WHO'S WHO 1992

WHO WAS WHO

Eight volumes containing the biographies removed from WHO'S WHO each year on account of death, with final details and date of death added. Also a Cumulated Index to the eight volumes giving name, years of birth and death, and the volume in which each entry is to be found.

VOL. I   1897-1915
VOL. II   1916-1928
VOL. III   1929-1940
VOL. IV   1941-1950
VOL. V   1951-1960
VOL. VI   1961-1970
VOL. VII   1971-1980
VOL. VIII   1981-1990
A CUMULATED INDEX 1897-1990

WHO'S WHO 1992

AN ANNUAL
BIOGRAPHICAL DICTIONARY

ONE HUNDRED AND FORTY FOURTH
YEAR OF ISSUE

A & C BLACK
LONDON

PUBLISHED BY A&C BLACK (PUBLISHERS) LIMITED, 35 BEDFORD ROW LONDON WC1R 4JH

COPYRIGHT © 1992 A&C BLACK (PUBLISHERS) LTD

"WHO'S WHO" IS A REGISTERED TRADE MARK IN THE UNITED KINGDOM

ISBN 0 7136 3514 2

The United States
ST MARTIN'S PRESS, NEW YORK

Australia
HODDER & STOUGHTON (AUSTRALIA) PTY LTD, RYDALMERE, NEW SOUTH WALES

New Zealand
RANDOM HOUSE (NZ) LTD, AUCKLAND

Canada
MAXWELL MACMILLAN (CANADA) INC.,
CAMBRIDGE, ONTARIO

Southern Africa
BOOK PROMOTIONS (PTY) LTD, CLAREMONT, CAPE TOWN

Middle East
EURAB LTD, CHORLEYWOOD, ENGLAND

India
ALLIED PUBLISHERS PRIVATE LTD, NEW DELHI

Hong Kong
UNITED PUBLISHERS SERVICES (HONG KONG) LTD.

Singapore
STP DISTRIBUTORS PTE LTD, SINGAPORE

Malaysia
STP DISTRIBUTORS (M) SDN BHD, KUALA LUMPUR

The publishers make no representation, express or implied,
with regard to the accuracy of the information contained
in this book and cannot accept any legal responsibility
for any errors or omissions that may take place.

TYPESET BY CLOWES COMPUTER COMPOSITION, PRINTED AND BOUND IN GREAT BRITAIN BY
WILLIAM CLOWES LIMITED, BECCLES AND LONDON

CONTENTS

INDEX TO ADVERTISERS

PREFACE

The first edition of *Who's Who* was published in 1849. It consisted of an almanac followed by thirty-nine lists of ranks and appointments and the names of those holding them. As might be expected, there were lists of peers, members of the House of Commons, judges, archbishops and bishops. Additionally, however, there were the names of the Governor and board of directors of the Bank of England, of British envoys abroad, of the directors of the East India Company and of the officers (including the actuaries) of the life and fire assurance companies in London.

The range of lists was expanded over the next half century to more than two hundred and fifty, to include, amongst others, the Police Commissioners, the officers of the principal railways, the members of the London School Board and the Crown Agents – together with the editors of significant newspapers and magazines whose names, the editor noted, were "given here, not for contributors, but that the public may know who lead public opinion".

In 1897 substantial changes were made to the nature and content of the book. The major change was the addition of a section of biographies in which details were given of the lives of some five and a half thousand leading figures of the day.

Now as then the book aims to list people who, through their careers, affect the political, economic, scientific and artistic life of the country. *Who's Who* places its emphasis on careers whilst giving opportunity for the inclusion of family and other individual details, such as the recreations which have become a distinctive feature of the book.

An invitation to appear in *Who's Who* has, on occasion, been thought of as conferring distinction; that is the last thing it can do. It recognises distinction and influence. The attitude of the present editorial board remains that of the editor of the 1897 edition, who stated in his preface that the book seeks to recognise people whose "prominence is inherited, or depending upon office, or the result of ability which singles them out from their fellows in occupations open to every educated man or woman".

ABBREVIATIONS USED IN THIS BOOK

Some of the designatory letters in this list are used merely for economy of
space and do not necessarily imply any professional or other qualification.

A

AA	Anti-Aircraft; Automobile Association; Architectural Association; Augustinians of the Assumption
AAA	Amateur Athletic Association; American Accounting Association
AAAL	American Academy of Arts and Letters (*now see* AAIL)
AA&QMG	Assistant Adjutant and Quartermaster-General
AAAS	American Association for the Advancement of Science
AAC	Army Air Corps
AACCA	Associate, Association of Certified and Corporate Accountants (*now see* ACCA)
AACE	Association for Adult and Continuing Education
AAF	Auxiliary Air Force (*now see* RAuxAF)
AAFCE	Allied Air Forces in Central Europe
AAG	Assistant Adjutant-General
AAI	Associate, Chartered Auctioneers' and Estate Agents' Institute (*now* (after amalgamation) *see* ARICS)
AAIL	American Academy and Institute of Arts and Letters
AAM	Association of Assistant Mistresses in Secondary Schools
AAMC	Australian Army Medical Corps (*now see* RAAMC)
A&AEE	Aeroplane and Armament Experimental Establishment
AASA	Associate, Australian Society of Accountants
AASC	Australian Army Service Corps
AAUQ	Associate in Accountancy, University of Queensland
AB	Bachelor of Arts (US); able-bodied seaman; airborne
ABA	Amateur Boxing Association; Antiquarian Booksellers' Association; American Bar Association
ABC	Australian Broadcasting Commission; American Broadcasting Companies
ABCA	Army Bureau of Current Affairs
ABCC	Association of British Chambers of Commerce
ABCFM	American Board of Commissioners for Foreign Missions
ABIA	Associate, Bankers' Institute of Australasia
ABINZ	Associate, Bankers' Institute of New Zealand
ABNM	American Board of Nuclear Medicine
ABP	Associated British Ports
Abp	Archbishop
ABPsS	Associate, British Psychological Society (*now see* AFBPsS)
ABRC	Advisory Board for the Research Councils
ABS	Associate, Building Societies' Institute (*now see* ACBSI)
ABSA	Association for Business Sponsorship of the Arts
ABSI	Associate, Boot and Shoe Institution
ABSM	Associate, Birmingham and Midland Institute School of Music
ABTA	Association of British Travel Agents
ABTAPL	Association of British Theological and Philosophical Libraries
AC	Companion, Order of Australia; *Ante Christum* (before Christ)
ACA	Associate, Institute of Chartered Accountants
Acad.	Academy
ACARD	Advisory Council for Applied Research and Development
ACAS	Advisory, Conciliation and Arbitration Service; Assistant Chief of the Air Staff
ACBSI	Associate, Chartered Building Societies Institute
ACC	Association of County Councils; Anglican Consultative Council
ACCA	Associate, Association of Certified Accountants
ACCM	Advisory Council for the Church's Ministry
ACCS	Associate, Corporation of Secretaries (formerly of Certified Secretaries)
ACDP	Australian Committee of Directors and Principals
ACDS	Assistant Chief of Defence Staff
ACE	Association of Consulting Engineers; Member, Association of Conference Executives
ACF	Army Cadet Force
ACFA	Army Cadet Force Association
ACFAS	Association Canadienne-Française pour l'avancement des sciences
ACFHE	Association of Colleges for Further and Higher Education
ACG	Assistant Chaplain-General
ACGI	Associate, City and Guilds of London Institute
ACGS	Assistant Chief of the General Staff
ACIArb	Associate, Chartered Institute of Arbitrators
ACIB	Associate, Chartered Institute of Bankers
ACII	Associate, Chartered Insurance Institute
ACIS	Associate, Institute of Chartered Secretaries and Administrators (*formerly* Chartered Institute of Secretaries)
ACIT	Associate, Chartered Institute of Transport
ACLS	American Council of Learned Societies
ACM	Association of Computing Machinery
ACMA	Associate, Chartered Institute of Management Accountants (*formerly* Institute of Cost and Management Accountants)

ACNS	Assistant Chief of Naval Staff
ACommA	Associate, Society of Commercial Accountants (*now see* ASCA)
ACORD	Advisory Committee on Research and Development
ACOS	Assistant Chief of Staff
ACOST	Advisory Council on Science and Technology
ACP	Association of Clinical Pathologists; Associate, College of Preceptors; African/Caribbean/Pacific
ACPO	Association of Chief Police Officers
ACRE	Action with Rural Communities in England
ACS	American Chemical Society; Additional Curates Society
ACSEA	Allied Command South East Asia
ACSM	Associate, Camborne School of Mines
ACT	Australian Capital Territory; Australian College of Theology; Associate, College of Technology; Association of Corporate Treasurers
ACTT	Association of Cinematograph, Television and Allied Technicians
ACTU	Australian Council of Trade Unions
ACU	Association of Commonwealth Universities
ACWA	Associate, Institute of Cost and Works Accountants (*now see* ACMA)
AD	Dame of the Order of Australia; *Anno Domini*; Air Defence
aD	ausser Dienst
ADAS	Agricultural Development and Advisory Service
ADB	Asian Development Bank; Associate of the Drama Board (Education)
ADB/F	African Development Bank/Fund
ADC	Aide-de-camp
ADCM	Archbishop of Canterbury's Diploma in Church Music
AD Corps	Army Dental Corps (*now* RADC)
ADC(P)	Personal Aide-de-camp to HM The Queen
ADEME	Assistant Director Electrical and Mechanical Engineering
Ad eund	*Ad eundem gradum*; and *see under* aeg
ADFManc	Art and Design Fellow, Manchester
ADFW	Assistant Director of Fortifications and Works
ADGB	Air Defence of Great Britain
ADGMS	Assistant Director-General of Medical Services
ADH	Assistant Director of Hygiene
Adjt	Adjutant
ADJAG	Assistant Deputy Judge Advocate General
ADK	Order of Ahli Darjah Kinabalu
Adm.	Admiral
ADMS	Assistant Director of Medical Services
ADOS	Assistant Director of Ordnance Services
ADP	Automatic Data Processing
ADPA	Associate Diploma of Public Administration
ADS&T	Assistant Director of Supplies and Transport
Adv.	Advisory; Advocate
ADVS	Assistant Director of Veterinary Services
ADWE&M	Assistant Director of Works, Electrical and Mechanical
AE	Air Efficiency Award
AEA	Atomic Energy Authority; Air Efficiency Award (*now see* AE)
AEAF	Allied Expeditionary Air Force
AEC	Agriculture Executive Council; Army Educational Corps (*now see* RAEC); Atomic Energy Commission
AECMA	Association Européenne des Constructeurs de Matériel Aérospatial
AEE	Atomic Energy Establishment
AEF	Amalgamated Union of Engineering and Foundry Workers (*now see* AEU); American Expeditionary Forces
aeg	*ad eundem gradum* (to the same degree — of the admission of a graduate of one university to the same degree at another without examination)
AEGIS	Aid for the Elderly in Government Institutions
AEI	Associated Electrical Industries
AEM	Air Efficiency Medal
AER	Army Emergency Reserve
AERE	Atomic Energy Research Establishment (Harwell)
Æt., Ætat.	*Ætatis* (aged)
AEU	Amalgamated Engineering Union
AFA	Amateur Football Alliance
AFAIAA	Associate Fellow, American Institute of Aeronautics and Astronautics
AFASIC	Association for All Speech Impaired Children
AFBPsS	Associate Fellow, British Psychological Society
AFC	Air Force Cross; Association Football Club
AFCAI	Associate Fellow, Canadian Aeronautical Institute
AFCEA	Armed Forces Communications and Electronics Association
AFCENT	Allied Forces in Central Europe
AFD	Doctor of Fine Arts (US)
AFDS	Air Fighting Development Squadron
AFHQ	Allied Force Headquarters
AFI	American Film Institute
AFIA	Associate, Federal Institute of Accountants (Australia)

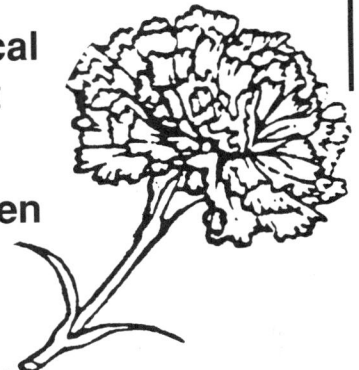

AFIAP	Artiste, Fédération Internationale de l'Art Photographique
AFIAS	Associate Fellow, Institute of Aeronautical Sciences (US) (*now see* AFAIAA)
AFICD	Associate Fellow, Institute of Civil Defence
AFIMA	Associate Fellow, Institute of Mathematics and its Applications
AFM	Air Force Medal
AFNORTH	Allied Forces in Northern Europe
AFOM	Associate, Faculty of Occupational Medicine
AFRAeS	Associate Fellow, Royal Aeronautical Society (*now see* MRAeS)
AFRC	Agricultural and Food Research Council
AFV	Armoured Fighting Vehicles
AG	Attorney-General
AGAC	American Guild of Authors and Composers
AGARD	Advisory Group for Aerospace Research and Development
AGH	Australian General Hospital
AGI	Artistes Graphiques Internationaux; Associate, Institute of Certificated Grocers
AGR	Advanced Gas-cooled Reactor
AGRA	Army Group Royal Artillery; Association of Genealogists and Record Agents
AGSM	Associate, Guildhall School of Music and Drama; Australian Graduate School of Management
AHA	Area Health Authority; American Hospitals Association; Associate, Institute of Health Service Administrators (*now see* AHSM)
AHA(T)	Area Health Authority (Teaching)
AHQ	Army Headquarters
AHSM	Associate, Institute of Health Services Management
AH-WC	Associate, Heriot-Watt College, Edinburgh
ai	*ad interim*
AIA	Associate, Institute of Actuaries; American Institute of Architects; Association of International Artists
AIAA	American Institute of Aeronautics and Astronautics
AIAgrE	Associate, Institution of Agricultural Engineers
AIAL	Associate Member, International Institute of Arts and Letters
AIArb	Associate, Institute of Arbitrators (*now see* ACIArb)
AIAS	Associate Surveyor Member, Incorporated Association of Architects and Surveyors
AIB	Associate, Institute of Bankers (*now see* ACIB)
AIBD	Associate, Institute of British Decorators
AIBP	Associate, Institute of British Photographers
AIBScot	Associate, Institute of Bankers in Scotland
AIC	Agricultural Improvement Council; Associate of the Institute of Chemistry (later ARIC, MRIC; *now see* MRSC)
AICA	Associate Member, Commonwealth Institute of Accountants; Association Internationale des Critiques d'Art
AICC	All-India Congress Committee
AICE	Associate, Institution of Civil Engineers
AICPA	American Institute of Certified Public Accountants
AICS	Associate, Institute of Chartered Shipbrokers
AICTA	Associate, Imperial College of Tropical Agriculture
AIDS	Acquired Immunity Deficiency Syndrome
AIE	Associate, Institute of Education
AIEE	Associate, Institute of Electrical Engineers
AIF	Australian Imperial Forces
AIG	Adjutant-Inspector-General
AIIA	Associate, Insurance Institute of America; Associate, Indian Institute of Architects
AIInfSc	Associate, Institute of Information Scientists
AIIRA	Associate, International Industrial Relations Association
AIL	Associate, Institute of Linguists
AILA	Associate, Institute of Landscape Architects (*now see* ALI)
AILocoE	Associate, Institution of Locomotive Engineers
AIM	Associate, Institution of Metallurgists (*now see* MIM); Australian Institute of Management
AIMarE	Associate, Institute of Marine Engineers
AIME	American Institute of Mechanical Engineers
AIMSW	Associate, Institute of Medical Social Workers
AInstM	Associate Member, Institute of Marketing
AInstP	Associate, Institute of Physics
AInstPI	Associate, Institute of Patentees and Inventors
AIP	Association of Independent Producers
AIPR	Associate, Institute of Public Relations
AIProdE	Associate, Institution of Production Engineers
AIQS	Associate Member, Institute of Quantity Surveyors
AIRTE	Associate, Institute of Road Transport Engineers
AIRTO	Association of Independent Research and Technology Organizations
AIS	Associate, Institute of Statisticians (*now see* MIS)
AISA	Associate, Incorporated Secretaries' Association
AIStructE	Associate, Institution of Structural Engineers
AITI	Associate, Institute of Translators and Interpreters
AITP	Associate, Institute of Town Planners, India
AJAG	Assistant Judge Advocate General
AJEX	Association of Jewish Ex-Service Men and Women
AK	Knight, Order of Australia
AKC	Associate, King's College London
ALA	Associate, Library Association; Association of London Authorities
Ala	Alabama (US)
ALAA	Associate, Library Association of Australia
ALAM	Associate, London Academy of Music and Dramatic Art
ALCD	Associate, London College of Divinity
ALCM	Associate, London College of Music
ALCS	Authors Lending and Copyright Society
ALFSEA	Allied Land Forces South-East Asia
ALI	Argyll Light Infantry; Associate, Landscape Institute
ALICE	Autistic and Language Impaired Children's Education
ALLC	Association for Literary and Linguistic Computing
ALP	Australian Labor Party
ALPSP	Association of Learned and Professional Society Publishers
ALS	Associate, Linnean Society
Alta	Alberta
ALVA	Association of Leading Visitor Attractions
AM	Albert Medal; Member, Order of Australia; Master of Arts (US); Alpes Maritimes
AMA	Association of Metropolitan Authorities; Assistant Masters Association; Associate, Museums Association; Australian Medical Association
AMARC	Associated Marine and Related Charities
Amb.	Ambulance; Ambassador
AMBIM	Associate Member, British Institute of Management (*now see* MBIM)
AMBritIRE	Associate Member, British Institution of Radio Engineers (*now see* AMIERE)
AMC	Association of Municipal Corporations
AMCST	Associate, Manchester College of Science and Technology
AMCT	Associate, Manchester College of Technology
AME	Association of Municipal Engineers
AMEME	Association of Mining Electrical and Mechanical Engineers
AMet	Associate of Metallurgy
AMF	Australian Military Forces
AMGOT	Allied Military Government of Occupied Territory
AMIAE	Associate Member, Institution of Automobile Engineers
AMIAgrE	Associate Member, Institution of Agricultural Engineers
AMIBF	Associate Member, Institute of British Foundrymen
AMICE	Associate Member, Institution of Civil Engineers (*now see* MICE)
AMIChemE	Associate Member, Institution of Chemical Engineers
AMIE(Aust)	Associate Member, Institution of Engineers, Australia
AMIED	Associate Member, Institution of Engineering Designers
AMIEE	Associate Member, Institution of Electrical Engineers (*now see* MIEE)
AMIE(Ind)	Associate Member, Institution of Engineers, India
AMIERE	Associate Member, Institution of Electronic and Radio Engineers
AMIH	Associate Member, Institute of Housing
AMIMechE	Associate Member, Institution of Mechanical Engineers (*now see* MIMechE)
AMIMinE	Associate Member, Institution of Mining Engineers
AMIMM	Associate Member, Institution of Mining and Metallurgy
AMInstBE	Associate Member, Institution of British Engineers
AMInstCE	Associate Member, Institution of Civil Engineers (*now see* MICE)
AmInstEE	American Institute of Electrical Engineers
AMInstR	Associate Member, Institute of Refrigeration
AMInstT	Associate Member, Institute of Transport (*now see* ACIT)
AMInstTA	Associate Member, Institute of Traffic Adminstration
AMINucE	Associate Member, Institution of Nuclear Engineers
AMIRSE	Associate Member, Institute of Railway Signalling Engineers
AMIStructE	Associate Member, Institution of Structural Engineers
AMN	Ahli Mangku Negara (Malaysia)
AMP	Advanced Management Program; Air Member for Personnel
AMRINA	Associate Member, Royal Institution of Naval Architects
AMS	Assistant Military Secretary; Army Medical Services
AMTE	Admiralty Marine Technology Establishment
AMTRI	Advanced Manufacturing Technology Research Institute
ANA	Associate National Academician (America)
ANAF	Arab Non-Arab Friendship
Anat.	Anatomy; Anatomical
ANC	African National Congress
ANECInst	Associate, NE Coast Institution of Engineers and Shipbuilders
ANGAU	Australian New Guinea Administrative Unit
Anon.	Anonymously
ANU	Australian National University
ANZAAS	Australian and New Zealand Association for the Advancement of Science
Anzac	Australian and New Zealand Army Corps
AO	Officer, Order of Australia; Air Officer
AOA	Air Officer in charge of Administration
AOC	Air Officer Commanding
AOC-in-C	Air Officer Commanding-in-Chief
AOD	Army Ordnance Department
AOER	Army Officers Emergency Reserve
APA	American Psychiatric Association
APACS	Association of Payment and Clearing Systems
APCK	Association for Promoting Christian Knowledge, Church of Ireland
APD	Army Pay Department
APEX	Association of Professional, Executive, Clerical and Computer Staff
APHA	American Public Health Association
APIS	Army Photographic Intelligence Service
APM	Assistant Provost Marshal
APMI	Associate, Pensions Management Institute
APR	Accredited Public Relations Practitioner
APS	Aborigines Protection Society; American Physics Society
APsSI	Associate, Psychological Society of Ireland
APSW	Association of Psychiatric Social Workers
APT&C	Administrative, Professional, Technical and Clerical
APTC	Army Physical Training Corps

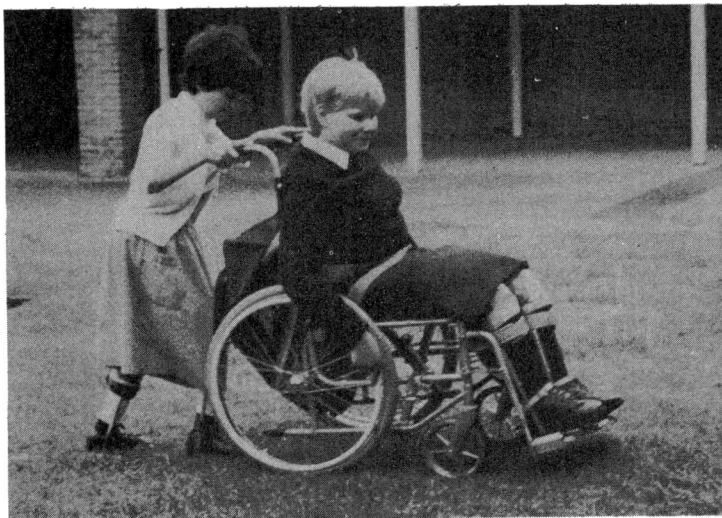

AQ	Administration and Quartering
AQMG	Assistant Quartermaster-General
AR	Associated Rediffusion (Television)
ARA	Associate, Royal Academy
ARACI	Associate, Royal Australian Chemical Institute
ARAD	Associate, Royal Academy of Dancing
ARAeS	Associate, Royal Aeronautical Society
ARAM	Associate, Royal Academy of Music
ARAS	Associate, Royal Astronomical Society
ARBA	Associate, Royal Society of British Artists
ARBC	Associate, Royal British Colonial Society of Artists
ARBS	Associate, Royal Society of British Sculptors
ARC	Architects' Registration Council; Agricultural Research Council (*now see* AFRC); Aeronautical Research Council
ARCA	Associate, Royal College of Art; Associate, Royal Canadian Academy
ARCamA	Associate, Royal Cambrian Academy of Art
ARCE	Academical Rank of Civil Engineer
ARCIC	Anglican-Roman Catholic International Commission
ARCM	Associate, Royal College of Music
ARCO	Associate, Royal College of Organists
ARCO(CHM)	Associate, Royal College of Organists with Diploma in Choir Training
ARCPsych	Associate Member, Royal College of Psychiatrists
ARCS	Associate, Royal College of Science
ARCST	Associate, Royal College of Science and Technology (Glasgow)
ARCUK	Architects' Registration Council of the United Kingdom
ARCVS	Associate, Royal College of Veterinary Surgeons
ARE	Associate, Royal Society of Painter-Etchers and Engravers; Arab Republic of Egypt; Admiralty Research Establishment
AREINZ	Associate, Real Estate Institute, New Zealand
ARELS	Association of Recognised English Language Schools
ARIAS	Associate, Royal Incorporation of Architects in Scotland
ARIBA	Associate, Royal Institute of British Architects (*now see* RIBA)
ARIC	Associate, Royal Institute of Chemistry (later MRIC; *now see* MRSC)
ARICS	Professional Associate, Royal Institution of Chartered Surveyors
ARINA	Associate, Royal Institution of Naval Architects
Ark	Arkansas (US)
ARLT	Association for the Reform of Latin Teaching
ARMS	Associate, Royal Society of Miniature Painters
ARP	Air Raid Precautions
ARPS	Associate, Royal Photographic Society
ARR	Association of Radiation Research
ARRC	Associate, Royal Red Cross
ARSA	Associate, Royal Scottish Academy
ARSCM	Associate, Royal School of Church Music
ARSM	Associate, Royal School of Mines
ARTC	Associate, Royal Technical College (Glasgow) (*now see* ARCST)
ARVIA	Associate, Royal Victoria Institute of Architects
ARWA	Associate, Royal West of England Academy
ARWS	Associate, Royal Society of Painters in Water-Colours
AS	Anglo-Saxon
ASA	Associate Member, Society of Actuaries; Associate of Society of Actuaries (US); Australian Society of Accountants; Army Sailing Asssociation
ASAA	Associate, Society of Incorporated Accountants and Auditors
ASAI	Associate, Society of Architectural Illustrators
ASAM	Associate, Society of Art Masters
AS&TS of SA	Associated Scientific and Technical Societies of South Africa
ASBAH	Association for Spina Bifida and Hydrocephalus
ASC	Administrative Staff College, Henley
ASCA	Associate, Society of Company and Commercial Accountants
ASCAB	Armed Services Consultant Approval Board
ASCAP	American Society of Composers, Authors and Publishers
ASCE	American Society of Civil Engineers
AScW	Association of Scientific Workers (*now see* ASTMS)
ASD	Armament Supply Department
ASE	Amalgamated Society of Engineers (*now see* AUEW)
ASEAN	Association of South East Asian Nations
ASH	Action on Smoking and Health
ASIAD	Associate, Society of Industrial Artists and Designers
ASIA(Ed)	Associate, Society of Industrial Artists (Education)
ASLDC	Association of Social and Liberal Democrat Councillors
ASLE	American Society of Lubrication Engineers
ASLEF	Associated Society of Locomotive Engineers and Firemen
ASLIB or Aslib	Association for Information Management (*formerly* Association of Special Libraries and Information Bureaux)
ASM	Association of Senior Members
ASME	American Society of Mechanical Engineers; Association for the Study of Medical Education
ASO	Air Staff Officer
ASSC	Accounting Standards Steering Committee
ASSET	Association of Supervisory Staffs, Executives and Technicians (*now see* ASTMS)
AssocISI	Associate, Iron and Steel Institute
AssocMCT	Associateship of Manchester College of Technology
AssocMIAeE	Associate Member, Institution of Aeronautical Engineers
AssocRINA	Associate, Royal Institution of Naval Architects
AssocSc	Associate in Science
Asst	Assistant
ASTC	Administrative Service Training Course

ASTMS	Association of Scientific, Technical and Managerial Staffs (now part of MSF)
ASVU	Army Security Vetting Unit
ASWDU	Air Sea Warfare Development Unit
ASWE	Admiralty Surface Weapons Establishment
ATA	Air Transport Auxiliary
ATAE	Association of Tutors in Adult Education
ATAF	Allied Tactical Air Force
ATC	Air Training Corps; Art Teacher's Certificate
ATCDE	Association of Teachers in Colleges and Departments of Education (*now see* NATFHE)
ATCL	Associate, Trinity College of Music, London
ATD	Art Teacher's Diploma
ATI	Associate, Textile Institute
ATII	Associate Member, Institute of Taxation
ato	Ammunition Technical Officer
ATPL (A) or (H)	Airline Transport Pilot's Licence (Aeroplanes), or (Helicopters)
ATS	Auxiliary Territorial Service (*now see* WRAC)
ATTI	Association of Teachers in Technical Institutions (*now see* NATFHE)
ATV	Associated TeleVision
AUA	American Urological Association
AUCAS	Association of University Clinical Academic Staff
AUEW	Amalgamated Union of Engineering Workers (*now see* AEU)
AUS	Army of the United States
AUT	Association of University Teachers
AVCC	Australian Vice-Chancellors' Committee
AVCM	Associate, Victoria College of Music
AVD	Army Veterinary Department
AVLA	Audio Visual Language Association
AVR	Army Volunteer Reserve
AWA	Anglian Water Authority
AWO	Association of Water Officers
AWRE	Atomic Weapons Research Establishment
aws	Graduate of Air Warfare Course

B

b	born; brother
BA	Bachelor of Arts
BAA	British Airports Authority
BAAB	British Amateur Athletic Board
BAAL	British Association for Applied Linguistics
BAAS	British Association for the Advancement of Science
BAB	British Airways Board
BAC	British Aircraft Corporation
BACM	British Association of Colliery Management
BACUP	British Association of Cancer United Patients
BAe	British Aerospace
BAED	Bachelor of Arts in Enviromental Design
B&FBS	British and Foreign Bible Society
BAFO	British Air Forces of Occupation
BAFPA	British Association of Fitness Promotion Agencies
BAFTA	British Academy of Film and Television Arts
BAG	Business Art Galleries
BAgrSc	Bachelor of Agricultural Science
BAI	*Baccalarius in Arte Ingeniaria* (Bachelor of Engineering)
BAIE	British Association of Industrial Editors
BALPA	British Air Line Pilots' Association
BAO	Bachelor of Art of Obstetrics
BAOMS	British Association of Oral and Maxillo-Facial Surgeons
BAOR	British Army of the Rhine (formerly *on* the Rhine)
BAOS	British Association of Oral Surgeons (*now see* BAOMS)
BAppSc(MT)	Bachelor of Applied Science (Medical Technology)
BARB	Broadcasters' Audience Research Board
BARC	British Automobile Racing Club
Bart	Baronet
BAS	Bachelor in Agricultural Science
BASc	Bachelor of Applied Science
BASCA	British Academy of Songwriters, Composers and Authors
BASEEFA	British Approvals Service for Electrical Equipment in Flammable Atmospheres
BASW	British Association of Social Workers
Batt.	Battery
BBA	British Bankers' Association; Bachelor of Business Administration
BB&CIRly	Bombay, Baroda and Central India Railway
BBB of C	British Boxing Board of Control
BBC	British Broadcasting Corporation
BBM	Bintang Bakti Masharakat (Public Service Star) (Singapore)
BBS	Bachelor of Business Studies
BC	Before Christ; British Columbia; Borough Council
BCAR	British Civil Airworthiness Requirements
BCC	British Council of Churches
BCE	Bachelor of Civil Engineering
BCh or BChir	Bachelor of Surgery
BCL	Bachelor of Civil Law
BCMF	British Ceramic Manufacturers' Federation
BCMS	Bible Churchmen's Missionary Society
BCOF	British Commonwealth Occupation Force
BCom or BComm	Bachelor of Commerce
BComSc	Bachelor of Commercial Science
BCS	Bengal Civil Service; British Computer Society
BCSA	British Constructional Steelwork Association

MOZART'S LEGACY HAS LASTED *200 YEARS*.

SO COULD YOURS.

Mozart left a legacy of masterpieces.

But he wrote no will.

When putting your affairs in order, please consider a legacy towards vital medical research.

Past successes include helping to develop the vaccines against polio and rubella, the ultrasound scanner, artificial hip replacement and many more.

Please call Action Research free on 0800 521533 for more legacy information.

You might give more pleasure than Mozart.

ACTION RESEARCH

Leading medical research for children

Registered Charity No. 208701

BCURA	British Coal Utilization Research Association
BCYC	British Corinthian Yacht Club
BD	Bachelor of Divinity
Bd	Board
BDA	British Dental Association
Bde	Brigade
BDS	Bachelor of Dental Surgery
BDSc	Bachelor of Dental Science
BE	Bachelor of Engineering; British Element
BEA	British East Africa; British European Airways; British Epilepsy Association
BEAMA	Federation of British Electrotechnical and Allied Manufacturers' Associations (formerly British Electrical and Allied Manufacturers' Association)
BE&A	Bachelor of Engineering and Architecture (Malta)
BEAS	British Educational Administration Society
BEC	Business Education Council (now see BTEC)
BEc	Bachelor of Economics
BEd	Bachelor of Education
Beds	Bedfordshire
BEE	Bachelor of Electrical Engineering
BEF	British Expeditionary Force; British Equestrian Federation
BEM	British Empire Medal
BEMAS	British Education Management and Administration Society
BEME	Brigade Electrical and Mechanical Engineer
BEO	Base Engineer Officer
Berks	Berkshire
BESO	British Executive Service Overseas
BFI	British Film Institute
BFMIRA	British Food Manufacturing Industries Research Association
BFPO	British Forces Post Office
BFSS	British Field Sports Society
BGS	Brigadier General Staff
Bhd	Berhad
BHF	British Heart Foundation
BHRA	British Hydromechanics Research Association
BHRCA	British Hotels, Restaurants and Caterers' Association
BHS	British Horse Society
BI	British Invisibles
BIBA	British Insurance Brokers' Association
BIBRA	British Industrial Biological Research Association
BICC	British Insulated Callender's Cables
BICERA	British Internal Combustion Engine Research Association (now see BICERI)
BICERI	British Internal Combustion Engine Research Institute
BICSc	British Institute of Cleaning Science
BIEC	British Invisible Exports Council (now see BI)
BIEE	British Institute of Energy Economics
BIF	British Industries Fair
BIFU	Banking Insurance and Finance Union
BIM	British Institute of Management
BIR	British Institute of Radiology
BIS	Bank for International Settlements
BISF	British Iron and Steel Federation
BISFA	British Industrial and Scientific Film Association
BISPA	British Independent Steel Producers Association
BISRA	British Iron and Steel Research Association
BITC	Business in the Community
BJ	Bachelor of Journalism
BJSM	British Joint Services Mission
BKSTS	British Kinematograph, Sound and Television Society
BL	Bachelor of Law
BLA	British Liberation Army
BLE	Brotherhood of Locomotive Engineers; Bachelor of Land Economy
BLESMA	British Limbless Ex-Servicemen's Association
BLitt	Bachelor of Letters
BM	British Museum; Bachelor of Medicine; Brigade Major; British Monomark
BMA	British Medical Association
BMedSci	Bachelor of Medical Science
BMEO	British Middle East Office
BMet	Bachelor of Metallurgy
BMEWS	Ballistic Missile Early Warning System
BMH	British Military Hospital
BMJ	British Medical Journal
BMM	British Military Mission
BMR	Bureau of Mineral Resources
BMRA	Brigade Major Royal Artillery
Bn	Battalion
BNAF	British North Africa Force
BNC	Brasenose College
BNEC	British National Export Council
BNFL	British Nuclear Fuels Ltd
BNOC	British National Oil Corporation; British National Opera Company
BNP	Banque Nationale de Paris
BNSC	British National Space Centre
BNSc	Bachelor of Nursing Science
BOAC	British Overseas Airways Corporation
BomCS	Bombay Civil Service
BomSC	Bombay Staff Corps
BoT	Board of Trade
Bot.	Botany; Botanical
BOTB	British Overseas Trade Board
Bp	Bishop
BPA	British Paediatric Association
BPG	Broadcasting Press Guild
BPharm	Bachelor of Pharmacy
BPIF	British Printing Industries Federation
BPMF	British Postgraduate Medical Federation
BPsS	British Psychological Society
BR	British Rail
Br.	Branch
BRA	Brigadier Royal Artillery; British Rheumatism & Arthritis Association
BRB	British Railways Board
BRCS	British Red Cross Society
BRE	Building Research Establishment
Brig.	Brigadier
BritIRE	British Institution of Radio Engineers (now see IERE)
BRNC	Britannia Royal Naval College
BRS	British Road Services
BRurSc	Bachelor of Rural Science
BS	Bachelor of Surgery; Bachelor of Science; British Standard
BSA	Bachelor of Scientific Agriculture; Birmingham Small Arms; Building Societies' Association
BSAA	British South American Airways
BSAP	British South Africa Police
BSC	British Steel Corporation; Bengal Staff Corps
BSc	Bachelor of Science
BScA	Bachelor of Science in Agriculture
BSc(Dent)	Bachelor of Science in Dentistry
BSc (Est. Man.)	Bachelor of Science in Estate Management
BScSoc	Bachelor of Social Sciences
BSE	Bachelor of Science in Engineering (US)
BSES	British Schools Exploring Society
BSF	British Salonica Force
BSFA	British Science Fiction Association
BSI	British Standards Institution
BSIA	British Security Industry Association
BSJA	British Show Jumping Association
BSME	Bachelor of Science in Mechanical Engineering
BSN	Bachelor of Science in Nursing
BSNS	Bachelor of Naval Science
BSocSc	Bachelor of Social Science
BSRA	British Ship Research Association
BSS	Bachelor of Science (Social Science)
BST	Bachelor of Sacred Theology
BT	Bachelor of Teaching; British Telecommunications
Bt	Baronet; Brevet
BTA	British Tourist Authority (formerly British Travel Association)
BTC	British Transport Commission
BTCV	British Trust for Conservation Volunteers
BTDB	British Transport Docks Board (now see ABP)
BTEC	Business and Technician Education Council
BTh	Bachelor of Theology
BTP	Bachelor of Town Planning
Btss	Baronetess
BUAS	British Universities Association of Slavists
BUGB	Baptist Union of Great Britain
BUPA	British United Provident Association
BV	Besloten Vennootschap
BVA	British Veterinary Association
BVM	Blessed Virgin Mary
BVMS	Bachelor of Veterinary Medicine and Surgery
Bucks	Buckinghamshire
BVetMed	Bachelor of Veterinary Medicine
BWI	British West Indies
BWM	British War Medal

C

(C)	Conservative; 100
c	child; cousin; circa (about)
CA	Central America; County Alderman; Chartered Accountant (Scotland and Canada)
CAA	Civil Aviation Authority
CAABU	Council for the Advancement of Arab and British Understanding
CAAV	(Member of) Central Association of Agricultural Valuers
CAB	Citizens' Advice Bureau; Commonwealth Agricultural Bureau
CACTM	Central Advisory Council of Training for the Ministry (now see ACCM)
CAER	Conservative Action for Electoral Reform
CALE	Canadian Army Liaison Executive
CAM	Communications, Advertising and Marketing
Cambs	Cambridgeshire
CAMC	Canadian Army Medical Corps
CAMRA	Campaign for Real Ale
CAMS	Certificate of Advanced Musical Study
CAMW	Central Association for Mental Welfare
Cantab	Cantabrigiensis (of Cambridge)
Cantuar	Cantuariensis (of Canterbury)
CARD	Campaign against Racial Discrimination
CARE	Cottage and Rural Enterprises
CARICOM	Caribbean Community
CARIFTA	Caribbean Free Trade Area (now see CARICOM)
CAS	Chief of the Air Staff
CASI	Canadian Aeronautics and Space Institute

- Andrea is mentally and physically handicapped and is cared for by loving members of her family.

- Crossroads care attendants work with Andrea's family to relieve some of the stress caused by giving constant attention to their daughter.

- 180 Crossroads schemes throughout the country currently help over 15,000 families care for physically or mentally handicapped people in their own homes, by giving the carers a break when they need it most.

- If you would like to help us to develop more schemes to help more families, please send your donations to:

Julia Scott, Appeals Director
CROSSROADS CARE
10 Regent Place
Rugby
Warwickshire CV21 2PN.

CROSSROADS
▶ C A R E ◀
Association of Crossroads Care Attendant Schemes limited

Reaching out
Meeting the need

Charity
Reg. No. 282102

DAME ANNA NEAGLE

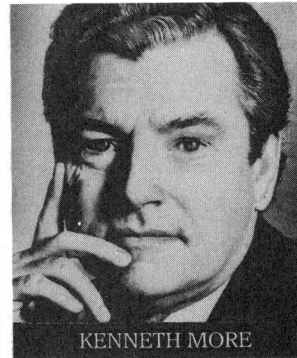
KENNETH MORE

A.J.P. TAYLOR

RAY KENNEDY

PARKINSON'S DISEASE CAN BE *ANYBODY'S* DISEASE.

It's often assumed that tremors are the only symptom of Parkinson's Disease. If only they were. Speech difficulty; inability to swallow; a face lacking expression; slow and clumsy movement; feet and legs that refuse to move.
They are all symptoms. There are over 100,000 sufferers in this country alone.
There is no known cure.
Parkinson's Disease Society seeks to ease the burden and find the cure for Parkinson's Disease.
We need *your* help. Please send a donation, a covenant or leave us a legacy. You can even phone your donation by Access or Visa to 071-383 3513.

HELP MAKE IT NOBODY'S DISEASE

Parkinson's Disease Society

22 Upper Woburn Place, London WC1H 0RA
Telephone: 071-383 3513

Patron: HRH The Princess of Wales

CAT	College of Advanced Technology
Cav.	Cavalry
CAWU	Clerical and Administrative Workers' Union (*now see* APEX)
CB	Companion, Order of the Bath; County Borough
CBC	County Borough Council
CBCO	Central Board for Conscientious Objectors
CBE	Commander, Order of the British Empire
CBI	Confederation of British Industry
CBIM	Companion, British Institute of Management
CBiol	Chartered Biologist
CBNS	Commander British Navy Staff
CBS	Columbia Broadcasting System
CBSA	Clay Bird Shooting Association
CBSI	Chartered Building Societies Institute
CC	Companion, Order of Canada; City Council; County Council; Cricket Club; Cycling Club; County Court
CCAB	Consultative Committee of Accountancy Bodies
CCAHC	Central Council for Agricultural and Horticultural Co-operation
CCBE	Commission Consultative des Barreaux de la Communauté Européenne
CCC	Corpus Christi College; Central Criminal Court; County Cricket Club
CCE	Chartered Civil Engineer
CCF	Combined Cadet Force
CCFM	Combined Cadet Forces Medal
CCG	Control Commission Germany
CCH	Cacique's Crown of Honour, Order of Service of Guyana
CChem	Chartered Chemist
CCHMS	Central Committee for Hospital Medical Services
CCIA	Commission of Churches on International Affairs
CCJ	Council of Christians and Jews
CCPR	Central Council of Physical Recreation
CCRA	Commander Corps of Royal Artillery
CCRE	Commander Corps of Royal Engineers
CCREME	Commander Corps of Royal Electrical and Mechanical Engineers
CCRSigs	Commander Corps of Royal Signals
CCS	Casualty Clearing Station; Ceylon Civil Service; Countryside Commission for Scotland
CCSU	Council of Civil Service Unions
CCTA	Commission de Coopération Technique pour l'Afrique
CCTS	Combat Crew Training Squadron
CD	Canadian Forces Decoration; Commander, Order of Distinction (Jamaica); Civil Defence
CDEE	Chemical Defence Experimental Establishment
CDipAF	Certified Diploma in Accounting and Finance
Cdo	Commando
CDRA	Committee of Directors of Research Associations
Cdre	Commodore
CDS	Chief of the Defence Staff
CDU	Christlich-Demokratische Union
CE	Civil Engineer
CEA	Central Electricity Authority
CECD	Confédération Européenne du Commerce de Détail
CECG	Consumers in European Community Group
CEDEP	Centre Européen d'Education Permanente
CEE	Communauté Economique Européenne
CEED	Centre for Economic and Environmental Development
CEF	Canadian Expeditionary Force
CEFIC	Conseil Européen des Fédérations de l'Industrie Chimique
CEGB	Central Electricity Generating Board
CEI	Council of Engineering Institutions
CEIR	Corporation for Economic and Industrial Research
CEM	Council of European Municipalities (*now see* CEMR)
CEMA	Council for the Encouragement of Music and the Arts
CEMR	Council of European Municipalities and Regions
CEMS	Church of England Men's Society
CEN	Comité Européen de Normalisation
CENELEC	European Committee for Electrotechnical Standardization
CEng	Chartered Engineer
Cento	Central Treaty Organisation
CEPT	Conférence Européenne des Postes et des Télécommunications
CERL	Central Electricity Research Laboratories
CERN	Organisation (*formerly* Centre) Européenne pour la Recherche Nucléaire
CERT	Charities Effectiveness Review Trust
Cert Ed	Certificate of Education
CertITP	Certificate of International Teachers' Program (Harvard)
CEST	Centre for Exploitation of Science and Technology
CET	Council for Educational Technology
CETS	Church of England Temperance Society
CF	Chaplain to the Forces
CFA	Canadian Field Artillery
CFE	Central Fighter Establishment
CFM	Cadet Forces Medal
CFR	Commander, Order of the Federal Republic of Nigeria
CFS	Central Flying School
CGA	Community of the Glorious Ascension; Country Gentlemen's Association
CGeol	Chartered Geologist
CGH	Order of the Golden Heart of Kenya (1st class)
CGIA	Insignia Award of City and Guilds of London Institute (*now see* FCGI)
CGLI	City and Guilds of London Institute
CGM	Conspicuous Gallantry Medal

CGRM	Commandant-General Royal Marines
CGS	Chief of the General Staff
CH	Companion of Honour
Chanc.	Chancellor; Chancery
Chap.	Chaplain
ChapStJ	Chaplain, Order of St John of Jerusalem (*now see* ChStJ)
CHAR	Campaign for the Homeless and Rootless
CHB	Companion of Honour of Barbados
ChB	Bachelor of Surgery
CHC	Community Health Council
Ch.Ch.	Christ Church
Ch.Coll.	Christ's College
CHE	Campaign for Homosexual Equality
ChLJ	Chaplain, Order of St Lazarus of Jerusalem
CHM	Chevalier of Honour and Merit (Haiti)
(CHM)	*See under* ARCO(CHM), FRCO(CHM)
ChM	Master of Surgery
Chm.	Chairman or Chairwoman
CHN	Community of the Holy Name
CHSC	Central Health Services Council
ChStJ	Chaplain, Most Venerable Order of the Hospital of St John of Jerusalem
CI	Imperial Order of the Crown of India; Channel Islands
CIA	Chemical Industries Association; Central Intelligence Agency
CIAD	Central Institute of Art and Design
CIAgrE	Companion, Institution of Agricultural Engineers
CIAL	Corresponding Member of the International Institute of Arts and Letters
CIArb	Chartered Institute of Arbitrators
CIB	Chartered Institute of Bankers
CIBS	Chartered Institution of Building Services (*now see* CIBSE)
CIBSE	Chartered Institution of Building Services Engineers
CIC	Chemical Institute of Canada
CICHE	Committee for International Co-operation in Higher Education
CICI	Confederation of Information Communication Industries
CID	Criminal Investigation Department
CIDEC	Conseil International pour le Développement du Cuivre
CIE	Companion, Order of the Indian Empire; Confédération Internationale des Etudiants
CIEx	Companion, Institute of Export
CIFRS	Comité International de la Rayonne et des Fibres Synthétiques
CIGasE	Companion, Institution of Gas Engineers
CIGRE	Conférence Internationale des Grands Réseaux Electriques
CIGS	Chief of the Imperial General Staff (*now see* CGS)
CIIA	Canadian Institute of International Affairs
CIM	China Inland Mission
CIMA	Chartered Institute of Management Accountants
CIMarE	Companion, Institute of Marine Engineers
CIMEMME	Companion, Institution of Mining Electrical and Mining Mechanical Engineers
CIMGTechE	Companion, Institution of Mechanical and General Technician Engineers
C-in-C	Commander-in-Chief
CINCHAN	Allied Commander-in-Chief Channel
CIOB	Chartered Institute of Building
CIPFA	Chartered Institute of Public Finance and Accountancy
CIPL	Comité International Permanent des Linguistes
CIPM	Companion, Institute of Personnel Management
CIR	Commission on Industrial Relations
CIRES	Co-operative Institute for Research in Environmental Sciences
CIRIA	Construction Industry Research and Information Association
CIRP	Collège Internationale pour Recherche et Production
CIS	Institute of Chartered Secretaries and Administrators (*formerly* Chartered Institute of Secretaries); Command Control Communications and Information Systems
CISAC	Confédération Internationale des Sociétés d'Auteurs et Compositeurs; Centre for International Security and Arms Control
CIT	Chartered Institute of Transport; California Institute of Technology
CIU	Club and Institute Union
CIV	City Imperial Volunteers
CJ	Chief Justice
CJM	Congregation of Jesus and Mary (Eudist Fathers)
CL	Commander, Order of Leopold
cl	*cum laude*
Cl.	Class
CLA	Country Landowners' Association
CLIC	Cancer and Leukemia in Children
CLIP	Common Law Institute of Intellectual Property
CLit	Companion of Literature (Royal Society of Literature Award)
CLJ	Commander, Order of St Lazarus of Jerusalem
CLP	Constituency Labour Party
CLRAE	Conference of Local and Regional Authorities of Europe
CM	Member, Order of Canada; Congregation of the Mission (Vincentians); Master in Surgery; Certificated Master; Canadian Militia
CMA	Canadian Medical Association; Cost and Management Accountant (NZ)
CMAC	Catholic Marriage Advisory Council
CMB	Central Midwives' Board
CMF	Commonwealth Military Forces; Central Mediterranean Force
CMG	Companion, Order of St Michael and St George

The Sue Ryder Foundation

In aid of the sick and disabled of all ages

Founder: Lady Ryder, of Warsaw, CMG, OBE

The Sue Ryder Foundation was established by Lady Ryder during the post-war years after she had been doing social relief work on the Continent. Its purpose was, and is, the relief of suffering on a wide scale by means of personal service, helping the sick and disabled everywhere, irrespective of race, religion or age, and thus serving as a **Living Memorial** to all those who suffered or died in the two World Wars and to those who undergo persecution or die in defence of human values today.

At present there are Homes in Britain in **Berkshire, Bedfordshire, Cambridgeshire, Cumbria, Gloucestershire, Hampshire, Hertfordshire, Lancashire, Leicestershire, Norfolk, Suffolk, Yorkshire, Berwickshire and West Lothian,** but many more are needed. They care for the **physically handicapped, cancer patients** both terminal and convalescent, patients suffering with **Huntington's Chorea** and the **elderly.**

Domiciliary care is also undertaken.

New homes are planned in Birmingham, Shropshire, The North-East, Kent, London and Nottinghamshire.

In addition to its work in Britain, the Foundation also works in many countries overseas where the needs are even greater.

These and all our patients desperately need your help—with a legacy, deed of covenant or donation in finance or kind. Also, the Foundation will be pleased to advise companies whose employees wish to contribute via the Give-As-You-Earn scheme.

Please write for any further information to

The Sue Ryder Foundation
Cavendish, Suffolk CO10 8AY

ROSEMARY FOR REMEMBRANCE

CMLJ	Commander of Merit, Order of St Lazarus of Jerusalem
CMM	Commander, Order of Military Merit (Canada)
CMO	Chief Medical Officer
CMP	Corps of Military Police (*now see* CRMP)
CMS	Church Missionary Society; Certificate in Management Studies
CMT	Chaconia Medal of Trinidad
CNAA	Council for National Academic Awards
CND	Campaign for Nuclear Disarmament
CNI	Companion, Nautical Institute
CNR	Canadian National Railways
CNRS	Centre National de la Recherche Scientifique
CO	Commanding Officer; Commonwealth Office (after Aug. 1966) (*now see* FCO); Colonial Office (before Aug. 1966); Conscientious Objector
Co.	County; Company
C of E	Church of England
C of S	Chief of Staff; Church of Scotland
Coal.L or Co.L	Coalition Liberal
Coal.U or Co.U	Coalition Unionist
COHSE	Confederation of Health Service Employees
COI	Central Office of Information
CoID	Council of Industrial Design (*now* Design Council)
Col	Colonel
Coll.	College; Collegiate
Colo	Colorado (US)
Col.-Sergt	Colour-Sergeant
Com	Communist
Comd	Command
Comdg	Commanding
Comdr	Commander
Comdt	Commandant
COMEC	Council of the Military Education Committees of the Universities of the UK
COMET	Committee for Middle East Trade
Commn	Commission
Commnd	Commissioned
CompAMEME	Companion, Association of Mining Electrical and Mechanical Engineers
CompICE	Companion, Institution of Civil Engineers
CompIEE	Companion, Institution of Electrical Engineers
CompIERE	Companion, Institution of Electronic and Radio Engineers
CompIGasE	Companion, Institution of Gas Engineers
CompIMechE	Companion, Institution of Mechanical Engineers
CompIWES	Companion, Institution of Water Engineers and Scientists
CompTI	Companion of the Textile Institute
Comr	Commissioner
Comy-Gen.	Commissary-General
CON	Commander, Order of the Niger
Conn	Connecticut (US)
Const.	Constitutional
Co-op.	Co-operative
COPA	Comité des Organisations Professionels Agricoles de la CEE
COPEC	Conference of Politics, Economics and Christianity
Corp.	Corporation; Corporal
Corresp. Mem.	Corresponding Member
COS	Chief of Staff; Charity Organization Society
COSA	Colliery Officials and Staffs Association
CoSIRA	Council for Small Industries in Rural Areas
COSLA	Convention of Scottish Local Authorities
COSPAR	Committee on Space Research
COSSAC	Chief of Staff to Supreme Allied Commander
COTC	Canadian Officers' Training Corps
CP	Central Provinces; Cape Province
CPA	Commonwealth Parliamentary Association; Chartered Patent Agent; Certified Public Accountant (Canada) (*now see* CA)
CPAG	Child Poverty Action Group
CPAS	Church Pastoral Aid Society
CPC	Conservative Political Centre
CPEng	Chartered Professional Engineer (of Institution of Engineers of Australia)
CPhys	Chartered Physicist
CPL	Chief Personnel and Logistics
CPM	Colonial Police Medal
CPR	Canadian Pacific Railway
CPRE	Council for the Protection of Rural England
CPSA	Civil and Public Services Association
CPSU	Communist Party of the Soviet Union
CPsychol	Chartered Psychologist
CPU	Commonwealth Press Union
CQSW	Certificate of Qualification in Social Work
CR	Community of the Resurrection
cr	created or creation
CRA	Commander, Royal Artillery
CRAC	Careers Research and Advisory Centre
CRAeS	Companion, Royal Aeronautical Society
CRASC	Commander, Royal Army Service Corps
CRC	Cancer Research Campaign; Community Relations Council
CRCP(C)	Certificant, Royal College of Physicians of Canada
CRE	Commander, Royal Engineers; Commission for Racial Equality; Commercial Relations and Exports
Cres.	Crescent
CRMP	Corps of Royal Military Police
CRNCM	Companion, Royal Northern College of Music
CRO	Commonwealth Relations Office (before Aug. 1966; *now see* FCO)

CS	Civil Service; Clerk to the Signet
CSA	Confederate States of America
CSAB	Civil Service Appeal Board
CSB	Bachelor of Christian Science
CSC	Conspicuous Service Cross; Congregation of the Holy Cross
CSCA	Civil Service Clerical Association (*now see* CPSA)
CSCE	Conference on Security and Co-operation in Europe
CSD	Civil Service Department; Co-operative Secretaries Diploma; Chartered Society of Designers
CSEU	Confederation of Shipbuilding and Engineering Unions
CSG	Companion, Order of the Star of Ghana; Company of the Servants of God
CSI	Companion, Order of the Star of India
CSIR	Commonwealth Council for Scientific and Industrial Research (*now see* CSIRO)
CSIRO	Commonwealth Scientific and Industrial Research Organization (Australia)
CSO	Chief Scientific Officer; Chief Signal Officer; Chief Staff Officer
CSP	Chartered Society of Physiotherapists; Civil Service of Pakistan
CSS	Companion, Star of Sarawak; Council for Science and Society
CSSB	Civil Service Selection Board
CSSp	Holy Ghost Father
CSSR	Congregation of the Most Holy Redeemer (Redemptorist Order)
CSTI	Council of Science and Technology Institutes
CStJ	Commander, Most Venerable Order of the Hospital of St John of Jerusalem
CSU	Christlich-Soziale Union in Bayern
CSV	Community Service Volunteers
CTA	Chaplain Territorial Army
CTB	College of Teachers of the Blind
CTC	Cyclists' Touring Club; Commando Training Centre
CText	Chartered Textile Technologist
CTR(Harwell)	Controlled Thermonuclear Research
CU	Cambridge University
CUAC	Cambridge University Athletic Club
CUAFC	Cambridge University Association Football Club
CUBC	Cambridge University Boat Club
CUCC	Cambridge University Cricket Club
CUF	Common University Fund
CUHC	Cambridge University Hockey Club
CUMS	Cambridge University Musical Society
CUNY	City University of New York
CUP	Cambridge University Press
CURUFC	Cambridge University Rugby Union Football Club
CV	Cross of Valour (Canada)
CVCP	Committee of Vice-Chancellors and Principals of the Universities of the United Kingdom
CVO	Commander, Royal Victorian Order
CVS	Council of Voluntary Service
CVSNA	Council of Voluntary Service National Association
CWA	Crime Writers Association
CWGC	Commonwealth War Graves Commission
CWS	Co-operative Wholesale Society

D

D	Duke
d	died; daughter
DA	Dame of St Andrew, Order of Barbados; Diploma in Anaesthesia; Diploma in Art
DAA&QMG	Deputy Assistant Adjutant and Quartermaster-General
DAAG	Deputy Assistant Adjutant-General
DA&QMG	Deputy Adjutant and Quartermaster-General
DAC	Development Assistance Committee
DACG	Deputy Assistant Chaplain-General
DAD	Deputy Assistant Director
DAdmin	Doctor of Administration
DADMS	Deputy Assistant Director of Medical Services
DADOS	Deputy Assistant Director of Ordnance Services
DADQ	Deputy Assistant Director of Quartering
DADST	Deputy Assistant Director of Supplies and Transport
DAG	Deputy Adjutant-General
DAgr	Doctor of Agriculture
DAMS	Deputy Assistant Military Secretary
D&AD	Designers and Art Directors Association
DAppSc	Doctor of Applied Science
DAQMG	Deputy Assistant Quartermaster-General
DArt	Doctor of Art
DASc	Doctor in Agricultural Sciences
DATA	Draughtsmen's and Allied Technicians' Association (later AUEW(TASS))
DATEC	Art and Design Committee, Technician Education Council
DBA	Doctor of Business Administration
DBE	Dame Commander, Order of the British Empire
DC	District Council; District of Columbia (US)
DCAe	Diploma of College of Aeronautics
DCAS	Deputy Chief of the Air Staff
DCB	Dame Commander, Order of the Bath
DCC	Diploma of Chelsea College
DCG	Deputy Chaplain-General
DCGRM	Department of the Commandant General Royal Marines
DCGS	Deputy Chief of the General Staff

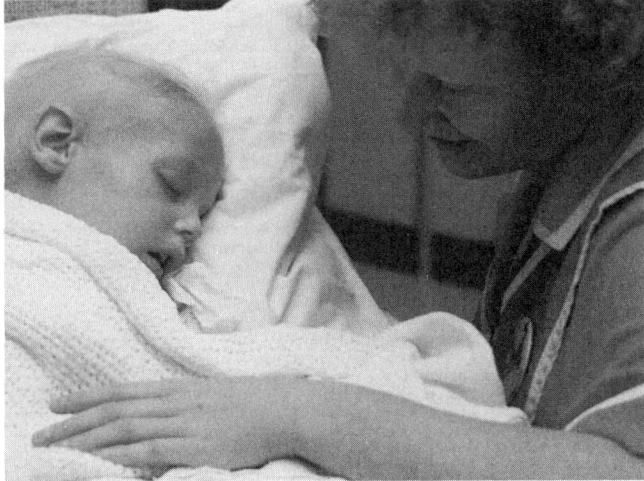

DCh	Doctor of Surgery
DCH	Diploma in Child Health
DCIGS	Deputy Chief of the Imperial General Staff (*now see* DCGS)
DCL	Doctor of Civil Law
DCLI	Duke of Cornwall's Light Infantry
DCLJ	Dame Commander, Order of St Lazarus of Jerusalem
DCM	Distinguished Conduct Medal
DCMG	Dame Commander, Order of St Michael and St George
DCMHE	Diploma of Contents and Methods in Health Education
DCnL	Doctor of Canon Law
DCO	Duke of Cambridge's Own
DComm	Doctor of Commerce
DCP	Diploma in Clinical Pathology; Diploma in Conservation of Paintings
DCS	Deputy Chief of Staff; Doctor of Commercial Sciences
DCSO	Deputy Chief Scientific Officer
DCT	Doctor of Christian Theology
DCVO	Dame Commander, Royal Victorian Order
DD	Doctor of Divinity
DDGAMS	Deputy Director General, Army Medical Services
DDL	Deputy Director of Labour
DDME	Deputy Director of Mechanical Engineering
DDMI	Deputy Director of Military Intelligence
DDMO	Deputy Director of Military Operations
DDMS	Deputy Director of Medical Services
DDMT	Deputy Director of Military Training
DDNI	Deputy Director of Naval Intelligence
DDO	Diploma in Dental Orthopaedics
DDPH	Diploma in Dental Public Health
DDPR	Deputy Director of Public Relations
DDPS	Deputy Director of Personal Services
DDR	Deutsche Demokratische Republik
DDRA	Deputy Director Royal Artillery
DDS	Doctor of Dental Surgery; Director of Dental Services
DDSc	Doctor of Dental Science
DDSD	Deputy Director Staff Duties
DDSM	Defense Distinguished Service Medal
DDST	Deputy Director of Supplies and Transport
DDWE&M	Deputy Director of Works, Electrical and Mechanical
DE	Doctor of Engineering
DEA	Department of Economic Affairs
decd	deceased
DEconSc	Doctor of Economic Science
DEd	Doctor of Education
Del	Delaware (US)
Deleg.	Delegate
DEME	Directorate of Electrical and Mechanical Engineering
DEMS	Defensively Equipped Merchant Ships
(DemU)	Democratic Unionist
DEng	Doctor of Engineering
DenM	Docteur en Médicine
DEOVR	Duke of Edinburgh's Own Volunteer Rifles
DEP	Department of Employment and Productivity; European Progressive Democrats
Dep.	Deputy
DES	Department of Education and Science
DèsL	Docteur ès lettres
DèsS or DèsSc	Docteur ès sciences
DesRCA	Designer of the Royal College of Art
DFA	Doctor of Fine Arts
DFC	Distinguished Flying Cross
DFH	Diploma of Faraday House
DFLS	Day Fighter Leaders' School
DFM	Distinguished Flying Medal
DG	Director General; Dragoon Guards
DGAA	Distressed Gentlefolks Aid Association
DGAMS	Director-General Army Medical Services
DGEME	Director General Electrical and Mechanical Engineering
DGLP(A)	Director General Logistic Policy (Army)
DGMS	Director-General of Medical Services
DGMT	Director-General of Military Training
DGMW	Director-General of Military Works
DGNPS	Director-General of Naval Personal Services
DGP	Director-General of Personnel
DGPS	Director-General of Personal Services
DGS	Diploma in Graduate Studies
DGStJ	Dame of Grace, Order of St John of Jerusalem (*now see* DStJ)
DGU	Doctor of Griffith University
DH	Doctor of Humanities
DHA	District Health Authority
Dhc	Doctor *honoris causa*
DHEW	Department of Health Education and Welfare (US)
DHL	Doctor of Humane Letters; Doctor of Hebrew Literature
DHM	Dean Hole Medal
DHMSA	Diploma in the History of Medicine (Society of Apothecaries)
DHQ	District Headquarters
DHSS	Department of Health and Social Security (*now see* DoH *and* DSS)
DHumLit	Doctor of Humane Letters
DIAS	Dublin Institute of Advanced Sciences
DIC	Diploma of the Imperial College
DICTA	Diploma of Imperial College of Tropical Agriculture
DIG	Deputy Inspector-General
DIH	Diploma in Industrial Health
DIMP	Darjah Indera Mahkota Pahang
Dio.	Diocese
DipAA	Diploma in Applied Art

DipAD	Diploma in Art and Design
DipAe	Diploma in Aeronautics
DipArch	Diploma in Architecture
DipASE	Diploma in Advanced Study of Education, College of Preceptors
DipAvMed	Diploma of Aviation Medicine, Royal College of Physicians
DipBA	Diploma in Business Administration
DipBS	Diploma in Fine Art, Byam Shaw School
DipCAM	Diploma in Communications, Advertising and Marketing of CAM Foundation
DipCC	Diploma of the Central College
DipCD	Diploma in Civic Design
DipCE	Diploma in Civil Engineering
DipEcon	Diploma in Economics
DipEd	Diploma in Education
DipEE	Diploma in Electrical Engineering
DipEl	Diploma in Electronics
DipESL	Diploma in English as a Second Language
DipEth	Diploma in Ethnology
DipFD	Diploma in Funeral Directing
DipFE	Diploma in Further Education
DipGSM	Diploma in Music, Guildhall School of Music and Drama
DipHA	Diploma in Hospital Administration
DipHSM	Diploma in Health Services Management
DipHum	Diploma in Humanities
DipLA	Diploma in Landscape Architecture
DipLib	Diploma of Librarianship
DipM	Diploma in Marketing
DipN	Diploma in Nursing
DipNEC	Diploma of Northampton Engineering College (*now* City University)
DipPA	Diploma of Practitioners in Advertising (*now see* DipCAM)
DipREM	Diploma in Rural Estate Management
DipSoc	Diploma in Sociology
DipTA	Diploma in Tropical Agriculture
DipT&CP	Diploma in Town and Country Planning
DipTh	Diploma in Theology
DipTP	Diploma in Town Planning
DipTPT	Diploma in Theory and Practice of Teaching
DistTP	Distinction in Town Planning
Div.	Division; Divorced
DJAG	Deputy Judge Advocate General
DJPD	Dato Jasa Purba Di-Raja Negeri Sembilan (Malaysia)
DJStJ	Dame of Justice, Order of St John of Jerusalem (*now see* DStJ)
DJur	*Doctor Juris*
DK	Most Esteemed Family Order (Brunei)
DL	Deputy Lieutenant
DLC	Diploma Loughborough College
DLES	Doctor of Letters in Economic Studies
DLI	Durham Light Infantry
DLit or DLitt	Doctor of Literature; Doctor of Letters
DLittS	Doctor of Sacred Letters
DLJ	Dame of Grace, Order of St Lazarus of Jerusalem
DLO	Diploma in Laryngology and Otology
DM	Doctor of Medicine
DMA	Diploma in Municipal Administration
DMD	Doctor of Medical Dentistry (Australia)
DME	Director of Mechanical Engineering
DMet	Doctor of Metallurgy
DMI	Director of Military Intelligence
DMin	Doctor of Ministry
DMJ	Diploma in Medical Jurisprudence
DMJ(Path)	Diploma in Medical Jurisprudence (Pathology)
DMLJ	Dame of Merit, Order of St Lazarus of Jerusalem
DMO	Director of Military Operations
DMR	Diploma in Medical Radiology
DMRD	Diploma in Medical Radiological Diagnosis
DMRE	Diploma in Medical Radiology and Electrology
DMRT	Diploma in Medical Radio-Therapy
DMS	Director of Medical Services; Decoration for Meritorious Service (South Africa); Diploma in Management Studies
DMSSB	Direct Mail Services Standards Board
DMT	Director of Military Training
DMus	Doctor of Music
DN	Diploma in Nursing
DNB	Dictionary of National Biography
DNE	Director of Naval Equipment
DNI	Director of Naval Intelligence
DO	Diploma in Ophthalmology
DOAE	Defence Operational Analysis Establishment
DObstRCOG	Diploma of Royal College of Obstetricians and Gynaecologists
DOC	District Officer Commanding
DocEng	Doctor of Engineering
DoE	Department of the Environment
DoH	Department of Health
DoI	Department of Industry
DOL	Doctor of Oriental Learning
Dom.	*Dominus*
DOMS	Diploma in Ophthalmic Medicine and Surgery
DOR	Director of Operational Requirements
DOrthRCS	Diploma in Orthodontics, Royal College of Surgeons
DOS	Director of Ordnance Services; Doctor of Ocular Science
Dow.	Dowager
DP	Data Processing
DPA	Diploma in Public Administration; Discharged Prisoners' Aid
DPD	Diploma in Public Dentistry

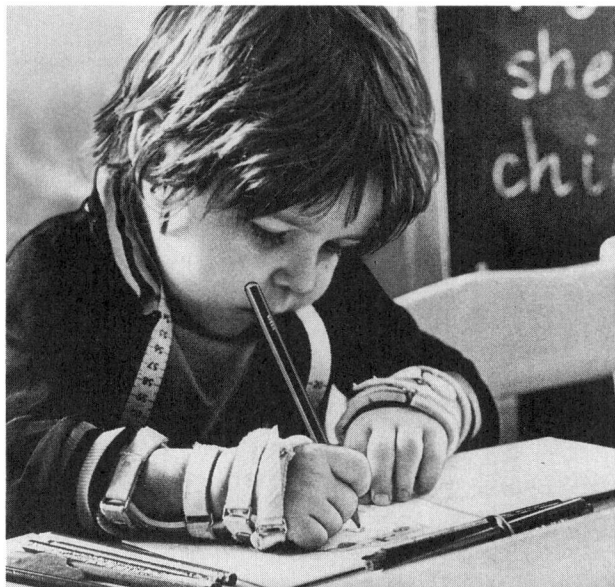

DPEc	Doctor of Political Economy
DPed	Doctor of Pedagogy
DPH	Diploma in Public Health
DPh or DPhil	Doctor of Philosophy
DPhysMed	Diploma in Physical Medicine
DPLG	Diplômé par le Gouvernement
DPM	Diploma in Psychological Medicine
DPMS	Dato Paduka Mahkota Selangor (Malaysia)
DPP	Director of Public Prosecutions
DPR	Director of Public Relations
DPS	Director of Postal Services; Director of Personal Services; Doctor of Public Service
DPSE	Diploma in Professional Studies in Education
DQMG	Deputy Quartermaster-General
Dr	Doctor
DRAC	Director Royal Armoured Corps
DRC	Diploma of Royal College of Science and Technology, Glasgow
DRD	Diploma in Restorative Dentistry
Dr ing	Doctor of Engineering
Dr jur	Doctor of Laws
DrŒcPol	*Doctor Œconomiæ Politicæ*
Dr rer. nat.	Doctor of Natural Science
DRS	Diploma in Religious Studies
DRSAMD	Diploma of the Royal Scottish Academy of Music and Drama
DS	Directing Staff; Doctor of Science
DSA	Diploma in Social Administration
DSAC	Defence Scientific Advisory Council
DSAO	Diplomatic Service Adinistration Office
DSC	Distinguished Service Cross
DSc	Doctor of Science
DScA	Docteur en sciences agricoles
DSCHE	Diploma of the Scottish Council for Health Education
DScMil	Doctor of Military Science
DSD	Director Staff Duties
DSIR	Department of Scientific and Industrial Research (later SRC; *now see* SERC)
DSL	Doctor of Sacred Letters
DSLJ	Dato Seri Laila Jasa Brunei
DSM	Distinguished Service Medal
DSNB	Dato Setia Negara Brunei
DSNS	Dato Setia Negeri Sembilan (Malaysia)
DSO	Companion of the Distinguished Service Order
DSocSc	Doctor of Social Science
DSP	Director of Selection of Personnel; Docteur en sciences politiques (Montreal)
dsp	*decessit sine prole* (died without issue)
DSS	Department of Social Security; Doctor of Sacred Scripture
Dss	Deaconess
DSSc	Doctor of Social Science
DST	Director of Supplies and Transport
DStJ	Dame of Grace, Most Venerable Order of the Hospital of St John of Jerusalem; Dame of Justice, Most Venerable Order of the Hospital of St John of Jerusalem
DTA	Diploma in Tropical Agriculture
DTD	Dekoratie voor Trouwe Dienst (Decoration for Devoted Service)
DTech	Doctor of Technology
DTH	Diploma in Tropical Hygiene
DTheol	Doctor of Theology
DThPT	Diploma in Theory and Practice of Teaching
DTI	Department of Trade and Industry
DTM&H	Diploma in Tropical Medicine and Hygiene
DU	Doctor of the University
Dunelm	*Dunelmensis* (of Durham)
DUniv	Doctor of the University
DUP	Docteur de l'Université de Paris
(DUP)	Democratic Unionist Party
DVA	Diploma of Veterinary Anaesthesia
DVH	Diploma in Veterinary Hygiene
DVLA	Driver and Vehicle Licensing Authority
DVLC	Driver and Vehicle Licensing Centre
DVM	Doctor of Veterinary Medicine
DVMS	Doctor of Veterinary Medicine and Surgery
DVR	Diploma in Veterinary Radiology
DVSc	Doctor of Veterinary Science
DVSM	Diploma in Veterinary State Medicine

E

E	East; Earl; England
e	eldest
EAA	Edinburgh Architectural Association
EAHY	European Architectural Heritage Year
EAP	East Africa Protectorate
EAW	Electrical Association for Women
EBC	English Benedictine Congregation
Ebor	*Eboracensis* (of York)
EBRD	European Bank for Reconstruction and Development
EBU	European Broadcasting Union
EC	Etoile du Courage (Canada); European Community; Emergency Commission
ECA	Economic Co-operation Administration; Economic Commission for Africa
ECAFE	Economic Commission for Asia and the Far East (*now see* ESCAP)

ECCTIS	Education Courses and Credit Transfer Information Systems
ECE	Economic Commission for Europe
ECGD	Export Credits Guarantee Department
ECLA	Economic Commission for Latin America
ECOVAST	European Council for the Village and Small Town
ECSC	European Coal and Steel Community
ECU	English Church Union
ED	Efficiency Decoration; Doctor of Engineering (US); European Democrat
ed	edited
EdB	Bachelor of Education
EDC	Economic Development Committee
EdD	Doctor of Education
EDF	European Development Fund
EDG	European Democratic Group
Edin.	Edinburgh
Edn	Edition
EDP	Executive Development Programme
Educ	Educated
Educn	Education
EEC	European Economic Community (*now see* EC); Commission of the European Communities
EEF	Engineering Employers' Federation; Egyptian Expeditionary Force
EETPU	Electrical Electronic Telecommunication & Plumbing Union
EETS	Early English Text Society
EFCE	European Federation of Chemical Engineering
EFTA	European Free Trade Association
eh	ehrenhalber (honorary)
EI	East Indian; East Indies
EIA	Engineering Industries Association
EIB	European Investment Bank
EICS	East India Company's Service
E-in-C	Engineer-in-Chief
EIS	Educational Institute of Scotland
EISCAT	European Incoherent Scatter Association
EIU	Economist Intelligence Unit
ELBS	English Language Book Society
ELSE	European Life Science Editors
ELT	English Language Teaching
EM	Edward Medal; Earl Marshal
EMBL	European Molecular Biology Laboratory
EMBO	European Molecular Biology Organisation
EMP	Electro Magnetic Pulse; Executive Management Program Diploma
EMS	Emergency Medical Service
Enc.Brit.	Encyclopaedia Britannica
Eng.	England
Engr	Engineer
ENO	English National Opera
ENSA	Entertainments National Service Association
ENT	Ear Nose and Throat
EO	Executive Officer
EOPH	Examined Officer of Public Health
EORTC	European Organisation for Research on Treatment of Cancer
EPP	European People's Party
er	elder
ER	Eastern Region (BR)
ERA	Electrical Research Association
ERC	Electronics Research Council
ERD	Emergency Reserve Decoration (Army)
ESA	European Space Agency
ESCAP	Economic and Social Commission for Asia and the Pacific
ESF	European Science Foundn
ESL	English as a Second Language
ESNS	Educational Sub-Normal Serious
ESRC	Economic and Social Research Council; Electricity Supply Research Council
ESRO	European Space Research Organization (*now see* ESA)
ESU	English-Speaking Union
ETA	Engineering Training Authority
ETH	Eidgenössische Technische Hochschule
ETUC	European Trade Union Confederation
EUDISED	European Documentation and Information Service for Education
Euratom	European Atomic Energy Community
Eur Ing	European Engineer
EUROM	European Federation for Optics and Precision Mechanics
EUW	European Union of Women
eV	eingetragener Verein
Ext	Extinct

F

FA	Football Association
FAA	Fellow, Australian Academy of Science; Fleet Air Arm
FAAAS	Fellow, American Association for the Advancement of Science
FAAO	Fellow, American Academy of Optometry
FAAP	Fellow, American Academy of Pediatrics
FAARM	Fellow, American Academy of Reproductive Medicine
FAAV	Fellow, Central Association of Agricultural Valuers
FAAVCT	Fellow, American Academy of Veterinary and Comparative Toxicology
FACC	Fellow, American College of Cardiology

"NOW IT'S GRANDPA'S HOUR OF NEED, IT'S THE RAF BENEVOLENT FUND THAT DESERVES A MEDAL"

"Grandpa was admired for many brave acts, but he won his DFM for his part in the Battle of Britain. Now he's been in the wars himself, he says it's the RAF Benevolent Fund that really deserves a medal."

Over 70,000 RAF men and women died for our country during the last War. Many thousands more were left disabled. Since 1945, too, the RAF has incurred casualties in its training, peace-preserving missions and operations.

From 1919, the Fund has been helping past and present RAF members of all ranks, their widows and children. In 1990, it expended over £7.9 million in making some 15,000 awards. Inflation and old age increases that figure annually.

Where does the money go? To helping families maintain a semblance of the life they had before, by providing housing and funds to overcome financial difficulties, by looking after the infirm in our rest homes and many other ways in which the Fund contributes to the well being of those who have an hour of need.

We urgently need your support to repay the debt we owe those who have suffered on our behalf. All donations will be gratefully received. We'll also be happy to advise on legacies, covenants and payroll giving. Please complete the coupon now.

Help MEDICINE
fight the evils of disease

HEART DISEASE, STROKE, SKIN CANCER... HELP US TO FIND THE ANSWERS.

At the Royal College of Physicians we are working to find the causes, cures and preventive treatments for these and other modern diseases. We carry out research into severe problems like the elderly mentally ill and alcohol abuse. We publish reports — "Smoking and Health" for example — which change and possibly <u>save</u> millions of lives. We carry out a continuous round of educational and training projects to maintain standards of Medicine in the community. Some of these meet the special needs of the day — such as equipping doctors to work on the problem of AIDS.

But all this costs enormous sums of money, and we rely entirely on charity. The solution? Our 'Help Medicine' appeal fund to finance our many projects. Please help us help medicine. You could be helping someone in your family. You could support a project in a field where you have had personal experience.

Help Medicine with a donation, a deed of covenant, or with a legacy (our programme is continuous). We will gladly send you details of current projects. Write to the Appeal Director, or telephone **071 935 1174**

FACCA	Fellow, Association of Certified and Corporate Accountants (*now see* FCCA)
FACCP	Fellow, American College of Chest Physicians
FACD	Fellow, American College of Dentistry
FACDS	Fellow, Australian College of Dental Surgeons (*now see* FRACDS)
FACE	Fellow, Australian College of Education
FACerS	Fellow, American Ceramic Society
FACI	Fellow, Australian Chemical Institute (*now see* FRACI)
FACMA	Fellow, Australian College of Medical Administrators (*now see* FRACMA)
FACOG	Fellow, American College of Obstetricians and Gynæcologists
FACOM	Fellow, Australian College of Occupational Medicine
FACP	Fellow, American College of Physicians
FACR	Fellow, American College of Radiology
FACRM	Fellow, Australian College of Rehabilitation Medicine
FACS	Fellow, American College of Surgeons
FACVT	Fellow, American College of Veterinary Toxicology (*now see* FAAVCT)
FAeSI	Fellow, Aeronautical Society of India
FAGO	Fellowship in Australia in Obstetrics and Gynaecology
FAGS	Fellow, American Geographical Society
FAHA	Fellow, Australian Academy of the Humanities
FAI	Fellow, Chartered Auctioneers' and Estate Agents' Institute (*now* (after amalgamation) *see* FRICS); Fédération Aéronautique Internationale
FAIA	Fellow, American Institute of Architects
FAIAA	Fellow, American Institute of Aeronautics and Astronautics
FAIAS	Fellow, Australian Institute of Agricultural Science
FAIB	Fellow, Australian Institute of Bankers
FAIBiol	Fellow, Australian Institute of Biology
FAIE	Fellow, Australian Institute of Energy
FAIEx	Fellow, Australian Institute of Export
FAIFST	Fellow, Australian Institute of Food Science and Technology
FAII	Fellow, Australian Insurance Institute
FAIM	Fellow, Australian Institute of Management
FAIP	Fellow, Australian Institute of Physics
FAMA	Fellow, Australian Medical Association
FAMI	Fellow, Australian Marketing Institute
FAmNucSoc	Fellow, American Nuclear Society
FAMS	Fellow, Ancient Monuments Society
F and GP	Finance and General Purposes
FANY	First Aid Nursing Yeomanry
FANZCP	Fellow, Australian and New Zealand College of Psychiatrists (*now see* FRANZCP)
FAO	Food and Agriculture Organization of the United Nations
FAPA	Fellow, American Psychiatric Association
FAPHA	Fellow, American Public Health Association
FAPI	Fellow, Australian Planning Institute (*now see* FRAPI)
FAPM	Fellow, Association of Project Managers
FAPS	Fellow, American Phytopathological Society
FArborA	Fellow, Arboricultural Association
FARE	Federation of Alcoholic Rehabilitation Establishments
FARELF	Far East Land Forces
FAS	Fellow, Antiquarian Society; Fellow, Nigerian Academy of Science
FASA	Fellow, Australian Society of Accountants (*now see* FCPA)
FASc	Fellow, Indian Academy of Sciences
fasc.	fascicule
FASCE	Fellow, American Society of Civil Engineers
FASI	Fellow, Architects' and Surveyors' Institute
FASSA	Fellow, Academy of the Social Sciences in Australia
FAusIMM	Fellow, Australasian Institute of Mining and Metallurgy
FAustCOG	Fellow, Australian College of Obstetricians and Gynæcologists (*now see* FRACOG)
FBA	Fellow, British Academy; Federation of British Artists
FBCO	Fellow, British College of Ophthalmic Opticians (Optometrists)
FBCS	Fellow, British Computer Society
FBEC(S)	Fellow, Business Education Council (Scotland)
FBHI	Fellow, British Horological Institute
FBHS	Fellow, British Horse Society
FBI	Federation of British Industries (*now see* CBI); Federal Bureau of Investigation
FBIA	Fellow, Bankers' Institute of Australasia (*now see* FAIB)
FBIBA	Fellow, British Insurance Brokers' Association
FBID	Fellow, British Institute of Interior Design
FBIM	Fellow, British Institute of Management
FBINZ	Fellow, Bankers' Institute of New Zealand
FBIPP	Fellow, British Institute of Professional Photography
FBIRA	Fellow, British Institute of Regulatory Affairs
FBIS	Fellow, British Interplanetary Society
FBKS	Fellow, British Kinematograph Society (*now see* FBKSTS)
FBKSTS	Fellow, British Kinematograph, Sound and Television Society
FBOA	Fellow, British Optical Association
FBOU	Fellow, British Ornithologists' Union
FBPICS	Fellow, British Production and Inventory Control Society
FBritIRE	Fellow, British Institution of Radio Engineers (*now see* FIERE)
FBPsS	Fellow, British Psychological Society
FBS	Fellow, Building Societies Institute (*now see* FCBSI)
FBSI	Fellow, Boot and Shoe Institution (*now see* FCFI)
FBSM	Fellow, Birmingham School of Music
FC	Football Club
FCA	Fellow, Institute of Chartered Accountants; Fellow, Institute of Chartered Accountants in Australia; Fellow, New Zealand Society of Accountants; Federation of Canadian Artists

FCAI	Fellow, New Zealand Institute of Cost Accountants; Fellow, Canadian Aeronautical Institute (*now see* FCASI)
FCAM	Fellow, CAM Foundation
FCAnaes	Fellow, College of Anaesthetists (*now see* FRCAnaes)
FCASI	Fellow, Canadian Aeronautics and Space Institute
FCBSI	Fellow, Chartered Building Societies Institute
FCCA	Fellow, Association of Certified Accountants
FCCEA	Fellow, Commonwealth Council for Educational Administration
FCCS	Fellow, Corporation of Secretaries (*formerly* of Certified Secretaries)
FCCT	Fellow, Canadian College of Teachers
FCEC	Federation of Civil Engineering Contractors
FCFI	Fellow, Clothing and Footwear Institute
FCGI	Fellow, City and Guilds of London Institute
FCGP	Fellow, College of General Practitioners (*now see* FRCGP)
FCH	Fellow, Coopers Hill College
FChS	Fellow, Society of Chiropodists
FCI	Fellow, Institute of Commerce
FCIA	Fellow, Corporation of Insurance Agents
FCIArb	Fellow, Chartered Institute of Arbitrators ·
FCIB	Fellow, Corporation of Insurance Brokers; Fellow, Chartered Institute of Bankers
FCIBS	Fellow, Chartered Institution of Building Services (*now see* FCIBSE)
FCIBSE	Fellow, Chartered Institution of Building Services Engineers
FCIC	Fellow, Chemical Institute of Canada (*formerly* Canadian Institute of Chemistry)
FCII	Fellow, Chartered Insurance Institute
FCILA	Fellow, Chartered Institute of Loss Adjusters
FCIM	Fellow, Chartered Institute of Marketing; Fellow, Institute of Corporate Managers (Australia)
FCIOB	Fellow, Chartered Institute of Building
FCIPA	Fellow, Chartered Institute of Patent Agents (*now see* CPA)
FCIS	Fellow, Institute of Chartered Secretaries and Administrators (*formerly* Chartered Institute of Secretaries)
FCISA	Fellow, Chartered Institute of Secretaries and Administrators (Australia)
FCIT	Fellow, Chartered Institute of Transport
FCM	Faculty of Community Medicine
FCMA	Fellow, Chartered Institute of Management Accountants (*formerly* Institute of Cost and Management Accountants)
FCMSA	Fellow, College of Medicine of South Africa
FCNA	Fellow, College of Nursing, Australia
FCO	Foreign and Commonwealth Office (departments merged Oct. 1968)
FCOG(SA)	Fellow, South African College of Obstetrics and Gynæcology
FCollH	Fellow, College of Handicraft
FCollP	Fellow, College of Preceptors
FCommA	Fellow, Society of Commercial Accountants (*now see* FSCA)
FCOphth	Fellow, College of Ophthalmologists
FCP	Fellow, College of Preceptors
FCPA	Fellow, Australian Society of Certified Practising Accountants
FCPath	Fellow, College of Pathologists (*now see* FRCPath)
FCPS	Fellow, College of Physicians and Surgeons
FCP(SoAf)	Fellow, College of Physicians, South Africa
FCPSO(SoAf)	Fellow, College of Physicians and Surgeons and Obstetricians, South Africa
FCPS (Pak)	Fellow, College of Physicians and Surgeons of Pakistan
FCRA	Fellow, College of Radiologists of Australia (*now see* FRACR)
FCS	Federation of Conservative Students
FCS or FChemSoc	Fellow, Chemical Society (now absorbed into Royal Society of Chemistry)
FCSD	Fellow, Chartered Society of Designers
FCSP	Fellow, Chartered Society of Physiotherapy
FCSSA or FCS(SoAf)	Fellow, College of Surgeons, South Africa
FCSSL	Fellow, College of Surgeons of Sri Lanka
FCST	Fellow, College of Speech Therapists
FCT	Federal Capital Territory (*now see* ACT); Fellow, Association of Corporate Treasurers
FCTB	Fellow, College of Teachers of the Blind
FCU	Fighter Control Unit
FCWA	Fellow, Institute of Cost and Works Accountants (*now see* FCMA)
FDF	Food and Drink Federation
FDI	Fédération Dentaire Internationale
FDP	Freie Demokratische Partei
FDS	Fellow in Dental Surgery
FDSRCPSGlas	Fellow in Dental Surgery, Royal College of Physicians and Surgeons of Glasgow
FDSRCS or FDS RCS	Fellow in Dental Surgery, Royal College of Surgeons of England
FDSRCSE	Fellow in Dental Surgery, Royal College of Surgeons of Edinburgh
FE	Far East
FEAF	Far East Air Force
FEANI	Fédération Européenne d'Associations Nationales d'Ingénieurs
FEBS	Federation of European Biochemical Societies
FECI	Fellow, Institute of Employment Consultants
FEE	Fédération des Expertes Comptables Européens
FEF	Far East Fleet

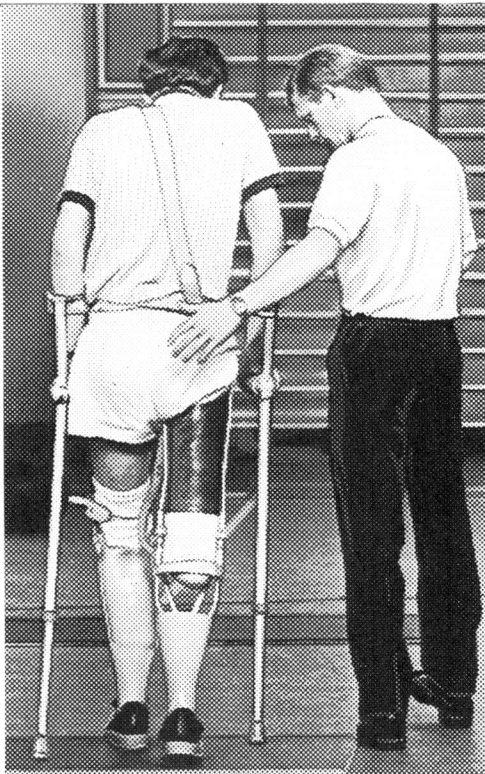

FEI	Fédération Equestre Internationale
FEIDCT	Fellow, Educational Institute of Design Craft and Technology
FEIS	Fellow, Educational Institute of Scotland
FELCO	Federation of English Language Course Opportunities
FEng	Fellow, Fellowship of Engineering
FES	Fellow, Entomological Society; Fellow, Ethnological Society
FESC	Fellow, European Society of Cardiology
FF	Fianna Fáil; Field Force
FFA	Fellow, Faculty of Actuaries (in Scotland); Fellow, Institute of Financial Accountants
FFARACS	Fellow, Faculty of Anaesthetists, Royal Australian College of Surgeons
FFARCS	Fellow, Faculty of Anaesthetists, Royal College of Surgeons of England
FFARCSI	Fellow, Faculty of Anaesthetists, Royal College of Surgeons in Ireland
FFAS	Fellow, Faculty of Architects and Surveyors, London (*now see* FASI)
FFA(SA)	Fellow, Faculty of Anaesthetists (South Africa)
FFB	Fellow, Faculty of Building
FFCM	Fellow, Faculty of Community Medicine (*now see* FFPHM)
FFCMI	Fellow, Faculty of Community Medicine of Ireland
FFDRCSI	Fellow, Faculty of Dentistry, Royal College of Surgeons in Ireland
FFF	Free French Forces
FFHC	Freedom from Hunger Campaign
FFHom	Fellow, Faculty of Homœopathy
FFI	French Forces of the Interior; Finance for Industry
FFOM	Fellow, Faculty of Occupational Medicine
FFOMI	Fellow, Faculty of Occupational Medicine of Ireland
FFPath, RCPI	Fellow, Faculty of Pathologists of the Royal College of Physicians of Ireland
FFPHM	Fellow, Faculty of Public Health Medicine
FFPM	Fellow, Faculty of Pharmaceutical Medicine
FFPS	Fauna and Flora Preservation Society
FFR	Fellow, Faculty of Radiologists (*now see* FRCR)
FG	Fine Gael
FGA	Fellow, Gemmological Association
FGCM	Fellow, Guild of Church Musicians
FGDS	Fédération de la Gauche Démocratique et Socialiste
FGGE	Fellow, Guild of Glass Engineers
FGI	Fellow, Institute of Certificated Grocers
FGS	Fellow, Geological Society
FGSM	Fellow, Guildhall School of Music and Drama
FGSM(MT)	Fellow, Guildhall School of Music and Drama (Music Therapy)
FHA	Fellow, Institute of Health Service Administrators (*formerly* Hospital Administrators; *now see* FHSM)
FHAS	Fellow, Highland and Agricultural Society of Scotland
FHCIMA	Fellow, Hotel Catering and Institutional Management Association
FHFS	Fellow, Human Factors Society
FHKIE	Fellow, Hong Kong Institution of Engineers
FHMAAAS	Foreign Honorary Member, American Academy of Arts and Sciences
FHS	Fellow, Heraldry Society; Forces Help Society and Lord Roberts Workshops
FHSA	Family Health Services Authority
FHSM	Fellow, Institute of Health Services Management
FH-WC	Fellow, Heriot-Watt College (*now* University), Edinburgh
FIA	Fellow, Institute of Actuaries
FIAA	Fellow, Institute of Actuaries of Australia
FIAAS	Fellow, Institute of Australian Agricultural Science
FIAA&S	Fellow, Incorporated Association of Architects and Surveyors
FIAgrE	Fellow, Institution of Agricultural Engineers
FIAI	Fellow, Institute of Industrial and Commercial Accountants
FIAL	Fellow, International Institute of Arts and Letters
FIAM	Fellow, International Academy of Management
FIAP	Fellow, Institution of Analysts and Programmers
FIArb	Fellow, Institute of Arbitrators (*now see* FCIArb)
FIArbA	Fellow, Institute of Arbitrators of Australia
FIAS	Fellow, Institute of Aeronautical Sciences (US) (*now see* FAIAA)
FIASc	Fellow, Indian Academy of Sciences
FIAWS	Fellow, International Academy of Wood Sciences
FIB	Fellow, Institute of Bankers (*now see* FCIB)
FIBA	Fellow, Institute of Business Administration, Australia (*now see* FCIM)
FIBD	Fellow, Institute of British Decorators
FIBiol	Fellow, Institute of Biology
FIBiotech	Fellow, Institute for Biotechnical Studies
FIBP	Fellow, Institute of British Photographers
FIBScot	Fellow, Institute of Bankers in Scotland
FIC	Fellow, Institute of Chemistry (*now see* FRIC, FRSC); Fellow, Imperial College, London
FICA	Fellow, Commonwealth Institute of Accountants; Fellow, Institute of Chartered Accountants in England and Wales (*now see* FCA)
FICAI	Fellow, Institute of Chartered Accountants in Ireland
FICD	Fellow, Institute of Civil Defence; Fellow, Indian College of Dentists
FICE	Fellow, Institution of Civil Engineers
FICeram	Fellow, Institute of Ceramics
FICFM	Fellow, Institute of Charity Fundraising Managers
FICFor	Fellow, Institute of Chartered Foresters
FIChemE	Fellow, Institution of Chemical Engineers
FICI	Fellow, Institute of Chemistry of Ireland; Fellow, International Colonial Institute

FICM	Fellow, Institute of Credit Management
FICMA	Fellow, Institute of Cost and Management Accountants
FICorrST	Fellow, Institution of Corrosion Science and Technology
FICS	Fellow, Institute of Chartered Shipbrokers; Fellow, International College of Surgeons
FICT	Fellow, Institute of Concrete Technologists
FICW	Fellow, Institute of Clerks of Works of Great Britain
FIDA	Fellow, Institute of Directors, Australia
FIDCA	Fellow, Industrial Design Council of Australia
FIDE	Fédération Internationale des Echecs; Fellow, Institute of Design Engineers
FIE(Aust)	Fellow, Institution of Engineers, Australia
FIEC	Fellow, Institute of Employment Consultants
FIED	Fellow, Institution of Engineering Designers
FIEE	Fellow, Institution of Electrical Engineers
FIEEE	Fellow, Institute of Electrical and Electronics Engineers (NY)
FIEHK	Fellow, Institution of Engineering, Hong Kong
FIElecIE	Fellow, Institution of Electronic Incorporated Engineers (*now see* FIEIE)
FIEI	Fellow, Institution of Engineering Inspection (*now see* FIQA); Fellow, Institution of Engineers of Ireland
FIEIE	Fellow, Institution of Electronics and Electrical Incorporated Engineers
FIEJ	Fédération Internationale des Editeurs de Journaux et Publications
FIERE	Fellow, Institution of Electronic and Radio Engineers (*now see* FIEE)
FIES	Fellow, Illuminating Engineering Society (later FIllumES; *now see* FCIBSE)
FIET	Fédération Internationale des Employés, Techniciens et Cadres
FIEx	Fellow, Institute of Export
FIExpE	Fellow, Institute of Explosives Engineers
FIFA	Fédération Internationale de Football Association
FIFF	Fellow, Institute of Freight Forwarders
FIFireE	Fellow, Institution of Fire Engineers
FIFM	Fellow, Institute of Fisheries Management
FIFor	Fellow, Institute of Foresters (*now see* FICFor)
FIFST	Fellow, Institute of Food Science and Technology
FIGasE	Fellow, Institution of Gas Engineers
FIGCM	Fellow, Incorporated Guild of Church Musicians
FIGD	Fellow, Institute of Grocery Distribution
FIGO	International Federation of Gynaecology and Obstetrics
FIH	Fellow, Institute of Housing; Fellow, Institute of the Horse
FIHE	Fellow, Institute of Health Education
FIHM	Fellow, Institute of Housing Managers (*now see* FIH)
FIHort	Fellow, Institute of Horticulture
FIHospE	Fellow, Institute of Hospital Engineering
FIHT	Fellow, Institution of Highways and Transportation
FIHVE	Fellow, Institution of Heating & Ventilating Engineers (later FCIBS and MCIBS; *now see* FCIBSE)
FIIA	Fellow, Institute of Industrial Administration (*now see* CBIM and FBIM); Fellow, Institute of Internal Auditors
FIIC	Fellow, International Institute for Conservation of Historic and Artistic Works
FIIM	Fellow, Institution of Industrial Managers
FIInfSc	Fellow, Institute of Information Scientists
FIInst	Fellow, Imperial Institute
FIIP	Fellow, Institute of Incorporated Photographers (*now see* FBIPP)
FIIPE	Fellow, Indian Institution of Production Engineers
FIL	Fellow, Institute of Linguists
FILA	Fellow, Institute of Landscape Architects (*now see* FLI)
FILDM	Fellow, Institute of Logistics and Distribution Management
FilDr	Doctor of Philosophy
Fil.Hed.	Filosofie Hedersdoktor
FILLM	Fédération Internationale des Langues et Littératures Modernes
FIllumES	Fellow, Illuminating Engineering Society (*now see* FCIBSE)
FIM	Fellow, Institute of Metals (*formerly* Institution of Metallurgists)
FIMA	Fellow, Institute of Mathematics and its Applications
FIMarE	Fellow, Institute of Marine Engineers
FIMatM	Fellow, Institute of Materials Management
FIMBRA	Financial Intermediaries, Managers and Brokers Regulatory Association
FIMC	Fellow, Institute of Management Consultants
FIMCB	Fellow, International Management Centre from Buckingham
FIMechE	Fellow, Institution of Mechanical Engineers
FIMfgE	Fellow, Institution of Manufacturing Engineers (*now see* FIEE)
FIMFT	Fellow, Institute of Maxillo-facial Technology
FIMGTechE	Fellow, Institution of Mechanical and General Technician Engineers
FIMH	Fellow, Institute of Materials Handling (*now see* FIMatM); Fellow, Institute of Military History
FIMI	Fellow, Institute of the Motor Industry
FIMinE	Fellow, Institution of Mining Engineers
FIMIT	Fellow, Institute of Musical Instrument Technology
FIMLS	Fellow, Institute of Medical Laboratory Sciences
FIMLT	Fellow, Institute of Medical Laboratory Technology (*now see* FIMLS)
FIMM	Fellow, Institution of Mining and Metallurgy
FIMMA	Fellow, Institute of Metals and Materials Australasia
FIMS	Fellow, Institute of Mathematical Statistics
FIMT	Fellow, Institute of the Motor Trade (*now see* FIMI)
FIMTA	Fellow, Institute of Municipal Treasurers and Accountants (*now see* IPFA)

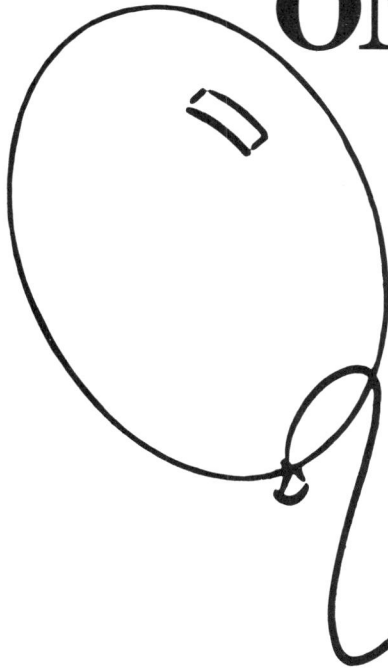

FIMunE	Fellow, Institution of Municipal Engineers (now amalgamated with Institution of Civil Engineers)
FIN	Fellow, Institute of Navigation (now see FRIN)
FINA	Fédération Internationale de Natation Amateur
FInstAM	Fellow, Institute of Administrative Management
FInstB	Fellow, Institution of Buyers
FInstBiol	Fellow, Institute of Biology (now see FIBiol)
FInstD	Fellow, Institute of Directors
FInstE	Fellow, Institute of Energy
FInstEnvSci	Fellow, Institute of Environmental Sciences
FInstF	Fellow, Institute of Fuel (now see FInstE)
FInstFF	Fellow, Institute of Freight Forwarders Ltd (now see FIFF)
FInstHE	Fellow, Institution of Highways Engineers (now see FIHT)
FInstLEx	Fellow, Institute of Legal Executives
FInstM	Fellow, Institute of Meat; Fellow, Institute of Marketing (now see FCIM)
FInstMC	Fellow, Institute of Measurement and Control
FInstMSM	Fellow, Institute of Marketing and Sales Management (later FInstM; now see FCIM)
FInstMet	Fellow, Institute of Metals (later part of Metals Society; now see FIM)
FInstNDT	Fellow, Institute of Non-Destructive Testing
FInstP	Fellow, Institute of Physics
FInstPet	Fellow, Institute of Petroleum
FInstPI	Fellow, Institute of Patentees and Inventors
FInstPS	Fellow, Institute of Purchasing and Supply
FInstSM	Fellow, Institute of Sales Management (now see FInstSMM)
FInstSMM	Fellow, Institute of Sales and Marketing Management
FInstW	Fellow, Institute of Welding (now see FWeldI)
FINucE	Fellow, Institution of Nuclear Engineers
FIOA	Fellow, Institute of Acoustics
FIOB	Fellow, Institute of Building (now see FCIOB)
FIOH	Fellow, Institute of Occupational Hygiene
FIOM	Fellow, Institute of Office Management (now see FIAM)
FIOP	Fellow, Institute of Printing
FIOSH	Fellow, Institute of Occupational Safety and Health
FIP	Fellow, Australian Institute of Petroleum
FIPA	Fellow, Institute of Practitioners in Advertising
FIPDM	Fellow, Institute of Physical Distribution Management (now see FILDM)
FIPENZ	Fellow, Institution of Professional Engineers, New Zealand
FIPG	Fellow, Institute of Professional Goldsmiths
FIPHE	Fellow, Institution of Public Health Engineers (now see FIWEM)
FIPlantE	Fellow, Institution of Plant Engineers (now see FIIM)
FIPM	Fellow, Institute of Personnel Management
FIPR	Fellow, Institute of Public Relations
FIProdE	Fellow, Institution of Production Engineers (later FIMfgE; now see FIEE)
FIQ	Fellow, Institute of Quarrying
FIQA	Fellow, Institute of Quality Assurance
FIQS	Fellow, Institute of Quantity Surveyors
FIRA	Furniture Industry Research Association
FIRA(Ind)	Fellow, Institute of Railway Auditors and Accountants (India)
FIRE(Aust)	Fellow, Institution of Radio Engineers (Australia) (now see FIREE(Aust)
FIREE(Aust)	Fellow, Institution of Radio and Electronics Engineers (Australia)
FIRI	Fellow, Institution of the Rubber Industry (now see FPRI)
FIRM	Fellow, Institute of Risk Management
FIRSE	Fellow, Institute of Railway Signalling Engineers
FIRTE	Fellow, Institute of Road Transport Engineers
FIS	Fellow, Institute of Statisticians
FISA	Fellow, Incorporated Secretaries' Association; Fédération Internationale des Sociétés d'Aviron
FISE	Fellow, Institution of Sales Engineers; Fellow, Institution of Sanitary Engineers
FISITA	Fédération Internationale des Sociétés d'Ingénieurs des Techniques de l'Automobile
FISP	Fédération Internationale des Sociétés de Philosophie
FIST	Fellow, Institute of Science Technology
FISTC	Fellow, Institute of Scientific and Technical Communicators
FISTD	Fellow, Imperial Society of Teachers of Dancing
FIStructE	Fellow, Institution of Structural Engineers
FISW	Fellow, Institute of Social Work
FITD	Fellow, Institute of Training and Development
FITE	Fellow, Institution of Electrical and Electronics Technician Engineers
FIW	Fellow, Welding Institute (now see FWeldI)
FIWE	Fellow, Institution of Water Engineers (later FIWES; now see FIWEM)
FIWEM	Fellow, Institution of Water and Environmental Management
FIWES	Fellow, Institution of Water Engineers and Scientists (now see FIWEM)
FIWM	Fellow, Institution of Works Managers (now see FIIM)
FIWPC	Fellow, Institute of Water Pollution Control (now see FIWEM)
FIWSc	Fellow, Institute of Wood Science
FIWSP	Fellow, Institute of Work Study Practitioners (now see FMS)
FJI	Fellow, Institute of Journalists
FJIE	Fellow, Junior Institution of Engineers (now see CIMGTechE)
FKC	Fellow, King's College London
FKCHMS	Fellow, King's College Hospital Medical School
FLA	Fellow, Library Association
Fla	Florida (US)
FLAI	Fellow, Library Association of Ireland
FLAS	Fellow, Chartered Land Agents' Society (now (after amalgamation) see FRICS)
FLCM	Fellow, London College of Music
FLHS	Fellow, London Historical Society
FLI	Fellow, Landscape Institute
FLIA	Fellow, Life Insurance Association
FLS	Fellow, Linnean Society
Flt	Flight
FM	Field-Marshal
FMA	Fellow, Museums Association
FMANZ	Fellow, Medical Association of New Zealand
FMES	Fellow, Minerals Engineering Society
FMF	Fiji Military Forces
FMS	Federated Malay States; Fellow, Medical Society; Fellow, Institute of Management Services
FMSA	Fellow, Mineralogical Society of America
FNA	Fellow, Indian National Science Academy
FNAEA	Fellow, National Association of Estate Agents
FNCO	Fleet Naval Constructor Officer
FNECInst	Fellow, North East Coast Institution of Engineers and Shipbuilders
FNI	Fellow, Nautical Institute; Fellow, National Institute of Sciences in India (now see FNA)
FNIA	Fellow, Nigerian Institute of Architects
FNZEI	Fellow, New Zealand Educational Institute
FNZIA	Fellow, New Zealand Institute of Architects
FNZIAS	Fellow, New Zealand Institute of Agricultural Science
FNZIC	Fellow, New Zealand Institute of Chemistry
FNZIE	Fellow, New Zealand Institution of Engineers
FNZIM	Fellow, New Zealand Institute of Management
FNZPsS	Fellow, New Zealand Psychological Society
FO	Foreign Office (now see FCO); Field Officer; Flying Officer
FODA	Fellow, Overseas Doctors' Association
FODC	Franciscan Order of the Divine Compassion
FOIC	Flag Officer in charge
FOMI	Faculty of Occupational Medicine of Ireland
FONA	Flag Officer, Naval Aviation
FONAC	Flag Officer Naval Air Command
FOR	Fellowship of Operational Research
For.	Foreign
FOREST	Freedom Organisation for the Right to Enjoy Smoking Tobacco
FOX	Futures and Options Exchange
FPA	Family Planning Association
FPC	Family Practitioner Committee (now see FHSA)
FPEA	Fellow, Physical Education Association
FPHM	Faculty of Public Health Medicine
FPhS	Fellow, Philosophical Society of England
FPI	Fellow, Plastics Institute (now see FPRI)
FPIA	Fellow, Plastics Institute of Australia
FPMI	Fellow, Pensions Management Institute
FPRI	Fellow, Plastics and Rubber Institute
FPS	Fellow, Pharmaceutical Society (now see FRPharmS); Fauna Preservation Society (now see FFPS)
FPhysS	Fellow, Physical Society
f r	fuori ruolo
FRA	Fellow, Royal Academy
FRACDS	Fellow, Royal Australian College of Dental Surgeons
FRACGP	Fellow, Royal Australian College of General Practitioners
FRACI	Fellow, Royal Australian Chemical Institute
FRACMA	Fellow, Royal Australian College of Medical Administrators
FRACO	Fellow, Royal Australian College of Ophthalmologists
FRACOG	Fellow, Royal Australian College of Obstetricians and Gynaecologists
FRACP	Fellow, Royal Australasian College of Physicians
FRACR	Fellow, Royal Australasian College of Radiologists
FRACS	Fellow, Royal Australasian College of Surgeons
FRAD	Fellow, Royal Academy of Dancing
FRAeS	Fellow, Royal Aeronautical Society
FRAgS	Fellow, Royal Agricultural Societies (ie of England, Scotland and Wales)
FRAHS	Fellow, Royal Australian Historical Society
FRAI	Fellow, Royal Anthropological Institute of Great Britain & Ireland
FRAIA	Fellow, Royal Australian Institute of Architects
FRAIB	Fellow, Royal Australian Institute of Building
FRAIC	Fellow, Royal Architectural Institute of Canada
FRAIPA	Fellow, Royal Australian Institute of Public Administration
FRAM	Fellow, Royal Academy of Music
FRAME	Fund for the Replacement of Animals in Medical Experiments
FRANZCP	Fellow, Royal Australian and New Zealand College of Psychiatrists
FRAPI	Fellow, Royal Australian Planning Institute
FRAS	Fellow, Royal Astronomical Society; Fellow, Royal Asiatic Society
FRASB	Fellow, Royal Asiatic Society of Bengal
FRASE	Fellow, Royal Agricultural Society of England
FRBS	Fellow, Royal Society of British Sculptors; Fellow, Royal Botanic Society
FRCA	Fellow, Royal College of Art
FRCAnaes	Fellow, Royal College of Anaesthetists
FRCCO	Fellow, Royal Canadian College of Organists
FRCD(Can.)	Fellow, Royal College of Dentists of Canada
FRCGP	Fellow, Royal College of General Practitioners
FRCM	Fellow, Royal College of Music
FRCN	Fellow, Royal College of Nursing

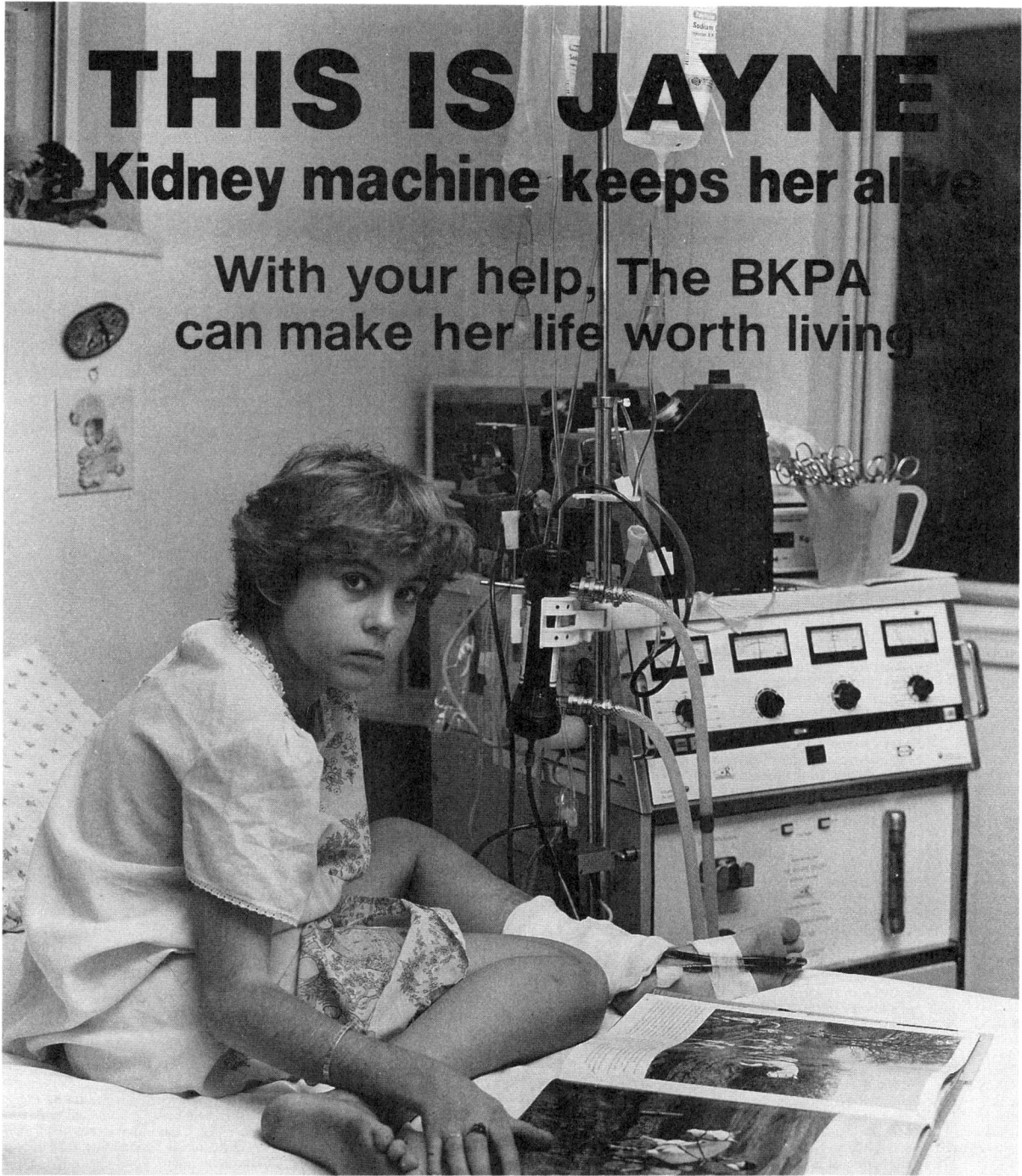

THIS IS JAYNE
a Kidney machine keeps her alive

With your help, The BKPA
can make her life worth living

FRCO	Fellow, Royal College of Organists
FRCO(CHM)	Fellow, Royal College of Organists with Diploma in Choir Training
FRCOG	Fellow, Royal College of Obstetricians and Gynaecologists
FRCP	Fellow, Royal College of Physicians, London
FRCPA	Fellow, Royal College of Pathologists of Australasia
FRCP&S (Canada)	Fellow, Royal College of Physicians and Surgeons of Canada
FRCPath	Fellow, Royal College of Pathologists
FRCP(C)	Fellow, Royal College of Physicians of Canada
FRCPE or FRCPEd	Fellow, Royal College of Physicians, Edinburgh
FRCPGlas	Fellow, Royal College of Physicians and Surgeons of Glasgow
FRCPI	Fellow, Royal College of Physicians of Ireland
FRCPS(Hon.)	Hon. Fellow, Royal College of Physicians and Surgeons of Glasgow
FRCPsych	Fellow, Royal College of Psychiatrists
FRCR	Fellow, Royal College of Radiologists
FRCS	Fellow, Royal College of Surgeons of England
FRCSCan	Fellow, Royal College of Surgeons of Canada
FRCSE or FRCSEd	Fellow, Royal College of Surgeons of Edinburgh
FRCSGlas	Fellow, Royal College of Physicians and Surgeons of Glasgow
FRCSI	Fellow, Royal College of Surgeons in Ireland
FRCSoc	Fellow, Royal Commonwealth Society
FRCUS	Fellow, Royal College of University Surgeons (Denmark)
FRCVS	Fellow, Royal College of Veterinary Surgeons
FREconS	Fellow, Royal Economic Society
FREI	Fellow, Real Estate Institute (Australia)
FRES	Fellow, Royal Entomological Society of London
FRFPSG	Fellow, Royal Faculty of Physicians and Surgeons, Glasgow (now see FRCPGlas)
FRG	Federal Republic of Germany
FRGS	Fellow, Royal Geographical Society
FRGSA	Fellow, Royal Geographical Society of Australasia
FRHistS	Fellow, Royal Historical Society
FRHS	Fellow, Royal Horticultural Society (now see MRHS)
FRHSV	Fellow, Royal Historical Society of Victoria
FRIAS	Fellow, Royal Incorporation of Architects of Scotland; Royal Institute for the Advancement of Science
FRIBA	Fellow, Royal Institute of British Architects (and see RIBA)
FRIC	Fellow, Royal Institute of Chemistry (now see FRSC)
FRICS	Fellow, Royal Institution of Chartered Surveyors
FRIH	Fellow, Royal Institute of Horticulture (NZ)
FRIN	Fellow, Royal Institute of Navigation
FRINA	Fellow, Royal Institution of Naval Architects
FRIPA	Fellow, Royal Institute of Public Administration (the Institute no longer has Fellows)
FRIPHH	Fellow, Royal Institute of Public Health and Hygiene
FRMCM	Fellow, Royal Manchester College of Music
FRMedSoc	Fellow, Royal Medical Society
FRMetS	Fellow, Royal Meteorological Society
FRMIA	Fellow, Retail Management Institute of Australia
FRMS	Fellow, Royal Microscopical Society
FRNCM	Fellow, Royal Northern College of Music
FRNS	Fellow, Royal Numismatic Society
FRPharmS	Fellow, Royal Pharmaceutical Society
FRPS	Fellow, Royal Photographic Society
FRPSL	Fellow, Royal Philatelic Society, London
FRS	Fellow, Royal Society
FRSA	Fellow, Royal Society of Arts
FRSAI	Fellow, Royal Society of Antiquaries of Ireland
FRSAMD	Fellow, Royal Scottish Academy of Music and Drama
FRSanI	Fellow, Royal Sanitary Institute (now see FRSH)
FRSC	Fellow, Royal Society of Canada; Fellow, Royal Society of Chemistry
FRS(Can)	Fellow, Royal Society of Canada (used when a person is also a Fellow of the Royal Society of Chemistry)
FRSCM	Fellow, Royal School of Church Music
FRSC (UK)	Fellow, Royal Society of Chemistry (used when a person is also a Fellow of the Royal Society of Canada)
FRSE	Fellow, Royal Society of Edinburgh
FRSGS	Fellow, Royal Scottish Geographical Society
FRSH	Fellow, Royal Society for the Promotion of Health
FRSL	Fellow, Royal Society of Literature
FRSM or FRSocMed	Fellow, Royal Society of Medicine
FRSNZ	Fellow, Royal Society of New Zealand
FRSSAf	Fellow, Royal Society of South Africa
FRST	Fellow, Royal Society of Teachers
FRSTM&H	Fellow, Royal Society of Tropical Medicine and Hygiene
FRTPI	Fellow, Royal Town Planning Institute
FRTS	Fellow, Royal Television Society
FRVA	Fellow, Rating and Valuation Association (now see IRRV)
FRVC	Fellow, Royal Veterinary College
FRVIA	Fellow, Royal Victorian Institute of Architects
FRZSScot	Fellow, Royal Zoological Society of Scotland
FS	Field Security
fs	Graduate, Royal Air Force Staff College
FSA	Fellow, Society of Antiquaries
FSAA	Fellow, Society of Incorporated Accountants and Auditors
FSAE	Fellow, Society of Automotive Engineers; Fellow, Society of Art Education
FSAI	Fellow, Society of Architectural Illustrators
FSAIEE	Fellow, South African Institute of Electrical Engineers
FSAM	Fellow, Society of Art Masters
FSArc	Fellow, Society of Architects (merged with the RIBA 1952)

FSaRS	Fellow, Safety and Reliability Society
FSAScot	Fellow, Society of Antiquaries of Scotland
FSASM	Fellow, South Australian School of Mines
FSBI	Fellow, Savings Banks Institute
fsc	Foreign Staff College
FSCA	Fellow, Society of Company and Commercial Accountants
FScotvec	Fellow, Scottish Vocational Educational Council
FSDC	Fellow, Society of Dyers and Colourists
FSE	Fellow, Society of Engineers
FSG	Fellow, Society of Genealogists
FSGT	Fellow, Society of Glass Technology
FSI	Fellow, Chartered Surveyors' Institution (now see FRICS)
FSIAD	Fellow, Society of Industrial Artists and Designers (now see FCSD)
FSLAET	Fellow, Society of Licensed Aircraft Engineers and Technologists
FSLCOG	Fellow, Sri Lankan College of Obstetrics and Gynaecology
FSLTC	Fellow, Society of Leather Technologists and Chemists
FSMA	Fellow, Incorporated Sales Managers' Association (later FInstMSM; now see FInstM)
FSMC	Freeman of the Spectacle-Makers' Company
FSME	Fellow, Society of Manufacturing Engineers
FSMPTE	Fellow, Society of Motion Picture and Television Engineers (USA)
FSRHE	Fellow, Society for Research into Higher Education
FSRP	Fellow, Society for Radiological Protection
FSS	Fellow, Royal Statistical Society
FSTD	Fellow, Society of Typographic Designers
FSVA	Fellow, Incorporated Society of Valuers and Auctioneers
FT	Financial Times
FTAT	Furniture, Timber and Allied Trades Union
FTC	Flying Training Command; Full Technological Certificate, City and Guilds of London Institute
FTCD	Fellow, Trinity College, Dublin
FTCL	Fellow, Trinity College of Music, London
FTI	Fellow, Textile Institute
FTII	Fellow, Institute of Taxation
FTP	Fellow, Thames Polytechnic
FTS	Fellow, Australian Academy of Technological Sciences and Engineering; Flying Training School; Fellow, Tourism Society
FTSC	Fellow, Tonic Sol-fa College
FUCUA	Federation of University Conservative and Unionist Associations (now see FCS)
FUMIST	Fellow, University of Manchester Institute of Science and Technology
FVRDE	Fighting Vehicles Reearch and Development Establshment
FWAAS	Fellow, World Academy of Arts and Sciences
FWACP	Fellow, West African College of Physicians
FWCMD	Fellow, Welsh College of Music and Drama
FWeldI	Fellow, Welding Institute
FWSOM	Fellow, Institute of Practitioners in Work Study, Organisation and Method (now see FMS)
FZS	Fellow, Zoological Society
FZSScot	Fellow, Zoological Society of Scotland (now see FRZSScot)

G

GA	Geologists' Association; Gaelic Athletic (Club)
Ga	Georgia (US)
GAI	Guild of Architectural Ironmongers
GAP	Gap Activity Projects
GAPAN	Guild of Air Pilots and Air Navigators
GATT	General Agreement on Tariffs and Trade
GB	Great Britain
GBA	Governing Bodies Association
GBE	Knight or Dame Grand Cross, Order of the British Empire
GBGSA	Governing Bodies of Girls' Schools Association (formerly Association of Governing Bodies of Girls' Public Schools)
GBSM	Graduate of Birmingham and Midland Institute School of Music
GC	George Cross
GCB	Knight or Dame Grand Cross, Order of the Bath
GCBS	General Council of British Shipping
GCCC	Gonville and Caius College, Cambridge
GCFR	Grand Commander, Order of the Federal Republic of Nigeria
GCH	Knight Grand Cross, Hanoverian Order
GCHQ	Government Communications Headquarters
GCIE	Knight Grand Commander, Order of the Indian Empire
GCLJ	Grand Cross, St Lazarus of Jerusalem
GCLM	Grand Commander, Order of the Legion of Merit of Rhodesia
GCM	Gold Crown of Merit (Barbados)
GCMG	Knight or Dame Grand Cross, Order of St Michael and St George
GCON	Grand Cross, Order of the Niger
GCSE	General Certificate of Secondary Education
GCSG	Knight Grand Cross, Order of St Gregory the Great
GCSI	Knight Grand Commander, Order of the Star of India
GCSJ	Knight Grand Cross of Justice, Order of St John of Jerusalem (Knights Hospitaller)
GCSL	Grand Cross, Order of St Lucia
GCStJ	Bailiff or Dame Grand Cross, Most Venerable Order of the Hospital of St John of Jerusalem
GCVO	Knight or Dame Grand Cross, Royal Victorian Order
g d	grand-daughter

GDBA	Guide Dogs for the Blind Association
GDC	General Dental Council
Gdns	Gardens
GDR	German Democratic Republic
Gen.	General
Ges.	Gesellschaft
GFD	Geophysical Fluid Dynamics
GFS	Girls' Friendly Society
g g d	great-grand-daughter
g g s	great-grandson
GGSM	Graduate in Music, Guildhall School of Music and Drama
GHQ	General Headquarters
Gib.	Gibraltar
GIMechE	Graduate Institution of Mechanical Engineers
GL	Grand Lodge
GLAA	Greater London Arts Association (*now see* GLAB)
GLAB	Greater London Arts Board
GLC	Greater London Council
Glos	Gloucestershire
GM	George Medal; Grand Medal (Ghana)
GMB	(Union for) General, Municipal, Boilermakers
GMBATU	General, Municipal, Boilermakers and Allied Trades Union (*now see* GMB)
GmbH	Gesellschaft mit beschränkter Haftung
GMC	General Medical Council; Guild of Memorial Craftsmen
GMIE	Grand Master, Order of the Indian Empire
GMSI	Grand Master, Order of the Star of India
GMWU	General and Municipal Workers' Union (later GMBATU; *now see* GMB)
GNC	General Nursing Council
GOC	General Officer Commanding
GOC-in-C	General Officer Commanding-in-Chief
GOE	General Ordination Examination
Gov.	Governor
Govt	Government
GP	General Practitioner; Grand Prix
GPDST	Girls' Public Day School Trust
GPO	General Post Office
GQG	Grand Quartier Général
Gr.	Greek
GRSM	Graduate of the Royal Schools of Music
GS	General Staff; Grammar School
g s	grandson
GSA	Girls' Schools Association
GSM	General Service Medal; (Member of) Guildhall School of Music and Drama
GSMD	Guildhall School of Music and Drama
GSO	General Staff Officer
GTCL	Graduate, Trinity College of Music
GTS	General Theological Seminary (New York)
GUI	Golfing Union of Ireland
GWR	Great Western Railway

H

HA	Historical Association; Health Authority
HAA	Heavy Anti-Aircraft
HAC	Honourable Artillery Company
Hants	Hampshire
HARCVS	Honorary Associate, Royal College of Veterinary Surgeons
Harv.	Harvard
HBM	His (or Her) Britannic Majesty (Majesty's); Humming Bird Gold Medal (Trinidad)
hc	*honoris causa*
HCEG	Honourable Company of Edinburgh Golfers
HCF	Honorary Chaplain to the Forces
HCIMA	Hotel, Catering and Institutional Management Association
HCSC	Higher Command and Staff Course
HDA	Hawkesbury Diploma in Agriculture (Australia)
HDD	Higher Dental Diploma
HDipEd	Higher Diploma in Education
HE	His (or Her) Excellency; His Eminence
HEC	Ecole des Hautes Etudes Commerciales; Higher Education Corporation
HEH	His (or Her) Exalted Highness
HEIC	Honourable East India Company
HEICS	Honourable East India Company's Service
Heir-pres.	Heir-presumptive
HEO	Higher Executive Officer
Herts	Hertfordshire
HFARA	Honorary Foreign Associate of the Royal Academy
HFRA	Honorary Foreign Member of the Royal Academy
HG	Home Guard
HGTAC	Home Grown Timber Advisory Committee
HH	His (or Her) Highness; His Holiness; Member, Hesketh Hubbard Art Society
HHA	Historic Houses Association
HHD	Doctor of Humanities (US)
HIH	His (or Her) Imperial Highness
HIM	His (or Her) Imperial Majesty
HJ	Hilal-e-Jurat (Pakistan)
HKIA	Hong Kong Institute of Architects
HKIPM	Hong Kong Institute of Personnel Management
HLD	Doctor of Humane Letters
HLI	Highland Light Infantry
HM	His (or Her) Majesty, or Majesty's

HMA	Head Masters' Association
HMAS	His (or Her) Majesty's Australian Ship
HMC	Headmasters' Conference; Hospital Management Committee
HMCIC	His (or Her) Majesty's Chief Inspector of Constabulary
HMCS	His (or Her) Majesty's Canadian Ship
HMHS	His (or Her) Majesty's Hospital Ship
HMI	His (or Her) Majesty's Inspector
HMIED	Honorary Member, Institute of Engineering Designers
HMMTB	His (or Her) Majesty's Motor Torpedo Boat
HMOCS	His (or Her) Majesty's Overseas Civil Service
HMS	His (or Her) Majesty's Ship
HMSO	His (or Her) Majesty's Stationery Office
HNC	Higher National Certificate
HND	Higher National Diploma
H of C	House of Commons
H of L	House of Lords
Hon.	Honourable; Honorary
HPk	Hilal-e-Pakistan
HQ	Headquarters
HQA	Hilal-i-Quaid-i-Azam (Pakistan)
(HR)	Home Rule
HRCA	Honorary Royal Cambrian Academician
HRGI	Honorary Member, The Royal Glasgow Institute of the Fine Arts
HRH	His (or Her) Royal Highness
HRHA	Honorary Member, Royal Hibernian Academy
HRI	Honorary Member, Royal Institute of Painters in Water Colours
HROI	Honorary Member, Royal Institute of Oil Painters
HRSA	Honorary Member, Royal Scottish Academy
HRSW	Honorary Member, Royal Scottish Water Colour Society
HSC	Health and Safety Commission
HSE	Health and Safety Executive
HSH	His (or Her) Serene Highness
Hum.	Humanity, Humanities (Classics)
Hunts	Huntingdonshire
HVCert	Health Visitor's Certificate
Hy	Heavy

I

I	Island; Ireland
Ia	Iowa (US)
IA	Indian Army
IAAF	International Amateur Athletic Federation
IAC	Indian Armoured Corps; Institute of Amateur Cinematographers
IACP	International Association of Chiefs of Police
IADR	International Association for Dental Research
IAEA	International Atomic Energy Agency
IAF	Indian Air Force; Indian Auxiliary Force
IAHM	Incorporated Association of Headmasters
IAM	Institute of Advanced Motorists; Institute of Aviation Medicine
IAMC	Indian Army Medical Corps
IAMTACT	Institute of Advanced Machine Tool and Control Technology
IAO	Incorporated Association of Organists
IAOC	Indian Army Ordnance Corps
IAPS	Incorporated Association of Preparatory Schools
IAPSO	International Association for the Physical Sciences of the Oceans
IARO	Indian Army Reserve of Officers
IAS	Indian Administrative Service; Institute of Advanced Studies
IASS	International Association for Scandinavian Studies
IATA	International Air Transport Association
IATUL	International Association of Technological University Libraries
IAU	International Astronomical Union
IAWPRC	International Association on Water Pollution Research and Control
ib. or ibid.	*ibidem* (in the same place)
IBA	Independent Broadcasting Authority; International Bar Association
IBG	Institute of British Geographers
IBRD	International Bank for Reconstruction and Development (World Bank)
IBRO	International Bank Research Organisation; International Brain Research Organisation
IBTE	Institution of British Telecommunications Engineers
i/c	in charge; in command
ICA	Institute of Contemporary Arts; Institute of Chartered Accountants in England and Wales
ICAA	Invalid Children's Aid Association
ICAI	Institute of Chartered Accountants in Ireland
ICAO	International Civil Aviation Organization
ICBP	International Council for Bird Preservation
ICBS	Irish Christian Brothers' School
ICC	International Chamber of Commerce
ICCROM	International Centre for Conservation at Rome
ICD	*Iuris Canonici Doctor;* Independence Commemorative Decoration (Rhodesia)
ICE	Institution of Civil Engineers
ICED	International Council for Educational Development
ICEF	International Federation of Chemical, Energy and General Workers' Unions

REMEMBER THOSE WHO WILL NEVER FORGET.

REMEMBER THEM IN YOUR WILL.

YOUR LEGACY WILL HELP US TO HELP THOSE WHO CANNOT HELP THEMSELVES.

THOSE WHO FOUGHT FOR THE FREEDOMS WE ENJOY TODAY.

SINCE THE FIRST WORLD WAR, HUNDREDS OF THOUSANDS OF BRITISH SERVICEMEN AND

WOMEN HAVE BEEN KILLED OR INJURED IN NUMEROUS CONFLICTS ALL OVER THE WORLD.

THE ROYAL BRITISH LEGION CARES FOR THEM, THEIR WIDOWS, AND THEIR DEPENDENTS.

(THERE ARE STILL 4,600 WAR PENSIONERS AND WIDOWS FROM THE FIRST WORLD WAR.)

AND WE'RE COMMITTED TO PROVIDING WELFARE SCHEMES FOR THEM ALL.

COMMITTED TO PROVIDING RESIDENTIAL AND CONVALESCENT HOMES, SHELTERED

EMPLOYMENT, CARING FOR THE DISABLED, PENSIONS COUNSELLING AND MUCH, MUCH MORE.

IN ALL, OVER 18 MILLION PEOPLE ARE ENTITLED TO ASK FOR OUR HELP. LAST YEAR MORE

THAN 100,000 DID.

WHICH IS WHY WE NEED ALL THE HELP WE CAN GET.

IF YOU WANT TO HELP, **PLEASE MAKE A BEQUEST TO THE ROYAL**

BRITISH LEGION POPPY APPEAL, ROYAL BRITISH LEGION VILLAGE,

MAIDSTONE, KENT ME20 7NX.

WE WON'T FORGET, IF YOU WON'T.

REGISTERED CHARITY NO. 219279.

Icel.	Icelandic
ICES	International Council for the Exploration of the Sea
ICF	International Federation of Chemical and General Workers' Unions (*now see* ICEF)
ICFC	Industrial and Commercial Finance Corporation (later part of Investors in Industry)
ICFTU	International Confederation of Free Trade Unions
ICHCA	International Cargo Handling Co-ordination Association
IChemE	Institution of Chemical Engineers
ICI	Imperial Chemical Industries
ICL	International Computers Ltd
ICM	International Confederation of Midwives
ICMA	Institute of Cost and Management Accountants (*now see* CIMA)
ICME	International Commission for Mathematical Education
ICOM	International Council of Museums
ICOMOS	International Council of Monuments and Sites
ICorrST	Institution of Corrosion Science and Technology
ICPO	International Criminal Police Organization (Interpol)
ICRC	International Committee of the Red Cross
ICRF	Imperial Cancer Research Fund
ICS	Indian Civil Service
ICSA	Institute of Chartered Secretaries and Administrators
ICSID	International Council of Societies of Industrial Design; International Centre for Settlement of Investment Disputes
ICSS	International Committee for the Sociology of Sport
ICSU	International Council of Scientific Unions
ICT	International Computers and Tabulators Ltd (*now see* ICL)
Id	Idaho (US)
ID	Independence Decoration (Rhodesia)
IDA	International Development Association
IDB	Internal Drainage Board
IDC	Imperial Defence College (*now see* RCDS); Inter-Diocesan Certificate
idc	completed a course at, or served for a year on the Staff of, the Imperial Defence College (*now see* rcds)
IDRC	International Development Research Centre
IDS	Institute of Development Studies; Industry Department for Scotland
IEA	Institute of Economic Affairs
IEC	International Electrotechnical Commission
IEE	Institution of Electrical Engineers
IEEE	Institute of Electrical and Electronics Engineers (NY)
IEEIE	Institution of Electrical and Electronics Incorporated Engineers (*now see* IEIE)
IEETE	Institution of Electrical and Electronics Technician Engineers (later IEEIE; *now see* IEIE)
IEI	Institution of Engineers of Ireland
IEIE	Institution of Electronics and Electrical Incorporated Engineers
IEME	Inspectorate of Electrical and Mechanical Engineering
IEng	Incorporated Engineer
IERE	Institution of Electronic and Radio Engineers
IES	Indian Educational Service; Institution of Engineers and Shipbuilders in Scotland
IExpE	Institute of Explosives Engineers
IFAC	International Federation of Automatic Control
IFAD	International Fund for Agricultural Development (UNO)
IFAW	International Fund for Animal Welfare
IFBWW	International Federation of Building Woodworkers
IFC	International Finance Corporation
IFIAS	International Federation of Institutes of Advanced Study
IFIP	International Federation for Information Processing
IFL	International Friendship League
IFLA	International Federation of Library Associations
IFORS	International Federation of Operational Research Societies
IFPI	International Federation of the Phonographic Industry
IFRA	World Press Research Association
IFS	Irish Free State; Indian Forest Service
IG	Instructor in Gunnery
IGasE	Institution of Gas Engineers
IGPP	Institute of Geophysics and Planetary Physics
IGS	Independent Grammar School
IGU	International Geographical Union; International Gas Union
IHA	Institute of Health Service Administrators
IHospE	Institute of Hospital Engineering
IHSM	Institute of Health Services Management
IHVE	Institution of Heating and Ventilating Engineers (*now see* CIBS)
IIM	Institution of Industrial Managers
IIMT	International Institute for the Management of Technology
IInfSc	Institute of Information Scientists
IIS	International Institute of Sociology
IISS	International Institute of Strategic Studies
IIT	Indian Institute of Technology
ILA	International Law Association
ILEA	Inner London Education Authority
ILEC	Inner London Education Committee
Ill	Illinois (US)
ILO	International Labour Office; International Labour Organisation
ILP	Independent Labour Party
ILR	Independent Local Radio; International Labour Review
IM	Individual Merit
IMA	International Music Association; Institute of Mathematics and its Applications
IMCB	International Management Centre from Buckingham

IMCO	Inter-Governmental Maritime Consultative Organization (*now see* IMO)
IMEA	Incorporated Municipal Electrical Association
IMechE	Institution of Mechanical Engineers
IMEDE	Institut pour l'Etude des Méthodes de Direction de l'Entreprise
IMF	International Monetary Fund
IMGTechE	Institution of Mechanical and General Technician Engineers
IMinE	Institution of Mining Engineers
IMM	Institution of Mining and Metallurgy
IMMLEP	Immunology of Leprosy
IMMTS	Indian Mercantile Marine Training Ship
IMO	International Maritime Organization
Imp.	Imperial
IMRO	Investment Management Regulatory Organisation
IMS	Indian Medical Service; Institute of Management Services; International Military Staff
IMTA	Institute of Municipal Treasurers and Accountants (*now see* CIPFA)
IMU	International Mathematical Union
IMunE	Institution of Municipal Engineers (now amalgamated with Institution of Civil Engineers)
IN	Indian Navy
Inc.	Incorporated
INCA	International Newspaper Colour Association
Incog.	Incognito
Ind.	Independent; Indiana (US)
Inf.	Infantry
INFORM	Information Network Focus on New Religious Movements
INSA	Indian National Science Academy
INSEA	International Society for Education through Art
INSEAD or Insead	Institut Européen d'Administration des Affaires
Insp.	Inspector
Inst.	Institute
InstBE	Institution of British Engineers
Instn	Institution
InstSMM	Institute of Sales and Marketing Management
InstT	Institute of Transport
INTELSAT	International Telecommunications Satellite Organisation
IOB	Institute of Building (*now see* CIOB)
IOC	International Olympic Committee; Intergovernmental Oceanographic Commission
IOCD	International Organisation for Chemical Science in Development
IODE	Imperial Order of the Daughters of the Empire
I of M	Isle of Man
IOGT	International Order of Good Templars
IOM	Isle of Man; Indian Order of Merit
IOOF	Independent Order of Odd-fellows
IOP	Institute of Painters in Oil Colours
IoW	Isle of Wight
IPA	International Publishers' Association
IPCS	Institution of Professional Civil Servants
IPFA	Member or Associate, Chartered Institute of Public Finance and Accountancy
IPHE	Institution of Public Health Engineers (*now see* IWEM)
IPI	International Press Institute; Institute of Patentees and Inventors
IPlantE	Institution of Plant Engineers (*now see* IIM)
IPM	Institute of Personnel Management
IPPA	Independent Programme Producers' Association
IPPF	International Planned Parenthood Federation
IPPS	Institute of Physics and The Physical Society
IProdE	Institution of Production Engineers (later Institution of Manufacturing Engineering; *now see* IEE)
IPS	Indian Police Service; Indian Political Service; Institute of Purchasing and Supply
IPU	Inter-Parliamentary Union
IRA	Irish Republican Army
IRAD	Institute for Research on Animal Diseases
IRC	Industrial Reorganization Corporation; Interdisciplinary Research Centre
IRCAM	Institute for Research and Co-ordination in Acoustics and Music
IRCert	Industrial Relations Certificate
IREE(Aust)	Institution of Radio and Electronics Engineers (Australia)
IRI	Institution of the Rubber Industry (*now see* PRI)
IRO	International Refugee Organization
IRPA	International Radiation Protection Association
IRRV	(Fellow/Member of) Institute of Revenues, Rating and Valuation
IRTE	Institute of Road Transport Engineers
IS	International Society of Sculptors, Painters and Gravers
Is	Island(s)
ISBA	Incorporated Society of British Advertisers
ISC	Imperial Service College, Haileybury; Indian Staff Corps
ISCM	International Society for Contemporary Music
ISCO	Independent Schools Careers Organisation
ISE	Indian Service of Engineers
ISI	International Statistical Institute
ISIS	Independent Schools Information Service
ISJC	Independent Schools Joint Council
ISM	Incorporated Society of Musicians
ISME	International Society for Musical Education
ISMRC	Inter-Services Metallurgical Research Council
ISO	Imperial Service Order; International Organization for Standardization

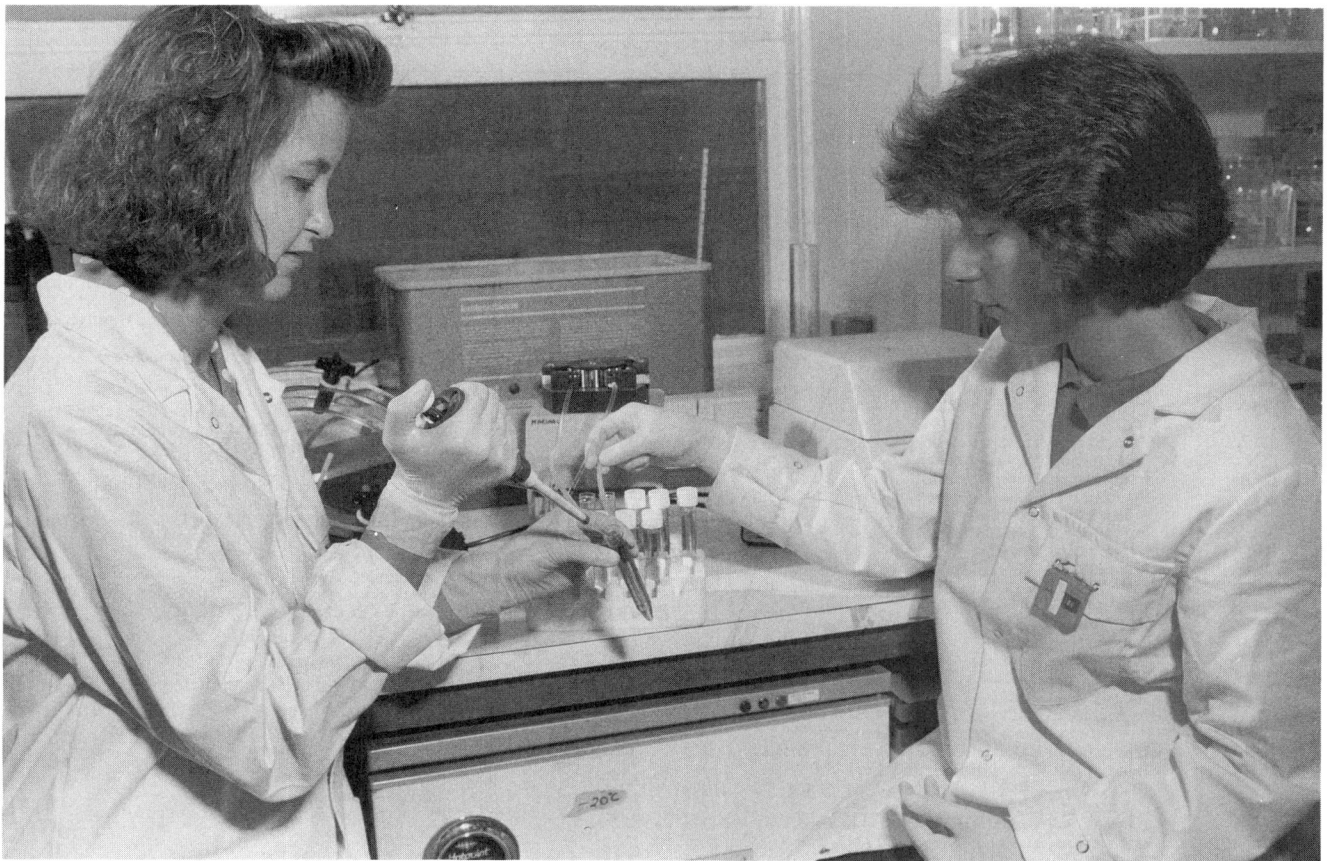

Purified populations of tumour cells being collected for use by ICR scientists investigating how oncogenes cause cancer.

'Genetic Engineering' and Cancer Research...

AT The Institute of Cancer Research's Laboratories, the latest 'genetic engineering' techniques are being applied to cancer research.

This involves the cloning, or isolation and propagation, of genes — the hereditary units of the body — and the study of alterations and rearrangements of genes in cancer cells. These genes, which play a crucial role in making a cell cancerous, are known as 'oncogenes'.

Research is currently centred on an oncogene found by Institute scientists to be active in certain human connective tissue tumours and leukaemias. Similar genes become activated in cells treated with cancer–causing chemicals. The oncogenes have aberrant products which cause cells to be cancerous. It is hoped that by learning how to block the activity of oncogenes the growth of cancer cells may be arrested.

Others in the Institute are working on the development of proteins, monoclonal antibodies, that can bind to the surfaces of cancer cells. By linking the antibodies with toxins, cancer cells should be selectively killed without harming normal tissues.

It is by research of this kind that our basic understanding of the nature of cancer is being extended and new approaches may be developed for cancer treatment and prevention.

Scientists at the Institute work side by side with clinicians at the Royal Marsden Hospital to form a specialised cancer centre. A particularly close relationship is maintained between doctor and researcher from laboratory to clinical trial, and from the bedside back to the laboratory.

Next time you are asked to advise on where a legacy or donation can best contribute to cancer research, remember that gifts to Charities do not attract Inheritance Tax. The Institute is a Charity recognised by the Inland Revenue as being exempt for taxation purposes. (Ref: X90004).

For more information about the work of The Institute of Cancer Research: Royal Cancer Hospital, please write to the Legacy Officer, 17A Onslow Gardens, London SW7 3AL. Tel:(071) 352–8133.

THE
INSTITUTE
of CANCER
RESEARCH
Royal Cancer Hospital

1991

Drug Development
Section

ISSTIP	International Society for Study of Tension in Performance
ISTC	Iron and Steel Trades Confederation; Institute of Scientific and Technical Communicators
ISTD	Imperial Society of Teachers of Dancing
IStructE	Institution of Structural Engineers
IT	Information Technology; Indian Territory (US)
ITA	Independent Television Authority (*now see* IBA)
ITAB	Information Technology Advisory Board
Ital. or It	Italian
ITB	Industry Training Board
ITC	International Trade Centre; Independent Television Commission
ITCA	Independent Television Companies Association Ltd (*now* Independent Television Association)
ITDG	Intermediate Technology Development Group
ITEME	Institution of Technician Engineers in Mechanical Engineering
ITF	International Transport Workers' Federation
ITN	Independent Television News
ITO	International Trade Organization
ITU	International Telecommunication Union
ITV	Independent Television
ITVA	International Television Association
IUA	International Union of Architects
IUB	International Union of Biochemistry
IUC	Inter-University Council for Higher Education Overseas (*now see* IUPC)
IUCN	International Union for the Conservation of Nature and Natural Resources
IUCW	International Union for Child Welfare
IUGS	International Union of Geological Sciences
IUHPS	International Union of the History and Philosophy of Science
IULA	International Union of Local Authorities
IUP	Association of Independent Unionist Peers
IUPAC	International Union of Pure and Applied Chemistry
IUPAP	International Union of Pure and Applied Physics
IUPC	Inter-University and Polytechnic Council for Higher Education Overseas
IUPS	International Union of Physiological Sciences
IUTAM	International Union of Theoretical and Applied Mechanics
IVF	In-vitro Fertilisation
IVS	International Voluntary Service
IWA	Inland Waterways Association
IWEM	Institution of Water and Environmental Management
IWES	Institution of Water Engineers and Scientists (*now see* IWEM)
IWGC	Imperial War Graves Commission (*now see* CWGC)
IWM	Institution of Works Managers (*now see* IIM)
IWPC	Institute of Water Pollution Control (*now see* IWEM)
IWSOM	Institute of Practitioners in Work Study Organisation and Methods (*now see* IMS)
IWSP	Institute of Work Study Practitioners (*now see* IMS)
IY	Imperial Yeomanry
IYRU	International Yacht Racing Union
IZ	I Zingari

J

JA	Judge Advocate
JACT	Joint Association of Classical Teachers
JAG	Judge Advocate General
Jas	James
JCB	*Juris Canonici* (or *Civilis*) *Baccalaureus* (Bachelor of Canon (or Civil) Law)
JCS	Journal of the Chemical Society
JCD	*Juris Canonici* (or *Civilis*) *Doctor* (Doctor of Canon (or Civil) Law)
JCI	Junior Chamber International
JCL	*Juris Canonici* (or *Civilis*) *Licentiatus* (Licentiate in Canon (or Civil) Law)
JCO	Joint Consultative Organisation (of AFRC, MAFF, and Department of Agriculture and Fisheries for Scotland)
JD	Doctor of Jurisprudence
JDipMA	Joint Diploma in Management Accounting Services
JG	Junior Grade
JInstE	Junior Institution of Engineers (*now see* IMGTechE)
jl(s)	journal(s)
JMB	Joint Matriculation Board
JMN	Johan Mangku Negara (Malaysia)
Joh. or Jno.	John
JP	Justice of the Peace
Jr	Junior
jsc	qualified at a Junior Staff Course, or the equivalent, 1942–46
JSD	Doctor of Juristic Science
JSDC	Joint Service Defence College
jsdc	completed a course at Joint Service Defence College
JSLS	Joint Services Liaison Staff
JSM	Johan Setia Mahkota (Malaysia)
JSPS	Japan Society for the Promotion of Science
JSSC	Joint Services Staff College
jssc	completed a course at Joint Services Staff College
jt, jtly	joint, jointly
JUD	*Juris Utriusque Doctor*, Doctor of Both Laws (Canon and Civil)
Jun.	Junior
Jun.Opt.	Junior Optime
JWS or jws	Joint Warfare Staff

K

KA	Knight of St Andrew, Order of Barbados
Kans	Kansas (US)
KAR	King's African Rifles
KBE	Knight Commander, Order of the British Empire
KC	King's Counsel
KCB	Knight Commander, Order of the Bath
KCC	Commander of Order of Crown, Belgium and Congo Free State
KCH	King's College Hospital; Knight Commander, Hanoverian Order
KCHS	Knight Commander, Order of the Holy Sepulchre
KCIE	Knight Commander, Order of the Indian Empire
KCL	King's College London
KCLJ	Knight Commander, Order of St Lazarus of Jerusalem
KCMG	Knight Commander, Order of St Michael and St George
KCSA	Knight Commander, Military Order of the Collar of St Agatha of Paterna
KCSG	Knight Commander, Order of St Gregory the Great
KCSI	Knight Commander, Order of the Star of India
KCSJ	Knight Commander, Order of St John of Jerusalem (Knights Hospitaller)
KCSS	Knight Commander, Order of St Silvester
KCVO	Knight Commander, Royal Victorian Order
KCVSA	King's Commendation for Valuable Services in the Air
KDG	King's Dragoon Guards
KEH	King Edward's Horse
KEO	King Edward's Own
KG	Knight, Order of the Garter
KGStJ	Knight of Grace, Order of St John of Jerusalem (*now see* KStJ)
KH	Knight, Hanoverian Order
KHC	Hon. Chaplain to the King
KHDS	Hon. Dental Surgeon to the King
KHNS	Hon. Nursing Sister to the King
KHP	Hon. Physician to the King
KHS	Hon. Surgeon to the King; Knight, Order of the Holy Sepulchre
K-i-H	Kaisar-i-Hind
KJStJ	Knight of Justice, Order of St John of Jerusalem (*now see* KStJ)
KLJ	Knight, Order of St Lazarus of Jerusalem
KM	Knight of Malta
KORR	King's Own Royal Regiment
KOSB	King's Own Scottish Borderers
KOYLI	King's Own Yorkshire Light Infantry
KP	Knight, Order of St Patrick
KPM	King's Police Medal
KRRC	King's Royal Rifle Corps
KS	King's Scholar
KSC	Knight of St Columba
KSG	Knight, Order of St Gregory the Great
KSJ	Knight, Order of St John of Jerusalem (Knights Hospitaller)
KSLI	King's Shropshire Light Infantry
KSS	Knight, Order of St Silvester
KStJ	Knight, Most Venerable Order of the Hospital of St John of Jerusalem
KStJ(A)	Associate Knight of Justice, Most Venerable Order of the Hospital of St John of Jerusalem
KT	Knight, Order of the Thistle
Kt	Knight
Ky	Kentucky (US)

L

(L)	Liberal
LA	Los Angeles; Library Association; Literate in Arts; Liverpool Academy
La	Louisiana (US)
LAA	Light Anti-Aircraft
(Lab)	Labour
LAC	London Athletic Club
LACSAB	Local Authorities Conditions of Service Advisory Board
LAMDA	London Academy of Music and Dramatic Art
LAMSAC	Local Authorities' Management Services and Computer Committee
LAMTPI	Legal Associate Member, Town Planning Institute (*now see* LMRTPI)
L-Corp. or Lance-Corp.	Lance-Corporal
Lancs	Lancashire
LARSP	Language Assessment, Remediation and Screening Procedure
Lautro	Life Assurance and Unit Trust Regulatory Organisation
LBC	London Broadcasting Company
LC	Cross of Leo
LCAD	London Certificate in Art and Design (University of London)
LCC	London County Council (later GLC)
LCh	Licentiate in Surgery
LCJ	Lord Chief Justice
LCL	Licentiate of Canon Law
LCP	Licentiate, College of Preceptors
LCSP	London and Counties Society of Physiologists

IMAGINE SEEING THE SEA AND NOT HEARING THE WAVES

DID YOU KNOW THERE ARE 8 MILLION HEARING IMPAIRED PEOPLE IN BRITAIN

A relative few are profoundly deaf and most are partially deaf, many quite severely. Some 4 million are hearing aid users and many more should be, if only hearing aid technology was as advanced as it could be.

● *BAHOH's expert Technical Committee lobbies Government and manufacturers to intensify hearing aid research.*

The NHS issues 200,000 aids to first time users per year and we estimate that a third of the recipients find them unsatisfactory and put them away in drawers, to start the long slide into isolation socially and at work.

● *BAHOH provides trained volunteers to give in-the-home support to help eradicate this problem.*

More and more young people are becoming affected by hearing impairment after learning communication by speech.

● *BAHOH has a Young Adults Hard Of Hearing section (YAHOH) and runs Noise Awareness Campaigns.*

All these schemes and projects need to be expanded and improved upon to meet the enormous demand.

● *BAHOH is planning a new, larger National Centre for Better Hearing.*

Just one of life's pleasures missed by the deaf

THE BRITISH ASSOCIATION OF THE
HARD OF HEARING

FOR FURTHER INFORMATION PLEASE WRITE TO:
THE DIRECTOR OF APPEALS,
BAHOH, PO BOX 18, NEWPORT, ISLE OF WIGHT, PO30 4QD.
OR PHONE PETER THOMPSON ON: 0983 78743
REG. CHARITY NO; 223322

OUR CREDIT CARD

The Sympathetic Hearing Scheme

People who show this card get consideration because the Sympathetic Hearing Scheme makes life easier for millions of hearing impaired people in the UK. Banks, Social Security offices, stores, small retailers and police stations, to mention a few, exhibiting the logo have been helped by the Scheme to instruct their staffs on methods of communication with the hard of hearing.

The Sympathetic Hearing Scheme is organised and funded by the BRITISH ASSOCIATION OF THE HARD OF HEARING (BAHOH) It is just one of the services BAHOH provides.

PLEASE HELP US TO ACHIEVE OUR AIMS BY REMEMBERING BAHOH IN YOUR WILL, OR JUST SEND A DONATION BY ANOTHER TAX EFFICIENT SCHEME, SUCH AS GIFT AID

CAMPAIGNING FOR ALL SUFFERERS OF THE INVISIBLE HANDICAP

AIDS HAS ALREADY LEFT ITS LEGACY.
(WHAT WILL YOU LEAVE?)

Lots of people would like to help an AIDS charity like the Terrence Higgins Trust.

But would rather not have to shout about it.

Sometimes it's because they're just embarrassed and don't want to be seen getting involved; more often than not, it's because they're worried. That's quite understandable – the media have had a field day. Everyone has seen the shock-horror headlines and read the stories. It's hard to separate the facts from the often sickening mire of misinformation.

But if it's the facts you're after, that's what the Terrence Higgins Trust is all about.

We were founded in 1983 to combat the total lack of information about AIDS and HIV infection.

We seek to not only educate, but increase people's understanding and awareness about AIDS and its associated problems.

And because AIDS doesn't discriminate, neither do we. Passing judgement is for those who seek to attribute blame and our time and money are too precious to waste.

We're not only there for those men, women and children who have become infected. We'll help individuals, organisations and even countries... Anyone who turns to us for help or advice will benefit from the straightforward and practical approach that has made us one of the world's leading AIDS organisations.

All this costs money, and we need to raise funds in many ways: surprisingly a Legacy is a good way to help. Because, far from being just a problem of today, AIDS is still going to be with us tomorrow. And in years to come, funds will be even more desperately needed.

For a free Legacy Advice Pack and more information which may be helpful to those clients who have expressed an interest, please contact us direct. Reg. Charity No. 288527

The Terrence Higgins Trust
ARRANGING YOUR AFFAIRS
MAKING A WILL

The Terrence Higgins Trust
52-54 Grays Inn Road, London WC1X 8JU
Phone: Administration 071-831 0330
Fax: 071-242 0121
Legal line: 071-405 2381 (7pm – 10pm Wed.)
Helpline: 071-242 1010 (3pm – 10pm Daily)

The Terrence Higgins Trust

HEALTH EDUCATION – COUNSELLING – SUPPORT GROUPS – BUDDYING – HELPLINE – ADVICE CENTRE – INFORMATION SERVICES.

LCST	Licentiate, College of Speech Therapists
LD	Liberal and Democratic; Licentiate in Divinity
LDDC	London Docklands Development Corporation
LDiv	Licentiate in Divinity
LDS	Licentiate in Dental Surgery
LDV	Local Defence Volunteers
LEA	Local Education Authority
LEPRA	British Leprosy Relief Association
LèsL	Licencié ès lettres
LG	Lady Companion, Order of the Garter
LGSM	Licentiate, Guildhall School of Music and Drama
LGTB	Local Government Training Board
LH	Light Horse
LHD	*Literarum Humaniorum Doctor* (Doctor of Literature)
LHSM	Licentiate, Institute of Health Services Management
LI	Light Infantry; Long Island
LIBA	Lloyd's Insurance Brokers' Association
Lib Dem	Liberal Democrat
LIBER	Ligue des Bibliothèques Européennes de Recherche
LicMed	Licentiate in Medicine
Lieut	Lieutenant
LIFFE	London International Financial Futures Exchange
Lincs	Lincolnshire
LIOB	Licentiate, Institute of Building
Lit.	Literature; Literary
LitD	Doctor of Literature; Doctor of Letters
Lit.Hum.	*Literae Humaniores* (Classics)
LittD	Doctor of Literature; Doctor of Letters
LJ	Lord Justice
LLA	Lady Literate in Arts
LLB	Bachelor of Laws
LLCM	Licentiate, London College of Music
LLD	Doctor of Laws
LLL	Licentiate in Laws
LLM	Master of Laws
LM	Licentiate in Midwifery
LMBC	Lady Margaret Boat Club
LMC	Local Medical Committee
LMCC	Licentiate, Medical Council of Canada
LMed	Licentiate in Medicine
LMH	Lady Margaret Hall, Oxford
LMR	London Midland Region (BR)
LMS	London, Midland and Scottish Railway; London Missionary Society
LMSSA	Licentiate in Medicine and Surgery, Society of Apothecaries
LMRTPI	Legal Member, Royal Town Planning Institute
(LNat)	Liberal National
LNER	London and North Eastern Railway
LOB	Location of Offices Bureau
L of C	Library of Congress; Lines of Communication
LP	Limited Partnership
LPH	Licentiate in Philosophy
LPO	London Philharmonic Orchestra
LPTB	London Passenger Transport Board (later LTE; *now see* LRT)
LRAD	Licentiate, Royal Academy of Dancing
LRAM	Licentiate, Royal Academy of Music
LRCP	Licentiate, Royal College of Physicians, London
LRCPE	Licentiate, Royal College of Physicians, Edinburgh
LRCPI	Licentiate, Royal College of Physicians of Ireland
LRCPSGlas	Licentiate, Royal College of Physicians and Surgeons of Glasgow
LRCS	Licentiate, Royal College of Surgeons of England
LRCSE	Licentiate, Royal College of Surgeons, Edinburgh
LRCSI	Licentiate, Royal College of Surgeons in Ireland
LRFPS(G)	Licentiate, Royal Faculty of Physicians and Surgeons, Glasgow (*now see* LRCPSGlas)
LRIBA	Licentiate, Royal Institute of British Architects (*now see* RIBA)
LRPS	Licentiate, Royal Photographic Society
LRT	London Regional Transport
LSA	Licentiate, Society of Apothecaries; Licence in Agricultural Sciences
LSE	London School of Economics and Political Science
LSHTM	London School of Hygiene and Tropical Medicine
LSO	London Symphony Orchestra
Lt	Lieutenant; Light
LT	London Transport (*now see* LRT); Licentiate in Teaching
LTA	Lawn Tennis Association
LTB	London Transport Board (later LTE; *now see* LRT)
LTCL	Licentiate of Trinity College of Music, London
Lt-Col	Lieutenant-Colonel
LTE	London Transport Executive (*now see* LRT)
Lt-Gen.	Lieutenant-General
LTh	Licentiate in Theology
(LU)	Liberal Unionist
LUOTC	London University Officers' Training Corps
LVO	Lieutenant, Royal Victorian Order (*formerly* MVO (Fourth Class))
LWT	London Weekend Television
LXX	Septuagint

M

M	Marquess; Member; Monsieur
m	married
MA	Master of Arts; Military Assistant

MAA	Manufacturers' Agents Association of Great Britain
MAAF	Mediterranean Allied Air Forces
MAAT	Member, Association of Accounting Technicians
MACE	Member, Australian College of Education; Member, Association of Conference Executives
MACI	Member, American Concrete Institute
MACM	Member, Association of Computing Machines
MACS	Member, American Chemical Society
MADO	Member, Association of Dispensing Opticians
MAE	Member, Academia Europaea
MAEE	Marine Aircraft Experimental Establishment
MAF	Ministry of Agriculture and Fisheries
MAFF	Ministry of Agriculture, Fisheries and Food
MAI	*Magister in Arte Ingeniaria* (Master of Engineering)
MAIAA	Member, American Institute of Aeronautics and Astronautics
MAICE	Member, American Institute of Consulting Engineers
MAIChE	Member, American Institute of Chemical Engineers
Maj.-Gen.	Major-General
Man	Manitoba (Canada)
MAO	Master of Obstetric Art
MAOT	Member, Association of Occupational Therapists
MAOU	Member, American Ornithologists' Union
MAP	Ministry of Aircraft Production
MAPsS	Member, Australian Psychological Society
MARAC	Member, Australasian Register of Agricultural Consultants
MArch	Master of Architecture
Marq.	Marquess
MASAE	Member, American Society of Agricultural Engineers
MASC	Member, Australian Society of Calligraphers
MASCE	Member, American Society of Civil Engineers
MASME	Member, American Society of Mechanical Engineers
Mass	Massachusetts (US)
MATh	Master of Arts in Theology
Math.	Mathematics; Mathematical
MATSA	Managerial Administrative Technical Staff Association
MAusIMM	Member, Australasian Institute of Mining and Metallurgy
MB	Medal of Bravery (Canada); Bachelor of Medicine
MBA	Master of Business Administration
MBASW	Member, British Association of Social Workers
MBC	Metropolitan/Municipal Borough Council
MBCS	Member, British Computer Society
MBE	Member, Order of the British Empire
MBFR	Mutual and Balanced Force Reductions (negotiations)
MBHI	Member, British Horological Institute
MBIFD	Member, British Institute of Funeral Directors
MBIM	Member, British Institute of Management (*now see* FBIM)
MBKS	Member, British Kinematograph Society (*now see* MBKSTS)
MBKSTS	Member, British Kinematograph, Sound and Television Society
MBOU	Member, British Ornithologists' Union
MBPICS	Member, British Production and Inventory Control Society
MBPS	Member, British Computer Society
MBritIRE	Member, British Institution of Radio Engineers (later MIERE; *now see* MIEE)
MBS	Member, Building Societies Institute (*now see* MCBSI)
MBSc	Master of Business Science
MC	Military Cross; Missionaries of Charity
MCAM	Member, CAM Foundation
MCB	Master in Clinical Biochemistry
MCBSI	Member, Chartered Building Societies Institute
MCC	Marylebone Cricket Club; Metropolitan County Council
MCCD RCS	Member in Clinical Community Dentistry, Royal College of Surgeons
MCD	Master of Civic Design
MCE	Master of Civil Engineering
MCFP	Member, College of Family Physicians (Canada)
MCh or MChir	Master in Surgery
MChE	Master of Chemical Engineering
MChemA	Master in Chemical Analysis
MChOrth	Master of Orthopaedic Surgery
MCIBS	Member, Chartered Institution of Building Services (*now see* MCIBSE)
MCIBSE	Member, Chartered Institution of Building Services Engineers
MCIM	Member, Chartered Institute of Marketing
MCIOB	Member, Chartered Institute of Building
M.CIRP	Member, International Institution for Production Engineering Research
MCIS	Member, Institute of Chartered Secretaries and Administrators
MCIT	Member, Chartered Institute of Transport
MCL	Master in Civil Law
MCMES	Member, Civil and Mechanical Engineers' Society
MCom	Master of Commerce
MConsE	Member, Association of Consulting Engineers
MCOphth	Member, College of Ophthalmologists
MCP	Member of Colonial Parliament; Master of City Planning (US)
MCPA	Member, College of Pathologists of Australia (*now see* MRCPA)
MCPath	Member, College of Pathologists (*now see* MRCPath)
MCPP	Member, College of Pharmacy Practice
MCPS	Member, College of Physicians and Surgeons
MCS	Madras Civil Service; Malayan Civil Service
MCSD	Member, Chartered Society of Designers
MCSEE	Member, Canadian Society of Electrical Engineers
MCSP	Member, Chartered Society of Physiotherapy

MCST	Member, College of Speech Therapists
MCT	Member, Association of Corporate Treasurers
MD	Doctor of Medicine; Military District
Md	Maryland (US)
MDC	Metropolitan District Council
MDes	Master of Design
MDS	Master of Dental Surgery
MDSc	Master of Dental Science
Me	Maine (US)
ME	Mining Engineer; Middle East; Master of Engineering
MEAF	Middle East Air Force
MEC	Member of Executive Council; Middle East Command
MEc	Master of Economics
MECAS	Middle East Centre for Arab Studies
Mech.	Mechanics; Mechanical
MECI	Member, Institute of Employment Consultants
Med.	Medical
MEd	Master of Education
MEF	Middle East Force
MEIC	Member, Engineering Institute of Canada
MELF	Middle East Land Forces
Mencap	Royal Society for Mentally Handicapped Children and Adults
MEng	Master of Engineering
MEO	Marine Engineering Officer
MEP	Member of the European Parliament
MetR	Metropolitan Railway
MetSoc	Metals Society (formed by amalgamation of Institute of Metals and Iron and Steel Institute; now merged with Institution of Metallurgists to form Institute of Metals)
MEXE	Military Engineering Experimental Establishment
MF	Master of Forestry
MFA	Master of Fine Arts
MFC	Mastership in Food Control
MFCM	Member, Faculty of Community Medicine (now see MFPHM)
MFGB	Miners' Federation of Great Britain (now see NUM)
MFH	Master of Foxhounds
MFHom	Member, Faculty of Homœopathy
MFOM	Member, Faculty of Occupational Medicine
MFPHM	Member, Faculty of Public Health Medicine
MGA	Major-General in charge of Administration
MGC	Machine Gun Corps
MGDS RCS	Member in General Dental Surgery, Royal College of Surgeons
MGGS	Major-General, General Staff
MGI	Member, Institute of Certificated Grocers
MGO	Master General of the Ordnance; Master of Gynaecology and Obstetrics
Mgr	Monsignor
MHA	Member of House of Assembly
MHCIMA	Member, Hotel Catering and Institutional Management Association
MHK	Member of the House of Keys
MHR	Member of the House of Representatives
MHRA	Modern Humanities Research Association
MHRF	Mental Health Research Fund
MHSM	Member, Institute of Health Services Management
MI	Military Intelligence
MIAeE	Member, Institute of Aeronautical Engineers
MIAgrE	Member, Institution of Agricultural Engineers
MIAM	Member, Institute of Administrative Management
MIAS	Member, Institute of Aeronautical Science (US) (now see MAIAA)
MIBF	Member, Institute of British Foundrymen
MIBiol	Member, Institute of Biology
MIBritE	Member, Institution of British Engineers
MIB(Scot)	Member, Institute of Bankers in Scotland
MICE	Member, Institution of Civil Engineers
MICEI	Member, Institution of Civil Engineers of Ireland
MICFor	Member, Institute of Chartered Foresters
Mich	Michigan (US)
MIChemE	Member, Institution of Chemical Engineers
MICM	Member, Institute of Credit Management
MICorrST	Member, Institution of Corrosion Science and Technology
MICS	Member, Institute of Chartered Shipbrokers
MIDPM	Member, Institute of Data Processing Management
MIE(Aust)	Member, Institution of Engineers, Australia
MIED	Member, Institution of Engineering Designers
MIEE	Member, Institution of Electrical Engineers
MIEEE	Member, Institute of Electrical and Electronics Engineers (NY)
MIEI	Member, Institution of Engineering Inspection
MIE(Ind)	Member, Institution of Engineers, India
MIERE	Member, Institution of Electronic and Radio Engineers (now see MIEE)
MIES	Member, Institution of Engineers and Shipbuilders, Scotland
MIEx	Member, Institute of Export
MIExpE	Member, Institute of Explosives Engineers
MIFA	Member, Institute of Field Archaeologists
MIFF	Member, Institute of Freight Forwarders
MIFireE	Member, Institution of Fire Engineers
MIFM	Member, Institute of Fisheries Management
MIFor	Member, Institute of Foresters (now see MICFor)
MIGasE	Member, Institution of Gas Engineers
MIGeol	Member, Institution of Geologists
MIH	Member, Institute of Housing
MIHM	Member, Institute of Housing Managers (now see MIH)
MIHort	Member, Institute of Horticulture
MIHT	Member, Institution of Highways and Transportation
MIHVE	Member, Institution of Heating and Ventilating Engineers (now see MCIBS)
MIIA	Member, Institute of Industrial Administration (now see FBIM)
MIIM	Member, Institution of Industrial Managers
MIInfSc	Member, Institution of Information Sciences
MIL	Member, Institute of Linguists
Mil.	Military
MILGA	Member, Institute of Local Government Administrators
MILocoE	Member, Institution of Locomotive Engineers
MIM	Member, Institute of Metals (formerly Institution of Metallurgists)
MIMarE	Member, Institute of Marine Engineers
MIMC	Member, Institute of Management Consultants
MIMechE	Member, Institution of Mechanical Engineers
MIMGTechE	Member, Institution of Mechanical and General Technician Engineers
MIMI	Member, Institute of the Motor Industry
MIMinE	Member, Institution of Mining Engineers
MIMM	Member, Institution of Mining and Metallurgy
MIMunE	Member, Institution of Municipal Engineers (now amalgamated with Institution of Civil Engineers)
Min.	Ministry
MIN	Member, Institute of Navigation (now see MRIN)
Minn	Minnesota (US)
MInstAM	Member, Institute of Administrative Management
MInstBE	Member, Institution of British Engineers
MInstCE	Member, Institution of Civil Engineers (now see FICE)
MInstD	Member, Institute of Directors
MInstE	Member, Institute of Energy
MInstEnvSci	Member, Institute of Environmental Sciences
MInstF	Member, Institute of Fuel (now see MInstE)
MInstHE	Member, Institution of Highway Engineers (now see MIHT)
MInstM	Member, Institute of Marketing (now see MCIM)
MInstMC	Member, Institute of Measurement and Control
MInstME	Member, Institution of Mining Engineers
MInstMet	Member, Institute of Metals (later part of Metals Society, now see MIM)
MInstP	Member, Institute of Physics
MInstPet	Member, Institute of Petroleum
MInstPI	Member, Institute of Patentees and Inventors
MInstPkg	Member, Institute of Packaging
MInstPS	Member, Institute of Purchasing and Supply
MInstR	Member, Institute of Refrigeration
MInstRA	Member, Institute of Registered Architects
MInstT	Member, Institute of Transport
MInstTM	Member, Institute of Travel Managers in Industry and Commerce
MInstW	Member, Institute of Welding (now see MWeldI)
MInstWM	Member, Institute of Wastes Management
MINucE	Member, Institution of Nuclear Engineers
MIOB	Member, Institute of Building (now see MCIOB)
MIOM	Member, Institute of Office Management (now see MIAM)
MIOSH	Member, Institution of Occupational Safety and Health
MIPA	Member, Institute of Practitioners in Advertising
MIPlantE	Member, Institution of Plant Engineers (now see MIIM)
MIPM	Member, Institute of Personnel Management
MIPR	Member, Institute of Public Relations
MIProdE	Member, Institution of Production Engineers (now see MIEE)
MIQ	Member, Institute of Quarrying
MIRE	Member, Institution of Radio Engineers (now see MIERE)
MIREE(Aust)	Member, Institution of Radio and Electronics Engineers (Australia)
MIRO	Mineral Industry Research Organisation
MIRT	Member, Institute of Reprographic Technicians
MIRTE	Member, Institute of Road Transport Engineers
MIS	Member, Institute of Statisticians
MISI	Member, Iron and Steel Institute (later part of Metals Society)
MIS(India)	Member, Institution of Surveyors of India
Miss	Mississippi (US)
MIStructE	Member, Institution of Structural Engineers
MIT	Massachusetts Institute of Technology
MITA	Member, Industrial Transport Association
MITD	Member, Institute of Training and Development
MITE	Member, Institution of Electrical and Electronics Technician Engineers
MITT	Member, Institute of Travel and Tourism
MIWE	Member, Institution of Water Engineers (later MIWES; now see MIWEM)
MIWEM	Member, Institution of Water and Environmental Management
MIWES	Member, Institution of Water Engineers and Scientists (now see MIWEM)
MIWM	Member, Institution of Works Managers (now see MIIM)
MIWPC	Member, Institute of Water Pollution Control (now see MIWEM)
MIWSP	Member, Institute of Work Study Practitioners (now see MMS)
MJA	Medical Journalists Association
MJI	Member, Institute of Journalists
MJIE	Member, Junior Institution of Engineers (now see MIGTechE)
MJS	Member, Japan Society

MJur	*Magister Juris*
ML	Licentiate in Medicine; Master of Laws
MLA	Member of Legislative Assembly; Modern Language Association; Master in Landscape Architecture
MLC	Member of Legislative Council
MLCOM	Member, London College of Osteopathic Medicine
MLitt	Master of Letters
Mlle	Mademoiselle (Miss)
MLM	Member, Order of the Legion of Merit (Rhodesia)
MLO	Military Liaison Officer
MLR	Modern Language Review
MM	Military Medal
MMA	Metropolitan Museum of Art
MMB	Milk Marketing Board
MME	Master of Mining Engineering
Mme	Madame
MMechE	Master of Mechanical Engineering
MMet	Master of Metallurgy
MMGI	Member, Mining, Geological and Metallurgical Institute of India
MMin	Master of Ministry
MMM	Member, Order of Military Merit (Canada)
MMS	Member, Institute of Management Services
MMSA	Master of Midwifery, Society of Apothecaries
MN	Merchant Navy
MNAS	Member, National Academy of Sciences (US)
MNECInst	Member, North East Coast Institution of Engineers and Shipbuilders
MNI	Member, Nautical Institute
MNSE	Member, Nigerian Society of Engineers
MO	Medical Officer; Military Operations
Mo	Missouri (US)
MoD	Ministry of Defence
Mods	Moderations (Oxford)
MOF	Ministry of Food
MOH	Medical Officer(s) of Health
MOI	Ministry of Information
MOMI	Museum of the Moving Image
Mon	Monmouthshire
Mont	Montana (US); Montgomeryshire
MOP	Ministry of Power
MOrthRCS	Member in Orthodontics, Royal College of Surgeons
MoS	Ministry of Supply
Most Rev.	Most Reverend
MoT	Ministry of Transport
MOV	Member, Order of Volta (Ghana)
MP	Member of Parliament
MPA	Master of Public Administration; Member, Parliamentary Assembly, Northern Ireland
MPBW	Ministry of Public Building and Works
MPH	Master of Public Health
MPIA	Master of Public and International Affairs
MPO	Management and Personnel Office
MPP	Member, Provincial Parliament
MPRISA	Member, Public Relations Institute of South Africa
MPS	Member, Pharmaceutical Society (*now see* MRPharmS)
MR	Master of the Rolls; Municipal Reform
MRAC	Member, Royal Agricultural College
MRACP	Member, Royal Australasian College of Physicians
MRACS	Member, Royal Australasian College of Surgeons
MRAeS	Member, Royal Aeronautical Society
MRAIC	Member, Royal Architectural Institute of Canada
MRAS	Member, Royal Asiatic Society
MRC	Medical Research Council
MRCA	Multi-Role Combat Aircraft
MRCGP	Member, Royal College of General Practitioners
MRC-LMB	Medical Research Council Laboratory of Molecular Biology
MRCOG	Member, Royal College of Obstetricians and Gynaecologists
MRCP	Member, Royal College of Physicians, London
MRCPA	Member, Royal College of Pathologists of Australia
MRCPE	Member, Royal College of Physicians, Edinburgh
MRCPGlas	Member, Royal College of Physicians and Surgeons of Glasgow
MRCPI	Member, Royal College of Physicians of Ireland
MRCPsych	Member, Royal College of Psychiatrists
MRCS	Member, Royal College of Surgeons of England
MRCSE	Member, Royal College of Surgeons of Edinburgh
MRCSI	Member, Royal College of Surgeons in Ireland
MRCVS	Member, Royal College of Veterinary Surgeons
MRE	Master of Religious Education
MRES or MREmpS	Member, Royal Empire Society
MRHS	Member, Royal Horticultural Society
MRI	Member, Royal Institution
MRIA	Member, Royal Irish Academy
MRIAI	Member, Royal Institute of the Architects of Ireland
MRIC	Member, Royal Institute of Chemistry (*now see* MRSC)
MRIN	Member, Royal Institute of Navigation
MRINA	Member, Royal Institution of Naval Architects
MRPharmS	Member, Royal Pharmaceutical Society
MRSanI	Member, Royal Sanitary Institute (*now see* MRSH)
MRSC	Member, Royal Society of Chemistry
MRSH	Member, Royal Society for the Promotion of Health
MRSL	Member, Order of the Republic of Sierra Leone
MRSM or MRSocMed	Member, Royal Society of Medicine
MRST	Member, Royal Society of Teachers

MRTPI	Member, Royal Town Planning Institute
MRUSI	Member, Royal United Service Institution
MRVA	Member, Rating and Valuation Association
MS	Master of Surgery; Master of Science (US)
MS, MSS	Manuscript, Manuscripts
MSA	Master of Science, Agriculture (US); Mineralogical Society of America
MSAE	Member, Society of Automotive Engineers (US)
MSAICE	Member, South African Institution of Civil Engineers
MSAInstMM	Member, South African Institute of Mining and Metallurgy
MS&R	Merchant Shipbuilding and Repairs
MSAutE	Member, Society of Automobile Engineers
MSC	Manpower Services Commission; Missionaries of the Sacred Heart; Madras Staff Corps
MSc	Master of Science
MScD	Master of Dental Science
MSD	Meritorious Service Decoration (Fiji)
MSE	Master of Science in Engineering (US)
MSF	(Union for) Manufacturing, Science, Finance
MSH	Master of Stag Hounds
MSIAD	Member, Society of Industrial Artists and Designers
MSINZ	Member, Surveyors' Institute of New Zealand
MSIT	Member, Society of Instrument Technology (*now see* MInstMC)
MSM	Meritorious Service Medal; Madras Sappers and Miners
MSN	Master of Science in Nursing
MSocIS	Member, Société des Ingénieurs et Scientifiques de France
MSocSc	Master of Social Sciences
MSR	Member, Society of Radiographers
MSTD	Member, Society of Typographic Designers
Mt	Mount, Mountain
MT	Mechanical Transport
MTA	Music Trades Association
MTAI	Member, Institute of Travel Agents
MTB	Motor Torpedo Boat
MTCA	Ministry of Transport and Civil Aviation
MTD	Midwife Teachers' Diploma
MTEFL	Master in the Teaching of English as a Foreign or Second Language
MTh	Master of Theology
MTIRA	Machine Tool Industry Research Association (*now see* AMTRI)
MTPI	Member, Town Planning Institute (*now see* MRTPI)
MTS	Master of Theological Studies
MUniv	Master of the University
MusB	Bachelor of Music
MusD	Doctor of Music
MusM	Master of Music
MV	Merchant Vessel, Motor Vessel (naval)
MVEE	Military Vehicles and Engineering Establishment
MVO	Member, Royal Victorian Order
MVSc	Master of Veterinary Science
MW	Master of Wine
MWA	Mystery Writers of America
MWeldI	Member, Welding Institute
MWSOM	Member, Institute of Practitioners in Work Study Organisation and Methods (*now see* MMS)

N

(N)	Nationalist; Navigating Duties
N	North
n	nephew
NA	National Academician (America)
NAACP	National Association for the Advancement of Colored People
NAAFI	Navy, Army and Air Force Institutes
NAAS	National Agricultural Advisory Service
NAB	National Advisory Body for Public Sector Higher Education
NABC	National Association of Boys' Clubs
NAC	National Agriculture Centre
NACCB	National Accreditation Council for Certification Bodies
NACF	National Art-Collections Fund
NACRO	National Association for the Care and Resettlement of Offenders
NADFAS	National Association of Decorative and Fine Arts Societies
NAE	National Academy of Engineering
NAEW	Nato Airborn Early Warning
NAHA	National Association of Health Authorities (*now see* NAHAT)
NAHAT	National Association of Health Authorities and Trusts
NALGO or Nalgo	National and Local Government Officers' Association
NAMAS	National Measurement and Accreditation Service
NAMCW	National Association for Maternal and Child Welfare
NAMH	MIND (National Association for Mental Health)
NAMMA	NATO MRCA Management Agency
NAPT	National Association for the Prevention of Tuberculosis
NASA	National Aeronautics and Space Administration (US)
NASDIM	National Association of Security Dealers and Investment Managers (*now see* FIMBRA)
NAS/UWT	National Association of Schoolmasters/Union of Women Teachers
NATCS	National Air Traffic Control Services (*now see* NATS)
NATFHE	National Association of Teachers in Further and Higher Education (combining ATCDE and ATTI)
NATLAS	National Testing Laboratory Accreditation Scheme
NATO	North Atlantic Treaty Organisation

NATS	National Air Traffic Services
Nat. Sci.	Natural Sciences
NATSOPA	National Society of Operative Printers, Graphical and Media Personnel (*formerly* of Operative Printers and Assistants)
NAYC	Youth Clubs UK (*formerly* National Association of Youth Clubs)
NB	New Brunswick
NBA	North British Academy
NBC	National Book Council (later NBL); National Broadcasting Company (US)
NBL	National Book League
NBPI	National Board for Prices and Incomes
NC	National Certificate; North Carolina (US)
NCA	National Certificate of Agriculture
NCARB	National Council of Architectural Registration Boards
NCB	National Coal Board
NCC	National Computing Centre; Nature Conservancy Council
NCCI	National Committee for Commonwealth Immigrants
NCCL	National Council for Civil Liberties
NCDAD	National Council for Diplomas in Art and Design
NCET	National Council for Educational Technology
NCLC	National Council of Labour Colleges
NCSE	National Council for Special Education
NCSS	National Council of Social Service
NCTA	National Community Television Association (US)
NCU	National Cyclists' Union
NCVCCO	National Council of Voluntary Child Care Organisations
NCVO	National Council for Voluntary Organisations
NCVQ	National Council for Vocational Qualifications
NDA	National Diploma in Agriculture
NDak	North Dakota (US)
ndc	National Defence College
NDD	National Diploma in Dairying; National Diploma in Design
NDH	National Diploma in Horticulture
NDIC	National Defence Industries Council
NDTA	National Defense Transportation Association (US)
NE	North-east
NEAC	New English Art Club
NEAF	Near East Air Force
NEARELF	Near East Land Forces
NEB	National Enterprise Board
Neb	Nebraska (US)
NEBSS	National Examinations Board for Supervisory Studies
NEC	National Executive Committee
NECCTA	National Educational Closed Circuit Television Association
NECInst	North East Coast Institution of Engineers and Shipbuilders
NEDC	National Economic Development Council; North East Development Council
NEDO	National Economic Development Office
NEH	National Endowment for the Humanities
NEL	National Engineering Laboratory
NERC	Natural Environment Research Council
Nev	Nevada (US)
New M	New Mexico (US)
NFC	National Freight Consortium (*formerly* Corporation, then Company)
NFER	National Foundation for Educational Research
NFMS	National Federation of Music Societies
NFS	National Fire Service
NFT	National Film Theatre
NFU	National Farmers' Union
NFWI	National Federation of Women's Institutes
NGO	Non-Governmental Organisation(s)
NGTE	National Gas Turbine Establishment
NH	New Hampshire (US)
NHBC	National House-Building Council
NHS	National Health Service
NI	Northern Ireland; Native Infantry
NIAB	National Institute of Agricultural Botany
NIACRO	Northern Ireland Association for the Care and Resettlement of Offenders
NIAE	National Institute of Agricultural Engineering
NIAID	National Institute of Allergy and Infectious Diseases
NICEC	National Institute for Careers Education and Counselling
NICG	Nationalised Industries Chairmen's Group
NICS	Northern Ireland Civil Service
NID	Naval Intelligence Division; National Institute for the Deaf; Northern Ireland District; National Institute of Design (India)
NIESR	National Institute of Economic and Social Research
NIH	National Institutes of Health (US)
NIHCA	Northern Ireland Hotels and Caterers Association
NII	Nuclear Installations Inspectorate
NILP	Northern Ireland Labour Party
NISTRO	Northern Ireland Science and Technology Regional Organisation
NJ	New Jersey (US)
NL	National Liberal; No Liability
NLCS	North London Collegiate School
NLF	National Liberal Federation
NLYL	National League of Young Liberals
NMR	Nuclear Magnetic Resonance
NNMA	Nigerian National Merit Award
NNOM	Nigerian National Order of Merit
Northants	Northamptonshire
NOTB	National Ophthalmic Treatment Board
Notts	Nottinghamshire

NP	Notary Public
NPA	Newspaper Publishers' Association
NPFA	National Playing Fields Association
NPk	Nishan-e-Pakistan
NPL	National Physical Laboratory
NRA	National Rifle Association; National Recovery Administration (US); National Rivers Authority
NRAO	National Radio Astronomy Observatory
NRCC	National Research Council of Canada
NRD	National Registered Designer
NRDC	National Research Development Corporation
NRPB	National Radiological Protection Board
NRR	Northern Rhodesia Regiment
NS	Nova Scotia; New Style in the Calendar (in Great Britain since 1752); National Society; National Service
ns	Graduate of Royal Naval Staff College, Greenwich
NSA	National Skating Association
NSAIV	Distinguished Order of Shaheed Ali (Maldives)
NSF	National Science Foundation (US)
NSM	Non-Stipendiary Minister
NSMHC	National Society for Mentally Handicapped Children (*now see* Mencap, RSMHCA)
NSPCC	National Society for Prevention of Cruelty to Children
NSRA	National Small-bore Rifle Association
N/SSF	Novice, Society of St Francis
NSTC	Nova Scotia Technical College
NSW	New South Wales
NT	New Testament; Northern Territory (Australia); National Theatre; National Trust
NT&SA	National Trust & Savings Association
NTDA	National Trade Development Association
NTUC	National Trades Union Congress
NUAAW	National Union of Agricultural and Allied Workers
NUBE	National Union of Bank Employees (*now see* BIFU)
NUFLAT	National Union of Footwear Leather and Allied Trades (*now see* NUKFAT)
NUGMW	National Union of General and Municipal Workers (*now see* GMBATU)
NUHKW	National Union of Hosiery and Knitwear Workers (*now see* NUKFAT)
NUI	National University of Ireland
NUJ	National Union of Journalists
NUJMB	Northern Universities Joint Matriculation Board
NUKFAT	National Union of Knitwear, Footwear and Apparel Trades
NUM	National Union of Mineworkers
NUMAST	National Union of Marine, Aviation and Shipping Transport Officers
NUPE	National Union of Public Employees
NUR	National Union of Railwaymen
NUT	National Union of Teachers
NUTG	National Union of Townswomen's Guilds
NUTN	National Union of Trained Nurses
NUU	New University of Ulster
NW	North-west
NWFP	North-West Frontier Province
NWP	North-Western Province
NWT	North-Western Territories
NY	New York
NYC	New York City
NYO	National Youth Orchestra
NZ	New Zealand
NZEF	New Zealand Expeditionary Force
NZIA	New Zealand Institute of Architects

O

O	Ohio (US)
o	only
OA	Officier d'Académie
O & E	Operations and Engineers (US)
O & M	organisation and method
O & O	Oriental and Occidental Steamship Co.
OAS	Organisation of American States; On Active Service
OAU	Organisation for African Unity
OB	Order of Barbados
ob	*obiit* (died)
OBE	Officer, Order of the British Empire
OBI	Order of British India
OC	Officer, Order of Canada (equivalent to former award SM)
o c	only child
OC or o/c	Officer Commanding
OCA	Old Comrades Association
OCDS or ocds Can	Overseas College of Defence Studies (Canada)
OCF	Officiating Chaplain to the Forces
OCSS	Oxford and Cambridge Shakespeare Society
OCTU	Officer Cadet Training Unit
OCU	Operational Conversion Unit
OD	Officer, Order of Distinction (Jamaica)
ODA	Overseas Development Administration
ODI	Overseas Development Institute
ODM	Ministry of Overseas Development
ODSM	Order of Diplomatic Service Merit (Lesotho)
OE	Order of Excellence (Guyana)
OEA	Overseas Education Association

OECD	Organization for Economic Co-operation and Development
OED	Oxford English Dictionary
OEEC	Organization for European Economic Co-operation (*now see* OECD)
OF	Order of the Founder, Salvation Army
OFEMA	Office Française d'Exportation de Matériel Aéronautique
OFM	Order of Friars Minor (Franciscans)
OFMCap	Order of Friars Minor Capuchin (Franciscans)
OFMConv	Order of Friars Minor Conventual (Franciscans)
OFR	Order of the Federal Republic of Nigeria
OFS	Orange Free State
OFT	Office of Fair Trading
Oftel	Office of Telecommunications
OGS	Oratory of the Good Shepherd
OHMS	On His (or Her) Majesty's Service
O i/c	Officer in charge
OJ	Order of Jamaica
OL	Officer, Order of Leopold; Order of the Leopard (Lesotho)
OLM	Officer, Legion of Merit (Rhodesia)
OM	Order of Merit
OMCS	Office of the Minister for the Civil Service
OMI	Oblate of Mary Immaculate
OMM	Officer, Order of Military Merit (Canada)
ON	Order of the Nation (Jamaica)
OND	Ordinary National Diploma
Ont	Ontario
ONZ	Order of New Zealand
OON	Officer, Order of the Niger
OP	*Ordinis Praedicatorum* (of the Order of Preachers (Dominican)); Observation Post
OPCON	Operational Control
OPCS	Office of Population Censuses and Surveys
OQ	Officer, National Order of Quebec
OR	Order of Rorima (Guyana); Operational Research
ORC	Orange River Colony
Ore	Oregon (US)
ORGALIME	Organisme de Liaison des Industries Métalliques Européennes
ORL	Otorhinolaryngology
ORS	Operational Research Society
ORSL	Order of the Republic of Sierra Leone
ORT	Organization for Rehabilitation by Training
ORTF	Office de la Radiodiffusion et Télévision Française
o s	only son
OSA	Order of St Augustine (Augustinian); Ontario Society of Artists
OSB	Order of St Benedict (Benedictine)
osc	Graduate of Overseas Staff College
OSFC	Franciscan (Capuchin) Order
O/Sig	Ordinary Signalman
OSNC	Orient Steam Navigation Co.
o s p	*obiit sine prole* (died without issue)
OSRD	Office of Scientific Research and Development
OSS	Office of Strategic Services
OStJ	Officer, Most Venerable Order of the Hospital of St John of Jerusalem
OSUK	Ophthalmological Society of the United Kingdom
OT	Old Testament
OTC	Officers' Training Corps
OTL	Officer, Order of Toussaint L'Ouverture (Haiti)
OTU	Operational Training Unit
OTWSA	Ou-Testamentiese Werkgemeenskap in Suider-Afrika
OU	Oxford University; Open University
OUAC	Oxford University Athletic Club
OUAFC	Oxford University Association Football Club
OUBC	Oxford University Boat Club
OUCC	Oxford University Cricket Club
OUDS	Oxford University Dramatic Society
OUP	Oxford University Press; Official Unionist Party
OURC	Oxford University Rifle Club
OURFC	Oxford University Rugby Football Club
OURT	Order of the United Republic of Tanzania
Oxon	Oxfordshire; *Oxoniensis* (of Oxford)

P

PA	Pakistan Army; Personal Assistant
Pa	Pennsylvania (US)
PAA	President, Australian Academy of Science
pac	passed the final examination of the Advanced Class, The Military College of Science
PACE	Protestant and Catholic Encounter
PAg	Professional Agronomist
P&O	Peninsular and Oriental Steamship Co.
P&OSNCo.	Peninsular and Oriental Steam Navigation Co.
PAO	Prince Albert's Own
PASI	Professional Associate, Chartered Surveyors' Institution (*now see* ARICS)
PBS	Public Broadcasting Service
PC	Privy Counsellor; Police Constable; Perpetual Curate; Peace Commissioner (Ireland); Progressive Conservative (Canada)
pc	*per centum* (in the hundred)
PCC	Parochial Church Council
PCE	Postgraduate Certificate of Education
PCEF	Polytechnic and Colleges Employers' Forum
PCFC	Polytechnics and Colleges Funding Council

PCMO	Principal Colonial Medical Officer
PdD	Doctor of Pedagogy (US)
PDG	Président Directeur Général
PDR	People's Democratic Republic
PDRA	post doctoral research assistant
PDSA	People's Dispensary for Sick Animals
PDTC	Professional Dancer's Training Course Diploma
PE	Procurement Executive
PEI	Prince Edward Island
PEN	Poets, Playwrights, Editors, Essayists, Novelists (Club)
PEng	Registered Professional Engineer (Canada); Member, Society of Professional Engineers
Penn	Pennsylvania
PEP	Political and Economic Planning (*now see* PSI)
PER	Professional and Executive Recruitment
PEST	Pressure for Economic and Social Toryism
PETRAS	Polytechnic Educational Technology Resources Advisory Service
PF	Procurator-Fiscal
PFA	Professional Footballers' Association
pfc	Graduate of RAF Flying College
PFE	Program for Executives
PGA	Professional Golfers' Association
PGCE	Post Graduate Certificate of Education
PH	Presidential Order of Honour (Botswana)
PHAB	Physically Handicapped & Able-bodied
PhB	Bachelor of Philosophy
PhC	Pharmaceutical Chemist
PhD	Doctor of Philosophy
Phil.	Philology, Philological; Philosophy, Philosophical
PhL	Licentiate of Philosophy
PHLS	Public Health Laboratory Service
PhM	Master of Philosophy (USA)
PhmB	Bachelor of Pharmacy
Phys.	Physical
PIARC	Permanent International Association of Road Congresses
PIB	Prices and Incomes Board (later NBPI)
PICAO	Provisional International Civil Aviation Organization (*now* ICAO)
pinx.	*pinxit* (he painted it)
PIRA	Paper Industries Research Association
PITCOM	Parliamentary Information Technology Committee
PJG	Pingat Jasa Gemilang (Singapore)
PJK	Pingkat Jasa Kebaktian (Malaysia)
Pl.	Place; Plural
PLA	Port of London Authority
PLC or plc	public limited company
Plen.	Plenipotentiary
PLI	President, Landscape Institute
PLP	Parliamentary Labour Party
PMA	Personal Military Assistant
PMC	Personnel Management Centre
PMD	Program for Management Development
PMG	Postmaster-General
PMN	Panglima Mangku Negara (Malaysia)
PMO	Principal Medical Officer
PMRAFNS	Princess Mary's Royal Air Force Nursing Service
PMS	Presidential Order of Meritorious Service (Botswana); President, Miniature Society
PNBS	Panglima Negara Bintang Sarawak
PNEU	Parents' National Educational Union
PNG	Papua New Guinea
PNP	People's National Party
PO	Post Office
POB	Presidential Order of Botswana
POMEF	Political Office Middle East Force
Pop.	Population
POUNC	Post Office Users' National Council
POW	Prisoner of War; Prince of Wales's
PP	Parish Priest; Past President
pp	pages
PPA	Periodical Publishers Association
PPCLI	Princess Patricia's Canadian Light Infantry
PPE	Philosophy, Politics and Economics
PPInstHE	Past President, Institution of Highway Engineers
PPIStructE	Past President, Institution of Structural Engineers
PPITB	Printing and Publishing Industry Training Board
PPP	Private Patients Plan
PPRA	Past President, Royal Academy
PPRBA	Past President, Royal Society of British Artists
PPRBS	Past President, Royal Society of British Sculptors
PPRE	Past President, Royal Society of Painter-Etchers and Engravers
PPROI	Past President, Royal Institute of Oil Painters
PPRTPI	Past President, Royal Town Planning Institute
PPS	Parliamentary Private Secretary
PPSIAD	Past President, Society of Industrial Artists and Designers
PQ	Province of Quebec
PR	Public Relations
PRA	President, Royal Academy
PRBS	President, Royal Society of British Sculptors
PRCS	President, Royal College of Surgeons
PRE	President, Royal Society of Painter-Etchers and Engravers
Preb.	Prebendary
PrEng.	Professional Engineer
Pres.	President
PRHA	President, Royal Hibernian Academy

PRI	President, Royal Institute of Painters in Water Colours; Plastics and Rubber Institute
PRIA	President, Royal Irish Academy
PRIAS	President, Royal Incorporation of Architects in Scotland
Prin.	Principal
PRISA	Public Relations Institute of South Africa
PRO	Public Relations Officer; Public Records Office
Proc.	Proctor; Proceedings
Prof.	Professor; Professional
PROI	President, Royal Institute of Oil Painters
PRO NED	Promotion of Non-Executive Directors
PRORM	Pay and Records Office, Royal Marines
Pro tem.	*Pro tempore* (for the time being)
Prov.	Provost; Provincial
Prox.	*Proximo* (next)
Prox.acc.	*Proxime accessit* (next in order of merit to the winner)
PRS	President, Royal Society; Performing Right Society Ltd
PRSA	President, Royal Scottish Academy
PRSE	President, Royal Society of Edinburgh
PRSH	President, Royal Society for the Promotion of Health
PRSW	President, Royal Scottish Water Colour Society
PRUAA	President, Royal Ulster Academy of Arts
PRWA	President, Royal West of England Academy
PRWS	President, Royal Society of Painters in Water Colours
PS	Pastel Society; Paddle Steamer
ps	passed School of Instruction (of Officers)
PSA	Property Services Agency; Petty Sessions Area
psa	Graduate of RAF Staff College
psc	Graduate of Staff College († indicates Graduate of Senior Wing Staff College)
PSD	Petty Sessional Division
PSGB	Pharmaceutical Society of Great Britain (*now see* RPSGB)
PSI	Policy Studies Institute
PSIAD	President, Society of Industrial Artists and Designers
PSM	Panglima Setia Mahkota (Malaysia)
psm	Certificate of Royal Military School of Music
PSMA	President, Society of Marine Artists
PSNC	Pacific Steam Navigation Co.
PSO	Principal Scientific Officer; Personal Staff Officer
PSOE	Partido Socialista Obrero Español
PSSC	Personal Social Services Council
PTA	Passenger Transport Authority; Parent-Teacher Association
PTE	Passenger Transport Executive
Pte	Private
ptsc	passed Technical Staff College
Pty	Proprietary
PUP	People's United Party
PVSM	Param Vishishc Seva Medal (India)
PWD	Public Works Department
PWE	Political Welfare Executive
PWO	Prince of Wales's Own
PWR	Pressurized Water Reactor

Q

Q	Queen
QAIMNS	Queen Alexandra's Imperial Military Nursing Service
QALAS	Qualified Associate, Chartered Land Agents' Society (*now* (after amalgamation) *see* ARICS)
QARANC	Queen Alexandra's Royal Army Nursing Corps
QARNNS	Queen Alexandra's Royal Naval Nursing Service
QBD	Queen's Bench Division
QC	Queen's Counsel
QCVSA	Queen's Commendation for Valuable Service in the Air
QEH	Queen Elizabeth Hall
QEO	Queen Elizabeth's Own
QFSM	Queen's Fire Service Medal for Distinguished Service
QGM	Queen's Gallantry Medal
QHC	Queen's Honorary Chaplain
QHDS	Queen's Honorary Dental Surgeon
QHNS	Queen's Honorary Nursing Sister
QHP	Queen's Honorary Physician
QHS	Queen's Honorary Surgeon
Qld	Queensland
Qly	Quarterly
QMAAC	Queen Mary's Army Auxiliary Corps
QMC	Queen Mary College, London (*now see* QMW)
QMG	Quartermaster-General
QMW	Queen Mary and Westfield College, London
QO	Qualified Officer
QOOH	Queen's Own Oxfordshire Hussars
Q(ops)	Quartering (operations)
QPM	Queen's Police Medal
Qr	Quarter
QRIH	Queen's Royal Irish Hussars
QRV	Qualified Valuer, Real Estate Institute of New South Wales
QS	Quarter Sessions
qs	RAF graduates of the Military or Naval Staff College
QSM	Queen's Service Medal (NZ)
QSO	Queen's Service Order (NZ)
QUB	Queen's University, Belfast
qv	*quod vide* (which see)

R

(R)	Reserve
RA	Royal Academician; Royal Artillery
RAA	Regional Arts Association
RAAF	Royal Australian Air Force
RAAMC	Royal Australian Army Medical Corps
RABI	Royal Agricultural Benevolent Institution
RAC	Royal Automobile Club; Royal Agricultural College; Royal Armoured Corps
RACDS	Royal Australian College of Dental Surgeons
RACGP	Royal Australian College of General Practitioners
RAChD	Royal Army Chaplains' Department
RACI	Royal Australian Chemical Institute
RACO	Royal Australian College of Ophthalmologists
RACOG	Royal Australian College of Obstetricians and Gynaecologists
RACP	Royal Australasian College of Physicians
RACS	Royal Australasian College of Surgeons; Royal Arsenal Co-operative Society
RADA	Royal Academy of Dramatic Art
RADAR	Royal Association for Disability and Rehabilitation
RADC	Royal Army Dental Corps
RADIUS	Religious Drama Society of Great Britain
RAE	Royal Australian Engineers; Royal Aerospace Establishment (formerly Royal Aircraft Establishment)
RAEC	Royal Army Educational Corps
RAeS	Royal Aeronautical Society
RAF	Royal Air Force
RAFA	Royal Air Force Association
RAFO	Reserve of Air Force Officers (*now see* RAFRO)
RAFRO	Royal Air Force Reserve of Officers
RAFVR	Royal Air Force Volunteer Reserve
RAI	Royal Anthropological Institute of Great Britain & Ireland; Radio Audizioni Italiane
RAIA	Royal Australian Institute of Architects
RAIC	Royal Architectural Institute of Canada
RAM	(Member of) Royal Academy of Music
RAMC	Royal Army Medical Corps
RAN	Royal Australian Navy
R&D	Research and Development
RANR	Royal Australian Naval Reserve
RANVR	Royal Australian Naval Volunteer Reserve
RAOC	Royal Army Ordnance Corps
RAPC	Royal Army Pay Corps
RARDE	Royal Armament Research and Development Establishment
RARO	Regular Army Reserve of Officers
RAS	Royal Astronomical Society; Royal Asiatic Society
RASC	Royal Army Service Corps (*now see* RCT)
RASE	Royal Agricultural Society of England
RAuxAF	Royal Auxiliary Air Force
RAVC	Royal Army Veterinary Corps
RB	Rifle Brigade
RBA	Member, Royal Society of British Artists
RBC	Royal British Colonial Society of Artists
RBK&C	Royal Borough of Kensington and Chelsea
RBS	Royal Society of British Sculptors
RBSA	(Member of) Royal Birmingham Society of Artists
RBY	Royal Bucks Yeomanry
RC	Roman Catholic
RCA	Member, Royal Canadian Academy of Arts; Royal College of Art; (Member of) Royal Cambrian Academy
RCAC	Royal Canadian Armoured Corps
RCAF	Royal Canadian Air Force
RCamA	Member, Royal Cambrian Academy
RCAS	Royal Central Asian Society (*now see* RSAA)
RCDS	Royal College of Defence Studies
rcds	completed a course at, or served for a year on the Staff of, the Royal College of Defence Studies
RCGP	Royal College of General Practitioners
RCHA	Royal Canadian Horse Artillery
RCHM	Royal Commission on Historical Monuments
RCM	(Member of) Royal College of Music
RCN	Royal Canadian Navy; Royal College of Nursing
RCNC	Royal Corps of Naval Constructors
RCNR	Royal Canadian Naval Reserve
RCNVR	Royal Canadian Naval Volunteer Reserve
RCO	Royal College of Organists
RCOG	Royal College of Obstetricians and Gynaecologists
RCP	Royal College of Physicians, London
RCPath	Royal College of Pathologists
RCPE or RCPEd	Royal College of Physicians, Edinburgh
RCPI	Royal College of Physicians of Ireland
RCPSG	Royal College of Physicians and Surgeons of Glasgow
RCPsych	Royal College of Psychiatrists
RCR	Royal College of Radiologists
RCS	Royal College of Surgeons of England; Royal Corps of Signals; Royal College of Science
RCSE or RCSEd	Royal College of Surgeons of Edinburgh
RCSI	Royal College of Surgeons in Ireland
RCT	Royal Corps of Transport
RCVS	Royal College of Veterinary Surgeons
RD	Rural Dean; Royal Naval and Royal Marine Forces Reserve Decoration
Rd	Road

RDA	Royal Defence Academy
RDC	Rural District Council
RDF	Royal Dublin Fusiliers
RDI	Royal Designer for Industry (Royal Society of Arts)
RDS	Royal Dublin Society
RE	Royal Engineers; Fellow, Royal Society of Painter-Etchers and Engravers; Religious Education
REACH	Retired Executives Action Clearing House
react	Research Education and Aid for Children with potentially Terminal illness
Rear-Adm.	Rear-Admiral
REconS	Royal Economic Society
Regt	Regiment
REME	Royal Electrical and Mechanical Engineers
REngDes	Registered Engineering Designer
REPC	Regional Economic Planning Council
RERO	Royal Engineers Reserve of Officers
RES	Royal Empire Society (*now* Royal Commonwealth Society)
Res.	Resigned; Reserve; Resident; Research
RETI	Association of Traditional Industrial Regions
Rev.	Reverend; Review
RFA	Royal Field Artillery
RFC	Royal Flying Corps (*now* RAF); Rugby Football Club
RFD	Reserve Force Decoration
RFH	Royal Festival Hall
RFN	Registered Fever Nurse
RFPS(G)	Royal Faculty of Physicians and Surgeons, Glasgow (*now see* RCPGlas)
RFR	Rassemblement des Français pour la République
RFU	Rugby Football Union
RGA	Royal Garrison Artillery
RGI	Royal Glasgow Institute of the Fine Arts
RGJ	Royal Green Jackets
RGN	Registered General Nurse
RGS	Royal Geographical Society
RGSA	Royal Geographical Society of Australasia
RHA	Royal Hibernian Academy; Royal Horse Artillery; Regional Health Authority
RHAS	Royal Highland and Agricultural Society of Scotland
RHB	Regional Hospital Board
RHBNC	Royal Holloway and Bedford New College, London
RHC	Royal Holloway College, London (*now see* RHBNC)
RHF	Royal Highland Fusiliers
RHG	Royal Horse Guards
RHistS	Royal Historical Society
RHR	Royal Highland Regiment
RHS	Royal Horticultural Society; Royal Humane Society
RHV	Royal Health Visitor
RI	(Member of) Royal Institute of Painters in Water Colours; Rhode Island
RIA	Royal Irish Academy
RIAI	Royal Institute of the Architects of Ireland
RIAM	Royal Irish Academy of Music
RIAS	Royal Incorporation of Architects in Scotland
RIASC	Royal Indian Army Service Corps
RIBA	(Member of) Royal Institute of British Architects
RIBI	Rotary International in Great Britain and Ireland
RIC	Royal Irish Constabulary; Royal Institute of Chemistry (*now see* RSC)
RICS	Royal Institution of Chartered Surveyors
RIE	Royal Indian Engineering (College)
RIF	Royal Inniskilling Fusiliers
RIIA	Royal Institute of International Affairs
RILEM	Réunion internationale des laboratoires d'essais et de recherches sur les matériaux et les constructions
RIM	Royal Indian Marines
RIN	Royal Indian Navy
RINA	Royal Institution of Naval Architects
RINVR	Royal Indian Naval Volunteer Reserve
RIPA	Royal Institute of Public Administration
RIPH&H	Royal Institute of Public Health and Hygiene
RIrF	Royal Irish Fusiliers
RLSS	Royal Life Saving Society
RM	Royal Marines; Resident Magistrate; Registered Midwife
RMA	Royal Marine Artillery; Royal Military Academy Sandhurst (*now incorporating Royal Military Academy, Woolwich*)
RMB	Rural Mail Base
RMC	Royal Military College Sandhurst (*now see* RMA)
RMCM	(Member of) Royal Manchester College of Music
RMCS	Royal Military College of Science
RMedSoc	Royal Medical Society, Edinburgh
RMetS	Royal Meterological Society
RMFVR	Royal Marine Forces Volunteer Reserve
RMIT	Royal Melbourne Institute of Technology
RMLI	Royal Marine Light Infantry
RMN	Registered Mental Nurse
RMO	Resident Medical Officer(s)
RMP	Royal Military Police
RMPA	Royal Medico-Psychological Association
RMS	Royal Microscopical Society; Royal Mail Steamer; Royal Society of Miniature Painters
RN	Royal Navy; Royal Naval
RNAS	Royal Naval Air Service
RNAY	Royal Naval Aircraft Yard
RNC	Royal Naval College
RNCM	(Member of) Royal Northern College of Music
RNEC	Royal Naval Engineering College
RNIB	Royal National Institute for the Blind
RNID	Royal National Institute for the Deaf
RNLI	Royal National Life-boat Institution
RNLO	Royal Naval Liaison Officer
RNR	Royal Naval Reserve
RNS	Royal Numismatic Society
RNSA	Royal Naval Sailing Association
RNSC	Royal Naval Staff College
RNT	Registered Nurse Tutor
RNTNEH	Royal National Throat, Nose and Ear Hospital
RNUR	Régie Nationale des Usines Renault
RNVR	Royal Naval Volunteer Reserve
RNVSR	Royal Naval Volunteer Supplementary Reserve
RNXS	Royal Naval Auxiliary Service
RNZAC	Royal New Zealand Armoured Corps
RNZAF	Royal New Zealand Air Force
RNZIR	Royal New Zealand Infantry Regiment
RNZN	Royal New Zealand Navy
RNZNVR	Royal New Zealand Naval Volunteer Reserve
ROC	Royal Observer Corps
ROF	Royal Ordnance Factories
R of O	Reserve of Officers
ROI	Member, Royal Institute of Oil Painters
RoSPA	Royal Society for the Prevention of Accidents
(Rot.)	Rotunda Hospital, Dublin (after degree)
RP	Member, Royal Society of Portrait Painters
RPC	Royal Pioneer Corps
RPMS	Royal Postgraduate Medical School
RPO	Royal Philharmonic Orchestra
RPR	Rassemblement pour la République
RPS	Royal Photographic Society
RPSGB	Royal Pharmaceutical Society of Great Britain
RRC	Royal Red Cross
RRE	Royal Radar Establishment (*now see* RSRE)
RRF	Royal Regiment of Fusiliers
RRS	Royal Research Ship
RSA	Royal Scottish Academician; Royal Society of Arts; Republic of South Africa
RSAA	Royal Society for Asian Affairs
RSAD	Royal Surgical Aid Society
RSAF	Royal Small Arms Factory
RSAI	Royal Society of Antiquaries of Ireland
RSAMD	Royal Scottish Academy of Music and Drama
RSanI	Royal Sanitary Institute (*now see* RSH)
RSC	Royal Society of Canada; Royal Society of Chemistry; Royal Shakespeare Company
RSCM	Royal School of Church Music
RSCN	Registered Sick Children's Nurse
RSE	Royal Society of Edinburgh
RSF	Royal Scots Fusiliers
RSFSR	Russian Soviet Federated Socialist Republic
RSGS	Royal Scottish Geographical Society
RSH	Royal Society for the Promotion of Health
RSL	Royal Society of Literature; Returned Services League of Australia
RSM	Royal School of Mines
RSM or **RSocMed**	Royal Society of Medicine
RSMA	Royal Society of Marine Artists
RSME	Royal School of Military Engineering
RSMHCA	Royal Society for Mentally Handicapped Children and Adults (*see* Mencap)
RSNC	Royal Society for Nature Conservation
RSO	Rural Sub-Office; Railway Sub-Office; Resident Surgical Officer
RSPB	Royal Society for Protection of Birds
RSPCA	Royal Society for Prevention of Cruelty to Animals
RSRE	Royal Signals and Radar Establishment
RSSAILA	Returned Sailors, Soldiers and Airmen's Imperial League of Australia (*now see* RSL)
RSSPCC	Royal Scottish Society for Prevention of Cruelty to Children
RSTM&H	Royal Society of Tropical Medicine and Hygiene
RSUA	Royal Society of Ulster Architects
RSV	Revised Standard Version
RSW	Member, Royal Scottish Society of Painters in Water Colours
RTE	Radio Telefis Eireann
Rt Hon.	Right Honourable
RTL	Radio-Télévision Luxembourg
RTO	Railway Transport Officer
RTPI	Royal Town Planning Institute
RTR	Royal Tank Regiment
Rt Rev.	Right Reverend
RTS	Religious Tract Society; Royal Toxophilite Society; Royal Television Society
RTYC	Royal Thames Yacht Club
RU	Rugby Union
RUC	Royal Ulster Constabulary
RUI	Royal University of Ireland
RUKBA	Royal United Kingdom Beneficent Association
RUR	Royal Ulster Regiment
RURAL	Society for the Responsible Use of Resources in Agriculture & on the Land
RUSI	Royal United Services Institute for Defence Studies (*formerly* Royal United Service Institution)
RVC	Royal Veterinary College
RWA or **RWEA**	Member, Royal West of England Academy

RWAFF	Royal West African Frontier Force
RWF	Royal Welch Fusiliers
RWS	(Member of) Royal Society of Painters in Water Colours
RYA	Royal Yachting Association
RYS	Royal Yacht Squadron
RZSScot	Royal Zoological Society of Scotland

S

(S)	(in Navy) Paymaster; Scotland
S	Succeeded; South; Saint
s	son
SA	South Australia; South Africa; Société Anonyme
SAAF	South African Air Force
SABC	South African Broadcasting Corporation
SAC	Scientific Advisory Committee
sac	qualified at small arms technical long course
SACEUR	Supreme Allied Commander Europe
SACLANT	Supreme Allied Commander Atlantic
SACSEA	Supreme Allied Command, SE Asia
SA de CV	sociedad anónima de capital variable
SADF	Sudanese Auxiliary Defence Force
SADG	Société des Architectes Diplômés par le Gouvernement
SAE	Society of Automobile Engineers (US)
SAMC	South African Medical Corps
SARL	Société à Responsabilité Limitée
Sarum	Salisbury
SAS	Special Air Service
Sask	Saskatchewan
SASO	Senior Air Staff Officer
SAT	Senior Member, Association of Accounting Technicians
SATRO	Science and Technology Regional Organisation
SB	Bachelor of Science (US)
SBAA	Sovereign Base Areas Administration
SBAC	Society of British Aerospace Companies (formerly Society of British Aircraft Constructors)
SBS	Special Boat Service
SBStJ	Serving Brother, Most Venerable Order of the Hospital of St John of Jerusalem
SC	Star of Courage (Canada); Senior Counsel (Eire, Guyana, South Africa); South Carolina (US)
sc	student at the Staff College
SCAO	Senior Civil Affairs Officer
SCAPA	Society for Checking the Abuses of Public Advertising
SCAR	Scientific Committee for Antarctic Research
ScD	Doctor of Science
SCDC	Schools Curriculum Development Committee
SCF	Senior Chaplain to the Forces; Save the Children Fund
Sch.	School
SCI	Society of Chemical Industry
SCL	Student in Civil Law
SCM	State Certified Midwife; Student Christian Movement
SCONUL	Standing Conference of National and University Libraries
Scot.	Scotland
ScotBIC	Scottish Business in the Community
SCOTVEC	Scottish Vocational Education Council
SD	Staff Duties
SDA	Social Democratic Alliance; Scottish Diploma in Agriculture; Scottish Development Agency
SDak	South Dakota (US)
SDB	Salesian of Don Bosco
SDF	Sudan Defence Force; Social Democratic Federation
SDI	Strategic Defence Initiative
SDLP	Social Democratic and Labour Party
SDP	Social Democratic Party
SE	South-east
SEAC	South-East Asia Command
SEALF	South-East Asia Land Forces
SEATO	South-East Asia Treaty Organization
SEC	Security Exchange Commission
Sec.	Secretary
SEE	Society of Environmental Engineers
SEN	State Enrolled Nurse
SEPM	Society of Economic Palaeontologists and Mineralogists
SERC	Science and Engineering Research Council
SERT	Society of Electronic and Radio Technicians (now see IEIE)
SESO	Senior Equipment Staff Officer
SFInstE	Senior Fellow, Institute of Energy
SFInstF	Senior Fellow, Institute of Fuel (now see SFInstE)
SFTA	Society of Film and Television Arts (now see BAFTA)
SFTCD	Senior Fellow, Trinity College Dublin
SG	Solicitor-General
SGA	Member, Society of Graphic Art
SGBI	Schoolmistresses' and Governesses' Benevolent Institution
Sgt	Sergeant
SHA	Secondary Heads Association; Special Health Authority
SHAC	London Housing Aid Centre
SHAEF	Supreme Headquarters, Allied Expeditionary Force
SH&MA	Scottish Horse and Motormen's Association
SHAPE	Supreme Headquarters, Allied Powers, Europe
SHHD	Scottish Home and Health Department
SIAD	Society of Industrial Artists and Designers (now see CSD)
SIAM	Society of Industrial and Applied Mathematics (US)
SIB	Shipbuilding Industry Board; Securities and Investments Board

SICOT	Société Internationale de Chirurgie Orthopédique et de Traumatologie
SID	Society for International Development
SIESO	Society of Industrial and Emergency Services Officers
SIMA	Scientific Instrument Manufacturers' Association of Great Britain
SIME	Security Intelligence Middle East
SIMG	Societas Internationalis Medicinae Generalis
SinDrs	Doctor of Chinese
SITA	Société Internationale de Télécommunications Aéronautiques
SITPRO	Simpler Trade Procedures Board (formerly Simplification of International Trade Procedures)
SJ	Society of Jesus (Jesuits)
SJAB	St John Ambulance Brigade
SJD	Doctor of Juristic Science
SL	Serjeant-at-Law
SLA	Special Libraries Association
SLAC	Stanford Linear Accelerator Centre
SLAET	Society of Licensed Aircraft Engineers and Technologists
SLAS	Society for Latin-American Studies
SLD	Social and Liberal Democrats
SLP	Scottish Labour Party
SM	Medal of Service (Canada) (now see OC); Master of Science; Officer qualified for Submarine Duties
SMA	Society of Marine Artists (now see RSMA)
SMB	Setia Mahkota Brunei
SME	School of Military Engineering (now see RSME)
SMHO	Sovereign Military Hospitaller Order (Malta)
SMIEEE	Senior Member, Institute of Electrical and Electronics Engineers (New York)
SMIRE	Senior Member, Institute of Radio Engineers (New York)
SMMT	Society of Motor Manufacturers and Traders Ltd
SMN	Seri Maharaja Mangku Negara (Malaysia)
SMO	Senior Medical Officer; Sovereign Military Order
SMP	Senior Managers' Program
SMPTE	Society of Motion Picture and Television Engineers (US)
SMRTB	Ship and Marine Requirements Technology Board
SNAME	Society of Naval Architects and Marine Engineers (US)
SNCF	Société Nationale des Chemins de Fer Français
SND	Sisters of Notre Dame
SNP	Scottish National Party
SNTS	Society for New Testament Studies
SO	Staff Officer; Scientific Officer
SOAS	School of Oriental and African Studies
Soc.	Society
Soc & Lib Dem	Social and Liberal Democrats (now see Lib Dem)
SocCE(France)	Société des Ingénieurs Civils de France
SODEPAX	Committee on Society, Development and Peace
SOE	Special Operations Executive
SOGAT	Society of Graphical and Allied Trades
SOLACE or Solace	Society of Local Authority Chief Executives
SOM	Society of Occupational Medicine
SOSc	Society of Ordained Scientists
SOTS	Society for Old Testament Study
sowc	Senior Officers' War Course
sp	sine prole (without issue)
SP	Self-Propelled (Anti-Tank Regiment)
SpA	Società per Azioni
SPAB	Society for the Protection of Ancient Buildings
SPCA	Society for the Prevention of Cruelty to Animals
SPCK	Society for Promoting Christian Knowledge
SPCM	Darjah Seri Paduka Cura Si Manja Kini (Malaysia)
SPD	Salisbury Plain District
SPDK	Seri Panglima Darjal Kinabalu
SPG	Society for the Propagation of the Gospel (now see USPG)
SPk	Sitara-e-Pakistan
SPMB	Seri Paduka Makhota Brunei
SPMK	Darjah Kebasaran Seri Paduka Mahkota Kelantan (Malaysia)
SPMO	Senior Principal Medical Officer
SPNC	Society for the Promotion of Nature Conservation (now see RSNC)
SPNM	Society for the Promotion of New Music
SPR	Society for Psychical Research
SPRC	Society for Prevention and Relief of Cancer
sprl	société de personnes à responsabilité limitée
SPSO	Senior Principal Scientific Officer
SPTL	Society of Public Teachers of Law
SPUC	Society for the Protection of the Unborn Child
Sq.	Square
sq	staff qualified
SQA	Sitara-i-Quaid-i-Azam (Pakistan)
Sqdn or Sqn	Squadron
SR	Special Reserve; Southern Railway; Southern Region (BR)
SRC	Science Research Council (now see SERC); Students' Representative Council
SRHE	Society for Research into Higher Education
SRIS	Science Reference Information Service
SRN	State Registered Nurse
SRNA	Shipbuilders and Repairers National Association
SRO	Supplementary Reserve of Officers
SRP	State Registered Physiotherapist
SRY	Sherwood Rangers Yeomanry
SS	Saints; Straits Settlements; Steamship
SSA	Society of Scottish Artists

SSAC	Social Security Advisory Committee
SSAFA or	
SS&AFA	Soldiers', Sailors', and Airmen's Families Association
SSBN	Nuclear Submarine, Ballistic
SSC	Solicitor before Supreme Court (Scotland); Sculptors Society of Canada; *Societas Sanctae Crucis* (Society of the Holy Cross); Short Service Commission
SSEB	South of Scotland Electricity Board
SSEES	School of Slavonic and East European Studies
SSF	Society of St Francis
SSJE	Society of St John the Evangelist
SSM	Society of the Sacred Mission; Seri Setia Mahkota (Malaysia)
SSO	Senior Supply Officer; Senior Scientific Officer
SSRC	Social Science Research Council (*now see* ESRC)
SSStJ	Serving Sister, Most Venerable Order of the Hospital of St John of Jerusalem
St	Street; Saint
STA	Sail Training Association
STB	*Sacrae Theologiae Baccalaureus* (Bachelor of Sacred Theology)
STC	Senior Training Corps
STD	*Sacrae Theologiae Doctor* (Doctor of Sacred Theology)
STh	Scholar in Theology
Stip.	Stipend; Stipendiary
STL	*Sacrae Theologiae Lector* (Reader or a Professor of Sacred Theology)
STM	*Sacrae Theologiae Magister* (Master of Sacred Theology)
STP	*Sacrae Theologiae Professor* (Professor of Divinity, old form of DD)
STRIVE	Society for Preservation of Rural Industries and Village Enterprises
STSO	Senior Technical Staff Officer
STV	Scottish Television
SUNY	State University of New York
Supp. Res.	Supplementary Reserve (of Officers)
Supt	Superintendent
Surg.	Surgeon
Surv.	Surviving
SW	South-west
SWET	Society of West End Theatre
SWlA	Society of Wildlife Artists
SWPA	South West Pacific Area
SWRB	Sadler's Wells Royal Ballet
Syd.	Sydney

T

T	Telephone; Territorial
TA	Telegraphic Address; Territorial Army
TAA	Territorial Army Association
TAF	Tactical Air Force
T&AFA	Territorial and Auxiliary Forces Association
T&AVR	Territorial and Army Volunteer Reserve
TANS	Territorial Army Nursing Service
TANU	Tanganyika African National Union
TARO	Territorial Army Reserve of Officers
TAS	Torpedo and Anti Submarine Course
TASS	Technical, Administrative and Supervisory Section of AUEW (now part of MSF)
TAVRA or	
TA&VRA	Territorial Auxiliary and Volunteer Reserve Association
TC	Order of the Trinity Cross (Trinidad and Tobago)
TCCB	Test and County Cricket Board
TCD	Trinity College, Dublin (University of Dublin, Trinity College)
TCF	Temporary Chaplain to the Forces
TCPA	Town and Country Planning Association
TD	Territorial Efficiency Decoration; Efficiency Decoration (T&AVR) (since April 1967); Teachta Dala (Member of the Dáil, Eire)
TDD	Tubercular Diseases Diploma
TEAC	Technical Educational Advisory Council
TEC	Technician Education Council (*now see* BTEC); Training and Enterprise Council
Tech(CEI)	Technician
TEFL	Teaching English as a Foreign Language
TEM	Territorial Efficiency Medal
TEMA	Telecommunication Engineering and Manufacturing Association
Temp.	Temperature; Temporary
TEng(CEI)	Technician Engineer (*now see* IEng)
Tenn	Tennessee (US)
TeolD	Doctor of Theology
TES	Times Educational Supplement
TET	Teacher of Electrotherapy
Tex	Texas (US)
TF	Territorial Force
TFR	Territorial Force Reserve
TFTS	Tactical Fighter Training Squadron
TGEW	Timber Growers England and Wales Ltd
TGO	Timber Growers' Organisation (*now see* TGEW)
TGWU	Transport and General Workers' Union
ThD	Doctor of Theology
THED	Transvaal Higher Education Diploma
THELEP	Therapy of Leprosy
THES	Times Higher Education Supplement

ThL	Theological Licentiate
ThSchol	Scholar in Theology
TIMS	The Institute of Management Sciences
TLS	Times Literary Supplement
TMMG	Teacher of Massage and Medical Gymnastics
TNC	Theatres National Committee
TOSD	Tertiary Order of St Dominic
TP	Transvaal Province
TPI	Town Planning Institute (*now see* RTPI)
Trans.	Translation; Translated
Transf.	Transferred
TRC	Thames Rowing Club
TRE	Telecommunications Research Establishment (*now see* RRE)
TRH	Their Royal Highnesses
TRIC	Televison and Radio Industries Club
Trin.	Trinity
TRRL	Transport and Road Research Laboratory
TS	Training Ship
TSB	Trustee Savings Bank
tsc	passed a Territorial Army Course in Staff Duties
TSD	Tertiary of St Dominic
TSSA	Transport Salaried Staffs' Association
TUC	Trades Union Congress
TULV	Trade Unions for a Labour Victory
TUS	Trade Union Side
TV	Television
TVEI	Technical and Vocational Education Initiative
TWA	Thames Water Authority
TYC	Thames Yacht Club (*now see* RTYC)

U

(U)	Unionist
u	uncle
UAE	United Arab Emirates
UAR	United Arab Republic
UAU	Universities Athletic Union
UBC	University of British Columbia
UBI	Understanding British Industry
UC	University College
UCCA	Universities Central Council on Admissions
UCET	Universities Council for Education of Teachers
UCH	University College Hospital (London)
UCL	University College London
UCLA	University of California at Los Angeles
UCMSM	University College and Middlesex School of Medicine
UCNS	Universities' Council for Non-academic Staff
UCNW	University College of North Wales
UCRN	University College of Rhodesia and Nyasaland
UCS	University College School
UCSD	University of California at San Diego
UCW	University College of Wales; Union of Communication Workers
UDC	Urban District Council; Urban Development Corporation
UDF	Union Defence Force; Union démocratique française
UDR	Ulster Defence Regiment; Union des Démocrates pour la Vème République (*now see* RFR)
UDSR	Union Démocratique et Socialiste de la Résistance
UEA	University of East Anglia
UED	University Education Diploma
UEFA	Union of European Football Associations
UF	United Free Church
UFAW	Universities Federation for Animal Welfare
UFC	Universities' Funding Council
UGC	University Grants Committee (*now see* UFC)
UIAA	Union Internationale des Associations d'Alpinisme
UICC	Union Internationale contre le Cancer
UIE	Union Internationale des Etudiants
UISPP	Union Internationale des Sciences Préhistoriques et Protohistoriques
UJD	*Utriusque Juris Doctor* (Doctor of both Laws, Doctor of Canon and Civil Law)
UK	United Kingdom
UKAC	United Kingdom Automation Council
UKAEA	United Kingdom Atomic Energy Authority
UKCC	United Kingdom Central Council for Nursing, Midwifery and Health Visiting
UKCIS	United Kingdom Chemical Information Service
UKIAS	United Kingdom Immigrants' Advisory Service
UKISC	United Kingdom Industrial Space Committee
UKLF	United Kingdom Land Forces
UKMF(L)	United Kingdom Military Forces (Land)
UKMIS	United Kingdom Mission
UKOOA	United Kingdom Offshore Operators Association
UKPIA	United Kingdom Petroleum Industry Association Ltd
UKSLS	United Kingdom Services Liaison Staff
ULCI	Union of Lancashire and Cheshire Institutes
UMDS	United Medical and Dental Schools
UMIST	University of Manchester Institute of Science and Technology
UN	United Nations
UNA	United Nations Association
UNCAST	United Nations Conference on the Applications of Science and Technology
UNCIO	United Nations Conference on International Organisation
UNCITRAL	United Nations Commission on International Trade Law

UNCSTD	United Nations Conference on Science and Technology for Development
UNCTAD or Unctad	United Nations Commission for Trade and Development
UNDP	United Nations Development Programme
UNDRO	United Nations Disaster Relief Organisation
UNECA	United Nations Economic Commission for Asia
UNEP	United Nations Environment Programme
UNESCO or Unesco	United Nations Educational, Scientific and Cultural Organisation
UNFAO	United Nations Food and Agriculture Organisation
UNFICYP	United Nations Force in Cyprus
UNHCR	United Nations High Commissioner for Refugees
UNICE	Union des Industries de la Communauté Européenne
UNICEF or Unicef	United Nations Children's Fund (formerly United Nations International Children's Emergency Fund)
UNIDO	United Nations Industrial Development Organisation
UNIDROIT	Institut International pour l'Unification du Droit Privé
UNIFIL	United Nations Interim Force in Lebanon
UNIPEDE	Union Internationale des Producteurs et Distributeurs d'Energie Electrique
UNISIST	Universal System for Information in Science and Technology
UNITAR	United Nations Institute of Training and Research
Univ.	University
UNO	United Nations Organization
UNRRA	United Nations Relief and Rehabilitation Administration
UNRWA	United Nations Relief and Works Agency
UNSCOB	United Nations Special Commission on the Balkans
UP	United Provinces; Uttar Pradesh; United Presbyterian
UPGC	University and Polytechnic Grants Committee
UPNI	Unionist Party of Northern Ireland
UPU	Universal Postal Union
(UPUP)	Ulster Popular Unionist Party
URC	United Reformed Church
URSI	Union Radio-Scientifique Internationale
US	United States
USA	United States of America
USAAF	United States Army Air Force
USAF	United States Air Force
USAID	United States Agency for International Development
USAR	United States Army Reserve
USC	University of Southern California
USDAW	Union of Shop Distributive and Allied Workers
USM	Unlisted Securities Market
USMA	United States Military Academy
USN	United States Navy
USNR	United States Naval Reserve
USPG	United Society for the Propagation of the Gospel
USPHS	United States Public Health Service
USR	Universities' Statistical Record
USS	United States Ship
USSR	Union of Soviet Socialist Republics
USVI	United States Virgin Islands
UTC	University Training Corps
(UU)	Ulster Unionist
(UUUC)	United Ulster Unionist Coalition
(UUUP)	United Ulster Unionist Party
UWIST	University of Wales Institute of Science and Technology
UWT	Union of Women Teachers

V

V	Five (Roman numerals); Version; Vicar; Viscount; Vice
v	versus (against)
v or vid.	vide (see)
Va	Virginia (US)
VAD	Voluntary Aid Detachment
V&A	Victoria and Albert
VAT	Value Added Tax
VC	Victoria Cross
VCAS	Vice-Chief of the Air Staff
VCDS	Vice-Chief of the Defence Staff
VCGS	Vice-Chief of the General Staff
VCNS	Vice-Chief of Naval Staff
VD	Royal Naval Volunteer Reserve Officers' Decoration (now VRD); Volunteer Officers' Decoration; Victorian Decoration
VDC	Volunteer Defence Corps
Ven.	Venerable
Vet.	Veterinary
VG	Vicar-General
VHS	Hon. Surgeon to Viceroy of India
VIC	Victoria Institute of Colleges
Vice-Adm.	Vice-Admiral
Visc.	Viscount
VM	Victory Medal
VMH	Victoria Medal of Honour (Royal Horticultural Society)

Vol.	Volume; Volunteers
VP	Vice-President
VPP	Volunteer Political Party
VPRP	Vice-President, Royal Society of Portrait Painters
VQMG	Vice-Quartermaster-General
VR	Victoria Regina (Queen Victoria); Volunteer Reserve
VRD	Royal Naval Volunteer Reserve Officers' Decoration
VSO	Voluntary Service Overseas
Vt	Vermont (US)
(VUP)	Vanguard Unionist Party

W

W	West
WA	Western Australia
WAAF	Women's Auxiliary Air Force (now see WRAF)
Wash	Washington State (US)
WCC	World Council of Churches
W/Cdr	Wing Commander
WEA	Workers' Educational Association; Royal West of England Academy
WES/PNEU	Worldwide Education Service of Parents' National Educational Union
WEU	Western European Union
WFSW	World Federation of Scientific Workers
WFTU	World Federation of Trade Unions
WhF	Whitworth Fellow
WHO	World Health Organization
WhSch	Whitworth Scholar
WI	West Indies; Women's Institute
Wilts	Wiltshire
WIPO	World Intellectual Property Organization
Wis	Wisconsin (US)
Wits	Witwatersrand
WJEC	Welsh Joint Education Committee
WLA	Women's Land Army
WLD	Women Liberal Democrats
WLF	Women's Liberal Federation
Wm	William
WMO	World Meteorological Organization
WNO	Welsh National Opera
WO	War Office; Warrant Officer
Worcs	Worcestershire
WOSB	War Office Selection Board
WR	West Riding; Western Region (BR)
WRAC	Women's Royal Army Corps
WRAF	Women's Royal Air Force
WRNS	Women's Royal Naval Service
WRVS	Women's Royal Voluntary Service
WS	Writer to the Signet
WSPU	Women's Social and Political Union
WUS	World University Service
WVa	West Virginia (US)
WVS	Women's Voluntary Services (now see WRVS)
WWF	World Wide Fund for Nature (formerly World Wildlife Fund)
Wyo	Wyoming (US)

X

X	Ten (Roman numerals)
XO	Executive Officer

Y

y	youngest
YC	Young Conservative
YCNAC	Young Conservatives National Advisory Committee
Yeo.	Yeomanry
YES	Youth Enterprise Scheme
YHA	Youth Hostels Association
YMCA	Young Men's Christian Association
Yorks	Yorkshire
YPTES	Young People's Trust for Endangered Species
yr	younger
yrs	years
YTS	Youth Training Scheme
YVFF	Young Volunteer Force Foundation
YWCA	Young Women's Christian Association

Z

ZANU	Zimbabwe African National Union
ZAPU	Zimbabwe African People's Union

OBITUARY

Deaths notified from September 1990 to September 1991.

Aarvold, His Honour Sir Carl Douglas, OBE, TD, 17 March 1991.
Abdul Rahman Putra, Tunku (Prince), CH, 6 Dec. 1990.
Acland, Sir Richard Thomas Dyke, 15th Bt, 24 Nov. 1990.
Adcock, Sir Robert Henry, CBE, 16 Oct. 1990.
Aldred, Cyril, 23 June 1991.
Alldritt, Walter, 27 July 1990.
Allen, Rev. Canon Derek William, 22 Jan. 1991.
Allerton, 3rd Baron; George William Lawies Jackson, 1 July 1991 (*ext*).
Allsebrook, Peter Winder, CBE, 14 March 1991.
Amwell, 2nd Baron; Frederick Norman Montague, 12 Oct. 1990.
Anderson, Prof. Carl David, 11 Jan. 1991.
Anderson, Prof. John Stuart, FRS, 25 Dec. 1990.
Andrewes, Edward David Eden, 20 Sept. 1990.
Annaly, 5th Baron; Luke Robert White, 30 Sept. 1990.
Anstey, Sidney Herbert, 5 Sept. 1991.
Arias, Dame Margot Fonteyn de, (Margot Fonteyn), DBE, 21 Feb. 1991.
Armstrong, John Anderson, CB, OBE, TD, 3 Oct. 1990.
Arrau, Claudio, 9 June 1991.
Ashburton, 6th Baron; Alexander Francis St Vincent Baring, KG, KCVO, 12 June 1991.
Ashcroft, Dame Peggy, (Edith Margaret Emily), DBE, 14 June 1991.
Ashtown, 6th Baron; Christopher Oliver Trench, 27 April 1990.
Ashworth, Prof. William, 19 March 1991.
Asprey, Algernon, 27 May 1991.
Atkinson, Colin Ronald Michael, CBE, 25 June 1991.
Atkinson, Frank, OBE, 5 Sept. 1991.
Attlee, 2nd Earl; Martin Richard Attlee, 27 July 1991.
Attwell, Rt Rev. Arthur Henry, 2 March 1991.

Badenoch, Alec William, 16 Feb. 1991.
Baker, Rt Rev. William Scott, 30 Nov. 1990.
Ballantyne, Colin Sandergrove, CMG, 2 July 1988.
Bank-Anthony, Sir Mobolaji, KBE, 26 May 1991.
Banks, Sir Maurice Alfred Lister, 11 Aug. 1991.
Barber, Prof. Michael, FRS, 8 May 1991.
Bardeen, Prof. John, 30 Jan. 1991.
Bardsley, Rt Rev. Cuthbert Killick Norman, CBE, 9 Jan. 1991.
Barley, Prof. Maurice Willmore, 23 June 1991.
Barnes, Prof. Winston Herbert Frederick, 15 Sept. 1990.
Batsford, Sir Brian Caldwell Cook, 5 March 1991.
Batt, Reginald Joseph Alexander, 13 June 1991.
Baxter, Jeremy Richard, 4 Jan. 1991.
Bazire, Rev. Canon Reginald Victor, 20 Oct. 1990.
Beaton, Arthur Charles, CMG, 29 Nov. 1990.
Beck, (Rudolph) Rolf, (Baron Rolf Beck), 25 April 1991.
Beckett, Noel George Stanley, 3 Sept. 1990.
Beckwith, John Gordon, FBA, FSA, 20 Feb. 1991.
Beddoe, Jack Eglinton, CB, 15 Dec. 1990.
Belam, Noël Stephen, 15 March 1991.
Belfrage, Leif Axel Lorentz, Hon. GBE, 30 Aug. 1990.
Bell, (Edward) Percy, OBE, 27 Feb. 1987.
Bell, John Stewart, FRS, 1 Oct. 1990.
Bellairs, Prof. Angus d'Albini, 26 Sept. 1990.
Bennett, Jill, 4 Oct. 1990.
Bennett, Joan, 7 Dec. 1990.
Bere, Rennie Montague, CMG, 23 March 1991.
Berkeley, (Augustus Fitzhardinge) Maurice, CB, 2 Sept. 1991.
Bernstein, Leonard, 14 Oct. 1990.
Bingham, James, 15 Oct. 1990.
Bishop, Instr Rear-Adm. Sir William Alfred, KBE, CB, 22 May 1991.
Black, Prof. Duncan, FBA, 14 Jan. 1991.
Blackwood, Prof. William, 3 Dec. 1990.
Blair, Rt Rev. James Douglas, CBE, 12 Jan. 1991.
Blankenhorn, Herbert, Hon. GCVO, 10 Aug. 1991.
Blaxter, Sir Kenneth Lyon, FRS, 18 April 1991.
Bloomfield, Hon. Sir John Stoughton, QC (Victoria), 30 June 1989.
Bolitho, Major Simon Edward, MC, 20 Feb. 1991.
Bourdillon, Henry Townsend, CMG, 14 Feb. 1991.
Bowen, Edward George, CBE, FRS, 12 Aug. 1991.
Bowen, Gordon, CB, CMG, 29 June 1991.
Bower, Air Marshal Sir Leslie William Clement, KCB, DSO, DFC, 17 Feb. 1991.
Bower, Norman, 7 Dec. 1990.

Bowers, Prof. Fredson Thayer, 11 April 1991.
Boyle, Andrew Philip More, 22 April 1991.
Boyle, John Sebastian, 2 April 1991.
Bretherton, Russell Frederick, CB, 11 Jan. 1991.
Brewster, George, CVO, 18 Jan. 1991.
Brickhill, Paul Chester Jerome, 23 April 1991.
Brodie, Very Rev. Peter Philip, 16 Oct. 1990.
Brown, Sir Edward Joseph, MBE, 27 Aug. 1991.
Brown, John Francis Seccombe, AO, MC, 8 Sept. 1989.
Brown, Sir Raymond Frederick, OBE, 3 Sept. 1991.
Browne, Coral Edith, (Mrs Vincent Price), 29 May 1991.
Bruce, Prof. Frederick Fyvie, FBA, 11 Sept. 1990.
Buchan, Norman Findlay, MP, 23 Oct. 1990.
Buchanan-Smith, Rt Hon. Alick Laidlaw, PC, MP, 29 Aug. 1991.
Buckley, George James, MP, 14 Sept. 1991.
Burch, Maj.-Gen. Geoffrey, CB, 13 Oct. 1990.
Burleigh, George Hall, 28 June 1991.
Burn, Andrew Robert, 17 June 1991.
Burns, Sir John Crawford, 25 July 1991.
Burt-Andrews, Stanley George, CMG, MBE, 28 Oct. 1990.
Burton, Neil Edward David, 6 June 1990.
Burton-Taylor, Sir Alvin, 29 May 1991.
Busk, Sir Douglas Laird, KCMG, 11 Dec. 1990.
Butler, Rt Rev. Arthur Hamilton, MBE, 6 July 1991.
Button, Air Vice-Marshal Arthur Daniel, CB, OBE, 27 May 1991.

Caccia, Baron (Life Peer); Harold Anthony Caccia, GCMG, GCVO, 31 Oct, 1990.
Cadbury, Kenneth Hotham, CBE, MC, 9 June 1991.
Caine, Sir Sydney, KCMG, 2 Jan. 1991.
Campbell of Airds, Brig. Lorne Maclaine, VC, DSO, OBE, TD, 25 May 1991.
Campoli, Alfredo, 27 March 1991.
Capra, Frank, DSM, Hon. OBE. 3 Sept. 1991.
Carew, William James, CBE, 5 April 1990.
Carr, Frank George Griffith, CB, CBE, 9 July 1991.
Carstairs, Dr George Morrison, 17 April 1991.
Case, Air Vice-Marshal Albert Avion, CB, CBE, 16 Nov. 1990.
Cayley, Henry Douglas, OBE, 31 March 1991.
Chadwick, Rt Rev. William Frank Percival, 12 Feb. 1991.
Chamberlain-Garrington, Rev. Elsie Dorothea, 10 April 1991.
Chapman, Hon. Sir Stephen, 23 March 1991.
Charles, Anthony Harold, ERD, TD, 25 Nov. 1990.
Chester, Prof. Theodore Edward, CBE, 8 Aug. 1991.
Chesterfield, Arthur Desborough, CBE, 21 July 1991.
Chesworth, Donald Piers, OBE, 24 May 1991.
Cheveley, Stephen William, OBE, 7 June 1991.
Chorley, (Charles) Harold, CB, 22 Dec. 1990.
Churston, 4th Baron; Richard Francis Roger Yarde-Buller, 9 April 1991.
Clapham, Prof. Arthur Roy, CBE, FRS, 18 Dec. 1990.
Claringbull, Sir (Gordon) Frank, 23 Nov. 1990.
Clark, Sir George Anthony, 3rd Bt, 20 Feb. 1991.
Clark, Sir John Douglas, 4th Bt, 17 Jan. 1991.
Claxton, John Francis, CB, 18 Jan. 1991.
Cleary, Rt Rev. Joseph Francis, 25 Feb. 1991.
Clutterbuck, Edmund Harry Michael, OBE, 20 Feb. 1991.
Coates, Patrick Devereux, 28 Oct. 1990.
Cohen, Ruth Louisa, CBE, 27 July 1991.
Colahan, Air Vice-Marshal William Edward, CB, CBE, DFC, 20 Feb. 1991.
Coleman, Donald Richard, CBE, MP, 14 Jan. 1991.
Collins, Maj.-Gen. Joseph Clinton, CB, CBE, 21 May 1991.
Colman, (Elijah) Alec, 25 July 1991.
Concannon, Terence Patrick, 15 Feb. 1990.
Conner, Rearden, (Patrick Reardon Connor), MBE, 29 Aug. 1991.
Cooke, (Roland) Cecil, CMG, CBE, 28 Feb. 1991.
Cooksley, Clarence Harrington, CBE, QPM, 19 May 1991.
Copland, Aaron, 2 Dec. 1990.
Corbett-Winder, Col John Lyon, OBE, MC, 20 Dec. 1990.
Cory, Sir Clinton James Donald, 4th Bt, 28 Aug. 1991.
Cosslett, Vernon Ellis, FRS, 21 Nov. 1990.
Cousins, Norman, 1 Dec. 1990.
Cowan, Prof. Ian Borthwick, 22 Dec. 1990.
Cox, Sir John William, CBE, 11 Dec. 1990.

Cox, Ronald, 15 July 1991.
Crawshaw, Sir (Edward) Daniel (Weston), QC (Aden), 4 April 1991.
Critchley, Thomas Alan, 28 June 1991.
Croft, Major Sir John Archibald Radcliffe, 5th Bt, 16 Nov. 1990.
Cromer, 3rd Earl of; George Rowland Stanley Baring, KG, GCMG, MBE, PC, 16 March 1991.
Cronne, Prof. Henry Alfred, 27 Sept. 1990.
Cross, Prof. Kenneth William, 10 Oct. 1990.
Crowe, Prof. Ralph Vernon, 20 Nov. 1990.
Cumber, Sir John Alfred, CMG, MBE, TD, 18 May 1991.
Cunliffe, Captain Robert Lionel Brooke, CBE, RN, 29 Nov. 1990.
Cunliffe-Jones, Rev. Prof. Hubert, 3 Jan. 1991.

Dahl, Murdoch Edgcumbe, 20 June 1991.
Dahl, Roald, 23 Nov. 1990.
Davenport, Rear-Adm. Dudley Leslie, CB, OBE, 27 Dec. 1990.
David, Brian Gurney, CBE, 27 June 1990.
Davies, Sir (David) Arthur, KBE, 13 Nov. 1990.
Davies, Sir David Joseph, 17 Aug. 1991.
Davies, Ernest Albert John, 16 Sept. 1991.
Davies, George Francis, CMG, 29 Aug. 1987.
Davies, Rev. Prof. John Gordon, 13 Dec. 1990.
Davies, Kenneth Arthur, CMG, OBE, 19 July 1991.
Davin, Daniel Marcus, (Dan Davin), CBE, 28 Sept. 1990.
Davis, Prof. Ralph Henry Carless, FBA, 12 March 1991.
Daymond, Douglas Godfrey, 27 Oct. 1990.
de Beer, Esmond Samuel, CBE, FBA, 3 Oct. 1990.
Dedijer, Vladimir, 1 Dec. 1990.
Deed, Basil Lingard, OBE, TD, 17 March 1991.
De L'Isle, 1st Viscount; William Philip Sidney, VC, KG, GCMG, GCVO, PC, 5 April 1991.
Dennys, Cyril George, CB, MC, 4 Sept. 1991.
Dent, (Robert) Stanley (Gorrell), RWS, RE, 29 April 1991.
De Saumarez, 6th Baron; James Victor Broke Saumarez, 20 Jan. 1991.
Devenport, Martyn Herbert, 9 May 1991.
Dick, Rear-Adm. Roger Mylius, CB, CBE, DSC, 23 April 1991.
Dickie, Rev. Edgar Primrose, MC, 28 June 1991.
Dickson, Dame Violet Penelope, DBE, 4 Jan. 1991.
Dixon, Sir John George, 3rd Bt, 7 Oct. 1990.
Dixon, Prof. Kendal Cartwright, 17 Dec. 1990.
Dossor, Rear-Adm. Frederick, CB, CBE, 4 Oct. 1990.
Dowding, Michael Frederick, CBE, 8 Feb. 1991.
Drake, Antony Elliot, CBE, 16 Oct. 1990.
Drake, John Edmund Bernard, CBE, DSC, 21 April 1991.
Drew, Lt-Gen. Sir (William) Robert (Macfarlane), KCB, CBE, 27 July 1991.
Dridan, Julian Randal, CMG   *[Deceased.*
Dring, Lt-Col Sir (Arthur) John, KBE, CIE, 16 June 1991.
Dring, (Dennis) William, RA, RWS, 27 Sept. 1990.
Drury, Hon. Charles Mills, OC, CBE, DSO, ED, 12 Jan. 1991.
Duff, Patrick William, 28 Aug. 1991.
Dugmore, Rev. Prof. Clifford William, 25 Oct. 1990.
Duly, Sidney John, 25 June 1991.
Duncan, James Stuart, CMG, 20 Dec. 1986.
Duncan, Michael John Freeman, 6 May 1991.
Dunderdale, Comdr Wilfred Albert, CMG, MBE, RNVR, 13 Nov. 1990.
Dunne, Most Rev. Patrick, 16 March 1988.
Dunpark, Hon. Lord; Alastair McPherson Johnston, TD, 31 Aug. 1991.
Dupuch, Sir (Alfred) Etienne (Jerome), OBE, 23 Aug. 1991.
Durrant, Maj.-Gen. James Thom, CB, DFC, 15 Oct. 1990.
Durrell, Lawrence George, 7 Nov. 1990.
Dürrenmatt, Friedrich, 14 Dec. 1990.

East, Gerald Reginald Ricketts, 1 June 1991.
Eastman, Ven. Derek Ian Tennent, MC, 7 Jan. 1991.
Easton, Air Cdre Sir James Alfred, KCMG, CB, CBE, 19 Oct. 1990.
Ebbisham, 2nd Baron; Rowland Roberts Blades, TD, 12 April 1991 (*ext*).
Edden, Alan John, CMG, 10 Aug. 1991.
Edwards, Donald Isaac, CBE, 14 Sept. 1991.
Eggleston, Hon. Sir Richard Moulton, 16 Jan. 1991.
Eldin-Taylor, Kenneth Roy, CVO, 28 Sept. 1990.
Elias, Dr Taslim Olawale, GCON, CFR, QC, 14 Aug. 1991.
Ellis, Wilfred Desmond, OBE, TD, 30 Dec. 1990.
Elton, Charles Sutherland, FRS, 1 May 1991.
Emett, (Frederick) Rowland, OBE, 13 Nov. 1990.
Emmett, Harold Leslie, 28 June 1991.
Emms, John Frederick George, 9 Oct. 1990.
Escritt, (Charles) Ewart, OBE, 31 Oct. 1990.
Evans, Prof. Dennis Frederick, FRS, 6 Nov. 1990.
Evans, Laurence James, CBE, 28 July 1991.
Evans, Phyllis Mary Carlyon, 27 Oct. 1990.

Fanshawe, Maj.-Gen. George Drew, CB, DSO, OBE, 20 Feb. 1991.
Farrell, Arthur Denis, CMG, 18 Dec. 1990.
Faulkner, Sir Percy, KBE, CB, 22 Sept. 1990.
Fawcett, Sir James Edmund Sandford, DSC, QC, 24 June 1991.
Fay, John David, CMG, 27 Aug. 1991.
Fergus, Most Rev. James, 24 March 1989.

Fergusson, James David, CB, 30 Aug. 1991.
ffrench-Beytagh, Rev. Canon Gonville Aubie, 11 May 1991.
Field, John, CBE, 3 Aug. 1991.
Fieldhouse, Sir Harold, KBE, CB, 20 March 1991.
Fieldhouse, (Richard) Arnold, 28 Sept. 1990.
Fielding, Frank Stanley, OBE, 29 Oct. 1990.
Figgures, Sir Frank Edward, KCB, CMG, 27 Nov. 1990.
Finniston, Sir (Harold) Montague, (Sir Monty), FRS, 2 Feb. 1991.
Fish, Anthony, CBE, 21 July 1991.
Fiske, Dudley Astley, 2 Jan. 1991.
Fitzgerald, Rev. (Sir) Edward Thomas, 3rd Bt, 13 Aug. 1988.
Fitzgerald, William Knight, CBE, 25 June 1991.
FitzRoy, Charles, 1989.
Flemington, Rev. William Frederick, 14 May 1991.
Fletcher, James Thomas, CBE, 23 Feb. 1990.
Fletcher, (Leopold) Raymond, 16 March 1991.
Foden, Air Vice-Marshal Arthur, CB, CBE, 23 Nov. 1990.
Forbes of Pitsligo, Sir Charles Edward Stuart-, 12th Bt, 28 March 1985.
Forbes of Craigievar, Hon. Sir Ewan, 11th Bt, 12 Sept. 1991.
Forbes, Muriel Rose, CBE, 18 April 1991.
Forty, Francis John, OBE, 22 Nov. 1990.
Franklin, Richard Harrington, CBE, 15 Sept. 1991.
Fraser, Sir Douglas Were, ISO, 2 Jan. 1988.
Freebody, Air Vice-Marshal Wilfred Leslie, CB, CBE, AFC, 8 May 1991.
Freeman, Ifan Charles Harold, CMG, TD, 2 Dec. 1990.
Freeman, His Eminence Sir James Darcy, Cardinal, KBE, 16 March 1991.
Fretwell, Sir George Herbert, KBE, CB, 16 March 1991.
Fröhlich, Herbert, FRS, 23 Jan. 1991.

Gale, George Stafford, 3 Nov. 1990.
Gale, Malcolm Ruthven, CBE, 23 Sept. 1990.
Gandhi, Rajiv, 21 May 1991.
García Robles, Alfonso, 3 Sept. 1991.
Gardham, Air Vice-Marshal Marcus Maxwell, CB, CBE, 5 May 1991.
Garnett-Orme, Ion, 10 Feb. 1991.
Garran, Sir (Isham) Peter, KCMG, 5 July 1991.
Garvey, Sir Ronald Herbert, KCMG, KCVO, MBE, 31 May 1991.
Gates, William Thomas George, CBE, 23 Nov. 1990.
Gibbons, Brig. Edward John, CMG, CBE, 8 Nov. 1990.
Gibbs, Rt Hon. Sir Humphrey Vicary, GCVO, KCMG, OBE, PC, 5 Nov. 1990.
Gilbertson, Sir Geoffrey, CBE, 2 Feb. 1991.
Gilkison, Sir Alan Fleming, CBE, 13 Jan. 1990.
Gillam, Group Captain Denys Edgar, DSO, DFC, AFC, 2 July 1991.
Gilliatt, Prof. Roger William, MC, 19 Aug. 1991.
Girling, Maj.-Gen. Peter Howard, CB, OBE, 9 July 1991.
Goadby, Hector Kenneth, 25 Sept. 1990.
Gooch, Sir Robert Douglas, 4th Bt, 6 May 1989.
Goolden, Barbara, 29 April 1990.
Gowing, Sir Lawrence Burnett, CBE, RA, 5 Feb. 1991.
Gowland, Rev. William, 23 May 1991.
Graham, Prof. Angus Charles, FBA, 26 March 1991.
Graham, David Alec, CBE, 19 April 1991.
Graham, Rev. Douglas Leslie, 1 July 1991.
Graham, Martha, 1 April 1991.
Graham, Sir Ralph Wolfe, 13th Bt, 1988.
Granit, Prof. Ragnar Arthur, 12 March 1991.
Grant, Maj.-Gen. Ferris Nelson, CB, 9 Sept. 1991.
Graveson, Prof. Ronald Harry, CBE, QC, 5 Jan. 1991.
Gray, Sylvia Mary, CBE, 27 April 1991.
Grayson, Sir Rupert Stanley Harrington, 4th Bt, 4 April 1991.
Green, Alan, CBE, 2 Feb. 1991.
Green, Sir George Ernest   *[Deceased.*
Green, Maj.-Gen. Kenneth David, CB, OBE, ED, 2 Oct. 1987.
Greene, Edward Reginald, CMG, 13 Nov. 1990.
Greene, Graham, OM, CH, CLit, 3 April 1991.
Greeves, Rev. Derrick Amphlet, 14 March 1991.
Greeves, Maj.-Gen. Sir Stuart, KBE, CB, DSO, MC, 11 Oct. 1989.
Grey, Sir Paul Francis, KCMG, 15 Dec. 1990.
Griffiths, Sir Reginald Ernest, CBE, 17 July 1991.
Grindle, Captain John Annesley, CBE, RN, 20 Feb. 1991.
Groom, Air Marshal Sir Victor Emmanuel, KCVO, KBE, CB, DFC, 6 Dec. 1990.
Groves, Ronald, 8 Feb. 1991.
Guise, Sir John, GCMG, KBE, MP (PNG), 7 Feb. 1991.
Gunston, Sir Richard Wellesley, 2nd Bt, 30 June 1991.

Hadden-Paton, Major Adrian Gerard Nigel, 6 Sept. 1991.
Hagen, John Peter, DSM, 26 Aug. 1990.
Hainsworth, Col John Raymond, CMG, CBE, 15 May 1991.
Hall, Edward, RP, 3 Sept. 1991.
Hall, Trevor Henry, 8 March 1991.
Hamilton, Anthony Norris, 2 Feb. 1991.
Hammer, Armand, 10 Dec. 1990.
Hancock, Lt-Col Sir Cyril Percy, KCIE, OBE, MC, 6 Nov. 1990.
Hanes, Prof. Charles Samuel, FRS, 6 July 1990.
Happold, Prof. Frank Charles, 4 March 1991.
Harcus, Rear-Adm. Ronald Albert, CB, 21 Aug. 1991.

Hardie, William Francis Ross, 30 Sept. 1990.
Harding, His Honour Rowe, 10 Feb. 1991.
Hardman, Amy Elizabeth, 2 Nov. 1990.
Hardman, Sir Fred, MBE, 6 March 1991.
Hardwick, Michael John Drinkrow, 4 March 1991.
Harley, Prof. John Laker, CBE, FRS, 13 Dec. 1990.
Harley, Sir Thomas Winlack, MBE, MC, 13 Jan. 1991.
Harmer, Sir (John) Dudley, OBE, 13 March 1991.
Harmood-Banner, Sir George Knowles, 3rd Bt, 23 Oct. 1990 (*ext*).
Harvie-Clark, Ven. Sidney, 13 Feb. 1991.
Hatfield, Hon. Richard Bennett, PC (Can.), 25 April 1991.
Haughton, Daniel Jeremiah, 5 July 1987.
Hawarden, 8th Viscount; Robert Leslie Eustace Maude, 6 Sept. 1991.
Hawker, Sir (Frank) Cyril, 22 Feb. 1991.
Hawkings, Sir (Francis) Geoffrey, 31 Oct. 1990.
Hawtrey, Stephen Charles, CB, 9 Oct. 1990.
Hayday, Sir Frederick, CBE, 26 Feb. 1990.
Heaney, Brig. Sheila Anne Elizabeth, CB, MBE, TD, 1 Feb. 1991.
Hearnshaw, Prof. Leslie Spencer, 10 June 1991.
Heffer, Eric Samuel, MP, 27 May 1991.
Hellings, Gen. Sir Peter William Cradock, KCB, DSC, MC, 2 Nov. 1990.
Hepburn, Bryan Audley St John, CMG, 30 May 1991.
Hewett, Sir John George, 5th Bt, MC, 17 Oct. 1990.
Hewitt, Captain John Graham, DSO, RN, 1 Feb. 1991.
Hewitt, Margaret, 7 June 1991.
Hilditch, Clifford Arthur, 24 Feb. 1991.
Hill, Sir Austin Bradford, CBE, FRS, 18 April 1991.
Hill, John Frederick Rowland, CMG, 12 April 1991.
Hill, Robert, FRS, 15 March 1991.
Hills, Lawrence Donegan, 20 Sept. 1990.
Hillyard, Patrick Cyril Henry, OBE, 2 March 1991.
Himsworth, Eric, CMG, 7 Aug. 1991.
Hobhouse, Sir Charles Chisholm, 6th Bt, TD, 5 Jan. 1991.
Hodkinson, William, CBE, 10 May 1991.
Hofstadter, Prof. Robert, 17 Nov. 1990.
Holden, Kenneth Graham, 5 Oct. 1990.
Holford, Rear-Adm. Frank Douglas, CB, DSC, 10 Jan. 1991.
Holland, Rt Rev. John Tristram, CBE, 9 Oct. 1990.
HolmPatrick, 3rd Baron; James Hans Hamilton, Feb. 1991.
Holt, Sir James Richard, KBE, 24 Nov. 1990.
Holttum, Richard Eric, 18 Sept. 1990.
Hood, Rev. Norman Arthur, 24 Sept. 1990.
Hopkins, Maj.-Gen. Ronald Nicholas Lamond, CBE, 26 Nov. 1990.
Hosford, John Percival, 10 Feb. 1991.
Hosking, Eric John, OBE, 22 Feb. 1991.
Hothfield, 5th Baron; George William Anthony Tufton, TD, 5 Feb. 1991.
Houston, Prof. William John Ballantyne, 17 Aug. 1991.
Howarth, David Armine, 2 July 1991.
Hsiung, Shih I., 15 Sept. 1991.
Hubback, David Francis, CB, 17 March 1991.
Hughes, William Reginald Noel, 10 July 1990.
Hulme, Henry Rainsford, 8 Jan. 1991.
Humphreys, Maj.-Gen. George Charles, CB, CBE, 8 April 1991.
Hunter, Adam, 9 April 1991.
Hunter, Prof. Archibald Macbride, 14 Sept. 1991.
Hurley, Sir John Garling, CBE, 17 Sept. 1990.
Hurll, Alfred William, CVO, CBE, 1 Jan. 1991.
Hutchinson, Rear-Adm. Christopher Haynes, CB, DSO, OBE, 24 Dec. 1990.
Huxtable, Rev. (William) John (Fairchild), 16 Nov. 1990.
Hyde White, Wilfrid, 6 May 1991.

Illingworth, Sir Charles Frederick William, CBE, 23 Feb. 1991.
Innes of Coxton, Sir Charles Kenneth Gordon, 11th Bt, 27 Dec. 1990.
Irving, Rear-Adm. Sir Edmund George, KBE, CB, 1 Oct. 1990.
Irving, Robert Augustine, DFC, 13 Sept. 1991.
Irwin, Sir James Campbell, OBE, ED, 24 July 1990.

Jackson, Prof. Daphne Frances, OBE, 8 Feb. 1991.
Jackson, Eric Stead, CB, 20 June 1991.
Jackson, Most Rev. George Frederic Clarence, 24 Dec. 1990.
Jackson, Prof. Kenneth Hurlstone, CBE, FBA, 20 Feb. 1991.
Jackson, Laura Riding, 2 Sept. 1991.
Jackson, Comdr Sir Robert Gillman Allen, AC, KCVO, CMG, OBE, 12 Jan. 1991.
Jacob, Very Rev. William Ungoed, 18 Dec. 1990.
Jamison, Robin Ralph, FRS, 18 March 1991.
Jardine, John Frederick James, 12 March 1990.
Johnson, Henry Leslie, 29 July 1991.
Johnston, Ninian Rutherford Jamieson, RSA, 12 Nov. 1990.
Johnstone, Prof. Alan Stewart, 5 Oct. 1990.
Jooste, Gerhardus Petrus, DMS, June 1990.
Joyce, Eileen Alannah, CMG, 25 March 1991.
Juma, Sa'ad   [*Deceased.*

Kaberry of Adel, Baron (Life Peer); Donald Kaberry, TD, 13 March 1991.
Karimjee, Sir Tayabali Hassanali Alibhoy, 14 July 1987.
Kelley, Richard   [*Deceased.*
Kelway, Col George Trevor, CBE, TD, 2 Nov. 1990.

Kempff, Wilhelm Walter Friedrich, 23 May 1991.
Kemsley, Col Sir Alfred Newcombe, KBE, CMG, MSM, ED, 24 Feb. 1987.
Kennon, Vice-Adm. Sir James Edward Campbell, KCB, CBE, 22 Jan. 1991.
Kerr, Rt Hon. Sir John Robert, AK, GCMG, GCVO, PC, 24 March 1991.
Kilmartin, Terence Kevin, CBE, 17 Aug. 1991.
Kiparsky, Prof. Valentin Julius Alexander   [*Deceased.*
Klien, Walter, 10 Feb. 1991.
Kohler, Foy David, 23 Dec. 1990.
Kosinski, Jerzy Nikodem, 3 May 1991.
Krestin, Dr David, 21 Aug. 1991.

Lance, Rev. Preb. John Du Boulay, MC, 4 Sept. 1991.
Land, Edwin Herbert, 1 March 1991.
Lang, Prof. David Marshall, 30 March 1991.
Langdon, Michael, CBE, 12 March 1991.
Large, Maj.-Gen. Stanley Eyre, MBE, 12 May 1991.
Lavington, His Honour Cyril Michael, MBE, 1 Dec. 1990.
Lawrence, Arnold Walter, 31 March 1991.
Lazarus, Robert Stephen, QC, 3 June 1991.
Lea, Lt-Gen. Sir George Harris, KCB, DSO, MBE, 27 Dec. 1990.
Lea, Sir (Thomas) Julian, 4th Bt, 17 Oct. 1990.
Lean, Sir David, CBE, 16 April 1991.
Lee, Gilbert Henry Clifton, 5 Jan. 1991.
Leech, William Charles, CBE, [Kt Jan. 1991], 23 Dec. 1990.
Leedale, Harry Heath, CBE, 10 Sept. 1991.
Lees, Air Marshal Sir Ronald Beresford, KCB, CBE, DFC, 18 May 1991.
Le Gallienne, Eva, 3 June 1991.
Lennon, Dennis, CBE, MC, 16 April 1991.
Leslie, Hon. John Wayland, 17 June 1991.
Lewis, Richard, CBE, 13 Nov. 1990.
Lewis, Sir (William) Arthur, 15 June 1991.
Le Witt, Jan, 21 Jan. 1991.
Lewy, Casimir, FBA, 8 Feb. 1991.
Leyton, (Robert) Nevil (Arthur), 1987.
Li, Choh-Ming, Hon. KBE, 21 April 1991.
Lincoln, Hon. Sir Anthony Leslie Julian; Hon. Mr Justice Lincoln, 12 Aug. 1991.
Lindsay, Kenneth Martin, 4 March 1991.
Lipson, Prof. Henry Solomon, CBE, FRS, 26 April 1991.
Little, Hon. Sir Douglas Macfarlan, 30 Nov. 1990.
Little, Prof. Kenneth Lindsay, 28 Feb. 1991.
Livingston, James Barrett, CBE, DSC, 12 Feb. 1991.
Lloyd of Kilgerran, Baron (Life Peer); Rhys Gerran Lloyd, CBE, QC, 30 Jan. 1991.
Lloyd, Glyn, CBE, 21 Jan. 1991.
Lloyd, Maj.-Gen. Richard Eyre, CB, CBE, DSO, 10 April 1991.
Lloyd Jones, David Elwyn, MC, 8 July 1991.
Loch, 4th Baron; Spencer Douglas Loch, MC, 24 June 1991 (*ext*).
Lockspeiser, Sir Ben, KCB, FRS, 18 Oct. 1990.
Lockwood, Sir Joseph Flawith, 6 March 1991.
Longland, Cedric James, LVO, 14 Jan. 1991.
Looker, Sir Cecil Thomas   [*Deceased.*
Loosley, Stanley George Henry, MC, 23 July 1991.
Lovell, Arnold Henry, 4 Oct. 1990.
Luard, (David) Evan (Trant), 8 Feb. 1991.
Lucet, Charles Ernest, 25 March 1990.
Lurgan, 5th Baron; John Desmond Cavendish Brownlow, OBE, 17 Sept. 1991 (*ext*).
Luria, Prof. Salvador Edward, 6 Feb. 1991.
Lusty, Sir Robert Frith, 23 July 1991.
Lyons, His Honour Sir Rudolph, QC, 25 Jan. 1991.
Lyttle, John Gordon, 27 April 1991.

Macara, Sir (Charles) Douglas, 3rd Bt   [*Deceased.*
McCone, John A., 14 Feb. 1991.
Macdonald, Alistair, 1 May 1991.
Macdonald, Donald Hardman, CMG, 3 Oct. 1990.
MacDougall, Brig. David Mercer, CMG, 13 May 1991.
MacFarlane, Donald, CBE, 28 March 1991.
McGrath, Peter William, 11 Oct. 1990.
McGuire, Robert Ely, CMG, OBE, 24 June 1991.
McInerney, Hon. Sir Murray Vincent, 23 Nov. 1988.
Mackay, Sir William Calder, OBE, MC, 19 June 1990.
Mackenzie, Keith Roderick Turing, OBE, MC, 7 Oct. 1990.
Mackenzie, Kenneth Roderick, CB, 4 Jan. 1991.
Mackey, Prof. William Arthur, TD, 27 Nov. 1990.
Mackintosh, Duncan Robert, CB, 14 Sept. 1991.
MacLaren, Sir Hamish Duncan, KBE, CB, DFC, 15 Oct. 1990.
MacLean, Captain Donald Murdo, DSC, RD, RNR, 4 April 1991.
MacLellan, Sir (George) Robin (Perronet), CBE, 12 June 1991.
MacLennan, Prof. Hugh, CC, 7 Nov. 1990.
MacLeod of Fuinary, Baron (Life Peer); Very Rev. George Fielden MacLeod, MC, 27 June 1991.
MacLeod, Angus, CBE, 18 Jan. 1991.
McMillan, Prof. Edwin Mattison, 7 Sept. 1991.
McNair, Air Vice-Marshal James Jamieson, 9 Oct. 1990.
McPetrie, Sir James Carnegie, KCMG, OBE, 26 Aug. 1991.
Maddox, Sir (John) Kempson, VRD, 27 July 1990.
Magarey, Sir (James) Rupert, 13 Oct. 1990.
Mahony, Lt-Col John Keefer, VC, 15 Dec. 1990.

Maidment, Kenneth John, 3 Oct. 1990.
Malet, Col Sir Edward William St Lo, 8th Bt, OBE, 9 Oct. 1990.
Manhood, Harold Alfred, 5 Jan. 1991.
Mann, Frederick (Francis) Alexander, CBE, FBA, 16 Sept. 1991.
Mansergh, Prof. (Philip) Nicholas (Seton), OBE, FBA, 16 Jan. 1991.
Mant, Sir Cecil George, CBE, 2 Nov. 1990.
Manzù, Giacomo, 17 Jan. 1991.
Marnan, His Honour John Fitzgerald, MBE, QC, 24 Nov. 1990.
Marshall of Leeds, Baron (Life Peer); Frank Shaw Marshall, 1 Nov. 1990.
Marshall, Prof. Herbert Percival James, 28 May 1991.
Martell, Edward Drewett, 3 April 1989.
Martin, Sir John Miller, KCMG, CB, CVO, 31 March 1991.
Martin, Rupert Claude, 17 Aug. 1991.
Mather, Leonard Charles, CBE, 8 May 1991.
Mathias, Sir Richard Hughes, 2nd Bt, 4 Jan. 1991 (*ext*).
Mathias, Winifred Rachel, CBE, 24 Sept. 1988.
Matilal, Prof. Bimal Krishna, 8 June 1991.
Matthews, Thomas Stanley, 4 Jan. 1991.
Maxwell, Col (Arthur) Terence, TD, 27 June 1991.
May, Dr Harry Blight, 21 June 1991.
Meinertzhagen, Daniel, 22 March 1991.
Mellor, Sir John Francis, 3rd Bt, 8 Nov. 1990 (*ext*).
Meyer, Prof. Alfred, 27 Sept. 1990.
Meyer, Rollo John Oliver, (Jack), OBE, 9 March 1991.
Michalopoulos, Prof. André, CBE   [*Deceased.*
Michener, Rt Hon. Roland, CC, CMM, CD, PC (Canada), QC (Canada),
     6 Aug. 1991.
Miles, Baron (Life Peer); Bernard James Miles, CBE, 14 June 1991.
Miller of Glenlee, Sir (Frederick William) Macdonald, 7th Bt, 19 June 1991.
Miller, Sir (Joseph) Holmes, OBE, 6 Feb. 1986.
Miller, Comdr William Ronald, OBE, RN, 26 May 1991.
Milne, Prof. Malcolm Davenport, FRS, 3 April 1991.
Minion, Stephen, OBE, 13 Oct. 1990.
Minogue, Hon. Sir John Patrick, QC, 19 Sept. 1989.
Mitchell, Harold Charles, CIE, 11 May 1991.
Mitchell, Prof. John Richard Anthony, 22 March 1991.
Mitchell, William Eric Marcus, MC, 27 Dec. 1990.
Mocatta, Sir Alan Abraham, OBE, 1 Nov. 1990.
Monroe, John George, 10 July 1991.
Montague, Francis Arnold, CMG, 16 June 1991.
Moon, Sir Peter James Scott, KCVO, CMG, 10 July 1991.
Moravia, Alberto, 26 Sept. 1990.
Morgan, Gwenda, RE, 9 Jan. 1991.
Morrah, Ruth, (Mrs Dermot Morrah), 4 Oct. 1990.
Morse, David A., 1 Dec. 1990.
Morton, Sir Brian, 27 July 1991.
Moss, Alfred Allinson, 28 Oct. 1990.
Moynihan, Rodrigo, CBE, RA, 6 Nov. 1990.
Muggeridge, Malcolm, 14 Nov. 1990.
Muir, John Gerald Grainger, CBE, DSC, 2 Oct. 1990.
Murdoch, Richard Bernard, 9 Oct. 1990.
Murray, Rear-Adm. Sir Brian Stewart, KCMG, AO, 4 June 1991.
Murray, Cecil James Boyd, 4 April 1991.
Myers, His Honour Mark, QC, 1 Dec. 1990.

Nathan, Kandiah Shanmuga, QC, 20 Nov. 1990.
Naylor, (Gordon) Keith, TD; His Honour Judge Naylor, 17 Dec. 1990.
Nelson, Campbell Louis, 11 Jan. 1991.
Nelson, Sir William Vernon Hope, 3rd Bt, OBE, 27 May 1991.
Newe, Rt Hon. Gerard Benedict, CBE, PC (NI)   [*Deceased.*
Nicholson, Sir Godfrey, 1st Bt, 14 July 1991 (*ext*).
Nicholson, (John) Leonard, 4 Dec. 1990.
Noble, Major Sir Marc Brunel, 5th Bt, CBE, 2 Jan. 1991.
Nock, Sir Norman Lindfield, 24 June 1990.
Norman, Baroness, (Priscilla), CBE, 5 April 1991.
Northbrook, 5th Baron; Francis John Baring, 4 Dec. 1990.
Norton, Sir Clifford John, KCMG, CVO, 6 Dec. 1990.
Oakeshott, Michael Joseph, FBA, 18 Dec. 1990.
O'Faolain, Sean, 21 April 1991.
Offler, Prof. Hilary Seton, FBA, 24 Jan. 1991.
Ogilvie, Lady, (Mary Helen), 10 Nov. 1990.
O'Gorman, Rev. Brian Stapleton, 20 Jan. 1991.
Oliver, Brig. James Alexander, CB, CBE, DSO, TD, 4 Oct. 1990.
Orr, Rt Hon. Sir Alan Stewart, OBE, PC, 3 April 1991.
O'Shea, Alexander Paterson, CMG, 24 Dec. 1990.
Oswald, Thomas, 23 Oct. 1990.
Ottley, Agnes May, 10 Nov. 1990.
Owen, Prof. Paul Robert, CBE, FRS, 11 Nov. 1990.

Pandit, Vijaya Lakshmi, (Mrs Ranjit S. Pandit), 1 Dec. 1990.
Pape, Hon. Sir George (Augustus), 15 June 1987.
Parham, Adm. Sir Frederick Robertson, GBE, KCB, DSO, 20 March 1991.
Parker, Dame Marjorie Alice Collett, DBE, 18 March 1991.
Parker, Sir (William) Alan, 4th Bt, 22 Nov. 1990.
Parrish, Alfred Sherwen, 1 Oct. 1990.
Partridge, Harry Cowderoy, 3 Oct. 1990.
Paterson, John Allan, 18 Jan. 1991.

Peacock, Sir Geoffrey Arden, CVO, 27 March 1991.
Pearce, Baron (Life Peer); Edward Holroyd Pearce, PC, 26 Nov. 1990.
Pearson, Sir Francis Fenwick, 1st Bt, MBE, 17 Feb. 1991.
Pedler, Sir Frederick Johnson, 6 April 1991.
Penney, Baron (Life Peer); William George Penney, OM, KBE, FRS, 3 March 1991.
Perth (Australia), Archbishop of (RC); Most Rev. William J. Foley, 10 Feb. 1991.
Phillips, Arthur, OBE, 16 May 1991.
Phillips, Sydney William Charles, CB, 5 May 1991.
Piper, Sir David Towry, CBE, 29 Dec. 1990.
Plaister, Sir Sydney, CBE, 25 March 1991.
Pollock, David Linton, 17 Sept. 1991.
Pollock, Sir George, QC, 28 April 1991.
Portal of Hungerford, Baroness (2nd in line); Rosemary Ann Portal,
     29 Sept. 1990 (*ext*).
Potts, Archie, 24 May 1991.
Potts, Kenneth Hampson, 20 March 1990.
Pouncey, Philip Michael Rivers, CBE, FBA, 12 Nov. 1990.
Pounder, Rafton John, 16 April 1991.
Powell, Prof. Herbert Marcus, FRS, 10 March 1991.
Powell, Roger, OBE, 16 Oct. 1990.
Powlett, Rear-Adm. Philip Frederick, CB, DSO, DSC, 15 Jan. 1991.
Prain, Sir Ronald Lindsay, OBE, 10 May 1991.
Prichard, Sir Montague Illtyd, CBE, MC, 12 June 1991.
Priestland, Gerald Francis, 20 June 1991.
Prime, Derek Arthur, RDI, 16 June 1990.
Pring, David Andrew Michael, CB, MC, 15 Aug. 1991.
Proudfoot, William, 19 Dec. 1990.
Purcell, (John) Denis, 1 Oct. 1990.

Raby, Sir Victor Harry, KBE, CB, MC, 7 Dec. 1990.
Rae, Charles Robert Angus, 28 Nov. 1990.
Rahimtoola, Habib Ibrahim, 2 Jan. 1991.
Ramsey, Leonard Gerald Gwynne, 14 May 1990.
Ranchhodlal, Sir Chinubhai Madhowlal, 2nd Bt, 28 Aug. 1990.
Raper, Vice-Adm. Sir (Robert) George, KCB, 30 Nov. 1990.
Ravensdale, Thomas Corney, CMG, 26 Dec. 1990.
Read, Prof. Margaret Helen, CBE, 19 May 1991.
Redesdale, 5th Baron; Clement Napier Bertram Mitford, 3 March 1991.
Rees, Prof. Garnet, 20 Oct. 1990.
Reid, Air Vice-Marshal Sir (George) Ranald Macfarlane, KCB, DSO, MC,
     19 May 1991.
Reid, Very Rev. George Thomson Henderson, MC, 5 Dec. 1990.
Reidy, Joseph Patrick Irwin, 10 Sept. 1991.
Reilly, Baron (Life Peer); Paul Reilly, 11 Oct. 1990.
Reilly, Noel Marcus Prowse, CMG, 22 April 1991.
Rhodes, Rev. Canon Cecil, 21 Nov. 1990.
Richards, Hon. Sir Edward Trenton, CBE, 13 May 1991.
Richardson, Ven. John Farquhar, 29 April 1991.
Richardson, Sir (Lionel) Earl (George), 10 Sept. 1990.
Riddoch, John Haddow, CMG, 6 May 1991.
Ripley, Sydney William Leonard, 7 June 1991.
Rishbeth, John, OBE, FRS, 1 June 1991.
Ritchie, Sir James Edward Thomson, 2nd Bt, TD, 20 March 1991 (*ext*).
Roberts, Emrys, CBE, 29 Oct. 1990.
Roberts, Dame Joan Howard, DBE, 22 June 1990.
Roberts, Thomas Arnold, OBE, TD, 12 March 1990.
Roberts, Wilfrid Hubert Wace, 26 May 1991.
Robertson, James, CBE, 18 May 1991.
Robertson, Dr Ronald Foote, CBE, 11 April 1991.
Robson, Sir Thomas Buston, MBE, 12 April 1991.
Roddan, Gilbert McMicking, CMG, 15 Dec. 1990.
Rodger, Sir William Glendinning, OBE, 23 July 1990.
Rogers, Hugh Charles Innes, 20 March 1991.
Rogers, Murray Rowland Fletcher, 28 March 1991.
Roijen, Jan Herman Van, 16 March 1991.
Rose, Sir Alec Richard, 11 Jan. 1991.
Rosenthal, Erwin Isak Jacob, 5 June 1991.
Roskill, Sir Ashton Wentworth, QC, 23 June 1991.
Ross, Alfred William, OBE, 8 Jan. 1991.
Ross, Sir Lewis Nathan, CMG, 26 April 1991.
Rostal, Prof. Max, CBE, 6 Aug. 1991.
Rostron, Sir Frank, MBE, 25 Aug. 1991.
Row, Comdr Sir Philip John, KCVO, OBE, RN, 28 Nov. 1990.
Rowe, Norman Lester, CBE, 4 Aug. 1991.
Rowntree, Sir Norman Andrew Forster, 22 July 1991.
Rucker, Sir Arthur Nevil, KCMG, CB, CBE, 12 July 1991.
Ruoff, Theodore Burton Fox, CB, CBE, 6 Nov. 1990.
Rydon, Prof. (Henry) Norman, 12 Sept. 1991.

Sainsbury, Richard Eric, CBE, 7 Sept. 1991.
St Clair-Ford, Captain Sir Aubrey, 6th Bt, DSO, RN, 8 April 1991.
St Davids, 2nd Viscount; Jestyn Reginald Austen Plantagenet Philipps, 10 June 1991.
Sakzewski, Sir Albert, 6 July 1991.
Sales, William Henry, 13 Feb. 1991.
Salt, Sir Anthony Houlton, 6th Bt, 16 Jan. 1991.
Sandbach, Prof. Francis Henry, FBA, 18 Sept. 1991.
Sanders, Christopher Cavania, RA, RP, Aug. 1991.

Santa Cruz, Victor Rafael Andrés, Hon. GCVO, 8 Sept. 1990.
Sayers, Eric Colin, CBE, 16 March 1991.
Schmitthoff, Prof. Clive Macmillan, 30 Sept. 1990.
Schreiber, Gaby, 3 July 1991.
Schultz, Sir Leo, (Joseph Leopold), OBE, 22 July 1991.
Scott, Sir (Charles) Hilary, 9 April 1991.
Scott, Douglas, RDI, 2 Oct. 1990.
Scott, George Barclay, 31 Oct. 1990.
Scott, Rev. Percy, 25 Jan. 1991.
Scott, Maj.-Gen. Robert, CB, 19 March 1991.
Scrutton, (Thomas) Hugh, CBE, 28 Aug. 1991.
Seddon, John, 13 July 1991.
Seebohm, Baron (Life Peer); Frederic Seebohm, TD, 15 Dec. 1990.
Serkin, Rudolf, 8 May 1991.
Seton, Anya, (Anya Seton Chase), 8 Nov. 1990.
Sharp, Brig. Mainwaring Cato Ensor, CBE, 13 Dec. 1990.
Sharp, Margery, 14 March 1991.
Sharrock, Prof. Roger Ian, 27 Dec. 1990.
Shaw, George Anthony Theodore, CBE, 25 May 1990.
Shields, Maj.-Gen. Ronald Frederick, OBE, 5 May 1991.
Shillito, Edward Alan, CB, 3 March 1991.
Sidey, John MacNaughton, DSO, 31 Oct. 1990.
Singer, Isaac Bashevis, 24 July 1991.
Sinnott, Ernest, 31 May 1989.
Skutsch, Prof. Otto, 8 Dec. 1990.
Slack, Prof. Geoffrey Layton, CBE, TD, 5 June 1991.
Smiley, Sir Hugh Houston, 3rd Bt, 1 Nov. 1990.
Smirk, Sir (Frederick) Horace, KBE, 17 May 1991.
Smith, Dr (Charles Edward) Gordon, CB, 4 Aug. 1991.
Smith, Charles Stuart, 13 July 1991.
Smith, Dodie, 24 Nov. 1990.
Smith, William French, 29 Oct. 1990.
Snell, Frederick Rowlandson, 19 April 1991.
Snell, Dr William Edward, 25 Oct. 1990.
Snoy et d'Oppuers, Comte Jean-Charles, Hon. KBE, 17 May 1991.
Somerville, Maj.-Gen. Ronald Macaulay, CB, OBE, 25 Jan. 1991.
Spofford, Charles Merville, DSM, Hon. CBE, 23 March 1991.
Stanford, Adm. Sir Peter Maxwell, GCB, LVO, 22 May 1991.
Stanley, Hon. Pamela Margaret, 30 June 1991.
Stanton-Jones, Richard, 23 Jan. 1991.
Steinberg, Jack, 14 July 1991.
Stevens, Frank Leonard, 15 April 1991.
Steward, Nigel Oliver Willoughby, OBE, 13 May 1991.
Stewart, Prof. Andrew, 14 July 1990.
Stewart, Air Vice-Marshal Colin Murray, CB, CBE, 24 Nov. 1990.
Stewart, James Gill, CB, CBE, 3 July 1991.
Stewart, Richard, CBE, 7 April 1991.
Stirling, Sir (Archibald) David, DSO, OBE, 4 Nov. 1990.
Stockdale, Group Captain George William, 27 Oct. 1990.
Strachan, Robert Martin   [*Deceased.*
Stradling Thomas, Sir John, MP, 29 March 1991.
Stuart, Malcolm Moncrieff, CIE, OBE, 30 April 1991.
Sultan, Syed Abdus, 11 March 1991.
Surridge, Sir (Ernest) Rex (Edward), CMG, 19 Dec. 1990.
Sutcliffe, Prof. Reginald Cockcroft, CB, OBE, FRS, 28 May 1991.
Sutcliffe, Air Cdre Walter Philip, CB, DFC, 9 Oct. 1990.
Sutton, Denys Miller, CBE, 25 Jan. 1991.
Swan, Lt-Col Sir William Bertram, KCVO, CBE, TD, 4 Dec. 1990.
Swann, Sir Anthony Charles Christopher, 3rd Bt, CMG, OBE, 3 Feb. 1991.
Sykes, Air Vice-Marshal William, OBE, 28 Jan. 1991.
Symons, Ernest Vize, CB, 5 Nov. 1990.

Tapp, Maj.-Gen. Sir Nigel Prior Hanson, KBE, CB, DSO, 9 Feb. 1991.
Tapper-Jones, Sydney, 2 Feb. 1991.
Taylor of Mansfield, Baron (Life Peer); Harry Bernard Taylor, CBE, 11 April 1991.
Taylor, John Ralph Carlisle, CIE, 28 June 1991.
Taylor, Sir Michael Goodiff, CBE, 31 July 1991.
Taylor, William Leonard, CBE, 4 Aug. 1991.
Teare, Dr (Hugo) Douglas, CVO, 9 June 1991.
Terry, Walter, 25 June 1991.
Thomas, Melbourne, QPM, 15 Sept. 1989.
Thompson, Charles, OBE, 28 Feb. 1991.
Thomson, Sir Ivo Wilfrid Home, 2nd Bt, 6 Jan. 1991.
Thomson, Peter, 23 April 1991.
Thoyts, Robert Francis Newman, 14 June 1991.
Thurburn, Brig. Roy Gilbert, CB, CBE, 5 Oct. 1990.
Thurlow, Very Rev. Alfred Gilbert Goddard, 24 April 1991.
Thwaites, Brig. Peter Trevenen, 23 May 1991.
Todd, (Alfred) Norman, 28 Dec. 1990.
Tooth, Hon. Sir (Seymour) Douglas   [*Deceased.*
Tortelier, Paul, 18 Dec. 1990.
Travancore, Rajpramukh of; Maj.-Gen. HH Sri Padmanabha Dasa Bala Rama Varma, GCSI, GCIE, 19 July 1991.
Trethowan, Sir (James) Ian (Raley), 12 Dec. 1990.
Trimlestown, 19th Baron; Charles Aloysius Barnewall, 9 Oct. 1990.
Trinder, Air Vice-Marshal Frank Noel, CB, CBE, 21 Aug. 1991.
Troughton, Sir Charles Hugh Willis, CBE, MC, TD, 13 May 1991.

Trythall, Rear-Adm. John Douglas, CB, OBE, 24 Feb. 1991.
Tucker, William Eldon, CVO, MBE, TD, 4 Aug. 1991.
Tweedie, Brig. John William, CBE, DSO, 27 July 1991.

Vancouver, Archbishop of, (RC); Most Rev. James F. Carney, 16 Sept. 1990.
Vaughan, Henry William Campbell, 11 March 1991.
Vercors, (Jean Bruller), 10 June 1991.
Veronese, Vittorino, 3 Sept. 1986.
Versey, Prof. Henry Cherry, 12 Nov. 1990.
Verykios, Panaghiotis Andrew, MM (Greece), 23 June 1990.
Vicars-Harris, Noël Hedley, CMG, 4 May 1991.
Vidler, Rev. Alexander Roper, 25 July 1991.
Vivian, 5th Baron; Anthony Crespigny Claude Vivian, 24 June 1991.
Vouel, Raymond, 12 Feb. 1987.

Wainwright, Robert Everard, CMG, 28 Nov. 1990.
Wainwright, Rear-Adm. Rupert Charles Purchas, CB, DSC, 15 Aug. 1991.
Wakeman, Sir (Offley) David, 5th Bt, 24 Feb. 1991.
Waley-Cohen, Sir Bernard Nathaniel, 1st Bt, 3 July 1991.
Walker, Frank Stockdale, MC, 26 June 1989.
Walker, Sebastian, 16 June 1991.
Wall, Ronald George Robert, CB, 8 Sept. 1991.
Wallis, Col Hugh Macdonell, OC, DSO, OBE, MC, VD, CD, 21 March 1991.
Walston, Baron (Life Peer); Henry David Leonard George Walston, CVO, 29 May 1991.
Walwyn, Fulke Thomas Tyndall, CVO, 18 Feb. 1991.
Ward, Sir John Guthrie, GCMG, 12 Jan. 1991.
Ward-Jackson, Adrian Alexander, CBE, 23 Aug. 1991.
Warman, Ven. Francis Frederic Guy, 25 July 1991.
Warren, Dr Wilfrid, 8 Jan. 1991.
Warrington, Anthony, CBE, 10 Dec. 1990.
Warwick, Prof. Roger, 14 Sept. 1991.
Watkins, Prof. Arthur Goronwy, CBE, 26 Dec. 1990.
Watkiss, Ronald Frederick, CBE, 21 April 1991.
Watson, Herbert James, CB, 26 May 1988.
Watson, Joseph Stanley, MBE, QC, 30 May 1991.
Watson, Air Cdre Michael, CB, CBE, 22 March 1991.
Watson, Sydney, OBE, 17 Feb. 1991.
Watt, Richard Lorimer, 27 June 1991.
Webber, Fernley Douglas, CMG, MC, TD, 13 Feb. 1991.
Weipers, Prof. Sir William Lee, 15 Dec. 1990.
Wells-Pestell, Baron (Life Peer); Reginald Alfred Wells-Pestell, CBE, 17 Jan. 1991.
Wetherall, Rev. Canon Theodore Sumner, 19 Oct. 1990.
Wheatley, Sir (George) Andrew, CBE, 21 May 1991.
Wheeler, Lt-Comdr Sir (Ernest) Richard, KCVO, MBE, RN, 9 Dec. 1990.
White, Arthur John Stanley, CMG, OBE, 8 Feb. 1991.
White, Erica, 5 Feb. 1991.
White, Patrick Victor Martindale, 30 Sept. 1990.
Wild, Rt Rev. Eric, 10 Aug. 1991.
Wilkes, His Honour Lyall, 28 March 1991.
Wilkinson, Kenneth Grahame, CBE, 21 Oct. 1990.
Williams, Dr Denis John, CBE, 26 Nov. 1990.
Williams, Rt Rev. Gwilym Owen, 23 Dec. 1990.
Williams, Rev. (Henry) Howard, 27 Feb. 1991.
Williams, Leslie Henry, 1 May 1991.
Williams-Thomas, Lt-Col Reginald Silvers, DSO, TD, 4 Nov. 1990.
Willoughby, Maj.-Gen. Sir John Edward Francis, KBE, CB, 23 Feb. 1991.
Wilson, Prof. Allan Charles, FRS, 21 July 1991.
Wilson, Sir Angus Frank Johnstone, CBE, CLit, 31 May 1991.
Wilson, Sir Austin George, OBE, 5 May 1987.
Wilson, Prof. Charles Henry, CBE, FBA, 1 Aug. 1991.
Wilson, (Henry) James, 28 July 1990.
Wilson, Sir (Mathew) Martin, 5th Bt, 20 March 1991.
Wilson, Prof. Roger Cowan, 31 July 1991.
Winstone, (Frank) Reece, 30 May 1991.
Wolfson, Sir Isaac, 1st Bt, FRS, 20 June 1991.
Wolters, Very Rev. Conrad Clifton, 7 Feb. 1991.
Womersley, J(ohn) Lewis, CBE, 28 Oct. 1990.
Woodd Walker, Geoffrey Basil, 28 May 1991.
Woodland, Austin William, CBE, 9 Nov. 1990.
Woodward, Geoffrey Royston, 7 Sept. 1991.
Worsley, Very Rev. Godfrey Stuart Harling, 10 Nov. 1990.
Wray, Martin Osterfield, CMG, OBE, 2 Sept. 1991.
Wright, (Edmund) Kenneth, 17 Feb. 1991.
Wright, Sir Rowland Sydney, CBE, 14 June 1991.
Wright, William Alan, CIE, AFC, 26 April 1990.
Wright, Most Rev. William Lockridge, 19 Jan. 1990.
Wroth, Prof. (Charles) Peter, 3 Feb. 1991.

Yarborough, 7th Earl of; John Edward Pelham, 21 March 1991.
Yates-Bell, John Geoffrey, 29 April 1991.
Yorke, Richard Michael, QC, 12 April 1991.
Young, Mark, 15 Aug. 1991.

THE ROYAL FAMILY

THE SOVEREIGN

	Born
Her Majesty Queen Elizabeth II, (Elizabeth Alexandra Mary)	21 April 1926

Succeeded her father, King George VI, 6 February 1952

Married 20 Nov. 1947, HRH The Duke of Edinburgh, *now* HRH The Prince Philip, Duke of Edinburgh, KG, KT, OM, GBE (*b* 10 June 1921; *s* of HRH Prince Andrew of Greèce (*d* 1944) and of HRH Princess Andrew of Greece (*d* 1969), *gg-d* of Queen Victoria; *cr* 1947, Baron Greenwich, Earl of Merioneth and Duke of Edinburgh)

Residences: Buckingham Palace, SW1A 1AA; Windsor Castle, Berkshire SL4 1NJ; Sandringham House, Norfolk PE35 6EN; Balmoral Castle, Aberdeenshire AB35 5TB.

SONS AND DAUGHTER OF HER MAJESTY

HRH The Prince of Wales, (Prince Charles Philip Arthur George), KG, KT, GCB; . . . 14 Nov. 1948

cr 1958, Prince of Wales and Earl of Chester; Duke of Cornwall; Duke of Rothesay, Earl of Carrick and Baron of Renfrew; Lord of the Isles and Great Steward of Scotland

Married 29 July 1981, Lady Diana Frances Spencer, *now* HRH The Princess of Wales (*b* 1 July 1961; *y d* of 8th Earl Spencer, *qv*), and has issue –

HRH PRINCE WILLIAM OF WALES, (PRINCE WILLIAM ARTHUR PHILIP LOUIS) . . . 21 June 1982

HRH PRINCE HENRY OF WALES, (PRINCE HENRY CHARLES ALBERT DAVID) . . . 15 Sept. 1984

Office: Buckingham Palace, SW1A 1AA; *residence:* Highgrove, Doughton, Tetbury, Gloucestershire GL8 8TN.

HRH The Duke of York, (Prince Andrew Albert Christian Edward), CVO; . . . . 19 Feb. 1960

cr 1986, Baron Killyleagh, Earl of Inverness and Duke of York

Married 23 July 1986, Sarah Margaret Ferguson (*b* 15 Oct. 1959; 2nd *d* of Major Ronald Ivor Ferguson, Life Guards (retired)), and has issue –

HRH PRINCESS BEATRICE OF YORK, (PRINCESS BEATRICE ELIZABETH MARY) . . . 8 Aug. 1988

HRH PRINCESS EUGENIE OF YORK, (PRINCESS EUGENIE VICTORIA HELENA) . . . 23 March 1990

Residences: Buckingham Palace, SW1A 1AA; Sunninghill Park, Ascot, Berkshire SL5 7TH.

HRH The Prince Edward (Antony Richard Louis), CVO . . . . 10 March 1964

HRH The Princess Royal, (Princess Anne Elizabeth Alice Louise), GCVO . . . . 15 Aug. 1950

Married 14 Nov. 1973, Captain Mark Anthony Peter Phillips, *qv*, and has issue –

PETER MARK ANDREW PHILLIPS . . . . 15 Nov. 1977

ZARA ANNE ELIZABETH PHILLIPS . . . . 15 May 1981

Office: Buckingham Palace, SW1A 1AA; *residence:* Gatcombe Park, Minchinhampton, Stroud, Gloucestershire GL6 9AT.

SISTER OF HER MAJESTY

HRH The Princess Margaret (Rose), Countess of Snowdon, CI, GCVO . . . . . 21 Aug. 1930

Married 6 May 1960, Antony Charles Robert Armstrong-Jones, *now* 1st Earl of Snowdon, *qv* (marriage dissolved, 1978), and has issue –

DAVID ALBERT CHARLES ARMSTRONG-JONES, (VISCOUNT LINLEY, *qv*) . . . . 3 Nov. 1961

SARAH FRANCES ELIZABETH ARMSTRONG-JONES, (LADY SARAH ARMSTRONG-JONES) . . 1 May 1964

Residence: Kensington Palace, W8 4PU.

MOTHER OF HER MAJESTY

Her Majesty Queen Elizabeth The Queen Mother, (Elizabeth Angela Marguerite), . . . 4 Aug. 1900

Lady of the Order of the Garter, Lady of the Order of the Thistle, CI, GCVO, GBE

Married 26 April 1923 (as Lady Elizabeth Bowes-Lyon, *d* of 14th Earl of Strathmore and Kinghorne), HRH The Duke of York (Prince Albert), who succeeded as King George VI, 11 Dec. 1936 and *d* 6 Feb. 1952

Residences: Clarence House, St James's, SW1A 1BA; Royal Lodge, The Great Park, Windsor, Berkshire; Birkhall, Ballater, Aberdeenshire; Castle of Mey, Caithness-shire.

WIDOW OF UNCLE OF HER MAJESTY

HRH Princess Alice (Christabel), Duchess of Gloucester, GCB, CI, GCVO, GBE, . . . 25 Dec. 1901
3rd *d* of 7th Duke of Buccleuch

Married 6 Nov. 1935, HRH The Duke of Gloucester (Prince Henry William Frederick Albert, *b* 31 March 1900, *d* 10 June 1974), and has issue –

HRH PRINCE WILLIAM OF GLOUCESTER, (PRINCE WILLIAM HENRY ANDREW FREDERICK), *b* 18 Dec. 1941; *d* 28 Aug. 1972

HRH THE DUKE OF GLOUCESTER, (PRINCE RICHARD ALEXANDER WALTER GEORGE) (*see below*)

Residences: Kensington Palace, W8 4PU; Barnwell Manor, Peterborough PE8 5PJ.

COUSINS OF HER MAJESTY

Child of HRH The Duke of Gloucester and of HRH Princess Alice Duchess of Gloucester (*see above*)

HRH The Duke of Gloucester, (Prince Richard Alexander Walter George), GCVO . . . 26 Aug. 1944
Married 8 July 1972, Brigitte Eva van Deurs, GCVO, *d* of Asger Preben Wissing Henriksen, and has issue –

ALEXANDER PATRICK GREGERS RICHARD, (EARL OF ULSTER, *qv*) . . . . 24 Oct. 1974
DAVINA ELIZABETH ALICE BENEDIKTE, (LADY DAVINA WINDSOR) . . . 19 Nov. 1977
ROSE VICTORIA BIRGITTE LOUISE, (LADY ROSE WINDSOR) . . . . 1 March 1980

Residences: Kensington Palace, W8 4PU; Barnwell Manor, Peterborough PE8 5PJ.

Children of HRH The Duke of Kent (Prince George Edward Alexander Edmund, *b* 20 Dec. 1902, *d* 25 Aug. 1942) and HRH Princess Marina, Duchess of Kent (*b* 13 Dec. 1906, *d* 27 Aug. 1968), *y d* of late Prince Nicholas of Greece

HRH The Duke of Kent, (Prince Edward George Nicholas Paul Patrick), KG, GCMG, GCVO   9 Oct. 1935
Married 8 June 1961, Katharine Lucy Mary Worsley, GCVO (*b* 22 Feb. 1933, *o d* of Sir William Worsley, 4th Bt) and has issue –

GEORGE PHILIP NICHOLAS, (EARL OF ST ANDREWS, *qv*) . . . . . 26 June 1962
NICHOLAS CHARLES EDWARD JONATHAN, (LORD NICHOLAS WINDSOR) . . . 25 July 1970
HELEN MARINA LUCY, (LADY HELEN WINDSOR) . . . . . . 28 April 1964

Residences: York House, St James's Palace, SW1A 1BQ; Crocker End House, Nettlebed, Henley-on-Thames, Oxon RG9 5BJ.

HRH Prince Michael of Kent, (Prince Michael George Charles Franklin) . . . . . 4 July 1942
Married 30 June 1978, Baroness Marie-Christine Agnes Hedwig Ida von Reibnitz, *d* of Baron Günther Hubertus von Reibnitz, and has issue –

FREDERICK MICHAEL GEORGE DAVID LOUIS, (LORD FREDERICK WINDSOR) . . . 6 April 1979
GABRIELLA MARINA ALEXANDRA OPHELIA, (LADY GABRIELLA WINDSOR) . . . 23 April 1981

Residences: Kensington Palace, W8 4PU; Nether Lypiatt Manor, Stroud, Gloucestershire GL6 7LS.

HRH Princess Alexandra (Helen Elizabeth Olga Christabel), The Hon. Lady Ogilvy, GCVO   25 Dec. 1936
Married 24 April 1963, Hon. Sir Angus (James Bruce) Ogilvy, *qv*, and has issue –

JAMES ROBERT BRUCE OGILVY . . . . 29 Feb. 1964
Married 30 July 1988, Julia, *d* of Charles Frederick Melville Rawlinson, *qv*
MARINA VICTORIA ALEXANDRA, (MRS PAUL MOWATT) . . . . . . 31 July 1966
Married 2 Feb. 1990, Paul Julian Mowatt, and has issue –
ZENOUSKA MOWATT . . . . 26 May 1990

Office: 22 Friary Court, St James's Palace, SW1A 1BP; *residence:* Thatched House Lodge, Richmond, Surrey TW10 5HP.

EDITORS' NOTE

A proof of each entry is posted to its subject every year for personal revision, but this cannot be sent unless an address is recorded. Addresses printed in *Who's Who* are those which the subjects of the entries have submitted for publication. It should be noted that the numbers given of the children of a marriage are, unless otherwise indicated, those of the sons and daughters now living; also, that it is the practice to print the names of London clubs unaccompanied by the word London. Forenames printed within brackets are those which the subject of the entry does not commonly use.

It cannot be stated too emphatically that inclusion in *Who's Who* has never at any time been a matter for payment or of obligation to purchase the volume.

A

AARONSON, Graham Raphael; QC 1982; *b* 31 Dec. 1944; *s* of late John Aaronson and of Dora Aaronson (*née* Franks); *m* 1967, Linda Esther Smith; two *s* one *d*. *Educ:* City of London Sch.; Trinity Hall, Cambridge (Thomas Waraker Law Schol.; MA). Called to the Bar, Middle Temple, 1966 (Bencher 1991); practised Revenue law, 1968–73 and 1978–. Advr on tax reform to Treasury, Israel, 1986–. Chm., Dietary Res. Foundn, 1989–. Founder, Standford Grange residential rehabilitation centre for ex-offenders, 1974; Man. Dir, Worldwide Plastics Development, 1974–77; Dir, Bridgend Group PLC, 1977–. *Publication:* contrib. Chitty on Contracts, 23rd edn 1968. *Recreations:* photography, sitting in the sun and staring at the sea. *Address:* Queen Elizabeth Building, Temple, EC4Y 9BS. *T:* 071–936 3131.

ABBADO, Claudio; Principal Conductor, Berlin Philharmonic Orchestra, since 1989; *b* 26 June 1933; *m*; two *s* one *d*. *Educ:* Conservatorio G. Verdi, Milan; Musical Academy, Vienna. Guest Conductor of principal orchestras in Europe and America: conductor at principal festivals and opera houses, 1961–. Music Dir, La Scala, Milan, 1968–86; Musical Dir, European Community Youth Orch., 1977–; Principal Conductor: Vienna Phil. Orch., 1971–; LSO, 1979–87; Music Director: Vienna State Opera, 1986–; Youth Orchestra, Gustav Mahler Foundn, 1986–; Generalmusikdir of Vienna, 1987–. Founder and Artistic Dir of Festival, Wien Modern, 1988. Dr *hc*: Aberdeen, 1986; Ferrara, 1990. Sergei Koussewitzky Prize, Tanglewood, 1958; Dimitri Mitropoulos Prize, 1963; Mozart-Medaille, Mozart-Gemeinde, Vienna, 1973; Goldmedaille der Internat. Gustav Mahler Gesellschaft, Vienna; winner of major international prizes for recordings (Diapason, Deutscher Schallplatten-Preis, Grand Prix du Disque, Grammy, USA, etc), 1965–. *Address:* Wiener Staatsoper, Opernring 2, A-1010, Vienna, Austria.

ABBOTT, Sir Albert (Francis), Kt 1981; CBE 1974; Mayor, City of Mackay, Queensland, 1970–88; *b* Marvel Loch, WA, 10 Dec. 1913; *s* of late Albert Victor and Diana Abbott; *m* 1941, Gwendoline Joyce Maclean; two *s* four *d*. *Educ:* Mount Martin and Mackay State Schs, Qld. Served RAAF, 1941–45. Sugar cane farmer, 1950–; has given twenty years service to sugar industry organisations. Member: Picture, Theatre and Films Commn, 1975–; Qld Local Govt Grants Commn, 1977–85. Returned Services League of Australia: Mem., 1946–; Pres., Mackay Sub-Br., 1960–65; Dist Pres., Mackay, 1965–74; Pres., Qld State, 1974–. President: N Qld Local Govt Assoc., 1975–84; Qld Local Govt Assoc., 1983–88; Aust. Local Govt Assoc., 1986–87. Mem., Mackay Rotary Club. Governor, Utah Foundn, 1975–. *Recreations:* golf, tennis, racing. *Address:* 2 Tudor Court, Mackay, Qld 4740, Australia. *Clubs:* United Services (Brisbane); RSL Ex-Services, Bowls, Golf, Trotting, Turf, Amateur Race, Diggers Race, Legacy (all in Mackay).

ABBOTT, Anthony Cecil, MC 1945; RDI 1972; RIBA; Senior Designer, BBC Television, since 1962 (Designer, 1954–62); *b* 21 Aug. 1923; *s* of Col Albert Leigh Abbott, MC, and Alice Elizabeth Abbott. *Educ:* Dulwich Coll.; Architectural Assoc. (AADip Hons). Served Army, 1939–45 (Captain). AA, 1946–51; Architects' Dept, LCC; private practice, designing new Kuwait, 1952–54. *Work includes: opera:* Billy Budd, 1966; Rigoletto, La Bohème, Faust, 1968; Otello, 1969; *drama:* Horror of Darkness, 1964; Brothers Karamazov, Poet Game, 1965; The Idiot, Somerset Maugham, 1984, Out of the Unknown, Ross, 1966; Richard II, Beyond the Sunrise, 1968; Rembrandt, Vortex, 1969; St Joan, The Tempest, Somerset Maugham, 1970; Traitor, The General's Day, Sextet, 1971; Oh Fat White Woman, The Grievance, The Merchant of Venice, Lady Windermere's Fan, 1972; Caucasian Chalk Circle, Loyalties, Secrets, An Imaginative Woman (film), Twelfth Night, 1973; The Applecart, Forget-Me-Not-Lane, Savages, 1974; A Story to Frighten the Children (film), Look Back in Anger, 1975; 84 Charing Cross Road, A Picture of Dorian Gray, Abide with Me (film), Rogue Male (film), 1976; Heartbreak House, She Fell Amongst Thieves (film), 1977; Beaux Stratagem, Richard II, Julius Caesar, 1978; Crime and Punishment, 1979; Dr Jekyll and Mr Hyde, The Crucible, The Fatal Spring, 1980; Timon of Athens, Little Eyolf, Baal, 1981; Accounts, 1982; Shibear–Going Home; A Fellow by the Name of (film); Mr Pye (film), 1985; *theatre work includes:* Hotel in Amsterdam, Time Present, This Story is Yours, Look Back in Anger, 1968; Fidelio (opera), The Marquise, So What About Love, 1969; The Entertainer, 1974; The Exorcism, 1975; Julius Caesar (opera) 1984. Awards: Guild of TV Directors and Producers: Designer of the Year, for The Idiot, 1984, Billy Budd, 1966; Pye Colour Award: Best Colour Prodn, for Otello, 1969; Soc. of Film and TV Arts: Designer of the Year, for Vortex, Rembrandt, 1970. *Recreations:* gardening, music, travel. *Address:* 116 Marine Parade, Kemp Town, Brighton, Sussex BN2 1DD.

ABBOTT, Diane Julie; MP (Lab) Hackney North and Stoke Newington, since 1987; *b* 27 Sept. 1953; *d* of late Reginald and Julia Abbott. *Educ:* Harrow County Girls' Grammar Sch.; Newnham Coll., Cambridge. Formerly: Admin. Trainee, Home Office; Race Relations Officer, NCCL; Researcher, Thames Television; Reporter, TV-am; Equality Officer, ACTT; Press and PR Officer, GLC; Principal Press Officer, Lambeth Borough Council. Joined Labour Party, 1971. Mem., Westminster City Council, 1982–86. *Address:* House of Commons, SW1A 0AA.

ABBOTT, James Alan, PhD; Manager and Director of Research, Koninklijk/Shell Laboratorium, Amsterdam, Shell Research BV, 1981–88, retired; *b* 2 Dec. 1928; *s* of George Oswald and Eva Abbott; *m* 1954, Rita Marjorie Galloway; one *s* one *d*. *Educ:* Ilkeston Grammar School; University of Nottingham (BSc, PhD). Post-doctoral research, Univ. of Durham, 1952–53; served Royal Air Force, 1953–56 (Flt Lt RAF Technical Coll., Henlow). Shell companies, UK and Holland, 1956–; Dir, Shell Research Ltd, Sittingbourne Research Centre, 1980–81. Officer, Order of Oranje-Nassau (The Netherlands), 1988. *Publications:* papers in Trans Faraday Soc., Proc. Royal Society. *Recreation:* golf. *Address:* Barn Heyes, Old Barnhill, Broxton, Cheshire CH3 9HL.

ABBOTT, Morris Percy; Deputy Chairman, Trinity Insurance Co. Ltd; Chairman, Trinity Reinsurance (Underwriting Management) Ltd; *b* 3 May 1922; *s* of Harry Abbott and Agnes Maud Breeze; *m* 1944, Marjorie Leven; one *s* one *d*. *Educ:* Rothesay Academy. MIB(Scot) Bank of Scotland, 1939–49. Served War as Pilot, 1941–46; Flight Lieut, RAF; seconded to US Navy at Pensacola Naval Air Station, Florida. Senior Executive with National Bank of India (now Grindlays Bank) in India and East Africa, 1949–59. Managing Director: Credit Insurance Assoc. Ltd, 1969; Hogg Robinson & Gardner Mountain Ltd, 1971; Hogg Robinson Group Ltd: Group Man. Dir, 1973; Chief Exec., 1974–83; Chm., 1977–83. *Recreations:* music, golf, tennis, sailing. *Address:* Castlemans, Sedlescombe, Battle, Sussex. *T:* Sedlescombe (0424) 870501. *Clubs:* City of London, Caledonian; Royal and Ancient Golf, Prestwick Golf, Rye Golf, Royal Calcutta Golf.

ABBOTT, Rear-Adm. Peter Charles; Assistant Chief of Naval Staff, since 1991; *b* 12 Feb. 1942; *s* of late Lieut-Col Dennis Abbott, Royal Garwhal Rifles and Delphine McConaghey; *m* 1965, Susan Phillippa Grey; three *d*. *Educ:* St Edward's Sch., Oxford. Queens' College, Cambridge (MA 1966). Articled Clerk, Blackburn, Robson Coates, 1963; 2nd Lieut, RMFVR 1963; Sub Lieut, RN 1964; Commanding Officer, HM Ships Chawton, 1972, Ambuscade, 1976, Ajax, 1983 (and First Frigate Sqdn); RCDS 1985; Flag Officer, Flotilla Two, 1989. *Address:* Ministry of Defence, Main Building, Whitehall, SW1A 2HB.

ABBOTT, Roderick Evelyn; Director, Directorate-General of External Relations, EEC Commission, Brussels, since 1982; *b* 16 April 1938; *e s* of Stuart Evelyn Abbott, OBE; *m* 1963, Elizabeth Isobel McLean; three *d*. *Educ:* Rugby Sch.; Merton Coll., Oxford. Board of Trade, 1962–68 (Private Sec. to Pres. of BoT, 1965–66; seconded to DEA, 1966–68); UK Mission to UN, Geneva, 1968–71; Foreign Office, London, 1971–73; EEC, 1973–75; EEC Delegation, Geneva, 1975–79; EEC, 1980–. *Recreation:* travel. *Address:* c/o EEC Commission, Berlaymont (DG I), 200 rue de la Loi, 1049 Brussels, Belgium. *Club:* Commonwealth Trust.

ABBOTT, Ronald William, CVO 1989; CBE 1979; FIA, ASA, FPMI; Consultant Partner, Bacon & Woodrow, Consulting Actuaries, since 1982 (Senior Partner, 1972–81); *b* 18 Jan. 1917; *s* of late Edgar Abbott and Susan Mary Ann Abbott; *m* 1st, 1948, Hilda Mary Hampson (*d* 1972), *d* of late William George Clarke and Emily Jane Clarke; two *d*; 2nd, 1973, Barbara Constance, *d* of late Gilbert Hugh Clough and Harriet Clough. *Educ:* St Olave's and St Saviour's Grammar Sch. FIA 1946; FPMI 1976. Actuarial Assistant: Atlas Assce Co., 1934–38; Friends Provident & Century Life Office, 1938–46; Sen. Actuary, Bacon & Woodrow, 1946, Partner 1948. Mem., Deptl Cttee on Property Bonds and Equity Linked Life Assce, 1971–73. Dep. Chm., 1973–82, Chm., 1982–87, Occupational Pensions Bd. Mem. Council: Inst. of Actuaries, 1966–74 (Hon. Treasurer, 1971–73); Indust. Soc., 1964–84; Pensions Management Inst., 1977–81 (Vice-Pres., 1978–80). Master, Worshipful Co. of Ironmongers, 1986–87. FRSA. Finlaison Medal, Inst. of Actuaries, 1988. *Publications:* contrib. to Jl of Inst. of Actuaries. *Recreation:* music. *Address:* 43 Rottingdean Place, Falmer Road, Rottingdean, E Sussex BN2 7FS. *T:* Brighton (0273) 303302. *Club:* Royal Automobile.

ABDALLAH, Abdelwaheb; with the Presidency, Tunis, since 1991; *b* 14 Feb. 1940; *s* of (Militant) Ameur Abdallah; *m* Alia Abdallah; four *s*. *Educ:* Univ. of Caen, France. Master Public Law and Pol. Sci.; Dipl. Inst. of Admin of Enterprises; Dr Pol. Sci. (Paris). Teacher: Higher Inst. of Management, Tunis, 1971; Law Faculty, Tunis, 1972–74; Press Inst., 1974–86. Attaché, Cabinet, Min. of Nat. Educn, 1971; Legal Adviser to Min. of Nat. Educn, 1971–74; Attaché, Cabinet, President of the Republic, 1974; Head of Office: Minister Dir, Pres. Office, 1974; Minister, Cultural Affairs, 1976; Minister, Information, 1978; Man. Dir, Nat. Printing Co., 1978; Editor, La Presse, Tunisia, 1979–86; Man. Dir, Nat. News Agency Tunis-Afrique-Presses, 1986; Minister of Information, 1987; MP Monastir, 1988; Mem., Central Cttee, RCD Party, 1988; Ambassador to UK, 1988–90. Kt, Order of Independence; Comdr, Order of the Republic; several foreign decorations. *Publications:* The Maghrebian Policy of Tunisia (thesis of Public Law), 1970; The Role of Governor in the Political and Administrative Life of Tunisia (Pol. Sci. thesis), 1973; Gaullism and Jacobinism (Univ. Study), 1972; The Re-Election of the President of the Republic of Tunisia, 1974; articles on political analysis. *Address:* Présidence de la République, Palais de Carthage, Tunis.

ABDELA, His Honour Jack Samuel Ronald, TD 1948; QC 1966; a Circuit Judge, Central Criminal Court (formerly Deputy Chairman, Inner London Quarter Sessions), 1970–86; *b* 9 Oct. 1913; *s* of Joseph and Dorothy Abdela, Manchester; *m* 1942, Enid Hope Russell, *y d* of Edgar Dodd Russell, London; one *s* (and one *s* decd). *Educ:* Manchester Gram. Sch.; Milton Sch., Bulawayo; Fitzwilliam House, Cambridge (MA). Called to the Bar, Gray's Inn, 1935. 2nd Lieut, Lancashire Fusiliers (TA), 1938; Lieut-Col. Comdt 55 Div. Battle School, 1943; 7th Bn Royal Welch Fusiliers, NW Europe, 1944–46; Major, Inns of Court Regt. (TA), 1946–52. Liveryman, The Worshipful Company of Painter-Stainers. *Recreations:* swimming, tennis, gardening. *Address:* Tall Trees Cottage, Shipton-under-Wychwood, Oxfordshire OX7 6DB. *Club:* Savage.

ABDUL AZIZ, Mahmood; High Commissioner for Singapore in London, since 1988; *b* 21 May 1935; *s* of Ghulam Mahmood and Fatimah Mohamad; *m* 1961, Fauziah Aziz; two *d*. *Educ:* Univ. of Malaya, Singapore (BA Hons Econ). Joined Singapore Civil Service, 1966; First Sec., Singapore High Commn, Canberra, 1966–68; Min. of Foreign Affairs (MFA), 1968–69; Chargé d'Affaires, Phnom Penh, 1969–70; MFA, 1970–73; Chargé d'Affaires, Paris, 1973–78; MFA, 1979–82; Ambassador to the Philippines, 1982–86; MFA as Dir-Gen., ASEAN Nat. Secretariat, Singapore, 1986–88. Public Admin. Medal (Silver), Singapore, 1986; Order of Sikatuna, Philippines, 1986. *Recreation:* golf. *Address:* Singapore High Commission, 9 Wilton Crescent, SW1X 8SA. *T:* 071–235 8315. *Clubs:* Highgate Golf; Tanah Merah Country (Singapore).

ABDUL JAMIL RAIS, Tan Sri Dato', PMN; Chairman, Penang Port Commission, since 1971; High Commissioner for Malaysia in the UK, 1967–71; *b* 14 Jan. 1912; *s* of Abdul Rais and Saodah; *m* 1936, Norhimah Abdul Jamil; four *s* six *d* (and one *s* decd). *Educ:* Clifford Sch.; Jesus Coll., Oxford. Joined Govt service, 1932; State Sec., Perlis, 1951–52; State Financial Officer, Selangor, 1954–55; State Sec., Selangor, 1955–56; Chief Minister, Selangor, 1957–59; Sec. to Treasury, 1961–64; Chief Sec. to Malaysian Govt and Sec. to Cabinet, 1964–67. *Recreations:* golf, tennis. *Address:* Jamnor, 32 Jalan Kia Beng, Kuala Lumpur, Malaysia.

ABDULAH, Frank Owen; Deputy Secretary-General, Caribbean Community Secretariat, Guyana, since 1989; *b* 8 Nov. 1928; *m*; four *d. Educ:* Queen's Royal Coll., Trinidad; Oxford (MA, DipEd Oxon). Held several govt posts, 1953–62, before entering Diplomatic Service at Trinidad and Tobago's Independence, 1962; Dep. Perm. Rep. (Minister Counsellor), 1970–73, Perm. Rep. (Ambassador), 1975–83, Trinidad and Tobago Perm. Mission to UN, NY; Perm. Sec. (Acting), Ministry of External Affairs, Port of Spain, 1973–75; High Comr for Trinidad and Tobago in London with concurrent accreditations as Ambassador to Denmark, Finland, France, FRG, Norway and Sweden, 1983–85; Permanent Sec., Min. of External Affairs and Internat. Trade, Trinidad and Tobago, 1985–88. *Recreations:* music, sports. *Address:* Caribbean Community Secretariat, Bank of Guyana Building, PO Box 10827, Georgetown, Guyana.

ABDULLAH bin Ali, Datuk; Director, Guthrie Ropel Berhad, since 1979; *b* Johore State, 31 Aug. 1922; *m* Datin Badariah binti Haji Abdul Aziz; two *s* two *d. Educ:* Raffles Coll., Singapore; ANU, Canberra. Entered Johore Civil Service, 1949, later Malayan Civil Service; with Independence of Malaysia joined Malaysian Foreign Service; served in India, Australia, Indonesia, Thailand, and as Head of Mission in Ethiopia, Morocco; Chief of Protocol and Dep. Sec.-Gen. (Admin and Gen Affairs), Min. of Foreign Affairs, Kuala Lumpur, 1969–71; High Comr to Singapore, 1971–74; Ambassador to Fed. Rep. of Germany, 1975; High Comr in London and Ambassador to Ireland, 1975–79. Has attended many foreign confs, incl. UNO in NY. Holds Orders: Panglima Setia DiRaja (Order of the Sovereign of Malaysia); Dato Paduka Mahkota Johore (Order of Crown of Johore, Malaysia); Kesatria Mangku Negara (Order of Upholder of Realm, Malaysia); Order of Sacred Heart (Japan). *Address:* c/o Ministry of Foreign Affairs, Wisma Putra, Jalan Wisma Putra, 50602 Kuala Lumpur, Malaysia.

ABDY, Sir Valentine (Robert Duff), 6th Bt *cr* 1850; European Representative, Smithsonian Institution, Washington DC, since 1983; *b* 11 Sept. 1937; *s* of Sir Robert Henry Edward Abdy, 5th Bt, and Lady Diana Bridgeman (*d* 1967), *e d* of 5th Earl of Bradford; *S* father, 1976; *m* 1971, Mathilde Coche de la Ferté (marr. diss. 1982); one *s. Educ:* Eton. *Heir:* *s* Robert Etienne Eric Abdy, *b* 22 Feb. 1978. Special Advr, Internat. Fund for Promotion of Culture, UNESCO. *Address:* Newton Ferrers, Callington, Cornwall; Bryanston, Clos du Petit Bois, St Martin's, Guernsey, Channel Islands; 13 villa Molitor, Paris 16, France. *Clubs:* Travellers', Jockey (Paris).

ABEL, Prof. Edward William, PhD, DSc; FRSC; Professor of Inorganic Chemistry, University of Exeter, since 1972 (Head of Department of Chemistry, 1977–88); *b* 3 Dec. 1931; *s* of Sydney and Donna Abel; *m* 1960, Margaret R. Edwards; one *s* one *d. Educ:* Bridgend Grammar Sch.; University Coll., Cardiff (BSc 1952); Northern Polytechnic, London (PhD 1957). Served Army, 1953–55. Research Fellow, Imperial Coll., 1957–59; Lectr, later Reader, Univ. of Bristol, 1957–71. Vis. Professor: Univ. of British Columbia, 1970; Japanese Soc. for Promotion of Science, 1971; Tech. Univ. of Braunschweig, 1973; ANU, Canberra, 1990. Royal Society of Chemistry: Mem. Council, 1977–82, 1983–87 and 1989– (Chm., Local Affairs Bd, 1983–87; Chm., Divl Affairs Bd, 1989–). Main Group Chem. Medal, 1976; Tilden Medal and Lectr, 1981; Dalton Div. Council, 1977–83, 1987–91 (Sec./Treasurer, 1977–82; Vice-Pres., 1983, 1989–91; Pres., 1987–89). Perm. Sec., Internat. Confs on Organometallic Chem., 1972–89; Mem., UGC, 1986–89 (Chm., Phys. Scis Sub-Cttee, 1986–89); Nat. Advr for Chem., UFC, 1989–; CNAA: Chm., Phys. Scis Cttee, 1987–91; Mem., Cttee for Academic Affairs, 1989–91. *Publications:* (ed jtly) Organometallic Chemistry, vols 1–16, 1970–; (exec. editor) Comprehensive Organometallic Chemistry, 9 vols, 1984; papers to learned jls. *Address:* 1A Rosebarn Avenue, Exeter EX4 6DY. *T:* Exeter (0392) 70272; Department of Chemistry, University of Exeter, Exeter EX4 4QD. *T:* Exeter (0392) 263489.

ABEL, Kenneth Arthur, CBE 1984; DL; Clerk and Chief Executive, Dorset County Council, 1967–91 (Clerk of the Peace, 1967–73); *b* 4 April 1926; *s* of late Arthur Abel, CBE and Frances Ethel Abel; *m* 1955, Sarah Matilda, *d* of late Capt. M. P. Poynor, TD and Norah Elizabeth Poynor; three *s. Educ:* Durham Sch.; Glasgow Univ.; Durham Univ. (LLB). Served RA, 1944–48. Admitted Solicitor, 1953; Assistant Solicitor: Warwicks CC, 1953–54; Leics CC, 1954–59; Sen. Asst Solicitor, Northants CC, 1959–63. Chm., Assoc. of County Chief Execs, 1982–83. DL Dorset, 1977. *Recreations:* golf, gardening. *Address:* Herne's Oak, Bradford Road, Sherborne, Dorset DT9 6BP. *T:* Sherborne (0935) 813200. *Clubs:* Sherborne Golf (Sherborne), Came Down Golf (Dorchester).

ABEL-SMITH, Prof. Brian; Professor of Social Administration, University of London, at the London School of Economics, since 1965; *b* 6 Nov. 1926; *s* of late Brig.-Gen. Lionel Abel-Smith. *Educ:* Haileybury Coll.; Clare Coll., Cambridge. MA, PhD, 1955. Served Army: Private 1945; commissioned Oxford and Bucks Light Inf., 1946; Mil. Asst to Dep. Comr, Allied Commn for Austria (Capt.), 1947–48. Res. Fellow, Nat. Inst. of Economic and Social Res., collecting economic evidence for Guillebaud Cttee (cost of NHS), 1953–55. LSE: Asst Lectr in Social Science, 1955; Lectr, 1957; Reader in Social Administration, University of London, 1961. Assoc. Prof., Yale Law Sch., Yale Univ., 1961. Consultant and Expert Adv. to WHO on costs of med. care, 1957–; Consultant: to Social Affairs Div. of UN, 1959, 1961; to ILO, 1967 and 1981–83; Special Adviser: to Sec. of State for Social Services, 1968–70, 1974–78; to Sec. of State for the Environment, 1978–79; Adviser to Comr for Social Affairs, EEC, 1977–80. Member: SW Metrop. Reg. Hosp. Bd, 1956–63; Cent. Health Services Coun. Sub-Cttee on Prescribing Statistics, 1960–64; Sainsbury Cttee (Relationship of Pharmaceut. Industry with NHS), 1965–67; Long-term Study Group (to advise on long-term develt of NHS), 1965–68; Hunter Cttee (Functions of Medical Administrators,) 1970–72; Fisher Cttee (Abuse of Social Security Benefits), 1971–73. Chm., Chelsea and Kensington HMC, 1961–62; Governor: St Thomas' Hosp., 1957–68; Maudsley Hosp. and Inst. of Psychiatry, 1963–67. Hon. MD Limburg, 1981. *Publications:* (with R. M. Titmuss) The Cost of the National Health Service in England and Wales, 1956; A History of the Nursing Profession, 1960; (with R. M. Titmuss) Social Policy and Population Growth in Mauritius, 1961; Paying for Health Services (for WHO), 1963; The Hospitals, 1800–1948, 1964; (with R. M. Titmuss *et al.*) The Health Services of Tanganyika, 1964; (with K. Gales) British Doctors at Home and Abroad, 1964; (with P. Townsend) The Poor and the Poorest, 1965; (with R. Stevens) Lawyers and the Courts, 1967; An International Study of Health Expenditure (for WHO), 1967; (with R. Stevens) In Search of Justice, 1968; (with M. Zander and R. Brooke) Legal Problems and the Citizen, 1973; People Without Choice, 1974; Value for Money in Health Services, 1976; Poverty Development and Health Policy, 1978; National Health Service: the first thirty years, 1978; (with P. Grandjeat) Pharmaceutical Consumption,

1978; (with A. Maynard) The Organisation, Financing and Cost of Health Care in the European Community, 1979; Sharing Health Care Costs, 1980; (with E. Mach) Planning the Finances of the Health Sector, 1984; Cost Containment in Health Care, 1984; (with Marios Raphael) Future Directions for Social Protection, 1986; (ed with Kay Titmuss) The Philosophy of Welfare: selected writings of Richard M. Titmuss, 1987; (with Andrew Creese) Recurrent Costs in the Health Sector, 1989; (jtly) Health Insurance for Developing Countries, 1990; the Finances of the Health Sector, 1984; Cost Containment in Health Care, 1984; pamphlets for Fabian Soc., 1953–; articles. *Recreations:* skiing, swimming. *Address:* London School of Economics, Houghton Street, WC2. *T:* 071–405 7686.

ABEL SMITH, Henriette Alice, (Lady Abel Smith), DCVO 1977 (CVO 1964); JP; an Extra Lady-in-Waiting to the Queen (formerly as HRH Princess Elizabeth), since 1987 (a Lady-in-Waiting, 1949–87); *b* 6 June 1914; *d* of late Comdr Francis Charles Cadogan, RN, and late Ruth Evelyn (*née* Howard, *widow* of Captain Gardner Sebastian Bazley); *m* 1st, 1939, Sir Anthony Frederick Mark Palmer, 4th Bt (killed in action, 1941); one *s* one *d*; 2nd, 1953, Sir Alexander Abel Smith, KCVO, TD (*d* 1980); one *s* one *d*. JP Tunbridge Wells 1955, Gloucestershire 1971. *Address:* The Garden House, Quenington, Cirencester, Glos GL7 5BN. *T:* Coln St Aldwyns (028575) 231.
See also Sir T. S. Bazley, Bt, Sir C. M. Palmer, Bt.

ABEL SMITH, Col Sir Henry, KCMG 1961; KCVO 1950; DSO 1945; DL; late Royal Horse Guards; Governor of Queensland, 1958–66; Administrator, Australian Commonwealth, during part of 1965; *b* 8 March 1900; *er s* of late Francis Abel Smith and Madeline St Maur, *d* of late Rev. Henry Seymour; *m* 1931, Lady May Cambridge, *o surv. c* of Earl of Athlone, KG, PC, GCB, GCMG, GCVO, DSO, FRS (*d* 1957), and Princess Alice, Countess of Athlone, VA, GCVO, GBE (*d* 1981); one *s* two *d. Educ:* RMC, Sandhurst. Entered RHG, 1919; Capt. 1930; Major, 1934; Temp. Lieut-Col 1941; Lieut-Col 1944; Acting Colonel, Corps of Household Cavalry, 1946; retired, 1950. ADC to Earl of Athlone, Governor-General of S Africa, 1928–31. DL Berks 1953. KStJ 1958; Hon. LLD Univ. of Queensland, 1962. Hon. Air Cdre, RAAF, 1966. *Recreations:* hunting, shooting, fishing, polo. *Address:* Barton Lodge, Winkfield, Windsor, Berks SL4 4RL. *T:* Winkfield Row (0344) 882632. *Club:* Turf.

ABELES, Sir (Emil Herbert) Peter, AC 1991; Kt 1972; Managing Director, Chief Executive and Deputy Chairman, TNT (formerly Thomas Nationwide Transport Ltd), Australia, and associated companies, since 1967; Joint Managing Director, since 1980 and Joint Chairman, since 1981, Ansett Transport Industries Ltd; *b* 25 April 1924; *s* of late Alexander Abel and Mrs Anna Deakin; *m* 1969, Katalin Ottilia (*née* Fischer); two *d. Educ:* Budapest. Scrap metal industry, Hungary; emigrated to Australia, Sept. 1949; formed Alltrans Pty Ltd, 1950. Director: Ansett Transport Industries Ltd Group; Bliss Corp.; Morael Pty Ltd Gp; Reserve Bank of Australia; TNT Ltd Gp; Union Shipping Gp. Trustee, Australian Cancer Foundn for Medical Res. *Recreations:* swimming, bridge. *Address:* TNT Ltd, Tower One, 10th Floor, TNT Plaza, Lawson Square, Redfern, NSW 2016, Australia. *Clubs:* Carlton; American National, Royal Automobile of Australia, Royal Motor Yacht, Tattersalls, Australian Jockey (Sydney).

ABELL, Sir Anthony (Foster), KCMG 1952 (CMG 1950); Gentleman Usher of the Blue Rod, in the Order of St Michael and St George, 1972–79; *b* 11 Dec. 1906; 2nd *s* of late G. F. Abell, JP, Foxcote Manor, Andoversford, Glos; unmarried. *Educ:* Repton; Magdalen Coll., Oxford. Joined Colonial Admin. Service, Nigeria, 1929. Resident, Oyo Province, Nigeria, 1949; Governor and C-in-C, Sarawak, 1950–59; High Commissioner, Brunei, 1950–58. Family Order of Brunei (First Class), 1954. *Address:* Gavel House, Wherwell, Andover, Hants. *Clubs:* MCC, Royal Over-Seas League, United Oxford & Cambridge University.

ABELL, Charles, OBE 1948; CEng, Hon. FRAeS; Consultant, British Airways Overseas Division, 1974–77; *b* 1 Dec. 1910; *s* of late Major George Henry Abell and Muriel Abell (*née* Griesbach); *m* 1st, 1939, Beryl Anne Boyce (*d* 1973); one *s*; 2nd, 1976, M. A. Newbery. *Educ:* Sherborne Sch. Imperial Airways, 1934–39; BOAC 1939–74: Manager No 3 Line, 1946–51; Dep. Operations Dir (Engineering), 1951–55; Chief Engineer, 1955–68; Engineering Dir, 1968–74; Board Mem., 1972–74; Chm., British Airways Engine Overhaul Ltd, 1972–74. Hon FRAeS (Pres., 1976–77; Vice-Pres., 1972–74); Hon. FSLAET (Pres. 1973–74). British Silver Medal for Aeronautics, RAeS, 1957. *Recreation:* sailing. *Address:* Five Oaks, Woodlands Road West, Virginia Water, Surrey GU25 4PL. *T:* Wentworth (0344) 2560. *Clubs:* Cruising Association; Royal Lymington Yacht.

ABELL, (John) David; Chairman and Chief Executive, Suter plc (formerly Suter Electrical), since 1981; *b* 15 Dec. 1942; *s* of Leonard Abell and Irene (*née* Anderson); *m* 1st, 1967, Anne Janette Priestley (marr. diss. 1977); three *s*; 2nd, 1981, Sandra Dawn Atkinson (marr. diss. 1986); one *s* one *d*; 3rd, 1988, Juliana, *d* of Prof. J. L. I. Fennell, *qv. Educ:* Univ. of Leeds (BAEcon); London School of Economics (Dip. Business Admin). Assistant to Cash and Investment Manager, Ford Motor Co., 1962–65; Asst, Treasurer's Office, AEI, 1965–67; British Leyland: Central Staffs, 1968–69; Manager, Investments and Banking, 1969–70; Chm. and Chief Exec., Prestcold Div., 1970–72; Corporate Treasurer, 1972; First Nat. Finance Corp., Nov. 1972–Aug. 1973; re-joined British Leyland as Man. Dir, Leyland Australia, 1974–75; Group Man. Dir, Leyland Special Products, 1975; Man. Dir, BL Commercial Vehicles, Chm. and Chief Exec., Leyland Vehicles Ltd, 1978–81. *Recreations:* horse racing and breeding, wine, tennis, music. *Address:* Suter plc, St Vincent's, Grantham, Lincs NG31 9EJ.

ABELL, John Norman; Chairman, Europe, CIBC Wood Gundy Inc., since 1990; Vice-Chairman, Wood Gundy Inc., London, since 1988; *b* 18 Sept. 1931; *s* of Sir George Edmond Brackenbury Abell; *m* 1957, Mora Delia (*née* Clifton-Brown); two *s* one *d. Educ:* Marlborough Coll.; Worcester Coll., Oxford (MA). Wood Gundy Ltd: joined in Vancouver, Canada, 1955; Internat. Man. Dir, Toronto, 1962; Director and Vice-Pres., 1966; Pres., Wood Gundy Inc., New York, 1966; Vice-Chm., Wood Gundy Ltd, Toronto, 1977; Dep. Chm. and Chief Exec., Orion Royal Bank Ltd, 1982, Chm. and Chief Exec. Officer, 1983–85; Vice-Chm., Wood Gundy Inc., Toronto, 1986–88; Director: Echo Bay Mines, Edmonton, Canada, 1980–; First Australia Prime Income Investment Co. Ltd, 1986–; Minerals & Resources Corp. Ltd, 1985–89; Euro-clear Clearance System, 1989–. Mem., Securities and Investments Bd, 1985–86; Gov., Toronto Stock Exchange, 1987–88. Chm., Arthritis Soc. of Canada, 1981–82. Dir, London House for Overseas Graduates, 1984; Mem. Council, Reading Univ., 1984. *Address:* Whittonditch House, Ramsbury, Marlborough, Wilts SN8 2PZ. *T:* (office) 071–234 7100. *Clubs:* Boodle's, City of London, MCC; Toronto, York (Toronto).

ABER, Prof. Geoffrey Michael, FRCP; Professor of Renal Medicine, University of Keele, since 1982; *b* 19 Feb. 1928; *s* of David and Hilda Aber; *m* 1964, Eleanor Maureen; one *s* one *d. Educ:* Leeds Grammar School; University of Leeds (MB, ChB, MD with distinction); PhD Birmingham. Leeds Gen. Infirmary, 1952–54; RAMC, 1954–56; Queen Elizabeth Hosp., Birmingham (Univ. of Birmingham), 1956–57, 1958–65; Brompton Hosp., London, 1957–58; Research Fellow: Univ. of Birmingham (Depts of Expt Path. and Medicine), 1958–59 and 1960–64; McGill Univ., 1959–60; Wellcome

Sen. Res. Fellow in Clinical Sci., 1964–65; Keele University: Prof. and Adviser in Clinical Res., 1979–82; Head of Dept. of Postgrad. Medicine, 1982–89; Dean of Postgrad. Medicine, 1989–91. *Publications:* contribs to: Recent Advances in Renal Medicine, 1983; Postgraduate Nephrology, 1985; Textbook of Genitourinary Surgery, 1985; scientific papers in learned jls. *Recreations:* music, sport, motor cars. *Address:* School of Postgraduate Medicine and Biological Sciences, University of Keele, North Staffordshire Hospital Centre, Thornburrow Drive, Hartshill, Stoke-on-Trent ST4 7QB. *T:* (Univ.) Stoke-on-Trent (0782) 49144; (home) Stoke-on-Trent (0782) 613692.

ABERCONWAY, 3rd Baron, *cr* 1911, of Bodnant; **Charles Melville McLaren**, Bt 1902; JP; President: John Brown & Co. Ltd, 1978–85 (Director, 1939–85; Chairman, 1953–78); English China Clays Ltd, since 1984 (Director, 1935–87; Chairman, 1963–84); President, Royal Horticultural Society, 1961–84, now President Emeritus; Commissioner-General, International Garden Festival of Liverpool 1984; Director, National Garden Festival (Stoke on Trent) 1986 Ltd; *b* 16 April 1913; *e s* of 2nd Baron Aberconway, CBE, LLD and Christabel (*d* 1974), *y d* of Sir Melville Macnaghten, CB; *S* father, 1953; *m* 1st, 1941, Deirdre Knewstub (marr. diss. 1949); one *s* two *d*; 2nd, 1949, Ann Lindsay Bullard, *o d* of Mrs A. L. Aymer, New York City; one *s*. *Educ:* Eton; New Coll., Oxford. Barrister, Middle Temple, 1937. Served War of 1939–45, 2nd Lieut RA. Deputy Chairman: Sun Alliance & London Insurance, 1976–85 (Dir, London Assurance, 1953); Westland Aircraft, 1979–84 (Dir, 1947–85); Dir, National Westminster Bank (formerly National Provincial Bank), 1953–83. JP Denbighshire 1946; High Sheriff of Denbighshire 1950. *Recreations:* gardening, travel. *Heir:* s Hon. Henry Charles McLaren [*b* 26 May 1948; *m* 1981, Sally, *yr d* of Captain C. N. Lentaigne; one *s* two *d*]. *Address:* 25 Egerton Terrace, SW3; Bodnant, Tal-y-cafn, Colwyn Bay, Clwyd.

ABERCORN, 5th Duke of, *cr* 1868; **James Hamilton**; Lord of Paisley, 1587; Lord of Abercorn, 1603; Earl of Abercorn and Lord of Hamilton, Mountcastle and Kilpatrick, 1606; Baron of Strabane, 1617; Viscount of Strabane, 1701; Viscount Hamilton, 1786; Marquess of Abercorn, 1790; Marquess of Hamilton, 1868; Bt 1660; Lord Lieutenant of Co. Tyrone, since 1987; company director; *b* 4 July 1934; *er s* of 4th Duke of Abercorn, and Lady Mary Kathleen Crichton (Dowager Duchess of Abercorn, GCVO) (*d* 1990); *S* father, 1979; *m* 1966, Anastasia Alexandra, *e d* of late Lt-Col Harold Phillips, Checkendon Court, Reading; two *s* one *d*. *Educ:* Eton Coll.; Royal Agricultural Coll., Cirencester, Glos. Joined HM Army, Oct. 1952; Lieut, Grenadier Guards. MP (UU) Fermanagh and South Tyrone, 1964–70. Dir, Northern Bank Ltd, 1970–. Chm., Laganside Develt Corp., 1989– (Laganside Ltd, 1986–89); Dir, NI Industrial Develt Bd, 1982–87. Member: Council of Europe, 1968–70; European Economic and Social Cttee, 1973–78. President: Royal UK Beneficent Assoc., 1979–; Building Socs Assoc., 1986–; Patron, Royal Ulster Agricl Soc., 1990. High Sheriff of Co. Tyrone, 1970. *Recreations:* shooting, ski-ing. *Heir: s* Marquess of Hamilton, qv. *Address:* Barons Court, Omagh, Northern Ireland BT78 4EZ. *T:* Newtownstewart (06626) 61470, *Fax:* Newtownstewart (06626) 62059; 10 Little Chester Street, SW1. *T:* 071-235 5518. *Clubs:* Royal Automobile, Brooks's.

ABERCROMBIE, Prof. David, FBA 1991; Professor of Phonetics, Edinburgh University, 1964–80, now Emeritus Professor; *b* 19 Dec. 1909; *e s* of Lascelles Abercrombie, FBA, and Catherine Abercrombie; *m* 1944, Mary, *d* of Eugene and Mary Marble, Carmel, Calif; no *c*. *Educ:* Leeds Grammar Sch.; Leeds Univ.; University Coll., London; Sorbonne. Asst Lectr in English, LSE, 1934–38; Dir of Studies, Inst. of English Studies, Athens, 1938–40; Lectr in English: Cairo Univ., 1940–45; LSE, 1945–47; Lectr in Phonetics, Leeds Univ., 1947–48; Edinburgh Univ.: Lectr in Phonetics, 1948–51; Sen. Lectr 1951–57; Reader, 1957–63. Lectr in Linguistics and Phonetics, Glasgow Univ., 1980–81. *Publications:* Isaac Pitman: a Pioneer in the Scientific Study of Language, 1937; Problems and Principles in Language Study, 1956; English Phonetic Texts, 1964; Studies in Phonetics and Linguistics, 1965; Elements of General Phonetics, 1967; Fifty Years in Phonetics: selected papers, 1991. *Address:* 13 Grosvenor Crescent, Edinburgh EH12 5EL. *T:* 031–337 4864.

ABERCROMBIE, Robert James, CMG 1964; General Manager, Bank of New South Wales, 1962–64, retired; *b* 9 July 1898; *s* of P. M. Abercrombie, Whitburn, Scotland; *m* 1924, Dorothy, *d* of H. F. Oldham; two *d*. *Educ:* Sydney Grammar School; Scotch Coll., Melbourne. Chairman, Consultative Council of Export Payments Insurance Corporation, 1958–64; Chairman, Australian Bankers' Assoc., 1964. *Recreation:* golf. *Address:* 1 Hillside Avenue, Vaucluse, NSW 2030, Australia. *Club:* Union (Sydney).

ABERCROMBY, Sir Ian George, 10th Bt *cr* 1636, of Birkenbog; *b* 30 June 1925; *s* of Robert Ogilvie Abercromby (*g s* of 5th Bt); *S* kinsman, 1972; *m* 1st, 1950, Joyce Beryl, *d* of Leonard Griffiths; 2nd, 1959, Fanny Mary, *d* of late Dr Graham Udale-Smith; one *d*; 3rd, 1976, Diana Marjorie, *d* of H. G. Cockell, and *widow* of Captain Ian Charles Palliser Galloway. *Educ:* Lancing Coll.; Bloxham Sch. *Heir:* none. *Address:* c/o National Westminster Bank, Sloane Square, SW1; Sitio Litre, Puerto de la Cruz, Tenerife, Canary Is. *Clubs:* Ski Club of Great Britain; Kandahar; Kildare Street (Dublin).

ABERDARE, 4th Baron, *cr* 1873, of Duffryn; **Morys George Lyndhurst Bruce,** KBE 1984; PC 1974; DL; Chairman of Committees, House of Lords, since 1976; *b* 16 June 1919; *s* of 3rd Baron Aberdare, GBE, and Margaret Bethune (*née* Black); *S* father 1957; *m* 1946, Maud Helen Sarah, *o d* of Sir John Dashwood, 10th Bt, CVO; four *s*. *Educ:* Winchester; New College, Oxford (MA). Welsh Guards, 1939–46. Minister of State, DHSS, 1970–74; Minister Without Portfolio, 1974. Chairman: Albany Life Assurance Co. Ltd, 1975–; Metlife (UK) Ltd, 1986–. Chm., The Football Trust, 1979–; President: Welsh Nat. Council of YMCAs; Kidney Res. Unit for Wales Foundn; Tennis and Rackets Assoc. Hon. LLD Wales, 1985. DL Dyfed, 1985. Bailiff Grand Cross, 1974, Prior for Wales, 1958–88, OStJ. *Publications:* The Story of Tennis, 1959; Willis Faber Book of Tennis and Rackets, 1980. *Recreations:* real tennis and rackets. *Heir: s* Hon. Alastair John Lyndhurst Bruce [*b* 2 May 1947; *m* 1971, Elizabeth Mary Culbert, *d* of John Foulkes; one *s* one *d*]. *Address:* 32 Elthiron Road, SW6 4BW. *T:* 071–736 0825. *Clubs:* Lansdowne, MCC, Queen's.

ABERDEEN, Bishop of, (RC), since 1977; **Rt. Rev. Mario Joseph Conti;** *b* Elgin, Moray, 20 March 1934; *s* of Louis Joseph Conti and Josephine Quintilia Panicali. *Educ:* St Marie's Convent School and Springfield, Elgin; Blairs Coll., Aberdeen; Pontifical Gregorian Univ. (Scots College), Rome. PhL 1955, STL 1959. Ordained, Rome, 1958; Curate, St Mary's Cathedral, Aberdeen, 1959–62; Parish Priest, St Joachim's, Wick and St Anne's, Thurso (joint charge), 1962–77. Chairman: Scottish Catholic Heritage Commn, 1980–; Commn for the Pastoral Care of Migrant Workers and Tourists (incl. Apostleship of the Sea, Scotland), 1978–85; Pres.-Treasurer, Scottish Catholic Internat. Aid Fund, 1978–85; Pres., National Liturgy Commn, 1981–85; Scottish Mem., Episcopal Bd, Internat. Commn for English in the Liturgy, 1978–87; Mem., Bishops' Jt Cttee for Bioethical Issues, 1982–; Pres., Nat. Christian Doctrine and Unity Commn, 1985–; Consultor-Mem., Secretariat, later Council, for Promotion of Christian Unity (Rome), 1984–; Convener, Action of Churches Together in Scotland, 1990–. Hon. DD Aberdeen, 1989. Commendatore, Order of Merit of the Italian Republic, 1982. *Recreations:* music, art,

book browsing, TV, travel, swimming. *Address:* 156 King's Gate, Aberdeen AB2 6BR. *T:* Aberdeen (0224) 319154.

ABERDEEN, (St Andrew's Cathedral), Provost of; *see* Wightman, Very Rev. W. D.

ABERDEEN AND ORKNEY, Bishop of, since 1978; **Rt. Rev. Frederick Charles Darwent,** JP; *b* Liverpool, 20 April 1927; *y s* of Samuel Darwent and Edith Emily Darwent (*née* Malcolm); *m* 1st, 1949, Edna Lilian (*d* 1981), *o c* of David Waugh and Lily Elizabeth Waugh (*née* McIndoe); twin *d*; 2nd, 1983, Roma Evelyn, *er d* of John Michie and Evelyn Michie (*née* Stephen). *Educ:* Warbreck Sch., Liverpool; Ormskirk Grammar Sch., Lancs; Wells Theological Coll., Somerset. Followed a Banking career, 1943–61 (War service in Far East with Royal Inniskilling Fusiliers, 1945–48). Deacon 1963; priest 1964, Diocese of Liverpool; Curate of Pemberton, Wigan, 1963–65 (in charge of St Francis, Kitt Green, 1964–65); Rector of: Strichen, 1965–71; New Pitsligo, 1965–78; Fraserburgh, 1971–78; Canon of St Andrew's Cathedral, Aberdeen, 1971; Dean of Aberdeen and Orkney, 1973–78. JP Aberdeen City, 1988. Hon. LTh, St Mark's Inst. of Theology, 1974. *Recreations:* amateur stage (acting and production), music (especially jazz), calligraphy. *Address:* Bishop's House, 107 Osborne Place, Aberdeen AB2 4DD. *T:* Aberdeen (0224) 646497. *Clubs:* Rotary International; Club of Deir (Aberdeens).

ABERDEEN AND ORKNEY, Dean of; *see* Stranraer-Mull, Very Rev. G.

ABERDEEN AND TEMAIR, 6th Marquess of, *cr* 1916; **Alastair Ninian John Gordon;** Bt (NS) 1642; Earl of Aberdeen, Viscount Formartine, Lord Haddo, Methlic, Tarves and Kellie, 1682 (Scot.); Viscount Gordon 1814, Earl of Haddo 1916 (UK); painter; *b* 20 July 1920; *s* of 3rd Marquess of Aberdeen and Temair, DSO, and Cécile Elizabeth (*d* 1948), *d* of George Drummond, Swaylands, Penshurst, Kent; *S* brother, 1984; *m* 1950, Anne, *d* of late Lt-Col Gerald Barry, MC; one *s* two *d*. *Educ:* Harrow. Served War of 1939–45, Captain Scots Guards. Member: Internat. Assoc. of Art Critics; Bach Choir, 1939–82. *Recreations:* wine, women and song. *Heir: s* Earl of Haddo, qv. *Address:* Quick's Green, near Pangbourne, Berks RG8 8SN. *Clubs:* Arts, MCC; Puffins (Edinburgh).

ABERDEEN AND TEMAIR, June Marchioness of; (Beatrice Mary) June Gordon, CBE 1989 (MBE 1971); DL; Musical Director and Conductor, Haddo House Choral and Operatic Society (formerly Haddo House Choral Society), since 1945; *d* of Arthur Paul Boissier, MA, and Dorothy Christina Leslie Smith; *m* 1939, David George Ian Alexander Gordon (later 4th Marquess of Aberdeen and Temair, CBE, TD) (*d* 1974); two adopted *s* two adopted *d*. *Educ:* Southlands School, Harrow; Royal Coll. of Music. GRSM, ARCM. Teacher of Music, Bromley High School for Girls, 1936–39. Director of Haddo House Choral and Operatic Soc. and Arts Centre, 1945–. Chairman: Scottish Children's League, 1969–; NE Scotland Music School, 1975–; Adv. Council, Scottish Opera, 1979–; Chm. (local), Adv. Cttee, Aberdeen Internat. Festival of Music and the Performing Arts, 1980–. Governor: Gordonstoun Sch., 1971–86; Royal Scottish Acad. of Music and Drama, 1979–82. FRCM 1967; FRSE 1983; FRSAMD 1985. DStJ 1977. DL Aberdeenshire, 1971. Hon. LLD Aberdeen, 1968. *Publications:* contribs to Aberdeen Univ. Jl, RCM magazine. *Address:* Haddo House, Aberdeen AB4 0ER. *T:* Tarves (06515) 216. *Club:* Naval & Military.

ABERDOUR, Lord; John Stewart Sholto Douglas; *b* 17 Jan. 1952; *s* and *heir* of 22nd Earl of Morton, qv; *m* 1985, Amanda, *yr d* of David Mitchell, Kirkcudbright; one *s* one *d*. *Educ:* Dunrobin Castle School. Studied Agriculture, Aberdeen Univ. *Heir: s* Master of Aberdour, qv. *Address:* Haggs Farm, Kirknewton, Midlothian.

ABERDOUR, Master of; Hon. John David Sholto Douglas; *b* 28 May 1986; *s* and *heir* of Lord Aberdour, qv.

ABERGAVENNY, 5th Marquess of, *cr* 1876; **John Henry Guy Nevill,** KG 1974; OBE 1945; JP; Baron Abergavenny, 1450; Earl of Abergavenny and Viscount Nevill, 1784; Earl of Lewes, 1876; Lt-Col late Life Guards; Lord-Lieutenant of East Sussex, 1974–89 (Vice-Lieutenant of Sussex, 1970–74); Chancellor, Order of the Garter, since 1977; *b* 8 Nov. 1914; *er s* of 4th Marquess and Isabel Nellie (*d* 1953), *d* of James Walker Larnach; *S* father, 1954; *m* 1938, Patricia (*see* Marchioness of Abergavenny); three *d* (and one *s* one *d* decd). *Educ:* Eton; Trinity Coll., Cambridge. Joined Life Guards, 1936; served War of 1939–45 (despatches, OBE); Lt-Col, retired 1946; Hon. Col, Kent & Co. of London Yeomanry, 1948–62. Director: Massey-Ferguson Holdings Ltd, 1955–85; Lloyds Bank Ltd, 1962–85; Lloyds Bank UK Management, 1962–85; Lloyds Bank SE Regional Bd (Chm.), 1962–85; Whitbread Investment Co. Trustee, Ascot Authority, 1953–; HM Representative at Ascot, 1972–82; President: Royal Assoc. of British Dairy Farmers, 1955 and 1963; Assoc. of Agriculture, 1961–63; Royal Agric. Soc. of England, 1967 (Dep. Pres. 1968, 1972); Hunters' Improvement Soc., 1959; British Horse Soc., 1970–71; Vice-Chm., Turf Bd, 1967–68; Mem. Nat. Hunt Cttee, 1942 (Senior Steward, 1953 and 1963); Mem. Jockey Club, 1952. Member: E Sussex CC, 1947–54 (Alderman 1954–62); E Sussex Agric. Cttee, 1948–54. JP Sussex, 1948; DL Sussex, 1955. KStJ 1976 (Pres. Council, Order of St John, Sussex, 1975). *Heir: nephew* Guy Rupert Gerard Nevill [*b* 29 March 1945; *s* of Lord Rupert Nevill, CVO (*d* 1982); *m* 1982, Lady Beatrix Lambton, *d* of Viscount Lambton, qv]. *Address:* (seat) Eridge Park, Tunbridge Wells, East Sussex. *T:* Tunbridge Wells (0892) 27378; Flat 2, 46 Pont Street, SW1. *T:* 071–581 3967. *Club:* White's. *See also* Earl of Cottenham.

ABERGAVENNY, Marchioness of; Mary Patricia Nevill, DCVO 1981 (CVO 1970); an Extra Lady of the Bedchamber to the Queen, 1960–66 and since 1987 (a Lady of the Bedchamber, 1966–87); *b* 20 Oct. 1915; *d* of late Lt-Col John Fenwick Harrison, Royal Horse Guards, and Hon. Margery Olive Edith, *d* of 3rd Baron Burnham, DSO; *m* 1938, Marquess of Abergavenny, qv; three *d* (and one *s* one *d* decd). *Address:* Eridge Park, Tunbridge Wells, East Sussex; Flat 2, 46 Pont Street, SW1.

ABERNETHY, William Leslie, CBE 1972; FCA, IPFA; Managing Trustee, Municipal Mutual Insurance Ltd, and Director of associated companies, 1973–87; Comptroller of Financial Services, Greater London Council, 1972–73 (Treasurer, 1964–72) and Chief Financial Officer, Inner London Education Authority, 1967–73; *b* 10 June 1910; *s* of Robert and Margaret Abernethy; *m* 1937, Irene Holden; one *s*. *Educ:* Darwen Grammar Sch., Lancs. Hindle & Jepson, Chartered Accts, Darwen, 1925–31; Borough Treasurer's Dept, Darwen, 1931–37; Derbyshire CC, Treasurer's Dept, 1937–48 (Dep. Co. Treas., 1944–48); 1st Treas., Newcastle upon Tyne Regional Hosp. Bd, 1948–50. LCC: Asst Comptroller, 1950–56; Dep. Comptroller, 1956–64; Comptroller, Sept. 1964–Mar. 1965. Hon. Life Mem., Roy. Inst. of Public Admin (Chm. Exec. Coun., 1959–60). Mem. Council, IMTA, 1966–73. *Publications:* Housing Finance and Accounts (with A. R. Holmes), 1953; Internal Audit in Local Authorities and Hospitals, 1957; Internal Audit in the Public Boards, 1957; contribs professional jls. *Address:* 6 Thornhill Close, Port Erin, Isle of Man. *T:* Port Erin (0624) 835316.

ABINGDON, Earl of; *see* Lindsey and Abingdon, Earl of.

ABINGER, 8th Baron, *cr* 1835; **James Richard Scarlett,** DL; Lt-Col, late Royal Artillery; farmer and company director; *b* 28 Sept. 1914; *e s* of 7th Baron and Marjorie

(*d* 1965), 2nd *d* of John McPhillamy, Blair Athol, Bathurst, NSW; *S* father, 1943; *m* 1957, Isla Carolyn, *o d* of late Vice-Adm. J. W. Rivett-Carnac, CB, CBE, DSC; two *s*. *Educ:* Eton; Magdalene College, Cambridge (MA 1952). India, France, Airborne Corps, and attached RAF; RNXS, 1968. DL Essex, 1968. KStJ. *Heir: s* Hon. James Harry Scarlett, *b* 28 May 1959. *Address:* Clees Hall, Bures, Suffolk. *T:* Bures (0787) 227227; 1a Portman Mansions, Chiltern Street, W1. *T:* 071–487 3585. *Clubs:* Carlton, Royal Automobile.
See also Hon. J. L. C. Scarlett.

ABNEY-HASTINGS, family name of **Countess of Loudoun.**

ABOU-SEÉDA, Hassan A. H.; Order of Merit, First Class (Egypt), 1979; Star of Honour (Egypt) and King Abdel Aziz Alsaud Order, First Class (for performance during 1973 October War), 1973; Order of Liberation (Egypt), 1957; fourteen military medals; Ambassador; Ministry of Defence, Arab Republic of Egypt; *b* 13 Oct. 1930; *s* of Aly Hassan Abou-Seéda and Fatimah Salamah; *m* 1973, Sohair A. A. el-Etriby; one *s*. *Educ:* Military College, Cairo (BA mil. sciences, MA mil. sciences). Fellow: Higher War Studies College; Nasser Academy. Military service with promotion all through command structure of Egyptian Armed Forces, 1949–79: Division Commander, 1971; Commander of an army, 1976; Chief of Military Operations and Dep. Chief of Staff of Armed Forces, 1978. Ambassador in Foreign Ministry, 1979; Ambassador to the UK, 1980–84. *Publications:* several research papers on the 1973 October War and on military strategy (Egypt). *Recreations:* reading (strategy, economics and history), chess, painting, tennis. *Address:* PO Box 636, Cairo, Egypt. *T:* Cairo (202) 355 6600. *Clubs:* Gezirah, Armed Forces Officers', Tahrir, Rotary (Cairo).

ABOYADE, Prof. Ojetunji, CON 1977; PhD; Professor of Economics, University of Ibadan, 1966–75 and 1978–81; *b* 9 Sept. 1931; *s* of Mr and Mrs Aboyade, Awe, Oyo, Nigeria; *m* 1961, Olabimpe (*née* Odubanjo); two *s* two *d*. *Educ:* The University, Hull (Groves Prize, Best Perf. Econs Dept, 1957; BSc Hons Econs 1st Cl.); Pembroke Coll., Cambridge (PhD 1960). Govt Scholar, 1953–60. Res. Asst, Nigerian National Income Accounts, Fed. Office of Statistics, Lagos, 1958–59; University of Ibadan, Nigeria: Lectr, Grade II and I, 1960–64; Sen. Lectr, 1964–66; Head, Dept of Econs, 1966–71; Dean of Social Sciences, 1972–74; Vice-Chancellor and Professor, Univ. of Ife, 1975–78. Head, National Econ. Planning, Fed. Govt of Nigeria (Econ. Develt), 1969–70. Vis. Asst Prof. and Res. Fellow, Dept of Econs, Univ. of Mich, Ann Arbor, 1963–64; Vis. Consultant (Econ.), World Bank, USA, 1971–72. Editor, Nigerian Jl of Economic and Social Studies, 1961–71. Pres., Nigerian Econ. Soc., 1973–74; Member: Bd of Trustees, Internat. Food Policy Research Inst., USA; Internat. Assoc. for Res. and Income, 1964–; Council, Assoc. of Commonwealth Univs; Chm., Tech. Cttee on Revenue Allocation, 1977. *Publications:* Foundations of an African Economy: a study of investment and growth in Nigeria, 1967 (USA); Issues in the Development of an African Economy, 1976 (Nigeria); chapters in and essay contribs to books, and articles in professional jls, 1961–75. *Recreations:* hobbies include farming. *Address:* c/o University of Ibadan, Ibadan, Nigeria.

ABOYNE, Earl of; Alistair Granville Gordon; *b* 26 July 1973; *s* and *heir* of Marquess of Huntly, *qv*. *Educ:* Harrow. *Address:* c/o Aboyne Castle, Aberdeenshire.

ABRAHAM, Ann; Chief Executive, National Association of Citizens Advice Bureaux, since 1991; *b* 25 Aug. 1952; *d* of John Kenneth and Kathleen Mary Marsden. *Educ:* Bedford Coll., Univ. of London (BA Hons German); Postgrad. DMS. MIH. Housing Manager, Local Govt, 1975–80; Ops Manager, Regional Dir and Ops Dir, Housing Corp., 1980–90. *Recreations:* walking, family, friends, football. *Address:* National Association of Citizens Advice Bureaux, Myddleton House, 115–123 Pentonville Road, N1 9LZ. *T:* 071–833 2181.

ABRAHAM, Sir Edward (Penley), Kt 1980; CBE 1973; FRS 1958; MA, DPhil (Oxon); Fellow of Lincoln College, Oxford, 1948–80, Honorary Fellow, since 1980; Professor of Chemical Pathology, Oxford, 1964–80, now Emeritus Professor; *b* 10 June 1913; *s* of Albert Penley Abraham and Mary Abraham (*née* Hearn); *m* 1939, Asbjörg Harung, Bergen, Norway; one *s*. *Educ:* King Edward VI School, Southampton; The Queen's College, Oxford (1st cl. Hons Sch. of Natural Science), Hon. Fellow 1973. Rockefeller Foundation Travelling Fellow at Universities of Stockholm (1939) and California (1948). Ciba lecturer at Rutgers University, NJ, 1957; Guest lecturer, Univ. of Sydney, 1960; Reader in Chemical Pathology, Oxford, 1960–64. Lectures: Rennebohm, Univ. of Wisconsin, 1966–67; Squibb, Rutgers Univ., 72; Perlman, Univ. of Wisconsin, 1985; A. L. P. Garrod, RCP, 1986; Sarton, Univ. of Gent, 1989. Hon. Fellow: Linacre Coll., Oxford, 1976; Lady Margaret Hall, Oxford, 1978; Wolfson Coll., Oxford, 1982; St Peter's Coll., Oxford, 1983. For. Hon. Mem., Amer. Acad. of Arts and Scis, 1983. Hon. DSc: Exeter, 1980; Oxon, 1984; Strathclyde, 1989. Royal Medal, Royal Soc., 1973; Mullard Prize and Medal, Royal Soc., 1980; Scheele Medal, Swedish Academy of Pharmaceut. Sciences, 1975; Chemical Soc. Award in Medicinal Chemistry, 1975; Internat. Soc. Chemotherapy Award, 1983; Sarton Medal, Gent, 1989. *Publications:* Biochemistry of Some Peptide and Steroid Antibiotics, 1957; Biosynthesis and Enzymic Hydrolysis of Penicillins and Cephalosporins, 1974; contribs to: Antibiotics, 1949; The Chemistry of Penicillin, 1949; General Pathology, 1957, 4th edn 1970; Cephalosporins and Penicillins, Chemistry and Biology, 1972; scientific papers on the biochemistry of natural products, incl. penicillins and cephalosporins; contrib. Biographical Memoirs of Fellows of Royal Society (Sir Ernst Chain, 1983; Lord Florey, 1991). *Recreations:* walking, ski-ing. *Address:* Badger's Wood, Bedwells Heath, Boars Hill, Oxford OX1 5JE. *T:* Oxford (0865) 735395; Sir William Dunn School of Pathology, South Parks Road, Oxford OX1 3RE. *T:* Oxford (0865) 275571. *Club:* Athenæum.

ABRAHAM, Maj.-Gen. (Sutton) Martin (O'Heguerty), CB 1973; MC 1942 and Bar, 1943; Secretary, Bedford College, University of London, 1976–82, retired; *b* 26 Jan. 1919; *s* of Capt. E. G. F. Abraham, CB, late Indian Civil Service, and Ruth Eostre Abraham; *m* 1950, Iona Margaret, *d* of Sir John Stirling, KT, MBE; two *s* one *d*. *Educ:* Durnford; Eton; Trinity Coll., Cambridge (BA Modern Languages). Commissioned in RA, 1939; transf. to 12th Royal Lancers, 1941; Egypt, 1941; Armoured Car Troop Leader, desert campaigns; Armoured Car Sqdn 2nd-in-Comd, Italian campaign, Sangro Valley, Rimini, Po Valley; accepted surrender of Trieste (Sqdn Ldr); Mil. Asst to C-in-C Austria, and accompanied him to BAOR, 1946; psc 1948; Mem. Chiefs of Staff Secretariat, 1949–52; Sqdn Ldr 12th Lancers, Malaya, 1953–54; Mem. Staff Coll. Directing Staff, 1955–57; 2nd-in-Comd 12th Lancers, 1957–58; CO 12th Lancers, 1958–62 (Cyprus, 1959–60); Asst Mil. Sec., Southern Comd, 1960–62; GSO1, Staff Coll. (Minley Div.), 1960–62; Comdr RAC (Brig.), 1st Brit. Corps, Germany, 1964–66; idc 1967; Dir, Combat Develt (Army), MoD, 1968–71; Chief of Jt Services Liaison Orgn, BAOR, 1971–73; Mil. Adviser to Arms Control and Disarmament Res. Unit and Western Organisations Dept, FCO, 1973–76, retd. Col, 9/12 Royal Lancers, 1977–81. Governor, Bedford Coll., 1982–85. *Recreations:* painting, reading, sundry practical country pursuits and chores, shooting. *Address:* c/o C. Hoare & Co., 37 Fleet Street, EC4. *T:* 071–353 4522. *Club:* Cavalry and Guards.

ABRAHAMS, Allan Rose, CMG 1962; *b* 29 Nov. 1908; *s* of late Mr and Mrs Frank Abrahams; *m* 1948, Norma Adeline Neita; one *s* two *d*. *Educ:* Jamaica College, Jamaica. Joined Civil Service, 1927; Permanent Secretary, Ministry of Communications and Works, Jamaica, 1955–64, retired. *Recreation:* gardening. *Address:* 20 Widcombe Road, Kingston 6, Jamaica. *T:* 78214. *Club:* Kingston (Kingston, Jamaica).

ABRAHAMS, Anthony Claud Walter; advocate and solicitor, Brunei Darussalam, since 1987; *b* 16 June 1923; *s* of late Rt Hon. Sir Sidney Abrahams, QC, and of Ruth Bowman; *m* 1st, 1950, Laila Myking; two *s* one *d*; 2nd, 1982, Elizabeth, *d* of late Comdr A. E. Bryant, RN. *Educ:* Bedford Sch.; Emmanuel Coll., Cambridge (MA). Barrister-at-law. Served War: Wavell Cadet, Bangalore, 1942–43; commnd 3/12 Royal Bn, Frontier Force Regt, 1943–45; India, N Africa, Italy, Greece (despatches). Called to the Bar, Middle Temple, 1951; practised Midland Circuit, 1951–64. Gov., 1966–88, Chm., 1978–88, Harpur Trust (the Bedford Charity). Centre for British Teachers: Founder, 1964; Dir, 1973–82; Life Pres., 1982; Chm., Colchester and Bedford English Study Centres, 1982–84 (Man. Dir, 1968–82). Mem., Educn Cttee, British-Malaysian Soc., 1986–. Liveryman, Worshipful Co. of Glaziers. *Recreations:* Rugby, cricket, golf, Rugby fives, English language learning. *Address:* Goldsmith Building, Temple, EC4Y 7BL. *T:* 071–353 7913. *Clubs:* Garrick, MCC, Jesters.

ABRAHAMS, Gerald Milton, CBE 1967; Chairman and Managing Director, Aquascutum Group, plc, since 1947; *b* 20 June 1917; *s* of late Isidor Abrahams; *m* 1st, 1946, Doris, *d* of Mark Cole, Brookline, Mass, USA; two *d*; 2nd, 1972, Marianne Wilson, *d* of David Kay, London. *Educ:* Westminster Sch. Served War of 1939–45, Major HAC, RHA, in Greece, W Desert and Ceylon. Member: Council, FBI, 1962–65, CBI, 1965–87; British Menswear Guild (Chm., 1959–61, 1964–66); Clothing Export Council (Chm., 1966–70; Vice-Pres., 1970–); Clothing Manufacturers Fedn of GB, 1960–82 (Chm., 1965–66); EDC for Clothing Industry, 1966–69; British Clothing Industry Assoc., 1982–87; BNEC Cttee for Exports to Canada, 1965–70; North American Adv. Gp, BOTB, 1978–87 (Vice Chm., 1983–87). FRSA 1972; CBIM 1973. *Recreations:* golf, tennis. *Address:* 100 Regent Street, W1A 2AQ. *T:* 071–734 6090. *Club:* Buck's.

ABRAHAMS, Ivor, RA 1991 (ARA 1989); sculptor; *b* 10 Jan. 1935; *s* of Harry Abrahams and Rachel Kalisky; *m* 1st, 1966, Victoria Taylor; one *s*; 2nd, 1974, Evelyne Horvais; one *s*. *Educ:* Wigan Grammar Sch.; St Martin's and Camberwell Schools of Art. NDD(ScSp). Visiting Lecturer: Birmingham College of Art, 1960–63; Coventry College of Art, 1963–66; RCA, Slade Sch., 1980–82. *Major Exhibitions:* Kölnischer Kunstverein, Cologne, 1973; Ikon Gall., Birmingham, 1976; Yorkshire Sculpture Park, Wakefield, 1984. *Public Collections:* Arts Council of GB; Bibliotheque Nat., Paris; Brit. Council; Denver Mus., Colorado; Metropolitan Mus., NY; Nat. Gall. of Australia, Canberra; Tate Gall.; Mus. of Modern Art, NY; V&A Mus.; Wilhelm Lembruck Mus., Duisburg, W Germany; Boymans Mus., Rotterdam, etc. Winston Churchill Fellow, 1990. *Publications:* E. A. Poe: poems and tales (foreword Norbert Lynton), 1976; Oxford Garden Sketchbook (foreword Robert Melville), 1977. *Recreations:* golf, photography. *Address:* 67 Bathurst Gardens, NW10 5JH. *T:* 081–969 2505. *Clubs:* Chelsea Arts, Colony Rooms.

ABRAHAMSEN, Egil; Comdr, Order of St Olav, 1987 (Kt Comdr 1979); Chairman: Norsk Hydro, since 1985; OPAK, since 1985; IKO Group, since 1988; *b* 7 Feb. 1923; *s* of Anker Christian Abrahamsen and Aagot (*née* Kjølberg); *m* 1950, Randi Wiborg; two *s* one *d*. *Educ:* Technical Univ. of Norway (Naval Architect, 1949); Durham Univ., King's Coll., Newcastle upon Tyne (post-grad. studies and res.); Univ. of Calif, Berkeley (post-grad. studies). Sales Engr, Maschienen-Fabrik Augsburg-Nürnberg, and Karlstads Mekaniska Verkstad AB, Sweden, 1949–50; projects and planning, A/S Rosenberg Mekanisk Verksted, Stavanger, 1951–52; Det Norske Veritas, 1952–85: Surveyor, 1952; Sen. Surveyor, 1954 (resp. for building up Res. Dept); Principal Surveyor, 1957; Dep. Pres., 1966; Vice Pres., 1967; Pres., 1967. Chairman: Norwegian Telecommunications Admin, 1980–; Royal Caribbean Cruise-Line, 1987–88; Kosmos, 1988–; Eikland, 1990–; Vice-Chm., IM Skaugen A/S, 1990–. Editor, European Shipbuilding, 1952—60. Fellow, Nat. Acad. of Engrg, USA, 1978; Member: Norwegian Acad. of Technical Scis, 1968; Royal Swedish Acad. of Engrg Scis, 1979; Hon. Mem., Soc. of Naval Architects and Marine Engrs, Norway, 1987. DTech *hc* Royal Inst. of Technol., Sweden, 1977. Owes Hon. Prize, for contribn to res. and educn, 1971. Grand Officer, Order of Infante Dom Henrique (Portugal), 1977; Comdr, Order of the Lion (Finland), 1982; Kt, Nat. Order of Merit (France), 1982. *Address:* Norsk Hydro A/S, Bygdov Allé 2, Oslo 2, Norway. *T:* 47–2–432454.

ABRAMS, Mark Alexander, PhD; Director of Research Unit, Age Concern, 1976–85; *b* 27 April 1906; *s* of Abram Abrams and Anne (*née* Jackson); *m* 1st, 1931, Una Strugnell (marr. diss. 1951); one *s* one *d*; 2nd, 1951, Jean Bird; one *d*. *Educ:* Latymer Sch., Edmonton; London Sch. of Economics, Univ. of London. Fellow, Brookings Institute, Washington, DC, 1931–33; Research Department, London Press Exchange, 1933–39; BBC Overseas Dept, 1939–41; Psychological Warfare Board and SHAEF, 1941–46; Man. Dir, then Chm., Research Services Ltd, 1946–70; Dir, Survey Res. Unit, SSRC, 1970–76. Vice-Pres., PSI, 1978– (Mem. Council, 1978–82); Member: Metrication Bd, 1969–79; Exec. Council, Austrian Soc. for Social Sci. Res.; Business Educn Council, 1974–77. *Publications:* Condition of the British People, 1911–1946, 1947; Social Surveys and Social Action, 1951; Beyond Three Score and Ten, 1980; People in Their Sixties, 1983. *Recreation:* listening to music. *Address:* 12 Pelham Square, Brighton, East Sussex BN1 4ET. *T:* Brighton (0273) 684537. *Club:* Civil Service.

ABRAMS, Dr Michael Ellis, FRCP, FFCM; Deputy Chief Medical Officer, Department of Health (formerly of Health and Social Security), since 1985; *b* 17 Sept. 1932; *s* of late Sam Philip and Ruhamah Emmie Abrams; *m* 1962, Rosalind J. Beckman; four *c*. *Educ:* King Edward's Sch., Birmingham; Univ. of Birmingham (BSc 1st Cl. Anat. and Physiol. 1953; MB ChB Distinction in Medicine 1956). FRCP 1972; MFCM (Founder Mem.) 1972, FFCM 1983. Ho. Officer posts in United Birmingham Hosps, 1957–58; Univ. Research Fellow, Dept of Exp. Pathology, Univ. of Birmingham, and Medical Registrar, Queen Elizabeth Hosp., Birmingham, 1959; Medical Registrar and MRC Clinical Res. Fellow, Queen Elizabeth Hosp., Birmingham, 1959–62; MRC Clin. Res. Fellow, Dept of Medicine, Guy's Hosp., London, 1962–63; Rockefeller Travelling Fellow, Cardiovascular Res. Inst., Univ. of California Med. Centre, San Francisco, 1963–64; Lectr/Sen. Lectr and Hon. Cons. Phys., Guy's Hosp., 1964–75; Chief Med. Adviser, Guy's Hosp./Essex Gen. Practice Computing Unit, 1968–73; Dir, Inter-Deptl Laboratory, Guy's Hosp., 1971–75; DHSS: SMO, 1975–78; PMO, 1978–79; SPMO, 1979–85. Hon. Cons. Phys. Emeritus, Guy's Hosp. and Hon. Lectr in Medicine, Guy's Hosp. Med. Sch.; Examr in Human Communication, London Univ., 1972–84. President, Section of Measurement in Medicine, RSM, 1981–83; Chm., Computer Cttee, RCP, 1981–89. *Publications:* (ed) Medical Computing Progress and Problems, 1970; (ed) Spectrum 71, 1971; (ed) The Computer in the Doctor's Office, 1980; articles on biomedical computing, pulmonary surfactant and glucose tolerance in diabetes. *Recreations:* reading, gardening, beachcombing. *Club:* Athenæum.

ABRAMSKY, Jennifer, (Mrs Alasdair Liddell); Editor, News and Current Affairs, BBC Radio, since 1987; *b* 7 Oct. 1946; *d* of Chimen Abramsky and Miriam (*née* Nirenstein); *m* 1976, Alasdair D. MacDuff Liddell, *qv*; one *s* one *d*. *Educ:* Holland Park

Sch.; Univ. of East Anglia (BA Hons English) (Dep. Chm., New Univs Fest., 1968). BBC: joined as Prog. Operations Asst, 1969; Producer, World at One, 1973; Jt Producer and Compiler of Special Prog. on 'Nixon', 1974; Editor: PM Prog., 1978–81; Radio Four Budget Prog., 1979–86; World at One, 1981–86; Today, 1986–87. *Recreations:* theatre, music. *Address:* BBC, Broadcasting House, Portland Place, W1A 1AA. *T:* 071–580 4468.

ABRAMSON, Sidney, CMG 1979; retired from Department of Trade (Under Secretary, 1972–81); *b* 14 Sept. 1921; *s* of Jacob and Rebecca Abramson; *m* 1st, 1946, Lerine Freedman (marr. diss. 1958); two *s*; 2nd, 1960, Violet Ellen Eatly. *Educ:* Emanuel Sch., London; Queen's Coll., Oxford. Joined Civil Service, 1948; served Board of Trade, later Dept of Trade, 1950–81, including delegns to OEEC and EFTA, and GATT Secretariat. *Recreations:* music, gardening, writing. *Address:* 26 Arlington, N12. *T:* 081–445 1264.

ABSE, Dr Dannie, FRSL; Specialist in charge of chest clinic, Central Medical Establishment, London, 1954–89; writer; *b* 22 Sept. 1923; *s* of Rudolph Abse and Kate (*née* Shepherd); *m* 1951, Joan (*née* Mercer); one *s* two *d*. *Educ:* St Illtyd's Coll., Cardiff; University Coll., Cardiff; King's Coll., London; Westminster Hosp., London. MRCS, LRCP. First book of poems accepted for publication, 1946. Qualified at Westminster Hosp., 1950; RAF, 1951–54, Sqdn Ldr; Sen. Fellow of the Humanities, Princeton Univ., 1973–74. Pres., Poetry Soc., 1978–. FRSL 1983. Hon. DLitt Wales, 1989. *Publications: poetry:* After Every Green Thing, 1948; Walking Under Water, 1952; Tenants of the House, 1957; Poems, Golders Green, 1962; A Small Desperation, 1968; Funland and other Poems, 1973; Collected Poems, 1977; Way Out in the Centre, 1981; Ask the Bloody Horse, 1986; White Coat, Purple Coat, 1989; Remembrance of Crimes Past, 1990; *prose:* Ash on a Young Man's Sleeve, 1954; Journals from the Ant Heap, 1986; *novels:* Some Corner of an English Field, 1957; O. Jones, O. Jones, 1970; There Was a Young Man from Cardiff, 1991; *autobiography:* A Poet in the Family, 1974; A Strong Dose of Myself, 1983; *plays:* House of Cowards, (first prod.) Questors Theatre, Ealing, 1960; The Dogs of Pavlov, (first prod.) Questors, 1969; Pythagoras, (first prod.) Birmingham Rep. Th., 1976; Gone in January, (first prod.) Young Vic, 1978; *anthologies edited:* (with Howard Sergeant) Mavericks, 1957; Modern European Verse, 1964; (with Joan Abse) Voices in the Gallery, 1986; (with Joan Abse) The Music Lover's Literary Companion, 1988; The Hutchinson Book of Post-War British Poets, 1989. *Recreations:* chess, watching Cardiff City FC. *Address:* 85 Hodford Road, NW11 8NH; Green Hollows, Craig-yr-Eos Road, Ogmore-by-Sea, Glamorgan, South Wales.
See also Leo Abse.

ABSE, Leo; *b* 22 April 1917; *s* of Rudolph and Kate Abse; *m* 1955, Marjorie Davies; one *s* one *d*. *Educ:* Howard Gardens High Sch.; LSE. Served RAF, 1940–45 (arrest for political activities in ME, 1944, precipitated parly debate). Solicitor; sen. partner in Cardiff law firm. Chm., Cardiff City Lab Party, 1951–53; Mem., Cardiff CC, 1953–58. Contested (Lab) Cardiff N, 1955. MP (Lab): Pontypool, Nov. 1958–1983; Torfaen, 1983–87. Chm., Welsh Parly Party, 1976–87. Mem., Home Office Adv. Cttees on the Penal System, 1968, on adoption, 1972; first Chm., Select Cttee on Welsh Affairs, 1980; Mem., Select Cttee on Abortion, 1975–76; Sec., British-Taiwan Parly Gp, 1983–87. Sponsor or co-sponsor of Private Mem.'s Acts relating to divorce, homosexuality, family planning, legitimacy, widows' damages, industrial injuries, congenital disabilities and relief from forfeiture; sponsored Children's Bill, 1973, later taken over by Govt to become Children's Act, 1975; sponsored Divorce Bill, 1983, later taken over by Govt to become Matrimonial and Family Proceedings Act, 1985; initiated first Commons debates on genetic engineering, Windscale, *in vitro* pregnancies. Led Labour anti-devolution campaign in Wales, 1979. Mem. Council, Inst. for Study and Treatment of Delinquency, 1964–; Chm., Winnicott Clinic of Psychotherapy, 1988– (Trustee, 1980–); Pres., National Council for the Divorced and Separated, 1974–; Vice-Pres., British Assoc. for Counselling, 1985–; Chm., Parly Friends of WNO, 1985–87. Gov., Nat. Mus. of Wales, 1981–87; Member of Court: Univ. of Wales, 1981–87; UWIST. Regents' Lectr, Univ. of Calif, 1984. Received best dressed man award of Clothing Fedn, 1962. Order of Brilliant Star (China), 1988. *Publications:* Private Member: a psychoanalytically orientated study of contemporary politics, 1973; (contrib.) In Vitro Fertilisation: past, present and future, 1986; Margaret, daughter of Beatrice: a psychobiography of Margaret Thatcher, 1989. *Recreations:* Italian wines, psycho-biography. *Address:* 54 Strand-on-the-Green, W4 3PD. *T:* 081–994 1166; Via Poggio di Mezzo, Nugola Vecchia, Livorno, Italy. *T:* Livorno 586 977022.
See also D. Abse.

ABUBAKAR, Prof. Iya; Wali of Mubi; Minister of Defence, Nigeria, 1979–82; *b* 14 Dec. 1934; *s* of Buba Abubakar, Wali of Mubi, and Fatima Abubakar; *m* 1963, Ummu; one *s* three *d*. *Educ:* Univ. of Ibadan (BSc London (External)); Cambridge Univ. (PhD). FRAS, FIMA. Ahmadu Bello Univ., Zaria, Nigeria: Prof. of Maths, 1967–75, 1978; Dean, Faculty of Science, 1968–69, 1973–75; Vice-Chancellor, 1975–78. Visiting Professor: Univ. of Michigan, 1965–66; City Univ. of New York, 1971–72. Chm., Natural Sciences Reg. Council of Nigeria, 1972–75. Mem., Nigerian Univs Commn, 1968–73. Dir, Central Bank of Nigeria, 1972–75. Hon. DSc Univ. of Ife, 1977. *Publications:* Entebbe Modern Mathematics, 1970; several research papers on mathematics in internat. jls. *Recreations:* chess, golf, horse riding. *Address:* c/o PO Box 221, Yola, Nigeria.

ABU BAKAR, Datuk Jamaluddin, PNBS 1977; JMN 1967; AMN 1965; High Commissioner for Malaysia in United Kingdom and Ambassador to Ireland, 1986–88; *b* Seremban, 19 May 1929; *m* Datin Rahmah Jamaluddin; one *s* two *d*. *Educ:* Univ. of Malaya (BA Hons History); LSE (Internat. Relns). Min. of For. Affairs, Malaya, 1957; Second Sec., Bangkok, 1958; Consul, Songkhla, 1961; First Sec., Cairo, 1963; Prin. Asst Sec., Min. of For. Affairs, 1966; Counsellor, Washington, 1969; Dep. Sec.-Gen. (Gen. Affairs), Min. of For. Affairs, Apr. 1971; Sec.-Gen. Min. of Culture, Youth and Sports, Nov. 1971; Sec.-Gen., Min. of Nat. Unity, 1973; Ambassador to Kuwait, 1974; High Comr to India, Feb. 1978; seconded to Bintulu Develt Authy, Sarawak, Oct. 1978; Ambassador to Tokyo, 1981. *Recreation:* sports, including golf and tennis. *Address:* c/o Ministry of Foreign Affairs, Wismaputra, Kuala Lumpur, Malaysia.

ABUSHAMA, Sayed El-Rashid Abushama Abdel Mahmoud; Sudanese Ambassador to the Court of St James's, since 1989; *b* 1937; *s* of Sheikh Abushama Abdel Mahmoud Abushama and Sara Ghulam Alla. Dr of Law, MA (Translation), Dip. Civil Engineering. Army Engineer Officer, 1960–70; Diplomat, 1970–. *Publications:* Matrimonial Relations in both Sudanese Islamic and Czechoslovak Family Laws; Conception of Islam (trans. into Arabic). *Recreations:* jogging, swimming. *Address:* Sudanese Embassy, 3 Cleveland Row, St James's, SW1A 1DD. *T:* 071–839 6817.

ACHEBE, Prof. Chinua, FRSL 1983; author; Professor Emeritus, University of Nigeria, since 1984; Pro-Chancellor and Chairman of Council, Anambra State University of Technology, Enugu, 1986–88; *b* 16 Nov. 1930; *s* of Isaiah and Janet Achebe; *m* 1961, Christiana Okoli; two *s* two *d*. *Educ:* Univ. of Ibadan. Nigerian Broadcasting Corp.: Talks Producer, 1954; Controller, 1959; Dir, 1961–66. Rockefeller Fellowship, 1960; Unesco Fellowship, 1963; Professor of English: Univ. of Massachusetts, 1972–75; Univ. of Connecticut, Storrs, 1975–76; Univ. of Nigeria, Nsukka, 1973–81. Fulbright Prof., Univ. of Massachusetts, 1987–88; Vis. Distinguished Prof. of English, City Coll., City Univ. of NY, 1989. Chairman: Soc. of Nigerian Authors, 1966; Assoc. of Nigerian Authors, 1982–86. Member: Council, Univ. of Lagos, 1966; Exec. Cttee, Commonwealth Arts Orgn, London, 1981–. Neil Gunn Internat. Fellowship, Scottish Arts Council, 1975; Hon. Fellow: Modern Language Assoc. of America, 1975; Amer. Acad. and Inst. of Arts and Letters, 1982. Editor, Okike, 1971–. Patron, Writers and Scholars Educnl Trust, London, and Writers and Scholars Internat., 1972–; Governor, Newsconcern Internat. Foundn, London, 1983–. Hon. DLitt: Dartmouth Coll., 1972; Southampton, 1975; Ife, 1978; Nigeria, 1981; Kent, 1982; Guelph and Mount Allison, 1984; Franklin Pierce Coll., 1985; Ibadan, 1989; Skidmore Coll., 1990; DUniv: Open, 1989; Stirling, 1975; Hon. LLD Prince Edward Island, 1976; Hon. DHL: Massachusetts, 1977; Westfield Coll., 1989; Georgetown Univ., 1990. Jock Campbell New Statesman Award, 1965; Commonwealth Poetry Prize, 1972; Commonwealth Foundn Sen. Vis. Practitioner Award, 1983. Nigerian Nat. Merit Award, 1979; Order of the Fed. Repub. (Nigeria), 1979. Chm. and Publisher, African Commentary Magazine. *Publications:* Things Fall Apart, 1958; No Longer at Ease, 1960; Arrow of God, 1964; A Man of the People, 1966; Beware Soul-brother (poems), 1971; Girls at War, 1972; Morning Yet on Creation Day (essays), 1975; The Trouble with Nigeria (essays), 1983; Anthills of the Savannah, 1987; Hopes and Impediments (essays), 1987; *for children:* Chike and the River, 1966; (jt) How the Leopard Got its Claws, 1971; The Flute, 1978; The Drum, 1978. *Recreation:* music. *Address:* PO Box 53, Nsukka, Nigeria.

ACHESON, family name of **Earl of Gosford.**

ACHESON, Sir (Ernest) Donald, KBE 1986; Chief Medical Officer, Departments of Health and of Social Security (formerly Department of Health and Social Security), Department of Education and Science and Home Office, 1984–91; *b* 17 Sept. 1926; *s* of Malcolm King Acheson, MC, MD, and Dorothy Josephine Rennoldson; *m* Barbara Mary Castle; one *s* four *d* (and one *d* decd). *Educ:* Merchiston Castle Sch., Edinburgh; Brasenose Coll., Oxford (Theodore Williams Schol. in pathology, 1946; MA, DM; Hon. Fellow, 1989); Middlesex Hospital (Sen. Broderip Schol. in Med., Surg. and Pathol., 1950). FRCP; FRCS; FFPHM; FFOM. Sqdn Leader, RAF Med. Br., 1953–55. Medical Practitioner, 1951; various clinical posts at Middlesex Hosp.; Radcliffe Trav. Fellow of University Coll., Oxford, 1957–59; Medical Tutor, Nuffield Dept of Medicine, Radcliffe Infirmary, Oxford, 1960; Dir, Oxford Record Linkage Study and Unit of Clin. Epidemiology, 1962; May Reader in Medicine, 1965; Fellow, Brasenose Coll., Oxford, 1968; Prof. of Clinical Epidemiology, Univ. of Southampton, and Hon. Consultant Physician, Royal South Hants Hosp., 1968–83; Foundation Dean, Faculty of Med., Southampton Univ., 1968–78; Dir, MRC Unit in Environmental Epidemiology, 1979–83. Member: Wessex Regional Hosp. Bd, 1968–74; Hampshire AHA (Teaching) 1974–78; Chm., SW Hants and Southampton DHA, 1981–83; Member: Adv. Cttee on Asbestos, Health and Safety Exec., 1978; Royal Commn on Environmental Pollution, 1979–83; UGC, 1982–83; GMC, 1984–91; MRC, 1984–91; Chairman: Slow Virus Group, DHSS, 1979–80; Primary Health Care Inner London Gp, DHSS, 1980–81; Enquiry into Public Health in England, 1988; UK Rep., Exec. Bd, WHO, 1988–. R. Samuel McLaughlin Vis. Prof., McMaster Univ., 1977; King's Fund Travelling Fellow, NZ Postgrad. Med. Fedn, 1979; Vis. Prof., Dept of Public Health and Policy, LSHTM, 1991–. Lectures: inaugural Adolf Streicher Meml, Stoke-on-Trent, 1978; Walter Hubert, British Assoc. for Cancer Res., 1981; Christie Gordon, Univ. of Birmingham, 1982; Edwin Chadwick Centennial, LSHTM, 1990, etc. Examiner in Community Medicine: Univ. of Aberdeen, 1971–74; Univ. of Leicester, 1981–82; Examiner in Medicine, Univ. of Newcastle upon Tyne, 1975. Mem., Assoc. of Physicians of GB and Ire, 1965– (Pres. 1979). Hon. Fellow, LSHTM. Hon. DM Southampton, 1984; Hon. DSc: Newcastle, 1984; Salford, 1991; Hon. MD: QUB, 1987; Nottingham, 1989; Birmingham, 1991; Hon. LLD Aberdeen, 1988. *Publications:* Medical Record Linkage, 1967; Multiple Sclerosis, a reappraisal, 1966; Medicine, an outline for the intending student, 1970; scientific papers on epidemiology of cancer and chronic disease, medical education and organisation of medical care. *Recreations:* family, gardening, music. *Address:* London School of Hygiene and Tropical Medicine, Keppel Street, WC1E 7HT. *Club:* Athenæum.
See also R. M. Acheson.

ACHESON, Prof. Roy Malcolm, ScD, DM; FRCP, FFCM, FFOM; Professor of Community Medicine, University of Cambridge, 1976–88, now Emeritus; Fellow, Churchill College, Cambridge, since 1976; *b* 18 Aug. 1921; *s* of Malcolm King Acheson, MC, MD and Dorothy Rennoldson; *m* 1950, Fiona Marigo O'Brien; two *s* one *d*. *Educ:* Merchiston Castle Sch., Edinburgh; TCD (MA, ScD); Brasenose Coll., Oxford (MA, DM); Radcliffe Infirmary, Oxford. FRCP 1973; FFCM 1972; FFOM (by distinction) 1984. Clin. and res. posts, Radcliffe Infirmary and Univ. of Oxford; Rockefeller Trav. Fellow, Western Reserve and Harvard Univs, 1955–56; Radcliffe Trav. Fellow, University Coll., Oxford, 1955–57; Lectr in Social Med., Univ. of Dublin, 1955–59; FTCD, 1957–59; Sen. Lectr, then Reader in Social and Preventive Med., Guy's Hosp. Med. Sch. and London Sch. of Hygiene and Trop. Med., 1959–62; Yale University: Associate Prof. of Epidemiology, 1962; Prof. of Epidemiology, 1964–72; Fellow, Jonathan Edwards Coll., 1966–75; London Sch. of Hygiene and Tropical Medicine: Commonwealth Fund Sen. Trav. Fellow in Med., 1968–69; Dir, Centre for Extension Trng in Community Med., 1972–76. Hon. Cons. in Community Med., NE Thames RHA (formerly NE Metrop. RHB), 1972–76, E Anglian RHA, 1976–88; Prof. of Health Service Studies, Univ. of London, 1974–76. Samuel R. McLaughlin Vis. Prof. in Med., McMaster Univ., Hamilton, Ont, 1976. Member: Exec. Cttee and Council, Internat. Epidemiol Soc., 1964–75; Expert Cttee, Methods in Chronic Disease Epidemiol., WHO, 1966; GMC, 1979–88 (Mem. Exec. Cttee, 1979–88; Mem. Educn Cttee, 1979–86); GDC, 1985–88 (Mem. Educn Cttee, 1985–88); Cambridge HA, 1986–88. Cons., Argentina, Colombia, Guatemala, India, Venezuela, WHO, 1965–. Faculty of Community Medicine: Mem. Bd, 1974–84; Sec. to Examrs, 1974–77; Vice Pres., 1986–88; and Mem., numerous cttees. Gov., Action in Internat. Medicine, 1989–; Councillor, Oral and Dental Res. Trust, 1989–. Hon. Fellow: Buenos Aires Acad. of Medicine, 1980; Singapore Acad. of Medicine, 1988. Hon. MA Yale, 1964. *Publications:* (ed) Comparability in International Epidemiology, 1965; Seminars in Community Medicine: (ed with L. Aird) I: Sociology, 1976; (ed with L. Aird and D. J. Hall) II: Health Information, Planning and Monitoring, 1971; (with S. Hagard) Health, Society and Medicine: an introduction to community medicine, 1985; (jtly) Costs and Benefits of the Heart Transplantation Programmes at Harefield and Papworth Hospitals, 1985. *Recreations:* golf (when time permits); country matters; meditating in the bath. *Address:* Churchill College, Cambridge CB3 0DS. *T:* Cambridge (0223) 336000. *Clubs:* United Oxford & Cambridge University; Gog Magog Golf.
See also Sir E. D. Acheson.

ACHONRY, Bishop of, (RC), since 1977; **Most Rev. Thomas Flynn,** DD; *b* 8 July 1931; *s* of Robert and Margaret Flynn. *Educ:* St Nathy's, Ballaghaderreen; Maynooth College. BD, LPh, MA. Diocesan Religious Inspector of Schools, 1957–64; teaching in St Nathy's College, Ballaghaderreen, 1964–73; President and Headmaster of St Nathy's Coll., 1973–77. DD 1977. *Recreations:* gardening, fishing, golf. *Address:* St Nathy's, Ballaghaderreen, Co. Roscommon, Eire. *T:* Ballaghaderreen (0907) 60021.

ACKERMANN, Georg K.; *see* Kahn-Ackermann.

ACKERS, Sir James George, Kt 1987; Chairman, Ackers Jarrett Leasing Ltd, since 1982; Chairman, West Midlands Regional Health Authority, since 1982; *b* 20 Oct. 1935; *s* of James Ackers and Vera Harriet Ackers (*née* Edwards). *Educ:* Oundle Sch., Northants; LSE. Bsc(Econ). Man. Dir, 1963–, Chm., 1974–, Ackers Jarrett Ltd; Vice Pres., Michael Doud Gill & Associates, Washington, DC, 1968–71. Pres., Walsall Chamber of Industry and Commerce, 1978; Association of British Chambers of Commerce, 1982–: Dep. Chm., 1982–84; Chm., 1984–86; Pres., 1986–90. Member: Cttee of Inquiry into Civil Service Pay, 1981–; Monopolies and Mergers Commn, 1981–; Nat. Trng Task Force, 1989–; NEDC, 1989–. Chm., Fedn of Univ. Conservative Assocs, 1958; Vice-Chm., Bow Group, 1962–63. Pres., Jerome K. Jerome Soc., 1985–. *Address:* 5 Wrekin Court, Walsall Road, Sutton Coldfield, West Midlands B74 4QN. *Club:* Carlton.

ACKLAND, Joss, (Sidney Edmond Jocelyn); actor; *b* 29 Feb. 1928; *s* of Major Norman Ackland, Journalist, Daily Telegraph and Morning Post, and Ruth Izod; *m* 1951, Rosemary Jean Kirkcaldy, actress; one *s* five *d* (and one *s* decd). *Educ:* Cork Grammar Sch.; Dame Alice Owens Sch.; Central Sch. of Speech Training and Dramatic Art. *Plays:* The Hasty Heart, Aldwych, 1945; The Rising Sun, Arts, 1946; Dir, Winterset, 20th Century, 1946; Shakespeare Fest., Stratford-on-Avon, 1947; various try-out plays at Irving, Q, and Watergate Theatres, and toured, with Easy Money, in Germany, 1948; acted for Anthony Hawtrey, Embassy, Buxton and Croydon; then Arts Council tour, first Pitlochry Fest.; tours, and Repertory at Windsor, Chesterfield and Coventry. Went, with family, to Malawi, Central Africa, to work as a tea planter, 1954. S Africa: acting, directing, script writing and disc-jockeying, 1955–57; returned to England and joined Oxford Playhouse Co., 1957. Old Vic Co.: (incl. tours of America, Canada, USSR, Yugoslavia and Poland) Falstaff, Toby Belch, Caliban, Pistol, etc, 1958–61; Associate Dir, Mermaid Theatre: casting, choosing plays, Dir, Plough and the Stars, and playing numerous leading rôles, 1961–63. In 1963 his house burnt down so concentrated on television and did not return to theatre until 1965. Leading rôles on London stage: The Professor, in The Professor, 1966; Jorrocks, in Jorrocks, 1967; Hotel in Amsterdam, 1968–69; Come As You Are, 1969–70; Brassbound, in Captain Brassbound's Conversion, 1971; The Collaborators, 1973; Mitch, in A Streetcar Named Desire, 1974; Frederick, in A Little Night Music, 1975–76; The Madras House, 1977; Juan Perón, in Evita, 1978; Falstaff, in Henry IV pts 1 and 2, RSC, opening of Barbican Theatre, 1982; Captain Hook and Mr Darling, in Peter Pan, Barbican, 1982; Romain Gary, in Jean Seberg, NT, 1983; Stewart, in Pack of Lies, 1984; Captain Hook in Peter Pan, 1985; Clarence Darrow, in Never the Sinner, Playhouse, 1990; tours: Petruchio, in The Taming of the Shrew, 1977; Sir, in The Dresser; Gaev in The Cherry Orchard, Chichester, 1981. *Films:* Seven Days to Noon, 1949; Crescendo, 1969; The House that Dripped Blood, Villain, 1970; The Happiness Cage, England Made Me, 1971; Penny Gold, The Little Prince, The Black Windmill, S-P-Y-S, The Three Musketeers, 1973; Great Expectations, One of our Dinosaurs is Missing, 1974; Operation Daybreak, Royal Flash, 1975; The Silver Bears, 1976; The End of Civilisation as we know it, The Greek Tycoon, Someone is killing the Great Chefs of Europe, 1977; Saint Jack, The Apple, Rough Cut, 1978; Lady Jane, 1984; A Zed and Two Noughts, 1985; Don Masino, in The Sicilian, 1987; Sir Jock Broughton, in White Mischief, The Colonel, in To Kill a Priest, 1988; Lethal Weapon II, The Hunt for Red October, To Forget Palermo, 1989; The Object of Beauty, The Sheltering Desert, The Bridge, A Murder of Quality, Bill and Ted Go to Hell, 1991. Numerous appearances on TV, incl. Alan Holly, in First and Last, C. S. Lewis in Shadowland, Barrett in The Barretts of Wimpole Street, Goering, in The Man Who Lived at the Ritz, Queenie (TV film), the photographer in When We Are Married; also TV series: Kipling; The Crezz; Tinker, Tailor, Soldier, Spy; Shroud for a Nightingale; Killing on the Exchange; The Colonel's Lady; Codename Kyril; A Quiet Conspiracy; The Justice Game. *Publication:* I Must Be in There Somewhere, 1989. *Recreations:* his children, writing, painting. *Club:* Garrick.

ACKLAND, Rodney; Playwright; *b* 18 May 1908; *m* 1952, Mab (*d* 1972), *d* of Frederick Lonsdale. First play, Improper People, Arts, 1929; Marionella, Players, 1930; Dance With No Music, Arts and Embassy, 1931; Strange Orchestra, Embassy and St Martin's, 1932; Ballerina, adapted from Lady Eleanor Smith's novel, Gaiety, 1933; Birthday, Cambridge, 1934; The Old Ladies, adapted from Sir Hugh Walpole's novel, New and St Martin's, 1935; After October, Criterion and Aldwych, 1936; Plot Twenty-One, Embassy, 1936; The White Guard, adapted from the Russian play by Michael Bulgakov, Phœnix, 1938; Remembrance of Things Past, Globe, 1938; Sixth Floor, adapted from the French play by Alfred Gehri, St James's, 1939; The Dark River, Whitehall, 1943; Crime and Punishment, adapted from Dostoevsky, New, 1946; (with Robert G. Newton) Cupid and Mars, Arts, 1947; Diary of a Scoundrel, based on a comedy by Ostrovsky, Arts, 1949; Before the Party, adapted from Somerset Maugham's short story, St Martin's, 1949, revived, Queen's and Apollo, 1980; The Pink Room, Lyric, Hammersmith, 1952; A Dead Secret, Piccadilly, 1957; adapted Farewell, Farewell, Eugene, Garrick, 1959; Smithereens, Theatre Royal, Windsor, 1985; adapted Ostrovsky's Too Clever By Half, Old Vic, 1988. *Publications:* Improper People; Dance With No Music; Strange Orchestra; The Old Ladies; Birthday; After October; The Dark River; Crime and Punishment; Cupid and Mars; Diary of a Scoundrel; Before the Party; Farewell, Farewell, Eugene; The Celluloid Mistress (autobiography); The Other Palace. *Address:* c/o Eric Glass Ltd, 28 Berkeley Square, W1X 6HD.

ACKNER, family name of **Baron Ackner.**

ACKNER, Baron *cr* 1986 (Life Peer), of Sutton in the county of West Sussex; **Desmond James Conrad Ackner**; Kt 1971; PC 1980; a Lord of Appeal in Ordinary, since 1986; *b* 18 Sept. 1920; *s* of Dr Conrad and Rhoda Ackner; *m* 1946, Joan, *d* of late John Evans, JP, and widow of K. B. Spence; one *s* two *d*. *Educ:* Highgate Sch.; Clare Coll., Cambridge (MA; Hon. Fellow, 1983). Served in RA, 1941–42; Admty Naval Law Br., 1942–45. Called to Bar, Middle Temple, 1945; QC 1961; Recorder of Swindon, 1962–71; Judge of Courts of Appeal of Jersey and Guernsey, 1967–71; a Judge of the High Court of Justice, Queen's Bench Div., 1971–80; Judge of the Commercial Court, 1973–80; Presiding Judge, Western Circuit, 1976–79; a Lord Justice of Appeal, 1980–86. Mem. Gen. Council of Bar, 1957–61, 1963–70 (Hon. Treas., 1964–66; Vice-Chm., 1966–68; Chm., 1968–70); Bencher Middle Temple, 1965, Dep. Treasurer, 1983, Treasurer, 1984; Mem. Senate of the Four Inns of Court, 1966–70 (Vice-Pres., 1968–70); Pres., Senate of the Inns of Court and the Bar, 1980–82. Chm., Law Adv. Cttee, British Council, 1980–90. Hon. Mem., Canadian Bar Assoc., 1973–. *Recreations:* swimming, gardening, theatre. *Address:* 7 Rivermill, 151 Grosvenor Road, SW1. *T:* 071–821 8068; Browns House, Sutton, near Pulborough, West Sussex. *T:* Sutton (Sussex) (07987) 206.

ACKRILL, Prof. John Lloyd, FBA 1981; Professor of the History of Philosophy, Oxford University, 1966–89, now Emeritus; Fellow of Brasenose College, Oxford, 1953–89, now Emeritus; *b* 30 Dec. 1921; *s* of late Frederick William Ackrill and Jessie Anne Ackrill; *m* 1953, Margaret Walker Kerr; one *s* three *d*. *Educ:* Reading School; St John's Coll., Oxford (Scholar) (1940–41 and 1945–48). War service (Royal Berks Regt and GS, Capt.), 1941–45. Assistant Lecturer in Logic, Glasgow Univ., 1948–49; Univ. Lectr in Ancient Philosophy, Oxford, 1951–52; Tutorial Fellow, Brasenose Coll., 1953–66. Mem., Inst. for Adv. Study, Princeton, 1950–51, 1961–62; Fellow Coun. of Humanities, and Vis. Prof., Princeton Univ., 1955, 1964. *Publications:* Aristotle's *Categories* and *De Interpretatione* (trans. with notes), 1963; Aristotle's Ethics, 1973; Aristotle the Philosopher, 1981; New Aristotle Reader, 1987; articles in philos. and class. jls. *Address:* 22 Charlbury Road, Oxford OX2 6UU. *T:* Oxford (0865) 56098.

ACKROYD, Sir John (Robert Whyte), 2nd Bt *cr* 1956; *b* 2 March 1932; *s* of Sir Cuthbert Lowell Ackroyd, 1st Bt, and Joyce Wallace (*d* 1979), *d* of Robert Whyte; *S* father, 1973; *m* 1956, Jennifer Eileen MacLeod, *d* of H. G. S. Bishop; two *s* two *d*. *Educ:* Bradfield Coll.; Worcester Coll., Oxford (BA 1955, MA 1958). Commissioned RA, 1951; Sword of Honour, Mons Officer Cadet Sch., 1951; served in Jordan, 1951–52. Oxford Univ., 1952; Steward, OUDS, 1954. Underwriting Mem. of Lloyd's, 1959–; joined Engineer Planning & Resources Ltd, 1968–75. Mem. Gen. Council, Victoria League for Commonwealth Friendship, 1973; Hon. Sec., The Pilgrims of GB, 1966; Hon. Sec., RCM, 1986– (Mem. Council, 1981–; FRCM 1988); Vice-Pres., Bromley Symphony Orch., 1979. Patron, London and Internat. Sch. of Acting, 1983–. Mem. Court, City Univ., 1989–. Church Warden: St Mary-le-Bow, Cheapside, 1973–87; The Church of All Hallows, 1973–87. FZS 1970 (Mem. Council, 1987–90); FRSA 1989. Freeman of the City of London; Liveryman Carpenters' Co. *Publication:* (ed) Jordan, 1978 (to commemorate Silver Jubilee of HM King Hussein of Jordan). *Recreations:* music, theatre. *Heir:* *er s* Timothy Robert Whyte Ackroyd, *b* 7 Oct. 1958. *Address:* Flat 1, 65 Ladbroke Grove, Holland Park, W11 2PD. *T:* 071–727 5465. *Clubs:* Garrick; (Life Mem.) Union Society (Oxford).

ACKROYD, Norman, RA 1991 (ARA 1988); RE 1985; artist (painter and etcher); Tutor in Etching, Central School of Arts, London, since 1965; *b* 26 March 1938; *s* of late Albert Ackroyd, master butcher, and Clara Briggs, weaver; *m* 1st, Sylvia Buckland (marr. diss. 1975); two *d*; 2nd, Penelope Hughes-Stanton; one *s* one *d*. *Educ:* Cockburn High Sch., Leeds; Leeds Coll. of Art; Royal Coll. of Art (ARCA 1964). Teaches occasionally at RA, Slade, RCA and in N. America. Over 40 one-man exhibns, 1970–, mainly in UK and USA; work in public collections includes: Tate Gall.; BM; V&A; Arts Council; British Council; Mus. of Modern Art, NY; Nat. Galls of Scotland, Norway, Canada, S Africa; Albertina, Vienna; Rijksmus. and Stedelyk, Amsterdam; Musée d'Art Histoire, Geneva. Mural commissions include: Albany, Glasgow, 1975; Haringey Cultural Centre, 1985; Lloyds Bank Technol. Centre, London, 1990; British Airways, 1991. TV work includes: Artists in Print (etching), BBC 2, 1981; A Prospect of Rivers, Channel 4, 1988. Awards: Bradford Internat. Biennale, 1972, 1982; Royal Soc. of Etchers and Engravers, 1984, 1985; Bronze Medal, Frechen, Germany, 1986. *Publications:* A Cumberland Journey, 1981; Travels with Copper and Zinc, 1983; (with Douglas Dunn) The Pictish Coast, 1988; St Kilda: the furthest land, 1989; Windrush, 1990; numerous collections of etchings from travels in the British Isles, occasionally with poets. *Recreations:* cricket, archæology. *Address:* Royal Academy of Arts, Piccadilly, W1V 0DS. *T:* 071–378 6001. *Clubs:* Chelsea Arts, Arts.

ACKROYD, Peter; writer; Chief Book Reviewer, The Times, since 1986; *b* 5 Oct. 1949; *s* of Graham Ackroyd and Audrey Whiteside. *Educ:* St Benedict's Sch., Ealing; Clare Coll., Cambridge (MA); Yale Univ. (Mellon Fellow). Literary Editor, 1973–77, Jt Managing Editor, 1978–82, The Spectator. FRSL 1984. *Publications: poetry:* London Lickpenny, 1973; Country Life, 1978; The Diversions of Purley, 1987; *novels:* The Great Fire of London, 1982; The Last Testament of Oscar Wilde, 1983 (Somerset Maugham Prize, 1984); Hawksmoor, 1985 (Whitbread Award; Guardian Fiction Prize); Chatterton, 1987; First Light, 1989; *non-fiction:* Notes for a New Culture, 1976; Dressing Up, 1979; Ezra Pound and his World, 1980; T. S. Eliot, 1984 (Whitbread Award; Heinemann Award); Dickens, 1990; Introduction to Dickens, 1991. *Address:* c/o Anthony Sheil Associates Ltd, 43 Doughty Street, WC1N 2LF. *T:* 071–405 9351.

ACKROYD, Rev. Prof. Peter Runham, MA, PhD Cantab, BD, MTh, DD London; Samuel Davidson Professor of Old Testament Studies, University of London, 1961–82, now Emeritus Professor; *b* 15 Sept. 1917; *s* of Jabez Robert Ackroyd and Winifred (*née* Brown); *m* 1940, Evelyn Alice Nutt (*d* 1990), BSc (Manch.), *d* of William Young Nutt; two *s* three *d*. *Educ:* Harrow County School for Boys; Downing and Trinity Colleges, Cambridge. Open Exhibition in Modern Languages, Downing Coll., Cambridge, 1935; Mod. and Med. Langs Tripos, Pt I, 1936, Pt II, 1938; BDHons London, 1940; Stanton Student, Trin. Coll., Cambridge, 1941–43; Dr Williams's Trust Exhibnr, 1941; MTh London, 1942; PhD Cambridge, 1945; DD London, 1970. Minister of: Roydon Congregational Church, Essex, 1943–47; Balham Congregational Church, London, 1947–48; Lectr in Old Testament and Biblical Hebrew, Leeds Univ., 1948–52; Cambridge University: Univ. Lectr in Divinity, 1952–61; Select Preacher, 1955; Mem. Council of Senate, 1957–61; Hulsean Lectr, 1960–62; Select Preacher, Oxford, 1962, 1981 (McBride Sermon); Dean of Faculty of Theology, King's Coll., London, 1968–69; FKC 1969; Mem. Senate, London Univ., 1971–79; Dean, Univ. Faculty of Theology, 1976–80. Vis. Professor: Lutheran Sch. of Theology, Chicago, 1967 and 1976; Univ. of Toronto, 1972; Univ. of Notre Dame, Indiana, 1982; Emory Univ., Atlanta, 1984. Lectures: Selwyn, NZ, 1970; Ethel M. Wood, Univ. of London, 1982; (first) Walter S. Williams, Denver, 1982; Tübingen, 1983; Haskell, Oberlin, Ohio, 1984; series of lectures, Japan, 1983. External Examiner, Belfast, Bristol, Durham, Cambridge, Edinburgh, Leeds, Nottingham, Exeter, West Indies. Ordained Deacon, 1957; Priest, 1958; Hon. Curate, Holy Trinity, Cambridge, 1957–61. Proctor in Convocation, Cambridge Univ., 1960–64. Pres., Soc. for Old Testament Study, 1972 (Foreign Sec., 1986–89); Hon. Mem., Soc. of Biblical Literature, 1982–; Chairman: Council, British Sch. of Archaeology in Jerusalem, 1979–83; Palestine Exploration Fund, 1986–90 (Hon. Sec., 1962–70). Hon. DD St Andrews, 1970. *Publications:* Freedom in Action, 1951; The People of the Old Testament, 1959, new edn 1981; Continuity, 1962; The Old Testament Tradition, 1963; Exile and Restoration, 1968; Israel under Babylon and Persia, 1970; 1 & 2 Chronicles, Ezra, Nehemiah, Ruth, Jonah, Maccabees, 1970; 1 Samuel (Cambridge Bible Commentary), 1971; I & II Chronicles, Ezra, Nehemiah (Torch Bible Commentary), 1973; 2 Samuel, 1977; Doors of Perception, 1978, new edn 1983; Studies in the Religious Tradition of the Old Testament, 1987; The Chronicler in His Age, 1991; articles and reviews in various learned jls, dictionaries, etc; *translations:* E. Würthein's The Text of the Old Testament, 1957; L. Köhler's Hebrew Man, 1957, repr. 1973; O. Eissfeldt's The Old Testament: An Introduction, 1965; *editor:* Bible Key Words, 1961–64; Society for Old Testament Study Book List, 1967–73; Palestine Exploration Quarterly, 1971–86; *joint editor:* SCM Press OT Library, 1960–80; Cambridge Bible Commentary, 1961–79; SCM Studies in Biblical Theol., 1962–77; Words and Meanings: Essays presented to D. W. Thomas, 1968; Cambridge History of the Bible; vol. I, 1970; Oxford Bible Series, 1979–; Cambridge Commentaries: Jewish and Christian Writings of the period 200 BC to AD 200, 1979–. *Recreations:* reading, music. *Address:* Lavender Cottage, Middleton, Saxmundham, Suffolk IP17 3NQ. *T:* Westleton (072873) 458.

ACLAND, Sir Antony (Arthur), GCMG 1986 (KCMG 1982; CMG 1976); GCVO 1991 (KCVO 1976); HM Diplomatic Service, retired; Provost of Eton, since 1991; *b* 12 March 1930; *s* of Brig. P. B. E. Acland, *qv*; *m* 1956, Clare Anne Verdon (*d* 1984); two *s* one *d*; *m* 1987, Jennifer McGougan (*née* Dyke). *Educ:* Eton; Christ Church, Oxford (MA 1956). Joined Diplomatic Service, 1953; ME Centre for Arab Studies, 1954; Dubai, 1955; Kuwait, 1956; FO, 1958–62; Asst Private Sec. to Sec. of State, 1959–62; UK Mission to UN, 1962–66; Head of Chancery, UK Mission, Geneva, 1966–68; FCO, 1968, Hd of Arabian Dept, 1970–72; Principal Private Sec. to Foreign and Commonwealth Sec., 1972–75; Ambassador to Luxembourg, 1975–77, to Spain, 1977–79; Deputy Under-Sec. of State, FCO, 1980–82, Perm. Under-Sec. of State, FCO, and Head of Diplomatic Service, 1982–86; Ambassador to Washington, 1986–91. Trustee, Nat. Portrait Gall., 1991–. Hon. DCL Exeter, 1988. *Address:* Provost's Lodge, Eton College, Windsor, Berks SL4 6DH. *Club:* Brooks's.

See also Maj.-Gen. Sir J. H. B. Acland.

ACLAND, Lt-Col Sir (Christopher) Guy (Dyke), 6th Bt *cr* 1890; MVO 1990; Lieutenant Colonel, RA; Staff Officer 1, Management Services Organisation 3, Ministry of Defence, since 1990; *b* 24 March 1946; *s* of Major Sir Antony Guy Acland, 5th Bt, and of Margaret Joan, *e d* of late Major Nelson Rooke; *S* father, 1983; *m* 1971, Christine Mary Carden, *y d* of Dr John Waring, Totland Bay, Isle of Wight; two *s*. *Educ:* Allhallows School; RMA Sandhurst. Commissioned RA, 1966; served BAOR (26 Field Regt), 1967–70; UK and Hong Kong, (3 RHA), 1970–73; BAOR and UK (22 AD Regt), 1974–77; Staff Coll., Camberley, 1978 (psc); served on Staff of HQ Eastern District, 1979–80; commanded Q (Sanna's Post) Bty in BAOR (5 Regt), 1981–83; SO2, Army Staff Duties Directorate, MoD, 1983–85; 2 i/c 1 RHA BAOR, 1986–88; Equerry to HRH the Duke of Edinburgh, 1988–90. *Recreations:* sailing, shooting, gardening. *Heir: s* Alexander John Dyke Acland, *b* 29 May 1973. *Clubs:* Royal Artillery Yacht; Royal Solent Yacht; Yarmouth Sailing.

ACLAND, Sir John Dyke, 16th Bt *cr* 1644, of Columb John, Devon; *S* father, 1990.

ACLAND, Maj.-Gen. Sir John (Hugh Bevil), KCB 1980; CBE 1978; DL; farmer; Director of Liaison Research, Allied Vintners, since 1982; *b* 26 Nov. 1928; *s* of Brig. Peter Acland, *qv*; *m* 1953, Myrtle Christian Euing, *d* of Brig. and Mrs Alastair Crawford, Auchentroig, Stirlingshire; one *s* one *d*. *Educ:* Eton. Enlisted Scots Guards, 1946; commnd, 1948; served with 1st or 2nd Bn in Malaya, Cyprus, Egypt, Germany, Kenya, Zanzibar and NI, 1949–70; Equerry to HRH the Duke of Gloucester, 1957–59; Staff Coll., 1959; Bde Major, 4th Guards Armoured Bde, 1964–66; CO 2nd Bn Scots Guards, 1968–71; Col GS ASD, MoD, 1971–74; BGS, MoD, 1975; Comd Land Forces and Dep. Comd British Forces Cyprus, 1976–78; GOC South West Dist, 1978–81; Comd Monitoring Force, Southern Rhodesia, and Military Advr to the Governor, 1979–80. Hon. Colonel: Exeter Univ. OTC, 1980–90; Royal Devon Yeomanry, 1983–; Royal Wessex Yeomanry, 1989–. Pres., Royal British Legion, Devon, 1982–90; Mem., Dartmoor National Park Authority, 1986. Chm., SW Regl Working Party on Alcohol, 1987–. Mem. Steering Gp, Schools Health Educn Unit, Exeter Univ., 1988–. Governor, Allhallows Sch., 1982–. DL Devon, 1984. *Publications:* articles in British Army Review and other jls. *Recreations:* fishing, arboriculture, destroying vermin. *Address:* c/o Messrs C. Hoare & Co., 37 Fleet Street, EC4. *Clubs:* MCC, Blue Seal.

See also Sir Antony Acland.

ACLAND, Brigadier Peter Bevil Edward, OBE 1945; MC 1941; TD; Vice-Lord-Lieutenant of Devon, 1962–78; *b* 9 July 1902; *s* of late Col A. D. Acland, CBE; *m* 1927, Bridget Susan Barnett (served ME, 1940–43; despatches), *d* of late Canon H. Barnett; two *s*. *Educ:* Eton; Christ Church, Oxford. Sudan Political Service, 1924–40. Served War of 1939–45: Abyssinia, Western Desert, Ægean (wounded, despatches). Comd Royal Devon Yeomanry, 1947–51, Hon. Col, 1953; Chairman, Devon AEC, 1948–58; Member, National Parks Commission, 1953–60; Chairman, Devon T&AFA, 1960. DL Devon, 1948; High Sheriff for Devon, 1961; JP 1962. 4th Class Order of the Nile; Greek War Cross. *Address:* Little Court, Feniton, Honiton, Devon EX14 0BE.

See also Sir A. A. Acland, Maj.-Gen. Sir J. H. B. Acland.

ACRES, Dr Douglas Ian, CBE 1987 (OBE 1981); JP; DL; Chairman of Council, Magistrates' Association, 1984–87; *b* Brockley, 21 Nov. 1924; *y s* of Sydney Herbert and Hilda Emily Acres; *m* Joan Marjorie, *o d* of William Charles and Alice Emily Bloxham, Benfleet. *Educ:* Westcliff High Sch.; Borland's, Victoria; London Hosp. Med. Coll. MRCS, LRCP 1949; DMJ (Clin.); MRCGP 1968. House Surgeon and Casualty Registrar, King George Hosp., Ilford, 1949–51; RAF Med. Branch, 1951–53 (Dep. Pres., Air Crew Med. Bd, Hornchurch; AOC's Commendation and Vote of Thanks, OStJ, East Coast Flood Disaster, 1953); gen. med. practice, Benfleet, 1953–84; MO, Remploy Ltd, 1965–. Med. Adviser, Congregational Fedn, 1985–; Member: Cttee on Mentally Abnormal Offenders, 1972–75; Barclay Cttee on Role and Task of Social Worker, 1979; Parole Bd, 1984–87; Sec., Fedn of Alcohol Rehab. Estabts, 1980–82; Mem., Exec. Cttee, Alcohol Concern, 1983–87; Chairman: Essex Council on Alcoholism, 1981–86; Out of Court (Alt. for Drunkenness Offenders), 1982–89; Churches' Council on Alcohol and Drugs, 1986–89; Mem., Interdeptl Cttee on Alcoholism, 1975–78; Chm., Educn Cttee, Inst. for Study and Treatment and Deliquency, 1985–89. Cropwood Fellow, Inst. of Criminology, 1973; Member: Medico-Legal Soc., British Acad. of Forensic Scis; Royal Soc. of Health; BMA (Chm., SE Essex Div., 1979). Magistrates' Association: Dep. Chm., 1983; Chm., Sentencing of Offenders Cttee, 1978–83; Chm., Essex and NE London Br., 1975–78; Chm., Trng Sub-Cttee, 1978–. JP Essex, 1958; Chm., Rochford Bench, 1974–84; Member: Lord Chancellor's Essex Adv. Cttee, 1973–87; Essex Magistrates' Courts Cttee, 1973– (Chm., Trng Sub-Cttee, 1978–); Essex Probation Cttee, 1972– (Chm., R&D Sub-Cttee, 1980–90); Pres., Essex Br., Nat. Assoc. of Probation Officers, 1983–89. Indep. Mem., Benfleet UDC, 1960–65 (Chm., Public Health Cttee). Mem., Board of Visitors, HM Borstal, Bullwood Hall, 1970–83 (Vice-Chm., 1976–82); Member, Governing Body: King John Sch., Thundersley, 1967–89 (Chm., 1971–89); SE Essex Sixth Form Coll., 1982–. Lay Pastor, Battlesbridge Free Church and Woodham Ferrers Congregational Church, 1984–. DL Essex 1978. CStJ. Med. corresp., SE Essex Evening Echo, 1968–. *Publications:* articles and chapters on medico-legal matters. *Address:* Thundersley Lodge, Runnymede Chase, Thundersley, Benfleet, Essex SS7 3DB. *T:* South Benfleet (0268) 793241. *Club:* Royal Society of Medicine.

ACTON, 4th Baron *cr* 1869, of Aldenham, Salop; **Richard Gerald Lyon-Dalberg-Acton;** Bt 1644; Hereditary Duke of Dalberg; Patrician of Naples; writer; *b* 30 July 1941; *s* of 3rd Baron Acton, CMG, MBE, TD and of Daphne, *o d* of 4th Baron Rayleigh, FRS and late Mary Hilda, 2nd *d* of 4th Earl of Leitrim; *S* father, 1989; *m* 1st, 1965, Hilary Juliet Sarah (*d* 1973), *d* of Dr Osmond Laurence Charles Cookson, Perth, WA; one *s*; 2nd, 1974, Judith (writer) (marr. diss. 1987), *d* of Hon. Sir Garfield Todd, *qv*; 3rd, 1988, Patricia (Law Professor and writer), *o d* of late M. Morey Nassif and of Mrs Nassif, Iowa, USA. *Educ:* St George's Coll., Salisbury, Rhodesia; Trinity Coll., Oxford (BA History 1963, MA 1988). Called to the Bar, Inner Temple, 1976. Dir, Coutts & Co., 1970–74. Senior Law Officer, Min. of Justice, Legal and Parly Affairs, Zimbabwe, 1981–85. *Publications:* contribs to newspapers and historical and literary jls. *Heir: s* Hon. John Charles Ferdinand Harold Lyon-Dalberg-Acton, *b* 19 Aug. 1966. *Address:* Marcham Priory, near Abingdon, Oxon. *T:* Frilford Heath (0865) 391260; 100 Red Oak Lane SE, Cedar Rapids, Iowa 52403, USA. *T:* (319) 362–6181.

ACTON, Sir Harold (Mario Mitchell), Kt 1974; CBE 1965; author; *b* 5 July 1904; *s* of Arthur Mario Acton and Hortense Mitchell, La Pietra, Florence. *Educ:* Eton Coll.; Christ Church, Oxford (BA). FRSL. Lectr in English Literature, National University of Peking and Peking Normal College, 1933–35. Lived for seven years in Peking, devoting much time to Chinese Classical Theatre. Served in RAF during War of 1939–45, chiefly in Far East. Hon. DLitt New York Univ., 1973. Grand Officer, Republic of Italy; Kt of the Constantinian Order. *Publications:* Aquarium, 1923; An Indian Ass, 1925; Five Saints and an Appendix, 1927; Humdrum, 1928; Cornelian, 1928; This Chaos, 1930; The Last Medici, 1932, new edn 1958; (in collab.) Modern Chinese Poetry, 1936; (in collab.) Famous Chinese Plays, 1937; Peonies and Ponies, 1941; Glue and Lacquer, 1941 (Four Cautionary Tales, 1947, reprint of former); Memoirs of an Aesthete, 1948; Prince Isidore, 1950; The Bourbons of Naples, 1956; The Last Bourbons of Naples, 1961; Florence (an essay), 1961; Old Lamps for New, 1965; More Memoirs of an Aesthete, 1970; Tit for Tat, 1972; Tuscan Villas, 1973, repr. as The Villas of Tuscany, 1984; Nancy Mitford: a memoir, 1975; (in collab.) The Peach Blossom Fan, 1976; The Pazzi Conspiracy, 1979; The Soul's Gymnasium (short stories), 1982; Three Extraordinary Ambassadors, 1984; (in collab.) Florence, a traveller's companion, 1986. *Recreations:* jettatura, hunting the Philistines. *Address:* La Pietra, Florence, Italy. *T:* 474448. *Club:* Savile.

ACTON, William Antony; *b* 8 April 1904; *o s* of late William Walter Acton, Wolverton Hall, Pershore, Worcs; *m* 1932, Joan, *o c* of late Hon. Francis Geoffrey Pearson; one *d*. *Educ:* Eton; Trinity College, Cambridge. HM Treasury, 1939–45. Managing Director, Lazard Bros & Co. Ltd, 1945–53; Director: The National Bank Ltd, 1945–70 (Chm., 1964–70); Bank of London and South America Ltd, 1953–70; Standard Bank Ltd, 1953–70; Ottoman Bank, 1953–58; Bank of London and Montreal Ltd., 1959–64; Bank of West Africa Ltd, 1954–70; Bank of Ireland, 1966–70; National Commercial Bank of Scotland, 1967–70; National and Commercial Banking Group Ltd, 1969–70; The Whitehall Trust, 1945–70. High Sheriff, County of London, 1955. *Recreation:* travelling. *Address:* Poste Restante, Corfu, Greece. *T:* Corfu 91–236. *Club:* White's.

ACWORTH, Brig. Robert William, CBE 1986; Registrar of St Paul's Cathedral, since 1991; *b* 11 Dec. 1938; *s* of Rev. Oswald Roney Acworth and Jean Margaret (*née* Coupland); *m* 1967, Elizabeth Mary, *e d* of J. N. S. Ridgers, *qv*; two *s* one *d*. *Educ:* St John's Sch., Leatherhead; RMA, Sandhurst. Commnd, Queen's Royal Regt, 1958; served in Germany, Holland, Norway, Gibraltar, Aden, Oman, Hong Kong, UK and NI; sc 1970; HQ AFNORTH, 1971–73; Instructor, Jun. Div., Staff Coll., 1975–77; GS01, Oman, 1979–81; 10 UDR, 1981–83; Asst COS, HQ NI, 1983–85; Coll. Comdr, RMA, Sandhurst, 1985–87; Asst COS (Intelligence), HQ AFCENT, 1987–90; Dep. Comdr and COS, SE Dist, 1990–91, retd. Dep. Col, Queen's Regt, 1986–. *Recreations:* gardening, shooting, fishing, tennis. *Address:* St Paul's Cathedral, EC4M 8AD. *T:* 071–236 4128. *Club:* Army and Navy.

ADAIR, Brian Campbell, TD 1979; NP 1975; Senior Partner, Adairs, Solicitors, Dumbarton, since 1973; President, Law Society of Scotland, May 1992–93; *b* 28 Aug. 1945; *s* of Alan William Adair and Helen Mary Scott or Adair; *m* 1969, Elaine Jean Morrison; one *s* two *d*. *Educ:* Milngavie Primary Sch.; High Sch., Glasgow; Glasgow Univ. (LLB). Apprentice Solicitor, McGrigor Donald, Glasgow, 1967–70; Solicitor, Dumbarton CC, 1970–73; constituted own firm, 1973. Mem. Council, Law Soc. of Scotland, 1980– (Vice Pres., 1991–May 1992). Elder, St Paul's Church, Milngavie. *Recreations:* holidaying in Arran, golf at Milngavie Golf Club. *Address:* (office) 3/13 Castle Street, Dumbarton G82 1QS. *T:* Dumbarton (0389) 67625; 21 James Watt Road, Milngavie, Glasgow G62 7JX. *T:* 041–956 3070.

ADAM, Sir Christopher Eric Forbes, 3rd Bt *cr* 1917; *b* 12 Feb. 1920; *s* of Eric Graham Forbes Adam, CMG (*d* 1925) (2nd *s* of 1st Bt) and of Agatha Perrin, *d* of Reginald Walter Macan; *S* uncle, 1982; *m* 1957, Patricia Ann Wreford, *y d* of late John Neville Wreford Brown; one adopted *d*. *Heir: cousin* Rev. (Stephen) Timothy Beilby Forbes Adam [*b* 19 Nov. 1923; *m* 1954, Penelope, *d* of George Campbell Munday, MC; four *d*]. *Address:* 46 Rawlings Street, SW3.

ADAM, (David Stuart) Gordon; Director, Barclays Bank UK, 1977–87; Chairman, International Trust Group Ltd, 1983–89; *b* 21 Dec. 1927; *o s* of late James Adam, RCNC and Florence (*née* Kilpatrick); *m* 1965, Rosanne, *er d* of late William Watson of Ardlamont; two *s* one *d*. *Educ:* Upper Canada College; Queen's Univ., Belfast (LLB); Trinity Hall, Cambridge (MA, LLM). Called to the Bar, Gray's Inn, 1951 (scholar and exhibnr). War Office, 1952–53; joined Barclays Bank, 1954; Southern and Central Africa, 1956–57; Local Dir, 1959, Gen. Man., 1968, Dep. Chm., 1977–82, Barclays Bank Trust Co.; Chm., Barclays Internat. Devlt Fund, 1985–87; Dir, various cos in Barclays' Group. Director: Henry Ansbacher Ltd, 1989–; Ansbacher International, 1989–. Mem. Council, CBI, 1972–77. Chairman: Council, Wycombe Abbey Sch., 1981–91; Girls Education Co., 1981– (Dir, 1977–). *Recreation:* getting others there. *Address:* Mulberry Hill, Wendover, Bucks HP22 6NQ. *T:* Wendover (0296) 623200. *Clubs:* Boodle's, Kandahar.

ADAM, Gordon; *see* Adam, D. S. G.

ADAM, Gordon Johnston, PhD; Member (Lab) Northumbria, European Parliament, since 1979; *b* 28 March 1934; *s* of John Craig Adam and Deborah Armstrong Johnston; *m* 1973, Sarah Jane Seely; one *s*. *Educ:* Leeds Univ. (BSc Hons, PhD). CEng, MIMinE. Mining Engr, NCB, 1959–79. Mem., Whitley Bay Bor. Council, 1971–74; Mem. 1973–80, and Dep. Leader 1975–80, North Tyneside Metrop. Bor. Council (Chm., 1973–74; Mayor, 1974–75). Chm., Whitley Bay Playhouse Theatre Trust, 1975–80; Vice-Chm., Energy, Res. and Technol. Cttee, Eur. Parlt, 1984–; Member: Northern Econ. Planning Council, 1974–79; Northern Arts Gen. Council, 1975–; Northern Sinfonia Management Cttee, 1978–80; Board Member: Newcastle Free Fest. 1989–; Northern Stage Co., 1989–. Parly Labour Candidate: Tynemouth, 1966; Berwick-upon-Tweed, Nov. 1973 (by-election), and Feb. 1974. *Recreation:* gardening. *Address:* The Old Farm House, East House Farm, Killingworth Village, Newcastle upon Tyne NE12 0BQ. *T:* 091–216 0154; (office) 10 Coach Road, Wallsend, Tyne and Wear NE28 6JA. *T:* 091-263 5838.

ADAM, Madge Gertrude, MA, DPhil; FRAS; University Lecturer (Astronomy), Department of Astrophysics, University Observatory, Oxford, 1947–79; Research Fellow of St Hugh's College, 1957–79, now Emeritus Fellow; *b* 6 March 1912; 2nd *d* of late John Gill Simpson and late Gertrude Adam; unmarried. *Educ:* Municipal High School, Doncaster; St Hugh's College, Oxford (Scholar). Research Scholar, Lady Margaret Hall, 1935–37; Junior British Scholarship, 1936–37; Assistant Tutor of St Hugh's College and Research Assistant at Oxford University Observatory, 1937; lately Fellow and Tutor, St Hugh's College. *Publications:* papers in Monthly Notices of Royal Astronomical Society from 1937. *Address:* 17 Dove House Close, Upper Wolvercote, Oxford OX2 8BG.

ADAM, Robert Wilson, (Robin); Deputy Chairman, General Accident, since 1987 (Director, since 1980); *b* 21 May 1923; *s* of R. R. W. Adam; *m* 1957, Marion Nancy Scott. *Educ:* Fettes, Edinburgh. Royal Scots, 1942; commnd RIASC 1942; served in India and Burma (Major). Chartered Accountant 1950. Joined British Petroleum Co. Ltd, 1950;

Pres., BP North America Inc. New York, 1969–72; Director: BP Canada, 1969–84 (Chm., 1981); BP Trading Ltd, 1973–75; The Standard Oil Co. (Sohio), 1972–76 and 1978–83; a Man. Dir, 1975–83, and Dep. Chm. 1981–83, British Petroleum Co. plc; Chairman: MEPC, 1984–88 (Dir, 1982–); London & Scottish Marine Oil, 1985–88; Director: Motherwell Bridge Holdings Ltd, 1984–; Royal Bank of Canada, 1984–88; TRW Inc., 1986–. Lay Mem., Stock Exchange Council, 1983–85. Mem., British N America Cttee, 1980–88; Trustee, Foundn for Canadian Studies, 1975–80. *Address:* 25 Onslow Square, SW7. *Clubs:* Brooks's, MCC; Berkshire Golf.

ADAM SMITH, Janet (Buchanan), (Mrs John Carleton), OBE 1982; author and journalist; *b* 9 Dec. 1905; *d* of late Very Rev. Sir George Adam Smith, Principal of Aberdeen Univ. and late Lady Adam Smith; *m* 1st, 1935, Michael Roberts (*d* 1948); three *s* one *d;* 2nd, 1965, John Carleton (*d* 1974). *Educ:* Cheltenham Ladies' College (scholar); Somerville College, Oxford (exhibitioner). BBC, 1928–35; Asst Editor, The Listener, 1930–35; Asst Literary Editor, New Statesman and Nation, 1949–52, Literary Editor, 1952–60. Virginia Gildersleeve Vis. Prof., Barnard Coll., New York, 1961 and 1964. Trustee, National Library of Scotland, 1950–85; Pres., Royal Literary Fund, 1976–84. Hon. LLD Aberdeen, 1962. *Publications:* Poems of Tomorrow (ed), 1935; R. L. Stevenson, 1937; Mountain Holidays, 1946; Life Among the Scots, 1946; Henry James and Robert Louis Stevenson (ed) 1948; Collected Poems of R. L. Stevenson (ed), 1950; Faber Book of Children's Verse (ed), 1953; Collected Poems of Michael Roberts (ed), 1958; John Buchan: a Biography, 1965; John Buchan and his World, 1979. *Recreation:* mountain walking. *Address:* 57 Lansdowne Road, W11 2LG. *T:* 071–727 9324. *Club:* Alpine (Vice-Pres., 1978–80).

See also E. A. Roberts.

ADAMI, Edward F.; *see* Fenech-Adami, E.

ADAMS, Dr Aileen Kirkpatrick, CBE 1988; FRCS; FFARCS; Emeritus Consultant Anaesthetist, Addenbrooke's Hospital, Cambridge, since 1983; *b* 5 Sept. 1923; *d* of F. Joseph Adams and M. Agnes Adams (*née* Munro). *Educ:* Farringtons School, Chislehurst; Sheffield Univ. MB ChB Sheffield, 1946; MA Cantab 1977; FFARCS 1954; FRCS 1988; FDSRCS 1989. Fellow in anaesthesia, Harvard Univ. and Mass. Gen. Hosp., Boston, 1955–57; Consultant Anaesthetist, Addenbrooke's Hosp., Cambridge, 1960–83; Associate Lectr, Univ. of Cambridge, 1977–85; Dean, Faculty of Anaesthetists, RCS, 1985–88. Sen. Lectr, Lagos Univ. Med. Sch., Nigeria, 1963–64. Mem., Cambridge Health Authy, 1978–82. Council Mem., RCS, 1982–88; President: Anaesthetic Sect., RSocMed, and other professional socs; History of Anaesthesia Soc., 1990–; former Examr, Cambridge Univ. and FFARCS. Hon. Mem., Assoc. of Anaesthetists, GB and Ire. FFA (SA) 1987. Mem., Editl Bd, Anaesthesia, 1972–85. Silver Jubilee Medal, 1977. *Publications:* book chapters and papers in med. jls on anaesthetic and related topics. *Recreations:* choral singing, outdoor activities, including walking, ski-ing, history. *Address:* 90 High Street, Great Abington, Cambridge CB1 6AE. *T:* Cambridge (0223) 891523.

ADAMS, Rt. Rev. (Albert) James; Acting Vicar, Ridgeway Team Ministry, Diocese of Salisbury, 1984–87; *b* 9 Nov. 1915; *s* of James and Evelyn Adams, Rayleigh, Essex; *m* 1943, Malvena Jones; three *s. Educ:* Brentwood Sch.; King's Coll., London; Community of St Andrew, Whittlesford, Cambridge. Ordained Deacon, 1942; Priest, 1943; Curate of Walkley, Sheffield, 1942–44; Succentor, 1944, Precentor, 1945–47, Sheffield Cathedral. Rector of Bermondsey, 1947–55; Rural Dean of Bermondsey, 1954–55; Rector of: Stoke Damerel, Devonport, 1955–63; Wanstead, 1963–71. Sub-Dean, Wanstead and Woodford, 1968–69; Asst Rural Dean, Redbridge, 1970–71; Archdeacon of West Ham, 1970–75; Bishop Suffragan of Barking, 1975–83. *Address:* 89 Hardens Mead, Chippenham, Wilts SN15 3AQ. *T:* Chippenham (0249) 660728.

ADAMS, Alec Cecil Stanley, CMG 1960; CBE 1952; HM Diplomatic Service, retired; *b* 25 July 1909; *e s* of late Stanley A. Adams. *Educ:* King's School, Canterbury; Corpus Christi Coll., Cambridge. One of HM Vice-Consuls in Siam, 1933; served in Portuguese East Africa (acting Consul at Beira, June 1936–Feb. 1937); local rank 2nd Secretary, Bangkok Legation, 1937; Acting Consul, Sourabaya, 1938; Bangkok Legation, 1939–40; Foreign Office, Ministry of Information, 1940; Consul, in Foreign Office, 1945; Bangkok, 1946, Acting Consul-General and Chargé d'Affaires, 1948; Consul, Cincinnati, 1949; HM Chargé d'Affaires in Korea, 1950; HM Consul-General at Houston, Texas, 1953–55; Counsellor and Consul-General at HM Embassy, Bangkok, 1956–62; Deputy Commissioner-General for South East Asia, 1962–63; Political Advisor to C-in-C (Far East) at Singapore, 1963–67; retired 1967. *Address:* Flat 513, 97 Southampton Row, WC1B 4HH. *Club:* Travellers'.

ADAMS, Prof. Anthony Peter, FFARCS, FCAnaes; FFARACS; Professor of Anaesthetics in the University of London, at the United Medical and Dental Schools of Guy's and St Thomas's Hospitals (formerly at Guy's Hospital Medical School), since 1979; Vice Chairman, Division of Anaesthetics, United Medical and Dental Schools, since 1989 (Chairman, 1984–89); *b* 17 Oct. 1936; *s* of late H. W. J. Adams and W. L. Adams; *m* 1973, Veronica Rosemary John; three *s* one *d. Educ:* Epsom College; London Univ. MB BS 1960, PhD 1970; DA 1962; MRCS 1960, LRCP 1960, FFARCS 1964, FFARACS 1987. Wellcome Res. Fellow, RPMS, 1964–66; Consultant Anaesthetist and Clinical Lectr, Nuffield Dept of Anaesthetics, Univ. of Oxford, 1968–79. Member: Standing Cttee, Bd of Studies in Surgery, London Univ., 1979–; Academic Bd of Medicine, London Univ., 1980–83; Jt Cttee for Higher Trng of Anaesthetists, 1985–90; Specialist Adv. Cttee on Accident and Emergency Medicine, Jt Cttee for Higher Trng in Medicine, 1986–90; Exec. Cttee, Fedn of Assocs of Clin. Profs, 1979–87; Exec. Cttee, Anaesthetic Res. Soc., 1983–; Council, Assoc. of Anaesthetists of GB and Ireland, 1984–89 (Chm., Safety Cttee, 1987–89); Council, Coll. of Anaesthetists, 1989–; Chm., Assoc. of Profs of Anaesthesia, 1984–88; Senator, Eur. Acad. of Anaesthesiology, 1985–. Regional Educnl Adviser (SE Thames RHA) to Faculty of Anaesthetists of RCS, 1980–87; Examiner: FFARCS, 1974–86; DVA, 1986–; DA and DM, Univ. of WI, 1986–88; PhD, Univ. of London, 1989; MB ChB Chinese Univ. of Hong Kong, 1990. Asst Editor, Anaesthesia, 1976–82; Associate Editor: Survey of Anesthesiology, 1984–; European Jl of Anaesthesiology, 1987–; Mem. Editl Bd, British Jl of Anaesthesia, 1984–. Mem., Bd of Govs, Sutton High Sch. for Girls, 1988–. *Publications:* Principles and Practice of Blood Gas Analysis, 1979, 2nd edn 1982; Intensive Care, 1984; (ed jtly) Recent Advances in Anaesthesia and Analgesia, 1984 and 1989; Emergency Anaesthesia, 1986; (ed jtly) Anaesthesia, Analgesia and Intensive Care, 1991; contribs to medical jls. *Recreations:* badger watching, English castles, history, tennis, croquet, cinema, theatre, ballet. *Address:* Department of Anaesthetics, Guy's Hospital, London Bridge, SE1 9RT. *T:* 071–955 4047. *Clubs:* Royal Society of Medicine; Halifax House (Oxford).

ADAMS, Bernard Charles; architect; *b* 29 Oct. 1915; *s* of late Charles Willoughby Adams and Emily Alice (*née* Ambrose); *m* 1st, 1942, Marjorie Barrett Weller (*d* 1986); one *d* (and two *d* decd); 2nd, 1989, Betty Isabel Tucker (*née* Feist). *Educ:* King James I Sch., Newport, IoW. ARIBA 1948, FRIBA 1968. TA, 1938–39; served 1939–41, 57 (Wessex) HAA Regt, RA; commissioned 1941; served 1941–46, 107 HAA Regt RA, France (Normandy), Belgium, Holland, Germany; Captain RA (despatches). Sen. Architect, Derbs CC, 1951–54; Asst County Architect, Kent CC, 1954–59; Dep. County Architect, Herts CC, 1959–60; County Architect, Somerset CC, 1960–80. Mem. Council, RIBA, 1963–69 and 1970–76 (Vice-Pres., 1970–72; Chm., S-W Regional Council, 1972–74); Chm., Structure of the Profession Study, RIBA, 1976–79; Mem., Nat. Consultative Council for Building and Civil Engrg Industries, 1974–80; Pres., County Architects' Soc., 1973–74 (Vice-Pres., 1971–73); Hon. Mem., Soc. of Ch. Architects of Local Authorities (founded 1974), 1983 (Sen. Vice-Pres., 1974–75; Pres. 1975–76); Architect Adviser to ACC, 1971–80; Mem., Bd of Architectural Studies, Bristol Univ., 1964–74; Founder Chm., Architects' Cttee, Consortium for Method Building, 1961–68. Chm., Taunton Theatre Trust, 1986–89 (Founder Mem., 1972). RIBA Architecture Award, 1970, and Commendation, 1974; Heritage Year Award (EAHY), 1975; Civic Trust Awards, 1962, 1968, 1971, and Commendation, 1965. FRSA 1972. *Publications:* contrib. Jl of RIBA and other jls. *Recreations:* arts, music, theatre, travel, languages. *Address:* Meadowside, Wild Oak Lane, Trull, Taunton, Somerset TA3 7JT. *T:* Taunton (0823) 272485.

ADAMS, Douglas Noël; author; *b* 11 March 1952; *s* of Christopher Douglas Adams and Janet Dora Adams (*née* Donovan, now Thrift). *Educ:* Brentwood Sch., Essex; St John's Coll., Cambridge (BA, MA). Radio and TV writer, 1974–78; BBC Radio Producer, 1978; BBV TV Script Editor, 1978–80; novelist, 1979–. *Publications:* The Hitch Hiker's Guide to the Galaxy, 1979; The Restaurant at the End of the Universe, 1980; Life, the Universe and Everything, 1982; So Long, and Thanks for all the Fish, 1984; (with John Lloyd) The Meaning of Liff, 1984; The Original Hitch Hiker Radio Scripts, 1985; Dirk Gently's Holistic Detective Agency, 1987; The Long Dark Tea Time of the Soul, 1988; (with Mark Carwardine) Last Chance to See . . ., 1990; (with John Lloyd) The Deeper Meaning of Liff, 1990. *Recreations:* buying equipment for recreations he thinks he would like to take up one day. *Address:* c/o Ed Victor Ltd, 162 Wardour Street, W1V 3AT. *T:* 071–734 4795. *Club:* Groucho.

ADAMS, Ernest Victor, CB 1978; Deputy Secretary and Commissioner, Inland Revenue, 1975–81; *b* 17 Jan. 1920; *s* of Ernest and Amelia Adams; *m* 1st, 1943, Joan Bastin, Halesworth, Suffolk (*d* 1985); one *s* one *d*; 2nd, 1987, Mavisse Evelyn Surtees, Henley-on-Thames. *Educ:* Manchester Grammar Sch.; Keble Coll., Oxford (MA). HM Forces, RA, 1940–45. Inland Revenue Dept, 1947; Sen. Inspector of Taxes, 1956; Principal Inspector of Taxes, 1961; Sen. Principal Inspector of Taxes, 1966; Dep. Chief Inspector of Taxes, 1969. *Address:* 5 Northfield Court, Henley-on-Thames RG9 2LH. *T:* Henley-on-Thames (0491) 572586. *Club:* Phyllis Court (Henley).

ADAMS, Frank Alexander, CB 1964; Member, Public Health Laboratory Service Board, 1968–79; *b* 9 July 1907; *m* 1928, Esther Metcalfe (*d* 1988); two *d*. *Educ:* Selhurst Grammar Sch.; London School of Economics, Univ. of London. HM Inspector of Taxes, 1928; Assistant Secretary, Board of Inland Revenue, 1945; Counsellor (Economic and Financial), UK Delegation to OEEC, Paris, 1957–59; Director, Civil Service Pay Research Unit, 1960–63; Under-Sec. (Finance) and Accountant-General, Min. of Health, 1963–67. Mem. Council, Hosp. Saving Assoc., 1968–89. *Address:* 6 Magpie Way, Winslow, Buckingham MK18 3JT. *T:* Winslow (029671) 3848. *Clubs:* Climbers'; Swiss Alpine (Geneva).

ADAMS, Frederick Baldwin, Jr; Director, Pierpont Morgan Library, 1948–69, now Emeritus; *b* 28 March 1910; *s* of Frederick B. Adams and Ellen Walters Delano; *m* 1st, 1933, Ruth Potter; 2nd, 1941, Betty Abbott; four *d*; 3rd, 1969, Marie-Louise de Croy. *Educ:* St Paul's Sch.; Yale Univ. (BA). Empl. Air Reduction Co. Inc., 1933–48. President: New-York Historical Soc., 1963–71; Bd Governors, Yale University Press, 1959–71; Hon. Pres., Assoc. Internationale de Bibliophilie (Pres., 1974–83); Trustee, Yale Univ., 1964–71; Fellow: Amer. Acad. Arts and Sciences; Amer. Philosophical Soc.; Amer. Antiquarian Soc.; Mass. Historical Soc.; Mem., Phi Beta Kappa. Hon. degrees: LittD: Hofstra Coll., 1959; Williams Coll., 1966; DFA, Union Coll., 1959; MA, Yale Univ., 1965; LHD, New York Univ., 1966. Chevalier, Légion d'Honneur, 1950; Comdr, Order of the Crown of Belgium, 1979. *Publications:* Radical Literature in America, 1939; One Hundred Influential American Books (with Streeter and Wilson), 1947; To Russia with Frost, 1963; contrib. to books and jls in bibliography, printing, collecting. *Address:* 208 rue de Rivoli, 75001 Paris, France. *Clubs:* Athenæum, Roxburghe; Century, Grolier (NY); Cercle Interallié (Paris).

See also S. H. Nowell-Smith.

ADAMS, Gerald Edward, PhD, DSc; Director, Medical Research Council Radiobiology Unit, Chilton, Oxon, since 1982; *b* 8 March 1930; *m* 1955, Margaret Ray; three *s. Educ:* Royal Technical Coll., Salford (BSc London, 1955); Univ. of Manchester (PhD 1958, DSc 1970). Post-doctoral Fellow, Argonne National Lab., USA, 1958–60; Vis. Scientist, Centre d'Etude Nucléaire, Saclay, France, 1961–62; Lectr, 1962–66, Sen. Lectr, 1966–70, Cancer Campaign Res. Unit in Radiobiol., Mount Vernon Hosp. (later CRC Gray Lab.); Dir of Molecular Radiobiol., 1970–72, Dep. Dir of Lab., 1972–76, CRC Gray Lab.; Prof. of Physics as Applied to Medicine, Inst. of Cancer Res. (Univ. of London), Sutton, 1976–82. Hon. Vis. Prof., Dept of Pharmacy, Univ. of Manchester, 1984–; Vis. Prof. of Radiobiol., Shanghai Med. Univ., 1986–87. Adrian Fellow, Univ. of Leicester, 1986–. Lectures: 2nd Milford Schulz Annual, Harvard Med. Sch., 1979; Maurice Lenz Annual, Columbia Univ., NY, 1981. Hon. Doctorate, Univ. of Bologna, 1982. Hon. FACR 1981. Radiation Res. Award, 1969, Failla Gold Medal, 1990, Radiation Res. Soc., USA; David Anderson-Berry Prize, RSE, 1969; Silvanus Thompson Medal, British Inst. of Radiol., 1979; Röntgen Medal, Soc. of Friends of German Röntgen Mus., 1989. Specialist Editor, Encyc. of Pharmacology and Therapeutics, 1975–; Member Editorial Board: Internat. Jl of Radiation Oncology, Biology and Physics, 1978–; British Jl of Cancer, 1981–; Internat. Jl of Radiation Biology, 1983–; Radiation Research, 1987–90. *Recreations:* music, golf, walking. *Address:* MRC Radiobiology Unit, Chilton, Didcot, Oxon OX11 0RD. *T:* Abingdon (0235) 834393.

ADAMS, Hervey Cadwallader, RBA 1932; FRSA 1951; landscape painter; lecturer on art; *b* Kensington, 1903; *o s* of late Cadwallader Edmund Adams and Dorothy Jane, *y d* of Rev. J. W. Knight; *m* 1928, Iris Gabrielle, (*d* 1984), *y d* of late F. V. Bruce, St Fagans, Glamorgan; two *s. Educ:* Charterhouse. Studied languages and singing in France and Spain, 1922–26; studied painting under Bernard Adams, 1929. Art Master, Tonbridge Sch., 1940–63. *Publications:* The Student's Approach to Landscape Painting, 1938; Art and Everyman, 1945; Eighteenth Century Painting, 1949; Nineteenth Century Painting, 1949; The Adventure of Looking, 1949. *Address:* Pummel, Houndscroft, near Stroud, Glos GL5 5DG.

ADAMS, Irene; *see* Adams, Katherine.

ADAMS, Rt. Rev. James; *see* Adams, Rt Rev. A. J.

ADAMS, Sir James; *see* Adams, Sir W. J.

ADAMS, Jennifer; Superintendent, Central Royal Parks, Department of the Environment, since 1983; *b* 1 Feb. 1948; *d* of Arthur Roy Thomas Crisp and Joyce Muriel Crisp (*née* Davey); *m* 1968, Terence William Adams. *Educ:* City of London School for Girls. Final Diploma, Inst. of Leisure and Amenity (FILAM DipPRA); FIHort. Various positions in

Parks Dept, London Borough of Wandsworth, 1971–83. *Recreations:* walking, gardening, nature conservation. *Club:* Soroptimists' International.

ADAMS, John Crawford, OBE 1977; MD, MS, FRCS; Honorary Consulting Orthopædic Surgeon, St Mary's Hospital, London; Hon. Civil Consultant in Orthopædic Surgery, Royal Air Force; Member, Council, Journal of Bone and Joint Surgery (formerly Production Editor); *m* 1st, 1940, Joan Bower Elphinstone (*d* 1981); 2nd, 1985, Valerie le Maistre (marr. diss. 1989); 3rd, 1990, Marguerite Kyle. MB, BS 1937; MRCS 1937; LRCP 1937; FRCS 1941; MD (London) 1943; MS (London) 1965. Formerly: Chief Asst, Orthopædic and Accident Dept, London Hosp.; Orthopædic Specialist, RAFVR; Resident Surgical Officer, Wingfield-Morris Orthopædic Hosp., Oxford. FRSM; Fellow, British Orthopædic Assoc. (Hon. Sec., 1959–62; Vice-Pres., 1974–75). OBE 1977. *Publications:* Outline of Orthopædics, 1956, 11th edn 1990; Outline of Fractures, 1957, 10th edn 1991; Ischio-femoral Arthrodesis, 1966; Arthritis and Back Pain, 1972; Standard Orthopaedic Operations, 1976, 3rd edn 1985; Recurrent Dislocation of Shoulder (chapter in Techniques in British Surgery, ed Maingot), 1950; Shakespeare's Physic, Lore and Love, 1989; Associate Editor and Contributor Operative Surgery (ed Rob and Smith); contributions to the Journal of Bone and Joint Surgery, etc. *Address:* 126 Harley Street, W1; 33 Denman's Lane, Lindfield, Sussex.

ADAMS, John Douglas Richard; Registrar of Civil Appeals, since 1982; *b* 19 March 1940; *o s* of late Gordon Arthur Richard Adams and Marjorie Ethel Adams (*née* Ongley); *m* 1966, Anne Easton Todd, *o d* of late Robert Easton Todd and Mary Ann Margaret Todd (*née* Isaac); two *d. Educ:* Watford Grammar School; Durham Univ. (LLB 1963). Called to Bar, Lincoln's Inn, 1967. Lecturer: Newcastle Univ., 1963–71; University College London, 1971–78; also practised at Revenue Bar until 1978; Special Comr of Income Tax, 1978–82. Hon. Lecturer, St Edmund Hall, Oxford, 1978–. *Publications:* (with J. Whalley) The International Taxation of Multinational Enterprises, 1977; (contrib.) Atkin's Court Forms, 1984; (ed jtly) Supreme Court Practice, 1985, 1991. *Recreations:* music, walking, dining. *Address:* Royal Courts of Justice, Strand, WC2A 2LL.

ADAMS, Rear-Adm. John Harold, CB 1967; LVO 1957; Director, DUO (UK) Ltd, since 1983; *b* Newcastle-on-Tyne, 19 Dec. 1918; *m* 1st, 1943, Mary Parker (marr. diss. 1961); one *s* decd; 2nd, 1961, Ione Eadie, MVO, JP; two *s* two *d. Educ:* Glenalmond. Joined Navy, 1936; Home Fleet, 1937–39; Western Approaches, Channel and N Africa, 1939–42 (despatches); Staff Capt. (D), Liverpool, 1943–45; Staff Course, Greenwich, 1945; jssc 1949; Comdr, HM Yacht Britannia, 1954–57; Asst Dir, Underwater Weapons Matériel Dept, 1957–58; Capt. (SM) 3rd Submarine Sqdn, HMS Adamant, 1958–60; Captain Supt, Underwater Detection Estab., Portland, subseq. Admty Underwater Weapons Estab., 1960–62; idc 1963; comd HMS Albion, 1964–66; Asst Chief of Naval Staff (Policy), 1966–68; retd 1968. Lieut 1941; Lieut-Comdr 1949; Comdr 1951; Capt. 1957; Rear-Adm. 1966. Dir, Paper and Paper Products Industry Training Bd, 1968–71; Dir, Employers' Federation of Papermakers and Boardmakers, 1972–73; Dir Gen., British Paper and Board Industry Fedn, 1974–83. FIPM 1975. Chm. Governors, Cheam Sch, 1975–87. *Recreations:* shooting, fishing, photography. *Address:* The Oxdrove House, Burghclere, Newbury, Berks RG15 9HJ. *T:* Burghclere (063527) 385. *Club:* Army and Navy.

ADAMS, John Kenneth; Editor of Country Life, 1958–73; Editorial Director, Country Life Ltd, 1959–73; *b* 3 June 1915; *o c* of late Thomas John Adams and late Mabel Adams (*née* Jarvis), Oxford; *m* 1944, Margaret, *o c* of late Edward Claude Fortescue, Banbury, Oxon. *Educ:* City of Oxford Sch.; Balliol Coll., Oxford. Asst Master, Stonyhurst Coll., 1939–40; served with RAFVR, 1940–41 (invalided); Asst Master, Wellington Coll., 1941–44; attached to Manchester Guardian as Leader-writer, 1942–44; Leader-writer, The Scotsman, 1944–46; joined editorial staff of Country Life, 1946; Asst Editor, 1952; Deputy Editor, 1956; Editor, 1958; Editorial Director, 1959. *Recreations:* gardening, ornithology, travel. *Address:* 95 Alleyn Park, West Dulwich, SE21 8AA. *T:* 081–693 1736. *Club:* Athenæum.

ADAMS, John Nicholas William B.; *see* Bridges-Adams.

ADAMS, John Roderick Seton; His Honour Judge Adams; a Circuit Judge, since 1990; *b* 29 Feb. 1936; *s* of George Adams and Winifred (*née* Wilson); *m* 1965, Pamela Bridget, *e d* of Rev. D. E. Rice, MC; three *s. Educ:* Whitgift Sch.; Trinity Coll., Cambridge. BA, 1959, MA 1963. Commnd, Seaforth Highlanders, 1955–56; Parachute Regt, TA, 1959–66. Legal Adviser in industry, 1960–66. Called to the Bar, Inner Temple, 1962; began practice at the Bar, 1967; Dep. Circuit Judge, 1978–80; a Recorder, 1980–90. *Recreations:* music, fishing, growing old roses. *Address:* 6 Pump Court, Temple, EC4. *T:* 071–583 6013; Melness House, Sutherland. *T:* Talmine (084756) 255.

ADAMS, Katherine, (Irene Adams); JP; MP (Lab) Paisley North, since Nov. 1990; *b* 1948; *m* 1968, Allen S. Adams (*d* 1990), MP Paisley North; one *s* two *d.* Councillor, Paisley Town, 1970. *Address:* c/o House of Commons, SW1A 0AA.

ADAMS, Major Kenneth Galt, CVO 1979; CBE 1989; Industry Fellow, Comino Foundation, since 1987; *b* 6 Jan. 1920; *s* of late William Adams, OBE, and Christina Elisabeth (*née* Hall); *m* 1988, Sally, *d* of late Col John Middleton and *widow* of Douglas Long. *Educ:* Doncaster Grammar Sch.; Staff Coll., Camberley (psc 1953). MA (Lambeth); CBIM, FRSA, FCIT. Served RASC, 1940–59: War Service, ME and N Africa; DADST WO. 1946–48; DAA&QMG, Aldershot, 1952; DAQMG HQ Northern Comd, 1954–56; Sen. Instr, RASC Officers Sch., 1956–59. Sec., S London Indust. Mission, 1959–61; Proprietors of Hay's Wharf Ltd, 1960–70, Exec. Dir, 1966–70; non-exec. dir and consultant, other cos, until 1985. St George's House, Windsor Castle: Dir of Studies, 1969–76; Fellow, 1976–82; Hon. Fellow, 1990. Comino Fellow, RSA, 1979–89. Chm., Indust. Christian Fellowship, 1977–86; Vice Chairman: Archbishops' Council on Evangelism, 1965–77; Southwark Cathedral Council, 1967–70; Member: Indust. Cttee, Bd for Social Responsibility of C of E, 1973–81; Bldg EDC, NEDC, 1977–81; Prof. Standards Cttee, BIM, 1976–81; Dept of Employment's Services Resettlement Cttee for SE England, 1967–77; Adv. Cttee, Christian Assoc. of Business Execs, 1975–; Adv. Cttee, Inst. of Business Ethics, 1986–; Trustee, Industrial Trng Foundn, 1980–. Hon. DPhil Internat. Management Centres, 1991. *Publications:* lectures and papers on developing an affirmative cultural attitude to industry in Britain. *Recreations:* 19th century novels, Border terriers. *Address:* 8 Datchet Road, Windsor, Berks SL4 1QE. *T:* Windsor (0753) 869708. *Club:* Army and Navy.

ADAMS, Surg. Rear-Adm. Maurice Henry, CB 1965; MB, BCh, DOMS; *b* 16 July 1908; *s* of Henry Adams and Dorothea (*née* Whitehouse); *m* 1938, Kathleen Mary (*née* Hardy); one *s* two *d. Educ:* Campbell Coll.; Queen's University, Belfast. MB, BCh, 1930. RN Medical Service 1933; HMS Cornwall, 1934; HMS Barham, 1936; Central Air Medical Board, 1940; HMS Activity, 1942; RN Hospital, Haslar, 1944; Med. Dept, Admiralty, 1946; RN Hospital: Malta, 1950; Chatham, 1952; MO i/c Trincomalee, 1957; Med. Dept, Admiralty, 1958; Medical Officer-in-Charge, Royal Naval Hosp., Malta, 1963; QHS, 1963–66; retd 1966. *Recreations:* sailing, golf. *Address:* Canberra, Rock, Cornwall PL27 6LF.

ADAMS, Air Vice-Marshal Michael Keith, CB 1986; AFC 1970; FRAeS; Director: UK, Thomson-CSF, since 1988; International Test Pilots School; *b* 23 Jan. 1934; *s* of late William Frederick Adams and Jean Mary Adams; *m* 1966, Susan (*née* Trudgian); two *s* one *d. Educ:* Bedford Sch.; City of London Sch. FRAeS 1978. Joined RAF, 1952; qualified Pilot, 1954; Flying Instr, 1960; Test Pilot, 1963; Staff Coll., Toronto, 1969; CO Empire Test Pilots' Sch., 1975; Dir of Operational Requirements, 1978–81; RCDS, 1982; ACAS (Op. Requirements), MoD, 1984; ACDS (Op. Requirements) Air, MoD, 1985–86; Sen. Directing Staff (Air), RCDS, 1987–88; retd. *Recreations:* walking, climbing, skiing.

ADAMS, Norman (Edward Albert), RA 1972 (ARA 1967); ARCA 1951; artist (painter); Keeper of the Royal Academy, since 1986; *b* 9 Feb. 1927; *s* of Albert Henry Adams and Winifred Elizabeth Rose Adams; *m* 1947, Anna Theresa; two *s. Educ:* Royal Coll. of Art. Head of Sch. of Painting, Manchester Coll. of Art and Design, 1962–70; Lectr, Leeds Univ., 1975–; Prof. of Fine Art, and Dir of King Edward VII Coll. (formerly Sch.), Univ. of Newcastle upon Tyne, 1981–86. Exhibitions in most European capitals, also in America (New York, Pittsburgh); Retrospective exhibns, Royal College of Art, 1969, Whitechapel Gall., RA, 1988. Paintings in collections of: most British Provincial Art Galleries; Tate Gall., London; Nat. Galls, New Zealand; work purchased by: Arts Coun. of Gt Brit.; Contemp. Art Soc.; Chantrey Bequest; various Educn Authorities. Murals at: Broad Lane Comprehensive Sch., Coventry; St Anselm's Church, S London; Our Lady of Lourdes, Milton Keynes. Decor for ballets, Covent Garden and Sadler's Wells. *Publications:* Alibis and Convictions, 1978; A Decade of Painting, 1971–81, 1981; (with A. Adams) Angels of Soho, 1988. *Address:* Butts, Horton-in-Ribblesdale, Settle, North Yorks. *T:* Horton-in-Ribblesdale (07296) 284; Royal Academy of Arts, W1.

ADAMS, Sir Philip (George Doyne), KCMG 1969 (CMG 1959); HM Diplomatic Service, retired; *b* 17 Dec. 1915; *s* of late George Basil Doyne Adams, MD, and Arline Maud Adams (*née* Dodgson); *m* 1954, Hon. (Mary) Elizabeth Lawrence, *e d* of Baron Trevethin and Oaksey (3rd and 1st Baron respectively); two *s* two *d. Educ:* Lancing Coll.; Christ Church, Oxford. Entered Consular Service, 1939; served at: Beirut, 1939; Cairo, 1941; Jedda, 1945; FO, 1947; First Sec., 1948; Vienna, 1951; Counsellor, Khartoum, 1954; Beirut, 1956; FO, 1959; Chicago, 1963; Ambassador to Jordan, 1966–70; Asst Under-Sec., FCO, 1970; Dep. Sec., Cabinet Office, 1971–72; Ambassador to Egypt, 1973–75. Dir, Ditchley Foundn, 1977–82. Member: Board, British Council, 1977–82; Marshall Aid Commem. Commn, 1979–88. *Address:* 78 Sussex Square, W2 2SS; The Malt House, Ditchley, Enstone, Oxford OX7 4EP. *Club:* Brooks's.

ADAMS, Richard Borlase, CBE 1983; Managing Director, Peninsular & Oriental Steam Navigation Co., 1979–84 (Director, 1970, Deputy Managing Director, 1974); *b* 9 Sept. 1921; *s* of James Elwin Cokayne Adams and Susan Mercer Porter; *m* 1951, Susan Elizabeth Lambert; two *s* one *d. Educ:* Winchester Coll.; Trinity Coll., Oxford, 1940. War service, Rifle Bde, 1940–46 (Major). Mackinnon Mackenzie Gp of Cos, Calcutta, New Delhi and Hongkong, 1947–63; Chm., Islay Kerr & Co. Ltd, Singapore, 1963–66; British India Steam Navigation Co. Ltd: Dir, 1966; Man. Dir, 1969; Chm., 1970. Dir, Clerical, Medical & General Life Assurance Soc., 1975–88. *Recreations:* gardening, tennis, golf. *Address:* Beacon House, Bethersden, Ashford, Kent TN26 3AE. *T:* Bethersden (023382) 247. *Club:* Oriental.

ADAMS, Richard George; author; *b* 9 May 1920; *s* of Evelyn George Beadon Adams, FRCS, and Lilian Rosa Adams (*née* Button); *m* 1949, Barbara Elizabeth Acland; two *d. Educ:* Bradfield Coll., Berks; Worcester Coll., Oxford (MA, Mod. Hist.). Entered Home Civil Service, 1948; retd as Asst Sec., DoE, 1974. Writer-in-residence: Univ. of Florida, 1975; Hollins Univ., Virginia, 1976. Pres., RSPCA, 1980–82. Carnegie Medal, 1972; Guardian Award for Children's Literature, 1972. FRSL 1975; FRSA. *Publications:* Watership Down, 1972 (numerous subseq. edns in various languages; filmed 1978); Shardik, 1974; Nature through the Seasons, 1975; The Tyger Voyage, 1976; The Ship's Cat, 1977; The Plague Dogs, 1977 (filmed 1982); Nature Day and Night, 1978; The Girl in a Swing, 1980 (filmed 1988); The Iron Wolf, 1980; (with Ronald Lockley) Voyage through the Antarctic, 1982; Maia, 1984; The Bureaucats, 1985; A Nature Diary, 1985; (ed and contrib.) Occasional Poets (anthology), 1986; The Legend of Te Tuna, 1986; Traveller, 1989; The Day Gone By (autobiog.), 1990. *Recreations:* folk-song, chess, country pursuits, fly-fishing, travel. *Address:* 26 Church Street, Whitchurch, Hants RG28 7AR.

ADAMS, Richard John Moreton G.; *see* Goold-Adams.

ADAMS, Sir (William) James, KCMG 1991 (CMG 1976); HM Diplomatic Service; Ambassador to Egypt, since 1987; *b* 30 April 1932; *s* of late William Adams and late Norah (*née* Walker); *m* 1961, Donatella, *d* of late Andrea Pais-Tarsilia; two *s* one *d. Educ:* Wolverhampton Grammar Sch.; Shrewsbury Sch.; Queen's Coll., Oxford. 2nd Lieut RA, MELF, 1950–51. Foreign Office, 1954; MECAS, 1955; 3rd Sec., Bahrain, 1956; Asst Political Agent, Trucial States, 1957; FO, 1958; 2nd Sec., 1959; Manila, 1960; 1st Sec. and Private Sec. to Minister of State, FO, 1963; 1st Sec. (Information), Paris, 1965–69; FCO, 1969; Counsellor, 1971; Head of European Integration Dept (2), FCO, 1971–72; seconded to Economic Commn for Africa, Addis Ababa, 1972–73; Counsellor (Developing Countries), UK Permanent Representation to EEC, 1973–77; Head of Chancery and Counsellor (Economic), Rome, 1977–80; Asst Under-Sec. of State (Public Depts, then Energy), FCO, 1980–84; Ambassador to Tunisia, 1984–87. Order of the Star of Honour (Hon.), Ethiopia, 1965; Order of the Two Niles (Hon.), Sudan, 1965. *Address:* c/o Foreign and Commonwealth Office, SW1A 2AH. *Club:* Reform.

ADAMS-SCHNEIDER, Rt. Hon. Sir Lancelot (Raymond), KCMG 1984; PC 1980; Ambassador of New Zealand to the United States, 1982–84; *b* Wellington, NZ, 11 Nov. 1919; *s* of A. A. Adams; *m* 1945, Shirley Lois, *d* of L. A. Brunton; two *s* one *d. Educ:* Mt Albert Grammar School. Served War of 1939–45, NZ Medical Corps. Formerly Gen. Manager of department store, Taumarunui; Mem. Borough Council and Pres., Chamber of Commerce, Taumarunui; Exec. Member, NZ Retailers' Fedn. Vice-Chm. of Nat. Party in Waitomo electorate; Mem. S Auckland Div. Exec.; MP for Hamilton, 1959–69, for Waikato, 1969–81; Minister of Broadcasting, and Assistant to Minister of Customs, 1969; Minister of Customs, Asst Minister of Industries and Commerce, 1969–72; Minister of Health, Social Security and Social Welfare, Feb.-Nov. 1972; Opposition Spokesman on Health and Social Welfare, 1972–75, and on Industry, Commerce and Customs, 1974–75; Minister of Trade and Industry, 1975–81. *Address:* 48 Rama Crescent, Khandallah, Wellington 4, New Zealand.

ADAMSON, Sir Campbell; *see* Adamson, Sir W. O. C.

ADAMSON, Hamish Christopher; Director (International), The Law Society, since 1987; *b* 17 Sept. 1935; *s* of John Adamson, Perth, Scotland, and Denise Adamson (*née* Colman-Sadd). *Educ:* Stonyhurst Coll.; Lincoln Coll., Oxford (Schol.; MA Hons Jurisprudence). Solicitor (Hons). Law Society: Asst Sec., then Sen. Asst Sec. (Law Reform), 1966–81; Sec., Law Reform and Internat. Relations, 1981–87. Sec., UK Delegn, Council of the Bars and Law Socs of EEC, 1981–; Exec. Sec., Commonwealth Lawyers' Assoc.,

1983–. *Publication:* The Solicitors Act 1974, 1975. *Recreations:* plants, books, travel. *Address:* 133 Hartington Road, SW8 2EY.

ADAMSON, Norman Joseph, CB 1981; QC (Scot.) 1979; Legal Secretary to the Lord Advocate and First Parliamentary Draftsman for Scotland, 1979–89, retired; Assistant Counsel to the Lord Chairman of Committees, House of Lords, since 1989; *b* 29 Sept. 1930; *o s* of Joseph Adamson, wine and spirit merchant, and Lily Thorrat, Glasgow; *m* 1961, Patricia Mary, *er d* of Walter Scott Murray Guthrie and Christine Gillies Greenfield, Edinburgh; four *d*. *Educ:* Hillhead High Sch., Glasgow; Glasgow Univ. MA (Hons Philosophy and Economics) 1952; LLB 1955; Faculty of Advocates, Scotland, 1957; called to English Bar, Gray's Inn, 1959. Army Legal Aid (Civil) (UK), 1956–57; practice at Scottish Bar, 1957–65; Standing Jun. Counsel, Bible Board, 1962; Standing Jun. Counsel, MoD (Army), 1963–65; Hon. Sheriff Substitute, 1963–65; Parly Draftsman and Legal Sec., Lord Advocate's Dept, London, 1965–89. Elder of the Church of Scotland. *Recreations:* music, theatre. *Address:* Whiteways, White Lane, Guildford, Surrey GU4 8PS. *T:* Guildford (0483) 65301. *Clubs:* Royal Over-Seas League (London and Edinburgh), College (Glasgow).

ADAMSON, Rt. Rev. Mgr. Canon Thomas; Residential Hospital Chaplain, Lourdes Hospital, Liverpool; Provost Emeritus, Liverpool Metropolitan Cathedral; *b* 30 Sept. 1901; *s* of George and Teresa Adamson, Alston Lane, near Preston. *Educ:* St Edward's College, Liverpool; Upholland College; Oscott College, Birmingham; Gregorian University, Rome. Ordained Priest, 1926; Beda College, Rome, 1926–28; Private Secretary to Archbishop of Liverpool, 1928–45; Parish Priest of St Clare's, Liverpool, 1945–88; Canon, Liverpool Metropolitan Cathedral 1950, Provost 1981–88; Privy Chamberlain to Pope Pius XI, 1932; Domestic Prelate to the Pope, 1955; Vicar General to Archbishops of Liverpool, 1955–65; Protonotary Apostolic to the Pope. *Address:* Lourdes Hospital, Greenbank Road, Liverpool L18 1HQ.

ADAMSON, Sir (William Owen) Campbell, Kt 1976; Chairman, Abbey National plc (formerly Abbey National Building Society), 1978–91; *b* 26 June 1922; *o s* of late John Adamson, CA; *m* 1st, 1945, Gilvray (*née* Allan) (marr. diss. 1984); two *s* two *d*; 2nd, 1984, Mrs J. (Mimi) Lloyd-Chandler. *Educ:* Rugby Sch.; Corpus Christi Coll., Cambridge. Royal Inst. of Internat. Affairs, 1944–45; Baldwins Ltd as Management Trainee, 1945; successive managerial appts with Richard Thomas & Baldwins Ltd and Steel Co. of Wales Ltd, 1947–69; Gen. Man. i/c of construction and future operation of Spencer Steelworks, Llanwern; Dir, Richard Thomas & Baldwins Ltd, 1959–69, seconded as Dep. Under-Sec. of State, and Co-ordinator of Industrial Advisers, DEA, 1967–69; Dir-Gen., CBI, 1969–76. Director: Imperial Group, 1976–86; Renold, 1976–86 (Dep. Chm., 1981–82; Chm., 1982–86); Lazard Bros & Co., 1977–87; Tarmac, 1980–90. Member: BBC Adv. Cttee, 1964–67 and 1967–75; SSRC (on formation), 1965–69; NEDC, 1969–76; Council, Industrial Soc.; Design Council, 1971–73; Council, Iron and Steel Inst., 1960–72; Iron and Steel Industry Delegn to Russia, 1956, and to India, 1968; Vice-Chm., National Savings Cttee for England and Wales, 1975–77. Vis. Fellow: Lancaster Univ., 1970–90; Nuffield Coll., Oxford, 1971–79. Governor: Rugby Sch., 1979–; Bedford Coll., London Univ., 1983–85. *Publications:* various technical articles. *Recreations:* walking, music, arguing. *Address:* 32 Grosvenor Square, W1X 9LL. *T:* 071–491 4616.

ADAMSON-MACEDO, Prof. Emeritus Colin, DSc; FIEE; engineering and higher education consultant; *b* 23 Nov. 1922; British; *m* 1983, Dr Elvidina Nabuco Macedo; one *s* (and one *s* one *d* of former marriage). *Educ:* Pocklington Sch., Yorks. BSc 1947, MSc(Eng.) 1952, London; DSc Manchester, 1961. REME (Capt.), 1942–46. Asst Lectr, then with A. Reyrolle & Co. (power systems analysis), 1946–52; Sen. Lectr, then Reader, in Electrical Power Systems Engrg, UMIST, 1952–61; Chm., Dept of Electrical Engineering and Electronics, Univ. of Manchester Institute of Science and Technology, 1961–70; Rector, The Polytechnic of Central London, 1970–83; Overseas Adviser to Univ. of Salford, 1983–86. Mem., Conference Internationale des Grands Réseaux Electriques; Chm. of Consultants, Educational Overseas Services, 1975–; Chm. of Panel 1 (and Mem. Council), British Calibration Service, 1969–83. Mem., Exec. Cttee, Inter-Univ. Council for Service Overseas, 1972–82. Mem., Bd of Trustees, Ecole Supérieure Interafricaine d'Electricité, Abidjan, 1979–; UN Team leader for Yarmouk Univ. of Technology, Jordan, 1978–80. Vis. Professor: Univ. of Roorkee, India, 1954–55; Univs of Washington and Wisconsin, 1959; Middle East Techn. Univ., Ankara, 1967–68; Univ. of Technology, Baghdad, 1975–83; Fed. Univ. of Rio de Janeiro, 1983– (UNESCO Energy Conslt to Coordenação dos Programas de Pós-graduação de Engenharia, 1986); Advisor to Rector, Mahidol Univ., Thailand, 1984–; NATO Fellow, Electrical/Electronics Res. Inst., ME Technical Univ., Ankara, 1987; Vis. Prof. and Energy Conslt, Inst. de Pesquisas Tecnológicas, Univ. of São Paulo, 1987–88. Mem. Governing Council, Polytechnic of Huddersfield HEC, 1989–. *Publications:* (jtly) High Voltage Direct Current Power Transmission, 1960; High Voltage DC Power Convertors and Systems, 1963; University Perspectives, 1970; UNESCO reports: Higher Technical Education (Egypt), 1972; Alternative University Structures (UK), 1973, 3rd edn 1977; Technical Higher Education (Iraq), 1974; Post-secondary Education for Persons Gainfully-employed, 1976 and 1977; contribs to Proc. IEE and other learned jls. *Recreations:* yachting, oriental science and technology. *Address:* 6A Offley Road, Kennington, SW9 0LS; Yetts o' Huaxu, Glendevon by Dollar, Clackmannanshire FK14 7JY. *T:* Muckhart (025981) 241; Rua Barata Ribeira 664/503, Copacabana, 20,000 Rio de Janeiro-RJ, Brazil. *Clubs:* Athenæum, Royal Automobile; Royal Mersey Yacht.

ADCOCK, Robert Wadsworth; DL; Chief Executive and Clerk, Essex County Council, since 1976; *b* 29 Dec. 1932; *s* of Sir Robert Adcock, CBE; *m* 1957, Valerie Colston Robins; one *s* one *d*. *Educ:* Rugby Sch. Solicitor. Asst Solicitor, Lancs CC, 1955–56; Asst Solicitor, Manchester City Council, 1956–59; Sen. Solicitor, Berks CC, 1959–63; Asst Clerk, later Dep. Clerk, Northumberland CC, 1963–70; Dep. Chief Exec., Essex CC, 1970–76; Clerk of Essex Lieutenancy, 1976–. Assoc. of County Councils: Advisor, Police Cttee, 1976–83; Advisor, Policy Cttee, 1983–; Chm., Officers Adv. Gp, 1987–. Hon. Sec., Assoc. of County Chief Executives, 1983–90; Chm., Officers Adv. Panel, SE Regional Planning Conference, 1984–88. DL Essex, 1978. *Recreations:* gardening, ornithology. *Address:* The Christmas Cottage, Great Sampford, Saffron Walden, Essex. *T:* Great Sampford (079986) 363. *Club:* Law Society.

ADDERLEY, family name of **Baron Norton.**

ADDINGTON, family name of **Viscount Sidmouth.**

ADDINGTON, 6th Baron *cr* 1887; **Dominic Bryce Hubbard;** *b* 24 Aug. 1963; *s* of 5th Baron Addington and of Alexandra Patricia, *yr d* of late Norman Ford Millar; *S* father, 1982. *Educ:* Aberdeen Univ. (MA Hons). *Heir: b* Hon. Michael Walter Leslie Hubbard, *b* 6 July 1965. *Address:* 9/11 Chalk Hill Road, Norwich NR1 1SL.

ADDISON, family name of **Viscount Addison.**

ADDISON, 3rd Viscount *cr* 1945 of Stallingborough; **Michael Addison;** Baron Addison 1937; *b* 12 April 1914; 2nd *s* of 1st Viscount Addison, KG, PC, MD, FRCS, and Isobel McKinnon (*d* 1934), *d* of late Archibald Gray; *S* brother, 1976; *m* 1936, Kathleen Amy, *d* of Rt Rev. and Rt Hon. J. W. C. Wand, PC, KCVO, and Amy Agnes Wiggins; one *s* two *d*. *Educ:* Hele's School, Exeter; Balliol Coll., Oxford. BA (PPE) 1935, MA 1965. Min. of Labour, 1935; War Damage Commission, 1940. Served RAFVR, 1941–45, FO Intell. Branch. War Damage Commn and Central Land Bd, 1945–51; Min. of Supply/Aviation, 1951–63; HM Treasury, 1963–65; Sen. Lectr, Polytechnic of Central London (School of Management Studies), 1965–76; retired, 1976. Member: Royal Inst. of Public Administration; Assoc. of Teachers of Management. *Recreation:* gardening. *Heir: s* Hon. William Matthew Wand Addison [*b* 13 June 1945; *m* 1970, Joanna Mary, *e d* of late J. I. C. Dickinson; one *s* two *d*]. *Address:* Old Stables, Maplehurst, Horsham, West Sussex RH13 6RD. *T:* Lower Beeding (0403) 891298. *Club:* Oxford Union Society.

ADDISON, Prof. Cyril Clifford, PhD, DSc (Dunelm); FRS 1970; FInstP; FRSC; Professor of Inorganic Chemistry, University of Nottingham, 1960–78, Dean of Faculty of Pure Science, 1968–71, Leverhulme Emeritus Fellow, 1978; *b* 28 Nov. 1913; *s* of late Edward Thomas Addison and Olive Clifford; *m* 1939, Marjorie Whineray Thompson; one *s* one *d*. *Educ:* Workington and Millom Grammar Schools, Cumberland; University of Durham (Hatfield College). Scientific Officer, British Launderers' Research Assoc., 1936–38; Lectr, Harris Inst., Preston, 1938–39; Ministry of Supply, Chemical Inspection Dept, 1939–45; Chemical Defence Research Establ., 1945; Univ. of Nottingham: Lectr, 1946; Reader in Inorganic Chemistry, 1952. Lectures: Corday-Morgan, E Africa, 1969; Liversidge, 1976; Dist. Vis. Prof., Auburn Univ., Alabama, 1979–80. Member: Chemical Soc. Council, 1954–57 (Pres. 1976–77); Inst. of Chemistry Council, 1948–51 and 1962–65 (Vice-Pres., 1965–67). Hon. DSc: Dunelm, 1977; Warwick, 1979. *Publications:* The Chemistry of the Liquid Alkali Metals, 1984. Numerous papers in Jl Chemical Soc., Trans. Faraday Soc., etc. *Recreations:* mountain walking, gardening. *Address:* Department of Chemistry, The University, Nottingham NG7 2RD. *T:* Nottingham (0602) 484848.

ADDISON, Kenneth George, OBE 1978; Director, 1971–89, and Deputy Chief General Manager, 1976–84, Sun Alliance & London Insurance Group; *b* 1 Jan. 1923; *s* of Herbert George Addison and Ruby (*née* Leathers); *m* 1945, Maureen Newman; one *s* one *d*. *Educ:* Felixstowe Grammar Sch. LLB Hons London. Served RAF, 1942–46. Joined Alliance Assurance Co. Ltd, 1939; various subsequent appts; Asst Sec., Law Fire Insurance Office, 1960–64; Gen. Manager, Sun Alliance & London Insurance Group, 1971. Chm., Bourne Home Develts Ltd, 1989–; Dir, Sabre Insurance Co. Ltd, 1990–. Chairman: Fire Insurers' Res. & Testing Orgn, 1977–84; Management Cttee, Associated Insurers (British Electricity), 1977–84; Internat. Oil Insurers, 1979–82; Dir, Insurance Technical Bureau, 1977–84; Advr to Med. Defence Union, 1986–. Chm., Hearing Aid Council, 1971–78. Dir, Croydon Community Trust, 1990–. FCIS; FCII (Pres., 1980); FCIArb (Pres., 1968–69). *Publications:* papers on insurance and allied subjects. *Recreations:* swimming, carpentry, gardening. *Address:* Ockley, 13 Hillcroft Avenue, Purley, Surrey. *T:* 081–660 2793.

ADDISON, Michael Francis; His Honour Judge Addison; a Circuit Judge, since 1987; *b* 14 Sept. 1942; *s* of Joseph Addison and Wendy Blyth Addison; *m* 1979, Rosemary Hardy; one *s*. *Educ:* Eton; Trinity College, Cambridge (BA). Called to the Bar, Inner Temple, 1965. *Recreation:* gardening. *Address:* 2 Harcourt Buildings, Temple, EC4Y 9DB. *T:* 071–353 2112.

ADDISON, Dr Philip Harold, MRCS, LRCP; Hon. Consulting Secretary, The Medical Defence Union, since 1974 (Secretary, 1959–74); *b* 28 June 1909; 2nd *s* of late Dr Joseph Bartlett Addison and Mauricia Renée Addison; *m* 1934, Mary Norah Ryan; one *s* one *d*. *Educ:* Clifton Coll., Bristol; St Mary's Hosp. Medical Sch. MRCS, LRCP 1933; Gold Medallist, Military Medicine and Bronze Medallist Pathology, Army Medical Sch., Millbank, SW1, 1935. Permanent Commission, IMS, 1935; served Burma Campaign, 1943–45 (despatches). Chm., Ethical Cttee of Family Planning Assoc., 1956–60; Vice-Pres., Medico-Legal Soc., 1965–74. *Publications:* Professional Negligence, in Compendium of Emergencies, 1971; The Medico-Legal Aspects of General Anaesthesia, in, Clinical Practice of General Anaesthesia, 1971; contrib. Brit. Med. Jl, Irish Med. Jl, Proc. R.Soc.Med, Medico-Legal Jl, Lancet. *Recreations:* fishing, golf, bridge. *Address:* Red-Wyn-Byn, Monkmead Lane, West Chiltington, Pulborough, West Sussex. *T:* West Chiltington (07983) 3047. *Clubs:* East India, Devonshire, Sports and Public Schools; Shark Angling Club of Gt Britain; West Sussex Golf; BMA Bridge (Founder Mem.).

ADDISON, Sir William (Wilkinson), Kt 1974; JP; DL; Chairman of Council, The Magistrates' Association, 1970–76; *b* Mitton, WR Yorks, 4 April 1905; *s* of Joseph Addison, Bashall Eaves; *m* 1929, Phoebe, *d* of Robert Dean, Rimington, WR Yorks. Verderer of Epping Forest, 1957–84. Chm., Epping Petty Sessions, 1955–, combined Epping and Ongar Petty Sessions, 1968–76; Magistrates' Assoc.: Mem. Coun., 1959–76; Dep. Chm. of Coun., 1966–70; Chm., Treatment of Offenders Cttee, 1961–68; Chm. Exec. Cttee, 1968–75. Member: Hill Hall Prison Board of Visitors, 1955–70; Chelmsford Prison, 1958–77; Bullwood Hall Borstal, 1962–76; Home Sec.'s Adv. Coun. on Probation and After-Care, 1964–67; Lord Chancellor's Adv. Coun. on Trng of Magistrates, 1964–73; Magistrates' Courts Rule Cttee, 1968–74; Council, Commonwealth Magistrates Assoc., 1970–75; Assessor to Deptl Cttee on Liquor Licensing, 1971. Member: Court, Univ. of Essex, 1965–; Adv. Council, Univ. of Cambridge Inst. of Criminology, 1972–78; Vice-Pres., 1980, Pres., 1985–, Assoc. of Genealogists and Records Agents; Mem. Council, Essex Archaeol Soc., 1949–71 (Pres., 1964–67); Vice-Pres., Council for the Protection of Rural England (Essex), 1984–; Pres. or Chm. of several bodies connected with local history and the preservation of antiquities in Essex, inc. Victoria County History and Friends of Essex Churches. JP 1949, DL 1973, Essex. FSA 1965; FRHistS 1965. *Publications:* Epping Forest, 1945; The English Country Parson, 1947; Essex Heyday, 1949; Suffolk, 1950; Worthy Dr Fuller, 1951; English Spas, 1951; Audley End, 1953; English Fairs and Markets, 1953; Thames Estuary, 1953; In the Steps of Charles Dickens, 1955; Wanstead Park, 1973; Essex Worthies, 1973; Portrait of Epping Forest, 1977; Understanding English Place-Names, 1978; Understanding English Surnames, 1978; The Old Roads of England, 1980; Local Styles of the English Parish Church, 1982; Farmhouses in the English Landscape, 1986; Epping Forest: figures in a landscape, 1991. *Recreation:* exploring the English countryside for evidence of local history. *Address:* Ravensmere, Epping, Essex. *T:* Epping (0378) 73439.

ADDYMAN, Peter Vincent, FSA; Director, York Archaeological Trust, since 1972; *b* 12 July 1939; *y s* of Erik Thomas Waterhouse Addyman and Evelyn Mary (*née* Fisher); *m* 1965, Shelton (*née* Oliver), Atlanta, Ga; one *s* one *d*. *Educ:* Sedbergh Sch.; Peterhouse, Cambridge (MA). MIFA 1982; FSA 1967. Asst Lectr in Archaeology, 1962–64, Lectr, 1964–67, QUB; Lectr in Archaeol., Univ. of Southampton, 1967–72. Hon. Fellow, Univ. of York, 1972–; Hon. Reader, Univ. of Bradford, 1974–81. Directed excavations: Maxey, 1960; Lydford, 1964–67; Ludgershall Castle, 1964–72; Chalton, 1970–72. Vice-President: Council for British Archaeol., 1981–85; Royal Archaeol. Inst., 1979–83; Chairman: Standing Conf. of Archaeol Unit Managers, 1975–78; Inst. of Field Archaeologists, 1983–85. Chm., Cultural Resource Management Ltd, 1989– (Dir, 1979–); Academic Dir, Heritage Projects Ltd, 1984–. Hon. DSc Bradford, 1984; DUniv York, 1985. *Publications:* (gen. editor) The Archaeology of York, vols 1–20, 1976–91; (ed with V. E. Black) Archaeological Papers from York, 1984; papers in archaeol jls. *Recreations:*

gardening, watercolours, travel. *Address:* 50 Bootham, York YO3 7BZ. *T:* York (0904) 624311; York Archaeological Trust, 1 Pavement, York YO1 2NA. *T:* York (0904) 643211. *Clubs:* Athenæum; Yorkshire (York).

ADEANE, Hon. (George) Edward, CVO 1985; an Extra Equerry to HRH the Prince of Wales, since 1985; Director: Hambros Bank Ltd, since 1986; Guardian Royal Exchange Assurance plc, since 1985; English and Scottish Investors plc, since 1986; *b* 4 Oct. 1939; *s* of Baron Adeane, GCB, GCVO, PC and of Lady Adeane. *Educ:* Eton; Magdalene College, Cambridge (MA). Called to Bar, Middle Temple, July 1962. Page of Honour to HM the Queen, 1954–55; Private Sec. and Treas. to HRH the Prince of Wales, 1979–85; Treas. to TRH the Prince and Princess of Wales, 1981–85; Private Sec. to HRH the Princess of Wales, 1984–85. *Address:* B4 Albany, Piccadilly, W1. *T:* 071–734 9410.

ADEBO, Simeon Olaosebikan, Chief; The Okanlomo of Itoko and Egbaland, CFR 1979; CMG 1959; Chancellor, University of Lagos, Nigeria, since 1984; *b* 5 Oct. 1913; *s* of late Chief Adebo, the Okanlomo of Itoko, Abeokuta; *m* 1941, Regina Abimbola, *d* of Chief D. A. Majekodunmi, Abeokuta; three *s* one *d*. *Educ:* St Peter's Sch., Ake, Abeokuta; Abeokuta Grammar Sch.; King's Coll., Lagos, Nigeria. BA Hons (London) 1939; LLB Hons (London) 1946. Called to Bar, Gray's Inn, 1949. Accountant in trg, Nigerian Rly, 1933; Admin. Officer Cadet, Nigerian Govt, 1942; Asst Fin. Sec. to Govt of Nigeria, 1954; Western Nigeria: Admin. Officer, Class I, 1955; Perm. Sec., Min. of Finance, 1957; Perm. Sec. to Treasury and Head of Civil Service, 1958; Head of Civil Service and Chief Secretary to Government, 1961; Permanent Representative of Nigeria at UN and Comr-Gen. for Economic Affairs, 1962–67; UN Under-Secretary-General and Exec. Dir of UNITAR, 1968–72. Chancellor, Univ. of Ife, 1982–84. Mem., Constituent Assembly on draft constitution of Nigeria, 1977. Chairman: Nat. Universities Commn of Nigeria, 1975–77; Bd of Govs, Nat. Inst. for Policy and Strategic Studies, 1979–82. Mem., Soc. for Internat. Develt. Hon. LLD: Western Michigan, 1963; Nigeria, Nsukka, 1965; Fordham, 1966; Lincoln, 1966; Beaver Coll., 1966; Ife, 1968; Ibadan, 1969; Columbia, 1971; Ahmadu Bello (Nigeria), 1973; Open Univ., 1975; Lagos, Nigeria, 1978; Hon. DCL, Union Coll., 1965. *Publications:* (with Sir Sydney Phillipson) Report on the Nigerianisation of the Nigerian Civil Service, 1953; Our Unforgettable Years, 1984; Our International Years, 1988. *Recreation:* swimming. *Address:* Abimbola Lodge, Ibara, PO Box 139, Abeokuta, Nigeria. *Clubs:* Commonwealth Trust; Nigeria Society (Lagos); Abeokuta (Nigeria).

ADELAIDE, Archbishop of, and Metropolitan of South Australia, since 1991; **Most Rev. Ian Gordon Combe George,** AM 1989; *b* 12 Aug. 1934; *s* of late Gordon Frank George and Kathleen Mary George (*née* Combe); *m* 1964, Barbara Dorothy (*née* Peterson); one *d* (one *s* decd). *Educ:* St Peter's Coll., Adelaide; Univ. of Adelaide (LLB 1957); Gen. Theol Seminary, NY (MDiv 1964). Judges' Associate, Supreme Court of S Australia, 1955–57; barrister and solicitor, Australia, 1957–61. Ordained deacon and priest, New York, 1964; Assistant Curate: St Thomas', Mamaroneck, NY, USA, 1964–65; St David's, Burnside, SA, 1966–67; Priest-in-charge, St Barbara's, Woomera, SA and Chaplain and Welfare Officer, Australian Regular Army, 1967–69; Sub-Warden and Chaplain, St George's Coll., 1969–73, Lectr in History, 1969–73, Univ. of W Australia; Dean of Brisbane, Qld, 1973–81; Senior Chaplain (Army), Qld, 1975–81; Archdeacon of Canberra, 1981–89; Rector, St John's Church, Canberra, 1981–89; Asst Bp, Dio. of Canberra and Goulburn, 1989–91. Art Critic, The News, Adelaide, 1965–67. Trustee, Qld Art Gall., 1974–81. Founding Pres., Alcohol and Drug Problems Assoc. of Qld, 1975–81. Hon. DD Gen. Theol Seminary, NY, 1990. *Publications:* Meditations on the Life of Jesus, 1991; Making Worship Work, 1991; many articles in theol, church and aesthetics jls on art and religion. *Recreations:* gardening, reading, the Arts, wine, ski-ing. *Address:* Bishop's Court, Palmer Place, North Adelaide, SA 5006, Australia. *T:* (08) 267 2364; Church Office, 44 Currie Street, Adelaide, SA 5000, Australia. *T:* (08) 231 2402, *Fax:* (08) 211 8748. *Club:* Adelaide.

ADELAIDE, Archbishop of, (RC), since 1985; **Most Rev. Leonard Anthony Faulkner;** *b* Booleroo Centre, South Australia, 5 Dec. 1926. *Educ:* Sacred Heart Coll., Glenelg; Corpus Christi Coll., Werribee; Pontifical Urban University, Rome. Ordained Propaganda Fide Coll., Rome, 1 Jan. 1950. Asst Priest, Woodville, SA, 1950–57; Administrator, St Francis Xavier Cathedral, Adelaide, 1957–67; Diocesan Chaplain, Young Christian Workers, 1955–67; Mem., Nat. Fitness Council of SA, 1958–67; Bishop of Townsville, 1967–83; Coadjutor Archbishop of Adelaide, 1983–85. Chm., Aust. Catholic Bishops' Conf. Cttee for Laity, 1982– (Sec., 1968–82). *Address:* Catholic Diocesan Centre, Box 1364 GPO, Adelaide, SA 5001, Australia.

ADELAIDE, Dean of; *see* Renfrey, Rt Rev. L. E. W.

ADELSTEIN, Abraham Manie, MD; FRCP; FFCM; Visiting Professor, London School of Hygiene and Tropical Medicine, 1981–84, retired 1985; *b* 28 March 1916; *s* of Nathan Adelstein and Rosa Cohen; *m* 1942, Cynthia Gladys Miller; one *s* one *d*. *Educ:* Univ. of Witwatersrand. MB, ChB, MD. SAMC, 1941–45; Health Officer (res. and medical statistics), SA Railways, 1947–61; Sen. Lectr, Univ. of Manchester, 1961–67; OPCS, 1967–81 (SPMO and Chief Medical Statistician, 1975–81). Donald Reid Medal, LSHTM, 1979; Bisset Hawkins Medal, RCP, 1982. *Publications:* Thesis on Accident Proneness, 1950; papers in scientific jls on the distribution and aetiology of various diseases (diseases of heart, nervous system, respiratory system, cancer, accidents) and of methods of collecting, analysing and publishing national statistics. *Address:* 21 Dunstan Road, NW11 8AG. *T:* 081–455 9983.

ADEMOLA, Rt. Hon. Sir Adetokunbo (Adegboyega), GCON 1972; CFR 1963; PC 1963; KBE 1963; Kt 1957; Chancellor, University of Nigeria, since 1975; *b* 1 Feb. 1906; *e s* of late Sir Ladapo Ademola, Alake of Abeokuta, KBE, CMG; *m* 1939, Kofoworola, *yr d* of late Eric Olawolu Moore, CBE; three *s* two *d*. *Educ:* King's Coll., Lagos, Nigeria; Selwyn Coll., Cambridge. Attached to Attorney-General's Chambers, Lagos, Nigeria, 1934–35; Assistant Secretary, Secretariat, Southern Provinces, Nigeria, 1935–36; private law practice, Nigeria, 1936–39; Magistrate, Nigeria, 1939; served on commn for Revision of Courts Legislation, Nigeria, 1948; served on commn to enquire into Enugu (Nigeria) disturbances, 1949; Puisne Judge, Nigeria, 1949; Chief Justice, Western Region, Nigeria, 1955–58; Chief Justice of Nigeria, 1958–72. Deputy Chm., United Bank for Africa, 1972–74. Hon. Bencher, Middle Temple, 1959–. Chairman: Commonwealth Foundn, 1978–; Adv. Cttee on Conventions and Regulations of the ILO (Mem., 1962–); Member: Internat. Commn of Jurists, 1961– (now Hon. Mem.); Internat. Olympic Cttee, 1963–. Hon. LLD Ahmadu Bello, Nigeria, 1962; Hon. DSc Benin, 1972. *Recreations:* golf, horse racing. *Address:* The Close, Adetokunbo Ademola Street, Victoria Island, Lagos, Nigeria. *T:* Lagos 52219. *Clubs:* Island, Metropolitan, Yoruba Tennis (Lagos); Ibadan Recreation, Ibadan (Ibadan).

ADETILOYE, Most Rev. Joseph Abiodun; *see* Nigeria, Metropolitan Archbishop and Primate of.

ADIE, Jack Jesson, CMG 1962; BA (Oxon); *b* 1 May 1913; *s* of late P. J. Adie; *m* 1940, Patricia McLoughlin; one *s* two *d*. *Educ:* Shrewsbury Sch.; Magdalen Coll., Oxford. Entered Colonial Administrative Service, 1938; served in Zanzibar, 1938–48 (on military service, 1940–42 in Kenya Regt, KAR and Occupied Territory Administration), posts included: Private Sec. to The Sultan, Private Sec. to British Resident and Sen. Asst Sec.; seconded to Colonial Office, 1949–51, as Principal; Asst Sec., Kenya, 1951; Sec. for Educn and Labour, Kenya, 1952; Sec. for Educn, Labour and Lands, Kenya, 1954; acted as Minister for Educn, Labour and Lands, Kenya, Sept. 1955–Feb. 1956; Chief Sec., Barbados, 1957; Perm. Sec. for Forest Development, Game and Fisheries, Kenya, April-Dec. 1958; for Agriculture, Animal Husbandry and Water Resources, and Chm. African Land Development Bd, Dec. 1958–July 1959; for Housing, and Chm. Central Housing Bd, Nov. 1959–April 1960; for Housing, Common Services, Probation and Approved Schools, April 1960–April 1961; for Labour and Housing, 1961–62; acted as Minister for Labour and Housing, Jan.-April 1962; Perm. Sec. for Labour, 1962–63; retd from HMOCS, Jan 1964; Temp. Principal, Min. of Overseas Develt, 1964–69. Brilliant Star of Zanzibar, 4th class, 1947. *Address:* 3 Braemar, Kersfield Road, Putney, SW15.

ADIE, Kathryn, (Kate); Chief News Correspondent, BBC TV, since 1989; *b* 19 Sept. 1945; *d* of John Wilfrid Adie and Maud Adie (*née* Fambely). *Educ:* Sunderland Church High Sch.; Newcastle Univ. (BA Hons Scandinavian Studies). Technician and Producer, BBC Radio, 1969–76; Reporter, BBC TV South, 1977–78; Reporter, TV News, 1979–81, Correspondent, 1982. Words, BBC Radio 3 series, 1991. Hon. MA: Bath, 1987; Newcastle upon Tyne, 1990; Hon. DLitt City, 1989. RTS News Award, 1981 and 1987, Judges' Award, 1989; Monte Carlo Internat. TV News Award, 1981 and 1990; BAFTA Richard Dimbleby Award, 1989. *Address:* c/o BBC TV, Wood Lane, W12. *T:* 081–576 7487.

ADIE, Rt. Rev. Michael Edgar; *see* Guildford, Bishop of.

ADISESHIAH, Dr Malcolm Sathianathan; Member of Parliament, Rajya Sabha, 1978–84; Vice-Chancellor, University of Madras, 1975–78; Director, Madras Institute of Development Studies, 1971–78, now Chairman and Fellow; *b* 18 April 1910; *s* of Varanasi Adiseshiah and Nesammah Adiseshiah; *m* 1951, Sanchu Pothan. *Educ:* Univ. of Madras (MA); LSE, London Univ. (PhD). Lectr in Econs, St Paul's Coll., Calcutta, 1931–36; Prof. of Econs, Madras Christian Coll., 1940–46; Associate Gen. Sec., World Univ. Service, Geneva, 1946–48; Unesco, Paris: Dep. Dir, Dept of Exchange of Persons, 1948–50; Dir, Dept of Tech. Assistance, 1950–54; Asst Dir-Gen., 1954–63; Dep. Dir-Gen., 1963–70. Chairman: Tamil Nadu State Council for Science and Technology, 1984–; Governing Bd, Internat. Inst. for Educnl Planning, 1981–. *Publications:* Demand for Money, 1938; Agricultural Development, 1941; Rural Credit, 1943; Planning Industrial Development, 1944; Non-political UN, 1964; Economics of Indian and Industrial Natural Resources, 1966; Education and National Development, 1967; Adult Education, 1968; Let My Country Awake, 1970; It is Time to Begin, 1972; Techniques of Perspective Planning, 1973; Plan Implementation Problems and Prospects for the Fifth Plan, 1974; Science in the Battle against Poverty, 1974; Literacy Discussion, 1976; Towards a Functional Learning Society, 1976; Backdrop to Learning Society: educational perspectives for Tamil Nadu, 1977; Adult Education faces Inequality, 1980; Mid Term Appraisal of the VI Plan, 1982; Mid Year Review of the Economy, 1976–83; Some Thoughts on the VII Five Year Plan 1985–86 to 1989–90, 1985; Shaping National Events—the economy, 1985; VII Plan Perspectives, 1985; Mid-Year Review of the Economy, 1985, 1986; Comments on the Black Economy, 1986; Role of Foreign Trade in the Indian Economy, 1986; Entrepreneur Development for Tamil Nadu, 1986; Mid Year Review of the Economy, 1987–88; Mid-Term Assessment of the VII Plans 1985–86 to 1989–90; Madras Development Seminar Series, 1971–. *Address:* 21 Cenotaph Road, Madras-600018, India. *T:* Madras 440144.

ADLER, George Fritz Werner, OBE 1982; FEng, FIMechE; FICE; Director of Research, British Hydromechanics Research Association, 1971–86; *b* 12 Jan. 1926; *s* of Fritz Jacob Sigismund Adler and Hildegard Julie Adler (*née* Lippmann); *m* 1949, June Moonaheim Margaret Nash; three *d*. *Educ:* Penarth County School; Cardiff Technical Coll.; University Coll., Cardiff; Imperial Coll., London. BSc (Eng), DIC. Design Engineer, 1948, Chief, Mechanical Develt, 1953, English Electric, Rugby; Chief Mechanical Engineer, 1958, Gen. Manager Mech. Products, Marconi, 1962; Manager, Mech. Products Div., English Electric, 1966. Dir, Fluid Engineering Products Ltd, 1982–84. Vice-Pres., 1979, Pres., 1983, IMechE; Chm., CDRA (Fedn of Technology Centres), 1981–83; Mem., Engineering Council, 1986–89; Treasurer, Fellowship of Engrg, 1988–. FBIM; FInstD. Eur Ing, FEANI, 1987. *Publications:* chapter, Water Turbines (jtly), in Kempe's Engineers' Year Book, 1956; articles in technical jls. *Recreations:* gardening, swimming, music. *Address:* The Haining, Orchard Close, Longburton, Sherborne, Dorset DT9 5PP. *T:* Holnest (096321) 641. *Club:* Carlton.

ADLER, Larry, (Lawrence Cecil Adler); mouth organist; *b* 10 Feb. 1914; *s* of Louis Adler and Sadie Hack; *m* 1st, 1938, Eileen Walser (marr. diss. 1961); one *s* two *d*; 2nd, 1969, Sally Cline (marr. diss. 1977); one *d*. *Educ:* Baltimore City Coll. Won Maryland Harmonica Championship, 1927; first stage appearance, 1928 (NY); first British appearance, 1934 (in C. B. Cochran's Streamline revue); first appearance as soloist with Symphony Orchestra, Sydney, Australia, 1939; jt recital tours with dancer Paul Draper, US, 1941–49; soloist with NY Philharmonic and other major US Orchestras, also orchestras in England, Japan and Europe; war tours for Allied Troops, 1943, 1944, 1945; Germany, 1947, 1949; Korea (Brit. Commonwealth Div.), 1951; Israel (Six Day War), 1967; (Yom Kippur War), 1973; articles and book reviews in Sunday Times, New Statesman, Spectator, New Society, Observer, Punch; restaurant critic: Harpers & Queen, London Portrait; Boardroom; Chamber Life; columnist: What's On in London, Jazz Express, Jewish Gazette; numerous TV One Man Shows; soloist, Edinburgh Festival, playing first performance of unpublished Gershwin quartet (MS gift to Adler from I. Gershwin, 1963; works composed for Adler by: Dr Ralph Vaughan Williams, Malcolm Arnold, Darius Milhaud, Arthur Benjamin, Gordon Jacob, Cyril Scott, Francis Chagrin, Joaquin Rodrigo and others. Hon. Diploma: Peabody Conservatory of Music, Baltimore, 1986; City Coll., Baltimore, 1986. *Compositions:* film scores: Genevieve; King and Country; High Wind in Jamaica; The Great Chase, etc; TV scores: Midnight Men (BBC serial); various TV plays and documentaries; music for TV commercials, children's records, stage plays, etc; concert music: Theme and Variations; Camera III; One Man Show, From Hand to Mouth, Edinburgh Festival, 1965 (other festivals, 1965–). *Publications:* How I Play, 1937; Larry Adler's Own Arrangements, 1960; Jokes and How to Tell Them, 1963; It Ain't Necessarily So (autobiog.), 1985. *Recreations:* tennis, journalism, cycling, conversation; obsession: writing letters to Private Eye. *Address:* c/o MBA Literary Agents Ltd, 45 Fitzroy Street, W1P 5HR. *T:* 071–387 2076. *Clubs:* Groucho, Scribes; Paddington Tennis.

ADLER, Prof. Michael William, MD; FRCP, FFCM; Professor of Genito Urinary Medicine, and Consultant Physician, Middlesex Hospital and Medical School, since 1979; *b* 12 June 1939; *s* of late Gerhard and of Hella Adler; *m* 1st, 1966, Susan Jean (marr. diss. 1978); 2nd, 1979, Karen Hope Dunnell; two *d*. *Educ:* Bryanston Sch.; Middlesex Hosp. Med. Sch. MB BS 1965, MD 1977; MRCP 1970, FRCP 1984; MFCM 1977, FFCM 1983. House Officer and Registrar in Medicine, Middlesex, Central Middlesex and Whittington Hosps, 1965–69; Lectr, St Thomas' Hosp. Med. Sch., 1970–75; Sen. Lectr,

Middlesex Hosp. Med. Sch., 1975–79. Advr in Venereology, WHO, 1983–; Mem., Expert Adv. Gp on AIDS, 1984–, Chief Scientist's Advr, Res. Liaison Gp (Child Health), 1985–, Mem., Sub-Gp on Monitoring and Surveillance, 1987–88, DHSS. Medical Research Council: Member: Res. Adv. Gp on Epidemiol Studies of Sexually Transmitted Diseases, 1975–80; Working Party to co-ordinate Lab. Studies on the Gonococcus, 1979–83; Working Party on AIDS, 1981–87; Sub-Cttee on Therapeutic Studies, 1985–87; Cttee on Epidemiol Studies on AIDS, 1985–; Cttee on Clinical Studies of Prototype Vaccines against AIDS, 1987–. Member: Med. Adv. Cttee, Brook Adv. Centres, 1984–; Working Gp on AIDS, European Commn, 1985–; AIDS Working Party, BMA, 1986–; Exec. Cttee, Internat. Union Against the Venereal Diseases and Treponematoses, 1986–. Mem., Specialist Adv. Cttee on Genito Urinary Medicine, Jt Cttee of Higher Med. Trng, 1981–86 (Sec., 1981–82; Chm., 1983–86) Royal College of Physicians: Member: Cttee on Genito Urinary Medicine, 1984– (Sec., 1984–87; Chm., 1987–); Working Gp on AIDS, FCM, 1985–; Mem. Council, Med. Soc. for the Study of Venereal Diseases. Dir, Terrence Higgins Trust, 1982–88; Trustee, Nat. AIDS Trust, 1987– (Chm., Grants and Gen. Purposes Cttee, 1988–); Adviser: AIDS Crisis Trust, 1986–; Parly All Party Cttee on AIDS, 1987–. Patron, Albany Soc., 1987–91. Evian Health Award, 1990. Member, Editorial Panel: Genito Urinary Medicine; Current Opinion on Infections Diseases; Enfermedades de Transmission Sexual; also Ed., AIDS, 1986–; Consultant Editor, AIDS Letter, RSM, 1987–89. *Publications:* ABC of Sexually Transmitted Diseases, 1984, 2nd edn 1990; (ed) ABC of AIDS, 1987, 2nd edn 1991; (ed) Diseases in the Homosexual Male, 1988; articles on sexually transmitted diseases and AIDS in med. jls. *Recreations:* yoga, jogging. *Address:* Academic Department of Genito Urinary Medicine, James Pringle House, Middlesex Hospital, W1N 8AA. *T:* 071–380 9146.

ADLEY, Robert James; MP (C) Christchurch, since 1983 (Bristol North East, 1970–74; Christchurch and Lymington, 1974–83); Director and Marketing Consultant, Commonwealth Holiday Inns of Canada Ltd; *b* 2 March 1935; *s* of Harry and Marie Adley; *m* 1961, Jane Elizabeth Pople; two *s*. *Educ:* Falconbury; Uppingham. Lived and worked in: Malaya, Singapore, Thailand; established Pearl & Dean (Thailand) Ltd, 1956; Sales Director, May Fair Hotel, 1960–64; Director: William Jacks plc, 1984–; Adley Pritchard Ltd, 1989–; Home Rouxl Ltd, 1990–. Chairman: Parly Tourism Cttee; British-Jordanian Parly Gp; British-ASEAN Parly Gp; British-Chinese Parly Gp; Pres., Western Area Young Conservatives, 1972. Member: Nat. Council, British Hotels, Restaurants and Caterers Assoc.; Railway Correspondence and Travel Soc.; Cttee, National Railway Museum; Founder and First Chm., Brunel Soc.; Trustee, Brunel Engineering Centre Trust; Patron, SS Great Britain Project. *Publications:* Hotels, the Case for Aid, 1966; One Man, No Vote, 1976; A Policy for Tourism, 1977; British Steam in Cameracolour 1962–68, 1979; Take It or Leave It, 1980; In Search of Steam, 1981; The Call of Steam, 1982; To China for Steam, 1983; All Change Hong Kong, 1984; In Praise of Steam, 1985; Wheels, 1987; Covering my Tracks, 1988; Out of Steam, 1990. *Recreations:* railway photography, railway enthusiast. *Address:* House of Commons, SW1A 0AA. *T:* 071–219 4438. *Club:* Carlton.

ADMANI, Dr Haji (Abdul) Karim, OBE 1987; JP; FRCPGlas; Consultant Physician, Sheffield Area Health Authority (Teaching), since 1970; Hon. Clinical Lecturer in Medicine, Sheffield University Medical School, since 1972; *b* 19 Sept. 1937; *s* of late Haji Abdul Razzak Admani (Electrical Engr in India), and of Hajiani Rahima Admani; *m* 1968, Seema (*née* Robson; Nursing Dir); one *s* one *d*. *Educ:* Gujarat Univ., India (BSc 1st Cl. Hons 1956); Karachi Univ., Pakistan (MB, BS 1962). DTM&H 1963; MRCPE (Neurology), 1967; FRCPE 1979; Associate MRCP; MRCPGlas 1987, FRCPGlas 1988; FRSM 1988. Sec. Med. Div., Northern Dist, Sheffield, 1972–75; Mem. Dist Med. Cttee, N Dist, 1975–; Area Rep. and Mem. Exec. Cttee, BMA, Sheffield, 1975–; Member: Sheffield AHA, 1977–82; GMC, 1979–; Chm., Overseas Doctors' Training Scheme, ODA, 1986–. Vis. Prof. of Medicine and Neurology, Quaid-e-Azam Med. Coll., Bhawalpur, Pakistan, 1989. President: British Red Cross Soc. for Co. of S Yorks, 1982– (County MO, 1974–82); Muslim Council of Sheffield, Rotherham and dist, 1977– (Chm., 1970–76); Sheffield and N Reg., Pakistan Med. Soc. in UK, 1972–; Anglo-Asian Soc., Sheffield, 1973–; Union of Pakistani Orgns in UK and Europe, 1979– (Sen. Vice Pres., 1978–79); Overseas Doctors' Assoc. in UK, 1987– (Vice-Chm., 1975–81, Chm., 1981–88; Chm. Post-grad. Med. Sub-Cttee, 1975; Chm. S Yorks Div., 1976–; Chm., Inf., Advice and Welfare Centre, 1977–82; Fellow, 1985). Chairman: Islamic Centre Man. Cttee, Sheffield, 1973–; BBC Radio Sheffield Adv. Council, 1982–. Vice-Chairman: National Org. of Afro-Asian-Caribbean People in UK, 1977; Sheffield Cttee for Racial Equality, 1981–. Member: Exec. Cttee, Standing Conf. of Pakistani Orgs in UK, 1976– (Chm. Standing Conf., 1974–76); Asian Action Cttee (National), 1976; Exec. Cttee, Sheffield Community Relations Council, 1974–76; Adv. Council, IBA for Radio Hallam, Sheffield, 1975–81; National Cttee for Campaign against Rickets and Osteomalacia, 1980– (Chm., Sheffield Cttee, 1981–); Central Cttee for Hosp. Med. Services in UK, 1979–. Pres., Sheffield Stroke Club, 1977. Member: British Geriatric Soc.; Medico-Chirurgical Soc. Sheffield; Abbeydale Rotary Club, Sheffield; BMA (Fellow 1988); Collegiate Cttee of Edinburgh; Magistrates' Assoc. JP City of Sheffield, 1974. *Publication:* (ed) Guidance for Overseas Doctors in National Health Service, 1982. *Recreations:* tennis, cricket, chess, football, golf, table tennis. *Address:* 1 Derriman Glen, Silverdale Road, Sheffield S11 9LQ. *T:* Sheffield (0742) 360465.

ADRIAN, family name of **Baron Adrian.**

ADRIAN, 2nd Baron, *cr* 1955, of Cambridge; **Richard Hume Adrian,** MD; FRCP 1987; FRS 1977; Professor of Cell Physiology, University of Cambridge, since 1978; Master of Pembroke College, since 1981; Vice-Chancellor, University of Cambridge, 1985–87; *b* 16 Oct. 1927; *o s* of 1st Baron Adrian, OM, FRS, FRCP, and Hester Agnes, DBE 1965 (*d* 1966), *o d* of late Hume C. and Dame Ellen Pinsent, DBE, Birmingham; *S* father, 1977; *m* 1967, Lucy Caroe, MA, PhD. *Educ:* Swarthmore High Sch., USA; Westminster Sch.; Trinity Coll., Cambridge (MA). MB, BChir Cantab. UCH, 1951; National Service, RAMC, 1952–54; Univ. of Cambridge: G. H. Lewes Student, Physiol Lab., 1954; Univ. Demonstr, 1956; Fellow, Corpus Christi Coll., 1956; Univ. Lectr, 1961; Reader in Exptl Biophysics, 1968; Fellow of Churchill Coll., 1961–81, Hon. Fellow 1985; Hon. Fellow, Darwin Coll., 1987. Mem., British Library Bd, 1987–; Trustee: British Museum, 1979–; British Museum (Nat. Hist.), 1984–88; Mem. Council, Royal Soc., 1984. For. Mem., Amer. Philosophical Soc. Prime Warden, Goldsmiths' Co., 1990–91. Docteur *hc* Poitiers, 1975. *Publications:* articles in Jl of Physiol. *Recreations:* sailing, skiing. *Address:* The Master's Lodge, Pembroke College, Cambridge CB2 1RF. *T:* Cambridge (0223) 338129; Umgeni, Cley, Holt, Norfolk NR25 7RY. *T:* Cley (0263) 740597.

ADRIEN, Sir J. F. M. L.; *see* Latour-Adrien.

ADSHEAD, Mary; *m* 1929, Stephen Bone (*d* 1958); two *s* one *d*. Trained at Slade School under Prof. Henry Tonks. Mural paintings in public and private buildings; illustrations, designs for GPO stamps. Chief works: murals in: Restaurant at Luton Hoo; St Peter's Church, Vauxhall Estate, Luton; Civic Centre, Plymouth; Town Hall, Totnes; Commonwealth Inst.; Messrs Costain & Sons; The Post House, Leicester; Beatson Mural, Beatson Walk Underpass, Rotherhithe, 1982 (mosaic mural depicting the return of the Fighting Temeraire to Rotherhithe; mediums used were mosaics, high fired tiles, cast iron; mould for canon and aluminium strip framework for ships; also various screeds; work carried out for Southwark Council in conjunction with Land Use Consultants); exhibn of easel pictures, Sally Hunter Gall., 1986; exhibn of watercolours, Sally Hunter Gall., 1989. *Recreations:* swimming, travel (has visited by car France and Italy, by air Western Canada, USA, Turkey, Russia and Sweden).

See also Q. Bone.

ADYE, John Anthony; Director, Government Communications Headquarters, since 1989; *b* 24 Oct. 1939; *s* of Arthur Francis Capel Adye and Hilda Marjorie Adye (*née* Elkes); *m* 1961, Anne Barbara, *d* of Dr John Aeschlimann, Montclair, NJ; two *s* one *d*. *Educ:* Leighton Park Sch.; Lincoln Coll., Oxford (MA). Joined GCHQ, 1962; Principal, 1968; British Embassy, Washington, 1973–75; Nat. Defence Coll., Latimer, 1975–76; Asst Sec., 1977–83; Under Sec., 1983–89. *Address:* Government Communications Headquarters, Priors Road, Cheltenham, Glos. *Club:* Naval and Military.

AGA KHAN (IV), His Highness Prince Karim, granted title His Highness by the Queen, 1957, granted title His Royal Highness by the Shah of Iran, 1959; *b* Creux-de-Genthod, Geneva, 13 Dec. 1936; *s* of late Prince Aly Salomon Khan and of Princess Joan Aly Khan, now Viscountess Camrose (*née* Joan Barbara Yarde-Buller, *e d* of 3rd Baron Churston, MVO, OBE); became Aga Khan, spiritual leader and Imam of Ismaili Muslims all over the world on the death of his grandfather, Sir Sultan Mohamed Shah, Aga Khan III, GCSI, GCIE, GCVO, 11 July 1957; *m* 1969, Sarah Frances Croker-Poole; two *s* one *d*. *Educ:* Le Rosey, Switzerland; Harvard University (BA Hons 1959). Leading owner and breeder of race horses in France, UK and Ireland; won Derby, 1981 (Shergar), 1986 (Shahrastani), 1988 (Kahyasi) and Prix de L'Arc de Triomphe, 1982 (Akiyda); Prix de Jockey Club: Charlottesville, 1980; Top Ville, 1979; Darshaan, 1984; Mouktar, 1985; Nanoun, 1987. President: Aga Khan Foundn, Geneva, 1967 (also branches in Bangladesh, Canada, Egypt, India, Kenya, Pakistan, Portugal, UK and US); Aga Khan Award for Architecture, 1976–; Inst. of Ismaili Studies, 1977–; Aga Khan Trust for Culture, Geneva, 1988. Founder and Chancellor, Aga Khan Univ., Pakistan, 1983. Doctor of Laws (*hc*): Peshawar Univ., Pakistan, 1967; Sind Univ., Pakistan, 1970; McGill Univ., Canada, 1983; Hon. DLitt London, 1989. Thomas Jefferson Meml Foundn Medal in Architecture, 1984; Amer. Inst. of Architects' Inst. Honor, 1984; Medalla de Oro, Consejo Superior de Colegios de Arquitectos, Spain, 1987. Commandeur, Ordre du Mérite Mauritanien, 1960; Grand Croix: Order of Prince Henry the Navigator, Portugal, 1960; l'Ordre National de la Côte d'Ivoire, 1965; l'Ordre National de la Haute-Volta, 1965; l'Ordre Malgache, 1966; l'Ordre du Croissant Vert des Comores, 1966; Grand Cordon, Order of the Taj, Iran, 1967; Nishan-i-Imtiaz, Pakistan, 1970; Cavaliere di Gran Croce della Republica Italiana, 1977; Grand Officier, l'Ordre National du Lion, Sénégal, 1982; Nishan-e-Pakistan, Pakistan, 1983; Grand Cordon, Ouissam-al Arch, Morocco, 1986; Cavaliere del Lavoro, Italy, 1988. *Recreations:* ski-ing, yachting. *Address:* Aiglemont, 60270 Gouvieux, France. *Clubs:* Royal Yacht Squadron; Yacht Club Costa Smeralda (Founder Pres.) (Sardinia); Pevero Golf (Founder Pres.) (Sardinia).

AGA KHAN, Prince Sadruddin; Consultant to the Secretary-General of the UN, since 1978; Co-ordinator, UN Humanitarian and Economic Assistance Programmes relating to Afghanistan, since 1988; Founding Member and President, Groupe de Bellerive; Founding Member and Chairman, Independent Commission on Internal Humanitarian Issues, 1983; *b* 17 Jan. 1933; *s* of His late Highness Sir Sultan Mohamed Shah, Aga Khan III, GCSI, GCIE, GCVO and of Andrée Joséphine Caron; *m* 1957, Nina Sheila Dyer (marr. diss., 1962); *m* 1972, Catherine Aleya Sursock. *Educ:* Harvard Univ. (BA); Harvard Grad. Sch. Arts and Sciences; Centre of Middle Eastern Studies. Unesco Consultant for Afro-Asian Projects, 1958; Head of Mission and Adviser to UN High Comr for Refugees, 1959–60; Unesco Special Consultant to Dir-Gen., 1961; Exec. Sec., Internat. Action Cttee for Preservation of Nubian Monuments, 1961; UN Dep. High Comr for Refugees, 1962–65; UN High Comr for Refugees, 1965–77. Vice Pres., WWF, 1986–. Dr *hc*: Fletcher Sch. of Law and Diplomacy, 1986; Univ. of Nice, 1988. Hon. Citizen Geneva, 1978. UN Human Rights Award, 1978; Hammarsköld Medal, German UN Assoc., 1979; Olympia Prize, Alexander S. Onassis Foundn, 1982; Man of Peace Award, 1989. Grand Cross: Order of St Silvestro (Papal), 1963; Order of Homayoun (Iran), 1967; Order of the Royal Star of Great Comoro (Comoro Is), 1970; Order of the Two Niles (First Class) Sudan, 1973; Commander's Cross with Star, Order of Merit of Polish People's Republic, 1977; Commandeur de la Légion d'Honneur (France), 1979. *Publications:* Lectures on refugee problems delivered to RSA and Acad. Internat. Law, The Hague; Violations of Human Rights and Mass Exodus, study for UN Commn on Human Rights, 1981. *Recreations:* Islamic art, sailing, ski-ing, hiking, kite-flying. *Address:* Château de Bellerive, 1245 Collonge-Bellerive, Canton of Geneva, Switzerland. *Clubs:* Travellers' (Paris); Knickerbocker (New York).

AGAR, family name of **Earl of Normanton.**

AGER, Rear-Adm. Kenneth Gordon, CB 1977; retired Royal Navy 1977; *b* 22 May 1920; *s* of Harold Stoddart Ager and Nellie Maud (*née* Tate); *m* 1944, Muriel Lydia Lanham; one *s* one *d*. *Educ:* Dulwich Central Sch. and Royal Navy. Called up for War Service, RN, 1940; Sub Lt (Special Br.) RNVR, 1943; Lieut (Electrical) RN, 1944; Weapons and Elect. Engr; Comdr (WE) 1958; Captain (E) 1966; Fleet Weapons and Elect. Engr Officer, 1969–71; Sen. Officers' War Course, 1971–72; CSO (Eng) to Flag Off. Scotland and NI, and Captain Fleet Maintenance, Rosyth, 1972–75; Rear-Adm. (E) 1975; Flag Off., Admiralty Interview Bd, 1975–77. *Recreations:* bowls, reading. *Club:* Royal Naval and Royal Albert Yacht (Portsmouth).

AGLIONBY, Francis John; His Honour Judge Aglionby; a Circuit Judge, since 1980; *b* 17 May 1932; *s* of Francis Basil and Marjorie Wycliffe Aglionby; *m* 1967, Susan Victoria Mary Vaughan; one *s* one *d*. *Educ:* Charterhouse; Corpus Christi Coll., Oxford (MA). Barrister, Inner Temple, 1956, Bencher, 1976; a Recorder of the Crown Court, 1975–80. Chancellor of Diocese: of Birmingham, 1971–; of Portsmouth, 1978–; of Carlisle, 1991–. Held Home Office enquiry into Horserace Totalisator Bd's bets transmissions procedures, 1979. *Recreations:* variable. *Address:* The Croft, Houghton, Carlisle, Cumbria CA3 0LD. *T:* Carlisle (0228) 23747; 8 King's Bench Walk, Temple EC4Y 7DU. *T:* 071–583 4306. *Club:* Brooks's.

AGNELLI, Dr Giovanni; industrialist; Chairman: Fiat, since 1966; Istituto Finanziario Industriale, since 1959; IFINT, SA, Luxembourg, since 1974; Giovanni Agnelli Foundation, since 1968; Chairman, Editrice La Stampa, since 1982; *b* Turin, Italy, 12 March 1921; *s* of Edoardo Agnelli, and *g s* of Giovanni Agnelli, founder of Fabbrica Italiana Automobili Torino (FIAT); *m* 1953, Princess Marella Caracciolo di Castagneto; one *s* one *d*. *Educ:* Turin. DrJur, Univ. of Turin, 1943. Member Board: Eurafrance, Paris; Mediobanca; Credito Italiano; Italian Stock Cos Assoc.; Turin Industrial Assoc.; Member: Exec. Bd, Confedn of Italian Industry; Internat. Adv. Cttee, Chase Manhattan Bank, NY; Atlantic Adv. Council, United Technologies Corp.; European Adv. Council, Merck; Adv. Bd, Petrofina; Internat. Indust. Conf., San Francisco; Exec. Cttee, Trilateral Commn,

Paris; Adv. Bd, Bilderberg Meetings; European Round Table of Industrialists. Vice-Chm., Assoc. for Monetary Union of Europe. Hon. Chm., Council for US and Italy. Romanes Lectr, Univ. of Oxford, 1991. Hon. Fellow, Magdalen Coll., Oxford, 1991. Corresp. Mem., Moral and Political Scis Acad., Institut de France. *Address:* 10 Corso Marconi, Turin, Italy. *T:* 65651.

AGNEW, Sir Anthony Stuart; *see* Agnew, Sir J. A. S.

AGNEW OF LOCHNAW, Sir Crispin Hamlyn, 11th Bt *cr* 1629; Chief of the Name and Arms of Agnew; Advocate; Rothesay Herald of Arms, since 1986; *b* 13 May 1944; *s* of (Sir) Fulque Melville Gerald Noel Agnew of Lochnaw, 10th Bt and of Swanzie, *d* of late Major Esmé Nourse Erskine, CMG, MC; *S* father, 1975; *m* 1980, Susan (journalist, broadcaster; formerly Advertising Exec.), *yr d* of J. W. Strang Steel, Logie, Kirriemuir, Angus; one *s* three *d*. *Educ:* Uppingham; RMA, Sandhurst. Major RARO (retd 1981), late RHF. Slains Pursuivant of Arms to Lord High Constable of Scotland, 1978–81; Unicorn Pursuivant of Arms, 1981–86. Leader: Army Expedn to E Greenland, 1968; Jt Services Expedn to Chilean Patagonia, 1972–73; Army Expedn to Api, NW Nepal, 1980; Member: RN Expedn to E Greenland, 1966; Jt Services to Elephant Island (Antarctica), 1970–71; Army Nuptse Expedn, 1975; Jt British and Royal Nepalese Army Everest Expedn, 1976 (reached the South Col). *Publications:* (jtly) Allan and Chapman, Licensing (Scotland) Act 1976, 2nd edn 1989; articles in newspapers and magazines, and in legal and heraldic jls. *Recreations:* mountaineering, sailing (Yacht Pippa's Song), heraldry. *Heir: s* Mark Douglas Noel Agnew, *b* 24 April 1991. *Address:* 6 Palmerston Road, Edinburgh EH9 1TN. *Club:* Army and Navy.

AGNEW, Sir Godfrey; *see* Agnew, Sir W. G.

AGNEW, Sir (John) Anthony Stuart, 4th Bt, *cr* 1895; *b* 25 July 1914; *s* of Sir John Stuart Agnew, 3rd Bt, TD, DL, and Kathleen (*d* 1971), *d* of late I. W. H. White, Leeds; *S* father, 1957. *Educ:* privately in Switzerland. *Heir: b* Major George Keith Agnew, TD [*b* 25 Nov. 1918; *m* 1948, Anne Merete Louise, *yr d* of Baron Johann Schaffalitzky de Muckadell, Fyn, Denmark; two *s*]. *Address:* c/o Blackthorpe Farm, Rougham, Bury St Edmunds, Suffolk.

AGNEW, Jonathan Geoffrey William; Chief Executive, Kleinwort Benson Group since 1989; Chairman, Kleinwort Benson Ltd, since 1989; *b* 30 July 1941; *er s* of Sir Geoffrey Agnew and Hon. Doreen Maud, *y d* of 1st Baron Jessel, CB, CMG; *m* 1st, 1966, Hon. Joanna Campbell (marr. diss. 1985); one *s* two *d*; 2nd, 1990, Marie-Claire, *d* of Bernard Dreesmann. *Educ:* Eton College; Trinity College, Cambridge (MA). The Economist, 1964–65; World Bank, 1965–67; Hill Samuel & Co., 1967–73, Dir, 1971; Morgan Stanley & Co., 1973–82, a Managing Dir, 1977; financial consultant, 1983–86; Chief Exec., ISRO, 1986–87; Kleinwort Benson, 1987–. *Address:* Flat E, 51 Eaton Square, SW1W 9BE. *T:* 071-235 7589. *Clubs:* White's; Automobile (Paris).

AGNEW, Peter Graeme, MBE 1946; BA; retired; Deputy Chairman, Bradbury Agnew & Co. Ltd (Proprietors of Punch), 1969–84; *b* 7 April 1914; *s* of late Alan Graeme Agnew; *m* 1937, Mary Diana (*née* Hervey); two *s* two *d*. *Educ:* Kingsmead, Seaford; Stowe School; Trinity College, Cambridge. Student Printer, 1935–37. Joined Bradbury Agnew & Co. Ltd, 1937. RAFVR 1937. Served War of 1939–45; Demobilised, 1945, as Wing Commander. *Recreations:* sailing, gardening. *Address:* The Old House, Manaccan, Helston, Cornwall TR12 6HR. *T:* Manaccan (032623) 468.

See also Col N.T. Davies.

AGNEW, Rudolph Ion Joseph; Chairman: Sealink Stena Line, since 1990; TVS Entertainment, since 1990; *b* 12 March 1934; *s* of Rudolph John Agnew and Pamela Geraldine (*née* Campbell); *m* 1980, Whitney Warren. *Educ:* Downside School. Commissioned officer, 8th King's Royal Irish Hussars, 1953–57. Joined Consolidated Gold Fields, 1957; Dep. Chm., 1978–82; Gp Chief Exec., 1978–89; Chm., 1983–89; Mem., Cttee of Man. Dirs, 1986–89. Dir, Hanson Trust, 1989–91. Vice President: Nat. Assoc. of Boys' Clubs; Game Conservancy (Fellow); Mem. Council, WWF (UK), 1989– (Trustee, 1983–89); Trustee, Hawk Trust. CBIM; FRSA. *Recreation:* shooting. *Address:* 1 The Park, Highgate, N6 4EU. *Club:* Cavalry and Guards.

AGNEW, Spiro Theodore, (Ted); *b* Baltimore, Md, 9 Nov. 1918; *s* of Theodore S. Agnew and Margaret Akers; *m* 1942, Elinor Isabel Judefind; one *s* three *d*. *Educ:* Forest Park High Sch., Baltimore; Johns Hopkins Univ.; Law Sch., Univ. Baltimore (LLB). Served War of 1939–45 with 8th and 10th Armd Divs, 1941–46, company combat comdr in France and Germany (Bronze Star). Apptd to Zoning Bd of Appeals of Baltimore County, 1957 (Chm., 1958–61); County Executive, Baltimore County, 1962–66; Governor of Maryland, 1967–68; Vice-President of the United States, 1969–73. Republican. With Pathlite Inc., Crofton, Md, 1974–. *Publication:* The Canfield Decision, 1976. *Recreations:* golf, tennis.

AGNEW, Stanley Clarke, CB 1985; FEng 1985; FICE; Chief Engineer, Scottish Development Department, 1976–87, retired; *b* 18 May 1926; *s* of Christopher Gerald Agnew and Margaret Eleanor Agnew (*née* Clarke); *m* 1950, Isbell Evelyn Parker (*née* Davidson); two *d*. *Educ:* Royal Belfast Academical Instn; Queen's Univ., Belfast (BSc Civil Eng., 1947). FIWEM. Service with contractors, consulting engineers and local authorities, 1947–62; Eng. Inspector, Scottish Develt Dept, 1962–68, Dep. Chief Engr, 1968–75. *Recreations:* golf, photography, motoring, gardening. *Address:* Duncraig, 52 Blinkbonny Road, Edinburgh EH4 3HX. *T:* 031–332 4072. *Club:* Murrayfield Golf (Edinburgh).

AGNEW, Sir (William) Godfrey, KCVO 1965 (CVO 1953); CB 1975; Chairman, Lady Clare Ltd, 1970–87 (Director, 1948–87); Vice-Chairman, Sun Life Assurance Society plc, 1983–84 (Director, 1974–84); Director, Sun Life Properties Ltd, 1980–84; *b* 11 Oct. 1913; *o s* of late Lennox Edelsten Agnew and Elsie Blyth (*née* Nott), Tunbridge Wells; *m* 1st, 1939, Ruth Mary (*d* 1962), *e d* of late Charles J. H. O'H. Moore, CVO, MC, and late Lady Dorothie Moore; three *s* three *d*; 2nd, 1965, Lady (Nancy Veronica) Tyrwhitt, *widow* of Adm. Sir St John Reginald Joseph Tyrwhitt, 2nd Bt, KCB, DSO, DSC; two step *s* one step *d*. *Educ:* Tonbridge. Solicitor, 1935; entered Public Trustee Office, 1936. Served RA and Surrey and Sussex Yeomanry, 1939–46; Major, 1945. Senior Clerk, Privy Council Office, 1946–51; Clerk of the Privy Council, 1953–74 (Deputy Clerk, 1951–53); Dep. Sec., Cabinet Office, 1972–74. Director: Seaway Shipping Agencies Ltd, 1971–80; Seaway Holdings Ltd, 1971–80; Artagen Properties Ltd, 1976–80. Chairman, Sembal Trust, 1967–73. Mem., Bd of Hon. Tutors, Council of Legal Educn, Univ. of WI, 1973–; Consultant: CEI, 1974–79; University Coll., Cardiff, 1982–84; Univ. of Wales Inst. of Science and Technol., 1982–84. Hon. FIMechE, 1968; Hon. FIMunE, 1974; Hon. FCIBSE (formerly Hon. FCIBS), 1975; Hon. FICE, 1984. *Clubs:* Army and Navy; Swinley Forest Golf; Rye Golf.

See also Sir J. M. H. Pollen, Bt, Sir Reginald Tyrwhitt, Bt.

AGNEW-SOMERVILLE, Sir Quentin (Charles Somerville), 2nd Bt *cr* 1957, of Clendry, Co. Wigtown; *b* 8 March 1929; *s* of Comdr Sir Peter Agnew, 1st Bt and Enid Frances (*d* 1982), *d* of late Henry Boan; assumed additional name of Somerville by Royal licence, 1950; *S* father, 1990; *m* 1963, Hon. April, *y d* and a *co-heiress* of 15th Baron Strange; one *s* two *d*. *Educ:* RNC Dartmouth. *Heir: s* James Lockett Charles Agnew-Somerville, *b* 26 May 1970. *Address:* Mount Auldyn, Jurby Road, Ramsey, Isle of Man.

AGUIRRE, Marcelino O.; *see* Oreja Aguirre.

ÁGÚSTSSON, Helgi, Hon. GCVO 1990; Icelandic Grand Order of the Falcon, 1990 (Order of the Falcon, 1979); Icelandic Ambassador to the Court of St James's, since 1989, and to Ireland, Holland and Nigeria, since 1990; *b* 16 Oct. 1941; *s* of Ágúst Pétursson and Helga Jóhannesdóttir; *m* 1963, Hervör Jónasdóttir; three *s* one *d*. *Educ:* Univ. of Iceland (Law degree 1970). Joined Foreign Ministry, 1970; served London, 1973–77; Counsellor, 1977; Dir, Defence Div., Foreign Min., 1979 and Chm., US-Icelandic Defence Council; Minister-Counsellor, 1980; served Washington, 1983–87; Dep. Permt Under-Sec., Foreign Min., 1987, in rank of Ambassador. Former Pres., Icelandic Basketball Fedn. Decorations from Finland, Denmark, Sweden, Italy, Spain. *Recreations:* theatre, music, reading, basketball. *Address:* Icelandic Embassy, 1 Eaton Terrace, SW1W 8EY. *T:* 071–730 5131. *Club:* Les Ambassadeurs.

AGUTTER, Jennifer Ann; actress; *b* 20 Dec. 1952; *d* of Derek and Catherine Agutter; *m* 1990, Johan Tham. *Educ:* Elmhurst Ballet School, Camberley. *Films:* East of Sudan, 1964; Ballerina, 1964; Gates of Paradise, 1967; Star, 1968; Walkabout, I Start Counting, The Railway Children, 1969 (Royal Variety Club Most Promising Artist, 1971); Logan's Run, 1975; The Eagle Has Landed, Equus (BAFTA Best Supporting Actress, 1977), The Man In The Iron Mask, 1976; Dominique, Clayton and Catherine, 1977; The Riddle of the Sands, Sweet William, 1978; The Survivor, 1980; An American Werewolf in London, 1981; Secret Places, 1983; Dark Tower, 1987; King of the Wind, 1989; Child's Play 2, 1990; *stage:* School for Scandal, 1972; Rooted, Arms and the Man, The Ride Across Lake Constance, 1973; National Theatre: The Tempest, Spring Awakening, 1974; Hedda, Betrayal, 1980; Royal Shakespeare Co.: Arden of Faversham, Lear, King Lear, The Body, 1982–83; Breaking the Silence, 1985; Shrew, The Unified Field, LA, 1987; Breaking the Code, NY, 1987; *television includes:* Long After Summer, 1967; The Wild Duck, The Cherry Orchard, The Snow Goose (Emmy Best Supporting Actress), 1971; A War of Children, 1972; School Play, 1979; Amy, 1980; Love's Labours Lost, This Office Life, 1984; Silas Marner, 1985; Murder She Wrote, 1986; The Equaliser, Magnum, 1988; The Outsiders, Dear John, 1989; Not a Penny More, Not a Penny Less, 1990. *Publication:* Snap, 1983. *Address:* c/o Namara Cowan Ltd, 45 Poland Street, W1V 3DF.

AH-CHUEN, Sir Moi Lin Jean (Etienne), Kt 1980; Minister of Local Government, Mauritius, 1969–76; Chairman: Chue Wing & Co. Ltd, since 1977; The Mauritius Union Assurance Co. Ltd, since 1977; *b* 22 Feb. 1911. *Educ:* De La Salle School; Mauritius. Mem., Mauritius Legislative Assembly, 1948–76. Founder (Chm. and Man. Dir), ABC Store (Chue Wing & Co. Ltd), 1931–68; Dir, Chinese Daily News, 1942–. Alternately Pres. and Vice-Pres., Chinese Chamber of Commerce, 1942–64. Chairman: Union Shipping Ltd; ABC Motors Co. Chm., Chinese Nat. Coll. Pres., Chinese Cultural Centre, 1968–; mem. or past-mem., various other social and charitable organisations. *Recreations:* bridge, travelling, sports. *Address:* 5 Reverend Lebrun Street, Rose Hill, Mauritius. *T:* 4–3804. *Clubs:* Mauritius Turf, Chinese Traders (Mauritius).

AHERN, Most Rev. John J.; *b* 31 Aug 1911; *s* of James Ahern and Ellen Mulcahy. *Educ:* St Colman's Coll., Fermoy; St Patrick's Coll., Maynooth; Irish Coll., Rome. Ordained, 1936. Prof. at St Colman's Coll., Fermoy, 1940–44; St Patrick's Coll., Maynooth, 1946–57; Bishop of Cloyne, 1957–87. *Address:* Nazareth House, Mallow, Co. Cork, Ireland.

AHERN, Hon. Michael John; MLA; company director; Premier of Queensland, Treasurer, and Minister for the Arts, 1987–89, Minister for State Development, 1989; *b* 2 June 1942; *s* of John James Ahern and Gwendoline May Thornton; *m* 1971, Andrea Maria Louise Meyer; one *s* four *d*. *Educ:* Downlands College, Toowoomba; Univ. of Queensland (BAgrScis 1963). MLA National Party (formerly Country Party) for Landsborough, 1968–; Minister for: Primary Industries, 1980–83; Industry, Small Business and Technology, 1983–86; Health and Environment, 1986–87. *Recreations:* theatre, ballet, tennis. *Address:* 3 Shelley Park, Caloundra, Qld 4551, Australia. *T:* (office) (071) 912780; (home) (071) 911645. *Clubs:* Brisbane, Tattersall's (Brisbane).

AHMAD, Khurshid; Chairman: Institute of Policy Studies, Islamabad, Pakistan, since 1979; Board of Trustees, Islamic Foundation, Leicester, since 1985; Member, Senate of Pakistan, since 1978; *b* 23 March 1934; three *s* three *d*. *Educ:* Karachi Univ. (LLB; MA Economics; MA Islamic Studies). Dir-Gen., Islamic Foundn, Leicester Univ., 1973–78; Federal Minister for Planning and Develt and Dep. Chm., Planning Commn, Govt of Pakistan, 1978–79. Chm., Internat. Inst. of Islamic Econs, Islamic Univ., Islamabad, 1983–87. Hon. PhD Educn, Nat. Univ. of Malaya. Islamic Develt Bank Laureate for dist. contribn to Islamic econs, 1988; King Faisal, Internat. Prize for service to Islam, 1990. *Publications:* Essays on Pakistan Economy (Karachi), 1958; An Analysis of Munir Report (Lahore), 1958; (ed) Studies in the Family Law of Islam (Karachi), 1960; (ed) The Quran: an Introduction (Karachi), 1966; The Prophet of Islam (Karachi), 1967; Principles of Islamic Education (Lahore), 1970; Fanaticism, Intolerance and Islam (Lahore), 1970; Islam and the West (Lahore), 1972; The Religion of Islam (Lahore), 1973; (ed) Islam: its meaning and message (London, Islamic Council of Europe), 1976; Development Strategy for the Sixth Plan (Islamabad), 1983; *for Islamic Foundation, Leicester:* Islam: Basic Principles and Characteristics, 1974; Family Life in Islam, 1974; Islamic Perspectives: Studies in honour of Maulana Mawdudi, 1979; The Quran: Basic Teachings, 1979; Studies in Islamic Economics, 1980; contrib. The Third World's Dilemma of Development, Non-Aligned Third World Annual, (USA) 1970. *Recreations:* travelling, reading. *Address:* Markfield Dawah Centre, Ratby Lane, Markfield, Leicester LE6 0RN. *T:* Markfield (0530) 244944; Institute of Policy Studies, Block 19, Markaz F-7, Islamabad, Pakistan. *T:* Islamabad 051-818230.

AHMED, Dr Haroon, FEng 1990; Reader in Microelectronics, Cavendish Laboratory, Cambridge, since 1984; Fellow of Corpus Christi College, Cambridge, since 1967; *b* 2 March 1936; *s* of Mohammad Nizam Ahmed and Bilquis Jehan Ahmed; *m* 1969, Evelyn Anne Travers; one *s* two *d*. *Educ:* St Patrick's Sch., Karachi; Imperial College London; King's College, Cambridge. GEC and Hirst Research Centre, 1958–59; Turner and Newall Res. Fellow, 1962–63; University of Cambridge: Univ. Demonstrator, Engineering Dept, 1963–66; Lectr, Engineering Dept, 1966–84. *Publications:* (with A. H. W. Beck) Introduction to Physical Electronics, 1968; (with P. J. Spreadbury) Electronics for Engineers, 1973, 2nd edn 1984. *Recreations:* golf, tennis, ski-ing. *Address:* Microelectronics Research Centre, Cavendish Laboratory, Madingley Road, Cambridge CB3 0HE. *T:* Cambridge (0223) 337557.

'AHO, Siaosi Taimani; High Commissioner for Tonga in London, 1986–89; concurrently Ambassador for Tonga to EEC, Belgium, FRG, France, USSR, Denmark, Italy, Luxemburg, USA; *b* 18 Jan. 1939; *s* of Tenita Kilisimari 'Aho and Otolose 'Aho; *m* 1984, Sitola 'Aho; one *s*. *Educ:* Auckland Grammar Sch.; Auckland Teachers' Coll., Auckland Univ. (BA). Asst Teacher, Tonga High Sch., 1965; Asst Sec., Min. of Health, 1972; 1st

Sec., Tonga High Commn, London, 1976; Asst Sec., Min. of For. Affairs, 1980; Sec. to Cabinet, 1982; Sec. for For. Affairs, 1983. *Recreations:* watching sports, playing snooker, fishing, gardening. *Address:* c/o Ministry for Foreign Affairs, Nuku'alofa, Tonga.

AHRENDS, Peter; Founding Partner, Ahrends Burton & Koralek, Architects, since 1961; *b* 30 April 1933; *s* of Steffen Bruno Ahrends and Margarete Marie Sophie Ahrends; *m* 1954, Elizabeth Robertson; two *d*. *Educ:* Architectural Assoc. Sch. of Architecture (Dipl., Hons). RIBA 1959. Steffen Ahrends & Partners, Johannesburg, 1957–58; Denys Lasdun & Partners, 1959–60; Julian Keable & Partners; major-projects, 1961–, include: *public buildings:* Redcar Liby, 1971; Maidenhead Liby, 1972; RC Chaplaincy, Oxford, 1972; Hampton Site, Nat. Gall. Extn, 1982 (comp. winning entry); St Mary's Hosp., Newport, IoW (nucleus low energy hosp.), 1991; *educational buildings:* Chichester Theol Coll., 1965; Berkeley Liby, TCD, 1967; Templeton Coll., Oxford; residential bldg, Keble Coll., Oxford, 1976 (RIBA Arch. Award, 1978); Arts Faculty Bldg, TCD, Portsmouth Poly. Liby, 1975–79; won internat. comp. for Univ. of Grenoble Campus, 1989; *residential buildings:* Dunstan Rd, Oxford, 1969; Nebenzahl House, Jerusalem, 1972; Chalvedon Housing, 1975–77; Whitmore Court Housing, 1975 (RIBA Good Design in Housing Award, 1977); Felmore Housing, 1975–80; *commercial/industrial buildings:* warehouse, showroom and offices, Habitat, 1974 (Structural Steel Design Award, FT Industrial Arch. Award, 1976); Cummins Engines develt plan, 1975–83 (Struct. Steel Design Award, 1980); John Lewis dept store, Kingston-upon-Thames, 1990; Sainsbury supermarket, Canterbury, 1984– (Struct. Steel Design Award, 1985); W. H. Smith offices, Greenbridge, 1985. Chair, UK Architects Against Apartheid, 1988–; Member: Design Council, 1988–; Council, AA, 1965–67. Bartlett Prof. of Arch., Bartlett Sch. of Arch. and Planning, UCL, 1986–89; part-time teaching posts and workshops at AA Sch. of Arch., Canterbury Sch. of Art, Edinburgh Univ., Winter Sch. Edinburgh, Plymouth Poly., Kingston Poly., and Plymouth Sch. of Art; vis. critic and/or ext. examr at Kumasi Univ., AA Sch. of Arch., Nova Scotia Tech. Univ., Kingston Poly., Strathclyde Univ. Exhibitions of drawings and works: RIBA Heinz Gall., 1980; Douglas Hyde Gall., Dublin, 1981; Braunschweig Tech. Univ., Tech. Univ. of Hanover, Museum of Finnish Arch.; Univ. of Oulu, Alvar Aalto Museum, Finland, 1982; AA HQ, Oslo, 1983. *Publications:* (contrib.) Ahrends Burton & Koralek, Architects (monograph), 1991; papers and articles in RIBA Jl and other prof. jls. *Recreations:* architecture, France. *Address:* (office) 7 Chalcot Road, NW1 8LH.

AIKEN, Joan Delano, (Mrs Julius Goldstein); writer of historical, mystery and children's novels, plays and poetry; *b* 4 Sept. 1924; *d* of Conrad Potter Aiken and Jessie McDonald; *m* 1st, 1945, Ronald George Brown (*d* 1955); one *s* one *d*; 2nd, 1976, Julius Goldstein. *Educ:* Wychwood Sch., Oxford. Inf. Officer, subseq. Librarian, UN London Inf. Centre, 1943–49; Features Editor, Argosy magazine, 1955–60; Copy-writer, J. Walter Thompson London office, 1960–61; time thereafter devoted to writing. Mem., Soc. of Authors. Guardian Award for Children's Literature, 1969; Lewis Carroll Award, 1970. *Publications:* (most also published in USA and as paperbacks): The Silence of Herondale, 1964; The Fortune Hunters, 1965; Trouble with Product X, 1966 (Beware of the Bouquet, USA 1966); Hate Begins at Home, 1967 (Dark Interval, USA 1967); The Ribs of Death, 1967 (The Crystal Crow, USA 1968); The Windscreen Weepers (stories), 1969; The Embroidered Sunset, 1970; The Butterfly Picnic, 1970 (A Cluster of Separate Sparks, USA 1972); Died on a Rainy Sunday, 1972; Voices in an Empty House, 1975; Castle Barebane, 1976; Last Movement, 1977; The Five-Minute Marriage, 1977; The Smile of the Stranger, 1978; A Touch of Chill (horror stories), 1979; The Lightning Tree, 1980 (The Weeping Ash, USA); The Girl from Paris, 1982; The Way to Write for Children, 1982; A Whisper in the Night, 1982; Foul Matter, 1983; Mansfield Revisited, 1984; Deception, 1987; Jane Fairfax, 1990; *for children:* (many also published in USA): All You've Ever Wanted (stories), 1953; More Than You Bargained For (stories), 1955; The Kingdom and the Cave, 1960; The Wolves of Willoughby Chase, 1962; Black Hearts in Battersea, 1964; Night Birds on Nantucket, 1966; The Whispering Mountain, 1968; A Necklace of Raindrops (stories), 1968; A Small Pinch of Weather (stories), 1969; Night Fall, 1969; Armitage, Armitage, Fly Away Home (stories), USA 1970; Smoke From Cromwell's Time, USA 1970; The Cuckoo Tree, 1971; The Kingdom Under the Sea (folktales), 1971; The Green Flash (fantasy and horror stories), USA 1971; A Harp of Fishbones (stories), 1972; Winterthing (play), USA 1972; The Mooncusser's Daughter (play), USA 1973; Winterthing & The Mooncusser's Daughter, 1973; Midnight is a Place, 1974; Arabel's Raven, USA 1974; Tales of Arabel's Raven, 1974; Not What You Expected (stories), USA 1974; Tale of a One-Way Street (stories), 1976; The Skin Spinners (poems), USA 1976; A Bundle of Nerves (horror stories), 1976; The Angel Inn (trans. from French), 1976; The Faithless Lollybird (stories), 1977; Mice and Mendelson, 1978; Go Saddle the Sea, 1978; Street (play), USA 1978; Arabel and Mortimer, 1979; The Shadow Guests, 1980; The Stolen Lake, 1981; Mortimer's Cross, 1983; Bridle the Wind, 1983; Up the Chimney Down and Other Stories, 1984; Fog Hounds, Wind Cat, Sea Mice, 1984; The Kitchen Warriors, 1984; The Last Slice of Rainbow, 1985; Mortimer Says Nothing, 1985; Dido and Pa, 1986; Past Eight O'Clock, 1986; A Goose on Your Grave, 1987; Beware of the Moon, 1987; The Teeth of the Gale, 1988; The Erl King's Daughter, 1988; Blackground, 1989; Give Yourself a Fright, 1989; Voices, 1989; A Foot in the Grave, 1990; A Fit of Shivers (horror stories), 1990. *Recreations:* listening to music, looking at art, travel, reading, gardening, walking, talking to friends. *Address:* The Hermitage, East Street, Petworth, West Sussex GU28 0AB. *T:* Petworth (0798) 42279. *Clubs:* Society of Authors, Writers' Guild, Crime Writers' Association, PEN; Mystery Writers of America.

AIKEN, Air Chief Marshal Sir John (Alexander Carlisle), KCB 1973 (CB 1967); Director General of Intelligence, Ministry of Defence, 1978–81; *b* 22 Dec. 1921; *s* of Thomas Leonard and Margaret Aiken; *m* 1948, Pamela Jane (*née* Bartlett); one *s* one *d*. *Educ:* Birkenhead School. Joined RAF, 1941; Fighter Sqdns, Europe and Far East, 1942–45; Fighter Comd, 1946–47; CFS, 1948; Staff of RAF Coll., Cranwell, 1948–50; OC Univ. of Birmingham Air Sqdn, 1950–52; Staff Coll., 1953; HQ Fighter Comd, 1954–55; OC 29 Fighter Sqdn, 1956–57; jssc 1958; Headquarters AF North, 1958–60; Air Min., 1960–63; Station Comdr, RAF Finningley, 1963–64; Air Cdre Intelligence, Min. of Defence, 1965–67; idc 1968; Dep. Comdr, RAF, Germany, 1969–71; Dir-Gen. Training, RAF, 1971–72; Head of Economy Project Team (RAF), 1972–73; AOC-in-C, NEAF, Comdr British Forces Near East, and Administrator, Sovereign Base Areas, Cyprus, 1973–76; Air Member for Personnel, 1976–78. Pres., RAFA, 1984–85 and 1987–88 (Chm., Central Council, 1981–84). Mem. Council, Chatham House, 1984–90. *Recreations:* walking, ski-ing, music. *Club:* Royal Air Force.

AIKENS, Richard John Pearson; QC 1986; *b* 28 Aug. 1948; *s* of late Basil Aikens and of Jean Eleanor Aikens; *m* 1979, Penelope Anne Hartley Rockley (*née* Baker); two *s* two step *d*. *Educ:* Norwich Sch.; St John's Coll., Cambridge (MA). Called to Bar, Middle Temple, 1973; Harmsworth scholarship, 1974; in practice, 1974–; a Junior Counsel to the Crown, Common Law, 1981–86. Mem., Supreme Court Rules Cttee, 1984–88. Dir, Bar Mutual Indemnity Fund Ltd, 1987–. Governor, Sedbergh Sch., 1988–. *Publication:* (contributing editor) Bullen and Leake and Jacob, Precedents of Pleading, 13th edn 1990. *Recreations:* music, gardening, wine. *Address:* Brick Court Chambers, 15/19 Devereux Court, WC2R 3JJ. *T:* 071-583 0777. *Club:* Leander.

AIKIN, Olga Lindholm, (Mrs J. M. Driver); Partner, Aikin Driver Partnership, since 1988; Visiting Lecturer, London Business School, since 1985; Council Member, Advisory Conciliation and Arbitration Service, since 1982; *b* 10 Sept. 1934; *d* of Sidney Richard Daly and Lilian May Daly (*née* Lindholm); *m* 1st, 1959, Ronald Sidney Aikin (marr. diss. 1979); one *d*; 2nd, 1982, John Michael Driver; one step *d*. *Educ:* London School of Economics (LLB); King's Coll., London. Called to Bar, Gray's Inn, 1956. Assistant Lecturer, King's Coll., London, 1956–59; Lecturer, London School of Economics, 1959–70; London Business School: Sloan Fellowship Programme, 1970–71; Vis. Lectr, 1971–79; Lectr in Law, 1979–85. Dir, Gen. Law Div., Lion Internat. (Keiser Enterprises Inc.), 1985–90. *Publications:* Employment, Welfare and Safety at Work, 1971 (with Judith Reid); articles in Personnel Management. *Recreation:* collecting cookery books and pressed glass. *Address:* 22 St Luke's Road, W11 1DP. *T:* 071-727 9791.
See also Hon. Francis Daly.

AIKMAN, Colin Campbell, CBE 1990; PhD; consultant; *b* 24 Feb. 1919; *s* of Colin Campbell Aikman and Bertha Egmont Aikman (*née* Harwood); *m* 1952, Betty Alicia, *d* of R. Y. James; three *d* (one *s* decd). *Educ:* Palmerston North Boys' High Sch.; Victoria University Coll., Wellington, NZ (LLM); London Sch. of Economics (PhD). Law Clerk in Legal Offices, 1935–41; Barrister and Solicitor of Supreme Court of New Zealand, 1940–41; Prime Minister's Dept and Dept of External Affairs (Legal Adviser, 1949–55), 1943–55; Mem. NZ Delgn to San Francisco Conf., 1945; Prof. of Jurisprudence and Constitutional Law, Victoria Univ. of Wellington (Dean of Law Faculty, 1957–59, 1962–67), 1955–68; Mem. Council, NZ Inst. of Internat. Affairs (Nat. Pres., 1960–63, Dir. 1979–84), 1955–; Advr to NZ Govt on Constitutional Develt of Cook Is, Western Samoa and Niue, 1956–68, 1975; Vice-Chancellor, The Univ. of the South Pacific, Suva, Fiji, 1968–74; NZ High Comr to India, accredited also to Bangladesh and Nepal, 1975–78. Member: Council of Volunteer Service Abroad (Inc.) (Chm. 1962–65), 1962–68; Adv. Cttee on External Aid and Develt, 1980–88. Trustee, Norman Kirk Meml Trust, 1979–. Silver Jubilee Medal, 1977. *Publications:* (co-author): A Report to Members of the Legislative Assembly of the Cook Islands on Constitutional Development, 1963; New Zealand, The Development of its Laws and Constitution (ed Robson), 1967 (2nd edn); New Zealand's Record in the Pacific Islands in the Twentieth Century (ed Angus Ross), 1969; contribs to NZ Internat. Review, Victoria Univ. of Wellington Law Review. *Recreations:* golf, cricket, carpentry. *Address:* 28 Korokoro Road, Petone, New Zealand. *T:* (04) 691518. *Clubs:* Wellington; Wellington Golf (Heretaunga).

AILESBURY, 8th Marquess of, *cr* 1821; **Michael Sydney Cedric Brudenell-Bruce;** Bt 1611; Baron Brudenell 1628; Earl of Cardigan 1661; Baron Bruce 1746; Earl of Ailesbury 1776; Earl Bruce 1821; Viscount Savernake 1821; 30th Hereditary Warden of Savernake Forest; Lt RHG, 1946; Member London Stock Exchange since 1954; *b* 31 March 1926; *e s* of 7th Marquess of Ailesbury and Joan (*d* 1937), *d* of Stephen Salter, Ryde, Isle of Wight; *S* father, 1974; *m* 1st, 1952, Edwina Sylvia de Winton (from whom he obtained a divorce, 1961), *yr d* of Lt-Col Sir (Ernest) Edward de Winton Wills, 4th Bt; one *s* two *d*; 2nd, 1963, Juliet Adrienne (marr. diss. 1974), *d* of late Hilary Lethbridge Kingsford and of Mrs Latham Hobrow, Marlborough; two *d*; 3rd, 1974, Mrs Caroline Elizabeth Romilly, *d* of late Commander O. F. M. Wethered, RN, DL, JP. *Educ:* Eton. *Heir: s* Earl of Cardigan, *qv*. *Address:* Stable Block, Tottenham House, near Marlborough, Wilts; 40 Munster Road, SW6.

AILSA, 7th Marquess of, *cr* 1831; **Archibald David Kennedy,** OBE 1968; Baron Kennedy, 1452; Earl of Cassillis, 1509; Baron Ailsa (UK), 1806; *b* 3 Dec. 1925; *s* of 6th Marquess of Ailsa and Gertrude Millicent (*d* 1957), *d* of Gervas Weir Cooper, Wordwell Hall, Bury St Edmunds; *S* father 1957; *m* 1954, Mary, 7th *c* of John Burn, Amble; two *s* one *d*. *Educ:* Nautical Coll., Pangbourne. Scots Guards, 1943–47; Royal Northumberland Fusiliers, 1950–52. National Trust for Scotland, 1953–56. Territorial Army, 1958–68; Hon. Col, Ayr and Renfrew Battalion ACF, 1980–. Patron, Isle of Man Railway Soc., 1978–; Chm., Scottish Assoc. of Boys Clubs, 1978–82. Chm., Anglo-Somali Soc., 1987. *Recreations:* walking, motoring, modelling, sailing. *Heir: s* Earl of Cassillis, *qv*. *Address:* Cassillis, Maybole, Ayrshire KA19 7JN. *Clubs:* Carlton; New (Edinburgh); Royal Yacht Squadron.
See also Rev. N. W. Drummond.

AINLEY, Sir (Alfred) John, Kt 1957; MC 1940; Chief Justice, Kenya, 1963–68; retired; Chairman of Industrial Tribunals, 1972–76; *b* 10 May 1906; *o s* of late Rev. A. Ainley, Cockermouth, Cumb; *m* 1935, Mona Sybil Wood (*d* 1981); one *s* two *d*. *Educ:* St Bees Sch.; Corpus Christi, Oxford. Called to Bar, 1928; Magistrate, Gold Coast, 1935; Crown Counsel (Gold Coast), 1936; Puisne Judge, Uganda, 1946–55; Chief Justice of Eastern Region, Nigeria, 1955–59; Combined Judiciary of Sarawak, N Borneo and Brunei, 1959–62. Served War of 1939–45, West African Forces, E Africa and Burma. *Address:* Horrock Wood, Watermillock, Penrith, Cumbria CA11 0JJ.

AINLEY, David Geoffrey, CEng, FIMechE, FRAeS; Deputy Director (Projects and Research), Military Vehicles and Engineering Establishment, Chertsey, 1978–84; *b* 5 July 1924; *s* of Cyril Edward and Constance Ainley; *m* 1st, 1948, Dorothy Emily (*née* Roberts); one *s* one *d*; 2nd, 1959, Diana Margery Hill (*née* Sayles); one *d*; 3rd, 1988, Joyce Dinah (*née* Jessett). *Educ:* Brentwood Sch., Essex; Queen Mary Coll., London Univ. (BSc, 1st Cl. Hons). Engine Dept, RAE, Farnborough, 1943–44; Power Jets (R&D) Ltd, 1944–46; National Gas Turbine Estabt, Pyestock, 1946–66; idc 1967; Dir of Engine Develt, MoD (Procurement Exec.), 1968–78. George Stephenson Research Prize, IMechE, 1953. *Publications:* contrib. books and learned jls on gas turbine technology. *Recreations:* painting, sketching, golf. *Address:* 20 Hampton Close, Church Crookham, Aldershot, Hants GU13 0LB. *T:* Fleet (0252) 622577.

AINLEY, Sir John; see Ainley, Sir A. J.

AINSCOW, Robert Morrison, CB 1989; Deputy Secretary, Overseas Development Administration, Foreign and Commonwealth Office, since 1986; *b* 3 June 1936; *s* of Robert M. Ainscow and Hilda Ainscow (*née* Cleminson); *m* 1965, Faye Bider; one *s* one *d*. *Educ:* Salford Grammar School; Liverpool Univ. (BA Econ Hons). Statistician: Govt of Rhodesia and Nyasaland, 1957–61; UN Secretariat, New York, 1961–65 and 1966–68; Dept of Economic Affairs, London, 1965–66. Ministry of Overseas Development: Economic Adviser, 1968–70; Senior Economic Adviser, 1971–76; Head, South Asia Dept, 1976–79; Under Secretary, FCO (ODA), 1979–86. Chm., OECD (DAC) Working Party on Financial Aspects of Develt Assistance, 1982–86. *Address:* Overseas Development Administration, Eland House, Stag Place, SW1E 5DH.

AINSWORTH, Sir David; see Ainsworth, Sir T. D.

AINSWORTH, (Mervyn) John, FCIS, FInstAM; Chief Executive and Secretary, Institute of Chartered Secretaries and Administrators, since 1990; *b* 28 Jan. 1947; *s* of late Gordon John Ainsworth and Eileen Ainsworth; *m* 1973, Marta Christina Marmolak; two *s* one *d*. *Educ:* Stanfields Technical High Sch., Stoke-on-Trent; Goldsmiths' Coll., Univ. of London (DipEd). Asst Clerk to Govs and Bursar, Dulwich Coll., 1969–74; Principal Assistant, Sec. and Solicitors' Dept, CEGB, 1974–77; Secretarial Asst, BTDB, 1977–78; Sec., 1978–83,

Sec. and Dir of Finance, 1983–84, BPIF; Sec. General, Inst. of Administrative Management, 1984–90. Member: Bd, Nat. Examining Bd for Supervisory Management, 1984–; Academic Bd, Greenwich Coll., 1984–; Court, Cranfield Inst. of Technology, 1990–. FBIM. Hon. Fellow, Canadian Inst. of Certified Administrative Managers, 1987. Freeman, Co. of Chartered Secs and Administrators. *Publications:* articles on management education and administrative systems. *Recreations:* sailing, gardening, family life. *Address:* 3 Silverdale Drive, SE9 4DH. *T:* 081–857 2630.

AINSWORTH, Sir (Thomas) David, 4th Bt *cr* 1916; *b* 22 Aug. 1926; *s* of Sir Thomas Ainsworth, 2nd Bt, and Marie Eleanor (May) (*d* 1969), *d* of Compton Charles Domvile; *S* half-brother, 1981; *m* 1957, Sarah Mary, *d* of late Lt-Col H. C. Walford; two *s* two *d*. *Educ:* Eton. Formerly Lt 11th Hussars. *Recreations:* shooting, fishing. *Heir: s* Anthony Thomas Hugh Ainsworth, *b* 30 March 1962. *Address:* 80 Elm Park Gardens, SW10 9PD; Ashley House, Wootton, Woodstock, Oxon OX7 1DX. *Club:* Cavalry and Guards.

AIRD, Captain Sir Alastair (Sturgis), KCVO 1984 (CVO 1977; LVO 1969); Comptroller to Queen Elizabeth the Queen Mother since 1974; *b* 14 Jan. 1931; *s* of Col Malcolm Aird; *m* 1963, Fiona Violet, LVO 1980, *d* of late Lt-Col Ririd Myddelton, MVO; two *d*. *Educ:* Eton; RMA Sandhurst. Commnd 9th Queen's Royal Lancers, 1951; served in BAOR; Adjt 9th Lancers, 1956–59; retd from Army, 1964. Equerry to Queen Elizabeth the Queen Mother, 1960; Asst Private Sec. to the Queen Mother, 1964. Mem. Council, Feathers Assoc. of Youth Clubs, 1973–; Trustee, RSAS Develt Trust, 1986–. *Recreations:* shooting, fishing, tennis. *Address:* 31B St James's Palace, SW1A 1BA. *T:* 071–839 6700.

AIRD, Sir (George) John, 4th Bt *cr* 1901; Chairman and Managing Director, Sir John Aird & Co Ltd, since 1969; *b* 30 Jan. 1940; *e s* of Sir John Renton Aird, 3rd Bt, MVO, MC, and of Lady Priscilla Aird, *yr d* of 2nd Earl of Ancaster; *S* father, 1973; *m* 1968, Margaret, *yr d* of Sir John Muir, Bt, *qv*; one *s* two *d*. *Educ:* Eton; Oxford Univ.; Harvard Business Sch. MICE. Trainee, Sir Alexander Gibb & Partners, 1961–65; Manager, John Laing & Son Ltd, 1967–69. *Recreations:* farming, skiing. *Heir: s* James John Aird, *b* 12 June 1978. *Address:* Grange Farm, Evenlode, Moreton-in-Marsh, Glos GL56 0NT. *T:* Moreton-in-Marsh (0608) 50607. *Club:* White's.

AIREDALE, 4th Baron, *cr* 1907; **Oliver James Vandeleur Kitson;** Bt, *cr* 1886; Deputy Chairman of Committees, House of Lords, since 1961; Deputy Speaker, House of Lords, since 1962; *b* 22 April 1915; *o s* of 3rd Baron Airedale, DSO, MC, and Sheila Grace (*d* 1935), *d* of late Frank E. Vandeleur, London; *S* father, 1958; unmarried. *Educ:* Eton; Trinity College, Cambridge. Major, The Green Howards. Called to the Bar, Inner Temple, 1941. *Heir:* none. *Address:* (seat) Ufford Hall, Stamford, Lincs.

AIREY OF ABINGDON, Baroness *cr* 1979 (Life Peer), of Abingdon in the County of Oxford; **Diana Josceline Barbara Neave Airey;** *b* 7 July 1919; *d* of late Thomas A. W. Giffard, MBE, JP, and late Angela Erskine Giffard (*née* Trollope); *m* 1942, Airey Middleton Sheffield Neave, DSO, OBE, MC (assassinated, March 1979), MP Abingdon; two *s* one *d*. *Educ:* privately and abroad. Quartermaster, RAF Hospital, 1939; later with Foreign Office (PWE) and Polish Ministry of Information, London. Then, in politics with her husband. Member: N Atlantic Assembly, 1983–84; Select Cttee on Eur. Communities (Sub-Cttee F), 1986–87. Trustee: Nat. Heritage Meml Fund, 1980–88; Imperial War Mus., 1984–90; Dorney Wood Trust, 1980–; Stansted Park Foundn, 1983–. Freedom, City of London, 1980. *Recreations:* reading, theatre, opera. *Address:* House of Lords, SW1.

AIREY, David Lawrence; Managing Director, Bunge & Co. Ltd, 1987–90, retired; *b* 28 April 1935; *s* of Samuel Airey and Helena Florence Lever; *m* 1961, Joan Mary Stewart; three *d*. *Educ:* Oldershaw Grammar Sch., Wallasey. J. Bibby & Sons Ltd: Management trainee, various sales/commercial management positions, 1952–74; Chief Exec., Edible Oils Div., 1974–78; Man. Dir, J. Bibby Edible Oils Ltd, 1979–86; Dep. Man. Dir, Bunge & Co. Ltd, 1986. Chm., Seed Crushers & Oil Processors Assoc., 1980–82. JP Liverpool, 1980–86. *Recreations:* Rubgy Union football (Birkenhead Park FC, 1955–66, Cheshire, 1958–65, North West Counties, 1964, Barbarians, 1965), fishing. *Address:* Darnley, Church Road, Woodborough, Pewsey, Wilts SN9 5PH. *T:* Marlborough (0672) 851647. *Clubs:* Birkenhead Park FC; Liverpool Racquet.

AIREY, Sir Lawrence, KCB 1978 (CB 1976); Chairman of the Board of Inland Revenue, 1980–86, retired; Director (non-executive), since 1987, and Deputy Chairman, since 1988, Standard Life Assurance Co.; Consultant, Drivers Jonas Partners, since 1986; *b* 10 March 1926; *s* of late Lawrence Clark Airey and Isabella Marshall Pearson; *m* 1953, Patricia Anne, *d* of late Edward George Williams and Mary Selway; two *s* one *d*. *Educ:* Newcastle Royal Grammar Sch.; Peterhouse, Cambridge. Served RM, 1945–47. Entered Civil Service, 1949; General Register Office, 1949–56; Cabinet Office, 1956–58; HM Treasury, 1958–79: Under-Sec., 1969–73; Dep. Sec., 1973–77; Second Perm. Sec., 1977–79. Research Fellow, Nuffield Coll., Oxford, 1961–62. Member: Bd of British Nat. Oil Corp., 1976–77; Govt Contracts Rev. Bd, 1986–. *Recreations:* collecting books; music. *Address:* Lions House, Berwick-on-Tweed, Northumberland. *T:* Berwick-on-Tweed (0289) 304384.

AIRLIE, 13th Earl of, *cr* 1639 (*de facto* 10th Earl, 13th but for the Attainder); **David George Coke Patrick Ogilvy,** KT 1985; GCVO 1984; PC 1984; JP; Baron Ogilvy of Airlie, 1491; Captain late Scots Guards; Lord Chamberlain of HM Household, since 1984; Chancellor, Royal Victorian Order, since 1984; Lord-Lieutenant of Angus, since 1989; *b* 17 May 1926; *e s* of 12th (*de facto* 9th) Earl of Airlie, KT, GCVO, MC, and Lady Alexandra Marie Bridget Coke (*d* 1984), *d* of 3rd Earl of Leicester, GCVO; *S* father, 1968; *m* 1952, Virginia Fortune Ryan (*see* Countess of Airlie); three *s* three *d*. *Educ:* Eton. Lieutenant Scots Guards, 1944; serving 2nd Battalion Germany, 1945; Captain, ADC to High Comr and C-in-C Austria, 1947–48; Malaya, 1948–49; resigned commission, 1950. Ensign, 1975–85, Lieutenant, 1985–, Queen's Body Guard for Scotland, Royal Company of Archers. Chairman: Schroders plc, 1977–84; Gen. Accident Fire & Life Assurance Corp., 1987– (Dir, 1962–; Dep. Chm., 1975–87); Ashdown Investment Trust Ltd, 1968–82; Director: J. Henry Schroder Wagg & Co. Ltd, 1961–84 (Chm., 1973–77); Scottish & Newcastle Breweries plc, 1969–83; The Royal Bank of Scotland Gp, 1983–; Stratton Investment Trust, 1986–. Hon. Pres., Scout Assoc. in Scotland, 1988–. DL Angus, 1964; JP Angus, 1990. Governor, Nuffield Nursing Homes Trust, 1985–89. Hon. LLD Dundee, 1990. *Heir: s* Lord Ogilvy, *qv*. *Address:* Cortachy Castle, Kirriemuir, Angus, Scotland. *T:* Cortachy (05754) 231; 5 Swan Walk, Chelsea SW3 4JJ.
See also Hon. Sir Angus Ogilvy, Sir Hereward Wake.

AIRLIE, Countess of; Virginia Fortune Ogilvy, CVO 1983; Lady of the Bedchamber to the Queen since 1973; *b* 9 Feb. 1933; *d* of John Barry Ryan, Newport, RI, USA; *m* 1952, Lord Ogilvy (now Earl of Airlie, *qv*); three *s* three *d*. *Educ:* Brearley School, New York City. Founder Governor, Cobham School, Kent, 1958. Mem., Industrial Design Panel, British Rail, 1974–. Trustee: Tate Gallery, 1983– (Chm. Friends of Tate Gallery, 1978–83); Amer. Mus. in Britain, 1985–89; Nat. Gallery, 1989–. Pres., Angus Br., BRCS, 1988. *Address:* Cortachy Castle, Kirriemuir, Angus, Scotland; 5 Swan Walk, SW3 4JJ.

AIRY, Maj.-Gen. Sir Christopher (John), KCVO 1989; CBE 1984; Private Secretary and Treasurer to TRH The Prince and Princess of Wales, 1990–91; *b* 8 March 1934; *m*; one *s* two *d*. 2nd Lieut, Grenadier Guards, 1954; Scots Guards, 1974. PMA to Sec. of State for War, 1960; DAAG, Regtl Adjt, 1967; Bde Major, 4th Guards Armoured Bde, 1971; CO, 1st Bn Scots Guards, 1974; Mil. Asst (GSO1) to Master Gen. of the Ordnance, 1976; Comdr 5th Field Force, 1979; ACOS, HQ UKLF, 1982; Sen. Army Mem., RCDS, 1983; GOC London District and Maj.-Gen. Comdg Household Div., 1986; retd 1989. Mem., Prince of Wales's Council, 1990–91.

AISHER, Sir Owen (Arthur), Kt 1981; Founder Member, Marley Ltd, 1934, Chairman, 1945–82, now Life President, Marley plc; *b* 28 May 1900; *s* of late Owen Aisher, Branksome Park, Poole; *m* 1921, Ann Allingham (*d* 1989); two *s* two *d*. Mem. Court of Paviors; Pres., RYA, 1970–75; has had many successes in off-shore racing, inc. Fastnet Race, 1951; was elected Yachtsman of the Year, 1958. *Recreations:* sailing, fishing, shooting. *Address:* Faygate, South Godstone, Surrey RH9 8JD. *Clubs:* Reform, City Livery; Royal Thames Yacht; RORC (Adm. 1969–75); Ranelagh Sailing; Little Ship (Pres.); Royal Southern Yacht (Hamble); Royal Yacht Squadron, Royal London Yacht, Island Sailing (Adm.) (Cowes); Bembridge Sailing; Royal Motor Yacht (Poole); New York YC, Seawanhaka Corinthian Yacht (USA); Royal St George Yacht (Eire); Royal Cape Yacht (South Africa).

AITCHISON, Sir Charles (Walter de Lancey), 4th Bt, *cr* 1938; Director: De Lancey Lands Ltd; Walter Willson Ltd; *b* 27 May 1951; *er s* of Sir Stephen Charles de Lancey Aitchison, 3rd Bt, and (Elizabeth) Anne (Milburn), *er d* of late Lt-Col Edward Reed, Ghyllheugh, Longhorsley, Northumberland; *S* father 1958; *m* 1984, Susan, *yr d* of late Edward Ellis; one *s* one *d*. Lieut, 15/19th The King's Royal Hussars, 1974; RARO 1974–78. ARICS. *Recreations:* fishing, shooting. *Heir: er s* Rory Edward de Lancey Aitchison, *b* 7 March 1986. *Address:* Whelprigg White House, Kirkby Lonsdale, Cumbria LA6 2LF. *Club:* Northern Counties.
See also R. A. Cookson.

AITCHISON, Craigie (Ronald John), RA 1988 (ARA 1978); painter; *b* 13 Jan. 1926; *yr s* of late Rt Hon. Lord Aitchison, PC, KC, LLD. *Educ:* Scotland; Slade Sch. of Fine Art. British Council Italian Govt Scholarship for painting, 1955; Edwin Austin Abbey Premier Scholarship, 1965; Lorne Scholarship, 1974–75. One-man Exhibitions: Beaux Arts Gall., 1959, 1960, 1964; Marlborough Fine Art (London) Ltd, 1968; Compass Gall., Glasgow, 1970; Basil Jacobs Gall., 1971; Rutland Gall., 1975; Knoedler Gall., 1977; Kettle's Yard Gall., Cambridge, 1979; Serpentine Gall. (major retrospective, 1953–81), 1981–82; Artis, Monte Carlo, Monaco, 1986; Albemarle Gall., 1987, 1989; Castlefield Gall., Manchester, 1990. Exhibited: Galouste Gulbenkian Internat. Exhibn, 1964; Il Tempo del imagine, 2nd Internat. Biennale, Bologna, 1967; Modern British Painters, Tokyo, Japan, 1969; 23rd Salon Actualité de l'Esprit, Paris, 1975; The Proper Study, British Council Lalit Kala Akademi, Delhi, 1984; Hard Won Image, Tate Gall., 1985; British Council Exhibn, Picturing People, Hong Kong and Zimbabwe, 1990; The Journey, Lincoln Cathedral, 1990; Nine Contemporary Painters, City of Bristol Mus. and Art Gall., 1990. Pictures in public collections: Tate Gall., Arts Council, Contemp. Art Soc., Scottish National Gall. of Modern Art, Glasgow Mus. and Art Gall., and Nat. Gall. of Melbourne, Australia. 1st Johnson Wax Prize, Royal Acad., 1982; Korn Ferry Internat. Award, Royal Acad., 1989. *Address:* 32 St Mary's Gardens, SE11. *T:* 071–582 3708; Montecastelli San Gusme, Siena, Italy.

AITCHISON, June Rosemary, (Mrs T. J. Aitchison); *see* Whitfield, J. R.

AITKEN, family name of **Baron Beaverbrook.**

AITKEN, Ian Levack; political columnist, The Guardian, since 1990 (Political Editor, 1975–90); *b* 19 Sept. 1927; *s* of George Aitken and Agnes Levack Aitken; *m* 1956, Dr Catherine Hay Mackie, *y d* of late Maitland Mackie, OBE; two *d*. *Educ:* King Alfred Sch., Hampstead; Regent Street Polytechnic; Lincoln Coll., Oxford (BA PPE; MA); LSE. Served Fleet Air Arm, 1945–48. HM Inspector of Factories, 1951; Res. Officer, CSEU, 1952; Industrial Reporter, Tribune, 1953–54; Industrial Reporter, subseq. Foreign Correspondent and Political Correspondent, Daily Express, 1954–64; political staff, The Guardian, 1964–. Gerald Barry Award for journalism, 1984. *Recreation:* music. *Address:* 52A North Hill, N6. *T:* 081–340 5914. *Clubs:* Garrick, Wig and Pen.
See also Baron John-Mackie, Baron Mackie of Benshie, Sir M. Mackie.

AITKEN, Prof. John Thomas; Professor of Anatomy, University of London at University College, 1965–80, now Emeritus; *b* 6 May 1913; *s* of David and Helen Aitken; *m* 1941, Doreen Violet Whitaker; two *s* two *d*. *Educ:* High School, Glasgow; Grammar School, Hull; Glasgow University. MB, ChB 1936, MD 1950. University College, London, 1940–80. *Publications:* Manual of Human Anatomy (in collab.); Essential Anatomy (in collab.); papers on regeneration of nerves and muscles, in various jls. *Recreation:* gardening. *Address:* Woodpeckers Cottage, Sway Road, Brockenhurst, Hants SO42 7RX. *T:* Lymington (0590) 22493.

AITKEN, Jonathan William Patrick; MP (C) Thanet South, since 1983 (Thanet East, Feb. 1974–1983); *b* 30 Aug. 1942; *s* of late Sir William Aitken, KBE and of Hon. Lady Aitken, MBE, JP; *m* 1979, Lolicia Olivera, *d* of Mr and Mrs O. Azucki, Zürich; one *s* two *d*. *Educ:* Eton Coll.; Christ Church, Oxford. MA Hons Law. Private Sec. to Selwyn Lloyd, 1964–66; Foreign Corresp., London Evening Standard, 1966–71; Man. Dir, Slater Walker (Middle East) Ltd, 1973–75; Dep. Chm., Aitken Hume Internat. PLC, 1990– (Co-founder, 1981; Chm., 1981–90); Dir, TV-am PLC, 1981–88. Mem., Select Cttee on Employment, 1979–82. *Publications:* A Short Walk on the Campus, 1966; The Young Meteors, 1967; Land of Fortune: A Study of Australia, 1969; Officially Secret, 1970; articles in Spectator, Sunday Telegraph, Sydney Morning Herald, Washington Post, The Independent, etc. *Recreations:* squash, cross-country ski-ing, marathon running. *Address:* House of Commons, SW1A 0AA. *Clubs:* Pratt's, Turf, Beefsteak.

AITKEN, Prof. Martin Jim, FRS 1983; FSA, FRAS; Professor of Archaeometry, 1985–89, and Deputy Director, Research Laboratory for Archaeology, 1957–89, Oxford University; Fellow of Linacre College, Oxford, 1965–89; *b* 11 March 1922; *s* of Percy Aitken and Ethel Brittain; *m* Joan Killick; one *s* four *d*. *Educ:* Stamford Sch., Lincs; Wadham Coll. and Clarendon Lab., Oxford Univ. (MA, DPhil). Served War, RAF Radar Officer, 1942–46 (Burma Star, 1945). Mem., Former Physical Soc., 1951–89; MRI, 1972–89. Editor, Archaeometry, 1958–89. *Publications:* Physics and Archaeology, 1961, 2nd edn 1974; Thermoluminescence Dating, 1985; Science-based dating in Archaeology, 1990. *Recreations:* sailing, dinghy-racing. *Address:* Ofslang House, Islip, Oxford OX5 2SZ; Le Garret, 63930 Augerolles, France. *T:* 73–72–61–20.

AITKEN, Sir Robert (Stevenson), Kt 1960; MD (New Zealand), DPhil (Oxford); FRCP, FRACP; DL; retired; *b* NZ; *s* of late Rev. James Aitken; *m* 1929, Margaret G. Kane (*d* 1991); one *s* two *d*. *Educ:* Gisborne High School, Gisborne, NZ; University of Otago, Dunedin, NZ; Oxford. Medical Qualification in New Zealand, 1922; Rhodes Scholar, Balliol College, Oxford, 1924–26; attached to Medical Unit, The London Hospital, 1926–34; Reader in Medicine, British Post-Graduate Medical School, Univ. of

London, 1935–38; Regius Prof. of Medicine, Univ. of Aberdeen, 1939–48; Vice-Chancellor, Univ. of Otago, Dunedin, NZ, 1948–53; Vice-Chancellor, Univ. of Birmingham, 1953–68. Vice-Chm. Association of Univs of the British Commonwealth, 1955–58; Dep. Chm., UGC, 1968–73; Chairman: Committee of Vice-Chancellors and Principals, 1958–61; Birmingham Repertory Theatre, 1962–74. DL Co. Warwick, 1967, West Midlands, 1974. Hon. FRCPE; Hon. FDSRCS; Hon. DCL Oxford; Hon. LLD: Dalhousie, Melbourne, Panjab, McGill, Pennsylvania, Aberdeen, Newfoundland, Leicester, Birmingham, Otago; Hon. DSc: Sydney, Liverpool. *Publications:* papers in medical and scientific journals. *Address:* 6 Hintlesham Avenue, Birmingham B15 2PH.

See also T. H. D. Arie.

AJAYI, Prof. Jacob Festus Ade; Professor of History, University of Ibadan, 1963–89, now Emeritus; ; *b* 26 May 1929; *s* of Chief E. Ade Ajayi and late Mrs C. Bolajoko Ajayi; *m* 1956, Christie Aduke Martins; one *s* four *d*. *Educ:* University College, Ibadan; University College, Leicester; Univ. of London; BA, PhD (London). Research Fellow, Inst. of Historical Research, London, 1957–58; Lectr, Univ. of Ibadan, 1958–62, Sen. Lectr, 1962–63; Dean, Faculty of Arts, 1964–66; Asst to Vice-Chancellor, 1966–68. Fellow, Centre for Advanced Study in the Behavioural Sciences, Stanford, Calif, 1970–71; Vice-Chancellor, Univ. of Lagos, 1972–78; Pro-Chancellor, Ondo State Univ., Ado-Ekiti, 1984–88. Member: UN University Council, 1974–80 (Chm., 1976–77); Nat. Archives Cttee, Nigeria, 1961–72; Nat. Antiquities Commn, Nigeria, 1970–74; Exec. Council, Internat. African Inst. London, 1971– (Chm., 1975–87); Exec. Bd, Assoc. of African Univs, 1974–80; Admin. Bd., Internat. Assoc. of Univs, 1980–90; Pres., Historical Soc. of Nigeria, 1972–81; Pres., Internat. Congress of African Studies, 1978–85. Hon. LLD Leicester, 1975; Hon. DLitt Birmingham, 1984. Fellow, Hist. Soc. of Nigeria, 1980; Overseas FRHistS, 1982. National Merit Award, Nigeria, 1986. Traditional titles, Bobapitan of Ikole-Ekiti and Onikoyi of Ife, 1983. *Publications:* Milestones in Nigerian History, 1962; (ed, with Ian Espie) A Thousand Years of West African History, 1964; (with R. S. Smith) Yoruba Warfare in the Nineteenth Century, 1964; Christian Missions in Nigeria: the making of a new elite, 1965; (ed, with Michael Crowder) A History of West Africa, vol. I, 1972; vol. II, 1974; (ed jtly) The University of Ibadan, 1948–73, 1973; (ed with Bashir Ikara) Evolution of Political Culture in Nigeria, 1985; (ed with M. Crowder) A Historical Atlas of Africa, 1985; (ed) Africa in the Nineteenth Century until the 1880s, vol. VI of Unesco General History of Africa, 1989; History and the Nation, and other Addresses, 1990; contribs to Jl Historical Soc. of Nigeria, Jl of African History, etc. *Recreations:* dancing, tennis. *Address:* 1 Ojobadan Avenue, Bodija, PO Box 14617, UI Post Office, Ibadan, Nigeria.

AKEHURST, Gen. Sir John (Bryan), KCB 1984; CBE 1976; Deputy Supreme Allied Commander, Europe, 1987–90; *b* 12 Feb. 1930; *s* of late Geoffrey and Doris Akehurst; *m* 1955, Shirley Ann, *er d* of late Major W. G. Webb, MBE, and of Ethel Webb; one *s* one *d* decd. *Educ:* Cranbrook Sch.; RMA, Sandhurst. Commnd Northamptonshire Regt, 1949; Malay Regt (despatches), 1952–55; Adjt, 5th Northamptonshire Regt (TA), 1959–60; Staff Coll., Camberley, 1961; Brigade Major, 12 Infantry Bde Gp, 1962–64; Instructor, Staff Coll., Camberley, 1966–68; commanded 2nd Royal Anglian Regt, 1968–70; Directing Staff, IDC/RCDS, 1970–72; Comdt, Jun. Div., Staff Coll., 1972–74; Comdr, Dhofar Bde, Sultan of Oman's Armed Forces, 1974–76; Dep. Mil. Sec. (A), MoD (Army), 1976–79; GOC 4th Armoured Div., BAOR, 1979–81; Comdt, The Staff Coll., Camberley, 1982–83; Comdr, UK Field Army, and Inspector Gen., TA, 1984–87. Sen. Mil. Visitor to Saudi Arabia, 1985–87; Dep. Col, 1981–86, Col, 1986–91, Royal Anglian Regt. Chm., Council, TA&VRA, 1990–; Mem. Council, RUSI, 1985–88. Chm., 1982–84, Pres., 1984–90, Army Golf Assoc.; Vice Patron, Army Officers' Golf Soc., 1986– (Pres., 1983–86). Gov., Royal Star and Garter Home, 1990–91. Governor: Harrow Sch., 1982– (Chm. of Govs, 1991–); John Lyon Sch., 1989–91. Order of Oman, 3rd Class (mil.), 1976. *Publication:* We Won a War, 1982. *Recreations:* golf, trout fishing, travel. *Address:* c/o Midland Bank, Minehead, Somerset TA24 5LH. *Clubs:* Army and Navy; Bath Golf.

AKENHEAD, Robert; QC 1989; *b* 15 Sept. 1949; *s* of late Edmund and of Angela Akenhead; *m* 1972, Elizabeth Anne Jackson; one *s* three *d*. *Educ:* Rugby School; Exeter Univ. (LLB). Called to the Bar, Inner Temple, 1972; in practice as barrister, 1973–. *Publication:* Site Investigation and the Law, 1984. *Recreations:* theatre, cricket, ski-ing. *Address:* 1 Atkin Building, Gray's Inn, WC1. *T:* 071–404 0102.

AKERLOF, Prof. George Arthur, PhD; teaching in Economics Department, University of California at Berkeley, since 1980; Cassel Professor of Economics, London School of Economics and Political Science, 1978–81; *b* 17 June 1940; *s* of Gosta C. Akerlof and Rosalie C. Akerlof; *m* 1978, Janet Yellen. *Educ:* Yale Univ. (BA 1962); MIT (PhD 1966). Fellowships: Woodrow Wilson, 1962–63; National Science Co-op., 1963–66; Fulbright, 1967–68; Guggenheim, 1973–74. Univ. of Calif, Berkeley: Asst Prof. of Econs, 1966–70; Associate Prof., 1970–77; Prof., 1977–78. Vis. Prof., Indian Statistical Inst., New Delhi, 1967–68. Sen. Economist, Council of Econ. Advisors, USA, 1973–74; Vis. Economist, Bd of Governors of Fed. Reserve System, USA, 1977–78. *Publications:* contrib. American Econ. Rev., Econ. Jl, Qly Jl Econs, Jl Polit. Econ., Rev. of Econ. Studies, Internat. Econ. Rev., Jl Econ. Theory, Indian Econ. Rev., and Rev. of Econs and Stats. *Address:* Economics Department, University of California, Berkeley, Calif 94720, USA. *Club:* Piggy (Center Harbor, NH, USA).

AKERS, John Fellows; Chairman, International Business Machines Corp., since 1986; *b* 1934; *m* 1960, Susan Davis; one *s* two *d*. *Educ:* Yale Univ. (BS). International Business Machines Corp., 1960–: Pres., Data Processing Div., 1974–76; IBM Vice Pres., Asst Gp Exec., plans and controls, Data Processing Product Gp, 1976–78; IBM Vice Pres., Gp Exec., Data Processing Marketing Gp, 1978–81, Inf. Systems and Communications Gp, 1981–82, IBM Sen. Vice Pres., 1982–83; Dir, IBM, 1983–; Pres., 1983–89; Chief Exec. Officer, 1985–. Dir, New York Times Co., 1985–. Member: President's Educn Policy Adv. Cttee; President's Adv. Cttee on Points of Light Initiative Foundn. Trustee: MMA; CIT; Chm., Bd of Governors, United Way of America. *Address:* (office) IBM Corp., Old Orchard Road, Armonk, NY 10504, USA.

AKERS-DOUGLAS, family name of **Viscount Chilston.**

AKERS-JONES, Sir David, KBE 1985; CMG 1978; Chief Secretary, Hong Kong, 1985–86; Acting Governor, Hong Kong, Dec. 1986–April 1987; Chairman, Hong Kong Housing Authority, since 1988; *b* 14 April 1927; *s* of Walter George and Dorothy Jones; *m* 1951, Jane Spickernell (MBE 1988); one *d* (one *s* decd). *Educ:* Worthing High Sch.; Brasenose Coll., Oxford (MA). British India Steam Navigation Co., 1945–49. Malayan Civil Service (studied Hokkien and Malay), 1954–57; Hong Kong Civil Service, 1957–86; Government Secretary: for New Territories, 1973–81; for City and New Territories, 1981–83; for Dist Admin, 1983–85. Advr to Gov., April-Sept. 1987. Chairman: WWF Hong Kong, 1986–; Hong Kong Housing Soc. Develt Cttee, 1981–; Hong Kong Artists' Guild, 1987–; Inst. for Res. and Consultancy, City Poly. of Hong Kong, 1989–. Pres., Outward Bound Trust, Hong Kong, 1986–; Vice-Patron, Hong Kong Football Assoc. Hon. DCL Kent, 1987; Hon. LLD Chinese Univ. of Hong Kong, 1988. *Recreations:* painting, gardening, walking, music. *Address:* Dragon View, Tsung Lung Tau, Castle Peak Road, New Territories, Hong Kong. *Clubs:* Athenæum, Royal Over-Seas League; Hong Kong, Kowloon, Dynasty (Hong Kong).

AKHTAR, Prof. Muhammad, FRS 1980; Professor of Biochemistry, since 1973, and Head of Department of Biochemistry, since 1978, University of Southampton; *b* 23 Feb. 1933; *m* 1963, Monika E. Schurmann; two *s*. *Educ:* Punjab Univ., Pakistan (MSc 1st class 1954); Imperial College, London (PhD, DIC 1959). Research Scientist, Inst. for Medicine and Chemistry, Cambridge, Mass, USA, 1959–63; University of Southampton: Lecturer in Biochemistry, 1963–66; Senior Lectr, 1966–68; Reader, 1968–73; Chm., Sch. of Biochem. and Physiol. Scis, 1983–87; Dir, SERC Centre for Molecular Recognition, 1990–. Chm., Inst. of Biomolecular Scis, 1989–90. Member: Chemical Soc. of GB; American Chemical Soc.; Biochemical Soc. of GB; Council, Royal Soc., 1983–85; Founding Fellow, Third World Acad. of Sciences, 1983. Sitara-I-Imtiaz (Pakistan), 1981. *Publications:* numerous works on: enzyme mechanisms; synthesis and biosynthesis of steroids and porphyrins; biochemistry of vision; synthesis of anti-microbial compounds. *Address:* Department of Biochemistry, University of Southampton, Southampton SO9 3TU. *T:* Southampton (0703) 595000.

AKIHITO, HM the Emperor of Japan; Collar, Supreme Order of Chrysanthemum, 1989; *b* Tokyo, 23 Dec. 1933; *e s* of His late Majesty Emperor Hirohito (Showa) and of HM Empress Dowager Nagako; *S* father, 1989; *m* 1959, Michiko Shoda; two *s* one *d*. *Educ:* Gakushuin Primary, Jun. and Sen. High Schs; Dept of Politics, Faculty of Politics and Econs, Gakushuin Univ. Official Investiture as Crown Prince of Japan, 1952. Res. Associate, Australian Mus.; Mem., Ichthyological Soc. of Japan; Hon. Mem., Linnean Soc. of London. *Heir: er s* Crown Prince Naruhito, *b* Tokyo, 23 Feb. 1960. *Publications:* (contrib. jtly) Fishes of the Japanese Archipelago, 1984; (jtly) The Fresh Water Fishes of Japan, 1987; 27 papers on gobies. *Recreation:* tennis. *Address:* Imperial Palace, 1-1 Chiyoda, Chiyoda-ku, Tokyo 100, Japan. *T:* (03) 3213–1111.

AKINKUGBE, Prof. Oladipo Olujimi, CON 1979; Officier de l'Ordre National de la République de Côte d'Ivoire, 1981; MD, DPhil; FRCP, FWACP, FAS; Professor of Medicine, University of Ibadan, Nigeria, since 1968; *b* 17 July 1933; *s* of late Chief David Akinbobola and of Chief (Mrs) Grace Akinkugbe; *m* 1965, Dr Folasade Modupeore Dina; two *s*. *Educ:* Univs of Ibadan, London (MD), Liverpool (DTM&H) and Oxford (DPhil). FRCP 1968; FWACP 1975; FAS 1980. House Surg., London Hosp., 1958; House Phys., King's Coll. Hosp., London, 1959; Commonwealth Res. Fellow, Balliol Coll. and Regius Dept of Medicine, Oxford, 1962–64; Head of Dept of Medicine, 1972, Dean of Medicine, 1970–74, and Chm., Cttee of Deans, 1972–74, Univ. of Ibadan; Vice-Chancellor: Univ. of Ilorin, 1977–78 (Principal, 1975–77); Ahmadu Bello Univ., Zaria, 1978–79. Rockefeller Vis. Fellow, US Renal Centres, 1966; Vis. Fellow in Medicine, Univs of Manchester, Cambridge and London, 1969; Vis. Prof. of Medicine, Harvard Univ., 1974–75; Vis. Fellow, Balliol Coll., Oxford, 1981–82. Adviser on Postgrad. Med. Educn to Fed. Govt of Nigeria, 1972–75; Pres., Nigerian Assoc. of Nephrology, 1987–90; Member: Univ. Grants Commn, Uganda Govt; OAU Scientific Panels on Health Manpower Develt; Council, Internat. Soc. of Hypertension, 1982–90; Bd of Trustees, African Assoc. of Nephrology, 1986–; internat. socs of hypertension, cardiology, and nephrology; Med. Res. Soc. of GB; Scientific Adv. Panel, Ciba Foundn; WHO Expert Adv. Panels on Cardiovascular Diseases, 1973–78, on Health Manpower 1979–; WHO Adv. Council on Health Res., 1990–; Sec. to WHO 1984 Technical Discussions. Pro-Chancellor, and Chm. of Council, Univ. of Port-Harcourt, Nigeria, 1986–90. Member, Editorial Bd: Jl of Hypertension, 1984–90; Jl of Human Hypertension, 1988–; Kidney International, 1990–. Hon. DSc Ilorin, 1982. Searle Dist. Res. Award, 1989. Traditional title, Atobase of Ife, 1991. *Publications:* High Blood Pressure in the African, 1972; (ed) Priorities in National Health Planning, 1974; (ed) Cardiovascular Disease in Africa, 1976; (ed jtly) Clinical Medicine in the Tropics Series, 1987–; papers on hypertension and renal disease in African, Eur. and Amer. med. jls, and papers on med. and higher educn. *Recreations:* music, gardening. *Address:* Department of Medicine, University of Ibadan, Ibadan, Nigeria. *T:* 400550. *Clubs:* Rotary International; Dining (Ibadan); Oxford and Cambridge (Nigeria).

ALANBROOKE, 3rd Viscount *cr* 1946; **Alan Victor Harold Brooke;** Baron Alanbrooke, 1945; *b* 24 Nov. 1932; *s* of 1st Viscount Alanbrooke, KG, GCB, OM, GCVO, DSO, and Benita Blanche (*d* 1968), *d* of Sir Harold Pelly, 4th Bt; *S* half-brother, 1972. *Educ:* Harrow; Bristol Univ. (BEd Hons 1976). Qualified teacher, 1975. Served Army, 1952–72; Captain RA, retired. *Heir:* none.

ALBEE, Edward; American dramatist; *b* 12 March 1928. *Publications: plays:* The Zoo Story, 1958; The Death of Bessie Smith, 1959; The Sandbox, 1959; The American Dream, 1960; Who's Afraid of Virginia Woolf?, 1962; (adapted from Carson McCullers' novella) The Ballad of the Sad Café, 1963; Tiny Alice, 1964; (adapted from the novel by James Purdy) Malcolm, 1965; A Delicate Balance, 1966 (Pulitzer Prize, 1967); (adapted from the play by Giles Cooper) Everything in the Garden, 1967; Box and Quotations from Chairman Mao Tse-Tung, 1968; All Over, 1971; Seascape, 1974 (Pulitzer Prize, 1975); Listening, 1975; Counting the Ways, 1976; The Lady from Dubuque, 1978; Lolita (adapted from V. Nabakov), 1979; The Man Who Had Three Arms, 1981; Finding the Sun, 1982; Walking, 1984; Marriage Play, 1986. *Address:* 14 Harrison Street, New York, NY 10013, USA.

ALBEMARLE, 10th Earl of, *cr* 1696; **Rufus Arnold Alexis Keppel;** Baron Ashford, 1696; Viscount Bury, 1696; *b* 16 July 1965; *s* of Derek William Charles Keppel, Viscount Bury (*d* 1968), and Marina, *yr d* of late Count Serge Orloff-Davidoff; *S* grandfather, 1979. *Heir: cousin* Crispian Walter John Keppel [*b* 29 Oct. 1948; *m* 1990, Tina Ammann]. *Address:* 20A Pembroke Square, W8 6PA.

ALBEMARLE, Countess of, (Diana Cicely), DBE 1956; Chairman: Development Commission, 1948–74; The Drama Board, 1964–78; *b* 6 Aug. 1909; *o c* of John Archibald Grove; *m* 1931, 9th Earl of Albemarle, MC (*d* 1979); one *d*. *Educ:* Sherborne Sch. for Girls. Norfolk County Organiser, WVS, 1939–44. Chairman: Exec. Cttee, Nat. Fedn of Women's Institutes, 1946–51; Departmental Cttee on Youth Service, 1958–60; Nat. Youth Employment Council, 1962–68. Vice-Chm., British Council, 1959–74. Member: Arts Council, 1951; Royal Commn on Civil Service, 1954; Harkness Fellowship Cttee of Award, 1963–69; UGC, 1956–70; Standing Commn on Museums and Galleries, 1958–71; English Local Govt Boundary Commn, 1971–77; Youth Develt Council, 1960–68; Council, Univ. of E Anglia, 1964–72. Life Trustee, Carnegie UK Trust (Chm., 1977–82); Trustee of: The Observer until 1977; Glyndebourne Arts Trust, 1968–80. RD Councillor, Wayland, Norfolk, 1935–46. Hon. DLitt Reading, 1959; Hon. DCL Oxon, 1960; Hon. LLD London, 1960. *Recreations:* gardening, reading. *Address:* Seymours, Melton, Woodbridge, Suffolk IP12 1LW. *T:* Woodbridge (03943) 2151.

See also Sir Hew Hamilton-Dalrymple.

ALBERT, Sir Alexis (François), Kt 1972; CMG 1967; VRD 1942; Chairman: Albert Investments Pty Ltd, since 1962; J. Albert & Son Pty Ltd, Sydney, since 1962; The Australian Broadcasting Company Pty Ltd, Sydney, since 1962; *b* 15 Oct. 1904; *s* of late M. F. and M. E. Albert, Sydney; *m* 1934, Elsa K. R. (decd), *d* of late Capt. A. E. Lundgren, Sydney; three *s*. *Educ:* Knox College, Sydney; St Paul's College, University of Sydney.

BEc 1930. Director: Amalgamated Television Services Pty Ltd, 1955–87; Australasian Performing Right Association Ltd, 1946–76. Underwriting Member of Lloyd's, 1944–74; President, Royal Blind Soc. of NSW, 1962–78; Fellow of Council, St Paul's Coll., Univ. of Sydney, 1965–; Council, Nat. Heart Foundn of Aust., NSW Div. 1959–. RANR, 1918–49; Lt-Comdr, retd. Hon. ADC to Governors of NSW, 1937–57. KStJ 1985. *Recreations:* swimming, yachting. *Address:* 25 Coolong Road, Vaucluse, NSW 2030, Australia; (office) 175 Macquarie Street, Sydney, NSW 2000. *T:* 232 2144. *Clubs:* Naval and Military; Australian, Union (Sydney); Royal Sydney Golf, Royal Sydney Yacht Squadron (Commodore 1971–75); New York Yacht.

ALBERT, Carl (Bert); Speaker, US House of Representatives, 1970–76; Member, Third Oklahoma District, 1947–76 (Democratic Whip, 1955–62; Majority Leader, 1962–71); *b* 10 May 1908, McAlester, Oklahoma; *s* of Ernest Homer and Leona Ann (Scott) Albert; *m* 1942, Mary Sue Greene Harmon; one *s* one *d*. *Educ:* Univ. of Oklahoma (AB 1931); Oxford Univ. (Rhodes Scholar, BA 1933, BCL 1934). Served US Army, 1941–46. Admitted Oklahoma Bar, 1935; Legal Clerk, Fed. Housing Admin, 1935–37; attorney and accountant, Sayre Oil Co., 1937–38; legal dept, Ohio Oil Co., 1939–40. Practised law: Oklahoma City, 1938; Mattoon, Ill, 1938–39; McAlester, Oklahoma, 1946–47. Bronze Star, 1945. *Recreation:* reading. *Address:* Route two, McAlester, Oklahoma 74501, USA.

ALBERTI, Prof. Kurt George Matthew Mayer, DPhil; FRCP, FRCPE, FRCPath; Professor of Medicine, University of Newcastle upon Tyne, since 1985; *b* 27 Sept. 1937; *s* of William Peter Matthew Alberti and Edith Elizabeth Alberti; *m* 1964; three *s*. *Educ:* Balliol Coll., Oxford (MA; DPhil 1964; BM, BCh 1965). FRCP 1978; FRCPath 1985; FRCPE 1988. Res. Fellow, Harvard Univ., Boston, USA, 1966–69; Res. Officer, Dept of Medicine, Oxford Univ., 1969–73; Prof. of Chemical Pathology and Human Metabolism, 1973–78, Prof. of Clinical Biochemistry and Metabolic Medicine, 1978–85, Univ. of Southampton. Vice-Pres., Internat. Diabetes Fedn, 1988–. Fellow, All India Inst. of Diabetes, 1976; Hon. Member: Hungarian Diabetes Assoc., 1986; Argentinian Diabetes Assoc., 1991. *Publications:* edited more than 30 medical books, including: Diabetes Annual, Vols 1–6; Recent Advances in Clinical Biochemistry, Vols 1–3; Internat. Textbook of Diabetes Mellitus, 1991; author of more than 600 pubns in learned jls. *Recreatioons:* hill walking, jogging, crime fiction, Mozart. *Address:* 25 Beverley Gardens, Cullercoats, North Shields, Tyne and Wear NE30 4NS. *T:* 091–252 2169.

ALBERTYN, Rt. Rev. Charles Henry; a Bishop Suffragan, Diocese of Cape Town, since 1983; *b* 24 Dec. 1928; *s* of Adam and Annie Albertyn; *m* 1965, Berenice Lategan; one *s* two *d*. *Educ:* Hewat Training College (Teacher's Diploma 1948); Diocesan Clergy School, Cape Town (LTh 1956). Teaching, 1948–52. Deacon 1955, priest 1956; Assistant, St Nicholas, Matroosfontein, 1955–60; Priest-in-charge, St Helena Bay, 1960–64; Assistant, St George's, Silvertown, 1965–70; Rector: Church of Holy Spirit, Heideveld, 1970–75; St Mary's, Kraaifontein, 1975–78; Church of Resurrection, Bonteheuwel, 1978–83; Canon of St George Cathedral, Cape Town, 1972–83; Archdeacon of Bellville, 1981–83. *Recreation:* watching soccer. *Address:* Bishopsholme, 18 Rue Ursula, Glenhaven, Bellville, Cape, S Africa. *T:* (021) 951 4277.

ALBERY, Tim; theatre and opera director; *b* 20 May 1952. *Theatre* productions include: War Crimes, ICA, 1981; Secret Gardens, Amsterdam and ICA, 1983; Venice Preserv'd, Almeida, 1983; Hedda Gabler, Almeida, 1984; The Princess of Cleves, ICA, 1985; Mary Stuart, Greenwich, 1988; As You Like It, Old Vic, 1989; Berenice, NT, 1990; *opera* productions include: for English National Opera: Billy Budd, 1988; Beatrice and Benedict, 1990; Peter Grimes, 1991; for Opera North: The Midsummer Marriage, 1985; The Trojans, 1986; La finta giardiniera, 1989; Don Giovanni, 1991; for Welsh National Opera: The Trojans, 1987; for Scottish Opera: The Midsummer Marriage, 1988; The Trojans, 1990; for Balignano Fest., Italy, The Turn of the Screw, 1983; for Bregenz, Austria, La Wally, 1990. *Address:* c/o Harriet Cruickshank, Cruickshank Cazenove, 97 Old South Lambeth Road, SW8 1XU.

ALBERY, Prof. Wyndham John, FRS 1985; FRSC; Master, University College, Oxford, since 1989; *b* 5 April 1936; *s* of late Michael James Albery, QC, and of Mary Lawton Albery. *Educ:* Winchester Coll.; Balliol Coll., Oxford (MA, DPhil). Weir Jun. Research Fellow, 1962, Fellow, 1963–78, University Coll., Oxford; Lectr, Phys. Chem., Univ. of Oxford, 1964–78; Imperial College, London: Prof., Phys. Chemistry, 1978–89; Staff Orator, 1980–83; Dean, RCS, 1986–89. Vis. Fellow, Univ. of Minnesota, 1965; Vis. Prof., Harvard Univ., 1976. Tilden Lectr, RSC, 1979; Sherman Fairchild Schol., Calif. Inst. of Tech., 1985. Chairman: SERC Chemistry Cttee, 1982–85; Electrochem. Gp, RSC, 1985–89. Mem. Council, Royal Instn, 1985–88. Writer for television series That Was The Week That Was, 1963–64; also (with John Gould) two musicals, Who Was That Lady?, and On The Boil. Curator, Oxford Playhouse, 1974–78; Governor, Old Vic, 1979–89; Burton Taylor Theatre Management Cttee, 1990–. Gov., Rugby Sch., 1987–. Fellow, Winchester Coll., 1989–. Hon. DSc Kent, 1990. *Publications:* Ring-Disc Electrodes, 1971; Electrode Kinetics, 1975; papers in jls: Faraday I, Nature, and Jls of Electrochemical Soc., Electroanalytical Chemistry, etc. *Recreations:* theatre, skiing. *Address:* Master's Lodgings, University College, Oxford OX1 4BH. *T:* Oxford (0865) 276600. *Club:* Garrick.

ALBROW, Desmond; an Assistant Editor, Sunday Telegraph, 1976–87; *b* 22 Jan. 1925; *er s* of Frederick and Agnes Albrow; *m* 1950, Aileen Mary Jennings; one *s* three *d*. *Educ:* St Bede's Grammar Sch., Bradford; Keble Coll., Oxford (MA). On the Editorial Staff of the Yorkshire Observer, 1950–51, Manchester Guardian, 1951–56, Daily Telegraph, 1956–60; Sunday Telegraph, 1960–66: Chief Sub-Editor, News Editor, and Night Editor; Editor, Catholic Herald, 1966–71; Features Editor, Sunday Telegraph, 1971–76. *Recreations:* drinking in moderation and talking to excess; watching other people cultivate their gardens. *Address:* Totyngton Cottage, 18 Victoria Road, Teddington, Mddx TW11 0BG. *T:* 081–977 4220. *Clubs:* Garrick, Presscala.

ALBU, Austen Harry, BSc (Eng.); FCGI, CEng; *b* London, 21 Sept. 1903; *s* of Ferdinand and Beatrice Rachel Albu; *m* 1st, 1929, Rose (*d* 1956), *d* of Simon Marks, Newcastle; two *s*; 2nd, 1958, Dr Marie Jahoda, *qv*. *Educ:* Tonbridge School; City and Guilds College (Imperial College of Science and Technology). Works Manager, Aladdin Industries, Greenford, 1930–46. Dep. Pres., Govtl Sub-Commn, CCG, 1946–47. Dep. Dir, British Institute of Management, Feb.-Nov. 1948. MP (Lab) Edmonton, 1948–Feb. 1974; Minister of State, Dept of Economic Affairs, 1965–67. Fellow, Imp. Coll. of Science and Technology. DUniv Surrey, 1966. *Address:* 17 The Crescent, Keymer, Sussex BN6 8RB.

ALBU, Sir George, 3rd Bt, *cr* (UK) 1912, of Grosvenor Place, City of Westminster, and Johannesburg, Province of Transvaal, South Africa; farmer; *b* 5 June 1944; *o s* of Major Sir George Werner Albu, 2nd Bt, and Kathleen Betty (*d* 1956), *d* of Edward Charles Dicey, Parktown, Johannesburg; *S* father, 1963; *m* 1969, Joan Valerie Millar, London; two *d*. *Recreations:* horse racing, tennis, golf. *Heir:* none. *Address:* Glen Hamish Farm, PO Box 62, Richmond, Natal, 3780, South Africa. *T:* Richmond (Natal) 2587. *Clubs:* Victoria (Pietermaritzburg, Natal); Richmond Country (Richmond, Natal).

ALBU, Marie, (Mrs A. H. Albu); *see* Jahoda, Prof. Marie.

ALCOCK, Prof. Leslie, OBE 1991; Hon. Professorial Research Fellow, University of Glasgow, since 1990; *b* 24 April 1925; *o s* of Philip John Alcock and Mary Ethel (*née* Bagley); *m* 1950, Elizabeth A. Blair; one *s* one *d*. *Educ:* Manchester Grammar Sch.; Brasenose Coll., Oxford. BA 1949, MA 1950. Supt of Exploration, Dept of Archaeology, Govt of Pakistan, 1950; Curator, Abbey House Museum, Leeds, 1952; Asst Lectr, etc, UC Cardiff, 1953; Professor of Archaeology: UC Cardiff, 1973; Univ. of Glasgow, 1973–90. Member: Bd of Trustees, Nat. Mus. of Antiquities, Scotland, 1973–85; Ancient Monuments Bd, Scotland, 1974–90; Royal Commn on Ancient and Historical Monuments of Scotland, 1977–90; Royal Commn on Ancient and Historical Monuments in Wales, 1986–90. President: Cambrian Archaeological Assoc., 1982; Glasgow Archaeological Soc., 1984–85; Soc. of Antiquaries, Scotland, 1984–87. Lectures: Jarrow, 1988; Rhind, Soc. of Antiquaries, Scotland, 1988–89. FSA 1957; FRHistS 1969; FRSE 1976–87. *Publications:* Dinas Powys, 1963; Arthur's Britain, 1971; Cadbury/Camelot, 1972; Economy, Society and Warfare, 1987; (co-ed) From the Baltic to the Black Sea, 1988; articles and reviews in British and Amer. jls. *Recreations:* mountain and coastal scenery, music. *Address:* 29 Hamilton Drive, Hillhead, Glasgow G12 8DN.

ALCOCK, Air Marshal Robert James Michael, CB 1989; Chief of Logistics Support, Royal Air Force, since 1991; *b* 11 July 1936; *s* of late William George and Doris Alcock; *m* 1965, Pauline Mary Oades; two *d*. *Educ:* Victoria College, Jersey; Royal Aircraft Establishment. CEng, FIMechE. Commissioned, Engineer Branch, RAF, 1959; RAF Tech. Coll., Henlow, 1961; Goose Bay, Labrador, 1964; Units in Bomber Comd, 1959–69; RAF Staff Coll., Bracknell, 1970; PSO to DGEng (RAF), 1971–73; OC Eng. Wing, RAF Coningsby, 1973–75; OC No 23 Maintenance Unit, RAF Aldergrove, 1975–77; Group Captain (Plans), HQ RAF Support Command, 1977–79; MoD, 1979–81; Dep. Comdt, RAF Staff Coll., Bracknell, 1981–84; RCDS, 1984; Dir Gen. of Communications, Inf. Systems and Orgn (RAF), 1985–88; AO Engrg, HQ Strike Comd, 1988–91. *Recreations:* golf, model aircraft, sailing. *Address:* c/o National Westminster Bank, Farnborough, Hants. *Clubs:* Royal Air Force; Berkshire Golf, Trevose Golf.

ALDAM, Jeffery Heaton, CBE 1980; MC 1945; County Education Officer, Hampshire, 1973–83, retired; *b* 11 Nov. 1922; *s* of William and Clara Ellen Aldam; *m* 1950, Editha Hilary Mary (*née* Preece); two *s* two *d*. *Educ:* Chesterfield Grammar Sch.; Trinity Coll., Cambridge (MA); Harvard Univ. (AM). Served 13th/18th Royal Hussars (QMO), 1942–45. Admin. Asst, Asst Educn Officer, then Sen. Asst Educn Officer, Norfolk CC, 1949–56; Dep. County Educn Officer, NR Yorks CC, 1957–62; Chief Educn Officer, East Suffolk CC, 1962–71; County Educn Officer, (former) Hampshire CC, 1972–73. Mem., Court and Council, Univ. of Southampton, 1972–. *Recreations:* reading, walking, gardening. *Address:* 18 Lynford Way, Weeke, Winchester SO22 6BW. *T:* Winchester (0962) 853594.

ALDENHAM, 6th Baron *cr* 1896, of Aldenham, Co. Hertford, **AND HUNSDON OF HUNSDON,** 4th Baron *cr* 1923, of Briggens, Co. Hertford; **Vicary Tyser Gibbs;** *b* 9 June 1948; *s* of 5th Baron Aldenham and of Mary Elizabeth, *o d* of late Walter Parkyns Tyser; *S* father, 1986; *m* 1980, Josephine Nicola, *er d* of John Richmond Fell, Lower Bourne, Farnham, Surrey; one *s* one *d*. *Educ:* Eton; Oriel College, Oxford; RAC, Cirencester. *Heir:* *s* Hon. Humphrey William Fell Gibbs, *b* 31 Jan. 1989. *Address:* Aldenham Wood Lodge, Watling Street, Elstree, Herts WD6 3AA.

ALDER, Lucette, (Mrs Alan Alder); *see* Aldous, Lucette.

ALDER, Michael; Controller, English Regional Television, British Broadcasting Corporation, 1977–86, retired; *b* 3 Nov. 1928; *s* of late Thomas Alder and Winifred Miller; *m* 1955, Freda, *d* of late John and Doris Hall; two *d*. *Educ:* Ranelagh Sch., Bracknell, Berks; Rutherford Coll., Newcastle-upon-Tyne. Newcastle Evening Chronicle, 1947–59; BBC North-East: Chief News Asst, Newcastle; Area News Editor, Newcastle; Representative, NE England, 1959–69; Head of Regional Television Development, BBC, 1969–77. Mem., Exec. Cttee, Relate (formerly Nat. Marriage Guidance Council), 1987– (Chm., S Warwicks, 1987–89; Chm., Appeals Cttee, 1988–). Mem., Incorporated Co. of Butchers, 1948. Freeman, City of Newcastle upon Tyne. *Recreations:* gardening, fishing, walking, country pursuits. *Address:* Red Roofs, Bates Lane, Tanworth-in-Arden, Warwicks B94 5AR. *T:* Tanworth-in-Arden (05644) 2403.

ALDERSLADE, Richard, FFPHM, Regional Director of Public Health and Regional Medical Officer, Trent Regional Health Authority, since 1988; *b* 11 Aug. 1947; *s* of Herbert Raymond Alderslade and Edna F. Alderslade; *m* 1974, Elizabeth Rose; two *s* one *d* (and one *d* decd). *Educ:* Chichester High Sch. for Boys; Christ Church, Oxford (BM BCh; MA); St George's Hosp. GP, 1974–76; Registrar in Community Medicine, 1976–78, Lectr, 1978–79; MO and SMO, DHSS, 1979–85; Specialist in Community Medicine, 1985–88 and Community Unit Gen. Manager, 1986–88, Hull HA. *Publications:* articles on public health, BMJ and other jls. *Recreations:* walking, railways, photography. *Address:* 85 Market Place, South Cave, Brough, N Humberside HU15 2AS. *T:* Howden (0430) 421362.

ALDERSON, Brian Wouldhave; freelance editor and writer; Children's Books Editor, The Times, since 1967; *b* 19 Sept. 1930; *s* of John William Alderson and Helen Marjory (*née* Hogg), *m* 1953, Valerie Christine (*née* Wells); three *s* (and two *s* decd). *Educ:* Ackworth Sch.; University College of the South-West, Exeter (BA Hons). Work in the book trade, 1952–63; Tutor-librarian, East Herts Coll. of Further Educn, 1963–65; Sen. Lectr, (on Children's Literature and on the Book Trade), Polytechnic of N London, 1965–83. Visiting Professor: Univ. of Southern Mississippi, 1985; UCLA, 1986. Founder and first Chmn., Children's Books Hist. Soc., 1969–78. Exhibition organiser: (with descriptive notes): Looking at Picture Books, NBL, 1973; Grimm Tales in England, British Library, 1985–86; (with full catalogue), Randolph Caldecott and the Art of the English Picture Book, 1986–87. Eleanor Farjeon Award, 1968. *Publications: translations:* Hürlimann, Three Centuries of Children's Books in Europe, 1967; Grimm, Popular Folk Tales, 1978; *edited:* The Juvenile Library, 1966–74; The Colour Fairy Books, by Andrew Lang, 1975–; Lear, a Book of Bosh, 1975; Children's Books in England, by F. J. Harvey Darton, 1982; Hans Christian Andersen and his Eventyr in England, 1982; Andersen and Drewsen, Christine's Picture Book, 1984; Sing a Song for Sixpence, 1986; (with Iona and Robert Opie) Treasures of Childhood, 1989. *Recreations:* bibliography, dale-walking. *Address:* 28 Victoria Road, Richmond, North Yorks DL10 4AS. *T:* Richmond (0748) 3648.

ALDERSON, Daphne Elizabeth, (Mrs J. K. A. Alderson); *see* Wickham, D. E.

ALDERSON, John Cottingham, CBE 1981; QPM 1974; writer and commentator on police and penal affairs; Chief Constable of Devon and Cornwall, 1973–82; *b* 28 May 1922; *e s* of late Ernest Cottingham Alderson and Elsie Lavinia Rose; *m* 1948, Irené Macmillan Stirling; one *s*. *Educ:* Barnsley Elem. Schs and Techn. College. Called to Bar, Middle Temple. British Meml Foundn Fellow, Australia, 1956; Extension Certif. in Criminology, Univ. of Leeds. Highland LI, 1938–41 (Corp.); Army Phys. Trng Corps, N Africa and Italy, 1941–46 (Warrant Officer). West Riding Constabulary as Constable,

1946; Police Coll., 1954; Inspector, 1955; Sub-Divisional Comd, 1960; Sen. Comd Course, Police Coll., 1963–64; Dep. Chief Constable, Dorset, 1964–66; Metropolitan Police, Dep. Comdr (Admin and Ops), 1966; 2nd-in-comd No 3 Police District, 1967; Dep. Asst Comr (Trng), 1968; Comdt, Police Coll., 1970; Asst Comr (Personnel and Trng), 1973. Consultant on Human Rights to Council of Europe, 1981–. Member: BBC Gen. Adv. Council, 1971–78; Royal Humane Soc. Cttee, 1973–81; Pres., Royal Life-Saving Soc., 1974–78. Vis. Prof. of Police Studies, Strathclyde Univ., 1983–89. Fellow Commoner, Corpus Christi Coll., Cambridge, 1982; Fellow, Inst. of Criminology, Cambridge, 1982; Gwilym Gibbon Res. Fellow, Nuffield Coll., Oxford, 1982–83; Australian Commonwealth Fellow, Australian Govt, 1987; Hon. Res. Fellow, Centre for Policy Studies, Univ. of Exeter, 1987–. Contested (L) Teignbridge, Devon, 1983. Hon. LLD Exeter, 1979; Hon. DLitt Bradford, 1982. *Publications:* (contrib.) Encyclopedia of Crime and Criminals, 1960; (ed jtly) The Police We Deserve, 1973; Policing Freedom, 1979; Law and Disorder, 1984; Human Rights and the Police, 1984; articles in professional jls and newspapers. *Recreations:* reading, writing, keeping fit.

ALDERSON, Margaret Hanne, (Maggie); Editor, Elle Magazine, since 1989; *b* 31 July 1959; *d* of Douglas Arthur Alderson and Margaret Dura Alderson (*née* Mackay); *m* 1991, Geoffrey Francis Laurence. *Educ:* Alleyne's Sch., Stone, Staffs; Univ. of St Andrews (MA Hons History of Art). Features Editor: Look Now, 1983; Honey, 1984; Commng Editor, You, 1985; Metropolitan Features Editor, Evening Standard, 1986; Editor, ES Magazine, 1988. British Society of Magazine Editors: Mem., 1988–; Editor of the Year, Colour Supplements, 1989. *Recreations:* reading, gardening, painting, travelling. *Address:* 13 Chalcot Road, NW1 8LH. *T:* 071–586 9343. *Club:* Groucho.

ALDERTON, John; actor (stage, films, television); *b* Gainsborough, Lincs, 27 Nov. 1940; *s* of Gordon John Alderton and Ivy Handley; *m* 1st, Jill Browne (marr. diss.); 2nd, Pauline Collins, *qv*; two *s* one *d*. *Educ:* Kingston High Sch., Hull. *Stage:* 1st appearance (Rep.) Theatre Royal, York, in Badger's Green, 1961; cont. Rep.; 1st London appearance, Spring and Port Wine, Mermaid (later Apollo), 1965; Dutch Uncle, RSC, Aldwych, 1969; The Night I chased the Women with an Eel, Comedy, 1969; Punch and Judy Stories, Howff, 1973; Judies, Comedy, 1974; The Birthday Party, Shaw, 1975; Confusions (4 parts), Apollo, 1976; Rattle of a Simple Man, Savoy, 1980; Special Occasions, Ambassadors, 1983; The Maintenance Man, Comedy, 1986; Waiting for Godot, NT, 1987; *films:* (1962–): incl. Duffy, Hannibal Brooks, Zardoz, It Shouldn't Happen to a Vet, Please Sir; *television:* series: Please Sir, No Honestly, My Wife Next Door, P. G. Wodehouse, The Upchat Line, Thomas and Sarah, Father's Day, Forever Green and various plays. *Address:* c/o James Sharkey Associates Ltd, 15 Golden Square, W1R 3AG. *Club:* Garrick.

ALDINGTON, 1st Baron, *cr* 1962; **Toby (Austin Richard William) Low,** PC 1954; KCMG 1957; CBE 1945 (MBE 1944); DSO 1941; TD and clasp, 1950; DL; Chairman, Leeds Castle Foundation, since 1984; Barrister-at-Law; *b* 25 May 1914; *s* of Col Stuart Low, DSO (killed at sea by enemy action, Dec. 1942), and of late Hon. Mrs Spear; *m* 1947, Araminta Bowman, *e d* of late Sir Harold MacMichael, GCMG, DSO; one *s* two *d*. *Educ:* Winchester; New Coll., Oxford (Hon. Fellow 1976). Called to the Bar, 1939. TA; 2nd Lieut 1934; Brig. BGS 5 Corps Italy, Aug. 1944–June 1945; served Greece, Crete, Egypt, Libya, Tunisia, Sicily, Italy, Austria (DSO, MBE, CBE, Croix de guerre avec palmes, Commander of Legion of Merit, USA); Hon. Col 288 LAA Regt RA (TA), 1947–59. MP (C) Blackpool North, 1945–62; Parliamentary Secretary, Ministry of Supply, 1951–54; Minister of State, Board of Trade, 1954–57; Dep. Chm., Cons. Party Organisation, Oct. 1959–63; Chm., H of L Select Cttee on Overseas Trade, 1984–85. Chm., GEC, 1964–68, Dep. Chm. 1968–84; Chairman: Grindlays Bank Ltd, 1964–76; Sun Alliance and London Insurance Co., 1971–85; Westland Aircraft, 1977–85 (Pres., 1985). Director: Lloyds Bank, 1967–85; Citicorp, 1969–83. Chairman: Port of London Authority, 1971–77; Jt Special Cttee on Ports Industry, 1972. Chairman: Cttee of Management, Inst. of Neurology, 1962–80; BBC Gen. Adv. Council, 1971–78; ISJC, 1986–89; Kent Foundn, 1986–; President: BSI, 1986–89; Brain Res. Trust, 1987– (Chm., 1974–87). Fellow, Winchester Coll., 1972–87 (Warden, 1979–87). DL Kent, 1973. *Recreation:* golf. *Heir: s* Hon. Charles Harold Stuart Low [*b* 22 June 1948; *m* 1989, Regine, *d* of late Erwin von Csongrady-Schopf; one *s*]. *Address:* Knoll Farm, Aldington, Ashford, Kent TN25 7BY. *T:* Aldington (023372) 292. *Clubs:* Beefsteak, Carlton.
See also Hon. P. J. S. Roberts.

ALDINGTON, Sir Geoffrey (William), KBE 1965 (OBE 1946); CMG 1958; HM Diplomatic Service, retired; *b* 1 June 1907; *s* of late Henry William Aldington; *m* 1932, Roberta Finch; two *d*. *Educ:* City of London School; Magdalen Coll., Oxford. Student Interpreter, China Consular Service, 1929; Vice-Consul (Grade II), China, 1931; Vice-Consul, Peking, 1931–33; Private Secretary to HM Minister, Peking, 1933–35; Foreign Office, 1936–37; Acting Consul, Chungking, 1937–39; Consul, Tsingtao, 1939–41; seconded to Min. of Information, 1943–45; Actg Consul-Gen., Hankow, 1945–46; Suptg Consul, Shanghai, 1946–47; Foreign Office, 1947–50; Political Adviser to Hong Kong Govt, 1950–53; Consul-Gen. Zagreb, Yugoslavia, 1954–56; Consul-General at Philadelphia, Pa, USA, 1956–61; HM Ambassador to Luxembourg, 1961–66; also Consul-General, Luxembourg, 1962–66. *Recreations:* riding, reading. *Address:* Rustlings, 4 Tudor Close, Barnmeadow Lane, Great Bookham, Surrey KT23 3DP. *T:* Bookham (0372) 54088. *Clubs:* Hong Kong (Hong Kong); Racquet (Philadelphia, USA).
See also S. J. G. Semple.

ALDISS, Brian Wilson; writer; critic; *b* 18 Aug. 1925; *s* of Stanley and Elizabeth May Aldiss; *m* 1965, Margaret Manson; one *s* one *d*, and one *s* one *d* by previous *m*. *Educ:* Framlingham Coll.; West Buckland School. FRSL 1990. Royal Signals, 1943–47; bookselling, 1947–56; writer, 1956–; Literary Editor, Oxford Mail, 1958–69. Pres., British Science Fiction Assoc., 1960–64. Editor, SF Horizons, 1964–. Chairman, Oxford Branch Conservation Soc., 1968–69; Vice Pres., The Stapledon Soc., 1975–; Jt Pres., European SF Cttees, 1976–79; Society of Authors: Mem., Cttee of Management, 1976–78, Chm., 1978; Chm., Cultural Exchanges Cttee, 1979–; Member: Arts Council Literature Panel, 1978–80; Internat. PEN, 1983–; Pres., World SF, 1982–84; Vice-President: H. G. Wells Soc., 1983–; Soc. for Anglo-Chinese Understanding, 1987–. Mem. Council, Council for Posterity, 1990–. Observer Book Award for Science Fiction, 1956; Ditmar Award for Best Contemporary Writer of Science Fiction, 1969; first James Blish Award, for SF criticism, 1977; Pilgrim Award, 1978; first Award for Distinguished Scholarship, Internat. Assoc. for the Fantastic in the Arts, Houston, 1986. *Publications:* The Brightfount Diaries, 1955; Space, Time and Nathaniel, 1957; Non-Stop, 1958 (Prix Jules Verne, 1977); Canopy of Time, 1959; The Male Response, 1961; Hothouse, 1962 (Hugo Award, 1961); Best Fantasy Stories, 1962; The Airs of Earth, 1963; The Dark Light Years, 1964; Introducing SF, 1964; Greybeard, 1964; Best SF Stories of Brian W. Aldiss, 1965; Earthworks, 1965; The Saliva Tree, 1966 (Nebula Award, 1965); Cities and Stones: A Traveller's Jugoslavia, 1966; An Age, 1967; Report on Probability A, 1968; Farewell, Fantastic Venus!, 1968; Intangibles Inc. and other Stories, 1969; A Brian Aldiss Omnibus, 1969; Barefoot in the Head, 1969; The Hand-Reared Boy, 1970; The Shape of Further Things, 1970; The Moment of Eclipse, 1971 (BSFA Award, 1972); A Soldier Erect, 1971; Brian Aldiss Omnibus II, 1971; Billion Year Spree: a history of science fiction, 1973 (Special BSFA Award, 1974; Eurocon Merit Award, 1976); Frankenstein Unbound, 1973; The Eighty-Minute Hour, 1974; (ed) Space Opera, 1974; (ed) Space Odysseys: an Anthology of Way-Back-When Futures, 1975; (ed) Hell's Cartographers, 1975; (ed) Evil Earths, 1975; Science Fiction Art: the fantasies of SF, 1975 (Ferrara Silver Comet, 1977); (ed with H. Harrison) Decade: the 1940s, 1976; (ed with H. Harrison) Decade: the 1950s, 1976; The Malacia Tapestry, 1976; (ed) Galactic Empires, vols 1 and 2, 1976; (ed with H. Harrison) The Year's Best Science Fiction No 9, 1976; Brothers of the Head, 1977; Last Orders, 1977; (ed with H. Harrison) Decade: the 1960's, 1977; A Rude Awakening, 1978; Enemies of the System, 1978; (ed) Perilous Planets, 1978; This World and Nearer Ones, 1979; New Arrivals, Old Encounters, 1979; Life in the West, 1980; Moreau's Other Island, 1980; Helliconia Spring, 1982 (BSFA Award, John W. Campbell Meml Award); Helliconia Summer, 1983; Seasons in Flight, 1984; Helliconia Winter, 1985; Helliconia Trilogy (boxed set of Helliconia Spring, Helliconia Summer, and Helliconia Winter), 1985; The Horatio Stubbs Saga, 1985; The Pale Shadow of Science, 1985; . . . And the Lurid Glare of the Comet, 1986; (with David Wingrove) Trillion Year Spree, 1986 (Hugo Award, 1987); Cracken at Critical, 1987; Ruins, 1987; Forgotten Life, 1988; Best SF Stories of Brian W. Aldiss, 1988; Science Fiction Blues, 1988; A Romance of the Equator, 1989; Bury My Heart at W. H. Smith's, 1990; Dracula Unbound, 1991 (filmed as Frankenstein Unbound, 1991). *Recreations:* fame, obscurity, trances. *Address:* Woodlands, Foxcombe Road, Boars Hill, Oxford OX1 5DL. *Clubs:* Groucho, Helen's.

ALDOUS, Alan Harold; Headmaster of Leeds Grammar School, 1970–75; *b* 14 Nov. 1923; *o s* of George Arthur and Agnes Bertha Aldous; *m*; one *s* one *d*, and one step *s*. *Educ:* Ilford County High Sch. for Boys; Jesus Coll., Oxford (MA). Royal Signals and Royal West African Frontier Force, 1943–46. Oxford Univ., 1942 and 1946–49; Asst Master, St Dunstan's Coll., Catford, 1949–54; Asst Master, Merchant Taylors' Sch., Crosby, 1954–59; Headmaster, King's Sch., Pontefract, 1959–70; Dir, Sixth Form Studies, Longsands Sch., subseq. Longsands Community Coll., St Neots, 1976–88. *Recreations:* music, walking. *Address:* Casterbridge, Madeley Court, Hemingford Grey, Huntingdon, Cambs PE18 9DF. *T:* St Ives (0480) 66153.

ALDOUS, Charles; QC 1985; *b* 3 June 1943; *s* of Guy Travers Aldous and Elizabeth Angela Aldous (*née* Paul); *m* 1969, Hermione Sara de Courcy-Ireland; one *s* two *d* (and one *d* decd). *Educ:* Harrow; University College London (LLB). Called to the Bar, Inner Temple, 1967. *Address:* Ravensfield Farm, Bures Hamlet, Suffolk.
See also Hon. Sir W. Aldous.

ALDOUS, Lucette; Head of Classical Dance, Dance Department, Western Australian Academy of Performing Arts; Senior Adjudicator, National Eisteddfods, since 1979; *b* 26 Sept. 1938; *d* of Charles Fellows Aldous and Marie (*née* Rutherford); *m* 1972, Alan Alder; one *d*. *Educ:* Toronto Public Sch., NSW; Brisbane Public Sch., Qld; Randwick Girls' High Sch., NSW. Awarded Frances Scully Meml Schol. (Aust.) to study at Royal Ballet Sch., London, 1955; joined Ballet Rambert, 1957, Ballerina, 1958–63; Ballerina with: London Fest. Ballet, 1963–66; Royal Ballet, 1966–71; Prima Ballerina, The Australian Ballet, 1971; Master Teacher, Australian Ballet Sch., 1979; Guest Teacher: Australian Ballet, 1988–; Royal NZ Ballet Co., 1988–; West Australian Ballet Co., 1988–. Rep. Australia, 1st Internat. Ballet Competition, Jackson, Miss, USA, 1979; Guest, Kirov Ballet and Ballet School, Leningrad, 1975–76. Guest appearances: Giselle, with John Gilpin, NY, 1968; Lisbon, 1969; with Rudolf Nureyev, in Don Quixote: Aust., 1970, NY, Hamburg and Marseilles, 1971; Carmen, Johannesburg, 1970; The Sleeping Beauty: E Berlin, 1970, Teheran, 1970, 1975; partnered Edward Villela at Expo '74, Spokane, USA. *Television:* title rôle, La Sylphide, with Fleming Flindt, BBC, 1960. *Films:* as Kitri, in Don Quixote, with Rudolf Nureyev and Robert Helpmann, Aust., 1972; The Turning Point, 1977. *Recreations:* music, reading, gardening, breeding Burmese cats. *Address:* c/o Dance Department, Western Australian Academy of Performing Arts, 2 Bradford Street, Mount Lawley, Perth, WA 6050, Australia.

ALDOUS, Hon. Sir William, Kt 1988; **Hon. Mr Justice Aldous;** a Judge of the High Court of Justice, Chancery Division, since 1988; *b* 17 March 1936; *s* of Guy Travers Aldous, QC; *m* 1960, Gillian Frances Henson; one *s* two *d*. *Educ:* Harrow; Trinity Coll., Cambridge (MA). Barrister, Inner Temple, 1960, Bencher, 1985. Jun. Counsel, DTI, 1972–76; QC 1976; appointed to exercise appellate jurisdiction of BoT under Trade Marks Act, 1981–88; Chm., Performing Rights Tribunal, 1986–88. *Address:* Royal Courts of Justice, Strand, WC2.
See also C. Aldous.

ALDRIDGE, Frederick Jesse; Member, Public Health Laboratory Service Board, 1977–83; Under-Secretary and Controller of Supply, Department of Health and Social Security, 1968–75; *b* 13 Oct. 1915; *s* of late Jesse and Clara Amelia Aldridge; *m* 1940, Grace Hetty Palser; two *d*. *Educ:* Westminster City Sch. Clerical Off., Air Min., 1933; Exec. Off., Min. of Health, 1935; RAF, 1940–46; Acct-General's Div., Min. of Health: Asst Acct-Gen., 1956; Dep. Acct-Gen., 1958; Asst Sec. for Finance and Dep. Acct-Gen., 1964; Asst Sec., Food, Health and Nutrition, also Civil Defence, 1966. *Recreation:* music. *Address:* High Trees, 17 Tanglewood Close, Croydon CR0 5HX. *T:* 081–656 3623.

ALDRIDGE, (Harold Edward) James; author; *b* 10 July 1918; *s* of William Thomas Aldridge and Edith Quayle Aldridge; *m* 1942, Dina Mitchnik; two *s*. With Herald and Sun, Melbourne, 1937–38; Daily Sketch, and Sunday Dispatch, London, 1939; subsequently Australian Newspaper Service and North American Newspaper Alliance (war correspondent), Finland, Norway, Middle East, Greece, USSR, until 1945; also correspondent for Time and Life, Teheran, 1944. Rhys Meml Award, 1945; Lenin Peace Prize, 1972. *Publications:* Signed With Their Honour, 1942; The Sea Eagle, 1944; Of Many Men, 1946; The Diplomat, 1950; The Hunter, 1951; Heroes of the Empty View, 1954; Underwater Hunting for Inexperienced Englishmen, 1955; I Wish He Would Not Die, 1958; Gold and Sand (short stories), 1960; The Last Exile, 1961; A Captive in the Land, 1962; The Statesman's Game, 1966; My Brother Tom, 1966; The Flying 19, 1966; (with Paul Strand) Living Egypt, 1969; Cairo: Biography of a City, 1970; A Sporting Proposition, 1973; The Marvellous Mongolian, 1974; Mockery in Arms, 1974; The Untouchable Juli, 1975; One Last Glimpse, 1977; Goodbye Un-America, 1979; The Broken Saddle, 1983; The True Story of Lilli Stubek, 1984; The True Story of Spit MacPhee, 1986 (Guardian Children's Fiction Prize). *Recreations:* trout fishing, etc. *Address:* c/o Curtis Brown, 162–168 Regent Street, W1R 5TA.

ALDRIDGE, Dr John Frederick Lewis, OBE 1990, FRCP, FRCPEd, FFOM; consultant in occupational medicine, since 1987; Civil Consultant in Occupational Medicine to the Royal Navy, since 1983; *b* 28 Dec. 1926; *s* of Dr Frederick James Aldridge and Kathleen Marietta Micaela (*née* White); *m* 1955, Barbara Sheila Bolland; three *s* one *d*. *Educ:* Gresham's Sch.; St Thomas's Hosp. Med. Sch. (MB, BS 1951). DIH 1963; FRCPEd 1980; FFOM 1981; FRCP 1984. Served RAMC, 1953–60 (retd, Major). Indust. MO, Reed Paper Gp, 1960–63; CMO, IBM United Kingdom Ltd, 1963–87; part-time Hon. Clin. Asst, Dept of Psychol Medicine, UCH, 1970–76. Faculty of Occupational Medicine, Royal Coll. of Physicians: Vice-Dean, 1984–86; Dean, 1986–88; Royal Soc. of Medicine: Fellow, 1964; Hon. Sec., 1970–72 and Vice-Pres., 1974–77, Occupl Medicine Section;

Soc. of Occupational Medicine: Mem., 1960–; Hon. Meetings Sec., 1969–71. Member: Specialist Adv. Cttee on Occupl Medicine, Jt Cttee of Higher Med. Trng, 1970–74; Nat. Occupl Health and Safety Cttee, RoSPA, 1979–81; Standing Med. Adv. Cttee, DHSS, 1986–88; Defence Med. Emergency Steering Cttee, 1986–88; Indust. Soc. Med. Adv. Cttee, 1986–89 (Chm., 1987–89); CEGB Med. Adv. Cttee, 1988–89. Mem., Council and Cttee of Management, Shipwrecked Mariners' Royal Benevolent Soc., 1987–; Dep. Chm., and Mem. Standing Cttee, W Sussex Assoc. for the Disabled, 1991–; Trustee, Southampton and Wessex Med. Sch. Trust, 1978–82. Liveryman, Worshipful Soc. of Apothecaries, 1984–. *Publications:* papers on occupl med. topics and occupl mental health. *Recreations:* 18th century English porcelain, watercolours, walking, shooting. *Address:* East House, Charlton, Chichester, W Sussex PO18 0HU. *T:* Singleton (024363) 392. *Clubs:* Lansdowne; Itchenor Sailing.

See also M. W. ff. Aldridge.

ALDRIDGE, Michael William ffolliott; actor; *b* 9 Sept. 1920; *s* of Dr Frederick James Aldridge and Kathleen M. M. Aldridge; *m* 1947, Kirsteen Rowntree; three *d. Educ:* Watford Grammar Sch.; Gresham's Sch., Holt, Norfolk. Served RAF, 1940–46 (Flight-Lieut). First professional appearance in French without Tears, Palace Theatre, Watford, 1939; in rep. at Bristol, Blackpool, Sunderland, Sheffield, Bradford and Amersham, 1939–40; first London appearance in This Way to the Tomb, Garrick, 1946; toured with Arts Council Midland Theatre Co., 1946–48; title rôle in Othello, Nottingham, 1948, Embassy, 1949; with Birmingham Rep., 1949; Old Vic Co. at New Theatre, 1949–50: Love's Labour's Lost, She Stoops to Conquer, The Miser, Hamlet; with Arts Council Midland Theatre Co., 1950; Bristol Old Vic, 1951–52: title rôle in Macbeth, Two Gentlemen of Verona, Of Mice and Men; Chichester Festival, 1966–69, 1971–72. London appearances include: Escapade, St James's, Strand, 1953–54; Salad Days, Vaudeville, 1954; Free As Air, Savoy, 1957; Moon for the Misbegotten, Arts, 1960; Vanity Fair, Queen's, 1962; The Fighting Cock, Duke of York's, 1966; Heartbreak House, Lyric, 1967; The Cocktail Party, Wyndham's, Haymarket, 1968; The Magistrate, Cambridge, 1969; Bequest to the Nation, Haymarket, 1970; Reunion in Vienna, Piccadilly, 1972; Absurd Person Singular, Criterion, 1973; The Tempest, RSC at The Other Place, 1974; Jeeves, Her Majesty's, 1975; Lies, Albery, 1975; The Bed before Yesterday, Lyric, 1976; Rosmersholm, Haymarket, 1977; The Old Country, Queen's, 1978; Bedroom Farce, Nat. Theatre at The Prince of Wales, 1978; The Last of Mrs Cheyney, Cambridge, 1980; Noises Off, Lyric, Hammersmith and Savoy, 1982; The Biko Inquest, Riverside, 1984; Relatively Speaking, Greenwich, 1986. *Films* include, 1946–: Nothing Venture; Bank Holiday Luck; The North Sea Bus; Murder in the Cathedral; A Life for Ruth; Chimes at Midnight; The Public Eye; Bullshot; Turtle Diary; Mussolini; Clockwise; Murder by the Book; Shanghai Surprise. *Television* plays and serials include: The Man in Room 17; Happy and Glorious; Bleak House; Sense and Sensibility; Fall of Eagles; Love for Lydia; Tinker, Tailor, Soldier, Spy; Love in a Cold Climate; Voyage Round My Father; Spy Ship; Reilly; Under the Hammer; Charlie; Charters and Caldicote; Last of the Summer Wine; The Understanding; Game, Set and Match; Chronicles of Narnia; Countdown to War. Mem., BAFTA. *Recreation:* sailing. *Address:* 11 Crooms Hill, Greenwich, SE10 8ER. *Club:* Little Ship.

See also J. F. L. Aldridge.

ALDRIDGE, Trevor Martin; solicitor; Law Commissioner, since 1984; *b* 22 Dec. 1933; *s* of Dr Sidney and Isabel Aldridge; *m* 1966, Joanna, *d* of C. J. v. D. Edwards; one *s* one *d. Educ:* Frensham Heights School; Sorbonne; St John's College, Cambridge (MA). Partner in Bower Cotton & Bower, 1962–84. Chairman: Conveyancing Standing Cttee, 1989 (Mem., 1985–89); Commonhold Working Gp, reported 1987. Chm. of Governors, Frensham Heights School, 1977–. General editor, Property Law Bulletin, 1980–84. *Publications:* Boundaries, Walls and Fences, 1962, 6th edn 1986; Finding Your Facts, 1963; Directory of Registers and Records, 1963, 4th edn 1984; Service Agreements, 1964, 4th edn 1982; Rent Control and Leasehold Enfranchisement, 1965, 9th edn 1989; Betterment Levy, 1967; Letting Business Premises, 1971, 6th edn 1989; Your Home and the Law, 1975, 2nd edn 1979; (jtly) Managing Business Property, 1978; Criminal Law Act 1977, 1978; Guide to Enquiries of Local Authorities, 1978, 2nd edn 1982; Guide to Enquiries Before Contract, 1978; Guide to National Conditions of Sale, 1979, 2nd edn 1981; Leasehold Law, 1980; Housing Act, 1980, and as amended 1984, 2nd edn 1984; (ed) Powers of Attorney, 6th edn 1986 to 8th edn 1991; Guide to Law Society's Conditions of Sale, 1981, 2nd edn 1984; Questions of Law: Homes, 1982; Law of Flats, 1982, 2nd edn 1989; Practical Conveyancing Precedents, 1984; Practical Lease Precedents, 1987; Companion to Standard Conditions of Sale, 1990; Companion to Property Information Forms, 1990; First Registration, 1991. *Address:* Conquest House, 37/38 John Street, Theobalds Road, WC1N 2BQ. *T:* 071–242 0861, *Fax:* 071–430 2976. *Club:* United Oxford & Cambridge University.

ALDRIN, Dr Buzz; President, Research and Engineering Consultants Inc., since 1972; *b* Montclair, NJ, USA, 20 Jan. 1930; *s* of late Col Edwin E. Aldrin, USAF retd, Brielle, NJ, and Marion Aldrin (*née* Moon); *m* 1988, Lois Driggs-Cannon; two *s* one *d* of former marriage. *Educ:* Montclair High Sch., Montclair, NJ (grad.); US Mil. Academy, West Point, NY (BSc); Mass Inst. of Technology (DSc in Astronautics). Received wings (USAF), 1952. Served in Korea (66 combat missions) with 51st Fighter Interceptor Wing. Aerial Gunnery Instr, Nellis Air Force Base, Nevada; attended Sqdn Officers Sch., Air Univ., Maxwell Air Force Base, Alabama; Aide to Dean of Faculty, USAF Academy; Flt Comdr with 36th Tactical Fighter Wing, Bitburg, Germany. Subseq. assigned to Gemini Target Office of Air Force Space Systems Div., Los Angeles, Calif; later transf. to USAF Field Office, Manned Spacecraft Center. One of 3rd group of astronauts named by NASA, Oct. 1963; served as back up pilot, Gemini 9 Mission and prime pilot, Gemini 12 Mission (launched into space, with James Lovell, 11 Nov. 1966), 4 day 59 revolution flight which brought Gemini Program to successful close; he established a new record for extravehicular activity and obtained first pictures taken from space of an eclipse of the sun; also made a rendezvous with the previously launched Agena; later assigned to 2nd manned Apollo flight, as back-up command module pilot; Lunar Module Pilot, Apollo 11 rocket flight to the Moon; first lunar landing with Neil Armstrong, July 1969; left NASA to return to USAF as Commandant, Aerospace Res. Pilots Sch., Edwards Air Force Base, Calif, 1971; retired USAF 1972. Mem., Soc. of Experimental Test Pilots; FAIAA; Tau Beta Pi, Sigma Xi. Further honours include Presidential Medal of Freedom, 1969; Air Force DSM with Oak Leaf Cluster; Legion of Merit; Air Force DFC with Oak Leaf Cluster; Air Medal with 2 Oak Leaf Clusters; and NASA DSM, Exceptional Service Medal, and Group Achievement Award. Various hon. memberships and hon. doctorates. *Publications:* Return to Earth (autobiography), 1973; Men From Earth. *Recreations:* athletics, scuba diving, skiing, etc. *Address:* 233 Emerald Bay, Laguna Beach, Calif 92651, USA.

ALDRIN, Dr Edwin E(ugene), Jr; *see* Aldrin, Dr Buzz.

ALEKSANDER, Prof. Igor, PhD; FEng 1989; Professor of Neural Systems Engineering, and Head of Department of Electrical Engineering, Imperial College of Science, Technology and Medicine, University of London, since 1988; *b* 26 Jan. 1937. *Educ:* Marist Brothers' Coll., S Africa; Univ. of the Witwatersrand (BSc Eng); Univ. of London (PhD). Section Head of STC, Footscray, 1958–61; Lectr, Queen Mary Coll., Univ. of London, 1961–65; Reader in Electronics, Univ. of Kent, 1965–74; Prof. of Electronics and Head of Electrical Engrg Dept, Brunel Univ., 1974–84; Prof. of Information Technology Management, Computing Dept, Imperial Coll., 1984–88. *Publications:* An Introduction to Logic Circuit Theory, 1971; Automata Theory: an engineering approach, 1976; The Human Machine, 1978; Reinventing Man, 1983 (USA 1984); Designing Intelligent Systems, 1984; Thinking Machines, 1987; An Introduction to Neural Computing, 1990; *c* 100 papers on computing and human modelling. *Recreations:* tennis, skiing, music, architecture. *Address:* c/o Department of Electrical Engineering, Imperial College of Science, Technology and Medicine, 180 Queen's Gate, SW7 2BZ. *T:* 071-589 5111.

ALEPOUDELIS, Odysseus; *see* Elytis, Odysseus.

ALEXANDER, family name of **Barons Alexander of Potterhill** and **Alexander of Weedon,** of **Earl Alexander of Tunis,** and of **Earl of Caledon.**

ALEXANDER, Viscount; Frederick James Alexander; *b* 15 Oct. 1990; *s* and *heir* of Earl of Caledon, *qv.*

ALEXANDER OF POTTERHILL, Baron *cr* 1974 (Life Peer), of Paisley; **William Picken Alexander,** Kt 1961; LHD, PhD, MEd, MA, BSc, FBPsS; General Secretary, Association of Education Committees (England, Wales, Northern Ireland, Isle of Man and Channel Islands), 1945–77; *b* 13 Dec. 1905; *y s* of Thomas and Joan Alexander; *m* 1949, Joan Mary, *d* of Robert and Margaret Williamson; one *s* (and one *s* decd). *Educ:* Paisley Grammar School; Glasgow Univ. Schoolmaster in Scotland, 1929–31; Asst Lectr in Education, Glasgow Univ., 1931–32; Rockefeller Research Fellow, 1932–33; Deputy Director of Education, Walthamstow, 1934–35; Director of Education, Margate, 1935–39, Sheffield, 1939–44. Joint Sec. to Management Panel of Burnham Committees and Associated Committees negotiating salaries of teachers, 1945–73. Hon. DLitt Leeds, 1977. *Publications:* Intelligence, Concrete and Abstract, 1935; The Educational Needs of Democracy, 1940; A Performance Scale for the Measurement of Technical Ability, 1947; A Parents' Guide to the Education Act, 1944, 1947; Education in England, 1953; Towards a new Education Act, 1969, etc. *Recreations:* golf and contract bridge. *Address:* 3 Moor Park Gardens, Pembroke Road, Northwood, Middlesex HA6 2LF. *T:* Northwood (09274) 21003. *Club:* Moor Park Golf (Herts).

ALEXANDER OF TUNIS, 2nd Earl *cr* 1952; **Shane William Desmond Alexander;** Viscount, 1946; Baron Rideau, 1952; Lieutenant Irish Guards, retired, 1958; Director: International Hospitals Group, since 1981; Pathfinder Financial Corporation, Toronto, since 1980; *b* 30 June 1935; *er s* of 1st Earl Alexander of Tunis, KG, PC, GCB, OM, GCMG, CSI, DSO, MC, and Lady Margaret Diana Bingham (Countess Alexander of Tunis), GBE, DStJ, DL (*d* 1977), *yr d* of 5th Earl of Lucan, PC, GCVO, KBE, CB; *S* father, 1969; *m* 1981, Hon. Davina Woodhouse (LVO 1991; Lady-in-Waiting to Princess Margaret, 1975–), *y d* of 4th Baron Terrington, *qv*; two *d. Educ:* Ashbury Coll., Ottawa, Canada; Harrow. A Lord in Waiting (Govt Whip), 1974. Chm., Canada Meml Foundn, 1989–; Pres., British-American Associates, 1989–. Patron, British-Tunisian Soc., 1979–. Liveryman, Mercers Company. *Heir: b* Hon. Brian James Alexander, *b* 31 July 1939. *Address:* c/o House of Lords, SW1. *Club:* MCC.

ALEXANDER OF WEEDON, Baron *cr* 1988 (Life Peer), of Newcastle-under-Lyme in the County of Staffordshire; **Robert Scott Alexander,** QC 1973; QC (NSW) 1983; Chairman, National Westminster Bank, since 1989 (Deputy Chairman, 1989); *b* 5 Sept. 1936; *s* of late Samuel James and of Hannah May Alexander; *m*; two *s* one *d* (and one *s* decd). *Educ:* Brighton Coll.; King's Coll., Cambridge. BA 1959, MA 1963. Called to Bar, Middle Temple, 1961; Bencher, 1979; Vice Chm., 1984–85, Chm., 1985–86, of the Bar Council. Chm., Panel on Takeovers and Mergers, 1987–89. Non-exec. Dir, RTZ Corp., 1991–. Chairman: Council, Justice, 1990–; Trustees, Crisis, 1990–. Trustee, National Gall., 1987–. Pres., King's Coll. Assoc., 1980–81; Mem., Council of Governors, Wycombe Abbey Sch., 1986–. FRSA 1991. Hon. LLD Sheffield, 1991. *Recreations:* tennis, gardening. *Address:* National Westminster Bank, 41 Lothbury, EC2P 2BP. *Club:* Garrick.

ALEXANDER, Prof. Albert Geoffrey, FDSRCS; Professor of Conservative Dentistry, University of London, since 1972; Dean, University College and Middlesex School of Dentistry (formerly University College Dental School), since 1977; *b* 22 Sept. 1932; *s* of William Francis Alexander and Muriel Katherine (*née* Boreham); *m* 1956, Dorothy Constance (*née* Johnson); one *d. Educ:* Bridlington Sch.; UCH Dental Sch., Univ. of London (BDS 1956; MDS 1968). LDSRCS 1955, FDSRCS 1961. Dental House Surgeon, Nat. Dental Hosp., 1955–56; Nat. Service, RADC, 1956–58; Clinical Asst, UCH Dental Dept, 1958; private dental practice, 1958–59; Lectr in Cons. Dentistry, 1959–62, Sen. Lectr in Cons. Dentistry and Periodontics, 1962–69, UCH Dental Sch.; Hon. Consultant, UCH Dental Hosp., 1967–; Vice-Dean of Dental Studies, UCL Dental Sch., 1974–77; Vice-Dean, Faculty of Clinical Sciences, UCM Sch. of Medicine, 1977–. Fellow, UCL, 1986; Member: Council, UCL, 1984–; Senate, Univ. of London, 1987–. Chm., Dental Educn Adv. Council, 1986–90; Member: GDC, 1986– (Treasurer, 1989–); Bloomsbury HA, 1981–90. Fellow, Internat. Coll. of Dentists, 1975. *Publications:* (co-ed) The Prevention of Periodontal Disease, 1971; (jtly) Self-Assessment Manual, No 3, Clinical Dentistry, 1978; (co-ed) Companion to Dental Studies, Vol. 3, 1986, Vol. 2, 1988; scientific, technical and clinical articles on dentistry and dental research. *Recreations:* photography, blue and white Chinese ceramics. *Address:* 18 Masefield View, Orpington, Kent BR6 8PH. *T:* Orpington (0689) 858852.

ALEXANDER, Sir Alexander Sandor, (Sir Alex), Kt 1974; Managing Director, Europe, Lehman Brothers International Ltd (formerly Shearson Lehman Hutton International Inc.), since 1989; Chairman, J. Lyons and Company, 1979–89; Vice-Chairman, 1982–88, Deputy Chairman, 1988–89, Allied-Lyons plc; *b* 21 Nov. 1916; *m* 1946, Margaret Irma; two *s* two *d. Educ:* Charles Univ., Prague. Dir, 1954–69, Man. Dir and Chief Exec., 1967–69, Chm. 1969, Ross Group Ltd; Chm., Imperial Foods Ltd, 1969–79; Dir, Imperial Group Ltd (formerly Imperial Tobacco Group Ltd), 1969–79. Director: National Westminster Bank Ltd, South East Region, 1973–84; Ransomes, Sims & Jefferies plc, 1974–83; Alfred McAlpine, 1978–; Unigate, 1978–89; Tate & Lyle, 1978–89; Arbor Acres Farms, USA, 1985–91; London Wall Holdings, 1986–; Hiram Walker-Gooderham and Worts, Canada, 1987–89; Olympia and York Canary Wharf, 1989–; Dep. Chm., British United Trawlers, 1969–81. President: Processors and Growers Research Orgn, 1978–82; British Food Export Council, 1973–76; Member: Eastern Gas Bd, 1963–72; Agric. Econ. Develt Cttee, 1974–78; Governor: British Nutrition Foundn, 1975–79; Royal Ballet, 1985–; Dir, Royal Opera House, Covent Garden, 1987–; Chairman: Royal Opera House Trust, 1987–; Theatre Royal (Norwich) Trust Ltd, 1969–84; Trustee, 1975–89, Vice Chm., 1978–89, Glyndebourne Arts Trust; Member: National Theatre Develt Council, 1984–; Court, UEA, 1963–; Trustee: Charities Aid Foundn, 1979–86; Thrombosis Res. Inst., 1988–; Friend of RCP, 1982–. FBIM; FRSA. High Sheriff, Norfolk, 1976. *Recreations:* tennis, shooting, painting, opera, ballet. *Address:* Westwick Hall, Westwick, Norwich. *T:* (office) 071–260 3069.

ALEXANDER, Andrew Clive; City Editor, Daily Mail, since 1984; Director, Mail Newspapers plc; *b* 12 May 1935; *s* of Ronald and Doreen Alexander. *Educ:* Lancing College. Leader Writer, Yorkshire Post, 1960–65; Parly Sketch-Writer, Daily Telegraph, 1966–72; Parly Sketch-Writer and Columnist, Daily Mail, 1972–84. Contested (C) Colne Valley, March 1963, 1964. *Publication:* (with Alan Watkins) The Making of the Prime Minister, 1970. *Recreations:* music, gardening, history, weight training. *Address:* c/o Daily Mail, New Carmelite House, Carmelite Street, EC4Y 0JA. *T:* 071–606 1234. *Club:* Reform.

ALEXANDER, Anthony George Laurence; Director, Hanson PLC, since 1976, and UK Chief Operating Officer, since 1986; *b* 4 April 1938; *s* of George and Margaret Alexander; *m* 1962, Frances, *d* of Cyril Burdett; one *s* two *d*. *Educ:* St Edward's School, Oxford. FCA. Chm., subsids of Hanson plc. Underwriting Member of Lloyd's. *Recreations:* tennis, golf. *Address:* Crafnant, Gregories Farm Lane, Beaconsfield, Bucks HP9 1HJ. *T:* Beaconsfield (0494) 672882.

ALEXANDER, Anthony Victor, CBE 1987; Director, Sedgwick Group, 1978–89; *b* 17 Sept. 1928; *s* of Aaron and Victoria Alexander; *m* 1958, Hélène Esther; one *d*. *Educ:* Harrow School; St John's Coll., Cambridge (BA, LLB, Mod. Langs and Law). FINucE. Sedgwick Collins & Co: joined 1954; Exec., UK Co., 1954–64; Dir, 1964–68; Sedgwick Collins Holdings Ltd: Dir, 1968–73, and Chm., SCUK; Sedgwick Forbes Holdings: Dir and Chm., SFUK, 1973–77; Dep. Chm., Sedgwick Forbes, 1977–78; Sedgwick Group: Chm., Underwriting Services and Special Services, 1978–84; Director: Securicor Group and Security Services, 1976–; ARV Aviation, 1985–88. Member: Overseas Projects Bd, 1978–79; British Invisible Exports Council, 1983–; Marketing of Investments Bd, 1985–86; Dir, Securities and Investments Bd, 1986–89. Chm., Trustees, Victor Adda Foundn and Fan Museum Trust; Chm., British Insurance Brokers Assoc., 1982–87 (Dep. Chm., 1981–82). *Recreations:* gardening, sailing, fishing, forestry, antique collecting. *Address:* 1 St Germans Place, Blackheath, SE3 0NH. *T:* 081–858 5509. *Clubs:* Lloyd's Yacht, Bar Yacht, Medway Yacht.

ALEXANDER, Bill, (William Alexander Paterson); Hon. Associate Director, Royal Shakespeare Company, since 1991 (Associate Director, 1984–91); *b* 23 Feb. 1948; *s* of Bill and Rosemary Paterson; *m* 1978, Juliet Harmer; two *d*. *Educ:* St Lawrence Coll., Ramsgate; Keele Univ. (BA Hons English/Politics). Seasons with The Other Company, Bristol Old Vic, Royal Court, 1972–78; Asst Dir, 1978–80, Resident Dir, 1980–84, RSC. *Productions directed:* 1972–78: *Bristol Old Vic:* The Ride Across Lake Constance; Twelfth Night; Old Times; Butley; How the Other Half Loves; *Royal Court:* Sex and Kinship in a Savage Society, 1976; Amy and the Price of Cotton, 1977; Class Enemy, 1978; Sugar and Spice, 1979; Entertaining Mr Sloane, Nottingham Playhouse, 1977; The Gingerbread Lady, Ipswich, 1977; The Last of the Knuckle Men, Edin. Fest. Fringe, 1977; Julius Caesar, Newcastle upon Tyne, 1979; One White Day, Soho Poly, 1976; Mates, Leicester Square, 1976; Betrayal, 1980; Anna Christie, 1981, Cameri Th., Tel Aviv; Talk of the Devil, Watford Palace, 1986; *Royal Shakespeare Company:* Factory Birds, 1977; Shout Across the River, The Hang of the Gaol, Captain Swing, 1978; Men's Beano, 1979; Bastard Angel, Henry IV tour, 1980; Accrington Pals, 1981; Money, Clay, Molière, 1982; Tartuffe, Valpone, 1983; Richard III, Today, The Merry Wives of Windsor, 1984; Crimes in Hot Countries, Downchild (co-dir), 1985; Country Dancing, A Midsummer Night's Dream, 1986; Cymbeline, Twelfth Night, The Merchant of Venice, 1987; The Duchess of Malfi, Cymbeline, 1989; Much Ado About Nothing, 1990; The Taming of the Shrew (dir, regional tour), 1990; Much Ado About Nothing, 1991. *Recreation:* tennis. *Address:* Rose Cottage, Tunley, Glos GL7 6LP. *T:* (office) 071–628 3351.

ALEXANDER, Sir Charles G(undry), 2nd Bt *cr* 1945; MA, AIMarE; Chairman, Alexander Shipping Co. Ltd, 1959–87; *b* 5 May 1923; *s* of Sir Frank Alexander, 1st Bt, and Elsa Mary (*d* 1959), *d* of Sir Charles Collett, 1st Bt; *S* father 1959; *m* 1st, 1944, Mary Neale, *o c* of S. R. Richardson; one *s* one *d*; 2nd, 1979, Eileen Ann Stewart. *Educ:* Bishop's Stortford College; St John's College, Cambridge. Served War as Lieut (E), RN, 1943–46. Chm., Governors Care Ltd, 1975–86; formerly Dep. Chm., Houlder Bros and Co. Ltd; Director: Furness-Houlder Insurance Ltd, until 1988; Furness-Houlder (Reinsurance Services) Ltd, until 1988; Inner London Region, National Westminster Bank Ltd, until 1987; Chm., Hull, Blyth & Co. Ltd, 1972–75. Chm., Bd of Governors, Bishop's Stortford College, until 1986. Mem. Court of Common Council, 1969; Alderman (Bridge Ward), 1970–76. Master, Merchant Taylors' Co., 1981–82; Prime Warden, Shipwrights' Co., 1983–84. *Heir:* *s* Richard Alexander [*b* 1 Sept. 1947; *m* 1971, Lesley Jane, *d* of Frederick William Jordan, Bishop's Stortford; two *s*]. *Address:* Hollytree Farmhouse, North Cadbury, Yeovil, Somerset BA22 7DD. *T:* North Cadbury (0963) 40159. *Club:* Royal Automobile.

ALEXANDER, Cherian; *see* Alexander, P. C.

ALEXANDER of Ballochmyle, Sir Claud Hagart-, 3rd Bt, *cr* 1886 of Ballochmyle; JP; Vice Lord-Lieutenant, Ayr and Arran, since 1983; *b* 6 Jan. 1927; *s* of late Wilfred Archibald Alexander (2nd *s* of 2nd Bt) and Mary Prudence, *d* of Guy Acheson; *S* grandfather, 1945; assumed additional surname of Hagart, 1949; *m* 1959, Hilda Etain, 2nd *d* of Miles Malcolm Acheson, Ganges, BC, Canada; two *s* two *d*. *Educ:* Sherborne; Corpus Christi Coll., Cambridge (BA 1948). MInstMC 1980. DL Ayrshire, 1973; JP Cumnock and Doon Valley, 1983. *Heir:* *s* Claud Hagart-Alexander, *b* 5 Nov. 1963. *Address:* Kingencleugh House, Mauchline, Ayrshire KA5 5JL. *T:* Mauchline (0290) 50217. *Club:* New (Edinburgh).

ALEXANDER, David; *see* Alexander, J. D.

ALEXANDER, Maj.-Gen. David Crichton, CB 1976; Commandant, Scottish Police College, 1979–87, retired; *b* 28 Nov. 1926; *s* of James Alexander and Margaret (*née* Craig); *m* 1957, Diana Joyce (Jane) (*née* Fisher); one *s* two *d* and one step *s*. *Educ:* Edinburgh Academy. Joined RM, 1944; East Indies Fleet; 45 Commando, Malaya, Malta, Canal Zone, 1951–54; Parade Adjt, Lympstone, 1954–57; Equerry and Acting Treasurer to Duke of Edinburgh, 1957–60; psc 1960; Directing Staff, Staff Coll., Camberley, 1962–65; 45 Commando (2IC), Aden, 1965–66; Staff of Chief of Defence Staff, incl. service with Sec. of State, 1966–69; CO 40 Commando, Singapore, 1969–70; Col GS to CGRM, 1970–73; ADC to the Queen, 1973–75; RCDS 1974; Comdr, Training Gp RM, 1975–77. Dir-Gen., English-Speaking Union, 1977–79. Governor, Corps of Commissionaires, 1978–; Member: Civil Service Final Selection Bd, 1978–88; MoD Police Review Cttee, 1985; Transport Users' Consultative Cttee for Scotland, 1989–. Dir, Edinburgh Acad., 1980–89 (Chm., 1985–89). Pres., SSAFA, Fife, 1990–. Freeman, City of London; Liveryman, Painter Stainers' Co., 1978. *Recreations:* fishing, gardening, golf. *Address:* Carnbee House, Carnbee, by Anstruther, Fife KY10 2RU. *T:* Arncroach (03338) 238. *Club:* Army and Navy.

ALEXANDER, Sir Douglas, 3rd Bt *cr* 1921; with Cowen & Co.; *b* 9 Sept. 1936; *s* of Lt-Comdr Archibald Gillespie Alexander (*d* 1978) (2nd *s* of 1st Bt), and of Margery Isabel, *d* of Arthur Brown Griffith; *S* uncle, 1983; *m* 1958, Marylon, *d* of Leonidas Collins Scatterday; two *s*. *Educ:* Rice Univ., Houston, Texas (MA 1961). PhD 1967 (Univ. of N Carolina). Formerly Assoc. Prof. and Chairman, French, State Univ. of New York at Albany. *Heir:* *s* Douglas Gillespie Alexander, *b* 24 July 1962. *Address:* 2499 Windsor Way Court, Wellington, Fla 33414, USA.

ALEXANDER, Ian Douglas Gavin; QC 1989; a Recorder of the Crown Court, since 1982; *b* 10 April 1941; *s* of late Dr A. D. P. Alexander, MB ChB, and of Mrs D. Alexander; *m* 1969, Rosemary Kirkbride Richards; one *s* one *d*. *Educ:* Tonbridge; University College London (LLB). Called to Bar, Lincoln's Inn, 1964; Recorder, Midland and Oxford Circuit, 1982–. *Recreations:* horses, sailing, gardening. *Address:* 13 King's Bench Walk, Temple, EC4Y 7EN. *T:* 071–353 7204. *Club:* Naval and Military.

ALEXANDER, (John) David, DPhil; Trustees' Professor, Pomona College, since 1991 (President, 1969–91); American Secretary, Rhodes Scholarship Trust, since 1981; *b* 18 Oct. 1932; *s* of John David Alexander, Sr and Mary Agnes McKinnon; *m* 1956, Catharine Coleman; one *s* two *d*. *Educ:* Southwestern at Memphis (BA); Louisville Presbyterian Theological Seminary; Oxford University (DPhil). Instructor to Associate Prof., San Francisco Theol Seminary, 1957–64; Pres., Southwestern at Memphis, 1965–69. Trustee, Teachers Insurance and Annuity Assoc., NY, 1970–; Director: Great Western Financial Corp., Beverly Hills, 1973–; KCET (Community Supported TV of S Calif.), 1979–89; Amer. Council on Educn, Washington DC, 1981–84; National Assoc. of Indep. Colls and Univs, 1984–88; British Inst., 1979–87 (Mem., Bd of Advrs, 1987–); Member: Nat. Panel on Academic Tenure, 1971–72; Assoc. of Amer. Med. Colls Panel on Gen. Professional Preparation of Physicians, 1981–84. Hon. LLD: Univ. of S California, 1970; Occidental Coll., 1970; Centre Coll. of Kentucky, 1971; Hon. LHD Loyola Marymount Univ., 1983; Hon. LittD Rhodes Coll., Memphis, 1986. *Publications:* articles in Biblical studies; articles and chapters on higher educn in USA. *Recreations:* music, book collecting. *Address:* 345 North College Avenue, Claremont, Calif 91711, USA. *T:* 714/624 7848. *Clubs:* Century Association (NY); California (Los Angeles); Bohemian (San Francisco).

ALEXANDER, Sir (John) Lindsay, Kt 1975; MA; Deputy Chairman, Lloyds Bank PLC, 1980–88 (Director, 1970–91); Director: British Petroleum Co. PLC, 1975–91; Hawker Siddeley plc, since 1981; *b* 12 Sept. 1920; *e s* of Ernest Daniel Alexander and Florence Mary Mainsmith; *m* 1944, Maud Lilian, 2nd *d* of Oliver Ernest and Bridget Collard; two *s* one *d*. *Educ:* Alleyn's Sch.; Brasenose Coll., Oxford (Thomas Wall Schol.; Hon. Fellow 1977). Royal Engineers, 1940–45 (Capt.); served Middle East and Italy. Chairman: The Ocean Steam Ship Co. Ltd, later Ocean Transport and Trading Ltd, 1971–80 (Man. Dir, 1955–71; Dir, 1955–86); Lloyds Bank Internat., 1980–85 (Dir, 1975–85; Dep. Chm., 1979–80); Lloyds Merchant Bank Hldgs, 1988 (Dep. Chm. and Dir, 1985–88). Director: Overseas Containers Holdings Ltd, 1971–82 (Chm., 1976–82); Jebsens Drilling PLC, 1980–86; Wellington Underwriting Holdings Ltd, 1986–; Wellington Underwriting Agencies Ltd, 1986–; Britoil, 1988–90; Abbey Life Gp, later Lloyds Abbey Life, 1988–91. Chairman: Liverpool Port Employers' Assoc., 1964–67; Cttee, European Nat. Shipowners' Assocs, 1971–73; Vice-Chm., Nat. Assoc. of Port Employers, 1965–69; President: Chamber of Shipping of UK, 1974–75 (Vice-Pres., 1973–74); Gen. Council, British Shipping Ltd, 1974–75. Hon. Mem., Master Mariners' Co., 1974–. FCIT (MInstT 1968); CBIM 1980 (FBIM 1972). JP Cheshire, 1965–75. Comdr, Royal Order of St Olav, Norway. *Recreations:* gardening, music, photography. *Address:* Lloyds Bank Plc, 71 Lombard Street, EC3P 3BS. *T:* 071–626 1500. *Club:* Brooks's.

ALEXANDER, Prof. John Malcolm; Emeritus Professor, University of Wales; *b* 14 Oct. 1921; *s* of Robert Henry Alexander and Gladys Irene Lightfoot Alexander (*née* Domville); *m* 1946, Margaret, *d* of F. A. Ingram; two *s*. *Educ:* Ipswich Sch.; City and Guilds Coll. DSc (Eng) London; PhD; FCGI; FICE; FIMechE; FIProdE; FIM; FEng; MASME; FRSA. REME commn, 1942–47; Aluminium Labs Ltd, 1953–55; English Electric, 1955–57; London University: Reader in Plasticity, 1957–63; Prof. of Engrg Plasticity, 1963–69; Chm. Board of Studies in Civil and Mech. Engrg, 1966–68; Prof. of Applied Mechanics, Imp. Coll., 1969–78; Prof. and Head of Dept of Mech. Engrg, University Coll. of Swansea, 1978–83. Stocker Vis. Prof. in Engrg and Technol., 1985–87, Adjunct Prof., 1987–, Univ. of Ohio. Chm., Applied Mechanics Gp, IMechE, 1963–65; Mem., CIRP, 1965–; Vice-President: Inst. of Metals, 1968–71; Inst. of Sheet Metal Engrg, 1979–. Gov., Ipswich Sch., 1977–86. Chm., British Cold Forging Gp, 1973–79. Assessor, Sizewell 'B' Public Inquiry, 1983–85; Mem., Adv. Cttee on Safe Transport of Radioactive Materials, 1985–89. Liveryman, Blacksmiths' Co., 1976. Series Editor, Ellis Horwood Ltd, 1970–; Mem. Editorial Board: Internat. Jl Mech. Sciences, 1968–; Internat. Jl Machine Tool Design and Research, 1973–. Joseph Bramah Medal, IMechE, 1970. *Publications:* Advanced Mechanics of Materials, Manufacturing Properties of Materials, 1963; Hydrostatic Extrusion, 1971; Strength of Materials, 1980; Manufacturing Technology, 1987; papers to Royal Soc., IMechE, Iron and Steel Inst., Inst. Metals, Metals Soc. *Recreations:* music, gardening. *Address:* Rowan Cottage, Furze Hill Road, Headley Down, Hants GU35 8NP. *Club:* Army and Navy.

ALEXANDER, Jonathan James Graham, DPhil; FBA 1985; FSA 1981; Professor of Fine Arts, Institute of Fine Arts, New York, since 1988; *b* 20 Aug. 1935; *s* of Arthur Ronald Brown and Frederica Emma Graham (who *m* 2nd, Boyd Alexander); *m* 1974, Mary Davey; one *s*. *Educ:* Magdalen Coll., Oxford (BA, MA, DPhil). Assistant, Dept of Western MSS, Bodleian Library, Oxford, 1963–71; Lecturer, 1971–73, Reader, 1973–87, History of Art Dept, Manchester Univ. Lyell Reader in Bibliography, Univ. of Oxford, 1982–83; Sen. Kress Fellow, Center for Adv. Study in Visual Arts, Nat. Gall. of Art, Washington DC, 1984–85; Sandars Reader in Bibliography, Cambridge Univ., 1984–85. *Publications:* (with Otto Pächt) Illuminated Manuscripts in the Bodleian Library, Oxford, 3 vols, 1966, 1970, 1973; (with A. C. de la Mare) Italian Illuminated Manuscripts in the Library of Major J. R. Abbey, 1969; Norman Illumination at Mont St Michel *c* 966–1100, 1970; The Master of Mary of Burgundy, A Book of Hours, 1970; Italian Renaissance Illuminations, 1977; Insular Manuscripts 6th-9th Century, 1978; The Decorated Letter, 1978; (with E. Temple) Illuminated Manuscripts in Oxford College Libraries, 1986; (ed with Paul Binski) Age of Chivalry: Art in Plantagenet England 1200–1400, 1987; articles in Burlington Magazine, Arte Veneta, Pantheon, etc. *Recreations:* music, gardening. *Address:* Institute of Fine Arts, 1 East 78th Street, New York, NY 10021, USA.

ALEXANDER, Sir Kenneth (John Wilson), Kt 1978; BSc (Econ.); FRSE 1978; Chancellor, University of Aberdeen, since 1986; *b* Edinburgh, 14 March 1922; *o s* of late William Wilson Alexander; *m* 1949, Angela-May, *d* of late Capt. G. H. Lane, RN; one *s* four *d*. *Educ:* George Heriot's Sch., Edinburgh; Sch. of Economics, Dundee. Research Asst, Univ. of Leeds, 1949–51; Lectr, Univ. of Sheffield, 1951–56; Lectr, Univ. of Aberdeen, 1957–62; Dean of Scottish Business Sch., 1973–75 (Chm., Acad. Exec. Cttee, 1972–73); Prof. of Econs, Strathclyde Univ., 1963–80, on leave of absence, 1976–80; Chm., Highlands and Islands Develt Bd, 1976–80; Principal and Vice-Chancellor, Stirling Univ., 1981–86. Mem. Adv. Cttee on University of the Air, 1965; Director: Fairfields (Glasgow) Ltd, 1966–68; Upper Clyde Shipbuilders Ltd, 1968–71; Scottish Television, 1982–; Stakis plc, 1987–; Aberdeen Univ. Press, 1989– (Chm., 1990); Scottish Daily Record and Sunday Mail (1986) Ltd, 1990–; Chairman: Govan Shipbuilders, 1974–76; Michael Kelly Associates, 1986–; Scottish Industrial Exhibitions Ltd, 1991–. Dir, Glasgow Chamber of

Commerce, 1969–73; Economic Consultant to Sec. of State for Scotland, 1968–; Chm., Cttee on Adult Educn in Scotland, 1970–73; Mem. Exec. Cttee, 1968–, Dep. Chm. 1982–, Scottish Council (Develt and Industry); Member: (part-time) Scottish Transport Gp, 1969–76; SSRC, 1975–76; Scottish Develt Agency, 1975–86; Bd, UK CEED, 1985–. Governor: Technical Change Centre, 1981–87; Newbattle Abbey Coll., 1967–73; President: Section F, British Assoc., 1974; Saltire Soc., 1975–81; Scottish Section, Town and Country Planning, 1982–; Hon. Pres., The Highland Fund, 1983–; Chairman: John Muir Trust, 1985–88; Edinburgh Book Fest., 1987–; Paxton Trust, 1989–; Trustee, Nat. Museums of Scotland, 1985–87. CBIM 1980; FEIS 1983; FBEC(S) 1984; FRIAS 1988. Hon. LLD: CNAA, 1976; Aberdeen, 1986; Dundee, 1986; DUniv: Stirling, 1977; Open 1985. *Publications:* The Economist in Business, 1967; Productivity Bargaining and the Reform of Industrial Relations, 1969; (with C. L. Jenkins) Fairfields, a study of industrial change, 1971; (ed) The Political Economy of Change, 1976; articles in Oxford Econ. Papers, Quarterly Jl of Econ., Scottish Jl of Pol. Econ., Economica, Yorkshire Bulletin Economics, and other jls. *Recreation:* Scottish antiquarianism. *Address:* 9 West Shore, Pittenweem, Fife KY10 2NV.

ALEXANDER, Sir Lindsay; *see* Alexander, Sir J. L.

ALEXANDER, Rt. Rev. Mervyn Alban Newman; *see* Clifton, Bishop of, (RC).

ALEXANDER, Michael Charles; writer; *b* 20 Nov. 1920; *s* of late Rear-Adm. Charles Otway Alexander and Antonia Geermans; *m* 1963, Sarah Wignall (marr. diss.); one *d*. *Educ:* Stowe; RMC, Sandhurst; Oflag IVC, Colditz. Served War: DCLI; 5 (Ski) Bn Scots Gds; 8 Commando (Layforce); HQ 13 Corps (GSO 3); Special Boat Section; (POW, 1942–44); 2nd SAS Regt; War Office (Civil Affairs). Intergovtl Cttee on Refugees, 1946; Editorial Dir, Common Ground Ltd, 1946–50. Located Firuzkoh, Central Afghanistan, 1952; Himalayan Hovercraft Expedn, 1972; Yucatan Straits Hovercraft Expedn, 1975; Upper Ganges Hovercraft Expedn, 1980; Promoter, Scottish Highlands & Is Inflatable Boat Race, 1990, 1991. Dir, Acorn Productions Ltd, 1977–. Founded: Woburn Safari Service, 1977; Chelsea Wharf Restaurant, 1983. FZS, FRGS; Fellow, Royal Soc. for Asian Affairs. Co-publisher, Wildlife magazine. *Publications:* The Privileged Nightmare (with Giles Romilly), 1952 (republ., as Hostages at Colditz, 1975); Offbeat in Asia, 1953; The Reluctant Legionnaire, 1955; The True Blue, 1957; Mrs Fraser on the Fatal Shore, 1972; Discovering the New World, 1976; Omai: Noble Savage, 1977; Queen Victoria's Maharajah, 1980; Delhi-Agra: a traveller's companion, 1987. *Address:* 48 Eaton Place, SW1. *T:* 071–235 2724; Skelbo House, Dornoch, Sutherland. *T:* Golspie (04083) 3180. *Clubs:* Chelsea Arts, Special Forces.

ALEXANDER, Sir Michael (O'Donel Bjarne), KCMG 1988 (CMG 1982); HM Diplomatic Service, retired; *b* 19 June 1936; *s* of late Conel Hugh O'Donel Alexander, CMG, CBE, and Enid Constance Crichton Neate; *m* 1960, Traute Krohn; two *s* one *d*. *Educ:* Foyle Coll., Londonderry; Hall Sch., Hampstead; St Paul's Sch. (Schol.); King's Coll., Cambridge (Schol.); Harkness Fellow (Yale and Berkeley) 1960–62. MA (Cantab), AM (Yale). Royal Navy, 1955–57. Entered HM Foreign (later Diplomatic) Service, 1962; Moscow, 1963–65; Office of Political Adviser, Singapore, 1965–68; FCO, 1968–72; Asst Private Sec. to Secretary of State (Rt Hon. Sir Alec Douglas-Home, MP, and Rt Hon. James Callaghan, MP) 1972–74; Counsellor (Conf. on Security and Co-operation in Europe) and later Head of Chancery, UK Mission, Geneva, 1974–77; Dep. Head, 1977–78, Head, 1978–79, Personnel Operations Dept, FCO; Private Sec. (Overseas Affairs) to the Prime Minister (Rt Hon. Margaret Thatcher, MP), 1979–81; Ambassador, Vienna, 1982–86; concurrently Hd of UK Delegn to the Negotiations on Mutual and Balanced Reduction of Forces and Armaments in Central Europe, 1985–86; Ambassador and UK Permanent Rep. on North Atlantic Council, Brussels, 1986–Jan. 1992 (Dean of Council, 1991–Jan. 1992). Organised: Britain in Vienna Fest., 1986; Grosses Goldenes Ehrenzeichen (Wien), 1986. Former Public Schools', British Universities' and National Junior Foil Champion; fenced for Cambridge Univ., 1957–60 (Captain, 1959–60); English Internat., 1958; Silver Medallist (Epée Team) Olympic Games, 1960; Gold Medallist, US Championships, 1961; Captained England, 1963. Represented Cambridge in Field Events Match with Oxford, 1959, 1960. *Publications:* articles on East/West relations and international security. *Recreations:* reading history; watching or participating in sport of any kind. *Address:* 6 Iverna Gardens, W8 6TN. *Clubs:* Athenæum, Garrick, Epée, All England Fencing; Hawks (Cambridge).

ALEXANDER, Sir Norman (Stanley), Kt 1966; CBE 1959. Professor of Physics: Raffles Coll., Singapore, 1936–49; Univ. of Malaya, Singapore, 1949–52; University Coll., Ibadan, Nigeria, 1952–60; Vice-Chancellor, Ahmadu Bello Univ., Nigeria, 1961–66.

ALEXANDER, Dr (Padinjarethalakkal) Cherian; Governor, Tamil Nadu, since 1988; *b* 20 March 1921; *m* 1942, Ackama Alexander; two *s* two *d*. *Educ:* India and Britain; MA (Hist. and Econ.); MLitt; DLitt. Indian Administrative Service, Kerala Cadre, 1948; Develt Comr, Small Scale Industries, 1960–63; Sen. Advr, Centre for Industrial Develt, UN HQ, NY, 1963–66; Chief, UN Project on Small Industries and Chief Advr to Govt of Iran, 1970–73; Develt Comr, Small Scale Industries, 1973–75; Sec., Foreign Trade, later Commerce Sec., 1975–78; Sen. Advr, later Exec. Dir and Asst Sec. Gen., Internat Trade Centre, UNCTAD-GATT, Geneva, 1978–81; Principal Sec. to Prime Minister of India, 1981–85; High Commissioner for India in London, 1985–88. *Publications:* The Dutch in Malabar; Buddhism in Kerala; Industrial Estates in India. *Address:* Raj Bhavan, Madras, Tamil Nadu, India.

ALEXANDER, Lt-Col Sir Patrick Desmond William C.; *see* Cable-Alexander.

ALEXANDER, Maj.-Gen. Paul Donald, CB 1989; MBE 1968; Policy Director (Army), Ministry of Defence, since 1989; *b* 30 Nov. 1934; *s* of Donald Alexander and Alice Louisa Alexander (*née* Dunn); *m* 1958, Christine Winifred Marjorie Coakley; three *s*. *Educ:* Dudley Grammar Sch.; RMA Sandhurst; Staff Coll., Camberley; NDC; RCDS. Enlisted 1953; commissioned Royal Signals, 1955; served Hong Kong, E Africa, Germany; Comd 1st Div. Signal Regt, 1974–76; MoD, 1977–79; Comdr, Corps Royal Signals, 1st (Br) Corps, 1979–81; Dep. Mil. Sec. (B), 1982–85; Signal Officer in Chief (Army), 1985–89, retired. Col Comdt, RCS, 1989–; Hon. Col, 35th Signal Regt, 1991–. Chm., Royal Signals Assoc., 1990–. *Publications:* occasional contribs to professional jls. *Recreations:* gardening, unstructured hedonism. *Clubs:* Army and Navy; Royal Signals Yacht (Adm., 1989–).

ALEXANDER, Richard Thain; MP (C) Newark, since 1979; *b* 29 June 1934; *s* of Richard Rennie Alexander and Gladys Alexander; *m* 1966, Valerie Ann Winn (marr. diss. 1985); one *s* one *d*; *m* 1987, Pat. *Educ:* Dewsbury Grammar Sch., Yorks; University Coll. London (LLB Hons). Articled with Sir Francis Hill, Messrs Andrew & Co., Lincoln, 1957–60; Asst Solicitor, Messrs McKinnell, Ervin & Holmes, Scunthorpe, 1960–64; Sen. Partner, Messrs Jones, Alexander & Co., Retford, 1964–85, Consultant, 1986–90. *Recreations:* tennis, bowls, horse riding. *Address:* 51 London Road, Newark, Notts. *Clubs:* Carlton; Newark Conservative.

ALEXANDER, Rear-Adm. Robert Love, CB 1964; DSO 1943; DSC 1944; *b* 29 April 1913; *o s* of Captain R. L. Alexander, Edinburgh; *m* 1936, Margaret Elizabeth, *o d* of late George Conrad Spring, and late Mrs Maurice House; one *s* three *d* (and one *d* decd). *Educ:* Merchiston Castle; Royal Naval College, Dartmouth. Joined RNC, 1927; Cadet HMS Repulse, 1930; Midshipman HMS Kent, 1931–33; Sub-Lieut, qualified in submarines, 1935. Served throughout War of 1939–45 in submarines; first command HMS H32, 1940; later commands: HMS Proteus, 1942; HMS Truculent, 1942–44; HMS Tuna, 1945. Second in command and in temp. command HMS Glory, Korean War, 1951–52; in command First Destroyer Squadron, 1957; Imperial Defence College, 1959; in command HMS Forth and 1st Submarine Squadron, 1960; Captain Submarines and Minesweepers, Mediterranean, and NATO Commander Submarines, Mediterranean, HMS Narvik, 1960–62. Vice Naval Deputy to the Supreme Allied Commander Europe, 1962–65. Lieut 1936; Comdr 1946; Capt. 1952; Rear-Adm. 1962; retd, 1965. *Address:* Tythe Barn, South Harting, Petersfield, Hants. *T:* Harting (073085) 505.

ALEXANDER, Prof. (Robert) McNeill, FRS 1987; FIBiol; Professor of Zoology, University of Leeds, since 1969; *b* 7 July 1934; *s* of Robert Priestley Alexander and Janet McNeill; *m* 1961, Ann Elizabeth Coulton; one *s* one *d*. *Educ:* Tonbridge School; Trinity Hall, Cambridge (MA, PhD); DSc Wales. Asst Lectr in Zoology, University Coll. of North Wales, 1958, Lectr 1961, Sen. Lectr 1968; Head, Dept of Pure and Applied Zoology, Univ. of Leeds, 1969–78 and 1983–87. Visiting Professor: Harvard, 1973; Duke, 1975; Nairobi, 1976, 1977, 1978; Basle, 1986. Mem., Biological Scis Cttee, SRC, 1974–77. Mem. Council, 1988–91, Vice Pres., 1990–91, Zool Soc. of London. Hon. Mem., Amer. Soc. of Zoologists, 1986. Scientific Medal, Zoological Soc., 1969; Linnean Medal, Linnean Soc., 1979. *Publications:* Functional Design in Fishes, 1967, 3rd edn 1974; Animal Mechanics, 1968, 2nd edn 1983; Size and Shape, 1971; The Chordates, 1975, 2nd edn 1981; Biomechanics, 1975; The Invertebrates, 1979; Locomotion of Animals, 1982; Optima for Animals, 1982; Elastic Mechanisms in Animal Movement, 1988; Dynamics of Dinosaurs and other Extinct Giants, 1989; Animals, 1990; The Human Machine, 1991; papers on mechanics of human and animal movement. *Recreations:* history of natural history, local history. *Address:* 14 Moor Park Mount, Leeds LS6 4BU. *T:* Leeds (0532) 759218.

ALEXANDER, Thomas John; Director for Social Affairs, Manpower and Education, OECD, Paris, since 1989; *b* 11 March 1940; *s* of late John Alexander and of Agnes Douglas Stewart (*née* Creedican); *m* 1961, Pamela Mason; two *s* one *d*. *Educ:* Royal High Sch., Edinburgh. Entered FO, 1958; MECAS, 1961; Third Sec. (Commercial), Kuwait, 1963; Asst Private Sec. to the Minister of State, FO, 1965; Second Sec. (Commercial), Tripoli, 1967; seconded to industry (ICI), 1970; Vice Consul (Commercial), Seattle, 1970; First Sec., FCO, 1974; special unpaid leave to act as Private Sec. to Sec.-Gen. of OECD, Paris, 1977–82; Counsellor and Head of Chancery, Khartoum, 1982–83; Dep. Head of Planning, 1984, Head of Private Office of Sec.-Gen., 1984–89, OECD. *Recreations:* squash, tennis. *Address:* c/o OECD, 2 rue André Pascal, 75016 Paris, France.

ALEXANDER, Walter Ronald, CBE 1984; Chairman, Walter Alexander plc, 1979–90 (Managing Director, 1973–79); company director; *b* 6 April 1931; *s* of Walter Alexander and Katherine Mary Turnbull; *m* 1st, 1956, Rosemary Anne Sleigh (marr. diss. 1975); two *s* two *d*; 2nd, 1979, Mrs Lorna Elwes, *d* of Lydia Duchess of Bedford. *Educ:* Loretto Sch.; Cambridge Univ. (MA Hons). Chm. and Man. Dir, Tayforth Ltd, 1961–71; Chm., Scottish Automobile Co. Ltd, 1971–73. Director: Scotcros plc, 1965–82 (Chm., 1972–82); Investors Capital Trust plc, 1967–; Clydesdale Bank plc, 1971–; RIT and Northern plc (formerly Great Northern Investment Trust plc), 1973–84; Dawson Internat. plc, 1979–. Chm., Scottish Appeals Cttee, Police Dependants' Trust, 1974–81; Pres., Public Schs Golfing Soc., 1973–79; Chm., PGA, 1982–85. Governor, Loretto Sch., 1961–89; Comr, Queen Victoria Sch., 1987–. Scottish Free Enterprise Award, 1977. *Recreation:* golf. *Address:* Moonzie Mill, Balmullo, St Andrews, Fife KY16 0AH. *T:* St Andrews (0334) 870864. *Clubs:* Royal and Ancient Golf (Captain, 1980–81; Chm., 1987–); Hon. Company of Edinburgh Golfers; Prestwick Golf; Royal St George's Golf; Pine Valley Golf, Augusta National Golf (USA).

ALEXANDER, William Gemmell, MBE 1945; *b* 19 Aug. 1918; *s* of Harold Gemmell Alexander and Winifred Ada Alexander (*née* Stott); *m* 1945, Janet Rona Page Alexander (*née* Elias); four *s* one *d*. *Educ:* Tre Arddur Bay Sch.; Sedbergh Sch.; Oxford Univ. (MA). Served War of 1939–45 (despatches, war stars and clasps): Driver Mechanic, 2nd Lieut, Lieut, Capt., Maj.; served in France, S Africa, Eritrea, Egypt, Middle East, Sicily, Italy, Algeria, NW Europe. HM Overseas Civil Service, 1946–59: Gilbert and Ellice Is, 1946–51; Mauritius, 1951–55; Cyprus, 1955–59; Man., Cooperative Wholesale Soc., Agricultural Dept, 1960–63; Dir, Internat. Cooperative Alliance, 1963–68; Dir-Gen., RoSPA, 1968–74; County Road Safety Officer, W Yorks MCC, 1974–78; Chm., W. H. Stott & Co. Ltd, 1979–83 (Dir, 1968–83). Mem., BSI Quality Assurance Council, 1975–83. Member: Bradford Dio. Bd of Finance; Ewecross Deanery Synod; Dent PCC. Clerk, Dent Parish Council, 1980–86. Chm., Bd of Govs, Dent GS. AMBIM 1963. *Recreations:* all sports and long distance walking. *Address:* Cross House, Dent, Cumbria LA10 5TF. *T:* Dent (05875) 228. *Club:* Commonwealth Trust.

ALEXANDER-SINCLAIR of Freswick, Maj.-Gen. David Boyd, CB 1981; retired 1982; *b* 2 May 1927; *s* of late Comdr M. B. Alexander-Sinclair of Freswick, RN and late Avril N. Fergusson-Buchanan; *m* 1958, Ann Ruth, *d* of late Lt-Col Graeme Daglish; two *s* one *d*. *Educ:* Eton. Commnd into Rifle Bde, 1946, served in Germany, Kenya, Cyprus; ADC to GOC South Malaya District and Maj.-Gen. Bde of Gurkhas, 1950–51; psc 1958; Bde Major, 6th Inf. Bde Gp, 1959–61; GSO2 (Dirg Staff) Staff Coll., 1963–65; comdg 3rd Bn Royal Green Jackets, 1967–69; MoD, 1965–67 and 1969–71; Comdr, 6th Armd Bde, 1971–73; Student, RCDS, 1974; GOC 1st Division, 1975–77; COS, UKLF, 1978–80; Comdt, Staff Coll., 1980–82.

AL-FAYED, Mohamed; Chairman: House of Fraser Holdings plc, since 1985; Harrods Ltd, since 1985; Chairman and Owner, Ritz Hotel, Paris, since 1979; *b* Egypt, Jan. 1933; *m*; five *c*. *Educ:* Alexandria Univ. Chevalier, Légion d'Honneur; La Grande Médaille de la Ville de Paris. *Address:* Harrods Ltd, Brompton Road, SW1 7XL.

ALFONSÍN, Dr Raúl Ricardo; President of Argentina, 1983–89; *b* 12 March 1927; *s* of Serafín Raúl Alfonsín and Ana María Foulkes; *m* 1949, María Lorenza Barreneche; three *s* three *d*. *Educ:* Regional Normal School, Chascomus; Gen. San Martín Mil. Acad.; Law Sch., Nat. Univ. of La Plata. Mem., Radical Civic Union, 1945, Pres., 1983–. Journalist, founder El Imparcial, Chascomus; Mem., Chascomus City Cttee, 1951, Councilman, 1954–55 (Pres., 1955 and 1959–61); Mem., Buenos Aires Provincial Legislature, 1952; Provincial Deputy, 1958–62; Deputy, Nat. Congress, 1963–66, 1973–76. Founder, Renovation and Change movement. Dr *hc* Univ. of New Mexico, 1985. Human Rights Prize (jtly), Council of Europe, 1986; numerous awards. *Publications:* La Cuestión Argentina, 1980; Ahora, mi Propuesta Política, 1983; Que es el Radicalismo?, 1983. *Address:* c/o President's Office, Buenos Aires, Argentina.

ALFORD, Ven. John Richard; Archdeacon of Halifax, 1972–84, now Emeritus; *b* 21 June 1919; *s* of Walter John and Gertrude Ellen Alford. *Educ:* Fitzwilliam House,

Cambridge (History Tri. Pts 1 and 2, BA 1941, MA 1947); Cuddesdon College, Oxford. Deacon 1943, priest 1944, Wakefield; Curate, St Paul, King Cross, Halifax, 1943–47; Curate, Wakefield Cathedral, 1947–50; Tutor, Wells Theological College, 1950–56; Priest Vicar, Wells Cathedral, 1950–56; Vice-Principal, The Queen's College, Birmingham, 1956–67; Exam. Chaplain to Bp of Kimberley and Kuruman, 1961–65; Domestic Chaplain, Director of Ordinands, and Exam. Chaplain to Bp of Chester, 1967–72; Vicar of Shotwick, Chester, 1967–72; Hon. Canon of Chester Cathedral, 1969–72, Emeritus, 1972; Canon Residentiary of Wakefield Cathedral, 1972–84, Emeritus 1985–; Examining Chaplain to Bp of Wakefield, 1972–84. Mem., General Synod of C of E, 1980–84; Vice-Pres., CEMS, 1980–86. *Recreations:* music, walking. *Address:* College of St Barnabas, Blackberry Lane, Lingfield, Surrey. *Club:* Royal Over-Seas League.

ALFORD, Richard Harding, OBE 1988; Director of Personnel, British Council, since 1989; *b* 28 Dec. 1943; *s* of Jack Harding Alford and Sylvia Alford; *m* 1968, Penelope Jane Wort; one *s* two *d*. *Educ:* Dulwich Coll.; Keble Coll., Oxford (BA; Diploma in History and Philosophy of Science). Asst Cultural Attaché, British Embassy, Prague, 1969–72; posts in ME Dept, Policy Res. Dept, and Educnl Contracts Dept, British Council, 1972–77; Project Planning Centre, Bradford Univ., 1977; Inst. of Educn, London Univ., 1978; British Council: Asst Rep., New Delhi, 1978–81; Dir, E Europe and N Asia Dept, 1982–85; Rep., Poland, 1985–89. *Recreations:* squash, theatre, walking the dog. *Address:* c/o The British Council, 10 Spring Gardens, SW1A 2BN. *T:* 071–930 8466. *Club:* Friends of Dulwich College Sports.

ALFRED, (Arnold) Montague; Deputy Chairman: Ward Lock Educational Co. Ltd, 1985–88; BLA Publishing Ltd, 1985–88; Ling Kee (UK) Ltd, 1985–88; retired; *b* 21 March 1925; *s* of Reuben Alfred and Bessie Alfred (*née* Arbesfield); *m* 1947, Sheila Jacqueline Gold; three *s*. *Educ:* Central Foundation Boys' Sch.; Imperial Coll., London; London Sch. of Economics. Head of Economics Dept, Courtaulds Ltd, 1953–69; Director, Nylon Div., Courtaulds Ltd, 1964–69; Dir, BPC Ltd, 1969–81; Chairman: BPC Publishing Ltd, 1971–81; Caxton Publishing Holdings Ltd, 1971–81; Second Permanent Sec., and Chief Exec., PSA, DoE, 1982–84. *Publications:* Discounted Cash Flow (jointly), 1965; Business Economics (jointly), 1968. Numerous articles in: Accountant, Textile Jl, Investment Analyst, etc. *Recreation:* active in Jewish community affairs. *Address:* c/o Institute of Directors, 168 Pall Mall, SW1Y 5ED.

ALFVÉN, Prof. Hannes Olof Gösta, PhD; Emeritus Professor of Plasma Physics, Royal Institute of Technology, Stockholm; *b* Sweden, 30 May 1908; *s* of Johannes Alfvén and Anna-Clara Romanus; *m* 1935, Kerstin Erikson, *d* of Rolf E. and Maria Uddenberg. *Educ:* Univ. of Uppsala (PhD 1934). Prof. of Theory of Electricity, 1940–45, of Electronics, 1945–63, and of Plasma Physics, 1963–73, Royal Inst. of Technology, Stockholm. Prof. (part-time), Univ. of California at San Diego, 1967–89. Pres., Pugwash Confs on Science and World Affairs, 1967–72; Member: Bd of Dirs, Swedish Atomic Energy Co., 1956–68; Science Adv. Council of Swedish Govt, 1961–67. Member: Swedish Acad. of Sciences; several foreign acads incl. Royal Society, London, 1980, Acad. of Sciences of the USSR, Nat. Acad. of Sciences, Washington, DC. Hon. DSc Oxon, 1977. Awarded Gold Medal of Royal Astronomical Soc. (Gt Britain), 1967; Nobel Prize for Physics, 1970; Lomonosov Medal, 1971; Franklin Medal, 1971. *Publications:* Cosmical Electrodynamics, 1948; On the Origin of the Solar System, 1956; Cosmical Electrodynamics: Fundamental Principles (jointly), 1963; World-Antiworlds (Eng. trans.), 1966; (as Olof Johannesson) The Tale of the Big Computer (Eng. trans.), 1968; Atom, Man and the Universe (Eng. trans.), 1969; (with Kerstin Alfvén) M70–Living on the Third Planet, 1971; (with G. Arrhenius) Evolution of the Solar System NASA SP-345, 1976; Cosmic Plasma, 1981; papers in physics and astrophysics. *Address:* c/o Department of Plasma Physics, Royal Institute of Technology, S-100 44 Stockholm, Sweden.

ALGOMA, Bishop of, since 1983; **Rt. Rev. Leslie Ernest Peterson;** *b* 4 Nov. 1928; *s* of late Ernest Victor Peterson and of Dorothy Blanche Peterson (*née* Marsh); *m* 1953, Yvonne Hazel Lawton; two *s* three *d*. *Educ:* Univ. of Western Ontario (BA 1952); Huron College (LTh 1954); Teachers' Coll., North Bay, Ont., 1970. Deacon 1954, priest 1955; Incumbent of All Saints', Coniston, Ont., 1954–59; St Peter's Elliot Lake, 1959–63; Rector, Christ Church, North Bay, 1963–78; Teacher, Marshall Park Elem. School, 1970–78; Rector, Trinity Church, Parry Sound, 1978–83; Coadjutor Bishop, June-Sept. 1983. *Recreations:* canoe tripping, gardening, skiing. *Address:* 134 Simpson Street, Sault Ste Marie, Ontario P6A 3V4, Canada. *T:* 705–256–7379, (office) 705–256–5061.

ALHEGELAN, Sheikh Faisal Abdul Aziz, Hon. GBE; Grand Cross and Cordon, Order of King Abdul Aziz, Saudi Arabia; Saudi Arabian diplomat; Minister of Health, Saudi Arabia, since 1984; *b* Riyadh, 7 Oct. 1929; *s* of Sheikh Abdulaziz Alhegelan and Fatima Al-Eissa; *m* 1961, Nouha Tarazi; three *s*. *Educ:* Faculty of Law, Fouad Univ., Cairo. Min. of Foreign Affairs, 1952–54; Saudi Arabian Embassy, Washington, USA, 1954–58; Chief of Protocol, Min. of Foreign Affairs, 1958–60; Polit. Adviser to King Sa'ud, 1960–61; Ambassador to: Spain, 1961–68; Venezuela and Argentina (concurrently), 1968–75; Denmark, 1975–76; Court of St James's, 1976–79; USA, 1979–83. Chm. Bd of Dirs, Saudi Red Crescent Soc., 1984–. Order of Isabel la Católica, Spain; Gran Cordon, Orden del Libertador, Venezuela; Grande Official, Orden Rio Branco, Brazil; May Grand Decoration, Argentina. *Recreations:* golf, bridge, collecting selective books and objets d'art. *Address:* c/o Ministry of Health, Riyadh, Saudi Arabia. *T:* 4011443, 4033567.

ALI, Rt. Rev. Dr Michael N.; *see* Nazir-Ali.

ALI, Lt-Gen. Mir Shawkat; High Comissioner of Bangladesh in London, since 1986; *b* 19 Jan. 1938; *s* of Mir Mahboob Ali and Begum Shahajadi; *m* 1963, Begum Tahmina Shawkat; one *s* three *d*. *Educ:* Military Acad., Kakul (commnd); Command and Staff Coll., Quetta (graduated). Chief of General Staff, Bangladesh Army, Principal Staff Officer to Supreme Comdr of Bangladesh Armed Forces, raised and commanded two Bdes and two Infantry Divs (Bir Uttam for gallantry in combat during liberation war in 1971); retd 1981. Ambassador to: Egypt, and concurrently to Sudan and Ethiopia, 1981–82; Federal Republic of Germany, and concurrently to Austria, 1982–86. Gold Medal for Agriculture, 1977; President's Gold Medal for contrib. to Sports, 1978. *Recreations:* reading, cuisine, outdoor sports. *Address:* High Commission for Bangladesh, 28 Queen's Gate, SW7 5JA. *T:* 071–584 0081.

ALISON, Rt. Hon. Michael James Hugh; PC 1981; MP (C) Selby, since 1983 (Barkston Ash, 1964–83); Second Church Estates Commissioner, since 1987; *b* 27 June 1926; *m* 1958, Sylvia Mary Haigh; two *s* one *d*. *Educ:* Eton; Wadham Coll., Oxford. Coldstream Guards, 1944–48; Wadham Coll., Oxford, 1948–51; Lazard Bros & Co. Ltd, 1951–53; London Municipal Soc., 1954–58; Conservative Research Dept, 1958–64. Parly Under-Sec. of State, DHSS, 1970–74; Minister of State: Northern Ireland Office, 1979–81; Dept of Employment, 1981–83; PPS to Prime Minister, 1983–87. *Publication:* (ed jtly) Christianity and Conservatism, 1990. *Address:* House of Commons, SW1A 0AA.

ALISON, William Andrew Greig, FLA; Director of Libraries, City of Glasgow, 1975–81; *b* 23 Oct. 1916; *m* 1942, Jessie Youngson Henderson; two *d*. *Educ:* Daniel Stewart's Coll., Edinburgh. Served War, Royal Air Force, 1940–46. Edinburgh Public Libraries, 1935–62: Assistant, 1935–46; Librarian, Fine Art Dept, 1946–55; Branch Librarian, 1955–61; Librarian, Scottish and Local History Depts, 1961–62; Glasgow City Libraries, 1962–81: Supt of District Libraries, 1962–64; Depute City Librarian, 1964–74; City Librarian, 1974–75. President: Scottish Library Assoc., 1975; Library Assoc., 1979 (also Mem. Council, 1979–82; Chm., Library Assoc. Publishing, 1981–82); Member: British Library Adv. Council, 1979–82; Nat. Library of Scotland Library Co-operation Cttee, 1974–81. British Council visits to: Zimbabwe, 1981; Bahrain, 1982; Syria, 1983. Church of Scotland elder and session clerk. Silver Jubilee Medal, 1977. *Publication:* (assoc. ed.) New Library Buildings 1984–1989, 1990. *Recreations:* travel, philately. *Address:* St Mawgan, 103 Mossgiel Road, Glasgow G43 2BY. *T:* 041–632 6036.

AL-KHALIFA, Shaikh Abdul-Rahman Faris; Ambassador in the Ministry of Foreign Affairs, Bahrain, since 1984; *b* 24 Feb. 1942; *s* of Shaikh Faris bin Khalifa Al-Khalifa and Shaikha Latifa Rashid Al-Khalifa; *m* 1969, Shaikha Latifa Salman Al-Khalifa; one *s* four *d*. *Educ:* Bahrain; Univ. of Cairo (BSc Economics and Commercial Subjects). Member of the Ruling Family of the State of Bahrain. Ambassador to UK, 1980–84. *Address:* Ministry of Foreign Affairs, PO Box 547, Bahrain. *Clubs:* Royal Automobile; Wentworth Golf, Hampstead Golf.

ALLAIRE, Paul Arthur; President, since 1986, and Chief Executive Officer, since 1990, Xerox Corporation, PO Box 1600, Stamford, Connecticut; *b* 21 July 1938; *s* of late Arthur E. Allaire and of Mrs G. P. Murphy; *m* 1963, Kathleen Buckley; one *s* one *d*. *Educ:* Worcester Polytechnic Inst., USA (BS Elect. Eng., 1960); Carnegie-Mellon Univ., USA (MS Industrial Admin, 1966). Engineer, Univac, 1960–62; Project Manager, General Electric, 1962–64; Manager Financial Planning and Pricing, Xerox Corp., 1966–70; Financial Controller, Rank Xerox Ltd, 1970–73; Xerox Corporation: Dir, Internat. Finance, 1973–74; Dir, Internat. Ops, 1974–75; Rank Xerox Ltd: Chief Staff Officer, 1975–79; Dep. Man. Dir, 1979–80; Man. Dir, 1980–83; Mem., Bd of Dirs; Sen. Vice-Pres., Xerox Corp., 1983–86; Member, Board of Directors: Fuji Xerox Co.; Sara Lee Corp. Mem., Council on For. Relations. Member: Bd of Dirs, NY City Ballet; Bd, Catalyst. Trustee, Nat. Planning Assoc.; Member, Board of Trustees: Carnegie Mellon Univ. (Mem., Business Adv. Council, Grad. Sch. of Indust. Admin); Worcester Polytechnic Inst., Mass. *Recreations:* horse riding, tennis.

ALLAIS, Prof. Maurice; Commandeur de la Légion d'honneur, 1989; Officier des Palmes académiques, 1949; Chevalier de l'économie nationale, 1962; French economist and engineer; *b* 31 May 1911; *s* of Maurice Allais and Louise (*née* Caubet); *m* 1960, Jacqueline Bouteloup; one *d*. *Educ:* Lycée Lakanal à Sceaux; Lycée Louis-le-Grand; Ecole Polytechnique; Ecole Nationale Supérieure des Mines de Paris. Engineer, Dept of Mines and Quarries, Nantes, 1937–43; Dir, Bureau de Documentation Minière, 1943–48; Prof. of Economic Analysis, Ecole Nationale Supérieure des Mines de Paris, 1944–88; Dir, Centre for Economic Analysis, 1946–; Prof. of Economic Theory, Inst. of Statistics, Univ. of Paris, 1947–68; research in economics, 1948–; Dir of Res., Centre National de la Recherche Scientifique, 1954–80; Prof., Graduate Inst. of Internat. Studies, Geneva, 1967–70; Dir, Clément Juglar Centre of Monetary Analysis, Univ of Paris, 1970–85. Fellow: Operations Res. Soc., 1958; Internat. Soc. of Econometrics, 1949. Mem. de l'Académie des Sciences Morales et Politiques, 1990; Hon. Mem., Amer. Econ. Assoc., 1976; Associate Foreign Mem., US Nat. Acad. of Scis, 1989. Dr *hc* Univ. of Groningen, 1964. Prizes from: L'Académie des Sciences, 1933; L'Académie des Sciences Morales et Politiques, 1954, 1959, 1983, 1984. Gravity Res. Foundn, 1959; also Lanchester Prize, Amer. Economic Assoc., 1958; Prix Galabert, 1959; Grand Prix André Arnoux, 1968; Gold Medal, Centre National de la Recherche Scientifique, 1978; Nobel Prize for Economics, 1988. *Publications* include: A la recherche d'une discipline économique, 1943; Abondance ou misère, 1946; Economie et Intérêt, 1947; Les fondements comptables de la macroéconomique, 1954; Manifeste pour une société libre, 1959; L'Europe unie, route de la prosperité, 1960; The Role of Capital in Economic Development, 1963; Growth without Inflation, 1968; Les théories de l'équilibre économique général et de l'éfficacité maximale, 1971; Inequality and Civilization, 1973; L'impôt sur le capital et la réforme monétaire, 1977; La théorie générale des surplus, 1980; Frequency, Probability and Chance, 1982; Determination of Cardinal Utility, 1985; Les conditions monétaires d'une économie de marché, 1987; Autoportraits, 1989; Pour l'indexation, 1990; Pour la réforme de la fiscalité, 1990; L'Europe face à son avenir, que faire, 1991. *Address:* (office) 60 boulevard Saint Michel, 75006 Paris, France.

ALLAM, Peter John; Architect Principal in private practice of Peter Allam, Chartered Architect, Dollar, 1964–68, 1971–78 and since 1981; *b* 17 June 1927; *er s* of late Leslie Francis Allam and Annette Farquharson (*née* Lawson); *m* 1961, Pamela Mackie Haynes; two *d*. *Educ:* Royal High Sch., Edinburgh; Glasgow Sch. of Architecture. War service, 1944–48, Far East; commnd in Seaforth Highlanders, 1946. Architectural trng, 1948–53. Bahrain Petroleum Co., Engrg Div., 1954–55; Asst in private architectural practices, 1956–64; Partner in private practice of Haswell-Smith & Partners, Edinburgh, 1978–79; Director, Saltire Soc., 1968–70; Dir of Sales, Smith & Wellstood Ltd, Manfg Ironfounders, 1979–81. ARIBA 1964; FRIAS 1985 (Associate, 1964). Red Cross Br. Trng Officer and Speaker on Internat. Humanitarian Law. *Recreations:* study and practice of conservation, both architectural and natural; music, painting, Rugby. *Address:* 4 Moir's Well, Dollar, Clackmannanshire FK14 7BQ. *T:* (home) Dollar (0259) 42973; (office) Dollar (0259) 42850.

ALLAN, Alexander Claud Stuart; Under Secretary (General Expenditure Policy Group), HM Treasury, since 1990; *b* 9 Feb. 1951; *s* of Lord Allan of Kilmahew, DSO, OBE and of Maureen (*née* Stuart Clark); *m* 1978, Katie Christine Clemson. *Educ:* Harrow Sch.; Clare College, Cambridge; University College London (MSc). HM Customs and Excise, 1973–76; HM Treasury, 1976–; secondments in Australia, 1983–84; Principal Private Sec. to Chancellor of the Exchequer, 1986–89; Under Sec. (Internat. Finance), 1989–90. *Recreations:* Grateful Dead music, sailing, computers. *Address:* HM Treasury, Parliament Street, SW1P 3AG. *T:* 071–270 4499. *Club:* Royal Ocean Racing.

ALLAN, Andrew Norman; Managing Director, Central Broadcasting Ltd, since 1990; *b* 26 Sept. 1943; *s* of Andrew Allan and Elizabeth (*née* Davison); *m* 1978, Joanna Forrest; two *s* one *d*, and two *d* of a former marriage. *Educ:* Birmingham Univ. (BA). Presenter, ABC Television, 1965–66; Producer: Thames Television, 1966–69; ITN, 1970; Thames TV, 1971–75; Head of News, Thames TV, 1976–78; Tyne Tees Television: Dir of Progs, 1978–83; Dep. Man. Dir, 1982–83; Man. Dir, 1983–84; Dir of Progs, Central Indep. TV, 1984–90. *Recreations:* reading, dining. *Address:* c/o Central Broadcasting Ltd, Central House, Broad Street, Birmingham B1 2JP. *T:* 021–643 9898.

ALLAN, Sir Anthony James Allan H.; *see* Havelock-Allan.

ALLAN, (Charles) Lewis (Cuthbert), MA, CEng, FICE, FIEE, FBIM; Chairman, South of Scotland Electricity Board, 1967–73 (Deputy Chairman, 1964–67); Member, North of Scotland Hydro-Electric Board, 1967–73; *b* 22 July 1911; *s* of Charles W. Allan, Edinburgh, and Isabella H. Young; *m* 1938, Kathleen Mary Robinson, Chesterfield, Derbyshire; one *s* three *d*. *Educ:* Merchiston Castle School, Edinburgh; Pembroke College, Cambridge (Mechanical Sciences Tripos). Bruce Peebles & Co. Ltd, Edinburgh, 1933–35;

Balfour Beatty & Co. Ltd, 1935–38; Central Electricity Board, 1938–41; Ipswich Corp. Electric Supply and Transport Dept, 1941–44; North of Scotland Hydro-Electric Board, 1944–63 (Chief Electrical and Mechanical Engineer, 1954–63). *Publications:* articles in the electrical technical press and for World Power Conference. *Recreations:* gardening, walking, fishing, piping, Church work. *Address:* 19 Bonaly Avenue, Colinton, Edinburgh EH13 0ET.

ALLAN, Colin Faulds, CB 1976; Chief Planning Inspector (Director of Planning Inspectorate), Department of the Environment, 1971–78, retired; *b* Newcastle upon Tyne, 1917; *s* of late Jack Stanley and Ruth Allan; *m* 1941, Aurea, 2nd *d* of Algernon Noble, Hexham; one *s* one *d. Educ:* Royal Grammar Sch., Newcastle upon Tyne; King's Coll. (Newcastle), Durham Univ. DipArch, ARIBA, DipTP (Distinction), FRTPI. Capt., RA, 1940–45; served in Iraq, India, Burma (despatches). Chief Asst to Dr Thomas Sharp, Planning Consultant, 1945–47; Area Planning Officer, Cumberland and Staffs CC, 1947–57; joined Housing and Planning Inspectorate, 1957; Chief Housing and Planning Inspector, DoE (formerly Min. of Housing and Local Govt), 1967–71. *Recreations:* walking, bird-watching, eighteenth-century wineglasses. *Address:* Fieldfares, Chinthurst Lane, Shalford, Guildford, Surrey. *T:* Guildford (0483) 61528.

ALLAN, Sir Colin (Hamilton), KCMG 1977 (CMG 1968); OBE 1959; FRAI 1950; Her Majesty's Overseas Civil Service, retired; *b* 23 Oct. 1921; *yr s* of late John Calder Allan, Cambridge, NZ; *m* 1955, Betty Dorothy, *e d* of late A. C. Evans, Brisbane, Australia; three *s. Educ:* Hamilton High Sch., NZ; College House, Canterbury Univ., NZ; Magdalene College, Cambridge. Military Service, NZ, 1942–44. Cadet, Colonial Admin. Service, British Solomon Is, 1945; District Comr, Western Solomons, 1946; District Comr, Malaita, 1950; Special Lands Comr, 1953; Sen. Asst Sec., Western Pacific High Commn, 1957; Asst Resident Comr, New Hebrides, 1959, British Resident Comr, 1966–73; Governor and C-in-C, Seychelles, 1973–76, and Comr, British Indian Ocean Territory, 1973–76; Governor, Solomon Is, and High Comr for Western Pacific, 1976–78. Delegate: Seychelles Constitutional Conf., 1975, 1976; Solomon Is Constitutional Conf., 1977. Vis. Fellow, Australian Nat. Univ., Research Sch. of Pacific Studies, 1979; Visiting Lecturer: Law Sch., Auckland Univ., 1981–; Univ. of NSW, Sydney, 1988; Univ. of Otago, 1989. Chm., Ranfurly Library Service, NZ, 1985–; Member: Leprosy Trust Bd (NZ), 1980–; NZ Adv. Council, Province of Melanesia, 1982–. Commandeur, l'Ordre Nationale du Mérite (France), 1966. *Publications:* Land Tenure in the British Solomon Islands Protectorate, 1958; Solomons Safari, 1989; papers on colonial administration. *Recreations:* malacology, collecting, reading The Times. *Address:* Glen Rowan, 17 Sale Street, Howick, Auckland, New Zealand. *Club:* Commonwealth Trust.

ALLAN, Diana Rosemary, (Mrs R. B. Allan); *see* Cotton, D. R.

ALLAN, Douglas; *see* Allan, J. D.

ALLAN, George Alexander, MA; Headmaster, Robert Gordon's College, Aberdeen, since 1978; *b* 3 Feb. 1936; *s* of William Allan and Janet Peters (*née* Watt); *m* 1962, Anne Violet Veevers; two *s. Educ:* Daniel Stewart's Coll., Edinburgh; Edinburgh Univ. (MA 1st Cl. Hons Classics; Bruce of Grangehill Scholar, 1957). Classics Master, Glasgow Acad., 1958–60; Daniel Stewart's College: Classics Master, 1960–63; Head of Classics, 1963–73; Housemaster, 1966–73; Schoolmaster Fellow, Corpus Christi Coll., Cambridge, 1972; Dep. Headmaster, Robert Gordon's Coll., 1973–77. Headmasters' Conference: Sec. 1980–86, Chm., 1988, 1989, Scottish Div.; Mem. Cttee, 1982, 1983; Mem., ISIS Scotland Cttee, 1984–; Council Mem., Scottish Council of Indep. Schs, 1988–. Governor, Welbeck Coll., 1980–89. *Recreations:* golf, gardening, music. *Address:* 24 Woodend Road, Aberdeen AB2 6YH. *T:* Aberdeen (0224) 321733. *Clubs:* East India, Devonshire Sports and Public Schools; Royal Northern & University (Aberdeen).

ALLAN, Gordon Buchanan, TD 1950; BA; CA; *b* 11 Aug. 1914; *s* of late Alexander Buchanan Allan, MIMechE, and Irene Lilian Allan, Glasgow; *m* 1971, Gwenda Jervis Davies, *d* of late John William and Elizabeth Davies, Porthcawl, Glam. *Educ:* Glasgow Academy; High Sch. of Glasgow; Glasgow Univ. Mem., Inst. of Chartered Accountants of Scotland, 1937. Commissioned into Royal Signals (TA), 1938. Served War of 1939–45, DAAG, GHQ, India, 1945, Major. Director: George Outram & Co. Ltd, 1960–75 (Dep. Man. Dir and Financial Dir, 1970–75); Holmes McDougall Ltd, 1966–72. Mem. Press Council, 1969–74. Vice-Pres., Scottish Daily Newspaper Soc., 1970, Pres. 1971–73; Dir, Glasgow Chamber of Commerce, 1971–75. Member: UK Newsprint Users' Cttee, 1972–75; Council, CBI, 1972–74; Finance Cttee, RIIA, 1975–77; Merchants' House of Glasgow, 1975–. Mem. Bd, Bield Housing Assoc. Ltd, 1978–. Trustee, Bield Housing Trust, 1975–. Governor, The Queen's College, Glasgow, 1976–89. *Recreations:* music, golf. *Address:* 3 Winchester Court, Glasgow G12 0JN. *T:* 041-334 2353. *Club:* Royal Scottish Automobile (Glasgow).

ALLAN, Rt. Rev. Hugh James Pearson, DD; Assistant Bishop of Nova Scotia, since 1991; *b* 7 Aug. 1928; *s* of Hugh Blomfield Allan and Agnes Dorothy (*née* Pearson); *m* 1955, Beverley Edith Baker; one *s* three *d. Educ:* St John's Coll., Univ. of Manitoba (LTh 1955, BA 1957). Deacon 1954, priest 1955; Assistant: St Aidan's, Winnipeg, 1954; All Saints, Winnipeg, 1955; Missionary, Peguis Indian Reserve, 1956–60; Rector, St Mark's, Winnipeg, 1960–68; Hon. Canon, Diocese of Rupert's Land, 1967; Rector, St Stephen's Swift Current, Sask., 1968–70; Rural Dean of Cypress, 1968–70; Dean of Qu'Appelle and Rector of St Paul's Cathedral, Regina, Sask., 1970–74; Bishop of Keewatin, 1974–91. Hon. DD, St John's Coll., Univ. of Manitoba, 1974. *Recreations:* ornithology, boating. *Address:* 5720 College Street, Halifax, NS B3H 1X3, Canada.

ALLAN, Ian; Chairman, Ian Allan Group Ltd, since 1962; *b* 29 June 1922; *s* of George A. T. Allan, OBE, and Mary Louise (*née* Barnes); *m* 1947, Mollie Eileen (*née* Franklin); two *s. Educ:* St Paul's Sch. Joined Southern Railway Co., 1939. Founded Ian Allan Ltd, Publishers, 1945; other cos co-ordinated into Ian Allan Group Ltd, 1962. Chm., Dart Valley Light Railway PLC, 1976–87. Governor, Christ's Hosp., 1944–, Almoner, 1980–89; Chm., King Edward's Sch., Witley, 1983– (Governor, 1975–); Treas., Bridewell Royal Hosp. 1983–. Vice Pres., Transport Trust, 1979–; Mem., Transport Users Consultative Cttee for London, 1982–84; Chm., Assoc. of Indep. Rlys, 1987–. *Publications:* compiled and edited many books on railways and transport subjects, 1939–. *Recreations:* swimming, touring, miniature railways. *Address:* Terminal House, Shepperton TW17 8AS. *T:* Walton-on-Thames (0932) 228950; The Jetty, Middleton-on-Sea, Bognor Regis, W Sussex. *T:* Middleton-on-Sea (024369) 3378.

ALLAN, James Nicholas, CMG 1989; CBE 1976; HM Diplomatic Service; Senior Directing Staff, Royal College of Defence Studies, since 1989; *b* 22 May 1932; *s* of late Morris Edward Allan and Joan Bach; *m* 1961, Helena Susara Crouse; one *s* one *d. Educ:* Gresham's Sch.; London Sch. of Economics. HM Forces, 1950–53. Asst Principal, CRO, 1956–58; Third, later Second Sec., Cape Town/Pretoria, 1958–59; Private Sec. to Parly Under-Sec., 1959–61; First Secretary: Freetown, 1961–64; Nicosia, 1964; CRO, later FCO, 1964–68; Head of Chancery, Peking, 1969–71; Luxembourg, 1971–73; Counsellor, seconded to Northern Ireland Office, Belfast, 1973–75; Counsellor, FCO, 1976; Head of

Overseas Inf. Dept., FCO, 1978–81 (Governor's Staff, Salisbury, Dec. 1979–March 1980); High Comr in Mauritius, 1981–85, concurrently Ambassador (non-resident) to the Comoros, 1984–85; Ambassador to Mozambique, 1986–89. *Address:* c/o Foreign and Commonwealth Office, SW1A 2AH. *Club:* Athenæum.

ALLAN, Dr James Wilson; Keeper of Eastern Art, Ashmolean Museum, Oxford, since 1991; Fellow of St Cross College, Oxford, since 1990; *b* 5 May 1945; *s* of John Bellerby Allan and Evelyn Mary Allan; *m* 1970, Jennifer Robin Hawksworth; two *s* two *d. Educ:* Marlborough Coll.; St Edmund Hall, Oxford (MA 1966; DPhil 1976). Eastern Art Department, Ashmolean Museum: Asst Keeper, 1966–88; Sen. Asst Keeper, 1988–91. *Publications:* Medieval Middle Eastern Pottery, 1971; Persian Metal Technology 700–1300 AD, 1978; Islamic Metalwork: the Nuhad Es-Said Collection, 1982; Nishapur: metalwork of the early Islamic period, 1982; Metalwork of the Islamic World: the Aron Collection, 1986; (ed) Creswell: A Short Account of Early Muslim Architecture, 1989. *Recreations:* music, ornithology, walking, travel. *Address:* Ashmolean Museum, Oxford OX1 2PH. *T:* Oxford (0865) 278068.

ALLAN, John Clifford, RCNC; Director, Manpower, Dockyards, 1975–79; *b* 3 Feb. 1920; *s* of James Arthur and Mary Alice Allan; *m* 1947, Dorothy Mary (*née* Dossett); two *d. Educ:* Royal Naval Coll., Greenwich. Entered Royal Corps of Naval Constructors, 1945; service at HM Dockyards: Portsmouth, Chatham, Devonport, Gibraltar, Singapore, 1950–75; Chief Constructor, Chief Executive Dockyard HQ, 1967–69, Asst Dir, 1969, Dir, 1975. *Recreations:* painting, tennis, squash (Pres., Lansdown Lawn Tennis & Squash Racquets Club). *Address:* 21 Henrietta Street, Bath, Avon BA2 6LP. *T:* Bath (0225) 446570.

ALLAN, (John) Douglas; Sheriff of South Strathclyde, Dumfries and Galloway at Lanark, since 1988; *b* 2 Oct. 1941; *s* of Robert Taylor Allan and late Christina Helen Blythe Reid or Allan; *m* 1966, Helen Elizabeth Jean Aiton or Allan; one *s* one *d. Educ:* George Watson's Coll.; Edinburgh Univ. (BL); Napier Coll., Edinburgh (DMS); FBIM. Solicitor and Notary Public. Solicitor, 1963–67; Depute Procurator Fiscal, 1967–71; Sen. Legal Asst, Crown Office, 1971–76; Asst Procurator Fiscal, Glasgow, 1976–77; Sen. Asst Procurator Fiscal, Glasgow, 1978–79; Asst Solicitor, Crown Office, 1979–83; Regl Procurator Fiscal for Lothian and Borders and Procurator Fiscal for Edinburgh, 1983–88. *Recreations:* youth work, church work, walking. *Address:* Sheriff Court, County Buildings, Lanark ML11 7NQ; Minard, 80 Greenbank Crescent, Edinburgh EH10 5SW. *T:* 031-447 2593.

ALLAN, John Gray, CBE 1975; Legal Adviser and Solicitor to the Crown Estate Commissioners, 1961–77; *b* 10 Nov. 1915; *s* of late John Allan, CB, FSA, FBA, LLD, and Ida Mary (*née* Law). *Educ:* Charterhouse; Oriel College, Oxford. Called to Bar, Middle Temple, 1940. War Service, 1940–46: The Black Watch, GSO2 (War Office and Allied Land Headquarters, Melbourne), 1942–46. Legal Branch, Min. of Agriculture, Fisheries and Food, 1946–57. Deputy Legal Adviser, Crown Estate Office, 1957. *Recreations:* golf, bridge. *Address:* 5 Rheidol Terrace, N1. *T:* 071-226 7616. *Club:* Boodle's.

ALLAN, Lewis; *see* Allan, C. L. C.

ALLAN, Richard Andrew; Director of Personnel, Department of Transport, since 1990; *b* 28 Feb. 1948; *s* of Kenneth and Mary Allan; *m* 1975, Katharine Mary Tait; one *s* one *d. Educ:* Bolton Sch.; Balliol Coll., Oxford (MA Mod. Hist.). VSO, Nigeria, 1970. Asst Principal, DTI, 1970; Asst British Trade Comr, Hong Kong, 1973; Department of Industry: Private Sec. to Perm. Sec., 1974–75; Principal, 1975–79; First Sec. (Civil Aviation and Shipping), Washington, 1980–84; Department of Transport: Asst Sec., 1984; Principal Private Sec. to Sec. of State for Transport, 1985–87; Under Sec., 1988; seconded to BRB, 1988–90. *Recreations:* choral singing, theatre, walking. *Address:* Department of Transport, Lambeth Bridge House, Albert Embankment, SE1 7SB.

ALLAN, William Roderick Buchanan; Arts Consultant to United Technologies Corporation, since 1983, currently working with Tate Gallery, National Portrait Gallery and National Maritime Museum; *b* 11 Sept. 1945; *s* of James Buchanan Allan and Mildred Pattenden; *m* 1973, Gillian Gail Colgan; two *s. Educ:* Stowe; Trinity Coll., Cambridge (MA Hons History, 1970). Joined staff of The Connoisseur, 1972, Editor 1976–80; Editorial Consultant to Ommific, 1980–83; Author of seven radio plays with nineteenth century historical themes. *Publications:* contrib. to several books dealing with British history; contrib. to History Today, The Connoisseur, and Antique Collector. *Recreations:* military history, cooking.

ALLANBRIDGE, Hon. Lord; William Ian Stewart; a Senator of the College of Justice in Scotland, since 1977; *b* 8 Nov. 1925; *s* of late John Stewart, FRIBA, and Mrs Maysie Shepherd Service or Stewart, Drimfearn, Bridge of Allan; *m* 1955, Naomi Joan Douglas, *d* of late Sir James Boyd Douglas, CBE, and of Lady Douglas, Barstibly, Castle Douglas; one *s* one *d. Educ:* Loretto; Glasgow and Edinburgh Univs. Sub-Lt, RNVR, 1944–46. Called to the Bar, 1951; QC (Scot.) 1965; Advocate-Depute, 1959–64; Mem., Criminal Injuries Compensation Bd, 1969–70; Home Advocate-Depute, 1970–72; Solicitor-General for Scotland, 1972–74; Temp. Sheriff-Principal of Dumfries and Galloway, Apr.-Dec. 1974. Mem., Criminal Injuries Compensation Bd, 1976–77. *Address:* 60 Northumberland Street, Edinburgh EH3 6JE. *T:* 031-556 2823. *Clubs:* New (Edinburgh); RNVR (Glasgow).

ALLANSON-WINN, family name of **Baron Headley.**

ALLARD, Sir Gordon (Laidlaw), Kt 1981; President, Royal Victorian Eye and Ear Hospital, 1964–80; *b* 7 Aug. 1909; *m* 1935, Cherry Singleton; one *s. Educ:* Scotch Coll., Melbourne. FCA; FCA (NZ). Joined Flack & Flack, later Price Waterhouse & Co., 1927; Partner, and a Sen. Partner, in Australia and NZ, 1942–74. Chm., AMI-Toyota Ltd, 1976–85 (Dir, 1975–86). Mem., Gen. Council, Inst. of Chartered Accountants in Australia, 1962–70 (Victorian Chm., 1962–64). *Recreations:* golf, bowls, gardening. *Address:* 4 St Martins Close, Kooyong, Vic 3144, Australia. *Clubs:* Melbourne, Australian (Melbourne); Royal Melbourne Golf, Frankston Golf.

ALLARD, General Jean Victor, CC (Canada) 1968; CBE 1946; DSO 1943 (Bars 1944, 1945); ED 1946; CD 1958; Chief of Canadian Defence Staff, 1966–69; Representative of the Province of Quebec in New York, Sept. 1969–June 1970; *b* Nicolet, PQ, 12 June 1913; *s* of late Ernest Allard and Victorine Trudel; *m* 1939, Simone, *d* of Gustave Piche, OBE; two *d. Educ:* St Laurent Coll., Montreal; St Jerome Coll., Kitchener, Ont. Joined Three Rivers Regt, 1933; Capt., 1938; Major, 1939; War of 1939–45: Co. of London Yeomanry, 1940–41; Canadian Army Staff Coll., Kingston, 1941–42 (Instructor, 1942); 5th Canadian Armoured Div.; second in command: Régt de la Chaudière; Royal 22e Regt, 1943 (Italy); Lt-Col 1944; CO Royal 22e Regt; Brig. 1945; Comd 6th Canadian Infantry Brigade, 1945 (Holland); Military Attaché Canadian Embassy, Moscow, 1945–48; Comd Eastern Quebec Area, 1948–50; idc 1951; Vice Quarter-Master Gen., Canada, 1952; Comdr, 25th Canadian Infantry Brigade Group, in Korea, 1953; Comdr 3rd Canadian Infantry Brigade, 1954; Comd Eastern Quebec Area, 1956; Maj.-Gen. 1958; Vice Chief of the General Staff, Canada, 1958; Comdr 4th Division, BAOR, 1961–63 (first Canadian to command a British Div.); Maj.-Gen. Survival, Ottawa, 1963;

Lt-Gen. 1964; Chief of Operational Readiness, Canada, 1964–65; Comdr, Mobile Command, Canada, Oct. 1965–June 1966; General, 1966; Col Comdt, 12 Regt Blindé du Canada; Col, Royal 22e Regt, 1985. Member: Royal 22e Regt Assoc.; La Régie du 22e; Royal Canadian Air Force Assoc.; Royal Canadian Naval Service Assoc.; Cercle Universitaire d'Ottawa; Chm. Bd of Governors, Ottawa Univ., 1966–69, Member Bd, 1969–. Hon. DSS Laval, 1958; Hon. LLD: Ottawa, 1959; St Thomas, 1966; St Mary's, Halifax, 1969; Hon. DScMil RMC Canada, 1970. FRSA. Bronze Lion (Netherlands), 1945; Légion d'Honneur and Croix de Guerre (France), 1945; Legion of Merit (US), 1954. Kt of Magistral Grace, Sovereign and Military Order of Malta, 1967. *Publication:* Mémoires, 1985. *Recreation:* music. *Address:* 3265 Boulevard du Carmel, Trois-Rivieres, Quebec, Canada.

ALLARDICE, William Arthur Llewellyn; His Honour Judge Allardice; DL; a Circuit Judge since 1972 (Midland and Oxford Circuit); *b* 18 Dec. 1924; *s* of late W. C. Allardice, MD, FRCSEd, JP, and late Constance Winifred Allardice; *m* 1956, Jennifer Ann, *d* of late G. H. Jackson; one *s* one *d*. *Educ:* Stonyhurst Coll.; University Coll., Oxford (MA). Open Schol., Classics, 1942; joined Rifle Bde, 1943, commnd 1944; served with 52nd LI, Europe and Palestine, 1945; Oxford, 1946–48; called to Bar, Lincoln's Inn, 1950; practised Oxford Circuit, 1950–71. DL Staffs, 1980. *Recreations:* local history, matters equestrian. *Address:* c/o Courts Administrator, Stafford. *T:* Stafford (0785) 55219.

ALLASON, Lt-Col James Harry, OBE 1953; *b* 6 Sept. 1912; *s* of late Brigadier-General Walter Allason, DSO; *m* 1946, Nuala Elveen (marr. diss. 1974), *d* of late J. A. McArevey, Foxrock, Co. Dublin; two *s*. *Educ:* Haileybury; RMA, Woolwich. Commissioned RA, 1932; transferred 3rd DG, 1937; War Service India and Burma, 1939–44; retired 1953. Member Kensington Borough Council, 1956–65. Contested (C) Hackney Central, General Election, 1955; MP (C) Hemel Hempstead, 1959–Sept. 1974; PPS to Sec. of State for War, 1960–64. *Address:* 82 Ebury Mews, SW1W 9NX. *T:* 071–730 1576. *Clubs:* White's; Royal Yacht Squadron.

See also R. W. S. Allason.

ALLASON, Rupert William Simon; MP (C) Torbay, since 1987; European Editor, Intelligence Quarterly, since 1985; *b* 8 Nov. 1951; *s* of Lt-Col J. H. Allason, *qv*; *m* 1979, Nicole Jane, *y d* of late M. L. Van Moppes; one *s* one *d*. *Educ:* Downside; Grenoble Univ.; London Univ. (external). Special Constable, 1975–82. BBC TV, 1978–82. Contested (C): Kettering, 1979; Battersea, 1983. *Publications:* The Branch: A History of the Metropolitan Police Special Branch 1883–1983, 1983; *as Nigel West:* non-fiction: Spy! (with Richard Deacon), 1980; MI5: British Security Service Operations 1909–45, 1981; A Matter of Trust: MI5 1945–72, 1982; MI6: British Secret Intelligence Service Operations 1909–45, 1983; Unreliable Witnesses: espionage myths of World War II, 1984; Garbo (with Juan Pujol), 1985; GCHQ: The Secret Wireless War, 1986; Molehunt, 1987; The Friends: Britain's post-war secret intelligence operations, 1988; Games of Intelligence, 1989; fiction: The Blue List, 1989; Cuban Bluff, 1990. *Recreation:* sailing close to the wind. *Address:* c/o House of Commons, SW1A 0AA. *Clubs:* White's, Special Forces; Royal Yacht Squadron (Cowes); Royal Torbay Yacht Club (Torquay).

ALLAUN, Frank; *b* 27 Feb. 1913; *s* of Harry and Hannah Allaun; *m* 1st, 1941, Lilian Ball (*d* 1986); one *s* one *d*; 2nd, 1989, Millie Bobker. *Educ:* Manchester Grammar Sch. BA (Com); ACA. Town Hall Correspondent, and later Industrial Correspondent, Manchester Evening News; Northern Industrial Correspondent, Daily Herald; Editor, Labour's Northern Voice, 1951–67. Mem., NUJ; formerly Mem. AEU and Shop Assistants' Union; Pres., Labour Action for Peace, 1965–; Vice-Pres., Campaign for Nuclear Disarmament, 1983–; helped organise first Aldermaston march. MP (Lab) East Salford, 1955–83; PPS to the Secretary of State for the Colonies, Oct. 1964–March 1965, resigned. Mem., Labour Party National Executive, 1967–83, Dep. Chm., 1977–78, Chm., 1978–79. *Publications:* Stop the H Bomb Race, 1959; Heartbreak Housing, 1966; Your Trade Union and You, 1950; No Place Like Home, 1972; The Wasted '30 Billions, 1975; Questions and Answers on Nuclear Weapons, 1981; Spreading the News: a guide to media reform, 1989; numerous broadcasts. *Recreations:* walking, swimming. *Address:* 11 Eastleigh Road, Prestwich, Manchester M25 8BQ. *T:* 061–740 5085.

ALLAWAY, Percy Albert, CBE 1973; FEng; Director, EMI Ltd, 1965–81; Chairman, EMI Electronics Ltd, 1968–81; Member, Executive Management Board, THORN EMI Ltd, 1980–81, Consultant, 1981–82; *b* 22 Aug. 1915; *s* of Albert Edward Allaway and Frances Beatrice (*née* Rogers); *m* 1959, Margaret Lilian Petyt. *Educ:* Southall Technical College. FEng 1980, FIProdE, FIEE, FIQA. Trained EMI Ltd, 1930–35, returned 1940; Man. Dir, 1961–81, Chm., 1969–81, EMI Electronics Ltd; Chairman: EMI-Varian Ltd, 1969–81; EMI-MEC Ltd, 1968–81; Director: Nuclear Enterprises Ltd, 1961–81; SE Labs (EMI) Ltd, 1967–81. Pres., EEA, 1969–70 (former Mem. Council). Chm., Defence Industries Quality Assurance Panel, 1971–78; Past Chm. and Hon. Mem., NCQR; Member: Nat. Electronics Council, 1965–80; Raby Cttee, 1968–69; Parly and Scientific Cttee, 1976–82; Pres., IERE, 1975; a Vice-Pres., and Mem. Council: Inst. of Industrial Managers; IQA; Member: Bd and Exec. Cttee, CEI, 1974–78 (Vice-Chm., 1979–80, Chm., 1980–81); Design Council, 1978–80; PO Engrg Adv. Cttee, 1977–81, British Telecom Engrg Adv. Cttee, 1981–82. Mem., Court and Council, Brunel Univ., 1976–82. Liveryman, 1978, and Mem. Court, 1981–86, Worshipful Co. of Scientific Instrument Makers. FRSA. DTech (hc) Brunel, 1973. *Address:* Kroller, 54 Howards Wood Drive, Gerrards Cross, Bucks. *T:* Gerrards Cross (0753) 885028.

ALLCHIN, Rev. Canon Arthur Macdonald; Director, St Theosevia Centre for Christian Spirituality, Oxford, since 1987; *b* 20 April 1930; *s* of late Dr Frank Macdonald Allchin and Louise Maude Allchin. *Educ:* Westminster Sch.; Christ Church, Oxford (BLitt, MA); Cuddesdon Coll., Oxford. Curate, St Mary Abbots, Kensington, 1956–60; Librarian, Pusey House, Oxford, 1960–69; Visiting Lecturer: General Theological Seminary, NY, 1967 and 1968; Catholic Theological Faculty, Lyons, 1980; Trinity Inst., NY, 1983; Vis. Prof., Nashotah House, Wisconsin, 1984; Warden, Community of Sisters of Love of God, Oxford, 1967–; Res. Canon of Canterbury, 1973–87, Hon. Canon, 1988–. Editor, Sobornost, 1960–77; Jt Editor, Christian, 1975–80. Hon. DD: Bucharest Theol Inst., 1977; Nashotah House, 1985. *Publications:* The Silent Rebellion, 1958; The Spirit and the Word, 1963; (with J. Coulson) The Rediscovery of Newman, 1967; Ann Griffiths, 1976; The World is a Wedding, 1978; The Kingdom of Love and Knowledge, 1979; The Dynamic of Tradition, 1981; A Taste of Liberty, 1982; The Joy of All Creation, 1984; (with E. de Waal) Threshold of Light, 1986; Participation in God, 1988; The Heart of Compassion, 1989; Landscapes of Glory, 1989; Praise Above All, 1991; contrib. Studia Liturgica, Irenikon, Theology, Eastern Churches Review, Worship, One in Christ. *Recreations:* music, poetry, walking in hill country. *Address:* 2 Canterbury Road, Oxford OX2 6LU. *T:* Oxford (0865) 310341.

See also F. R. Allchin.

ALLCHIN, Frank Raymond, PhD; FBA 1981; Fellow of Churchill College, since 1963, and Reader in Indian Studies, 1972–90, University of Cambridge; Reader Emeritus, since 1990; *b* 9 July 1923; *s* of Frank MacDonald Allchin and Louise Maude Wright; *m* 1951, Bridget Gordon; one *s* one *d*. *Educ:* Westminster Sch.; Regent Street Polytechnic; Sch. of Oriental and African Studies, London Univ. (BA, PhD 1954); MA Cantab. Lectr in Indian Archaeology, SOAS, 1954–59; Univ. Lectr in Indian Studies, Cambridge, 1959–72. Jt Dir, Cambridge Univ. (British) Archaeol Mission to Pakistan, 1975–. Treas., Ancient India and Iran Trust, 1978–; Vice Chm., British Assoc. for Conservation of Cultural Heritage of Sri Lanka, 1982–. Consultant: UNESCO, 1969, 1972, 1975; UNDP, 1971. Chm., Broads Tours, Wroxham, Ltd, 1975–86 (Dir, 1964–86). *Publications:* Piklihal Excavations, 1960; Utnur Excavations, 1961; Neolithic Cattle Keepers of South India, 1963; Kavitāvalī, 1964; The Petition to Rām, 1966; (with B. Allchin) Birth of Indian Civilization, 1968; (with N. Hammond) The Archaeology of Afghanistan, 1978; (with D. K. Chakrabarti) Sourcebook of Indian Archaeology, vol. 1, 1979; (with B. Allchin) The Rise of Civilization in India and Pakistan, 1982; contribs to learned journals. *Recreations:* gardening, walking. *Address:* Westgate House, 3 Orwell Road, Barrington, Cambridge CB2 5SE. *T:* Cambridge (0223) 870494. *Clubs:* Royal Over-Seas League; Indian International Centre (New Delhi).

See also Rev. Canon A. M. Allchin.

ALLDAY, Coningsby, CBE 1971; BSc (Hons); Chairman and Chief Executive, British Nuclear Fuels plc, 1983–86 (Managing Director, 1971–83); Director, Allday Nuclear Consultants Ltd, since 1986; *b* 21 Nov. 1920; *s* of late Esca and Margaret Allday; *m* 1945, Iris Helena (Bobbin) Adams; one *s* one *d*. *Educ:* Solihull Sch.; BSc (Hons) Chemistry, London. CEng, FIChemE 1979; CBIM 1984. ICI, 1939–59; UKAEA, 1959–71: Chief Chemist, Technical Dir, Commercial Dir, Dep. Man. Dir; Mem. UKAEA, 1976–86. Chairman, NIMTECH NW, 1986–90; Director: North Region, National Westminster Bank, 1985–; Sonomatic Ltd, 1988–90. FRSA. Hon. DSc Salford, 1985. Chevalier, Légion d'Honneur, 1983. *Address:* 54 Goughs Lane, Knutsford, Cheshire WA16 8QN.

ALLDIS, Air Cdre Cecil Anderson, CBE 1962; DFC 1941; AFC 1956; RAF (retd); *b* 28 Sept. 1918; 2nd *s* of John Henry and Margaret Wright Alldis, Birkenhead; *m* 1942, Jeanette Claire Tarrant, *d* of Albert Edward Collingwood and Aida Mary Tarrant, Johannesburg; no *c*. *Educ:* Birkenhead Institute; Emmanuel Coll., Cambridge (MA). Served War, 1939–45 (despatches, DFC): Pilot, Wing Comdr, RAF, Bomber Command. Asst Air Attaché, Moscow, 1947–49; Flying and Staff appts, RAF, 1949–59; Dir of Administrative Planning, Air Ministry, 1959–62; Air Attaché, Bonn, 1963–66. Retd from RAF and entered Home Civil Service, 1966; MoD, 1966–69; seconded to HM Diplomatic Service, 1969; Counsellor (Defence Supply), HM Embassy, Bonn, 1969–80; retired from Home Civil Service, 1980. Sec. Gen., The Air League, 1982–90. *Recreations:* golf, fishing, beagling. *Address:* Tudor Cottage, Oxshott Way, Cobham, Surrey KT11 2RU. *T:* Cobham (0932) 66092. *Club:* Naval and Military.

ALLDIS, John; conductor; *b* 10 Aug. 1929; *s* of W. J. and N. Alldis; *m* 1960, Ursula Margaret Mason; two *s*. *Educ:* Felsted School; King's Coll., Cambridge (MA). ARCO. Formed John Alldis Choir, 1962; formed and conducted London Symphony Chorus, 1966–69; Conductor, London Philharmonic Choir, 1969–82; Joint Chief Conductor, Radio Denmark, 1971–77; Conductor, Groupe Vocal de France, 1979–. FGSM 1976; Fellow, Westminster Choir Coll., Princeton, NJ, 1978. Chevalier des Arts et des Lettres (France), 1984. *Address:* 3 Wool Road, Wimbledon, SW20 0HN. *T:* 081–946 4168.

ALLEN, family name of **Baron Allen of Abbeydale** and **Baron Croham.**

ALLEN OF ABBEYDALE, Baron *cr* 1976 (Life Peer), of the City of Sheffield; **Philip Allen,** GCB 1970 (KCB 1964; CB 1954); Member, Security Commission, since 1973; *b* 8 July 1912; *yr s* of late Arthur Allen and Louie Tipper, Sheffield; *m* 1938, Marjorie Brenda Coe. *Educ:* King Edward VII Sch., Sheffield; Queens' Coll., Cambridge (Whewell Schol. in Internat. Law, 1934; Hon. Fellow 1974). Entered Home Office, 1934; Offices of War Cabinet, 1943–44; Commonwealth Fellowship in USA, 1948–49; Deputy Chm. of Prison Commn for England and Wales, 1950–52; Asst Under Sec. of State, Home Office, 1952–55; Deputy Sec., Min. of Housing and Local Govt, 1955–60; Deputy Under-Sec. of State, Home Office, 1960–62; Second Sec., HM Treasury, 1963–66; Permanent Under-Sec. of State, Home Office, 1966–72. Chairman: Occupational Pensions Bd, 1973–78; Nat. Council of Social Service, 1973–77; Gaming Bd for GB, 1977–85 (Mem., 1975); Mencap, 1982–88. Member Royal Commissions: on Standards of Conduct in Public Life, 1974–76; on Civil Liability and Compensation for Personal Injury, 1973–78; Mem., tribunal of inquiry into Crown Agents, 1978–82. Chief Counting Officer, EEC Referendum, 1975. *Address:* Holly Lodge, Middle Hill, Englefield Green, Surrey TW20 0JP. *T:* Egham (0784) 432291.

ALLEN, Anthony John; Chief Executive, and Clerk to the Lieutenancy, Royal County of Berkshire, since 1986; *b* 7 Oct. 1939; *s* of late Raymond Houghton Allen and Elsie Zillah Allen; *m* 1st, 1964, Suzanne Myfanwy Davies; two *s*; 2nd, 1987, Helen Leah Graney. *Educ:* Battersea Grammar Sch.; Univ. of Exeter (LLB 1961). Admitted Solicitor, 1964. Asst Solicitor: Hendon Bor. Council, 1964–65; Barnet Bor. Council, 1965; Watford Bor. Council, 1966–68; Asst Town Clerk, Coventry CBC, 1968–71; Asst. Chief Exec., Lewisham Bor. Council, 1971–72; Solicitor to the Council and Dep. Town Clerk, Southwark Bor. Council, 1972–76; Chief Exec., Hammersmith and Fulham Bor. Council, 1976–86. Organizer, London Youth Games, 1979–85; Promoter and Dir, London Youth Games Ltd, 1985–. *Publications:* (contrib.) Practical Corporate Planning, ed John Skitt, 1975. *Recreations:* golf, travel. *Address:* The Fifteenth, 7 Broadlands Close, Calcot Park, Reading, Berks RG3 5RP. *T:* Reading (0734) 427310.

ALLEN, His Honour Anthony Kenway, OBE 1946; a Circuit Judge, 1978–90; *b* 31 Oct. 1917; *s* of Charles Valentine Allen and Edith Kenway Allen; *m* 1975, Maureen Murtough. *Educ:* St George's Coll., Weybridge, Surrey; St John's Coll., Cambridge (BA Hons); Freiburg and Grenoble Univs. Served War, RAF Special Intelligence, 1939–45 (Wing Comdr). Called to the Bar, Inner Temple, 1947. *Recreations:* gardening, walking, music. *Address:* 73 Downswood, Epsom Downs, Surrey.

ALLEN, Arnold Millman, CBE 1977; Chairman, UKAEA, 1984–86; *b* 30 Dec. 1924; *s* of Wilfrid Millman and Edith Muriel Allen; *m* 1947, Beatrice Mary Whitaker; three *s* one *d*. *Educ:* Hackney Downs Sec. Sch.; Peterhouse, Cambridge (Scholar). Entered HM Treasury, 1945; Private Sec. to Financial Secretary, 1951–52; Principal, HM Treasury, 1953–55; Private Sec. to Chm. of UKAEA (Lord Plowden), 1956–57; HM Treasury, 1958; Dir of Personnel and Admin., Development and Engineering Group (subseq. Reactor Group), UKAEA, 1959–63; Gen. Manager, British Waterways Bd, 1963–68, and Mem. of Bd 1965–68; UKAEA: Personnel Officer, 1968–69; Personnel and Programmes Officer, 1970; Secretary and Mem. for Administration, 1971; Mem. for Finance and Admin, 1976–84; Dep. Chm., 1981–84; Chief Exec., 1982–84. *Address:* Duntish Cottage, Duntish, Dorchester, Dorset DT2 7DR. *T:* Buckland Newton (03005) 258.

ALLEN, Colin Mervyn Gordon, CBE 1978; General Manager, Covent Garden Market Authority, 1967–89; *b* 17 April 1929; *s* of late Cecil G. Allen and late Gwendoline L. Allen (*née* Hutchinson); *m* 1953, Patricia, *d* of late William and late Doris Seddon; two *s* one *d*. *Educ:* King Edward's Sch., Bath. BA Open, 1985; MA London, 1986. FInstPS. Naval Store Dept, Admiralty, 1948–56; National Coal Board: London HQ, 1956–59;

Area Stores Officer, NE Div., 1959–64; Covent Garden Market Authority: Planning Officer, 1964–66; Asst Gen. Man., 1967. President: Assoc. of Wholesale Markets within Internat. Union of Local Authorities, 1972–78; IPS, 1982–83. Chm., Vauxhall Cross Amenity Trust, 1982–83. *Publications:* various papers on horticultural marketing and allied topics, and on supply and logistics matters. *Recreation:* archaeology. *Address:* 10 Whitecroft Way, Beckenham, Kent BR3 3AG. *T:* 081–650 0787.

ALLEN, Rear-Adm. Sir David, KCVO 1991; CBE 1985; Defence Services Secretary, 1988–91; Chief Naval Supply and Secretariat Officer, 1988–91; retired; *b* 14 June 1933; *s* of late A. V. Allen and G. M. Allen; *m* 1962, Margaret Gwendolin Todd; two *s*. *Educ:* Hutcheson's Grammar School, Glasgow; BRNC Dartmouth. Joined RN 1949; Supply Officer, HMS Fife, 1970–72; MoD, 1973–75; Fleet Supply Officer, Staff of C-in-C Fleet, 1975–77; Sec. to Chief of Staff, Fleet, 1977–78; Sec. to Controller of the Navy, 1978–81; Chief Staff Officer (Personnel), Naval Air Comd, 1981–82; Sec. to Chief of Naval Staff and First Sea Lord, 1982–85; HMS Cochrane in Comd and Flag Captain to FO Scotland and NI, 1985–87; Staff of Chief of Defence Staff, 1987–88. *Recreations:* family and friends, reading, gardening, sheep breeding, shooting, fishing, house maintenance. *Address:* c/o National Westminster Bank, Cowes, Isle of Wight. *Clubs:* Farmers', Landsdowne.

ALLEN, Prof. Deryck Norman de Garrs; Professor of Applied Mathematics in the University of Sheffield, 1955–80, now Emeritus; Warden of Ranmoor House, 1968–82; *b* 22 April 1918; *s* of Leonard Lincoln Allen and Dorothy Allen (*née* Asplin). *Educ:* King Edward VII School, Sheffield; Christ Church, Oxford. Messrs Rolls Royce, 1940; Research Asst to Sir Richard Southwell, FRS, 1941; Lectr in Applied Mathematics at Imperial Coll., London, 1945; Visiting Prof. in Dept of Mechanical Engineering, Massachusetts Inst. of Technology, 1949; Reader in Applied Mathematics at Imperial Coll. in Univ. of London, 1950. Pro-Vice-Chancellor, Sheffield Univ., 1966–70; Chm., Jt Matriculation Bd, 1973–76. *Publications:* Relaxation Methods, 1954 (US); papers on Applied Maths and Engineering Maths in: Proc. Royal Soc.; Philosophical Trans. of Royal Soc.; Quarterly Jl of Mechanics and Applied Maths; Jl of Instn of Civil Engineers. *Recreation:* travel. *Address:* 18 Storth Park, Fulwood Road, Sheffield S10 3QH. *T:* Sheffield (0742) 308751.

ALLEN, Donald George, CMG 1981; Deputy Parliamentary Commissioner for Administration (Ombudsman), 1982–90; Member, Broadcasting Complaints Commission, since 1990; *b* 26 June 1930; *s* of Sidney George Allen and Doris Elsie (*née* Abercombie); *m* 1955, Sheila Isobel Bebbington; three *s*. *Educ:* Southall Grammar School. Foreign Office, 1948; HM Forces, 1949–51; FO, 1951–54; The Hague, 1954–57; 2nd Sec. (Commercial), La Paz, 1957–60; FO, 1961–65: 1st Sec. 1962; Asst Private Sec. to Lord Privy Seal, 1961–63 and to Minister without Portfolio, 1963–64; 1st Sec., Head of Chancery and Consul, Panama, 1966–69; FCO, 1969–72; Counsellor on secondment to NI Office, Belfast, 1972–74; Counsellor and Head of Chancery, UK Permanent Delegn to OECD, Paris, 1974–78; Inspector, 1978–80; Dir, Office of Parly Comr (Ombudsman), 1980–82, on secondment. *Recreations:* squash, tennis, golf. *Address:* 99 Parkland Grove, Ashford, Mddx TW15 2JF. *T:* Ashford (0784) 255617. *Club:* Royal Automobile.

ALLEN, Fergus Hamilton, CB 1969; ScD, MA, MAI; First Civil Service Commissioner, Civil Service Department, 1974–81; *b* 3 Sept. 1921; *s* of Charles Winckworth Allen and late Marjorie Helen, *d* of F. J. S. Budge; *m* 1947, Margaret Joan, *d* of Prof. M. J. Gorman; two *d*. *Educ:* Newtown Sch., Waterford; Trinity Coll., Dublin. ScD 1966. Asst Engineer, Sir Cyril Kirkpatrick and Partners, 1943–48; Port of London Authority, 1949–52; Asst Director, Hydraulics Research Station, DSIR, 1952–58; Dir of Hydraulics Research, DSIR, 1958–65; Chief Scientific Officer, Cabinet Office, 1965–69; Civil Service Comr, 1969–74; Scientific and Technological Advr, CSD, 1969–72. Consultant, Boyden Internat. Ltd, 1982–86. Instn Civil Engrs: Mem., 1947–57; Fellow, 1957–86; Telford Gold Medal, 1958; Mem. Council, 1962–67, 1968–71. *Publications:* papers in technical journals; poems. *Address:* Dundrum, Wantage Road, Streatley, Berks RG8 9LB. *T:* Goring-on-Thames (0491) 873234. *Club:* Athenæum.

ALLEN, Francis Andrew; His Honour Judge Francis Allen; a Circuit Judge, since 1979; *b* 7 Dec. 1933; *s* of Andrew Eric Allen and Joan Elizabeth Allen; *m* 1961, Marjorie Pearce; one *s* three *d*. *Educ:* Solihull School; Merton College, Oxford. MA. 2nd Lieut, Highland Light Infantry, 1957; called to the Bar, Gray's Inn, 1958. A Recorder of the Crown Court, 1978–79. *Recreation:* walking. *Club:* Mountain Bothies Association (Scottish Highlands).

ALLEN, Frank Graham, CB 1984; Clerk of the Journals, House of Commons, 1975–84; *b* 13 June 1920; *s* of Percy and Gertrude Allen; *m* 1947, Barbara Caulton; one *d* (one *s* decd). Educ: Shrewsbury Sch. (Schol.); Keble Coll., Oxford (Exhibr, BA). 7th Bn Worcs Regt, 1940–46, India, 1942–44. Asst Clerk, House of Commons, 1946; Principal Clerk, 1973. Mem., House of Laity, Gen. Synod, 1970–80. Silver Jubilee Medal, 1977. *Recreation:* involvement in Chorleywood CARE and in St Andrew's old people's day centre. *Address:* March Mount, Haddon Road, Chorleywood, Herts. *T:* Chorleywood (0923) 282709. *Club:* Rhinefield Owners (Brockenhurst).

ALLEN, Gary James, CBE 1991; Managing Director, IMI plc, since 1986; *b* 30 Sept. 1944; *s* of Alfred and Alice Allen; *m* 1966, Judith Anne Nattrass; three *s*. *Educ:* King Edward VI Grammar School, Aston, Birmingham; Liverpool University (BCom). FCMA. Managing Dir, IMI Range, 1973–77; Dir, IMI, 1978–; Chm., IMI Components, 1981–85; Asst Man. Dir, IMI, 1985–86; Chairman: Optilon, 1979–84; Eley, 1981–85; Director: (non-exec.) NV Bekaert SA, Belgium, 1987–; Marley, 1989–; Birmingham European Airways, 1989–. Mem. Council, CBI, 1986– (Mem., W Midlands Regional Council, 1983–89); Mem. Council, Birmingham Chamber of Industry & Commerce, 1983– (Vice-Pres., 1989–). Mem. Council, Univ. of Birmingham, 1985–90 (Hon. Life Mem., Court, 1984). CBIM; FRSA. Midland Businessman of the Year, 1989. *Recreations:* sport, reading. *Address:* IMI plc, PO Box 216, Birmingham B6 7BA. *T:* 021–356 4848.

ALLEN, Prof. Sir Geoffrey, Kt 1979; PhD; FRS 1976; FRSC; FInstP; CEng; Head of Research, Unilever PLC, 1981–90 (Director, Unilever PLC and NV, 1982–90); Director, Courtaulds, since 1987; Executive Adviser, Kobe Steel Ltd, since 1990; *b* 29 Oct. 1928; *s* of John James and Marjorie Allen; *m* 1973, Valerie Frances Duckworth; one *d*. *Educ:* Clay Cross Tupton Hall Grammar Sch.; Univ. of Leeds (BSc, PhD). FInstP 1972; FPRI 1974. Postdoctoral Fellow, Nat. Res. Council, Canada, 1952–54; Lectr, Univ. of Manchester, 1955–65, Prof. of Chemical Physics, 1965–75; Prof. of Polymer Science, 1975–76, Prof. of Chemical Technology, 1976–81, Imperial Coll. of Science and Technology (Fellow, 1986); Vis. Fellow, Robinson Coll., Cambridge, 1980–. Mem., Science Research Council, 1976, Chm., 1977–81; Pres., PRI, 1990–. Hon. FCGI 1990. Hon. MSc Manchester; DUniv Open, 1981; Hon. DSc: Durham, East Anglia, 1984; Bath, Bradford, Loughborough, 1985; Essex, Keele, Leeds, 1986; Cranfield, 1988; Surrey, 1989. *Publications:* papers on chemical physics of polymers in Trans Faraday Soc., Polymer. *Recreations:* walking, talking and eating.

ALLEN, Graham William; MP (Lab) Nottingham North, since 1987; *b* 11 Jan. 1953; *s* of William and Edna Allen. *Educ:* Robert Shaw Primary Sch.; Forest Fields Grammar Sch.; City of London Polytechnic; Leeds Univ. Warehouseman, Nottingham, 1971–72; Labour Party Res. Officer, 1978–83; Local Govt Officer, GLC, 1983–84; Trades Union National Co-ordinator, Political Fund Ballots Campaign, 1984–86; Regional Res. and Educn Officer, GMBATU, 1986–87. Member: Public Accounts Cttee; Procedure Cttee; 1990 Financial Bill Cttee. Chm., PLP Treasury Cttee, 1990–. *Recreation:* cricket. *Address:* House of Commons, SW1A 0AA. *T:* 071–219 4343. *Clubs:* Long Eaton Labour, Strelley Social, Beechdale Community Centre, Bulwell Community Centre, Dunkirk Cricket (Nottingham).

ALLEN, Hamish McEwan, CB 1984; Head of Administration Department, House of Commons, 1981–85; *b* 7 Sept. 1920; *s* of late Ernest Frank Allen and Ada Florence Allen (*née* Weeks); *m* 1951, Peggy Joan Fifoot; one *s*. *Educ:* City of Bath Sch.; Portsmouth Southern Secondary Sch. Served RAF, 1941–46. Air Ministry: Clerical Officer, 1938; Exec. Officer, 1948; House of Commons: Asst Accountant, 1959; Dep. Accountant, 1962; Head of Estabs Office, 1968. *Address:* 124 Ridge Langley, South Croydon, Surrey CR2 0AS.

ALLEN, (Harold) Norman (Gwynne), CBE 1965; FEng; retired 1977; *b* 30 April 1912; *yr s* of Harold Gwynne Allen and Hilda Margaret Allen (*née* Langley), Bedford; *m* 1938, Marjorie Ellen (*née* Brown); one *s* three *d*. *Educ:* Westminster Sch.; Trinity Coll., Cambridge, BA 1933, MA 1936, Cantab; FEng 1979, FICE, FIMechE, FRINA, FIMarE, FIProdE. Engrg trng, John Samuel White & Co. Ltd, Cowes, John Brown & Co. Ltd, Clydebank, and in Merchant Navy, 1933–37; W. H. Allen Sons & Co. Ltd, Bedford: progressive staff appts, 1937–43; Dir 1943–77; Techn. Dir 1945–52; Jt Man. Dir 1952–; Dep. Chm. 1962–70; Chm. 1970–77; Amalgamated Power Engrg Ltd, Bedford: Techn. Dir 1968–70; Dep. Chm. 1970–77. Belliss & Morcom Ltd, Birmingham, 1968–77. Mem. Bedfordshire CC, 1947–50. Mem. Council: British Internal Combustion Engrg Res. Assoc., 1952–60 (Chm. 1953–54); British Hydromechanics Res. Assoc., 1947–59; IMechE, 1952–70 (Vice-Pres. 1959–65, Pres. 1965); Mem. Adv. Cttee, Nat. Engrg Lab., 1971–73 (Mem. Steering Cttee 1962–68); Mem. British Transport Commn Res. Adv. Council, 1958–60; Vice-Chm. of Council, Mander Coll., Bedford, 1958–74; Governor, Coll. of Aeronautics, Cranfield, 1955–69 (Vice-Chm. 1962–69); Charter Pro-Chancellor, Cranfield Inst. of Technology, 1969–75; Mem. Bd, Council of Engrg Instns, 1964–66; Mem. Exec. Bd, BSI, 1970–76. Provost, Buffalo Hunt of Manitoba, 1960. Dir, Son et Lumière, Woburn Abbey, 1957. Hon. DSc Bath, 1967; Hon. DSc Cranfield, 1977. *Publications:* papers in jls of IMarE, S African IMechE, Engrg Inst. Canada, IMechE. *Recreations:* gardening (MRHS), countryside (Mem. Nat. Trust), magic (Mem. Magic Circle). *Address:* 45 Berry Hill Crescent, Cirencester, Glos GL7 2HF.

ALLEN, Prof. Harry Cranbrook, MC 1944; Professor of American Studies, 1971–80, now Emeritus, and Dean of the School of English and American Studies, 1974–76, University of East Anglia; *b* 23 March 1917; *s* of Christopher Albert Allen and Margaret Enid (*née* Hebb); *m* 1947, Mary Kathleen Andrews; one *s* two *d*. *Educ:* Bedford School; Pembroke College, Oxford (Open Scholar; 1st cl. hons Modern History; MA). Elected Fellow, Commonwealth Fund of New York, 1939 (held Fellowship, Harvard Univ., Jan-Sept. 1946). Served War of 1939–45, with Hertfordshire and Dorsetshire Regts, in France and Germany (Major); comdt 43rd Division Educational Coll., June-Nov. 1945. Fellow and Tutor in Modern History, Lincoln College, Oxford, 1946–55; Commonwealth Fund Prof. of American History, University Coll., 1955–71, and Dir, Inst. of United States Studies, 1966–71, Univ. of London; Senior Research Fellow, Austr. Nat. Univ., Canberra, and Visiting Scholar, Univ. of California, Berkeley, 1953–54; Schouler Lecturer, The Johns Hopkins University, April 1956; American Studies Fellow, Commonwealth Fund of New York, 1957, at the University of Virginia; Vis. Mem., Inst. for Advanced Study, Princeton, NJ, 1959; Vis. Professor: Univ. of Rochester, New York, 1963; Univ. of Michigan, Ann Arbor, 1966. Member: Dartmouth Royal Naval College Review Cttee, 1958, Naval Education Adv. Cttee, 1960–66; Academic Planning Board, Univ. of Essex, 1962; Chm., British Assoc. for American Studies, 1974–77; Pres., European Assoc. for American Studies, 1976–80. *Publications:* Great Britain and the United States, 1955; Bush and Backwoods, 1959; The Anglo-American Relationship since 1783, 1960; The Anglo-American Predicament, 1960; The United States of America, 1964; Joint Editor: British Essays in American History, 1957; Contrast and Connection, 1976. *Recreation:* travel (when practicable!). *Address:* 1 Shepard Way, Chipping Norton, Oxon OX7 5BE. *T:* Chipping Norton (0608) 644381. *Club:* Athenæum.

ALLEN, Prof. Ingrid Victoria, (Mrs Alan Barnes), MD, DSc, FRCPath, FRCPI, FRCPG; Professor of Neuropathology, Queen's University of Belfast, since 1979; *b* 30 July 1932; *d* of Rev. Robert Allen, MA, PhD, DD and Doris V. Allen; *m* 1972, Alan Watson Barnes, MA, ARIBA, Past Pres., RSUA. *Educ:* Cheltenham Ladies College; QUB. House Officer, Royal Victoria Hosp., Belfast, 1957–58; Musgrave Res. Fellow, Tutor in Path., Calvert Res. Fellow, QUB, 1958–64; Sen. Registrar, RVH, 1964–65; Sen. Lectr and Consultant in Neuropath., QUB/RVH, 1966–78; Reader and Consultant, 1978–79; Head, NI Regional Neuropath. Service, RVH, Belfast, 1979–. Mem., MRC, 1989– (Chm., Neuroscis Bd, 1989–); Vice-Pres., Internat. Soc. of Neuropath. DL Belfast 1989. Mem. editl bds of various scientific jls. *Publications:* (contrib.) Greenfield's Neuropathology, 1984; (contrib.) McAlpine's Multiple Sclerosis, 1990; contribs to jls on neuropathology, demyelinating diseases, neurovirology and neuro-oncology. *Recreations:* tennis, sailing, reading, history, architecture. *Address:* Regional Neuropathology Laboratories, Institute of Pathology, Grosvenor Road, Belfast BT12 6BA. *T:* Belfast (0232) 240503. *Clubs:* Royal Society of Medicine; Royal Ulster Yacht.

ALLEN, Janet Rosemary; Headmistress of Benenden School, Kent, 1976–85; *b* 11 April 1936; *d* of John Algernon Allen and Edna Mary Allen (*née* Orton). *Educ:* Cheltenham Ladies' Coll.; University Coll., Leicester; Hughes Hall, Cambridge. BA London 1958; CertEd Cambridge 1959. Asst Mistress, Howell's Sch., Denbigh, North Wales, 1959: Head of History Dept, 1961; in charge of First Year Sixth Form, 1968; Housemistress, 1968 and 1973–75. Member: E-SU Scholarship Selection Panel, 1977–85; South East ISIS Cttee, 1978–84; Boarding Schs Assoc. Cttee, 1980–83; GSA Educnl sub-cttee, 1983–85. Vice-Pres., Women's Career Foundn (formerly Girls of the Realm Guild), 1981–. Gov., St Catherine's Sch., Bramley, 1986–. *Recreations:* music, drama, dogwalking, swimming, reading. *Address:* Bourne Rise, Queen's Square, Winchcombe, Cheltenham, Glos GL54 5LR. *Club:* Royal Over-Seas League.

ALLEN, Prof. John Anthony, PhD, DSc; FIBiol; FRSE; Professor of Marine Biology, University of London, and Director, University Marine Biological Station, Millport, Isle of Cumbrae, 1976–91, now Professor Emeritus; *s* of George Leonard John Allen and Dorothy Mary Allen; *m* 1st, 1952, Marion Ferguson Crow (marr. diss. 1983); one *s* one *d*; 2nd, 1983, Margaret Porteous Aitken. *Educ:* High Pavement Sch., Nottingham; London Univ. (PhD, DSc). FIBiol 1969; FRSE 1968 (Mem. Council, 1970–73). Served in Sherwood Foresters, 1945–46, and RAMC, 1946–48. Asst Lectr, Univ. of Glasgow, 1951–54; John Murray Student, Royal Soc., 1952–54; Lectr/Sen. Lectr in Zool., then Reader in Marine Biol., Univ. of Newcastle upon Tyne, 1954–76. Post Doctoral Fellow and Guest Investigator, Woods Hole Oceanographic Instn, USA, 1965–; Vis. Prof., Univ. of Washington, 1968, 1970, 1971; Royal Soc. Vis. Prof., Univ. of West Indies, 1976. Member: NERC, 1977–83 (Chm., Univ. Affairs Cttee, 1978–83); Council, Scottish

Marine Biol Assoc., 1977–83; Council, Marine Biol Assoc. UK, 1981–83, 1990–; Life Sciences Bd, CNAA, 1981–84; Nature Conservancy Council, 1982–90 (Chm., Adv. Cttee Sci., 1984–90); British Nat. Cttee for Oceanic Res., 1988–90. Pres., Malacological Soc. of London, 1982–84. *Publications:* many papers on decapod crustacea and molluscs, and deep sea benthos, in learned jls. *Recreations:* travel, appreciation of gardens, publunching. *Address:* Drialstone, Millport, Isle of Cumbrae, Scotland KA28 0EP. *T:* Millport (0475) 530479.

ALLEN, Very Rev. John Edward; Provost of Wakefield, since 1982; *b* 9 June 1932; *s* of Rev. Canon Ronald and Mrs Isabel Allen; *m* 1957, Eleanor (*née* Prynne); one *s* three *d*. *Educ:* Rugby; University Coll., Oxford (MA); Fitzwilliam Coll., Cambridge (MA); Westcott House. Colonial Service, Kenya, 1957–63; Sales and Marketing, Kimberly-Clark Ltd, 1963–66; Theological College, 1966–68; Curate, Deal, Kent, 1968–71; Senior Chaplain to Univ. of Bristol and Vicar of St Paul's, Clifton, 1971–78; Vicar of Chippenham, Wilts, 1978–82. Mem., Gen. Synod of C of E, 1985–. *Recreations:* walking, fishing and people. *Address:* 1 Cathedral Close, Margaret Street, Wakefield, West Yorkshire WF1 2DQ. *T:* Wakefield (0924) 372402.

ALLEN, Prof. John Frank, FRS 1949; Professor of Natural Philosophy in the School of Physical Sciences, University of St Andrews, 1947–78, now Emeritus; *b* 6 May 1908; *s* of late Prof. Frank Allen, FRSC; *m* 1933, Elfriede Hiebert (marr. diss. 1951); one *s*. *Educ:* Public schools of Winnipeg, Canada. BA (University of Manitoba, 1928), MA (University of Toronto, 1930), PhD (University of Toronto, 1933). Bursar, Student and Fellow of National Research Council of Canada, 1930–33; Fellow of National Research Council of USA, 1933–35; Research Assistant, Royal Society Mond Laboratory, Cambridge, 1935–44; MA Cantab, 1936; Lecturer in Physics, Univ. of Cambridge and Fellow and Lecturer of St John's College, Cambridge, 1944–47. Hon. DSc: Manitoba, 1979; Heriot-Watt, 1984. *Publications:* numerous scientific papers and articles, mainly on experimental low temperature physics. *Recreations:* scientific cinefilms, golf. *Address:* 2 Shorehead, St Andrews, Fife KY16 9RG. *T:* St Andrews (0334) 72717.

See also W. A. Allen.

ALLEN, Maj.-Gen. John Geoffrey Robyn, CB 1976; Lay Observer attached to Lord Chancellor's Department, 1979–85; *b* 19 Aug. 1923; *s* of R. A. Allen and Mrs Allen (*née* Youngman); *m* 1959, Ann Monica (*née* Morford); one *s* one *d*. *Educ:* Haileybury. Commissioned KRRC, 1942; trans. RTR, 1947; Bt Lt-Col, 1961; Lt-Col, CO 2 RTR, 1963; Mil. Asst (GSO1) to CGS, MoD, 1965; Brig., Comd 20 Armd Bde, 1967; IDC, 1970; Dir of Operational Requirements 3 (Army), MoD, 1971; Maj.-Gen., Dir-Gen., Fighting Vehicles and Engineer Equipment, MoD, 1973–74; Dir, RAC, 1974–76; Sen. Army Directing Staff, RCDS, 1976–78; retired 1979. Col Comdt, RTR, 1976–80; Hon. Colonel: Westminster Dragoons, 1982–87; Royal Yeomanry, 1982–87. Member: Adv. Cttee on Legal Aid, 1979–86; Booth Cttee on Procedure in Matrimonial Causes, 1982–85. *Recreation:* dinghy sailing. *Address:* Meadowleys, Charlton, Chichester, W Sussex PO18 0HU. *T:* Singleton (024363) 638. *Clubs:* Army and Navy; Bosham Sailing.

ALLEN, John Hunter, OBE 1978; company director; Mayor of Antrim, since 1973; *s* of John Allen and Jane Kerr Hunter; *m* 1952, Elizabeth Irwin Graham; three *d*. *Educ:* Larne Grammar Sch., NI; Orange's Acad., NI. Served RAF, pilot, 1942–47. Civil Service Excise, 1947–59; Proprietor: Ulster Farm Feeds Ltd, 1959–76; Antrim Feeds Ltd, 1959–76; Roadway Transport Ltd, 1959–; Aldergrove Farms Ltd, 1965–; A.B. Fuels, 1969–; Downtown Developments Ltd, 1975–; Allen Service Stns, 1977–; Century Supplies, 1984–. Chm., NI Sports Council, 1977–84. Chm., Antrim Royal British Legion. Member: Ulster Games Foundn, 1983–; NI Gen. Consumers Council, 1984–. Life Mem., Royal Ulster Agricl Soc, 1972. *Recreations:* Rugby, sailing, boxing, tennis. *Address:* The Grange, Muckamore, Antrim, Co. Antrim. *Clubs:* Royal Air Force; Antrim Rugby (Pres.); Antrim Hockey (Pres.); Antrim Boxing (Pres.); Antrim Boat (Trustee); Muckamore Cricket (Life Member).

ALLEN, John Piers, OBE 1979; *b* 30 March 1912; *s* of Percy Allen and Marjorie Nash; *m* 1937; two *s*; *m* 1945; two *s* two *d*; *m* 1982. *Educ:* Aldenham Sch. Old Vic Theatre, 1933–35; Victor Gollancz Ltd, 1936–37; London Theatre Studio, 1937–39; RNVR, 1940–45; Dir, Glyndebourne Children's Theatre, 1945–51; writer-producer, BBC, 1951–61; Adjudicator, Dominion Drama Festival, Canada, 1956; UNESCO Drama Specialist. Australia, 1959, 1961; HM Inspector of Schs, 1961–72. Principal, Central School of Speech and Drama, 1972–78. Vis. Prof. of Drama, Westfield Coll., Univ. of London, 1979–83; Vis. Lectr, Centre for Arts, City Univ., 1979–83. Vice-Chm., British Theatre Assoc., 1978–83; Chairman: Accreditation Bd, Nat. Council of Drama Trng, 1979–83; Council of Dance Educn and Trng, 1982– (Chm., Accreditation Bd, 1979–82); Mem., CNAA Dance and Drama Panels, 1979–82; Vice-Pres., British Centre, Internat. Amateur Theatre Assoc., 1982–. *Publications:* Going to the Theatre, 1949; Great Moments in the Theatre, 1949; Masters of British Drama, 1957; Masters of European Drama, 1962; Drama in Schools, 1978; Theatre in Europe, 1981; A History of the Theatre in Europe, 1983; (ed) Three Medieval Plays, 1956. *Address:* The Old Orchard, Lastingham, York YO6 6TQ. *T:* Lastingham (07515) 334.

ALLEN, Prof. John Robert Lawrence, DSc; FRS 1979; Professor of Sedimentology (formerly of Geology), since 1972, and Director, Postgraduate Research Institute for Sedimentology, since 1988, University of Reading; *b* 25 Oct. 1932; *s* of George Eustace Allen and Alice Josephine (*née* Formby); *m* 1960, Jean Mary (*née* Wood); four *s* one *d*. *Educ:* St Philip's Grammar Sch., Birmingham; Univ. of Sheffield (BSc, DSc). Academic career in University of Reading, 1959–. FGS 1955. Lyell Medal, Geolog. Soc., 1980; David Linton Award, British Geomorphological Research Group, 1983; Twenhofel Medal, Soc. of Economic Paleontologists and Mineralogists, 1987; G. K. Warren Prize, Nat. Acad. of Scis, USA, 1990. *Publications:* Current Ripples, 1968; Physical Processes of Sedimentation, 1970; Sedimentary Structures, 1982; Principles of Physical Sedimentology, 1985; numerous contribs to professional jls. *Recreations:* cooking, music, opera. *Address:* 17c Whiteknights Road, Reading RG1 2BY. *T:* Reading (0734) 64621.

ALLEN, Prof. Joseph Stanley; (first) Professor and Head of Department of Town and Country Planning, University of Newcastle upon Tyne (formerly King's College, Durham University), 1946–63 (developing first University Degree Course in Town and Country Planning); now Professor Emeritus; *b* 15 March 1898; *s* of late Harry Charles Allen and of Elizabeth S. Allen; *m* 1931, Guinevere Mary Aubrey Pugh (*d* 1974); one *s* one *d*; *m* 1977, Meryl, *d* of late Charles and Eveline Watts. *Educ:* Liverpool Collegiate School; Liverpool University; post-graduate study in USA. RIBA Athens Bursar. Lectr, Liverpool Univ., 1929–33; Head, Leeds School of Architecture, 1933–45; founded Leeds Sch. of Town and Country Planning, 1934. Vice-Chm. RIBA Bd of Architectural Education and Chm. Recognised Schools Cttee, 1943–45; Member of Council RIBA, 1943–50; Pres. Royal Town Planning Institute, 1959–60 (Vice-Pres. 1957–59). Architect and Town Planning Consultant; undertakings include: Develt Plan for Durham Univ.; Quadrangle, King's College, Newcastle; Courthouse, Chesterfield; Nat. Park Residential Study Centre, Maentwrog; Science Wing, Durham Univ. Consultant, Snowdonia National Park, 1957–74; Member, North of England Regional Advisory Committee, Forestry Commission, 1951–74; Member Diocesan Committees for Care of Churches: Ripon, Newcastle and York Dioceses. Hon. DLitt Heriot-Watt, 1978. *Publications:* (with R. H. Mattocks): Report and Plan for West Cumberland; Report and Plan for Accrington (Industry and Prudence), 1950. Founder-Editor, Planning Outlook (founded 1948); contrib. to professional journals on architecture and town and country planning. *Recreations:* motoring and walking in the countryside, music, farming and breeding Welsh ponies. *Address:* Bleach Green Farm, Ovingham, Northumberland NE42 6BL. *T:* Prudhoe (0661) 32340.

ALLEN, Sir Kenneth; *see* Allen, Sir William Kenneth G.

ALLEN, Prof. Kenneth William; Professor of Nuclear Structure, 1963–91, Professor Emeritus, since 1991, and Head of Department of Nuclear Physics, 1976–79 and 1982–85, University of Oxford; Fellow, since 1963 and Estates Bursar, 1980–83 and since 1991, Balliol College; *b* 17 Nov. 1923; *m* 1947, Josephine E. Boreham; two *s*. *Educ:* Ilford County High School; London University (Drapers' Scholar); St Catharine's College, Cambridge University. PhD (Cantab) 1947. Physics Division, Atomic Energy of Canada, Chalk River, 1947–51; Leverhulme Research Fellow and Lecturer, Liverpool University, 1951–54; Deputy Chief Scientist, UKAEA, 1954–63. Sen. Vis. Scientist, Lawrence Berkeley Lab., Univ. of California, 1988–89. Mem., Nuclear Physics Bd, SRC, 1970–73. *Publications:* contribs to Nuclear Physics, Physical Review, Review of Scientific Instruments, Nature, etc. *Recreations:* music, chess. *Address:* Ridgeway, Lincombe Lane, Boars Hill, Oxford OX1 5DZ. *T:* Oxford (0865) 739327.

ALLEN, Mark Echalaz, CMG 1966; CVO 1961; HM Diplomatic Service, retired; *b* 19 March 1917; *s* of late Lancelot John Allen and Eleanor Mary (*née* Carlisle); *m* 1948, Elizabeth Joan, *d* of late Richard Hope Bowdler and Elsie (*née* Bryning); two *s* one *d* (and one *d* decd). *Educ:* Charterhouse; Christ Church, Oxford (MA). Appointed Asst Principal, Dominions Office, 1939. Served War of 1939–45 in Western Desert, Sicily and Italy. Dublin, 1945; Bombay, 1948; United Nations, New York, 1953; Madras, 1960; New Delhi, 1961; Diplomatic Service Inspector, 1964; Dep. Chief of Administration, DSAO, 1966; Minister (Econ. and Social Affairs), UK Mission to UN, New York, 1968; Ambassador to Zaïre and Burundi, 1971, and to Congo Republic, 1973; Permanent UK Rep. to Disarmament Conf., Geneva, 1974–77, retired from Diplomatic Service, 1977. Mem., Jt Inspection Unit, UN, 1978–84. *Address:* The Gate House, 65 Albion Street, Stratton, Cirencester, Glos GL7 2HT. *T:* Cirencester (0285) 653510.

ALLEN, Norman; *see* Allen, H. N. G.

ALLEN, Prof. Percival, FRS 1973; Professor of Geology, and Head of Geology Department, University of Reading, 1952–82, now Emeritus Professor; Director, Sedimentology Research Laboratory, 1965–82; *b* 15 March 1917; *s* of late Norman Williams Allen and Mildred Kathleen Hoad; British; *m* 1941, Frances Margaret Hepworth, BSc; three *s* one *d*. *Educ:* Brede Council Sch.; Rye Grammar School; University of Reading. BSc 1939, PhD 1943, Reading. Univ. Demonstrator, 1942–45, Univ. Asst Lectr, 1945–46, Reading; University Demonstrator, 1946–47, Univ. Lectr, 1947–52, Cambridge; Dean of Science Faculty, Reading, 1963–66. Vis. Prof., Univ. of Kuwait, 1970. Served War of 1939–45. In Royal Air Force, 1941–42. Sedgwick Prize, Univ. of Cambridge, 1952; Daniel Pidgeon Fund, Geological Soc. of London, 1944; Leverhulme Fellowships Research Grant, 1948, 1949. Geological Soc. of London: Mem. Council, 1964–67; Lyell Medal, 1971; Pres., 1978–80; Royal Society: Mem. Council, 1977–79; a Vice-Pres., 1977–79; Chairman: Expeditions Cttee, 1974–; British Nat. Cttee for Geology, 1982; Sectional Cttee 5, 1983–88; Actg Chm., Earth Sciences Res. Priorities, 1987–89. Chm., Scottish Regional Cttee and Mem., Nat. and Eastern Reg. Cttees, UGC Earth Sciences Rev., 1987–90; Council Mem., NERC, 1971–74 and Royal Soc. Assessor, 1977–80; Chm., vis. group to Palaeont. Dept in British Mus. (Nat. Hist.), 1975, and Univ. of Strathclyde, 1982; External Appraiser (Geol. Depts): Meml Univ., Newfoundland, 1968; Jadavpur Univ., India, 1977; Univ. of Western Ontario, 1982; Univ. of London, 1982; Univ. of Malaya, 1983; Adv. Panel, UNDP Project on Nile Delta, 1972–; UNESCO/UNDP Geology Consultant, India, 1976–77. UK Editor, Sedimentology, 1961–67; Jt Editor, OUP Monographs in Geology and Geophysics series, 1980–87. Chm., Org. Cttees: VII Internat. Sedimentological Congress, 1967; first European Earth and Planetary Physics Colloquium, 1971; first Meeting European Geological Socs, 1975; UK Delegate to Internat. Union of Geol Sciences, Moscow, 1984; UK Corresp., IGCP Project 245, 1986–. Sec.-Gen., Internat. Assoc. Sedimentologists, 1967–71; Pres., Reading Geol. Soc., 1976–78, 1987–88; Chm., British Inst. for Geological Conservation, 1987–. Algerian Sahara Glacials Expedn, 1970; Sec., Philpots Quarry Ltd. Hon. Member: American Soc. of Economic Paleontologists and Mineralogists; Bulgarian Geological Soc.; Geologists' Assoc.; Internat. Assoc. of Sedimentologists; For. Fellow, Indian Nat. Sci. Acad., 1979. *Publications:* papers on wealden (lower cretaceous) and torridonian (proterozoic) in various scientific journals. *Recreations:* chess, natural history, gardening, cycling. *Address:* Orchard End, Hazeley Bottom, Hartley Wintney, Hants RG27 8LU. *T:* Hartley Wintney (025126) 2229; Postgraduate Research Institute for Sedimentology, University of Reading, Reading RG6 2AB. *T:* Reading (0734) 875123.

ALLEN, Hon. Sir Peter (Austin Philip Jermyn), Kt 1987; High Court Judge, Lesotho, 1987–89; *b* 20 Oct. 1929; *yr s* of late Donovan Jermyn Allen and of Edith Jane Bates. *Educ:* Headlands School, Swindon. LLB London. Army service, 1947–55, Lieut RA, 1952–55. HM Overseas Police Service, Asst Supt Uganda Police, 1955–62; ADC to Governor of Uganda, 1957; called to the Bar, Gray's Inn, 1964; Lectr, 1962–64, Principal, 1964–70, Uganda Law School; Judicial Adviser, Buganda Kingdom, 1964; Advocate, High Court of Uganda, 1965; Chief Magistrate, Uganda, 1970–73; Judge, Uganda High Court, 1973–85; Chief Justice (Head of Uganda Judiciary, Chm., Judicial Service Commn), 1985–86. Member: Uganda Law Reform Commn, 1964–68; Foundn Cttee, Uganda YMCA, 1959; Dir, Mbarara Branch, YMCA, 1970–73; Chm., Presidential Commn of Inquiry into Kampala City Council, 1971; Mem., Uganda Law Soc., 1964–70. Uganda Independence Medal, 1962. *Publications:* An Introduction to the Law of Uganda (co-author), 1968; Days of Judgment, 1987. *Address:* PO Box 38, Savannah, Grand Cayman, Cayman Islands, British West Indies. *Club:* Commonwealth Trust.

ALLEN, Sir Peter (Christopher), Kt 1967; MA, BSc (Oxon); Advisory Director, New Perspective Fund, 1973–85; *b* Ashtead, Surrey, 8 Sept. 1905; *s* of late Sir Ernest King Allen and Florence Mary (*née* Gellatly); *m* 1st, 1931, Violet Sylvester Wingate-Saul (*d* 1951); two *d*; 2nd, 1952, Consuelo Maria Linares Rivas (*d* 1991). *Educ:* Harrow; Trinity Coll., Oxford (Hon. Fellow 1969). Joined Brunner, Mond & Co., Ltd, 1928; Chm., Plastics Div. of ICI Ltd, 1948–51 (Man. Dir, 1942–48); Pres. and Chm., ICI of Canada Ltd, 1961–68; Chm., ICI Ltd, 1968–71 (Dir, 1951–63, a Dep. Chm., 1963–68); Dir, British Nylon Spinners Ltd, 1954–58; Pres., Canadian Industries Ltd, 1959–62, Chm., 1962–68; Director: Royal Trust Co., Canada, 1961–64; Bank of Montreal, 1968–75; BICC, 1971–81. Vice-President: Inst. of Manpower Studies, 1968–76; Manufacturing Chemists' Assoc., USA, 1961–62 (Dir, 1959–62); Mem. and Vice-Chairman: Council of Assoc. of Brit. Chem. Manufacturers, 1963–65; Bd of Dirs, Société de Chimie Industrielle, 1968; Chm., Chem. Ind. Assoc., 1966–67; President: Plastics Inst., 1950–52; Brit. Plastics

Fedn, 1963–65; Univ. of Manchester Inst. of Sci. and Technology, 1968–71; Vice-Pres., British Assoc. for Commercial and Industrial Educn, 1969–; Mem. of Council, CBI, 1965–67. Chm., BNEC, 1970–71 (Mem., 1964–67; Chm., Cttee for Exports to Canada, 1964–67); Mem., British Overseas Trade Bd, 1972–75. Governor, Nat. Coll. of Rubber Technology, 1964–68; Member: Court, British Shippers' Council, 1968–70; Export Council for Europe, 1962–65; Overseas Development Inst. Council, 1963–64; Iron and Steel Holding and Realisation Agency, 1963–67; NEDC for Chemical Industry, 1964–67; Commonwealth Export Council, 1964–67; Industrial Policy Group, 1969–71. Pres., Transport Trust, 1967–88. FBIM 1968; FInstD 1969; FRGS 1980. Hon. Member: Chemical Industries Assoc., 1968– (Pres., 1965–67; Mem. Council, 1967–68); Canadian Chemical Producers' Assoc., 1962–. Chm., Anglo-Spanish Soc., 1973–80. Trustee, Civic Trust, 1970–76. Governor, Harrow School, 1969–82. Freeman, City of London, 1978. Knight Grand Cross, Spanish Order of Civil Merit, 1981. *Publications:* The Railways of the Isle of Wight, 1928; Locomotives of Many Lands, 1954; On the Old Lines, 1957; (with P. B. Whitehouse) Narrow Gauge Railways of Europe, 1959; (with R. A. Wheeler) Steam on the Sierra, 1960; (with P. B. Whitehouse) Round the World on the Narrow Gauge, 1966; (with Consuelo Allen) The Curve of Earth's Shoulder, 1966; (with A. B. MacLeod) Rails in the Isle of Wight, 1967; Famous Fairways, 1968; Play the Best Courses, 1973, 2nd edn 1988; (with P. B. Whitehouse) Narrow Gauge the World Over, 1976; The 91 Before Lindbergh, 1985; The Sunley Book of Royal Golf, 1989. *Recreations:* foreign travel, railways, golf, writing. *Address:* Telham Hill House, near Battle, E Sussex TN33 0SN. *Clubs:* Carlton; Royal and Ancient; Royal Cinque Ports, Rye, Royal St George's; Oxford and Cambridge Golfing Soc.; Augusta National (Ga, USA); Pine Valley (NJ, USA).

ALLEN, Peter William, FCA; Deputy Chairman, Coopers & Lybrand Deloitte, since 1990; *b* 22 July 1938; *s* of late Alfred William Allen, Sittingbourne, Kent, and Myra Nora (*née* Rogers); *m* 1965, Patricia Mary, *d* of Joseph Frederick Dunk, FCA, Sheffield; three *d*. *Educ:* Cambridge Univ. (MA). Served RAF, 1957–59. Joined Coopers & Lybrand, 1963; qualified CA, 1966; Partner, 1973; Chm., Internat. Personnel Cttee, 1975–78; Partner in Charge, London Office, 1983; Man. Partner, 1984–90. Member: UK Management Cttee, 1984–; Internat. Exec. Cttee, 1988–90. Freeman, City of London, 1988; Liveryman, Co. of Glaziers and Painters of Glass, 1989. *Recreations:* golf, bridge. *Address:* John O'Gaddesden's House, Little Gaddesden, Berkhamsted, Herts HP4 1PF; Coopers & Lybrand Deloitte, Plumtree Court, EC4A 4HT. *T:* 071–822 4501. *Club:* Reform.

ALLEN, (Philip) Richard (Hernaman); Director, Internal Taxes and Commissioner of Customs and Excise, since 1990; *b* 26 Jan. 1949; *s* of late Philip Hernaman Allen and of Dorothy Allen (*née* Modral); *m* 1970, Vanessa (*née* Lampard); two *d*. *Educ:* Loughborough Grammar Sch.; Merton Coll., Oxford (BA (Hons) Mod. History). Asst Principal, HM Customs and Excise, 1970; Assistant Private Secretary: to Paymaster Gen., 1973; to Chancellor of the Duchy of Lancaster, 1974; HM Customs and Excise: Principal, 1975; Asst Sec., 1984. *Recreations:* music, badminton, gardening. *Address:* HM Customs and Excise, New King's Beam House, 22 Upper Ground, SE1. *T:* 071–865 5015.

ALLEN, Sir Richard (Hugh Sedley), KCMG 1960 (CMG 1953); retired; *b* 3 Feb. 1903; *s* of late Sir Hugh Allen, GCVO; *m* 1945, Juliet Home Thomson (*d* 1983); one step *s* (and one *s* decd). *Educ:* Royal Naval Colleges, Osborne and Dartmouth; New College, Oxford. Junior Asst Sec., Govt of Palestine, 1925–27. Entered Foreign Office and Diplomatic Service, 1927; Second Sec., 1932; First Sec., 1939; Counsellor, 1946; Minister, British Embassy, Buenos Aires, 1950–54; Minister to Guatemala, 1954–56; British Ambassador to Burma, 1956–62. *Publications:* Malaysia: Prospect and Retrospect, 1968; A Short Introduction to the History and Politics of Southeast Asia, 1970; Imperialism and Nationalism in the Fertile Crescent, 1974. *Recreation:* sailing. *Address:* 42 Somerstown, Chichester, Sussex PO19 4AL. *T:* Chichester (0243) 781182. *Clubs:* Athenæum; Royal Naval Sailing Association, Bosham and Itchenor Sailing.

ALLEN, Richard Ian Gordon; Under Secretary and Head of Local Government Group, HM Treasury, since 1990; *b* 13 Dec. 1944; *s* of Reginald Arthur Hill Allen and Edith Alice Allen (*née* Manger); *m* 1988, Lynn Conroy. *Educ:* Edinburgh Academy; Edinburgh Univ. (MA); York Univ. (BPhil). Consultant, UN Economic Commn for Europe, Geneva, 1970; Research Officer, NIESR, 1971–75; Economic Adviser: Dept of Energy, 1975–78; HM Treasury, 1978–81; Senior Economic Adviser, later Asst Sec., HM Treasury, 1981–85; Counsellor (Economic), Washington, 1985–87; Press Sec. to Chancellor of the Exchequer, 1987–88; Under Sec., Overseas Finance, European Communities Gp, HM Treasury, 1988–90. Mem., Bd of Dirs, EIB, 1988–90. *Recreations:* music, theatre, golf. *Address:* 29 Cleveland Square, W2 6DD. *Club:* Royal Wimbledon Golf.

ALLEN, Rowland Lancelot, CB 1968; Principal Assistant Treasury Solicitor, 1963–69, retired; *b* 17 Feb. 1908; *s* of Rowland Allen and Maud Annie Allen (*née* Bacon); *m* 1934, Elizabeth Ethel (*née* Lewis) (*d* 1982); two *s* one *d*. *Educ:* Eton College. Called to the Bar, Inner Temple, 1931; Public Trustee Office, 1934; Treasury Solicitor's Dept, 1940; Foreign Compensation Commission, 1950–53; Treasury Solicitor's Dept, 1953. *Recreation:* golf. *Address:* 12 Raeburn Court, St John's Hill, Woking, Surrey GU21 1QW. *T:* Woking (0483) 724326.

ALLEN, Thomas, CBE 1989; singer; *b* 10 Sept. 1944; *s* of Thomas Boaz Allen and Florence Allen; *m* 1968, Margaret Holley (marr. diss. 1986); one *s*; *m* 1988, Jeannie Gordon Lascelles. *Educ:* Robert Richardson Grammar Sch., Ryhope; Royal College of Music. ARCM; FRCM 1988. Welsh Nat. Opera, 1969–72; Principal Baritone, Royal Opera, Covent Garden, 1972–78; appearances include: Glyndebourne Fest. Opera; English Opera Group; Paris Opera; Florence; Teatro Colon, Buenos Aires; Met. Opera, NY; Hamburg; La Scala, Milan; BBC TV (The Gondoliers, The Marriage of Figaro); all major orchestras and various concert engagements abroad. Major rôles include: Figaro in Barber of Seville; Figaro and the Count in Marriage of Figaro; Paolo Albiani in Simon Boccanegra; Papageno in The Magic Flute; Billy Budd; Marcello in La Bohême; Belcore in l'Elisir d'Amore; Sid in Albert Herring; Tarquinius in Rape of Lucretia; Guglielmo in Così fan Tutte; Demetrius in A Midsummer Night's Dream; Valentin in Faust; Dr Falke in Die Fledermaus; King Arthur; The Count in Voice of Ariadne; Silvio in Pagliacci; Pelléas in Pelléas and Mélisande; Germont in La Traviata; Don Giovanni; title rôle in Il ritorno d'Ulisse, and many others. Hon. RAM, 1988. Hon. MA Newcastle, 1984; Hon. DMus Durham, 1988. *Recreations:* gardening, golf, sailing, reading, ornithology. *Address:* c/o John Coast, Manfield House, 376/9 Strand, WC2R 0LR.

ALLEN, Walter Ernest, author and literary journalist; *b* Birmingham, 23 Feb. 1911; 4th *s* of Charles Henry Allen and Annie Maria Thomas; *m* 1944, Peggy Yorke, 3rd *d* of Guy Lionel Joy and Dorothy Yorke Maundrell, Calne, Wilts; two *s* two *d*. *Educ:* King Edward's Grammar School, Aston, Birmingham; Birmingham University. Assistant Master, King Edward's Grammar School, Aston, Birmingham, 1934; Visiting Lecturer in English, State University of Iowa, USA, 1935; Features Editor, Cater's News Agency, Birmingham, 1935–37; Assistant Technical Officer, Wrought Light Alloys Development Assoc., 1943–45. Asst Literary Editor, New Statesman, 1959–60, Literary Editor, 1960–61. Margaret Pilcher Vis. Prof. of English, Coe Coll., Iowa, 1955–56; Visiting Professor of English: Vassar College, New York, 1963–64; Univ. of Kansas, 1967; Univ. of Washington, 1967; Prof. of English, New Univ. of Ulster, 1967–73; Berg Prof. of English, New York Univ., 1970–71; Vis. Prof. of English, Dalhousie Univ., Halifax, NS, 1973–74; C. P. Miles Prof. of English, Virginia Polytechnic Inst. and State Univ., 1974–75. FRSL. *Publications: novels:* Innocence is Drowned, 1938; Blind Man's Ditch, 1939; Living Space, 1940; Rogue Elephant, 1946; Dead Man Over All, 1950; Get Out Early, 1986; Accosting Profiles, 1989; *topography:* The Black Country, 1946; *literary criticism:* Writers on Writing, 1948; Arnold Bennett, 1948; Reading a Novel, 1949; The English Novel A Short Critical History, 1954; Six Great Novelists, 1955; All in a Lifetime, 1959; Tradition and Dream, 1964; George Eliot, 1964; The Urgent West: an Introduction to the Idea of the United States, 1969; Transatlantic Crossing: American visitors to Britain and British visitors to America in the nineteenth century, 1971; The Short Story in English, 1981; As I Walked Down New Grub Street, 1981. *Address:* 4B Alwyne Road, N1 2HH. *T:* 071–226 7085.

ALLEN, Walter John Gardener; Controller, Capital Taxes Office (formerly Estate Duty Office), Inland Revenue, 1974–78; *b* 8 Dec. 1916; *s* of late John Gardiner Allen and late Hester Lucy Allen, Deal, Kent; *m* 1944, Irene (*d* 1983), *d* of late John Joseph and Sarah Henderson, Lisburn, N Ireland; one *s* one *d*. *Educ:* Manwoods, Sandwich; London Univ. (LLB). Entered Inland Revenue, 1934. Served RAF, 1940–46 (Flying Officer). FGS 1982. *Recreations:* amateur geologist; gardening. *Address:* 43 The Chase, Eastcote, Pinner, Mddx HA5 1SH. *T:* 081–868 7101.

ALLEN, William Alexander, CBE 1980; RIBA; Founder Chairman, Bickerdike Allen Partners, architects, 1962–89, retired; *b* 29 June 1914; *s* of late Professor Frank Allen, FRSC; *m* 1938, Beatrice Mary Teresa Pearson; two *s* one *d*. *Educ:* public schools in Winnipeg; University of Manitoba. Royal Architectural Inst. of Canada Silver Medal, 1935. Univ. Gold Medal in Architecture, 1936. Appointed to Building Research Station, Watford, 1937; Chief Architect, Bldg Res. Stn, 1953–61; Principal of the Architectural Assoc. School of Architecture, 1961–66. Mem. Council, RIBA, 1953–72, 1982–89 (Chm. various cttees); ARIBA 1937; FRIBA 1965; Chm., Fire Research Adv. Cttee, 1973–83, Visitor, 1983–88; President: Institute of Acoustics, 1975–76; Ecclesiastic Arch. Assoc., 1980. Hon. Associate NZIA, 1965; Hon. Fellow, American Inst. Of Architects, 1984. Hon. LLD Manitoba, 1977. Commander, Ordem do Mérito, Portugal, 1972. *Publications:* (with R. Fitzmaurice) Sound Transmission in Buildings, 1939. Papers, etc, on scientific and technical aspects of architecture and urban design, professionalism, and modern architectural history and education. *Recreations:* writing, drawing, music. *Address:* 4 Ashley Close, Welwyn Garden City, Herts AL8 7LH. *T:* Welwyn Garden (0707) 324178. *Club:* Athenæum.

See also Prof. J. F. Allen.

ALLEN, William Anthony; Head of Foreign Exchange Division, Bank of England, since 1990; *b* 13 May 1949; *s* of Derek William Allen and Margaret Winifred Allen (*née* Jones); *m* 1972, Rosemary Margaret Eminson; one *s* two *d*. *Educ:* King's College Sch., Wimbledon; Balliol College, Oxford (BA); LSE (MScEcon). Joined Bank of England, 1972; Economic Intell. Dept, 1972–77; Gold and Foreign Exchange Office, 1977–78; seconded to Bank for Internat. Settlements, Basle, 1978–80; Asst Adviser, Economics Div., Bank of England (working on monetary policy), 1980–82; Manager, Gilt-Edged Div., 1982–86; Hd of Money Market Operations Div., 1986–90. *Publications:* articles in economics jls. *Recreations:* gardening, jazz. *Address:* Bank of England, Threadneedle Street, EC2R 8AH. *T:* 071–601 4444.

ALLEN, Sir William (Guilford), Kt 1981; Chairman, family group of companies; *b* 22 April 1932; *s* of Sir William Guilford Allen, CBE, and Mona Maree Allen; *m* 1959, Elaine Therese Doyle; two *s* one *d*. *Educ:* Downlands Coll., Toowoomba, Qld. In grazing industry, Merino sheep; Principal, Historic Malvern Hills Registered Merino Stud; stud Santa Gertrudis cattle breeder. Commercial broadcasting industry. Treasurer and Trustee, Nat. Party, Qld. Councillor, Longreach Shire. Chm., Qld Transport and Technology Centre, 1984–; Chairman: Suncorp Insurance Corp., 1989– (Dir, 1985–); Suncorp Building Soc., 1989– (Dir, 1985–); Dir, Power Brewing Co., 1988–. Fellow, GAPAN. *Recreation:* aviation. *Address:* Toorak House, Hipwood Road, Hamilton, Brisbane, Qld 4007, Australia. *T:* Brisbane 2624111. *Clubs:* Brisbane, Tattersalls, Australian, Royal Queensland Golf, Longreach, Queensland Turf, Brisbane Amateur Turf (Brisbane); Australian, Royal Sydney Golf (Sydney).

ALLEN, Sir (William) Kenneth (Gwynne), Kt 1961; DL; *b* 23 May 1907; *er s* of Harold Gwynne Allen and Hilda Allen, Bedford; *m* 1931, Eleanor Mary (*née* Eeles) (*d* 1990); one *s* one *d*. *Educ:* Westminster Sch.; Univ. of Neuchâtel, Switzerland. Started as engineering pupil, Harland & Wolff Ltd, Glasgow and Belfast; subsequently at W. H. Allen, Sons & Co. Ltd, Bedford; Dir, 1937–70, Man. Dir, 1946–70, Chm., 1955–70, W. H. Allen, Sons & Co. Ltd; Chm., Amalgamated Power Engineering, 1968–70; Director: Whessoe Ltd, 1954–65; Electrolux, 1970–78. Chm., Brit. Internal Combustion Engine Manufacturers' Assoc., 1955–57; Pres., British Engineers' Assoc., 1957–59 (now British Mechanical Engineering Fedn); Chm., BEAMA, 1959–61; Pres., Engineering Employers' Fedn, 1962–64; Chm., Labour and Social Affairs Cttee of CBI, 1965–67. FIMarE; MRINA. Freeman of City of London. Liveryman, Worshipful Company of Shipwrights. Mem. Beds CC, 1945–55; High Sheriff Beds, 1958–59; DL Beds, 1978. *Address:* Manor Close, Aspley Guise, Milton Keynes, Bedfordshire MK17 8HZ. *T:* Milton Keynes (0908) 583161.

ALLEN, Maj.-Gen. William Maurice, CB 1983; FCIT, FIMI, FILDM, FBIM, MInstPet; Managing Director: Fortis International Ltd; Pulsar Aviation Ltd; *b* 29 May 1931; *s* of William James Allen and Elizabeth Jane Henrietta Allen; *m* 1955, Patricia Mary (*née* Fletcher); one *d* decd. *Educ:* Dunstable Sch. FCIT 1972; FIMI 1982; FILDM (FIPDM 1982); FBIM 1983; MInstPet 1982. Commnd RASC, 1950; RCT, 1965; regtl and staff appts, Korea, Cyprus, Germany and UK; Student, Staff Coll., Camberley, 1961; Instructor, Staff Coll., Camberley and RMCS Shrivenham, 1968–70; Student, RCDS, 1976; Asst Comdt, RMA Sandhurst, 1979–81; Dir Gen. of Transport and Movements (Army), 1981–83. Dir of Educn and Trng, Burroughs Machines Ltd, 1983–85. Jt Man. Dir, Marina Moraira Yacht Brokers, 1989– (Dir, 1988–); Sen. Mil. Consultant to Mondial & Co., 1985–; Director: Govt Projects, Unisys Corp. (formerly Systems Develt Corp.), Heidelberg, 1985–86; Fortis Aviation Gp, Spain, 1988–89; European Management Information, 1989–. Member, Council: IAM, 1982–85; NDTA, 1983–. Chm., Milton Keynes Information Technol. Trng Centre, 1983–85. Associate, St George's House. Freeman, City of London, 1981; Hon. Liveryman, Worshipful Co. of Carmen, 1981. *Recreations:* economics, trout fishing, squash, gardening, rough shooting, ocean cruising. *Address:* c/o Royal Bank of Scotland, Holts Farnborough Branch, Lawrie House, 31–37 Victoria Road, Farnborough, Hants GU14 7NR. *Club:* Bristol Channel Yacht (Swansea).

ALLEN, Prof. William Sidney, MA, PhD (Cantab); FBA 1971; Professor of Comparative Philology in the University of Cambridge, 1955–82; Fellow of Trinity College, since

1955; *b* 18 March 1918; *er s* of late W. P. Allen and Ethel (*née* Pearce); *m* 1955, Aenea, *yr d* of late Rev. D. McCallum and Mrs McCallum, Invergordon. *Educ:* Christ's Hosp.; Trinity Coll., Cambridge (Classical Scholar); Porson Scholarship, 1939. War of 1939–45: RTR and General Staff (Int) (despatches). Lecturer in Phonetics, 1948–51, and in Comparative Linguistics, 1951–55, School of Oriental and African Studies, Univ. of London. Dialect research in India, 1952; Fellow of Rockefeller Foundation, USA, 1953; Brit. Council visitor, Univ. of W Indies, 1959. Linguistic Soc. of America's Professor, 1961; Collitz Professor, Linguistic Institute, USA, 1962; Ida Beam Lectr, Univ. of Iowa, 1983. Pres., Philological Soc., 1965–67. Hon. Fellow, Soc. for Cycladic Studies (Athens), 1977. Chm. Editorial Bd, CUP linguistic series, 1969–82; Editor, Lingua, 1963–85. *Publications:* Phonetics in Ancient India, 1953; On the Linguistic Study of Languages (inaugural lecture), 1957; Sandhi, 1962; Vox Latina, 1965; Vox Graeca, 1968, 3rd edn 1987; Accent and Rhythm, 1973; articles on general and comparative linguistics, phonetics, metrics and classical, Indian and Caucasian languages, Aegean cartography. *Address:* 24 Sherlock Road, Cambridge CB3 0HR. *T:* Cambridge (0223) 356739.

ALLEN, Woody; writer, actor, director; *b* Brooklyn, 1 Dec. 1935; *s* of Martin and Nettie Konigsberg; *m* 1966, Louise Lasser (marr. diss.); one *s* by Mia Farrow, *qv*. TV script writer, 1953–64, and appeared as a comedian in nightclubs and on TV shows. Sylvania Award, 1957. *Plays:* (writer) Don't Drink the Water, 1966; (writer and actor) Play It Again Sam, 1969 (filmed 1972); The Floating Light Bulb, 1990. *Films:* (writer and actor) What's New Pussycat?, 1965; (actor): Casino Royale, 1967; Scenes from a Mall, 1991; (writer, actor and director): What's Up Tiger Lily?, 1966; Take the Money and Run, 1969; Bananas, 1971; Everything You Always Wanted to Know About Sex But Were Afraid to Ask, 1972; Sleeper, 1973; Love and Death, 1975; The Front, 1976; Annie Hall (Academy Award), 1977; Manhattan, 1979; Stardust Memories, 1980; A Midsummer Night's Sex Comedy, 1982; Zelig, 1983; Broadway Danny Rose, 1984; Hannah and her Sisters (Academy Award), 1986; New York Stories, 1989; (writer and director): Interiors, 1978; The Purple Rose of Cairo, 1985; Radio Days, 1987; September, 1988; Another Woman, 1989; Crimes and Misdemeanours, 1989; Alice, 1990. *Publications:* Getting Even, 1971; Without Feathers, 1975; Side Effects, 1981; contribs to New Yorker, etc.

ALLEN-JONES, Air Vice-Marshal John Ernest, CBE 1966; Director of RAF Legal Services, 1961–70, retired; *b* 13 Oct. 1909; *s* of Rev. John Allen-Jones, Llanyblodwel Vicarage, Oswestry; *m* 1st, 1937, Margaret Rix (*d* 1973), Sawbridgeworth; one *s* two *d*; 2nd, 1973, Diana Gibbons. *Educ:* Rugby; Worcester Coll., Oxford (MA). Solicitor (Honours), 1934; Partner with Vaudrey, Osborne & Mellor, Manchester. Joined RAF, 1939. Air Vice-Marshal, 1967. Gordon-Shepherd Memorial Prizeman, 1963. *Recreations:* tennis, bridge. *Address:* Hartfield, Duton Hill, Dunmow, Essex CM6 2DX. *T:* Great Easton (037184) 554.

ALLENBY, family name of **Viscount Allenby.**

ALLENBY, 3rd Viscount *cr* 1919, of Megiddo and of Felixstowe; **Michael Jaffray Hynman Allenby;** Lieutenant-Colonel, The Royal Hussars, retired 1986; Chairman, Quickrest Ltd, since 1987; *b* 20 April 1931; *s* of 2nd Viscount Allenby and of Mary Lethbridge Allenby (*d* 1988), *d* of Edward Champneys; *S* father, 1984; *m* 1965, Sara Margaret, *d* of Lt-Col Peter Milner Wiggin; one *s*. *Educ:* Eton; RMA Sandhurst. Commnd 2/Lieut 11th Hussars (PAO), 1951; served Malaya, 1953–56; ADC to Governor, Cyprus, 1957–58; Bde Major, 51 Brigade, Hong Kong, 1967–70; comd Royal Yeomanry (TA), 1974–77; GS01 Instructor, Nigerian Staff Coll., Kaduna, 1977–79. *Recreations:* horses, sailing. *Heir:* *s* Hon. Henry Jaffray Hynman Allenby, *b* 29 July 1968. *Club:* Cavalry and Guards.

ALLENBY, Rt. Rev. (David Howard) Nicholas; Assistant Bishop, Diocese of Worcester since 1968; *b* 28 Jan. 1909; *s* of late William Allenby; unmarried. *Educ:* Kelham Theological College. MA (Lambeth), 1957. Deacon, 1934; Priest, 1935. Curate of St Jude, West Derby, Liverpool, 1934–36; Tutor, Kelham Theological College and Public Preacher, Diocese of Southwell, 1936–44; Rector of Averham with Kelham, 1944–57; Mem., Southwell RDC, 1944–52; Proctor in Convocation, Southwell, 1950–57; Editor of Diocesan News and Southwell Review, 1950–55; Hon. Canon of Southwell, 1953–57, Canon Emeritus, 1957–62; Personal Chaplain to Bishop of Southwell, 1954–57; Rural Dean of Newark, 1955–57; Provincial of Society of Sacred Mission in Australia, 1957–62; Commissary, Melanesia, 1958–62; Warden of Community of Holy Name, City and Diocese of Melbourne, 1961–62; Bishop of Kuching, 1962–68; Commissary, Kuching, 1969. Chaplain, St Oswald's Almshouses, Worcester, 1973–84. *Publication:* Pray with the Church, 1937 (jointly). *Recreations:* reading, painting, cooking. *Address:* 16 Woodbine Road, Barbourne, Worcester WR1 3JB. *T:* Worcester (0905) 27980. *Club:* Commonwealth Trust.

ALLENDALE, 3rd Viscount, *cr* 1911; **Wentworth Hubert Charles Beaumont,** DL; Baron, 1906; *b* 12 Sept. 1922; *e s* of 2nd Viscount Allendale, KG, CB, CBE, MC, and Violet (*d* 1979), *d* of Sir Charles Seely, 2nd Bt; *S* father 1956; *m* 1948, Hon. Sarah Ismay (marr. diss.), 2nd *d* of 1st Baron Ismay, KG, PC, GCB, CH, DSO; three *s*. *Educ:* Eton. RAFVR, 1940; Flight-Lieutenant 1943; ADC to Viceroy of India, 1946–47. DL Northumberland, 1961. *Heir:* *s* Hon. Wentworth Peter Ismay Beaumont [*b* 13 Nov. 1948; *m* 1975, Theresa Mary, *d* of F. A. More O'Ferrall; one *s* three *d*]. *Address:* Bywell Hall, Stocksfield on Tyne, Northumberland. *T:* Stocksfield (0661) 3169; Allenheads, Hexham, Northumberland. *T:* Allenheads (043485) 205. *Clubs:* Turf, White's; Northern Counties (Newcastle upon Tyne).

See also Earl of Carlisle, Hon. E. N. C. Beaumont.

ALLERTON, Air Vice-Marshal Richard Christopher, CB 1989; Director General of Supply, Royal Air Force, 1987–90, retired; *b* 7 Dec. 1935; *er s* of late Air Cdre Ord Denny Allerton, CB, CBE, and of Kathleen Allerton; *m* 1964, Marie Isobel Campbell Mackenzie, *er d* of Captain Sir Roderick Mackenzie, 11th Bt, CBE, DSC, RN, and of Marie, Lady Mackenzie; two *s*. *Educ:* Stone House, Broadstairs; Stowe Sch. Commissioned RAF, 1954; served, 1955–78: RAF Hullavington, Oakington, Feltwell, Kinloss, RAF Unit HQ Coastal Command, Hereford, Little Rissington; Instructor, RAF Coll., Cranwell; Student, RAF Staff Coll., Bracknell; Staff, HQ RAF Germany; Chief Instructor, Supply and Secretarial Trng, RAF Coll., Cranwell; Student, Nat. Defence Coll., Latimer; MoD Harrogate; Dep. Dir, RAF Supply Policy, MoD, 1978–80; Station Comdr, RAF Stafford, 1980–82; RCDS 1983; Air Cdre, Supply and Movements, HQ Strike Comd, 1983–86. ADC to the Queen, 1980–82. Pres., RAF Cricket Assoc., 1987–89. *Recreations:* shooting, fishing, cricket. *Address:* c/o Lloyds Bank, 13 Broad Street, Launceston, Cornwall. *Club:* Royal Air Force.

ALLEY, Ronald Edgar; artist; Keeper of the Modern Collection, Tate Gallery, London, 1965–86; *b* 12 March 1926; *s* of late Edgar Thomas Alley; *m* 1955, Anthea Oswell (marr. diss.) (now painter and sculptor, as Anthea Alley); two *d*. *Educ:* Bristol Grammar School; Courtauld Institute of Art, London University. Tate Gallery staff as Asst Keeper II, 1951–54; Deputy Keeper, 1954–65. Member: Museum Board, Cecil Higgins Art Gallery, Bedford, 1957; Art Cttee, Ulster Museum, Belfast, 1962; Art Panel of Arts Council, 1963–70. *Publications:* Tate Gallery: Foreign Paintings, Drawings and Sculpture, 1959; Gauguin, 1962; William Scott, 1963; Ben Nicholson, 1963; Francis Bacon (with Sir John Rothenstein), 1964; British Painting since 1945, 1966; Picasso's "Three Dancers" 1967; Barbara Hepworth, 1968; Recent American Art, 1969; Abstract Expressionism, 1974; Catalogue of the Tate Gallery's Collection of Modern Art, other than works by British Artists, 1981. *Recreation:* ornithology. *Address:* 61 Deodar Road, SW15. *T:* 081–874 2016. *Club:* Institute of Contemporary Arts.

ALLEYNE, Sir George (Allanmore Ogarren), Kt 1990; MD, FRCP; Assistant Director, Pan American Health Organization, since 1990; *b* 7 Oct. 1932; *s* of Clinton O. Alleyne and Eileen A. Alleyne (*née* Gaskin); *m* 1958, Sylvan Ionie (*née* Chen); two *s* one *d*. *Educ:* Harrison College, Barbados; University College of the West Indies (MB BS London 1977, MD). Completed training as physician in Barbados and UCH, London, 1958–62; Sen. Med. Registrar, UCH, Jamaica, 1962–63; Res. Fellow, Sen. Res. Fellow, MRC Tropical Metabolism Res. Unit, 1963–72; Prof. of Medicine, Univ. of W Indies, 1972–81 (Chm., Dept of Medicine, 1976–81); Pan American Health Organization: Head of Res. Unit, 1981–83; Dir of Health Programs Develt, 1983–90. Sir Arthur Sims Travelling Prof., 1977. Hon. FACP. Hon. DSc Univ. of W Indies, 1989. Jamaica Assoc. of Scientists Award, 1979. Jamaica Centenary Medal, 1980. *Publications:* contribs to learned jls on medicine, renal physiology and biochemistry, health and develt issues. *Recreations:* reading, gardening. *Address:* Pan American Health Organization, 525 23rd Street NW, Washington, DC 20037, USA. *T:* (202) 861–3404.

ALLEYNE, Rev. Sir John (Olpherts Campbell), 5th Bt *cr* 1769; Rector of Weeke, Diocese of Winchester, since 1975; *b* 18 Jan. 1928; *s* of Captain Sir John Meynell Alleyne, 4th Bt, DSO, DSC, RN, and Alice Violet (*d* 1985), *d* of late James Campbell; *S* father, 1983; *m* 1968, Honor, *d* of late William Albert Irwin, Belfast; one *s* one *d*. *Educ:* Eton; Jesus Coll., Cambridge (BA 1950, MA 1955). Deacon 1955, priest 1956; Curate, Southampton, 1955–58; Chaplain: Coventry Cathedral, 1958–62; Clare Coll., Cambridge, 1962–66; to Bishop of Bristol, 1966–68; Toc H Area Sec., SW England, 1968–71; Vicar of Speke, 1971–73, Rector, 1973–75. *Heir:* *s* Richard Meynell Alleyne, *b* 23 June 1972. *Address:* The Rectory, 44 Cheriton Road, Winchester, Hants SO22 5AY.

ALLEYNE, Selwyn Eugene, CBE 1986; Hong Kong Commissioner in London, 1987–89, retired; *b* 4 Dec. 1930; *s* of Gilbert Sydney Alleyne and Dorothy Alleyne; *m* 1956, Ellie Lynn Wong, MBE. *Educ:* Queen's Royal Coll., Trinidad; Jesus Coll., Oxford (MA). Joined Hong Kong Govt, 1956; Dep. Dir of Urban Services, 1974; Dep. Sec. for Civil Service, 1979; Dir of Social Welfare, and MLC, 1980; Dep. Financial Sec., 1983–87. *Recreations:* tennis, chess, collecting Chinese ceramics. *Address:* 118 Whitehall Court, SW1A 2EL. *Club:* Commonwealth Trust.

ALLFORD, David, CBE 1984; FRIBA; architect, retired; Senior Partner, YRM Partnership, 1975–87 (Partner since 1958); Chairman, YRM plc, 1987–89; Visiting Professor, Bartlett School of Architecture, University College London, since 1989; *b* 12 July 1927; *s* of Frank Allford and Martha Blanche Allford; *m* 1953, Margaret Beryl Roebuck; one *s* three *d*. *Educ:* High Storrs Grammar Sch., Sheffield; Univ. of Sheffield (BA Hons Architecture, 1952). FRIBA 1969. Served RAF, 1945–48. Joined Yorke Rosenberg Mardall, Architects (now YRM), 1952; Partner i/c architectural projects: schools, univs (principally Univ. of Warwick), Newcastle Airport, hosps and commercial projs in UK and overseas. Mem. Council, Architectural Assoc., 1970–71 and 1977–78. *Publications:* articles in architectural press and related jls. *Recreations:* drawing, painting, following Sheffield Wednesday Football Club. *Address:* 39 Belsize Road, NW6 4RX. *T:* 071–722 6724. *Clubs:* Garrick, Arts, MCC.

ALLHUSEN, Major Derek Swithin, CVO 1984; DL; farmer; Standard Bearer, HM's Body Guard of Honourable Corps of Gentlemen at Arms, 1981–84; *b* 9 Jan. 1914; 2nd *s* of late Lt-Col F. H. Allhusen, CMG, DSO, Fulmer House, Fulmer, Bucks; *m* 1937, Hon. Claudia Violet Betterton, *yr d* of 1st and last Baron Rushcliffe, PC, GBE (*d* 1949); one *s* one *d* (and one *s* decd). *Educ:* Eton; Chillon Coll., Montreux, Switzerland; Trinity Coll., Cambridge (MA). Lieut, 9th Queen's Royal Lancers, 1935. Served War of 1939–45: France, 1940, North Africa, Italy (wounded twice) (Silver Star Medal of USA, 1944); Major 1942; 2 i/c 1945–47; retired, 1949. One of HM's Body Guard of Hon. Corps of Gentlemen at Arms, 1963–84. Chm., Riding for the Disabled, Norwich and Dist. Gp, 1968– (Vice-Pres., Eastern Region); President: Royal Norfolk Agric. Assoc., 1974; Nat. Pony Soc., 1982; Cambridge Univ. Equestrian Club; Norfolk Schs Athletic Assoc.; Pres., British Horse Soc., 1986–88 (Mem. Council, 1962–). Freeman, City of London; Hon. Yeoman, Worshipful Co. of Saddlers, 1969; Hon. Freeman, Worshipful Co. of Farriers, 1969. High Sheriff, 1958, DL 1969, Norfolk. *Recreations:* riding, shooting, skiing. Represented GB: Winter Pentathlon Olympic Games, 1948; Equestrianism European Championships Three-Day Event, 1957, 1959, 1965, 1967, 1969 (Winners of Team Championship, 1957, 1967, 1969); Olympic Games, Mexico, 1968 (Gold Medal, Team; Silver Medal, Individual); lent his horse Laurieston to British Olympic Equestrian Team, Munich, 1972 (individual and team Gold Medals). *Address:* Manor House, Claxton, Norwich, Norfolk. *T:* Thurton (050843) 228. *Clubs:* Cavalry and Guards, Army and Navy.

ALLIANCE, Sir David, Kt 1989; CBE 1984; Chairman: Coats Viyella, since 1989 (Group Chief Executive, 1975–90); N. Brown Group, since 1968; Tootal Group, since 1991; *b* June 1932. *Educ:* Iran. First acquisition, Thomas Hoghton (Oswaldtwistle), 1956; acquired Spirella, 1968, then Vantona Ltd, 1975, to form Vantona Group, 1975; acquired Carrington Viyella to form Vantona Viyella, 1983, Nottingham Manufacturing, 1985, Coats Patons to form Coats Viyella, 1986. CBIM 1985; CompTI 1984. FRSA 1988. Hon. Fellow UMIST 1988; Hon. LLD Manchester 1989. *Address:* Coats Viyella, 28 Savile Row, W1X 2DD. *T:* 071–734 4030.

ALLIBONE, Thomas Edward, CBE 1960; DSc Sheffield; FRS 1948; FEng; External Professor of Electrical Engineering, University of Leeds, 1967–79, now Emeritus; Visiting Professor of Physics, City University, since 1971; also Robert Kitchin (Saddlers) Research Professor, since 1983, and first Frank Poynton Professor, Physics Department, since 1984, City University; *b* 11 Nov. 1903; *s* of Henry J. Allibone; *m* 1931, Dorothy Margery, LRAM, ARCM, *d* of Frederick Boulden, BSc, MEng, MIMechE; two *d*. *Educ:* Central Sch., Sheffield (Birley Scholar); Sheffield Univ. (Linley Scholar); Gonville and Caius Coll., Cambridge (Wollaston Scholar). PhD Sheffield; PhD Cantab. 1851 Exhibition Sen. Student, Cavendish Laboratory, Cambridge, 1926–30; i/c High-Voltage Laboratory, Metropolitan-Vickers Electrical Co., Manchester, 1930–46; Director: Res. Laboratory, AEI, Aldermaston, 1946–63; AEI (Woolwich) Ltd, 1948–63; Scientific Adviser, AEI, 1963; Chief Scientist, Central Electricity Generating Bd, 1963–70. Mem., British Mission on Atomic Energy, Berkeley, Calif, and Oakridge, Tenn, 1944–45; Visitor: BISRA, 1949–55; ASLIB, 1955–62. Lectures: Faraday, 1946, 1956; Royal Instn Christmas, 1959; Wm Menelaus, 1959; Bernard Price, 1959; Trotter Patterson, 1963; Fison Memorial, 1963; Royal Soc. Rutherford Memorial, 1964 and 1972; Baird Memorial, 1967; Melchett, 1970. President: Section A, British Assoc., 1958; EIBA, 1958–59; Inst. of Information Scientists, 1964–67. Vice-President: Inst. of Physics, 1948–52; Royal Instn, 1955–57, 1970–72. Chm., Res. Cttee, British Electrical and Allied Industries Res. Assoc., 1955–62. Member: Council, British Inst. of Radiology, 1935–38; Council, IEE, 1937–40, 1946–49,

1950–53; Cttee, Nat. Physical Laboratory, 1950–60; Govt Cttee on Copyright, 1951; DSIR (Mem., Industrial Grants Cttee, 1950–58); Council, Physical Soc., 1953–56; Council, Southern Electricity Bd, 1953–62; Adv. Council, Science Museum; Adv. Council, RMC; Adv. Court, AEA; Nuclear Safety Adv. Council, Min. of Power, 1959–88. Trustee, British Museum, 1968–74. Governor, Downe House, 1959–69; Chm. Governors, Reading Technical Coll., 1959–68. Lord of the Manor, Aldermaston, 1953–87. Mem. Court, Worshipful Co. of Broderers, 1985– (Liveryman, 1967). FInstP; Founder FEng; Hon. FIEE; Fellow, Amer. Inst. of Electrical Engineers. Hon. DSc: Reading, 1960; City, 1970; Hon. DEng Sheffield, 1969. Röntgen Medal, British Inst. of Radiology; Thornton and Cooper Hill Medals, IEE; Melchett Medal, Inst. of Fuel. *Publications:* The Release and Use of Nuclear Energy, 1961; Rutherford: Father of Nuclear Energy (Rutherford Lecture 1972), 1973; The Royal Society and its Dining Clubs, 1975; Lightning: the long spark, 1977; Cockcroft and the Atom, 1983; Metropolitan-Vickers Electrical Co. and the Cavendish Laboratory, 1984; The Making of Physicists, 1987; Philately and the Royal Society, 1990; papers on high voltage and transient electrical phenomena, fission and fusion. *Recreations:* photography, travel, gardening, philately. *Address:* York Cottage, Lovel Road, Winkfield, Windsor, Berks. *T:* Winkfield Row (0344) 884501.

ALLIN, George, RCNC; Director General Ship Refitting, Ministry of Defence, since 1989; *b* 21 June 1933; *s* of late Henry Richard Allin and Mary Elizabeth Allin (*née* Wyatt); *m* 1st, 1956, Barbara May Short (marr. diss.); two *s*; 2nd, 1977, Janice Annette Richardson-Sandell. *Educ:* Devonport High Sch.; Devonport Dockyard Tech. Coll.; RNEC Manadon; RNC Greenwich. WhSch, BSc, CEng, MIEE, FIIM. Asst Elect. Engineer, 1957–59; HMS Belfast, 1959; Admiralty, Bath, 1959–62; Elect. Engineer, MoD (Navy), Bath, 1963–68; HM Dockyard, Devonport: Line Manager, 1968–70; Project Manager Frigates, 1970–71; Supt Elect. Engineer, Dep. Personnel Manager, 1971–74; Industrial Relations Manager, 1975; Org. and Develt. Div., Dockyard HQ, Bath, 1975–79; HM Dockyard, Rosyth: Project Manager, SSBN Refit, 1980–81; Production Dir, 1981–83; Dockyard HQ, Bath: Management Systems and Audit Div., 1984–85; Principal Dir, Policy and Plans, 1985–86; Principal Dir, Ship Refitting, MoD (Navy), Bath, 1986–87; Dir, Aldermaston Projects, Brown & Root (on secondment), 1987–89. FBIM. *Recreations:* chess, music, squash, snooker. *Address:* c/o DGSR, Ministry of Defence, Carpenter House, Bath. *T:* Bath (0225) 472285. *Club:* Bath and County (Bath).

ALLINSON, Sir Leonard; *see* Allinson, Sir W. L.

ALLINSON, Sir (Walter) Leonard, KCVO 1979 (MVO 1961); CMG 1976; HM Diplomatic Service, retired; *b* 1 May 1926; *o s* of Walter Allinson and Alice Frances Cassidy; *m* 1951, Margaret Patricia Watts; three *d* (of whom two are twins). *Educ:* Friern Barnet Grammar Sch.; Merton Coll., Oxford. First class in History, 1947; MA. Asst Principal, Ministry of Fuel and Power (Petroleum Div.), 1947–48; Asst Principal, later Principal, Min. of Education, 1948–58 (Asst Private Sec. to Minister, 1953–54); transf. CRO, 1958; First Sec. in Lahore and Karachi, 1960–62, Madras and New Delhi, 1963–66; Counsellor and Head of Political Affairs Dept, March 1968; Dep. Head, later Head, of Permanent Under Secretary's Dept, FCO, 1968–70; Counsellor and Head of Chancery, subsequently Deputy High Comr, Nairobi, 1970–73; RCDS, 1974; Diplomatic Service Inspectorate, 1975; Dep. High Comr and Minister, New Delhi, 1975–77; High Comr, Lusaka, 1978–80; Asst Under-Sec. of State (Africa), 1980–82; High Comr in Kenya and Ambassador to UN Environment Programme, 1982–86. Vice Pres., Royal African Soc., 1982–; Mem. Council, East Africa Inst., 1986–; Vice Chm., Kenya Soc., 1989–. *Address:* c/o National Westminster Bank, 6 Tothill Street, SW1. *Club:* Oriental.

ALLIOTT, Hon. Sir John (Downes), Kt 1986; **Hon. Mr Justice Alliott;** Judge of the High Court of Justice, Queen's Bench Division, since 1986; Presiding Judge, South Eastern Circuit, since 1989; *b* 9 Jan. 1932; *er s* of late Alexander Clifford Alliott and Ena Kathleen Alliott (*née* Downes); *m* 1957, Patsy Jennifer, *d* of late Gordon Beckles Willson; two *s* one *d*. *Educ:* Charterhouse; Peterhouse, Cambridge (Schol., BA). Coldstream Guards, 1950–51; Peterhouse, 1951–54; called to Bar, Inner Temple, 1955, Bencher 1980; QC 1973. Dep. Chm., E Sussex QS, 1970–71; Recorder, 1972–86; Leader of the SE Circuit, 1983–86. Mem., Home Office Adv. Bd on Restricted Patients, 1983–86. *Recreations:* rural pursuits, France and Italy, military history. *Address:* Royal Courts of Justice, Strand, WC2.

ALLISON, Brian George; Director: BIS Group Ltd (formerly Business Intelligence Services), since 1964 (Executive Chairman, 1985–87); NYNEX Network Systems Co. (Brussels) SA, since 1991; *b* 4 April 1933; *s* of Donald Brian Allison and Edith Maud Allison (*née* Humphries); *m* 1958, Glennis Mary Taylor; one *s* one *d*. *Educ:* Hele's Sch., Exeter; University Coll. London (BSc Econ). FCIM 1981. Flying Officer, RAF, 1955–58. Economist Statistician, Shell-Mex & BP, 1958; Marketing Res. Manager, Spicers, 1958–64; Business Intelligence Services: Dir and Gen. Manager, 1964–69; Man. Dir and Dep. Chm., 1969–74; Chm. and Man. Dir, 1974–81; Chm. and Chief Exec., 1981–85. Director: ECC Gp (formerly English China Clays), 1984–; NYNEX Inf. Solutions Gp, 1987–90; Brammer plc, 1988–; Electra Corporate Ventures, 1989–; London, Halifax Building Soc., 1991–. Vis. Prof., Univ. of Surrey, 1976–. Mem., ESRC, 1986–90. Distinguished Scholar, QUB, 1989. *Recreations:* tennis, travel, motoring, restoring historic properties. *Club:* Reform.

ALLISON, Charles Ralph, MA; Secretary, Lord Kitchener National Memorial Fund, 1968–83; Headmaster of Brentwood School, 1945–65; *b* 26 May 1903; *s* of Harry A. Allison, FCA, and Gertrude Wolfsberger; *m* 1930, Winifred Rita, *d* of A. C. Williams; two *s* one *d*. *Educ:* Caterham Sch.; University Coll., London; St Catharine's College, Cambridge (Exhibitioner). Assistant Master, Worksop College, 1928; Malvern College, 1929–36; English Tutor, Stowe School, 1936–38; Headmaster of Reigate Grammar School, 1938–40, and Alleyn's School, 1940–45. Formerly Mem. Cttee, Headmasters' Conf. (Vice-Chm. 1965). Governor: Sidney Perry Foundation (Chm., 1961–87; Pres., 1987; Jt Pres., 1988); Lindisfarne Coll., Ruabon, 1954–81; Brentwood Sch., 1970–85; Stowe Sch., 1965–80. Vice-Chm., Commonwealth Youth Exchange Cttee, 1970–72; Vice-Pres., Eastern Region, UNA, 1965–83. Mem., Nat. Commn for UNESCO, 1954–65; UK Delegate to Gen. Confs, 1958 and 1960. Member: Cttee, Governing Bodies' Assoc., 1972–79, 1980–83; Essex Education Cttee, 1967–74. Reader in the Parish of: St Mary's, Great Warley, 1967–83; St Alban, Tattenhall, 1985–. *Address:* Groom's Cottage, Chester Road, Tattenhall, Cheshire CH3 9AH. *T:* Tattenhall (0829) 70827. *Club:* East India, Devonshire, Sports and Public Schools.

ALLISON, Air Vice-Marshal Dennis, CB 1987; Chief Executive, North Western Regional Health Authority, since 1990 (General Manager, 1986–90); *b* 15 Oct. 1932; *m* 1964, Rachel Anne, *d* of Air Vice-Marshal J. G. Franks, *qv*; one *s* four *d*. *Educ:* RAF Halton; RAF Coll., Cranwell. Commnd, 1954; No 87 Sqdn, 1955–58; cfs 1958; Flying Instructor and Coll. Adjt, RAF Coll., 1958–61; CO, RAF Sharjah, 1961–62; Indian Jt Services Staff Coll., 1965; MoD Central Staffs, 1968–70; ndc, 1973; MoD Central Staffs, 1973–74; CO, RAF Coningsby, 1974–76; Canadian Nat. Defence Coll., 1977; MoD Central Staffs, 1978–79; Comdt, Central Flying Sch., 1979–83; Dir of Training (Flying), MoD, 1983–84; Dir of Management and Support of Intelligence, MoD, 1985–86; retired 1987. Member: NHS Trng Authority, 1988–91; Standing Cttee on Postgrad. Educn, 1988–; Steering Cttee on Pharmacist Postgrad. Educn, 1991–. Gov., Salford Coll. of Technology, 1987–89. QCVSA 1959. *Recreations:* bridge, golf. *Address:* The Old Forge, Castle Bytham, Grantham, Lincs NG33 4RU. *T:* Castle Bytham (078081) 372. *Club:* Royal Air Force.

ALLISON, John, CBE 1975; JP, DL; company director; *b* 4 Oct. 1919; *m* 1948, Elvira Gwendoline Lewis; one *s* two *d*. *Educ:* Morriston Elementary Sch.; Glanmor Secondary Sch.; Swansea Tech. Coll. In family business of quarrying to 1968, and musical instrument retailing, 1957–. Mem. (Lab) Swansea City Council, 1957–74, Leader, 1967–74 (Dep. Mayor, 1966–67 and 1972–73); Mem. (Lab) W Glamorgan County Council, 1974–89, Leader, 1977–89 (Chm., 1975–76); Chm., ACC, 1986–88. Contested (Lab) Barry, 1970. Chm., S Wales Police Authority, 1987–89. DL W Glam 1975; JP Swansea 1966. *Recreations:* fishing, gardening. *Address:* Penbryn, 155 Vicarage Road, Morriston, Swansea SA6 6DT. *T:* Swansea 71331. *Clubs:* Royal Over-Seas League; Morriston Golf.

ALLISON, Air Vice-Marshal John Shakespeare, CBE 1986 (MBE 1971); Assistant Chief of Defence Staff Operational Requirements (Air), Ministry of Defence, 1989–91; *b* 24 March 1943; *o s* of Walter Allison and Mollie Emmie Allison (*née* Poole); *m* 1966, Gillian Patricia Middleton; two *s* three *d*. *Educ:* Royal Grammar Sch., Guildford; RAF College, Cranwell; psc, rcds. Commissioned 1964; flying and staff appts include: 5 Sqn; 226 OCU; 310 TFTS (USAF), Arizona; OC 228 OCU; Station Comdr, RAF Wildenrath; Sec., Chiefs of Staff Cttee; Dir, Air Force Plans and Programmes, 1987–89. *Recreations:* air display flying, gliding, preservation of old cars and aircraft. *Address:* c/o National Westminster Bank, 24 Broadgate, Coventry CV1 1NB. *Club:* Royal Air Force.

ALLISON, Roderick Stuart; Director, Special Hazards Division, Health and Safety Executive, since 1989; *b* 28 Nov. 1936; *s* of Stuart Frew Allison and Poppy (*née* Hodges); *m* 1968, Anne Sergeant; one *s* one *d*. *Educ:* Manchester Grammar Sch.; Balliol Coll., Oxford. Entered Ministry of Labour, 1959; Private Sec. to Perm. Sec., 1963–64; Principal, 1964; Civil Service Dept, 1969–71; Asst Sec., 1971, Under Sec., 1977, Dept of Employment. Chm., Adv. Cttee on Dangerous Substances, HSC, 1989–. *Recreations:* reading, music, sailing. *Address:* c/o Health and Safety Executive, Baynards House, 1 Chepstow Place, Westbourne Grove, W2 4TF.

ALLISON, Ronald William Paul, CVO 1978; journalist, broadcaster; television consultant; Chairman, Television Barter International, since 1990; *b* 26 Jan. 1932. *Educ:* Weymouth Grammar Sch.; Taunton's Sch., Southampton. Reporter, Hampshire Chronicle, 1952–57; Reporter, BBC, 1957–67; freelance broadcaster, 1968–69; special correspondent, BBC, 1969–73; Press Sec. to Queen, 1973–78; regular presenter and commentator, Thames TV, 1978–; Controller of Sport and Outside Broadcasts, 1980–85, Dir of Corporate Affairs, 1986–89, Thames TV. *Publications:* Look Back in Wonder, 1968; The Queen, 1973; Charles, Prince of our Time, 1978; The Country Life Book of Britain in the Seventies, 1980. *Recreations:* photography, watching football. *Clubs:* Royal Automobile; Stage Golf Soc.; Old Tauntonians (Southampton).

ALLISON, Rt. Rev. Sherard Falkner, MA, DD, LLD; *b* 19 Jan. 1907; *s* of Reverend W. S. Allison; *m* 1936, Ruth Hills; one *s* two *d* (and one *s* decd). *Educ:* Dean Close School, Cheltenham; Jesus Coll., Cambridge (Scholar); Ridley Hall, Cambridge. 1st Cl. Classical Tripos, Parts I and II; 2nd Class Theological Tripos, Part I and Jeremie Septuagint Prize; Curate of St James', Tunbridge Wells, 1931–34; Chaplain of Ridley Hall, Cambridge, and Examining Chaplain to Bishop of Bradford, 1934–36; Vicar of Rodbourne Cheney, Swindon, 1936–40; Vicar of Erith, 1940–45; Principal of Ridley Hall, Cambridge, 1945–50; Bishop of Chelmsford, 1951–61; Bishop of Winchester, and Prelate of the Most Noble Order of the Garter, 1961–74. Examining Chaplain to Bishop of Rochester, 1945, and to Bishop of Ely, 1947; Select Preacher: Univ. of Cambridge, 1946, 1955, 1962; Univ. of Oxford, 1953–55, 1963; Proctor in Convocation, Diocese of Ely, 1949. Hon. Fellow, Jesus College, Cambridge, 1963. DD, Lambeth, 1951; Hon. DD: Occidental Coll., Los Angeles, 1959; Wycliffe Coll., Toronto, 1959; Hon. STD, Church Divinity Sch. of the Pacific, 1959; Hon. LLD: Sheffield, 1960; Southampton, 1974. *Publication:* The Christian Life, 1938 (Joint). *Recreations:* sailing, water-colour sketching, bird watching, gardening. *Address:* Winton Lodge, Alde Lane, Aldeburgh, Suffolk IP15 5DZ. *T:* Aldeburgh (0728) 452485.

ALLISS, Peter; golfer; television commentator; *b* 28 Feb. 1931; *s* of Percy Alliss and Dorothy Alliss (*née* Rust); *m* 1st, 1953, Joan; one *s* one *d*; 2nd, 1969, Jacqueline Anne; two *s* one *d*. *Educ:* Queen Elizabeth's Grammar Sch., Wimborne; Crosby House, Bournemouth. Nat. Service, RAF Regt, 1949–51. Professional golfer, 1946; played in 8 Ryder Cup matches and 10 Canada Cup (now World Cup) matches; winner of 21 major events; open championships of Spain, Portugal, Italy, Brazil. Past Pres., Ladies' PGA and British Green Keepers' Assoc.; twice Captain, British PGA; golf course architect. *Publications:* Easier Golf (with Paul Trevillion), 1969; Bedside Golf, 1980; Shell Book of Golf, 1981; The Duke, 1983; Play Golf with Peter Alliss, 1983; The Who's Who of Golf, 1983; (with Michael Hobbs) The Open, 1984; Golfer's Logbook, 1984; Lasting the Course, 1984; More Bedside Golf, 1984; Peter Alliss' Most Memorable Golf, 1986; Peter Alliss' Supreme Champions of Golf, 1986; (ed) Winning Golf, 1986; Yet More Bedside Golf, 1986; Play Better Golf with Peter Alliss, 1989; (with Michael Hobbs) Peter Alliss' Best 100 Golfers, 1989; (with Bob Ferrier) The Best of Golf, 1989; *autobiography:* Alliss in Wonderland, 1964; Peter Alliss: an autobiography, 1981. *Recreation:* talking and taking wine with chums. *Address:* Bucklands, Hindhead, Surrey GU26 6HY. *Clubs:* Lansdowne, Crockfords, Ritz Casino.

ALLNUTT, Ian Peter, OBE; MA; *b* 26 April 1917; *s* of Col E. B. Allnutt, CBE, MC, and Joan C. Gainsford; *m* 1946, Doreen Louise Lenagan; four *d*. *Educ:* Imperial Service Coll., Windsor; Sidney Sussex Coll., Cambridge. HM Colonial Service, 1939–46, Nigeria, with break, 1940–45, for service in World War II, Nigeria Regt, RWAFF (despatches). Service with the British Council in Peru, E Africa, Colombia, Argentina, Malta, London and Mexico, 1946–77. OBE 1976; Insignia of Aztec Eagle, 1975. *Recreations:* rowing, swimming, pre-Columbian America, the Hispanic world. *Club:* Leander (Henley-on-Thames).

ALLOTT, Prof. Antony Nicolas, JP; Professor of African and Comparative Law, University of Buckingham, since 1987; *b* 30 June 1924; *s* of late Reginald William Allott and Dorothy Allott (*née* Dobson); *m* 1952, Anna Joan Sargant, *d* of late Tom Sargant, OBE, and of Marie Černy; two *s* two *d*. *Educ:* Downside Sch.; New Coll., Oxford. Lieut Royal Northumberland Fusiliers and King's African Rifles, 1944–46. BA Oxon (1st class Hons Jurisprudence), 1948; PhD London 1954. Lecturer in African Law, School of Oriental and African Studies, London, 1948–60; Reader in African Law, 1960–64, Prof. of African Law, 1964–86, Univ. of London. Vis. Prof., Université de Paris I, 1984. Hon. Director, Africa Centre, 1963–66; Pres., African Studies Assoc. of UK, 1969–70 (past Hon. Treas.); Vice-Pres., Internat. African Law Assoc., 1967. Académicien associé, Académie Internat. de Droit Comparé, 1982–; Corresponding Mem., Académie Royale des Sciences d'Outre-Mer, Belgium, 1980. Vice-Chm., Governing Body, Plater Coll.,

Oxford; Govr, St Bartholomew's Hosp. Med. Sch. Member: Senate, Univ. of London, 1978–86; Council, Commonwealth Magistrates' and Judges' Assoc. (formerly Commonwealth Magistrates' Assoc.), 1972–; Chm., Mddx Magistrates' Cts Cttee, 1982–86. Chm., Barnet Petty Sessional Area, 1986. JP: Middlesex 1969–86 (Chm., Gore Div., 1985–86); Oxfordshire 1987–. KSG 1990. *Publications:* Essays in African Law, with special reference to the Law of Ghana, 1960; (ed) Judicial and Legal Systems in Africa, 1962, 2nd edn 1970; New Essays in African Law, 1970; The Limits of Law, 1980; (ed with G. Woodman) People's Law and State Law, 1985; articles in legal and other jls. *Recreations:* music, gardening, silviculture. *Address:* School of Law, University of Buckingham, Buckingham MK18 1EG.
See also R. M. Allott.

ALLOTT, Air Cdre Molly Greenwood, CB 1975; *b* 28 Dec. 1918; *d* of late Gerald William Allott. *Educ:* Sheffield High Sch. for Girls. Served War of 1939–45: joined WAAF, 1941; served in: Egypt, Singapore, Germany. Staff of AOC-in-C: RAF Germany, 1960–63; Fighter Command, 1963–66; Training Command, 1971–73; Dir, WRAF, 1973–76. ADC 1973–76; Nat. Chm., Girls' Venture Corps, 1977–82; Member: Council, Union Jack Club, 1977–; Main Grants Cttee, RAF Benevolent Fund, 1977–82. FBIM. *Recreations:* travel, fine and decorative arts. *Address:* 15 Camden Hurst, Milford-on-Sea, Lymington, Hants SO41 0WL. *Clubs:* Royal Air Force, Royal Lymington Yacht.

ALLOTT, Robin Michael; Under-Secretary, Establishment Personnel Division, Departments of Industry and Trade, 1978–80; *b* 9 May 1926; *s* of Reginald William Allott and Dorothy (*née* Dobson). *Educ:* The Oratory Sch., Caversham; New Coll., Oxford; Sheffield Univ. Asst Principal, BoT, 1948; UK Delegn to OECD, Paris, 1952; Private Sec. to Sec. for Overseas Trade, 1953; Principal, Office for Scotland, Glasgow, 1954; UK Delegn to UN Conf. on Trade and Devel, Geneva, 1964; Asst Sec., BoT, 1965; Counsellor, UK Delegn to EEC, Brussels, 1971; sabbatical year, New Coll., Oxford, 1974–75; Dept of Industry (motor industry), 1975; Under-Sec., Dept of Trade, 1976. *Publications:* The Physical Foundation of Language, 1973; The Motor Theory of Language Origin, 1989. *Recreations:* studying the evolutionary relation of language, perception and action; computer programming. *Address:* 5 Fitzgerald Park, Seaford, East Sussex BN25 1AX. *T:* Seaford (0323) 896022.
See also A. N. Allott.

ALLPORT, Denis Ivor; Chairman, 1979–85 and Chief Executive, 1977–85, Metal Box Ltd (Director, 1973–85, Managing Director, 1977–79, Deputy Chairman, 1979); *b* 20 Nov. 1922; *s* of late A. R. Allport and late E. M. Allport (*née* Mashman); *m* 1949, Diana (*née* Marler); two *s* one *d*. *Educ:* Highgate School. Served War, Indian Army, 1941–46; joined Metal Box Ltd, 1946; various appts in UK, Singapore and Pakistan; Man. Dir, Metal Box Co. of India, 1969–70; Dir, Metal Box Overseas Ltd, 1970–74. Chm., Castle Underwriting Agents Ltd, 1989– (Dir, 1988–); Director: Beecham Gp plc, 1981–88; Marley plc, 1985–. Member: Nat. Enterprise Bd, 1980–83; NRDC, 1981–83; Neill Cttee of Enquiry into Regulatory Arrangements at Lloyd's, 1986. Gov., Highgate Sch., 1981–. FBIM 1977. *Recreation:* golf. *Address:* The Barn, Highmoor, Henley-on-Thames, Oxon RG9 5DH. *T:* Nettlebed (0491) 641283. *Clubs:* MCC, Oriental.

ALLSOP, Peter Henry Bruce, CBE 1984; FRSA; FBIM; Publishing Consultant, Publishers' Management Advisers, since 1983; *b* 22 Aug. 1924; *s* of late Herbert Henry Allsop and of Elsie Hilpern (*née* Whitaker); *m* 1950, Patricia Elizabeth Kingwell Bown; two *s* one *d*. *Educ:* Haileybury; Caius Coll., Cambridge (MA). Called to Bar, Lincoln's Inn, 1948, Bencher, 1989. Temp. Asst Principal, Air Min., 1944–48; Barrister in practice, 1948–50; Sweet & Maxwell: Editor, 1950–59; Dir, 1960–64; Man. Dir, 1965–73; Chm., 1974–80; Dir, Associated Book Publishers, 1963, Asst Man. Dir, 1965–67, Man. Dir, 1968–76, Chm., 1976–88. Chm., Teleordering Ltd, 1978–91; Trustee and Vice-Chm., Yale University Press, 1984– (Dir, 1981–84); Director: J. Whitaker & Sons, 1987–; Lloyd's of London Press, 1991–. Mem. Council, Publishers Assoc., 1969–81 (Treasurer, 1973–75, 1979–81; Pres., 1975–77; Vice-Pres., 1977–78; Trustee, 1982–); Member: Printing and Publishing Industry Trng Bd, 1977–79; Publishers' Adv. Cttee, British Council, 1980–85; Chm., Management Cttee, Book House Training Centre, 1980–86; Dir, Woodard Schools (Western Div.) Ltd, 1985–. Chm., Social Security Appeal Tribunal, 1982–87 (Mem., 1979–82). Chm., Book Trade Benevolent Soc., 1986– (Trustee, 1976–85; Dir, 1985). Mem., St Albans City Council, 1955–58. Chm., Diocesan Adv. Cttee, Bath and Wells, 1985–; Trustee, St Andrews Conservation Trust, Wells, 1987–. Chm. Council, King's Coll., Taunton, 1986– (Mem., 1983–86). Editor, later Editor Emeritus: Current Law, 1952–90; Criminal Law Review, 1954–90. *Publications:* (ed) Bowstead's Law of Agency, 11th edn, 1951. *Recreations:* gardening, hill walking, theatre. *Address:* Manor Farm, Charlton Mackrell, Somerton, Somerset TA11 7BQ. *Clubs:* Garrick, Farmers'.

ALLSOPP, family name of **Baron Hindlip.**

ALLSOPP, Bruce; *see* Allsopp, H. B.

ALLSOPP, Hon. Charles (Henry); Chairman, Christie, Manson & Woods, since 1986; Director, Christies International, since 1986; *b* 5 Aug. 1940; *e s* and *heir* of 5th Baron Hindlip, *qv*; *m* 1968, Fiona Victoria Jean Atherley, *d* of late Hon. William Johnston McGowan, 2nd *s* of 1st Baron McGowan, KBE; one *s* three *d*. *Educ:* Eton. Coldstream Guards, 1959–62; joined Christie's, 1962; Gen. Manager, Christie's New York, 1965–70; Christie, Manson & Woods: Dir, 1970; Dep. Chm., 1985. Member of Lloyd's. *Recreations:* painting, shooting, ski-ing. *Address:* Christie, Manson & Woods, 8 King Street, St James's, SW1Y 6QT. *T:* 071–839 9060; 9 Cottesmore Gardens, W8. *T:* 071–937 6038; The Cedar House, Inkpen, Berks. *Clubs:* White's, Pratt's.

ALLSOPP, (Harold) Bruce, BArch, DipCD, FSA, MRTPI; author and artist; *b* Oxford, 4 July 1912; *s* of Henry Allsopp and Elizabeth May Allsopp (*née* Robertson); *m* 1935, Florence Cyrilla Woodroffe, ARCA; two *s*. *Educ:* Manchester Grammar Sch.; Liverpool School of Architecture. BArch (1st Cl. Hons), Liverpool, 1933; Rome Finalist, 1934; Diploma in Civic Design 1935; ARIBA 1935; AMTPI 1936; FRIBA 1955; FSA 1968. Asst Architect in Chichester and London, 1934–35; Lecturer, Leeds Coll. of Art, 1935–40. War Service 1940–46, N Africa, Italy, Captain RE. Lecturer in Architecture, Univ. of Durham, 1946; Sen. Lecturer, 1955; Sen. Lecturer, Univ. of Newcastle upon Tyne, 1963, Dir of Architectural Studies, 1965–69; Sen. Lecturer in History of Architecture, 1969–73; Reader, 1973–77. Chm., Oriel Press Ltd, 1962–87; Dir, Routledge & Kegan Paul Books Ltd, 1974–85. Chairman: Soc. of Architectural Historians of GB, 1959–65; Independent Publishers Guild, 1971–73; Master, Art Workers Guild, 1970; Pres., Fedn of Northern Art Socs, 1980–83. Presenter, TV films, including Fancy Gothic, 1974; The Bowes Museum, 1977; Country Houses and Landscape of Northumberland, 1979. *Publications:* Art and the Nature of Architecture, 1952; Decoration and Furniture, Vol. 1 1952, Vol. 2 1953; A General History of Architecture, 1955; Style in the Visual Arts, 1957; Possessed, 1959; The Future of the Arts, 1959; A History of Renaissance Architecture, 1959; The Naked Flame, 1962; Architecture, 1964; To Kill a King, 1965; A History of Classical Architecture, 1965; Historic Architecture of Newcastle upon Tyne, 1967; Civilization, the Next Stage, 1969; The Study of Architectural History, 1970; Modern Architecture of Northern England, 1970; Inigo Jones on Palladio, 1970; Romanesque Architecture, 1971; Ecological Morality, 1972; The Garden Earth, 1973; Towards a Humane Architecture, 1974; Return of the Pagan, 1974; Cecilia, 1975; Inigo Jones and the Lords A'Leaping, 1975; A Modern Theory of Architecture, 1977; Appeal to the Gods, 1980; Should Man Survive?, 1982; The Country Life Companion to British and European Architecture, 1985; Social Responsibility and the Responsible Society, 1985; Guide de l'Architecture, 1985; Larousse Guide to European Architecture, 1985; (with Ursula Clark): Architecture of France, 1963; Architecture of Italy, 1964; Architecture of England, 1964; Photography for Tourists, 1966; Historic Architecture of Northumberland, 1969; Historic Architecture of Northumberland and Newcastle, 1977; English Architecture, 1979; (with U. Clark and H. W. Booton): The Great Tradition of Western Architecture, 1966; articles in Encyclopedia Americana, Encyclopaedia Britannica, Jl of RSA, etc. *Recreations:* piano and organ, gardening. *Address:* Woodburn, 3 Batt House Road, Stocksfield, Northumberland NE43 7QZ. *T:* Stocksfield (0661) 842323. *Club:* Athenæum.

ALLUM, Sarah Elizabeth Royle, (Mrs R. G. Allum); *see* Walker, S. E. R.

AL-MASHAT, Mohamed Sadiq, PhD; Ambassador of the Republic of Iraq to the United States of America, since 1989; *b* 15 Dec. 1930; *s* of Mohamed Sadiq Al-Mashat and Fakhria Issa; *m* 1972, Mrs Sammar Hadid; two *s* one *d*. *Educ:* College of Law, Baghdad Univ. (grad. in Law); Univ. of California-Berkeley (BA, MA Criminology); Univ. of Maryland (PhD Sociology). Dir of Fellowship and Scholarship, Min. of Educn, and Lectr, Univ. of Baghdad, 1961–63; Under Sec., Min. of Educn, 1963; Professor: Univ. of Baghdad, 1963–64; Mohamed V Univ., Rabat, 1964–66; Prof. of Sociology, Baghdad Univ., 1966–68; Under Sec., Min. of Labour and Social Affairs, 1968–69; Amb. to France, 1969–70; Pres., Mosul Univ., Iraq, 1970–77; Minister of Higher Educn and Sci. Researches, 1977–78; Ambassador: to Austria, 1978–81; to France, 1982–87; to UK, 1987–89. Grand Cross (Austria), 1982. *Publication:* Introduction to Sociology, 1967. *Recreations:* swimming, tennis, reading. *Address:* Embassy of Iraq, 1801 P Street NW, Washington, DC 20036, USA. *Clubs:* Al-Sayid Hunting, Al-A'alwiya (Baghdad).

ALMENT, Sir (Edward) Anthony (John), Kt 1980; FRCOG; Consultant Obstetrician and Gynaecologist, Northampton, 1960–85, retired; *b* 3 Feb. 1922; *s* of Edward and Alice Alment; *m* 1946, Elizabeth Innes Bacon. *Educ:* Marlborough Coll.; St Bartholomew's Hosp. Med. Coll. MRCS, LRCP 1945; FRCOG 1967 (MRCOG 1951); FRCPI 1979; FRCPE 1981; FRCGP 1982. Served RAFVR, 1947–48. Trng appointments: St Bartholomew's Hosp., 1945–46 and 1954–60; Norfolk and Norwich Hosp., 1948; Queen Charlotte's Hosp. and Chelsea Hosp. for Women, 1949–50; London Hosp., 1951–52. Royal Coll. of Obstetricians and Gynaecologists: Mem. Council, 1961–67; Hon. Sec., 1968–73; Pres., 1978–81. Chm., Cttee of Enquiry into Competence to Practise, 1973–76; Member: Oxford Reg. Hosp. Bd, 1968–74 (Chm., Med. Adv. Cttee, 1972–74); Oxford RHA, 1973–75; Central Midwives Bd, 1967–68; UK Central Council for Nursing, Midwifery and Health Visiting, 1980–83. Examiner: RCOG; Univs of Cambridge, Leeds and Dar-es-Salaam. Hon. Fellow, Amer. Assoc. of Obstetricians and Gynaecologists, 1973 (Joseph Price Oration, 1972); Hon. FRACOG 1984. Hon. DSc Leicester, 1982. *Publications:* Competence to Practise, 1976; contrib. to med. jls; articles on wine-related subjects. *Recreations:* wine, fishing, engineering, church architecture. *Address:* Winston House, Boughton, Northampton NN2 8RR.

ALMOND, Thomas Clive, OBE 1989; HM Diplomatic Service; Assistant Marshal of the Diplomatic Corps and Assistant Head of Protocol Department, since 1988; *b* 30 Nov. 1939; *s* of late Thomas and Eveline Almond; *m* 1965, Auriol Gala Elizabeth Annette Hendry. *Educ:* Bristol Grammar Sch. Entered HM Diplomatic Service, 1967; Accra, 1968; Paris, 1971; FCO, 1975; Brussels, 1978; Jakarta, 1980; Brazzaville, 1983; Ambassador to People's Republic of the Congo, 1987–88. *Recreations:* travelling, golf. *Address:* c/o Foreign and Commonwealth Office, King Charles Street, SW1A 2AH.

AL-NIMR, Nabih; Ambassador of Jordan to Egypt, since 1988; *b* 26 Oct. 1931; *m* 1961, Rabab Al-Nimr; one *s* one *d*. *Educ:* Univ. of Alexandria. Attaché in Ankara, Karachi, Bonn, 1955–62; Third Sec., Tunisia, 1962–65; First Sec., London, 1967–71; Counsellor: Kuwait, 1971–73; Damascus, 1973–74; Ambassador to Syrian Arab Republic, 1974–78; Amb. to Fed. Rep. of Germany and non-resident Amb. to Sweden, Denmark, Norway, Luxembourg, 1978–81; Amb. to Tunisia and Perm. Rep. of Jordan to Arab League, 1981–85; Amb. to UK, 1985–87; Sec. Gen., Min. of Foreign Affairs, 1987–88. Decorations from Jordan, Syria, Germany, Tunisia, Italy, Belgium, Ethiopia. *Address:* c/o Ministry of Foreign Affairs, Amman, Jordan.

ALPHAND, Hervé; Grand Officier, Légion d'Honneur, 1968; *b* 1907; *s* of Charles Hervé and Jeanne Alphand; *m* 1958, Nicole Merenda (*d* 1979). *Educ:* Lycée Janson de Sailly; Ecole des Sciences Politiques. Inspector of Finances and Dir Dept of Treaties, Min. of Commerce, 1937–38; Financial Attaché to Embassy, Washington, 1940–41; Dir of Economic Affairs for French National Cttee in London, 1941–44; Director-General, Economic, Financial and Technical Affairs (Min. of Foreign Affairs), 1945; French Ambassador to OEEC; French Dep. to Atlantic Council, 1950, and Mem. NATO Perm. Council, 1952–54; Ambassador: to UN, 1955–56; to USA, 1956–65; Secretary-General, Min. of Foreign Affairs, France, 1965–73. *Publication:* L'étonnement d'être, 1978. *Address:* 122 rue de Grenelle, 75007 Paris, France.

ALPORT, family name of **Baron Alport.**

ALPORT, Baron, *cr* 1961, of Colchester (Life Peer); **Cuthbert James McCall Alport,** PC 1960; TD 1949; DL; *b* 22 March 1912; *o s* of late Prof. Arthur Cecil Alport, MD, FRCP, and of Janet, *y d* of James McCall, Dumfriesshire; *m* 1945, Rachel Cecilia (*d* 1983), *o d* of late Lt-Col R. C. Bingham, CVO, DSO, and late Dorothy Louisa Pratt; one *s* two *d*. *Educ:* Haileybury; Pembroke Coll., Cambridge. MA History and Law; Pres., Cambridge Union Society, 1935. Tutor Ashridge Coll., 1935–37. Barrister-at-Law, Middle Temple. Joined Artists Rifles, 1934. Served War of 1939–45: Hon. Lieut-Col; Director Conservative Political Centre, 1945–50. MP (C) Colchester division of Essex, 1950–61; Chairman Joint East and Central African Board, 1953–55; Governor, Charing Cross Hospital, 1954–55. Asst Postmaster-General, Dec. 1955–Jan. 1957; Parliamentary Under-Secretary of State, Commonwealth Relations Office, 1957–59; Minister of State, Commonwealth Relations Office, Oct. 1959–March 1961; British High Commissioner in the Federation of Rhodesia and Nyasaland, 1961–63; Mem. of Council of Europe, 1964–65; British Govt Representative to Rhodesia, June-July 1967. A Dep. Speaker, House of Lords, 1971–82, 1983–. Adviser to the Home Secretary, 1974–82. Chm., New Theatre Trust, 1970–83; Pres., Minories Art Gall., Colchester, 1978–88. Life Governor, Haileybury Coll. Master, Skinners' Co., 1969–70, 1982–83. Pro-Chancellor, City Univ., 1972–79. Chm., Acad. Adv. Cttee, Gresham Coll., 1984–86. High Steward of Colchester, 1967–; DL Essex 1974. Hon. DCL City Univ., 1979. *Publications:* Kingdoms in Partnership, 1937; Hope in Africa, 1952; The Sudden Assignment, 1965. *Address:* The Cross House, Layer de la Haye, Colchester, Essex CO2 0JG. *T:* Layer de la Haye (020634) 217. *Clubs:* Pratt's, Farmers'.
See also I. C. Taylor.

AL-QARAGULI, Dr Wahbi Abdul Razaq Fattah; Ambassador of Iraq to Austria, since 1985; *b* Baghdad, 1929; *m* Mrs Suhaila Al-Khatib; two *s* one *d*. *Educ:* Univ. of Baghdad (BA Econs 1954); Univ. of Neuchâtel, Switzerland (PhD 1962). Dep. Perm. Rep., UN, Geneva, 1964–68; Counsellor: Algeria, 1968; China, 1970; Minister Plenipotentiary, Lebanon, 1972–76; Dep. Gen. Dir, Econs Dept, Min. of Foreign Affairs, Baghdad, 1977; Ambassador to Indonesia and (non-resident) to Australia, NZ, Singapore and PNG, 1977; Chief of Protocol, Presidential Palace, Baghdad, 1978; Ambassador: to Malaysia and (non-resident) to Philippines, 1980–82; to UK, 1982–85. *Address:* Iraqi Embassy, Johannes Gasse 26, A-1010 Vienna, Austria.

AL-SABAH, Shaikh Saud Nasir; Ambassador of Kuwait to the United States of America, and to Canada and Venezuela, since 1981; *b* 3 Oct. 1944; *m* 1962, Shaikha Awatif Al-Sabah; three *s* two *d*. Barrister-at-law, Gray's Inn. Entered Legal Dept, Min. of Foreign Affairs, Kuwait. Representative of Kuwait: to 6th Cttee of UN Gen. Assembly, 1969–74; to Seabed Cttee of UN, 1969–73; Vice-Chm., Delegn of Kuwait to Conf. of Law of the Sea, 1974–75; Rep. of Delegn to Conf. of Law of Treaties, 1969; Ambassador to the Ct of St James's, and to Norway, Sweden and Denmark, 1975–80. *Address:* Embassy of Kuwait, 2940 Tilden Street NW, Washington, DC 20008, USA.

AL SABBAGH, Salman Abdul Wahab; Ambassador of the State of Bahrain to the Court of St James's, 1984–90; *b* 1932; *m* Mrs Sharifa Ahmed Abdulla. *Educ:* Western Elem. Sch.; Manama Secondary Sch.; Cairo Univ. (BA Accountancy). Chief Auditor, MoD, Kuwait, 1962–66; Accountant, Bank of Bahrain, Bahrain, 1967–69; Gen. Man., Agency of General Motors & Commodities, 1969–72; Min. of Foreign Affairs, Bahrain: posts held in Iraq, France and UK, 1972–84. *Address:* c/o Ministry of Foreign Affairs, Manama, State of Bahrain.

AL-SALIHI, Dr Azmi Shafeeq; Iraq Ambassador to the Court of St James's, 1989–91; *b* 1934; *m* 1965, Najla A. F. Mohamad Al-Salihi; three *s* two *d*. *Educ:* Univ. of London (PhD Political Literature). Dir Gen., Cinema and Theatre, Ministry of Information, 1968–70; Dean, Al-Mustansiria Univ., 1970–72; post-graduate student, London Univ., 1972–76; Dir of Languages Dept, Educn Coll., Baghdad Univ., 1976–79; Dir Gen., Dep. Prime Minister's Office, 1979–83; Ambassador and Dir Gen., Dept of Research, Min. of Foreign Affairs, 1983–89; Dir Gen., Inf. and Research Centre, Revolutionary Command Council, 1985–87; Acting Dean, Inst. of External Service, Min. of Foreign Affairs, 1987–89. Rapporteur, Rewrite History of Iraq Cttee; Member: High Commn for Enhancement of Arabic Language; Editl Cttee, Al-Dhad; Central Cttee for Publishing; Union of Iraqi Authors. *Publications:* On the Aesthetics, 1969; The Islamic Poet Al-Tirmmah Al-Tai'i, 1972; The Origin of the Theatre, 1975. *Recreations:* writing books, reading. *Address:* c/o Ministry of Foreign Affairs, Karradat Mariam, Baghdad, Iraq.

AL SHAKAR, Karim Ebrahim; Ambassador of the State of Bahrain to the Court of St James's, since 1990; *b* 23 Dec. 1945; *m* Fatima Al Mansouri; three *d*. *Educ:* primary and secondary educn, Bahrain; Delhi Univ. (BA political science 1970). Attaché, Min. of Foreign Affairs, 1970; Mem., Perm. Mission to UN, later Min. of Foreign Affairs, 1972–76; First Sec., 1978; Counsellor, 1981; Perm. Rep. to UN, Geneva and Consul-Gen., 1982–87 (non-resident Ambassador to Germany and Austria and to UN, Vienna, 1984); Ambassador and Perm. Rep to UN, New York, 1987–90. *Recreation:* travelling. *Address:* Embassy of the State of Bahrain, 98 Gloucester Road, SW7 4AU. *T:* 071–370 5132.

AL-SHAWI, Hisham Ibrahim; Ambassador of the Republic of Iraq to Canada, since 1985 (non-resident Ambassador to Jamaica, since 1986, to Grenada, since 1987); *b* Baghdad, 16 March 1931; *s* of Maj.-Gen. Ibrahim Al-Shawi and Najia Al-Shawi; *m* 1966, Hadia Al-Atia; one *s* one *d*. *Educ:* Baghdad (High Sch. Certif., Lit. Section, 1948); Amer. Univ. of Beirut (BA with Distinction Pol. Science, 1952); Univ. of Oxford (MLitt Internat. Relations, 1956). Asst Instructor, Instructor, then Asst Prof. and Head of Dept of Politics, Univs of Baghdad and Al-Mustansyria, 1958–70; Dean, Coll. of Law and Politics, Mustansyria Univ., 1970–72; Ambassador, Min. of Foreign Affairs, 1972; Perm. Rep. at UN, Geneva, 1972; Minister of Higher Educn and Scientific Res., 1972–74; Minister of State, 1974–75; Minister of State for For. Affairs, 1975–76; Ambassador, Min. of For. Affairs, 1976–77; Perm. Rep. at UN, New York, 1977; Head, Diwan of Presidency of Republic, 1977–78; Ambassador, Min. of For. Affairs, 1978; Ambassador to UK, 1978–82, to Austria, 1982–85. First President: Iraqi Political Science Assoc.; Iraqi UN Assoc.; Chm., Iraqi Atomic Energy Commn, 1972–74; Mem., UN Sub-Commn on Prevention of Racial Discrimination and Protection of Minorities, 1972–74; Rep. on Commn on Human Rights, 26th–30th Sessions. Gov. for Iraq, IAEA, 1974–76. Statue of Victory Personality of the Year, Centro Studi e Ricerche delle Nazioni, Parma, Italy, 1984. *Publications:* From the Essence of the Matter: a collection of articles, 1966; The Art of Negotiation, 1967; An Introduction in Political Science, 1967 (new edn 1978). *Recreations:* horse riding, hunting. *Address:* Embassy of the Republic of Iraq, 215 McLeod Street, Ottawa, Ont. K2P 0Z8, Canada. *Club:* Iraqi Hunting (Iraq).

ALSTEAD, Stanley, CBE 1960; MD, FRCP; Professor Emeritus, Regius Chair of Materia Medica, University of Glasgow; formerly Senior Visiting Physician, Stobhill Hospital, Glasgow; *b* 6 June 1905; *s* of late Robert Alstead, OBE, sometime MP, and Anne Alstead; *m* 1st, 1932, Nora (*d* 1980), 2nd *d* of late M. W. Sowden and late Nell Sowden; one *s*; 2nd, 1982, Dr Jessie, (Janet), McAlpine Pope. *Educ:* Wigan Grammar Sch.; Liverpool Univ. Held various appts in north of England; appointed Pollok Lecturer in Pharmacology, Univ. of Glasgow, 1932, and became interested in clinical aspects of subject; Cons. Physician, Highlands and Islands, based Inverness, 1947; Regius Prof. of Materia Medica and Therapeutics, Univ. of Glasgow, 1948–70. Hon. Prof., Univ. of East Africa (Makerere University Coll.) and Hon. Physician to Kenyatta Nat. Hosp., Nairobi, Kenya, 1965–66. Served War of 1939–45, in RAMC as medical specialist to 5 CCS in Tunisia and Sicily, and in Belgium and Egypt as Officer in Charge of Med. Div. 67 Gen. Hosp. and 63 Gen. Hosp. with rank of Lt-Col (despatches). MD Liverpool (N. E. Roberts Prize); FRCP; FRCPGlas; FRCPE; FRSE. Pres. RFPSG (now RCPSGlas), 1956–58 (Hon. Fellow, 1979). Member: British Pharmacopœia Commn, 1953–57; Standing Jt Cttee on Classification of Proprietary Preparations; Commn. on Spiritual Healing (General Assembly of Church of Scotland). Jt Editor, Textbook of Medical Treatment. *Publications:* papers in med. jls on results of original research in clinical pharmacology. *Recreations:* gardening, music (violin) and reading poetry. *Address:* Glenholme, Glen Road, Dunblane, Perthshire FK15 0DJ. *T:* Dunblane (0786) 822466. *Club:* College (Glasgow).

ALSTON, (Arthur) Rex; freelance broadcaster and journalist with The Daily Telegraph, retired 1988; BBC Commentator, 1943–61; *b* 2 July 1901; *e s* of late Arthur Fawssett Alston, Suffragan Bishop of Middleton, and late Mary Isabel Alston; *m* 1st, 1932, Elspeth (*d* 1985), *d* of late Sir Stewart Stockman and Lady Stockman; one *s* one *d*; *m* 2nd, 1986, Joan, *widow* of T. C. A. Wilson, dental surgeon. *Educ:* Trent College; Clare College, Cambridge. Assistant Master, Bedford School, 1924–41. Joined BBC, Jan. 1942. *Publications:* Taking the Air, 1950; Over to Rex Alston, 1953; Test Commentary, 1956; Watching Cricket, 1962. *Recreations:* golf, gardening. *Address:* Garlands, Ewhurst, Cranleigh, Surrey GU6 7QA. *T:* Cranleigh (0483) 277315. *Clubs:* East India, Devonshire, Sports and Public Schools, MCC.

ALSTON, Rt. Rev. Mgr. J(oseph) Leo; Parish Priest, Sacred Heart Church, Ainsdale, Southport, since 1972; *b* 17 Dec. 1917; *s* of Benjamin Alston and Mary Elizabeth (*née* Moss). *Educ:* St Mary's School, Chorley; Upholland College, Wigan; English Coll., Rome; Christ's College, Cambridge. Priest, 1942; Licentiate in Theology, Gregorian Univ., Rome, 1942; BA (1st Cl. Hons Classics) Cantab 1945. Classics Master, Upholland Coll., Wigan, 1945–52, Headmaster, 1952–64; Rector, Venerable English Coll., Rome, 1964–71. Protonotary Apostolic, 1988. *Recreation:* music. *Address:* 483 Liverpool Road, Ainsdale, Southport, Merseyside. *T:* Southport (0704) 77527.

ALSTON, Rex; *see* Alston, A. R.

ALSTON, Richard John William; Artistic Director, Rambert Dance Company (formerly Ballet Rambert), since 1986 (Resident Choreographer, 1980–86); *b* 30 Oct. 1948; *s* of Gordon Walter Alston and Margot Alston (*née* Whitworth). *Educ:* Eton; Croydon Coll. of Art. Choreographed for London Contemporary Dance Theatre, 1970–72; founded Strider, 1972; worked in USA, 1975–77. Principal Ballets: Nowhere Slowly; Tiger Balm; Blue Schubert Fragments; Soft Verges; Rainbow Bandit; Doublework; Soda Lake; for Ballet Rambert: Bell High, 1980; Landscape, 1980; Rainbow Ripples, 1980; The Rite of Spring, 1981; Night Music, 1981; Apollo Distraught, 1982; Chicago Brass, 1983; Voices and Light Footsteps, 1984; Wildlife, 1984; Dangerous Liaisons, 1985; Java, 1985; Zansa, 1986; Dutiful Ducks, 1986; Pulcinella, 1987; Strong Language, 1987; Rhapsody in Blue, 1988; Hymnos, 1988; Cinema, 1989; Pulau Dewata, 1989; Mythologies, 1989; Roughcut, 1990; Dealing with Shadows, 1990. Created: The Kingdom of Pagodas, for Royal Danish Ballet, 1982; Midsummer, first work for Royal Ballet, 1983. *Recreations:* music, reading. *Address:* Rambert Dance Company, 94 Chiswick High Road, W4 1SH. *T:* 081–995 4246.

ALSTON, Robert John, CMG 1987; HM Diplomatic Service; seconded to Home Civil Service, since 1990; *b* 10 Feb. 1938; *s* of Arthur William Alston and Rita Alston; *m* 1969, Patricia Claire Essex; one *s* one *d*. *Educ:* Ardingly Coll.; New Coll., Oxford (BA Mod. Hist.). Third Sec., Kabul, 1963; Eastern Dept, FO, 1966; Head of Computer Study Team, FCO, 1969; First Sec. (Econ.), Paris, 1971; First Sec. and Head of Chancery, Tehran, 1974; Asst Head, Energy Science and Space Dept, FCO, 1977; Head, Joint Nuclear Unit, FCO, 1978; Political Counsellor, UK Delegn to NATO, 1981; Head, Defence Dept, FCO, 1984; Ambassador to Oman, 1986–90. *Recreations:* gardening, travel, music. *Address:* c/o Foreign and Commonwealth Office, King Charles Street, SW1A 2AH.

ALSTON, Prof. Robin Carfrae, FSA; Professor of Library Studies, London University, and Director, School of Library, Archive and Information Studies, University College London, since 1990; *b* 29 Jan. 1933; *s* of Wilfred Louis Alston; *m* 1957, Joanna Dorothy Ormiston; two *s* one *d*. *Educ:* Rugby Sch.; Univs of British Columbia (BA), Oxford (MA), Toronto (MA) and London (PhD). Teaching Fellow, University Coll., Toronto, 1956–58; Lectr, New Brunswick Univ., 1958–60; Lectr in English Lit., Leeds Univ., 1964–76; Consultant to British Library, 1977–; Editor-in-Chief, 18th Century Short Title Catalogue, 1978–89; Advr to Develt and Systems Office, Humanities and Social Scis (formerly Ref. Div.), British Library, 1984–; Editl Dir, The Nineteenth Century, series of microfiche texts 1801–1900, 1985–. Hon. Res. Fellow, UCL, 1987–. Klein Vis. Prof., Univ of Texas, 1990. David Murray Lectr, Univ. of Glasgow, 1983; Guest Lectr, Univ. of London, 1983, Sorbonne, 1984, Tokyo Symposium on micro-reproduction, 1984; Cecil Oldman Lectr, Leeds Univ., 1988, 1989; Maurice Bird Meml Lectr, 1991. Jt Editor, Leeds Studies in English and Leeds Texts and Monographs, 1965–72; Editor, Studies in Early Modern English, 1965–72; Jt Editor, The Direction Line, 1976–; Editor: Special Pubns, Bibliographical Soc., 1983–; Libraries and Archives (series), 1991–. Founder, Chm. and principal Editor, Scolar Press Ltd, 1966–72, Man. Dir, 1984–; Founder, Janus Press, devoted to original art prints, 1973. Member: Adv. Cttee, British Library, 1975–; Adv. Cttee, MLA of America for the Wing Project, 1980–; Adv. Panel, Aust. Research Grants Cttee, 1983–; Adv. Bd, Cambridge Hist. of the Book in Britain, 1989–. Member: Organising Cttee, 18th Century Short Title Catalogue, 1976–; Cttee, British Book Trade Index, 1984–. Mem. Council, Bibliographical Soc., 1967– (Vice-Pres., 1978–88, Pres., 1988–90); Founding Mem. Council, Ilkley Literature Festival, 1973–; Founder, Frederic Madden Soc., 1989–. Consultant, Consortium of Univ. Research Libraries, 1985–86; Advr to Govt of Pakistan on estabt of Nat. Liby of Pakistan, 1988. FSA 1987; Hon. FLA, 1986. Samuel Pepys Gold Medal, Ephemera Soc., 1984; Smithsonian Instn award, 1985. *Publications:* An Introduction to Old English, 1961 (rev. edn 1966); A Catalogue of Books relating to the English Language (1500–1800) in Swedish Libraries, 1965; English Language and Medieval English Literature: a Select Reading-List for Students, 1966; A Bibliography of the English Language from the Invention of Printing to the Year 1800: Vol. I, 1965; Vols V and VIII, 1966; Vols VII and IV, 1967; Vol. II, 1968; Vol. VI, 1969; Vol. III, 1970; Vol. IX, 1971; Vol. X, 1972; Vol. XI, 1978; Vol. XII part 1, 1987; Vol. XII part 2, 1988; Alexander Gil's Logonomia Anglica (1619): a translation into Modern English, 1973; (jtly) The Works of William Bullokar, Vol. I, 1966; English Studies (rev. edn of Vol. III, Cambridge Bibl. Eng. Lit.), 1968; English Linguistics 1500–1800: a Collection of Texts in Facsimile (365 vols), 1967–72; European Linguistics 1500–1700: a Collection of Texts in Facsimile (12 vols), 1968–72; A Checklist of the works of Joseph Addison, 1976; Bibliography MARC and ESTC, 1978; Eighteenth-Century Subscription Lists, 1983; ESTC: the British Library Collections, 1983; The arrangement of books in the British Museum Library 1843–1973, and the British Library 1973–1985, 1987; The Nineteenth Century: subject scope and principles of selection, 1987; Index to Pressmarks in use in the British Museum Library and the British Library, 1987; Index to the Classification Schedules of the Map Collections in the British Library, 1987; Computers and Libraries, 1987; The British Library: past, present, future, 1989; Women Writers of Fiction, Verse and Drama: a checklist of works published between 1801 and 1900 in the collections of the British Library, 1990; Handlist of unpublished finding aids to the London Collections of the British Library, 1991; Handlist of catalogues and book lists in the Department of Manuscripts, British Library, 1991; numerous articles, printed lectures, reviews, etc. *Recreations:* music, photography. *Address:* 16 Medburn Street, NW1 1RJ.

ALSTON-ROBERTS-WEST, Lt-Col George Arthur; *see* West.

AL-TAJIR, Mohamed Mahdi; Special Adviser to HH The Ruler; *b* 26 Dec. 1931; *m* 1956, Zohra Al-Tajir; five *s* one *d*. *Educ:* Al Tajir Sch., Bahrain; Preston Grammar Sch., Lancs, England. Dir, Dept of Port and Customs, Govt of Bahrain, 1955–63; Dir, Dept of HH the Ruler's Affairs and Petroleum Affairs, 1963–; Director: Nat. Bank of Dubai Ltd, 1963–; Dubai Petroleum Co., 1963–; Dubai Nat. Air Travel Agency, 1966–; Qatar-Dubai Currency Bd, 1965–73; United Arab Emirates Currency Bd, 1973–; Dubai Dry Dock Co., 1973–; Chm., S Eastern Dubai Drilling Co., 1968–. Amb. of UAE to UK, 1972–86, and France, 1972–77. Hon. Citizen of State of Texas, USA, 1963. *Address:* Department of HH Ruler's Affairs and Petroleum Affairs, PO Box 207, Dubai, United Arab Emirates.

ALTAMONT, Earl of; Jeremy Ulick Browne; *b* 4 June 1939; *s* of 10th Marquess of Sligo, *qv*: *m* 1961, Jennifer June, *d* of Major Derek Cooper, Dunlewey, Co. Donegal, and Mrs C. Heber Percy, Pophleys, Radnage; five *d*. *Educ:* St Columba's College, Eire; Royal Agricultural College, Cirencester. *Address:* Westport House, Co. Mayo, Eire.

ALTHAUS, Sir Nigel (Frederick), Kt 1989; Senior Broker to the Commissioners for the Reduction of the National Debt (Government Broker), 1982–89; *b* 28 Sept. 1929; *er s* of late Frederick Rudolph Althaus, CBE and Margaret Frances (*née* Twist); *m* 1958, Anne, *d* of P. G. Cardew; three *s* one *d*. *Educ:* Eton; Magdalen Coll., Oxford (Roberts Gawen Scholar; 2nd Cl. Lit. Hum. 1954). National Service, 60th Rifles, 1948–50. Joined Pember and Boyle (Stockbrokers), 1954; Partner, 1955–75, Sen. Partner, 1975–82; Sen. Partner, Mullens and Co., 1982–86. Mem., Stock Exchange, 1955–89; Chm., Stock Exchange Benevolent Fund, 1975–82. Master, Skinners' Co., 1977–78; Chm. Governors, Skinners' Co. Sch. for Boys, Tunbridge Wells, 1982–89. Chm., British Library of Tape Recordings for Hosp. Patients, 1975–. Comr, Royal Hosp., Chelsea, 1988–. Queen Victoria's Rifles (TA), 1950–60; Hon. Col, 39 Signal Regt (TA), 1982–88. *Publication:* (ed) British Government Securities in the Twentieth Century, 1976. *Recreations:* golf, shooting, music. *Address:* c/o Bank of England, Threadneedle Street, EC2R 8AH. *Clubs:* Boodle's, Beefsteak; Swinley Forest Golf (Ascot).

ALTHORP, Viscount; Charles Edward Maurice Spencer; Contributing Correspondent, NBC News, since 1987; *b* 20 May 1964; *s* and *heir* of 8th Earl Spencer, *qv*; *m* 1989, Victoria, *d* of John Lockwood; one *d*. *Educ:* Maidwell Hall; Eton College; Magdalen Coll., Oxford. Page of Honour to HM the Queen, 1977–79. *Address:* Althorp, Northampton NN7 4HG. *Clubs:* Brooks's, White's.

ALTMAN, Lionel Phillips, CBE 1979; adviser and consultant to public bodies and private sector; Director, Equity & General plc, since 1978 (Chairman, 1978–91); *b* 12 Sept. 1922; *s* of late Arnold Altman and Catherine Phillips; *m* Diana; one *s* two *d* by previous marriages. *Educ:* University Coll. and Business Sch., also in Paris. FIMI; FInstM; MIPR. Served war, 1942–46, special intelligence duties, War Office and Political Intelligence Dept, FO (UK and Far East). Director: Carmo Holdings Ltd, 1947–63; Sears Holdings Motor Gp, 1963–72; Sears Finance, 1965–71; C. & W. Walker Holdings Ltd, 1974–77; H. P. Information plc, 1985–91; Motor Agents Assoc. Ltd, 1986–89 (Mem., Nat. Council, 1965–; Pres., 1975–77); Chm. and Chief Exec., Pre-Divisional Investments Ltd, 1972–. Chairman: Motor Industry Educnl Consultative Council Industry Working Party, producing Altman Report on recruitment and training, 1968; Retail Motor Industry Working Party on Single European Market, 1988–. Vice-Pres., and Mem. Council, Inst. of Motor Industry, 1970–78. Chairman: Publicity Club of London, 1961–62; Industry Taxation Panel, 1977–86; United Technologists Estabt, 1980–; Member: Council, CBI, 1977–88; CBI Industrial Policy Cttee, 1979–85; Dun & Bradstreet Industry Panel, 1982–86. Chm., Automotive VIP Club, 1988–. Freeman: City of London, 1973; City of Glasgow, 1974; Liveryman and former Hon. Treas., Coachmakers' and Coach Harness Makers' Co.; Burgess Guild Brother, Cordwainers' Co. *Publications:* articles, TV and radio broadcasts. *Address:* (office) 44 Ennismore Gardens, Knightsbridge, SW7 1AQ. *T:* 071–581 8187.

ALTMAN, Robert; film director; *b* Kansas City, 20 Feb. 1925; *m* 3rd, Kathryn Altman; one *s* and one adopted *s* (and two *s* one *d* by previous marriages). *Educ:* Univ. of Missouri. Served US Army, 1943–47. Industrial film maker, Calvin Co., Kansas City, 1950–57. Television writer, producer and director, 1957–65. Films directed: That Cold Day in the Park, 1969; M*A*S*H*, 1970 (Grand Prix, Cannes, 1970); Brewster McCloud, 1971; McCabe and Mrs Miller, 1971; Images, 1972; The Long Goodbye, 1973; Thieves Like Us, 1974; California Split, 1974; Nashville, 1975; Buffalo Bill and the Indians, 1976; 3 Women, 1977; A Wedding, 1978; Quintet, 1979; A Perfect Couple, 1979; Health, 1979; Popeye, 1980; Come Back to the 5 & Dime Jimmy Dean, Jimmy Dean, 1982; Streamers, 1983; Fool for Love, 1986; Beyond Therapy, 1987; (jtly) Aria, 1987; Vincent & Theo, 1990; directed and produced: Secret Honor, 1984; Tanner '88, 1988 (series); produced: Welcome to LA, 1977; The Late Show, 1977; Remember My Name, 1978; Rich Kids, 1979. *Address:* c/o Sandcastle 5 Productions, Inc., 502 Park Avenue #15-G, New York City, NY 10022, USA.

ALTON, David Patrick; MP Mossley Hill Division of Liverpool, since 1983 (Edge Hill Division, March 1979–1983) (L 1979–88, Soc & Lib Dem since 1988); *b* 15 March 1951; *s* of Frederick and Bridget Alton; *m* 1988, Dilys Elizabeth, *yr d* of Rev. Philip Bell; one *s* one *d*. *Educ:* Edmund Campion Sch., Hornchurch; Christ's College of Education, Liverpool. Elected to Liverpool City Council as Britain's youngest City Councillor, 1972; CC, 1972–80; Deputy Leader of the Council and Housing Chairman, 1978; Vice-Pres., AMA, 1979–. MP (L) Liverpool, Edge Hill (by-election), with a 32 per cent swing, March 1979 (youngest member of that parliament); Liberal Party spokesman on: the environment and race relations, 1979–81; home affairs, 1981–82; NI, 1987–88 (Alliance spokesman on NI, 1987); Chief Whip, Liberal Party, 1985–87; Mem., Select Cttee on the Environment, 1981–85. Chm., Liberal Candidates Cttee, 1985. Nat. Pres., Nat. League of Young Liberals, 1979. Founder, Movement for Christian Democracy, 1990. Former Chm., Council for Educn in Commonwealth. Nat. Vice-Pres., Life; Pres., Liverpool Old People's Hostels Assoc.; Vice-Pres., Liverpool YMCA. Dir, Florence Inst., Liverpool. Vice-Pres., Assoc. of Councillors. Trustee: Crisis at Christmas; Liverpool Hostels for Victims of Violent Crime; Western Care Assoc. Patron: Jubilee Campaign for the release of prisoners of conscience, 1986–; Belfast Trust for Integrated Educn. Mem., Inst. of Journalists. Columnist: Catholic Pictorial, 1982–; The Universe, 1989–. *Publications:* What Kind of Country?, 1987; Whose Choice Anyway?, 1988; Faith in Britain, 1991. *Recreations:* theatre, reading, walking. *Address:* 25 North Mossley Hill Road, Liverpool L18 8BL. *T:* 051–724 6106.

ALTON, Euan Beresford Seaton, MBE 1945; MC 1943; Under Secretary, Department of Health and Social Security, 1968–76; *b* 22 April 1919; *y s* of late William Lester St John Alton and Ellen Seaton Alton; *m* 1953, Diana Margaret Ede; one *s* one *d*. *Educ:* St Paul's Sch.; Magdalen Coll., Oxford (Exhibnr; MA). Served with Army, 1939–45; Major RA. Admin. Officer, Colonial Service and HM OCS, Gold Coast and Ghana, 1946–58; Admin. Officer, Class 1, 1957. Entered Civil Service as Asst Principal, Min. of Health, 1958; Principal, 1958; Asst Sec., 1961; Under Sec., 1968. *Recreations:* sailing, walking. *Address:* Spindlehurst, School Lane, Brantham, Manningtree, Essex CO11 1QE. *T:* Colchester (0206) 393419. *Clubs:* Cruising Association; Stour Sailing (Manningtree).

ALTRINCHAM, Barony of, *cr* 1945, of Tormarton; title disclaimed by 2nd Baron. *Heir to barony:* Hon. Anthony Ulick David Dundas Grigg [*b* 12 Jan. 1934; *m* 1965, Eliane de Miramon; two *s* one *d*].

ALUN-JONES, Sir (John) Derek, Kt 1987; Chairman, Spectrum Energy & Information Technology Ltd; *b* 6 June 1933; *s* of Thomas Alun-Jones, LLB and Madge Beatrice Edwards; *m* 1960, Gillian Palmer; two *s* three *d*. *Educ:* Lancing College; St Edmund Hall, Oxford (MA Hons Jurisp.). Philips Electrical, 1957–59; H. C. Stephens, 1959–60; Expandite, 1960–71 (Man. Dir, 1966–71); Man. Dir, Burmah Industrial Products, 1971–74; Man. Dir and Chief Exec., 1975–87, Chm., 1987–90, Ferranti, subseq. Ferranti Internat. Signal, then Ferranti Internat.; Director: Burmah Oil Trading, 1974–75; Royal Insurance, 1981–; Throgmorton Trust, 1978–84; SBAC, 1982–90; Reed International PLC, 1984–90; GKN plc, 1986–88; Consolidated Gold Fields PLC, 1988–89. *Recreations:* shooting, fishing, golf. *Address:* The Willows, Effingham Common, Surrey KT24 5JE. *T:* Bookham (0372) 458158.

ALVAREZ, Alfred; poet and author; *b* London, 1929; *s* of late Bertie Alvarez and Katie Alvarez (*née* Levy); *m* 1st, 1956, Ursula Barr (marr. diss. 1961); one *s*; 2nd, 1966, Anne Adams; one *s* one *d*. *Educ:* Oundle Sch.; Corpus Christi Coll., Oxford. BA (Oxon) 1952, MA 1956. Research Schol., CCC, Oxon, and Research Schol. of Goldsmiths' Company, 1952–53, 1954–55. Procter Visiting Fellowship, Princeton, 1953–54; Vis. Fellow of Rockefeller Foundn, USA, 1955–56, 1958; gave Christian Gauss Seminars in Criticism, Princeton, and was Lectr in Creative Writing, 1957–58; D. H. Lawrence Fellowship, New Mexico, 1958; Poetry Critic, The Observer, 1956–66. Visiting Professor: Brandeis Univ., 1960; New York State Univ., Buffalo, 1966. Vachel Lindsay Prize for Poetry (from Poetry, Chicago), 1961. *Publications:* The Shaping Spirit (US title, Stewards of Excellence), 1958; The School of Donne, 1961; The New Poetry (ed and introd), 1962; Under Pressure, 1965; Beyond All This Fiddle, 1968; Lost (poems), 1968; Penguin Modern Poets, No 18, 1970; Apparition (poems, with paintings by Charles Blackman), 1971; The Savage God, 1971; Beckett, 1973; Hers (novel), 1974; Hunt (novel), 1978; Autumn to Autumn and Selected Poems 1953–76, 1978; Life After Marriage, 1982; The Biggest Game in Town, 1983; Offshore, 1986; Feeding the Rat, 1988; Rain Forest (with paintings by Charles Blackman), 1988; Day of Atonement (novel), 1991. *Recreations:* rock-climbing, poker, music. *Address:* c/o Aitken & Stone, 29 Fernshaw Road, SW10 0TG. *Clubs:* Beefsteak, Climbers', Alpine.

ALVES, Colin, OBE 1990; General Secretary: General Synod Board of Education, 1984–90; National Society for Promoting Religious Education, 1984–90; *b* 19 April 1930; *s* of Donald Alexander Alves and Marjorie Alice (*née* Marsh); *m* 1953, Peggy (*née* Kember); two *s* one *d*. *Educ:* Christ's Hospital, Horsham; Worcester Coll., Oxford (MA). School teaching, 1952–59; Lectr, King Alfred's Coll., Winchester, 1959–68; Head of Dept, Brighton Coll. of Educn, 1968–74; Dir, RE Centre, St Gabriel's Coll., 1974–77; Colleges Officer, General Synod Bd of Educn, 1977–84. Mem., Durham Commn on RE, 1967–70; Chm., Schs Council RE Cttee, 1971–77; Sec., Assoc. of Voluntary Colls, 1978–84; Member: Adv. Cttee on Supply and Educn of Teachers, 1980–85; Nat. Adv. Body for Public Sector Higher Educn, 1983–88; Voluntary Sector Consultative Council, 1984–88. MLitt Lambeth, 1989. *Publications:* Religion and the Secondary School, 1968; The Christian in Education, 1972; The Question of Jesus, 1987; contrib. various symposia on RE. *Recreations:* music, walking, gardening. *Address:* 9 Park Road, Haywards Heath, Sussex RH16 4HY. *T:* Haywards Heath (0444) 454496. *Club:* Commonwealth Trust.

ALVEY, John, CB 1980; FEng 1984; Chairman, SIRA Ltd, since 1987; *b* 19 June 1925; *s* of George C. V. Alvey and Hilda E. Alvey (*née* Pellatt); *m* 1955, Celia Edmed Marson; three *s*. *Educ:* Reeds Sch.; London Univ.; BSc (Eng), DipNEC. FIEE; MBCS. London Stock Exchange, to 1943. Royal Navy, 1943–46; Royal Naval Scientific Service, 1950; Head of Weapons Projects, Admiralty Surface Weapons Estabt, 1968–72; Dir-Gen. Electronics Radar, PE, MoD, 1972–73; Dir-Gen., Airborne Electronic Systems, PE, MoD, 1974–75; Dir, Admiralty Surface Weapons Estabt, 1976–77; Dep. Controller, R&D Estabts and Res. C, and Chief Scientist (RAF), MoD, 1977–80; Senior Dir, Technology, 1980–83, Man. Dir, Develt and Procurement, and Engr-in-Chief, 1983–86, British Telecom. Dir (non-exec.), LSI Logic Ltd, 1986–. Member Council: Fellowship of Engrg, 1985– (Vice-Pres., 1989–); Foundn for Sci. and Technology, 1986–90; City Univ., 1985–. Hon. Fellow, Queen Mary and Westfield Coll. (formerly QMC), London, 1988. Hon. DSc City, 1984; Hon. DTech CNAA, 1991. *Recreations:* reading, Rugby, skiing, theatre going. *Address:* SIRA Ltd, South Hill, Chislehurst, Kent BR7 5EH.

ALVINGHAM, 2nd Baron, *cr* 1929, of Woodfold; **Maj.-Gen. Robert Guy Eardley Yerburgh,** CBE 1978 (OBE 1972); *b* 16 Dec. 1926; *s* of 1st Baron and Dorothea Gertrude (*d* 1927), *d* of late J. Eardley Yerburgh; *S* father 1955; *m* 1952, Beryl Elliott, *d* of late W. D. Williams; one *s* one *d*. *Educ:* Eton. Commissioned 1946, Coldstream Guards; served UK, Palestine, Farelf, British Guiana; Head of Staff, CDS, 1972–75; Dep. Dir, Army Staff Duties, 1975–78; Dir of Army Quartering, 1978–81, retired. *Heir: s* Captain Hon. Robert Richard Guy Yerburgh, 17th/21st Lancers, retired [*b* 10 Dec. 1956; *m* 1981, Vanessa, *yr d* of Captain Duncan Kirk; two *s*].

AMBARTSUMIAN, Victor; Hero of Socialist Labour (twice); Order of Lenin (five times); Order of Labour Red Banner (twice); President, Academy of Sciences of Armenia, since 1947; *b* 18 Sept. 1908; *m* 1931, Vera Ambartsumian; two *s* two *d*. *Educ:* Univ. of Leningrad. Lecturer in Astronomy, 1931–34, Prof. of Astrophysics, 1934–44, Univ. of Leningrad; Prof. of Astrophysics, Univ. of Erevan, 1944–. Full Mem., Academy of Sciences of USSR, 1953–. Pres., Internat. Council of Scientific Unions, 1968–72. Hon. Dr of Science: Univs of Canberra, 1963; Paris, 1965; Liege, 1967; Prague, 1967; Torun, 1973; La Plata, 1974; Foreign Member of Academies of Science: Washington, Paris, Rome, Vienna, Berlin, Amsterdam, Copenhagen, Sofia, Stockholm, Boston, New York, New Delhi, Cordoba, Prague, Budapest; Foreign Member of Royal Society, London. *Publications:* Theoretical Astrophysics, 1953 (in Russian; trans. into German, English, Spanish, Chinese); about 100 papers in learned jls. *Address:* Academy of Sciences of Armenia, Marshal Bagramian Avenue 24, Erevan, Armenia, USSR.

AMBERLEY, Viscount; Nicholas Lyulph Russell; *b* 12 Sept. 1968; *s* and *heir* of Earl Russell, *qv*.

AMBLER, Eric, OBE 1981; novelist and screenwriter; *b* 28 June 1909; *s* of Alfred Percy and Amy Madeleine Ambler; *m* 1st, 1939, Louise Crombie; 2nd, 1958, Joan Harrison. *Educ:* Colfe's Grammar Sch.; London Univ. Apprenticeship in engineering, 1927–28; advertisement copywriter, 1929–35; professional writer, 1936–. Served War of 1939–45: RA, 1940; commissioned, 1941; served in Italy, 1943; Lt-Col, 1944; Asst Dir of Army Kinematography, War Office, 1944–46. US Bronze Star, 1946. Wrote and produced film, The October Man, 1947 and resumed writing career. Diamond Dagger Award, CWA, 1986. Screenplays include: The Way Ahead, 1944; The October Man, 1947; The Passionate Friends, 1948; Highly Dangerous, 1950; The Magic Box, 1951; Gigolo and Gigolette, in Encore, 1952; The Card, 1952; Rough Shoot, 1953; The Cruel Sea, 1953; Lease of Life, 1954; The Purple Plain, 1954; Yangtse Incident, 1957; A Night to Remember, 1958; Wreck of the Mary Deare, 1959; Love Hate Love, 1970. *Publications:* The Dark Frontier, 1936; Uncommon Danger, 1937; Epitaph for a Spy, 1938; Cause for Alarm, 1938; The Mask of Dimitrios, 1939; Journey into Fear, 1940; Judgment on Deltchev, 1951; The Schirmer Inheritance, 1953; The Night-comers, 1956; Passage of Arms, 1959; The Light of Day, 1962; The Ability to Kill (essays), 1963; (ed and introd) To Catch a Spy, 1964; A Kind of Anger, 1964 (Edgar Allan Poe award, 1964); Dirty Story, 1967; The Intercom Conspiracy, 1969; The Levanter, 1972 (Golden Dagger award, 1973); Doctor Frigo, 1974 (MWA Grand Master award, 1975); Send No More Roses, 1977; The Care of Time, 1981; Here Lies (autobiog.), 1985. *Address:* c/o Campbell Thomson & McLaughlin Ltd, 31 Newington Green, N16 9PU. *Club:* Garrick.

AMBLER, John Doss; Vice-President, since 1980, Vice-President, Human Resources, since 1989, Texaco Inc.; *b* 24 July 1934; *m*; one *s* one *d*. *Educ:* Virginia Polytechnic Inst. (BSc Business Admin). Texaco Inc., USA: various assignments, Marketing Dept, Alexandra, Va, 1956–65; Dist Sales Manager, Harrisburg, Pa, 1965–67; Asst Divl Manager, Norfolk, Va, 1967–68; Staff Asst to Gen. Man. Marketing US, New York, 1968; various assignments, Chicago and New York, 1969–72; Gen. Man., Texaco Olie Maatschappij BV, Rotterdam, 1972–75; Man. Dir, Texaco Oil AB, Stockholm, 1975–77; Asst to Pres. of Texaco Inc., USA, 1977–80; Pres., Texaco Europe, New York, 1981–82; Chm. and Chief Exec. Officer, Texaco Ltd, 1982–89. *Recreations:* hunting, fishing, tennis, photography. *Address:* Texaco Inc., 2000 Westchester Avenue, White Plains, New York, NY 10650, USA.

AMBO, Rt. Rev. George Somboba, KBE 1988 (OBE 1978); Archbishop of Papua New Guinea, 1983–89; Bishop of Popondota, 1977–89; Chairman, South Pacific Anglican Council, 1986–89; *b* Gona, Nov. 1925; *s* of late J. O. Ambo, Gona; *m* 1946, Marcella O., *d* of Karau; two *s* two *d*. *Educ:* St Aidan's College, Dogura; Newton Theological Coll., Dogura. Deacon, 1955; Priest, 1958. Curate of: Menapi, 1955–57; Dogura, 1957–58; Priest in charge of Boianai, Diocese of New Guinea, 1958–63; Missionary at Wamira, 1963–69; an Asst Bishop of Papua New Guinea, 1960 (first Papuan-born Anglican Bishop). *Publication:* St John's Gospel in Ewage. *Recreations:* reading, carpentry. *Address:* c/o Anglican Diocesan Office, PO Box 26, Popondetta, Papua New Guinea.

AMBRASEYS, Prof. Nicholas, FEng 1985, FICE; Professor of Engineering Seismology, University of London, at Imperial College, since 1973; Head of Engineering Seismology Section, since 1969; *b* 19 Jan. 1929; *s* of Neocles Ambraseys, Athens, and Cleopatra Jambany; *m* 1955, Xeni, *d* of A. Stavrou. *Educ:* National Technical Univ. of Athens (DipEng); Univ. of London (DIC; PhD; DSc 1980). Lectr in Civil Engineering, Imperial Coll., 1958–62; Associate Prof. of Civil Engrg, Univ. of Illinois, 1963; Prof. of Hydrodynamics, Nat. Tech. Univ., Athens, 1964; Imperial College: Lectr, 1965–68; Univ. Reader in Engrg Seismology, 1969–72. Chm., British Nat. Cttee for Earthquake Eng., 1961–71; Dir, Internat. Assoc. for Earthquake Engrg, 1961–77; Vice-Pres., European Assoc. for Earthquake Engrg, 1964–75; Mem., 1969–78, Vice-Chm., 1979–81, Unesco Internat. Adv. Cttee of Earthquake Risk; leader, UN/Unesco earthquake reconnaissance missions to Pakistan, Iran, Turkey, Romania, Jugoslavia, Italy, Greece, Algeria, Nicaragua, East and Central Africa; Chm., Internat. Commn for earthquake protection of historical monuments, 1977–81; Royal Soc. rep., British Nat. Cttee for Geodesy and Geophysics, 1975–85; consultant to Binnie & Partners, UN/Unesco. Decennial Award, European Assoc. for Earthquake Engrg, 1975; Busk Medal, RGS, 1975. *Publications:* A History of Persian Earthquakes (with C. Melville), 1982; papers on engrg seismology, soil mechanics, tectonics, historical seismicity. *Recreations:* history, philately. *Address:* Imperial College, SW7 2BU. *T:* 071–589 5111; 19 Bede House, Manor Fields, SW15 3LT. *T:* 081–788 4219.

AMBROSE, Prof. Edmund Jack, MA (Cantab), DSc (London); Professor of Cell Biology, University of London, Institute of Cancer Research, 1967–76, now Emeritus Professor; Staff of Chester Beatty Research Institute, Institute of Cancer Research: Royal Cancer Hospital, 1952–75; *b* 2 March 1914; *s* of Alderman Harry Edmund Ambrose and Kate (*née* Stanley); *m* 1943, Andrée (*née* Huck), Seine, France; one *s* one *d*. *Educ:* Perse Sch., Cambridge; Emmanuel Coll., Cambridge. Wartime research for Admiralty on infra-red detectors, 1940–45; subseq. research on structure of proteins using infra-red radiation at Courtauld Fundamental Research Laboratory. Formerly Convener of Brit. Soc. for Cell Biology. Formerly Special Adviser in Cancer to Govt of India at Tata Meml Centre, Bombay. Special Adviser in Leprosy, Foundn for Med. Res., Bombay, 1978– (awarded St Elizabeth Meml Medal, Order of St John, Paris, 1981 for leprosy work); Adviser, Regional Cancer Centre, Kerala, India, 1984–. Pres., Internat. Cell Tissue and Organ Culture Group. Research on structure of proteins, on structure of normal and cancer cells, and on characteristics of surface of cancer cells, cell biology and microbiology of leprosy, using labelled metabolites. *Publications:* Cell Electrophoresis, 1965; The Biology of Cancer, 1966, 2nd edn 1975; The Cancer Cell *in vitro*. 1967; (jtly) Cell Biology, 1970, rev. edn 1976; Nature of the Biological World, 1982; The Mirror of Creation; publications on Protein Structure and Cell Biology, in Proc. Royal Soc., biological jls. *Recreation:* sailing. *Club:* Royal Bombay Yacht.

AMBROSE, James Walter Davy; Judge, Supreme Court Singapore, 1958–68; *b* 5 Dec. 1909; *s* of Samuel Ambrose; *m* 1945, Theresa Kamala Ambrose; no *c*. *Educ:* Free Sch., Penang; Oxford Univ. Asst Official Assignee, Singapore, 1936; Police Magistrate and Asst District Judge, Malacca, 1940; Registrar, Superior Court, Malacca, 1945; Dep. Public Prosecutor, 1946; Sen. Asst Registrar, Supreme Courts of Ipoh, Penang, and Kuala Lumpur, 1947–52; President, Sessions Court, Penang, 1953; Acting District Judge and First Magistrate, Singapore, 1955; Official Assignee, Public Trustee, and Comr of Estate Duties, Singapore 1957. *Address:* Block 10B, Apartment 04–06, Braddell Hill, Singapore 2057.

AMERY, Colin Robert; architectural writer, critic and historian; *b* 29 May 1944; *yr s* of Kenneth George Amery and Florence Ellen Amery (*née* Young). *Educ:* King's College London; Univ. of Sussex (BA Hons). Editor and Inf. Officer, TCPA, 1968–70; Asst Editor and Features Editor, Architectural Review, 1970–79; Architecture Corresp., Financial Times, 1979–. Advr for Sainsbury Wing, Nat. Gall., 1985–; Arch. consultant to J. Sainsbury plc, 1985–. Vis. Fellow, Jesus Coll., Cambridge, 1989. Member: Arts Panel, Arts Council, 1984–86; Exec. Cttee, Georgian Gp, 1985–; Architecture Panel, NT, 1986–; London Adv. Cttee, English Heritage, 1987–; Building Cttee, Nat. Gallery, 1988–; Adv. Cttee, Geffrye Mus., 1985–87; Dir, Sir John Soane Soc., 1987–; Chairman: Organising Cttee, Lutyens Exhibn, 1981–82; Lutyens Trust, 1984–; Trustee: Spitalfields Trust, 1977–85; Brooking Collection, 1985–; Nat. Museums and Galls on Merseyside, 1988–. *Publications:* Period Houses and Their Details, 1974; (jtly) The Rape of Britain, 1975; Three Centuries of Architectural Craftsmanship, 1977; (jtly) The Victorian Buildings of London 1837–1887, 1980; (compiled jtly) Lutyens 1869–1944, 1981; (contrib.) Architecture of the British Empire, 1986; Wren's London, 1988; articles in professional jls. *Address:* c/o Financial Times, 1 Southwark Bridge, SE1 9HL. *Club:* Travellers'.

AMERY, Rt. Hon. Julian, PC 1960; MP (C) Brighton Pavilion since 1969; *b* 27 March 1919; *s* of late Rt Hon. Leopold Amery, PC, CH; *m* 1950, Lady Catherine (*d* 1991), *d* of 1st Earl of Stockton, OM. PC, FRS; one *s* three *d*. *Educ:* Summerfields; Eton; Balliol Coll., Oxford. War Corresp. in Spanish Civil War, 1938–39; Attaché HM Legation, Belgrade, and on special missions in Bulgaria, Turkey, Roumania and Middle East, 1939–40; Sergeant in RAF, 1940–41; commissioned and transferred to army, 1941; on active service, Egypt, Palestine and Adriatic, 1941–42; liaison officer to Albanian resistance movement, 1944; served on staff of Gen. Carton de Wiart, VC, Mr Churchill's personal representative with Generalissimo Chiang Kai-Shek, 1945. Contested Preston in Conservative interest, July 1945; MP (C) Preston North, 1950–66; Delegate to Consultative Assembly of Council of Europe, 1950–53 and 1956. Member Round Table Conference on Malta, 1955. Parly Under-Sec. of State and Financial Sec., War Office, 1957–58; Parly Under-Sec. of State, Colonial Office, 1958–60; Sec. of State for Air, Oct. 1960–July 1962; Minister of Aviation, 1962–64; Minister of Public Building and Works, June-Oct. 1970; Minister for Housing and Construction, DoE, 1970–72; Minister of State, FCO, 1972–74. Pres., Horn of Africa and Aden Council, 1984–. Kt Comdr, Order of Phœnix, Greece; Grand Cordon, Order of Scanderbeg, Albania; Order of Oman, first class. *Publications:* Sons of the Eagle, 1948; The Life of Joseph Chamberlain: vol. IV, 1901–3: At the Height of his Power, 1951; vols V and VI, 1901–14: Joseph Chamberlain and the Tariff Reform Campaign, 1969; Approach March (autobiog.), 1973; articles in National Review, Nineteenth Century and Daily Telegraph. *Recreations:* ski-ing, mountaineering, travel. *Address:* 112 Eaton Square, SW1W 9AE. *T:* 071–235 1543, 071–235 7409; Forest Farm House, Chelwood Gate, Sussex. *Clubs:* White's, Beefsteak, Carlton, Buck's.

AMES, Mrs Kenneth; *see* Gainham, S. R.

AMESS, David Anthony Andrew; MP (C) Basildon, since 1983; Chairman, Accountancy Aims, since 1990; *b* Plaistow, 26 March 1952; *s* of late James Henry Valentine Amess and of Maud Ethel Martin; *m* 1983, Julia Monica Margaret Arnold; one *s* three *d*. *Educ:* St Bonaventure's Grammar Sch.; Bournemouth Coll. of Technol. (BScEcon Hons 2.2., special subject Govt). Teacher, St John the Baptist Jun. Mixed Sch., Bethnal Green, 1970–71; Jun. Underwriter, Leslie & Godwin Agencies, 1974–77; Sen. Manager of Temporary Div., Accountancy Personnel, 1977–80. Mem., Redbridge Council, 1982–86 (Vice Chm., Housing Cttee, 1982–85). Contested (C) Newham NW, 1979. Parliamentary Private Secretary: to Parly Under-Secs of State (Health), DHSS, 1987–88; to Minister of State and Parly Under-Sec. of State, Dept of Transport, 1988–90; to Minister of State, DoE, 1990–. *Publications:* contrib. magazines and pamphlets. *Recreations:* gardening, music, sport, animals, theatre, antiques. *Address:* c/o House of Commons, SW1A 0AA. *Clubs:* Carlton; Kingswood Squash and Racketball (Basildon).

AMHERST, family name of **Earl Amherst.**

AMHERST, 5th Earl, *cr* 1826; **Jeffery John Archer Amherst,** MC 1918; Baron Amherst of Montreal, 1788; Viscount Holmesdale, 1826; Major, late Coldstream Guards; Manager, External Affairs, BEA, 1946; later Director of Associated Companies, retd, Dec. 1966; Hon. Commission as Wing Commander, RAF, 1942; *b* 13 Dec. 1896; *e s* of 4th Earl and Hon. Eleanor Clementina St Aubyn (*d* 1960), *d* of 1st Baron St Levan; *S* father, 1927. *Educ:* Eton; RMC Sandhurst. Served European War, 1914–18, with Coldstream Guards (MC); placed on RARO 1921; recalled 1940, served Middle East, 1940–44. Reportorial Staff, New York Morning World, 1923–29; Commercial Air Pilot and General Manager Air Line Company, 1929–39; Asst Air Adviser to British Railways, 1945–46. Dir, BEA associated cos, 1946–66. *Publication:* Wandering Abroad (autobiog.), 1976. *Clubs:* Cavalry and Guards, Travellers', Pratt's, Garrick.

AMHERST OF HACKNEY, 4th Baron *cr* 1892; **William Hugh Amherst Cecil;** Director, E. A. Gibson Shipbrokers Ltd, 1978–90; *b* 28 Dec. 1940; *s* of 3rd Baron Amherst of Hackney, CBE, and of Margaret Eirene Clifton Brown, *d* of late Brig.-Gen. Howard Clifton Brown; *S* father, 1980; *m* 1965, Elisabeth, *d* of Hugh Humphrey Merriman, DSO, MC, TD, DL; one *s* one *d*. *Educ:* Eton. *Heir:* *s* Hon. Hugh William Amherst Cecil, *b* 17 July 1968. *Address:* Hillside House, Hyde, near Fordingbridge, Hants SP6 2HD. *Clubs:* Royal Yacht Squadron, Royal Ocean Racing.

AMIES, Sir (Edwin) Hardy, KCVO 1989 (CVO 1977); RDI 1964; FRSA 1965; Dressmaker by Appointment to HM The Queen, since 1955; Director Hardy Amies Ltd, since 1946; Design Consultant to manufacturers in the UK, EEC, USA, Canada, Australia, New Zealand, Japan, and Korea; *b* 17 July 1909; *s* of late Herbert William Amies and Mary (*née* Hardy). *Educ:* Brentwood. Studied languages in France and Germany, 1927–30; trainee at W. & T. Avery Ltd, Birmingham, 1930–34; managing designer at Lachasse, Farm Street, W1, 1934–39. War Service, 1939–45: joined Intelligence Corps, 1939, becoming Lt-Col and head of Special Forces Mission to Belgium, 1944; founded dressmaking business, 1946. Chairman, Incorporated Society of London Fashion Designers, 1959–60 (Vice-Chm., 1954–56). Awards: Harper's Bazaar, 1962; Caswell-Massey, 1962, 1964, 1968; Ambassador Magazine, 1964; Sunday Times Special Award, 1965; Personnalité de l'Année (Haute Couture), Paris, 1986; Hall of Fame Award, British Fashion Council, 1989. Officier de l'Ordre de la Couronne (Belgium), 1946. *Publications:* Just So Far, 1954; ABC of Men's Fashion, 1964; Still Here, 1984. *Recreations:* lawn tennis, gardening, opera. *Address:* The Old School, Langford, near Lechlade, Glos GL7 3LF; Hardy Amies Ltd, 14 Savile Row, W1X 2JN. *T:* 071–734 2436. *Clubs:* Queen's, Buck's.

AMIS, Sir Kingsley, Kt 1990; CBE 1981; author; *b* 16 April 1922; *o c* of William Robert and Rosa Amis; *m* 1st, 1948, Hilary Ann, *d* of Leonard Sidney and Margery Bardwell; two *s* one *d*; 2nd, 1965, Elizabeth Jane Howard, *qv* (marr. diss. 1983). *Educ:* City of London School; St John's, Oxford (Hon. Fellow, 1976). Served in Army, 1942–45. Lectr in English, University Coll. of Swansea, 1949–61 (Hon. Fellow, 1985); Fellow of Peterhouse, Cambridge, 1961–63. Cholmondeley Award, 1990. *Publications: novels:* Lucky Jim, 1954 (filmed, 1957); That Uncertain Feeling, 1955 (filmed as Only Two Can Play, 1962, televised, 1986); I Like it Here, 1958; Take a Girl Like You, 1960; One Fat Englishman, 1963; (with Robert Conquest) The Egyptologists, 1965; The Anti-Death League, 1966; (as Robert Markham) Colonel Sun, 1968; I Want it Now, 1968; The Green Man, 1969 (televised, 1990); Girl, 20, 1971; The Riverside Villas Murder, 1973; Ending Up, 1974; Jake's Thing, 1978; Russian Hide-and-Seek, 1980; Stanley and the Women, 1984; The Old Devils (Booker Prize), 1986 (adapted for stage, 1989); The Crime of the Century, 1987; Difficulties with Girls, 1988; The Folks that Live on the Hill, 1990; *short stories:* My Enemy's Enemy, 1962; Collected Short Stories, 1980, enlarged edn, 1987; *verse:* A Frame of Mind, 1953; A Case of Samples, 1956; A Look Round the Estate, 1967; Collected Poems 1944–1979, 1979; *belles-lettres:* New Maps of Hell, 1960; The James Bond Dossier, 1965; (as William Tanner) The Book of Bond, or Every Man His Own 007, 1966; What Became of Jane Austen?, 1970; *non-fiction:* On Drink, 1972; Rudyard Kipling and his World, 1975; The Alteration, 1976; Every Day Drinking, 1983; How's Your Glass?, 1984; (with J. Cochrane) Great British Songbook, 1986; Memoirs, 1991; *edited:* G. K. Chesterton selected stories, 1972; Tennyson, 1972; Harold's Years, 1977; The New Oxford Book of Light Verse, 1978; The Faber Popular Reciter, 1978; The Golden Age of Science Fiction, 1981; The Amis Anthology, 1988; The Crime of the Century, 1989; The Amis Collection, 1990. *Recreations:* music, thrillers, television. *Address:* c/o Jonathan Clowes, Iron Bridge House, Bridge Approach, NW1 8BD. *Club:* Garrick.

See also M. L. Amis.

AMIS, Martin Louis; author; special writer for The Observer, since 1980; *b* 25 Aug. 1949; *s* of Sir Kingsley Amis, *qv* and Hilary Bardwell; *m* 1984, Antonia Phillips; two *s*. *Educ:* various schools; Exeter Coll., Oxford (BA Hons 1st cl. in English). Fiction and Poetry Editor, TLS, 1974; Literary Editor, New Statesman, 1977–79. *Publications:* The Rachel Papers, 1973 (Somerset Maugham Award, 1974); Dead Babies, 1975; Success, 1978; Other People: a mystery story, 1981; Money, 1984; The Moronic Inferno and Other Visits to America, 1986; Einstein's Monsters (short stories), 1987; London Fields,

1989. *Recreations:* tennis, chess, snooker. *Address:* c/o Peters Fraser & Dunlop, 5th Floor, The Chambers, Chelsea Harbour, Lots Road, SW10 0XF. *Club:* United Oxford & Cambridge University.

AMLOT, Roy Douglas; QC 1989; barrister; *b* 22 Sept. 1942; *s* of Douglas Lloyd Amlot and Ruby Luise Amlot; *m* 1969, Susan Margaret (*née* McDowell); two *s. Educ:* Dulwich Coll. Called to the Bar, Lincoln's Inn, 1963, Bencher, 1986. Second Prosecuting Counsel to the Inland Revenue, Central Criminal Court and London Crown Courts, 1974; First Prosecuting Counsel to the Crown, Inner London Crown Court, 1975; Jun. Prosecuting Counsel to the Crown, Central Criminal Court, 1977, Sen. Prosecuting Counsel, 1981; First Sen. Prosecuting Counsel, 1987. *Publication:* (ed) 11th edn, Phipson on Evidence. *Recreations:* skiing, squash, music. *Address:* 6 King's Bench Walk, Temple, EC4Y 7DR. *T:* 071–583 0410.

AMOORE, Rt. Rev. Frederick Andrew; Provincial Executive Officer, Church of the Province of South Africa, 1982–87, retired; *b* 6 June 1913; *s* of Harold Frederick Newnham Amoore and Emily Clara Amoore, Worthing; *m* 1948, Mary Dobson; three *s. Educ:* Worthing Boys' High Sch.; University of Leeds. BA (Hons Hist) Leeds, 1934. Curate of: Clapham, London, 1936; St Mary's, Port Elizabeth, S Africa, 1939; Rector of St Saviour's, E London, S Africa, 1945; Dean of St Albans Cathedral, Pretoria, 1950; Exec. Officer for Church of Province of S Africa, 1962–67; Bishop of Bloemfontein, 1967–82. *Recreations:* music, italic script. *Address:* 503 Salwood Court, Main Road, Rondebosch, CP, 7700, South Africa. *Club:* City and Civil Service (Cape Town).

AMORY; *see* Heathcoat Amory and Heathcoat-Amory.

AMOS, Alan Thomas; MP (C) Hexham, since 1987; *b* 10 Nov. 1952; *s* of William Edmond Amos and Cynthia Florence Kathleen Amos. *Educ:* St Albans Sch.; St John's Coll., Oxford (MA(PPE) Hons); London Univ. Inst. of Educn (PGCE 1976). Pres., Oxford Univ. Cons. Assoc., 1974–75. Dir of Studies, Hd of Sixth Form, Hd of Econs and Politics Dept, Dame Alice Owen's Sch., Potters Bar, 1976–84; Hd of Agric. and Environment Sect., Cons. Res. Dept, 1984–86; Asst Prin., College of Further Educn, 1986–87. Councillor, 1978–90, Dep. Leader, and Chm. Educn Cttee, 1983–87, Enfield Bor. Council; Chm., London Boroughs Assoc. Educn Cttee, 1986–87. Contested (C): Tottenham, GLC, 1981; Walthamstow, 1983. Mem., Agriculture Select Cttee, 1989–; Chairman: Cons. backbench Forestry Cttee, 1987–; Parly ASH Gp, 1991–; Secretary: Cons. backbench Transport Cttee, 1988–; Cons. backbench Educn Cttee, 1989–; British-Bulgarian All Party Gp, 1991–. Sec., Nat. Agricl and Countryside Forum, 1984–86. A Vice-Pres., Gtr London YCs, 1981–. Member: ESU, 1982–; ASH, 1987–; SPUC, 1987–. *Recreations:* travel, badminton, USA politics, bibliophilia. *Address:* c/o House of Commons, SW1A 0AA.

AMOS, Air Comdt Barbara Mary D.; *see* Ducat-Amos.

AMOS, Francis John Clarke, CBE 1973; BSc(Soc); DipArch, SPDip, ARIBA, PPRTPI; Chief Executive, Birmingham City Council, 1973–77; Senior Fellow, University of Birmingham, since 1977; *b* 10 Sept. 1924; *s* of late Frank Amos, FALPA (Director, H. J. Furlong & Sons, Ltd, London), and Alice Mary Amos; *m* 1956, Geraldine Mercy Sutton, MBE, JP, BSc (Econ), MRTPI; one *s* one *d* (and one *d* decd). *Educ:* Alleyns Sch., and Dulwich Coll., London; Sch. of Architecture, The Polytechnic, London (DipArch); Sch. of Planning and Regional Research, London (SPDip); LSE and Birkbeck Coll., Univ. of London (BSc(Soc)). Served War: Royal Corps of Signals, 1942–44; RIASC, 1944–47. Harlow Develt Corp, 1951; LCC, Planning Div., 1953–58; Min. of Housing and Local Govt, 1958–59 and 1962–63; Adviser to Imperial Ethiopian Govt, 1959–62; Liverpool Corp. City Planning Dept, 1962–74, Chief Planning Officer 1966–74; Chairman: Planning Sub-Cttee, Merseyside Area Land Use/Transportation Study, 1967–73; Working Gp, Educnl Objectives in Urban and Regional Planning, Centre for Environmental Studies, 1970–72; Examination in Public Buckinghamshire Structure Plan, 1981–82. Consultant, Halcrow Fox and Associates , 1984–. Member: Exec. Cttee, Internat. Centre for Regional Planning and Develt, 1954–59; various Cttees, Liverpool Council of Social Services, 1965–72; Exec. Cttee, Town and Country Planning Summer Sch., 1969–70; Planning, Architecture and Bldg Studies Sub-Cttee, UGC, 1968–74; Community Work Gp of Calouste Gulbenkian Foundn, 1970–82; Constitution Cttee, Liverpool Community Relations Council, 1970–73; Planning and Transport Res. Adv. Council, DoE, 1971–77; Town and Country Planning Council and Exec. Cttee, 1972–74; Adv. Cttee, Bldg Res. Estabt, 1972–77 (Chm., Planning Cttee, 1972–80); SSRC Planning and Human Geography and Planning Cttees, 1972–76; Social Studies Sub-Cttee, UGC, 1974–76; W Midlands Economic Planning Council, 1974–77; Environmental Bd, DoE, 1975–78; Trustee, Community Projects Foundn, 1978–88; Council of Management, Action Resource Centre, 1978–86; Study Commn on Family, 1978–83; Arts Council Regional Cttee, 1979–; Exec. Cttee, Watt Cttee on Energy, 1980–82; Planning Cttee, CNAA, 1980–83. Comr, London and Metropolitan Govt Staff Commn, 1984–87; Asst Comr, Local Govt Boundary Commn, 1986–. Chm., Birmingham Gp, Internat. Year for Shelter for the Homeless 1987. Special Prof. of Planning Practice and Management, Univ. of Nottingham, 1979–; Vis. Prof., QUB, 1991–. External Examiner in Planning: Univs of: Liverpool, 1967–70; Newcastle, 1968–71; Aston (Birmingham), 1970–71; Queen's (Belfast), 1972–74; Heriot-Watt, 1972–74; Nottingham, 1973–76; UCL 1975–77; Sheffield, 1979–82; Glasgow, 1979–82; Hong Kong, 1982–85; Polytechnics of: Leeds, 1967–68; Central London, 1967–70; Birmingham, 1975–79; Liverpool, 1977–82. Since 1977, has acted as adviser to govts in aid programmes: Bangladesh (UN); Ghana (UN); Hong Kong (UK); India (ODA); Iraq; Laos; Poland; Tanzania (ODA); Trinidad and Tobago (UN); Turkey (OECD); Venezuela (IBRD); Kenya, Pakistan and Zimbabwe (UN); Uganda (ODA); Zambia (British Council). Mem., County Exec. Cttee, Scout Assoc., 1977–85. Mem., Court, Univ. of Nottingham, 1975–. Chm., Sir Herbert Manzoni Scholarship Trust, 1975–. Adviser to AMA Social Services Cttee, 1974–77; Chm., W Midlands Area, 1978–82, Mem. Nat. Exec., 1982–86, Nat. Assoc. of CAB. Member: Jt Land Requirements Cttee, 1983–; Nuffield Inquiry into Town and Country Planning, 1984–86. Pres., Royal Town Planning Inst., 1971–72 (AMTPI, 1955; Fellow 1967; Hon. Sec., 1979–); Architect RIBA, 1951. FRSA 1977. Freeman of City of London, 1968. *Publications:* Education for Planning (CES Report), 1973; various reports on Liverpool incl.: Annual Reviews of Plans, Study of Social Malaise; RTPI Report on Future of Planning, 1971, 1977; (part) City Centre Redevelopment; (part) Low Income Housing in the Developing World; articles on Planning and Management in Local Govt in various professional jls. *Recreations:* travel; unsystematic philately and unskilled building. *Address:* Grindstones, 20 Westfield Road, Edgbaston, Birmingham B15 3QG. *T:* 021–454 5661; The Coach House, Ashton Gifford Lane, Codford St Peter, Warminster, Wilts BA12 0NJ. *T:* Warminster (0985) 50610.

AMOS, Valerie; Chief Executive, Equal Opportunities Commission, since 1989; *b* 13 March 1954; *d* of E. Michael Amos and Eunice Amos. *Educ:* Univ. of Warwick (BA Sociol.); Univ. of Birmingham (MA Cultural Studies); Univ. of E Anglia (doctoral research). With London Boroughs: Lambeth, 1981–82; Camden, 1983–85; Hackney, 1985–89 (Head of Trng; Head of Management Services); Management Consultant, 1984–89. Mem., Adv. Bd, Centre for Educnl Develt Appraisal and Res; Ext. Examr (MA Equal Opportunities), Newcastle Polytechnic. Trustee, Runnymede Trust. *Publications:* various articles on race and gender issues. *Address:* Equal Opportunities Commission, Overseas House, Quay Street, Manchester M3 3HN.

AMPLEFORTH, Abbot of; *see* Barry, Rt. Rev. N. P.

AMPTHILL, 4th Baron *cr* 1881; **Geoffrey Denis Erskine Russell,** CBE 1986; Deputy Chairman of Committees, since 1980, Deputy Speaker, since 1983, House of Lords; *b* 15 Oct. 1921; *s* of 3rd Baron Ampthill, CBE, and Christabel, Lady Ampthill (*d* 1976); *S* father, 1973; *m* 1st, 1946, Susan Mary (marr. diss. 1971), *d* of late Hon. Charles John Frederic Winn; two *s* one *d* (and one *s* decd); 2nd, 1972, Elisabeth Anne Marie (marr. diss. 1987), *d* of late Claude Henri Gustave Mallon. *Educ:* Stowe. Irish Guards, 1941–46; 2nd Lt 1941, Captain 1944. Gen. Manager, Fortnum and Mason, 1947–51; Chairman, New Providence Hotel Co. Ltd, 1951–64; Director: United Newspapers plc, 1981–; Dualvest plc, 1981–87; Express Newspapers plc, 1985–. Managing Director of theatre owning and producing companies, 1953–81. Dir, Leeds Castle Foundn, 1980–82. Chm., Select Cttee on Channel Tunnel Bill, 1987. *Heir: s* Hon. David Whitney Erskine Russell [*b* 27 May 1947; *m* 1980, April McKenzie Arbon, *y d* of Paul Arbon, New York; two *d*]. *Address:* 51 Sutherland Street, SW1V 4JX.

AMRITANAND, Rt. Rev. Joseph; Bishop of Calcutta, 1970–82; *b* Amritsar, Punjab, India, 17 Feb. 1917; *m* 1943, Catherine Phillips; one *s* one *d. Educ:* District Board School, Toba Tek Singh, Punjab; Forman Christian Coll., Lahore, Punjab Univ. (BA); Bishop's College, Calcutta; Wycliffe Hall, Oxford. Deacon 1941, priest 1943; Missionary-in-charge of CMS Mission Field, Gojra, 1946–48; Bishop of Assam, 1949–62; Bishop of Lucknow, 1962–70; translated, after inauguration of Church of North India, Nov. 1970; first Bishop of Durgapur, 1972–74. *Recreations:* reading, bird watching, visiting, helping anyone in need on the road, intercessional ministering. *Address:* 182 Civil Lines, Bareilly, UP 243001, India.

AMWELL, 3rd Baron *cr* 1947, of Islington; **Keith Norman Montague;** Associate with Brian Colquhoun and Partners, Consulting Engineers, since 1984; *b* 1 April 1943; *o s* of 2nd Baron Amwell and of Kathleen Elizabeth Montague (*née* Fountain); *S* father, 1990; *m* 1970, Mary, *d* of Frank Palfreyman; two *s. Educ:* Ealing Grammar Sch. for Boys; Nottingham Univ. BSc (Civil Engineering); CEng; MICE; MIHT; FGS. Consulting civil engineer, 1965–. *Publications:* papers to international construction confs. *Recreations:* walking, photography, badminton. *Heir: s* Hon. Ian Keith Montague, *b* 20 Sept. 1973.

AMY, Dennis Oldrieve, OBE 1984; HM Diplomatic Service; Ambassador to the Democratic Republic of Madagascar, since 1990, and Ambassador (non-resident) to Federal Islamic Republic of the Comoros, since 1991; *b* 21 Oct. 1932; *s* of late George Arthur Amy and Isabella Thompson (*née* Crosby); *m* 1956, Helen Rosamunde, *d* of Wilfred Leslie Clemens; one *s* one *d. Educ:* Southall Grammar Sch. Served RM, 1951–53. Entered HM Foreign, later HM Diplomatic Service, 1949; FO, 1949–51 and 1953–58; Athens, 1958–61; Second Sec. and Vice Consul, Moscow, 1961–63; FO, 1963–65; DSAO, 1965; Second Sec. and Passport Officer, Canberra, 1966–70; First Sec., Ibadan, 1971–74; seconded to Dept of Trade, 1974–75; FCO, 1976–78; First Sec. (Commercial), Santiago, 1978–83 (Chargé d'Affaires, 1979); FCO, 1983–86 (Counsellor, 1985–86); Consul Gen., Bordeaux, 1986–89. *Recreations:* Scottish country dancing, golf, gardening. *Address:* c/o Foreign and Commonwealth Office, SW1A 2AH. *Club:* Commonwealth Trust.

AMYOT, Léopold Henri, CVO 1990; Secretary to Governor General of Canada and Secretary General of Order of Canada and of Order of Military Merit, since 1985; Herald Chancellor of Canada, since 1988; *b* 25 Aug. 1930; *s* of S. Eugène Amyot and Juliette Gagnon; *m* 1958, (Marie Jeanne) Andrée Jobin; one *s* two *d. Educ:* Laval Univ., Québec (BLSc, BScSoc); Ottawa Univ. (BA); Geneva Univ. (course on Internat. Instns). Joined External Affairs, 1957; Second Secretary: Canberra, 1960; New Delhi, 1961; Counsellor, Paris, 1968; Amb. to Lebanon (with accredn to Syria, Jordan, Iraq), 1974; Dep. Sec. Gen., Agence de Co-opération culturelle et technique, Paris, 1976; Chief of Protocol, Ext. Affairs, Ottawa, 1980; Exec. Dir, Task Force, on Pope's Visit to Canada, 1983; Amb. to Morocco, 1983. Chm., Official Residences Collections (formerly Official Residences Arts) Adv. Cttee, 1985–. Member: Professional Assoc. of For. Service Officers, Ottawa, 1957–; l'Inst. canadien des Affaires internat., Québec, 1985–. Prix d'honneur (Sect. de Québec) l'Inst. canadien des Affaires internat., 1985. *Recreations:* tennis, golf, swimming, contemporary art collector. *Address:* Government House, 1 Sussex Drive, Ottawa, Ontario K1A 0A1, Canada. *T:* (613) 993–0259.

AMYOT, René, QC; barrister; Counsel, Jolin, Fournier, Morisset; *b* Quebec City, 1 Nov. 1926; *s* of Omer Amyot and Caroline L'Espérance (*née* Barry); *m* 1954, Monique, *d* of Fernand Boutin; two *s* two *d. Educ:* Collège des Jésuites de Québec (BA 1946); Laval Univ. Law Sch. (LLL 1949); Harvard Univ. Grad. Sch. of Business Admin (MBA 1951). Called to Bar of Québec, 1949; QC Canada 1965. Joined Procter & Gamble, Montreal, 1951; Bouffard & Associates, Quebec, 1952; Asst Prof., Faculty of Admin. Scis, Laval Univ., 1954–69; Asst Prof., Fiscal Law, Laval Univ. Law Sch., 1960–70; Consul for Belgium, 1966–82. Dir, and Mem. Exec. Cttee, Centre de Recherche Industrielle de Québec, 1971–76; Pres., Quebec Dist Chamber of Commerce, 1972; Founding Pres., Centre Internat. Recherches et Etudes en Management, 1972; Chairman, Air Canada, 1981–83; Director: Bank of Nova Scotia, 1972–81; Logistec Corp.; Rothmans Inc.; Palmar Inc.; Ressources Robex Inc.; Ressources Orcar Inc., Ressources Veinor Inc.; Fidusco Ltd; Ferme Charlevoix Inc. Dir, Council for Business and the Arts in Canada. Member: Canadian Bar Assoc.; Québec Bar Assoc.; Canadian Tax Foundn; Cttee, Internat. Chamber; Assoc. des MBA du Québec. Gov., Faculty of Administrative Scis, Laval Univ. Chevalier de l'Ordre de Léopold (Belgium), 1985. *Recreations:* skiing, swimming, tennis, farming. *Address:* Jolin, Fournier, Morisset, Edifice Iberville 3, Suite 500, 2960 Boulevard Laurier, Sainte-Foy, Québec G1V 4S1, Canada. *Clubs:* Québec Garrison, Toronto.

ANCHORENA, Dr Manuel de; Argentine Ambassador to the Court of St James's, 1974–76; *b* 3 June 1933; *s* of Norberto de Anchorena and Ena Arrotea; *m* 1st, 1955, Elvira Peralta Martinez (*d* 1977); three *s* one *d*; 2nd, 1978, Anne Margaret Clifford. *Educ:* Univ. of Buenos Aires. Doctorate in Law, Buenos Aires, 1955. Landowner, politician, and historian. *Publications:* several articles contrib. to jl of Inst. of Historic Investigation, Argentina; articles on wild life and natural preservation. *Recreations:* polo, tennis, squash, fencing. *Address:* Estancia La Corona, Villanueva 7225, F.C. Roca, Provincia de Buenos Aires, Argentina. *Clubs:* Hurlingham, Royal Automobile; Circulo de Caza Mayor (Buenos Aires) (former Pres.).

ANCRAM, Earl of; Michael Andrew Foster Jude Kerr; DL; advocate; *b* 7 July 1945; *s* and *heir* of 12th Marquess of Lothian, *qv*; *m* 1975, Lady Jane Fitzalan-Howard, *y d* of 16th Duke of Norfolk, KG, PC, GCVO, GBE, TD, and of Lavinia Duchess of Norfolk, *qv;* two *d. Educ:* Ampleforth; Christ Church, Oxford (BA); Edinburgh Univ. (LLB). Advocate, Scottish Bar, 1970. Contested (C) Edinburgh S, 1987. MP (C): Berwickshire and East Lothian, Feb.-Sept. 1974; Edinburgh S, 1979–87. Parly Under-Sec. of State, Scottish Office, 1983–87. Mem., Select Cttee on Energy, 1979–83. Chm., Cons. Party in

Scotland, 1980–83 (Vice-Chm., 1975–80). Chm., Northern Corporate Communications; Dir, CSM Parly Consultants; Mem. Bd, Scottish Homes, 1988–90. DL Roxburgh, Ettrick and Lauderdale, 1990. *Recreations:* ski-ing, photography, folksinging. *Address:* Fairfield House, Pewsey, Wilts; Monteviot, Jedburgh, Scotland. *Club:* Turf.

ANDERSEN, Valdemar Jens, CMG 1965; OBE 1960 (MBE 1955); VRD 1962; Resident Commissioner, Gilbert and Ellice Islands Colony, 1962–70, retired; *b* 21 March 1919; 2nd *s* of Max Andersen, Maraenui, NZ; *m* 1946, Alison Leone, 2nd *d* of G. A. Edmonds, Remuera, Auckland, NZ; one *s* one *d*. *Educ:* Napier Boys High Sch. NZ; Auckland University Coll. (BSc). Lieut, RNZNVR, 1940–46; Lieut, RANVR, 1947–62. British Solomon Islands Protectorate: Administrative Officer, 1947; Class A, Administrative Officer, 1954; Secretary Protectorate Affairs, 1958. *Recreations:* drama, gardening. *Address:* McKinney Road, Warkworth, New Zealand.

ANDERSON, family name of **Viscount Waverley.**

ANDERSON, Maj.-Gen. Alistair Andrew Gibson, CB 1980; *b* 26 Feb. 1927; *s* of Lt-Col John Gibson Anderson and Margaret Alice (*née* Scott); *m* 1953, Dr Margaret Grace Smith; one *s* two *d*. *Educ:* George Watson's Boys Coll., Edinburgh; University Coll. of SW of England, Exeter (Short Univ. Course, 1944); Staff Coll., Camberley; Jt Services Staff Coll., Latimer. Enlisted 1944; commnd Royal Corps of Signals, 1946; comd 18 Signal Regt, 1967–69; Defence Ops Centre, 1969–72; staff of Signal Officer-in-Chief, 1972–74; Comdt, Sch. of Signals, 1974–76; Signal Officer-in-Chief (Army), 1977–80, retired; Dir, Communications and Electronics Security Gp, GCHQ, 1980–85. Col Comdt, Royal Corps of Signals, 1980–86; Chm., Royal Signals Assoc., 1982–87. *Recreations:* hill walking, sailing, gardening. *Club:* Army and Navy.
See also Sir J. E. Anderson.

ANDERSON, Anthony John; QC 1982; *b* 12 Sept. 1938; *s* of late A. Fraser Anderson and Margaret Anderson; *m* 1970, Fenja Ragnhild Gunn. *Educ:* Harrow; Magdalen Coll., Oxford. MA. 2nd Lieut, The Gordon Highlanders, 1957–59. Called to the Bar, Inner Temple, 1964. *Recreation:* golf. *Address:* 2 Mitre Court Buildings, Temple, EC4Y 7BX. *T:* 071–583 1380; 33 Abinger Road, Bedford Park, W4. *T:* 081–994 2857. *Club:* Garrick.

ANDERSON, Dr Arthur John Ritchie, (Iain), CBE 1984; MA; MRCGP; General Medical and Hospital Practitioner, Trainer, since 1961; *b* 19 July 1933; *s* of Dr John Anderson and Dorothy Mary Anderson; *m* 1959, Janet Edith Norrish; two *s* one *d*. *Educ:* Bromsgrove Sch.; Downing Coll., Cambridge; St Mary's Hospital Medical Sch. MA, MB BChir (Cantab). MRCS; LRCP; DCH; DObstRCOG. Various hospital posts, 1958–61. Hemel Hempstead RDC, 1967–74, Vice-Chm., 1970–74; Councillor, Hertfordshire CC, 1973–, Vice-Chm., 1985–87 (Leader, 1977–83), Chief Whip, Cons. Gp, 1989–. Chm., Herts Police Authority, 1984–87; Member: NW Thames Regional Health Authority, 1978–84; Regional Planning Council for South East, 1977–79. President, Hertfordshire Branch, BMA, 1973–74. Member, various governing bodies of primary, secondary, further and higher educn instns. Chm., Crouchfield Trust, 1989–. FRSM 1984. *Publications:* numerous articles, mainly in periodicals. *Recreations:* writing, hockey, walking. *Address:* Leaside, Rucklers Lane, King's Langley, Herts WD4 9NQ. *T:* King's Langley (09277) 62884. *Club:* Herts 100.

ANDERSON, Beverley Jean; education consultant, since 1989, and broadcaster; *b* 9 Dec. 1940; *d* of Arthur Benjamin Phillpotts and Sylvia Tomlinson Phillpotts; *m* 1st, 1968, Angus Walker, *qv* (marr. diss. 1976); 2nd, 1976, Andrew Anderson (marr. diss. 1986); one *s*. *Educ:* Wellesley Coll., Mass (BA History, and Politics 1962); London Univ. (PGCE 1967). Jamaican Foreign Service, Kingston and Washington, 1963–66; primary sch. teacher, London, 1968–71, Oxfordshire primary schs, 1971–81; Headteacher, Berwood First Sch., Oxford, 1981–83; Sen. Lectr in Educn, Oxford Poly., 1985–89; Lectr in Educn, Warwick Univ., 1989–. Chairman: Equal Opportunities Wkg Gp, NAB, 1987–88; CNAA Steering Cttee on Accesss Courses to HE Framework, 1988–89; Member: Nat. Curriculum Council, 1989–91; Council, ABSA, 1989–; Arts Council, 1990–; Governor: BFI, 1985–; Oxford Stage Co. Bd, 1986–; S Bank Bd, 1989–. Mem., Nuffield Council on Bioethics, 1991–; Chm. Council, Charter '88, 1989–. Columnist, TES, 1989–. Television includes: Presenter: Black on Black, 1982–83; Nothing but the Best; Sixty Minutes; After Dark, 1989–90; Behind the Headlines, 1990–91. FRSA 1991. *Publications:* Learning with Logo: a teacher's guide, 1985; numerous articles on education, social issues and media education. *Recreations:* plays, paintings, poems, movies, dancing, music. *Address:* c/o Arts Council, 14 Great Peter Street, SW1P 3NQ. *T:* 071–333 0100.

ANDERSON, Brian David Outram, FRS 1989; Professor of Systems Engineering, Australian National University, since 1981; *b* 15 Jan. 1941; *s* of David Outram Anderson and late Nancy Anderson; *m* 1968, Dianne, *d* of M. Allen; three *d*. *Educ:* Sydney Univ.; Stanford Univ.; California Univ. Res. Asst, Stanford Electronics Labs, 1964; Lectr in Electrical Engrg, Stanford Univ., 1965; Asst Prof. and Staff Consultant, Vidar Corp., Mount View, Calif., 1966; Hd of Dept, 1967–75, Prof., 1967–81, Dept of Electrical Engrg, Univ. of Newcastle. Mem., Scientific Adv. Bd, CRA Ltd, 1982–; Dir, Telectronics Hldgs Ltd, 1986–. Member: Aust. Res. Grants Cttee, 1972–77; Aust. Science and Technology Council, 1977–82; UNESCO Nat. Commn, 1982–83; Aust. Industrial Res. and Develt Incentives Bd, 1984–86. FAA; FTS; FIEEE; Hon. FIE(Aust). *Publications* include: Linear Optimal Control, 1971; Network Analysis and Synthesis, 1975; Optimal Filtering, 1980; Optimal Control, 1990. *Address:* c/o Department of Systems Engineering, Australian National University, GPO Box 4, Canberra, ACT 2601, Australia.

ANDERSON, Campbell McCheyne; Managing Director, since 1985, and Chief Executive Officer, since 1986, Renison Goldfields Consolidated; Director, Minora Resources NL, since 1987; *b* 17 Sept. 1941; *s* of Allen Taylor Anderson and Ethel Catherine Rundle; *m* 1965, Sandra Maclean Harper; two *s* one *d*. *Educ:* The Armidale Sch., NSW, Aust.; Univ. of Sydney (BEcon). AASA. Trainee and General Administration, Boral Ltd, Australia, 1962–69; Gen. Manager/Man. Dir, Reef Oil NL, Australia, 1969–71; Asst Chief Representative, Burmah Oil Australia Ltd, 1972; Corporate Development, Burmah Oil Incorporated, New York, 1973; Corporate Development, 1974; Finance Director and Group Planning, Burmah Oil Trading Ltd, UK, 1975; Special Projects Dir, 1976, Shipping Dir, 1978, Industrial Dir, 1979, Man. Dir, 1982–84, Burmah Oil Co. Dir, Consolidated Gold Fields, 1985–89. Director: Aust. Mines and Metals Assoc., 1985–; World Gold Council, 1986–; Councillor: Aust. Mining Industry Council, 1985–; Business Council of Aust., 1986–. *Recreations:* golf, swimming, horse-racing, shooting. *Address:* 77 Drumalbyn Road, Bellevue Hill, Sydney, NSW 2023, Australia. *Clubs:* Oil Industries; Frilford Heath Golf; Australian; Royal Sydney Golf; Australian Jockey; Elanora Country (NSW).

ANDERSON, Rear-Adm. (Charles) Courtney, CB 1971; Flag Officer, Admiralty Interview Board, 1969–71, retired; *b* 8 Nov. 1916; *s* of late Lt-Col Charles Anderson, Australian Light Horse, and Mrs Constance Powell-Anderson, OBE, JP; *m* 1940, Pamela Ruth Miles; three *s*. *Educ:* RNC, Dartmouth. Joined RN, 1930. Served War of 1939–45: in command of Motor Torpedo Boats, Destroyers and Frigates. Naval Intelligence, 1946–49 and 1955–57; Commanded HMS Contest, 1949–51; Comdr, 1952; BJSM, Washington, 1953–55; Capt., 1959; Naval Attaché, Bonn, 1962–65; Director, Naval Recruiting, 1966–68; ADC to Queen, 1968; Rear-Adm., 1969. Editor, The Board Bulletin, 1971–78. *Publications:* The Drum Beats Still, 1951. Numerous articles and short stories. *Recreations:* gardening, do-it-yourself. *Address:* Bybrook Cottage, Bustlers Hill, Sherston, Malmesbury, Wilts SN16 0ND.

ANDERSON, (Clarence) Eugene; Chairman and Chief Executive, Ferranti International plc, since 1990; *b* 31 Aug. 1938; *s* of Clarence Leslie Anderson and Wilda Faye Anderson; *m* 1977, Daniela Leopolda Proche; one *s* three *d*. *Educ:* Univ. of Texas (BSc Chem. Engrg, 1961); Harvard Univ. (MBA 1963). Process Engr, New Orleans, 1961, Ops Analyst, Houston, 1963–66, Tenneco Oil Co.; Man. Dir, Globe Petroleum Sales Ltd, Lincs, 1966–69; Dir, Supply and Transportation, Houston, 1969–72, Dir, Operational Planning, Houston, 1972, Tenneco Oil Co.; Vice Pres., Tenneco International Co., Houston, 1973; Exec. Dir, Albright & Wilson Ltd, London, 1973–75; Vice Pres., Corporate Develt, Tenneco Inc., Houston, 1975–78; Dep. Man. Dir, Ops, Albright & Wilson Ltd, London, 1979–81; Pres., Celanese International Co., and Vice Pres., Celanese Corp., New York, 1981–85; Chief Exec., Johnson Matthey PLC, London, 1985–89. *Publication:* (jtly) report on microencapsulation. *Recreations:* music, literature, theatre, various sports. *Address:* Ferranti International plc, Bridge House, Park Road, Gatley, Cheadle, Cheshire SK8 4HZ. *T:* 061–428 3644.

ANDERSON, Courtney; *see* Anderson, (Charles) Courtney.

ANDERSON, Rev. David; Principal Lecturer in Religious Studies, Hertfordshire College of Higher Education (formerly Wall Hall College), Aldenham, Herts, 1974–84 (Senior Lecturer, 1970–74); *b* 30 Oct. 1919; *s* of William and Nancy Anderson, Newcastle upon Tyne; *m* 1953, Helen Finlay Robinson, 3rd *d* of Johnson and Eleanor Robinson, Whitley Bay, Northumberland; one *s* two *d*. *Educ:* Royal Grammar Sch. Newcastle upon Tyne; Selwyn Coll., Cambridge. Served in RA, 1940–42, Intelligence Corps, 1942–46, Lieut. Deacon, 1949, Priest, 1950; Curate of parish of St Gabriel, Sunderland, 1949–52; Tutor of St Aidan's Coll., Birkenhead, 1952–56; Warden of Melville Hall, Ibadan, Nigeria, 1956–58; Principal of: Immanuel Coll., Ibadan, Nigeria, 1958–62; Wycliffe Hall, Oxford, 1962–69. Examining Chaplain: to Bishop of Liverpool, 1969–75; to Bishop of St Albans, 1972–80. *Publications:* The Tragic Protest, 1969; Simone Weil, 1971; contrib: Religion and Modern Literature, 1975; William Golding: some critical considerations, 1978; The Passion of Man, 1980. *Recreations:* listening to music, hi-fi gramophones. *Address:* 6 Flassburn Road, Durham DH1 4LX. *T:* Durham (091) 3843063.

ANDERSON, David Colville, VRD 1947, and Clasp, 1958; QC (Scotland) 1957; *b* 8 Sept. 1916; *yr s* of late J. L. Anderson of Pittormie, Fife, solicitor and farmer, and late Etta Colville; *m* 1948, Juliet, *yr d* of late Hon. Lord Hill Watson, MC, LLD; two *s* one *d*. *Educ:* Trinity Coll., Glenalmond; Pembroke Coll., Oxford; Edinburgh Univ. BA (Hons) Oxford 1938; LLB (Distinction) 1946. Thow Scholar, Maclagan Prizeman, Dalgety Prizeman, Edinburgh Univ. Lecturer in Scots Law, Edinburgh Univ., 1947–60; Advocate, 1946; Standing Junior Counsel to Ministry of Works, 1954–55, and to War Office, 1955–57. Contested (C) Coatbridge and Airdrie, 1955, and East Dunbartonshire, 1959; MP (C) Dumfries, Dec. 1963–Sept. 1964. Solicitor-General for Scotland, 1960–64; Vice-Chairman, Commissioners of Northern Lighthouses, 1963–64; Hon. Sheriff-Substitute, Lothians and Peebles, 1965–; Chm., Industrial Tribunals (Scotland), 1971–72; Chief Reporter for Public Inquiries and Under Sec., Scottish Office, 1972–74. Joined RNVR, 1935. In VIII awarded Ashburton Shield, Bisley, 1933 (Trinity Coll., Glenalmond; schools event); Inter-Services XX at Bisley, 1936–38. Served War of 1939–45 in destroyers (despatches); Lieut 1940; Egerton Prizeman in Naval Gunnery, 1943; Flotilla Gunnery Officer, Rosyth Escort Force, 1943–45; led special operation N Norway, 1945; Lt-Comdr 1948. King Haakon VII Liberty Medal, 1946. *Relevant Play:* The Case of David Anderson QC by John Hale (Manchester, and Traverse Theatre, Edinburgh, 1980; Lyric Studio Hammersmith, 1981). *Address:* 8 Arboretum Road, Edinburgh EH3 5PD. *T:* 031–552 3003. *Club:* New (Edinburgh).

ANDERSON, David Heywood, CMG 1982; HM Diplomatic Service; Second Legal Adviser, Foreign and Commonwealth Office, since 1989; Barrister-at-Law; *b* 14 Sept. 1937; *s* of late Harry Anderson; *m* 1961, Jennifer Ratcliffe; one *s* one *d*. *Educ:* King James' Grammar Sch., Almondbury. LLB (Leeds); LLM (London). Called to Bar, Gray's Inn, 1963. Asst Legal Adviser, FCO, 1960–69; Legal Adviser, British Embassy, Bonn, 1969–72; Legal Counsellor, FCO, 1972–79; Legal Adviser, UK Mission to UN, NY, 1979–82; Legal Counsellor, FCO, 1982–87; Dep. Legal Advr, FCO, 1987–89. *Recreations:* reading, gardening. *Address:* c/o Foreign and Commonwealth Office, King Charles Street, SW1A 2AH.

ANDERSON, David Munro; Chairman, E. D. & F. Man International Ltd, since 1986; *b* 15 Dec. 1937; *s* of Alexander Anderson and Jessica Anderson (*née* Vincent-Innes); *m* 1965, Veronica Jane (*née* Stevens); two *s* one *d*. *Educ:* Morrison's Academy, Perthshire; Strathallan, Perthshire. Commissioned Black Watch; served W Africa; tea production with James Finlay & Co., India, 1959–62; London Chamber of Commerce and Industry, 1962–63; joined E. D. & F. Man Ltd, 1963; formed Anderson Man Ltd, 1981; formed E. D. & F. Man International Ltd, 1985; Man. Dir, Commodity Analysis Ltd, 1968; numerous directorships. Chairman, formation cttees: Internat. Petroleum Exchange; Baltic Internat. Freight Futures Exchange (jtly); former Vice-Chm., London Commodity Exchange; Member: Securities and Investments Bd, 1986–87; Futures and Commodity Exchanges. *Recreations:* ski-ing, shooting. *Address:* The Old Rectory, Lamarsh, Bures, Suffolk CO8 5EU. *T:* Bures (0787) 227271. *Club:* Caledonian.

ANDERSON, Brig. David William, CBE 1976 (OBE 1972); Chief Executive, Cumbernauld Development Corporation, 1985–88; *b* 4 Jan. 1929; *s* of David Anderson and Frances Anderson; *m* 1954, Eileen Dorothy Scott; one *s* two *d*. *Educ:* St Cuthbert's Grammar Sch., Newcastle on Tyne. Black Watch, 1946; RMA, Sandhurst, 1947; commnd HLI, 1948; served ME and Malaya; RHF, Staff Coll., Trucial Oman Scouts, Sch. of Inf., I RHF, Germany, and HQ NORTHAG, 1959–66; Instr, Staff Coll., 1967–69; CO I RHF, Scotland, N Ireland, Singapore, 1969–72; Colonel GS: MoD, 1972–73; HQ Dir of Inf., 1974; Comdr, 3 Inf. Bde, N Ireland, 1975–76; Comdt, Sch. of Infantry, 1976–79; Comdr, Highlands, 1979–81, Comdr 51 Highland Bde, 1982; ADC to the Queen, 1981–82. Chief Exec., NE Fife DC, 1982–85. Hon. Colonel: Aberdeen Univ. OTC, 1982–87; 1/52 Lowland Vol., 1987–88; Member: RHF Council, 1970–88; Highland TA&VRA, 1984–88; Lowland TA & VRA, 1987–88. Chm., Fife Area Scout Council, 1985–86. Mem., St John Assoc., 1984–85. Hon. Vice-Pres., Cumbernauld Br., Royal British Legion (Scotland), 1985–88. *Recreations:* moving house, Scottish history.

ANDERSON, Prof. Declan John; Professor of Oral Biology, University of Bristol, 1966–85, now Professor of Physiology Emeritus; Director, The Oral and Dental Research Trust, since 1989; *b* 20 June 1920; *s* of Arthur John Anderson and Katherine Mary Coffey; *m* 1947, Vivian Joy Dunkerton; four *s* three *d*. *Educ:* Christ's Hospital; Guy's Hospital Medical School, Univ. of London. BDS (London) 1942; LDSRCS 1943, BSc 1946, MSc 1947, PhD 1955. Prof. of Physiology, Univ. of Oregon, USA, 1957–58; Prof.

of Physiology in Relation to Dentistry, Univ. of London, 1963–66. *Publications:* Physiology for Dental Students, 1952; scientific papers in professional jls. *Recreations:* silversmithing, forging, music. *Address:* Little Dene, Stonequarry Road, Chelwood Gate, East Sussex RH17 7LS.

ANDERSON, Donald; MP (Lab) Swansea East, since Oct. 1974; barrister-at-law; *b* 17 June 1939; *s* of David Robert Anderson and Eva (*née* Mathias); *m* 1963, Dr Dorothy Trotman, BSc, PhD; three *s. Educ:* Swansea Grammar Sch.; University Coll. of Swansea (Hon. Fellow, 1985). 1st cl. hons Modern History and Politics, Swansea, 1960. Barrister; called to Bar, Inner Temple, 1969. Member of HM Foreign Service, 1960–64: Foreign Office, 1960–63; 3rd Sec., British Embassy, Budapest, 1963–64; lectured in Dept of Political Theory and Govt, University Coll., Swansea, 1964–66. Councillor, Kensington and Chelsea, 1971–75. MP (Lab) Monmouth, 1966–70; Mem. Estimates Cttee, 1966–69; Vice-Chm., Welsh Labour Group, 1969–70, Chm., 1977–78; PPS to Min. of Defence (Administration), 1969–70; PPS to Attorney General, 1974–79; opposition front-bench spokesman on foreign affairs, 1983–. Chairman: Parly Lab. Party Environment Gp, 1974–79; Welsh Lab. Gp, 1977–78; Select Cttee on Welsh Affairs, 1981–83 (Mem., 1980–83); British-Zimbabwe Parly Gp, 1989–. Vice-Chairman: Exec., IPU, 1985–88 (Treas., 1988–90); CPA, 1986– (Treas., 1990–); British-French Parly Gp, 1984–; British-Norwegian Parly Gp, 1988–; Jt Hon. Sec., British-German Parly Gp, 1975–; Treas., Anglo-Austrian Soc., 1988–; Sen. Vice-Pres., Assoc. of W European Parliamentarians for Action against Apartheid, 1984–. Pres., Gower Soc., 1976–78. Chairman: Parly Christian Fellowship, 1990; Nat. Prayer Breakfast, 1989. Local preacher. Commander's Cross, Order of Merit (FRG), 1986. *Recreations:* church work, walking and talking. *Address:* House of Commons, SW1A 0AA.

ANDERSON, Prof. Donald Thomas, AO 1986; PhD, DSc; FRS 1977; Challis Professor of Biology, University of Sydney, since 1984 (Professor of Biology, 1972–84); *b* 29 Dec. 1931; *s* of Thomas and Flora Anderson; *m* 1960, Joanne Trevathan (*née* Claridge). *Educ:* King's Coll., London Univ. DSc London, 1966; DSc Sydney, 1983. Lectr in Zoology, Sydney Univ., 1958–61; Sen. Lectr, 1962–66; Reader in Biology, 1967–71. Clarke Medal, Royal Soc. of NSW, 1979. *Publication:* Embryology and Phylogeny, of Annelids and Arthropods, 1973; papers in zool. jls. *Recreations:* gardening, photography. *Address:* 52 Spruson Street, Neutral Bay, NSW 2089, Australia. *T:* (home) 929.7583; (office) 692.2438.

ANDERSON, Prof. Ephraim Saul, CBE 1976; FRCP, FRS 1968; Director, Enteric Reference Laboratory, Public Health Laboratory Service, 1954–78; *b* 1911; *e s* of Benjamin and Ada Anderson, Newcastle upon Tyne; *m* 1959, Carol Jean (*née* Thompson) (marr. diss.); three *s. Educ:* Rutherford Coll., and King's Coll. Med. Sch. (Univ. of Durham), Newcastle upon Tyne. MB, BS 1934; MD Durham, 1953; Dip.Bact. London, 1948; Founder Fellow, Royal Coll. of Pathologists, 1963. GP, 1935–39; RAMC, 1940–46; Pathologist, 1943–46; Registrar in Bacteriology, Postgrad. Med. Sch., 1946–47; Staff, Enteric Reference Lab., 1947–52, Dep. Dir, 1952–54. WHO Fellow, 1953; FIBiol 1973; FRCP 1975. Hon. Chm., Internat. Fedn for Enteric Phage Typing of Internat. Union of Microbiol. Socs, 1986– (Jt Chm., 1958–66; Chm., 1966–86); Dir, Internat. Ref. Lab. for Enteric Phage Typing of Internat. Fedn for Enteric Phage Typing, 1954–78; Dir, Collab. Centre for Phage Typing and Resistance of Enterobacteria of WHO, 1960–78; Mem., WHO Expert Adv. Panel for Enteric Diseases. Vis. Prof., Sch. of Biol Sciences, Brunel Univ., 1973–77. Lectures: Scientific Basis of Medicine, British Postgrad. Med. Fedn, 1966; Almroth Wright, Wright-Fleming Inst. of Microbiol., 1967; Holme, UCH, 1970; Cutter, Sch. of Public Health, Harvard, 1972; Marjory Stephenson Meml, Soc. for Gen. Microbiol., 1975. Hon. DSc Newcastle, 1975. *Publications:* contrib. to: The Bacteriophages (Mark Adams), 1959; The World Problem of Salmonellosis (Van Oye), 1964; Ciba Symposium: Bacterial Episomes and Plasmids, 1969; numerous articles on bacteriophage typing and its genetic basis, microbial ecology, transferable drug resistance in bacteria, its evolution, and epidemiology. *Recreations:* music, photography. *Address:* 10 Rosecroft Avenue, NW3 7QB.

ANDERSON, Eric; *see* Anderson, W. E. K.

ANDERSON, Eugene; *see* Anderson, C. E.

ANDERSON, Sir Ferguson; *see* Anderson, Sir W. F.

ANDERSON, Dame Frances Margaret; *see* Anderson, Dame Judith.

ANDERSON, Rev. Prof. George Wishart, FRSE 1977; FBA 1972; Professor of Old Testament Literature and Theology, 1962–68, of Hebrew and Old Testament Studies, 1968–82, University of Edinburgh; *b* 25 Jan. 1913; *s* of George Anderson and Margaret Gordon Wishart; *m* 1st, 1941, Edith Joyce Marjorie Walter (decd); one *s* one *d*; 2nd, 1959, Anne Phyllis Walter. *Educ:* Arbroath High Sch.; Univs of St Andrews, Cambridge, Lund. United Coll., St Andrews: Harkness Scholar; MA 1st Cl. Hons Classics, 1935. Fitzwilliam House and Wesley House, Cambridge: 1st Cl. Theol Tripos Part I, 1937; 2nd Cl. Theol Tripos Part II, 1938; BA 1937; MA 1946. Asst Tutor, Richmond Coll., 1939–41. Chaplain, RAF, 1941–46; Tutor in OT Lang. and Lit., Handsworth Coll., 1946–56; Lecturer in OT Lit. and Theol., Univ. of St Andrews, 1956–58; Prof. of OT Studies, Univ. of Durham, 1958–62. Hon. Sec., Internat. Organization of Old Testament Scholars, 1953–71 (Pres., 1971–74); Mem. Editorial Bd of Vetus Testamentum, 1950–75; Editor, Book List of Soc. for OT Study, 1957–66; President, Soc. for OT Study, 1963; Hon. Sec. (Foreign Correspondence), Soc. for OT Study, 1964–74; Charles Ryder Smith Meml Lectr, 1964; Fernley-Hartley Lectr, 1969; Speaker's Lectr in Biblical Studies, Univ. of Oxford, 1976–80; Henton Davies Lectr, 1977; A. S. Peake Meml Lectr, 1984. Hon. DD St Andrews, 1959; Hon. TeolD Lund, 1971. Burkitt Medal for Biblical Studies, British Acad., 1982. *Publications:* He That Cometh (trans. from Norwegian of S. Mowinckel), 1956; A Critical Introduction to the Old Testament, 1959; The Ras Shamra Discoveries and the Old Testament (trans. from Norwegian of A. S. Kapelrud, US 1963, UK 1965); The History and Religion of Israel, 1966 (trans. Chinese 1990); (ed) A Decade of Bible Bibliography, 1967; (ed) Tradition and Interpretation, 1979; articles in: The Old Testament and Modern Study (ed H. H. Rowley), 1951; The New Peake Commentary (ed M. Black and H. H. Rowley), 1962; The Cambridge History of the Bible, Vol. I (ed P. R. Ackroyd and C. F. Evans), 1970, and in various learned jls. *Recreations:* reading, music, walking. *Address:* 51 Fountainhall Road, Edinburgh EH9 2LH.

ANDERSON, Gordon Alexander, CA, FCMA; Chartered Accountant; *b* 9 Aug. 1931; *s* of Cecil Brown Anderson and Janet Davidson Bell; *m* 1958, Eirené Cochrane Howie Douglas; two *s* one *d. Educ:* High School of Glasgow. Qualified as Chartered Accountant, 1955; FCMA 1984. National Service, RN, 1955–57. Partner: Moores Carson & Watson, 1958 (subseq. McClelland Moores & Co., Arthur Young McClelland Moores & Co., Arthur Young (Chm., 1987–89), and Ernst & Young (Dep. Sen. Partner, 1989–90)); McLintock Moores & Murray, 1963–69. Chm., Bitmac Ltd, 1990– (Dir, 1984–); Director: Douglas Firebrick Co. Ltd, 1961–70; High School of Glasgow Ltd, 1975–81, and 1990–; Mem., Scottish Milk Marketing Bd, 1979–85. Mem., Council on Tribunals, 1990– (Mem., Scottish Cttee, 1990–). Institute of Chartered Accountants of Scotland: Mem. Council, 1980–84; Vice-Pres., 1984–86; Pres., 1986–87. *Recreations:* golf, gardening, Rugby football. *Address:* Ardwell, 41 Manse Road, Bearsden, Glasgow G61 3PN. *T:* 041–942 2803. *Clubs:* Caledonian; Western (Glasgow); Glasgow Golf; Buchanan Castle Golf (Captain 1979–80).

ANDERSON, H(ector) John, FRCP; Physician: St Thomas' Hospital, since 1948 (Special Trustee, 1972–81); Lambeth Hospital, since 1960; South Western Hospital, since 1948; French Hospital, since 1950; *b* Central Provinces, India, 5 Jan. 1915; *s* of H. J. Anderson; *m* 1st, 1940, Frances Pearce (marr. diss.), *er d* of Rev. W. P. Putt; one *s* one *d*; 2nd, 1956, Pauline Mary, *d* of A. Hammond; one *d. Educ:* Exeter Sch.; St Catharine's Coll., Cambridge; St Thomas' Hospital. MA, MB (Cantab), FRCP 1950. Medical Registrar and Res. Asst Physician, St Thomas' Hospital, 1941 and 1942. Hon. Lt-Col RAMC; served MEF, 1944–47. Kitchener Scholar; Mead Prizeman, St Thomas' Hospital; Murchison Scholar, RCP, 1942; Goulstonian Lectr, RCP, 1951; Examiner: MB London; Medicine, Conjoint Bd, London and England; RCP. Mem. AHA, Lambeth, Southwark, Lewisham Area (T). Member: Assoc. of Physicians of Gt Britain; Thoracic Soc.; FRSoc.Med. *Publications:* Brim of Day, 1944; contrib. to medical literature. *Address:* Churchill Clinic, 80 Lambeth Road, SE1. *T:* 01–928 5633; 102 Lambeth Road, SE1. *T:* 071–928 1533.

ANDERSON, Rev. Prof. Hugh, MA, BD, PhD, DD, FRSE; Professor of New Testament Language, Literature and Theology, University of Edinburgh, 1966–85, now Professor Emeritus; *b* 18 May 1920; *s* of Hugh Anderson and Jeannie Muir; *m* 1945, Jean Goldie Torbit; one *s* one *d* (and one *s* decd). *Educ:* Galston Sch.; Kilmarnock Acad.; Univ. of Glasgow (MA (Hons Classics and Semitic Langs I), BD (Dist. New Testament); PhD); post-doctoral Fellow, Univs of Oxford and Heidelberg. FRSE 1987. Chaplain, Egypt and Palestine, 1945–46; Lectr in Old Testament, Univ. of Glasgow, 1946–51; Minister, Trinity Presb. Church, Glasgow, 1951–57; A. B. Bruce Lectr, Univ. of Glasgow, 1954–57; Prof. of Biblical Criticism, Duke Univ., N Carolina, 1957–66. Dir, Postgrad. Studies in Theology, Univ. of Edinburgh, 1968–72; Select Preacher, Oxford Univ., 1970; Haskell Lectr, Oberlin Coll., Ohio, 1971; McBride Vis. Prof. of Religion, Bryn Mawr Coll., Pa, 1974–75; Vis. Prof. of Religion, Meredith Coll., N Carolina, 1982; James A. Gray Lectr, 1982, Kenneth Willis Clark Meml Lectr, 1985, Duke Univ., N Carolina; Scholar-in-res., Florida Southern Coll., Lakeland, Fla, 1983; Warner Hall Lectr, St Andrews Presbyterian Coll., N Carolina, 1985; Bishop E. J. Pendergrass Prof. of Religion, Florida Southern Coll., 1986; J. Wallace Hamilton Lectr, Fla, 1988. Convener of Ch. of Scotland's Special Commn on Priorities of Mission in 70s and 80s, 1969–71; Chm., Internat. Selection Council for Albert Schweitzer Internat. Prizes, 1972–. Hon. DD Glasgow, 1970. *Publications:* Psalms I-XLV, 1951; Historians of Israel, 1957; Jesus and Christian Origins, 1964; The Inter-Testamental Period in The Bible and History (ed W. Barclay), 1965; (ed with W. Barclay) The New Testament in Historical and Contemporary Perspective, 1965; Jesus, 1967; The Gospel of Mark, 1976; Commentary on 3 and 4 Maccabees, Doubleday Pseudepigrapha Vol. 2, 1982; (with Walter Weaver) Perspectives on Christology, 1989; contribs to Religion in Life, Interpretation, Scottish Jl of Theology, Expos. Times. *Recreations:* golf, gardening, music. *Address:* 5 Comiston Springs Avenue, Edinburgh EH10 6NT. *T:* 031–447 1401. *Clubs:* Greek (Edinburgh); Luffness Golf (E Lothian).

ANDERSON, Iain; *see* Anderson, A. J. R.

ANDERSON, James Frazer Gillan, CBE 1979; JP; DL; Member, Scottish Development Agency, 1986–89; *b* 25 March 1929; *m* 1956, May Harley; one *s* one *d. Educ:* Maddiston Primary Sch.; Graeme High Sch., Falkirk. Member: Stirling CC, 1958–75 (Convener, 1971–75); Central Regional Council, Scotland, 1974– (Convener, 1974–86). Mem., Health and Safety Commission, 1974–80. OStJ. DUniv Stirling, 1987. *Recreations:* gardening, walking.

ANDERSON, Prof. Sir (James) Norman (Dalrymple), Kt 1975; OBE (mil.) 1945 (MBE 1943); BA 1930, LLB 1931, MA 1934, LLD 1955 (Cantab); Hon. DD St Andrews 1974; FBA 1970; QC 1974; Professor of Oriental Laws in the University of London, 1954–75, now Emeritus Professor; Director of the Institute of Advanced Legal Studies in the University of London, 1959–76; *b* 29 Sept. 1908; *s* of late William Dalrymple Anderson; *m* 1933, Patricia Hope, *d* of A. Stock Givan; one *s* and two *d* decd. *Educ:* St Lawrence Coll., Ramsgate; Trinity Coll., Cambridge (Senior Scholar). 1st Class, Law Tripos Parts I and II (distinction in Part I); 1st Class LLB. Called to the Bar, Gray's Inn, 1965. Missionary, Egypt General Mission, 1932; served War of 1939–45 in Army as Arab Liaison Officer, Libyan Arab Force, 1940; Sec. for Sanusi Affairs, Civil Affairs Branch, GHQ, MEF, 1941; Sec. for Arab Affairs, 1943; Political Sec., 1943; Chief Sec. (Col), 1944; Lectr in Islamic Law, Sch. of Oriental and African Studies, 1947; Reader in Oriental Laws in Univ. of London, 1951–53; Hd of Dept of Law, SOAS, 1953–71, now Hon. Fellow, SOAS; Dean of Faculty of Laws, Univ. of London, 1965–69. President, Soc. of Public Teachers of Law, 1968–69. Chm. UK Nat. Cttee of Comparative Law, 1957–59; Vice-Chm. Internat. African Law Assoc.; Visiting Prof., Princeton Univ. and New York Univ. Law Sch., 1958; Harvard Law Sch., 1966. Conducted survey of application of Islamic Law in British African possessions for Colonial Office, 1950–51. President: BCMS, 1963–86; CPAS, 1974–86; Scripture Union, 1975–80; Victoria Inst., 1978–85; Lawyers' Christian Fellowship, 1987–89. First Chairman, House of Laity in Gen. Synod of Church of England, 1970–79 (Mem., 1970–80; Mem. former Church Assembly, 1965–70); Anglican delegate to the World Council of Churches. Hon. LittD Wheaton Coll., 1980. Libyan Order of Istiqlal, Class II, 1959. *Publications:* Al-'Aql wa'l Iman (in Arabic), 1939; Islamic Law in Africa, 1954; Islamic Law in the Modern World, 1959; Into the World: The Need and Limits of Christian Involvement, 1968; Christianity: the witness of history, 1969; Christianity and Comparative Religion, 1970; Morality, Law and Grace (Forwood Lectures), 1972; A Lawyer among the Theologians, 1973; Law Reform in the Muslim World, 1976; Issues of Life and Death, 1976; Liberty, Law and Justice (Hamlyn Lectures), 1978; The Mystery of the Incarnation (Bishop John Prideaux Lectures), 1978; The Law of God and the Love of God, 1980; God's Word for God's World, 1981; The Teaching of Jesus, 1983; Christianity and World Religions: the challenge of pluralism, 1984; Jesus Christ: the witness of history, 1984; An Adopted Son (autobiog.), 1986; Freedom Under Law, 1987; Islam in the Modern World: a Christian perspective, 1990; Editor: The World's Religions, 1950, 4th edn 1975; Changing Law in Developing Countries, 1963; Family Law in Asia and Africa, 1968; numerous articles in periodicals. *Address:* 9 Larchfield, Gough Way, Cambridge. *T:* Cambridge (0223) 358778. *Club:* Athenæum.

ANDERSON, Prof. John, MD, FRCP; Professor of Medicine, King's College Hospital Medical School, 1964–86, now Emeritus; *b* 11 Sept. 1921; *s* of James and Margaret Anderson; *m* 1952, Beatrice May Venner; three *s. Educ:* Durham Univ. BA Hons, Dunelm (Mod. Hist.) 1942; MB, BS Hons, 1950; BSc Hons, 1952 (Physiology); MA (Mod. Hist.), MD. Served War, Lt, RA (Field) (Ayrshire Yeomanry), 1940–45. MRC Fellow in Clin. Med., Univ. Coll. Hosp., London, 1952–55; Rockefeller Travelling Fellowship, 1956–57; Reader in Medicine, King's Coll. Hosp. Med. Sch., Med. Unit, 1962–64. Mem., Med. Research Soc. FRCP 1962; FBCS 1969; FIBiol 1977. *Publications:* A New Look at Medical Education, 1965; Information Processing of Medical Records, 1970; articles in Lancet and BMJ, on: nutron activation, medical computing, cancer, endocrinology, med. educn. *Recreations:* sailing, fishing. *Address:* 14 Styles Way, Park Langley, Beckenham, Kent. *T:* (office) 071–274 6222. *Club:* University (Durham).

ANDERSON, Prof. John, FRCP; FRCOG; Postgraduate Dean and Director, Regional Postgraduate Institute for Medicine and Dentistry, and Professor of Medical Education, University of Newcastle upon Tyne, since 1985; *b* 2 Feb. 1936; *s* of John and Norah Anderson, Newcastle upon Tyne; *m* Mary Bynon, Whitley Bay; one *s* one *d. Educ:* Royal Grammar Sch., Newcastle upon Tyne; Med. Sch., King's Coll., Univ. of Durham (MB, BS 2nd Cl. Hons). FRCP 1973 (MRCP 1961); FRCOG (*ad eundem*) 1983. Med. Registrar, Royal Victoria Inf., Newcastle upon Tyne, 1962–64; Res. Fellow, Univ. of Virginia, Charlottesville, 1965–66; University of Newcastle upon Tyne: First Asst in Medicine 1967–68; Sen. Lectr in Medicine 1968–85; Academic Sub-Dean, Med. Sch., 1975–85. Hon. Cons. Phys., Newcastle HA, 1968–. Mem. Council, RCP, 1974–77; Member: Assoc. of Phys of GB and Ire., 1976–; Exec. Cttee, ASME, 1979– (Hon. Treas., 1980–88; Gen. Sec., 1990–); GMC, 1981–. *Publications:* The Multiple Choice Question in Medicine, 1976, 2nd edn 1982; numerous chapters in books, and papers in sci. jls on medicine, diabetes and med. educn. *Recreations:* listening to music, watching cricket, reading, thinking. *Address:* 6 Wilson Gardens, Newcastle upon Tyne NE3 4JA. *T:* 091–285 4745. *Clubs:* Yorkshire CC; Close House Golf (Wylam).

ANDERSON, Prof. John Allan Dalrymple, TD 1967; DL; FRCP; FRCGP; FFPHM; FFOM; Professor of Community Medicine, University of London, at United Medical and Dental Schools (Guy's Campus), 1975–90, now Professor Emeritus; Professor and Chairman, Department of Public Health and Occupational Medicine, University of the United Arab Emirates, since 1990; *b* 16 June 1926; *s* of John Allan Anderson and Mary Winifred (*née* Lawson); *m* 1965, Mairead Mary MacLaren; three *d. Educ:* Loretto Sch.; Worcester Coll., Oxford (MA); Edinburgh Univ. (MD); London Univ. (DPH); DObstRCOG. Lectr in gen. practice, 1954–59, Dir, Industrial Survey Unit, 1960–63, Univ. of Edinburgh; Sen. Lectr, Social Medicine, LSHTM, 1963–69; Dir, Dept of Community Medicine, Guy's Hosp. Med. Sch., 1970–90; Hon. Consultant Guy's Hosp., 1970–90. Dir, Occupational Health Service, Lewisham and N Southwark HA, 1984–90. Acad. Registrar, FCM, RCP, 1983–89. OC London Scot. Co. 1/51 Highland Vols, TA, 1967–70; CO 221 Fd Amb. (TA), 1978–81; TA Col HQ Lond. Dist, 1981–84; Regtl Col Lond. Scot. Regt, 1983–89. Hon. Civilian Consultant to the Army in Public Health Medicine, 1990–. Elder, Ch. of Scotland, 1977–; Area Surg., SJAB, SW Lond., 1984–90. DL Greater London, 1985; Rep. DL, Borough of Richmond, 1986–90. *Publications:* A New Look at Community Medicine, 1965; Self Medication, 1982; (with Dr R. Grahame) Bibliography of Low Back Pain, 1982; Epidemiological, Sociological and Environmental Aspects of Rheumatic Diseases, 1987; sci. papers on public health and occupational med. and rheumatology. *Recreations:* hill walking, golf, bridge. *Address:* 24 Lytton Grove, Putney, SW15 2HB. *T:* 081–788 9420. *Clubs:* Hurlingham; New (Edinburgh).

ANDERSON, Maj.-Gen. Sir John (Evelyn), KBE 1971 (CBE 1963); CEng, FIEE; CBIM; Associate and Director, Space and Maritime Applications Inc., since 1988; *b* 28 June 1916; *e s* of Lt-Col John Gibson Anderson, Christchurch, NZ, and Margaret (*née* Scott), Edinburgh; *m* 1944, Jean Isobel, *d* of Charles Tait, farmer, Aberdeenshire; one *s* one *d. Educ:* King's Sch., Rochester; RMA, Woolwich. Commissioned in Royal Signals, 1936; Lt-Col 1956; Col 1960; Brig. 1964; Maj.-Gen. 1967; Signal Officer in Chief (Army), MoD, 1967–69; ACDS (signals), 1969–72. Col Comdt, Royal Corps of Signals, 1969–74. Hon. Col 71st (Yeomanry) Signal Regt TAVR, 1969–76; Hon. Col Women's Transport Corps (FANY), 1970–76. Dir Gen., NATO Integrated Communications System Management Agency, 1977–81; Exec. Dir, Europe Gp, AFCEA, 1981–88. Pres., Piscatorial Soc., 1981–87. *Recreation:* fishing. *Address:* The Beeches, Amport, Andover, Hampshire. *Clubs:* Army and Navy, Flyfishers'.
See also Maj.-Gen. A. A. G. Anderson.

ANDERSON, John Graeme, CBE 1989, CEng, FInstE; Deputy Chairman, Northern Engineering Industries plc, 1986–89; Director, Tyne and Wear Development Corporation, since 1987; *b* 3 June 1927; *s* of John Anderson and Ella (*née* Pusey); *m* 1953, Nancy Clarice Taylor Johnson; one *s* twin *d. Educ:* Merchant Taylors' Sch., Sandy Lodge; London Univ. (BScEng Hons). MIMechE. Served RN, Fleet Air Arm, 1945–48. International Combustion Ltd: graduate apprentice, 1952; Dir, 1968; Dep. Chief Exec., 1969; Man. Dir, 1974; Northern Engineering Industries: Man. Dir, NEI-Internat. Combustion Ltd, 1977; Managing Director: Mechanical Gp, 1980; Power Gp, 1982; Internat. and Projects Gp, 1984. Chm., Internat. Combustion-HUD Hong Kong, 1978–82; Dir, British Nuclear Associates, 1985–88; Alternate Dir, Nat. Nuclear Corp., 1986–88; Dir, The Newcastle Initiative, 1988–90. Mem., Duke of Kent's BOTB mission to Turkey, 1984. Chairman: Solid Waste Assoc., 1972–74; Watertube Boilermakers' Assoc., 1976–80; Member: Process Plant Assoc., 1968–87; Process Plant, EDC, 1972–76; Heavy Electrical, EDC, 1976–80. Gov., Derby Coll. of Technology, 1969–74. Chm., Upstage, 1977–79. *Recreations:* shooting, painting, music, fell walking. *Address:* Trinity Barns, Corbridge, Northumberland NE45 5HP. *T:* Hexham (0434) 633228.

ANDERSON, Prof. John Kinloch, FSA; Professor of Classical Archaeology, University of California, Berkeley, since 1958; *b* 3 Jan. 1924; *s* of late Sir James Anderson, KCIE, and of Lady Anderson; *m* 1954, Esperance, *d* of Guy Batham, Dunedin, NZ; one *s* two *d. Educ:* Trinity Coll., Glenalmond; Christ Church, Oxford (MA). Served War, in Black Watch (RHR) and Intelligence Corps, 1942–46 (final rank, Lieut). Student, British Sch. at Athens, 1949–52; Lecturer in Classics, Univ. of Otago, NZ, 1953–58. FSA 1976. Award for Distinction in Teaching, Phi Beta Kappa (N Calif. Chapter), 1988. *Publications:* Greek Vases in the Otago Museum, 1955; Ancient Greek Horsemanship, 1961; Military Theory and Practice in the Age of Xenophon, 1970; Xenophon, 1974; Hunting in the Ancient World, 1985; articles and reviews in Annual of British Sch. at Athens; Jl of Hellenic Studies, etc. *Recreations:* gardening, riding (Qualified Riding Mem., Calif Dressage Soc.). *Address:* 1020 Middlefield Road, Berkeley, California 94708, USA. *T:* Berkeley 841–5335.

ANDERSON, Sir John (Muir), Kt 1969; CMG 1957; Commissioner of State Savings Bank of Victoria, 1962–83, Chairman of Commissioners, 1967; *b* 14 Sept. 1914; *s* of John Weir Anderson; *m* 1949, Audrey Drayton Jamieson; one *s* one *d. Educ:* Brighton Grammar Sch.; Melbourne Univ. 2/6th Commando Co., 1941; Lieut, 1st Australian Parachute Bn, 1944; served SE Asia, 1941–45. Established John M. Anderson & Co. Pty Ltd, Manufacturers, Agents and Importers, 1951; Managing Director, King Oscar Fine Foods Pty Ltd. Pres. of Liberal and Country Party of Victoria, 1952–56 (Treasurer, 1957–61, 1978–80). Comr, Melbourne Harbour Trust, 1972–83. Trustee, Melbourne Exhibn, 1960, Chm. of Trustees, 1968. *Recreations:* swimming, fishing. *Address:* 25 Cosham Street, Brighton, Vic 3186, Australia. *T:* 592–4790.

ANDERSON, Professor John Neil; (first) Professor of Dental Prosthetics, 1964–82 (now Emeritus), (first) Dean of Dentistry, 1972–76, 1980–82, University of Dundee; *b* 11 Feb. 1922; *m* 1945, Mary G. Croll; one *s* one *d. Educ:* High Storrs Gram. Sch., Sheffield; Sheffield Univ. Asst Lectr, Sheffield Univ., 1945–46; Lectr, Durham Univ., 1946–48; Lectr, Birmingham Univ., 1948–52; Sen. Lectr, St Andrews Univ., 1952–64. External Examiner, Univs of Malaya, Baghdad, Newcastle upon Tyne, Bristol, Birmingham, Liverpool, RCSI. *Publications:* Applied Dental Materials, 1956; (with R. Storer) Immediate and Replacement Dentures, 1966, 3rd edn, 1981; contribs to leading dental jls. *Recreations:* music, gardening, carpentry. *Address:* Wyndham, Derwent Drive, Baslow, Bakewell, Derbyshire.

ANDERSON, Prof. John Russell, CBE 1980; Professor of Pathology at the Western Infirmary, Glasgow University, 1967–83, retired; *b* 31 May 1918; *s* of William Gregg Anderson and Mary Gordon Adam; *m* 1956, Audrey Margaret Shaw Wilson; two *s* two *d. Educ:* Worksop Coll.; St Andrews Univ. BSc (St Andrews) 1939, MB, ChB (St Andrews) 1942, MD (St Andrews) 1955; MRCP 1961; FRCPGlas 1965; FRCPath 1966; FRSE 1968. RAMC, 1944–47 (Emergency Commn). Lecturer and Senior Lecturer in Pathology, Glasgow Univ., 1947–65; George Holt Prof. of Pathology, Liverpool Univ., 1965–67. Rockefeller travelling fellowship in Medicine, at Rochester, NY, 1953–54. Pres., RCPath, 1978–81 (Vice-Pres., 1975). Hon. FRCPI, 1981. Hon. LLD Dundee, 1981. *Publications:* Autoimmunity, Clinical and Experimental (jtly), 1967; (ed) Muir's Textbook of Pathology, 9th edn 1972 to 12th edn 1985; various papers on immunopathology in scientific jls. *Recreations:* golf, ski-ing, gardening. *Address:* 3 Connell Crescent, Milngavie, Glasgow G62 6AR.

ANDERSON, Josephine, (Mrs Ande Anderson); *see* Barstow, J.

ANDERSON, Dame Judith, DBE 1960; **(Dame Frances Margaret Anderson);** Actress; *b* Adelaide, South Australia, 10 Feb. 1898; *d* of James Anderson Anderson and Jessie Saltmarsh; *m* 1937, Prof. B. H. Lehman (marr. diss. 1939); *m* 1946, Luther Greene (marr. diss. 1950). *Educ:* Norwood High Sch., South Australia. Started Theatre with Julius Knight; toured Australia and America, 1918; has played in: The Dove, 1925; Behold the Bridegroom, 1927; Strange Interlude, 1930; Mourning becomes Electra, 1931; Come of Age, 1934; The Old Maid, 1935; Hamlet, 1936; Macbeth (London), 1937; Family Portrait, 1939; Three Sisters, 1942; Medea (New York, 1947–48; toured America, 1948–49; Paris Internat. Drama Festival, 1955); The Seagull, Edin. Fest., 1960, Sept. at Old Vic; The Oresteia, 1966; Hamlet, 1970. *Films:* Rebecca, Edge of Darkness, Laura, King's Row, Spectre of the Rose, The Red House, Pursued, Tycoon, Cat on a Hot Tin Roof, Macbeth, Don't Bother to Knock, A Man Called Horse, Star Trek III; TV: The Chinese Prime Minister, 1974. *Recreation:* gardening.

ANDERSON, Julian Anthony; Director General, Country Landowners' Association, since 1990; *b* 12 June 1938; *s* of Sir Kenneth Anderson, *qv. Educ:* King Alfred Sch.; Wadham Coll., Oxford (MA). Entered MAFF as Asst Principal, 1961; Asst Private Sec. to Minister of Agriculture, 1964–66; Principal, 1966; seconded to FCO, 1970–73; Asst Sec., 1973, Under Sec., 1982–90, MAFF; seconded as Minister (Food and Agriculture), UK Perm. Rep. to EEC, 1982–85. *Recreations:* music, sport, travel, photography, gardening, DIY. *Address:* c/o Country Landowners' Association, 16 Belgrave Square, SW1X 8PQ. *Clubs:* United Oxford & Cambridge University, Civil Service.

ANDERSON, Sir Kenneth, KBE 1962 (CBE 1946); CB 1955; *b* 5 June 1906; *s* of Walter Anderson, Exmouth; *m* 1932, Helen Veronica Grose (*d* 1986); one *s* one *d. Educ:* Swindon Secondary Sch.; Wadham Coll., Oxford (MA). Entered India Office, 1928; Asst Sec., 1942; Dep. Financial Adviser to British Military Governor, Germany, 1947–48; Imperial Defence Coll., 1949; Under-Sec., HM Treasury, 1950–51; Dep. Director-General, 1954–66 and Comptroller and Accountant-General, 1952–66, GPO. Officer, Order of Orange-Nassau, 1947. *Address:* 7 Milton Close, N2 0QH. *T:* 081–455 8701. *Club:* United Oxford & Cambridge University.
See also J. A. Anderson.

ANDERSON, Hon. Sir Kevin (Victor), Kt 1980; Judge of the Supreme Court of Victoria, 1969–84; *b* 4 Sept. 1912; *s* of Robert Victor Anderson and Margaret Anderson (*née* Collins); *m* 1942, Claire Margaret Murphy; six *d. Educ:* Xavier Coll., Kew; Melbourne Univ. (LLB). Victorian Crown Law Dept, 1929–42: Courts Branch, 1929–35; Professional Asst, Crown Solicitor's Office, 1935–42; Lt, RAN, 1942–46; Victorian Bar, 1946–69; QC (Victoria) 1962. Chm., Bd of Inquiry into Scientology, 1963–65. Chm., Victorian Bar Council, 1966–67; Treasurer, Australian Law Council, 1966–68. Kt, Australian Assoc. of SMO of Malta, 1979. *Publications:* Stamp Duties in Victoria, 1949, 2nd edn 1968; joint author: Price Control, 1947; Landlord and Tenant Law, 1948, 3rd edn 1958; Victorian Licensing Law, 1952; Victoria Police Manual, 1956, 2nd edn 1969; Workers' Compensation, 1958, 2nd edn 1966; Fossil in the Sandstone: the Recollecting Judge, 1986; (ed) Victorian Law Reports, 1956–69. *Recreations:* yachting, woodworking. *Address:* 12 Power Avenue, Toorak, Victoria 3142, Australia. *T:* 822–2901. *Clubs:* Victoria Racing, Royal Automobile of Victoria, Celtic, Essoign (Melbourne).

ANDERSON, Lindsay (Gordon); film and theatre director; *b* 17 April 1923; 2nd *s* of late Maj.-Gen. A. V. Anderson and Estelle Bell Sleigh. *Educ:* Cheltenham Coll.; Wadham Coll., Oxford. Associate Artistic Director, Royal Court Theatre, 1969–75. Governor, British Film Institute, 1969–70. *Films include:* Wakefield Express, 1953; Thursday's Children (with Guy Brenton), 1954; O Dreamland, 1954; Every Day Except Christmas, 1957; This Sporting Life, 1963; The White Bus, 1966; Raz, Dwa, Trzy (The Singing Lesson), for Warsaw Documentary Studio, 1967; If . . . ., 1968 (Grand Prix, Cannes Fest., 1969); O Lucky Man!, 1973 (Film Critics' Guild award for best film of 1973); In Celebration, 1974; Britannia Hospital, 1982; If You Were There . . ., 1985; The Whales of August, 1988; Glory! Glory!, 1989. *Productions in theatre:* The Waiting of Lester Abbs, 1957; The Long and the Short and the Tall; Progress to the Park; Jazzetry; Serjeant Musgrave's Dance, 1959; The Lily White Boys; Billy Liar; Trials by Logue, 1960; The Fire-Raisers, 1961; The Diary of a Madman, 1963; Andorra, 1964; Julius Caesar, 1964; The Cherry Orchard, 1966, 1983; first Polish production of Inadmissible Evidence (Nie Do Obrony), Warsaw, 1966; In Celebration, 1969; The Contractor, 1969; Home (also NY), 1970; The Changing Room, 1973; The Farm, 1974; Life Class, 1974; What the Butler Saw, 1975; The Sea Gull, 1975; The Bed Before Yesterday, 1975; The Kingfisher, 1977 (NY, 1978); Alice's Boys, 1978; Early Days, 1980; Hamlet, 1981; The Holly and the Ivy, NY, 1982; The Playboy of the Western World, 1984; In Celebration, NY, 1984; Hamlet, Washington, DC, 1985; Holiday, 1987; The March on Russia, 1989; Jubilee, 1990. *Video plays:* Home, 1971; Look Back in Anger, NY, 1980. *Television play:* The Old Crowd, 1979. Editor, film quarterly, Sequence, 1947–51. *Publications:* Making a Film, 1952; About John Ford, 1981; contrib. to Declaration, 1957. *Address:* 9 Stirling Mansions, Canfield Gardens, NW6 3JT.

ANDERSON, Marian, (Mrs Orpheus H. Fisher); American contralto; *b* Philadelphia, Pa, 27 Feb. 1902; *m* 1943, Orpheus H. Fisher. *Educ:* Philadelphia; New York; Chicago; and in Europe. MusD Howard Univ., 1938. Singing career began in 1924; 1st prize at Lewisohn Stadium competition, New York, 1925. Has made numerous tours in the United States, Europe, Japan, Israel, India, Pakistan, Korea, etc. Ulrica in Verdi's The Masked Ball, Metropolitan Opera House, New York, 1955. US Delegate to UN, 1958. Has made many recordings. Holds numerous American and other hon. doctorates; Bok Award, 1940. Finnish decoration, 1940; Litteris et Artibus Medal, Sweden, 1952; Yukusho Medal, Japan, 1953; Gimbel Award, 1958; Gold Medal, US Inst. of Arts and Sciences,

1958; US Presidential Medal of Freedom, 1963; Congressional Gold Medal, 1978. *Publication:* My Lord, What a Morning, 1957.

ANDERSON, Brig. Hon. Dame Mary Mackenzie; *see* Pihl, Brig. Hon. Dame M. M.

ANDERSON, Mary Margaret, FRCOG; Consultant Obstetrician and Gynaecologist, Lewisham Hospital, since 1967; *b* 12 Feb. 1932; *d* of William Anderson and Lily Adams. *Educ:* Forres Acad.; Edinburgh Univ. (MB, ChB 1956). FRCOG 1974. Jun. hosp. posts in Scotland and England, including Hammersmith Hosp., and St Mary's Hosp., London (Sen. Registrar); Chm., Div. of Obst. and Gynaecol., Lewisham Hosp., 1984. Consultant Advr, CMO, 1990–. Royal College of Obstetricians and Gynaecologists: Chm., Hosp. Recognition Cttee, 1987–89; Jun. Vice Pres., 1989–. Chm., SE Thames Specialist Sub Cttee, 1986–88; Member: Scientific Cttee, National Birthday Trust, 1990–; Council, Med. Defence Union, 1987–. *Publications:* Anatomy and Physiology of Obstetrics, 1979; Handbook of Obstetrics and Gynaecology, 1981; The Menopause, 1983; Pregnancy after Thirty, 1984; An A–Z of Gynaecology, 1986; Infertility, 1987; (contrib.) Ten Teachers in Obstetrics and Gynaecology, 1990. *Recreations:* reading, music, gardening. *Address:* Green Roof Cottage, 1 Heathway, Blackheath, SE3 7AN; 96 Harley Street, W1N 1AF. *T:* 071–487 4146.

ANDERSON, Prof. Michael, FRSE; FBA 1989; Professor of Economic History, University of Edinburgh, since 1979; *b* 21 Feb. 1942; *s* of Douglas Henry and Rose Lillian Anderson; *m* 1966, Rosemary Elizabeth Kitching; one *s* one *d. Educ:* Kingston Grammar Sch.; Queens' Coll., Cambridge (BA 1964; MA 1968; PhD 1969). FRSE 1990. University of Edinburgh: Department of Sociology: Asst Lectr, 1967; Lectr, 1969; Reader, 1975; Department of Economic and Social History, 1979; Dean, Faculty of Social Scis, 1985–89; Vice-Principal, 1989–. Member: Economic and Social History Cttee, SSRC, 1974–78; Computing Cttee, SSRC, 1980–82; ESRC, 1990– (Member: Res. Resources and Methods Cttee, 1982–84; Society and Politics Res. Develt Gp, 1989–91). *Publications:* Family Structure in Nineteenth Century Lancashire, 1981; (ed) Sociology of the Family, 1972; Approaches to the History of the Western Family 1500–1914, 1981; The 1851 Census: a national sample of the enumerators returns, 1987; Population Change in Northwestern Europe 1750–1850, 1988. *Recreations:* natural history, gardening, study of ancient civilizations. *Address:* 30 Kings Park, Longniddry, East Lothian EH32 0QL.

ANDERSON, Vice Adm. Sir Neil (Dudley), KBE 1982 (CBE 1976); CB 1979; Chief of Defence Staff (NZ), 1980–83; *b* 5 April 1927; *s* of Eric Dudley Anderson and Margaret Evelyn (*née* Craig); *m* 1951, Barbara Lillias Romaine Wright; two *s. Educ:* Hastings High Sch.; BRNC. Joined RNZN, 1944; trng and sea service with RN, 1944–49; Korean War Service, 1950–51; qual. as navigation specialist; Navigator: HMS Vanguard, 1952–53; HMNZS Lachlan, 1954; HMS Saintes, 1958–59; Commanding Officer, HMNZS: Taranaki, 1961–62; Waikato, 1968–69; Philomel, 1969–70; Dep. Chief of Def. Staff, 1976–77; Chief of Naval Staff, 1977–80. Lieut 1949, Lt-Comdr 1957, Comdr 1960, Captain 1968, Cdre 1972, Rear Adm. 1977, Vice Adm. 1980. *Recreations:* golf, fishing. *Address:* 36 Beauchamp Street, Karori, Wellington, New Zealand. *T:* 766 257. *Club:* Wellington (Wellington, NZ).

ANDERSON, Sir Norman; *see* Anderson, Sir J. N. D.

ANDERSON, Prof. Philip Warren; Joseph Henry Professor of Physics, Princeton University, New Jersey, since 1975; *b* 13 Dec. 1923; *s* of Prof. H. W. Anderson and Mrs Elsie O. Anderson; *m* 1947, Joyce Gothwaite; one *d. Educ:* Harvard Univ. BS 1943; MA 1947; PhD 1949, Harvard. Naval Res. Lab., Washington, DC, 1943–45 (Chief Petty Officer, USN). Mem., Technical Staff, 1949–76, Dir, 1976–84, Bell Telephone Labs. Fulbright Lectr, Tokyo Univ., 1952–53; Overseas Fellow, Churchill Coll., Cambridge, 1961–62; Vis. Prof. of Theoretical Physics, Univ. of Cambridge, 1967–75, and Fellow of Jesus College, Cambridge, 1969–75, Hon. Fellow, 1978–; Cherwell-Simon Meml Lectureship, Oxford, 1979–80. Member: Amer. Acad. of Arts and Sciences, 1966; Nat. Acad. of Sciences, US, 1967; Foreign Member: Royal Society, London, 1980; Japan Acad., 1988; Indian Nat. Acad. of Scis, 1990; Foreign Associate, Accademia Lincei, Rome, 1985. Hon. FInstP, 1986. Hon. DSc Illinois, 1978. O. E. Buckley Prize, Amer. Phys. Soc., 1964; Dannie Heinemann Prize, Akad. Wiss. Göttingen, 1975; (jtly) Nobel Prize for Physics, 1977; Guthrie Medal, Inst. of Physics, 1978; Nat. Medal of Science, US, 1984. *Publications:* Concepts in Solids, 1963; Basic Notions of Condensed Matter Physics, 1984; numerous articles in scholarly jls. *Recreations:* go (Japanese game), rank sho-dan, walking. *Address:* 74 Aunt Molly Road, Hopewell, NJ 08525, USA.

ANDERSON, Reginald, CMG 1974; Chairman, A. B. Jay Ltd, since 1981; *b* 3 Nov. 1921; *s* of late Herbert Anderson and late Anne Mary (*née* Hicks); *m* 1945, Audrey Gabrielle Williams; two *d. Educ:* Palmers, Grays, Essex. Cabinet Office, 1938–40. Served War, RAF, Flt Lt, 1941–46. Ministry of: Supply, 1947–57; Supply Staff, Australia, 1957–59; Aviation, 1960–67; Counsellor, British Embassy, Washington, 1967–70; Asst Under-Sec. of State, 1970–76, Dep. Under-Sec. of State, 1976–81, MoD. *Recreations:* tennis, badminton, golf. *Address:* Reynosa, Heronway, Shenfield, Essex CM13 2LX. *T:* Brentwood (0277) 213077. *Club:* Royal Air Force.

ANDERSON, Robert Geoffrey William; Director, British Museum, since 1992; *b* 2 May 1944; *er s* of Herbert Patrick Anderson and Kathleen Diana Anderson (*née* Burns); *m* 1973, Margaret Elizabeth Callis Lea; two *s. Educ:* Woodhouse Sch., London; St John's Coll., Oxford (Casberd exhibitioner) (BSc, MA, DPhil). FRSC 1984; FSA 1986; FRSE 1990. Assistant Keeper: Royal Scottish Museum, 1970–75; Science Museum, 1975–78; Dep. Keeper, Wellcome Museum of History of Medicine, and Sec., Adv. Council, Science Museum, 1978–80; Keeper, Dept of Chemistry, Science Mus., 1980–84; Director: Royal Scottish Mus., 1984–85; Nat. Museums of Scotland, 1985–91. Sec., Royal Scottish Soc. of Arts, 1973–75; Member Council: Soc. for History of Alchemy and Chemistry, 1978–; Gp for Scientific, Technological and Medical Collections, 1979–83; British Soc. History of Science, 1981–84 (Pres., 1988–90); Scottish Museums, 1984–; Museums Assoc., 1988–; Mem., British Nat. Cttee for Hist. of Science, 1985–89; Pres., Scientific Instrument Commn, IUHPS, 1982–. Member Editorial Board: Annals of Science, 1981–; Annali di Storia della Scienza, 1986–. Dexter Prize, Amer. Chemical Soc., 1986. *Publications:* The Mariner's Astrolabe, 1972; Edinburgh and Medicine, 1976; (ed) The Early Years of the Edinburgh Medical School, 1976; The Playfair Collection and the Teaching of Chemistry at the University of Edinburgh, 1978; (contrib.) The History of Technology, Vol. VI, ed T. I. Williams, 1978; Science in India, 1982; (ed) Science, Medicine and Dissent: Joseph Priestley (1733–1804), 1987. *Recreation:* books. *Address:* British Museum, WC1B 3DG. *T:* 071-636 1555. *Club:* Athenæum.

ANDERSON, Prof. Robert Henry; Joseph Levy Professor of Paediatric Cardiac Morphology, National Heart and Lung Institute (formerly Cardiothoracic Institute), University of London, since 1979; *b* 4 April 1942; *s* of Henry Anderson and Doris Amy Anderson (*née* Callear); *m* 1966, Christine (*née* Ibbotson); one *s* one *d. Educ:* Wellington Grammar Sch., Shropshire; Manchester Univ. BSc (Hons); MD; FRCPath. House Officer, Professorial Surgical Unit, 1966, Medical Unit, 1967, Manchester Royal Infirmary; Asst Lectr in Anatomy, 1967–69, Lectr, 1969–73, Manchester Univ.; MRC Travelling Fellow,

Dept of Cardiology, Univ. of Amsterdam, 1973–74; Cardiothoracic Institute, University of London: British Heart Foundn Sen. Res. Fellow and Sen. Lectr in Paediatrics, 1974–77; Joseph Levy Reader in Paediatric Cardiac Morphology, 1977–79. Hon. Prof. of Surgery, Univ. of N Carolina, USA, 1984–; Visiting Professor: Univ. of Pittsburgh, Pa, 1985–; Liverpool Univ., 1989–. Excerpta Medica Travel Award, 1977; British Heart Foundn Prize for Cardiovascular Research, 1984. Associate Editor, Internat. Jl of Cardiology, 1985–; Internat. Consultant, Cardiology in the Young, 1991–. *Publications:* (ed jtly) Paediatric Cardiology, 1977, vol. 3, 1981, vol. 5, 1983, vol. 6, 1986; (with A. E. Becker) Cardiac Anatomy, 1980; (with E. A. Shinebourne) Current Paediatric Cardiology, 1980; (with A. E. Becker) Pathology of Congenital Heart Disease, 1981; (with M. J. Davies and A. E. Becker) Pathology of the Conduction Tissues, 1983; (jtly) Morphology of Congenital Heart Disease, 1983; (with A. E. Becker) Cardiac Pathology, 1984; (with G. A. H. Miller and M. L. Rigby) The Diagnosis of Congenital Heart Disease, 1985; (with B. R. Wilcox) Surgical Anatomy of the Heart, 1985; (with F. J. Macartney, E. A. Shinebourne and M. Tynan) Paediatric Cardiology, 2 vols, 1987; over 200 invited chapters in published books and over 350 papers in jls. *Recreations:* golf, tennis, music, wine. *Address:* 60 Earlsfield Road, SW18 3DN. *T:* 081-870 4368. *Club:* Roehampton.

ANDERSON, Robert (Woodruff); playwright; *b* NYC, 28 April 1917; *s* of James Hewston Anderson and Myra Esther (*née* Grigg); *m* 1st, 1940, Phyllis Stohl (*d* 1956); 2nd, 1959, Teresa Wright (marr. diss. 1978). *Educ:* Phillips Exeter Acad.; Harvard Univ. AB (*magna cum laude*) 1939, MA 1940. Served USNR, 1942–46 (Lt); won prize (sponsored by War Dept) for best play written by a serviceman, Come Marching Home, 1945, subseq. prod, Univ. of Iowa and Blackfriars Guild, NY. Rockefeller Fellowship, 1946; taught playwrighting, American Theatre Wing Professional Trng Prog., 1946–50; organized and taught Playwright's Unit, Actors Studio, 1955; Writer in Residence, Univ. of N Carolina, 1969; Faculty: Salzburg Seminar in Amer. Studies, 1968; Univ. of Iowa Writers' Workshop, 1976. Member: Playwrights Co., 1953–60; Bd of Governors, American Playwrights Theatre, 1963–; Council, Dramatists Guild, 1954– (Pres., 1971–73); New Dramatists Cttee, 1949– (Pres., 1955–57); Fac., Salzburg Seminar in American Studies, 1968; Vice-Pres., Authors' League of America; Chm., Harvard Bd of Overseers' Cttee to visit the Performing Arts, 1970–76. Wrote and adapted plays for TV and Radio, 1948–53. Elected to Theater Hall of Fame, 1980. *Plays:* Eden Rose, 1948; Love Revisited, 1952; Tea and Sympathy, 1953; All Summer Long, 1954; Silent Night, Lonely Night, 1959; The Days Between, 1965; You Know I Can't Hear You When the Water's Running (four short plays), 1967; I Never Sang For My Father, 1968; Solitaire/Double Solitaire, 1971; Free and Clear, 1983; The Kissing was Always the Best, 1987; The Last Act is a Solo, 1989; *screenplays:* Tea and Sympathy, 1956; Until They Sail, 1957; The Nun's Story, 1959; The Sand Pebbles, 1965; I Never Sang For My Father, 1970 (Writers Guild Award for Best Screenplay, 1971); The Patricia Neal Story, TV, 1981; Absolute Strangers, TV, 1991; The Last Act is a Solo, TV, 1991. *Publications: novels:* After, 1973; Getting Up and Going Home, 1978; *anthology:* (jtly) Elements of Literature, 6 vols, 1988. *Recreations:* photography, tennis. *Address:* Roxbury, Conn 06783, USA. *Club:* Harvard (New York City).

ANDERSON, Roy Arnold; Chairman Emeritus, Lockheed Corporation, since 1989; *b* Ripon, Calif, 15 Dec. 1920; *s* of Carl Gustav Anderson and Esther Marie Johnson; *m* 1948, Betty Leona Boehme; two *s* two *d. Educ:* Ripon Union High Sch.; Humphreys Sch. of Business; Stanford Univ. AB 1947; MBA 1949; Phi Beta Kappa; CPA. Served War, USNR, 1942–46 and 1950–52. Westinghouse Electric Corporation: Manager, Factory Accounting, 1952–56; Lockheed Missiles and Space Co.: Manager, Accounting and Finance, and Dir, Management Controls, 1956–65; Lockheed Georgia Co.: Dir of Finance, 1965–68; Lockheed Corporation: Asst Treas., 1968–69; Vice-Pres. and Controller, 1969–71; Sen. Vice-Pres., Finance, 1971–75; Vice-Chm. of Board, also Chief Financial and Admin. Officer, 1975–77; Chm. and Chief Exec. Officer, 1977–85; Chm., Exec. Cttee, Dir and Consultant, 1985–88. Director of cos in California. *Recreation:* tennis. *Address:* c/o Lockheed Corporation, PO Box 551, Burbank, California 91520, USA. *T:* (818) 847–6452; (office) 2555 N Hollywood Way, Burbank, California 91520, USA.

ANDERSON, Prof. Roy Malcolm, FRS 1986; Professor, since 1982, and Head of Department of Biology, since 1984, Imperial College, London University; *b* 12 April 1947; *s* of James Anderson and Betty Watson-Weatherburn; *m* 1975, Dr Mary Joan Anderson (marr. diss. 1989); *m* 1990, Dr Claire Baron. *Educ:* Duncombe Sch., Bengeo; Richard Hale Sch., Hertford; Imperial Coll., London (BSc, ARCS, PhD, DIC). CBiol, FIBiol; FSS. IBM Research Fellow, Univ. of Oxford, 1971–73; Lectr, King's Coll., London, 1973–77; Lectr, 1977–80, Reader, 1980–82, Imperial Coll. Vis. Prof., McGill Univ., 1982–; Alexander Langmuir Vis. Prof., Harvard, 1990–. Member: NERC, 1988–91 (Chm., Services and Facilities Cttee, 1989–90); ACOST, 1989– (Chm., Standing Cttee on Envmt, 1990–); Council: Zoological Soc., 1988–90; Royal Soc., 1989–; RSTM&H, 1989–. Chm., Infection and Immunity Grant Panel, Wellcome Trust. Zoological Soc. Scientific Medal, 1982; Huxley Meml Medal, 1983; Wright Meml Medal, 1986; David Starr Jordan Medal, 1986; Chalmers Medal, 1988; Weldon Medal, 1989; John Hill Grundy Medal, 1990. *Publications:* (ed) Population Dynamics of Infectious Disease Agents: theory and applications, 1982; (ed jtly) Population Biology of Infectious Diseases, 1982; (with R. M. May) Infectious Diseases of Humans: dynamics and control, 1991. *Recreations:* hill walking, croquet, natural history, photography. *Club:* Athenæum.

ANDERSON, Walter Charles, CBE 1968; Solicitor; General Secretary, National and Local Government Officers Association, 1957–73; Member, IBA, 1973–78; *b* 3 Dec. 1910; *s* of William Walter John Anderson and Mary Theresa McLoughlin; *m* 1941, Doris Jessie Deacon; two *s. Educ:* Bootle Grammar Sch. and Wigan Grammar Sch.; Liverpool Univ. (LLB). Articled Clerk, J. W. Wall & Co., Solicitors, Bootle, Liverpool, 1930–33; Asst Solicitor, Bootle, 1933–34; Dep. Town Clerk, Heywood, 1934–37; Asst Solicitor, Nalgo, 1937–41; Royal Air Force, 1941–45; Legal Officer, Nalgo, 1945–50; Dep. Gen. Sec., Nalgo, 1950–57; Mem., Gen. Council of TUC, 1965–73. Member: Fulton Cttee on Civil Service Recruitment, Structure, Management and Training, 1966–68; Nat. Insurance Adv. Cttee, 1970–74; Industrial Injuries Adv. Council, 1970–74; Nat. Inst. of Econ. and Social Res., 1970–76; Industrial Arbitration Bd, Workpeople's Rep., 1972; Royal Commn on Civil Liability and Compensation for Personal Injury, 1973–78. *Publication:* Simonds' Local Government Superannuation Act, 1937 (rev. and ed), 1947. *Recreations:* sport, gardening. *Address:* 1 The Comyns, Bushey, Watford WD2 1HN. *T:* 081–950 3708.

ANDERSON, (William) Eric (Kinloch), MA, BLitt, DLitt, FRSE; Headmaster of Eton College, since 1980; *b* 27 May 1936; *er s* of W. J. Kinloch Anderson, Edinburgh; *m* 1960, Poppy, *d* of W. M. Mason, Skipton; one *s* one *d. Educ:* George Watson's Coll.; Univ. of St Andrews (MA; Hon. DLitt); Balliol Coll., Oxford (BLitt; Hon. Fellow, 1989). Asst Master: Fettes Coll., 1960–64; Gordonstoun, 1964–66; Asst Master, Fettes Coll., and Housemaster, Arniston House, 1967–70; Headmaster: Abingdon Sch., 1970–75; Shrewsbury Sch., 1975–80. Pres., Edinburgh Sir Walter Scott Club, 1981. FRSE 1985. *Publications:* The Written Word, 1964; (ed) The Journal of Sir Walter Scott, 1972; (ed) The Percy Letters, vol IX, 1988; articles and reviews. *Recreations:* golf, fishing. *Address:* Eton College, Windsor, Berks. *Club:* Leander (Henley).

ANDERSON, Professor Sir (William) Ferguson, Kt 1974; OBE 1961; David Cargill Professor of Geriatric Medicine, University of Glasgow, 1965–79; *b* 8 April 1914; *s* of James Kirkwood Anderson, Capt. 7th Scottish Rifles (killed on active service Gaza 1917) and late Sarah Barr Anderson; *m* 1940, Margaret Battison Gebbie; one *s* two *d*. *Educ:* Merchiston Castle Sch.; Glasgow Academy; Glasgow Univ. (MB Hons 1936; MD Hons 1942, with Bellahouston Gold Medal). FRFPSG 1939 (now FRCPG); FRCPE 1961; FRCP 1964; FRCPI 1975; FRCP (C) 1976. Med. Registrar, Univ. Med. Clinic, 1939–41; Army Service, 1941–46, Major (Med. Specialist). Sen. Lectr, Dept of Materia Medica and Therapeutics, Univ. of Glasgow, and Asst Phys., Univ. Med. Clinic, Stobhill Hosp., Glasgow, 1946–49; Sen. Univ. Lectr, Medical Unit, also Hon. Cons. Phys., Cardiff Royal Infirmary, 1949–52; Physician in Geriatric Medicine, Stobhill Gen. Hosp., Adviser in Diseases of Old Age and Chronic Sickness, Western Reg. Hosp. Bd, Scotland, 1952–74. Mem., adv. panel on organization of medical care, WHO, 1973–83. Fogarty Internat. Scholar, Nat. Inst. on Aging, Bethesda, 1979. President: RCPGlas, 1974–76; British Geriatric Soc., 1975–78; BMA, 1977–78. Vice-President: Age Concern (Scotland); Abbeyfield Soc. Hon. Vice-Pres., Scottish Retirement Council; Hon. Pres., Crossroads (Scotland) Care Attendant Schemes. Hon. Chairman: St Mungo's Old Folks' Club, Glasgow; European Clin. Sect., Internat. Assoc. Gerontology. Mem., Turnberry Trust. Fellow, Australasian Coll. of Biomedical Scientists (formerly Australasian Coll. of Technologists), 1971; Hon. Fellow, Amer. Coll. of Physicians, 1980. St Mungo Prize, Glasgow, 1968; Brookdale Award, Gerontological Soc. of America, 1984. KStJ 1974. *Publications:* Practical Management of the Elderly, 1967, 5th edn (with Dr B. Williams) 1989; Current Achievements in Geriatrics (ed with Dr B. Isaacs), 1964; articles on Geriatric Medicine and Preventive aspects of Geriatrics in current med. jls. *Recreation:* walking. *Address:* Rodel, Moor Road, Strathblane, Glasgow G63 9EX. *T:* Blanefield (0360) 70862. *Clubs:* University Staff, Royal Scottish Automobile (Glasgow).

ANDERTON, Sir (Cyril) James, Kt 1991; CBE 1982; QPM 1977; DL; Chief Constable, Greater Manchester Police Force, 1976–91 (Deputy Chief Constable, 1975); *b* 24 May 1932; *o s* of late James Anderton and late Lucy Anderton (*née* Occleshaw); *m* 1955, Joan Baron; one *d*. *Educ:* St Matthew's Church Sch., Highfield; Wigan Grammar Sch. Certif. Criminology, Manchester Univ., 1960; Sen. Comd Course, Police Coll., 1967. Corps of Royal Mil. Police, 1950–53; Constable to Chief Inspector, Manchester City Police, 1953–67; Chief Supt, Cheshire Constab., 1967–68; Asst Chief Constable, Leicester and Rutland Constab., 1968–72; Asst to HM Chief Inspector of Constab. for England and Wales, Home Office, London, 1972–75; Dep. Chief Constable, Leics Constabulary, 1975. President: Manchester and Dist RSPCA, 1984– (Vice-Pres., 1981–84); Manchester Br., BIM, 1984–; British Coll. of Accordionists, 1984– (Chm. Governing Council, 1972–77; Vice-Pres., 1977–84); Leics Bn, Boys' Bde, 1972–76; Manchester NSPCC Jun. League, 1979–; Christian Police Assoc., 1979–81; Wythenshawe Hosp. League of Friends, 1991–; Member: ACPO, 1968–91 (Pres., 1986–87); Manchester Adv. Bd, Salvation Army, 1977–; Exec. Cttee, Manchester NSPCC, 1979–; NW Regional Bd, BIM, 1985–90 (Chm., 1986–90); Bd, Henshaws Soc. for the Blind, 1991–; Comdr, St John Amb. Assoc., Greater Manchester, 1989– (County Dir, 1976–89); Vice-President: Manchester YMCA, 1976–91; Manchester and District RLSS, 1976–; Adelphi Lads' Club, Salford, 1979–; Sharp Street Ragged Sch., Manchester, 1982–; Manchester Schools Football Assoc., 1976–91; Greater Manchester East Scout Council, 1977–91; Greater Manchester Fedn of Boys' Clubs, 1984–; 318 (Sale) Sqn, ATC, 1985–; Wigan Hospice, 1990–; Hon. National Vice-Pres., The Boys' Bde, 1983–. Patron: NW Counties Schs ABA, 1980–91; NW Campaign for Kidney Donors, 1983–; NW Eye Res. Trust, 1982–91; N Manchester Hosp. Broadcasting Service, 1983–; Internat. Spinal Res. Trust (Greater Manchester Cttee), 1983–91; Sale RNLI, 1986–; Wigan and Dist RSPCA, 1987–; Stockport Canal Trust, 1989–; Disabled Living Services, Manchester, 1991–; Trustee, Manchester Olympic Bid Cttee, 1985–. CBIM 1980; Hon. FBCA 1976; Hon. RNCM 1984. Member: RSCM; RSPB; NT; Corps of Royal Mil. Police Assoc.; National Geographical Soc.; St Andrew's Soc. of Manchester; Manchester Lit. and Phil. Soc. Mancunian of The Year, 1980. DL Greater Manchester, 1989. Freeman, City of London, 1990. KStJ 1989 (OStJ 1978; CStJ 1982). Cross Pro Ecclesia et Pontifice, 1982. Chevalier de la Confrérie des Chevaliers du Tastevin, 1985. *Recreations:* home and family. *Address:* 9 The Avenue, Sale, Cheshire M33 4PB. *Clubs:* Commonwealth Trust, Royal Over-Seas League, St John House.

ANDERTON, James, CBE 1966 (OBE 1956); CEng, MIMinE; *b* 3 Nov. 1904; *s* of Richard and Rebecca Anderton; *m* 1st, 1931, Margaret Asbridge (*d* 1945); no *c*; 2nd, 1949, Lucy Mackie; no *c*. *Educ:* Wigan and District Mining and Technical Coll. Manager of various collieries. On nationalisation of mining industry in 1947 became Asst Agent for a group of collieries in St Helens, Lancs; later made Prod. Man., St Helens Area, N Western Div.; Area Gen. Man., St Helens Area, 1949; Dep. Chm., Scottish Div., NCB, 1958. Chm., North Western Div., NCB, 1961–67. Gullick Ltd, Wigan: Dir, 1967–70; Mining Consultant, 1970–81. Hon. MIMinE, 1968. Medal, Instn of Mining Engineers, 1965. Alfried Krupp von Bohlen und Halbach Prize for Energy Research, 1979. *Recreation:* golf. *Address:* The Knoll, Mere Road, Newton-le-Willows, Merseyside. *T:* Newton-le-Willows (09252) 5901.

ANDERTON, Sir James; *see* Anderton, Sir C. J.

ANDOVER, Viscount; Alexander Charles Michael Winston Robsahm Howard; *b* 17 Sept. 1974; *s* and *heir* of 21st Earl of Suffolk and Berkshire, *qv*.

ANDREAE-JONES, William Pearce; QC 1984; a Recorder of the Crown Court, since 1982; *b* 21 July 1942; *s* of Willie and Minnie Charlotte Andreae-Jones; *m* 1977, Anne Marie Cox; one *s*. *Educ:* Canford Sch.; Corpus Christi Coll., Cambridge (BA Hons). Called to the Bar, Inner Temple, 1965. *Address:* 6 King's Bench Walk, Temple, EC4; Coleridge Chambers, The Citadel, Corporation Street, Birmingham.

ANDREOTTI, Giulio; Prime Minister (President of the Council of Ministers) of Italy, 1972–73, 1976–79 and since 1989; *b* 14 Jan. 1919; *s* of Filippo and Rosa Andreotti; *m* 1945, Livia Danese; two *s* two *d*. *Educ:* Univ. of Rome. Mem. for Rome Latina Viterbo Frosinone, Chamber of Deputies, 1946–. Under Sec. of State, Council of Ministers, 1947–54; Minister of Interior, 1954; Minister of Finance, 1955–58; Minister of the Treasury, 1958–59; Minister of Defence, 1959–65; Minister of Industry and Commerce, 1966–68; Chm., Christian Democrats, 1968–72; Minister of Defence, March–Oct. 1974; Minister for Budget and Economic Planning, 1974–76; Minister of Foreign Affairs, 1983–89. Founder, and Editor, Concretezza (political weekly), 1955–76. Hon. Dr: Sorbonne; Loyola Univ., Chicago; Copernican Univ. of Torun, Poland; La Plata; Salamanca; St John's, NY; Warsaw; Univ. of Sci. and Technol., Beijing; New York; Jewish Theol Seminary, NY. Bancarella Prize, 1985. *Publications* include: Pranzo di magro per il cardinale, 1954; De Casperi e il suo tempo, 1965; La Sciarada di Papa Mastai, 1967; Ore 13: il Ministro deve morire, 1975; Ad Ogni morte di Papa, 1980; Il diario 1976–79, 1981; De Gasperi visto da vicino, 1986; Visti da vicino (3 vols of profiles): Onorevole, stia zitto, 1987, L'URSS vista da vicino, 1988, Gli USA visti da vicino, 1989; Il potere logora . . . ma è meglio non perderlo, 1990; many articles. *Address:* Office of the Prime Minister, Palazzo Chigi, Piazza Colonna 370, 00100 Rome, Italy.

ANDRESKI, Prof. Stanislav Leonard; Professor of Sociology, University of Reading, 1964–84, now Emeritus; Professor of Comparative Sociology, Polish University in London, since 1982; *b* 18 May 1919; two *s* two *d*. *Educ:* Secondary sch. in Poznan, 1928–37; Univ. of Poznan (Faculty of Economics and Jurisprudence), 1938–39; London Sch. of Economics, 1942–43. Military service in Polish Army (with exception of academic year 1942–43), 1937–38 and 1939–47 (commissioned, 1944). Lectr in Sociology, Rhodes Univ., SA, 1947–53; Sen. Research Fellow in Anthropology, Manchester Univ., 1954–56; Lectr in Economics, Acton Technical Coll., London, 1956–57; Lectr in Management Studies, Brunel Coll. of Technology, London, 1957–60; Prof. of Sociology, Sch. of Social Sciences, Santiago, Chile, 1960–61; Sen. Res. Fellow, Nigerian Inst. of Social and Economic Research, Ibadan, Nigeria, 1962–64; Hd, Dept of Sociology, Univ. of Reading, 1964–82. Vis. Prof. of Sociology and Anthropology, City Coll., City Univ. of New York, 1968–69; Vis. Prof. of Sociology, Simon Frazer Univ., Vancouver, 1976–77. *Publications:* Military Organization and Society (Internat. Library of Sociology and Social Reconstruction), 1954 (2nd aug. edn, 1968, USA, 1968, paperback, 1969); Class Structure and Social Development (with Jan Ostaszewski and others), (London), 1964 (in Polish); Elements of Comparative Sociology (The Nature of Human Society Series), 1964, Spanish edn 1972; The Uses of Comparative Sociology (American edn of the foregoing), 1965, paperback 1969; Parasitism and Subversion: the case of Latin America, 1966 (NY, 1967, rev. edn 1968, etc; Buenos Aires (in Spanish with a postscript), 1968; paperback edn, London, 1970); The African Predicament: a study in pathology of modernisation, 1968 (USA, 1969); Social Sciences as Sorcery, 1972, Spanish edn 1973, German edn 1974, French edn 1975, Italian edn 1977, Japanese edn 1982; Prospects of a Revolution in the USA, 1973; The Essential Comte, 1974; Reflections on Inequality, 1975; Max Weber's Insights and Errors, 1984; Syphilis, Puritanism and Witch-Hunts, 1989; Editor: Herbert Spencer, Principles of Sociology, 1968; Herbert Spencer, Structure, Function and Evolution, 1970; Max Weber on Capitalism, Bureaucracy and Religion, 1983; contribs to: A Dictionary of the Social Sciences (UNESCO); A Dictionary of Sociology (ed D. Mitchell); Brit. Jl of Sociology; Japanese Jl of Sociology; The Nature of Fascism (ed S. Woolf); Science Jl, Man, European Jl of Sociology, Encounter, etc. *Recreations:* sailing, horse-riding. *Address:* Farriers, Village Green, Upper Basildon, Berkshire RG8 8LS. *T:* Upper Basildon (0491) 671318.

ANDREW, Dr Christopher Maurice, FRHistS; Reader in Modern and Contemporary History, University of Cambridge, since 1989; Fellow, Corpus Christi College, Cambridge, since 1967; *b* 23 July 1941; *s* of Maurice Viccars Andrew and Freda Mary (*née* Sandall); *m* 1962, Jennifer Ann Alicia Garratt; one *s* two *d*. *Educ:* Norwich Sch.; Corpus Christi Coll., Cambridge (MA, PhD). FRHistS 1976. Res. Fellow, Gonville and Caius Coll., Cambridge, 1965–67; Dir of Studies in History, 1967–81 and 1988–, Sen. Tutor, 1981–87, Corpus Christi Coll., Cambridge; Univ. Lectr in History, Cambridge, 1972–89. Ext. Examr in History, NUI, 1977–84. Specialist Adviser, H of C Select Cttee on Educn, Science and the Arts, 1982–83. Visiting Fellow: ANU, 1987; Wilson Center, Washington, 1987. TV Presenter: The Fatal Attraction of Adolf Hitler, 1989; Hess: an edge of conspiracy, 1990; The Cambridge Moles, 1990; All the King's Jews, 1990. Editor: The Historical Journal, 1976–85; Intelligence and National Security, 1986–. *Publications:* Théophile Delcassé and the making of the Entente Cordiale, 1968; The First World War: causes and consequences, 1970 (vol. 19 of Hamlyn History of the World); (with A. S. Kanya-Forstner) France Overseas: the First World War and the climax of French imperial expansion, 1981; (ed with Prof. D. Dilks) The Missing Dimension: governments and intelligence communities in the Twentieth Century, 1984; Secret Service: the making of the British Intelligence Community, 1985; Codebreaking and Signals Intelligence, 1985; (ed with Jeremy Noakes) Intelligence and International Relations 1900–1945, 1987; (with Oleg Gordievsky) KGB: the inside story of its foreign operations from Lenin to Gorbachev, 1990; broadcasts and articles on mod. history, Association football, secret intelligence, internat. relations. *Address:* 67 Grantchester Meadows, Cambridge CB3 9JL. *T:* Cambridge (0223) 353773.

ANDREW, Prof. Colin, FIMechE; Professor of Manufacturing Engineering, Cambridge University, since 1986; Fellow, Christ's College, Cambridge, since 1986; Managing Director, Bristol Technical Developments Ltd, since 1985; *b* 22 May 1934; *s* of Arnold Roy and Kathleen Andrew; *m* 1952, Ruth E. Probert; two *s* two *d*. *Educ:* Bristol Grammar Sch.; Christ's Coll., Cambridge Univ. MA; PhD. Res. Engr, Rolls-Royce, 1955–58; research, Cambridge, 1958–60; Develt Engr, James Archdale & Co., 1960–61; Bristol University: Lectr, 1961–68; Reader, 1968–71; Prof. of Applied Mechanics, 1971–82; Hon. Prof., 1982–86. Man. Dir, Flamgard Ltd, 1982–85. Chairman: Engrg Processes Cttee, SERC, 1981–83; Production Cttee, SERC, 1983–84; Member: Technology Sub-Cttee, UGC, 1986–89; Engrg Council, 1991–. *Publications:* (jtly) Creep Feed Grinding, 1985; papers in scientific jls. *Address:* 17 High Street, Orwell, Cambs. *T:* Cambridge (0223) 207662; Christ's College, Cambridge, CB2 3BU.

ANDREW, Prof. Edward Raymond, MA, PhD, ScD (Cambridge); FRS 1984; CPhys; FInstP; FRSE; Graduate Research Professor, University of Florida, since 1983; *b* Boston, Lincs, 27 June 1921; *o s* of late Edward Richard Andrew and Anne (*née* Henderson); *m* 1948, Mary Farnham (*decd* 1965); two *d*; *m* 1972, Eunice Tinning. *Educ:* Wellingborough Sch.; Christ's (Open Scholarship) and Pembroke Colls, Univ. of Cambridge. Scientific Officer, Royal Radar Establishment, Malvern, 1942–45; Cavendish Laboratory, Cambridge, 1945–48; Stokes Student, Pembroke Coll., Cambridge, 1947–49; Commonwealth Fund Fellow, Harvard Univ., 1948–49; Lectr in Natural Philosophy, Univ. of St Andrews, 1949–54; Prof. of Physics, University of Wales, Bangor, 1954–64; Lancashire-Spencer Prof. of Physics, 1964–83, and Dean of Faculty of Science, 1975–78, Univ. of Nottingham; Fellow, Christ's Coll., Cambridge, 1989. Vis. Prof. of Physics, Univ. of Florida, 1969–70. President: Groupement Ampère, 1974–80 (Hon. Pres., 1980–); Internat. Soc. of Magnetic Resonance, 1984–87; Chm., Standing Conf. of Profs of Physics, 1976–79; Mem. Council, European Physical Soc., 1976–79; Chm., British Radio Spectroscopy Gp, 1981–83 (Founder-Chm., 1956–59); Mem., Bd of Trustees, Soc. of Magnetic Resonance in Medicine, 1983–; Planning Cttee, US Nat. High Magnetic Field Lab., Fla, 1990–. Selby Fellow, Aust. Academy of Sci., 1989; Fellow, Amer. Physical Soc., 1989. Hon. DSc: Univ. of Turku, Finland, 1980; Leipzig Univ., 1990; Dr *hc* Adam Mickiewicz Univ., Poznan, Poland, 1989. Wellcome Medal and Prize, Royal Soc., 1984. Editor, Physics Reports, 1974–90; Editor-in-Chief, Magnetic Resonance in Medicine, 1983–; Mem., Editorial Bd, Chemical Physics Letters, 1984–87. *Publications:* Nuclear Magnetic Resonance, 1955; (jtly) Clinical Magnetic Resonance, 1990; scientific papers in learned jls. *Recreation:* travel. *Address:* Department of Physics, University of Florida, 215 Williamson Hall, Gainesville, Florida 32611, USA.

ANDREW, Herbert Henry; QC 1982; **His Honour Judge Andrew;** a Circuit Judge, since 1984; *b* 26 July 1928; *s* of Herbert Henry Andrew and Nora Andrew (*née* Gough); *m* 1966, Annette Josephine Colbert; two *s* two *d*. *Educ:* Preston Grammar Sch.; Queens' Coll., Cambridge (BA). Called to the Bar, Gray's Inn, 1952; practised on Northern Circuit, 1953–84; a Recorder, 1978–84. *Recreation:* fell walking. *Address:* Peel House, 5/7 Harrington Street, Liverpool L2 9QA. *T:* 051–236 4321. *Club:* Liverpool Racquet.

ANDREW, Sir Robert (John), KCB 1986 (CB 1979); Director, Esmée Fairbairn Trust, since 1989; *b* 25 Oct. 1928; *s* of late Robert Young Andrew and Elsie (*née* Heritage); *m*

1963, Elizabeth Bayley; two *s*. *Educ:* King's College Sch., Wimbledon; Merton Coll., Oxford (MA). Intelligence Corps, 1947–49. Joined Civil Service, 1952: Asst Principal, War Office, Principal, 1957; Min. of Defence, 1963; Asst Sec., 1965; Defence Counsellor, UK Delegn to NATO, 1967–70. Private Sec. to Sec. of State for Defence, 1971–73; Under-Sec., CSD, 1973–75; Asst Under-Sec. of State, MoD, 1975–76; Dep. Under-Sec. of State, Home Office, 1976–83; Perm. Under-Sec. of State, NI Office, 1984–88; Cabinet Office, Review of Govt Legal Services, 1988. Conservator of Wimbledon and Putney Commons, 1973–. Governor, King's College Sch., 1975– (Chm., 1990–). Mem. Council, RHBNC, 1989–. *Recreations:* walking, carpentry. *Club:* United Oxford & Cambridge University.

ANDREW, Sydney Percy Smith, FRS 1976; FEng, FIChemE, MIMechE; consultant chemical engineer; ICI Senior Research Associate, 1976–88; *b* 16 May 1926; *s* of Harold C. Andrew and Kathleen M. (*née* Smith); *m* 1986, Ruth Harrison Kenyon (*née* Treanor). *Educ:* Barnard Castl Sch.; King's Coll., Durham Univ. (Open Schol.; BSc); Trinity Hall, Cambridge (Schol. and Prizeman; MA). Joined ICI Billingham Div., 1950; Chemical Engrg Res., 1951; Plant Engr, 1953; Section Manager: Reactor Res., 1955; Process Design, 1959; Gp Man., Catalysts and Chemicals Res., 1963–76. Vis. Prof., Univ. of Bath, 1988–. Chm., Res. Cttee, IChemE. Hon. DSc Leeds, 1979. Soc. of Chemical Industry Medal, 1989. *Publications:* Catalyst Handbook, 1970; various papers in chemical engrg, applied chemistry and plant physiology. *Recreations:* archaeology, ancient and medieval history. *Address:* 1 The Wynd, Stainton in Cleveland, Middlesbrough TS8 9BP. *T:* Middlesbrough (0642) 596348.

ANDREWS, Air Cdre Charles Beresford Eaton B.; *see* Burt-Andrews.

ANDREWS, David Roger Griffith, CBE 1981; Chairman, Gwion Ltd, since 1986; *b* 27 March 1933; *s* of C. H. R. Andrews and G. M. Andrews; *m* 1963, Dorothy Ann Campbell; two *s* one *d*. *Educ:* Abingdon Sch.; Pembroke Coll., Oxford (MA). ACMA, CBIM. Pirelli-General, 1956–59; Ford Motor Company, 1960–69: Controller: Product Engrg, 1965–66; Transmission and Chassis Div., 1967; European Sales Ops, 1967–69; Asst Controller, Ford of Europe, 1969; BLMC: Controller, 1970; Finance Dir, Austin Morris, 1971–72; Man. Dir, Power and Transmission Div., 1973–75; British Leyland Ltd: Man. Dir, Leyland International, 1975–77; Exec. Vice Chm., BL Ltd, 1977–82; Chm., Leyland Gp and Land Rover Gp, 1981–82; Chm. and Chief Exec., Land Rover-Leyland, 1982–86. Director: Clarges Pharmaceutical Trustees Ltd, 1983–; Glaxo Trustees Ltd, 1983–; Ex-Cell-O Ltd, 1987–88; Foundn for Sci. and Technology, 1990– (Mem. Council and Hon. Treas.). Member: CBI Council, 1981–86; Exec. Cttee, SMMT, 1981–86; Open Univ. Visiting Cttee, 1982–85. FRSA. *Recreations:* reading, sailing. *Address:* Gainford, Mill Lane, Gerrards Cross, Bucks SL9 8BA. *T:* Gerrards Cross (0753) 884310.

ANDREWS, Sir Derek (Henry), KCB 1991 (CB 1984); CBE 1970; Permanent Secretary, Ministry of Agriculture, Fisheries and Food, since 1987; *b* 17 Feb. 1933; *s* of late Henry Andrews and Emma Jane Andrews; *m* 1956, Catharine May (*née* Childe) (*d* 1982); two *s* one *d*. *Educ:* LSE. BA (Hons) 1955. Ministry of Agriculture, Fisheries and Food: Asst Principal, 1957; Asst Private Sec. to Minister of Agriculture, Fisheries and Food, 1960–61; Principal, 1961; Asst Sec., 1968; Private Sec. to Prime Minister, 1966–70; Harvard Univ., USA, 1970–71; Under-Sec., 1973; Dep. Sec., 1981. *Address:* Ministry of Agriculture, Fisheries and Food, Whitehall Place, SW1.

ANDREWS, Hon. Sir Dormer (George), Kt 1987; Chief Justice of Queensland, 1985–89; *b* 8 April 1919; *s* of Miles Dormer Andrews and Margaret Mary Andrews (*née* Robertson); *m* 1943, Joan Merle Tear; three *s*. *Educ:* University of Queensland (BA, LLB). Flying Officer, RAAF, served UK and ME, 1940–44. Admitted Queensland Bar, 1947; District Court Judge, Queensland, 1959; Chm., District Courts, 1965; Judge, 1971, Senior Puisne Judge, 1982, Supreme Court of Queensland. Chm., Law Reform Commn, Queensland, 1973–82. *Recreations:* walking, reading. *Address:* 2 Gleneagle Street, Kenmore, Brisbane, Queensland, Australia. *T:* 378–4298. *Clubs:* Queensland, Tattersalls, United Service (Brisbane).

ANDREWS, Brig. George Lewis Williams, CBE 1960; DSO 1944; *b* 1 July 1910; *o s* of Captain C. G. W. Andrews, The Border Regt (killed in action, 1914) and of late Mrs Diana Gambier-Parry (*née* Norrington); *m* 1938, Marianne, *d* of late Carl Strindberg, Stockholm and late Fru Greta Winbergh (*née* Skjöldebrand); one *s*. *Educ:* Haileybury; Sandhurst. Commissioned 2nd Lieut, The Seaforth Highlanders, 1930; active service, Palestine, 1936. Served War of 1939–45; BEF, 1939, MEF, 1941–43, BLA, 1944–45; Comd 2nd Bn The Seaforth Highlanders, 1943–45. Comd 1st Bn Seaforth Highlanders, 1953–54; Comd 152nd Highland Infantry Brigade (TA), 1954–57; Assistant Commandant, RMA Sandhurst, 1957–60. Hon. Col, 2nd Bn 51st Highland Volunteers, 1975–79. Lieut-Col, 1953; Colonel, 1955; Hon. Brig., 1960; psc 1940; jssc 1948. Chevalier, Order of Leopold, Belgium, 1945; Croix de Guerre with palm, Belgium, 1945. *Address:* West Kingsteps, Nairn, Scotland IV12 5LF. *T:* Nairn (0667) 53231.

ANDREWS, Lt-Col Harold Marcus E.; *see* Ervine-Andrews.

ANDREWS, James Roland Blake F.; *see* Fox-Andrews.

ANDREWS, John Hayward, CMG 1988; Chairman, Queensland Sugar Corporation (formerly Sugar Board (Queensland)), since 1986; Director, Logan Motorway Group (formerly Logan Toll Motorway Group), since 1988; *b* 9 Nov. 1919; *s* of James Andrews and Florence Elizabeth Andrews; *m* 1947; one *s* one *d* (and one *s* decd). *Educ:* Univ. of Queensland (BEc). FIE(Aust); FAIM; DipT&CP; DipCE. Served Royal Aust. Engineers, 1940–45. Local Govt City Engineer, Wagga Wagga and Tamworth, NSW, 1946–60; Deputy Commissioner, Main Roads Dept, Queensland, 1961–78; Administrator, Gold Coast City, 1978–79; private practice, 1979–81; Agent-Gen. for Qld, 1981–84; Chm., Electoral Redistribution Commn for Qld, 1985–86. Director: White Industries Ltd, 1986–88; Logan Toll Road Co., 1987. *Recreations:* golf, painting, walking. *Address:* 7/34 Sandford Street, St Lucia, Brisbane, Qld 4067, Australia. *Clubs:* Brisbane, Toowong RSL, Indooroopilly Golf (Queensland).

ANDREWS, Julie (Elizabeth); Actress; *b* 1 Oct. 1935; *m* 1st, Anthony J. Walton (marr. diss. 1968); one *d*; 2nd, 1969, Blake Edwards; one step *s* one step *d*, and two adopted *d*. *Educ:* Woodbrook Girls' Sch., Beckenham and private governess. Appeared in The Boy Friend, Broadway, New York, 1954; My Fair Lady: New York, 1956, London, 1958; Camelot, New York, 1960. *Films:* (Walt Disney) Mary Poppins, 1963 (Academy Award, 1964); Americanisation of Emily, 1964; Sound of Music, 1964; Hawaii, 1965; Torn Curtain, 1966; Thoroughly Modern Millie, 1966; Star, 1967; Darling Lili, 1970; The Tamarind Seed, 1973; "10", 1980; Little Miss Marker, 1980; S.O.B., 1981; Victor/Victoria, 1982; The Man Who Loved Women, 1983; Duet for One, 1987; That's Life, 1987. *TV:* The Julie Andrews Hour, 1972–73; The Sound of Christmas (Emmy Award), 1987. *Publications:* (as Julie Andrews Edwards) Mandy, 1972; Last of the Really Great Whangdoodles, 1973. *Recreations:* boating, ski-ing, riding.

ANDREWS, Prof. Kenneth Raymond, FBA 1986; Professor of History, University of Hull, 1979–88 (part-time, 1986–88), now Emeritus; *b* 26 Aug. 1921; *s* of Arthur Walter and Marion Gertrude Andrews; *m* 1969, Ottilie Kalman, Olomouc, Czechoslovakia; two step *s*. *Educ:* Henry Thornton Sch., Clapham; King's College London (BA 1948, PhD 1951). Lectr, Univ. of Liverpool, 1963–64; Lectr and Sen. Lectr, Univ. of Hull, 1964–79; active research in English maritime history. *Publications:* English Privateering Voyages to the West Indies, 1959; Elizabethan Privateering, 1964; Drake's Voyages, 1967; The Last Voyage of Drake and Hawkins, 1972; The Spanish Caribbean, 1978; Trade, Plunder and Settlement, 1984; Ships, Money and Politics, 1991; articles in learned jls. *Recreations:* chess, cookery, 20th century painting. *Address:* 8 Grange Drive, Cottingham, North Humberside HU16 5RE.

ANDREWS, Peter John; QC 1991; a Recorder of the Crown Court, since 1990; *b* 14 Nov. 1946; *s* of Reginald and Dora Andrews; *m* 1976, Ann Chavasse; two *d*. *Educ:* Bishop Vesey Grammar Sch.; Bristol Univ. (LLB); Christ's Coll., Cambridge (Dip. Criminology). Called to the Bar, Lincoln's Inn, 1970; Junior, Midland and Oxford Circuit, 1973–74; Asst Recorder, 1986–90. *Address:* 3 Fountain Court, Steelhouse Lane, Birmingham B4 6DR. *T:* 021–236 5854.

ANDREWS, Raymond Denzil Anthony, MBE 1953; VRD 1960; Senior Partner, Andrews, Downie & Partners, Architects, since 1960; *b* 5 June 1925; *s* of Michael Joseph Andrews, BA, and Phylis Marie Andrews (*née* Crowley); *m* 1958, Gillian Whitlaw Small, BA; one *s* one *d*. *Educ:* Highgate Sch.; Christ's Coll., Cambridge; University Coll. London (DipArch, DipTP); Univ. of Michigan (MArch). RIBA. Lieut, Royal Marines, 1943–46; RM Reserve, 1948–68 (Major). King George VI Meml Fellow of English-Speaking Union of US, 1954–55; Chm., London Region, RIBA, 1968–72; Vice-Pres., RIBA, 1972–74, 1978–81; Chm., Festival of Architecture, 1984; Pres., Architectural Assoc., 1975–77. Civic Trust Award, 1971 and 1978; 1st Prize, Royal Mint Square Housing Competition, GLC, 1974. Order of Al Rafadain (Iraq), 1956. *Recreation:* sailing. *Address:* 6 Addison Avenue, W11 4QR. *T:* 071–602 7701. *Clubs:* Bosham Sailing; RIBA Sailing (Cdre, 1983–87).

ANDREWS, Robert Graham M.; *see* Marshall-Andrews.

ANDREWS, Stuart Morrison; Head Master of Clifton College, 1975–90; *b* 23 June 1932; *s* of William Hannaford Andrews and Eileen Elizabeth Andrews; *m* 1962, Marie Elizabeth van Wyk; two *s*. *Educ:* Newton Abbot Grammar Sch.; St Dunstan's Coll.; Sidney Sussex Coll., Cambridge (MA). Nat. service with Parachute Bde, 1952–53. Sen. History Master and Librarian, St Dunstan's Coll., 1956–60; Chief History Master and Librarian, Repton Sch., 1961–67; Head Master, Norwich Sch., 1967–75. Chm., Direct-grant Sub-cttee of Headmasters' Conf., 1974–75; Dep. Chm., Assisted Places Cttee, 1982–; Nat. Rep., HMC, 1986–87. Editor, Conference, 1972–82. *Publications:* Eighteenth-century Europe, 1965; Enlightened Despotism, 1967; Methodism and Society, 1970; articles in various historical jls. *Recreations:* walking, writing. *Address:* 34 St Thomas Street, Wells, Somerset. *Club:* East India, Devonshire, Sports and Public Schools.

ANDREWS, William Denys Cathcart, CBE 1980; WS; Partner, Shepherd & Wedderburn, WS, Edinburgh, since 1962; *b* 3 June 1931; *s* of Eugene Andrews and Agnes Armstrong; *m* 1955, May O'Beirne; two *s* two *d*. *Educ:* Girvan High Sch.; Worksop Coll.; Edinburgh Univ. (BL). Served RASC, 1950–52. Law Society of Scotland: Mem. Council, 1972–81; Vice Pres., 1977–78; Pres., 1978–79. Examr in Conveyancing, Edinburgh Univ., 1974–77. Pt-time Mem., Lands Tribunal for Scotland, 1980–. Fiscal to Soc. of Writers to HM Signet, 1987–. *Recreation:* gardening. *Address:* Auchairne, Ballantrae, South Ayrshire KA26 0NX. *T:* Ballantrae (046583) 344. *Club:* New (Edinburgh).

ANDRIESSEN, Dr Frans, (Franciscus H. J. J.), Kt, Order of Dutch Lion; Officer, Order of Orange-Nassau; LLD; Member, since 1981, Vice-President, since 1985, the European Commission (responsible for external relations); *b* Utrecht, 2 April 1929; *m*; four *c*. *Educ:* Univ. of Utrecht (LLD). Served at Catholic Housing Institute, latterly as Director, 1954–72. Member: Provincial Estates of Utrecht, 1958–67; Lower House of the States-General, initially as specialist in housing matters, 1967–77; Chairman, KVP party in Lower House, 1971–77; Minister of Finance, 1977–80; Member, Upper House of States-General (Senate), 1980. *Address:* Commission of the European Communities, 200 rue de la Loi, 1049 Brussels, Belgium.

ANDRUS, Francis Sedley, LVO 1982; Beaumont Herald of Arms Extraordinary, since 1982; *b* 26 Feb. 1915; *o s* of late Brig.-Gen. Thomas Alchin Andrus, CMG, JP, and Alice Loveday (*née* Parr); unmarried. *Educ:* Wellington Coll.; St Peter's Hall (now Coll.), Oxford (MA). Entered College of Arms as Member of Staff, 1938; Bluemantle Pursuivant of Arms, 1970–72; Lancaster Herald of Arms, 1972–82. Freeman, City of London, 1988. *Address:* 8 Oakwood Rise, Longfield, Kent DA3 7PA. *T:* Longfield (04747) 5424.

ANFINSEN, Dr Christian Boehmer; Professor of Biology, Johns Hopkins University, since 1982; *b* Monessen, Pa, 26 March 1916; *s* of Christian Boehmer Anfinsen and Sophie (*née* Rasmussen); *m* 1941, Florence Bernice Kenenger; one *s* two *d*; *m* 1979, Libby Esther Shulman. *Educ:* Swarthmore Coll. (BA); Univ. of Pennsylvania (MS); Harvard (PhD). Amer.-Scand. Foundn Fellow, Carlsberg Lab., Copenhagen, 1939; Sen. Cancer Res. Fellow, Nobel Inst. Medicine, Stockholm, 1947; Asst Prof. of Biological Chemistry, Harvard Medical Sch., 1948–50; Head of Lab. of Cellular Physiology and Metabolism, Nat. Heart Inst., Bethesda, Md, 1950–62; Prof. of Biochemistry, Harvard Med. Sch., 1962–63; Head of Lab. of Chem. Biol., Nat. Inst. of Arthritis, Metabolism and Digestive Diseases, Bethesda, 1963–82. Rockefeller Fellow, 1954–55; Guggenheim Fellow, Weizmann Inst., Rehovot, Israel, 1958. Mem., Bd of Governors, Weizmann Inst., Rehovot, 1960–. Member: Amer. Soc. of Biol Chemists (Pres., 1971–72); Amer. Acad. of Arts and Scis; Nat. Acad. of Scis; Royal Danish Acad.; Washington Acad. of Scis; Fedn Amer. Scientists (Vice-Chm., 1958–59, and 1974–75); Pontifical Acad., 1980. Hon. DSc: Swarthmore, 1965; Georgetown, 1967; Pennsylvania, 1973; NY Med. Coll., Gustavus Adolphus Coll., 1975; Brandeis, 1977; Providence Coll., 1978; Hon. MD Naples, 1982. (Jtly) Nobel Prize for Chemistry, 1972. *Publication:* The Molecular Basis of Evolution, 1959. *Address:* Department of Biology, Johns Hopkins University, Baltimore, Md 21218, USA.

ANFOM, Emmanuel E.; *see* Evans-Anfom.

ANGEL, Gerald Bernard Nathaniel Aylmer; Senior District Judge, Family Division of the High Court, since 1991 (Registrar, 1980–90; District Judge, 1991); *b* 4 Nov. 1937; *s* of late Bernard Francis and Ethel Angel; *m* 1968, Lesley Susan Kemp; three *s* one *d* (and one *s* decd). *Educ:* St Mary's Sch., Nairobi. Served Kenya Regt, 1956–57. Called to Bar, Inner Temple, 1959; Advocate, Kenya, 1960–62; practice at Bar, 1962–80. Member: Judicial Studies Bd, 1989–90 (Mem., Civil and Family Cttee, 1985–90); Supreme Ct Procedure Cttee, 1990–; Matrimonial Causes Rule Cttee, 1991. *Publications:* (ed) Industrial Tribunals Reports, 1966–78; (contrib.) Atkin's Court Forms (Adv. Editor), 1988. *Recreations:* reading, walking. *Address:* 9 Lancaster Avenue, SE27 9EL. *T:* 081–670 7184.

ANGEL, Heather, FRPS, FBIPP; professional wildlife photographer, author and lecturer; *b* 21 July 1941; *d* of Stanley Paul Le Rougetel and Hazel Marie Le Rougetel (*née* Sherwood); *m* 1964, Martin Vivian Angel; one *s*. *Educ:* 14 schools in England and NZ; Bristol Univ. (BSc Hons (Zoology) 1962; MSc 1965). FRPS 1972; FBIPP 1974. One-man Exhibitions: The Natural History of Britain and Ireland, Sci. Mus., 1981; Nature in Focus, Natural Hist. Mus., 1987; The Art of Wildlife Photography, Gloucester, 1989. Television: demonstrating photographic techniques, Me and My Camera I, 1981; Me and My Camera II, 1983; Gardener's World, 1983; Nature, 1984; Nocon on Photography, 1988. Led British Photographic Delegn to China, 1985. Photos used worldwide in books, magazines, on TV, advertising, etc, 1972–. Hon. FRPS 1986 (Pres., 1984–86). Hon. DSc Bath, 1986. Hood Medal, RPS, 1975; Médaille de Salverte, Soc. Française de Photographie, 1984. *Publications:* Nature Photography: its art and techniques, 1972; All Colour Book of Ocean Life, 1975; Photographing Nature: Trees, 1975, Insects, 1975, Seashore, 1975, Flowers, 1975, Fungi, 1975; Seashore Life on Rocky Shores, 1975; Seashore Life on Sandy Beaches, 1975; Seashells of the Seashore, 1976; Wild Animals in the Garden, 1976; Life in the Oceans, 1977; Life in our Estuaries, 1977; Life in our Rivers, 1977; British Wild Orchids, 1977; The Countryside of the New Forest, 1977; The Countryside of South Wales, 1977; Seaweeds of the Seashore, 1977; Seashells of the Seashore, Book 1, 1978, Book 2, 1978; The Countryside of Devon, 1980; The Guinness Book of Seashore Life, 1981; The Natural History of Britain and Ireland, 1981; The Family Water Naturalist, 1982; The Book of Nature Photography, 1982; The Book of Close-up Photography, 1983; Heather Angel's Countryside, 1983; A Camera in the Garden, 1984; Close-up Photography, 1986; Kodak Calendar, The Thames, 1987; A View from a Window, 1988; Nature in Focus, 1988; Landscape Photography, 1989; Animal Photography, 1991; *for children:* Your Book of Fishes, 1972; The World of an Estuary, 1975; Fact Finder—Seashore, 1976; The World of a Stream, 1976; Fungi, 1979; Lichens, 1980; Mosses and Ferns, 1980. *Recreation:* travelling to remote parts of the world to photograph wilderness areas and unusual aspects of animal behaviour. *Address:* Highways, 6 Vicarage Hill, Farnham, Surrey GU9 8HJ. *T:* Farnham (0252) 716700, *Fax:* Farnham (0252) 727464.

ANGELES, Victoria de los; *see* de los Angeles.

ANGELL-JAMES, John, CBE 1967; MD, FRCP, FRCS; Hon. Consulting Surgeon in Otolaryngology, United Bristol Hospitals, 1966–87; *b* 23 Aug. 1901; *s* of Dr John Angell James, MRCS, LRCP and Emily Cormell (*née* Ashwin), Bristol; *m* 1930, Evelyn Miriam Everard, *d* of Francis Over and Ada Miriam Everard, Birmingham; one *s* two *d*. *Educ:* Bristol Grammar Sch.; Univ. of Bristol; London Hosp.; Guy's Hosp. MB ChB 1st Cl. Hons 1924, Bristol; MBBS London (Hons) 1924; MD 1927; FRCS 1928; FRCP 1965. Res. appts, 1924–28, Bristol and London; Hon. ENT Registrar, Bristol Royal Infirmary, 1928–29; Hon. ENT Surg., Bristol Children's Hosp., 1928–48; Cons. ENT Surg., 1948–66; Hon. Asst ENT Surg., later Hon. ENT Surg., Bristol Royal Infirmary, 1929–48; Clin. Tutor, Univ. of Bristol, 1928–55, Lectr and Head of Dept of Otolaryngology, 1955–66; Cons. ENT Surg., United Bristol Hosps, 1948–66. Lt-Col RAMC, 1942–46; Adviser in Otorhinolaryngol., MEF, 1945. Hunterian Prof., RCS, 1962; Semon Lectr in Laryngol., Univ. of London, 1965; James Yearsley Lectr, 1966; Sir William Wilde Meml Lectr, Irish Otolaryngol. Soc., 1966; Vis. Lectr, Univs of Toronto, Vermont, Cornell, Baylor and Chicago. Royal Soc. of Medicine: Former Fellow, Hon. FRSM 1976; Hon. Mem., Sections of Laryngol. (Pres., 1955) and otology. Member: SW Laryngolog. Assoc. (Chm. 1956); Brit. Medical Assoc. (Pres. Sect. of Otolaryngol., 1959; Chm. Bristol Div., 1966–67; Pres., Bath, Bristol and Som Br., 1968–69); Bristol Med.-Chirurg. Soc. (Pres. 1961); Visiting Assoc. of ENT Surgs of GB, 1948 (Pres. 1965–66); Brit. Assoc. of Otolaryngologists, 1942 (Pres. 1966–69); Collegium Oto-Rhino-Laryngologicum Amicitiae Sacrum, 1948 (Councillor, 1966–74; Pres., 1974); Barany Soc.; Pres., Otolaryngological Res. Soc., 1978. Extern. Examr, Univ. of Manchester, 1964. Hon. Member: Irish Otolaryngol. Soc.; S Africa Soc. of Otolaryngol.; Corresp. Mem., Deutsche Gesellschaft für Hals-Nasen-Ohren-Heilkunde Kopf-und Hals-Chirurgie. Hon. FRCSE 1971; Jobson Horne Prize, BMA, 1962; Colles Medal, RCSI, 1963; Dalby Prize, RSM, 1963; W. J. Harrison Prize in Laryngology, RSM, 1968. President: Gloucester Soc., 1977; Colston Soc., 1983–84. Chm. Editorial Cttee, Clinical Otolaryngology. *Publications:* Chapters in: British Surgical Practice, 1951; Diseases of the Ear, Nose and Throat, 1952 (2nd edn 1966); Ultrasound as a diagnostic and surgical tool, 1964; Clinical Surgery, 1966; Ménière's Disease, 1969; Family Medical Guide, 1980; articles in learned jls in Eng., USA, Canada, Germany and Sweden. *Recreations:* farming; shooting. *Address:* The Leaze, Sundayshill Lane, Falfield, Wotton-under-Edge, Glos GL12 8DQ.

ANGLESEY, 7th Marquess of, *cr* 1815; **George Charles Henry Victor Paget;** Baron Paget, of Beau Desert, 1549; Earl of Uxbridge, 1784; Bt 1730; Lord-Lieutenant of Gwynedd, 1983–89; *b* 8 Oct. 1922; *o s* of 6th Marquess of Anglesey, GCVO, and Lady Victoria Marjorie Harriet Manners (*d* 1946), *d* of 8th Duke of Rutland; *S* father, 1947; *m* 1948, Elizabeth Shirley Vaughan Morgan (*see* Marchioness of Anglesey); two *s* three *d*. *Educ:* Wixenford, Wokingham; Eton Coll. Major, RHG, 1946. Div. Dir, Wales, Nationwide Building Soc., 1973–89. President: Anglesey Conservative Assoc., 1948–83; Nat. Museum of Wales, 1962–68; Friends of Friendless Churches, 1966–84; Ancient Monuments Soc., 1979–84. Treasurer, Danilo Dolci Trust (Britain), 1964–86. Vice-Chm., Welsh Cttee, Nat. Trust, 1975–85; Member: Historic Buildings Council for Wales, 1953– (Chm., 1977–); Royal Fine Art Commn, 1965–71; Redundant Churches Fund, 1969–78; Royal Commn on Historical Manuscripts, 1984–; Council, Soc. of Army Historical Research; Trustee: Nat. Portrait Gall., 1979–; Nat. Heritage Memorial Fund, 1980–. Hon. Prof., UCW, 1986. FSA 1952; FRSL 1969; Hon. FRIBA, 1971; FRHistS, 1975. Anglesey: CC, 1951–67; JP, 1959–68, 1983–89; DL, 1960, Vice-Lieut, 1960. Hon. Fellow, Royal Cambrian Acad. Freeman of the City of London. Hon. DLitt Wales, 1984. CStJ 1984. *Publications:* (ed) The Capel Letters, 1814–1817, 1955; One-Leg: the Life and Letters of 1st Marquess of Anglesey, 1961; (ed) Sergeant Pearman's Memoirs, 1968; (ed) Little Hodge, 1971; A History of the British Cavalry, 1816–1919, vol I, 1973, vol. II, 1975, vol. III, 1982, vol. IV, 1986. *Recreations:* gardening, music. *Heir:* *s* Earl of Uxbridge, *qv*. *Address:* Plâs-Newydd, Llanfairpwll, Anglesey LL61 6DZ. *T:* Llanfairpwll (0248) 714330.

ANGLESEY, Marchioness of; (Elizabeth) Shirley Vaughan Paget, DBE 1983 (CBE 1977); Chairman, Drama and Dance Advisory Committee, since 1981 and Member of Board, since 1985, British Council; Chairman, Broadcasting Complaints Commission, since 1987; *b* 4 Dec. 1924; *d* of late Charles Morgan and Hilda Vaughan (both novelists); *m* 1948, Marquess of Anglesey, *qv*; two *s* three *d*. *Educ:* Francis Holland Sch., London; St James', West Malvern; Kent Place Sch., USA. Personal Secretary to Gladwyn Jebb, FO, until marriage. Dep. Chm., Prince of Wales Cttee, 1970–80. Member: Civic Trust for Wales, 1967–76; Arts Council, 1972–81 (Chm., Welsh Arts Council, 1975–81); Royal Commn on Environmental Pollution, 1973–79; IBA, 1976–82; Radioactive Waste Management Adv. Cttee, 1981–; Vice-Chairman: Museums and Galls Commn, 1989– (Mem., 1981–); Govt Working Party on Methods of Sewage Disposal, 1969–70. Chm., NFWI, 1966–69. Trustee, Pilgrim Trust, 1982–. Hon. Fellow, UCNW, Bangor, 1990. Hon. LLD Wales, 1977. *Address:* Plâs-Newydd, Llanfairpwll, Gwynedd LL61 6DZ. *T:* Llanfairpwll (0248) 714330.

See also R. H. V. C. Morgan.

ANGLIN, Prof. Douglas (George); Professor of Political Science, Carleton University, Ottawa, Canada, 1958–89, Adjunct Professor, since 1989; *b* Toronto, Canada, 16 Dec. 1923; *s* of George Chambers Anglin, MD, and Ruth Cecilia Cale, MD; *m* 1948, Mary Elizabeth Watson; two *d*. *Educ:* Toronto Univ.; Corpus Christi and Nuffield Colls, Oxford Univ. BA Toronto; MA, DPhil Oxon. Lieut, RCNVR, 1943–45. Asst (later Associate) Prof. of Polit. Sci. and Internat. Relations, Univ. of Manitoba, Winnipeg, 1951–58; Associate Prof. (later Prof.), Carleton Univ., 1958–89. Vice-Chancellor, Univ. of Zambia, Lusaka, Zambia, 1965–69; Associate Research Fellow, Nigerian Inst. of Social and Economic Research, Univ. of Ibadan, Ibadan, Nigeria, 1962–63; Research Associate, Center of Internat. Studies, Princeton Univ., 1969–70; Pres., Canadian Assoc. of African Studies, 1973–74. *Publications:* The St Pierre and Miquelon Affairs of 1941: a study in diplomacy in the North Atlantic quadrangle, 1966; Zambia's Foreign Policy: studies in diplomacy and dependence, 1979; edited jointly: Africa: Problems and Prospects 1961; Conflict and Change in Southern Africa, 1978; Canada, Scandinavia and Southern Africa, 1978; articles on Internat. and African affairs in a variety of learned jls. *Address:* Carleton University, Colonel By Drive, Ottawa, Ontario K1S 5B6, Canada.

ANGLIN, Eric Jack; HM Diplomatic Service, retired; Consul-General, Melbourne, 1979–83; *b* 9 Aug. 1923; *m* 1954, Patricia Farr; three *s*. Joined Foreign Service (subseq. Diplomatic Service), 1948; FO, 1948–52; HM Missions in: Damascus, 1952–56; Rangoon, 1956–59; Madrid, 1960–64; FO, 1964–67; La Paz, 1967–70; Khartoum, 1970–72; Inspector, Diplomatic Service, FCO, 1973–76; Buenos Aires, 1976–78; Chargé d'Affaires and Consul-Gen., Santiago, 1978–79. Dir, Aberdeen Sea Products Ltd, 1989–. *Recreations:* auctions, lecturing. *Address:* Treetops, The Glade, Kingswood, Tadworth, Surrey KT20 6LH. *T:* Mogador (0737) 832858.

ANGUS, Rev. (James Alexander) Keith, LVO 1990; TD; Minister of Braemar and Crathie Parish Churches, since 1979; Domestic Chaplain to the Queen, since 1979; *b* 16 April 1929; *s* of late Rev. Walter C. S. Angus and late Margaret I. Stephen; *m* 1956, Alison Jane Daly; one *s* one *d*. *Educ:* High School of Dundee; Univ. of St Andrews (MA). National Service, Army, 1947–49; served with TA, 1950–76; Captain RA (TA), 1955; Chaplain to 5, KOSB (TA), 1957–67, to 154 Regt, RCT (V), 1967–76. Assistant Minister, The Cathedral, Glasgow, 1955–56; Minister: Hoddam Parish Church, 1956–67; Gourock Old Parish Church, 1967–79. Convener, Gen. Assembly's Cttee on Chaplains to HM Forces, 1981–85. *Recreations:* fishing, hill walking, golf. *Address:* The Manse of Crathie, Crathie, near Ballater, Aberdeenshire AB3 5UL. *T:* Crathie (03397) 42208. *Club:* New (Edinburgh).

ANGUS, Sir Michael (Richardson), Kt 1990; Chairman, Unilever PLC, 1986–May 1992 (Director, 1970–92); Vice Chairman, Unilever NV, 1986–May 1992 (Director, 1970–92); Deputy Chairman, Jan.–July 1992, Chairman from Aug. 1992, Whitbread plc (Director, since 1986); a Deputy Chairman, National Westminster Bank, since 1991; *b* 5 May 1930; *s* of William Richardson Angus and Doris Margaret Breach; *m* 1952, Eileen Isabel May Elliott; two *s* one *d*. *Educ:* Marling Sch., Stroud, Glos; Bristol Univ. (BSc Hons). CBIM 1979. Served RAF, 1951–54. Unilever, 1954–92: Marketing Dir, Thibaud Gibbs, Paris, 1962–65; Man. Dir, Res. Bureau, 1965–67; Sales Dir, Lever Brothers UK, 1967–70; Toilet Preparations Co-ordinator, 1970–76; Chemicals Co-ordinator, 1976–80; Regional Dir, N America, 1979–84; Chairman and Chief Exec. Officer: Unilever United States, Inc., New York, 1980–84; Lever Brothers Co., New York, 1980–84. Jt Dep. Chm., British Airways, 1989– (Dir, 1988–); non-exec. Dir, Thorn EMI plc, 1988–. Jt Chm., Netherlands-British Chamber of Commerce, 1984–89; Internat. Counsellor and Trustee, The Conference Board, 1984–. Dep. Pres., CBI, 1991–. Vis. Fellow, Nuffield Coll., Oxford, 1986–. Trustee, Leverhulme Trust, 1984–. Governor, Ashridge Management Coll., 1974–; Mem. Court of Govs, LSE, 1985–. Hon. DSc Bristol, 1990. Holland Trade Award, 1990. *Recreations:* countryside, wine, puzzles. *Address:* (until May 1992) c/o Unilever PLC, PO Box 68, EC4P 4BQ. *T:* 071–822 5252; (from May 1992) Whitbread plc, The Brewery, Chiswell Street, EC1Y 4SD. *T:* 071–606 4455. *Clubs:* Athenæum; University, Knickerbocker (New York).

ANNALY, 6th Baron *cr* 1863; **Luke Richard White;** *b* 29 June 1954; *o s* of 5th Baron Annaly and Lady Marye Isabel Pepys (*d* 1958), *d* of 7th Earl of Cottenham; *S* father, 1990; *m* 1983, Caroline Nina, *yr d* of Col Robert Garnett, MBE: one *s* two *d*. *Educ:* Eton; RMA Sandhurst. Commnd Royal Hussars, 1974–78, RARO. *Heir:* *s* Hon. Luke Henry White, *b* 20 Sept. 1990. *Address:* House of Lords, SW1A 0PW.

ANNAN, family name of **Baron Annan.**

ANNAN, Baron, *cr* 1965 (Life Peer); **Noël Gilroy Annan,** OBE 1946; Chairman, Board of Trustees, National Gallery, 1980–85 (Trustee, 1978–85); *b* 25 Dec. 1916; *s* of late James Gilroy Annan; *m* 1950, Gabriele, *d* of Louis Ferdinand Ullstein, Berlin; two *d*. *Educ:* Stowe Sch.; King's Coll., Cambridge (Exhibitioner and Scholar). Served War of 1939–45: WO, War Cabinet Offices, and Military Intelligence, 1940–44; France and Germany, 1944–46; GSO1, Political Div. of British Control Commn, 1945–46. University of Cambridge: Fellow of King's Coll., 1944–56, 1966; Asst Tutor, 1947; Lectr in Politics, 1948–66; Provost of King's Coll., 1956–66; Provost of University Coll., London, 1966–78; Vice-Chancellor, Univ. of London, 1978–81. Romanes Lectr, Oxford, 1965. Chairman: Departmental Cttee on Teaching of Russian in Schools, 1960; Academic Planning Bd, Univ. of Essex, 1965–70; Cttee on Future of Broadcasting, 1974–77, report published 1977. Member: Academic Adv. Cttee, Brunel Coll., 1966–73; Academic Planning Bd, Univ. of East Anglia, 1964–71; Public Schools Commn, 1966–70. Chm., Enquiry on the disturbances in Essex Univ. (report published 1974). Sen. Fellow Eton Coll., 1956–66. Governor: Stowe Sch., 1945–66; Queen Mary Coll., London, 1956–60. Trustee: Churchill Coll., Cambridge, 1958–76; British Museum, 1963–80; Pres., London Library, 1980–. Dir, Royal Opera House, Covent Garden, 1967–78; Gulbenkian Foundation: Mem., Arts Cttee, 1957–64; Chm., Educn Cttee, 1971–76. FRHistS; Fellow, Berkeley Coll., Yale, 1963; Hon. Fellow: UCL, 1968; Churchill Coll., Cambridge, 1988; Emer. Fellow, Leverhulme Trust, 1984. For. Hon. Mem., Amer. Acad. of Arts and Sciences, 1973. Hon. DLitt: York, Ontario, 1966; New York, 1981; DUniv Essex, 1967; Hon. LLD Pennsylvania, 1980, Le Bas Prize, 1948; Diamond Jubilee Medal, Inst. of Linguists, 1971; Clerk Kerr Medal, Univ. of Calif, Berkeley, 1985. Comdr, Royal Order of King George I of the Hellenes (Greece), 1962. *Publications:* Leslie Stephen: his thought and character in relation to his time, 1951 (awarded James Tait Black Memorial Prize, 1951), rev. edn 1984; The Intellectual Aristocracy (in Studies in Social History, a tribute to G. M. Trevelyan, 1956); Kipling's Place in the History of Ideas (in Kipling's Mind and Art, 1964); The Curious Strength of Positivism in English Political Thought, 1959; Roxburgh of Stowe, 1965; Our Age: portrait of a generation, 1990; articles in Victorian Studies and other periodicals. *Recreation:* writing English prose. *Address:* 16 St John's Wood Road, NW8 8RE. *Club:* Brooks's.

ANNAND, John Angus; Under Secretary, Welsh Office, 1975–85; *b* 13 May 1926; *s* of James Annand and Lilias Annand (*née* Smith); *m* 1971, Julia Dawn Hardman (marr. diss. 1986). *Educ:* Hillhead High Sch., Glasgow; Glasgow Univ. (MA, 1st Cl. Hons); Brasenose Coll., Oxford (MLitt). Lecturer: Univ. of Ceylon; Univ. of South Australia, 1951–53;

Asst Dir, Civil Service Commn, 1953–57; Principal, 1957, Asst Sec., 1967, HM Treasury; Civil Service Dept, 1968; Welsh Office, 1971; Under Sec., Health and Social Work Dept, Welsh Office, 1975; Economic Policy Gp, 1978. Mem., GMC, 1986–90. *Address:* 21 Fairwater Road, Llandaff, Cardiff CF5 2LD.

ANNAND, Richard Wallace, VC 1940; DL; Personnel Officer at Finchale Abbey Training Centre for the Disabled, near Durham, 1948–79; late Captain Durham Light Infantry (RARO); *b* 5 Nov. 1914; *s* of Lt-Comdr Wallace Moir Annand, Royal Naval Division (killed Gallipoli 1915), and late Dora Elizabeth Chapman, South Shields; *m* 1940, Shirley Osborne, JP 1957. *Educ:* Pocklington, East Yorks. Staff of National Provincial Bank, 1933–37; commissioned in RNVR 1933 (Tyne and London Divisions); transferred to Durham Light Infantry, Jan. 1938; served in France and Belgium, 1939–40 (wounded, VC). Invalided, Dec. 1948. Hon. Freeman Co. Borough of South Shields, 1940; Hon. Representative of The Officers' Assoc.; DL Co. of Durham, 1956. *Recreations:* Rugby football, golf; interest: general welfare of the deafened. *Address:* Springwell House, Whitesmocks, Durham City DH1 4LL. *Club:* County (Durham).

ANNANDALE AND HARTFELL, 11th Earl of, *cr* 1662 (S) with precedence to 1643; **Patrick Andrew Wentworth Hope Johnstone of Annandale and of that Ilk,** DL; Earl of the territorial earldom of Annandale and Hartfell, and of the Lordship of Johnstone; Hereditary Steward of the Stewartry of Annandale; Hereditary Keeper of the Castle of Lochmaben; Chief of the Name and Arms of Johnstone; landowner; *b* 19 April 1941; *s* of Major Percy Wentworth Hope Johnstone of Annandale and of that Ilk, TD (*d* 1983) (*de jure* 10th Earl) and of Margaret Jane (now Margaret Countess of Annandale and Hartfell), *d* of Herbert William Francis Hunter-Arundell; claim to earldom admitted by Committee for Privileges, House of Lords, 1985; *m* 1969, Susan Josephine, *d* of late Col Walter John Macdonald Ross, CB, OBE, MC, TD, Netherhall, Castle Douglas; one *s* one *d*. *Educ:* Stowe School; RAC, Cirencester. Member: Dumfries CC, 1970–75; Dumfries and Galloway Regional Council, 1974–86; Scottish Valuation Advisory Council, 1983–85. Director: Bowring Members Agency, 1985–88; Murray Lawrence Members Agency, 1988–; Solway River Purification Bd, 1970–86; Chm., Royal Jubilee and Prince's Trusts for Dumfries and Galloway, 1984–88. Underwriting Member of Lloyds, 1976–. DL Nithsdale and Annandale and Eskdale, 1987. *Recreations:* golf, shooting. *Heir:* *s* Lord Johnstone, *qv*. *Address:* House of Lords, SW1. *Clubs:* Brooks's; Puffin's (Edinburgh).

ANNENBERG, Walter H., KBE (Hon.) 1976; US Ambassador to the Court of St James's, 1969–74; *b* 13 March 1908; *s* of M. L. Annenberg; *m* 1951, Leonore Cohn; one *d*. *Educ:* Peddie Sch.; Univ. of Pennsylvania. President, Triangle Publications Inc., Philadelphia, Pa; Publisher: Seventeen Magazine; TV Guide; Daily Racing Form. Hon. Bencher, Middle Temple; Hon. Old Etonian, 1990; Trustee, Winston Churchill Traveling Fellowships. Medal of Freedom, 1986; holds foreign decorations. *Address:* Llanfair Road, Wynnewood, Pa 19096, USA; Suite A200, St Davids Center, 150 Radnor-Chester Road, St Davids, Pa 19087, USA. *Clubs:* White's; Racquet, Rittenhouse (Philadelphia); Lyford Cay (Bahamas); National Press (Washington, DC); Swinley Forest Golf.

ANNESLEY, family name of **Earl Annesley** and **Viscount Valentia.**

ANNESLEY, 10th Earl *cr* 1789; **Patrick Annesley;** Baron Annesley, 1758; Viscount Glerawly, 1766; *b* 12 August 1924; *e s* of 9th Earl Annesley, and of Nora, *y d* of late Walter Harrison; *S* father, 1979; *m* 1947, Catherine, *d* of John Burgess, Edinburgh; four *d*. *Heir:* *b* Hon. Philip Harrison Annesley [*b* 29 March 1927; *m* 1951, Florence Eileen, *o d* of late John Arthur Johnston]. *Address:* 35 Spring Rise, Egham, Surrey.

ANNESLEY, Hugh Norman, QPM 1986; Chief Constable, Royal Ulster Constabulary, since 1989; *b* 22 June 1939; *s* of late William Henry Annesley and of Agnes Annesley (*née* Redmond); *m* 1970, Elizabeth Ann (*née* MacPherson); one *s* one *d*. *Educ:* St Andrew's Prep. Sch., Dublin; Avoca Sch. for Boys, Blackrock. Joined Metropolitan Police, 1958; Chief Supt, 1974; Police Staff College: Special Course, 1963; Intermed. Comd Course, 1971; Sen. Comd Course, 1975; Asst Chief Constable, Personnel and Ops, Sussex Police, 1976; RCDS 1980; Metropolitan Police, Deputy Assistant Commissioner: Central and NW London, 1981; Personnel, 1983; Dir, Force Re-organisation Team, 1984; Assistant Commissioner: Personnel and Training, 1985; Specialist Ops, 1987. Member: Nat. Exec. Inst., FBI, 1986–; Exec. Cttee, Interpol (British Rep.), 1987–90. *Recreations:* hockey, sailing. *Address:* Brooklyn, Knock Road, Belfast BT5 6LE.

ANNETT, David Maurice, MA; Headmaster of King's School, Worcester, 1959–79; *b* 27 April 1917; *s* of late M. W. Annett and Marguerite, *d* of Rev. W. M. Hobson; *m* 1953, Evelyn Rosemary, *d* of late W. M. Gordon, Headmaster of Wrekin Coll., and *widow* of R. E. Upcott; one *d* (one step-*s* two step-*d*). *Educ:* Haileybury Coll.; Queens' Coll., Cambridge. Head of Classical Dept at Oundle Sch., 1939–53, and Housemaster, 1948–53; Headmaster of Marling Sch., Stroud, 1953–59. Served with 27th Field Regt, RA, in India and Burma (Capt.), 1941–45. *Address:* The Old Shop, Whitbourne, Worcester WR6 5SR. *T:* Knightwick (0886) 21727.

ANNING, Raymon Harry, CBE 1982; QPM 1975; Commissioner of Police, The Royal Hong Kong Police Force, 1985–90; Director, Securicor Consultancy Ltd, since 1990; *b* 22 July 1930; *s* of Frederick Charles Anning and Doris Mabel Anning (*née* Wakefield); *m* 1949, Beryl Joan Boxall; one *s* one *d*. *Educ:* Richmond and East Sheen Grammar School. Army (East Surrey Regt and Royal Military Police), 1948–50. Metropolitan Police, 1952–79: Constable to Chief Supt, Divisions and Headquarters, 1952–69; Officer i/c Anguilla Police Unit, W Indies, 1969; Chief Supt i/c Discipline Office, New Scotland Yard, 1970–72; Commander i/c A 10 (Complaints Investigation) Branch, NSY, 1972–75; seconded to Hong Kong Govt, 1974; Dep. Asst Commissioner C (CID) Dept, 1975–78; Inspector of Metropolitan Police (Dep. Asst Comr), 1979; HM Inspector of Constabulary for England and Wales, 1979–83; Dep. Comr of Police, Hong Kong, 1983–85. Graduate of Nat. Exec. Inst., FBI Academy, Quantico, Virginia, USA, 1979. *Recreation:* walking. *Address:* Sutton Park House, 15 Carshalton Road, Sutton, Surrey SM1 4LE. *Clubs:* Royal Over-Seas League; Royal Hong Kong Golf Club.

ANNIS, David, MD; FRCS; Senior Research Fellow, University of Liverpool, since 1981 (Science and Engineering Research Council Senior Research Fellow, Institute of Medical and Dental Engineering, 1981–86); *b* 28 Feb. 1921; *s* of Harold and Gertrude Annis; *m* 1948, Nesta Roberts; three *s* one *d*. *Educ:* Manchester Grammar Sch.; Univ. of Liverpool. ChM 1953, MD 1959; FRCS 1946. Res. Fellow in Exptl Surgery, Mayo Clinic, Minn., 1949–51. Liverpool University: Sen. Lectr in Surgery, 1951–54; Dir of Studies, Surg. Sci., 1964–69; Dir, Bioengineering Unit, Dept of Surgery, 1969-85; Consultant Gen. Surgeon, Royal Liverpool Hosp., 1954–81. Member: Biomaterials Sub-Cttee, SRC, 1978–80; Physiolog. Systems and Disorders Bd, MRC, 1980–. Mem. Ct of Examrs, RCS, 1963–69; Examiner in Surgery, Univs of Leeds, Glasgow, Cardiff, Dundee, Liverpool and Lagos. Member, Editorial Committee: Bioengineering Jl, 1980–; British Jl of Surgery, 1965–80. *Publications:* contribs to: Wells and Kyle, Scientific Foundations of Surgery, 1967, 3rd edn 1982; Cuschieri, Moosa and Giles, Companion to Surgical Practice, 1982; papers on surgical and med. bioengrg subjects in learned jls. *Recreation:* countryside. *Address:* Little Hey, Dibbinsdale Road, Bromborough, Merseyside L63 0HQ. *T:* 051–334 3422.

ANNIS, Francesca; actress; *b* 1945. *Theatre:* Royal Shakespeare Company: Romeo and Juliet, 1976; Troilus and Cressida, 1976; Luciana in Comedy of Errors, 1976; Natalya in A Month in the Country, Nat. Theatre, 1981; Masha in Three Sisters, Albery, 1987; Melitta in Mrs Klein, NT, 1988. *Films:* Penny Gold, 1972; Macbeth, 1973; Krull, 1983; Dune, 1984; The Golden River; Under the Cherry Moon. *Television:* A Pin to see the Peepshow, 1973; Madame Bovary, 1975; Stronger than the Sun, 1977; The Ragazza, 1978; Lillie (series), 1978; Partners in Crime (series), 1983; Inside Story (series), 1986; Parnell and the Englishwoman, Absolute Hell, 1991. *Address:* c/o Dennis Selinger, ICM, 388–396 Oxford Street, W1.

ANNIS, Philip Geoffrey Walter; Manager, Regimental History Project, Royal Regiment of Artillery, since 1986; *b* 7 Feb. 1936; *s* of Walter and Lilian Annis; *m* 1967, Olive, *d* of Mr & Mrs E. W. A. Scarlett; one *s*. *Educ:* Sale Grammar Sch.; Kelsick Grammar Sch., Ambleside; Manchester Univ. FSA 1973; FRHistS 1975. Served RA, 1957–59, and RA (TA), 1961–66. Board of Inland Revenue, 1959–62. Joined National Maritime Museum, 1962; Head of Museum Services, 1971; Dep. Dir, 1979–86. Mem., British Commn, Internat. Commn for Maritime History, 1980–88. Comdr, Order of Lion of Finland, 1986. *Publications:* Naval Swords, 1970; (with Comdr W. E. May) Swords For Sea Service, 1970; articles on the history of naval uniform. *Recreation:* gardening. *Address:* The Royal Artillery Institution, Old Royal Military Academy, Woolwich, SE18 4DN. *T:* 081–854 2242.

ANSBRO, David Anthony; Partner, Hepworth & Chadwick, solicitors, since 1991; *b* 3 April 1945; *s* of late David T. Ansbro and of Kathleen Mary Ansbro (*née* Mallett); *m* 1967, Veronica Mary (*née* Auton); two *d*. *Educ:* Xaverian Coll., Manchester; Leeds Univ. (LLB Hons). Articled to Town Clerk, Leeds, 1966–69; admitted Solicitor, 1969; Solicitor, Leeds City Council, 1969–73; Asst Dir of Admin, 1973–77, Dep. Dir of Admin, 1977–81, W Yorks County Council; Town Clerk and Chief Exec., York City Council, 1981–85; Chief Exec., Kirklees Council, 1985–87; Rees & Co., Solicitors, Huddersfield, 1987–88; Chief Exec., Leeds City Council, 1988–91. Papal Medal Pro Ecclesia et Pontifice, 1982. *Recreations:* family, friends, watching Manchester City. *Address:* Cloth Hall Court, Infirmary Street, Leeds LS1 2JB. *T:* Leeds (0532) 430391. *Club:* Honley Cricket.

ANSCOMBE, Gertrude Elizabeth Margaret, FBA 1967; Professor of Philosophy, University of Cambridge, 1970–86; Fellow, New Hall, Cambridge, 1970–86, Hon. Fellow, since 1986; *b* 1919; *d* of Allen Wells Anscombe and Gertrude Elizabeth Anscombe (*née* Thomas); *m* 1941, Prof. Peter Thomas Geach, *qv*; three *s* four *d*. *Educ:* Sydenham High Sch.; St Hugh's Coll., Oxford (Schol.); Newnham Coll., Cambridge. 2nd cl. Hon. Mods 1939, 1st cl. Greats 1941, Oxford. Research studentships, Oxford and Cambridge, 1941–44; research fellowships, Somerville Coll., Oxford, 1946–64; Fellow, Somerville Coll., 1964–70, Hon. Fellow, 1970–; Hon. Fellow, St Hugh's Coll., Oxford, 1972. Hon. Dr Laws Notre Dame Univ., 1986; Hon. DPhil and Letters Navarra Univ., 1989. For. Hon. Mem., Amer. Acad. of Arts and Sciences, 1979. Ehrenkreuz Pro Litteris et Artibus (Austria), 1978; Forschungspreis, Alexander von Humboldt Stiftung, 1983. *Publications:* Intention, 1957; An Introduction to Wittgenstein's Tractatus, 1959; (with Peter Geach) Three Philosophers, 1961; Collected Papers: 1, Parmenides to Wittgenstein, 2, Metaphysics and the Philosophy of Mind, 3, Ethics, Religion and Politics, 1981; translator and co-editor of posthumous works of Ludwig Wittgenstein. *Address:* 3 Richmond Road, Cambridge.

ANSELL, Dr Barbara Mary, CBE 1982; Consultant Physician (Rheumatology), Wexham Park Hospital, Slough, 1985–88; Head of Division of Rheumatology, Clinical Research Centre, Northwick Park Hospital, Harrow, 1976–88; *b* 30 Aug. 1923; *m* A. H. Weston, MB, FRCGP. *Educ:* Kings High Sch. for Girls, Warwick; Birmingham Univ. (MD 1969). MRCP 1951, FRCP 1967. Consultant Physician (Rheumatol.), Canadian Red Cross Hosp., Taplow, 1962–85. Mem., Cttee for the Review of Medicines, 1979–82. Member: British Assoc. for Rheumatism and Rehabilitation (Mem. Council, 1978–81); Arthritis and Rheumatism Council (Member: Educn Cttee, 1961–77 (Chm., 1966–68); Scientific Co-ordinating Cttee, 1981–; Exec. Cttee, 1987–); RCP Cttee on Rheumatology, 1972–82; Warnock Cttee of Enquiry into Educn of Handicapped Children, 1975; Exec. Cttee, British League Against Rheumatism, 1976–; Standing Cttee, European League Against Rheumatism, 1979– (Chm., Cttee on Paediatric Rheumatology, 1979–); Heberden Soc. (Pres., 1976); Council, RCP, 1987–88 (2nd Vice-Pres.); Rheumatology Chm., RCP Cttee on Higher Med. Trng, 1977–79. Hon. FRCS, 1984; Hon. FRSM, 1989. Hon. Member: Amer. Coll. of Physicians; American, Australian, Finnish, French, German and South African Rheumatism Associations; Spanish Soc. of Rheumatology. Editor, Medicine, 1974, 1976, 1978–79. *Publications:* (ed) Clinics in Rheumatic Diseases, 1976; Chronic Ailments in Childhood, 1976; (ed jtly) Surgical Management of Juvenile Chronic Polyarthritis, 1978; Rheumatic Disorders in Childhood, 1980; Inflammatory Disorders of Muscle, 1984. *Recreations:* travelling, cooking. *Address:* Dumgoyne, Templewood Lane, Stoke Poges, Bucks SL2 4BG. *T:* Fulmer (02816) 2321; (consulting rooms) 9 Beaumont Road, Windsor, Berks SL4 1HY. *Club:* Royal Society of Medicine.

ANSELL, Sir Michael Picton, Kt 1968; CBE 1951; DSO 1944; DL; First President/Chairman, British Equestrian Federation, 1972–76; Show Director, Royal International Horse Show, and Horse of the Year Show, 1949–75; *b* 26 March 1905; *s* of Lieut-Col G. K. Ansell and K. Cross; *m* 1st, 1936, Victoria Jacintha Fleetwood Fuller (*d* 1969); two *s* one *d*; 2nd, 1970, Eileen (*née* Stanton) (*d* 1971), *widow* of Maj.-Gen. Roger Evans, CB, MC. *Educ:* Wellington; RMC Sandhurst. Gazetted 5th Royal Inniskilling Dragoon Guards, 1924, Col, 1957–62. War of 1939–45: Lieut-Col to command 1st Lothian & Border Yeo., 1940 (severely wounded and prisoner, 1940); discharged disabled, 1944. Chairman: British Show Jumping Assoc., 1945–64, 1970–71 (Pres., 1964–66); (first) British Horse Soc. Council, 1963–72 (Hon. Dir, British Horse Soc., 1952–73). Yeoman, Worshipful Co. of Saddlers, 1963; Freeman: Worshipful Co. of Farriers, 1962, Worshipful Co. of Loriners, 1962. Mem. Council, St Dunstan's, 1958– (a Vice-Pres., 1970, Vice-Chm., 1975–77, Pres., 1977–86). DL 1966, High Sheriff 1967, Devon. Chevalier, Order of Leopold, Belgium, 1932; Commander's Cross, Order of Merit, German Federal Republic, 1975; Olympic Order, Silver, IOC, 1977. *Publications:* Soldier On (autobiog.), 1973; Riding High, 1974; Leopard, the Story of My Horse, 1980. *Recreations:* show jumping (International, 1931–39), polo International, fishing. *Address:* Pillhead House, Bideford, N Devon EX39 4NF. *T:* Bideford (0237) 472574. *Club:* Cavalry and Guards.

See also N. G. P. Ansell.

ANSELL, Maj.-Gen. Nicholas George Picton, OBE 1980; Senior Directing Staff, Army, Royal College of Defence Studies, since 1990; *b* 17 Aug. 1937; *s* of Col Sir Michael Ansell, *qv*; *m* 1961, Vivien, *e d* of Col Anthony Taylor, DSO, MC; two *s* one *d*. *Educ:* Wellington Coll.; Magdalene Coll., Cambridge (MA). Commnd into 5th Royal Inniskilling Dragoon Guards, 1956; served BAOR, Libya, Cyprus; sc Camberley, 1970; Bde Major RAC HQ 1 (BR) Corps, 1971–72; Instructor Staff Coll., 1976–77; CO 5th Royal Inniskilling Dragoon Guards, 1977–80; Col GS Staff Coll., 1980–81; comd 20

Armd Bde, 1982–83; RCDS, 1984; Dep. Chief of Staff HQ BAOR, 1985–86; Dir, RAC, 1987–89. *Recreations:* country pursuits—horses, fishing, shooting, birdwatching. *Address:* c/o Lloyds Bank, Bideford, Devon EX39 2AD. *Club:* Cavalry and Guards.

ANSON, family name of **Earl of Lichfield.**

ANSON, Viscount; Thomas William Robert Hugh Anson; *b* 19 July 1978; *s* and *heir* of Earl of Lichfield, *qv.*

ANSON, Charles Vernon, LVO 1983; Press Secretary to the Queen, since 1990; *b* 11 March 1944; *s* of Philip Vernon Anson and Stella Anson (*née* Parish); *m* 1976, Clarissa Rosamund Denton; one *s* one *d. Educ:* Lancing College; Jesus College, Cambridge (BA History). Joined Diplomatic Service, 1966; Third, later Second Sec. (Commercial), Washington, 1968–71; FO, 1971–74; Asst Private Sec. to Minister of State, 1974–76; Second Sec. (Commercial), Tehran, 1976–79; seconded to Press Office, 10 Downing St., 1979–81; First Sec. (Inf.), Washington, 1981–85; FO, 1985–87; Dir of Public Relations, Kleinwort Benson, 1987–90. *Address:* c/o Buckingham Palace, SW1A 1AA. *Club:* Hurlingham.

ANSON, Vice-Adm. Sir Edward (Rosebery), KCB 1984; FRAeS 1982; Senior Naval Adviser, British Aerospace plc, 1989–91, retired; *b* 11 May 1929; *s* of Ross Rosebery Anson and Ethel Jane (*née* Green); *m* 1960, Rosemary Anne Radcliffe; one *s* one *d. Educ:* Prince of Wales Sch., Nairobi, Kenya; BRNC, Dartmouth; Empire Test Pilots Sch., Farnborough (grad. 1957). Served, 1952–64: Naval Air Sqdns, and 700X and 700Z Flts (Blackburn Aircraft Ltd, 1959–61); comd HMS Eskimo, 1964–66; Commander (Air): RNAS Lossiemouth, 1967–68; HMS Eagle, 1969–70; comd Inter Service Hovercraft Trials Unit, 1971; Naval and Air Attaché, Tokyo and Seoul, 1972–74; comd HMS Juno and Captain F4, 1974–76; comd HMS Ark Royal, 1976–78; Flag Officer, Naval Air Command, 1979–82 C of S to C-in-C Fleet, 1982–84, retired. Exec. Dir, Sales, BAe Bristol Div., 1985–86; Pres. and Chief Exec. Officer, BAe, Washington, 1986–89. *Recreations:* walking, golf, tennis, photography. *Address:* c/o Lloyds Bank, High Street, Yeovil, Somerset.

ANSON, Elizabeth Audrey, (Lady Anson), JP, DL; an Adjudicator, Immigration Appeals, since 1987; *b* 9 Jan. 1931; *d* of late Rear-Adm. Sir Philip Clarke, KBE, CB, DSO, and Audrey (*née* White); *m* 1955, Rear-Adm. Sir Peter Anson, Bt, *qv;* two *s* two *d. Educ:* Weirfield Sch., Taunton; Royal Naval Sch., Haslemere; King's Coll., London (LLB). Called to Bar, Inner Temple, 1952; joined Western Circuit, 1952; practice at Bar, 1952–56; part-time Adjudicator, Immigration Appeals, 1977–87. Chm., Ind. Appeals Authority for Sch. Examinations, 1990–. Councillor, Waverley Bor. Council, 1974–, Mayor, 1987–88. Association of District Councils of England and Wales: Mem., 1983–; Chm., Housing and Environmental Health Cttee, 1987–; Mem., Local Govt Audit Commn, 1987–90. Chm., Nat. Mobility Scheme, 1987–88. JP 1977, DL 1984, Surrey. *Recreations:* travel, needlecraft. *Address:* Rosefield, Rowledge, Farnham, Surrey GU10 4AT. *T:* Frensham (025125) 2724.

ANSON, Sir John, KCB 1990 (CB 1981); Second Permanent Secretary (Public Expenditure), HM Treasury, 1987–90; *b* 3 Aug. 1930; *yr s* of Sir Edward Anson, 6th Bt, and of Dowager Lady Anson; *m* 1957, Myrica Fergie-Woods; two *s* two *d. Educ:* Winchester, Magdalene Coll., Cambridge (MA; Smith's Prize). Served in HM Treasury, 1954–68; Financial Counsellor, British Embassy, Paris, 1968–71; Asst Sec., 1971–72, Under-Sec., 1972–74, Cabinet Office; Under-Sec., 1974–77, Dep. Sec., 1977–87, HM Treasury; Economic Minister, British Embassy, Washington, and UK Exec. Dir, IMF and World Bank, 1980–83. Mem. Bd, Public Finance Foundn, 1989–. Hon. Treas., Council of Churches for Britain and Ireland, 1991–. *Address:* 18 Church Road, Barnes, SW13 9HN. *T:* 081–748 6557.

    See also Sir Peter Anson, Bt.

ANSON, Malcolm Allinson; Chairman, Wessex Water Authority, 1982–87; Chairman, Cancer Help Centre, since 1983; *b* 23 April 1924; *s* of Sir Wilfrid Anson, MBE, MC, and Dinah Anson (*née* Bourne); *m* 1950, Alison Lothian (separated 1990), *d* of late Sir Arthur Lothian, KCIE, CSI; three *s* one *d. Educ:* Winchester; Trinity College, Oxford (MA). War Service, Royal Horse Artillery, 1943–46. Joined Imperial Tobacco Co. (of GB & Ireland) Ltd, 1948; Dir, 1968; Dep. Chm., Imperial Gp Ltd, 1979–80, Chm. 1980–81. Director: Bristol Waterworks Co., 1981–82; Nat. Westminster Bank, 1981–85. Chairman: Bristol Assoc. of Youth Clubs, 1963–71; Endeavour Training, 1969–76; Avon Enterprise Fund, 1984–90. Dir, Oxford Univ. Business Summer Sch., 1966; Chm., Careers Adv. Bd, Bristol Univ., 1971–; Vice-Chm., Clifton Coll. Council, 1978–; Dir, Ullswater Outward Bound Mountain Sch., 1971–83. High Sheriff of Avon, 1977–78. Master, Society of Merchant Venturers, Bristol, 1979–80. *Recreations:* ski-ing, sailing, shooting, golf. *Address:* Drax House, Tilshead, Salisbury, Wilts SP3 4SJ. *T:* Shrewton (0980) 620473. *Club:* Cavalry and Guards.

ANSON, Rear-Adm. Sir Peter, 7th Bt, *cr* 1831; CB 1974; CEng, FIEE; Chairman, Marconi Space Systems, since 1985 (Managing Director, 1984–85); *b* 31 July 1924; *er s* of Sir Edward R. Anson, 6th Bt, and Alison, *o d* of late Hugh Pollock; *S* father 1951; *m* 1955, Elizabeth Audrey Clarke (*see* E. A. Anson); two *s* two *d. Educ:* RNC, Dartmouth. Joined RN 1938; Lieut 1944. Served War of 1939–45, HMS Prince of Wales, HMS Exeter. Lieut-Comdr, 1952; Comdr 1956. Commanding Officer, HMS Alert, 1957–58; Staff of RN Tactical Sch., Woolwich, 1959–61; Commanding Officer, HMS Broadsword, 1961–62; Captain, 1963; Director Weapons, Radio (Naval), 1965–66 (Dep. Director, 1963–65); CO HMS Naiad and Captain (D) Londonderry Squadron, 1966–68; Captain, HM Signal School, 1968–70; Commodore, Commander Naval Forces Gulf, 1970–72; ACDS (Signals), 1972–74, retired 1975. Divisional Manager, Satellites, Marconi Space and Defence Systems Ltd, 1977–84. Chm., UK Industrial Space Cttee, 1980–82. FIERE 1972. *Heir: s* Philip Roland Anson, *b* 4 Oct. 1957. *Address:* Rosefield, Rowledge, Farnham, Surrey GU10 4AT. *T:* Frensham (025125) 2724.

    See also Sir John Anson.

ANSTEE, Margaret Joan; Under-Secretary-General of the United Nations (Director-General, UN Office at Vienna, and concurrently Director, Centre for Social Development and Humanitarian Affairs), since 1987; Special Representative of the Secretary-General for Bolivia, since 1982; *b* 25 June 1926; *d* of Edward Curtis Anstee and Anne Adaliza (*née* Mills). *Educ:* Chelmsford County High Sch. for Girls; Newnham Coll., Cambridge (MA; 1st cl. Hons, Mod. and Med. Langs Tripos); BSc(Econ) London. Lectr in Spanish, QUB, 1947–48; Third Sec., FO, 1948–52; Admin. Officer, UN Technical Assistance Bd, Manila, Philippines, 1952–54; Spanish Supervisor, Cambridge Univ., 1955–56; UN Technical Assistance Board: O i/c Bogotá, Colombia, 1956–57; Resident Rep., Uruguay, 1957–59; Resident Rep., UN Tech. Assistance Bd, Dir of Special Fund Progs, and Dir of UN Inf. Centre, Bolivia, 1960–65; Resident Rep., UNDP, Ethiopia, and UNDP Liaison Officer with UN Econ. Commn for Africa, 1965–67; Sen. Econ. Adviser, Prime Minister's Office, UK, 1967–68; Sen. Asst to Comr i/c Study of Capacity of UN Develt System, 1968–69; Resident Rep., UNDP, Morocco, 1969–72; Resident Rep., UNDP, Chile, and UNDP Liaison Officer with UN Econ. Commn for Latin America, 1972–74; Dep. to UN Under

Sec.-Gen. i/c UN Relief Operation to Bangladesh, and Dep. Co-ordinator of UN Emergency Assistance to Zambia, June–Dec. 1973; United Nations Development Programme, New York: Dep. Asst Adminr, and Dep. Reg Dir for Latin America, 1974–76; Dir, Adminr's Unit for Special Assignments, Feb.–July 1976; Asst Dep. Adminr, July–Dec. 1976; Asst Adminr and Dir, Bureau for Prog. Policy and Evaluation, 1977–78; Asst Sec.-Gen. of UN (Dept of Technical Co-operation for Develt), NY, 1978–87; Special Rep. of the Sec.-Gen. for co-ordination of internat. assistance to Mexico following the earthquake, 1985–87; Chm., Adv. Gp on review of World Food Council, UN, 1985–86; Special Co-ordinator of UN Sec.-Gen. to ensure implementation of Gen. Assembly resolution on financial and admin. reform of UN, 1986–87; Co-ordinator for all UN Drug-Control-Related Activities, 1987–90; Rep. of Sec.-Gen., UN Conf. for adoption of convention against illicit traffic in narcotic drugs and psychotropic substances, 1988; Sec.-Gen., 8th UN Congress on Prevention of Crime and Treatment of Offenders, 1990. Comdr, Order of Ouissam Alaouite, Morocco, 1972; Gran Cruz de Dama, Condor of the Andes, Bolivia, 1986. *Publications:* The Administration of International Development Aid, USA 1969; Gate of the Sun: a prospect of Bolivia, 1970 (USA 1971); (ed with R. K. A. Gardiner and C. Patterson) Africa and the World (Haile Selassie Prize Trust Symposium), 1970. *Recreations:* writing, gardening, hill-walking (preferably in the Andes), bird-watching, swimming. *Address:* United Nations Office at Vienna, Room E–1400, Vienna International Centre, PO Box 500, A–1400 Vienna, Austria. *T:* (43–222) 2631–5001. *Club:* United Oxford & Cambridge University (Lady Associate Member).

ANSTEY, Edgar, MA, PhD; Deputy Chief Scientific Officer, Civil Service Department, and Head of Behavioural Sciences Research Division, 1969–77; *b* 5 March 1917; British; *s* of late Percy Lewis Anstey and Dr Vera Anstey; *m* 1939, Zoë Lilian Robertson; one *s. Educ:* Winchester Coll.; King's Coll, Cambridge. Assistant Principal, Dominions Office, 1938; Private Sec. to Duke of Devonshire, 1939. 2nd Lieut Dorset Regt, 1940; Major, War Office (DSP), 1941. Founder-Head of Civil Service Commission Research Unit, 1945; Principal, Home Office, 1951; Senior Principal Psychologist, Min. of Defence, 1958; Chief Psychologist, Civil Service Commn, 1964–69. Pres., N Cornwall Democrat Assoc., 1988– (N Cornwall Liberal Assoc., 1985–88). *Publications:* Interviewing for the Selection of Staff (with Dr E. O. Mercer), 1956; Staff Reporting and Staff Development, 1961; Committees-How they work and how to work them, 1962; Psychological Tests, 1966; The Techniques of Interviewing, 1968; (with Dr C. A. Fletcher and Dr. J. Walker) Staff Appraisal and Development, 1976; An Introduction to Selection Interviewing, 1978; articles in Brit. Jl of Psychology, Occupational Psychology, etc. *Recreations:* fell-walking, surfing, golf, bridge. *Address:* Sandrock, 3 Higher Tristram, Polzeath, Wadebridge, Cornwall PL27 6TF. *T:* Trebetherick (0208) 863324. *Club:* Commonwealth Trust.

ANSTEY, Brig. Sir John, Kt 1975; CBE 1946; TD; DL; President and Chairman, National Savings Committee, 1975–78 (a Vice-Chairman, 1968–75); retired as Chairman and Managing Director, John Player & Sons; Director, Imperial Tobacco Co., Ltd, 1949–67; *b* 3 Jan. 1907; *s* of late Major Alfred Anstey, Matford House, Exeter, Devon; *m* 1935, Elizabeth Mary (*d* 1990), *d* of late William Garnett, Backwell, Somerset; one *s* one *d. Educ:* Clifton; Trinity Coll., Oxford. Served War of 1939–45: N Africa, France, SEAC (despatches); Lt-Col 1944; Brig. 1944. Mem. Council, Nottingham Univ. (Treasurer, 1979–81; Pro-Chancellor, 1982–); Member: (part-time) East Midlands Gas Board, 1968–72; Univ. Authorities Panel, 1979–82. Governor, Clifton Coll. Mem. Council, The Queen's Silver Jubilee Appeal, 1976. High Sheriff of Nottinghamshire, 1967; DL Notts 1970. Hon. LLD Nottingham, 1975. Legion of Honour; Croix de Guerre (France); Legion of Merit (USA). *Address:* Southwell, Notts.

ANSTRUTHER of that Ilk, Sir Ralph (Hugo), 7th Bt, *cr* 1694 (S), of Balcaskie, and 12th Bt *cr* 1700 (S), of Anstruther; KCVO 1976 (CVO 1967); MC 1943; DL; Hereditary Carver to the Queen; Equerry to the Queen Mother since 1959, also Treasurer, since 1961; *b* 13 June 1921; *o s* of late Capt. Robert Edward Anstruther, MC, The Black Watch, *o s* of 6th Bt; *S* grandfather, 1934, and cousin, Sir Windham Eric Francis Carmichael-Anstruther, 11th Bt, 1980. *Educ:* Eton; Magdalene Coll., Cambridge (BA). Major (retd), Coldstream Gds. Served Malaya, 1950 (despatches). Mem. Queen's Body Guard for Scotland (Royal Co. of Archers). DL Fife, 1960, Caithness-shire, 1965. *Heir: cousin,* Ian Fife Campbell Anstruther, Capt. late Royal Corps of Signals [*b* 11 May 1922; *m* 1st, 1951, Honor (marr. diss. 1963), *er d* of late Capt. Gerald Blake, MC; one *d*; 2nd, 1963, Susan Margaret Walker, *e d* of H. St J. B. Paten; two *s* three *d*]. *Address:* Balcaskie, Pittenweem, Fife; Watten, Caithness.

    See also Sir T. D. Erskine.

ANSTRUTHER-GOUGH-CALTHORPE, Sir Euan (Hamilton), 3rd Bt *cr* 1929; student; *b* 22 June 1966; *s* of Niall Hamilton Anstruther-Gough-Calthorpe (*d* 1970) and of Martha Rodman (who *m* 2nd, 1975, Charles C. Nicholson), *d* of Stuart Warren Don; *S* grandfather, 1985. *Educ:* Hawtreys, Savernake Forest; Harrow School; Royal Agricultural Coll., Cirencester. *Heir: uncle* John Austen Anstruther-Gough-Calthorpe [*b* 14 July 1947; *m* 1st, 1977, Lady Mary Gaye Georgiana Lorna Curzon (marr. diss. 1986), *d* of 5th Earl Howe, PC, CBE; one *s* two *d*; 2nd, 1987, Vanessa Mary Theresa, *y d* of Lt-Comdr Theodore Bernard Peregrine Hubbard, RN; one *d*].

    See also Sir J. N. Nicholson, Bt.

ANTALPÉTER, Tibor; Hungarian Ambassador to the Court of St James's, since 1990; *b* 4 Feb. 1930; *s* of late István Antalpéter and Viktória Dobai; *m* 1956, Adél; two *d. Educ:* Univ. of Economics, Budapest; graduated 1954. Importtex, foreign trade co., 1954; Commercial Sec. in London, 1956–60; Department of International Commercial Relations, Ministry of Foreign Trade: Head of Section, 1960; Dir of Dept, 1964; Dep. Dir-Gen., 1968–73; Dir-Gen. of Dept, 1977–88; Commercial Counsellor, London, 1973–77, 1988–90. Internat. volley-ball player, 1947–56; Chm., Hungarian Volley-ball Assoc. and Mem., Hungarian Olympic Cttee, 1980–86. Order of Merit for Labour, Bronze 1966, Gold 1979. *Recreations:* sport, music. *Address:* Hungarian Embassy, 35 Eaton Place, SW1X 8BY. *T:* 071–235 4048. *Club:* Athenæum.

ANTCLIFFE, Kenneth Arthur; Director of Education, City of Liverpool, 1975–89. *Recreations:* reading, writing, walking, bird watching, gardening, bridge. *Address:* 56 Alderley Road, Hoylake, Wirral L47 2BA.

ANTHONY, Metropolitan, of Sourozh; Head of the Russian Orthodox Patriarchal Church in Great Britain and Ireland (Diocese of Sourozh); *né* André Borisovich Bloom; *b* Lausanne, Switzerland, 19 June 1914; *o c* of Boris Edwardovich Bloom (Russian Imperial Diplomatic Service) and Xenia Nikolaevna Scriabin (sister of the composer Alexander Scriabin). *Educ:* Lycée Condorcet and Sorbonne, Paris. Dr of Med., Sorbonne, 1943. Army service, med. corps French Army and Resistance, 1939–45. Gen. Practitioner, 1945–49. Took monastic vows, 1943; Priest, Russian Orthodox Church in Paris, 1948; Chaplain to Fellowship of St Alban and St Sergius, London, 1949–50; Vicar, Russian Orthodox Church of St Philip, London, 1950; apptd Hegumen, 1953, Archimandrite, 1956; consecrated Bishop of Sergievo, Suffragan Bishop, Exarchate of Western Europe, 1957; Archbishop of Sourozh, 1960, acting Exarch, 1962–65; Metropolitan of Sourozh and Exarch of the Patriarch of Moscow and All Russia in Western Europe, 1965–74. Member:

Ecumenical Commn of Russian Orthodox Church; Central Cttee and Christian Medical Commn of World Council of Churches, 1968. Hulsean Preacher, Cambridge, 1972–73; Preacher, Lambeth Conf., 1978; Firth Lectures, Nottingham Univ., 1982; Eliot Lectures, Kent Univ., 1982; Constantinople Lecture, 1982. Médaille de Bronze de la Société d'encouragement au bien (France), 1945; Browning Award (for spreading of the Christian gospel), USA, 1974. Orders of: St Vladimir 1st Cl. (Russia), 1962; St Andrew (Ecumenical Patriarchate), 1963; St Sergius (Russia), 1977. Lambeth Cross, 1975. Hon. DD (Aberdeen), 1973. *Publications:* Living Prayer, 1965; School for Prayer, 1970; God and Man, 1971; Meditations on a Theme, 1972; Courage to Pray, 1973. *Address:* Russian Orthodox Cathedral, Ennismore Gardens, SW7. *T:* 01–584 0096.

ANTHONY, Rt. Hon. Douglas; *see* Anthony, Rt Hon. J. D.

ANTHONY, Evelyn, (Mrs Michael Ward-Thomas); author; *b* 3 July 1928; *d* of Henry Christian Stephens, inventor of the Dome Trainer in World War II, and Elizabeth (*née* Sharkey); *g g d* of Henry Stephens of Cholderton, Wilts, inventor of Stephens Ink; *m* 1955, Michael Ward-Thomas; four *s* two *d*. *Educ:* Convent of Sacred Heart, Roehampton. Freeman, City of London, 1987; Liveryman, Needlemakers' Co., 1987. *Publications:* Imperial Highness, 1953; Curse Not the King, 1954; Far Fly the Eagles, 1955; Anne Boleyn, 1956 (US Literary Guild Award); Victoria, 1957 (US Literary Guild Award); Elizabeth, 1959; Charles the King, 1961; Clandara, 1963; The Heiress, 1964; Valentina, 1965; The Rendezvous, 1967; Anne of Austria, 1968; The Legend, 1969; The Assassin, 1970; The Tamarind Seed, 1971; The Poellenberg Inheritance, 1972; The Occupying Power, 1973 (Yorkshire Post Fiction Prize); The Malaspiga Exit, 1974; The Persian Ransom, 1975; The Silver Falcon, 1977; The Return, 1978; The Grave of Truth, 1979; The Defector, 1980; The Avenue of the Dead, 1981; Albatross, 1982; The Company of Saints, 1983; Voices on the Wind, 1985; No Enemy But Time, 1987; The House of Vandekar, 1988; The Scarlet Thread, 1989; The Relic, 1991. *Recreations:* racing (National Hunt), gardening, going to sale rooms, preferably Christie's. *Address:* Horham Hall, Thaxted, Essex CM6 2NN.

ANTHONY, Graham George, CEng; Director, Industry and Regions, Engineering Council, 1983–90; *b* 25 Oct. 1931; *s* of George Alfred and Dorothy Anthony; *m* 1957, Thelma Jane Firmstone; two *s* one *d*. *Educ:* Fletton Grammar Sch.; King's College London (BSc Eng). Projects Manager, ICI Fibres, 1956; Works Engineer, ICI India, 1964; Chief Engineer, Ilford Ltd, 1968; Gen. Manager, Bonded Structures, 1975; Commercial Dir, Ciba-Geigy (UK) Ltd, 1979. FRSA. *Recreations:* offshore sailing, woodworking. *Address:* 38 Morpeth Terrace, SW1P 1ET. *T:* 071–828 0272.

ANTHONY, Rt. Hon. (John) Douglas, CH 1982; PC 1971; company director and farmer; Chairman: Pan Australian Mining Ltd, since 1986; Resource Finance Corporation, since 1987; Baskin Robbins 31 Flavours Pty Ltd, since 1987; Director: John Swires & Sons Pty Ltd (Australia), since 1987; Clyde Agriculture Ltd, since 1988; *b* 31 Dec. 1929; *s* of late H. L. Anthony; *m* 1957, Margot Macdonald Budd; two *s* one *d*. *Educ:* Murwillumbah Primary and High Schs, The King's Sch., Parramatta; Queensland Agricultural Coll. (QDA). MP, Country Party, later National Party, Richmond, NSW, 1957–84, (Mem., Exec. Council, 1963–72, 1975–83). Minister for Interior, 1964–67; Minister for Primary Industry, 1967–71; Dep. Prime Minister and Minister for Trade and Industry, 1971–72; Minister for Overseas Trade, Minerals and Energy, Nov.-Dec. 1975; Dep. Prime Minister and Minister for Trade and Resources, 1975–83. Dep. Leader, Aust. Country Party, 1966–71; Leader, Nat. Country Party, later Nat. Party, 1971–84. Hon. LLD Victoria Univ. of Wellington, NZ, 1983. Council Gold Medal, Qld Agricl Coll., 1985. NZ Commemorative Medal, 1990. *Recreations:* golf, tennis, fishing, swimming. *Address:* Sunnymeadows, Murwillumbah, NSW 2484, Australia. *Clubs:* Union, Royal Sydney Golf (Sydney); Queensland (Brisbane).

ANTHONY, Ronald Desmond; consultant in safety and engineering, since 1986; Chief Inspector of Nuclear Installations, Health and Safety Executive, 1981–85; *b* 21 Nov. 1925; *s* of William Arthur Anthony and Olive Frances Anthony (*née* Buck); *m* 1948, Betty Margaret Croft; four *d*. *Educ:* Chislehurst and Sidcup Grammar School; City and Guilds Coll., Imperial Coll. of Science and Technology (BSc, ACGI). CEng, FIMechE, MRAeS. Vickers Armstrongs (Supermarine), 1950; Nuclear Power Plant Co., 1957; Inspectorate of Nuclear Installations, 1960; Deputy Chief Inspector, 1973; Dir, Safety Policy Div., 1977, Hazardous Installations Gp, 1981–82, Health and Safety Exec. *Publications:* papers in technical journals. *Recreations:* gardening, golf. *Address:* 3 Mereside, Orpington, Kent BR6 8ET. *T:* Farnborough (Kent) (0689) 57565.

ANTHONY, Vivian Stanley; Secretary, Headmasters' Conference, since 1990; *b* 5 May 1938; *s* of Captain and Mrs A. S. Anthony; *m* 1969, Rosamund Anne MacDermot Byrn; one *s* one *d*. *Educ:* Cardiff High Sch.; LSE (1st Div. 2nd Cl. Hons BSc Econ); Fitzwilliam Coll., Cambridge (DipEd); Merton Coll., Oxford (schoolmaster student). Asst Master, Leeds Grammar Sch., 1960–64; Asst Master and Housemaster, Tonbridge Sch., 1964–69; Lectr in Educn, Univ. of Leeds, 1969–71; Dep. Headmaster, The King's Sch., Macclesfield, 1971–76; Headmaster, Colfe's Sch., London, 1976–90. Asst Examr, Econ. Hist., London Univ., 1964–71; Asst Examr, Econs, Oxford and Cambridge Bd, 1970–76, Chief Examr (Awarder), Econs, 1976–; Ext. Examr, Educn, Univs of Manchester, 1972–75, Birmingham, 1975–78, and Lancaster, 1977–79. Chm., Econs Assoc., 1974–77; Member: Schools Council Social Science Cttee, 1976–83; London Univ. Schs Examinations Cttee, 1981–85; Secondary Examinations Council Economics Panel, 1984–89; CBI/Schools Panel, 1984–88; Court, Univ. Kent, 1985–90. Sabbatical tour, US indep. schools, 1983. Chm., London Area, 1988–89, Mem. Council, 1989–, SHA; elected Headmasters' Conf., 1980, Chm., Academic Policy Cttee, 1988–90 (Mem., 1983–), Member, Professional Develt Cttee, 1985–89, Teacher Shortage Wkg Party, 1987–88, Assisted Places Cttee, 1987–89, Chm., Records of Achievement Wkg Party, 1987–. Comr, Inland Revenue, 1989–. Hon. Freeman, Leathersellers' Co., 1990. FCP 1991. *Publications:* Monopoly, 1968, 3rd edn 1976; Overseas Trade, 1969, 4th edn 1981; Banks and Markets, 1970, 3rd edn 1979; (contrib.) The Teaching of Economics in Secondary Schools, 1970; Objective Tests in A Level Economics, 1971, 2nd edn 1974; (contrib.) Curriculum Development in Secondary Schools, 1973; (contrib.) Control of the Economy, 1974; Objective Tests in Introductory Economics, 1975, 3rd edn 1983; History of Rugby Football at Colfe's, 1980; US Independent Schools, 1984; (contrib.) Comparative Economics, in Teaching Economics, 1984; 150 Years of Cricket at Colfe's, 1986; articles in Economics. *Recreations:* choral singing, Rugby football, squash, tennis. *Address:* 130 Regent Road, Leicester LE1 7PG. *T:* Leicester (0533) 854810, *Fax:* Leicester (0533) 471152. *Clubs:* East India, Devonshire, Sports and Public Schools, Old Colfeians Association.

ANTICO, Sir Tristan, AC 1983; Kt 1973; Founding Chairman, 1949, and Managing Director, 1949–88, Pioneer International Ltd (formerly Pioneer Concrete Services); *b* 25 March 1923; *s* of Terribile Giovanni Antico and Erminia Bertin; *m* 1950, Dorothy Brigid Shields; three *s* four *d*. *Educ:* Sydney High Sch. Began career as Accountant; subseq. became Company Secretary, Melocco Bros; Founder of Pioneer Concrete Services Ltd. Chairman: Ampol Ltd; Ampol Exploration; Papuan Oil Search. Dir, Société Générale Australia Hldgs. AC and Knighthood awarded for services to industry and the community. Comdr, Order of Star of Solidarity (Italy), 1967. *Recreations:* horse breeding and horse racing, swimming, yachting. *Address:* 161 Raglan Street, Mosman, NSW 2088, Australia. *T:* 969 4070. *Clubs:* Tattersall's, Australian Jockey, Sydney Turf, American National, Royal Sydney Yacht Squadron (Sydney); Manly Golf.

ANTIGUA (diocese); *see* North-Eastern Caribbean and Aruba.

ANTON, Alexander Elder, CBE 1973; FRSE 1977; FBA 1972; *b* 1922; *m* 1949, Doris May Lawrence; one *s*. *Educ:* Aberdeen Univ. (MA, LLB with dist.). Solicitor, 1949; Lectr, Aberdeen, 1953–59; Prof. of Jurisprudence, Univ. of Glasgow, 1959–73. Hon. Vis. Prof., 1982–84, Hon. Prof., 1984, Aberdeen Univ. Mem., Scottish Law Commission, 1966–82. Literary Dir, Stair Soc., 1960–66; Chm., Scottish Rights of Way Soc., 1988–. *Publications:* Private International Law, 1967, 2nd edn (with P. R. Beaumont), 1990; Civil Jurisdiction in Scotland, 1984; contribs to legal and historical jls. *Recreation:* hill walking. *Address:* 9 Baillieswells Terrace, Bieldside, Aberdeen AB1 9AR.

ANTONIO; *see* Ruiz Soler, Antonio.

ANTONIONI, Michelangelo; Film Director; *b* Ferrara, Italy, 29 Sept. 1912; *s* of Ismaele and Elisabetta Roncagli; *m* (marr. diss.). *Educ:* degree in Economics and Commerce, Univ. of Bologna. Formerly an Asst Dir, Film Critic to newspapers, and Script Writer. Films directed include: 8 documentaries, etc, 1943–50; subseq. long films: Cronaca di un Amore, 1950; one episode in Amore in Città, 1951; I Vinti, 1952; La Signora Senza Camelie, 1953; Le Amiche, 1955; Il Grido, 1957; L'Avventura, 1959–60; La Notte, 1961; L'Eclisse, 1962; Il Deserto Rosso, 1964; one episode in I Tre Volti, 1965; Blow-Up, 1967; Zabriskie Point, 1969; Chung Kuo-China, 1972; The Passenger, 1974; Il Mistero di Oberwald, 1979; Identificazione di una Donna, 1981; documentaries: Fumbha Mela, Roma, 1989. *Recreations:* collecting blown glass, tennis, ping-pong. *Address:* Via Vincenzo Tiberio 18, Rome, Italy.

ANTRIM, 14th Earl of, *cr* 1620; **Alexander Randal Mark McDonnell;** Viscount Dunluce; Head of Collection Services, Tate Gallery, since 1990; *b* 3 Feb. 1935; *er s* of 13th Earl of Antrim, KBE, and Angela Christina (*d* 1984), *d* of Sir Mark Sykes, 6th Bt; *S* father, 1977 (but continues to be known as Viscount Dunluce); *m* 1963, Sarah Elizabeth Anne (marr. diss. 1974), 2nd *d* of St John Harmsworth; one *s* two *d*; *m* 1977, Elizabeth, *d* of late Michael Moses Sacher; one *d*. *Educ:* Downside; Christ Church, Oxford; Ruskin Sch. of Art. Restorer, the Ulster Museum, 1969–71; Restorer, 1965–75, Keeper of Conservation, 1975–90, Tate Gall. Dir, Ulster Television, 1982–. Mem., Exec. Cttee, City and Guilds Art School, 1983–. FRSA 1984. *Recreations:* painting, vintage cars. *Heir:* *s* Hon. Randal Alexander St John McDonnell, *b* 2 July 1967. *Address:* Glenarm Castle, Glenarm, Co. Antrim, N Ireland. *T:* Glenarm (057484) 1229. *Club:* Beefsteak.

ANTROBUS, Sir Philip Coutts, 7th Bt, *cr* 1815; *b* 10 April 1908; *s* of late Geoffrey Edward Antrobus and Mary Atherstone, *d* of Hilton Barber, JP, Halesowen, Cradock, Cape Province; *S* cousin, 1968; *m* 1st, 1937, Dorothy Margaret Mary (*d* 1973), *d* of late Rev. W. G. Davis; two *s* one *d*; 2nd, 1975, Doris Primrose (*d* 1986), *widow* of Ralph Dawkins. Served War, 1939–45 (POW). *Heir:* *s* Edward Philip Antrobus [*b* 28 Sept. 1938; *m* 1966, Janet (*d* 1990), *d* of Philip Sceales; one *s* two *d*]. *Address:* West Amesbury House, West Amesbury, near Salisbury, Wilts SP4 7BH. *T:* Amesbury (0980) 623860.

ANWAR, Mohamed Samih; Order of the Republic, 2nd Class (Egypt), 1958; Order of Merit, 1st Class (Egypt), 1968; *b* 10 Dec. 1924; *s* of Ahmed Fouad Anwar and Aziza Tewfik; *m* 1953, Omayma Soliman Hazza; one *s* one *d*. *Educ:* Cairo Univ. (Bachelor of Law, 1945). Min. of Justice, 1946–54; First Sec., Min. of Foreign Affairs, 1954; apptd to Egyptian Embassies in Moscow, 1957, and London, 1963; Ambassador to Kuwait, 1966; Under Sec., Min. of Foreign Affairs, 1968; Ambassador to Iran, 1970; Minister of State for Foreign Affairs, 1974; Ambassador to UK, 1975–79, to USSR, 1979–80. Order of Hamayon, 1st Cl. (Iran), 1974; Order of the Flag (Yugoslavia), 1970. *Recreations:* rowing, tennis. *Address:* Ministry of Foreign Affairs, Cairo, Egypt. *Clubs:* Royal Automobile, Hurlingham; Al Ahly (Cairo).

ANWYL, Shirley Anne, (Mrs R. H. C. Anwyl); *see* Ritchie, S. A.

ANWYL-DAVIES, Marcus John, MA, QC 1967; **His Honour Judge Anwyl-Davies;** a Circuit Judge, since 1972; *b* 11 July 1923; *s* of late Thomas Anwyl-Davies and Kathleen Beryl Anwyl-Davies (*née* Oakshott); *m* 1st, 1954, Eva Hilda Elisabeth Paulson (marr. diss. 1974); one *s* one *d*; 2nd, 1983, Myrna Dashoff. *Educ:* Harrow Sch.; Christ Church, Oxford. Royal Artillery, including service with Hong Kong and Singapore RA, 1942–47 (despatches 1945). Called to Bar, Inner Temple, 1949. Legal Assessor, GMC and GDC, 1969–72; Liaison Judge to Herts Magistrates, 1972; Resident Judge, St Albans Crown Court, 1977–82. Vice-Pres., Herts Magistrates' Assoc., 1975; Pres., Council of HM's Circuit Judges, 1989. *Recreation:* photography. *Club:* Reform.

ANYAOKU, Eleazar Chukwuemeka, (Emeka), CON 1982; Ndichie Chief Adazie of Obosi; Secretary-General of the Commonwealth, since 1990; *b* 18 Jan. 1933; *e s* of late Emmanuel Chukwuemeka Anyaoku, Ononukpo of Okpuno Ire, Obosi, Nigeria, and Cecilia Adiba (*née* Ogbogu); *m* 1962, Ebunola Olubunmi, *yr d* of late barrister Olusola Akanbi Solanke, of Abeokuta, Nigeria; three *s* one *d*. *Educ:* Merchants of Light Sch., Oba; Univ. of Ibadan (Schol.), Nigeria; courses in England and France.Exec. Asst, Commonwealth Develt Corp., in London and Lagos, 1959–62. Joined Nigerian Diplomatic Service, 1962; Mem. Nigerian Permanent Mission to the UN, New York, 1963–66; seconded to Commonwealth Secretariat as Asst Dir, 1966–71, and Dir, 1971–75, Internat. Affairs Div.; Asst Sec.-Gen., 1975–77, Dep. Sec.-Gen. (Political), 1977–83 and 1984–90, of the Commonwealth. Minister of External Affairs, Nigeria, Nov.-Dec. 1983. Served as Secretary: Review Cttee on Commonwealth inter-governmental organisations, June-Aug., 1966; Commonwealth Observer Team for Gibraltar Referendum, Aug.-Sept., 1967; Anguilla Commn, WI, Jan.-Sept. 1970; Leader, Commonwealth Mission for Mozambique, 1975; Commonwealth Observer, Zimbabwe Talks, Geneva, 1976; accompanied Commonwealth Eminent Persons Gp, SA, 1986. Vice-Pres., Royal Commonwealth Society, London, 1975–; Mem. Council, Overseas Develt Inst., 1979–90. Mem., Governing Council: SCF, 1984–90; IISS, London, 1987–. Hon. DLitt Ibadan, 1990; Hon. DPhil Ahmadu Bello, 1991; Hon LLD Nigeria, 1991. *Publication:* The Racial Factor in International Politics, 1977. *Recreations:* tennis, swimming, reading. *Address:* Commonwealth Secretariat, Marlborough House, Pall Mall, SW1Y 5HX. *T:* 071–839 3411; Orimili, Obosi, Anambra State, Nigeria. *Clubs:* Commonwealth Trust, Africa Centre, Travellers'; Metropolitan (Lagos).

AOTEAROA, Bishop of, since 1981; **Rt. Rev. Whakahuihui Vercoe,** MBE 1970; *b* 4 June 1928; *s* of Joseph and Wyness Vercoe; *m* 1951, Dorothy Eivers; three *s*. *Educ:* Torere Primary; Feilding Agricultural High School; College House Theological Coll.; Canterbury Univ. LTh 1985. Curate, St John's Church, Feilding, 1951–53; Priest-in-Charge, Wellington Pastorate, 1953–54; Pastor: Wairarapa, 1954–57; Rangitikei, 1957–61; Chaplain: Armed Forces, Malaya, 1961–64; Papakura Military Camp, 1964–65; ANZAC Brigade, Vietnam, 1968–69; Burnham Mil. Camp, 1965–71; Principal, Te Waipounamu Girls' School, 1971–76; Vicar: Ohinemutu Pastorate,

1976–78; Te Rohe o Whakaari, 1978–81; Archdeacon of Tairawhiti and Vicar-General to Bishopric of Aotearoa, 1978–81. *Recreations:* Rugby, golf, reading, tennis, cricket, fishing. *Address:* PO Box 146, Rotorua, New Zealand. *T:* (home) 479–241, (office) 86–093.

APEL, Dr Hans Eberhard; Social-democratic Member of Bundestag, 1965–90 (Deputy-Chairman of Group, 1969–72); *b* Hamburg, 25 Feb. 1932; *m* 1956, Ingrid Schwingel; two *d. Educ:* Hamburg Univ. Diplom-Volkswirt, 1957, Dr.rer.pol, 1960. Apprentice in Hamburg export and import business, 1951–54; Sec., Socialist Group in European Parlt, 1958–61; Head of Economics, Finance and Transportation Dept of European Parlt, 1962–65. Chm., Bundestag Cttee on Transportation, 1969–72. Mem. Nat. Bd, Social-democratic Party (SPD), 1970–88; Parly Sec. of State, Min. for Foreign Affairs, 1972–74; Federal Minister of Finance, 1974–78, of Defence, 1978–82. *Publications:* Edwin Cannan und seine Schüler (Doct. Thesis), 1961; Raumordnung der Bundesrepublik, in: Deutschland 1975, 1964; Europas neue Grenzen, 1964; Der deutsche Parlamentarismus, 1968; Bonn, den ..., Tagebuch eines Bundestagsabgeordneten, 1972. *Recreations:* sailing, soccer. *Address:* Rögenfeld 42c, 2000 Hamburg 67, Germany.

APLEY, Alan Graham, FRCS; Consulting Editor, Journal of Bone and Joint Surgery, since 1989 (Editor, 1983–89); *b* 10 Nov. 1914; *s* of Samuel Apley and Mary Tanis; *m* 1st, 1939, Janie Kandler (decd); one *s* one *d*; 2nd, 1988, Violet Chambers. *Educ:* Regent Street Polytechnic; University Coll. London; University College Hosp., London (MB BS); MRCS, LRCP 1938, FRCS 1941; Hon. FRCSE 1987. Served RAMC, 1944–47. Cons. Surg., Rowley Bristow Orthopaedic Hosp., Pyrford, 1947; Dir of Accident and Emergency Centre, St Peter's Hosp., Chertsey, 1964; Hon. Dir, Dept of Orthopaedics, St Thomas' Hosp., London, 1972; Mem. Council, 1973–85, Vice-Pres. 1984–85, RCS; Pres., Orthopaedic Sect., RSM, 1979. *Publications:* System of Orthopaedics and Fractures, 1959, 6th edn 1982; (jtly) Replacement of the Knee, 1984; (jtly) Atlas of Skeletal Dysplasias, 1985; (ed) Recent Advances in Orthopaedics, 1969; (ed) Modern Trends in Orthopaedics, 1972; (jtly) A Concise System of Orthopaedics and Fractures, 1988; various articles in surg. jls. *Recreations:* music, ski-ing, travelling. *Address:* Singleton Lodge, West Byfleet, Surrey KT14 6PW. *T:* Byfleet (09323) 43353; (office) 071-405 7227.

APPEL, Karel Christian; Netherlands Artist (Painter); *b* 25 April 1921; *s* of Jan Appel and Johanna Chevallier. *Educ:* Royal Academy of Art, Amsterdam. Began career as artist in 1938. Has had one-man exhibitions in Europe and America including the following in London: Inst. of Contemporary Art, 1957; Gimpel Fils, 1959, 1960, 1964. UNESCO Prize, Venice Biennale, 1953; Lissone Prize, Italy, 1958; Acquisition Prize, Sao Paulo Biennale, Brazil, 1959; Graphique Internat. Prize, Ljubljana, Jugoslavia, 1959; Guggenheim National Prize, Holland, 1961; Guggenheim International Prize, 1961. *Publications:* Illustrations: De Blijde en Onvoorziene Week, by Hugo Claus, 1950; Atonaal, by Simon Vinkenoog, 1951; De Ronde Kant van de Aarde, by Hans Andreus, 1952; Het Bloed Stroomt Door, by Bert Schierbeek, 1954; Haine, by E. Looten, 1954; Cogne Ciel, by E. Looten, 1954; Rhapsodie de ma Nuit, by E. Looten, 1958; Unteilbare Teil, by André Frénaud, 1960; Een Dier Heeft een Mens Getekend, by B. Schierbeek, 1961.

APPLEBY, Brian John, QC 1971; **His Honour Judge Appleby;** a Circuit Judge, since 1988; *b* 25 Feb. 1930; *s* of Ernest Joel and Gertrude Appleby; *m* 1958, Rosa Helena (*née* Flitterman); one *s* one *d. Educ:* Uppingham; St John's Coll., Cambridge (BA). Called to Bar, Middle Temple, 1953; Bencher, 1980. Dep. Chm., Notts QS, 1970–71; a Recorder, 1972–88. Mem., Nottingham City Council, 1955–58 and 1960–63. District Referee, Nottinghamshire Wages Conciliation Board, NCB, 1980–. *Recreations:* watching good football (preferably Nottingham Forest: Mem. Club Cttee, 1965–82, Life Mem., 1982; Vice-Chm., 1972–75, Chm., 1975–78); swimming, reading and enjoying, when possible, company of wife and children. *Address:* The Poplars, Edwalton Village, Notts. *T:* Nottingham (0602) 232814.

APPLEBY, Douglas Edward Surtees; farmer; retired as Managing Director, The Boots Co. Ltd; *b* 17 May 1929; *s* of late Robert Appleby, MSc and Muriel (*née* Surtees); *m* 1952 (marr. diss. 1990); one *s* one *d. Educ:* Durham Johnston Sch.; Univ. of Nottingham. BSc London, BSc Nottingham, 1950. Chartered Accountant, 1957. Commissioned, RAF, Cranwell, 1950–54. Moore, Stephens & Co., Chartered Accountants, London, 1954–57; Distillers Co. Ltd, 1957–58; Corn Products Co., New York, 1959–63; Wilkinson Sword Ltd, 1964–68; The Boots Co Ltd, 1968–81 (Finance Dir, 1968–72, Man. Dir, 1973–81). Regional Dir, Nat. Westminster Bank, 1979–88; Chairman: John H. Mason Ltd, 1982–87; Meadow Farm Produce plc, 1984–86; Sims Food Gp plc, 1987–89. Member Council: Inst. Chartered Accountants, 1971–75; Loughborough Univ., 1973–75; CBI, 1977–81. *Address:* Craigend of Aldbar, by West Drums, Brechin, Angus DD9 6ST.

APPLEBY, (Lesley) Elizabeth, (Mrs Michael Kenneth Collins), QC 1979; barrister-at-law; a Recorder, since 1989; *b* 12 Aug. 1942; *o d* of Arthur Leslie Appleby and late Dorothy Evelyn Appleby (*née* Edwards); *m* 1978, Michael Kenneth Collins, OBE, BSc, MICE; one *s* one *d. Educ:* Dominican Convent, Brewood, Staffs; Wolverhampton Girls' High Sch.; Manchester Univ. (LLB Hons). Called to Bar, Gray's Inn, 1965 (Richardson Schol.); *ad eundem* Lincoln's Inn, 1975, Bencher, 1986; in practice at Chancery Bar, 1966–; Member, Senate of Inns of Court and Bar, 1977–80, 1981–82. *Recreations:* sailing, swimming, music, golf, gardening. *Address:* 4/5 Gray's Inn Square, Gray's Inn, WC1R 5AY. *T:* 071–404 5252; 32 Pembroke Road, W8. *T:* 071–602 4141; The Glebe House, The Green, Chiddingfold, Surrey. *T:* Wormley (042879) 4671. *Club:* Royal Lymington Yacht.

APPLEBY, Malcolm Arthur; engraver designer; *b* 6 Jan. 1946; *s* of James William and Marjory Appleby. *Educ:* Haws Down County Secondary Modern School for Boys; Beckenham Sch. of Art; Ravensbourne Coll. of Art and Design; Central Sch. of Arts and Crafts; Sir John Cass Sch. of Art; Royal Coll. of Art. Set up trade, 1968; bought Crathes station, 1970; developed fresh approaches to engraving on silver, forging after engraving; works designed and executed include: engraving on Prince of Wales coronet; model of moon (subseq. gift to first moon astronauts); steel and gold cylinder box for Goldsmiths' Co.; steel, gold, ivory and silver chess set, 1977; 500th anniv. silver for London Assay Office; King George VI Diamond Stakes trophy, 1978; seal for the Board of Trustees, V & A; silver condiment set for 10 Downing Street, commnd by Silver Trust; major silver commn for Royal Mus. of Scotland; sporting guns, silver bowls, jewels, prints. Work in collections: Aberdeen Art Gallery; Royal Scottish Museum; Scottish Craft Collection; East Midlands Arts; British Museum; Goldsmiths' Co., V&A; Crafts Council; Contemporary Arts Soc.; Tower of London Royal Armouries. Founder, British Art Postage Stamp Soc., 1986; Mem., British Art Medal Soc., 1987–. Mem., Crathes Drumoak Community Council (Chm., 1981). Life Member: NT for Scotland, 1971; SPAB, 1989. *Recreations:* work, walking, looking at garden, drinking tea with friends, acting in pantomime, cats (Joan, a big bouncing tom, Edith), conservation matters, supporter of NE Mountain Trust, breeding silver spangled Hamburg bantam hens. *Address:* Crathes Station, Banchory, Kincardineshire. *T:* Crathes (033044) 642.

APPLEBY, Dom Raphael; National Chaplain to Catholic Students' Council, since 1974; *b* 18 July 1931; *s* of Harold Thompson Appleby and Margaret Morgan. *Educ:* Downside; Christ's Coll., Cambridge (MA). Downside novitiate, 1951. Housemaster at Downside, 1962–75, Head Master, 1975–80; Nat. Co-ordinator for RC Chaplains in Higher Educn, 1980–87. Diocesan Youth Chaplain, Clifton Dio., 1983–89. *Publication:* Dear Church, What's the Point?, 1984. *Recreations:* books, music. *Address:* Downside Abbey, Bath BA3 4RH.

APPLEBY, Robert, CBE 1969; Chairman, Black & Decker Ltd, 1956–75 (Managing Director, 1956–72); *b* 1913; *s* of Robert James Appleby; *m* 1957, Elisabeth Friederike (*d* 1975), *d* of Prof. Eidmann. *Educ:* Graham Sea Training and Engineering Sch., Scarborough. Dep. Chm., Black & Decker Manufacturing Co., Maryland, 1968–72. Mem., Post Office Bd, 1972–73. CEng, FIProdE; FBIM.

APPLETON, Rt. Rev. George, CMG 1972; MBE 1946; *b* 20 Feb. 1902; *s* of Thomas George and Lily Appleton; *m* 1929, Marjorie Alice (*d* 1980), *d* of Charles Samuel Barrett; one *s* two *d. Educ:* County Boys' School, Maidenhead; Selwyn Coll., Cambridge; St Augustine's Coll., Canterbury. BA Cantab 1924 (2nd Cl. Math. Trip. pt 1, 1st Cl. Theological Trip. pt I); MA 1929. Deacon, 1925; Priest, 1926. Curate, Stepney Parish Church, 1925–27; Missionary in charge SPG Mission, Irrawaddy Delta, 1927–33; Warden, Coll. of Holy Cross, Rangoon, 1933–41; Archdeacon of Rangoon, 1943–46; Director of Public Relations, Government of Burma, 1943–46; Vicar of Headstone, 1947–50; Sec., Conf. of Brit. Missionary Societies, 1950–57; Rector of St Botolph, Aldgate, 1957–62; Archdeacon of London and Canon of St Paul's Cathedral, 1962–63; Archbishop of Perth and Metropolitan of W Australia, 1963–69; Archbishop in Jerusalem and Metropolitan, 1969–74. Buber-Rosenzweig Medal, Council of Christians and Jews, 1975. *Publications:* John's Witness to Jesus, 1955; In His Name, 1956; Glad Encounter, 1959; On the Eightfold Path, 1961; Daily Prayer and Praise, 1962; Acts of Devotion, 1963; One Man's Prayers, 1967; Journey for a Soul, 1974; Jerusalem Prayers, 1974; The Word is the Seed, 1976; The Way of a Disciple, 1979; The Practice of Prayer, 1980; Glimpses of Faith, 1982; Praying with the Bible, 1982; Prayers from a Troubled Heart, 1983; The Quiet Heart, 1983; (ed) The Oxford Book of Prayer, 1985; Hour of Glory, 1985; Entry into Life, 1985; The Heart of the Bible, 1986; Understanding the Psalms, 1987; 100 Personal Prayers for Today, 1988; Prayer in a Troubled World, 1988; Paul the Interpreter, 1989; Unfinished—a critical autobiography, 1990. *Address:* 112A St Mary's Road, Oxford OX4 1QF.

APPLEYARD, Leonard Vincent, CMG 1986; HM Diplomatic Service; Deputy Secretary, Cabinet Office, since 1989 (on secondment); *b* 2 Sept. 1938; *s* of Thomas William Appleyard; *m* 1964, Elizabeth Margaret West; two *d. Educ:* Read School, Drax, W Yorks; Queens' Coll., Cambridge (MA). Foreign Office, 1962; Third Secretary, Hong Kong, 1964; Second Secretary, Peking, 1966; Second, later First, Secretary, Foreign Office, 1969; First Secretary, Delhi, 1971, Moscow, 1975; HM Treasury, 1978; Financial Counsellor, Paris, 1979–82; Head of Economic Relations Dept, FCO, 1982–84; Principal Private Sec. to Sec. of State for Foreign and Commonwealth Affairs, 1984–86; Ambassador to Hungary, 1986–89. *Recreations:* music, reading, tennis. *Address:* c/o Foreign and Commonwealth Office, SW1. *Club:* Brooks's.

APPLEYARD, Sir Raymond (Kenelm), KBE 1986; PhD; Director-General for Information Market and Innovation, Commission of the European Communities, 1981–86; *b* 5 Oct. 1922; *s* of late Maj.-Gen. K. C. Appleyard, CBE, TD, DL, and Monica Mary Louis; *m* 1947, Joan Greenwood; one *s* two *d. Educ:* Rugby; Cambridge. BA 1943, MA 1948, PhD 1950. Instructor, Yale Univ., 1949–51; Fellow, Rockefeller Foundn, California Inst. of Technology, 1951–53; Research Officer, Atomic Energy of Canada Ltd, 1953–56; Sec., UN Scientific Cttee on effects of atomic radiation, 1956–61; Dir, Biology Services, Commn of European Atomic Energy Community, 1961–73; Dir-Gen. for Scientific and Tech. Information and Information Management, EEC Commn, 1973–80. Exec. Sec., European Molecular Biology Organisation, 1965–73; Sec., European Molecular Biology Conf., 1969–73; President: Inst. of Information Scientists, 1981–82; Inst. of Translation and Interpreting, 1989–. Hon. Dr.med Ulm, 1977. *Publications:* contribs to: Nature, Jl Gen. Microbiol., Genetics. *Recreations:* bridge, tennis, squash. *Clubs:* Athenæum; Fondation Universitaire (Brussels).

APPLEYARD, Dr William James, FRCP; Consultant Paediatrician, Canterbury and Thanet Health District, since 1971; *b* 25 Oct. 1935; *s* of late E. R. Appleyard and Maud Oliver Collingwood (*née* Marshall); *m* 1964, Elizabeth Anne Ward; one *s* two *d. Educ:* Canford Sch.; Exeter College, Oxford (BM BCh, MA); Guy 's Hosp. Med. Sch., Univ. of London. DObstRCOG; FRCP 1978. Junior paediat. posts, Guy's and Gt Ormond St; Resident in Pediat., Univ. of Louisville, 1964–66; Dyers' Co. Res. Registrar, St Thomas' Hosp., 1968–69. Treasurer, BPA, 1983–88; Mem., GMC, 1984–; Mem. Council, RCP, 1988– (Member: Standing Cttee, 1970–72; Res. Cttee, 1971–74; Paed. Cttee, 1987–); Mem. Council, BMA, 1973– (Mem., Jt Consultants Cttee, 1979–83; Dep. Chm., Consultants Cttee, 1979–83, Repr. Body, 1989–91); Member: Health Service Inf. Steering Gp, Korner Cttee, 1985; DoH Inf. Adv. Gp, 1986–; London Univ. Nominee, Kent AHA, 1974–78. Hon. Tutor in Paed., Guy's Hosp.; Hon. Lectr in Paed., St Thomas' Hosp.; Associate Prof. of Paed. (UK), St George's Univ. Sch. of Medicine, Grenada, 1985– (Chm., Senate, 1991–). Patron, Dyspraxia Trust, 1988–. Liveryman, Apothecaries' Soc., 1983. Alumnus Award for Paed. Res., Univ. of Louisville, 1965. *Publications:* contribs to med. jls. *Recreations:* lawn tennis, photography, erstwhile allotment digger. *Address:* 20 St Stephen's Road, Canterbury, Kent CT2 7HT. *T:* Canterbury (0227) 455883. *Clubs:* Athenæum, Penn.

ap REES, Prof. Thomas; Professor of Botany and Head of Department of Plant Sciences, since 1991 and Fellow of Gonville and Caius College, Cambridge; *b* 19 Oct. 1930; *s* of Elfan Rees and Frances Rees (*née* Boston); *m* 1955, Wendy Ruth, *d* of late Reginald Holroyde and Marjorie Holroyde; three *s. Educ:* Llandovery Coll., Dyfed; Lincoln Coll., Oxford (BA 1955; MA, DPhil 1958); ScD Cantab 1983. Nat. service, commnd Royal Signals, 1949–51. Lectr in Mycology, Univ. of Sydney, 1959–61; res. officer and sen. res. officer, CSIRO, 1961–64; University of Cambridge: Lectr in Botany, 1964–91; Reader in Plant Biochem., 1991; Gonville and Caius College: Fellow, 1965–91, Professorial Fellow, 1991–; College Lectr, 1965–91; Dir of Studies in Biol Scis, 1986–91. Science and Engineering Research Council: Mem., Plant Sci. and Microbiol. Cttee, 1982–87 (Chm., 1985–87); Mem., Biol Scis Cttee, 1984–87. Trustee, Llandovery Coll., 1966–. *Publications:* (jtly) Plant Biochemistry, 1964; sci. papers in learned jls. *Recreations:* mountaineering, gardening. *Address:* Department of Plant Sciences, Downing Site, Downing Street, Cambridge CB2 3EA. *T:* Cambridge (0223) 333900; The Elms, High Street, Little Eversden, Cambridge CB3 7HE.

ap ROBERT, Hywel Wyn Jones; His Honour Judge ap Robert; a Circuit Judge, since 1975, now Judge of Mid-Glamorgan, Neath and Port Talbot, Brecon and Llandrindod Wells group of County Courts; *b* 19 Nov. 1923; *s* of Rev. Robert John Jones, BA, BD and Mrs Jones (*née* Evans); *m* 1956, Elizabeth Davies; two *d. Educ:* Cardiff High Sch.; Corpus Christi Coll., Oxford (MA). War Service, FO and Intell. Corps. 1942–46, in Britain and India. Called to Bar, Middle Temple, 1950. A Recorder of the Crown Court, 1972–75; Stipendiary Magistrate, Cardiff, later S Glamorgan, 1972–75.

Contested (Plaid Cymru) Cardiganshire, 1970. Hon. Mem., Gorsedd of Bards, 1973. *Recreations:* Welsh literature, classical and modern languages. *Address:* Law Courts, Cardiff. *Club:* Cardiff and County (Cardiff).

APSLEY, Lord; Allen Christopher Bertram Bathurst; *b* 11 March 1961; *s* and *heir* of 8th Earl Bathurst, *qv*; *m* 1986, Hilary, *d* of John F. George, Weston Lodge Albury, Guildford; one *s*. *Heir: s* Hon. Benjamin George Henry Bathurst, *b* 6 March 1990. *Address:* Cirencester Park, Cirencester, Glos GL7 2BT.

APTHORP, John Dorrington; Chairman, Wizard Wine, Borehamwood, since 1989; *b* 25 April 1935; *s* of late Eric and Mildred Apthorp; *m* 1959, Jane Frances Arnold; three *s* one *d*. *Educ:* Aldenham School. FBIM 1977; FInstD 1978; FIGD 1981. Sub-Lieut RNVR, 1953–55. Family business, Appypak, 1956–68; started Bejam Group, 1968, Exec. Chm., 1968–87, non-exec. Chm., 1987–88. Guardian Young Business Man of Year, 1974. Councillor, London Bor. of Barnet, 1968–74. Liveryman, Butchers' Company, 1974–. Commandeur d'Honneur pour Commanderie du Bontemps de Medoc et des Graves, 1977. *Recreations:* shooting, wine. *Address:* The Field House, Newlands Avenue, Radlett, Herts WD7 8EL. *T:* Radlett (0923) 855201. *Clubs:* St Hubert's, Radlett Tennis and Squash (Pres., 1982–).

AQUILECCHIA, Prof. Giovanni; Professor of Italian, University of London, 1970–89, now Emeritus (Bedford College, 1970–85; Royal Holloway and Bedford New College, 1985–89); Hon. Research Fellow, University College London, since 1984; *b* Nettuno, Rome, 28 Nov. 1923; *s* of late Gen. Vincenzo Aquilecchia and Maria L. Filibeck; *m* 1951, Costantina M. Bacchetta (marr. diss. 1973); two *s* one *d*. *Educ:* Liceo T. Tasso, Rome; Univ. of Rome. Dott. Lett., 1946, Diploma of Perfezionamento in Filologia Moderna, 1948, Univ. of Rome. Asst in Italian, Univ. of Rome, 1946–49; Boursier du Gouvernement Français at Collège de France, Univ. of Paris, 1949–50; British Council Scholar, Warburg Inst., Univ. of London, 1950–51; Asst, Dept of Italian Studies, Univ. of Manchester, 1951–53; Asst Lectr in Italian, University Coll., London, 1953–55, Lectr, 1955–59; Libero Docente di Letteratura Italiana, Univ. of Rome, 1958–; Reader in Italian, Univ. of London, at University Coll., 1959–61; Prof. of Italian Lang. and Lit., Univ. of Manchester, 1961–70. Corr. Fellow, Arcadia, 1961. Visiting Professor: Univ. of Melbourne, 1983; Univ. of Naples, 1990. MA (Manchester) 1965. *Publications:* Giordano Bruno, 1971; Schede di italianistica, 1976; Le opere italiane di Giordano Bruno: critica testuale e dintorni, 1991; Il dilemma matematico di Bruno tra atomismo e infinitismo, 1991; critical editions of: Giordano Bruno: La Cena de le Ceneri, 1955; Due Dialoghi sconosciuti, 1957; Dialoghi Italiani, 1958, repr. 1972, 1985; Praelectiones geometricæ e Ars deformationum, 1964; De la causa, principio et uno, 1973; Pietro Aretino: Sei Giornate, 1969, 2nd edn with Introduction, 1975, reprint 1980; Giovanni Villani: Cronica con le continuazioni di Matteo e Filippo, 1979; G. B. Della Porta: Metoposcopia, 1990; (co-editor) Collected essays on Italian Language and Literature, 1971; contrib.: Atti dell'Accad. Nazionale Lincei, Atti e Memorie dell'Arcadia, Bull. dell'Accad. della Crusca, Bull. John Rylands Library, Cultura Neolatina, Dizionario Biografico degli Italiani, Enciclopedia Dantesca, Encyclopædia Britannica, English Miscellany, Filologia e critica, Giornale critico della filosofia italiana, Giornale storico della letteratura italiana, Italian Studies, Lingua Nostra, Quaderni veneti, Storia della cultura veneta, Studi Secenteschi, Studi Tassiani, etc. *Address:* Department of Italian, University College, Gower Street, WC1.

AQUINO, Maria Corazón Cojuangco, (Cory Aquino); President of the Philippines, since 1986; *b* 25 Jan. 1933; *d* of late José and Demetria Cojuangco; *m* 1954, Benigno S. Aquino (*d* 1983); one *s* four *d*. *Educ:* St Scholastica's Coll. and Assumption Convent, Manila; Ravenhill Acad., Philadelphia; Notre Dame Sch., NY; Mount St Vincent Coll., NY (BA); Far Eastern Univ., Manila. Numerous honours, awards and hon. degrees from Philippine and overseas bodies. *Address:* Malacañang, Manila, Philippines.

ARAIN, Shafiq; Ugandan politician and diplomat; Director, Equatorial Bank plc, since 1989; *b* 20 Nov. 1933; *s* of late Din Mohd Arain; *m* 1966, Maria Leana Godinho; one *s* two *d*. *Educ:* Government Sch., Kampala; Regent's Polytechnic, London; Nottingham Univ. MP (UPC), 1962–71; Member, E African Legislative Assembly, 1963–71; E African Minister for Common Market and Economic Affairs, later E African Minister for Communications, Research and Social Services; Chairman: Minimum Wages Commission, 1964; Statutory Commn on Cooperative Movement, 1967. Uganda's Delegate to UN General Assembly, 1965–66; Leader, Uganda Delegn to Canada and CPA Conf., Trinidad and Tobago, 1969. Member, Governing Council, Univ. of Dar es Salaam, 1967–68; Chm., Commonwealth Parly Assoc., Uganda Br., 1969–70. Pres., Uganda Cricket Assoc., 1968–69. Left for exile in London following coup in 1971; returned to Uganda, 1979; elections were held in Dec. 1980; Minister without Portfolio, President's Office, and High Comr for Uganda to London, 1980–85. *Recreations:* golf, walking, reading. *Address:* 30 Roland Way, SW7 3RE. *T:* 071–835 1277. *Clubs:* Uganda, Commonwealth Trust, Mark's.

ARBER, Prof. Werner; Professor of Molecular Microbiology, Basle University, since 1971. Discovered restriction enzymes at Geneva in 1960's; Nobel Prize in Physiology or Medicine (jointly), 1978. *Address:* Department of Microbiology, Biozentrum der Universität Basel, 70 Klingelbergstrasse, CH 4056, Basel, Switzerland.

ARBUTHNOT, Andrew Robert Coghill; Missioner, London Healing Mission, since 1983; Director, Sun Alliance and London Insurance Ltd, since 1970; *b* 14 Jan. 1926; *s* of Robert Wemyss Muir Arbuthnot and Mary Arbuthnot (*née* Coghill); *m* 1952, Audrey Dutton-Barker; one *s* one *d*. *Educ:* Eton. Served 1944–47, Captain, Scots Guards, wounded. Dir, Arbuthnot Latham & Co. Ltd, 1953–82; Chm. and Chief Exec., Arbuthnot Latham Holdings, 1974–81; Chm., Arbuthnot Insurance Services, 1968–83. Contested (C) Houghton-le-Spring, 1959. Ordained Deacon, 1974; Priest, 1975. *Publications:* (with Audrey Arbuthnot) Love that Heals, 1986; Christian Prayer and Healing, 1989. *Recreations:* water colour painting, walking. *Address:* Monksfield House, Tilford, Farnham, Surrey GU10 2AL. *T:* Runfold (02518) 2233.

ARBUTHNOT, James Norwich; MP (C) Wanstead and Woodford, since 1987; *b* 4 Aug. 1952; 2nd *s* of Sir John Arbuthnot, Bt, *qv*; *m* 1984, Emma Louise Broadbent; one *s* one *d*. *Educ:* Wellesley House, Broadstairs; Eton Coll. (Captain of School); Trinity Coll., Cambridge. MA. Called to the Bar, 1975. Practising barrister, 1977–. Councillor, Royal Bor. of Kensington and Chelsea, 1978–87. Contested (C) Cynon Valley, 1983, May 1984. PPS to Minister of State for Armed Forces, 1988–90, to Sec. of State, DTI, 1990–. Pres., Cynon Valley Cons. Assoc., 1983–. *Recreations:* playing guitar, ski-ing, theatre. *Address:* House of Commons, SW1A 0AA. *T:* 071–219 4541. *Club:* West Essex Conservative.

ARBUTHNOT, Sir John (Sinclair-Wemyss), 1st Bt *cr* 1964; MBE 1944; TD 1951; *b* 11 Feb. 1912; *s* of late Major K. W. Arbuthnot, the Seaforth Highlanders; *m* 1943, Margaret Jean, *yr d* of late Alexander G. Duff; two *s* three *d*. *Educ:* Eton; Trinity Coll., Cambridge. MA Hons in Nat. Sciences. Served throughout War of 1939–45, in RA, Major (wounded); Dep. Inspector of Shell, 1942–45; hon. pac 1944. Prospective Conservative candidate, Don Valley Div. of Yorks, 1934–35, Dunbartonshire, 1936–45, Dover Div. of Kent, 1945–50, contesting elections in 1935 and 1945. MP (C) Dover Div. of Kent, 1950–64; PPS to Parly Sec., Min. of Pensions, 1952–53, to Minister of Pensions, 1953–56, and to Minister of Health, 1956–57; a Chm. of Committees and a Temporary Chm. of the House, 1958–64; Second Church Estates Comr, 1962–64; Church Comr for England and Mem., Bd of Governors, 1962–77 (Dep Chm., Assets Cttee, 1966–77); Mem., Church Assembly and Gen. Synod of Church of England, 1955–75 (Panel of Chairmen, 1970–72); Trustee, Lambeth Palace Library, 1964–77; Chm., Archbp of Canterbury's Commn to inquire into the organisation of the Church by dioceses in London and the SE of England, 1965–67. Member: Crathorne Cttee on Sunday Observance, 1961–64; Hodson Commn on Synodical Government for the Church of England, 1964–66; Parliamentary Chm., Dock & Harbour Authorities Assoc., 1962–64; Member: Public Accounts Cttee, 1955–64; Standing Cttee, Ross Inst., 1951–62. Member Parliamentary Delegations: to the Iron and Steel Community, 1955; to West Africa, 1956; to USA, 1957; to The West Indies, 1958; to Zanzibar, Mauritius and Madagascar, 1961; Leader of Parliamentary Delegation to Bulgaria, 1963. A Vice Pres., Trustee Savings Banks Assoc., 1962–76; in business in tea industry concerned with India, Ceylon and the Cameroons, 1934–74; Chairman: Estates & Agency Holdings Ltd, 1955–70; Folkestone and District Water Co., 1974–87; Joint Hon. Sec. Assoc. of British Chambers of Commerce, 1953–59. *Recreation:* gardening. *Heir: s* William Reierson Arbuthnot, *b* 2 Sept. 1950. *Address:* Poulton Manor, Ash, Canterbury, Kent CT3 2HW. *T:* Ash (0304) 812516. *Clubs:* Carlton, Commonwealth Trust.
See also J. N. Arbuthnot.

ARBUTHNOT, Sir Keith Robert Charles, 8th Bt *cr* 1823, of Edinburgh; *b* 23 Sept. 1951; *s* of Sir Hugh Fitz-Gerald Arbuthnot, 7th Bt and Elizabeth Kathleen (*d* 1972), *d* of late Sqdn-Ldr G. G. A. Williams; *S* father, 1983; *m* 1982, Anne, *yr d* of Brig. Peter Moore; two *s* one *d*. *Educ:* Wellington; Univ. of Edinburgh. BSc (Soc. Sci.). *Heir: s* Robert Hugh Peter Arbuthnot, *b* 2 March 1986. *Address:* Whitebridge, Peebles, Peeblesshire EH45 9HS.

ARBUTHNOTT, family name of **Viscount of Arbuthnott.**

ARBUTHNOTT, 16th Viscount of, *cr* 1641; **John Campbell Arbuthnott,** CBE 1986; DSC 1945; FRSE 1984; Lord-Lieutenant Grampian Region (Kincardineshire), since 1977; Lord High Commissioner to General Assembly, Church of Scotland, 1986, 1987; Chairman, Aberdeen and Northern Marts, since 1986 (Director, since 1973); Director: Scottish Widows' Fund and Life Assurance Society, since 1978 (Deputy Chairman, 1982–84 and 1987–88; Chairman, 1984–87); Clydesdale Bank, since 1985 (Northern Area, 1975–85); Britoil plc, 1988–90; British Petroleum Scottish Advisory Board, since 1990; *b* 26 Oct. 1924; *e s* of 15th Viscount of Arbuthnott, CB, CBE, DSO, MC, and Ursula Collingwood (*d* 1989); *S* father, 1966; *m* 1949, Mary Elizabeth Darley (*née* Oxley); one *s* one *d*. *Educ:* Fettes Coll.; Gonville and Caius Coll., Cambridge. Served RNVR (Fleet Air Arm), 1942–46; Near and Far East, British Pacific Fleet, 1945. Cambridge University, 1946–49 (Estate Management), MA 1967. Chartered Surveyor and Land Agent; Agricultural Land Service, 1949–55; Land Agent (Scotland), The Nature Conservancy, 1955–67; Member: Countryside Commn for Scotland, 1967–71; Aberdeen Univ. Court, 1978–84; Royal Commn on Historical MSS, 1987–; Chm., Red Deer Commn, 1969–75; President: British Assoc. for Shooting and Conservation (formerly Wildfowlers Assoc. of GB and Ireland), 1973–; The Scottish Landowners' Fedn, 1974–79 (Convener, 1971–74); Royal Zool Soc. of Scotland, 1976–; Scottish Agricl Orgn Soc., 1980–83; RSGS, 1983–87; Fedn of Agricl Co-operatives (UK) Ltd, 1983–87; Dep. Chm., Nature Conservancy Council, 1980–85, Chm., Adv. Cttee for Scotland, 1980–85. FRSA. KStJ 1982, Prior of Scotland, OStJ, 1983. *Recreations:* countryside activities, historical research. *Heir: s* Master of Arbuthnott, *qv*. *Address:* Arbuthnott House, by Laurencekirk, Kincardineshire, Scotland AB30 1PA. *T:* Inverbervie (05616) 1226. *Clubs:* Army and Navy; New (Edinburgh).

ARBUTHNOTT, Master of; Hon. John Keith Oxley Arbuthnott; *b* 18 July 1950; *s* and *heir* of 16th Viscount of Arbuthnott, *qv*; *m* 1974, Jill Mary, *er d* of Captain Colin Farquharson, *qv*; one *s* two *d*. *Educ:* Fettes College; Aberdeen Univ. *Address:* Kilternan, Arbuthnott, Laurencekirk, Kincardineshire AB3 1NA. *T:* Inverbervie (0561) 61203.

ARBUTHNOTT, Hugh James, CMG 1984; HM Diplomatic Service; Ambassador to Portugal, since 1989; *b* 27 Dec. 1936; *m*; two *s* (and one *s* decd). *Educ:* Ampleforth Coll., Yorks; New Coll., Oxford. Nat. Service, Black Watch, 1955–57. Joined Foreign (subseq. Diplomatic) Service, 1960; 3rd Sec., Tehran, 1962–64; 2nd, later 1st Sec., FO, 1964–66; Private Sec., Minister of State for Foreign Affairs, 1966–68; Lagos, 1968–71; 1st Sec. (Head of Chancery), Tehran, 1971–74; Asst, later Head of European Integration Dept (External), FCO, 1974–77; Counsellor (Agric. and Econ.), Paris, 1978–80; Head of Chancery, Paris, 1980–83; Under Sec., Internat. Div., ODA, 1983–85; Amb. to Romania, 1986–89. *Publication:* Common Man's Guide to the Common Market (ed with G. Edwards), 1979, 2nd edn (co-author with G. Edwards), 1989. *Address:* c/o Foreign and Commonwealth Office, SW1A 2AH.

ARBUTHNOTT, Prof. John Peebles, PhD, ScD; FIBiol; Principal and Vice Chancellor, University of Strathclyde, since 1991; *b* 8 April 1939; *s* of James Anderson Arbuthnott and Jean (*née* Kelly); *m* 1962, Elinor Rutherford Smillie; one *s* two *d*. *Educ:* Univ. of Glasgow (BSc 1960; PhD 1964); Trinity Coll., Dublin (ScD 1984). FIBiol 1988. University of Glasgow: Lectr, Dept of Bacteriology, 1963–67; Alan Johnston, Lawrence and Moseley Res. Fellow of Royal Soc., 1968–72; Sen. Lectr, Dept of Microbiol., 1972–73; Sen. Lectr, Dept of Bacteriol., 1973–75; Professor of Microbiology: TCD, 1976–88 (Bursar, 1983–86); Univ. of Nottingham, 1988–91. Vis. Lectr, Dept of Microbiol., New York Univ. Med. Centre, 1966–67. Hon. Microbiologist, Public Health Service, 1988–. Treasurer, Soc. for Gen. Microbiol., 1987–92. MRIA 1985; FRSA 1989. *Publications:* edited: (jtly) Isoelectric Focusing, 1975; (jtly) The Determinants of Bacterial and Viral Pathogencity, 1983; (jtly) Foodborne Illness: a Lancet review, 1991; more than 100 in prestigious scientific learned jls and books. *Recreations:* Scottish country dancing, golf, attending soccer matches. *Address:* University of Strathclyde, Glasgow G1 1XQ. *T:* 041–552 4400.

ARBUTHNOTT, Robert, CBE 1991; Minister (Cultural Affairs), British High Commission (British Council Division), India, since 1988; *b* 28 Sept. 1936; *s* of late Archibald Arbuthnott, MBE, ED, and of Barbara Joan (*née* Worters); *m* 1962, Sophie Robina (*née* Axford); one *s* two *d*. *Educ:* Sedbergh Sch. (scholar); Emmanuel Coll., Cambridge (exhibnr; BA Mod Langs, MA). Nat. service, 1955–57 (2nd Lieut The Black Watch RHR). British Council, 1960–: Karachi, 1960–62; Lahore, 1962–64; London, 1964–67; Representative, Nepal, 1967–72; London Inst. of Education, 1972–73; Representative, Malaysia, 1973–76; Director, Educational Contracts Dept, 1976–77; Controller, Personnel and Staff Recruitment Div., 1978–81; Representative, Germany, 1981–85; RCDS, 1986; Controller, America, Pacific and S Asia Div., 1987. *Recreations:* music-making, the arts, sport. *Club:* United Oxford & Cambridge University.

ARCHDALE, Sir Edward (Folmer), 3rd Bt, *cr* 1928; DSC 1943; Captain, RN, retired; *b* 8 Sept. 1921; *s* of Vice-Adm. Sir Nicholas Edward Archdale, 2nd Bt, CBE, and Gerda (*d* 1969), 2nd *d* of late F. C. Sievers, Copenhagen; *S* father 1955; *m* 1954, Elizabeth Ann Stewart (marr. diss. 1978), *d* of late Maj.-Gen. Wilfrid Boyd Fellowes Lukis, CBE; one *s* two *d*. *Educ:* Royal Naval Coll., Dartmouth. Joined Royal Navy, 1935; served War of 1939–45 (despatches, DSC). Mem. (UU) Ards BC, 1989–. *Recreation:* civilization. *Heir:* *s* Nicholas Edward Archdale, *b* 2 Dec. 1965. *Address:* 19 Dermott Road, Comber, Co. Down BT23 5LG.

ARCHER, Albert, MBE 1980; Member, Royal Commission on Environmental Pollution, 1981–85; *b* 7 March 1915; *s* of Arthur Archer and Margaret Alice Norris; *m* 1st, 1939; two *s*; 2nd, 1975, Peggy, *widow* of John F. Marsh; two step *s*. *Educ:* Manchester Grammar Sch.; Manchester Coll. of Technology. Fellow, Instn of Environmental Health Officers, 1961. Chief Public Health Inspector, Bor. of Halesowen, 1943–73; City of Birmingham: Environmtl Protection Officer, 1973–75; Dep. City Environmtl Officer, 1975–76; City Environmtl Officer, 1976–80. Mem., govt working parties on air pollution. Pres., Inst. of Environmental Health Officers, 1979–83. *Publications:* articles on air pollution in technical jls. *Recreation:* watching cricket. *Address:* 8 Portland Drive, Stourbridge, West Midlands DY9 0SD. *T:* Hagley (0562) 883366.

ARCHER, Gen. Sir (Arthur) John, KCB 1976; OBE 1964; Chief Executive, Royal Hong Kong Jockey Club, 1980–86, retired; *b* 12 Feb. 1924; *s* of Alfred and Mildred Archer, Fakenham; *m* 1950, Cynthia Marie, *d* of Col Alexander and Eileen Allan, Swallowcliffe, Wilts; two *s*. *Educ:* King's Sch., Peterborough; St Catharine's Coll., Cambridge. Entered Army, 1943; commnd 1944; regular commn Dorset Regt, 1946; psc 1956; jssc 1959; GSO1 3rd Div., 1963–65; CO 1 Devon and Dorset Regt, 1965–67; Comdr Land Forces Gulf, 1968–69; idc 1970; Dir of Public Relations (Army), 1970–72; Comdr 2nd Div., 1972–74; Dir of Army Staff Duties, 1974–76; Comdr British Forces Hong Kong, 1976–78 and Lt-Gen. Brigade of Gurkhas, 1977–78; C-in-C, UKLF, 1978–79. CBIM. Col, Devonshire and Dorset Regt, 1977–79. *Recreations:* light aviation, gliding, sailing. *Address:* c/o Lloyds Bank, 38 Blue Boar Row, Salisbury, Wilts SP1 1DB. *Clubs:* Army and Navy; Royal Motor; Hong Kong, Royal Hong Kong Jockey (Hong Kong).

ARCHER, Bruce; *see* Archer, L. B.

ARCHER, Sir Clyde Vernon Harcourt, Kt 1962; Judge of the Court of Appeal, Bahamas, 1971–75; *b* 12 Nov. 1904. *Educ:* Harrison Coll., Barbados; Cambridge Univ. Barrister-at-Law, Gray's Inn; clerk to the Attorney-General, Barbados, 1930; police magistrate Barbados, 1935; Judge, Bridgetown Petty Debt Court, 1938; Legal Draftsman, Trinidad and Tobago, 1944; Solicitor-General, Trinidad and Tobago, 1953; Puisne Judge, Trinidad and Tobago, 1954; Chief Justice of the Windward Islands and Leeward Islands, 1958; a Federal Justice, WI, 1958–62. *Publication:* (jointly) Revised Edition of the Laws of Barbados, 1944. *Address:* 40 Graeme Hall Terrace, Christchurch, Barbados.

ARCHER, Frank Joseph, RE 1960 (ARE 1940); RWS 1976 (ARWS 1972); ARCA 1937; Head of School of Fine Art, Kingston Polytechnic, Kingston upon Thames (formerly Kingston College of Art), 1962–73, retired; *b* 30 June 1912; *s* of Joseph and Alberta Archer; *m* 1939, Celia Cole; one *s* one *d*. *Educ:* Eastbourne Grammar Sch.; Eastbourne Sch. of Art; Royal Coll. of Art. ARCA 1937; Rome Scholar, Engraving, 1938; British Sch. at Rome, 1938. Paintings bought by numerous local authorities and private collectors. *Address:* Flat 1, Stony Down, 8 Milnthorpe Road, Eastbourne, East Sussex BN21 4ND. *T:* Eastbourne (0323) 23381.

ARCHER, Graham Robertson; HM Diplomatic Service; Counsellor, Foreign and Commonwealth Office, since 1990; *b* 4 July 1939; *s* of late Henry Robertson Archer and Winifred Archer; *m* 1963, Pauline Cowan; two *d*. *Educ:* Judd School, Tonbridge. Joined Commonwealth Relations Office, 1962; British High Commission, New Delhi, 1964; Vice Consul, Kuwait, 1966; CRO (later FCO), 1967; Second Secretary (Commercial), Washington, 1970; First Secretary: FCO, 1972; Wellington, NZ, 1975; FCO, 1979; Counsellor: Pretoria, 1982; The Hague, 1986. *Recreations:* listening to music, gardening, hill walking. *Address:* c/o Foreign and Commonwealth Office, Whitehall, SW1A 2AP.

ARCHER, Mrs Jean Mary; Under-Secretary, Ministry of Agriculture, Fisheries and Food, 1973–86; *b* 24 Aug. 1932; *e d* of late Reginald R. and D. Jane Harvey, Braiseworth Hall, Tannington, Suffolk; *m* 1954, G. Michéal D. Archer, MB, BChir, FFARCS, *er s* of Maj.-Gen. G. T. L. Archer, CB; two *d*. *Educ:* Fleet House, Felixstowe; St Felix Sch., Southwold; Newnham Coll., Cambridge. MA Econs 1954. Asst Principal, Min. of Agriculture, 1954; Private Sec. to successive Perm. Secs, MAFF, 1956–59; Principal 1960; Sec., Reorganisation Commn for Eggs, 1967; Asst Sec. 1968; Under-Sec. i/c Food Policy Gp, MAFF, 1973; Under-Sec., Dept of Prices and Consumer Protection, 1974–76; returned to MAFF, as Under-Sec., Milk and Marketing Group, 1976; Under-Sec., Meat, Poultry and Eggs Div., 1980. *Recreations:* travel, music, tennis, watching sport, swimming administration (Team Man., Chelsea/Kensington Swimming Club; Hon. Sec., Swimmers' Parents' and Supporters' Assoc.). *Address:* Friary Cottage, Mendlesham, Suffolk. *T:* Stowmarket (0449) 766395. *Club:* Hurlingham.
See also Rt Hon. Sir A. J. D. McCowan.

ARCHER, Jeffrey Howard; politician and author; *b* 15 April 1940; *s* of William Archer and Lola Archer (*née* Cook); *m* 1966, Mary Weeden (*see* M. D. Archer); two *s*. *Educ:* by my wife since leaving Wellington Sch., Somerset; Brasenose Coll., Oxford. Athletics Blues, 1963–65, Gymnastics Blue, 1963, Pres. OUAC 1965; ran for Great Britain (never fast enough); Oxford 100 yards record (9.6 sec.), 1966. Mem. GLC for Havering, 1966–70; MP (C) Louth, Dec. 1969–Sept. 1974. Dep. Chm., Cons. Party, 1985–86. Trustee, RWS, 1989–. Pres., Somerset AAA, 1973; Hon. Pres., Glasgow Univ. Dialectic Soc., 1984–. FRSA 1973. *Plays:* Beyond Reasonable Doubt, Queen's, 1987; Exclusive, Queen's, 1990. *Publications:* Not a Penny More, Not a Penny Less, 1975 (televised, 1990); Shall We Tell the President?, 1977; Kane and Abel, 1979 (televised, 1986); A Quiver Full of Arrows, 1980; The Prodigal Daughter, 1982; First Among Equals, 1984 (televised, 1986); A Matter of Honour, 1986; A Twist in the Tale (short stories), 1988; As the Crow Flies, 1991. *Recreations:* theatre, watching Somerset play cricket (represented Somerset CCC in benefit match, 1981; Pres., Somerset Wyverns, 1983). *Address:* Alembic House, 93 Albert Embankment, SE1 7TY; The Old Vicarage, Grantchester. *Clubs:* MCC; Louth Working Men's.

ARCHER, Sir John; *see* Archer, Sir A. J.

ARCHER, John Francis Ashweek, QC 1975; a Recorder of the Crown Court since 1974; *b* 9 July 1925; *s* of late George Eric Archer, FRCSE, and late Frances Archer (*née* Ashweek); *m* 1960, Doris Mary Hennessey (*d* 1988). *Educ:* Winchester Coll., 1938–43; New Coll., Oxford, 1947–49 (BA 1949). Served War of 1939–45, 1944–47; Lieut RA, 1948. Called to Bar, Inner Temple, 1950, Bencher, 1984. Mem., Criminal Injuries Compensation Bd, 1987–. *Recreations:* motoring, bridge. *Address:* 7 King's Bench Walk, Temple, EC4.

ARCHER, John Norman; Managing Director, International Tanker Owners Pollution Federation Ltd, 1979–86; *b* 27 Feb. 1921; *s* of late Clifford Banks Archer and Grace Archer; *m* 1st, 1952, Gladys Joy (*née* Barnes) (*d* 1985); one step *d*; 2nd, 1986, Mrs Anne L. M. Appleby (*née* Padwick). *Educ:* Wandsworth School. Served with RA, 1939–46 (Major). Entered Civil Service, Board of Educn, 1937; Asst Principal 1947, Principal 1949, Min. of Educn; attended Admin. Staff Coll., Henley, 1960; Asst Sec. (Joint Head, Architects and Buildings Br.), 1962; technical assistance assignments etc educn, Nigeria, Yugoslavia, Tunisia, 1961–63; Asst Sec., Treasury, O&M Div., 1964; Civil Service Department: Asst Sec., Management Services Development Div., 1968; Under-Sec., Management Services, 1970; Under-Sec., Marine Div., DTI, later Dept of Trade, 1972–79. Member: Cttee of Management, RNLI; Council, Marine Soc.; Internat. Lawn Tennis Club of GB. Freeman, City of London, 1985; Liveryman, Shipwrights' Co., 1986–. *Recreations:* lawn tennis, bridge, watching cricket. *Address:* 17 Sovereign House, Draxmont, Wimbledon Hill Road, SW19 7PG. *T:* 081–946 6429. *Clubs:* All England Lawn Tennis, Hurlingham, MCC; Kent CC; Frinton Lawn Tennis.

ARCHER, Prof. (Leonard) Bruce, CBE 1976; DrRCA; CEng, MIMechE; Director of Research, Royal College of Art, 1985–88, now Emeritus Professor; Director and Secretary, Southwood House Estate Residents Co. Ltd, since 1986; *b* 22 Nov. 1922; *s* of Leonard Castella Archer and Ivy Hilda Archer; *m* 1950, Joan Henrietta Allen; one *d*. *Educ:* Henry Thornton Sch., London; City Univ., London. MIED, ASIA(Ed). Served, Scots Guards, 1941–44. City Univ., 1946–50. Various posts in manufacturing industry, 1950–57; Lectr, Central Sch. of Art and Design, London, 1957–60; Guest Prof., Hochschule für Gestaltung, Ulm, 1960–61; Research Fellow, later Prof., Royal Coll. of Art, 1961–88; Hd of Dept of Design Research, RCA, 1968–85. Various public appointments in design, educn and industrial and scientific policy, 1968–; Member: Design Council, 1972–80; Internat. Science Policy Foundn, 1979–; Council, Assoc. of Art Instns, 1980–; Chm., Confedn of Art and Design Assocs, 1981–88. Director: Gore Projects Ltd, 1982–90; Design Research Innovation Centre Ltd, 1982–86. Hon. DSc City, 1986. *Publications:* varied, on the theory and practice of research, design, develt and educn. *Recreations:* music, the theatre. *Address:* 60 Jackson's Lane, N6 5SX. *T:* 081–340 2918.

ARCHER, Dr Mary Doreen; scientist; *b* 22 Dec. 1944; *d* of late Harold Norman Weeden and of Doreen Weeden (*née* Cox); *m* 1966, Jeffrey Howard Archer, *qv*; two *s*. *Educ:* Cheltenham Ladies' College; St Anne's Coll., Oxford (Nuffield Schol.; MA 1972); Imperial Coll., London Univ. (PhD 1968); MA Cantab 1976. FRSC 1987. Junior Res. Fellow, St Hilda's Coll., Oxford, 1968–71; temp. Lectr in Chemistry, Somerville Coll., Oxford, 1971–72; Res. Fellow, Royal Instn of GB, 1972–76 (Dewar Fellow, 1975–76); Lector in Chemistry, Trinity Coll., Cambridge, 1976–86; Fellow and Coll. Lectr in Chem., Newnham Coll., Cambridge, 1976–86 (Bye-Fellow, 1987–). Vis. Prof., Leicester Polytechnic, 1990–. Trustee, Science Mus., 1990–. Mem. Bd of Dirs, Internat. Solar Energy Soc., 1975–81 (Sec., UK Section, 1973–76); Manager, 1982–84, Mem. Council, 1984–85, Royal Instn; Chm., Nat. Energy Foundn, 1990–. Director: Anglia Television Gp, 1987–; Mid Anglia Radio, 1988–; Cambridge & Newmarket FM Radio, 1988–; Mem. Council of Lloyd's, 1989–. Pres., Guild of Church Musicians, 1989–. Fitzwilliam Mus. Trust, 1984–. *Publications:* Rupert Brooke and the Old Vicarage, Grantchester, 1989; contribs to chem. jls. *Recreations:* village choirmistress, theatre, squash, cats, picking up litter. *Address:* The Old Vicarage, Grantchester, Cambridge CB3 9ND. *T:* Cambridge (0223) 840213.

ARCHER, Dr Mildred Agnes, (Mrs W. G. Archer), OBE 1979; in charge of Prints and Drawings Section, India Office Library, London, 1954–80; *b* 28 Dec. 1911; *d* of V. A. Bell, MBE; *m* 1934, William George Archer (*d* 1979); one *s* one *d*. *Educ:* St Hilda's College, Oxford (MA, DLitt 1978; Hon. Fellow 1978). Art historian (British period, India); resided India, 1934–47; revisited India (study tours), 1966, 1972, 1976, 1981–82, 1984, 1989. *Publications:* Patna Painting, 1947; (with W. G. Archer) Indian Painting for the British, 1955; Tippoo's Tiger, 1959; Natural History Drawings in the India Office Library, 1962; Indian Miniatures and Folk Paintings, 1967; Indian Architecture and the British, 1968; British Drawings in the India Office Library (2 vols), 1969; Indian Paintings from Court, Town and Village, 1970; Company Drawings in the India Office Library, 1972; Artist Adventurers in Eighteenth Century India, 1974; Indian Popular Painting, 1977; India and British Portraiture, 1770–1825, 1979; (with John Bastin) The Raffles Drawings in the India Office Library, 1979; Early Views of India, 1980; (with T. Falk) Indian Miniatures in the India Office Library, 1981; (with R. Lightbown) India Observed, 1982; Oil Paintings and Sculpture in the India Office Collection, 1986; Visions of India: the sketchbooks of William Simpson 1859–62, 1986; (with T. Falk) India Revealed: the art and adventures of James and William Fraser 1801–35, 1989; articles in Country Life, Apollo, Connoisseur, History Today, Geographical Mag. *Recreations:* grandchildren, gardening, travel. *Address:* 18A Provost Road, Hampstead, NW3 4ST. *T:* 071–722 2713; 5 Frog Meadow, Dedham, Colchester, Essex. *T:* Colchester (0206) 323099.

ARCHER, Rt. Hon. Peter (Kingsley), PC 1977; QC 1971; MP (Lab) Warley West, since 1974 (Rowley Regis and Tipton, 1966–74); a Recorder of the Crown Court, since 1982; *b* 20 Nov. 1926; *s* of Cyril Kingsley Archer and May (*née* Baker); *m* 1954, Margaret Irene (*née* Smith); one *s*. *Educ:* Wednesbury Boys' High Sch.; LSE; University Coll., London (Fellow 1978). Called to Bar, Gray's Inn, 1952; Bencher, 1974; commenced practice, 1953. PPS to Attorney-Gen., 1967–70; Solicitor General, 1974–79; chief Opposition spokesman on legal affairs, 1979–82, on trade, 1982–83, on N Ireland, 1983–87. UK Deleg. to UN Gen. Assembly (Third Cttee), 1969. Chm., Amnesty International (British Section), 1971–74; Chm., Parly Gp for World Govt, 1970–74; Chm., Soc. of Labour Lawyers, 1971–74, 1979–; Vice-Chm., Anti-Slavery Soc., 1970–74; Mem., Exec. Cttee, Fabian Soc., 1974–86 (Chm., 1980–81). Ombudsman for Mirror Group Newspapers, 1989–. *Publications:* The Queen's Courts, 1956; ed Social Welfare and the Citizen, 1957; Communism and the Law, 1963; (with Lord Reay) Freedom at Stake, 1966; Human Rights, 1969; (jtly) Purpose in Socialism, 1973; The Role of the Law Officers, 1978; contributions to: Trends in Social Welfare, 1965; Atkin's, Court Forms, 1965; The International Protection of Human Rights, 1967; Renewal, 1983; Fabian Centenary Essays, 1984; (ed) More Law Reform Now, 1984. *Recreations:* music, writing, talking. *Address:* House of Commons, SW1A 0AA.

ARCHIBALD, Barony of, *cr* 1949, of Woodside, Glasgow; title disclaimed by 2nd Baron; *see under* Archibald, George Christopher.

ARCHIBALD, George Christopher, FRSC 1979; Professor of Economics, University of British Columbia, since 1970; *b* 30 Dec. 1926; *s* of 1st Baron Archibald, CBE, and Dorothy Holroyd Edwards (*d* 1960); *S* father, 1975, as 2nd Baron Archibald, but disclaimed his peerage for life; *m* 1st, 1951, Liliana Barou (marr. diss. 1965); 2nd, 1971, Daphne May Vincent. *Educ:* Phillips Exeter Academy, USA; King's Coll., Cambridge (MA); London Sch. of Economics (BSc Econ.). Served in Army, 1945–48, Captain RAEC. Formerly: Prof. of Economics, Univ. of Essex; Lectr in Economics, Otago Univ. and LSE; Leon Fellow, London Univ. Fellow, Econometric Soc., 1976. *Publications:* (ed) Theory of the Firm, 1971; (with R. G. Lipsey) Introduction to a Mathematical Treatment of Economics, 1973. *Address:* c/o Department of Economics, University of British Columbia, Vancouver, BC V6T 1W5, Canada.

ARCHIBALD, Dr (Harry) Munro, CB 1976; MBE 1945; Deputy Chief Medical Officer (Deputy Secretary), Department of Health and Social Security, 1973–77; *b* 17 June 1915;

s of James and Isabella Archibald; unmarried. *Educ:* Hillhead High Sch.; Univ. of Glasgow. MB, ChB 1938; DPH 1956. War Service: RAMC, 1940–43; IMS/IAMC, 1943–46; Lt-Col; Italian Campaign (despatches). Colonial Medical Service, Nigeria, 1946–62: Senior Specialist (Malariologist), 1958; Principal Med. Officer, Prevent. Services, N Nigeria, 1960; Med. Officer, Min. of Health, 1962; Sen. Med. Off., 1964; Principal Med. Off., DHSS, 1970; Sen. Principal Med. Off., 1972. Mem. Bd, Public Health Laboratory Service, 1975–77. Fellow, Faculty of Community Medicine, 1973. *Recreation:* travel. *Address:* 1 Camborne House, Camborne Road, Sutton, Surrey SM2 6RL. *T:* 081–643 1076. *Club:* Caledonian.

ARCHIBALD, Liliana; Director, Holman Wade Ltd, since 1989; *b* 25 May 1928; *d* of late Noah and Sophie Barou; *m* 1951, George Christopher Archibald (marr. diss. 1965). *Educ:* Kingsley Sch.; Geneva University. Univ. Lectr, Otago Univ., 1952–55; Director: Const & Co. Ltd, 1955–73, 1977–; Credit Consultants Ltd, 1957–73, 1977–85; Adam Brothers Contingency Ltd, 1957–73, 1977–85; Fenchurch Gp Internat., 1985–88; Head of Division (Credit Insurance and Export Credit), EEC, 1973–77; EEC Advr to Lloyd's and the British Insurance Brokers Assoc., 1978–85; Internat. Affairs Advr to Lloyd's, 1981–85; Advr to Internat. Gp of Protection & Indemnity Clubs, 1980–85. Frequent lecturer on insurance-related problems. Member: Liberalisation of Trade in Services Cttee, British Invisible Exports Council, 1981–; British Export Finance Adv. Council, 1982–91; Action Resource Centre, 1986–91; Govt Inquiry into Shops Act—Sunday and Late-Night Trading, 1984–85; Review Cttee, Banking Law Services, 1987–88; Vice-Chm., ICC Insurance Commn, 1982–87; Chm., Insurance Cttee, British Nat. Cttee, ICC, 1983–87. Member of Lloyd's, 1973–. *Publications:* (trans. and ed) Peter the Great, 1958; (trans. and ed) Rise of the Romanovs, 1970; contrib. Bankers Magazine. *Recreations:* driving fast cars, ski-ing, gardening. *Address:* 21 Langland Gardens, NW3 6QE.
See also A. Kennaway.

ARCHIBALD, Munro; *see* Archibald, H. M.

ARCTIC, Bishop of The, since 1991; **Rt. Rev. (John) Christopher (Richard) Williams;** *b* 22 May 1936; *s* of Frank Harold and Ceridwen Roberts Williams; *m* 1964, Rona Macrae (*née* Aitken); one *s* one *d.* *Educ:* Manchester Grammar Sch.; Univ. of Manchester (BA Comm); Univ. of Durham, Cranmer Hall (DipTh). Ordained: deacon, Stretford, England, 1960; priest, Sugluk, PQ, 1962; Missionary, diocese of The Arctic: Sugluk, PQ, 1961–72; Cape Dorset, NWT, 1972–75; Baker Lake, NWT, 1975–78; Archdeacon of The Keewatin, 1975–87; Rector, Yellowknife, NWT, 1978–87; Bp Suffragan, 1987–90, Coadjutor Bp, 1990, dio. of The Arctic. *Recreations:* walking, cross country ski-ing. *Address:* PO Box 164, Iqaluit, NWT X0A 0H0, Canada. *T:* (819) 979 4745.

ARCULUS, Sir Ronald, KCMG 1979 (CMG 1968); KCVO 1980; HM Diplomatic Service, retired; Director, Glaxo Holdings, since 1983; *b* 11 Feb. 1923; *s* of late Cecil and Ethel L. Arculus; *m* 1953, Sheila Mary Faux; one *s* one *d.* *Educ:* Solihull; Exeter Coll., Oxford (MA; Hon. Fellow, 1989). 4th Queen's Own Hussars (now Queen's Royal Irish Hussars), 1942–45 (Captain). Joined HM Diplomatic Service, 1947; FO, 1947; San Francisco, 1948; La Paz, 1950; FO, 1951; Ankara, 1953; FO, 1957; Washington, 1961; Counsellor, 1965; New York, 1965–68; IDC, 1969; Head of Science and Technology Dept, FCO, 1970–72; Minister (Economic), Paris, 1973–77; Ambassador and Permt Leader, UK Delegn to UN Conf. on Law of the Sea, 1977–79; Ambassador to Italy, 1979–83. Special Advr to Govt on Channel Tunnel trains, 1987–88. Consultant: Trusthouse Forte, 1983–86; London and Continental Bankers Ltd, 1985–90. Dir of Appeals, King's Med. Res. Trust, 1984–88. Governor, British Institute, Florence, 1983–. FBIM 1984. Freeman, City of London, 1981. Kt Grand Cross, Order of Merit, Italy, 1980. *Recreations:* travel, music and fine arts. *Address:* 20 Kensington Court Gardens, W8 5QF. *Clubs:* Army and Navy, Hurlingham.

ARDAGH AND CLONMACNOISE, Bishop of, (RC), since 1983; **Most Rev. Colm O'Reilly;** *b* 11 Jan. 1935; *s* of John and Alicia O'Reilly. *Address:* St Michael's, Longford, Ireland. *T:* Longford 46432.

ARDEE, Lord; John Anthony Brabazon; *b* 11 May 1941; *e s* of 14th Earl of Meath, *qv*; *m* 1973, Xenia Goudime; one *s* two *d.* *Educ:* Harrow. Page of Honour to the Queen, 1956–57. Served Grenadier Guards, 1959–62. *Heir:* *s* Hon. Anthony Jaques Brabazon, *b* 30 Jan. 1977. *Address:* Ballinacor, Rathdrum, Co. Wicklow, Ireland.

ARDEN, Andrew Paul Russel; QC 1991; *b* 20 April 1948; *m* 1991, Joanne Leahy. *Educ:* Stowe; University College Sch.; University Coll. London (LLB). Called to the Bar, Gray's Inn, 1974; Dir, Small Heath Community Law Centre, Birmingham, 1976–78; Inquiry into Housing Assocs for GLC, 1982–83; Inquiry into Housing Improvement Grants for Bristol CC, 1985; Inquiry into Freemasonary and Institutional Deficiencies of the Authority for Hackney London BC, 1985–87. General Editor: Encyclopaedia of Housing Law, 1978–; Housing Law Reports, 1981–. *Publications:* Manual of Housing Law, 1978, 4th edn 1989; Housing Act 1980 (annotations), 1980; (with Prof. M. Partington) Quiet Enjoyment, 1980, 2nd edn 1985; Housing Law, 1983, 2nd edn 1991; (with Prof. J. T. Farrand) Rent Acts & Regulations, amended and annotated, 1981; (with C. Cross) Housing & Building Control Act 1984 (annotations), 1984; Private Tenants Handbook, 1985, 2nd edn 1989; Public Tenants Handbook, 1985, 2nd edn 1989; (with S. McGrath) Landlord & Tenant Act 1985 (annotations), 1986; Housing Act 1985 (annotations), 1986; (with J. Ramage) Housing Associations Act 1985 (annotations), 1986; Homeless Persons Handbook, 1986, 2nd edn 1988; Homeless Persons: Part III, Housing Act 1985, 3rd edn 1988; (with C. Hunter) Housing Act 1988 (annotations), 1989; (with Sir Robert Megarry) Assured Tenancies, Vol. 3, The Rent Acts, 11th edn 1989; (with C. Hunter) Local Government & Housing Act 1989 (annotations), 1990; *fiction:* The Motive Not The Deed, 1974; No Certain Roof, 1985; The Object Man, 1986; four thrillers under pseudonym, 1990–91. *Recreations:* Southern Comfort, Hill Street Blues, Camel cigarettes. *Address:* Gray's Inn Chambers, Gray's Inn, WC1R 5JA. *T:* 071–404 1111.

ARDEN, Rt. Rev. Donald Seymour, CBE 1981; Assistant Bishop in Willesden, since 1981, and voluntary assistant priest, St Alban's, North Harrow, since 1986; *b* 12 April 1916; *s* of Stanley and Winifred Arden; *m* 1962, Jane Grace Riddle; two *s.* *Educ:* St Peter's Coll., Adelaide; University of Leeds (BA); College of the Resurrection, Mirfield. Deacon, 1939; Priest, 1940. Curate of: St Catherine's, Hatcham, 1939–40; Nettleden with Potten End, 1941–43; Asst Priest, Pretoria African Mission, 1944–51; Director of Usuthu Mission, Swaziland, 1951–61; Bishop of Nyasaland, 1961 (name of diocese changed, when Nyasaland was granted independence, July 1964); Bishop of Malaŵi, 1964–71, of Southern Malaŵi, 1971–81; Archbishop of Central Africa, 1971–80; Priest-in-charge of St Margaret's, Uxbridge, 1981–86. Commissary, dio. of Niassa, Mozambique, 1989–. *Publication:* Out of Africa Something New, 1976. *Recreations:* photography, farming. *Address:* 6 Frobisher Close, Eastcote, Mddx HA5 1NN. *T:* 081–866 6009.

ARDEN, John; playwright; *b* 26 Oct. 1930; *s* of C. A. Arden and A. E. Layland; *m* 1957, Margaretta Ruth D'Arcy; four *s* (and one *s* decd). *Educ:* Sedbergh Sch.; King's Coll., Cambridge; Edinburgh Coll. of Art. *Plays produced include:* All Fall Down, 1955; The Life of Man, 1956; The Waters of Babylon, 1957; Live Like Pigs, 1958; Serjeant Musgrave's Dance, 1959; Soldier, Soldier, 1960; Wet Fish, 1962; The Workhouse Donkey, 1963; Ironhand, 1963; Armstrong's Last Goodnight, 1964; Left-Handed Liberty, 1965; The True History of Squire Jonathan and his Unfortunate Treasure, 1968; The Bagman, 1970; Pearl, 1978; To Put It Frankly, 1979; Don Quixote, 1980; Garland for a Hoar Head, 1982; The Old Man Sleeps Alone, 1982; *with Margaretta D'Arcy:* The Business of Good Government, 1960; The Happy Haven, 1960; Ars Longa Vita Brevis, 1964; Friday's Hiding, 1966; The Royal Pardon, 1966; The Hero Rises Up, 1968; Island of the Mighty, 1972; The Ballygombeen Bequest, 1972; The Non-Stop Connolly Cycle, 1975; Vandaleur's Folly, 1978; The Little Gray Home in the West, 1978; The Manchester Enthusiasts, 1984; Whose is the Kingdom?, 1988. *Publications:* To Present the Pretence (essays), 1977; Silence Among the Weapons (novel), 1982; Books of Bale (novel), 1988; (with Margaretta D'Arcy) Awkward Corners, 1988. *Recreations:* antiquarianism, mythology. *Address:* c/o Margaret Ramsay Ltd, 14 Goodwin's Court, WC2.

ARDEN, Mary Howarth, (Mrs J. H. Mance); QC 1986; *b* 23 Jan. 1947; *d* of late Lt-Col E. C. Arden, LLB, TD and of M. M. Arden (*née* Smith); *m* 1973, Jonathan Hugh Mance, *qv*; one *s* two *d.* *Educ:* Huyton College; Girton College, Cambridge (MA, LLM); Harvard Law School (LLM). Called to the Bar, Gray's Inn, 1971 (Arden and Birkenhead Scholarships, 1971); admitted *ad eundem* to Lincoln's Inn, 1973. Bar Mem., Law Society's Standing Cttee on Company Law, 1976–. DTI Inspector, Rotaprint PLC, 1988–91. *Publications:* Negligence and the Public Accountant (contrib.), 1972; Legal Editor, Current Accounting Law and Practice, by Robert Willott, 1976; (with George Eccles) Tolley's Companies Act 1980, 1980; Legal Consultant Editor: Tolley's Companies Act 1981, 1981; Tolley's Accounting Problems of the Companies Acts, 1984; Accounting Provisions of the Companies Act 1985, 1985; Coopers & Lybrand Deloitte Manual of Accounting, vols 1 and 2, 1990; Jt Gen. Editor and Contributor, Buckley on the Companies Acts, 14th edn: Special Bulletin, 1990. *Recreations:* family activities, reading, swimming.

ARDWICK, Baron *cr* 1970 (Life Peer), of Barnes; **John Cowburn Beavan;** Member of European Parliament, 1975–79; *b* 29 April 1910; *s* of late Silas Morgan Beavan and Alderman Emily Beavan, JP; *m* 1934, Gladys (*née* Jones); one *d.* *Educ:* Manchester Grammar Sch. Blackpool Times, 1927; Evening Chronicle, Manchester, 1928; Manchester Evening News, 1930; London staff, Manchester Evening News, 1933; News Editor, Manchester Evening News, Manchester, 1936; Asst Editor, Londoner's Diary, Evening Standard, and leader writer, 1940; News Editor and Chief Sub, Observer, 1942; Editor, Manchester Evening News, 1943; Dir, Manchester Guardian and Evening News Ltd, 1943–55; London Editor, Manchester Guardian, 1946–55; Asst Dir, Nuffield Foundation, 1955; Editor, Daily Herald, 1960–62; Political Adviser to the Daily Mirror Group, 1962–76; Mem. Editorial Bd, The Political Quarterly, 1978–; Chm., Press Freedom Cttee, Commonwealth Press Union, 1980–; Hon. Sec., British Cttee, Internat. Press Inst., 1972–76. Chm., Industrial Sponsors, 1975–. Chm., Back Benchers' Co-ordinating Cttee, 1986–. A Pres., European Movement, 1989. *Address:* 10 Chester Close, SW13. *T:* 081–789 3490. *Clubs:* Garrick, Roehampton.
See also M. J. Symonds.

ARGENT, Eric William, FCA; FCBSI; Director, Nationwide Anglia Building Society, 1987–88, retired (Joint General Manager, 1978–81, Director, 1978–87, Anglia Building Society); *b* 5 Sept. 1923; *s* of Eric George Argent and Florence Mary Argent; *m* 1949, Pauline Grant; two *d.* *Educ:* Chiswick Grammar Sch. FCA 1951. War Service, 1942–47. With City Chartered Accountants, 1940–42 and 1947–51; with London Banking House, Antony Gibbs & Sons Ltd, 1951–59; Hastings & Thanet Building Society, 1959–78: Sec. and Chief Accountant, 1962; Dep. Gen. Man., 1964; Gen. Man. and Sec., 1966; Dir and Gen. Man., 1976. *Recreations:* reading, gardening, travel. *Address:* Fairmount, 104 Longcliffe Road, Grantham, Lincs NG31 8DY. *T:* Grantham (0476) 591433.

ARGENT, Malcolm, CBE 1985; Secretary, since 1984, and Director, since 1989, British Telecommunications plc; *b* 14 Aug. 1935; *s* of Leonard James and Winifred Hilda Argent; *m* 1st, 1961, Mary Patricia Addis Stimson (marr. diss. 1983); one *s* one *d*; 2nd, 1986, Thelma Hazel Eddleston. *Educ:* Palmer's Sch., Grays, Essex. General Post Office, London Telecommunications Region: Exec. Officer, 1953–62; Higher Exec. Officer, 1962–66; Principal, PO Headquarters, 1966–70; Private Sec., Man. Dir, Telecommunications, 1970–74; Personnel Controller, External Telecommun. Exec., 1974–75; Dir, Chairman's Office, PO Central Headquarters, 1975–77; Dir, Eastern Telecommun. Region, 1977; Secretary: of the Post Office, 1978–81; of British Telecommunications Corp., 1981–; Trustee, British Telecom Staff Superannuation Fund, 1981–. Dir, McCaw Cellular Communications Inc., 1989–. Freeman, City of London, 1987. CBIM 1991 (FBIM 1980). *Recreation:* tennis. *Address:* 4 Huskards, Fryerning, Ingatestone, Essex CM4 0HR.

ARGENTINA, Bishop of, since 1990; **Rt. Rev. David Leake;** Presiding Bishop, Province of the Anglican Church of the Southern Cone of America, 1982–89; *b* 26 June 1935; *s* of Rev. Canon William Alfred Leake and Dorothy Violet Leake; *m* 1961, Rachel Yarham; two *s* one *d.* *Educ:* St Alban's Coll., Buenos Aires; London Coll. of Divinity. ALCD 1959 (LTh). Deacon 1959, priest 1960; Assistant Bishop: Paraguay and N Argentina, 1969–73; N Argentina, 1973–79; Bishop of Northern Argentina, 1979–89. *Recreations:* observing people's behaviour at airports, railway stations and bus terminals. *Address:* Casilla Correo 4293, 1000 Correo Central, Buenos Aires, Argentina.

ARGOV, Shlomo; Ambassador of Israel to the Court of St James's, 1979–82; *b* 1929; *m* Hava Argov; one *s* two *d.* *Educ:* Georgetown Univ., USA (BSc Pol. Science); London School of Economics (Internat. Relns) (MSc Econ; Hon. Fellow, 1983). Israel Defence Force, 1947–50; Prime Minister's Office, Jerusalem, 1955–59; Consul General of Israel, Lagos, 1959–60; Counsellor, Accra, 1960–61; Consul, Consulate General of Israel, New York, 1961–64; Dep. Director, United States Div., Min. of Foreign Affairs, Jerusalem, 1965–68; Minister, Embassy of Israel, Washington, 1968–71; Ambassador of Israel, Mexico, 1971–74; Asst Dir Gen. (Dir of Israel Information Services), Min. of Foreign Affairs, Jerusalem, 1974–77; Ambassador of Israel, Netherlands, 1977–79. *Address:* c/o Ministry of Foreign Affairs, Jerusalem, Israel.

ARGYLE, His Honour Major Michael Victor, MC 1945; QC 1961; a Circuit Judge (formerly an Additional Judge of the Central Criminal Court), 1970–88; *b* 31 Aug. 1915; *e s* of late Harold Victor Argyle and Elsie Marion, Repton, Derbyshire; *m* 1951, Ann Norah, *d* of late Charles Newton and M. Newton, later Mrs Jobson; three *d.* *Educ:* Shardlow Hall, Derbyshire; Westminster Sch.; Trinity Coll., Cambridge (MA). Served War of 1939–45: with 7th QO Hussars in India, ME and Italy (immediate MC), 1939–47. Called to Bar, Lincoln's Inn, 1938, Bencher, 1967, Treasurer, 1984; resumed practice at Bar, 1947 (Midland Circuit); Recorder of Northampton, 1962–65, of Birmingham, 1965–70; Dep. Chm., Holland QS, 1965–71; Lay Judge, Arches Court, Province of Canterbury, 1968–. General Elections, contested (C) Belper, 1950, and Loughborough, 1955. Master, Worshipful Co. of Makers of Playing Cards, 1984–85. *Publications:* (ed) Phipson on Evidence, 10th edn. *Recreations:* chess, boxing. *Address:* The Red House, Fiskerton, near Southwell, Notts NG25 0UL. *Clubs:* Carlton, Kennel.

ARGYLL, 12th Duke of, *cr* 1701 (Scotland), 1892 (UK); **Ian Campbell;** DL; Marquess of Lorne and Kintyre; Earl of Campbell and Cowal; Viscount Lochow and Glenyla; Baron Inveraray, Mull, Morvern, and Tiry, 1701; Baron Campbell, 1445; Earl of Argyll, 1457; Baron Lorne, 1470; Baron Kintyre, 1633 (Scotland); Baron Sundridge, 1766; Baron Hamilton of Hameldon, 1776; Bt 1627; 36th Baron and 46th Knight of Lochow; Celtic title, Mac Cailein Mhor, Chief of Clan Campbell (from Sir Colin Campbell, knighted 1280); Hereditary Master of the Royal Household, Scotland; Hereditary High Sheriff of the County of Argyll; Admiral of the Western Coast and Isles; Keeper of the Great Seal of Scotland and of the Castles of Dunstaffnage, Dunoon, and Carrick and Tarbert; *b* 28 Aug. 1937; *e s* of 11th Duke of Argyll, TD, and Louise (*d* 1970), *o d* of Henry Clews; *S* father, 1973; *m* 1964, Iona Mary, *d* of Captain Sir Ivar Colquhoun, *qv*; one *s* one *d*. *Educ:* Le Rosey, Switzerland; Glenalmond; McGill Univ., Montreal. Captain (retd) Argyll and Sutherland Highlanders. Member, Queen's Body Guard for Scotland, the Royal Company of Archers, 1960–. Chm., Beinn Bhuidhe Holdings, 1977–; Director: S. Campbell & Son, 1982–; Aberlour Glenlivet Distillery Co.; White Heather Distillers; Muir, MacKenzie & Co., 1973–; Visual Sound Programmes, 1970–. President: Royal Caledonian Schs; Argyll Scouts Assoc.; Highland Soc. of London, 1985–90. Hon. Col, Argyll and Sutherland Highlanders Bn (ACF). DL Argyll and Bute, 1987. KStJ 1975. *Heir: s* Marquess of Lorne, *qv*. *Address:* Inveraray Castle, Inveraray, Argyll PA32 8XF. *T:* Inveraray (0499) 2275, *Fax:* (0499) 2421. *Clubs:* White's; New (Edinburgh).

ARGYLL AND THE ISLES, Bishop of, since 1977; **Most Rev. George Kennedy Buchanan Henderson,** MBE 1974; Primus of the Episcopal Church in Scotland, since 1990; *b* 5 Dec. 1921; *s* of George Buchanan Henderson and Anna Kennedy Butters; *m* 1950, Isobel Fergusson Bowman. *Educ:* Oban High School; University of Durham (BA, LTh). Assistant Curate, Christ Church, Glasgow, 1943–48; Priest in Charge, St Bride's, Nether Lochaber, 1948–50; Chaplain to Bishop of Argyll and The Isles, 1948–50; Rector, St Andrew's, Fort William, 1950–77; Canon, St John's Cathedral, Oban, 1960; Synod Clerk, 1964–73; Dean of Argyll and The Isles, 1973–77. JP of Inverness-shire, 1963–; Hon. Sheriff, 1971–; Provost of Fort William, 1962–75; Hon. Burgess of Fort William, 1973. *Address:* Benvoulin, Achnalea, Onich, by Fort William PH33 6SA. *T:* Onich (08553) 240.

ARGYLL AND THE ISLES, Bishop of, (RC), since 1991; **Rt. Rev. Roderick Wright;** *b* 28 June 1940. *Educ:* St Mary's Coll., Blairs, Grampian; St Peter's Coll., Cardross, Strathclyde. Ordained 1964; Assistant Priest: St Laurence's, Drumchapel, 1964–66; St Jude's, Barlanark, 1966–69; Procurator, Blairs Coll., Grampian, 1969–74; Assistant Priest: Dunoon, Argyll, 1974–76; Fort William, 1976–80; Parish priest: Ardkenneth, South Uist, 1980–87; St Anne's Corpach and St John the Evangelist, Caol, 1987–91. Mem., Cttee on local and regl ecumenism of Action of Churches Together in Scotland. *Address:* Bishop's House, Esplanade, Oban, Argyll PA34 5AB.

ARGYLL AND THE ISLES, Dean of; *see* Macleay, Very Rev. J. H. J.

ARGYLL AND THE ISLES, Provosts in; *see* McCubbin, Very Rev. D.; Maclean, Very Rev. A. M.

ARGYRIS, Prof. John, DScEng, DE Munich; FRS 1986; FEng 1990; FRAeS 1955; Professor of Aeronautical Structures in the University of London, at Imperial College of Science and Technology, 1955–75, Visiting Professor 1975–78, now Emeritus Professor; Director, Institute for Computer Applications, Stuttgart, since 1984; *b* 19 Aug. 1916; *s* of Nicolas and Lucie Argyris; *m* 1953, Inga-Lisa (*née* Johansson); one *s*. *Educ:* 3rd Gymnasium, Athens; Technical Universities, Athens, Munich and Zurich. With J. Gollnow u. Son, Stettin, Research in Structures, 1937–39; Royal Aeronautical Soc., Research and Technical Officer, 1943–49; Univ. of London, Imperial Coll. of Science and Technology, Dept of Aeronautics: Senior Lecturer, 1949; Reader in Theory of Aeronautical Structures, 1950; Hon. FIC 1985. Dir, Inst. for Statics and Dynamics, Stuttgart, 1959–84. Principal Editor, Jl of Computer Methods in Applied Mechanics and Engineering, 1972–. Hon. Professor: Northwestern Polytech. Univ., Xian, China, 1980; Tech. Univ. of Beijing, 1983; Qinghua Univ., Beijing, 1984. Corresp. Mem., Acad. of Scis, Athens, 1973; Life Mem., ASME, 1981; Hon. Life Mem., NY Acad. of Scis, 1983; Foreign Associate, US Nat. Acad. of Engrg, 1986. FAIAA 1983; FAAAS 1985; Hon. Fellow, Groupe pour l'Avancement des Méthodes Numériques de l'Ingénieur, Paris, 1974; Hon. FCGI 1976; Hon. Fellow, Aeronautical Soc. of India, 1985; Hon. FRAeS 1986. Hon. Dott Ing Genoa, 1970; Hon. dr.tech Trondheim, 1972; Hon. Dr Ing Tech. Univ. of Hanover, 1983; Hon. Tek. Dr Univ. Linköping, 1986; Hon. DSc (Maths), Athens Univ., 1989. Silver Medal, RAeS, 1971; Von Kármán Medal, ASCE, 1975; Copernicus Medal, Polish Acad. of Scis, 1979; Timoshenko Medal, ASME, 1981; I. B. Laskowitz Award with Gold Medal in Aerospace Engrg, NY Acad. of Scis, 1982; World Prize in Culture, and election as Personality of the Year 1984, Centro Studi e Ricerce delle Nazione, Acad. Italia, 1983; Royal Medal, Royal Soc., 1985; Daidalus Gold Medal, Sir George Cayley Inst., 1988. Gold Medal, Land Baden-Württemberg, 1980; Grand Cross of Merit, FRG, 1985; Grand Cross of Merit with Star, FRG, 1989. *Publications:* Handbook of Aeronautics, Vol. I, 1952: Energy Theorems and Structural Analysis, 1960; Modern Fuselage Analysis and the Elastic Aircraft, 1963; Recent Advances in Matrix Methods of Structural Analysis, 1964; Introduction into the Finite Element Method, vols I, II and III, 1986–88; Dynamics of Structures, 1991; An overview of aerolasticity, 1992; The Dynamics of Chaos, 1992; articles and publications in Ingenieur Archiv, Reports and Memoranda of Aeronautical Research Council, Journal of Royal Aeronautical Society and Aircraft Engineering, CMAME, Jl of AIAA, etc; over 350 scientific publications. *Recreations:* reading, music, hiking, archæology. *Address:* Institute for Computer Applications, 27 Pfaffenwaldring, D-7000 Stuttgart 80, Federal Republic of Germany. *T:* 010–49711 6853594; c/o Department of Aeronautics, Imperial College, Prince Consort Road, SW7. *T:* 071–589 5111. *Club:* English-Speaking Union.

ARIAS-SALGADO Y MONTALVO, Fernando; Consul-General for Spain in Zürich, since 1985; Barrister-at-Law; *b* 3 May 1938; *s* of Gabriel Arias-Salgado y Cubas and Maria Montalvo Gutierrez; *m* 1969, Maria Isabel Garrigues Lopez-Chicheri; one *s* one *d*. *Educ:* Univ. of Madrid. Mem., Illustrious Coll. of Lawyers of Madrid. Entered Diplomatic Sch., 1963; Sec., Permanent Rep. of Spain to UN, 1966; Advr, UN Security Council, 1968–69; Asst Dir Gen., Promotion of Research, 1971, Asst Dir Gen., Internat. Co-operation, 1972, Min. of Educn and Science; Legal Advr (internat. matters), Legal Dept, Min. of Foreign Affairs, 1973; Counsellor, Spanish Delegn to Internat. Court of Justice, 1975; Tech. Sec. Gen., Min. of Foreign Affairs, 1976; Dir Gen., Radiotelevisión Española, 1977; Ambassador to the Court of St James's, 1981–83; Dir, Internat. Legal Dept, Min. of Foreign Affairs, 1983–85. Comendador: Orden de Isabel la Católica; Orden del Merito Civil; Orden de San Raimundo de Peñafort; Caballero, Orden de Carlos III. *Address:* Stampfenbachstrasse 85, CH-8035 Zürich, Switzerland; Roncal 7, Madrid 2, Spain.

ARIAS SÁNCHEZ, Oscar, PhD; President of Costa Rica, 1986–90; *b* 13 Sept. 1941; *m* Margarita; one *s* one *d*. *Educ:* Univ. of Costa Rica; LSE; Univ. of Essex. Prof., Sch. of Political Sciences, Univ. of Costa Rica, 1969–72; Financial Adviser to President, 1970–72; Minister of Nat. Planning and Economic Policy, 1972–77; Sec., 1975, Gen. Sec., 1979–86, Liberación Nacional Party; Congressman, 1978–82. Member: Board of Central Bank, 1972–77 (Vice-Pres., 1970–72); Commn, Heredia's Nat. Univ., 1972–75; Board of Tech. Inst., 1974–77; Rector's Nat. Council, 1974–77; Board, Internat. Univ. Exchange Fund, Geneva, 1976; formulated Central American Peace Agreement, 1986–87. Mem. Bd of Dirs, WWF. Hon. PhD: Harvard, 1988; Essex, 1988. Nobel Peace Prize, 1987; Prince of Asturias Prize, 1988; Nat. Audubon Soc. Prize, 1988. *Publications:* Pressure Groups in Costa Rica, 1970; Who Governs Costa Rica?, 1976; Latin American Democracy, Independence and Society, 1977; Roads for Costa Rica's Development, 1977; New Ways for Costa Rican Development, 1980. *Address:* c/o Office of the President, San José, Costa Rica.

ARIE, Prof. Thomas Harry David, FRCPsych, FRCP, FFCM; Foundation Professor of Health Care of the Elderly, University of Nottingham, since 1977, and Hon. Consultant Psychiatrist, Nottingham Health Authority; *b* 9 Aug. 1933; *s* of late Dr O. M. Arie and Hedy (*née* Glaser); *m* 1963, Eleanor, MRCP, *yr d* of Sir Robert Aitken, *qv*; two *d* one *s*. *Educ:* Reading Sch.; Balliol Coll., Oxford (Open Exhibnr in Classics; 1st cl. Hons, Classical Mods); MA, BM 1960; DPM. Training, Radcliffe Infirmary, Oxford, and Maudsley and London Hosps; Consultant Psychiatrist, Goodmayes Hosp., 1969–77; Sen. Lectr in Social Medicine, London Hosp. Med. Coll.; Hon. Sen. Lectr in Psychiatry, UCH Med. Sch. Royal College of Psychiatrists: Vice-Pres., 1984–86; Chm., Specialist Section on Psychiatry of Old Age, 1981–86; Jt Cttee on Higher Psychiatric Training, 1978–84; Royal College of Physicians: Geriatrics Cttee, 1984–90; Examining Bd for Dipl. in Geriatric Medicine. Member: Central Council for Educn and Trng in Social Work, 1975–81; Standing Med. Adv. Cttee, DHSS, 1980–84; Cttee on Review of Medicines, 1981–; Res. Adv. Council, Nat. Inst. for Social Work, 1982–90; Adv. Council, Centre for Policy on Ageing, 1985–89; Med. Adv. Cttee to Registrar General, 1990–. Fotheringham Lectr, Univ. of Toronto, 1979; Vis. Prof., NZ Geriatrics Soc., 1980; Dozor Vis. Prof., Univ. of the Negev, Israel, 1988; Fröhlich Vis. Prof., UCLA, 1991. Chm., Geriatric Psych. Section, World Psych. Assoc., 1989–. *Publications:* (ed) Health Care of the Elderly, 1981; (ed) Recent Advances in Psychogeriatrics, 1985; articles in med. jls and chapters in other people's books. *Address:* Department of Health Care of the Elderly, Queen's Medical Centre, Nottingham NG7 2UH. *T:* Nottingham (0602) 709408.

ARIFIN, Dr Sjahabuddin; Adviser to the Minister of Foreign Affairs, Indonesia, since 1986; *b* 3 March 1928; *m* Siti Asiah; three *s*. *Educ:* Rechts- und Wirtschaftswissenschaftl. Fakultät, Universität Bern, Switzerland (Dr of Econs). Indonesian Embassy, Bern, Switzerland, 1951–57; Econ. Expert, Dept of Foreign Affairs, Jakarta, 1957–62; Lectr, Sch. of Econs, Pajajaran Univ., Bandung, 1960–62; Counsellor, Indonesian Embassy, Washington, USA, 1962–63; Ambassador to Iran, 1963–67; Dept of Foreign Affairs, Jakarta: Head of Directorate, Econ. Multilateral Co-operation, 1967–71; Dir Gen., Foreign Econ., Social and Cultural Relations, 1971–77; Sec. Gen., 1977–81; Ambassador to UK, 1981–85. *Recreations:* reading, walking, golf. *Address:* 10L Jalan Susukan, Kemang, Jakarta 12730, Indonesia. *T:* (021) 794398. *Club:* Jakarta Golf (Indonesia).

ARIS, John Bernard Benedict, TD 1967; Director, IMPACT Programme, since 1990; *b* 6 June 1934; *s* of John (Jack) Woodbridge Aris and Joyce Mary (*née* Williams). *Educ:* Eton (King's Schol.); Magdalen Coll., Oxford (MA). FBCS; FInstD; FRSA. LEO Computers, 1958–63; English Electric Computers, 1963–69; ICL, 1969–75; Imperial Group, 1975–85 (Man., Gp Management Services, 1982–85); Dir, NCC, 1985–90. Non-exec. Dir, NCC, 1981–85; Chairman: FOCUS Private Sector Users Cttee (DTI), 1984–85; Alvey IT User Panel, 1985–88; Mem., IT 86 Cttee, 1986. Founder Freeman, Co. of Information Technologists, 1987. *Recreations:* travel, music, art, scuba diving, gastronomy.

ARKELL, John Hardy, MA; Headmaster, Gresham's School, Holt, since 1991; *b* 10 July 1939; *s* of Hardy Arkell and Vivienne (*née* Le Sueur); *m* 1963, Jean Harding; two *s* one *d*. *Educ:* Stowe Sch.; Selwyn Coll., Cambridge (BA Hons English Tripos; MA). National Service, HM Submarines, 1958–60 (Sub Lieut). Asst Master, Abingdon Sch., 1963–64; Head of VI form English, Framlingham Coll., 1964–70; Fettes College, 1970–83: Head of English Dept, 1972–73 and 1976–78; Founder Headmaster, Fettes Jun. Sch., 1973–79; Housemaster, Glencorse House, 1979–83; Headmaster, Wrekin Coll., 1983–91. Chm., ISIS, Central England, 1989–91. *Recreations:* tennis, sailing, motor cars, drama. *Address:* Lockhart House, Gresham's School, Holt, Norfolk NR25 6DZ. *T:* Holt (0263) 713739.

ARKELL, John Heward, CBE 1961; TD; MA; CBIM, FIPM; Director of Administration, BBC, 1960–70; *b* 20 May 1909; *s* of Rev. H. H. Arkell, MA, and Gertrude Mary Arkell; *m* 1st, 1940, Helen Birgit Huitfeldt; two *s* one *d*; 2nd, 1956, Meta Bachke Grundtvig (marr. diss.); one *s*. *Educ:* Dragon Sch.; Radley Coll.; Christ Church, Oxford (MA). Sir Max Michaelis (Investment) Trust, 1931–37. Asst Sec., CPRE, 1937–39, Mem. of Exec. Cttee, 1945–75, Vice-Chm., 1967–74, Vice-Pres., 1975–. Commissioned Territorial Officer, 1st Bn Queen's Westminsters, KRRC, 1939; Instructor, then Chief Instructor, Army Infantry Signalling Sch., 1940; served in BLA as special infantry signalling liaison officer, 1944; demobilised 1945, Major. Personnel Manager, J. Lyons, 1945–49; BBC: Controller, Staff Admin, 1949–58; Dir, Staff Admin, 1958–60. Director: The Boots Co. Ltd, 1970–79; UK Provident Instn, 1971–80; Sen. Associate, Kramer Internat. Ltd, 1980–86. Chm., Air Transport and Travel ITB, 1970–80. Lay Mem., Nat. Industrial Relations Ct, 1971–74. Lectr on indust. subjects; occasional indep. management consultancies include P&O and Coates Group of Cos (Dir, 1970–76). Founder, Exec. Pres. then Jt Pres., and former Gen. Hon. Sec., then Chm., Christ Church (Oxford) United Clubs (Community Centre, SE London), 1932–. Chm. Council, British Institute of Management, 1972–74 (Fellow, 1964–, now Companion; Vice-Chm., 1966–72; Chm. Exec. Cttee, 1966–69; Vice Pres., 1974–); Chm. BIM/CBI Educl Panel, 1971–72; Dir, BIM Foundn, 1976–81; Member Council: CBI, 1973–75; Industry for Management Educn, 1971–; Foundn for Management Educn, 1971–75; National Trust, 1971–84 (Chm., NT Council's Adv. Cttee on the Trust, its members and public, 1982–83); Adv. Council, Business Graduates Assoc., 1973–85; Action Resources Centre, 1975–86 (special advr, 1986–90). Mem., later Dir, Christian Frontier Council, 1955–65; Chm., Cttee of British Council of Churches responsible for report on further educn of young people, 1960–61; Member: Finance Cttee, C of E Bd of Finance, 1960–68; CS Deptl Cttee to consider application of Fulton Report to Civil Service, 1968–70; Final Selection Bd, CS Commn, 1978–81. Trustee, Visnews, 1960–69; Vis. Fellow, Henley Management Coll. (formerly Administrative Staff Coll.), 1971–; Governor, Radley Coll., 1965–70; Chm., Radley Coll. War Meml Cttee, 1963–88. Chm., Ringstead Bay Protection Soc., 1983–. FRSA. *Publications:* composer of light music (The Leander Waltz, Bless Them Lord, Seringa, Candlelight and others); contrib. to jls on management and indust. subjects. *Recreations:* walking, swimming, music. *Address:* Pinnocks, Fawley, near Henley-on-Thames, Oxon RG9 6JH. *T:* Henley (0491) 573017; Glen Cottage, Ringstead Bay, Dorchester, Dorset. *T:* Warmwell (0305) 852686. *Clubs:* Savile, Lansdowne; Leander.

ARKFELD, Most Rev. Leo, CBE (Hon.) 1976; Archbishop of Madang, (RC), 1976–87; *b* 4 Feb. 1912; *s* of George Arkfeld and Mary Siemer. *Educ:* St Mary's Seminary, Techny, Ill., USA (BA). Bishop of Wewak, Papua New Guinea, 1948–76; Administrator Apostolic of Wewak, 1976. *Address:* Box 750, Madang, Papua New Guinea. *T:* 82–2707.

ARLOTT, (Leslie Thomas) John, OBE 1970; wine and general writer, The Guardian; topographer; broadcaster; *b* Basingstoke, 25 Feb. 1914; *s* of late William John and Nellie Jenvey Arlott; *m* 1st, Dawn Rees; one *s* (and one *s* decd); 2nd, Valerie France (*d* 1976); one *s* (one *d* decd); 3rd, 1977, Patricia Hoare. *Educ:* Queen Mary's Sch., Basingstoke. Clerk in Mental Hospital, 1930–34; Police (Detective, eventually Sergeant), 1934–45; Producer, BBC, 1945–50; General Instructor, BBC Staff Training School, 1951–53. Contested (L) Epping Division, Gen. Election, 1955 and 1959. President: Cricketers' Assoc., 1968–; Hampshire Schools Cricket Assoc., 1966–80. Hon. MA Southampton, 1973. Sports Journalist of 1979 (British Press Award); Sports Personality of 1980 (Soc. of Authors' Pye Radio Award); Sports Presenter of the Year, 1980 (TV and Radio Industries Club Award). DUniv. Open, 1981. *Publications:* (with G. R. Hamilton) Landmarks, 1943; Of Period and Place (poems), 1944; Clausentum (poems), 1945; First Time In America (anthology), 1949; Concerning Cricket, 1949; How to Watch Cricket, 1949, new edn, 1983; Maurice Tate, 1951; Concerning Soccer, 1952; (ed) Cricket (Pleasures of Life series), 1953; The Picture of Cricket, 1955; English Cheeses of the South and West, 1956; Jubilee History of Cricket, 1965; Vintage Summer, 1967; (with Sir Neville Cardus) The Noblest Game, 1969; Fred: portrait of a fast bowler, 1971; The Ashes, 1972; Island Camera: the Isles of Scilly in the photography of the Gibson family, 1973, repr. 1983; The Snuff Shop, 1974; (ed) The Oxford Companion to Sports and Games, 1975; (with Christopher Fielden) Burgundy, Vines and Wines, 1976; Krug: House of Champagne, 1977; (with Patrick Eagar) An Eye for Cricket, 1979; Jack Hobbs: a profile of The Master, 1981; A Word From Arlott (ed David Rayvern Allen), 1983; (ed) Wine, 1984; Arlott on Cricket, 1984; (with Patrick Eagar) Botham, 1985; (with Mike Brearley) Arlott in Conversation with Mike Brearley, 1986; John Arlott's 100 Greatest Batsmen, 1986; Arlott on Wine, 1986; The Essential John Arlott, 1989; Basingstoke Boy, 1990. *Recreations:* watching cricket, drinking wine, talking, sleeping, collecting aquatints, engraved glass, and wine artefacts. *Address:* c/o The Guardian, 119 Farringdon Road, EC1R 3ER. *Clubs:* National Liberal, MCC (Hon. Life Mem., 1980); Master's; Forty, Somerset CCC (Hon. Life Mem., 1982), Hampshire CCC (Hon. Life Mem., 1984).

ARMAGH, Archbishop of, and Primate of All Ireland, since 1986; **Most Rev. Robert Henry Alexander Eames;** *b* 27 April 1937; *s* of William Edward and Mary Eleanor Thompson Eames; *m* 1966 Ann Christine Daly; two *s*. *Educ:* Belfast Royal Acad.; Methodist Coll., Belfast; Queen's Univ., Belfast (LLB (hons), PhD); Trinity Coll., Dublin. Research Scholar and Tutor, Faculty of Laws, QUB, 1960–63; Curate Assistant, Bangor Parish Church, 1963–66; Rector of St Dorothea's, Belfast, 1966–74; Examining Chaplain to Bishop of Down, 1973; Rector of St Mark's, Dundela, 1974–75; Bishop of Derry and Raphoe, 1975–80; Bishop of Down and Dromore, 1980–86. Select Preacher, Oxford Univ., 1987. Irish Rep., 1984, Mem. Standing Cttee, 1985, ACC; Chairman: Commn on Communion and Women in the Episcopate, 1988–; Commn on Inter-Anglican Relations, 1988–. Governor, Church Army, 1985–. Hon. LLD QUB, 1989. *Publications:* A Form of Worship for Teenagers, 1965; The Quiet Revolution—Irish Disestablishment, 1970; Through Suffering, 1973; Thinking through Lent, 1978; Through Lent, 1984; contribs to New Divinity, Irish Legal Quarterly, Criminal Law Review. The Furrow. *Address:* The See House, Cathedral Close, Armagh, Co. Armagh BT61 7EE.

ARMAGH, Archbishop of, (RC), and Primate of All Ireland, since 1990; **His Eminence Cardinal Cahal Brendan Daly;** *b* 1917. *Educ:* St Malachy's, Belfast; Queen's Univ., Belfast (BA Hons, Classics, MA); St Patrick's, Maynooth (DD); Institut Catholique, Paris (LPh). Ordained, 1941. Lecturer in Scholastic Philosophy, Queen's Univ., Belfast, 1946–62; Reader, 1962–67; consecrated Bishop, 1967; Bishop of Ardagh and Clonmacnois, 1967–82; Bishop of Down and Connor, 1982–90. Cardinal, 1991. *Publications:* Morals, Law and Life, 1962; Natural Law Morality Today, 1965; Violence in Ireland and Christian Conscience, 1973; Theologians and the Magisterium, 1977; Peace the Work of Justice, 1979; chapters in: Prospect for Metaphysics, 1961; Intellect and Hope, 1968; New Essays in Religious Language, 1969; Understanding the Eucharist, 1969; The Price of Peace, 1991. *Address:* Ara Coeli, Armagh, Ireland.

ARMAGH, Dean of; *see* Cassidy, Very Rev. H.

ARME, Prof. Christopher, PhD, DSc; CBiol, FIBiol; Professor of Zoology, University of Keele, since 1979; *b* 10 Aug. 1939; *s* of Cyril Boddington and Monica Henrietta Arme; *m* 1962, Mary Hancock; three *s*. *Educ:* Heanor Grammar Sch.; Univ. of Leeds (BSc 1961; PhD 1964); Univ. of Keele (DSc 1985). FIBiol 1980; CBiol 1980. SRC/NATO Res. Fellow, Univ. of Leeds, 1964–66; Res. Associate, Rice Univ., Texas, 1966–68; Lectr, later Reader, QUB, 1968–76; Head of Biology Gp, N Staffs Polytechnic, 1976–79; Head, Dept of Biol Scis, Univ. of Keele, 1981–88. British Society for Parasitology: Hon. Gen. Sec., 1980–83; Silver Jubilee Lectr, 1987; Vice Pres., 1988–90; Pres., 1990–Apr. 1992. Chm., Heads of Zool. Depts of Univs Gp, 1981–82; Hon. Treasurer and Chm., Finance Cttee, Inst. of Biol., 1986–91; Mem., Biol Scis Cttee, and Chm., Animal Scis and Psychol. Sub-Cttee, SERC, 1989–Sept. 1992. Hon. Mem., Czechoslovakian Parasitological Soc., 1989. Jt Editor, Parasitology, 1987–. *Publications:* (ed jtly) Biology of the Eucestoda, Vols I and II, 1983; (ed) Molecular Transfer across Parasite Membranes, 1988; contribs to parasitological jls. *Address:* Department of Biological Sciences, University of Keele, Keele, Staffs ST5 5BG. *T:* Newcastle (Staffs) (0782) 621111.

ARMFIELD, Diana Maxwell, (Mrs Bernard Dunstan), RA 1991 (ARA 1989); RWS 1983 (ARWS 1977); RWA; NEAC; painter, since 1965; *b* 11 June 1920; *d* of Joseph Harold Armfield and Gertrude Mary Uttley; *m* 1949, Bernard Dunstan, *qv*; three *s*. *Educ:* Bedales; Bournemouth Art Sch.; Slade Sch.; Central School of Arts and Crafts. MCSD. Textile/wallpaper designer, 1949–65; work in Fest. of Britain, 1951, and Permanent Collection, V&A Mus. Regular one woman exhibns, Browse & Darby (London), 1979–; Artist in Residence: Perth, WA, 1985; Jackson, Wyoming, 1989. Work in Permanent Collections: Govt picture collection, RWA; Yale Center for British Art; Nat. Trust; Contemporary Art Soc. for Wales; RWS collection, BM. Commissions: Reuters, Nat. Trust, 1989; Prince of Wales, 1989. *Recreations:* music, gardening, travel. *Address:* 10 High Park Road, Kew, Richmond, Surrey TW9 4BH; Llwynhir, Parc, Bala, Gwynedd, North Wales LL23 7YU. *Club:* Arts.

ARMIDALE, Bishop of, since 1976; **Rt. Rev. Peter Chiswell;** *b* 18 Feb. 1934; *s* of Ernest and Florence Ruth Chiswell; *m* 1960, Betty Marie Craik; two *s* one *d*. *Educ:* Univ. of New South Wales (BE); Moore Theological College (BD London, Th. Schol.). Vicar of Bingara, 1961–68; Vicar of Gunnedah, 1968–76; Archdeacon of Tamworth, 1971–76. *Address:* Bishopscourt, Armidale, NSW 2350, Australia. *T:* 067–724555.

ARMITAGE, Edward, CB 1974; Comptroller-General, Patent Office and Industrial Property and Copyright Department, Department of Trade (formerly Trade and Industry), 1969–77; *b* 16 July 1917; *s* of Harry and Florence Armitage; *m* 1940, Marjorie Pope; one *s* two *d*. *Educ:* Huddersfield Coll.; St Catharine's Coll., Cambridge. Patent Office, BoT: Asst Examr 1939; Examr 1944; Sen. Examr 1949; Principal Examr 1960; Suptg Examr 1962; Asst Comptroller 1966. Governor, Centre d'Etudes Internationales de la Propriété Industrielle, Strasbourg, 1975–; Mem. Council, Common Law Inst. of Intellectual Property, 1981–90. *Recreations:* tennis, bowls, bridge, gardening. *Address:* Lynwood, Lascot Hill, Wedmore, Somerset BS28 4AE. *T:* Wedmore (0934) 712079.
See also Peter Armitage.

ARMITAGE, Maj.-Gen. Geoffrey Thomas Alexander, CBE 1968 (MBE 1945); *b* 5 July 1917; *s* of late Lt-Col H. G. P. Armitage and late Mary Madeline (*née* Drought); *m* 1949, Monica Wall Kent (*widow, née* Poat); one *s* one step *d*. *Educ:* Haileybury Coll.; RMA, Woolwich (Sword of Honour). Commissioned Royal Artillery, 1937. Served War of 1939–45 (despatches, MBE), BEF, Middle East, Italy, NW Europe. Transferred to Royal Dragoons (1st Dragoons), 1951, comd 1956–59; Instructor (GSO1), IDC, 1959–60; Col GS, War Office, 1960–62; Comdt RAC Centre, 1962–65; Chief of Staff, HQ1 (BR) Corps, 1966–68; Dir, Royal Armoured Corps, 1968–70; GOC Northumbrian Dist, 1970–72; retd 1973. Dir, CLA Game Fair, 1974–80. *Recreations:* writing, some field sports. *Address:* Clyffe, Tincleton, near Dorchester, Dorset DT2 8QR. *Clubs:* Army and Navy, Kennel.

ARMITAGE, Henry St John Basil, CBE 1978 (OBE 1968); HM Diplomatic Service, retired; Middle East consultant; Honorary Secretary to British/Saudi Arabian Parliamentary Group; *b* 5 May 1924; *s* of Henry John Armitage and late Amelia Eleanor Armitage; *m* 1956, Jennifer Gerda Bruford, *d* of Prof. W. H. Bruford, FBA; one *s* one *d*. *Educ:* St Bede's and Bradford Grammar Schs; Lincoln Christ's Hosp.; Trinity Coll., Cambridge. Served Army, 1943–49; Arab Legion, 1946; British Mil. Mission to Saudi Arabia, 1946–49. Mil. Adviser to Saudi Arabian Minister of Defence, 1949–51; Desert Locust Control, Kenya and Aden Protectorates, 1952; in mil. service of Sultan of Muscat and Oman in Oman and Dhofar, 1952–59; Resident Manager, Gen. Geophysical Co. (Houston), Libya, 1959–60; Oil Conslt, Astor Associates, Libya, 1960–61; Business conslt, Beirut, 1962; joined HM Diplomatic Service, 1962; First Secretary (Commercial): Baghdad, 1963–67; Beirut, 1967–68; First Sec., Jedda, 1968 and 1969–74; Chargé d'Affaires: Jedda, 1969 and 1973; Abu Dhabi, 1975, 1976 and 1977; Counsellor and Consul Gen. in charge British Embassy, Dubai, 1974–78. Director: Soc. Commissionaire et Financière, Geneva, 1979–86; SCF (Equity) Ltd, 1979–89. Mem., Editl Adv. Bd, 8 Days, 1978–79. *Recreations:* reading, travel. *Address:* The Old Vicarage, East Horrington, Wells, Somerset BA5 3EA. *Club:* Travellers'.

ARMITAGE, John Vernon, PhD; Principal, College of St Hild and St Bede, Durham, since 1975; *b* 21 May 1932; *s* of Horace Armitage and Evelyn (*née* Hauton); *m* 1963, Sarah Catherine Clay; two *s*. *Educ:* Rothwell Grammar Sch., Yorks; UCL (BSc, PhD); Cuddesdon Coll., Oxford. Asst Master: Pontefract High Sch., 1956–58; Shrewsbury Sch., 1958–59; Lectr in Maths, Univ. of Durham, 1959–67; Sen. Lectr in Maths, King's Coll., London, 1967–70; Prof. of Mathematical Educn, Univ. of Nottingham, 1970–75; Special Prof., Nottingham Univ., 1976–79. Chm., Math. Instruction Sub-Cttee, Brit. Nat. Cttee for Maths, Royal Soc., 1975–78. *Publications:* A Companion to Advanced Mathematics (with H. B. Griffiths), 1969; papers on theory of numbers in various jls. *Recreations:* railways, cricket and most games inexpertly. *Address:* The Principal's House, Leazes Lane, Durham DH1 1TB. *T:* Durham (091) 3743050. *Club:* Athenæum.

ARMITAGE, Kenneth, CBE 1969; sculptor; *b* 18 July 1916; *m* 1940. Studied at Slade Sch., London, 1937–39. Served War of 1939–45 in the Army. Teacher of Sculpture, Bath Academy of Art, 1946–56. *One-man exhibitions:* Gimpel Fils, London, regularly 1952–; New York, 1954–58, the last at Paul Rosenberg & Co.; Marlborough Fine Art London, 1962, 1965; Arts Council Exhibn touring 10 English cities, 1972–73; Gall. Kasahara, Osaka, 1974, 1978 and Fuji Telecasting Gall., Tokyo, and Gal. Humanite, Nagoya; Stoke-on-Trent City Mus. and Art Gall., 1981; Sala Mendoza, Caracas, Venezuela, 1982; Taranman Gall., London, 1982; Retrospective Exhibn, Artcurial, Paris, 1985. Gregory Fellowship in sculpture, Leeds Univ., 1953–55; *Guest Artist:* Caracas, Venezuela, 1963; City of Berlin, 1967–69. *Work shown in:* Exhibn of Recent Sculpture in British Pavilion at 26th Venice Biennale, 1952; Internat. Open-Air Exhibns of sculpture in Antwerp, London, Sonsbeek, Varese, and Sydney; British Council Exhibns of sculpture since 1952, which have toured Denmark, Germany, Holland, Norway, Sweden, Switzerland, Canada, USA, and S America; New Decade Exhibn, Museum of Modern Art, New York, 1955; British Section of 4th Internat. São Paulo Biennial, Brazil, 1957; 5th Internat. Exhibn of Drawings and Engravings, Lugano, 1958 (prize-winner); British Pavilion at 29th Venice Biennale, 1958; Art since 1945, Kassel Exhibition, 1959; work in British Sculpture in the 'Sixties' exhibition, Tate Gallery, 1965; Internat. Open-air Exhibn, Hakone, Japan, 1969, 1971; 24 English Sculptors, Burlington House, 1971; Jubilee sculpture exhibn, Battersea Park, 1977; World Expo 88, Brisbane, Australia. Work represented in: Victoria and Albert Museum, Tate Gallery; Museum of Modern Art, New York; Musée D'Art Moderne, Paris; Galleria Nazionale d' Arti Moderne, Rome; Hakone Open-Air Sculpture Museum, Japan, and other galleries throughout the world. *Address:* 22a Avonmore Road, W14 8RR.

ARMITAGE, Air Chief Marshal Sir Michael (John), KCB 1983; CBE 1975; Commandant, Royal College of Defence Studies, 1988–89; *b* 25 Aug. 1930; *m* 1st, 1955 (marr. diss. 1969); three *s*; 2nd, 1970, Gretl Renate Steinig. *Educ:* Newport Grammar Sch., IW; Halton Apprentice; RAF Coll., Cranwell. psc 1965, jssc 1970, rcds 1975. Commnd 1953; flying and staff appts, incl. 28 Sqn, Hong Kong, and No 4 and No 1 Flying Trng Schools; Personal Staff Officer to Comdr 2ATAF, 1966; OC 17 Sqdn, 1967–70; Stn Comdr, RAF Luqa, Malta, 1972–74; Dir Forward Policy, Ministry of Defence (Air Force Dept), 1976–78; Dep. Comdr, RAF Germany, 1978–80; Senior RAF Mem., RCDS, 1980–81; Dir of Service Intelligence, 1982; Dep. Chief of Defence Staff (Intelligence), 1983–84; Chief of Defence Intelligence, 1985–86; Air Mem. for Supply and Orgn, Air Force Dept, MoD, 1986–87. Mem. Council, RUSI, 1986. Lectures on air power, defence and internat. affairs. *Publications:* (jtly) Air Power in the Nuclear Age, 1982; Unmanned Aircraft, 1988; contrib. prof. jls. *Recreations:* military history, shooting, reading, writing. *Address:* c/o Lloyds Bank, Cox & King's Branch, 7 Pall Mall, SW1. *Club:* Royal Air Force.

ARMITAGE, Prof. Peter, CBE 1984; Professor of Applied Statistics (formerly of Biomathematics), 1976–90, now Emeritus, and Fellow, St Peter's College, University of Oxford, 1976–90, now Emeritus Fellow; *b* 15 June 1924; *s* of Harry and Florence Armitage, Huddersfield; *m* 1947, Phyllis Enid Perry, London: one *s* two *d*. *Educ:* Huddersfield Coll.; Trinity Coll., Cambridge. Wrangler, 1947; MA Cambridge, 1952; PhD London, 1951; Ministry of Supply, 1943–45; National Physical Laboratory, 1945–46; Mem. Statistical Research Unit of Med. Research Council, London Sch. of Hygiene and Trop. Med., 1947–61; Prof. of Medical Statistics, Univ. of London, 1961–76. President: Biometric Soc., 1972–73; Royal Statistical Soc., 1982–84 (Hon. Sec., 1958–64); Internat. Soc. for Clinical Biostatistics, 1990–91; Mem., International Statistical Institute, 1961. (Jtly) J. Allyn Taylor Prize, John P. Roberts Res. Inst., London, Ont, 1987; Guy Medals in bronze, silver and gold, 1962, 1978, 1990. Editor, Biometrics, 1980–84. *Publications:* Sequential Medical Trials, 1960, 2nd edn 1975; Statistical Methods in Medical Research, 1971, 2nd edn (with G. Berry), 1987; papers in statistical and medical journals. *Recreation:* music. *Address:* 71 High Street, Drayton, Abingdon, Oxon OX14 4JW. *T:* Abingdon (0235) 531763.
See also Edward Armitage.

ARMITAGE, (William) Kenneth; *see* Armitage, Kenneth.

ARMOUR, Mary Nicol Neill, RSA 1958 (ARSA 1940); RSW 1956; RGI 1977 (Vice-President, 1982; Hon. President, 1983); Teacher of Still Life, Glasgow School of Art, 1952–62 (Hon. Life President, 1982); *b* 27 March 1902; *d* of William Steel; *m* 1927, William Armour, RSA, RSW, RGI (*d* 1979). *Educ:* Glasgow Sch. of Art. Has exhibited at Royal Academy, Royal Scottish Academy, Soc. of Scottish Artists, and Royal Glasgow Institute. Work in permanent collections: Glasgow Municipal Gallery; Edinburgh Corporation; Art Galleries of Aberdeen, Perth, Dundee, Newport, Paisley, Greenock and Victoria (Australia). Hon. Life Vice Pres., Paisley Inst., 1983; Hon. LLD Glasgow, 1980. *Recreations:* weaving, gardening. *Address:* 2 Gateside, Kilbarchan, Renfrewshire PA10 2LY. *T:* Kilbarchan (05057) 2873.

ARMSON, (Frederick) Simon (Arden); Chief Executive, The Samaritans, since 1990; *b* 11 Sept. 1948; *s* of late Frank Gerald Arden Armson and of Margaret Fenella Armson (*née* Newton); *m* 1975, Marion Albinia (*née* Hamilton-Russell); one *s* two *d*. *Educ:* Denstone Coll. Various administrative and managerial posts, NHS, 1970–84; Asst Gen. Sec. 1984–89, Gen. Sec. 1989, The Samaritans. *Recreations:* music, photography, cycling (cross country), walking. *Address:* Broad Oak, Hurley, Maidenhead, Berkshire SL6 5LW. *T:* Littlewick Green (0628) 824322.

ARMSON, Rev. Canon John Moss; Canon Residentiary, Rochester Cathedral, since 1989; *b* 21 Dec. 1939; *s* of Arthur Eric Armson and Edith Isobel Moss. *Educ:* Wyggeston Sch.; Selwyn Coll., Cambridge (MA); St Andrews Univ. (PhD); College of the Resurrection, Mirfield. Curate, St John, Notting Hill, 1966; Chaplain and Fellow, Downing Coll., Cambridge, 1969; Chaplain, 1973–77, Vice-Principal, 1977–82, Westcott House, Cambridge; Principal, Edinburgh Theol Coll., 1982–89. *Recreation:* gardening. *Address:* Easter Garth, King's Orchard, Rochester, Kent ME1 1SX.

ARMSON, Simon; *see* Armson, F. S. A.

ARMSTRONG, family name of **Baron Armstrong of Ilminster.**

ARMSTRONG OF ILMINSTER, Baron *cr* 1988 (Life Peer), of Ashill in the county of Somerset; **Robert Temple Armstrong,** GCB 1983 (KCB 1978; CB 1974); CVO 1975; Secretary of the Cabinet, 1979–87, and Head of the Home Civil Service, 1983–87 (Joint Head, 1981–83), retired; Chairman, Biotechnology Investments Ltd, since 1989; director of companies; *b* 30 March 1927; *o s* of Sir Thomas (Henry Wait) Armstrong, *qv*; *m* 1st, 1953, Serena Mary Benedicta (marr. diss. 1985), *er d* of Sir Roger Chance, 3rd Bt, MC; two *d*; 2nd, 1985, Mary Patricia, *d* of late C. C. Carlow. *Educ:* Dragon Sch., Oxford; Eton; Christ Church, Oxford (Hon. Student 1985). Asst Principal, Treasury, 1950–55; Private Secretary to: Rt Hon. Reginald Maudling, MP (when Economic Sec. to Treasury), 1953–54; Rt Hon. R. A. Butler, CH, MP (when Chancellor of the Exchequer), 1954–55; Principal, Treasury, 1955–57; Sec., Radcliffe Cttee on Working of Monetary System, 1957–59; returned to Treasury as Principal, 1959–64; Sec., Armitage Cttee on Pay of Postmen, 1964; Asst Sec., Cabinet Office, 1964–66; Sec. of Kindersley Review Body on Doctors' and Dentists' Remuneration and of Franks Cttee on Pay of Higher Civil Service, 1964–66; Asst Sec., Treasury, 1967–68; Jt Prin. Private Sec. to Rt Hon. Roy Jenkins, MP (Chancellor of the Exchequer), 1968; Under Secretary (Home Finance), Treasury, 1968–70; Principal Private Sec. to Prime Minister, 1970–75; Dep. Sec., 1973; Dep. Under-Sec. of State, Home Office, 1975–77, Permt Under Sec. of State, 1977–79. Director: BAT Industries, 1988–; Bristol & West Building Soc., 1988–; Inchcape, 1988–; Lucas Industries, 1989–; N. M. Rothschild & Sons, 1988–; RTZ Corporation, 1988–; Shell Transport & Trading Co., 1988–; Mem., Supervisory Bd, Robeco Gp, 1988–. Chm., Bd of Trustees, V & A Museum, 1988–; Trustee, Leeds Castle Foundn, 1988–; Member: Governing Body, RAM, 1975– (Hon. Fellow 1985); Council of Management, Royal Philharmonic Soc., 1975–; Rhodes Trust, 1975–; Bd of Dirs, Royal Opera House, Covent Garden, 1988– (Sec., 1968–88). Fellow of Eton Coll., 1979–. Hon. Bencher, Inner Temple, 1986. *Recreation:* music. *Address:* House of Lords, SW1.

ARMSTRONG, Alan Gordon; Senior Lecturer in Economics, University of Bristol, since 1977; *b* 11 Feb. 1937; *s* of late Joseph Gordon Armstrong and of Evelyn Armstrong (*née* Aird); *m* 1963, Margaret Louise Harwood; one *s* one *d*. *Educ:* Bede Grammar Sch., Sunderland; Queens' Coll., Cambridge (MA). Economist, Reed Paper Gp, 1960–62; Res. Officer, Dept of Applied Econs, Univ. of Cambridge, 1962–69; Lectr in Econs, Univ. of Bristol, 1970–77. Part-time Mem., Monopolies and Mergers Commn, 1989–; Consultant on Economic Statistics to: UN Statistical Office, OECD, EEC, UK Central Statistical Office, DTI, NEDO, various times, 1970–. *Publications:* Input–Output Tables and Analysis, 1973; Structural Change in UK, 1974; Review of DTI Statistics, 1989; res. papers and jl articles on input–output, nat. accounts and the motor industry. *Recreations:* gardening (by necessity), badminton, cricket, church affairs. *Address:* Rock House, King's Hill, Nailsea, Bristol BS19 2AU. *T:* Bristol (0275) 853197.

ARMSTRONG, Sir Andrew (Clarence Francis), 6th Bt *cr* 1841, of Gallen Priory, King's County; CMG 1959; Permanent Secretary, Ministry of Mines and Power, Federation of Nigeria, retired; *b* 1 May 1907; *s* of E. C. R. Armstrong (*d* 1923) (*g s* of 1st Bt), FSA, MRIA, Keeper of Irish Antiquities and later Bluemantle Pursuivant, Herald's Coll., and Mary Frances (*d* 1953), *d* of Sir Francis Cruise; *S* cousin, 1987; *m* 1st, 1930, Phyllis Marguerite (*d* 1930), *e d* of Lt-Col H. Waithman, DSO; 2nd, 1932, Laurel May (*d* 1988), *d* of late A. W. Stuart; one *s* (and one *s* decd). *Educ:* St Edmund's Coll., Old Hall, Ware; Christ's Coll., Cambridge; BA. Colonial Administrative Service : Western Pacific, 1929; Nigeria, 1940. *Recreation:* croquet. *Heir: s* Christopher John Edmund Stuart Armstrong, MBE, Lt-Col RCT [*b* 15 Jan. 1940; *m* 1972, Georgina Elizabeth Carey, *d* of Lt-Col W. G. Lewis; three *s* one *d*]. *Address:* 15 Ravenscroft Road, Henley-on-Thames, Oxon RG9 2DH. *T:* Henley-on-Thames (0491) 577635. *Club:* Phyllis Court.

ARMSTRONG, Anne Legendre, (Mrs Tobin Armstrong); Member, Board of Directors: General Motors, and Halliburton Company, since 1977; Boise Cascade Corporation, since 1978; American Express, 1975–76 and since 1981; Glaxo Holding plc, since 1991; *b* New Orleans, Louisiana, 27 Dec. 1927; *d* of Armant Legendre and Olive Martindale; *m* 1950, Tobin Armstrong; three *s* two *d*. *Educ:* Foxcroft Sch., Middleburg, Va; Vassar Coll., NY (BA). Deleg. Nat. Conventions, 1964, 1968, 1972, 1980, 1984; Mem. Republican Nat. Cttee, 1968–73 (Co-Chm., 1971–73); Counselor to the President, with Cabinet rank, 1973–74; Ambassador to the Court of St James's, 1976–77. Co-Chm., Reagan/Bush Campaign, 1980; Chm., President's Foreign Intelligence Adv. Bd, 1981–90. Chm., Bd of Trustees, Center for Strategic and Internat. Studies, Georgetown Univ., 1987–. Member: Council on Foreign Relations, 1977–; Chm. E-SU of the US, 1977–80. Trustee: Southern Methodist Univ., 1977–86; Economic Club of NY, 1978–81 (Mem., 1982–); Amer. Associates of the Royal Acad. Citizen Regent, Smithsonian Instn, 1978–. Hon. Mem., City of London Br., Royal Soc. of St George, 1978; Mem. and Governor, Ditchley Foundn, 1977–87. Pres., Blair House Restoration Fund, 1985–. Hon. LLD: Bristol, 1976; Washington and Lee, 1976; Williams Coll., 1977; St Mary's Univ., 1978; Tulane, 1978; Hon. LHD: Mt Vernon Coll., 1978; Ripon Coll., 1986; Hamilton Coll., 1990. Gold Medal, Nat. Inst. Social Scis, 1977. Josephine Meredith Langstaff Award, Nat. Soc. Daughters of British Empire in US, 1978; Republican Woman of the Year Award, 1979; Texan of the Year Award, 1981; Texas Women's Hall of Fame, 1986; Presidential Medal of Freedom, 1987; Golden Plate Award, Amer. Acad. of Achievement, 1989. Phi Beta Kappa. *Address:* Armstrong Ranch, Armstrong, Texas 78338, USA. *Club:* Pilgrims (New York).

ARMSTRONG, Prof. Arthur Hilary, MA Cantab; FBA 1970; Emeritus Professor, University of Liverpool, since 1972; Visiting Professor of Classics and Philosophy, Dalhousie University, Halifax, Nova Scotia, 1972–83; *b* 13 Aug. 1909; *s* of the Rev. W. A. Armstrong and Mrs E. M. Armstrong (*née* Cripps); *m* 1933, Deborah, *d* of Alfred Wilson and Agnes Claudia Fox Pease; two *s* two *d* (and one *d* decd). *Educ:* Lancing Coll.; Jesus Coll., Cambridge. Asst Lectr in Classics, University Coll., Swansea, 1936–39; Professor of Classics, Royal University of Malta, Valletta, 1939–43; Classical VIth Form Master, Beaumont Coll., Old Windsor, Berks, 1943–46; Lectr in Latin, University Coll., Cardiff, 1946–50; Gladstone Professor of Greek, Univ. of Liverpool, 1950–72. Killam Sen. Fellow, Dalhousie Univ., 1970–71. *Publications:* The Architecture of the Intelligible Universe in the Philosophy of Plotinus, 1940, repr. 1967 (French trans. with new preface, 1984); An Introduction to Ancient Philosophy, 1947 (American edn, 1949, 4th edn, 1965, last repr. 1981); Plotinus, 1953 (American edn, 1963); Christian Faith and Greek Philosophy (with R. A. Markus), 1960 (American edn, 1964); Plotinus I–VII (Loeb Classical Library), 1966–88; Cambridge History of Later Greek and Early Mediæval Philosophy (Editor and part author), 1967, repr. 1970; St Augustine and Christian Platonism, 1968; Plotinian and Christian Studies, 1979; Classical Mediterranean Spirituality (Vol. 15 of World Spirituality) (Editor and part author), 1986; Hellenic and Christian Studies, 1990; contribs to Classical Qly, Jl Hellenic Studies, Jl Theological Studies, etc. *Recreations:* travel, gardening. *Address:* Minia, Livesey Road, Ludlow, Shropshire SY8 1EX. *T:* Ludlow (0584) 872854.

ARMSTRONG, Rt. Hon. Ernest, PC 1979; *b* 12 Jan. 1915; *s* of John and Elizabeth Armstrong; *m* 1941, Hannah P. Lamb; one *s* one *d*. *Educ:* Wolsingham Grammar Sch. Schoolmaster, 1937–52; Headmaster, 1952–64. Chm., Sunderland Educn Cttee, 1960–65. MP (Lab) NW Durham, 1964–87. Asst Govt Whip, 1967–69; Lord Comr, HM Treasury, 1969–70; an Opposition Whip, 1970–73; Parly Under-Sec. of State, DES, 1974–75, DoE, 1975–79; Dep. Chm., Ways and Means and Dep. Speaker, 1981–87. Vice-Pres., Methodist Conf., 1974–75. Dep. Chm., Municipal Mutual Insurance Ltd, 1982–. Pres., Northern Football League. *Recreation:* walking. *Address:* Penny Well, Witton-le-Wear, Bishop Auckland, Co. Durham DL14 0AR. *T:* Witton-le-Wear (038888) 397.

See also H. J. Armstrong.

ARMSTRONG, Frank William, FEng 1991; FIMechE; FRAeS; independent technical consultant, since 1991; *b* 26 March 1931; *s* of Frank Armstrong and Millicent L. Armstrong; *m* 1957, Diane T. Varley; three *d*. *Educ:* Stretford Grammar Sch.; Royal Technical Coll., Salford; Queen Mary Coll., Univ. of London (BSc Eng; MSc Eng 1956). Massey-Harris Ltd, 1947–51; De Havilland Engine Co., 1956–58; Admiralty Engineering Lab., 1958–59; NGTE, 1959–78; Engine Div., MoD (PE), 1978–81; Dep. Dir, R&D, NGTE, 1981–83; Royal Aircraft, later Royal Aerospace, Establishment: Head of Propulsion Dept, 1983–87, Dep. Dir (Aircraft), 1987–88, Dep. Dir, 1988–90, Dir, 1990–91, Aerospace Vehicles. *Publications:* contribs on aeronautics research, gas turbines and aircraft propulsion to learned jls. *Recreations:* mountaineering, music, aviation history. *Address:* 6 Corringway, Crookham, Fleet, Hants GU13 0AN. *T:* Fleet (0252) 616526.

ARMSTRONG, Hilary Jane; MP (Lab) Durham North West, since 1987; *b* 30 Nov. 1945; *d* of Rt Hon. Ernest Armstrong, *qv*. *BSc* Monkwearmouth Comp. Sch., Sunderland; West Ham Coll. of Technology (BSc Sociology); Univ. of Birmingham (Dip in Social Work). VSO, Murray Girls' High Sch., Kenya, 1967–69; Social Worker, Newcastle City Social Services Dept, 1970–73; Community Worker, Southwick Neighbourhood Action Project, Sunderland, 1973–75; Lectr, Community and Youth Work, Sunderland Polytechnic, 1975–86. Frontbench spokesperson on education, 1988– (under-fives, primary, and special educn). *Recreations:* reading, knitting. *Address:* House of Commons, Westminster, SW1A 0AA. *T:* 071–219 5076; (constituency) Bishop Auckland 767065.

ARMSTRONG, Jack; *see* Armstrong, J. A.

ARMSTRONG, Rt. Rev. John, CB 1962; OBE 1942; Assistant Bishop in the Diocese of Exeter, 1969–88; *b* 4 Oct. 1905; *y s* of late John George and Emily Armstrong; *m* 1942, Diana Gwladys Prowse (*d* 1989), *widow* of Lieut Geoffrey Vernon Prowse, and 2nd *d* of late Admiral Sir Geoffrey Layton, GBE, KCB, KCMG, DSO; one step *s*. *Educ:* Durham School and St Francis Coll., Nundah, Brisbane, Qld. LTh, 2nd Class Hons, Australian College of Theology, 1932. Ordained 1933; Mem. Community of Ascension, Goulburn, 1932–33; Curate, St Martin, Scarborough, 1933–35; Chaplain RN, HMS Victory, 1935; Courageous, 1936–39; 6th Destroyer Flotilla, 1939–41 (despatches 1940); RM Div., 1941–43; Commando Group, 1943–45; HMS Nelson, 1945; Sen. Naval Chaplain, Germany, 1946–48; Excellent, 1948–50; RM Barracks, Portsmouth, 1950–53; Indomitable, 1953; RN Rhine Sqdn, 1953–54; HMS Vanguard, 1954; Tyne, 1954; HM Dockyard, Malta, and Asst to Chaplain of the Fleet, Mediterranean, 1955–57; HMS Bermuda, 1957–59; RM Barracks, Portsmouth, 1959–60; Chaplain of the Fleet and Archdeacon of the Royal Navy, 1960–63; Bishop of Bermuda, 1963–68; Vicar of Yarcombe, Honiton, 1969–73. QHC, 1958–63. Life Mem., Guild of Freemen of City of London. *Address:* c/o Lady Riches, 34 Cheriton Road, Winchester SO22 5AY. *Club:* Naval and Military.

ARMSTRONG, John Archibald, (Jack), OC 1983; retired; Chief Executive Officer, 1973–82, and Chairman, 1974–82, Imperial Oil Ltd; *b* Dauphin, Manitoba, 24 March 1917. *Educ:* Univ. of Manitoba (BSc Geol.); Queen's Univ. at Kingston (BSc Chem. Engrg). Worked for short time with Geol Survey of Canada and in mining industry; joined Imperial Oil Ltd as geologist, Regina, 1940; appts as: exploration geophysicist, western Canada, and with affiliated cos in USA and S America; Asst Reg. Manager, Producing Dept, 1949; Asst Co-ordinator, Producing Dept of Standard Oil Co. (NJ), New York; Gen. Man., Imperial's Producing Dept, Toronto, 1960; Dir, 1961; Dir resp. for Marketing Ops, 1963–65; Exec. Vice-Pres., 1966, Pres. 1970, Chief Exec. Officer, 1973, Chm., 1974. Chm., Commonwealth Study Conf. Assoc. Life Mem., Fraser Inst. Hon. LLD: Winnipeg, 1978; Calgary, 1980. *Address:* 1235 Bay Street, Suite 601, Toronto, Ont M5R 3K4, Canada.

ARMSTRONG, Neil A.; Chairman, CTA Inc., since 1982; formerly NASA Astronaut (Commander, Apollo 11 Rocket Flight to the Moon, 1969); *b* Wapakoneta, Ohio, USA, 5 Aug. 1930; *s* of Stephen and Viola Armstrong, Wapakoneta; *m* 1956, Janet Shearon, Evanston, Ill; two *s*. *Educ:* High Sch., Wapakoneta, Ohio; Univ. of Southern California (MS); Purdue Univ. (BSc). Pilot's licence obtained at age of 16. Served in Korea (78 combat missions) being a naval aviator, 1949–52. He joined NASA's Lewis Research Center, 1955 (then NACA Lewis Flight Propulsion Lab.) and later transf. to NASA High Speed Flight Station at Edwards Air Force Base, Calif, as an aeronautical research pilot for NACA and NASA; in this capacity, he performed as an X-15 project pilot, flying that aircraft to over 200,000 feet and approximately 4,000 miles per hour; other flight test work included piloting the X-1 rocket airplane, the F-100, F-101, F-102, F-104, F5D, B-47, the paraglider, and others; as pilot of the B-29 "drop" aircraft, he participated in the launches of over 100 rocket airplane flights. Selected as an astronaut by NASA, Sept. 1962; served as backup Command Pilot for Gemini 5 flight; as Command Pilot for Gemini 8 mission, launched 16 March 1966; he performed the first successful docking of 2 vehicles in space; served as backup Command Pilot for Gemini 11 mission; assigned as backup Comdr for Apollo VIII Flight, 1969; Dep. Associate Administrator of Aeronautics, NASA HQ, Washington, 1970–71; University Prof. of Aerospace Engrg, Univ. of Cincinnati, 1971–79; Chm., Cardwell International Ltd, 1980–82. Director: Cincinnati Gas and Electric Co.; Eaton Corp.; Cincinnati Milacron; UAL Inc. Mem., Nat. Acad. of Engrg. Fellow, Soc. of Experimental Test Pilots; FRAeS. Honours include NASA Exceptional Service Medal, and AIAA Astronautics Award for 1966; RGS Gold Medal, 1970. Presidential Medal for Freedom, 1969.

ARMSTRONG, Richard; conductor; *b* 7 Jan. 1943. *Educ:* Wyggeston School, Leicester; Corpus Christi College, Cambridge. Music staff, Royal Opera House, Covent Garden, 1966–68; Welsh National Opera: head of music staff, 1968–73; Musical Director, 1973–86; Principal Guest Conductor, 1987–; Principal Guest Conductor, Frankfurt Opera, 1987–90. Janáček Medal, 1978. *Recreations:* walking, food. *Address:* c/o Ingpen & Williams, 14 Kensington Court, W8 5DN.

ARMSTRONG, Robert George, CBE 1972; MC 1946; TD 1958; Deputy Director and Controller, Savings Bank, Department for National Savings, 1969–74, retired (Deputy Director and Controller, Post Office Savings Bank, 1964); *b* 26 Oct. 1913; *s* of late George William Armstrong; *m* 1947, Clara Christine Hyde; one *s* one *d*. *Educ:* Marylebone Grammar Sch.; University Coll., London. Post Office Engineering Dept, 1936–50. Served War of 1939–45, Royal Signals. Principal, PO Headquarters, 1950; Asst Sec., 1962; Dep. Dir of Savings, 1963; Under-Sec., 1972. *Address:* Barryleigh, Wheelers Lane, Brockham, Betchworth, Surrey RH3 7HJ. *T:* Betchworth (0737) 843217.

ARMSTRONG, Sheila Ann; soprano; *b* 13 Aug. 1942; *m* 1980, Prof. D. E. Cooper. *Educ:* Hirst Park Girls' Sch., Ashington, Northumberland; Royal Academy of Music, London. Debut Sadler's Wells, 1965 Glyndebourne, 1966, Covent Garden, 1973. Sings all over Europe, Far East, N and S America; has made many recordings. K. Ferrier and Mozart Prize, 1965; Hon. RAM 1970, FRAM 1973. Hon. MA Newcastle, 1979. *Recreations:* interior decoration, collecting antique keys, swimming.

ARMSTRONG, Dr Terence Edward; Founder Fellow, Clare Hall, since 1964, Vice-President, 1985–87, and Reader in Arctic Studies, 1977–83, now Emeritus, Cambridge University; *b* 7 April 1920; *s* of Thomas Mandeville Emerson Armstrong and Jane Crawford (*née* Young); *m* 1943, Iris Decima Forbes; two *s* two *d*. *Educ:* Winchester; Magdalene Coll., Cambridge (BA 1941; MA 1947; PhD 1951). Served Army, 1940–46 (Intelligence Corps, parachutist, wounded at Arnhem). Scott Polar Research Institute: Res. Fellow in Russian, 1947–56; Asst Dir of Res. (Polar), 1956–77; Actg Dir, 1982–83; Tutor, Clare Hall, Cambridge, 1967–74. Extensive travel in Arctic and sub-Arctic, incl. voyage through NW Passage, 1954. US Nat. Sci. Foundn Sen. For. Scientist Fellowship, Univ. of Alaska, 1970; Vis. Prof. of Northern Studies, Trent Univ., Ontario, 1988. Chm., Wkg Gp on Arctic Science Policy, NERC, 1987–88. Jt Hon. Sec., Hakluyt Soc., 1965–90. Hon. LLD McGill, 1963; Hon. DSc Alaska, 1980. Cuthbert Peek Award, RGS, 1954; Victoria Medal, RGS, 1978. *Publications:* The Northern Sea Route, 1952; Sea Ice North of the USSR, 1958; The Russians in the Arctic, 1958; Russian Settlement in the North, 1965; (ed) Yermak's Campaign in Siberia, 1975; (jtly) The Circumpolar North, 1978; contribs to jls on socio-economic problems of Arctic and sub-Arctic regions. *Recreations:* making music, walking, foreign travel. *Address:* Harston House, Harston, Cambridge CB2 5NH. *T:* Cambridge (0223) 870262.

ARMSTRONG, Sir Thomas Henry Wait, Kt 1958; MA, DMus; FRCM; Hon. FRCO, Hon. RAM; Principal, Royal Academy of Music, 1955–68; Organist of Christ Church, Oxford, 1933–55; Student of Christ Church, 1939–55, Student Emeritus, 1955, Hon. Student, 1981; Choragus of the University and University lecturer in music, 1937–54; Conductor of the Oxford Bach Choir and the Oxford Orchestral Society; Musical Director of the Balliol Concerts; Trustee, The Countess of Munster Musical Trust; *b* 15 June 1898; *o s* of A. E. Armstrong, Peterborough, Northants; *m* 1926, Hester (*d* 1982), 2nd *d* of late Rev. W. H. Draper; one *s* one *d*. *Educ:* Choir Sch., Chapel Royal, St James's; King's Sch., Peterborough; Keble Coll., Oxford; Royal Coll. of Music. Organist, Thorney Abbey, 1914; sub-organist, Peterborough Cathedral, 1915; Organ Scholar, Keble Coll., Oxford 1916, Hon. Fellow, 1955; served in RA, BEF, France, 1917–19; sub-organist, Manchester Cathedral, 1922; organist, St Peter's, Eaton Square, 1923; organist of Exeter Cathedral, 1928. Cramb Lectr in music, Univ. of Glasgow, 1949. A Dir, Royal Opera House, 1958–69. Former Chairman: Fedn of Music Socs; Musicians Benevolent Fund, 1963; Royal Philharmonic Soc., 1964–68; Former Mem., Vic-Wells and Sadler's Wells Bd of Govs. Pres., ISM, 1946 and 1961. Sen. Music Advr to Delius Trust, 1961–. Many broadcasts to schools and on musical subjects; has been on juries of many internat. competitions and examined in many universities. Hon. FTCL. Hon. DMus: Edinburgh; Royal Univ. of Brazil, 1963. *Compositions:* various, the larger ones remain unpublished. *Publications:* include choral music, songs and church music, together with many occasional writings on music. *Address:* 1 East Street, Olney, Bucks MK46 4AP. *Club:* Garrick.

See also Baron Armstrong of Ilminster.

ARMSTRONG-JONES, family name of **Earl of Snowdon.**

ARMYTAGE, Captain David George, CBE 1981; Royal Navy, retired; Secretary General, British Diabetic Association, 1981–91; *b* 4 Sept. 1929; *e s* of late Rear-Adm. Reginald William Armytage, GC, CBE and of Mrs Sylvia Beatrice Armytage; *heir* to Sir (John) Martin Armytage, Bt, *qv*; *m* 1954, Countess Cosima Antonia de Bosdari; two *s* one *d*. *Educ:* RNC, Dartmouth. Comd Motor Torpedo Boats, 1952–53; Direction Officer: 809 Sqn, 1956–58; HMS Chichester, 1958–59; Action Data Automation Project Team, 1959–64; Direction Officer, HMS Eagle, 1964–66; Directorate, Navigation and Tactical Control, 1966–68; comd HMS Minerva, 1968–70; Defence Policy Staff, 1970–72; Naval Asst to First Sea Lord, 1972–74; Internat. Mil. Staff, Brussels, 1975–76; comd, HMS Scylla, 1976 and HMS Jupiter, 1977–78. Capt., 7th Frigate Sqn, 1976–78; Dep. Dir, Naval Warfare, 1978–80; comd, NATO Standing Naval Force Atlantic, 1980–81. ADC to the Queen, 1981. *Recreations:* sailing, gardening, shooting. *Address:* Sharcott Manor, Pewsey, Wilts SN9 5PA. *T:* Marlborough (0672) 63485. *Club:* Oriental.

ARMYTAGE, Sir (John) Martin, 9th Bt *cr* 1738, of Kirklees, Yorkshire; *b* 26 Feb. 1933; *s* of Sir John Lionel Armytage, 8th Bt, and of Evelyn Mary Jessamine, *d* of Edward Herbert Fox, Adbury Park, Newbury; *S* father, 1983. *Heir: cousin* Captain David George Armytage, *qv*. *Address:* Halewell Close, Withington, Glos GL54 4BN. *T:* Withington (024289) 238. *Club:* Naval and Military.

ARMYTAGE, Prof. Walter Harry Green; Professor of Education, University of Sheffield, 1954–82, now Emeritus Professor; Gerald Read Professor of Education, Kent State University, Ohio, 1982–85; *b* 22 Nov. 1915; *e s* of Walter Green Armytage and Harriet Jane May Armytage; *m* 1948, Lucy Frances Horsfall; one *s*. *Educ:* Redruth County School; Downing Coll., Cambridge. 1st Cl. Hist. Trip. 1937, Cert. in Educ., 1938. History Master, Dronfield Grammar Sch., 1938–39; served War of 1939–45 (despatches); Captain, London Irish Rifles. Univ. of Sheffield: Lectr, 1946; Sen. Lectr, 1952; Pro-Vice-Chancellor, 1964–68. Visiting Lecturer: Univ. of Michigan, USA, 1955, 1959, 1961, 1963, 1975; Newcastle, NSW, 1977; Lectures: Ballard-Matthews, University Coll. of North Wales, 1973; Cantor, RSA, 1969; Hawkesley, IMechE, 1969; S. P. Thompson, IEE, 1972; Galton, Eugenics Soc., 1974; Clapton, Leeds Univ., 1979. Hon. DLitt: NUU, 1977; Hull, 1980. *Publications:* A. J. Mundella 1825–1897; The Liberal Background of the Labour Movement, 1951; Thomas Hughes: The Life of the Author of Tom Brown's Schooldays, 1953 (with E. C. Mack); Civic Universities: Aspects of a British Tradition, 1955; Sir Richard Gregory: his Life and Work, 1957; A Social History of Engineering, 1961; Heavens Below: Utopian Experiments in England, 1560–1960, 1962; Four Hundred Years of English Education, 1964; The Rise of the Technocrats, 1965; The American Influence on English Education, 1967; Yesterday's Tomorrows: A Historical Survey of Future Societies, 1968; The French Influence on English Education, 1968; The German Influence on English Education, 1969; The Russian Influence on English Education, 1969; (ed jtly) Perimeters of Social Repair, 1978. *Recreations:* walking, gardening. *Address:* 3 The Green, Totley, Sheffield, South Yorks. *T:* Sheffield (0742) 362515. *Clubs:* National Liberal; University Staff (Sheffield).

ARNDT, Ulrich Wolfgang, MA, PhD; FRS 1982; Member, Scientific Staff of Medical Research Council Laboratory of Molecular Biology, Cambridge, since 1962; *b* 23 April 1924; *o s* of E. J. and C. M. Arndt; *m* 1958, Valerie Howard, *e d* of late Maj.-Gen. F. C. Hilton-Sergeant, CB, CBE, QHP; three *d*. *Educ:* Dulwich Coll.; King Edward VI High Sch., Birmingham; Emmanuel Coll., Cambridge (MA, PhD). Metallurgy Dept, Birmingham Univ., 1948–49; Davy-Faraday Laboratory of Royal Instn, 1950–63; Dewar Fellow of Royal Instn, 1957–61; Univ. of Wisconsin, Madison, 1956; Institut Laue-Langevin, Grenoble, 1972–73. *Publications:* (with B. T. M. Willis) Single Crystal Diffractometry, 1966; (with A. J. Wonacott) The Rotation Method in Crystallography, 1977; papers in scientific jls. *Recreations:* walking, reading. *Address:* 28 Barrow Road, Cambridge CB2 2AS. *T:* Cambridge (0223) 350660.

ARNELL, Richard Anthony Sayer; Hon. FTCL; composer; conductor; poet; Principal Lecturer, Trinity College of Music, 1981–87 (Teacher of Composition, 1949–81); *b* 15 Sept. 1917; *s* of late Richard Sayer Arnell and of Hélène Marie Sherf; *m* 1981, Audrey Millar Paul. *Educ:* The Hall, Hampstead; University Coll. Sch., NW3; Royal Coll. of Music. Music Consultant, BBC North American Service, 1943–46; Lectr, Royal Ballet Sch., 1958–59. Editor, The Composer, 1961–64; Chairman: Composers' Guild of GB, 1965, 1974–75; Young Musicians' Symph. Orch. Soc., 1973–75. Vis. Lectr (Fulbright Exchange), Bowdoin Coll., Maine, 1967–68; Vis. Prof. Hofstra Univ., New York, 1968–70. Music Dir and Board Mem., London Internat. Film Sch., 1975–89 (Chm., Film Sch. Trust, 1981–87; Chm., Friends of LIFS, 1982–87, Vice-Pres., 1988–); Music Dir, Ram Filming Ltd, 1980–; Director: Organic Sounds Ltd, 1982–87; A plus A Ltd, 1984–89. Chm., Friends of TCM-Junior Dept, 1986–87 (Vice-Pres., 1987–). Chm., Tadcaster Civic Soc. Music and Arts Cttee, 1988–. Composer of the Year 1966 (Music Teachers Assoc. Award); Tadcaster Town Council Merit Award, 1990. Compositions include: 6 symphonies; 2 concertos for violin; concerto for harpsichord; 2 concertos for piano; 6 string quartets; 2 quintets; piano trio; piano works; songs; cantatas; organ works; music for string orchestra, wind ensembles, brass ensembles, song cycles; electronic music. *Opera:* Love in Transit; Moonflowers. *Ballet scores:* Punch and the Child, for Ballet Soc., NY, 1947; Harlequin in April, for Arts Council, 1951; The Great Detective, for Sadler's Wells Theatre Ballet, 1953; The Angels, for SWRB, 1957; Giselle (Adam) re-orchestrated, for Ballet Rambert, 1965. *Film scores:* The Land, 1941; The Third Secret, 1963; The Visit, 1964; The Man Outside, 1966; Topsail Schooner, 1966; Bequest for a Village, 1969; Second Best, 1972; Stained Glass, 1973; Wires Over the Border, 1974; Black Panther, 1977; Antagonist, 1980; Dilemma, 1981; Doctor in the Sky, 1983; Toulouse Lautrec, 1984. *Other works:* Symphonic Portrait, Lord Byron, for Sir Thomas Beecham, 1953; Landscapes and Figures, for Sir Thomas Beecham, 1956; Petrified Princess, puppet operetta (libretto by Bryan Guinness), for BBC, 1959; Robert Flaherty, Impression for Radio Eireann, 1960; Musica Pacifica for Edward Benjamin, 1963; Festival Flourish, for Salvation Army, 1965; 2nd piano concerto, for RPO, 1967; Overture, Food of Love, for Portland Symph. Orch., 1968; My Ladye Greene Sleeves, for Hofstra Univ., 1968; Life Boat Voluntary, for RNLI, 1974; Call, for LPO, 1980; Ode to Beecham, for RPO, 1986; War God II, 1987. *Mixed media:* Nocturne: Prague, 1968; I Think of all Soft Limbs, for Canadian Broadcasting Corp., 1971; Astronaut One, 1973; Gesualdo, 1989; Not Wanted on Voyage, 1990. *Address:* 5 Wharfe Bank Terrace, Tadcaster, N Yorks LS24 9BA. *Club:* Savage.

ARNOLD, Mrs Elliott; *see* Johns, Glynis.

ARNOLD, Rt. Rev. George Feversham, DD; *b* 30 Dec. 1914; *s* of Arnold Feversham and Elsie Mildred Arnold; *m* 1940, Mary Eleanor Sherman Holmes; one *s* one *d*. *Educ:* Univ. of King's Coll., Halifax, NS (LTh 1937, BD 1944); Dalhousie Univ. (BA 1935, MA 1938). Rector: Louisbourg, 1938–41; Mahone Bay, 1941–50; St John's, Fairview, 1950–53; Windsor, 1953–58; Clerical Sec. and Diocesan Registrar, 1958–67; Exam. Chaplain to Bishop of Nova Scotia, 1947–70; Hon. Canon of All Saints Cathedral, 1959–63, Canon, 1963–67; Bishop Suffragan of Nova Scotia, 1967–75, Bishop Coadjutor, May-Sept. 1975; Bishop of Nova Scotia, 1975–79. Hon. DD, King's Coll., Halifax, 1968. *Recreation:* yachting. *Address:* 56 Holmes Hill Road, Hantsport, NS B0P 1P0, Canada.

ARNOLD, Jacques Arnold; MP (C) Gravesham, since 1987; *b* London, 27 Aug. 1947; *s* of late Samuel Arnold and Eugenie (*née* Patentine); *m* 1976, Patricia Anne, *er d* of Dennis Maunder, of Windsor; one *s* two *d*. *Educ:* schools in Brazil and by correspondence; London School of Economics (BSc (Econ) 1972). Asst Gp Rep., Midland Bank, São Paulo, 1976–78; Regl Dir, Thomas Cook Gp, 1978–84; Asst Trade Finance Dir, Midland Bank, 1984–85; Dir, American Express Europe Ltd, 1985–87; has travelled to over 70 countries on business. County Councillor for Oundle, Northants, 1981–85. Contested (C) Coventry SE, 1983. Mem., Educn, Arts and Sci. Select Cttee, 1989–; Sec., Cons. Backbench Cttee on Foreign and Commonwealth Affairs, 1990–. Sec., British-Latin-American Parly Gp, 1987–. Chm., LSE Cons. Soc., 1971–72; Treasurer, Nat. Assoc. of Cons. Graduates, 1974–76; Chm., Hyde Park Tories, 1975–76; Vice-Chairman: Croydon NE Cons. Assoc., 1974–76; Corby Cons. Assoc., 1983–85. Trustee, Environment Foundn, 1989–. *Publications:* various political articles and pamphlets. *Recreations:* family life, gardening, philately. *Address:* House of Commons, SW1A 0AA. *T:* 071–219 4150; Fairlawn, 243 London Road, West Malling, Kent ME19 5AD. *T:* West Malling (0732) 848573. *Club:* Carlton.

ARNOLD, Rt. Hon. Sir John Lewis, Kt 1972; PC 1979; President of Family Division, 1979–88; a Judge in the Division, 1972–88; *b* 6 May 1915; *s* of late A. L. Arnold and E. K. Arnold; *m* 1940, Alice Margaret Dorothea (*née* Cookson) (marr. diss., 1963); one *s* one *d*; *m* 1963, Florence Elizabeth, *d* of H. M. Hague, Montreal; one *s* two *d*. *Educ:* Wellington

Coll.; abroad. Called to Bar, Middle Temple, 1937; served War of 1939–45 in Army (despatches, 1945); resumed practice at Bar, 1946; QC 1958; Chm. Bar Council, 1970–72, Chm., Plant Variety Rights Tribunal for proceedings in England and Wales, 1969–72. Hon. DLitt Reading, 1982. *Recreations:* cricket, travel. *Address:* Villa La Pergola, Via B. Bonci 14, Vagliagli 53010, Siena, Italy.

ARNOLD, Very Rev. John Robert; Dean of Durham, since 1989; *b* 1 Nov. 1933; *s* of John Stanley and Ivy Arnold; *m* 1963, Livia Anneliese Franke; one *s* two *d*. *Educ:* Christ's Hospital; Sidney Sussex Coll., Cambridge (MA); Westcott House Theol College. Curate of Holy Trinity, Millhouses, Sheffield, 1960–63; Sir Henry Stephenson Fellow, Univ. of Sheffield, 1962–63; Chaplain and Lectr, Univ. of Southampton, 1963–72; Secretary, Board for Mission and Unity, General Synod of the Church of England, 1972–78; Dean of Rochester, 1978–89. Hon. Canon of Winchester Cathedral, 1974–78; Mem., General Synod, 1980–. Mem., European Ecumenical Commn for Church and Society, 1986–; Pres. and Vice-Chm., Conference of European Churches, 1986–. Order of Saint Vladimir (Russian Orthodox Church), 1977. *Publications:* (trans.) Eucharistic Liturgy of Taizé, 1962; (contrib.) Hewitt, Strategist for the Spirit, 1985; Rochester Cathedral, 1987; contribs to Theology, Crucible, St Luke's Journal of Theology. *Recreations:* music; European languages and literature. *Address:* The Deanery, Durham DH1 3EQ. *T:* Durham (091) 3847500. *Clubs:* Commonwealth Trust, Christ's Hospital.

ARNOLD, Rt. Rev. Keith Appleby; Bishop Suffragan of Warwick, 1980–90; *b* 1 Oct. 1926; *s* of Dr Frederick Arnold, Hale, Cheshire, and Alice Mary Appleby Arnold (*née* Holt); *m* 1955, Deborah Noreen Glenwright; one *s* one *d*. *Educ:* Winchester; Trinity Coll., Cambridge (MA); Westcott House, Cambridge. Served as Lieut, Coldstream Guards, 1944–48. Curate: Haltwhistle, Northumberland, 1952–55; St John's, Princes St, Edinburgh, 1955–61; Chaplain, TA, 1956–61; Rector of St John's, Edinburgh, 1961–69; Vicar of Kirkby Lonsdale, Cumbria, 1969–73; Team Rector of Hemel Hempstead, 1973–80. Vice-Pres., Abbeyfield Soc., 1981–; Chairman: Housing Assocs Charitable Trust, 1980–86; English Villages Housing Assoc., 1987–. Pres., Warwicks Marriage Guidance Council, subseq. Relate, 1980–90. *Recreations:* skiing, gardening. *Address:* White Lodge, Dunstan, Alnwick, Northumberland NE66 3TB. *T:* Alnwick (0665) 76485.

ARNOLD, Malcolm, CBE 1970; FRCM; composer; *b* 21 Oct. 1921; *s* of William and Annie Arnold, Northampton; *m*; two *s* one *d*. *Educ:* Royal Coll. of Music, London (Schol., 1938). FRCM 1983. Principal Trumpet, London Philharmonic Orchestra, 1941–44; served in the Army, 1944–45; Principal Trumpet, London Philharmonic Orchestra, 1945–48; Mendelssohn Schol. (study in Italy), 1948; Coronation Ballet, Homage to the Queen, performed Royal Opera House, 1953. Awarded Oscar for music for film Bridge on the River Kwai, 1957; Ivor Novello Award for outstanding services to British Music, 1985; Wavendon Allmusic Composer of the Year, 1987. Bard of the Cornish Gorsedd, 1969. Hon. RAM; Hon. Mem., Schubert Soc., 1988. Hon. DMus: Exeter, 1970; Durham, 1982; Leicester, 1984; Hon. Dr Arts and Humane Letters, Miami Univ., Ohio, 1990. Hon. Freeman, Borough of Northampton, 1989. *Publications: symphonies:* No 1, 1949; No 2, 1953; No 3, 1957; No 4, 1960; No 5, 1961; No 6, 1967; No 7, 1973; No 8, 1978; Symphony for Brass Instruments, 1979; *other works:* Beckus the Dandipratt, overture, 1943; Tam O'Shanter, overture, 1955; Peterloo, overture, 1967; eighteen concertos; five ballets; two one-act operas; two string quartets; two brass quintets; vocal, choral and chamber music. *Recreations:* reading and foreign travel. *Club:* Savile.

ARNOLD, Dr Richard Bentham; Executive Vice-President, International Federation of Pharmaceutical Manufacturers' Associations, since 1984; *b* 29 Aug. 1932; *s* of George Benjamin and Alice Arnold; *m* 1956, Margaret Evelyn Racey; one *s* one *d*. *Educ:* Stamford Sch.; King Edward VII Sch., King's Lynn; Nottingham Univ. BSc, PhD. Joined May & Baker Ltd, 1959; Commercial Manager, Pharmaceuticals Div., 1974–76; Dir Designate, 1976, Dir, 1977–83, Assoc. of British Pharmaceutical Industry. *Recreations:* golf, fishing, bird watching. *Address:* IFPMA Secretariat, 67 rue de St Jean, 1201 Geneva, Switzerland.

ARNOLD, Simon Rory; Chairman and Chief Executive, Bain Clarkson Ltd, since 1986; Main Board Director, Inchcape plc, since 1988; *b* 10 Sept. 1933; *s* of R. W. Arnold and R. A. Arnold; *m* 1960, (Janet) Linda May; one *s* one *d*. *Educ:* Diocesan Coll., Cape Town. J. H. Minet & Co. Ltd: S. Africa, 1952; London, 1955; Chm. and Chief Exec., 1979; Gp Man. Dir, Minet Holdings, 1983; Chief Exec., Bain Dawes Ltd, 1984. Chm., Lloyd's Brokers Cttee, 1986– (Mem., 1979–); Mem. Council, Lloyd's, 1991–. *Recreations:* ski-ing, walking, golf, tennis. *Address:* Meadows, Ditchling Common, Ditchling, Sussex BN6 8TN. *T:* Hassocks (0273) 4246.

ARNOLD, Sir Thomas (Richard), Kt 1990; MP (C) Hazel Grove, since Oct. 1974; *b* 25 Jan. 1947; *s* of Thomas Charles Arnold and Helen Breen; *m* 1984, Elizabeth Jane, *widow* of Robin Smithers; one *d*. *Educ:* Bedales Sch.; Le Rosey, Geneva; Pembroke Coll., Oxford (MA). Theatre producer; publisher. Contested (C): Manchester Cheetham, 1970; Hazel Grove, Feb. 1974; PPS to Sec. of State for NI, 1979–81, to Lord Privy Seal, FCO, 1981–82. Vice-Chm., Conservative Party, 1983–. *Address:* House of Commons, SW1A 0AA. *T:* 071–219 4096. *Clubs:* Carlton, Royal Automobile.

ARNOLD, Vere Arbuthnot, CBE 1970; MC 1945; TD 1953; JP; DL; Chairman, Ross T. Smyth & Co. Ltd, 1957–80; *b* 23 May 1902; *s* of Rev. H. A. Arnold, Wolsingham Rectory, Co. Durham; *m* 1928, Joan Kathleen, *d* of C. J. Tully, Wairarapa, NZ; one *s* one *d*. *Educ:* Haileybury Coll.; Jesus Coll., Cambridge (BA). Ross T. Smyth & Co. Ltd, 1924, Director, 1931; Pres., Liverpool Corn Trade Association, 1947–48 and 1951–52. Chm., Runcorn Develt Corp., 1964–74. Served War of 1939–45 as Major (MC, TD). JP County of Chester, 1949; High Sheriff, Cheshire, 1958; DL Cheshire, 1969. *Recreations:* shooting, fishing. *Address:* Ardmore, Great Barrow, near Chester CH3 7JM. *T:* Tarvin (0829) 40257.

ARNOLD, William; Head of Courts and Legal Services Act Implementation Division, Lord Chancellor's Department, since 1989; *b* 13 May 1953; *s* of Rev. William and Mrs Ruth Arnold. *Educ:* Bury Grammar Sch.; King's Coll., Cambridge (MA Classics). Joined Lord Chancellor's Department, 1974: Asst Private Sec. to Lord Chancellor, 1977–79; Principal, 1979; Head of Legal Services Div., 1987; Head of Remuneration and Competition Div., 1988. Reader, St Margaret's Church, Putney, 1989–. *Recreations:* ski-ing, swimming, squash, long-distance trekking, opera, ballet, choral singing. *Address:* Lord Chancellor's Department, Trevelyan House, 30 Great Peter Street, SW1P 2BY. *T:* 071–210 8789.

ARNOLD-BAKER, Charles, OBE 1966; Deputy Eastern Traffic Commissioner, 1978–90; Consultant Lecturer, since 1978, and Visiting Professor, since 1985, City University; occasional broadcaster; *b* 25 June 1918; *s* of Baron Albrecht v. Blumenthal and Alice Wilhelmine (*née* Hainsworth); *m* 1943, Edith (*née* Woods); one *s* one *d*. *Educ:* Winchester Coll.; Magdalen Coll., Oxford. BA 1940. Called to Bar, Inner Temple, 1948. Army (Private to Captain), 1940–46. Admty Bar, 1948–52; Sec., Nat. Assoc. of Local Councils, 1953–78; Mem., Royal Commn on Common Lands, 1955–58; Mem. European Cttee, Internat. Union of Local Authorities, 1960–78; a Deleg. to European Local Govt Assembly, Strasbourg, 1960–78. Gwylim Gibbons Award, Nuffield Coll., Oxford, 1959. King Haakon's Medal of Freedom (Norway), 1945. *Publications:* Norway (pamphlet), 1946; Everyman's Dictionary of Dates, 1954; Parish Administration, 1958; New Law and Practice of Parish Administration, 1966; The 5000 and the Power Tangle, 1967; The Local Government Act 1972, 1973; Local Council Administration, 1975, 3rd rev. edn 1989; The Local Government, Planning and Land Act 1980, 1981; Practical Law for Arts Administrators, 1983; The Five Thousand and the Living Constitution, 1986; many contribs to British and European local govt and legal jls. *Recreations:* travel, history, writing, music, cooking, journalism, wine and doing nothing. *Address:* Top Floor, 2 Paper Buildings, Inner Temple, EC4Y 7ET. *T:* 071–353 3490. *Club:* Union (Oxford).

ARNOTT, Sir Alexander John Maxwell, 6th Bt *cr* 1896, of Woodlands, Shandon, Co. Cork; *b* 18 Sept. 1975; *s* of Sir John Robert Alexander Arnott, 5th Bt, and of Ann Margaret, *d* of late T. A. Farrelly, Kilcar, Co. Cavan; *S* father, 1981. *Heir:* *b* Andrew John Eric Arnott, *b* 20 June 1978. *Address:* 11 Palmerston Road, Dublin 6, Ireland.

ARNOTT, Sir Melville; *see* Arnott, Sir W. M.

ARNOTT, Prof. Struther, FRS 1985; Principal and Vice-Chancellor, University of St Andrews, since 1986; *b* 25 Sept. 1934; *s* of Charles McCann and Christina Struthers Arnott; *m* 1970, Greta Edwards (BA); two *s*. *Educ:* Hamilton Academy, Lanarkshire; Glasgow Univ. (BSc, PhD). FRSC 1970; FIBiol 1987; FRSE 1988. King's College London: scientist, MRC Biophysics Research Unit, 1960–70; demonstrator in Physics. 1960–67; dir of postgraduate studies in Biophysics, 1967–70; Purdue University: Prof. of Molecular Biology, 1970–; Head, Dept of Biol Scis, 1975–80; Vice-Pres. for Research and Dean, Graduate Sch., 1980–86. Oxford University: Sen. Vis. Fellow, Jesus Coll., 1980–81; Nuffield Res. Fellow, Green Coll., 1985–86. Guggenheim Meml Foundn Fellow, 1985. *Publications:* papers in learned jls on structures of fibrous biopolymers, especially nucleic acids and polysaccharides, and techniques for visualizing them. *Recreations:* bird watching, botanizing. *Address:* College Gate, St Andrews, Fife KY16 9AJ. *T:* St Andrews (0334) 76161; The Principal's House, 9 The Scores, St Andrews, Fife KY16 9AR. *T:* St Andrews (0334) 72492. *Clubs:* Athenæum, Caledonian; Royal and Ancient (St Andrews).

ARNOTT, Sir (William) Melville, Kt 1971; TD (and clasps) 1944; MD; FRCP; FRCPE, FRCPath; FRSE; British Heart Foundation Professor of Cardiology, University of Birmingham, 1971–74, now Emeritus Professor of Medicine; Physician, United Birmingham Hospitals, 1946–74; Hon. Consultant Physician, Queen Elizabeth Hospital, Birmingham, since 1974; *b* 14 Jan. 1909; *s* of Rev. Henry and Jeanette Main Arnott; *m* 1938, Dorothy Eleanor, *er d* of G. F. S. Hill, Edinburgh; one *s*. *Educ:* George Watson's Coll., Edinburgh; Univ. of Edinburgh. MB, ChB (Hons), 1931, BSc (1st Cl. Hons Path.), 1934, MD (Gold Medal and Gunning Prize in Path.), 1937, Edinburgh; McCunn Res. Schol. in Path., 1933–35, Crichton Res. Schol. in Path., 1935, Shaw Macfie Lang Res. Fellow, 1936–38, Edinburgh. MD Birmingham, 1947. 2nd Lieut RA, 1929; TA 1929–39; War of 1939–45, served as specialist physician; five years foreign service (Siege of Tobruk; despatches, NW Europe); Lt-Col 1942. Asst Physician, Edinburgh Municipal Hosps, 1934–36; Hon. Asst Physician: Church of Scotland Deaconess Hosp., Edinburgh, 1938–46; Edinburgh Royal Infirmary, 1946. Dir, Post-grad. studies in Medicine, Edinburgh Univ., 1945–46; William Withering Prof. of Medicine, Univ. of Birmingham, 1946–71. Consultant Adviser in Research to W Midlands RHA, 1974–79. Associate Examr in Medicine, London Univ., 1948–49; Examr in Medicine, to Univs of Cambridge, 1950–56, London, 1951–54, Wales, 1954–57, Queen's, Belfast, 1956–59, Edinburgh, 1959–62, Leeds, 1959–62, St Andrews, 1961–63, Oxford, 1961–68, Newcastle, 1964–67, Manchester, 1964–67, Singapore, 1965, East Africa, 1965, Malaysia, 1973, NUI, 1975–77. Member: UGC, 1954–63; MRC, 1965–69; Council, University Coll. of Rhodesia, 1964–70; UGC Hong Kong, 1966–75; Home Office Cttee (Brodrick) on Death Registration and Coroners, 1965–71; Tropical Medicine Res. Bd, 1967–71. Dep. Pres., First Internat. Conf. on Med. Educn, 1953. Editor, Clinical Science, 1953–58, Member, Editorial Board: Brit. Jl of Social Medicine; Brit. Jl of Industrial Medicine and Cardiovascular Research. RCPE: Mem., 1933; Fellow, 1937; John Matheson Shaw Lectr, 1958; Cullen Prize, 1958. RCP: Mem., 1947; Fellow, 1951; Mem. Council, 1954–56; Oliver-Sharpey Lectr, 1955; Examr for Membership, 1957–66; Croonian Lectr, 1963; Censor, 1969–71; Sen. Vice-Pres., and Sen. Censor, 1973. Foundation Fellow, Royal Coll. of Pathologists. FRMedSoc 1929 (late Senior Pres.); Hon. FRCP(C), 1957; Hon. FACP, 1968 (Lilly Lectr, 1968); FRSE 1971. Member: Assoc. of Physicians; Physiological Soc.; Pathological Soc.; Med. Res. Soc.; Cardiac Soc.; Thoracic Soc.; Internat. Soc. of Internal Medicine. Sir Arthur Sims Commonwealth Trav. Prof. of Medicine, 1957. Lectures: Frederick Price, Trinity Coll., Dublin, 1959; Hall, Cardiac Soc. of Aust. and NZ, 1962; Henry Cohen, Hebrew Univ. of Jerusalem, 1964; Alexander Brown Meml, Univ. of Ibadan, 1972; John Snow, Soc. of Anaesthetists, 1973. President: Edinburgh Harveian Soc., 1955; British Lung Foundation, 1984–87. Research: Originally into experimental path. of renal hypertension and peripheral vascular disease; at present, into physiology and path. of cardio-respiratory function. Hon. DSc: Edinburgh, 1975; Chinese Univ. of Hong Kong, 1983; Hon. LLD: Rhodesia, 1976; Dundee, 1976. *Publications:* some 50 scientific papers, principally in Lancet, Jl of Physiol., Jl of Path., Brit. Jl of Social Medicine, Edinburgh Med. Jl, etc. *Recreation:* travel. *Address:* 40 Carpenter Road, Edgbaston, Birmingham B15 2JJ. *T:* 021–440 2195. *Club:* Naval and Military.

ARONSOHN, Lotte Therese; *see* Newman, L. T.

ARONSON, Geoffrey Fraser, CB 1977; retired solicitor; Legal Adviser and Solicitor to Ministry of Agriculture, Fisheries and Food, to Forestry Commission, and to (EEC) Intervention Board for Agricultural Produce, 1974–79; *b* 17 April 1914; *er s* of late Victor Rees Aronson, CBE, KC, and Annie Elizabeth Aronson (*née* Fraser); *m* 1940, Marie Louise, *e d* of late George Stewart Rose-Innes; one *s* two *d*. *Educ:* Haileybury. Solicitor (Honours) 1936. Legal Dept, Min. of Agriculture and Fisheries, 1938; served War of 1939–45, Flying Control Officer, RAFVR; promoted Asst Solicitor, MAFF, 1960; Under-Sec. (Principal Asst Solicitor), 1971, when chiefly concerned with UK accession to EEC. Part-time consultant to Law Commn, 1979–84. Co-Founder, 1959, and Chm., 1959–74, Epsom Protection Soc. *Recreations:* environmental, travel, gardening. *Address:* 4 The Oaks, Downs Avenue, Epsom, Surrey KT18 5HH. *T:* Epsom (0372) 722431; 30 Eastergate Green, Rustington, W Sussex. *T:* Rustington (0903) 775736. *Clubs:* Commonwealth Trust, Royal Automobile.

ARONSON, Hazel Josephine, (Mrs John A. Cosgrove); Sheriff of Lothian and Borders at Edinburgh, since 1983; *b* 12 Jan. 1946; *d* of late Moses Aron Aronson and Julia Tobias; *m* 1967, John Allan Cosgrove, dental surgeon; one *s* one *d*. *Educ:* Glasgow High Sch. for Girls; Univ. of Glasgow (LLB). Advocate at the Scottish Bar. Admitted to Fac. of Advocates, 1968; Standing Junior Counsel to Dept of Trade, 1977–79; Sheriff of Glasgow and Strathkelvin, 1979–83. Mem., Parole Bd for Scotland, 1988–; Chm., Mental Welfare Commn for Scotland, 1991–. Vice Chm., Edinburgh Friends of Israel, 1980–. *Recreations:* foreign travel, opera, walking, reading, langlauf. *Address:* 14 Gordon Terrace, Edinburgh EH16 5QR.

ARRAN, 9th Earl of, *cr* 1762, of the Arran Islands, Co. Galway; **Arthur Desmond Colquhoun Gore;** Bt 1662; Viscount Sudley, Baron Saunders, 1758; Baron Sudley

(UK), 1884; Parliamentary Under Secretary of State for the Armed Forces, Ministry of Defence, since 1989; *b* 14 July 1938; *er s* of 8th Earl of Arran and of Fiona Bryde, *er d* of Sir Iain Colquhoun of Luss, 7th Bt, KT, DSO; *S* father, 1983; *m* 1974, Eleanor, *er d* of Bernard van Cutsem and Lady Margaret Fortescue; two *d*. *Educ:* Eton; Balliol College, Oxford. 2nd Lieutenant, 1st Bn Grenadier Guards (National Service). Asst Manager, Daily Mail, 1972–73; Man. Dir, Clark Nelson, 1973–74; Asst Gen. Manager Daily and Sunday Express, June-Nov. 1974. Co-Founder, Gore Publishing Ltd, 1980. A Lord in Waiting (Govt Whip), 1987–89. Co-Chm., Children's Country Holidays Fund. *Recreations:* tennis, shooting, gardening, croquet. *Address:* c/o House of Lords, SW1A 0PW. *Clubs:* Pratt's, Turf, Beefsteak.

ARRINDELL, Sir Clement Athelston, GCMG 1984; GCVO 1985; Kt 1982; QC; Governor-General, St Christopher and Nevis, since 1983 (Governor, St Kitts-Nevis, 1981–83); *b* Basseterre, 19 April 1931. *Educ:* private school; Basseterre Boys' Elementary Sch.; St Kitts-Nevis Grammar Sch. (Island Scholar). Called to the Bar, Lincoln's Inn, 1958. Post-grad. studies; in practice as barrister and solicitor, 1959–66; Acting Magistrate, 1964–66; Magistrate, 1966–71; Chief Magistrate, 1972–78; Judge, WI Associated States Supreme Court, 1978–81. *Recreations:* piano-playing, classical music, gardening. *Address:* Government House, Basseterre, St Christopher, West Indies. *T:* 2315.

ARROW, Kenneth Joseph; Professor of Economics and Operations Research, Stanford University, since 1979; *b* 23 Aug. 1921; *s* of Harry I. and Lillian Arrow; *m* 1947, Selma Schweitzer; two *s*. *Educ:* City College (BS in Social Science 1940); Columbia Univ. (MA 1941, PhD 1951). Captain, US AAF, 1942–46. Research Associate, Cowles Commn for Research in Economics, Univ. of Chicago, 1947–49; Actg Asst Prof., Associate Prof. and Prof. of Economics, Statistics and Operations Research, Stanford Univ., 1949–68; Prof. of Econs, later University Prof., Harvard Univ., 1968–79. Staff Mem., US Council of Economic Advisers, 1962. Consultant, The Rand Corp., 1948–. Fellow, Churchill Coll., Cambridge, 1963–64, 1970, 1973, 1986. President: Internat. Economic Assoc., 1983–86; Internat. Soc. for Inventory Res., 1984–90; Member: Inst. of Management Sciences (Pres., 1963); Nat. Acad. of Sciences; Amer. Inst. of Medicine; Amer. Philosoph. Soc.; Fellow: Econometric Soc. (Pres., 1956); Amer. Acad. of Arts and Sciences; Amer. Assoc. for Advancement of Science (Chm., Section K, 1982); Amer. Statistical Assoc.; Dist. Fellow: Amer. Econ. Assoc. (Pres., 1972); Western Econ. Assoc. (Pres., 1980–81); Corresp. Fellow, British Acad., 1976; Foreign Hon. Mem., Finnish Acad. of Sciences. John Bates Clark Medal, American Economic Assoc., 1957; Nobel Meml Prize in Economic Science, 1972; von Neumann Prize, Inst. of Management Scis and Ops Res. Soc. of America, 1986. Hon. LLD: Chicago, 1967; City Univ. of NY, 1972; Univ. of Pennsylvania, 1976; Washington Univ., St Louis, Missouri, 1989; Hon. Dr Soc. and Econ. Sciences, Vienna, 1971; Hon. ScD Columbia, 1973; Hon. DSocSci, Yale, 1974; Hon. Dr: Paris, 1974; Hebrew Univ. of Jerusalem, 1975; Helsinki, 1976; Aix-Marseille III, 1985; Hon. LittD Cambridge, 1985. Order of the Rising Sun (2nd class), Japan, 1984. *Publications:* Social Choice and Individual Values, 1951, 2nd edn 1963; (with S. Karlin and H. Scarf) Studies in the Mathematical Theory of Inventory and Production, 1958; (with M. Hoffenberg) A Time Series Analysis of Interindustry Demands, 1959; (with L. Hurwicz and H. Uzawa) Studies in Linear and Nonlinear Programming, 1959; Aspects of the Theory of Risk Bearing, 1965; (with M. Kurz) Public Investment, the Rate of Return, and Optimal Fiscal Policy, 1971; Essays in the Theory of Risk-Bearing, 1971; (with F. Hahn) General Competitive Analysis, 1972; The Limits of Organization, 1974; (with L. Hurwicz) Studies in Resource Allocation Processes, 1977; Collected Papers, Vols 1–6, 1984–86; (with H. Raynaud) Social Choice and Multicriterion Decision-Making, 1986; 170 articles in jls and collective vols. *Address:* Department of Economics, Fourth Floor, Encina Hall, Stanford University, Stanford, Calif 94305, USA.

ARROWSMITH, Sir Edwin (Porter), KCMG 1959 (CMG 1950); *b* 23 May 1909; *s* of late Edwin Arrowsmith and of Kathleen Eggleston Arrowsmith (*née* Porter); *m* 1936, Clondagh, *e d* of late Dr W. G. Connor; two *d*. *Educ:* Cheltenham Coll.; Trinity Coll., Oxford (MA). Assistant District Commissioner, Bechuanaland Protectorate, 1932; in various District posts, Bechuanaland Protectorate, 1933–38; Commissioner, Turks and Caicos Islands, BWI, 1940–46; Administrator, Dominica, BWI, 1946–52; Resident Commissioner, Basutoland, 1952–56; Governor and Commander-in-Chief, Falkland Islands, 1957–64, and High Commissioner, British Antarctic Territory, 1962–64; Dir of Overseas Services Resettlement Bureau, 1965–79. Mem. Council, St Dunstan's, 1965–. Vice-Pres., Royal Commonwealth Soc. for the Blind, 1985– (Chm., 1970–85). Vice-Pres., Freshwater Biol Assoc., 1984– (Pres., 1977–83). *Recreation:* flyfishing. *Address:* 25 Rivermead Court, SW6 3RU. *T:* 071–736 4757. *Clubs:* Flyfishers', Hurlingham, Commonwealth Trust.

ARROWSMITH, Pat; pacifist and socialist; has worked at Amnesty International, since 1971, now an assistant editor; *b* 2 March 1930; *d* of late George Ernest Arrowsmith and late Margaret Vera (*née* Kingham); *m* Mr Gardner, 11 Aug. 1979, separated 11 Aug. 1979; lesbian partnership with Wendy Butlin, 1962–76. *Educ:* Farringtons; Stover Sch.; Cheltenham Ladies' Coll.; Newnham Coll., Cambridge (BA history); Univ. of Ohio; Liverpool Univ. (Cert. in Social Science). Has held many jobs, incl.: Community Organizer in Chicago, 1952–53; Cinema Usher, 1953–54; Social Caseworker, Liverpool Family Service Unit, 1954; Child Care Officer, 1955 and 1964; Nursing Asst, Deva Psychiatric Hosp., 1956–57; Reporter for Peace News, 1965; Gardener for Camden BC, 1966–68; Researcher for Soc. of Friends Race Relations Cttee, 1969–71; Case Worker for NCCL, 1971; and on farms, as waiter in cafes, in factories, as a toy demonstrator, as a 'temp' in numerous offices, as asst in children's home, as newspaper deliverer and sales agent, as cleaner, as bartender, and in a holiday camp. Organizer for Direct Action Cttee against Nuclear War, Cttee of 100 and Campaign for Nuclear Disarmament, 1958–68; gaoled 11 times as political prisoner, 1958–85 (adopted twice as Prisoner of Conscience by Amnesty International); awarded Holloway Prison Green Band, 1964; awarded Girl Crusaders knighthood, 1940. Contested: Fulham, 1966 (Radical Alliance) and 1970 (Hammersmith Stop the SE Asia War Cttee), on peace issues; Cardiff South East (Independent Socialist), 1979. Member: War Resisters' Internat.; Campaign for Nuclear Disarmament; Socialist Movement; TGWU. *Publications:* Jericho (novel), 1965; Somewhere Like This (novel), 1970; To Asia in Peace, 1972; The Colour of Six Schools, 1972; Breakout (poems and drawings from prison), 1975; On the Brink (anti-war poems with pictures), 1981; The Prisoner (novel), 1982; Thin Ice (anti-nuclear poems), 1984; Nine Lives (poems and pictures), 1990. *Recreations:* water colour painting (has held and contrib. exhibns), swimming, writing poetry. *Address:* 132c Middle Lane, N8. *T:* 081–340 2661.

ARTHINGTON-DAVY, Humphrey Augustine, LVO 1977; OBE 1965; HM Diplomatic Service, retired; High Commissioner to Tonga, 1973–80, and Western Samoa, 1973–77; *b* 1920. *Educ:* Eastbourne Coll.; Trinity Coll., Cambridge. Indian Army, 1941; Indian Political Service, 1946; Civil Service of Pakistan, 1947; CRO, 1958; British Representative in the Maldives, 1960; Deputy High Commissioner: Botswana, 1966; Mauritius, 1968; Tonga, 1970. *Recreation:* travel. *Address:* c/o Grindlays Bank, 13 St James's Square, SW1; PO Box 56, Nuku' Alofa, Tonga, South Pacific. *Club:* Naval and Military.

ARTHUR, family name of **Baron Glenarthur.**

ARTHUR, Allan James Vincent, MBE 1948; DL; Vice Lord-Lieutenant of Essex, 1978–85; *b* 16 Sept. 1915; *s* of late Col Sir Charles Arthur, MC, VD, and late Lady (Dorothy Grace) Arthur; *m* 1940, Joan Deirdre Heape (marr. diss. 1948); *m* 1949, Dawn Rosemary Everil, *d* of Col F. C. Drake, OBE, MC, DL; two *s* two *d*. *Educ:* Rugby Sch.; Magdalene Coll., Cambridge (MA). Indian Civil Service (Punjab), 1938–47; Sub Divl Officer, Murree, 1941, Kasur, 1942–43; Dep. Comr, Attock, 1944–46, Multan, 1946–47; Sudan Political Service, 1948–54; District Comr, Khartoum, 1949–51, Shendi, 1951–54; Dep. Governor, Northern Province, 1954; J. V. Drake and Co. Ltd, Sugar Brokers, 1954–60; Woodhouse, Drake, and Carey Ltd, Commodity Merchants, 1960–75 (Chm., 1972–75). Member, Chelmsford Borough Council, 1973–79, Mayor, 1977–78; Governor: London Hosp. Med. Coll., 1956–74; Chigwell Sch., 1972–82; Brentwood Sch., 1973–85. Pres., Chelmsford Medical Educn and Res. Trust, 1981–88. Trustee, Friends of Essex Youth Orchestras, 1985–. Member: Bd of Visitors, HM Prison, Chelmsford, 1973–79; Council, Univ. of Essex, 1980–87. Pres., Old Rugbeian Soc., 1982–84. High Sheriff of Essex, 1971–72; DL Essex, 1974. *Publications:* contrib. to: The District Officer in India, 1930–47, 1980; Set under Authority, by K. D. D. Henderson, 1987. *Recreations:* swimming, shooting, gardening. *Address:* Mount Maskall, Boreham, Chelmsford CM3 3HW. *T:* Chelmsford (0245) 467776. *Clubs:* Oriental; Hawks (Cambridge).

ARTHUR, Prof. Geoffrey Herbert; Emeritus Professor of Veterinary Surgery, University of Bristol, since 1980; *b* 6 March 1916; *s* of William Gwyn Arthur and Ethel Jessie Arthur; *m* 1948, Lorna Isabel Simpson; four *s* one *d*. *Educ:* Abersychan Secondary Sch.; Liverpool Univ. BVSc 1939; MRCVS 1939; MVSc 1945; DVSc 1957; FRCVS 1957. Lectr in Veterinary Medicine, Liverpool Univ., 1941–48; Reader in Veterinary Surgery, Royal Veterinary Coll., 1949–51; Reader in Veterinary Surgery and Obstetrics, Univ. of London, 1952–65; Prof. of Veterinary Obstetrics and Diseases of Reproduction, Univ. of London, 1965–73; Prof. and Head of Dept of Vet. Surgery, Bristol Univ., 1974–79. Examiner to Univs of Cambridge, Dublin, Edinburgh, Glasgow, Liverpool, London, Reading, Bristol and Ceylon. Visiting Professor: Univ. of Khartoum, 1964; Pahlavi Univ., 1976; Nairobi Univ., 1979; Clinical Prof., King Faisal Univ., Saudi Arabia, 1980–84. *Publications:* Wright's Veterinary Obstetrics (including Diseases of Reproduction, 3rd edn), 1964, 5th edn, as Veterinary Reproduction and Obstetrics, 1982, 6th edn 1989; papers on medicine and reproduction in Veterinary Record, Veterinary Jl, Jl of Comparative Pathology, Jl Reprod. Fert., Equine Vet. Jl and Jl Small Animal Pract. (Editor). *Recreations:* observing natural phenomena and experimenting. *Address:* Fallodene, Stone Allerton, Axbridge, Som BS26 2NH.

ARTHUR, James Stanley, CMG 1977; HM Diplomatic Service, retired; British High Commissioner in Bridgetown, 1978–82, also British High Commissioner (non-resident) to Dominica, 1978–82, to St Lucia and St Vincent, 1979–82, to Grenada, 1980–82, to Antigua and Barbuda, 1981–82, and concurrently British Government Representative to West Indies Associated State of St Kitts-Nevis; retired 1983; *b* 3 Feb. 1923; *s* of Laurence and Catherine Arthur, Lerwick, Shetland; *m* 1950, Marion North; two *s* two *d*. *Educ:* Trinity Academy, Edinburgh; Liverpool Univ. (BSc). Scientific Civil Service, 1944–46; Asst Principal, Scottish Educn Dept, 1946; Min. of Educn/Dept of Educn and Science, 1947–66: Private Sec. to Parly Sec., 1948–50; Principal Private Sec. to Minister, 1960–62; Counsellor, FO, 1966; Nairobi, 1967–70; Dep. High Comr, Malta, 1970–73; High Comr, Suva, 1974–78, and first High Comr (non-resident), Republic of Nauru, 1977–78. Member: Court, Liverpool Univ., 1987–; Central Council, Royal Commonwealth Soc., 1988–. *Recreations:* golf, music. *Address:* Moreton House, Longborough, Moreton-in-Marsh, Glos GL56 0QQ. *T:* Cotswold (0451) 30774. *Club:* Commonwealth Trust.

ARTHUR, Lt-Gen. Sir (John) Norman (Stewart), KCB 1985; DL; General Officer Commanding Scotland and Governor of Edinburgh Castle, 1985–88, retired; *b* 6 March 1931; *s* of Col Evelyn Stewart Arthur and Mrs E. S. Arthur (*née* Burnett-Stuart); *m* 1960, Theresa Mary Hopkinson; one *s* one *d* (and one *s* decd). *Educ:* Eton Coll.; RMA, Sandhurst. rcds, jssc, psc. Commnd Royal Scots Greys, 1951; commanded: Royal Scots Dragoon Guards, 1972–74 (despatches, 1974); 7th Armoured Bde, 1976–77; GOC 3rd Armoured Div., 1980–82; Dir of Personal Services (Army), MoD, 1983–85. Col Comdt, Military Provost Staff Corps, 1985–88; Col, The Royal Scots Dragoon Gds (Carabiniers and Greys), 1984–; Hon. Col 205 (Scottish) Gen. Hosp., RAMC(V), 1988–. Officer, Royal Co. of Archers, Queen's Body Guard for Scotland. Chm., Scotland, Army Benevolent Fund, 1988–; Vice Pres., Edinburgh and Borders, Riding for the Disabled Assoc., 1988–; Dir, Edinburgh Mil. Tattoo Co., 1988–; Pres., Scottish Conservation Projects, 1989–; Mem., Automobile Assoc. Cttee, 1990–. Mem., British Olympic Team, Equestrian Three-Day Event, 1960. DL Stewartry, 1989. *Recreations:* field and country sports and pursuits, horsemanship, military history. *Address:* Newbarns, Dalbeattie, Kirkcudbrightshire DG5 4PY. *T:* Rockcliffe (055663) 227. *Clubs:* Cavalry and Guards; Caledonian Hunt.

ARTHUR, John Rhys, DFC 1944; JP; **His Honour Judge Arthur;** a Circuit Judge, since 1975; *b* 29 April 1923; *s* of late John Morgan Arthur and Eleanor Arthur; *m* 1951, Joan Tremearne Pickering; two *s* one *d*. *Educ:* Mill Hill; Christ's Coll., Cambridge (MA). Commnd RAF, 1943, demobilised 1946. Cambridge, 1946–48; called to Bar, Inner Temple, 1949. Asst Recorder, Blackburn QS, 1970; Dep. Chm., Lancs County QS, 1970–71; a Recorder, 1972–75. JP Lancs 1970. *Address:* Orovales, Caldy, Wirral L48 1LP. *T:* 051–625 8624. *Clubs:* MCC, Old Millhillians; Athenæum (Liverpool).

ARTHUR, Michael Anthony; HM Diplomatic Service; Head of European Community Department (Internal), Foreign and Commonwealth Office, since 1988; *b* 28 Aug. 1950; *s* of late John Richard Arthur and of Mary Deirdre (*née* Chaundy); *m* 1974, Plaxy Gillian Beatrice (*née* Corke); two *s* two *d*. *Educ:* Rugby; Balliol Coll., Oxford. Entered HM Diplomatic Service, 1972; UK Mission to UN, NY, 1972; FCO, 1973; 3rd, later 2nd Sec., UK Perm. Representation to Eur. Communities, 1974–76; 2nd Sec., Kinshasa, 1976–78; FCO, 1978–83; Private Secretary: to Lord Privy Seal, 1981; to Minister of State, FCO, 1982; 1st Sec., Bonn, 1984–88. *Recreations:* music, travel, books. *Address:* c/o Foreign and Commonwealth Office, King Charles Street, SW1A 2AH.

ARTHUR, Lt-Gen. Sir Norman; *see* Arthur, Lt-Gen. Sir J. N. S.

ARTHUR, Peter Bernard; Deputy Chairman and Chairman of the Sub-Committees of Classification, Lloyd's Register of Shipping, 1976–84; *b* 29 Aug. 1923; *s* of Charles Frederick Bernard Arthur and Joan (*née* Dyer); *m* 1954, Irène Susy (*née* Schüpbach); one *s* two *d*. *Educ:* Oundle Sch. Commnd 1943; Mahratta LI, 1943–47 (mentioned in despatches, Italy, 1945); RA, 1947–53. Underwriting Mem. of Lloyd's, 1954–; Mem. Cttee, Lloyd's Register of Shipping, and Vice-Chm., Sub-Cttees of Classification, 1967. Dir, Bolton Steam Shipping Co. Ltd, 1958–84; Chairman: London Deep Sea Tramp Shipowners' Assoc., 1970–71; Deep Sea Tramp Sect., Chamber of Shipping of UK, 1972–73; Bolton Maritime Management Ltd, 1982–83. *Recreations:* golf, music, water colour painting, gardening. *Address:* Lower Terrace, 37A Peter Avenue, Oxted, Surrey RH8 9LG. *T:* Oxted (0883) 712962. *Club:* Tandridge Golf.

ARTHUR, Rt. Rev. Robert Gordon; *b* 17 Aug. 1909; *s* of George Thomas Arthur and Mary Arthur; *m* Marie Olive Cavell Wheen; two *s* two *d*. *Educ:* Launceston and Devonport High Schs, Tasmania; Queen's Coll., Univ. of Melbourne. MA (Hons) 1932. Rector of: Berridale, NSW, 1950–53; St John's, Canberra, ACT, 1953–60; Wagga Wagga, NSW, 1960–61; Archdeacon of Canberra, 1953–60; Asst Bp of Canberra and Goulburn, 1956–61; Bishop of Grafton, NSW, 1961–73; Rector of St Philip's, Canberra, 1973–74; Priest-in-charge of Bratton, Wilts, 1975–78, and Rural Dean of Heytesbury, 1976–78; Hon. Asst Bishop of Sheffield, 1978–80. *Address:* 4 Berry Street, Downer, Canberra, ACT 2602, Australia.

ARTHUR, Sir Stephen (John), 6th Bt *cr* 1841, of Upper Canada; *b* 1 July 1953; *s* of Hon. Sir Basil Malcolm Arthur, 5th Bt, MP, and of Elizabeth Rita, *d* of late Alan Mervyn Wells; *S* father, 1985; *m* 1978, Carolyn Margaret (marr. diss.), *d* of Burney Lawrence Daimond, Cairns, Queensland; one *s* two *d*. *Educ:* Timaru Boys' High School. *Heir: s* Benjamin Nathan Arthur, *b* 27 March 1979. *Address:* No 3 RD, Seadown, Timaru, New Zealand. *T:* Timaru 47721.

ARTHURE, Humphrey George Edgar, CBE 1969; MD, FRCS, FRCOG; Consulting Obstetric and Gynæcological Surgeon: Charing Cross Hospital; Queen Charlotte's Hospital; Mount Vernon Hospital. MRCS, LRCP 1931; MB, BS 1933; FRCS 1935; MD London 1938; FRCOG 1950 (Hon. Sec. 1949–56; Vice-Pres. 1964–67); FRSM (Pres., Section of Obstetrics and Gynaecology, 1969); co-opted Mem. Council, RCS 1960; Pres., West London Medico-Chirurgical Soc., 1964; Formerly: Chm., Central Midwives Board, and Adviser, Obstetrics and Gynæcology, DHSS; Mem., Standing Maternity and Midwifery Advisory Cttee; Resident Obstetric Officer and Obstetrical Registrar, Charing Cross Hospital; Resident Medical Officer, Chelsea Hospital for Women. Served War of 1939–45, temp. Lt-Col, RAMC. *Publications:* Simpson Oration, 1972; (jtly) Sterilisation, 1976; contribs med. jls. *Address:* 12 Eyot Green, Chiswick Mall, W4 2PT. *T:* 081–994 7698.

ARTHURS, Prof. Harry William, OC 1989; FRSC 1982; President, York University, Canada, since 1985; *b* 9 May 1935; *s* of Leon and Ellen Arthurs; *m* 1974, Penelope Geraldine Ann Milnes; two *s*. *Educ:* Univ. of Toronto (BA, LLB); Harvard Univ. (LLM). Barrister and Solicitor, 1961. Asst Prof. 1961, Associate Prof. 1964, Associate Dean 1967, Prof. 1968, Dean 1972–77, Osgoode Hall Law Sch., York Univ. Mem., Economic Council of Can., 1978–82; Bencher, Law Soc. of Upper Can., 1979–84; Chm., Consultative Gp on Res. and Educn in Law, 1981–84; Arbitrator, Mediator in Labour Disputes, 1962–84; Chair, Council of Ontario Univs, 1987–89. Visitor: Univs of Toronto, 1965, and McGill, 1967; Clare Hall, Cambridge, 1971; Inst. for Socio-Legal Res., Oxford, 1977–78; UCL, 1984. Hon. LLD: Sherbrooke, 1986; Brock, 1986; Law Soc. of Upper Can., 1987. *Publications:* Law and Learning, 1983; (jtly) Industrial Relations and Labour Law in Canada, 1979, 3rd edn 1988; Without the Law, 1985. *Address:* Office of the President, York University, 4700 Keele Street, North York, Ontario M3J 1P3, Canada. *T:* (416) 736 5200. *Club:* University (Toronto).

ARTIS, Prof. Michael John, FBA 1988; Professor of Economics, Manchester University, since 1975; *b* 29 June 1938; *s* of Cyril John and Violet Emily Artis; *m* 1st, 1961, Lilian Gregson (marr. diss. 1982); two *d*; 2nd, 1983, Shirley Knight. *Educ:* Baines Grammar Sch., Poulton-le-Fylde, Lancs; Magdalen Coll., Oxford. BA Hons (PPE) Oxon. Assistant Research Officer, Oxford Univ., 1959; Lectr in Economics, Adelaide Univ., 1964; Lectr and Sen. Lectr in Economics, Flinders Univ., 1966; Research Officer and Review Editor, Nat. Inst. of Economic and Social Research, London, 1967; Prof. of Applied Economics, Swansea Univ. Coll., 1972. *Publications:* Foundations of British Monetary Policy, 1964; (with M. K. Lewis) Monetary Control in the United Kingdom, 1981; Macroeconomics, 1984; (with S. Ostry) International Economic Policy Co-ordination, 1986; (with M. K. Lewis) Money in Britain, 1991; contribs on economics, economic policy to books and learned jls. *Recreation:* eating out. *Address:* 76 Bexton Road, Knutsford, Cheshire WA16 0DX. *T:* Knutsford (0565) 633204. *Club:* Reform.

ARTON, Major A. T. B.; *see* Bourne-Arton.

ARTRO MORRIS, John Evan; District Judge, Principal Registry of the Family Division (formerly a Registrar of the Supreme Court, Family Division), since 1977; *b* 17 Feb. 1925; *s* of Tudor and Mabel Artro Morris; *m* 1961, Karin Ilsa Alida Russell; two *s*. *Educ:* Liverpool Coll.; The Queen's Coll., Oxford. BA Oxon. Served RN, 1943–47. Called to the Bar, Middle Temple, 1952. *Recreations:* D-I-Y, Rugby (spectator), fishing. *Address:* 69 Gowan Avenue, SW6 6RH. *T:* 071-736 6492. *Club:* London Welsh RFC.

ARTUS, Ronald Edward, CBE 1991; non-executive Director: Celltech Ltd, since 1980; Imperial Cancer Research Technology Ltd, since 1988; Prudential Corporation PLC, since 1990; Electrocomponents plc, since 1990; GEC, since 1990; The Solicitors Indemnity Fund Ltd, since 1990; *b* 8 Oct 1931; *s* of late Ernest and of Doris Artus; *m* 1st, 1956, Brenda M. Touche (marr. diss.); three *s* one *d*; 2nd, 1987, Dr Joan M. Mullaney, MD. *Educ:* Sir Thomas Rich's Sch., Gloucester; Magdalen Coll., Oxford (MA). Joined Prudential, 1954; Head of Economic Intelligence Dept, 1958–71; Sen. Asst Investment Manager, 1971–73; Dep. Investment Manager, 1973–75; Jt Sec. and Chief Investment Manager, 1975–79; Dep. Chm., 1985–90; Prudential Corp. PLC: Gp Chief Investment Manager, 1979–90; an Exec. Dir, 1984–90; Chairman: Prudential Portfolio Managers, 1981–90; Prudential Property Services, 1986–90; a Dir of various cos, Prudential Gp, until 1990. Director: Keyser Ullmann Holdings Ltd, 1972–80; Charterhouse Gp Ltd, 1980–82. Member: City Capital Markets Cttee, 1982–90 (Chm., 1988–90); Accounting Standards Cttee, 1982–86; Council, Inst. for Fiscal Studies, 1988–; CBI City Industry Task Force, 1987; indep. Mem. Bd, Securities Assoc. Ltd, 1990–. Mem. Finance Cttee, ICRF, 1975–. Hon. Fellow, Soc. of Investment Analysts, 1980 (Mem. Council, 1964–76; Chm., 1973–75); FRSA. *Publications:* contrib. various jls on economic and investment matters. *Recreations:* music (esp. opera), learning about art (esp. British Sch. and English watercolours). *Address:* Prudential Corporation, 1 Stephen Street, W1P 2AP. *T:* 071–405 9222. *Club:* MCC.

ARUNDEL AND BRIGHTON, Bishop of, (RC), since 1977; **Rt. Rev. Cormac Murphy-O'Connor;** *b* 24 Aug. 1932; *s* of late Dr P. G. Murphy-O'Connor and Ellen (*née* Cuddigan). *Educ:* Prior Park Coll., Bath; English Coll., Rome; Gregorian Univ. PhL, STL. Ordained Priest, 1956. Asst Priest, Portsmouth and Fareham, 1957–66; Sec. to Bp of Portsmouth, 1966–70; Parish Priest, Parish of the Immaculate Conception, Southampton, 1970–71; Rector, English College, Rome, 1971–77. Chairman: Bishops' Cttee for Europe, 1978–83; Cttee for Christian Unity, 1983–; Jt Chm., ARCIC-II, 1983–. *Recreations:* music, sport. *Address:* St Joseph's Hall, Storrington, Pulborough, Sussex RH20 4HE.

ARUNDEL AND SURREY, Earl of; Edward William Fitzalan-Howard; *b* 2 Dec. 1956; *s* and *heir* of 17th Duke of Norfolk, *qv*; *m* 1987, Georgina, *y d* of Jack and Serena Gore; one *s* one *d*. *Educ:* Ampleforth Coll., Yorks; Lincoln Coll., Oxford. *Recreations:* skiing, motor-racing, shooting. *Heir: s* Lord Maltravers, *qv*. *Address:* Arundel Castle, Sussex. *T:* Arundel (0903) 882173; 25 Brynmaer Road, SW11. *T:* 071–622 2972; Scar House, Arkengarthdale, Reeth, N Yorks. *T:* Richmond (0748) 84726. *Club:* British Racing Drivers (Silverstone).

ARUNDELL; *see* Monckton-Arundell, family name of Viscount Galway.

ARUNDELL, family name of **Baron Talbot of Malahide**.

ARVILL, Robert; *see* Boote, R. E.

ASAAD, Prof. Fikry Naguib M.; *see* Morcos-Asaad.

ASANTE, Kwaku Baprui, GM 1976; MOV 1978; High Commissioner for Ghana in London, since 1991; *b* 26 March 1924; *s* of Kweku Asante and Odorso Amoo; *m* 1958, Matilda Dzagbele Anteson; two *s* two *d*. *Educ:* Achimota Coll.; Durham Univ. (BSc); Final Exam., Inst. Statisticians (AIS), London. Sen. Maths Master, Achimota, 1954–56; joined Ghana Foreign Service, 1956; 2nd Sec., London, 1957–58; Chargé d'Affaires, Tel Aviv, 1958–60; Principal Sec., African Affairs Secretariat, Office of Pres., 1960–66; Head of Admin., OAU, 1966–67; Ambassador to Switzerland and Austria and Permanent Delegate to UN Office, Geneva, 1967–72; Principal Sec., Min. of Foreign Affairs, 1972; Sen. Principal Sec., Ministries of Trade and Tourism, and Economic Planning, 1973–76; Ambassador to Belgium, Luxembourg and EEC, 1976–79; Sec.-Gen., Social Democratic Front, 1979–81; Sec. (Minister) for Trade and Tourism, 1982; Private Consultant, 1982–88; Sec. (Minister) for Educn, 1988–91. *Publications:* articles in Ghanaian and foreign newspapers and jls. *Recreations:* music, cricket. *Address:* 41 Avenue Road, St John's Wood, NW8 6BS. *T:* 071–722 4568.

ASCHERSON, (Charles) Neal; journalist and author; *b* 5 Oct. 1932; *s* of Stephen Romer Ascherson and Evelyn Mabel Ascherson; *m* 1st, 1958, Corinna Adam (marr. diss. 1982); two *d*; 2nd, 1984, Isabel Hilton; one *s* one *d*. *Educ:* Eton College; King's College, Cambridge (MA). Served RM, 1950–52. Reporter and leader writer, Manchester Guardian, 1956–58; Commonwealth corresp., Scotsman, 1959–60; The Observer: reporter, 1960–63; Central Europe corresp., 1963–68; Eastern Europe corresp., 1968–75; foreign writer, 1979–85; columnist, 1985–90; Associate Editor, 1985–89; columnist, The Independent on Sunday, 1990–. Scottish politics corresp., Scotsman, 1975–79. Hon. DLitt Strathclyde, 1988; Hon. DSc(SocSci) Edinburgh, 1990. Reporter of the Year 1982, Journalist of the Year 1987, Granada Awards; James Cameron Award, 1989. *Publications:* The King Incorporated, 1963; The Polish August, 1981; The Struggles for Poland, 1987; Games with Shadows, 1988. *Address:* 27 Corsica Street, N5. *Club:* Ognisko Polskie (Polish Hearth Club).

ASFA WOSSEN HAILE SELLASSIE, HIH Merd Azmatch; GCMG (Hon.) 1965; GCVO (Hon.) 1930; GBE (Hon.) 1932; Crown Prince of Ethiopia, since 1930; *b* 27 July 1916; *e s* and *heir* of late Emperor Haile Sellassie, KG, and Empress Menen; *m* 1st, Princess Wallatta Israel; one *d* decd; 2nd, Princess Madfariash Wark Abebe; one *s* three *d*. *Educ:* privately; Liverpool Univ. Governor of Wollo province; Mem., Crown Council. Fought in Italo-Ethiopian War, 1935–36. Grand Cross: Légion d'Honneur; Belgian Order of Leopold; Order of the Netherlands; Order of Rising Sun, Japan; Order of White Elephant, Siam. *Heir: s* Prince Zara Yacob, *b* 18 Aug. 1953.

ASH, Brian Maxwell; QC 1990; *b* 31 Jan. 1941; *s* of late Carl Ash and of Irene Ash (*née* Atkinson); *m* 1971, Barbara Anne Maxwell, creator and editor of BBC TV Question Time; two *s* one *d*. *Educ:* Mercers' Sch.; City of London Sch.; New Coll., Oxford (Open Exhibnr; BA). BBC TV Current Affairs Producer, Reporter and Programme Presenter, 1967–73; called to the Bar, Gray's Inn, 1975. Chm. of Panel, Examination in Public of First Alteration to Devon Structure Plan, 1986. *Recreations:* golf, sailing, ski-ing, music. *Address:* 4/5 Gray's Inn Square, WC1R 5AY. *T:* 071–404 5252. *Clubs:* Royal Mid-Surrey Golf; Royal Norwich Golf.

ASH, Sir Eric (Albert), Kt 1990; CBE 1983; FRS 1977; FEng 1978; Rector, Imperial College of Science, Technology and Medicine (formerly of Science and Technology), since 1985; *b* 31 Jan. 1928; *s* of Walter and Dorothea Ash; *m* 1954, Clare (*née* Babb); five *d*. *Educ:* University College Sch.; Imperial Coll. of Science and Technology. BSc(Eng), PhD, DSc; FCGI, DIC. FIEE; FIEEE; FInstP. Research Fellow: Stanford Univ., Calif, 1952–54; QMC, 1954–55; Res. Engr, Standard Telecommunication Laboratories Ltd, 1955–63; Sen. Lectr, 1963–65, Reader, 1965–67, Prof., 1967–85, Pender Prof. and Head of Dept, 1980–85, Dept of Electronic and Electrical Engrg, UCL (Hon. Fellow, 1985). Dir (non-exec.), British Telecom, 1987–. Pres., IEE, 1987–88 (Vice-Pres., 1980–83; Dep. Pres., 1984–86); Member: Royal Soc. Cttees; Exec. Bd, Fellowship of Engrg, 1981–84; ABRC, 1989–; Chm., BBC Science Advisory Cttee, 1987–. Trustee: Science Mus., 1987–; Wolfson Foundn, 1988–. Sec., Royal Instn, 1984–88 (Vice Pres., 1980–82, Manager, 1980–84). Marconi International Fellowship, 1984. Dr *hc*: Aston; Leicester; Edinburgh; Institut National Polytechnique de Grenoble. Faraday Medal, IEE, 1980; Royal Medal, Royal Soc., 1986. *Publications:* patents; papers on topics in physical electronics in various engrg and physics jls. *Recreations:* music, skiing, swimming. *Address:* Imperial College of Science, Technology and Medicine, SW7 2AZ.

ASH, Maurice Anthony, BSc (Econ); Vice President, Town and Country Planning Association, since 1987 (Chairman of Executive, 1969–83; Chairman of Council, 1983–87); *b* 31 Oct. 1917; *s* of Wilfred Cracroft and Beatrice Ash; *m* 1947, Ruth Whitney Elmhirst (*d* 1986); three *d* (one *s* decd). *Educ:* Gresham's Sch., Holt; LSE; Yale. Served War of 1939–45, armoured forces in Western Desert, Italy, Greece (despatches 1944). Mem., SW Regl Economic Planning Council, 1965–68; Chm., Green Alliance, 1978–83. Trustee, Dartington Hall, 1964– (Chm., 1972–84); Mem., Henry Moore Foundn, 1980–89. *Publications:* The Human Cloud, 1962; Who are the Progressives Now?, 1969; Regions of Tomorrow, 1969; A Guide to the Structure of London, 1972; Green Politics, 1980; New Renaissance, 1987; Journey into the Eye of a Needle, 1989; articles on land use, education and environment. *Recreation:* applying Wittgenstein. *Address:* Sharpham House, Ashprington, Totnes, Devon TQ9 7UT. *T:* Harbertonford (080423) 216. *Club:* Reform.

ASH, Raymond; former Director, Business Statistics Office, retired from Civil Service, 1986; Director, Business and Trade Statistics Ltd, since 1986; *b* 2 Jan. 1928; *s* of late Horace Ash and Gladys Ash; *m* 1947, Mavis (*née* Wootton); two *s* one *d*. *Educ:* Wolverhampton Grammar Sch. Civil Service, 1949–86: professional statistician and senior manager working on health, labour, overseas trade, and business statistics. *Publications:* contrib. learned jls. *Recreations:* country walks, tourism, historical studies. *Address:* 20 Taliesin Close, Rogerstone, Newport, Gwent NP1 0DD. *T:* Newport (0633) 895470.

ASH, Rear-Admiral Walter William Hector, CB 1962; WhSch; CEng; FIEE; *b* Portsmouth, Hants, 2 May 1906; *s* of Hector Sidney and Mabel Jessy Ash; *m* 1932, Louisa Adelaide Salt, Jarrow-on-Tyne; three *d*. *Educ:* City & Guilds Coll., Kensington; Royal Naval Coll., Greenwich. Whitworth Scholar, 1926; John Samuel Scholar, 1927. Asst Elect. Engr, Admiralty (submarine design), 1932–37; Elect. Engr, Admiralty (battleship design), 1937–39; Fleet Elect. Engr, Staff C-in-C Med., 1939–40; Supt Elect. Engr,

Admiralty (supply and prod.), 1940–45; Supt Elect. Engr, HM Dockyard, Hong Kong, 1945–48; Supt Elect. Engr, Admiralty Engineering Lab., 1948–49; Comdr RN, HMS Montclare, 1950–51; Capt. RN, Admiralty (weapon control design), 1951–54; Capt. RN, Elect. Engr Manager, HM Dockyard, Devonport, 1954–58; Capt. RN, Ship Design Dept, Admiralty, 1959–60; Rear-Adm. 1960; subseq. Ship Dept Directorate, Admty, retd Aug. 1963. Vis. Lectr in electrical machinery design, RN Coll., Greenwich, 1934–37. Chairman IEE, SW Sub Centre, 1957–58. ADC to the Queen, 1958–60. *Recreation:* music (piano and organ). *Address:* 4 Vavasour House, North Embankment, Dartmouth, Devon TQ6 9PW. *T:* Dartmouth (0803) 834630.

ASH, Rear-Adm. William Noel, CB 1977; LVO 1959; *b* 6 March 1921; *s* of late H. Arnold Ash, MRCS, LRCP; *m* 1951, Pamela, *d* of late Harry C. Davies, Hawkes Bay, NZ; one *s* one *d*. *Educ:* Merchant Taylors' School. Joined RN, 1938; HM Yacht Britannia, 1955–58; Captain 1965; Canadian NDC, 1965–66; Staff of SACLANT (NATO), 1966–69; Cabinet Office, 1969–71; comd HMS Ganges, 1971–73; Rear-Adm. 1974; Dir of Service Intelligence, 1974–77. Sec. Defence Press and Broadcasting Cttee, 1980–84. *Address:* c/o National Bank of New Zealand, PO Box 25051, St Heliers, Auckland, New Zealand. *Club:* Commonwealth Trust.

ASHBEE, Paul; Archaeologist, University of East Anglia, 1969–83; *b* 23 June 1918; *s* of Lewis Ashbee and Hannah Mary Elizabeth Ashbee (*née* Brett); *m* 1952, Richmal Crompton Lamburn Disher; one *s* one *d*. *Educ:* sch. in Maidstone, Kent; Univ. of London; Univ. of Leicester (MA; DLitt 1984). Post-grad. Dip. Prehistoric Archaeology, London. Royal W Kent Regt and REME, 1939–46; Control Commn for Germany, 1946–49; Univ. of London, Univ. of Bristol (Redland Coll.), 1949–54; Asst Master and Head of History, Forest Hill Sch., 1954–68. Excavation of prehistoric sites, mostly barrows both long and round for then Min. of Works, 1949–76; Co-dir with R. L. S. Bruce-Mitford of BM excavations at Sutton-Hoo, 1964–69; Mem., Sutton Hoo Research Cttee, 1982–. Mem. Council and Meetings Sec., Prehistoric Soc., 1960–74; Sec. (Wareham Earthwork), British Assoc. Sub-Cttee for Archaeological Field Experiment, 1961–; one-time Sec., Neolithic and Bronze Age Cttee, Council for British Archaeology; Mem. Royal Commn on Historical Monuments (England), 1975–85; Mem., Area Archaeological Adv. Cttee (DoE) for Norfolk and Suffolk, 1975–79. Pres., Cornwall Archæol Soc., 1976–80, Vice-Pres., 1980–84; Chm., Scole Cttee for E Anglian Archaeology, 1979–84. FSA 1958; FRSAI 1987. *Publications:* The Bronze Age Round Barrow in Britain, 1960; The Earthen Long Barrow in Britain, 1970, 2nd edn 1984; Ancient Scilly, 1974; The Ancient British, 1978; chapter in Sutton Hoo, Vol. I, 1976; Wilsford Shaft, 1989; numerous papers, articles and reviews in Archaeologia, Antiquaries Jl, Archaeological Jl, Proc. Prehistoric Soc., Antiquity, Cornish Archaeology, Arch. Cantiana, Proc. Dorset Arch. and Nat. Hist. Soc., Proc. Hants FC, Wilts Archaeol Magazine, Yorks Arch. Jl, etc. *Recreations:* East Anglia, historical architecture, bibliophilia, dog ownership. *Address:* The Old Rectory, Chedgrave, Norfolk NR14 6ND. *T:* Loddon (0508) 20595.

ASHBOURNE, 4th Baron *cr* 1885; **Edward Barry Greynville Gibson;** Lieut-Comdr RN, retired; home civil service; *b* 28 Jan. 1933; *s* of 3rd Baron Ashbourne, CB, DSO, and of Reta Frances Manning, *e d* of E. M. Hazeland, Hong Kong; *S* father, 1983; *m* 1967, Yvonne Georgina, *d* of Mrs Flora Ham, of Malin, County Donegall; three *s*. *Educ:* Rugby. Pres., Petersfield Br., East Hants Cons. Assoc.; Vice-President: Hampshire Autistic Soc.; (Europe) Hope Now Internat. Ministries; Chm., Joshua Christian Trust. *Heir:* *s* Hon. Edward Charles d'Olier Gibson, *b* 31 Dec. 1967. *Address:* 107 Sussex Road, Petersfield, Hants.

ASHBROOK, 10th Viscount, *cr* 1751 (Ire.); **Desmond Llowarch Edward Flower,** KCVO 1977; MBE 1945; DL; Baron of Castle Durrow, 1733; Member of Council of Duchy of Lancaster, 1957–77; *b* 9 July 1905; *o s* of 9th Viscount and late Gladys, *d* of late Gen. Sir George Wentworth A. Higginson, GCB, GCVO; *S* father, 1936; *m* 1934, Elizabeth, *er d* of late Capt. John Egerton-Warburton, and of late Hon. Mrs Waters; two *s* one *d*. *Educ:* Eton; Balliol Coll., Oxford (BA 1927). Served War of 1939–45, RA. Formerly a Chartered Accountant. JP, 1946–67, DL 1949–, Vice-Lieutenant, 1961–67, Cheshire. *Heir:* *s* Hon. Michael Llowarch Warburton Flower, *qv*. *Address:* Woodlands, Arley, Northwich, Cheshire.

ASHBROOK, Kate Jessie; General Secretary, Open Spaces Society, since 1984; *b* 1 Feb. 1955; *d* of John Ashbrook and Margaret Balfour. *Educ:* Benenden Sch., Kent; Exeter Univ. (BSc). Member, Executive Committee: Open Spaces Soc., 1978–84; Ramblers' Assoc., 1982–; Council for National Parks, 1983–; Mem., Common Land Forum, 1984–86; Footpath Sec., Bucks and W Middx, Ramblers' Assoc., 1986–; Hon. Sec., Dartmoor Preservation Assoc., 1981–84. Editor, Open Space, 1984–. *Publications:* (contrib.) The Walks of South-East England, 1975; (contrib.) Severnside: a guide to family walks, 1976; pamphlets; contribs to The Countryman and various jls. *Recreations:* pedantry, finding illegally blocked footpaths. *Address:* Telfer's Cottage, Turville, Henley-on-Thames RG9 6QL. *T:* Henley-on-Thames (0491) 63396.

ASHBURNER, Prof. Michael, PhD, ScD; FRS 1990; Professor of Biology, University of Cambridge, since 1991; Extraordinary Fellow, Churchill College, Cambridge, since 1990; *b* 23 May 1942; *s* of Geoffrey Staton Ashburner and Diane Ashburner (*née* Leff); *m* 1963, Francesca Ryan, *d* of Desmond Francis Ryan and Isabel Ryan; one *s* two *d*. *Educ:* Royal Grammar Sch., High Wycombe; Churchill Coll., Cambridge (BA 1964, PhD 1968, ScD 1978). FRES 1975. University of Cambridge: Asst in Research, 1966–68; Univ. Demonstrator, 1968–73; Univ. Lectr, 1973–80; Reader in Developmental Genetics, 1980–91; Sen. Res. Fellow, Churchill Coll., 1980–90. Gordon Ross Res. Fellow, Calif. Inst. of Technology, 1968–69; Vis. Prof., Univ. of California Sch. of Medicine, San Francisco, 1977–78; Vis. Prof., Univ. of Crete, 1985; Goldschmidt Lectr, Hebrew Univ., Jerusalem, 1985; Miller Vis. Prof., Univ. of California at Berkeley, 1986; Vis. Prof., Univ. of Pavia, Italy, 1990–. Mem., EMBO 1977, Council, 1988–. Mem., Academia Europaea, 1989. *Publications:* (ed) The Genetics and Biology of Drosophila, 1976–86, 12 vols; (ed) Insect Cytogenetics, 1980; (ed) Heat Shock: from bacteria to man, 1982; Drosophila: a laboratory handbook and manual, 2 vols, 1989; contribs to scientific jls. *Recreations:* walking, watching birds. *Address:* 5 Bateman Street, Cambridge CB2 1NB. *T:* Cambridge (0223) 64706; Department of Genetics, Downing Street, Cambridge CB2 3EH. *T:* Cambridge (0223) 333969.

ASHBURNHAM, Captain Sir Denny Reginald, 12th Bt *cr* 1661; Captain South Staffordshire Regiment; *b* 24 March 1916; *o surv. s* of Sir Fleetwood Ashburnham, 11th Bt, and Elfrida, *d* of late James Kirkley, JP, Cleadon Park, Co. Durham; *S* father 1953; *m* 1946, Mary Frances, *d* of Major Robert Pascoe Mair, Wick, Udimore, Sussex; two *d* (one *s* decd). *Heir:* *g s* James Fleetwood Ashburnham, *b* 17 Dec. 1979. *Address:* Little Broomham, Guestling, Hastings, East Sussex.

ASHBURTON, 7th Baron *cr* 1835; **John Francis Harcourt Baring,** KCVO 1990 (CVO 1980); Kt 1983; Chairman: Barings plc, 1985–89 (non-executive Director, since 1989); Baring Brothers & Co. Ltd, 1974–89 (a Managing Director, 1955–74); Lord Warden of the Stannaries, Duchy of Cornwall, since 1990 (Receiver-General, 1974–90); *b* 2 Nov. 1928; *er s* of 6th Baron Ashburton, KG, KCVO and Hon. Doris Mary Thérèse Harcourt (*d* 1981), *e d* of 1st Viscount Harcourt; *S* father, 1991; *m* 1st, 1955, Susan Mary Renwick (marr. diss. 1984), *e d* of 1st Baron Renwick, KBE, and Mrs John Ormiston; two *s* two *d*; 2nd, 1987, Mrs Sarah Crewe, *d* of J. G. Spencer Churchill, *qv*. *Educ:* Eton (Fellow, 1982); Trinity Coll., Oxford (MA; Hon. Fellow 1989). Dep. Chm., Royal Insurance Co. Ltd, 1975–82 (Dir, 1964–82); Chairman: Outwich Investment Trust Ltd, 1968–86; Stratton Investment Trust, 1986–; Director: Dunlop Holdings Ltd, 1981–84; British Petroleum, 1982–; Bank of England, 1983–91; Jaguar, 1989–. Vice-Pres., British Bankers' Assoc., 1977–81; Pres., Overseas Bankers' Club, 1977–78. Chm., Accepting Houses Cttee, 1977–81; Chm., Cttee on Finance for Industry, NEDC, 1980–86. Member: British Transport Docks Bd, 1966–71; President's Cttee, CBI, 1976–79; Hon. Treas., Police Foundn, 1989–; Mem. Exec. Cttee, NACF, 1989–. Trustee: Rhodes Trust, 1970– (Chm., 1987–); Nat. Gall., 1981–87. Hon. Fellow, Hertford Coll., Oxford, 1976. *Heir:* *s* Hon. Mark Francis Robert Baring [*b* 17 Aug. 1958; *m* 1983, Miranda Caroline, *d* of Captain Charles St John Graham Moncrief; one *d*]. *Address:* Lake House, Northington, Alresford, Hants SO24 9TG. *T:* Alresford (0962) 734293; 3 Stanley House, 13 Stanley Crescent, W11 2NA. *T:* 071–727 3007. *Clubs:* Pratt's, Flyfishers'.

ASHBY, family name of **Baron Ashby.**

ASHBY, Baron *cr* 1973 (Life Peer), of Brandon, Suffolk; **Eric Ashby,** Kt 1956; FRS 1963; DSc London, MA Cantab; DIC; Chancellor, Queen's University, Belfast, 1970–83; Fellow of Clare College, Cambridge, 1958, Life Fellow since 1975; *b* 1904; *s* of Herbert Charles Ashby, Bromley, Kent, and Helena Chater; *m* 1931, Elizabeth Helen Farries, Castle-Douglas, Scotland; two *s*. *Educ:* City of London Sch.; Imperial Coll. of Science, Univ. of London; Univ. of Chicago. Demonstrator at Imperial Coll., 1926–29; Commonwealth Fund Fellow in Univ. of Chicago and Desert Laboratory of Carnegie Institution, 1929–31; Lectr, Imperial Coll. of Science, 1931–35; Reader in Botany, Bristol Univ., 1935–37; Prof. of Botany, Univ. of Sydney, Australia, 1938–46; Harrison Prof. of Botany and Dir of Botanical Labs, Univ. of Manchester, 1946–50; Pres. and Vice-Chancellor, Queen's Univ., Belfast, 1950–59; Master of Clare College, Cambridge, 1959–75; Vice-Chancellor, Univ. of Cambridge, 1967–69. Chm., Aust. National Research Council, 1940–42; Chm., Professorial Board, Univ. of Sydney, 1942–44; Mem., Power Alcohol Committee of Enquiry, 1940–41; conducted enquiry for Prime Minister into enlistment of scientific resources in war, 1942; Trustee, Aust. Museum, 1942–46; Dir, Scientific Liaison Bureau, 1942–43; Counsellor and Chargé d'Affaires at Australian Legation, Moscow, USSR, 1945–46; Member of: Advisory Council on Scientific Policy, 1950–53; Nuffield Provincial Hospitals Trust, 1951–59; Advisory Council on Scientific and Industrial Research, 1954–60; Chairman: Scientific Grants Cttee, DSIR, 1955–56; Postgraduate Grants Cttee, DSIR, 1956–60; Northern Ireland Adv. Council for Education, 1953–58; Adult Education Cttee, 1953–54; Cttee of Award of Commonwealth Fund, 1963–69 (Member, 1956–61); Royal Commn on Environmental Pollution, 1970–73; Member: Univ. Grants Cttee, 1959–67; Commonwealth Scholarship Commn, 1960–69; Council of Royal Soc., 1964–65; Governing Body, Sch. of Oriental and African Studies, Univ. of London, 1965–70; Chm., Commn for post-secondary and higher education in Nigeria, 1959–61; Chm., working party on pollution control in connection with UN conf. on the Environment, Stockholm, June 1972. Vice-Chm. Assoc. of Univs of Brit. Commonwealth, 1959–61; Pres., Brit. Assoc. for the Advancement of Science, 1963. Walgreen Prof., Michigan, 1975–77; Lectures: Godkin, Harvard Univ., 1964; Whidden, McMaster Univ., 1970; Bernal, Royal Soc., 1971; Prof-at-large, Cornell Univ., 1967–72; Trustee: Ciba Foundation, 1966–79; British Museum, 1969–77; Fellow: Imperial Coll. of Science; Davenport Coll., Yale Univ.; Hon. Fellow, Clare Hall; Hon. FRSE; Hon. FRIC. Hon. Foreign Mem., Amer. Acad. of Arts and Sciences. Hon. LLD: St Andrews; Aberdeen; Belfast; Rand; London; Wales; Columbia; Chicago; Michigan; Windsor; Western Australia; Manchester; Johns Hopkins; Liverpool; Hon. ScD Dublin; Hon. DSc: NUI; Univ. of Nigeria; Southampton; Hon. DLitt: W Ont; Sydney; Hon. DPhil Tech. Univ. Berlin; Hon. DCL East Anglia; Hon. DHL: Yale; Utah. Jephcott Medal, RSM, 1976. Order of Andrés Bello, first class, Venezuela, 1974. *Publications:* Environment and Plant Development, translated from German, 1931; German-English Botanical Terminology (with Elizabeth Helen Ashby), 1938; Food Shipment from Australia in Wartime; Challenge to Education, 1946; Scientist in Russia, 1947 (German trans., 1950); Technology and the Academics, 1958 (Japanese trans., 1963; Spanish trans, 1970); Community of Universities, 1963; African Universities and Western Tradition, 1964 (French trans. 1964); Universities: British, Indian, African (with Mary Anderson), 1966 (Spanish trans. 1972); Masters and Scholars, 1970; (with Mary Anderson) The Rise of the Student Estate, 1970; Any Person, Any Study, 1971; (with Mary Anderson) Portrait of Haldane, 1974; Reconciling Man with the Environment, 1978 (Spanish trans. 1981); (with Mary Anderson) The Politics of Clean Air, 1981. *Recreation:* chamber music. *Address:* 22 Eltisley Avenue, Cambridge CB3 9JG.

See also M. F. Ashby.

ASHBY, David Glynn; MP (C) North-West Leicestershire, since 1983; barrister; *b* 14 May 1940; *s* of Robert M. Ashby and Isobel A. Davidson; *m* 1965, Silvana Morena; one *d*. *Educ:* Royal Grammar Sch., High Wycombe; Bristol Univ. (LLB Hons). Called to the Bar, Gray's Inn, 1963; in practice on SE Circuit. Member: Hammersmith Bor. Council, 1968–71; for W Woolwich, GLC, 1977–81; ILEA, 1977–81. *Recreations:* gardening, skiing, music. *Address:* House of Commons, SW1A 0AA.

ASHBY, Francis Dalton, OBE 1975; Director, National Counties Building Society, 1980–90; retired; *b* 20 Jan. 1920; *s* of late John Frederick Ashby and late Jessie Ashby; *m* 1948, Mollie Isabel Mitchell; one *s* one *d* (and one *d* decd). *Educ:* Watford Grammar Sch. Diploma in Govt Admin. War Service, Royal Signals, 1940–46: POW, Far East, 1942–45. National Debt Office: Exec. Officer, 1938; Asst Comptroller and Estabt Officer, 1966–76; Comptroller-General, 1976–80. *Recreations:* local voluntary work, walking. *Address:* Moorfield, Carpenters Wood Drive, Chorleywood, Herts.

ASHBY, Rt. Rev. Godfrey William Ernest Candler; Assistant Bishop of Leicester, since 1988; *b* 6 Nov. 1930; *s* of late William Candler Ashby and Vera Fane Ashby (*née* Hickey); *m* 1957, Sally Hawtree; four *s* two *d*. *Educ:* King's School, Chester; King's Coll., London (BD, AKC, PhD). Deacon 1955, priest 1956; Assistant Curate: St Peter, St Helier, Morden, 1955–57; Clydesdale Mission, 1958; Priest-in-charge, St Mark's Mission, 1958–60; Subwarden, St Paul's Coll., Grahamstown, 1960–65; Rector of Alice and Lectr, Federal Theological Seminary, 1966–68; Sen. Lecturer, Old Testament and Hebrew, Rhodes Univ., Grahamstown, 1969–75; Assoc. Professor, 1974–75; Overseas Visiting Scholar, St John's Coll., Cambridge, 1975; Dean and Archdeacon, Cathedral of St Michael and St George, Grahamstown, 1976–80; Bishop of St John's (Transkei and S Africa), 1980–84; Prof. of Divinity, Univ. of Witwatersrand, Johannesburg, 1985–88. *Publications:* Theodoret of Cyrrhus as Exegete of the Old Testament, 1970; Sacrifice, 1988; articles in theological jls. *Recreation:* ornithology. *Address:* Bishopsmead, 554 Bradgate Road, Newtown Linford, Leicester LE6 0HB. *T:* Markfield (0530) 242955.

ASHBY, Prof. Michael Farries, FRS 1979; Royal Society Research Professor, Department of Engineering, University of Cambridge, since 1989 (Professor of Engineering Materials, 1973–89); *b* 20 Nov. 1935; *s* of Lord Ashby, *qv*; *m* 1962, Maureen Ashby; two *s* one *d*.

Educ: Campbell Coll., Belfast; Queens' Coll., Cambridge (BA, MA, PhD). Post-doctoral work, Cambridge, 1960–62; Asst, Univ. of Göttingen, 1962–65; Asst Prof., Harvard Univ., 1965–69; Prof. of Metallurgy, Harvard Univ., 1969–73. Mem., Akad. der Wissenschaften zu Göttingen, 1980–. Hon. MA Harvard, 1969. Editor, Acta Metallurgica, 1974–. *Recreations:* music, design. *Address:* 51 Maids Causeway, Cambridge CB5 8DE. *T:* Cambridge (0223) 64741.

ASHCOMBE, 4th Baron, *cr* 1892; **Henry Edward Cubitt;** late RAF; Chairman, Cubitt Estates Ltd; *b* 31 March 1924; *er s* of 3rd Baron Ashcombe; *S* father, 1962; *m* 1955, Ghislaine (marr. diss. 1968), *o d* of Cornelius Willem Dresselhuys, Long Island, New York; *m* 1973, Hon. Virginia Carington, *yr d* of Baron Carrington, *qv*; *m* 1979, Mrs Elizabeth Dent-Brocklehurst. *Educ:* Eton. Served War of 1939–45, RAF. Consul-General in London for the Principality of Monaco, 1961–68. *Heir: cousin* Mark Edward Cubitt, *b* 29 Feb. 1964. *Address:* Sudeley Castle, Winchcombe, Cheltenham, Glos GL54 5JD. *Club:* White's.

See also Earl of Harrington.

ASHCROFT, David, TD 1957; MA Cantab; Headmaster, Cheltenham College, 1959–78; *b* 20 May 1920; *s* of late A. H. Ashcroft, DSO; *m* 1949, Joan Elizabeth Young; two *s* three *d. Educ:* Rugby Sch.; Gonville and Caius Coll., Cambridge. War Service, 1940–46 (despatches). Asst Master, Rossall Sch., 1946–50; Asst Master, Rugby Sch., 1950–59. *Address:* London House, Ashton Keynes, Swindon, Wilts SN6 6NX. *T:* Cirencester (0285) 861319.

ASHCROFT, James Geoffrey, CB 1988; Deputy Under Secretary of State, Finance, Ministry of Defence, 1985–88; *b* 19 May 1928; *s* of James Ashcroft and Elizabeth (*née* Fillingham); *m* 1953, Margery (*née* Barratt); one *s. Educ:* Cowley Sch., St Helens; Peterhouse, Cambridge. BA (Hons Hist.). Min. of Supply, 1950–59; Min. of Aviation, 1959–61, 1964–65; Min. of Defence, 1961–64, 1965–68, 1970–73; Inst. of Strategic Studies, 1968–70; Under-Sec., Pay Board, 1973–74; Asst Under Sec. of State, Management Services, PE, 1974–76; Asst Under Sec. of State, Gen. Finance, MoD, 1976–84. *Publications:* papers on international collaboration in military logistics. *Recreation:* golf. *Address:* 39 Hill Rise, Hinchley Wood, Esher, Surrey KT10 0AL. *T:* 081–398 5637.

ASHCROFT, John Kevin, CBE 1990; Chairman, Coloroll Group, 1986–90; *b* 24 Dec. 1948; *s* of Cumania Manion and late John Ashcroft; *m* 1972, Jennifer Ann (*née* King); two *s* one *d. Educ:* Upholland Grammar School; LSE (BSc Econ Hons). Marketing Trainee, Tube Investments, 1970; Brand Manager, Crown Wallcoverings Internat. Div., 1974; Marketing Dir, Crown Wallcoverings French Subsidiary, 1976; Man. Dir, Coloroll, 1978–82, Dep. Chm. and Chief Exec., 1982–86. Young Business Man of the Year, The Guardian, 1987. *Recreations:* fine arts, opera, sports, shooting, wine, sheep breeding. *Club:* Mosimann's.

ASHCROFT, Ven. Lawrence; retired as Archdeacon of Stow and Vicar of Burton-on-Stather (1954–62); *b* 1901; *s* of Lawrence Ashcroft; *m* 1927, Barbara Louise Casson; two *s* three *d. Educ:* University Coll., Durham; Lichfield Theological Coll. Deacon, 1926; Priest, 1927; Curate of Ulverston, 1926–29, of Egremont, 1929–30; District Sec., Brit. and Foreign Bible Society, 1930–33; Southwell Minster, 1930–33; Vicar of St Saviour's, Retford, 1934–40; Chaplain to the Forces (Emergency Commission), 1940–43, now Hon. Chaplain; Rector of St Michael Stoke, Coventry, 1943; Rural Dean of Coventry, 1949–53; Hon. Canon of Coventry, 1952–53; Hon. Canon of Lincoln, 1954–62; Proctor in Convocation, Canterbury, 1955–62; Chaplain to High Sheriff of Lincolnshire, 1958, to British Embassy, Oslo, 1967, Luxembourg, 1968; Rector, St Philip's, Antigua, 1969, Manvers St Crispin, Toronto, 1970–79. Mem., Church Assembly, 1955–62. Governor, De Aston Grammar Sch., 1955–62; Founder and Chm., Brigg Church Sch., 1956–62.

ASHCROFT, Philip Giles; Legal Consultant, Registry of Friendly Societies and Building Societies Commission, since 1988; *b* 15 Nov. 1926; *s* of Edmund Samuel Ashcroft and Constance Ruth Ashcroft (*née* Giles); *m* 1st, 1968, Kathleen Margaret Senior (marr. diss. 1983); one *s*; 2nd, 1985, Valerie May Smith, *d* of late E. T. G. Smith. *Educ:* Royal Grammar Sch., Newcastle upon Tyne; Durham Univ. Admitted solicitor, 1951. Joined Treasury Solicitor's Dept, 1955; Asst Legal Adviser, Land Commn, 1967; Asst Treasury Solicitor, 1971; Under-Sec. (Legal), DTI, 1973; Legal Adviser, Dept of Energy, 1974–80; Dep. Solicitor to the Post Office, 1980–81; Solicitor, British Telecommunications, 1981–87, retired. *Recreations:* reading, listening to music, walking. *Address:* 24A Rudd's Lane, Haddenham, Aylesbury, Bucks HP17 8JP. *T:* Haddenham (0844) 291921.

ASHDOWN, Rt. Hon. Jeremy John Durham, (Paddy); PC 1989; MP Yeovil (L 1983–88, Lib Dem since 1988); Leader of the Social and Liberal Democrats, since 1988; *b* 27 Feb. 1941; *s* of John W. R. D. Ashdown and Lois A. Ashdown; *m* 1961, Jane (*née* Courtenay); one *s* one *d. Educ:* Bedford Sch. Served RM, 1959–71: 41 and 42 Commando; commanded 2 Special Boat Section; Captain RM; HM Diplomatic Service, 1st Sec., UK Mission to UN, Geneva, 1971–76; Commercial Manager's Dept, Westlands Gp, 1976–78; Sen. Manager, Morlands Ltd, 1978–81; employed by Dorset CC, 1982–83. L spokesman for Trade and Industry, 1983–86; Lib/SDP Alliance spokesman on education and science, 1987; Lib Dem spokesman on NI, 1988–. *Publication:* Citizen's Britain, 1989. *Recreations:* walking, gardening, wine making. *Address:* Vane Cottage, Norton sub Hamdon, Som TA14 6SG. *T:* Chiselborough (093588) 491. *Club:* National Liberal.

ASHE, Sir Derick (Rosslyn), KCMG 1978 (CMG 1966); HM Diplomatic Service, retired 1979; Ambassador and Permanent UK Representative to Disarmament Conference, Geneva, 1977–79 and Permanent Head of UK Delegation to UN Special Session on Disarmament, New York, 1977–78; *b* 20 Jan. 1919; *s* of late Frederick Allen Ashe and late Rosalind Ashe (*née* Mitchell); *m* 1957, Rissa Guinness, *d* of late Capt. Hon. Trevor Tempest Parker, DSC, Royal Navy and Mrs Parker; one *s* one *d. Educ:* Bradfield Coll.; Trinity Coll., Oxford. HM Forces, 1940–46 (despatches 1945). Second Sec., Berlin and Frankfurt-am-Main, 1947–49; Private Sec. to Permanent Under-Sec. of State for German Section of FO, 1950–53; First Sec., La Paz, 1953–55; FO, 1955–57; First Sec. (Information), Madrid, 1957–61; FO, 1961–62; Counsellor and Head of Chancery: Addis Ababa, 1962–64; Havana, 1964–66; Head of Security Dept, FCO (formerly FO), 1966–69; Minister, Tokyo, 1969–71; Ambassador to: Romania, 1972–75; Argentina, 1975–77. Knight of the Order of Orange-Nassau (with swords), 1945. *Recreations:* gardening, antiques. *Address:* Dalton House, Hurstbourne Tarrant, Andover, Hants SP11 0AX. *T:* Hurstbourne Tarrant (026476) 276. *Clubs:* White's, Travellers', Beefsteak.

ASHE LINCOLN, Fredman; *see* Lincoln, F. A.

ASHENHURST, Maj.-Gen. Francis Ernest; QHDS 1989; Director, Defence Dental Services, since 1990; *b* 1 April 1933; *s* of Charles Ashenhurst and Margaret Jane (*née* MacLaine); *m* 1959, Hilary Chapman; two *d. Educ:* Methodist Coll., Belfast; Queen's Univ., Belfast (BDS); London Univ. (MSc). Commnd RADC, 1963; OC Rhine Area Dental Unit, 1964–66; Instr and Chief Instr, Depot and Trng Estabt, RADC, 1967–71; Commanding Officer: Army Dental Centres, Hong Kong, 1971–73; 6 Dental Gp, UKLF, 1973–76; postgrad. studies, 1976–77; Asst Dir, Army Dental Service, 1977–78; 1 Dental Gp, BAOR, 1978–81; Dep. Dir, Army Dental Service, 1981–84; Comdt, HQ and Central Gp, RADC, 1984; Dep. Comdr, Med. (Dentistry), BAOR, 1984–86; Comdr, HQ and Tech. Services, RADC, BAOR, 1986–88; Dir, Army Dental Service, 1989–90; OStJ 1974. *Recreations:* gardening, listening to music, cooking, being idle. *Address:* DMSD, First Avenue House, High Holborn, WC1V 6HE. *T:* 071–430 5733. *Club:* Army and Navy.

ASHER, Jane; actress and writer; *b* 5 April 1946; *d* of Richard A. J. Asher, MD, FRCP and Margaret Asher (*née* Eliot); *m* Gerald Scarfe, *qv*; two *s* one *d. Educ:* North Bridge House; Miss Lambert's PNEU. *Stage:* Will You Walk a Little Faster, Duke of York's, 1960; Wendy in Peter Pan, Scala, 1961; Bristol Old Vic, 1965; Romeo and Juliet and Measure for Measure, NY, 1967; Look Back in Anger, Royal Court, 1969; The Philanthropist, Mayfair and NY, 1970; Treats, Royal Court, 1975; National Theatre, 1976; Whose Life is it Anyway?, Mermaid and Savoy, 1978; Before the Party, Queen's, 1978; Blithe Spirit, Vaudeville, 1986; Henceforward, Vaudeville, 1988; The School for Scandal, NT, 1990; *films include:* Mandy, 1951; Greengage Summer, 1961; Alfie, 1966; Deep End, 1970; Henry VIII and his Six Wives, 1970; Runners, 1984; Dream Child, 1985; Paris by Night, 1988; *television includes:* Brideshead Revisited, 1981; The Mistress, 1986; Wish Me Luck, 1987–89; Eats for Treats, 1990; Tonight at 8.30, Murder Most Horrid, 1991; numerous plays for radio; Radio Actress of the Year Award, 1986. Trustee: WWF; Child Accident Prevention Trust; Ford Martin Trust for Cancer in Children. Governor, Molecule Theatre. Opened shop, Jane Asher's Party Cakes, London, 1990. *Publications:* Jane Asher's Party Cakes, 1982; Jane Asher's Fancy Dress, 1983; Silent Nights for You and Your Baby, 1984; Jane Asher's Quick Party Cakes, 1986; The Moppy Stories, 1987; Easy Entertaining, 1987; Keep Your Baby Safe, 1988; Children's Parties, 1988; Calendar of Cakes, 1989; Eats for Treats, 1990; journalism for newspapers and magazines. *Recreations:* reading, skiing. *Address:* c/o Chatto & Linnit, Prince of Wales Theatre, Coventry Street, W1.

ASHFORD, (Albert) Reginald, CMG 1962; Assistant Secretary, Board of Customs and Excise, 1952–73; *b* 30 June 1914; *s* of Ernest and Ethel Ashford; *m* 1946, Mary Anne Ross Davidson (*d* 1990); one *s. Educ:* Ealing Grammar Sch.; London Sch. of Economics (BSc Econ). Entered Civil Service, 1931 as Clerical Officer, MoT; Exec. Officer, Customs and Excise, 1934; Private Sec. to Chm. of Bd, 1943–46; Principal, 1946; UK deleg. and sometime Chm. working parties to internat. confs on reduction of barriers to trade inc. GATT, 1946–60: Geneva, 1947; Annecy, 1949; Torquay, 1950; Havana Conf. and intermediate meetings, 1947–48; Econ. Commn for Europe, 1948–56 (TIR Convention, 1949); UNESCO Conv., Geneva and Florence, 1950; Chm., Customs Co-operation Council, 1953–60 (Chm. Permanent Tech. Cttee, 1954 and Finance Cttee, 1958–59); European Tariff discussions and European Free Trade Area Agreement, Brussels, Paris, Stockholm, 1953–60; transferred by choice to home div., 1960. Vice Chm., Bucks Assoc. for Blind, 1979–81. *Address:* 4 Tithe Green, Rustington, West Sussex BN16 3QX. *T:* Rustington (0903) 776545.

ASHFORD, George Francis, OBE 1945; retired; *b* 5 July 1911; *s* of G. W. Ashford and L. M. Redfern; *m* 1950, Eleanor Vera Alexander; two *s. Educ:* Malvern Coll.; Trinity Hall, Cambridge; Birmingham Univ. Served War of 1939–45, Army, N Africa and Italy (despatches 1944). Distillers Co. Ltd, 1937–67: Solicitor, 1937; Legal Adviser, 1945; Dir, 1956; Management Cttee, 1963–67; Dir, BP Co. Ltd, 1967–73, Man. Dir, 1969–73; Dir, Albright & Wilson Ltd, 1973–79. Mem., Monopolies and Mergers Commn, 1973–80. Pres., British Plastics Fedn, 1966–67; Vice-President: Soc. of Chemical Industry, 1966–69; Chem. Ind. Assoc., 1967–70. Mem. Economic Policy Cttee for Chemical Industry, 1967–74; Chm., Working Party on Industrial Review, 1973. Organiser, Meals on Wheels, Woodley and Sonning, 1983–86. *Recreation:* gardening. *Address:* The Old House, Sonning, Berks RG4 0UR. *T:* Reading (0734) 692122.

ASHFORD, Ven. Percival Leonard; Chaplain to the Queen, since 1982; *b* 5 June 1927; *s* of late Edwin and Gwendoline Emily Ashford; *m* 1955, Dorothy Helen Harwood; two *s. Educ:* Kemp Welch Sch., Poole; Bristol Univ.; Tyndale Hall Theol Coll., Bristol. Asst Curate, St Philip and St James, Ilfracombe, 1954; Curate-in-Charge, Church of Good Shepherd, Aylesbury, 1956; Vicar, St Olaf's, Poughill, Bude, 1959; HM Prison Service: Asst Chaplain, Wormwood Scrubs, 1965; Chaplain: Risley Remand Centre, 1966; Durham, 1969; Wandsworth, 1971; Winchester, 1975; SW Reg. Chaplain of Prisons, 1977; Chaplain General of Prisons, 1981–85; Archdeacon to the Prison Service, 1982–85; Vicar of Hambledon, 1985–87; Permission to officiate, dio. Sarum. Mem. Gen. Synod, C of E, 1985. Exam. Chaplain to Bishop of Portsmouth, 1986. Selector Chm., ACCM, 1988–. *Recreations:* choral and classical music, reading. *Address:* Applewood, 14 South Hill, Alderholt, Fordingbridge, Hants SP6 3AS. *T:* Fordingbridge (0425) 654379.

ASHFORD, Reginald; *see* Ashford, A. R.

ASHFORD, Air Vice-Marshal Ronald Gordon, CBE 1978; Senior Traffic Commissioner, Western Traffic Area and Licensing Authority, since 1991; *b* 2 May 1931; *s* of Richard Ashford and Phyllis Lancaster; *m* 1966, Patricia Ann Turner; two *d. Educ:* Ilfracombe Grammar Sch.; Bristol Univ. (LLB). Joined RAF, 1952; qualified as Navigator, 1953; OC No 115 Squadron, 1971–72; OC RAF Finningley, 1976–77; RCDS, 1978; Air Cdre Intelligence, 1979–83; Comdr, Southern Maritime Air Region, 1983–84; Dir Gen., Personal Services (RAF), MoD, 1984–85; retired. Chm., Metropolitan Traffic Comrs, 1985–91. *Recreation:* golf. *Address:* Alborough Lodge, Packhorse Road, Gerrards Cross SL9 8JD. *Club:* Royal Air Force.

ASHFORD, William Stanton, OBE 1971; HM Diplomatic Service, retired; *b* 4 July 1924; *s* of Thomas and May Ashford; *m* 1957, Rosalind Anne Collett; two *s. Educ:* Winchester Coll.; Balliol Coll., Oxford. Served RAF, 1943–47; Air Ministry, 1948; Commonwealth Relations Office, 1961; Director of British Information Services, Sierra Leone, 1961, Ghana, 1962; Acting Consul-General, Tangier, 1965; Regional Information Officer, Bombay, 1966; Head of Chancery, British Government Office, Montreal, 1967; seconded to Northern Ireland Office, 1972; FCO, 1974; Consul-General, Adelaide, 1977; High Comr, Vanuatu, 1980–82. *Recreations:* 18th Century music, backyard farming. *Address:* c/o Lloyds Bank, Fore Street, Bodmin, Cornwall PL31 2HP. *T:* Bodmin (0208) 3434.

ASHIOTIS, Costas; High Commissioner of Cyprus in London, 1966–79; Cyprus Ambassador to Denmark, Sweden, Norway and Malta, 1966–79; *b* 1908; *m. Educ:* Pancyprian Gymnasium, Nicosia; London Sch. of Economics. Journalist and editor; joined Govt Service, 1942; Asst Comr of Labour, 1948; Dir-Gen., Min. of Foreign Affairs, 1960. Mem. Cyprus delegns to UN and to internat. confs. Retired from Foreign Service, 1979. MBE 1952. *Publications:* Labour Conditions in Cyprus during the War Years, 1939–45; literary articles. *Address:* 10 Ev. Pallikarides Street, Nicosia, Cyprus.

ASHKEN, Kenneth Richard; Director, Policy and Communications Group, Crown Prosecution Service, since 1990; *b* 13 June 1945; *s* of Karol and Dulcinea Ashken; *m* 1969, Linda Salemink (separated); two *s* one *d. Educ:* Whitgift Sch., Croydon; London Univ. (LLB Hons); Cambridge Inst. of Criminology (DipCrim). Office of Director of Public Prosecutions, 1972; Asst Dir of Public Prosecutions, 1984; Hd of Policy and Inf. Div.,

Crown Prosecution Service, 1986. *Address:* Crown Prosecution Service, 4–12 Queen Anne's Gate, SW1H 9AZ. *T:* 071–273 8124.

ASHKENAZY, Vladimir; concert pianist; conductor; Music Director, Royal Philharmonic Orchestra, since 1987; Chief Conductor, Berlin Radio Symphony Orchestra, since 1989; *b* Gorky, Russia, 6 July 1937; *m* 1961, Thorunn Johannsdottir, *d* of Johann Tryggvason, Iceland; two *s* three *d. Educ:* Central Musical Sch., Moscow; Conservatoire, Moscow. Studied under Sumbatyan; Lev Oborin class, 1955: grad 1960. Internat. Chopin Comp., Warsaw, at age of 17 (gained 2nd prize); won Queen Elizabeth Internat. Piano Comp., Brussels, at age of 18 (gold medal). Joint winner (with John Ogdon) of Tchaikovsky Piano Comp., Moscow, 1962. London debut with London Symph. Orch. under George Hurst, and subseq, solo recital, Festival Hall, 1963. Has played in many countries. Makes recordings. Hon. RAM 1972. Icelandic Order of the Falcon, 1971. *Publication:* (with Jasper Parrott) Beyond Frontiers, 1985. *Address:* Käppelistrasse 15, 6045 Meggen, Switzerland.

ASHLEY, Lord; Anthony Nils Christian Ashley-Cooper; *b* 24 June 1977; *s* and *heir* of Earl of Shaftesbury, *qv*.

ASHLEY, Sir Bernard (Albert), Kt 1987; FCSD; Chairman, Laura Ashley Holdings plc, since 1985 (Chairman, Laura Ashley Ltd (formerly Ashley, Mountney Ltd), since 1954); *b* 11 Aug. 1926; *s* of Albert Ashley and Hilda Maud Ashley; *m* 1st, 1949, Laura Mountney (*d* 1985); two *s* two *d*; 2nd, 1990, Mme Regine Burnell. *Educ:* Whitgift Middle Sch., Croydon, Surrey. Army commission, 1944; Royal Fusiliers, 1944–46, seconded 1 Gurkha Rifles, 1944–45. Incorporated Ashley, Mountney Ltd, 1954. Chm., Assoc. Laura Ashley Companies Overseas. Hon. DScEcon Wales, 1986. *Recreations:* sailing, flying. *Address:* 43 rue Ducale, Brussels 1000, Belgium. *Clubs:* Royal Thames Yacht (Southampton), Army Sailing Association; Lyford Cay (Bahamas).

ASHLEY, Cedric, CBE 1984; PhD; automotive engineering consultant; Chairman, Cedric Ashley and Associates, since 1989; Chief Executive, British Internal Combustion Engine Research Institute, since 1989; *b* 11 Nov. 1936; *s* of Ronald Ashley and Gladys Fincher; *m* 1st, 1960, Pamela Jane Turner (decd); one *s*; 2nd, 1965, (Marjorie) Vivien Gooch (marr. diss. 1991); one *s* one *d*; 3rd, 1991, Auriol Mary Keogh. *Educ:* King Edward's Sch., Birmingham; Mech. Engrg Dept, Univ. of Birmingham (BSc 1958, PhD 1964). FIMechE 1978. Rolls-Royce Ltd, Derby, 1955–60; Univ. of Birmingham, 1960–73: ICI Res. Fellow, 1963; Lectr, 1966; Internat. Technical Dir, Bostrom Div., Universal Oil Products Ltd, 1973–77; Dir, Motor Industry Res. Assoc., 1977–87; Man. Dir, Lotus Engineering, 1987. Chairman: SEE, 1970–72; RAC Tech. Cttee, 1980–87; Member: SMMT Technical Bds, 1977–87; Board, Assoc. Ind. Contract Res. Orgns, 1977–86 (Pres., 1982–84); Coventry and District Engineering Employers Assoc., 1978–85; Board, Automobile Div., IMechE, 1978– (Chm., 1990–91); Court, Cranfield Inst. of Technol., 1977–87; Engine and Vehicles Cttee, DTI, 1980–88; Three-Dimensional Design Bd, CNAA, 1981–87. FRSA 1983. Cementation Muffelite Award, SEE, 1968; Design Council Award, 1974. TA, 1959–68. *Publications:* (contrib.) Infrasound and Low Frequency Vibration, ed Tempest, 1976; papers on electro-hydraulics, vehicle ride, and effect of vibration and shock on man and buildings, in learned jls. *Recreations:* travel, reading. *Address:* 29 High Street, Burnham, Bucks SL1 7JD. *T:* Maidenhead (0628) 662399. *Clubs:* Royal Automobile, Anglo-Belgian.

ASHLEY, Rt. Hon. Jack, CH 1975; PC 1979; MP (Lab) Stoke-on-Trent, South, since 1966; *b* 6 Dec. 1922; *s* of John Ashley and Isabella Bridge; *m* 1951, Pauline Kay Crispin; three *d. Educ:* St Patrick's Elem. Sch., Widnes, Lancs; Ruskin Coll., Oxford; Gonville and Caius Coll., Cambridge. Labourer and cranedriver, 1936–46; Shop Steward Convener and Nat. Exec. Mem., Chemical Workers' Union, 1946; Scholarship, Ruskin Coll., 1946–48 and Caius Coll., 1948–51 (Chm. Cambridge Labour Club, 1950; Pres. Cambridge Union, 1951); BBC Radio Producer, 1951–57; Commonwealth Fund Fellow, 1955; BBC Senior Television Producer, 1957–66; Mem., General Advisory Council, BBC, 1967–69, 1970–74. Parliamentary Private Secretary to: Sec. of State for Econ. Affairs, 1967–68; Sec. of State, DHSS, 1974–76. Mem., Lab. Party Nat. Exec. Cttee, 1976–78. Founder and Pres., Hearing and Speech Trust, 1985–. Councillor, Borough of Widnes, 1945. *Publication:* Journey into Silence, 1973. *Address:* House of Commons, SW1A 0AA.

ASHLEY, Maurice Percy, CBE 1978; *b* 4 Sept. 1907; *s* of Sir Percy Ashley, KBE, and Lady Ashley (*née* Hayman); *m* 1st, 1935, Phyllis Mary Griffiths (*d* 1987); one *s* one *d*; 2nd, 1988, Patricia Ann Entract. *Educ:* St Paul's Sch., London; New Coll., Oxford (History Scholar). 1st Class Hons Modern History; DPhil Oxon; DLitt Oxon, 1979. Historical Research Asst to Sir Winston Churchill, 1929–33; Editorial Staff, The Manchester Guardian, 1933–37; Editorial Staff, The Times, 1937–39; Editor, Britain Today, 1939–40. Served in Army, 1940–45 (Major, Intelligence Corps). Deputy Editor, The Listener, 1946–58, Editor, 1958–67; Research Fellow, Loughborough Univ. of Technology, 1968–70. Pres. Cromwell Association, 1961–77. *Publications include:* Financial and Commercial Policy under the Cromwellian Protectorate, 1934 (revised, 1962); Oliver Cromwell, 1937; Marlborough, 1939; Louis XIV and the Greatness of France, 1946; John Wildman: Plotter and Postmaster, 1947; Mr President, 1948; England in the Seventeenth Century, 1952, rev. edn, 1978; Cromwell's Generals, 1954; The Greatness of Oliver Cromwell, 1957 (revised 1967); Oliver Cromwell and the Puritan Revolution, 1958; Great Britain to 1688, 1961; The Stuarts in Love, 1963; Life in Stuart England, 1964; The Glorious Revolution of 1688, 1966 (revised, 1968); Churchill as Historian, 1968; A Golden Century, 1598–1715, 1969; (ed) Cromwell: great lives observed, 1969; Charles II: the man and the statesman, 1971; Oliver Cromwell and his World, 1972; The Life and Times of King John, 1972; The Life and Times of King William I, 1973; A History of Europe 1648–1815, 1973; The Age of Absolutism 1648–1775, 1974; A Concise History of the English Civil War, 1975, rev. edn 1990; Rupert of the Rhine, 1976; General Monck, 1977; James II, 1978; The House of Stuart, 1980; The People of England: a short social and economic history, 1982; Charles I and Oliver Cromwell, 1987; The Battle of Naseby and the Fall of Charles I, 1991. *Recreations:* bridge, gardening. *Address:* 2 Elm Court, Cholmeley Park, N6 5EJ. *T:* 081–340 3659. *Club:* Reform.

ASHLEY-COOPER, family name of **Earl of Shaftesbury.**

ASHLEY-MILLER, Dr Michael, DPH; FFCM; FRCPE; FRCP; Secretary, Nuffield Provincial Hospitals Trust, London, since 1986; *b* 1 Dec. 1930; *s* of Cyril and Marjorie Ashley-Miller; *m* 1958, Yvonne Townend; three *d. Educ:* Charterhouse; Oxford Univ.; King's Coll. Hosp.; London Sch. of Hygiene and Tropical Med. MA Oxon; BM BCh; DObstRCOG. FRCP 1990. Ho. Surg., Ho. Phys., King's Coll. Hosp., 1956–57; SMO, Dulwich Hosp., 1957; MO/SMO, RAF, 1958–61; SMO, IoW CC, 1961–64; MO/SMO, MRC (HQ Staff), 1964–74; PMO, SPMO, Scottish Home and Health Dept, 1974–86. Hon. MRCP 1986. *Publications:* (invited contributor to) Vol. III, Textbook of Public Health, 1985; (jt ed) Screening for Risk of Coronary Heart Disease, 1987; articles in The Practitioner, Public Health, The Medical Officer, Health Bull. *Recreations:* tennis, golf, reading, visiting cathedrals. *Address:* 28 Fitzwarren Gardens, N19 3TP. *T:* 071–272 7017. *Club:* Royal Society of Medicine.

ASHLEY-SMITH, Jonathan, PhD; FMA; Keeper, Department of Conservation, Victoria and Albert Museum, since 1977; *b* 25 Aug. 1946; *s* of Ewart Trist and Marian Tanfield Ashley-Smith; *m* 1967, Diane Louise (*née* Wagland); one *s* one *d. Educ:* Sutton Valence Public Sch.; Bristol Univ. (BSc (Hons), PhD). FMA 1988. Post-doctoral research, Cambridge Univ., 1970–72; Victoria and Albert Museum, 1973–. Member: UK Inst. for Conservation, 1974– (Mem., Exec Cttee, 1978–; Vice-Chm., 1980–); Crafts Council, 1980–83; Conservation Cttee, Crafts Council, 1978–83; Council for Care of Churches Conservation Cttee, 1978–85; Board of Governors, London Coll. of Furniture, 1983–85; Chm., UK Inst. for Conservation, 1983–84. FRSC 1987; FIIC 1985. Scientific Editor, Science for Conservators (Crafts Council series), 1983–84. *Publications:* articles in learned jls on organometallic chemistry, spectroscopy and scientific examination of art objects. *Recreations:* loud music, good beer. *Address:* Victoria and Albert Museum, Exhibition Road, SW7 2RL. *T:* 071–589 6371.

ASHMOLE, (Harold) David; Senior Principal Dancer, Australian Ballet, since 1984; *b* 31 Oct. 1949; *s* of Richard Thomas Ashmole and Edith Ashmole. *Educ:* Sandye Place, Beds; Royal Ballet Sch. Solo Seal, Royal Acad. of Dancing; ARAD. Joined Royal Ballet Co., 1968; Soloist, 1972; Principal, 1975; transf. to Sadler's Wells Royal Ballet, 1976, Sen. Principal, 1978–84. Appeared in: Dame Alicia Markova's Master Classes, BBC Television, 1980; Maina Gielgud's Steps, Notes and Squeaks, Aberdeen Internat. Festival, 1981. Guest appearances with Scottish Ballet, 1981, with Bolshoi (for UNESCO Gala), 1986, with Sadlers Wells Royal Ballet at Royal Opera House, 1986 (season) and in Japan, Germany, S Africa and France. *Classical ballets include:* La Bayadère, Coppélia, Daphnis and Chloe, Giselle, Nutcracker, Raymonda, The Seasons, Sleeping Beauty, Swan Lake, La Sylphide; *other ballets include:* (choreography by Ashton): Cinderella, The Two Pigeons, La Fille Mal Gardée, Les Rendezvous, The Dream, Lament of the Waves, Symphonic Variations, Birthday Offering; (Balanchine): Apollo, Prodigal Son, Serenade, The Four Temperaments, Agon, Tchaikovsky Pas de Deux; (Béjart): Gaîté Parisienne, Webern Opus 5, Songs of a Wayfarer, Le Concours; (Bintley): Night Moves, Homage to Chopin, The Swan of Tuonela; (Cranko): Brouillards, Pineapple Poll, The Taming of the Shrew, Onegin; (Darrell): The Tales of Hoffmann; (de Valois): Checkmate, The Rake's Progress; (Fokine): Les Sylphides, Petrushka; (Hynd): Papillon; (Lander): Etudes; (Lifar): Suite en Blanc; (MacMillan): Concerto, Elite Syncopations, Romeo and Juliet, Quartet, Song of the Earth, Symphony; (Massine): La Boutique Fantasque; (Miller-Ashmole): Snugglepot-and-Cuddlepie; (Nijinska): Les Biches; (Nureyev): Don Quixote; (Robbins): Dances at a Gathering, Requiem Canticles, In the Night, Concert; (Seymour): Intimate Letters, Rashamond; (Samsova): Paquita; (Tetley): Gemini, Laborintus, Orpheus; (van Manen): Grosse Fugue, 5 Tangos; (Wright): Summertide; (Prokovsky): The Three Musketeers; (Tudor): Spartacus. *Recreations:* Moorcroft pottery collection, gardening, shooting, fishing. *Address:* c/o Australian Ballet, 2 Kavanagh Street, South Melbourne, Vic 3205, Australia.

ASHMORE, Dr Alick, CBE 1979; Director, Daresbury Laboratory, Science Research Council, 1970–81; *b* 7 Nov. 1920; *s* of Frank Owen Ashmore and Beatrice Maud Swindells; *m* 1947, Eileen Elsie Fuller; two *s* three *d. Educ:* King Edward VII Sch., Lytham; King's Coll., London. Experimental Officer, RRDE, Malvern, 1941–47; Lecturer in physics, University of Liverpool, 1947–59; Queen Mary Coll., London: Reader in experimental physics, 1960–64; Prof. of Nuclear Physics, 1964–70, also Head of Physics Dept, 1968–70. *Publications:* research publications on nuclear and elementary-particle physics in Proc. Phys. Soc., Nuclear Physics, Physical Review. *Recreations:* walking, travel. *Address:* Farnham House, Hesket Newmarket, Wigton, Cumbria CA7 8JG. *T:* Caldbeck (06998) 414.

ASHMORE, Admiral of the Fleet Sir Edward (Beckwith), GCB 1974 (KCB 1971; CB 1966); DSC 1942; Director, Racal Electronics plc, since 1978; *b* 11 Dec. 1919; *er s* of late Vice-Admiral L. H. Ashmore, CB, DSO and late Tamara Vasilevna Shutt, Petrograd; *m* 1942, Elizabeth Mary Doveton Sturdee, *d* of late Rear-Admiral Sir Lionel Sturdee, 2nd Bt, CBE; one *s* one *d* (and one *d* decd). *Educ:* RNC, Dartmouth. Served HMS Birmingham, Jupiter, Middleton, 1938–42; qualified in Signals, 1943; Staff of C-in-C Home Fleet, Flag Lieut, 4th Cruiser Sqdn, 1944–45; qualified Interpreter in Russian, 1946; Asst Naval Attaché, Moscow, 1946–47; Squadron Communications Officer, 3rd Aircraft Carrier Squadron, 1950; Commander 1950; comd HMS Alert, 1952–53; Captain 1955; Captain (F) 6th Frigate Sqdn, and CO HMS Blackpool, 1958; Director of Plans, Admiralty and Min. of Defence, 1960–62; Commander British Forces Caribbean Area, 1963–64; Rear-Adm., 1965; Asst Chief of the Defence Staff, Signals, 1965–67; Flag Officer, Second-in-Command, Far East Fleet, 1967–68; Vice-Adm. 1968; Vice-Chief, Naval Staff, 1969–71; Adm. 1970; C-in-C Western Fleet, Sept.-Oct. 1971; C-in-C, Fleet, 1971–74; Chief of Naval Staff and First Sea Lord, 1974–77; First and Principal Naval Aide-de-Camp to the Queen, 1974–77; CDS, Feb.-Aug. 1977. Dep. Chm. of Govs, Suttons Hosp. in Charterhouse. *Recreations:* usual. *Club:* Naval and Military.
See also Vice-Adm. Sir P. W. B. Ashmore, Sir John Sykes, Bt.

ASHMORE, Vice-Adm. Sir Peter (William Beckwith), KCB 1972 (CB 1968); KCVO 1980 (MVO (4th Class) 1948); DSC 1942; Extra Equerry to the Queen, since 1952; *b* 4 Feb. 1921; *yr s* of late Vice-Adm. L. H. Ashmore, CB, DSO and late Tamara Vasilevna Schutt, Petrograd; *m* 1952, Patricia Moray Buller, *o d* of late Admiral Sir Henry Buller, GCVO, CB and of Lady Hermione Stuart; one *s* three *d. Educ:* Yardley Court; RN Coll., Dartmouth. Midshipman, 1939. Served War of 1939–45, principally in destroyers (despatches); Lieut, 1941; Equerry (temp.) to King George VI, 1946–48; Extra Equerry, 1948; Comdr, 1951; Captain, 1957; Deputy Director, RN Staff Coll., Greenwich, 1957; Captain (F) Dartmouth Training Squadron, 1960–61; Imperial Defence Coll., 1962; Admiralty, Plans Division, 1963; Rear-Adm. 1966; Flag Officer, Admiralty Interview Board, 1966–67; Chief of Staff to C-in-C Western Fleet and to NATO C-in-C Eastern Atlantic, 1967–69; Vice-Adm. 1969; Chief of Allied Staff, NATO Naval HQ, S Europe, 1970–72, retired 1972. Master of HM's Household, 1973–86. *Recreations:* fishing, golf. *Address:* Netherdowns, Sundridge, near Sevenoaks, Kent TN14 6AR.
See also Adm. of the Fleet Sir E. B. Ashmore.

ASHMORE, Prof. Philip George; Professor of Physical Chemistry, The University of Manchester Institute of Science and Technology, 1963–81, now Professor Emeritus; *b* 5 May 1916; *m* 1943, Ann Elizabeth Scott; three *s* one *d. Educ:* Emmanuel Coll., Cambridge. Fellow, Asst Tutor and Dir of Studies of Natural Sciences, Emmanuel Coll., Cambridge, 1949–59; Lecturer in Physical Chem., Univ. of Cambridge, 1953–63; Fellow and Tutor to Advanced Students, Churchill Coll., Cambridge, 1959–63. Vice-Principal Acad. Affairs, UMIST, 1973, 1974. Course Consultant, Open Univ., 1981–85. *Publications:* The Catalysis and Inhibition of Chemical Reactions, 1963; (ed) Reaction Kinetics, 1975; RIC Monographs for Teachers: No 5 and No 9; many papers in: TFS, International Symposium on Combustion, Jl of Catalysis. *Address:* 30 Queen Edith's Way, Cambridge CB1 4PN. *T:* Cambridge (0223) 248225.

ASHTON, family name of **Baron Ashton of Hyde.**

ASHTON OF HYDE, 3rd Baron *cr* 1911; **Thomas John Ashton,** TD; Director, Barclays Bank PLC and subsidiary companies, 1969–87; *b* 19 Nov. 1926; *s* of 2nd Baron Ashton of Hyde and of Marjorie Nell, *d* of late Hon. Marshall Jones Brooks; *S* father, 1983; *m* 1957, Pauline Trewlove, *er d* of late Lt-Col R. H. L. Brackenbury, OBE; two *s* two *d*. *Educ:* Eton; New Coll., Oxford (BA 1950, MA 1955). Sen. Exec. Local Dir, Barclays Bank, Manchester, 1968–81. Major retd, Royal Glos Hussars (TA). JP Oxon, 1965–68. *Heir: s* Hon. Thomas Henry Ashton, [*b* 18 July 1958; *m* 1987, Emma, *d* of Colin Allinson]. *Address:* Fir Farm, Upper Slaughter, Bourton-on-the-Water GL54 2JR. *Club:* Boodle's.

ASHTON, Anthony Southcliffe; *b* 5 July 1916; *s* of late Prof. Thomas Southcliffe Ashton, FBA, and of Mrs Marion Hague Ashton; *m* 1939, Katharine Marion Louise Vivian; two *d*. *Educ:* Manchester Grammar Sch.; Hertford Coll., Oxford (MA). Economist, Export Credits Guarantee Dept, 1937. Served War of 1939–45, as driver and Lt-Col, RASC. Asst Financial Editor, Manchester Guardian, 1945; Dep. Asst Dir of Marketing, NCB, 1947; Manager, various depts of Vacuum Oil Co. (later Mobil Oil Co.), 1949; attended Advanced Management Programme, Harvard Business Sch., 1961; Treasurer, 1961, Finance Director, 1967–69, Esso Petroleum Co.; Mem. Bd (Finance and Corporate Planning), Post Office Corp., 1970–73. Director: Tyzack and Partners Ltd, 1974–79; Provincial Insce Co., 1974–86. Member: Shipbuilding Industry Bd, 1967–71; Council of Manchester Business Sch., 1968–81; Dir, Oxford Univ. Business Summer Sch., 1974 (Mem., Steering Cttee, 1978–81). Trustee: PO Pension Fund, 1975–83; Tyzack Employee Trust, 1979–84; Dir, Exeter Trust, 1980–86 (Chm., 1982–86). Vice-Pres., Hertford Coll. Soc., 1977–. *Address:* Quarry Field, Stonewall Hill, Presteigne, Powys LD8 2HB. *T:* Presteigne (0544) 267447. *Club:* Army and Navy.

ASHTON, George Arthur, CEng; FIMechE; engineering and management consultant, retired; *b* 27 Nov. 1921; *s* of Lewis and Mary Ashton; *m* 1st, 1948, Joan Rutter (decd); one *s*; 2nd, 1978, Pauline Jennifer Margett. *Educ:* Llanidloes Grammar Sch.; Birmingham Central Tech. Coll. Student Engrg Apprentice, Austin Motor Co., 1939–42. HM Forces, 1943–47 (Temp. Major, REME). Works Dir, Tubes Ltd, 1958; Tech. Dir, 1962, Dep. Man. Dir, 1966, TI Steel Tube Div.; Dir, Tube Investments, 1969; Man. Dir, Machine Div., 1974, Technical Dir and Business Area Chm., 1978–84, TI Group plc; Chm., Seamless Tubes Ltd, 1983–86. Dir, A. Lee & Sons plc, 1981–. Dep. Chm., Steering Cttee, WINTECH, Welsh Develt Agency, 1984–87. Pres., BISPA, 1974–75; Vice-Pres., AMTRI, 1986– (Chm. Council, 1982–86). FRSA 1981; CBIM. *Recreations:* gardening, walking, theatre-going. *Address:* Barn Cottage, Longford, Derby DE6 3DT. *T:* Great Cubley (0335) 330561. *Club:* Naval and Military.

ASHTON, John Russell, CB 1988; retired engineer; *b* 28 Feb. 1925; *s* of Jessie Florence and John William Ashton; *m* 1951, Isobel Burbury; two *d*. *Educ:* Canberra Grammar School; Sydney University. BE (Civil Engineering). Hydro-Electric Commission, Tasmania: Engineer, 1947–54; System Development Engineer, 1954–71; Dep. Engineer for Civil Investigation, 1971–72; Asst to Comr, 1972–77; Commissioner, 1977–87. In-service training Fellowship with US Bureau of Reclamation, 1960. *Recreations:* golf, photography, carpentry, gardening. *Address:* 3 Lanrick Court, Lindisfarne, Tasmania 7015, Australia. *T:* 002–438758. *Club:* Royal Hobart Golf.

ASHTON, Joseph William; MP (Lab) Bassetlaw Division of Notts since Nov. 1968; journalist; *b* 9 Oct. 1933; *s* of Arthur and Nellie Ashton, Sheffield; *m* 1957, Margaret Patricia Lee; one *d*. *Educ:* High Storrs Grammar Sch.; Rotherham Technical Coll. Engineering Apprentice, 1949–54; RAF National Service, 1954–56; Cost Control Design Engineer, 1956–68; Sheffield City Councillor, 1962–69. PPS to Sec. of State for Energy, formerly Sec. of State for Industry, 1975–76; an Asst Govt Whip, 1976–77; Opposition Spokesman on Energy, 1979–81. Member, Select Committee: on Trade and Industry, 1987–89; on Home Affairs, 1989–90. Columnist for: Sheffield Star, 1970–75, 1979–80; Labour Weekly, 1971–82; Daily Star, 1979–87; Sunday People, 1987–88; Plus magazine, 1988–89. Columnist of the Year, What the Papers Say, Granada TV, 1984. *Publications:* Grass Roots, 1977; A Majority of One (stage play), 1981. *Recreations:* being a Director of Sheffield Wednesday and Vice-Pres. of supporters' club, reading, do-it-yourself, motoring, films, theatre. *Address:* 16 Ranmoor Park Road, Sheffield. *T:* Sheffield (0742) 301763. *Clubs:* Foundry Working Men's (Sheffield); Doncaster Road Working Men's (Langold); various Miners' Institutes, etc.

ASHTON, Kenneth Bruce; General Secretary, National Union of Journalists, 1977–85; *b* 9 Nov. 1925; *m* 1955, Amy Anne Sidebotham; four *s*. *Educ:* Latymer Upper School. Served Army, 1942–46. Reporter: Hampstead and Highgate Express, 1947–50; Devon and Somerset News, Mansfield Reporter, Sheffield Star, 1950–58; Sub-Editor, Sheffield Telegraph, Daily Express, London and Daily Mail, Manchester, 1958–75. Nat. Exec. Cttee Mem., NUJ, 1968–75, Pres., 1975, Regional Organiser, 1975–77. Member: TUC Printing Industries' Cttee, 1975—86; Printing and Publishers' Industry Training Bd, 1977–83; British Cttee, Journalists in Europe, 1980–86; Communications Adv. Cttee, UK Nat. Commn for Unesco, 1981–86; consultative Mem., Press Council, 1977–80; Pres., Internat. Fedn of Journalists, 1982–86. *Address:* High Blean, Raydaleside, Askrigg, Leyburn, N Yorks DL8 3DJ.

ASHTON, Rt. Rev. Leonard (James), CB 1970; Bishop in Cyprus and The Gulf, 1976–83; Hon. Assistant Bishop, Diocese of Oxford, since 1984; *b* 27 June 1915; *s* of late Henry Ashton and Sarah Ashton (*née* Ing). *Educ:* Tyndale Hall, Bristol. Ordained, Chester, 1942; Curate, Cheadle, 1942–45; Chap. RAF, 1945–; N Wales, 1945; AHQ Malaya and Singapore, 1946; BC Air Forces, Japan, 1947–48; Halton, 1948–49; Feltwell, 1949–50; Chap. and Lectr, RAF Chap. Sch., Cheltenham, 1950–53; Sen. Chap., AHQ Iraq, 1954–55; RAF Coll., Cranwell, 1956–60; Br. Forces Arabian Peninsular and Mid. East Command, 1960–61; Asst Chap. Chief, Trng Commands, 1962–65; Res. Chap., St Clement Danes, Strand, 1965–69; Chaplain-in-Chief, (with relative rank of Air Vice-Marshal) RAF, and Archdeacon of RAF, 1969–73; QHC, 1967–73; Hon. Canon and Prebendary of St Botolph, Lincoln Cathedral, 1969–73, Canon Emeritus, 1973–; Asst Bishop in Jerusalem, 1974–76; Episcopal Canon: St George's Cathedral, Jerusalem, 1976–83; St Paul's Cath., Nicosia, Cyprus, 1989–; Hon. Asst Bishop, Jerusalem and Middle East, 1983–84; Commissary for Bishop in Iran and Bishop in Jerusalem, 1984–. ChStJ 1976. *Publication:* Winged Words, 1990. *Recreations:* gardening, photography. *Address:* 60 Lowndes Avenue, Chesham, Bucks HP5 2HJ. *T:* Chesham (0494) 782952. *Club:* Royal Air Force.

ASHTON, Prof. Norman (Henry), CBE 1976; DSc (London); FRS 1971; FRCP, FRCS, FRCPath, FCOphth; Professor of Pathology, University of London, 1957–78, now Emeritus; Director, Department of Pathology, Institute of Ophthalmology, University of London, 1948–78; Consultant Pathologist, Moorfields Eye Hospital, 1948–78; *b* 11 Sept. 1913; 2nd *s* of Henry James and Margaret Ann Ashton. *Educ:* West Kensington Central Sch.; King's Coll. and Westminster Hosp. Med. Sch., Univ. of London. Westminster Hospital: Prize in Bacteriology, 1938; Editor Hosp. Gazette, 1939–40; House Surg., House Phys., Sen. Casualty Officer and RMO, 1939–41. Asst Pathologist, Princess Beatrice Hosp., 1939; Dir of Pathology, Kent and Canterbury Hosp., and Blood Transfusion Officer of East Kent, 1941. Lieut-Col RAMC, Asst Dir of Pathology and Officer i/c Central Pathological Lab., Middle East, 1946. Pathologist to the Gordon Hosp., 1947; Reader in Pathology, Univ. of London, 1953; Fellow in Residence, Johns Hopkins Hosp., Baltimore, 1953, and Visiting Prof. there, 1959. Emeritus Fellow, Leverhulme Trust. Vis. Research Fellow, Merton Coll., Oxford, 1980. Lectures: Walter Wright, 1959; Banting, 1960; Clapp (USA), 1964; Proctor (USA), 1965; Bradshaw (RCP), 1971; Montgomery, 1973; Foundation, RCPath, 1974; Jackson (USA), 1978; Foundn, Assoc. of Clinical Pathologists, 1985. Chm., Fight for Sight Appeal; Trustee, Sir John Soane's Museum, 1977–82. Member, Board of Governors: Moorfields Eye Hosp., 1963–66 and 1975–78; Hosp. for Sick Children, Gt Ormond St, 1977–80; Royal Nat. Coll. for the Blind, 1977–; Member: Brit. Nat. Cttee for Prevention of Blindness, 1973–78; Royal Postgrad. Med. Sch. Council, 1977–80; Council, RCPath, 1963–66 and 1976–78 (Founder Fellow); Governing Body, Brit. Postgrad. Med. Fedn, 1967–82, and Cent. Acad. Council, 1957–78 (Chm., 1967–70); Council, RSM, 1971–79, and Exec. Cttee, 1976–81; Med. Adv. Bd, British Retinitis Pigmentosa Soc.; Pathological Soc. of Great Britain and Ireland; European Assoc. for Study of Diabetes; Chapter Gen. and Hosp. Cttee of St John; Oxford Ophthalmological Congress; Medical Art Soc.; Member, Cttee of Management: Inst. of Ophthalmology, 1953–78, 1984–; Inst. of Child Health, 1960–65; Cardio-Thoracic Inst., 1972–78; Inst. of Rheumatology, 1973–77; Mem. Bd of Governors, Brendoncare Foundn, 1984–. President: Ophth. Sect., RSM, 1972–74; Assoc. of Clinical Pathologists, 1978–79; Ophth. Soc. of UK, 1979–81; Chm., Brit. Diab. Assoc. Cttee on Blindness in Diabetes, 1967–70. Fellow, Inst. of Ophthalmology. Hon. Life Mem., British Diabetic Association; Life Pres. European Ophth. Pathology Soc.; Pres. Brit. Div. Internat. Acad. of Pathology, 1962. Hon. Member: Assoc. for Eye Research; Hellenic Ophth. Soc.; British Div., Internat. Acad. of Pathology; Amer. Ophth. Soc.; Gonin Club. Hon. Fellow: RSocMed; Coll. of Ophthalmologists; Coll. of Physicians, Philadelphia; Amer. Acad. Ophthal. and Otolaryng. Mem. Ed. Bd, Brit. Jl Ophthalmology, 1963–78, and Jl Histopathology. FRSocMed; Master, Soc. of Apothecaries of London, 1984–85; Freeman, City of London. Hon. DSc Chicago. KStJ. Edward Nettleship Prize for Research in Ophthalmology, 1953; BMA Middlemore Prize, 1955; Proctor Medal for Research in Ophthalmology (USA), 1957; Doyne Medal (Oxford), 1960; William Julius Mickle Fellow, Univ. London, 1961; Bowman Medal, 1965; Donder's Medal, 1967; Wm Mackenzie Memorial Medal, 1967; Gonin Medal, 1978; 1st Jules Stein Award, USA, 1981; Francis Richardson Cross Medal, 1982; Lord Crook Gold Medal, Spectacle Makers' Co., 1989. *Publications:* contrib. to books and numerous scientific articles in Jl of Pathology and Bacteriology, Brit. Jl of Ophthalmology, and Amer. Jl of Ophthalmology. *Recreations:* painting, gardening. *Address:* 4 Blomfield Road, Little Venice, W9 1AH. *T:* 071–286 5536. *Clubs:* Athenæum, Garrick.

ASHTON, Rev. Canon Patrick Thomas, LVO 1963; Chaplain to the Queen, 1955–86; *b* 27 July 1916; *s* of Lieut-Col S. E. Ashton, OBE; *m* 1942, Mavis St Clair Brown, New Zealand; three *d* (one *s* decd). *Educ:* Stowe; Christ Church, Oxford (MA); Westcott House, Cambridge. Served War of 1939–45 as Captain, Oxfordshire Yeomanry; Curate, St Martin-in-the-Fields, 1947–51; Rector of All Saints, Clifton, Beds, 1951–55; Rector of Sandringham with West Newton and Appleton, and Domestic Chaplain to the Queen, 1955–70; Rector: Sandringham Gp of Eight Parishes, 1963–70; Swanborough Team of Parishes, 1970–73; Priest-in-charge of Avebury with Winterbourne Monkton and Berwick Bassett, 1974–77; Rector, Upper Kennet team of Parishes, 1975–77; a Canon of Salisbury Cathedral, 1975; Rural Dean of Marlborough, 1976–77. *Address:* Field Cottage, Bottlesford, Pewsey, Wilts SN9 6LU. *T:* Woodborough (067285) 340.

ASHTON, Prof. Robert, PhD; Professor of English History, University of East Anglia, 1963–89, now Emeritus; *b* 21 July 1924; *s* of late Joseph and late Edith F. Ashton; *m* 1946, Margaret Alice Sedgwick; two *d*. *Educ:* Magdalen Coll. Sch., Oxford; University Coll., Southampton (1942–43, 1946–49); London Sch. of Economics (1949–52). BA 1st Cl. hons (London) 1949; PhD (London) 1953; Asst Lecturer in Economic History, Univ. of Nottingham, 1952; Lecturer, 1954; Senior Lecturer, 1961; Vis. Associate Prof. in History, Univ. of California, Berkeley, 1962–63; Prof. of English History, 1963, and Dean of Sch. of English Studies, 1964–67, Univ. of East Anglia. Vis. Fellow, All Souls Coll., Oxford, 1973–74 and 1987; James Ford Special Lectr in History, Oxford, 1982; Leverhulme Emeritus Fellow, 1989–90. FRHistS 1960 (Vice-Pres., 1983–86). *Publications:* The Crown and the Money Market, 1603–1640, 1960; Charles I and the City, in Essays in the Economic and Social History of Tudor and Stuart England in honour of R. H. Tawney (ed F. J. Fisher), 1961; James I by his Contemporaries, 1969; The Civil War and the Class Struggle, in The English Civil War and After 1642–1658 (ed R. H. Parry), 1970; The English Civil War: Conservatism and Revolution 1603–49, 1978, 2nd edn 1989; The City and the Court 1603–1643, 1979; Reformation and Revolution 1558–1660, 1984; articles in learned periodicals. *Recreations:* music, looking at old buildings, wine. *Address:* The Manor House, Brundall, Norwich NR13 5JY. *T:* Norwich (0603) 713368.

ASHTON, Roy; a Recorder of the Crown Court, since 1979; barrister-at-law; *b* 20 Oct. 1928; *s* of Charles and Lilian Ashton; *m* 1954, Brenda Alice Dales; one *s* one *d*. *Educ:* Boston Grammar Sch.; Nottingham Univ. (LLB Hons). National Service, Directorate of Legal Services, RAF, 1951–53. Called to the Bar, Lincoln's Inn, 1954. Dep. Chairman, Agricultural Land Tribunal, 1978–. *Recreations:* reading, chess, film collecting. *Address:* (chambers) 22 Albion Place, Northampton. *Club:* Northampton and County.

ASHTON, Ruth Mary, (Mrs E. F. Henschel), OBE 1991; RGN, RM, MTD; General Secretary, Royal College of Midwives, since 1980; *b* 27 March 1939; *d* of Leigh Perry Ashton and Marion Lucy Ashton (*née* Tryon); *m* 1984, E. Fred Henschel. *Educ:* Kenya High Sch. for Girls; Clarendon Sch. (lately Abergele). London Hosp. and Queen Mother's Hosp., Glasgow; High Coombe Midwife Teachers' Training College (RN 1964; RM 1967; MTD 1970). Staff Midwife and Midwifery Sister, Queen Mother's Hosp., Glasgow, 1967–69; Nursing Officer and Midwifery Tutor, King's College Hosp., 1971–75; Tutor, 1975–79 and Professional Officer, 1979, Royal College of Midwives. Temp. Prof., March of Dimes, Los Angeles, 1982. OStJ 1988. *Publications:* midwifery related articles. *Recreations:* gardening, sailing, travel. *Address:* Royal College of Midwives, 15 Mansfield Street, W1M 0BE. *T:* 071–580 6523. *Club:* Queenborough Yacht.

ASHTON HILL, Norman, MBE (mil.) 1945; TD; Consultant, Ashton Hill Bond, Solicitors and Commissioners for Oaths, 1981 (Principal Partner, 1948–81); *b* 1 March 1918; *s* of Sydney and Marguerite Ashton Hill, Bewdley, Worcs; *m* 1971, Ireina Hilda Marie; (one *s* two *d* by former *m*). *Educ:* Uppingham Sch.; Birmingham Univ. (LLB Hons). Served War, 1939–45: commnd 2nd Lieut TA, 1939; BEF, BLA, BAOR; Staff Coll. (psc), mentioned in despatches; NW Europe War Crimes, 1945–46; Hon. Lt-Col, Royal Warwickshire Regt. Enrolled Gibraltar Bar, 1971. Chm., Radio Trent Ltd, 1973–79; Dir, 1971–78, Vice-Chm., 1972–78, Bonser Engrg Ltd. Director: Lunn Poly (formerly Sir Henry Lunn Ltd) (Vice-Chm., 1954–68); Eagle Aviation Ltd, and Cunard Eagle Airways Ltd and Group, 1952–68; North Midland Construction Plc, 1971–85; Morgan Housing Co. Ltd and Group, 1962–81; Derby Music Finance Ltd, 1978–84; Cooper & Roe Ltd, 1979–80. Chairman: Air Transport Cttee, ABCC, 1958–82 (a Vice-Pres. ABCC, 1977–88); Air Transp. Cttee, ICC UK (formerly British National Chamber of Internat. Chamber of Commerce), 1970–88; Air Transport Users Cttee, 1980–82 (Mem., 1976–82; Dep. Chm., 1978–79; Hon. Consultant, 1982–86); Fedn of Air Transport Users Representatives in the Economic Community, 1982–86 (Hon. Pres., 1987); Rapporteur to Internat. Foundn of Airline Passengers Assoc., 1986–. CRAeS 1980.

NSPCC: Hon. Vice-Pres., and formerly Hon. Gen. and Cases Sec., Nottingham Br.; Mem. Central Exec. Cttee, 1955–80, Vice-Chm., 1974–80; Hon. Vice-Pres. Hon. Vice-Consul for Norway, Notts, 1955–80. Assistant, Glaziers Co., 1978–87. FRSA. Kt (1st Cl.), Order of St Olav, Norway, 1972. *Recreations:* gardening, shooting, humanities. *Address:* Apartado 435, Estepona, Málaga 29680, Spain. *T:* (34) 52–793719. *Club:* Royal Aero.

ASHTOWN, 7th Baron *cr* 1800; **Nigel Clive Cosby Trench,** KCMG 1976 (CMG 1966); HM Diplomatic Service, retired; *b* 27 Oct. 1916; *s* of Clive Newcome Trench (*d* 1964), *g s* of 2nd Baron, and Kathleen (*d* 1979), 2nd *d* of Major Ivar MacIvor, CIE; *S* cousin, 1990; *m* 1939, Marcelle Catherine Clotterbooke Patyn; one *s*. *Educ:* Eton; Univ. of Cambridge. Served in KRRC, 1940–46 (despatches). Appointed a Member of the Foreign (subseq. Diplomatic) Service, 1946; Lisbon, 1946; First Secretary, 1948; returned Foreign Office, 1949; First Secretary (Commercial) Lima, 1952; transf. Foreign Office, 1955; Counsellor, Tokyo, 1961; Counsellor, Washington, 1963; Cabinet Office, 1967; HM Ambassador to Korea, 1969–71; CS Selection Board, 1971–73; Ambassador to Portugal, 1974–76. Mem., Police, Prison and Fire Service Selection Bds, 1977–86. Sungrye Medal, Order of Distinguished Diplomatic Service Merit (Korea), 1984. *Heir: s* Hon. Roderick Nigel Godolphin Trench [*b* 17 Nov. 1944; *m* 1st, 1967, Janet (*d* 1971), *d* of Harold Hamilton-Faulkner; one *s*; 2nd, 1973, Susan Barbara, *d* of L. F. Day, FRCS, DLO; one *d*]. *Address:* 4 Kensington Court Gardens, Kensington Court Place, W8 5QE. *Clubs:* Naval and Military, MCC.

ASHWORTH, Prof. Graham William, CBE 1980; DL; Professor of Urban Environmental Studies, University of Salford, 1973–87, part-time Research Professor, since 1987; Director General, Tidy Britain (formerly Keep Britain Tidy) Group, since 1987; *b* 14 July 1935; *s* of Frederick William Ashworth and Ivy Alice Ashworth; *m* 1960, Gwyneth Mai Morgan-Jones; three *d*. *Educ:* Devonport High Sch., Plymouth; Univ. of Liverpool (Master of Civic Design, BArch). RIBA, PPRTPI, FRSA, FInstEnvSci, FBIM. LCC (Hook New Town Project), 1959–61; consultancy with Graeme Shankland, 1961–64; architect to Civic Trust, 1964–65; Dir, Civic Trust for North-West, 1965–73 (Chm., Exec. Cttee, 1973–87); Director: Univ. of Salford Environmental Inst., 1978–87; CAMPUS (Campaign to Promote Univ. of Salford), 1981–87. Member: Skeffington Cttee on Public Participation in Planning, 1969; North-West Adv. Council of BBC, 1970–75 (Chm.); NW Economic Planning Council (and Sub-gp Chm.), 1968–79; Countryside Commn, 1974–77; Merseyside Urban Develt Corp., 1981–; (non-exec.) North Western Electricity Bd, 1985–88; Chm., Ravenhead Renaissance, 1988–. Governor, Northern Baptist Coll., 1966–82; Pres., Royal Town Planning Inst., 1973–74; Chm., Instn of Environmental Sciences, 1980–82. Member: Council, St George's House, Windsor, 1982–88; Council, Baptist Union, 1983–. Trustee, Manchester Mus. of Science and Industry, 1988–. Editor, Internat. Jl of Environmental Educn, 1981–. DL Lancs 1991. *Publication:* An Encyclopædia of Planning, 1973. *Recreations:* gardening, painting, church and social work. *Address:* Manor Court Farm, Preston New Road, Samlesbury, Preston PR5 0UP. *Clubs:* Athenæum, National Liberal.

ASHWORTH, Sir Herbert, Kt 1972; Chairman: Nationwide Building Society, 1970–82 (Deputy-Chairman, 1968–70); Nationwide Housing Trust, 1983–87; *b* 30 Jan. 1910; *s* of Joseph Hartley Ashworth; *m* 1936, Barbara Helen Mary, *d* of late Douglas D. Henderson; two *s* one *d*. *Educ:* Burnley Grammar Sch.; London Univ. (grad. econ. and law). General Manager, Portman Building Soc., 1938–50; General Manager, Co-operative Permanent Building Soc., 1950–61; Director and General Manager, Hallmark Securities Ltd, 1961–66. Dep. Chm., 1964–68, Chm., 1968–73, Housing Corp. Dir, The Builder Ltd, 1975–80. Chm., Surrey and W Sussex Agricl Wages Cttee, 1974–87. Vice-Pres., Building Socs Assoc. *Publications:* Housing in Great Britain, 1951; Building Society Work Explained, (current edn), 1977; The Building Society Story, 1980. *Address:* 8 Tracery, Park Road, Banstead, Surrey SM7 3DD. *T:* Burgh Heath (0737) 352608.

ASHWORTH, Ian Edward; Circuit Administrator, Western Circuit, Lord Chancellor's Office (Under Secretary), 1970–87; *b* 3 March 1930; *s* of late William Holt and Cicely Ashworth, Rochdale; *m* Pauline, *er d* of late Maurice James Heddle, MBE, JP, and of Gladys Heddle, Westliff-on-Sea; two *s* one *d*. *Educ:* Manchester Grammar Sch.; The Queen's Coll., Oxford (BCL, MA). Admitted Solicitor, 1956; FGA 1983. Asst Solicitor, Rochdale, 1956–58; Dep. Town Clerk, Dep. Clerk of Peace, Canterbury, 1958–63; Town Clerk, Clerk of Peace, Deal, 1963–66; Town Clerk, Rugby, 1966–70. *Recreations:* music, gemmology, gardening. *Address:* Westdale Edge, Beer Road, Seaton, Devon EX12 2PT. *T:* Seaton (0297) 21212. *Club:* United Oxford & Cambridge University.

ASHWORTH, James Louis, FIMechE, FIEE, ARTC (Salford); Full-Time Member for Operations, Central Electricity Generating Board, 1966–70, retired; *b* 7 March 1906; *s* of late James and late Janet Ashworth; *m* 1931 Clara Evelyn Arnold; one *s* two *d*. *Educ:* Stockport Grammar Sch.; Salford Royal Coll. of Technology. Apprenticeship with Mirrlees, Bickerton & Day Ltd, Stockport (Diesel Oil Engine Manufrs), 1924–29; Metro-Vickers Electrical Co. Ltd, 1929; Manchester Corp. Elec. Dept, Stuart Street Gen. Stn, 1930–32; Hull Corp. Elec. Dept, 1932–35; Halifax Corp. Elec. Dept, 1935–40; Mersey Power Co. Ltd, Runcorn, 1940–48; British Elec. Authority, N West: Chief Generation Engr (O), 1948–57; Dep. Divisional Controller, 1957–58; Central Elec. Gen. Bd, N West, Merseyside and N Wales Region: Dep. Regional Dir, 1958–62; Regional Dir, 1962–66. *Recreations:* gardening, photography, travel, reading. *Address:* Chase Cottage, 23 The Chase, Reigate, Surrey. *T:* Redhill (0737) 61279.

ASHWORTH, Brig. John Blackwood, CBE 1962; DSO 1944; retired 1965; *b* 7 Dec. 1910; *s* of Lieut-Col H. S. Ashworth, Royal Sussex Regt (killed in action, 1917) and late Mrs E. M. Ashworth; *m* 1944, Eileen Patricia, *d* of late Major H. L. Gifford (Royal Ulster Rifles) and of Lady Gooch; one *d*. *Educ:* Wellington Coll.; RMC, Sandhurst. Commissioned Royal Sussex Regt, 1930; Instructor RMC, 1938; War of 1939–45 (despatches twice); OC Training Centre, 1942; OC 1/5 Queen's Royal Regt (wounded, DSO), 1944; GSO1, War Office, 1944; OC 4/5 Royal Sussex, 1945; OC 1st Royal Sussex, 1946; GSO1, Brit. Middle East Office, 1947; AMS War Office, 1948; OC 1st Royal Sussex, 1951; Comdt Joint Sch. of Chemical Warfare, 1954; Commander 133rd Inf. Bde (TA), 1957; Director of Military Training, War Office, 1959–62; Inspector of Boys' Training, War Office, 1962–65. ADC to the Queen, 1961–65. Col The Royal Sussex Regt, 1963–66; Dep. Col, The Queen's Regt (Royal Sussex), 1967–68. DL Sussex 1972–83. OStJ 1950. Grand Officer, Order of House of Orange, 1967. *Address:* 16 Castlegate, New Brook Street, Ilkley, W Yorks LS29 8DF. *T:* Ilkley (0943) 602404.

ASHWORTH, Dr John Michael, FIBiol; Director, London School of Economics and Political Science, since 1990; Chairman, National Computing Centre, since 1983; *b* 27 Nov. 1938; *s* of late Jack Ashworth and late Constance Mary Ousman; *m* 1st, 1963, Ann Knight (*d* 1985); one *s* three *d*; 2nd, 1988, Auriol Stevens. *Educ:* West Buckland Sch., N Devon; Exeter Coll., Oxford (MA, DSc; Hon. Fellow, 1983); Leicester Univ. (PhD). FIBiol 1974. Dept of Biochemistry, Univ. of Leicester: Res. Demonstr, 1961–63; Lectr, 1963–71; Reader, 1971–73; Prof. of Biology, Univ. of Essex, 1974–79 (on secondment to Cabinet Office, 1976–79); Under-Sec., Cabinet Office, 1979–81 and Chief Scientist, Central Policy Review Staff, 1976–81; Vice-Chancellor, Univ. of Salford, 1981–90. Harkness Fellow of Commonwealth Fund, NY, at Brandeis Univ. and Univ. of Calif, 1965–67. NEDO: Chm., Information Technology EDC, 1983–86; Mem., Electronics EDC, 1983–86. Chm., Nat. Accreditation Council for Certification Bodies, BSI, 1984–88. Director: Granada TV, 1987–89; Granada Group, 1990–. Colworth Medal, Biochem. Soc., 1972. *Publications:* Cell Differentiation, 1972; (with J. Dee) The Slime Moulds, 1976; over 100 pubns in prof. jls on biochem., genet., cell biolog. and educnl topics. *Recreation:* windsurfing. *Address:* London School of Economics and Political Science, Houghton Street, Aldwych, WC2A 2AE.

ASHWORTH, Peter Anthony Frank; Director, Leeds Permanent Building Society, since 1971 (President, 1978); *b* 24 Aug. 1935; *s* of Peter Ormerod and Dorothy Christine Ashworth; *m* 1964, Elisabeth Crompton; one *s* one *d*. *Educ:* Leeds Grammar School. Articled to Hollis & Webb, Chartered Surveyors, Leeds (now Weatherall, Green & Smith), 1953–56; Partner, 1961–80. FRICS; ACIArb. *Recreations:* golf, gardening. *Address:* 4 Bridge Paddock, Collingham, Wetherby LS22 5BN. *T:* Collingham Bridge (0937) 572953. *Club:* Alwoodley Golf (Leeds).

ASHWORTH, Piers, QC 1973; a Recorder of the Crown Court, since 1974; *b* 27 May 1931; *s* of Tom and Mollie Ashworth; *m* 1st, 1959, Iolene Jennifer (marr. diss. 1978), *yr d* of W. G. Foxley; three *s* one *d*; 2nd, 1980, Elizabeth, *er d* of A. J. S. Aston. *Educ:* Christ's Hospital; Pembroke Coll., Cambridge (scholar). Commnd Royal Signals, 1951. BA (Cantab) 1955; Harmsworth Law Scholar, 1956; called to Bar, Middle Temple, 1956, Bencher, 1984; Midland and Oxford circuit. Gov. and Almoner, Christ's Hosp, 1986–. *Recreations:* sailing, squash, tennis, bridge. *Address:* 2 Harcourt Buildings, Temple, EC4Y 9DB. *T:* 071–583 9020.

ASIMOV, Prof. Isaac, PhD; Professor of Biochemistry, University of Boston, since 1979; author; *b* 2 Jan. 1920; *s* of Judah Asimov and Anna Rachel (*née* Berman); *m* 1st, 1942, Gertrude Blugerman; one *s* one *d*; 2nd, 1973, Dr Janet Jeppson. *Educ:* Columbia Univ. (BS 1939, MA 1941, PhD 1948, all in chemistry). Joined faculty of Boston Univ. Sch. of Medicine, 1949; retd from academic labors, 1958, but retained title. First professional sale of short story, 1938; first book published, 1950; 400th book published, 1988. *Publications:* over 400 books, including: I, Robot, 1950; The Human Body, 1963; Asimov's Guide to Shakespeare, 1970; Asimov's Guide to Science, 1972; Murder at the ABA, 1976; The Collapsing Universe, 1977; In Memory Yet Green (autobiog., vol. 1), 1979; A Choice of Catastrophes, 1979; In Joy Still Felt (autobiog., vol. 2), 1980; In the Beginning, 1981; Foundation's Edge, 1982; The Robots of Dawn, 1983; Asimov's New Guide to Science, 1984; Asimov's Guide to Halley's Comet, 1985; Robots and Empire, 1985. *Recreation:* a man's work is his play: my recreation is writing. *Address:* 10 West 66th Street, New York, NY 10023, USA. *T:* 212–362–1564.

ASIROGLU, Vahap; Turkish Ambassador to the Court of St James's, 1978–81; *b* Karamürsel, 1916; *m*; one *c*. *Educ:* Galatasaray High Sch.; Istanbul Univ. (Faculty of Law). Third Sec., Second Political Dept, Min. of Foreign Affairs, 1943–46; successively, Third, Second, First Sec., Turkish Embassy, Prague, 1946–51; First Sec., Dept of Internat. Economic Affairs, MFA, 1951–53; First Sec. and Counsellor, Turkish Perm. Mission to UN, 1953–59; Asst Dir Gen., Dept of Internat. Econ. Affairs, MFA, 1959–60; Asst Dir Gen. and Dir Gen., Personnel and Admin. Dept, MFA, 1960; Dir Gen., UN and Internat. Instns Dept, MFA, 1960–62; Asst Perm. Rep., Turkish Perm. Mission to UN, 1962–65; Turkish Ambassador: to Copenhagen, 1965–68; to Jakarta, 1968–71; Sec. Gen., Reg. Cooperation for Develt (a reg. org. between Turkey, Iran and Pakistan), 1971–74; Sen. Counsellor, MFA, 1974; Director General: Dept of Consular Affairs, MFA, 1974–75; Dept of Cultural Affairs, MFA, 1975–76; Asst Sec. Gen. for Inf. and Cultural Affairs, MFA, 1976. Mem., UN Human Rights Commn, 1953–56; Turkish Rep., ICAO Conf., Montreal, 1956–57; Head of Turkish Delegn, GATT Conf., Tokyo, 1959; Asst Chm., Conf. on Immunities and Diplomatic Relns, Vienna, 1961; Chm., Fifth Commn, UN Gen. Assembly, 1967. *Address:* Tahran Caddesi 6–3, Kavaklidere, 06700 Ankara, Turkey.

ASKE, Rev. Sir Conan, 2nd Bt *cr* 1922; Assistant Curate of St John-in-Bedwardine, Worcester, 1972–80; *b* 22 April 1912; *s* of Sir Robert William Aske, 1st Bt, TD, QC, LLD, and Edith (*d* 1918), *d* of Sir Walter Herbert Cockerline; *S* father 1954; *m* 1st, 1948, Vera Faulkner (*d* 1960); 2nd, 1965, Rebecca, *d* of Hugh Grant, Wick, Caithness. *Educ:* Rugby; Balliol Coll., Oxford. TA, London Irish Rifles, 1939; served, 1939–49, with East York Regt, Sudan Defence Force, Somalia Gendarmerie. Major, Civil Affairs Officer, Reserved Area of Ethiopia and The Ogaden, 1949–51; Schoolmaster, Hillstone, Malvern, 1952–69; Asst Curate, Hagley, Stourbridge, 1970–72. Hon. Padre, Worcs Br., 1940 Dunkirk Veterans' Assoc., 1988–. *Heir: b* Robert Edward Aske [*b* 21 March 1915; *m* 1940, Joan Bingham, *o d* of Captain Bingham Ackerley, Cobham; one *s*]. *Address:* 167 Malvern Road, Worcester WR2 4NN. *T:* Worcester (0905) 422817.

ASKEW, Barry Reginald William; journalist, broadcaster and public relations consultant; *b* 13 Dec. 1936; *s* of late Reginald Ewart Askew and Jane Elizabeth Askew; *m* 1st, 1958, June Roberts (marr. diss. 1978), *d* of Vernon and late Betty Roberts; one *s* one *d*; 2nd, 1980, Deborah Parker, *d* of Harold and Enid Parker. *Educ:* Lady Manners Grammar Sch., Bakewell, Derbys. Trainee reporter upwards, Derbyshire Times, 1952–57; Reporter and sub-ed., Sheffield Telegraph, 1957–59; reporter, feature writer and broadcaster, Raymonds News Agency, Derby, 1959–61; Editor, Matlock Mercury, 1961–63; Industrial Correspondent, Asst Ed., Dep. Ed., Sheffield Telegraph, later Morning Telegraph, Sheffield, 1964–68; Associate Ed., The Star, Sheffield, 1968; Editor, 1968–81, Dir, 1978–81, Lancashire Evening Post; Editor, News of the World, 1981. Presenter and anchor man: ITV, 1970–81; BBC Radio 4, 1971–72; BBC 1, 1972; BBC 2, 1972–76. Consultant in TV, radio, PR and commerce, 1982–91. Mem., Davies Cttee to reform hosp. complaints procedures in UK, 1971–73. Campaigning Journalist of 1971, IPC Nat. Press Awards; Journalist of 1977, British Press Awards; Crime Reporter of 1977, Witness Box Awards. *Recreations:* Rugby, chess, reading military history, golf. *Address:* School House Cottage, Rosemary Lane, Bartle, Preston, Lancs. *T:* Preston (0772) 731817, (office) Preston (0772) 690459. *Club:* Preston Grasshoppers RF.

ASKEW, Sir Bryan, Kt 1989; Personnel Director, Samuel Smith Old Brewery (Tadcaster), since 1982; Chairman, Yorkshire Regional Health Authority, since 1983; *b* 18 Aug. 1930; *s* of John Pinkney Askew and Matilda Askew; *m* 1955, Millicent Rose Holder; two *d*. *Educ:* Wellfield Grammar Sch., Wingate, Co. Durham; Fitzwilliam Coll., Cambridge (MA Hons History). ICI Ltd, 1952–59; Consett Iron Co. Ltd (later part of British Steel Corporation), 1959–71; own consultancy, 1971–74; Samuel Smith Old Brewery (Tadcaster), 1974–. Member, Consett UDC, 1967–71; contested (C) General Elections: Penistone, 1964 and 1966; York, 1970. Mem., Duke of Edinburgh's Third Commonwealth Study Conf., Australia, 1968. Mem., Working Gp on Young People and Alcohol, Home Office Standing Conf. on Crime Prevention, 1987. Mem. Court, 1985–, Mem. Council, 1988–, Univ. of Leeds. FRSA 1986; FRSM 1988. *Recreations:* listening to music, reading, walking, particularly in Northumberland. *Address:* The Old Brewery, Tadcaster LS24 9SB. *T:* Tadcaster (0937) 832225. *Club:* Royal Society of Medicine.

ASKEW, John Marjoribanks Eskdale, CBE 1974; *b* 22 Sept. 1908; *o s* of late William Haggerston Askew, JP, Ladykirk, Berwicks, and Castle Hills, Berwick-on-Tweed; *m* 1st,

1933, Lady Susan Egerton (marr. diss., 1966), 4th *d* of 4th Earl of Ellesmere, MVO; one *s* one *d*; *m* 1976, Priscilla Anne, *e d* of late Algernon Ross-Farrow. *Educ*: Eton; Magdalene Coll., Cambridge (BA). Lieut 2 Bn Grenadier Guards, 1932; Capt. 1940; Major 1943; served NW Europe 1939–40 and 1944–45. Brigadier, Royal Company of Archers, Queen's Body Guard for Scotland. Convener: Berwicks CC, 1961; Border Regional Council, 1974–82. *Address*: Ladykirk, Berwicks. *T*: Berwick (0289) 82229; Castle Hills, Berwick-on-Tweed. *Clubs*: Boodle's; New (Edinburgh).
See also Baron Faringdon, Duke of Sutherland.

ASKEW, Rev. Canon Reginald James Albert; Dean of King's College, London, since 1988; Canon Emeritus, Salisbury Cathedral, since 1988; *b* 16 May 1928; *s* of late Paul Askew and Amy Wainwright; *m* 1953, Kate, *yr d* of late Rev. Henry Townsend Wigley; one *s* two *d*. *Educ*: Harrow; Corpus Christi Coll., Cambridge (MA); Lincoln Theological College. Curate of Highgate, 1957–61; Tutor and Chaplain of Wells Theol. Coll., 1961–65, Vice-Principal 1966–69; Priest Vicar of Wells Cath., 1961–69; Vicar of Christ Church, Lancaster Gate, London, 1969–73; Principal, Salisbury and Wells Theol Coll., 1973–87; Canon of Salisbury Cathedral and Prebendary of Grantham Borealis, 1975–87. Proctor, London Univ.; Mem., Gen. Synod of C of E, 1990–. Mem., Corrymeela Community. *Publication*: The Tree of Noah, 1971. *Recreations*: music, gardening, cricket. *Address*: King's College, Strand, WC2R 2LS. *T*: 071–873 9028; Carters Cottage, North Wootton, Somerset BA4 4AF.

ASKONAS, Brigitte Alice, PhD; FRS 1973; Head of Division of Immunology, MRC, National Institute for Medical Research, London, 1977–88; with Institute of Molecular Medicine (Molecular Immunology), John Radcliffe Hospital, Oxford, since 1989 (part-time); *b* 1 April 1923; *d* of late Charles F. Askonas and Rose Askonas. *Educ*: McGill Univ., Montreal (BSc, MSc); Cambridge Univ. (PhD; Hon. Fellow, New Hall and Girton Coll.). Research student, Sch. of Biochemistry, Univ. of Cambridge, 1949–52; Immunology Div., NIMR, 1953–89; Dept of Bacteriology and Immunology, Harvard Med. Sch., Boston, 1961–62; Basel Inst. for Immunology, Basel, Switzerland, 1971–72. Hon. Member: Amer. Soc. of Immunology; Soc. française d'Immunologie. Hon. DSc McGill, 1987. *Publications*: contrib. scientific papers to various biochemical and immunological jls and books. *Recreations*: art, travel. *Address*: 23 Hillside Gardens, N6 5SU. *T*: 081–348 6792; Institute of Molecular Medicine (Molecular Immunology), John Radcliffe Hospital, Headington, Oxford OX3 9DU. *T*: Oxford (0865) 752336.

ASKWITH, Hon. Betty Ellen, FRSL; *b* 26 June 1909; *o d* of late Baron Askwith, KCB, KC, LLD, and Lady Askwith, CBE; *m* 1950, Keith Miller Jones (*d* 1978). *Educ*: Lycée Français, London; North Foreland Lodge, Broadstairs. *Publications*: First Poems, 1928; If This Be Error, 1932; Poems, 1933; Green Corn, 1933; Erinna, 1937; Keats, 1940; The Admiral's Daughters, 1947; A Broken Engagement, 1950; The Blossoming Tree, 1954; The Tangled Web, 1960; A Step Out of Time, 1966; Lady Dilke, 1969; Two Victorian Families, 1971; The Lytteltons, 1975; A Victorian Young Lady, 1978; Piety and Wit: Harriet Countess Granville 1785–1862, 1982; Crimean Courtship, 1985; with Theodora Benson: Lobster Quadrille, 1930; Seven Basketfuls, 1932; Foreigners, 1935; Muddling Through, 1936; How to Be Famous, 1937. *Translations*: The Tailor's Cake, 1947; A Hard Winter, 1947; Meeting, 1950. *Recreation*: reading Victorian novels. *Address*: 9/105 Onslow Square, SW7. *T*: 071–589 7126.

ASLET, Clive William; Deputy Editor, Country Life, since 1989; *b* 15 Feb. 1955; *s* of Kenneth and Monica Aslet; *m* 1980, Naomi Roth. *Educ*: King's College Sch., Wimbledon; Peterhouse, Cambridge. Joined Country Life, 1977, Architectural Editor, 1984–88. Founding Hon. Sec., Thirties Soc., 1979–87. *Publications*: The Last Country Houses, 1982; (with Alan Powers) The National Trust Book of the English House, 1985; Quinlan Terry, the Revival of Architecture, 1986; The American Country House, 1990; Countryblast, 1991. *Recreations*: opera, writing, travel, living in London. *Address*: c/o Country Life, King's Reach Tower, Stamford Street, SE1 9LS. *T*: 071–261 6969. *Club*: Garrick.

ASPEL, Michael Terence; broadcaster and writer; *b* 12 Jan. 1933; *s* of late Edward and of Violet Aspel; *m* 1st, 1957, Dian; one *s* (and one *s* decd); 2nd, 1962, Ann; twin *s* and *d*; 3rd 1977, Elizabeth; two *s*. *Educ*: Emanuel School. Tea boy, publishers, 1949–51. Nat. Service, KRRC and Para Regt, TA, 1951–53. Radio actor, 1954–57; television announcer, 1957–60, newsreader, 1960–68; freelance broadcaster, radio and TV, 1968–; presenter: Aspel and Company, 1984–; This is Your Life, 1988–; occasional stage appearances. Pres., Stackpole Trust, 1985–; Vice-President: BLISS (Baby Life Support Systems), 1981–; ASBAH (Assoc. for Spina Bifida and Hydrocephalus), 1985–; Patron, Plan International, 1986–. Member: Equity, 1955–; Lord's Taverners; RYA. FZS. *Publications*: Polly Wants a Zebra (autobiog.), 1974; Hang On! (for children), 1982; (with Richard Hearsey) Child's Play, 1985; regular contribs to magazines. *Recreations*: water sports, theatre, cinema, eating, travel. *Address*: c/o Bagenal Harvey Organisation, 141–143 Drury Lane, WC2B 5TB.

ASPELL, Col Gerald Laycock, TD (2 clasps); DL; FCA; Vice Lord-Lieutenant of Leicestershire, 1984–90; *b* 10 April 1915; *s* of Samuel Frederick Aspell and Agnes Maude (*née* Laycock); *m* 1939, Mary Leeson Carroll, *d* of Rev. Ion Carroll, Cork; one *s* two *d*. *Educ*: Uppingham Sch. FCA 1938. Commnd 2nd Lieut, 4th Bn Leicestershire Regt, TA, 1933; served War of 1939–45 in UK and Burma, RE, RA, RAF; commanded 579 Light Anti-Aircraft Regt, RA (TA), 1946–51. Partner, Coopers & Lybrand, 1952–78; mem. of various nat. and local cttees of Inst. of Chartered Accountants during that time. Dir, 1964–85, Chm., 1978–85, Leicester Building Soc.; Dep. Chm., Alliance and Leicester Building Soc., 1985; Local Dir, Eagle Star Insce Gp, 1949–84 (Chm., Midlands Bd, 1970–84). Chairman: Leicester and Dist Local Employment Cttee, then Leics Dist Manpower Cttee, 1971–79. Mem., Leicester Diocesan Bd of Finance, 1952–77. Civil Defence Controller, then Sub-Regl Dir CD, Leics, Rutland and Northants, 1956–65. Member: Leics and Rutland TAA, then E Midlands TAVRA, 1947–80 (Chm., Leics Cttee, 1969–80). Hon. Colonel: Royal Anglian Regt (Leics), 1972–79; Leics and Northants ACF, 1979–84. Grand Treasurer, United Grand Lodge of England, 1974–75. Trustee, Uppingham Sch., 1964–87 (Chm., 1977–87). DL Leics, 1952. *Recreations*: cricket, tennis, squash, fishing, charitable involvements. *Address*: Laburnum House, Great Dalby, Melton Mowbray, Leics LE14 2HA. *T*: Melton Mowbray (0664) 63604. *Club*: Leicestershire (Leicester).

ASPIN, Norman, CMG 1968; HM Diplomatic Service, retired; Adviser and Secretary, East Africa Association, 1981–84; *b* 9 Nov. 1922; *s* of Thomas and Eleanor Aspin; *m* 1948, Elizabeth Irving; three *s*. *Educ*: Darwen Grammar Sch.; Durham Univ. (MA). War Service, 1942–45, Lieut RNVR. Demonstrator in Geography, Durham Univ., 1947–48; Asst Principal, Commonwealth Relations Office, 1948; served in India, 1948–51; Principal, Commonwealth Relations Office, 1952; served in Federation of Rhodesia and Nyasaland, 1954–57; British Deputy High Commissioner in Sierra Leone, 1961–63; Commonwealth Relations Office, 1963–65; British Embassy, Tel Aviv, 1966–69; IDC 1970; Head of Personnel Policy Dept, FCO, 1971–73; Under-Sec., FCO, 1973–76; Comr, British Indian Ocean Territory, 1976; British High Comr in Malta, 1976–79; Asst Under-Sec. of State, FCO, 1979–80. *Recreations*: sailing, tennis. *Address*: Mounsey Bank, Dacre, Cumbria CA11 0HL.

ASPINALL, John Victor; Chairman of the Trustees, Howletts and Port Lympne Foundation, since 1984; *b* 11 June 1926; *s* of late Col Robert Aspinall and Mary (*née* Horn, later Lady Osborne); *m* 1st, 1956, Jane Gordon Hastings (marr. diss. 1966); one *s* one *d*; 2nd, 1966, Belinda Musker (marr. diss. 1972); 3rd, 1972, Lady Sarah Courage (*née* Curzon); one *s*. *Educ*: Rugby Sch.; Jesus Coll., Oxford. Founded: Howletts Zoo Park, 1958; Clermont Club, 1962; Port Lympne Zoo Park, 1973; Aspinall's Club, 1978; Aspinall Curzon Club, 1984. Won gaming case Crown *v* Aspinall, 1958. *Publications*: The Best of Friends, 1976, Amer. edn 1977, German edn 1978; (contrib.) Primates: the road to self-sustaining populations; contribs to Jl of Reproduction and Fertility, Ecologist. *Recreations*: wild animals, gambling. *Address*: 64 Sloane Street, SW1X 9SH. *T*: 071–235 2768.

ASPINALL, Wilfred; Member, European Economic and Social Consultative Assembly, since 1986; Principal and Partner, Aspinall & Associates, Eurolink Professionals in Europe, European Communities Advisers, since 1988; Executive Director, Federation of Managerial, Professional and General Associations, since 1978; parliamentary and industrial relations consultant; Vice-President, Confédération International des Cadres, since 1979; *b* 14 Sept. 1942; *s* of late Charles Aspinall and Elizabeth Aspinall; *m* 1973, Judith Mary, *d* of late Leonard James Pimlott and Kathleen Mary Pimlott; one *d*. *Educ*: Poynton Secondary Modern; Stockport Coll. for Further Educn. Staff, National Provincial Bank Ltd, 1960–69; Asst Gen. Sec., National Westminster Staff Assoc., 1969–75; Dep. Sec. (part-time), Council of Bank Staff Assocs, 1969–75; Mem., Banking Staff Council, 1970–77; Gen. Sec., Confedn of Bank Staff Assocs, 1975–79. Member: N Herts DHA, 1981–86; NW Thames RHA, 1986–88; Hammersmith and Queen Charlotte's SHA, 1981–90; Professions Allied to Medicine, Whitley Management Negotiating Cttee, 1983–87. *Recreations*: motoring, travel—particularly to places of historical interest, social affairs and political history. *Address*: The Croft, Shillington Road, Pirton, Hitchin, Herts. *T*: Hitchin (0462) 712316; (office) Tavistock House, Tavistock Square, WC1. *T*: 071–383 7783; Economic and Social Consultative Assembly, rue Ravenstein 2, Brussels 1000, Belgium. *T*: 519 9498; (Brussels private office) Boîte 49, 34 rue de Montagne, Brussels 1000. *T*: 511 2720.

ASPINWALL, Jack Heywood; MP (C) Wansdyke, since 1983 (Kingswood, 1979–83); company director; *b* Feb. 1933; *m* Brenda Jean Aspinwall. *Educ*: Prescot Grammar School, Lancs; Marconi College, Chelmsford. Served RAF, 1949–56. Director, investment co. Mem., Avon County Council. Contested (L) Kingswood, Feb. and Oct. 1974. *Publication*: (comp.) Kindly Sit Down!: best after-dinner stories from both Houses of Parliament, 1983. *Address*: House of Commons, SW1A 0AA; 154 Bath Road, Willsbridge, Bristol.

ASPRAY, Rodney George, FCA; Chief Executive Officer, Norwest Cooperative Society, since 1969; *b* 1934. Secretary, Manchester and Salford Cooperative Society, 1965–69; Director: Co-operative Bank, 1980–89 (Chm., 1986–89); Co-operative Wholesale Soc. Ltd, 1980–89; Mersey Docks & Harbour Co., 1987–; Piccadilly Radio Plc, 1989–90. Mem., Monopolies and Mergers Commn, 1975–81. FCA 1960. *Address*: Kambara, 4 Green Lane, Higher Poynton, Cheshire SK12 1TJ.

ASQUITH, family name of **Earl of Oxford and Asquith**.

ASQUITH, Viscount; Raymond Benedict Bartholomew Michael Asquith; HM Diplomatic Service; Foreign and Commonwealth Office, since 1980; *b* 24 Aug. 1952; *er s* and *heir* of 2nd Earl of Oxford and Asquith, *qv*; *m* 1978, Mary Clare, *e d* of Francis Pollen; one *s* four *d*. *Educ*: Ampleforth; Balliol College, Oxford. FCO, 1980–83; First Sec., Moscow, 1983–85. *Heir*: *s* Hon. Mark Julian Asquith, *b* 13 May 1979. *Address*: Little Claveys, Mells, Frome, Somerset.

ASSCHER, Prof. (Adolf) William, MD, FRCP; Dean, St George's Hospital Medical School, London University, since 1988; Hon. Consultant Physician, St George's Hospital, since 1988; *b* 20 March 1931; *s* of William Benjamin Asscher and Roosje van der Molen; *m* 1st, 1959, Corrie van Welt (*d* 1961); 2nd, 1962, Dr Jennifer Lloyd, *d* of Wynne Llewelyn Lloyd, CB; two *d*. *Educ*: Maerlant Lyceum, The Hague; London Hosp. Med. Coll. BSc 1954; MB 1957; MD 1963; MRCP 1959, FRCP 1971. Nat. service, Lieut RE, 1949–51. Jun. appts, London Hosp., 1957–59; Lectr in Medicine, London Hosp. Med. Coll., 1959–64; Welsh National School of Medicine, later University of Wales College of Medicine: Sen. Lectr, 1964–70, and Hon. Cons. Physician, Royal Inf., Cardiff; Reader, 1970–76; Prof. of Medicine, 1976–80; Head of Dept of Renal Medicine, 1980–88. Chairman: Cttee on Review of Medicines, DHSS, 1985–87; Cttee on Safety of Medicines, DHSS, 1987– (Mem., 1984–87); Member: Medicines Commn, DHSS, 1981–84; SW Thames RHA, 1987–90; Welsh Arts Council, 1985–88. Regl Advr, 1976–79, Mem. Council, 1977–80, RCP. Examnr, Final MB, Wales, London, Bristol and Edinburgh. Pres., Renal Assoc., 1986–89. *Publications*: Urinary Tract Infection, 1973 (with W. Brumfitt); the Challenge of Urinary Tract Infections, 1980; (with D. B. Moffat and E. Sanders) Nephrology Illustrated, 1982; (with D. B. Moffat) Nephro-Urology, 1983; (with W. Brumfitt) Microbial Diseases in Nephrology, 1986; (with S. R. Walker) Medicines and Risk-Benefit Decisions, 1986; (with J. D. Williams) Clinical Atlas of the Kidney, 1991; papers on nephrology in learned jls. *Recreations*: visual arts, golf, tennis. *Address*: Dean's Office, St George's Hospital Medical School, Cranmer Terrace, Tooting, SW17 0RE. *T*: 081–672 3122. *Club*: Reform.

ASSHETON, family name of **Baron Clitheroe**.

ASTAIRE, Jarvis Joseph; Deputy Chairman, Wembley Stadium, since 1984; Chairman, Viewsport Ltd, since 1964; *b* 6 Oct. 1923; *s* of late Max and of Esther Astaire; *m* 1st, 1948, Phyllis Oppenheim (*d* 1974); one *s* one *d*; 2nd, 1981, Nadine Hyman (*d* 1986). *Educ*: Kilburn Grammar Sch., London. Dir, Lewis & Burrows Ltd, 1957–60; Managing Director: Mappin & Webb Ltd, 1958–60; Hurst Park Syndicate, 1962–71; Director: Perthpoint Investments Ltd, 1959–70; Associated Suburban Properties Ltd, 1963–81; Anglo-Continental Investment & Finance Co. Ltd, 1964–75; William Hill Org., 1971–82; First Artists Prodns Inc. (USA), 1976–79; Wembley PLC (formerly GRA Gp), 1987–; Greyhound Racing Assoc., 1991–. Introduced into UK showing of sporting events on large screen in cinemas, 1964. Chm., Royal Free Hosp. and Med. Sch. Appeal Trust, 1974; Hon. Treas., London Fedn of Boys' Clubs, 1976–. Chm., Associated City Properties, 1981–. Chief Barker (Pres.), Variety Club of GB, 1983; Pres., Variety Clubs Internat. (Worldwide), 1991–. *Recreations*: playing tennis, watching cricket and football. *Address*: Broughton House, 6–8 Sackville Street, W1X 1DD. *T*: 071–287 4601. *Clubs*: East India, MCC; Friars (USA).

ASTILL, Michael John; His Honour Judge Astill; a Circuit Judge, since 1984; *b* 31 Jan. 1938; *s* of Cyril Norman Astill and Winifred Astill; *m* 1968, Jean Elizabeth, *d* of Dr J. C. H. Mackenzie; three *s* one *d*. *Educ*: Blackfriars School, Laxton, Northants. Admitted solicitor, 1962; called to the Bar, Middle Temple, 1972; a Recorder, 1980–84. A Pres., Mental Health Tribunals, 1986–. *Recreations*: music, reading, sport. *Address*: Colborough House, Halstead, Tilton-on-the-Hill, Leics. *T*: Tilton (053754) 608.

ASTLEY, family name of **Baron Hastings.**

ASTLEY, Sir Francis Jacob Dugdale, 6th Bt, *cr* 1821; Head of Classics Department, The Atlantic College, St Donat's Castle, Glamorgan, 1962–69, retired; *b* 26 Oct. 1908; *s* of Rev. Anthony Aylmer Astley (6th *s* of 2nd Bt); *S* kinsman 1943; *m* 1934, Brita Margareta Josefina Nyström, Stockholm; one *d*. *Educ:* Marlborough; Trinity Coll., Oxford. Sen. Lectr, University Coll. of Ghana, 1948–61. *Heir:* none. *Address:* 16 Doulton Mews, Lymington Road, NW6 1XY. *T:* 071–435 9945.

ASTLEY, Philip Sinton, LVO 1979; HM Diplomatic Service; Deputy Head of Mission, Copenhagen, since 1990; *b* 18 Aug. 1943; *s* of Bernard Astley and Barbara Astley (*née* Sinton); *m* 1966, Susanne Poulsen; two *d*. *Educ:* St Albans Sch.; Magdalene Coll., Cambridge (BA 1965). Asst Representative, British Council, Madras, 1966–70; British Council, London, 1970–73; First Sec., FCO, 1973–76, Copenhagen, 1976–79; First Sec. and Head of Chancery, East Berlin, 1980–82; First Sec., FCO, 1982–84; Counsellor and Head of Management Review Staff, FCO, 1984–86; Econ. Counsellor and Consul Gen., Islamabad, 1986–90. Kt, Order of Dannebrog (Denmark), 1979. *Recreations:* oriental textiles, gardening. *Address:* c/o Foreign and Commonwealth Office, SW1A 2AH.

ASTLING, Alistair Vivian; Chief Executive, Dudley Metropolitan Borough Council, since 1988; *b* 6 Sept. 1943; *s* of Alec William and Barbara Grace Astling; *m* 1967, Hazel Ruth Clarke. *Educ:* Glyn Grammar Sch., Epsom; Sheffield Univ. (LLB 1965; LLM 1967); Birmingham Univ. (MSocSci 1973). West Bromwich County Borough Council: articled clerk, 1967; Asst Solicitor, 1971; Asst Town Clerk, 1973; Walsall Metropolitan Borough Council: Corporate Planner, 1974; Chief Exec. and Town Clerk, 1982; Clerk to W Midlands Police Authy, 1988–; Sec. to Birmingham Internat. Airport Shareholders' Forum, 1988–. *Recreations:* squash, theatre, music. *Address:* Dudley Metropolitan Borough Council, Council House, Dudley DY1 1HF. *T:* Dudley (0384) 453201; 16 Knighton Drive, Sutton Coldfield, W Midlands B74 4QP.

ASTON, Archdeacon of; *see* Barton, Ven. C. J. G.

ASTON, Sir Harold (George), Kt 1983; CBE 1976; Chairman and Chief Executive, Bonds Coats Patons Ltd, 1981–87 (Deputy Chairman, 1970–80); Director, Central Sydney Area Health Service, since 1988; *b* Sydney, 13 March 1923; *s* of Harold John Aston and Annie Dorothea McKeown; *m* 1947, Joyce Thelma Smith; one *s* one *d*. *Educ:* Crown Street Boys' Sch., Sydney, Australia. Manager, Buckinghams Ltd, Sydney, 1948–55; Bonds Industries Ltd: Merchandising Manager, 1955–63; Gen. Man., 1963–67; Man. Dir, 1967–70; Director: Bonds Coats Patons Ltd (formerly Bonds Industries Ltd); Manufacturers Mutual Insurance, 1982–; Downard-Pickfords Pty Ltd, 1983–89 (Chm.); Australian Guarantee Corp. Ltd, 1983–88; Australian Manufacturing Life Assce Ltd, 1984–88; Rothmans Hldgs Ltd, 1986–; Westpac Banking Corp., 1988–; Consultant, Pacific Dunlop Ltd, 1987–. President: Textile Council of Australia, 1973–80 (Life Mem., 1984); Confedn of Aust. Industry, 1980–82; Hon. Trustee, Cttee for Econ. Develt of Australia, 1988–; Governor: Aesop Foundn, 1988–; (Founding), Heart Inst. of Australia, 1986–. CompTI 1984; FCFI 1986; OStJ 1987 (Dep. Receiver-Gen., Finance Cttee, 1985–). *Recreations:* bowls, swimming, walking, gardening. *Address:* 44 Greenway Drive, Pymble, NSW 2073, Australia. *Clubs:* American, Australian, Royal Sydney Yacht Squadron (Sydney); Concord Golf.
See also Sir William Aston.

ASTON, Prof. Peter George, DPhil; Professor of Music, University of East Anglia, since 1974; *b* 5 Oct. 1938; *s* of late George William Aston and Elizabeth Oliver Smith; *m* 1960, Elaine Veronica Neale; one *s*. *Educ:* Tettenhall Coll.; Birmingham Sch. of Music (GBSM); Univ of York (DPhil); FTCL, ARCM. Lectr in Music, 1964–72, Sen. Lectr, 1972–74, Univ. of York; Dean, Sch. of Fine Arts and Music, UEA, 1981–84. Dir, Tudor Consort, 1958–65; Conductor: English Baroque Ensemble, 1968–70; Aldeburgh Festival Singers, 1975–88; Jt Artistic Dir, Norwich Fest. of Contemporary Church Music, 1981–; Chorus Master, Norfolk and Norwich Triennial Fest., 1982–88. Chairman: Eastern Arts Assoc. Music Panel, 1976–81; Norfolk Assoc. for the Advancement of Music, 1990–; Pres., Trianon Music Gp, 1984–. Patron, Lowestoft Choral Soc., 1986–. Gen. Editor, UEA Recording Series, 1979–. FRSA 1980. Hon. Fellow, Curwen Inst., 1987. *Compositions:* song cycles, chamber music, choral and orchestral works, church music, opera. *Publications:* George Jeffreys and the English Baroque, 1970; The Music of York Minster, 1972; Sound and Silence (jtly), 1970, German edn 1972, Italian edn 1979, Japanese edn 1982; (ed) The Collected Works of George Jeffreys, 3 vols, 1977; contrib. to internat. music jls. *Recreations:* Association football, cricket, bridge, chess. *Address:* University of East Anglia, Music Centre, School of Art History and Music, Norwich NR4 7TJ. *T:* Norwich (0603) 56161. *Clubs:* Athenæum; Norfolk (Norwich).

ASTON, Hon. Sir William (John), KCMG 1970; JP; Speaker, House of Representatives, Australia, 1967–73; MP for Phillip, 1955–61, 1963–72; Chairman, Kolotex Holdings Ltd; Director, Neilson McCarthy & Partners; *b* 19 Sept. 1916; *s* of Harold John Aston and Dorothea (*née* McKeown); *m* 1941, Beatrice Delaney Burrett; one *s* two *d*. *Educ:* Randwick Boys' High School. Served War, 1939–45, AIF in New Guinea, Lieut. Mayor of Waverley, 1952–53. Dep. Govt Whip, 1959–61 and 1963–64; Chief Govt Whip, 1964–67; Trustee, Parlt Retiring Allowances, 1964–67; Mem. and Dep. Chm., Joint Select Cttee on New and Perm. Parlt House, 1965–72; Chairman: House of Reps Standing Orders Cttee, 1967–72; Joint House Cttee, 1967–72; Library Cttee, 1967–72; Joint Cttee on Broadcasting of Parly Proceedings, 1967–72; Jt Chm., Inter-Parliamentary Union (Commonwealth of Aust. Br.) and Commonwealth Parly Assoc. (Aust. Br.), 1967–72; Leader, Aust. Delegn to IPU Conf., Ottawa, 1964; Convenor and Chm., First Conf. of Aust. Presiding Officers, 1968; rep. Australia at: opening of Zambian Parlt Bldg; Funeral of Israeli Prime Minister Eshkol and IPU Symposium, Geneva, 1968; Conf. of Commonwealth Presiding Officers, Ottawa, 1969, New Delhi, 1971; opened Aust. House, Mt Scopus, Univ. of Israel, 1971; led Parly delegn to Turkey, Yugoslavia, UK and to Council of Europe, 1971. JP NSW 1954. Korean Order of Distinguished Service Merit (1st Class), 1969. *Recreations:* cricket, golf, football, fishing, bowls. *Address:* 55 Olola Avenue, Vaucluse, NSW 2030, Australia. *T:* 337–5992. *Clubs:* Royal Automobile of Australia (Sydney); Waverley Bowling, Royal Sydney Golf.
See also Sir H. G. Aston.

ASTOR, family name of **Viscount Astor** and **Baron Astor of Hever.**

ASTOR, 4th Viscount, *cr* 1917, of Hever Castle; Baron *cr* 1916; **William Waldorf Astor;** a Lord in Waiting (Government Whip), since 1990; *b* 27 Dec. 1951; *s* of 3rd Viscount Astor; *S* father 1966; *m* 1976, Annabel Sheffield, *d* of T. Jones; two *s* one *d*. *Educ:* Eton Coll. *Heir:* *s* Hon. William Waldorf Astor, *b* 18 Jan. 1979. *Address:* Ginge Manor, Wantage, Oxon OX12 8QT. *Clubs:* White's, Turf.

ASTOR OF HEVER, 3rd Baron *cr* 1956, of Hever Castle; **John Jacob Astor;** *b* 16 June 1946; *s* of 2nd Baron Astor of Hever and of Lady Irene Haig, *d* of Field Marshal 1st Earl Haig, KT, GCB, OM, GCVO, KCIE; *S* father, 1984; *m* 1st, 1970, Fiona Diana Lennox Harvey (marr. diss. 1990), *d* of Captain Roger Harvey; three *d*; 2nd, 1990, Hon. Elizabeth, *d* of 2nd Viscount Mackintosh of Halifax, OBE, BEM; one *s*. *Educ:* Eton College. Lieut Life Guards, 1966–70, Malaysia, Hong Kong, Ulster. Director: Terres Blanches Services Sarl, 1975–77; Valberg Plaza Sarl, 1977–82; Electro-Nucleonics, Inc., 1984–; Man. Dir, Honon et Cie, 1982–; President: Astor Enterprises Inc., 1983–; Vitesse Washington Inc., 1986–; Chm., Astor Enterprises Ltd, 1986–. Chm., Council of St John, Kent, 1987–. *Heir:* *s* Hon. Charles Gavin John Astor, *b* 10 Nov. 1990. *Address:* Frenchstreet House, Westerham, Kent TN16 1PW. *Clubs:* White's, Cavalry and Guards.
See also Hon. H. W. Astor.

ASTOR, David Waldorf; farmer, since 1973; Chairman, Council for the Protection of Rural England, since 1983; *b* 9 Aug. 1943; *s* of late Michael Langhorne Astor and Barbara Mary (*née* McNeil); *m* 1968, Clare Pamela St John; two *s* two *d*. *Educ:* Eton Coll.; Harvard Univ. Short service comm in Royal Scots Greys, 1962–65. United Newspapers, 1970–72; Housing Corp., 1972–75; Head of Develt, National Th., 1976–77. Director: Jupiter Tarbutt Merlin, 1985–; Sinclair-Stevenson Ltd, 1990–; Priory Investments Holdings, 1990–; Chm., Classic FM, 1989–. Contested (SDP/Alliance) Plymouth Drake, 1987. FRSA. *Recreations:* books, sport. *Address:* Bruern Grange, Milton under Wychwood, Oxford OX7 6HA. *T:* Shipton-under-Wychwood (0993) 830413. *Clubs:* Brook's, MCC.

ASTOR, Hon. (Francis) David (Langhorne); Editor of The Observer, 1948–75; Director, The Observer, 1976–81; *b* 5 March 1912; *s* of 2nd Viscount Astor and Nancy, Viscountess Astor, CH, MP (*d* 1964); *m* 1st, 1945, Melanie Hauser; one *d*; 2nd, 1952, Bridget Aphra Wreford; two *s* three *d*. *Educ:* Eton; Balliol, Oxford. Yorkshire Post, 1936. Served War of 1939–45, with Royal Marines, 1940–45. Foreign Editor of the Observer, 1946–48. Croix de Guerre, 1944. *Publication:* (with V. Yorke) Peace in the Middle East: super powers and security guarantees, 1978. *Address:* 9 Cavendish Avenue, St John's Wood, NW8 9JD. *T:* 071–286 0223; Manor House, Sutton Courtenay, Oxon. *T:* Abingdon (0235) 848221. *Clubs:* Athenæum, Reform.

ASTOR, Hon. Hugh Waldorf, JP; Director, Hambro's plc, since 1960; *b* 20 Nov. 1920; 2nd *s* of 1st Baron Astor of Hever; *m* 1950, Emily Lucy, *d* of Sir Alexander Kinloch, 12th Bt; two *s* three *d*. *Educ:* Eton; New Coll., Oxford. Served War of 1939–45; Intelligence Corps, Europe and SE Asia (Lieut-Col). Joined The Times as Asst Middle East Correspondent, 1947; elected to Board of The Times, 1956; Dep. Chm., 1959, resigned 1967 on merger with Sunday Times; Chm., The Times Book Co. Ltd, 1960, resigned 1967 on merger with Sunday Times. Chairman: Times Trust, 1967–82; Trust Houses Forte Council, 1971– (Mem. Council, 1962–); Exec. Vice Chm., Olympia Ltd, 1971–73; Director: Winterbottom Energy Trust plc, 1961–86; Phoenix Assurance plc, 1962–85. Dep. Chm., Middlesex Hosp., 1965–74; Chm., King Edward's Hospital Fund for London, 1983–88. Governor, Peabody Trust (Chm., Peabody Donation Fund, 1981); Hon. Treasurer: Franco-British Soc., 1969–76; Marine Biol Assoc. UK, 1968–78; has served on Council or governing body of: RNLI; RYA; RORC; Air League. Mem. Ct of Assts, Fishmongers' Co. (Prime Warden, 1976–77). In partnership with Sir William Dugdale participated in air races, London-Sydney 1969, London-Victoria 1971. JP Berks, 1953; High Sheriff of Berks, 1963. *Recreations:* sailing, flying, shooting, diving. *Address:* Folly Farm, Sulhamstead, Berks. *T:* Reading (0734) 302326. *Clubs:* Brooks's, Buck's, Pratt's; Royal Yacht Squadron, Royal Ocean Racing.
See also Baron Astor of Hever.

ASTOR, Major Hon. Sir John (Jacob), Kt 1978; MBE 1945; ERD 1989; DL; Major, Life Guards; *b* 29 Aug. 1918; 4th *s* of 2nd Viscount Astor; *m* 1st, 1944, Ana Inez (marr. diss. 1972), *yr d* of Señor Dr Don Miguel Carcano, KCMG, KBE; one *s* one *d*; 2nd, 1976, Susan Sheppard (marr. diss. 1985), *d* of Major M. Eveleigh; 3rd, 1988, Marcia de Savary. *Educ:* Eton; New Coll., Oxford. Served War of 1939–45 (MBE, Legion of Honour, French Croix de Guerre). Contested (C) Sutton Div. of Plymouth, 1950; MP (C) Sutton Div. of Plymouth, 1951–Sept. 1959. PPS to Financial Sec. of Treasury, 1951–52. Chairman: Governing Body of Nat. Inst. of Agricultural Engineering, 1963–68; Agric. Res. Council, 1968–78; NEDC for Agricultural Industry, 1978–83. Member: Horserace Totalisator Bd, 1962–68; Horserace Betting Levy Bd, 1976–80. Steward of Jockey Club, 1968–71 and 1983–85. DL 1962, JP, Cambs, 1960–74. *Address:* The Dower House, Hatley Park, Hatley St George, Sandy, Beds SG19 3HL. *T:* Gamlingay (0767) 50266. *Club:* White's.

ASTWOOD, Hon. Sir James (Rufus), Kt 1982; JP; Chief Justice of Bermuda, since 1977; *b* 4 Oct. 1923; *s* of late James Rufus Astwood, Sr, and Mabel Winifred Astwood; *m* 1952, Gloria Preston Norton; one *s* two *d*. *Educ:* Berkeley Inst., Bermuda; Univ. of Toronto, Canada. Called to the Bar, Gray's Inn, London, Feb. 1956, Hon. Bencher, 1985; admitted to practice at Jamaican Bar, Oct. 1956; joined Jamaican Legal Service, 1957; Dep. Clerk of Courts, 1957–58; Clerk of Courts, Jamaica, 1958–63; Stipendiary Magistrate and Judge of Grand Court, Cayman Islands (on secondment from Jamaica), 1958–59; Resident Magistrate, Jamaica, 1963–74; Puisne Judge, Jamaica, during 1971 and 1973; retd from Jamaican Legal Service, 1974. Sen. Magistrate, Bermuda, 1974–76; Solicitor General, 1976–77; Acting Attorney General, during 1976 and 1977; Acting Dep. Governor for a period in 1977. Has served on several cttees, tribunals and bds of enquiry, both in Bermuda and Jamaica. *Recreations:* golf, cricket, photography, reading, bridge, travel, cycling. *Address:* (home) Clifton, 8 Middle Road, Devonshire DVO3, Bermuda; PO Box HM 1674, Hamilton HMGX, Bermuda; (office) Chief Justice's Chambers, Supreme Court, Bermuda. *Clubs:* Kingston Cricket (Kingston, Jamaica); Castle Harbour Golf, Bermuda Senior Golfers Society, Royal Hamilton Amateur Dinghy, Coral Beach and Tennis, Mid Ocean (Bermuda).

ASTWOOD, Lt-Col Sir Jeffrey (Carlton), Kt 1972; CBE 1966; OBE (mil.) 1946; ED 1942; Speaker of House of Assembly, Bermuda, 1968–72, retired; *b* 5 Oct. 1907; *s* of late Jeffrey Burgess Astwood, Neston, Bermuda, and Lilian Maude (*née* Searles); *m* 1928, Hilda Elizabeth Kay (*née* Onions); one *s* one *d*. *Educ:* Saltus Grammar School, Bermuda. Served local TA, 1922–60; retired as Lt-Col, having commanded since 1943. House of Assembly, Bermuda, 1948–72; Minister of Agriculture, of Immigration and Labour, of Health; Member of Exec. Council; Dep. Speaker, 1957–68. President: Exec. Cttee, Sandys Grammar Sch., 1950–57 (Chm. Trustees, 1950–); Bermuda Sea Cadet Assoc., 1974–78; Chm., St James' Church Vestry. President: Atlantic Investment and Development Co. Ltd; J. B. Astwood & Son Ltd; Belfield-in-Somerset Ltd; Aberfeldy Nurseries Ltd. FInstD. *Recreations:* theatre, horticulture. *Address:* Greenfield, Somerset MA03, Bermuda. *T:* (business) Hamilton 292–2245; (home) 234–1729. *Clubs:* Royal Bermuda Yacht, Sandys Boat, Somerset Lawn Tennis (Bermuda).

ATCHERLEY, Sir Harold Winter, Kt 1977; Chairman: Toynbee Hall, 1985–90 (Member, Management Committee, since 1979); Aldeburgh Foundation, since 1989 (Deputy Chairman, 1988–89); *b* 30 Aug. 1918; *s* of L. W. Atcherley and Maude Lester (*née* Nash); *m* 1st, 1946, Anita Helen (*née* Leslie) (marr. diss. 1990); one *s* two *d*; 2nd, 1990, Mrs Elke Jessett, *d* of late Dr Carl Langbehn. *Educ:* Gresham's Sch.; Heidelberg and Geneva Univs. Joined Royal Dutch Shell Gp, 1937. Served War: Queen's Westminster Rifles, 1939; commissioned Intelligence Corps, 1940; served 18th Infty Div., Singapore; PoW, 1942–45. Rejoined Royal Dutch Shell Gp, 1946: served Egypt, Lebanon, Syria, Argentina, Brazil, 1946–59. Personnel Co-ordinator, Royal Dutch Shell Group, 1964–70, retd. Recruitment Advisor to Ministry of Defence, 1970–71. Chm., Tyzack & Partners, 1979–85; Dir, British Home Stores Ltd, 1973–87. Chairman: Armed Forces Pay Review Body, 1971–82; Police Negotiating Bd, 1983–86 (Dep. Chm., 1982); Member: Top Salaries Review Body, 1971–87; Nat. Staff Cttee for Nurses and Midwives, 1973–77; Cttee of Inquiry into Pay and Related Conditions of Service of Nurses, 1974; Cttee of Inquiry into Remuneration of Members of Local Authorities, 1977. Vice-Chm., Suffolk Wildlife Trust, 1987–90; Mem. Management Cttee, Suffolk Rural Housing Assoc., 1984–. Empress Leopoldina Medal (Brazil), 1958. *Recreations:* music, skiing, good food. *Address:* Conduit House, The Green, Long Melford, Suffolk. *T:* Sudbury (0787) 310897.

ATHA, Bernard Peter, OBE 1991; Principal Lecturer in Business Studies, Huddersfield Technical College, 1973–90; *b* 27 Aug. 1928; *s* of Horace Michael Atha and Mary Quinlan; unmarried. *Educ:* Leeds Modern Sch.; Leeds Univ. (LLB Hons). Barrister-at-law, Gray's Inn. Commn, RAF, 1950–52. Variety artist on stage; Mem. Equity; films and TV plays. Elected Leeds City Council, 1957; Chm., Leeds Leisure Services Cttee, 1988–; former Chairman: Watch Cttee; Social Services Cttee; Educn Cttee. Vice-Chm., W Leeds HA, 1988–90. Contested (Lab): Penrith and the Border, 1959; Pudsey, 1964. Pres., Leeds Co-op. Soc.; Chm., Leeds Playhouse and Leeds Grand Theatre; Dir, Opera North. Member: Arts Council, 1979–82; Ministerial Working Party: on Sport and Recreation, 1974; on Sport for the Disabled, 1989; Vice-Chm., Sports Council, 1976–80; Chairman: Yorks and Humberside Reg. Sports Council, 1966–76; Nat. Water Sports Centre, 1978–84; UK Sports Assoc. for People with Mental Handicap; British Paralympics Assoc., 1989; Yorks Dance Centre Trust; Red Ladder Theatre Co.; Vice-Chm., Leeds Festival; Dir, St James' Univ. Hosp. Trust, 1990. Governor, Sports Aid Foundn. FRSA. *Recreations:* sport, the arts, travel. *Address:* 25 Moseley Wood Croft, Leeds, West Yorks LS16 7JJ. *T:* Leeds (0532) 672485.

ATHABASCA, Bishop of, since 1983; **Rt. Rev. Gary Frederick Woolsey;** *b* 16 March 1942; *s* of William and Doreen Woolsey; *m* 1967, Marie Elaine Tooker; two *s* two *d*. *Educ:* Univ. of Western Ontario (BA); Huron Coll., London, Ont. (BTh); Univ. of Manitoba (Teacher's Cert.). Deacon, 1967; Priest-pilot, Diocese of Keewatin, 1967–68; Rector: St Peter's, Big Trout Lake, Ont., 1968–72; St Mark's, Norway House, Manitoba, 1972–76; St Paul's, Churchill, Man., 1976–80; Program Director and Archdeacon of Keewatin, 1980–83. *Recreations:* fishing, hunting, boating, camping, photography, flying. *Address:* Box 6868, Peace River, Alberta T8S 1S6, Canada. *T:* (home) (403) 624–5607, (office) (403) 624–2767.

ATHERTON, Alan Royle, CB 1990; Member, Letchworth Garden City Corporation; Chairman, Queen Elizabeth II Conference Centre Board; Director, Argyll Investments Ltd; *b* 25 April 1931; *s* of Harold Atherton and Hilda (*née* Royle); *m* 1959, Valerie Kemp; three *s* one *d*. *Educ:* Cowley Sch., St Helens; Sheffield Univ. (BSc (Hons Chem.)). ICI Ltd, 1955–58; DSIR, 1959–65; Min. of Housing and Local Govt, 1965–70; Ordnance Survey, 1970–74; Under-Sec., 1975–87, Dep. Sec., 1987–91, DoE. *Recreations:* walking, opera, Rugby, tennis. *Clubs:* Arts, Civil Service.

ATHERTON, David; Music Director, Hong Kong Philharmonic Orchestra, since 1989; Musical Director, London Sinfonietta, 1967–73 and since 1989 (Founder, 1967); *b* 3 Jan. 1944; *s* of Robert and Lavinia Atherton; *m* 1970, Ann Gianetta Drake; one *s* two *d*. *Educ:* Cambridge Univ. (MA). LRAM, LTCL. Repetiteur, Royal Opera House, Covent Garden, 1967–68; Resident Conductor, Royal Opera House, 1968–79; Principal Conductor and Artistic Advr, 1980–83, Principal Guest Conductor, 1983–86, Royal Liverpool Philharmonic Orch.; Music Dir and Principal Conductor, San Diego Symphony Orch., 1980–87; Artistic Dir and Conductor: London Stravinsky Fest., 1979–82; Ravel/Varese Fest., 1983–84; Principal Guest Conductor, BBC Symphony Orch., 1985–89. Became youngest conductor in history of Henry Wood Promenade Concerts at Royal Albert Hall, and also at Royal Opera House, 1968; Royal Festival Hall debut, 1969; from 1970 performances in Europe, Middle East, Far East, Australasia, N America. Adapted and arranged Pandora by Roberto Gerhard for Royal Ballet, 1975. Conductor of the year award (Composers' Guild of GB), 1971; Edison award, 1973; Grand Prix du Disque award, 1977; Koussevitzky Award, 1981; Internat. Record Critics Award, 1982; Prix Caecilia, 1982. *Publications:* (ed) The Complete Instrumental and Chamber Music of Arnold Schoenberg and Roberto Gerhard, 1973; (ed) Pandora and Don Quixote Suites by Roberto Gerhard, 1973; contrib., The Musical Companion, 1978, The New Grove Dictionary, 1981. *Recreations:* travel, squash, theatre. *Address:* c/o Harold Holt Ltd, 31 Sinclair Road, W14 0NS.

ATHERTON, James Bernard; Secretary-General, British Bankers' Association, 1982–85; *b* 3 Dec. 1927; *s* of late James Atherton and Edith (*née* Atkinson); *m* 1953, Eileen Margaret Birch; two *s*. *Educ:* Alsop High Sch., Liverpool. Served RAF, 1946–48; Martins Bank, 1943–46 and 1948–69 (Asst Chief Accountant, 1966–69); Barclays Bank, 1969–82 (Chief Clearing Manager, 1969–73, Asst Gen. Manager, 1973–78, Divl Gen. Manager, 1978–82). *Recreations:* opera, gardening. *Address:* Spring House, Empshott, Liss, Hants. *T:* Blackmoor (04207) 231.

ATHOLL, 10th Duke of, *cr* 1703; **George Iain Murray;** DL; Lord Murray of Tullibardine, 1604; Earl of Tullibardine, Lord Gask and Balquhidder, 1606; Earl of Atholl, 1629; Marquess of Atholl, Viscount Balquhidder, Lord Balvenie, 1676; Marquess of Tullibardine, Earl of Strathtay, Earl of Strathardle, Viscount Glenalmond, Viscount Glenlyon, 1703—all in the peerage of Scotland; Representative Peer for Scotland in the House of Lords, 1958–63; *b* 19 June 1931; *s* of Lieut-Col George Anthony Murray, OBE, Scottish Horse (killed in action, Italy, 1945), and Hon. Mrs Angela Campbell-Preston, (*d* 1981), *d* of 2nd Viscount Cowdray (she *m* 2nd, 1950, Robert Campbell-Preston of Ardchattan, *qv*); *S* kinsman 1957. *Educ:* Eton; Christ Church, Oxford. Director: Westminster Press (Chm., 1974–); BPM Holdings, 1972–83; Pearson Longman Ltd, 1975–83. Pres., Scottish Landowners Fedn, 1986– (Vice-Convener, 1971–76, Convener, 1976–79); Chm., RNLI, 1979–89 (Dep. Chm., 1972–79); Member: Cttee on the Preparation of Legislation, 1973–75; Exec. Cttee, Nat. Trust for Scotland (Vice-Pres., 1977–); Red Deer Commn, 1969–83. DL Perth and Kinross, 1980. *Heir: cousin* John Murray [*b* 19 Jan. 1929; *m* 1956, Margaret Yvonne, *o d* of late Ronald Leonard Leach; two *s* one *d*]. *Address:* Blair Castle, Blair Atholl, Perthshire. *T:* Blair Atholl (079681) 212; 31 Marlborough Hill, NW8. *Clubs:* Turf, White's; New (Edinburgh).

ATIYAH, Sir Michael (Francis), Kt 1983; MA, PhD Cantab; FRS 1962; FRSE 1985; Master of Trinity College, Cambridge, since 1990; President of the Royal Society, since 1990; Director, Isaac Newton Institute for Mathematical Sciences, Cambridge, since 1990; *b* 22 April 1929; *e s* of late Edward Atiyah and Jean Levens; *m* 1955, Lily Brown; three *s*. *Educ:* Victoria Coll., Egypt; Manchester Grammar Sch.; Trinity Coll., Cambridge. Research Fellow, Trinity Coll., Camb., 1954–58, Hon. Fellow, 1976; First Smith's Prize, 1954; Commonwealth Fund Fellow, 1955–56; Mem. Inst. for Advanced Study, Princeton, 1955–56, 1959–60, 1967–68, 1987; Asst Lectr in Mathematics, 1957–58, Lectr 1958–61, Univ. of Cambridge; Fellow Pembroke Coll., Cambridge, 1958–61 (Hon. Fellow, 1983); Reader in Mathematics, Univ. of Oxford, and Professorial Fellow of St Catherine's Coll., Oxford, 1961–63; Savilian Prof. of Geometry, and Fellow of New College, Oxford, 1963–69; Prof. of Mathematics, Inst. for Advanced Study, Princeton, NJ, 1969–72; Royal Soc. Res. Prof., Mathematical Inst., Oxford, and Professorial Fellow, St Catherine's Coll., Oxford, 1973–90. Visiting Lecturer, Harvard, 1962–63 and 1964–65. Member: Exec. Cttee, Internat. Mathematical Union, 1966–74; SERC, 1984–89; President: London Mathematical Soc., 1975–77; Mathematical Assoc., 1981–82; Chm., European Mathematical Council, 1978–90. Foreign Member: Amer. Acad. of Arts and Scis; Swedish Royal Acad.; Leopoldina Acad.; Nat. Acad. of Scis, USA; Acad. des Sciences, France; Royal Irish Acad.; Czechoslovak Union of Mathematicians and Physicists. Hon. DSc: Bonn, 1968; Warwick, 1969; Durham, 1979; St Andrew's, 1981; Dublin, 1983; Chicago, 1983; Edinburgh, 1984; Essex, 1985; London, 1985; Sussex, 1986; Ghent, 1987; Reading, Helsinki, 1990; Hon. ScD Cantab, 1984. Fields Medal, Internat. Congress of Mathematicians, Moscow, 1966; Royal Medal, Royal Soc., 1968; De Morgan Medal, London Mathematical Soc., 1980; Antonio Feltrinelli Prize for mathematical sciences, Accademia Nazionale dei Lincei, Rome, 1981; King Faisal Foundn Internat. Prize for Science, Saudi Arabia, 1987; Copley Medal, Royal Soc., 1988; Gunning Victoria Jubilee Prize, RSE, 1990. *Publications:* Collected Works, 5 vols, 1988; The Geometry and Physics of Knots, 1990; papers in mathematical journals. *Recreation:* gardening. *Address:* Master's Lodge, Trinity College, Cambridge CB2 1TQ. *Clubs:* Athenæum, United Oxford & Cambridge University.

See also P. S. Atiyah.

ATIYAH, Prof. Patrick Selim, DCL; FBA 1978; QC 1989; Professor of English Law, and Fellow of St John's College, Oxford University, 1977–88, Hon. Fellow, 1988; *b* 5 March 1931; *s* of Edward Atiyah and D. J. C. Levens; *m* 1951, Christine Best; four *s*. *Educ:* Woking County Grammar Sch. for Boys; Magdalen Coll., Oxford (MA 1957, DCL 1974). Called to the Bar, Inner Temple, 1956. Asst Lectr, LSE, 1954–55; Lectr, Univ. of Khartoum, 1955–59; Legal Asst, BoT, 1961–64; Fellow, New Coll., Oxford, 1964–69; Professor of Law: ANU, 1970–73; Warwick Univ., 1973–77; Visiting Professor: Univ of Texas, 1979; Harvard Law Sch., 1982–83; Duke Univ., 1985. Lectures: Lionel Cohen, Hebrew Univ., Jerusalem, 1980; Oliver Wendell Holmes, Harvard Law Sch., 1981; Cecil Wright Meml, Univ. of Toronto, 1983; Viscount Bennett, Univ. of New Brunswick, 1984; Chorley, LSE, 1985; Hamlyn, Leeds Univ., 1987. Hon. LLD Warwick, 1989. General Editor, Oxford Jl of Legal Studies, 1981–86. *Publications:* The Sale of Goods, 1957, 8th edn 1990; Introduction to the Law of Contract, 1961, 3rd edn 1981; Vicarious Liability, 1967; Accidents, Compensation and the Law, 1970, 4th edn (ed Peter Cane), 1987; The Rise and Fall of Freedom of Contract, 1979; Promises, Morals and Law, 1981 (Swiney Prize, RSA/RSP, 1984); Law and Modern Society, 1983; Essays on Contract, 1987; Pragmatism and Theory in English Law, 1987; (with R. S. Summers) Form and Substance in Anglo-American Law, 1987; articles in legal jls. *Recreations:* gardening, cooking. *Address:* 9 Sheepway Court, Iffley, Oxford OX4 4JL. *T:* Oxford (0865) 717637.

See also Sir M. F. Atiyah.

ATKIN, Alec Field, CBE 1978; FEng, FIMechE, FRAeS; Managing Director, Marketing, Aircraft Group, British Aerospace, 1981–82, retired; Director, AWA (Consultancy) Ltd, since 1983; *b* 26 April 1925; *s* of Alec and Grace Atkin; *m* 1948, Nora Helen Darby (marr. diss. 1982); two *s* one *d*; *m* 1982, Wendy Atkin. *Educ:* Riley High Sch.; Hull Technical Coll. (DipAe); Hull Univ. (BSc Hons). FIMechE 1955; FRAeS 1952. English Electric Co., Preston: Aerodynamicist, 1950; Dep. Chief Aerodyn., 1954; Head of Exper. Aerodyns, 1957; Asst Chief Engr, then Proj. Manager, 1959; Warton Div., British Aircraft Corporation Ltd: Special Dir, 1964; Dir, 1970; Asst Man. Dir, 1973–75; Dep. Man. Dir, 1975–76; Man. Dir, 1976–77; Man. Dir (Mil.), Aircraft Gp of British Aerospace, and Chm., Warton, Kingston-Brough and Manchester Divs, 1978–81. FRSA. *Recreation:* sailing. *Address:* Les Fougères d'Icart, Icart Road, St Martin, Guernsey, Channel Islands.

ATKINS, family name of **Baron Colnbrook.**

ATKINS, Eileen, CBE 1990; actress; *b* 16 June 1934; *d* of Arthur Thomas Atkins and late Annie Ellen (*née* Elkins); *m* Bill Shepherd. *Educ:* Latymers Grammar Sch., Edmonton; Guildhall Sch. of Music and Drama. *Stage appearances include:* Twelfth Night, Richard III, The Tempest, Old Vic, 1962; The Killing of Sister George, Bristol Old Vic, transf. Duke of York's, 1965 (Best Actress, Standard Awards); The Cocktail Party, Wyndham's, transf. Haymarket, 1968; Vivat! Vivat Regina!, Piccadilly, 1970; Suzanne Andler, Aldwych, 1973; As You Like It, Stratford, 1973; St Joan, Old Vic, 1977; Passion Play, Aldwych, 1981; Medea, Young Vic, 1986; The Winter's Tale, Cymbeline, Mountain Language, NT, 1988; A Room of One's Own, Hampstead, 1989; Exclusive, Strand, 1989; Prin, NY, 1990; *films include:* Equus, 1974; The Dresser, 1984; Let Him Have It, 1990; *TV appearances include:* The Duchess of Malfi; Sons and Lovers; Smiley's People; Nelly's Version; The Burston Rebellion; Breaking Up; The Vision; Mrs Pankhurst in In My Defence (series), 1990; A Room of One's Own, 1990. BAFTA Award, 1985. *Address:* c/o Duncan Heath Associates, 162–170 Wardour Street, W1V 3AT.

ATKINS, Henry St J., DSc; President, University College, Cork, 1954–63, retired; *b* 19 March 1896; *s* of Patrick Atkins and Agnes Egan, Cork; *m* 1929, Agnes E. O'Regan (*d* 1960), MB, BCh; one *s* one *d*. *Educ:* Christian Brothers, North Monastery, Cork; University Coll., Cork. BSc (Math. Science) 1915; post-grad. scholar, MSc 1923. Prof. of Pure Maths, University Coll., Cork, 1936–54; Registrar, 1943–54. Hon. DSc 1955. MRIA 1957. *Recreations:* golf, fishing. *Address:* Knockrea Park, Cork. *T:* Cork 32448. *Clubs:* National University of Ireland; Cork City and County (Cork).

ATKINS, Leonard B. W.; *see* Walsh-Atkins.

ATKINS, Rt. Rev. Peter Geoffrey; Dean, Provincial Theological College of St John the Evangelist, Auckland, since 1991; *b* 29 April 1936; *s* of late Lt-Col Owen Ivan Atkins and Mrs Mary Atkins; *m* 1968, Rosemary Elizabeth (*née* Allen); one *d*. *Educ:* Merchant Taylors' School, Crosby, Liverpool; Sidney Sussex Coll., Cambridge; St John's Coll., Auckland, NZ. MA (Cantab), BD (Otago), LTh (NZ). Deacon 1962, priest 1963; Curate, Karori Parish, Wellington, 1962–66; Priest-Tutor, St Peter's Theological Coll., Siota, Solomon Is, 1966–67; Curate, Dannevirke Parish, dio. Waiapu, 1968–70; Vicar of Waipukurau Parish, 1970–73; Diocesan Sec. and Registrar, Diocese of Waiapu, 1973–79; Canon of St John's Cathedral, Napier, 1974–79; Vicar of Havelock North, 1979–83; Archdeacon of Hawkes Bay, 1979–83; Vicar-Gen., Diocese of Waiapu, 1980–83; Commissary to Archbishop of NZ, 1983; Bishop of Waiapu, 1983–90. *Recreations:* gardening, tennis, music. *Address:* Dean's Lodge, St John's College, 200 St John's Road, Meadow Bank, Auckland 5, New Zealand. *T:* (home) 09–5287086; (office) 09–5212725.

ATKINS, Robert James; MP (C) South Ribble, since 1983 (Preston North, 1979–83); Parliamentary Under-Secretary of State (Minister for Sport), Department of Education and Science, since 1990; *b* 5 Feb. 1946; *s* of late Reginald Alfred and of Winifred Margaret Atkins; *m* 1969, Dulcie Mary (*née* Chaplin); one *s* one *d*. *Educ:* Highgate School. Councillor, London Borough of Haringey, 1968–77; Vice-Chm., Greater London Young Conservatives, 1969–70, 1971–72. Contested (C) Luton West, Feb. 1974 and Oct. 1974 general elections. PPS to Minister of State, DoI, then DTI, 1982–84, to Minister without

Portfolio, 1984–85, to Sec. of State for Employment, 1985–87; Parly Under Sec. of State, DTI, 1987–89, Dept of Transport, 1989–90. Vice-Chm., Cons. Aviation Cttee, 1979–82; Jt Sec., Cons. Defence Cttee, 1979–82. President: Cons. Trade Unionists, 1984–87; Lancs Young Conservatives, 1984–86. Member: Victorian Soc.; Sherlock Holmes Soc. of London. Freeman, City of London, 1989. *Publication:* (contrib.) Changing Gear, 1981. *Recreations:* cricket, ecclesiology, wine. *Address:* c/o House of Commons, SW1A 0AA. *T:* 071–219 5080. *Clubs:* MCC, Middlesex County Cricket, Lords and Commons Cricket, Lancashire County Cricket.

ATKINS, Ronald Henry; *b* Barry, Glam, 13 June 1916; *s* of Frank and Elizabeth Atkins; *m*; three *s* two *d*. *Educ:* Barry County Sch.; London Univ. (BA Hons). Teacher, 1949–66 (latterly Head, Eng. Dept, Halstead Sec. Sch.); Lectr, Accrington Coll. of Further Educn, 1970–74. Member: Braintree RDC, 1952–61; Preston Dist Council, 1974–76, 1980–. Contested (Lab) Lowestoft, 1964; MP (Lab) Preston North, 1966–70 and Feb. 1974–1979. *Recreations:* jazz, dancing, walking. *Address:* 38 James Street, Preston, Lancs. *T:* Preston (0772) 51910.

ATKINSON, Sir Alec; *see* Atkinson, Sir J. A.

ATKINSON, Prof. Anthony Barnes, FBA 1984; Professor of Economics, London School of Economics and Political Science, 1980–Sept. 1992; Professor of Political Economy, and Fellow of Churchill College, Cambridge, from Oct. 1992; *b* 4 Sept. 1944; *s* of Norman Joseph Atkinson and Esther Muriel Atkinson; *m* 1965, Judith Mary (*née* Mandeville); two *s* one *d*. *Educ:* Cranbrook Sch.; Churchill Coll., Cambridge (MA). Fellow, St John's Coll., Cambridge, 1967–71; Prof. of Econs, Univ. of Essex, 1971–76; Prof. and Hd of Dept of Political Economy, UCL, 1976–79. Vis. Prof. MIT, 1973. Member: Royal Commn on Distribution of Income and Wealth, 1978–79; Retail Prices Index Adv. Cttee, 1984–. President: European Econ. Assoc., 1989 (Vice-Pres., 1986–88); Internat. Econ. Assoc., 1989–Aug. 1992; Vice-Pres., British Acad., 1988–90. Fellow, Econometric Soc., 1975 (Vice-Pres., 1986–87, Pres., 1988). Hon. Mem., Amer. Econ. Assoc., 1985. Hon. Dr Rer. Pol. Univ. of Frankfurt, 1987; Hon. Dr en Sci. Econ., Univ. of Lausanne, 1988; Hon. Dr Univ. of Liège, 1989. Scientific Prize, Union des Assurances de Paris, 1986. Editor, Jl of Public Economics, 1972–. *Publications:* Poverty in Britain and the Reform of Social Security, 1969; Unequal Shares, 1972; The Tax Credit Scheme, 1973; Economics of Inequality, 1975; (with A. J. Harrison) Distribution of Personal Wealth in Britain, 1978; (with J. E. Stiglitz) Lectures on Public Economics, 1980; Social Justice and Public Policy, 1982; (jtly) Parents and Children, 1983; (with J. Micklewright) Unemployment Benefits and Unemployment Duration, 1985; Poverty and Social Security, 1989; articles in Rev. of Econ. Studies, Econ. Jl, Jl of Public Econs, Jl of Econ. Theory. *Address:* 33 Hurst Green, Brightlingsea, Colchester, Essex. *T:* Colchester (0206) 302253.

ATKINSON, Arthur Kingsley Hall, CB 1985; Chief Executive, Intervention Board for Agricultural Produce, 1980–86; *b* 24 Dec. 1926; *er s* of Arthur Hall Atkinson and Florence (*née* Gerrans). *Educ:* Priory Sch., Shrewsbury; Emmanuel Coll., Cambridge (MA). RAF, 1948; MAFF: Asst Principal 1950; Private Sec. 1953; Principal 1956; Asst Sec. 1965; Under Sec., 1973; Cabinet Office, 1976–78; MAFF, 1978–80. *Recreations:* travel, music, gardening.

ATKINSON, Prof. Bernard, FEng, FIChemE; Director, Brewing Research Foundation, since 1981; *b* 17 March 1936; *s* of late Thomas Atkinson and of Elizabeth Ann (*née* Wilcox); *m* 1957, Kathleen Mary Richardson; two *s*. *Educ:* Farnworth Grammar Sch.; Univ. of Birmingham (BSc); Univ. of Manchester Inst. of Science and Technology; PhD Univ. of Manchester. FEng 1980. Post-Doctoral Fellow and Asst Prof., Rice Univ., Houston, Texas, 1960–63; Lectr, Sen. Lectr in Chem. Engrg, and latterly Reader in Biochem. Engrg, University Coll. of Swansea, 1963–74; Prof. and Head of Dept of Chem. Engrg, UMIST, 1974–81; Visiting Professor: UMIST, 1981–86; Swansea, 1986–. Editor, Biochemical Engineering Journal, 1983–. Senior Moulton Medal, IChemE, 1976; Gairn EEC Medal, Soc. of Engrs, 1985; Presidential Award, Master Brewers' Assoc. of the Americas, 1988. *Publications:* Biochemical Reactors, 1974, trans. Japanese, Russian, Spanish; (with P. F. Cooper) Biological Fluidised Bed Treatment of Water and Waste Water, 1981; (with F. Mavituna) Biochemical Engineering and Biotechnology Handbook, 1982; (ed) Research and Innovation in the 1990s: the chemical engineering challenge, 1986; (with C. Webb and G. M. Black) Process Engineering Aspects of Immobilised Cell Systems, 1986; numerous contribs to chemical engrg and biochemical engrg jls. *Recreations:* cycling, sailing, walking. *Address:* Brewing Research Foundation, Lyttel Hall, Nutfield, Surrey RH1 4HX. *T:* Nutfield Ridge (0737) 822272; Little Mieders, Borers Arms Road, Copthorne, Crawley, West Sussex RH10 3LJ. *T:* Copthorne (0342) 713181.

ATKINSON, David Anthony; MP (C) Bournemouth East, since Nov. 1977; *b* 24 March 1940; *s* of late Arthur Joseph Atkinson and of Joan Margaret Atkinson (*née* Zink); *m* 1968, Susan Nicola Pilsworth; one *s* one *d*. *Educ:* St George's Coll., Weybridge; Coll. of Automobile and Aeronautical Engrg, Chelsea. Diplomas in Auto. Engrg and Motor Industry Management. Member: Southend County Borough Council, 1969–72; Essex CC, 1973–78. Mem., Council of Europe, 1979–86, 1987–. PPS, 1979–87, to Rt Hon. Paul Channon, MP (Minister of State, Civil Service Dept, 1979–81, Minister for the Arts, 1981–83, Minister of State, DTI, 1983–86, Sec. of State for Trade and Industry, 1986–87). Nat. Chm., Young Conservative Orgn, 1970–71; President: Christian Solidarity Internat. (UK), 1983– (Chm., 1979–83); Internat. Soc. for Human Rights (UK), 1985–. *Recreations:* mountaineering, art and architecture, travel. *Address:* House of Commons, SW1A 0AA.

ATKINSON, David Rowland; Regional Chairman, British Gas East Midlands, since 1987; *b* 18 June 1930; *s* of late Rowland Hodgson Atkinson and Nora Marian (*née* Coleman); *m* 1956, Marian Eileen Sales; one *d*. *Educ:* Wrekin College. FCA, CBIM, CompIGasE. National Coal Board: NW Div., 1955; E Midlands Div., 1961; Chief Accountant, W Midlands Gas, 1969; Dir of Finance, E Midlands Gas, 1977; Dep. Chm., SE Gas, 1983; Dir of Finance, British Gas, 1985. *Recreations:* Rugby, gardening, ciné photography. *Address:* Russetts, 124 The Ridings, Rothley, Leics LE7 7SL. *T:* Leicester (0533) 535600.

ATKINSON, Air Marshal Sir David (William), KBE 1982; FFOM; FRCPE; FFPHM; Director-General, Chest, Heart and Stroke Association, since 1985; Director-General, RAF Medical Services, 1981–84; *b* 29 Sept. 1924; *s* of late David William Atkinson and of Margaret Atkinson; *m* 1948, Mary (*née* Sowerby); one *s*. *Educ:* Edinburgh Univ. (MB, ChB 1948). DPH and DIH, London; FFPHM (FFCM 1976); MFOM 1978, FFOM 1983; FRCPE 1983. Joined RAF, 1949; med. officer appts, UK, Jordan and Egypt, 1949–63; Student, RAF Staff Coll., 1963–64; SMO, RAF Brüggen, Germany, 1964–67; Dep. PMO, HQ Air Support Comd, 1967–70; PMO, HQ Brit. Forces Gulf, Bahrain, 1970–71; OC RAF Hosp., Wegberg, Germany, 1971–73; Dir of Health and Research (RAF), 1974–78; QHP 1977–84; PMO, RAF Strike Command, 1978–81. Freeman, City of London, 1984; Liveryman, Soc. of Apothecaries. CStJ 1981. *Publication:* (jtly) Double Crew Continuous Flying Operations: a study of aircrew sleep patterns, 1970. *Recreations:* walking, gardening, reading, looking at pictures. *Address:* 39 Brim Hill, N2 0HA. *Club:* Royal Air Force.

ATKINSON, Frank, OBE 1980; FSA; FMA; museum, leisure and tourism consultant; Director, Beamish North of England Open Air Museum, 1970–87; *b* 13 April 1924; *s* of Ernest Atkinson and Elfrida (*née* Bedford); *m* 1953, Joan Peirson; three *s*. *Educ:* Holgate Grammar Sch., Barnsley; Sheffield Univ. (BSc). Director: Wakefield City Art Gall. and Mus., 1949; Halifax Museums, 1951; Bowes Mus. and Durham Co. Mus. Service, 1958. Member: Working Party on Preservation of Technolog. Material, 1970–71; Wright Cttee on Provincial Museums and Galls, 1971–73; Working Party of Standing Commn on Museums and Galls (Drew Report), 1975–78; Museums and Galleries Commn, 1987–. Chm., Thomas Bewick Birthplace Trust, 1985–91. Pres., Museums Assoc., 1974–75. Hon. MA Newcastle upon Tyne, 1971; Hon. DCL Durham, 1987. *Publications:* Aspects of the 18th century Woollen and Worsted Trade, 1956; The Great Northern Coalfield, 1966, 3rd edn 1979; Industrial Archaeology of North East England, 1974; Life and Traditions in Northumberland and Durham, 1977, 2nd edn 1986; North East England: people at work 1860–1950, 1980; Victorian Britain: North East England, 1989; Northern Life, 1991; contribs to Trans Newcomen Soc., Procs of British Spel. Soc., Antiquaries Jl, Museums Jl, etc. *Recreations:* pot-holing (now only in retrospect), computer programming. *Address:* The Old Vicarage, Ovingham, Prudhoe, Northumberland NE42 6BW. *T:* Prudhoe (0661) 35445.

ATKINSON, Sir Frederick John, (Sir Fred Atkinson), KCB 1979 (CB 1971); Hon. Fellow of Jesus College, Oxford, since 1979; *b* 7 Dec. 1919; *s* of George Edward Atkinson and of late Elizabeth Sabina Cooper; *m* 1947, Margaret Grace Gibson; two *d*. *Educ:* Dulwich Coll.; Jesus Coll., Oxford; Hon. Fellow, Jesus Coll., 1979. Lectr, Jesus and Trinity Colls, Oxford, 1947–49; Economic Section, Cabinet Office, 1949–51; British Embassy, Washington, 1952–54; HM Treasury, 1955–62; Economic Adviser, Foreign Office, 1962–63; HM Treasury, 1963–69 (Dep. Dir, Economic Section, Treasury, 1965–69); Controller, Economics and Statistics, Min. of Technology, 1970; Chief Econ. Adviser, DTI, 1970–73; an Asst Sec.-Gen., OECD, Paris, 1973–75; Dep. Sec. and Chief Econ. Advr, Dept of Energy, 1975–77; Chief Economic Adviser, HM Treasury, and Head of Govt Econ. Service, 1977–79. *Publication:* (with S. Hall) Oil and the British Economy, 1983. *Recreation:* reading. *Address:* 26 Lee Terrace, Blackheath, SE3 9TZ. *T:* 081–852 1040; Tickner Cottage, Aldington, Kent TN25 7EG. *T:* Aldington (0233) 720514.

ATKINSON, Brig. Geoffrey Arthur; Executive Secretary, Fellowship of Engineering, since 1990; *b* 17 March 1931; *s* of Arthur Vivian Atkinson and Flora Muriel Atkinson (*née* Lucas); *m* 1952, Joyce Eileen Pavey; one *s* one *d*. *Educ:* Berkhamsted Sch.; Royal Military College of Science (BScEng); Manchester Business Sch. CEng, FIMechE; FBIM. Commnd REME, 1950; Regtl and technical employment, UK, Malaya, BAOR, 1950–60; EME, Queen's Own Hussars, 1960; Instr, RMA Sandhurst, 1962; Technical Staff trng, RMCS, 1963; BEME 20 Armd Bde, 1965; Weapons Staff, Army Sch. of Transport, 1967; CO 7 Armd Workshop, 1970; GSO1(W) DGFVE, 1972; ADEME 1/3 HQ DEME, 1975; Mil. Dir of Studies, Weapons and Vehicles, RMCS, 1977; CCREME HQ 1 BR Corps, BAOR, 1978; Dir of Equipment Engrg, HQ DGEME, 1981; Comdr HQ REME TA, 1983, retired 1984. Hon. Col REME Specialist Units TA, 1986–89. Dep. Sec., Fellowship of Engineering, 1984. Freeman, City of London, 1990; Liveryman, Co. of Engineers, 1991. *Recreations:* sailing, antique furniture restoration. *Address:* Fellowship of Engineering, 2 Little Smith Street, SW1P 3DL. *T:* 071–222 2688. *Club:* Army and Navy.

ATKINSON, Harry Hindmarsh, PhD; Under Secretary, Director (Special Responsibilities), Science and Engineering Research Council, since 1988; *b* 5 Aug. 1929; *s* of late Harry Temple Atkinson and Constance Hindmarsh Atkinson (*née* Shields); *m* 1958, Anne Judith Barrett; two *s* one *d*. *Educ:* Nelson Coll., Nelson, NZ; Canterbury University Coll., NZ (BSc, sen. schol.; MSc (1st cl. Hons)), 1948–52. Asst Lectr, Physics, CUC, 1952–53; Research Asst, Cornell Univ., USA, 1954–55; Corpus Christi Coll. and Cavendish Laboratory, Cambridge Univ., 1955–58 (PhD); Sen. Research Fellow, AERE, Harwell, 1958–61; Head, General Physics Group, Rutherford Laboratory, 1961–69; Staff Chief Scientific Adviser, Cabinet Office, 1969–72; Dep. Chief Scientific Officer and Head of Astronomy, Space and Radio Division, SRC, 1972–78; Dir (Astronomy, Space and Radio, and Nuclear Physics), SRC later SERC, 1979–83; Dir Science, SERC, 1983–88. Chm. Council, ESA, 1984–87 (Vice-Chm., 1981–84, UK Deleg., 1974–87); UK Member: EISCAT Council, 1976–86; Bd, Anglo-Aust. Telescope, 1979–88; Council, European Synchrotron Radiation Facility, 1986–88; Chairman: Cttee on Netherlands/UK Astronomy Collaboration, 1981–88; Steering Cttee, Inst. Laue-Langevin, Grenoble, 1984 and 1987 (UK deleg., 1983–88); Assessor, UGC, 1987–89; Member: NI Cttee, UFC, 1989–; Working Gp on Internat. Collaboration (Cabinet Office), ACOST, 1989; Chief Scientist, Loss Prevention Council, 1990–. *Publications:* papers on various branches of physics and on science policy. *Address:* Bampton, Oxon. *Club:* Athenæum.

ATKINSON, Prof. James; Founder Director, Centre for Reformation Studies, Sheffield, since 1983; Professor of Biblical Studies, University of Sheffield, 1967–79, now Emeritus; *b* 27 April 1914; *s* of Nicholas Ridley Atkinson and Margaret (*née* Hindhaugh); *m* 1939, Laura Jean Nutley (decd); one *s* one *d*. *Educ:* Tynemouth High Sch.; Univ. of Durham. MA 1939, MLitt 1950 Durham; DrTheol, Münster, Germany, 1955. Curate, Newcastle upon Tyne, 1937; Precentor, Sheffield Cath., 1941; Vicar, Sheffield, 1944; Fellow, Univ. of Sheffield, 1951; Canon Theologian: Leicester, 1954–70; Sheffield, 1971–; Reader in Theology, Univ. of Hull, 1956; Vis. Prof., Chicago, 1966; Public Orator, Univ. of Sheffield, 1972–79; Consultant Prof. with Evangelical Anglican Res. Centre, Latimer House, Oxford, 1981–84. Examining Chaplain to: Bp of Leicester, 1968–79; Bp of Derby, 1978–88. Member: Anglican-Roman Catholic Preparatory Commission, 1967–; Gen. Synod of Church of England, 1975–80; Marriage Commn, 1976–78. Pres., Soc. for Study of Theology, 1978–80; Mem., Acad. Internat. des Sciences Religieuses, 1980–. *Publications:* Library of Christian Classics, Vol. XVI, 1962; Rome and Reformation, 1965; Luther's Works, Vol. 44, 1966; Luther and the Birth of Protestantism, 1968; (trans. Spanish 1971, Italian 1983); The Reformation, Paternoster Church History, Vol. 4, 1968; The Trial of Luther, 1971; Martin Luther: Prophet to the Church Catholic, 1983; The Darkness of Faith, 1987; contribs to learned jls, also essays and parts of books. *Recreations:* gardening, music. *Address:* Leach House, Hathersage, Derbyshire. *T:* Hope Valley (0433) 50570; Centre for Reformation Studies, St George's Hall, Portobello, Sheffield S1 4DP. *T:* Sheffield (0742) 768555, ext. 5015.

See also Sir Robert Atkinson.

ATKINSON, Sir John Alexander, (Sir Alec Atkinson), KCB 1978 (CB 1976); DFC 1943; Second Permanent Secretary, Department of Health and Social Security, 1977–79; *b* 9 June 1919; *yr s* of late Rev. R. F. Atkinson and late Harriet Harrold Atkinson, BSc (*née* Lowdon); *m* 1945, Marguerite Louise Pearson, MA; one *d*. *Educ:* Kingswood Sch.; Queen's Coll., Oxford. Served in RAF, 1939–45. Asst Prin., 1946, Prin., 1949, Min. of Nat. Insce; Cabinet Office, 1950–52; Prin. Private Sec. to Minister of Pensions and Nat. Insce, 1957–58; Asst Sec., 1958; Under-Sec., Min. of Social Security, later DHSS, 1966–73; Dep. Sec., DHSS, 1973–76. Member: Panel of Chairmen, CSSB, 1979–88; Occupational Pensions Bd, 1981–88. Pres., Kingswood Assoc., 1983. *Address:* Bleak House, The Drive, Belmont, Sutton, Surrey SM2 7DH. *T:* 081–642 6479. *Club:* United Oxford & Cambridge University.

ATKINSON, Kenneth Neil, FIPM; Director, Association of British Travel Agents' National Training Board, since 1989; *b* 4 April 1931; *s* of William Atkinson and Alice Reid. *Educ:* Kingussie High Sch., Inverness-shire. ARCM 1961; FIPM 1986. Various appts, Min. of Labour and Dept of Employment, 1948–67; Dep. Chief Conciliation Officer, Dept of Employment, 1968–72; Dir, Industry Trng Bd Relations, MSC, 1973–78; Manpower Services Dir, Scotland, 1979–82; Dir of Youth Training, Training Agency (formerly Manpower Services/Training Commn), 1983–89. Chm., Prince's Trust Community Venture. *Recreations:* tennis, choral and solo singing, conducting. *Address:* 57 St Andrews Wharf, 12 Shad Thames, SE1 2YN. *T:* 071–407 7491. *Club:* Royal Scottish Automobile (Glasgow).

ATKINSON, Leonard Allan, CMG 1963; *b* 6 Dec. 1906; *s* of L. Atkinson; *m* 1933, Annie R., *d* of A. E. Wells; one *s* two *d*. *Educ:* Wellington Coll. and Victoria Univ. of Wellington, New Zealand. Joined Customs Dept, 1924; Inspector, Public Service Commission, 1941–44; Sec., 1944–47; Asst Comr, 1947–54; Commission Member, 1954–58; Chm., 1958–62; Chm., State Services Commission, NZ, 1963–66. *Recreation:* bowls. *Address:* 181 The Parade, Island Bay, Wellington, NZ. *Club:* Wellington (NZ).

ATKINSON, Leslie, CMG 1965; OBE 1961; Managing Director, Leslie Atkinson Pty Ltd, 1960; Member of Export Development Council, Sydney, 1959; *b* 11 Jan. 1913; *s* of J. Atkinson; *m* 1935, Ellen, *d* of J. Kinsey; one *s* one *d*. *Educ:* Wollongong Technical Sch. Controller, Nock and Kirby Ltd, 1943–49, Associate Dir, 1949–53; Dir and General Manager, Carr and Elliott, 1953–59. Pres., Sydney Junior Chamber of Commerce, 1946–47; Vice-Pres. and Hon. Treasurer, Sydney Chamber of Commerce, 1949–53, Pres., 1953–54, 1957–58; Vice-Pres., Associated Chambers of Commerce of the Commonwealth of Australia, 1956–57 (Pres., 1964–65). Mem. of Standing Cttee, NSW Methodist Conference, 1957–62. *Address:* 47 Woniora Road, Hurstville, NSW 2220, Australia.

ATKINSON, Mary; *see under* Hardwick, Mollie.

ATKINSON, Michael William, CMG 1985; MBE 1970; HM Diplomatic Service; Ambassador to Romania, since 1989; *b* 11 April 1932; *m* 1963, Veronica Bobrovsky; two *s* one *d*. *Educ:* Purley County Grammar School; Queen's College, Oxford (BA Hons). Served FO, Vientiane, Buenos Aires, British Honduras, Madrid; FCO 1975; NATO Defence Coll., 1976; Counsellor, Budapest, 1977–80, Peking, 1980–82; Hd of Consular Dept, FCO, 1982–85; Ambassador to Ecuador, 1985–89. *Address:* c/o Foreign and Commonwealth Office, King Charles Street, SW1A 2AH.

ATKINSON, Norman; *b* 25 March 1923; *s* of George Atkinson, Manchester; *m* 1948, Irene Parry. *Educ:* elementary and technical schs. Served apprenticeship, Metropolitan Vickers Ltd, Trafford Park. Member of Manchester City Council, 1945–49. Chief Design Engineer, Manchester University, 1957–64. Contested (Lab) Wythenshawe, 1955, Altrincham and Sale, 1959. MP (Lab) Tottenham, 1964–87. Treasurer, Labour Party, 1976–81. Mem., Governing Body, Imperial Coll., London, 1975–. *Recreations:* walking, cricket, football, oil painting. *Address:* 4 Willow Court, 31 Willow Place, SW1. *Club:* Arts.

ATKINSON, Rev. Canon Peter Gordon; Principal, Chichester Theological College, since 1991; *b* 26 Aug. 1952; *m* 1983, Lynne Wilcock; one *s* one *d*. *Educ:* St John's Coll., Oxford (BA 1974; MA 1978); Westcott House, Cambridge. Ordained: deacon, 1979; priest, 1980; Asst Curate, Clapham, Old Town Team Ministry, 1979–83; Priest-in-charge, St Mary, Tatsfield, 1983–90; Rector, Holy Trinity, Bath, 1990–91; Bursalis Preb., Chichester Cathedral, 1991–. *Publication:* (contrib.) Stepping Stones: joint essays on Anglican Catholic and Evangelical Unity, ed C. Baxter, 1987. *Recreations:* reading, walking, painting. *Address:* Theological College, Chichester, West Sussex PO19 1SG. *T:* Chichester (0243) 783369.

ATKINSON, Reay; *see* Atkinson, W. R.

ATKINSON, Prof. Richard John Copland, CBE 1979; MA; FSA 1946; Professor of Archaeology, University College, Cardiff, 1958–83, now Emeritus; *b* 22 Jan. 1920; *e s* of Roland Cecil Atkinson and Alice Noel Herbert Atkinson (*née* Wright); *m* 1st, 1942, Hester Renée Marguerite Cobb (*d* 1981); three *s*; 2nd, 1981, Judith Marion O'Kelly. *Educ:* Sherborne School; Magdalen College, Oxford. Asst Keeper, Department of Antiquities, Ashmolean Museum, Oxford, 1944–49; Lectr in Prehistoric Archæology, Univ. of Edinburgh, 1949–58; Dep. Principal, UC Cardiff, 1970–74. Member: Ancient Monuments Board for Wales, 1959–86; Cttee of Enquiry into Arrangements for Protection of Field Monuments, 1966–68; Science-Based Archaeology Cttee, SRC, 1977–81 (UGC Assessor, SERC, 1981–86); Royal Commission: on Ancient and Historical Monuments in Wales, 1963–86 (Chm., 1984–86); on Historical Monuments (England), 1968–86 (acting Chm., 1984); UGC, 1973–82 (Vice Chm., 1976–77; Chm., Arts Sub-cttee, 1978–82). Vice-President: Prehistoric Society, 1963–67; Council for British Archæology, 1970–73 (Hon. Sec., 1964–70); Dir, BBC Silbury Hill project, 1967–70; Chm., York Minster Excavation Cttee, 1975–86. *Publications:* Field Archæology, 1946; Stonehenge, 1956; Stonehenge and Avebury, 1959; Archæology, History and Science, 1960; Stonehenge and Neighbouring Monuments, 1979; The Prehistoric Temples of Stonehenge and Avebury, 1980; articles in archæological journals. *Recreation:* reading. *Address:* Warren House, Mountain Road, Pentyrch, Cardiff CF4 8QP.

ATKINSON, Sir Robert, Kt 1983; DSC 1941; RD 1947; FEng; Chairman: Lyons Holdings Ltd, since 1990; British Shipbuilders, 1980–84; *b* 7 March 1916; *s* of Nicholas and Margaret Atkinson; *m* 1st, 1941, Joyce Forster (*d* 1973); one *s* one *d*; 2nd, 1977, Margaret Hazel Walker. *Educ:* London Univ. (BSc(Eng) Hons). MIMechE, CEng, FEng 1983. Served War 1939–45 (DSC 1941 and two Bars, 1st, 1943, 2nd, 1944, mentioned in Despatches, 1943). Managing Director: Wm Doxford, 1957–61; Tube Investments (Eng), 1961–67; Unicorn Industries, 1967–72; Chm., Aurora Holdings, Sheffield, 1972–83; Dir, Stag Furniture Hldgs, 1973–. *Publications:* The Design and Operating Experience of an Ore Carrier Built Abroad, 1957; The Manufacture of Steel Crankshafts, 1960; Some Crankshaft Failures: Investigation into Causes and Remedies, 1960; technical papers. *Recreations:* salmon fishing, walking, gardening. *Address:* Southwood House, Itchen Abbas, Winchester, Hants SO21 1AT. *Club:* Royal Thames Yacht.

See also Prof. James Atkinson.

ATKINSON, Rowan Sebastian; actor and writer; *b* 6 Jan. 1955; *s* of late Eric Atkinson and of Ella May Atkinson; *m* 1990, Sunetra Sastry. *Educ:* Durham Cathedral Choristers' Sch.; St Bees Sch.; Newcastle Univ.; Oxford Univ. (BSc, MSc). *Stage:* Beyond a Joke, Hampstead, 1978; Oxford Univ. Revues at Edinburgh Festival Fringe; youngest person to have a one-man show in the West End of London, 1981; The Nerd, 1984; The New Revue, 1986; The Sneeze, 1988; *television:* Not the Nine O'clock News, 1979–82; The Black Adder, 1983; Blackadder II, 1985; Blackadder the Third, 1987; Blackadder goes Forth, 1989; Mr Bean, The Return of Mr Bean, The Curse of Mr Bean, 1990–91; *films:* The Tall Guy, 1989; The Appointment of Dennis Jennings, 1989; The Witches, 1990. *Recreations:* motor cars, motor sport. *Address:* c/o PBJ Management Ltd, 47 Dean Street, W1V 5HL. *T:* 071–434 0672.

ATKINSON, Prof. Thomas, PhD, DSc, DEng; FEng 1987; Professor and Head of Department of Mining Engineering, Nottingham University, 1977–88; Chairman, Consolidated Coalfields Ltd, since 1986; *b* 23 Jan. 1924; *s* of Thomas Bell and Elizabeth Atkinson; *m* 1948, Dorothy; one *d* (two *s* decd). *Educ:* Imperial Coll., London. DIC; PhD London, 1973; DSc Nottingham, 1988; DEng Witwatersrand, 1989. FIMM, FIMinE, FIEE, FIMechE. FRSA. Served RN, 1942–46. Charlaw and Sacriston Collieries Ltd, Durham, 1938–42; NCB, 1946–49; Andrew Yule, India, 1949–53; KWPR, Australia, 1953–56; Mining Engr, Powell Duffryn Technical Services Ltd, 1956–68; Sen. Lectr, Imperial Coll., 1968–73; Head of Coal Mining Div., Shell Internat. Petroleum Maatschappij BV, Holland, 1973–77. Dir, British Mining Consultants Ltd, 1969–88. Chm., Nat. Awards Tribunal, British Coal (formerly NCB), 1984–. *Publications:* contribs to Mining Engrg, Mineral Econs, Mine Electrics, etc. *Recreation:* painting. *Address:* 27 Kirk Lane, Ruddington, Nottingham NG11 6NN. *T:* Nottingham (0602) 842400. *Club:* Chaps.

ATKINSON, William Christopher; Stevenson Professor of Hispanic Studies in University of Glasgow, 1932–72; Director, Institute of Latin-American Studies, 1966–72; *b* Belfast, 9 Aug. 1902; *s* of Robert Joseph Atkinson; *m* 1928, Evelyn Lucy (*d* 1990), *d* of C. F. Wakefield, Hampstead; one *s* three *d*. *Educ:* Univs of Belfast and Madrid. Lectr in Spanish at Armstrong Coll., Newcastle upon Tyne, 1926–32; Hon. Sec., Modern Humanities Research Assoc., 1929–36; Head of Spanish and Portuguese sections, Foreign Research and Press Service of Royal Institute of International Affairs, 1939–43; Visiting British Council Lecturer to Latin America, 1946, 1960, 1971; Hon. Prof. National Univ. of Colombia, 1946; Chm. 1st Scottish cultural delegation to USSR, 1954; Carnegie Research Fellow visiting US Univs, 1955; Member, Hispanic Society of America, 1955 (Corres. Mem., 1937); Rockefeller Fellow visiting Latin-American Univs, 1957; Visiting Prof. of Portuguese Studies, University Coll. of Rhodesia and Nyasaland, 1963. Commander, Order of Prince Henry the Navigator, Portugal, 1972. *Publications:* Spain, A Brief History, 1934; The Lusiads of Camoens, 1952; The Remarkable Life of Don Diego, 1958; A History of Spain and Portugal, 1960; The Conquest of New Granada, 1961; The Happy Captive, 1977; contributions to Encyclopædia Britannica, learned periodicals and reviews, and to composite works on Spanish and Portuguese studies. *Recreations:* travel and tramping. *Address:* 361 Albert Drive, Glasgow G41 5PH. *T:* 041–427 6173.

ATKINSON, (William) Reay, CB 1985; FBCS; Under Secretary, 1978–86, and Regional Director, North Eastern Region, 1981–86, Department of Industry; *b* 15 March 1926; *s* of William Edwin Atkinson and Lena Marion (*née* Haselhurst); *m*; one *s* two *d*; *m* 1983, Rita Katherine (*née* Bunn). *Educ:* Gosforth Grammar Sch., Newcastle upon Tyne; King's Coll., Durham Univ.; Worcester Coll., Oxford. Served RNVR, 1943–46. Entered Civil Service as Inspector of Taxes, 1950; Principal, 1958, Asst. Sec., 1965; Secretaries Office, Inland Revenue, 1958–61 and 1962–69; Asst Sec., Royal Commn on the Press, 1961–62; Civil Service Dept, 1969; Under Sec., and Dir, Central Computer Agency, CSD, 1973–78. Chm., Northern Development Co. Ltd, 1986–90; Director: English Estates Corp., 1986–; Northern Rock Building Soc., 1987–; Belasis Hall Technol. Park, 1989–; Maryport Develt Co. Ltd, 1989–. Chm of Governors, Newcastle-upon-Tyne Polytechnic. (Hon. Fellow, 1987). *Recreations:* fell walking, music. *Address:* High Dryburn, Garrigill, near Alston, Cumbria CA9 3EJ.

ATTALLAH, Naim Ibrahim; Book Publisher and Proprietor: Quartet Books, since 1976; The Women's Press, since 1977; Robin Clark, since 1980; Financial Director and Joint Managing Director, Asprey of Bond Street, since 1979; Managing Director, Mappin & Webb, since 1990; Executive Director, Garrard, since 1990; *b* 1 May 1931; *s* of Ibrahim and Genevieve Attallah; *m* 1957, Maria Attallah (*née* Nykolyn); one *s*. *Educ:* Battersea Polytechnic. Foreign Exchange Dealer, 1957; Financial Consultant, 1966; Dir of cos, 1969–; Magazine Proprietor: The Literary Review, 1981–; The Wire, 1984–. Launched Parfums Namara, Avant L'Amour and Après L'Amour, 1985, Naïdor, 1987, L'Amour de Namara, 1990. *Theatre:* co-presenter, Happy End, Lyric, 1975; presented and produced, The Beastly Beatitudes of Balthazar B, Duke of York's, 1981; co-prod, Trafford Tanzi, Mermaid, 1982; *films:* co-prod (with David Frost), The Slipper and the Rose, 1974–75; exec. producer, Brimstone and Treacle, 1982; also prod and presented TV docs. *Publications:* Women, 1987; Singular Encounters, 1990; articles in The Literary Review. *Recreations:* classical music, opera, theatre, cinema, photography. *Address:* Namara House, 45–46 Poland Street, W1V 4AU. *T:* 071-439 6750. *Clubs:* Arts, Academy.

ATTENBOROUGH, Sir David (Frederick), Kt 1985; CVO 1991; CBE 1974; FRS 1983; broadcaster and naturalist; *b* 8 May 1926; *s* of late Frederick Levi Attenborough; *m* 1950, Jane Elizabeth Ebsworth Oriel; one *s* one *d*. *Educ:* Wyggeston Grammar Sch. for Boys, Leicester; Clare Coll., Cambridge (Hon. Fellow, 1980). Served in Royal Navy, 1947–49. Editorial Asst in an educational publishing house, 1949–52; joined BBC Television Service as trainee producer, 1952; undertook zoological and ethnographic filming expeditions to: Sierra Leone, 1954; British Guiana, 1955; Indonesia, 1956; New Guinea, 1957; Paraguay and Argentina, 1958; South West Pacific, 1959; Madagascar, 1960; Northern Territory of Australia, 1962; the Zambesi, 1964; Bali, 1969; Central New Guinea, 1971; Celebes, Borneo, Peru and Colombia, 1973; Mali, British Columbia, Iran, Solomon Islands, 1974; Nigeria, 1975; Controller, BBC-2, BBC Television Service, 1965–68; Dir of Programmes, Television, and Mem., Bd of Management, BBC, 1969–72. Writer and presenter, BBC series: Tribal Eye, 1976; Life on Earth, 1979; The Living Planet, 1984; The First Eden, 1987; Lost Worlds, Vanished Lives, 1989; The Trials of Life, 1990. Huw Wheldon Meml Lecture, RTS, 1987. Mem., Nature Conservancy Council, 1973–82. Trustee: WWF UK, 1965–69, 1972–82, 1984–90; WWF Internat., 1979–86; British Museum, 1980–; Science Museum, 1984–87; Royal Botanic Gardens, Kew, 1986–. Corresp. Mem., Amer. Mus. Nat. Hist., 1985. Fellow, BAFTA 1980. Hon. Fellow: Manchester Polytechnic, 1976; UMIST, 1980; Hon. FRCP 1991. Special Award, SFTA, 1961; Silver Medal, Zool Soc. of London, 1966; Silver Medal, RTS, 1966; Desmond Davis Award, SFTA, 1970; Cherry Kearton Medal, RGS, 1972; Kalinga Prize, UNESCO, 1981; Washburn Award, Boston Mus. of Sci., 1983; Hopper Day Medal, Acad. of Natural Scis, Philadelphia, 1983; Founder's Gold Medal, RGS, 1985; Internat. Emmy Award, 1985; Encyclopaedia Britannica Award, 1987; Livingstone Medal, RSGS, 1990. Hon. DLitt: Leicester, 1970; City, 1972; London, 1980; Birmingham, 1982; Hon. DSc: Liverpool, 1974; Heriot-Watt, 1978; Sussex, 1979; Bath, 1981; Ulster, Durham, 1982; Keele, 1986; Oxford, 1988; Hon. LLD: Bristol, 1977; Glasgow, 1980; DUniv: Open Univ., 1980; Essex, 1987; Hon. ScD Cambridge, 1984. Hon. Freeman, City of Leicester, 1990. Comdr of Golden Ark (Netherlands), 1983. *Publications:* Zoo Quest to Guiana, 1956; Zoo Quest for a Dragon, 1957; Zoo Quest in Paraguay, 1959; Quest in Paradise, 1960; Zoo Quest to Madagascar, 1961; Quest under Capricorn, 1963; The Tribal Eye, 1976; Life on Earth, 1979; The Living Planet, 1984, rev. edn 1985; The First Eden, 1987; The Trials of Life, 1990. *Recreations:* music, tribal art, natural history. *Address:* 5 Park Road, Richmond, Surrey.

See also Sir R. S. Attenborough.

ATTENBOROUGH, John Philip, CMG 1958; CBE 1953 (OBE 1946); retired; *b* 6 Nov. 1901; *s* of late Frederick Samuel and Edith Attenborough; *m* 1947, Lucie Blanche

Woods, *y d* of late Rev. J. R. and Mrs Prenter and *widow* of late Dr P. P. Murphy; one step *s. Educ:* Manchester Grammar Sch.; Corpus Christi Coll., Oxford (MA). Superintendent of Education, Northern Nigeria, 1924–30; Lecturer and Senior Inspector, Education Dept, Palestine, 1930–37; Dir of Education, Aden, 1937–46; Deputy Dir of Education, Palestine, 1946–48; Asst Educational Adviser, Colonial Office, 1948; Dir of Education, Tanganyika, 1948–55; Mem. for Social Services, Tanganyika, 1955–57; Min. for Social Services, Tanganyika, 1957–58; Consultant: UNICEF, 1963–65; UNESCO, 1967; Devon, CC, 1961–68; Mem. SW Regional Hosp. Bd, 1965–71. Pres. Torbay Conservative Assoc., 1967–79. *Address:* 21 Thorncliff Close, Torquay, Devon TQ1 2QW. *T:* Torquay (0803) 297291.

ATTENBOROUGH, Peter John; Headmaster of Charterhouse, since 1982; *b* 4 April 1938; *m* 1967, Alexandra Deidre Campbell Page; one *s* one *d. Educ:* Christ's Hospital; Peterhouse, Cambridge. BA Classics 1960, MA 1964. Asst Master, Uppingham Sch., 1960–75 (Housemaster, Senior Classics Master); Asst Master, Starehe Boys' Centre, Nairobi, 1966–67; Headmaster, Sedbergh Sch., 1975–81. Chairman: Common Entrance Cttee of Independent Schs, 1983–88; Schools Arabic Project, 1986–87; Mem., HMC Cttee, 1986–90. Almoner, Christ's Hosp., 1987–; Governor: Ashdown House, 1983–; Haslemere Prep. Sch., 1986–; St Edmund's Sch., 1986–; Brambletye Sch., 1989–; Caldicott Sch., 1990–. Freeman, City of London, 1965; Liveryman, Skinners' Co., 1978. *Address:* Charterhouse, Godalming, Surrey GU7 2DF. *T:* Guildford (0483) 426796.

ATTENBOROUGH, Philip John; publisher; Chairman: Hodder & Stoughton Ltd and Hodder & Stoughton Holdings Ltd, since 1975; The Lancet Ltd, since 1977; *b* 3 June 1936; *er s* of John Attenborough, CBE, and Barbara (*née* Sandle); *m* 1963, Rosemary, *y d* of Dr W. B. Littler, *qv*; one *s* one *d. Educ:* Rugby; Trinity Coll., Oxford. Christmas postman (parcels), 1952–54; Nat. Service, Sergeant 68th Regt RA, Oswestry, 1956; lumberjack, Blind River, Ont, 1957; joined Hodder & Stoughton, 1957: Export Manager, 1960; Dir, 1963; Sales Dir, 1969. Dir, Book Tokens Ltd, 1985–. Publishers Association: Mem. Council, 1976– (Treasurer, 1981–82; Vice-Pres., 1982–83, 1985–86; Pres., 1983–85); Leader, delegns of Brit. publishers to China, 1978, to Bangladesh, India and Pakistan, 1986, to India, 1990; Mem. Exec. Cttee, IPA, 1988–; Chairman: Book Develt Council, 1977–79; PA Freedom to Publish Cttee, 1987–; Member: British Council Publishers Adv. Cttee, 1977– (Chm., 1989–); British Library Adv. Council, 1986–89; Fédération des Editeurs Européens, 1986–. Gov., Judd Sch., Tonbridge, 1987–. Liveryman, Skinners' Co., 1970 (extra Mem. Court, 1985–88). *Recreations:* trout fishing, playing golf and tennis, watching cricket. *Address:* Coldhanger, Seal Chart, near Sevenoaks, Kent TN15 0EJ. *T:* Sevenoaks (0732) 61516. *Clubs:* Garrick, MCC; Kent CC, Rye Golf.

ATTENBOROUGH, Sir Richard (Samuel), Kt 1976; CBE 1967; actor, producer and director; Goodwill Ambassador for UNICEF, since 1987; *b* 29 Aug. 1923; *s* of late Frederick L. Attenborough; *m* 1945, Sheila Beryl Grant Sim; one *s* two *d. Educ:* Wyggeston Grammar Sch., Leicester. Leverhulme Schol. to Royal Acad. of Dramatic Art, 1941 (Bancroft Medal). First stage appearance as Richard Miller in Ah Wilderness, Intimate Theatre, Palmers Green, 1941; Ralph Berger in Awake and Sing, Arts Theatre (West End début), 1942; The Little Foxes, Piccadilly Theatre, 1942; Brighton Rock, Garrick, 1943. Joined RAF 1943; seconded to RAF Film Unit for Journey Together, 1944; demobilised, 1946. Returned to stage in The Way Back (Home of the Brave), Westminster, 1949; To Dorothy, a Son, Savoy, 1950, Garrick, 1951; Sweet Madness, Vaudeville, 1952; The Mousetrap, Ambassadors, 1952–54; Double Image, Savoy, 1956–57, St James's, 1957; The Rape of the Belt, Piccadilly, 1957–58. *Film: appearances:* In Which We Serve (screen début), 1942; School for Secrets, The Man Within, Dancing With Crime, Brighton Rock, London Belongs to Me, The Guinea Pig, The Lost People, Boys in Brown, Morning Departure, Hell is Sold Out, The Magic Box, Gift Horse, Father's Doing Fine, Eight O'Clock Walk, The Ship That Died of Shame, Private's Progress, The Baby and the Battleship, Brothers in Law, The Scamp, Dunkirk, The Man Upstairs, Sea of Sand, Danger Within, I'm All Right Jack, Jet Storm, SOS Pacific; The Angry Silence (also co-prod), 1959; The League of Gentlemen, 1960; Only Two Can Play, All Night Long, 1961; The Dock Brief, The Great Escape, 1962; Séance On a Wet Afternoon (also prod; Best actor, San Sebastian Film Fest. and British Film Acad.), The Third Secret, 1963; Guns at Batasi (Best actor, British Film Acad.), 1964; The Flight of the Phœnix, 1965; The Sand Pebbles (Hollywood Golden Globe), 1966; Dr Dolittle (Hollywood Golden Globe), The Bliss of Mrs Blossom, 1967; Only When I Larf, 1968; The Last Grenade, A Severed Head, David Copperfield, Loot, 1969; 10 Rillington Place, 1970; And Then There Were None, Rosebud, Brannigan, Conduct Unbecoming, 1974; The Chess Players, 1977; The Human Factor, 1979; *produced:* Whistle Down the Wind, 1961; The L-Shaped Room, 1962; *directed:* Young Winston (Hollywood Golden Globe), 1972; A Bridge Too Far (Evening News Best Drama Award), 1976; Magic, 1978; A Chorus Line, 1985; *produced and directed:* Oh! What a Lovely War (16 Internat. Awards incl. Hollywood Golden Globe and SFTA UN Award), 1968; Gandhi (8 Oscars, 5 BAFTA Awards, 5 Hollywood Golden Globes, Dirs' Guild of America Award for Outstanding Directorial Achievement), 1980–81; Cry Freedom (Berlinale Kamera), 1987; Formed: Beaver Films with Bryan Forbes, 1959; Allied Film Makers, 1960. Chairman: Goldcrest Films & Television Ltd, 1982–87; Channel Four Television, 1987– (Dep. Chm., 1980–86); Capital Radio, 1972–; Duke of York's Theatre, 1979–. Dir, Chelsea Football Club, 1969–82. Chairman: Actor's Charitable Trust, 1956–88 (Pres., 1988–); Combined Theatrical Charities Appeals Council, 1964–88 (Pres., 1988–); BAFTA (formerly SFTA), 1969–70 (Vice-Pres., 1971–); RADA, 1970– (Mem. Council, 1963–); UK Trustees, Waterford-Kamhlaba Sch., Swaziland, 1976– (Gov., 1987–); BFI, 1981–; Cttee of Inquiry into the Arts and Disabled People, 1983–85; British Screen Adv. Council, 1987–; European Script Fund, 1988–; Member: British Actors' Equity Assoc. Council, 1949–73; Cinematograph Films Council, 1967–73; Arts Council of GB, 1970–73. Gov., Nat. Film Sch., 1970–81. Pres., Muscular Dystrophy Gp of GB, 1971– (Vice-Pres., 1962–71); Dir, Young Vic, 1974–84. Trustee: Help a London Child, 1975–; Tate Gall., 1976–82 (Tate Foundn, 1986–). Gov., Motability, 1977–. Patron, Kingsley Hall Community Centre, 1982–. President: The Gandhi Foundn, 1983–; Brighton Festival, 1984–; British Film Year, 1984–86; Arts for Health, 1989–. Pro-Chancellor, Sussex Univ., 1970–. Fellow, BAFTA, 1983. Freeman, City of Leicester, 1990. Hon. DLitt: Leicester, 1970; Kent, 1981; Sussex, 1987; Hon. DCL Newcastle, 1974; Hon. LLD, Dickinson, Penn., 1983. Evening Standard Film Award, 40 years service to British Cinema, 1983; Award of Merit for Humanitarianism in Film Making, European Film Awards, 1988. Martin Luther King, Jr Peace Prize, 1983. Padma Bhushan (India), 1983; Commandeur, Ordre des Arts et des Lettres (France), 1985; Chevalier, Légion d'Honneur (France), 1988. *Publications:* In Search of Gandhi, 1982; (with Diana Carter) Richard Attenborough's Chorus Line, 1986; Cry Freedom, A Pictorial Record, 1987. *Recreations:* collecting paintings and sculpture, listening to music, watching football. *Address:* Old Friars, Richmond Green, Surrey. *Clubs:* Garrick, Beefsteak, Green Room.

See also Sir D. F. Attenborough.

ATTERTON, David Valentine, CBE 1981; PhD; FEng; FIM; Chairman, Foseco Minsep plc, 1979–86; *b* 13 Feb. 1927; *s* of Frank Arthur Shepherd Atterton and Ella Constance (*née* Collins); *m* 1948, Sheila Ann McMahon; two *s* one *d. Educ:* Bishop Wordsworth's Sch., Salisbury; Peterhouse, Cambridge. MA, PhD Cantab. Post-doctorate research, Cambridge, 1950–52; joined Foundry Services Ltd, 1952; Managing Director: Foseco Ltd, 1966; Foseco Minsep Ltd, 1969. Dep. Chm., Associated Engineering plc, 1979–86 (Dir 1972–); Director: Investors in Industry plc (formerly Finance Corp. for Industry and FFI), 1974–; IMI plc, 1976–89; Barclays Bank UK Ltd, 1982–84; Bank of England, 1984–; Barclays Bank, 1984–; (part-time) British Coal, 1986–; Marks and Spencer plc, 1987–; Rank Organisation, 1987–; Dimex Ltd, 1988–89. Chm., NEDO Iron and Steel Sector Working Party, 1977–82; Member: Bd of Governors, United World Coll. of the Atlantic, 1968–85 (Chm., 1973–79); Adv. Council for Applied R&D, 1982–85; Pres., Birmingham Chamber of Commerce and Industry, 1974–75. *Publications:* numerous scientific papers in learned jls. *Recreations:* cartography, notaphilia, Japanese language, photography. *Address:* Cathedral Green House, Wells, Somerset BA5 2UB. *T:* Wells (0749) 74907.

ATTEWELL, Brian; HM Diplomatic Service; Commercial Counsellor, Brussels, since 1988; *b* 29 May 1937; *s* of late William John Geldard Attewell and of Marie Evelyn Attewell; *m* 1963, Mary Gillian Tandy; two *s* one *d. Educ:* Dulwich Coll.; London School of Economics and Political Science (BScEcon 1961). BoT, 1956–58, 1961–66; Private Sec. to Parly Sec., 1964–66; transf. to Diplomatic Service, 1966: Washington, 1967–70; Buenos Aires, 1970–73; FCO, 1974–78; Canberra, 1978–80; FCO, 1980–83; Dubai, 1984–87. *Recreations:* golf, tennis, walking, listening to music (classical and jazz), following fortunes of Charlton Athletic. *Address:* c/o Foreign and Commonwealth Office, King Charles Street, SW1A 2AH. *Club:* Cercle Gaulois (Brussels).

ATTLEE, family name of **Earl Attlee.**

ATTLEE, 3rd Earl *cr* 1955; **John Richard Attlee;** Viscount Prestwood, 1955; *b* 3 Oct. 1956; *s* of 2nd Earl Attlee and Anne Barbara, *er d* of late James Henderson, CBE; *S* father, 1991. *Educ:* Stowe.

ATTLEE, Air Vice-Marshal Donald Laurence, CB 1978; LVO 1964; DL; fruit farmer, since 1977; *b* 2 Sept. 1922; *s* of Major Laurence Attlee; *m* 1952, Jane Hamilton Young; one *s* two *d. Educ:* Haileybury. Pilot trng in Canada, 1942–44; Flying Instructor, 1944–48; Staff, Trng Comd, 1949–52; 12 Sqdn, 1952–54; Air Ministry, Air Staff, 1954–55; RAF Staff Coll., 1956; 59 Sqdn, 1957–59; CO, The Queen's Flight (W/Cdr), 1960–63; HQ, RAF Germany, 1964–67; CO, RAF Brize Norton, 1968–69; IDC, 1970; MoD Policy Staff, 1971–72; Dir of RAF Recruiting, 1973–74; Air Cdre, Intell., 1974–75; AOA Trng Comd, 1975–77, retired. Chm., Mid-Devon Business Club, 1985–87; Mem. Bd, Mid-Devon Enterprise Agency, 1983–. Mem., Mid-Devon DC, 1982– (Vice-Chm., 1987–89; Chm., 1989–91). DL Devon, 1991. *Recreations:* genealogy, Do-it-Yourself, gardening. *Address:* Jerwoods, Culmstock, Cullompton, Devon EX15 3JU. *T:* Hemycock (0823) 680317. *Club:* Royal Air Force.

ATTRIDGE, Elizabeth Ann Johnston, (Mrs John Attridge); Under Secretary, Animal Health Group, Ministry of Agriculture, Fisheries and Food, since 1989; *b* 26 Jan. 1934; *d* of late Rev. John Worthington Johnston, MA, CF, and Mary Isabel Giraud (*née* McFadden); *m* 1956, John Attridge; one *s. Educ:* Richmond Lodge Sch., Belfast; St Andrews Univ., Fife. Assistant Principal, Min. of Education, NI, 1955, reappointed on marriage (marriage bar), MAFF, London, 1956; assisted on Agriculture Acts, 1957 and 1958; Head Plant Health Br., 1963–66, Finance, 1966–69, External Relations (GATT) Br., 1969–72; Assistant Secretary: Animal Health I, 1972–75; Marketing Policy and Potatoes, 1975–78; Tropical Foods Div., 1978–83; Under Secretary: European Community Group, 1983–85; Emergencies, Food Quality and Pest Control, 1985–89. Chairman, International Coffee Council, 1982–83. *Recreations:* collecting fabric, opera. *Address:* Ministry of Agriculture, Fisheries and Food, Whitehall Place, SW1A 2HH.

ATTWOOD, Thomas Jaymril; Chairman, Cargill, Attwood and Thomas Ltd, Management Consultancy Group, since 1965; *b* 30 March 1931; *s* of George Frederick Attwood and Avril Sandys (*née* Cargill, NZ); *m* 1963, Lynette O. E. Lewis; one *s* one *d. Educ:* Haileybury and Imperial Service Coll.; RMA Sandhurst; Harvard Grad. Sch. of Business Admin; INSEAD, Fontainebleau. Pres., Internat. Consultants' Foundn, 1978–81. Conducted seminars for UN Secretariat, European Commn and World Council of Churches, 1970–80; presented papers to Eur. Top Management Symposium, Davos, Internat. Training Conf. and to World Public Relations Conf. Mem. Exec. Cttee, Brit. Management Training Export Council, 1978–85; Chm., Post Office Users National Council, 1982–83. Mem. Court, Worshipful Company of Marketors, 1985– (Liveryman, 1980). FCIM; FIMC; FBIM; Fellow, Inst. of Dirs. Mem., Richmond upon Thames Borough Council, 1969–71. *Publications:* (jtly) Bow Group pubn on United Nations, 1961; contrib. to reference books, incl. Systems Thinking, Innovation in Global Consultation, Handbook of Management Development, and Helping Across Cultures; articles on marketing, management and business topics. *Recreations:* travel, music, City of London, cricket. *Address:* 8 Teddington Park, Teddington, Mddx TW11 8DA. *T:* 081–977 8091. *Clubs:* City Livery, MCC, Lord's Taverners.

ATTYGALLE, Gen. Don Sepala, Hon. LVO 1954; High Commissioner for Democratic Socialist Republic of Sri Lanka in London, since 1990; *b* 14 Oct. 1921; *m* 1958, Ithali Mercia Attygalle; one *s. Educ:* Royal College, Colombo; psc 1953, idc 1966. Commissioned into Army, 1940; Ceylon Light Infantry; Extra ADC to Governor-General of Ceylon, 1952–65; CO, Ceylon Armoured Corps, 1955; Comdr, Sri Lanka Army, 1967–77; Chief Co-Ordinating Authority, 1977, Sec., 1983–90, Min. of Defence. Deshamanya, 1990. *Recreations:* sports. *Address:* Sri Lanka High Commission, 13 Hyde Park Gardens, W2 2LU. *T:* 071–262 1841.

ATWELL, Sir John (William), Kt 1976; CBE 1970; FEng; FIMechE, FRSE; Chairman, Omega Software Ltd, 1982–84; *b* 24 Nov. 1911; *s* of William Atwell and Sarah Workman; *m* 1945, Dorothy Hendry Baxter, *d* of J. H. Baxter and Janet Muir; no *c. Educ:* Hyndland Secondary Sch., Glasgow; Royal Technical Coll., Glasgow (ARTC); Cambridge Univ. (MSc). General Management, Stewarts and Lloyds Ltd, 1939–54; Dir 1955–61, Man. Dir 1961–68, G. & J. Weir Ltd; Dir, The Weir Group Ltd, 1961–74, and Chm., Engineering Div., 1968–74; Mem., BRB (Scottish), 1975–81. Chm., Scottish Offshore Partnership, 1975–81; Director: Anderson Strathclyde Ltd, 1975–78; Govan Shipbuilders Ltd, 1975–79. Mem., Bd of Royal Ordnance Factories, 1974–79. Chm., Requirements Bd for Mechanical Engineering and Machine Tools, DTI, 1972–76. Member: University Grants Cttee, 1965–69; NEDC Mech. Eng Cttee, 1969–74; Court, Strathclyde Univ., 1967–83 (Chm., 1975–80); Council, RSE, 1974–85 (Treas., 1977–82; Pres., 1982–85); Exec. Cttee, Scottish Council of Develt and Industry, 1972–77; Adv. Council for Applied R&D, 1976–80; Scottish Hosps Res. Trust, 1972–84; Council, Scottish Business Sch., 1972–80. Vice-Pres., IMechE, 1966–73, Pres., 1973–74; Vice-Chm., 1977–78, Chm., 1978–79, CEI. Hon. Fellow, Strathclyde Univ., 1990. Hon. LLD Strathclyde, 1973. *Recreation:* golf. *Address:* Elmfield, Buchanan Drive, Rutherglen, Glasgow G73 3PE. *T:* 041–647 1824. *Clubs:* New (Edinburgh); Western (Glasgow).

ATWILL, Sir (Milton) John (Napier), Kt 1979; Deputy Chairman, David Jones Ltd, since 1975 (Board Member, since 1971); Director, MEPC Australia Ltd, since 1980; *b* 16

Jan. 1926; s of Milton Spencer Atwill and Isabella Caroline Atwill; m 1955, Susan Playfair; two d. Educ: Cranbrook Sch., Sydney; Geelong Church of England Grammar Sch.; Jesus Coll., Cambridge (MA). Called to the Bar, Gray's Inn, 1953, NSW Bar, 1953. President, NSW Division, Liberal Party of Australia, 1970–75; Hon. Treas., 1968–69; Federal Pres., Liberal Party, 1975–82; Chm., Pacific Democrat Union, 1982; Vice-Chm., Internat. Democrat Union, 1983. Recreations: cricket, tennis. Address: 5 Fullerton Street, Woollahra, NSW 2025, Australia. T: (02) 32–1570. Clubs: Australian, Union, Royal Sydney Golf, Melbourne.

ATWOOD, Barry Thomas; Principal Assistant Solicitor (Under Secretary), Ministry of Agriculture, Fisheries and Food, since 1989; b 25 Feb. 1940; s of Percival Atwood and Vera Fanny Atwood (née Stoneham); m 1965, Jennifer Ann Burgess; two s. Educ: Bristol Grammar Sch.; Bristol Univ. (LLB); University College London. Solicitor. Articled John Robinson and Jarvis, Isle of Wight, 1961; Solicitor with Robert Smith & Co., Bristol, 1965; Legal Dept, Ministry of Agriculture, Fisheries and Food: conveyancing, 1966; food legislation, 1970; Common Agricultural Policy, 1977; i/c European Court litigation, 1982; Agricultural Commodities and Food Safety Bill, 1986. Recreations: family, music, swimming, walking, France. Address: Ministry of Agriculture, Fisheries and Food, 55 Whitehall, SW1A 2EY. T: 071–270 8339.

ATWOOD, Margaret, CC (Can.) 1981; FRSC 1987; writer; b Ottawa, 18 Nov. 1939. Educ: Univ. of Toronto (BA 1961); Radcliffe Coll., Cambridge, Mass (AM 1962); Harvard Univ., Cambridge, Mass. Lectr in English, Univ. of BC, Vancouver, 1964–65; Instructor in English: Sir George Williams Univ., Montreal, 1967–68; Univ. of Alberta, 1969–70; Asst Prof. of English, York Univ., Toronto, 1971–72; Writer-in-Residence: Univ. of Toronto, 1972–73; Tuscaloosa, Alabama, 1985; Berg Prof., New York Univ., 1986; Macquarie Univ., Australia, 1987. Holds hon. degrees from univs and colls; recipient of awards, medals and prizes for writing. TV scripts: The Servant Girl, 1974; Snowbird, 1981; (with Peter Pearson) Heaven on Earth, 1986; radio script, The Trumpets of Summer, 1964. Publications: poetry: Double Persephone, 1961; Kaleidoscopes Baroque: a poem, 1965; Talismans for Children, 1965; Speeches for Doctor Frankenstein, 1966; The Circle Game, 1966; The Animals in That Country, 1969; The Journals of Susanna Moodie, 1970; Procedures for Underground, 1970; Power Politics, 1971; You Are Happy, 1974; Selected Poems, 1976; Marsh, Hawk, 1977; Two-Headed Poems, 1978; True Stories, 1981; Notes Towards a Poem that Can Never be Written, 1981; Snake Poems, 1983; Interlunar, 1984; Selected Poems II, 1986; Selected Poems 1966–84, 1990; Margaret Atwood Poems, 1991; fiction: The Edible Woman, 1969; Surfacing, 1972; Lady Oracle, 1976; Dancing Girls (short stories), 1977; Up in the Tree (for children), 1978; Anna's Pet (for children), 1980; Life Before Man, 1979; Bodily Harm, 1981; Encounters with the Element Man, 1982; Murder in the Dark, 1983; Bluebeard's Egg, 1983; Unearthing Suite, 1983; The Handmaid's Tale, 1986 (Governor General's Award, 1986; filmed 1990); Cat's Eye, 1989; (ed with Shannon Ravenel) The Best American Short Stories, 1989; For the Birds (for children), 1990; non-fiction: Survival: a thematic guide to Canadian literature, 1972; Days of the Rebels 1815–1840, 1977; Second Words: selected critical prose, 1982. Address: c/o Jonathan Cape, 32 Bedford Square, WC1B 3EL.

AUBEE, Caleb Babatunde; High Commissioner for Sierra Leone in the United Kingdom, since 1987; b 1 Nov. 1942; m; three c. Educ: W. A. M. Collegiate Secondary Sch., Sierra Leone; Wilmington Coll., Ohio, USA; Wayne State Univ., Michigan, USA. BA, MA. Editor, political jl The Task Ahead, 1969–71; Dir, West African Consultancy Ltd, 1975–78; Dep. High Comr for Sierra Leone in UK, 1978–81; Ambassador to People's Republic of China, 1981–87. Mem., Central Cttee, Ruling All People's Congress Party, 1985–. Recreations: soccer, music. Address: Sierra Leone High Commission, 33 Portland Place, W1N 3AG.

AUBREY, John Melbourn, CBE 1979; b 5 March 1921; s of Melbourn Evans Aubrey and Edith Maria Aubrey; m 1949, Judith Christine Fairbairn; two s two d (and one s decd). Educ: St Paul's Sch.; Corpus Christi Coll., Cambridge (Mech. Sciences Tripos). FCIPA 1952. Armstrong Siddeley Motors Ltd, 1942–43; RE, 1943–47; Tootal Broadhurst Lee Co., 1947–49; Gill Jennings and Every, Chartered Patent Agents, 1949–55; Courtaulds Ltd, 1955–81, Consultant 1982–86. Chm., Baptist Insurance Co. Ltd, 1980– (Dir, 1971–); Mem. Council, Baptist Union of GB and Ireland, 1970–89. Recreations: gardening, sailing, swimming, skiing. Address: Clarence Cottage, 45 Clarence Hill, Dartmouth TQ6 9NY. T: Dartmouth (0803) 833194. Clubs: United Oxford & Cambridge University, Ski of GB; Dartmouth Yacht.

AUBREY-FLETCHER, family name of **Baroness Braye.**

AUBREY-FLETCHER, Sir John (Henry Lancelot), 7th Bt cr 1782; a Recorder of the Crown Court, 1972–74; Metropolitan Magistrate, 1959–71; b 22 Aug. 1912; s of Major Sir Henry Aubrey-Fletcher, 6th Bt, CVO, DSO, and Mary Augusta (d 1963), e d of Rev. R. W. Chilton; S father, 1969; m 1939, Diana Fynvola, d of late Lieut-Col Arthur Egerton (killed in action, 1915), Coldstream Guards, and late Mrs Robert Bruce; one s (one d decd). Educ: Eton; New Coll., Oxford. Called to Bar, 1937. Served War of 1939–45, Grenadier Guards, reaching rank of temp. Lieut-Col and leaving Army with rank of Hon. Major. Dep. Chm., Bucks Quarter Sessions, 1959–71. High Sheriff, Bucks, 1961. Heir: s Henry Egerton Aubrey-Fletcher [b 27 Nov. 1945; m 1976, Roberta Sara, d of late Major Robert Buchanan, Blackpark Cottage, Evanton, Ross-shire, and of Mrs Ogden White; three s]. Address: The Gate House, Chilton, Aylesbury, Bucks HP18 9LR. T: Long Crendon (0844) 347.

AUCHINCLOSS, Louis Stanton; author; Partner, Hawkins Delafield and Wood, NYC, since 1957 (Associate, 1954–57); b NY, 27 Sept. 1917; s of J. H. Auchincloss and P. Stanton; m 1957, Adèle Lawrence; three s. Educ: Groton Sch.; Yale Univ.; Univ. of Virginia (LLB). Lieut USNR; served, 1941–45. Admitted to NY Bar, 1941; Associate Sullivan and Cromwell, 1941–51. Mem. Exec. Cttee, Assoc. of Bar of NY City. Pres., Museum of City of NY, 1967; Trustee, Josiah Macy Jr Foundn. Mem., Nat. Inst. of Arts and Letters. Publications: The Indifferent Children, 1947; The Injustice Collectors, 1950; Sybil, 1952; A Law for the Lion, 1953; The Romantic Egoists, 1954; The Great World and Timothy Colt, 1956; Venus in Sparta, 1958; Pursuit of the Prodigal, 1959; The House of Five Talents, 1960; Reflections of a Jacobite, 1961; Portrait in Brownstone, 1962; Powers of Attorney, 1963; The Rector of Justin, 1964; Pioneers and Caretakers, 1966; The Embezzler, 1966; Tales of Manhattan, 1967; A World of Profit, 1969; Second Chance: tales to two generations, 1970; Edith Wharton, 1972; I Come as a Thief, 1972; Richelieu, 1972; The Partners, 1974; A Writer's Capital, 1974; Reading Henry James, 1975; The Winthrop Covenant, 1976; The Dark Lady, 1977; The Country Cousin, 1978; The House of the Prophet, 1980; The Cat and the King, 1981; Watch Fires, 1982; Honourable Men, 1986; Diary of a Yuppie, 1987; The Golden Calves, 1989; Fellow Passengers, 1990; pamphlets on American writers. Address: 1111 Park Avenue, New York, NY 10028, USA; (office) 67 Wall Street, New York, NY 10005. Club: Century Association (NY).

AUCKLAND, 9th Baron (cr Irish Barony, 1789; British 1793); **Ian George Eden;** Non-executive Director: C. J. Sims & Co. Ltd; George S. Hall & Co. Ltd; b 23 June 1926; s of

8th Baron Auckland; S father 1957; m 1954, Dorothy Margaret, d of H. J. Manser, Eastbourne; one s two d. Educ: Blundell's Sch. Royal Signals, 1945–48; 3/4 County of London Yeomanry (Sharpshooters) (TA), 1948–53. Underwriting Mem. of Lloyd's, 1956–64. Pres., Inst. of Insurance Consultants, 1977–89. Member: New Zealand Soc.; Anglo-Finnish Parly Gp. Pres., Surrey Co. Br., Royal British Legion; Council, RoSPA. Master, Broderers' Co., 1967–68; Hon. Mem., Court of Assistants, Blacksmiths' Co. Knight, 1st cl., White Rose (Finland), 1984. Recreations: music, theatre, tennis and walking. Heir: s Hon. Robert Ian Burnard Eden, b 25 July 1962. Address: Tudor Rose House, 30 Links Road, Ashtead, Surrey. T: Ashtead (03722) 74393. Clubs: City Livery, World Traders.

AUCKLAND (Dio. Durham), **Archdeacon of;** see Hodgson, Ven. J. D.

AUCKLAND (NZ), Bishop of, since 1985; **Rt. Rev. Bruce Carlyle Gilberd;** b 22 April 1938; s of Carlyle Bond Gilberd and Dorothy Annie Gilberd; m 1963, Patricia Molly Tanton; two s one d. Educ: King's College, Auckland; Auckland Univ. (BSc); St John's Coll., Auckland (LTh Hons, STh). Deacon 1962, priest 1963, Auckland; Assistant Curate: Devonport, 1962–64; Ponsonby and Grey Lynn, 1965; Panmure, 1965–68; Vicar of Avondale, 1968–71. Trainee Industrial Chaplain, Tees-side Industrial Mission, and Asst Curate of Egglescliffe, 1971–73; visited industrial missions in UK and Europe. Director, Interchurch Trade and Industrial Mission, Wellington, 1973–79; founding Mem., Wellington Industrial Relations Soc.; Hon. Asst Curate, Lower Hutt 1973–77, Waiwhetu 1977–79; Lectr, St John's Coll., Auckland, 1980–85. Mem. Gen. Synod, NZ. Has travelled widely in UK, Europe, China, USA and S Africa. NZ Commemorative Medal, 1990. Publication: (ed) Christian Ministry: a definition, 1984. Recreations: fishing, surfing, sailing. Address: PO Box 37 023, Parnell, Auckland 1, New Zealand. T: 771 989.

AUCKLAND (NZ), Bishop of, (RC), since 1983; **Rt. Rev. Denis George Browne;** b 21 Sept. 1937; s of Neville John Browne and Catherine Anne Browne (née Moroney). Educ: Holy Name Seminary, Christchurch, NZ; Holy Cross College, Mosgiel, NZ. Assistant Priest: Gisborne, 1963–67; Papatoetoe, 1968–71; Remuera, 1972–74; Missionary in Tonga, 1975–77; Bishop of Rarotonga, 1977–83. Hon. DD. Recreation: golf. Address: Pompallier Diocesan Centre, Private Bag, Ponsonby, Auckland, New Zealand. T: (09) 784380.

AUCKLAND (NZ), Assistant Bishop of; see Buckle, Rt Rev. E. G.

AUDLAND, Sir Christopher (John), KCMG 1987 (CMG 1973); HM Diplomatic Service and Commission of the European Communities, retired; b 7 July 1926; s of late Brig. Edward Gordon Audland, CB, CBE, MC, and Violet Mary, d of late Herbert Shepherd-Cross, MP; m 1955, Maura Daphne Sullivan; two s one d. Educ: Winchester Coll. RA, 1944–48 (Temp. Capt.). Entered Foreign (subseq. Diplomatic) Service, 1948; served in: Bonn; British Representation to Council of Europe, Strasbourg; Washington; UK Delegn to negotiations for British Membership of European Communities, Brussels, 1961–63; Buenos Aires; Head of Science and Technology Dept, FCO, 1968–70; Counsellor (Head of Chancery), Bonn, 1970–72; seconded to Commn of Eur. Communities, 1973: Dep. Sec.-Gen., 1973–81; Dir-Gen. for Energy, 1981–86. Head, UK Delegn to 1st UN Conf. on Seabed and Ocean Floor, 1968; Dep. Head, UK Delegn to Four-Power Negotiations on Berlin, 1970–72. Hon. Fellow, Faculty of Law, and Vis. Lectr on European Instns, Edinburgh Univ., 1986–. President: Internat. Castles Inst., 1990– (Vice Pres., 1988–90); Vice Pres., Europa Nostra, 1989–; Dep. Chm., National Trust Lake Dist Appeal, 1987–90; Member: NW Regl Cttee, National Trust, 1987–; European Strategy Bd, ICL, 1988–; Lake District Nat. Park Authority, 1989–; Pro-Chancellor, Lancaster Univ., 1990– (Mem., Council, 1988–). Address: The Old House, Ackenthwaite, Milnthorpe, Cumbria LA7 7DH. T: Milnthorpe (05395) 62202. Club: United Oxford & Cambridge University.

AUDLEY, 25th Baron cr 1312–13; **Richard Michael Thomas Souter;** Director, Graham Miller & Co. Ltd, retired 1983; b 31 May 1914; s of Sir Charles Alexander Souter, KCIE, CSI (d 1958) and Lady Charlotte Dorothy Souter (née Jesson) (d 1958); S kinswoman, Baroness Audley (24th in line), 1973; m 1941, Pauline, d of D. L. Eskell; three d. Educ: Uppingham. Fellow, CILA. Military Service, 1939–46; Control Commission, Germany, 1946–50. Insurance Broker until 1955; Loss Adjuster, 1955–84. Recreations: shooting, gardening. Heir: three co-heiresses. Address: Friendly Green, Cowden, near Edenbridge, Kent TN8 7DU. T: Cowden (0342) 850682.

AUDLEY, Sir (George) Bernard, Kt 1985; Chairman: Caverswall Holdings, since 1990; Pergamon AGB plc, 1988–90; Founder, and Chairman, AGB Research PLC, 1973–88; b Stockton Brook, N Staffs, 24 April 1924; s of late Charles Bernard Audley and Millicent Claudia Audley; m 1950, Barbara, d of late Richard Arthur Heath; two s one d. Educ: Wolstanton Grammar Sch.; Corpus Christi Coll., Oxford (MA). Lieut, Kings Dragoon Guards, 1943–46. Asst Gen. Man., Hulton Press Ltd, 1949–57; Man. Dir, Television Audience Measurement Ltd, 1957–61; founded AGB Research, 1962. Chairman: Netherhall Trust, 1962–; Industry and Commerce Adv. Cttee, William and Mary Tercentenary Trust, 1985–89; Arts Access, 1986–; St Bride's Appeal for Restoration and Develt, 1987–; Pres., EUROPANEL, 1966–70; Vice-Pres., Periodical Publishers Assoc., 1989– (Pres., 1985–89). Vis. Prof. in Business and Management, Middlesex Polytechnic, 1989–. Governor, Hong Kong Coll., 1984–. FRSA 1986. Freeman of City of London, 1978; Liveryman, Gold and Silver Wyre Drawers' Company, 1975–. Recreations: golf, reading, travel. Address: Capstone, Willenhall Avenue, New Barnet, Herts EN5 1JN. T: 081–449 2030; Le Collet du Puits, Montauroux, 83440 Fayence, France. T: (94) 765287. Clubs: Cavalry and Guards, MCC; Rye Golf, Hadley Wood Golf.

AUDLEY, Prof. Robert John, PhD; FBPsS; Professor of Psychology, since 1965, Head of Psychology Department, since 1979, and Vice-Provost, since 1988, University College London; b 15 Dec. 1928; s of Walter Audley and Agnes Lilian (née Baker); m 1952, Patricia Mary Bannister (marr. diss. 1977); two s; m 1990, Vera Elyashiv Bickerdike. Educ: Battersea Grammar Sch.; University Coll. London (BSc 1st Cl. Hons Psychology, 1952; PhD 1955). Fullbright Scholar and Res. Asst, Washington State Univ., 1952; University College London: Res. Worker, MRC Gp for Exptl Investigation of Behaviour, 1955–57; Lectr in Psychology, 1957–64; Reader in Psychology, 1964; Dean, Faculty of Science, 1985–88; Fellow, 1989. Vis. Prof., Columbia Univ., NY, 1962; Vis. Miller Prof., Univ. of Calif, Berkeley, 1971; Vis Fellow, Inst. for Advanced Study, Princeton, 1970. Member: UGC Social Studies Sub-Cttee, 1975–82; UGC Equipment Sub-Cttee, 1982–89; Computer Bd for Univs and Res. Councils, 1986–90. President: British Psychological Soc., 1969–70; Exptl Psychology Soc., 1975–76. Editor, British Jl of Math. and Stat. Psychology, 1965–70. Publications: papers on choice, judgement, medical mishaps. Recreations: crosswords, cooking, the arts. Address: Psychology Department, University College London, Gower Street, WC1E 6BT. T: 071–380 7558.

AUDLEY-CHARLES, Prof. Michael Geoffrey, PhD; Yates-Goldsmid Professor of Geology and Head of the Department of Geological Sciences, University College London, since 1982; b 10 Jan. 1935; s of Lawrence Geoffrey and Elsie Ada Audley-Charles; m 1965, Brenda Amy Cordeiro; one s one d. Educ: Royal Wanstead Sch.; Chelsea Polytechnic

(BSc); Imperial Coll., London (PhD). Geologist with mining and petroleum cos, Canada and Australia, 1957–62; Imperial Coll. of Science and Technology, London: research in geology, 1962–67; Lectr in Geol., 1967–73; Reader in Geol., 1973–77; Prof. of Geol. and Head of Dept of Geol Sciences, Queen Mary Coll., London, 1977–82. *Publications:* geological papers dealing with stratigraphy of British Triassic, regional geol. of Indonesia and Crete and evolution of Gondwanaland, in learned jls. *Recreation:* gardening. *Address:* Shambrooks, Hurst Green, Etchingham, East Sussex TN19 7QT. *T:* Hurst Green (058086) 297.

AUDU, Rev. Ishaya Shu'aibu, FRCPE; Medical Director, Savannah Polyclinic, Zaria, since 1984; *b* 1 March 1927; *s* of Malam Bulus Audu and Malama Rakiya Audu; *m* 1958, Victoria Abosede Ohiorhenuan; two *s* five *d.* *Educ:* Ibadan and London Univs. House Officer, Sen. House Officer, Registrar in Surgery, Medicine, Obstetrics and Gynæcology and Pædiatrics, King's Coll. Hosp., London and Univ. Coll. Hosp., Ibadan, 1954–58; postgrad. studies, UK, 1959–60; Specialist Physician, Pædiatrician to Govt of Northern Nigeria and Personal Physician to Premier of North Region Govt, 1960–62; Lectr to Associate Professorship in Pæds, Univ. of Lagos Med. Sch., 1962–66; Vis. Res. Associate Prof., Univ. of Rochester Med. Sch., NY, 1964–65; Dep. Chm., Lagos Univ. Teaching Hosp. Man. Bd and Mem. Council, Univ. Lagos Med. Coll., 1962–66; Mem. Senate, Lagos Univ., 1963–66; Vice-Chancellor, Ahmadu Bello Univ., 1966–1975; Prof. of Medicine, 1967–77; Sen. Medical Officer, Ashaka Cement Co. Ltd, 1977–79; Minister of External Affairs, Fed. Republic of Nigeria, 1979–83; Ambassador and Perm. Rep. of Nigeria to UN, 1983–84. Pres., Christian Health Assoc. of Nigeria, 1986–. Ordained Minister, United Church of Christ in Nigeria, 1986. Hon. LHD Ohio, 1968; Hon DSc Nigeria, 1971; Hon. LLD Ibadan, 1973; FMC (Pæd) Nigerian Med. Council; FRSocMed. *Publications:* contribs to learned jls. *Recreations:* walking, table tennis. *Address:* (office) Sarki Road, Samaru, Zaria, Nigeria; (home) 23a Circular Road, GRA, Zaria.

AUDUS, Prof. Leslie John, MA, PhD, ScD Cantab; FLS, FInstBiol; Hildred Carlile Professor of Botany, Bedford College, University of London, 1948–79; *b* 9 Dec. 1911; English; *m* 1938, Rowena Mabel Ferguson (*d* 1987); two *d.* *Educ:* Downing Coll., Cambridge Univ. Downing Coll. Exhibitioner, 1929–31; Frank Smart Research Student (Cambridge Univ.), 1934–35; Lecturer in Botany, University Coll., Cardiff, 1935–40. Served War of 1939–45: RAFVR (Technical, Radar, Officer), 1940–46; PoW South Pacific, 1942–45. Scientific Officer, Agricultural Research Council, Unit of Soil Metabolism, Cardiff, 1946–47; Monsanto Lecturer in Plant Physiology, University Coll., Cardiff, 1948. Recorder, 1961–65, Pres., 1967–68, Section K, British Assoc. for the Advancement of Science. Vis. Prof. of Botany: Univ. of California, Berkeley, 1958; Univ. of Minnesota, Minneapolis, 1965; Vice-Pres. Linnean Soc. of London, 1959–60; Life Mem. New York Academy of Sciences, 1961. Editor, Journal Exp. Botany, 1965–74. *Publications:* Plant Growth Substances, 1953, 3rd edn 1972; (ed) The Physiology and Biochemistry of Herbicides, 1964; (ed) Herbicides: physiology, biochemistry and ecology, 1976; original research on plant respiration, hormones, responses to gravity, soil microbiology in relation to pesticides, etc in Annals of Botany, New Phytologist, Nature, Journal of Experimental Botany, Weed Research, etc. *Recreations:* furniture construction and restoration, electronics, amateur radio. *Address:* 38 Belmont Lane, Stanmore, Middlesex HA7 2PT.

AUERBACH, Charlotte, PhD, DSc; FRS 1957; FRSE; Professor of Genetics in the University of Edinburgh (Institute of Animal Genetics), 1967, Emeritus 1969 (Lecturer, 1947–57; Reader, 1957–67). Has done pioneering work on the chemical induction of mutations. Hon. Mem., Genetics Soc., Japan, 1966; Foreign Mem., Kongelige Danske Videnskabernes Selskab, 1968; Foreign Associate, Nat. Acad. of Sciences, USA, 1970. Hon. Dr: Leiden, 1975; Bloomington, Indiana, 1985; Hon. ScD: Dublin, 1977; Cambridge, 1977. Darwin Medal, Royal Soc., 1976. *Publications:* Genetics in the Atomic Age, 1956; The Science of Genetics, 1961; Mutation Pt 1–Methods, 1962; Heredity, 1965; Mutation Research, 1976; papers in various genetical journals. *Address:* Tyne Lodge, 131 Grange Loan, Edinburgh EH9 2HB.

AUERBACH, Frank Helmuth; painter; *b* 29 April 1931; *s* of Max Auerbach, lawyer, and Charlotte Norah Auerbach; *m* 1958, Julia Wolstenholme; one *s.* *Educ:* privately; St Martin's Sch. of Art; Royal Coll. of Art. *One-man exhibitions:* Beaux Arts Gallery, 1956, 1959, 1961, 1962, 1963; Marlborough Fine Art, 1965, 1967, 1971, 1974, 1977, 1983, 1987, 1990; Marlborough-Gerson, New York, 1969; Villiers, Sydney, Australia, 1972; Bergamini, Milan, 1973; Univ. of Essex, 1973; Mun. Gall. of Modern Art, Dublin, 1974; Marlborough, Zurich, 1976; Anthony D'Offay, London; Arts Council Retrospective, Hayward Gall., 1978; Edinburgh, 1978; Jacobson, NY, 1979; Marlborough, NY, 1982; Anne Berthoud, London, 1983; Venice Biennale, British Pavilion, 1986 (Golden Lion Prize); Kunstverein, Hamburg; Museum Folkwang, Essen; Centro de Arte Reina Sofia, Madrid, 1986–87; Rijksmuseum Vincent van Gogh, Amsterdam, 1989. *Mixed exhibitions:* Carnegie International, Pittsburgh, 1958, 1962; Dunn International, Fredericton, 1963; Gulbenkian International, Tate Gallery, 1964; European Painting in the Seventies, USA, 1976; Annual Exhbn, part I, Hayward Gall., 1977; Westkunst, Cologne, 1981; Internat. Survey, Moma, NY, 1984; The Hard Won Image, Tate Gall., 1984; The British Show, Australia, 1985; British Art in the Twentieth Century, RA, 1987; Current Affairs, Mus. of Modern Art, Oxford, and tour, 1987; A School of London, Kunstnernes Hus. Oslo, and tour, 1987–88; *public collections:* Arts Council; Brit. Council; Brit. Museum; Tate Gallery, London; Metropolitan Museum, NY; Mus. of Modern Art, NY; National Gallery of Victoria, Melbourne; Nat. Galls of Australia, W Australia and NSW; County Museum of LA, Calif; Cleveland Mus., Ohio; Univ. of Cincinnati; Aberdeen, Bedford, Bolton, Edinburgh, Hartlepool, Huddersfield, Hull, Leeds, Leicester, Manchester, Nottingham, Oldham, Rochdale, Sheffield, Southampton Galls; Arts Council, Contemporary Art Soc., etc. *Address:* c/o Marlborough Fine Art, 6 Albemarle Street, W1X 4BY.

AUGER, Pierre Victor, Grand Croix, Legion of Honour; retired as Director-General European Space Research Organisation (ESRO); Professor, Faculty of Sciences, University of Paris, since 1937; *b* 14 May 1899; *s* of Victor E. Auger, Prof., Univ. of Paris, and Eugénie Blanchet; *m* 1921, Suzanne Motteau; two *d.* *Educ:* Ecole Normale Supérieure, Paris; Univ. of Paris. Université de Paris (Faculté des Sciences): Asst 1927; Chef de Travaux, 1932; Maître de Conférences, 1937. Research Associate, Univ. of Chicago, 1941–43; Head of Physics Div., joint Anglo-Canadian research project on atomic energy, 1942–44; Dir of Higher Education, Min. of Education, France, 1945–48; Mem. exec. Board of UNESCO, 1946–48; Membre du comité de l'Energie Atomique, France, 1946–48; Dir, Natural Sciences Dept, UNESCO, 1948–59; Special Consultant, UNO and UNESCO, 1959–60; Chm., French Cttee on Space Research, 1960–62. Mem., French Academy of Sciences, 1977. Feltrinelli International Prize, 1961; Kalinga Internat. Prize, 1972; Gaede-Langmuir Award, 1979. FRSA. *Publications:* Rayons cosmiques, 1941; L'Homme microscopique, 1952; Current Trends in Scientific Research, 1961; scientific papers on physics (X-rays, neutrons, cosmic rays), 1923–; papers on philosophy of science, 1949–. *Address:* 12 rue Emile Faguet, 75014 Paris, France. *T:* 45 40 96 34.

AUGUSTINE, Fennis Lincoln; High Commissioner for Grenada in London, 1979–84; *b* 22 April 1932; *s* of late Mr Augustine and of Festina Joseph; *m* 1973, Oforiwa Augustine; one *s* one *d.* *Educ:* London Univ. (LLB); Ruskin Coll., Oxford (Labour Studies). Called to the Bar, Inner Temple, 1972. *Recreations:* cricket, music. *Address:* c/o Augustine & Augustine Chambers, Lucas Street, St George's, Grenada.

AUKIN, David; Head of Drama, Channel 4 Television, since 1990; *b* 12 Feb. 1942; *s* of Charles and Regina Aukin; *m* 1969, Nancy Meckler, theatre director; two *s.* *Educ:* St Paul's Sch., London; St Edmund Hall, Oxford (BA). Admitted Solicitor, 1965. Literary Advr, Traverse Theatre Club, 1970–73; Administrator, Oxford Playhouse Co., 1974–75; Administrator, 1975–79, Dir, 1979–84, Hampstead Theatre; Dir, Leicester Haymarket Theatre, 1984–86; Exec. Dir, NT, 1986–90. FRSA 1989. *Recreation:* golf. *Address:* c/o Channel 4 Television, 60 Charlotte Street, W1P 2AX. *T:* 071–631 4444. *Club:* Garrick.

AULD, Alasdair Alpin, FMA; Director, Glasgow Museums and Art Galleries, 1979–88, retired; *b* 16 Nov. 1930; *s* of Herbert Bruce Auld and Janetta Isabel MacAlpine; *m* 1959, Mary Hendry Paul; one *s* one *d.* *Educ:* Shawlands Acad., Glasgow; Glasgow Sch. of Art (DA). FMA 1971. Glasgow Museums and Art Galleries: Asst Curator, 1956–72; Keeper of Fine Art, 1972–76; Depute Dir, 1976–79. Pres., Scottish Fedn of Museums and Art Galls, 1981–84. FRSA. *Publications:* catalogues; articles on museum subjects. *Recreations:* golf, travel. *Address:* 3 Dalziel Drive, Pollokshields, Glasgow G41 4JA. *T:* 041–427 1720. *Club:* Art (Glasgow).

AULD, Margaret Gibson, RGN, RM; FRCN; MPhil; Chief Nursing Officer, Scottish Home and Health Department, 1977–88, retired; *b* 11 July 1932; *d* of late Alexander John Sutton Auld and Eleanor Margaret Ingram. *Educ:* Glasgow; Cardiff High Sch. for Girls; Radcliffe Infirm., Oxford (SRN 1953); St David's Hosp., Cardiff; Queen's Park Hosp., Blackburn (SCM 1954). Midwife Teacher's Dipl., 1962; Certif. of Nursing Admin, 1966, MPhil 1974, Edinburgh. Queen's Park Hosp., Blackburn, 1953–54; Staff Midwife, Cardiff Maternity Hosp., 1955, Sister, 1957; Sister, Queen Mary Hosp., Dunedin, NZ, 1959–60; Deptl Sister, Cardiff Maternity Hosp., 1960–66; Asst Matron, Simpson Meml Maternity Pavilion, Edinburgh, 1966–68, Matron, 1968–73; Actg Chief Reg. Nursing Officer, S-Eastern Reg. Hosp. Bd, Edinburgh, 1973; Chief Area Nursing Off., Borders Health Bd, 1973–76. Life Vice Pres., Royal Coll. of Midwives of UK, 1988. Member: GNC (Scotland), 1973–76; Central Midwives Bd (Scotland), 1972–76; Cttee on Nursing (Briggs), 1970–72; Maternity Services Cttee, Integration of Maternity Work (Tennent Report), 1972–73; Human Fertilization and Embryol. Authy, 1990–; Cttee on Ethics of Gene Therapy, 1990–91. Gov., Queen Margaret Coll., Edinburgh, 1989–. FRCN 1981; CBIM 1983. Hon. DSc CNAA, 1987. *Recreations:* reading, music, entertaining. *Address:* Staddlestones, Neidpath Road, Peebles EH45 8NN. *T:* Peebles (0721) 29594.

AULD, Hon. Sir Robin Ernest, Kt 1988; **Hon. Mr Justice Auld;** a Judge of the High Court of Justice, Queen's Bench Division, since 1987; Presiding Judge, Western Circuit, since 1991; *b* 19 July 1937; *s* of late Ernest Auld; *m* 1963, Catherine Eleanor Mary, *er d* of late David Henry Pritchard; one *s* one *d.* *Educ:* Brooklands Coll.; King's Coll., London (LLB, PhD; FKC 1987). Called to Bar, Gray's Inn, 1959 (Macaskie Schol., Lord Justice Holker Sen. Schol.), Bencher, 1984; SE Circuit; in practice at English Bar, 1959–87; admitted to Bar, State of NY, USA, 1984. Prosecuting Counsel to Dept of Trade, 1969–75; QC 1975; a Recorder, 1977–87. Legal Assessor, GMC and GDC, 1982–87; Mem., Judicial Studies Bd, 1989–91 (Chm., Criminal Cttee, 1989–91). Mem., Commn of Inquiry into Casino Gambling in the Bahamas, 1967; Chm., William Tyndale Schools' Inquiry, 1975–76; Dept of Trade Inspector, Ashbourne Investments Ltd, 1975–79; Counsel to Inquiry into Brixton Disorders, 1981; Chm., Home Office Cttee of Inquiry into Sunday Trading, 1983–84. Master, Woolmen's Co., 1984–85. *Address:* Royal Courts of Justice, Strand, WC2. *Club:* Athenæum.

AUSENDA, Marco; Editor: World Magazine, since 1987; Geographical Magazine, since 1988; *b* 16 July 1955; *s* of Giorgio Ausenda and Antonia Fattori; *m* 1988, Valentina Pozzo. *Educ:* Università Bocconi, Milan (business and admin. degree, 1981). Sub-editor, then dep. editor, Italian nature and travel magazines, Airone, Aqua and Silva, 1982–87. *Address:* c/o World Publications Ltd, 5 Manfred Road, SW15 2RS. *T:* 081–877 1080.

AUST, Anthony Ivall; Legal Counsellor, Foreign and Commonwealth Office, 1984–88 and since 1991; *b* 9 March 1942; *s* of Ivall George Aust and Jessie Anne Salmon; *m* 1st, 1969, Jacqueline Antoinette Thérèse Paris (marr. diss. 1987); two *d*; 2nd, 1988, Dr Kirsten Kaarre Jensen. *Educ:* Wilson Central Sch., Reading; Stoneham Grammar Sch., Reading; London Sch. of Econs and Pol Science (LLB 1963, LLM 1967). Admitted Solicitor, 1967. Asst Legal Adviser, FCO (formerly CO), 1967–76; Legal Adviser, British Mil. Govt, Berlin, 1976–79; Asst Legal Adviser, FCO, 1979–84; Counsellor (Legal Advr) UK Mission to UN, NY, 1988–91. *Recreations:* architecture, cinema, black and white photography, parlour games. *Address:* c/o Foreign and Commonwealth Office, SW1A 2AH.

AUSTEN-SMITH, Air Marshal Sir Roy (David), KBE 1979; CB 1975; DFC 1953; retired; a Gentleman Usher to HM the Queen, since 1982; *b* 28 June 1924; *m* 1951, Ann (*née* Alderson); two *s.* *Educ:* Hurstpierpoint College. Pilot trng, Canada, 1943–44; 41 Sqn (2 TAF), 1945; 33 Sqdn, Malaya, 1950–53; Cranwell, 1953–56; 73 Sqdn, Cyprus, 1956–59; Air Min., 1960–63; 57 Sqdn, 1964–66; HQ 2 ATAF, 1966–68; CO, RAF Wattisham; MoD, 1970–72; AOC and Comdt, RAF Coll., Cranwell, 1972–75; SASO Near East Air Force, 1975–76; Comdr British Forces, Cyprus, AOC Air HQ Cyprus and Administrator, Sovereign Base Areas, Cyprus, 1976–78; Hd of British Defence Staff, Washington, and Defence Attaché, 1978–81. *Recreation:* golf. *Address:* c/o National Westminster Bank, Swanley, Kent. *Club:* Royal Air Force.

AUSTERBERRY, Ven. Sidney Denham; Archdeacon of Salop, 1959–79, now Archdeacon Emeritus; *b* 28 Oct. 1908; *s* of late Mr and Mrs H. Austerberry; *m* 1934, Eleanor Jane Naylor; two *s* two *d.* *Educ:* Hanley High Sch.; Egerton Hall, Manchester. Curate, Newcastle-under-Lyme Parish Church, 1931–38; Vicar of S Alkmund, Shrewsbury, 1938–52; Vicar of Brewood, 1952–59; Hon. Clerical Sec., Lichfield Diocesan Conf., 1954–70; Rural Dean of Penkridge, 1958–59; Vicar of Great Ness, 1959–77. Hon. Canon, Lichfield Cathedral, 1968–79. *Address:* 6 Honeysuckle Row, Sutton Park, Shrewsbury SY3 7TW. *T:* Shrewsbury (0743) 68080.

AUSTICK, David; Senior Partner, Austicks Bookshops, Leeds; *b* 8 March 1920; *m* 1944, Florence Elizabeth Lomath. Member: Leeds City Council (for W Hunslet), 1969–74, Hon. Alderman, 1988; Leeds Metropolitan District Council (for Hunslet), 1974–75; W Yorkshire County Council (for Otley and Lower Wharfedale), 1974–79. MP (L) Ripon, July 1973–Feb. 1974; Contested (L) Ripon, 1974, (L) Cheadle, 1979, (L) Leeds, European Parlt, 1979. Member: Electoral Reform Soc. (Exec. Chm., 1984–86; Co-Sec., 1985–); European Movement; Fellowship of Reconciliation. Co. and Financial Sec., E. R. Ballot Services Ltd, 1989–91. *Address:* Austicks Bookshops, 57 Great George Street, Leeds LS1 3BN; 31 Cross Green, Otley, West Yorks; Electoral Reform Society, 6 Chancel Street, SE1 0UX. *Club:* National Liberal.

AUSTIN, Brian Patrick; HM Diplomatic Service; Counsellor, Stockholm, since 1989; *b* 18 March 1938; *s* of Edward William Austin and Winifred Alice Austin; *m* 1968, Augusta Francisca Maria Lina; one *s* one *d.* *Educ:* St Olave's Grammar Sch.; Clare Coll.,

Cambridge. National Service, 1956–58. Joined CRO, 1961; Central African Office, 1962; Lagos, 1963; The Hague, 1966; First Sec., FCO, 1969; Montreal, 1973; FCO, 1978; Dep. High Comr, Kaduna, 1981–84; Counsellor, FCO, 1984–88. *Recreation:* birdwatching. *Address:* c/o Foreign and Commonwealth Office, SW1A 2AH.

AUSTIN, Dr Colin François Lloyd, FBA 1983; Director of Studies in Classics and Fellow, Trinity Hall, Cambridge, since 1965; Reader in Greek Language and Literature, University of Cambridge, since 1988; *b* Melbourne, Australia, 26 July 1941; *s* of Prof. Lloyd James Austin, *qv*; *m* 1967, Mishtu Mazumdar, Calcutta, India; one *s* one *d*. *Educ:* Lycée Lakanal, Paris; Manchester Grammar Sch.; Jesus Coll., Cambridge (Scholar; MA 1965); Christ Church, Oxford (Sen. Scholar; MA, DPhil 1965); Freie Universität, West Berlin (Post-grad. Student). Univ. of Cambridge: John Stewart of Rannoch Scholar in Greek and Latin, 1960; Battie Scholar, Henry Arthur Thomas Scholar and Hallam Prize, 1961; Sir William Browne Medal for a Latin Epigram, 1961; Porson Prize, 1962; Prendergast Greek Student, 1962; Res. Fellow, Trinity Hall, 1965–69; Asst Univ. Lectr in Classics, 1969–73, Lectr, 1973–88; Leverhulme Res. Fellow, 1979 and 1981. Treasurer: Jt Cttee, Greek and Roman Socs, London, 1983–; Cambridge Philological Soc., 1971–. *Publications:* De nouveaux fragments de l'Erechthée d'Euripide, 1967; Nova Fragmenta Euripidea, 1968; (with Prof. R. Kasser) Papyrus Bodmer XXV et XXVI, 2 vols, 1969; Menandri Aspis et Samia, 2 vols, 1969–70; Comicorum Graecorum Fragmenta in papyris reperta, 1973; (with Prof. R. Kassel) Poetae Comici Graeci: vol. IV, Aristophon—Crobylus, 1983, vol. III 2, Aristophanes, Testimonia et Fragmenta, 1984, vol. V, Damoxenus—Magnes, 1986, vol. VII, Menecrates-Xenophon, 1989, vol. II, Agathenor—Aristonymus, 1991; notes and reviews in classical periodicals. *Recreations:* cycling, philately, wine tasting. *Address:* 7 Park Terrace, Cambridge CB1 1JH. *T:* Cambridge (0223) 62732; Trinity Hall, Cambridge CB2 1TJ.

AUSTIN, Prof. Colin Russell, FAA; Charles Darwin Professor of Animal Embryology, and Fellow of Fitzwilliam College, University of Cambridge, 1967–81, now Professor Emeritus; *b* 12 Sept. 1914; *s* of Ernest Russell Austin and Linda Mabel King; *m* 1941, Patricia Constance Jack; two *s*. *Educ:* Univ. of Sydney, Australia (BVSc 1936; DSc 1954); MA Cantab 1967. FAA 1987; FAIBiol 1987. Mem. Research Staff, CSIRO, Australia, 1938–54; Mem. Scientific Staff of MRC, UK, 1954–64; Editor, Jl of Reproduction and Fertility, 1959–64; Head of Genetic and Developmental Disorders Research Program, Delta Regional Primate Research Center, and Prof. of Embryology, Tulane Univ., New Orleans, 1964–67. F. R. Lillie Meml Fellow, Marine Biol Lab, Woods Hole, Mass, 1961. Goding Lectr, Australian Soc. for Reproductive Biol., 1991. Editor: Reproduction in Mammals, 1972–86; Biological Reviews, 1981–84. Hon. Mem., Amer. Assoc. Anatomists, 1984; Hon. Member: Soc. Chilena Reprod. y Desarrollo, 1989; Eur. Soc. of Human Reproduction and Embryol., 1990. Medal and Citation, Istituto Sperimentale Italiano Lazzaro Spallanzani, 1972; Marshall Medal, Soc. for Study of Fertility, 1981. *Publications:* The Mammalian Egg, 1961; Fertilization, 1965; Ultrastructure of Fertilization, 1968; Human Embryos: the debate on assisted reproduction, 1989; numerous research papers. *Recreations:* gardening, swimming, tennis. *Address:* 47 Dixon Road, Buderim, Qld 4556, Australia.

AUSTIN, Ven. George Bernard; Archdeacon of York, since 1988; *b* 16 July 1931; *s* of Oswald Hulton Austin and Evelyn Austin; *m* 1962, Roberta Anise Thompson; one *s*. *Educ:* St David's Coll., Lampeter (BA); Chichester Theological Coll. Deacon 1955, priest 1956; Assistant Curate: St Peter's, Chorley, 1955–57; St Clement's, Notting Dale, 1957–59; Asst Chaplain, Univ. of London, 1960; Asst Curate, Dunstable Priory, 1961–64; Vicar: St Mary the Virgin, Eaton Bray, 1964–70; St Peter, Bushey Heath, 1970–88. Hon. Canon: St Albans, 1978–88; York, 1988–. Proctor in Convocation, 1970–; a Church Commr, 1978–. *Publications:* Life of our Lord, 1960; WCC Programme to Combat Racism, 1979; (contrib.) When will ye be Wise?, 1983; (contrib.) Building in Love, 1990. *Recreations:* cooking, theatre. *Address:* 7 Lang Road, Bishopthorpe, York YO2 1QJ. *T:* York (0904) 709541. *Club:* Athenæum.

AUSTIN, Hon. Jacob, (Jack), PC (Canada) 1981; QC (Canada) 1970; Member of the Senate, Canadian Parliament, since 1975; *b* 2 March 1932; *s* of Morris Austin and Clara Edith (*née* Chetner); *m* (marr. diss.); three *d*; *m* 1978, Natalie Veiner Freeman. *Educ:* Univ. of British Columbia (BA, LLB); Harvard Univ. (LLM). Barrister and Solicitor, BC and Yukon Territory. Asst Prof. of Law, Univ. of Brit. Columbia, 1955–58; practising lawyer, Vancouver, BC, 1958–63; Exec. Asst to Minister of Northern Affairs and Nat. Resources, 1963–65; contested (Liberal) Vancouver-Kingsway, Can. Federal Election, 1965; practising lawyer, Vancouver, BC, 1966–70; Dep. Minister, Dept of Energy, Mines and Resources, Ottawa, 1970–74; Principal Sec. to Prime Minister, Ottawa, May 1974–Aug. 1975; Minister of State, 1981–82; Minister of State for Social Develt, responsible for Canada Develt Investment Corp., 1982–84; Chm., Ministerial Sub-Cttee on Broadcasting and Cultural Affairs, 1982–84. Pres., Internat. Div., Bank of British Columbia, 1985–86; Associate Counsel, Swinton & Co., 1986–; Chairman of Board and Director: Elite Insurance Management Ltd, 1986–90. Hon. DSocSc Univ. East Asia, 1987. *Publications:* articles on law and public affairs in Canadian Bar Rev., Amer. Soc. of Internat. Law and other publns. *Recreations:* sailing, tennis, reading, theatre. *Address:* Suite 304, 140 Wellington Street, The Senate, Ottawa, Ontario K1A 0A4, Canada. *T:* (613) 992–1437. *Clubs:* Rideau (Ottawa); Cercle Universitaire d'Ottawa; University Club of Vancouver (Vancouver, BC); Metropolitan (NY).

AUSTIN, Professor Lloyd James; FBA 1968; Emeritus Fellow of Jesus College, Cambridge; Emeritus Drapers Professor of French; *b* 4 Nov. 1915; *s* of late J. W. A. Austin and late Mrs J. E. Austin (*née* Tymms), Melbourne, Australia; *m* 1939, Jeanne Françoise Guérin, Rouen, France; three *s* one *d*. *Educ:* Melbourne Church of England Grammar Sch.; Univ. of Melbourne; Univ. of Paris. French Government Scholar, Paris, 1937–40; Lecturer in French, Univ. of Melbourne, 1940–42. Active Service as Lieut (Special Branch) RANVR, SW Pacific area, 1942–45. Lecturer in French, Univ. of Melbourne, 1945–47; Lecturer in French, Univ. of St Andrews, 1947–51; Research work in Paris, 1951–55; Fellow of Jesus Coll., Cambridge, 1955–56, 1961–80; Professor of Modern French Literature, Univ. of Manchester, 1956–61; Lecturer in French, Univ. of Cambridge, 1961–66, Reader, 1966–67, Drapers Prof. of French, 1967–80; Librarian, Jesus Coll., Cambridge, 1965–68, 1972–73. Hon. Sen. Res. Fellow, Inst. of Romance Studies, Univ. of London, 1990. Herbert F. Johnson Visiting Prof., Inst. for Research in the Humanities, Univ. of Wisconsin, 1962–63; Mem., Editorial Bd, French Studies, 1964–80, Gen. Editor, 1967–80, Mem. Adv. Bd, 1980–; Pres., Assoc. Internat. des Etudes Françaises, 1969–72 (Vice-Pres., 1966–69). Hon. FAHA 1985; Hon. Member: Soc. for French Studies, 1980–; Société d'Histoire Littéraire de la France, 1980; Mem., Acad. Royale de Langue et de Littérature Françaises de Belgique, 1980. Docteur *hc* Paris-Sorbonne, 1973. Prix Henri Mondor, Acad. française, 1981; Prix internat. des amitiés françaises, Soc. des Poètes français, 1982. Chevalier de l'Ordre des Arts et des Lettres, 1971; Officier de l'Ordre National du Mérite, 1976. *Publications:* Paul Bourget, 1940; (ed) Paul Valéry: Le Cimetière marin, 1954; L'Univers poétique de Baudelaire, 1956; (ed with E. Vinaver and G. Rees) Studies in Modern French Literature, presented to P. Mansell-Jones, 1961; (ed with H. Mondor) Les Gossips de Mallarmé, 1962; (ed with H. Mondor) Stéphane Mallarmé: Correspondance (1871–1898), 11 vols, 1965–85; (ed) Baudelaire: L'Art romantique, 1968; Poetic Principles and Practice, 1987; (ed) Mallarmé: Poésies, 1989; (contrib.) The Symbolist Movement in the Literature of European Languages, 1982; contrib. to French Studies, Modern Languages, Modern Language Review, Forum for Modern Language Studies, Bulletin of the John Rylands Library, Mercure de France, Nouvelle Revue Française, Revue des Sciences Humaines, Revue d'Histoire littéraire de la France, Revue de littérature comparée, Romanic Review, Studi francesi, Synthèses, Revue de l'Université de Bruxelles, L'Esprit créateur, Comparative Literature Studies, Wingspread Lectures in the Humanities, Encyclopædia Britannica, Yale French Studies, Meanjin Quarterly, Australian Jl for French Studies, AUMLA, Quadrant, etc. *Recreations:* watching cricket, tennis, looking at pictures, listening to music, travel. *Address:* 2 Park Lodge, Park Terrace, Cambridge CB1 1JJ. *T:* Cambridge (0223) 359630; Jesus College, Cambridge.
See also C. F. L. Austin.

AUSTIN, Sir Michael (Trescawen), 5th Bt *cr* 1894, of Red Hill, Castleford, W Riding; General Commissioner of Inland Revenue, 1965–86; *b* 27 Aug. 1927; *s* of Sir William Ronald Austin, 4th Bt and Dorothy Mary (*d* 1957), *d* of L. A. Bidwell, FRCS; *S* father, 1989; *m* 1951, Bridget Dorothea Patricia, *d* of late Francis Farrell; three *d*. *Educ:* Downside. Served War of 1939–45 with RNVR. MFH for 10 years. *Heir: b* Anthony Leonard Austin [*b* 30 Sept. 1930; *m* 1st, 1956, Mary Annette (marr. diss. 1966), *d* of Richard Kelly; two *s* one *d*; 2nd, 1967, Aileen Morrison Hall, *d* of William Hall Stewart; one *d*]. *Address:* Idestone, Barton, Dunchideock, Exeter, Devon EX2 9UE.

AUSTIN, Vice-Adm. Sir Peter (Murray), KCB 1976; Managing Director, Mastiff Electronic Systems, since 1990 (Director, since 1987); *b* 16 April 1921; *er s* of late Vice-Adm. Sir Francis Austin, KBE, CB, and late Lady (Marjorie) Austin (*née* Barker); *m* 1959, Josephine Rhoda Ann Shutte-Smith; three *s* one *d*. *Educ:* RNC, Dartmouth. Cadet, Dartmouth, 1935. Served War of 1939–45: at sea in HMS Cornwall, 1939–40; destroyers, 1941–45. Qualif. as pilot in FAA, 1946; served in 807 Sqdn, 1947–49; CO 736 Sqdn, 1950–52; grad. from RAF Flying Coll., Manby, 1953; comd 850 Sqdn in HMAS Sydney, incl. Korea, 1953–54; Lt-Cmdr (Flying), HMS Bulwark, 1954–56; Comdr (Air), RNAS Brawdy, 1956–58; Comdr (Air), HMS Eagle, 1958–59; Captain, 1961; Captain F7 in HMS Lynx, 1963–65; CO, RNAS Brawdy, 1965–67; Staff of SACLANT, 1967–69; comd aircraft carrier, HMS Hermes, 1969–70; Rear-Adm., 1971; Asst Chief of Naval Staff (Ops and Air), 1971–73; Flag Officer, Naval Air Comd, 1973–76, retired; Vice-Adm., 1974. Operations Dir, Mersey Docks and Harbour Co., 1976–80; Dir, Avanova Internat. Consultants, 1980–89; Chm., Special Training Services, 1984–90. Vice-Chm. Council, Air League, 1987–. Liveryman, GAPAN, 1987–. CBIM. *Recreations:* golf, ski-ing, sailing, walking, swimming. *Clubs:* Army and Navy; Royal Yacht Squadron.

AUSTIN, Air Vice-Marshal Roger Mark, AFC 1973; FRAeS; Air Officer Commanding and Commandant, Royal Air Force College, Cranwell, since 1989; *b* 9 March 1940; *s* of Mark and Sylvia Joan Austin; *m* 1st, 1963, Carolyn de Recourt Martyn (marr. diss. 1981); two *s* one *d*; 2nd, 1986, Glenys Amy Beckley (*née* Roberts); two step *d*. *Educ:* King Alfred's Grammar Sch., Wantage. Commissioned in RAF, 1957; flying appts as Qualified Flying Instructor and with Nos 20 and 54 Sqns, 1960–68; commanded No 54 Sqn, 1969; flying appt with No 4 Sqn, 1970–72; Staff Coll., Camberley, 1973; commanded 233 OCU, 1974–77; PSO to AOC-in-C Strike Command, 1977–80; commanded RAF Chivenor, 1980–82; ADC to the Queen, 1980–82; Staff of HQ Strike Command, 1982–84; Dir of Op. Requirements, 1984–85; RCDS, 1986; AO i/c Central Tactics and Trials Orgn, 1987; DG Aircraft 1, MoD (PE), 1987–89. *Recreations:* walking, transport systems. *Address:* c/o National Westminster Bank, 3 Newbury Street, Wantage, Oxon OX12 8BX. *Club:* Royal Air Force.

AUSTIN-SMITH, Michael Gerard; QC 1990; a Recorder, since 1986; *b* 4 Sept. 1944; *s* of late Cyril John Austin-Smith and of Joyce Austin-Smith; *m* 1971, Stephanie Maddocks; one *s* one *d*. *Educ:* Hampton Grammar Sch.; Exeter Univ. (LLB Hons). Called to the Bar, Inner Temple, 1969. DTI Inspector, 1988–89 and 1989–90. *Address:* 36 Essex Street, Strand, WC2 3AS.

AUSTRALIA, North-West, Bishop of, since 1981; **Rt. Rev. Gerald Bruce Muston;** *b* 19 Jan. 1927; 3rd *s* of Stanley John and Emily Ruth Muston; *m* 1951, Laurel Wright; one *s* one *d*. *Educ:* N Sydney Chatswood High School; Moore Theological College, Sydney. ThL (Aust. Coll. of Theology). Rector, Wallerawang, NSW, 1951–53; Editorial Secretary, Church Missionary Society (Aust.), 1953–58; Rector, Tweed Heads, NSW, 1958–61; Vicar, Essendon, Vic, 1961–67; Rural Dean of Essendon, 1963–67; Rector of Darwin, NT, and Archdeacon of Northern Territory, 1967–69; Federal Secretary, Bush Church Aid Society of Aust., 1969–71; Bishop Coadjutor, dio. Melbourne (Bishop of the Western Region), 1971–81. *Recreations:* golf, reading. *Address:* Bishop's House, 11 Mark Way, Tarcoola, Geraldton, WA 6530, Australia. *Club:* Melbourne (Melbourne).

AUSTWICK, Prof. Kenneth, JP; Professor of Education, Bath University, since 1966; *b* 26 May 1927; *s* of Harry and Beatrice Austwick; *m* 1956, Gillian Griffin; one *s* one *d*. *Educ:* Morecambe Grammar Sch.; Sheffield Univ. BSc Maths, DipEd, MSc, PhD Sheffield. Fellow, Royal Statistical Soc.; FRSA. Schoolmaster, Bromsgrove, Frome and Nottingham, 1950–59; Lectr/Sen. Lectr, Sheffield Univ., 1959–65; Dep. Dir, Inst. of Educn, Reading Univ., 1965–66; Pro-Vice-Chancellor, Bath Univ., 1972–75. Vis. Lecturer: Univ. of BC, 1963; Univ. of Michigan, 1963; Univ. of Wits., 1967. Consultant, OECD, 1965; Adviser, Home Office, 1967–81; Chm., Nat. Savings SW Regional Educn, 1975–78. JP Bath 1970. *Publications:* Logarithms, 1962; Equations and Graphs, 1963; (ed) Teaching Machines and Programming, 1964; (ed) Aspects of Educational Technology, 1972; Maths at Work, 1985; Mathematics Connections, 1985; articles and contribs on maths teaching and educnl technology. *Recreations:* gardening, wine making. *Address:* Brook House, Combe Hay, near Bath. *T:* Combe Down (0225) 832541. *Club:* Commonwealth Trust.

AUTY, Richard Mossop, CBE 1978 (OBE 1968); retired British Council officer; *b* 29 Jan. 1920; *s* of Rev. Thomas Richard Auty and Mrs Edith Blanche Auty (*née* Mossop); *m* 1st, 1944, Noreen Collins (marr. diss. 1949); one *d*; 2nd, 1956, (Anne) Marguerite Marie Poncet; one *s* one *d*. *Educ:* Hanley High Sch.; LSE, Univ. of London. Planning Br., Min. of Agriculture and Fisheries, 1942–46; Bureau of Current Affairs, 1946–49; Lectr, Goldsmiths' Coll. and Morley Coll., 1947–49; British Council, 1949–80: Lectr, Milan, 1949–57; Head, Overseas Students Centre, London, 1957–61; Reg. Rep., S India, 1961–65; Cultural Attaché, Brit. Embassy, Budapest, 1965–68; Director: S Asia Dept, 1968–70; Personnel Dept, 1970–72; Controller, European Div., 1972–76; Rep., France, and Cultural Counsellor, British Embassy, Paris, 1976–80. *Recreations:* literature, theatre, cinema. *Address:* 4 Thurlow Road, NW3. *T:* 071–435 8982.

AVEBURY, 4th Baron *cr* 1900; **Eric Reginald Lubbock;** Bt 1806; *b* 29 Sept. 1928; *s* of Hon. Maurice Fox Pitt Lubbock (6th *s* of 1st Baron) (*d* 1957), and Hon. Mary Katherine Adelaide Stanley (*d* 1981), *d* of 5th Baron Stanley of Alderley; *S* cousin, 1971; *m* 1953, Kina Maria (marr. diss. 1983) (*see* Lady Avebury); two *s* one *d*; 2nd, 1985, Lindsay Stewart; one *s*. *Educ:* Upper Canada Coll.; Harrow Sch.; Balliol Coll., Oxford (BA Engineering; boxing blue). Welsh Guards (Gdsman, 2nd Lieut), 1949–51; Rolls Royce Ltd, 1951–56; Grad. Apprentice; Export Sales Dept; Tech. Assistant to Foundry Manager.

Management Consultant: Production Engineering Ltd, 1953–60; Charterhouse Group Ltd, 1960. MP (L) Orpington, 1962–70; Liberal Whip in House of Commons, 1963–70. Dir, C. L. Projects Ltd, 1966–; Consultant, Morgan-Grampian Ltd, 1970–. President: Data Processing Management Assoc., 1972–75; Fluoridation Soc., 1972–84; Conservation Soc., 1973–83. Member: Council, Inst. of Race Relations, 1972–74; Royal Commn on Standards of Conduct in Public Life, 1974–76; Chm., British Parly Human Rights Gp, 1976–. Pres., London Bach Soc. and Steinitz Bach Players, 1984–. MIMechE. *Recreations:* listening to music, reading. *Heir:* *s* Hon. Lyulph Ambrose Jonathan Lubbock [*b* 15 June 1954; *m* 1977, Susan (*née* MacDonald); one *s* one *d*]. *Address:* House of Lords, SW1.

AVEBURY, Lady; Kina-Maria Lubbock, (Kina Lady Avebury); Mental Health Planner, Tower Hamlets Social Services, since 1986; *b* 2 Sept. 1934; *d* of late Count Joseph O'Kelly de Gallagh and of Mrs M. Bruce; *m* 1953, 4th Baron Avebury, *qv* (marr. diss. 1983); two *s* one *d*. *Educ:* Convent of the Sacred Heart, Tunbridge Wells; Goldsmiths' College (BScSoc Hons) and LSE, Univ. of London. Lectr, Royal Coll. of Nursing, 1970–74; campaign organizer, European Movement, 1975; Asst Dir, Nat. Assoc. for Mental Health, 1976–82; Sociologist, Dept of Psychiatry, London Hosp. Med. Coll., 1983–85. Chairman: Nat. Marriage Guidance Council, 1975–82; Family Service Units, 1984–87; Avebury Working Party, 1982–84 (produced Code of Practice for Residential Care for DHSS); Mem., Central Council for Educn and Trng in Social Work, 1986–. JP Kent, 1974–79. *Publications:* Volunteers in Mental Health, 1985; articles on mental health and related social policy. *Recreations:* painting, opera, cooking.

AVELING, Alan John, CB 1986; Consultant, Mott Macdonald Group, since 1988; Under Secretary, Director of Home Regional Services, Property Services Agency, Department of the Environment, 1980–88; *b* 4 Jan. 1928; *s* of late Herbert Ashley Aveling and Ethel Aveling; *m* 1960, Stella May Reed; one *s* one *d*. *Educ:* Fletton Grammar Sch.; Rugby Technical Coll. CEng; FIEE, FIMechE, FCIBSE. Air Min. Works Dir, Newmarket, 1951–52; RAF Airfield Construction, 2nd Allied Tactical Air Force, 1952–55; Air Min. HQ, 1955–61; Sen. Engr, War Office Works Dept, 1961–63; BAOR Services, Germany, MPBW, 1963–66; Directorate Personnel, MPBW, 1966–67; Superintending Engr, Overseas Defence and FCO Services, 1967–72; Reg. Works Officer, later Regional Dir, British Forces, Germany, PSA/DoE, 1972–76; Dir of Estate Management Overseas, 1976–78; Dir Eastern Region, PSA/DoE, 1978–80. *Recreations:* aviculture, ski-ing. *Club:* Royal Air Force.

AVERY, Gillian Elise, (Mrs A. O. J. Cockshut); writer; *b* 1926; *d* of late Norman and Grace Avery; *m* 1952, A. O. J. Cockshut; one *d*. *Educ:* Dunottar Sch., Reigate. Chm., Children's Books History Soc., 1987–90; Mem., American Antiquarian Soc., 1988. *Publications: children's fiction:* The Warden's Niece, 1957; Trespassers at Charlcote, 1958; James without Thomas, 1959; The Elephant War, 1960; To Tame a Sister, 1961; The Greatest Gresham, 1962; The Peacock House, 1963; The Italian Spring, 1964; The Call of the Valley, 1966; A Likely Lad, 1971 (Guardian Award, 1972); Huck and her Time Machine, 1977; *adult fiction:* The Lost Railway, 1980; Onlookers, 1983; *non-fiction:* 19th Century Children: heroes and heroines in English children's stories (with Angela Bull), 1965; Victorian People in Life and Literature, 1970; The Echoing Green: memories of Regency and Victorian youth, 1974; Childhood's Pattern, 1975; Children and Their Books: a celebration of the work of Iona and Peter Opie (ed with Julia Briggs), 1989; The Best Type of Girl: a history of girls' independent schools, 1991. Ed, Gollancz revivals of early children's books, 1967–70, and anthologies of stories and extracts from early children's books. *Recreations:* walking, growing vegetables, cooking. *Address:* 32 Charlbury Road, Oxford OX2 6UU.

AVERY, Graham John Lloyd; a Director, Commission of the European Communities, Brussels, since 1987; *b* 29 Oct. 1943; *s* of Rev. Edward Avery and Alice Avery; *m* 1967, Susan Steele; two *s*. *Educ:* Kingswood Sch., Bath; Balliol Coll., Oxford (MA). Fellow, Center for Internat. Affairs, Harvard Univ. Joined MAFF, 1965; Principal responsible for negotiations for British entry to European Communities, 1969–72; PPS to Ministers, Frederick Peart, John Silkin, 1976; Commission of the European Communities, Brussels: Member of Cabinets: of President, Roy Jenkins, 1977–80; of Vice-Pres. for External Relns, Christopher Soames, 1973–76; of Comrs for Agric., Finn Gundelach 1981, Poul Dalsager 1981, Frans Andriessen 1985—86; served in Directorate Gen. for Agric. as Hd of Div. for Econ. Affairs and Gen. Problems, 1981–84, as Dir for Agricl Structures, 1987–89, as Dir for Rural Develt, 1989–90; served in Directorate Gen. for External Relations as Dir for relns with USA, Canada, Australia, NZ and S Africa, 1990–. *Publications:* articles in Internat. Affairs, World Today, Europ. Affairs, Common Mkt Law Rev., Jl of Agricl Econs, Europ. Environment Rev., etc. *Address:* European Commission, 1049 Brussels, Belgium. *T:* Brussels 235.49.07.

AVERY, James Royle, (Roy Avery); Headmaster, Bristol Grammar School, 1975–86; *b* 7 Dec. 1925; *s* of Charles James Avery and Dorothy May Avery; *m* 1954, Marjorie Louise (*née* Smith); one *s* one *d*. *Educ:* Queen Elizabeth's Hosp., Bristol; Magdalen Coll., Oxford; Bristol Univ. MA Oxon, CertifEd Bristol; FRSA. Asst History Master, Bristol Grammar Sch., 1951–59; Sen. History Master, Haberdashers' Aske's Sch. at Hampstead, then Elstree, 1960–65; Head Master, Harrow County Boys' Sch., 1965–75. *Publications:* The Story of Aldenham House, 1961; The Elstree Murder, 1962; The History of Queen Elizabeth's Hospital 1590–1990, 1990; contrib. Dictionary of World History, 1973; articles, reviews in educnl jls. *Recreations:* reading, walking, sport, music, the Ecumenical Movement, international studies. *Address:* First Floor Flat, 4 Rockleaze, Sneyd Park, Bristol BS9 1ND. *T:* Bristol (0272) 686805.

AVERY, John Ernest; Deputy Parliamentary Commissioner for Administration, since 1990; *b* 18 April 1940; *s* of Ernest Charles Avery and Pauline Margaret Avery; *m* 1966, Anna Meddings; two *d*. *Educ:* Plymouth Coll.; Leeds Univ. (BSc). Called to the Bar, Gray's Inn, 1972. Patent Examiner, Bd of Trade, 1964–72; Office of Fair Trading, 1972–76; Dept of Industry, later DTI, 1976–89; Dir of Investigations, Office of Parly Comr for Admin (Ombudsman), 1989–90. *Recreations:* squash, theatre. *Address:* Office of Parliamentary Commissioner for Administration, Church House, Great Smith Street, SW1P 3BW. *T:* 071–276 2119.

AVERY, Percy Leonard; Chairman, staff side, Civil Service National Whitley Council, 1977–80; General Secretary, Association of Government Supervisors and Radio Officers, 1951–79; *b* 10 March 1915; *s* of Percy James Avery and Frances Elisabeth Avery; *m* 1940, Joan Mahala Breakspear; one *s* one *d* (and one *d* decd). *Educ:* Woolwich Polytechnic. Served War: Navigator, RAF Bomber Comd, 1941–45; Flt Lieut. Exec. Sec., Internat. Fedn of Air Traffic Electronics Assoc., 1972–79. Member: Kent Area Health Authority, 1973–79; MoD Management Review Body, 1975–76; Civil Service Pay Rev. Board, 1978–79; CS Deptl Whitley Councils (various), 1949–77. Dir of Admin, British Karate Bd, 1979–82; Dir, Internat. Amateur Karate Fedn, 1983–; Treasurer: English Karate Council, 1981–82; European Amateur Karate Fedn, 1982–. Governor, Ruskin Coll; Mem., Kent Age Concern, 1980–83. *Recreations:* athletics, Rugby, music, gardening. *Address:* Edificio Oromar no 136, Piso 9, Avenida Columbretes, Oropesa del Mar, Castellon, Spain. *T:* Castellon 31.10.17.

AVERY, Roy; *see* Avery, J. R.

AVERY JONES, Sir Francis, Kt 1970; CBE 1966; FRCP; retired; Consulting Physician, Gastroenterological Department, Central Middlesex Hospital (Physician, 1940–74); Consulting Gastroenterologist: St Mark's Hospital (Consultant, 1948–78); Royal Navy (Consultant, 1950–78); Hon. Consulting Physician, St Bartholomew's Hospital, 1978; *b* 31 May 1910; *s* of Francis Samuel and Marion Rosa Jones; *m* 1st, 1934, Dorothea Pfirter (*d* 1983); one *s*; 2nd, 1983, K. Joan Edmunds. *Educ:* Sir John Leman Sch., Beccles; St Bartholomew's Hosp. Baly Research Scholarship, St Bart's, 1936; Julius Mickle Fellowship, University of London, 1952. Goulstonian Lecturer, Royal College of Physicians, 1947; Lumleian Lectr, RCP; Nuffield Lectr in Australia, 1952; First Memorial Lectr, Amer. Gastroenterological Assoc., 1954; Croonian Lectr, RCP, 1969; Harveian Orator, RCP, 1980. Formerly Examiner: RCP; Univ. of London; Univ. of Leeds. Chairman: Emergency Bed Service, 1967–72; Med. Records Cttee, Dept of Health and Social Security; Medical Adv. Cttee, British Council, 1973–79; Member: Med. Sub-cttee, UGC, 1966–71; Brent and Harrow AHA, 1975–78; Dep. Chm., Management Cttee, King Edward VII Hosp. Fund, 1976–79; Mem. Council, Surrey Univ., 1975–82. Pres., United Services Section, RSM, 1974–75 (formerly Pres., section of Proctology); 2nd Vice-Pres., RCP, 1972–73; President: Medical Soc. of London, 1977–78; Medical Artists Assoc., 1980–; British Digestive Foundn, 1981–. Editor of Gut, 1965–70. Hon. FRCS 1981; Hon. FACP 1985; Hon. Mem., Amer., Canadian, French, Scandinavian and Australian Gastroenterological Assocs. Master, Worshipful Co. of Barbers, 1977–78. Hon. MD Melbourne, 1952; DUniv Surrey, 1980. Ambuj Nath Bose Prize, RCP, 1971; Moxon Medal, RCP, 1978; Fothergillian Gold Medal, Med. Soc., London, 1980; Henry L. Bockus Medal, World Orgn of Gastroenterology, 1982. *Publications:* Clinical Gastroenterology (jt author), 2nd edn 1967; Editor of Modern Trends in Gastroenterology First and Second Series, 1952 and 1958; many articles on Gastroenterology in the Medical Press. *Recreation:* water-side and herb gardening. *Address:* Mill House, Nutbourne, Pulborough, West Sussex RH20 2HE. *T:* West Chiltington (0798) 813314. *Club:* Athenæum.

See also J. F. Avery Jones.

AVERY JONES, John Francis, CBE 1987; FTII; Senior Partner, Speechly Bircham, since 1985; *b* 5 April 1940; *s* of Sir Francis Avery Jones, *qv*. *Educ:* Rugby Sch.; Trinity Coll., Cambridge (MA, LLM). Solicitor, 1966; Partner in Bircham & Co., 1970. Member: Meade Cttee, 1975–77; Keith Cttee, 1980–84. Pres., Inst. of Taxation, 1980–82; Chm., Law Soc.'s Revenue Law Cttee, 1983–87; Member Council: Law Soc., 1986–90; Inst. for Fiscal Studies, 1988–; Exec. Cttee, Internat. Fiscal Assoc., 1988– (Chm., British Br., 1989–); Mem., Bd of Trustees, Internat. Bureau of Fiscal Documentation, 1989–. Vis. Prof. of Taxation, LSE, 1988–. Mem. Bd of Governors, Voluntary Hosp. of St Bartholomew, 1984–; Chm., Addington Soc., 1985–87. Master, Co. of Barbers, 1985–86. Consulting Ed., Encyclopedia of VAT (Gen. Ed., 1972); Jt Editor, British Tax Review, 1974–; Mem. Editl Bd, Simon's Taxes, 1977–. *Publications:* (ed) Tax Havens and Measures Against Tax Avoidance and Evasion in the EEC, 1974; numerous articles on tax. *Recreations:* music, particularly opera. *Address:* 65 Castlebar Road, W5 2DA. *T:* 081–998 2143. *Club:* Athenæum.

AVNER, Yehuda; Inspector General of the Foreign Service, Israel, since 1990; *b* 30 Dec. 1928; *m* Miriam Avner; one *s* three *d*. *Educ:* High School, Manchester. Editor of publications, Jewish Agency, Jerusalem, 1956–64; Editor of Political Publications, Min. of Foreign Affairs, and Asst to Prime Minister Levi Eshkol, 1964–67; Consul, New York, 1967–68; First Sec. then Counsellor, Washington, 1968–72; Dir of Foreign Press Bureau, Foreign Ministry, and Asst to PM Golda Meir, 1972–74; seconded to PM's Bureau, and Adviser to PM Yitzhak Rabin, 1974–77; Adviser to PM Menachem Begin, 1977–83; Ambassador to UK, 1983–88; Dir Gen., Clore Foundn, Israel, 1989–90. *Publication:* The Young Inheritors: a portrait of Israeli youth, 1982. *Address:* Ministry of Foreign Affairs, Hakirya, Romema, Jerusalem 91950, Israel.

AVONSIDE, Rt. Hon. Lord; Ian Hamilton Shearer, PC 1962; a Senator of the College of Justice in Scotland, 1964–84; *b* 6 Nov. 1914; *s* of Andrew Shearer, OBE, and Jessie Macdonald; *m* 1st, 1942; one *s* one *d*; 2nd, 1954, Janet Sutherland Murray (*see* Lady Avonside). *Educ:* Dunfermline High Sch.; Glasgow Univ.; Edinburgh Univ. MA Glasgow, 1934; LLB Edinburgh, 1937. Admitted to Faculty of Advocates, 1938; QC (Scotland) 1952. Served War of 1939–45, RA; Major; released 1946, Emerg. R of O. Standing Counsel: to Customs and Excise, Bd of Trade and Min. of Labour, 1947–49; to Inland Revenue, 1949–51; to City of Edinburgh Assessor, 1949–51; Junior Legal Assessor to City of Edinburgh, 1951; Sheriff of Renfrew and Argyll, 1960–62; Lord Advocate, 1962–64. Mem., Lands Valuation Court, 1964 (Chm., 1975–84). Chm. Nat. Health Service Tribunal, Scotland, 1954–62; Mem. Scottish Cttee of Coun. on Tribunals, 1958–62; Chm. Scottish Valuation Advisory Coun., 1965–68; Mem., Scottish Univs Cttee of the Privy Council, 1971–. Pres., Stair Soc., 1975–87. *Publications:* Purves on Licensing Laws, 1947; Acta Dominorum Concilii et Sessionis, 1951. *Recreations:* golf, gardening. *Address:* The Mill House, Samuelston, East Lothian. *T:* Haddington (062082) 2396. *Club:* New (Edinburgh).

AVONSIDE, Lady; Janet Sutherland Shearer, OBE 1958; Scottish Governor, BBC, 1971–76; *b* 31 May 1917; *d* of William Murray, MB, ChB, and Janet Harley Watson; *m* 1954, Ian Hamilton Shearer, Rt Hon. Lord Avonside, *qv*. *Educ:* St Columba's Sch., Kilmacolm; Erlenhaus, Baden Baden; Univ. of Edinburgh. LLB, Dip. of Social Science. Asst Labour Officer (Scot.), Min. of Supply, 1941–45; Sec. (Scot.), King George's Fund for Sailors, 1945–53; Hon. Sec. (Scot.), Federal Union and United Europe, 1945–64; Scottish Delegate: Congress of Europe, 1947; Council of Europe, Strasburg, 1949. Contested (C), elections: Maryhill, Glasgow, 1950; Dundee East, 1951; Leith, 1955. Lectr in Social Studies, Dept of Educational Studies, Univ. of Edinburgh, 1962–70. Governor, Queen Margaret Coll., Edinburgh, 1986–89. *Recreation:* gardening. *Address:* The Mill House, Samuelston, East Lothian, Scotland. *T:* Haddington (062082) 2396. *Clubs:* Caledonian (Associate Mem.); New (Edinburgh).

AWAD, Muhammad Hadi; Ambassador of the Yemeni Republic (formerly People's Democratic Republic of Yemen) to Tunisia and Permanent Representative to The Arab League, since 1980; *b* 5 May 1934; Yemeni; *m* 1956, Adla; one *s* three *d*. *Educ:* Murray House Coll. of Educn. DipEd, Certif. Social Anthrop. Edinburgh. Teacher, 1953–59; Educn Officer, 1960–62; Chief Inspector of Schs, 1963–65; Vice-Principal, As-Shaab Coll., 1965–67; Perm. Rep. to Arab League, Ambassador to UAR and non-resident Ambassador to Sudan, Lebanon, Libya and Iraq, 1968–70; Perm. Sec., Min. of For. Affairs, 1970–73; Ambassador to London, 1973–80, to Sweden and Spain, 1974–80, to Denmark, Portugal and the Netherlands, 1975–80. *Recreation:* photography. *Address:* Embassy of the Yemeni Republic, Tunis, Tunisia.

AWAK, Shehu, OFR 1981; High Commissioner for Nigeria in the UK, 1981–84; *b* Awak, 14 May 1932; *m* 1953, A'ishatu Shehu Awak; four *s* seven *d*. *Educ:* Nigerian Coll.; Manchester Univ. (DCPA 1966); London Sch. of Economics. ASTC IV, Zaria, 1961. Nigerian Foreign Service: Admin. Officer, 1961–70; actg Perm. Sec., 1970–73; Perm.

Sec., 1973–78; Sec. to Mil. Govt, 1978–79, and Head of CS, 1978–81, Bauchi State. *Recreations:* table tennis, walking, gaming.

AWDRY, Daniel (Edmund), TD; DL; *b* 10 Sept. 1924; *s* of late Col Edmund Portman Awdry, MC, TD, DL, Coters, Chippenham, Wilts, and Mrs Evelyn Daphne Alexandra Awdry, JP (formerly French); *m* 1950, Elizabeth Cattley; three *d. Educ:* Winchester Coll. RAC, OCTU, Sandhurst, 1943–44 (Belt of Honour). Served with 10th Hussars as Lieut, Italy, 1944–45; ADC to GOC 56th London Div., Italy, 1945; Royal Wilts Yeo., 1947–62; Major and Sqdn Comdr, 1955–62. Qualified Solicitor, 1950. Mayor of Chippenham, 1958–59; Pres., Southern Boroughs Assoc., 1959–60. MP (C) Chippenham, Wilts, Nov. 1962–1979; PPS to Minister of State, Board of Trade, Jan.-Oct. 1964; PPS to Solicitor-Gen., 1973–74. Director: BET Omnibus Services, 1966–80; Sheepbridge Engineering, 1968–79; Rediffusion Ltd, 1973–85; Colonial Mutual Life Assurance Ltd, 1974–89. DL Wilts, 1979. *Recreation:* chess. *Address:* Old Manor, Beanacre, near Melksham, Wilts. *T:* Melksham (0225) 702315.

AWDRY, Rev. Wilbert Vere; Church of England clergyman, and author; *b* 15 June 1911; *s* of Rev. Vere Awdry and Lucy Louisa (*née* Bury); *m* 1938, Margaret Emily (*née* Wale); one *s* two *d. Educ:* Dauntsey's, W Lavington, Wilts; St Peter's Hall. Oxford (MA); Wycliffe Hall, Oxford (DipTh). Asst Master, St George's Sch., Jerusalem, 1933–36; Curate: Odiham, Hants, 1936–38; W Lavington, 1938–40; King's Norton, Birmingham, 1940–46; Rector, Elsworth with Knapwell, Cambs, 1946–53; Rural Dean, Bourn, Cambs, 1950–53; Vicar, Emneth, Wisbech, 1953–65; authorised to officiate in Dio. of Gloucester, 1965–. *Publications: for children:* The Three Railway Engines, 1945; Thomas the Tank-engine, 1946; James the Red Engine, 1948; Tank-engine Thomas again, 1949; Troublesome Engines, 1950; Henry the Green Engine, 1951; Toby the Tram Engine, 1952; Gordon the Big Engine, 1953; Edward the Blue Engine, 1954; Four Little Engines,, 1955; Percy the Small Engine, 1956; The Eight Famous Engines, 1957; Duck & the Diesel Engine, 1958; Belinda the Beetle, 1958; The Little Old Engine, 1959; The Twin Engines, 1960; Branch Line Engines, 1961; Belinda beats the Band, 1961; Gallant Old Engine, 1962; Stepney the Bluebell Engine, 1963; Mountain Engines, 1964; Very Old Engines, 1965; Main Line Engines, 1966; Small Railway Engines, 1967; Enterprising Engines, 1968; Oliver the Western Engine, 1969; Duke the Lost Engine, 1970; Tramway Engines, 1972; Thomas' Christmas Party, 1984; Map of the Island of Sodor, 1958, 4th edn 1988; (jtly) The Island of Sodor: its people, history and railways, 1987; *non fiction:* (ed) Industrial Archaeology in Gloucestershire, 1973, 3rd edn 1983; (jt ed) A Guide to Steam Railways of Great Britain, 1979, 3rd edn 1984; (jtly) The Birmingham and Gloucester Railway, 1987. *Recreations:* reading, railway modelling, photography, family history. *Address:* Sodor, 30 Rodborough Avenue, Stroud, Glos GL5 3RS. *T:* Stroud (0453) 762321.

AXELROD, Julius, PhD; Guest Researcher, Laboratory of Cell Biology, since 1984, Chief, Section on Pharmacology, Laboratory of Clinical Science, 1955–84 (Acting Chief, Jan.-Oct. 1955), National Institute of Mental Health, USA; Laboratory of Cell Biology, since 1984; *b* NYC, 30 May 1912; *s* of Isadore Axelrod, Michaliev, Poland, and Molly Liechtling, Striej, Poland (formerly Austria); *m* 1938, Sally (*née* Taub); two *s. Educ:* George Washington Univ., Wash., DC (PhD); New York Univ. (MA); New York City Coll. (BS). Lab. Asst Dept Bacteriology, NY Univ. Med. Sch., 1933–35; Chemist, Lab. Industrial Hygiene, 1935–46; Res. Associate, Third NY Univ.; Research Div., Goldwater Memorial Hosp., 1946–49; Nat. Heart Inst., NIH: Associate Chemist, Section on Chem. Pharmacology, 1949–50; Chemist, 1950–53; Sen. Chemist, 1953–55. Jt Nobel Prize for Physiology-Medicine, 1970; Mem., Nat. Academy of Sciences, 1971; Fellow, Amer. Acad. of Arts and Sciences; Senior Mem., Amer. Inst. of Medicine, 1979. Thudicum Medal and Lecture, British Biochem Soc., 1989. Foreign Member: Royal Society, 1979; Deutsche Akademie der Naturforscher, 1984. Hon. LLD: George Washington, 1971; College City, NY, 1972; Hon. DSc: Chicago, 1966; Med. Coll., Wisconsin, 1971; New York, 1971; Pennsylvania Coll. of Med., 1973; Hahnemann Univ., 1987; McGill Univ., 1988; Doctor *hc* Panama, 1972; DPhil *hc:* Ripon Coll., 1984; Tel Aviv Univ., 1984. Winner of 15 awards; holds 23 hon. lectureships; Member: 13 editorial boards; 5 Sci. Adv. Cttees. *Publications:* (with Richard J. Wurtman and Douglas E. Kelly) The Pineal, 1968; numerous original papers and contribs to jls in Biochem., Pharmacol. and Physiology. *Recreations:* reading and listening to music. *Address:* 10401 Grosvenor Place, Rockville, Maryland 20852, USA. *T:* (301) 493–6376.

AXFORD, David Norman, PhD, CEng, FIEE; Deputy Secretary-General, World Meteorological Organisation, since 1989; *b* 14 June 1934; *s* of Norman Axford and Joy Alicia Axford (*née* Williams); *m* 1st, 1962, Elizabeth Anne (*née* Stiles) (marr. diss. 1980); one *s* two *d;* 2nd, 1980, Diana Rosemary Joan (*née* Bufton); three step *s* one step *d. Educ:* Merchant Taylors' School, Sandy Lodge; Plymouth Coll.; St John's Coll., Cambridge (Baylis Open Scholarship in Maths; BA 1956, MA 1960, PhD (Met.) 1972); MSc (Electronics) Southampton 1963; FIEE 1982. Entered Met. Office, 1958; Flying Officer, RAF, 1958–60; Meteorological Office: Forecasting and Research, 1960–68; Met. Research Flight, and Radiosondes, 1968–76; Operational Instrumentation, 1976–80; Telecommunications, 1980–82; Dep. Dir, Observational Services, 1982–84; Dir of Services, 1984–89. Chm., Cttee on Operational World Weather Watch Systems Evaluation, N Atlantic (CONA), 1985–89. Pres., N Atlantic Observing Stations (NAOS) Bd, 1983–86; Vice Pres., RMetS, 1989– (Mem. Council and Hon. Gen. Sec., 1983–88). L. G. Groves 2nd Meml Prize for Met., 1970. *Publications:* papers in learned jls on met. and aspects of met. instrumentation in GB and USA. *Recreations:* home and garden, music, travel, good food. *Address:* c/o World Meteorological Organisation, Case Postale No 2300, CH-1211 Genève 2, Switzerland; Rudgewick Cottage, Binfield Heath, Henley-on-Thames, Oxon RG9 4JY. *T:* Henley-on-Thames (0491) 574423. *Club:* Phyllis Court (Henley-on-Thames).

AXFORD, Dr William Ian, FRS 1986; Director, Max Planck Institut für Aeronomie, Katlenburg-Lindau, West Germany, 1974–82 and since 1985; *b* 2 Jan. 1933; *s* of John Edgar Axford and May Victoria Axford; *m* 1955, Catherine Joy; two *s* two *d. Educ:* Univ. of Canterbury, NZ (MSc Hons, ME Dist.); Univ. of Manchester (PhD); Univ. of Cambridge. NZ Defence Science Corps, 1957–63; seconded to Defence Res. Bd, Ottawa, 1960–62; Associate Prof. of Astronomy, 1963–66, Prof. of Astronomy, 1966–67, Cornell Univ., Ithaca, NY; Prof. of Physics and Applied Physics, Univ. of Calif at San Diego, 1967–74; Vice-Chancellor, Victoria Univ. of Wellington, NZ, 1982–85. Pres., COSPAR, 1986–; Vice-Pres., Scientific Cttee on Solar-Terrestrial Physics, 1986–90. Hon. Prof., Göttingen Univ., 1978; Appleton Meml Lectr, URSI, 1969. Pres., European Geophysical Soc., 1990–92. Fellow, Amer. Geophysical Union, 1971; ARAS 1981; For. Associate, US Nat. Acad. of Scis, 1983; Member: Internat. Acad. of Astronautics, 1985; Academia Europaea, 1989. Space Science Award, AIAA, 1970; John Adam Fleming Medal, Amer. Geophysical Union, 1972; Tsiolkovsky Medal, Kosmonautical Fedn, USSR, 1987. *Publications:* about 200 articles in scientific jls on aspects of space physics and astrophysics. *Address:* Max Planck Institut für Aeronomie, Postfach 20, D-3411 Katlenburg-Lindau, West Germany. *T:* 5556–401414; Alte Post Strasse 2, D-3410 Northeim, West Germany. *T:* 5551–1567; 2 Gladstone Road, Napier, New Zealand. *T:* 70–352188.

AXISA, John Francis, MBE 1950; *b* 20 Nov. 1906; *s* of late Emmanuel Axisa and Vincenzina (*née* Micallef); *m* 1939, Ariadne Cachia; three *s* one *d. Educ:* St Paul's Sch.,

Malta and privately. Joined Malta Civil Service, 1927; Dir of Emigration, 1947–56; Dir of Technical Education, 1956–59; Dir of Emigration, Labour and Social Welfare, 1959–60; Under-Sec., 1960–61; Commissioner-Gen. for Malta in London, 1961–64; Malta's first High Commissioner on Malta's Independence, 1964–69; Ambassador of Malta to: France, 1966–69; Fed. Republic of Germany, 1967–69; Libya, 1966–68; Belgium, 1967–68; Netherlands, 1968–69. Chm., Bd of Govs, St Edward's Coll., Malta, 1985–. *Recreations:* carpentry, fishing, reading. *Address:* 5/8 Tower Road, Sliema, Malta, GC. *Club:* Union (Malta).

AXTON, Henry Stuart, (Harry), FCA; Chairman, Brixton Estate plc, since 1983; *b* 6 May 1923; *s* of Wilfrid George Axton and Mary Louise Laver; *m* 1947, Constance Mary Godefroy; one *d. Educ:* Rock Ferry. RMC, Sandhurst, commissioned 1942; served: N Africa, Royal Tank Regt, NW Europe, Fife and Forfar Yeo.; wounded three times, invalided out, 1945. Articles, G. E. Holt & Son; Chartered Accountant 1948. Treas., United Sheffield Hosps and other hosp. appts, 1948–55; Company Sec., Midland Assurance, 1955–61; Brixton Estate, 1961–: Man. Dir, 1964–83; Dep. Chm., 1971–83; Chm., Investment Cos in Australia and Switzerland. Pres., British Property Fedn, 1984–86 (Mem. Council, 1974–; Vice-Pres., 1983–84). Dep. Chm., Audit Commn, 1987–91 (Mem., 1986–). Chairman: Council, St George's Hosp. Med. Sch., 1977– (Mem., 1969–; Dep. Chm. 1974–77); St George's New Hosp. Bldg Cttee, 1972– (Mem., 1969–); Nuffield Hosps, 1976– (Governor, 1968–; Dep. Chm. 1975–76); BUPA Medical Centre, 1973–82 (Governor, 1970–82); Mem., Chichester HA, 1985–87; Governor: BUPA, 1969–80; St George's Hosp., 1970–74, Special Trustee, 1974–77. Chm., Chichester Festivities, 1989–. Dir, Cathedral Works Organisation (Chichester), 1985–91. Mem., Archbp's Council for Church Urban Fund, 1990–. *Recreations:* sailing, music. *Address:* Hook Place, Aldingbourne, near Chichester, Sussex PO20 6TS. *T:* Eastergate (0243) 542291. *Clubs:* Royal Thames Yacht, Royal Ocean Racing.

AXWORTHY, Geoffrey (John); Artistic Director of Sherman Theatre, University College, Cardiff, 1970–88, retired; *b* Plymouth, England, 10 Aug. 1923; *s* of William Henry Axworthy and Gladys Elizabeth Kingcombe; *m* 1st, 1951, Irene Dickinson (*d* 1976); two *s* one *d;* 2nd, 1977, Caroline Griffiths; one *s* one *d. Educ:* Exeter Coll., Oxford (MA). On staff of: Univ. of Baghdad 1951–56; Univ. of Ibadan, Nigeria, 1956–67. First Director, Univ. of Ibadan Sch. of Drama, 1962–67. Principal, Central School of Speech and Drama, London, 1967–70. Founded Univ. of Ibadan Travelling Theatre, 1961. *Address:* 22 The Walk, West Grove, Cardiff CF2 3AF. *T:* Cardiff (0222) 490696.

AYALA, Jaime Z. de; *see* Zobel de Ayala.

AYCKBOURN, Alan, CBE 1987; playwright; Artistic Director, Stephen Joseph Theatre-in-the-Round, Scarborough; *b* 12 April 1939; *s* of Horace Ayckbourn and Irene Maude (*née* Worley); *m* 1959, Christine Helen (*née* Roland); two *s. Educ:* Haileybury. Worked in repertory as Stage Manager/Actor at Edinburgh, Worthing, Leatherhead, Oxford, and with late Stephen Joseph's Theatre-in-the-Round Co., at Scarborough. Founder Mem., Victoria Theatre, Stoke-on-Trent, 1962. BBC Radio Drama Producer, Leeds, 1964–70; Co. Dir, NT, 1986–87. Vis. Prof. of Drama, and Fellow, St Catherine's Coll., Oxford, 1991–92. Has written numerous full-length plays. London productions: Mr Whatnot, Arts, 1964; Relatively Speaking, Duke of York's, 1967, Greenwich, 1986 (televised, 1969, 1989); How the Other Half Loves, Lyric, 1970, Duke of York's, 1988; Time and Time Again, Comedy, 1972 (televised, 1976); Absurd Person Singular, Criterion, 1973 (Evening Standard Drama Award, Best Comedy, 1973) (televised, 1985); The Norman Conquests (Trilogy), Globe, 1974 (Evening Standard Drama Award, Best Play; Variety Club of GB Award); Plays and Players Award) (televised, 1977); Jeeves (musical, with Andrew Lloyd Webber), Her Majesty's, 1975; Absent Friends, Garrick, 1975 (televised, 1985); Confusions, Apollo, 1976; Bedroom Farce, Nat. Theatre, 1977 (televised, 1980); Just Between Ourselves, Queen's, 1977 (Evening Standard Drama Award, Best Play) (televised, 1978); Ten Times Table, Globe, 1978; Joking Apart, Globe, 1979 (Plays and Players Award); Sisterly Feelings, Nat. Theatre, 1980; Taking Steps, Lyric, 1980; Suburban Strains (musical with Paul Todd), Round House, 1981; Season's Greetings, Apollo, 1982; Way Upstream, Nat. Theatre, 1982 (televised, 1988); Making Tracks (musical with Paul Todd), Greenwich, 1983; Intimate Exchanges, Ambassadors, 1984; A Chorus of Disapproval, Nat. Theatre, 1985 (Standard Drama Award, Best Comedy; Olivier Award, Best Comedy; Drama Award, Best Comedy, 1985), transf. Lyric, 1986 (filmed, 1989); Woman in Mind, Vaudeville, 1986; A Small Family Business, Nat. Theatre, 1987 (Evening Standard Drama Award, Best Play); Henceforward ..., Vaudeville, 1988 (Evening Standard Drama Award, Best Comedy, 1989); Man of the Moment, Globe, 1990 (Evening Standard Drama Award, Best Comedy, 1990); Invisible Friends, Nat. Theatre, 1991; Scarborough: Mr A's Amazing Maze Plays, 1988; The Revengers' Comedies, 1989; Body Language, 1990; Callisto 5 (play for children), 1990; Wildest Dreams, 1991. Plays directed: Nat. Theatre: Tons of Money, 1986; A View from the Bridge, 1987; A Small Family Business, 1987; 'Tis Pity She's a Whore, 1988. Hon. DLitt: Hull, 1981; Keele, 1987; Leeds, 1987. *Publications:* The Norman Conquests, 1975; Three Plays (Absurd Person Singular, Absent Friends, Bedroom Farce), 1977; Joking Apart and Other Plays (Just Between Ourselves, Ten Times Table), 1979; Sisterly Feelings, and Taking Steps, 1981; A Chorus of Disapproval, 1986; Woman in Mind, 1986; A Small Family Business, 1987; Henceforward ..., 1988; Mr A's Amazing Maze Plays, 1989; Man of the Moment, 1990; Invisible Friends, 1991. *Recreations:* music, reading, cricket, films. *Address:* c/o Margaret Ramsay Ltd, 14a Goodwin's Court, St Martin's Lane, WC2N 4LL. *T:* 071–240 0691. *Club:* Garrick.

AYERS, John Gilbert; Keeper, Far Eastern Department, Victoria and Albert Museum, 1970–82; *b* 27 July 1922; *s* of H. W. Ayers, CB, CBE; *m* 1957, Bridget Elspeth Jacqualine Fanshawe; one *s* two *d. Educ:* St Paul's Sch.; St Edmund Hall, Oxford. Served in RAF, 1941–46 (Sgt). Asst Keeper, Dept of Ceramics, Victoria and Albert Museum, 1950, Dep. Keeper 1963. Pres., Oriental Ceramic Soc., 1984–87. *Publications:* The Seligman Collection of Oriental Art, II, 1964; The Baur Collection: Chinese Ceramics, I-IV, 1968–74, Japanese Ceramics, 1982; (with R. J. Charleston) The James A. de Rothschild Collection: Meissen and Oriental Porcelain, 1971; Oriental Ceramics, The World's Great Collections: Victoria and Albert Museum, 1975; (with J. Rawson) Chinese Jade throughout the Ages, exhbn catalogue, 1975; (with D. Howard) China for the West, 2 vols, 1978; (with D. Howard) Masterpieces of Chinese Export Porcelain, 1980; Oriental Art in the Victoria and Albert Museum, 1983; (ed) Chinese Ceramics in the Topkapi Saray Museum, Istanbul, 3 vols, 1986; (with O. Impey and J. V. G. Mallet) Porcelain for Palaces: the fashion for Japan in Europe 1650–1750, 1990; From Cauldron to Teapot: the evolution of ceramic tea vessels in China, 1991. *Address:* 3 Bedford Gardens, W8 7ED. *T:* 071–229 5168.

AYERST, Rev. Edward Richard; Chaplain to the Queen, since 1987; *m* 1959, Pauline Clarke; one *s* two *d. Educ:* Coopers' Company's School; Leeds Univ. (BA Hons 1951); College of the Resurrection, Mirfield. Vicar of St Mary with St John, Edmonton, N18, 1960–66; Rector of East Cowes with Whippingham, IoW, 1966–77; Vicar of Bridgwater, 1977–90. Mem., Philosophical Soc., 1981. *Recreations:* sailing; helping the Sea Cadet Corps. *Address:* 56 Maple Drive, Burnham-on-Sea, Somerset TA8 1DH. *T:* Burnham-on-Sea (0278) 780701.

AYKROYD, Sir Cecil William, 2nd Bt, *cr* 1929; *b* 23 April 1905; *e s* of Sir Frederic Alfred Aykroyd, 1st Bt and late Lily May, *e d* of Sir James Roberts, 1st Bt, LLD, of Strathallan Castle, Perthshire, and Fairlight Hall, near Hastings; *S* father 1949; unmarried. *Educ:* Charterhouse; Jesus Coll., Cambridge. BA 1926. Dir, Nat. Provincial Bank Ltd, 1958–69 (Dir Bradford and District Bd, 1946–69). *Recreations:* fishing and shooting. *Heir: nephew* James Alexander Frederic Aykroyd [*b* 6 Sept. 1943; *m* 1973, Jennifer, *d* of Frederick William Marshall; two *d*]. *Address:* Birstwith Hall, near Harrogate, North Yorks. *T:* Harrogate (0423) 770250.

AYKROYD, Sir William Miles, 3rd Bt *cr* 1920; MC 1944; *b* 24 Aug. 1923; *s* of Sir Alfred Hammond Aykroyd, 2nd Bt, and Sylvia Ambler Aykroyd (*née* Walker), *widow* of Lieut-Col Foster Newton Thorne; *S* father, 1965. *Educ:* Charterhouse. Served in 5th Royal Inniskilling Dragoon Guards, Lieut, 1943–47. Dir, Hardy Amies Ltd, 1950–69. *Heir: cousin* Michael David Aykroyd [*b* 14 June 1928; *m* 1952, Oenone Gillian Diana, *o d* of Donald George Cowling, MBE; one *s* three *d*]. *Address:* Buckland Newton Place, Dorchester, Dorset. *T:* Buckland Newton (03005) 259. *Club:* Boodle's.

AYLARD, Comdr Richard John; RN, retired; Private Secretary and Treasurer to the Prince of Wales, since 1991; *b* 10 April 1952; *s* of John and Joy Aylard; *m* 1st, 1977, Sally Williams (marr. diss. 1984); 2nd, 1984, Suzanne Walker; two *d*. *Educ:* Queen Elizabeth's Grammar Sch., Barnet; Reading Univ. (BSc Hons Applied Zoology with Maths). Joined RN as university cadet, 1972; served HM Ships Shavington, Ark Royal, Fox, 1974–77; Staff of Flag Officer Submarines, 1977–79; Flag Lieut to Dep. SACLANT, Norfolk, USA, 1979–81; Capt's Sec., HMS Invincible, 1981–83; Supply Officer, HMS Brazen, 1984–85; Equerry to the Princess of Wales, 1985–88; Asst Private Sec. and Comptroller to the Prince and Princess of Wales, 1988–91; Comdr RN, 1987; RN retd, 1989. *Recreations:* sailing, fishing, gardening, ski-ing. *Address:* Wren House, Kensington Palace, W8 4PU.

AYLEN, Rear-Adm. Ian Gerald, CB 1962; OBE 1946; DSC 1942; CEng; FIMechE; *b* 12 Oct. 1910; *s* of late Commander A. E. Aylen, RN and Mrs S. C. M. Aylen; *m* 1937, Alice Brough Maltby; one *s* two *d*. *Educ:* Blundell's, Tiverton. RNE Coll., Keyham, 1929–33; served in HMS Rodney; Curacoa; Galatea, 1939–40; Kelvin, 1940–42; 30 Assault Unit, 1945; Cossack; Fleet Engineer Officer, Home Fleet, 1957–58; CO HMS Thunderer, RNE Coll., 1958–60; Rear-Admiral, 1960; Admiral Superintendent, HM Dockyard, Rosyth, 1960–63; Dep. Sec., Instn Mechanical Engineers, 1963–65; Asst Sec., Council of Engineering Instns, 1966–71, retired 1971. *Address:* Tracey Mill Barn, Honiton, Devon.

AYLEN, Walter Stafford; QC 1983; a Recorder, since 1985; *b* St Helena, 21 May 1937; *s* of late Rt Rev. Charles Arthur William Aylen and Elisabeth Margaret Anna (*née* Hills); *m* 1967, Peggy Elizabeth Lainé Woodford; three *d*. *Educ:* Summer Fields Sch.; Winchester Coll. (schol.); New Coll., Oxford (schol., sen. schol.; BCL; MA). Commnd 2nd Lieut KRRC, 1956–57. Called to the Bar, Middle Temple, 1962 (Bencher 1991); Asst Recorder, 1982. Bishop's Commnd Asst, Christian Stewardship Dept, Dio. of Southwark, 1970–. FRSA 1989. *Recreations:* reading novels (especially his wife's), theatre, music. *Address:* 27 Gauden Road, SW4 6LR. *T:* 071–622 7871; Hardwicke Building, New Square, Lincoln's Inn, WC2A 3SB. *T:* 071–242 2523.

AYLESFORD, 11th Earl of; **Charles Ian Finch-Knightley,** JP; Baron Guernsey, 1703; Lord-Lieutenant of West Midlands, since 1974; *b* 2 Nov. 1918; *er s* of 10th Earl of Aylesford; *S* father, 1958; *m* 1946, Margaret Rosemary Tyer (*d* 1989); one *s* two *d*. *Educ:* Oundle. Lieut RSF, 1939; Captain Black Watch, 1947. Regional Dir, Birmingham and W Midlands Bd, Lloyds Bank, 1982–88. Mem., Water Space Amenity Commn, 1973–83. County Comr for Scouts, 1949–74, Patron 1974–. JP 1948, DL 1954, Vice-Lieutenant 1964–74, Warwicks. KStJ 1974. Hon. LLD 1989. *Recreations:* wild life and nature conservation. *Heir: s* Lord Guernsey, *qv*. *Address:* Packington Old Hall, Coventry, West Midlands CV7 7HG. *T:* (home) Meriden (0676) 23273; (office) Meriden (0676) 22585. *Club:* Warwickshire CC (President, 1980–).

AYLESTONE, Baron *cr* 1967 (Life Peer), of Aylestone; **Herbert William Bowden;** PC 1962; CH 1975; CBE 1953; Chairman, Independent Broadcasting Authority (formerly Independent Television Authority), 1967–75; *b* 20 Jan. 1905; *m* 1928, Louisa Grace, *d* of William Brown, Cardiff; one *d*. RAF, 1941–45. MP (Lab) S Leicester, 1945–50, S-W Div. of Leicester, 1950–67. PPS to Postmaster-Gen., 1947–49; Asst Govt Whip, 1949–50; a Lord Comr of the Treasury, 1950–51; Dep. Chief Oppn Whip, 1951–55; Chief Oppn Whip, 1955–64; Lord Pres. of the Council and Leader of the House of Commons, 1964–66; Secretary of State for Commonwealth Affairs, 1966–67; joined SDP, 1981; Dep. Speaker, House of Lords, 1984–. Gold Medal, RTS, 1975. *Address:* c/o House of Lords, SW1.

AYLING, Peter William, OBE 1989; BSc, CEng, FRINA; Secretary, Royal Institution of Naval Architects, 1967–89; *b* 25 Sept. 1925; *s* of late William Frank and Edith Louise Ayling; *m* 1949, Sheila Bargery; two *s* two *d*. *Educ:* Royal Dockyard Sch., Portsmouth; King's Coll., Univ. of Durham (BSc). Shipwright apprentice, HM Dockyard, Portsmouth, 1942–47; King's Coll., Univ. of Durham, 1947–50; Research and Principal Research Officer, British Ship Research Assoc., London, 1950–65; Principal Scientific Officer, Ship Div., Nat. Physical Laboratory, Feltham (now British Maritime Technology Ltd), 1965–67. *Publications:* papers on ship strength and vibration, Trans RINA, NECInst and IESS. *Recreations:* music, gardening, walking, motoring. *Address:* Royal Institution of Naval Architects, 10 Upper Belgrave Street, SW1X 8BQ. *T:* 071–235 4622; (home) Oakmead, School Road, Camelsdale, Haslemere, Surrey. *T:* Haslemere (0428) 644474.

AYLING, Air Vice-Marshal Richard Cecil, CB 1965; CBE 1961 (OBE 1948); Adjudicator, Immigration Appeals, 1970–88; *b* 7 June 1916; *s* of A. C. Ayling, LDS, Norwood, London; *m* 1st, 1941, Patricia Doreen Wright (*d* 1966); one *s* one *d*; 2nd, 1971, Virginia, *d* of Col Frank Davis, Northwood; two *d*. *Educ:* Dulwich Coll. No 3(F) Sqdn, 1936–39. Served RNZAF, 1940–43; Comd No 51 Sqdn (Bomber Comd), 1944; Station Comdr, Bomber Comd, 1944–45; Staff Coll., 1945. Staff of Central Bomber Estabt, 1946–48; Air Staff (Plans) Far East, 1948–50; Air Min. (OR1 and Dep. Dir Policy Air Staff), 1951–54; Station Comdr, Bomber Comd, 1954–58; Asst Chief of Defence Staff, Min. of Defence, 1958–59; Dir of Organisation (Estabts), Air Min., 1960–61; SASO, Flying Training Command, 1962–65; Min. of Defence, 1965–66; AOA, RAF Air Support (formerly Transport) Comd, 1966–69; retd, 1969. *Recreations:* ski-ing, sailing, gardening. *Address:* Buckler's Spring, Buckler's Hard, Beaulieu, Hants SO42 7XA. *T:* Buckler's Hard (0590) 616204. *Club:* Royal Lymington Yacht.

AYLMER, family name of **Baron Aylmer.**

AYLMER, 13th Baron *cr* 1718; **Michael Anthony Aylmer;** Bt 1662; *b* 27 March 1923; *s* of Christopher Aylmer (*d* 1955) and Marjorie (*d* 1981), *d* of Percival Ellison Barber, surgeon, Sheffield; *S* cousin, 1982; *m* 1950, Countess Maddalena Sofia, *d* of late Count Arbeno Attems, Aiello del Friuli, Italy; one *s* one *d*. *Educ:* privately and Trinity Hall, Cambridge (Exhibnr, MA, LLM). Admitted a solicitor, 1948. Employed in Legal Dept of Equity & Law Life Assurance Society plc, 1951 until retirement, 1983. *Recreations:* reading and music. *Heir: s* Hon. (Anthony) Julian Aylmer [*b* 10 Dec. 1951; *m* 1990, Belinda Rosemary, *d* of Maj. Peter Parker; one *s*]. *Address:* 42 Brampton Grove, NW4 4AQ. *T:* 081–202 8300.

AYLMER, Dr Gerald Edward, FBA 1976; Master of St Peter's College, Oxford, 1978–91, Hon. Fellow, 1991; *b* 30 April 1926; *s* of late Captain E. A. Aylmer, RN, and Mrs G. P. Aylmer (*née* Evans); *m* 1955, Ursula Nixon; one *s* one *d*. *Educ:* Winchester; Balliol Coll., Oxford (MA, DPhil). Served RN, 1944–47. Jane Eliza Proctor Vis. Fellow, Princeton Univ., NJ, USA, 1950–51; Jun. Res. Fellow, Balliol Coll., Oxford, 1951–54; Asst Lectr in History, Univ. of Manchester, 1954–57, Lectr, 1957–62; Prof. of History and Head of Dept of History, Univ. of York, 1963–78; Mem., Oxford History Faculty, 1978–. Vis. Mem., Inst. for Advanced Study, Princeton, 1975. Mem., Royal Commn on Historical Manuscripts, 1978– (Chm., 1989–). Pres., RHistS, 1984–88 (Hon. Vice Pres., 1988–). Mem., Editorial Bd, History of Parliament, 1969– (Chm., 1989–). *Publications:* The King's Servants, 1961 (2nd edn 1974); (ed) The Diary of William Lawrence, 1962; The Struggle for the Constitution, 1963 (5th edn 1975); (ed) The Interregnum, 1972 (2nd edn 1974); The State's Servants, 1973; (ed) The Levellers in the English Revolution, 1975; (ed with Reginald Cant) A History of York Minster, 1978; Rebellion or Revolution?: England 1640–1660, 1986; articles and revs in learned jls. *Address:* 18 Albert Street, Jericho, Oxford, OX2 6AZ; The Old Captains, Hereford Road, Ledbury, Herefordshire HR8 2PX.

AYLMER, Sir Richard John, 16th Bt *cr* 1622, of Donadea, Co. Kildare; writer; *b* 23 April 1937; *s* of Sir Fenton Gerald Aylmer, 15th Bt and Rosalind Boultbee (*d* 1991), *d* of J. Percival Bell; *S* father, 1987; *m* 1962, Lise, *d* of Paul Demers; one *s* one *d*. *Educ:* Lower Canada Coll., Montreal; Western Ontario, London, Canada; Harvard Univ., Cambridge, Mass, USA. *Heir: s* Fenton Paul Aylmer, *b* 31 Oct. 1965. *Address:* 3573 Lorne Avenue, Montreal, Quebec H2X 2A4, Canada.

AYOUB, John Edward Moussa, FRCS; Consulting Surgeon, Moorfields Eye Hospital, since 1973 (Surgeon, 1950–73); Consulting Ophthalmic Surgeon, London Hospital, since 1973 (Surgeon, 1947–73); Consulting Ophthalmic Surgeon, Royal Masonic Hospital, since 1973 (Consultant, 1967–73); Consulting Ophthalmic Surgeon, Royal Navy; *b* 7 Sept. 1908; British; *m* 1939, Madeleine Marion Coniston Martin; one *s* one *d*. *Educ:* St Paul's Sch.; Lincoln Coll., Oxford; St Thomas' Hospital. BM, BCh Oxon 1933; FRCS 1935. Fellow, and past Vice-Pres. Section of Ophthalmology, RSM; Past Mem. Council, Faculty of Ophthalmologists (Vice-Pres., 1959–). Served War of 1939–45, Surg. Lieut-Comdr RNVR, specialist in ophthalmology. Visiting consultant ophthalmologist to Western Memorial Hosp., Newfoundland, 1974–. *Publications:* contributions to medical journals. *Recreation:* gardening. *Address:* 2 Clarendon Road, Boston Spa, near Wetherby, West Yorks LS23 6NG. *Clubs:* Leander; Royal Cruising.

AYRES, Gillian, OBE 1986; RA 1991 (ARA 1982); painter, artist; *b* 3 Feb. 1930; *d* of Stephen and Florence Ayres; *m* Henry Mundy (marr. diss.); two *s*. *Educ:* St Paul's Girls' Sch.; Camberwell Sch. of Art. Student, 1946–50; taught, 1959–81 (incl. Sen. Lectr, St Martin's Sch. of Art, and Head of Painting, Winchester Sch. of Art, 1978–81). One-woman Exhibitions include: Gallery One, 1956; Redfern Gall., 1958; Moulton Gall., 1960 and 1962; Kasmin Gall., 1965, 1966 and 1969; William Darby Gall., 1976; Women's Internat. Centre, New York, 1976; Knoedler Gall., 1979, 1982, 1987; Mus. of Mod. Art, Oxford, 1981; retrospective exhibn, Serpentine Gall., 1983; also exhibited: Redfern Gall., 1957; 1st Paris Biennale, 1959; Hayward Gall., 1971; Hayward Annual Exhibn, 1974 and 1980; Silver Jubilee Exhibn, RA, 1977; Knoedler Gall., NY, 1985. Works in public collections: Tate Gall.; Mus. of Mod. Art, NY; Olinda Mus., Brazil; Gulbenkian Foundn, Lisbon; V&A Mus.; British Council. Prize winner: Tokyo Biennale, 1963; John Moores 2nd Prize, 1982; Major Arts Council Bursary, 1979. *Recreation:* gardening. *Address:* Tall Trees, Gooseham, near Bude, Cornwall. *T:* Morwenstow (028883) 206.

AYRTON, Norman Walter; international theatre and opera director; Dean, British American Drama Academy, London, since 1986; *b* London, 25 Sept. 1924. Served War of 1939–45, RNVR. Trained as an actor at Old Vic Theatre School under Michael Saint Denis, 1947–48; joined Old Vic Company, 1948; repertory experience at Farnham and Oxford, 1949–50; on staff of Old Vic Sch., 1949–52; rejoined Old Vic Company for 1951 Festival Season; opened own teaching studio, 1952; began dramatic coaching for Royal Opera House, Covent Garden, 1953; apptd Asst Principal of London Academy of Music and Dramatic Art, 1954; taught at Shakespeare Festival, Stratford, Ont, and Royal Shakespeare Theatre, Stratford-upon-Avon, 1959–62; apptd GHQ Drama Adviser to Girl Guide Movement, 1960–74; Principal, LAMDA, 1966–72; Dean, World Shakespeare Study Centre, Bankside, 1972; Dir of Opera, Royal Acad. of Music, 1986–90. *Director:* Artaxerxes, for Handel Opera Soc., Camden Festival, 1963; La Traviata, Covent Garden, 1963; Manon, Covent Garden, 1964; Sutherland-Williamson Grand Opera Season, in Australia, 1965; Twelfth Night at Dallas Theatre Center, Texas, 1967; The Way of the World, NY, 1976; Lakmé, Sydney Opera House, 1976; Der Rosenkavalier, Sydney Opera House, 1983; *Guest Director:* Australian Council for Arts, Sydney and Brisbane, 1973; Loeb Drama Center, Harvard (and teacher), 1974, 1976, 1978; Faculty, Juillard Sch., NY, 1974–85; Melbourne Theatre Co., 1974–; Nat. Inst. of Dramatic Art, Sydney, 1974; Vancouver Opera Assoc., 1975–; Sydney Opera House, 1976–81, 1983; Williamstown Festival, USA, 1977; Hartford Stage Co. and Amer. Stage Fest., 1978–; Missouri Rep. Theatre, 1980–81; Nat. Opera Studio, London, 1980–81; Spoleto Fest., USA, 1984; Resident Stage Director: Amer. Opera Center, NY, 1981–85; Vassar Coll., NY, 1990–91. *Recreations:* reading, music, travel. *Address:* 40A Birchington Road, NW6 4LJ.

AZIKIWE, Rt. Hon. Nnamdi, GCFR 1980; PC 1960; LLD, DLitt, MA, MSc; Ndichie Chief Owelle of Onitsha, 1973; Leader, Nigeria People's Party, since 1979; (First) President of the Federal Republic of Nigeria, 1963–66; Governor-General and Commander-in-Chief of Nigeria, 1960–63; *b* Zungeru, Northern Nigeria, 16 Nov. 1904; *s* of Obededom Chukwuemeka and Rachel Chinwe Azikiwe; *m* 1936, Flora Ogbenyeanu Ogoegbunam, *d* of Chief Ogoegbunam, the Adazia of Onitsha (Ndichie Chief); three *s* one *d*. *Educ:* CMS Central Sch., Onitsha; Methodist Boys' High Sch., Lagos; Storer Coll., Harpers Ferry, W Va, USA; Howard Univ., Washington, DC; Lincoln Univ., Pa; Univ. of Pennsylvania. Overseas Fellow, Inst. Journalists, London, 1962 (Mem., 1933–). Editor-in-Chief, African Morning Post, Accra, 1934–37; Editor-in-Chief, West African Pilot, 1937–45; Correspondent for Associated Negro Press, 1944–47; Gen. Sec., Nat. Council of Nigeria and the Cameroons, 1944–46 (Pres., 1946–60); Correspondent for Reuter's, 1944–46; Chm. African Continental Bank Ltd, 1944–53. MLC Nigeria, 1947–51; Mem. Foot Commission for Nigerianisation of Civil Service, 1948. Leader of Opposition in the Western House of Assembly, 1952–53; Mem. Eastern House of Assembly, 1954–59; MHR 1954; Minister, Eastern Nigeria, 1954–57; Leader, Educational Missions to UK and USA, for establishment of Univ. of Nigeria, 1955 and 1959; Premier of Eastern Nigeria, 1954–59; Pres., Exec. Council of Govt of E Nigeria, 1957–59; President of Senate of Federation, Jan-Nov. 1960. NPP Candidate, Presidential Election, 1979. Mem., Council of State, 1979–83. Ndichie Chief Ozizani Obi of Onitsha, 1963–72. Chm., Provisional Council of Univ. of Nigeria, 1960–61; Chancellor of Univ. of Nigeria, 1961–66, of Univ. of Lagos, 1970–76. Jt Pres., Anti-Slavery Soc. for Human Rights,

London, 1970– (Vice-Pres., 1966–69). (Life) FREconS; (Life) FRAI; (Life) Mem. British Association for Advancement of Science; Member: American Soc. of International Law; American Anthropological Assoc. Pres. numerous sporting assocs and boards, 1940–60; Mem., Nigerian Olympic Cttee, 1950–60. Hon. DCL Liberia, 1969; Hon. DSc Lagos, 1972. KStJ 1960–66. *Publications:* Liberia in World Politics, 1934; Renascent Africa, 1937; The African in Ancient and Mediaeval History, 1938; Land Tenure in Northern Nigeria, 1942; Political Blueprint of Nigeria, 1943; Economic Reconstruction of Nigeria, 1943; Economic Rehabilitation of Eastern Nigeria, 1955; Zik: a selection of speeches, 1961; Meditations: a collection of poems, 1965; My Odyssey, 1971; Military Revolution in Nigeria, 1972; Dialogue on a New Capital for Nigeria, 1974; Treasury of West African Poetry; Democracy with Military Vigilance, 1974; Onitsha Market Crisis, 1975; Civil War Soliloquies: further collection of poems, 1976; Ideology for Nigeria, 1978. *Recreations:* athletics, boxing, cricket, soccer, swimming, tennis, reading. *Address:* Onuiyi Haven, PO Box 7, Nsukka, Nigeria.

AZIZ, Suhail Ibne; international management consultant, since 1981; Chairman and Managing Director, Brettonwood Partnership Ltd, since 1990; *b* Bangladesh (then India), 3 Oct. 1937; permanently resident in England, since 1966; *s* of Azizur Rahman and Lutfunnessa Khatoon; *m* 1960, Elizabeth Ann Pyne, Dartmouth, Devon; two *d*. *Educ:* Govt High Sec. Sch., Sylhet; Murarichand Coll., Dacca Univ., Sylhet (Intermed. in Science, 1954); Jt Services Pre-Cadet Trng Sch., Quetta; Cadet Trng Sch., PNS Himalaya, Karachi; BRNC, Dartmouth (Actg Sub-Lieut 1958); (mature student) Kingston upon Thames Polytechnic and Trent Polytech., Nottingham (Dipl. in Man. Studies, 1970); (ext. student) London Univ. (BScEcon Hons 1972); (internal student) Birkbeck Coll., London Univ., (MScEcon 1976). FBIM; MIMC 1986. Sub-Lieut and Lieut, Pakistan Navy Destroyers/Mine Sweeper (Exec. Br.), 1954–61. Personnel and indust. relations: Unilever (Pakistan); Royal Air Force; Commn on Indust. Relations, London; Ford Motor Co. (GB); Mars Ltd, 1963–78; Dir of Gen. Services Div., CRE, 1978–81; Dep. Dir of Econ. Devlt, London Borough of Lewisham, 1984–88; Management Consultant, Fullemploy Consultancy Ltd, 1989–90. Mem., London Electricity Consumer Cttee, 1991–. Leading Mem., Bangladesh Movement in UK, 1971. Member: Exec., Standing Conf. of Asian Orgs in UK, 1972–; N Metropol. Conciliation Cttee, Race Relations Bd, 1971–74; Exec., Post Conf. Constituent Cttee, Black People in Britain—the Way Forward, 1975–76; Adv.

Cttee to Gulbenkian Foundn on Area Resource Centre and Community Support Forum, 1976–81; Exec., Nottingham and Dist Community Relations Council, 1975–78; Dept of Employment Race Relations Employment Adv. Gp, 1977–78; BBC Asian programme Adv. Cttee, 1977–81; Industrial Tribunals, 1977–; Exec., Nat. Org. of African, Asian and Caribbean Peoples, 1976–77; Home Sec.'s Standing Adv. Council on Race Relations, 1976–78; Steering Cttee, Asian Support Forum, 1984–86; Jt Consultative Cttee with Ethnic Minorities, Merton BC, 1985–; Plunkett Foundn for Co-operative Studies, 1985–; "One World", 1986–; Adv. Gp, City of London Polytechnic Ethnic Minority Business Devlt Unit, 1987–; Res. Adv. Bd, QMC, London Univ., 1988–; (co-opted), Exec. Cttee, Tower Hamlets Assoc. for Racial Equality, 1988– (Mem., Action Tower Hamlets, 1987); Bangladeshis in Britain—a Response Forum, 1987–; Chairman: Jalalabad Overseas Orgn in UK, 1983–; London Boroughs Bangladesh Assoc., 1984–; Founder Chm., East London Bangladeshi Enterprise Agency, 1985–. CRE Bursary to study Minority Business Devlt initiatives in USA, 1986. Mem., Labour Econ. Finance Taxation Assoc., 1973–80; Institute of Management Consultants: Chm., Third World Specialist Gp, 1984–; Treasurer, London Reg., 1985–87. Jt Trustee, United Action-Bangladesh Relief Fund, 1971–; Trustee, Brixton Neighbourhood Assoc., 1979–82. Deeply interested in community and race relations and believes profoundly that future health of Brit. society depends on achieving good race relations. *Recreations:* travelling, seeing places of historical interest, meeting people, reading (*eg* political economy). *Address:* 126 St Julian's Farm Road, West Norwood, SE27 0RR. *Clubs:* Royal Air Force; Sudan (Khartoum).

AZNAM, Raja Tan Sri bin Raja Haji Ahmad; Malaysian High Commissioner in London, 1979–82; *b* Taiping, 21 Jan. 1928; *s* of Raja Haji Ahmad and Hajjah Zainab; *m* 1954, Tengku Puan Sri Zailah Btd T. Zakaria; one *s* two *d*. *Educ:* King Edward VII Coll., Taiping; Malay Coll., Kuala Kangsar; Univ. of Malaya in Singapore. Joined Malayan Civil Service 1953, Foreign Service 1956; Second Sec., Bangkok, 1957; First Sec., Cairo, 1960–62; Principal Asst Sec., Min. of Foreign Affairs, 1962–65; Dep. Perm. Rep to UN, 1965–68; High Comr in India, 1968–71; Ambassador to Japan, 1971–74, to USSR, Bulgaria, Hungary, Mongolia, Poland and Romania, 1974–77, to France, Morocco, Portugal and Spain, 1977–79. *Recreations:* reading, golf. *Address:* c/o Ministry of Foreign Affairs, Wismaputre, Kuala Lumpur, Malaysia.

B

BABCOCK, Horace Welcome; Director, Mount Wilson and Palomar Observatories, 1964–78, retired; *b* 13 Sept. 1912; *s* of Harold D. Babcock and Mary G. (*née* Henderson); *m* 1st, 1940; one *s* one *d*; 2nd, 1958, Elizabeth M. Aubrey; one *s*. *Educ:* California Institute of Technology (BS); Univ. of California (PhD). Instructor, Yerkes and McDonald Observatories, 1939–41; Radiation Laboratory, Mass Inst. of Tech., 1941–42; Calif Inst. of Tech., 1942–45; Staff Mem., Mount Wilson Observatory, 1946–51; Astronomer, Mount Wilson and Palomar Observatories, 1951–80; Founding Dir, Las Campanas Observatory, Chile, of Carnegie Instn, Washington, 1968–78. Elected to: National Acad. of Sciences, 1954 (Councillor, 1973–76); American Acad. of Arts and Sciences, 1959; American Philosophical Soc., 1966; Corres. Mem., Société Royale des Sciences de Liège, 1968; Associate, Royal Astronomical Soc., 1969; Member: American Astronomical Soc.; Astronomical Soc. of the Pacific; Internat. Astronomical Union. Hon. DSc Univ. of Newcastle upon Tyne, 1965. US Navy Bureau of Ordnance Development Award, 1945; Eddington Gold Medal, RAS, 1958; Henry Draper Medal of the National Acad. of Sciences, 1957; Bruce Medal, Astronomical Soc. of the Pacific, 1969; Gold Medal, RAS, 1970. *Publications:* scientific papers in Astrophysical Jl, Publications of the Astronomical Soc. of the Pacific, Jl of Optical Soc. of America, etc, primarily on magnetic fields of the stars and sun, astrophysics, diffraction gratings, adaptive optics, and astronomical instruments. *Address:* The Observatories, Carnegie Institution of Washington, 813 Santa Barbara Street, Pasadena, California 91101, USA. *T:* (818) 577–1122.

BABER, Ernest George, CBE 1987; Judge of the Supreme Court of Hong Kong, 1973–86; *b* 18 July 1924; *s* of late Walter Averette Baber and Kate Marion (*née* Pratt); *m* 1960, Dr Flora Marion, *y d* of late Dr Raymond Bisset Smith and Mrs Jean Gemmell Bisset Smith (*née* Howie); one *s* two *d*. *Educ:* Brentwood; Emmanuel Coll., Cambridge (MA, LLM). Served RN, 1942–47 (Lieut (S)). Called to Bar, Lincoln's Inn, 1951. Resident Magistrate, Uganda, 1954–62; Magistrate and President of Tenancy Tribunal, Hong Kong, 1962; Senior Magistrate, 1963–67; District Judge, 1967–73. *Recreations:* children, music, walking. *Address:* 18 Cumnor Hill, Oxford OX2 9HA. *Club:* Hong Kong (Hong Kong).

BABINGTON, His Honour Anthony Patrick; a Circuit Judge, 1972–87; *b* 4 April 1920; 2nd *s* of late Oscar John Gilmore Babington, MAI, AMICE, Monkstown, Co. Cork. *Educ:* Reading Sch. Served with Royal Ulster Rifles and Dorset Regt, 1939–45 (wounded twice); Croix de Guerre with Gold Star (France), 1944. Called to the Bar, Middle Temple, 1948; Bencher, 1977; South Eastern Circuit; Prosecuting Counsel to Post Office, SE Circuit (South), 1959–64; Metropolitan Stipendiary Magistrate, 1964–72. Mem., Home Office Working Party on Bail, 1971–73. Mem., Nat. Exec. Cttee, Internat. PEN English Centre, 1979–82. *Publications:* No Memorial, 1954; The Power to Silence, 1968; A House in Bow Street, 1969; The English Bastille, 1971; The Only Liberty, 1975; For the Sake of Example, 1983; Military Intervention in Britain, 1990; The Devil to Pay, 1991. *Recreations:* music, theatre, reading. *Address:* 3 Gledhow Gardens, South Kensington, SW5 0BL. *T:* 071–373 4014; Thydon Cottage, Chilham, near Canterbury, Kent CT4 8BX. *T:* Canterbury (0227) 730300. *Clubs:* Garrick, Special Forces.

BABINGTON, Robert John, DSC 1943; QC (NI) 1965; **His Honour Judge Babington;** appointed County Court Judge for Fermanagh and Tyrone, 1978; *b* 9 April 1920; *s* of David Louis James Babington and Alice Marie (*née* McClintock); *m* 1952, Elizabeth Bryanna Marguerite Alton, *d* of Dr E. H. Alton, Provost of Trinity College, Dublin; two *s* one *d*. *Educ:* St Columba's Coll., Rathfarnham, Dublin; Trinity Coll., Dublin (BA). Called to the Bar, Inn of Court of NI, 1947. MP North Down, Stormont, 1968–72. *Recreations:* golf, bird-watching. *Address:* Royal Courts of Justice, Chichester Street, Belfast BT1 3JF. *Clubs:* Special Forces; Tyrone County (Omagh); Fermanagh County (Enniskillen); Royal Belfast Golf.

BABINGTON, William, CBE 1972; QFSM 1969; Chief Officer, Kent County Fire Brigade, 1966–76, retired; *b* 23 Dec. 1916; *s* of William and Annie Babington; *m* 1940, Marjorie Perdue Le Seelleur; one *d*. *Educ:* King Edward's Grammar Sch., Birmingham. Addtl Supt of Police, Assam, India, 1942–44; Instructor, Fire Service Coll., 1951–53; Divl Officer, Hampshire Fire Service, 1954–59; Asst Chief Officer, Suffolk and Ipswich Fire Service, 1959–62; Dep. Chief Officer, Lancashire Fire Brigade, 1962–66. *Recreations:* sailing, travel. *Address:* Alpine Cottage, Grouville, Jersey, CI. *T:* Jersey (0534) 52737.

BABINGTON-BROWNE, Gillian Brenda, (Mrs K. J. Wilson); a Metropolitan Stipendiary Magistrate, since 1991; *b* 20 May 1949; *d* of Derek Keith Babington-Browne and Olive Maude (*née* Seymour); *m* 1983, Kenneth John Wilson. *Educ:* Coll. of Law, London. Admitted Solicitor, 1973; Asst Solicitor with Arnold, Tuff & Grimwade, Rochester, 1973–74; Assistant with Ronald A. Prior, 1974, with Edward Lewis Possart, London, 1974–78; own practice, 1978–89; freelance advocate and consultant, 1989–91. *Publications:* contribs to legal jls. *Recreations:* gardening, interior design/decorating, reading. *Address:* c/o Bow Street Magistrates' Court, WC2E 7AS. *T:* 071–379 4713.

BACHE, Andrew Philip Foley; HM Diplomatic Service; on secondment to Civil Service Selection Board, since 1990; *b* 29 Dec. 1939; *s* of late Robert Philip Sidney Bache, OBE and Jessie Bache; *m* 1963, Shân Headley; two *s* one *d*. *Educ:* Shrewsbury Sch.; Emmanuel Coll., Cambridge (MA). Joined HM Diplomatic Service, 1963; 3rd Sec., Nicosia, 1964–66; Treasury Centre for Admin. Studies, 1966; 2nd Sec., Sofia, 1966–68; FCO, 1968–71; 1st Sec., Lagos, 1971–74; FCO, 1974–78; 1st Sec. (Commercial), Vienna, 1978–81; Counsellor and Head of Chancery, Tokyo, 1981–85; Counsellor, Ankara, 1985–87; Hd of Personnel Services Dept, FCO, 1988–90. *Recreations:* diverse, including travel, history, ornithology, fine arts, squash, tennis, cricket. *Address:* c/o Foreign and Commonwealth Office, King Charles Street, SW1. *Club:* MCC.

BACK, Mrs J. H.; *see* Harrison, Kathleen.

BACK, Kenneth John Campbell, AO 1984; MSc, PhD; Executive Director, International Development Program of Australian Universities and Colleges Ltd, since 1986; *b* 13 Aug. 1925; *s* of J. L. Back; *m* 1950, Patricia, *d* of R. O. Cummings; two *d*. *Educ:* Sydney High Sch.; Sydney Univ. (MSc); Univ. of Queensland (PhD). Res. Bacteriologist, Davis Gelatine (Aust.) Pty Ltd, 1947–49; Queensland University: Lectr in Bacteriology, 1950–56; Sen. Lectr in Microbiology, 1957–61; Actg Prof. of Microbiology, 1962; Warden, University Coll. of Townsville, Queensland, 1963–70; Vice-Chancellor, James Cook Univ. of N Queensland, 1970–85. Chm., Standing Cttee, Australian Univs Internat. Develt Prog. (formerly Australian-Asian Univs Co-operation Scheme), 1977–85. Hon. DSc Queensland, 1982. *Publications:* papers on microbiological metabolism. *Recreations:* golf, bridge, sailing. *Address:* International Development Program of Australian Universities and Colleges Ltd, GPO Box 2006, Canberra, ACT 2601, Australia; 13 Steinwedel Street, Farrer, ACT 2607, Australia. *T:* (062) 865014. *Clubs:* Commonwealth, Royal Canberra Golf (Canberra).

BACK, Patrick, QC 1970; a Recorder of the Crown Court, since 1972; *b* 23 Aug. 1917; *s* of late Ivor Back, FRCS, and Barbara Back (*née* Nash). *Educ:* Marlborough; Trinity Hall, Cambridge. Captain, 14th Punjab Regt, 1941–46. Called to Bar, 1940; Bencher, Gray's Inn, 1978. Commenced practice, Western Circuit, 1948, Leader, 1984–89; Dep. Chm., Devon QS, 1968. *Recreation:* fly-fishing. *Address:* Paddock Edge, Broadwindsor, Dorset. *T:* Broadwindsor (0308) 644; 3 Paper Buildings, Temple, EC4Y 7EU; Flat 3, Marquess House, 74 Marquess Road, N1. *T:* 071–226 0991.

BACKETT, Prof. Edward Maurice; Foundation Professor of Community Health, University of Nottingham, 1969–81, now Professor Emeritus; *b* 12 Jan. 1916; *o s* of late Frederick and Louisa Backett; *m* 1940, Shirley Paul-Thompson; one *s* two *d*. *Educ:* University Coll., London; Westminster Hospital. Operational Research with RAF; Nuffield Fellow in Social Medicine; Research Worker, Medical Research Council; Lecturer, Queen's Univ., Belfast; Senior Lecturer, Guy's Hospital and London Sch. of Hygiene and Tropical Medicine; Prof. and Head of Dept of Public Health and Social Medicine, Univ. of Aberdeen, 1958–69. Hon. Member: Internat. Epidemiol Assoc., 1984; Soc. for Social Medicine, 1986. *Publications:* The Risk Approach to Health Care, 1984; papers in scientific journals. *Recreations:* swimming, walking, sailing. *Address:* Lidstones, South Town, Dartmouth, Devon TQ6 9BU. *T:* Dartmouth (0803) 833788.

BACKHOUSE, David Miles; Chairman, Henderson Administration Group PLC, since 1990; *b* 30 Jan. 1939; *s* of Jonathan Backhouse and Alice Joan (*née* Woodroffe); *m* 1969, Sophia Ann (*née* Townsend); one *s* one *d*. *Educ:* Summerfields, Oxford; Eton Coll. Commenced career in banking with Schroders PLC, 1966. Non-executive Director: TSB Group, 1985–; Witan Investment Company, 1985–; RAC, Cirencester, 1987; Bradstock Group, 1990–. *Recreations:* tennis, riding. *Address:* South Farm, Fairford, Glos GL7 3PN. *T:* Cirencester (0285) 712225; 54 Cadogan Place, SW1X 9RT. *T:* 071–235 5997. *Clubs:* Boodle's, City of London; Vanderbilt Racquet.

BACKHOUSE, Jonathan; retired; *b* 16 March 1907; 2nd *s* of late Lieut-Col M. R. C. Backhouse, DSO, TD, and of Olive Backhouse; *m* 1934, Alice Joan Woodroffe (*d* 1984); two *s* one *d*. *Educ:* RNC Dartmouth. Served War of 1939–45, Royal Artillery. Merchant Bank, 1924–28; Stock Exchange, 1928–50; Merchant Bank, 1950–70. *Recreations:* shooting, etc. *Address:* Breewood Hall, Great Horkesley, Colchester, Essex CO6 4BW. *T:* Colchester (0206) 271260. *Club:* Royal Thames Yacht.
See also D. M. Backhouse.

BACKHOUSE, Sir Jonathan Roger, 4th Bt, *cr* 1901; formerly Managing Director, W. H. Freeman & Co. Ltd, Publishers; *b* 30 Dec. 1939; *s* of Major Sir John Edmund Backhouse, 3rd Bt, MC, and Jean Marie Frances, *d* of Lieut-Col G. R. V. Hume-Gore, MC, The Gordon Highlanders; *S* father, 1944. *Educ:* Oxford. *Heir: b* Oliver Richard Backhouse [*b* 18 July 1941; *m* 1970, Gillian Irene, *o d* of L. W. Lincoln, Northwood, Middx].

BACKHOUSE, Roger Bainbridge; QC 1984; *b* 8 March 1938; *s* of Leslie Bainbridge Backhouse and Jean Backhouse; *m* 1962, Elizabeth Constance, *d* of Comdr J. A. Lowe, DSO, DSC; two *s* one *d*. *Educ:* Liverpool Coll.; Trinity Hall, Cambridge (History Tripos parts I & II). Nat. Service, RAF, 1956–58 (Pilot Officer). Worked in family business, 1961–62; Schoolmaster, 1962–64; called to the Bar, Middle Temple, 1965. *Recreations:* shooting, golf, opera. *Address:* Preston House, Colebrook Street, Winchester, Hants SO23 9LH. *T:* Winchester (0962) 63053; (chambers) 1 Middle Temple Lane, WC2 9AA. *Clubs:* Royal Air Force; Hampshire (Winchester).

BACON, family name of **Baroness Bacon.**

BACON, Baroness *cr* 1970 (Life Peer), of Leeds and Normanton; **Alice Martha Bacon,** PC 1966; CBE 1953; DL; *d* of late County Councillor B. Bacon, miner. *Educ:* Elementary Schs, Normanton, Yorks; Normanton Girls' High Sch.; Stockwell Training Coll.; external student of London Univ. Subsequently schoolmistress. MP (Lab) NE Leeds, 1945–55, SE Leeds, 1955–70; Minister of State: Home Office, 1964–67; Dept of Educn and Science, 1967–70. Mem. National Executive Cttee of Labour Party, 1941–70; Chm., Labour Party, 1950–51. DL W Yorkshire 1974. Hon. LLD Leeds, 1972. *Address:* 53 Snydale Road, Normanton, West Yorks WF6 1NY. *T:* Wakefield (0924) 893229.

BACON, Francis, artist; *b* Dublin, 28 Oct. 1909; English parents. Self-taught. Exhibited furniture and rugs of his own design, Queensbury Mews studio, began painting, 1929; destroyed nearly all earlier works, 1941–44; rep. GB with Ben Nicholson and Lucian Freud, 27th Venice Biennale, 1954. *One-man exhibitions:* Hanover Gall., London, 1949, 1950, 1951, 1952, 1954, 1957, 1959; Durlacher Bros, NY 1953; ICA, 1955; Galerie Rive Droite, Paris, 1957; Galleria Galatea, Turin, 1958, 1970; Marlborough Fine Art, London,

1960, 1963, 1965, 1967, 1983, 1985, 1989; Tate Gall., 1962 (retrospective) (travelled to Mannheim, Turin, Zürich, Amsterdam, 1962), 1985 (retrospective) (travelled to Stuttgart, Berlin, 1985–86); Solomon R. Guggenheim Mus., NY, 1963 (retrospective) (travelled to Chicago, Houston, 1963); Kunstverein, Hamburg, 1965 (retrospective) (travelled to Stockholm, Dublin, 1965); Galerie Maeght, Paris, 1966, 1984, (Lelong Gall.) 1987; Oberes Schloss, Siegen, 1967; Marlborough Gall., NY, 1968, 1980, 1984, 1987, 1990; Grand Palais, Paris, 1971 (retrospective) (travelled to Düsseldorf, 1972); Metrop. Mus. of Art, NY, 1975; Marlborough Gal, Zürich, 1975; Musée Cantini, Marseilles, 1976; Galerie Claude Bernard, Paris, 1977; Mus. de Arte Moderno, Mexico, 1977 (travelled to Caracas, 1977–78); Fundación Juan March, Madrid, 1977 (travelled to Barcelona, 1978); Nat. Mus. of Modern Art, Tokyo, 1983 (retrospective) (travelled to Kyoto, Nagoya, 1983); Galerie Beyeler, Basle, 1987; Central Hall of Artists, Moscow, 1988; Marlborough Gall., Tokyo, 1988–89; Hirshhorn Mus., Washington, 1989–90 (retrospective) (travelled to LA, NY, 1990); Tate Gall., Liverpool, 1990–91. *Important works include:* Three Studies for Figures at the Base of a Crucifixion, 1944; Figure in a Landscape, Fig. Study II, 1945–46; Painting, 1946; Head I, 1948; Two Figures, 1953; Man in Blue, 1954; Study for a Portrait of Van Gogh, 1957; Three Studies for a Crucifixion, 1962; Three Figures in a Room, 1964; Crucifixion, 1965; Triptych, 1971, 1972, 1973, 1974; Study for Self Portrait—Triptych, 1985–86. Paintings acquired by major museum collections throughout the world. Rubens Prize, 1967; Painting Prize, Carnegie Inst., Pittsburgh, 1967. *Address:* c/o Marlborough Fine Art, 6 Albemarle Street, W1X 4BY.

BACON, Francis Thomas, OBE 1967; FRS 1973; FEng 1976; consultant on fuel cells, retired; *b* 21 Dec. 1904; 2nd *s* of T. W. Bacon, Ramsden Hall, Billericay; *m* 1934, Barbara Winifred, *y d* of G. K. Papillon, Manor House, Barrasford; one *s* one *d* (and one *s* decd). *Educ:* Eton Coll.; Trinity Coll., Cambridge. CEng, MIMechE 1947. With C. A. Parsons & Co. Ltd, Newcastle-on-Tyne, 1925–40 (i/c production of silvered glass reflectors, 1935–39); experimental work on hydrogen/oxygen fuel cell at King's Coll., London, for Merz & McLellan, 1940–41; Temp. Exper. Off. at HM Anti-Submarine Experimental Estbt, Fairlie, 1941–46; exper. work on hydrogen/oxygen fuel cell at Cambridge Univ., 1946–56 (for ERA); Consultant to: NRDC on fuel cells at Marshall of Cambridge Ltd, 1956–62; Energy Conversion Ltd, Basingstoke, 1962–71; Fuel Cells Ltd, AERE, 1971–72; Johnson Matthey PLC, 1984–. British Assoc. Lecture, 1971; Bruno Breyer Meml Lecture and Medal, Royal Aust. Chem. Inst., 1976. S. G. Brown Award and Medal (Royal Soc.), 1965; British Silver Medal (RAeS), 1969; Churchill Gold Medal, Soc. of Engineers, 1972; Melchett Medal, Inst. of Fuel, 1972; Vittorio de Nora Diamond Shamrock Award and Prize, Electrochemical Soc. Inc., 1978. Hon. FSE, 1972. Hon. DSc Newcastle upon Tyne, 1980. *Publications:* chapter 5 in Fuel Cells (ed G. J. Young), 1960; chapter 4 in Fuel Cells (ed W. Mitchell), 1963; papers on fuel cells for World Power Conf., Royal Instn, Nature, two UN Confs, Amer. Inst. of Chem. Eng., Inst. of Fuel, Electrochimica Acta, Royal Soc., 5th World Hydrogen Energy Conf. *Recreations:* hill walking, music, photography, gardening. *Address:* Trees, 34 High Street, Little Shelford, Cambridge CB2 5ES. *T:* Cambridge (0223) 843116. *Club:* Athenæum.

BACON, Prof. George Edward, MA, ScD Cantab, PhD London; Professor of Physics, University of Sheffield, 1963–81, now Emeritus; *b* 5 Dec. 1917; *s* of late George H. Bacon and Lilian A. Bacon, Derby; *m* 1945, Enid Trigg; one *s* one *d. Educ:* Derby Sch.; Emmanuel Coll., Cambridge (Open and Sen. Schol.); CPhys. Air Ministry, Telecommunications Research Estabt, 1939–46. Dep. Chief Scientific Officer, AERE, Harwell, 1946–63; Dean, Faculty of Pure Science, Sheffield Univ., 1969–71. Leverhulme Emeritus Fellow, 1988. FInstP. *Publications:* Neutron Diffraction, 1955; Applications of Neutron Diffraction in Chemistry, 1963; X-ray and Neutron Diffraction, 1966; Neutron Physics, 1969; Neutron Scattering in Chemistry, 1977; The Architecture of Solids, 1981; Fifty Years of Neutron Diffraction, 1987; many scientific pubns on X-ray and neutron crystallographic studies in Proc. Royal Society, Acta Cryst., etc. *Recreations:* gardening, photography, travel. *Address:* Windrush Way, Guiting Power, Cheltenham GL54 5US. *T:* Guiting Power (0451) 850631.

BACON, Jennifer Helen; Director of Resources and Strategy (Grade 2), Department of Employment, since 1991; *b* 16 April 1945; *d* of Dr Lionel James Bacon and Joyce Bacon (*née* Chapman). *Educ:* Bedales Sch., Petersfield; New Hall, Cambridge (BA Hons 1st cl.). Joined Civil Service as Asst Principal, Min. of Labour, 1967; Private Sec. to Minister of State for Employment, 1971–72; Principal, 1972–78, worked on health and safety and industrial relations legislation; Principal Private Sec. to Sec. of State for Employment, 1977–78; Asst Sec., Controller of Trng Services, MSC, 1978–80; sabbatical, travelling in Latin America, 1980–81; Asst Sec., Machinery of Govt Div., CSD, later MPO, 1981–82; Under Sec., Dir of Adult (formerly Occupational) Trng, MSC, 1982–86; Under Sec., School Curriculum and Exams, DES, 1986–89; Prin. Finance Officer (Grade 3), Dept of Employment, 1989–91. Vis. Fellow, Nuffield Coll., Oxford, 1989–. *Recreations:* classical music especially opera, travelling, walking.

BACON, Sir Nicholas (Hickman Ponsonby), 14th Bt of Redgrave, *cr* 1611, and 15th Bt of Mildenhall, *cr* 1627; Premier Baronet of England; *b* 17 May 1953; *s* of Sir Edmund Castell Bacon, 13th and 14th Bt, KG, KBE, TD and of Priscilla Dora, *d* of Col Sir Charles Edward Ponsonby, 1st Bt, TD; *S* father, 1982; *m* 1981, Susan, *d* of Raymond Dinnis, Edenbridge, Kent; three *s. Educ:* Eton; Dundee Univ. (MA). Barrister-at-law, Gray's Inn. A Page of Honour to the Queen, 1966–69. *Heir: s* Henry Hickman Bacon, *b* 23 April 1984. *Address:* Raveningham Hall, Norfolk NR14 6NS. *Club:* Pratt's.

BACON, Sir Sidney (Charles), Kt 1977; CB 1971; BSc(Eng); FEng, FIMechE, FIProdE, FTP; Managing Director, Royal Ordnance Factories, 1972–79; Deputy Chairman, Royal Ordnance Factories Board, 1972–79; *b* 11 Feb. 1919; *s* of Charles and Alice Bacon. *Educ:* Woolwich Polytechnic; London Univ. Military Service, 1943–48, Capt. REME. Royal Arsenal, Woolwich, 1933–58; Regional Supt of Inspection, N Midland Region, 1958–60; Asst Dir, ROF, Nottingham, 1960–61; Director, ROF: Leeds, 1961–62; Woolwich, 1962–63; Birtley, 1965; idc, 1964; Dir of Ordnance Factories, Weapons and Fighting Vehicles, 1965–66; Dep. Controller, ROFs, 1966–69; Controller, ROFs, 1969–72. Dir, Short Brothers Ltd, 1980–89. Pres., IProdE, 1979; Mem. Council, CGLI, 1979–91. Hon. FCGI. *Recreations:* golf, listening to music. *Address:* 228 Erith Road, Bexleyheath, Kent DA7 6HP. *Club:* Shooters Hill Golf.

BADCOCK, Maj.-Gen. John Michael Watson, CB 1976; MBE 1969; DL; Chairman, S. W. Mount & Sons, 1982–86; *b* 10 Nov. 1922; *s* of late R. D. Badcock, MC, JP and Mrs J. D. Badcock; *m* 1948, Gillian Pauline (*née* Attfield); one *s* two *d. Educ:* Sherborne Sch.; Worcester Coll., Oxford. Enlisted in ranks (Army), 1941; commnd Royal Corps of Signals, 1942; war service UK and BAOR; Ceylon, 1945–47; served in UK, Persian Gulf, BAOR and Cyprus; Comdr 2 Inf. Bde and Dep. Constable of Dover Castle, 1968–71; Dep. Mil. Sec., 1971–72; Dir of Manning (Army), 1972–74; Defence Advr and Head of British Defence Liaison Staff, Canberra, 1974–77; retired. psc, jssc, idc. Col Comdt, Royal Signals, 1974–80 and 1982–90; Master of Signals, 1982–90; Hon. Col, 31 (London) Signal Regt (Volunteers), 1978–83. Chm., SE TA&VRA, 1979–85. Chief Appeals Officer, CRC, 1978–82. DL Kent, 1980. *Recreations:* Rugby football, cricket, hockey, most field sports less horsemanship. *Address:* c/o RHQ Royal Signals, 56 Regency Street, SW1P 4AD. *T:* 071–414 8243. *Club:* Army and Navy.

BADDELEY, Dr Alan David; Director, Applied Psychology Unit, Medical Research Council, Cambridge, since 1974; Senior Research Fellow, Churchill College, Cambridge, since 1988; *b* 23 March 1934; *s* of Donald and Nellie Baddeley; *m* 1964, Hilary Ann White; three *s. Educ:* University Coll., London (BA); Princeton Univ. (MA). PhD Cantab. Walker Fellow, Princeton Univ., 1956–57; Scientist, MRC Applied Psychology Unit, Cambridge, 1958–67; Pembroke Coll., Cambridge, 1959–62; Lectr then Reader, Sussex Univ., 1969–72; Prof. of Psychology, Stirling Univ., 1972–74. Vis. Fellow, Univ. of California, San Diego, 1970–71; Visiting Professor: Harvard Univ., 1984; Univ. of Queensland, 1990; Univ. of Texas, Austin, 1991. President: Experimental Psychology Soc., 1984–86; European Soc. for Cognitive Psychology, 1986–90. Mem., Academia Europaea, 1989. *Publications:* The Psychology of Memory, 1976; Your Memory: a user's guide, 1982; Working Memory, 1986; Human Memory: theory and practice, 1990. *Recreations:* walking, reading, travel. *Address:* MRC Applied Psychology Unit, 15 Chaucer Road, Cambridge CB2 2EF. *T:* Cambridge (0223) 355294.

BADDELEY, Sir John (Wolsey Beresford), 4th Bt *cr* 1922; Finance Director, Mentzendorff & Co. Ltd, since 1986; *b* 27 Jan. 1938; *s* of Sir John Beresford Baddeley, 3rd Bt, and of Nancy Winifred, *d* of late Thomas Wolsey; *S* father, 1979; *m* 1962, Sara Rosalind Crofts; three *d. Educ:* Bradfield College, Berks. FCA. Qualified as Chartered Accountant, 1961. *Recreations:* inland waterways, tennis, squash. *Heir: cousin* Mark David Baddeley, *b* 10 May 1921.

BADDELEY, Very Rev. William Pye, BA; Dean Emeritus of Brisbane, 1981; *b* 20 March 1914; *s* of W. H. Clinton-Baddeley and Louise Bourdin, Shropshire; *m* 1947, Mary Frances Shirley, *d* of Col E. R. C. Wyatt, CBE, DSO; one *d. Educ:* Durham Univ.; St Chad's Coll., Durham; Cuddesdon Coll., Oxford. Deacon, 1941; Priest, 1942; Curate of St Luke, Camberwell, 1941–44; St Anne, Wandsworth, 1944–46; St Stephen, Bournemouth, 1946–49; Vicar of St Pancras (with St James and Christ Church from 1954), 1949–58; Dean of Brisbane, 1958–67; Rector of St James's, Piccadilly, 1967–80; RD of Westminster (St Margaret's), 1974–79; Commissary to: Archbishop of Brisbane, 1967–; Bishop of Wangaratta, 1970–; Archbishop of Papua New Guinea, 1972–80; Bishop of Newcastle, NSW, 1976–. Member: London Diocesan Synod, 1970–80; Bishop of London's Council, 1975–80. Chaplain: Elizabeth Garrett Anderson Hospital, London, 1949–59; St Luke's Hostel, 1952–54; Qld Univ. Anglican Soc., 1960–64; St Martin's Hosp., Brisbane, 1960–67; London Companions of St Francis, 1968–80; Lord Mayor of Westminster, 1968–69 and 1974–75; Actors' Church Union, 1968–70; Royal Acad. of Arts, 1968–80; Vis. Chaplain, Westminster Abbey, 1980–. Hon. Chaplain to: Archbishop of Brisbane (Diocesan Chaplain, 1963–67); Union Soc. of Westminster, 1972–80. President: Brisbane Repertory Theatre, 1961–64; Qld Univ. Dramatic Soc., 1961–67; Qld Ballet Co., 1962–67; Dir, Australian Elizabethan Theatre Trust, 1963–67; Mem. Council of Management, Friends of Royal Academy, 1978–; Chairman: Diocesan Radio and Television Council, 1961–67; weekly television Panel "Round Table", 1962–66; monthly television Panel "What Do YOU Think", 1960–67; Pres., Connard and Seckford Players, 1984–. Governor: Burlington Sch., 1967–76; Archbishop Tenison's Sch., 1967–80; Chairman: Assoc. for Promoting Retreats, 1967–80; Malcolm Sargent Cancer Fund for Children, 1968–; Cttee for Commonwealth Citizens in China, 1970–73; Mem. Council, Metropolitan Hosp. Sunday Fund, 1968–78; Vice-Pres., Cancer Relief Appeal, 1977–. Life Governor of Thomas Coram Foundation, 1955–. Mem. Chapter-Gen., OStJ, 1974–. ChStJ 1971 (SBStJ 1959). *Recreations:* theatre, music, photography. *Address:* Cumberland House, Woodbridge, Suffolk IP12 4AH. *T:* Woodbridge (03943) 4104. *Clubs:* East India, Carlton, Arts.

BADDILEY, Prof. Sir James, Kt 1977; PhD, DSc, ScD; FRS 1961; FRSE 1962; Professor of Chemical Microbiology, 1977–83, now Emeritus, and Director, Microbiological Chemistry Research Laboratory, 1975–83, University of Newcastle upon Tyne; SERC Senior Research Fellow, and Fellow of Pembroke College, University of Cambridge, 1981–85, now Emeritus; *b* 15 May 1918; *s* of late James Baddiley and Ivy Logan Cato; *m* 1944, Hazel Mary, *yr d* of Wesley Wilfrid Townsend and Ann Rayner Townsend (*née* Kilner); one *s. Educ:* Manchester Grammar Sch.; Manchester University (BSc 1941, PhD 1944, DSc 1953; Sir Clement Royds Meml Schol., 1942, Beyer Fellow, 1943–44); MA 1981, ScD 1986, Cantab. Imperial Chemical Industries Fellow, University of Cambridge, 1945–49; Swedish Medical Research Council Fellow, Wenner-Grens Institute for Cell Biology, Stockholm, 1947–49; Mem. of Staff, Dept of Biochemistry, Lister Institute of Preventive Medicine, London, 1949–55; Rockefeller Fellowship, Mass. Gen. Hosp., Harvard Med. Sch., 1954; Prof. of Organic Chem., King's Coll., Univ. of Durham, 1955–77 (later Univ. of Newcastle upon Tyne); Head of Sch. of Chemistry, Newcastle upon Tyne Univ., 1968–78. Member: Council, Chemical Soc., 1962–65; Cttee, Biochemical Soc., 1964–67; Council, Soc. of Gen. Microbiol., 1973–75; Council, SERC (formerly SRC), 1979–81 (Mem., Enzyme Chem. and Technol Cttee, 1972–75, Biol Scis Cttee, 1976–79; Mem., Science Bd, 1979–81); Council, Royal Soc., 1977–79; Editorial Boards, Biochemical Preparations, 1960–70, Biochimica et Biophysica Acta, 1970–77. Karl Folkers Vis. Prof. in Biochem., Illinois Univ., 1962; Tilden Lectr, Chem. Soc., 1959; Special Vis. Lectr, Dept of Microbiology, Temple Univ., Pa, 1966; Leeuwenhoek Lectr, Royal Society, 1967; Pedler Lectr, Chem. Soc., 1978; Endowment Lectr, Bose Inst., Calcutta, 1980. Hon. Mem., Amer. Soc. Biochem. and Molecular Biol. Hon. DSc Heriot Watt, 1979; Bath, 1986. Meldola Medal, RIC, 1947; Corday-Morgan Medal, Chem. Soc., 1952; Davy Medal, Royal Soc., 1974. *Publications:* numerous in Journal of the Chemical Society, Nature, Biochemical Journal, etc; articles in various microbiological and biochemical reviews. *Recreations:* photography, music. *Address:* Hill Top Cottage, Hildersham, Cambridge CB1 6DA. *T:* Cambridge (0223) 893055; Department of Biochemistry, University of Cambridge, Tennis Court Road, Cambridge CB2 1QW. *T:* Cambridge (0223) 333600.

BADEN, (Edwin) John, CA; Director, Girobank plc, since 1987 (Deputy Chairman, 1989–90; Chief Executive, 1989–91; Managing Director, 1990–91); *b* 18 Aug. 1928; *s* of Percy Baden and Jacoba (*née* de Blank); *m* 1952, Christine Irene (*née* Grose); two *s* three *d. Educ:* Winchester Coll.; Corpus Christi Coll., Cambridge (MA Econ and Law). Mem. Inst. of Taxation. Audit Clerk, Deloitte Haskins & Sells, CA, 1951–54; Financial Dir/Co. Sec., H. Parrot & Co., Wine Importer, 1954–61; Dir of various subsids, C & A Modes, 1961–63; a Man. Dir, Samuel Montagu & Co. Ltd, 1963–78; Man. Dir/Chief Exec., Italian International Bank Plc, 1978–89. Dir, Alliance & Leicester Building Soc., 1990–. Mem., Review Panel, Financial Reporting Council, 1990–. Cavaliere Ufficiale, Order of Merit, Italian Republic, 1986. *Recreations:* reading, sailing, shooting. *Address:* The Old Manor House, Chilworth, Guildford, Surrey GU4 8NE. *T:* Guildford (0483) 61203.

BADEN-POWELL, family name of **Baron Baden-Powell.**

BADEN-POWELL, 3rd Baron, *cr* 1929, of Gilwell; **Robert Crause Baden-Powell;** Bt, *cr* 1922; Vice-President, Scout Association, since 1982; Chairman, Quarter Horse

Racing UK, since 1985; *b* 15 Oct. 1936; *s* of 2nd Baron and Carine Crause Baden-Powell (*née* Boardman); *S* father, 1962; *m* 1963, Patience Hélène Mary Batty (*see* Lady Baden-Powell). *Educ:* Bryanston (Blandford). Chief Scouts Comr, 1965–82; Pres., West Yorks Scout Council, 1972–88; Mem., 1965–, Mem. Cttee, 1972–78, Council, Scout Assoc. Mem. Council, British Quarter Horse Assoc., 1984–90 (Chm., 1990); Chm., Quarter Horse Racing UK, 1985–88. *Recreation:* breeding racing Quarter Horses. *Heir: b* Hon. David Michael Baden-Powell [*b* 11 Dec. 1940; *m* 1966, Joan Phillips, *d* of H. W. Berryman, Melbourne, Australia; three *s*]. *Address:* Grove Heath Farm, Ripley, Woking, Surrey GU23 6ES. *T:* Guildford (0483) 224262.

BADEN-POWELL, Lady; Patience Hélène Mary Baden-Powell, CBE 1986; Vice President, The Girl Guides Association, since 1990; President, Commonwealth Youth Exchange Council, 1982–86; *b* 27 Oct. 1936; *d* of Mr and Mrs D. M. Batty, Zimbabwe; *m* 1963, Baron Baden-Powell, *qv. Educ:* St Peter's Diocesan Sch., Bulawayo. Internat. Comr, 1975–79, Chief Comr, 1980–85, Girl Guides Assoc. Director: Laurentian Financial Gp, 1986–; Britannia Cable Systems Surrey; Fieldguard. President: Surrey Council for Voluntary Youth Services, 1986–; National Playbus Assoc.; Patron: Woodlarks Camp Site for the Disabled; Surrey Antiques Fair. *Address:* Grove Heath Farm, Ripley, Woking, Surrey GU23 6ES. *T:* Guildford (0483) 224262.

BADENOCH, (Ian) James (Forster); QC 1989; a Recorder, since 1987; *b* 24 July 1945; *s* of Sir John Badenoch, *qv*; *m* 1979, Marie-Thérèse Victoria Cabourn-Smith; two *s* one *d*. *Educ:* Dragon Sch., Oxford; Rugby Sch.; Magdalen Coll., Oxford (MA). Called to the Bar, Lincoln's Inn, 1968; Mem., Inner Temple. *Publication:* (contrib.) Medical Negligence, 1990. *Recreations:* family, tennis, garden, travel. *Address:* 1 Crown Office Row, Temple, EC4Y 7HH. *T:* 071–353 1801.

BADENOCH, Sir John, Kt 1984; DM; FRCP, FRCPE; Hans Sloane Fellow, Royal College of Physicians, 1985; Emeritus Fellow, Merton College, Oxford University, 1987; *b* 8 March 1920; *s* of William Minty Badenoch, MB, and Ann Dyer Badenoch (*née* Coutts); *m* 1944, Anne Newnham, *d* of Prof. Lancelot Forster; two *s* two *d*. *Educ:* Rugby Sch.; Oriel College, Oxford. MA; DM 1952; FRCP 1959; FRCPE 1982. Rockefeller Med. Studentship, Cornell Univ. Med. Coll., 1941. Res. Asst, Nuffield Dept of Clin. Medicine, Oxford, 1949–56; Dir, Clin. Studies, Univ. of Oxford, 1954–65; Consultant Phys., Oxfordshire HA, 1956–85; Univ. Lectr in Medicine, Univ. of Oxford, 1956–85. Former Mem., Board of Governors of United Oxford Hosps; Mem. Board, Oxford AHA(T), 1974–83; Mem., GMC, 1984–89. Royal College of Physicians: Pro-Censor and Censor, 1972–73; Sen. Censor and Sen. Vice-Pres., 1975–76; Goulstonian Lectr, 1960; Lumleian Lectr, 1977. Examiner in Medicine at various times for the Universities of: Oxford, Cambridge, Manchester, QUB and NUI. Member: Assoc. of Physicians of GB and Ireland; Med. Res. Soc.; British Soc. of Haematology; British Soc. of Gastroenterology. Liveryman, Soc. of Apothecaries. *Publications:* (ed jtly) Recent Advances in Gastroenterology, 1965, 2nd edn 1972; various papers in the field of gastroenterology and medicine. *Recreations:* reading, walking, natural history. *Address:* 21 Hartley Court, 84 Woodstock Road, Oxford OX2 7PF. *T:* Oxford (0865) 511311.

See also I. J. F. Badenoch.

BADGE, Peter Gilmour Noto; a Metropolitan Stipendiary Magistrate, since 1975; Chairman, Inner London Juvenile Panel, since 1979; a Recorder of the Crown Court, since 1980; *b* 20 Nov. 1931; *s* of late Ernest Desmond Badge, LDS and Marie Benson Badge (*née* Clough); *m* 1956, Mary Rose Noble; four *d*. *Educ:* Univ. of Liverpool (LLB). National Service, 1956–58: RNVR, lower deck and commnd; UK, ME and FE; RNR, 1958–62. Solicitor, 1956; Mem., Solicitor's Dept, New Scotland Yard, 1958–61; Asst Solicitor and later Partner, 1961–75, Kidd, Rapinet, Badge & Co.; Notary Public, Clerk to Justices, Petty Sessional Div. of Marlow, 1967–74; Sen. Solicitor to Comr and Detention Appeals Tribunal, NI, 1973–75. Member: Cttee on Criminal Law, Law Soc., 1971–79; Lord Chancellor's Adv. Cttee for Inner London; Magisterial Cttee, Judicial Studies Bd; Chm., Legal Cttee, Magistrates' Assoc., 1990–. Contested (L) Windsor and Maidenhead, 1964. *Publications:* articles on coracles. *Address:* Thames Magistrates' Court, 58 Bow Road, E3 4DJ.

BADGER, Sir Geoffrey Malcolm, Kt 1979; AO 1975; PhD, DSc; FRSC, FRACI, FACE, FTS, FAA; Chairman, Australian Science and Technology Council, 1977–82; *b* 10 Oct. 1916; *s* of J. McD. Badger; *m* 1941, Edith Maud, *d* of Henry Chevis. *Educ:* Geelong Coll.; Gordon Inst. of Technology; Univs of Melbourne, London (PhD), Glasgow (DSc). Instructor Lieut, RN, 1943–46. Finney-Howell Research Fellow, London, 1940–41; Research Chemist, ICI, 1941–43; Research Fellow, Glasgow, 1946–49. Univ. of Adelaide: Sen. Lectr, 1949–51; Reader, 1951–54; Prof. of Organic Chemistry, 1955–64, now Emeritus Professor; Dep. Vice-Chancellor, 1966–67; Vice-Chancellor, 1967–77; Res. Professor, 1977–79. Mem. Executive, CSIRO, 1964–65. President: Aust. Acad. of Science, 1974–78; Aust. and NZ Assoc. for Advancement of Science, 1979–80; Chm., Order of Australia Assoc., 1989–. DUniv Adelaide. *Publications:* Structures and Reactions of Aromatic Compounds, 1954; Chemistry of Heterocyclic Compounds, 1961; The Chemical Basis of Carcinogenic Activity, 1962; Aromatic Character and Aromaticity, 1969; (ed) Captain Cook, 1970; The Explorers of the Pacific, 1988; numerous papers in Jl Chem. Soc., etc. *Address:* 1 Anna Court, West Lakes, SA 5021, Australia. *T:* (08) 49–4594. *Club:* Adelaide (Adelaide).

BADHAM, Douglas George, CBE 1975; JP; HM Lord-Lieutenant for Mid Glamorgan, 1985–89; company director; Chairman, Hamell (West) Ltd, since 1968; *b* 1 Dec. 1914; *s* of late David Badham, JP; *m* 1939, Doreen Spencer Phillips; two *d*. *Educ:* Leys Sch., Cambridge. CA. Exec. Director: Powell Duffryn Gp, 1938–69; Pascoe Hldgs, 1983–88; Alignrite, 1984–87; T. H. Couch, 1984–88; World Trade Centre Wales, 1984–; Chairman: Powell Duffryn Wagon Co., 1965–85; T. T. Pascoe, 1983–89; Economic Forestry Gp PLC, 1981–88 (Dir, 1978–88). Chm., Nat. Health Service Staff Commn, 1972–75; Mem., 1978–84, Dep. Chm., 1980–84, Welsh Develt Agency. Member: Wales and the Marches Telecommunications Bd, 1973–80; British Gas Corp., 1974–83; Forestry Commn, S Wales Reg. Adv. Cttee, 1946–76 (Chm., 1973–76); Western Region Adv. Bd, BR, 1977–82; Welsh Council (Chm., Industry and Planning Panel), 1971–80; Nature Conservancy Council Adv. Cttee for Wales; Council, UWIST, 1975–80; Develt Corp. for Wales, 1965–83 (Chm., 1971–80). JP Glamorgan, 1962; DL, 1975–82, High Sheriff, 1976, Lieut, 1982, Mid Glamorgan. *Recreations:* forestry, trout breeding. *Address:* Swyn-y-Coed, Watford Road, Caerphilly, Mid Glamorgan CF8 1NE. *T:* Caerphilly (0222) 882094. *Club:* Cardiff and County (Cardiff).

BADHAM, Leonard; Vice Chairman, J. Lyons & Company Ltd, 1984–87; Director, Allied-Lyons PLC (formerly Allied Breweries), 1978–87; *b* 10 June 1923; *s* of John Randall Badham and Emily Louise Badham; *m* 1944, Joyce Rose Lowrie; two *d*. *Educ:* Wandsworth Grammar Sch. Commnd E Surrey Regt, 1943; Royal W Kent Regt, 5th Indian Div., 1944–46; SO II Stats, Burma Comd, 1946–47. J. Lyons & Co. Ltd: Management Trainee, 1939; Main Bd, 1965; Chief Comptroller, 1965; Tech. and Commercial Co-ordinator, 1967; Exec. Dir, Finance and Admin, 1970; Asst Gp Man. Dir, 1971; Dep. Gp Man. Dir, 1975; Man Dir, 1977. Gov., S Thames Coll., 1990–. FHCIMA; CBIM. *Recreations:* bridge, gardening. *Address:* 26 Vicarage Drive, East Sheen, SW14 8RX. *T:* 081–876 4373.

BADIAN, Ernst, FBA 1965; Professor of History, since 1971, John Moors Cabot Professor, since 1982, Harvard University; *b* 8 Aug. 1925; *s* of Joseph Badian and Sally (*née* Horinger), Vienna (later Christchurch, NZ); *m* 1950, Nathlie Anne (*née* Wimsett); one *s* one *d*. *Educ:* Christchurch Boys' High Sch.; Canterbury Univ. Coll., Christchurch, NZ; University Coll., Oxford (Hon. Fellow 1987). MA (1st cl. hons), NZ, 1946; LitD, Victoria, NZ, 1962. University of Oxford: Chancellor's Prize for Latin Prose, 1950; Craven Fellow, 1950; Conington Prize, 1959; BA (1st cl. hons Lit. Hum.) 1950; MA 1954; DPhil 1956. Asst Lectr in Classics, Victoria University Coll., Wellington, 1947–48; Rome Scholar in Classics, British Sch. at Rome, 1950–52; Asst Lectr in Classics and Ancient History, Univ. of Sheffield, 1952–54; Lectr in Classics, Univ. of Durham, 1954–65; Prof. of Ancient History, Univ. of Leeds, 1965–69; Prof. of Classics and History, State Univ. of NY at Buffalo, 1969–71. John Simon Guggenheim Fellow, 1985; Fellow, Nat. Humanities Center, 1988. Vis. Professor: Univs of Oregon, Washington and California (Los Angeles), 1961; Univ. of S Africa, 1965, 1973; Harvard, 1967; State Univ. of NY (Buffalo), 1967–68; Heidelberg, 1973; Univ. of California (Sather Prof.), 1976; Univ. of Colorado, 1978; Univ. of Tel-Aviv, 1981; Martin Classical Lectr, Oberlin Coll., 1978; lecturing visits to Australia, Canada, France, Germany, Holland, Israel, Italy, NZ, Rhodesia, Switzerland, and S Africa. Fellow: Amer. Acad. of Arts and Sciences, 1974; Amer. Numismatic Soc., 1987; Corresponding Member: Austrian Acad. of Scis, 1975; German Archaeol Inst., 1981; Foreign Mem., Finnish Acad. of Sci. and Letters, 1985. Hon. Mem., Soc. for Promotion of Roman Studies, 1983. Editor, Amer. Jl of Ancient History. *Publications:* Foreign Clientelae (264–70 BC), 1958; Studies in Greek and Roman History, 1964; (ed) Ancient Society and Institutions, 1966; Polybius (The Great Histories Series), 1966; Roman Imperialism in the Late Republic, 1967 (2nd edn 1968); Publicans and Sinners, 1972; (ed) Sir Ronald Syme, Roman Papers, Vols 1–2, 1979; contribs to collections, dictionaries and encyclopaedias and to classical and historical journals. *Recreations:* travelling, reading. *Address:* Department of History, Harvard University, Cambridge, Mass 02138, USA.

BAELZ, Very Rev. Peter Richard; Dean of Durham, 1980–88, Dean Emeritus since 1988; *b* 27 July 1923; 3rd *s* of Eberhard and Dora Baelz; *m* 1950, Anne Thelma Cleall-Harding; three *s*. *Educ:* Dulwich Coll.; Cambridge Univ. BA 1944, MA 1948, BD 1971; DD Oxon 1979. Asst Curate: Bournville, 1947–50; Sherborne, 1950–52; Asst Chap. Ripon Hall, Oxford, 1952–53; Rector of Wishaw, Birmingham, 1953–56; Vicar of Bournville, 1956–60; Fellow and Dean, Jesus Coll., Cambridge, 1960–72; University Lectr in Divinity, Cambridge, 1966–72; Canon of Christ Church and Regius Prof. of Moral and Pastoral Theology, Univ. of Oxford, 1972–79. Hulsean Lectr, 1965–66; Bampton Lectr, 1974. *Publications:* Prayer and Providence, 1968; Christian Theology and Metaphysics, 1968; The Forgotten Dream, 1975; Ethics and Belief, 1977; Does God Answer Prayer?, 1982; contributor to: Traditional Virtues Reassessed, 1964; Faith, Fact and Fantasy, 1964; The Phenomenon of Christian Belief, 1970; Christianity and Change, 1971; Christ, Faith and History, 1972; Is Christianity Credible?, 1981; God Incarnate: story and belief, 1981; By What Authority?, 1987; Embracing the Chaos, 1990; The Weight of Glory, 1991; edited and contributed to: Choices in Childlessness, 1982; Perspectives on Economics, 1984; Ministers of the Kingdom, 1985; Call to Order, 1989. *Recreations:* walking, motoring. *Address:* 36 Brynteg, Llandrindod Wells, Powys LD1 5NB. *T:* Llandrindod Wells (0597) 825404.

BAER, Jack Mervyn Frank; Managing Director, Hazlitt, Gooden & Fox, since 1973; *b* 29 Aug. 1924; *yr s* of late Frank and Alix Baer; *m* 1st, 1952, Jean St Clair (marr. diss. 1969; she *d* 1973), *o c* of late L. F. St Clair and Evelyn Synnott; one *d*; 2nd, 1970, Diana Downes Baillieu, *yr d* of Aubrey Clare Robinson and Mollie Panter-Downes, *qv*; two step *d*. *Educ:* Bryanston; Slade Sch. of Fine Art, University Coll., London. Served RAF (Combined Ops), 1942–46. Joined Hazlitt Gallery as Partner, 1948, Man. Dir, 1957, Chm. 1960–82. Chm., Fine Arts and Antiques Export Adv. Cttee to Dept of Trade, 1971–73 (Vice-Chm., 1969–71). Pres., Fine Art Provident Institution, 1972–75. Chm., Soc. of London Art Dealers, 1977–80 (Vice Chm. 1974–77). *Publications:* numerous exhibition catalogues; articles in various jls. *Recreation:* drawing. *Address:* 9 Phillimore Terrace, W8 6BJ. *T:* 071–937 6899. *Clubs:* Brooks's, Buck's, Beefsteak.

BAERLEIN, Richard Edgar; Racing Writer: The Observer, since 1963; The Guardian, since 1968; *b* 15 Sept. 1915; *s* of Edgar Baerlein and Dorothy Baerlein (*née* Dixon); *m* 1948, Lillian Laurette de Tankerville Chamberlain. *Educ:* Eton; Sidney Sussex Coll., Cambridge. Sporting Chronicle, 1936–39. Served RAF, Sqdn Ldr, 1940–47 (despatches). Racing writer, Evening Standard, 1947–57; started farm and stud, 1948; Racing Manager to Basil Mavrolem. *Publications:* Nijinsky, 1972; Shergar, 1983; Joe Mercer, 1987. *Recreations:* shooting, golf. *Address:* Shergar, 2nd Avenue, Summerley, Felpham, near Middleton-on-Sea, West Sussex PO22 7LJ. *Clubs:* Clermont; Sunningdale.

BAGGE, Sir (John) Jeremy (Picton), 7th Bt *cr* 1867, of Stradsett Hall, Norfolk; *b* 21 June 1945; *s* of Sir John Bagge, 6th Bt, ED, DL and of Elizabeth Helena, *d* of late Daniel James Davies, CBE; *S* father, 1990; *m* 1979, Sarah Margaret Phipps, *d* of late Maj. James Shelley Phipps Armstrong; two *s* one *d*. *Educ:* Eton. FCA 1968. *Heir: s* Alfred James John Bagge, *b* 1 July 1980. *Address:* Stradsett Hall, King's Lynn, Norfolk PE33 9HA.

BAGGLEY, Charles David Aubrey, CBE 1980; MA; Headmaster of Bolton School, 1966–83; *b* 1 Feb. 1923; *s* of A. C. and M. Baggley, Bradford, Yorks; *m* 1st, 1949, Marjorie Asquith Wood (marr. diss. 1983), *d* of M. H. Wood, Harrogate; one *s* one *d*; 2nd, 1983, Julia Hazel Yorke, *d* of S. Morris, Sonning-on-Thames. *Educ:* Bradford Grammar Sch.; King's Coll., Cambridge (1942 and 1945–47) (Exhibitioner in Classics, Scholar in History; Class I, Part II of Historical Tripos, 1947; BA 1947, MA 1952). Temp. Sub. Lieut, RNVR, 1942–45. History Master, Clifton Coll., 1947–50; Head of History Side, Dulwich Coll., 1950–57; Headmaster, King Edward VII Sch., Lytham, 1957–66. Chm., HMC, 1978. Schools Liaison Advr, Salford Univ., 1983–91. Mem., Bolton Civic Trust. Gov., Giggleswick School. *Recreations:* walking, gardening, reading. *Address:* Martin's Farm, Broadhead, Turton, Bolton, Lancs BL7 0JQ. *T:* Turton (0204) 852568.

BAGIER, Gordon Alexander Thomas; DL; *b* 7 July 1924; *m* 1949, Violet Sinclair; two *s* two *d*. *Educ:* Pendower Secondary Technical Sch., Newcastle upon Tyne. Signals Inspector, British Railways; Pres., Yorks District Council, NUR, 1962–64. Mem. of Keighley Borough Council, 1956–60; Mem. of Sowerby Bridge Urban Council, 1962–65. MP (Lab) Sunderland South, 1964–87. PPS to Home Secretary, 1968–69. Chm., Select Cttee on Transport, 1985–87. DL Tyne and Wear, 1988. *Recreation:* golf. *Address:* Rahana, Whickham Highway, Dunston, Gateshead, Tyne and Wear NE11 9QH. *Club:* Westerhope Golf (Newcastle upon Tyne).

BAGLIN, Richard John; Managing Director, New Businesses, Abbey National plc (formerly Abbey National Building Society), since 1988; *b* 30 Oct. 1942; *s* of F. W. and C. C. Baglin; *m* 1964, Anne Christine; one *d*. *Educ:* Preston Manor County Grammar Sch.; St John's Coll., Cambridge (MA). Various posts with Abbey National BS, 1964–:

Gen. Man., 1981–88; Dir, various subsidiaries, 1987–. *Recreations:* theatre, the arts. *Address:* Abbey House, Baker Street, NW1 6XL. *T:* 071–486 5555.

BAGNALL, Kenneth Reginald, QC 1973; QC (Hong Kong) 1983; Chairman, Brookfield House Estates plc, since 1989; *b* 26 Nov. 1927; *s* of Reginald and Elizabeth Bagnall; *m* 1st, 1955, Margaret Edith Wall; one *s* one *d*; 2nd, 1963, Rosemary Hearn; one *s* one *d*. *Educ:* King Edward VI Sch., Birmingham; Univ. of Birmingham. LLB (Hons). Yardley Scholar. Served Royal Air Force; Pilot Officer, 1947, Flt Lt, 1948. Called to the Bar, Gray's Inn, 1950; a Dep. Judge of Crown Court, 1975–83. Co-founder, 1980, Chm., 1980–82, and Life Govr, 1983, Anglo-American Real Property Inst. Mem., Crafts Council, 1982–85; Co-founder, Bagnall Gall., Crafts Council, 1982. Co-founder, Residential Recovery Co., I of M, 1990–; Chm., New Law Publishing Co., 1991–. Mem., Inst. of Dirs. Freeman, City and Corp. of London, 1972; Freeman and Liveryman, Barber-Surgeons' Co., 1972. Chm. Editl Bd, New Property Cases, 1986–. *Publications:* Guide to Business Tenancies, 1956; Atkins Court Forms and Precedents (Town Planning), 1973; (with K. Lewison) Development Land Tax, 1978; Judicial Review, 1985. *Recreations:* yachting, motoring, travel. *Address:* Brookfield House, Wentworth, Surrey GU25 4JZ. *Clubs:* Carlton, 1900.

BAGNALL, Field Marshal Sir Nigel (Thomas), GCB 1985 (KCB 1981); CVO 1978; MC 1950 and Bar 1953; Chief of the General Staff, 1985–88; *b* 10 Feb. 1927; *s* of Lt-Col Harry Stephen Bagnall and Marjory May Bagnall; *m* 1959, Anna Caroline Church; two *d*. *Educ:* Wellington Coll. Joined Army, 1945; commnd Green Howards, 1946; Palestine, 1946–48, 6th Airborne Div.; Malaya, 1949–53, Green Howards; GSO1 (Intell.), Dir of Borneo Ops, 1966–67; comd 4/7 Royal Dragoon Guards, NI and BAOR, 1967–69; Sen. Directing Staff (Army), Jt Services Staff Coll., 1970; comd Royal Armoured Corps HQ 1 (Br.) Corps, 1970–72; Defence Fellow, Balliol Coll., Oxford, 1972–73; Sec., Chief of Staff Cttee, 1973–75; GOC 4th Div., 1975–77; ACDS (Policy), MoD, 1978–80; Comdr, 1 (Br.) Corps, 1980–83; C-in-C BAOR and Comdr, Northern Army Gp, 1983–85. Col Comdt, APTC, 1981–88, RAC, 1985–88; ADC Gen. to the Queen, 1985–88. Hon. Fellow, Balliol Coll., Oxford, 1986. *Publication:* The Punic Wars, 1991. *Recreations:* writing, reading, gardening. *Address:* c/o Royal Bank of Scotland, Kirkland House, SW1.

BAGNALL, Richard Maurice, MBE 1945; Deputy Chairman, Tube Investments Ltd, 1976–81, Managing Director, 1974–81, Director, 1969–81; *b* 20 Nov. 1917; *s* of late Francis Edward Bagnall, OBE and Edith Bagnall; *m* 1946, Irene Pickford; one *s* one *d*. *Educ:* Repton. Served War, 1939–45: RA, Shropshire Yeomanry, 1939–43 (despatches); Bde Major, 6 AGRA Italy, 1943–45. Joined Tube Investments Ltd, 1937. Chm., Round Oak Steel Works Ltd, 1976–81 (Dir, 1974–81). Governor, King's Sch., Worcester, 1977–81. Bronze Star, USA, 1945. *Recreations:* golf, gardening, photography. *Address:* Vila da Chypre, Carvoeiro, 8400 Lagoa, Algarve, Portugal. *Club:* MCC.

BAGOT, family name of **Baron Bagot.**

BAGOT, 9th Baron *cr* 1780; **Heneage Charles Bagot;** Bt 1627; *b* 11 June 1914; *s* of Charles Frederick Heneage Bagot (*d* 1939) (4th *s* of *g s* of 1st Baron) and of Alice Lorina, *d* of Thomas Farr; *S* half-brother, 1979; *m* 1939, Muriel Patricia Moore, *y d* of late Maxwell James Moore Boyle; one *s* one *d*. *Educ:* Harrow. Formerly Major, QEO 6th Gurkha Rifles. *Recreations:* shooting, skiing, sailing. *Heir: s* Hon. Charles Hugh Shaun Bagot [*b* 23 Feb. 1944; *m* 1986, Mrs Sally A. Stone, *d* of D. G. Blunden]. *Address:* Llithfaen, near Pwllheli, Gwynedd; 16 Barclay Road, SW6. *Clubs:* Alpine Ski; Himalayan.

BAGSHAWE, Prof. Kenneth Dawson, CBE 1990; MD; FRCP; FRCR; FRS 1989; Professor of Medical Oncology in the University of London at Charing Cross and Westminster Medical School (formerly Charing Cross Hospital Medical School), 1974–90, now Emeritus; Consultant Physician, Charing Cross Hospital, since 1961; *b* 17 Aug. 1925; *s* of Harry Bagshawe and Gladys (*née* Dawson); *m* 1st, 1946, Ann Kelly; one *s* one *d*; 2nd, 1977, Sylvia Dorothy Lawler (*née* Corben). *Educ:* Harrow County Sch.; London Sch. of Econs and Pol Science; St Mary's Hosp. Med. Sch. (MB, BS 1952; MD 1964). FRCP 1969; FRCR 1983; FRCOG *ad eundem* 1978. Served RN, 1942–46. Fellow, Johns Hopkins Univ., Baltimore, USA, 1955–56; Sen. Registrar, St Mary's Hosp., 1956–60. Visiting Professor: Down State Univ., NY, 1977; Univ. of Hong Kong, 1982. Chm., DHSS Wkg Gp on Acute Cancer Services, 1980–84. Cancer Research Campaign: Chm., Scientific Cttee, 1983–85; Chm., Exec. Cttee, 1988–90; Vice Chm. Bd, 1988–. Hon. DSc Bradford, 1990. *Publications:* Choriocarcinoma, 1969; Medical Oncology, 1975; 300 papers on cancer chemotherapy, tumour markers, drug targeting, etc. *Recreations:* (passive) music, art; (active) demolition, conservation. *Address:* 115 George Street, W1H 5TA. *T:* 071–262 6033, (office) 081–846 7517. *Club:* Athenæum.

BAILES, Alyson Judith Kirtley; HM Diplomatic Service; Consul-General and Deputy Head of Mission, Oslo, since 1990; *b* 6 April 1949; *d* of John-Lloyd Bailes and Barbara (*née* Martin). *Educ:* Belvedere Sch., Liverpool; Somerville Coll., Oxford (MA Modern Hist.). Entered Diplomatic Service, 1969; Budapest, 1970–74; UK Delgn to NATO, 1974–76; FCO, 1976–78; Asst to EC 'Cttee of Wise Men' (which reported on ways of improving functioning of EC instns), 1979; on loan to MoD, 1979–81; Bonn, 1981–84; Dep. Head of Planning Staff, FCO, 1984–86; Counsellor, Peking, 1987–89; on attachment to RIIA, 1990. *Recreations:* music, nature, travel. *Address:* c/o Foreign and Commonwealth Office, SW1A 2AF. *T:* (home) 071–373 1259.

BAILEY, family name of **Baron Glanusk.**

BAILEY, Sir Alan (Marshall), KCB 1986 (CB 1982); Permanent Secretary, Department of Transport, 1986–91; *b* 26 June 1931; *s* of John Marshall Bailey and Muriel May Bailey; *m* 1st, 1959, Stella Mary Scott (marr. diss. 1981); three *s*; 2nd, 1981, Shirley Jane Barrett. *Educ:* Bedford Sch.; St John's and Merton Colls, Oxford (MA, BPhil). Harmsworth Senior Scholarship, 1954; Harkness Commonwealth Fellowship, USA, 1963–64. Principal Private Sec. to Chancellor of the Exchequer, 1971–73; Under-Sec., HM Treasury, 1973–78, Dep. Sec., 1978–83 (Central Policy Review Staff, Cabinet Office, 1981–82), 2nd Perm. Sec., 1983–85. *Address:* 11 Park Row, SE10 9NG. *T:* 081–858 3015.

BAILEY, Prof. Allen Jackson, FRSC; Professor of Biochemistry, University of Bristol, 1980 and since 1991; *b* 31 Jan. 1931; *s* of late Horace Jackson Bailey and Mabel Bailey (*née* Young); *m* 1956, Beryl Lee; twin *s* two *d*. *Educ:* Eccles Grammar Sch. BSc London (Chem.) 1954; MSc (Physics) 1958, PhD (Chem.) 1960, Birmingham; MA 1967, ScD 1973, Cambridge. FIFST. Shell Chemicals, 1954–57; Low Temp. Res. Station, Univ. of Cambridge, 1960–67; Harkness Fellow, Commonwealth Fund, Biol. Dept, CIT, 1963–65; joined AFRC Meat Res. Inst., Bristol, 1967: SPSO (Special Merit), 1972; Head of Biochem. Dept, 1977–79; Director (DCSO), 1979–85; Hd of Lab., AFRC Inst. of Food Res., Bristol, 1985–90. Scott Robertson Meml Lectr, QUB, 1986; Proctor Meml Lectr, Leeds, 1991. Hon. Fellow, British Connective Tissue Soc. Senior Medal Food Science, RSC, 1987; Internat. Lectureship Award, Amer. Meat Sci. Assoc., 1989. Mem. Editl Bds, sci. jls. *Publications:* Recent Advances in Meat Science, 1985; Collagen as a Food, 1987; Connective Tissue in Meat and Meat Products, 1989; sci. papers in learned jls. *Recreations:* travel, photography. *Address:* Seasons, Bridgwater Road, Winscombe, Avon BS25 1NA. *T:* Winscombe (093484) 3447. *Club:* Farmers'.

BAILEY, Sir Brian (Harry), Kt 1983; OBE 1976; JP; DL; Chairman, Television South West Ltd, since 1980; Deputy Chairman, Channel Four Television, since 1989 (Director, since 1985); Director, Oracle Teletext Ltd, since 1983; *b* 25 March 1923; *s* of Harry Bailey and Lilian (*née* Pulfer); *m* 1948, Nina Olive Sylvia (*née* Saunders); two *d*. *Educ:* Lowestoft Grammar Sch. RAF, 1941–45. SW Dist Organisation Officer, NALGO, 1951–82; South Western Reg. Sec., TUC, 1968–81. Chairman: South Western RHA, 1975–82; Health Educn Council, 1983–87; Health Educn Authority, 1987–89; Member: Somerset CC, 1966–84; SW Econ. Planning Council, 1969–79; Central Health Services Council, 1978–80; MRC, 1978–86; Adv. Cttee on Severn Barrage, Dept of Energy, 1978–81; Business Educn Council, 1980–84; NHS Management Inquiry Team, 1983–84. Chm. Council, Indep. Television Assoc., 1991–; Vice-Chm., BBC Radio Bristol Adv. Council, 1971–78; Member: BBC West Reg. Adv. Council, 1973–78; Council, ITCA, 1982–86; South and West Adv. Bd, Legal and General Assurance Soc. Ltd, 1985–87. Director: Independent Television Publications Ltd, 1985–90; Western Orchestral Soc. Ltd, 1982–. SW Regl Pres., MENCAP, 1984–90; Nat. Pres., Hosp. Caterers Assoc., 1987–. Trustee, EEC Chamber Orchestra, 1987–. Gen. Governor, British Nutrition Foundn, 1987–. JP Somerset, 1964 (Chm., Taunton Deane Magistrates Bench, 1987–); DL Somerset, 1988. *Recreations:* football, cricket and tennis (watching), music, fishing and golf (playing). *Address:* Runnerstones, 32 Stonegallows, Taunton, Somerset TA1 5JP. *T:* Taunton (0823) 461265. *Club:* Enmore Park Golf.

BAILEY, D(avid) R(oy) Shackleton, LittD; FBA 1958; Pope Professor of the Latin Language and Literature, Harvard University, 1982–88, now Emeritus; *b* 10 Dec. 1917; *y s* of late Rev. J. H. Shackleton Bailey, DD, and Rosamund Maud (*née* Giles); *m* 1967, Hilary Ann (marr. diss. 1974), *d* of Leonard Sidney and Margery Bardwell. *Educ:* Lancaster Royal Grammar Sch.; Gonville and Caius Coll., Cambridge. Fellow of Gonville and Caius Coll., 1944–55, Praelector, 1954–55; Fellow and Dir of Studies in Classics, Jesus Coll., Cambridge, 1955–64; Visiting Lecturer in Classics, Harvard Coll., 1963; Fellow and Dep. Bursar, Gonville and Caius Coll., 1964; Senior Bursar 1965–68; Univ. Lectr in Tibetan, 1948–68; Prof. of Latin, Univ. of Michigan, 1968–74; Prof. of Greek and Latin, Harvard Univ., 1975–82. Andrew V. V. Raymond Vis. Prof., State Univ. of NY at Buffalo, 1973–74; Vis. Fellow of Peterhouse, Cambridge, 1980–81; Nat. Endowment of Humanities Fellowship, 1980–81. Mem., Amer. Philosophical Soc., 1977. Fellow, Amer. Acad. of Arts and Sciences, 1979. Editor, Harvard Studies in Classical Philology, 1978–84. Hon. LittD Dublin, 1984. Charles J. Goodwin Award of Merit, Amer. Philol Assoc., 1978; Kenyon Medal, British Acad., 1985. *Publications:* The Śatapañcāśatka of Mātrceta, 1951; Propertiana, 1956; Towards a Text of Cicero, *ad Atticum*, 1960; Ciceronis Epistulae ad Atticum IX-XVI, 1961; Cicero's Letters to Atticus, Vols I and II, 1965; Vol. V, 1966, Vol. VI, 1967, Vols III and IV, 1968, Vol. VII, 1970; Cicero, 1971; Two Studies in Roman Nomenclature, 1976; Cicero: *Epistulae ad Familiares*, 2 vols, 1977; (trans.) Cicero's Letters to Atticus, 1978; (trans.) Cicero's Letters to his Friends, 2 Vols, 1978; Towards a Text of *Anthologia Latina*, 1979; Selected Letters of Cicero, 1980; Cicero: *Epistulae ad Q. Fratrem et M. Brutum*, 1981; Profile of Horace, 1982; Anthologia Latina, I.1, 1982; Horatius, 1985; Cicero: Philippics, 1986; (trans.) Cicero, Selected Letters, 1986; Ciceronis Epistulae, 4 vols, 1987–88; Lucanus, 1988; Onomasticon to Cicero's speeches, 1988; Quintilianus: *Declamationes minores*, 1989; Martialis, 1990; Back from Exile, 1991; articles in Classical and Orientalist periodicals. *Recreation:* cats. *Address:* 303 North Division, Ann Arbor, Michigan 48104, USA.

BAILEY, David, FRPS, FCSD; photographer, film director; *b* 2 Jan. 1938; *s* of William Bailey and Agnes (*née* Green); *m* 1st, 1960, Rosemary Bramble; 2nd, 1967, Catherine Deneuve, *qv*; 3rd, 1975, Marie Helvin (marr. diss. 1985); 4th, 1986, Catherine Dyer; one *s* one *d*. *Educ:* self taught. FRPS 1972; FSIAD 1975. Photographer for Vogue, 1959–; Dir of television commercials, 1966–, Dir of documentaries, 1968–. Exhibitions: Nat. Portrait Gall., 1971; one-man retrospective, V&A, 1983; Internat. Centre of Photograph, NY, 1984; Photographs from the Sudan, ICA and tour, 1985; Bailey Now!, Nat. Centre of Photography, Bath, 1989. *Publications:* Box of Pinups, 1964; Goodbye Baby and Amen, 1969; Warhol, 1974; Beady Minces, 1974; Papua New Guinea, 1975; Mixed Moments, 1976; Trouble and Strife, 1980; David Bailey's London NW1, 1982; Black and White Memories, 1983; Nudes 1981–84, 1984; Imagine, 1985; If We Shadows, 1991. *Recreations:* aviculture, photography, travelling, painting. *Address:* 24–26 Brownlow Mews, WC1N 2LA.

BAILEY, Dennis, RDI 1980; ARCA; graphic designer and illustrator; Partner, Bailey and Kenny; *b* 20 Jan. 1931; *s* of Leonard Charles Bailey and Ethel Louise Funnell; *m* 1985, Nicola Anne Roberts; one *s* one *d*. *Educ:* West Tarring Sec. Mod. Sch.; West Sussex Sch. of Art, Worthing; Royal College of Art. Asst Editor, Graphis magazine, Zürich, 1956; free-lance graphic design and illustrator, London, 1957–60; Vis. Lectr in Typography, Central Sch. of Art, 1959–60; worked on film projects, advertising and art direction, Paris, 1961–64; Art Dir, Town magazine, London, 1964–66; Lectr in graphic design, Chelsea Sch. of Art, 1970–81, Middlesex Polytechnic, 1985–89. *Clients and work include:* Economist Newspaper: covers and typographic advisor; Economist Publications: The World in 1989, 1990, 1991 and 1992; Architectural Assoc.: art dir of magazine AA Files; Arts Council of GB: design of exhibn catalogues and posters for Dada and Surrealism Reviewed, 1978, Picasso's Picassos, 1981, Renoir, 1985, Torres-Garcia, 1985, Le Corbusier, 1987; Royal Academy: catalogue and graphics for Pompeii AD 79, 1977, graphics and publicity for The Genius of Venice, 1984, Inigo Jones, 1989, Frans Hals, 1990, Egon Schiele, 1990; Imperial War Museum: graphics for Cabinet War Rooms, Whitehall, 1984; RSA: housestyle, 1989; A. d'Offay Gallery: catalogues and housestyle, 1990–91; design of business print for Cons. Gold Fields, Ultramar, London Merchant Securities and N. M. Rothschild & Sons. Illustrations for The Economist, Esquire, Harpers Bazaar (USA), Harpers and Queen, Illustrated London News, Listener, Nova, Observer, Olympia (Paris), Town; book jackets for Jonathan Cape, Penguin Books and Anglo-German Foundn. *Address:* Cunningham Place, NW8. *T:* (studio) 071–377 5483.

BAILEY, Sir Derrick Thomas Louis, 3rd Bt, *cr* 1919; DFC; *b* 15 Aug. 1918; 2nd *s* of Sir Abe Bailey, 1st Bt, KCMG; *S* half-brother, 1946; *m* 1st, 1946, Katharine Nancy Stormonth Darling; four *s* one *d*; 2nd, 1980, Mrs Jean Roscoe. *Educ:* Winchester. Engaged in farming. *Recreations:* all sports, all games. *Heir: s* John Richard Bailey [*b* 11 June 1947; *m* 1977, Jane, *o d* of John Pearson Gregory; two *s* one *d*]. *Address:* Lappingford, Worminghall, Aylesbury, Bucks; Bluestones, Alderney, CI. *Club:* Rand (Johannesburg).

BAILEY, His Honour Desmond Patrick; a Circuit Judge (formerly Judge of County Courts), 1965–79; *b* 6 May 1907; 3rd *s* of Alfred John Bailey, Bowdon, Cheshire, and of Ethel Ellis Johnson; unmarried. *Educ:* Brighton Coll.; Queens' Coll., Cambridge (BA, LLB). Called to Bar, Inner Temple, 1931. Northern Circuit. Served War of 1939–45: Rifle Brigade, Lancashire Fusiliers, Special Operations Executive, North Africa, Italy (Major). Recorder of Carlisle, 1963–65. *Address:* c/o Davies Wallis Foyster, 37 Peter Street, Manchester M2 5GB.

BAILEY, Air Vice-Marshal Dudley Graham, CB 1979; CBE 1970; Deputy Managing Director, Services Sound and Vision (formerly Services Kinema Corporation), since 1980; *b* 12 Sept. 1924; *s* of P. J. Bailey and D. M. Bailey (*née* Taylor); *m* 1948, Dorothy Barbara

Lovelace-Hunt; two *d*. Pilot trng, Canada, 1943–45; Intell. Officer, Air HQ Italy, 1946–47 and HQ 23 Gp, 1948–49; Berlin Airlift, 1949; Flt Comdr No 50 and 61 Sqdns, Lincolns, 1950–52; exchange duties, USAF, B-36 aircraft, 1952–54; Canberra Sqdn: Flt Comdr, 1955; Sqdn Comdr, 1956; Air Min., 1956–58; Army Staff Coll., Camberley, 1959; OC No 57 (Victor) Sqdn, 1960–62; Air Warfare course, Manby, 1962; Wing Comdr Ops, HQ Air Forces Middle East, 1963–65; MoD Central Staffs, 1965–66; MoD (Air) Directorate of Air Staff Plans, 1966–68; OC RAF Wildenrath, 1968–70; Sen. Personnel Staff Officer, HQ Strike Comd, 1970–71; Royal Coll. of Defence Studies, 1972; Dir of Personnel (Air), RAF, 1972–74; SASO, RAF Germany, 1974–75; Dep. Comdr, RAF Germany, 1975–76; Dir Gen., Personal Services (RAF), MoD, 1976–80, retired. *Address:* Firs Corner, Abbotswood, Speen, Bucks HP17 0SR. *T:* High Wycombe (0494) 488462. *Club:* Royal Air Force.

BAILEY, Eric; Director, Plymouth Polytechnic, 1970–74, retired; *b* 2 Nov. 1913; *s* of Enoch Whittaker Bailey, Overton Hall, Sandbach, Cheshire; *m* 1942, Dorothy Margaret Laing, Stockport; one *s* one *d*. *Educ:* King's Sch., Macclesfield; Manchester Univ. BSc Hons; CEng, FRIC, MIChemE; DipEd. Lectr, Stockport Coll. of Technology, 1936–41; Industrial Chemist, 1941–45; Lectr, Enfield Coll. of Technology, 1945–46; Vice-Principal, Technical Coll., Worksop, 1946–51; Principal: Walker Technical Coll., Oakengates, Salop, 1951–59; Plymouth Coll. of Technology, 1959–69. *Recreations:* putting colour into gardens, photography, pursuing leisure and voluntary activities. *Address:* 3 St Bridget Avenue, Crownhill, Plymouth, Devon PL6 5BB. *T:* Plymouth (0752) 771426. *Club:* Rotary (Plymouth).

BAILEY, Harold, CMG 1960; Under-Secretary, Department of Trade and Industry, 1970–74, retired; *b* 26 Feb. 1914; *yr s* of late John Bailey and Elizabeth Watson, Preston, Lancashire; *m* 1946, Rosemary Margaret, *d* of Harold and Irene Brown, Shotesham St Mary, Norfolk; two *s* one *d*. *Educ:* Preston Grammar Sch.; Christ Church, Oxford. Asst Principal Air Ministry, 1937; Principal, Min. of Aircraft Production, 1942; Served, Royal Air Force, 1942–45; Private Sec. to Minister of Supply and Aircraft Production, 1945–47; Asst Sec., 1947; Min. of Supply Rep. and Adviser (Defence Supplies) to UK High Comr, Ottawa, 1953–55; Under-Secretary: Ministry of Supply, 1957; BoT, 1958; British Senior Trade Comr in India, and Economic Adviser to the British High Comr, 1958–63. *Address:* Hollies, Hurstbourne Tarrant, Hants. *T:* Hurstbourne Tarrant (026476) 482.

BAILEY, Sir Harold (Walter), Kt 1960; FBA 1944; MA, W Aust.; MA, DPhil Oxon; Professor of Sanskrit, Cambridge Univ., 1936–67, Professor Emeritus, 1967; *b* Devizes, Wilts, 16 Dec. 1899. Was Lecturer in Iranian Studies at Sch. of Oriental Studies. Member of: Danish Academy, 1946; Norwegian Academy, 1947; Kungl. Vitterhets Historie och Antikvitets Akademien, Stockholm, 1948; Governing Body, SOAS, Univ. of London, 1946–70; L'Institut de France, Associé étranger, Académie des Inscriptions et Belles-Lettres, 1968. President: Philological Soc., 1948–52; Royal Asiatic Society, 1964–67 (Gold Medal, RAS, 1972); Soc. for Afghan Studies, 1972–79; Soc. of Mithraic Studies (1971), 1975–; Council, Corpus inscriptionum iranicarum, 1985–; Chm., Anglo-Mongolian Soc., 1979–81. Chm., Ancient India and Iran Trust, 1978–. FAHA 1971; Hon. Fellow: SOAS, London Univ., 1963–; Queens' Coll., Cambridge, 1967; St Catherine's Coll., Oxford, 1976. Hon. Mem., Bhandarkar Oriental Res. Inst., Poona, 1968. Hon. DLitt: W Aust., 1963; ANU, 1970; Oxon, 1976; Hon. DD Manchester, 1979. *Publications:* in Bulletin of Sch. of Oriental Studies, Journal of Royal Asiatic Soc., Zeitschrift der Deutschen Morgenländischen Gesellschaft, etc. Codices Khotanenses, 1938; Zoroastrian Problems in the Ninth Century Books, 1943, 2nd edn 1971; Khotanese Texts I, 1945; Khotanese Buddhist Texts, 1951; Indoscythian Studies, Khotanese Texts II, 1953; III, 1956; IV, 1961; V, 1963; VI, 1967; VII, 1985; Corpus inscriptionum iranicarum, Saka Documents, Portfolios I-IV, 1960–67; Saka Documents, text volume, 1968; Dictionary of Khotan Saka, 1979; Bibliotheka Persica: the culture of the Sakas in ancient Iranian Khotan, 1982. *Address:* Queens' College, Cambridge.

BAILEY, Jack Arthur; Secretary, MCC, 1974–87; Secretary, International Cricket Conference, 1974–87; *b* 22 June 1930; *s* of Horace Arthur and Elsie Winifred Bailey; *m* 1957, Julianne Mary Squier; one *s* two *d*. *Educ:* Christ's Hospital; University Coll., Oxford (BA). Asst Master, Bedford Sch., 1958–60; Reed Paper Group, 1960–67; Rugby Football Correspondent, Sunday Telegraph, 1962–74; Asst Sec., MCC, 1967–74. Regular contributor to The Times, 1987–. *Publication:* Conflicts in Cricket, 1989. *Recreations:* cricket (played for Essex and for Oxford Univ.), golf. *Address:* 32 Elgin Mansions, Elgin Avenue, W9 1JG. *T:* 071–289 5186. *Clubs:* Wig and Pen, MCC; Vincent's (Oxford).

BAILEY, John; *see* Bailey, W. J. J.

BAILEY, Sir John Bilsland, KCB 1987 (CB 1982); HM Procurator General and Treasury Solicitor, 1984–88; *b* 5 Nov. 1928; *o s* of late Walter Bailey and Ethel Edith Bailey, FRAM (who *m* 2nd, Sir Thomas George Spencer); *m* 1952, Marion Rosemary (*née* Carroll); two *s* one *d*. *Educ:* Eltham Coll.; University Coll., London (LLB). Solicitor of Supreme Court. Legal Asst, Office of HM Treasury Solicitor, 1957; Sen. Legal Asst, 1962; Asst Treasury Solicitor, 1971; Principal Asst Treasury Solicitor, 1973; Under-Sec. (Legal), Dept of HM Procurator General and Treasury Solicitor, 1973–77; Legal Dir, Office of Fair Trading, 1977–79; Dep. Treasury Solicitor, 1979–84. Chief Adjudicator, Cttee for Supervision of Standards of Telephone Inf. Services, 1989–. Gov., Anglo-European Coll. of Chiropractic, 1990–. *Recreations:* walking, reading, listening to music. *Club:* Reform.

BAILEY, John Everett Creighton, CBE 1947; Executive Chairman, Difco Laboratories (UK) Ltd, 1970–75; Chairman and Managing Director, Baird & Tatlock Group of Cos, 1941–69; *b* 2 Nov. 1905; *s* of late John Edred Bailey and late Violet Constance Masters; *m* 1928, Hilda Anne Jones (*d* 1982); one *s* four *d*. *Educ:* Brentwood Sch. Peat Marwick Mitchell & Co., 1925–31; Director: Derbyshire Stone Ltd, 1959–69; Tarmac Derby Ltd, 1969–70; G. D. Searle & Co., 1969–70, and other companies. Mem., Admlty Chemical Adv. Panel, 1940–50; Pres. Scientific Instrument Manufacturers Assoc., 1945–50; Chm. Brit. Laboratory Ware Assoc., 1950–52, Pres., 1974–83; Chm. Brit. Sci. Instr. Research Assoc., 1952–64 (Pres. 1964–71), first Companion, SIRA Inst.; Mem., Grand Council FBI, 1945–58; Mem. BoT Exhibns Adv. Cttee, 1957–65, and Census of Production Adv. Cttee, 1960–68. Formerly Special Member, Prices and Incomes Board. Master, 1957–58 and 1974–75, Worshipful Co. of Scientific Instrument Makers; Master, Worshipful Co. of Needlemakers, 1981–83; Freeman of City of London. Fellow, Inst. of Export; MRI; CBIM. *Recreation:* golf. *Address:* Wayford Manor, Wayford, Crewkerne, Somerset TA18 8QG. *Club:* Athenæum.

BAILEY, Ven. Jonathan Sansbury; Archdeacon of Southend, since 1982; Bishop's Officer for Industry and Commerce, diocese of Chelmsford, since 1982; *b* 24 Feb. 1940; *s* of Walter Eric and Audrey Sansbury Bailey; *m* 1965, Susan Mary Bennett-Jones; three *s*. *Educ:* Quarry Bank High School, Liverpool; Trinity College, Cambridge (MA). Assistant Curate: Sutton, St Helens, Lancs, 1965–68; St Paul, Warrington, 1968–71; Warden, Marrick Priory, 1971–76; Vicar of Wetherby, Yorks, 1976–82. *Address:* 136 Broomfield Road, Chelmsford, Essex CM1 1RN. *T:* Chelmsford (0245) 258257, *Fax:* Chelmsford (0245) 250845.

BAILEY, Norman Stanley, CBE 1977; operatic and concert baritone; *b* Birmingham, 23 March 1933; *s* of late Stanley and Agnes Bailey; *m* 1st, 1957, Doreen Simpson (marr. diss. 1983); two *s* one *d*; 2nd, 1985, Kristine Ciesinski. *Educ:* Rhodes Univ., S Africa; Vienna State Academy. BMus; Performer's and Teacher's Licentiate in Singing; Diplomas, opera, lieder, oratorio. Principal baritone, Sadler's Wells Opera, 1967–71; regular engagements at world's major opera houses and festivals, including: La Scala, Milan; Royal Opera House, Covent Garden; Bayreuth Wagner Festival (first British Hans Sachs in Meistersinger, 1969); Vienna State Opera (first British Wanderer in Siegfried, 1976); Metropolitan Opera, NY; Paris Opera; Edinburgh Festival; Hamburg State Opera; Munich State Opera. BBC Television performances in Falstaff, La Traviata, The Flying Dutchman, Macbeth. Recordings include The Ring (Goodall); Meistersinger and Der Fliegende Holländer (Solti); Walküre (Klemperer), among others. Hon. RAM, 1981; Hon. DMus, Rhodes, 1986. *Recreations:* Mem., Baha'i world community; chess, notaphily, golf, microcomputing. *Address:* c/o Music International, 13 Ardilaun Road, Highbury, N5 2QR.

BAILEY, Patrick Edward Robert; Director, Dan-Air Associated Services, since 1985; *b* 16 Feb. 1925; *s* of late Edward Bailey and Mary Elizabeth Bailey; *m* 1947, Rowena Evelyn Nichols; two *s* three *d*. *Educ:* Clapham Coll.; St Joseph's Coll., Mark Cross; LSE. BSc(Econ). MIPM; FCIT 1971 (Mem. Council, 1982–85 and 1987–89). RAPC and RAEC (Captain), 1943–48; Labour Management, Min. of Supply and Army Department: ROF Glascoed, 1951–54; RAE Farnborough, 1954–58; RSAF Enfield, 1958–59; ROF Radway Green, 1959–61; ROFs Woolwich, 1961–66. British Airports Authority: Dep. Personnel Dir, 1966; Personnel Dir, 1970; Airport Services Dir, 1974; Dir, Gatwick and Stansted Airports, 1977–85. Chm. Trustees, British Airports Authority Superannuation Scheme, 1975–86. Mem., Air Transport and Travel Industry Trng Bd, 1971–76; Mem. Bd, Internat. Civil Airports Assoc., 1974–77. Mem., Mid-Sussex DC, 1986–. *Address:* 17 Lucastes Lane, Haywards Heath, W Sussex RH16 1LE.

BAILEY, Paul, (christened **Peter Harry**); freelance writer, since 1967; radio broadcaster; *b* 16 Feb. 1937; *s* of Arthur Oswald Bailey and Helen Maud Burgess. *Educ:* Sir Walter St John's Sch., London; Central School of Speech and Drama. Actor, 1956–64: appeared in first productions of Ann Jellicoe's The Sport of My Mad Mother, 1958, and John Osborne's and Anthony Creighton's Epitaph for George Dillon, 1958. Literary Fellow at Univ. of Newcastle and Univ. of Durham, 1972–74; Bicentennial Fellowship, 1976; Visiting Lectr in English Literature, North Dakota State Univ., 1977–79. Frequent radio broadcaster, mainly on Radio 3; has written and presented programmes on Karen Blixen, Henry Green, I. B. Singer and Primo Levi, among others. FRSL, 1982–84. E. M. Forster Award, 1974; George Orwell Meml Prize, 1978, for broadcast essay The Limitations of Despair. *Publications:* At the Jerusalem, 1967 (Somerset Maugham Award, 1968; Arts Council Prize, 1968); Trespasses, 1970; A Distant Likeness, 1973; Peter Smart's Confessions, 1977; Old Soldiers, 1980; An English Madam, 1982; Gabriel's Lament, 1986; An Immaculate Mistake: scenes from childhood and beyond (autobiog.), 1990; Hearth and Home, 1990; contribs to Observer, TLS, Daily Telegraph. *Recreations:* visiting churches, opera, watching tennis. *Address:* 79 Davisville Road, W12 9SH. *T:* 081–749 2279.

BAILEY, Reginald Bertram, CBE 1976; Member, Employers' Panel, Industrial Tribunals in England and Wales, 1977–85; *b* 15 July 1916; *s* of late George Bertram Bailey and Elizabeth Bailey, Ilford; *m* 1942, Phyllis Joan Firman; one *s* one *d*. *Educ:* Owen's School. Served War of 1939–45: RAPC, 1940–42; RE, 1942–46 (Captain). Entered Post Office as Exec. Officer, 1935; Higher Exec. Officer, 1947; Sen. Exec. Officer, 1948; Principal, 1950; Instructor, Management Trng Centre, 1957; Staff Controller, SW Region, 1958; Comdt, Management Trng Centre, 1962; Asst Sec., 1965; Dir, Wales and the Marches Postal Region, 1967; Dir, South-Eastern Postal Region, 1970–76. *Recreations:* walking, gardening, philately, old railway timetables. *Address:* 21 Preston Paddock, Rustington, Littlehampton, West Sussex BN16 2AA. *T:* Rustington (0903) 772451.

BAILEY, Sir Richard (John), Kt 1984; CBE 1977; Chairman: British Ceramic Research Limited, 1982–83 and 1987–90; Royal Doulton Ltd, 1980–87; Royal Crown Derby Porcelain Co. Ltd, 1983–87; *b* 8 July 1923; *s* of Philip Bailey and Doris Margaret (*née* Freebody); *m* 1945, Marcia Rachel Cureton Webb; one *s* three *d*. *Educ:* Newcastle; Shrewsbury. FICeram 1955 (Founder Fellow). Served RNVR 1942–46 (Lieut). Doulton Fine China Ltd: Technical Dir, 1955–63; Man. Dir, 1963–72; Dir, Doulton & Co., 1967–82; Man. Dir, Royal Doulton Tableware Ltd, 1972–80. Dir, Central Independent Television plc, 1986–. Member: Ceramics Industry Nat. Jt Council, 1961–84 (Jt Chm., 1969–84); Ceramic Industry Training Bd, 1967–70; Dir, W Midlands Industrial Develt Assoc., 1983–87; President: BCMF, 1973–74; British Ceramic Soc., 1980–81; Chm., North Staffs Business Initiative, 1981–. Hon. Freeman, City of Stoke-on-Trent, 1987. Hon. Fellow, Staffordshire Poly., 1988. MUniv Keele, 1983. FRSA 1977. *Recreations:* golf, walking, gardening. *Address:* Lea Cottage, School Lane, Aston, near Market Drayton, Shropshire TF9 4JD.

BAILEY, Ronald William, CMG 1961; HM Diplomatic Service, retired; *b* 14 June 1917; *o s* of William Staveley and May Eveline Bailey, Southampton; *m* 1946, Joan Hassall, *d* of late A. E. Gray, JP, Stoke-on-Trent; one *s* one *d*. *Educ:* King Edward VI Sch., Southampton; Trinity Hall, Cambridge (Wootton Isaacson Scholar in Spanish). Probationer Vice-Consul, Beirut, 1939–41; HM Vice-Consul, Alexandria, 1941–45; Asst Oriental Sec., British Embassy, Cairo, 1945–48; Foreign Office, 1948–49; 1st Sec., British Legation, Beirut, 1949–52 (acted as Chargé d'Affaires, 1949, 1950 and 1951); 1st Sec., British Embassy, Washington, 1952–55; Counsellor, Washington, 1955–57; Khartoum, 1957–60 (acted as Chargé d'Affaires in each of these years); Chargé d'Affaires, Taiz, 1960–62; Consul-Gen., Gothenburg, 1963–65; Minister, British Embassy, Baghdad, 1965–67; Ambassador to Bolivia, 1967–71; Ambassador to Morocco, 1971–75. Mem. Council, Anglo-Arab Assoc., 1978–85. Vice-Pres., 1975–87, Pres., 1987–89, Hon. Life Vice-Pres., 1989, Soc. for Protection of Animals in N Africa; Chm., Black Down Cttee, Nat. Trust, 1982–87; Hon. Life Pres., British-Moroccan Soc., 1989. *Publication:* (ed) Records of Oman 1867–1947 (8 vols), 1989. *Recreations:* walking, photography, gardening. *Address:* Redwood, Tennyson's Lane, Haslemere, Surrey GU27 3AF. *T:* Haslemere (0428) 642800. *Club:* Oriental.

BAILEY, Sir Stanley (Ernest), Kt 1986; CBE 1980; QPM 1975; DL; Chief Constable of Northumbria, 1975–91; Regional Police Commander, No 1 Home Defence Region, retired; *b* 30 Sept. 1926; *m* 1954, Marguerita Dorothea Whitbread. Joined Metropolitan Police, 1947; Asst Chief Constable, Staffs, 1966; Dir, Police Res., Home Office, 1970–72; Dep. Chief Constable, Staffs, 1973–75. Mem., IACP (Chairman: Adv. Cttee on Internat. Policy, 1984–89; Europ. Sub-Cttee, 1984–89; Mem. Exec. Cttee, 1986–91); Rep., ICPO, 1986–88. Pres., ACPO, England, Wales & NI, 1985–86 (Vice-Pres., 1984–85; Immediate Past Pres., 1986–87; Chm., Crime Prevention Sub-cttee, 1986–91); Vice Pres., Police Mutual Assce Soc., 1986–. Chairman: Cttee on Burglar Alarms, BSI, 1975–; Organising Cttee, 1st Internat. Police Exhibn and Conf., London, 1987; Founder and Jt Chm., Centre for Res. into Crime, Community and Policing, Univ. of Newcastle upon Tyne, 1989–; Vice Chm., Crime Concern, 1989– (Mem., Adv. Bd); Member: Home Office Standing

Conf. on Crime Prevention, 1977–91; Bd, Northumbria Coalition Against Crime, 1989–; Chm. of cttees and working parties on crime prevention, intruder alarms, criminal intelligence, computer privacy, and physical stress in police work. Observer, VIII UN Congress on Crime Prevention, Havana, 1990 (Organiser and Chm., First UN Meeting of Sen. Police Officials). Police Advr, AMA, 1987–. Has presented papers etc in USA, Denmark, France, Hong Kong, NZ, Japan, Germany, Spain, Thailand, China, Holland, Portugal, Italy, Belgium and USSR on community crime prevention, measurement of effectiveness, and Private Security industry. Mem., Bd of Govs, Internat. Inst. of Security, 1990–. Grad., Nat. Exec. Inst., FBI Washington, 1984. Freeman, City of London, 1988. CBIM 1987. DL Tyne and Wear, 1986. OStJ 1981. *Publications:* articles in learned jls on policy issues. *Recreations:* gardening, travel. *Address:* 2 Hadrian Court, Darras Hall, Ponteland, Newcastle upon Tyne NE20 9JU.

BAILEY, Thomas Aubrey, MBE 1959; Director, Peter Cox Ltd, Building Restoration Specialists (Member of SGB Group of Cos), 1970–76; *b* 20 Jan. 1912; *o s* of late Thomas Edward Bailey and Emma Bailey; *m* 1944, Joan Woodman, *d* of late John Woodman Hooper; one *s. Educ:* Adams' Grammar Sch., Newport, Shropshire; Regent Street Polytechnic Sch. of Architecture. Entered HM Office of Works, Ancient Monuments Br., 1935; Asst Architect, 1945–49; Architect, London and E Anglia, 1949–54; Sen. Architect in charge Ancient Monuments Br., Eng., Wales and Overseas, Min. of Public Building and Works, 1954–69; Architectural Adv. to Oxford Historic Bldgs Fund, 1963–69. Served on various cttees on stone decay and preservation; seconded to Sir Giles G. Scott, OM, RA, for Rebuilding of House of Commons, 1944–49. *Principal works:* Direction of MPBW Survey for Oxford Historic Bldg Appeal, 1957–62 and Cambridge Appeal, 1963; re-erection of fallen Trilithons at Stonehenge, 1958–64; Conservation of Claudian Aqueduct and Aurelian Wall, Brit. Embassy at Rome, 1957–69; etc. Resigned professional membership of RIBA and ARCUK, to enter specialised Bldg Industry, 1969. Mem. Conservation Cttee, for Council for Places of Worship, 1968; Mem. Council, Ancient Monuments Soc., 1970–. FSA 1957; FRSA 1969; Fellow of Faculty of Bldg, 1970. Freeman of City of London, 1967; Freeman and Liveryman, Worshipful Company of Masons, 1973. Hon. MA Oxon, 1963. *Publications:* (jointly) The Claudian Aqueduct in the Grounds of the British Embassy, Rome, 1966; many technical reports on conservation of Historic Monuments. *Recreations:* music, photography, travel, motoring. *Address:* 32 Anne Boleyn's Walk, Cheam, Sutton, Surrey SM3 8DF. *T:* 081–642 3185. *Club:* City Livery.

BAILEY, Wilfrid; Chairman, Southern Gas Region (formerly Southern Gas Board), 1969–75; Chartered Accountant; *b* 9 March 1910; *s* of late Harry Bailey and Martha Bailey (*née* Pighills); *m* 1934, Vera (*née* Manchester); two *s* one *d. Educ:* Keighley Grammar Sch. Borough Treasurer, Bexley BC, 1945–47; Chief Financial Officer, Crawley Development Corp., 1947–49; Gas Council: Chief Accountant, 1949–58; Secretary, 1958–61; Dep. Chm., Southern Gas Bd, 1961–69. FCA 1935. *Recreations:* cricket, motoring, music, photography, gardening. *Address:* (home) Bramble Way, Clease Way, Compton Down, near Winchester. *T:* Twyford (0962) 713382.

BAILEY, (William) John (Joseph); journalist; *b* 11 June 1940; *s* of Ernest Robert Bailey and Josephine Smith; *m* 1963, Maureen Anne, *d* of James Gibbs Neenan and Marjorie Dorema Wrigglesworth; five *s* three *d. Educ:* St Joseph's, Stanford-le-Hope, Essex; Campion Hall, Jamaica; St George's Coll., Kingston, Jamaica; St Chad's Coll., Wolverhampton. Reporter: Southend Standard, Essex, and Essex and Thurrock Gazette, 1960–63; Northern Daily Mail, 1963–64; Chief Reporter, Billingham and Stockton Express, 1964–72; Sub-Editor, Mail, Hartlepool, 1972–75; Features Editor, Echo, Sunderland, 1975–. Member: Press Council, 1974–80; Complaints Cttee, 1974–76, 1977–; Cttee for Evidence to Royal Commission on Press, 1975–76; Gen. Purposes Cttee, 1976–77; Secretariat Cttee, 1976–. Nat. Union of Journalists: Mem., Nat. Exec. Council, 1966–82; Vice-Pres., 1972–73; Pres., 1973–74; Gen. Treasurer, 1975–83. Sec., Hartlepool People Ltd, 1985–. Provincial Journalist of the Year (jtly with Carol Roberton), British Press Awards, 1977 (commended, 1979); Special award Northern Cross, Tom Cordner North East Press Awards, 1984–85, 1989. *Address:* 225 Park Road, Hartlepool, Cleveland TS26 9NG. *T:* Hartlepool (0429) 264577. *Club:* Press (Glasgow).

BAILHACHE, Philip Martin; QC (Jersey) 1989; Attorney-General for Jersey, since 1986; *b* 28 Feb. 1946; *s* of Jurat Lester Vivian Bailhache (Lieut-Bailiff of Jersey, 1980–82) and Nanette Ross (*née* Ferguson); *m* 1st, 1967 (marr. diss. 1982); two *s* two *d*; 2nd, 1984, Linda (*née* Le Vavasseur dit Durell); one *s* one *d. Educ:* Charterhouse; Pembroke Coll., Oxford. Called to the Bar, Middle Temple, 1968; called to the Jersey Bar, 1969. In private practice as Advocate, Jersey, 1969–74; States of Jersey Dep. for Grouville, 1972–74; Solicitor-Gen., Jersey, 1975–85. Chm., Jersey Arts Council, 1987–89. *Recreations:* books, wine, gardening, the arts. *Address:* L'Anquetinerie, Grouville, Jersey, Channel Islands. *T:* Jersey (0534) 52533. *Clubs:* Reform; United (Jersey).

BAILIE, Rt. Hon. Robin John, PC (N Ire) 1971; Solicitor of the Supreme Court of Judicature, Northern Ireland, since 1961; *b* 6 March 1937; *m* 1961, Margaret F. (*née* Boggs); one *s* three *d. Educ:* Rainey Endowed Sch. Magherafelt, Co. Londonderry; The Queen's Univ. of Belfast (LLB). MP (N Ire) for Newtonabbey, 1969–72; Minister of Commerce, Govt of NI, 1971–72. Chm., Fine Wine Wholesalers; Director: Goodyear Tyre & Rubber Co. (GB); Jones Engrg Services Ltd. *Recreations:* wine drinking, ski-ing, squash, golf, tennis. *Address:* 5 Thurloe Close, SW7. *T:* 071–581 4898; Timbers, Park Wall Lane, Lower Basildon, Berkshire.

BAILLIE, family name of **Baron Burton.**

BAILLIE, Alastair Turner; HM Diplomatic Service, retired; Deputy High Commissioner in Calcutta, 1987–91; *b* 24 Dec. 1932; *s* of late Archibald Turner Baillie and Margaret Pinkerton Baillie; *m* 1st, 1965, Wilma Noreen Armstrong (marr. diss. 1974); one *s*; 2nd, 1977, Irena Maria Gregor; one step *s* one step *d. Educ:* Dame Allan's Sch., Newcastle upon Tyne; Christ's Coll., Cambridge (BA). National Service, commissioned Queen's Own Cameron Highlanders, 1951–53. HMOCS: North Borneo, subseq. Sabah, Malaysia, 1957–67; joined HM Diplomatic Service, 1967; FCO, 1967–73; Consul (Commercial), Karachi, 1973–77; First Sec. and Head of Chancery, Manila, 1977–80; Counsellor, Addis Ababa, 1980–81; Counsellor (Commercial), Caracas, 1981–83; Governor of Anguilla, 1983–87. *Recreations:* sport, reading, travelling. *Club:* Commonwealth Trust.

BAILLIE, Sir Gawaine George Hope, 7th Bt, of Polkemmet, *cr* 1823; *b* 8 March 1934; *s* of Sir Adrian Baillie, 6th Bt, and Hon. Olive Cecilia (*d* 1974), *d* of 1st Baron Queenborough, GBE; *S* father, 1947; *m* 1966, Margot, *d* of Senator Louis Beaubien, Montreal; one *s* one *d. Heir: s* Adrian Louis Baillie, *b* 26 March 1973. *Address:* Freechase, Warninglid, Sussex.

BAILLIE, Ian Fowler, CMG 1966; OBE 1962; Director, The Thistle Foundation, Edinburgh, 1970–81; *b* 16 Feb. 1921; *s* of late Very Rev. Principal John Baillie, CH, DLitt, DD, LLD and Florence Jewel (*née* Fowler); *m* 1951, Sheila Barbour (*née* Mathewson); two *s* one *d. Educ:* Edinburgh Acad,; Corpus Christi Coll., Oxford (MA). War service, British and Indian Armies, 1941–46. HM Overseas Civil Service (formerly Colonial Service), 1946–66: Admin. Officer (District Comr), Gold Coast, 1946–54; Registrar of Co-operative Socs and Chief Marketing Officer, Aden, 1955; Protectorate Financial Sec., Aden, 1959; Dep. British Agent, Aden, 1962; Brit. Agent and Asst High Comr, Aden, 1963; Dir, Aden Airways 1959–66; Sen. Research Associate and Administrative Officer, Agricultural Adjustment Unit, Dept of Agricultural Economics, Univ. of Newcastle upon Tyne, 1966–69. *Publication:* (ed with S. J. Sheehy) Irish Agriculture in a Changing World, 1971. *Recreation:* angling. *Address:* 4 Grange Loan Gardens, Edinburgh EH9 2EB. *T:* 031–667 2647.

BAILLIE, Prof. John, CA; Visiting Professor of Accountancy, Heriot-Watt University, since 1989; Partner, KPMG Peat Marwick McLintock; *b* 7 Oct. 1944; *s* of Arthur and Agnes Baillie; *m* 1972, Annette Alexander; one *s* one *d. Educ:* Whitehill Sch. CA 1967 (Gold Medal and Distinction in final exams). Partner, Thomson McLintock & Co., later Peat Marwick McLintock, then KPMG Peat Marwick McLintock, 1978–. Johnstone-Smith Prof. of Accountancy, Univ. of Glasgow, 1983–88. Mem. various technical and professional affairs cttees, Inst. of Chartered Accountants of Scotland. Hon. MA Glasgow, 1983. *Publications:* Systems of Profit Measurement, 1985; Consolidated Accounts and the Seventh Directive, 1985; technical and professional papers; contribs to Accountants' Magazine and other professional jls. *Recreations:* keeping fit, reading, music, golf. *Address:* The Glen, Glencairn Road, Kilmacolm, Renfrewshire PA13 4PB. *T:* Kilmacolm (050587) 3254. *Club:* Western (Glasgow).

BAILLIE, William James Laidlaw, RSA 1979 (ARSA 1968); PRSW 1974 (RSW 1963); painter; Senior Lecturer in Drawing and Painting, Edinburgh College of Art, since 1968; Treasurer, Royal Scottish Academy, since 1980; *b* 19 April 1923; *s* of James and Helen Baillie; *m* 1961, Helen Gillon; one *s* two *d. Educ:* Dunfermline High Sch.; Edinburgh College of Art (Andrew Grant Schol., 1941–50; Dip. Drawing and Painting 1950). Studies interrupted by war service with Royal Corps of Signals, mainly in Far East, 1942–47. Taught in Edinburgh schools, 1951–60; Mem., Teaching Staff, Edin. College of Art, 1960–; Visiting Tutor, National Gallery of Canada Summer Sch., near Ottawa, 1955. Exhibits at Gall. 10, London, but mostly in Scotland, mainly at Scottish Gall., Edinburgh; first retrospective exhibn in Kirkcaldy Art Gallery, 1977. *Recreations:* music, travel. *Address:* 6A Esslemont Road, Edinburgh EH16 5PX. *T:* 031–667 1538.

BAILLIE-HAMILTON, family name of **Earl of Haddington.**

BAILLIEU, family name of **Baron Baillieu.**

BAILLIEU, 3rd Baron *cr* 1953, of Sefton, Australia and Parkwood, Surrey; **James William Latham Baillieu;** Assistant Director, Standard Chartered Asia Ltd; *b* 16 Nov. 1950; *s* of 2nd Baron Baillieu and Anne Bayliss, *d* of Leslie William Page, Southport, Queensland; *S* father, 1973; *m* 1st, 1974, Cornelia Masters Ladd (marr. diss.), *d* of W. Ladd; one *s*; 2nd, 1987, Clare Stephenson, *d* of Peter Stephenson of Benalla, Victoria. *Educ:* Radley College; Monash Univ., Melbourne (BEc 1977). Short Service Commission, Coldstream Guards, 1970–73. Manager Asst, Banque Nationale de Paris, Melbourne, 1980; Rothschild Australia Ltd, 1980–88 (Manager, 1983; Sen. Manager, 1984; Associate Dir, 1985); Rothschild Australia Asset Management Ltd, 1980–88 (Associate Dir, 1985); Dir, Manufacturers Hanover Australia Ltd, 1988–90. *Heir: s* Hon. Robert Latham Baillieu, *b* 2 Feb. 1979. *Address:* c/o Mutual Trust Pty Ltd, 360 Collins Street, Melbourne, Victoria 3000, Australia. *Clubs:* Boodle's; Australian (Melbourne).

BAILLIEU, Colin Clive; Member, Monopolies and Mergers Commission, since 1984; Chairman, Gresham Underwriting Agencies, since 1990; *b* 2 July 1930; *s* of Ian Baillieu and Joanna Baillieu (*née* Brinton); *m* 1st, 1955, Diana Robinson (marr. diss. 1968); two *d*; 2nd, 1968, Renata Richter; two *s. Educ:* Dragon Sch.; Eton. Commissioned Coldstream Guards, 1949. Local newspaper, Evening Standard, 1951–52; British Metal Corp., 1952–58; British Aluminium, 1958–60; Monsanto Fibres, 1960–66; Arthur Sanderson, 1966–68; Ultrasonic Machines, 1968–76. Mem., Council of Lloyd's, 1983–88. Contested (C) Rossendale, Lancs, 1964 and 1966. *Recreations:* skiing, tennis, teaching boys to play polo, theology, 17th Century history *Address:* Hoyle Farm, Heyshott, Midhurst, West Sussex GU29 0DY. *T:* Graffham (07986) 230. *Clubs:* Travellers', Beefsteak, Shikar, MCC.

BAIN, Andrew David, FRSE 1980; Group Economic Adviser, Midland Bank, 1984–90; *b* 21 March 1936; *s* of Hugh Bain and Kathleen (*née* Eadie); *m* 1st, 1960, Anneliese Minna Frieda Kroggel (marr. diss. 1988); three *s*; 2nd, 1989, Eleanor Riches. *Educ:* Glasgow Academy; Christ's Coll., Cambridge. PhD Cantab 1963. Junior Res. Officer, Dept of Applied Econs, Cambridge Univ., 1958–60; Res. Fellow, Christ's Coll., Cambridge, 1960; Instructor, Cowles Foundn, Yale Univ., 1960–61; Lectr, Cambridge, 1961–66; Fellow, Corpus Christi Coll., Cambridge, 1962; on secondment to Bank of England, 1965–67; Prof. of Econs, 1967–70, Esmee Fairbairn Prof. of Econs of Finance and Investment, 1970–77, Univ. of Stirling; Walton Prof. of Monetary and Financial Econs, Univ. of Strathclyde, 1977–84; Vis. Prof. of Political Econ., Glasgow Univ., 1991–. Member: Cttee to Review the Functioning of Financial Institutions, 1977–80; (part-time) Monopolies and Mergers Commn, 1981–82; Bd, Scottish Enterprise, 1991–. *Publications:* The Growth of Television Ownership in the United Kingdom (monograph), 1964; The Control of the Money Supply, 1970; Company Financing in the UK, 1975; The Economics of the Financial System, 1981; articles on demand analysis, monetary policy and other subjects. *Address:* 1 Stafford Street, Helensburgh, Glasgow G84 9HU. *Club:* Reform.

BAIN, Douglas John; Industrial Adviser to the Secretary of State for Scotland, 1983–85; *b* 9 July 1924; *s* of Alexander Gillan Bain and Fanny Heaford; *m* 1946, Jean Wallace Fairbairn; three *d. Educ:* Pollokshields Secondary School; Royal Technical Coll. (now Strathclyde Univ.), Glasgow (DRTC). ATI. Royal Tech. Coll., 1941–43 and 1948–51. RAF, 1943–48. J. & P. Coats Ltd, 1951–83: graduate trainee, 1951–55; overseas management, 1955–60; central management, 1960–68; Director, 1968–83; seconded to Scottish Office (Scottish Econ. Planning Dept) as Under Sec., 1979–82. *Recreations:* golf, walking, geology, flying. *Address:* 49 Bimbadeen Crescent, Yallambie, Melbourne, Vic 3085, Australia.

BAIN, Prof. George Sayers, DPhil; Principal, London Business School, since 1989; *b* 24 Feb. 1939; *s* of George Alexander Bain and Margaret Ioleen Bamford; *m* 1st, 1962, Carol Lynn Ogden White (marr. diss. 1987); one *s* one *d*; 2nd, 1988, Frances Gwynneth Rigby (*née* Vickers). *Educ:* Univ. of Manitoba (BA Hons 1961, MA 1964); Oxford Univ. (DPhil 1968). Lectr in Econs, Univ. of Manitoba, 1962–63; Res. Fellow, Nuffield Coll., Oxford, 1966–69; Frank Thomas Prof. of Indust. Relations, UMIST, 1969–70; University of Warwick: Dep. Dir, 1970–74, Dir, 1974–81, SSRC Industrial Relations Res. Unit; Pressed Steel Fisher Prof. of Industrial Relations, 1979–89; Chm., Sch. of Industrial and Business Studies, 1983–89. Member: Mech. Engrg Econ. Develt Cttee, NEDO, 1974–76; Cttee of Inquiry on Indust. Democracy, Dept of Trade (Chm., Lord Bullock), 1975–76; Research Staff: Royal Commn on Trade Unions and Employers' Assocs (Donovan Commn), 1966–67; Canadian Task Force on Labour Relations, 1968. Member Council: ESRC, 1986–91; Nat. Forum for Management Educn and Develt, 1987–90; Chm. Council,

Univ. Management Schs, 1987–90. Member: Bd of Trustees, European Foundn for Management Develt, 1990–; Internat. Affairs Cttee, Amer. Assembly of Collegiate Schs of Business, 1990–. Consultant, NBPI, 1967–69; acted as Consultant to Dept of Employment, and to the Manitoba and Canada Depts of Labour; frequently acts as arbitrator and mediator in indust. disputes. FRSA. *Publications:* Trade Union Growth and Recognition, 1967; The Growth of White-Collar Unionism, 1970; (jtly) The Reform of Collective Bargaining at Plant and Company Level, 1971; (jtly) Social Stratification and Trade Unionism, 1973; (jtly) Union Growth and the Business Cycle, 1976; (jtly) A Bibliography of British Industrial Relations, 1979; (jtly) Profiles of Union Growth, 1980; (ed) Industrial Relations in Britain, 1983; (jtly) A Bibliography of British Industrial Relations 1971–1979, 1985; contrib. prof. and learned jls. *Address:* London Business School, Sussex Place, Regent's Park, NW1 4SA. *T:* 071–262 5050.

BAIN, Iain Andrew; Editor, Nairnshire Telegraph, since 1987; *b* 25 Feb. 1949; *s* of Alistair I. R. Bain and Jean R. Forrest; *m* 1974, Maureen Beattie; three *d*. *Educ:* Nairn Acad.; Univ. of Aberdeen (MA). Research, Univ. of Durham, 1971–74; Sub-editor, 1974, Asst Editor, 1980, Editor, 1981–87, The Geographical Magazine. *Publications:* Mountains and People, 1982; Water on the Land, 1983; Mountains and Earth Movements, 1984; various articles. *Recreations:* reading, walking, photography, gardening. *Address:* Rosebank, Leopold Street, Nairn IV12 4BE. *Club:* Geographical.

BAIN, John Taylor, CBE 1975; Director of Education, Glasgow, 1968–75; Lay Observer (Solicitors Act) in Scotland, 1977–83; *b* 9 May 1912; *m*; one *s* two *d*. *Educ:* St Andrews Univ. (BSc, MA); Edinburgh Univ. (BEd). War Service, RAF (Technical Br.). Entered educational administration in 1947. JP Glasgow, 1971. *Recreation:* golf.

BAIN, Margaret Anne; *see* Ewing, M. A.

BAIN, Neville Clifford, FCA, FCIS; Group Chief Executive, Coats Viyella PLC, since 1989; *b* 14 July 1940; *s* of Charles Alexander Bain and Gertrude Mae Bain; *m* 1987, Anne Patricia; one step *d*, and one *s* one *d* by previous marriage. *Educ:* King's High Sch., Dunedin, NZ; Otago Univ., Dunedin. BCom Acctcy 1964; BCom Econ 1966; MCom Hons 1968. CMA; ACA 1959, FCA 1989; FCIS 1962. Trainee Inspector, Inland Revenue, NZ, 1957–59; Manager, Anderson & Co., Chartered Accountants, NZ, 1960–62; Cadbury Schweppes Hudson: Cost Accountant, subseq. Financial Controller, and Co. Sec., NZ, 1963–68; Finance Dir, NZ, 1968–75; Cadbury Schweppes: Group Chief Exec., S Africa, 1975–80; Group Strategic Planning Dir, 1980–83 (apptd to Main Bd, 1981); Managing Director: Cadbury Ltd, 1983–86; Cadbury World Wide, 1986–89; Dep. Group Chief Exec. and Finance Dir, Cadbury Schweppes Plc, 1989–90. CBIM 1988. *Recreations:* sport, walking, music. *Address:* 28 Savile Row, W1X 2DD. *T:* 071–734 4030, *Fax:* 071–437 2016.

BAINBRIDGE, Beryl, FRSL; actress, writer; *b* 21 Nov. 1934; *d* of Richard Bainbridge and Winifred Baines; *m* 1954, Austin Davies (marr. diss.); one *s* two *d*. *Educ:* Merchant Taylors' Sch., Liverpool; Arts Educational Schools, Ltd, Tring. Weekly columnist, Evening Standard, 1987–. FRSL 1978. Hon. LittD Liverpool, 1986. *Plays:* Tiptoe Through the Tulips, 1976; The Warrior's Return, 1977; Its a Lovely Day Tomorrow, 1977; Journal of Bridget Hitler, 1981; Somewhere More Central (TV), 1981; Evensong (TV), 1986. *Publications:* A Weekend with Claud, 1967, revd edn 1981; Another Part of the Wood, 1968, rev. edn 1979; Harriet Said. . . ., 1972; The Dressmaker, 1973 (film, 1989); The Bottle Factory Outing, 1974 (Guardian Fiction Award); Sweet William, 1975 (film, 1980); A Quiet Life, 1976; Injury Time, 1977 (Whitbread Award); Young Adolf, 1978; Winter Garden, 1980; English Journey, 1984 (TV series, 1984); Watson's Apology, 1984; Mum and Mr Armitage, 1985; Forever England, 1986 (TV series, 1986); Filthy Lucre, 1986; An Awfully Big Adventure, 1989. *Recreations:* painting, sleeping. *Address:* 42 Albert Street, NW1 7NU. *T:* 071–387 3113.

BAINBRIDGE, Cyril, FJI; author and journalist; *b* 15 Nov. 1928; *o s* of late Arthur Herman and Edith Bainbridge; *m* 1952, Barbara Hannah (*née* Crook); one *s* two *d*. *Educ:* privately (Negus Coll., Bradford). Served Army, staff of CGS, WO, 1947–49. Entered journalism as Reporter, Bingley Guardian, 1944–45; Telegraph and Argus, and Yorkshire Observer, Bradford, 1945–54; Press Assoc., 1954–63; joined The Times, 1963: Asst News Editor, 1967; Dep. News Editor, 1967–69; Regional News Editor, 1969–77; Managing News Editor, 1977–82; Asst Managing Editor, 1982–86; Editorial Data Manager, Times Newspapers, 1986–88. Vice-Pres., 1977–78, Pres., 1978–79, Fellow, 1986, Inst. of Journalists; Member: Press Council, 1980–90; Nat. Council for Trng of Journalists, 1983–86. Mem. Editorial Adv. Bd, Thomson Foundn, 1983–. *Publications:* Taught With Care: a Century of Church Schooling, 1974; The Brontës and their Country, 1978, 2nd edn 1990; Brass Triumphant, 1980; North Yorkshire and North Humberside, 1984, 2nd edn 1989; (ed) One Hundred Years of Journalism, 1984; Pavilions on the Sea, 1986. *Recreations:* reading, brass bands, collecting old bookmarks. *Address:* 98 Mayfield Avenue, North Finchley, N12 9JE. *T:* 081–445 4178.

BAINBRIDGE, Maj.-Gen. Henry, CB 1948; CBE 1944; psc; retired; late Corps of Royal Engineers; *b* 1903. 2nd Lieut Royal Engineers, 1923. Served War of 1939–45, 1939–44 (despatches twice, CBE). Dir of Man-power Planning, War Office, 1949–52; Dep. QMG, War Office, 1952–55, retired 1955. *Address:* Brizlee, Hoe Lane, Peaslake, Surrey GU5 9SW.

BAINES, Anthony Cuthbert, DLitt; FBA 1980; *b* 6 Oct. 1912; *s* of Cuthbert Edward Baines and Margaret Clemency Lane Poole; *m* 1960, Patricia Margaret Stammers. *Educ:* Westminster Sch. (KS); Christ Church Oxford; Royal College of Music. BA 1933, MA 1970, DLitt 1977, Oxon. Member, London Philharmonic Orchestra, 1935–39, 1946–49. Commissioned Royal Tank Regt, 1940–45. Associate Conductor, International Ballet Co., 1950–53; Member, Music Staff: Uppingham Sch., 1954–65; Dean Close Sch., 1965–70; Curator, Bate Collection of Historical Wind Instruments, Oxford Univ., 1970–80, retired. Fellow, University Coll., Oxford, 1974–80, retired. Editor, Galpin Society Jl, 1956–63 and 1970–84. *Publications:* Woodwind Instruments and their History, 1957, 5th edn 1977; Bagpipes, 1960, 4th edn 1979; ed and contrib. Musical Instruments through the Ages, 1961, 6th edn 1978; Victoria and Albert Museum, Catalogue of Musical Instruments, vol. II, Non-Keyboard, 1968; European and American Musical Instruments, 1966, 2nd edn 1981; Brass Instruments, their History and Development, 1976, 3rd edn 1980. *Recreations:* folk music, wild life. *Address:* 8 Lynette Avenue, SW4 9HD.

BAINES, Sir George G.; *see* Grenfell-Baines.

BAINES, Prof. John Robert, MA, DPhil; Professor of Egyptology, Oxford University and Fellow of Queen's College, Oxford, since 1976; *b* 17 March 1946; *o s* of late Edward Russell Baines and of Dora Margaret Jean (*née* O'Brien); *m* 1971, Jennifer Christine Ann, *e d* of S. T. Smith; one *s* one *d*. *Educ:* Winchester Coll.; New Coll., Linacre Coll., Worcester Coll., Oxford (BA 1967, MA, DPhil 1976). Lectr in Egyptology, Univ. of Durham, 1970–75; Laycock Student, Worcester Coll., Oxford, 1973–75. Visiting Professor: Univ. of Arizona, 1982, 1988; Univ. of Michigan, 1989; Fellow, Humboldt-Stiftung, 1982, 1989. *Publications:* (trans. and ed) H. Schäfer, Principles of Egyptian Art, 1974, rev. edn 1986; (with J. Málek) Atlas of Ancient Egypt, 1980; (trans. and ed) E. Hornung, Conceptions of God in Ancient Egypt, 1982; Fecundity Figures, 1985; (ed jtly) Pyramid Studies and Other Essays presented to I. E. S. Edwards, 1988; articles in collections and in Acta Orientalia, American Anthropologist, Art History, Encyclopaedia Britannica, Jl Egypt. Archaeol., Man, Orientalia, Studien altägypt. Kultur, etc. *Address:* Oriental Institute, Pusey Lane, Oxford OX1 2LE.

BAINS, Lawrence Arthur, CBE 1983; DL; Director: Bains Brothers Ltd; Crowland Leasings Ltd; Bains Finance Management Ltd, and associated companies; Chairman, Haringey District Health Authority, since 1982; *b* 11 May 1920; *s* of late Arthur Bains and Mabel (*née* Payn); *m* 1954, Margaret, *d* of late Sir William and Lady Grimshaw; two *s* one *d*. *Educ:* Stationers' Company's School. Served War, 1939–46: Middlesex Yeomanry, 1939; N Africa, 1940; POW, 1942, escaped, 1943. Member of Lloyd's. Hornsey Borough Council: Mem., 1949–65; Dep. Leader, 1958–64; Mayor, 1964–65; Council, London Borough of Haringey: Mem., 1964–74; Finance Chm., 1968–71; Greater London Council: Chm., 1977–78; Mem. for Hornsey/Haringey, 1967–81; Chm., South Area Planning Bd, 1970–73; Dep. Leader, Housing Policy Cttee, 1979–81; Chm., GLC/Tower Hamlets Jt Management Cttee, 1979–81; Mem., Lee Valley Regional Park Authority, 1968–81 (Chm., 1980–81). Liveryman, Worshipful Co. of Basketmakers. DL Greater London, 1978 (Rep. DL for Borough of Barnet, 1983). Order of St Lazarus of Jerusalem. *Address:* Crowland Lodge, 100 Galley Lane, Arkley, Barnet EN5 4AL. *T:* 081–440 3499. *Club:* City Livery.

BAINS, Malcolm Arnold; JP, DL; Clerk of the Kent County Council and Clerk to the Lieutenancy of Kent, 1970–74; *b* 12 Sept. 1921; *s* of Herbert Bains, Newcastle-upon-Tyne; *m* 1st, 1942, Winifred Agnes Davies (marr. diss. 1961); three *s*; 2nd, 1968, Margaret Hunter. *Educ:* Hymers Coll.; Durham Univ. (LLB (Hons)); Solicitor. Commnd as Pilot in RAF, 1942–46. Solicitor with Taunton and Sunderland and with Notts and Hants County Councils, 1946–55; Dep. Clerk of Hants County Council and Dep. Clerk of the Peace, 1955–60; Dep. Clerk of Kent County Council, 1960–70; Chm., Working Group which advised Secretary of State for Environment on future management of Local Authorities, 1971–73. Chm., Local Govt Review Bd of Victoria, 1978–79. Fellow, ANU and Advr to NSW Govt, 1977–78. Head of Norfolk Island Public Service, 1979–82. FRSA 1976. DL Kent 1976; JP Norfolk Is, 1980. *Publications:* The Bains Report, 1972; Management Reform in English Local Government, 1978; Local Government in NSW, 1980. *Recreations:* swimming, tennis. *Address:* 77 Langham Road, Teddington, Middlesex; PO Box 244, Norfolk Island, 2899, via Australia.

BAIRD, Anthony; *see* Baird, E. A. B.

BAIRD, Charles Fitz; Chairman and Chief Executive Officer, Inco Ltd, 1980–87, retired; *b* 4 Sept. 1922; *s* of George White and Julia (Fitz) Baird; *m* 1947, Norma Adele White; two *s* two *d*. *Educ:* Middlebury Coll. (BA); New York Univ. (Grad. Sch. of Bus. Admin); Harvard Univ. (Advanced Management Program). US Marine Corps, 1943–46, 1951–52 (Capt.). Standard Oil Co. (NJ), now Exxon, 1948–65: Dep. European Financial Rep., London, 1955–58; Asst Treas., 1958–62; Dir, Esso Standard SA Française, 1962–65; Asst Sec., Financial Man., US Navy, 1965–67, Under Secretary, 1967–69; Internat. Nickel Co. of Canada Ltd (Inco Ltd): Vice Pres. Finance, 1969–72, Sen. Vice Pres., 1972–76; Dir, 1974–; Vice Chm., 1976–77; Pres., 1977–80. Director: Bank of Montreal, 1975–; Aetna Life and Casualty Co., 1982–. Nat. Advr, Council on Oceans and Atmosphere, 1972–74; Member: Presidential Commn on Marine Sci. Engrg and Resources, 1967–69; Council on Foreign Relations. Mem., Bd of Trustees, Bucknell Univ., 1969– (Chm., 1976–82); Trustee, Center for Naval Analyses, Logistic Management Inst. Hon. LLD Bucknell Univ. 1976. US Navy Distinguished Civilian Service Award, 1969. *Recreations:* tennis, platform tennis, golf. *Clubs:* Chevy Chase (Washington, DC); Maidstone (E Hampton, NY); Short Hills Tennis (NJ).

BAIRD, Sir David Charles, 5th Bt of Newbyth, *cr* 1809; *b* 6 July 1912; *s* of late William Arthur Baird, of Lennoxlove, and Lady Hersey Baird; *S* uncle, 1941. *Educ:* Eton; Cambridge. *Heir: nephew* Charles William Stuart Baird [*b* 8 June 1939; *m* 1965, Jane Joanna, *d* of late Brig. A. Darley Bridge; three *d*]. *Address:* 52 High Street, Kirkcudbright DG6 4JX.

BAIRD, Prof. David Tennent, FRCPE; FRCOG: Medical Research Council Clinical Research Professor of Reproductive Endocrinology, Edinburgh University, since 1985; *b* 13 March 1935; *s* of Sir Dugald Baird, MD, FRCOG and Lady (May) Baird (*née* Tennent), CBE; *m* 1965, Frances Diana Lichtveld (separated); two *s*. *Educ:* Aberdeen Grammar Sch., Aberdeen Univ.; Trinity Coll., Cambridge (BA); Edinburgh Univ. (MB, ChB; DSc). Junior med. posts, Royal Infirmary, Edinburgh, 1959–65; MRC Travelling Research Fellow, Worcester Foundn of Experimental Biology, USA, 1965–68; Lectr, later Sen. Lectr, Dept of Obstetrics, Univ. of Edinburgh, 1968–72; Dep. Dir, MRC Unit of Reproductive Biology, Edinburgh, 1972–77; Prof. of Obst. and Gyn., Univ. of Edinburgh, 1977–85. Consultant Gynaecologist, Royal Infirmary, Edinburgh, 1970–. FRSE 1990. *Publications:* Mechanism of Menstrual Bleeding, 1985; contribs in med. and sci. jls on reproductive endocrinology. *Recreations:* ski mountaineering, golf. *Address:* 22 India Street, Edinburgh EH3 6HB. *T:* 031–225 3962. *Club:* Royal Society of Medicine.

BAIRD, (Eric) Anthony (Bamber); Director, Institute for Complementary Medicine, since 1980; *b* 11 Dec. 1920; *s* of Oswald Baird and Marion Bamber; *m* 1st, 1952, Margareta Toss (marr. diss. 1957); 2nd, 1959, Inger Bohman (marr. diss. 1977); two *d*. *Educ:* LSE (BScEcon). Served RA, 1941–46. Swedish Broadcasting Corp., 1950–65; Public Relations Ltd, 1965–72; Civil Service, 1973–78; Inst. for Complementary Medicine, 1979–. *Publications:* Notes on Canada, 1962; (jtly) The Charm of Sweden, 1962. *Recreations:* writing children's stories, gardening. *Address:* 24 Backwoods Lane, Lindfield, Haywards Heath, West Sussex RH16 2ED. *T:* Lindfield (04447) 2018.

BAIRD, James Hewson; Chief Executive and Company Secretary, British Veterinary Association, since 1987; *b* 28 March 1944; *s* of James Baird, MBE, MRCVS and Ann Sarah Baird (*née* Hewson); *m* 1969, Clare Rosalind (*née* Langstaff); three *d*. *Educ:* Austin Friars; Creighton, Carlisle; Newcastle upon Tyne Univ. (BSc Hons Agric). MIWES. Hydrologist, Essex River Authy, 1968–75; Policy Officer, Nat. Water Council, 1975–80 (Mem., DoE/NWC Waste of Water Gp, 1978–80). Inst. of Civil Engineers: Asst Dir, 1980–81; Dir of Admin., 1981–86; Mem., Infrastructure Planning Gp, 1982–86; Dir, Assoc. of Municipal Engineers, 1984–86; Dir, External Affairs, Fedn of Civil Engineering Contractors, 1986–87; Sec., London and SE Section, FCEC, 1986–87. *Recreations:* Rugby, gardening, farming, countryside. *Address:* British Veterinary Association, 7 Mansfield Street, W1M 0AT. *T:* 071–636 6541. *Clubs:* Royal Society of Medicine, Rugby of London.

BAIRD, Lt-Gen. Sir James (Parlane), KBE 1973; MD, FRCP, FRCPEd; Medical Adviser, National Advice Centre for Postgraduate Education, 1977–84; *b* 12 May 1915; *s* of Rev. David Baird and Sara Kathleen Black; *m* 1948, Anne Patricia Anderson; one *s* one *d*. *Educ:* Bathgate Academy; Univ. of Edinburgh. FRCPEd 1952, MD 1958, FRCP 1959. Commissioned, RAMC, 1939; Lt-Col 1956; Prof. of Military Medicine, Royal Army Medical Coll., 1965; Cons. Physician, BAOR, 1967; Dir of Medicine and

Consulting Physician to the Army, 1969–71; Comdt and Dir of Studies, Royal Army Med. Coll., 1971–73; Dir Gen., Army Medical Services, 1973–77. QHP 1969. QHA (Pakistan), 1982. *Publications:* Tropical Diseases Supplement to Principles and Practice of Medicine, 1968; (contrib.) The Oxford Companion to Medicine, 1986. *Recreation:* golf. *Address:* c/o Royal Bank of Scotland, Whitehall, SW1A 2EB. *Club:* West Sussex Golf.

BAIRD, Sir James Richard Gardiner, 10th Bt *cr* 1695; MC 1945; *b* 12 July 1913; *er s* of Captain William Frank Gardiner Baird (killed in action 1914) (2nd *s* of 8th Bt) and Violet Mary (*d* 1947), *d* of late Richard Benyon Croft; *S* uncle, Sir James Hozier Gardiner Baird, 9th Bt, 1966; *m* 1941, Mabel Ann (Gay), *d* of A. Algernon Gill; two *s* one *d. Educ:* Eton. Served War of 1939–45. Lieut, Royal Artillery, 1940; Captain, Kent Yeomanry, 1944. *Recreation:* shooting. *Heir: s* James Andrew Gardiner Baird [*b* 2 May 1946; *m* 1984, Jean Margaret (marr. diss. 1988), *yr d* of Brig. Sir Ian Jardine, 4th Bt; one *s. Educ:* Eton]. *Address:* Church Farm House, Guist, Norfolk NR20 5AJ. *T:* Foulsham (036284) 808. *Club:* Naval and Military.

BAIRD, Joyce Elizabeth Leslie, OBE 1991; Joint General Secretary, Assistant Masters and Mistresses Association, 1978–90; *b* 8 Dec. 1929; *d* of Dr J. C. H. Baird and Mrs J. E. Baird. *Educ:* The Abbey School, Reading; Newnham College, Cambridge (MA); secretarial training. FEIS 1987. Secretary to Sir Austin Robinson and editorial assistant, Royal Economic Soc., 1952–60; Senior Geography Mistress, Hertfordshire and Essex High School, Bishop's Stortford, 1961–77 (Dep. Head, 1973–75). President: Assoc. of Assistant Mistresses, 1976–77; Internat. Fedn of Secondary Teachers, 1981–85; Vice Pres., NFER, 1991–. *Recreations:* walking, thinking about gardening, travel. *Address:* 26 Fulbrooke Road, Cambridge CB3 9EE. *T:* Cambridge (0223) 354909. *Club:* University Women's.

BAIRD, Kenneth William; Music Director, Arts Council, since 1988; *b* 14 July 1950; *s* of William and Christine Baird. *Educ:* Uppingham School; St Andrews Univ. (MA); Royal College of Music. LRAM, ARCM. English National Opera, 1974–82; Gen. Manager, Aldeburgh Foundn, 1982–88. Chm., Snape Historical Trust, 1986–. *Address:* c/o Arts Council, 14 Great Peter Street, SW1P 3NQ. *Club:* Chelsea Arts.

BAIRD, Ronald; Director, Saatchi & Saatchi Compton, since 1974; *b* 9 Dec. 1930; *s* of Richard Baird and Emma Baird (*née* Martin); *m* 1957, Helen Lilian, *d* of His Honour Judge John and Lilian Charlesworth. *Educ:* Grammar School, Blyth, Northumberland; King's College, Univ. of Durham. 13th/18th Royal Hussars (QMO), 1949–51. Saward Baker & Co., 1954–63; Chief Exec. Officer, Stuart Advtg, 1963–68; Man. Dir, Holmwood Advtg, 1968–74; Dir, Notley Advtg, 1970–74. Member: Derwent Howe Steering Group (Cumbria), 1982–; Council, Think British, 1980–; Board, Nat. Theatre, 1984– (Vice-Chm., Nat. Theatre Develt Council, 1985); Leverhulme Cttee, RCS; Small Animal Health Trust; Royal Soc. for Nature Conservation; Royal Life Saving Soc. (Vice-Pres.); St Mary's Coronary Flow Trust; London Fedn of Boys' Clubs. *Recreations:* Irish wolfhounds, music, painting, fell walking, field sports. *Address:* Berry Corner, Berry Lane, Chorleywood, Herts WD3 5EY. *T:* Chorleywood (09278) 3251; Spout House, Gosforth, Cumbria.

BAIRD, Susan, CBE 1991; JP; Lord Provost and Lord-Lieutenant of Glasgow, since 1988; *b* 26 May 1940; *d* of Archie and Susan Reilly; *m* 1957, George Baird; three *s* one *d. Educ:* St Mark's Secondary School, Glasgow. Mem. Labour Party, 1969; Glasgow District Council: Mem. (Lab), 1974–; Bailie of the City, 1980–84; Convener, Manpower Cttee, 1980–84; Vice-Convener, Parks and Recreation Cttee, 1984–88. JP Glasgow, 1977. *Recreations:* reading, walking. *Address:* 138 Downfield Street, Parkhead, Glasgow G32 8RZ. *T:* 041–778 7641.

BAIRD, Vice-Adm. Sir Thomas (Henry Eustace), KCB 1980; DL; *b* Canterbury, Kent, 17 May 1924; *s* of Geoffrey Henry and Helen Jane Baird; *m* 1953, Angela Florence Ann Paul, Symington, Ayrshire; one *s* one *d. Educ:* RNC, Dartmouth. Served HM Ships: Trinidad, in support of convoys to Russia, 1941, Midshipman; Bermuda, Russian convoys and landings in N Africa, and Orwell, Russian convoys and Atlantic escort force, 1942; Howe, E Indies, 1943, Sub-Lt; Rapid, E Indies, 1944 until VJ Day, Lieut; St James, Home Fleet, 1946; Ganges, Ratings' New Entry Trng, 1948; Plucky, Exec. Officer, mine clearance in Mediterranean, 1950; Lt Comdr 1952; Veryan Bay, Exec. Officer, W Indies and Falkland Is., 1953; O-in-C, Petty Officers' Leadership Sch., Malta, 1954; Exec. Officer, HMS Whirlwind, Home Fleet and Med., for Suez Op., 1956; Comd, HMS Acute, Dartmouth Trng Sqdn, 1958; Comdr 1959; Comd, HMS Ulysses, Home Fleet, 1960; Staff, C-in-C, Home Fleet, Northwood, 1961; Exec. Officer, Jt Anti-Sub. Sch., Londonderry, 1963; EO, HMS Bulwark, Far East, 1965; Ch. Staff Officer to Cdre, Naval Drafting, 1966; Captain 1967; Dep. Dir, Naval Equipment, Adm., Bath, 1967; Captain: Mine Countermeasures; Fishery Protection and HMS Lochinvar (comd), 1969; Comd, HMS Glamorgan, Far East, W Indies, S Amer., Med., and UK Waters, 1971; Captain of the Fleet, 1973; Rear Adm. 1976; Chief of Staff to C-in-C Naval Home Comd, 1976–77; Dir Gen., Naval Personal Services, 1978–79; Vice-Adm. 1979; Flag Officer Scotland and NI, 1979–82. Chm. Exec. Cttee, Erskine Hosp., 1986–. DL Ayr and Arran, 1982. *Recreations:* cricket, golf, shooting, fishing. *Address:* Craigrethill, Symington, Ayrshire KA1 5QN. *Clubs:* Army and Navy; Prestwick Golf (Prestwick).

BAIRD, Dr Thomas Terence, CB 1977; Chief Medical Officer, Department of Health and Social Services, Northern Ireland, 1972–78, retired; *b* 31 May 1916; *s* of Thomas Baird, Archdeacon of Derry, and Hildegarde Nolan; *m* 1st, 1940, Joan Crosbie; two *d*; 2nd, 1982, Mary Wilson Powell. *Educ:* Haileybury Coll.; Queen's Univ. of Belfast. MB, BCh, BAO, 1939; DPH, 1947; FFPHM (FFCM (RCP), 1972); MRCPI 1973, FRCPI 1975; MRCPEd 1975; FFCM Ireland (Founder Fellow), 1977. Ho. Surg./Ho. Phys., North Lonsdale Hosp., Barrow-in-Furness, 1939–40. Served War, RNVR, 1940–46. Queen's Univ. of Belfast, DPH course, 1946–47. Berks CC: Asst MO, 1947–49; Dep. County MO and Dep. Principal Sch. MO, 1949–54. Welsh Bd of Health: MO, 1954–57; Sen. MO, 1957–62; Min. of Health and Local Govt, Northern Ireland: PMO, 1962–64; Dep. Chief MO, 1964–68; Min. of Health and Social Services, NI, Sen. Dep. Chief MO, 1968–72. Chairman: NI Med. Manpower Adv. Cttee; NI Adv. Cttee on infant mortality and handicaps. Member: GMC, 1973–79; Faculty of Medicine, QUB; NI Council for Postgrad. Med. Educn; Bd, Faculty of Community Medicine, RCPI. Chief Surgeon for Wales, St John Ambulance Bde, 1959–62. QUB Boat Club: Capt. of Boats, 1937–38; Vice-Pres., 1989–90. QHP 1974–77. CStJ 1959. *Publications:* (jtly) Infection in Hospital—a code of practice, 1971; papers in various learned jls. *Recreations:* fishing, forestry. *Address:* 2 Kensington Road, Belfast BT5 6NF. *T:* Belfast (0232) 798020; Port-a-Chapel, Greencastle, Co. Donegal. *T:* Greencastle (077) 81038. *Club:* Carlton.

BAIRD, William; Under Secretary, Scottish Home and Health Department, 1978–87; *b* 13 Oct. 1927; *s* of Peter and Christina Baird, Airdrie; *m* 1954, Anne Templeton Macfarlane; two *d. Educ:* Airdrie Academy; Glasgow Univ. Entered Scottish Home Dept, 1952; Private Sec. to Perm. Under-Sec. of State, Scottish Office, 1957; Principal, Scottish Educn Dept, 1958–63; Private Sec. to Minister of State and successive Secs of State for Scotland, 1963–65; Asst Sec., Scottish Educn Dept, 1965–66; Dept of Agriculture and Fisheries for Scotland, 1966–71; Scottish Office Finance Div., 1971–73; Registrar General for Scotland, 1973–78. *Address:* 8 Strathearn Road, North Berwick EH39 5BZ. *T:* North Berwick (0620) 3190.

BAIRSTO, Air Marshal Sir Peter (Edward), KBE 1981 (CBE 1973); CB 1980; AFC 1957; Military Aviation Adviser, Ferranti Defence Systems Ltd (formerly Scottish Group, Ferranti plc), Edinburgh, since 1984; *b* 3 Aug. 1926; *s* of late Arthur Bairsto and Beatrice (*née* Lewis); *m* 1947, Kathleen (*née* Clarbour); two *s* one *d. Educ:* Rhyl Grammar Sch. Pilot, FAA, 1944–46; 1946–62: FO RAF Regt, Palestine, Aden Protectorate; Flying Instr; Fighter Pilot, Fighter Comd and Near East; Flight Comdr, 43 Sqdn, and Leader, RAF Aerobatic Team; Sqdn Comdr, 66 Sqdn; RAF Staff Coll.; Wing Comdr, Flying, Nicosia, 1963–64; Op. Requirements, MoD, 1965–67; JSSC Latimer, 1967; Instr, RAF Staff Coll., 1968–70; Stn Comdr, RAF Honington, 1971–73; Dir, Op. Requirements, MoD, 1974–77; AOC Training Units, Support Command, 1977–79; Comdr, Northern Maritime Air Region, 1979–81; Dep. C-in-C, Strike Command, 1981–84. Vice-Chm. (Air), Highland TAVRA, 1984–90. Hon. Col, Northern Gp Field Sqns RE (ADR) (Vol.), 1989–. Mem., Scottish Sports Council, 1985–90. HM Comr, Queen Victoria Sch., Dunblane, 1984–; Chm. Management Bd, RAF Benevolent Fund Home, Alastrean House, Tarland, 1984–. Mem., St Andrews Links Trust, 1989–. Queen's Commendation for Valuable Services in the Air, 1955 and 1960. CBIM. *Recreations:* golf, fishing, shooting, gardening. *Address:* Lucklaw House, Logie, by Cupar, Fife. *T:* Balmullo (0334) 870546. *Clubs:* Royal Air Force; New (Edinburgh); Royal and Ancient Golf, New Golf (St Andrews).

BAIRSTOW, John; Founder, 1968, Chairman, since 1972, Queens Moat Houses PLC (formerly Queens Modern Hotels Ltd); *b* 25 Aug. 1930; *m*; four *d. Educ:* City of London Sch. FSVA. Founded: Bairstow, Eves and Son, Valuers and Estate Agents, 1953. Dir of cos. *Recreation:* salmon fishing. *Address:* Queens Moat Houses PLC, Queens Court, 9–17 Eastern Road, Romford, Essex RM1 3NG. *T:* Romford (0708) 730522.

BAKER, Prof. Alan, FRS 1973; Professor of Pure Mathematics, University of Cambridge, since 1974; Fellow of Trinity College, Cambridge, since 1964; *b* 19 Aug. 1939; *o c* of Barnet and Bessie Baker. *Educ:* Stratford Grammar Sch.; University Coll. London; Trinity Coll., Cambridge. BSc (London); MA, PhD (Cantab). Mem., Dept of Mathematics, UCL, 1964–65 and Fellow, UCL, 1979; Research Fellow, 1964–68, and Dir of Studies in Mathematics, 1968–74, Trinity Coll., Cambridge; Mem., Dept of Pure Maths and Math. Statistics, Univ. of Cambridge, 1966–; Reader in Theory of Numbers, 1972–74. Visiting Professor: Univs of Michigan and Colorado, 1969; Stanford Univ., 1974; Royal Soc. Kan Tong Po Prof., Univ. of Hong Kong, 1988; ETH, Zürich, 1989; Mem., Inst. for Advanced Study, Princeton, 1970; First Turán Lectr, J. Bolyai Math. Soc. Hungary, 1978. For. Fellow, Indian Nat. Sci. Acad., 1980. Fields Medal, Internat. Congress of Mathematicians, Nice, 1970; Adams Prize of Univ. of Cambridge, 1971–72. *Publications:* Transcendental Number Theory, 1975; (ed jtly) Transcendence Theory: advances and applications, 1977; A Concise Introduction to the Theory of Numbers, 1984; (ed) New Advances in Transcendence Theory, 1988; papers in various mathematical jls. *Recreation:* travel. *Address:* Trinity College, Cambridge CB2 1TQ. *T:* Cambridge (0223) 338400.

BAKER, Alex Anthony, CBE 1973; MD, MRCP, DPM; FRCPsych; Consultant Psychiatrist with special interest in the elderly to Gloucestershire Clinical Area, 1973–77, retired; *b* 22 March 1922; *m* 1944; two *s* two *d. Educ:* St Mary's Hosp. Med. Sch. Consultant Psychiatrist: Banstead Hosp., 1955; Mother and Baby Unit, Downview Hosp., 1958; St Mary Abbotts Hosp., 1967; Medical Administrator, Banstead Hosp., 1964; sometime Consultant to WHO; Sen. Principal Medical Officer, Dept of Health, 1968; Dir, NHS Hospital Adv. Service, 1969–73. *Publications:* (jtly) Psychiatric Services and Architecture, 1958; (jtly) Social Psychiatry; Psychiatric Disorders in Obstetrics, 1967; Comprehensive Psychiatric Care, 1976; chapters in sundry books; papers in numerous jls on research, psychiatric treatment, organisation of psychiatric services, etc. *Address:* Pineholm, High Close, Bovey Tracey, Devon TQ13 9EX.

BAKER, Alexander Shelley, CB 1977; OBE 1958; DFC 1944; Assistant Under Secretary of State, Home Office, 1973–77, retired; *b* 5 June 1915; *s* of late Rev. William Shelley Baker and Mrs Winifred Baker, Staines and Stratford E15; *m* 1944, Cynthia, 2nd *d* of late Charles Mould, Great Easton, Leics; two *d. Educ:* West Ham Secondary School. Served RAF, 1939–65 (despatches, 1944; 2 citations French Croix de Guerre); comd Nos 4, 16, 37 and 224 Sqdns and RAF North Front Gibraltar; retd as Group Captain. Principal, Home Office, 1965; Asst Sec., 1969–73. Reader, Church of England. *Recreations:* gardening, bridge. *Address:* High View, Foxearth, near Sudbury, Suffolk CO10 7JB. *T:* Sudbury (0787) 72548. *Club:* Royal Air Force.

BAKER, Sir (Allan) Ivor, Kt 1972; CBE 1944; JP; DL; Chairman, Baker Perkins Holdings Ltd, 1944–75; *b* 2 June 1908; *s* of late Allan Richard Baker; *m* 1935, Josephine, *d* of late A. M. Harley, KC; three *s* one *d. Educ:* Bootham, York; King's Coll., Cambridge; Harvard, USA. Baker Perkins: Student apprentice, 1931; Director, 1935–; Jt Man. Dir., 1942–67; Chm., 1944–75. British Engineers' Assoc.: Mem. Council, 1943–68; Pres., 1960–61; Director: Lloyds Bank Ltd, 1973–79; Lloyds Bank Eastern Region, 1953–73 (Chm., 1973–79); Mitchell Construction Holdings Ltd, 1963–85. Member: Economic Planning Council for East Anglia, 1965–69; Peterborough Development Corp., 1968–78. JP 1954; High Sheriff, 1968–69, DL 1973, Cambridgeshire. *Recreations:* golf, gardening. *Address:* 214 Thorpe Road, Peterborough PE3 6LW. *T:* Peterborough (0733) 262437.

BAKER, Ann Maureen, (Mrs D. R. Baker); *see* Jenner, A. M.

BAKER, Anthony Baxter, CBE 1983; JP; Regional Administrator, Northern Regional Health Authority, 1973–83; *b* 12 June 1923; *s* of late Anthony Thurlbeck Baker and Robina Frances Jane (*née* Baxter); *m* 1st, 1946, Mary Margherita Patterson (*d* 1978); one *s* three *d*; 2nd, 1981, Judith Margaret Ayers, JP. *Educ:* Tynemouth High Sch.; Durham Univ. DPA; FHA. RAFVR, UK, Canada and Iceland, 1942–46. Admin. Asst, later Dep. Sec., SE Northumberland HMC, 1949–60; Asst Sec., later Principal Asst Sec., Newcastle Regional Hosp. Bd, 1960–73. JP Tynemouth 1965; former Chm., North Tyneside PSD. *Recreations:* Rugby football (PP Percy Park RFC; PP Northumberland RFU), golf. *Address:* 59 Broadway, Tynemouth, North Shields NE30 2LJ. *T:* Tyneside 091–257 4660.

BAKER, Anthony Castelli, LVO 1980; MBE 1975; HM Diplomatic Service, retired; *b* 27 Dec. 1921; *s* of late Alfred Guy Baker and of Luciana (*née* Castelli). *Educ:* Merchant Taylors' Sch., Northwood, Mddx. Served War: munitions worker, 1940–41; volunteered for RAFVR and served in UK, ME and Italy, 1941–46 (Flt Lieut). Joined HM Diplomatic Service, 1946; served in Rome and Paris, 1946–50; Third Sec., Prague, 1951; Hamburg, 1953; Vice-Consul, Milan, 1954; Third, later Second Sec., Athens, 1959; Second Sec., Beirut, 1963; First Sec., Cairo, 1965; Naples, 1968; Turin, 1970; First Sec. Commercial, Calcutta, 1972; Consul, Montreal, 1975; First Sec. Commercial, Port of Spain, 1976; Consul, Genoa, 1979–81. Officer, Order of Merit (Italy), 1980. *Recreations:* tennis, watching cricket, travelling, jazz music. *Address:* c/o Flat 2, 44 Elsworthy Road, NW3 3BU; Box 91, 17100 La Bisbal, Gerona, Spain. *Clubs:* Royal Air Force, MCC; Gloucestershire CC.

BAKER, Arthur John, CBE 1981; Principal, Brockenhurst Tertiary College (formerly Brockenhurst Grammar School, then Brockenhurst Sixth Form College), 1969–88, retired; *b* 29 Nov. 1928; *s* of Arthur Reginald and Ruth Baker; *m* 1953, June Henrietta Dunham; one *s* two *d. Educ:* Southampton Univ. (BSc; DipEd). Mathematics Master, Hampton Grammar Sch., 1952–55; Dep. Head, Sunbury Grammar Sch., 1955–61; Headmaster, Christchurch Grammar Sch., 1961–69. *Recreations:* walking, gardening, travel. *Address:* 93 New Forest Drive, Brockenhurst, Hampshire SO42 7QT. *T:* Lymington (0590) 23138.

BAKER, Cecil John; Chairman, Alliance & Leicester Building Society (formerly Alliance Building Society), 1981–91 (Director, since 1970); *b* 2 Sept. 1915; *s* of late Frederick William Baker and Mildred Beatrice Palmer; *m* 1st, 1942, Kathleen Cecilia Henning (marr. diss. 1965); one *s*; 2nd, 1971, Joan Beatrice Barnes; one *d. Educ:* Whitgift Sch.; LSE (LLB 1939; BSc(Econ) 1949); Inst. of Actuaries. FIA 1948; ACII 1937. Sec., Insurance Inst. of London, 1945–49; Investment Manager, London Assurance, 1950–64; Investment Consultant, Hambros Bank Ltd, 1964–74; Chairman: Pension Fund Property Unit Trust, 1966–87; Charities Property Unit Trust, 1967–87; Agricl Property Unit Trust for Pension Funds and Charities, 1976–87; Victory Insurance Holdings Ltd, 1979–85; British American Property Unit Trust, 1982–87; United Real Property Trust plc, 1983–86 (Dir, 1982–86); Hunting Gate Group, 1980–90; Dir, Abbey Life Group plc, 1985–88. *Recreations:* golf, travel. *Address:* 3 Tennyson Court, 12 Dorset Square, NW1 6QB. *T:* 071–724 9716. *Club:* Savile.

BAKER, Charles A.; *see* Arnold-Baker.

BAKER, Air Vice-Marshal Christopher Paul, CB 1991; FBIM; FInstPS; Director General of Support Management, Royal Air Force, since 1989; *b* 14 June 1938; *er s* of late Paul Hocking Baker, FCA and Kathleen Minnie Florence Baker; *m* 1st, 1961, Heather Ann Laity (decd), *d* of late Cecil Henry Laity and Eleanor Hocking Laity; three *s*; 2nd, 1981, Francesca R. Aghabi, *er d* of George Khalil Aghabi and Elizabeth Maria Regina Aghabi; one *s. Educ:* Bickley Hall, Kent; Tonbridge School. FInstPS 1989. Commnd RAF, 1958; served 1958–61: RAF Khormaksar (Air Movements), Aden; Supply Sqdn, RAF Coll., Cranwell; RAF Labuan, N Borneo; No 389 Maintenance Unit, RAF Seletar, Singapore; MoD Harrogate; student, RAF Staff Coll., Bracknell; OC Supply Sqdn, RAF Linton-on-Ouse; 2nd ATAF, SHAPE; ndc; Directing Staff, RAF Staff Coll., Bracknell; HQ RAF Support Comd; Dep. Dir, RAF Supply Systems, MoD; Comd Supply Movements Officer, HQ Strike Comd, RAF High Wycombe, 1982–85; RCDS, 1985; Dir, Supply Systems, MoD, 1986–88; Dir, Supply Policy and Logistics Plans, MoD, 1988–89. FBIM 1979. Freeman, City of London; Liveryman, Bakers' Co. *Publications:* papers on the crisis of authority, oil potential of the Arctic Basin, and German reunification. *Recreations:* Rugby, rowing, ski-ing, modern history. *Address:* Lloyds Bank, Cox's & King's Branch, PO Box 1190, 7 Pall Mall, SW1Y 5NA. *T:* 071–839 1333. *Club:* Royal Air Froce.

BAKER, Derek; *see* Baker, L. G.

BAKER, Douglas Robert Pelham, FCA; Chairman: Portman Building Society, since 1990; Hardy Oil and Gas plc, since 1989; Deputy Chairman, London International Group, since 1989; *b* 21 May 1929. With Touche Ross & Co., Chartered Accountants, 1945–47 and 1949–89 (Chm., 1984–88). Dep. Chm., 1987–88, Chm., 1988–90, Regency and W of England Building Soc. (merged with Portman Wessex Building Soc., 1990); Dir, Merrett Hldgs, 1988–. Royal Naval Service, 1947–49. Chm., Brighton HA, 1988–. *Address:* Hamsey Manor, Hamsey, E Sussex BN8 5TD.

BAKER, Hon. Francis Edward N.; *see* Noel-Baker.

BAKER, Francis Eustace, CBE 1984 (OBE 1979); business interests in property, farming and the automotive industry; Partner, Crossroads Motors, since 1988; *b* 19 April 1933; *s* of Stephen and Jessica Wilhelmina Baker; *m* 1957, Constance Anne Shilling; two *s* two *d. Educ:* Borden Grammar Sch.; New Coll., Oxford (MA). Nat. Service, RN, 1955–57 (Sub Lieut). Admin. Officer, HMOCS, 1957; Solomon Is, 1958–63; farming, 1963–67; Admin. Officer, Condominium of New Hebrides, 1967–79; Chief Sec. to Falkland Is Govt, 1979–83; Gov. and C-in-C, St Helena and Dependencies, 1984–88. Silver Jubilee Medal, 1977. *Recreations:* swimming, reading, farming, interesting motor cars. *Address:* Dark Orchard, Primrose Lane, Bredgar, near Sittingbourne, Kent ME9 8EH. *T:* Wormshill (062784) 295.

BAKER, Geoffrey, QC 1970; **His Honour Judge Geoffrey Baker;** a Circuit Judge, since 1978; *b* 5 April 1925; *er s* of late Sidney and Cecilia Baker, Bradford; *m* 1948, Sheila (*née* Hill); two *s* one *d. Educ:* Bradford Grammar Sch.; Leeds Univ.; LLB (Hons). Called to Bar, Inner Temple, 1947. Recorder: of Pontefract, 1967–71; of Sunderland, 1971; a Recorder of the Crown Court, 1972–78. Pres., Leeds and WR Medico-Legal Soc., 1984–85 (Mem. Cttee, 1980–). Chm., Standing Council, Convocation of Leeds Univ., 1986– (Mem. 1980–); Member: Adv. Cttee on Law, Leeds Univ., 1983–; Court, Leeds Univ., 1984–; Pres., Leeds Univ. Law Graduates' Assoc., 1981–. *Recreations:* gardening, painting, photography. *Address:* c/o Courts Administrator, Bank House, Park Place, Leeds LS1 5QS.

BAKER, Geoffrey Hunter, CMG 1962; HM Diplomatic Service, retired; *b* 4 Aug. 1916; *s* of late Thomas Evelyn Baker and Gladys Beatrice Baker (*née* Marsh); *m* 1963, Anita Wägeler; one *d. Educ:* Haberdashers' Aske's Hampstead Sch.; Royal Masonic Sch., Bushey, Herts; Gonville and Caius Coll., Cambridge (Scholar). Joined Consular Service, 1938; Vice-Consul at Hamburg, 1938, Danzig, 1939, Bergen, 1939; captured by German forces there, April 1940; Vice-Consul, Basra, 1942, Jedda, 1942; Foreign Office, 1945–47; First Sec., Rangoon, 1947–51, Tehran, 1951–52; FO, 1953–54; NATO Def. Coll., Paris, 1954; Consul-Gen., Hanoi, 1954–56; UK Delegation, UN, Nov. 1956–March 1957; Cabinet Office, 1957–60; UK Delegation to the European Free Trade Association, Geneva, 1960–66; Consul-General, Munich, 1966–71, Zagreb, 1971–74. Order of Merit (Bavaria), 1971. *Recreations:* reading, listening to music. *Address:* 10 Leigh Road, Highfield, Southampton SO2 1EF. *Clubs:* United Oxford & Cambridge University; Cambridge University Cruising (Cambridge).

BAKER, George William, CBE 1977 (OBE 1971); VRD 1952 (Clasp 1979); HM Diplomatic Service, retired; *b* 7 July 1917; *e s* of late George William Baker and of Lilian Turnbull Baker; *m* 1942, Audrey Martha Elizabeth, *e d* of Harry and Martha Day; two *d. Educ:* Chigwell Sch.; Hertford Coll., Oxford (Colonial Service Second Devonshire Course). London Div., RNVR, 1937–62; served War, RN, 1939–45. Colonial Admin. Service, Tanganyika, 1946–62: Asst Colonial Attaché, Washington (incl. service in UK Delegn to Trusteeship Council at UN), 1957; Defence Sec., Tanganyika, 1959; Head of Tanganyika Govt Information Dept, 1959–62; retd after Tanganyika Independence, 1962. Joined CRO, 1962; Head of Chancery, First Sec. (Information) and Dir of British Inf. Services, British High Commn, Freetown, 1962–65; served in FCO (Consular and Defence Depts), 1965–69; First Sec. and Head of Chancery, Kinshasa, 1969–72; Dep. British Govt Rep., St Vincent and Grenada, Windward Is, 1972–74; British Commissioner, Port Moresby, Papua New Guinea, 1974–75, High Comr to Papua New Guinea, 1975–77. Mem., E Sussex Cttee, VSO, 1984– (Chm., 1980–84). A Vice-Pres., Royal African Soc., 1973–; Hon. Mem. and Foreign Affairs Advr, Scientific Exploration Soc., 1965–; Consultant to Operation Raleigh, 1987–. Chm., Heathfield Cttee, Sussex Housing Assoc. for Aged, 1979–84; Chm., Waldron Br., Wealden Cons. Assoc. and Vice-Chm., Constituency Political Cttee, 1983–84. Mem. Guild of Freemen of City of London, 1980–; Freeman, City of London, 1980; Liveryman, Clockmakers' Co., 1984– (Mem., 1981–; Steward, 1987–; Ed., Clockmaker's Times, 1987–). Mem., Queenhithe Ward Club, City of London. Member: Exeter Flotilla (Chm., 1987–90); Hertford Soc.; Cttee, Devon Br., Oxford Soc.; E Devon Luncheon Club (Chm., 1989–); sundry E Devon clubs and socs. *Publications:* official booklets and contribs to learned jls. *Recreations:* photography, fishing, sailing, climbing, tennis, Rugby Union, cricket, flying, clock and cabinet-making. *Address:* Crosswinds, Coreway, Sidford, Sidmouth, Devon EX10 9SD. *T:* Sidmouth (0395) 578845. *Club:* MCC.

See also Baron Coleridge.

BAKER, Gordon Meldrum; HM Diplomatic Service; Head of West Indian and Atlantic Department, Foreign and Commonwealth Office, since 1991; *b* 4 July 1941; *o s* of Walter John Ralph Gordon Baker and Kathleen Margaret Henrietta Dawe Baker (*née* Meldrum); *m* 1978, Sheila Mary Megson. *Educ:* St Andrew's Sch., Bawdrip, near Bridgwater. MSc Bradford 1976. Lord Chancellor's Dept, 1959–66; transf. to HM Diplomatic Service, 1966; Commonwealth Office, 1966–68; FO (later FCO), 1968–69; Lagos, 1969–72; First Sec., FCO, 1973–75 (Resident Clerk, 1974–75); sabbatical at Postgrad. Sch. of Studies in Industrial Technol., Univ. of Bradford, 1975–76; FCO, 1976–78 (Res. Clerk, 1976–78); First Sec. (Chancery/Information), subseq. First Sec., Head of Chancery and Consul, Brasilia, 1978–81; Asst Head, Mexico and Central America Dept, FCO, 1982–84; Counsellor, 1984; on secondment to British Aerospace, 1984–86; Counsellor, Head of Chancery then Dep. Hd of Mission, and Consul-General, Santiago, 1986–89, Chargé d'Affaires, 1986, 1987 and 1989; RCDS, 1990–91. *Recreations:* walking, watching birds, amateur dramatics, browsing. *Address:* c/o Foreign and Commonwealth Office, King Charles Street, SW1A 2AH.

BAKER, Howard Henry, Jr; Chief of Staff at the White House, 1987–88; Senior Partner, Vinson and Elkins, and Baker, Worthington, Crossley, Stansberry & Woolf, law firms; *b* 15 Nov. 1925; *s* of Howard H. Baker and Dora Ladd; *m* 1951, Joy Dirksen; one *s* one *d. Educ:* McCallie Sch.; Tulane Univ.; Univ. of Tennessee (LLB 1949). Served USN, 1943–46. Director: AT & T; Gannett Co. Inc.; MCA. Former Chm. of Bd, First Nat. Bank, Oneida, Tenn. US Senate: Senator from Tennessee 1967–85; Minority Leader, 1977–81; Majority Leader, 1981–85; former Co-Chm., Senate Select Cttee on Presidential Campaign Activities, and mem. other Senate cttees. Member: Adv. Bd, Merrill Lynch; Trustees Bd, Mayo Clinic. Mem., Amer. Bar Assoc. Presidential Medal of Freedom, 1984. *Address:* Huntsville, Tenn 37756, USA.

BAKER, Maj.-Gen. Ian Helstrip, CBE 1977 (MBE 1965); rcds, psc; Secretary, University College London, since 1982; General Officer Commanding, North East District, 1980–82; *b* 26 Nov. 1927; *s* of late Henry Hubert Baker and Mary Clare Baker (*née* Coles); *m* 1956, Susan Anne, *d* of Major Henry Osmond Lock, York House, Dorchester, Dorset; one *s* one *d* (and one *s* decd). *Educ:* St Peter's Sch., York; St Edmund Hall, Oxford; RMA, Sandhurst. Commnd 2nd Lieut, RA, 1948; 10th Fd Regt RA, 1949–51; Lieut 1950; 2nd Regt RHA, 1951–53; Capt. 1953; RAC Centre, 1953–55; transf. RTR, 1955; 4th Royal Tank Regt, 1955–57; HQ 10th Inf. Bde, 1957–58; Staff Coll., Camberley, 1959; Major 1960; DAAG HQ 17 Gurkha Div., Overseas Commonwealth Land Forces, Malaya and Singapore, 1960–62; OC Parachute Sqdn RAC (C Sqdn 2nd Royal Tank Regt), 1962–65; Instr Staff Coll., Camberley, and Bt Lt-Col, 1965; GSO1 and Asst Sec., Chiefs of Staff Cttee, MoD, 1966–67; Lt-Col 1966; CO, 1st Royal Tank Regt, UK and BAOR, 1967–69; Col 1970; Col, RTR, 1970–71; Brig. 1972; Comdr, 7th Armoured Bde, BAOR, 1972–74; RCDS, 1974; Brig. Gen. Staff, HQ UKLF, 1975–77; Service Fellow, St Catharine's Coll., Cambridge, 1977; Maj.-Gen., 1978; Asst Chief of the Gen. Staff, 1978–80. Member: Army Combat Develt Cttee, MoD, 1975–80; MoD Op. Requirements Cttee, 1978–80; Hd, UK Delegn, NATO talks on weapons and equipment policy, 1978–80. Col Comdt, Royal Tank Regt, 1981–86. Member: Organising Cttee for 4th Internat. Conf. of Univ. Administrators, Delhi, 1985, for 5th Internat. Conf., Sydney, 1987, for 6th Internat. Conf., Maryland, USA, 1989, for 7th Internat. Conf., Twente, The Netherlands, 1991; Univ. of London Mil. Educn Cttee, 1987–. Hon. President: Medical and Dental Students Soc., UCL, 1983–88; UCL Boat Club, 1986–. Mem., RAC Benevolent Fund Cttee, 1985–89. Governor, Welbeck Coll., 1980–82. *Publications:* contribs to service and university papers and journals. *Recreations:* skiing, sailing, outdoor pursuits. *Address:* University College London, Gower Street, WC1E 6BT. *T:* 071–380 7000; c/o Barclays Bank, 10 South Street, Dorchester, Dorset DT1 1BT.

BAKER, Ian Michael; Metropolitan Stipendiary Magistrate, since 1990; *b* 8 May 1947; *s* of late David Ernest Baker and of Phyllis Hinds; *m* 1st, 1976, Sue Joel (marr. diss. 1985); one *s*; 2nd, 1991, Jill Sack. *Educ:* Cynffig Grammar Sch., Mid Glam; St Catharine's Coll., Cambridge (MA). Articled, then Asst Solicitor to John Clitheroe, Kingsley Napley, 1972–76; Partner, Heninghem, Ambler & Gildener, York, 1976–79; Assistant Solicitor: Claude, Hornby & Cox, 1979; Seifert Sedley, 1980–83; Clinton Davis, 1984–87; Partner, T. V. Edwards, 1987–90. Trustee, Nat. Council for Welfare of Prisoners Abroad, 1986–. *Recreations:* jazz, travel, kitchen gardening, theatre, photography, cooking, bird-watching. *Address:* Wells Street Magistrates' Court, 59–65 Wells Street, W1A 3AE. *Clubs:* Ronnie Scott's, Jazz Café.

BAKER, Sir Ivor; *see* Baker, Sir A. I.

BAKER, James Addison, III; Secretary of State, United States of America, since 1989; *b* 28 April 1930; *s* of James A. Baker, Jr and late Bonner Means Baker; *m* 1973, Susan Garrett; eight *c. Educ:* Princeton Univ. (BA); Univ. of Texas at Austin (law degree). Served US Marine Corps, 1952–54. Practised law, firm of Andrews, Kurth, Campbell and Jones, Houston, Texas, 1957–75, 1977–81. Under Sec. of Commerce, US Govt, 1975; National Chairman: President Ford's re-elecn campaign, 1976; George Bush for President Cttee, 1979–80; Dep. Dir, Reagan–Bush Transition and Sen. Advr to 1980 Reagan–Bush Cttee, 1980–Jan. 1981; Chief of Staff to US President, 1981–85; Sec. of US Treasury, 1985–88. Numerous hon. degrees. *Recreations:* hunting, fishing, tennis, golf. *Address:* Secretary of State, 2201 C Street NW, Washington, DC 20520, USA. *T:* (202) 647–4910. *Clubs:* numerous social, civic and paternal.

BAKER, Dame Janet (Abbott), DBE 1976 (CBE 1970); professional singer; *b* 21 Aug. 1933; *d* of Robert Abbott Baker and May (*née* Pollard); *m* 1957, James Keith Shelley. *Educ:* The College for Girls, York; Wintringham, Grimsby. Mem., Munster Trust. Chancellor, Univ. of York, 1991–. Daily Mail Kathleen Ferrier Award, 1956; Queen's Prize, Royal College of Music, 1959; Shakespeare Prize, Hamburg, 1971; Copenhagen Sonning Prize, 1979. Hon. DMus: Birmingham, 1968; Leicester, 1974; London, 1974; Hull, 1975; Oxon, 1975; Leeds, 1980; Lancaster, 1983; York, 1984; Hon. MusD Cantab, 1984; Hon. LLD Aberdeen, 1980; Hon. DLitt Bradford, 1983. Hon. Fellow: St Anne's Coll., Oxford, 1975; Downing Coll., Cambridge, 1985. FRSA 1979. Gold Medal, Royal

Philharmonic Soc., 1990. *Publication:* Full Circle (autobiog.), 1982. *Recreations:* reading, tennis, walking. *Address:* Carlyon House, Mount Park Road, Harrow, Mddx HA1 3JS.

BAKER, John Arnold, DL; **His Honour Judge Baker;** a Circuit Judge, since 1973; *b* Calcutta, 5 Nov. 1925; *s* of late William Sydney Baker, MC and Hilda Dora Baker (*née* Swiss); *m* 1954, Edith Muriel Joy Heward; two *d. Educ:* Plymouth Coll.; Wellington Sch., Somerset; Wadham Coll., Oxford (MA, BCL). Treas., Oxford Union, 1948. Admitted Solicitor, 1951; called to Bar, Gray's Inn, 1960. A Recorder, 1972–73. Chm., Nat. League of Young Liberals, 1952–53; contested (L): Richmond, 1959 and 1964; Dorking, 1970; Vice-Pres., Liberal Party, 1968–69; Chm., Liberal Party Exec., 1969–70. Pres., Medico-Legal Soc., 1986–88. DL Surrey, 1986. *Recreations:* music, boating. *Address:* c/o The Crown Court, Canbury Park Road, Kingston upon Thames, Surrey KT2 6JV. *T:* 081–549 5241.

BAKER, Rt. Rev. John Austin; *see* Salisbury, Bishop of.

BAKER, John B.; *see* Brayne-Baker.

BAKER, John Burkett, QC 1975; **His Honour Judge J. Burkett Baker;** a Circuit Judge, since 1978; *b* 17 Sept. 1931; *s* of Philip and Grace Baker; *m* 1955, Margaret Mary Smeaton; two *s* seven *d* (and one *s* decd). *Educ:* Finchley Catholic Grammar Sch.; White Fathers, Bishops Waltham; UC Exeter. LLB London. RAF, 1955–58. Called to Bar, Gray's Inn, 1957; practised from 1958. Prosecuting Counsel to Dept of Health and Social Security, 1969–75; Dep. Chm., Shropshire QS, 1970–71; a Recorder of the Crown Court, 1972–78. Marriage Counsellor, Catholic Marriage Adv. Council, 1970–87 (Chm., 1981–83); Pres., Barnet, Haringey and Hertsmere Marriage Guidance Council, 1982–. Governor: Bedford Coll., London, 1983–85; Holy Family Convent, Enfield, 1984–89. Papal Cross Pro Ecclesia et Pontifice, 1986. *Recreation:* theatre. *Address:* 43 The Ridgeway, Enfield, Mddx EN2 8PD.

BAKER, Prof. John Hamilton, LLD; FBA 1984; Professor of English Legal History, Cambridge University, since 1988; Fellow of St Catharine's College, since 1971; *b* 10 April 1944; *s* of Kenneth Lee Vincent Baker, QPM and Marjorie (*née* Bagshaw); *m* 1968, Veronica Margaret, *d* of Rev. W. S. Lloyd; two *d. Educ:* King Edward VI Grammar School, Chelmsford; UCL (LLB 1965 (Andrews Medal), PhD 1968; Fellow 1990); MA Cantab 1971, LLD 1984, Yorke Prize, 1975. FRHistS 1980. Called to the Bar, Inner Temple, 1966 (Hon. Bencher 1988), *aeg* Gray's Inn, 1978. Asst Lectr, Faculty of Laws, UCL, 1965–67, Lectr, 1967–71; Cambridge University: Librarian, Squire Law Library, 1971–73; Univ. Lectr in Law, 1973–83; Reader in English Legal History, 1983–88; Junior Proctor, 1980–81. Visiting Professor: European Univ. Inst., Florence, 1979; Yale Law Sch., 1987; NY Univ. Law Sch., 1988–; Vis. Lectr, Harvard Law Sch., 1982; Mellon Senior Res. Fellow, H. E. Huntington Lib., San Marino, Calif., 1983; Ford Special Lectr, Oxford Univ., 1984. Jt Literary Dir, Selden Soc., 1981–. Ames Prize, Harvard, 1985. *Publications:* An Introduction to English Legal History, 1971, 3rd edn 1990; English Legal Manuscripts, vol. I, 1975, vol. II, 1978; The Reports of Sir John Spelman, 1977–78; (ed) Legal Records and the Historian, 1978; Manual of Law French, 1979, 2nd edn 1990; The Order of Serjeants at Law, 1984; English Legal Manuscripts in the USA, vol. I 1985, vol. II 1991; The Legal Profession and the Common Law, 1986; (with S. F. C. Milsom) Sources of English Legal History, 1986; The Notebook of Sir John Port, 1986; (ed) Judicial Records, Law Reports and the Growth of Case Law, 1989; Readings and Moots in the Inns of Court, vol. II, 1990; articles in legal and hist. jls. *Address:* 75 Hurst Park Avenue, Cambridge CB4 2AB. *T:* Cambridge (0223) 62251; St Catharine's College, Cambridge CB2 1RL. *T:* Cambridge (0223) 338317.

BAKER, John William; Chief Executive, National Power plc, since 1990; *b* 5 Dec. 1937; *s* of Reginald and Wilhelmina Baker; *m* 1st, 1962, Pauline (*née* Moore); one *s*; 2nd, 1975, Gillian (*née* Bullen). *Educ:* Harrow Weald County Grammar Sch.; Oriel Coll., Oxford. Served Army, 1959–61. MoT, 1961–70; DoE, 1970–74; Dep. Chief Exec., Housing Corp., 1974–78; Sec., 1979–80, Bd Mem., 1980–89, Corporate Man. Dir, 1986–89, CEGB. *Recreations:* tennis, bridge, music, theatre. *Address:* National Power plc, Sudbury House, 15 Newgate Street, EC1A 7AU. *T:* 071–634 5111.

BAKER, Rt. Hon. Kenneth (Wilfred); PC 1984; MP (C) Mole Valley, since 1983 (St Marylebone, Oct. 1970–1983; Acton, March 1968–1970); Secretary of State for the Home Department, since 1990; *b* 3 Nov. 1934; *s* of late W. M. Baker, OBE and of Mrs Baker (*née* Harries); *m* 1963, Mary Elizabeth Gray-Muir; one *s* two *d. Educ:* St Paul's Sch.; Magdalen Coll., Oxford. Nat. Service, 1953–55: Lieut in Gunners, N Africa; Artillery Instructor to Libyan Army. Oxford, 1955–58 (Sec. of Union). Served Twickenham Borough Council, 1960–62. Contested (C): Poplar, 1964; Acton, 1966. Parly Sec., CSD, 1972–74; PPS to Leader of Opposition, 1974–75; Minister of State and Minister for Information Technology, DTI, 1981–84; a Minister for Local Govt, DoE, 1984–85; Sec. of State for the Environment, 1985–86; Sec. of State for Educn and Sci., 1986–89; Chancellor of the Duchy of Lancaster, 1989–90; Chm., Conservative Party, 1989–90. Mem., Public Accounts Cttee, 1969–70. Mem. Exec., 1922 Cttee. Chm., Hansard Soc., 1978–81. Sec. Gen., UN Conf. of Parliamentarians on World Population and Development, 1978. *Publications:* (ed) I Have No Gun But I Can Spit, 1980; (ed) London Lines, 1982; (ed) The Faber Book of English History in Verse, 1988; (ed) Unauthorized Versions: poems and their parodies, 1990. *Recreation:* collecting books. *Address:* House of Commons, SW1. *Clubs:* Athenæum, Carlton, Garrick.

BAKER, Prof. (Leonard Graham) Derek, MA, BLitt; Professor of History, since 1986, Director, Institute for Medieval Renaissance and Hispanic Studies, since 1989, Director, Centre for Undergraduate Study and Research, since 1990, University of Texas; *b* 21 April 1931; *s* of Leonard and late Phoebe Caroline Baker; *m* 1970, Jean Dorothy Johnston; one *s* one *d. Educ:* Christ's Hospital; Oriel Coll., Oxford (1st Class Hons Modern History 1955, MA, BLitt). Captain, Royal Signals, 1950–52. Senior History Master, The Leys School, 1956–66; Lecturer in Medieval History, Univ. of Edinburgh, 1966–79; Headmaster, Christ's Hosp., 1979–85. Editor, Ecclesiastical History Soc., 1969; Pres., British Sub-Commission, Commission Internationale d'Histoire Ecclésiastique Comparée, 1971. Dir, Exec. Cttee, Haskins Soc., 1990–. FRHistS 1969. *Publications:* Portraits and Documents, Vol. 1 1967, Vol. 2 1969; Partnership in Excellence, 1974; (ed) Studies in Church History, 7–17, 1970–80 (subsidia 1–2, 1978–79); numerous articles in historical jls. *Recreations:* singing; climbing, mountaineering, pot-holing, camping; good company; food and wine; travel. *Address:* 5 Allendale, Southwater, Horsham, Sussex RH13 7UE. *T:* Southwater (0403) 731459; 30 Dick Place, Edinburgh EH9 2JB. *T:* 031–667 5920; 1300 Dallas Drive, #1023, Denton, Texas 76201, USA. *T:* 817–387–3282. *Clubs:* National Liberal; Leander (Henley-on-Thames).

BAKER, Mark Alexander Wyndham; Executive Director, Corporate Affairs and Personnel, Nuclear Electric plc, since 1989; *b* 19 June 1940; *s* of late Lt-Comdr Alexander Arthur Wyndham Baker, RN and Renée Gavrelle Stenson (*née* Macnaghten); *m* 1964, Meriel, *yr d* of Capt. Hugh Chetwynd-Talbot, MBE and Cynthia Chetwynd-Talbot; one *s* one *d. Educ:* Prince Edward Sch., Salisbury, S Rhodesia; University Coll. of Rhodesia & Nyasaland (Beit Schol.; BA London); Christ Church, Oxford (Rhodes Schol.; MA). United Kingdom Atomic Energy Authority, 1964–89: Sec., 1976–78, Gen. Sec., 1978–81, AERE, Harwell; Dir of Personnel and Admin, Northern Div., 1981–84; Authority Personnel Officer, 1984–86; Authority Sec., 1986–89. *Recreations:* bridge, gardening, squash, walking, words. *Address:* Nuclear Electric plc, Barnett Way, Barnwood, Gloucester GL4 7RS. *T:* Gloucester (0452) 654250. *Clubs:* United Oxford & Cambridge University; Antrobus Dining (Cheshire).

BAKER, Martyn Murray; Head of Overseas Trade Division 4, Department of Trade and Industry, since 1990; *b* 10 March 1944; *s* of Norman and Constance Baker; *m* 1970, Rosemary Caroline Holdich. *Educ:* Dulwich Coll.; Pembroke Coll., Oxford (MA). Asst Principal, Min. of Aviation, 1965–67; Asst Private Sec. to Minister of State, Min. of Technology, 1968–69; Private Sec. to Parly Under Secs of State, Min. of Technology, Min. of Aviation Supply, DTI, 1969–71; Principal, 1971; Principal Private Sec. to Sec. of State for Trade, 1977–78; Asst Sec., Dept of Trade, 1978; Counsellor, Civil Aviation and Shipping, Washington, 1978–82; Department of Trade and Industry: Asst Sec., Air Div., 1982–85; Projects and Export Policy Div., 1985–86; Under Sec., 1986; Regl Dir, NW, 1986–88; Dir, Enterprise and Deregulation Unit, 1988–90. Mem., Export Guarantees Advisory Council, 1985–86. Leader, Manchester-Salford City Action Team, 1986–88. Hon. Vis. Sen. Fellow, Manchester Business Sch., 1988–. FRSA 1988. *Address:* Department of Trade and Industry, 1–19 Victoria Street, SW1H 0ET.

BAKER, Maurice S.; Managing Director, F. W. Woolworth & Co. Ltd, 1967–71, retired; *b* 27 Jan. 1911; *s* of Sidney B. Baker and Ellen Elizabeth (*née* Airey); *m* 1st, 1935, Helen Johnstone (*née* Tweedie) (*d* 1977); one *s*; 2nd, 1978, Kirsten Randine (*née* Haugen). *Educ:* Lowestoft Grammar School. Trainee Manager, F. W. Woolworth & Co. Ltd, 1928; RAOC, 1940–46 (Major); rejoined company; Dir 1962. Officer, Legion of Merit (US), 1945. *Recreation:* bowls (Pres., 1975, Hon. Life Mem., 1983, Surrey County Bowling Assoc.).

BAKER, Michael Findlay; QC 1990; a Recorder, since 1991; *b* 26 May 1943; *s* of Rt Hon. Sir George Baker, PC, OBE; *m* 1973, Sarah Hartley Overton; two *d. Educ:* Haileybury; Brasenose Coll., Oxford. Called to the Bar, Inner Temple, 1966. Sec., National Reference Tribunals for the Coal-mining Industry, 1973–. *Recreations:* mountain climbing and walking, cross country running. *Address:* Fountain Court, Temple, EC4Y 9DH. *T:* 071–583 3335. *Clubs:* Alpine; Thames Hare and Hounds.
See also Hon. Sir T. S. G. Baker.

BAKER, Prof. Michael John, TD 1971; Professor of Marketing, since 1971, Deputy Principal since, 1984, Strathclyde University; Chairman, Westburn Publishers Ltd, since 1984; *b* 5 Nov. 1935; *s* of John Overend Baker and Constance Dorothy (*née* Smith); *m* 1959, Sheila (*née* Bell); one *s* two *d. Educ:* Worksop Coll.; Gosforth and Harvey Grammar Schs; Durham Univ. (BA); London Univ. (BScEcon); Harvard Univ. (CertITP, DBA); DipM. FCIM; FCAM; FRSA; FScotvec. 2nd Lieut, RA, 1956–57. Salesman, Richard Thomas & Baldwins (Sales) Ltd, 1958–64; Asst Lectr, Medway Coll. of Technology, 1964–66; Lectr, Hull Coll. of Technology, 1966–68; Foundn for Management Educn Fellow, 1968–71, Res. Associate, 1969–71, Harvard Business Sch.; Dean, Strathclyde Bus. Sch., 1978–84. Mem., Vice Chm. and Chm., Scottish Bus. Educn Council, 1973–85; Pres., Marketing Educn Gp, 1986– (Chm., 1973–86); Member: Food and Drink, EDC, 1976–78; SSRC Management and Industrial Relns Cttee, 1976–80; Nat. Councillor, Inst. of Marketing, 1977, Vice Chm. 1984–86, Chm. 1987. Member: Scottish Hosps Endowment Res. Trust, 1983–; Chief Scientist's Cttee, SHHD, 1985–; Bus. and Management Sub-Cttee, UGC, 1985–89. Director: Stoddard Sekers International (formerly Stoddard Hldgs) PLC, 1983–; Scottish Transport Gp, 1986–90; ARIS plc, 1990–; Reid Gp, 1989–; SGBS Ltd, 1990–. Founding Editor, Jl of Marketing Management, 1985. *Publications:* Marketing, 1971, 5th edn 1991; Marketing New Industrial Products, 1975; (with R. McTavish) Product Policy, 1976; (ed) Marketing in Adversity, 1976; (ed) Marketing Theory and Practice, 1976, 2nd edn 1983; (ed) Industrial Innovation, 1979; Market Development, 1983; (ed) Dictionary of Marketing, 1984, 2nd edn 1990; Marketing Strategy and Management, 1985; (with S. T. Parkinson) Organisational Buying Behaviour, 1986; (ed) The Marketing Book, 1987; (with D. Ughanwa) The Role of Design in International Competitiveness, 1989; (with S. Hart) Marketing and Competitive Success, 1989; Research for Marketing, 1991; (ed) Perspectives on Marketing Management, vol. 1, 1991. *Recreations:* hill walking, sailing, foreign travel. *Address:* Westburn, Helensburgh G84 9NH. *T:* Helensburgh (0436) 74686. *Club:* Royal Over-Seas League.

BAKER, Michael John David; His Honour Judge Michael Baker; a Circuit Judge, since 1988; *b* 17 April 1934; *s* of late Ernest Bowden Baker and of Dulcie Baker; *m* 1958, Edna Harriet Lane; one *s* one *d. Educ:* Trinity Sch. of John Whitgift; Bristol Univ. (LLB Hons). Admitted solicitor, 1957. Flying Officer, RAF, 1957–60. Joined firm of Glanvilles, Solicitors, Portsmouth, 1960; Partner, 1963–88; a Recorder, 1980–88. Coroner, S Hampshire, 1973–88 (Asst Dep. Coroner, 1971; Dep. Coroner, 1972). Pres., Southern Coroners Soc., 1975–76; Mem. Council, Coroners Soc. of England and Wales, 1979–88 (Jun. Vice-Pres., 1987–88). *Recreations:* walking, tennis, the theatre, music (particularly choral singing), photography. *Address:* c/o 131 London Road, Waterlooville, Hants PO7 7SS. *T:* Waterlooville (0705) 251414. *Clubs:* Royal Air Force, Law Society; Emsworth Sailing.

BAKER, Nicholas Brian; MP (C) North Dorset, since 1979; a Lord Commissioner of HM Treasury (Government Whip), since 1990; *b* 23 Nov. 1938; *m* 1970, Penelope Carol d'Abo; one *s* one *d. Educ:* Clifton Coll.; Exeter Coll., Oxford (MA). Partner in Frere Cholmeley, solicitors, WC2, 1973–. Parliamentary Private Secretary to: Minister of State for the Armed Forces, 1981–83, for Defence Procurement, MoD, 1983–84; Sec. of State for Defence, MoD, 1984–86; Sec. of State for Trade and Industry, 1987–88; an Asst Govt Whip, 1989–90. *Publications:* pamphlets. *Recreations:* exercise, music, English countryside. *Address:* House of Commons, SW1. *Clubs:* Wimborne Conservative, Blandford Constitutional.

BAKER, Nigel Robert James; QC 1988; a Recorder, since 1985; *b* 21 Dec. 1942; *s* of late Herbert James Baker and of Amy Beatrice Baker; *m* 1973, Stephanie Joy Stephenson; one *s. Educ:* Norwich Sch.; Univ. of Southampton (BA Law); Queens' Coll., Cambridge (LLM). Lectr in Law, Univ. of Leicester, 1968–70; called to the Bar, Middle Temple, 1969; practice on Midland and Oxford Circuit. Mem., Bar Council, 1985. *Recreations:* football, fell walking, gardening. *Address:* 2 Crown Office Row, Temple, EC4. *T:* 071–353 1365.

BAKER, Paul Vivian; His Honour Judge Paul Baker; a Circuit Judge, since 1983; *b* 27 March 1923; *er s* of Vivian Cyril Baker and Maud Lydia Baker; *m* 1957, Stella Paterson Eadie, *d* of William Eadie, MD; one *s* one *d. Educ:* City of London Sch.; University Coll., Oxford (BCL, MA). Called to Bar, Lincoln's Inn, 1950, Bencher, 1979; QC 1972. Editor, Law Quarterly Review, 1971–87. *Recreations:* music, gardening. *Address:* 9 Old Square, Lincoln's Inn, WC2A 3SR. *T:* 071–242 2633. *Clubs:* Athenæum, Authors'.

BAKER, Peter Maxwell; QC 1974; **His Honour Judge Peter Baker;** a Circuit Judge, since 1983; *b* 26 March 1930; *s* of late Harold Baker and of Rose Baker; *m* 1954, Jacqueline Mary Marshall; three *d*; *m* 1988, Sandra Elizabeth Hughes. *Educ:* King Edward VII Sch., Sheffield; Exeter Coll., Oxford. MA Oxon. Called to Bar, Gray's Inn, 1956 (Holker Senior Exhibitioner); Junior, NE Circuit, 1960; a Recorder of the Crown Court, 1972–83. *Recreations:* yachting, music, watching others garden. *Address:* c/o Circuit Administrator, 17th Floor, West Riding House, Albion Street, Leeds LS1 5AA. *Club:* Sheffield (Sheffield).

BAKER, Richard Douglas James, OBE 1976; RD 1979; broadcaster and author; Member, Broadcasting Standards Council, since 1988; *b* Willesden, London, 15 June 1925; *s* of Albert and Jane Isobel Baker; *m* 1961, Margaret Celia Martin; two *s*. *Educ:* Kilburn Grammar Sch.; Peterhouse, Cambridge (MA). Served War, Royal Navy, 1943–46. Actor, 1948; Teacher, 1949; Third Programme Announcer, 1950–53; BBC TV Newsreader, 1954–82; Commentator for State Occasion Outside Broadcasts, 1967–70; TV Introductions to Promenade Concerts, 1960–; Panellist on BBC2's Face the Music, 1966–79; Presenter, Omnibus, BBC TV, 1983; on Radio 4: Presenter of Start the Week with Richard Baker, 1970–87; These You Have Loved, 1972–77; Baker's Dozen, 1978–87; Rollercoaster, 1984; Music in Mind, 1987–88; Comparing Notes, 1987–; on Radio 3: Mainly for Pleasure, 1986–; on Radio 2: Presenter of Melodies for You, 1986–. Columnist, Now! Magazine, 1979–80. Dir. Youth and Music; Mem., Exec. Cttee, Friends of Covent Garden; Trustee, D'Oyly Carte Opera Co., 1985–; Governor, NYO of GB, 1985–. TV Newscaster of the Year (Radio Industries Club), 1972, 1974, 1979; BBC Radio Personality of the Year (Variety Club of GB), 1984. Hon. FLCM 1974; Hon. RCM 1988. Hon. LLD: Strathclyde, 1979; Aberdeen, 1983. *Publications:* Here is the News (broadcasts), 1966; The Terror of Tobermory, 1972; The Magic of Music, 1975; Dry Ginger, 1977; Richard Baker's Music Guide, 1979; Mozart, 1982; London, a theme with variations, 1989. *Recreations:* gardening, the gramophone. *Address:* c/o Bagenal Harvey Organisation, 141–143 Drury Lane, WC2B 5TB. *T:* 071–379 4625. *Club:* Garrick.

BAKER, Richard Hugh; HM Diplomatic Service; Civilian Member, Senior Directing Staff, Royal College of Defence Studies, since 1986; *b* 22 Oct. 1935; *s* of Hugh Cuthbert Baker and Muriel Lovenda Baker (*née* Owens); *m* 1963, Patricia Marianne Haigh Thomas; one *s* three *d*. *Educ:* Marlborough Coll.; New Coll., Oxford. Army (2nd Lieut RA), 1954–56. Plebiscite Officer, UN Plebiscite, S Cameroons, 1960–61; joined Diplomatic Service, 1962; 3rd, later 2nd, then 1st Sec., Addis Ababa, 1963–66; Foreign Office, 1967; Private Sec. to Permanent Under-Sec. of State, Foreign Office (later FCO), 1967–70; 1st Sec. and Head of Chancery, Warsaw, 1970–72; FCO, 1973–76; RCDS 1977; Econ. and Financial Counsellor, and Dep. Head, UK Perm. Delegn to OECD, Paris, 1978–82; Dep. High Comr, Ottawa, 1982–86. *Recreations:* music, painting, literature. *Address:* c/o Foreign and Commonwealth Office, SW1.

BAKER, Sir Robert George Humphrey S.; *see* Sherston-Baker.

BAKER, Scott; *see* Baker, T. S. G.

BAKER, Stephen, OBE 1987; consultant; Managing Director, British Electricity International Ltd, 1978–86; *b* 27 March 1926; *s* of late Arthur and Nancy Baker; *m* 1950, Margaret Julia Wright; one *s* two *d*. *Educ:* Epsom Coll.; Clare Coll., Cambridge (MA). FIMechE. Engr Officer, RN, 1944–47; Apprentice, Davy United Engineering Co. Ltd, 1947–49; Works Engr, John Baker & Bessemer Ltd, 1949–51; Davy United Engrg Co. Ltd, 1951: Dir of Prodn, 1960; Gen. Man., 1961; Dir, Davy Ashmore Ltd, 1963; Dir of Ops, Davy-Ashmore Engrg Ltd, 1964; Chm. and Chief Exec. of Davy United Engrg Co. Ltd, Ashmore Benson Pease Ltd and Loewy Robertson Engrg Co. Ltd, 1968; Man. Dir, Kearney & Trecker Ltd, 1970; Co-ordinator of Industrial Advrs, Depts of Trade and Industry, 1974–78. *Recreations:* fishing, gardening. *Address:* 75 Slayleigh Lane, Sheffield S10 3RG.

BAKER, Very Rev. Thomas George Adames, MA; DD Lambeth, 1987; Dean of Worcester, 1975–86, Dean Emeritus since 1986; *b* 22 Dec. 1920; *s* of late Walter and Marion Baker, Southampton; unmarried. *Educ:* King Edward VI Sch., Southampton; Exeter Coll., Oxford; Lincoln Theological Coll. Curate of All Saints, King's Heath, Birmingham, 1944–47; Vicar of St James, Edgbaston, 1947–54; Sub-Warden of Lincoln Theological Coll., 1954–60; Principal of Wells Theological College and Prebendary of Combe II in Wells Cathedral, 1960–71; Archdeacon of Bath, 1971–75. Canon Theologian of Leicester Cathedral, 1959–66. Select Preacher, Univ. of Cambridge, 1963, Univ. of Oxford, 1973. Recognised Teacher, Bristol Univ., 1969–74. *Publications:* What is the New Testament?, 1969; Questioning Worship, 1977. *Recreation:* music. *Address:* 21 Brooklyn Road, Bath BA1 6TE. *T:* Bath (0225) 337243.

BAKER, Hon. Sir (Thomas) Scott (Gillespie), Kt 1988; **Hon. Mr Justice Scott Baker;** a Judge of the High Court of Justice, Family Division, since 1988; Family Division Liaison Judge (Wales and Chester Circuit), since 1990; Presiding Judge, Wales and Chester Circuit, since 1991; *b* 10 Dec. 1937; *s* of late Rt Hon. Sir George Baker, PC, OBE and Jessie McCall Baker; *m* 1973, Margaret Joy Strange; two *s* one *d*. *Educ:* Haileybury; Brasenose Coll., Oxford. Called to the Bar, Middle Temple, 1961 (Astbury Schol.), Bencher 1985; a Recorder, 1976–88; QC 1978. Member: Senate, Inns of Court, 1977–84; Bar Council, 1988. Mem., Govt Cttee of Inquiry into Human Fertilisation (Warnock Cttee), 1982–84. Mem., Chorleywood UDC, 1965–68. Dep. Chm., Cricket Council Appeals Cttee, 1986–88. *Recreations:* golf, fishing, shooting. *Address:* Royal Courts of Justice, Strand, WC2A 2LL. *Clubs:* MCC; Denham Golf.
    See also M. F. Baker.

BAKER, Wallis James, CB 1989; Chairman, Land Administration Commission, Queensland, 1983–89, retired; *b* 19 March 1931; *s* of James Campbell Baker and Doris Isabel (*née* Nowland); *m* 1960, Eileen Merle Seeney; one *s* one *d*. *Educ:* Downlands Coll., Toowoomba, Qld. Admitted Solicitor, Supreme Court of Qld, 1954; called to the Bar, Qld, 1969. Practised as Solicitor, Monto, Qld, 1955–68; entered Qld Public Service as career public servant, 1968. *Recreations:* tennis, ancient history, rock collecting. *Address:* 61 Montrose Street, Gordon Park, Brisbane, Qld 4031, Australia. *T:* 357 6618.

BAKER, Willfred Harold Kerton, TD; *b* 6 Jan. 1920; *o s* of late W. H. Baker; *m* 1st, 1945, Kathleen Helen Sloan (*née* Murray Bisset) (*d* 1987); one *s* two *d*; 2nd, Jean Gordon Scott (*née* Skinner). *Educ:* Hardye's Sch.; Edinburgh Univ.; Cornell Univ., USA. Joined TA, and served War of 1939–45 (Major). Edinburgh Univ. (BSc Agriculture), 1946–49. MP (C) Banffshire, 1964–Feb. 1974. *Recreations:* golf, fishing, philately. *Address:* Ashdown, 42 Southfield Avenue, Paignton, South Devon TQ3 1LH. *T:* Paignton (0803) 550861.

BAKER, Wilson, FRS 1946; FRSC; BSc, MSc, PhD, DSc (Manchester); MA (Oxon.); retired; Alfred Capper Pass Professor of Organic Chemistry, University of Bristol, 1945–65 (Dean of the Faculty of Science, 1948–51; Emeritus Professor, University of Bristol, 1965); *b* 24 Jan. 1900; *yr s* of Harry and Mary Baker, Runcorn, Cheshire; *m* 1927, Juliet Elizabeth, *d* of Henry and Julia R. Glaisyer, Birmingham; one *s* two *d*. *Educ:* Liverpool Coll. Upper Sch.; Victoria Univ. of Manchester (Mercer Schol., Baeyer Fellow and Dalton Scholar). Asst Lecturer in Chemistry, Univ. of Manchester, 1924–27; Tutor

in Chemistry, Dalton Hall, Manchester, 1926–27; Univ. Lecturer and Demonstrator in Chemistry, Univ. of Oxford, 1927–44; Fellow and Praelector in Chemistry, The Queen's Coll., Oxford, 1937–44. Vice-Pres. of the Chemical Society, 1957–60. *Publications:* numerous original papers on organic chemistry, dealing chiefly with the synthesis of natural products, the development of synthetical processes, compounds of abnormal aromatic type, organic inclusion compounds, and the preparation of large-ring compounds, and the chemistry of penicillin, published mainly in Journal of the Chemical Society; (with T. W. J. Taylor) 2nd Edition of Professor N. V. Sidgwick's The Organic Chemistry of Nitrogen, 1937. *Recreations:* walking, gardening, music, mineralogy. *Address:* Lane's End, 54 Church Road, Winscombe, Avon. *T:* Winscombe (093484) 3112.

BAKER-BATES, Merrick Stuart; HM Diplomatic Service; Head of South Atlantic and Antarctic Department, Foreign and Commonwealth Office, and Commissioner, British Antarctic Territory, since 1989; *b* 22 July 1939; *s* of late E. T. Baker-Bates, MD, FRCP, and of Norah Stuart (*née* Kirkham); *m* 1963, Chrystal Jacqueline Goodacre; one *s* one *d*. *Educ:* Shrewsbury Sch.; Hertford Coll., Oxford (MA); College of Europe, Bruges. Journalist, Brussels, 1962–63; entered HM Diplomatic Service, 1963; 3rd, later 2nd Sec., Tokyo, 1963–68; 1st Secretary: FCO, 1968–73; (Inf.), Washington, 1973–76; (Commercial), Tokyo, 1976–79; Counsellor (Commercial), Tokyo, 1979–82. Dir, Cornes & Co., Tokyo, 1982–85; Representative Dir, Gestetner Ltd (Japan), 1982–85; Dep. High Comr and Counsellor (Commercial/Econ.), Kuala Lumpur, 1986–89. *Recreations:* photography, golf, cycling. *Address:* c/o Foreign and Commonwealth Office, SW1A 2AH. *Clubs:* Brooks's; Tokyo (Tokyo).

BAKER-CARR, Air Marshal Sir John (Darcy), KBE 1962 (CBE 1951); CB 1957; AFC 1944; Controller of Engineering and Equipment, Air Ministry, 1962–64, retired; *b* 13 January 1906; *s* of late Brigadier-General C. D. Baker-Carr, CMG, DSO and Sarah Quinan; *m* 1934, Margery Dallas; no *c*. *Educ:* England and USA. Entered RAF as Pilot Officer, 1929; No 32 Fighter Sqdn 1930, Flying Officer; Flying Boats at home and overseas, 1931; Armament Specialist Course, 1934; Flight-Lieut; Armament and Air Staff appts, 1935–38; Sqdn Ldr, 1938; Armament Research and Development, 1939–45 (AFC); Wing Comdr, 1940; Gp Captain, 1942; Central Fighter Estab., 1946–47; Dep. Dir Postings, Air Min., 1947–48; Air Cdre, 1948; Dir of Armament Research and Development, Min. of Supply, 1948–51 (CBE); idc 1952; Comdt RAF, St Athan, 1953–56; Senior Technical Staff Officer, HQ Fighter Command, RAF, 1956–59; Air Vice-Marshal, 1957; Air Officer Commanding, No 41 Group, Maintenance Command, 1959–61; Air Marshal, 1962. *Recreations:* sailing and carpentry. *Address:* Thatchwell Cottage, King's Somborne, Hants SO20 6PH. *Club:* Royal Air Force Yacht (Hamble, Hants).

BAKER WILBRAHAM, Sir Richard, 8th Bt *cr* 1776; Director, J. Henry Schroder Wagg & Co. Ltd, 1969–89; Deputy Chairman, Bibby Line Group, since 1989; *b* 5 Feb. 1934; *s* of Sir Randle Baker Wilbraham, 7th Bt, and Betty Ann, CBE (*d* 1975), *d* of W. Matt Torrens; *S* father, 1980; *m* 1962, Anne Christine Peto, *d* of late Charles Peto Bennett, OBE; one *s* three *d*. *Educ:* Harrow. Welsh Guards, 1952–54. J. Henry Schroder Wagg & Co. Ltd, 1954–89. Director: Westpool Investment Trust, 1974–; Brixton Estate, 1985–; The Really Useful Group plc, 1985–90; Charles Barker Group, 1986–89; Grosvenor Estates Hldgs, 1989– (Dep. Chm., 1989–); Severn Trent, 1989–; Majedie Investments, 1989–; Christie Hosp. NHS Trust, 1990–. Mem., Gen. Council, King Edward's Hosp. Fund for London, 1986–. Gov., Nuffield Hosps, 1990–. Trustee, Grosvenor Estate, 1981–. Governor: Harrow Sch., 1982–; The King's Sch., Macclesfield, 1986–. High Sheriff, Cheshire, 1991–92. *Recreations:* field sports. *Heir:* *s* Randle Baker Wilbraham, *b* 28 May 1963. *Address:* Rode Hall, Scholar Green, Cheshire ST7 3QP. *T:* Alsager (0270) 882961. *Clubs:* Brooks's, Pratt's.

BAKEWELL, Joan Dawson; broadcaster and writer; *b* 16 April 1933; *d* of John Rowlands and Rose Bland; *m* 1st, 1955, Michael Bakewell (marr. diss. 1972); one *s* one *d*; 2nd, 1975, Jack Emery. *Educ:* Stockport High Sch. for Girls; Newnham Coll., Cambridge (BA History and Econs). Pres., Soc. of Arts Publicists. *BBC Television incl.* Meeting Point, 1964; The Second Sex, 1964; Late Night Line Up, 1965–72; The Youthful Eye, 1968; Moviemakers at the National Film Theatre, 1971; Film 72, and Film 73, 1972–73; For the Sake of Appearance, Where is Your God?, Who Cares?, and The Affirmative Way (series), 1973; Holiday '74, '75, '76, '77 and '78 (series); What's it all About? (2 series) and Time Running Out (series), 1974; The Shakespeare Business, The Brontë Business, and Generation to Generation (series), 1976; My Day with the Children, 1977; The Moving Line, 1979; Arts UK: OK?, 1980; Arts Correspondent, 1981–87; The Heart of the Matter, 1988–. *ITV incl.* Sunday Break, 1962; Home at 4.30, 1964; (writer and producer) Thank You, Ron (documentary), 1974; Fairest Fortune and Edinburgh Festival Report, 1974; Reports Action (4 series), 1976–78. *Radio:* Away from it All, 1978–79; PM, 1979–81; plays: There and Back; Parish Magazine. *Theatre:* Brontës: The Private Faces, Edinburgh Fest., 1979. *Publications:* (with Nicholas Garnham) The New Priesthood: British television today, 1970; (with John Drummond) A Fine and Private Place, 1977; The Complete Traveller, 1977; journalism for Punch, Radio Times; Television Critic of the Times, 1978–81; columnist, Sunday Times, 1988–. *Recreations:* theatre, travel, talk. *Address:* c/o Heart of the Matter, BBC TV Centre, W12.

BALCAZAR-MONZON, Dr Gustavo; Gran Cruz, Order of Boyaca, Colombia; Orden del Mérito Militar, General José Maria Córdoba, Colombia; Ciudades Confederadas Gran Cauca, Colombia; Senator of the Republic of Colombia, since 1962; *b* 10 Aug. 1927; *m* 1952, Bolivia Ramos de Balcázar; two *d*. *Educ:* Universidad Javeriana, Bogotá, Colombia (Dr in Econ. and Jurid. Sciences). Municipal Civil Judge, Cali, 1949–51; Attorney of the City of Cali, 1951–52. Member, House of Representatives, 1958–62, President, 1960; Governor of the Valle, 1962–64; Minister of Agriculture, 1964–65; President of the Senate, 1975; President Designate of the Republic, 1978–80; Colombian Ambassador to the Court of St James's, 1979–81. Member, Liberal Party Nat. Governing Body, 1970–71, 1974–77 and 1978; a Director of the Liberal Party, 1978. *Publications:* La Ciudad, el Urbanismo y el Impuesto de Valorización (The City, Urban Planning and the Tax for Increase in Value), 1950; La Reforma Tributaria de 1960 (The Tax Reform of 1960), 1961; several articles for the press. *Recreation:* apiculture. *Address:* Calle 10 Norte 9AN-10, Cali, Colombia; Senado de la República, Capitolio Nacional, Bogotá, Colombia. *Clubs:* Royal Automobile, Travellers'; Les Ambassadeurs.

BALCHIN, John Alfred; General Manager, Stevenage Development Corporation, 1969–76, retired; *b* 8 Aug. 1914; *er s* of Alfred and Florence Balchin; *m* 1st, 1940, Elsie Dormer (*d* 1982); one *s* two *d*; 2nd, 1986, Edna Bilton (*née* Morgan). *Educ:* Sir Walter St John's Sch., Battersea; Sir John Cass Coll., City of London. DPA (London), DMA, FCIS, FIH. LCC Clerk's Dept, 1932–38; civil defence co-ordination work, 1938–45; to Housing Dept, 1946–65; Principal Clerk, 1952; Asst Dir (Finance), 1960; Asst Dir (Housing Management), 1963; Sen. Asst Dir of Housing, GLC, 1965–69. Assoc. Sen. Lectr, for Housing Management and Administration, Brunel Univ., 1969–71. Member: Housing Services Adv. Gp, DoE, 1976–80; North British Housing Assoc., 1976–89; Auriol Housing Foundn, 1986–88. *Publications:* Housing: programming and development of estates, 1971, revd edn 1978; Housing Management: history, principles and practice,

1972; Housing Studies, 1st series, 1979, 2nd series, 1980, revd edn 1981; First New Town: an autobiography of the Stevenage Development Corporation, 1980. *Address:* Westwards, Perran Downs, Goldsithney, Cornwall TR20 9HL. *T:* Penzance (0736) 710449.

BALCHIN, Robert George Alexander; Chairman, The Grant-Maintained Schools Foundation, since 1991; *b* 31 July 1942; *s* of late Leonard George and Elizabeth Balchin; *m* 1970, Jennifer, SSStJ, BA (Mus), ACP, *d* of late Bernard Kevin Kinlay, Cape Town; twin *s*. *Educ:* Bec Sch.; Univs of London and Hull. MEd, Adv. DipEd; FCP. Asst Master, Chinthurst Sch., 1964–68; Hd of English Dept, Ewell Sch., 1968–69; Res., Univ. of Hull Inst. of Educn, 1969–71; Headmaster, Hill Sch., Westerham, 1972–80; Company Director, 1980–; Chm., Pardoe-Blacker (Publishing) Ltd, 1989–. St John Ambulance: Nat. Schs Advr, 1978–82; Asst Dir-Gen., 1982–84; Dir-Gen., 1984–90; Mem. Chapter-Gen., Order of St John, 1984–. Standing Conf. on Sch. Sci. and Technol., 1976–79; Treasurer: Coll. of Preceptors, 1979–87; Catch 'em Young Project Trust, 1984–; Chm./Founder, Campaign for a Gen. Teaching Council, 1981–85; Chm., Nat. Schs Project, 1990; Mem. Editorial Bd, Education Today, 1981–87; Mem., Centre for Policy Studies, 1982–; Lecture Sec., Heraldry Soc., 1982–88; Trustee, Adeline Genée Th., 1982–87; Gov., Oxted County Sch., 1985. Mem., Surrey CC, 1981–85 (Mem., Educn and Social Services Cttees); Vice-Pres., Lambeth Cons. Assoc., 1976–81; Treas., E Surrey Cons. Assoc., 1982–85; Cons. Party Dep. Area Treas., 1983–86; Cons. Vice-Chm. (SE Area), 1986–89; Cons. Bd of Finance, 1990–; Cons. Party Treas. for SE England, 1990–; Consultant-Dir, Cons. Central Office, 1988–. Hon. Mem. CGLI, 1983. Hon. FCP 1987; Hon. FHS 1987. Hon. DPhil Northland Open Univ., Canada, 1985. Freeman, 1980, Liveryman, 1987, Goldsmiths' Co. KStJ 1984. Cross of Merit (Comdr), SMO Malta, 1987. *Publications:* Emergency Aid in Schools, 1984; New Money, 1985, 2nd edn 1989; (jtly) Choosing a State School, 1989; (jtly) Emergency Aid at Work, 1990; numerous articles on educn/politics. *Address:* New Place, Lingfield, Surrey RH7 6EF. *T:* Lingfield (Surrey) (0342) 834543; 7 Ashley Court, Westminster, SW1. *Clubs:* Athenæum, Carlton, St Stephen's Constitutional.

BALCHIN, Prof. William George Victor, MA, PhD; FKC; FRGS, FRMetS; Emeritus Professor of Geography in the University of Wales (Swansea), 1978 (Professor of Geography, 1954–78); *b* 20 June 1916; *s* of Victor Balchin and Ellen Winifred Gertrude Chapple; *m* 1939, Lily Kettlewood; one *s* one *d* (and one *d* decd). *Educ:* Aldershot County High Sch. (State Scholar and County Major Scholar, 1934); St Catharine's Coll., Cambridge (1st Cl. Pt I Geographical Tripos, 1936; College Prize for Geography, 1936; BA 1937; MA 1941). PhD KCL 1951; FKC 1984. FRGS 1937; FRMetS 1945. Jun. Demonstrator in Geog., Univ. of Cambridge, 1937–39 (Geomorphologist on Spitsbergen Expedn, 1938); Hydrographic Officer, Hydrographic Dept, Admiralty, 1939–45 (also part-time Lectr for Univ. of Bristol Regional Cttee on Educn and WEA Tutor and Lectr); Lectr in Geog., KCL, 1945–54 (Geomorphologist on US Sonora-Mohave Desert Expedn, 1952); University Coll. of Swansea, Univ. of Wales: Head, Dept of Geog., 1954–78; Dean, Faculty of Pure and Applied Science, 1959–61; Vice-Principal, 1964–66 and 1970–73. Leverhulme Emeritus Fellow, 1982. Royal Geographical Society: Open Essay Prize, 1936; Gill Meml Award, 1954; Mem. Council, 1962–65, 1975–82, 1984–88; Chm., Educn Cttee, 1975–88; Vice-Pres., 1978–82; Chm., Ordnance Survey Cons. Cttee for Educn, 1983–. Geographical Association: Hon. Annual Conf. Organiser, 1950–54; Mem. Council, 1950–81; Trustee, 1954–77; Pres., 1971; Hon. Mem., 1980. Pres., Section E (Geog.), BAAS, 1972. Member: Met. Res. Cttee, MoD, 1963–69; British Nat. Cttee for Cartography, 1961–71 and 1976–79, for Geography, 1964–70 and 1976–78; Council, British Geography, 1988–. Treasurer, Second Land Utilisation Survey of Britain, 1961–; Chm., Land Decade Educnl Council, 1978–83. Mem., Nature Conservancy Cttee for Wales, 1959–68; Vice-Pres., Glam Co. Naturalists' Trust, 1961–80. Member: Hydrology Cttee, ICE, 1962–76; Bradford Univ. Disaster Prevention and Limitation Unit, 1989–. Member, Court of Governors: Nat. Mus. of Wales, 1966–74; UCW, Swansea, 1980–; Mem. Council, St David's UC, 1968–80. *Publications:* (ed) Geography and Man (3 vols), 1947; (with A. W. Richards) Climatic and Weather Exercises, 1949; (with A. W. Richards) Practical and Experimental Geography, 1952; Cornwall (The Making of the English Landscape Series), 1954; (ed and contrib.) Geography: an outline for the intending student, 1970; (ed and contrib.) Swansea and its Region, 1971; (ed and contrib.) Living History of Britain, 1981; Concern for Geography, 1981; The Cornish Landscape, 1983; over 150 res. papers, articles and contribs on geomorphology, climatology, hydrology, econ. geography and cartography in learned jls. *Recreations:* travel, writing. *Address:* 10 Low Wood Rise, Ben Rydding, Ilkley, West Yorks LS29 8AZ. *T:* Ilkley (0943) 600768. *Clubs:* Commonwealth Trust, Geographical.

BALCOMBE, Rt. Hon. Sir (Alfred) John, Kt 1977; PC 1985; **Rt. Hon. Lord Justice Balcombe;** a Lord Justice of Appeal, since 1985; *b* 29 Sept. 1925; *er s* of late Edwin Kesteven Balcombe; *m* 1950, Jacqueline Rosemary, *yr d* of late Julian Cowan; two *s* one *d*. *Educ:* Winchester (schol.); New Coll., Oxford (exhibnr). Served, 1943–47: Royal Signals; commnd 1945. BA 1949 (1st class Hons Jurisprudence), MA 1950. Called to Bar, Lincoln's Inn, 1950, Bencher 1977; QC 1969; practised at Chancery Bar, 1951–77; Judge of the High Court of Justice, Family Div., 1977–85; Judge of the Employment Appeal Tribunal, 1983–85. Mem., Gen. Council of the Bar, 1967–71. Chm., London Marriage Guidance Council, 1982–88. Master, Worshipful Company of Tin Plate Workers, 1971–72. *Publications:* Exempt Private Companies, 1953; (ed) Estoppel, in Halsbury's Laws of England, 4th edn. *Address:* Royal Courts of Justice, Strand, WC2A 2LL. *Club:* Garrick.

BALCOMBE, Frederick James; Lord Mayor of Manchester, 1974–75, Deputy Lord Mayor, 1975–76; *b* 17 Dec. 1911; *s* of late Sidney and late Agnes Balcombe; *m* 1st, 1936, Clarice (*née* Cassel) (*d* 1949); two *s* (and two *c* decd); 2nd, 1956, Rhoda (*née* Jaffe) (*d* 1989); one *d*. *Educ:* St Anthony's RC Sch., Forest Gate; West Ham Secondary Central Sch., Stratford, London. Served War of 1939–45, RAF (commnd). Chm., family co. of insurance loss assessors. President: Manchester and District Fedn of Community Assocs, 1962–78; Manchester and District Allotments Council, 1963–78; Higher Blackley Community Assoc., 1963–; Vice-President: Blackley Prize Band, 1964–; formerly Mem. Cttee and Hon. Treas., Crumpsall Hosp., 1964–70, League of Friends, 1966–; connected with 199th Manchester Scout Gp. Mem. Manchester City Council, Crumpsall Ward, subseq. St Peter's Ward, Collegiate Church Ward, 1958–82; served as Chm. Central Purchasing Cttee, 1964–67, Gen. and Parly (now Policy), Markets, 1958–82, Airports, 1971–82 (Chm.), Parks, 1958–67, and Finance, 1964–73, Cttees (Dep. Chm.). Chm., Manchester Internat. Airport, 1975–79. Mem., Airport Owners' Assoc., 1979–82. Founder, Hillel House, Manchester Univ, 1958 (Hon. Sec., 1958–68, now Sen. Life Vice-Pres.); Chm. of Governors, Coll. of Building, Manchester, 1964–67; Mem. Council, BBC Radio Manchester, 1970–76; Mem. Council, Manchester and Salford Police Authority, 1968–74; Mem., AMC Rating Cttee, 1973–74. Mem., Bd of Deputies of British Jews, 1956–64; Mem., Council, Manchester and Salford Jews, 1958– (Exec. Mem., 1963–68); Founder Mem., Manchester Jewish Blind Soc., 1956– (Hon. Sec. 13 years, now Vice-Pres.); Adjutant, Jewish Lads' Brigade and Club, Manchester, 1946–49, Chm. 1972–78. Trustee/Mem., NW Liver Research, 1986–. Governor, King David Schs, Manchester, 1954–84; Vice-Pres., Fedn of Boys' Clubs, 1969–; President: Manchester Cttee, Central British Fund, 1969–; RAFA Manchester South, 1981–84; Manchester City Swimming Club, 1981–. Founder Mem., Variety Club of Israel, 1972; Barker of Variety Club, 1970– (Chm. Manchester Cttee, 1976). JP Manchester, 1967–. Mem. Jewish Faith. Life long blood donor. *Recreations:* family, communal endeavour, swimming, walking. *Address:* 16 Spath Road, Didsbury, Manchester M20 8GA. *T:* 061–434 2555; (office) 061–941 6231.

BALCOMBE, Rt. Hon. Sir John; *see* Balcombe, Rt. Hon. Sir A. J.

BALCON, Dr Raphael, MD; FRCP, FACC; Consultant Cardiologist, Royal Brompton and National Heart Hospitals, Victoria Park, since 1970; *b* 26 Aug. 1936; *s* of Henry and Rhoda Balcon; *m* 1959, Elizabeth Ann Henry; one *d*. *Educ:* King's Coll., London; King's Coll. Hosp. Med. Sch. (MB, BS 1960, MD 1969). LRCP, MRCS 1960, MRCP 1965, FRCP 1977; FACC 1973. House Phys., Med. Unit, KCH, 1960; House Surg., KCH, Dulwich, 1960; House Phys., London Chest Hosp., 1961; Sen. House Officer, St Stephen's Hosp., 1962; Public Health Fellow in Cardiology, Wayne State Univ. Med. Sch., USA, 1963; British Heart Foundn Fellow, Dept of Cardiol., KCH, 1964, Med. Registrar 1965; Registrar, then Sen. Registrar, National Heart Hosp., 1966–70. Dean, Cardiothoracic Inst., 1976–80. Hon. Treasurer, British Cardiac Soc. *Publications:* contrib. books on cardiological subjects; papers in BMJ, Lancet, Brit. Heart Jl, Amer. Jl of Cardiol., Circulation, Eur. Jl of Cardiol., Acta Medica Scandinavica. *Recreations:* ski-ing, tennis, mountain walking.

BALDERSTONE, Sir James (Schofield), Kt 1983; company director and grazier; Chairman: Australian Mutual Provident Society, since 1990 (Director, since 1979); Chase AMP Bank, since 1990 (Director, since 1985); Broken Hill Proprietary Co. Ltd, 1984–89 (Director, 1971–89); Stanbroke Pastoral Co., since 1982 (Managing Director, 1964–81); *b* 2 May 1921; *s* of James Schofield and Mary Essendon Balderstone; *m* 1946, Mary Henrietta Tyree; two *s* two *d*. *Educ:* Scotch College, Melbourne. Service with RANR, WWII, 1940–45. General Manager for Aust., Thos Borthwick & Sons, 1953–67; Chm., Squatting Investment Co., 1966–73; Director: Commercial Bank of Australia, 1970–81; Westpac Banking Corp. (after merger), 1981–84; NW Shelf Develt Pty, 1976–83; Woodside Petroleum, 1976–83; ICI (Australia), 1981–84; Vic. Br.., AMP Soc., 1962– (Chm., 1984–89). Founding Chm., Australian Meat Exporters' Fed. Council, 1963–64; Member: Australian Meat Bd, 1964–67; Export Develt Council, 1968–71. Pres., Inst. of Public Affairs, 1981–84; Chm., Commonwealth Govt's Working Gp on Agricl Policy: Issues and Options for the 1980s, 1981–82. DUniv Newcastle, NSW, 1985. *Recreations:* farming, reading, watching sport. *Address:* 115 Mont Albert Road, Canterbury, Victoria 3126, Australia. *T:* 03–836–3137. *Clubs:* Australian, Melbourne (Melbourne); Union (Sydney); Queensland (Brisbane).

BALDOCK, Brian Ford; Director, since 1986, Group Managing Director, since 1989, Guinness PLC; *b* 10 June 1934; *s* of Ernest A. and Florence F. Baldock; *m* 1st, 1956, Mary Lillian Bartolo (marr. diss. 1966); two *s*; 2nd, 1968, Carole Anthea Mason; one *s*. *Educ:* Clapham Coll., London. Army Officer, 1952–55. Procter & Gamble, 1956–61; Ted Bates Inc., 1961–63; Rank Orgn, 1963–66; Smith & Nephew, 1966–75; Revlon Inc., 1975–78; Imperial Group, 1978–86. Chm., Portman Group. Freeman, City of London, 1989. FInstM 1976; Fellow, Marketing Soc., 1988. FRSA 1987. *Recreations:* theatre (opera), cricket. *Address:* The White House, Donnington, Newbury, Berks RG13 2JT. *T:* Newbury (0635) 41200. *Clubs:* Mark's, Lord's Taverners (Mem. Council).

BALDOCK, John Markham, VRD 1949; Lieutenant Commander RNVR 1948; Chairman Lenscrete Ltd, 1949; Director CIBA-GEIGY (UK) Ltd; *b* 19 Nov. 1915; *s* of late Captain W. P. Baldock, and Mrs H. Chalcraft; *m* 1949, Pauline Ruth Gauntlett; two *s*. *Educ:* Rugby Sch.; Balliol Coll., Oxford. Agric. degree, 1937. Served War of 1939–45, with Royal Navy, Atlantic, Mediterranean, Indian Ocean; Russian convoys, 1942–43. Lloyds, EC3, 1945. Joined Board of Lenscrete, 1946. MP (C) Harborough Div. of Leics, 1950–Sept. 1959, retd, also as Parl. Private Sec. to Rt Hon. D. Ormsby Gore (Minister of State, Foreign Office). Founder, Hollycombe steam collection and steam fair. *Recreations:* country life, sailing, steam engines, industrial archæology, theatre. *Address:* Duffryn, Wheatsheaf Enclosure, Liphook, Hants GU30 7EJ. *T:* Liphook (0428) 723233; 17 Aylesford Street, SW1. *T:* 071–821 8759. *Club:* Farmers'.

BALDOCK, Lionel Trevor; Agent-General for Victoria, since 1990; *b* 26 Nov. 1936; *s* of late Lionel Vernon Baldock and of Alice Thelma Baldock; *m* 1967, Carolynne Cutting; one *s* one *d*. *Educ:* Melbourne Univ. (BCom). Man. Dir, Evasoft Leather Co., 1958–73; General Manager: Tecnicast Pty Ltd, 1974–80; (also Dir) Centrifugal Castings Australia Pty Ltd, 1974–80; J. C. & Howard Wright Pty Ltd, 1983–84; Pacific Dunlop Ltd (NSW), 1984–85; Sen. Trade Comr, Australian Trade Commn, Paris, 1985–90. *Recreations:* swimming, ski-ing, sailing, walking. *Address:* Victoria House, Melbourne Place, Strand, WC2B 4LG. *T:* 071–836 2656. *Clubs:* Royal Automobile, Royal Overseas League; Royal Automobile, Royal South Yarra Lawn Tennis (Melbourne).

BALDRY, Antony Brian, (Tony); MP (C) Banbury, since 1983; Parliamentary Under Secretary of State, Department of the Environment, since 1990; *b* 10 July 1950; *e s* of Peter Edward Baldry and Oina (*née* Paterson); *m* 1979, Catherine Elizabeth, 2nd *d* of Captain James Weir, RN and Elizabeth Weir; one *s* one *d*. *Educ:* Leighton Park Sch., Reading; Univ. of Sussex (BA, LLB). Called to the Bar, Lincoln's Inn, 1975; barrister. Director: New Opportunity Press, 1975–90; Newpoint Publishing Gp, 1983–90. Contested (C) Thurrock, 1979. PPS to Minister of State for Foreign and Commonwealth Affairs, 1986–87, to Lord Privy Seal and Leader of the House, 1987–89, to Sec. of State for Energy, 1989–90; Parly Under-Sec. of State, Dept of Energy, 1990. Mem., Parly Select Cttee on Employment, 1983–86. Joined Sussex Yeomanry, 1971; TA Officer, resigned 1990. Robert Schuman Silver Medal, Stiftung FVS Hamburg, 1978. *Recreations:* walking in the country, reading historical biography, gardening, cricket, beagling. *Address:* House of Commons, SW1A 0AA. *Clubs:* Carlton; Brass Monkey; Banbury Conservative.

BALDRY, Prof. Harold Caparne; Emeritus Professor of Classics, University of Southampton; *b* 4 March 1907; *s* of William and Gertrude Mary Baldry, Nottingham; *m* 1934, Carina Hetley (*née* Pearson) (*d* 1985); one *s* two *d*. *Educ:* Nottingham High Sch.; Trinity Hall, Cambridge (Warr Schol., MA). Editor Cambridge Review, 1931. Educational Staff, Trinity Hall, Cambridge, 1931–34; Asst Lecturer in Classics, University Coll. of Swansea, 1934–35; Univ. of Cape Town: Lecturer in Classics, 1936–48, Prof. of Classics, 1948–54; Univ. of Southampton: Prof. of Classics, 1954–72; Dean of Faculty of Arts, 1959–62; Dep. Vice-Chancellor, 1963–66; Public Orator, 1959–67. Chm., Council of University Classical Depts, 1969–72; Pres., Orbilian Soc., 1970; Vice-Pres., Classical Assoc., 1972–; Mem., Arts Council of GB, 1973–78 (Chm. Regional Cttee, 1975–78); Chm., Southern Arts Assoc., 1972–74. Hon. DLitt Southampton, 1975. *Publications:* The Classics in the Modern World (an Inaugural Lecture), 1949; Greek Literature for the Modern Reader, 1951; Ancient Utopias (an Inaugural Lecture), 1956; The Unity of Mankind in Greek Thought, 1965; Ancient Greek Literature in its Living Context, 1968; The Greek Tragic Theatre, 1971; The Case for the Arts, 1981; articles and reviews in classical journals. *Address:* 19 Uplands Way, Southampton SO2 1QW. *T:* Southampton (0703) 555290.

BALDRY, Jack Thomas; Director, Purchasing and Supplies, Post Office, 1969–72; *b* 5 Oct. 1911; *s* of late John and Ellen Baldry; *m* 1936, Ruby Berenice (*née* Frost); three *d*.

Educ: Framlingham Coll. Post Office: Asst Traffic Supt, 1930; Asst Surveyor, 1935; Asst Princ., 1940; Princ., 1947 (Private Sec. to PMG, 1950–53); Asst Sec., 1953; Dep. Dir, External Telecommunications, 1960; Dir of Personnel, 1967. *Recreations:* farming, foreign travel. *Address:* Village End, Bruisyard Road, Badingham, Woodbridge IP13 8NA. *T:* Badingham (072875) 331.

BALDRY, Tony; *see* Baldry, A. B.

BALDWIN, family name of **Earl Baldwin of Bewdley.**

BALDWIN OF BEWDLEY, 4th Earl *cr* 1937; **Edward Alfred Alexander Baldwin;** Viscount Corvedale, 1937; *b* 3 Jan. 1938; *o s* of 3rd Earl Baldwin of Bewdley and Joan Elspeth, *y d* of late C. Alexander Tomes, New York, USA; *S* father, 1976; *m* 1970, Sarah MacMurray, *er d* of Evan James, *qv;* three *s. Educ:* Eton; Trinity Coll., Cambridge (MA, PGCE). Mem., Res. Council for Complementary Medicine, 1988–. *Heir: s* Viscount Corvedale, *qv. Address:* Manor Farm House, Upper Wolvercote, Oxford OX2 8AJ. *Club:* MCC.

BALDWIN, Alan Charles; Metropolitan Stipendiary Magistrate, since 1990; *b* 14 April 1948; *s* of Frederick Baldwin and Millicent Baldwin (*née* McCarthy); *m* 1974, Denise Maureen Jagger; two *s.* Admitted Solicitor, 1976. *Address:* Magistrates' Court, Bow Street, WC2E 7AS.

BALDWIN, David Arthur, CBE 1990; Chairman, Hewlett-Packard Ltd, since 1988; *b* 1 Sept. 1936; *s* of late Isaac Arthur Baldwin and Edith Mary Baldwin (*née* Collins); *m* 1961, (Jacqueline) Anne Westcott; one *s* one *d. Educ:* Twickenham Technical Coll.; Wimbledon Technical Coll. (qualified electronic engineer). CEng. R&D Engineer, EMI, 1954–63; Sales Engineer, Solartron, 1963–65; Hewlett-Packard: Sales Engineer and Sales Manager, 1965–73; European Marketing Manager, 1973–78; Man. Dir, 1978–88. Hon. Dr Strathclyde, 1990. *Recreations:* golf, ski-ing, photography, painting, sailing. *Address:* Hewlett-Packard Ltd, Cain Road, Bracknell, Berks RG12 1HN. *T:* Bracknell (0344) 360000. *Club:* Royal Automobile.

BALDWIN, Captain George Clifton, CBE 1968; DSC 1941 and Bar 1944; RN (retd); Member: Press Council, 1973–78; Press Council Appointments Commission, 1978–90; *b* 17 Jan. 1921; *s* of late George and late Louisa Baldwin; *m* 1947, Hasle Mary McMahon; three *s. Educ:* Sleaford Grammar Sch., Lincs; Hitchin Grammar Sch., Herts. Served War: joined RN, 1939, Pilot in Fleet Air Arm; in comd: 807 Sqdn, 1943; No 4 Naval Fighter Wing, 1944–45. Qual. at Empire Test Pilots' Sch., 1946; in comd, 800 Sqdn, 1952; in comd, RN Air Station, Lossiemouth, 1961–62; IDC course, 1963; Dir, Naval Air Warfare, MoD, 1964–66; in comd, RN Air Station, Yeovilton, 1966–68; ADC, 1967; retd, 1968. Mem., Royal United Services Inst., 1968. Chm., Fleet Air Arm Officers' Assoc., 1973–78 (Vice Pres., 1978–). *Address:* Three Greens, Level Mare Lane, Eastergate, Chichester PO20 6SB. *T:* Chichester (0243) 543040.

BALDWIN, Prof. Jack Edward, PhD; FRS 1978; Waynflete Professor of Chemistry and Fellow of Magdalen College, University of Oxford, since 1978; *b* 8 Aug. 1938; *s* of Frederick Charles Baldwin and Olive Frances Headland; *m* 1977, Christine Louise, *d* of William B. Franchi. *Educ:* Lewes County Grammar Sch.; Imperial Coll., London Univ. (BSc, DIC, PhD). ARCS. Asst Lectr in Chem., Imperial Coll., 1963, Lectr, 1966; Asst Prof. of Chem., Pa State Univ., 1967, Associate Prof., 1969; Alfred P. Sloan Fellow, 1969–70, Associate Prof. of Chem., 1970, Prof., 1972, MIT; Daniell Prof. of Chem., King's Coll., London, 1972; Prof. of Chem., MIT, 1972–78. Lectures: Tilden, RSC, 1979; Simonsen, RSC, 1982. Corresp. Mem., Academia Scientiarum Gottingensis, Göttingen, 1988. Hon. DSc: Warwick, 1988, Strathclyde, 1989. Corday Morgan Medal and Prize, Chem. Soc., 1975; Medal and Prize for Synthetic Organic Chemistry, RSC, 1980; Paul Karrer Medal and Prize, Zürich Univ., 1984; Medal and Prize for Natural Product Chemistry, RSC, 1984; Hugo Müller Medal, RSC, 1987; Max Tischler Award, Harvard Univ., 1987; Dr Paul Jansen Prize for Creativity in Organic Synthesis, Belgium, 1988. *Publications:* res. pubns in Jl of Amer. Chem. Soc., Jl of Chem. Soc., Tetrahedron. *Address:* Dyson Perrins Laboratory, South Parks Road, Oxford OX1 3QY.

BALDWIN, John, OBE 1978; National Secretary, Amalgamated Engineering Union (formerly Amalgamated Union of Engineering Workers) Workers/Construction Section, since 1976; *b* 16 Aug. 1923; *s* of Stephen John Baldwin and Elizabeth (*née* Hutchinson); *m* 1945, Grace May Florence (*née* Wilson); two *d. Educ:* Laindon High Road Sen. Sch., Essex. Boy service, RN, HMS Ganges, 1938; returned to civilian life, 1948; Steel Erector, CEU, 1950; played active part as Shop Steward and Site Convenor; elected full-time official, 1957; Asst Gen. Sec., AUEW/Construction Sect., 1969–76. Chm., Mechanical Handling Sector Working Party of NEDO; Member: Engrg Construction EDC, 1975–; Construction Equipment and Mobile Cranes Sector Working Party of NEDO; National Jt Council for the Engrg Construction Industry. Prominent Mem., Labour Party, 1962–. *Recreations:* most sports. *Address:* 7 Ridge Langley, Sanderstead, South Croydon, Surrey. *T:* 081–651 1643.

BALDWIN, Prof. John Evan, PhD; FRS 1991; Professor of Radioastronomy, and Fellow of Queens' College, University of Cambridge, since 1989; Head of Mullard Radio Astronomy Observatory, Cavendish Laboratory, since 1987; *b* 6 Dec. 1931; *s* of Evan Baldwin and Mary Wild; *m* 1969, Joyce Cox. *Educ:* Merchant Taylors', Crosby; Queens' Coll., Cambridge (MA; Clerk Maxwell Student, 1955–57; PhD 1956). Cambridge University: Research Fellow, later Fellow, Queens' Coll., 1956–74; Univ. Demonstrator in Physics, 1957–62; Asst Dir of Research, 1962–81; Reader, 1981–89. *Publications:* contribs to scientific jls. *Recreations:* gardening, mountain walking. *Address:* Cavendish Laboratory, Madingley Road, Cambridge CB3 0HE. *T:* Cambridge (0223) 337299.

BALDWIN, Maj.-Gen. Peter Alan Charles; Chief Executive, Radio Authority, since 1991; *b* 19 Feb. 1927; *s* of Alec Baldwin and Anne Dance; *m* 1st, 1953, Judith Elizabeth Mace; 2nd, 1982, Gail J. Roberts. *Educ:* King Edward VI Grammar Sch., Chelmsford. Enlisted 1942; commnd R Signals 1947; early service included Berlin, 1948–49 (during airlift), and Korean War, 1950; Staff Coll., 1960; JSSC, 1964; Borneo operations (despatches, 1967); Directing Staff, Staff Coll., 1967–69; Comdr, 13 Signal Regt, BAOR, 1969–71; Sec. for Studies, NATO Defence Coll., 1971–74; Comdr, 2 Signal Group, 1974–76; ACOS Jt Exercises Div., Allied Forces Central Europe, 1976–77; Maj.-Gen. and Chief Signal Officer, BAOR, 1977–79. Dep. Dir of Radio, 1979–87, Dir of Radio, 1987–90, IBA. *Recreations:* tennis, cricket, music, theatre. *Address:* c/o Lloyds Bank, 6 Pall Mall, SW1. *Clubs:* Army and Navy, MCC.

BALDWIN, Sir Peter (Robert), KCB 1977 (CB 1973); MA; Chairman, SE Thames Regional Health Authority, 1983–91; *b* 10 Nov. 1922; *s* of Charles Baldwin and Katie Baldwin (*née* Field); *m* 1951, Margaret Helen Moar; two *s. Educ:* City of London Sch.; Corpus Christi Coll., Oxford (Hon. Fellow, 1980). Foreign Office, 1942–45; Gen. Register Office, 1948–54; HM Treasury, 1954–62; Cabinet Office, 1962–64; HM Treasury, 1964–76; Principal Private Sec. to Chancellor of Exchequer, July 1966–Jan. 1968; Under-Sec., HM Treasury, 1968–72; Dep. Sec., HM Treasury, 1972–76; Second Permanent Sec., DoE, 1976; Permanent Sec., Dept of Transport, 1976–82. Dir, Mitchell Cotts, 1983–87; Chairman: Rural Village Develt Foundn, 1983–85 (Vice-Chm., 1985–90); Community Transport, 1985–87; Tripscope, 1986–; Disabled Persons Transport Adv. Cttee, 1986–; Brent Dial-a-Ride, 1983–85; Westminster Dial-a-Ride, 1984–87; President: Readibus, 1981–84; Disability Action Westminster, 1986– (Chm., 1983–86); Hearing Dogs for the Deaf, 1986– (Chm., 1983–86); Vice-President: RNID, 1983–; Disabled Drivers Motoring Club, 1985–; PHAB, 1988– (Vice-Chm., 1981, Chm., 1982–88); Member: Exec. Cttee, RADAR, 1983–; Cttee, AA, 1983– (Vice-Chm., 1990–; Chm., AA Road Safety Res. Foundn, 1990–); Nat. Railway Mus. Cttee, 1983–87; Bd, Public Finance Foundn, 1984–; Bd, Charities Aid Foundn, 1988–; Bd, RSA Exams, 1989–; Bd, City Lit. Inst., 1990–. Chairman: Council, Royal Soc. of Arts, 1985–87 (Vice-Pres., 1987–; FRSA); Delegacy, KCH Med. and Dental Sch., 1991–. Life Vice-Pres., Civil Service Sports Council, 1982– (Chm., 1978–82; Vice-Chm., 1974–78). Chm., St Catherine's Home and Sch., Ventnor, 1961–78; Governor, Eltham Coll., 1984–85. Trustee, Pets as Therapy, 1990–. FCIT; Hon. FIHT; CBIM. *Recreations:* painting, watching cricket. *Address:* 123 Alderney Street, SW1V 4HE. *T:* 071–821 7157. *Club:* Reform.

BALES, Kenneth Frederick, CBE 1990; Regional Managing Director (formerly Regional General Manager), West Midlands Regional Health Authority, since 1984; *b* 2 March 1931; *s* of Frederick Charles Bales and Deborah Alice Bales; *m* 1958, Margaret Hazel Austin; two *s* one *d. Educ:* Buckhurst Hill Grammar Sch.; LSE; Univ. of Manchester. BScSoc; DipSocAdmin. Hosp. Sec., Newhall & Hesketh Park Hosps, 1958–62; Regional Trng Officer, Birmingham Regional Hosp. Bd, 1962–65; Regional Staff Officer, Birmingham Regional Staff Cttee, 1965–68; Group Sec., W Birmingham HMC, 1968–73; Regional Administrator, W Midlands RHA, 1973–84. Associate, Inst. Health Service Management. *Recreations:* painting, sport. *Address:* 25 South Road, West Hagley, West Midlands DY9 0JT. *T:* Hagley (0562) 882550.

BALFE, Richard Andrew; Member (Lab) London South Inner, European Parliament, since 1979, also Labour spokesman on human rights, and the Third World, and Rapporteur on Turkey and Bangladesh; Chair, Co-operative Wholesale Society, South East Branch, since 1987; *b* 14 May 1944; *s* of Dr Richard J. Balfe and Mrs Dorothy L. Balfe (*née* de Cann); *m* 1986, Susan Jane Honeyford; one *d,* and one *s* by a previous marriage. *Educ:* Brook Secondary Sch., Sheffield; LSE (BSc Hons 1971). Fellow Royal Statistical Soc., 1972. HM Diplomatic Service, 1965–70; Res. Officer, Finer Cttee on One Parent Families, 1970–73; Political Sec., RACS, 1973–79; Dir, RACS and associated cos, 1978–85. Parly Candidate (Labour), Paddington South, 1970. Mem., GLC for Southwark/Dulwich, 1973–77; Chairman: Thamesmead New Town Cttee, 1973–75; GLC Housing Cttee, 1975–77. Member: Exec. Cttee, Fabian Soc., 1981–82; London Labour Party Exec., 1973– (Chair Policy Cttee, 1983–85). Member: Ct of Governors, LSE, 1973–; RIIA, 1982–. *Publications:* Housing: a new Socialist perspective, 1976; Role and Problems of the Co-operative Movement in the 1980s (with Tony Banks), 1977. *Recreations:* collecting books and pamphlets on political and social history topics, music. *Address:* 132 Powis Street, SE18 6NL. *T:* (office) 081–855 2128; (home) 081–761 2510. *Clubs:* Reform; Lewisham Labour.

BALFOUR, family name of **Earl of Balfour** and **Barons Balfour of Inchrye, Kinross** and **Riverdale.**

BALFOUR, 4th Earl of, *cr* 1922; **Gerald Arthur James Balfour;** Viscount Traprain 1922; JP; *b* 23 Dec. 1925; *er s* of 3rd Earl of Balfour and Jean (*d* 1981), 4th *d* of late Rev. Canon J. J. Cooke-Yarborough; *S* father, 1968; *m* 1956, Natasha Georgina, *d* of late Captain George Anton. *Educ:* Eton; HMS Conway. Holds Master Mariner's certificate. Mem., E Lothian CC, 1960–75. JP East Lothian, 1970. *Heir: cousin* Eustace Arthur Goschen Balfour [*b* 26 May 1921; *m* 1st, 1946, Anne, *d* of late Major Victor Yule; two *s;* 2nd, 1971, Mrs Paula Cuene-Grandidier]. *Address:* The Tower, Whittingehame, Haddington, Scotland EH41 4QA. *Clubs:* English-Speaking Union; International Association of Cape Horners.

BALFOUR OF BURLEIGH, Lord *cr* 1607 (*de facto* 8th Lord, 12th but for the Attainder); **Robert Bruce,** CEng, FIEE; FRSE; Director: Scottish Investment Trust plc, since 1971; William Lawson Distillers Ltd, since 1984; UAPT Infolink plc, since 1991; Edinburgh Book Festival, since 1981 (Chairman, 1981–87); Chairman: The Turing Institute, since 1983; Cablevision (Scotland) plc, since 1983; Canongate Press plc, since 1991; Chancellor, Stirling University, since 1988; *b* 6 Jan. 1927; *e s* of 11th Lord Balfour of Burleigh and Dorothy (*d* 1977), *d* of late R. H. Done; *S* father, 1967; *m* 1971, Mrs Jennifer Brittain-Catlin, *d* of late E. S. Manasseh; two *d. Educ:* Westminster Sch. Served RN, 1945–48, as Ldg Radio Electrician's Mate. Joined English Electric Co. Ltd, 1951; graduate apprentice, 1951–52; Asst Foreman, Heavy Electrical Plant Dept, Stafford Works, 1952–54; Asst Superintendent, Heavy Electrical Plant Dept, Netherton Works, Liverpool, 1954–57; Manager, English Electric Co. of India (Pvt) Ltd, Madras, 1957–60; Dir and Gen. Manager, English Electric Co. India Ltd, 1960–64; Dep. Gen. Manager, English Electric Co. Ltd, Netherton, Liverpool, 1964–65, Gen. Manager 1965–66; Dir and Gen. Manager, D. Napier & Son Ltd, 1966–68; Dep. Gov., Bank of Scotland, 1977–91 (Dir, 1968–91). Chairman: Viking Oil, 1971–80; NWS Bank (formerly North West Securities), 1978–91; Dir, Tarmac, 1981–90; Member: British Railways (Scottish) Board, 1982–; Forestry Commn, 1971–74. Chm., Fedn of Scottish Bank Employers, 1977–86. Chairman: Scottish Arts Council, 1971–80; NBL Scotland, 1981–85; Mem. Council, ABSA, 1976– (Chm., Scotland Cttee., 1990–). Pres., Friends of Vellore, 1973–. Vice-Pres., RNID, 1987–; Treasurer: Royal Scottish Corp., 1967–; RSE, 1989–. Hon. FRIAS, 1982. DUniv Stirling, 1988. *Recreations:* music, climbing, woodwork. *Heir: d* Hon. Victoria Bruce, *b* 7 May 1973. *Address:* Canongate Press plc, 14 Frederick Street, Edinburgh EH2 2HB. *T:* 031–220 3800.

See also G. J. D. Bruce.

BALFOUR OF INCHRYE, 2nd Baron *cr* 1945, of Shefford; **Ian Balfour;** *b* 21 Dec. 1924; *s* of 1st Baron Balfour of Inchrye, PC, MC and Diana Blanche (*d* 1982), *d* of Sir Robert Grenville Harvey, 2nd Bt; *S* father, 1988; *m* 1953, Josephine Maria Jane, *d* of late Morogh Percy Wyndham Bernard and of the Hon. Mrs Bernard; one *d. Educ:* Eton, spasmodically, and Magdalen College, Oxford (MA). Business consultant, author and composer. *Publication:* Famous Diamonds, 1987. *Recreations:* watching cricket and Association football, walking, writing, thinking, drinking, dreaming. *Address:* 10 Limerston Street, SW10 0HH. *T:* 071–351 0343.

BALFOUR, David Mathers, CBE 1970; MA; CEng, MICE; Director, R. M. Douglas Construction Ltd, 1975–83; Chairman, Balfour, Beatty & Co. Ltd, 1971–74 (Managing Director, 1966–72); *b* 11 Jan. 1910; *s* of late George Balfour, MP and Margaret (*née* Mathers); *m* 1938, Elisabeth, *d* of John Murdoch Beddall; two *s* one *d. Educ:* Shrewsbury Sch.; Pembroke Coll., Cambridge (MA). Served War of 1939–45, Lt-Col RE. Joined Balfour, Beatty & Co. Ltd, as Civil Engineer, 1930 (Dir, 1942); Chairman: Power Securities Corporation Ltd, 1971–74; Balfour Kilpatrick Ltd, 1971–72 (Dir, 1971–75); Exec. Dir, British Insulated Callender's Cables Ltd, 1970–72. Chairman: Export Gp for the Constructional Industries, 1963–65; Fedn of Civil Engineering Contractors, 1966–67. *Recreations:* golf, shooting. *Address:* Little Garnstone Manor, Seal, Sevenoaks, Kent TN15

0HY. *T:* Sevenoaks (0732) 61221. *Clubs:* East India, Devonshire, Sports and Public Schools; Rye Golf (Rye); Wildernesse Golf (Sevenoaks).

BALFOUR, (Elizabeth) Jean, CBE 1981; FRSE 1980; FRSA; FICFor; FIBiol; JP; Chairman, Countryside Commission for Scotland, 1972–82; *b* 4 Nov. 1927; 2nd *d* of late Maj.-Gen. Sir James Syme Drew, KBE, CB, DSO, MC, and late Victoria Maxwell of Munches; *m* 1950, John Charles Balfour, *qv;* three *s. Educ:* Edinburgh Univ. (BSc). Partner/Owner, Balbirnie Home Farms; Dir, A. & J. Bowen & Co. Ltd. Pres., Royal Scottish Forestry Soc., 1969–71; Mem., Fife CC, 1958–70; Chm., Fife County and City and Royal Burgh of Dunfermline Joint Probation Cttee, 1967–69; Governor, East of Scotland Coll. of Agriculture, 1958–88, Vice Pres. 1982–88; Dir, Scottish Agricl Colls, 1987–88, Dir, Council, 1974–87; Member: Scottish Agric. Develt Council, 1972–77; Verney Working Party on Natural Resources, 1971–72; Nature Conservancy Council, 1973–80; Oil Develt Council, 1973–78; Scottish Economic Council, 1978–83; Vice-Chm., Scottish Wildlife Trust, 1968–72 (Founder Council Mem.); Chairman: Regional Adv. Cttee, East (Scotland) Forestry Commn, 1976–85; Regional Adv. Cttee, Mid (Scotland) Forestry Commn, 1988–; Food and Farming Adv. Cttee, Scottish Cons. and Unionist Assoc., 1985–88; Crarae Gardens Charitable Trust, 1986–. Dep. Chm., Seafish Industry Authority, 1987–90. Mem., Cttee of Enquiry on handling of geographical information, 1985–87. Trustee, Buckland Foundn, 1989. Mem. Council, RSE, 1983–86; Mem. Council and Chm., Policy and Legislation Cttee, Inst. of Chartered Foresters, 1986–88. Hon. Vice-Pres., Scottish YHA, 1983–. Mem. Court, St Andrews Univ., 1983–87 (Chm. Ct Cttee, Estates and Buildings, 1983–87). JP Fife, 1963. FRSA 1981; FRZSScot 1983; FIBiol 1988. Hon. DSc St Andrews, 1977. Report to Government, A New Look at the Northern Ireland Countryside, 1984–85. *Recreations:* hill walking, fishing, painting, exploring arctic vegetation, shooting. *Address:* Kirkforthar House, Markinch, Fife KY7 6LS. *T:* Glenrothes (0592) 752233; Scourie, by Lairg, Sutherland. *Clubs:* Farmers', Commonwealth Trust; (Assoc. Mem.) New (Edinburgh).

BALFOUR, Rear-Adm. George Ian Mackintosh, CB 1962; DSC 1943; *b* 14 Jan. 1912; *yr s* of late Dr T. Stevenson Balfour, Chard, Som, and Mrs Balfour; *m* 1939, Pamela Carlyle Forrester, *y d* of late Major Hugh C. C. Forrester, DL, JP, Tullibody House, Cambus, and late Mrs Forrester; two *s* one *d. Educ:* Royal Naval Coll., Dartmouth. Served in China, 1930–32; South Africa, 1935–37. Commanded Destroyers for most of War of 1939–45, on various stations. Mediterranean, 1948, Far East, 1949–50, USA 1951–53, Captain (D) 2nd Destroyer Flotilla, 1956–58; Dir of Officer Appointments, 1958–59; Senior Naval Mem., Imperial Defence Coll., 1960–63; retired list, 1963. Chief Appeals Officer, Cancer Res. Campaign, 1963–77. *Address:* Westover, Farnham Lane, Haslemere, Surrey GU27 1HD. *T:* Haslemere (0428) 643876.

BALFOUR, Rear-Adm. Hugh Maxwell, CB 1990; LVO 1974; Commander, Sultan of Oman's Navy, 1985–90; *b* 29 April 1933; *s* of Ronald Hugh Balfour and Ann Smith; *m* 1958, Sheila Ann Weldon; one *s* two *d. Educ:* Ardvreck; Crieff; Kelly College, Tavistock. Joined RN 1951; qualified as Signal Officer, 1959; Commanded HM Ships Sheraton, Phoebe, Whitby and Fifth Destroyer Squadron in HMS Exeter, to 1985 (Exec. Officer, HM Yacht Britannia, 1972–74). Order of Oman, 1990. *Recreations:* sailing, shooting, gardening. *Club:* Naval and Military.

BALFOUR, Jean; *see* Balfour, E. J.

BALFOUR, John Charles, OBE 1978; MC 1943; JP; Vice Lord-Lieutenant for Fife, since 1988; Chairman, Fife Area Health Board, 1983–87 (Member, 1981–87); *b* 28 July 1919; *s* of late Brig. E. W. S. Balfour, CVO, DSO, OBE, MC, and Lady Ruth Balfour, CBE; *m* 1950, (Elizabeth) Jean Drew (*see* (Elizabeth) Jean Balfour); three *s. Educ:* Eton Coll.; Trinity Coll., Cambridge (BA). Served war, Royal Artillery, 1939–45 (Major), N Africa and Europe. Member, Royal Company of Archers, Queen's Body Guard for Scotland, 1949–. Member: Inter-departmental Cttee on Children and Young Persons, Scotland (Chm., Lord Kilbrandon), 1961–64; Scottish Council on Crime, 1972–75; Chairman: Children's Panel, Fife County, 1970–75, Fife Region 1975–77; Scottish Assoc. of Youth Clubs, 1968–79. JP 1957, DL 1958, Fife. *Recreations:* shooting, fishing. *Address:* Kirkforthar House, Markinch, Glenrothes, Fife KY7 6LS. *T:* Glenrothes (0592) 752233. *Club:* New (Edinburgh).
See also P. E. G. Balfour.

BALFOUR, Hon. Mark Robin; Chairman: Finglands Services Ltd, since 1981; Light Trades House Ltd, since 1973; *b* 16 July 1927; *s* and *heir* of 2nd Baron Riverdale, *qv;* *m* 1959, Susan Ann Phillips; one *s* two *d. Educ:* Aysgarth Sch., Yorks; Lisgar Collegiate, Ottawa, Canada; Trinity Coll. Sch., Port Hope, Ont; Millfield Sch.; Rotherham Technical Coll. (Intermediate Cert. in Metallurgy). Served RN, 1944–47. Arthur Balfour & Co. Ltd: Dir, 1955; Manager, London Office, Home and Export, 1957; Asst Man. Dir, 1959; negotiated merger with Darwins Group Ltd, 1960; Man. Dir, Balfour Darwins Ltd, 1961, Chm. 1971–75; following formation of Sheffield Rolling Mills Ltd (consortium of BSC, James Neill subsid., Balfour Darwins Ltd subsid.), 1969, Chm. 1970–74; non-exec. Dir, Special Steels Div., BSC, 1971–73; negotiated sale of Sheffield Rolling Mills Ltd to BSC, 1973; Dir, Overseas Ops, Edgar Allen Balfour Ltd (formed by merger of Balfour Darwins Ltd and Edgar Allen Ltd), 1975–79. British Independent Steel Producers' Association: Mem., Exec. Cttee, 1969–75; Mem., Product Group (Special Steels), 1962–75 (Chm., 1970–71); Mem., Steelmakers' Cttee, 1970–75. Pres., National Fedn of Engineers' Tool Manufrs, 1974–76; Member: EDC for Machine Tools, 1976–78; Council, Fedn of British Hand Tool Manufrs, 1972–77; Econs and Management Cttee, Iron and Steel Inst., 1970–75; Iron and Steel Industry Regional Trng Bd, 1964–68; Sheffield and Dist Br. Cttee, Inst. of Dirs, 1969–77; Council, Sheffield Chamber of Commerce, 1959– (Pres., 1978); Australian British Trade Assoc. Council, BOTB, 1975–85; ANZ Trade Adv. Cttee, BOTB, 1975–85. Chm., Ashdell Schs Trust, 1985–. Master, Cutlers' Co. of Hallamshire, 1969–70; Mem., Worshipful Co. of Blacksmiths, 1972–; Freeman, City of London, 1972. High Sheriff, S Yorks, 1986–87. Vice-Consul for Finland in Sheffield, 1962–; Order of the Lion, Finland, 1975. Silver Jubilee Medal, 1977. *Recreations:* fishing, shooting. *Address:* Fairways, Saltergate, Bamford, Derbyshire S30 2BE. *T:* Hope Valley (0433) 51314. *Club:* The Club (Sheffield).

BALFOUR, Michael John; JP; Chairman: IMI Capital Markets (UK) Ltd, since 1987; IMI Securities Ltd, since 1988; Deputy Chairman, IMI Bank (International), since 1987; *b* 17 Oct. 1925; *s* of Duncan and Jeanne Germaine Balfour; *m* 1951, Mary Campbell Penney, *d* of Maj.-Gen. Sir (William) Ronald Campbell Penney, KBE, CB, DSO, MC; two *s* one *d* (and *e s* decd). *Educ:* Eton Coll.; Christ Church, Oxford (MA Hons Modern Languages 1949). War service, RAF, 1944–47. Entered Bank of England, 1950: Senior Adviser, European affairs, 1973, Chief Adviser, 1976; Asst Dir, 1980–85. Alternate Director, Bank for International Settlements, 1972–85; Member, EEC Monetary Cttee, 1974–85. Director, Balgonie Estates Ltd, 1955–. JP Roxburgh, 1988. *Recreations:* music, fishing, boating, etc. *Address:* Harrietfield, Kelso, Roxburghshire TD5 7SY. *T:* Kelso (0573) 24825; 17 Shrewsbury Mews, W2 5PN. *T:* 071-229 8013.

BALFOUR, Nancy, OBE 1965; President, Contemporary Art Society, since 1984 (Chairman, 1976–82); *b* 1911; *d* of Alexander Balfour and Ruth Macfarland Balfour. *Educ:* Wycombe Abbey Sch.; Lady Margaret Hall, Oxford (MA). Foreign Office Research Dept, 1941–45; BBC N American Service, 1945–48; Economist Newspaper, 1948–72: Asst Editor with responsibility for American Survey, 1954–72; Fellow, Inst. of Politics, Kennedy Sch. of Govt, Harvard Univ., 1973–74. Member: Council, RIIA, 1963–84; Bd, British–American Arts Assoc., 1980–; Hon. Treasurer, Contemporary Art Soc., 1971–76; Chm., Art Services Grants, 1982–89; Vice-Chm., Crafts Council, 1983–85 (Mem., 1980–85); Chairperson, Southern Arts Craft Panel, 1986–90. Trustee, Public Art Develt Trust, 1983–. FRSA 1985. *Recreations:* sightseeing, ancient and modern; viewing work by living artists. *Address:* 36E Eaton Square, SW1W 9DH. *T:* 071-235 7874. *Club:* Arts.

BALFOUR, Neil Roxburgh; Chairman: York Trust Group plc, since 1986; York Mount Group Plc, since 1986; Yorkshire General Unit Trust, since 1985; *b* 12 Aug. 1944; *s* of Archibald Roxburgh Balfour and Lilian Helen Cooper; *m* 1st, 1969, HRH Princess Elizabeth of Yugoslavia; one *s;* 2nd, 1978, Serena Mary Churchill Russell; one *s* one *d. Educ:* Ampleforth Coll., Yorks; University Coll., Oxford Univ. (BA History); called to the Bar, Middle Temple, 1969. Baring Brothers & Co., 1968–74; European Banking Co. Ltd, 1974–83 (Exec. Dir, 1980–83); Man. Dir, York Trust Ltd, 1983–86. Mem. (C) N Yorks, European Parlt, 1979–84. *Publication:* Paul of Yugoslavia (biography), 1980. *Recreations:* bridge, golf, tennis, shooting, fishing. *Address:* Dawyck, Stobo, Peebles, Tweeddale EH45 9JU. *T:* Stobo (07216) 242. *Clubs:* Turf, Pratt's; Royal St George's (Sandwich).

BALFOUR, Peter Edward Gerald, CBE 1984; Chairman, Charterhouse plc, 1985–90; a Vice-Chairman, Royal Bank of Scotland, 1985–90 (Director, 1971–90); Director, Royal Bank of Scotland Group, 1978–91; *b* 9 July 1921; *y s* of late Brig. Edward William Sturgis Balfour, CVO, DSO, OBE, MC and Lady Ruth Balfour, CBE, MB; *m* 1st, 1948, Grizelda Davina Roberta Ogilvy (marr. diss. 1967); two *s* one *d;* 2nd, 1968, Diana Rosemary Wainman; one *s* one *d. Educ:* Eton College. Scots Guards, 1940–54. Joined Wm McEwan & Co. Ltd, 1954; Chm. and Chief Exec., Scottish & Newcastle Breweries, 1970–83. Director: British Assets Trust Ltd; Selective Assets Trust (formerly Edinburgh American Assets Trust), 1962– (Chm., 1978–); First Charlotte Assets Trust (Chm., 1981–). Chm., Scottish Council for Develt and Industry, 1978–85. Mem., Hansard Soc. Commn on Electoral Reform, 1975–76. *Address:* Scadlaw House, Humbie, East Lothian. *T:* Humbie (087533) 252. *Clubs:* Cavalry and Guards; New (Edinburgh).
See also J. C. Balfour.

BALFOUR, Raymond Lewis, MVO 1965; HM Diplomatic Service, retired; Counsellor, Kuwait, 1979–83; *b* 23 April 1923; *s* of Henry James Balfour and Vera Alice (*née* Dunford); *m* 1975, Vanda Gaye Crompton. RMA Sandhurst, 1942; commnd RAC; served with IV Queen's Own Hussars, 1942–47. Diplomatic Service, 1947–87; served at Munich, Beirut, Gdansk (Poland), Baghdad, Khartoum, Geneva, Damascus; Counsellor, Tripoli, 1976–79. Order of the Blue Nile, Sudan, 1965. *Recreations:* travel, gardening. *Address:* 25 Chenery Drive, Sprowston, Norwich, Norfolk NR7 8RR. *Clubs:* Commonwealth Trust, Players Theatre.

BALFOUR, Richard Creighton, MBE 1945; retired; *b* 3 Feb. 1916; *s* of Donald Creighton Balfour and Muriel Fonçeca; *m* 1943, Adela Rosemary Welch; two *s. Educ:* St Edward's Sch., Oxford (Pres., Sch. Soc., 1985–86). FIB. Joined Bank of England, 1935; Agent, Leeds, 1961–65; Deputy Chief Cashier, 1965–70; Chief Accountant, 1970–75. Dir, Datasaab Ltd, 1975–81. Naval Service, Lt-Comdr RNVR, 1939–46. President: Royal National Rose Soc., 1973 and 1974; World Fedn of Rose Socs, 1983–85 (Vice-Pres. for Europe, 1981–83; Chm., Classification Cttee, 1981–88); Chairman: 1976—The Year of the Rose; Internat. Rose Conf., Oxford, 1976; organiser and designer of the British Garden at Montreal Floralies, 1980. Master, Worshipful Co. of Gardeners, 1991–92; Freeman, City of London. DHM 1974. Gold Medal, World Fedn of Rose Socs, 1985; Australian Rose Award, 1989. *Publications:* articles in many horticultural magazines and photographs in many publications. *Recreations:* roses, gardening, photography, dancing, sea floating, collecting rocks and hat pins, travel, watching sport. *Address:* Albion House, Little Waltham, Chelmsford, Essex CM3 3LA. *T:* Chelmsford (0245) 360410.

BALFOUR, Sir Robert George Victor FitzGeorge; *see* FitzGeorge-Balfour.

BALFOUR-PAUL, (Hugh) Glencairn, CMG 1968; HM Diplomatic Service, retired; Director General, Middle East Association, 1978–79; Research Fellow, University of Exeter, since 1979; *b* 23 Sept. 1917; *s* of late Lt-Col J. W. Balfour Paul, DSO; *m* 1st, 1950, Margaret Clare Ogilvy (*d* 1971); one *s* three *d;* 2nd, 1974, Janet Alison Scott; one *s* one *d. Educ:* Sedbergh; Magdalen Coll., Oxford. Served War of 1939–45, Sudan Defence Force. Sudan Political Service, Blue Nile and Darfur, 1946–54; joined Foreign Office, 1955; Santiago, 1957; Beirut, 1960; Counsellor, Dubai, 1964; Dep. Political Resident, Persian Gulf, 1966; Counsellor, FO, attached St Antony's Coll., Oxford, 1968; Ambassador to Iraq, 1969–71; Ambassador to Jordan, 1972–75; Ambassador to Tunisia, 1975–77. *Publication:* The End of Empire in the Middle East, 1990. *Recreations:* archaeology, modern poetry, carpentry. *Address:* Uppincott Barton, Shobrooke, Crediton, Devon EX17 1BE. *T:* Crediton (03632) 2104.

BALGONIE, Lord; David Alexander Leslie Melville; Director: Wood Conversion Ltd, since 1984; The Treske Shop Ltd, since 1988; *b* 26 Jan. 1954; *s* and *heir* of Earl of Leven and Melville, *qv;* *m* 1981, Julia Clare, *yr d* of Col I. R. Critchley, Lindores, Muthill, Perthshire; one *s* one *d. Educ:* Eton. Lieut (acting Captain), Queen's Own Highlanders (GSM for N Ireland); RARO 1979–89. *Heir: s* Hon. Alexander Ian Leslie Melville, *b* 29 Nov. 1984. *Address:* Old Farmhouse, West Street, Burghclere, Newbury, Berkshire RG15 9LB.

BALKWILL, Bryan Havell; conductor; Professor of Conducting, Indiana University, Bloomington, since 1977; *b* 2 July 1922; *s* of Arthur William Balkwill and Dorothy Silver Balkwill (*née* Wright); *m* 1949, Susan Elizabeth Roberts; one *s* one *d. Educ:* Merchant Taylors' Sch.; Royal Academy of Music. Asst Conductor, New London Opera Co., 1947–48; Associate Conductor, Internat. Ballet, 1948–49; Musical Director and Principal Conductor, London Festival Ballet, 1950–52; Music staff and subseq. Associate Conductor, Glyndebourne Opera, 1950–58; Musical Dir, Arts Council 'Opera For All', 1953–63; Resident Conductor, Royal Opera House, Covent Garden, 1959–65; Musical Director: Welsh Nat. Opera Company, 1963–67; Sadler's Wells Opera, 1966–69; free-lance opera and concert conducting in N America, Europe and GB, 1970–. Guest Conductor: Royal Opera House, Covent Garden, English Nat. Opera, Glyndebourne, Wexford Festival, Aldeburgh, RPO, LPO, BBC. Mem. Royal Philharmonic Society; FRAM. *Recreation:* open air. *Address:* 8 The Green, Wimbledon Common, SW19 5AZ. *T:* 081-947 4250.

BALL, Air Marshal Sir Alfred (Henry Wynne), KCB 1976 (CB 1967); DSO 1943; DFC 1942; Vice-Chairman (Air), Council of Territorial, Auxiliary and Volunteer Reserve Associations, 1979–84; *b* 18 Jan. 1921; *s* of Captain J. A. E. Ball, MC, BA, BE; *m* 1942, Nan McDonald; three *s* one *d. Educ:* Campbell Coll., Belfast; RAF Coll., Cranwell; idc, jssc, psc, pfc. Served War of 1939–45 (Despatches twice; US Air Medal 1943); Sqdn Ldr 1942; Wing Comdr 1944; air operations, Lysanders, Spitfires, Mosquitoes;

commanded: 4 Photo. Reconn. Unit; 682, 542, 540 and 13 Photo. Reconn. Sqdns in N Africa, UK, France and Middle East; E Africa, 1947; Bomber Comd, 1952; BJSM, Washington, 1959; Comdr, Honington V Bomber Base, 1963–64; Air Officer, Administration, Aden, 1965; IDC, 1967; Dir of Operations, (RAF), MoD, 1967–68; Air Vice-Marshal, 1968; ACOS, Automatic Data Processing Div., SHAPE, 1968–71; Dir-Gen. Organisation (RAF), 1971–75; Air Marshal, 1975; UK Rep., Perm. Mil. Deputies Gp, Cento, 1975–77; Dep. C-in-C, RAF Strike Command, 1977–79, retired 1979. Mil. Affairs Advr, Internat. Computers Ltd, 1979–83. Hon. Air Cdre, No 2624 (Co. of Oxford) RAuxAF Regt Sqdn, 1984–90. Hon. FBCS 1974. *Recreations*: golf, bridge. *Clubs*: Royal Air Force; Phyllis Court; Huntercombe.

BALL, Anthony George, (Tony Ball), MBE 1986; FCIM; FIMI; ACIArb; Chairman, Tony Ball Associates plc, since 1983; Deputy Chairman: Lumley Insurance Consultants Ltd, since 1985; Lumley Warranty Services Ltd, since 1985; *b* 14 Nov. 1934; *s* of Harry Ball and Mary Irene Ball, Bridgwater; *m* 1957, Ruth Parry Davies; two *s* one *d*. *Educ*: Dr Morgan's Grammar Sch., Bridgwater. Indentured engineering apprentice, Austin Motor Co., 1951–55; UK sales executive, Austin Motor Co., 1959–62; responsible for launch of Mini, 1959; Commercial Vehicle Sales Manager, 1962–64, Car Sales Manager, 1964–66, Austin Motor Co.; Sales and Marketing Exec., British Motor Corp., 1966–67; Chm. and Man. Dir, Barlow Rand UK Motor Gp, 1967–78; Managing Director: Barlow Rand Ford, S Africa, 1971–73; Barlow Rand European Operations, 1973–78; Barlow Handling Ltd, 1975–78; returned to British Leyland as Man. Dir, Overseas Trading Operations, 1978; Director: Leyland Australia, Leyland S Africa, Leyland Kenya and all BL African subsids; Dep. Man. Dir, Austin Morris Ltd, 1979; Chm. and Man. Dir, BL Europe & Overseas, 1979–82; Director, 1979–82: BL Cars Ltd (World Sales Chief, 1979–82); Austin Morris Ltd; Rover Triumph Ltd; Jaguar Rover Triumph Inc. (USA); Dir, Jaguar Cars Ltd, 1980–82. Chm., Nuffield Press, 1978–80. Chief Exec. and Gp Man. Dir, Henlys plc, 1982–83. Director: Harry Ball (Bridgwater) Ltd, 1960–84; Lumley Insurance Ltd, 1983–; LIC Management Ltd, 1983–; Midas Holdings Ltd, 1983–88; Customer Concern Ltd, 1986–; Jetmaster UK, 1989–; Jetmaster Internat., 1989–. Responsible for: conducting BL's Buy British campaign and launch of the Austin Metro in 1980; staging General Motors' UK launch of Vauxhall Astra, 1984, Vauxhall range, 1985, GM Europe Conf., 1986–87, AWD/Bedford launch, 1988, Lada Samara/Proton Cars launches, 1989, Mercedes-Benz and Fiat Uno launches, 1990, Proton Live Link TV promotion and opening ceremony of Rugby World Cup, Twickenham, 1991. Dir, producer and stager of 'Industrial Theatre' Motivational confs, sponsorship, marketing, promotions and new product launches, 1983–. Apptd special Marketing Adviser: to Sec. of State for Agric. on launch of Food from Britain campaign, 1982; to Sec. of State for Energy, 1984–87 (responsible for staging Nat. Energy Management Confs and Exhibns, 1985 and 86); to Sec. of State for Wales, 1988– (with responsibility for review of Welsh craft and giftware industry); created and devised "Wales—Land of Quality" corporate marketing theme. Lectr, public and after dinner speaker; TV and radio broadcasts on motoring, marketing and industrial subjects include: The Money Programme, Today, Top Gear, Going Places, World in Action, Focus, World at One, Gloria Hunniford show; After Dark; documentaries Moving the Metal, The Edwardes Years; panellist, BBC, Any Questions, Start the Week. Mason Meml Lecture, Birmingham Univ., 1983. Governor, N Worcs Coll., 1984–. Freeman of City of London, 1980; Liveryman: Worshipful Co. of Coach Makers and Coach Harness Makers, 1980; Worshipful Co. of Carmen, 1982. Fellowship of Inst. of Marketing awarded 1981, for launch of the Metro and services to Brit. Motor Industry; Hon. Mem. CGLI, 1982, for services to technical and vocational educn; Prince Philip Medal, CGLI, 1984, for outstanding contribution to marketing and the motor industry. *Publications*: (contrib.) Tales out of School, 1983; A Marketing Study of the Welsh Craft Industry (Welsh Office report, 1988); (contrib.) Making Better Business Presentations, 1988; contribs to numerous industrial, management and marketing books and jls. *Recreations*: theatre, British military history, golf, good humour. *Address*: Tony Ball Associates, 174–178 North Gower Street, NW1 2NB; Blythe House, Bidford-on-Avon, Warwickshire B50 4BY. *T*: Bidford-on-Avon (0789) 778015. *Club*: Oriental.

BALL, Arthur Beresford, OBE 1973; HM Diplomatic Service, retired; Consul-General, Perth, Western Australia, 1978–80; *b* 15 Aug. 1923; *s* of Charles Henry and Lilian Ball; *m* 1961, June Stella Luckett; one *s* two *d*. *Educ*: Bede Collegiate Boys' Sch., Sunderland; Univ. of E Anglia (BA Hons 1987; MA 1989). Joined HM Diplomatic Service, 1949: Bahrain, 1949; Tripoli, 1950; Middle East Centre for Arab Studies, 1952; Ramullah, 1953; Damascus, 1954; Foreign Office, 1957; Kuwait, 1959; HM Consul, New Orleans, 1963; Jedda, 1965; FO, 1967; São Paulo, 1969; Lisbon, 1972; Ankara, 1975. *Recreations*: sailing, ice skating, historical studies. *Address*: 15 Eccles Road, Holt, Norfolk NR25 6HJ.

BALL, Sir Charles (Irwin), 4th Bt *cr* 1911; Deputy Chairman, Associated British Ports Holdings, since 1982; *b* 12 Jan. 1924; *s* of Sir Nigel Gresley Ball, 3rd Bt, and of Florine Isabel, *d* of late Col Herbert Edwardes Irwin; *S* father, 1978; *m* 1950, Alison Mary Bentley (marr. diss. 1983); one *s* one *d*. *Educ*: Sherborne Sch. FCA 1960. Served RA, 1942–47. Chartered Accountant, 1950; Peat, Marwick, Mitchell & Co., 1950–54; joined Robert, Benson, Lonsdale & Co. Ltd (now Kleinwort, Benson Ltd), 1954; Director: Kleinwort, Benson Ltd, 1964–76 (Vice-Chm., 1974–76); Kleinwort, Benson, Lonsdale Ltd, 1974–76; Cadbury Schweppes Ltd, 1971–76; Chubb & Son Ltd, 1971–76; Sun Alliance and London Insurance Ltd, 1971–83; Telephone Rentals plc, 1971–89 (Vice-Chm., 1978–81, Chm., 1981–89); Tunnel Holdings Ltd, 1976–82; Barclays Bank Ltd, 1976–77 (Chm., Barclays Merchant Bank Ltd, 1976–77); Rockware Group plc, 1978–84; Peachey Property Corporation plc, 1978–88 (Chm., 1981–88); British Transport Docks Bd, 1971–82; Chm., Silkolene plc, 1989–. Liveryman, 1960, Mem. Ct of Assts, 1979–87, Master, 1985, Clockmakers' Co. *Heir*: *s* Richard Bentley Ball, *b* 29 Jan. 1953. *Address*: Appletree Cottage, Heath Lane, Ewshot, near Farnham, Surrey GU10 5AW. *T*: Aldershot (0252) 850208.

BALL, Sir Christopher (John Elinger), Kt 1988; MA; Royal Society of Arts Fellow in Continuing Education, since 1989; *b* 22 April 1935; *er s* of late Laurence Elinger Ball, OBE, and Christine Florence Mary Ball (*née* Howe); *m* 1958, Wendy Ruth Colyer, *d* of Cecil Frederick Colyer and Ruth Colyer (*née* Reddaway); three *s* three *d*. *Educ*: St George's School, Harpenden; Merton College, Oxford (Harmsworth Scholar 1959; Hon. Fellow, 1987); 1st Cl. English Language and Literature, 1959; Dipl. in Comparative Philology, 1962; MA Oxon, 1963. 2nd Lieut, Parachute Regt, 1955–56. Lectr in English Language, Merton Coll., Oxford, 1960–61; Lectr in Comparative Linguistics, Sch. of Oriental and African Studies (Univ. of London), 1961–64; Fellow and Tutor in English Language, Lincoln Coll., Oxford, 1964–79 (Sen. Tutor and Tutor for Admissions, 1971–72; Bursar, 1972–79; Hon. Fellow, 1981); Warden, Keble College, Oxford, 1980–88 (Hon. Fellow, 1989). Founding Fellow, Kellogg Forum for Continuing Educn, Univ. of Oxford, 1988–89; Vis. Prof. in Higher Educn, Leeds Poly., 1989–. Sec., Linguistics Assoc. of GB, 1964–67; Pres., Oxford Assoc. of University Teachers, 1968–71; Publications Sec., Philological Soc., 1969–75; Chairman: Oxford Univ. English Bd, 1977–79; Bd of NAB, 1982–88; Higher Educn Inf. Services Trust, 1987–90; Education—Industry Forum (Industry Matters), RSA, 1988–90; Member: General Bd of the Faculties, 1979–82; Hebdomadal Council, 1985–89; CNAA, 1982–88 (Chm., English Studies Bd, 1973–80, Linguistics Bd, 1977–82); BTEC, 1984–89 (Chm., Quality Assurance & Control Cttee, 1989–90); IT Skills Shortages Cttee (Butcher Cttee), 1984–85; CBI IT Skills Agency, 1985–88; CBI Task Force, 1988–89. Chairman: NICEC, 1989–; Pegasus, 1989–. Member: Council and Exec., Templeton Coll., Oxford, 1981–; Centre for Medieval and Renaissance Studies, Oxford, 1987–90; Brathay Hall Trust, 1988– (Chm, 1990–); Manchester Polytechnic, 1989– (Hon. Fellow, 1988). Pres., ACFHE, 1990–. Gov., St George's Sch., Harpenden, 1985–89. Jt Founding Editor (with late Angus Cameron), Toronto Dictionary of Old English, 1970; Member Editorial Board: Oxford Rev. of Education, 1984–; Science and Public Affairs, 1989–. FRSA 1987. Hon. DLitt CNAA, 1989. *Publications*: Fitness for Purpose, 1985; Aim Higher, 1989; (ed jtly) Higher Education in the 1990s, 1989; various contributions to philological, linguistic and educational jls. *Address*: 45 Richmond Road, Oxford OX1 2JJ. *T* and *Fax*: Oxford (0865) 310800. *Club*: United Oxford & Cambridge University.

BALL, Christopher John Watkins; Chief Executive, The Private Bank & Trust Co. Ltd, since 1989; *b* 2 Nov. 1939; *s* of Clifford George and Cynthia Lindsay Watkins-Ball; *m* 1968, Susan Anne Nellist; one *s* two *d*. *Educ*: St John's Coll., Johannesburg; Univ. of the Witwatersrand (Dipl. Iuris 1963); Jesus Coll., Cambridge (MA Econs 1967). Outwich South Africa Ltd, 1968–72, Dir 1970; Barclays Group, 1972–89: Barclays Nat. Merchant Bank, S Africa, 1972–78; Manager, Corporate Finance, 1972–75; Gen. Manager, 1975–78; Man. Dir, Barclays Nat. Western Bank, S Africa, 1978–80; Regional Gen. Manager, London, Barclays Bank, 1980–83; Barclays Nat. Bank Ltd (now First Nat. Bank of Southern Africa), S Africa, 1983, Man. Dir, 1984–89. Pres., Clearing Bankers' Assoc. of S Africa, 1985. *Recreations*: golf, tennis. *Address*: The Private Bank & Trust Co. Ltd, Lansdowne House, Berkeley Square, W1X 5DG; Mayertorne Manor, Wendover Dean, Bucks HP22 6QA. *T*: Wendover (0296) 625226. *Clubs*: Marks; Leander.

BALL, Denis William, MBE 1971; industrial and financial consultant; Director: Perkins Foods PLC, since 1987; Western Bloodstock Ltd, since 1987; Redbridge Properties Ltd, since 1990; *b* 20 Oct. 1928; *er s* of William Charles Thomas and Dora Adelaide Ball, Eastbourne; *m* 1972, Marja Tellervo Lumijärvi (*d* 1987), *er d* of Osmo Kullervo and Leila Tellervo Lumijärvi, Toijala, Finland; two *s* one *d*. *Educ*: Brunswick Sch.; Tonbridge Sch. (Scholar); Brasenose Coll., Oxford (MA). Sub-Lt, RNR, 1953; Lieut 1954; Lt-Comdr 1958. Asst Master, 1953–72, Housemaster, 1954–72, The King's Sch., Canterbury; Headmaster, Kelly Coll., 1972–85. Dir, James Wilkes plc, 1977–78; Cons., Throgmorton Investment Management, 1977–78. Trustee, Tavistock Sch., 1972–85; Vice-Chm. of Governors, St Michael's Sch., Tawstock Court, 1974– (Headmaster during interregnum, 1986); Mem., Political and PR Sub-Cttee, HMC, 1979–84. Treas., Ickham PCC, 1990–. Mem., Johnson Club, 1987–. *Recreations*: Elizabethan history, cryptography, literary and mathematical puzzles, cricket, real tennis, squash (played for Oxford Univ. and Kent), golf. *Address*: Ickham Hall, Ickham, Canterbury, Kent CT3 1QT. *Clubs*: East India, Devonshire, Sports and Public Schools, MCC.

BALL, Dr Harold William; Keeper of Palæontology, British Museum (Natural History), 1966–86; *b* 11 July 1926; *s* of Harold Ball and Florence (*née* Harris); *m* 1955, Patricia Mary (*née* Silvester); two *s* two *d*. *Educ*: Yardley Gram. Sch.; Birmingham Univ. BSc 1947, PhD 1949, Birmingham. Geologist, Nyasaland Geological Survey, 1949–51; Asst Lectr in Geology, King's Coll., London, 1951–54; Dept of Palæontology, British Museum (Nat. Hist.), 1954–86: Dep. Keeper, 1965; Keeper, 1966. Adrian Vis. Fellow, Univ. of Leicester, 1972–77. Sec., 1968–72, Vice-Pres., 1972–73, 1984–86, Geological Soc. of London; Pres., 1981–84, Vice-Pres., 1984–86, Soc. for the History of Natural History. Wollaston Fund, Geological Soc. of London, 1965. *Publications*: papers on the stratigraphy of the Old Red Sandstone and on the palæontology of the Antarctic in several scientific jls. *Recreations*: music, wine, gardening. *Address*: Wilderbrook, Dormans Park, East Grinstead, West Sussex. *T*: Dormans Park (034287) 426.

BALL, Sir James; *see* Ball, Sir R. J.

BALL, Prof. John Geoffrey, CEng; consultant metallurgist; Professor of Physical Metallurgy, Imperial College, University of London, 1956–80, now Emeritus (Head of Metallurgy Department, 1957–79; Senior Research Fellow, 1980–86); *b* 27 Sept. 1916; *s* of late I. H. Ball and late Mrs E. M. Ball; *m* 1941, Joan C. M., *d* of late Arthur Wiltshire, JP, Bournemouth. *Educ*: Wellington (Salop) High Sch.; Univ. of Birmingham. British Welding Res. Assoc., 1941–49; Sen. Metallurgist, 1945–49; AERE, Harwell, 1949–56; Head of Reactor Metallurgy, 1953–56. Min. of Tech. Visitor to British Non-Ferrous Metals Res. Assoc., 1962–72. Dean, Royal Sch. of Mines, Imperial Coll., 1962–65 and 1971–74; Dean, Faculty of Engineering, Univ. of London, 1970–74. Chairman: Res. Bd, 1964–74, and Mem. of Council Br. Welding Res. Assoc., 1964–81; Engrg Physics Sub-Cttee, Aeronautical Res. Council, 1964–68; Metallurgy Bd, CNAA, 1965–71; Metallurgy and Materials Cttee and Univ. Science and Technology Bd, SRC, 1967–70; Engrg Bd, SRC, 1969–71; Manpower Utilisation Working Party, 1967–69; Mem., Light Water Reactor Pressure Vessel Study Gp, Dept of Energy, 1974–77. Consultant on Materials, SERC, 1983–84. President: Inst. of Welding, 1965–66; Instn of Metallurgists, 1966–67 (Mem. Council 1951–56, 1958–70); Member: Council, Br. Nuclear Forum, 1964–71; Manpower Resources Cttee, 1965–68; Council, Inst. of Metals, 1965; Council, Iron and Steel Inst., 1965; Council, City Univ., 1966–90; Brain Drain Cttee, 1966–67; Public Enquiry into loss of "Sea Gem", 1967; Materials and Structures Cttee, 1967–70; Technology Sub-Cttee of UGC, 1968–73; Chartered Engineer Section Bd, CEI, 1978–83; Mem., Group IV Exec. Cttee, Engineering Council, 1983–. Governor, Sir John Cass Coll., 1958–67. Hon. ARSM 1961. Brooker Medal, Welding Inst., 1979; Freedom of Inst. and Distinguished Service Award, Indian Inst. of Technology, Delhi, 1985. *Recreations*: gardening, painting, travel. *Address*: 3 Sylvan Close, Limpsfield, Surrey RH8 0DX. *T*: Oxted (0883) 713511.

BALL, Prof. John Macleod, DPhil; FRS 1989; FRSE; Professor of Applied Analysis, Department of Mathematics, Heriot-Watt University, since 1982; *b* 19 May 1948; *s* of Ernest Frederick Ball and Dorothy Forbes Ball; *m* 1973, Mary Judith Hodges (marr. diss. 1977). *Educ*: Mill Hill Sch.; St John's Coll., Cambridge (BA Maths, 1969); Univ. of Sussex (DPhil 1972). FRSE 1980. SRC Postdoctoral Res. Fellow, Dept of Maths, Heriot-Watt Univ., and Lefschetz Center for Dynamical Systems, Brown Univ., USA, 1972–74; Lectr in Maths, 1974–78, Reader in Maths, 1978–82, SERC Sen. Fellow, 1980–85, Heriot-Watt Univ. Visiting Professor: Dept of Maths, Univ. of Calif, Berkeley, 1979–80; Laboratoire d'Analyse Numérique, Université Pierre et Marie Curie, Paris, 1987–88. Member: Edinburgh Mathematical Soc., 1972– (Pres., 1989–90); London Math. Soc., 1982–; Amer. Math. Soc., 1987–; Soc. for Nat. Phil., 1978–. Whittaker Prize, Edinburgh Math. Soc., 1981; Jun. Whitehead Prize, London Math. Soc., 1982; Keith Prize, RSE, 1990. Exec. Editor, Proc. A, RSE, 1987–; Member Editorial Boards: Archive for Rational Mechanics and Analysis, 1984–; Analyse Non Linéaire, 1984–; Physica D, 1986–; Jl Elasticity, 1987–; Dynamics and Differential Equations, 1989–; Proc. A, Royal Soc., 1989–. *Publications*: articles in math. and scientific jls. *Recreations*: travel, music, chess. *Address*: 11 Gloucester Place, Edinburgh EH3 6EE. *T*: 031-226 4384.

BALL, Rt. Rev. Michael Thomas; *see* Truro, Bishop of.

BALL, Rt. Rev. Peter John; *see* Lewes, Bishop Suffragan of.

BALL, Rev. Canon Peter William; Canon Emeritus, St Paul's Cathedral, since 1990 (Residentiary Canon, 1984–90); Public Preacher, diocese of Salisbury, since 1990; *b* 17 Jan. 1930; *s* of Leonard Wevell Ball and Dorothy Mary Ball; *m* 1956, Angela Jane Dunlop; one *s* two *d*. *Educ*: Aldenham School; Worcester Coll., Oxford (MA); Cuddesdon Coll., Oxford. Asst Curate, All Saints, Poplar, 1955; Vicar, The Ascension, Wembley, 1961; Rector, St Nicholas, Shepperton, 1968; Area Dean of Spelthorne, 1972–83; Prebendary of St Paul's Cathedral, 1976. Dir, Post Ordination Trng and Continuing Ministerial Educn, Kensington Episcopal Area, 1984–87. Chaplain: Rediffusion Television, 1961–68; Thames Television, 1970–. First Dir, Brent Samaritans, 1965–68; Dep. Dir, NW Surrey Samaritans, 1973–79. Mem., European Conf. on the Catechumenate, 1975– (Chm., 1983). *Publications*: Journey into Faith, 1984; Adult Believing, 1988. *Recreations*: gardening, walking, music. *Address*: Whittonedge, Whittonditch Road, Ramsbury, Marlborough, Wilts SN8 2PX.

BALL, Prof. Sir (Robert) James, Kt 1984; MA, PhD; Professor of Economics, London Business School, since 1965; Chairman, Legal & General Group, since 1980; Director: IBM UK Holdings Ltd, since 1979; London and Scottish Marine Oil, since 1988; Royal Bank of Canada, since 1990; Economic Adviser, Touche Ross & Co., since 1984; *b* 15 July 1933; *s* of Arnold James Hector Ball; *m* 1st, 1954, Patricia Mary Hart Davies (marr. diss. 1970); one *s* three *d* (and one *d* decd); 2nd, 1970, Lindsay Jackson (*née* Wonnacott); one step *s*. *Educ*: St Marylebone Grammar Sch.; The Queen's College, Oxford; Styring Schol.; George Webb Medley Junior Schol. (Univ. Prizeman), 1956. BA 1957 (First cl. Hons PPE), MA 1960; PhD Univ. of Pennsylvania, 1973. RAF 1952–54 (Pilot-Officer, Navigator). Research Officer, Oxford University Inst. of Statistics, 1957–58; IBM Fellow, Univ. of Pennsylvania, 1958–60; Lectr, Manchester Univ., 1960, Sen. Lectr, 1963–65; London Business School: Governor, 1969–84; Dep. Principal, 1971–72; Principal, 1972–84. Director: Ogilvy and Mather Ltd, 1969–71; Economic Models Ltd, 1971–72; Barclays Bank Trust Co., 1973–86. Part-time Mem., Nat. Freight Corporation, 1973–77; Dir, Tube Investments, 1974–84. Member: Cttee to Review National Savings (Page Cttee), 1971–73; Economics Cttee of SSRC, 1971–74; Cttee on Social Forecasting, SSRC, 1971–72; Cttee of Enquiry into Electricity Supply Industry (Plowden Cttee), 1974–75; Chm., Treasury Cttee on Policy Optimisation, 1976–78. Marshall Aid Commemoration Comr, 1987–. Governor, NIESR, 1973–. Member Council: REconS, 1973–79; BIM, 1974–82 (Chm., Economic and Social Affairs Cttee, 1979–82); British–N American Cttee, 1985–. Pres., Sect. F, BAAS, 1991. Trustee: Foulkes Foundn, 1984–; Civic Trust, 1986–; The Economist, 1987–. Fellow, Econometric Soc., 1973; CBIM 1974; FIAM 1985. Freedom, City of London, 1987. Hon. DSc Aston, 1987; Hon. DSocSc Manchester, 1988. *Publications*: An Econometric Model of the United Kingdom, 1961; Inflation and the Theory of Money, 1964; (ed) Inflation, 1969; (ed) The International Linkage of National Economic Models, 1972; Money and Employment, 1982; (with M. Albert) Toward European Economic Recovery in the 1980s (report to European Parliament), 1984; articles in professional jls. *Recreations*: fishing, chess. *Address*: London Business School, Sussex Place, Regent's Park, NW1 4SA. *T*: 071–262 5050. *Club*: Royal Automobile.

BALLANTINE, (David) Grant, FFA; Directing Actuary, Government Actuary's Department, since 1991; *b* 24 March 1941; *s* of James Williamson Ballantine and Robertha (*née* Fairley); *m* 1969, Marjorie Campbell Brown; one *s* one *d*. *Educ*: Daniel Stewart's Coll.; Edinburgh Univ. (BSc 1st Cl.). Scottish Widows' Fund, 1963–68; Asst Vice-Pres., Amer. Insce Gp (Far East), 1968–73; Government Actuary's Department, 1973–: Actuary, 1973–82; Chief Actuary, 1983–90. Mem. Council, Faculty of Actuaries, 1991–. *Publications*: articles in trade and professional jls. *Address*: Government Actuary's Department, 22 Kingsway, WC2B 6LE. *T*: 071–242 6828.

BALLARAT, Bishop of, since 1975; **Rt. Rev. John Hazlewood**, SSC; *b* 19 May 1924; *s* of George Harold Egerton Hazlewood and Anne Winnifred Edeson; *m* 1961, Dr Shirley Shevill; two *s*. *Educ*: Nelson Coll., New Zealand; King's Coll., Cambridge (BA 1948, MA 1952); Cuddesdon Coll., Oxford. Deacon 1949, priest 1950, Southwark; Asst Curate: SS Michael and All Angels, Camberwell, 1949–50, 1953–55; St Jude, Randwick, Sydney, 1950–51; Holy Trinity, Dubbo, NSW, 1951–53; Vice-Principal, St Francis Coll., Brisbane, 1955–60; Asst Lectr in Ecclesiastical History, Univ. of Queensland, 1959–60; Dean of Rockhampton, Qld, 1960–68; Dean of Perth, WA, 1968–75. Chaplain to Victorian Br., Order of St Lazarus of Jerusalem, 1984–. Mem., Australian Anglican Nat. Doctrine Commn, 1978–89. Mem., Soc. of Holy Cross (SSC), 1985–. *Recreations*: travelling, music, gardening, reading, theatre, art. *Address*: Bishopscourt, 454 Wendouree Parade, Ballarat, Victoria 3350, Australia. *T*: 053–392370. *Clubs*: Melbourne, Royal Automobile of Victoria (Melbourne).

BALLARAT, Bishop of, (RC), since 1971; **Most Rev. Ronald Austin Mulkearns**, DD, DCL; *b* 11 Nov. 1930. *Educ*: De La Salle Coll., Malvern; Corpus Christi Coll., Werribee; Pontifical Lateran Univ., Rome. Ordained, 1956; Coadjutor Bishop, 1968–71. *Address*: 1444 Sturt Street, Ballarat, Victoria 3350, Australia.

BALLARD, Prof. Clifford Frederick; Professor Emeritus in Orthodontics, University of London; Hon. Consultant, Eastman Dental Hospital, London; *b* 26 June 1910; *s* of Frederick John Ballard and Eliza Susannah (*née* Wilkinson); *m* 1937, Muriel Mabel Burling; one *s* one *d*. *Educ*: Kilburn Grammar Sch.; Charing Cross Hosp. and Royal Dental Hospital. LDS 1934; MRCS, LRCP 1940. Hd of Dept of Orthodontics, Inst. of Dental Surgery, British Post-Grad. Med. Fedn, Univ. of London, 1948–72; Prof. of Orthodontics, London Univ., 1956–72; Dental Surgeon, Victoria Hosp. for Children, SW3, 1948–64; Tooting, 1964–71. Pres. of Brit. Soc. for the Study of Orthodontics, 1957, Senior Vice-Pres., 1963, 1964; Mem. Council of Odontological Section of Royal Society Med., 1954–56, 1959–62 (Sec., 1957, Vice-Pres., 1969–72); Mem. Board, Faculty of Dental Surgery, RCS, 1966–74. FDS 1949; Diploma in Orthodontics, 1954 (RCS); FFDRCS Ire., 1964. Charles Tomes Lectr, RCS, 1966; Northcroft Memorial Lectr, Brit. Soc. for Study of Orthodontics, 1967. Hon. Life Mem., British Dental Assoc., 1982; Hon. Member: British Soc. for Study of Orthodontics; Israel Orthodontic Soc.; NZ Orthodontic Soc.; European Orthodontic Soc.; Membre d'Honneur, Société Française d'Orthopédie Dento-faciale. Colyer Gold Medal, RCS, 1975; (first recipient) C. F. Ballard Award, Consultant Orthodontists' Gp, 1990. *Publications*: numerous contributions to learned journals, 1948–. *Recreations*: golf, gardening. *Address*: Flat 20, The Maltings, Salisbury, Wilts SP1 1BD. *T*: Salisbury (0722) 335099.

BALLARD, James Graham; novelist and short story writer; *b* 15 Nov. 1930; *s* of James Ballard and Edna Ballard (*née* Johnstone); *m* 1954, Helen Mary Matthews (*d* 1964); one *s* two *d*. *Educ*: Leys School, Cambridge; King's College, Cambridge. *Publications*: The Drowned World, 1963; The 4–Dimensional Nightmare, 1963 (re-issued as The Voices of Time, 1985); The Terminal Beach, 1964; The Drought, 1965; The Crystal World, 1966; The Disaster Area, 1967; The Atrocity Exhibition, 1970; Crash, 1973; Vermilion Sands, 1973; Concrete Island, 1974; High Rise, 1975; Low-Flying Aircraft, 1976; The Unlimited Dream Company, 1979; Myths of the Near Future, 1982; Empire of the Sun, 1984 (filmed, 1988); The Venus Hunters, 1986; The Day of Creation, 1987; Running Wild,

1988; War Fever, 1990. *Address*: 36 Old Charlton Road, Shepperton, Middlesex. *T*: Walton-on-Thames (0932) 225692.

BALLARD, John Frederick; Director, Housing Associations and the Private Sector, Department of the Environment, since 1990; *b* 8 Aug. 1943; *s* of Frederick and Margaret Ballard; *m* 1976; one *s* two *d*. *Educ*: Roundhay Grammar Sch., Leeds; Ifield Grammar Sch., W Sussex; Southampton Univ. (BA); Exeter Univ. (CertEd). Academic Registrar's Dept, Univ. of Surrey, 1965–69; Asst Principal, MoT, 1969; Principal, DoE, 1972; Treasury, 1976; Asst Sec. 1978, Sec., Top Salaries Review Body and Police Negotiating Bd; DoE, 1979; Prin. Private Sec. to Sec. of State for the Environment, 1983–85; Under Sec., DoE and Dept of Transport, and Regl Dir, Yorks and Humberside Region, 1986. *Recreations*: squash, singing, reading. *Address*: 2 Marsham Street, SW1P 3EB. *T*: 071–276 3120.

BALLARD, Ronald Alfred; Head of Technical Services of the Central Computers and Telecommunications Agency, HM Treasury (formerly Civil Service Department), 1980–85; Consultant, since 1985; voluntary work, Help the Aged, since 1989; *b* 17 Feb. 1925; *s* of Joseph William and Ivy Amy Ballard; *m* 1948, Eileen Margaret Edwards; one *d*. *Educ*: Univ. of Birmingham (BSc (Hons) Physics). National Service, RN, 1945–47. Admiralty Surface Weapons Establishment, Portsmouth: Scientific Officer, then Sen. Scientific Officer, Research and Development Seaborne Radar Systems, 1948–55; Application of Computers to Naval Comd and Control Systems, 1955–69; PSO, 1960, responsibilities for Action Data Automation (ADA), on HMS Eagle and destroyers; SPSO, to Head Computer Systems and Techniques in Civil Service Dept (Central Computers Agency in 1972), 1969; Head of Central Computers Facility, 1972–76; DCSO, to Head Technical Services Div. of Central Computers Agency, 1977; CSO(B), 1980–85. Treas., Sutton Assoc. for the Blind, 1985–; Asst Treas., League of Friends, Queen Mary's Hosp., Carshalton, 1986–.

BALLENTYNE, Donald Francis, CMG 1985; HM Diplomatic Service, retired; Consul-General, Los Angeles, 1985–89; *b* 5 May 1929; *s* of late Henry Q. Ballentyne and Frances R. MacLaren; *m* 1950, Elizabeth Heywood, *d* of Leslie A. Heywood; one *s* one *d*. *Educ*: Haberdashers' Aske's Hatcham Sch. FO, 1950–53; Berne and Ankara, 1953–56; Consul: Munich, 1957; Stanleyville, 1961; Cape Town, 1962; First Secretary: Luxembourg, 1965–69, Havana, 1969–72; FCO, 1972–74; Counsellor (Commercial), The Hague, 1974–78, Bonn, 1978–81; Counsellor, E Berlin, 1982–84. *Recreations*: sailing, riding. *Address*: Orford, Suffolk.

BALLESTEROS, Severiano; golfer; *b* Santander, Spain, 9 April 1957; *m* 1988, Carmen Botin; one *s*. Professional golfer, 1974–; won Spanish Young Professional title, 1975, 1978; French Open, 1977, 1982, 1985, 1986; Japan Open, 1977, 1978; Swiss Open, 1977, 1978, 1989; German Open, 1978, 1988; Open Champion, Lytham St Anne's, 1979 and 1988, St Andrews, 1984; won US Masters, 1980, 1983; World Matchplay Champion, Wentworth, 1981, 1982, 1984, 1985; Australian PGA Championship, 1981; Spanish Open, 1985; Dutch Open, 1986; numerous other titles in Europe, USA, Australasia; Mem. Ryder Cup team, 1979, 1983, 1985, 1987, 1989. Prince of Asturias prize for sport, 1989. *Address*: Houston Palace, 7 Avenue Princess Grace, Monte Carlo, Monaco.

BALLS, Alastair Gordon; Chief Executive, Tyne and Wear Development Corporation, since 1987; *b* 18 March 1944; *s* of Dr Ernest George Balls and Mrs Elspeth Russell Balls; *m* 1978, Beryl May Nichol; one *s* one *d*. *Educ*: Hamilton Acad.; Univ. of St Andrews (MA); Univ. of Manchester (MA). Economist: Treasury, Govt of Tanzania, 1966–68; Min. of Transport, UK, 1969–74; Sec., Adv. Cttee on Channel Tunnel, 1974–75; Sen. Econ. Adviser, HM Treasury, 1976–79; Asst Sec., Dept of Environment, 1979–83; Regl Dir, Depts of Environment and Transport (Northern Region), 1984–87. *Recreations*: sailing, cycling, walking, camping in the company of my family. *Address*: Tyne and Wear Development Corporation, Scotswood House, Newcastle Business Park, Newcastle upon Tyne NE4 7YL. *T*: 091–226 1234, *Fax*: 091–226 1388.

BALMER, Sir Joseph (Reginald), Kt 1965; JP; Retired Insurance Official; *b* 22 Sept. 1899; *s* of Joseph Balmer; *m* 1927, Dora, *d* of A. Johnson; no *c*. *Educ*: King Edward's Grammar Sch., Birmingham. North British and Mercantile Insurance Co. Ltd, 1916–60; National Chairman Guild of Insurance Officials, 1943–47. Pres. Birmingham Borough Labour Party, 1946–54; elected to Birmingham City Council, 1945, 1949, 1952; Alderman 1952–74; Chairman Finance Cttee, 1955–64; Lord Mayor of Birmingham, 1954–55; Hon. Alderman, 1974; City Magistrate, 1956. Hon. Life Mem. Court, Birmingham Univ.; formerly Governor, King Edward VI Schs, Birmingham; Member or ex-member various cttees. Served European War, 1914–18, overseas with RASC and Somerset Light Infantry. *Recreation*: reading. *Address*: 26 Stechford Lane, Ward End, Birmingham B8 2AN. *T*: 021–783 3198.

BALMFORTH, Ven. Anthony James; Archdeacon of Bristol, 1979–90; *b* 3 Sept. 1926; *s* of Joseph Henry and Daisy Florence Balmforth; *m* 1952, Eileen Julia, *d* of James Raymond and Kitty Anne Evans; one *s* two *d*. *Educ*: Sebright School, Wolverley; Brasenose Coll., Oxford (BA 1950, MA 1951); Lincoln Theological Coll. Army service, 1944–48. Deacon 1952, priest 1953, dio. Southwell; Curate of Mansfield, 1952–55; Vicar of Skegby, Notts, 1955–61; Vicar of St John's, Kidderminster, Worcs, 1961–65; Rector of St Nicolas, King's Norton, Birmingham, 1965–79; Hon. Canon of Birmingham Cathedral, 1975–79; RD of King's Norton, 1973–79; Examining Chaplain to: Bishop of Birmingham, 1978–79; Bishop of Bristol, 1981–. Hon. Canon of Bristol Cathedral, 1979–. Mem., Gen. Synod of C of E, 1982–90. *Recreations*: cricket, gardening. *Address*: Slipper Cottage, Stag Hill, Yorkley, near Lydney, Glos GL15 4TB. *T*: Dean (0594) 564016.

BALNIEL, Lord; **Anthony Robert Lindsay**; Director, J. O. Hambro Investment Management, since 1987; *b* 24 Nov. 1958; *s* and *heir* of Earl of Crawford and Balcarres, *qv*; *m* 1989, Nicola A., *y d* of Antony Bicket; one *s*. *Educ*: Eton Coll.; Univ. of Edinburgh. *Heir*: *s* Master of Lindsay, *qv*. *Address*: 82 Onslow Gardens, SW7. *Clubs*: New (Edinburgh); XII.

BALSTON, Antony Francis; **His Honour Judge Balston**; a Circuit Judge, since 1985; *b* 18 Jan. 1939; *s* of Comdr E. F. Balston, DSO, RN, and D. B. L. Balston (*née* Ferrers); *m* 1966, Anne Marie Judith Ball; two *s* one *d*. *Educ*: Downside; Christ's Coll., Cambridge (MA). Served Royal Navy, 1957–59; Univ. of Cambridge, 1959–62; admitted Solicitor, 1966. Partner, Herington Willings & Penry Davey, Solicitors, Hastings, 1967–85; a Recorder of the Crown Court, 1980–85; Hon. Recorder, Hastings, 1984–. *Recreation*: gardening.

BALTIMORE, Prof. David, PhD; President, The Rockefeller University, since 1990; *b* New York, 7 March 1938; *s* of Richard and Gertrude Baltimore; *m* 1968, Alice Huang; one *d*. *Educ*: Swarthmore Coll. (BA 1960); Rockefeller Univ. (PhD 1964). Postdoctoral Fellow, MIT, 1963–64; Albert Einstein Coll. of Med., NY, 1964–65; Research Associate, Salk Inst., La Jolla, Calif, 1965–68; Massachusetts Institute of Technology: Associate Prof., 1968–72; Amer. Cancer Soc. Prof. of Microbiol., 1973–83; Prof. of Biology, 1972–90; Dir, Whitehead Inst., 1982–90. FAAAS 1980. Member: Nat. Acad. of Scis, 1974; Amer. Acad. of Arts and Scis, 1974; Pontifical Acad. of Scis, 1978; Foreign Mem., Royal Soc.,

1987. Eli Lilly Award in Microbiology and Immunology, 1971; US Steel Foundn Award in Molecular Biology, 1974; (jtly) Nobel Prize for Physiology or Medicine, 1975. *Address:* The Rockefeller University, 1230 York Avenue, New York, NY 10021-6399, USA.

BAMBERG, Harold Rolf, CBE 1968; Chairman, Bamberg Group Ltd and other companies, including Glos Air Aviation PLC, Eagle Aircraft Services Ltd and Eagle Aerotech; *b* 17 Nov. 1923; *m* 1957, June Winifred Clarke; one *s* two *d* (and one *s* one *d* of a former marriage). *Educ:* Fleet Sch.; William Ellis Sch., Hampstead. FRSA. *Recreations:* polo, bloodstock breeding. *Address:* Harewood Park, Sunninghill, Berks.

BAMBOROUGH, John Bernard; Principal of Linacre College, Oxford, 1962–88; Pro-Vice-Chancellor, Oxford University, 1966–88; *b* 3 Jan. 1921; *s* of John George Bamborough; *m* 1947, Anne, *d* of Olav Indrehus, Indrehus, Norway; one *s* one *d*. *Educ:* Haberdashers' Aske's Hampstead Sch. (Scholar); New College, Oxford (Scholar). 1st Class, English Language and Literature, 1941; MA 1946. Service in RN, 1941–46 (in Coastal Forces as Lieut RNVR; afterwards as Educ. Officer with rank of Instructor Lieut, RN). Junior Lectr, New Coll., Oxford, 1946; Fellow and Tutor, Wadham Coll., Oxford, 1947–62 (Dean, 1947–54; Domestic Bursar, 1954–56; Sen. Tutor, 1957–61); Univ. Lectr in English, 1951–62; Mem. Hebdomadal Council, Oxford Univ., 1961–79. Hon. Fellow: New Coll., Oxford, 1967; Linacre Coll., Oxford, 1988; Wadham Coll., Oxford, 1988. Editor, Review of English Studies, 1964–78. Cavaliere Ufficiale, Order of Merit (Italy). *Publications:* The Little World of Man, 1952; Ben Jonson, 1959; (ed) Pope's Life of Ward, 1961; Jonson's Volpone, 1963; The Alchemist, 1967; Ben Jonson, 1970; (ed) Burton's Anatomy of Melancholy, 1989. *Address:* 18 Winchester Road, Oxford OX2 6NA. *T:* Oxford (0865) 59886.

BAMFIELD, Clifford, CB 1981; Deputy Chairman, Civil Service Appeal Board, since 1989 (Member, since 1982); Civil Service Commission Panel of Selection Board Chairmen, since 1982; *b* 21 March 1922; *s* of G. H. Bamfield. *Educ:* Wintringham Grammar Sch., Grimsby; Manchester Business Sch., 1966. Served War, RNVR, 1941–46. Customs and Excise: Exec. Officer, 1946; Private Sec. to Chm., 1959–61; Principal, 1961; Asst Sec., 1967; Under Sec., Comr and Dir of Estabs, 1973; Under Sec., CSD, 1974–80. *Address:* 15 The Linkway, Sutton, Surrey SM2 5SE. *T:* 081–642 5377. *Club:* Army and Navy.

BAMFORD, Alan George, CBE 1985; Principal, Homerton College, Cambridge, 1985–91; *b* 12 July 1930; *s* of James Ross and Margaret Emily Bamford; *m* 1954, Joan Margaret, *e d* of Arthur W. Vint; four *s*. *Educ:* Prescot Grammar School; Borough Road College, London; Liverpool University (DipEd, MEd); MA Cantab; Cert. Ed. London. Teacher and Dep. Headmaster, Lancashire primary schs, 1952–62; Lectr in Primary Educn, Liverpool Univ., 1962–63; Sen. Lectr in Educn, Chester Coll., 1963–66; Principal Lectr and Head of Educn Dept, St Katharine's Coll., Liverpool, 1966–71; Principal, Westhill Coll., Birmingham, 1971–85. Pres., Birmingham Council of Christian Educn, 1972–74, Vice-Pres., 1974–91; Vice-Pres., Colls of Educn Christian Union, 1965–86, Pres., 1966–67, 1972–73; Chm., Birmingham Assoc. of Youth Clubs, 1972–85, Vice-Pres., 1985–; Trustee, Invest in Youth Trust, 1973–79; Member: Standing Conf. on Studies in Educn, 1974– (Exec. Cttee and Editl Bd, 1978–87, Sec., 1982–84); Council of Nat. Youth Bureau, 1974–80 (Exec. Cttee, 1978–80); Adv. Cttee on religious broadcasts, BBC Radio Birmingham, 1972–80; Educn Cttee, Free Church Fed. Council, 1978–89; BCC Standing Cttee on Theol Educn, 1979–82; Council, British and Foreign School Soc., 1979–85; Exec. Cttee, Assoc. of Voluntary Colls, 1979–86; Standing Cttee on Educn and Training of Teachers, 1985– (Vice-Chm., 1988; Chm. , 1989); Cttee, Standing Conf. of Principals and Dirs of Colls and Insts of Higher Educn, 1986–91; Voluntary Sector Consultative Council, 1987–88; Cambridge HA, 1987–90 (Trustee, 1988–90); Chairman: Colls Cttee, NATFHE, 1981–82; Central Register and Clearing House Cttee, 1981–82 (Mem. Council of Management, 1982–). Governor: London Bible Coll., 1981–89; Cambridge Inst. of Educn, 1985–. JP Birmingham 1977–85. FRSA. Hon. MA Birmingham, 1981. *Publications:* articles on educn and church-related subjects. *Recreations:* travel, photography. *Address:* Homerton College, Cambridge CB2 2PH. *Clubs:* Commonwealth Trust, United Oxford & Cambridge University.

BAMFORD, Sir Anthony (Paul), Kt 1990; DL; Chairman and Managing Director, J. C. Bamford Group, since 1975; *b* 23 Oct. 1945; *s* of Joseph Cyril Bamford, *qv*; *m* 1974, Carole Gray Whitt; two *s* one *d*. *Educ:* Ampleforth Coll.; Grenoble Univ. Joined JCB on shop floor, 1962; led company's only takeover so far, Chaseside Engineering, 1968. Dir, Tarmac, 1987. Member: Design Council, 1987–; President's Cttee, CBI, 1986–. Pres., Staffs Agricl Soc., 1987–88. Pres., Burton on Trent Cons. Assoc., 1987–. High Sheriff, Staffs, 1985–86. DL Staffs, 1989. Hon. MEng Birmingham, 1987; DUniv Keele, 1988. Young Exporter of the Year, 1972; Young Businessman of the Year, 1979. Chevalier, l'Ordre National du Mérite (France), 1989. *Recreations:* riding, farming. *Address:* c/o J. C. Bamford Excavators Ltd, Rocester, Uttoxeter, Staffs ST14 5JP. *Clubs:* Pratt's, British Racing Drivers'.

BAMFORD, Prof. Clement Henry, FRS 1964; MA, PhD, ScD Cantab; CChem, FRSC; Honorary Senior Fellow, Institute of Medical and Dental Bioengineering, University of Liverpool, since 1980; Campbell Brown Professor of Industrial Chemistry, University of Liverpool, 1962–80, now Emeritus Professor; *b* 10 Oct. 1912; *s* of Frederic Jesse Bamford and Catherine Mary Bamford (*née* Shelley), Stafford; *m* 1938, Daphne Ailsa Stephan, BSc Sydney, PhD Cantab, of Sydney, Australia; one *s* one *d*. *Educ:* St Patrick's and King Edward VI Schs, Stafford; Trinity Coll., Cambridge (Senior Scholar, 1931). Fellow, Trinity Coll., Cambridge, 1937; Dir of Studies in Chemistry, Emmanuel Coll., Cambridge, 1937. Joined Special Operations Executive, 1941; joined Fundamental Research Laboratory of Messrs Courtaulds Ltd, at Maidenhead, 1945; head of laboratory, 1947–62; Liverpool University: Dean, Faculty of Science, 1965–68; Pro-Vice-Chancellor, 1972–75. Member: Council, Chem. Soc., 1972–75; Council, Soc. Chem. Ind., 1974–75. Pres., British Assoc. Section B (Chemistry), 1975–76; Vice-Pres., 1977–81, Pres., 1981–85, Macromolecular Div., Internat. Union of Pure and Applied Chemistry. Vis. Professor: Kyoto Univ., 1977; Univ. of NSW, 1981. Mem. Edit. Bd, Polymer, 1958–; European Ed., Jl of Biomaterials Sci., 1988–. Hon. DSc: Bradford, 1980; Lancaster, 1988. Meldola Medal, Royal Inst. of Chemistry, 1941; Macromolecules and Polymers Award, Chemical Soc., 1977; Award for dist. service in advancement of polymer science, Soc. of Polymer Science, Japan, 1989. *Publications:* Synthetic Polypeptides (with A. Elliott and W. E. Hanby), 1956; The Kinetics of Vinyl Polymerization by Radical Mechanisms (with W. G. Barb, A. D. Jenkins and P. F. Onyon), 1958; (ed with late C. F. H. Tipper and R. G. Compton) Comprehensive Chemical Kinetics, 26 vols, 1969–86; papers on physical chemistry, polymer science and biomaterials science in learned journals. *Recreations:* music, especially violin playing, hill walking, gardening. *Address:* Broom Bank, Tower Road, Prenton, Birkenhead, Merseyside L42 8LH. *T:* 051–608 3979.

BAMFORD, Joseph Cyril, CBE 1969; formerly Chairman and Managing Director: J. C. Bamford Excavators Ltd; JCB Farms Ltd; JCB Research Ltd; JCB Sales Ltd; JCB Service; JCB Earthmovers Ltd; *b* 21 June 1916; *m* 1941, Marjorie Griffin; two *s*. *Educ:* St John's, Alton, Staffs; Stonyhurst Coll. Founded J. C. Bamford Excavators Ltd, 1945; more than seventy per cent of total production now goes to export market. Hon. DTech Loughborough Univ. of Technol., 1983. *Recreations:* yacht designing, landscaping, landscape gardening. *Address:* Les Tourelles, Bon Port 15, CH 1820 Montreux-Territet, Switzerland.

See also Sir A. P. Bamford.

BAMFORD, Louis Neville Jules; Legal Executive with Margetts & Ritchie, Solicitors, Birmingham, since 1960; *b* 2 July 1932; *s* of Neville Barnes Bamford and Elise Marie Bamford; unmarried. *Educ:* local schools in Birmingham. Member (Lab): Birmingham CC, 1971–74; W Midlands CC, 1974–86 (Chm., 1981–82; Chm., Legal and Parly Cttee, 1974–77; Mem. of various cttees); Birmingham CC, 1986– (Mem. various cttees incl. Gen. Purposes, Envmtl Health and Trading Services (Vice-Chm.)). Chm., Birmingham Convention and Visitors Bureau. *Recreations:* football, music. *Address:* 15 Chilton Court, Park Approach, Erdington, Birmingham B23 7XY.

BAMPFYLDE, family name of **Baron Poltimore.**

BANANA, Rev. Dr Canaan Sodindo; President of Zimbabwe, 1980–87; *b* Esiphezini, Matabeleland, 5 March 1936; *s* of Aaron and Jese Banana; *m* 1961, Janet Mbuyazwe; three *s* one *d*. *Educ:* Mzinyati Mission; Tegwani Trng Inst.; Epworth Theol Coll., Salisbury; Kansai Industrial Centre, Japan; Wesley Theol Seminary, Washington, DC; Univ. of S Africa. Dip. in Urban and Industrial Mission, Kansai, 1970; MTS Hons, Wesley Theol Seminary, 1974; BA Hons Univ. of SA, 1980. Methodist Minister and Manager of Schools: Wankie Area, 1963–64; Plumtree Area, 1965–66 (Sch. Chaplain, Tegwani High Sch.); Methodist Minister, Fort Viet Area, 1967–68; Methodist Minister, Bulawayo and Chm., Bulaway Council of Churches, 1969–70; with Mambo Press as Promotion Officer for Moto, Catholic newspaper, 1971; Founder Mem. and first Vice Pres., ANC, Zimbabwe, 1971–73; ANC Rep. in N America and UN, 1973–75; Chaplain, American Univ., 1974–75; Publicity Sec., People's Movement Internal Co-ordinating Cttee (ZANU-PF), 1976–77; Reg. Co-ordinator, Matabeleland N and S Provinces, 1979–80. Chm., Southern Africa Contact Gp, 1970–73; Mem., Adv. Cttee, WCC, 1970–80. Hon. LLD: Amer. Univ., 1981; Univ. of Zimbabwe, 1983. *Publications:* The Zimbabwe Exodus, 1974; The Gospel According to the Ghetto, 1974, 3rd edn 1980; The Woman of my Imagination, 1980 (also in Ndebele and Shona versions); Theology of Promise, 1982; The Ethos of Socialism, 1988; various articles. *Recreations:* tennis, table tennis; soccer (player, referee and coach); volley ball (umpire); music. *Address:* c/o State House, Box 368, Harare, Zimbabwe. *T:* Harare 26666.

BANBURY, family name of **Baron Banbury of Southam.**

BANBURY OF SOUTHAM, 3rd Baron *cr* 1924, of Southam; **Charles William Banbury;** Bt 1902; *b* 29 July 1953; *s* of 2nd Baron Banbury of Southam and of Hilda Ruth, *d* of late A. H. R. Carr; *S* father, 1981; *m* 1984, Lucinda Trehearne (marr. diss. 1986). *Educ:* Eton College. *Heir:* none. *Address:* The Mill, Fossebridge, Glos.

BANBURY, (Frederick Harold) Frith; theatrical director, producer and actor; *b* 4 May 1912; *s* of Rear-Adm. Frederick Arthur Frith Banbury and Winifred (*née* Fink); unmarried. *Educ:* Stowe Sch.; Hertford Coll., Oxford; Royal Academy of Dramatic Art. First stage appearance in "If I Were You", Shaftesbury Theatre, 1933; for next 14 years appeared both in London and Provinces in every branch of theatre from Shakespeare to revue. Appearances included: Hamlet, New Theatre, 1934; Goodness How Sad, Vaudeville, 1938; (revue) New Faces, Comedy, 1939; Uncle Vanya, Westminster, 1943; Jacobowsky and the Colonel, Piccadilly, 1945; Caste, Duke of York's, 1947. During this time he also appeared in numerous films including The Life and Death of Colonel Blimp and The History of Mr Polly, and also on the television screen. Since 1947 he has devoted his time to production and direction, starting with Dark Summer at Lyric, Hammersmith (later transferred St Martin's), 1947; subseq. many, in both London and New York, including The Holly and the Ivy, Duchess, 1950; Waters of the Moon, Haymarket, 1951; The Deep Blue Sea, Duchess, 1951, and Morosco, New York, 1952; A Question of Fact, Piccadilly, 1953; Marching Song, St Martin's, 1954; Love's Labour's Lost, Old Vic, 1954; The Diary of Anne Frank, Phoenix, 1956; A Dead Secret, Piccadilly, 1957; Flowering Cherry, Haymarket, 1957, and Lyceum, New York, 1959; A Touch of the Sun, Saville, 1958; The Ring of Truth, Savoy, 1959; The Tiger and the Horse, Queen's, 1960; The Wings of the Dove, Lyric, 1963; The Right Honourable Gentleman, Billy Rose, New York, 1965; Howards End, New, 1967; Dear Octopus, Haymarket, 1967; Enter A Free Man, St Martin's, 1968; A Day In the Death of Joe Egg, Cameri Theatre, Tel Aviv, 1968; Le Valet, Théâtre de la Renaissance, Paris, 1968; On the Rocks, Dublin Theatre Festival, 1969; My Darling Daisy, Lyric, 1970; The Winslow Boy, New, 1970; Captain Brassbound's Conversion, Cambridge, 1971; Reunion in Vienna, Chichester Festival, 1971, Piccadilly, 1972; The Day After the Fair, Lyric, 1972, Shubert, Los Angeles, 1973; Glasstown, Westminster, 1973; Ardèle, Queen's, 1975; On Approval, Canada and SA, 1976, Vaudeville, 1977; directed in Australia, Kenya, USA, 1978–79; Motherdear, Ambassadors, 1980; Dear Liar, Mermaid, 1982; The Aspern Papers, Haymarket, 1984; The Corn is Green, Old Vic, 1985; The Admirable Crichton, Haymarket, 1988; Screamers, Arts, 1989. *Recreation:* playing the piano.

BANBURY, Frith; *see* Banbury, Frederick Harold F.

BANCROFT, family name of **Baron Bancroft.**

BANCROFT, Baron *cr* 1982 (Life Peer), of Coatham in the county of Cleveland; **Ian Powell Bancroft,** GCB 1979 (KCB 1975; CB 1971); Head of the Home Civil Service and Permanent Secretary to the Civil Service Department, 1978, retired Nov. 1981; *b* 23 Dec. 1922; *s* of A. E. and L. Bancroft; *m* 1950, Jean Swaine; two *s* one *d*. *Educ:* Coatham Sch.; Balliol Coll., Oxford (Scholar; Hon. Fellow 1981). Served Rifle Brigade, 1942–45. Entered Treasury, 1947; Private Secretary: to Sir Henry Wilson Smith, 1948–50; to Chancellor of the Exchequer, 1953–55; to Lord Privy Seal, 1955–57; Cabinet Office, 1957–59; Principal Private Sec. to successive Chancellors of the Exchequer, 1964–66; Under-Sec., HM Treasury, 1966–68, Civil Service Dept, 1968–70; Dep. Sec., Dir Gen. of Organization and Establishments, DoE, 1970–72; a Comr of Customs and Excise, and Dep. Chm. of Bd, 1972–73; Second Permanent Sec., CSD, 1973–75; Permanent Sec., DoE, 1975–77. Mem., Adv. Council on Public Records, 1983–88. Dep. Chm., Sun Life Corp. plc, 1987– (Dir, 1983–; a Vice-Chm., 1986–87); Director: Rugby Group (formerly Rugby Portland Cement), 1982–; Bass Plc, 1982–; ANZ Grindlays Bank plc, 1983–; Bass Leisure Ltd, 1984–; ANZ Merchant Bank, 1987–. Pres., Building Centre Trust, 1987–; a Vice-Pres., BSA, 1984–. Vis. Fellow, Nuffield Coll., Oxford, 1973–81; Chm. Trustees, Mansfield Coll., Oxford, 1988– (Chm. Council, 1981–88). Chm., Royal Hosp. and Home, Putney, 1984–88 (Mem., Management Board, 1988–); Governor, Cranleigh Sch., 1983–. *Address:* House of Lords, SW1A 0PW. *T:* 071–219 3000. *Clubs:* United Oxford & Cambridge University, Civil Service.

BAND, David; Chief Executive, Barclays de Zoete Wedd, since 1988; Director: Barclays PLC, since 1988; Barclays Bank PLC, since 1988; *b* 14 Dec. 1942; *s* of David Band and Elisabeth Aitken Band; *m* 1973, Olivia Rose (*née* Brind); one *s* one *d*. *Educ:* Rugby; St Edmund Hall, Oxford (MA). Joined J. P. Morgan & Co. in London, 1964; General

Manager: Singapore, 1976; Paris, 1978; Sen. Vice Pres., Morgan Guaranty Trust Co., New York, 1981; Man. Dir, Morgan Guaranty Ltd, London, 1986; Exec. Vice Pres., Morgan Guaranty Trust Co., and Chm., J. P. Morgan Securities Ltd, London, 1987. Dep. Chm., Securities Assoc., 1986–88. *Recreation:* tennis. *Address:* 20 Ilchester Place, W14 8AA. *T:* 071–602 2124.

BAND, Robert Murray Niven, MC 1944; QC 1974; **His Honour Judge Band;** a Circuit Judge, since 1978; *b* 23 Nov. 1919; *s* of Robert Niven Band and Agnes Jane Band; *m* 1948, Nancy Margery Redhead; two *d. Educ:* Trinity Coll., Glenalmond; Hertford Coll., Oxford (MA). Served in Royal Artillery, 1940–46. Called to the Bar, Inner Temple, 1947; Junior Treasury Counsel in Probate Matters, 1972–74; Chm. Family Law Bar Assoc., 1972–74; a Recorder of the Crown Court, 1977–78. Chm., St Teresa's Hosp., Wimbledon, 1969–83. *Recreations:* the countryside, gardens, old buildings, treen.

BAND, Thomas Mollison, FSAScot; FTS; Chief Executive, Scottish Tourist Board, since 1987; *b* 28 March 1934; *s* of late Robert Boyce Band and Elizabeth Band; *m* 1959, Jean McKenzie Brien; one *s* two *d. Educ:* Perth Academy. National Service, RAF, 1952–54. Joined Civil Service, 1954; Principal, BoT, 1969; Sen. Principal, Dept of Industry, 1973; Scottish Econ. Planning Dept, 1975, Asst Sec., 1976; Scottish Development Dept, 1978; Scottish Office, Finance, 1981; Dir, Historic Bldgs and Monuments, Scottish Develt Dept, 1984–87. Dir, Taste of Scotland, 1988–; Dep. Chm., Forth Bridge Centenary Trust, 1989–; Director: Edinburgh Chamber of Commerce, 1989–; Edinburgh Marketing Ltd, 1990–. *Recreations:* skiing, gardening, beating. *Address:* Heathfield, Pitcairngreen, Perthshire. *T:* Almondbank (0738) 83403.

BANDA, Hastings Kamuzu, MD, **(His Excellency Ngwazi Dr H. Kamuzu Banda);** President of Malaŵi since 1966, Life President, 1971; Chancellor, University of Malaŵi, since 1965; Life President, Malaŵi Congress Party; *b* Nyasaland, 1905. *Educ:* Meharry Medical Coll., Nashville, USA (MD); Universities of Glasgow and Edinburgh. Further degrees: BSc, MB, ChB, LRCSE; and several hon. degrees awarded later. Practised medicine in Liverpool and on Tyneside during War of 1939–45 and in London, 1945–53. Returned to Africa, 1953, and practised in Gold Coast. Took over leadership of Nyasaland African Congress in Blantyre, 1958, and became Pres.-Gen.; was imprisoned for political reasons, 1959; unconditionally released, 1960; Minister of Natural Resources and Local Government, Nyasaland, 1961–63; Prime Minister of Malaŵi (formerly Nyasaland), 1963–66. *Address:* Office of the President, Private Bag 388, Capital City, Lilongwe 3, Malaŵi.

BANDARANAIKE, Mrs Sirimavo; President, Sri Lanka Freedom Party, since 1960; Member of Parliament of Sri Lanka, 1960–80; Prime Minister of Sri Lanka (Ceylon until 1972), 1960–65, and 1970–77, also Minister of Defence and Foreign Affairs, of Planning and Economic Affairs, and of Plan Implementation; *b* 17 April 1916; *d* of Barnes Ratwatte, Ratemahatmaya of Ratnapura Dist, Mem. of Ceylon Senate; *m* 1940, Solomon West Ridgeway Dias Bandaranaike (*d* 1959), Prime Minister of Ceylon, 1956–59; one *s* two *d. Educ:* Ratnapura Ferguson Sch.; St Bridget's Convent, Colombo. Assisted S. W. R. D. Bandaranaike in political career. Campaigned for Sri Lanka Freedom Party in election campaigns, March and July 1960. Formerly Pres. and Treasurer, Lanka Mahila Samiti. Prime Minister of Ceylon, also Minister of Defence and External Affairs, 1960–65; Minister of Information and Broadcasting, 1964–65; Leader of the Opposition, 1965–70. Chm., Non Aligned Movt, 1976–77. Ceres Medal, FAO, 1977. *Address:* Horagolla, Nittambuwa, Sri Lanka.

BANFIELD, Ven. David John; Archdeacon of Bristol, since 1990; *b* 25 June 1933; *s* of Norman Charles Banfield and Muriel Gladys Honor Banfield (*née* Pippard); *m* 1967, Rita (*née* Woolhouse); three *d. Educ:* Yeovil Sch.; London Coll. of Divinity, London Univ. (ALCD). RAF, 1951–53. Deacon 1957, priest 1958; Curate, Middleton, Manchester, 1957–62; Chaplain and Asst Warden, Scargill House, Yorks, 1962–67; Vicar of Addiscombe, Croydon, 1967–80; Vicar of Luton, Beds, 1980–90. *Recreations:* travel, walking, music, gardening. *Address:* 10 Great Brockeridge, Westbury-on-Trym, Bristol BS9 3TY. *T:* Bristol (0272) 622438.

BANGEMANN, Dr Martin; a Vice-President, Commission of the European Community, since 1989; *b* 15 Nov. 1934; *s* of Martin Bangemann and Lotte Telge; *m* 1962, Renate Bauer; three *s* two *d. Educ:* Univ. of Tübingen; Univ. of Munich (DJur). Lawyer, 1962. Mem., Bundestag, 1973–79 and 1987–89; Mem., European Parliament, 1979–84; Minister of Econs, FRG, 1984–88. Freie Demokratische Partei: Mem., 1963–; Chm., 1985–88. *Address:* Rue de la Loi 200, 1049 Brussels, Belgium.

BANGHAM, Alec Douglas, MD; FRS 1977; retired; Research Worker, Agricultural Research Council, Institute of Animal Physiology, Babraham, 1952–82 and Head, Biophysics Unit, 1971–82; *b* 10 Nov. 1921; *s* of Dr Donald Hugh and Edith Bangham; *m* 1943, Rosalind Barbara Reiss; three *s* one *d. Educ:* Bryanston Sch.; UCL and UCH Med. Sch. (MD). Captain, RAMC, 1946–48. Lectr, Dept of Exper. Pathology, UCH, 1949–52; Principal Scientific Officer, 1952–63, Senior Principal Scientific Officer (Merit Award), 1963–82, ARC, Babraham. Fellow, UCL, 1981–. *Publications:* contrib. Nature, Biochim. Biophys. Acta, and Methods in Membrane Biol. *Recreations:* horticulture, photographic arts, sailing. *Address:* 17 High Green, Great Shelford, Cambridge. *T:* Cambridge (0223) 843192.

BANGOR, 7th Viscount *cr* 1781; **Edward Henry Harold Ward;** Baron, 1770; free-lance journalist (as Edward Ward); *b* 5 Nov. 1905; *s* of 6th Viscount Bangor, PC (Northern Ireland), OBE and Agnes Elizabeth (*d* 1972), 3rd *d* of late Dacre Hamilton of Cornacassa, Monaghan; *S* father, 1950; *m* 1st, 1933, Elizabeth (who obtained a divorce, 1937), *e d* of T. Balfour, Wrockwardine Hall, Wellington, Salop; 2nd, 1937, Mary Kathleen (marr. diss. 1947), *d* of W. Middleton, Shanghai; 3rd, 1947, Leila Mary (marr. diss. 1951; she died, 1959), *d* of David R. Heaton, Brookfield, Crownhill, S Devon; one *s*; 4th, 1951, Mrs Marjorie Alice Simpson (*d* 1991), *d* of late Peter Banks, St Leonards-on-Sea; one *s* one *d. Educ:* Harrow; RMA, Woolwich. Formerly Reuter's correspondent in China and the Far East; BBC War Correspondent in Finland, 1939–40, ME, 1940–41, and Foreign Correspondent all over world, 1946–60. *Publications:* 1940 Despatches from Finland, 1946; Give Me Air, 1946; Chinese Crackers, 1957; The New Eldorado, 1957; Oil is Where They Find It, 1959; Sahara Story, 1962; Number One Boy, 1969; I've Lived like a Lord, 1970. With his wife, Marjorie Ward: Europe on Record, 1950; The US and Us 1951; Danger is Our Business, 1955. *Heir: s* Hon. William Maxwell David Ward [*b* 9 Aug. 1948; *m* 1976, Mrs Sarah Bradford]. *Address:* 59 Cadogan Square, SW1X 0HZ. *T:* 071–235 3202. *Clubs:* Savile, Garrick.

BANGOR, Bishop of, 1983–Sept. 1992; **Rt. Rev. John Cledan Mears;** *b* 8 Sept. 1922; *s* of Joseph and Anna Lloyd Mears; *m* 1949, Enid Margaret; one *s* one *d. Educ:* Univ. of Wales, Aberystwyth (BA Philosophy 1943); Wycliffe Hall, Oxford; St Deiniol's Library, Hawarden. MA Wales 1948 (research, Blaise Pascal). Deacon 1947, priest 1948, St Asaph; Curate: Mostyn, 1947–49; Rhosllannerchrugog, 1949–55; Vicar of Cwm, 1955–58; Lecturer, St Michael's Coll., Llandaff and Univ. of Wales, Cardiff, 1959–73; Chaplain, 1959–67; Sub-warden, 1967–73; Vicar of St Mark's, Gabalfa, Cardiff, 1973–82. Examining Chaplain, 1960–73; Hon. Canon of Llandaff Cathedral, 1981–82; Sec. of Governing Body, Church in Wales, 1977–82. *Publications:* reviews in Theology, articles in Efrydiau Athronyddol, Diwynyddiaeth, and Barn. *Recreations:* hiking, mountaineering. *Address:* (until Sept. 1992) Ty'r Esgob, Bangor, Gwynedd LL57 2SS. *T:* Bangor (0248) 362895; 25 Avon Ridge, Thornhill, Cardiff.

BANGOR, Dean of; *see* Edwards, Very Rev. T. E. P.

BANHAM, Mrs Belinda Joan, CBE 1977; JP; Part time Consultant, Health Division, Business Sciences Ltd; *d* of late Col Charles Unwin and Winifred Unwin; *m* 1939, Terence Middlecott Banham; two *s* two *d. Educ:* privately; West Bank Sch.; Brussels. BSc (Hons) London; Dip. Social Studies London. RGN. Work in health services, 1937–; work in theory and practice on aspects of social deviance and deprivation, Cornwall CC, 1954–67; Mem., SW RHB, 1965–74; Chairman: Cornwall and Isles of Scilly HMC, 1967–74 (Mem., 1964–77); Cornwall and Isles of Scilly AHA, 1974–77; Kensington, Chelsea and Westminster FPC, 1979–85 (Mem. 1977–79); Paddington and N Kensington DHA, 1981–86; Mem., Lambeth, Southwark and Lewisham FPC, 1987–90; Vice Chm., Lambeth, Southwark and Lewisham FHSA, 1990–; Mem., MRC, 1980–87 (Chm., Standing Cttee on Use of Medical Inf. in Research, 1980–87). Mem., Industrial Tribunals, 1974–87. Marriage Guidance Councillor, 1960–72. A Vice-Chm., Disabled Living Foundn, 1984– (Dir, then Hon. Dir, 1977–83); Vice-Pres. KIDS, 1987– (Chm., 1982–87); Trustee, Wytham Hall, 1985– (Vice Chm., 1990–); Vice-Pres., AFASIC, 1990–. JP Cornwall, 1972. Special interests: social deprivation and deviance, Health Service management and use of resources. *Publications:* (jtly) (paper) Systems Science in Health Care (NATO Conf., Paris, 1977); (jtly) (report) Partnership in Action: a study of healthcare services for elderly and physically handicapped in Newcastle, 1989. *Recreations:* gardening, plant biology, theatre. *Address:* Ponsmaen, St Feock, Truro, Cornwall TR3 6QG. *T:* Truro (0872) 862 275; 81 Vandon Court, Petty France, SW1. *T:* 071–222 1414.

See also J. M. M. Banham.

BANHAM, John Michael Middlecott; Director General, Confederation of British Industry, 1987–Oct. 1992; *b* 22 Aug. 1940; *s* of Terence Middlecott Banham, FRCS and Belinda Joan Banham, *qv*; *m* 1965, Frances Barbara Molyneux Favell; one *s* two *d. Educ:* Charterhouse; Queens' Coll., Cambridge (Foundn Schol.; BA 1st cl. in Natural Scis, 1962; Hon. Fellow, 1989). Asst Principal, HM Foreign Service, 1962–64; Dir of Marketing, Wallcoverings Div., Reed International, 1965–69; McKinsey & Co. Inc., 1969–83: Associate, 1969–75; Principal, 1975–80; Dir, 1980–83; Controller, Audit Commn, 1983–87. Mem., BOTB, 1989–Oct. 1992; Dir and Mem. Bd, Business in the Community, 1989–. Member Council: PSI, 1986–; BESO, 1991–. Member: Council of Management, PDSA, 1982–; Governing Body, London Business Sch., 1987–; Managing Trustee, Nuffield Foundn, 1988–; Hon. Treas., Cancer Res. Campaign, 1991–. Hon. LLD Bath, 1987; Hon. DSc Loughborough, 1989. *Publications:* Future of the British Car Industry, 1975; Realizing the Promise of a National Health Service, 1977; numerous reports for Audit Commn on education, housing, social services and local government finance, 1984–87, and for CBI on UK economy, skills, transport, the infrastructure and urban regeneration. *Recreations:* ground clearing, cliff walking in W Cornwall, ocean sailing. *Address:* c/o CBI, Centre Point, 103 New Oxford Street, WC1A 1DU. *T:* 071–379 7400, *Fax:* 071–836 0645. *Clubs:* Travellers', Oriental.

BANISTER, Stephen Michael Alvin; Secretary, British and Foreign School Society, since 1978; Director, Taylor and Francis Ltd, since 1978; Editor, Transport Reviews, since 1981; *b* 7 Oct. 1918; *s* of late Harry Banister and Idwen Banister (*née* Thomas); *m* 1944, Rachel Joan Rawlence; four *s. Educ:* Eton; King's Coll., Cambridge (MA). With Foreign Office, 1939–45; Home Guard (Major, 1944). Asst Principal, Min. of Civil Aviation, 1946; Principal, 1947; Private Sec. to six successive Ministers of Transport and Civil Aviation, 1950–56; Asst Sec., Min. of Transport and BoT, 1956–70; Under Sec., DoE, 1970–76, Dept of Transport, 1976–78. UK Shipping Delegate, UNCTAD, 1964; UK Dep., European Conf. of Ministers of Transport, 1976–78. Mem., Nat. Insurance Tribunal, Kingston upon Thames, 1979–85. *Compositions:* (amateur) for singers, including Bluebeard. *Recreations:* countryside, walking, singing (formerly in opera, now in choirs); formerly cricket (Cambridge Crusader); played for CU *v* Australians, 1938. *Address:* Bramshaw, Lower Farm Road, Effingham, Surrey KT24 5JJ. *T:* Bookham (0372) 52778.

BANKS, family name of **Baron Banks.**

BANKS, Baron *cr* 1974 (Life Peer), of Kenton in Greater London; **Desmond Anderson Harvie Banks,** CBE 1972; President, Liberal European Action Group, 1971–87; *b* 23 Oct. 1918; *s* of James Harvie Banks, OBE and Sheena Muriel Watt; *m* 1948, Barbara Wells (OBE 1987); two *s. Educ:* Alpha Prep. Sch.; University College Sch. Served with KRRC and RA, 1939–46, Middle East and Italy (Major); Chief Public Relations Officer to Allied Mil. Govt, Trieste, 1946. Joined Canada Life Assce Co., subseq. Life Assoc. of Scotland; life assce broker from 1959; Director: Tweddle French & Co. (Life & Pensions Consultants) Ltd, 1973–82; Lincoln Consultants Ltd, 1982–89. Liberal Party: Pres., 1968–69; Chm. Exec., 1961–63 and 1969–70; Dir of Policy Promotion, 1972–74; Chm. Res. Cttee, 1966; Hon. Sec., Home Counties Liberal Fedn, 1960–61; Chairman: Working Party on Machinery of Govt, 1971–74; Liberal Summer Sch. Cttee, 1979–; Member: For. Affairs Panel, 1961–88 (sometime Vice-Chm.); Social Security Panel, 1961–88; Hon. Sec., Liberal Candidates Assoc., 1947–52; contested (L): Harrow East, 1950; St Ives, 1955; SW Herts, 1959. Vice-Chm., Liberal Party Standing Cttee, 1973–79; Dep. Liberal Whip, House of Lords, 1977–83; spokesman on: social security, 1975–89; social services, 1977–83; Vice-Pres., European Atlantic Gp, 1985– (Vice Chm., 1979–85); a Pres., British Council, European Movement, 1986– (Vice-Chm., 1979–86). Elder, United Reformed Church. *Publications:* Clyde Steamers, 1947, 2nd edn 1951; numerous political pamphlets. *Recreations:* pursuing interest in Gilbert and Sullivan opera and in Clyde river steamers; reading. *Address:* Lincoln House, The Lincolns, Little Kingshill, Great Missenden, Bucks HP16 0EH. *T:* Great Missenden (02406) 6164. *Club:* National Liberal (President, 1981–).

BANKS, Alan George; HM Diplomatic Service, retired; *b* 7 April 1911; *s* of George Arthur Banks and Sarah Napthen; *m* 1946, Joyce Frances Telford Yates; two *s. Educ:* Preston Gram. Sch. Served in HM Forces, 1939–43; at Consulate-Gen., Dakar, 1943–45; Actg Consul, Warsaw, 1945–48; HM Vice-Consul: Bordeaux, 1948–50; Istanbul, 1950–52; Zagreb, 1952–55; FO, 1955–58; HM Consul, Split, 1958–60; 1st Sec. and Consul, Madrid, 1960–62; 1st Sec., FO, 1962–67; Consul-General, Alexandria, 1967–71. *Recreations:* classical music, gardening, photography. *Address:* Ferney Field, Parkgate Road, Newdigate, Dorking, Surrey RH5 5AH. *T:* Newdigate (030677) 434. *Club:* MCC.

BANKS, Colin; Founder Partner, Banks and Miles, graphic designers, London, since 1958, Hamburg, since 1990 and Brussels, since 1991; *b* 16 Jan. 1932; *s* of William James Banks and late Ida Jenny (*née* Hood); *m* 1961, Caroline Grigson, PhD; one *s* (one *d* decd). Prodn Editor (with John Miles) of Which? and other Consumers' Assoc. magazines, 1964–. Design Consultant to: Zool Soc., 1962–82; British Council, 1968–83; E Midlands Arts Assoc., 1974–77; English National Opera, 1975–76; Direct Election Campaign, European Parlt, 1978, 1984; (new visual identity for) Post Office: Royal Mail, Telecommunications, etc, 1972–; British Telecom., 1980; US Govt Social Marketing Project, Family Planning in Indonesia, 1985–; NERC, 1986; City Univ., 1987; CNAA, 1988; IMechE, 1988; Fondation Roi Baudouin, 1988–; SERC, 1989. Designer/Design Adviser to: City and Guilds; Commn for Racial Equality; LRT; other instns and commercial cos. Exhibitions: London, Paris, Amsterdam, Glasgow, Brussels, Kyoto. Vice-Pres., SIAD, 1974–76. Pres., Soc. of Typographic Designers, 1988–; Design and Industries Assoc. Manager, Blackheath Sch. of Art, 1981–89; Treas., Project Mala for children's educn and welfare, India, 1989–. Lectured in Europe, India, Japan, SE Asia, USA. FRSA. Fifty Best German Printed Books, W Germany, 1989; Internationalen Buchkunst Ausstellung Medal, Leipzig, 1971, 1989; Gold Medal, Brno Biennale, 1986; RSA Environment Award, 1989; BBC Envmtl Design Prize, 1990. *Publications:* Social Communication, 1979; (with E. Schumacher Gebler) 26 Letters, Vol. I 1989, Vol. II 1992; contrib. jls, London, Budapest, Copenhagen, USA etc. *Recreation:* India. *Address:* 1 Tranquil Vale, Blackheath, SE3 0BU. *T:* 081–318 1131; Little Town, Wilts. *Clubs:* Arts; Double Crown (Chm.), Wynkyn de Worde; Type Directors (New York).

BANKS, Frank David, FCA; business consultant; Chairman, H. Berkeley (Holdings) Ltd, 1984–90; *b* 11 April 1933; *s* of Samuel and Elizabeth Banks; *m* 1st, 1955, Catherine Jacob; one *s* two *d*; 2nd, 1967, Sonia Gay Coleman; one *d*. *Educ:* Liverpool Collegiate Sch.; Carnegie Mellon Univ. (PFE); Open Univ. (BA 1988). British Oxygen Co. Ltd, 1957–58; Imperial Chemical Industries Ltd, 1959–62; English Electric Co. Ltd, 1963–68; Finance Dir, Platt International Ltd, 1969–71; Industrial Advr, DTI, 1972–73; Constructors John Brown Ltd, 1974–80; Man. Dir, Agribusiness Div., Tate & Lyle Ltd, 1981–83. *Recreations:* music, history. *Address:* 8 Lewes Crescent, Kemp Town, Brighton BN2 1FH.

BANKS, Mrs Gillian Theresa, CB 1990; Director, Carnegie Inquiry into the Third Age, since 1990; *b* 7 Feb. 1933; *d* of Percy and Enid Brimblecombe; *m* 1960, John Anthony Gorst Banks; one *s* two *d*. *Educ:* Walthamstow Hall Sch., Sevenoaks; Lady Margaret Hall, Oxford (BA). Asst Principal, Colonial Office, 1955; Principal, Treasury, 1966; Department of Health and Social Security: Asst Sec., 1972; Under Sec. 1981; Dir, Health Authy Finance, 1985; Dir, OPCS and Registrar Gen. for Eng. and Wales, 1986. *Recreation:* hill walking. *Address:* 16 Chalcot Square, NW1 8YA. *T:* 071–722 3962.

BANKS, John, FEng, FIEE; Consultant Chairman, Adacom 3270 Communications Ltd, 1986–90; *b* 2 Dec. 1920; *s* of John Banks and Jane Dewhurst; *m* 1943, Nancy Olive Yates; two *s*. *Educ:* Univ. of Liverpool (BEng Hons, Elec. Engrg). FEng 1983; FIEE 1959. Chief Engr, Power Cables Div., BICC, 1956–67; Divl Dir and Gen Man., Supertension Cables Div., BICC, 1968–74; Exec. Dir, 1975–78, Chm., 1978–84, BICC Research and Engineering Ltd; Exec. Dir, BICC, 1979. Vis. Prof., Liverpool Univ., 1987–. Pres., IEE, 1982–83. *Recreations:* golf, swimming, music and the arts. *Address:* Flat B1 Marine Gate, Marine Drive, Brighton BN2 5TQ. *T:* Brighton (0273) 690756. *Club:* Seaford Golf.

BANKS, Lynne Reid; writer; *b* 1929; *d* of Dr James Reid-Banks and Muriel (Pat) (*née* Alexander); *m* Chaim Stephenson, sculptor; three *s*. *Educ:* schooling mainly in Canada; RADA. Actress, 1949–54; reporter for ITN, 1955–62; English teacher in kibbutz in Western Galilee, Israel, 1963–71; full-time writer, 1971–; writing includes plays for stage, television and radio. *Publications: plays:* It Never Rains, 1954; All in a Row, 1956; The Killer Dies Twice, 1956; Already, It's Tomorrow, 1962; *fiction:* The L-Shaped Room, 1960 (trans. 10 langs; filmed 1962); An End to Running, 1962 (trans. 2 langs); Children at the Gate, 1968; The Backward Shadow, 1970; Two is Lonely, 1974; Defy the Wilderness, 1981; The Warning Bell, 1984; Casualties, 1986; *biographical fiction:* Dark Quartet: the story of the Brontes, 1976 (Yorks Arts Lit. Award, 1977); Path to the Silent Country: Charlotte Bronte's years of fame, 1977; *history:* Letters to my Israeli Sons, 1979; Torn Country, USA 1982; *for young adults:* One More River, 1973; Sarah and After, 1975; My Darling Villain, 1977 (trans. 3 langs); The Writing on the Wall, 1981; Melusine, 1988 (trans 3 langs); *for children:* The Adventures of King Midas, 1976; The Farthest-Away Mountain, 1977; I, Houdini, 1978; The Indian in the Cupboard, 1980 (trans. 11 langs) (Pacific NW Choice Award, 1984; Calif. Young Readers Medal, 1985; Va Children's Choice, 1988; Rebecca Caudill Award, Mass. Children's Choice, 1988; Arizona Children's Choice, 1989); Maura's Angel, 1984 (trans. 2 langs); The Fairy Rebel, 1985; Return of the Indian, 1986; The Secret of the Indian, 1989; The Magic Hare, 1991; short stories; articles in The Times, The Guardian, Sunday Telegraph, Observer, TES, TLS, Jewish Chronicle, Spectator, and in overseas periodicals. *Recreations:* theatre, gardening, teaching ESL abroad. *Address:* c/o Watson, Little Ltd, 12 Egbert Street, NW1 8LJ. *T:* 071–722 9514.

BANKS, Richard Alford, CBE 1965; *b* 11 July 1902; *s* of William Hartland Banks, Hergest Croft, Kington, Hereford; *m* 1st, 1937, Lilian Jean (*d* 1974), *d* of Dr R. R. Walker, Presteigne, Radnorshire; two *s* one *d*; 2nd, 1976, Rosamund Gould. *Educ:* Rugby; Trinity Coll., Cambridge (BA). Dir of Imperial Chemical Industries Ltd, 1952–64; Chm. of the Industrial Training Council, 1962–64; Mem., Water Resources Bd, 1964–74. Veitch Meml Medal, RHS, 1983. JP Hereford, 1963–73. *Recreations:* arboriculture, gardening and travel. *Address:* Haywood Cottages, Kington, Herefordshire HR5 3EJ.

BANKS, Robert George; MP (C) Harrogate, since Feb. 1974; *b* 18 Jan. 1937; *s* of late George Walmsley Banks, MBE, and of Olive Beryl Banks (*née* Tyler); *m* 1967, Diana Margaret Payne Crawfurd; four *s* one *d* (of whom one *s* one *d* are twins). *Educ:* Haileybury. Lt-Comdr RNR. Jt Founder Dir, Antocks Lairn Ltd, 1963–67. Member of Lloyd's. Mem., Alcohol Educn and Res. Council, 1982–. Mem., Paddington BC, 1959–65. PPS to Minister of State and to Under-Sec. of State, FCO, 1979–82. Member: Council of Europe, 1977–81; WEU, 1977–81; N Atlantic Assembly, 1981–. Jt Sec., Cons. Defence Cttee, 1976–79; Vice-Chm., All-Party Tourism Gp, 1979–; Chm., All-Party Anglo-Sudan Gp, 1982– (Sec., 1978–82); Mem., Select Cttee on Foreign Affairs (and its Overseas Develt Sub-Cttee), 1982–83. Introd Licensing (Alcohol Educn and Res.) Act, 1981; sponsored Licensing (Restaurants Meals) Act, 1987. Reports: for Mil. Cttee of WEU, Report on Nuclear, Biol. and Chem. Protection, adopted by WEU Assembly April 1980; North Atlantic Assembly document, The Technology of Military Space Systems, 1982; New Jobs from Pleasure, report on tourism, 1985. *Publications:* (jtly) Britain's Home Defence Gamble (pamphlet), 1979; committee reports. *Recreations:* travel, farming, architecture, contemporary art. *Address:* House of Commons, SW1A 0AA.

BANKS, Tony; MP (Lab) Newham North West, since 1983. *Educ:* St John's Primary Sch., Brixton; Archbishop Tenison's Grammar Sch., Kensington; York Univ. (BA); London School of Economics. Former trade union research worker; Head of Research, AUEW, 1969–75; an Asst Gen. Sec., Assoc. of Broadcasting and Allied Staffs, 1976–83. Political Advr to Minister for Overseas Develt, 1975. Joined Labour Party, 1964; Greater London Council: Mem. for Hammersmith, 1970–77, for Tooting, 1981–86; Chairman: Gen. Purposes Cttee, 1975–77; Arts and Recreation Cttee, 1981–83; GLC, 1985–86. Contested (Lab): E Grinstead, 1970; Newcastle upon Tyne N, Oct. 1974; Watford, 1979. Member: Select Cttee, HM Treasury, 1986–87; Select Cttee on Procedure, 1987–; Standing Orders Cttee, 1987–; Jt Lords/Commons Cttee on Private Bill Procedure, 1987–88. Chairman: London Gp, Labour MP's, 1987–; Britain-Nicaragua IPU Gp, 1987–. Member: ENO Bd, 1981–83; London Festival Ballet Bd, 1981–83; Nat. Theatre Bd, 1981–85. *Address:* 306 High Street, Stratford, E15. *T:* 081–555 0036.

BANKS, William Hartley; Member, West Yorkshire County Council, 1977–86 (Chairman, 1982–83); *b* 5 July 1909; *s* of Hartley and Edith Banks; *m* 1935, Elsie Kendrew; four *s* one *d* (and one *s* decd). *Educ:* Holbeck Technical Sch. Entered local politics, 1947; Mem., Divl Educn Exec., 1948; Mem., Rothwell UDC, 1959–74 (Chm., 1972–73); Chairman: Sch. Governors, Rothwell, 1964–68; Rothwell Primary Schs, 1974–; Rothwell Secondary Schs, 1982–. Chairman: Rothwell Accident Prevention Cttee, 1960–72; Rothwell Road Safety Cttee, 1987– (Vice-Chm., 1974–87); Sec., Rothwell and Dist Civic Soc., 1974–77; President: Rothwell Athletic Club, 1974– (Treasurer, 1951–74); Rothwell Cricket Club, 1960–; Rothwell Civic Soc., 1980–; Rothwell Pensioners' Assoc., 1986–; Chm., Rothwell Gateway Club, 1980–88; Rothwell Theatre Gp, 1986–; Leader, Rothwell Windmill Youth Club, 1950–55. *Recreations:* classical music, most sports. *Address:* 6 Prospect Place, Rothwell, Leeds LS26 0AL. *T:* Leeds (0532) 821502.

BANNENBERG, Jon, RDI 1978; AMRINA; *b* Australia, 8 July 1929; *s* of Henryk and Kay Bannenberg; *m* 1960, Beaupré Robinson; two *s*. *Educ:* Canterbury High Sch., Sydney; Sydney Conservatorium of Music. RDI (Motor Yacht Design) 1978. Designed: 'Siècle d'Elégance' Exhibn, Louvre, Paris, 1959; CINOA Exhibn, V&A Museum, London, 1960; Motor and Sail Boat Designs include: Queen Elizabeth 2, 1967; Tiawana, Tamahine, 1968; Carinthia V, Anemos II, 1969; Benedic, 1970; Carinthia VI, Arjuna, Aetos, 1971; Blue Lady, Yellowbird, Firebird, Heron 21, 1972; Stilvi, Pegasus III, 1973; My Gail, Xiphas, Mediterranean Sky, 1974; Boule Dogue, Southern Breeze, 1975; Solitaire, 1976; Majestic, 1977; Rodis Island, Nabila, Cimba, 1979; My Gail II, Nahema, 1981; Acajou, Azteca, Paraiso Bobbara, Three Y's, 1983; My Gail III, Cedar Sea, Shirley B, Highlander, Sterling One, Oceanfast, Garuda, 1985. Member, RYA. *Recreations:* running, swimming, sailing, music, Polynesian and Pacific history. *Address:* 35 Carlyle Square, Chelsea, SW3 6HA. *T:* 071–352 6129; 6 Burnsall Street, SW3 3ST. *T:* 071–352 8444.

BANNER, Mrs Delmar; *see* Vasconcellos, J. de.

BANNERMAN, Sir David (Gordon), 15th Bt, *cr* 1682 (NS), of Elsick, Kincardineshire; OBE 1977; with Ministry of Defence, since 1963; *b* 18 Aug. 1935; *s* of Lt-Col Sir Donald Arthur Gordon Bannerman, 13th Bt and of Barbara Charlotte, *d* of late Lt-Col Alexander Cameron, OBE, IMS; *S* brother, Sir Alexander Patrick Bannerman, 14th Bt, 1989; *m* 1960, Mary Prudence, *d* of Rev. Philip Frank Ardagh-Walter; four *d*. *Educ:* Gordonstoun; New Coll., Oxford (MA). 2nd Lieut Queen's Own Cameron Highlanders, 1954–56. HMOCS (Tanzania), 1960–63. *Recreations:* painting, ornithology, tennis, squash. *Address:* c/o Royal Bank of Scotland, Holt's Whitehall Branch, Kirkland House, Whitehall, SW1A 2EB.

BANNISTER, Sir Roger (Gilbert), Kt 1975; CBE 1955; DM (Oxon); FRCP; Master of Pembroke College, Oxford, since 1985; Hon. Consultant Physician, National Hospital for Nervous Diseases, Queen Square, WC1 (formerly Consultant Physician); Hon. Consultant Neurologist: Oxford Regional and District Health Authorities; St Mary's Hospital, W2 (formerly Consultant Neurologist); *b* 23 March 1929; *s* of late Ralph and of Alice Bannister, Harrow; *m* 1955, Moyra Elver, *d* of late Per Jacobsson, Chairman IMF; two *s* two *d*. *Educ:* City of Bath Boys' Sch.; University Coll. Sch., London; Exeter and Merton Colls, Oxford; St Mary's Hospital Medical Sch., London. Amelia Jackson Studentship, Exeter Coll., Oxford, 1947; BA (hons) Physiology, Junior Demonstrator in Physiology, Harmsworth Senior Scholar, Merton Coll., Oxford, 1950; Open and State Schol., St Mary's Hosp., 1951; MSc Thesis in Physiology, 1952; MRCS, LRCP, 1954; BM, BCh Oxford, 1954; DM Oxford, 1963. William Hyde Award for research relating physical education to medicine; MRCP 1957. Junior Medical Specialist, RAMC, 1958; Radcliffe Travelling Fellowship from Oxford Univ., at Harvard, USA, 1962–63. Consultant Neurologist, Western Ophthalmic Hosp., 1963–85. Chm., Hon. Consultants, King Edward VII Convalescent Home for Officers, Osborne, 1979–87. Chm., Medical Cttee, St Mary's Hosp., 1983–85; Deleg., Imperial Coll., representing St Mary's Hosp. Med. Sch., 1988–. President: National Fitness Panel, NABC, 1956–59; Alzheimer's Disease Soc., 1982–84. Mem. Council, King George's Jubilee Trust, 1961–67; Pres., Sussex Assoc. of Youth Clubs, 1972–79; Chm., Res. Cttee, Adv. Sports Council, 1965–71; Mem., Min. of Health Adv. Cttee on Drug Dependence, 1967–70; Chm., Sports Council, 1971–74; Pres., Internat. Council for Sport and Physical Recreation, 1976–83. Mem., Management Cttee, 1979–84, Council, 1984–, King Edward's Hosp. Fund for London; Trustee: King George VI and Queen Elizabeth Foundn of St Catharine's, Cumberland Lodge, Windsor, 1985–; Henry and Proctor Amer. Fellowships, 1987–; Winston Churchill Fellowships, 1988–; Mem. of Commn, Marshall Fellowships; Governor: Atlantic Coll., 1985–; Sherborne Sch., 1989–. Saville Lectr, West End Hosp., London, 1970; Chadwick Trust Lectr, 1972; George Cecil Clarke Lectr, Univ. of Nottingham, 1982; Goodman Lectr, 1987; Tetelman Lectr, Yale Univ., 1990. Winner Oxford *v* Cambridge Mile, 1947–50; Pres. OUAC, 1948; Capt. Oxford & Cambridge Combined American Team, 1949; Finalist, Olympic Games, Helsinki, 1952; British Mile Champion, 1951, 1953, 1954; World Record for One Mile, 1954; British Empire Mile title and record, 1954; European 1500 metres title and record, 1954. Hon. FUMIST, 1974; Hon. Fellow: Exeter Coll., Oxford, 1979; Merton Coll., Oxford, 1986. Hon. LLD Liverpool, 1972; Hon. DLitt Sheffield, 1978; Hon. Doctorates: Univ. of Jyvaskyla, Finland; Univ. Bath, 1984; Univ. Rochester, NY, 1985; Univ. of Pavia, Italy, 1986; Williams Coll., USA, 1987. Hans-Heinrich Siegbert Prize, 1977. *Publications:* First Four Minutes, 1955; (ed) Brain's Clinical Neurology, 3rd edn 1969 to 6th edn 1985, 7th edn 1990 (as Brain and Bannister's Clinical Neurology); (ed) Autonomic Failure, 1983, 2nd edn 1988; papers on physiology of exercise, heat illness and neurological subjects. *Address:* Master's Lodgings, Pembroke College, Oxford OX1 1DW. *T:* Oxford (0865) 276401. *Clubs:* Athenæum, United Oxford & Cambridge University; Vincent's (Oxford).

BANNON, John Kernan, ISO 1969; Director of Services, Meteorological Office, 1973–76; *b* 26 April 1916; *s* of Frederick J. Bannon, Clerk in Holy Orders and Eveline Bannon, Muckamore, NI; *m* 1947, Pauline Mary Roch Thomas, Pembroke; one *s* one *d*. *Educ:* Royal Sch., Armagh; Emmanuel Coll., Cambridge (Braithwaite Batty Scholar). BA (Wrangler) 1938. Technical Officer, Meteorological Office, 1938; commnd RAFVR, 1943–46 (Temp. Sqdn Ldr); Met. Office, 1946–76; idc 1963. *Publications:* some official scientific works; articles in meteorological jls. *Recreations:* walking, gardening. *Address:* 18 Courtenay Drive, Emmer Green, Reading RG4 8XH. *T:* Reading (0734) 473696.

BANTOCK, Prof. Geoffrey Herman; Emeritus Professor of Education, University of Leicester, 1975; *b* 12 Oct. 1914; *s* of Herman S. and Annie Bantock; *m* 1950, Dorothy Jean Pick; no *c*. *Educ:* Wallasey Grammar Sch.; Emmanuel Coll., Cambridge. BA 1936, MA 1942, Cantab. Taught in grammar schs, training coll.; Lectr in Educn, University Coll. of Leicester, 1950–54; Reader in Educn, University Coll., Leicester, later Univ. of Leicester, 1954–64; Prof. of Educn, 1964–75; Leverhulme Emeritus Fellow, 1976–78. Vis. Prof., Monash Univ., Melbourne, 1971. *Publications:* Freedom and Authority in Education, 1952 (2nd edn 1965); L. H. Myers: a critical study, 1956; Education in an

Industrial Society, 1963 (2nd edn 1973); Education and Values, 1965; Education, Culture and the Emotions, 1967; Education, Culture and Industrialization, 1968; T. S. Eliot and Education, 1969 (paperback 1970); Studies in the History of Educational Theory: Vol. I, Artifice and Nature 1350–1765, 1980, Vol. II, The Minds and the Masses 1760–1980, 1984 (Book Prize, Standing Conf. on Studies in Educn, 1985); Dilemmas of the Curriculum, 1980; The Parochialism of the Present, 1981. *Recreations:* music, art, foreign travel. *Address:* c/o The University, Leicester.

BANTOCK, John Leonard; Assistant Under Secretary of State, Home Office Police Department, 1980–84; *b* 21 Oct. 1927; *s* of Edward Bantock and Agnes Bantock; *m* 1947, Maureen McKinney; two *s*. *Educ:* Colfe's Sch., SE13; King George V Sch., Southport, Lancs; LSE, London Univ. (LLB 1951). Unilever Ltd, 1943–45; Army, 1945–48 (Staff Captain); Colonial Office, 1951–52; Inland Revenue, 1952–69; Secretariat, Royal Commn on Constitution, 1969–73; Cabinet Office, 1973–76; Sec., Cttee of Privy Counsellors on Recruitment of Mercenaries, 1976; Asst Under Sec. of State, Home Office Radio Regulatory Dept, 1976–79 (Head, UK Delegn, World Admin. Radio Conf., 1979). *Club:* MCC.

BANTON, Prof. Michael Parker; JP; PhD, DSc; Professor of Sociology, since 1965, and Pro-Vice-Chancellor, 1985–88, University of Bristol; *b* 8 Sept. 1926; *s* of Francis Clive Banton and Kathleen Blanche (*née* Parkes); *m* 1952, Rut Marianne (*née* Jacobson), Luleå; two *s* two *d*. *Educ:* King Edward's Sch., Birmingham; London Sch. of Economics. BSc Econ. 1950; PhD 1954; DSc 1964. Midn, then Sub-Lieut RNVR, 1945–47. Asst, then Lecturer, then Reader, in Social Anthropology, University of Edinburgh, 1950–65. Dir, SSRC Res. Unit on Ethnic Relations, 1970–78. Visiting Professor: MIT, 1962–63; Wayne State Univ., Detroit, 1971; Univ. of Delaware, 1976; ANU, 1981; Duke Univ., 1982. Editor, Sociology, 1966–69. President: Section N, 1969–70 and Section H, 1985–86, BAAS; Royal Anthropological Inst., 1987–89; Mem., Vetenskapssocieteten, Lund, Sweden, 1972; Member: Royal Commn on Criminal Procedure, 1978–80; Royal Commn on Bermuda, 1978; UK National Commn for UNESCO, 1963–66 and 1980–85; UN Cttee for the Elimination of Racial Discrimination, 1986–; SW Regl Hosp. Board, 1966–70. JP Bristol, 1966. FRSA 1981. *Publications:* The Coloured Quarter, 1955; West African City, 1957; White and Coloured, 1959; The Policeman in the Community, 1964; Roles, 1965; Race Relations, 1967; Racial Minorities, 1972; Police-Community Relations, 1973; (with J. Harwood) The Race Concept, 1975; The Idea of Race, 1977; Racial and Ethnic Competition, 1983; Promoting Racial Harmony, 1985; Investigating Robbery, 1985; Racial Theories, 1987; Racial Consciousness, 1988. *Address:* The Court House, Llanvair Discoed, Gwent NP6 6LX. *T:* Penhow (0633) 400208.

BANWELL, Derick Frank, CBE 1978; Member: BCAR (Housing) Ltd (Chairman, 1979–89); BCAR (Homes) Ltd (Chairman, 1979–86); *b* 19 July 1919; *s* of Frank Edward Banwell; *m* 1945, Rose Kathleen Worby; two *s* one *d*. *Educ:* Kent Coll., Canterbury. RA, 1939–46. Admitted as Solicitor, 1947; Asst Solicitor, Southend-on-Sea Co. Borough Coun., 1947–48; Sen. Asst Solicitor, Rochdale Co. Borough Coun., 1948–51; Chief Common Law Solicitor, City of Sheffield, 1951–56; Sen. Asst Solicitor, 1956–59, Asst Town Clerk, 1959–60, Southend-on-Sea Co. Borough Coun.; Dep. Town Clerk and Dep. Clerk of the Peace, Swansea Co. Borough Council, 1960–64; Gen. Manager, Runcorn Develt Corp., 1964–78. Sec., Church Bldgs Cttee, United Reformed Church, 1978–85. *Recreations:* history, music, model railways. *Address:* 57 Broad Street, Canterbury, Kent CT1 2LS.

BÁNYÁSZ, Dr Rezső; Order of Merit for Labour, 1955, 1984; Hungarian Ambassador to Canada, since 1988; *b* 9 Jan. 1931; *m* 1951, Irén Horváth; two *s*. *Educ:* Univ. of Budapest. Foreign Editor, "Magyar Ifjuság" (Hungarian Youth) daily, "Népszava" (People's Voice) daily, 1950–61; entered Min. of Foreign Affairs, 1961; First Sec., Press Attaché, Stockholm, 1962–68; Counsellor and Dep. Head of Press Dept, Budapest, 1968–70, Head of Press Dept, 1970–72; Sen. Counsellor and Dep. Perm. Rep. of Hungary to UN, NY, 1972–76; Vice-Chm., Hungarian Delegn to Belgrade Meeting of CSCE, 1977; Head, Press Dept, 1978–81; Ambassador to London, 1981–84; State Sec., and Pres., Inf. Office of Hungarian Govt, 1984–88. Commenda da Orden do Infante D. Henrique (Portugal), 1979. *Recreation:* gardening. *Address:* Hungarian Embassy, 7 Delaware Avenue, Ottawa, Ont K2P 0Z2, Canada.

BARBACK, Ronald Henry; Consultant, Confederation of British Industry, since 1981; *b* 31 Oct. 1919; *s* of late Harry Barback and Winifred Florence (*née* Norris); *m* 1950, Sylvia Chambers; one *s* one *d*. *Educ:* Woodside Sch., Glasgow; Univ. Coll., Nottingham (BScEcon); Queen's and Nuffield Colls, Oxford (MLitt). Asst Lectr in Econs, Univ. of Nottingham, 1946–48; Lectr in Econs, subseq. Sen. Lectr, Canberra University Coll., Australia, 1949–56; Univ. of Ibadan (formerly University Coll., Ibadan): Prof. of Econs and Social Studies, 1956–63; Dean, Faculty of Arts, 1958–59; Dean, Faculty of Econs and Social Studies, 1959–63; Dir, Nigerian (formerly W African) Inst. of Social and Econ. Res., 1956–63; Sen. Res. Fellow, Econ. Res. Inst., Dublin, 1963–64; Prof. of Econs, TCD, 1964–65; Univ. of Hull: Prof. of Econs, 1965–76; Dean, Faculty of Social Sciences and Law, 1966–69; Head, Dept of Econs and Commerce, 1971–74. Dep. Econ. Dir and Head, Econ. Res., CBI, 1977–81. Nigeria: Mem., Ibadan Univ. Hosp. Bd of Management, 1958–63; Mem., Jt Econ. Planning Cttee, Fedn of Nigeria, 1959–61; Sole Arbitrator, Trade Disputes in Ports and Railways, 1958; Chm., Fed. Govt Cttee to advise on fostering a share market, 1959. UK Official Delegate, FAO meeting on investment in fisheries, 1970; Mem., FAO mission to Sri Lanka, 1975. Consultant, Div. of Fisheries, Europ. Commn Directorate-Gen. of Agriculture, 1974. Commonwealth Scholarships Commn Adviser on Econs, 1971–76; Mem., Schools Council Social Sciences Cttee, 1971–80; Chm., Schs Council Econs and Business Studies Syllabus Steering Gp, 1975–77. Member: Hull and Dist Local Employment Cttee, 1966–73; N Humberside Dist Manpower Cttee, 1973–76; CNAA Business and Management Studies Bd, 1978–81, Economics Bd, 1982–; Ct, Brunel Univ., 1979–; Editorial Bd, Bull. of Economic Research (formerly Yorks Bull. of Social and Economic Research), 1965–76 (Jt Editor, 1966–67); Editorial Adv. Bd, Applied Economics, 1969–80. Editor, Humberside Statistical Bull., nos 1–3, 1974, 1975, 1977. Specialist adviser, House of Lords Select Cttee on the European Communities, 1980–. *Publications:* (contrib.) The Commonwealth in the World Today, ed J. Eppstein, 1956; (ed with Prof. Sir Douglas Copland) The Conflict of Expansion and Stability, 1957; (contrib.) The Commonwealth and Europe (EIU), 1960; The Pricing of Manufactures, 1964; (contrib.) Insurance Markets of the World, ed M. Grossmann 1964; (contrib.) Webster's New World Companion to English and American Literature, 1973; Forms of Co-operation in the British Fishing Industry, 1976; (with M. Breimer and A. F. Haug) Development of the East Coast Fisheries of Sri Lanka, 1976; contrib. New Internat. Encyc., FAO Fisheries Reports, and jls. *Recreations:* walking, music. *Address:* 14a Calverley Park Gardens, Tunbridge Wells, Kent TN1 2JN. *T:* Tunbridge Wells (0892) 33290. *Club:* Commonwealth Trust.

BARBARA, Agatha, Companion of Honour, National Order of Merit (Malta), 1990; social/welfare worker; President of the Republic of Malta, 1982–87; Chairperson, The Samaritans – Malta, since 1988; *b* Zabbar, 11 March 1923. *Educ:* Government Grammar School. School teacher, 1945; entered politics, 1946; first woman Member of Parliament, 1947; became first woman Minister, in Labour Govt, 1955, as Minister of Education; also Minister of Educn, 1971–74; Minister of Labour, Culture, and Welfare, 1974–81. Was Acting Prime Minister on various occasions, and elected President of the Republic, 16 Feb. 1982. Hon. President: Malta-USSR Cultural & Friendship Soc.; Malta-Czechoslovakia Cultural & Friendship Soc. Patron: Ad Vitam St Michael's Band Club, Zabbar; Malta-China Friendship and Cultural Soc. Hon. Academician, Accademia Universale A. Magno, Prato, Italy; Hon. PhD Univ. of Beijing, China, 1984. Stara Planina, 1st cl. with ribbon (Bulgaria), 1983; Order of National Flag 1st Class (Democratic People's Republic of Korea), 1985; Hishan-e-Pakistan (Islamic Republic of Pakistan), 1986. Keys and Freedom of: Lahore, Buenos Aires, Lima, San José, Bogotà and Montevideo, 1986; Aden, 1987. *Recreations:* philately, classical and modern music. *Address:* Kenn Taghna, Wied Il-Ghajn Street, Zabbar, Republic of Malta.

BARBARITO, Most Rev. Luigi, DD, JCD; Titular Archbishop of Fiorentino; Apostolic Pro-Nuncio to the Court of St James's, since 1986; *b* Atripalda, Avellino, Italy, 19 April 1922; *s* of Vincenzo Barbarito and Alfonsina Armerini. *Educ:* Pontifical Seminary, Benevento, Italy; Gregorian Univ., Rome (JCD); Papal Diplomatic Academy, Rome (Diploma). Priest, 1944; served Diocese of Avellino, 1944–52; entered Diplomatic Service of Holy See, 1953; Sec., Apostolic Delegn, Australia, 1953–59; Secretariat of State of Vatican (Council for Public Affairs of the Church), 1959–67; Counsellor, Apostolic Nunciature, Paris, 1967–69; Archbishop and Papal Nuncio to Haiti and Delegate to the Antilles, 1969–75; Pro-Nuncio to Senegal, Bourkina Fasso, Niger, Mali, Mauretania, Cape Verde Is and Guinea Bissau, 1975–78; Apostolic Pro-Nuncio to Australia, 1978–86. Mem., Mexican Acad. of Internat. Law. Grand Cross, National Order of Haiti, 1975; Grand Cross, Order of the Lion (Senegal), 1978; Knight Commander, Order of Merit (Italy), 1966, (Portugal), 1967. *Recreations:* music, walking, snooker. *Address:* Apostolic Nunciature, 54 Parkside, Wimbledon, SW19 5NF. *T:* 081–946 1410.

BARBER, family name of **Baron Barber.**

BARBER, Baron *cr* 1974 (Life Peer), of Wentbridge; **Anthony Perrinott Lysberg Barber,** PC 1963; TD; DL; Chairman, Standard Chartered Bank plc, 1974–87; *b* 4 July 1920; *s* of John Barber, CBE, Doncaster; *m* 1st, 1950, Jean Patricia (*d* 1983), *d* of Milton Asquith, Wentbridge, Yorks; two *d*; 2nd, 1989, Mrs Rosemary Youens, *d* of Rev. Canon Fearnly Youens. *Educ:* Retford Grammar Sch.; Oriel Coll., Oxford Univ. (PPE, MA) (Hon. Fellow 1971). Served War of 1939–45: commnd in Army (Dunkirk); seconded to RAF as pilot, 1940–45 (despatches; prisoner of war, 1942–45, took Law Degree with 1st Class Hons while POW, escaped from Poland, prisoner of the Russians). Barrister-at-law, Inner Temple, 1948 (Inner Temple Scholarship). MP (C): Doncaster, 1951–64; Altrincham and Sale, Feb. 1965–Sept. 1974; PPS to the Under-Sec. of State for Air, 1952–55; Asst Whip, 1955–57; a Lord Comr of the Treasury, 1957–58; PPS to the Prime Minister, 1958–59; Economic Sec. to the Treasury, 1959–62; Financial Sec. to the Treasury, 1962–63; Minister of Health and Mem. of the Cabinet, 1963–64; Chancellor of the Duchy of Lancaster, June-July 1970; Chancellor of the Exchequer, 1970–74. Chm., Conservative Party Organisation, 1967–70. Dir, BP, 1979–88. Mem., Falkland Islands Inquiry (Franks Cttee), 1982. British Mem., Eminent Persons Gp on S Africa, 1986. Chm. Council, Westminster Med. Sch., 1975–84. DL W Yorks, 1987. *Address:* House of Lords, SW1. *Club:* Carlton.

BARBER, Chris; *see* Barber, D. C.

BARBER, Sir Derek (Coates), Kt 1984; Environment Consultant to Humberts, Chartered Surveyors, since 1972; Chairman: Countryside Commission, 1981–91; Booker Countryside Advisory Board, since 1990; *s* of Thomas Smith-Barber and Elsie Coates; 1st marr. diss. 1981; *m* 2nd, 1983, Rosemary Jennifer Brougham, *o d* of late Lt-Comdr Randolph Brougham Pearson, RN, and of Hilary Diana Mackinlay Pearson (*née* Bennett). *Educ:* Royal Agricl Coll., Cirencester (MRAC; Gold Medal, Practical Agriculture). Served War: invalided, Armed Forces, 1942. Farmed in Glos Cotswolds; Mem., Cheltenham Rural District Council, 1948–52; Dist Adv. Officer, National Agricl Adv. Service, MAFF, 1946–57; County Agricl Advisor, Glos, 1957–72; MAFF Assessor: Pilkington Cttee on Agric. Educ., 1966; Agric. and Hort. Trng Bd, 1968. Chairman: BBC's Central Agricl Adv. Cttee, 1974–80 (*ex officio* Mem., BBC's Gen. Adv. Council, 1972–80); New National Forest Adv. Bd. Royal Soc. for Protection of Birds: Mem., 1970–75, Chm., 1976–81, Council; Chm., Educn Cttee, 1972–75; Vice-Pres., 1982; Pres., 1990–. President: RASE, 1991–92; Rare Breeds Survival Trust, 1991– (Mem. Council, 1987–); Glos Naturalists' Soc., 1981–; Vice-Pres., Ornithol Soc. of Mid-East, 1987–; Mem. Council, British Trust for Ornithology, 1987–90; Founder Mem., 1969, Farming and Wildlife Adv. Gp of landowning, farming and wildlife conservation bodies; Member: Ordnance Survey Adv. Bd, 1982–85; Bd, Responsible Use of Resources in Agriculture and on the Land Council, 1983–; Bd, Centre for Environmental and Econ. Develt, 1984–; Centre for Agricl Strategy, 1985–; Dep. Chm., Bd, Groundwork Foundn, 1985–91. Associate Mem., Guild of Agricl Journalists, 1981. Hon. FRAgS, 1986. Hon. DSc Bradford, 1986. First Recipient, Summers Trophy for services to agric. in practice or science, 1955; Bledisloe Gold Medal for distinguished service to UK agriculture, 1967; RSPB Gold Medal for services to bird protection, 1982; Massey-Ferguson Award for services to agric., 1989; RASE Gold Medal, for distinguished service to UK agric., 1991. Silver Jubilee Medal, 1977. Editor, Humberts Commentary, 1973–88; columnist, Power Farming, 1973–91; Spec. Correspondent, Waitaki NZR Times, 1982–88. *Publications:* (with Keith Dexter) Farming for Profits, 1961, 2nd edn 1967; (with J. G. S. and Frances Donaldson) Farming in Britain Today, 1969, 2nd edn 1972; (ed) Farming with Wildlife, 1971; A History of Humberts, 1980; contrib. farming and wildlife conservation jls. *Recreations:* birds, wildlife conservation, farming, hill walking. *Address:* Chough House, Gotherington, Glos GL52 4QU. *T:* Cheltenham (0242) 673908. *Club:* Farmers'.

BARBER, (Donald) Chris(topher), OBE 1991; band leader, Chris Barber's Jazz and Blues Band; *b* 17 April 1930; *s* of Henrietta Mary Evelyn Barber, MA Cantab and Donald Barber, CBE, BA Cantab; *m* Renate M. Hilbich; one *s* one *d*. *Educ:* King Alfred School; St Paul's School. Formed first amateur band, 1949; present band commenced on professional basis, 1954; plays trombone, trumpet, baritone horn, contra bass. Hon. Citizen, New Orleans. Numerous recordings, including over 100 LPs, with records in the hit parade of over 40 countries world wide. *Recreations:* motor racing, snooker. *Address:* c/o Cromwell Management, The Coach House, 9A The Broadway, St Ives, Huntingdon, Cambs PE17 4BX. *T:* Huntingdon (0480) 65695, *Fax:* Huntingdon (0480) 495382.

BARBER, Hon. Sir (Edward Hamilton) Esler, Kt 1976; Puisne Judge, Supreme Court of Victoria, Australia, 1965–77; *b* Hamilton, Vic., 26 July 1905; *s* of late Rev. John Andrew Barber and Maggie Rorke; *m* 1954, Constance, *d* of Captain C. W. Palmer; one *s* one *d*. *Educ:* Hamilton Coll., Victoria; Scots Coll., Sydney; Scotch Coll., Melbourne; Melbourne Univ. Barrister-at-law, 1929; QC (Vic.) 1955, Tas. 1956; Judge, County Court, Vic., 1957–65; Actg Judge, 1964–65. Chm., Royal Commn into Failure of King's Bridge, 1962–63; Dep. Chm. Parole Bd, Vic., Nov. 1969–77; Mem. Council of Legal Educn, 1968–77; Chm., Royal Commn into West Gate Bridge Disaster, 1970–71; Chm., Bd of Inquiry into causes and origins of bush and grass fires in Vic. during Jan.-Feb. 1977,

1977–. *Publications:* articles on Matrimonial Law, incl. Divorce—the Changing Law, 1968. *Address:* 1 St George's Court, Toorak, Vic 3142, Australia. *T:* 24–5104. *Club:* Australian (Melbourne).

BARBER, Frank; Partner, Morgan, Fentiman & Barber, since 1968; Deputy Chairman of Lloyd's, 1983, 1984; *b* 5 July 1923; *s* of Sidney Barber and Florence (*née* Seath); *m* 1945, Gertrude Kathleen Carson; one *s* one *d* (and one *s* decd). *Educ:* West Norwood Central School. Pilot, RAFVR, 1942–46; Underwriter, Lloyd's syndicate, Frank Barber & others, 1962–81; Member: Cttee of Lloyd's, 1977–80, 1982–85 and 1987. Council of Lloyd's, 1983–85 and 1987; Dep. Chm., Lloyd's Underwriters' Non-Marine Assoc., 1971, Chm., 1972; Dep. Chm., British Insurers' European Cttee, 1983. *Recreations:* music, walking, sailing. *Address:* Doiley Hill House, Hurstbourne Tarrant, Andover, Hants SP11 0ER. *T:* Hurstbourne Tarrant (026476) 595.

BARBER. Giles Gaudard; Librarian, Taylor Institution, University of Oxford, since 1970; Fellow, Linacre College, Oxford, since 1963 (Vice-Principal, 1988–90); *b* 15 Aug. 1930; *s* of Eric Arthur Barber and Madeleine Barber (*née* Gaudard); *m* 1st, 1958, Monique Fluchère (*d* 1969); one *d*; 2nd, 1970, Gemma Miani; two *s* one *d*. *Educ:* Dragon Sch., Oxford; Leighton Park Sch.; St John's Coll., Oxford (MA, BLitt). Asst, Bodleian Library, 1954–70; Univ. Lectr in Continental Bibliography, Oxford, 1969–. Mem. Council, Internat. Soc. for 18th Century Studies, 1979–83; Vice-Pres., Bibliographical Soc., 1983–; Chm., Voltaire Foundn, 1987–89. Vis. Lectr, Univ. of Paris IV (Sorbonne), 1980; Lectures: 1st Graham Pollard Meml, 1984; Moses Tyson Meml, Manchester Univ., 1985; Panizzi, British Library, 1988. Gordon Duff Prize in Bibliography, 1962. *Publications:* Fine Bindings 1500–1700, 1968 (ed jtly); A checklist of French printing manuals, 1969; Textile and embroidered bookbindings, 1971; (ed) Book making in Diderot's Encyclopédie, 1973; (ed) Contat, Anecdotes typographiques, 1980; (ed jtly) Buch und Buch-handel in Europa im achtzehnten Jahrhundert, 1981; Daphnis and Chloe, 1989; articles in learned jls. *Recreations:* book-collecting, gardening. *Address:* 2 Linton Road, Oxford OX2 6UG. *T:* Oxford (0865) 511500.

BARBER, Dr James Peden, JP; Master, Hatfield College, Durham, since 1980; Pro-Vice-Chancellor, since 1987 and Sub Warden, since 1990, Durham University; *b* 6 Nov. 1931; *s* of John and Carrie Barber; *m* 1955, Margaret June (*née* McCormac); three *s* one *d*. *Educ:* Liverpool Inst. High Sch.; Pembroke Coll., Cambridge (MA, PhD); The Queen's Coll., Oxford. Served RAF, 1950–52 (Pilot Officer). Colonial Service, Uganda: Dist Officer, subseq. Asst Sec. to Prime Minister and Clerk to the Cabinet, 1956–63; Lectr, Univ. of NSW, Australia, 1963–65; Lectr in Govt, Univ. of Exeter, 1965–69 (seconded to University Coll. of Rhodesia, 1965–67); Prof. of Political Science, Open Univ., 1969–80. Advr, Commons Select Cttee on Foreign Affairs, 1990–91. Mem. RIIA; Part-time Dir, Chatham House study, Southern Africa in Conflict, 1979–81. Mem., Amnesty International. President: Durham Univ. Soc. of Fellows, 1988; Durham Univ. Hockey Club, 1981–. JP Bedford, 1977–80. *Publications:* Rhodesia: the road to rebellion, 1967; Imperial Frontier, 1968; South Africa's Foreign Policy, 1973; European Community: vision and reality, 1974; The Nature of Foreign Policy, 1975; Who Makes British Foreign Policy?, 1977; The West and South Africa, 1982; The Uneasy Relationship: Britain and South Africa, 1983; South Africa: the search for status and security, 1990; The Prime Minister since 1945, 1991. *Recreations:* choral music, all kinds of sport, walking the dog. *Address:* Kingsgate House, Bow Lane, Durham DH1 3ER. *T:* Durham (091) 3848651. *Club:* Commonwealth Trust.

BARBER, Rear-Adm. John L.; *see* Lee-Barber.

BARBER, John Norman Romney; company director and business consultant; *s* of George Ernest and Gladys Eleanor Barber; *m* 1941, Babette Chalu; one *s*. *Educ:* Westcliff. Served with Army, 1939–46 (Capt.). Min. of Supply, 1946–55 (Princ.). Joined Ford Motor Co. Ltd, 1955, Finance Dir, 1962; Chm., Ford Motor Credit Co. Ltd, 1963; Dir, Henry Ford & Son Ltd, Cork, 1963; Dir Autolite Motor Products Ltd, 1963; Finance Dir, AEI Ltd, 1965; Chm., Telephone Cables Ltd, 1967; Dir of Finance and Planning, 1968–71, Dep. Man. Dir, 1971–73, Dep. Chm. and Man. Dir, 1973–75, British Leyland Motor Corp. Ltd; Chairman, 1973–75: British Leyland International Ltd; Leyland Innocenti, SpA; Leyland Motor Corp. of Australia Ltd; Director: Leyland España SA; Automóviles de Turismo Hispano Ingleses SA; NZ Motor Corp. Ltd; British Leyland Motors Inc.; Metalurgica de Santa Ana SA; Chairman: Pullmaflex International Ltd, 1976–79; Aberhurst Ltd, 1976–88; A. C. Edwards Engineering Ltd, 1976–81; Cox & Kings Financial Services Ltd, 1980–85; C & K Executive Search Ltd, 1980–85; C & K Consulting Group Ltd, 1982–88; Director: Acrow plc, 1977–84; Good Relations Group plc, 1979–86; Amalgamated Metal Corp. Ltd, 1980–81; Spear & Jackson International plc, 1980–85; Economists Advisory Group Ltd, 1981–; UK Investments Ltd, 1985–; The Communications Group plc, 1990–; Deputy Chairman: Cox & Kings Ltd, 1980–81; John E. Wiltshier Group plc, 1980–88 (Dir, 1979–88). Mem., Royal Commn on Medical Educn, 1965–68; Chm., Adv. Cttee to BoT on Investment Grants, 1967–68; Mem., Adv. Council for Energy Conservation, 1974–75. Vice Pres., SMMT, 1974–76. CBIM; Mem. Council BIM, 1967–71. *Publications:* papers on management subjects in various jls. *Recreations:* motor sport, forestry, photography. *Address:* 38 Spring Street, W2 1JA. *Club:* British Automobile Racing.

BARBER, Nicholas Charles Faithorn; Chief Executive, Ocean Group (formerly Ocean Transport & Trading) plc, since 1987 (Director since 1980; Group Managing Director, 1986–87); *b* 7 Sept. 1940; *s* of Bertram Harold and Nancy Lorraine Barber; *m* 1966, Sheena Macrae Graham; two *s* one *d*. *Educ:* Ludgrove Sch.; Shrewsbury Sch.; Wadham Coll., Oxford (MA); Columbia Univ., New York, 1969–71 (MBA). Lectr, Marlboro Coll., Vermont, USA, 1963–64; joined Ocean Transport and Trading, 1964; Divl Dir, NEB, 1977–79. Director: Costain Gp, 1990–; Royal Insurance Hldgs, 1990–. Mem., NW Industrial Develt Bd, 1982–85; Trustee, Nat. Museums and Galls on Merseyside, 1986–; Mem., Adv. Cttee, Tate Gall., Liverpool, 1988–. Governor, Shrewsbury Sch., 1983–; Mem. Council: Liverpool Univ., 1985–88; Centre for Business Strategy, London Business School, 1988–; Vice-Pres., Liverpool Sch. of Tropical Medicine, 1988–; Dir, Liverpool Playhouse, 1982–87. *Recreations:* hill-walking, cricket, destructive gardening. *Address:* 47 Russell Square, WC1B 4JP. *Clubs:* United Oxford & Cambridge University, MCC.

BARBER, Rt. Rev. Paul Everard; *see* Brixworth, Bishop Suffragan of.

BARBER, Col Sir William (Francis), 2nd Bt *cr* 1960; TD; JP; CEng, MIMinE; *b* 20 Nov. 1905; *yr* and *o* surv. *s* of Sir (Thomas) Philip Barber, 1st Bt, DSO, TD, JP, DL, and of Beatrice Mary (*d* 1962), *d* of Lieut-Col W. Ingersoll Merritt; *S* father, 1961; *m* 1st, 1936, Diana Constance (marr. diss. 1978; she *d* 1984), *d* of late Lieut-Col Thomas Owen Lloyd, CMG, Minard Castle, Argyll; one *s* one *d*; 2nd, 1978, Jean Marie, *widow* of Dr H. C. Nott, Adelaide, S Australia. *Educ:* Eton Coll. South Nottinghamshire Hussars Yeomanry (Commnd, 1924). Royal Horse Artillery; served in Palestine, Egypt, North Africa, NW Europe; Lieut-Col 1947. Hon. Col, South Nottinghamshire Hussars Yeomanry, 1961–66. JP Notts, 1952; High Sheriff, Notts, 1964. *Heir:* *s* (Thomas) David Barber [*b* 18 Nov. 1937; *m* 1st, 1972, Amanda Mary (*née* Rabone) (marr. diss. 1976), *widow* of Maj. Michael Healing; one *s*; 2nd, 1978, Jeannine Mary Boyle, *d* of Captain T. J. Gurney; one *s* one *d*]. *Address:* Lamb Close, Eastwood, Notts NG16 3QX. *T:* Langley Mill (0773) 712011.

BARBER, Prof. William Joseph, Hon. OBE 1981; Professor of Economics, Wesleyan University, Middletown, Conn, USA, since 1965; *b* 13 Jan. 1925; *s* of Ward Barber; *m* 1955, Sheila Mary Marr; three *s*. *Educ:* Harvard Univ. (AB); Balliol Coll., Oxford. BA, 1st Cl. Hons, 1951, MA 1955; DPhil (Nuffield Coll.) 1958. Served War, US Army, 1943–46. Lectr in Econs, Balliol Coll., Oxford, 1956; Wesleyan University: Dept of Economics, 1957–; Asst Prof., 1957–61; Associate Prof., 1961–65; Prof., 1965–; Andrews Prof., 1972–; Acting Pres., Aug.–Oct. 1988. Research Associate: Oxford Univ. Inst. of Economics and Statistics, 1962–63; Twentieth Century Fund, South Asian Study, 1961–62. Amer. Sec., Rhodes Scholarship Trust, 1970–80. Pres., Hist. of Econs Soc., 1989–90. *Publications:* The Economy of British Central Africa, 1961; A History of Economic Thought, 1967; contributor to Asian Drama: an inquiry into the poverty of nations (with Gunnar Myrdal and others), 1968; British Economic Thought and India 1600–1858, 1975; (jtly) Exhortation and Controls: the search for a wage-price policy, 1975; Energy Policy in Perspective, 1981; From New Era to New Deal: Herbert Hoover, the economists, and American economic policy 1921–1933, 1985; (ed, and jt author) Breaking the Academic Mould: economists and American higher learning in the nineteenth century, 1988; (ed) Perspectives on the History of Economic Thought, vols V and VI, 1991; contribs to professional jls. *Address:* 306 Pine Street, Middletown, Conn 06457, USA. *T:* 203–346–2612.

BARBIERI, Margaret Elizabeth, (Mrs M. E. Barbieri-Webb); Senior Principal, Sadler's Wells Royal Ballet, 1974–89; freelance ballet teacher and coach, Royal Ballet School and London Studio Centre; *b* 2 March 1947; *d* of Ettore Barbieri and Lea Barbieri; *m* 1983, Iain Webb, soloist SWRB; one *s*. *Educ:* Convent High Sch., Durban, S Africa. Trained with Iris Manning and Brownie Sutton, S Africa; Royal Ballet Sen. Sch., 1963; joined Royal Ballet, 1965; Principal, 1970. Gypsy Girl, Two Pigeons, 1966; 1st Giselle, Covent Garden, 1968; 1st Sleeping Beauty, Leeds, 1969; 1st Swan Lake, Frankfurt, 1977, Covent Garden, 1983; 1st Romeo and Juliet, Covent Garden, 1979; 1st Sleeping Beauty, Covent Garden, 1985. Other roles with Royal Ballet: La Fille mal Gardée, Two Pigeons, The Dream, Façade, Wedding Bouquet, Rendezvous (Ashton); Lady and the Fool, Card Game, Pineapple Poll (Cranko); The Invitation, Solitaire, (Summer) The Four Seasons (MacMillan); Checkmate, The Rake's Progress (de Valois); Grosse Fugue, Tilt (van Manen); Lilac Garden (Tudor); Fête Etrange (Howard); Grand Tour (Layton); Summer Garden (Hynd); Game Piano (Thorpe), 1978; Cinderella (Killar), 1978; Cinderella (Rodrigues), 1979; Papillon, The Taming of the Shrew, 1980; Coppélia, Les Sylphides, Raymonda Act III, Spectre de la Rose; La Vivandière, 1982; Petrushka, 1984. Roles created: Knight Errant (Tudor), 1968; From Waking Sleep (Drew), 1970; Ante-Room (Cauley), 1971; Oscar Wilde (Layton), 1972; Sacred Circles and The Sword (Drew), 1973; The Entertainers (Killar), 1974; Charlotte Brontë (Hynd), 1974; Summertide (Wright), 1977; Metamorphosis (Bintley), 1984; Flowers of the Forest (Bintley), 1985; The Wand of Youth (Corder), 1985. Guest appearances, Birmingham Royal Ballet, 1990, 1991. Recreated: Pavlova's Dragonfly Solo, 1977; The Dying Swan, produced by Dame Alicia Markova after Fokine, 1985. Travelled with Royal Ballet to Australia, Canada, China, Egypt, Far East, France, Germany, Greece, Holland, Israel, Italy, Japan, New Zealand, Portugal, Spain, Switzerland, Yugoslavia, India and North and South America; guest appearances, USA, Germany, S Africa, France, Norway, Czechoslovakia. TV Appearances in: Spectre de la Rose; Grosse Fugue; Giselle; Coppelia; Checkmate; Markova master classes. *Recreations:* music (classical), theatre, gardening. *Address:* Chiswick.

BARBOUR, Very Rev. Prof. Robert Alexander Stewart, KCVO 1991; MC 1945; Professor of New Testament Exegesis, University of Aberdeen, 1971–82; Master of Christ's College, Aberdeen, 1977–82; an Extra Chaplain to the Queen in Scotland since 1991 (Chaplain-in-Ordinary to the Queen, 1976–91); Dean of the Chapel Royal in Scotland, 1981–91; Prelate of the Priory of Scotland of the Order of St John, since 1977; *b* 11 May 1921; *s* of George Freeland Barbour and Helen Victoria (*née* Hepburne-Scott); *m* 1950, Margaret Isobel Pigot; three *s* one *d*. *Educ:* Rugby Sch.; Balliol Coll., Oxford (MA 1946); Univ. of St Andrews (BD 1952); Yale Univ. (STM 1953). Sec., Edinburgh Christian Council for Overseas Students, 1953–55; Lectr and Sen. Lectr in NT Lang., Lit. and Theol., Univ. of Edinburgh, 1955–71. Hensley Henson Lectr, Univ. of Oxford, 1983–84. Moderator, Gen. Assembly of Church of Scotland, 1979–80. Chm., Scottish Churches' Council, 1982–86. Hon. Sec., Studiorum Novi Testamenti Societas, 1970–77. Chm. Governors, Rannoch Sch., 1973–79. Hon. DD St Andrews, 1979. *Publications:* The Scottish Horse 1939–45, 1950; Traditio-Historical Criticism of the Gospels, 1972; What is the Church for?, 1973; articles in various jls. *Recreations:* music, walking, forestry. *Address:* Fincastle, Pitlochry, Perthshire PH16 5RJ. *T:* Pitlochry (0796) 3209. *Club:* New (Edinburgh).

BARBOUR, Walworth; US Ambassador to Israel, 1961–73; *b* 4 June 1908; *s* of Samuel Lewis Barbour and Clara Hammond; unmarried. *Educ:* Harvard Coll., USA. Vice Consul, Naples, 1932; Athens, 1933; Baghdad, 1936; Sofia, 1939; Dip. Sec., Cairo, 1941; Athens, 1944; Dept of State, Washington, 1945–49; Minister, Moscow, 1949–51; Dept of State, Washington, 1951–55; Deputy Asst Sec. of State for European Affairs, 1954–55; American Minister, London, 1955–61. Hon. Fellow, Weizmann Inst. of Sci., 1970. Hon. PhD: Tel Aviv, 1971; Hebrew Univ. of Jerusalem, 1972; Hon. LLD Dropsie, Pa, 1973. *Recreation:* golf. *Clubs:* Swinley Forest (Surrey); Chevy Chase (Md, USA).

BARBOZA, Mario G.; *see* Gibson-Barboza.

BARCLAY, Christopher Francis Robert, CMG 1967; Secretary, Government Hospitality Fund, 1976–80; *b* 8 June 1919; *s* of late Captain Robert Barclay, RA (retired) and late Annie Douglas Dowdeswell Barclay (*née* Davidson); *m* 1st, 1950, Clare Justice Troutbeck (marr. diss., 1962); two *s* one *d*; 2nd, 1962, Diana Elizabeth Goodman; one *s* one *d*. *Educ:* Eton Coll.; Magdalen Coll., Oxford (MA). 2nd Lieut The Rifle Bde, 1940; Capt. 1942; Major 1943; served in Middle East; Political Officer, Northern Iraq, 1945; Brit. Embassy, Baghdad, 1946. Foreign Office, 1946; Second Sec., British Embassy, Cairo, 1947; First Sec., Foreign Office, 1950; Brit. Embassy, Bonn, 1953; FO, 1956; Regional Information Officer, Beirut, 1960; FO, 1961; Counsellor and Head of Information Research Dept, 1962–66; Head of Personnel Dept (Training and General), FCO, 1967–69; Asst Sec., CSD, 1969–73, DoE, 1973–76. Chm., Jt Nat. Horse Educn and Trng Council, 1988–90. Mem. Council, City Univ., 1976–84. Master, Saddlers' Co., 1983–84. FRSA 1984. *Recreations:* fishing, gardening. *Address:* Croft Edge, Painswick, Glos GL6 6XH. *T:* Painswick (0452) 812332. *Club:* Army and Navy.

BARCLAY, Sir Colville Herbert Sanford, 14th Bt, *cr* 1668; Painter; *b* 7 May 1913; *s* of late Rt Hon. Sir Colville Adrian de Rune Barclay, 3rd *s* of 11th Bt, and Sarita Enriqueta, *d* of late Herbert Ward; *S* uncle, 1930; *m* 1949, Rosamond Grant Renton Elliott; three *s*. *Educ:* Eton, Trinity Coll., Oxford. Third Sec., Diplomatic Service, 1937–41; enlisted in Navy, Nov. 1941; Sub-Lieut RNVR 1942; Lieut 1943; Lieut Commander 1945; demobilised, 1946. Exhibitor: Royal Academy, RBA, London Group, Bradford City and

Brighton Art Galleries. Chm. Royal London Homoeopathic Hospital, 1970–74 (Vice-Chm., 1961–65; Chm., League of Friends, 1974–84). Plant-hunting expedns to Crete, Turkey, Cyprus, Réunion, Mauritius and Nepal, 1966–81. *Publications:* Crete: checklist of the vascular plants, 1986; articles in botanical jls. *Recreations:* gardening, plant-hunting. *Heir: s* Robert Colraine Barclay [*b* 12 Feb. 1950; *m* 1980, Lucilia Saboia, *y d* of Carlos Saboia de Albuquerque, Rio de Janeiro; one *s* one *d*]. *Address:* Pitshill, Petworth, West Sussex GU28 9AZ. *T:* Lodsworth (07985) 341. *Club:* Naval.

BARCLAY, Hugh Maben; Clerk of Public Bills, House of Commons, since 1988; *b* 20 Feb. 1927; *s* of late William Barclay, FRCS, and late Mary Barclay; *m* 1956, Hilda Johnston; one *s* one *d*. *Educ:* Fettes Coll., Edinburgh (exhbnr); Gonville and Caius Coll., Cambridge (schol.). Served Royal Artillery, 1948. House of Commons: Asst Clerk, 1950; Sen. Clerk, 1955; Dep. Principal Clerk, 1967; Principal Clerk, 1976; Clerk of Standing Cttees, 1976; Clerk of Private Bills, 1982. *Address:* 37 Stockwell Green, SW9 9HZ. *T:* 071–274 7375.

BARCLAY, James Christopher; Chairman, Cater Allen Holdings PLC, since 1985 (Deputy Chairman, 1981–85); *b* 7 July 1945; *s* of late Theodore David Barclay and of Anne Barclay; *m* 1974, Rolleen Anne, *d* of late Lt-Col Arthur Forbes and of Joan Forbes; one *s* one *d*. *Educ:* Harrow. Served 15th/19th The King's Royal Hussars, 1964–67. Chm., Cater Ryder & Co. Ltd, 1981. Chm., London Discount Market Assoc., 1988–90. *Recreations:* fresh air pursuits. *Address:* Rivers Hall, Waldringfield, Woodbridge, Suffolk IP12 4QX; (office) 20 Birchin Lane, EC3V 9DJ. *Club:* Pratt's.

BARCLAY, Peter Maurice, CBE 1984; Partner, Beachcrofts, Solicitors, 1974–88, retired; *b* 6 March 1926; *s* of George Ronald Barclay and Josephine (*née* Lambert); *m* 1953, Elizabeth Mary Wright; one *s* two *d*. *Educ:* Bryanston Sch.; Magdalene Coll., Cambridge (MA). Served RNVR, 1944–46. Admitted Solicitor, 1952; Senior Partner, Beachcroft & Co., 1964–74. Chairman: Cttee on Roles and Tasks of Social Workers, 1981–82; Social Security Adv. Cttee, 1984–. Pres. National Inst. for Social Work, 1988 (Chm., 1973–85); Chairman: St Pancras Housing Assoc., 1983–; Horticultural Therapy, 1989–. Trustee, Joseph Rowntree Memorial Trust, 1972–; Governor, Bryanston Sch., 1972–88; Council Mem., PSI, 1989–. *Recreations:* gardening, painting, golf. *Address:* 4/43 Ladbroke Grove, W11 3AR. *T:* 071–727 4613.

BARCLAY, Sir Roderick (Edward), GCVO 1966 (KCVO 1957; CVO 1953); KCMG 1955 (CMG 1948); HM Diplomatic Service, retired; *b* 22 Feb. 1909; *s* of late J. Gurney Barclay and Gillian (*née* Birkbeck); *m* 1934, Jean Cecil, *d* of late Sir Hugh Gladstone; one *s* three *d*. *Educ:* Harrow; Trinity Coll., Cambridge. Entered Diplomatic Service, 1932. Served at HM Embassies at Brussels, Paris, Washington and in FO; Counsellor in FO 1946; Principal Private Sec. to Sec. of State for Foreign Affairs, 1949–51; Asst Under-Sec. of State, 1951; Dep. Under-Sec. of State, 1953–56; HM Ambassador to Denmark, 1956–60; Adviser on European Trade Questions, Foreign Office, and Dep. Under-Sec. of State for Foreign Affairs, 1960–63; Ambassador to Belgium, 1963–69. Director: Slough Estates, 1969–84; Barclays Bank SA, 1969–79 (Chm., 1970–74); Barclays Bank Internat., 1971–77; Banque de Bruxelles, 1971–77. Knight Grand Cross of the Dannebrog (Denmark) and of the Couronne (Belgium). *Publication:* Ernest Bevin and the Foreign Office 1932–69, 1975; contrib. Country Life, etc. *Recreations:* shooting, fishing. *Address:* Great White End, Latimer, Chesham, Bucks HP5 1UJ. *T:* Little Chalfont (0494) 762050. *Club:* Brooks's.

See also A. E. Palmer.

BARCLAY, Yvonne Fay, (Mrs William Barclay); *see* Minton, Y. F.

BARCROFT, Prof. Henry, FRS 1953; MA; MD; FRCP; Professor of Physiology, St Thomas's Hospital Medical School, London, 1948–71, Emeritus since 1971; a Wellcome Trustee, 1966–75; *b* 18 Oct. 1904; *s* of late Sir Joseph Barcroft, CBE, FRS; *m* 1933, Bridget Mary (*d* 1990), *d* of late A. S. Ramsey; three *s* one *d*. *Educ:* Marlborough Coll.; King's Coll. Cambridge; Exhibitioner, 1923. Natural Science Tripos Class I, Parts I and II; Harold Fry and George Henry Lewes studentships at Cambridge, 1927–29; Gedge Prize, 1930; Harmsworth Scholar, St Mary's Hospital, London, 1929–32; Lectr in Physiology, University Coll., London, 1932–35; Dunville Prof. of Physiology, Queen's Univ., Belfast, 1935–48. Arris and Gale Lectr, RCS, 1945; Bertram Louis Abrahams Lectr, RCP, 1960; Robert Campbell Meml Orator, Ulster Med. Soc., 1975; Bayliss-Starling Meml Lectr, Physiological Soc., 1976; Vis. Prof., Univ. of Adelaide, 1963. Chairman: Editorial Bd, Monographs of Physiological Soc., 1957–65; Research Defence Soc., 1968–71, Sec. 1972–77, Vice-Pres., 1978–. Hon. Member: Academic Adv. Cttee, Loughborough Coll. of Technology, 1964–66; Société Française d'Angiologie; Japanese Coll. of Angiology; Czechoslovak Med. Soc. J. E. Purkinje. Hon. DSc Univ. Western Australia, 1963; Hon. MD Leopold-Franzens Univ., Innsbruck, 1969; Hon. DSc QUB, 1975. Pro meritis médaille in silver, Karl Franzens Univ., Graz. *Publications:* (with H. J. C. Swan) Sympathetic Control of Human Blood Vessels, 1953; papers in the Journal of Physiology. *Recreations:* sailing, golf. *Address:* 73 Erskine Hill, NW11 6EY. *T:* 081–458 1066. *Club:* Athenæum.

BARD, Dr Basil Joseph Asher, CBE 1968; Innovation consultant, retired; Director, Scanning Technology Ltd, since 1984; *b* London, 20 Aug. 1914; *s* of late Abram Isaac Bard and Anita Bard; *m* 1942, Ena Dora Birk; three *s*. *Educ:* Owen's Sch.; RCS (Imperial Coll.). BSc(Chem.), ARCS 1934, DIC (Chem. Engrg and Fuel Technology) 1935, PhD (Chem. Constitution of Coal) 1936, London; Bar Finals (1st cl. hons) and Studentship, Coun. of Legal Educn, 1937; called to Bar, Gray's Inn (Birkenhead and William Shaw Schol.), 1938. Practised at Bar, 1938–39; Legal Dept, Coal Commn, 1939–41; Explosives Prodn Dept, Min. of Supply, 1941–43; Materials Dept, Min. of Aircraft Production, 1943–45; Depts of Industrial Res., Educn, Design, etc, FBI, 1945–49; NRDC, 1950–74; in turn, Commercial Man., Techn. Dir and Exec. Dir, Dept of Applied Science; Mem., NRDC, 1956–73, Man. Dir, 1971–73; Exec. Dir, First National Finance Corp., 1974–76; Chm., Birmingham Mint Ltd, 1977–81. Director: Allied Insulators Ltd, 1975–77; Interflex Group, 1984–89; Chairman: NPM Gp, 1977–83; Xtec Ltd, 1983–86 (Dir, 1981–86); ProMicro Ltd, 1985–91. Founder and Chm., 1968–70, subsequently Vice-Pres., UK Licensing Execs Soc. (awarded Gold Medal 1973; Hon. Life Member, 1989). Consultant to UNIDO, 1972–74; Hon. Mem., Foundn for Sci. and Technol., 1990– (Hon. Treasurer, 1984–90); has served on various Govt Cttees. Pres., Jewish Meml Council, 1982–89; Vice-Pres., Anglo-Jewish Assoc., 1983– (Pres., 1977–83). *Publications:* (ed) Industry and Research, 1947; (ed) The Patent System, 1975; various articles on science, technology, patents, industry, commerce and their inter-relationships. *Recreations:* music, bridge, chess, social life. *Address:* 23 Mourne House, Maresfield Gardens, Hampstead, NW3 5SL. *T:* 071–435 5340; (office) c/o 1/3 Canfield Place, NW6 3BT. *T:* 071–328 8183. *Club:* Athenæum.

BARDEN, Prof. Laing, CBE 1990; PhD, DSc; Director, Newcastle upon Tyne Polytechnic, since 1978; *b* 29 Aug. 1931; *s* of Alfred Eversfield Barden and Edna (*née* Laing); *m* 1956, Nancy Carr; two *s* one *d*. *Educ:* Washington Grammar Sch.; Durham Univ. (BSc, MSc). R. T. James & Partners, 1954–59. Liverpool Univ., 1959–62 (PhD); Manchester Univ., 1962–69 (DSc); Strathclyde Univ., 1969–74; Newcastle Polytechnic, 1974–. Director: Microelectronics Applications Res. Inst. Ltd, 1980–90; Tyne and Wear Enterprise Trust Ltd, 1982–; Newcastle Technology Centre Ltd, 1985–90; Newcastle Initiative, 1988–. Mem., Council for Industry and Higher Educn, 1987–. *Publications:* contribs to Geotechnique, Proc. ICE, Jl Amer. Soc. CE, Qly Jl Eng. Geol. *Recreations:* cricket, soccer, snooker. *Address:* 7 Westfarm Road, Cleadon, Tyne and Wear SR6 7UG. *T:* Wearside (091) 5362317. *Clubs:* National Liberal; Mid Boldon (Boldon).

BARDER, Brian Leon; HM Diplomatic Service; High Commissioner to Australia, since 1991; *b* 20 June 1934; *s* of Harry and Vivien Barder; *m* 1958, Jane Maureen Cornwell; one *s* two *d*. *Educ:* Sherborne; St Catharine's Coll., Cambridge (BA). 2nd Lieut, 7 Royal Tank Regt, 1952–54. Colonial Office, 1957; Private Sec. to Permanent Under-Sec., 1960–61; HM Diplomatic Service, 1965; First Secretary, UK Mission to UN, 1964–68; FCO, 1968–70; First Sec. and Press Attaché, Moscow, 1971–73; Counsellor and Head of Chancery, British High Commn, Canberra, 1973–77; Canadian Nat. Defence Coll., Kingston, Ontario, 1977–78; Head of Central and Southern, later Southern African Dept, FCO, 1978–82; Ambassador to Ethiopia, 1982–86; Ambassador to Poland, 1986–88; High Comr to Nigeria, and concurrently Ambassador to Benin, 1988–91. CON 1989. *Address:* c/o Foreign and Commonwealth Office, SW1A 2AH. *Clubs:* United Oxford & Cambridge University, Commonwealth Trust.

See also E. L. Wen.

BARDSLEY, Andrew Tromlow; JP; Principal, Westgate Development Consultancy; Director, Holbank Securities Ltd; *b* 7 Dec. 1927; *o s* of Andrew and Gladys Ada Bardsley; *m* 1954, June Patricia (*née* Ford); one *s* one *d*. *Educ:* Ashton-under-Lyne Grammar Sch.; Manchester Coll. of Art. CEng, FICE. Royal Navy, 1947–49. Entered Local Govt (Municipal Engrg), 1950; various appts leading to Borough Engr and Surveyor, Worksop MB, 1962–69; Director of Technical Services: Corby New Town, 1969–71; Luton CBC, 1971–73; Gen. Manager and Chief Exec., Harlow Develt Corp., 1973–80. Gen. Comr of Taxes in England and Wales, 1987–. JP Essex, 1975 (Dep. Chm., Harlow Bench, 1987–). *Publications:* papers on engrg and associated matters incl. housing and town centre re-development. *Recreations:* golf, music, gardening, most spectator sports. *Address:* 19 Copper Court, Sawbridgeworth, Herts CM21 9ER. *T:* Bishops Stortford (0279) 723210; Poole (0202) 537954. *Club:* Ferndown Golf.

BARENBOIM, Daniel; pianist and conductor; Musical Director, Chicago Symphony Orchestra, since 1991; *b* Buenos Aires, 15 Nov. 1942; *s* of Enrique Barenboim and Aida Barenboim (*née* Schuster); *m* 1st, 1967, Jacqueline du Pré (*d* 1987); 2nd, 1988, Elena Bashkirova; two *s*. *Educ:* Santa Cecilia Acad., Rome; studied with his father; coached by Edwin Fischer, Nadia Boulanger, and Igor Markevitch. Debut as pianist with: Israel Philharmonic Orchestra, 1953; Royal Philharmonic Orchestra, 1956; Berlin Philharmonic Orchestra, 1963; NY Philharmonic Orchestra, 1964; Musical Dir, Orchestre de Paris, 1975–88; tours include: Australia, North and South America, Far East; regular appearances at Bayreuth, Edinburgh, Lucerne, Prague and Salzburg Festivals. Many recordings as conductor and pianist. Beethoven Medal, 1958; Paderewski Medal, 1963; subsequently other awards. Legion of Honour (France), 1987. *Address:* c/o Daniel Barenboim Secretariat, 5 place de la Fusterie, 1204 Génève, Switzerland.

BARFETT, Ven. Thomas; Archdeacon of Hereford and Canon Residentiary of Hereford Cathedral, 1977–82, now Emeritus; Prebendary of Colwall and Treasurer, 1977–82; Chaplain to the Queen, 1975–86; *b* 2 Oct. 1916; *s* of Rev. Thomas Clarence Fairchild Barfett and Dr Mary Deborah Barfett, LRCP, LRCS, MA; *m* 1945, Edna, *d* of Robert Toy; one *s* one *d*. *Educ:* St John's Sch., Leatherhead; Keble Coll., Oxford (BA 1938; MA 1942); Wells Theol Coll. Ordained deacon, Portsmouth, 1939; priest, 1940; Curate: Christ Church, Gosport, 1939–44; St Francis of Assisi, Gladstone Park, London, 1944–47; St Andrew Undershaft with St Mary Axe, City of London, 1947–49; Asst Sec., London Diocesan Council for Youth, 1944–49; Vicar, St Paul, Penzance, dio. of Truro, 1949–55; Rector of Falmouth, 1955–77; Officiating Chaplain, 1102 Marine Craft Unit, RAF, 1957–75; Sec., Truro Diocesan Conf., 1952–67; Proctor in Convocation, dio. of Truro, 1958–76; Hon. Canon, Truro, 1964–77. Chm., House of Clergy, and Vice-Pres., Truro Diocesan Synod, 1970–76; Mem., Gen. Synod, 1977–82. Chaplain to lay Sheriff, City of London, 1976–77. Church Comr, 1975–82; Mem. C of E Central Bd of Finance, 1969–77, Pensions Board, 1973–86. Chm., Cornwall Family History Soc., 1985–88. Freeman, City of London, 1973; Freeman and Liveryman, Scriveners Co., 1976. Sub ChStJ, 1971 (Asst ChStJ, 1963). Silver Jubilee Medal, 1977. *Publication:* Trebarfoote: a Cornish family, 1975, 2nd edn 1989. *Recreations:* heraldry, genealogy. *Address:* Treberveth, 57 Falmouth Road, Truro, Cornwall TR1 2HL. *T:* Truro (0872) 73726. *Club:* United Oxford & Cambridge University.

BARFORD, Sir Leonard, Kt 1967; Deputy Chairman, Horserace Totalisator Board, 1974–77 (Member, 1973–77); Chief Inspector of Taxes, Board of Inland Revenue, 1964–73; Commissioner of Inland Revenue, 1970–73; *b* 1 Aug. 1908; *s* of William and Ada Barford, Finsbury Park; *m* 1939, Betty Edna Crichton, Plymouth; two *s*. *Educ:* Dame Alice Owen's Sch.; St Catharine's Coll., Cambridge Univ. (Exhibitioner in History). Asst Inspector of Taxes, 1930; Administrative Staff Coll., Henley, 1948; President, Assoc. of HM Inspectors of Taxes, 1951–53; Principal Inspector of Taxes, 1953; Senior Principal Inspector of Taxes, 1957; Deputy Chief Inspector, 1960. *Publication:* (jointly) Essay on Management in Tax Offices, 1950. *Recreations:* badminton, tennis, chess, bridge. *Address:* Harley House, 79 Sutton Road, Seaford, East Sussex BN25 4QH. *T:* Seaford (0323) 893364. *Club:* Civil Service.

BARING, family name of **Baron Ashburton,** of **Earl of Cromer,** of **Baron Howick of Glendale,** of **Baron Northbrook,** and of **Baron Revelstoke.**

BARING, Sir John (Francis), 3rd Bt *cr* 1911, of Nubia House, Isle of Wight; *b* 21 May 1947; *s* of Raymond Alexander Baring (*d* 1967) (2nd *s* of 1st Bt) and of Margaret Fleetwood Baring (who *m* 1991, Earl of Malmesbury, *qv*), *d* of late Col R. W. P. C. Campbell-Preston; *S* uncle, 1990; *m* 1971, Elizabeth Anne, *yr d* of Robert D. H. Pillitz; two *s* one *d*. *Educ:* Eton Coll.; Royal Agricl Coll.; London Sch. of Economics. Hackman Baring & Co.; Citibank NA, 1971–72; Chemical Bank, 1972–84; Kidder, Peabody & Co. Inc., 1984–89; GPA Group Ltd, 1989. *Recreation:* gardening. *Heir: s* Julian Alexander David Baring, *b* 10 Feb. 1975. *Address:* June Road, North Salem, NY 10560, USA. *T:* (914) 669 5750; 17 East 96th Street, New York, NY 10128, USA. *T:* (212) 722 5920. *Club:* Union (New York).

BARING, Nicholas Hugo; Chairman, Commercial Union plc, since 1990 (Director, since 1968; Deputy Chairman, 1983–90); *b* 2 Jan. 1934; *er s* of late Francis Anthony Baring (killed in action, 1940) and of Lady Rose Baring, *qv*; *m* 1972, Elizabeth Diana, *d* of late Brig. Charles Crawfurd; three *s*. *Educ:* Eton (King's Schol.); Magdalene Coll., Cambridge (exhibnr, BA). Nat. service, 2nd Lieut Coldstream Guards, 1952–54. ADC to Governor of Kenya, 1957–58; joined Baring Brothers, 1958; Man. Dir, Baring Brothers & Co., 1963–86; Dir, Barings plc, 1985– (Dep. Chm., 1986–89). Mem., City Capital Markets Cttee, 1983–89 (Chm., 1983–87). Pres., Liverpool Sch. of Tropical Medicine, 1989–. Chm., Bd of Trustees, Nat. Gall., 1992– (Trustee, 1989–). National Trust: Mem. Exec. Cttee, 1965–69 and 1979–; Mem. Council, 1978–; Chm., Finance Cttee, 1980–91.

Member: Council, Baring Foundn, 1969–; Council of Management, Architectl Heritage Fund, 1987–. *Address:* St Helen's, 1 Undershaft, EC3P 3DQ. *Club:* Brooks's.
See also P. Baring.

BARING, Peter; Chairman, Barings plc, since 1989; *b* 28 Oct. 1935; *yr s* of Francis Anthony Baring (killed in action, 1940) and of Lady Rose Baring, *qv*; *m* 1960, Teresa Anne Bridgeman; three *s*. *Educ:* Magdalene College, Cambridge (MA English). Joined Baring Brothers & Co., 1959, Director, 1967; Dir, Inchcape, 1978–. Dep. Chm., Provident Mutual Life Assurance Assoc., 1989–; Dir, British Invisibles, 1990–. *Address:* Barings plc, 8 Bishopsgate, EC2N 4AE. *T:* 071–280 1000.
See also N. H. Baring.

BARING, Lady Rose (Gwendolen Louisa), DCVO 1972 (CVO 1964); Extra Woman of the Bedchamber to the Queen, since 1973; *b* 23 May 1909; *er d* of 12th Earl of Antrim and of Margaret, *y d* of late Rt Hon. J. G. Talbot; *m* 1933, Francis Anthony Baring (killed in action, 1940); two *s* one *d*. Woman of the Bedchamber to the Queen, 1953–73. *Address:* 43 Pembroke Square, W8.
See also N. H. Baring, P. Baring.

BARK, Evelyn (Elizabeth Patricia), CMG 1967; OBE 1952; retired as Director International Affairs Department of British Red Cross (1950–66); *b* 26 Dec. 1900; *e d* of late Frederick William Bark. *Educ:* privately. On staff of Swedish Match Co. (at home and abroad) until 1939, when joined British Red Cross. Served War, 1939–44, VAD (Stars: of 1939–45, of France, and of Germany; Defence Medal, and War Medal, 1939–45). Foreign Relations Officer, 1944–48. Commissioner, NW Europe, 1948–49; Foreign Relations and Relief Adviser, 1950 (title later changed to Dir International Affairs). Serving Sister of St John's, 1953; British Red Cross Certificate First Class, 1966. *Publication:* No Time to Kill, 1960. *Recreations:* reading, music, nordic languages. *Address:* c/o 15 Holly Hill Drive, Banstead, Surrey SM7 2BD.

BARKER, family name of **Baroness Trumpington.**

BARKER, Sir Alwyn (Bowman), Kt 1969; CMG 1962; BSc, BE; CEng, FIEAust; Chairman, Kelvinator Australia Ltd, 1967–80 (Managing Director, 1952–67); *b* 5 Aug. 1900; *s* of late A. J. Barker, Mt Barker, South Australia; *m* 1926, Isabel Barron Lucas, *d* of late Sir Edward Lucas; one *d* (one *s* decd). *Educ:* St Peter's Coll., Adelaide; Geelong C of E Grammar Sch.; Univ. of Adelaide. British Thomson Houston Co. Ltd, England, 1923–24; Hudson Motor Car Co., Detroit, 1924–25; Production Manager, Holden's Motor Body Builders Ltd, Adelaide, 1925–30; Works Manager, Kelvinator Aust. Ltd, Adelaide, 1931–40; Gen. Man., Chrysler Aust. Ltd, Adelaide, 1940–52; Chm., Municipal Tramways Trust SA, 1953–68; Dir, public companies. Mem. Faculty of Engineering, Univ. of Adelaide, 1937–66 (Lectr in Industrial Engineering, 1929–53). Chm., Industrial Develt Adv. Council, 1968–70; Fellow, Internat. Acad. of Management; Member: Manufacturing Industries Adv. Council, 1958–72; Res. and Develt Adv. Cttee, 1967–72. Hon. Life Mem., Australian Mineral Foundn; Hon. Fellow Australian Inst. of Management (Federal Pres., 1952–53, 1959–61; Pres. Adelaide Div., 1952–54); Pres., Australian Council, Inst. of Prodn Engrs, 1970–72. John Storey Meml Medal, 1965; Jack Finlay Nat. Award, 1964. *Publications:* Three Presidential Addresses, 1954; William Queale Memorial Lecture, 1965. *Recreations:* pastoral. *Address:* 51 Hackney Road, Hackney, SA 5069, Australia. *T:* 362.2838. *Club:* Adelaide.

BARKER, Anne Judith, (Mrs B. J. Barker); *see* Rafferty, A. J.

BARKER, Anthony; QC 1985; a Recorder, since 1985; *b* 10 Jan. 1944; *s* of Robert Herbert Barker and Ellen Doreen Barker; *m* 1st, 1969, (marr. diss. 1980); two *d*; 2nd, 1983, Mrs Valerie Ann Ellis; one step *s*. *Educ:* Newcastle-under-Lyme High Sch.; Clare Coll., Cambridge (BA Hons). Called to the Bar, Middle Temple, 1966. Asst Recorder, 1981. *Recreations:* gardening, walking, music. *Address:* Hilderstone House, Hilderstone, near Stone, Staffs ST15 8SF. *T:* Hilderstone (0889) 505331.

BARKER, Arthur Vincent, CBE 1974 (OBE 1955); Chartered Accountant; financial planning consultant; *b* 10 Nov. 1911; *e s* of late Arthur and Susannah Mary Barker; *m* 1936, Dorothy Drew; one *d*. *Educ:* Whitley and Monkseaton High Sch.; London Sch. of Economics. Qual. as CA, 1934; with Price Waterhouse & Co., 1934–35; with NAAFI in Middle East and UK, 1935–62 (Jt Gen. Man., 1955); Asst Gen. Man., Southern Region, British Railways, and Mem., Southern Railway Bd, 1962; Asst Gen. Man., London Midland Region, British Railways, and Mem., LMR Bd, 1965; Chairman: Shipping and Internat. Services Div., British Railways, 1968–69; British Rail Hovercraft, 1970–71; British Transport Hotels Ltd, 1968–74; Mem., British Railways Bd, 1968–74. *Recreation:* fly-fishing. *Address:* 24 West Mount, The Mount, Guildford, Surrey GU2 5HL. *T:* Guildford (0483) 39524.

BARKER, Audrey Lilian; writer; *b* 13 April 1918; *d* of Harry and Elsie Barker. *Educ:* County secondary schools in Beckenham, Kent and Wallington, Surrey. Editorial office, Amalgamated Press, 1936; Publisher's reader, Cresset Press, 1947; BBC, 1949–78. Atlantic Award in Literature, 1946; Somerset Maugham Award, 1947; Cheltenham Festival of Literature Award, 1963; SE Arts Creative Book Award, 1981. FRSL 1970; Mem. Exec. Cttee, PEN, 1981–85; Member Panel of Judges: Katherine Mansfield Prize, 1984; Macmillan Silver Pen Award for Fiction, 1986 and 1989. *Publications: collected stories:* Innocents, 1947; Novelette, 1951; Lost Upon the Roundabouts, 1964; Femina Real, 1971; Life Stories, 1981; No Word of Love, 1985; Any Excuse for a Party, 1991; *novels:* Apology for a Hero, 1950; The Joy-Ride (three novellas), 1963; A Case Examined, 1965; The Middling, 1967; John Brown's Body, 1969 (shortlisted for Booker Prize, 1969); A Source of Embarrassment, 1974; A Heavy Feather, 1978; Relative Successes, 1984; The Gooseboy, 1987; The Woman Who Talked to Herself, 1989. *Address:* 103 Harrow Road, Carshalton, Surrey SM5 3QF.

BARKER, Barry, MBE 1960; FCIS; Secretary and Chief Executive, Institute of Chartered Secretaries and Administrators (formerly Chartered Institute of Secretaries), 1976–89; *b* 1929; *s* of late Francis Walter Barker and of Amy Barker; *m* 1954, Dr Vira Dubash; two *s*. *Educ:* Ipswich Sch.; Trinity Coll., Oxford (MA Class. Greats). Secretary: Bombay Chamber of Commerce and Industry, 1956–62; The Metal Box Co. of India Ltd, 1962–67. Dir, Shipbuilding Industry Bd, 1967–71; Consultant at Dept of Industry, 1972; Sec., Pye Holdings Ltd, 1972–76. Chm., Consultative Council of Professional Management Orgns, 1981–90. Member: BTEC, 1985–; RSA Exams Bd, 1987–; Nat. Forum for Management Educn and Develt, 1989–; Bd of Management, Young Vic Co., 1984–90. *Recreations:* the theatre and the arts. *Address:* 82 Darwin Court, Gloucester Avenue, NW1 7BQ. *T:* 081–528 0570. *Club:* Oriental.

BARKER, Brian John; QC 1990; a Recorder of the Crown Court, since 1985; *b* 15 Jan. 1945; *s* of William Barker and Irene Barker (*née* Gillow); *m* 1977, Anne Judith Rafferty, *qv*; three *d* (and one *d* decd). *Educ:* Strode's School, Egham; Univ. of Birmingham (LLB); Univ. of Kansas (MA). Called to the Bar, Gray's Inn, 1969. Mem., Senate and Bar Council, 1976–79. Freeman, City of London; Liveryman, Coopers' Co., 1989. *Recreations:* occasional gardening and golf. *Address:* Queen Elizabeth Building, Temple, EC4Y 9BS. *T:* 071–583 5766. *Clubs:* City Livery; Royal Mid-Surrey Golf, Pett Cricket.

BARKER, Rt. Rev. Clifford Conder, TD 1970; Bishop Suffragan of Selby, 1983–91; *b* 22 April 1926; *s* of Sidney and Kathleen Alice Barker; *m* 1952, Marie Edwards (*d* 1982); one *s* two *d*; 2nd, 1983, Mrs Audrey Gregson; two step *s* one step *d*. *Educ:* Oriel Coll., Oxford (BA 1950, MA 1955); St Chad's Coll., Durham (Dip. in Theol. 1952). Emergency Commun, The Green Howards, 1944–48; deacon 1952, priest 1953; Curate: All Saints', Scarborough, 1952–55; Redcar, 1955–57; Vicar: All Saints', Sculcoates, Hull, 1957–63; Rudby-in-Cleveland, 1963–70; RD of Stokesley, 1965–70; Vicar, St Olave with St Giles, York, 1970–76; RD of York, 1971–76; Canon of York, 1973–76; Bishop Suffragan of Whitby, 1976–83. CF (TA), 1958–74. *Recreations:* golf, gardening, music. *Address:* Wylde Green, 15 Oak Tree Close, Strensall, York YO2 5TE. *T:* York (0904) 490406. *Club:* Yorkshire (York).

BARKER, Sir Colin, Kt 1991; Chairman, British Technology Group, since 1983 (Chief Executive, 1983–85); *b* 20 Oct. 1926; *m* 1951, Beryl; three *s* one *d*. *Educ:* Hull Grammar Sch.; Londodn and Edinburgh Univs. Ford UK, 1960–67 (Finance Dir, 1967); Finance Director: Blue Circle, 1968–70; STC, 1970–80; British Steel Corp., 1980–83. Chairman: CIN Management, 1985–; British Investment Trust, 1985–; MCD (UK), 1990–; Anglian Windows, 1991–; Director: Reed Internat., 1983–; British Coal Corp., 1984–91; Edinburgh Fund Managers, 1988–. *Address:* British Technology Group, 101 Newington Causeway, SE1 6BU. *T:* 071–403 6666.

BARKER, David, QC 1976; a Recorder of the Crown Court, since 1974; *b* 13 April 1932; *s* of late Frederick Barker and of Amy Evelyn Barker; *m* 1957, Diana Mary Vinson Barker (*née* Duckworth); one *s* three *d*. *Educ:* Sir John Deane's Grammar Sch., Northwich; University Coll., London; Univ. of Michigan. 1st cl. hons LLB London; LLM Michigan. RAF, 1956–59. Called to Bar, Inner Temple, 1954, Bencher, 1985; practised Midland and Oxford Circuit; Mem., Senate of Inns of Court and the Bar, 1981–84. Mem., Criminal Injuries Compensation Bd, 1990–. Contested (Lab) Runcorn, 1955. *Recreations:* gardening, walking, sailing. *Address:* Nanhill, Woodhouse Eaves, Leics LE12 8TL. *T:* Woodhouse Eaves (0509) 890224; Francis Taylor Building, Temple, EC4Y 7BY. *T:* 071–353 7768. *Club:* Western (Glasgow).

BARKER, Prof. David (Faubert), MA, DPhil, DSc; Professor of Zoology, University of Durham, 1962–87, now Professor Emeritus; *b* 18 Feb. 1922; *s* of Faubert and Doreen Barker; *m* 1st, 1945, Kathleen Mary Frances Pocock; three *s* two *d*; 2nd, 1978, Patricia Margaret Drake; one *s* one *d*. *Educ:* Bryanston Sch.; Magdalen Coll., Oxford. DSc 1972. Senior Demy of Magdalen Coll., 1946; Leverhulme Research Scholar, Royal Coll. of Surgeons, 1946; Demonstrator in Zoology and Comparative Anatomy, Oxford, 1947; DPhil 1948; Rolleston Prizeman, 1948; Prof. of Zoology, Univ. of Hong Kong, 1950–62; led scientific expeditions to Tunisia, 1950, North Borneo, 1952; Dean of Faculty of Science, Hong Kong, 1959–60; Public Orator, Hong Kong, 1961; Sir Derman Christopherson Fellow, Durham Univ. Research Foundn, 1984–85. Emeritus Fellow, Leverhulme Trust, 1989–92. *Publications:* (Founder) Editor, Hong Kong Univ. Fisheries Journal, 1954–60; Editor, Symposium on Muscle Receptors, 1962; scientific papers, mostly on muscle innervation. *Address:* Department of Biological Sciences, Science Laboratories, South Road, Durham DH1 3LE. *T:* Durham (091) 3743342.

BARKER, Edward, OBE 1966; QPM 1961; Chief Constable of Sheffield and Rotherham Constabulary, 1967–72; *b* 1 Nov. 1909; *s* of George and Gertrude Barker; *m* 1935, Clare Garth; one *d*. *Educ:* The Grammar School, Malton. Joined Preston Borough Police, 1931; transf. Lancs Constabulary, 1938; Inspector/Chief Inspector, Comdt of Constabulary Trng Sch., 1946–51; Supt 1954; Vis. Lectr to Bermuda Police, 1955; Chief Supt 1956; Asst Comdt, Police Coll., Bramshill, 1956–57; Chief Constable: Bolton Borough Police, 1957; Sheffield City Police, 1964. Hon. Fellow, Sheffield Poly., 1973. Police Long Service and Good Conduct Medal, 1953. SBStJ. *Recreations:* golf, gardening, watching field sports. *Address:* 21 Woodstock Road, Aberdeen AB2 4ET. *T:* Aberdeen (0224) 318484. *Club:* Deeside Golf.

BARKER, George Granville; writer; *b* 26 Feb. 1913; *s* of George Barker and Marion Frances Barker (*née* Taaffe); *m* 1964, Elspeth Langlands. *Educ:* Marlborough Road London County Council Sch., Chelsea. Prof. of English Literature at Imperial Tohoku Univ., Japan, 1939; visited America, 1940; returned to England, 1943; lived in Rome, 1960–65. Arts Fellow York Univ., 1966–67; Vis. Prof., Florida Internat. Univ., 1974. *Publications:* Thirty Preliminary Poems, 1933; Alanna Autumnal, 1933; Poems, 1935; Janus, 1935; Calamiterror, 1937; Lament and Triumph, 1940; Eros in Dogma, 1944; News of the World, 1950; The Dead Seagull, 1950; The True Confession of George Barker, 1950; A Vision of Beasts and Gods, 1954; Collected Poems, 1930–55, 1957; The True Confession of George Barker, Book II, 1957; Two Plays, 1958; The View from a Blind I, 1962; Dreams of a Summer Night, 1966; The Golden Chains, 1968; Essays, 1970; Runes & Rhymes & Tunes & Chimes, 1970; To Aylsham Fair, 1970; At Thurgarton Church, 1970; Poems of Places and People, 1971; The Alphabetical Zoo, 1972; In Memory of David Archer, 1973; Dialogues etc, 1976; Villa Stellar, 1978; Anno Domini, 1983; Collected Poems, 1987; Seventeen, 1988. *Address:* Bintry House, Itteringham, Aylsham, Norfolk NR11 7AT. *T:* Saxthorpe (026387) 240.

BARKER, Prof. Graeme William Walter, FSA; Professor and Head of School of Archaeological Studies, Leicester University, since 1988; *b* 23 Oct. 1946; *s* of Reginald Walter Barker and Kathleen (*née* Walton); *m* 1976, Sarah Miranda Buchanan (marr. diss. 1991); one *s* one *d*. *Educ:* Alleyn's Sch., Dulwich; St John's Coll., Cambridge (Henry Arthur Thomas Schol., 1965–67; MA, PhD). FSA 1979. Rome Schol. in Classical Studies, British Sch. at Rome, 1969–71; Lectr, 1972–81, Sen. Lectr, 1981–88, in Prehist. and Archaeol., Sheffield Univ.; Dir., British Sch. in Rome, 1984–88. Dir, Molise survey and excavation project, S Italy, 1974–78; Co-Director: UNESCO Libyan Valleys Survey, 1979–; Tuscania Project, 1986–. *Publications:* Landscape and Society: Prehistoric Central Italy, 1981, Italian edn 1984; (with R. Hodges) Archaeology and Italian Society, 1981; Prehistoric Communities in Northern England, 1981; (jtly) La Casatico di Marcaria, 1983; (jtly) Cyrenaica in Classical Antiquity, 1984; Prehistoric Farming in Europe, 1985; (with C. S. Gamble) Beyond Domestication in Prehistoric Europe: Investigations in Subsistence Archaeology and Social Complexity, 1985; (with J. A. Lloyd) Roman Landscapes, 1991; contribs, esp. on archaeol survey, archaeozool. and ancient agric., to learned jls. *Address:* School of Archaeological Studies, University of Leicester, University Road, Leicester LE1 7RH. *T:* Leicester (0533) 708132.

BARKER, Harold; retired; Keeper, Department of Conservation and Technical Services, British Museum, 1975–79; Member: Council for Care of Churches, 1976–81; Crafts Council, 1979–80; *b* 15 Feb. 1919; *s* of William Frampton Barker and Lily (*née* Pack); *m* 1942, Everilda Alice Whittle; one *s* one *d*. *Educ:* City Secondary Sch., Sheffield; Sheffield Univ. (BSc). Experimental Asst, 1940, Experimental Officer, 1942, Chemical Inspectorate, Min. of Supply; British Museum: Experimental Officer, Research Lab., 1947; Sen. Experimental Officer, 1953; Chief Experimental Officer, 1960; Principal Scientific Officer, 1966; Acting Keeper, 1975. *Publications:* papers on radiocarbon dating and scientific examination of antiquities in various jls. *Recreations:* music, walking, videography. *Address:* 27 Westbourne Park, Falsgrave, Scarborough, N Yorks YO12 4AS. *T:* Scarborough (0723) 370967.

BARKER, Sir Harry Heaton, KBE 1978 (CBE 1972; OBE 1964); JP; New Zealand Journalist; chairman various organisations; *b* Nelson, NZ, 18 July 1898; *s* of J. H. Barker; *m* 1926, Anita (MBE), *d* of H. Greaves; no *c. Educ:* Wellington and Auckland; New Plymouth Boys' High Sch. Served NZEF, 1917–19. Entered journalism, working with NZ Herald and country newspapers, 1916–17, 1919–23; Gisborne Herald: joined, 1923; sub-editor, 1926; Leader Writer, Associate Editor, 1930; Editor, 1935–43, resigned. Mayor of Gisborne, 1950; re-elected, 1953, 1956, 1959, 1962, 1965, 1968, 1971, 1974. Contested Gisborne seat, 1943, 1946. Member: Cook Hospital Board, 1944–71; King George V Health Camps Federation Board, 1953–69; Exec., Dist Roads Council, 1953–78; East Coast Planning Council, 1972–77. Chairman: Barrington Miller Educnl Trust, 1950–77; Gisborne Airport Cttee, 1958–77; cttee organising nat. celebration, Cook Bicentenary celebration, 1969. Executive, NZ Municipalities Assoc., and Dir, Municipalities Insurance Co., 1959–69. Knighted for services to the City of Gisborne, NZ, and local government. *Publications:* To-Days and Yesterdays, 1978; political articles. *Recreations:* reading, writing, gardening. *Address:* Leighton House, Cheeseman Road, Gisborne, New Zealand. *T:* 8677697. *Club:* Victoria League.

BARKER, Howard; playwright and poet; *b* 28 June 1946. *Educ:* Univ. of Sussex (MA). Theatre productions, 1970–, include: *Royal Court:* No End of Blame, 1981; Victory, 1983; version of Thomas Middleton's Women Beware Women, 1986; The Last Supper, 1988; Golgo, 1990; *RSC* at The Pit: The Castle, 1985; Downchild: a fantasy, 1985; The Bite of the Night, 1988; other productions: A Passion in Six Days, Crucible, Sheffield, 1983; The Power of the Dog, Hampstead, 1985; Possibilities, Almeida, 1988. TV and radio plays include: Scenes from an Execution, Radio 3, 1984 (Best Drama Script, Sony Radio Awards, 1985; Prix Italia, 1985; perf. Almeida, 1990); Pity in History, BBC 2, 1985. Formed The Wrestling School (company to perform own work), 1989. *Publications: plays:* Stripwell, and Claw, 1977; Fair Slaughter, 1978; Love of a Good Man, and All Bleeding, 1981; That Good Between Us, and Credentials of a Sympathiser, 1981; No End of Blame: scenes of overcoming, 1981; Two Plays for the Right: Birth on a Hard Shouder, and The Loud Boy's Life, 1982; Hang of the Gaol, 1982; Victory: choices in reaction, 1983; The Castle, and Scenes from an Execution, 1984; Crimes in Hot Countries, and Fair Slaughter, 1984; Power of the Dog, 1985; A Passion in Six Days, and Downchild, 1985; The Last Supper: a New Testament, 1988; Lullabies for the Impatient, 1988; Possibilities, 1988; Pity in History, 1989; Seven Lears, and Golgo, 1990; Europeans, and Judith, 1990; Collected Plays, vol. I, 1990; *poetry:* Don't Exaggerate (Desire and Abuse), 1985; Breath of the Crowd, 1986; Gary the Thief/Gary Upright, 1987; The Ascent of Monte Grappa, 1991; *essays:* Arguments for a Theatre, 1989. *Address:* c/o Judy Daish Associates, 83 Eastbourne Mews, W2 6LQ.

BARKER, John Francis Holroyd, CB 1984; Consultant, Cabinet Office, since 1985; *b* 3 Feb. 1925; *s* of Rev. C.H. Barker and B.A. Barker (*née* Bullivant); *m* 1954, Felicity Ann (*née* Martindale); three *d. Educ:* King Edward's School, Stourbridge; Oriel College, Oxford. RNVR, 1943–46. Director of Music, Abingdon School, 1950–54; War Office/Ministry of Defence, 1954–85. *Recreation:* music. *Address:* c/o Coutts & Co., 440 Strand, WC2. *Club:* Athenæum.

BARKER, Air Vice-Marshal John Lindsay, CB 1963; CBE 1946; DFC 1945; RAF (retired); *b* 12 Nov. 1910; *s* of Abraham Cockroft Barker and Lilian Alice (*née* Woods); *m* 1948, Eleanor Margaret Hannah; one *s. Educ:* Trent Coll., Derbys; Brasenose Coll., Oxford. Called to the Bar, Middle Temple, 1947. RAFO, 1930, RAF, 1933. Served War of 1939–45: France, 1939–40; N Africa, 1942–44; Bomber Command, 1944–45; Far East, 1945–46; Palestine, 1946–48; Egypt, 1950–53; Air Attaché, Rome, 1955–58; Cmdr Royal Ceylon Air Force, 1958–63. Air Vice-Marshal, 1959. Retd, 1963. Order of Merit, Italy, 1958. *Recreations:* golf, photography, sailing. *Address:* The Old Cider Press, Mill Court, Frogmore, Kingsbridge, S Devon TQ7 2PB. *T:* Frogmore (0548) 531746. *Club:* Royal Air Force.

BARKER, John Michael Adrian; His Honour Judge Barker; a Circuit Judge, since 1979; *b* 4 Nov. 1932; *s* of Robert Henry Barker and Annie Robson Barker (*née* Charlton); *m* 1971, Gillian Marsha (*née* Greenstone). *Educ:* Marist Coll., Hull Univs of Sheffield and Hull. BSc, LLB. Called to Bar, Middle Temple, 1959. Schoolmaster, Stonyhurst Coll., 1957–59; Lectr in Law, Univ. of Hull, 1960–63. A Recorder of the Crown Court, 1974–79. Mem., Hull CC, 1965–71. *Publications:* articles in Conveyancer and Property Lawyer, Solicitors' Jl, Criminal Law Review and Solicitor. *Recreations:* walking, gardening. *Address:* 2 Harcourt Buildings, Temple, EC4. *Club:* Lansdowne.

BARKER, Rear-Adm. John Perronet, CB 1985; RN retired, 1986; Administration Secretary, Missions to Seamen, since 1987; *b* 24 June 1930; *s* of late Gilbert Barker and Dorothy G. Barker (*née* Moore); *m* 1955, Priscilla, *d* of late Sir William Christie, KCIE, CSI, MC; two *s. Educ:* Edgbaston Prep. Sch., Birmingham; Nautical Coll., Pangbourne; BRNC, Dartmouth. Entered RN, 1948; served, 1949–72: HMS King George V, Glory, Condor, Ceres, Lagos, Hampshire and Centurion; staff of C-in-C Home Fleet, of C-in-C Nore and of Comdr British Navy Staff, Washington; Sec. to ACNS (OR), MoD (Navy), to Flag Officer 2FEF, and to Flag Officer Plymouth; Sec. to Controller of the Navy, 1972–76; Student, RCDS, 1977; Dir, Fleet Supply Duties, MoD (Navy), 1978–80; Cdre, HMS Centurion, 1980–83; Chief of Staff to C-in-C, Naval Home Command, 1983–85. Chairman: IYRU World Youth Sailing, 1986–; Assoc. of RN Officers, 1987–; Life Rear Cdre, RNSA, 1986. Liveryman, Worshipful Co. of Shipwrights, 1983. *Recreations:* sailing, gardening. *Address:* c/o Lloyds Bank, 125 Colmore Row, Birmingham B3 3AD. *Clubs:* Royal Yacht Squadron (Cowes); Royal Naval Sailing Association (Portsmouth); Midland Sailing (Birmingham).

BARKER, Kenneth; Director, Leicester Polytechnic, since 1987 (Deputy Director/Director Designate, 1986–87); *b* 26 June 1934; *s* of Thomas William and Lillian Barker; *m* 1958, Jean Ivy Pearl; one *s* one *d. Educ:* Royal Coll. of Music; King's Coll., London (BMus); Sussex Univ. (MA). Schoolmaster, 1958–62; lectr and university teacher, 1962–75; Principal, Gipsy Hill Coll., 1975; Pro-Dir, Kingston Polytechnic, 1975–86. *Publications:* contribs to jls. *Recreations:* music, theatre, watching Rugby. *Address:* Leicester Polytechnic, PO Box 143, Leicester LE1 9BH; 20 Albany Mews, Kingston upon Thames KT2 5SL. *T:* 081-541 1438. *Clubs:* Reform, Institute of Directors.

BARKER, Nicolas John; Deputy Keeper, British Library, since 1976; Editor, Book Collector, since 1965; *b* 6 Dec. 1932; *s* of Sir Ernest Barker, FBA, and Olivia Stuart Horner; *m* 1962, Joanna Mary Sophia Nyda Cotton; two *s* three *d. Educ:* Westminster Sch.; New Coll., Oxford (MA). With Bailliere, Tindall & Cox, 1959 and Rupert Hart-Davis, 1959; Asst Keeper, National Portrait Gallery, 1964; with Macmillan & Co. Ltd, 1965; with OUP, 1971. William Andrews Clark Vis. Prof, UCLA, 1986–87. President: Amici Thomae Mori, 1978–89; Double Crown Club, 1980–81; Bibliographical Soc., 1981–85; Member: Publication Bd of Dirs, RNIB, 1969–; London Library Cttee, 1971–; BBC and ITV Appeals Adv. Cttee, 1977–86; Nat. Trust Arts Panel, 1979–; Trustee, The Pilgrim Trust, 1977–; Chm., Laurence Sterne Trust, 1984–. *Publications:* The Publications of the Roxburghe Club, 1962; The Printer and the Poet, 1970; Stanley Morison, 1972; (ed) Essays and Papers of A. N. L. Munby, 1977; (ed) The Early Life of James McBey: an autobiography, 1883–1911, 1977; Bibliotheca Lindesiana, 1977; The Oxford University Press and the Spread of Learning 1478–1978, 1978; (with John Collins) A Sequel to an Enquiry, 1983; Aldus Manutius and the Development of Greek Script and Type, 1985; The Butterfly Books, 1987; Two East Anglian Picture Books, 1988; (ed) Treasures of the British Library, 1989; (ed) S. Morison, Early Italian Writing-Books, 1990. *Address:* 22 Clarendon Road, W11 3AB. *T:* 071–727 4340. *Clubs:* Garrick, Beefsteak, Roxburghe; Roxburghe (San Francisco); Zamorano (Los Angeles).

BARKER, Paul; writer and broadcaster; *b* 24 Aug. 1935; *s* of Donald and Marion Barker; *m* 1960, Sally, *e d* of James and Marion Huddleston; three *s* one *d. Educ:* Hebden Bridge Grammar Sch.; Calder High Sch.; Brasenose Coll., Oxford (Hulme Exhibr), MA. Intell. Corps (commn), 1953–55. Lecteur, Ecole Normale Supérieure, Paris, 1958–59; The Times, 1959–63; New Society, staff writer, 1964; The Economist, 1964–65; New Society: Assistant Editor, 1965–68; Editor, 1968–86; Social Policy Ed., Sunday Telegraph, 1986–88; Associate Ed., The Independent Magazine, 1988–90. Townscape and arts columnist, Evening Standard, 1987–; social and political columnist, Sunday Times, 1990–91. Gen. Editor, Towards a New Society, book series, 1971–78; Dir and Adv. Editor, The Fiction Magazine, 1982–87. Dir, Pennine Heritage, 1978–86. Vis. Fellow, Centre for Analysis of Social Policy, Univ. of Bath, 1986–. FRSA 1990. (Jtly) BPG Award for outstanding radio prog., My Country, Right or Wrong, 1988. *Publications:* (ed) A Sociological Portrait, 1972; (ed and contrib.) One for Sorrow, Two for Joy, 1972; (ed) The Social Sciences Today, 1975; (ed and contrib.) Arts in Society, 1977; (ed and contrib.) The Other Britain, 1982; (ed) Founders of the Welfare State, 1985; (contrib.) Britain in the Eighties, 1990. *Recreation:* driving along an empty motorway to a baroque church, with the radio on. *Address:* 15 Dartmouth Park Avenue, NW5 1JL. *T:* 071–485 8861.

BARKER, Peter William, CBE 1988; DL; Chairman, Fenner (formerly J. H. Fenner (Holdings)) PLC, since 1982; *b* 24 Aug. 1928; *s* of William Henry George and Mabel Irene Barker; *m* 1961, Mary Rose Hainsworth, JP; one *s* one *d. Educ:* Royal Liberty Sch., Romford; Dorking County High Sch.; South London Polytechnic. CBIM; FIIM; FInstD; FCIM. J. H. Fenner & Co., 1953–67; Jt Managing Dir, Fenner International, 1967–71; Chief Exec., J. H. Fenner (Holdings), 1971–82. Non-exec. Dir, Neepsend plc, 1984–. Member: Yorks and Humberside Regional Council, CBI, 1981– (Vice-Chm., 1988–); National Council, CBI, 1985–; Yorks and Humberside Regional Indust. Develt Bd, 1981–. FRSA. DL 1990. *Recreations:* sailing, ski-ing, tennis, music. *Address:* Swanland Rise, West Ella, North Humberside HU10 7SF. *T:* Hull (0482) 653050. *Clubs:* Oriental, Hurlingham; Royal Yorkshire Yacht.

BARKER, Richard Philip; Headmaster, Sevenoaks School, since 1981; *b* 17 July 1939; *s* of late Philip Watson Barker and Helen May Barker; *m* 1966, Imogen Margaret Harris; two *s* one *d. Educ:* Repton; Trinity Coll., Cambridge (MA 1962); Bristol Univ. (Cert. Ed. 1963). Head of Geography, Bedales Sch., 1963–65; Dir, A level business studies project, 1966–73; Lectr, Inst. of Education, London Univ., 1973–74; Housemaster, Marlborough Coll., 1973–81. Mem., RSA. *Publications:* (ed) Understanding Business Series, 1976–91. *Recreations:* fishing, sailing, travelling. *Address:* Headmaster's House, Sevenoaks School, Kent TN13 1HU. *T:* Sevenoaks (0732) 455133.

BARKER, Ronald Hugh, PhD, BSc; CEng, FIEE, FIMechE; Deputy Director, Royal Armament Research and Development Establishment, 1965–75, retired; *b* 28 Oct. 1915; *s* of E. W. Barker and L. A. Taylor; *m* 1943, W. E. Hunt; two *s. Educ:* University of Hull. Physicist, Standard Telephones and Cables, 1938–41; Ministry of Supply, 1941–59; Dep. Dir, Central Electricity Research Laboratories, 1959–62; Technical Dir, The Pullin Group Ltd, 1962–65. *Publications:* various, on servomechanisms and control systems. *Address:* Cramond, 17 Dewlands Way, Verwood, Dorset BH21 6JN.

BARKER, Ronnie, (Ronald William George Barker), OBE 1978; actor, retired 1987; *b* 25 Sept. 1929; *s* of Leonard and Edith Barker; *m* 1957, Joy Tubb; two *s* one *d. Educ:* Oxford High Sch. Started acting career, Aylesbury Rep. Co., 1948. *Plays (West End):* Mourning Becomes Electra, 1955; Summertime, 1955; Listen to the Wind, 1955; Double Image, 1956; Camino Real, 1957; Lysistrata, 1958; Irma la Douce, 1958; Platanov, 1960; On the Brighter Side, 1961; Midsummer Night's Dream, 1962; Real Inspector Hound, 1968; The Two Ronnies, Palladium, 1978. *Films include:* Robin and Marian, 1975; Picnic, 1975; Porridge, 1979. *Television: series:* Seven Faces of Jim, 1965; Frost Report, 1966–67; Hark at Barker, 1968–69; Six Dates with Barker, 1970; The Two Ronnies, 10 series, 1971–86; Twenty Years of the Two Ronnies, 1986; Porridge, 1974, 1975, 1976, 1977; Open All Hours, 1976, 1981, 1982; Going Straight, 1978; Clarence, 1987. Awards: Variety Club, 1969, 1974, 1980; SFTA, 1971; Radio Industries Club, 1973, 1974, 1977, 1981; Water Rats, 1975; British Acad. Award, 1975, 1977, 1978; Royal Television Society's award for outstanding creative achievement, 1975. *Publications:* Book of Bathing Beauties, 1974; Book of Boudoir Beauties, 1975; It's Goodnight From Him, 1976; Sauce, 1977; Gentlemen's Relish, 1979; Sugar and Spice, 1981; Ooh-la-la!, 1983; Pebbles on the Beach, 1985; A Pennyworth of Art, 1986. *Recreations:* writing song lyrics, collecting postcards.

BARKER, Susan Vera; *see* Cooper, Susie.

BARKER, Prof. Theodore Cardwell, PhD, FRHistS; Professor of Economic History, University of London, 1976–83, now Emeritus and engaged in research; *b* 19 July 1923; *s* of Norman Humphrey Barker and Louie Nettleton Barker; *m* 1955, Joy Marie (Judith) Pierce. *Educ:* Cowley Sch., St Helens; Jesus Coll., Oxford (MA); Manchester Univ. (PhD). FRHistS 1963. Econ. History staff, LSE, 1953–64; first Prof. of Econ. and Social Hist., Univ. of Kent at Canterbury, 1964–76. President: Econ. Hist. Soc., 1986–89 (Hon. Sec., 1960–86); Railway and Canal Hist. Soc., 1986–88; Internat. Historical Congress, 1990– (Chm., British Nat. Cttee, 1978–); Chairman: Management Cttee, Inst. of Historical Res., London Univ., 1977–88; Hist. Bd, CNAA, 1977–81; Management Cttee, London Univ. Business History Unit, 1979–86; Debrett's Business History Research Ltd, 1984–89; Athlone Press, 1988–. Chm., Oral Hist. Soc., 1973–76. Mem. Council, RHistS, 1967–70 and 1974–77. *Publications:* A Merseyside Town in the Industrial Revolution (with J. R. Harris), 1954; A History of the Girdlers Company, 1957; Pilkington Brothers and the Glass Industry, 1960; (with R. H. Campbell, Peter Mathias and B. S. Yamey) Business History, 1960, 2nd edn 1970; (with R. M. Robbins) A History of London Transport: Vol. I, 1963, Vol. II, 1974; (ed with J. C. McKenzie and John Yudkin) Our Changing Fare: two hundred years of British food habits, 1966; (with B. W. E. Alford) A History of the Worshipful Company of Carpenters, 1968; (ed) The Long March of Everyman, 1974; (with M. J. Hatcher) A History of British Pewter, 1974; (with C. I. Savage) An Economic History of Transport, 1975; The Glassmakers, 1977; The Transport Contractors of Rye, 1982; (ed with Michael Drake) The Population Factor, 1982; (ed) The Economic and Social Effects of the Spread of Motor Vehicles, 1987; Moving Millions, 1990. *Recreations:* walking, motoring. *Address:* Minsen Dane, Brogdale Road, Faversham, Kent ME13 8YA. *T:* Faversham (0795) 3523. *Club:* Reform.

BARKER, Thomas Christopher; HM Diplomatic Service, retired; Secretary to Trustees, Scottish National War Memorial, Edinburgh, since 1987 (Curator, 1978–87); *b* 28 June 1928; *m* 1960, Griselda Helen Cormack; two *s* one *d*. *Educ:* Uppingham (Schol.); New Coll., Oxford (Schol.). MA, Lit Hum, 1952; Gaisford Prize for Greek Verse. FSA Scot. 2nd Lt, 1st Bn, The Worcestershire Regt, 1947–48. HM Foreign (now Diplomatic) Service, 1952; Third Sec., Paris, 1953–55; Second Sec., Baghdad, 1955–58; FO, 1958–62; First Sec., Head of Chancery and Consul, Mexico City, 1962–67; FO, 1967–69; Counsellor and Head of Chancery, Caracas, 1969–71; FCO, 1971–75; seconded as Under Sec., NI Office, Belfast, 1976. *Address:* Carmurie, South Street, Elie, Fife KY9 1DN.

BARKER, Timothy Gwynne; Deputy Chief Executive, Kleinwort Benson Group plc, since 1990 (Director, since 1988); Vice Chairman, Kleinwort Benson Ltd, since 1989 (Director, since 1973); *b* 8 April 1940; *s* of Frank Richard Peter Barker and Hon. Olwen Gwynne (*née* Philipps); *m* 1964, Philippa Rachel Mary Thursby-Pelham; one *s* one *d*. *Educ:* Eton Coll.; McGill Univ., Montreal; Jesus Coll., Cambridge (MA). Director-General: City Panel on Take-overs and Mergers, 1984–85; Council for the Securities Industry, 1984–85. *Address:* 20 Fenchurch Street, EC3P 3DB. *T:* 071-623 8000.

BARKER, Trevor; Chairman: Alpha Consolidated Holdings Ltd, since 1988; Micklegate Group, since 1989; Deputy Chairman, Blanchards PLC, since 1988; *b* 24 March 1935; *s* of Samuel Lawrence Barker and Lilian Barker (*née* Dawson); *m* 1957, Joan Elizabeth Cross; one *s* one *d*. *Educ:* Acklam Hall Grammar School. FCA. Price Waterhouse & Co., 1957–58; Cooper Brothers, 1958–62; sole practitioner, 1962–70; Chm. and Chief Exec., Gold Case Travel, 1964–77; Dir, Ellerman Wilson Lines, 1977–80; Chairman: John Crowther Gp, 1980–88; William Morris Fine Arts plc, 1981–88. FRSA 1989. Liveryman, Co. of Woolmen, 1986. *Recreations:* breeding and racing thoroughbred horses, opera, music, literature, the arts. *Address:* Windways, 323 Coniscliffe Road, Darlington, Co. Durham DL3 8AH. *T:* Darlington (0325) 350436.

BARKER, Sir William, KCMG 1967 (CMG 1958); OBE 1949; Bowes Professor of Russian, University of Liverpool, 1969–76, now retired; *b* 19 July 1909; *s* of Alfred Barker; *m* 1939, Margaret Beirne; one *s* one *d*. *Educ:* Universities of Liverpool and Prague. Employed in Foreign Office, 1943; First Sec., Prague, 1945; Foreign Service Officer, Grade 7, Senior Branch of Foreign Service, 1946; Chargé d'Affaires, Prague, 1947; transferred Moscow, Aug. 1947; granted rank of Counsellor, Dec. 1948; Grade 6, 1950; Counsellor, Oslo, 1951, also Chargé d'Affaires; Consul-Gen., Boston, Mass, Sept. 1954; Counsellor, Washington, 1955; Minister, Moscow, 1960–63; Fellow, Center for Internat. Affairs, Harvard Univ., 1963–64. Asst Under-Sec. of State, FO, 1965–66; British Ambassador to Czechoslovakia, 1966–68. *Address:* 19 Moors Way, Woodbridge, Suffolk IP12 4HQ.

BARKING, Area Bishop of, since 1991; **Rt. Rev. Roger Frederick Sainsbury;** *b* 2 Oct. 1936; *s* of Frederick William Sainsbury and Lillian Maude Sainsbury; *m* 1960, Jennifer Marguerite Carey. *Educ:* High Wycombe Royal Grammar School; Jesus Coll., Cambridge (MA); Clifton Theological Coll., Curate, Christ Church, Spitalfields, 1960–63; Missioner, Shrewsbury House, Liverpool, 1963–74; Warden, Mayflower Family Centre, Canning Town, 1974–81; Priest-in-Charge, St Luke, Victoria Dock, 1978–81; Vicar of Walsall, 1981–86; Archdeacon of West Ham, 1988–91. Alderman, London Borough of Newham, 1976–78. Chairman: Frontier Youth Trustees, 1985–; Evangelical Coalition for Urban Mission, 1988–; London Churches Docklands Gp, 1989–. *Publications:* From a Mersey Wall, 1970; Justice on the Agenda, 1985; Lifestyle, 1986; Rooted and Grounded in Love, 1988; God of New Beginnings, 1990. *Recreations:* cricket, football supporting, stone polishing. *Address:* Barking Lodge, 110 Capel Road, Forest Gate, E7 0JS. *T:* 081–478 2456. *Club:* Sion College.

BARKLEY, Rev. Prof. John Montieth; retired; Principal, Union Theological College, Belfast, 1978–81; *b* 16 Oct. 1910; *s* of Rev. Robert James Barkley, BD, and Mary Monteith; *m* 1st, 1936, Irene Graham Anderson (*d* 1987); one *d*; 2nd, 1988, Caroline Margaret Barnett. *Educ:* Magee Univ. Coll. Derry; Trinity Coll., Dublin; The Presbyterian Coll., Belfast. BA 1934, MA 1941, BD 1944, PhD 1946, DD 1949, Trinity Coll., Dublin; BA 1952, MA 1953, Queen's Univ., Belfast. Thompson Memorial Prizeman in Philosophy, 1934; Larmour Memorial Exhibitioner in Theology, 1944; Paul Memorial Prizeman in History, 1953; Carey Lecturer, 1954–56; Lecturer in Ecclesiastical History, Queen's Univ., Belfast, 1951–54; Prof. in Ecclesiastical Hist., 1954–79, Vice-Principal, 1964–76, Principal, 1976–78, Presbyterian Coll., Belfast, until amalgamated with Magee Coll. to form Union Theological Coll. FRHistS. Ordained, Drumreagh Presbyterian Church, 1935; installed in II Ballybay and Rockcorry, 1939; installed in Cooke Centenary, Belfast, 1949. *Publications:* Handbook on Evangelical Christianity and Romanism, 1949; Presbyterianism, 1951; Westminster Formularies in Irish Presbyterianism, 1956; History of the Presbyterian Church in Ireland, 1959; Weltkirchenlexikon (arts), 1960; History of the Sabbath School Society for Ireland, 1961; The Eldership in Irish Presbyterianism; The Baptism of Infants, 1963; The Presbyterian Orphan Society, 1966; Worship of the Reformed Church, 1966; St Enoch's 1872–1972, 1972; (ed) Handbook to Church Hymnary, 3rd edn, 1979; Fasti of the Presbyterian Church in Ireland 1840–1910, 1987; articles in Scottish Journal of Theology, Verbum Caro, Biblical Theology, Dictionary of Worship. *Recreations:* bowls, golf. *Address:* 14 Clonallon Park, Belfast BT4 2BZ. *T:* Belfast (0232) 650842.

BARKSHIRE, John; *see* Barkshire, R. R. St J.

BARKSHIRE, Robert Hugh, CBE 1968; *b* 24 Oct. 1909; *yr s* of late Lt-Col Charles Robert Barkshire, OBE; *m* 1934, Emily Blunt, *er d* of A. S. Blunt, Bedford; one *s*. *Educ:* King's Sch., Bruton. Bank of England, 1927–55: Private Sec. to the Governor (C. F. Cobbold, later Lord Cobbold), 1949–53; Sec. to Cttee of London Clearing Bankers, British Bankers' Assoc., Bankers' Clearing House, and Mem., various inter-Bank Cttees, 1955–70; Hon. Sec., Meetings of Officers of European Bankers' Assocs, 1959–72; Gen. Comr of Income Tax for City of London, 1969–78; Governor, NIESR, 1970–78. FCIB (FIB 1960). Freeman, City of London. *Address:* The Boat House, Fowey, Cornwall PL23 1BH. *T:* Fowey (0726) 833389. *Clubs:* Royal Thames Yacht; Royal Fowey Yacht.

See also R. R. St J. Barkshire.

BARKSHIRE, Robert Renny St John, (John), CBE 1990; TD; JP; DL; farmer; Chairman, International Commodities Clearing House Ltd, 1986–90; *b* 31 Aug. 1935; *s* of Robert Hugh Barkshire, *qv*; *m* 1st, 1960, Margaret Elizabeth Robinson (marr. diss. 1990); two *s* one *d*; 2nd, 1990, Audrey Mary Anne Witham. *Educ:* Bedford School. ACIB. Served Duke of Wellington's Regt, 2nd Lt, 1953–55; HAC, 1955–74 (CO, 1970–72; Regtl Col, 1972–74). Joined Cater Ryder & Co., 1955, Jt Man. Dir, 1963–72; Chm., Mercantile House Holdings plc, 1972–87; Non-exec. Dir, Extel Gp PLC, 1979–87 (Dep. Chm., 1986–87); Chm., CL-Alexanders Laing & Cruickshank Hldgs Ltd, 1984–88. Chm., Financial Futures Wkg Pty, 1980, later LIFFE Steering Cttee, 1981–82; Dir, LIFFE, 1982–91 (Chm., 1982–85); Mem., Adv. Bd, Internat. Monetary Market Div., Chicago Mercantile Exchange, 1981–84. Director: Household Mortgage Corp., 1985–; Savills, 1988–; Sun Life Assce Soc., 1988–; London Adv. Bd, Bank Julius Baer, 1988–; Chm., Uplink Ltd (EPN Satellite Service), 1988–90. Chm., Cttee on Market in Single Properties, 1985–. Gen. Comr for Income Tax, City of London, 1981–. Chairman: Reserve Forces Assoc., 1983–87; Sussex TA Cttee, 1983–85; SE TAVRA, 1985–91; Dep. Chm., TA Sport Bd, 1983– (Mem., 1979–). Fin. Advisor, Victory Services Club, 1981–; Dir, Officers' Pensions Soc. Investment Co. Ltd, 1982–; Mem., Regular Forces Employment Assoc. Council, 1986–. Chm., E. Sussex Br., Magistrates' Assoc., 1986–91. Mem., Chiddingly Parish Council, 1979–86; Chm., Chiddingly & Dist Royal British Legion, 1982–87; Treas., Chiddingly PCC, 1976–86. Governor: Harpur Trust, 1984–89 (Chm., Bedford Sch. Cttee, 1984–89); Eastbourne Coll., 1980– (Vice Chm., 1983–); Roedean Sch., 1984–89; Comr, Duke of York's Royal Military Sch., 1986–. Hon. Col, 6/7 Bn Queen's Regt, 1986–91. Freeman, City of London, 1973; Liveryman, Worshipful Co. of Farmers, 1981. JP Lewes, 1980; DL E Sussex, 1986. *Recreations:* sailing, shooting. *Address:* Hazelhurst Farm, Three Leg Cross, Ticehurst, East Sussex TN5 7LF. *T:* Ticehurst (0580) 200382. *Clubs:* City of London, Cavalry and Guards; MCC; Royal Fowey Yacht (Cornwall).

BARKWORTH, Peter Wynn; actor, since 1948; director, since 1980; *b* 14 Jan. 1929; *s* of Walter Wynn Barkworth and Irene May Barkworth. *Educ:* Stockport Sch.; Royal Academy of Dramatic Art. Folkestone and Sheffield Repertory Cos, 1948–51. West End plays include: A Woman of No Importance, Savoy, 1953; Roar Like a Dove, Phoenix, 1957–60; The School for Scandal, Haymarket, 1962; Crown Matrimonial, Haymarket, 1972; Donkeys' Years, Globe, 1976; Can You Hear Me at the Back?, Piccadilly, 1979; A Coat of Varnish, Haymarket, 1982; Siegfried Sassoon, Apollo, 1987; Hidden Laughter, Vaudeville, 1990. Director: Night and Day, Leatherhead, 1980; Sisterly Feelings, nat. tour, 1982; The Eight O'Clock Muse, Riverside Studios, 1989. Television serials: The Power Game, 1966; Manhunt, 1969; Telford's Change, 1979; Winston Churchill: the wilderness years, 1981; The Price, 1985; Late Starter, 1985; The Gospel According to St Matthew, 1986. Film: Champions, 1984. Awards: Best Actor, BAFTA, 1974 and 1977; Royal TV Soc. and Broadcasting Press Guild, 1977 (both 1977 awards for Professional Foul). *Publications:* About Acting, 1980; First Houses, 1983; More About Acting, 1984. *Recreations:*walking, gardening, music, looking at paintings. *Address:* 47 Flask Walk, NW3 1HH. *T:* 071–794 4591. *Club:* British Academy of Film and Television Arts.

BARLING, Gerald Edward; QC 1991; practising in EEC Law, London and Brussels, since 1981; *b* 18 Sept. 1949; *s* of Banks Hubert Barling and Barbara Margarita (*née* Myerscough); *m* 1983, Myriam Frances (*née* Ponsford); three *d*. *Educ:* St Mary's Coll., Blackburn; New Coll., Oxford (Burnett Open Exhibnr in Classics, 1968; Hons Sch. of Jurisprudence (1st Cl.), 1971; MA). Called to the Bar, Middle Temple, 1972 (Harmsworth Entrance Exhibnr, 1971; Astbury Law Scholar, 1973). Practised at Common Law Bar, Manchester, 1973–81; an Asst Recorder, 1990–. Lectr in Law, New Coll., Oxford, 1972–77. *Publications:* (contrib.) Butterworth's European Court Practice, 1991; papers on different aspects of EEC Law. *Recreations:* fishing, tennis, cathedrals. *Address:* 15/19 Devereux Court, WC2R 3JJ. *T:* 071–583 0777; avenue de la Joyeuse Entrée 8, B1040 Brussels, Belgium.

BARLOW, Sir Christopher Hilaro, 7th Bt, *cr* 1803; architect; *b* 1 Dec. 1929; *s* of Sir Richard Barlow, 6th Bt, AFC, and Rosamund Sylvia, *d* of late F. S. Anderton (she *m* 2nd, 1950, Rev. Leonard Haslet Morrison, MA); *S* father, 1946; *m* 1952, J. C. de M. Audley, *e d* of late J. E. Audley, Cheshire; one *s* two *d* (and one *s* decd). *Educ:* Eton; McGill Univ., Montreal. BArch. MRAIC. Past Pres., Newfoundland Architects' Assoc. Lt Governor's Silver Medal, 1953. *Heir:* *s* Crispian John Edmund Audley Barlow, Inspector, Royal Hong Kong Police, [*b* 20 April 1958; *m* 1981, Anne Waiching Siu]. *Address:* 18 Winter Avenue, St John's, Newfoundland A1A 1T3, Canada.

BARLOW, Prof. David Hearnshaw, MD; Nuffield Professor of Obstetrics and Gynaecology, University of Oxford, since 1990; Fellow, Oriel College, Oxford, since 1990; *b* 26 Dec. 1949; *s* of Archibald and Anne Barlow; *m* 1973, Norma Christie Woodrow; one *s* one *d*. *Educ:* Clydebank High Sch.; Univ. of Glasgow (BSc Hons Biochem. 1971; MB ChB 1975; MD 1982); MA Oxon 1985. MRCOG 1980. MRC Trng Fellowship, 1977–78; Hall Tutorial Fellow, Univ. of Glasgow, 1979–81; Sen. Registrar, Queen Mother's Hosp., Glasgow, 1981–84; Clinical Reader in Obstetrics and Gynaecology, Univ. of Oxford, 1984–90; Fellow, Green Coll., Oxford, 1984–90, Hon. Sen. Associate Mem., 1990; Hon. Consultant Obstetrician and Gynaecologist, John Radcliffe Hosp., Oxford, 1984–. Blair Bell Meml Lectr, RCOG, 1985. *Publications:* scientific publications in field of reproduction, particularly on endometriosis, the menopause and IVF. *Recreations:* wide-ranging interest in music, painting. *Address:* Nuffield Department of Obstetrics and Gynaecology, John Radcliffe Hospital, Headington, Oxford OX3 9DU. *T:* Oxford (0865) 221008.

BARLOW, David John; Controller, Information Services and International Relations, BBC, since 1991; *b* 20 Oct. 1937; *s* of Ralph and Joan Barlow; *m* 1981, Sanchia Béatrice Oppenheimer; two *s* one *d*, and three *s* of previous marr. *Educ:* Leighton Park Sch.; The Queen's Coll., Oxford; Leeds Univ. MA, DipEd (Oxon); DipESL (Leeds). British Council, 1962–63; BBC, 1963–: Producer, African Service; Schools Broadcasting, 1965–67; Programme Organiser, Hindi, Tamil, Nepali and Bengali Service, 1967–70; Further Educn Radio, 1970–71; UNESCO, British Council Consultancies, 1970–73; Head of Liaison Internat. Relations, 1974–76; Chief Asst Regions, 1977–79; Gen. Sec., ITCA, 1980–81; BBC: Sec., 1981–84; Controller: Public Affairs and Internat. Relations, 1984–86; Public Affairs, 1986–87; Regional Broadcasting, 1987–90; seconded to EBU as Co-ordinator for Audio Visual Eureka Project, 1990–91. *Recreations:* photography, bird watching, mountain walking, book collecting. *Address:* 1 St Joseph Close, Olney, Bucks MK46 5HD. *T:* Bedford (0234) 712960. *Club:* English-Speaking Union.

BARLOW, David Michael Rigby; Under Secretary, Government Legal Service, since 1989; *b* 8 June 1936; *s* of late Samuel Gordon Barlow and of Eunice Hodson Barlow; *m* 1973, Valeree Elizabeth Rush-Smith; one *s*; one *d* by previous marr. *Educ:* Shrewsbury Sch.; Christ Church, Oxford (MA Law). National Service: Midshipman RNVR in Submarine Br. of RN, 1954–56; Sub-Lieut and Lieut in permanent RNR, 1956–61. Solicitor, England and Wales, 1965, NI, 1991. Appointments as a lawyer in the public service, 1965–73; Asst Sec. in Govt Legal Service, 1973–89. *Recreations:* Spanish language and culture, sailing, cinema. *Address:* Royal Courts of Justice, Chichester Street, Belfast BT1 4NX. *T:* Belfast (0232) 235111.

BARLOW, Donald Spiers Monteagle, MS London; FRCS; Consulting Surgeon: Hospitals for Diseases of the Chest, since 1971 (Consultant Surgeon 1947–71); Southend Group of Hospitals, since 1970 (Consultant Surgeon 1936–70); Luton Group of Hospitals, since 1970 (Consultant Surgeon 1940–70); Italian Hospital, since 1970 (Hon. Consultant Thoracic Surgeon 1955–70); Penrose-May Surgical Tutor to the Royal College of Surgeons of England, since 1969 (Surgical Tutor, 1962–69); *b* 4 July 1905; *s* of late Leonard Barlow, MIEE, and Katharine Barlow; *m* 1934, Violet Elizabeth (*née* Maciver); one *s* three *d* (and one *d* decd). *Educ:* Whitgift Sch.; University Coll. Hospital and Medical Sch. MRCS, LRCP 1927; MB, BS London 1928; MS London 1930; FRCS 1930. Formerly: RMO, Wimbledon Hosp., 1927; House Phys., UCH, 1928; House Surg., UCH, 1929; Ho. Surg., Norfolk and Norwich Hosp., 1930–31; Resident Asst Surg., West London Hosp., 1931–35; Surg. Registrar London Lock Hosp., 1936; Research work at

UCL, 1936–37; Hon. Surg., St John's Hosp., Lewisham, 1937–47; Cons. Thoracic Surg., LCC, 1945–48. Teacher, 1964–67, Lectr, 1967–71, Inst. of Diseases of the Chest, Univ. of London. Chm., S Beds' Div., BMA, 1971–72. Coronation Medal, 1953. *Publications:* contribs to: Progress of Clinical Surgery, 1960 (ed Rodney Smith); Operative Surgery, 2nd edn 1969 (ed Rob and Smith). Many publications in learned jls mostly concerning diseases of oesophagus, chest and abdomen. Also 3 reports (Ceylon Govt White Papers), 1952, 1954, 1967. *Recreations:* golf (Captain, Harpenden Golf Club, 1971–72, Pres., 1976–79), painting. *Address:* Deacons Field, High Elms, Harpenden, Herts AL5 2JU. *T:* Harpenden (05827) 3400.

See also Michael Miller.

BARLOW, Prof. Frank, CBE 1989; MA, DPhil; FBA 1970; FRSL 1971; Professor of History and Head of Department, University of Exeter, 1953–76, now Emeritus Professor; *b* 19 April 1911; *e s* of Percy Hawthorn and Margaret Julia Barlow; *m* 1936, Moira Stella Brigid Garvey; two *s*. *Educ:* Newcastle High Sch.; St John's Coll., Oxford. Open Schol., St John's Coll., Oxford, 1929; 1st Cl. Hons Sch. of Modern History, 1933; Bryce Student, 1933; Oxford Senior Student, 1934.; BLitt, 1934; Fereday Fellow, St John's Coll., Oxford, 1935–38; DPhil 1937. Asst Lecturer, University Coll., London, 1936–40; War service in the Army, 1941–46, commissioned into Intelligence Corps, demobilised as Major; Lecturer 1946, Reader 1949, Dep. Vice-Chancellor, 1961–63, Public Orator, 1974–76, University of Exeter. Hon. DLitt Exon, 1981. *Publications:* The Letters of Arnulf of Lisieux, 1939; Durham Annals and Documents of the Thirteenth Century, 1945; Durham Jurisdictional Peculiars, 1950; The Feudal Kingdom of England, 1955; (ed and trans.) The Life of King Edward the Confessor, 1962; The English Church, 1000–1066, 1963; William I and the Norman Conquest, 1965; Edward the Confessor, 1970; (with Martin Biddle, Olof von Feilitzen and D. J. Keene) Winchester in the Early Middle Ages, 1976; The English Church 1066–1154, 1979; The Norman Conquest and Beyond (selected papers), 1983; William Rufus, 1983; Thomas Becket, 1986; Introduction to Devonshire Domesday Book, 1991. *Recreation:* gardening. *Address:* Middle Court Hall, Kenton, Exeter EX6 8NA. *T:* Starcross (0626) 890438.

BARLOW, George Francis, FRICS; Director, Peabody Trust, since 1987; *b* 26 May 1939; *s* of Agnes Barlow and late George Barlow; *m* 1969, Judith Alice Newton; one *s* two *d*. *Educ:* Wimbledon Coll.; Hammersmith Sch. of Art and Building; Polytechnic of Central London. Surveyor, Building Design Partnership, 1962–67; Develt Surveyor, GLC Housing Dept, 1967–70; The Housing Develt Officer, London Borough of Camden, 1970–76; Dir/Sec., Metropolitan Housing Trust, 1976–87 (incl. Winding-up Sec. of Omnium (Central) and Strongbridge & SE Regional Housing Assocs). External Examiner, Polytechnic of Central London, 1989–90. Sec., Metropolitan Home Ownership Ltd, 1981–87; Chm., London Housing Assocs Council, 1978–82; Member: Central YMCA Housing Assoc., 1982–85; Council, Nat. Fedn of Housing Assocs, 1985–89; Housing Cttee, RICS, 1986–; Council, Business in the Community, 1989–; Cttee, Community Self Build Agency, 1989–; Cttee, Broomleigh Housing Trust, 1989–; Trustee, Kent Community Housing Trust, 1989–. *Publications:* articles in Housing Review and Voluntary Housing. *Recreations:* swimming, music, supporter of Crystal Palace FC. *Address:* (office) 207 Waterloo Road, SE1 8XW. *T:* 071–928 7811.

BARLOW, Sir (George) William, Kt 1977; BSc Tech, FEng, FIMechE, FIEE; Chairman: BICC plc, 1984–91 (Director, since 1980); Ericsson Ltd, since 1981; SKF (UK) Ltd, since 1990; Director, Racal Telecom plc, since 1988; *b* 8 June 1924; *s* of Albert Edward and Annice Barlow; *m* 1948, Elaine Mary Atherton (*née* Adamson); one *s* one *d*. *Educ:* Manchester Grammar Sch.; Manchester Univ. (Kitchener Schol., Louis Atkinson Schol.; BSc Tech. 1st cl. Hons Elec. Engrg, 1944). Served as Elec. Lt, RNVR, 1944–47. Various appts, The English Electric Co. Ltd (in Spain, 1952–55, Canada, 1958–62); Gen. Manager, Liverpool and Netherton, 1964–67; Managing Director: English Electric Domestic Appliance Co. Ltd, 1965–67; English Electric Computers Ltd, 1967–68. Gp Chief Exec., 1969–77, Chm., 1971–77, Ransome Hoffman Pollard Ltd. Chm., Post Office, 1977–80, organized separation of Post Office and British Telecom, 1980. Chm., NICG, 1980–. Member: Industrial Develt Adv. Bd, 1972–79; Electronics EDC, 1981–83; Council, IEE, 1969–72 (Vice-Pres., 1978–80, Dep. Pres., 1983–84; Hon. Fellow, 1990); Council, IMechE, 1971–74; National Electronics Council, 1982–; President: IWM, 1976–77; BEAMA, 1986–87; ORGALIME, 1990–; Fellowship of Engrg, 1991–; Chm., Ferrous Foundries Adv. Cttee, 1975–78; Vice Pres., City and Guilds of London Inst., 1982–. Chairman: Design Council, 1980–86; Engineering Council, 1988–90. Trustee, Brain Res. Trust, 1987–. Governor, London Business Sch., 1979–. Liveryman, Worshipful Company of Glaziers; Master, Worshipful Company of Engineers, 1986–87. CBIM 1971. Hon. FUMIST 1978; Hon. FICE 1991. Hon. DSc: Cranfield, 1979; Bath, 1986; Aston, 1988; City, 1989; Hon. DTech CNAA, 1988. *Recreation:* golf. *Address:* 4 Parkside, Henley-on-Thames, Oxon RG9 1TX. *Clubs:* Army and Navy, Brooks's; Huntercombe, Royal Birkdale Golf.

BARLOW, Dr Horace Basil, FRS 1969; Royal Society Research Professor, Physiological Laboratory, Cambridge University, 1973–87; *b* 8 Dec. 1921; *s* of Sir (James) Alan (Noel) Barlow, 2nd Bt, GCB, KBE and Nora Barlow (*née* Darwin); *m* 1st, 1954, Ruthala (marr. diss., 1970), *d* of Dr M. H. Salaman, *qv*; four *d*; 2nd, 1980, Miranda, *d* of John Weston Smith; one *s* two *d*. *Educ:* Winchester; Trinity Coll., Cambridge. Research Fellow, Trinity Coll., 1950–54, Lectr, King's Coll., Cambridge, 1954–64. Demonstrator and Asst Dir of Research, Physiological Lab., Cambridge, 1954–64; Prof. of Physiological Optics and Physiology, Univ. of Calif, Berkeley, 1964–73. *Publications:* several, on neurophysiology of vision in Jl of Physiology, and elsewhere. *Address:* Trinity College, Cambridge CB2 1TQ.

See also Sir T. E. Barlow, Bt.

BARLOW, Sir John (Kemp), 3rd Bt *cr* 1907, of Bradwall Hall, Sandbach; merchant banker and farmer; Chairman: Thomas Barlow and Bro. Ltd; Barlow Services Ltd; Majedie Investments plc; Director of other companies; *b* 22 April 1934; *s* of Sir John Denman Barlow, 2nd Bt and Hon. Diana Helen (*d* 1986), *d* of 1st Baron Rochdale, CB and *sister* of Viscount Rochdale, *qv*; *S* father, 1986; *m* 1962, Susan, *er d* of Col Sir Andrew Horsbrugh-Porter, *qv*; four *s*. *Educ:* Winchester; Trinity Coll., Cambridge (MA 1958). Chm., Rubber Growers' Assoc., 1974. Steward of the Jockey Club, 1988–90. High Sheriff, Cheshire, 1979. *Recreations:* steeplechasing, hunting, shooting. *Heir:* *s* John William Marshall Barlow, *b* 12 March 1964. *Address:* Bulkeley Grange, Malpas, Cheshire SY14 8BT. *Clubs:* Brooks's, City of London, Jockey.

BARLOW, Patrick; actor, writer, director; *b* 18 March 1947; *s* of Edward Morgan and Sheila Maud Barlow; two *s*. *Educ:* Uppingham Sch.; Birmingham Univ. (BA 1968). Founder mem., Inter-Action Community Arts, 1968–72; Dir, Lancaster Young People's Theatre, 1972–74; Founder Dir, Solent People's Theatre, 1974–76; created Henrietta Sluggett and appeared nationwide in clubs, streets, theatres, incl. Crucible, Sheffield, Haymarket, Leicester and NT, 1976–79; created *National Theatre of Brent*, 1980, appeared in and wrote jointly: stage: Charge of the Light Brigade, 1980; Zulu!, 1981; Black Hole of Calcutta, 1982; Götterdämmerung, 1982; Messiah, 1983; Complete Guide to Sex, 1984; Greatest Story Ever Told, 1987; television: Messiah, 1983; Mighty Moments from World History, Lawrence of Arabia, Dawn of Man, Boadicea, Arthur and Guinevere, 1985; Revolution!!, 1989; *other stage appearances* incl.: Truscott, in Loot, Manchester Royal Exchange, 1987; Humphry, in Common Pursuit, Phoenix, 1988; Pseudolus, in A Funny Thing Happened on the Way to the Forum, Manchester Liby Th., 1988; Sidney, in Silly Cow, Haymarket, 1991; *television* incl.: Talk to Me, 1983; All Passion Spent, 1986; Thank You Miss Jones, 1987; also series, Victoria Wood As Seen On TV, French and Saunders, Riotous Assembly, Growing Pains of Adrian Mole; frequent radio broadcasts. Writer for television: The Ghost of Faffner Hall (jtly), 1989; adaptation, The Growing Pains of Adrian Mole, 1986; screenplay, Van Gogh (Prix Futura, Berlin Film Fest.), 1990; also libretto, Judgement of Paris, Garden Venture, Royal Opera, 1991. *Publication:* All the World's a Globe, 1987 (adapted for radio (Sony Radio award), 1990). *Address:* London Management, 235 Regent Street, W1R 7AG. *T:* 071–493 1610.

BARLOW, Roy Oxspring; solicitor; a Recorder of the Crown Court, since 1975; *b* 13 Feb. 1927; *s* of George and Clarice Barlow; *m* 1957, Kathleen Mary Roberts; two *s* one *d*. *Educ:* King Edward VII Sch., Sheffield; Queen's Coll., Oxford; Sheffield Univ. (LLB). Local Government, 1952–62; solicitor in private practice, 1962–. *Recreations:* farming, walking, reading. *Address:* The Cottage, Oxton Rakes, Barlow, Sheffield S18 5TH. *T:* Sheffield (0742) 890652.

BARLOW, Sir Thomas (Erasmus), 3rd Bt *cr* 1902; DSC 1945; DL; *b* 23 Jan. 1914; *s* of Sir Alan Barlow, 2nd Bt, GCB, KBE, and Nora (*d* 1989), *d* of late Sir Horace Darwin, KBE; *S* father, 1968; *m* 1955, Isabel, *d* of late Dr T. M. Body, Middlesbrough, Yorks; two *s* two *d*. *Educ:* Winchester College. Entered RN as cadet, 1932; qualified Submarines, 1937; served in Submarines in Atlantic, Mediterranean, Indian Ocean and Far East during War of 1939–45; Naval Staff Course, 1946; Joint Services Staff Course, 1947, Commander, 1950. British Joint Services Mission, Washington, 1950–53; Captain 1954; Imperial Defence Coll., 1957; Chief Staff Officer to Flag Officer Submarines, 1960–62; Commodore, HMS Drake, Devonport, 1962–64; retired, 1964. Actively concerned in Wildlife and Countryside Conservation: Royal Soc. for Nature Conservation; Berks, Bucks and Oxfordshire Naturalists' Trust; Charles Darwin Foundn for Galapogos Is. DL Bucks, 1977. *Recreations:* bird watching, the countryside. *Heir:* *s* James Alan Barlow, *b* 10 July 1956. *Address:* 45 Shepherds Hill, Highgate, N6 5QJ. *T:* 081–340 9653. *Clubs:* Athenæum, Savile.

See also H. B Barlow.

BARLOW, Sir William; *see* Barlow, Sir G. W.

BARLTROP, Roger Arnold Rowlandson, CMG 1987; CVO 1982; HM Diplomatic Service, retired; Ambassador to Fiji, 1988–89 (High Commissioner, 1982–88) and High Commissioner (non-resident) to Republic of Nauru and to Tuvalu, 1982–89; *b* 19 Jan. 1930; *s* of late Ernest William Barltrop, CMG, CBE, DSO, and Ethel Alice Lucy Barltrop (*née* Baker); *m* 1962, Penelope Pierrepont Dalton; two *s* two *d*. *Educ:* Solihull Sch.; Leeds Grammar Sch.; Exeter Coll., Oxford. MA. Served RN, 1949–50, RNVR/RNR, 1950–64 (Lt-Comdr 1962). Asst Principal, CRO, 1954–56; Second Sec., New Delhi, 1956–57; Private Sec. to Parly Under-Sec. of State and Minister of State, CRO, 1957–60; First Sec., E Nigeria, 1960–62; Actg Dep. High Comr, W Nigeria, 1962; First Sec., Salisbury, Rhodesia, 1962–65; CO and FO, later FCO, 1965–69; First Sec. and Head of Chancery, Ankara, 1969–70; Dep. British Govt Rep., WI Associated States, 1971–73; Counsellor and Head of Chancery, Addis Ababa, 1973–77; Head of Commonwealth Coordination Dept, FCO, 1978–82. Mem., Commonwealth Observer Gp for Bangladesh elections, Feb. 1991. *Recreations:* sailing, genealogy, opera. *Address:* c/o Commonwealth Trust, 18 Northumberland Avenue, WC2N 5BJ. *Clubs:* Commonwealth Trust; Royal Suva Yacht (Suva).

BARNA, Prof. Tibor, CBE 1974; Professor of Economics, University of Sussex, 1962–82, Professor Emeritus 1984; Member, Monopolies and Mergers Commission, 1963–78; *b* 1919. *Educ:* London School of Economics. Lecturer, London School of Economics, 1944; Official Fellow, Nuffield College, Oxford, 1947; senior posts in UN Economic Commission for Europe, 1949; Assistant Director, National Institute of Economic and Social Research, London, 1955. *Publications:* Redistribution of Income through Public Finance in 1937, 1945; Investment and Growth Policies in British Industrial Firms, 1962; Agriculture towards the Year 2000, 1979; European Process Plant Industry, 1981; papers in Jl Royal Statistical Soc., Economic Jl, European Econ. Review. *Address:* Beanacre, Westmeston, Hassocks, West Sussex BN6 8XE. *T:* Hassocks (07918) 2384.

BARNARD, 11th Baron, *cr* 1698; **Harry John Neville Vane,** TD 1960; Landowner; Lord-Lieutenant and Custos Rotulorum of County Durham, 1970–88; a Vice-Chairman, Council, British Red Cross Society, since 1987 (Member Council 1982–85); *b* 21 Sept. 1923; *er s* of 10th Baron Barnard, CMG, OBE, MC, TD, and Sylvia Mary, *d* of Herbert Straker; *S* father, 1964; *m* 1952, Lady Davina Mary Cecil, DStJ, *e d* of 6th Marquess of Exeter, KCMG; one *s* four *d*. *Educ:* Eton. MSc Durham, 1986. Served War of 1939–45, RAFVR, 1942–46 (Flying Officer, 1945). Northumberland Hussars (TA), 1948–66; Lt-Col Commanding, 1964–66. Vice-Pres., N of England TA&VRA, 1970 and 1977–88, Pres., 1974–77. Hon. Col, 7 (Durham) Bn The Light Infantry, 1979–89. County Councillor, Durham, 1952–61. Member: Durham Co. AEC, 1953–72 (Chm., 1970–72); N Regional Panel, MAFF, 1972–76; CLA Council, 1950–80; Dir, NE Housing Assoc., 1964–77. President: Durham Co. Br., BRCS, 1969–87; Farmway Ltd, 1965–; Durham Co. Br., CLA, 1965–89; Durham Co. St John Council, 1971–88; Durham Co. Scouts Assoc., 1972–88; Durham and Cleveland Co. Br. RBL, 1973–; Durham Wildlife Trust (formerly Durham Co. Conservation Trust), 1984–. DL Durham, 1956, Vice-Lieutenant, 1969–70; JP Durham, 1961. Joint Master of Zetland Hounds, 1963–65. KStJ 1971. *Heir:* *s* Hon. Henry Francis Cecil Vane, *b* 11 March 1959. *Address:* Raby Castle, PO Box 50, Staindrop, Darlington, Co. Durham DL2 3AY. *T:* Staindrop (0833) 60751. *Clubs:* Brooks's; Durham County (Durham); Northern Counties (Newcastle upon Tyne).

BARNARD, Sir (Arthur) Thomas, Kt 1958; CB 1954; OBE 1946; Director-General of Inspection, Ministry of Supply, 1956–58, retired; *b* 28 Sept. 1893; *s* of late Arthur Barnard; *m* 1921, Grace (*d* 1986), *d* of William Magerkorth, Belvedere, Kent. *Educ:* Erith Technical Coll. Is a Chartered Civil Engineer. Chief Superintendent, Royal Ordnance Factories, Woolwich, 1951–55; Dep. Dir-Gen., Royal Ordnance Factories, Adelphi, London, 1955–56.

BARNARD, Prof. Christiaan Neethling, MD, MMed, PhD; Professor of Surgical Science, Cape Town University, 1968–83, Professor Emeritus, 1984; Senior Consultant and Scientist in Residence, Oklahoma Heart Centre, Baptist Medical Centre, since 1985; *b* 8 Nov. 1922; *s* of Adam Hendrik Barnard and Maria Elizabeth Barnard (*née* De Swart); *m* 1st, 1948, Aletta Gertruida Louw (marr. diss. 1970); one *d* (one *s* decd); 2nd, 1970, Barbara Maria Zoellner (marr. diss. 1982); two *s*; 3rd, 1988, Karin Setzkorn; one *s*. *Educ:* Beaufort West High Sch.; Univs of Cape Town and Minnesota. MB, ChB 1946, MD 1953, Cape Town; MS, PhD 1958, Minnesota. Private practice, Ceres, CP, 1948–51; Sen. Resident MO, City Hosp., Cape Town, 1951–53; subseq. Registrar, Groote Schuur Hosp.; Registrar, Surgery Dept, Cape Town Univ.; Charles Adams Meml Schol. and Dazian Foundn Bursary for study in USA; US Public Health Grant for further res. in cardiac surgery; Specialist Cardio-Thoracic Surgeon, Lectr and Dir of Surg. Res., Cape Town Univ. and Groote Schuur Hosp., 1958; Head of Cardio-Thoracic Surgery, Cape Town Univ. Teaching Hosps, 1961; Assoc. Prof., Cape Town Univ., 1962. Oppenheimer Meml Trust Bursary for overseas study, 1960. Performed world's first human heart transplant operation, 3 Dec. 1967, and world's first double-heart transplant, 25 Nov. 1974. Holds numerous hon. doctorates, foreign orders and awards, hon. citizenships and freedoms, medallions, etc; Dag Hammarskjöld Internat. Prize and Peace Prize, Kennedy Foundn Award, Milan Internat. Prize for Science, etc; hon. fellow or member various colleges, societies, etc. FACS 1963; Fellow NY Cardiological Soc. 1965; FACC 1967. *Publications:* (with V. Schrire) Surgery of Common Congenital Cardiac Malformations, 1968; One Life, 1969; Heart Attack: You Don't Have to Die, 1971; The Unwanted, 1974; South Africa: Sharp Dissection, 1977; In The Night Season, 1977; Best Medicine, 1979; Good Life—Good Death, 1980; (jtly) The Arthritis Handbook, 1984; numerous contribs to med. jls. *Recreations:* viticulture, ornithology, farming. *Address:* PO Box 988, Cape Town 8000, Republic of South Africa.

BARNARD, Prof. Eric Albert, PhD; FRS 1981; Director, MRC Molecular Neurobiology Unit, Cambridge, since 1985; *b* 2 July 1927; *m* 1956, Penelope J. Hennessy; two *s* two *d*. *Educ:* Davenant Foundn Sch.; King's Coll., London. BSc, PhD 1956. King's College, London: Nuffield Foundn Fellow, 1956–59; Asst Lectr, 1959–60; Lectr, 1960–64. State University of New York at Buffalo: Associate Prof. of Biochemical Pharmacol., 1964–65; Prof. of Biochemistry, 1965–76; Head of Biochemistry Dept, 1969–76; Imperial College of Science and Technology, London: Rank Prof. of Physiol Biochemistry, 1976–85; Chm., Div. of Life Sciences, 1977–85; Head, Dept of Biochem., 1979–85. Rockefeller Fellow, Univ. of Calif, Berkeley, 1960–61; Guggenheim Fellow, MRC Lab. of Molecular Biol., Cambridge, 1971. Vis. Prof., Univ. of Marburg, Germany, 1965; Vis. Scientist, Inst. Pasteur, France, 1973. Member: Amer. Soc. Biol Chemists; Internat. Soc. Neurochem; Committee Member: MRC; CNRS. Josiah Macy Faculty Scholar Award, USA, 1975; Medal of Polish Acad. of Scis, 1980; Ciba Medal and Prize, 1985. *Publications:* editor of five scientific books; mem., editorial bds of four scientific jls; numerous papers in learned jls. *Recreation:* the pursuit of good claret. *Address:* MRC Molecular Neurobiology Unit, MRC Centre, University of Cambridge, Hills Road, Cambridge CB2 2QH. *T:* Cambridge (0223) 248011.

BARNARD, Surg. Rear Adm. Ernest Edward Peter, DPhil; FFCM; Surgeon Rear Admiral, Operational Medical Services, 1982–84; retired 1984; *b* 22 Feb. 1927; *s* of Lionel Edward Barnard and Ernestine (*née* Lethbridge); *m* 1955, Dr Joan Barnard (*née* Gunn); one *s* one *d*. *Educ:* schools in England and Australia; Univ. of Adelaide; St Mary's Hosp., Univ. of London (MB, BS 1955); St John's Coll., Univ. of Oxford (student, 1966–68; DPhil 1969). MRCS, LRCP 1955; MFOM 1979; FFCM 1980. After house appts, joined RN, 1956; served, 1957–76: HMS Bulwark, Reclaim and Dolphin; RN Physiol Lab.; RN Med. Sch.; Inst. of Naval Medicine; Dept of Med. Dir Gen. (Naval); exchange service with US Navy at Naval Med. Res. Inst., Bethesda, Md, 1976–78; Inst. of Naval Medicine, 1978–80; QHP 1980–84; Dep. Med. Dir Gen. (Naval), 1980–82; Surgeon Rear-Adm., Inst. of Naval Medicine, and Dean of Naval Medicine, 1982. FRSM 1962. *Publications:* papers on underwater medicine and physiology. *Recreations:* gardening, literature, photography. *Address:* c/o Barclays Bank, 12 The Square, Wickham, Hants PO17 5JQ.

BARNARD, Prof. George Alfred, MA, DSc; Emeritus Professor of Mathematics, University of Essex; statistical consultant to various organisations; *b* 23 Sept. 1915; *s* of Frederick C. and Ethel C. Barnard; *m* 1st, 1942, Helen J. B. Davies; three *s*; 2nd, 1949, Mary M. L. Jones; one *s*. *Educ:* Sir George Monoux Grammar Sch., Walthamstow; St John's Coll., Cambridge. Math. Trip., Pt III, 1936, Res. Studentship, St John's Coll., spent at Grad. Sch. Princeton, NJ, USA, 1937–39. Plessey Co., Ilford, as Math. Consultant, 1940–42; Ministry of Supply Adv. Unit, 1942–45; Maths Dept, Imperial Coll., London: Lectr, 1945–47; Reader in Math. Statistics, 1948–54, Professor, 1954–66; Prof. of Mathematics, Univ. of Essex, 1966–75; Prof. of Statistics, Univ. of Waterloo, 1975–81. Visiting Professor: Yale, 1966; Univ. of Waterloo, 1972–73; Univ. of Nottingham, 1975–77. Member: UGC, 1967–72; Computer Bd, 1970–72; SSRC, 1971–74. Royal Statistical Society: Council Mem. and Vice-Pres., 1952, 1962, Pres. 1971–72 (Chm. Res. Sect., 1958; Guy Medal in Silver, 1958, in Gold, 1975); Mem. Internat. Statistical Inst., 1952; Statistical Adviser, Brit. Standards Instn (with Prof. E. S. Pearson), 1954; Chm. Inst. of Statisticians, 1960–62; President: Operational Res. Soc., 1962–64; Inst. of Mathematics and its Applications, 1970–71 (Gold Medal, 1986); Fellow: Amer. Statistical Assoc.; Inst. of Mathematical Statistics; Amer. Assoc. for Advancement of Science. Hon. Dr Math. Waterloo, 1983; DUniv Open, 1986. *Publications:* (ed) The Foundations of Statistical Inference, 1962; papers in Jl Royal Statistical Society; Technometrics; Biometrika. *Recreations:* viola playing, boating. *Address:* Mill House, Hurst Green, Brightlingsea, Essex CO7 0EH. *T:* Brightlingsea (020630) 2388.

See also D. E. C. Wedderburn.

BARNARD, Captain Sir George (Edward), Kt 1968; Deputy Master of Trinity House, 1961–72; *b* 11 Aug. 1907; 2nd *s* of Michael and Alice Louise Barnard; *m* 1940, Barbara Emma Hughes (*d* 1976); one *s*. Apprenticed at sea, 1922; 1st Command, Blue Star Line, 1945. Elder Brother of Trinity House, 1958–. Trustee, Nat. Maritime Museum, 1967–74; Treasurer, Internat. Assoc. of Lighthouse Authorities, 1961–72; Hon. Sec., King George's Fund for Sailors, 1967–75; first Chm., Nautical Inst., 1972–73, Pres., 1973–75, Fellow, 1975; former Mem. Cttee of Management, RNLI. FRSA 1969. *Address:* Warden, Station Road, Much Hadham, Herts SG10 6AX. *T:* Much Hadham (027984) 3133.

BARNARD, Prof. John Michael; Professor of English Literature, School of English, University of Leeds, since 1978; *b* Folkestone, 13 Feb. 1936; *s* of John Claude Southard Barnard and Dora Grace Barnard; *m* 1961, Katherine Buckham (marr. diss. 1973); one *s* two *d*; partner 1975, Hermione Lee. *Educ:* Wadham Coll., Oxford (BA (Hons) Eng. Lang. and Lit.; BLitt; MA). Res. Asst, English Dept, Yale Univ., 1961–64; Vis. Lectr, English Dept, Univ. of California at Santa Barbara, 1964–65; Leeds University: Lectr and Sen. Lectr, Sch. of English, 1965–78; Actg Dir, Inst. of Bibliography and Textual Criticism, Sch. of English, 1982–. Member: British Cttee, Eighteenth Century Short Title Catalogue, 1983–89; Council, Bibliographical Soc., 1989–. British Academy Warton Lecture, 1989. Gen. Editor, Longman Annotated Poets, 1976–. *Publications:* (ed) William Congreve, The Way of the World, 1972; (ed) Pope: The Critical Heritage, 1973; (ed) John Keats: the complete poems, 1973, 3rd edn 1988; (ed) Etherege: The Man of Mode, 1979; John Keats, 1987; (ed) John Keats: selected poems, 1988; articles in Brit. and Amer. learned jls, occasional reviews, etc. *Recreations:* travel, cricket. *Address:* Lane End, Weeton Lane, Weeton, near Leeds LS17 0AN. *T:* Harrogate (0423) 734814. *Club:* Johnson.

BARNARD, Sir Joseph (Brian), Kt 1986; JP; DL; Vice-Chairman, National Union of Conservative and Unionist Associations, since 1988 (Chairman, Yorkshire Area, 1983–88); *b* 22 Jan. 1928; *s* of Joseph Ernest Barnard and Elizabeth Loudon (*née* Constantine); *m* 1959, Suzanne Hamilton Bray; three *s* (incl. twins). *Educ:* Bramcote School, Scarborough; Sedbergh School. Served Army, 1946–48, commissioned KRRC. Director: Joseph Constantine Steamship Line, 1952–66; Teesside Warehousing Co., 1966–. Farms at East Harlsey. Dir, Northern Electric (formerly NE Electricity Bd), 1986–90; Chm., NE Electricity Cons. Council, 1986–90; Mem., Electricity Consumers' Council, 1986–90. Chm. Governors, Ingleby Arncliffe C of E Primary School, 1979–; Patron, St Oswald's, E Harlsey. JP Northallerton, 1973; Chm., Northallerton (formerly Allertonshire PSD), 1981–; Mem., N Yorks Magistrates' Courts Cttee, 1981–. DL N Yorks, 1988. *Recreations:* walking, shooting, gardening. *Address:* Harlsey Hall, Northallerton, N Yorks DL6 2BL. *T:* Northallerton (0609) 82203. *Club:* Carlton.

BARNARD, Hon. Lance Herbert, AO 1979; retired; Director, Office of Australian War Graves, Department of Veterans' Affairs, Commonwealth of Australia, 1981–83; *b* 1 May 1919; *s* of Hon. H. C. Barnard and M. M. Barnard (*née* McKenzie); *m* 2nd, 1962, Jill Denise Carstairs, *d* of Senator H. G. J. Cant; one *s* two *d* (and one *d* decd); also one *d* by a former marriage. *Educ:* Launceston Technical Coll. Served War, overseas, AIF 9th Div., 1940. Formerly teacher, Tasmanian Educn Dept. Elected to House of Representatives as Member for Bass, 1954, 1955, 1958, 1961, 1963, 1966, 1969, 1972, 1974. From Dec. 1972: Minister of Defence, Navy, Army, Air, Supply, Postmaster-Gen., Labour and National Service, Immigration, Social Services, Repatriation, Health, Primary Industry, National Development, and of the Interior. Dep. Leader, Federal Parliamentary Labor Party, 1967–72; Deputy Prime Minister, 1972–74; Minister for Defence (Navy, Army, Air and Supply), 1973–75. Australian Ambassador to Sweden, Norway and Finland, 1975–78. Captain, Aust. Cadet Corps, post War of 1939–45. State Pres., Tasmanian Br., Aust. Labor Party; Tasmanian deleg., Federal Exec., Aust. Labor Party. *Publication:* Labor's Defence Policy, 1969. *Recreation:* gardening. *Address:* 6 Bertland Court, Launceston, Tasmania 7250, Australia.

BARNARD, Sir Thomas; *see* Barnard, Sir A. T.

BARNE, Major Nicholas Michael Lancelot; Private Secretary, Comptroller and Equerry to Princess Alice, Duchess of Gloucester, and to the Duke and Duchess of Gloucester, since 1989; *b* 25 Nov. 1943; *m* 1974, Hon. Janet Elizabeth, *d* of Baron Maclean, KT, GCVO, KBE, PC; two *s*. *Educ:* Eton Coll. Regular officer, Scots Guards, 1965–79; fruit farming, 1979–84; Co. Comdt, Norfolk Army Cadet Force, 1985–89. *Recreations:* golf, ski-ing, shooting. *Address:* Blofield House, Blofield, Norwich, Norfolk NR13 4RW; Tower Flat, Kensington Palace, W8 4PU.

BARNEBY, Lt-Col Henry Habington, TD 1946; retired from HM Forces 1955; Vice Lord-Lieutenant of Hereford and Worcester, 1974–77; *b* 19 June 1909; *er s* of Richard Hicks Barneby, Longworth Hall, Hereford; *m* 1st, 1935, Evelyn Georgina Heywood; 2nd, 1944, Angela Margaret Campbell (*d* 1979); four *s* one *d* (and one *s* decd). *Educ:* Radley Coll.; RMC Sandhurst. QALAS 1939. 2nd Lieut KSLI 1929, retd 1935; Lieut Hereford Regt TA 1936; commanded: Hereford Regt (TA), 1945–46; Hereford LI (TA), 1947–51; Jamaica Bn, 1951–53; regranted commn in KSLI as Major, 1947; retd 1955. Mem., Herefordshire T&AFA, 1955–68; Mem., W Midlands T&AVR, 1968–77. Member: Hereford RDC, 1955–67 (Chm., 1964–67); Dore and Bredwardine RDC, 1966–73; S Herefordshire RDC, 1973–76. DL Herefordshire 1958–83, Vice Lieut, 1973–74, High Sheriff 1972; JP Hereford County PSD, 1957–79 (Chm., 1977–79). *Address:* Llanerch-y-Coed, Dorstone, Herefordshire HR3 6AG. *T:* Clifford (04973) 215.

BARNES; *see* Oppenheim-Barnes.

BARNES, family name of **Baron Gorell.**

BARNES, Adrian Francis Patrick; Remembrancer of the City of London, since 1986; *b* 25 Jan. 1943; *s* of Francis Walter Ibbetson Barnes, *qv* and Heather Katherine (*née* Tamplin); *m* 1980, Sally Eve Whatley; one *s* one *d*. *Educ:* St Paul's School; MA City of London Polytechnic 1981. Called to the Bar, Gray's Inn, 1973; Solicitor's Dept, DTI, 1975; Dep. Remembrancer, Corp. of London, 1982. Liveryman, Merchant Taylors' Co., 1989–. *Recreations:* music, cricket, biography, circuit training, swimming, City lore. *Address:* Guildhall, EC2P 2EJ. *T:* 071–260 1200, *Fax:* 071–260 1895.

BARNES, Alan Robert, CBE 1976; JP; Headmaster, Ruffwood School, Kirkby, Liverpool, 1959–87; Field Officer, Secondary Heads Association, since 1987; Schools Liaison Officer, University of Essex, since 1988; *b* 9 Aug. 1927; *s* of Arthur Barnes and Ida Barnes; *m* 1951, Pearl Muriel Boughton; (two *s* decd). *Educ:* Enfield Grammar Sch.; Queens' Coll., Cambridge (MA). National Service, RAEC. Wallington County Grammar Sch., 1951–55; Churchfields Sch., West Bromwich, 1955–59. Pres., Headmasters' Assoc., 1974, Treas., 1975–77; Chm., Jt Four Secondary Assocs, 1978; Treas., Secondary Heads Assoc., 1978–82; Vice-Chm., British Educn Management and Admin Soc., 1980–82, Chm. 1982–84. JP Knowsley, Merseyside, 1967. *Publications:* (contrib.) Going Comprehensive (ed Halsall), 1970; (contrib.) Management and Headship in the Secondary School (ed Jennings), 1978; contrib. to: Education, BEMAS Jl, SHA publications. *Recreation:* bridge. *Address:* 2 Lark Valley Drive, Fornham St Martin, Bury St Edmunds, Suffolk IP28 6UF.

BARNES, Dame (Alice) Josephine (Mary Taylor), (Dame Josephine Warren), DBE 1974; FRCP, FRCS, FRCOG; Consulting Obstetrician and Gynaecologist, Charing Cross Hospital and Elizabeth Garrett Anderson Hospital; President, Women's National Cancer Control Campaign, since 1974 (Chairman 1969–72; Vice-President, 1972–74); *b* 18 Aug. 1912; *er d* of late Rev. Walter W. Barnes, MA(Oxon), and Alice Mary Ibbetson, FRCO, ARCM; *m* 1942, Sir Brian Warren, *qv* (marr. diss. 1964); one *s* two *d*. *Educ:* Oxford High Sch.; Lady Margaret Hall, Oxford (Hon. Fellow, 1980); University College Hosp. Med. Sch. 1st class Hons Physiology, Oxford, BA 1934, MA, BM, BCh 1937, DM 1941. University College Hospital: Goldschmid Scholar; Aitchison Scholar; Tuke Silver Medal; Fellowes Silver Medal; F. T. Roberts Prize; Suckling Prize. Various appointments at UCH, Samaritan Hosp., Queen Charlotte's Hosp., and Radcliffe Infirmary, Oxford; Dep. Academic Head, Obstetric Unit, UCH, 1947–52; Surgeon, Marie Curie Hosp., 1947–67. Medical Women's Federation: Hon. Sec., 1951–57; Pres., London Assoc., 1958–60; Pres., 1966–67. Royal Society of Medicine: Mem. Council, 1949–50; Pres., Sect. of Obstetrics and Gynaecology, 1972–73; Hon. Editor, Sect. of Obstetrics, 1951–71; Hon. Fellow, 1988. President: W London Medico-Chirurgical Soc., 1969–70; Nat. Assoc. of Family Planning Doctors, 1976–; Obstetric Physiotherapists Assoc., 1976–; BMA, 1979–80 (Pres.-elect, 1978–79); Union Professionnelle Internationale de Gynécologie et d'Obstétrique, 1977–79; Royal Medical Benevolent Fund, 1982–. Examiner in Obstetrics and Gynaecology: Univ. of London; RCOG; Examining Bd in England, Queen's Univ., Belfast; Univ. of Oxford; Univ. of Kampala; Univ. of Ibadan; Univ. of Maiduguri. Member: Council, Med. Defence Union, 1961–82 (Vice-Pres. 1982–87; Hon. Fellow 1988); Royal Commn on Med. Educn, 1965–68; Council, RCOG, 1965–71 (Jun. Vice-Pres., 1972–74, Sen. Vice-Pres., 1974–75); MRC Cttee on Analgesia in Midwifery; Min. of Health Med. Manpower Cttee; Medico-Legal Soc.; Population Investigation Cttee, Eugenics Soc.; Cttee on the Working of the Abortion Act, 1971–73; Standing Med. Adv. Cttee, DHSS, 1976–80; Council, Advertising Standards Authority, 1980–; DHSS Inquiry into Human Fertilisation and Embryology, 1982–84; Vice-Pres., Nat. Union of Townswomen's Guilds, 1979–82; President: Nat. Assoc. of Family Planning Nurses, 1980–; Osler Club of London, 1988–89; Friends of GPDST, 1988–. Mem. of Honour,

French Gynaecological Soc., 1945; Hon. Member: Italian Soc. of Obstetrics and Gynaecology, 1979; Nigerian Soc. of Gynaecology and Obstetrics, 1981; Corresp. Mem., Royal Belgian Soc. of Obstetricians and Gynaecologists, 1949. Governor: Charing Cross Hosp.; Chelsea Coll. of Science and Technology, 1958–85; Member Council: Benenden Sch.; Bedford Coll., 1976–85; King's Coll., London, 1985– (FKC 1985); Mem. Court of Patrons, RCOG, 1984. Lectures: Fawcett, Bedford Coll., 1969; Rhys-Williams, Nat. Birthday Trust, 1970; Winston Churchill Meml, Postgrad. Med. Centre, Canterbury, 1971; Bartholomew Mosse, Rotunda Hosp., Dublin, 1975; Simpson Oration, RCOG, 1977; Annual, Liverpool Med. Instn, 1979; Sophia, Univ. of Newcastle upon Tyne, 1980; Ann Horler, Newcastle upon Tyne, 1984; Helena Wright Meml, 1988; Margaret Jackson Meml, 1988. Hon. FRCPI 1977; Hon. Fellow, Edinburgh Obstetrical Soc., 1980; Hon. Fellow, RHBNC, London Univ., 1986. Hon. MD: Liverpool, 1979; Southampton, 1981; Hon. DSc: Leicester, 1980; Oxon, 1990. Commandeur du Bontemps de Médoc et des Graves, 1966. *Publications:* Gynaecological Histology, 1948; The Care of the Expectant Mother, 1954; Lecture Notes on Gynaecology, 1966; (ed, jtly) Scientific Foundations of Obstetrics and Gynaecology, 1970; Essentials of Family Planning, 1976; numerous contribs to med. jls, etc. *Recreations:* music, gastronomy, motoring, foreign travel; formerly hockey (Oxford Univ. Women's Hockey XI, 1932, 1933, 1934). *Address:* 8 Aubrey Walk, W8 7JG. *T:* 071–727 9832.

See also F. W. I. Barnes, A. I. Holden, M. G. J. Neary.

BARNES, Anthony Hugh; Director, Redundant Churches Fund, since 1984; *b* 16 June 1931; *s* of Sir George Barnes and Anne Barnes; *m* 1st, 1956, Susan Dempsey; two *s* one *d*; 2nd, 1984, Jennifer Carey. *Educ:* King's Coll., Cambridge (MA). FIPM. Schweppes Ltd, 1954–66; Royal Opera House, 1966–70; ICI, 1970–82; self-employed, 1982–84. *Recreations:* none have been observed. *Address:* 69 Oxford Gardens, W10 5UJ. *T:* 081–968 8020.

BARNES, Christopher John Andrew; Under Secretary, Arable Crops and Horticulture Group, Ministry of Agriculture, Fisheries and Food, since 1990; *b* 11 Oct. 1944; *s* of late Eric Vernon Barnes and of Joan Mary Barnes; *m* 1978, Carolyn Elizabeth Douglass Johnston (*d* 1990); two *s*; *m* 1990, Susan Elizabeth Bird; one *s*. *Educ:* City of London Sch.; London School of Economics (BScEcon). Exec. Officer, MAFF, 1962; Asst Principal, 1967; Private Sec. to Parly Sec., 1969–71; Principal, 1971; Sec. to Northfield Cttee on Agricultural Land Ownership and Occupancy, 1977–79; Asst Sec., 1980; Chief Reg. Officer, Nottingham and Reading, 1980–83; Hd of Personnel and R&D Requirements Divs, 1983–90; 'Barnes Review' of near market R&D, 1988; Under Sec. (Grade 3), 1990. Non-exec. Dir, Booker Food Services, 1987–90. *Recreations:* off-road racing, country living, France. *Address:* Ministry of Agriculture, Fisheries and Food, Whitehall Place, SW1A 2HH. *T:* 071–270 8139.

BARNES, Clive Alexander, CBE 1975; Associate Editor and Chief Drama and Dance Critic, New York Post, since 1977; *b* London, 13 May 1927; *s* of Arthur Lionel Barnes and Freda Marguerite Garratt; *m* 1958, Patricia Winckley; one *s* one *d*. *Educ:* King's Coll., London; St Catherine's Coll., Oxford. Served RAF, 1946–48. Admin. Officer, Town Planning Dept, LCC, 1952–61; concurrently freelance journalist; Chief Dance Critic, The Times, 1961–65; Exec. Editor, Dance and Dancers, Music and Musicians, and Plays and Players, 1961–65; a London Correspondent, New York Times, 1963–65, Dance Critic, 1965–77, Drama Critic (weekdays only), 1967–77; a NY correspondent, The Times, 1970–. Knight of the Order of Dannebrog (Denmark), 1972. *Publications:* Ballet in Britain since the War, 1953; (ed, with others) Ballet Here and Now, 1961; Frederick Ashton and his Ballets, 1961; Dance Scene, USA (commentary), 1967; (ed with J. Gassner) Best American Plays, 6th series, 1963–67, 1971, and 7th series, 1974; (ed) New York Times Directory of the Theatre, 1973; Nureyev, 1983; contribs to jls, inc. Punch, The New Statesman, The Spectator, The New Republic. *Recreations:* eating, drinking, walking, theatregoing. *Address:* c/o New York Post, 210 South Street, New York, NY 10002, USA. *Club:* Century (NY).

BARNES, Rev. Cyril Arthur; *b* 10 Jan. 1926; *s* of Reginald William and Mary Adeline Barnes; *m* 1951, Patricia Patience Allen. *Educ:* Penistone Grammar School; Edinburgh Theological Coll. (GOE 1950). King's Own Scottish Borderers and RAEC, 1944–47. Curate, St John's, Aberdeen, 1950–53; Rector, St John's, Forres, 1953–55; Priest-in-Charge, Wentbridge, Yorks, 1955–58; Vicar, St Bartholomew's, Ripponden with St John's, Rishworth, 1958–67, also St John's, Thorpe, 1966–67; Rector, Christ Church, Huntly with St Marnan's, Aberchirder, 1967–84, also Holy Trinity, Keith, 1974–84; Canon of Inverness Cathedral, 1971–80; Synod Clerk, 1977–80; Dean of Moray, Ross and Caithness, 1980–84. Editor, Huntly Express, 1985–91. *Recreations:* gardening, do-it-yourself. *Address:* Tillytarmont Cottage, Bridge of Isla, Huntly, Aberdeenshire AB5 4SP.

BARNES, Daniel Sennett, CBE 1977; CEng, FIEE; Chairman, Berkshire and Oxfordshire Manpower Board, 1983–88; *b* 13 Sept. 1924; *s* of Paula Sennett Barnes and John Daniel Barnes; *m* 1955, Jean A. Steadman; one *s*. *Educ:* Dulwich Coll.; Battersea Polytechnic (BScEng, 1st Cl. Hons). Apprenticeship at Philips, 1941–46; served REME, 1946–48; Battersea Polytechnic, 1948–51; Sperry Gyroscope, 1951–82: Dir of Engineering, 1962–68; Manager, Defence Systems, 1968–70; Gen. Manager, 1970–71; Man. Dir, 1971–82; British Aerospace PLC (formerly Sperry Gyroscope): Man. Dir, Electronic Systems and Equipment Div., 1982–85; HQ Dir, 1985–86; Director: Sperry Ltd UK, 1971–82; Sperry AG Switzerland, 1979–83. Pres., Electronic Engrg Assoc., 1981–82. *Recreations:* sailing, joinery, music and ballet, gardening.

BARNES, David; *see* Barnes, J. D. F.

BARNES, (David) Michael (William), QC 1981; a Recorder, since 1985; *b* 16 July 1943; *s* of David Charles Barnes and Florence Maud Barnes; *m* 1970, Susan Dorothy Turner; three *s*. *Educ:* Monmouth Sch.; Wadham Coll., Oxford. Called to Bar, Middle Temple, 1965, Bencher, 1989. Hon. Research Fellow, Lady Margaret Hall, Oxford, 1979. Chm., Hinckley Point 'C' Public Inquiry, 1988. *Publications:* Leasehold Reform Act 1967, 1967; Hill and Redman's Law of Landlord and Tenant, 15th edn 1970– 18th edn 1988. *Recreations:* walking, crime fiction. *Address:* 2 Paper Buildings, Temple, EC4Y 7ET.

BARNES, Sir Denis (Charles), KCB 1967 (CB 1964); Director: Glynwed Ltd; General Accident, Fire & Life Assurance Corporation, 1976–85; President, Manpower Society, since 1976; *b* 15 Dec. 1914; *s* of Frederick Charles Barnes; *m* 1938, Patricia Abercrombie. *Educ:* Hulme Gram. Sch., Manchester; Merton Coll., Oxford. Chambers Postmaster, Merton Coll., Oxford, 1933–37. BA, 1st Cl. Mod. History, 1936; PPE 1937. Entered Min. of Labour, 1937; Private Sec. to Minister of Labour, 1945–47; Dep. Sec., Min. of Labour, 1963, Permanent Sec. 1966; Permanent Sec., Dept of Employment, 1968–73; Chairman: Manpower Services Commn, 1974–76; Member: Council, Manchester Business Sch., 1975; Council, Zoological Soc. of London, 1978–81. FIPM 1974. Commonwealth Fellowship, 1953. *Publication:* Governments and Trade Unions, 1980. *Address:* The Old Inn, 30 The Street, Wittersham, Kent TN30 7ED. *T:* Wittersham (07977) 528. *Club:* Savile.

BARNES, Edward Campbell; independent television producer/director and television consultant, since 1986; Head of Children's Programmes, BBC Television, 1978–86; *b* 8 Oct. 1928; *s* of Hubert Turnbull Barnes and Annie Mabel Barnes; *m* 1950, Dorothy Smith; one *s* two *d*. *Educ:* Wigan Coll. British Forces Network, Vienna, 1946–49; stage management, provincial and West End theatre, 1949–55; BBC Television: studio management, 1955–62; Producer, Blue Peter, 1962–70; Dep. Head of Children's Progs, 1970–78, incl.: original Editor, John Craven's Newsround; Producer: Blue Peter Royal Safari with Princess Anne; 6 series of Blue Peter Special Assignments; Producer and Director: Treasure Houses, 1986; All Our Children, 1987–90. Mem. Bd, Children's Film and Television Foundn Ltd, 1983–. Mem., RTS (Mem., Awards Cttee, 1989–). SFTA Award, 1969; RTS Silver Medal, 1986; Pye Television Award, 1985. *Publications:* 25 Blue Peter Books and 8 Blue Peter Mini Books, 1964–; 6 Blue Peter Special Assignment Books, 1973–75; Blue Peter Royal Safari, 1971; Petra: a dog for everyone, 1977; Blue Peter: the inside story, 1989; numerous articles for nat. press. *Recreations:* cricket, Mozart, Venice, Bali. *Clubs:* BAFTA; Tewin Irregulars Cricket.

BARNES, Rev. Edwin Ronald; Principal of St Stephen's House, Oxford, since 1987; *b* 6 Feb. 1935; *s* of Edwin and Dorothy Barnes; *m* 1963, Jane Elizabeth (*née* Green); one *s* one *d*. *Educ:* Plymouth College; Pembroke Coll., Oxford (MA). Rector of Farncombe, Surrey, 1967–78; Vicar of Hessle, dio. York, 1978–87. Proctor in Convocation, Canterbury 1975–78, York 1985–87; Mem., General Synod of C of E, 1990–. *Address:* St Stephen's House, 16 Marston Street, Oxford OX4 1JX. *T:* Oxford (0865) 247874.

BARNES, Hon. Eric Charles; Hon. Mr Justice Barnes; High Court Judge, Hong Kong, since 1981; *b* 12 Sept. 1924; *m* 1st, Estelle Fay Barnes (*née* Darnell); four *s* one *d*; 2nd, 1978, Judianna Wai Ling Barnes (*née* Chang); one *s* one *d*. *Educ:* Univ. of Queensland (LLB). *Recreations:* tennis, racing (horse), sports. *Address:* 2B Eastview, 3 Cox's Road, Kowloon, Hong Kong. *T:* 3–679221. *Clubs:* United Services Recreation, Kowloon Cricket, Royal Hong Kong Jockey (Hong Kong); Tattersall's (Brisbane).

BARNES, Sir (Ernest) John (Ward), KCMG 1974; MBE (mil.) 1946; HM Diplomatic Service, retired; *b* 22 June 1917; *er s* of Rt Rev. Ernest William Barnes, 3rd Bishop of Birmingham, and Adelaide, *d* of Sir Adolphus Ward, Master of Peterhouse, Cambridge; *m* 1948, Cynthia Margaret Ray (JP E Sussex, CStJ), *d* of Sir Herbert Stewart, CIE; two *s* three *d*. *Educ:* Dragon Sch., Oxford; Winchester; Trinity Coll., Cambridge. Classical Tripos, Pts I and II, Class I; Porson Scholar, 1939. Royal Artillery, 1939–46 (Lt-Col, MBE, US Bronze Star). HM Foreign Service, 1946; served Washington, Beirut, Bonn and Harvard Univ. (Center for International Affairs); Ambassador to Israel, 1969–72; Ambassador to the Netherlands, 1972–77. Director: Alliance Investment Co., 1977–87; Whiteaway Laidlaw Ltd, 1979–88. Chairman: Sussex Rural Community Council, 1982–87; Governors, Hurstpierpoint Coll., 1983–87. Member: Chichester Diocesan Synod, 1978–90; Council, Sussex Univ., 1981–85 (Vice-Chm. 1982–84). *Publication:* Ahead of his Age, 1979. *Address:* Hampton Lodge, Hurstpierpoint, Sussex BN6 9QN; 20 Thurloe Place Mews, SW7 2HL. *Clubs:* Athenæum, Beefsteak, Brooks's; MCC.

BARNES, Francis Walter Ibbetson; Chairman, Industrial Tribunals, 1976–87 (Resident Chairman, Exeter, 1984–87); *b* 10 May 1914; *e s* of late Rev. Walter W. Barnes, MA (Oxon) and Alice Mary Ibbetson, FRCO, ARCM; *m* 1st, 1941, Heather Katherine (marr. diss. 1953), *d* of Frank Tamplin; two *s*; 2nd, 1955, Sonia Nina (Nina Walker, pianist), *d* of late Harold Higginbottom; two *s* one *d*. *Educ:* Dragon Sch., Oxford; Mill Hill Sch.; Balliol Coll., Oxford. BA Jurisprudence (Hons), Oxford, 1937; MA 1967. Called to Bar, Inner Temple, 1938. Profumo Prize, Inner Temple, 1939. Served War, 1939–46 in Army (Middlesex Regt) and Home Office and Military Fire Services; Sen. Company Officer NFS and Capt. comdg military Fire Fighting Co. on BLA; later Staff Capt. in Amsterdam, and in JAG (War Crimes Section), GHQ Germany. After release from Army, functioned as Judge Advocate or Prosecutor in various trials of war criminals in Germany, 1947–48. Recorder of Smethwick, 1964–66; Dep. Chm., Oxfordshire QS, 1965–71; Recorder of Warley, 1966–71, Hon. Recorder, 1972; a Recorder of the Crown Court, 1972–76. Life Governor, Mill Hill Sch., 1939–; Mem., Dame Henrietta Barnett Bd (Educnl Trust), 1951–. Elected to Bar Council, 1961. Bar Council's rep. (observer) on Cons. cttee of Lawyers of the Common Market countries, 1962–71; contrib. to Common Market Law Review. Union Internat. des Avocats: Mem. Council, 1964–; Rapporteur Général at Vienna Congress, 1967; Rapporteur National at Paris Congress, 1971. Mem., Exec. Cttee, Friends of Farnham Park Rehabilitation Centre, 1988–; Dir, Farnham Park Ltd, 1989–. *Recreations:* music, languages, gardening. *Address:* 83 St George's Drive, Ickenham, Mddx UB10 8HR. *T:* Ruislip (0895) 672532.

See also A. F. P. Barnes, Dame A. J. M. T. Barnes.

BARNES, Geoffrey Thomas, CBE 1989; Secretary for Security, Hong Kong Government, 1988–90; *b* 18 Aug. 1932; *s* of late Thomas Arthur Barnes and Ethel Maud (*née* Walker); *m* 1962, Agnete Scot Madsen; three *s* one *d*. *Educ:* Dover College; St Catharine's College, Cambridge (MA). Nat. Service, 2nd Lieut QO Royal West Kent Regt; served Malaya, 1951–52; Lieut, Royal Warwickshire Regt, TA, 1952–55. Admin Officer, HMOCS Sarawak, 1956–68; City and Guilds of London, 1968–70; HMOCS Hong Kong: Asst Defence Sec., 1970–72; Police Civil Sec., 1972–76; Asst Dir, Commerce and Industry Dept, 1976–77; Dep. Sec. for Security, 1977–81, for Health and Welfare, 1981–84; Comr, Indep. Commn Against Corruption, 1985–88; Official Mem., Hong Kong Legislative Council, 1988–90. JP Hong Kong, 1980. *Recreations:* walking, painting, photography. *Address:* Alloways, Cranleigh Road, Ewhurst, Surrey GU6 7RJ. *T:* Cranleigh (0483) 276490. *Clubs:* Royal Over-Seas League; Hong Kong (Hong Kong).

See also K. J. Barnes.

BARNES, Harold, (Harry); MP (Lab) Derbyshire North East, since 1987; *b* 22 July 1936; *s* of Joseph and Betsy Barnes; *m* 1963, Elizabeth Ann Stephenson; one *s* one *d*. *Educ:* Ruskin Coll., Oxford (Dip. Econs and Political Science); Hull Univ. (BA Philosophy and Political Studies). National Service, 1954–56. Railway clerk, 1952–54 and 1956–60; adult student, 1960–65; further educn lectr, 1965–66; Lectr, Sheffield Univ., 1966–87. Mem., National Admin. Council, Ind. Labour Publications, 1977–80 and 1982–85. *Publications:* pamphlets on local govt and on the public face of Militant; articles and reviews in Labour Leader, London Labour Briefing, Tribune, Morning Star, Local Socialism, New Socialist, Derbyshire Miner, Leeds Weekly Citizen, Sheffield Forward, Industrial Tutor, Political Studies. *Address:* 16 Gosforth Lane, Dronfield, Sheffield S18 6PR. *T:* Dronfield (0246) 412588; (office) 071–219 4521. *Clubs:* Dronfield Contact; Chesterfield Labour.

BARNES, Ingrid Victoria, (Mrs Alan Barnes); *see* Allen, I. V.

BARNES, (James) David (Francis), CBE 1987; Executive Director, Imperial Chemical Industries plc, since 1986; *b* 4 March 1936; *s* of Eric Cecil Barnes, CMG, and of Jean Margaret Barnes; *m* 1963, Wendy Fiona Mary (*née* Riddell); one *s* one *d*. *Educ:* Shrewsbury Sch.; Liverpool Univ. FInstD; CBIM. National Service, commnd 'N' Battery (Eagle Troop), 2nd Regt RA, 1958–60 (Malaya). Overseas Dir 1971–77, Dep. Chm. 1977–83, ICI Pharmaceuticals Div.; Chm., Paints Div., 1983–86; Non-Exec. Dir, Thorn-EMI, 1987–. Chairman: Pharmaceuticals EDC, NEDO, 1983–; Biotechnology Industries

Working Party, NEDO, 1989–. Vice-Pres., Thames Valley Hospice, 1986–. FRSA 1988. *Recreations:* fishing, shooting, walking. *Address:* c/o ICI plc, 9 Millbank, SW1P 3JF.

BARNES, James Edwin; Under-Secretary, Small Firms and Regional Development Grants, Department of Industry, 1974–75; retired; *b* 23 Nov. 1917; *s* of James Barnes and Kate (*née* Davies); *m* 1943, Gloria Parkinson; two *s* one *d*. *Educ:* King Edward VI Sch., Nuneaton. Joined Civil Service as Executive Officer, War Office, 1936; Higher Executive Officer, Min. of Supply, 1942; Sen. Exec. Officer 1945, Principal, 1946, Asst Sec. 1952; Under-Secretary: Min. of Aviation, 1964–66; BoT, 1966–70; DTI, 1970–74. Coronation Medal, 1953. *Address:* 28 Sandown Road, Deal, Kent CT14 6PG. *T:* Deal (0304) 369308.

BARNES, James Frederick, CB 1982; Stewardship Adviser, Diocese of Monmouth, since 1989; Deputy Chief Scientific Adviser, and Head of Profession for the Science Group, Ministry of Defence, 1987–89; *b* 8 March 1932; *s* of Wilfred and Doris M. Barnes; *m* 1957, Dorothy Jean Drew; one *s* two *d*. *Educ:* Taunton's Sch., Southampton; Queen's Coll., Oxford. BA 1953, MA 1957; CEng, FRAeS. Bristol Aeroplane Co. (Engine Div.), 1953; Min. of Supply, Nat. Gas Turbine Estabt: Sci. Officer 1955; Sen. Sci. Off. 1957; Principal Sci. Off. 1962; Sen. Principal Sci. Off. (Individual Merit) 1965; Min. of Aviation Supply, Asst Dir, Engine R&D, 1970; seconded to HM Diplomatic Service, Counsellor (Science and Technology), British Embassy, Washington, 1972; Under-Sec., MoD, 1974; Dir Gen. Res. (C), MoD (Procurement Exec.), 1974–77; Dep. Dir (Weapons), RAE, 1978–79; Dep. Chief Scientific Adviser (Projs), MoD, 1979–82; Dep. Controller, Establishments Resources and Personnel, MoD, 1982–84; Dep. Controller, Estabts and Res., MoD, 1984–86. Chm., MoD Individual Merit Promotion Panel, 1990–. Mem., Council on Christian Approaches to Defence and Disarmament, 1980–; Lay Member: Guildford Diocesan Synod, 1978–84; Winchester Diocesan Synod, 1985–89; Chm., Deanery Finance Cttee, 1987–89; Co-opted Mem., Monmouth Diocesan Conf.; Churchwarden, All Saints', Farringdon, 1985–89. Chm. of Govs, Yateley Manor Prep. Sch., 1981–89. James Clayton Fund Prize, IMechE, 1964. *Publications:* contrib. books and learned jls on mech. engrg, esp. gas turbine technology, heat transfer and stress analysis. *Recreation:* making things. *Address:* 64 Caerau Road, Newport, Gwent NP9 4HJ.

BARNES, Sir James George, Kt 1976; MBE (mil.) 1946; JP; Mayor of Dunedin, New Zealand, 1968–77; sharebroker; *b* Dunedin, NZ, 1908; *s* of Richard R. Barnes; *m* 1938, Elsie, *d* of James D. Clark; one *d*. *Educ:* King Edward Technical High Sch. Served War, RNZAF 75 Sqdn, 1940–46 (POW, 1942–45). Mem., Dunedin City Council, 1947–53 and 1959–80 (Dep. Mayor 1951–53 and 1959–68); MP, 1951–57. Exec. Mem.: Otago Peninsula Trust; NZ Fedn for the Blind; Chm., Bd of Ocean Beach Domain. Past Pres., Otago Savings Bank. Chm. or Dir, Sch. Bds and Youth orgs. NZ mile champion, 1932; NZ Cross Country Champion, 1933; Manager NZ Empire Games Team, 1950; Asst Man., NZ Olympic Team, 1956; Past Pres., NZ AAA; Mem. Otago AAA; Mem. NZ Trotting Conf. (Pres., 1979–80); Sen. Vice Pres., Aust. Trotting Council, 1977–80; Exec. Mem., World Trotting Congress, 1980; Past Pres., Forbury Park Trotting Club. CStJ 1979. *Recreations:* golf, trotting. *Address:* 35 Cliffs Road, Dunedin, New Zealand; PO Box 221, Dunedin.

BARNES, Sir John; *see* Barnes, Sir E. J. W.

BARNES, John Alfred; Director-General, City and Guilds of London Institute, since 1985; *b* 29 April 1930; *s* of John Joseph and Margaret Carr Barnes; *m* 1954, Ivy May (*née* Walker); two *d*. *Educ:* Bede Boys Grammar Sch., Sunderland; Durham Univ. (MA, BSc, MEd). Teacher, Grangefield Grammar Sch., Stockton-on-Tees, 1953–57; Asst Educn Officer, Barnsley, 1957–61; Dep. Dir, then Dir of Educn, City of Wakefield, 1963–68; Chief Educn Officer, City of Salford, 1968–84. Mem. Council, Assoc. of Colls of Further and Higher Educn, 1976–82 (Chm. 1980–81); Chairman: Northern Examining Assoc., 1979–82; Associated Lancs Schs Examg Bd, 1972–84; Member: Associated Examg Bd, Nat. Exams Bd for Supervisory Studies, 1985–; Further Educn Unit Management Bd, 1986–89; YTS Certification Bd, 1986–89; various ind. trng bds, 1969–78, and MSC cttees, 1978–84; Review of Vocational Qualifications Working Gp, 1985–86; Task Gp on Assessment and Testing, 1987–88; Exec. Mem., Standing Conf. on Sch. Sci. and Technol., 1985–89 (Chm., Exec. Cttee, 1988–89). Mem., Nat. Exec. Cttee, Soc. of Educn Officers, 1979–84; Sec., Assoc. of Educn Officers, 1977–84; Treas., NFER, 1979–84; Pres., Educnl Develt Assoc., 1980–85. Chm., Sir Isaac Pitman Ltd, 1990–; Sec., UK Skills, 1990–. Mem. Council, City Technology Colls Trust, 1990–; Gov., Imperial Coll., 1987–. FRSA 1973; FITD 1986. *Publications:* occasional papers in educnl press. *Recreations:* cultural activities, foreign travel. *Address:* 37 Woodfield Park, Amersham, Bucks HP6 5QH. *T:* Amersham (02043) 6120. *Clubs:* Athenæum, Rotary.

BARNES, Prof. John Arundel, DSC 1944; FBA 1981; Fellow of Churchill College, Cambridge, since 1969; Visiting Fellow, Sociology, Research School of Social Sciences, Australian National University, since 1985; *b* Reading, 9 Sept. 1918; *s* of T. D. and M. G. Barnes, Bath; *m* 1942, Helen Frances, *d* of Charles Bastable; three *s* one *d*. *Educ:* Christ's Hosp.; St John's Coll., Cambridge; Sch. of African Studies, Univ. of Cape Town; Balliol Coll., Oxford. Fellow, St John's Coll., Cambridge, 1950–53; Simon Research Fellow, Manchester Univ., 1951–53; Reader in Anthropology, London Univ., 1954–56; Prof. of Anthropology, Sydney Univ., 1956–58; Prof. of Anthropology, Inst. of Advanced Studies, ANU, Canberra, 1958–69; Overseas Fellow, Churchill Coll., Cambridge, 1965–66; Prof. of Sociology, Univ. of Cambridge, 1969–82, now Emeritus. *Publications:* Marriage in a Changing Society, 1951; Politics in a Changing Society, 1954; Inquest on the Murngin, 1967; Sociology in Cambridge, 1970; Three Styles in the Study of Kinship, 1971; Social Networks, 1972; The Ethics of Inquiry in Social Science, 1977; Who Should Know What?, 1979; Models and interpretations, 1990. *Address:* Sociology Program, Research School of Social Sciences, Australian National University, GPO Box 4, Canberra, ACT 2601, Australia.

BARNES, Prof. Jonathan, FBA 1987; Professor of Ancient Philosophy, since 1989 and Fellow of Balliol College, since 1978, University of Oxford; *b* 1942; *m* 1965, Jennifer Postgate; two *d*. *Educ:* City of London Sch.; Balliol Coll., Oxford. Fellow, Oriel Coll., Oxford, 1968–78. Visiting posts at: Inst. for Advanced Study, Princeton, 1972; Univ. of Texas, 1981; Wissenschaftskolleg zu Berlin, 1985; Univ. of Alberta, 1986; Univ. of Zurich, 1987; Instituto Italiano per gli studi filosofici, 1988. *Publications:* The Ontological Argument, 1972; Aristotle's Posterior Analytics, 1975; The Presocratic Philosophers, 1979; Aristotle, 1982; Early Greek Philosophy, 1987. *Address:* 19 St Margaret's Road, Oxford. *T:* Oxford (0865) 54418.

BARNES, Joseph Harry George; Director, J. Sainsbury plc, since 1969 (Joint Managing Director, 1988–90); *b* 24 July 1930; *s* of William Henry Joseph Barnes and Dorothy Eleanor Barnes; *m* 1958, Rosemary Gander; two *s*. *Educ:* John Ruskin Grammar Sch., Croydon. FCA 1963. Articled clerk, Lever Honeyman & Co., 1946–52. National Service, 2nd Lieut RAPC, 1953–55. Joined J. Sainsbury plc, 1956. *Recreations:* tennis, fishing. *Address:* Tudor Court, 29 Grimwade Avenue, Croydon, Surrey CR0 5DJ. *T:* 081–654 5696.

BARNES, Dame Josephine; *see* Barnes, Dame A. J. M. T.

BARNES, Julian Patrick; writer; *b* 19 Jan. 1946; *m* Pat Kavanagh. *Educ:* City of London Sch.; Magdalen Coll., Oxford. Lexicographer, OED Supplement, 1969–72; freelance journalist; Contributing Ed., New Review, 1977; Asst Literary Ed., 1977–79, TV Critic, 1977–81, New Statesman; Dep. Literary Ed., Sunday Times, 1980–82; TV Critic, Observer, 1982–86. *Publications:* Metroland, 1980 (Somerset Maugham Award, 1981); Before She Met Me, 1982; Flaubert's Parrot, 1984 (Prix Médicis, 1986); Staring at the Sun, 1986; A History of the World in 10½ Chapters, 1989; Talking it Over, 1991; (as Dan Kavanagh): Duffy, 1980; Fiddle City, 1981; Putting the Boot In, 1985; Going to the Dogs, 1987. *Address:* c/o A. D. Peters, The Chambers, Chelsea Harbour, Lots Road, SW10 0XF.
See also Jonathan Barnes.

BARNES, Sir Kenneth, KCB 1977 (CB 1970); Permanent Secretary, Department of Employment, 1976–82; *b* 26 Aug. 1922; *s* of Arthur and Doris Barnes, Accrington, Lancs; *m* 1948, Barbara Ainsworth; one *s* two *d*. *Educ:* Accrington Grammar Sch.; Balliol Coll., Oxford. Entered Ministry of Labour, 1948; Under-Sec., Cabinet Office, 1966–68; Dep. Sec., Dept of Employment, 1968–75. *Address:* South Sandhills, Sandy Lane, Betchworth, Surrey RH3 7AA. *T:* Betchworth (0737) 842445. *Club:* United Oxford & Cambridge University.

BARNES, Kenneth James, CBE 1969 (MBE 1964); Advisor (Finance), Directorate General for Development, Commission of the European Communities, 1982–87; *b* 8 May 1930; *s* of late Thomas Arthur Barnes and Ethel Maude Barnes; *m* 1st, 1953, Lesley Dawn Grummett Wright (*d* 1976); two *s* one *d*; 2nd, 1981, Anna Elisabeth Gustaf Maria Vanoorlé (marr. diss. 1988). *Educ:* Guilford and Hale Schs, Perth, WA; Dover Coll.; St Catharine's Coll., Cambridge (Crabtree exhibnr; MA); London Univ. Pilot Officer, RAF, 1949–50; Flying Officer, RAFVR, 1950–53. Administrative Officer, HMOCS Eastern Nigeria, 1954–60; Asst Sec., Min. of Finance, Malaŵi, 1960–64, Sen. Asst Sec., 1965, Dep. Sec., 1966, Permanent Sec., 1967–71; Asst Sec., British Steel Corp., 1971–73; EEC: Principal Administrator, Directorate-Gen. for Develt, 1973–75; Head of Div. for Ind. Co-operation, Trade Promotion and Regional Co-operation, 1976–78; Hd of Div. for Caribbean, Indian and Pacific Oceans, 1979–80; Advr (Political), 1981–82; Advr (Finance), 1983–87. *Recreations:* reading, esp. history, listening to music, mediaeval fortifications, strengthening European Community links, charities for the disabled. *Address:* 29 Bearwater, Charnham Street, Hungerford, Berks RG17 0NM. *T:* Hungerford (0488) 684329. *Club:* Commonwealth Trust.
See also G. T. Barnes.

BARNES, Melvyn Peter Keith, OBE 1990; ALA; Guildhall Librarian and Director of Libraries and Art Galleries, Corporation of London, since 1984; *b* 26 Sept. 1942; *s* of Harry and Doris Barnes; *m* 1965, Judith Anne Leicester; two *s*. *Educ:* Chatham House Sch., Ramsgate; North-Western Polytechnic, London. ALA 1965; DMA 1972; FBIM 1980; FRSA 1983. Public library posts in Kent, Herts and Manchester, 1958–68; Dep. Bor. Librarian, Newcastle-under-Lyme, 1968–72; Chief Librarian, Ipswich, 1972–74; Bor. Librarian and Arts Officer, Kensington and Chelsea, 1974–80; City Librarian, Westminster, 1980–84. Hon. Librarian to Clockmakers' Co., Gardeners' Co., Disabled Living Foundn. Member: LA Council, 1974– (Chm. Exec. Cttee, 1987–; Vice-Pres., 1991–); Liby and Inf. Services Council, 1984–89; Brit. Liby Adv. Council, 1986–; Brit. Liby SRIS Adv. Cttee, 1986–. Pres., Internat. Assoc. of Metropolitan City Libraries, 1989–; Dep. Chm., Liby Services Trust and Liby Services Ltd, 1983–. Hon. Treas., Victoria County History of Inner Middlesex, 1979–90. Gov., St Bride Inst., 1984–. Liveryman, Clockmakers' Co., 1990–. Editorial Cons., Journal of Librarianship, 1980–. *Publications:* Youth Library Work, 1968, 2nd edn 1976; Best Detective Fiction, 1975; Murder in Print, 1986; Dick Francis, 1986; (ed) Deerstalker series of classic crime fiction reprints, 1977–82; contributor to numerous books and jls in fields of librarianship and crime fiction criticism. *Recreations:* reading and writing, going to the theatre, studying the history of the movies and stage musicals, performing amateur operatics. *Address:* Guildhall Library, Aldermanbury, EC2P 2EJ. *T:* 071–260 1850.

BARNES, Michael; *see* Barnes, D. M. W.

BARNES, Michael Cecil John; Legal Services Ombudsman for England and Wales, since 1991; *b* 22 Sept. 1932; *s* of late Major C. H. R. Barnes, OBE and of Katherine Louise (*née* Kennedy); *m* 1962, Anne Mason; one *s* one *d*. *Educ:* Malvern; Corpus Christi Coll., Oxford. Nat. Service, 2nd Lieut, Wilts Regt, served in Hong Kong, 1952–53. MP (Lab) Brentford and Chiswick, 1966–Feb. 1974; an Opposition Spokesman on food and food prices, 1970–71; Chairman: Parly Labour Party Social Security Group, 1969–70; ASTMS Parly Cttee, 1970–71; Jt Hon. Sec., Labour Cttee for Europe, 1969–71; Mem., Public Accounts Cttee, 1967–74. Contested (Lab): Wycombe, 1964; Brentford and Isleworth, Feb. 1974; Mem. Labour Party, 1957–79; helped form SDP, 1981; rejoined Labour Party, 1983–. Chm., Electricity Consumers' Council, 1977–83; Dir, UKIAS, 1984–90. Member: Council of Management, War on Want, 1972–77; Nat. Consumer Council, 1975–80; Arts Council Trng Cttee, 1977–83; Energy Commn, 1977–79; Internat. Cttee of Nat. Council for Voluntary Organisations, 1977–83; Advertising Standards Authority, 1979–85; Direct Mail Services Standards Bd, 1983–86; Data Protection Tribunal, 1985–90; Investigation Cttee, Solicitors' Complaints Bureau, 1987–90; Chairman: UK Adv. Cttee on EEC Action Against Poverty Programme, 1975–76; Notting Hill Social Council, 1976–79; West London Fair Housing Gp Ltd, 1980–87; Vice Chm., Bangabandhu Soc., 1980–90; Organising Secretary: Gulbenkian Foundn Drama Trng Inquiry, 1974–75; Music Trng Inquiry, 1976–77; Sec., Nat. Council for Drama Trng, 1976–84; Chm., Hounslow Arts Trust, 1974–82; Trustee, Project Hand Trust, 1974–77; Governor, Internat. Musicians Seminar, Prussia Cove, 1978–81. *Recreations:* walking, swimming, dogs. *Address:* 45 Ladbroke Grove, W11 3AR. *T:* 071–727 2533.

BARNES, Prof. Michael Patrick; Professor of Scandinavian Philology, University College London, since 1983; *b* 28 June 1940; *s* of William Edward Clement Barnes and Gladys Constance Barnes (*née* Hooper); *m* 1970, Kirsten Heiberg (*née* Røer); one *s* three *d*. *Educ:* University College London (BA, MA); Univ. of Oslo. Asst Lectr, Lectr and Reader in Scandinavian Philology, UCL, 1964–83. Visiting Professor: Tórshavn, Faroe Islands, 1979; Uppsala Univ., 1984. Mem., Gustav Adolfs Akademien, Uppsala, 1984 (Corresp. Mem., 1977). Mem., Editl Bd, North-Western European Language Evolution, 1989– (Mem. Adv. Bd, 1981–88); Jt Hon. Sec., Viking Soc. for Northern Research, 1982– (Mem. Editl Bd, 1970–76, Chief Editor, 1977–83, Saga Book of the Viking Soc.). *Publications:* Draumkvæde: an edition and study, 1974; articles in learned jls. *Recreations:* badminton, being with family, walking disused railways. *Address:* 93 Longland Drive, N20 8HN. *T:* 081–445 4697.

BARNES, Peter; dramatist; *b* 10 Jan. 1931; *s* of Frederick and Martha Barnes; *m* 1958, Charlotte (*née* Beck). *Educ:* Stroud Grammar Sch. 1st Play, Sclerosis, 1965. Adapted and co-directed: Wedekind's Lulu, 1970; The Bewitched, 1974; adapted and dir., Feydeau's The Purging, 1976; directed: Wedekind's The Singer, 1976; Jonson's Bartholomew Fair, 1978, 1987; Marston's Antonio, 1979; Wedekind's The Devil Himself, 1980; adapted Jonson's The Devil is an Ass, 1977; directed: For All Those Who Get Despondent, 1977;

Laughter!, 1978; Somersaults, 1981; Red Noses, 1985; adapted Feydeau's Scenes from a Marriage, 1986; dir, The Spirit of Man (TV plays), 1989; Sunsets and Glories, 1990; *radio plays:* My Ben Jonson, 1973; Eastward Ho, from Jonson, Chapman and Marston, 1974; Lulu, from Wedekind, 1976; Antonio, from Marston, 1977; The Two Hangmen, from Wedekind and Brecht, 1979; A Chaste Maid in Cheapside, from Middleton, 1979; Eulogy on Baldness, from Synesius of Cyrene, 1980; For the Conveyance of Oysters, from Gorki, 1981; The Soldier's Fortune, from Otway, 1981; The Atheist, from Otway, 1981; Barnes' People One, 1981; The Magician, from Gorki, 1982; The Singer, from Wedekind, 1982; The Dutch Courtesan, from Marston, 1982; A Mad World My Masters, from Middleton, 1983; Barnes' People Two, 1983; The Primrose Path, from Feydeau, 1984; A Trick to Catch the Old One, from Middleton, 1985; The Old Law, from Middleton, Rowley and Massinger, 1986; Barnes' People Three, 1986; Women of Paris, 1987; Don Juan and Faust, from Grabbe, 1987; The Magnetic Lady, from Jonson, 1987; The Devil is an Ass, from Jonson, 1987. John Whiting Award, 1968; Evening Standard Award, 1969; Giles Cooper Radio Award, 1981; Laurence Olivier Award for Best Play, 1985. *Publications:* The Ruling Class, 1969; Leonardo's Last Supper, 1970; Noonday Demons, 1970; Lulu, 1971; The Bewitched, 1974; The Frontiers of Farce, 1976; Laughter!, 1978; The Collected Plays, 1981; Barnes' People Two, 1984; Red Noses, 1985; The Real Long John Silver (Barnes' People Three), 1986. *Address:* 7 Archery Close, Connaught Street, W2 2BE. *T:* 071–262 9205.

BARNES, Peter Robert, CB 1982; Deputy Director of Public Prosecutions, 1977–82; President, Video Appeals Committee, since 1985; *b* 1 Feb. 1921; *s* of Robert Stanley Barnes and Marguerite (*née* Dunkels); *m* 1955, Pauline Belinda Hannen; two *s* one *d*. *Educ:* Eton Coll.; Trinity Coll., Cambridge (BA). Called to Bar, Inner Temple, 1947. Dir. of Public Prosecutions: Legal Asst, 1951; Sen. Legal Asst, 1958; Asst Solicitor, 1970; Asst Director, 1974; Principal Asst Dir, 1977. *Recreation:* bridge. *Address:* The Old Vicarage, Church Lane, Witley, Surrey GU8 5PN.

BARNES, Dr Robert Sandford; Chairman, Robert S. Barnes Consultants Ltd, since 1978; Principal, Queen Elizabeth College, Kensington, London University, 1978–85, Fellow, 1985; *b* 8 July 1924; *s* of William Edward and Ada Elsie Barnes (*née* Sutherst); *m* 1952, Julia Frances Marriott Grant; one *s* three *d*. *Educ:* Univ. of Manchester. BSc Hons 1948, MSc 1959, DSc 1962. Radar Research, Admiralty Signals Estab., Witley, Surrey, 1944–47; AERE, Harwell: Metallurgical Research, 1948–62; Head of Irradiation Branch, 1962–65; Vis. Scientist, The Science Center, N Amer. Aviation Co., Calif, 1965; Head of Metallurgy Div., AERE, Harwell, 1966–68; Dep. Dir, BISRA, 1968–69; Dir, BISRA, 1969–70; Dir R&D, British Steel Corp., 1970–75; Chief Scientist, BSC, 1975–78. Technical Adviser: Bd of BOC Ltd, 1978–79; Bd of BOC International Ltd, 1979–81; Bd of New Ventures Secretariat, 1978–80. Chm., Ruthner Continuous Crop Systems Ltd, 1976–78. Member: CBI Res. and Technol. Cttee, 1968–75; Adv. Council on R&D for Iron and Steel, 1970–75; Materials Science and Technol. Cttee, SRC, 1975–79; European Industrial Res. Management Assoc., 1970 (Vice-Pres., 1974–78); Parly and Scientific Cttee, 1970–80, 1983–85; Foundn for Science and Technology, 1984–; Chm., Material Technology Panel, Internat. Tin Res. Inst., 1988–. Member: Council, Welding Inst., 1970–75; Council, Instn of Metallurgists, 1970–75 and 1979–85 (Vice Pres., 1979; Sen. Vice Pres., 1982; Pres., 1983–85); Council, Metals Soc., 1974–80, 1982–85 (Chairman: Coordinating Cttee, 1976–78, Executive Cttee, 1976–80). Institute of Metals: Mem., Steering Gp, 1983–84; Mem. Council, 1985–; Mem. Exec. Cttee, 1985–; Past Pres., 1985–; Chm., Professional Bd, 1985–. Chairman: Combined Operations Working Party, 1980–81; European Nuclear Steel-making Club, 1973–76; UK Representative: Commn de la Recherche Technique Sidérurgique, 1972–78; Conseil d'Association Européenne pour la Promotion de la Recherche Technique en Sidérurgie, 1972–78; Adv. Council on Energy Conservation, Industry Group, 1977–78; Council, Backpain Assoc., 1979–. Hon. Mem. Council, Iron and Steel Inst., 1969–73. Governor, Sheffield Polytechnic, 1968–72; Member: Court of Univ. of Surrey, 1968–80; Collegiate Council, Univ. of London, 1978–85; Jt Finance and Gen. Purposes Cttee, Univ. of London, 1978–85; Senate, Univ. of London, 1980–85; Member Council: King's Coll. London, 1982–85; Chelsea Coll., 1983–85; Bd Mem., CSTI, 1984–88. Lectures: Hatfield Meml, Iron and Steel Inst., 1973; John Player, IMechE, 1976. Freeman, City of London, 1984; Liveryman, Worshipful Co. of Engrs, 1985. Rosenhain Medallist, Inst. of Metals, 1964. FInstP 1961; FIM 1965; FRSA 1976; FKC 1985; Life Mem., Royal Instn, 1986. CEng 1977. *Publications:* chapters in specialist books of science; scientific papers in various learned jls. *Recreations:* yachting, gardening. *Address:* Pigeon Forge, Daneshill, The Hockering, Woking, Surrey GU22 7HQ. *T:* Woking (0483) 761529. *Clubs:* Athenæum, Cruising Association.

BARNES, Roland, CBE 1970; BSc, MB, ChB, FRCS, FRCSE, FRCSGlas; Professor of Orthopaedic Surgery, University of Glasgow, 1959–72, now Professor Emeritus; *b* 21 May 1907; *y s* of Benjamin Barnes and Mary Ann Bridge, Accrington, Lancs.; *m* 1938, Mary Mills Buckley; one *s* two *d*. *Educ:* University of Manchester. BSc 1927; MB, ChB 1930; Medical and Surgical Clinical prizes. Usual resident appointments; Resident Surgical Officer, Manchester Royal Infirmary, 1934–35; Dickinson Travelling Scholar, Univ. of Manchester, 1935–36; visited orthopaedic clinics in USA; Fellow, Hospital for Ruptured and Crippled, New York. Chief Asst to Sir Harry Platt, Bt, Orthopaedic Department, Royal Infirmary, Manchester, 1937–39; Surgeon in Charge of Orthopædic and Peripheral Nerve Injury Centre, EMS Hospital, Winwick, Lancs, 1940–43. Past Pres., British Orthopædic Assoc.; Hon. Mem. French, Finnish, German and S African Orthopædic Assocs; Corresp. Mem. Amer. Orthopædic Assoc. *Publications:* papers on injuries of the peripheral nerves and spine, fractures of neck of femur, and on tumours of bone. *Recreation:* gardening. *Address:* 12 St Germains, Bearsden, Glasgow G61 2RS. *T:* 041–942 2699.

BARNES, Rosemary Susan, (Rosie); MP Greenwich, since Feb. 1987 (SDP, 1987–90; Social Democrat, since 1990); *b* 16 May 1946; *d* of Alan Allen and Kathleen (*née* Brown); *m* 1967, Graham Barnes; two *s* one *d*. *Educ:* Bilborough Grammar School.; Birmingham Univ. (BSocSci Hons). Management Trainee, Research Bureau Ltd, 1967–69; Product Manager, Yardley of London Ltd, 1969–72; primary teacher (briefly), 1972; freelance market researcher, 1973–87. *Recreations:* motherhood and politics leave little time. *Address:* 21 Egerton Drive, Greenwich, SE10 8JR. *T:* 081–692 8452.

BARNES, Timothy Paul; QC 1986; a Recorder, since 1987; *b* 23 April 1944; *s* of Arthur Morley Barnes and Valerie Enid Mary Barnes; *m* 1969, Patricia Margaret Gale; one *s* three *d*. *Educ:* Bradfield Coll., Berkshire; Christ's Coll., Cambridge (MA). Called to Bar, Gray's Inn, 1968, Hilbery Exhibn; practises Midland and Oxford Circuit; Asst Recorder, 1983. *Recreations:* gardening, hockey. *Address:* The White House, Crooms Hill, SE10 8HH. *T:* 081–858 1185. *Club:* MCC.

BARNETT, family name of **Baron Barnett.**

BARNETT, Baron *cr* 1983 (Life Peer), of Heywood and Royton in Greater Manchester; **Joel Barnett;** PC 1975; JP; chairman and director of a number of companies; Vice-Chairman, Board of Governors, BBC, since 1986; *b* 14 Oct. 1923; *s* of Louis and Ettie Barnett, both of Manchester; *m* 1949, Lilian Goldstone; one *d*. *Educ:* Derby Street Jewish Sch.; Manchester Central High Sch. Certified accountant. Served RASC and British Military Govt in Germany. Mem. of Prestwich, Lancs, Borough Council, 1956–59; JP Lancs 1960; Hon. Treas. Manchester Fabian Society, 1953–65. Contested (Lab) Runcorn Div. of Cheshire, Oct. 1959; MP (Lab) Heywood and Royton Div., Lancs, 1964–83. Member: Public Accounts Cttee, 1965–71 (Chm., 1979–83); Public Expenditure Cttee, 1971–74; Select Cttee on Tax Credits, 1973–74; Chm. Parly Labour Party Economic and Finance Group, 1967–70 and 1972–74 (Vice-Chm., 1966–67); Opposition Spokesman on Treasury matters, 1970–74; Chief Sec. to the Treasury, 1974–79 (Cabinet Mem., 1977–79); Opposition spokesman on the Treasury in House of Lords, 1983–86. Hon. Visiting Fellow, Univ. of Strathclyde, 1980–. Chm., British Screen Finance Ltd (formerly British Screen Finance Consortium), 1985–. Mem., Internat. Adv. Bd, Unisys, 1989–. Chm., Building Societies' Ombudsman Council, 1987–. Trustee, V&A Museum, 1984–. Mem., Hallé Cttee, 1982–. Chm., Hansard Soc. for Parly Govt, 1984–90. Pres., RIPA, 1989–. Hon. LLD Strathclyde, 1983. *Publication:* Inside the Treasury, 1982. *Recreations:* walking, conversation and reading; good food. *Address:* Flat 92, 24 John Islip Street, SW1; 7 Hillingdon Road, Whitefield, Manchester M25 7QQ.

BARNETT, Dr Christopher Andrew; Headmaster, Whitgift School, Croydon, since 1991; *b* 1 Feb. 1953; *s* of Peter Alan Barnett and Jean Barnett (*née* Cullis); *m* 1976, Hon. Laura Miriam Elizabeth, *o c* of Baron Weidenfeld, *qv*; three *s* one *d*. *Educ:* Cedars Sch., Leighton Buzzard; Oriel Coll., Oxford (Exhibnr; BA Hons History 1974; MA 1978; DPhil 1981). Lectr in Econs, Brunel Univ., 1975–77; Head of History Dept, Bradfield Coll., Berks, 1978–87; Second Master, Dauntsey's Sch., Wilts, 1987–91. Evelyn Wrench Scholar, ESU, 1990. *Recreations:* opera, political Victoriana, hill-walking, travel, horse-racing (steeplechases). *Address:* Whitgift School, Haling Park, South Croydon CR2 6YT. *T:* 081–688 9222.

BARNETT, Christopher John Anthony; His Honour Judge Barnett; a Circuit Judge, since 1988; QC 1983; *b* 18 May 1936; *s* of Richard Adrian Barnett and Phyllis Barnett (*née* Cartwright); *m* 1959, Sylvia Marieliese (*née* Pritt); two *s* one *d*. *Educ:* Repton Sch., Derbyshire; College of Law, London. Called to the Bar, Gray's Inn, 1965. District Officer (Kikuyu Guard) and Kenya Government Service, 1955–60; a District Officer in HM Overseas Civil Service, serving in Kenya, 1960–62; in practice as barrister, 1965–88; a Recorder, 1982–88. Chm., SE Circuit Area Liaison Cttee, 1985–88. Mem., Court of Essex Univ., 1983–. *Recreations:* cricket, tennis. *Address:* 4 Paper Buildings, Temple, EC4Y 7EX. *T:* 071–583 7765.

BARNETT, Colin Michael; international business consultant, since 1990; Regional Secretary, North-West Regional Council of the Trades Union Congress, 1976–85; Divisional Officer, North-West Division of the National Union of Public Employees, 1971–84; *b* 27 Aug. 1929; *s* of Arthur Barnett and Kathleen Mary Barnett; *m* 1st, 1953, Margaret Barnett (marr. diss. 1980); one *s* one *d*; 2nd, 1982, Hilary Carolyn Hodge, PhD; one *s* one *d*. *Educ:* St Michael's Elem. Sch., Southfields; Wandsworth Grammar Sch.; London Sch. of Econs and Polit. Science; WEA classes. Area Officer, NUPE, 1959, Asst Divl Officer 1961. Chm. Gp H, Duke of Edinburgh Conf. on Industry and Society, 1974. Secretary: NW Peace Council, 1979–; NW Cttee Against Racism, 1980–. Chm., MSC Area Bd, Gtr Manchester and Lancashire, 1978–83. Member: Merseyside District Manpower Bd, 1983–86; Industrial Tribunal, Manchester, 1974–; Liverpool Social Security Appeal Tribunal, 1986–. Dir, AT4 Community Prog. Agency, 1986–. Debt and Industrial Advr, St Helens CAB, 1984–; Marriage Guidance Counsellor, 1984–. Organised: People's March for Jobs, 1981; (jtly) People's March for Jobs, 1983. British Representative: Leningrad Business Forum; Leningrad Independent Humanitarian Foundn. Employment Advr, This is Your Right, Granada TV, 1970–89. Governor, William Temple Foundn, 1980–87. *Recreations:* walking, reading, laughing. *Address:* 14 Elm Grove, Eccleston Park, Prescot, Merseyside L34 2AX. *T:* 051–426 4045, *Fax:* 091–426 0100.

BARNETT, Correlli (Douglas); author; Keeper of the Churchill Archives Centre, and a Fellow, Churchill College, Cambridge, since 1977; *b* 28 June 1927; *s* of D. A. Barnett; *m* 1950, Ruth Murby; two *d*. *Educ:* Trinity Sch., Croydon; Exeter Coll., Oxford. Second class hons, Mod. Hist. with Mil. Hist. and the Theory of War as a special subject; MA 1954. Intell. Corps, 1945–48. North Thames Gas Bd, 1952–57; Public Relations, 1957–63. Vice-Pres., E Arts Assoc., 1978– (Chm. Literature Panel, and Mem. Exec. Cttee, 1972–78); Pres., East Anglian Writers, 1969–88; Member: Council, Royal Utd Services Inst. for Defence Studies, 1973–85; Cttee, London Library, 1977–79 and 1982–84. Leverhulme Res. Fellowship, 1976; apptd Lectr in Defence Studies, Univ. of Cambridge, 1980; resigned in order to devote more time to writing, 1983. Winston Churchill Meml Lectr, Switzerland, 1982. FRSL; FRHistS. *Publications:* The Hump Organisation, 1957; The Channel Tunnel (with Humphrey Slater), 1958; The Desert Generals, 1960, new enlarged edn, 1983; The Swordbearers, 1963; Britain and Her Army, 1970 (RSL award, 1971); The Collapse of British Power, 1972; Marlborough, 1974; Bonaparte, 1978; The Great War, 1979; The Audit of War, 1986 (US edn as The Pride and the Fall, 1987); Engage the Enemy More Closely: the Royal Navy in the Second World War, 1991; (historical consultant and writer to) BBC Television series: The Great War, 1963–64; The Lost Peace, 1965–66; The Commanders, 1972–73; reviews Mil. Hist. for The Sunday Telegraph; contrib. to: The Promise of Greatness (a symposium on the Great War), 1968; Governing Elites (a symposium), 1969; Decisive Battles of the Twentieth Century, 1976; The War Lords, 1976; The Economic System in the UK, 1985; Education for Capability, 1986; (ed) Hitler's Generals, 1989. *Recreations:* gardening, interior decorating, idling, eating, mole-hunting. *Address:* Catbridge House, East Carleton, Norwich NR14 8JX. *T:* Mulbarton (0508) 410.

BARNETT, Air Chief Marshal Sir Denis Hensley Fulton, GCB 1964 (KCB 1957; CB 1956); CBE 1945; DFC 1940; RAF, retired; Member for Weapons Research and Development, Atomic Energy Authority, 1965–72; *b* 11 Feb. 1906; *y s* of late Sir Louis Edward Barnett; *m* 1939, Pamela, OBE, *y d* of late Sir Allan John Grant; one *s* two *d*. *Educ:* Christ's Coll., NZ; Clare Coll., Cambridge (BA 1929, MA 1935). Perm. Commn, RAF, 1929; Flt Lieut, 1934; Sqdn Ldr 1938; comd 84 Sqdn, Shaibah, 1938. Served War of 1939–45; Sqdn Comdr, Stn Comdr and G/C Ops, Bomber Comd, 1939–44; Dep. Dir Bomber Ops, Air Min., 1944; Dep. SASO at HQ Bomber Comd, 1945; Actg Wing Cdr, 1940; Gp Capt., 1941; Air Cdre, 1945; Dir of Ops at Air Min., 1945–46; Air Staff, India, 1946–47; Jt Services Staff Coll., 1948; Comdt Central Bomber Estabt, 1949; Dir of Ops Air Min., 1950–52; idc, 1952; Representative of UK Chiefs of Staff at HQ, UN Command, Tokyo, 1952–54; AOC, No. 205 Group, Middle East Air Force, 1954–56; Commandant, RAF Staff Coll., Bracknell, 1956; Commander Allied Air Task Force, Near East, 1956; Air Secretary, Air Ministry, 1957–59; AOC-in-C, RAF Transport Command, 1959–62; Air Officer Commanding-in-Chief, RAF Near East; Commander, British Forces Cyprus, and Administrator of the Sovereign Base Areas, 1962–64; Subst. Air Commodore, 1950; Air Vice-Marshal, 1953; Air Marshal, 1959; Air Chief Marshal, 1962. Comdr, US Legion of Merit, 1954; French Légion d'Honneur (Commandeur) and Croix de Guerre, 1958. *Address:* River House, Rushall, Pewsey, Wilts SN9 6EN.

See also G. G. F. Barnett, J. S. Peel.

BARNETT, Geoffrey Grant Fulton; Director, Baring Brothers & Co. Ltd, since 1979; *b* 9 March 1943; *s* of Air Chief Marshal Sir Denis H. F. Barnett, *qv*; *m* 1968, Fiona

Katharine Milligan; two *s* two *d*. *Educ:* Winchester; Clare Coll., Cambridge (MA). Courtaulds Ltd, 1964–67; The Economist Intelligence Unit, 1967–70; British Printing Corp., 1970–71; Baring Brothers & Co. Ltd, 1971–; Man. Dir, Baring Brothers Asia, Hong Kong, 1979–83; seconded as Dir Gen., Panel on Takeovers and Mergers, 1989–91. Hon. Treas., VSO, 1984–; Mem. Cttee, London and Quadrant Housing Trust, 1985–. *Recreations:* Scotland, walking, music, bird watching. *Address:* 2 Mill Hill Road, SW13 0HR. *T:* 081–878 6975.

BARNETT, Jenifer W.; *see* Wilson-Barnett.

BARNETT, Jeremy John, OBE 1982; British Council Director (formerly Representative) and Cultural Counsellor, British Embassy, Cairo, since 1989; *b* 26 Jan. 1941; *s* of late Audrey Wickham Barnett and Lt-Comdr Charles Richard Barnett, RN; *m* 1968, Maureen Janet Cullum; one *s* one *d*. *Educ:* St Edward's Sch., Oxford; St Andrews Univ. (MA); Leeds Univ. (Dip TEFL). Joined British Council, 1964; teaching, Victory Coll., Cairo, 1965–67; Lectr, Inst. of Educn, Istanbul, 1967–69; MECAS, Lebanon, 1969–70; Dir of Studies, Turco-British Assoc., Ankara, 1970–72; British Council Rep., Riyadh, 1972–75; Dir, ME Dept, 1975–78; Counsellor for British Council and Cultural Affairs, Ankara, 1978–82; British Council Rep., Warsaw, 1982–85; Dir, E Europe and N Asia Dept, 1985–88; Controller, S and W Asia Div., 1988–89. *Recreation:* hill walking. *Address:* Oakdene Station Road, Groombridge, Tunbridge Wells, Kent TN3 9NB. *T:* Langton (0892) 864626.

BARNETT, Joseph Anthony, CBE 1983 (OBE 1975); Director (formerly Representative), British Council, Tokyo, 1983–91; *b* 19 Dec. 1931; *s* of Joseph Edward Barnett and Helen Johnson; *m* 1960, Carolina Johnson Rice; one *s* one *d*. *Educ:* St Albans Sch.; Pembroke Coll., Cambridge (BA (Hons) English and Psychology); Edinburgh Univ. (Diploma in Applied Linguistics). Served Army, 1950–51 (2nd Lieut). Teaching, Aylesford House, St Albans, 1954–55; Unilever Ltd, 1955–58; apptd British Council, 1958; Asst Educn Officer, Dacca, Pakistan, 1958; trng at Sch. of Applied Linguistics, Edinburgh Univ., 1960; Educn Officer, Dacca, 1961; seconded to Inst. of Educn, London Univ., 1963; Head, English Language Teaching Inst., London, 1964; Dir of Studies, Regional Inst. of English, Bangalore, India, 1968; Representative, Ethiopia, 1971; Controller, English Language Teaching Div., 1975; Representative, Brazil, 1978–82. *Publications:* (jtly) Getting on in English, 1960; Success with English (language laboratory materials), Books 1–3, 1966–69. *Recreation:* sport (tennis, cricket, riding). *Address:* The Thatch, Stebbing Green, Dunmow, Essex. *T:* Stebbing (037186) 352. *Club:* Athenæum.

BARNETT, Kenneth Thomas, CB 1979; Director, Abbey Data Systems Ltd, since 1984; *b* 12 Jan. 1921; *yr s* of late Frederick Charles Barnett and Ethel Barnett (*née* Powell); *m* 1943, Emily May Lovering; one *d*. *Educ:* Howard Gardens High Sch., Cardiff. Entered Civil Service (Min. of Transport), 1937; Sea Transport Office, Port Said, 1951–54; Asst Sec., 1965; Under-Sec., Cabinet Office (on secondment), 1971–73; Under-Sec., DoE, 1970–76, Dep. Sec., 1976–80. *Recreations:* gardening, watching Rugby football. *Address:* The Stone House, Frith End, Bordon, Hants GU35 0RA. *T:* Bordon (0420) 472856.

BARNETT, Sir Oliver (Charles), Kt 1968; CBE 1954 (OBE 1946); QC 1956; *b* 7 Feb. 1907; *er s* of Charles Frederick Robert Barnett, 2nd Lieut Gloucestershire Regt (TA) (killed in action, 1915), and late Cicely Frances Barnett (*née* Cornish); *m* 1945, Joan, *o surv c* of Capt. W. H. Eve, 13th Hussars (killed in action, 1917), *o s* of late Rt Hon. Sir Harry Trelawney Eve, a Judge of the High Court. *Educ:* Eton. Called to Bar, Middle Temple, 1928; Bencher, Middle Temple, 1964, Oxford Circuit; Central Criminal Court Sessions; Dep. Chm., Somerset QS, 1967–71. Dir of Public Prosecutions Office, 1931; Legal Asst, Judge Advocate General's Office, 1934; Second Deputy Judge Advocate, 1937; First Deputy Judge Advocate, 1938; RAF, 1939–47 (OBE); Wing Comdr (RAFVR); Asst Judge Advocate Gen. (RAF), 1942–47; Asst Judge Advocate Gen. (Army and RAF), 1947–54; Deputy Judge Advocate Gen. (Army and RAF) BAOR, BTA and 2nd TAF, 1953–54; Vice Judge Advocate Gen., 1955–62; Judge Advocate Gen., 1963–68. *Address:* The Almonry, Stogumber, Taunton, Somerset TA4 3SZ. *T:* Stogumber (0984) 56291. *Clubs:* Brooks's, Pratt's.

BARNETT, Rt. Rev. Paul William, PhD; Bishop of North Sydney, and an Assistant Bishop, Diocese of Sydney, since 1990; *b* 23 Sept. 1935; *s* of William and Edna Barnett; *m* 1963, Anita Janet Simpson; two *s* two *d*. *Educ:* Univ. of London (BD Hons 1963, PhD 1978); Univ. of Sydney (MA Hons 1975). Deacon, 1963; priest, 1965; Lectr, Moore Theol Coll., 1964–67; Rector, St Barnabas, Broadway, 1967–73; Rector, Holy Trinity, Adelaide, 1973–79; Master, Robert Menzies Coll., Macquarie Univ., 1980–90. Lecturer, part time: Macquarie Univ., 1980–86; Univ. of Sydney, 1982–. Vis. Prof., Regent Coll., Vancouver, 1987, 1991. Vis. Fellow in History, Macquarie Univ., 1987–. Highly commended author, Christian Booksellers Conf., 1990. *Publications:* Is the New Testament History?, 1986; The Message of 2 Corinthians, 1988; Bethlehem to Patmos, 1989; Apocalypse Now and Then, 1990; The Two Faces of Jesus, 1990; The Servant King, 1991. *Recreations:* tennis, swimming, fishing, fine music. *Address:* Diocese of Sydney, St Andrew's House, Sydney Square, Sydney, NSW 2001, Australia. *T:* (02) 4196761.

BARNETT, William Evans; QC 1984; barrister; a Recorder of the Crown Court, since 1981; *b* 10 March 1937; *s* of late Alec Barnett and late Esmé (*née* Leon); *m* 1976, Lucinda Jane Gilbert, JP, MA, ARCM; two *s*. *Educ:* Repton; Keble Coll., Oxford (BA Jurisprudence, 1961; MA 1965). National Service, RCS, 1956–58. Called to the Bar, Inner Temple, 1962; Major Scholarship, Inner Temple, 1962. Mem., Personal Injuries Litigation Procedure Wkg Pty, 1976–78. *Recreations:* golf, photography, gardening. *Address:* Carleon, 6 Castlemaine Avenue, South Croydon, Surrey CR2 7HQ. *T:* 081–688 9559; 12 King's Bench Walk, Temple, EC4Y 7EL. *T:* 071–583 0811. *Clubs:* Royal Automobile; Surrey Tennis and Country.

BARNEVIK, Percy; President and Chief Executive Officer, ABB Asea Brown Boveri Ltd, Zürich, Switzerland, since 1988; *b* Simrishamn, Sweden, 1941. *Educ:* Sch. of Econs, Gothenburg, Sweden (MBA 1964); Stanford Univ. Johnson Group, 1966–69; Sandvik AB: Group Controller, 1969–75; Pres. of Sandvik, USA, 1975–79; Exec. Vice Pres., 1979–80; Chm., 1983–; Pres. and Chief Exec. Officer, Asea, 1980–87. Member Board: Flakt, 1983–; Providentia, 1987–; Skanska, 1986–. Hon. DTech, Linköping, Sweden, 1989. *Address:* ABB Asea Brown Boveri Ltd, PO Box 8131, CH-8050, Zürich, Switzerland.

BARNEWALL, family name of **Baron Trimlestown.**

BARNEWALL, Sir Reginald Robert, 13th Bt, *cr* 1622; cattle breeder and orchardist at Mount Tamborine; *b* 1 Oct 1924; *o s* of Sir Reginald J. Barnewall, 12th Bt and of Jessie Ellen, *d* of John Fry; *S* father 1961; *m* 1st, 1946, Elsie Muriel (*d* 1962), *d* of Thomas Matthews-Frederick, Brisbane; three *d* (one *s* decd); 2nd, 1962, Maureen Ellen, *d* of William Joseph Daly, South Caulfield, Vic; one *s*. *Educ:* Xavier Coll., Melbourne. Served War of 1939–45, overseas with Australian Imperial Forces. Served with Citizen Military Forces Unit, Royal Australian Armoured Corps, 1948–56. Managing Dir, Southern Airlines Ltd of Melbourne, 1953–58; Operation Manager, Polynesian Airlines, Apia, Western Samoa, 1958–62; Managing Dir, Orchid Beach (Fraser Island) Pty Ltd, 1962–71; Dir, Island Airways Pty Ltd, Pialba, Qld, 1964–68; owner and operator, Coastal-Air Co. (Qld), 1971–76; Dir and Vice-Chm., J. Roy Stevens Pty Ltd, to 1975. *Heir:* *s* Peter Joseph Barnewall, *b* 26 Oct. 1963. *Address:* Mount Tamborine, Queensland 4272, Australia. *Clubs:* United Service (Brisbane); RSL (Surfers Paradise).

BARNSLEY, Thomas Edward, OBE 1975; FCA; Director, H. P. Bulmer Holdings, 1980–87; a Managing Director, Tube Investments Ltd, 1974–82; *b* 1 Sept. 1919; *s* of Alfred E. Barnsley and Ada F. Nightingale; *m* 1947, Margaret Gwyneth Llewellin; one *s* one *d*. *Educ:* Wednesbury Boys' High Sch. ACMA. Friends' Ambulance Unit, 1940–45. Price Waterhouse Peat & Co., South America, 1948–49; Asst Sec., 1958–62, Group Financial Controller, 1962–65, Tube Investments Ltd; Chm. and Man. Dir, Raleigh Industries Ltd, 1968–74. Chm., Nat. Industrial Cttee, Nat. Savings Movement, 1975–78. *Recreation:* gardening. *Address:* The Old Rectory, Llanelidan, near Ruthin, Clwyd LL15 2PT.

BARNSTAPLE, Archdeacon of; *see* Lloyd, Ven. B. T.

BARON, Alexander; *see* Baron, J. A.

BARON, Franklin Andrew Merrifield; Dominican High Commissioner to London, 1986–88; Permanent Representative to United Nations and to Organisation of American States, 1982–88; *b* 19 Jan. 1923; *m* 1973, Sybil Eva McIntyre. *Educ:* Portsmouth Govt Sch., Dominica Grammar Sch.; St Mary's Acad. A. A. Baron & Co.: entered firm, 1939; Partner, 1945; sole owner, 1978–. Member: Roseau Town Council, 1945–47 and 1961–63; Legislative and Exec. Councils, 1954–66; Leader, United People's Party, 1954–66; Minister of Trade and Production, 1957; Chief Minister and Minister of Finance, 1960–61. Ambassador to USA, 1982–86. Chairman: National Commercial Bank, 1986–; Fort Young Hotel Co., 1986–; Dir, New Chronicle, 1984–. Member: Public Services Commn, 1976–78; Electoral Commn, 1979–; Dominica Boundaries Commn, 1979–; Bd, Dominca Electricity Services, 1981– (Chm., 1983–); Bd, Industrial Develt Corp., 1984–; Chm., Dominica Public Library, 1985–. *Recreations:* horticulture, reading, travel. *Address:* 14 Cork Street, Roseau, Dominica. *T:* 809 448 2445.

BARON, (Joseph) Alexander; writer; *b* 4 Dec. 1917; *s* of Barnet Baron and Fanny Levinson; *m* 1960, Delores Salzedo; one *s*. *Educ:* Hackney Downs Sch., London. Asst Editor, The Tribune, 1938–39. Served War of 1939–45, Army. Editor, New Theatre, 1946–49. *Publications: novels:* From the City, From the Plough, 1948; There's No Home, 1950; Rosie Hogarth, 1951; With Hope, Farewell, 1952; The Human Kind, 1953; The Golden Princess, 1954; Queen of the East, 1956; Seeing Life, 1958; The Lowlife, 1963; Strip Jack Naked, 1966; King Dido, 1969; The In-Between Time, 1971; Gentle Folk, 1976; Franco is Dying, 1977; also film scripts and television plays. *Address:* c/o Unna and Durbridge, 24 Pottery Lane, W11 4LZ.

BARON, Dr (Ora) Wendy; Curator, Government Art Collection, since 1978; *b* 20 March 1937; *d* of Dr S. B. Dimson and Gladys Felicia Dimson, *qv*; *m* 1st, 1960, Jeremy Hugh Baron (marr. diss.); one *s* one *d*; 2nd, 1990, David Joseph Wyatt, *qv*. *Educ:* St Paul's Girls' Sch.; Courtauld Institute of Art (BA, PhD). *Publications:* Sickert, 1973; Miss Ethel Sands and her Circle, 1977; The Camden Town Group, 1979; exhibn catalogues, articles and reviews in professional jls in the field of modern British art. *Address:* c/o Office of Arts and Libraries, Horse Guards Road, SW1P 3AL.

BARÓN CRESPO, Enrique Carlos; lawyer; Member, European Parliament, since 1986 (President, 1989–91); *b* Madrid, 27 March 1944; *m*; one *s*. *Educ:* Univ. of Madrid (LLL); Inst. Católico de Dirección de Empresas (Lic. en Ciencias Empresariales); Ecole Supérieure des Scis Econ. et Commerciales, Paris (Dip.). Lectr in Agricl Econs, Inst. Nacional de Estudios Agrarios, Valladolid, and in Structural Econs, Univ. of Madrid, 1966–70; lawyer in private practice, 1970–77. Mem. (PSOE), Congress of Deputies, Spain, 1977–; spokesman on econ. and budgetary affairs, 1977–82; Minister of Transport, Tourism and Communications, 1982–85. European Parliament: a Vice-Pres., 1987–89; Pres., Spanish Socialist Gp. Pres., Internat. European Movt, 1987–. *Publications:* Población y Hambre en el Mundo; El Final del Campesinado; La Civilización del Automóvil; Europa 92: el rapto del futuro; contribs on economic and social questions to major Spanish periodicals. *Address:* European Parliament, 1040 Brussels, Belgium; Centre Européen, Plateau de Kirchberg, L-2929, Luxembourg.

BARR, A. W. Cleeve, CBE 1972; retired 1977; *b* 1910; *s* of Albert John Barr and Ellen (*née* Cleeve); *m* 1st, 1935, Edith M. Edwards, BA (*d* 1965); one *s* one *d* (and one *s* decd); 2nd, 1966, Mrs Mary W. Harley (*widow*). *Educ:* Borlase, Marlow; Liverpool Univ. Private offices (Charles Holden and Paul Mauger); Herts CC (schools) and LCC (housing). Dep. Housing Architect, LCC, 1956–57; Development Architect, Ministry of Education, 1957–58; Chief Architect, Min. of Housing and Local Govt, 1959–64. Dir, Nat. Building Agency, 1964–77 (Man. Dir, 1967–77); Dir, Nat. Building Agency Film Unit, 1977–80; Vice-Pres., UK Housing Trust, 1981–89. Hon. Sec. RIBA, 1963–65. *Recreation:* painting. *Address:* 72 Eastwick Road, Walton-on-Thames, Surrey KT12 5AR.

BARR, David; a Metropolitan Stipendiary Magistrate, since 1976; *b* Glasgow, 15 Oct. 1925; *s* of late Walter and Betty Barr; *m* 1960, Ruth Weitzman; one *s* one *d*. *Educ:* Haberdashers' Aske's Hampstead Sch.; Brookline High Sch., Boston, USA; Edinburgh Univ.; University Coll., London (LLB). Royal Navy, 1943–47. Solicitor, 1953; private practice, 1953–76 (Partner, Pritchard Englefield & Tobin). JP Inner London Area, 1963–76; Chm., Inner London Juvenile Panel, 1969–76; Dep. Chm., N Westminster PSD, 1968–76. Manager, Finnart House Sch., Weybridge, 1955–73 (Trustee, 1973–, Chm., 1985–). *Recreations:* book collecting, bridge. *Address:* Highbury Corner Magistrates' Court, Holloway Road, N7 8JA. *Clubs:* Garrick, MCC.

BARR, Ian; Chairman, Scottish Post Office Board (formerly Post Office Scotland), 1984–88; Board Member, National Girobank Scotland, 1984–88; *b* 6 April 1927; *s* of late Peter McAlpine Barr and Isobel Baillie; *m* 1st, 1951, Gertrud Karla (marr. diss. 1988), *d* of late August Otto Odefey, Schleswig-Holstein; two *d*; 2nd, 1988, cousin Margaret Annie McAlpine, *d* of late Andrew McAlpine Barr and Ann Jane Brodie-Scott. *Educ:* Boroughmuir High Sch., Edinburgh. Post Office: Asst Postal Controller, N Western Region, 1955; Inspector of Postal Services, 1957; Asst Controller, Planning, 1962; Principal, 1966; Mem., CS Selection Bd, 1966–71; Post Office: Asst Sec., 1971; Regional Dir, Eastern Region, 1976; Dir, Bldgs, Mechanisation and Transport, 1978; Dir, Estates Exec., 1981–84. Chairman: PO National Arts Cttee, 1976–87; Scottish Cttee, Assoc. for Business Sponsorship of the Arts, 1986–88; CEPT (Bâtiments), 1982–86; Saltire Soc., 1986–87; Member: British Materials Handling Board, 1978–81; Scottish Council, CBI, 1984–88. Director: St Mary's Music School, Edinburgh, 1987– (Chm., Management Cttee, 1988–90); Friedman Camerata of St Andrew, 1988–89; Scottish Nat. Orch., 1988–90; Mem., Edinburgh Fest. Council, 1988–89. Mem., Scottish Convention Cttee, 1988, leading to establishment of Scottish Constitutional Convention, 1989– (report, A Claim of Right for Scotland, 1988). Director: Endocrine Res. Trust, Western Gen. Hosp., Edinburgh, 1987–; Lamp of Lothian Collegiate Trust, Haddington, 1988–. *Recreations:* composing serial music, constructing a metaphysical system. *Address:* Scott House, Newcastleton, Roxburghshire TD9 0QU.

BARR, Rev. Prof. James, MA, BD, DD; FBA 1969; Professor of Hebrew Bible, Vanderbilt University, Nashville, Tennessee, since 1989; *b* 20 March 1924; *s* of Rev. Prof. Allan Barr, DD; *m* 1950, Jane J. S. Hepburn, MA; two *s* one *d.* *Educ:* Daniel Stewart's Coll., Edinburgh; Edinburgh Univ. (MA 1948, BD 1951); MA 1976, BD DD 1981, Oxon. Served War of 1939–45 as pilot in RNVR (Fleet Air Arm), 1942–45. Minister of Church of Scotland, Tiberias, Israel, 1951–53; Prof. of New Testament Literature and Exegesis, Presbyterian Coll., Montreal, 1953–55; Prof. of Old Testament Literature and Theology, Edinburgh Univ., 1955–61; Prof. of Old Testament Literature and Theology, Princeton Theological Seminary, 1961–65; Prof. of Semitic Languages and Literatures, Manchester Univ., 1965–76; Oriel Prof. of the Interpretation of Holy Scripture, and Fellow of Oriel Coll., Oxford Univ., 1976–78 (Hon. Fellow, 1980); Regius Prof. of Hebrew, Oxford Univ., and Student of Christ Church, 1978–89. Visiting Professor: Hebrew Univ., Jerusalem, 1973; Chicago Univ., 1975, 1981; Strasbourg Univ., 1975–76; Brown Univ., Providence, RI, 1985; Univ. of Otago, NZ, 1986; Univ. of South Africa, 1986; Vanderbilt Univ., Nashville, Tenn, 1987–88; lectured in Princeton Univ., 1962–63; in Union Theol. Seminary, New York, 1963; Lectures: Currie, Austin Theol. Seminary, Texas, 1964; Cadbury, Birmingham Univ., 1969; Croall, Edinburgh Univ., 1970; Grinfield, on the Septuagint, Oxford Univ., 1974–78; Firth, Nottingham Univ., 1978; Sprunt, Richmond, Va, 1982; Sanderson, Ormond Coll., Melbourne, 1982; Faculty, Cardiff, 1986; Schweich, British Acad., 1986; Cole, Vanderbilt, 1988; Sarum, Oxford, 1989; Guggenheim Memorial Fellowship for study in biblical semantics, 1965. Mem., Inst. for Advanced Study, Princeton, NJ, 1985. Editor: Jl of Semitic Studies, 1965–76; Oxford Hebrew Dictionary, 1974–80. President: Soc. for OT Studies, 1973; British Assoc. for Jewish Studies, 1978. FRAS 1969. Hon. Fellow, SOAS, 1975. Hon. DD: Knox Coll., Toronto, 1964; Dubuque, 1974; St Andrews, 1974; Edinburgh, 1983; Victoria Univ., Toronto, 1988; Hon. DTheol: Univ. of South Africa, 1986; Protestant Theol Faculty, Paris, 1988; Hon. MA Manchester, 1969. Corresp. Mem., Göttingen Acad. of Sciences, 1976; Mem., Norwegian Acad. of Science and Letters, 1977; Hon. Mem., Soc. of Biblical Lit. (USA), 1983. *Publications:* The Semantics of Biblical Language, 1961; Biblical Words for Time, 1962; Old and New in Interpretation, 1966; Comparative Philology and the Text of the Old Testament, 1968; The Bible in the Modern World, 1973; Fundamentalism, 1977; The Typology of Literalism, 1979; Explorations in Theology 7: The Scope and Authority of the Bible, 1980; Holy Scripture: Canon, Authority, Criticism, 1983; Escaping from Fundamentalism, 1984; The Variable Spellings of the Hebrew Bible, 1988; articles in Semitic and biblical journals. *Recreation:* bird watching. *Address:* 4400 Belmont Park Terrace, no 203, Nashville, Tenn 37215, USA; 6 Fitzherbert Close, Iffley, Oxford OX4 4EN. *T:* Oxford (0865) 772741; 11 Résidence Galawa, Quai Nord-Est, 34340 Marseillan (Hérault), France; C. Aspret 21, 03792 Orba (Alicante), Spain.

BARR, Maj.-Gen. John Alexander James Pooler, CBE 1989; Engineer-in-Chief (Army), since 1991; *b* 29 Jan. 1939. 2nd Lieut, RE, 1960; Lt-Col, 1978; GSO1 (DS) SC, 1978; Brig. 1983; Comdt, Royal Sch. of Mil. Engrg, Chatham, 1983–87; Dir of Army Staff Duties, MoD, 1987–89; DCS (Support), HQ Allied Forces Northern Europe, 1989–91. *Address:* Northumberland House, Northumberland Avenue, WC2N 5BP.

BARR, Kenneth Glen; Sheriff of South Strathclyde, Dumfries and Galloway at Dumfries, since 1976; *b* 20 Jan. 1941; *o s* of Rev. Gavin Barr and Mrs Catherine McLellan Barr (*née* McGhie); *m* 1970, Susanne Crichton Keir. *Educ:* Ardrossan Acad.; Royal High Sch.; Edinburgh Univ. (MA, LLB). Admitted to Faculty of Advocates, 1964. *Address:* Sheriff Court House, Dumfries DG1 2AN.

BARR, Prof. Murray Llewellyn, OC (Canada) 1968; FRS 1972; Professor of Anatomy, University of Western Ontario, 1949–79, now Emeritus Professor; *b* 20 June 1908; Canadian; *m* 1934, Ruth Vivian King; three *s* one *d.* *Educ:* Univ. of Western Ontario (BA, MD, MSc). FRSC 1958; FRCP(C) 1964; FACP 1965; FRCOG 1972. Served War of 1939–45 as MO, RCAF (Wing Comdr). Univ. of Western Ontario: Instructor in Anatomy, 1936–45; Associate Prof. of Anatomy, 1945–49 (Chm., Dept of Anatomy, 1951–67). Hon. Degrees: LLD Queen's, 1963; LLD Toronto, 1964; Drmed Basel, 1966; LLD Alberta, 1967; LLD Dalhousie, 1968; LLD Saskatchewan, 1973; DSc Western Ontario, 1974. *Publications:* The Human Nervous System: an anatomical viewpoint, 1972, 5th edn (with J. A. Kiernan) 1988; A Century of Medicine at Western, 1977; numerous scientific papers. *Address:* 452 Old Wonderland Road, London, Ontario, Canada N6K 3R2. *T:* (519) 471–5618. *Club:* Harvey (London, Ont.).

BARR, His Honour Judge Reginald Alfred; a Circuit Judge (formerly Judge of County Courts), since 1970; *b* 21 Nov. 1920; *s* of Alfred Charles Barr; *m* 1946, Elaine, 2nd *d* of James William Charles O'Bala Morris, Llanstephan, Carmarthenshire. *Educ:* Christ's Hospital; Trinity Coll., Oxford (MA). Served War, 1941–46, Middle East and Burma. Called to Bar, Middle Temple, 1954; Standing Counsel to Registrar of Restrictive Trading Agreements, 1962–70. Mem. Review Bd for Govt Contracts, 1969–70. *Address:* 42 Bathurst Mews, Hyde Park, W2. *T:* 071–262 5731.

BARR, William Greig, DL; Rector, Exeter College, Oxford, 1972–82; *b* 10 June 1917; *s* of late William S. Barr, Glasgow; *m* 1954, Helen Georgopoulos (*d* 1988); two *s.* *Educ:* Sedbergh Sch.; Magdalen Coll., Oxford. Stanhope Prize, 1938; 1st cl., Hon. Sch. of Modern History, 1939. Served War, 1939–45: Lt-Col, Royal Devon Yeomanry. Exeter College, Oxford: Fellow, 1945–72; Sub-Rector, 1947–54; Sen. Tutor, 1960–66; Hon. Fellow, 1982; Oxford University: Lectr in Modern History, 1949–72; Jun. Proctor, 1951–52; Pro-Vice-Chancellor, 1980–82. Hon. Treas., Oxford Univ. Rugby Football Club, 1948–73. A Rhodes Trustee, 1975–87. Visiting Prof. of Hist., Univ. of South Carolina, 1968. Pres., Brighton Coll. DL Oxon 1974. *Address:* 24 Northmoor Road, Oxford OX2 6UR. *T:* Oxford (0865) 58253.

BARR YOUNG, Gavin Neil; His Honour Judge Barr Young; a Circuit Judge, since 1988; *b* 14 Aug. 1939; *s* of Dr James Barr Young and Elsie Barr Young (*née* Hodgkinson); *m* 1969, Barbara Elizabeth Breckon; two *d.* *Educ:* Loretto Sch., Musselburgh; Leeds Univ. (LLB). Called to the Bar, Gray's Inn, 1963; Member, North Eastern Circuit, 1964–88 (North Eastern Circuit Junior, 1968); a Recorder of the Crown Court, 1979–88. *Recreations:* gardening, music, sailing. *Address:* Flaxbourne House, Great Ouseburn, York YO5 9RG. *T:* Boroughbridge (0423) 330629. *Club:* Lansdowne.

BARRACK, William Sample, Jr; Senior Vice-President, Texaco Inc., NY, since 1983; *b* 26 July 1929; *s* of William Sample Barrack and Edna Mae Henderson; *m* 1953, Evelyn Irene Ball; one *s* one *d.* *Educ:* Pittsburgh Univ. BSc (Engr) 1950. FInstPet 1981. Comdr, USN, 1950–53. Joined Texaco Inc., 1953; marketing and management positions in USA, 1953–67; in Europe, 1967–71; Vice-President: in NY, 1971–80; Marketing Dept, Europe, 1971–76; Producing Dept, Eastern Hemisphere, 1976–77; Personnel and Corporate Services Dept, 1977–80; Chm. and Chief Exec., Texaco Ltd, London, 1980–82. Director: Caltex Petroleum Corp.; Texaco Foundn Inc. Governor, Foreign Policy Assoc.; Mem., US Naval War College Foundn; Trustee, Manhattanville College. *Address:* Texaco Inc., 2000 Westchester Avenue, White Plains, New York, NY 10650, USA. *Clubs:* Woodway Country; Ox Ridge Hunt; Ida Lewis Yacht; North Sea (Belgium); Clambake (Newport, RI).

BARRACLOUGH, Air Chief Marshal Sir John, KCB 1970 (CB 1969); CBE 1961; DFC 1942; AFC 1941 (despatches twice); FRAeS; FRSA, FIPM, FBIM, MIPR; Hon. Inspector General, Royal Auxiliary Air Force, 1984–89; Gentleman Usher to the Sword of State, 1980–88; Vice-Chairman: British Export Finance Advisory Council, 1982–89; Commonwealth War Graves Commission, 1981–86 (Commissioner 1974–86); company director; *b* 2 May 1918; *s* of late Horatio and Marguerite Maude Barraclough; *m* 1946, Maureen (*née* McCormack), niece of George Noble, Count Plunkett; one *d.* *Educ:* Cranbrook Sch. Service Artists' Rifles, 1935–38. Commissioned RAF, 1938. Air Vice-Marshal, 1964; Air Marshal, 1970; Air Chief Marshal, 1973. Served Near, Middle and Far East; first single-engined jet flight to S Africa, 1951. Examining Wing, Central Flying Sch., 1948–51; Staff of IDC, 1952–54; Station Commander, RAF Biggin Hill, 1952–54 and Middleton St George, 1954–56; GC Ops, FEAF, 1958–61; Dir of Public Relations, Air Ministry, 1961–64; AOC No 19 Group, and NATO Air Comdr, Central Sub-Area, Eastern Atlantic Comd, 1964–67; Harvard Business Sch., AMP, 1967; AOA, Bomber Command, 1967–68; AOA, Strike Comd, 1968–70; Vice-Chief of Defence Staff, 1970–72; Air Secretary, 1972–74; Comdt, Royal Coll. of Defence Studies, 1974–76, retired. Underwriting Mem. of Lloyd's, 1979–. Hon. Air Cdre, No 3 (County of Devon) Maritime HQ Unit, RAuxAF, 1979–90. Mem., RAF Training and Educn Adv. Bd, 1976–79; Vice Chm., Air League Council, 1977–81; Chm., RUSI Council, 1977–80, Vice-Pres., 1980–90; President: Air Public Relations Assoc., 1976–; West Devon Area, St John Ambulance, 1977–85. OStJ 1985. Past President: RAF Modern Pentathlon Assoc.; Combined Services Equitation Assoc. Editl Dir, 1978–81, Vice-Chm. of Editl Bd, 1981–86, NATO's Sixteen Nations. *Publications:* (jtly) The Third World War, 1978; contrib. to The Third World War: The Untold Story, 1982; contribs to professional jls. *Recreations:* country pursuits, sailing (Irish Admiral's Cup Team, 1973). *Address:* c/o Hoare and Co., Fleet Street, EC4. *Clubs:* Boodle's, Royal Air Force; Bath and County; Royal Western Yacht.

BARRACLOUGH, Sir Kenneth (James Priestley), Kt 1978; CBE 1967 (OBE 1945); TD; JP; Chief Metropolitan Magistrate 1975–78, retired; *b* 1907; *s* of Herbert Barraclough, Leeds; *m* 1931, Gladys Evelyn, *d* of Charles Henderson, Liverpool and Rio de Janeiro; two *s* one *d.* *Educ:* Oundle Sch.; Clare Coll., Cambridge. Barrister, Middle Temple, 1929 (Master of the Bench, 1975), North Eastern Circuit; Inns of Court Regt, TA, 1938; Col 1945. HQ, 21st Army Group (despatches). Metropolitan Magistrate, 1954; Dep. Chm. Appeals Cttee, Hampshire QS, 1957–62; Chm., HO Poisons Board, 1958–76. Member: Adv. Cttee on Drug Dependence, 1966–70; Adv. Council on the Misuse of Drugs, 1972–73; Medicines Commn, 1969–75. JP Hampshire, 1957. *Address:* 18 Fitzroy Road, Fleet, Hants GU13 8JJ.

BARRAN, Sir David Haven, Kt 1971; Chairman, Midland Bank Ltd, 1980–82 (Deputy Chairman, 1975–80); *b* 23 May 1912; *s* of Sir John Barran, 2nd Bt and Alice Margarita (*née* Parks); *m* 1944, Jane Lechmere Macaskie; four *s* three *d.* *Educ:* Winchester; Trinity Coll., Cambridge. BA 1934. Joined Asiatic Petroleum Co., 1934; served in Egypt, Palestine, Sudan, India, 1935–46. Pres., Asiatic Petroleum Corp., New York, 1958; Managing Dir, Royal Dutch/Shell Group, 1961–72; Chm., Shell Oil Co., 1970–72; Director: Shell Transport and Trading Co. Ltd, 1961–83 (Dep. Chm., 1964–67; Chm., 1967–72; Man. Dir, 1964–73); General Accident Insurance; BICC; Glaxo Hldgs. Chairman: CBI Cttee on Inflation Accounting, 1973–74; Adv. Cttee on Appt of Advertising Agents, 1975–78 (Mem., 1973–78); Ct of Governors, Administrative Staff Coll., 1971–76; Governor, Centre for Environmental Studies, 1972–75. Comdr, Order of Oranje Nassau, 1971; Comdr, Order of Merit, Fed. Repub. of Germany, 1980. *Recreations:* gardening, shooting, embroidery (Pres., Embroiderers' Guild, 1982–87). *Address:* 36 Kensington Square, W8. *T:* 071–937 5664; Brent Eleigh Hall, Suffolk. *T:* Lavenham (0787) 247202. *Club:* River (New York).

BARRAN, Sir John (Napoleon Ruthven), 4th Bt *cr* 1895; Head of Information Technology, Central Office of Information, 1985–87, retired; *b* 14 Feb. 1934; *s* of Sir John Leighton Barran, 3rd Bt, and Hon. Alison Mary (*d* 1973), 3rd *d* of 9th Baron Ruthven, CB, CMG, DSO; *S* father, 1974; *m* 1965, Jane Margaret, *d* of Sir Stanley Hooker, CBE, FRS; one *s* one *d.* *Educ:* Heatherdown Sch., Ascot; Winchester Coll. National Service, 1952–54, Lieut, 5th Roy. Inniskilling Dragoon Guards; served Canal Zone. Asst Account Executive: Dorland Advertising Ltd, 1956–58; Masius & Fergusson Advertising Ltd, 1958–61; Account Executive, Ogilvy, Benson & Mather (New York) Inc., 1961–63; Overseas TV News Service, COI, 1964; First Sec. (Information), British High Commission, Ottawa, 1965–67; Central Office of Information: Home Documentary Film Section, 1967–72; Overseas TV and Film News Services, 1972–75; TV Commercials and Fillers Unit, 1975–78; Head of Viewdata Unit, 1978–85. *Recreations:* entertaining, gardening, shooting. *Heir:* *s* John Ruthven Barran, *b* 10 Nov. 1971. *Address:* 17 St Leonard's Terrace, SW3 4QG. *T:* 071–730 2801; The Hermitage, East Bergholt, Suffolk; Middle Rigg Farm, Sawley, North Yorks. *Club:* Royal Automobile.

BARRASS, Gordon Stephen; HM Diplomatic Service; Under Secretary, Cabinet Office, since 1991; *b* 5 Aug. 1940; *s* of James and Mary Barrass; *m* 1965, Alice Cecile Oberg (*d* 1984). *Educ:* Hertford Grammar Sch.; LSE (BSc (Econs)); SOAS (postgrad.). FCO, 1965–67; Chinese Language student, Hong Kong Univ., 1967–69; in Office of HM Chargé d'Affaires, Peking, 1970–72; Cultural Exchange Dept, FCO, 1972–74; UKMIS Geneva, 1974–78; Planning Staff, FCO, 1979–82; RCDS, 1983; seconded to MoD, 1984, Cabinet Office, 1987. *Recreations:* Chinese and Western art, classical archaeology, opera, travel, books. *Address:* c/o Foreign and Commonwealth Office, SW1A 2AH. *Club:* Athenæum.

BARRATT, Francis Russell, CB 1975; Director, Amdahl (UK), since 1983; Member, Review Board for Government Contracts, since 1984; *b* 16 Nov. 1924; *s* of Frederick Russell Barratt; *m* 1st, 1949, Janet Mary Sherborne (marr. diss. 1978); three *s*; 2nd, 1979, Josephine Norah Harrison (*née* McCririck). *Educ:* Durban High Sch., SA; Clifton; University Coll., Oxford. War Service, 1943–46; Captain, Intelligence Corps, 1946. Asst Principal, HM Treasury, 1949; Principal, 1953; First Sec., UK High Commission, Karachi, 1956–58; Asst Sec., 1962, Under Sec., 1968, Dep. Sec., 1973–82, HM Treasury. *Recreations:* reading, golf, music. *Address:* Little Paddocks, Smallhythe Road, Tenterden, Kent TN30 7LY. *T:* Tenterden (05806) 3734. *Club:* Athenæum.

BARRATT, Gilbert Alexander; Master of the Supreme Court, Chancery Division, since 1980; *b* 1930; *s* of Arthur Walter Barratt and Frances Erskine Barratt (*née* Scott); *m* 1964, Fiona MacDermott; one *s* one *d.* *Educ:* Winchester; New Coll., Oxford. BA Modern History. Qualified as Solicitor, 1957; Partner: Stitt & Co., 1960–63; Thicknesse & Hull, 1963–67; Lee Bolton & Lee, 1967–78; Winckworth & Pemberton, 1978–80. *Recreation:* travel. *Address:* The Old School, Clungunford, Craven Arms, Shropshire SY7 0PN. *Club:* Travellers'.

BARRATT, Herbert George Harold, OBE 1966; General Secretary, Confederation of Shipbuilding and Engineering Unions, 1957–70; *b* 12 Jan. 1905; *m* 1926; one *s* three *d.*

Educ: Vicarage Street Church of England Sch., Nuneaton. Nuneaton Borough Councillor, 1945–47; Mem. Nat. Cttee AEU, 1943–48; Delegate to USSR, 1946. Chm. Nuneaton Labour Party, 1944–46; Coventry Dist. Cttee AEU, 1943–49; Shop Steward Convener, Daimler Motors, 1940–49; Appeals Board Assessor during war years; Nat. Insurance Tribunal Assessor; elected Nat. Organiser AEU, 1949–57. Formerly Member: Gas Adv. Council; Shipbuilding and Ship repairing Council; Nat. Adv. Council for the Motor Manufacturing Industry; Motor Industry Joint Labour Council; British Railways Productivity Council; Econ. Develt Cttee for Mech. Engrg Industry; Econ. Develt Cttee for Electrical Engrg Industry; Econ. Develt Cttee for Motor Manufacturing Industry; Industrial Training Board, Engrg; Industrial Training Board, Shipbuilding; British Productivity team to Swedish Shipyards, 1959; visited German Federal Railways, 1960; Exchange Leader Scheme visitor to USA, 1961; Vice-Chm., Sub-Cttee on Programme and Planning, Metal Trades Cttee, ILO, Geneva, 1965. *Recreation:* gardening. *Address:* 7 Rosebery Close, Sittingbourne, Kent ME10 3DB.

BARRATT, Sir Lawrence (Arthur), (Sir Lawrie Barratt), Kt 1982; FCIS; Chairman, Barratt Developments PLC, and subsidiary companies, 1962–88, and since 1991 (Managing Director, 1962–88; Life President, since 1989); *b* Newcastle, 14 Nov. 1927; *m* 1st, 1951 (marr. diss. 1984); two *s*; 2nd, 1984, Mary Sheila (*née* Brierley). Founded Barratt Developments, as a private co., 1958. *Recreations:* golf, shooting, sailing. *Address:* Barratt Developments, Wingrove House, Ponteland Road, Newcastle upon Tyne NE5 3DP.

BARRATT, Michael Fieldhouse; communications consultant; broadcaster on radio and television; Chairman: Commercial Video Ltd, since 1981; Michael Barratt Ltd, since 1977; Director, Travel and Leisure Communications Ltd, since 1982; *b* 3 Jan. 1928; *s* of late Wallace Milner Barratt and Doris Barratt; *m* 1st, 1952, Joan Francesca Warner (marr. diss.); three *s* three *d*; 2nd, 1977, Dilys Jane Morgan; two *s* one *d*. *Educ:* Rossall and Paisley Grammar Sch. Entered journalism, Kemsley Newspapers, 1944; Editor, Nigerian Citizen, 1956; *television:* Reporter, Panorama, 1963; Presenter: 24 Hours, 1965–69; Nationwide, 1969–77; Songs of Praise, 1977–82; Reporting London, 1983–88; *radio:* Question-Master, Gardeners' Question Time, 1973–79. Rector, Aberdeen Univ., 1973. Hon. LLD Aberdeen, 1975. FRHS. *Publications:* Michael Barratt, 1973; Michael Barratt's Down-to-Earth Gardening Book, 1974; Michael Barratt's Complete Gardening Book, 1977; Golf with Tony Jacklin, 1978. *Recreations:* golf, cricket, listening. *Address:* 5/7 Forlease Road, Maidenhead, Berks SL6 1RP. *T:* Maidenhead (0628) 770800. *Clubs:* Reform, Lord's Taverners.

BARRATT, Prof. Michael George; Professor of Mathematics, Northwestern University, Illinois, since 1974; *b* 26 Jan. 1927; *e s* of George Bernard Barratt and Marjorie Holloway Barratt (*née* Oldham); *m* 1952, Jenepher Hudson; one *s* four *d*. *Educ:* Stationers' Company's Sch.; Magdalen Coll., Oxford. Junior Lecturer, Oxford Univ., 1950–52; Fellow, Magdalen Coll., Oxford, 1952–56; Lectr, Brasenose Coll., Oxford, 1955–59; Sen. Lectr and Reader, 1959–63, Prof. of Pure Maths, 1964–74, Manchester Univ. Vis. Prof., Chicago Univ., 1963–64. *Publications:* papers in mathematical jls. *Address:* Department of Mathematics, Northwestern University, Lunt Building, Evanston, Ill 60201, USA.

BARRATT, Sir Richard (Stanley), Kt 1988; CBE 1981; QPM 1974; HM Chief Inspector of Constabulary, 1987–90; *b* 11 Aug. 1928; *s* of Richard Barratt and Mona Barratt; *m* 1952, Sarah Elizabeth Hale; one *s* two *d*. *Educ:* Saltley Grammar Sch., Birmingham. CBIM. Birmingham City Police (Constable to Chief Inspector), 1949–65; Dir, Home Office Crime Prevention Centre, Stafford, 1963; seconded to Home Office (Res. and Develt), 1964; Sen. Comd Course, Police Coll., 1964; Supt, Cheshire Constab., 1965, Chief Supt, 1966; Asst Chief Constable, Manchester City Police, 1967; Asst Chief Constable, Manchester and Salford Police, 1968, Dep. Chief Constable, 1972; Dep. Chief Constable, Greater Manchester Police, 1974; Chief Constable, S Yorks Police, 1975–78; HM Inspector of Constabulary, 1978–87. Review of the Royal Bahamas Police, 1985. Led Police delegns to China, 1987, Pakistan, 1990. Assessor, Guildford and Woolwich Inquiry, 1990–. Mem., Gaming Bd for GB, 1991–. OStJ 1978. *Recreations:* reading, gardening, golf. *Address:* c/o Home Office, Room 565, Queen Anne's Gate, SW1H 9AT.

BARRATT, Robin Alexander; QC 1989; *b* 24 April 1945; *s* of Harold and Phyllis Barratt; *m* 1972, Gillian Anne Ellis; one *s* three *d*. *Educ:* Charterhouse; Worcester Coll., Oxford (Exhibnr; BA Hons, MA). Harmsworth Entrance Exhibnr, 1965, Schol. 1969; called to the Bar, Middle Temple, 1970. Lectr in Law, Kingston Polytechnic, 1968–71; Western Circuit, 1971. Councillor (C), London Bor. of Merton, 1978–86. *Recreations:* squash, fell walking, music. *Address:* 2 Mitre Court Buildings, Temple, EC4Y 7BX. *T:* 071–583 1355.

BARRATT-BOYES, Sir Brian (Gerald), KBE 1971 (CBE 1966); Surgeon-in-Charge, Cardio-Thoracic Surgical Unit, Greenlane Hospital, Auckland, 1964–88, now Hon. Consultant; Hon. Senior Cardio-Thoracic Surgeon, Mercy (formerly Mater Misericordiae) Hospital, Auckland, 1966–89; *b* 13 Jan. 1924; *s* of Gerald Cave Boyes and Edna Myrtle Boyes (*née* Barratt); *m* 1st, 1949, Norma Margaret Thompson (marr. diss. 1986); five *s*; 2nd, 1986, Sara Rose Monester. *Educ:* Wellington Coll.; Univ. of Otago. MB, ChB 1946; FRACS 1952; FACS 1960; ChM 1962. Lectr in Anatomy, Otago Univ. Med. Sch., 1947; House Surg. and Registrar, Wellington Hosp., 1948–50; Surgical Registrar and Pathology Registrar, Palmerston North Hosp., 1950–52; Fellow in Cardio-Thoracic Surgery, Mayo Clinic, USA, 1953–55; Nuffield Trav. Fellowship UK (Bristol Univ.), 1956; Sen. Cardio-Thoracic Surg., Greenlane Hosp., 1957. Hon. Prof. of Surgery, Auckland Univ., 1971; Sir Arthur Sims Commonwealth Travelling Prof., 1982. FRSNZ 1970. Hon. FACS 1977; Hon. FRCS 1985; Hon. Fellow, Royal Coll. of Surgeons of Thailand, 1987; Hon. FACC 1988. Hon. DSc, 1985. R. T. Hall Prize for Disting. Cardiac Surgery in Austr. and NZ, 1966; René Leriche Prize, Société Internationale de Chirurgie, 1987. *Publications:* Heart Disease in Infancy: diagnosis and surgical treatment, 1973; (jtly) Cardiac Surgery, 1986; numerous in med. jls throughout the world. *Recreations:* farming, trout fishing. *Address:* Greenhills, Main Road, Waiwera, New Zealand. *Club:* Northern (Auckland).

BARRAULT, Jean-Louis; Officer of the Legion of Honour; actor, director, producer; Director: Odéon-Théâtre de France, 1959–68; Théâtre des Nations, Paris, 1965–67, and since 1971; *b* Vésinet, France, 8 Sept. 1910; *m* Madeleine Renaud, *qv*. *Educ:* public sch., Paris; Collège Chaptal. Taught at Collège Chaptal, 1931; Atelier Dramatic Sch. and Theatre (schol.), 1931–35; formed experimental theatrical company. Served War of 1939–40. With Comédie-Française as producer-director, 1940–46. At instigation of French Govt formed company with Madeleine Renaud, Marigny Theatre. Has appeared at Venice; Edinburgh Festival, 1948, 1957 and 1985; St James's Theatre, London, 1951; Palace Theatre, London, 1956, etc.; produced Duel of Angels, Apollo, 1958; World Theatre Season, Aldwych, 1965, 1968; toured Western Europe, S America, Canada, and US. Films include: Les Beaux Jours, Hélène, Les Perles de la couronne, La Symphonie fantastique, Les Enfants du Paradis, D'Hommes à hommes, Versailles, Chappaqua, Le Puritain, La route de Varennes. *Publications:* Une Troupe et ses auteurs, 1950; Reflections on the Theatre (autobiography), 1951; Rabelais, 1971 (prod, Paris 1968–69, tours in Japan and USA, 1969, London 1971); Memories for Tomorrow: the memoirs of Jean-Louis Barrault, 1974; articles in theatrical publications. *Address:* 18 avenue du Président Wilson, 75116 Paris, France.

BARRE, Raymond; Chevalier de la Légion d'Honneur, Chevalier de l'Ordre National du Mérite agricole, Officier des Palmes Académiques; Grand Croix de l'Ordre National du Mérite, 1977; Député, Rhône, French National Assembly; *b* Saint-Denis, Réunion, 12 April 1924; *s* of René Barre and Charlotte Déramond; *m* 1954, Eve Hegedüs; two *s*. *Educ:* Lycée Leconte-de-Lisle, Saint-Denis-de-la-Réunion; Faculté de Droit, Paris; Institut d'Etudes Politiques, Paris. Professor at Faculté de Droit et des Sciences Economiques: Caen, 1950; Paris (Chair of Political Economy), 1963–. Econs Res. Dir Foundation Nat. des Scis Politiques, 1958. Professor at Institut d'Etudes Politiques, Paris, 1961–. Director of Cabinet of Mr J.-M. Jeanneney (Minister of Industry), 1959–62; Member: Cttee of Experts (Comité Lorain) studying financing of investments in France, 1963–64; Gen. Cttee on Economy and Financing of Fifth Plan, 1966; Vice-Chm., Commn of European Communities (responsible for Economic and Financial Affairs), 1967–72; Minister of Foreign Trade, Jan.–Aug. 1976; Prime Minister, 1976–81; elected to National Assembly, from Rhône, 1978. Mem. Gen. Council, Banque de France, 1973; Chm. Cttee for studying Housing Financing Reform, 1975–76. *Publications:* Economie Politique, vol. 1, 1961, vol. 2, 1965; Une Politique pour l'Avenir, 1981; Refléxions pour Demain, 1984; Au Tournant du Siècle, 1987; Questions de Confiaure, 1988. *Address:* 4–6 avenue Emile-Acollas, 75007 Paris, France.

BARRELL, Anthony Charles, FEng; Chief Executive, North Sea Safety, Department of Energy, since 1990; *b* 4 June 1933; *s* of William Frederick Barrell and Ruth Eleanor Barrell (*née* Painter); *m* 1963, Jean, *d* of Francis Henry Hawkes and Clarice Jean (*née* Silke); one *s* one *d*. *Educ:* Friars Sch., Bangor; Kingston Grammar Sch.; Birmingham Univ.; Imperial Coll. BSc Hons chem. eng. CEng, FEng 1990; FIChemE 1984; EurIng 1988. Chemist, Ministry of Supply, later War Dept, 1959–64; Commissioning Engineer, African Explosives and Chemical Industries, 1964–65; Shift Manager, MoD, 1965–66; Chemical Inspector, then Supt. Specialist Inspector, HM Factory Inspectorate, 1966–78; Head of Major Hazards Assessment Unit, HSE, 1978–85; Dir, Technology, HSE, 1985–90. Mem. Council, IChemE, 1989–. *Publications:* papers on assessment and control of major hazards, on offshore safety and on fire and explosion risks. *Recreations:* off-shore sailing, fell walking, reading (anything). *Address:* Sanderling, Baskervyle Road, Gayton, Wirral L60 8NJ. *T:* 051–342 8255.

BARRER, Prof. Richard Maling, FRS 1956; PhD Cantab; DSc (NZ); ScD Cantab; FRSC (FRIC 1939); Hon. ARCS, 1959; Senior Research Fellow, Imperial College of Science and Technology, since 1977; Professor of Physical Chemistry, Imperial College of Science and Technology, University of London, 1954–77, now Emeritus; Head of Department of Chemistry, 1955–76; *b* 16 June 1910; *s* of T. R. Barrer, 103 Renall Street, Masterton, New Zealand; *m* 1939, Helen Frances Yule, Invercargill, NZ; one *s* three *d*. *Educ:* Canterbury University Coll., NZ (MSc); Clare Coll., Cambridge (1851 Exhibition Scholar). PhD Cantab, 1935; DSc NZ, 1937; ScD Cantab, 1948. Major Research Student, 1935–37, Research Fellow, 1937–39, Clare Coll.; Head of Chemistry Dept, Technical Coll., Bradford, 1939–46; Reader in Chemistry, London Univ., 1946–49; Prof. of Chemistry, Aberdeen Univ., 1949–54. Dean, Royal Coll. of Science, 1964–66. Member Council: Faraday Soc., 1952–55; Chemical Soc., 1956–59, 1974–77; Royal Institute of Chemistry, 1961–64; Soc. of Chemical Industry, 1965–68. Governor, Chelsea Coll. of Sci. and Technol., 1960–81. Hon. ARCS 1959; Hon. FRSNZ 1965; Hon. FNZIC 1987; Hon. DSc: Bradford, 1967; Aberdeen, 1983. *Publications:* Diffusion in and through Solids, 1941; Zeolites and Clay Minerals as Sorbents and Molecular Sieves, 1978; Hydrothermal Chemistry of Zeolites, 1982; research papers in British and foreign scientific journals. *Recreations:* tennis and interest in athletics. Full Blue for cross-country running, 1934. *Address:* Flossmoor, Orpington Road, Chislehurst, Kent BR7 6RA. *Clubs:* Hawks (Cambridge); Achilles.

BARRETT, (Arthur) Michael, PhD; FIBiol; Vice-Chancellor, University of Buckingham, 1985–91; *b* 1 April 1932; *s* of Arthur Cowley Barrett and late Doris Annie Barrett; *m* 1960, Patricia Lillian Harris (*d* 1989); one *s* one *d*. *Educ:* Cheltenham Grammar Sch.; Sch. of Pharmacy, Univ. of London (BPharm 1st Cl. Hons, PhD). Cleveland, Ohio, Rotary Foundn Fellow, Western Reserve Univ., 1956–57; Asst Lectr in Pharmacology, 1958–59, Lectr, 1959–61, Sch. of Pharmacy, London Univ.; Res. Pharmacologist, Pharmaceuticals Div., ICI Ltd, 1961–70; Head of Pharmacology, Organon Internat. BV, 1970; Prof. and Hd of Dept of Pharmacology, 1970–84, Pro Vice Chancellor, 1979–81, Leeds Univ. Chm., Leeds Eastern Health Authority, 1981–84; Vice-Chairman: Kirklees AHA, 1978–79 (Mem., 1974–79); Aylesbury Vale HA, 1990–; Mem., Gen. Sales List Cttee, Medicines Commn, DHSS, 1971–74; Assessor to Inquiry on LD50 Test, Home Office, 1977–79. Sec. Gen., Internat. Union of Pharmacology, 1981–87; Member: British Pharmacol Soc., 1963– (Meetings Sec., 1977–79; Gen. Sec., 1980–82); Soc. for Endocrinology, 1959–. Mem. Bd Governors, 1985–, Chm., Academic Bd, 1987–89, RAC, Cirencester; Mem. Academic Adv. Cttee, Bellerby's Coll., Hove; Governor: Beachborough Sch., Westbury, 1986–; Dixon's City Technology Coll., Bradford, 1989–; Chm. Trustees, Lorch Foundn, 1986–91; Trustee, Lloyd's of London Tercentenary Foundn, 1988–. FIBiol 1984; FRSA 1985. *Publications:* The Pharmacology of Beta-adrenoceptor blockade, 1975; papers in pharmacol and endocrinol jls. *Recreations:* models, gardening, music. *Address:* Thene House, Shalstone, Buckingham MK18 5LU. *T:* Brackley (0280) 700551.

BARRETT, Rev. Prof. Charles Kingsley, DD; FBA 1961; Professor of Divinity, Durham University, 1958–82; *b* 4 May 1917; *s* of Rev. F. Barrett and Clara (*née* Seed); *m* 1944, Margaret E. Heap, Calverley, Yorks; one *s* one *d*. *Educ:* Shebbear Coll.; Pembroke Coll., Cambridge; Wesley House, Cambridge. DD Cantab, 1956. Asst Tutor, Wesley Coll., Headingley, 1942; Methodist Minister, Darlington, 1943; Lecturer in Theology, Durham Univ., 1945. Lectures: Hewett, USA, 1961; Shaffer, Yale, 1965; Delitzsch, Münster, 1967; Cato, Australia, 1969; Tate-Willson, Dallas, 1975; McMartin, Ottawa, 1976; Sanderson, Melbourne, and West-Watson, Christchurch, NZ, 1983; Alexander Robertson, Univ. of Glasgow, 1984; K. W. Clark, Duke, USA, 1987; Ryan, Asbury Seminary, Kentucky, 1988; Dominican-Chalmers, Ottawa, 1990; Woodruff Vis. Prof., Emory Univ., Atlanta, 1986. Vice-Pres., British and Foreign Bible Soc.; Pres., Studiorum Novi Testamenti Societas, 1973; Hon. Mem., Soc. of Biblical Literature, USA. Hon. DD: Hull, 1970; Aberdeen, 1972; Hon. DrTheol Hamburg, 1981. Burkitt Medal for Biblical Studies, 1966; von Humboldt Forschungspreis, 1988. *Publications:* The Holy Spirit and the Gospel Tradition, 1947; The Gospel according to St John, 1955, 2nd edn 1978; The New Testament Background: Selected Documents, 1956, 2nd edn 1987; Biblical Preaching and Biblical Scholarship, 1957; The Epistle to the Romans, 1957, 2nd edn 1991; Westcott as Commentator, 1959; Yesterday, Today and Forever: The New Testament Problem, 1959; Luke the Historian in Recent Study, 1961; From First Adam to Last, 1962; The Pastoral Epistles, 1963; Reading Through Romans, 1963; History and Faith: the Story of the Passion, 1967; Jesus and the Gospel Tradition, 1967; The First Epistle to the Corinthians, 1968; The Signs of an Apostle, 1970; Das Johannesevangelium und das Judentum, 1970; The Prologue of St John's Gospel, 1971; New Testament Essays,

1972; The Second Epistle to the Corinthians, 1973; The Fourth Gospel and Judaism, 1975; (ed) Donum Gentilicium, 1978; Essays on Paul, 1982; Essays on John, 1982; Freedom and Obligation, 1985; Church, Ministry and Sacraments in the New Testament, 1985; contributions to learned journals and symposia in Britain, the Continent, Australia and USA. *Address:* 22 Rosemount, Plawsworth Road, Pity Me, Durham DH1 5GA. *T:* Durham (091) 3861340.

BARRETT, David; MP for Esquimalt Tuan de Fuca, since 1988; broadcaster, writer and political commentator on national and provincial media, since 1985; Premier and Minister of Finance, Province of British Columbia, Canada, 1972–75; *b* Vancouver, 2 Oct. 1930; *s* of Samuel Barrett and Rose (*née* Hyatt); father a business man in East Vancouver, after war service; *m* 1953, Shirley Hackman, West Vancouver; two *s* one *d. Educ:* Britannia High Sch., Vancouver; Seattle Univ.; St Louis Univ. BA(Phil) Seattle, 1953; Master of Social Work, St Louis, 1956. Personnel and Staff Trng Officer, Haney Correctional Inst., 1957–59; also gained experience in a variety of jobs. Fellow, Inst. of Politics, Harvard Univ., 1987; Vis. Schol., McGill Univ., 1988. Elected: MLA for Dewdney, Sept. 1960 and 1963; to re-distributed riding of Coquitlam 1966, 1969 and 1972; Vancouver East, by-election 1976, 1979; New Democratic Party Leader, June 1970–84 (first Social Democratic Govt in history of Province); Leader, Official Opposition, British Columbia, 1970–72 and 1975–84. Dr of Laws, *hc*, St Louis Univ., 1974; Hon. DPhil Simon Fraser Univ., BC, 1986. *Address:* 1179 Monro Street, Victoria, British Columbia V9A 5P5, Canada.

BARRETT, Lt-Gen. Sir David William S.; *see* Scott-Barrett.

BARRETT, Denis Everett; a Special Commissioner of Income Tax, 1967–71; *b* 7 Jan. 1911; *o s* of late Walter Everett Barrett, London, and Julia Barrett (*née* MacCarthy), Cork; *m* 1947, Eilish (*d* 1974), *y d* of late William and Margaret Phelan, Co. Laois; one *s* two *d. Educ:* Wimbledon Coll.; London Univ. Entered Inland Revenue Dept, 1930; Asst Sec., 1948. *Address:* c/o The Pump House, Bone Mill Lane, Enborne, Newbury, Berks RG15 0EU.

BARRETT, Sir Dennis Charles T.; *see* Titchener-Barrett.

BARRETT, Edmond Fox, OBE 1981; HM Diplomatic Service, retired; First Secretary, Foreign and Commonwealth Office, 1986–88; *b* 24 Aug. 1928; *s* of late Edmond Henry Barrett and Ellen Mary Barrett (*née* Fox); *m* 1959, Catherine Wendy Howard (*née* Slater). *Educ:* St Brendan's Coll., Bristol. Dominions Office, 1946; Royal Navy, 1947–49; CRO, 1949–50; Karachi, 1950–52; New Delhi, 1952–54; CRO, 1954–55; Admiralty, 1955–60; Foreign Office, 1960–63; Bucharest, 1963–65; Rio de Janeiro, 1965–68; Boston, 1968–70; Mexico City, 1971–73; FCO, 1973–76; Santo Domingo, 1976–79; Tehran, 1979–81; Consul Gen., Bilbao, 1981–86. *Recreations:* reading, golf, gardening. *Address:* 10 Greenheys Place, Woking, Surrey GU22 7JD.

BARRETT, Ernest; Chairman: Henry Barrett & Sons Ltd, 1982–87 (Joint Managing Director, 1968–85); Steel Stockholding Division, Henry Barrett & Sons Ltd, 1967–85; Henry Lindsay Ltd, since 1974; *b* 8 April 1917; *s* of Ernest Barrett and Marian Conyers; *m* 1940, Eileen Maria Peel; one *d. Educ:* Charterhouse. Joined Henry Barrett & Sons Ltd, Bradford, 1934. Served War, RA, and commissioned, 1940; served in Mediterranean Theatre, with 1st Army, 1943–46 (despatches, 1944); Major 1945. Apptd Dir, Henry Barrett & Sons Ltd, 1946. Pres., Nat. Assoc. of Steel Stockholders, 1977–79 (Chm., Yorks Assoc., 1964–66; Vice-Pres., 1975–77); Pres., Engineering Industries Assoc., 1971 (Chm. Yorks Region, 1960–65; Vice-Pres. of Assoc., 1965–71). *Recreation:* gardening. *Address:* West Ghyll, Victoria Avenue, Ilkley, W Yorks. *T:* Ilkley (0943) 609294.

BARRETT, Jack Wheeler, CBE 1971; PhD; FEng; CChem; FIC; Chairman, Cole Group plc, 1979–86 (Director, 1978); *b* 13 June 1912; *s* of John Samuel Barrett, Cheltenham; *m* 1935, Muriel Audley Read; two *s* two *d. Educ:* Cheltenham Grammar Sch.; Imperial Coll., Univ. of London. BSc, PhD, CChem, FRSC, FEng, FIChemE. Chief Chemist, London Essence Co. Ltd, 1936–41; joined Monsanto Chemicals Ltd, 1941; Dir of Research, 1955–71; Dir, Monsanto Ltd, 1955–78; Chm., Info-line Ltd, 1976–80. President: IChemE, 1971–72; Chem. Soc., 1974–75; IInfSc, 1976–79; ICSU Abstracting Bd, 1974–77; Chm., Chemical Divl Council, BSI, 1973–79; Mem., British Library Bd, 1973–79. *Publications:* articles in Jl Chem. Soc., Chemistry and Industry, Jl ASLIB, Chemistry in Britain. *Recreation:* gardening. *Address:* West Manor House, Bourton-on-the-Water, Cheltenham, Glos GL54 2AP. *T:* Cotswold (0451) 20296. *Club:* Athenæum.

BARRETT, Rev. John Charles Allanson; Headmaster, The Leys School, Cambridge, since 1990; *b* 8 June 1943; *s* of Leonard Wilfred Allanson Barrett and Marjorie Joyce Barrett; *m* 1967, Sally Elisabeth Hatley; one *s* one *d. Educ:* Culford Sch.; Univ. of Newcastle upon Tyne (BA Hons); Fitzwilliam Coll., Cambridge; Wesley House, Cambridge. MA Cantab. Ordained Methodist Minister. Chaplain and Lectr in Divinity, Westminster Coll., Oxford, 1968–69; Asst Tutor, Wesley Coll., Bristol, 1969–71; Circuit Minister, Hanley Trinity Circuit, Stoke on Trent, and actg Hd of Religious Studies, Birches High Sch., Hanley, 1971–73; Chaplain and Hd of Religious and Gen. Studies, Kingswood Sch., Bath, 1973–83; Headmaster, Kent Coll., Pembury, 1983–90. World Methodist Council: Mem. Exec. Cttee, 1981–; Sec., Brit. Cttee, 1986–. Mem. Steering Cttee, Bloxham Project, 1986–. *Publications:* What is a Christian School?, 1981; Family Worship in Theory and Practice, 1983; Methodist Education in Britain, 1990; sections on Methodism in Encyc. Britannica Year Books, 1988–91. *Recreations:* golf, water colour painting. *Address:* The Leys School, Cambridge CB2 2AD. *T:* Cambridge (0223) 355327.

BARRETT, John Edward; international tennis promotions director; Consultant, Dunlop Slazenger International; *b* 17 April 1931; *s* of Alfred Edward Barrett and Margaret Helen Barrett (*née* Walker); *m* 1967, (Florence) Angela (Margaret) Mortimer; one *s* one *d. Educ:* University College Sch., Hampstead; St John's Coll., Cambridge (MA History). Joined Slazengers as management trainee, 1957; Tournament Dir, 1975; Dir, 1978; Consultant, 1981– (now Dunlop Slazenger International). Consultant, David Lloyd Sports Clubs. Tennis career: RAF champion, 1950, 1951; Captain of Cambridge, 1954; Nat. Indoor Doubles champion (with D. Black), 1953; Davis Cup, 1956–57, non-playing Captain, 1959–62; Dir, LTA Trng Squad (Barrett Boys), 1965–68; qualified LTA coach, 1969; Founded: BP Internat Tennis Fellowship, 1968–80 (and directed); BP Cup (21-and-under), 1973–80; Junior Internat. Series, 1975–79. Financial Times: tennis corresp., 1963–; crossword contribs, 1986–. TV tennis commentator: BBC, 1971–; Australian networks, 1981–; USA and Hong Kong. *Publications:* Tennis and Racket Games, 1975; Play Tennis with Rosewall, 1975; 100 Wimbledon Championships, 1986; (with Dan Maskell) From Where I Sit, 1988; (with Dan Maskell) Oh, I Say, 1989; (ed and contrib.) World of Tennis, annually, 1969–. *Recreations:* music, theatre, reading. *Address:* All England Lawn Tennis Club, Church Road, Wimbledon, SW19 5AE. *Clubs:* United Oxford & Cambridge University, All England Lawn Tennis (Mem. Cttee), International Lawn Tennis (Chm.), Queen's.

BARRETT, Prof. Michael; *see* Barrett, Prof. A. M.

BARRETT, Sir Stephen Jeremy, KCMG 1991 (CMG 1982); HM Diplomatic Service, retired; Ambassador to Poland, 1988–91; *b* 4 Dec. 1931; *s* of late W. P. Barrett and Dorothy Barrett; *m* 1958, Alison Mary Irvine; three *s. Educ:* Westminster Sch.; Christ Church, Oxford (MA). FO, 1955–57; 3rd, later 2nd Sec., Political Office with Middle East Forces, Cyprus, 1957–59; Berlin, 1959–62; 1st Sec., FO, 1962–65; Head of Chancery, Helsinki, 1965–68; 1st Sec., FCO, 1968–72; Counsellor and Head of Chancery, Prague, 1972–74; Head of SW European Dept, FCO, later Principal Private Sec. to Foreign and Commonwealth Sec., 1975; Head of Science and Technology Dept, FCO, 1976–77; Fellow, Center for Internat. Affairs, Harvard, 1977–78; Counsellor, Ankara, 1978–81; Head of British Interests Section, Tehran, 1981; Asst Under-Sec. of State, FCO, 1981–84; Ambassador to Czechoslovakia, 1985–88. *Recreations:* climbing small mountains, reading. *Clubs:* Travellers'; Ausable (St Huberts, NY).

BARRETT, William Spencer, FBA 1965; Fellow of Keble College, Oxford, 1952–81 and Tutor in Classics, 1939–81, Hon. Fellow, 1981; Reader in Greek Literature, University of Oxford, 1966–81; *b* 29 May 1914; *o s* of William Barrett and Sarah Jessie Barrett (*née* Robbins); *m* 1939, Georgina Margaret Elizabeth (*d* 1989), *e d* of William and Alma Georgina Annie Hill; one *s* one *d. Educ:* Derby Sch; Christ Church, Oxford (Scholar). Ireland and Craven Schol. 1933; 1st Class Classical Hon. Mods, 1934; Gaisford Prize for Greek Verse, 1934; de Paravicini Schol., 1934; 1st Class Lit. Hum., 1937; Derby Schol., 1937; Charles Oldham Prize, 1938. Lectr, Christ Church, Oxford, 1938–39; Lectr, Keble Coll. 1939–52; Librarian, 1946–66; Univ. Lectr in Greek Literature, 1947–66; Sub Warden, Keble Coll., 1968–76. Temp. Civilian Officer, Admty (Naval Intelligence Div.), 1942–45. *Publications:* (ed) Euripides, Hippolytos, 1964; Sophocles, Niobe (in Papyrus Fragments of Sophocles, ed R. Carden), 1974; articles in learned jls. *Address:* 8 The Avenue, Clifton, Bristol BS8 3HE. *T:* Bristol (0272) 743321.

BARRETT-LENNARD, Rev. Sir Hugh (Dacre), 6th Bt *cr* 1801; Priest, London Oratory; *b* 27 June 1917; *s* of Sir Fiennes Cecil Arthur Barrett-Lennard (*d* 1963) and Winifrede Mignon (*d* 1969), *d* of Alfred Berlyn; *S* cousin, 1977. *Educ:* Radley College, Berks; Pontifical Beda College, Rome. Teaching, 1936. Served War of 1939–45, NW Europe (despatches); enlisted London Scottish, Jan. 1940; commissioned 2nd Lt, Oct. 1940; Captain Essex Regt, 1945. Entered Brompton Oratory, 1946; ordained Priest in Rome, 1950. *Recreations:* on Isle of Eigg, Hebrides. *Heir: cousin* Richard Fynes Barrett-Lennard, *b* 6 April 1941. *Address:* The Oratory, South Kensington, SW7 2RW. *T:* 071–589 4811.

BARRIE, Herbert, MD, FRCP; Consultant Paediatrician: Parkside Hospital, Wimbledon, since 1983; Ashtead Hospital, Surrey, since 1986; Hon. Consultant Paediatrician, Charing Cross Hospital, since 1987 (Consultant Paediatrician, 1966–84; Physician in charge, 1984–86); *b* 9 Oct. 1927; *m* 1963, Dinah Barrie, MB, BS, FRCPath; one *s* one *d. Educ:* Wallington County Grammar School; University College and Med. Sch., London. MB, BS 1950; MD 1952; MRCP 1957, FRCP 1972. Registrar, Hosp. for Sick Children, Gt Ormond St, 1955–57; Research Fellow, Harvard Univ., Children's Med. Center, 1957; Sen. Registrar and Sen. Lectr, Dept of Paediatrics, St Thomas' Hosp., 1959–65; Consultant Paediatrician, Moor House Sch. for Speech Disorders, 1968–74. Vis. Prof., Downstate Univ. Med. Center, NY, 1976. Member: London Med. Soc.; British Paediatric Assoc.; British Assoc. of Perinatal Paediatrics; Neonatal Soc.; Perinatal Visiting Club; BMA. Member, Editorial Board: Midwife; Health Visitor and Community Nurse; Maternity and Mothercraft. *Publications:* numerous contribs to books and jls on paediatric and neonatal topics, esp. resuscitation of newborn and neonatal special care. *Recreations:* tennis, writing, wishful thinking. *Address:* 3 Burghley Avenue, New Malden, Surrey KT3 4SW. *T:* 081–942 2836.

BARRINGTON, Sir Alexander (Fitzwilliam Croker), 7th Bt *cr* 1831; retired; *b* 19 Nov. 1909; *s* of Sir Charles Burton Barrington, 5th Bt, and Mary Rose (*d* 1943), *d* of Sir Henry Hickman Bacon, 10th and 11th Bt; *S* brother, 1980. *Educ:* Castle Park, Dalkey, Co. Dublin; Shrewsbury School; Christ Church, Oxford. Director of various private companies, 1932–39. Served in Army as Captain, Intelligence Corps, 1939–42; prisoner of war, Singapore and Thailand, 1942–45. Book publishers' executive, editor and production manager, 1946–72. *Recreations:* gardening, travel. *Heir: cousin* John William Barrington, Major retd, Royal Irish Fusiliers [*b* 20 Oct. 1917; *m* 1st, 1949, Annie Wetten (*d* 1985); two *s* one *d*; 2nd, 1986, Evelyn Carol Paterson, *d* of late Oscar Broten]. *Address:* 11 Tedworth Square, SW3 4DU.

BARRINGTON, Sir Nicholas John, KCMG 1990 (CMG 1982); CVO 1975; HM Diplomatic Service; High Commissioner to Pakistan, since 1989 (Ambassador, 1987–89); *b* 23 July 1934; *s* of late Eric Alan Barrington and Mildred (*née* Bill). *Educ:* Repton; Clare Coll., Cambridge (MA 1957). HM Forces, RA, 1952–54. Joined Diplomatic Service, 1957; Tehran (language student), 1958; Oriental Sec., Kabul, 1959; FO, 1961; 2nd Sec., UK Delegn to European Communities, Brussels, 1963; 1st Sec., Rawalpindi, 1965; FO, 1967; Private Sec. to Permanent Under Sec., Commonwealth Office, April 1968; Asst Private Sec. to Foreign and Commonwealth Sec., Oct. 1968; Head of Chancery, Tokyo, 1972–75 (promoted Counsellor and for a period apptd Chargé d'Affaires, Hanoi, 1973); Head of Guidance and Information Policy (subsequently Information Policy) Dept, FCO, 1976–78; Counsellor, Cairo, 1978–81; Minister and Head of British Interests Section, Tehran, 1981–83; Supernumary Ambassador attached to UK Mission to UN, NY, for Gen. Assembly, autumn 1983; Co-ordinator for London Econ. Summit, 1984; Asst Under-Sec. of State (Public Depts), FCO, 1984–87. FRSA 1984. 3rd Cl., Order of the Sacred Treasure, Japan, 1975. *Recreations:* theatre, drawing, tennis, prosopography. *Address:* c/o Foreign and Commonwealth Office, King Charles Street, SW1; 33 Gilmerton Court, Trumpington, Cambridge. *Clubs:* Athenæum, Commonwealth Trust.

BARRINGTON-WARD, Rt. Rev. Simon; *see* Coventry, Bishop of.

BARRITT, Rev. Dr Gordon Emerson, OBE 1979; Principal, National Children's Home, 1969–86; President of the Methodist Conference, 1984–85; *b* 30 Sept. 1920; *s* of Norman and Doris Barritt; *m* 1947, Joan Mary Alway (*d* 1984); two *s* one *d. Educ:* William Hulme's Grammar Sch., Manchester; Manchester Univ.; Cambridge Univ. (Wesley House and Fitzwilliam Coll.). Served War, RAF, 1942–45 (despatches). Methodist Minister: Kempston Methodist Church, Bedford, 1947–52; Westlands Methodist Church, Newcastle-under-Lyme, 1952–57; Chaplain, Univ. of Keele, 1953–57. Dir, Enfield Counselling Service, 1986–89; Treasurer, 1969–86, Chm., 1970–72, Nat. Council of Voluntary Child Care Organisations; Member: Home Office Adv. Council on Child Care, 1968–71; Brit. Assoc. of Social Workers, 1960–; Nat. Children's Bureau, 1964– (Treasurer, 1989–); Internat. Union for Child Welfare, 1969–86; Chm., Kids, 1986–; Chm., CQSW Course Adv. Cttee, Selly Oak Colls, Birmingham, 1970– (Fellow, 1987); Governor: Farringtons Sch. (Chm. of Govs, 1986–); Queenswood Sch., 1986–. DUniv Keele, 1985. *Publications:* The Edgworth Story, 1972; (ed) Many Pieces—One Aim, 1975; (ed) Family Life, 1979; Residential Care, 1979; contrib.: Caring for Children, 1969; Giving Our Best, 1982. *Recreations:* music, do-it-yourself. *Address:* 10 Cadogan Gardens, Grange Park, N21 1ER. *T:* 081–360 8687.

BARRON, Brian Munro; Asia Correspondent, BBC News and Current Affairs, since 1986; *b* 28 April 1940; *s* of Albert and Norah Barron; *m* 1974, Angela Lee, MA; one *d*. *Educ:* Bristol Grammar School. Junior Reporter, Western Daily Press, Bristol, 1956–60; Dep. Chief Sub-editor, Evening World, Bristol, 1960–61; Sub-editor, Daily Mirror, 1961–63; Dep. Chief Sub-editor, Evening Post, Bristol, 1963–65; Sub-editor, BBC External Services, London, 1965–67; Correspondent, BBC Radio: Aden, 1967–68; ME, Cairo, 1968–69; SE Asia, Singapore, 1969–71; Reporter, BBC TV News, 1971–73; Correspondent, BBC TV: Far East, Hong Kong, 1973–76; Africa, Nairobi, 1976–81; Ireland, 1981–83; Washington, 1983–86. Royal Television Society: Journalist of the Year, 1979–80; Internat. Reporting Award, 1985. *Recreations:* opera, theatre, tennis. *Address:* British Broadcasting Corporation, Asia Bureau, 1141 Telecom House, 3 Gloucester Road, Hong Kong. *T:* (852) 5280 527. *Clubs:* Nairobi (E Africa): Kenwood Country (Md, USA); Foreign Correspondents (Hong Kong).

BARRON, Derek Donald; Chairman and Chief Executive, Ford Motor Co. Ltd, since 1986; Chairman, Ford Motor Credit Co., since 1986; *b* 7 June 1929; *s* of Donald Frederick James Barron and Hettie Barbara Barron; *m* 1963, Rosemary Ingrid Brian; two *s*. *Educ:* Beckenham Grammar School; University College London (Intermediate LLB). Joined Ford Motor Co. Sales, 1951; Tractor Group, 1961; Tractor Manager, Ford Italiana 1963; Marketing Associate, Ford Motor Co. USA, 1970; Gen. Sales Manager, Overseas Markets, 1971; Man. Dir, Ford Italiana, 1973; Group Dir, Southern European Sales, Ford of Europe, 1977; Sales and Marketing Dir, Ford Brazil, 1979; Vice-Pres., Ford Motor de Venezuela, 1982; Dir-Vice-Pres., Operations, Ford Brazil, 1985. DUniv Essex, 1989. *Recreation:* sailing. *Address:* c/o Ford Motor Co. Ltd, Eagle Way, Brentwood, Essex CM13 3BW. *T:* Brentwood (0277) 253000. *Club:* Royal Automobile.

BARRON, Sir Donald (James), Kt 1972; DL; Chairman, Joseph Rowntree Foundation, since 1981; *b* 17 March 1921; *o s* of Albert Gibson Barron and Elizabeth Macdonald, Edinburgh; *m* 1956, Gillian Mary, *o d* of John Saville, York; three *s* two *d*. *Educ:* George Heriot's Sch., Edinburgh; Edinburgh Univ. (BCom). Member, Inst. Chartered Accountants of Scotland. Joined Rowntree Mackintosh Ltd, 1952; Dir, 1961; Vice-Chm., 1965; Chm., 1966–81. Dir, 1972, Vice-Chm., 1981–82, Chm., 1982–87, Midland Bank plc. Dep. Chm., CLCB, 1983–85; Chm., Cttee of London and Scottish Bankers, 1985–87. Director: Investors in Industry, subseq. 3i, Gp, 1980–91; Canada Life Assurance Co. of GB Ltd, 1980– (Chm., 1991–); Canada Life Unit Trust Managers Ltd, 1980–; Canada Life Assurance Co., Toronto, 1980–; Clydesdale Bank, 1986–87. Mem., Bd of Banking Supervision, 1987–89. Dir, BIM Foundn, 1977–80 and Mem. Council, BIM, 1978–80; Trustee, Joseph Rowntree Foundn (formerly Meml Trust), 1966–73, 1975– (Chm., 1981–); Treasurer, 1966–72, a Pro-Chancellor, 1982–, York Univ.; Member: Council of CBI, 1966–81 (Chm., CBI Educn Foundn, 1981–85); SSRC, 1971–72; UGC, 1972–81; Council, PSI, 1978–85; Council, Inst. of Chartered Accountants of Scotland, 1980–81; NEDC, 1983–85. Governor, London Business Sch., 1982–88. DL N Yorks (formerly WR Yorks and City of York), 1971. Hon. doctorates: Loughborough, 1982; Heriot-Watt, 1983; CNAA, 1983; Edinburgh, 1984; Nottingham, 1985; York, 1986. *Recreations:* golf, tennis, gardening. *Address:* Greenfield, Sim Balk Lane, Bishopthorpe, York YO2 1QH. *T:* York (0904) 705675. *Clubs:* Athenæum; Yorkshire (York).

BARRON, Douglas Shield, CIE 1945; Chairman, Godfrey Phillips, India, Ltd, retired 1973; *b* 18 March 1904; *s* of Thomas Barron; *m* 1934, Doris Katherine (*d* 1970), *o d* of late Henry Deakin; no *c*. *Educ:* Holgate Grammar Sch.; Corpus Christi Coll., Cambridge. Joined Indian Civil Service, 1926; retired, 1948. *Address:* Sundial Cottage, Cross Lanes, Mockbeggar, Ringwood, Hants BH24 3NQ. *T:* Ringwood (0425) 3885. *Club:* Bombay Yacht.

BARRON, Iann Marchant; Chairman, Division Ltd, since 1990; *b* 16 June 1936; *s* of William A. Barron and Lilian E. Barron; *m* 1961, Jacqueline R. Almond (marr. diss. 1989); two *s* two *d*. *Educ:* University College School; Christ's College, Cambridge (exhibitioner; MA). Elliott Automation, 1961–65; Managing Director: Computer Technology Ltd, 1965–72; Microcomputer Analysis Ltd, 1973–78; Exec. Dir, 1978–89, Chief Strategic Officer, 1984–89, INMOS International; Man. Dir, INMOS, 1981–88. Vis. Prof., Westfield Coll., London, 1976–78; Vis. Indust. Prof., Bristol Univ., 1985–; Vis. Fellow: QMC, 1976; Science Policy Res. Unit, 1977–78. Mem. Council, UCS, 1983–. Distinguished FBCS, 1986. Hon. DSc: Bristol Polytechnic, 1988; Hull, 1989. R. W. Mitchell Medal, 1983; J. J. Thompson Medal, IEE, 1986. *Publications:* The Future with Microelectronics (with Ray Curnow), 1977; technical papers. *Address:* Barrow Court, Barrow Gurney, Bristol BS19 3RW.

BARRON, Prof. John Penrose, MA, DPhil, FSA; Master of St Peter's College, Oxford, since 1991; *b* 27 Apr. 1934; *s* of George Barron and Minnie Leslie Marks; *m* 1962, Caroline Mary, *d* of late W. D. Hogarth, OBE; two *d*. *Educ:* Clifton Coll.; Balliol Coll., Oxford (Hon. Exhibnr). 1st Cl., Class. Hon. Mods, 1955; Lit. Hum., 1957; MA 1960, DPhil 1961; Thomas Whitcombe Greene Prizeman, 1955, and Scholar, 1957; Barclay Head Prizeman, 1959; Cromer Prize, British Academy, 1965. London University: Asst Lectr in Latin, Bedford Coll., 1959–61, and Lectr, 1961–64; Lectr in Archaeology, UCL, 1964–67; Reader in Archaeology and Numismatics, 1967–71; Prof. of Greek Lang. and Lit., 1971–91, and Head of Dept of Classics, 1972–84, KCL; Dean, Faculty of Arts, 1976–80; Dir, Inst. of Classical Studies, 1984–91; Dean, Insts for Advanced Study, 1989–91. Mem. Senate, 1977–81, 1987–, Mem. Academic Council, 1977–81, 1985–89; Public Orator, 1978–81, 1986–88; Pro-Vice-Chancellor, 1987–89. Mem., UFC, 1989–. FKC 1988. Vis. Mem., Inst. for Advanced Study, Princeton, 1973. Blegen Distinguished Vis. Res. Prof., Vassar Coll., NY, 1981; T. B. L. Webster Vis. Prof., Stanford Univ., 1986. Lectures: Eberhard L. Faber, Princeton, 1985; Woodward, Yale, 1985; Sotheby, Edinburgh, 1986; Dill, QUB, 1986. Pres., Soc. for Promotion of Hellenic Studies, 1990– (Trustee, 1970–; Hon. Sec., 1981–90); Mem., Academia Europaea, 1990. Almoner, Christ's Hosp., 1975–80. *Publications:* Greek Sculpture, 1965 (new and rev. edn 1981); Silver Coins of Samos, 1966; articles in Classical Quarterly, Jl of Hellenic Studies, Bulletin of Inst. of Classical Studies, etc. *Recreations:* travel, gardens. *Address:* St Peter's College, Oxford OX1 2DL. *Club:* Athenæum.

BARRON, Kevin John; MP (Lab) Rother Valley, since 1983; *b* 26 Oct. 1946; *s* of Richard Barron; *m* 1969; one *s* two *d*. *Educ:* Maltby Hall Secondary Modern Sch.; Ruskin Coll., Oxford. NCB, 1962–83. PPS to Leader of the Opposition, 1985–88; Opposition spokesman on energy, 1988–. Pres., Rotherham and Dist TUC. *Address:* House of Commons, SW1A 0AA.

BARRON, Rt. Rev. Patrick Harold Falkiner; *b* 13 Nov. 1911; *s* of Albert Harold and Mary Isabel Barron; *m* 1942, Kathleen May Larter; two *s* one *d*. *Educ:* King Edward VII Sch., Johannesburg; Leeds Univ. (BA); College of the Resurrection, Mirfield. Curate: Holy Redeemer, Clerkenwell, London, 1938–40; Boksburg, S Africa, 1940–41; CF (S African), 1941–46; Rector: Zeerust, S Africa, 1946–50; Potchefstroom, 1950–51; Blyvooruitzicht, 1951–55. St Cyprian's Mission, Johannesburg, 1956–59; Archdeacon of Germiston, 1957–58; Dean of Johannesburg, 1959–64; Bishop Suffragan of Cape Town, 1965–66; Bishop of George, 1966–77. *Recreation:* gardening. *Address:* E37 Edingight, Queen Road, Rondebosch, 7700, South Africa. *T:* 689.1820.

BARRON, Maj.-Gen. Richard Edward; Director Royal Armoured Corps, since 1989; *b* 22 Nov. 1940; *s* of John Barron and Lorna Frances Barron; *m* 1968, Margaret Ann Eggar; one *s* one *d*. *Educ:* Oundle; RMA. Commissioned Queen's Royal Irish Hussars, 1962; Staff College, 1973; DAA&QMG 7th Armoured Brigade, 1974–76; Instructor, Staff Coll., 1978–81; CO, QRIH, 1981–84; Comdr, 7th Armoured Brigade, 1984–86; RCDS 1987; QMG's Staff, 1988–89. *Recreations:* gardening, fishing. *Address:* c/o HQ DRAC, Bovington Camp, near Wareham, Dorset BH20 6JA. *Clubs:* Cavalry and Guards, MCC.

BARRON, (Thomas) Robert, CBE 1980; Member, British Railways Board, 1978–81; *b* 27 Dec. 1918; *s* of late Robert and Florence May Barron; *m* 1942, Constance Lilian Bolter; one *s* three *d*. *Educ:* Dame Allan's Sch., Newcastle-on-Tyne; King's Coll., Durham Univ. BA 1st class Hons (Econ.). Served RA and 1st Airborne Div., 1940–46. Joined LNER as Traffic Apprentice, 1946; Asst Gen. Manager, London Midland Region, 1966, Western Region, 1967; British Railways Board: Dir Management Staff, 1970; Controller of Corporate Planning, 1972; Dir of Planning and Investment, 1977. Exec. Dir, Channel Tunnel, 1981–82. Mem., NW Economic Planning Council, 1965–67. *Recreations:* music, fishing, watching sport. *Address:* 25 Shotford Road, Harleston, Norfolk IP20 9JN. *T:* Harleston (0379) 853625.

BARRONS, John Lawson; Vice-Chairman: Northern Press Ltd, since 1986; Northumberland Gazette Ltd, since 1986; *b* 10 Oct. 1932; *s* of late William Cowper Barrons, MBE and Amy Marie Barrons (*née* Lawson); *m* 1st, 1957, Caroline Anne (marr. diss. 1986), *d* of late George Edward Foster; three *s*; 2nd, 1987, Lauren Ruth, *d* of late Robert Z. Friedman. *Educ:* Caterham Sch. Nat. Service, 1st Bn Northamptonshire Regt, 1952–54. Journalist, UK and USA, 1950–57; Gen. Manager, Nuneaton Observer, 1957; Managing Editor, Northampton Chronicle & Echo, 1959; Gen. Manager, Edinburgh Evening News, 1961; Gen. Manager, 1965–76, Man. Dir, 1976–85, Westminster Press. Director: Pearson Longman, 1979–83; Stephen Austin Newspapers, 1986–; Lincolnshire Standard Gp plc, 1987–88; President: Westminster (Florida) Inc., 1980–85; Westminster (Jacksonville) Inc., 1982–85. Dir, Evening Newspaper Advertising Bureau, 1978–81 (Chm. 1979–80); Founder Dir, Reg. Newspaper Advertising Bureau, 1980– (Chm. 1982–84); Dir, The Press Association Ltd, 1985–86; Chm., Printing Industry Res. Assoc., 1983–85 (Mem. Council, 1978, a Vice-Chm., 1979–83); Mem. Bd of Management, Internat. Electronic Publishing Res. Centre, 1981–85. Member, Council: Newspaper Soc., 1975–87 (Pres., 1981–82; Hon. Vice-Pres., 1983–); CPU, 1970–86. *Recreations:* walking, fishing. *Address:* 3 Chesterford Gardens, Hampstead, NW3 7DD. *Club:* Flyfishers'.

BARROW, Prof. Geoffrey Wallis Steuart, FBA 1976; Sir William Fraser Professor of Scottish History and Palæography, University of Edinburgh, since 1979; *b* Headingley, Leeds, 28 Nov. 1924; *s* of late Charles Embleton Barrow and Marjorie, *d* of Donald Stuart; *m* 1951, Heather Elizabeth, *d* of James McLeish Lownie; one *s* one *d*. *Educ:* St Edward's Sch., Oxford; Inverness Royal Acad.; St Andrews Univ.; Pembroke Coll., Oxford. FRSE 1977. Lecturer in History, University Coll., London, 1950–61; Prof. of Mediaeval Hist., King's Coll., Univ. of Durham, later Univ. of Newcastle upon Tyne, 1961–74; Prof. of Scottish History, Univ. of St Andrews, 1974–79. Mem., Royal Commn on Historical MSS, 1984–. Ford's Lectr, Univ. of Oxford, 1977; Rhind Lectr, Soc. of Antiquaries of Scotland, 1985. Hon. DLitt Glasgow, 1988. *Publications:* Feudal Britain, 1956; Acts of Malcolm IV, King of Scots, 1960; Robert Bruce and the Community of the Realm of Scotland, 1965; Acts of William I, King of Scots, 1971; Kingdom of the Scots, 1973; (ed) The Scottish Tradition, 1974; The Anglo-Norman Era in Scottish History, 1980; Kingship and Unity, 1981; contrib. Scottish Historical Review, etc. *Recreation:* hill walking. *Address:* Department of Scottish History, 17 Buccleuch Place, Edinburgh EH8 9LN.

BARROW, Jocelyn, OBE 1972; Deputy Chairman, Broadcasting Standards Council, since 1989; *b* 15 April 1929; *d* of Charles Newton Barrow and Olive Irene Barrow (*née* Pierre); *m* 1970, Henderson Downer. *Educ:* Univ. of London. Mem., Taylor Cttee on School Governors; Gen. Sec., later Vice-Chm., Campaign Against Racial Discrimination, 1964–69; Vice-Chm., Internat. Human Rights Year Cttee, 1968; Member: CRC, 1968–72; Parole Bd, 1983–87. A Governor, BBC, 1981–88. Mem., Econ. and Social Cttee, EC, 1990–. Nat. Vice-Pres., Nat. Towns-women's Guilds, 1978–80, 1987–; Pres. and Founder, Community Housing Assoc.; Governor, Farnham Castle. FRSA. *Recreations:* theatre, music, cooking, reading. *Address:* c/o Broadcasting Standards Council, 5–8 The Sanctuary, SW1P 3JS. *T:* 071–233 0408. *Club:* Reform.

BARROW, John Frederick; HM Diplomatic Service, retired; *b* 28 Dec. 1918; *s* of Frederick William and Caroline Barrow; *m* 1947, Mary Roberta Young; two *d*. *Educ:* King Edward VII Sch., King's Lynn. Home Civil Service, 1936–39; war service in British and Indian Armies, 1939–46 (Major); rejoined Home Civil Service, 1946; Treasury, 1952–62; FCO, 1962; service overseas at Delhi, Kuala Lumpur, Jesselton, Prague, Washington, Hong Kong; retired as Counsellor, 1977. *Address:* Willow Down, Dental Street, Hythe, Kent CT21 5LH. *T:* Hythe (0303) 264830.

BARROW, Captain Michael Ernest, DSO 1982; RN; Clerk to the Worshipful Company of Haberdashers, since 1983; *b* 21 May 1932; *s* of late Captain Guy Runciman Barrow, OBE, RN and late Barbara Barrow; *m* 1962, Judith Ann (*née* Cooper); two *s* one *d*. *Educ:* Wellesley House; RNC, Dartmouth. Served in HM Ships: Devonshire, Liverpool (trng, 1950–52); Agincourt, Euryalus, 1952–53; HM Yacht Britannia, 1954–56; Camperdown, 1958–59; Flag Lt to Cdre Hong Kong, 1956–58; commanded: Caunton, 1960; Laleston, 1961–62; Mohawk, 1963–64; Torquay, 1967–69; Diomede, 1973–75; Glamorgan, 1980–83; RN Staff Course, 1966; Staff Flag Officer, Malta, 1970–71; Comdr RNC, Dartmouth, 1971–73; Dep. Dir, Recruiting, 1975–77; Asst Chief of Staff (Ops) to Comdr, Allied Naval Forces Southern Europe, Naples, 1978–80; ADC to the Queen, 1982–83; retired 1983. Gentleman Usher to Her Majesty, 1984–. *Recreations:* sailing, skiing, gardening, do-it-yourself. *Address:* Heathfield, Shear Hill, Petersfield, Hampshire GU31 4BB. *T:* Petersfield (0730) 64198. *Clubs:* Royal Naval Sailing; Royal Naval Ski.

BARROW, Dame Nita; *see* Barrow, Dame R. N.

BARROW, Captain Sir Richard John Uniacke, 6th Bt *cr* 1835; *b* 2 Aug. 1933; *s* of Sir Wilfrid John Wilson Croker Barrow, 5th Bt and (Gwladys) Patricia (*née* Uniacke); *S* father 1960; *m* 1961, Alison Kate (marr. diss. 1974), *yr d* of late Capt. Russell Grenfell, RN, and of Mrs Lindsay-Young; one *s* two *d*. *Educ:* Abbey Sch., Ramsgate; Beaumont Coll., Old Windsor. Commnd 2nd Lieut Irish Guards, 1952; served: Germany, 1952–53; Egypt, 1953–56; Cyprus, 1958; Germany, 1959–60; retired, 1960; joined International Computers and Tabulators Ltd; resigned 1973. *Heir: s* Anthony John Grenfell Barrow, *b* 24 May 1962.

BARROW, Dame (Ruth) Nita, DA 1980; GCMG 1990; FRCN 1980; Governor General of Barbados, since 1990; *b* 15 Nov. 1916. *Educ:* St Michael's Girls' School; Basic Nursing, Barbados (SRN), 1935–41; Midwifery Preparation, Trinidad Registered

Midwife, 1941–42; Public Health Diploma, 1943–44, Nursing Educn, 1944–45, Univ. of Toronto; Sister Tutor's Diploma, Edinburgh, 1951–52; BSc Nursing, Columbia Univ., NY, 1962–63. Staff Nurse, Barbados Gen. Hosp., Private Duty Nursing, 1940–41; Nursing Instr, Basic Sch. of Public Health, Jamaica, 1945–51; Sister Tutor, Kingston Sch. of Nursing, Jamaica, 1952–54; Matron, UCH, Jamaica, 1954–56; Principal Nursing Officer, Jamaica, 1956–63; WHO Nursing Advr, Caribbean Area, Region of the Americas, 1964–71; Associate Dir, 1971–75, Dir, 1975–81, Med. Commn, WCC. Ambassador Extraordinary and Plenipotentiary and Permanent Rep. of Barbados to UN, 1986–90. Mem., Editl Bd, Contact, Christian Med. Commn, Geneva. Gamaliel Lectr, Wisconsin, 1983. Hon. LLD: Univ. of W Indies, 1975; Toronto, 1987; Winnipeg, 1988; Spelman Coll., Atlanta; Hon. DSc McMaster, 1983; Hon. DHum: Maurice Brown, Ga, 1987; Mount St Vincent, 1988; numerous honours and awards from local and national organizations, including Presidential Medal, Brooklyn Coll., 1988; Christiane Reiman Award, Internat. Council of Nurses, Geneva, 1989. *Publications:* papers on Nursing Educn and Primary Health Care. *Recreations:* travel, reading. *Address:* Government House, Barbados. *Club:* Cosmopolitan (NY).

BARROWCLOUGH, Sir Anthony (Richard), Kt 1988; QC 1974; Parliamentary Commissioner for Administration, and Health Service Commissioner for England, Wales and Scotland, 1985–90; *b* 24 June 1924; *m* 1949, Mary Agnes Pery-Knox-Gore; one *s* one *d. Educ:* Stowe; New Coll., Oxford. Served RNVR, 1943–46 (Sub-Lieut and later Lieut). Called to the Bar, Inner Temple, 1949, Bencher 1982; Recorder, 1972–84. Part-time Member, Monopolies Commn, 1966–69; Mem., Council on Tribunals (and Mem., Scottish Cttee), 1985–90. *Recreation:* country pursuits. *Address:* The Old Vicarage, Winsford, near Minehead, Somerset.

BARRY, Prof. Brian Michael, FBA 1988; Professor of Political Science, London School of Economics and Political Science, since 1987; *b* 7 Aug. 1936; *s* of James Frederick and Doris Rose Barry; *m* 1960, Joanna Hill Scroggs (marr. diss. 1988); one *s. Educ:* Taunton's Sch., Southampton; Queen's Coll., Oxford (MA; DPhil 1965). Lloyd-Muirhead Res. Fellow, Univ. of Birmingham, 1960–61; Rockefeller Fellow in Legal and Political Philosophy, and Fellow of Harvard College, 1961–62; Asst Lectr, Keele Univ., 1962–63; Lectr, Univ. of Southampton, 1963–65; Tutorial Fellow, University Coll., Oxford, 1965–66; Official Fellow, Nuffield Coll., Oxford, 1966–69 and 1972–75; Prof., Univ. of Essex, 1969–72 (Dean of Social Studies, 1971–72); Prof., Univ. of British Columbia, 1975–76; Fellow, Center for Advanced Study in the Behavioral Scis, 1976–77; Professor: Univ. of Chicago, 1977–82; California Inst. of Technology, 1982–86; European Univ. Inst., Florence, 1986–87. Fellow, Amer. Acad. of Arts and Scis, 1978. Founding Editor, British Jl of Political Science, 1971–72; Editor, Ethics, 1979–82. *Publications:* Political Argument, 1965; Sociologists, Economics and Democracy, 1970; The Liberal Theory of Justice, 1973; (with Russell Hardin) Rational Man and Irrational Society?, 1982; Theories of Justice, vol. 1 of A Treatise on Social Justice, 1989; Democracy, Power and Justice: collected essays, 1989; articles in learned jls. *Recreations:* playing the piano, cooking, London. *Address:* London School of Economics, Houghton Street, WC2A 2AE. *T:* 071–405 7686.

BARRY, Daniel, CB 1988; Permanent Secretary, Department of the Environment for Northern Ireland, 1983–88; *b* 4 March 1928; *s* of William John Graham Barry and Sarah (*née* Wilkinson); *m* 1951, Florence (*née* Matier); two *s* one *d. Educ:* Belfast Mercantile Coll. FCIS, FSCA, FIHT. Local Government Officer with various NI Councils, 1944–68; Town Clerk, Carrickfergus Borough Council, 1968–73; Asst Sec. (Roads), Dept of the Environment for NI, 1973–76, Dep. Sec., 1976–80; Dep. Sec., Dept of Educn for NI, 1980–83. *Recreations:* golf, gardening, tobacco producing, wine making.

BARRY, Sir Edward; *see* Barry, Sir L. E. A. T.

BARRY, Edward Norman, CB 1981; Under Secretary, Northern Ireland Office, 1979–81, retired 1981; *b* 22 Feb. 1920; *s* of Samuel and Matilda (*née* Legge); *m* 1952, Inez Anna (*née* Elliott); one *s* two *d. Educ:* Bangor Grammar Sch. Northern Ireland Civil Service: Department of Finance: Establishment Div., 1940–51; Works Div., 1951–60; Treasury Div., 1960–67; Establishment Officer, 1967–72; Min. of Home Affairs, 1972–74; Asst Sec., N Ireland Office, 1974–79. *Recreations:* golf, Irish Football Association Ltd (Hon. Treasurer). *Address:* Allied Irish Banks Ltd, 697/703 Upper Newtownards Road, Dundonald, Belfast.

BARRY, James Edward; Stipendiary Magistrate for South Yorkshire, since 1985; a Recorder of the Crown Court, since 1985; *b* 27 May 1938; *s* of James Douglas Barry and Margaret Elizabeth (*née* Thornton); *m* 1963, Pauline Pratt; three *s. Educ:* Merchant Taylors' Sch., Crosby; Brasenose Coll., Oxford (schol.; MA Jurisp.). Called to the Bar, Inner Temple, 1963; in practice, NE Circuit, 1963–85. *Recreations:* reading, domestic pursuits. *Address:* Law Courts, Doncaster, S Yorks DN1 3HT.

BARRY, Sir (Lawrence) Edward (Anthony Tress), 5th Bt *cr* 1899; Baron de Barry in Portugal *cr* 1876; *b* 1 Nov. 1939; *s* of Sir Rupert Rodney Francis Tress Barry, 4th Bt, MBE, and Diana Madeline (*d* 1948), *o d* of R. O'Brien Thompson; *S* father, 1977; *m* 1968, Fenella Hoult; one *s* one *d. Educ:* Haileybury. Formerly Captain, Grenadier Guards. *Heir: s* William Rupert Philip Tress Barry, *b* 13 Dec. 1973. *Address:* 3 Sunnyside Cottages, Warehorne Road, Ham Street, Kent TN26 2JW. *T:* Ham Street (023373) 2454.

BARRY, Rt. Rev. (Noel) Patrick, OSB; Abbot of Ampleforth, since 1984; *b* 6 Dec. 1917; 2nd *s* of Dr T. St J. Barry, Wallasey, Cheshire. *Educ:* Ampleforth Coll.; St Benet's Hall, Oxford. Housemaster, Ampleforth Coll., 1954–64, Headmaster 1964–79. First Asst to Abbot Pres. of English Benedictine Congregation, 1985–. Chairman: Conference of Catholic Colleges, 1973–75; HMC, 1975; Union of Monastic Superiors, 1989–. *Address:* Ampleforth Abbey, York YO6 4EN.

BARRY, Peter; TD (FG) Cork South Central; *b* Cork, 10 Aug. 1928; *s* of Anthony Barry and Rita Costello; *m* 1958, Margaret O'Mullane; four *s* two *d. Educ:* Christian Brothers' Coll., Cork. Alderman of Cork Corp., 1967–73; Lord Mayor of Cork, 1970–71. TD: Cork City SE, 1969–82; Cork South Central, 1982–; opposition spokesman on labour and public services, 1972–73; Minister for: Transport and Power, 1973–76; Education, 1976–77; opposition spokesman on finance and economic affairs, 1977–81; Minister for the Environment, 1981–82; opposition spokesman on the environment, 1982; Minister for Foreign Affairs, 1982–87; opposition spokesman on foreign affairs, 1987–. Dep. Leader of Fine Gael Party; Chm., Nat. Exec., 1982–84. Co-Chm., Anglo-Irish Conf., 1982–87. *Address:* Sherwood, Blackrock, Co. Cork.

BARRY, Sir Philip Stuart M.; *see* Milner-Barry.

BARRY, Maj.-Gen. Richard Hugh, CB 1962; CBE 1953 (OBE 1943); retired; *b* 9 Nov. 1908; *s* of Lieut-Col Alfred Percival Barry and Helen Charlotte (*née* Stephens); *m* 1st, 1940, Rosalind Joyce Evans (*d* 1973); one *s* two *d*; 2nd, 1975, Elizabeth Lucia Middleton. *Educ:* Winchester; Sandhurst. 2nd Lieut Somerset LI, 1929; Staff Coll., Camberley, Capt., 1938; served War of 1939–45; BEF, SOE, AFHQ, Algiers. Military Attaché, Stockholm, 1947; Deputy Chief of Staff Western Europe Land Forces, 1948; Dir, Standing Group, NATO, 1952; Chief of Staff, HQ British Troops in Egypt, 1954–56; Imperial Defence Coll., 1957; Standing Group Representative, North Atlantic Council, 1959–62; retired, 1962. Maj.-Gen. 1959. Africa Star, 1943; 1939–45 Star; Defence, Victory Medals, 1945. *Recreation:* hunting. *Address:* Little Place, Farringdon, Alton, Hants GU34 3EH. *T:* Tisted (042058) 216. *Club:* Army and Navy.

BARSTOW, Josephine Clare, (Mrs Ande Anderson), CBE 1985; opera singer, free-lance since 1971; *b* Sheffield, 27 Sept. 1940; *m* 1969, Ande Anderson; no *c. Educ:* Birmingham Univ. (BA). Debut with Opera for All, 1964; studied at London Opera Centre, 1965–66; Opera for All, 1966; Glyndebourne Chorus, 1967; Sadler's Wells Contract Principal, 1967–68, sang Cherubino, Euridice, Violetta; *Welsh Nat. Opera:* Contract Principal, 1968–70, sang Violetta, Countess, Fiordiligi, Mimi, Amelia, Simon Boccanegra; Don Carlos, 1973; Jenufa, 1975; Peter Grimes, 1978, 1983; Tatyana in Onegin, 1980; Tosca, 1985; Un Ballo in Maschera, 1986; *Covent Garden:* Denise, world première, Tippett's The Knot Garden, 1970 (recorded 1974); Falstaff, 1975; Salome, 1982; Santuzza, 1982; Peter Grimes, 1988; Attila, 1990; *Glyndebourne:* Lady Macbeth (for TV), 1972; Idomeneo, 1974; Fidelio, 1981; *English Nat. Opera:* has sung all parts in Hoffman, Emilia Marty (Makropulos Case), Natasha (War and Peace) and Traviata; Der Rosenkavalier, 1975, 1984; Salome, 1975; Don Carlos, 1976, 1986; Tosca, 1976, 1987; Forza del Destino, 1978; Aida, 1979; Fidelio, Arabella, 1980; The Flying Dutchman, La Bohème, 1982; The Valkyrie, 1983; Don Giovanni, 1986; Lady Macbeth of Mtsensk, 1987, 1991. Other appearances include: Alice in Falstaff, Aix-en-Provence Festival, 1971; Nitocris in Belshazzar, Geneva, 1972; Jeanne, British première, Penderecki's The Devils, 1973; Marguerite, world première, Crosse's The Story of Vasco, 1974; Fidelio, Jenufa, Scottish Opera, 1977; Gayle, world première, Tippett's The Ice Break, 1977; US debut as Lady Macbeth, Miami, 1977; Musetta in La Bohème, NY Met., 1977; Salome, East Berlin, 1979 (Critics Prize), San Francisco, 1982; Abigaille in Nabucco, Miami, 1981; debut in Chicago as Lady Macbeth, 1981; new prod. of Jenufa, Cologne, 1981; La Voix Humaine and Pagliacci, Chicago, 1982; The Makropulos Case (in Italian), Florence, 1983; Gutrune, Göterdämmerung, Bayreuth, 1983; Die Fledermaus, San Francisco, 1984; Peter Grimes, 1984, La Traviata, 1985, Salome, 1987, Der Rosenkavalier, 1990, Houston; Benigna, world première, Penderecki's Die Schwarze Maske, Salzburg, 1986, Vienna Staatsoper, 1986; Manon Lescaut, USA, 1986; Tosca, Bolshoi, Tiblisi, 1986; Tosca, and Macbeth, Bolshoi, Riga, 1986; Macbeth, Zurich, 1986, Munich, 1987; Medea, Boston, 1988; Prokofiev's The Fiery Angel, Adelaide, 1988; Un Ballo in Maschera, Salzburg, 1989, 1990; Fanciulla del West, Toulouse, 1991. Sings in other opera houses in USA, Canada and Europe. Recordings include: Un Ballo in Maschera; Verdi arias; scenes from Salome, Medée, Makropulos case and Turandot; Kiss Me Kate; Kurt Weill's Street Scene. Fidelio medal, Assoc. of Internat. Opera Directors, 1985. *Recreation:* farm which she runs with her husband (she breeds pure-bred Arabian horses). *Address:* c/o John Coast, Manfield House, 376/9 Strand, Covent Garden, WC2R 0LR.

BARSTOW, Stan; writer; *b* 28 June 1928; *s* of Wilfred Barstow and Elsie Gosnay; *m* 1951, Constance Mary Kershaw; one *s* one *d. Educ:* Ossett Grammar Sch. Employed in Engineering Industry, 1944–62, mainly as Draughtsman. Best British Dramatisation, Writers' Guild of GB, 1974; Royal TV Soc. Writers' Award, 1975. Hon. Fellow, Bretton Coll., 1985. Hon. MA Open Univ., 1982. *Television:* dramatisations: A Raging Calm, 1974; South Riding, 1974; Joby, 1975; The Cost of Loving, 1977; Travellers, 1978; A Kind of Loving (from A Kind of Loving, The Watchers on the Shore, The Right True End), 1982; A Brother's Tale, 1983; *Publications:* A Kind of Loving, 1960; The Desperadoes, 1961; Ask Me Tomorrow, 1962; Joby, 1964; The Watchers on the Shore, 1966; A Raging Calm, 1968; A Season with Eros, 1971; The Right True End, 1976; A Brother's Tale, 1980; A Kind of Loving: The Vic Brown Trilogy, 1982; The Glad Eye, 1984; Just You Wait and See, 1986; B-Movie, 1987; Give Us This Day, 1989; Next of Kin, 1991; *plays:* Listen for the Trains, Love, 1970; Joby (TV script), 1977; An Enemy of the People (ad. Ibsen), 1978; The Human Element, and Albert's Part (TV scripts), 1984; (with Alfred Bradley): Ask Me Tomorrow, 1966; A Kind of Loving, 1970; Stringer's Last Stand, 1972. *Address:* c/o Lemon, Unna & Durbridge Ltd, 24 Pottery Lane, W11 4LZ.

BART, A. S.; *see* Schwarz-Bart.

BART, Lionel; composer, lyricist and playwright; *b* 1 Aug. 1930. Wrote lyrics for Lock Up Your Daughters, 1959; music and lyrics for Fings Ain't Wot They Used T'be, 1959; music, lyrics and book for Oliver!, 1960; music, lyrics and direction of Blitz!, also co-author of book with Joan Maitland, 1962; music and lyrics of Maggie May, 1964; music of Lionel, 1977. Has also written several film scores and many individual hit songs. *Films:* Serious Charge; In the Nick; Heart of a Man; Let's Get Married; Light up the Sky; The Tommy Steele Story; The Duke Wore Jeans; Tommy the Toreador; Sparrers Can't Sing; From Russia with Love; Man in the Middle; Oliver (gold disc for sound track, 1969); The Optimists of Nine Elms. Ivor Novello Awards as a song writer: three in 1957; four in 1959; two in 1960; Jimmy Kennedy, for life long achievement, 1985. Variety Club Silver Heart as Show Business Personality of the Year, 1960. Broadway, USA; Tony (Antoinette Perry) Award, etc (for Oliver!), best composer and lyricist, 1962. *Address:* c/o 8–10 Bulstrode Street, W1M 6AH.

BARTELL, Anne, (Mrs John Bartell); *see* Gibson, A.

BARTELL, Lt-Col (Hon.) Kenneth George William, CBE 1977; FCIB; Past President, British Chambers of Commerce in Continental Europe; Past President (twice) and Honorary Vice-President, British Chamber of Commerce, France; *b* 5 Dec. 1914; *s* of William Richard Aust Bartell and Daisy Florence (*née* Kendall); *m* 1955, Lucie Adèle George (*d* 1990). *Educ:* Cooper's Company's Sch. BCom London. Westminster Bank Ltd, London, 1933. Served war, RAOC: France, 1939–40, Egypt and Middle East, 1940–46 (despatches twice); demobilised Hon. Lt-Col. Westminster Bank Ltd, London, 1946–49; Westminster Foreign Bank Ltd: Paris, 1950–51; Lyons, 1952–53; Bordeaux, 1954–55; Manager, State Commercial Bank, Rangoon, Burma, 1955–59; Man., then Chief Man., Westminster Foreign Bank, Paris, 1960–74; Gen. Man., Internat. Westminster Bank Ltd, France, 1974–76, retired. Freeman: Coopers' Co., 1981; City of London, 1981. *Recreations:* swimming, bridge. *Address:* 5 avenue Saint-Honoré-d'Eylau, Paris 75116, France. *T:* (1) 45 53 69 48. *Clubs:* Army and Navy, Royal Automobile; Cercle de l'Union Interalliée (Paris).

BARTHOLOMEW, Prof. David John, PhD; FBA 1987; Professor of Statistics, London School of Economics, since 1973 (Pro-Director, 1988–91); *b* 6 Aug. 1931; *s* of Albert and Joyce Bartholomew; *m* 1955, Marian Elsie Lake; two *d. Educ:* University College London (BSc, PhD). Scientist, NCB, 1955–57; Lectr in Stats, Univ. of Keele, 1957–60; Lectr, then Sen. Lectr, UCW, Aberystwyth, 1960–67; Prof. of Stats, Univ. of Kent, 1967–73. Treasurer, Royal Statistical Soc., 1989– (Hon. Sec., 1976–82); Vice-Pres., Manpower Soc. *Publications:* (jtly) Backbench Opinion in the House of Commons 1955–1959, 1961; Stochastic Models for Social Processes, 1967, 3rd edn 1982; (jtly) Let's Look at the Figures: the quantitative approach to human affairs, 1971; (jtly) Statistical Inference Under Order Restrictions, 1972; (with A. F. Forbes) Statistical Techniques for Manpower Planning,

1979, 2nd edn 1991; Mathematical Methods in Social Science, 1981; God of Chance, 1984; Latent Variable Models and Factor Analysis, 1987; papers in statistical and social science jls. *Recreations:* gardening, steam railways, theology. *Address:* Department of Statistical and Mathematical Sciences, London School of Economics, Houghton Street, WC2A 2AE. *T:* 071–405 7686.

BARTLE, Ronald David; a Metropolitan Stipendiary Magistrate since 1972; *b* 14 April 1929; *s* of Rev. George Clement Bartle and late Winifred Marie Bartle; *m* 1st, 1963; one *s* one *d*; 2nd, 1981, Hisako (*née* Yagi). *Educ:* St John's Sch., Leatherhead; Jesus Coll., Cambridge (MA). Nat. Service, 1947–49 (Army Athletic Colours). Called to Bar, Lincoln's Inn, 1954. Contested (C) Islington North, 1958 and 1959. A Dep. Circuit Judge, 1975–79; A Chm., Inner London Juvenile Courts, 1975–79. Member: Home Office Council on Drug Abuse, 1987–; Home Office Cttee on Magistrates' Court Procedure, 1989–. Liveryman, Basketmaker's Co., 1976. Freeman, City of London, 1976 (Mem., Guild of Freemen, 1979); Member: Royal Soc. of St George; Lawyers' Christian Fellowship. *Publications:* Introduction to Shipping Law, 1958; The Police Officer in Court, 1984; Crime and the New Magistrate, 1985; The Law and the Lawless, 1987. *Recreations:* music, reading, swimming. *Address:* Bow Street Magistrates' Court, WC2E 7AS. *Clubs:* Garrick, Lansdowne.

BARTLEET, Rt. Rev. David Henry; *see* Tonbridge, Bishop Suffragan of.

BARTLES-SMITH, Ven. Douglas Leslie; Archdeacon of Southwark, since 1985; *b* 3 June 1937; *s* of Leslie Charles and Muriel Rose Bartles-Smith; *m* 1967, Patricia Ann Coburn; two *s* one *d*. *Educ:* Shrewsbury School; St Edmund Hall, Oxford (MA); Wells Theol Coll. Nat. Service (2nd Lieut, RASC), 1956–58. Curate of St Stephen's, Rochester Row, SW1, 1963–68; Curate-in-charge, St Michael and All Angels with Emmanuel and All Souls, Camberwell, 1968–72; Vicar, 1972–75; Vicar of St Luke, Battersea, 1975–85; RD of Battersea, 1981–85. *Publication:* (co-author) Urban Ghetto, 1976. *Recreations:* Shrewsbury Town Football Club, reading, walking, travel. *Address:* 1a Dog Kennel Hill, East Dulwich, SE22 8AA. *T:* 071–274 6767.

BARTLETT, Charles; *see* Bartlett, Harold Charles.

BARTLETT, George Robert; QC 1986; a Recorder, since 1990; *b* 22 Oct. 1944; *s* of late Commander H. V. Bartlett, RN and of Angela (*née* Webster); *m* 1972, Dr Clare Virginia, *y d* of G. C. Fortin; three *s*. *Educ:* Tonbridge Sch.; Trinity Coll., Oxford (MA). Called to the Bar, Middle Temple, 1966. *Publication:* (ed) Ryde on Rating, 1991–. *Recreations:* cricket and other games. *Address:* 2 Mitre Court Buildings, Temple, EC4Y 7BX. *T:* 071–583 1380.

BARTLETT, (Harold) Charles, ARCA 1949; RE 1961 (ARE 1950); RWS 1970 (ARWS 1959); President, Royal Society of Painters in Water Colours, since 1987; painter and printmaker; *b* Grimsby, 23 Sept. 1921; *s* of Charles Henry and Frances Kate Bartlett; *m*; one *s*. *Educ:* Eastbourne Grammar Sch.; Eastbourne Sch. of Art; Royal College of Art. First one man exhibition in London, 1960. *Recreations:* music, sailing. *Address:* St Andrews, Fingringhoe, near Colchester, Essex. *T:* Rowhedge (0206) 729406.

BARTLETT, Henry Francis, CMG 1975; OBE 1964; painter; HM Diplomatic Service, retired; *b* 8 March 1916; *s* of F. V. S. and A. G. Bartlett, London; *m* 1940, A. D. Roy. *Educ:* St Paul's Sch.; Queen's Coll., Oxford; Ruskin Sch. of Drawing; Univ. of California (Commonwealth Fellow). Min. of Inf., 1940–45; Paris, 1944–47; Vice-Consul Lyons, 1948–49; FO, 1949–50; Vice-Consul, Szczecin, 1950; Second, later First, Sec., Warsaw, 1951–53; FO, 1953–55; First Sec. (Commercial), Caracas, 1955–60; First Sec. (Inf.), Mexico City, 1960–63; Consul, Khorramshahr, 1964–67; Dep. High Comr, Brisbane, 1967–69; Counsellor, Manila, 1969–72 (Chargé d'Affaires, 1971); Ambassador to Paraguay, 1972–75. Hon. Prof., Nat. Univ. of Asunción, 1975. Exec. Officer, Utah Foundation, Brisbane, 1976–89. Exhibitions of painting: Paris, 1947; London, 1950; Caracas, 1957, 1959; Mexico City, 1962; Brisbane, 1969, 1978, 1981, 1983, 1985, 1988, 1990. Represented: Commonwealth Art Bank; Queensland and S Aust. State Galleries; Queensland Univ. of Technol.; Brisbane Civic Art Gall.; Bendigo Art Gall. Trustee: Queensland Art Gallery, 1977–87; Qld Cultural Centre Trust, 1980–87. *Recreations:* painting, book reviewing. *Address:* 14 Bowen Place, 341 Bowen Terrace, New Farm, Brisbane, Qld 4005, Australia.

BARTLETT, Sir John (Hardington), 4th Bt *cr* 1913, of Hardington Mandeville, Somerset; Chairman and Director of various companies; *b* 11 March 1938; *s* of Sir (Henry) David (Hardington) Bartlett, 3rd Bt, MBE and of Kathleen Rosamund, *d* of late Lt-Col W. H. Stanbury; *S* father, 1989; *m* 1st, 1966, Susan Elizabeth Waldock (*d* 1970); one *d*; 2nd, 1971, Elizabeth Joyce, *d* of George Raine; two *s*. *Educ:* St Peter's Grammar Sch., Guildford. Career in engineering and construction. *Recreations:* joinery, woodwork, construction, fine wine. *Heir:* *s* Andrew Alan Bartlett, *b* 26 May 1973. *Address:* Hardington House, Ermyn Way, Leatherhead, Surrey KT22 8TW. *Club:* Naval.

BARTLETT, Maj.-Gen. John Leonard, CB 1985; Paymaster-in-Chief and Inspector of Army Pay Services, 1983–86, retired; *b* 17 Aug. 1926; *s* of late F. Bartlett and E. Bartlett; *m* 1952, Pauline (*née* Waite); two *s*. *Educ:* Holt Grammar Sch., Liverpool. MBCS, FBIM, jssc, psc, pfc. Commissioned Royal Army Pay Corps, 1946; served Hong Kong, Singapore, BAOR, War Office, Washington, Malta, Libya, HQ MELF, 1966–67 (despatches 1968); Staff Pmr and O i/c FBPO Berlin, 1968–69; GSO1 (Secretary) NATO Mil. Agency for Standardisation, 1969–71; Comd Pmr, Hong Kong, 1972–74; Col GS, MoD (ADP Coord.), 1974–76; Chief Pmr ADP and Station Comdr, Worthy Down, 1976–79; Chief Pmr, BAOR, 1980–82. Col Comdt, RAPC, 1987–90. Freeman, City of London, 1984. *Recreation:* golf. *Address:* c/o Lloyds Bank, The Square, Wickham, Hants PO17 5JQ. *Club:* Lansdowne.

BARTLETT, John Vernon, CBE 1976; MA; FEng, FICE, FASCE, FIE Aust.; Consulting Engineer; Consultant, Mott MacDonald Group (formerly Mott, Hay and Anderson), since 1988; *b* 18 June 1927; *s* of late Vernon F. Bartlett and Olga Bartlett (*née* Testrup); *m* 1951, Gillian, *d* of late Philip Hoffmann, Sturmer Hall, Essex; four *s*. *Educ:* Stowe; Trinity Coll., Cambridge. Served 9th Airborne Squadron, RE, 1946–48; Engineer and Railway Staff Corps, TA, 1978; Col 1986. Engineer with John Mowlem & Co. Ltd, 1951–57; joined staff of Mott, Hay & Anderson, 1957; Partner, 1966–88; Chm., 1973–88. Pres., ICE, 1983–84 (Vice-Pres., 1979–82; Mem. Council, 1974–77); Chm., British Tunnelling Soc., 1977–79. FRSA 1975. Mem. Council, Fellowship of Engrg, 1982–86. Sen. Warden, Engineers' Co., 1991– (Mem., Court of Assts, 1986–). Telford Gold Medal, (jointly) 1971, 1973; S. G. Brown Medal, Royal Soc., 1973. *Publications:* Tunnels: Planning Design and Construction (with T. M. Megaw), vol. 1, 1981, vol. 2, 1982; contrib. various papers to ICE, ASCE, etc. *Recreation:* sailing. *Address:* c/o Mott MacDonald, 20/26 Wellesley Road, Croydon, Surrey CR9 2UL. *T:* 081–686 5041. *Clubs:* Hawks (Cambridge); Harlequin Football; Royal Engineers Yacht.

BARTLETT, Prof. Maurice Stevenson, FRS 1961; MA Cambridge, DSc London; Professor of Bio-mathematics in the University of Oxford, 1967–75, now Emeritus; *b* 18 June 1910; *s* of W. S. Bartlett, Scrooby; *m* 1957, Sheila, *d* of C. E. Chapman; one *d*. *Educ:* Latymer Upper Sch.; Queens' Coll., Cambridge. Wrangler, 1932; Rayleigh Prize, 1934. Asst Lectr in Statistics, University Coll., London, 1933–34; Statistician, Imperial Chemical Industries, Ltd, 1934–38; Lectr in Mathematics, Univ. of Cambridge, 1938–47. National Service, Min. of Supply, 1940–45. Visiting Prof. of Mathematical Statistics, Univ. of North Carolina, 1946; Prof. of Mathematical Statistics, Univ. of Manchester, 1947–60; Prof. of Statistics, Univ. of London (University Coll.), 1960–67. Mem. Internat. Statistical Institute, 1949, Hon. Mem., 1980; President: Manchester Statistical Soc., 1959–60; Biometric Soc. (Brit. Reg.), 1964–66; Internat. Assoc. Statistics Phys. Sci., 1965–67; Royal Statistical Society, 1966–67. Hon. DSc: Chicago, 1966; Hull, 1976. Gold Medal, Royal Statistical Soc., 1969; Weldon Prize and Medal, Oxford, 1971. *Publications:* An Introduction to Stochastic Processes, 1955; Stochastic Population Models in Ecology and Epidemiology, 1960; Essays in Probability and Statistics, 1962; Probability, Statistics and Time, 1975; Statistical Analysis of Spatial Pattern 1976; Selected Papers, 3 vols, 1988; papers on statistical and biometrical theory and methodology. *Address:* Overcliff, 4 Trefusis Terrace, Exmouth, Devon EX8 2AX.

BARTLETT, Prof. Neil, FRS 1973; FRSC; Professor of Chemistry, University of California, Berkeley, since 1969, and Principal Investigator, Chemical Sciences Division, Lawrence Berkeley Laboratory, since 1969; *b* Newcastle upon Tyne, 15 Sept. 1932; *s* of Norman Bartlett and Ann Willins Bartlett (*née* Vock), both of Newcastle upon Tyne; *m* 1957, Christina I., *d* of J. W. F. Cross, Guisborough, Yorks; three *s* one *d*. *Educ:* Heaton Grammar Sch., Newcastle upon Tyne; King's Coll., Univ. of Durham, Newcastle upon Tyne. BSc 1954, PhD 1958. Senior Chemistry Master, The Duke's Sch., Alnwick, Northumberland, 1957–58; Mem. Faculty (Dept of Chemistry), Univ. of British Columbia, 1958–66; Prof. of Chemistry, Princeton Univ., and Scientist, Bell Telephone Laboratories, Murray Hill, NJ, USA, 1966–69. For. Associate, Nat. Acad. of Sciences, USA, 1979. Member: Deutsche Akademie der Naturforscher Leopoldina, 1969; Der Akademie der Wissenschaften in Göttingen, 1977; Amer. Chem. Soc., etc.; Associé Etranger, Acad. des Sciences, France. Sigma Xi. Visiting Miller Prof., Univ. of Calif, Berkeley, 1967–68; Brotherton Vis. Prof., Univ. of Leeds, 1981, etc. Erskine Fellow, Univ. of Canterbury, NZ, 1983; Vis. Fellow, All Souls, Oxford, 1984. Hon. DSc: Univ. of Waterloo, Canada, 1968; Colby Coll., Maine, USA, 1972; Univ. of Newcastle, 1981; Dr *hc*: Univ. of Bordeaux, 1976; Univ. of Ljubljana, 1989; Univ. of Nantes, 1990. Fellow: Amer. Acad. of Arts and Scis, 1977; Chem. Inst. of Canada; Chem. Soc. (London). Corday-Morgan Medal and Prize of Chem. Soc., 1962; Robert A. Welch Award, 1976; Medal of Inst. Jožef Stefan, Ljubljana, 1980; W. H. Nichols Medal, NY Section, ACS, 1983; Prix Moissan, 1988; Amer. Chem. Soc. Award for Distinguished Service to Inorganic Chemistry, 1989; Pauling Medal, 1989; various overseas awards and prizes, 1965–. *Publications:* The Chemistry of the Monatomic Gases, 1975; scientific papers to: Jl of Chem. Soc., Inorganic Chem., etc; Mem. various editorial advisory bds in Gt Britain, France and USA. *Recreations:* water colour painting; walking in high country; gardening. *Address:* 6 Oak Drive, Orinda, Calif 94563, USA; Chemistry Department, University of California, Berkeley, Calif 94720, USA. *T:* (business) (415) 642–7259.

BARTON, Anne; *see* Barton, B. A.

BARTON, Prof. (Barbara) Anne, PhD; FBA 1991; Professor of English, Cambridge University, since 1984; Fellow of Trinity College, Cambridge, since 1986; *b* 9 May 1933; *d* of Oscar Charles Roesen and Blanche Godfrey Williams; *m* 1st, 1957, William Harvey Righter; 2nd, 1969, John Bernard Adie Barton, *qv*. *Educ:* Bryn Mawr College, USA. BA 1954 (*summa cum laude*); PhD Cantab 1960. Lectr in History of Art, Ithaca Coll., NY, 1958–59; Girton College, Cambridge: Rosalind Lady Carlisle Research Fellow, 1960–62; Official Fellow in English, 1962–72; Dir of Studies in English, 1963–72; Univ. Asst Lectr, later Univ. Lectr in English, Cambridge, 1962–72; Hildred Carlile Prof. of English and Head of Dept, Bedford Coll., London, 1972–74; Fellow and Tutor in English, New Coll., Oxford and CUF Lectr, 1974–84. Lectures: British Acad. Chatterton, 1967; Alexander Meml, Univ. Coll., Toronto, 1983; British Acad. Shakespeare, 1991; Hon. Fellow: Shakespeare Inst., Univ. of Birmingham, 1982; New Coll., Oxford, 1989. Member Editorial Advisory Boards: Shakespeare Survey, 1972–; Shakespeare Quarterly, 1981–; Studies in English Literature, 1976–. *Publications:* Shakespeare and the Idea of the Play, 1962, 4th edn 1977, trans. Japanese 1982; Ben Jonson, Dramatist, 1984; The Names of Comedy, 1990; essays and studies in learned jls. *Recreations:* opera, fine arts, travel. *Address:* Trinity College, Cambridge CB2 1TQ. *T:* Cambridge (0223) 338466; Leverington Hall, Wisbech, Cambs PE13 5DE.

BARTON, Ven. (Charles) John Greenwood; Archdeacon of Aston, since 1990; *b* 5 June 1936; *s* of Charles William Greenwood Barton and Doris Lilian Leach. *Educ:* Battersea Grammar Sch.; London Coll. of Divinity (ALCD). Asst Curate, St Mary Bredin, Canterbury, 1963–66; Vicar, Whitfield with West Langdon, dio. Canterbury, 1966–75; Vicar, St Luke, South Kensington, 1975–83; Area Dean, Chelsea, 1980–83; Chief Broadcasting Officer, Church of England, 1983–90. *Address:* 26 George Road, Edgbaston, Birmingham B15 1PJ. *T:* 021–454 5525. *Club:* National Liberal.

BARTON, Sir Derek Harold Richard, Kt 1972; FRS 1954; FRSE 1956; Professor of Chemistry, Texas A and M University, since 1985; *b* 8 Sept. 1918; *s* of William Thomas and Maude Henrietta Barton; *m* 1st, 1944, Jeanne Kate Wilkins; one *s*; 2nd, 1969, Christiane Cognet. *Educ:* Tonbridge Sch.; Imperial Coll., Univ. of London (Fellow, 1980). BSc Hons (1st Class) 1940; Hofmann Prizeman; PhD (Organic Chemistry) 1942; DSc London 1949. Research Chemist: on Govt project, 1942–44. Albright and Wilson, Birmingham, 1944–45; Asst Lectr, Dept of Chemistry, Imperial Coll., 1945–46, ICI Research Fellow, 1946–49; Visiting Lectr in Chemistry of Natural Products, Harvard Univ., USA, 1949–50; Reader in Organic Chemistry, Birkbeck Coll., 1950, Prof. of Organic Chemistry, 1953–55; Regius Prof. of Chemistry, Glasgow Univ., 1955–57; Prof. of Organic Chem., 1957–70, Hofmann Prof. of Organic Chem., 1970–78, Imperial Coll.; Emeritus Prof. of Organic Chem., Univ. of London, 1978; Dir, Institut de Chimie des Substances Naturelles, CNRS, France, 1978–85. Arthur D. Little Vis. Prof., MIT, 1958; Karl Folkers Vis. Prof., Univs of Illinois and Wisconsin, 1959; Cecil H. and Ida Green Vis. Prof., Univ. of British Columbia, 1977; Firth Vis. Prof. in Chemistry, Univ. of Sheffield, 1978. Lectures: Tilden, Chem. Soc., 1952; Max Tischler, Harvard Univ., 1956; First Simonsen Memorial, Chem. Soc., 1958; Falk-Plaut, Columbia Univ., 1961; Aub, Harvard Med. Sch., 1962; Renaud, Michigan State Univ., 1962; Inaugural 3 M's, Univ. of Western Ontario, 1962; 3 M's, Univ. of Minnesota, 1963; Hugo Müller, Chem. Soc., 1963; Pedler, Chem. Soc., 1967; Sandin, Univ. of Alberta, 1969; Robert Robinson, Chem. Soc., London, 1970; Bakerian, Royal Society, 1970; Bose Endowment, Bose Inst., Calcutta, 1972; Stieglitz, Chicago Univ., 1974; Bachmann, Michigan, 1975; Woodward, Yale, 1975; First Smissman, Kansas, 1976; Benjamin Rush and Priestley, Pennsylvania State Univ., 1977; Romanes, Edinburgh, 1979; (first) Hirst, St Andrews Univ., 1980. President: Section B, British Assoc. for the Advancement of Science, 1969; Organic Chemistry Div., Internat. Union of Pure and Applied Chemistry, 1969; Perkin Div., Chem. Soc., 1971; Pres., Chem. Soc., 1973–74. Mem., Council for Scientific Policy, 1965–68. Hon. Member: Sociedad Quimica de Mexico, 1969; Belgian Chem. Soc., 1970; Chilean Chem. Soc., 1970; Polish Chem. Soc., 1970; Pharmaceutical Soc. of Japan, 1970; Royal Acad. Exact

Scis, Madrid, 1971; Acad. of Pharmaceutical Scis, USA, 1971; Danish Acad. Scis, 1972; Argentinian Acad. Scis, 1973; Societa Italiana per il Progresso delle Scienze, 1976; Chem. Soc. of Japan, 1982; Corresp. Mem., Argentinian Chem. Soc., 1970; Foreign Member: Acad. das Ciencias de Lisboa, 1971; Academia Nazionale dei Lincei, Rome, 1975; Foreign Hon. Mem. American Academy of Arts and Sciences, 1960; Foreign Associate: Nat. Acad. of Sciences, USA, 1970; l'Académie des Sciences, Institute de France, 1978. Hon. Fellow: Deutsche Akad. der Naturforscher Leopoldina, 1967; Birkbeck Coll., 1970; ACS Centennial Foreign Fellow, 1976; Hon. FRSC 1985. Hon. DSc: Montpellier Univ., 1962; Dublin, 1964; St Andrews, Columbia NYC, 1970; Coimbra, 1971; Oxon, Manchester, 1972; South Africa, 1973; City, 1975; Hon. Dr: La Laguna, 1975; Univ. of Western Virginia, 1975; Sydney, 1976; Univs of Valencia, Sheffield, Western Ontario, 1979; Frankfurt, 1980; Metz, 1981; Lyon, 1983; London, 1984; Debrechen, 1986; Hon. DrEng Stevens Inst. of Technol., 1984. Harrison Memorial Prize, Chem. Soc., 1948; First Corday-Morgan Medallist, Chemical Soc., 1951; Fritzsche Medal, Amer. Chem. Soc., 1956; First Roger Adams Medal, Amer. Chem. Soc., 1959; Davy Medal, Royal Society, 1961; Nobel Prize for Chemistry (jointly), 1969; First award in Natural Product Chemistry, Chem. Soc. of London, 1971; Longstaff Medal, Chem. Soc., 1972; B. C. Law Gold Medal, Indian Assoc. for Cultivation of Science, 1972; Medal, Soc. of Cosmetic Chem. of GB, 1972; Royal Medal, Royal Soc., 1972; Second Centennial of Priestly Chemistry Award, Amer. Chem. Soc., 1974; Medal of Union of Sci. Workers, Bulgaria, 1978; Univ. of Sofia Medal, 1978; Acad. of Scis, Bulgaria Medal, 1978; Copley Medal, Royal Soc., 1980; Hanbury Meml Medal, PSGB, 1981. Order of the Rising Sun (2nd class), Japan, 1972; Officier, Légion d'Honneur, 1986 (Chevalier, 1974). *Publications:* numerous, in Journal of Chemical Society and Tetrahedron. *Address:* Department of Chemistry, Texas A and M University, College Station, Texas 77843–3255, USA.

BARTON, Maj.-Gen. Eric Walter, CB 1983; MBE 1966; BSc, FBIM, FRGS; Director, Caravan Club Ltd, since 1984; *b* 27 April 1928; *s* of Reginald John Barton and Dorothy (*née* Bradfield); *m* 1963 (marr. diss. 1983); two *s*; *m* 1984, Mrs Pamela Clare Frimann, *d* of late Reginald D. Mason and of Doris Mason, Winchelsea. *Educ:* St Clement Danes Sch., London; Royal Military Coll. of Science (BScEng 1955). Dip. in Photogrammetry, UCL, 1960. FBIM 1979; FRGS 1979. Commnd RE, 1948; served Mid East, 1948–50; Arab Legion, 1951–52; seconded to Dir, Overseas Surveys, E Africa, 1957–59; Sen. Instr, Sch. of Mil. Survey, 1961–63; OC 13 Fd Survey Sqdn, Aden, 1965–67; Dir, Surveys and Prodn, Ordnance Survey, 1977–80; Dir of Mil. Survey, 1980–84. Major 1961, Lt-Col 1967, Col 1972, Brig. 1976, Maj.-Gen. 1980. Col Comdt, RE, 1982–87; Hon. Col, Field Survey Sqn, later 135 Indep. Topographic Sqn RE (V) TA, 1984–89. Pres., Field Survey Assoc., 1991– (Chm., 1984–86); Member: Council, Photogrammetric Soc., 1979–82; Nat. Cttee for Photogrammetry, 1979–84; Council, RGS, 1980–83; Council, British Schs Exploring Soc., 1980–84; Nat. Cttee for Geography, 1981–84. *Recreations:* swimming, water sports, ski-ing, numismatics. *Address:* c/o Barclays Bank, Winchester, Hants. *Clubs:* Army and Navy, Geographical.

BARTON, Maj.-Gen. Francis Christopher, CB 1966; CBE 1964; *b* 17 Jan. 1916; *s* of Rev. John Bernard Barton, Elphinstone House, Hastings; *m* 1939, Olivia Mary Darroll-Smith; two *d*. *Educ:* Haileybury Coll. 2nd Lieut, Royal Marines, 1934; Lieut-Col, 1956; Brig., 1961; Maj.-Gen., 1964. Comd 45 Commando, RM, 1958–60; Comd 3 Commando Brigade, RM, 1962–63; Comdt, Joint Warfare Establishment, Old Sarum, 1964–66; retired, 1966. Voluntary Help Organiser, Royal Victoria Hospitals, Bournemouth, 1967–80; Chm., Standing Conf., Voluntary Help Organisers, 1971–72. *Address:* Moorcroft, Blissford, Fordingbridge, Hants SP6 2HY.

BARTON, Rev. Prof. John, DPhil, DLitt; Oriel and Laing Professor of the Interpretation of Holy Scripture, University of Oxford, since 1991; Fellow of Oriel College, Oxford, since 1991; *b* 17 June 1948; *s* of Bernard Arthur Barton and Gwendolyn Harriet Barton; *m* 1973, Mary Burn; one *d*. *Educ:* Latymer Upper Sch., Hammersmith; Keble Coll., Oxford (MA; DPhil 1974; DLitt 1988). University of Oxford: Jun. Res. Fellow, Merton Coll., 1973–74; Official Fellow, St Cross Coll., 1974–91; University Lectr in Theology (OT), 1974–89; Reader in Biblical Studies, 1989–91; Chaplain, St Cross Coll., 1979–91. *Publications:* Amos's Oracles against the Nations, 1980; Reading the Old Testament: method in biblical study, 1984; Oracles of God: perceptions of ancient prophecy in Israel after the Exile, 1986; People of the Book?—the authority of the Bible in Christianity, 1988; Love Unknown: meditations on the Death and Resurrection of Jesus, 1990; What is the Bible?, 1991. *Address:* Oriel College, Oxford OX1 4EW.

BARTON, John Bernard Adie, CBE 1981; Associate Director, Royal Shakespeare Company, since 1964; *b* 26 Nov. 1928; *s* of late Sir Harold Montague Barton and Joyce Wale; *m* 1968, Anne Righter (*see* B. A. Barton). *Educ:* Eton Coll.; King's Coll., Cambridge (BA, MA). Fellow, King's Coll., Cambridge, 1954–60 (Lay Dean, 1956–59). Joined Royal Shakespeare Company, 1960; Associate Dir, 1964. Has adapted texts and directed or co-directed many plays for Royal Shakespeare Company, including: The Taming of the Shrew, 1960; The Hollow Crown, 1961; The Art of Seduction, 1962; The Wars of the Roses, 1963–64; Henry IV, Parts I and II, and Henry V, 1964–66; Love's Labour's Lost, 1965; Coriolanus and All's Well That Ends Well, 1967; Julius Caesar and Troilus and Cressida, 1968; Twelfth Night and When Thou Art King, 1969; Measure for Measure and The Tempest, 1970; Richard II, Henry V, and Othello, 1971; Richard II, 1973; King John, Cymbeline, and Dr Faustus, 1974; Perkin Warbeck, 1975; Much Ado About Nothing, The Winter's Tale, and Troilus and Cressida, 1976; A Midsummer Night's Dream, Pillars of the Community, 1977; The Way of the World, The Merchant of Venice, Love's Labour's Lost, 1978; The Greeks, 1979; Hamlet, 1980; The Merchant of Venice, Titus Andronicus and The Two Gentlemen of Verona, 1981; La Ronde, 1982; Life's a Dream, 1983; The Devils, 1984; Waste, Dream Play, 1985; The Rover, 1986; Three Sisters, 1988; Coriolanus, 1989. Directed: The School for Scandal, Haymarket, 1983, Duke of York's, 1983; The Vikings at Helgeland, Den Nationale Scene, Bergen, 1983; Peer Gynt, Oslo, 1990. Wrote and presented Playing Shakespeare, LWT, 1982, Channel 4, 1984; narrated Morte d'Arthur, BBC2, 1984. *Publications:* The Hollow Crown, 1962 (and 1971); The Wars of the Roses, 1970; The Greeks, 1981. *Recreations:* travel, chess, work. *Address:* 14 DeWalden Court, 85 New Cavendish Street, W1. *T:* 071–580 6196.

BARTON, Ven. John Greenwood; *see* Barton, Ven. C. J. G.

BARTON, Margaret, LRAM; writer; *b* 1897; *y d* of Thomas Lloyd Barton and Fanny Roberta Isaacs. *Educ:* St Paul's Girls' Sch.; Royal Academy of Music. *Publications:* Tunbridge Wells, 1937; Garrick, 1948; (with Sir Osbert Sitwell) Sober Truth, 1930; Victoriana, 1931; Brighton, 1935. *Address:* 8 Penywern Road, SW5 9ST.

BARTON, Roger; Member (Lab) Sheffield, European Parliament, since 1989; *b* 6 Jan. 1945; *s* of late Joseph and Doreen Barton; *m* 1965; two *s*. *Educ:* Burngreave Secondary Modern Sch.; Granville Coll. (Engrg Technician's Cert.). Fitter, 1961–81; Sheffield TUC and Labour Party Sec., 1981–89. Mem., Sheffield CC, 1971–. *Recreations:* walking, gentle cycling, water sports. *Address:* Labour European Office, 48 Pinstone Street, Sheffield S1 2HN. *Clubs:* Trades and Labour, Wortley Hall Labour (Sheffield); Labour (Chesterfield).

BARTON-CHAPPLE, Dorothy, (Mrs Derek Barton-Chapple); *see* Tutin, Dorothy.

BARTOSIK, Rear-Adm. Josef C., CB 1968; DSC 1943; *b* 20 July 1917; *m* 1st, 1943, Cynthia Pamela Bowman; three *s* one *d*; 2nd, 1969, Jeannine Scott (*née* Bridgeman). Joined Polish Navy, 1935; served in Polish destroyers under British operational control, 1939–46; transf. to RN, 1948; commanded: HMS Comus, 1955–56; HMS Scarborough and 5th Frigate Sqn, 1960–61; HMS Seahawk (RN Air Station Culdrose), 1962–63, HMS London, 1964–65; Rear-Adm. 1966; Asst Chief of Naval Staff (Ops), 1966–68; retired 1968. Coordinating Dir, European Jt Org., Australia Europe Container Service and Australia NZ Europe Container Service, 1969–81, retired 1981. *Recreation:* picture framing. *Address:* 33 Cheval Place, SW7 1EW.

BARTTELOT, Col Sir Brian Walter de Stopham, 5th Bt, *cr* 1875; OBE 1983; DL; psc; Colonel, Foot Guards, since 1989; Regimental Lieutenant-Colonel Commanding Coldstream Guards, since 1986; *b* 17 July 1941; *s* of Lt-Col Sir Walter de Stopham Barttelot, 4th Bt, and Sara Patricia (who *m* 2nd, 1965, Comdr James Barttelot, RN retd), *d* of late Lieut-Col H. V. Ravenscroft; *S* father, 1944; *m* 1969, Hon. Mary Angela Fiona Weld Forester, *y d* of 7th Baron Forester, and of Marie Louise Priscilla, CStJ, *d* of Sir Herbert Perrott, 6th Bt, CH, CB; four *d*. *Educ:* Eton; RMA, Sandhurst. Commnd Coldstream Guards, 1961; Temp. Equerry to HM the Queen, 1970–71. Camberley Staff Coll., 1974; GSO2, Army Staff Duties Directorate, MoD, 1975–76; Second in comd, 2nd Bn, Coldstream Guards, 1977–78; Mil. Sec. to Maj.-Gen. comdg London Dist and Household Div., 1978–81; GSO1, MoD, 1981–82; CO 1st Bn Coldstream Gds, 1982–85; GSO1, HQ BAOR, 1985–86. Liveryman, Gunmakers' Co., 1981. DL W Sussex, 1988. *Heir:* *b* Robin Ravenscroft Barttelot [*b* 15 Dec. 1943; *m* 1987, Theresa, *er d* of late Kenneth Greenlees; one *s* one *d*]. *Address:* Stopham Park, Pulborough, W Sussex RH20 1EB. *Clubs:* Cavalry and Guards, Pratt's, Farmers', Buck's.

BARWELL, David John Frank; HM Diplomatic Service; Foreign and Commonwealth Office, since 1989; *b* 12 Oct. 1938; *s* of James Howard and Helen Mary Barwell; *m* 1968, Christine Sarah Carter; one *s*. *Educ:* Lancing College; Trinity College, Oxford; Institut des Hautes Etudes Internationales, Geneva. FCO, 1965; served: Aden, 1967; Baghdad, 1968; Bahrain, 1971; Cairo, 1973; FCO, 1976; Nicosia, 1982; Paris, 1985. *Recreations:* gardening, singing. *Address:* c/o Foreign and Commonwealth Office, SW1.

BARWICK, David Robert, CBE 1976; QC 1977; Governor of British Virgin Islands, 1982–86; *b* 20 Oct. 1927; *s* of Jack Barwick and Kathleen Barwick (*née* Gould); *m* 1951, Margaret (*née* Funnell); one *s* two *d*. *Educ:* Christchurch Boys' High Sch.; Univ. of New Zealand (LLB). Barrister and Solicitor of the Supreme Court of New Zealand. Private practice, NZ, 1953–56; Asst Attorney-General, Judicial Comr, British Solomon Islands, 1956–62; Judge of the High Court of Western Pacific, Gilbert and Ellice Islands, 1962–67; Parliamentary Draftsman, Solicitor-General, Secretary for Justice, Actg Attorney-General, Malawi, 1967–76; Attorney-General: Solomon Islands, 1976; Cayman Islands, 1976–82. *Recreations:* painting, conchology, music, golf. *Address:* PO Box 83, Savannah Post Office, Grand Cayman, Cayman Islands. *T:* 71583. *Club:* Commonwealth Trust.

BARWICK, Rt. Hon. Sir Garfield (Edward John), AK 1981; GCMG 1965; Kt 1953; PC 1964; QC (Australia); Chief Justice of Australia, 1964–81; *b* 22 June 1903; *s* of late Jabez Edward Barwick and Lilian Grace Ellicott; *m* 1929, Norma Mountier Symons; one *s* one *d*. *Educ:* Fort Street Boys' High Sch., Sydney; University of Sydney, BA 1923; LLB (Hons) 1926. New South Wales Bar, 1927; KC 1941; Victorian Bar, 1945; KC (Vic) 1945; Queensland Bar, 1958; QC Queensland, 1958. Practised extensively in all jurisdictions: Supreme Court, High Court of Australia and Privy Council. Pres. NSW Bar Assoc., 1950–52 and 1955–56; Attorney-Gen. Commonwealth of Australia, Dec. 1958–Feb. 1964; Minister for External Affairs, Dec. 1961–April 1964. Judge ad hoc, Internat. Court of Justice, 1973–74. President: Law Council of Australia, 1952–54; Australian Inst. of Internat. Affairs, 1972–83. Hon. Bencher, Lincoln's Inn, 1964. Leader: Australian Delegation, SEATO Council, Bangkok, 1961, Paris, 1963; UN Delegation, 1960, 1962–64; Australian Delegation to ECAFE, Manila, 1963; Australian Delegation, ANZUS, Canberra, 1962, Wellington, 1963. Chancellor, Macquarie Univ., 1967–78. Pres., NSW Inst. for Deaf and Blind Children, 1976–. Hon. LLD: Sydney, 1972; Macquarie, 1987. *Recreations:* fishing, yachting. *Address:* 71 The Cotswolds, Curagul and Bobbin Head Roads, North Turramurra, NSW 2074, Australia. *Clubs:* Australian (Sydney); Royal Sydney Yacht Squadron; Hon. Member: Pioneers' (Australasian); Tattersalls; City Tattersalls; Middle Harbour Yacht.

BARYSHNIKOV, Mikhail; ballet dancer; *b* 28 Jan. 1948; *s* of Nicolai Baryshnikov and Alexandra (*née* Kisselov). *Educ:* Ballet Sch. of Riga, Latvia; Kirov Ballet Sch., Leningrad. Soloist, Kirov Ballet Co., 1969–74; Principal Dancer, NY City Ballet, 1978–79; Artistic Dir, 1980–89, Principal Dancer, 1974–78 and 1980–89, American Ballet Theater. Guest Artist, 1974–, with: Royal Ballet; National Ballet of Canada; Hamburg Ballet; Ballet Victoria, Aust.; Stuttgart Ballet; Alvin Ailey Dance Co., and Eliot Feld Ballet, New York; Spoleto Festival. Repertoire includes: Shadowplay (Tudor); Le Jeune Homme et la Morte (Petit); Sacré du Printemps (Tetley); Prodigal Son, Apollo, Theme and Variations (Balanchine); Afternoon of a Faun (Robbins); Romeo and Juliet, Wild Boy (MacMillan); Configurations (Choo San Goh); Les Patineurs, A Month in the Country (Ashton); Spectre de la Rose, Le Pavillon d'Armide, Petrouchka (Fokine); Santa Fe Saga (Feld); La Sylphide, La Bayadère, Coppélia, La Fille mal gardée (Bournonville); Swan Lake (Sergeyev and Bruhn); The Nutcracker, Don Quixote (own choreography). Works created: Medea (Butler), 1975; Push Comes to Shove, and, Once More Frank (Tharp), Connotations on Hamlet (Neumeier), Pas de Duke (Ailey), Other Dances (Robbins), 1976; Variations on America (Feld), 1977; Rubies (Balanchine), Opus Nineteen (Robbins), 1979; Rhapsody (Ashton), 1980. Gold Medal: Varna Competition, Bulgaria, 1966; 1st Internat. Ballet Comp., Moscow, 1968 (also awarded Nijinsky Prize by Paris Acad. of Dance); Dance Magazine Award, NYC, 1978. *Films:* The Turning Point, 1978; White Nights, 1986; Dancers, 1987. *Publication:* (with Charles Engell France, photographs by Martha Swope) Baryshnikov at Work, 1976. *Recreation:* fishing. *Address:* c/o Edgar Vincent Associates, 124 East 40th Street, #304, New York, NY 10016, USA. *T:* (212) 687–5105.

BARZEL, Dr Rainer C.; Member of the Bundestag, Federal Republic of Germany, since 1957; *b* 20 June 1924; *s* of Dr Candidus Barzel, Senior Asst Master, and Maria Barzel. *Educ:* studied Jurisprudence and Political Economy, Univ. of Cologne (Referendar, Dr jur.). With Govt of North Rhine-Westphalia, 1949–56; Federal Minister in the Adenauer Govt, for all-German affairs, Dec. 1962–Oct. 1963; Chairman: Cttee on Economic Affairs, German Fed. Parlt, 1977–79; Cttee on Foreign Affairs, 1980–82; Fed. Minister for Inter-German Affairs, 1982–83; Pres. of Bundestag, 1983–84. Coordinator for German-French cooperation, Feb.-Dec. 1980. Chm., CDU, 1971–73 and Chm., CDU/CSU Group in German Federal Parlt, 1964–73. Pres., German-French Inst., 1980–83. *Publications:* (all publ. in Germany): Die geistigen Grundlagen der politischen Parteien, 1947; Die deutschen Parteien, 1952; Gesichtspunkte eines Deutschen, 1968; Es ist noch nicht zu spät, 1976; Auf dem Drahtseil, 1978; Das Formular, 1979; Unterwegs—Woher und wohin, 1982. *Recreation:* skating. *Address:* Bundeshaus, 5300 Bonn, Germany.

BARZUN, Jacques; University Professor Emeritus, Columbia University; *b* 30 Nov. 1907; *s* of Henri Barzun and Anna-Rose Martin; *m* 1936, Mariana Lowell (*d* 1979); two *s* one *d*; *m* 1980, Marguerite Davenport. *Educ:* Lycée Janson de Sailly; Columbia Univ. Instructor in History, Columbia Univ., 1929; Research Fellow, American Council of Learned Socs, 1933–34; Columbia University: Asst Prof., 1938; Associate Prof., 1942; Prof. of History, 1945–75; University Prof., 1967; Dean of Grad. Faculties, 1955–58; Dean of Faculties and Provost, 1958–67. Director: Council for Basic Educn; NY Soc. Library; Mem. Adv. Council, Univ. Coll. at Buckingham. Membre Associé de l'Académie Delphinale, Grenoble, 1952; Member: Amer. Acad. of Arts and Letters, USA (President, 1972–75, 1977–79); Amer. Acad. of Arts and Sciences; American Historical Assoc.; Amer. Philos. Soc.; FRSA, USA (Benjamin Franklin Fellow). Seth Low Prof. of History, Columbia Univ., 1960; Extraordinary Fellow, Churchill Coll., Cambridge, 1961–. Literary Advisor, Charles Scribner's Sons Ltd, 1975–; Mem. Bd of Editors, Encyclopaedia Britannica, 1962–. Chevalier de la Légion d'Honneur. *Publications:* The French Race: Theories of its Origins, 1932; Race: A Study in Superstition, 1937 (revd, 1965); Of Human Freedom, 1939 (revd, 1964); Darwin, Marx, Wagner, 1941 (revd, 1958); Teacher in America, 1945 (revd, 1981); Berlioz and the Romantic Century, 1950 (4th edn 1982); Pleasures of Music, 1951, rev. edn 1977; Selected Letters of Byron, 1953 (2nd edn 1957); Nouvelles Lettres de Berlioz, 1954, 2nd edn 1974; God's Country and Mine, 1954; Music in American Life, 1956; The Energies of Art, 1956; The Modern Researcher (with Henry F. Graff), 1957, 4th edn 1985; The House of Intellect, 1959 (2nd edn 1961); Classic, Romantic and Modern, 1961; Science: The Glorious Entertainment, 1964; (ed) Follett's Modern American Usage, 1967; The American University, 1968 (2nd edn 1970); (with W. H. Taylor) A Catalogue of Crime, 1971, rev. edn 1989; On Writing, Editing and Publishing, 1971; Berlioz's Evenings with the Orchestra, 1956, 2nd edn 1973; The Use and Abuse of Art, 1974; Clio and the Doctors, 1974; Simple and Direct, 1975; Critical Questions, 1982; A Stroll with William James, 1983; A Word Or Two Before You Go, 1986; The Culture We Deserve, 1989; Begin Here, 1991; An Essay on French Verse for Readers of English Poetry, 1991; contrib. to leading US journals. *Address:* 1170 Fifth Avenue, New York, NY 10029, USA. *T:* 289–4070. *Club:* Century (New York).

BASARAH, Air Chief Marshal Saleh; Indonesian Ambassador to the Court of St James's, 1978–81; *b* 14 Aug. 1928; *m* 1955, Sartini Kartina; two *s* three *d*. *Educ:* Air Force Staff and Command College. Sqdn Comdr, 1960; AO for Operation No 001 Trng Wing, 1963; Actg Wing Comdr, CO Wing, No 001 Trng Wing, 1964–66; Dir of Operation Air HQ, 1966–68; Comdr, Fifth Regional Air Comd, 1966–69; Comdr, Air Force Special Troop Comd, 1967–69; Asst CoS for Operation, 1969–70; CoS, Deptl Affairs, Dept of Defence and Security, 1970–73; CoS of Air Force, 1973–77. 11 Medals and Satya Lencana Orders of Merit. *Recreations:* golf, soccer, boxing.

BASHAM, Brian Arthur; Managing Director, Warwick Corporate Ltd, since 1991; *b* 30 July 1943; *s* of Arthur Edgar Basham and Gladys Florence Alice (*née* Turner); *m* 1st, 1968, Charlotte Blackman; two *d*; 2nd, 1988, Eileen Wise. *Educ:* Brownhill Road Primary Sch., Catford; Catford Secondary Sch. GEC Export Clerk, 1961; Daily Mail City Office: Stock Exchange prices collector, 1962; City Press reporter, then chief sub-editor, 1963; Prodn Editor, Daily Mail City Page, 1964; Financial Journalist: Daily Telegraph, 1966; The Times, 1968; Fund Man., Cornhill Consolidated, 1971; Associate Dir, John Addey Associates, 1973; Founder, 1976, subseq. Dep. Chm., Broad Street Gp. *Recreations:* physical work, family life. *Address:* c/o Warwick Corporate Ltd, 12–13 Clerkenwell Green, EC1R 0DP. *T:* 071–253 3300.

BASHFORD, Humphrey John Charles, MA; Headmaster, Hessle High School, 1964–81, retired; *b* 5 Oct. 1920; *s* of late Sir Henry Bashford, MD, FRCP, and late Margaret Eveline Sutton; *m* 1942, Alyson Margaret Liddle; one *s* three *d* (and one *s* decd). *Educ:* Sherborne Sch.; Clare Coll., Cambridge. MA Cambridge 1950. Served War of 1939–45: commissioned 2nd Bn Oxford Bucks LI, 1941; GSO3 HQ Airborne Corps 1944–46. Senior History Master, Leys Sch., Cambridge, 1947; Part-time Tutor, WEA, 1950; Headmaster, Wellingborough Sch., 1956–64. *Recreations:* gardening, fly-fishing. *Address:* 16 Main Street, Hotham, York YO4 3UF.

BASING, 5th Baron *cr* 1887; **Neil Lutley Sclater-Booth;** *b* 16 Jan. 1939; *s* of 4th Baron Basing and Jeannette (*d* 1957), *d* of late Neil Bruce MacKelvie, New York; *S* father, 1983; *m* 1967, Patricia Ann, *d* of late George Bryan Whitfield, New Haven, Conn; two *s*. *Educ:* Eton; Harvard Univ. (BA). *Heir: s* Hon. Stuart Whitfield Sclater-Booth, *b* 18 Dec. 1969.

BASINGSTOKE, Bishop Suffragan of, since 1977; **Rt. Rev. Michael Richard John Manktelow;** *b* 23 Sept. 1927; *s* of late Sir Richard Manktelow, KBE, CB, and late Helen Manktelow; *m* 1966, Rosamund Mann; three *d*. *Educ:* Whitgift School, Croydon; Christ's Coll., Cambridge (MA 1952); Chichester Theological Coll. Deacon 1953, priest 1954, Lincoln; Asst Curate of Boston, Lincs, 1953–57; Chaplain of Christ's Coll., Cambridge, 1957–61; Chaplain of Lincoln Theological Coll., 1961–64, Sub-Warden, 1964–66; Vicar of Knaresborough, 1966–73; Rural Dean of Harrogate, 1972–77; Vicar of St Wilfrid's, Harrogate, 1973–77; Hon. Canon of Ripon Cathedral, 1975–77; Canon Residentiary, 1977–91, Vice-Dean, 1987–91 and Hon. Canon, 1991, Winchester Cathedral. President: Anglican and Eastern Churches Assoc., 1980–; Assoc. for Promoting Retreats, 1982–87. *Publication:* Forbes Robinson: Disciple of Love, 1961. *Recreations:* music, walking. *Address:* Bishop's Lodge, Skippetts Lane West, Basingstoke, Hants RG21 3HP. *T:* Basingstoke (0256) 468193.

BASINGSTOKE, Archdeacon of; *see* Knight, Ven. A. F.

BASINSKI, Prof. Zbigniew Stanislaw, OC 1985; DPhil, DSc; FRS 1980; FRSC; Research Professor, Department of Materials Science and Engineering, McMaster University, Ont, since 1987; *b* Wolkowysk, Poland, 28 April 1928; *s* of Antoni Basinski and Maria Zofia Anna Hilferding Basinska; *m* 1952, Sylvia Joy Pugh; two *s*. *Educ:* Lyceum of Krzemieniec, Poland; Polish Army Cadet Sch., Camp Barbara, Palestine, 1943–47; Univ. of Oxford (BSc, MA, DPhil, DSc). Research Asst, Univ. of Oxford, 1951–54; Staff Member, Dept of Mech. Engrg (Cryogenic Lab.), Massachusetts Inst. of Technol., 1954–56; Nat. Res. Council of Canada, 1956–87, latterly as Principal Res. Officer and Head of Materials Physics (Div. of Physics). Ford Distinguished Vis. Prof., Carnegie Inst. of Technol., Pittsburgh, USA, 1964–65; Commonwealth Vis. Prof., Univ. of Oxford, Fellow of Wolfson Coll., Oxford, 1969–70; Adjunct Prof., Carleton Univ., Ottawa, 1975–77, 1981–; Overseas Fellow, Churchill Coll., Cambridge, 1980–81. *Publications:* many original research papers, mainly related to crystal defects and the mechanical properties of metals, in learned jls. *Recreations:* computer design, the stock market, winemaking, general reading. *Address:* Institute for Materials Research, McMaster University, 1280 Main Street West, Hamilton, Ontario L8S 4M1, Canada. *T:* (416) 525 9140 (ext. 3498). *Clubs:* Oxford Union, Halifax House (Oxford).

BASKER, Prof. Robin Michael, DDS; Professor of Dental Prosthetics, since 1978, and Chairman, Board of the Faculty of Medicine, since 1990, University of Leeds; Consultant in Restorative Dentistry, Leeds Western Health Authority, since 1978; *b* 26 Dec. 1936; *s* of Caryl Ashbourne Basker and Edna Crowden (*née* Russell); *m* 1961, Jacqueline Mary Bowles; one *s* one *d*. *Educ:* Wellingborough Sch.; London Hosp. Med. Coll., Univ. of London (BDS 1961); Birmingham Univ. (DDSc 1969). LDSRCS 1961, MGDSRCS 1979. General dental practice, 1961–63; Lectr and Sen. Lectr, Univ. of Birmingham, 1963–78; Dean, Sch. of Dentistry, Univ. of Leeds, 1985–90. Hon. Scientific Advr, British Dental Jl, 1980–; British Standards Expert Advr, ISO TC/106, 1982–. Member: Dental Cttee, Med. Defence Union, 1985–; GDC, 1986–; President: British Soc. for Study of Prosthetic Dentistry, 1988 (Mem. Council and Sec., 1978–81); Yorks Br., BDA, 1991–92. Ext. Examr in Dental Subjects, Univs of Birmingham, Bristol, Dundee, London, Manchester, Newcastle upon Tyne, Sheffield and Wales; Examr for Membership of Gen. Dental Surgery, RCS, 1979–84 (Chm. Examrs, 1987–92). FRSocMed. *Publications:* Prosthetic Treatment of the Edentulous Patient, 1976, 3rd edn 1991; Overdentures in General Dental Practice, 1983, 2nd edn 1988; A Colour Atlas of Removable Partial Dentures, 1987. *Recreations:* choral singing, walking. *Address:* 124 Leadhall Lane, Harrogate, North Yorks HG2 9PA. *T:* Harrogate (0423) 871867.

BASOV, Prof. Nikolai Gennadievich; Orders of Lenin, 1967, 1969, 1972, 1975, 1982; Hero of Socialist Labour, 1969, 1982; Order of the Patriotic War, II degree, 1985; Physicist, USSR; Member of the Praesidium of the Academy of Sciences of USSR, 1967–90; Adviser, since 1990; Deputy of USSR Supreme Soviet, 1974–89; Member of the Praesidium of the USSR Supreme Soviet, 1982–89; Director, Quantum Radiophysics Division, P. N. Lebedev Physical Institute, since 1989; Professor, Moscow Institute of Physical Engineers; *b* 1922; *s* of Prof. Gennady Fedorovich Basov and Zinaida Andreevna Molchanova; *m* 1950, Ksenia Tikhonovna Nazarova Basova; two *s*. *Educ:* secondary; Kiev Military-medical Sch.; Institute of Physical Engineers, Moscow. Joined the P. N. Lebedev Physical Institute, Moscow, 1948: Vice-Dir, 1958–73; Dir, 1973–89; Head, Lab. of Quantum Radiophysics, 1963–. Hon. Chm., All-Union Soc., Znanie, 1990– (Chm. Bd, 1978–90); Vice-Pres., WFSW, 1983–90 (Hon. Mem., 1990–; Vice-Pres., Exec. Council, 1976). Editor: Priroda (Nature), Popular Sciences Magazine, 1967–90; Soviet Jl of Quantum Electronics, 1971–. Corresponding Mem. USSR Acad. of Sciences, 1962; Academician, 1966. Fellow: Optical Soc. of America, 1974 (Mem. 1972); Indian Nat. Acad. of Sci., 1987; Member: Acad. of Sciences of GDR, 1967; German Acad. of Natural Scis, Leopoldina, 1971; Bulgarian Acad. of Scis, 1974; Swedish Royal Acad. of Engineering Sciences, 1975; Polish Acad. of Scis, 1977; Czechoslovakian Acad. of Scis, 1977 (Gold Medal, 1975); Hon. Member: Bulgarian Phys. Soc., 1972; Urania Soc., GDR, 1980; Eur. Acad. of Arts, Scis and Humanities, 1980; TIT Soc. (Soc. for Dissemination of Natural Scis), Hungary, 1981; Internat. Acad. of Sciences, 1989. Hon. Mem., Mark Twain Soc., USA, 1977. Hon. Dr: Polish Mil.-Tech. Acad., 1972; Jena Univ., 1974; Prague Polytechnic Inst., 1975; Pavia Univ., 1977; Madrid Polytechnic Univ., 1985; Karl-Marx Stadt Technical Univ., 1988. Awarded Lenin Prize, 1959; Nobel Prize for Physics (jointly with Prof. A. M. Prokhorov of the P. N. Lebedev Physical Institute, Moscow, and Prof. C. H. Townes of MIT Cambridge, Mass, USA), 1964; A. Volta Gold Medal, Italian Physical Soc., 1977; E. Henkel Gold Medal, GDR, 1986; Kalinga Prize, UNESCO, 1986; Gold Medal, Slovakian Acad. of Sciences, 1988; M. V. Lomonosov Gold Medal, Acad. of Sciences of USSR, 1989; State Prize, USSR, 1989. Order of Kirill and Mephodii (Bulgaria), 1981; Comdr's Cross, Order of Merit (Poland), 1986. *Address:* P. N. Lebedev Physical Institute, Academy of Sciences of the USSR, Lenin Prospekt 53, Moscow, USSR.

BASS; *see* Hastings Bass, family name of Earl of Huntingdon.

BASS, Bryan Geoffrey; Headmaster, City of London School, since 1990; *b* 23 March 1934; *s* of Leslie Horace Bass and Mary Joyce Light; *m* 1956, Cecilia Manning; one *s* two *d*. *Educ:* Wells Cathedral School; Christ Church, Oxford (BA Hons English 1956; MA 1983). Teacher, Manchester Grammar School; Headmaster, Hymers College, Hull, 1983–90. *Recreations:* making music, cooking for friends. *Address:* City of London School, Queen Victoria Street, EC4V 3AL. *T:* 071–489 0291.

BASS, Harry Godfrey Mitchell, CMG 1972; HM Diplomatic Service, retired; *b* 26 Aug. 1914; *s* of late Rev. Arthur Edward Bass and Mildred Bass; *m* 1948, Monica Mary, *d* of late Rev. H. F. Burroughs (and eponym of the orchid *Oncidium flexuosum* x *Rodriguezia fragrans*); two *s* one *d*. *Educ:* Marlborough Coll.; Gonville and Caius Coll., Cambridge; St John's Coll., Oxford (BA (Oxon) 1937, MA (Cantab) 1940). British Museum, Dept of Egyptian and Assyrian Antiquities, 1939; Admiralty, 1940; Dominions Office, 1946; Asst Sec., Office of UK High Commissioner, Australia, 1948–51; Mem. of Secretariat, Commonwealth Economic Conference, 1952 and Meeting of Commonwealth Prime Ministers, 1953; Counsellor, Office of UK High Commissioner, Calcutta, 1954–57; Dep. UK High Commissioner, Federation of Rhodesia and Nyasaland, 1959–61; British Minister (Pretoria and Cape Town) in the Republic of S Africa, 1961–62; seconded to Central African Office, 1963–64; British Dep. High Commissioner, Ibadan, 1965–67; Head of Consular Dept, FCO, 1967–70; High Comr in Lesotho, 1970–73. Chapter Clerk, St George's Chapel, Windsor, 1974–77. Silver Jubilee Medal, 1977. *Recreation:* birdwatching. *Address:* Tyler's Mead, Reepham, Norfolk NR10 4LA.

See also Baron Crofton.

BASS, Rear-Adm. Paul Eric, CB 1981; CEng, FIMechE, MIMarE; *b* 7 March 1925; *s* of C. H. P. Bass, Ipswich; *m* 1948, Audrey Bruce Tomlinson; one *s*. *Educ:* Northgate School, Ipswich; Royal Naval Engineering Coll., Keyham. Served as Midshipman in HM Ships Cambrian, Mauritius, Premier and Rodney; Lieut in Belfast, Phoebe and Implacable; Lt Comdr in Ulysses; Comdr in Lion and Tiger; Naval Staff Course, 1962; Captain, Weapons Trials, 1969–72; NATO Defense Course, 1972–73; Asst Chief of Staff (Intelligence), SACLANT, 1973–75; Dir, Naval Manning and Training (Engineering), 1975–78; Flag Officer, Portsmouth and Port Admiral, Portsmouth, 1979–81, retired 1981. *Recreations:* sailing, fishing. *Address:* c/o National Westminster Bank, 68 Palmerston Road, Southsea, Hants PO5 3PN. *Clubs:* Royal Yacht Squadron; Royal Naval Sailing Association; Royal Naval and Royal Albert Yacht (Portsmouth).

BASSET, Bryan Ronald; CBE 1988; Chairman, Royal Ordnance plc, 1985–87; *b* 29 Oct. 1932; *s* of late Ronald Lambart Basset and of Lady Elizabeth Basset, *qv*; *m* 1960, Lady Carey Elizabeth Coke, *d* of 5th Earl of Leicester; three *s*. *Educ:* Eton; RMA Sandhurst. Captain, Scots Guards, 1952–57. Stockbroker, Toronto, Canada, 1957–59; Panmure Gordon & Co., Stockbrokers, 1959–72; Managing Director, Philip Hill Investment Trust, 1972–85. *Recreations:* farming, shooting, fishing. *Address:* 10 Stack House, Cundy Street, SW1. *T:* 071–730 2785; Quarles, Wells-next-the-Sea, Norfolk. *T:* Fakenham (0328) 738105. *Clubs:* White's, Pratt's.

BASSET, Lady Elizabeth, DCVO 1989 (CVO 1976); Woman of the Bedchamber to Queen Elizabeth the Queen Mother, since 1981 (Extra Woman of the Bedchamber, 1959–81); *b* 5 March 1908; *d* of 7th Earl of Dartmouth, GCVO, TD and Ruperta, Countess of Dartmouth; *m* 1931, Ronald Lambart Basset (*d* 1972); one *s* (and one *s* decd). *Educ:* at home. *Publications: anthologies:* Love is My Meaning, 1973, 2nd edn 1988; Each in His Prison, 1978; The Bridge is Love, 1981. *Recreations:* riding, gardening, reading, writing, needlework. *Address:* 67 Cottesmore Court, Kelso Place, W8 5QW. *T:* 071–937 1803.

See also B. R. Basset.

BASSETT, Douglas Anthony; Director, National Museum of Wales, 1977–86; *b* 11 Aug. 1927; *s* of Hugh Bassett and Annie Jane Bassett; *m* 1955, Elizabeth Menna Roberts; three *d. Educ:* Llanelli Boys' Grammar Sch.; University Coll. of Wales, Aberystwyth. Asst Lectr and Lectr, Dept of Geology, Glasgow Univ., 1952–59; Keeper, Dept of Geology, Nat. Museum of Wales, 1959–77. Member: Water Resources Bd, 1965–73; Nature Conservancy Council (and Chm., Adv. Cttee for Wales), 1973–85; Secretary of State for Wales' Celtic Sea Adv. Cttee, 1974–79; Ordnance Survey Rev. Cttee, 1978–79; Founder Mem. and first Chm., Assoc. of Teachers of Geology, 1967–68; Chm., Royal Soc. Cttee on History of Geology, 1972–82. Dir, Nat. Welsh-American Foundn, 1980–. Prince of Wales' Cttee, 1977–86; Adv. Cttee for Wales, British Council, 1983–. Hon. Professorial Fellow, University Coll., Cardiff, 1977. Editor: Nature in Wales, 1982–87; Manual of Curatorship, Museums Assoc., 1983–. Aberconway Medal, Institn of Geologists, 1985; Silver Medal, Czechoslavakian Soc. for Internat. Relns, 1985. Mem. White Order of Bards of GB, 1979; Officier de l'Ordre des Arts et des Lettres (received from Min. of Culture, Paris), 1983. *Publications:* Bibliography and Index of Geology and Allied Sciences for Wales and the Welsh Borders, 1897–1958, 1961; A Source-book of Geological, Geomorphological and Soil Maps for Wales and the Welsh Borders (1800–1966), 1967; contribs to various geological, museum and historical jls. *Recreations:* bibliography, chronology. *Address:* 4 Romilly Road, Cardiff CF5 1FH.

BASSETT, Nigel F.; *see* Fox Bassett.

BASSINGTHWAIGHTE, Keith; His Honour Judge Bassingthwaighte; a Circuit Judge, since 1991; *b* 19 Jan. 1943; *s* of Reginald and Barbara Bassingthwaighte; *m* 1966, Olwyn Burn. *Educ:* Ashford (Middx) County Grammar Sch. Admitted solicitor, 1967. Served RAF Legal Branch as Flt Lt, 1968, Sqdn Ldr 1973, Wing Comdr 1978 and Gp Capt. 1981; retired 1984. Chm., Industrial Tribunals (London Central and S regions), part-time 1984–85, full-time 1985–91; a Recorder of the Crown Court, 1987–91. *Recreations:* golf, tennis, bridge. *Address:* c/o Barclays Bank, Sloane Square, SW1W 8AF. *Clubs:* Royal Air Force; Worplesdon Golf (Woking).

BASTEN, Sir Henry (Bolton), Kt 1966; CMG 1947; MA Oxon and Adelaide; retired, 1982; University of Adelaide, 1953–67, Vice-Chancellor, 1958–67. Formerly Chairman and General Manager, Singapore & Penang Harbour Boards. Investigated conditions in Australian ports for Commonwealth Government, 1951–52, report published, 1952. Chm., Aust. Univs Commn, 1968–71; Foundn Chm., Council, Australian Inst. of Marine Science, 1972–77. Hon. DLitt Flinders Univ. (S Australia), 1967. *Address:* Unit 34, Lindfield Garden Village, 2 Ulmarra Place, East Lindfield, NSW 2070, Australia.

BASTIN, Prof. John Andrew, MA, PhD; FRAS; Professor, since 1971, and Head of Department of Physics, 1975–80, Queen Mary College, London University; *b* 3 Jan. 1929; *s* of Lucy and Arthur Bastin; *m*; one *s* one *d*; *m* 1985, Aida Baterina Delfino. *Educ:* George Monoux Grammar Sch., London; Corpus Christi Coll., Oxford. MA, PhD. Univ. of Ibadan, Nigeria, 1952–56; Univ. of Reading, 1956–59; Queen Mary Coll., Univ. of London, 1959–. Initiated a group in far infrared astronomy at Queen Mary College, 1960–70. *Publications:* papers on far infrared astronomy and lunar evolution. *Recreations:* English water colours, architecture, Renaissance and Baroque music, tennis. *Address:* 27 Endwell Road, SE4 2NE.

BATCHELOR, Prof. George Keith, FRS 1957; Emeritus Professor of Applied Mathematics, University of Cambridge, 1983; *b* Melbourne, 8 March 1920; *s* of George Conybere Batchelor and Ivy Constance Batchelor (*née* Berneye); *m* 1944, Wilma Maud Rätz, MBE; three *d. Educ:* Essendon and Melbourne High Schs; Univ. of Melbourne. BSc 1940, MSc 1941, Melbourne; PhD 1948, Adams Prize, 1951, Univ. of Cambridge. Research Officer, Aeronautical Research Laboratory, Melbourne, 1940–44; Fellow of Trinity Coll., Cambridge, 1947–; Lectr, Univ. of Cambridge, 1948–59, Reader in Fluid Dynamics, 1959–64, and Head of Dept of Applied Mathematics and Theoretical Physics, 1959–83; Prof. of Applied Maths, Univ. of Cambridge, 1964–83. Chairman: European Mechanics Cttee, 1964–87; Nat. Cttee for Theoretical and Applied Mechanics, 1967–72. Editor, Cambridge Monographs on Mechanics and Applied Mathematics, 1953–; Editor, Journal of Fluid Mechanics, 1956–. Mem. Council, Royal Soc., 1986–87; Mem., Royal Soc. of Sciences, Uppsala, 1972. Foreign Hon. Member: Amer. Acad. of Arts and Scis, 1959; Polish Acad. of Scis, 1974; French Acad. of Sci., 1984; Aust. Acad. of Sci., 1990. Dr *hc*: Univ. of Grenoble, 1959; Tech. Univ. of Denmark, 1974; McGill Univ., 1986; Univ. of Michigan, 1990. Agostinelli Prize, Accad. Nazionale de Lincei, Rome, 1986; Royal Medal, Royal Soc., 1988; Timoshenko Medal, Amer. Soc. Mech. Engrs, 1988. *Publications:* The Theory of Homogeneous Turbulence, 1953; An Introduction to Fluid Dynamics, 1967; (ed) The Scientific Papers of G. I. Taylor, vol. 1, 1958, vol. 2, 1960, vol. 3, 1963, vol. 4, 1971; papers on fluid mechanics and its applications in scientific jls. *Address:* Cobbers, Conduit Head Road, Cambridge CB3 0EY. *T:* Cambridge (0223) 356387.

BATCHELOR, Sir Ivor (Ralph Campbell), Kt 1981; CBE 1976; FRCPE, DPM, FRSE, FRCPsych; Professor of Psychiatry, University of Dundee, 1967–82, now Emeritus Professor; *b* 29 Nov. 1916; *s* of Ralph C. L. Batchelor, FRCSE, FRCPE, and Muriel (*née* Shaw); *m* 1941, Honor Wallace Williamson; one *s* three *d. Educ:* Edinburgh Academy; Edinburgh Univ. MB ChB. FRCPsych 1971 (Hon. 1984). RAFVR, 1941–46; Sqdn Ldr, Comd Neuro-psychiatrist, CMF. Asst Phys. and Dep. Phys. Supt, Royal Edinburgh Hosp., and Sen. Lectr in Psychiatry, Univ. of Edinburgh, 1947–56; Phys. Supt, Dundee Royal Mental Hosp., 1956–62; Prof. of Psychiatry, Univ. of St Andrews, 1962–67. Member: Gen. Nursing Council for Scotland (Chm. Educn Cttee), 1964–71; Standing Med. Adv. Cttee, Scot., 1967–74; Adv. Cttee on Med. Research, Scotland, 1969–73; Scottish Council for Postgraduate Med. Educn, 1970–79; Chief Scientist Cttee, Scotland, 1973–82. Mem., Med. Services Review (Porritt) Cttee, 1958–62; Chm., Cttee on Staffing Mental Deficiency Hosps, 1967–70; Member: Cttee on Nursing (Briggs Cttee), 1970–72; Cttee on the Working of the Abortion Act (Lane Cttee), 1971–74; MRC (Chm. Clinical Research Bd, 1973–74, Chm. Neuro-Sciences Bd, 1974–75), 1972–76; MRC Health Services Res. Panel, 1981–82; Royal Commn on the Nat. Health Service, 1976–79; Indep. Sci. Cttee on Smoking and Health, 1980–86; UK Central Council for Nursing, Midwifery and Health Visiting, 1980–83; Scottish Hosp. Endowments Res. Trust, 1984–90. Chm. Trustees, Orchar Art Gall., Dundee, 1980–87. *Publications:* (with R. N. Ironside) Aviation Neuro-Psychiatry, 1945; Henderson and Gillespie's Textbook of Psychiatry, 8th edn 1956 and subseq. edns to 10th edn 1969; papers on clinical psychiatry and health services. *Recreation:* field natural history. *Address:* 55 Hepburn Gardens, St Andrews, Fife KY16 9LS. *T:* St Andrews (0334) 73130. *Clubs:* Athenæum; Royal and Ancient Golf (St Andrews).

BATCHELOR, Prof. (John) Richard; Professor of Immunology, Royal Postgraduate Medical School, Hammersmith Hospital, since 1979; *b* 4 Oct. 1931; *s* of B. W. Batchelor, CBE and Mrs C. E. Batchelor; *m* 1955, Moira Ann (*née* McLellan); two *s* two *d. Educ:* Marlborough Coll.; Emmanuel Coll., Cambridge; Guy's Hospital, London. MB, BChir Cantab, 1955; MD Cantab 1965. Nat. Service, RAMC, 1957–59; Dept of Pathology, Guy's Hospital: Res. Fellow, 1959–61; Lectr and Sen. Lectr, 1961–67. Prof. of Transplantation Research, RCS, 1967; Dir, McIndoe Res. Unit, Queen Victoria Hosp., East Grinstead, 1967–78. Pres., Transplantation Soc., 1988–90 (Hon. Sec., then Vice-Pres. (E Hemisphere), 1976–80); Member Council, Nat. Kidney Res. Fund, 1979–86; Chm., Scientific Co-ord. Cttee, Arthritis and Rheumatism Council, 1988–. MRSocMed. Mem. Court, Skinners' Company. European Editor, Transplantation, 1964–. *Publications:* scientific articles upon tissue transplantation research in various special jls. *Recreations:* sailing; tennis; walking. *Address:* Little Ambrook, Nursery Road, Walton-on-the-Hill, Tadworth, Surrey. *T:* Tadworth (0737) 2028. *Clubs:* Brooks's, Queen's.

BATE, Sir David (Lindsay), KBE 1978 (CBE 1968); Chief Judge, Benue and Plateau States of Nigeria, 1975–77; Senior Puisne Judge, High Court of Justice, Northern States of Nigeria, 1968–75 (Puisne Judge 1957–68); *b* 3 March 1916; *m* 1948, Thadeen June, *d* of late R. F. O'Donnell Peet; two *s. Educ:* Marlborough; Trinity Coll., Cambridge. Called to Bar, Inner Temple, 1938. Commissioned, Royal Artillery, 1939 and served, Royal Artillery, 1939–46. Entered Colonial Legal Service, 1947; Crown Counsel, Nigeria, 1947–52; Senior Crown Counsel, Nigeria, 1952–54; Senior Crown Counsel, Northern Nigeria 1954–56; Solicitor-Gen., Northern Nigeria, 1956. *Recreations:* shooting, fishing. *Address:* 4029 Lanchaster Road, RR2, Duncan, British Columbia V9L 1N9, Canada.

BATE, Sir (Walter) Edwin, Kt 1969; OBE 1955; Barrister, Solicitor and Notary Public, Hastings, New Zealand, since 1927; *b* 12 March 1901; *s* of Peter and Florence Eleanor Bate; *m* 1925, Louise Jordan; two *s* one *d. Educ:* Victoria Univ., Wellington. LLM (first class hons), 1922. Admitted Barrister and Solicitor, 1922; practised: Taumarunui, NZ, 1923; Hastings, NZ, 1927. Mayor, City of Hastings, NZ, 1953–59; Chm., Hawke Bay Hosp. Bd, 1941–74; Pres., Hosp. Bds Assoc. of NZ, 1953–74; Pres., Associated Trustee Savings Banks of NZ, 1968 and 1969. OStJ 1961. Grand Master of Freemasons in NZ, 1972–74. *Recreation:* gardening. *Address:* 38 Busby Hill, Havelock North, New Zealand. *T:* 8777448.

BATE, Prof. Walter Jackson; Kingsley Porter University Professor, Harvard University, since 1980; *b* 23 May 1918; *s* of William George Bate. *Educ:* Harvard Univ. AB 1939, PhD 1942. Harvard University: Associate Prof. of English, 1949–55; Prof. of English, 1955–62; Chm., Dept of English, 1955–62; Abbott Lawrence Lowell Prof. of the Humanities, 1962–80. Corresp. Fellow, British Acad., 1978. Member: Amer. Acad. of Arts and Sciences; Amer. Philosophical Soc.; Cambridge Scientific Soc. Christian Gauss Award, 1956, 1964, 1970; Pulitzer Prize for Biography, 1964, 1978; Nat. Book Award, 1978; Nat. Book Critics Award, 1978. *Publications:* Stylistic Development of Keats, 1945; From Classic to Romantic, 1946; Criticism: The Major Texts, 1952; The Achievement of Samuel Johnson, 1955; Prefaces to Criticism, 1959; Yale Edition of Samuel Johnson, Vol. II, 1963, Vols III-V, 1969; John Keats, 1963; Coleridge, 1968; The Burden of the Past and The English Poet, 1971; Samuel Johnson, 1977; (ed) Coleridge, *Biographia Literaria,* 1982; (ed) British and American Poets: Chaucer to the present, 1985. *Recreation:* farming. *Address:* 3 Warren House, Cambridge, Mass 02138, USA. *Club:* Saturday (Boston, Mass).

BATE, Maj.-Gen. William, CB 1974; OBE 1963; DL; Secretary to the Council of TAVR Associations, 1975–86 (Deputy Secretary, 1973–75); *b* 6 June 1920; *s* of S. Bate, Warrington; *m* 1946, Veronica Mary Josephine (*née* Quinn); two *s* two *d.* Commnd, 1941; war service in Burma, 1941–46 (despatches); Senior Instructor, RASC Officers Sch., 1947–50; Co. Comd 7th and 11th Armoured Divs, 1951–53; psc 1954; DAA&QMG Q (Ops), WO, 1955–57; jssc 1957; Admin. Staff Coll., Henley, 1958; Directing Staff, Staff Coll., Camberley, 1958–60; AA&QMG, Ops and Plans, HQ BAOR, 1961–63; CO, 2 Div. Column, BAOR, 1963–65; Col GS, Staff Coll., Camberley, 1965–67; Brig. Q (Maint.), MoD, 1967–68; ADC to the Queen, 1969; idc 1969; Dir of Admin. Planning (Army), 1970; Dir of Movements (Army), MoD, 1971–73. Col Comdt, 1974–86, Rep. Col Comdt, RCT, 1975, 1977, 1982, 1986. Hon. Col, 163 Movement Control Regt, RCT(V), TAVR, 1974–79. FCIT 1967. DL Surrey, 1980. *Recreations:* cricket, tennis. *Address:* Netherbury, 14 Belton Road, Camberley, Surrey GU15 2DE. *T:* Camberley (0276) 63529. *Clubs:* East India, Devonshire, Sports and Public Schools, MCC.

BATELY, Prof. Janet Margaret, (Mrs L. J. Summers), FBA 1990; Professor of English Language and Medieval Literature, King's College, University of London, since 1977; *b* 3 April 1932; *d* of late Alfred William Bately and Dorothy Maud Bately (*née* Willis); *m* 1964, Leslie John Summers, sculptor; one *s. Educ:* Greenhead High Sch., Huddersfield; Westcliff High Sch. for Girls; Somerville Coll., Oxford (Shaw Lefevre Scholar). BA 1st cl. hons English 1954, Dip. in Comparative Philology (with distinction) 1956, MA 1958; FKC 1986. Asst Lectr in English, Birkbeck Coll., Univ. of London, 1955–58, Lectr, 1958–69, Reader, 1970–76. Lectures: Sir Israel Gollancz Meml, British Acad., 1978; Toller Meml, Manchester Univ., 1987. Chm., Scholarships Cttee, Univ. of London, 1988–. Member: Council, EETS, 1981–; Exec. Cttee, Fontes Anglo-Saxonici (formerly Sources of Anglo-Saxon Literature), 1985–; Adv. Cttee, Internat. Soc. of Anglo-Saxonists, 1986–; Adv. Cttee, Sources of Anglo-Saxon Lit. and Culture, 1987–. Governor, Cranleigh Sch., 1982–88. Gen. Ed., King's Coll. London Medieval Studies, 1987–. *Publications:* The Old English Orosius, 1980; The Literary Prose of King Alfred's Reign: Translation or Transformation, 1980; (ed) The Anglo-Saxon Chronicle: MS.A, 1986; contribs to: England Before the Conquest, 1971; Saints, Scholars and Heroes (ed M. H. King and W. M. Stevens), 1979; Five Hundred Years of Words and Sounds (ed E. G. Stanley and Douglas Grey), 1983; Learning and Literature in Anglo-Saxon England (ed M. Lapidge and H. Gneuss), 1985; Medieval English Studies (ed D. Kennedy, R. Waldron and J. Wittig), 1988; Words for Robert Burchfield's Sixty-Fifth Birthday (ed E. G. Stanley and T. F. Hoad), 1988; Leeds Studies in English, Reading Medieval Studies, Eichstätter Beiträge, Medium Aevum, Rev. of English Studies, Anglia, English Studies, Essays and Studies, Classica et Mediaevalia, Scriptorium, Studies in Philology, Mediev. Arch., Notes and Queries, Archaeologia, Anglo-Saxon England, The Dickensian, Jl Soc. of Archivists, Bull. John Rylands Library, etc. *Recreations:* music, gardening. *Address:* 86 Cawdor Crescent, W7 2DD. *T:* 081-567 0486.

BATEMAN, Sir Cecil (Joseph), KBE 1967 (MBE 1944); Chairman, G. Heyn & Sons Ltd, 1971–87; Director: Nationwide Building Society, 1970–84; Allied Irish Banks, 1970–80; Allied Irish Investment Bank Ltd, 1971–80; *b* 6 Jan. 1910; *s* of Samuel and Annie Bateman; *m* 1938, Doris M. Simpson; one *s* one *d. Educ:* Queen's Univ., Belfast. Served War of 1939–45, Royal Artillery (Major). Entered NI Civil Service, Nov. 1927. Dir of Establishments, Min. of Finance, 1958–63; Sec. to Cabinet and Clerk of Privy Council of N Ireland, 1963–65; Permanent Sec., Min. of Finance, and Head of Northern Ireland Civil Service, 1965–70. *Recreations:* golf, reading. *Address:* 26 Schomberg Park, Belfast BT4 2HH. *T:* Belfast (0232) 763484. *Club:* Shandon Park Golf.

BATEMAN, Sir Geoffrey (Hirst), Kt 1972; FRCS; Surgeon, Ear, Nose and Throat Department, St Thomas' Hospital, London, 1939–71; *b* 24 Oct. 1906; *s* of Dr William Hirst Bateman, JP, Rochdale, Lancs; *m* 1931, Margaret, *d* of Sir Samuel Turner, Rochdale; three *s* one *d. Educ:* Epsom Coll.; University Coll., Oxford. Theodore Williams Schol. in Anat., Oxford Univ., 1926; BA Oxon, Hons sch. Physiol., 1927; Epsom schol. to King's Coll. Hosp., 1927; BM, BCh Oxon, 1930; FRCS, 1933; George Herbert Hunt Trav. Schol., Oxford Univ., 1933. RAFVR, Wing Comdr, 1939–45. Mem., Bd Governors, St

Thomas' Hosp., 1948; Mem. Collegium Otolaryngologica Amicitiæ Sacrum, 1949; Hon. Corr. Mem. Amer. Laryngological Assoc., 1960; Past Mem. Council, RCS; Editor, Jl of Laryngology and Otology, 1961–77; Formerly Hon. Cons. on Oto-rhino-laryngology to the Army; Cons. Adviser in Otolaryngology, Dept of Health and Social Security. Pres., British Assoc. of Otolaryngologists, 1970–71 (Vice-Pres., 1967–70). Hon. FRSM 1978. *Publications:* Diseases of the Nose and Throat (Asst Editor to V. E. Negus, 6th edn), 1955; contributor various jls, etc. *Recreations:* golf, fishing. *Address:* Thorney, Graffham, Petworth, West Sussex GU28 0QA. *T:* Graffham (07986) 314.

See also Sir R. M. Bateman.

BATEMAN, Leslie Clifford, CMG 1965; FRS 1968; Secretary-General, International Rubber Study Group, 1976–83; *b* 21 March 1915; *s* of Charles Samuel Bateman; *m* 1st, 1945, Marie Louise Pakes (*d* 1967); two *s*; 2nd, 1973, Mrs Eileen Joyce Jones (*née* Henwood); one step *s* one step *d*. *Educ:* Bishopshalt Sch., Uxbridge; University Coll., London. BSc, 1st cl. Hons Chem., 1935; PhD and Ramsey Memorial Medal, 1938; DSc 1955; Fellow, 1974. Oriel Coll., 1940–41; Chemist, Natural Rubber Producers Research Assoc., 1941–53; Dir of Research, 1953–62; Controller of Rubber Res., Malaysia, 1962–74; Chm., Internat. Rubber R&D Board, 1962–74. Mem., Malaysian Govt Task Force on Rubber Industry, 1983. Hon. DSc: Malaya, 1968; Aston, 1972. Colwyn Medal, 1963, and Jubilee Foundn Lectr, 1971, Inst. of Rubber Industry. Hon. PSM, Malaysia, 1974. *Publications:* (ed and contrib.) The Chemistry and Physics of Rubber-like Substances, 1963; numerous scientific papers in Jl Chem. Soc., etc, and articles on technical-economic status of natural rubber and its developments. *Recreations:* cricket, golf and other outdoor activities. *Address:* 3 Palmerston Close, Welwyn Garden City, Herts. *T:* Welwyn Garden (0707) 322391.

BATEMAN, Mary-Rose Christine, (Mrs R. D. Farley), MA; Administrator, Women's National Cancer Control Campaign, 1989; *b* 16 March 1935; *d* of Comdr G. A. Bateman, RN, and Mrs G. A. Bateman; *m* 1990, R. D. Farley. *Educ:* The Abbey, Malvern Wells, Worcs; St Anne's Coll., Oxford (MA); CertEd Cambridge. Assistant English Mistress: Westonbirt Sch., Tetbury, Glos, 1957–60; Ashford Sch., Kent, 1960–61; Lady Eleanor Holles Sch., Mddx, 1961–64; Head of English Department: Westonbirt Sch., Glos, 1964–69; Brighton and Hove High Sch., GPDST, 1969–71; Headmistress: Berkhamsted School for Girls, Herts, 1971–80; Perse Sch. for Girls, Cambridge, 1980–89. *Address:* Yerdley House, Long Compton, Shipston on Stour, Warwickshire CV36 5LH. *T:* Long Compton (060884) 231.

BATEMAN, Paul Terence; Chief Executive, Save and Prosper Group Ltd, since 1988; *b* 28 April 1946; *s* of Nelson John Bateman and Frances Ellen (*née* Johnston); *m* 1970, Moira (*née* Burdis); two *s*. *Educ:* Westcliff High Sch. for Boys; Univ. of Leicester (BSc). Save and Prosper Gp Ltd, 1967: graduate, secretarial dept, 1967–68; asst to Gp Actuary, 1968–73; Marketing Manager, 1973–75; Gp Marketing Manager, 1975–80; Gp Marketing and Develt Manager, 1980–81; Exec. Dir, Marketing and Develt, 1981–88. *Recreations:* yachting, squash. *Address:* Save and Prosper Group Ltd, 1 Finsbury Avenue, EC2M 2QY. *T:* 071–588 1717; 25 Plymtree, Thorpe Bay, Essex SS1 3RA. *T:* Southend-on-Sea (0702) 587152. *Club:* Royal Burnham Yacht.

BATEMAN, Sir Ralph (Melton), KBE 1975; MA Oxon; Chairman, Stothert and Pitt, 1977–85; President, Confederation of British Industry, 1974–76 (Deputy President, 1973–74); *b* 15 May 1910; 3rd *s* of William Hirst Bateman, MB, BCh, and of Ethel Jane Bateman, Rochdale, Lancs; *m* 1935, Barbara Yvonne, 2nd *d* of Herbert Percy Litton and Grace Vera Litton, Heywood, Lancs; two *s* two *d*. *Educ:* Epsom Coll.; University Coll., Oxford. Turner & Newall Ltd: joined as management trainee, 1931; held various directorships in Group, 1942–76; Dir, 1957; Dep. Chm., 1959; Chm., 1967–76. Mem., NEDC, 1973–76. Mem. Council, Manchester Business Sch., 1972–76; Vice-Pres., Ashridge Management Coll.; Chm. of Council, University Coll. at Buckingham, 1976–79; Member Court: Manchester Univ.; Salford Univ. FCIS, CBIM; FRSA 1970. Hon. Fellow, UMIST, 1977. Hon. DSc: Salford, 1969; Buckingham, 1983. *Recreations:* family and social affairs. *Address:* 2 Bollin Court, Macclesfield Road, Wilmslow, Cheshire SK9 2AP. *T:* Wilmslow (0625) 530437.

See also Sir G. H. Bateman.

BATEMAN, Richard George Saumarez La T.; *see* La Trobe-Bateman.

BATES, Alan (Arthur); actor; *b* 17 Feb. 1934; *m* 1970, Victoria Ward; one *s* (one twin *s* decd). *Educ:* Herbert Strutt Grammar Sch., Belper, Derbyshire; RADA. *Theatre:* English Stage Co. (Royal Court Theatre, London): The Mulberry Bush; Cards of Identity; Look Back in Anger; The Country Wife; In Celebration; London (West End): Long Day's Journey into Night; The Caretaker; The Four Seasons; Hamlet; Butley, London and NY (Evening Standard Best Actor award, 1972; Antoinette Perry Best Actor award, 1973); Poor Richard, NY; Richard III and The Merry Wives of Windsor, Stratford, Ont.; Venice Preserved, Bristol Old Vic; Taming of the Shrew, Stratford-on-Avon, 1973; Life Class, 1974; Otherwise Engaged, Queen's, 1975 (Variety Club of GB Best Stage Actor award, 1975); The Seagull, Duke of York's, 1976; Stage Struck, Vaudeville, 1979; A Patriot for Me, Chichester, Haymarket, 1983, transf. Ahmanson, LA (Variety Club of GB Best Stage Actor award, 1983); Victoria Station, and One for the Road, Lyric Studio, 1984; The Dance of Death, Riverside Studios, Hammersmith, 1985; Yonadab, NT, 1985; Melon, Haymarket, 1987; Ivanov, and Much Ado About Nothing, Strand, 1989. *Films:* The Entertainer, Whistle Down the Wind, A Kind of Loving, The Running Man, The Caretaker, Zorba the Greek, Nothing but the Best, Georgie Girl, King of Hearts, Far from the Madding Crowd, The Fixer (Oscar nomination), Women in Love, The Three Sisters (National Theatre Co.), A Day in the Death of Joe Egg, The Go-Between, Second Best (also prod.), Impossible Object, Butley, In Celebration, Royal Flash, An Unmarried Woman, The Shout, The Rose, Nijinsky, Quartet, The Return of the Soldier, The Wicked Lady, Duet for One, Prayer for the Dying, We Think the World of You, Mr Frost, Dr M, Hamlet, Shuttlecock. *Television:* various plays; Plaintiff and Defendant, Two Sundays, The Collection, 1977; The Mayor of Casterbridge, 1978; Very Like a Whale, The Trespasser, 1980; A Voyage Round my Father, Separate Tables, An Englishman Abroad, 1983 (BAFTA Best TV Actor award, 1984); Dr Fisher of Geneva, 1984; One for the Road, 1985; Pack of Lies, 1988; The Dog It Was that Died, 1988; 102 Boulevard Haussmann, 1991. *Recreations:* swimming, squash, driving, riding, water ski-ing, reading. *Address:* c/o Chatto & Linnit, Prince of Wales Theatre, Coventry Street, W1V 7FE.

BATES, Alfred; researcher and presenter since 1980, and an assistant producer since 1983, BBC Television; *b* 8 June 1944; *s* of Norman and Alice Bates; single. *Educ:* Stretford Grammar Sch. for Boys; Manchester Univ. (BSc); Corpus Christi Coll., Cambridge. Lectr in Maths, De La Salle Coll. of Educn, Middleton, 1967–74. MP (Lab) Bebington and Ellesmere Port, Feb. 1974–1979; PPS to Minister of State for Social Security, 1974–76; Asst Govt Whip, 1976–79; a Lord Comr, HM Treasury, 1979. *Recreation:* cricket umpiring. *Address:* 116 Jackson Street, Stretford, Manchester M32 8BB.

BATES, Allan Frederick, CMG 1958; BA (Hons); *b* 15 July 1911; *s* of John Frederick Lawes and Ethel Hannah Bates; *m* 1937, Ena Edith, *d* of John Richard Boxall; three *s*. *Educ:* Woolwich Central Sch.; London Univ. Qualified as Certified Accountant, 1938; practised in London, 1938–44. Joined Colonial Service (now Overseas Civil Service), 1944; Deputy Comptroller Inland Revenue, Cyprus, 1944–48; Comptroller Inland Revenue, Cyprus, 1948–52; Financial Secretary: Cyprus, 1952–60; Mauritius, 1960–64; Man. Dir, Develt Bank of Mauritius, 1964–70; Financial Advr (IMF) to Govt of Bahamas, 1971–75; Budget Advr (IMF) to Govt of Lesotho, 1975–76. Accounts Adviser, British Exec. Service Overseas, to Govt of Belize, 1982. Fellow Inst. of Taxation 1950; Mem., Inst. of Directors. *Recreations:* painting, carving. *Address:* 5 Redford Avenue, Coulsdon, Surrey. *T:* 081–660 7421. *Club:* Commonwealth Trust.

BATES, Air Vice-Marshal David Frank, CB 1983; RAF retired; *b* 10 April 1928; *s* of late S. F. Bates, MusB, FRCO, and N. A. Bates (*née* Story); *m* 1954, Margaret Winifred (*née* Biles); one *s* one *d*. *Educ:* Warwick Sch.; RAF Coll., Cranwell. Commnd, 1950; served Egypt, Innsworth, UKSLS Australia, HQ Transport Comd, RAF Technical Coll., Staff Coll., Lyneham, El Adem, Staff Coll., Jt Services Staff Coll., Innsworth, and RCDS, 1950–73; Stn Comdr, Uxbridge, 1974–75; Dir of Personnel Ground, 1975–76; Dir of Personnel Management (ADP), 1976–79; AOA, RAF Support Comd, 1979–82. Bursar, Warwick Sch., 1983–85. Pres., Adastrian Cricket Club, 1977–82. *Recreations:* cricket, most sports, gardening, model railways. *Address:* c/o Lloyds Bank, 73 Parade, Leamington Spa, Warwicks CV32 4BB. *Clubs:* Royal Air Force, MCC.

BATES, Prof. Sir David (Robert), Kt 1978; MSc; DSc; FRS 1955; MRIA; *b* Omagh, Co. Tyrone, N Ireland, 18 Nov. 1916; *s* of late Walter Vivian Bates and of Mary Olive Bates; *m* 1956, Barbara Bailey Morris; one *s* one *d*. *Educ:* Royal Belfast Academical Institution; Queen's Univ., Belfast; University Coll., London. Engaged at Admiralty Research Laboratory, 1939–41, and at Mine Design Department, 1941–45; Lecturer in Mathematics, University Coll., London, 1945–50; Consultant at US Naval Ordnance Test Station, Inyokern, Calif., 1950; Reader in Physics, University Coll., London, 1951; Queen's Univ., Belfast: Prof. of Applied Mathematics, 1951–68; Prof. of Theoretical Physics, 1968–74; Research Prof., 1976–82, now Emeritus; Smithsonian Regent's Fellow, Center for Astrophysics, Cambridge, Mass, Vis. Scholar in Atmospheric Scis, Harvard Univ., 1982–83. Chm., Adv. Bd Postgrad. Awards, NI Dept of Educn, 1974–82; Mem., UGC Working Party on Higher Educn in NI, 1983–87. Vice-Pres., RIA, 1976–77; Pres., Section A, British Assoc., 1987. Lectures: Chapman Meml, Univ. of Colorado, 1973; Kistiakowsky, Harvard Univ., 1983; Larmor, QUB, 1990. Hon. Pres., Sanibel Symposium, Florida, 1983. Vice-Pres., Alliance Party of NI, 1971–. Mem., Internat. Acad. Astronautics, 1961; Sen. Mem., Internat. Acad. of Quantum Molecular Sci., 1985; Hon. Foreign Mem., Amer. Acad. of Arts and Scis, 1974; Associate Mem., Royal Acad., Belgium, 1979; Foreign Associate, Nat. Acad. of Scis, USA, 1984. Hon. DSc: Ulster, 1972; NUI, 1975; York (Ontario), 1983; QUB, 1984; Hon. ScD Dublin, 1979; Hon. LLD Glasgow, 1979; DUniv: York, 1983; Stirling, 1986; Essex, 1989. Hughes Medal, Royal Soc., 1970; Chree Medal, Inst. Physics, 1973; Gold Medal, Royal Astron. Soc., 1977; Fleming Medal, Amer. Geophys. Union, 1987. *Publications:* papers in astrophysical, geophysical and physical journals. Editor-in-Chief, Planetary and Space Science; (ed with B. Bederson) Advances in Atomic, Molecular and Optical Physics. *Recreations:* reading and listening to radio. *Address:* 1 Newforge Grange, Belfast BT9 5QB. *T:* Belfast (0232) 665640.

BATES, Sir Dawson; *see* Bates, Sir J. D.

BATES, Maj.-Gen. Sir (Edward) John (Hunter), KBE 1969 (OBE 1952); CB 1965; MC 1944; Director, Thomson Regional Newspapers, 1969–77; *b* 5 Dec. 1911; *s* of Ernest Bates, FRIBA; *m* 1947, Sheila Ann Norman; two *s* two *d*. *Educ:* Wellington Coll.; Corpus Christi Coll., Cambridge. BA 1933; MA 1963. Commissioned, 1932; Pre-war service in UK and Malaya; War Service in Africa, Middle East, Sicily, Italy and Greece; Senior Army Instructor, JSSC, 1954–57; Student, IDC, 1958; CRA, 2 Div., 1959; CCRA 1 (British) Corps, 1960–61; Dir, RA, War Office, 1961–64; Comdt of RMCS, 1964–67; Dir, Royal Defence Acad., 1967–68. Special Comr, Duke of York's Royal Military Sch., 1972–. Col Comdt, RA 1966–76. Mem. Ct of Assts, 1972–, Warden, 1977, Master, 1979, Worshipful Co. of Haberdashers. Chm., RUSI, 1976–78. *Recreation:* fishing. *Address:* Chaffenden, Frensham Road, Rolvenden Layne, Cranbrook, Kent. *T:* Cranbrook (0580) 241536. *Clubs:* Army and Navy; Rye Golf.

See also Hon. Sir J. D. Waite.

BATES, Eric; Chairman, Midlands Electricity Board, 1969–72; *b* 1 Nov. 1908; *s* of late John Boon Bates and late Edith Anne Bates; *m* 1933, Beatrice, *d* of late William Henry Herapath and late Beatrice Herapath; one *s* two *d*. Trained Ilford Elec. Dept.; Asst, County of London Elec. Supply Co., 1929–32; Consumers' Engr: West Kent Electric Co., 1933–36; Isle of Thanet Elec. Supply Co., 1937–42; Elec. Engr, Kennedy & Donkin, 1942–44; Consumers' Engr, Luton Elec. Dept, 1944–48; Sect. Head, Eastern Elec. Bd, 1948–49; Dep. Chief Commercial Officer, Eastern Elec. Bd, 1949–57; North Eastern Electricity Board: Chief Commercial Officer, 1957–62; Dep. Chm., 1962–67; Chm., 1967–69. *Publications:* contribs to Proc. IEE. *Recreation:* golf. *Address:* Broadstairs, Kent.

BATES, Sir Geoffrey Voltelin, 5th Bt, *cr* 1880; MC 1942; *b* 2 Oct. 1921; *s* of Major Cecil Robert Bates, DSO, MC (3rd *s* of 2nd Bt) and Hylda, *d* of Sir James Heath, 1st Bt; *S* uncle, 1946; *m* 1st, 1945, Kitty Kendall Lane (*d* 1956); two *s*; 2nd, 1957, Olivia Gwyneth Zoë (*d* 1969) *d* of Capt. Hon. R. O. FitzRoy (later 2nd Viscount Daventry); one *d* (and one *d* decd); 3rd, 1971, Mrs Juliet Eleanor Hugolyn Whitelocke-Winter, *widow* of Edward Colin Winter and *d* of late Comdr G. C. A. Whitelocke, RN retd, and Mrs S. H. Whitelocke. *Educ:* Radley. High Sheriff, Flintshire, 1969. *Recreations:* hunting, shooting, fishing. *Heir:* *s* Edward Robert Bates, *b* 4 July 1946. *Address:* Gyrn Castle, Llanasa, near Holywell, Clwyd CH8 9BG. *T:* Prestatyn (07456) 3500.

BATES, Rt. Rev. Gordon; *see* Whitby, Bishop Suffragan of.

BATES, James P. M.; *see* Martin-Bates.

BATES, Maj.-Gen. Sir John; *see* Bates, Maj.-Gen. Sir E. J. H.

BATES, Sir John (David), Kt 1969; CBE 1962; VRD; Australian Consul-General in New York, 1970–73; *b* 1 March 1904; *s* of H. W. Bates, Plymouth, Devon; *m* 1930, Phyllis Helen Muller; one *s*. *Educ:* Plymouth. Joined sea staff of Orient Line, 1925; transf. to shore staff, in Australia, 1929; RANVR, 1932–57, Comdr; Gen. Manager in Australia of Orient Line, 1954–60; Dep. Chm., P & O Lines of Australia, 1960–67; Chm., Hon. Bd of Australian Nat. Travel Assoc., 1956–67; Chm. Australian Tourist Commn, 1967–69. Federal Pres., Navy League of Australia, 1950–56; Trustee, Art Gallery of NSW, 1962–70; Lay Member, Trade Practices Tribunal, 1968–70. *Recreations:* reading, walking. *Address:* 23/10 Kenburn Avenue, Cherrybrook, NSW 2021, Australia. *Club:* Union (Sydney).

BATES, Sir (John) Dawson, 2nd Bt, *cr* 1937; MC 1943; Regional Director of the National Trust, retired 1981; *b* 21 Sept. 1921; *o s* of Sir (Richard) Dawson Bates, 1st Bt, PC, and Muriel (*d* 1972), *d* of late Sir Charles Cleland, KBE, MVO, LLD; *S* father, 1949; *m* 1953, Mary Murray, *o d* of late Lieut-Col Joseph M. Hoult, Norton Place, Lincoln; two *s* one *d*. *Educ:* Winchester; Balliol. BA 1949. FRICS. Served War of 1939–45, Major, Rifle Brigade (MC). *Heir:* *s* Richard Dawson Hoult Bates, *b* 12 May 1956. *Address:* Butleigh House, Butleigh, Glastonbury, Somerset.

BATES, John Gerald Higgs; Solicitor, Office of Inland Revenue, since 1990; *b* 28 July 1936; *o s* of Thomas William Bates and Winifred Alice Higgs; *m* 1971, Antoinette Lotery (*d* 1984); two *s*. *Educ:* Kettering Grammar Sch.; St Catharine's Coll., Cambridge (MA); Harvard Law Sch. (LLM). Called to the Bar, Middle Temple, 1959. Practised at the Bar, 1962–66; Office of Solicitor of Inland Revenue, 1966–: Under Sec. (Legal), 1990. *Recreations:* cooking, wine, music. *Address:* Solicitor's Office, Inland Revenue, Somerset House, Strand, WC2R 1LB. *T:* 071–438 6228.

BATES, Merrick Stuart B.; *see* Baker-Bates.

BATES, Rev. Canon Paul Spencer; Residentiary Canon of Westminster Abbey, since 1990; *b* 1 Jan. 1940; *s* of Rev. John Spencer Bates and Margaret Annie Bates (*née* Harwood); *m* 1964, Freda Ann Spillard; two *s*. *Educ:* St Edmund's Sch., Canterbury; Corpus Christi Coll., Cambridge (MA); Lincoln Theol Coll. Deacon 1965, priest 1966; Asst Curate, Hartcliffe, Bristol, 1965–69; Chaplain, Winchester Coll., 1970–80; Dir of Training, dio. of Winchester, 1980–90. *Publications:* contrib. SPCK Taleteller series. *Recreations:* cricket, modern novels, gardening. *Address:* 5 Little Cloister, Westminster Abbey, SW1P 3PL. *T:* 071–222 6939.

BATES, Peter Edward Gascoigne, CBE 1987; Director, General Technology Systems Ltd, since 1986; Chairman, British Defence Market Intelligence Ltd, since 1986; *b* 6 Aug. 1924; *s* of James Edward Bates and Esmé Grace Gascoigne Bates (*née* Roy); *m* 1947, Jean Irene Hearn, *d* of late Brig. W. Campbell Grant; two *s* one *d*. *Educ:* Kingston Grammar Sch.; School of Oriental and African Studies, Univ. of London; Lincoln Coll., Oxford. Served War, Intelligence Corps, SEAC and Japan, 1943–46; Captain 1945. Malayan CS, 1947–55; Rolls-Royce, Aero Engine Div., 1955–57; Bristol Aircraft (later British Aircraft Corp.), 1957–64, Special Director, 1963; joined Plessey Co., 1964: Gen. Man., Plessey Radar, 1967–71; Man. Dir, Radar Div., 1971–76; Dep. Chm., Plessey Electronic Systems Ltd, 1976–86. Member: CBI Overseas Cttee, 1981–86; BOTB, 1984–87. Member: Council, Electronic Engrg Assoc., 1973–86 (Pres. 1976); Council, SBAC, 1978–86 (Pres. 1983–84); Pres., AECMA, 1985–86. *Recreations:* golf, gardening, theatre, reading history and biography. *Address:* 12 Lindisfarne Road, Wimbledon, SW20 0NW. *T:* 081–946 0345. *Clubs:* Army and Navy; Royal Wimbledon Golf.

BATES, Ralph; *b* Swindon, Wilts, 3 Nov. 1899; *s* of Henry Roy and Mabel Stevens Bates; *m* 1940, Eve Salzman; one *s*. *Educ:* Swindon and North Wilts. Secondary Sch. After service in 16th Queen's Royal West Surreys, 1917–19, worked in Great Western Railway Factory at Swindon; in Spain, 1930–37; took active part in Republican politics in Spain; began literary career in 1933 as consequence of unemployment; Capt. in the Spanish Loyalist Army and in the International Brigade, Madrid sector, 1936–37; lecture tour in USA 1937–38; one year resident in Mexico, 1938–39; Adjunct Prof. of Literature, New York Univ. 1948–68, now Professor Emeritus of Literature. *Publications:* Sierra, 1933; Lean Men, 1934, Schubert, 1934, The Olive Field, 1936; Rainbow Fish, 1937; The Miraculous Horde, 1939; The Fields of Paradise, 1941; The Undiscoverables, 1942; The Journey to the Sandalwood Forest, 1947; The Dolphin in the Wood, 1949. *Recreations:* small boating, music. *Address:* 37 Washington Square West, New York, NY 10011, USA. *T:* (212) 254–4149.

BATES, Stewart Taverner, QC 1970; **His Honour Judge Bates;** a Circuit Judge, since 1989; *b* 17 Dec. 1926; *s* of John Bates, Greenock; *m* 1950, Anne Patricia, *d* of David West, Pinner; two *s* four *d*. *Educ:* Univs of Glasgow and St Andrews; Corpus Christi Coll., Oxford. Officers' Trng Sch., Bangalore, 1946, commnd Argyll and Sutherland Highlanders. Called to Bar, Middle Temple, 1954, Bencher, 1975; a Recorder, 1981–89. Mem. Bar Council, 1962–66. Chm., Barristers' Benevolent Assoc., 1983–89; Member: Goodman Cttee on Charity Law and Voluntary Organisations, 1976; Cttee of Management, Inst. of Urology, Univ. of London, 1978–89; Chm., St Peter's Hosp. Special Cttee, 1986–89. *Recreations:* theatre, sailing, ski-ing. *Address:* The Grange, Horsington, Templecombe, Somerset BA8 0EF. *T:* Templecombe (0963) 70521. *Club:* Garrick.

BATES, William Stanley, CMG 1971; HM Diplomatic Service, retired; *b* 7 Sept. 1920; *m* 1970, Suzanne Elston. *Educ:* Christ's Hospital; Corpus Christi Coll., Cambridge. Asst Principal, Colonial Office, 1948; Principal, 1951; Commonwealth Relations Office, 1956; Canberra, 1956–59; Asst Sec., 1962. British Deputy High Commissioner, Northern Nigeria, 1963–65; Imperial Defence Coll., 1966; Head of Communications Dept, FCO, 1967–70; High Comr in Guyana, 1970–75; Ambassador to Korea, 1975–80. *Address:* 3 Houndean Close, Lewes, East Sussex BN7 1EZ.

BATESON; *see* de Yarburgh-Bateson, family name of Baron Deramore.

BATESON, Andrew James, QC 1971; *b* 29 June 1925; *m* 1954, Janette Mary Poupart (*d* 1970); one *s* three *d*. *Educ:* Eton. Called to the Bar, Middle Temple, 1951; Bencher, 1977. *Recreations:* shooting, fishing, gardening. *Address:* Little Foxwarren, Redhill Road, Cobham, Surrey KT11 1EG. *Club:* Flyfishers'.

BATESON, John Swinburne, FIHT; Group Chief Executive, AMEC plc, since 1988; *b* 11 Jan. 1942; *s* of William Swinburne Bateson and Katherine Urquart (*née* Lyttle); *m* Jean Vivien Forsyth; one *s* two *d*. *Educ:* Appleby Grammar Sch.; Lancaster Royal Grammar Sch. FIHT 1986. Family business and associated activities, 1959–61; Harbour & General Works Ltd: Trainee Quantity Surveyor, 1961; Quantity Surveyor, 1966; Site Quantity Surveyor, Marples Ridgway Ltd, 1966–68; Leonard Fairclough Ltd: Site Quantity Surveyor, 1969; Contracts Surveyor, 1971; Chief Quantity Surveyor, Scotland, 1974; Fairclough Civil Engineering Ltd: Asst to Chief Exec., 1977; Man. Dir, Southern Div., 1979; Fairclough Construction Group Ltd: Asst to Chief Exec., 1980; Dir, 1981–; AMEC plc: Dir, 1982–86; Dep. Chief Exec., 1986–88. *Recreations:* gardening, aviation, reading, photography, chess, bridge, antiques. *Address:* Clayton Croft, Ribchester Road, Clayton-le-Dale, Blackburn, Lancs BB1 9EE. *T:* Blackburn (0254) 240748.

BATESON, Prof. (Paul) Patrick (Gordon), FRS 1983; Professor of Ethology, University of Cambridge, since 1984; Provost of King's College, Cambridge, since 1988 (Fellow, 1964–84; Professorial Fellow, 1984–88); *b* 31 March 1938; *s* of Richard Gordon Bateson and Sölvi Helene Berg; *m* 1963, Dusha Matthews; two *d*. *Educ:* Westminster Sch.; King's Coll., Cambridge (BA 1960, PhD 1963, MA 1965, ScD 1977). Harkness Fellow, Stanford Univ. Medical Centre, Calif, 1963–65; Sen. Asst in Res., Sub-Dept of Animal Behaviour, Univ. of Cambridge, 1965–69; Lectr in Zoology, Univ. of Cambridge, 1969–78; Dir, Sub-Dept of Animal Behaviour, 1976–88; Reader in Animal Behaviour, 1978–84. Pres., Assoc. for the Study of Animal Behaviour, 1977–80; Council for Sci. and Soc., 1989–; Council, Zool Soc. of London, 1989–. Trustee, Inst. for Public Policy Studies, 1988–. Scientific Medal, Zool Soc. of London, 1976. *Publications:* (ed with P. H. Klopfer) Perspectives in Ethology, Vols 1–8, 1973–89; (ed with R. A. Hinde) Growing Points in Ethology, 1976; (ed) Mate Choice, 1983; (contrib.) Defended to Death, 1983; (with Paul Martin) Measuring Behaviour, 1986; (ed with D. S. Turner) The Domestic Cat: the biology of its behaviour, 1988. *Recreations:* cooking, dreaming. *Address:* Provost's Lodge, King's College, Cambridge CB2 1ST. *T:* Cambridge (0223) 355949.

BATH, 6th Marquess of, *cr* 1789; **Henry Frederick Thynne,** Bt 1641; Viscount Weymouth and Baron Thynne, 1682; Major Royal Wiltshire Yeomanry; JP; *b* 26 Jan. 1905; *o surv. s* of 5th Marquess, KG, PC, CB and Violet Caroline (*d* 1928), *d* of Sir Charles Mordaunt, 10th Bt; *S* father, 1946; *m* 1st, 1927, Hon. Daphne (marr. diss., 1953; she *m* 2nd, 1953, Major A. W. Fielding, DSO), *er d* of 4th Baron Vivian, DSO; two *s* one *d* (and one *s* decd); 2nd, 1953, Mrs Virginia Penelope Tennant, *d* of late Alan L. R. Parsons; one *d*. *Educ:* Harrow; Christ Church, Oxford. MP (U) Frome Division, Som., 1931–35. Served War of 1939–45 (wounded). Chm., Football Pools Panel, 1967–87. Life-long interest in forestry; Longleat has some of the best private woodland in the country. *Heir:* *s* Viscount Weymouth, *qv*. *Address:* Job's Mill, Warminster, Wilts BA12 8BB. *T:* Warminster (0985) 212279; Longleat, Warminster, Wilts. *Club:* White's.
See also Duke of Beaufort.

BATH and WELLS, Bishop of, since 1991; **Rt. Rev. James Lawton Thompson;** *b* 11 Aug. 1936; *s* of Bernard Isaac and Marjorie May Thompson; *m* 1965, Sally Patricia Stallworthy; one *s* one *d*. *Educ:* Dean Close School, Cheltenham; Emmanuel Coll., Cambridge (MA 1964). FCA 1959. 2nd Lt, 3rd Royal Tank Regt, 1959–61. Deacon, 1966; Curate, East Ham, 1966–68; Chaplain, Cuddesdon Coll., Oxford, 1968–71; Rector of Thamesmead and Ecumenical Team Leader, 1971–78; Suffragan, then Area, Bishop of Stepney, 1978–91. Mem., House of Bishops, Gen. Synod of C of E, 1988–. Chairman: Cttee for Relations with People of Other Faiths, BCC, 1983–89; Learning Foundn, 1984–; Interfaith Network (UK), 1987–; Church at Work, London, 1989–; Social Policy Cttee, Bd for Social Responsibility, 1990–; London Churches Broadcasting Gp. Hon. Fellow, QMC, 1986. Hon. DLitt E London Poly., 1989. (Jointly) Sir Sigmund Sternberg Award for Christian-Jewish Relations, 1987. *Publications:* Halfway: reflections in midlife, 1986; (contrib.) Trevor Huddleston, ed D. D. Honoré, 1989; The Lord's Song, 1990; Stepney Calling, 1991. *Recreations:* painting, a horse, sport. *Address:* The Palace, Wells, Somerset BA5 2PD. *T:* Wells (0749) 72341.

BATH, Archdeacon of; *see* Burgess, Ven. J. E.

BATH, Alan Alfred; Director, Education and Training, Commission of the European Communities, 1973–80; *b* 3 May 1924; *s* of Alfred Edward Bath and Doris Ellen Lawson; *m* 1st, 1946, Joy Roselle Thornton (*d* 1979), *d* of George Jeune, St Saviour, Jersey; one *s* two *d*; 2nd, 1987, Jill Diana Lesley Pearce, *d* of Eric and Nancy Douglas, Blandford Forum, Dorset. Educ: Frays Coll., Uxbridge; Queen's Univ., Belfast (BSc Econ). RAF, 1942–46. Asst Lectr in Econs, QUB, 1950–53; Admin. Officer, Assoc. of Univs of British Commonwealth, 1953–58; Imperial Coll., Univ. of London, 1958–62 (Develt Sec., 1960–62); Sec., Cttee of Vice-Chancellors and Principals of Univs of UK, 1964–73; Sec., UK Nat. Delegn to Council of Europe Cttee for Higher Educn and Research, 1969–73. *Publication:* A Survey of the Work of the Winston Churchill Memorial Trust, 1985. *Recreations:* music, sailing, gardening. *Address:* 6 Sleepers Hill Gardens, Winchester, Hants SO22 4NT. *T:* Winchester (0962) 65848. *Clubs:* Athenæum, Royal Air Force.

BATHO, Sir Peter (Ghislain), 3rd Bt *cr* 1928, of Frinton, Essex; *b* 9 Dec. 1939; *s* of Sir Maurice Benjamin Batho, 2nd Bt and of Antoinette Marie, *d* of Baron d'Udekem d'Acoz; *S* father, 1990; *m* 1966, Lucille Mary, *d* of Wilfrid F. Williamson; three *s*. *Educ:* Ampleforth Coll.; Writtle Agricl Coll. Career in agriculture. Mem., Suffolk CC, 1989–. *Heir:* *s* Rupert Sebastian Ghislain Batho, *b* 26 Oct. 1967. *Address:* Park Farm, Saxmundham, Suffolk, IP17 1DQ. *T:* Saxmundham (0728) 602132.

BATHO, Walter James Scott; Regional Director and Chairman of the Regional Board for the Eastern Region, Departments of the Environment and Transport, 1983–85; Chairman: London and Quadrant Housing Trust, since 1989; Department of the Environment Noise Review Working Party, since 1990; *b* 13 Nov. 1925; *er s* of Walter Scott Batho and Isabella Laidlaw Batho (*née* Common); *m* 1951, Barbara Kingsford; two *s* two *d*. *Educ:* Epsom County Grammar Sch.; Univ. of Edinburgh (MA Eng. Lit. and Lang.). Served War, RNVR, 1943–46. Air Min., 1950–53; WO, 1953–63 (Private Sec. to Perm. Under Sec. of State, 1956–57); MPBW, 1963–70; DoE, 1970–85, Under Sec., 1979–85. Pres., Ashtead Choral Soc. *Recreations:* singing, reading, gardening. *Address:* Bushpease, Grays Lane, Ashtead, Surrey KT21 1BU. *T:* Ashtead (0372) 273471. *Club:* Naval.

BATHURST, family name of **Earl Bathurst** and **Viscount Bledisloe.**

BATHURST, 8th Earl, *cr* 1772; **Henry Allen John Bathurst,** DL; Baron Bathurst of Battlesden, Bedfordshire, 1712; Baron Apsley of Apsley, Sussex, 1771; Earl Bathurst of Bathurst, Sussex, 1772; Capt. Royal Gloucestershire Hussars (TA); TARO, 1959; *b* 1 May 1927; *s* of late Lord Apsley, DSO, MC, MP (killed on active service, 1942), and late Lady Apsley, CBE; *g s* of 7th Earl; *S* grandfather, 1943; *m* 1st 1959, Judith Mary (marr. diss. 1977), *d* of Mr and Mrs A. C. Nelson, Springfield House, Foulridge, Lancs; two *s* one *d*; 2nd, 1978, Gloria, *widow* of David Rutherston and *o d* of Harold Edward Clarry, Vancouver, BC. *Educ:* Ridley Coll., Canada; Eton; Christ Church, Oxford, 1948–49. Late Lieut 10th Royal Hussars (PWO). Capt., Royal Glos. Hussars, TA, 1949–57. Hon. Sec. Agricultural Cttee (Conservative), House of Lords, 1957; a Lord-in-Waiting, 1957–61; Joint Parliamentary Under-Sec. of State, Home Office, 1961–July 1962. Governor, Royal Agricultural Coll.; Pres. Glos Branch CPRE. Chancellor, Primrose League, 1959–61. Dir, Forestor Gp, 1986–. Member: CLA Council, 1965 (Chm., Glos Branch of CLA, 1968–71); Timber Growers' Organisation (TGO) Council, 1966; President: Royal Forestry Soc., 1976–78; InstSMM, 1982–; Assoc. of Professional Foresters, 1983–87. DL County of Gloucester, 1960. *Heir:* *s* Lord Apsley, *qv*. *Address:* Manor Farm House, Sapperton, near Cirencester, Glos GL7 6LE. *Clubs:* White's, Cavalry and Guards.

BATHURST (NSW), Bishop of, since 1989; **Rt. Rev. Bruce Winston Wilson;** *b* 23 Aug. 1942; *s* of Alick Bruce Wilson and Maisie Catherine (*née* Pye); *m* 1966, Zandra Robyn Parkes; one *s* one *d*. *Educ:* Canterbury Boys' High School; Univ. of Sydney (MA); London Univ. (BD); Univ. of NSW (BA); Australian Coll. of Theology (ThL). Curacies, Darling Point and Beverly Hills, Sydney, 1966–69; Anglican Chaplain, Univ. of NSW, 1970–75; Rector of St George's, Paddington, Sydney, 1975–83; Director, St Mark's Theol Coll., Canberra, 1984–89; Asst Bishop, Diocese of Canberra and Goulburn, 1984–89. *Publications:* The Human Journey: Christianity and Modern Consciousness, 1981; Can God Survive in Australia?, 1983. *Recreations:* jogging, motor car restoration, reading, cooking. *Address:* Bishopscourt, 16 McKell Street, Bathurst, NSW 2795, Australia. *T:* (063) 31 1175.

BATHURST, Adm. Sir (David) Benjamin, GCB 1991 (KCB 1987); Vice Chief of the Defence Staff, since 1991; *b* 27 May 1936; *s* of late Group Captain Peter Bathurst, RAF and Lady Ann Bathurst; *m* 1959, Sarah Peto; one *s* three *d*. *Educ:* Eton College; Britannia RN College, Dartmouth. Joined RN, 1953; qualified as Pilot, 1960, as Helicopter Instructor, 1964; Fleet Air Arm appts incl. 2 years' exchange with RAN, 723 and 725 Sqdns; Senior Pilot, 820 Naval Air Sqdn; CO 819 Naval Air Sqdn; HMS Norfolk, 1971; Naval Staff, 1973; CO, HMS Ariadne, 1975; Naval Asst to First Sea Lord, 1976; Captain, 5th Frigate Sqdn, HMS Minerva, 1978; RCDS 1981; Dir of Naval Air Warfare, 1982; Flag Officer, Second Flotilla, 1983–85; Dir.-Gen., Naval Manpower and Training,

1985–86; Chief of Fleet Support, 1986–89; C-in-C Fleet, Allied C-in-C Channel, and C-in-C Eastern Atlantic Area, 1989–91. Liveryman, GAPAN. *Recreations:* gardening, shooting, fishing. *Address:* c/o Coutts and Co., 440 Strand, WC2. *Clubs:* Army and Navy, MCC.

BATHURST, Sir Frederick Peter Methuen Hervey-, 6th Bt, *cr* 1818; *b* 26 Jan. 1903; *s* of Sir Frederick Edward William Hervey-Bathurst, 5th Bt, DSO and Hon. Moira O'Brien, 2nd *d* of 14th Baron Inchiquin; *S* father 1956; *m* 1st, 1933, Maureen (marr. diss. 1956), *d* of Charles Gordon, Boveridge Park, Salisbury; one *s* one *d*; 2nd, 1958, Mrs Cornelia Shepard Riker, *widow* of Dr John Lawrence Riker, Rumson, NJ, USA. *Educ:* Eton. Served War of 1939–45, Capt. Grenadier Guards. *Recreations:* sailing, riding, skiing, flying. *Heir: s* Frederick John Charles Gordon Hervey-Bathurst [*b* 23 April 1934; *m* 1957, Caroline Myrtle, *d* of Lieut-Col Sir William Starkey, 2nd Bt, and late Irene Myrtle Francklin; one *s* two *d*]. *Address:* Bellevue Avenue, Rumson, New Jersey 07760, USA. *T:* 842–0791. *Clubs:* Cavalry and Guards, Royal Ocean Racing.

See also Sir J. F. Portal, Bt.

BATHURST, Joan Caroline, (Lady Bathurst); *see* Petrie, J. C.

BATHURST, Sir Maurice (Edward), Kt 1984; CMG 1953; CBE 1947; QC 1964; *b* 2 Dec. 1913; *o s* of late Edward John James Bathurst and Annie Mary Bathurst; *m* 1941, Dorothy (marr. diss. 1963), *d* of late W. S. Stevens, LDS, RCS; one *s*; *m* 1968, Joan Caroline Petrie, *qv*. *Educ:* Haberdashers' Aske's, Hatcham; King's Coll., London; Gonville and Caius Coll., Cambridge; Columbia Univ. LLB, First Class Hons. (London), 1937; University Law Schol. (London), 1937; Post-Grad. Research Studentship (London), 1938; Bartle Frere Exhibitioner (Camb.), 1939; Tutorial Fellow (Chicago), 1939; Special Fellow (Columbia), 1940; LLM (Columbia), 1941; Hon. DCL (Sacred Heart, NB), 1946; PhD (Camb.), 1949; LLD (London), 1966. Solicitor of Supreme Court, 1938–56. Called to Bar, Gray's Inn, 1957; Master of the Bench, 1970; Master of the Library, 1978–81. Legal Adviser, British Information Services, USA, 1941–43; Legal Adviser, British Embassy, Washington, 1943–46 (First Sec., 1944; Counsellor, 1946); Legal Member, UK Delegation to United Nations, 1946–48; UK Representative, Legal Advisory Cttee, Atomic Energy Commission, 1946–48; Legal Adviser to British Chm., Bipartite Control Office, Frankfurt, 1949; Dep. Legal Adviser, CCG, 1949–51; Legal Adviser, UK High Commn, Germany, 1951–55; Judge, Supreme Court, British Zone, Germany, 1953–55; Legal Adviser, British Embassy, Bonn, 1955–57; British Judge, Arbitral Commn, Germany, 1968–69; Mem., Panel of Arbitrators, Internat. Centre for Settlement of Investment Disputes, 1968–87; a Pres., Arbitral Tribunals, Internat. Telecommunication's Satellite Orgn, 1974–78; Judge, Arbitral Tribunal and Mixed Commn for Agreement on German External Debts, 1977–88. Mem. UK Delegations to UNRRA; United Nations San Francisco Conference; Bermuda Civil Aviation Conference; PICAO; Washington Financial Talks; UN Gen. Assembly; FAO; WHO; Internat. Tin Study Group; UK-US Double Taxation Treaty Negotiations; London Nine-Power Conf.; Paris Conf. on W Eur. Union; NATO Status of Forces Conf., Bonn. Internat. Vice-Pres. UN League of Lawyers; Vice President: Brit. Inst. of International and Comparative Law; Brit. Acad. of Experts, 1988–91. Member: UK Cttee, UNICEF, 1959–84; Ct of Assistants, Haberdashers' Co. (Fourth Warden, 1973–74; Second Warden, 1978–79; First Warden, 1979–80; Master, 1980–81); Editorial Cttee, British Yearbook of International Law; *ad eundem*, Inner Temple; Gen. Council of the Bar, 1970–71; Senate of Inns of Court, 1971–73; Council of Legal Educn, 1971–79; Senate of the Inns of Court and the Bar, 1974–77. Hon. Vis. Prof. in Internat. Law, King's Coll., London, 1967–77; Hon. Fellow, King's Coll., London. Chm. Governors, Haberdashers' Aske's Hatcham Schools, 1972–80. Pres., British Insurance Law Assoc., 1971–75. Freeman of the City of London and of the City of Bathurst, NB. *Publications:* Germany and the North Atlantic Community: A Legal Survey (with J. L. Simpson), 1956; (ed, jtly) Legal Problems of an Enlarged European Community, 1972; notes and articles in legal jls, etc., British and American. *Recreation:* theatre. *Address:* Airlie, The Highlands, East Horsley, Surrey KT24 5BG. *T:* East Horsley (04865) 3269. *Club:* Garrick.

BATHURST NORMAN, George Alfred; His Honour Judge Bathurst Norman; a Circuit Judge, since 1986; *b* 15 Jan. 1939; *s* of Charles Phipps Bathurst Norman and Hon. Doreen Albinia de Burgh Norman (*née* Gibbs); *m* 1973, Susan Elizabeth Ball; one *s* one *d*. *Educ:* Harrow Sch.; Magdalen Coll., Oxford (BA). Called to the Bar, Inner Temple, 1961; SE Circuit, 1962; Dep. Circuit Judge, 1975; a Metropolitan Stipendiary Magistrate, 1981–86; a Recorder, 1986. Mem., Home Office Working Party on Coroners Rules, 1976–81. Mem., Gen. Council of the Bar, 1968–70. *Recreations:* wildlife, ornithology, cricket, travel. *Address:* 3 Hare Court, Temple, EC4. *Club:* MCC.

BATISTE, Spencer Lee; MP (C) Elmet, since 1983; solicitor in private practice, since 1970; *b* 5 June 1945; *m* 1969, Susan Elizabeth (*née* Atkin); one *s* one *d*. *Educ:* Carmel Coll.; Sorbonne, Paris; Cambridge Univ. (MA). PPS to Minister of State for Industry and IT, 1985–87, to Minister of State for Defence Procurement, 1987–89; to Sir Leon Brittan, Vice-Pres. of EC Commn, 1989–. Mem., Select Cttee on Energy, 1985; Vice-Chairman: Cons. Space Cttee, 1986– (Sec., 1983–85); Cons. Trade and Industry Cttee, 1989–. Chm., Yorks Cons. Trade Unionists, 1984–87, Nat. Vice-Chm., 1987–. Vice-Chm., Small Business Bureau, 1983–. Law Clerk to the Guardians of the Standard of Wrought Plate within the Town of Sheffield, 1973–. Mem. Council, Univ. of Sheffield, 1982–. *Recreations:* gardening, reading, photography, stamp collecting. *Address:* House of Commons, SW1A 0AA. *Club:* The Club (Sheffield).

BATLEY, John Geoffrey, OBE 1987; CEng; Consultant, Dan-Rail, Copenhagen, since 1988; *b* 21 May 1930; *s* of John William and Doris Batley; *m* 1953, Cicely Anne Pindar; one *s* one *d*. *Educ:* Keighley Grammar School. MICE, MCIT. British Rail: trained and qualified as a chartered engineer in NE Region, 1947–53; Asst Divl Engr, Leeds, 1962; Management Services Officer, BR HQ, London, 1965; Dep. Principal, British Transport Staff Coll., Woking, 1970; Divl Manager, Leeds, 1976; Dep. Chief Secretary, BRB, London, 1982; Sec., BRB, 1984–87; Project Co-ordinator, World Bank/Tanzanian Railway Corp., 1988–90. *Recreations:* walking, golf, gardening. *Address:* Wentworth Cottage, Old Lodge Hill, Ilkley, West Yorkshire LS29 0BB. *T:* Ilkley (0943) 601396. *Clubs:* Farmers', Savile.

BATTEN, Sir John (Charles), KCVO 1987; MD, FRCP; Physician to the Queen, 1974–89 (Physician to HM Royal Household, 1970–74), and Head of HM Medical Household, 1982–89; Physician: King Edward VII Hospital for Officers, 1968–89; King Edward VII Hospital, Midhurst, 1969–89; Hon. Physician to: St Dunstan's, since 1960; St George's Hospital, since 1980; Brompton Hospital, since 1986; Chief Medical Officer, Confederation Life, since 1974 (Deputy Chief Medical Referee, 1958–74); *b* 11 March 1924; *s* of late Raymond Wallis Batten, JP and Gladys (*née* Charles); *m* 1950, Anne Mary Margaret, *d* of late John Oriel, CBE, MC; one *s* two *d* (and one *d* decd). *Educ:* Mill Hill School; St Bartholomew's Medical School. MB, BS 1946 London Univ.; MRCP 1950; MD London 1951; FRCP 1964. Junior appts, St George's Hosp. and Brompton Hosp., 1946–58. Surgeon Captain, Royal Horse Guards, 1947–49. Physician: St George's Hospital, 1958–79; Brompton Hosp., 1959–86. Dorothy Temple Cross Research Fellow, Cornell Univ. Medical Coll., New York, 1954–55. Examiner in Medicine, London Univ., 1968; Marc Daniels Lectr, RCP, 1969; Croonian Lectr, RCP, 1983. Member: Board of Governors, Brompton Hosp., 1966–69; St George's Hosp. Medical School Council, 1969; Management Cttee, King Edward VII Hosp. Fund; Council, RSocMed, 1970; Royal College of Physicians: Censor, 1977–78; Senior Censor, 1980–81; Vice-Pres., 1980–81. President: Cystic Fibrosis Res. Trust, 1986–; British Lung Foundn, 1987–; Medical Protection Soc., 1988–. *Publications:* contributions to medical books and journals. *Recreations:* music and sailing. *Address:* 7 Lion Gate Gardens, Richmond, Surrey TW9 2DF. *T:* 081–940 3282. *Club:* Oriental.

BATTEN, Mark Wilfrid, RBA 1962; FRBS 1952 (ARBS 1950); Sculptor, direct carver in stone; *s* of Edward Batten; *m* 1933, Elsie May Owston Thorneloe (*d* 1961); one *d*. *Educ:* Chelsea Sch. of Art. Commenced to experiment individually with stone carving, 1927; exhibited only drawings and paintings until 1934; combined experiment in sculpture with learning craft of stone carving mainly in granite mason's yards in Cornwall; first exhibited sculpture, 1936; FRSA 1936. Collaborated with Eric Gill, 1939; first exhibited sculpture at Royal Academy, 1939. War service in Life Guards, 1940–45. Exhibited Paris Salon, 1949, and thereafter frequently at RA and many sculpture exhibitions in Paris, London and provincial cities. Many commissions for stone sculptures on public buildings; works in museums and art galleries. President, RBS 1956–61; Council, 1953–; Council, RBA, 1964–. Société des Artistes Français: Gold Medal for Sculpture, 1977 (Silver Medal, 1952); Associate, 1970. Hon. Mem. National Sculpture Soc. of the USA, 1956; Syracuse Univ., USA, estab. Mark Batten Manuscripts Collection, 1965, also Wichita State Univ., 1971. *Publications:* Stone Sculpture by Direct Carving, 1957; Direct Carving in Stone, 1966; articles in art magazines. *Recreations:* country life, travel, contemplation of other men's sculptures. *Address:* 22c Grosvenor Road, W4 4EH. *Club:* Chelsea Arts.

BATTEN, Stephen Duval; QC 1989; barrister; a Recorder, since 1988; *b* 2 April 1945; *s* of Brig. Stephen Alexander Holgate Batten, CBE and of Alice Joan Batten, MBE, *d* of Sir Ernest Royden, 3rd Bt; *m* 1976, Valerie Jean Trim; one *s* one *d*. *Educ:* Uppingham; Pembroke Coll., Oxford (BA). Called to the Bar, Middle Temple, 1968. *Recreations:* golf, sheep farming. *Address:* 3 Raymond Buildings, Gray's Inn, WC1R 5BH. *T:* 071–831 5833.

BATTERBURY, Paul Tracy Shepherd, TD 1972 (2 bars); DL; **His Honour Judge Batterbury;** a Circuit Judge, since 1983; *b* 25 Jan. 1934; only *s* of late Hugh Basil John Batterbury and of Inez Batterbury; *m* 1962, Sheila Margaret, *d* of John Watson; one *s* one *d*. *Educ:* St Olave's Grammar Sch., Southwark; Univ. of Bristol (LLB). Served RAF, 1952–55, TA, 1959–85 (Major, RA). Called to Bar, Inner Temple, 1959; practising barrister, 1959–83; Dep. Circuit Judge, 1975–79; a Recorder of the Crown Court, 1979–83. Councillor: Chislehurst and Sidcup UDC, 1960–62; London Borough of Greenwich, 1968–71 (Chm., Housing Cttee, 1970–71). Founder Trustee, St Olave's Sch., SE9, 1970; Chm., Gallipoli Meml Lects, 1986 (Founder Chm.), 1989. Vice-Pres., SE London, SJAB, 1988–91. DL Greater London, 1986; rep. DL, London Borough of Havering, 1989–. *Recreations:* photography, walking, caravanning. *Address:* 5 Paper Buildings, Temple, EC4Y 9HB. *T:* 071–583 9275.

BATTERSBY, Prof. Alan Rushton, MSc, PhD, DSc, ScD; FRS 1966; Professor of Organic Chemistry, University of Cambridge, since 1969; Fellow of St Catharine's College, Cambridge; Director, Schering Agrochemicals Ltd; *b* Leigh, 4 March 1925; *s* of William and Hilda Battersby; *m* 1949, Margaret Ruth, *d* of Thomas and Annie Hart, Whaley Bridge, Cheshire; two *s*. *Educ:* Grammar Sch., Leigh; Univ. of Manchester (Mercer and Woodiwis Schol.); Univ. of St Andrews. MSc Manchester; PhD St Andrews; DSc Bristol; ScD Cantab. Asst Lectr in Chemistry, Univ. of St Andrews, 1948–53; Commonwealth Fund Fellow at Rockefeller Inst., NY, 1950–51 and at Univ. of Illinois, 1951–52; Lectr in Chemistry, Univ. of Bristol, 1954–62; Prof. of Organic Chemistry, Univ. of Liverpool, 1962–69. Mem. Council, Royal Soc., 1973–75. Mem. Deutsche Akademie der Naturforscher Leopoldina, 1967. Pres., Bürgenstock Conf., 1976. Chm., Exec. Council, Ciba Foundn, 1983–90. Lectures: Treat Johnson, Yale, 1969; Pacific Coast, USA, 1971; Karl Folkers, Wisconsin, 1972; N-E Coast, USA, 1974; Andrews, NSW, 1975; Middle Rhine, 1976; Tishler, Harvard, 1978; August Wilhelm von Hoffmann, Ges. Deutscher Chem., 1979; Pedler, Chem. Soc., 1980–81; Rennebohm, Wisconsin, 1981; Kharasch, Chicago, 1982; Bakerian, Royal Soc., 1984; Baker, Cornell, 1984; Lady Masson Meml, Melbourne, 1987; Atlantic Coast, USA, 1988; Nehru Centenary, Seshadri Meml and Zaheer Meml, India, 1989; Marvel, Illinois, 1989; Gilman, Iowa, 1989; Visiting Professor: Cornell Univ., 1969; Virginia Univ., 1971; Tohoku Univ., Japan, 1974; ANU, 1975; Technion, Israel, 1977; Univ. of Canterbury, NZ, 1980; Melbourne Univ., 1987; Univ. of Auckland, NZ, 1989; Univ. of NSW, 1990. Chemical Society: Corday-Morgan Medal, 1959; Tilden Medal and Lectr, 1963; Hugo Müller Medal and Lectr, 1972; Flintoff Medal, 1975; Award in Natural Product Chemistry, 1978; Longstaff Medal, 1984; Robert Robinson Lectr and Medal, 1986. Paul Karrer Medal and Lectr, Univ. Zürich, 1977; Davy Medal, 1977, Royal Medal, 1984, Royal Soc.; Roger Adams Award in Organic Chemistry, ACS, 1983; Havinga Medal, Holland, 1984; Antoni Feltrinelli Internat. Prize for Chemistry, Rome, 1986; Varro Tyler Lect. and Award, Purdue, 1987; Adolf Windaus Medal, Göttingen, 1987; Wolf Prize, Israel, 1989. Honorary Member: Soc. Royale de Chimie, Belgium, 1987; Amer. Acad. of Arts and Scis, 1988. Hon. LLD St Andrews, 1977; Hon. DSc: Rockefeller Univ., USA, 1977; Sheffield, 1986; Heriot-Watt, 1987. *Publications:* papers in chemical jls, particularly Jl Chem. Soc. *Recreations:* music, camping, sailing, fly fishing, gardening. *Address:* University Chemical Laboratory, Lensfield Road, Cambridge CB2 1EW. *T:* Cambridge (0223) 336400.

BATTERSBY, Robert Christopher, CBE 1990 (MBE 1971); *b* 14 Dec. 1924; *s* of late Major Robert Luther Battersby, MM, RFA, late Indian Army, and Dorothea Gladys (*née* Middleton); *m* 1st, 1949, June Scriven (marr. diss.); one *d*; 2nd, 1955, Marjorie Bispham; two *s* one *d*. *Educ:* Firth Park Grammar Sch., Sheffield; Edinburgh Univ. (Gen. Sciences); Fitzwilliam House, Cambridge; Sorbonne; Toulouse Univ. BA Cantab (Hons Russian and Modern Greek) 1950; Cert. of Educn 1952; MA Cantab 1954; Cert. de Langue française, Toulouse, 1953; FIL 1958. Served Royal Artillery (Field) and Intelligence Corps, 1942–47 (Italian Campaign, Greece and Crete 1944, Central and Western Macedonia 1945–47); TA to 1952; Lieut RARO. With Dowsett Gp of shipbuilding and civil engrg cos on major distant water trawler and pre-stressed concrete plant export contracts, 1953–63; Manager, Eastern Trade Dept, Glacier Metal Co. Ltd, 1963–66; Sales Dir, Associated Engrg Export Services Ltd, 1966–71; Sales Dir, GKN Contractors Ltd, 1971–73. Responsible for negotiating and installing USSR, Polish, Czechoslovak and Romanian plain bearing industries, Polish diesel engine component industry, and several other metallurgical and machining plants in E Europe; Export, Financial and Commercial Adviser to various UK and USA cos. Mem. CBI and Soc. of British Engrs delegns to China, Poland, Yugoslavia and Singapore. Mem. Exec. Council, Russo-British Chamber of Commerce, and of London Chamber of Commerce Russian and Polish sections, 1968–73; Adviser to E European Trade Council, 1969–71. Principal Administrator: Credit and Investments Directorate-Gen., EEC Commn, Luxembourg, 1973–75; Agriculture Directorate-Gen., 1975–76; Fisheries Directorate-Gen., Brussels, 1976–79;

Mem., first EEC Vice-Presidential delegn to Poland, 1977. MEP (C) Humberside, 1979–89; Mem., Agriculture and Budgetary Control Cttees, 1979; Chm., Fisheries Working Gp, 1979–84; Vice-Chairman: Fisheries Sub-Cttee, 1984–87; Budgetary Control, 1984–89; Vice-Pres., Eur. Parlt Delegn to China, 1981, 1984, and 1987, Eur. Parlt Delegn to USSR, 1987–89; Chief Whip, EDG, 1987–89. Contested (C) Humberside, Eur. Parly Elecn, 1989. Special Advr on E Europe, Cons. Party, 1990–. Vice Pres., Yorkshire and Humberside Develt Assoc., 1980–87. Chm., Friends of Poland Assoc., Eur. Parlt, 1982–. Occasional lectr at Farnham Castle on East/West trade, and in Poland and USSR on automotive component manufg technology; broadcaster. Member: RIIA; Anglo-Hellenic Soc. Silver Medal for European Merit, Luxembourg, 1981. FBIM 1982. *Publications*: works in English and Russian on distant water trawler operation; articles on fishing technology, shipbuilding and East/West trade; translations from Greek, Russian and other languages. *Recreations*: politics, European and Oriental languages, history, opera, music, travel. *Address*: West Cross, Rockshaw Road, Merstham, Surrey RH1 3BZ. *T*: Merstham (07374) 3783. *Club*: Carlton.

BATTISCOMBE, Christopher Charles Richard; HM Diplomatic Service; Ambassador to Algeria, since 1990; *b* 27 April 1940; *s* of late Lt-Col Christopher Robert Battiscombe and Karin Sigrid (*née* Timberg); *m* 1972, Brigid Melita Theresa Lunn; one *s* one *d*. *Educ*: Wellington Coll.; New Coll., Oxford (BA Greats). Entered FO, 1963; ME Centre for Arabic Studies, Shemlan, Lebanon, 1963–65; Third/Second Sec., Kuwait, 1965–68; FCO, 1968–71; First Secretary: UK Delegn, OECD, Paris, 1971–74; UK Mission to UN, New York, 1974–78; Asst Head, Eastern European and Soviet Dept, FCO, 1978–80; Commercial Counsellor: Cairo, 1981–84; Paris, 1984–86; Counsellor, FCO, 1986–90. *Recreations*: golf, skiing, tennis. *Address*: c/o Foreign and Commonwealth Office, SW1A 2AH. *Club*: Kandahar.

BATTISCOMBE, Mrs (Esther) Georgina, BA; FRSL 1964; author; *b* 21 Nov. 1905; *d* of late George Harwood, MP, Master Cotton Spinner, Bolton, Lancs, and Ellen Hopkinson, *d* of Sir Alfred Hopkinson, KC, MP, First Vice-Chancellor of Manchester Univ.; *m* 1932, Lt-Col Christopher Francis Battiscombe, OBE, FSA (*d* 1964), Grenadier Guards; one *d*. *Educ*: St Michael's Sch., Oxford; Lady Margaret Hall, Oxford. *Publications*: Charlotte Mary Yonge, 1943; Two on Safari, 1946; English Picnics, 1949; Mrs Gladstone, 1956; John Keble (James Tait Black Memorial Prize for best biography of year), 1963; Christina Rossetti (Writers and their Work), 1965; ed, with M. Laski, A Chaplet for Charlotte Yonge, 1965; Queen Alexandra, 1969; Shaftesbury, 1974; Reluctant Pioneer: The Life of Elizabeth Wordsworth, 1978; Christina Rossetti: a divided life, 1981; The Spencers of Althorp, 1984. *Recreation*: looking at churches. *Address*: 40 Phyllis Court Drive, Henley-on-Thames, Oxfordshire RG9 2HU. *T*: Henley (0491) 574830.

BATTISHILL, Sir Anthony (Michael William), KCB 1989; Chairman, Board of Inland Revenue, since 1986 (Deputy Chairman, 1985); *b* 5 July 1937; *s* of William George Battishill and Kathleen Rose Bishop; *m* 1961, Heather Frances Lawes; one *d*. *Educ*: Taunton Sch.; Hele's Sch., Exeter; London Sch. of Economics. BSc (Econ). 2nd Lieut, RAEC, 1958–60. Inland Revenue, 1960–63; HM Treasury, 1963–65; Inland Revenue, 1965–76, Asst Sec., 1970; Central Policy Review Staff, 1976–77; Principal Private Sec. to Chancellor of the Exchequer, HM Treasury, 1977–80; Under Sec., HM Treasury, 1980–82, 1983–85, Inland Revenue, 1982–83. Mem. Ct of Governors, LSE, 1987–. *Recreations*: gardening, old maps. *Address*: The Board Room, Somerset House, WC2R 1LB. *T*: 071–438 7711.

BATTLE, Dennis Frank Orlando; Commissioner and Director of Personnel, HM Customs and Excise, since 1990; *b* 17 Dec. 1942; *s* of Frank William Orlando and Marion Kathleen Battle; *m* 1965, Sandra Moule; one *s* one *d*. *Educ*: Bedford Modern School. Joined Customs and Excise as Exec. Officer, 1962; Higher Exec. Officer, NBPI, 1967; Sen. Exec. Officer, CS Coll., 1972; returned to Customs and Excise, 1975, Grade 7 1978, Asst Sec. 1985. *Recreation*: watching Aldershot play football.

BATTLE, John Dominic; MP (Lab) Leeds West, since 1987; *b* 26 April 1951; *s* of John and Audrey Battle; *m* 1977, Mary Meenan; one *s* two *d*. *Educ*: Leeds Univ. (BA Hons (1st cl.) 1976). Training for RC Priesthood, Upholland Coll., 1969–72; Leeds Univ., 1973–77; Res. Officer to Derek Enright, MEP, 1979–83; Nat. Co-ordinator, Church Action on Poverty, 1983–87. Main political interests are housing policy, economic affairs and poverty at home and abroad. *Recreation*: poetry. *Address*: 26 Victoria Park Avenue, Leeds LS5 3DG. *T*: Leeds (0532) 789094.

BATTY, Peter Wright; television and film producer, director and writer; Chief Executive, Peter Batty Productions, since 1970; *b* 18 June 1931; *s* of late Ernest Faulkner Batty and Gladys Victoria Wright; *m* 1959, Anne Elizabeth Stringer; two *s* one *d*. *Educ*: Bede Grammar Sch., Sunderland; Queen's Coll., Oxford. Feature-writer, Financial Times, 1954–56; freelance journalist, 1956–58; Producer, BBC TV, 1958–64: mem. original Tonight team, other prodns incl. The Quiet Revolution, The Big Freeze, The Katanga Affair, Sons of the Navvy Man; Editor, Tonight, 1963–64; Exec. Producer and Associate Head of Factual Programming, ATV, 1964–68: prodns incl. The Fall and Rise of the House of Krupp (Grand Prix for Documentary, Venice Film Fest., 1965; Silver Dove, Leipzig Film Fest., 1965), The Road to Suez, The Suez Affair, Vietnam Fly-in, Battle for the Desert; freelance work for BBC TV, ITV and Channel 4, 1968–. Progs dir., prod and scripted incl. The Plutocrats, The Aristocrats, Battle for Cassino, Battle for the Bulge, Birth of the Bomb, Farouk: last of the Pharaohs, Operation Barbarossa, Superspy, Sunderland's Pride and Passion, A Rothschild and his Red Gold, Search for the Super, Spy Extraordinary, Story of Wine, World of Television, The Rise and Rise of Laura Ashley, The Gospel According to St Michael, Battle for Warsaw, Battle for Dien Bien Phu, Nuclear Nightmares, A Turn Up in a Million, Il Poverello, Swindle!, The Algerian War, Fonteyn and Nureyev: the perfect partnership, The Divided Union, A Time for Remembrance, Swastika over British Soil; prod and scripted 6 episodes World at War series. *Publications*: The House of Krupp, 1966; (with Peter Parish) The Divided Union, 1987; La Guerre d'Algérie, 1989. *Recreations*: walking, reading, listening to music. *Address*: Claremont House, Renfrew Road, Kingston, Surrey KT2 7NT. *T*: 081–942 6304. *Club*: White Elephant.

BATTY, Mrs Ronald; see Foyle, C. A. L.

BATTY, Sir William (Bradshaw), Kt 1973; TD 1946; Chairman, Ford Motor Co. Ltd, 1972–75, retired (Managing Director, 1968–73); *b* 15 May 1913; *s* of Rowland and Nellie Batty; *m* 1946, Jean Ella Brice; one *s* one *d* (and one *s* decd). *Educ*: Hulme Grammar Sch., Manchester. Served War of 1939–45, RASC (Lt-Col). Apprentice toolmaker, Ford Motor Co. Ltd, Trafford Park, Manchester, 1930; Co. trainee, 1933; Press liaison, Advertising Dept, 1936; Service Dept, 1937; Tractor Sales Dept, 1945; Asst Man., Tractor Dept, 1948; Man., Tractor and Implement Product Planning, 1953; Man., Tractor Div., 1955; Gen. Man., Tractor Gp, 1961; Dir, Tractor Gp, 1963; Dir, Car and Truck Gp, 1964; Exec. Dir, 1963–75. Chairman: Ford Motor Credit Co. Ltd, 1968 (Dir, 1963–); Automotive Finance Ltd, 1970–75; Director: Henry Ford & Son Ltd, Cork, 1965–75; Ford Lusitana SARL, Portugal, 1973–75. Mem., Engineering Industries Council, 1975–76. Pres., SMMT, 1975–76. Hon. LLD Manchester, 1976. FBIM. *Recreations*: golf, sailing,

gardening. *Address*: Glenhaven Cottage, Riverside Road West, Newton Ferrers, South Devon. *Club*: Royal Western Yacht.

BAUER, family name of **Baron Bauer.**

BAUER, Baron *cr* 1982 (Life Peer), of Market Ward in the City of Cambridge; **Peter Thomas Bauer,** MA; DSc; FBA; Professor of Economics (with special reference to economic development and under-developed countries) in the University of London, at the London School of Economics, 1960–83, now Emeritus Professor of Economics; Fellow of Gonville and Caius College, Cambridge, 1946–60, and since 1968; *b* 6 Nov. 1915; unmarried. *Educ*: Scholae Piae, Budapest; Gonville and Caius Coll., Cambridge. Reader in Agricultural Economics, University of London, 1947–48; University Lecturer in Economics, Cambridge Univ., 1948–56; Smuts Reader in Commonwealth Studies, Cambridge Univ., 1956–60. *Publications*: books and articles on applied economics. *Address*: House of Lords, Westminster, SW1A 0PW. *Clubs*: Garrick, Beefsteak.

BAUGH, John Trevor; Director General of Supplies and Transport (Naval), Ministry of Defence, since 1986; *b* 24 Sept. 1932; *s* of late Thomas Harold Baugh and of Nellie Baugh (*née* Machin); *m* 1st, 1956, Pauline Andrews (decd); three *s*; 2nd, 1981, Noreen Rita Rosemary Sykes; two step *s*. *Educ*: Queen Elizabeth's Hospital, Bristol. MCIT 1956. Asst Naval Store Officer, Devonport, 1953; Dep. Naval Store Officer, Admiralty, 1959; Armament Supply Officer, Alexandria, 1966; Principal, MoD, Bath, 1970; Supt, RN Store Depot, Copenacre, 1974; Asst Sec., MoD (Navy), 1976, Exec. Dir, 1979; MoD (Army), 1983, Asst Under Sec. of State 1985. *Recreations*: bridge, golf. *Address*: c/o Ministry of Defence, Ensleigh, Bath BA1 5AB. *T*: Bath (0225) 467707. *Clubs*: Athenæum; Bath Golf.

BAUGHAN, Julian James; QC 1990; a Recorder, since 1985; *b* 8 Feb. 1944; *s* of Prof. E. C. Baughan, CBE, and late Mrs E. C. Baughan. *Educ*: Eton Coll. (King's Schol.); Balliol Coll., Oxford (Brassey Italian Schol.; BA History). Called to Bar, Inner Temple, 1967 (Profumo Schol., Philip Teichman Schol., Major Schol.); Prosecuting Counsel to DTI, 1983. *Address*: 13 King's Bench Walk, Temple, EC4Y 7EN.

BAUGHEN, Rt. Rev. Michael Alfred; see Chester, Bishop of.

BAUM, Prof. (John) David, MD; FRCP; Professor of Child Health, since 1985, and Founding Director, Institute of Child Health, since 1988, University of Bristol; *b* 23 July 1940; *s* of Isidor and Mary Baum; *m* 1967, Angela Rose Goschalk; four *s*. *Educ*: Univ. of Birmingham. MB ChB, MA, MSc, MD, DCH. Royal Postgrad. Med. Sch., 1967; Lectr then Clinical Reader in Paed., Oxford, 1972; Professorial Fellow, St Catherine's Coll., Oxford, 1977. Vis. Prof., Univ. of Colorado Med. Center, 1969. Founding Chm., Nat. Assoc. for Care of Children with Life Threatening Diseases and their Families, 1990–; Trustee: MusicSpace, Cancer & Leukemia in Childhood Trust; Arts in Hospital Trust; Bristol Family Conciliation Service. FRSA. Inventor, Silver Swaddler, 1968. Guthrie Medal, BPA, 1976. *Publications*: Clinical Paediatric Physiology, 1979; Care of the Child with Diabetes, 1985; (ed jtly) Listen, my child has a lot of living to do: caring for children with life-threatening conditions, 1990; numerous papers on child care. *Recreations*: visual arts, politics of child health, the environment. *Address*: 19 Charlotte Street, Bristol BS1 5PZ. *T*: Bristol (0272) 260448. *Club*: Oxford University Choolant Society.

See also M. Baum.

BAUM, Prof. Michael, ChM; FRCS; Professor of Surgery, Institute of Cancer Research, Royal Marsden Hospital, London, since 1990; *b* 31 May 1937; *s* of Isidor and Mary Baum; *m* 1965, Judith (*née* Marcus); one *s* two *d*. *Educ*: Univ. of Birmingham (MB, ChB; ChM). FRCS 1965. Lecturer in Surgery, King's College Hosp., 1969–72; Research Fellow, Univ. of Pittsburgh, USA, 1971–72; Reader in Surgery, Welsh National Sch. of Medicine, Cardiff, 1972–78; Hon. Cons. Surgeon, King's College Hosp., 1978–80. Prof. of Surgery, KCH Med. Sch., London, 1980–90. Chairman: SE Thames Regional Cancer Organisation, 1988–; British Breast Gp, 1989–; Breast Cancer Trials Cttee, 1989–; UK Co-ordinating Cttee for Cancer Research, 1989–. Mem., Adv. Cttee on Breast Cancer Screening, DHSS, 1987–. Hon. MD Göteborg, 1986. *Publications*: Breast Cancer—The Facts, 1981, rev. edn 1987; multiple pubns on breast cancer, cancer therapy, cancer biology and the philosophy of science. *Recreations*: painting, theatre, reading, philosophizing. *Address*: 22 Red Post Hill, SE24 9JQ. *T*: 071–733 6229. *Clubs*: Athenæum, Royal Society of Medicine.

BAUMAN, Robert Patten; Chief Executive, SmithKline Beecham, since 1989 (Chairman and Chief Executive, Beecham Group, 1986–89); *b* 27 March 1931; *s* of John Nevan Bauman Jr and Lucille Miller Patten; *m* 1961, Patricia Hughes Jones; one *s* one *d*. *Educ*: Ohio Wesleyan Univ. (BA); Harvard Sch. of Business (MBA). Served USAF, 1955–57. General Foods Corp., 1958–81: Corp. Vice-Pres., 1968; Group Vice-Pres., 1970; Exec. Vice-Pres. and Corp. Dir, 1972–81; Pres., Internat. Ops, 1974–81; Dir, Avco Corp., 1980, Chm. and Chief Exec., 1981–85; Vice-Chm. and Dir, Textron Inc., 1985–86. Director: Cap Cities/ABC Inc., 1986–; Union Pacific Corp., 1987–; CIONA Corp., 1990–. Mem., MRC, 1991–. Trustee: Ohio Wesleyan Univ., 1982–; Royal Botanic Gardens, Kew, 1990–. *Publication*: Plants as Pets, 1982. *Recreations*: growing orchids, tennis, photography, golf. *Address*: c/o SmithKline Beecham, Beecham House, Great West Road, Brentford, Middx TW8 9BD. *T*: 081–560 5151. *Clubs*: Queen's; Blind Brook (New York); Walton Heath Golf.

BAUR, Christopher Frank; writer; Editor, The Scotsman, 1985–87; *b* 28 May 1942; *s* of Mrs Marty Stewart (*née* Sigg) and Frank Baur; *m* 1965, Jaqueline Gilchrist; four *s*. *Educ*: Dalhousie Prep. Sch.; Strathallan Sch., Perthshire. Joined Scotsman as copy boy, 1960; trained as journalist; Scotsman's Industrial Reporter, 1963; additionally Scottish Politics, 1972; Financial Times, Scottish corresp., 1973; Scottish political corresp., BBC, 1976; Asst Editor, Scotsman, 1978, writing on politics and economic affairs; Dep. Editor, Scotsman, 1983–85. *Recreation*: creating. *Address*: 29 Edgehead Village, near Pathhead, Midlothian. *T*: Ford (0875) 320476.

BAVERSTOCK, Donald Leighton; Executive Producer, Television, BBC Manchester, 1975–77; *b* 18 Jan. 1924; *s* of Thomas Philip Baverstock and Sarah Ann; *m* 1957, Gillian Mary, *d* of late Mrs Kenneth Darrell Waters (Enid Blyton); one *s* two *d*. (and one *s* decd). *Educ*: Canton High Sch., Cardiff; Christ Church, Oxford (MA). Served with RAF, 1943–46; completed tour of operations Bomber Command, 1944; Instructor, Navigation, 1944–46. History Master, Wellington Coll., 1949. Producer, BBC General Overseas Service, 1950–54; Producer, BBC Television Service, 1954–57; Editor, Tonight Programme, 1957–61; Asst Controller, Television Programmes, BBC, 1961–63; Chief of Programmes BBC TV (1), 1963–65; Partner, Jay, Baverstock, Milne & Co., 1965–67; Dir of Programmes, Yorkshire TV, 1967–73; Man. Dir, Granada Video Ltd, 1974–75. *Address*: Low Hall, Middleton, Ilkley, Yorks. *T*: Ilkley (0943) 608037.

BAVIN, Alfred Robert Walter, CB 1966; Deputy Secretary, Department of Health and Social Security, 1968–73 (Ministry of Health, 1966–68); *b* 4 April 1917; *s* of late Alfred and late Annie Bavin; *m* 1947, Helen Mansfield (*d* 1987); one *s* three *d*. *Educ*: Christ's Hosp.; Balliol Coll., Oxford. 1st cl. Hon. Mods 1937; 1st cl. Lit. Hum. 1939. Min. of Health, Asst Principal, 1939, Principal, 1946; Cabinet Office, 1948–50; Min. of Health,

Principal Private Sec. to Minister, 1951; Asst Sec. 1952; Under-Sec. 1960. Nuffield Home Civil Service Travelling Fellowship, 1956. *Address:* 86 Chapel Lane, Sands, High Wycombe, Bucks HP12 4BS. *Clubs:* Athenæum, MCC.

BAVIN, Rt. Rev. Timothy John; *see* Portsmouth, Bishop of.

BAWDEN, Prof. Charles Roskelly, FBA; Professor of Mongolian, University of London, 1970–84, now Emeritus Professor; *b* 22 April 1924; *s* of George Charles Bawden and Eleanor Alice Adelaide Bawden (*née* Russell); *m* 1949, Jean Barham Johnson; three *s* one *d. Educ:* Weymouth Grammar School; Peterhouse, Cambridge (MA, PhD, Dipl. in Oriental Languages). War Service, RNVR, 1943–46. Asst Principal, German Section, Foreign Office, 1948–49; Lectr in Mongolian, SOAS, 1955; Reader in Mongolian, 1962, and Prof., 1970, Univ. of London; Head of Dept of Far East, SOAS, 1970–84; Pro-Director, SOAS, 1982–84. FBA 1971–80, 1985; Mem. corresp., Soc. Finno-Ougrienne 1975. *Publications:* The Mongol Chronicle Altan Tobči, 1955; The Jebtsundamba Khutukhtus of Urga, 1961; The Modern History of Mongolia, 1968, 2nd edn 1989; The Chester Beatty Library: a catalogue of the Mongolian Collection, 1969; Shamans Lamas and Evangelicals: the English missionaries in Siberia, 1985; articles and reviews in SOAS Bull., Central Asiatic Jl, Zentralasiatische Studien and other periodicals. *Address:* c/o School of Oriental and African Studies, University of London, Thornhaugh Street, Russell Square, WC1H 0XG.

BAWDEN, Nina Mary, (Mrs A. S. Kark), MA; FRSL; JP; novelist; *b* 19 Jan. 1925; *d* of Charles and Ellalaine Ursula May Mabey; *m* 1st, 1946, Henry Walton Bawden; one *s* (and one *s* decd); 2nd, 1954, Austen Steven Kark, *qv*; one *d. Educ:* Ilford County High Sch.; Somerville Coll., Oxford (BA). Asst, Town and Country Planning Assoc., 1946–47. JP Surrey, 1968. Mem., ALCS. Pres., Soc. of Women Writers and Journalists. *Publications: novels:* Who Calls the Tune, 1953; The Odd Flamingo, 1954; Change Here for Babylon, 1955; Devil by the Sea, 1958, 2nd edn 1972 (abridged for children, 1976); The Solitary Child, 1956; Just Like a Lady, 1960; In Honour Bound, 1961; Tortoise by Candlelight, 1963; Under the Skin, 1964; A Little Love, a Little Learning, 1965; A Woman of My Age, 1967; The Grain of Truth, 1969; The Birds on the Trees, 1970; Anna Apparent, 1972; George beneath a Paper Moon, 1974; Afternoon of a Good Woman, 1976 (Yorkshire Post Novel of the Year, 1976); Familiar Passions, 1979; Walking Naked, 1981; The Ice House, 1983; Circles of Deceit, 1987 (televised, 1990); Family Money, 1991; *for children:* The Secret Passage; On the Run; The White Horse Gang; The Witch's Daughter; A Handful of Thieves; The Runaway Summer; Squib; Carrie's War; The Peppermint Pig (Guardian award, 1976); Rebel on a Rock, 1978; The Robbers, 1979; Kept in the Dark, 1982; The Finding, 1985; Princess Alice, 1985; Keeping Henry, 1988; The Outside Child, 1989. *Recreations:* travelling, reading, politics, friends. *Address:* 22 Noel Road, N1 8HA. *T:* 071–226 2839; 19 Kapodistriou, Nauplion, Greece 21100. *Clubs:* Oriental, Lansdowne, PEN, Society of Authors.

BAWN, Cecil Edwin Henry, CBE 1956; FRS 1952; BSc, PhD; Brunner Professor of Physical Chemistry in the University of Liverpool, 1969–Dec. 1973, now Emeritus (Grant-Brunner Professor of Inorganic and Physical Chemistry, 1948–69); *b* 6 Nov. 1908; British; *m* 1934, Winifred Mabel Jackson; two *s* one *d. Educ:* Cotham Grammar Sch., Bristol. Graduated, Univ. of Bristol, 1929; PhD in Chemistry (Bristol), 1932; Asst Lectr in Chemistry, Univ. of Manchester, 1931–34; Lectr in Chemistry, 1934–38; Lectr in Physical Chemistry, Univ. of Bristol, 1938–45; Reader in Physical Chemistry, 1945–49. During War of 1939–45 was in charge of a Physico-Chemical Section in Armament Research Dept, Min. of Supply. Mem., Univ. Grants Cttee, 1965–74. Swinburne Gold Medal, 1966. Hon. DSc: Bradford, 1966; Birmingham, 1968; Bristol, 1974. *Publications:* The Chemistry of High Polymers, 1948; papers in chemical journals. *Address:* Springfields, Stoodleigh, near Tiverton, Devon EX16 9PT. *T:* Oakford (03985) 220.

BAWTREE, Rear Adm. David Kenneth, EurIng, CEng, FIMechE, FIEE; Flag Officer, Portsmouth, since 1990; *b* 1 Oct. 1937; *s* of Kenneth Alfred Bawtree and Dorothy Constance Bawtree (*née* Allen); *m* 1962, Ann Cummins; one *s* one *d. Educ:* Christ's Hospital; Royal Naval Engineering College. BSc(Eng). Served in HM Ships Maidstone, Jutland, Diamond, Defender, Rothesay, Bristol, and MoD, 1965–76; Staff of C-in-C Fleet, 1979, of DG Weapons, 1981; Dep. Dir, Naval Analysis, 1983; RCDS 1985; Dep. Dir, Op. Requirements (Navy), 1986; Dir, Naval Manning and Training (Eng), 1987–90. *Recreations:* squash, organs and their music, miniature furniture. *Address:* HM Naval Base, Portsmouth, Hants PO1 3LT. *T:* Portsmouth (0705) 822351.

BAXANDALL, David Kighley, CBE 1959; Director of National Galleries of Scotland, 1952–70, retired; *b* 11 Oct. 1905; *m* 1931, Isobel (*d* 1990), *d* of Canon D. J. Thomas; one *s* twin *d. Educ:* King's Coll. Sch., Wimbledon; King's Coll., University of London. Asst Keeper, 1929–39, and Keeper of the Department of Art, 1939–41, National Museum of Wales. Served in RAF, 1941–45. Dir of Manchester City Art Galleries, 1945–52. *Publications:* Ben Nicholson, 1962; numerous articles, gallery handbooks, catalogues and broadcast talks. *Address:* 24 Guardian Court, Ferrers Street, Hereford HR1 2LP. *T:* Hereford (0432) 357881.

See also M. D. K. Baxandall.

BAXANDALL, Prof. Michael David Kighley, FBA 1982; Professor of the History of Art, University of California, Berkeley, since 1987; *b* 18 Aug. 1933; *o s* of David Baxandall, *qv*; *m* 1963, Katharina Simon; one *s* one *d. Educ:* Manchester Grammar Sch.; Downing Coll., Cambridge (MA); Univs of Pavia and Munich. Jun. Res. Fellow, Warburg Inst., 1959–61; Asst Keeper, Dept of Architecture and Sculpture, Victoria and Albert Museum, 1961–65; Warburg Institute, University of London: Lectr in Renaissance Studies, 1965–73; Reader, 1973–81; Prof., History of the Classical Tradition, 1981–88. Slade Prof. of Fine Art, Univ. of Oxford, 1974–75; A. D. White Prof.-at-Large, Cornell Univ., 1982–88. *Publications:* Giotto and the Orators, 1971; Painting and Experience in Fifteenth-Century Italy, 1972; South German Sculpture 1480–1530 in the Victoria and Albert Museum, 1974; The Limewood Sculptors of Renaissance Germany, 1980; Patterns of Intention, 1985. *Address:* 405 Doe Library, University of California, Berkeley, Calif 94720, USA.

BAXENDELL, Sir Peter (Brian), Kt 1981; CBE 1972; FEng 1978; FIC 1983; Chairman, Hawker Siddeley Group PLC, since 1986 (Director, since 1984; Deputy Chairman, Jan–April 1986); Director: Shell Transport and Trading Co., since 1973 (Chairman, 1979–85); Inchcape PLC, since 1986; Sun Life Assurance Co. of Canada, since 1986; *b* 28 Feb. 1925; *s* of Lesley Wilfred Edward Baxendell and Evelyn Mary Baxendell (*née* Gaskin); *m* 1949, Rosemary (*née* Lacey); two *s* two *d. Educ:* St Francis Xavier's, Liverpool; Royal School of Mines, London (ARSM, BSc; FIC 1983). Joined Royal Dutch/Shell Group, 1946; Petroleum Engr in Egypt, 1947, and Venezuela, 1950; Techn. Dir, Shell-BP Nigeria, 1963; Head of SE Asia Div., London, 1966; Man. Dir, Shell-BP Nigeria, 1969; Man. Dir, 1973–75, Chm., 1974–79, Shell UK; Man. Dir, 1973, Chm., Cttee of Man. Dirs, 1982–85, Royal Dutch/Shell Gp of Cos; Chm., Shell Canada Ltd, 1980–85; Dir, Shell Oil Co., USA, 1982–85. Mem., UGC, 1983–89. Hon. DSc: Heriot-Watt, 1982; QUB, 1986; London, 1986; Loughborough, 1987. Commander, Order of Orange–Nassau, 1985. *Publications:* articles on petroleum engrg subjects in scientific jls. *Recreations:* tennis, fishing. *Address:* Shell Centre, SE1 7NA. *T:* 071–934 2772.

BAXTER, Maj.-Gen. Ian Stuart, CBE 1982 (MBE 1973); antiques dealer, since 1990; *b* 20 July 1937; *s* of Charles Baxter and Edith (*née* Trinder); *m* 1961, Meg Bullock; three *d. Educ:* Ottershaw Sch. Commissioned RASC, 1958; RCT, 1965; regtl and staff appts UK, NI, Kenya, India, Germany and Falkland Is; sc, Camberley, 1970; ndc, Latimer, 1974; DS, Staff Coll., Camberley, 1975–78; CO, 2nd Armoured Div., Regt RCT, 1978–80; Col AQ Commando Forces, RM, 1980–83 (incl. Falklands Campaign); RCDS, 1984; Dir, Army Recruiting, 1985–87; ACDS (Logistics), 1987–90, retd. Col Comdt, RCT, 1989–. Dir (non-exec.), Cornwall Community Healthcare NHS Trust, 1990–. *Recreations:* antique restoration, Rugby. *Address:* c/o Barclays Bank, 17/21 High Street, East Grinstead, West Sussex RH19 3AH.

BAXTER, John Lawson; DL; *b* 25 Nov. 1939; *s* of John Lawson Baxter and Enid Maud Taggart; *m* 1967; three *s. Educ:* Trinity Coll., Dublin; Queen's Univ., Belfast; BA, BComm, LLB; LLM Tulane Univ., New Orleans. Solicitor. Mem. (U) N Ireland Assembly, for N Antrim, 1973–75; Minister of Information, N Ireland Executive, 1974. Chm. (part-time), Industrial Tribunals (NI), 1980–83; Mem., Northern Health and Social Services Board, 1982–. DL Co Londonderry, 1988. *Recreations:* golf, fishing. *Address:* Beardiville, Cloyfin, Coleraine, N Ireland. *T:* Bushmills (02657) 31552.

BAXTER, John Walter, CBE 1974; Consultant, G. Maunsell & Partners (Partner, 1955, Senior Partner, 1959–80); *b* 4 June 1917; *s* of late J. G. Baxter and late D. L. Baxter (*née* Phelps); *m* 1941, Jessie, *d* of late T. Pimblott; one *d. Educ:* Westminster City Sch.; City and Guilds Engrg College. BSc(Eng), FCGI, FEng, FICE, FRSA. Civil Engineer: Trussed Concrete Steel Co. Ltd, 1936–41; Shell Refining Co. Ltd, 1941–52; Maunsell Posford & Pavry, 1952–55. President: ICE, 1976–77 (Vice-Pres., 1973–76, Mem. Council, 1963–68 and 1970–79); Smeatonian Soc. of Civil Engrs, 1986; Vice-Chm., ACE, 1979–80, Chm., 1980–81. *Publications:* contrib. Proc. ICE. *Address:* The Down Side, Itchen Abbas, Hants SO21 1AZ.

BAXTER, Prof. Murdoch Scott, PhD, CChem, FRSC; FRSE; Director, International Laboratory of Marine Radioactivity, Monaco, since 1990; *b* 12 March 1944; *s* of John Sawyer Napier Baxter and Margaret Hastie Baxter (*née* Murdoch); *m* 1968, Janice Henderson; one *s. Educ:* Univ. of Glasgow. BSc Hons Chem. 1966, PhD Geochem. 1969. Research Fellow, State Univ. of NY (Noble gas history of lunar rocks and meteorites), 1969–70; Lectr, Dept of Chemistry, Univ. of Glasgow (geochem., radiochem. and envtl radioactivity), 1970–85; Vis. Consultant, IAEA (nuclear waste disposal), 1981–82; Dir, Scottish Univs Res. and Reactor Centre, 1985–90; Personal Chair, Univ. of Glasgow, 1985–90. Member: Challenger Soc. for Marine Sci.; Scottish Marine Biol Assoc.; NERC Coger Cttee. FRSE 1989. Exec. Editor, JL of Envtl Radioactivity; Mem., Editl Bd, Jl of Radioanalytical and Nuclear Chem. *Publications:* numerous papers to professional jls. *Recreations:* hill walking, golf, sport watching, caravanning, keeping dogs. *Address:* International Laboratory of Marine Radioactivity, International Atomic Energy Agency, 19 Avenue des Castellans, Monaco 98000.

BAXTER, Raymond Frederic, FRSA; broadcaster and writer; *b* 25 Jan. 1922; *s* of Frederick Garfield Baxter and Rosina Baxter (*née* Rivers); *m* 1945, Sylvia Kathryn (*née* Johnson), Boston, Mass; one *s* one *d. Educ:* Ilford County High Sch. Joined RAF, 1940; flew Spitfires with 65, 93 and 602 Sqdns, in UK, Med. and Europe. Entered Forces Broadcasting in Cairo, still as serving officer, 1945; civilian deputy Dir BFN BBC, 1947–49; subseq. short attachment West Region and finally joined Outside Broadcast Dept, London; with BBC until 1966; Dir, Motoring Publicity, BMC, 1967–68. Member Cttee of Management: RNLI, 1979– (Vice Pres., 1987–); Air League, 1980–85. Hon. Freeman, City of London, 1978; Liveryman, GAPAN, 1983. Hon. Admiral, Assoc. of Dunkirk Little Ships, 1982–. *Publications:* (with James Burke and Michael Latham) Tomorrow's World, Vol. 1, 1970, Vol. 2, 1971; Farnborough Commentary, 1980; film commentaries, articles and reports on motoring and aviation subjects, etc. *Recreations:* motoring, riding, boating. *Address:* The Green Cottage, Wargrave Road, Henley-on-Thames, Oxon RG9 3HX. *T:* Henley-on-Thames (0491) 571081. *Clubs:* Royal Air Force, British Racing Drivers, etc.

BAXTER, Prof. Rodney James, FRS 1982; FAA 1977; Professor in the Departments of Theoretical Physics and Mathematics, Institute of Advanced Studies, Australian National University, since 1981; *b* 8 Feb. 1940; *s* of Thomas James Baxter and Florence A. Baxter; *m* 1968, Elizabeth Phillips; one *s* one *d. Educ:* Bancroft's Sch., Essex; Trinity Coll., Cambridge; Australian National Univ. Reservoir Engineer, Iraq Petroleum Co., 1964–65; Research Fellow, ANU, 1965–68; Asst Prof., Mathematics Dept, Massachusetts Inst. of Technology, 1968–70; Fellow, ANU, 1970–81. Pawsey Medal, Aust. Acad. of Science, 1975; Boltzmann Medal, IUPAP, 1980; Heineman Prize, Amer. Inst. of Physics, 1987. *Publications:* Exactly Solved Models in Statistical Mechanics, 1982; contribs to Proc. Royal Soc., Jl of Physics A, Physical Rev., Statistical Physics, Annals of Physics. *Recreation:* theatre. *Address:* Theoretical Physics IAS, Australian National University, Canberra, ACT 2601, Australia. *T:* (062) 492968.

BAXTER, Roger George, PhD; FRAS, FRSA; Headmaster of Sedbergh School, since 1982; *b* 21 April 1940; *s* of Rev. Benjamin George Baxter and Gweneth Muriel Baxter (*née* Causer); *m* 1967, Dorothy Ann Cook; one *s* one *d. Educ:* Handsworth Grammar Sch., Birmingham; Univ. of Sheffield (BSc, PhD). Junior Research Fellow, Univ. of Sheffield, 1965–66, Lectr, Dept of Applied Mathematics, 1966–70; Asst Mathematics Master, Winchester Coll., 1970–81, Under Master, 1976–81. Governor: Bramcote Sch., Scarborough, 1982–; Hurworth Hse Sch., Darlington, 1982–; Cathedral Choir Sch., Ripon, 1984–; Mowden Hall Sch., Northumberland, 1984–; Cundall Manor Sch., York, 1988–. Member: HMC Academic Policy Cttee, 1985–90; Common Entrance Board, 1989–. *Publications:* various papers on numerical studies in magnetoplasma diffusion with applications to the F-2 layer of the ionosphere. *Recreations:* opera, music, cooking, wine. *Address:* Birksholme, Sedbergh, Cumbria LA10 5HQ. *T:* Sedbergh (05396) 20491.

BAXTER, Walter; author; *b* 1915. *Educ:* St Lawrence, Ramsgate; Trinity Hall, Cambridge. Worked in the City, 1936–39; served War of 1939–45, with KOYLI in Burma; afterwards, in India, ADC to General Slim, and on Staff of a Corps HQ during re-conquest of Burma. After completion of first novel, returned to India to work temporarily on a mission. *Publications:* Look Down in Mercy, 1951; The Image and The Search, 1953. *Address:* 119 Old Brompton Road, SW7 3RN.

BAXTER, William T., BCom Edinburgh; Professor of Accounting, London School of Economics, 1947–73, Hon. Fellow 1980; *b* 27 July 1906; *s* of W. M. Baxter and Margaret Threipland; *m* 1st, 1940, Marjorie Allanson (*d* 1971); one *s* one *d*; 2nd, 1973, Leena-Kaisa Laitakari-Kaila. *Educ:* George Watson's Coll.; Univ. of Edinburgh. Chartered Accountant (Edinburgh), 1930; Commonwealth Fund Fellow, 1931, at Harvard Univ.; Lectr in Accounting, Univ. of Edinburgh, 1934; Prof. of Accounting, Univ. of Cape Town, 1937. Hon. DLitt: Kent at Canterbury, 1974; Heriot-Watt, 1976; Hon. DSc Buckingham, 1983; Hon. DSc(Econ) Hull, 1977. *Publications:* Income Tax for Professional Students,

1936; The House of Hancock, 1945; Depreciation, 1971; Accounting Values and Inflation, 1975; Collected Papers on Accounting, 1979; Inflation Accounting, 1984. *Address:* 1 The Ridgeway, NW11. *T:* 081–455 6810.

BAYDA, Hon. Edward Dmytro; Chief Justice of Saskatchewan, since 1981; *b* 9 Sept. 1931; *s* of Dmytro Andrew Bayda and Mary Bilinski; *m* 1953, Marie-Thérèse Yvonne Gagné; one *s* five *d.* *Educ:* Univ. of Saskatchewan (BA 1951, LLB 1953). Called to the Bar, Saskatchewan, 1954; QC (Sask) 1966. Senior Partner, Bayda, Halvorson, Scheibel & Thompson, 1966–72. Judge, Court of Queen's Bench, 1972; Justice, Court of Appeal, 1974. Hon. LLD 1989. KM 1975. *Address:* (home) 9 Turnbull Place, Regina, Sask S4S 4H2, Canada. *T:* 586–2126; (chambers) Court House, 2425 Victoria Avenue, Regina, Sask S4P 3V7. *T:* 787–5415.

BAYFIELD, Rabbi Anthony Michael; Director, Sternberg Centre for Judaism (Manor House Trust), London, since 1982; *b* 4 July 1946; *s* of Ronald Bayfield and Sheila (*née* Mann); *m* 1969, Linda Gavinia (*née* Rose); one *s* two *d.* *Educ:* Royal Liberty Sch., Gidea Park; Magdalene Coll., Cambridge (MA (Hons) Law); Leo Baeck Coll., London (Rabbinic degree). Rabbi, NW Surrey Synagogue, 1972–82; Dir, Advancement of Jewish Educn Trust, 1987–; Co-ordinator of Supervisors, Leo Baeck Coll., 1987–. Chairman: Assembly of Rabbis, Reform Synagogues of GB, 1980–82; Council of Reform and Liberal Rabbis, 1984–86. Founder Editor, Manna (Qly Jl of Progressive Judaism), 1983–. *Publications:* Churban: the murder of the Jews of Europe, 1981; articles in European Judaism, Brit. Jl of Religious Educn, Church Times. *Recreations:* family life, reading, walking, Essex CCC, suffering with West Ham United FC. *Address:* Sternberg Centre for Judaism, The Manor House, 80 East End Road, Finchley, N3 2SY. *T:* 081–346 2288.

BAYLEY, Gordon Vernon, CBE 1976; FIA, FIMA, FSS, CBIM; Chairman, Swiss Reinsurance Co. (UK) Ltd, since 1985; Director, National Provident Institution, since 1970; *b* 25 July 1920; *s* of late Capt. Vernon Bayley, King's Regt, and Mrs Gladys Maud Bayley; *m* 1945, Miriam Allenby, *d* of late Frederick Walter Ellis and Miriam Ellis, Eastbourne; one *s* two *d.* *Educ:* Abingdon. Joined HM Forces, 1940; commissioned Royal Artillery, Major 1945. Asst Actuary, Equitable Life Assurance Soc., 1949; Partner, Duncan C. Fraser and Co. (Actuaries), 1954–57; National Provident Institution: Assistant Sec., 1957, Joint Sec. 1959; Gen. Manager and Actuary 1964–85. Dir, TR Industrial and Gen. Trust PLC, 1983–88. Mem., Occupational Pensions Bd, 1973–74. Member: Cttee to Review the Functioning of Financial Institutions, 1977–80; Companies House Steering Bd, 1988–90. Institute of Actuaries: Fellow, 1946; Hon. Sec., 1960–62; Vice-Pres., 1964–67; Pres., 1974–76; Chm., Life Offices Assoc., 1969–70 (Dep. Chm., 1967–68). Chm., Bd of Governors, Abingdon Sch., 1979–83. *Publications:* contribs to Jl Inst. Actuaries, Jl Royal Statistical Soc. *Recreations:* ski-ing, sailing. *Address:* The Old Manor, Witley, Surrey. *T:* Wormley (042879) 2301. *Clubs:* Athenæum, English Speaking Union; Sea View Yacht.

BAYLEY, Dame Iris; *see* Murdoch, Dame J. I.

BAYLEY, Prof. John Oliver, FBA 1990; Warton Professor of English Literature, and Fellow of St Catherine's College, University of Oxford, 1974–Sept. 1992; *b* 27 March 1925; *s* of F. J. Bayley; *m* 1956, Dame Jean Iris Murdoch, *qv.* *Educ:* Eton; New Coll., Oxford. 1st cl. hons English Oxon 1950. Served in Army, 1943–47. Mem., St Antony's and Magdalen Colls, Oxford, 1951–55; Fellow and Tutor in English, New Coll., Oxford, 1955–74. *Publications:* In Another Country (novel), 1954; The Romantic Survival: A Study in Poetic Evolution, 1956; The Characters of Love, 1961; Tolstoy and the Novel, 1966; Pushkin: A Comparative Commentary, 1971; The Uses of Division: unity and disharmony in literature, 1976; An Essay on Hardy, 1978; Shakespeare and Tragedy, 1981; The Order of Battle at Trafalgar, 1987; The Short Story: Henry James to Elizabeth Bowen, 1988.

BAYLEY, Nicola Mary; writer, artist and illustrator; *b* 18 Aug. 1949; *d* of Percy Harold Bayley and Ann Barbara Crowder; *m* 1978, Alan John Howard Hilton, *qv*; one *s.* *Educ:* Farnborough Hill Convent College; St Martin's Sch. of Art (DipAD); Royal College of Art (MA Illus.). *Publications: written and illustrated:* Nicola Bayley's Book of Nursery Rhymes, 1975; One Old Oxford Ox, 1977; Copy Cats (5 books), 1984; As I was Going Up and Down, 1985; Hush-a-bye Baby, 1985; *illustrated:* Tyger Voyage, 1976; Puss in Boots, 1976; La Corona and the Tin Frog, 1979; The Patchwork Cat, 1981; The Mouldy, 1983; Merry Go Rhymes (4 books), 1987; The Mousehole Cat, 1990. *Recreations:* watching the garden, opera, sleeping, cats. *Address:* c/o Walker Books, 87 Vauxhall Walk, SE11 5HJ. *Club:* Art Workers Guild.

BAYLEY, Lt-Comdr Oscar Stewart Morris, RN retd; *b* 15 April 1926; *s* of late Rev. J. H. S. Bayley; *m* Pamela Margaret Harrison (one *s* one *d* by a former marriage). *Educ:* St John's Sch., Leatherhead; King James's Grammar Sch., Knaresborough. Called to Bar, Lincoln's Inn, 1959. Entered RN, 1944: Ceylon, 1956–58; Supply Off., HMS Narvik and Sqdn Supply Off., 5th Submarine Div., 1960–62; Sec. to Comdr British Forces Caribbean Area, 1962–65; retd from RN at own request, 1966. Legal Asst (Unfair Competition), The Distillers Co. Ltd, 1966–68; Clerk, Fishmongers' Co., 1968–73; Accountant, Hawker Siddeley Gp, 1978–81, John Lewis Partnership, 1981–82. Dir, Seed Oysters (UK) Ltd. Clerk to Governors of Gresham's Sch., Holt; Hon. Sec., Salmon and Trout Assoc. and of Shellfish Assoc. of Great Britain; Vice-Chm., National Anglers' Council; Secretary: Atlantic Salmon Research Trust; City and Guilds of London Art Sch. Ltd, 1968–73; Nat. Assoc. of Pension Funds Investment Protection Cttee, 1974–75. Dir and Chief Sec., The Royal Life Saving Soc., 1976–78. Reader, All Saints Church, Footscray, Kent, 1989; Chm., Sidcup Council of Churches, 1990. *Address:* 244 Bexley Lane, Sidcup, Kent DA14 4JG.

BAYLEY, Peter Charles; Emeritus Professor, University of St Andrews; Emeritus Fellow, University College, Oxford, since 1988; *b* 25 Jan. 1921; *y s* of late William Charles Abell Bayley and Irene (*née* Heath); *m* 1951, Patience (marr. diss. 1980), *d* of late Sir George (Norman) Clark and Lady Clark; one *s* two *d.* *Educ:* Crypt Sch., Gloucester; University Coll., Oxford (Sidgwick Exhibnr; MA 1st Cl. Hons English, 1947). Served RA and Intell. Corps, India, 1941–45. Jun. Fellow, University Coll., Oxon, 1947; Fellow and Praelector in English, 1949–72 (at various times Domestic Bursar, Tutor for Admissions, Librarian, Editor of University Coll. Record); Univ. Lectr in English, 1952–72; Proctor, 1957–58; Oxford Univ. Corresp., The Times, 1960–63; Master of Collingwood Coll. and Lectr, Dept of Engish, Univ. of Durham, 1971–78; Berry Prof. and Head of Dept of English, Univ. of St Andrews, 1978–85. Vis. Reader, Birla Inst., Pilani, Rajasthan, India, 1966; Vis. Lectr, Yale Univ., and Robert Bates Vis. Fellow, Jonathan Edwards Coll., 1970; Brown Distinguished Vis. Prof., Univ. of the South, Sewanee, Tenn, 1978; Brown Distinguished Vis. Lectr in British Studies, Vanderbilt Univ., Sewanee, Rhodes, Birmingham-Southern, Millsaps etc., 1985. *Publications:* Edmund Spenser, Prince of Poets, 1971; 'Casebook' on Spenser's The Faerie Queene, 1977; Poems of Milton, 1982; An ABC of Shakespeare, 1985; edited: Spenser, The Faerie Queene: Book II, 1965; Book I, 1966; Loves and Deaths: short stories by 19th century novelists, 1972. *Address:* 63 Oxford Street, Woodstock, Oxford OX7 1TJ.

BAYLEY, Prof. Peter James; Drapers Professor of French, since 1985, and Fellow of Gonville and Caius College, since 1971, Cambridge University; *b* 20 Nov. 1944; *s* of John Henry Bayley and Margaret Burness, Portreath, Cornwall. *Educ:* Redruth County Grammar Sch.; Emmanuel Coll., Cambridge (Kitchener Schol., 1963–66; 1st cl. Hons Mod. and Med. Langs Tripos, 1964 and 1966; MA 1970; PhD 1971); Ecole Normale Supérieure, Paris (French Govt Schol., 1967–68). Cambridge University: Fellow of Emmanuel Coll., 1969–71; Coll. Lectr, Gonville and Caius Coll., 1971–85; Tutor, 1973–79; Praelector Rhetoricus, 1980–86; Univ. Asst Lectr in French, 1974–78; Univ. Lectr, 1978–85 (Actg Head, Dept of French, 1983–85). Vice-Pres., Assoc. of Univ. Profs of French, 1989–. Pres., Soc. for French Studies, 1990–. Officier des Palmes Académiques, 1988. *Publications:* French Pulpit Oratory 1598–1650, 1980; (ed with D. Coleman) The Equilibrium of Wit: essays for Odette de Mourgues, 1982; (ed) Selected Sermons of the French Baroque, 1983; contributions to: Critique et création littéraires en France (ed Fumaroli), 1977; Bossuet: la Prédication au XVIIe siècle (ed Collinet and Goyet), 1980; Catholicism in Early Modern History: a guide to research (ed O'Malley), 1988; Convergences: rhetoric and poetic in Seventeenth-Century France (ed Rubin and McKinley), 1989; Cambridge Rev., Dix-Septième Siècle, French Studies, Mod. Lang. Rev., etc. *Recreations:* Spain, food and wine, gardening, English ecclesiastical history. *Address:* Gonville and Caius College, Cambridge CB2 1TA. *T:* Cambridge (0223) 332439; (vacations) The White House, Hackleton, Northants NN7 2AD. *T:* Northampton (0604) 870059.

BAYLEY, Stephen Paul; Founding Director, Arts Foundation, since 1990; Founder, EYE-Q Ltd, 1990; *b* 13 Oct. 1951; *s* of Donald and Anne Bayley; *m* 1981, Flo Fothergill; one *s* one *d.* *Educ:* Quarry Bank Sch., Liverpool; Manchester Univ.; Liverpool Univ. Sch. of Architecture. Lecturer: Hist. of Art, Open Univ., 1974–76; Hist. and Theory of Art, Univ. of Kent, 1976–80; Dir, Conran Foundn, 1981–89; formerly Dir, Boilerhouse Project, in V&A Mus.; Founding Dir, later Chief Exec., Design Mus. A Contributing Editor, GQ, 1991–. Mem., Design Cttee, LRT, 1989–. Vis. Lectr, Art Coll. Center of Design (Europe), La Tour-de-Peilz, Switzerland, 1987–; has lectured at: Nat. Inst. of Design, Ahmedabad; India Inst. of Technol., Bombay; Art Gall. of WA, Perth; Nat. Gall. of Victoria, Melbourne; Salon de l'Automobile, Geneva; Sony Design Center, Tokyo; Internat. Expo, Nagoya; RIBA; RSA; RCA; and at univs, colls and museums throughout Britain and Europe. Gov., History of Advertising Trust, 1985–. Chevalier de l'Ordre des Arts et des Lettres (France), 1989. *Publications:* In Good Shape, 1979; The Albert Memorial, 1981; Harley Earl and the Dream Machine, 1983; The Conran Directory of Design, 1985; Sex, Drink and Fast Cars, 1986; Twentieth Century Style and Design, 1986; Commerce and Culture, 1989; Taste, 1991; numerous Open Univ. books, and Boilerhouse/Design Mus. catalogues inc. Art and Industry, 1982; Sony Design, 1982; Taste, 1983; Robots, 1984; National Characteristics, 1985; Coke, 1986. *Recreations:* indistinguishable from work, but both involve words, pictures, food, drink, sport and travel. *Address:* 74 Fentiman Road, SW8 1LA. *T:* 071–587 3882. *Clubs:* Savile, Hurlingham, Academy.

BAYLIS, Clifford Henry, CB 1971; Controller, HM Stationery Office, and Queen's Printer of Acts of Parliament, 1969–74; *b* 20 March 1915; *s* of late Arthur Charles and Caroline Jane Baylis, Alcester, Warwicks; *m* 1st, Phyllis Mary Clark; two *s*; 2nd, Margaret A. Hawkins. *Educ:* Alcester Grammar Sch.; Keble Coll., Oxford. Harrods Ltd, 1937–39. Served with HM Forces, 1940–46: Major RASC. Principal, Board of Trade, 1947; Asst Sec., UK Trade Commissioner, Bombay, 1955; Export Credits Guarantee Dept, 1963–66; Under-Sec., Board of Trade, 1966–67; Under-Sec., Min. of Technology, 1967–69. Dir, Shipbuilders' and Repairers' Nat. Assoc., 1974–77; Clerk, Shipwrights' Co., 1977–86. *Address:* 38 Cleaver Street, SE11 4DP. *T:* 071–587 0817.

BAYLIS, Rear-Adm. Robert Goodwin, CB 1984; OBE 1963; CEng; FIEE; Chief Executive, R. G. Baylis & Associates, since 1984; Director, Reliability Consultants Ltd, since 1988; Consultant, GEC Avionics; *b* 29 Nov. 1925; *s* of Harold Goodwin Baylis and Evelyn May (*née* Whitworth); *m* 1949, Joyce Rosemary Churchill; two *s* one *d.* *Educ:* Highgate Sch.; Edinburgh Univ.; Loughborough Coll.; RN Engrg Coll.; Trinity Coll., Cambridge. MA Cantab. MRAeS. Joined Royal Navy, 1943; various appts at sea in Far East and Home Fleet and ashore in research and develt and trng establishments; Staff of C-in-C, S Atlantic and S America, 1958; British Navy Staff, Washington, and Special Projects (Polaris), 1964; Defence Fellow, Southampton Univ., 1969; Naval ADC to HM the Queen, 1978; Staff of Vice Chief of Defence Staff, 1979; President, Ordnance Board, 1981–84. Comdr 1961, Captain 1970, Rear-Adm. 1979. Chm., Nuffield Theatre Bd, 1989–. Mem. (Emeritus), Australian Ordnance Council; Mem. Council, IEE, 1984–86; Member: Social Scis Faculty Adv. Gp, Southampton Univ., 1986–; Euro-Atlantic Gp, 1989–. *Recreations:* tennis, sailing. *Address:* Broadwaters, 4 Cliff Road, Hill Head, Fareham, Hants PO14 3JS. *Clubs:* Lansdowne; Owls (Cape Town).

BAYLISS, Frederic Joseph; Special Professor, Department of Adult Education, University of Nottingham, since 1988; *b* 15 April 1926; *s* of Gordon and Gertrude Bayliss; *m* 1948, Mary Provost; two *d.* *Educ:* Ashby de la Zouch Grammar Sch.; Hertford Coll., Oxford. PhD Nottingham 1960. RAF, 1944–47. Tutor in Economics, Oxford Univ. Tutorial Classes Cttee, 1950–57; Lectr in Industrial Relations, Dept of Adult Education, Univ. of Nottingham, 1957–65; Industrial Relations Advr, NBPI, 1965–69; Asst Sec., CIR, 1969–71; Sen. Economic Advr, Dept of Employment, 1971–73; Under Sec., Pay Board, 1973–74; Sec., Royal Commn on the Distribution of Income and Wealth, 1974–77; Acct Gen., Dept of Employment, 1977–86. Chm., Campaign for Work, 1988–. Hon. Fellow, City Univ. Business Sch., 1989–. *Publications:* British Wages Councils, 1962; The Standard of Living, 1965. *Recreations:* gardening, walking. *Address:* 11 Deena Close, Queens Drive, W3 0HR. *T:* 081–992 1126; Department of Adult Education, University of Nottingham, Nottingham NG7 2RD. *Club:* Reform.

BAYLISS, John; Managing Director (Retail Operations), Abbey National plc (formerly Abbey National Building Society), since 1988; *b* 22 Jan. 1934; *s* of Athol Thomas Bayliss and late Elizabeth Rose Bayliss; *m* 1954, Maureen (*née* Smith); one *d.* *Educ:* Haberdashers' Aske's, Hatcham. Westminster Bank, 1950; Abbey National, 1957–: Regional Man., 1969; Personnel Man., 1972; Asst Gen. Man., 1974; General Manager: Field Operations, 1976; Housing, 1981; Marketing, 1983. *Recreations:* France, sail-boarding. *Address:* (office) Abbey House, Baker Street, NW1 6XL. *T:* 071–486 5555; 7 Wood Drive, Chislehurst, Kent BR7 5EU. *T:* 081–467 7102.

BAYLISS, Sir Noel (Stanley), Kt 1979; CBE 1960; PhD, FRACI, FAA; Professor of Chemistry, University of Western Australia, 1938–71, Emeritus Professor, 1972; *b* 19 Dec. 1906; *s* of Henry Bayliss and Nelly Stothers; *m* 1933, Nellie Elise Banks; two *s.* *Educ:* Queen's Coll., Univ. of Melbourne (BSc 1927); Lincoln Coll., Oxford (BA 1930); Univ. of Calif, Berkeley (PhD 1933). FRACI 1942; FAA 1954. Victorian Rhodes Scholar, 1927–30; Commonwealth Fund (Harkness) Fellow, Univ. of Calif, 1930–33; Sen. Lectr in Chem., Univ. of Melbourne, 1933–37. Chm., Murdoch Univ. Planning Bd, 1970–73; Member: Australian Univs Commn, 1959–70; Hong Kong Univ. and Polytech. Grants Cttee, 1966–73. Hon. FACE 1965; Hon. DSc Univ. of WA, 1968; Hon. DUniv Murdoch Univ., 1975. *Publications:* over 70 original papers in scientific jls. *Recreations:* golf, music.

Address: 104 Thomas Street, Nedlands, WA 6009, Australia. *T:* (09) 386 1453. *Club:* Royal Perth Yacht (WA).

BAYLISS, Sir Richard (Ian Samuel), KCVO 1978; MD, FRCP; consulting physician; Physician to the Queen, 1970–81, and Head of HM Medical Household, 1973–81; Consultant Physician, King Edward VII's Hospital for Officers, 1964–87; Consultant Physician, Westminster Hospital, since 1981; Assistant Director, Royal College of Physicians Research Unit, 1982–88; *b* 2 Jan. 1917; *o s* of late Frederick William Bayliss, Tettenhall, and late Muryel Anne Bayliss; *m* 1st, 1941, Margaret Joan Lawson (marr. diss. 1956); one *s* one *d*; 2nd, 1957, Constance Ellen, *d* of Wilbur J. Frey, Connecticut; two *d*; 3rd, 1979, Marina de Borehgrave d'Altena, *widow* of Charles Rankin. *Educ:* Rugby; Clare Coll., Cambridge (Hon. Fellow, 1983); St Thomas' Hosp., London. MB, BChir Cambridge 1941; MRCS, LRCP 1941; MRCP 1942; MD Cambridge 1946; FRCP 1956. Casualty Officer, Ho.-Phys., Registrar, Resident Asst Phys., St Thomas' Hosp.; Off. i/c Med. Div., RAMC, India; Sen. Med. Registrar and Tutor, Hammersmith Hosp.; Rockefeller Fellow in Medicine, Columbia Univ., New York, 1950–51; Lectr in Medicine and Physician, Postgrad. Med. Sch. of London; Dean, Westminster Med. Sch., 1960–64; Physician to HM Household, 1964–70; Consulting Physician: Westminster Hosp., 1954–81; King Edward VII Hosp., Midhurst, 1973–82; Civilian Consultant in Medicine, RN, 1975–82. Hon. Sec., Assoc. of Physicians, 1958–63, Cttee 1965–68, Pres., 1980–81; Pres., Section of Endocrinology, RSM, 1966–68; Examr in Medicine, Cambridge and Oxford Univs; Examr, MRCP. Member: Bd of Governors, Westminster Hosp., 1960–64, 1967–74; Council, Westminster Med. Sch., 1960–75; Soc. for Endocrinology (Council, 1956–60); Brit. Cardiac Soc., 1952; Council, RCP, 1968–71 (Second Vice-Pres., 1983–84); Bd of Advrs, Merck Inst. of Therapeutic Res., 1972–76. Med. Dir, Swiss Reinsurance Co. (UK), 1968–85; Director: Private Patients Plan, 1979–89; JS Pathology plc, 1984–90; Hon. Med. Adviser, Nuffield Nursing Home Trust, 1981–88. Harveian Orator, RCP, 1983. *Publications:* Thyroid Disease: the facts, 1982, 2nd edn 1991; Practical Procedures in Clinical Medicine, 3rd edn; various, in med. jls and textbooks, on endocrine, metabolic and cardiac diseases. *Recreations:* ski-ing, music. *Address:* Flat 7, 61 Onslow Square, SW7 3LS. *T:* 071–589 3087. *Club:* Garrick.

BAYLISS, Valerie June; Under Secretary and Director of Education Programmes, Department of Employment, since 1991; *b* 10 June 1944; *d* of George and Ellen Russell; *m* 1971, Derek Andrew Bayliss; one *s*. *Educ:* Wallington County Grammar Sch. for Girls; Univ. of Wales (1st cl. hons History, BA 1965; MA 1967). Research Student, LSE, 1966–68; Dept of Employment, 1968; Manpower Services Commission, subseq. Training Agency: Head of Job Centre Services, 1978–82; Head, YTS Policy, 1982–85; Dir, Field Ops, 1985–87; Dir, Resources and Personnel, 1987–90. Mem. Council, Univ. of Sheffield, 1988–; Chm., Univ. of Sheffield Careers Adv. Bd, 1988–. FRSA 1990. *Recreations:* walking, reading, listening to music. *Address:* Department of Employment, Moorfoot, Sheffield S1 4PQ. *T:* Sheffield (0742) 594573.

BAYLY, Christopher Alan, DPhil; FBA 1990; Reader in Modern Indian History, since 1988 and Fellow of St Catharine's College, since 1970, Cambridge University; *b* 18 May 1945; *s* of Roy Ernest and Elfreda Madeleine Bayly; *m* 1981, Susan Banks Kaufmann. *Educ:* Skinners School, Tunbridge Wells; Balliol College, Oxford (MA); St Antony's, Oxford (DPhil 1970). Stanhope Prize, Oxford, 1965. Dir of Studies in History, St Catharine's Coll., Cambridge, 1970– (Tutor, 1977–80); Smuts Reader in Commonwealth Studies, Univ. of Cambridge, 1981–87. Directeur d'Etudes associé, CNRS, Ecole des Hautes Etudes, Paris, 1986. Vis. Prof., Univ. of Virginia, Charlottesville, 1975. *Publications:* The Local Roots of Indian Politics: Allahabad 1880–1920, 1975; Rulers, Townsmen and Bazaars: North Indian society in the age of British Expansion 1770–1870, 1983, 2nd edn 1988; Indian Society and the Making of the British Empire, 1988; Imperial Meridian: the British Empire and the world 1780–1830, 1989; (ed) The Raj: India and the British 1600–1947, 1990; contribs to jls. *Recreation:* travelling. *Address:* St Catharine's College, Cambridge CB2 1RL. *T:* Cambridge (0223) 338321.

BAYLY, Vice-Adm. Sir Patrick (Uniacke), KBE 1968; CB 1965; DSC 1944, and 2 bars, 1944, 1951; *b* 4 Aug. 1914; *s* of late Lancelot F. S. Bayly, Nenagh, Eire; *m* 1945, Moy Gourlay Jardine, *d* of Robert Gourlay Jardine, Newtonmearns, Scotland; two *d*. *Educ:* Aravon, Bray, Co. Wicklow; RN Coll., Dartmouth, Midshipman, 1932; Sub-Lieut, 1934; Lieut, 1935; South Africa, 1936; China station, 1938; Combined operations, 1941–44, including Sicily and Salerno; Lieut-Comdr 1944; HMS Mauritius, 1946; Comdr 1948, Naval Staff, 1948; Korean War, 1952–53, in HMS Alacrity and Constance; Captain 1954, Naval Staff; Imperial Defence Coll., 1957; Capt. (D) 6th Destroyer Sqdn, 1958; Staff of SACLANT, Norfolk, Va, 1960; Chief of Staff, Mediterranean, 1962; Rear-Admiral, 1963; Flag Officer, Sea Training, 1963; Adm. Pres., RN Coll., Greenwich, 1965–67; Vice-Adm., 1967; Chief of Staff, COMNAVSOUTH, Malta, 1967–70; retd, 1970. Dir, Maritime Trust, 1971–88. US Legion of Merit, 1951. *Recreation:* golf. *Address:* Dunning House, Liphook, Hants GU30 7EH.

BAYNE, Brian Leicester, PhD; FIBiol; Director, Plymouth Marine Laboratory, Natural Environment Research Council, since 1988; *b* 24 July 1938; *s* of John Leonard and Jean Leicester Bayne; *m* 1961, Marianne Middleton; two *d*. *Educ:* Ardingly Coll.; Univ. of Wales (BSc, PhD). Post-doctoral res., Univ. of Copenhagen and Fisheries Laboratory, Conwy, 1963–68; Lectr, Sch. of Biology, Univ. of Leicester, 1968–73; Institute for Marine Environmental Research, Plymouth: Res. Scientist, 1973–83; Dir, 1983–88. Hon. Professorial Fellow, Sheffield Univ. *Publications:* Marine Mussels: ecology and physiology, 1976; res. papers in marine sci. jls, *eg* Jl of Experimental Marine Biol. and Ecol. *Recreation:* sailing. *Address:* Plymouth Marine Laboratory, Prospect Place, West Hoe, Plymouth, Devon PL1 3DH. *T:* Plymouth (0752) 222772.

BAYNE, John; Advocate; Sheriff of Glasgow and Strathkelvin, 1975–79; Sheriff (formerly Sheriff-Substitute) of Lanarkshire at Glasgow, 1959–74. *Address:* Winsford, 7 Milrig Road, Rutherglen G73 2NQ.

BAYNE, Nicholas Peter, CMG 1984; HM Diplomatic Service; Deputy Under-Secretary of State, Foreign and Commonwealth Office, since 1988; *b* 15 Feb. 1937; *s* of late Captain Ronald Bayne, RN and Elisabeth Ashcroft; *m* 1961, Diana Wilde; two *s* (and one *s* decd). *Educ:* Eton Coll.; Christ Church, Oxford (MA, DPhil). Entered Diplomatic Service, 1961; served at British Embassies in Manila, 1963–66, and Bonn, 1969–72; seconded to HM Treasury, 1974–75; Financial Counsellor, Paris, 1975–79; Head of Financial, later Economic Relations, Dept, FCO, 1979–82; attached to RIIA, 1982–83; Ambassador to Zaire, 1983–84, also accredited to the Congo, Rwanda and Burundi, 1984; seconded to CSSB, 1985; Ambassador and UK Perm. Rep. to OECD, Paris, 1985–88. *Publication:* (with R. D. Putnam) Hanging Together: the Seven-Power Summits, 1984, rev. edn 1987 (trans. German, Japanese, Italian). *Recreations:* reading, sightseeing. *Address:* c/o Foreign and Commonwealth Office, King Charles Street, SW1A 2AH. *Club:* Travellers'.

BAYNE-POWELL, Robert Lane, CB 1981; Senior Registrar of the Family Division, High Court of Justice, 1976–82, retired (Registrar, 1964–76); *b* 10 Oct. 1910; 2nd *s* of William Maurice and Rosamond Alicia Bayne-Powell; *m* 1938, Nancy Geraldine (*d* 1979), *d* of late Lt-Col J. L. Philips, DSO; one *s* two *d*. *Educ:* Charterhouse; Trinity Coll., Cambridge (BA). Called to Bar, Middle Temple, 1935; Mem., Senate of Inns of Court and the Bar, 1978–81. Served War of 1939–45, Intell. Corps; Major 1944; Allied Commn for Austria, 1945. Mem., Reviewing Cttee on Export of Works of Art, 1975–81; Hon. Keeper of the Miniatures, Fitzwilliam Museum, Cambridge, 1980–. *Publications:* (special editor) Williams and Mortimer on Executors and Probate, 1970; Catalogue of Miniatures in the Fitzwilliam Museum, Cambridge, 1985. *Recreations:* gardening, miniature collecting, wine-tasting. *Address:* The Mount, Borough Green, Sevenoaks, Kent. *T:* Borough Green (0732) 882045. *Club:* Athenæum.

BAYNES, Sir John (Christopher Malcolm), 7th Bt *cr* 1801; Lt-Col retd; *b* 24 April 1928; *s* of Sir Rory Malcolm Stuart Baynes, 6th Bt and Ethel Audrey (*d* 1947), *d* of late Edward Giles, CIE; *S* father, 1979; *m* 1955, Shirley Maxwell, *o d* of late Robert Allan Dodds; four *s*. *Educ:* Sedbergh School; RMA Sandhurst; Edinburgh Univ. (MSc). Commissioned Cameronians (Scottish Rifles), 1949; served Malaya, 1950–53 (despatches); Aden, 1966; Defence Fellow, Edinburgh Univ., 1968–69; comd 52 Lowland Volunteers (TAVR), 1969–72; retired, 1972. Order of the Sword, 1st Class (Sweden), 1965. *Publications:* Morale, 1967, new edn 1987; The Jacobite Rising of 1715, 1970; History of the Cameronians, Vol. IV, 1971; The Soldier in Modern Society, 1971; Soldiers of Scotland, 1988; The Forgotten Victor, 1989; (ed jtly) A Tale of Two Captains, 1990; The British Soldier in the 1990s, 1991; Urquhart of Arnhem, 1992; contribs to military and sporting jls. *Recreations:* shooting, fishing, golf. *Heir:* *s* Christopher Rory Baynes, *b* 11 May 1956. *Address:* Talwrn Bach, Llanfyllin, Powys SY22 5LQ. *T:* Llanfyllin (069184) 576. *Club:* Army and Navy.

BAYNES, Pauline Diana, (Mrs F. O. Gasch); designer and book illustrator; *b* 9 Sept 1922; *d* of Frederick William Wilberforce Baynes, CIE and Jessie Harriet Maud Cunningham; *m* 1961, Fritz Otto Gasch (*d* 1988). *Educ:* Beaufront Sch., Camberley; Farnham Sch. of Art; Slade Sch. of Art. MSIA 1951. Mem., Women's Internat. Art Club, 1938. Voluntary worker, Camouflage Develt and Trng Centre, RE, 1940–42; Hydrographic Dept, Admty, 1942–45. Designed world's largest crewel embroidery, Plymouth Congregational Church, Minneapolis, 1970. Kate Greenaway Medal, Library Assoc., 1968. *Publications: illustrated:* Farmer Giles of Ham, and subseq. books and posters by J. R. R. Tolkien, 1949; The Lion, the Witch and the Wardrobe, and subseq. Narnia books by C. S. Lewis, 1950; The Arabian Nights, 1957; The Puffin Book of Nursery Rhymes by Iona and Peter Opie, 1963; Recipes from an Old Farmhouse by Alison Uttley, 1966; Dictionary of Chivalry, 1968; Snail and Caterpillar, 1972; A Companion to World Mythology, 1979; The Enchanted Horse, 1981; Frog and Shrew, 1981; All Things Bright and Beautiful, 1986; The Story of Daniel by George MacBeth, 1986; Noah and the Ark, 1988; numerous other children's books, etc.; *written and illustrated:* Victoria and the Golden Bird, 1948; How Dog Began, 1985; King Wenceslas, 1987. *Recreation:* going for walks with dogs. *Address:* Rock Barn Cottage, Dockenfield, Farnham, Surrey GU10 4HH. *T:* Headley Down (0428) 713306.

BAYNHAM, Prof. Alexander Christopher; Principal, Cranfield Institute of Technology Campus (Shrivenham), since 1989; *b* 22 Dec. 1935; *s* of Alexander Baynham and Dulcie Rowena Rees; *m* 1961, Eileen May Wilson; two *s* one *d*. *Educ:* Marling Sch.; Reading Univ. (BSc); Warwick Univ. (PhD); Royal Coll. of Defence Studies (rcds). Joined Royal Signals and Radar Estab., Malvern, 1955; rejoined, 1961 (univ. studies, 1958–61); Head, Optics and Electronics Gp, 1976; RCDS, 1978; Scientific Adviser to Asst Chief Adviser on Projects, 1979; Dep. Dir, 1980–83, Dir, 1984–86, RSRE; Dir, RARDE, 1986–89. *Publications:* Plasma Effects in Semi-conductors, 1971; assorted papers in Jl of Physics, Jl of Applied Physics and in Proc. Phys. Soc. *Recreations:* church activities, music. *Address:* Cranfield Institute of Technology, Shrivenham Campus, Swindon, Wilts SN6 8LA.

BAYS, Rt. Rev. Eric; *see* Qu'Appelle, Bishop of.

BAYTON, Rt. Rev. John, AM 1983; Bishop of Geelong, since 1989 (Assistant Bishop of the Diocese of Melbourne); *b* 24 March 1930; *s* of Ernest Bayton and Jean Bayton (*née* Edwards); *m* 1959, Elizabeth Anne, *d* of Rt Rev. J. A. G. Housden, *qv*; one *s* two *d*. *Educ:* Univ. of Queensland (Dip. AA); Aust. Coll. of Theology, ACT (ThL (Hons)); St Francis Theol Coll., Brisbane. Ordained deacon 1956, priest 1957; Rector, Longreach, Qld, 1958–63; Rector and Sub-dean, Thursday Island (Canon in Residence), 1963–65; Rector, Auchenflower, 1965–68; Dean of St Paul's Cathedral, Rockhampton, 1968–79; Vicar, St Peter's, Eastern Hill, 1980–89; Archdeacon of Malvern, 1986–89. Chm., Division of Community Care, 1990–. Founder, Inst. for Spiritual Studies, Melbourne, 1981. Solo Art Exhibitions: Brisbane 1967, 1976, 1978; Rockhampton 1975, 1976; Melbourne 1981, 1984, 1986, 1987. Represented in public and private collections Australia, USA and UK. KCSJ 1988. *Publications:* Cross over Carpentaria, 1965; Coming of the Light, 1971; The Icon, 1980; (ed) Anglican Spirituality, 1982. *Recreations:* painting, sketching, sculpting, reading, walking. *Address:* The Bishop's House, 364 Shannon Avenue, Newtown, Geelong, Vic 3220, Australia. *T:* (052) 298625, *Fax:* (052) 222378. *Clubs:* Melbourne, Naval and Military (Melbourne).

BAYÜLKEN, Ümit Halûk; President, Turkish Atlantic Treaty Association, since 1984; *b* 7 July 1921; *s* of Staff Officer H. Hüsnü Bayülken and Mrs Melek Bayülken; *m* 1952, Mrs Valihe Salci; one *s* one *d*. *Educ:* Lycée of Haydarpasa, Istanbul; Faculty of Political Science (Diplomatic Sect.), Univ. of Ankara. Joined Min. of For. Affairs, 1944; 3rd Sec., 2nd Political Dept; served in Private Cabinet of Sec.-Gen.; mil. service as reserve Officer, 1945–47; Vice-Consul, Frankfurt-on-Main, 1947–49; 1st Sec., Bonn, 1950–51; Dir of Middle East Sect., Ankara, 1951–53; Mem. Turkish Delegn to UN 7th Gen. Assembly, 1952; Political Adviser, 1953–56, Counsellor, 1956–59, Turkish Perm. Mission to UN; rep. Turkey at London Jt Cttee on Cyprus, 1959–60; Dir-Gen., Policy Planning Gp, Min. of Foreign Affairs, 1960–63; Minister Plenipotentiary, 1963; Dep. Sec.-Gen. for Polit. Affairs, 1963–64; Sec.-Gen. with rank of Ambassador, 1964–66; Ambassador to London, 1966–69, to United Nations, 1969–71; Minister of Foreign Affairs, 1971–74; Secretary-General, Cento, 1975–77; Sec.-Gen., Presidency of Turkish Republic, 1977–80; Minister of Defence, 1980–83; MP, Antalya, 1983–87. Mem., Turkish Delegns to 8th-13th, 16th-20th Gen. Assemblies of UN; rep. Turkey at internat. confrs, 1953–66; Leader of Turkish Delegn: at meeting of For. Ministers, 2nd Afro-Asian Conf., Algiers, 1965. Univ. of Ankara: Mem., Inst. of Internat. Relations; Lectr, Faculty of Polit. Scis, 1963–66. Hon. Gov., Sch. of Oriental and African Studies, London; Hon. Mem., Mexican Acad. of Internat. Law. Isabel la Católica (Spain), 1964; Grand Cross of Merit (Germany), 1965; Hon. GCVO, 1967; Sitara-i-Pakistan (Pakistan), 1970; Star, Order One (Jordan), 1972; Sirdar-i-Ali (Afghanistan), 1972. Tunisia, 1973; UAR, 1973; UN, 1975; Turkish Pres., 1980. *Publications:* lectures, articles, studies and essays on subject of minorities, Cyprus, principles of foreign policy, internat. relations and disputes. *Recreations:* music, painting, reading. *Address:* Nergiz, Sokak no 15/20, Çankaya, Ankara, Turkey.

BAZALGETTE, Rear-Adm. Derek Willoughby, CB 1976; Independent Inquiry Inspector, since 1983; *b* 22 July 1924; *yr s* of late H. L. Bazalgette; *m* 1947, Angela Hilda Vera, *d* of late Sir Henry Hinchliffe, JP, DL; four *d*. *Educ:* RNC Dartmouth. Served War of 1939–45; specialised in Gunnery, 1949; HMS Centaur, 1952–54; HMS Birmingham, 1956–58; SO 108th Minesweeping Sqdn and in comd HMS Houghton, 1958–59; HMS

Centaur, 1963–65; Dep. Dir Naval Ops, 1965–67; comd HMS Aurora, 1967–68; idc 1969; Chief Staff Officer to Comdr British Forces Hong Kong, 1970–72; comd HMS Bulwark, 1972–74; Admiral President, RNC Greenwich, 1974–76; Comdr 1958; Captain 1965; Rear-Adm. 1974. ADC 1974. HQ Comr for Water Activities, Scout Assoc., 1976–87; Principal, Netley Waterside House, 1977–83. Lay Canon, Portsmouth Cathedral, 1984–; Mem., General Synod, 1985–90. Treas., Corp. of Sons of the Clergy, 1988–. Chm., Portsmouth Housing Trust, 1989–. Liveryman, Shipwrights' Co., 1986. Freeman, City of London, 1976. FBIM 1976. *Address:* The Glebe House, Newtown, Fareham, Hants. *Club:* Lansdowne.

BAZLEY, Most Rev. Colin Frederick; *see* Chile, Bishop of.

BAZLEY, Sir Thomas Stafford, 3rd Bt, *cr* 1869; *b* 5 Oct. 1907; *s* of Captain Gardner Sebastian Bazley, DL, *o s* of 2nd Bt (*d* 1911) and Ruth Evelyn (*d* 1962), *d* of late Sir E. S. Howard (she *m* 2nd, Comdr F. C. Cadogan, RN, retd; he *d* 1970); *S* grandfather, 1919; *m* 1945, Carmen, *o d* of late J. Tulla; three *s* two *d. Educ:* Harrow; Magdalen Coll., Oxford. *Heir: s* Thomas John Sebastian Bazley, *b* 31 Aug. 1948. *Address:* Eastleach Downs Farm, near Eastleach, Cirencester, Glos.
See also H. A. Abel Smith.

BEACH; *see* Hicks-Beach, family name of Earl St Aldwyn.

BEACH, Gen. Sir (William Gerald) Hugh, GBE 1980 (OBE 1966); KCB 1976; MC 1944; Chairman, Church Army, since 1990; *b* 20 May 1923; *s* of late Maj.-Gen. W. H. Beach, CB, CMG, DSO; *m* 1951, Estelle Mary Henry (*d* 1989); three *s* one *d. Educ:* Winchester; Peterhouse, Cambridge (MA; Hon. Fellow 1982). Active service in France, 1944 and Java, 1946; comd: 4 Field Sqn, 1956–57; Cambridge Univ. OTC, 1961–63; 2 Div. RE, 1965–67; 12 Inf. Bde, 1969–70; Defence Fellow, Edinburgh Univ. (MSc), 1971; Dir, Army Staff Duties, MoD, 1971–74; Comdt, Staff Coll., Camberley, 1974–75; Dep. C-in-C, UKLF, 1976–77; Master-Gen. of the Ordnance, 1977–81; Chief Royal Engr, 1982–87; Warden, St George's House, Windsor Castle, 1981–86. Dir, Council for Arms Control, 1986–89. Vice Lord-Lieut for Greater London, 1981–87. Kermit Roosevelt Vis. Lectr to US Armed Forces, 1977; Mountbatten Lectr, Edinburgh Univ., 1981; Gallipoli Meml Lectr, 1985; Wilfred Fish Meml Lectr, GDC, 1986. Colonel Commandant: REME, 1976–81; RPC, 1976–80; RE, 1977–87; Hon. Colonel, Cambridge Univ. OTC, TAVR, 1977–87; Chm., CCF Assoc., 1981–87; Chm., MoD Study Gp on Censorship, 1983. Mem., Security Commn, 1982–. Chairman: Rochester Cathedral Develt Trust, 1986–; Winchester Diocesan Adv. Cttee for Care of Churches, 1988–; Foundn Cttee, Gordon's Sch., 1988–; Gov., Bedales Sch., 1991–. Patron, Venturers Search and Rescue, 1985–. CBIM; FRSA. Hon. Fellow CIBSE, 1988. Hon. DCL Kent, 1990. *Publications: chapters on:* nuclear weapons in the defence of North-West Europe, in Unholy Warfare (ed Martin and Mullen), 1983; where does the nuclear-free path lead, in The Cross and the Bomb (ed Francis Bridger), 1983; disarmament and security in Europe, in Armed Peace (ed O'Connor Howe), 1984; military implications of 'No First Use', in Dropping the Bomb (ed John Gladwin), 1985. *Recreations:* sailing, ski-ing. *Address:* The Ropeway, Beaulieu, Hants. *T:* Beaulieu (0590) 612269. *Clubs:* Farmers'; Royal Lymington Yacht.

BEACH, Surgeon Rear-Adm. William Vincent, CB 1962; OBE 1949; MRCS; LRCP; FRCSE; Retd; *b* 22 Nov. 1903; *yr s* of late William Henry Beach; *m* 1931, Daphne Muriel, *yr d* of late Eustace Ackworth Joseph, ICS; two *d. Educ:* Seaford Coll.; Guy's Hospital, London. Joined RN Medical Service, 1928. Served War of 1939–45 as Surgical specialist in Hospital ships, Atlantic and Pacific Fleets. Surgical Registrar, Royal Victoria Infirmary, Newcastle upon Tyne; Senior Specialist in Surgery, RN Hospitals, Chatham, Haslar, Malta, Portland; Senior Medical Officer, RN Hospital, Malta; Medical Officer i/c RN Hospital, Portland; Sen. Medical Officer, Surgical Division, RN Hospital, Haslar; Medical Officer in charge of Royal Naval Hospital, Chatham, and Command MO on staff of C-in-C the Nore Command, 1960–61; MO i/c RN Hospital, Malta, and on staff of C-in-C, Mediterranean and as Medical Adviser to C-in-C, Allied Forces, Mediterranean, 1961–63. Surg. Rear-Admiral, 1960. QHS 1960. Senior Surgeon i/c Shaw Savill Passenger Liners, 1966–75. Fellow, Assoc. of Surgeons of Great Britain and Ireland, 1947, Senior Fellow, 1963. *Publications:* Urgent Surgery of the Hand, 1940; Inguinal Hernia—a new operation, 1946; The Treatment of Burns, 1950. *Recreations:* shooting, fishing. *Address:* Cherrytree Cottage, Easton, Winchester SO21 1EG. *T:* Itchen Abbas (096278) 222. *Club:* Naval and Military.

BEACHAM, Prof. Arthur, OBE 1961; MA, PhD; Deputy Vice-Chancellor, Murdoch University, Western Australia, 1976–79 (Acting Vice-Chancellor, 1977–78); *b* 27 July 1913; *s* of William Walter and Maud Elizabeth Beacham; *m* 1938, Margaret Doreen Moseley (*d* 1979); one *s* one *d. Educ:* Pontywaun Grammar Sch.; University Coll. of Wales (BA 1935); Univ. of Liverpool (MA 1937); PhD Belfast 1941. Jevons Res. Student, Univ. of Liverpool, 1935–36; Leon Res. Fellow, Univ. of London, 1942–43; Lectr in Economics, Queen's Univ. of Belfast, 1938–45; Sen. Lectr, University Coll. of Wales, 1945–47; Prof. of Indust. Relations, University Coll., Cardiff, 1947–51; Prof. of Economics, University Coll. of Wales, Aberystwyth, 1951–63; Vice-Chancellor, Univ. of Otago, Dunedin, New Zealand, 1964–66; Gonner Prof. of Applied Econs, Liverpool Univ., 1966–75. Chairman: Mid-Wales Industrial Develt Assoc., 1957–63; Post Office Arbitration Tribunal, 1972–73; Member: Advisory Council for Education (Wales), 1949–52; Transp. Consultative Cttee for Wales, 1948–63 (Chm. 1961–63); Central Transp. Consultative Cttee, 1961–63; Economics Cttee of DSIR, 1961–63; North West Economic Planning Council, 1966–74; Merseyside Passenger Transport Authority, 1969–71; Council, Royal Economic Soc., 1970–74. Chm., Cttees on Care of Intellectually Handicapped, Australia, 1982–85; Dir, Superannuation Scheme for Aust. Univs, 1982–83. Hon. LLD Otago, 1969; Hon. DUniv Murdoch, 1982. *Publications:* Economics of Industrial Organisation, 1948 (5th edn 1970); Industries in Welsh Country Towns, 1950. Articles in Econ. Jl, Quarterly Jl of Economics, Oxford Econ. Papers, etc. *Recreations:* golf, gardening. *Address:* 10 Mannersley Street, Carindale, Qld 4152, Australia. *T:* 398 6524. *Clubs:* Dunedin (Dunedin, NZ); Cricketers' (Qld).

BEAGLEY, Thomas Lorne, CB 1973; Hon. Secretary, Chartered Institute of Transport, since 1983; President, European Society of Transport Institutes, since 1985; *b* 2 Jan. 1919; *s* of late Captain T. G. Beagley, Royal Montreal Regt; *m* 1942, Heather Blanche Osmond; two *s* one *d. Educ:* Bristol Grammar Sch.; Worcester Coll., Oxford (MA). Served War: 2nd Lieut, Northamptonshire Regt, 1940; Lt-Col, AQMG (Movements), AFHQ, Italy, 1945. Joined Min. of Transport, 1946; Cabinet Office, 1951–52; Min. of Defence, 1952–54; UK Delegn to NATO, 1954–57; UK Shipping Rep., Far East, 1960–63; Asst Under-Sec. of State, Dept of Economic Affairs, 1966–68; Under-Sec., Min. of Transport, 1968–71; Dep. Sec., Transport Industries, DoE, 1972–76; Dep. Chief Exec., PSA, 1976–79. Member: Nat. Ports Council, 1979–81; Dover Harbour Bd, 1980–89. Chartered Institute of Transport: FCIT, 1972; Pres., 1977; Award of Merit, 1988. Hon. FIRTE 1979. Viva Award for Transport Improvement, Carmen's Co, 1985. *Recreations:* golf, galleries, gardening. *Address:* 3 Sheen Common Drive, Richmond, Surrey. *T:* 081–876 1216. *Clubs:* Travellers'; Richmond Golf, St Enodoc Golf.

BEAL, Anthony Ridley; publishing consultant; Chairman: Heinemann Educational Books, 1979–84; Heinemann International, 1984–85; Managing Director, Heinemann Educational Books (International), 1979–84; *b* 28 Feb. 1925; *s* of Harold and Nesta Beal; *m* 1958, Rosemary Jean Howarth (*d* 1989); three *d*; *m* 1990, Carmen Dolores Carter (*née* Martinez). *Educ:* Haberdashers' Aske's Hampstead School; Downing College, Cambridge (scholar); 1st class English Tripos 1948. RNVR, 1943–46; Lectr in English, Eastbourne Training Coll., 1949; joined William Heinemann, 1949; Dep. Man. Dir, Heinemann Educational Books, 1962–73, Man. Dir, 1973–79; Dir, Heinemann Group of Publishers, 1973–85; Chairman: Heinemann Publishers (NZ), 1980–85; Heinemann Publishers Australia Pty, 1981–85; Ginn & Co., 1979–84. Chm., Educational Publishers' Council, 1980–83 (Vice-Chm., 1978–80); Mem. Council, Publishers' Assoc., 1982–86. *Publications:* D. H. Lawrence: Selected Literary Criticism, 1956; D. H. Lawrence, 1961; contribs to books on literature, education and publishing. *Recreations:* reading maps, travelling, thinking while gardening. *Address:* 19 Homefield Road, Radlett, Herts WD7 8PX. *T:* Radlett (0923) 834567. *Club:* Garrick.

BEAL, Rt. Rev. Robert George; *see* Wangaratta, Bishop of.

BEALE, Anthony John; Solicitor and Legal Adviser, Welsh Office, 1980–91; Under Secretary (Legal), Welsh Office, 1983–91; *b* 16 March 1932, *o s* of late Edgar Beale and Victoria Beale; *m* 1969, Helen Margaret Owen-Jones; one *s* one *d. Educ:* Hitchin Grammar Sch.; King's Coll. London (LLB; AKC). Solicitor of the Supreme Court, 1956. Legal Asst, 1960, Sen. Legal Asst, 1966, Min. of Housing and Local Govt and Min. of Health; Consultant, Council of Europe, 1973; Asst Solicitor, DoE 1974. LRPS. *Recreations:* photography, golf, collecting old cheques.

BEALE, Edward; *see* Beale, T. E.

BEALE, Prof. Geoffrey Herbert, MBE 1947; FRS 1959; PhD; Royal Society Research Professor, Edinburgh University, 1963–78; *b* 11 June 1913; *s* of Herbert Walter and Elsie Beale; *m* 1949, Betty Brydon McCallum (marr. diss. 1969); three *s. Educ:* Sutton County Sch.; Imperial Coll. of Science, London. Scientific Research Worker, John Innes Horticultural Institution, London, 1935–40. Served in HM Forces (1941–46). Research worker, department of Genetics, Carnegie Institute, Cold Spring Harbor, New York, 1947; Rockefeller Fellow, Indiana Univ., 1947–48; Lecturer, Dept of Animal Genetics, 1948–59, Reader in Animal Genetics, 1959–63, Edinburgh Univ. Research Worker (part-time), Chulalongkorn Univ., Bangkok, 1976–. *Publications:* The Genetics of Paramecium aurelia, 1954; (with Jonathan Knowles) Extranuclear Genetics, 1978. *Address:* 23 Royal Terrace, Edinburgh EH7 5AH. *T:* 031–557 1329.

BEALE, Josiah Edward Michael; lately Assistant Secretary, Department of Trade and Industry; *b* 29 Sept. 1928; *s* of late Mr and Mrs J. E. Beale, Upminster, Essex; *m* 1958, Jean Margaret McDonald; two *d* (and one *d* decd). *Educ:* Brentwood Sch.; Jesus Coll., Cambridge. UK Shipping Adviser, Singapore, 1968–71. Assistant Secretary, Monopolies and Mergers Commission, 1978–81. Hon. Sec., Friends of Historic Essex, 1987–. *Address:* The Laurels, The Street, Great Waltham, Chelmsford, Essex CM3 1DE.

BEALE, Maj.-Gen. Peter John, QHP 1987; FRCP; Director General, Army Medical Services, since 1990; *b* 18 March 1934; *s* of Basil and Eileen Beale; *m* 1959, Julia Mary Beale; four *s* one *d* (and one *d* decd). *Educ:* St Paul's Cathedral Choir Sch.; Felsted Sch. (Music Schol.); Gonville and Caius Coll., Cambridge (Choral Schol.; BA); Westminster Hosp. MB BChir 1958. MFCM, DTM&H. Commissioned RAMC, 1960; medical training, 1964–71; Consultant Physician, Army, 1971; served Far East, Middle East, BAOR; Community Physician, Army, 1981; served BAOR and UK; Comdr Medical, HQ UKLF, 1987–90. OStJ. *Publications:* contribs to professional jls on tropical and military medicine. *Recreations:* music (conductor, tenor, pianist, French Horn player); sport (golf, squash, tennis); bridge. *Address:* The Old Bakery, Avebury, Marlborough, Wilts. *T:* Avebury (06723) 315.

BEALE, (Thomas) Edward, CBE 1966; JP; Chairman, Beale's Ltd, 1934–90; *b* 5 March 1904; *s* of late Thomas Henderson Beale, London; *m* Beatrice May (*d* 1986), *d* of William Steele McLaughlin, JP, Enniskillen; one *s. Educ:* City of London Sch. Mem. Bd, British Travel Assoc., 1950–70, Dep. Chm. 1965–70. Vice-Pres. and Fellow, Hotel and Catering Inst., 1949–71; Chm., Caterers' Assoc. of Gt Britain, 1949–52; Pres., Internat. Ho-Re-Ca (Union of Nat. Hotel, Restaurant & Caterers Assocs), 1954–64. Chm., Treasury Cttee of Enquiry, House of Commons Refreshment Dept, 1951. Master, Worshipful Co. of Bakers, 1955. Mem., Islington Borough Council, 1931–34. Creator, Beale Arboretum, West Lodge Park, 1965. JP Inner London, 1950 (Chm. EC Div., Inner London Magistrates, 1970–73). FRSH 1957; FRSA 1968; Hon FHCIMA 1974. Médaille d'Argent de Paris, 1960. *Recreation:* arboriculture. *Address:* West Lodge Park, Hadley Wood, Herts EN4 0PY. *Club:* Carlton.

BEALE, Sir William (Francis), Kt 1956; OBE 1945; *b* 27 Jan. 1908; *y s* of late George and Elizabeth Beale, Potterspury Lodge, Northants; *m* 1934, Dèva Zaloudek; one *s* one *d. Educ:* Downside Sch., Pembroke Coll., Cambridge. Joined Green's Stores (Ilford) Ltd, Dir, 1929–63 (Chm., 1950–63). Navy, Army and Air Force Institutes, UK, 1940–41, Dir, 1949–61 (Chm. 1953–61). EFI, GHQ West Africa, 1942–43; EFI, 21st Army Gp, 1944–46. *Recreations:* hunting, shooting; formerly Rugby football (Eastern Counties Cap, 1932). *Address:* The Old Rectory, Woodborough, Pewsey, Wilts SN9 5PH. *Club:* Army and Navy.

BEALES, Prof. Derek Edward Dawson, PhD, LittD; FRHistS; FBA 1989; Professor of Modern History, University of Cambridge, since 1980; Fellow of Sidney Sussex College, Cambridge, since 1958; *b* 12 June 1931; *s* of late Edward Beales and of Dorothy Kathleen Beales (*née* Dawson); *m* 1964, Sara Jean (*née* Ledbury); one *s* one *d. Educ:* Bishop's Stortford Coll.; Sidney Sussex Coll., Cambridge (MA, PhD, LittD). Sidney Sussex College: Research Fellow, 1955–58; Tutor, 1961–70; Vice-Master, 1973–75; University Asst Lectr, Cambridge, 1962–65; Lectr, 1965–80; Chairman, Faculty Board of History, Cambridge, 1979–81; Member: Cambridge Univ. Liby Syndicate, 1982–88; Gen. Bd of Faculties, Cambridge, 1987–89. Vis. Lectr, Harvard Univ., 1965; Founder's Meml Lectr, St Deiniol's Liby, Hawarden, 1990. Mem. Council, RHistS, 1984–88. Editor, 1971–75, Chm. Editl Bd, 1990–, Historical Jl. *Publications:* England and Italy 1859–60, 1961; From Castlereagh to Gladstone, 1969; The Risorgimento and the Unification of Italy, 1971; History and Biography, 1981; (ed with Geoffrey Best) History, Society and the Churches, 1985; Joseph II: in the shadow of Maria Theresa 1741–80, 1987; articles in learned jls. *Recreations:* playing keyboard instruments and bridge, walking, not gardening. *Address:* Sidney Sussex College, Cambridge CB2 3HU. *T:* Cambridge (0223) 338833.

BEALES, Peter Leslie; Chairman and Managing Director, Peter Beales Roses, since 1967; *b* 22 July 1936; *s* of E. M. Howes; *m* 1961, Joan Elizabeth Allington; one *s* one *d. Educ:* Aldborough School, Norfolk; Norwich City Tech. Coll. MIHort. Apprenticed E. B. LeGrice Roses (1st apprentice, Horticultural Apprentice Scheme), 1952–57; Nat. Service, RA, 1957–59; Manager, Rose Dept, Hillings Nurseries, Chobham, 1959–66; founded Peter Beales Roses, 1967. Lecturer, UK and overseas, 1985–. Chm., Attleborough Chamber of Commerce, 1988–89. Hon. Life Mem., Bermuda Rose Soc., 1987; Life

Mem., N. Ireland Rose Soc., 1985. Lester E. Harrell Award for significant contrib. to heritage roses, USA, 1988. *Publications:* Georgian and Regency Roses, 1981; Early Victorian Roses, 1981; Late Victorian Roses, 1981; Edwardian Roses, 1981; Classic Roses, 1985; Twentieth-Century Roses, 1988. *Recreations:* photography, rose breeding, travelling, sport, book collecting. *Address:* Peter Beales Roses, London Road, Attleborough, Norfolk NR17 1AY. *T:* Attleborough (0953) 454707. *Club:* Attleborough Rotary (Pres., 1989–90).

BEALEY, Prof. Frank William; Professor of Politics, University of Aberdeen, 1964–90, now Emeritus; *b* Bilston, Staffs, 31 Aug. 1922; *er s* of Ernest Bealey and Nora (*née* Hampton), both of Netherton, Dudley; *m* 1960, Sheila Hurst; one *s* two *d*. *Educ:* Hill Street Elem. Sch.; King Edward VI Grammar Sch., Stourbridge; London Sch. of Economics. Seaman in RN, 1941–46; Student, LSE, 1946–48 (1st cl. Hons Govt; DSc Econ. 1990); Finnish Govt Scholar, 1948–49; Research Asst for Passfield Trust, 1950–51; Extra-Mural Lectr, University of Manchester (Burnley Area), 1951–52; Lectr, University of Keele, 1952–64. Vis. Fellow, Yale, 1980. Treas., Soc. for Study of Labour Hist., 1960–63. Organiser, Parly All-Party Gp, Social Sci. and Policy, 1984–89. FRHistS 1974. *Publications:* (with Henry Pelling) Labour and Politics, 1958, 2nd edn 1982; (with J. Blondel and W. P. McCann) Constituency Politics, 1965; The Social and Political Thought of the British Labour Party, 1970; The Post Office Engineering Union, 1976; (with John Sewel) The Politics of Independence, 1981; Democracy in the Contemporary State, 1988; articles in academic jls. *Recreations:* reading poetry, eating and drinking, watching football and cricket, darts. *Address:* 2 Morag House, Oyne, Insch, Aberdeenshire AB52 6QT. *T:* Insch (0464) 5457. *Club:* Economicals Association Football and Cricket.

BEAM, Jacob D.; US Ambassador to USSR, 1969–73; *b* Princeton, NJ, 24 March 1908; *s* of Jacob Newton Beam and Mary Prince; *m* 1952, Margaret Glassford; one *s*. *Educ:* Kent Sch., USA; Princeton Univ. (BA 1929); Cambridge Univ., England (1929–30). Vice-Consul, Geneva, 1931–34; Third Sec., Berlin, 1934–40; Second Sec., London, 1941–45; Asst Political Adviser, HQ, US Forces, Germany, 1945–47; Chief of Central European Div., Dept of State, 1947–49; Counsellor and Consul-Gen., US Embassy, Djakarta, 1949–51; Actg US Rep., UN Commn for Indonesia, 1951; Counsellor, Belgrade, 1951–52; Minister-Counsellor, US Embassy, Moscow, 1952–53 (actg head); Dep. Asst Sec. of State, 1953–57; US Ambassador to Poland, 1957–61; Asst Dir, Internat. Relations Bureau, Arms Control and Disarmament Agency, USA, 1962–66; US Ambassador to Czechoslovakia, 1966–68. Chm., US Delegn to Internat. Telecomm. Union Plenipotentiary Conf., Malaga, 1973. Dir, Radio Free Europe, 1974–77. LLB *hc* Princeton, 1970. *Publication:* Multiple Exposure, 1978. *Address:* 3129 'O' Street NW, Washington, DC 20007, USA. *Club:* Metropolitan (Washington, DC).

BEAMENT, Sir James (William Longman), Kt 1980; ScD; FRS 1964; Drapers Professor of Agriculture, University of Cambridge, 1969–89, now Emeritus; Life Fellow, Queens' College, Cambridge, since 1989; *b* 17 Nov. 1921; *o c* of late T. Beament, Crewkerne, Somerset; *m* 1962, Juliet, *y d* of late Prof. Sir Ernest Barker, Cambridge; two *s*. *Educ:* Crewkerne Grammar Sch.; Queens' Coll., Cambridge; London Sch. of Tropical Medicine. Exhibitioner, Queens' Coll., 1941; BA 1943; MA 1946; PhD London 1945; ScD Cantab 1960. Research Officer with Agricultural Research Council, Cambridge, 1946; Cambridge University: Univ. Lectr, 1961; Reader in Insect Physiology, 1966; Hd of Dept of Applied Biol., 1969–89; Queens' College, Cambridge: Fellow and Tutor, 1961; Vice-Pres., 1981–86. Member: Adv. Bd for the Res. Councils, 1977; NERC, 1970–83 (Chm., 1977–80). Mem., Composers' Guild of Great Britain, 1967. Scientific Medal of Zoological Soc., 1963. *Publications:* many papers on insect physiology in scientific journals; Editor of several review volumes. *Recreations:* acoustics, playing the double-bass. *Address:* 19 Sedley Taylor Road, Cambridge CB2 2PW. *T:* Cambridge (0223) 243695; Queens' College, Cambridge CB3 9ET. *T:* Cambridge (0223) 335511. *Clubs:* Farmers'; Amateur Dramatic (Cambridge).

BEAMISH, Adrian John, CMG 1988; HM Diplomatic Service; Assistant Under Secretary of State (Americas, Australasia and Oceania), Foreign and Commonwealth Office, since 1989; *b* 21 Jan. 1939; *s* of Thomas Charles Constantine Beamish and Josephine Mary (*née* Lee); *m* 1965, Caroline Lipscomb; two *d*. *Educ:* Christian Brothers' Coll., Cork; Prior Park Coll., Bath; Christ's Coll., Cambridge (BA); Università per gli Stranieri, Perugia. Third, later Second Secretary, Tehran, 1963–66; Foreign Office, 1966–69; First Sec., UK Delegn, OECD, Paris, 1970–73; New Delhi, 1973–76; FCO, 1976–78; Counsellor, Dep. Head, Personnel Operations Dept, FCO, 1978–80; Counsellor (Economic), Bonn, 1981–85; Hd, Falkland Is Dept, FCO, 1985–87; Ambassador to Peru, 1987–89. *Recreations:* people, books, plants. *Address:* c/o Foreign and Commonwealth Office, SW1.

BEAMISH, Air Vice-Marshal Cecil Howard, CB 1970; FDSRCS; Director of Dental Services, Royal Air Force, 1969–73; *b* 31 March 1915; *s* of Frank George Beamish, Coleraine; *m* 1955, Frances Elizabeth Sarah Goucher; two *s*. *Educ:* Coleraine Acad.; Queen's Univ., Belfast. Joined Royal Air Force, 1936; Group Capt., 1958; Air Cdre, 1968; Air Vice-Marshal, 1969. QHDS 1969–73. *Recreations:* Rugby football, golf, squash. *Address:* East Keal Manor, Spilsby, Lincs PE23 4AS.

BEAMONT, Wing Comdr Roland Prosper, CBE 1969 (OBE 1953); DSO 1943, Bar 1944; DFC 1941, Bar 1943; DFC (US) 1946; FRAeS; author, aviation consultant; *b* 10 Aug. 1920; *s* of Lieut-Col E. C. Beamont and Dorothy Mary (*née* Haynes); *m* 1st, 1942, Shirley Adams (*d* 1945); one *d*; 2nd, 1946, Patricia Raworth; two *d*. *Educ:* Eastbourne Coll. Commissioned in RAF, 1939; served War of 1939–45, Fighter Command, RAF, BEF, Battle of Britain (despatches), Battle of France and Germany. Attached as Test Pilot to Hawker Aircraft Ltd during rest periods, in 1941–42 and 1943–44; Experimental Test Pilot, Gloster Aircraft Co. Ltd, 1946; Chief Test Pilot, English Electric Co., 1947–61; Special Dir and Dep. Chief Test Pilot, BAC, 1961–64; Director, Flight Operations, BAC Preston, later British Aerospace, Warton Division, 1965–78; Dir of Flight Operations, Panavia (Tornado testing), 1971–79. Events while Chief Test Pilot, English Electric Co. Ltd: 1st British pilot to fly at speed of sound (in USA), May 1948; 1st Flight of Britain's 1st jet bomber (the Canberra), May 1949; holder of Atlantic Record, Belfast-Gander, 4 hours 18 mins. Aug. 1951 and 1st two-way Atlantic Record, Belfast-Gander-Belfast, 10 hrs 4 mins Aug. 1952 (in a Canberra); first flight of P1, 1954 (Britain's first fully supersonic fighter); first British pilot in British aircraft to fly faster than sound in level flight, 1954, and first to fly at twice the speed of sound, Nov. 1958; first flight of Lightning supersonic all-weather fighter, 1957; first flight of TSR2, Sept. 1964 (Britain's first supersonic bomber). Britannia Trophy for 1953; Derry and Richards Memorial Medal, 1955; R. P. Alston Memorial Medal, RAeS, 1960; British Silver Medal for Aeronautics, 1965. Pres., Popular Flying Assoc., 1979–84. Master Pilot and Liveryman, Guild of Air Pilots. Hon. Fellow, Soc. of Experimental Testpilots, USA, 1985. DL Lancashire 1977–81. *Publications:* Phoenix into Ashes, 1968; Typhoon and Tempest at War, 1975; Testing Years, 1980; English Electric Canberra, 1984; English Electric P1 Lightning, 1985; Fighter Test Pilot, 1986; My Part of the Sky, 1989; Testing Early Jets, 1990. *Recreation:* fly-fishing. *Address:* Cross Cottage, Pentridge, Salisbury, Wilts SP5 5QX. *Club:* Royal Air Force.

BEAN, Basil, CBE 1985; Chief Executive (formerly Director-General), National House Building Council, since 1985; *b* 2 July 1931; *s* of Walter Bean and Alice Louise Bean; *m* 1956, Janet Mary Brown; one *d*. *Educ:* Archbishop Holgate Sch., York. Mem. CIPFA. York City, 1948–53; West Bromwich Borough, 1953–56; Sutton London Bor., 1957–62; Skelmersdale Develt Corp., 1962–66; Havering London Bor., 1967–69; Northampton Develt Corp., 1969–80 (Gen. Manager, 1977–80); Chief Exec., Merseyside Develt Corp., 1980–85; overseas consultancies. Mem., British Waterways Bd, 1985–88. Hon. FIAA&S. *Publications:* financial and technical papers. *Recreations:* reading, walking, travel. *Address:* NHBC, Buildmark House, Chiltern Avenue, Amersham, Bucks HP6 5AP. *T:* Amersham (0494) 434477; The Forge, Manor Farm, Church Lane, Princes Risborough, Bucks. *T:* Princes Risborough (08444) 6133. *Clubs:* Commonwealth Trust; Northampton and County (Northampton).

BEAN, Hugh (Cecil), CBE 1970; violinist (freelance); Professor of Violin, Royal College of Music, since 1954; *b* 22 Sept. 1929; *s* of Cecil Walter Claude Bean and Gertrude Alice Chapman; *m* 1963, Mary Dorothy Harrow; one *d*. *Educ:* Beckenham Grammar Sch. Studied privately, and at RCM, London (principal prize for violin) with Albert Sammons, 1938–57; Boise Trav. Schol., 1952; at Brussels Conservatoire with André Gertler (double premier prix for solo and chamber music playing), 1952–53. National Service, Gren. Gds, 1949–51. Formerly Leader of Harvey Phillips String Orch. and Dennis Brain Chamber Orch.; Leader of Philharmonia and New Philharmonia Orch., 1957–67; Associate Leader, BBC Symph. Orch., 1967–69; Co-Leader, Philharmonia Orch., 1990. Member: Bean-Parkhouse Duo; Music Gp of London. Has made solo commercial records, and has performed as soloist with many major orchestras. Hon. ARCM 1961, FRCM 1968. *Recreations:* design and construction of flying model aircraft; steam-driven passenger hauling model railways; gramophone record collection. *Address:* Rosemary Cottage, 30 Stone Park Avenue, Beckenham, Kent. *T:* 081–650 8774.

BEAN, Rev. Canon John Victor; Vicar, St Mary, Cowes, Isle of Wight, 1966–91, and Priest-in-charge, All Saints, Gurnard, IoW, 1978–91; Chaplain to the Queen, since 1980; *b* 1 Dec. 1925; *s* of Albert Victor and Eleanor Ethel Bean; *m* 1955, Nancy Evelyn Evans; two *s* one *d* (and one *d* died in infancy). *Educ:* local schools; Grammar Sch., Gt Yarmouth; Downing Coll., Cambridge (MA); Salisbury Theological Coll., 1948. Served War, RNVR, 1944–46; returned to Cambridge, 1946–48. Assistant Curate: St James, Milton, Portsmouth, 1950–55; St Peter and St Paul, Fareham, 1955–59; Vicar, St Helen's, IoW, 1959–66. Rural Dean of West Wight, 1968–73; Clergy Proctor for Diocese of Portsmouth, 1973–80; Hon. Canon, Portsmouth Cathedral, 1970–91, Canon Emeritus, 1991. *Recreations:* photography, boat-watching, tidying up. *Address:* 4 Parkmead Court, Park Road, Ryde, Isle of Wight PO33 2HD. *Club:* Gurnard Sailing (Gurnard).

BEAN, Leonard, CMG 1964; MBE (mil.) 1945; MA; Secretary, Southern Gas Region, 1966–79, retired; *b* 19 Sept. 1914; *s* of late Harry Bean, Bradford, Yorks, and late Agnes Sherwood Beattie, Worcester; *m* 1938, Nancy Winifred (*d* 1990), *d* of Robert John Neilson, Dunedin, NZ; one *d*. *Educ:* Canterbury Coll., NZ; Queens' Coll., Cambridge. Served War of 1939–45: Major, 2nd NZ Div. (despatches, MBE). Entered Colonial Service, N Rhodesia, 1945; Provincial Comr, 1959; Perm. Sec. (Native Affairs), 1961; acted as Minister for Native Affairs and Natural Resources in periods, 1961–64; Permanent Secretary: to Prime Minister, 1964; also to President, 1964. Adviser to President, Zambia, 1964–66. *Recreations:* golf, gardening. *Address:* Squirrels Gate, 20 Ashley Park, Ringwood, Hants BH24 2HA. *T:* Ringwood (0425) 475262. *Clubs:* MCC; Bramshaw Golf.

BEAN, Marisa; *see* Robles, Marisa.

BEAR, Leslie William, CBE 1972; Editor of Official Report (Hansard), House of Commons, 1954–72; *b* 16 June 1911; *s* of William Herbert Bear, Falkenham, Suffolk; *m* 1st, 1932, Betsy Sobels (*d* 1934), Lisse, Holland; 2nd, 1936, Annelise Gross (*d* 1979), Trier, Germany; two *s*. *Educ:* Gregg Sch., Ipswich. Served War, 1943–44, Royal Air Force. Mem. of Official Reporting Staff, League of Nations, Geneva, 1930–36; joined Official Report (Hansard), House of Commons, 1936; Asst Ed., 1951. *Recreations:* music, gardening, reading. *Address:* Medleys, Ufford, Woodbridge, Suffolk. *T:* Eyke (0394) 460358.

BEARD, Allan Geoffrey, CB 1979; Under Secretary, Department of Health and Social Security, 1968–79 (Ministry of Social Security 1966–68); *b* 18 Oct. 1919; *s* of late Major Henry Thomas Beard and Florence Mercy Beard; *m* 1945, Helen McDonagh; one *d*. *Educ:* Ormskirk Grammar Sch. Clerical Officer, Air Min., 1936; Exec. Off., Higher Exec. Off., Asst Principal, Assistance Board, 1938–47; Army Service, 1940–46 (Capt., RE); Principal, Nat. Assistance Board, 1950; Asst Sec., 1962. Hon. Treasurer, Motability, 1985–. *Recreations:* gardening, do-it-yourself. *Address:* 51 Rectory Park, Sanderstead, Surrey CR2 9JR. *T:* 081–657 4197. *Club:* Royal Automobile.

BEARD, (Christopher) Nigel; Senior Consultant, Imperial Chemical Industries Ltd, since 1979; *b* 10 Oct. 1936; *o s* of Albert Leonard Beard, Castleford, Yorks, and Irene (*née* Bowes); *m* 1969, Jennifer Anne, *d* of T. B. Cotton, Guildford, Surrey; one *s* one *d*. *Educ:* Castleford Grammar Sch., Yorks; University Coll. London. BSc Hons, Special Physics. Asst Mathematics Master, Tadcaster Grammar Sch., Yorks, 1958–59; Physicist with English Electric Atomic Power Div., working on design of Hinckley Point Nuclear Power Station, 1959–61; Market Researcher, Esso Petroleum Co., assessing future UK Energy demands and market for oil, 1961. MoD: Scientific Officer, later Principal Scientific Officer, in Defence Operational Analysis Estabt (engaged in analysis of central defence policy and investment issues), 1961–68, and Supt of Studies pertaining to Land Ops; responsible for policy and investment studies related to Defence of Europe and strategic movement of the Army, Dec. 1968–72; Chief Planner, Strategy, GLC, 1973–74; Dir, London Docklands Develt Team, 1974–79. Mem., SW Thames RHA, 1978–86; Mem. Bd, Royal Marsden Hosp., 1982–90. Contested (Lab): Woking, 1979; Portsmouth N, 1983. FRSA. *Publication:* The Practical Use of Linear Programming in Planning and Analysis, 1974 (HMSO). *Recreations:* reading, walking, sailing, the theatre. *Address:* Lanquhart, The Ridgway, Pyrford, Woking, Surrey. *T:* Byfleet (09323) 48630. *Club:* Athenæum.

BEARD, Derek, CBE 1979; Director, Westminster Democratic Studies Ltd, since 1988; *b* 16 May 1930; *s* of Walter Beard and Lily Beard (*née* Mellors); *m* 1st, 1953, Ruth Davies (marr. diss. 1966); two *s*; 2nd, 1966, Renate Else, *d* of late W. E. Kautz, Berlin and Mecklenburg; two *s*. *Educ:* Hulme Grammar Sch., Oldham; Brasenose Coll., Oxford (MA, DipEd). Stand Grammar Sch., Whitefield, 1954–56; HMOCS, Nyasaland, 1956–59; Asst Educn Officer, WR Yorks, 1959–61; Sen. Asst, Oxfordshire, 1961–63; British Council, Pakistan, 1963–65; Producer, BBC Overseas Educnl Recordings Unit, 1965–66; British Council: Dir, Appts, Services Dept, 1966–70; Dep. Rep., India, 1970–73; Controller, Educn and Science Div., 1973–77; Rep. in Germany, 1977–81, Belgium, 1981–84; Asst Dir Gen., 1984–87. Adviser, 21st Century Trust, 1987–88; Academic Dir, Oxford Internat. Summer Sch., 1988. MInstD. *Publications:* articles on educn and cultural relns. *Recreations:* sculpture, music, travel. *Address:* 3 College Avenue, Epsom, Surrey KT17 4HN. *Club:* Anglo-Belgian.

BEARD, Nigel; *see* Beard, C. N.

BEARD, Prof. Richard William, MD 1971; FRCOG 1972; Professor and Head of Department of Obstetrics and Gynaecology, St Mary's Hospital Medical School, since 1972; *b* 4 May 1931; *s* of late William and of Irene Beard; *m* 1st, 1957, Jane; two *s*; 2nd, 1979, Irène Victoire Marie de Marotte de Montigny; one *s*. *Educ:* Westminster Sch.; Christ's Coll., Cambridge (MA, MB Chir); St Bartholomew's Hosp. Obstetrician and Gynaecologist, RAF Changi, Singapore, 1957–60; Chelsea Hosp. for Women, 1961–62; UCH, 1962–63; Senior Lecturer/Hon. Consultant: Queen Charlotte's and Chelsea Hosps, 1964–68; King's Coll. Hosp., 1968–72. Advr to Social Services Select Cttee, H of C (2nd Report on Perinatal and Neonatal Mortality), 1978–80; Civil Consultant in Obstetrics and Gynaecology to RAF, 1983–; Consultant Advr in Obst. and Gyn. to DHSS, 1985–. Mem., Acad. Royale de Medécine de Belgique, 1983. *Publications:* Fetal Physiology and Medicine, 1976, 2nd edn 1983; contribs to learned jls. *Recreations:* tennis, sailing, Chinese history. *Address:* 64 Elgin Crescent, W11 2JJ. *T:* 071–221 1930. *Club:* Garrick.

BEARDMORE, Alexander Francis, OBE 1987; FEng, FIMechE, FIEE; Engineer in Chief, Post Office, 1981–91, retired; *b* 20 Feb. 1931; *s* of Alexander Beardmore and Alice Beardmore (*née* Turner); *m* 1959, Pamela Anne Cozens; two *d*. *Educ:* Mitcham County Grammar School; London Univ. (BScEng, MSc). FIMatM. Nat. Service, Royal Signals, 1954–56. Post Office, 1948–91: Research Engineer, 1948–68; Controller Marketing, London Postal Region, 1972–77; Asst Dir, equipment provision, 1977–81. Chm., Unit Load Tech. Cttee, British Materials Handling Board, 1983–89. FBIM. *Recreations:* Lions International, gardening, DIY, walking. *Address:* Three Gables, Cheltenham Road, Baunton, Cirencester, Glos GL7 7BE. *T:* Cirencester (0285) 654361.

BEARDMORE, Prof. John Alec, CBiol, FIBiol; Professor of Genetics, since 1966 and Head, School of Biological Sciences, since 1988, University College of Swansea; *b* 1 May 1930; *s* of George Edward Beardmore and Anne Jean (*née* Warrington); *m* 1953, Anne Patricia Wallace; three *s* one *d* (and one *s* decd). *Educ:* Burton on Trent Grammar Sch.; Birmingham Central Tech. Coll.; Univ. of Sheffield. BSc (1st Cl. Botany) 1953, PhD (Genetics) 1956. Research Demonstrator, Dept of Botany, Univ. of Sheffield, 1954–56; Commonwealth Fund Fellow, Columbia Univ., 1956–58; Vis. Asst Prof. in Plant Breeding, Cornell Univ., 1958; Lectr in Genetics, Univ. of Sheffield, 1958–61; Prof. of Genetics and Dir, Genetics Inst., Univ. of Groningen, 1961–66; Nat. Science Foundn Senior Foreign Fellow, Pennsylvania State Univ., 1966; Dean of Science, University Coll. of Swansea, 1974–76, Vice-Principal, 1977–80, Dir, Inst. of Marine Studies, 1983–87. Member: NERC Aquatic Life Scis Cttee, 1982–87 (Chm., 1984–87); CNAA: Life Scis Cttee, 1979–85; Cttee for Science, 1985–87; Bd, Council of Sci. and Technology Insts, 1983–85 (Chm., 1984–85); Council, Galton Inst. (formerly Eugenics Soc.), 1980– (Chm., Res. Cttee, 1979–87); British Nat. Cttee for Biology, 1983–87; Council, Linnean Soc., 1989–; Vice-Pres., Inst. of Biol., 1985–87 (Mem. Council, 1976–79; Hon. Sec., 1980–85); UK rep., Council of European Communities Biologists Assoc., 1980–87. FRSA; FLS. Darwin Lectr, Inst. of Biol. and Eugenics Soc, 1984. Univ. of Helsinki Medal, 1980. *Publications:* (ed with B. Battaglia) Marine Organisms: genetics ecology and evolution, 1977; articles on evolutionary genetics, human genetics and biological educn. *Recreations:* bridge, fell walking. *Address:* 153 Derwen Fawr Road, Swansea SA2 8ED. *T:* Swansea (0792) 206232. *Club:* Athenæum.

BEARDS, Paul Francis Richmond; *b* 1 Dec. 1916; *s* of late Dr Clifford Beards and Dorothy (*née* Richmond); *m* 1950, Margaret Elizabeth, *y d* of late V. R. Aronson, CBE, KC; one *s* one *d*. *Educ:* Marlborough; Queen's Coll., Oxford (Open Scholar; 1st cl. hons Mod. Hist.). Entered Admin. Class of Home Civil Service, 1938; Asst Princ., War Office; served in Army, 1940–44; Principal War Office, 1945; Asst Private Sec. to successive Prime Ministers, 1945–48; Princ. Private Sec. to successive Secs of State for War, 1951–54; Asst Sec., 1954; Imp. Def. Coll., 1961; Asst Under-Sec. of State, MoD, 1964–69; Comr for Administration and Finance, Forestry Commn, 1969; retd, 1970. Coronation Medal, 1953. *Recreations:* fishing, gardening, archæology. *Address:* Thrale Cottage, Budleigh Salterton, Devon EX9 6EA. *T:* Budleigh Salterton (03954) 2084. *Club:* Commonwealth Trust.

BEARDSWORTH, Maj.-Gen. Simon John, CB 1984; consultant, defence industries; *b* 18 April 1929; *s* of late Paymaster-Captain Stanley Thomas Beardsworth, RN and Pearl Sylvia Emma (Biddy) Beardsworth (*née* Blake); *m* 1954, Barbara Bingham Turner; three *s*. *Educ:* RC Sch. of St Edmund's Coll., Ware; RMA Sandhurst; RMCS. BSc. Commissioned Royal Tank Regt, 1949; Regtl service, staff training and staff appts, 1950–69; CO 1st RTR, 1970–72; Project Manager, Future Main Battle Tank, 1973–77; Student, Royal Naval War College, 1977; Dir of Projects, Armoured Fighting Vehicles, 1977–80; Dep. Comdt, RMCS, 1980–81; Vice Master Gen. of the Ordnance, 1981–84, retired. *Recreations:* game shooting, travel, support to equestrian events, authorship. *Address:* c/o Lloyds Bank, Chard, Somerset. *Club:* Army and Navy.

BEARE, Robin Lyell Blin, MB, BS; FRCS; Hon. Consultant Plastic Surgeon: Queen Victoria Hospital, East Grinstead, since 1960; Brighton General Hospital and Brighton and Lewes Group of Hospitals, since 1960; Hon. Consulting Plastic Surgeon, St Mary's Hospital, London, since 1976 (Consultant Plastic Surgeon, 1959–76); *b* 31 July 1922; *s* of late Stanley Samuel Beare, OBE, FRCS, and late Cecil Mary Guise Beare (*née* Lyell); *m* 1947, Iris Bick; two *s* two *d*. *Educ:* Radley (scholar). Middlesex Hosp. Medical Sch. MB, BS (Hons) 1952 (dist. Surg.); FRCS (Eng) 1955. Served with RAF Bomber Command (Aircrew) 1940–46. Formerly Ho. Surg., Casualty Officer, Asst Pathologist and Surgical Registrar, The Middlesex Hosp., 1952–56. Surg. Registrar, Plastic Surgery and Jaw Injuries Centre, Queen Victoria Hosp., East Grinstead, 1957–60. Examr in gen. surgery for FRCS, 1972–78. Fellow Assoc. of Surgeons of Gt Britain and Ireland; Fellow Royal Society Med.; Mem. Brit. Assoc. of Plastic Surgeons; Mem. of Bd of Trustees, McIndoe Memorial Research Unit, E Grinstead; Hon. Mem. Société Française de Chirurgie Plastique et Reconstructive. *Publications:* various on surgical problems in BMJ, Amer. Jl of Surgery, etc. *Recreations:* fishing, shooting. *Address:* Scraggs Farm, Cowden, Kent. *T:* Cowden (0342) 850386.

BEARE, Stuart Newton; Partner, Richards Butler, Solicitors, since 1969 (Senior Partner, 1988–91); *b* 6 Oct. 1936; *s* of Newton Beare and Joyce (*née* Atkinson); *m* 1974, Cheryl Wells. *Educ:* Clifton Coll.; Clare Coll., Cambridge (MA, LLB). Nat. Service, commnd Royal Signals, attached RWAFF, 1956–57. Plebiscite Supervisory Officer, N Cameroons, 1960–61; admitted solicitor, 1964. *Recreations:* mountain walking, ski-ing. *Addresses:* 24 Ripplevale Grove, N1 1HU. *T:* 071–609 0766. *Clubs:* Alpine, City of London, Oriental.

BEARN, Prof. Alexander Gordon, MD; FRCP, FRCPEd, FACP; Professor of Medicine, Cornell University Medical College, 1966–89, now Professor Emeritus (Stanton Griffis Distinguished Medical Professor, 1976–79); Attending Physician, The New York Hospital, since 1966; Adjunct Professor and Visiting Professor, Rockefeller University, 1966–88, Hon. Physician, since 1988; *b* 29 March 1923; *s* of E. G. Bearn, CB, CBE; *m* 1952, Margaret, *d* of Clarence Slocum, Fanwood, NJ, USA; one *s* one *d*. *Educ:* Epsom Coll.; Guy's Hosp., London. Postgraduate Medical Sch. of London, 1949–51. Rockefeller Univ., 1951–66; Hon. Research Asst, University Coll. (Galton Laboratory), 1959–60; Prof. and Sen. Physician, Rockefeller Univ., 1964–66; Chm., Dept of Medicine, Cornell Univ. Med. Coll., 1966–77; Physician-in-Chief, NY Hosp., 1966–77; Sen. Vice Pres., Medical and Scientific Affairs, Merck Sharp and Dohme Internat., 1979–88. Woodrow Wilson Foundn Vis. Fellow, 1979–80. Trustee: Rockefeller Univ., 1970–; Howard Hughes Medical Inst., 1987–; Dir, Josiah Macy Jr Foundn, 1981–. Mem. Editorial Bd, several scientific and med. jls. Lectures: Lowell, Harvard, 1958; Medical Research Soc., 1969; Lilly, RCP, 1973; Harvey, 1975; Lettsomian, Med. Soc., 1976. Macy Faculty Scholar Award, 1974–75. Alfred Benzon Prize, Denmark, 1979. Member: Nat. Acad. Science; Amer. Philosophical Soc.; Foreign Mem., Norwegian Acad. Science and Letters. Hon. MD Catholic Univ., Korea, 1968; Docteur *hc* Paris, 1975. *Publications:* articles on human genetics and liver disease, 1950–; (Co-Editor) Progress in Medical Genetics, Vol. 2 and subsequent annual vols, 1962–85; (Associate Editor) Cecil and Loeb: Textbook of Medicine. *Recreations:* biography, collecting snuff-mulls, travel. *Address:* 1225 Park Avenue, New York, NY 10128, USA. *T:* 212–534–2495. *Clubs:* Knickerbocker, Century (NY); Crail Golf.

BEARNE, Air Vice-Marshal Guy, CB 1956; *b* 5 Nov. 1908; *y s* of late Lieut-Col L. C. Bearne, DSO, AM; *m* 1933, Aileen Cartwright, *e d* of late H. J. Randall, Hove; one *s* two *d*. Commissioned RAF, 1929; served in various Bomber Sqdns, 1930–33; specialist armament course, 1933; armament duties, 1934–44; Bomber Command, 1944–45 (despatches twice); Staff Officer i/c Administration, RAF Malaya, 1946; Joint Services Staff Coll., 1947; Dep. Dir Organisation (Projects), 1947–49; Command of Central Gunnery Sch., 1949–51; SASO, Rhodesian Air Training Gp, 1951–52; AOC Rhodesian Air Training Gp, 1953; Dir of Organisation (Establishments), Air Ministry, 1954–56; Air Officer in Charge of Administration, Technical Training Command, 1956–61; retd, 1961. *Address:* 2 Mill Close, Hill Deverill, Warminster, Wilts BA12 7EE. *T:* Warminster (0985) 40533.

BEARSTED, 4th Viscount *cr* 1925, of Maidstone; **Peter Montefiore Samuel,** MC 1942; TD 1951; Bt 1903; Baron 1921; Banker; Director, Hill Samuel Group, 1965–87 (Deputy Chairman, after merger with Philip Hill, Higginson & Co., 1965–82); Chairman: Dylon International Ltd, 1958–84; Hill Samuel & Co. (Ireland) Ltd, 1964–84; *b* 9 Dec. 1911; second *s* of Viscount Bearsted and Dorothea, *e d* of late E. Montefiore Micholls; *S* brother, 1986; *m* 1st, 1939, Deirdre du Barry (marr. diss. 1942); 2nd, 1946, Hon. Elizabeth Adelaide Pearce Serocold (*d* 1983), *d* of late Baron Cohen, PC; two *s* one *d*; 3rd, 1984, Nina Alice Hilary, *widow* of Michael Pocock, CBE. *Educ:* Eton; New College, Oxford (BA). Served Warwickshire Yeo, Middle East and Italy, 1939–45. Director: M. Samuel & Co. Ltd, 1935 (Dep. Chm. 1948); Shell Transport & Trading Co. Ltd, 1938–82; Samuel Properties Ltd, 1961–86 (Chm., 1982–86); Mayborn Group PLC, 1946– (Chm., 1946–88); Trades Union Unit Trust Managers Ltd, 1961–82; General Consolidated Investment Trust Ltd, 1975–83. President, Norwood Home for Jewish Children, 1962–79; Hon. Treas., Nat. Assoc. for Gifted Children, 1968–81; Chairman: Council, Royal Free Hospital of Medicine, 1973–82 (Mem., 1948–); Bd of Governors, Royal Free Hosp., 1956–68 (Governor, 1939–). *Recreation:* shooting. *Heir:* *s* Hon. Nicholas Alan Samuel [*b* 22 Jan. 1950; *m* 1975, Caroline Jane, *d* of Dr David Sacks; one *s* four *d*]. *Address:* 9 Campden Hill Court, W8 7HX; Farley Hall, Farley Hill, near Reading, Berkshire RG7 1UL. *T:* Eversley (0734) 733242. *Club:* White's.

BEASLEY, John T.; *see* Telford Beasley.

BEASLEY, Michael Charles, IPFA, FCA, FCCA; County Treasurer, Royal County of Berkshire, 1970–88; *b* 20 July 1924; *y s* of late William Isaac Beasley and Mary Gladys (*née* Williams), Ipswich, Suffolk; *m* 1955, Jean Anita Mary, *o d* of late Reginald John Webber and of Margaret Dorothy (*née* Rees), Penarth, S Glamorgan; one *s*. *Educ:* Northgate Grammar Sch., Ipswich. BScEcon London. Treasurer's Dept, East Suffolk County Council, 1940–48; served Royal Navy, 1943–46; Treasurer's Dept, Staffordshire CC, 1948–51; Educn Accountant, Glamorgan CC, 1951–54; Asst County Treasurer, Nottinghamshire CC, 1954–61; Dep. County Treasurer, Royal County of Berkshire, 1961–70, Acting Chief Exec., 1986. Examiner, CIPFA, 1963–66; Financial Adviser, Assoc. of County Councils and former County Councils Assoc., 1971–87; Hon. Treasurer, Soc. of County Treasurers, 1984–88 (Hon. Sec., 1972–80, Vice-Pres., 1980–81, Pres., 1981–82); Mem., Treasury Cttee on Local Authority Borrowing, 1972–87; Member Council: Local Authorities Mutual Investment Trust, 1974–75; RIPA, 1976–82. *Publications:* contribs to jls on local govt finance and computers. *Recreations:* pottering and pondering. *Address:* Greenacre, Hyde End Road, Spencers Wood, Berkshire RG7 1BU. *T:* Reading (0734) 883868.

BEASLEY, Prof. William Gerald, CBE 1980; BA, PhD; FRHistS; FBA 1967; Professor of the History of the Far East, University of London, 1954–83; Head of Japan Research Centre, School of Oriental and African Studies, 1978–83; *b* 1919; *m* 1955, Hazel Polwin; one *s*. *Educ:* Magdalen Coll. Sch., Brackley; University Coll., London. Served War, 1940–46, RNVR. Lecturer, Sch. of Oriental and African Studies, University of London, 1947. Mem., 1961–68, British Chm., 1964–68, Anglo-Japanese Mixed Cultural Commn. Vice-Pres., British Acad., 1974–75, Treasurer, 1975–79. Hon. Mem., Japan Acad., 1984. Hon. DLitt Hong Kong, 1978. Order of the Rising Sun (Third Class), Japan, 1983. *Publications:* Great Britain and the opening of Japan, 1951; Select Documents on Japanese foreign policy, 1853–1868, 1955; The Modern History of Japan, 1963; The Meiji Restoration, 1972; Japanese Imperialism 1894–1945, 1987; The Rise of Modern Japan, 1990. *Address:* 172 Hampton Road, Twickenham TW2 5NJ.

BEASLEY-MURRAY, George Raymond, DD, PhD; Senior Professor of New Testament Interpretation, Southern Baptist Theological Seminary, Louisville, Kentucky, since 1980; *b* 10 Oct. 1916; *s* of George Alfred Beasley; *m* 1942, Ruth Weston; three *s* one *d*. *Educ:* City of Leicester Boys' Sch.; Spurgeon's Coll. and King's Coll., London; Jesus Coll., Cambridge (MA). BD 1941, MTh 1945, PhD 1952, DD 1964, London; DD Cambridge, 1989. Baptist Minister, Ilford, Essex, 1941–48; Cambridge, 1948–50; New Testament Lectr, Spurgeon's Coll., 1950–56; New Testament Prof., Baptist Theological Coll., Rüschlikon, Zürich, 1956–58; Principal, Spurgeon's Coll., 1958–73; Buchanan-Harrison Prof. of New Testament Interpretation, Southern Baptist Theol Seminary, Louisville, Ky, 1973–80. Pres., Baptist Union of Great Britain and Ireland, 1968–69. Hon. DD McMaster, 1973; Hon. LLD CNAA, 1989. *Publications:* Christ is Alive, 1947; Jesus and the Future, 1954; Preaching the Gospel from the Gospels, 1956; A Commentary on Mark Thirteen, 1957; Baptism in the New Testament, 1962; The Resurrection of Jesus Christ, 1964; Baptism Today and Tomorrow, 1966; Commentary on 2 Corinthians (Broadman Commentary), 1971; The Book of Revelation (New Century Bible), 1974; The Coming of God, 1983; Jesus and the Kingdom of God, 1986; Commentary on the Gospel of John (Word Commentary), 1987; Word Biblical Themes: John, 1989. *Recreation:* music. *Address:* 4 Holland Road, Hove, E Sussex BN3 1JJ.

See also Rev. Dr P. Beasley-Murray.

BEASLEY-MURRAY, Rev. Dr Paul; Principal of Spurgeon's College, since 1986; *b* 14 March 1944; *s* of Rev. Dr George R. Beasley-Murray, *qv*; *m* 1967, Caroline (*née* Griffiths); three *s* one *d*. *Educ:* Trinity School of John Whitgift; Jesus Coll., Cambridge (MA); Northern Baptist Coll. and Manchester Univ. (PhD); Baptist Theol Seminary, Rüschlikon and Zürich Univ. Baptist Missionary Soc., Zaire (Professor at National Univ., Theol. Faculty), 1970–72; Pastor of Altrincham Baptist Church, Cheshire, 1973–86. *Publications*: (with A. Wilkinson) Turning the Tide, 1981; Pastors Under Pressure, 1989; Dynamic Leadership, 1990; (ed) Mission to the World, 1991; Faith and Festivity, 1991. *Recreations*: music, walking. *Address*: Spurgeon's College, South Norwood Hill, SE25 6DJ. *T*: 081–653 1235.

BEASTALL, John Sale; Treasury Officer of Accounts, since 1987; *b* 2 July 1941; *s* of Howard and Marjorie Betty Beastall (*née* Sale). *Educ*: St Paul's School; Balliol College, Oxford (BA 1963). Asst Principal, HM Treasury, 1963–67 (Asst Private Sec. to Chancellor of the Exchequer, 1966–67); Principal: HM Treasury, 1967–68 and 1971–75 (Private Sec. to Paymaster General, 1974–75); CSD, 1968–71; Assistant Secretary: HM Treasury, 1975–79 and 1981–85; CSD, 1979–81; DES, 1985–87. *Recreation*: Christian youth work. *Address*: c/o HM Treasury, Parliament Street, SW1P 3AG. *Club*: United Oxford & Cambridge University.

BEATON, Chief Superintendent James Wallace, GC 1974; LVO 1987; Chief Superintendent, Metropolitan Police, since 1985; *b* St Fergus, Aberdeenshire, 16 Feb. 1943; *s* of J. A. Beaton and B. McDonald; *m* 1965, Anne C. Ballantyne; two *d*. *Educ*: Peterhead Acad., Aberdeenshire. Joined Metropolitan Police, 1962; Notting Hill, 1962–66; Sergeant, Harrow Road, 1966–71; Station Sergeant, Wembley, 1971–73; Royalty Protection Officer, 'A' Division, 1973; Police Officer to The Princess Anne, 1973–79; Police Inspector, 1974; Chief Inspector, 1979; Superintendent, 1983. Director's Honor Award, US Secret Service, 1974. *Recreations*: reading, keeping fit.

BEATSON, Jack; Law Commissioner for England and Wales, since 1989; Fellow and Tutor in Law, Merton College, Oxford, since 1973; *b* 3 Nov. 1948; *s* of late John James Beatson and of Miriam Beatson (*née* White); *m* 1973, Charlotte, *y d* of Lt-Col J. A. Christie-Miller; one *s* one *d*. *Educ*: Whittingehame Coll., Brighton; Brasenose Coll., Oxford (BCL, MA). Called to the Bar, Inner Temple, 1972; Lectr in Law, Univ. of Bristol, 1972–73. Visiting Professor: Osgoode Hall Law Sch., Toronto, 1979; Univ. of Virginia Law Sch., 1980, 1983; Vis. Sen. Teaching Fellow, Nat Univ. of Singapore, 1987. *Publications*: (ed jtly) Chitty on Contract, 25th edn 1982, 26th edn 1989; (with M. H. Matthews) Administrative Law: Cases and Materials, 1983, 2nd edn 1989; The Use and Abuse of Restitution, 1991; articles on administrative law and restitution in legal jls. *Recreations*: gardening, travelling.

BEATTIE, Hon. Sir Alexander (Craig), Kt 1973; President, The Eryldene Trust, 1983–89; *b* 24 Jan. 1912; *e s* of Edmund Douglas and Amie Louisa Beattie; *m* 1st, 1944, Joyce Pearl Alder (*d* 1977); two *s*; 2nd, 1978, Joyce Elizabeth de Groot. *Educ*: Fort Street High Sch., Sydney; Univ. of Sydney (BA, LLB; Hon. LLD). Admitted to NSW Bar, 1936. Served War of 1939–45: Captain, 2nd AIF, Royal Australian Armoured Corps, New Guinea and Borneo. Pres., Industrial Commn of NSW, 1966–81 (Mem., 1955). Trustee, Royal Botanic Gardens and Govt Domain, Sydney, 1976–82, Chm. 1980–82. *Recreations*: gardening, bowls. *Club*: Australian (Sydney).

BEATTIE, Anne Heather; *see* Steel, A. H.

BEATTIE, Prof. Arthur James, FRSE 1957; Professor of Greek at Edinburgh University, 1951–81; Dean of the Faculty of Arts, 1963–65; *b* 28 June 1914, *e s* of Arthur John Rait Beattie. *Educ*: Montrose Academy; Aberdeen Univ.; Sidney Sussex Coll., Cambridge. Wilson Travelling Fellowship, Aberdeen, 1938–40. Served War, 1940–45; RA 1940–41; Int. Corps, 1941–45; Major GS02; despatches, 1945. Fellow and Coll. Lectr, Sidney Sussex Coll., 1946–51; Faculty Asst Lectr and Univ. Lectr in Classics, Cambridge, 1946–51. Chm. Governors, Morrison's Acad., Crieff, 1962–75; Governor, Sedbergh Sch., 1967–78. Comdr, Royal Order of the Phœnix (Greece), 1966. *Publications*: articles contributed to classical jls. *Recreations*: walking, bird-watching. *Club*: New (Edinburgh).

BEATTIE, Charles Noel, QC 1962; retired; *b* 4 Nov. 1912; *s* of Michael William Beattie and Edith Beattie (*née* Lickfold); *m*; three *d*. *Educ*: Lewes Grammar Sch. LLB (London). Admitted a solicitor, 1938. Served War of 1939–45 (despatches), Capt. RASC. Called to the Bar, Lincoln's Inn, 1946; Bencher 1971. *Publication*: My Wartime Escapades, 1987. *Address*: 27 Old Buildings, Lincoln's Inn, WC2A 3UJ. *T*: 071–404 4931.

BEATTIE, David, CMG 1989; HM Diplomatic Service; Minister and Deputy UK Permanent Representative to NATO, Brussels, since 1987; *b* 5 March 1938; *s* of George William David Beattie and Norna Alice (*née* Nicolson); *m* 1966, Ulla Marita Alha, *d* of late Allan Alha and of Brita-Maja (*née* Tuominen), Helsinki, Finland; two *d*. *Educ*: Merchant Taylors' Sch., Crosby; Lincoln Coll., Oxford (BA 1964, MA 1967). National Service, Royal Navy, 1957–59; Sub-Lieut RNR, 1959; Lieut RNR 1962–67. Entered HM Foreign (now Diplomatic) Service, 1963; FO, 1963–64; Moscow, 1964–66; FO, 1966–70; Nicosia, 1970–74; FCO, 1974–78; Counsellor, later Dep. Head, UK Delegn to Negotiations on Mutual Reduction of Forces and Armaments and Associated Measures in Central Europe, Vienna, 1978–82; Counsellor (Commercial), Moscow, 1982–85; Head of Energy, Science and Space Dept, FCO, 1985–87. Freeman, City of London, 1989. FIL 1990. *Recreations*: bridge, walking, history of the House of Stuart. *Address*: c/o Foreign and Commonwealth Office, SW1A 2AH. *Club*: Travellers'.

BEATTIE, Hon. Sir David (Stuart), GCMG 1980; GCVO 1981; QSO 1985; Governor-General of New Zealand, 1980–85; Chairman, New Zealand International Festival of the Arts, since 1987; *b* Sydney, Australia, 29 Feb. 1924; *s* of Joseph Nesbitt Beattie; *m* 1950, Norma Macdonald, QSO, *d* of John Macdonald; three *s* four *d*. *Educ*: Dilworth Sch.; Univ. of Auckland (LLB). Served War of 1939–45, Naval Officer. Barrister and Solicitor; President Auckland Dist Law Soc., 1964; QC 1965; Judge of Supreme Court, 1969–80; Chairman, Royal Commission on the Courts, 1977–78. Chm., NZ Meat Industry Assoc. (Inc.), 1988–90; Pres., NZ Olympic and Commonwealth Games Assoc., 1989–. Chairman: Sir Winston Churchill Memorial Trust Board, 1975–80; Trustees, NZ Sports Foundn, 1977–80. Hon. LLD Auckland, 1983. *Publications*: legal articles. *Address*: 18 Golf Road, Heretaunga, Wellington, New Zealand.

BEATTIE, Thomas Brunton, CMG 1981; OBE 1968; HM Diplomatic Service, retired 1982; *b* 17 March 1924; *s* of Joseph William Beattie and Jessie Dewar (*née* Brunton), Rutherglen; *m* 1st, 1956, Paula Rahkola (marr. diss. 1981); one *d*; 2nd, 1982, Josephine Marion Collins. *Educ*: Rutherglen Acad.; Pembroke Coll., Cambridge. MA. Served RAF, 1943–47. Jt Press Reading Service, British Embassy, Moscow, 1947; Finnish Secretariat, British Legation, Helsinki, 1951; FO, 1954; Second Sec., Madrid, 1956; FO, 1960; First Sec., Athens, 1964; First Sec., later Counsellor, FCO, 1969; Counsellor, Rome, 1977, FCO 1981. Mem., Inst. of Translation and Interpreting, 1991. Treas., Scottish Covenanter Memls Assoc., 1991–. *Publications*: translated: Viktor Suvorov, Icebreaker, 1990; Vladimir Kuzichkin, Inside the KGB, 1990. *Recreations*: unremarkable. *Address*: Cairnside, Kirkland of Glencairn, Moniaive, Dumfriesshire DG3 4HD. *Clubs*: Carlton; Royal Scottish Automobile (Glasgow).

BEATTIE, William John Hunt Montgomery, MA Cantab; MD, FRCS, FRCOG, FRCGP; Consultant Gynæcologist and Obstetric Surgeon, St Bartholomew's Hospital; Gynæcologist: Leatherhead Hospital; Florence Nightingale Hospital; retired. *Educ*: Cambridge Univ.; London Univ. MRCS; LRCP 1927; BCh (Cantab) 1928; FRCS 1929; MB 1930; MD 1933; FRCOG 1942; Examiner: Central Midwives' Board; Univs. of Oxford, Cambridge and London (Obst. and Gynæcol.); Conjoint Board (Midwifery and Gynæcol.). *Publications*: (jt) Diseases of Women by Ten Teachers, 1941; articles in medical journals. *Address*: 89 West Street, Reigate, Surrey RH2 9DA.

BEATTY, 3rd Earl *cr* 1919; **David Beatty;** Viscount Borodale of Wexford, Baron Beatty of the North Sea and of Brooksby, 1919; *b* 21 Nov. 1946; *s* of 2nd Earl Beatty, DSC, and Dorothy Rita, *d* of late M. J. Furey, New Orleans, USA; *S* father, 1972; *m* 1971, Anne (marr. diss. 1983), *d* of A. Please, Wokingham; two *s*; *m* 1984, Anoma Corinne Wijewardene. *Educ*: Eton. *Heir*: *s* Viscount Borodale, *qv*. *Address*: c/o House of Lords, SW1A 0PW.

BEATTY, Hon. (Henry) Perrin; PC; MP (Progressive C) Wellington-Grey-Dufferin-Simcoe, since 1972; Minister of National Health and Welfare, Canada, since 1989; *b* 1950; *m* Julia Kenny; two *s*. *Educ*: Upper Canada College; Univ. of Western Ontario (BA 1971). Minister of State for Treasury Bd, 1979; Minister of Nat. Revenue and for Canada Post Corp., 1984; Solicitor General, 1985; Minister of Nat. Defence, 1986–89. Former Mem., Special Jt Cttee on Constitution of Canada; Chm., Commonwealth Delegated Legislation Cttee. *Address*: House of Commons, Ottawa, Ont K1A 0A6, Canada.

BEAUCHAMP, Sir Christopher Radstock Proctor-, 9th Bt *cr* 1744; solicitor with Gilbert H. Stephens & Sons, Exeter; *b* 30 Jan. 1935; *s* of Rev. Sir Ivor Cuthbert Proctor-Beauchamp, 8th Bt, and Caroline Muriel (*d* 1987), *d* of late Frank Densham; *S* father, 1971; *m* 1965, Rosalind Emily Margot, 3rd *d* of G. P. Wainwright, St Leonards-on-Sea; two *s* one *d*. *Educ*: Rugby; Trinity College, Cambridge (MA). *Heir*: *s* Charles Barclay Proctor-Beauchamp, *b* 7 July 1969. *Address*: The White House, Harpford, near Sidmouth, East Devon.

BEAUCLERK, family name of **Duke of St Albans.**

BEAUFORT, 11th Duke of, *cr* 1682; **David Robert Somerset;** Earl of Worcester, 1514; Marquess of Worcester, 1642; Chairman, Marlborough Fine Art Ltd, since 1977; *b* 23 Feb. 1928; *s* of late Captain Henry Robert Somers Fitzroy de Vere Somerset, DSO (*d* 1965) (*g g s* of 8th Duke) and late Bettine Violet Somerset (*née* Malcolm) (*d* 1973); *S* cousin, 1984; *m* 1950, Lady Caroline Jane Thynne, *d* of Marquess of Bath, *qv*; three *s* one *d*. *Educ*: Eton. Formerly Lieutenant, Coldstream Guards. Pres., British Horse Soc., 1988–90. *Heir*: *s* Marquess of Worcester, *qv*. *Address*: Badminton, Avon GL9 1DB.

BEAUMONT, family name of **Viscount Allendale** and **Baron Beaumont of Whitley.**

BEAUMONT OF WHITLEY, Baron *cr* 1967 (Life Peer), of Child's Hill; **Rev. Timothy Wentworth Beaumont,** MA (Oxon); priest and writer; Vicar, St Philip and All Saints, with St Luke, Kew, 1986–91; *b* 22 Nov. 1928; *o s* of Major and Hon. Mrs M. W. Beaumont; *m* 1955, Mary Rose Wauchope; one *s* two *d* (and one *s* decd). *Educ*: Gordonstoun; Christ Church, Oxford; Westcott House, Cambridge. Asst Chaplain, St John's Cathedral, Hong Kong, 1955–57; Vicar, Christ Church Kowloon Tong, Hong Kong, 1957–59; Hon. Curate, St Stephen's Rochester Row, London, 1960–63; resigned orders, 1973; resumed orders, 1984. Editor: Prism, 1960–63 and 1964; New Outlook, 1964, 1972–74; Chm., Studio Vista Books Ltd, 1963–68; Proprietor of New Christian, 1965–70. Food Columnist, Illustrated London News, 1976–80. Asst Dir (Public Affairs), Make Children Happy, 1977–78; Co-ordinator, The Green Alliance, 1978–80. Liberal Party Organisation: Jt Hon. Treas., 1962–63; Chm., Liberal Publications Dept, 1963–64; Head of Org., 1965–66; Chm., Liberal Party's Org. Cttee, 1966; Chm., Liberal Party, 1967–68; Pres., Liberal Party, 1969–70; Vice-Chm., Liberal Party Exec. and Dir, Policy Promotion, 1980–83; Liberal spokesman on education and the arts, House of Lords, 1968–78, 1980–; Alternate Mem., Assemblies of Council of Europe and WEU, 1973–77, Leader of Liberal Delegn, 1977–78, Vice-Chm., Liberal Gp, 1977–78. Pres., British Fedn of Film Socs, 1973–79. Chairman: Albany Trust, 1969–71; Inst. of Res. into Mental and Multiple Handicap, 1971–73; Exit, 1980–81. Mem., Exec. Cttee, British Council, 1974–78. Mem. Exec., Church Action on Poverty, 1983–86. *Publications*: (ed) Modern Religious Verse, 1965; ed and contrib., The Liberal Cookbook, 1972; (ed) New Christian Reader, 1974; (ed) The Selective Ego: the diaries of James Agate, 1976; Where shall I place my cross?, 1987. *Address*: 40 Elms Road, SW4 9EX. *T*: 071–498 8664.

BEAUMONT, Bill; *see* Beaumont, W. B.

BEAUMONT, Christopher; *see* Beaumont, H. C.

BEAUMONT, Christopher Hubert; a Recorder of the Crown Court, since 1981; *b* 10 Feb. 1926; *s* of Hubert and Beatrix Beaumont; *m* 1st, 1959, Catherine Sanders Clark (*d* 1971); two *s*; 2nd, 1972, Sara Patricia Magee; one *d*. *Educ*: West Monmouth Sch., Pontypool; Balliol Coll., Oxford (MA). Served RN, 1944–47 (Sub-Lieut RNVR). Called to Bar, Middle Temple, 1950. Asst Dep. Coroner, Inner West London, 1963–81. Chm., Agricultural Land Tribunal, Eastern Area, 1985– (Dep. Chm., 1979–85). *Publications*: Law Relating to Sheriffs, 1968; Town and Country Planning Act 1968, 1969; Housing Act 1969, 1969; Town and Country Planning Acts 1971 and 1972, 1973; (with W. G. Nutley) Land Compensation Act 1973, 1973; (with W. G. Nutley) Community Land Act 1975, 1976; (ed with W. G. Nutley) Planning Appeal Decisions, 1986–. *Address*: Rose Cottage, Lower Eashing, Godalming, Surrey GU7 2QG. *T*: Godalming (0483) 416316; 2 Harcourt Buildings, Temple, EC4Y 9DB. *T*: 071–353 8415.

BEAUMONT, David Colin Baskcomb; HM Diplomatic Service; Head of Protocol Department, Foreign and Commonwealth Office, since 1989; *b* 16 Aug. 1942; *s* of Colin Baskcomb Beaumont and Denise Heather Smith; *m* 1965, Barbara Enid Morris; two *s* one *d*. *Educ*: St Benedict's Sch., Ealing. Joined CRO, 1961; Private Sec. to Special Rep. in Africa, Nairobi, 1965; Third Sec., Bahrain, 1967; Second Sec., FCO, 1970; Second Sec. (Commercial), Accra, 1974; First Sec., FCO, 1977; First Sec. (Develt), Kathmandu, 1981; First Sec. and Head of Chancery, Addis Ababa, 1983; First Sec., later Counsellor, FCO, 1986. *Recreations*: tennis, squash, walking, cooking. *Address*: c/o Foreign and Commonwealth Office, King Charles Street, SW1A 2AH. *Club*: MCC.

BEAUMONT, Captain Hon. (Edward) Nicholas (Canning), CVO 1986 (LVO 1976); Vice Lord-Lieutenant of Berkshire, since 1989; Clerk of the Course and Secretary to Ascot Authority, since 1969; *b* 14 Dec. 1929; 3rd *s* of 2nd Viscount Allendale, KG, CB, CBE, MC and Violet (*d* 1979), *d* of Sir Charles Seely, 2nd Bt; *m* 1953, Jane Caroline, *d* of Alexander Lewis Paget Falconer Wallace, of Candacraig, Strathdon, Aberdeenshire; two *s*. *Educ*: Eton. Joined Life Guards, 1948; Captain 1956; retired 1960. Assistant to Clerk of the Course, Ascot, 1964. Pres., Berks SJAB, 1988. DL Berks 1982. *Address*: Royal Enclosure Lodge, Ascot, Berks SL5 7JN. *T*: Ascot (0344) 23127. *Club*: White's.

BEAUMONT, Sir George Howland Francis, 12th Bt, *cr* 1661; late Lieutenant 60th Rifles; *b* 24 Sept. 1924; *s* of 11th Bt and Renée Muriel (*d* 1987), 2nd *d* of late Maj.-Gen. Sir Edward Northey, GCMG, CB; *S* father 1933; *m* 1949, Barbara Singleton (marr.

annulled, 1951); *m* 1963, Henrietta Anne (marr. diss. 1986), *d* of late Dr A. Waymouth and Mrs J. Rodwell, Riverside Cottage, Donnington, Berks; twin *d. Educ:* Stowe Sch. *Address:* The Corner House, Manor Court, Stretton-on-Fosse, near Moreton-in-Marsh, Glos GL56 9SB. *T:* Shipston-on-Stour (0608) 62845. *Club:* Lansdowne.

BEAUMONT, His Honour (Herbert) Christopher, MBE 1948; a Circuit Judge, 1972–85; *b* 3 June 1912; *s* of late Gerald Beaumont, MC and bar, and Gwendolene Beaumont (*née* Haworth); *m* 1940, Helen Margaret Gordon Smail, *d* of William Mitchell Smail; one *s* two *d. Educ:* Uppingham Sch.; Worcester Coll., Oxford. Indian Civil and Political Services, 1936–47; Private Sec. to Lord Radcliffe, Chm. of Indo-Pakistan Boundary Commn, 1947; Foreign Office, 1948–52. Called to the Bar, Inner Temple, 1951; Metropolitan Magistrate, 1962–72. Chm. of the London Juvenile Courts, 1964; Dep. Chm., North Riding QS, 1966–71; temp. Resident Judge, Cyprus, 1986. Mem., Parole Bd, 1974–76; a Chm., Police (Disciplinary) Appeal Tribunal, 1988–90. *Recreations:* travel in Europe, growing vegetables. *Address:* Minskip Lodge, Boroughbridge, Yorks YO5 9JF. *T:* Boroughbridge (0423) 322365. *Clubs:* Brooks's; Yorkshire (York).
See also G. M. Waller.

BEAUMONT, (John) Michael; Seigneur of Sark since 1974; *b* 20 Dec. 1927; *s* of late Lionel (Buster) Beaumont and Enid Beaumont (*née* Ripley), and *g s* of Dame Sibyl Hathaway, Dame of Sark; *m* 1956, Diana (*née* La Trobe-Bateman); two *s. Educ:* Loughborough Coll. (DLC). Aircraft Design Engr, 1952–70; Chief Techn. Engr, Beagle Aircraft, 1969–70; Design Engr, BAC GW Div., 1970–75. *Recreations:* theatre, music, gardening. *Heir: s* Christopher Beaumont, Major RE, *b* 4 Feb. 1957. *Address:* La Seigneurie, Sark, Channel Islands. *T:* Sark (048183) 2017.

BEAUMONT, Hon. Nicholas; *see* Beaumont, Hon. E. N. C.

BEAUMONT, Peter John Luther; QC 1986; **His Honour Judge Beaumont;** a Circuit Judge, since 1989; *b* 10 Jan. 1944; *s* of S. P. L. Beaumont, OBE, and D. V. Beaumont; *m* 1970, Ann Jarratt; one *s* one *d. Educ:* Peterhouse, Zimbabwe; Univ. of Zimbabwe (BScEcon Hons). Called to the Bar, Lincoln's Inn, 1967; practised South Eastern Circuit; a Recorder, 1986. *Recreations:* cricket, tennis, gardening. *Address:* Chelmsford Crown Court. *T:* Chelmsford (0245) 358222.

BEAUMONT, Sir Richard Ashton, KCMG 1965 (CMG 1955); OBE 1949; HM Diplomatic Service, retired; Chairman, Arab-British Chamber of Commerce, since 1980; *b* 29 Dec. 1912; *s* of A. R. Beaumont, FRCS, Uppingham, and Evelyn Frances (*née* Rendle); *m* 1st, 1942, Alou (*d* 1985), *d* of M. Camran, Istanbul; one *d;* 2nd, 1989, Melanie Anns, *d* of H. Brummell. *Educ:* Repton; Oriel Coll., Oxford. Joined HM Consular Service, 1936; posted Lebanon and Syria, 1936–41. Served War, 1941–44. Returned to Foreign Office, 1944; served in London, Iraq, Venezuela; Imperial Defence Coll., 1958; Head of Arabian Department, Foreign Office, 1959; Ambassador: to Morocco, 1961–65; to Iraq, 1965–67; Dep. Under-Sec. of State, FO, 1967–69; Ambassador to the Arab Republic of Egypt, 1969–72. Dir-Gen., Middle East Assoc., 1973–77; Chairman: Arab British Centre, 1976–77; Anglo-Arab Assoc., 1979–. Governor, SOAS, 1973–78. Trustee, Thomson Foundn, 1974–. *Recreation:* golf. *Address:* 14 Cadogan Square, SW1X 0JU. *Club:* United Oxford & Cambridge University.

BEAUMONT, William Anderson, CB 1986; OBE (mil.) 1961; AE 1953; Speaker's Secretary, House of Commons, 1982–86; *b* 30 Oct. 1924; *s* of late William Lionel Beaumont and Mrs E. Taverner; *m* 1st, 1946, Kythé (*d* 1988), *d* of late Major K. G. Mackenzie, Victoria, BC; one *d;* 2nd, 1989, Rosalie, *widow* of Judge Michael Underhill, QC. *Educ:* Terrington Hall, York; Cranleigh Sch. (Entrance Exhibnr); Christ Church, Oxford (MA, DipEd). Served RAF, Navigator, 1942–47, 355 Sqdn, 232 Sqdn, SEAC (Flt Lt); RAuxAF 3507 (Co. of Somerset) FCU, 1948–54; 3609 (W Riding) FCU, 1954–61 (Wing Comdr CO, 1958–61); Observer Comdr, No 18 (Leeds) Gp, Royal Observer Corps, 1962–75 (ROC Medal 1975). Asst Master, Bristol Grammar Sch., 1951–54; Beaumont and Smith Ltd, Pudsey, 1954–66 (Man. Dir, 1958–66); Henry Mason (Shipley) Ltd (Man. Dir, 1966–76); Principal, Welsh Office, 1976–79; Asst Sec., Welsh Office, 1979–82. A Chm. of Assessors, CSSB, 1988–. Dir, St David's Forum, 1986–; Sec., Prince of Wales Award Gp, 1987–90; Awards Cttee, RAF Benevolent Fund, 1990–; Vice-Chm., Franco-British Soc., 1991–. FRSA 1977. *Recreations:* inland waterways, reluctant gardening, walking. *Address:* 28 Halford Road, Richmond, Surrey TW10 6AP. *T:* 081–940 2390. *Clubs:* Royal Air Force; Civil Service; United Services Mess (Cardiff).

BEAUMONT, William Blackledge, (Bill), OBE 1982; Rugby Union footballer, retired; sports broadcaster and writer; Director, J. Blackledge & Son Ltd, since 1981; *b* 9 March 1952; *s* of Ronald Walton Beaumont and Joyce Beaumont; *m* 1977, Hilary Jane Seed; two *s. Educ:* Ellesmere Coll., Shropshire. Joined family textile business, 1971. First played Rugby Union for England, 1975; 34 caps (20 caps as Captain); Mem., British Lions, NZ tour, 1977; Captain, British Lions, S Africa tour, 1980; played for Lancashire Barbarians, retd 1982. Television includes A Question of Sport (BBC TV), 1982–. *Publications:* Thanks to Rugby 1982; Bill Beaumont's Tackle Rugby, 1983; Bill Beaumont's Sporting Year Book, 1984. *Recreations:* tennis, golf, water-skiing. *Clubs:* East India, MCC; Fylde Rugby Union Football; Royal Lytham St Anne's Golf.

BEAUMONT-DARK, Anthony Michael; MP (C) Birmingham, Selly Oak, since 1979; investment analyst; *b* Birmingham, 11 Oct. 1932; *s* of Leonard Cecil Dark; *m* 1959, Sheelagh Irene, *d* of R. Cassey; one *s* one *d. Educ:* Birmingham Coll. of Arts and Crafts; Birmingham Univ. Mem., Birmingham Stock Exchange, 1958–; Consultant, Smith, Keen, Cutler, 1958– (Partner, 1959–85); Director: Wigham Poland (Midlands) Ltd, 1960–75; Nat. Exhibition Centre Ltd, 1971–73; Cope Allman Internat. Ltd, 1972–83; Birmid Qualcast PLC, 1983–89; J. Saville Gordon PLC, 1989–; TR High Income Trust PLC, 1990–; Birmingham Executive Airways (Chm., 1983–86). Mem., Central Housing Adv. Cttee, DoE, 1970–76. Member: Birmingham City Council, 1956–67 (Alderman, 1967–74, Hon. Alderman, 1976); W Midlands CC, 1973–87 (Chm., Finance Cttee, 1977–83). Contested (C) Birmingham, Aston, 1959, 1964. Mem., Treasury and Civil Service Select Cttee, 1979–. Governor: Aston Univ., 1980–; Birmingham Univ., 1984–. Trustee, Birmingham Copec Housing Trust, 1975–. *Address:* House of Commons, SW1; 124 Lady Byron Lane, Copt Heath, Solihull, Birmingham B93 9BA. *Club:* Carlton.

BEAUREPAIRE, Dame Beryl (Edith), DBE 1981 (OBE 1975); *b* 24 Sept. 1923; *d* of late E. L. Bedggood; *m* 1946, Ian Francis Beaurepaire, *qv;* two *s. Educ:* Fintona Girls' Sch., Balwyn, Victoria; Univ. of Melbourne. ASO, WAAAF, 1942–45. Mem. Nat. Exec., YWCA Australia, 1969–77. Liberal Party of Australia: Chm., Victorian Women's Sect., 1973–76; Chm., Federal Women's Sect., 1974–76; Vice-Pres., Victorian Div., 1976–86; Convenor, Nat. Women's Adv. Council, Australia, 1978–82. Member: Council, Australian War Memorial, 1982– (Chm., 1985–); Australian Children's Television Foundation Bd, 1982–. Chm., Bd of Management, Fintona Girls' Sch., 1973–87. Jubilee Medal, 1977. *Recreations:* golf, swimming. *Address:* 18 Barton Drive, Mount Eliza, Vic 3930, Australia. *T:* 787 1129. *Clubs:* Alexandra (Melbourne); Peninsula Country Golf (Frankston).

BEAUREPAIRE, Ian Francis, CMG 1967; Director, Pacific Dunlop Ltd (formerly Dunlop Olympic Ltd), since 1980; Chairman, Olex Ltd, since 1973; *b* 14 Sept. 1922; *s* of late Sir Frank and Lady Beaurepaire; *m* 1946, Beryl Edith Bedggood (*see* Dame Beryl Beaurepaire); two *s. Educ:* Carey Grammar Sch., Scotch Coll., Melbourne; Royal Melbourne Inst. of Technology. Served RAAF (Flying Officer), 1942–45. Man. Dir, Beaurepaire Tyre Service Pty Ltd, 1953–55; Gen. Man., The Olympic Tyre & Rubber Co. Pty Ltd, 1955–61; Chm., 1959–78, Man. Dir, 1959–75, Chief Exec., 1975–78, Exec. Chm., 1978–80, Olympic Consolidated Industries Ltd. Mem., Melbourne Underground Rail Loop Authority, 1971–83, Chm., 1981–83. Member: Melbourne City Council, 1956–75 (Lord Mayor of Melbourne, 1965–67); Management Cttee of Royal Victorian Eye and Ear Hosp., 1966–88 (Pres., 1982–88). *Recreations:* golf, grazing. *Address:* 18 Barton Drive, Mount Eliza, Victoria 3930, Australia. *Clubs:* Athenæum, Naval and Military, Melbourne (Melbourne); Peninsula Country Golf (Frankston).

BEAVAN, family name of **Baron Ardwick.**

BEAVEN, John Lewis, CMG 1986; CVO 1983 (MVO 1974); HM Diplomatic Service, retired; Ambassador to Sudan, 1986–90; *b* 30 July 1930; *s* of Charles and Margaret Beaven; *m* 1960, Jane Beeson (marr. diss.); one *s* one *d;* *m* 1975, Jean McComb Campbell. *Educ:* Newport (Gwent) High Sch. BoT, 1946; RAF, 1948–50; Asst Trade Comr, British High Commn, Karachi, 1956–60; Second Secretary (Commercial), British High Commn, Freetown, 1961–64; First Secretary (Commercial): British High Commn, Nicosia, 1964–66; Nairobi, 1966–68; FCO, 1969–72; Head of Chancery, British Embassy, Jakarta, 1972–74; Counsellor (Economic and Commercial), British High Commn, Lagos, 1975–77; Dep. Consul General and Dir, British Trade Develt Office, NY, 1978–82; Consul-General, San Francisco, 1982–86. US Rep., SCF, 1990–. *Recreations:* music, needlepoint, walking, computing. *Address:* Scannell Road, Ghent, NY 12075, USA. *T:* 518.392.2152. *Clubs:* Reform; Brook (New York).

BEAVERBROOK, 3rd Baron *cr* 1917, of Beaverbrook, New Brunswick, and of Cherkley, Surrey; **Maxwell William Humphrey Aitken;** Bt 1916; Chairman, Beaverbrook Foundation, since 1985; Treasurer: Conservative Party, since 1990; European Democratic Union, since 1990; *b* 29 Dec. 1951; *s* of Sir (John William) Max Aitken, 2nd Bt, DSO, DFC, and of Violet, *d* of Sir Humphrey de Trafford, 4th Bt, MC; *S* to disclaimed barony of father, 1985; *m* 1974, Susan Angela More O'Ferrall; two *s* two *d. Educ:* Charterhouse; Pembroke Coll., Cambridge. Beaverbrook Newspapers Ltd, 1973–77; Trustee, Beaverbrook Foundation, 1974–; Dir, Ventech, 1983–86; Chm., Ventech Healthcare Inc., 1986, 1988–. Govt spokesman for Home Office and DTI, H of L, 1986; a Lord in Waiting (Government Whip), 1986–88; Dep. Treas., Cons. Party, 1988. Chm., Nat. Assoc. of Boys' Clubs, 1989–. Mem. Council, Homeopathic Trust, 1986–. *Recreations:* sailing, motor cars. *Heir: s* Hon. Maxwell Francis Aitken, *b* 17 March 1977. *Address:* House of Lords, SW1. *Clubs:* White's; Royal Yacht Squadron.

BEAVIS, Air Chief Marshal Sir Michael (Gordon), KCB 1981; CBE 1977 (OBE 1969); AFC 1962; Deputy Chairman, Tubular Edgington Group, since 1988; *b* 13 Aug. 1929; *s* of Walter Erle Beavis and Mary Ann (*née* Sarjantson); *m* 1950, Joy Marion (*née* Jones); one *s* one *d. Educ:* Kilburn Grammar School. Joined RAF 1947; commnd 1949; served Fighter Comd Squadrons 1950–54, RNZAF 1954–56; flew Vulcan aircraft, Bomber Comd, 1958–62; Staff Coll., 1963; MoD, 1964–66; OC No 10 Squadron (VC10s), 1966–68; Group Captain Flying, Akrotiri, Cyprus, 1968–71; Asst Dir, Defence Policy, MoD, 1971–73; RCDS, 1974; RAF Germany, 1975–77 (SASO 1976–77); Dir Gen. RAF Training, 1977–80; Comdt, RAF Staff Coll, 1980–81; AOC-in-C, RAF Support Comd, 1981–84; Dep. Comdr, AFCENT, 1984–86. CBIM. Freeman, City of London, 1980; Liveryman, GAPAN, 1983. *Recreations:* golf, ski-ing, travel. *Address:* c/o Lloyds Bank, 202 High Street, Lincoln. *Club:* Royal Air Force.

BEAZER, Brian Cyril; Chairman and Chief Executive, Beazer (formerly C. H. Beazer (Holdings)) PLC, since 1983; *b* 22 Feb. 1935; *s* of late Cyril Henry George Beazer and of Ada Vera Beazer; *m* 1958, Patricia (*née* White); one *d. Educ:* Wells Cathedral School. Joined C.H. Beazer, 1958; Man. Dir, 1968; apptd Chm. and Chief Exec. on death of his father in 1983. *Recreations:* walking, reading. *Address:* The Weavers House, Castle Combe, Wiltshire SN14 7HX.

BEAZLEY, Christopher John Pridham; Member (C) Cornwall and Plymouth, European Parliament, since 1984; *b* 5 Sept. 1952; *s* of Peter George Beazley, *qv. Educ:* Shrewsbury, Bristol Univ. Formerly Nuffield Research Fellow, School of European Studies, Sussex Univ. Vice Chm., Lewes and Eastbourne branch, European Movement, 1980; Wealden DC, 1979–83. *Address:* The Grange, Devoran, near Truro, Cornwall TR3 6PF. *Club:* Oriental.

BEAZLEY, Hon. Kim Christian; MP (ALP) Swan, Perth, Australia, since 1980; Minister of State for Telecommunications, since 1990; *b* 14 Dec. 1948; *s* of Hon. Kim Edward Beazley and Betty Beazley; *m* 1st, 1974, Mary (marr. diss. 1989), *d* of Hon. Sir Shane Paltridge, KBE; two *d;* 2nd, 1990, Susannah. *Educ:* Univ. of Western Australia (MA); Oxford Univ. (Rhodes Scholar; MPhil). Tutor in Social and Political Theory, Murdoch Univ., WA, 1976–79, Lectr 1980. Minister of State for Aviation, and Minister Assisting the Minister for Defence, 1983–84; Special Minister of State, 1983–84; Minister of State for Defence, 1984–90. *Publication:* (with I. Clark) The Politics of Intrusion: the Super-Powers in the Indian Ocean, 1979. *Recreations:* swimming, reading. *Address:* Parliament House, Canberra, ACT 2600, Australia. *T:* (062) 73 3955.

BEAZLEY, Peter George; Member (C) Bedfordshire South, European Parliament, since 1984 (Bedfordshire, 1979–84); *b* 9 June 1922; *s* of Thomas Alfred and Agnes Alice Mary Beazley; *m* 1945, Joyce Marion Sulman; one *s* two *d* (and one *d* decd). *Educ:* Highgate Sch.; St John Baptist Coll., Oxford. 2nd Cl. Final Hons PPE, MA Oxon. Captain, Rifle Brigade, served in N Africa, Italy, Austria, 1942–47. Joined ICI, 1947; served in UK, Portugal, Germany, Belgium and S Africa as Manager, Gen. Manager, Divl Bd Dir, Vice Chm. and Man. Dir of associated cos, 1948–77; retd from ICI 1978. Member: European Democratic Gp Bureau, 1982–83; Economic and Monetary Affairs and Industrial Policy Cttee, European Parlt, 1984– (Vice Chm., 1984–89); European Parlt Portuguese Parlt Jt delegn, 1979–84; European Parlt Japanese delegn, 1985–89; Vice Chm., SE Asia delegn, 1989–. MRI; Mem., RIIA (Res. Fellow, 1977–78). *Publication:* The Role of Western Technology Transfer in the Development of the Soviet Union's Chemical Industry (with V. Sobeslavsky), 1979. *Recreations:* golf, gardening. *Address:* Rest Harrow, 14 The Combe, Ratton, Eastbourne, East Sussex BN20 9DB. *T:* Eastbourne (0323) 504460; 4 Bridgewater Court, Little Gaddesden, Herts. *T:* Little Gaddesden (044284) 3548. *Club:* Oriental.
See also C. J. P. Beazley.

BECHER, Major Sir William Fane Wrixon-, 5th Bt, *cr* 1831; MC 1943; Temp. Major, Rifle Brigade (SRO); *b* 7 Sept. 1915; *o s* of Sir Eustace W. W. W. Becher, 4th Bt, and Hon. Constance Gough-Calthorpe, *d* of 6th Baron Calthorpe; *S* father, 1934; *m* 1st, 1946, Vanda (marr. diss. 1960; she *m* 1962, Rear-Adm. Viscount Kelburn, later 9th Earl of Glasgow; she *d* 1984), *d* of 4th Baron Vivian; one *s* one *d;* 2nd, 1960, Hon. Mrs Yvonne Mostyn. *Educ:* Harrow; Magdalene Coll., Cambridge (BA). Served War of 1939–45; Western Desert and Tunisian Campaigns, 1940–43 (MC, wounded twice); Liaison Officer to Comdr, 7th Armoured Div., Lt-Gen. W. H. Gott, 1941 (taken prisoner at battle of Sidi

Rezegh, Nov. 1941, and escaped); Italian Campaign, 1944; ADC to FM Lord Wilson, Supreme Allied Comdr Mediterranean. Lloyd's Underwriter, 1950. Member: British Boxing Bd of Control, 1961–82; Nat. Playing Fields Assoc., 1953–65 (Pres., Wiltshire Branch, NPFA, 1950–56). *Recreations:* golf and cricket (played cricket for Sussex, 1939, captained Wiltshire, 1949–53). *Heir: s* John William Michael Wrixon-Becher, *b* 29 Sept. 1950. *Address:* 37 Clabon Mews, SW1X 0EQ. *T:* 071–589 7780. *Clubs:* MCC, White's, Royal Green Jackets; I Zingari (Sec., 1952–).

BECK, Prof. Arnold Hugh William, BSc (Eng), MA; Professor of Engineering, 1966–83, Head of Electrical Division, 1971–81, University of Cambridge, now Emeritus Professor; Life Fellow of Corpus Christi College, Cambridge, since 1983 (Fellow, 1962); Fellow of University College, London, since 1979; *y s* of Major Hugh Beck and Diana L. Beck; *m* 1947, Katharine Monica, *y d* of S. K. Ratcliffe; no *c. Educ:* Gresham's Sch., Holt; University Coll., London. Research Engr, Henry Hughes & Sons, 1937–41; seconded to Admty Signal Estab., 1941–45; Standard Telephones & Cables, 1947–58; Lectr, Cambridge Univ., 1958–64; Reader in Electrical Engrg, 1964–66. FIEEE 1959. *Publications:* Velocity Modulated Thermionic Tubes, 1948; Thermionic Valves, 1953; Space-charge Waves, 1958; Words and Waves, 1967; (with H. Ahmed) Introduction to Physical Electronics, 1968; Handbook of Vacuum Physics, Vol. 2, Parts 5 and 6, 1968; Statistical Mechanics, Fluctuations and Noise, 1976; papers in Jl IEE, Inst. Radio Engrs, etc. *Address:* 18 Earl Street, Cambridge. *T:* Cambridge (0223) 62997.

BECK, Rev. Brian Edgar, MA; Secretary of the Methodist Conference, since 1984; *b* 27 Sept. 1933; *o s* of A. G. and late C. A. Beck; *m* 1958, Margaret Ludlow; three *d. Educ:* City of London School; Corpus Christi College, Cambridge (1st Cl. Classical Tripos pts 1 and 2); Wesley House, Cambridge (1st Cl. Theol. Tripos pt 2). BA 1955, MA 1959. Ordained Methodist Minister, 1960; Asst Tutor, Handsworth Coll., 1957–59; E Suffolk Circuit Minister, 1959–62; St Paul's United Theological Coll., Limuru, Kenya, 1962–68; Tutor, Wesley House, Cambridge, 1968–80, Principal 1980–84. Sec., E African Church Union Consultation Worship and Liturgy Cttee, 1963–68; Mem., World Methodist Council, 1966–71, 1981–; Co-Chm., Oxford Inst. of Methodist Theol. Studies, 1976–. Fernley-Hartley Lectr, 1978. *Publications:* (contrib.) Christian Belief, a Catholic-Methodist statement, 1970; (contrib.) Unity the Next Step? (ed P. Morgan), 1972; Reading the New Testament Today, 1977; (contrib.) Suffering and Martyrdom in the New Testament (ed Horbury and McNeile), 1981; Christian Character in the Gospel of St Luke, 1989; articles in NT Studies, Epworth Review. *Recreations:* walking, DIY. *Address:* 1 Central Buildings, SW1H 9NH. *T:* 071–222 8010; 76 Beaumont Road, Purley, Croydon, Surrey CR8 2EG. *T:* 081–645 9162.

BECK, Clive; Deputy Chairman, John Mowlem & Co., since 1986; *b* 12 April 1937; *s* of Sir Edgar Beck, *qv*, and Mary Agnes Beck; *m* 1960, Philippa Flood, three *s* three *d. Educ:* Ampleforth College. 2nd Lieut, The Life Guards, 1956–57; John Mowlem & Co., 1957–67; SGB Group, 1967–86. *Recreations:* golf, shooting, fishing. *Address:* (office) Lion Court, Swan Street, Isleworth, Middx. *T:* 081–568 9111. *Clubs:* Buck's; Royal Wimbledon Golf, Swinley Forest Golf.

See also Sir E. P. Beck.

BECK, Sir Edgar (Charles), Kt 1975; CBE 1967; MA; FEng 1977; Chairman, John Mowlem & Company Ltd, 1961–79, President, since 1981; *b* 11 May 1911; *s* of Edgar Bee Beck and Nellie Stollard Beck (*née* Osborne); *m* 1933, Mary Agnes Sorapure (marr. diss. 1972); three *s* two *d*; *m* 1972, Anne Teresa Corbould. *Educ:* Lancing Coll.; Jesus Coll., Cambridge (MA). Joined John Mowlem & Co. Ltd as Engineer, 1933: Dir 1940; Man. Dir 1958. Director: Scaffolding Great Britain Ltd, 1942–85 (Chm., 1958–78); Builders' Accident Insce Ltd, 1959, Dep. Chm., 1969; Mem., ECGD Adv. Council, 1964–69; President, Fedn of Civil Engrg Contractors, 1971–75 (Chm., 1958–59); Chairman: Export Gp for the Constructional Industries, 1959–63; Brit. Hosps Export Council, 1964–75. Under-writing Mem. of Lloyd's, 1955–. FEng; FICE. *Recreations:* golf, salmon fishing. *Address:* 13 Eaton Place, SW1. *T:* 071–235 7455. *Clubs:* Buck's; Swinley Forest Golf.

See also C. Beck, Sir E. P. Beck.

BECK, Sir (Edgar) Philip, Kt 1988; Chairman, John Mowlem & Co., since 1979; *b* 9 Aug. 1934; *s* of Sir Edgar Charles Beck, *qv*; *m* 1957, Thomasina Joanna Jeal (marr. diss.); two *s*; *m* 1991, Bridget Cockerell (*née* Heathcoat-Amory). *Educ:* Ampleforth College; Jesus College, Cambridge (MA). Dir, John Mowlem, 1964, Dep. Chm., 1978–79. Chairman: FCEC, 1982–83; Export Group for Constructional Industries, 1986–88. *Address:* John Mowlem & Co., Lion Court, Swan Street, Isleworth, Middx. *T:* 081-568 9111. *Clubs:* Buck's; Royal Yacht Squadron.

See also C. Beck.

BECK, (James Henry) John; Director of Industries and Farms, Prison Department, Home Office, 1976–80; *b* 5 April 1920; *s* of James Henry and Elizabeth Kate Beck; *m* 1942, Doris Peacock; one *d* (and one *d* decd). *Educ:* Polytechnic Secondary Sch., Regent Street, W1. Entered Home Office as Clerical Officer, 1937; HM Forces, 1939; returned to Home Office as Executive Officer, 1946; Higher Exec. Officer, 1950; Sen. Exec. Officer, 1958; Principal, 1963; Asst Sec., 1968. *Address:* Scarlet Oaks, Ridgway, Pyrford, Woking, Surrey GU22 8PN. *T:* Byfleet (0932) 346064.

BECK, Prof. (John) Swanson, FRSE 1984; Professor of Pathology, University of Dundee, since 1971; Consultant Pathologist, Tayside Health Board, since 1974; *b* 22 Aug. 1928; *s* of late Dr John Beck and Mary (*née* Barbour); *m* 1960, Marion Tudhope Paterson; one *s* one *d. Educ:* Glasgow Acad.; Univ. of Glasgow. BSc, MB, ChB, MD, FRCPG, FRCPE, FRCPath, FIBiol, CBiol. Lectr in Pathology, Univ. of Glasgow, 1958–63; Sen. Lectr in Pathology, Univ. of Aberdeen, 1963–71. Consultant Pathologist: N Eastern Regional Hosp. Bd, 1963–71; Eastern Regional Hosp. Bd, 1971–74. Chairman: Breast Tumour Panel, MRC, 1979–90; Biomedical Res. Cttee, SHHD, 1983–91 (Mem. 1975–79). Member: Cell Biology and Disorders Bd, MRC, 1978–82; Health Services Res. Panel, MRC, 1981–82; Chief Scientist's Cttee, SHHD, 1983–; Tayside Health Bd, 1983–; Nat. Biol Standards Bd, 1988–; Med. Adv. Bd, LEPRA, 1988–. Mem. Council, RSE, 1987–90. *Publications:* various papers in Jl of Pathology and other medical and scientific jls. *Recreations:* walking, gardening, sailing. *Address:* 598 Perth Road, Dundee DD2 1QA. *T:* Dundee (0382) 562298. *Club:* Commonwealth Trust.

BECK, Sir Philip; *see* Beck, Sir E. P.

BECK, (Richard) Theodore, FRIBA, FSA, FRSA, MRTPI; architect; *b* 11 March 1905; *s* of Alfred Charles Beck and Grace Sophia Beck (*née* Reading); *m* 1950, Margaret Beryl Page; one *s* one *d. Educ:* Haileybury; Architectural Association Sch. Past Mem. Council, Royal Archaeological Inst.; Past Master: Broderers Company; Barber-Surgeons Company; Parish Clerks Co.; Mem. Court of Common Council, Corporation of London, 1963–82; Dep., Ward of Farringdon Within, 1978–82; Sheriff, City of London, 1969–70; former Dep. Chm., Central Criminal Court Extension Cttee. Chm., Governors, City of London Sch., 1971–75, Dep. Chm., 1976 (Hon. Mem., John Carpenter Club); Chm., Schools Cttee, Corporation of London, 1977, Dep. Chm., 1978. Former Governor: Bridewell Royal Hosp.; King Edward's Sch., Witley; Christ's Hospital (Aldermanic Almoner); Reeves Foundn. Vicary Lectr, 1969; Prestonian Lectr, 1975. *Publication:* The Cutting Edge: early history of the surgeons of London, 1975. *Recreations:* gardening, archaeology. *Address:* Blundens House, Upper Froyle, Alton, Hants GU34 4LB. *T:* Bentley (0420) 23147. *Clubs:* Guildhall, City Livery.

BECK, Swanson; *see* Beck, J. S.

BECKE, Mrs Shirley Cameron, OBE 1974; QPM 1972; Vice-Chairman, 1976–83 and Regional Administrator, London Region, 1974–79, Women's Royal Voluntary Service, retired; *b* 29 April 1917; *er d* of late George L. Jennings, AMIGasE and Marion Jennings; *m* 1954, Rev. Justice Becke, MBE, TD, FCA (*d* 1990); no *c. Educ:* privately; Ealing Co. Gram. Sch. Trained in Gas Engineering, 1935–40. Joined Metropolitan Police as Constable, 1941; served in various ranks; Woman Commander, 1969–74. OStJ 1975. *Recreations:* reading, keeping cats. *Address:* 51 St Pancras, Chichester, Sussex PO19 4LT. *T:* Chichester (0243) 784295.

BECKE, Lt-Col William Hugh Adamson, CMG 1964; DSO 1945; *b* 24 Sept. 1916; *er s* of late Brig.-Gen. J. H. W. Becke, CMG, DSO, AFC, and late Mrs A. P. Becke (*née* Adamson); *m* 1945, Mary Catherine, 3rd *d* of late Major G. M. Richmond, Kincairney, Murthly, Perthshire. *Educ:* Charterhouse; RMC Sandhurst. Commissioned in The Sherwood Foresters, 1937. British Military Mission to Greece, 1949–52; Asst Military Adviser to the High Commissioner for the UK in Pakistan, 1957–59; Military Attaché, Djakarta, 1962–64; retd 1966. Private Sec. and Comptroller to Governor of Victoria, 1969–74; Personnel Officer, Gas and Fuel Corp. of Vic, 1974–82. *Address:* 3 Chambers Street, South Yarra, Vic 3141, Australia. *Clubs:* Army and Navy; Melbourne, Victoria Racing (Melbourne).

BECKERMAN, Wilfred, PhD, DPhil; Fellow of Balliol College, Oxford, 1975–Sept. 1992; Reader in Economics, Oxford University, 1978–Sept. 1992; *b* 19 May 1925; *s* of Morris and Mathilda Beckerman; *m* 1952, Nicole Geneviève Ritter (*d* 1979); one *s* two *d. Educ:* Ealing County Sch.; Trinity Coll., Cambridge (MA, PhD); MA, DPhil Oxon. RNVR, 1943–46. Trinity Coll., Cambridge, 1946–50; Lecturer in Economics, Univ. of Nottingham, 1950–52; OEEC and OECD, Paris, 1952–61; National Inst. of Economic and Social Research, 1962–63. Fellow of Balliol Coll., Oxford, 1964–69; Prof. of Political Economy, Univ. of London, and Head of Dept of Political Economy, UCL, 1969–75; The Economic Adviser to the Pres. of the Board of Trade (leave of absence from Balliol), 1967–69. Mem., Royal Commn on Environmental Pollution, 1970–73. Member: Exec. Cttee, NIESR, 1973–; Council, Royal Economic Soc., 1990–. Elie Halévy Vis. Prof. Institut d'Etudes Politiques, Paris, 1977; Resident Scholar, Woodrow Wilson Internat. Center for Scholars, Washington, DC, 1982. Consultant: World Bank; OECD; ILO. Pres., Section F (Economics), BAAS, 1978. *Publications:* The British Economy in 1975 (with associates), 1965; International Comparisons of Real Incomes, 1966; An Introduction to National Income Analysis, 1968; (ed and contrib.) The Labour Government's Economic Record, 1972; In Defence of Economic Growth, 1974; Measures of Leisure, Equality and Welfare, 1978; (ed and contrib.) Slow Growth in Britain: Causes and Consequences, 1979; Poverty and the Impact of Income Maintenance Programmes, 1979; (with S. Clark) Poverty and the Impact of Social Security in Britain since 1961, 1982; (ed and contrib.) Wage Rigidity and Unemployment, 1986; articles in Economic Jl, Economica, Econometrica, Review of Economic Studies, Review of Economics and Statistics, etc. *Recreations:* various. *Address:* Balliol College, Oxford OX1 3BJ. *T:* Oxford (0865) 277713. *Club:* Reform.

BECKETT, family name of **Baron Grimthorpe.**

BECKETT, Prof. Arnold Heyworth, OBE 1983; Professor of Pharmacy, Chelsea College (University of London), 1959–85, now Emeritus; *b* 12 Feb. 1920; *m* 1st, 1942, Miriam Eunice Webster; one *s* one *d*; 2nd, Susan Yvonne Harris. *Educ:* Baines Grammar Sch., Poulton-le-Fylde; Sch. of Pharmacy and Birkbeck Coll., University of London. FRPharmS (FPS 1942); BSc 1947; PhD 1950; DSc London, 1959. Head, Dept of Pharmacy, Chelsea Coll. of Sci. and Technology, 1959–79. Chm., Med. Commn, Internat. Tennis Fedn; Mem., Med. Commn, Internat. Olympic Cttee, 1968–; former Mem., British Olympic Assoc. Med. Commn; Chm., Bd of Pharmaceutical Sciences, Fédération Internat. Pharmaceutique, 1960–80; Mem. Council, Pharmaceutical, later Royal Pharmaceutical, Soc. of GB, 1965– (Pres., 1981–82). Vis. Prof. to Univs, USA and Canada. Examr in Pharmaceut. Chem., Univs in UK, Nigeria, Ghana, Singapore. Pereira Medal, 1942; STAS Medal, Belg. Chem. Soc., 1962; Hanbury Meml Medal, 1974; Charter Gold Medal, 1977; Mem. of Olympic Order, Silver Medal, 1980. Hon. DSc: Heriot-Watt, 1976; Uppsala, 1977; Leuven, 1982. *Publications:* (co-author) Practical Pharmaceutical Chemistry, 1962; Part 1, 3rd edn, 1975, Part 2, 3rd edn, 1976; founder Co-editor, Jl of Medicinal Chemistry; research contribs to jls. *Recreations:* travel, sport, photography. *Address:* 20 Braybrooke Gardens, Upper Norwood, SE19 2UN.

BECKETT, Bruce Probart, FRIBA, FRIAS, FRTPI, FCIOB; Chartered Architect, Town and Country Planner and Building Consultant in private practice, since 1984; *b* 7 June 1924; *s* of J. D. L. Beckett and Florence Theresa (*née* Probart); *m* 1957, Jean McDonald; two *s* three *d* (incl. twin *s* and *d*). *Educ:* Rondebosch Boys' High Sch., Cape Town; Univ. of Cape Town (BArch with distinction, 1950); University Coll. London (Diploma in Town Planning, 1963). Active Service SA Navy, 1943; Midshipman, 1943; Sub-Lieut, 1944; seconded RN, 1944; Lieut, 1946. ARIBA 1950, FRIBA 1968; FRIAS 1968. Mem. Inst. S African Architects, 1950; FRTPI (AMTPI 1966); FCIOB 1979. Private practice in S Africa, 1952–59, London, 1960. Sen. Architect, War Office, 1961; Superintending Grade Arch., Directorate-Gen. of Res. and Development, 1963–67; Chief Architect, 1967–84 and Dir of Bldg, 1978–84, Scottish Office, retd. Partner, Hutchison Locke & Monk, 1984–87. Dep. Leader, Timber Trade Mission to Canada, 1964. A Vice-Pres., RIBA, 1972–73, 1975–76, 1976–77; Hon. Librarian, 1976–78. Sec. of State for Scotland's nominee on ARCUK, 1970–85, RIBA nominee, 1985–; Member Council: EAA, 1970–78; RIAS, 1971–78, 1984–87; RIBA, 1972–78; Member: Sec. of State for Environment's Construction and Housing Res. Adv. Council, 1968–79; Building Res. Estabt Adv. Cttees in England and Scotland, 1970–84; York Adv. Cttee for continuing educn for building professions, 1975–80. Assessor, to Scottish Cttee of Design Council, 1974–84; Civic Trust Adjudicator, 1985–87. *Publications:* papers on industrialised building, contract procedure, etc, in various jls; HMSO publications on Scottish housing, educational and health buildings. *Recreations:* sailing, walking. *Address:* Summerfield, Vines Cross Road, Horam, near Heathfield, East Sussex TN21 0HE. *T:* Horam Road (04353) 2042; 4/4 Liddesdale Place, Glenogle Road, Edinburgh EH3 5WJ. *T:* 031–556 2867. *Clubs:* Arts; New (Edinburgh); Western Province Sports (Kelvin Grove, Cape Town).

BECKETT, Maj.-Gen. Denis Arthur, CB 1971; DSO 1944; OBE 1960; *b* 19 May 1917; *o s* of late Archibald Beckett, Woodford Green, Essex; *m* 1946, Elizabeth (marr. diss. 1974), *er d* of late Col Guy Edwards, Upper Slaughter, Glos; one *s*; *m* 1978, Nancy Ann Hitt. *Educ:* Forest Sch.; Chard Sch. Joined Hon. Artillery Co., 1939; commnd into Essex Regt, 1940; served in W Africa, Middle East, Italy and Greece, 1940–45; DAA &

QMG and Bde Major, Parachute Bdes, 1948–50; Instructor: RMA Sandhurst, 1951–53; Staff Coll., Camberley, 1953–56; Second in Comd 3rd Bn Para. Regt, 1956–58; comd 2nd Bn Para. Regt, 1958–60; Directing Staff, JSSC, 1960–61; comd 19 Bde, 1961–63; idc 1964; DAG, BAOR, 1965–66; Chief of Staff, Far East Land Forces, 1966–68; Dir of Personal Services (Army), 1968–71, retired 1971. *Address:* 12 Wellington House, Eton Road, NW3. *Clubs:* Army and Navy, Lansdowne.

BECKETT, Maj.-Gen. Edwin Horace Alexander, CB 1988; MBE 1974; Head of British Defence Staff, Washington, 1988–91, retired; *b* 16 May 1937; *s* of William Alexander Beckett and Doris Beckett; *m* 1963, Micaela Elizabeth Benedicta, *d* of Col Sir Edward Malet, Bt, OBE; three *s* one *d*. *Educ:* Henry Fanshawe School; RMA Sandhurst; ndc, psc, sq. Commissioned 1957 West Yorks Regt; regtl service in Aden (despatches 1968), Gibraltar, Germany and N Ireland; DAA&QMG 11 Armd Brigade, 1972–74; CO 1 PWO, 1976–78 (despatches 1977); GSO1 (DS) Staff Coll., 1979; Comdt Junior Div., Staff Coll., 1980; Comdr UKMF and 6 Field Force, 1981; Comdr UKMF, 1 Inf. Brigade and Tidworth Garrison, 1982; Director: Concepts, MoD, 1983–84; Army Plans and Programmes, MoD, 1984–85; C of S, HQ BAOR, 1985–88. Col Comdt, The King's Div., 1988–. *Recreations:* fishing, picture framing, farming for fun. *Address:* Lloyds Bank, Cox's & King's Branch, 6 Pall Mall, SW1. *Club:* Naval and Military.

BECKETT, Prof. James Camlin, MA; Professor of Irish History, Queen's University of Belfast, 1958–75; *b* 8 Feb. 1912; 3rd *s* of Alfred Beckett and Frances Lucy Bushell. *Educ:* Royal Belfast Academical Instn; Queen's Univ., Belfast. History Master, Belfast Royal Academy, 1934; Lectr in Modern History, Queen's Univ., Belfast, 1945, Reader in Modern History, 1952. Fellow Commoner, Peterhouse, Cambridge, 1955–56; Cummings Lectr, McGill Univ., Montreal, 1976; Mellon Prof., Tulane Univ., New Orleans, 1977; Member: Irish Manuscripts Commn, 1959–86; Royal Commission on Historical Manuscripts, 1960–86. Hon. DLitt: New Univ. of Ulster, 1979; NUI, 1990; Hon. DLit Queen's Univ. of Belfast, 1980. FRHistS; MRIA. *Publications:* Protestant Dissent in Ireland, 1687–1780, 1948; Short History of Ireland, 1952; (ed with T. W. Moody) Ulster since 1800: a Political and Economic Survey, 1954; (ed with T. W. Moody) Ulster since 1800: a Social Survey, 1957; (with T. W. Moody) Queen's Belfast, 1845–1949, 1959; The Making of Modern Ireland 1603–1923, 1966; (ed with R. E. Glasscock) Belfast: the Origin and Growth of an Industrial City, 1966; (ed) Historical Studies VII, 1969; Confrontations, 1973; The Anglo-Irish Tradition, 1976; The Cavalier Duke, 1990; contrib. The Ulster Debate, 1972; articles, reviews, etc., in English Hist. Rev., History, Irish Hist. Studies and other jls. *Recreations:* chess, walking. *Address:* 19 Wellington Park Terrace, Belfast, N Ireland BT9 6DR. *Club:* Ulster Reform (Belfast).

BECKETT, John Michael; Chairman and Chief Executive, Woolworth Holdings plc, 1982–86; *b* 22 June 1929; *yr s* of H. N. Beckett, MBE, and C. L. Beckett; *m* 1955, Joan Mary, *o d* of Percy and F. M. Rogerson; five *d*. *Educ:* Wolverhampton Grammar Sch.; Magdalen Coll., Oxford (BA 1953, MA 1957). Nat. Service and Reg. Commn RA, 1947–50; TA 1950–60. Called to Bar, Gray's Inn, 1954. Bar, 1954–55; Tootal Ltd, 1955–58; Tarmac Ltd, 1958–75; Dir, 1963–82 (non-exec., 1975–82); Chief Exec., British Sugar Corp. Ltd, 1975–82. Dir, Johnson Matthey, 1985–86. Hon. FIQ; FRSA; CBIM.
See also Sir T. N. Beckett.

BECKETT, Margaret M., (Mrs L. A. Beckett); MP (Lab) Derby South, since 1983; *b* Jan. 1943; *d* of Cyril and Winifred Jackson; *m* 1979, Lionel A. Beckett; two step *s*. *Educ:* Notre Dame High Sch., Norwich; Manchester Coll. of Sci. and Technol. Formerly: engrg apprentice (metallurgy), AEI, Manchester; exptl officer, Manchester Univ.; Labour Party res. asst; political adviser, Minister for Overseas Develt, 1974; Principal Researcher, Granada TV, 1979–83. Contested (Lab) Lincoln, Feb. 1974; MP (Lab) Lincoln, Oct. 1974–1979; PPS to Minister for Overseas Develt, 1974–75; Asst Govt Whip, 1975–76; Parly Under-Sec. of State, DES, 1976–79; Opposition front bench spokesman on health and social security, 1984–89, on Treasury affairs, 1989–. Mem. NEC, Labour Party, 1980–81, 1985–86, 1988–. *Address:* Rose Cottage, 102 Village Street, Old Normanton, Derby DE3 8DF.

BECKETT, Sir Martyn Gervase, 2nd Bt, *cr* 1921; MC 1945; RIBA; Architect; *b* 6 Nov. 1918; *s* of Hon. Sir Gervase Beckett, 1st Bt, and Lady Marjorie Beckett (*d* 1964), *e d* of 5th Earl of Warwick; *S* father, 1937; *m* 1941, Hon. Priscilla Brett, *y d* of 3rd Viscount Esher, GBE; two *s* one *d*. *Educ:* Eton; Trinity Coll., Cambridge (BA). Enlisted in Green Howards, 1939; commnd Welsh Guards, 1940; served War of 1939–45 (MC); Lieut (temp. Captain). DipArch 1951, ARIBA 1952. Built or reconstructed several country houses and housing estates, hotels, libraries etc; works to various scheduled buildings and for National Trust. Architect to King's College Chapel, Cambridge, 1960– (internal alterations and renovations to the Chapel, 1968); Cons. Architect to: Gordonstoun, 1954–58; Savoy Hotel Gp, 1981–; Temple Bar Trust, 1983–; Charterhouse, 1983–; Ampleforth Coll., 1984; Eton Coll., 1986–; Rank Laboratories, 1987. Exhibited: RA, London, provinces; one man exhibitions: Clarges Gall., 1980 and 1983; Soar Gall., 1986, 1988 and 1990. Trustee: The Wallace Collection, 1972– (Chm. 1976–); British Museum, 1978–88; CPRE Trust, 1983–90; Chm., Yorkshire Regional Cttee, Nat. Trust, 1980–85; Member: N York Moor Nat. Park Cttee, 1972–78; Council of Management, Chatsworth House Trust, 1981–; President: Ryedale Br., CPRE, 1964–; Friends of York Art Gall., 1970–83. Mem. Council, RSPB, 1985–87. Trustee, D'Oyly Carte Charity Trust, 1988–. FRSA 1982; FAMS 1955. Freeman, City of London, 1986. *Recreations:* painting, photography, piano. *Heir:* *s* Richard Gervase Beckett, *qv*. *Address:* 3 St Albans Grove, W8 5PN. *T:* 071–937 7834; Kirkdale Farm, Nawton, Yorks. *Clubs:* Brooks's, MCC.

BECKETT, Richard Gervase; QC 1988; barrister; *b* 27 March 1944; *s* and *heir* of Sir Martyn Beckett, Bt, *qv*; *m* 1976, Elizabeth Ann, *d* of Major Hugo Waterhouse; one *s* three *d*. *Educ:* Eton. Diploma in Economics (Oxford). Called to the Bar, Middle Temple, 1965; practice at the Bar, 1966–. *Recreation:* landscape. *Address:* 33 Groveway, SW9 0AH. *T:* 071–735 3350. *Clubs:* Pratt's, Portland.

BECKETT, Sir Terence (Norman), KBE 1987 (CBE 1974); Kt 1978; FEng; Member, Top Salaries Review Body, since 1987; Adviser to Joint Committee of Milk Marketing Board and Dairy Trade Federation, since 1987; *b* 13 Dec. 1923; *s* of late Horace Norman Beckett, MBE and late Clarice Lillian (*née* Allsop); *m* 1950, Sylvia Gladys Asprey; one *d*. *Educ:* London Sch. of Econs. BScEcon, FIMechE, CBIM, FIMI. Captain REME, British Army (UK, India, Malaya), 1945–48; RARO, 1949–62. Company Trainee, Ford Motor Co. Ltd, 1950; Asst in office of Dep. Chm. and Man. Dir, 1951; Man., Styling, Briggs Motor Bodies Ltd (Ford subsid.), 1954; Admin Man., Engrg, Briggs, 1955; Manager, Product Staff, 1955; Gen. Man., Product Planning Staff, 1961 (responsible for Cortina, Transit Van, 'D' series truck); Manager, Marketing Staff, 1963; Dir, Car Div., 1964; Exec. Dir, Ford Motor Co. Ltd, 1966 and Dir of Sales, 1968; Vice-Pres., European and Overseas Sales Ops, Ford of Europe Inc., 1969; Man. Dir and Chief Exec., 1974–80 and Chm., 1976–80, Ford Motor Co. Ltd; Chm., Ford Motor Credit Co. Ltd, 1976–80; Director: ICI, 1976–80; Automotive Finance Ltd, 1974–77. Dir Gen. CBI, 1980–87 (Mem. Council, 1976–80); Dep. Chm., CEGB, 1990 (Dir, 1987–90). Member: NEDC, 1980–87; Engineering Industries Council, 1975–80; BIM Council, 1976–77; Grand Council, Motor and Cycle Trades Benevolent Fund (BEN), 1976–80; SMMT Council and Exec. Cttee, 1974–80; Council, Automobile Div., IMechE, 1979–80; Vice Pres. and Hon. Fellow, Inst. of the Motor Industry, 1974–80; Vice-Pres., Conference on Schs, Sci. and Technol., 1979–80; Chm., Governing Body, London Business Sch., 1979–86; Mem. Court, Cranfield Inst. of Technology, 1977–82; Pro-Chancellor and Chm. Council, Univ. of Essex, 1989– (Mem. Court, 1985–); Governor, Nat. Inst. of Econ. and Social Res., 1978–; Governor and Mem. Court, LSE, 1978–; Mem. Court of Assts, Worshipful Co. of Engineers, 1983–85. Pres., IVCA, 1987–91. Patron: MSC Award Scheme for Disabled People, 1979–80; AIESEC, 1985. Lectures: Stamp, London Univ., 1982; Pfizer, Kent at Canterbury Univ., 1983. Hon. Fellow: Sidney Sussex Coll., Cambridge, 1981; London Business Sch., 1988; Hon. DSc: Cranfield, 1977; Heriot-Watt, 1981; Hon. DSc (Econ.) London, 1982; Hon. DTech Brunel, 1991. FRSA 1984. Hambro Businessman of the Year, 1978; BIM Gold Medal, 1980. *Recreations:* ornithology, music. *Address:* c/o Barclays Bank plc, 74 High Street, Ingatestone, Essex CM4 9BW. *Club:* Athenæum.
See also J. M. Beckett.

BECKETT, William Cartwright, CB 1978; LLM; Solicitor to the Corporation of Lloyd's, since 1985; *b* 21 Sept. 1929; *s* of late William Beckett and Emily (*née* Cartwright); *m* 1st, 1956, Marjorie Jean Hoskin; two *s*; 2nd, 1974, Lesley Margaret Furlonger. *Educ:* Salford Grammar Sch.; Manchester Univ. (LLB 1950, LLM 1952). Called to Bar, Middle Temple, 1952. Joined Treasury Solicitor's Dept, 1956; Board of Trade, 1965; Asst Solicitor, DEP, 1969; Under-Sec., DTI, 1972; Dep.-Sec. 1977; Legal Secretary, Law Officers' Dept, 1975–80; Solicitor, DTI, 1980–84. *Recreations:* music, golf. *Address:* Park House, Bradwell, near Braintree, Essex. *T:* Braintree (0376) 561109. *Club:* Reform.

BECKINGHAM, Prof. Charles Fraser, FBA 1983; Professor of Islamic Studies, University of London, 1965–81, now Emeritus; International Director, Fontes Historiae Africanae Project, Union Académique Internationale, since 1986; *b* 18 Feb. 1914; *o c* of Arthur Beckingham, ARBA and Alice Beckingham, Houghton, Hunts; *m* 1946, Margery (*d* 1966), *o d* of John Ansell; one *d*. *Educ:* Grammar Sch., Huntingdon; Queens' Coll., Cambridge (scholar, Members' English prizeman, 1934). Dept of Printed Books, British Museum, 1936–46. Seconded to military and naval Intelligence, 1942–46. Foreign Office (GCHQ), 1946–51; Lectr in Islamic History, Manchester Univ., 1951–55; Sen. Lectr, 1955–58; Prof. of Islamic Studies, 1958–65. Pres., Hakluyt Soc., 1969–72; Treas., Royal Asiatic Soc., 1964–67, Pres., 1967–70, 1976–79, Hon. Fellow, Sri Lanka Branch, 1978. Chm., St Marylebone Soc., 1980–84. Jt Editor, 1961–64, Editor, 1965, Jl of Semitic Studies; Editor, Jl of RAS, 1984–87. Sir Percy Sykes Meml Medal, RSAA, 1987. *Publications:* contribs to Admiralty Handbook of Western Arabia, 1946; (with G. W. B. Huntingford) Some Records of Ethiopia, 1954; Introduction to Atlas of the Arab World and Middle East, 1960; (with G. W. B. Huntingford) A True Relation of the Prester John of the Indies, 1961; Bruce's Travels (ed and selected), 1964; The Achievements of Prester John, 1966; (ed) Islam, in, Religion in the Middle East (ed A. J. Arberry), 1969; (with E. Ullendorff) The Hebrew Letters of Prester John, 1982; Between Islam and Christendom, 1983; (ed) The Itinerário of Jerónimo Lobo, 1984; articles in learned jls. *Address:* 3 Pipe Passage, Lewes, E Sussex BN7 1YG. *Clubs:* Travellers', Beefsteak.

BECKLAKE, Ernest John Stephen, PhD; CEng; Head of Technology Group (formerly Keeper, Department of Engineering), Science Museum, since 1985; *b* 24 June 1943; *s* of Ernest and Evelyn Becklake; *m* 1965, Susan Elizabeth (*née* Buckle), BSc; two *s*. *Educ:* Bideford Grammar Sch.; Exeter Univ. (BSc, PhD). CEng 1988; MIEE 1988. Engr, EMI Electronics, Wells, 1967–69; Post-Doctoral Fellow, Victoria Univ., BC, Canada, 1969–70; Sen. Scientist, Marconi Space and Def. Systems, Frimley, 1970–72; Science Museum: Asst Keeper, Dept of Earth and Space Sciences, 1972–80; Keeper, Dept of Elect. Engrg, Communications and Circulation, 1980–85. Mem., Internat. Acad. of Astronautics, 1988–. *Publications:* Man and the Moon, 1980; The Climate Crisis, 1989; The Population Explosion, 1990; Pollution, 1990; (series editor) Exploration and Discovery, 1980–; technical pubns in Electronics Letters, Jl of Physics D, Jl of British Interplanetary Soc., and Spaceflight. *Recreations:* gardening, golf, rugby. *Address:* Tree Wood, Robin Hood Lane, Sutton Green, Guildford, Surrey GU7 4QY. *T:* Woking (0483) 766931. *Club:* Puttenham Golf.

BECKMAN, Michael David, QC 1976; *b* 6 April 1932; *s* of Nathan and Esther Beckman; *m* 1990, Jennifer (*née* Redmond); two *d* from former marriage. *Educ:* King's Coll., London (LLB (Hons)). Called to the Bar, Lincoln's Inn, 1954. *Recreations:* various. *Address:* Bullards, Widford, Herts SG12 8RQ. *T:* Much Hadham (027984) 2669; (chambers) 19 Old Buildings, Lincoln's Inn, WC2 3UR; 3 East Pallants, Chichester PO19 1TR.

BECKWITH, Prof. Athelstan Laurence Johnson, FRS 1988; FAA; FRACI; Professor of Organic Chemistry, since 1981, and Dean, since 1989, Research School of Chemistry, Australian National University; *b* 20 Feb. 1930; *s* of Laurence Alfred Beckwith and Doris Grace Beckwith; *m* 1953, Phyllis Kaye Marshall, Perth, WA; one *s* two *d*. *Educ:* Perth Modern Sch.; Univ. of WA (BSc Hons); Oxford Univ. (DPhil 1956). FAA 1973; FRACI 1973. Lectr in Chemistry, Adelaide Univ., 1953; CSIRO Overseas Student, 1954; Res. Officer, CSIRO Melbourne, 1957; Adelaide University: Lectr in Organic Chemistry, 1958; Prof., 1965–81; Dean of Science, 1972–73. Temp. Lectr, Imperial Coll., London, 1962–63; Vis. Lectr, Univ. of York, 1968; Carnegie Fellow, 1968. Federal Pres., RACI, 1965 (Rennie Medal, 1960; H. G. Smith Meml Medal, 1981); Vice-Pres., Aust. Acad. of Sci., 1985–86. *Publications:* numerous articles in Jl of Chem. Soc., Jl of Amer. Chem. Soc., etc. *Recreations:* golf, music, walking. *Address:* 2/14 Currie Crescent, Kingston, ACT 2604, Australia. *T:* (06) 249 4012; (06) 295 3694.

BECKWITH, John Lionel, FCA; Founder Chairman, London & Edinburgh Trust PLC, since 1971; *b* 19 March 1947; *s* of Col Harold Beckwith and Agnes Camilla McMichael (*née* Duncan); *m* 1975, Heather Marie Robbins; two *s* one *d*. *Educ:* Harrow Sch. FCA 1970; ATII 1970. Articled Clerk: Beresford Lye & Co., 1967–69; Arthur Andersen & Co., 1969–71; with London & Edinburgh Trust PLC, 1971–. *Recreations:* sport, music, ballet. *Address:* 243 Knightsbridge, SW7 1DH. *T:* 071–581 1322. *Clubs:* Annabel's; Old Harrovian Football; Royal Mid-Surrey Golf, St George's Hill Golf; Riverside Racquet Centre.
See also P. M. Beckwith.

BECKWITH, Peter Michael; Deputy Chairman, London and Edinburgh Trust, since 1987; *b* 20 Jan. 1945; *s* of Col Harold Andrew Beckwith and Agnes Camilla McMichael Beckwith; *m* 1968, Paula Gay Bateman; two *d*. *Educ:* Harrow School; Emmanuel College, Cambridge (MA Hons). Qualified Solicitor, 1970; Asst Solicitor, Norton Rose Botterell & Roche; London & Edinburgh Trust: Joint Founder and shareholder, 1972; Managing Director, 1983–86. FRSA. *Recreations:* tennis, ski-ing, opera, dogs, gardening. *Address:* 243 Knightsbridge, SW7 1DH. *T:* 071–581 1322. *Clubs:* Riverside Racquets; Down Hill Only (Wengen).
See also J. L. Beckwith.

BECTIVE, Earl of; Thomas Michael Ronald Christopher Taylour; estate agent, with Egerton, London; *b* 10 Feb. 1959; *s* and *heir* of 6th Marquis of Headfort, *qv*; *m* 1987, Susan Jane, *er d* of late C. A. Vandervell and of Mrs Vandervell; two *s*. *Educ:* Harrow;

RAC Cirencester. *Heir:* s Lord Kenlis, *qv.* *Address:* Northfields Farmhouse, Kirk Andreas, Ramsey, Isle of Man. *Clubs:* Lansdowne; Royal Dublin Society (Dublin).

BEDBROOK, Sir George (Montario), Kt 1978; OBE 1963; FRCS; FRACS; Director, Prevention of Spinal Injuries Programme, Royal Perth Rehabilitation Hospital, since 1990; *b* 8 Nov. 1921; *s* of Arthur Bedbrook and Ethel (*née* Prince); *m* 1946, Jessie Violet (*née* Page); two *s* three *d.* *Educ:* University High Sch., Melbourne; Medical Sch., Univ. of Melbourne (MB BS (Hons) 1944, J. P. Ryan Schol. in Surgery, MS 1950). FRACS 1950; FRCS (England) 1951; DPRM (Sydney) 1970. Resident MO, Royal Melb. Hosp., Vic, 1944–45; Lectr in Anatomy, Univ. of Melb., Vic, 1946–50; Resident MO, Nat. Orthopaedic Hosp., London, 1951; Registrar, Orthopaedic Dept, Croydon Gp Hosps, 1951–53; private practice in Perth, WA; Mem. Orthopaedic Dept, Royal Perth Hosp., 1953; began Paraplegic Service, Royal Perth Hosp., 1954; Head, Dept of Paraplegia, Royal Perth Rehabilitation Hosp., 1954–72, resigned; Royal Perth Hospital and Royal Perth Rehabilitation Hospital: Chm., Dept of Orthopaedic Surgery, 1965–79; Sen. Surgeon, Spinal Unit, 1972–86; Sen. Orthopaedic Consultant, 1972–86, now Consultant Emeritus; Clinical Sub-Dean, Royal Perth Hosp. and Univ. of WA, 1987–89. Pres., Aust. Orthopaedic Assoc., 1977; Vice Chm., Nat. Adv. Council for the Handicapped, 1975–83; Vice-Pres., Australian Council for the Rehabilitation of the Disabled (ACROD), 1970–80; Pres., Internat. Med. Soc. of Paraplegia, 1981–84; Chm., W Australian Cttee, Internat. Year of Disabled Persons, 1981. Hon. FRCSE 1981; Hon. Fellow, Coll. of Rehabilitation Medicine, 1987; Hon. MD, WA, 1973; Hon. DTech Curtin Univ., 1984. OStJ 1972. Betts Medal, Aust. Orthopaedic Assoc., 1972. *Publications:* Care and Management of Spinal Cord Injuries, 1981; Lifetime Care of the Paraplegic Patient, 1985; numerous (114) papers and contribs to medical and scientific jls, espec. relating to spinal injuries with paraplegia. *Recreations:* reading, music, travel, sports for the disabled. *Address:* (home) 29 Ulster Road, Floreat Park, WA 6014, Australia. *T:* 387.3582; (office) 13 Colin Grove, West Perth, WA 6005, Australia. *T:* 321.7543.

BEDBROOK, Jack Harry, CEng, FRINA; FBIM; RCNC; Managing Director, HM Dockyard, Devonport, 1979–84; *b* 8 Aug. 1924; *s* of Harry Bedbrook and Emma Bedbrook; *m* 1963, Janet Bedbrook; three *d.* *Educ:* Technical Coll., Portsmouth; RNC, Greenwich. Dir Gen. Ships Dept, Admiralty, 1946–51; Asst Constructor, Devonport, 1951–54; Dockyard Dept, Bath, 1954–56; Constructor, Gibraltar Dockyard, 1956–58; Admiralty Exptl Works, Haslar, 1958–62; Dir Gen. Ships Dept, 1962–65; Chief Constructor, Portsmouth, 1965–71; Project Manager, Rosyth, 1971–74; Prodn Dir, Devonport, 1974–77; Man. Dir, HM Dockyard, Rosyth, 1977–79. *Recreations:* badminton, sailing, gardening, music. *Address:* Laxtons, Cargreen, Saltash, Cornwall PL12 6PA. *T:* Saltash (0752) 844519.

BEDDALL, Hugh Richard Muir; Chairman, Muir Beddall & Co. Ltd, since 1964; Member of Lloyd's, since 1943; *b* 20 May 1922; *s* of Herbert Muir Beddall and Jennie Beddall (*née* Fowler); *m* 1946, Monique Henriette (*née* Haefliger); three *s* one *d.* *Educ:* Stowe; Ecole de Commerce, Neuchatel, Switzerland. Employee of Muir Beddall & Co., 1939–41. Served War of 1939–45; Royal Marines, 2nd Lieut, 1941; subseq. Captain A Troop 45 RM Commando and No 1 Commando Bde HQ; demob., 1946. Employee, Muir Beddall, Mise & Cie, Paris, 1946–47; returned as employee of Muir Beddall & Co. Ltd, 1947; Dir, 1949; Dep. Chm., 1960; Chm., 1964. FCII. Dir, Muir Beddall Mise & Cie, Paris. *Recreations:* shooting, fishing, racing. *Address:* Flat 4, 53 Cadogan Square, SW1X 0HY. *T:* 071-235 9461. *Clubs:* Buck's, East India, Devonshire, Sports and Public Schools.

BEDDARD, Nicholas Elliot; His Honour Judge Beddard; a Circuit Judge, since 1986; *b* 26 April 1934; *s* of Terence Elliot Beddard and Ursula Mary Hamilton Howard; *m* 1964, Gillian Elisabeth Vaughan Bevan, 2nd *d* of Llewellyn and Molly Bevan; two *s* one *d.* *Educ:* Eton. National Service, 1952–54; commissioned, Royal Sussex Regt, 1953; TA (Royal Sussex Regt), 1955–64. United Africa Co., 1955–58; Asst Public Policy Executive, RAC, 1958–68; called to the Bar, Inner Temple, 1967; A Recorder, 1986. *Recreations:* choral singing, squash, golf. *Address:* Farrar's Building, Temple, EC4Y 7BD. *T:* 071-583 9241. *Clubs:* Lansdowne; Orford Sailing.

BEDDINGTON, Charles Richard; Metropolitan Magistrate, 1963–80; *b* 22 Aug. 1911; *s* of late Charles Beddington, Inner Temple, and Stella (*née* de Goldschmidt); *m* 1939, Debbie, *d* of late Frederick Appleby Holt and Rae Vera Franz, *d* of Sir George Hutchinson; two *s* one *d.* *Educ:* Eton (scholar); Balliol Coll., Oxford. Barrister, Inner Temple, 1934. Joined TA, 1939; served RA, 1939–45, Major. Practised at the Bar in London and on SE Circuit. Mem. Mental Health Review Tribunal (SE Metropolitan Area), 1960–63. *Address:* 21 Mytten Close, Cuckfield, West Sussex RH17 5LN. *T:* Haywards Heath (0444) 454063; 1 Temple Gardens, Temple, EC4.

BEDDOES, Air Vice-Marshal John Geoffrey Genior, CB 1981; FRAeS; aviation consultant; *b* 21 May 1925; *s* of Algernon Geoffrey Beddoes and Lucy Isobel (*née* Collier); *m* 1948, Betty Morris Kendrick; three *s.* *Educ:* Wirral Grammar Sch., Bebington, Cheshire. Pilot training in Rhodesia and Egypt, 1943–45; No 114 Sqdn, Italy and Aden, Bostons and Mosquitos, 1945–46; No 30 Sqdn, Abingdon and Berlin Airlift, Dakotas, 1947–49; Central Flying Sch., 1949; Flying Instr, RAF Coll., Cranwell and Central Flying Sch., 1950–55; Flight Comdr, No 57 Sqdn, Canberras, 1955; Air Ministry, 1956–57; Flying Coll., 1958; Flt Comdr No 57 Sqdn, Victor Mk 1, 1959–61; sc Bracknell, 1962; OC No 139 (Jamaica) Sqdn, Victor Mk 2, 1963–64; Wing Comdr Ops HQ No 3 Gp, 1965–67; Directing Staff Coll. of Air Warfare, 1968–69; OC RAF Laarbruch, 1969–71; MoD Dep. Dir, Operational Requirements, 1971–73; HQ 2 ATAF Asst COS Offensive Operations, 1974–75; MoD Director of Operational Requirements, 1975–78; Dir Gen. Aircraft (2), MoD PE, 1978–80; retired RAF, 1981. Mem., Norfolk CC, 1989–. Chm., St Gregory's Trust, Norwich, 1988–. FBIM. *Recreations:* music, cricket, DIY, golf, gardening. *Address:* White Stables, Stow Bedon, Norfolk NR17 1HP. *T:* Caston 524. *Club:* Royal Air Force.

BEDFORD, 13th Duke of, *cr* 1694; **John Robert Russell;** Marquess of Tavistock, 1694; Earl of Bedford, 1550; Baron Russell of Chenies, 1540; Baron Russell of Thornhaugh, 1603; Baron Howland of Streatham, 1695; *b* 24 May 1917; *er s* of 12th Duke and Louisa Crommelin Roberta (*d* 1960), *y d* of Robert Jowitt Whitwell; *S* father 1953; *m* 1st, 1939, Clare Gwendolen Hollway, *née* Bridgman (*d* 1945); two *s*; 2nd, Lydia (marr. diss., 1960), *widow* of Capt. Ian de Hoghton Lyle, 3rd *d* of 3rd Baron Churston and late Duchess of Leinster; one *s*; 3rd, 1960, Mme Nicole Milinaire, *d* of Paul Schneider. Coldstream Guards, 1939; invalided out, 1940. *Publications:* A Silver-Plated Spoon, 1959; (with G. Mikes) Book of Snobs, 1965; The Flying Duchess, 1968; (with G. Mikes) How to Run a Stately Home, 1971. *Heir:* *s* Marquess of Tavistock, *qv.* *Address:* Château des Ligures, 2 rue Honoré Labande, Monte Carlo, MC 98000, Monaco. *Clubs:* Brooks's, Pratt's.

BEDFORD, Bishop Suffragan of, since 1981; **Rt. Rev. David John Farmbrough;** *b* 4 May 1929; 2nd *s* of late Charles Septimus and late Ida Mabel Farmbrough; *m* 1955, Angela Priscilla Hill, DL; one *s* three *d.* *Educ:* Bedford Sch.; Lincoln Coll., Oxford (BA 1951, MA 1953); Westcott House, Cambridge, 1951–53. Deacon, 1953, priest, 1954; Curate of Bishop's Hatfield, 1953–57; Priest-in-charge, St John's, Hatfield, 1957–63; Vicar of Bishop's Stortford, 1963–74; Rural Dean of Bishop's Stortford, 1973–74; Archdeacon of St Albans, 1974–81. Mem., Gen. Synod, 1972–81. *Publications:* In Wonder, Love and Praise, 1966; Belonging, Believing, Doing, 1971. *Recreations:* sailing, gardening. *Address:* 168 Kimbolton Road, Bedford MK41 8DN. *T:* Bedford (0234) 357551.

BEDFORD, Archdeacon of; *see* Bourke, Ven. M.

BEDFORD, Alfred William, (Bill), OBE 1961; AFC 1945; FRAeS; Aerospace consultant, since 1986; *b* 18 Nov. 1920; *m* 1941, Mary Averill; one *s.* *Educ:* Loughborough College School, Leics. Electrical engineering apprenticeship, Blackburn Starling & Co. Ltd. RAF 1940–51: served Fighter Sqdns, 605 (County of Warwick) Sqdn, 1941; 135 Sqdn, 1941–44; 65 Sqdn, 1945. Qualified Flying Instructor, Upavon, 1945, and Instructor, Instrument Rating Examiner, until 1949; Graduate Empire Flying School all-weather course. Awarded King's Commendation, 1949; Graduate and Tutor, Empire Test Pilots' School, 1949–50; Test Pilot, RAE Farnborough, 1950–51; Experimental Test Pilot, Hawker Aircraft Ltd, 1951–56; Chief Test Pilot, Hawker Aircraft Ltd, 1956–63; Chief Test Pilot (Dunsfold); Hawker Siddeley Aviation Ltd, 1963–67; Sales Man., Hawker Siddeley Aviation, 1968–78; British Aerospace: Divisional Mktg Manager, 1978–83; Regional Exec., SE Asia, 1983–86. London-Rome and return world speed records, 1956. Made initial flight, Oct. 1960, on the Hawker P1127 (the World's first VTOL strike fighter), followed by first jet V/STOL operations of such an aircraft from an Aircraft Carrier (HMS Ark Royal) on 8 Feb. 1963; Harrier first flight, Aug. 1966. First UK holder of Internat. Gold 'C' with two diamonds; held British and UK national gliding records of 257 miles and altitude of 21,340 ft (19,120 ft gain of height); awarded BGA trophies: de Havilland (twice), Manio, and Wakefield, 1950–51. Approved Air Registration Bd glider test pilot. Chm. and founder Mem., Test Pilots' Group, RAeS, 1964–66. Member SBAC Test Pilots' Soc., 1956–67. Member Society of Experimental Test Pilots. RAeS Alston Memorial Medal, 1959; Guild of Air Pilots and Air Navigators Derry Richards Memorial Medal, 1959–60; Segrave Trophy, 1963; Britannia Trophy, 1964; Air League Founders Medal, 1967; C. P. Robertson Meml Trophy, Air Pubns Assoc., 1987. First Class Wings, Indonesian Air Force, for services to the Republic, 1982. *Recreations:* squash, sail-plane flying. *Address:* The Chequers, West End Lane, Esher, Surrey KT10 8LF. *T:* Esher (0372) 62285. *Clubs:* Royal Air Force; Esher Squash.

BEDFORD, David; Youth Music Director, English Sinfonia, since 1986; Chairman, Association of Professional Composers, since 1991; *b* 4 Aug. 1937; *s* of late Leslie Herbert Bedford and Lesley Florence Keitley Duff; *m* 1st, 1958, Maureen Parsonage; two *d*; 2nd, 1969, Susan Pilgrim; two *d.* *Educ:* Lancing College; Royal Acad. of Music; Trinity Coll. London (LTCL). Guy's Hosp. porter, 1956; teacher, Whitefield Sch., Hendon, 1965; teacher, 1968–80, and composer-in-residence, 1969–81, Queen's Coll., London. ARAM. Mem. Exec. Cttee, Soc. for the Promotion of New Music, 1982–88; Pres., British Music Information Centre, 1988–89. Patron, Barnet Schs Music Assoc., 1987. Numerous compositions, many commissioned by major London orchestras and BBC; numerous recordings. *Recreations:* squash, table tennis, cricket, astronomy, ancient history, philosophy, horror films. *Address:* 39 Shakespeare Road, Mill Hill, NW7 4BA. *T:* 081-959 3165. *Clubs:* Ridgeway Table Tennis, Mill Hill Squash.

See also S. J. R. Bedford.

BEDFORD, Eric, CB 1959; CVO 1953; Chief Architect, Ministry of Works, 1952–70 (Chief Architect, Directorate General of Works, Ministry of Public Building and Works, 1963–70). ARIBA 1933; Grissell Gold Medal of Royal Institute of British Architects, 1934. Was responsible for Ministry of Works decorations for the Coronation, 1953.

BEDFORD, Steuart John Rudolf; freelance conductor; Co-Artistic Director, English Music Theatre Co. since 1976; Artistic Director, English Sinfonia, since 1981; *b* 31 July 1939; *s* of late L. H. Bedford and Lesley Florence Keitley Duff; *m* 1st, 1969, Norma Burrowes, *qv*; 2nd, 1980, Celia, *er d* of Mr and Mrs G. R. Harding; two *d.* *Educ:* Lancing Coll., Sussex; Royal Acad. of Music. Fellow, RCO; FRAM; BA. Artistic Dir, Aldeburgh Festival, 1974, and (jtly), 1987. Royal Acad. of Music, 1965; English Opera Gp, now English Music Theatre, 1967–. Debut at Metropolitan, NY, 1974 (Death in Venice); new prodn of The Marriage of Figaro, 1975. Has conducted regularly with English Opera Gp and Welsh National Opera; also at Royal Opera House, Covent Garden (operas incl. Owen Wingrave and Death in Venice, by Benjamin Britten, and Cosi Fan Tutte); also in Santa Fe, Buenos Aires, France, Belgium, Holland, Canada, Vienna, etc. *Recreations:* golf, gardening. *Address:* c/o Harrison Parrott Ltd, 12 Penzance Place, W11 4PA.

See also D. Bedford.

BEDFORD, Sybille, OBE 1981; author; *b* 16 March 1911; *d* of Maximilian von Schoenebeck and Elizabeth Bernard; *m* 1935, Walter Bedford. *Educ:* privately, in Italy, England and France. Career in writing and literary journalism. Vice-Pres., PEN, 1979. FRSL. *Publications:* The Sudden View, A Visit to Don Otavio, 1953, new edn 1982; A Legacy, 1956, 6th edn 1984, televised 1975; The Best We Can Do (The Trial of Dr Adams), 1958, new edn 1989; The Faces of Justice, 1961; A Favourite of the Gods, 1962, new edn 1984; A Compass Error, 1968, new edn 1984; Aldous Huxley, a Biography, Vol I, 1973, Vol II, 1974, new edn 1987; Jigsaw, 1989; As It Was (essays), 1990. *Recreations:* wine, reading, travel. *Address:* c/o Messrs Coutts, 1 Old Park Lane, W1Y 4BS. *Clubs:* Reform, PEN.

BEDINGFELD; *see* Paston-Bedingfeld.

BEDINGFIELD, Christopher Ohl Macredie, TD 1968; QC 1976; a Recorder of the Crown Court, since 1972; *b* 2 June 1935; *s* of late Norman Macredie Bedingfield, Nantygroes, Radnorshire and of Mrs Macredie Bedingfield. *Educ:* Rugby; University Coll., Oxford (MA). Called to Bar, Gray's Inn, 1957, Bencher, 1986; Wales and Chester Circuit. Commnd 2 Mon R; NS 24th Regt; Staff Captain TA, 1960–64; Coy Comdr 4 RWF, 1964–69; Lt-Col TAVR, 1973–76, Co. Comdt Denbigh and Flint ACF 1973, Clwyd ACF 1974–76 (resigned on appt as QC). *Recreations:* riding, squash. *Address:* 21 Whitefriars, Chester CH1 1NZ. *T:* Chester (0244) 342020; (residence) Nantygroes, near Knighton, Powys. *T:* Whitton (05476) 220. *Clubs:* Reform; Bristol Channel Yacht (Swansea).

BEDNORZ, J. George, PhD; Physicist at IBM Research Laboratory, Zürich, since 1982; *b* 16 May 1950. *Educ:* Swiss Federal Institute of Technology, Zürich. (Jtly) Nobel Prize for Physics, 1987. *Publications:* papers in learned jls on new super-conducting materials. *Address:* IBM Zürich Research Laboratory, Säumerstrasse 4, CH-8803 Rüschlikon, Zürich, Switzerland.

BEDSER, Alec Victor, CBE 1982 (OBE 1964); PR Consultant; *b* 4 July 1918; twin *s* of late Arthur and Florence Beatrice Bedser. *Educ:* Monument Hill Secondary Sch., Woking. Served with RAF in UK, France (BEF), N Africa, Sicily, Italy, Austria, 1939–46. Joined Surrey County Cricket Club, as Professional, 1938; awarded Surrey CCC and England caps, 1946, 1st Test Match v India, created record by taking 22 wickets in first two Tests; toured Australia as Member of MCC team, 1946–47, 1950–51, 1954–55; toured S Africa with MCC, 1948–49; held record of most number of Test wickets (236), since beaten, 1953; took 100th wicket against Australia (first English bowler since 1914 to do this),

1953; Asst Man. to Duke of Norfolk on MCC tour to Australia, 1962–63; Manager: MCC team to Australia, 1974–75; England team tour of Australia and India, 1979–80; Member: England Cricket Selection Cttee, 1961–85 (Chm., 1968–81); MCC Cttee, 1982–85. Pres., Surrey CCC, 1987–88. Founded own company (office equipment and supplies) with Eric Bedser, 1955. Freeman, City of London, 1968; Liveryman, Worshipful Co. of Environmental Cleaners, 1988. *Publications*: (with E. A. Bedser) Our Cricket Story, 1951; Bowling, 1952; (with E. A. Bedser) Following On, 1954; Cricket Choice, 1981; (with Alex Bannister) Twin Ambitions (autobiog.), 1986. *Recreations*: cricket, golf. *Address*: c/o Initial Contract Services, Lincoln House, 33/34 Hoxton Square, N1 6NN. *Clubs*: MCC (Hon. Life), East India, Devonshire, Sports and Public Schools; Surrey County Cricket (Hon. Life Mem.); West Hill Golf.

BEEBY, Clarence Edward, ONZ 1987; CMG 1956; PhD; International Consultant, 1969–87, and Director Emeritus, since 1986, New Zealand Council for Educational Research; *b* 16 June 1902; *s* of Anthony and Alice Beeby; *m* 1926, Beatrice Eleanor, *d* of Charles Newnham; one *s* one *d*. *Educ*: Christchurch Boys' High Sch.; Canterbury Coll., University of NZ (MA); University Coll., London; University of Manchester (PhD). Lectr in Philosophy and Education, Canterbury Univ. Coll., University of NZ, 1923–34; Dir, NZ Council for Educational Research, 1934–38; Asst Dir of Education, Education Dept, NZ, 1938–40; Dir of Education, NZ, 1940–60 (leave of absence to act as Asst Dir-Gen. of UNESCO, Paris, 1948–49); NZ Ambassador to France, 1960–63; Research Fellow, Harvard Univ., 1963–67; Commonwealth Visiting Prof., Univ. of London, 1967–68; Consultant: to Australian Govt in Papua and New Guinea, 1969; to Ford Foundn in Indonesia, 1970–77; to UNDP in Malaysia, 1976; to World Bank, Washington, DC, 1983; to Aga Khan Foundn, Tanzania, 1987; External Consultant to Univ. of Papua New Guinea, 1982. Leader of NZ Delegs. to Gen. Confs of UNESCO, 1946, 1947, 1950, 1953, 1954, 1956, 1958, 1960, 1962. Hon. Counsellor of UNESCO, 1950; Mem., Exec. Bd, UNESCO, 1960–63 (Chm., Exec. Bd, 1963); Mem., Council of Consultant Fellows, Internat. Inst. for Educnl Planning, Paris, 1971–77. For. associate, US Nat. Acad. of Educn, 1981. Hon. Fellow, NZ Educnl Inst., 1971. Hon. LLD Otago, 1969; Hon. LittD Wellington, 1970. Mackie Medal, ANZAAS, 1971. Grand Cross, Order of St Gregory, 1964. *Publications*: The Intermediate Schools of New Zealand, 1938; (with W. Thomas and M. H. Oram) Entrance to the University, 1939; The Quality of Education in Developing Countries, 1966; (ed) Qualitative Aspects of Educational Planning, 1969; Assessment of Indonesian Education: a guide in planning, 1978; articles in educational periodicals. *Recreations*: gardening, fishing, cabinet-making. *Address*: 73 Barnard Street, Wellington 6001, New Zealand.

BEEBY, George Harry, CBE 1974; PhD; BSc; CEng, FIChemE, CChem, FRSC; Chairman, Inveresk Research Foundation, 1977–84; *b* 9 Sept. 1902; *s* of George Beeby and Lucy Beeby (*née* Monk); *m* 1929, Helen Elizabeth Edwards; one *d*. *Educ*: Loughborough Grammar Sch.; Loughborough Coll. BSc Hons 1922; PhD 1924, London Univ. Various appts in rubber and chemical industries, 1924–84; Chm., Thorium Ltd and Radiochemical Centre (later Amersham Internat.), 1949–57; Divisional Chm., ICI, 1954–57; Chm., British Titan Ltd, 1957–69. Chairman: EDC for Chemical Industry, 1964–67; Nat. Sulphuric Acid Assoc., 1963–65; British Standards Instn, 1967–70 (Dep. Pres. 1970–73). Pres., Soc. of Chemical Industry, 1970–72 (Vice-Pres., 1966–69); Vice-Pres., RoSPA, 1969–84; Hon. Mem., Chemical Industries Assoc. Member: Robens Cttee on Safety and Health at Work, 1970–72; Parly and Sci. Cttee, 1971–83; Windeyer Cttee on lead poisoning, 1972. FRSA 1969. Hon. DTech Loughborough Univ. of Technology, 1969. Soc. of Chemical Industry Medal, 1973. *Publications*: contribs to various jls on industrial safety, industrial economics and business administration. *Address*: The Laurels, Sandy Drive, Cobham, Surrey KT11 2ET. *T*: Oxshott (0372) 842346.

BEECH, Patrick Mervyn, CBE 1970; Controller, English Regions, BBC, 1969–72, retired; *b* 31 Oct. 1912; *s* of Howard Worcester Mervyn Beech and Stella Patrick Campbell; *m* 1st, 1935, Sigrid Gunnel Christenson (*d* 1959); two *d*; 2nd, 1960, Merle-Mary Barnes; one *d*. *Educ*: Stowe; Exeter Coll., Oxford. Joined BBC as Producer, West Region, 1935; News Editor, West Region, 1945; Asst Head of programmes, West Region, 1954; Controller, Midland Region, 1964–69. *Recreations*: photography, music, theatre. *Address*: Mill Bank, Cradley, near Malvern, Worcs. *T*: Ridgway Cross (0886) 880234.

BEECHAM, Jeremy Hugh; Member, Newcastle upon Tyne City Council, since 1967, Leader since 1977; Partner, Allan Henderson Beecham & Peacock, since 1968; *b* 17 Nov. 1944; *s* of Laurence and Florence Beecham; *m* 1968, Brenda Elizabeth (*née* Woolf); one *s* one *d*. *Educ*: Royal Grammar Sch., Newcastle upon Tyne; University Coll., Oxford (First Cl. Hons Jurisprudence; MA). Chm., OU Labour Club, 1964. Admitted Solicitor, 1968. Dir, Northern Develt Co., 1986–91. Newcastle upon Tyne City Council: Chairman: Social Services Cttee, 1973–77; Policy and Resources Cttee, 1977–; Finance Cttee, 1979–85. Chm., AMA, 1991– (Dep. Chm., 1984–86; Vice Chm., 1986–91); Vice Chm., Northern Regl Councils Assoc., 1986–91. Member: RTPI Working Party on Public Participation in Planning, 1980–82; Historic Bldgs and Monuments Commn for England, 1983–87; Local and Regional Govt Sub-Cttee, Labour Party NEC, 1971–83; Labour Party NEC/Shadow Cabinet Wkg Pty on Future of Local Govt, 1984–87; Local and Central Govt Relns Res. Cttee, Joseph Rowntree Meml Trust, 1987–; President's Cttee, Business in the Community, 1988–; Bd of Trustees, NE Civic Trust, 1989–. Participant, Königswinter Conf., 1986. Member: Council of Management, Neighbourhood Energy Action, 1987–89; Council of Common Purpose, 1989–. Contested (Lab) Tynemouth, 1970. Hon. Fellow, Newcastle upon Tyne Polytechnic, 1989. *Recreations*: reading, history, music, very amateur photography, the Northumbrian countryside. *Address*: (office) 7 Collingwood Street, Newcastle upon Tyne NE1 1JE; 39 The Drive, Gosforth, Newcastle upon Tyne NE3 4AJ. *T*: 091–285 1888. *Club*: Manors Social (Newcastle upon Tyne).

BEECHAM, John Stratford Roland; *S* father as 4th Bt (*cr* 1914), 1982, but has declined to prove his claim and does not use the title. *Heir*: *b* Robert Adrian Beecham [*b* 6 Jan. 1942; *m* 1969, Daphne Mattinson; one *s* one *d*].

BEEDHAM, Brian James, CBE 1989; Associate Editor, The Economist, since 1989; *b* 12 Jan. 1928; *s* of James Victor Beedham and Nina Beedham (*née* Zambra); *m* 1960, Ruth Barbara Zollikofer. *Educ*: Leeds Grammar Sch.; The Queen's Coll., Oxford. RA, 1950–52. Asst Editor, Yorkshire Post, 1952–55; The Economist, 1955– : Washington correspondent, 1958–61; Foreign Editor, 1964–89. Commonwealth Fellowship, 1956–57. Fellow, Royal Geographical Society. *Recreations*: hillwalking, music, Kipling and Wodehouse. *Address*: 9 Hillside, SW19 4NH. *T*: 081–946 4454. *Club*: Travellers'.

BEELEY, Sir Harold, KCMG 1961 (CMG 1953); CBE 1946; *b* 15 Feb. 1909; *s* of Frank Arthur Beeley; *m* 1st, 1933, Millicent Mary Chinn (marr. diss., 1953); two *d*; 2nd, 1958, Mrs Patricia Karen Brett-Smith; one *d*. *Educ*: Highgate; Queen's Coll., Oxford. 1st Cl. in Modern History, 1930. Asst Lectr in Modern History, Sheffield Univ., 1930–31; University Coll., London, 1931–35; Junior Research Fellow and Lecturer, Queen's Coll., Oxford, 1935–38; Lecturer in Charge of History Dept, University Coll., Leicester, 1938–39. Mem. of wartime organisation of Royal Institute of International Affairs, and subsequently of Foreign Office Research Dept, 1939–45. Mem. of Secretariat of San

Francisco Conf. and of Preparatory Commission of UN, 1945; Sec. of Anglo-American Cttee of Enquiry on Palestine, 1946. Entered Foreign Service, 1946; Counsellor of Embassy, Copenhagen, 1949–50; Baghdad, 1950–53; Washington, 1953–55; Ambassador to Saudi Arabia, during 1955; Asst Under-Sec., Foreign Office, 1956–58; Dep. UK Representative to UN, New York, 1958–61; UK Representative, Disarmament Conf., Geneva, 1964–67; Ambassador to the United Arab Republic, 1961–64, 1967–69. Lectr in History, Queen Mary Coll., Univ. of London, 1969–75. Pres., Egypt Exploration Soc., 1969–88; Chairman: World of Islam Festival Trust, 1973–; Egyptian-British Chamber of Commerce, 1981–. *Address*: 38 Slaidburn Street, SW10 0JW. *Club*: Reform.

BEENSTOCK, Prof. Michael, PhD; Professor of Economics, Hebrew University, Jerusalem, since 1989; *b* 18 June 1946; *s* of Sidney and Taubie Beenstock; *m* 1968, Ruchi Hager; one *s* four *d*. *Educ*: London Sch. of Econs and Political Science (BSc, MSc; PhD 1976). Econ. Advisor, HM Treasury, 1970–76; Economist, World Bank, Washington, DC, 1976–78; Sen. Res. Fellow, London Business Sch., 1978–81; Esmée Fairbairn Prof. of Finance and Investment, City Univ. Business Sch., 1981–87; Lady Davis Prof. of Econs, Hebrew Univ., Jerusalem, 1987–89. *Publications*: The Foreign Exchange Market, 1978; A Neoclassical Analysis of Macroeconomic Policy, 1980; Health, Migration and Development, 1980; The World Economy in Transition, 1983, 2nd edn 1984; Insurance for Unemployment, 1986; Work, Welfare and Taxation, 1986; Modelling the Labour Market, 1988. *Recreations*: music, astronomy. *Address*: Kefar Etzion 35/4, Jerusalem, Israel. *T*: Jerusalem 723184.

BEER, Prof. (Anthony) Stafford; international consultant cybernetics in management; Chairman, Syncho Ltd (UK), since 1986; Visiting Professor of Cybernetics at Manchester University (Business School), since 1969; Research Professor of Managerial Cybernetics, European Business School, University College of Swansea, since 1990; *b* London, 25 Sept. 1926; *er s* of late William John and of Doris Ethel Beer; *m* 1st, 1947, Cynthia Margaret Hannaway; four *s* one *d*; 2nd, 1968, Sallie Steadman (*née* Child); one *s* two *d*. *Educ*: Whitgift Sch.; University Coll., London. MBA Manchester. Lieut, 9th Gurkha Rifles 1945; Captain, Royal Fusiliers 1947. Man. of Operational Res. and Prodn Controller, S. Fox & Co., 1949–56; Head of Op. Res. and Cybernetics, United Steel, 1956–61; Man. Dir, SIGMA Science in General Management Ltd and Dir, Metra International, 1961–66; Develt Dir, International Publishing Corp.; Dir, International Data Highways Ltd; Chm., Computaprint Ltd, 1966–69; Advisor in Cybernetics to Ernst and Whinney (Canada), 1970–87; Dir, Metapraxis Ltd (UK), 1984–87; Chm., Viable Systems Internat. (USA), 1987–88. Vis. Prof. of Gen. Systems, Open Univ., 1970–71; Scientific Dir, Project Cybersyn, Chile, 1971–73; Adjunct Prof. of Stats and Operations Res., Pennsylvania Univ. (Wharton Sch.), 1972–81, and of Social Systems Scis, 1981–87; Co-Dir, Project Urucib, Uruguay, 1986–87. Ex-Pres., Operational Res. Soc.; Ex-Pres., Soc. for Gen. Systems Res. (USA); Pres., World Orgn of Systems and Cybernetics (formerly of Gen. Systems and Cybernetics), 1981–; Mem. UK Automation Council, 1957–69; Mem. Gen. Adv. Council of BBC, 1961–69. Governor, Internat. Council for Computer Communication, 1973–. Hon. Chm., The Stafford Beer Foundn, 1986–. Hon. Prof., Orgnl Transformation, Sch. of Inf. Sci. and Technol., Liverpool Poly., 1990. FWA 1986. Hon. Fellow, St David's UC, Wales, 1989. Hon. LLD Concordia, Montreal, 1988. Silver Medal, Royal Swedish Acad. for Engrg Scis, 1958; Lanchester Prize (USA) for Ops Res., 1966; McCulloch Award (USA) for Cybernetics, 1970; Wiener Meml Gold Medal for Cybernetics, World Orgn of Gen. Systems and Cybernetics, 1984. *Publications*: Cybernetics and Management, 1959; Decision and Control, 1966; Management Science, 1967; Brain of the Firm, 1972 (new edn, 1981); Designing Freedom, 1974; Platform for Change, 1975; Transit (poems), 1977, extended edn 1983; The Heart of Enterprise, 1979; Diagnosing the System, for organizations, 1985; Pebbles to Computers: the thread, 1986; To Someone or Other (paintings), 1988; chapters in numerous other books. *Recreations*: spinning, yoga, classics, staying put. *Address*: Cwarel Isaf, Pont Creuddyn, Llanbedr Pont Steffan, Dyfed, Wales SA48 8PG; 34 Palmerston Square, Toronto, Ontario M6G 2S7, Canada. *Club*: Athenæum.

See also I. D. S. Beer.

BEER, Prof. Gillian Patricia Kempster, (Mrs J. B. Beer), FBA 1991; Professor of English, University of Cambridge, since 1989; Fellow of Girton College, since 1965; *b* 27 Jan. 1935; *d* of Owen Kempster Thomas and Ruth Winifred Bell; *m* 1962, John Bernard Beer, *qv*; three *s*. *Educ*: St Anne's Coll., Oxford (MA, BLitt); LittD Cambridge. Asst Lectr, Bedford Coll., London, 1959–62; part-time Lectr, Liverpool Univ., 1962–64; Asst Lectr 1966–71, Lectr, subseq. Reader in Literature and Narrative, 1971–89, Univ. of Cambridge. *Publications*: Meredith: a change of masks, 1970; The Romance, 1970; Darwin's Plots, 1983; George Eliot, 1986; Arguing with the Past, 1989. *Recreations*: singing, travel, conversation. *Address*: Girton College, Cambridge CB3 0JG. *T*: Cambridge (0223) 338999 and 356384. *Club*: University Women's.

BEER, Ian David Stafford, MA; JP; Head Master of Harrow, 1981–91; *b* 28 April 1931; *s* of late William Beer and Doris Ethel Beer; *m* 1960, Angela Felce, *d* of Col E. S. G. Howard, MC, RA; two *s* one *d*. *Educ*: Whitgift Sch.; St Catharine's Coll., Cambridge (Exhibitioner). E-SU Walter Page Scholar, 1968. Second Lieut in 1st Bn Royal Fusiliers, 1950. Bursar, Ottershaw Sch., 1955; Guinness Ltd, 1956–57; House Master, Marlborough Coll., Wilts, 1957–61; Head Master: Ellesmere Coll., Salop, 1961–69; Lancing Coll., Sussex, 1969–81. Chairman: HMC Academic Cttee, 1977–79; HMC, 1980; Adv. Cttee, ISJC, 1988–; Physical Educn Working Gp for Nat. Curriculum, 1990–. Mem. Council, Winston Churchill Meml Trust, 1990–; Trustee, RMC Welfare Trust, 1983–. Evelyn Wrench Lectr, E-SU, 1988, 1990. Governor, Whitgift Sch., 1986–. Chm. Editorial Bd, Rugby World and Post, 1977–. JP Shropshire, 1963–69, JP W Sussex, 1970–81, JP Mddx, 1981–. Hon. FCP 1990. *Recreations*: Rugby Football Union Cttee (Mem. Exec. Cttee, 1984–) (formerly) played Rugby for England; CURFC (Capt.), Harlequins, Old Whitgiftians), swimming, reading, zoology, meeting people. *Address*: c/o Harrow School, Harrow-on-the-Hill, Mddx. *Clubs*: East India, Devonshire, Sports and Public Schools; Hawks (Cambridge).

See also A. S. Beer.

BEER, James Edmund; Consultant: Citicorps Insurance Brokers, since 1986; Citicorps Investment Managers, since 1989; *b* 17 March 1931; *s* of Edmund Huxtable Beer and Gwendoline Kate Beer; *m* 1953, Barbara Mollie (*née* Tunley); two *s* one *d*. *Educ*: Torquay Grammar School. IPFA, FRVA, MBCS, MBIM. Torquay Borough Council, 1951–54; Chatham, 1954–56; Wolverhampton, 1956–58; Doncaster, 1958–60; Chief Accountant, Bedford, 1960–62; Asst Borough Treas., Croydon, 1963–65; Dep. Treas., Leeds, 1965; Chief Financial Officer, Leeds, 1968; Dir of Finance, Leeds City Council, 1973–78. Director: Short Loan and Mortgage Co. Ltd, 1978–88; Short Loan (Leasing) Ltd, 1979–88; London Financial Futures Co. Ltd, 1982–88. Mem. Local Govt Financial Exec., CIPFA, 1974–78; Financial Adviser to AMA, 1974–78; Treas., Soc. of Metropolitan Treasurers, 1974–78; Member: LAMSAC Computer Panel, 1972–78; Yorks and Humberside Develt Assoc. London Section, 1970–; Past Examr, CIPFA; Adviser on Rate Support Grant, AMA, 1974–78; Treas., Leeds Grand Theatre & Opera House Ltd, 1974–78; Governor, Leeds Musical Festival, 1979–84. Freeman, City of London, 1972;

Liveryman, Basketmakers Co., 1982. *Publications:* contrib. professional jls. *Recreations:* theatre, swimming, Rugby (past playing mem., Torquay Athletic RUFC). *Address:* 48 High Ash Avenue, Alwoodley, Leeds LS17 8RG. *T:* Leeds (0532) 683907. *Club:* City Livery.

BEÉR, Prof. János Miklós, DSc, PhD, FEng; Professor of Chemical and Fuel Engineering, Massachusetts Institute of Technology (MIT), since 1976; Programme Director for Combustion, MIT Energy Laboratory, since 1976; Science Director, MIT Combustion Research Facilities, since 1980; *b* Budapest, 27 Feb. 1923; *s* of Sándor Beér and Gizella Trismai; *m* 1944, Marta Gabriella Csató. *Educ:* Berzsenyi Dániel Gymnasium, Budapest; Univ. of Budapest (Dipl-Ing 1950). PhD (Sheffield), 1960, DSc(Tech) Sheffield, 1967. Heat Research Inst., Budapest: Research Officer, 1949–52; Head, Combustion Dept, 1952–56; Princ. Lectr (part-time), University of Budapest, 1953–56; Research Engr, Babcock & Wilcox Ltd, Renfrew, 1957; Research Bursar, University of Sheffield, 1957–60; Head, Research Stn, Internat. Flame Research Foundn, Ijmuiden, Holland, 1960–63; Prof., Dept of Fuel Science, Pa State Univ., 1963–65; Newton Drew Prof. of Chemical Engrg and Fuel Technology and Head of Dept, Univ. of Sheffield, 1965–76; Dean, Faculty of Engineering, Univ. of Sheffield, 1973–75. Member: Adv. Council on R&D for Fuel and Power, DTI, later Dept of Energy, 1973–76; Adv. Bd, Safety in Mines Research, Dept of Energy, 1974–76; Clean Air Council, DoE, 1974–76; Bd of Directors, The Combustion Inst., Pittsburgh, USA, 1974–86; Mem., Adv. Cttee, Italian Nat. Res. Council, 1974–; Chm., Clean Coal Utilization Project, US Nat. Acad. of Scis, 1987–88. Gen. Superintendent of Research, Internat. Flame Research Foundn, 1972–89. Australian Commonwealth Vis. Fellow, 1972; Fellow ASME, 1978 (Moody Award, 1964; Percy Nicholls Award, 1988); FEng 1979. Hon. Mem., Hungarian Acad. of Scis, 1986. Foreign Mem., Finnish Acad. of Technology, 1989. Dr *hc* Miskolc, Hungary, 1987. Melchett Medal, Inst. Energy, London, 1985; Coal Science Gold Medal, BCURA, 1986; Alfred Edgerton Gold Medal, Combustion Inst., 1986. Editor, Fuel and Energy Science Monograph Series, 1966–. *Publications:* (with N. Chigier) Combustion Aerodynamics, 1972; (ed with M. W. Thring) Industrial Flames, 1972; (ed with H. B. Palmer) Developments in Combustion Science and Technology, 1974; (ed with N. Afgan) Heat Transfer in Flames, 1975; contribs to Nature, Combustion and Flame, Basic Engrg Jl, Amer. Soc. Mech. Engrg, Jl Inst. F, ZVDI, Internat. Gas Wärme, Proc. Internat. Symposia on Combustion, etc. *Recreations:* swimming, rowing, reading, music. *Address:* Department of Chemical Engineering, Massachusetts Institute of Technology, Cambridge, Mass 02139, USA. *T:* 617–253–6661.

BEER, Prof. John Bernard; Professor of English Literature, since 1987, and Fellow of Peterhouse, since 1964, University of Cambridge. *b* 31 March 1926; *s* of John Bateman Beer and Eva Chilton; *m* 1962, Gillian Patricia Kempster Thomas (*see* G. P. K. Beer); three *s*. *Educ:* Watford Grammar Sch.; St John's Coll., Cambridge (MA, PhD). Research Fellow, St John's Coll., Cambridge, 1955–58; Lectr, Manchester Univ., 1958–64; Univ. Lectr, Cambridge, 1964–78; Reader in English Literature, Cambridge, 1978–87. British Acad. Chatterton Lectr, 1964; Vis. Prof., Univ. of Virginia, 1975; numerous lecture tours abroad. Pres., Charles Lamb Soc., 1989–. *Publications:* Coleridge the Visionary, 1959; The Achievement of E. M. Forster, 1962; (ed) Coleridge's Poems, 1963; Blake's Humanism, 1968; Blake's Visionary Universe, 1969; (ed) Coleridge's Variety: bicentenary studies, 1974; Coleridge's Poetic Intelligence, 1977; Wordsworth and the Human Heart, 1978; Wordsworth in Time, 1979; (ed with G. K. Das) E. M. Forster: a human exploration, 1979; (ed) A Passage to India: essays in interpretation, 1985; articles and reviews. *Recreation:* walking in town and country. *Address:* Peterhouse, Cambridge CB2 1RD. *T:* Cambridge (0223) 338254.

BEER, Patricia, (Mrs J. D. Parsons); freelance writer; *b* 4 Nov. 1924; *yr d* of Andrew William and Harriet Beer, Exmouth, Devon; *m* 1964, John Damien Parsons. *Educ:* Exmouth Grammar Sch.; Exeter Univ. (BA, 1st cl. Hons English); St Hugh's Coll., Oxford (BLitt). Lecturer: in English, Univ. of Padua, 1947–49; British Inst., Rome, 1949–51; Goldsmiths' Coll., Univ. of London, 1962–68. *Publications: poetry:* Loss of the Magyar, 1959; The Survivors, 1963; Just Like The Resurrection, 1967; The Estuary, 1971; (ed) New Poems 1975, 1975; Driving West, 1975; (ed jtly) New Poetry 2, 1976; Selected Poems, 1980; The Lie of the Land, 1983; Collected Poems, 1989; *novel:* Moon's Ottery, 1978; *non-fiction:* Wessex, 1985; *autobiog.:* Mrs Beer's House, 1968; *criticism:* Reader, I Married Him, 1974; contrib. The Listener, London Review of Books. *Recreations:* travelling, cooking. *Address:* Tiphayes, Up Ottery, near Honiton, Devon. *T:* Up Ottery (040486) 255.

BEER, Air Vice-Marshal Peter George, CBE 1987 (OBE 1979); LVO 1974; Commander British Forces, Falkland Islands, since 1991; *b* 16 July 1941; *s* of Herbert George Beer and Kathleen Mary Beer; *m* 1975, Fiona Georgina Hamilton Davidson; two *s*. *Educ:* Hugh Sexey's Sch., Bruton. Equerry to HM the Queen, 1971–74; Officer Commanding: No 55 Sqdn, 1977–79; RAF Brize Norton, 1984–86; Dir, RAF Plans and Programmes, 1989–91. *Recreations:* cricket (Pres. Adastrian Cricket Club), squash, opera, hockey (Pres. RAF Hockey Assoc.). *Club:* Royal Air Force.

BEER, Prof. Stafford; *see* Beer, Prof. A. S.

BEERLING, John William; Controller, BBC Radio 1, since 1985; *b* 12 April 1937; *s* of Raymond Starr and May Elizabeth Julia Beerling; *m* 1959, Carol Ann Reynolds; one *s* one *d*. *Educ:* Sir Roger Manwood's Grammar Sch., Sandwich, Kent. National Service, RAF, wireless fitter, 1955–57. Joined BBC, 1957; Studio Manager, 1958; Producer, 1962; Head of Radio 1 Programmes, 1983. *Publication:* Emperor Rosko's D. J. Handbook, 1976. *Recreations:* photography, fishing. *Address:* (office) Room 228, Egton House, Portland Place, W1A 1AA.

BEESLEY, Ian Blake; Partner, Price Waterhouse, since 1986; *b* 11 July 1942; *s* of Frank and Catherine Beesley; *m* 1st, 1964, Birgitte (*née* Smith) (marr. diss. 1982); 2nd, 1983, Elizabeth (*née* Wigley); one *s* two *d*. *Educ:* Manchester Grammar School; St Edmund Hall, Oxford (PPE). MA; Cert. in Statistics. Central Statistical Office, 1964–76; Chief Statistician, HM Treasury, 1976–78; Dep. Head, Unit supporting Lord Rayner, PM's adviser on efficiency, 1981–83; Under Sec. and Official Head of PM's Efficiency Unit, 1983–86. Alternate Mem., Jarratt Cttee on efficiency in universities, 1984–85; Mem., Croham Cttee to review function and operation of UGC, 1985–87. Mem., Council, Surrey Univ., 1986–. FRSA 1990. *Publications:* Policy analysis and evaluation in British Government (RIPA seminary papers), 1983; contribs to Jl Royal Statistical Soc. *Address:* c/o Price Waterhouse, 1 Moor Lane, EC2Y 9PB.

BEESLEY, Prof. Michael Edwin, CBE 1985; PhD; Professor of Economics, 1965–90, and Director, PhD Programme, 1985–90, London Business School, now Emeritus Professor; *b* 3 July 1924; *s* of late Edwin S. and Kathleen D. Beesley; *m* 1947, Eileen Eleanor Yard; three *s* two *d*. *Educ:* King Edward's Grammar Sch., Five Ways, Birmingham; Univ. of Birmingham (BCom Div. 1, 1945; PhD 1951). Lectr in Commerce, Univ. of Birmingham, 1951–60; Rees Jeffreys Res. Fellow, LSE, 1961–64; Sir Ernest Cassel Reader in Econs, with special ref. to transport, Univ. of London tenable at LSE, 1964–65. Vis. Associate Prof., Univ. of Pennsylvania, 1959–60; Vis. Prof., Harvard Univ., 1974; Vis. Prof. and Commonwealth Fellow: Univ. of BC, 1968; Macquarie Univ., Sydney, 1979–80. Chief Econ. Adviser, Min. of Transport, 1964–68; Special Adviser, Treasury and CS Cttee, Nationalised Industry Financing, 1981; Mem., Monopolies and Mergers Commn, 1988–. Chm., Inst. of Public Sector Management, 1983–87 (Dir, 1978–83). Formerly Member: Cttee on Road Pricing (Smeed Cttee); Cttee on Transport in London; Cttee on Transport Planning (Lady Sharp Cttee); Urban Motorways Inter-Deptl Cttee; Standing Adv. Cttee on Trunk Road Assessment (Sir George Leitch Cttee). Managing Editor, Jl of Transport Economics and Policy, 1975–88. *Publications:* Urban Transport: studies in economic policy, 1973; (ed with D. C. Hague) Britain in the Common Market: a new business opportunity, 1974; (ed) Productivity and Amenity: achieving a social balance, 1974; (ed) Industrial Relations in a Changing World, 1975; (with T. C. Evans) Corporate Social Responsibility: a reassessment, 1978; Liberalisation of the Use of British Telecommunications Network: an independent economic enquiry, 1981; (with P. B. Kettle) Improving Railway Financial Performance, 1985; (with B. Laidlaw) The Future of Telecommunications, 1989. *Recreations:* music, table tennis, golf. *Address:* 59 Canons Drive, Edgware, Mddx HA8 7RG. *T:* 081–952 1320. *Club:* Reform.

BEESON, Prof. Paul Bruce, Hon. KBE 1973; FRCP; Professor of Medicine, University of Washington, 1974–82, now Emeritus; *b* 18 Oct. 1908; *s* of John Bradley Beeson, Livingston, Mont; *m* 1942, Barbara Neal, *d* of Ray C. Neal, Buffalo, NY; two *s* one *d*. *Educ:* Univ. of Washington, McGill Univ. Med. Sch. MD, CM, 1933. Intern, Hosp. of Univ. of Pa, 1933–35; Gen. practice of medicine, Wooster, Ohio, 1935–37; Asst Rockefeller Inst., 1937–39; Chief Med. Resident, Peter Bent Brigham Hosp., 1939–40; Instructor in Med., Havard Med. Sch., and Chief Phys., American Red Cross-Harvard Field Hosp. Unit, Salisbury, 1940–42; Asst and Assoc. Prof. of Med., Emory Med. Sch., 1942–46; Prof. of Med. Emory Med. Sch., 1946–52; Prof. of Med. and Chm. Dept of Med., Yale Univ., 1952–65; Nuffield Prof. of Clinical Med., Oxford Univ., and Fellow of Magdalen Coll., 1965–74, Hon. Fellow, 1975; Hon. Fellow RSM, 1976. Vis. Investigator, Wright-Fleming Inst., St Mary's Hosp., 1958–59. Pres., Assoc. Amer. Physicians, 1967; Master, Amer. Coll. of Physicians, 1970. Phillips Award, Amer. Coll. Physicians, 1975; Flexner Award, Assoc. Amer. Med. Colls, 1977. *Alumnus Summa Laude Dignatus*, Univ. of Washington, 1968; Hon. DSc: Emory Univ., 1968; McGill Univ., 1971; Yale Univ., 1975; Albany Med. Coll., 1975; Ohio Med. Coll., 1979. *Publications:* (ed jtly) The Oxford Companion to Medicine, 1986; edited: Cecil-Loeb Textbook of Medicine, 1959–82; Yale Journal Biology and Medicine, 1959–65; Journal Amer. Geriatric Soc., 1981–84; numerous scientific publications relating to infectious disease, pathogenesis of fever, pyelonephritis and mechanism of eosinophilia. *Address:* 21013 NE 122nd Street, Redmond, Washington 98053, USA.

BEESON, Very Rev. Trevor Randall; Dean of Winchester, since 1987; *b* 2 March 1926; *s* of late Arthur William and Matilda Beeson; *m* 1950, Josephine Grace Cope; two *d*. *Educ:* King's Coll., London (AKC 1950; FKC 1987); St Boniface Coll., Warminster. RAF Met Office, 1944–47. Deacon, 1951; Priest, 1952; Curate, Leadgate, Co. Durham, 1951–54; Priest-in-charge and subseq. Vicar of St Chad, Stockton-on-Tees, 1954–65; Curate of St Martin-in-the-Fields, London, 1965–71; Vicar of Ware, Herts, 1971–76; Canon of Westminster, 1976–87; Treasurer, Westminster, 1978–82; Rector of St Margaret's, Westminster, 1982–87; Chaplain to Speaker of House of Commons, 1982–87. Chaplain of St Bride's, Fleet Street, 1967–84. Chm., Christian Action, 1988–. Gen. Sec., Parish and People, 1962–64; Editor, New Christian, and Man. Dir, Prism Publications Ltd, 1965–70; European Corresp. of The Christian Century (Chicago), 1970–83; Chm., SCM Press Ltd, 1978–87. Hon. MA (Lambeth) 1976. *Publications:* New Area Mission, 1963; (jtly) Worship in a United Church, 1964; An Eye for an Ear, 1972; The Church of England in Crisis, 1973; Discretion and Valour: religious conditions in Russia and Eastern Europe, 1974; Britain Today and Tomorrow, 1978; Westminster Abbey, 1981; A Vision of Hope: the churches and change in Latin America, 1984; (contrib.) God's Truth, 1988; contrib. to DNB, Oxford Dictionary of the Church. *Recreations:* cricket, gardening. *Address:* The Deanery, The Close, Winchester, Hants SO23 9LS.

BEESTON, Prof. Alfred Felix Landon, MA, DPhil; FBA 1965; Laudian Professor of Arabic, Oxford, 1955–78; Emeritus Fellow, St John's College, Oxford, 1978 (Fellow, 1955–78); *b* 1911; *o s* of Herbert Arthur Beeston and Edith Mary Landon. *Educ:* Westminster Sch.; Christ Church, Oxford. James Mew Arabic Scholarship, Oxford, 1934; MA (Oxford), 1936; DPhil (Oxford), 1937. Asst in Dept of Oriental Books, Bodleian Library, Oxford, 1935–40; Sub-Librarian and Keeper of Oriental Books, Bodleian Library, 1946–55. Mem., Governing Body, SOAS, Univ. of London, 1980–84 (Hon. Fellow 1980). Lidzbarski Medal for Semitic Epigraphy, Deutsche Morgenländische Ges., 1983. *Publications:* Baidāwī's Commentary on Sūrah 12, 1963; Written Arabic, 1968; The Arabic Language Today, 1970; Selections from the Poetry of Baššār, 1977; Samples of Arabic Prose, 1977; The 'Epistle on Singing Girls' of Jāhiz, 1980; Sabaic Grammar, 1984; many articles. *Address:* St John's College, Oxford OX1 3JP.

BEETHAM, Marshal of the Royal Air Force Sir Michael (James), GCB 1978 (KCB 1976); CBE 1967; DFC 1944; AFC 1960; DL; FRAeS; Chief of the Air Staff, 1977–82; Air ADC to the Queen, 1977–82; *b* 17 May 1923; *s* of Major G. C. Beetham, MC; *m* 1956, Patricia Elizabeth Lane; one *s* one *d*. *Educ:* St Marylebone Grammar School. Joined RAF, 1941; pilot trng, 1941–42; commnd 1942; Bomber Comd: 50, 57 and 35 Sqdns, 1943–46; HQ Staff, 1947–49; 82 (Recce) Sqdn, E Africa, 1949–51; psa 1952; Air Min. (Directorate Operational Requirements), 1953–56; CO 214 (Valiant) Sqdn Marham, 1958–60; Gp Captain Ops, HQ Bomber Comd, 1962–64; CO RAF Khormaksar, Aden, 1964–66; idc 1967; Dir Ops (RAF), MoD, 1968–70; Comdt, RAF Staff Coll., 1970–72; ACOS (Plans and Policy), SHAPE, 1972–75; Dep. C-in-C, Strike Command, 1975–76; C-in-C RAF Germany, and Comdr, 2nd Tactical Allied Air Force, 1976–77. Chm., GEC Avionics Ltd, 1986–90 (Dir, 1984–91); Dir, Brixton Estate PLC, 1983–. Chm., Trustees, RAF Museum, 1983–. FRSA 1979; FRAeS 1982. DL Norfolk, 1989. *Recreations:* golf, tennis. *Clubs:* Royal Air Force; Royal West Norfolk Golf.

BEETHAM, Roger Campbell, LVO 1976; HM Diplomatic Service; Ambassador to Senegal, since 1990; concurrently Ambassador (non-resident) to Cape Verde, Guinea, Guinea-Bissau and Mali, since 1990; *b* 22 Nov. 1937; *s* of Henry Campbell and Mary Beetham; *m* 1st 1965, Judith Rees (marr. diss. 1986); 2nd, 1986, Christine Marguerite Malerme. *Educ:* Peter Symonds Sch., Winchester; Brasenose Coll., Oxford (MA). Entered HM Diplomatic Service, 1960; FO, 1960–62; UK Delegation to Disarmament Conference, Geneva, 1962–65; Washington, 1965–68; News Dept, FCO, 1969–72; Head of Chancery, Helsinki, 1972–76; FCO, 1976; seconded to European Commission, Brussels, as Spokesman of the President, Rt Hon. Roy Jenkins, 1977–80; Counsellor (Econ. and Commercial), New Delhi, 1981–85; Head of Maritime, Aviation and Envmt Dept, FCO, 1985–90. Order of the White Rose of Finland, 1976. *Recreations:* oenology, cooking, travel. *Address:* c/o Foreign and Commonwealth Office, SW1A 2AH. *Club:* Travellers'.

BEETON, David Christopher; Chief Executive, Historic Royal Palaces, since 1989; *b* 25 Aug. 1939; *s* of Ernest Beeton and Ethel Beeton; *m* 1968, Brenda Lomax; two *s*. *Educ:* Ipswich Sch.; King's Coll., London Univ. (LLB). Solicitor. Chief Exec., Bath CC,

1973–85; Sec., National Trust, 1985–89. *Recreations:* swimming, historic buildings, cooking. *Address:* Hampton Court Palace, Surrey KT8 9AU. *T:* 081–977 7222.

BEEVOR, Antony Romer; Executive Director, Hambros Bank Ltd, since 1985; *b* 18 May 1940; *s* of Miles Beevor, *qv* and Sybil (*née* Gilliat); *m* 1970, Cecilia Hopton; one *s* one *d. Educ:* Winchester; New Coll., Oxford (BA). Admitted Solicitor, 1965. Ashurst Morris Crisp & Co., 1962–72 (on secondment, Panel on Takeovers and Mergers, 1969–71); joined Hambros Bank, 1972; Dir, 1974; on secondment, as Dir-Gen., Panel on Takeovers and Mergers, 1987–89; Dir, Hambros plc, 1990–. *Recreations:* ski-ing, sailing. *Address:* 20 Radipole Road, SW6 5DL. *T:* 071-731 8015. *Club:* Hurlingham.

BEEVOR, Miles; retired Solicitor and Director of Companies; *b* 8 March 1900; 2nd *s* of Rowland Beevor; *m* 1st, 1924, Margaret Florence Platt (*d* 1934); one *s* (and one *d* decd); 2nd, 1935, Sybil Gilliat (*d* 1991); two *s* one *d. Educ:* Winchester (Scholar); New Coll., Oxford (Scholar), BA 1921. Admitted a Solicitor, 1925. Served European War, 1914–18, in Army (RE Officer Cadet Battalion), 1918; War of 1939–45, RAFVR (Flt-Lieut Admin. and Special Duties Br.), 1941–43. Chief Legal Adviser, LNER, 1943–47; Actg Chief General Manager, LNER, 1947; Chief Sec. and Legal Adviser, British Transport Commission, 1947–51; Managing Dir, Brush Electrical Engineering Co. Ltd (which became The Brush Group Ltd), 1952–56; Deputy Chm. and Joint Managing Dir, 1956–57. *Address:* 44 Mill Lane, Welwyn, Herts. *T:* Welwyn (043871) 5103.
See also A. R. Beevor.

BEEVOR, Sir Thomas Agnew, 7th Bt, *cr* 1784; *b* 6 Jan. 1929; *s* of Comdr Sir Thomas Beevor, 6th Bt, and Edith Margaret Agnew (who *m* 2nd, 1944, Rear-Adm. R. A. Currie, *qv*, and *d* 1985); *S* father 1943; *m* 1st, 1957, Barbara Clare (marr. diss., 1965), *y d* of Capt. R. L. B. Cunliffe, RN (retd); one *s* two *d*; 2nd, 1966, Carola, *d* of His Honour J. B. Herbert, MC; 3rd, 1976, Mrs Sally Bouwens, White Hall, Saham Toney, Norfolk. *Heir: s* Thomas Hugh Cunliffe Beevor [*b* 1 Oct. 1962; *m* 1988, Charlotte Louise, *e d* of Keith E. Harvey]. *Address:* Hargham Hall, Norwich.

BEEZLEY, Frederick Ernest; His Honour Judge Beezley; a Circuit Judge, since 1976; *b* 30 Jan. 1921; *s* of Frederick William Beezley and Lilian Isabel (*née* Markham); *m* 1969, Sylvia Ruth (*née* Locke). *Educ:* Acton County Sch. Served War, Royal Signals, Combined Operations, 1940–46. Called to Bar, Gray's Inn, 1947; Res. Judge, Cambridge Crown Court, 1987–. *Recreations:* fly-fishing, horse racing, musician with Ely Mil. Band. *Address:* c/o The Crown Court, 10 Downing Street, Cambridge CB2 3DS. *T:* Cambridge (0223) 64436.

BEFFA, Jean-Louis Guy Henri; Chevalier de la Légion d'Honneur; Officier de l'Ordre National du Mérite; Chairman and Chief Executive Officer, Compagnie de Saint-Gobain, since 1987; *b* 11 Aug. 1941; *m* 1967, Marie-Madeleine Brunel; two *s* one *d. Educ:* Ecole Polytechnique (Ing. au Corps des Mines); Dip. de l'Inst. d'Etudes Politiques de Paris. Compagnie de Saint-Gobain: Vice-Pres., Corporate Planning, 1974–77; Pres., Pipe Div., 1978–82; Chief Operating Officer, 1982–86. Order of Merit (Germany); Order of Rio Branco (Brazil). *Recreations:* golf, classical music. *Address:* Compagnie de Saint-Gobain, Les Miroirs, 18 avenue d'Alsace Cédex 27, 92096 Paris La Défense, France. *T:* 47.62.33.10.

BEGG, Dr Sir Neil (Colquhoun), KBE 1986 (OBE 1973); Director of Medical Services, Royal New Zealand Plunket Society, 1956–76, retired; *b* 13 April 1915; *s* of Charles Mackie Begg, CB, CMG, Croix de Guerre, and Lillian Helen Lawrence Begg; *m* 1942, Margaret Milne MacLean; two *s* two *d. Educ:* John McGlashan Coll., Dunedin, NZ; Otago Univ. Med. Sch. (MB ChB 1940); postgrad. paediatrics, London and Edinburgh, 1947–48. DCH, MRCP London, MRCPE. Served 2 NZ Expedn Force, 1942–46, Med. Corps, ME and Italy. Paediatrician, Dunedin Public Hosp., 1949–56. Chm., NZ Historic Places Trust, 1978–86. Hon. FRCPE 1958, Hon. FRCP 1977. *Publications:* Dusky Bay (with A. C. Begg), 1966; (with A. C. Begg) James Cook and New Zealand, 1969; Child and his Family, 1970, 8th edn 1975; (with A. C. Begg) Port Preservation, 1973; (with A. C. Begg) The World of John Boultbee, 1979; The Intervening Years, 1991; contribs to NZ Med. Jl. *Recreation:* trout fishing. *Address:* 86 Newington Avenue, Dunedin 9001, New Zealand. *T:* 467–2089.

BEGG, Robert William, CBE 1977; MA; CA; FRSA; Consultant, Moores Rowland, Chartered Accountants, since 1987 (Partner, 1951–86, Consultant, 1986–87, Mann Judd Gordon); *b* 19 Feb. 1922; *s* of late David Begg, CA, FFA, and of Elizabeth Young Thomson; *m* 1948, Sheena Margaret Boyd; two *s. Educ:* Greenock Acad.; Glasgow Univ. (MA 1942). Served Royal Navy, 1942–46, Lieut RNVR (despatches). Mem., Institute of Chartered Accountants of Scotland, 1948. Member: Glasgow Univ. General Council Business Cttee, 1973–76; Court, Glasgow Univ., 1986–90. Hon. Treasurer: Royal Philosophical Soc. of Glasgow, 1952–62; Royal Glasgow Inst. of Fine Arts, 1975–86 (Pres., 1987–90); Mem. Bd of Governors, Glasgow School of Art, 1955–77, Chm., 1970–76; Trustee: RIAS Hill House Trust, 1977–82; Pollok Trust, 1987–; Member: Bd of Trustees, National Galleries of Scotland, 1974– (Chm., 1980–87); Council, National Trust for Scotland, 1984–90 (Mem. Exec. Cttee, 1985–90); Museums and Galls Commn, 1988–. DUniv Glasgow, 1990. *Recreation:* painting. *Address:* Allan House, 25 Bothwell Street, Glasgow G2 6NL. *T:* 041–221 6991; (home) 3 Colquhoun Drive, Bearsden, Glasgow G61 4NQ. *T:* 041–942 2436. *Clubs:* Art, XIII (Glasgow); New (Edinburgh).

BEGG, Admiral of the Fleet Sir Varyl (Cargill), GCB 1965 (KCB 1962; CB 1959); DSO 1952; DSC 1941; Governor and Commander-in-Chief of Gibraltar, 1969–73; *b* 1 Oct. 1908; *s* of Francis Cargill Begg and Muriel Clare Robinson; *m* 1943, Rosemary Cowan, CStJ; two *s. Educ:* St Andrews Sch., Eastbourne; Malvern Coll. Entered RN, special entry, 1926; Qualified Gunnery Officer, 1933; HMS Glasgow, 1939–40; HMS Warspite, 1940–43; Comdr Dec. 1942; Capt. 1947; commanded HM Gunnery Sch., Chatham, 1948–50; 8th Destroyer Flotilla, 1950–52; HMS Excellent, 1952–54; HMS Triumph, 1955–56; idc 1954; Rear-Adm. 1957; Chief of Staff to C-in-C Portsmouth 1957–58; Flag Officer Commanding Fifth Cruiser Squadron and Flag Officer Second-in-Command, Far East Station, 1958–60; Vice-Adm. 1960; a Lord Commissioner of the Admiralty and Vice-Chief of Naval Staff, 1961–63; Admiral, 1963; C-in-C, British Forces in the Far East, and UK Military Adviser to SEATO, 1963–65; C-in-C, Portsmouth, and Allied C-in-C, Channel, 1965–66; Chief of Naval Staff and First Sea Lord, 1966–68. KStJ 1969. PMN 1966. *Recreations:* fishing, gardening. *Address:* Copyhold Cottage, Chilbolton, Stockbridge, Hants SO20 6BA. *Club:* Army and Navy.

BEGGS, Roy; MP (UU) East Antrim, since 1983 (resigned seat Dec. 1985 in protest against Anglo-Irish Agreement; re-elected Jan. 1986); *b* 20 Feb. 1936; *s* of John Beggs; *m* 1959, Wilma Lorimer; two *s* two *d. Educ:* Ballyclare High Sch.; Stranmillis Trng Coll. (Certificate/Diploma in Educn). Teacher, 1957–78, Vice-Principal, 1978–83, Larne High Sch. Mem., 1973–, Vice-Chm., 1981–, NE Educn and Library Bd; Pres., Assoc. of Educn and Liby Bds, NI, 1984–85 (Vice-Pres., 1983–84). Mem., Larne Borough Council, 1973–; Mayor of Larne, 1978–83; Mem. for N Antrim, NI Assembly, 1982–86. Mem., Public Accounts Commn, 1984–. *Address:* House of Commons, SW1; 9 Carnduff Road, Ballyvernstown, Larne, Co. Antrim. *T:* Larne 73258.

BEGIN, Menachem, MJr; Prime Minister, State of Israel, 1977–83; *b* Brest-Litovsk, Poland, 16 Aug. 1913; *s* of Ze'ev-Dov and Hassia Begin; *m* 1939, Aliza Arnold (*d* 1982); one *s* two *d. Educ:* Mizrachi Hebrew Sch.; Polish Gymnasium (High Sch.); Univ. of Warsaw (MJr). Belonged to Hashomer Hatza'ir scout movement as a boy, joining Betar, the Zionist Youth Movement, when 16; head of Organization Dept of Betar for Poland, 1932; also delegated to Czechoslovakia to head movement there; returned to Poland, 1937, and after spell of imprisonment for leading demonstration against British policy in Eretz Israel became head of the movement in Poland, 1939. On outbreak of World War II, arrested by Russian NKVD and later confined in concentration camps in Siberia, 1941–42; subseq. released under Stalin-Sikorski agreement; joined Polish Army, 1942, his brigade being posted to Eretz Israel; after demobilization assumed comd of IZL, the National Military Organization, directing from underground headquarters operations against the British; met members of UN Inquiry Cttee and foreign press, secretly, to explain his movement's outlook. After estabt of State of Israel, 1948, he and his colleagues founded the Herut Movement and he headed that party's list of candidates for the Knesset; a member of the Knesset from the first elections; on eve of Six Day War, I June 1967, joined Govt of Nat. Unity, serving as Minister without Portfolio, until Aug. 1970; presented his Coalition to the Knesset, June 1977, winning necessary vote of confidence to become Prime Minister; re-elected Prime Minister following nat. elections, June 1981. Nobel Peace Prize (jtly, with Mohamed Anwar El-Sadat), 1978. *Publications:* White Nights (describing his wartime experience in Europe); The Revolt, trans. several languages; numerous articles. *Address:* c/o Herut Movement Headquarters, Beit Jabotinsky, 38 King George Street, Tel Aviv, Israel.

BEHNE, Edmond Rowlands, CMG 1974; Managing Director, Pioneer Sugar Mills Ltd, Queensland, 1952–76; *b* 20 Nov. 1906; *s* of late Edmund Behne; *m* 1932, Grace Elizabeth Ricketts; two *s* one *d. Educ:* Bendigo Sch. of Mines; Brisbane Boys' Coll.; Univ. of Queensland. BSc and MSc (App.); ARACI. Bureau of Sugar Experiment Stations, 1930–48 (Director, 1947); Pioneer Sugar Mills Ltd, 1948–80. *Recreation:* bowls. *Address:* Craigston, 217 Wickham Terrace, Brisbane, Qld 4000, Australia. *T:* 831 5657. *Club:* Johnsonian (Brisbane).

BEHR, Norman Isaac, FRICS; Vice President, London Rent Assessment Panel, since 1988 (Valuer Member, 1983–87); *b* 28 Sept. 1922; *s* of Moses and Sarah Behr; *m* 1950, Anne Laurette Hilton. *Educ:* Haberdashers' Aske's Sch.; College of Estate Management. Chartered Surveyor. Articled, De Groot & Co., 1939–42; served War, RAOC, REME, 1942–46; joined Valuation Office, 1948; District Valuer and Valuation Officer, Westminster, 1965–67, City of London, 1967–70; Superintending Valuer, 1970; Asst Chief Valuer, 1977; Dep. Chief Valuer (Rating), 1981–83. First Prize, Chartered Auctioneers and Estate Agents Inst., 1941; Wainwright Prize, Royal Instn of Chartered Surveyors, 1950. *Recreations:* opera, cooking, computers. *Address:* 43 Netherhall Gardens, NW3 5RL. *T:* 071–435 9391.

BEIGHTON, Leonard John Hobhouse; Director General, Board of Inland Revenue, since 1988; *b* 20 May 1934; *s* of John Durant Kennedy Beighton and Leonora Hobhouse; *m* 1962, Judith Valerie Bridge (decd); one *s* one *d. Educ:* Tonbridge Sch.; Corpus Christi College, Oxford (MA PPE). Inland Revenue, 1957; seconded HM Treasury, 1968–69 (Private Sec. to Chief Sec.), and 1977–79. *Address:* Board of Inland Revenue, Somerset House, WC2R 1LB. *T:* 071–438 6622.

BEILL, Air Vice-Marshal Alfred, CB 1986; Appeals Secretary, King Edward VII's Hospital for Officers, since 1987; *b* 14 Feb. 1931; *s* of late Group Captain Robert Beill, CBE, DFC and of Sophie Beill; *m* 1953, Vyvian Mary Crowhurst Archer; four *d. Educ:* Rossall Sch.; RAF Coll., Cranwell. FCIT 1980; FBIM 1976; FInstPS 1985. Commnd RAF, 1952; served, 1952–64: RAF Marham, Stafford and Fauld; HQ Air Forces ME, Aden; RAF Supply Control Centre, Hendon; student, RAF Staff Coll., Andover, 1964; HQ FEAF, Singapore, 1965–67; student, JSSC, Latimer, 1968; OC Supply and Movements Sqdn, RAF Scampton, 1968–69; HQ Maintenance Comd, 1969–70; DS JSSC (later NDC), 1970–73; Comd Supply Officer, HQ NEAF, Cyprus, 1973–75; Dir of Engrg and Supply Policy (RAF), 1976–78; student, RCDS, 1978; Dir of Movements (RAF), 1979–82; Dir of Supply Policy and Logistics Plans (RAF), 1982–84; Dir Gen. of Supply (RAF), 1984–87, retired. ADC to the Queen, 1974–75. Life Vice Pres., RAF Swimming Assoc., 1987– (Pres., 1982–87). *Address:* c/o Lloyds Bank, Cox's & King's Branch, 7 Pall Mall, SW1Y 5NA. *Club:* Royal Air Force.

BEISHON, (Ronald) John, DPhil; CPsychol, CEng; Chief Executive, Consumers' Association, and Director, Association for Consumer Research; *b* 10 Nov. 1930; *s* of Arthur and Irene Beishon; *m* 1955, Gwenda Jean Solway; two *s* two *d. Educ:* Battersea Polytechnic; Univ. of London (BSc); Univ. of Birmingham; Univ. of Oxford (DPhil). MIM, MWeldI, AFBPsS. National Service, RASC, 1951–53; Technical Officer, ICI Ltd, 1954–58; Section Leader, BICC Ltd, 1958–61; Sen. Res. Asst, Oxford Univ., 1961–64; Lectr, Bristol Univ., 1964–68; Reader, Sussex Univ., 1968–71; Professor of Systems, Open Univ., 1971–80; Dir, Poly. of South Bank, 1980–85; seconded as actg Dir, 1985, Permanent Dir, 1986–87, Poly. of North London; Dir, Consumers' Assoc., 1987. Member, Executive Committee: Internat. Organisation Consumer Unions, 1987–; NHBC, 1988–. FRSA. *Publications:* (ed with G. Peters) Systems Behaviour, 1973, 2nd edn 1976; articles in various jls. *Recreation:* squash. *Address:* 421 Ditchling Road, Brighton, Sussex BN1 6XB. *Club:* Wig and Pen.

BEIT, Sir Alfred Lane, 2nd Bt, *cr* 1924; Trustee of the Beit Trust; Trustee of Beit Fellowships for scientific research; *b* London, 19 Jan. 1903; *o* surv. *s* of 1st Bt and Lilian (*d* 1946), *d* of late T. L. Carter, New Orleans, USA; *S* father, 1930; *m* 1939. Clementine, 2nd *d* of late Major the Hon. Clement Mitford, DSO and Lady Helen Nutting. *Educ:* Eton; Christ Church, Oxford. Contested West Islington in LCC election 1928; South-East St Pancras (C) in general election, 1929; MP (U) St Pancras South-East, 1931–45. Pres., Wexford Fest. Opera; Mem., Board of Governors and Guardians, Nat. Gallery of Ireland. Hon. LLD Nat. Univ. of Ireland, 1979. *Heir:* none. *Address:* Russborough, Blessington, Co. Wicklow, Eire. *Clubs:* Brooks's, Carlton; Kildare Street and University (Dublin); Civil Service (Cape Town).

BEITH, Alan James; MP, Berwick-upon-Tweed since Nov. 1973 (L 1973–88, Lib Dem since 1988); spokesman on the Treasury, since 1987; *b* 20 April 1943; *o s* of James and Joan Beith, Poynton, Ches; *m* 1965, Barbara Jean Ward; one *s* one *d. Educ:* King's Sch., Macclesfield; Balliol and Nuffield Colls, Oxford. BLitt, MA Oxon. Lectr, Dept of Politics, Univ. of Newcastle upon Tyne, 1966–73. Vice-Chm., Northumberland Assoc. of Parish Councils, 1970–71 and 1972–73; Jt Chm., Assoc. of Councillors, 1974–79; Member: Gen. Adv. Council of BBC, 1974–84; Hexham RDC, 1969–74; Corbridge Parish Council, 1970–74; Tynedale District Council, 1973–74; BBC NE Regional Adv. Council, 1971–74; NE Transport Users' Consultative Cttee, 1970–74. Mem., House of Commons Commn, 1979–; UK Rep. to Council of Europe and WEU, 1976–84. Liberal Chief Whip, 1976–85; Dep. Leader, Liberal Party, 1985–88; spokesman on Educn, 1977–83; spokesman on parly and constitutional affairs, 1983–87; Lib. spokesman on foreign affairs, 1985–87 (Alliance spokesman on foreign affairs, 1987); Lib Dem Treasury spokesman,

1988–. Methodist Local Preacher. *Publications:* The Case for the Liberal Party and the Alliance, 1983; (jtly) Faith and Politics, 1987; chapter in The British General Election of 1964, ed Butler and King, 1965. *Recreations:* walking, music, looking at old buildings. *Address:* 28 Castle Terrace, Berwick-upon-Tweed TD15 1NZ. *T:* Berwick (0289) 330039. *Clubs:* National Liberal; Union Society (Oxford); Shilbottle Working Men's (Alnwick).

BEITH, Sir John, KCMG 1969 (CMG 1959); HM Diplomatic Service, retired; *b* 4 April 1914; *s* of late William Beith and Margaret Stanley, Toowoomba, Qld; *m* 1949, Diana Gregory-Hood (*d* 1987), *d* of Sir John Little Gilmour, 2nd Bt; one *s* one *d* (and one *d* decd), (one step *s* one step *d*). *Educ:* Eton; King's Coll., Cambridge. Entered Diplomatic Service, 1937, and served in FO until 1940; 3rd Sec., Athens, 1940–41; 2nd Sec., Buenos Aires, 1941–45; served Foreign Office, 1945–49; Head of UK Permanent Delegation to the UN at Geneva, 1950–53; Head of Chancery at Prague, 1953–54; Counsellor, 1954; Counsellor and Head of Chancery, British Embassy, Paris, 1954–59; Head of Levant Dept, FO, 1959–61; Head of North and East African Dept, Foreign Office, 1961–63; Ambassador to Israel, 1963–65; an Asst Sec.-Gen., NATO, 1966–67; Asst Under-Sec. of State, FO, 1967–69; Ambassador to Belgium, 1969–74. *Recreations:* music, racing, books. *Address:* Dean Farm House, Winchester SO21 2LP. *T:* Sparsholt (096272) 326. *Clubs:* White's, Anglo-Belgian.

BEITH, John William, CBE 1972; Director Special Duties, Massey Ferguson Holdings Ltd, 1971–74, retired; *b* 13 Jan. 1909; *s* of John William Beith and Ana Theresia (*née* Denk); *m* 1931, Dorothy (*née* Causbrook) (*d* 1986); two *s*. *Educ:* Spain, Chile, Germany; Llandovery Coll., S Wales. Joined Massey Harris (now Massey Ferguson), 1927, London; occupied senior exec. positions in Argentina, Canada, France and UK; Vice-Pres., Canadian parent co., 1963; Chm., Massey Ferguson (UK) Ltd, 1970. Pres., Agricl Engrs Assoc. Ltd, 1970. *Recreations:* ancient and contemporary history; follower of Rugby; swimming. *Address:* Torre Blanca, 22 Calle de S Hortet, 07669 Cala Serena, Mallorca. *T:* Baleares 657830. *Club:* Oriental.

BÉJART, Maurice (Jean); choreographer; Director, Béjart Ballet Lausanne, since 1987; *b* 1 Jan. 1927; *s* of Gaston and Germaine Berger. *Educ:* Lycée de Marseilles. Début as ballet dancer with Marseilles Opéra, 1945; International Ballet, 1949–50; Royal Opera, Stockholm, 1951–52; co-founded Les Ballets de l'Etoile, later Ballet-Théâtre de Paris, 1954 (Dir, 1954–59); Director: Twentieth Century Ballet Co., 1959–87; Mudra Sch., 1972. Grand Prix National de la Musique, 1970; Prix Erasme de la danse, 1974. Chevalier des Arts et des Lettres; Commandeur de l'Ordre de Léopold (Belgium), 1982; Ordre du Soleil Levant (Japan), 1986; Grand Officier de l'Ordre de la Couronne (Belgium), 1988. Principal works include: La Belle au Boa, Symphonie pour un homme seul, 1955; Orphée, 1958; Le sacre du printemps, 1959; Boléro, 1961; The Tales of Hoffman, 1962; The Merry Widow, The Damnation of Faust, l'Oiseau de Feu, 1964; Romeo and Juliet, 1966; Messe pour le temps présent, 1967; Firebird, 1970; Song of a Wayfarer, Nijinsky: clown de Dieu, 1971; Le Marteau sans Maître, La Traviata, 1973; Ce que l'amour me dit, 1974; Notre Faust, 1975; Heliogabale, Pli selon Pli, 1976; Petrouchka, 1977; Gaîté Parisienne, Ce que la Mort me dit, 1978; Mephisto Waltzer, 1979; Casta Diva, Eros Thanatos, 1980; The Magic Flute, Les Chaises, Light, Les Uns et les Autres (film), Adagietto, 1981; Wien Wien nur du Allein, Thalassa Mare Nostrum, 1982; Salome, Messe pour le Temps Futur, Vie et mort d'une marionnette humaine, 1983; Dionysos, 1984; Le Concours, la Chauve Souris, 1985; Arepo, Malraux ou la Métamorphose des Dieux, 1986; Trois Etudes pour Alexandre, Souvenir de Léningrad, Après-midi d'un Faune, Fiche Signalétique, 1987; Patrice Chéreau . . ., Dibouk, Et Valse, Piaf, Paris-Tokyo, A force de partir . . ., 1988; 1789 et nous, Elégie pour elle, L . . ., aile, 1989; Ring um den Ring, Nijinsky Clown de dieu (theatrical version), Pyramides, Mozart Tangos, 1990. *Publications:* Mathilde, ou le temps perdu (novel), 1963; La Reine Verte (play), 1963; L'autre chant de la danse, 1974; Un instant dans la vie d'autrui, 1979; La Mort Subite, 1991. *Address:* Béjart Ballet Lausanne, Case Postale 25, 1000 Lausanne 22, Switzerland.

BEKER, Prof. Henry Joseph, PhD; Executive Chairman, Zergo Ltd, since 1989 (Managing Director, 1988–89); Visiting Professor of Information Technology, Royal Holloway and Bedford New College (formerly Royal Holloway College), University of London, since 1984; *b* 22 Dec. 1951; *s* of Jozef and Mary Beker; *m* 1976, Mary Louise (*née* Keilthy); two *d*. *Educ:* Kilburn Grammar Sch.; Univ. of London (BSc Maths 1973, PhD 1976); Open Univ. (BA 1982). CEng, MIEE, 1984; MIS, 1977; AFIMA, 1978. Sen. Res. Asst, Dept of Statistics, University Coll. of Swansea, 1976–77; Principal Mathematician, Racal-Comsec Ltd, 1977–80, Chief Mathematician, 1980–83; Dir of Research, Racal Research Ltd, 1983–85; Dir of Systems, Racal-Chubb Security Systems Ltd, 1985–86; Man. Dir, Racal-Guardata Ltd, 1986–88. Vis. Prof. of IT, Westfield Coll., Univ. of London, 1983–84. Vice Pres., Inst of Mathematics and its Applications, 1988–89. FRSA. *Publications:* Cipher Systems, 1982; Secure Speech Communications, 1985. *Recreations:* music, reading, travel. *Address:* Communications House, Winchester Road, Basingstoke, Hants RG22 4AA. *T:* Basingstoke (0256) 818800, *Fax:* Basingstoke (0256) 812901.

BEKOE, Dr Daniel Adzei; Regional Director, International Development Research Centre, Nairobi, since 1986; Member, Pontifical Academy of Sciences, since 1983; *b* 7 Dec. 1928; *s* of Aristocles Silvanus Adzete Bekoe and Jessie Nadu (*née* Awuletey); *m* 1958, Theresa Victoria Anyisaa Annan (marr. diss. 1983); three *s* (and one *s* decd); *m* 1988, Bertha Augustina Ashia Randolph. *Educ:* Achimota Sch.; University Coll. of Gold Coast (BSc London); Univ. of Oxford (DPhil). Jun. Res. Asst, Univ. of Calif, LA, 1957–58; Univ. of Ghana (formerly University Coll. of Ghana): Lectr, 1958–63; Sen. Lectr, 1963–65; Associate Prof., 1965–74; Prof. of Chemistry, 1974–83; Vice-Chancellor, 1976–83; Dir, UNESCO Regl Office for Sci. and Technol. for Africa, 1983–85. Sabbatical year, Univ. of Calif, LA, 1962–63; Vis. Associate Prof., Univ. of Ibadan, 1966–67. Member: UN Univ. Council, 1980–83; UN Adv. Cttee on Science and Technology for Develt, 1980–82. Pres., ICSU, 1980–83. *Publications:* articles on molecular structures in crystallographic and chemical jls; gen. articles in Proc. Ghana Acad. of Arts and Sciences. *Recreations:* music, walking. *Address:* International Development Research Centre, PO Box 62084, Nairobi, Kenya. *T:* Nairobi 330850.

BELCH, Alexander Ross, CBE 1972; FRSE 1977; FRINA; CBIM; Chairman: Capelrig Ltd, since 1980; Jebsens Travel Ltd, since 1981; Altnacraig Shipping plc, since 1988; Kelvin Travel Ltd, since 1984; Murray Hotels (Crieff) Ltd, since 1974; Orico Systems Ltd, since 1987; Amprotech Ltd, since 1990; Ferguson Marine plc, since 1991; Ferguson Shipbuilders Ltd, since 1991; *b* 13 Dec. 1920; *s* of Alexander Belch, CBE, and Agnes Wright Ross; *m* 1947, Janette Finnie Murdoch (*d* 1988); four *d*. *Educ:* Morrison's Acad., Crieff, Perthshire; Glasgow Univ. (BSc Naval Arch. 1st Cl. Hons). Lithgows Ltd: Dir and Gen. Manager, 1954–59; Asst Man. Dir, 1959–64; Man. Dir, 1964–69; Scott Lithgow Ltd: Man. Dir, 1969–80; Chm., 1978–80. Dir, Jebsen Carriers Ltd. Pres., Shipbuilders and Repairers Nat. Assoc., 1974–76. Chm., Council of Trustees, Scottish Maritime Museum, 1983–. CBIM 1981. Hon. LLD Strathclyde, 1978. *Address:* Altnacraig House, Lyle Road, Greenock, Renfrewshire PA16 7XT. *T:* Greenock (0475) 21124.

BELCHER, John Rashleigh, MS 1945; FRCS 1942; Consultant Thoracic Surgeon, NE Metropolitan Regional Hospital Board, 1950–82; Surgeon, London Chest Hospital, 1951–82; Thoracic Surgeon, Middlesex Hospital, 1955–82; *b* 11 Jan. 1917; *s* of late Dr Ormonde Rashleigh Belcher, Liverpool; *m* 1940, Jacqueline Mary, *d* of late C. P. Phillips; two *s* one *d*. *Educ:* Epsom Coll.; St Thomas' Hosp. MB 1939; FRCS 1942; MS 1945; Resident appointments at St Thomas' Hospital, 1939–40. RAF, 1940–46: Medical Service; general duties and surgical specialist; Squadron Leader. Resident and Asst posts at St Thomas', Brompton, London Chest, and Middlesex Hosps; followed by consultant appointments; co-editor, Brit. Jl of Diseases of the Chest. Pres., Assoc. of Thoracic Surgeons, 1980; Member: Thoracic Soc.; Cardiac Soc.; Amer. Coll. of Chest Physicians. Toured: for British Council, Far East 1969, Cyprus and Greece 1973; for FCO, Indonesia 1971, Bolivia 1975; Yugoslavia 1977. Hunterian Prof., RCS, 1979. *Publications:* Thoracic Surgical Management, 1953; chapters in standard text-books; papers in British and foreign medical journals. *Recreations:* photography, picture framing, grandchildren, opera. *Address:* 23 Hornton Court, Hornton Street, W8 7RT. *T:* 071–937 7006.

BELCHER, Ronald Harry, CMG 1958; Under-Secretary, Ministry of Overseas Development, 1965–75; *b* 5 Jan 1916; *s* of Harry Albert Belcher; *m* 1948, Hildegarde (*née* Hellyer-Jones); one *s*. *Educ:* Christ's Hosp., Horsham; Jesus Coll., Cambridge; Brasenose Coll., Oxford. BA (Hons Classics) Cantab 1937; Dipl. Class. Arch. Cantab 1938; BA Oxon 1938. Indian Civil Service, Punjab, 1939–48; Commonwealth Relations Office, 1948–65; seconded to Foreign Office for service in British Embassy, Washington, 1951–53; Private Sec., 1953–54; Asst Sec., 1954; Deputy High Commissioner for the UK in S Africa, 1956–59; Asst Under Sec. of State, CRO, 1960–61; British Dep. High Comr, Delhi, 1961–65. *Address:* Fieldview, Lower Road, Fetcham, Surrey KT22 9EJ. *Club:* Commonwealth Trust.

BELDAM, Rt. Hon. Sir (Alexander) Roy (Asplan), Kt 1981; PC 1989; **Rt. Hon. Lord Justice Beldam;** a Lord Justice of Appeal, since 1989; *b* 29 March 1925; *s* of George William Beldam and Margaret Frew Shettle (formerly Beldam, *née* Underwood); *m* 1953, Elisabeth Bryant Farr; two *s* one *d*. *Educ:* Oundle Sch.; Brasenose Coll., Oxford. Sub-Lt, RNVR Air Branch, 1943–46. Called to Bar, Inner Temple, 1950; Bencher, 1977; QC 1969; a Recorder of the Crown Court, 1972–81; Presiding Judge, Wales and Chester Circuit, Jan.–Oct. 1985; a Judge of the High Court of Justice, QBD, 1981–89. Chm., Law Commn, 1985–89. *Recreations:* sailing, cricket, naval history. *Address:* Royal Courts of Justice, Strand, WC2.

BELFAST, Earl of; Arthur Patrick Chichester; farmer; *b* 9 May 1952; *s* and *heir* of 7th Marquess of Donegall, *qv*; *m* 1989, Caroline, *er d* of Major Christopher Philipson; one *s*. *Educ:* Harrow; Royal Agricl Coll., Cirencester. Coldstream Guards. *Recreations:* hunting, shooting, fishing. *Heir:* *s* Viscount Chichester, *qv*. *Address:* Dunbrody Park, Arthurstown, Co. Wexford, Eire.

BELFAST, Dean of; *see* Shearer, Very Rev. John.

BELHAM, David Ernest, CB 1975; Principal Assistant Solicitor (Under Secretary), Department of Employment, 1970–77, retired; *b* 9 Aug. 1914; *s* of Ernest George Belham and Grace Belham (*née* Firth); *m* 1938, Eunice Monica (*née* Vine); two *s* two *d*. *Educ:* Whitgift Sch.; Law Society's Sch. of Law. Solicitor (Hons), 1937. Private practice, 1937–39. Served War, RAFVR, 1940–46. Entered Solicitor's Department, Min. of Labour, 1946; Asst Solicitor, 1962. *Address:* 26 The Chase, Findon, Worthing, W Sussex BN14 0TT. *T:* Findon (0903) 873771.

BELHAVEN and STENTON, 13th Lord, *cr* 1647; **Robert Anthony Carmichael Hamilton;** farming; *b* 27 Feb. 1927; *o s* of 12th Lord; *S* father, 1961; *m* 1st, 1952, Elizabeth Ann, *d* of late Col A. H. Moseley, Warrawee, NSW; one *s* one *d*; 2nd, 1973, Rosemary Lady Mactaggart (marr. diss. 1986), *o d* of Sir Herbert Williams, 1st Bt, MP; one *d* (adopted); 3rd, 1986, Malgorzata Maria, *d* of Pobog Tadeusz Hruzik-Mazurkiewicz, Krakow, Poland; one *d*. *Educ:* Eton. Commissioned, The Cameronians, 1947. *Recreation:* cooking. *Heir:* *s* Master of Belhaven, *qv*. *Address:* 16 Broadwater Down, Tunbridge Wells, Kent; 710 Howard House, Dolphin Square, SW1. *Club:* Army and Navy.

BELHAVEN, Master of; Hon. Frederick Carmichael Arthur Hamilton; *b* 27 Sept. 1953; *s* of 13th Lord Belhaven and Stenton, *qv*; *m* 1981, Elizabeth Anne, *d* of S. V. Tredinnick, Wisborough Green, Sussex; two *s*. *Educ:* Eton.

BELICH, Sir James, Kt 1990; Mayor of Wellington, New Zealand, since 1986; *b* 25 July 1927; *s* of Yakov Belich and Maria (*née* Batistich); *m* 1951, Valerie Frances Anzulovich; one *s* two *d*. *Educ:* Otahuhu Coll.; Auckland Univ. (BA Hons Econs); Victoria Univ. of Wellington; IBM Fellow, Massey Univ. Consular/Internat. Trade, Auckland, Sydney, Wellington, 1948–56; Economist, Market Res. Manager, Dir, Chief Exec. and Chm., Research, Marketing, Public Relns, Advertising, 1956–86. Member: Wellington Harbour Bd; Wellington Regional Council. Director: Air NZ, 1987–89; Lambton Harbour Overview Ltd (Chm.); Wellington Internat. Airport. Pres. and Exec., various orgns incl.: Pres., UNA, Wellington and NZ; Founder Pres., UNICEF, NZ. FInstD; Fellow, Inst. of Advertising. *Recreations:* reading, walking, bowls. *Address:* Wellington City Council, PO Box 2199, Wellington, New Zealand; 4 Indus Street, Khandallah, Wellington 4, New Zealand. *T:* 793–339. *Clubs:* Wellington, Wellington Central Rotary (Wellington).

BELISLE, Denton; High Commissioner for Belize in London, 1986–87; *b* 18 March 1948; *s* of George Nathaniel and Laura Ianthe Belisle; *m* 1974, Barrette Johnissa (*née* Sanz); three *s*. *Educ:* Univ. of West Indies (BSc Hons); Univ. of Newcastle upon Tyne. Agricl Officer, 1970–78; Projects Officer (Agric.), 1978–81; Investment Promotion Officer, 1981–83; Dep. Perm. Rep. to UN, 1983–84; Hd, Econs Div., Develt Finance Corp., 1984–85; Chargé d'Affaires *ai*, Washington, 1985; Actg High Comr, London, 1985–86. *Recreations:* tennis, reading. *Address:* 24 Mango Street, Belmopan, Belize, Central America. *Club:* Belmopan Tennis.

BELL, Alexander Gilmour, CB 1991; Chief Reporter for Public Inquiries, Scottish Office, since 1979; *b* 11 March 1933; *s* of Edward and Daisy Bell; *m* 1966, Mary Chisholm; four *s*. *Educ:* Hutchesons' Grammar Sch.; Glasgow Univ. (BL). Admitted Solicitor, 1954. After commercial experience in Far East and in private practice, entered Scottish Office, as Legal Officer, 1967; Dep. Chief Reporter, 1973. *Recreations:* casual outdoor pursuits, choral music. *Address:* Woodend, Haddington, East Lothian EH41 4PE. *T:* Haddington (062082) 3514.

BELL, (Alexander) Scott; Managing Director, Standard Life Assurance Co., since 1988; *b* 4 Dec. 1941; *s* of William Scott Bell and Irene Bell; *m* 1965, Veronica Jane (*née* Simpson); two *s* one *d*. *Educ:* Daniel Stewart's College, Edinburgh. FFA, FPMI. Standard Life Assurance Co.: Asst Actuary for Canada, 1967; Dep. Actuary, 1972; South Region Manager, 1974; Asst Gen. Manager (Finance), 1979; Gen. Manager (Finance), 1985–88. Director: Bank of Scotland, 1988–; Hammerson Property Investment and Development Corporation plc, 1988–; Scottish Financial Enterprise, 1989–. *Recreations:* travel, golf, tennis, reading. *Address:* 28 Barnton Avenue East, Edinburgh. *Clubs:* New (Edinburgh); Bruntsfield Links Golfing Society.

BELL, Alistair Watson; His Honour Judge Bell; a Circuit Judge, since 1978; *b* Edinburgh, 31 March 1930; *s* of Albert William Bell and Alice Elizabeth Watson; *m* 1957, Patricia Margaret Seed; one *s* two *d*. *Educ:* Lanark Grammar Sch.; George Watson's Coll.; Univs of Edinburgh (MA) and Oxford (MA, BCL). 2nd Lieut RASC, 1955. Called to Bar, Middle Temple, 1955; Harmsworth Scholar, 1956; entered practice, Northern Circuit, 1957; a Recorder of the Crown Court, 1972–78. Hon. Recorder, Carlisle, 1990. Contested (L) Chorley, 1964 and Westmorland, 1966. *Recreation:* hill walking, with or without golf clubs. *Address:* The Crown Court, The Citadel, Carlisle.

BELL, Andrew Montgomery; Sheriff of Lothian and Borders, since 1990; *b* 21 Feb. 1940; *s* of James Montgomery Bell and Mary Bell (*née* Cavaye), Edinburgh; *m* 1969, Ann Margaret Robinson; one *s* one *d*. *Educ:* Royal High Sch., Edinburgh; Univ. of Edinburgh (BL). Solicitor, 1961–74; called to Bar, 1975; Sheriff of S Strathclyde, Dumfries and Galloway at Hamilton, 1979–84; Sheriff of Glasgow and Strathkelvin, 1984–90. *Address:* 5 York Road, Trinity, Edinburgh EH5 3EJ. *T:* 031–552 3859.

BELL, Archibald Angus, QC (Scot.) 1961; Sheriff of Glasgow and Strathkelvin (formerly Lanark) at Glasgow, since 1973; *b* 13 April 1923; *o s* of James Dunlop Bell, Solicitor, Ayrshire, and Katherine Rachel Gordon Miller; *m* 1949, Dorothy, *d* of Dr Pollok Donald, Edinburgh, and Mrs Dorothy Donald; two *s*. *Educ:* The Leys Sch., Cambridge; Univ. of St Andrews; Univ. of Glasgow. Served War, Royal Navy, 1941–45; Sub-Lieut RNVR. MA, St Andrews, 1947; LLB, Glasgow, 1949; admitted to Faculty of Advocates, 1949; Reporter, Court of Session Cases, 1952–55. Contested (C and U) Maryhill Div. of Glasgow, Gen. Elec., 1955. Standing Junior Counsel in Scotland: to Board of Trade, 1955–57; to War Dept, 1957–61. Pres., Scottish Cricket Union, 1975. *Recreations:* watching the sun rise, getting fun out of games. Formerly: hockey and cricket blue, St Andrews, and Pres. UAU and Dramatic Soc. *Clubs:* Royal Scots (Edinburgh); MCC; Royal and Ancient (St Andrews); RNVR (Scotland).

BELL, Arthur; *see* Bell, E. A.

BELL, (Charles) Trevor; General Secretary, Colliery Officials and Staffs Area of the National Union of Mineworkers, 1979–89; Member, National Executive Committee of the National Union of Mineworkers, 1979–89; *b* 22 Sept. 1927; *s* of Charles and Annie Bell; *m* 1974, Patricia Ann Tappin. *Educ:* state schools; Technical Coll. (City and Guilds Engrg); Coleg Harlech, N Wales (Trades Union scholarship, 1955). Craftsman in coal mining industry, 1941. Mem., Bd of Trustees, Jim Conway Meml Foundn for Res. and Educn, 1989–. Mem., Labour Party, 1946–. *Recreations:* gardening, golf. *Address:* Wakefield, West Yorks WF2 6SH.

BELL, Dr Donald Atkinson, CEng; Head of Research and Development, Strathclyde Institute, Glasgow, since 1990; *b* 28 May 1941; *s* of late Robert Hamilton Bell and Gladys Mildred Bell; *m* 1967, Joyce Louisa Godber; two *s*. *Educ:* Royal Belfast Academical Instn; Queen's Univ., Belfast (BSc); Southampton Univ. (PhD). FIMechE; MIEE; FBCS. National Physical Lab., 1966–77; Dept of Industry, 1978–82; Dir, Nat. Engrg Lab., 1983–90. Vis. Prof., Univ. of Strathclyde, 1986–. *Address:* Strathclyde Institute, 229 George Street, Glasgow G1 1RX. *T:* 041–552 4011.

BELL, Donald L.; *see* Lynden-Bell.

BELL, Prof. Donald Munro; international concert and opera artist; freelance; Associate Professor of Music, Calgary University, since 1982; *b* 19 June 1934; one *s*. *Educ:* South Burnaby High Sch., BC, Canada. Made Wigmore Hall Debut, 1958; since then has sung at Bayreuth Wagner Festival, 1958, 1959, 1960; Lucerne and Berlin Festivals, 1959; Philadelphia and New York debuts with Eugene Ormandy, 1959; Israel, 1962; Russia Recital Tour, 1963; Glyndebourne Festival, 1963, 1973, 1974, 1982; with Deutsche Oper am Rhein, Düsseldorf, 1964–66; Scottish National Opera, 1974; Scottish Opera, 1978; Basler Kammer Orchestre, 1978; Australian Tour (Musica Viva), 1980. Prof. and Head of Vocal Dept, Ottawa Univ., 1979–82. Now has Opera Workshop at Univ. of Calgary. Dir, Alberta Br., Nat. Opera Assoc, 1986–. Member: Nat. Assoc. of the Teachers Singing, 1985–; Nat. Opera Assoc., 1985– (Dir for Canada, 1988–). Has made recordings. Arnold Bax Medal, 1955. *Address:* University of Calgary, Faculty of Fine Arts, Department of Music, 1500 University Drive NW, Calgary, Alberta T2N 1N4, Canada.

BELL, Douglas Maurice, CBE 1972; Chairman and Chief Executive, Tioxide Group Ltd (formerly British Titan Ltd), 1973–78; Chairman, Tinsley Wire Industries Group, 1981–87 (Director, since 1978); *b* Shanghai, China, 15 April 1914; *s* of Alexander Dunlop Bell; *m* 1947, Elizabeth Mary Edelsten; one *s* two *d*. *Educ:* The Edinburgh Academy; St Andrews Univ. War Dept, Chemist, Woolwich Arsenal, 1936. Imperial Chemical Industries: Dyestuffs Div., 1937–42; Regional Sales Manager, 1946–53; Billingham Dir, 1953; Billingham Man. Dir, 1955–57; Heavy Organic Chemicals Managing Dir, 1958–61; Chm. of European Council, Imperial Chemical Industries Ltd, 1960–65; Chief Executive, ICI (Europa) Ltd, 1965–72. Director: British Titan Products Ltd, 1968–78; Tioxide Australia Pty Ltd, 1973–78; Tioxide of Canada Ltd, 1973–78; Tioxide SA, 1973–78; Titanio SA, 1973–78. Hon. Dir, NV Bekaert SA, 1979–. FBIM 1974; FRSA 1976; Soc. of Chemical Industry: Vice-Pres., 1975–76; Pres., 1976–78; Mem. Council, Chemical Industry Assoc., 1973–78. Member, Governing Board: British Sch. of Brussels, 1971–; Maison de la Chemie Française, 1972–. Hon. FIChemE, 1977. Hon. LLD St Andrews, 1977. Comendador de Numero de la Orden de Merito Civil (Spain), 1967; Commandeur, Ordre de Léopold II (Belgium), 1973. *Recreations:* sports and gardens. *Address:* Stocks Cottage, Church Street, West Chiltington, Sussex. *T:* West Chiltington (07983) 2284. *Clubs:* Anglo-Belgian; Cercle Royal Gaulois (Brussels); Royal Waterloo Golf, West Sussex Golf.

BELL, Edith Alice, OBE 1981; Chief Nursing Officer, Welsh Office, 1972–81; *b* 14 Sept. 1919; *d* of George and Alice Bell. *Educ:* Girls' Grammar Sch., Lancaster. SRN University Hosp., Leeds; SCM St Luke's Hosp., Bradford; Cert. Royal Medico Psychological Assoc., Westwood Hosp., Bradford; Registered Nurse, Mentally Subnormal, Aston Hall, Derby. Ward Sister, Aston Hall Hosp., Derby, 1941–43; Asst Matron, Royal Albert Hosp., Lancaster, 1943–46; Dep. Matron, Darenth Park Hosp., Dartford, 1946–48; Gp Matron, Fountain Gp HMC, London, 1948–60; Management Services Officer, SE RHB, Scotland, 1960–63; Chief Regional Nursing Officer, E Anglian RHB, 1963–72. WHO Fellowship, 1951. Past Member: Gen. Nursing Council, England and Wales; Nat. Council of Nurses; Standing Nursing Adv. Cttee; Services Cttee, Internat. Council of Nurses; Jt Bd, Clinical Nursing Studies; Council, Queen's Inst. of Dist Nursing Service; SW Metrop. RHB: Nursing, Research and Trng Cttees. Chairman: Mental Nurses Cttee; Jt Organizations; Reg. Nursing Officers Gp; Royal Coll. of Nursing Br. Mem., NHS Reorganization Steering Cttee. Hon. Sec., Mental Hosp. Matrons Assoc.; Pres., Inst. of Religion and Medicine. Chairman: CS Retirement Fellowship Gp, 1987– (Chm., N Lancs Br., 1989–; Mem., Cttee of Management, 1988–); Old Girls' Assoc., Girls' Grammar Sch., Lancaster, 1987–. *Publications:* contribs to professional jls. *Recreations:* reading, travel, gardening, supporting ecumenical activities, local Abbeyfield Society. *Address:* Tyla Teg, 51 Farmdale Road, Newlands, Lancaster LA1 4JB. *Club:* Civil Service.

BELL, (Edward) Percy, OBE 1974; Member for Newham South, Greater London Council, 1973–81 (for Newham, 1964–73); *b* 3 April 1902; *m* 1932, Ethel Mary Bell. (*d* 1974). *Educ:* Rutherford Coll., Newcastle upon Tyne; King's Coll., London. Teacher in the service of West Ham County Borough, 1922–64; Headmaster, Shipman County Secondary School, West Ham, 1951–64. Chairman: Planning Cttee of GLC, 1973–74; Town Development Cttee, 1974–75; Docklands Jt Cttee, 1974–77. *Recreations:* foreign travel; local and national social history. *Address:* 151c Ham Park Road, E7 9LE. *T:* (private) 081–472 8897.

BELL, Prof. (Ernest) Arthur, CB 1988; PhD; FLS, CChem, FRSC; FIBiol; Visiting Professor: King's College London, since 1982; University of Texas at Austin, since 1988; *b* 20 June 1926; *s* of Albert Bell and Rachel Enid (*née* Williams), Gosforth, Northumberland; *m* 1952, Jean Swinton Ogilvie; two *s* one *d*. *Educ:* Dame Allan's Sch., Newcastle upon Tyne; Univ. of Durham (King's Coll., Newcastle upon Tyne) BSc; Trinity Coll., Univ. of Dublin (MA, PhD; Hon. Fellow, 1990). CChem, FRIC (now FRSC) 1961; FIBiol 1987. Res. Chemist, ICI, Billingham, 1946; Demonstr and holder of Sarah Purser Med. Res. Award, TCD, 1947; Asst to Prof. of Biochem., TCD, 1949; Lectr in Biochem., KCL, 1953; Reader in Biochem., Univ. of London, 1964–68; Prof. of Botany, Univ. of Texas, 1968–72; Prof. of Biology, London Univ., and Hd of Dept of Plant Scis, KCL, 1972–81; FKC 1982; Dir, Royal Botanic Gardens, Kew, 1981–88. Sen. Foreign Scientist Fellow, Nat. Sci. Foundn, USA, and Vis. Prof. of Biol., Univ. of Kansas, 1966; Visiting Professor: Univ. of Sierra Leone, 1977; Univ. of Reading, 1982–88; Cecil H. and Ida Green Vis. Prof., Univ. of British Columbia, 1987; Vis. Commonwealth Fellow, Australia, 1980. Scientific Dir, Texas Botanical Gardens Soc., 1988–. Consultant Dir, CAB-Internat. Mycological Inst. (formerly Commonwealth Mycol. Inst.), 1982–88; Mem., Working Party on Naturally Occurring Toxicants in Food, 1983–. Hon. Botanical Adviser, Commonwealth War Graves Commn, 1983–89. President: Section K (Plant Biol.), BAAS, 1985–86; KCL Assoc., 1986–88; Vice Pres., Linnean Soc., 1983–85 (Mem. Council, 1980–85); Mem. Council, RHS, 1985–89; Hon. Mem., Phytochemical Soc. of Europe, 1985. *Publications:* contribs on plant biochem., chemotaxonomy, and chem. ecology to Phytochemistry, and Biochem. Jl. *Recreations:* walking, travel. *Address:* 3 Hillview, Wimbledon, SW20 0TA. *Club:* Athenæum.

BELL, Sir Ewart; *see* Bell, Sir W. E.

BELL, Prof. Frank, DSc, PhD; FRSC; FSAScot; FRSE; Professor of Chemistry, Heriot-Watt University (formerly College), Edinburgh, 1950–66 (now Emeritus); *b* 24 Dec. 1904; *o s* of Thomas Bell, Derby; *m* 1930, May Perryman; one *s* one *d*. *Educ:* Crypt Grammar Sch., Glos; Queen Mary Coll., University of London. Head of Science Dept, Blackburn Tech. Coll. 1935–41; Principal, Lancaster Tech. Coll., 1941–46; Prof. of Chemistry, Belfast Coll. of Tech., 1947–50. *Publications:* original papers mainly in Journal of Chemical Soc. *Recreations:* numismatics, walking and field-club activities (Past Pres., Cotteswold Naturalists' Field Club; Past Pres., Edinburgh Natural History Soc.). *Address:* Hilcot, Finchcroft Lane, Prestbury, Cheltenham, Glos.

BELL, Sir Gawain (Westray), KCMG 1957; CBE 1955 (MBE mil. 1942); Secretary-General, South Pacific Commission, 1966–70; *b* 21 Jan. 1909; *s* of late William Westray Bell; *m* 1945, Silvia, *d* of Major Adrian Cornwell-Clyne; three *d*. *Educ:* Winchester; Hertford Coll., Oxford. Sudan Political Service, 1931; seconded to the Government of Palestine, 1938 (attached Palestine Police, DSP). 2nd Lt TA, 1929–32; Military Service in Middle East, 1941–45; Kaimakam (Col): Arab Legion, 1942–45; RARO, 1949–59. District Comr, Sudan Political Service, 1945–49; Dep. Sudan Agent, Cairo, 1949–51; Dep. Civil Sec., Sudan Government, 1953–54; Permanent Under-Sec., Ministry of the Interior, 1954–55; HM Political Agent, Kuwait, 1955–57; Governor, Northern Nigeria, 1957–62; Sec Gen., Council for Middle East Trade, 1963–64; engaged, with Sir Ralph Hone, as Constitutional Adviser to Govt of Fedn of S Arabia, 1965–66. Various missions to Arab world, 1970–. Vice-President: LEPRA, 1984– (Chm. Exec. Cttee, 1972–84); Anglo-Jordanian Soc., 1985–. Member: Governing Body, SOAS, London Univ., 1971–81; part-time Chm., CS Selection Bds, 1972–77; Chapter Gen., Order of St John, 1964–66, 1970– (KStJ 1958). Order of Independence 3rd Class (Trans Jordan), 1944. *Publications:* Shadows on the Sand, 1984; An Imperial Twilight, 1989; contribs to DNB, and learned jls. *Recreations:* walking, riding, shooting, rifle shooting (Capt. Oxford Univ., 1931; shot for Sudan). *Address:* 6 Hildesley Court, East Ilsley, Berks RG16 0LA. *T:* Newbury (0635) 28554. *Club:* Army and Navy.

BELL, Geoffrey Lakin; Chairman, Guinness Mahon Holdings, since 1987; *b* 8 Nov. 1939; *s* of Walter Lakin Bell and Ann (*née* Barnes); *m* 1973, Joan Abel; one *d*. *Educ:* Grimsby Technical Sch.; London School of Economics and Political Science. Economic Asst, HM Treasury, 1961–63; Vis. Scholar, Fed. Reserve System, principally with Federal Reserve Bank of St Louis, 1963–64; HM Treasury, also Special Lectr at LSE, 1964–66; Economic Advr, British Embassy, Washington, 1966–69; 1969–82: Asst to Chm., J. Henry Schroder Wagg; Dir, Schroder Wagg; Exec. Vice Pres., Schroder Internat. and Sen. Advr, Schroder Bank and Trust Co., NY; Special Columnist on Econs and Finance, The Times, 1969–74; Exec. Sec. and Mem., Gp of Thirty, 1978–; Pres., Geoffrey Bell and Co., NY, 1982–. Cons. Editor, International Reports, 1983–. *Publications:* The Euro-Dollar Market and the International Financial System, 1973; numerous articles on internat. econs and finance in UK and USA. *Address:* 17 Abbotsbury House, Abbotsbury Road, W14. *T:* 071–603 9408; 300 East 56th Street, New York, NY, USA. *T:* 212/838–1193. *Club:* Reform.

BELL, George Douglas Hutton, CBE 1965; FRS 1965; PhD; Director, Plant Breeding Institute, Cambridge, 1947–71, retired; a Vice President, Royal Society, 1976–78; *b* 18 Oct. 1905; *er s* of George Henry and Lilian Mary Matilda Bell; *m* 1934, Eileen Gertrude Wright; two *d*. *Educ:* Bishop Gore's Grammar Sch., Swansea; Univ. Coll. of North Wales, Bangor (BSc 1928); University of Cambridge. PhD 1931. Research Officer, Plant Breeding Inst., 1931; University Demonstrator, Cambridge, 1933, Lectr, 1944; Fellow of Selwyn Coll., Cambridge, 1944–54, Hon. Fellow, 1965. Research Medal, Royal Agricultural Soc. of England, 1956; Royal Society Mullard Medal, 1967. Hon. DSc: Reading Univ., 1968; Univ. Wales, 1968; Liverpool Univ., 1970; Hon. ScD Cambridge, 1978. Massey-Ferguson National Award, 1973. *Publications:* Cultivated Plants of the Farm, 1948; The Breeding of Barley Varieties in Barley and Malt, 1962; Cereal Breeding in Vistas in Botany, Vol. II, 1963; Phylogeny of Temperate Cereals in Crop Plant Evolution, 1965; (contrib.) Wheat Breeding: the scientific basis, 1987; papers on barley and breeding in Jl of Agricultural Science, etc. *Recreations:* natural history; theatre, music. *Address:* 6 Worts Causeway, Cambridge CB1 4RL. *T:* Cambridge (0223) 247449.

BELL, Sir (George) Raymond, KCMG 1973; CB 1967; Vice-President, European Investment Bank, 1973–78, retired; Hon. Vice-President, European Investment Bank, 1978; *b* 13 March 1916; *e s* of late William Bell and Christabel Bell (*née* Appleton); *m* 1944, Joan Elizabeth, *o d* of late W. G. Coltham and Christina Coltham; two *s* two *d*. *Educ:* Bradford Grammar Sch.; St John's Coll., Cambridge (Scholar). Entered Civil Service, Assistant Principal, 1938; Min. of Health, 1938; transf. Treasury, 1939; served War 1941–44, Royal Navy (Lieut RNVR). Principal, Civil Service, 1945; Asst Sec.,

1951; Under-Sec., 1960; Dep. Sec., 1966; Dep. Sec. HM Treasury, 1966–72. Sec. (Finance), Office of HM High Commissioner for the UK in Canada, 1945–48; Counsellor, UK Permanent Delegn to OEEC/NATO, Paris, 1953–56; Principal Private Sec. to Chancellor of Exchequer, 1958–60. Mem. UK Delegation to Brussels Conference, 1961–62 and 1970–72. *Recreations:* music, reading, travel. *Address:* Quartier des Bories, Aouste-sur-Sye, 26400 Crest, Drôme, France. *T:* 75 25 26 94. *Club:* Athenæum.

BELL, Griffin B.; Attorney-General, USA, 1977–79; *b* Americus, Georgia, 31 Oct. 1918; *s* of A. C. Bell and Thelma Pilcher; *m* 1943, Mary Foy Powell; one *s*. *Educ:* Southwestern Coll., Ga; Mercer Univ. (LLB *cum laude* 1948, LLD 1967). Served AUS, 1941–46, reaching rank of Major. Admitted to Georgia Bar, 1947; practice in Savannah and Rome, 1947–53. Partner in King and Spalding, Atlanta, 1953–59, 1976–77, 1979–, Managing Partner, 1959–61; United States Judge, 5th Circuit, 1961–76. Chairman: Atlanta Commn on Crime and Delinquency, 1965–66; CSCE, 1980. Mem., Vis. Cttee, Law Sch., Vanderbilt Univ.; Trustee, Mercer Univ.; Member: Amer. Law Inst.; Amer. Coll. of Trial Lawyers (Pres., 1985–86). *Address:* 206 Townsend Place NW, Atlanta, Ga 30327, USA.

BELL, Guy Davies, CEng; Director, BAA plc, 1988–89; Managing Director, Gatwick Airport Ltd, 1985–89; *b* 19 May 1933; *s* of Percival and Margaret Bell; *m* 1958, Angela Mary Joan Bickersteth; two *s* one *d* (and one *s* decd). *Educ:* Sedbergh Sch. MICE. British Transport Docks Bd, 1963–68; British Airports Authority, 1968–86, Engrg Dir, 1977–85; BAA, 1986–89. *Recreations:* gardening, open air, music. *Club:* Royal Automobile.

BELL, Ian Wright, CBE 1964; HM Diplomatic Service, retired; *b* Radlett, Herts, 21 Aug. 1913; *s* of late T. H. D. Bell; *m* 1940, Winifred Mary Ruth Waterfield, *y d* of late E. H. Waterfield, ICS; three *s*. *Educ:* Canford Sch.; St Peter's Hall, Oxford. Vice-Consul: Valparaiso, 1938; Montevideo, 1940; Foreign Office, 1946; First Sec., 1947; First Sec., Addis Ababa, 1949, Chargé d'Affaires, 1949, 1950, 1952 and 1953; Consul, Innsbruck, 1953; First Sec., Prague, 1954, Chargé d'Affaires, 1954 and 1956; Counsellor and Consul-Gen., Jedda, 1956; Counsellor and Official Sec., UK High Commission, Canberra, 1957; HM Consul-Gen., Lyons, 1960–65; Ambassador, Santo Domingo, 1965–69; Consul-Gen., Stuttgart, 1969–73. FRGS. *Publications:* The Scarlet Flower (Poems), 1947; The Dominican Republic, 1981; reviews and articles in various periodicals. *Recreations:* painting, drama, music, walking. *Address:* 4A Fisher Lane, Bingham, Nottingham NG13 8BQ.

BELL, James Steven, CMG 1989; CBE 1964; DFC 1946; QPM 1956; CPM 1950; Director General, Ministry of the Interior, Bahrain; *b* 30 Sept. 1914; *s* of Lachlan Steven Bell and Mary (*née* Bertram). *Educ:* Whitehaven School. Grenadier Guards A Cadet, 1933–35; Kent County Constabulary, 1935–41; RAF, 1941–46; Nigeria Police, 1946–64; Bahrain Public Security, Ministry of the Interior, 1966–. Nigerian Police Medal, 1960; Order of Bahrain 1st Cl., 1983; Bahrain Public Security Medal for Distinguished Service, 1988. *Recreations:* walking, reading, travel. *Address:* Ministry of the Interior, Bahrain, Arabian Gulf.

BELL, Jocelyn; *see* Bell Burnell, S. J.

BELL, Rear-Adm. John Anthony, CB 1977; Research Fellow, Exeter University, 1986–89, retired; Director, Naval Education Service, 1975–78; Chief Naval Instructor Officer, 1978–79; *b* 25 Nov. 1924; *s* of Mathew Bell, Dundee, and Mary Ann Ellen Bell (*née* Goss), London; *m* 1946, Eileen Joan Woodman; three *d*. *Educ:* St Ignatius Coll., Stamford Hill; London Univ. BA, BSc, LLB. Barrister, Gray's Inn, 1970. RM 1943–45; Schoolmaster, RN, Instr Lt, Courses, Reserve Fleet, service with RAN, 1945–52; HMS Implacable, Theseus, Admiralty, HMS Excellent, 1952–59; HMS Centaur, RN Staff Course, Staff of SACLANT, USA, Directing Staff, RN Staff Course, Western Fleet, 1959–69; Naval Educn Service, Dir, Dept of Naval Oceanography and Meteorology, 1969–75; Instr Captain 1969, Rear-Adm. 1975. Educn Sec. of the BBC, 1979–83; Dep. Chairman: Police Complaints Bd, 1983–85; (Discipline), Police Complaints Authority, 1985–86; Vice Chm., Educn Foundn for Visual Aids, 1986–88; Member: BEC Educn Cttee, 1975–79; C&G Policy Cttee, 1975–79; TEC, 1976–79; Cert. of Extended Educn Cttee, DES, 1978–79. Governor, SOAS, 1975–79; Vice-Chm., Court of Governors, City of London Polytechnic, 1984–; Pres., SCC, Gravesend, 1982–84; Vice-Pres., United Services Catholic Assoc., 1979–; Nat. Vice-Pres., RN Assoc., 1983. Chairman: Kent EC Cttee, 1982–84; RNLI, Wellington, 1988–. Governor: Somerset Coll. of Art and Technology, 1987– (Vice-Chm. of Govs, 1989–); London Coll. of Furniture, 1988–90. Editor-in-Chief, Education Media International, 1988–. KSG 1983. *Recreations:* swimming, wines, travelling, France.

BELL, Sir John Lowthian, 5th Bt *cr* 1885; *b* 14 June 1960; *s* of Sir Hugh Francis Bell, 4th Bt and of Lady Bell (Mary Howson, MB, ChB, *d* of late George Howson, The Hyde, Hambledon); *S* father, 1970; *m* 1985, Venetia, *d* of J. A. Perry, Taunton; one *s* one *d*. *Recreations:* shooting, fishing. *Heir:* *s* John Hugh Bell, *b* 29 July 1988. *Address:* Arncliffe Hall, Ingleby Cross, Northallerton, N Yorks.

BELL, Joseph Denis Milburn; Chairman, North Western Electricity Board, 1976–85; *b* 2 Sept. 1920; *s* of John Bell, BEM, and Ann Bell; *m* 1949, Wilhelmina Maxwell Miller; one *s* one *d*. *Educ:* Bishop Auckland Grammar Sch.; St Edmund Hall, Oxford (MA). Served War, RAF, 1941–45. Contested (Lab) Canterbury, 1945. Lectr in Modern Econ. History, Univ. of Glasgow, 1946; National Coal Board: Indust. Relations Dept, 1954; Dep. Indust. Relations Dir, Durham Div., 1963; Electricity Council: Statistical Officer, Indust. Relations Dept, 1966; Dep. Indust. Relations Adviser (Negotiating), 1967; Indust. Relations Adviser, 1972. *Publications:* Industrial Unionism: a critical analysis, 1949 (repr. in Trade Unions: selected readings, ed W. E. J. McCarthy, 1972); (contrib.) The Scottish Economy (ed A. K. Cairncross), 1953; (contrib.) The System of Industrial Relations in Great Britain (ed A. Flanders and H. A. Clegg), 1954; (contrib.) The Lessons of Public Enterprise (ed M. Shanks), 1963. *Address:* Rossways, Broad Lane, Hale, Altrincham, Cheshire WA15 0DH. *T:* 061–980 4451. *Club:* United Oxford & Cambridge University.

BELL, Prof. Kathleen Myra, CBE 1978; Professor of Social Studies in the University of Newcastle upon Tyne, 1971–83, now Professor Emeritus; *b* 6 March 1920; *d* of late Walter Petty and late Myra Petty; *m* 1945, Rev. Jack Martin Bell; one *s* one *d*. *Educ:* St Joseph's Coll., Bradford; Univ. of Manchester (Prize in Public Admin. 1940). Asst Personnel Officer, later Trng Officer, Min. of Supply ROF, 1942–45; Tutor and Lectr in Univ. Depts of Extra-Mural Studies, 1945–63; University of Newcastle upon Tyne: Lectr in Social Studies, 1963–67; Sen. Tutor, 1967–69; Sen. Lectr, 1969–71. Member: Lord Chancellor's Council on Tribunals, 1963–81 (Ch. person, Cttee on Functions of the Council, 1977–81); Social Admin. Cttee of Jt Univ. Council for Public and Social Admin., 1965–83; BBC Programmes Complaints Commn, 1978–81; Academic Adviser (apptd by Govt Chief Scientist) to DHSS Social Security Res. Policy Cttee, 1976–83; Expert Adviser to OECD Directorate for Social Affairs and Educn, for their project, Role of Women in the Economy, 1976–77; Mem., AHA for N Tyneside, 1974–77; Mem., Davies Cttee on Hosp. Complaints Procedure, 1971–73; Member Editorial Board: Jl of Social Policy, 1971–78; Jl of Social Welfare Law, 1977–. *Publications:* Tribunals in the Social Services, 1969; Disequilibrium in Welfare, 1973; Research Study on Supplementary Benefit Appeal Tribunals—Review of Main Findings, Conclusions and Recommendations, 1975; The Functions of the Council on Tribunals, 1980; various papers in Jl of Social Policy, Econ. and Social Admin, and other jls. *Address:* Silverton, 86 Trinity Road, Edinburgh EH5 3JU.

BELL, Leslie Gladstone, CEng, FRINA; RCNC; Director of Naval Ship Production, Ministry of Defence, 1977–79, retired; *b* 20 Oct. 1919; *s* of late John Gladstone Bell and Jessie Gray Bell (*née* Quigley); *m* 1963, Adriana Agatha Jacoba van den Berg; one *s* one *d*. *Educ:* Portsmouth Dockyard Tech. Coll.; Royal Naval Engineering Coll., Keyham; Royal Naval Coll., Greenwich. Staff Constructor Cdr, Home Fleet, 1953–56; Aircraft Carrier Design, 1956–59; Chief Constructor, Weapon Development, 1959–67; IDC, 1968; Asst Dir, Submarine Design, 1969–72; Director, Submarine Project Team, 1972–77. *Recreations:* gardening, golf, music. *Address:* Haytor, Old Midford Road, Bath, Avon. *T:* Bath (0225) 833357. *Club:* Bath Golf.

BELL, Martin; Berlin Correspondent, BBC TV News, since 1989; *b* 31 Aug. 1938; *s* of late Adrian Hanbury Bell and Marjorie H. Bell; *m* 1971, Nelly Lucienne Gourdon; two *d*; *m* 1985, Rebecca D. Sobel. *Educ:* The Leys Sch., Cambridge; King's Coll., Cambridge (MA). BBC TV News: Reporter, 1965–77; Diplomatic Correspondent, 1977–78; Chief Washington Correspondent, 1978–89. Pool TV Reporter, 7th Armoured Bde, Gulf War, 1991. Royal Television Society Reporter of the Year, 1977. *Address:* c/o BBC, 103A Hohenzollerndamm, 1000 Berlin 33, Germany. *T:* 049 30 8245033.

BELL, Martin George Henry: Senior Partner, Ashurst Morris Crisp, since 1986; *b* 16 Jan. 1935; *s* of Leonard George Bell and Phyllis Bell (*née* Green); *m* 1965, Shirley Wrightson; two *s*. *Educ:* Charterhouse. Admitted Solicitor, 1961. Joined Ashurst Morris Crisp, 1961; Partner, 1963. *Address:* Mulberry, Woodbury Hill, Loughton, Essex IG10 1JB. *T:* 081–508 1188.

BELL, Michael John Vincent; Deputy Under-Secretary of State (Finance), Ministry of Defence, since 1988; *b* 9 Sept. 1941; *e s* of C. R. V. Bell, OBE and late Jane Bell, MBE; *m* 1983, Mary Shippen, *o d* of late J. W. Shippen and Mrs Margaret Shippen; one *s* two *d*. *Educ:* Winchester Coll.; Magdalen Coll., Oxford (BA Lit. Hum.). Res. Associate, Inst. for Strategic Studies, 1964; Ministry of Defence: Asst Principal, 1965; Principal, 1969; Asst Sec., 1975; on loan to HM Treasury, 1977–79; Asst Under Sec. of State (Resources and Programmes), 1982–84; Dir Gen. of Management Audit, MoD, 1984–86; Asst Sec. Gen. for Defence Plannning and Policy, NATO, 1986–88. *Recreations:* motorcycling, military history. *Address:* Ministry of Defence, Main Building, Whitehall, SW1A 2HB.

BELL, Prof. Peter Robert; Emeritus Professor of Botany, University of London; *b* 18 Feb. 1920; *s* of Andrew and Mabel Bell; *m* 1952, Elizabeth Harrison; two *s*. *Educ:* Simon Langton School, Canterbury; Christ's Coll., Cambridge (MA 1949). University College London: Asst Lecturer in Botany, 1946; Lectr in Botany, 1949; Reader in Botany, 1967; Prof. of Botany, 1967; Quain Prof. of Botany and Head of Dept of Botany and Microbiol., 1978–85. Visiting Professor: Univ. of California, Berkeley, 1966–67; Univ. of Delhi, India, 1970. British Council Distinguished Visitor, NZ, 1976; many other visits overseas, including exploration of Ecuadorian Andes. Vice-Pres., Linnean Soc., 1962–65; Mem. Biological Sciences Cttee, 1974–79 (Chm. Panel 1, 1977–79), SRC. *Publications:* Darwin's Biological Work, Some Aspects Reconsidered, 1959; (with C. F. Woodcock) The Diversity of Green Plants, 1968, 3rd edn 1983; (trans., with D. E. Coombe) Strasburger's Textbook of Botany, 8th English edn, 1976; scientific papers on botanical topics, particularly reproductive cells of land plants, and on history of botany. *Recreation:* mountains. *Address:* 13 Granville Road, Barnet, Herts EN5 4DU. *T:* 081–449 9331.

BELL, Prof. Peter Robert Frank, MD; FRCS, FRCSGlas; Professor of Surgery, University of Leicester, since 1974; *b* 12 June 1938; *s* of Frank and Ruby Bell; *m* 1961, Anne Jennings; one *s* two *d*. *Educ:* Univ. of Sheffield (MB, ChB Hons 1961; MD 1969). FRCS 1965; FRCSGlas 1968. Postgrad. surg. career in Sheffield hosps, 1961–65; Lectr in Surgery, Univ. of Glasgow, 1965–68; Sir Henry Wellcome Travelling Fellow, Univ. of Colorado, 1968–69; Consultant Surgeon and Sen. Lectr, Western Infirm., Glasgow, 1969–74. Pres., Surgical Res. Soc., 1986–88. *Publications:* Surgical Aspects of Haemodialysis, 1974, 2nd edn 1983; Operative Arterial Surgery, 1982; pubns on vascular disease, transplantation and cancer in med. and surg. jls. *Recreations:* horticulture, oil painting, tennis. *Address:* Department of Surgery, Clinical Sciences Building, PO Box 65, Royal Infirmary, Leicester LE2 7LX. *Club:* Leicestershire (Leicester).

BELL, Prof. Quentin (Claudian Stephen), FRSA; FRSL; Emeritus Professor of the History and Theory of Art, Sussex University; painter, sculptor, potter, author, art critic; *b* 19 Aug. 1910; 2nd *s* of late Clive and Vanessa Bell; *m* 1952, Anne Olivier Popham; one *s* two *d*. *Educ:* Leighton Park. Exhibitions, 1935, 1947, 1949, 1972, 1977, 1981, 1982, 1986. Political warfare executive, 1941–43. Lectr in Art Education, King's Coll., Newcastle, 1952; Senior Lecturer, 1956; Prof. of Fine Art, University of Leeds, 1962–67 (Head of Dept of Fine Art, 1959); Slade Professor of Fine Art, Oxford Univ., 1964–65; Ferens Prof. of Fine Art, University of Hull, 1965–66; Prof. of History and Theory of Art, Sussex Univ., 1967–75. Commissioned Sculpture for Univ. of Leeds. MA Dunelm, 1957. Regular contributor to Listener, 1951–60. *Publications:* On Human Finery, 1947, rev. edn 1976; Those Impossible English (with Helmut Gernsheim), 1951; Roger Montané, 1961; The Schools of Design, 1963; Ruskin, 1963; Victorian Artists, 1967; Bloomsbury, 1968; Virginia Woolf, a Biography, 2 vols, 1972 (James Tait Black Meml Prize; Duff Cooper Meml Prize); A New and Noble School, 1982; Techniques of Terracotta, 1983; The Brandon Papers (novel), 1985; Bad Art, 1989. *Address:* 81 Heighton Street, Firle, Sussex BN8 6NZ. *T:* Glynde (0273) 858201.

BELL, Sir Raymond; *see* Bell, Sir G. R.

BELL, Robert Donald Murray, CB 1966; *b* 8 Oct. 1916; *s* of Robert William and Mary Caroline Bell; *m* 1941, Karin Anna Smith; one *s* one *d*. *Educ:* Christ's Hosp.; Clare Coll., Cambridge. First Class Honours, Natural Sciences Tripos (Physics), 1938. Joined Scottish Office, 1938. War of 1939–45: Royal Artillery, 1940–45 (Mil. Coll. of Science, Bury, 1943). Principal, Scottish Home Dept, 1946; Private Sec. to Sec. of State for Scotland, 1947–50; Under-Secretary in Scottish Depts, 1959–76.

BELL, Prof. Robert Edward, CC (Canada) 1971; FRS 1965; FRSC 1955; Emeritus Professor of Physics, McGill University, Montreal, since 1983; *b* 29 Nov. 1918; *s* of Edward Richardson Bell and Edith E. Rich, British Columbia; *m* 1947, Jeanne Atkinson; one *d*. *Educ:* Univ. of British Columbia (BA 1939, MA 1941); McGill Univ. (PhD 1948). Wartime Radar development, Nat. Research Council, Ottawa, 1941–45; Sen. Research Officer, Chalk River Nuclear Laboratories, 1946–56; McGill University: seconded to Foster Radiation Lab., 1952–56; Assoc. Prof. of Physics, 1956–60; Dir, Foster Radiation Lab., 1960–69; Vice-Dean for Physical Scis, 1964–67; Dean, Fac. of Grad. Studies and Research, 1969–70; Rutherford Prof. of Physics, 1960–83; Principal and Vice-Chancellor, 1970–79; Dir, Arts, Sciences and Technol. Centre, Vancouver, 1983–85. Visiting scientist, Copenhagen Univ. Inst. for Theoretical Physics, under Niels Bohr, 1958–59. President: Royal Society of Canada, 1978–81 (Sec., Section III (Science), 1962–64); Canadian Assoc.

of Physicists, 1965–66. Fellow, American Physical Soc. Hon. DSc: Univ. of New Brunswick, 1971; Université Laval, 1973; Université de Montréal, 1976; Univ. of BC, 1978; McMaster Univ., McGill Univ., 1979; Carleton Univ., 1980; Hon. LLD: Univ. of Toronto, 1971; Concordia Univ., 1979; Hon. DCL Bishop's Univ., 1976. *Publications:* contribs to books: Annual Reviews of Nuclear Science, 1954; Beta and Gamma Ray Spectroscopy, 1955; Alpha, Beta and Gamma Ray Spectroscopy, 1964; papers on nuclear physics and allied topics in scientific jls. *Address:* 822 Tsawwassen Beach, Delta, BC V4M 2J3, Canada. *T:* (604) 943–0667.

BELL, Rodger, QC 1982; a Recorder of the Crown Court, since 1980; Legal Member, Mental Health Review Tribunals, since 1983; *b* 13 Sept. 1939; *s* of John Thornton Bell and Edith Bell; *m* 1969, Sylvia Claire Tatton Brown; one *s* three *d. Educ:* Brentwood Sch.; Brasenose Coll., Oxford (BA). Called to the Bar, Middle Temple, 1963. Mem., Parole Board, 1990–. *Recreations:* running, rowing. *Address:* 1 Crown Office Row, Temple, EC4Y 7HH. *T:* 071–353 1801.

BELL, Prof. Ronald Leslie, CB 1988; CEng, FIM, FInstP, FIAgrE; Director-General, Agricultural Development and Advisory Service and the Regional Organisation, and Chief Scientific Adviser, Ministry of Agriculture, Fisheries and Food, 1984–89; *b* 12 Sept. 1929; *s* of Thomas William Alexander Bell and Annie (*née* Mapleston); *m* 1954, Eleanor Joy (*née* Lancaster); one *s* two *d. Educ:* The City School, Lincoln; Univ. of Birmingham (BSc, PhD). Research Fellow, Royal Radar Estabt, Malvern, 1954–57; Imperial College, Univ. of London: Lectr in Metallurgy, 1957–62; Reader in Metallurgy, 1962–65; University of Southampton: Prof. of Engrg Materials, 1965–77; Head of Dept of Mech. Engrg, 1968; Dean of Faculty of Engrg and Applied Scis, 1970–72; Dep. Vice Chancellor, 1972–76; Dir, NIAE, 1977–84. Vis. Prof., Cranfield Inst. of Technology, 1979–89. Pres., British Crop Protection Council, 1985–89; Member: AFRC, 1984–89; Council, RASE, 1984–89. Hon. DSc Southampton, 1985. *Publications:* papers in learned jls dealing with twinning and brittle fracture of metals, grain boundary sliding and creep in metals, dislocations in semi-conductors, agricultural engineering. *Recreations:* music, painting, Association football, gardening. *Address:* 3 Old Garden Court, Mount Pleasant, St Albans AL3 4RQ. *Club:* Farmers'.

BELL, Ronald Percy, MA; FRS 1944; FRSE 1968; FRSC; Professor of Chemistry, University of Stirling, 1967–75, now Emeritus; Hon. Research Professor of Chemistry, University of Leeds, 1976–82; *b* 1907; *e s* of E. A. Bell, Maidenhead; *m* 1931, Margery Mary West; one *s. Educ:* County Boys' Sch., Maidenhead; Balliol Coll., Oxford. Bedford Lecturer in Physical Chemistry, Balliol Coll., 1932; Fellow of Balliol Coll., 1933 (Vice-Master, 1965); Hon. Fellow, 1967; Univ. Lecturer and Demonstrator, Oxford Univ., 1938; Univ. Reader, Oxford Univ., 1955. George Fisher Baker Lectr, Cornell Univ., 1958; Nat. Science Foundn Fellow, Brown Univ., 1964; Visiting Professor: Weizmann Inst. of Sci., Israel, 1973; Tech. Univ. of Denmark, Lyngby, 1976. President: Faraday Soc., 1956; Chemistry Section, British Assoc. Meeting, Durham, 1970; Vice-Pres. Chemical Soc., 1958 (Tilden Lectureship, 1941; Liversidge Lectureship, 1973–74; Spiers Meml Lectureship, 1975). Foreign Mem. Royal Danish Acad. of Arts and Sciences, 1962; Foreign Associate, Nat. Acad. of Sciences, USA, 1972; Foreign Hon. Mem., Amer. Acad. of Arts and Scis, 1974. Hon. LLD Illinois Inst. of Techn., 1965; Hon. DTech, Tech. Univ. of Denmark, 1969; Hon. DSc Kent, 1974; Hon. DUniv. Stirling, 1977. Leverhulme Emeritus Fellow, 1976. Meldola Medal, Inst. of Chemistry, 1936; Chem. Soc. Award in Kinetics and Mechanism, 1974. *Publications:* Acid-Base Catalysis, 1941; Acids and Bases, 1952, 2nd edn 1969; The Proton in Chemistry, 1959, 2nd edn 1973; The Tunnel Effect in Chemistry, 1980; papers in scientific journals. *Address:* Flat 5, Park Villa Court, Roundhay, Leeds LS8 1EB. *T:* Leeds (0532) 664236.

BELL, Scott; *see* Bell, Alexander Scott.

BELL, Stewart Edward; QC (Scot.) 1982; Sheriff Principal of Grampian, Highland and Islands, 1983–88; *b* 4 Aug. 1919; *yr s* of late Charles Edward Bell, shipowner, and Rosalind Stewart; *m* 1st, 1948, Isla (*d* 1983), 2nd *d* of late James Spencer and Adeline Kelly; three *d*; 2nd, 1985, Mavis Kydd, *d* of late A. St Clair Jameson, WS, and *widow* of Sheriff R. R. Kydd; two step *d. Educ:* Kelvinside Academy, Glasgow; Trinity Hall, Cambridge; Glasgow Univ. Trinity Hall, 1937–39 and 1946 (MA Cantab), Glasgow Univ., 1946–48 (LLB). Commissioned, Loyal Regt, 1939; served with 2nd Bn in Singapore and Malaya, 1940–42 (wounded, POW in Singapore and Korea, 1942–45). Admitted Advocate, 1948; practised: in Malacca, Malaya as Advocate and Solicitor, 1949–51; at Scottish Bar, 1951–61; Sheriff of Lanarks at Glasgow, later of Glasgow and Strathkelvin, 1961–82. Chm., Scottish Far East POW Assoc., 1988–. *Publication:* (contrib.) The Laws of Scotland: Stair Memorial Encyclopedia, vol. 17, 1989. *Recreation:* Highland bagpipe (Hon. Pipe-major, The Royal Scottish Pipers' Soc., 1975–77). *Address:* 14 Napier Road, Edinburgh EH10 5AY. *T:* 031–229 9822. *Clubs:* New (Edinburgh); Highland (Inverness).

BELL, Stuart; MP (Lab) Middlesbrough, since 1983; barrister; *b* High Spen, Co. Durham, 16 May 1938; *s* of Ernest and Margaret Rose Bell; *m* 1st, 1960, Margaret, *d* of Mary Bruce; one *s* one *d*; 2nd, 1980, Margaret, *d* of Edward and Mary Allan; one *s. Educ:* Hookergate Grammar Sch. Formerly colliery clerk, newspaper reporter, typist and novelist. Called to the Bar, Gray's Inn, 1970. Conseil Juridique and Internat. Lawyer, Paris, 1970–77. Member: Newcastle City Council, 1980–83 (Mem., Finance, Health and Environment, Arts and Recreation Cttees; Chm., Youth and Community Cttee; Vice-Chm., Educn Cttee); Educn Cttee, AMA; Council of Local Educn Authorities; Newcastle AHA (T), 1980–83. Contested (Lab) Hexham, 1979. PPS to Dep. Leader of Opposition, Rt Hon. Roy Hattersley, 1983–84; Opposition front bench spokesman on NI, 1984–87. Founder Mem., British–Irish Inter Parly Body, 1990–; Exec. Mem., IPU British Gp, 1990–. Member: Fabian Soc.; Soc. of Lab. Lawyers; GMBATU. *Publications:* Paris 69 (novel), 1973; Days That Used To Be (novel), 1975; How to Abolish the Lords (Fabian Tract), 1981; Valuation for United States Customs Purposes, 1981; When Salem Came to the Boro: the true story of the Cleveland child abuse crisis, 1989; Annotation of The Children Act, 1989. *Recreation:* writing. *Address:* House of Commons, SW1A 0AA.

BELL, Sir Timothy John Leigh, (Sir Tim), Kt 1990; Chairman, Lowe Bell Communications, since 1987; Director, Centre for Policy Studies, since 1991; *b* 18 Oct. 1941; *s* of Arthur Leigh Bell and Greta Mary Bell (*née* Findlay); *m* 1988, Virginia Wallis Hornbrook; one *d. Educ:* Queen Elizabeth's Grammar Sch., Barnet, Herts. FIPA. ABC Television, 1959–61; Colman Prentis & Varley, 1961–63; Hobson Bates, 1963–66; Geers Gross, 1966–70; Man. Dir, Saatchi & Saatchi, 1970–75; Chm. and Man. Dir, Saatchi & Saatchi Compton, 1975–85; Gp Chief Exec., Lowe Howard-Spink Campbell Ewald, 1985–87; Dep. Chm., Lowe Howard-Spink & Bell, 1987–89. Special Adviser to: Chm. NCB, 1984–86; South Bank Bd, 1985–86. Chairman: Charity Projects; Compass Theatre; Upstart Productions, 1991–. Member: Industry Cttee, SCF; Public Affairs Cttee, WWF, 1985–88; Public Relations Cttee, Greater London Fund for the Blind, 1979–86; Council, Royal Opera House, 1982–85; Steering Cttee, Percent Club. Governor: BFI, 1983–86; Sports Aid Foundn, 1991–; Council Mem., Sch. of Communication Arts, 1985–87. *Address:* (office) 7 Hertford Street, W1Y 7DY.

BELL, Trevor; *see* Bell, C. T.

BELL, Walter (Fancourt), CMG 1967; *b* 7 Nov. 1909; *s* of Canon George Fancourt Bell; *m* 1948, Katharine Spaatz, Washington, DC, USA; no *c. Educ:* Tonbridge Sch. Barrister, Inner Temple. Vice-Consul (Acting): New York, 1935–40; Mexico City, 1940–41; New York, 1941–42; Foreign Office, London, 1942–45; 1st Sec., Brit. Embassy, Washington, DC, 1946–48; attached E Africa High Commn, Nairobi, Kenya, 1949–52; 1st Sec., Brit. High Commn, New Delhi, 1952–55; attached War Office, London, 1956–57; Adviser, Federal Govt, W Indies, 1957–60; attached Govt of Kenya, 1961–63; Counsellor, British High Commn, Nairobi, Kenya, 1963–67. US Medal of Freedom with Bronze Palm, 1946. *Recreation:* walking. *Address:* 6 Onslow Square, SW7 3NP. *Club:* Travellers'.

BELL, William Archibald Ottley Juxon; Chairman, Heritage of London Trust, since 1980; *b* 7 July 1919; *s* of Maj. William Archibald Juxon Bell and Mary Isabel Maude Bell (*née* Ottley); *m* 1947, Belinda Mary (*née* Dawson); three *s* three *d. Educ:* Eton; Trinity College, Oxford (MA(Hist.)). Temp. Captain, Welsh Guards, 1940–45. Entered HM Foreign Service, 1945; Political Private Sec. to Sir Terence Shone, UK High Comr in India, 1946–47; Sec. to Exec. Dirs, British S Africa Co., 1947–50; Partner and Dir, King & Shaxson Ltd (Bill-brokers), 1950–. Mem. of Lloyd's, 1970. Mem., for Chelsea, GLC and ILEA, 1970–86. Chairman: Diocesan Bd of Finance for Oxon, 1973–76; GLC Historic Bldgs Cttee, 1977–81; Oxfordshire Buildings Trust, 1987–; English Heritage Commemorative Plaques Working Gp, 1990–; Member: UK Cttee for European Architectural Heritage Year, 1973–75; London Adv. Cttee, English Heritage, 1986–90; Cttee, Oxfordshire Historic Churches Trust. High Sheriff, Oxon, 1978–79. *Recreations:* shooting, golf, music. *Address:* Cottisford House, near Brackley, Northants. *T:* Finmere (02804) 247; 165 Cranmer Court, SW3. *T:* 071–589 1033. *Clubs:* White's, Pratt's.

BELL, William Bradshaw; JP; Chairman, Northern Ireland Gas Employers' Board, 1984–87; *b* 9 Oct. 1935; *s* of Robert Bell and Mary Ann Bell; *m* 1969, Leona Maxwell; one *s* three *d. Educ:* Fane Street Primary School, Belfast; Grosvenor High School, Belfast. Member: for N Belfast, NI Constitutional Convention, 1975–76; Belfast City Council, 1976–85 (Unionist spokesman on housing, 1976–79); for S Antrim, NI Assembly, 1982–86 (Dep. Chm., Finance and Personnel Cttee, 1984–86). Lord Mayor of Belfast, 1979–80; JP Belfast, 1985. *Recreations:* music, motoring, gardening.

BELL, William Edwin, CBE 1980; Chairman, Enterprise Oil plc, since 1984; *b* 4 Aug. 1926; *s* of late Cuthbert Edwin Bell and Winifred Mary Bell (*née* Simpson); *m* 1952, Angela Josephine Vaughan; two *s* two *d. Educ:* Birmingham University (BSc Civil Eng.); Royal School of Mines, Imperial College. Joined Royal Dutch Shell Group, 1948; tech. and managerial appts, Venezuela, USA, Kuwait, Indonesia; Shell International Petroleum Co. (Middle East Coordination), 1965–73; Gen. Man., Shell UK Exploration and Production and Dir, Shell UK, 1973; Man. Dir, Shell UK, 1976–79; Middle East Regional Coordinator and Dir, Shell International Petroleum Co., 1980–84, retired; non-exec. Dir, Costain Group, 1982–. Pres., UK Offshore Operators Assoc., 1975–76. *Publications:* contribs to internat. tech. jls, papers on offshore oil industry develts. *Recreations:* golf, sailing. *Address:* Fordcombe Manor, near Tunbridge Wells, Kent. *Club:* Nevill Golf.

BELL, Sir (William) Ewart, KCB 1982 (CB 1978); Head of Northern Ireland Civil Service, 1979–84 and Second Permanent Secretary, Northern Ireland Office, 1981–84, retired; Director, Ulster Bank Ltd, since 1985; *b* 13 Nov. 1924; *s* of late Rev. Dr Frederick G. Bell and late Margaret Jane Ewart; *m* 1957, Kathleen Ross Boucher; two *d. Educ:* Methodist Coll., Belfast; Wadham Coll., Oxford (MA). Asst Master, Cheltenham Coll., 1946–48; Northern Ireland Civil Service, 1948–84; Min. of Health and Local Govt, 1948–52; Min. (later Dept) of Commerce, 1952–76; Asst Sec., 1963–70; Dep. Sec., 1970–73; Sec., 1973–76; Permanent Sec., Dept of Finance, 1976–79. Hon. Treas., QUB, 1985–. Pres., Irish RFU, 1986–87. *Recreations:* gardening, golf, Rugby football (Irish Rugby International, 1953).

BELL, Sir William H. D. M.; *see* Morrison-Bell.

BELL, William Lewis, CMG 1970; MBE 1945; retired; Information Officer, University of Oxford, 1977–84; *b* 31 Dec. 1919; *s* of Frederick Robinson Bell and Kate Harper Bell (*née* Lewis); *m* 1943, Margaret Giles; one *s* one *d. Educ:* Hymers Coll., Hull; Oriel Coll., Oxford. Served The Gloucestershire Regt (Major), 1940–46. Colonial Administrative Service, Uganda, 1946–63: Dep. Sec. to the Treasury, 1956–58; Perm. Sec., Min. of Social Services, 1958–63; Fellow, Economic Develt Inst., World Bank, 1958. Chm., Uganda National Parks, 1962; Pres., Uganda Sports Union, 1961–62. Director, Cox & Danks Ltd (Metal Industries Group), 1963–64. Sec. to the Governors, Westfield Coll., Univ. of London, 1964–65; Founding Head of British Develt Div. in the Caribbean, ODA, 1966–72; UK Dir, Caribbean Develt Bank, 1970–72; Dir-Gen., Technical Educn and Training Org. for Overseas Countries, 1972–77. *Recreations:* cricket, Caribbeana. *Address:* Hungry Hatch, Fletching, E Sussex TN22 3SH. *Clubs:* MCC; Vincent's (Oxford).

BELL, William Rupert Graham, CB 1978; Under Secretary, Department of Industry, 1975–80; *b* 29 May 1920; *m* 1950, Molly Bolton; two *d. Educ:* Bradford Grammar Sch.; St John's Coll., Cambridge (Scholar). Served Royal Artillery, 1940–45 (despatches). Asst Principal, Min. of Fuel and Power, 1948; Principal, 1949; Asst Sec., 1959; Under-Sec., Min. of Power, 1966–70, DTI, 1970–72; Deputy Principal, Civil Service Coll., 1972–75. Imperial Defence Coll., 1965. *Address:* 47 Chiswick Staithe, Hartington Road, W4 3TP. *T:* 081–994 2545.

BELL BURNELL, (Susan) Jocelyn, PhD; FRAS; astronomer; Grade 7, Royal Observatory, Edinburgh, since 1989; *b* 15 July 1943; *d* of G. Philip and M. Allison Bell; *m* 1968, Martin Burnell (separated 1989); one *s. Educ:* The Mount Sch., York; Glasgow Univ. (BSc); New Hall, Cambridge (PhD). FRAS 1969. Res. Fellowships, Univ. of Southampton, 1968–73; Res. Asst, Mullard Space Science Lab., UCL, 1974–82; Sen. Res. Fellow, 1982–86, SSO, 1986–89, Royal Observatory, Edinburgh. An Editor, The Observatory, 1973–76. Mem., IAU, 1979–. Michelson Medal, Franklin Inst., Philadelphia (jtly with Prof. A. Hewish), 1973; J. Robert Oppenheimer Meml Prize, Univ. of Miami, 1978; Rennie Taylor Award, Amer. Tentative Soc., NY, 1978; (first) Beatrice M. Tinsley Prize, Amer. Astronomical Soc., 1987; Herschel Medal, RAS, 1989. *Publications:* Broken for Life, 1989; papers in Nature, Astronomy and Astrophysics, Jl of Geophys. Res., Monthly Notices of RAS. *Recreations:* Quaker interests, walking. *Address:* Royal Observatory, Blackford Hill, Edinburgh EH9 3HJ.

BELL DAVIES, Vice-Adm. Sir Lancelot (Richard), KBE 1977; Chairman, Sea Cadet Council, since 1983; *b* 18 Feb. 1926; *s* of late Vice-Adm. R. Bell Davies, VC, CB, DSO, AFC, and Mrs Bell Davies, Lee on Solent, Hants; *m* 1949, Emmeline Joan (*née* Molengraaff), Wassenaar, Holland; one *s* two *d. Educ:* Boxgrove Preparatory Sch., Guildford; RN Coll., Dartmouth. War of 1939–45: Midshipman, HMS Norfolk, 1943 (Scharnhorst sunk); joined Submarines, 1944. First Command, HMS Subtle, 1953; subseq. commands: HMS Explorer, 1955; Comdr, HMS Leander, 1962; Captain: HMS Forth, also SM7, 1967, and HMS Bulwark, 1972; Rear-Adm., 1973. Ministry of Defence Posts: (Comdr) Naval Staff, 1960; (Captain) Naval Asst to Controller, 1964; Director of Naval Warfare, 1969; Comdr, British Naval Staff, Washington, and UK Rep. to Saclant, 1973–75; Supreme Allied Commander Atlantic's Rep. in Europe, 1975–78; Comdt, Nato

Defence Coll., Rome, 1978–81. CBIM (FBIM 1977). *Recreations:* sailing, skiing, gardening. *Address:* Holly Hill Lodge, 123 Barnes Lane, Sarisbury Green, Southampton SO3 6BH. *T:* Locks Heath (0489) 573131. *Clubs:* Naval and Military; Royal Yacht Squadron, Royal Naval Sailing Association.

BELLAK, John George; Chairman, Severn Trent plc (formerly Severn-Trent Water Authority), since 1983; *b* 19 Nov. 1930; *m* 1960, Mary Prudence Marshall; three *s* one *d*. *Educ:* Uppingham; Clare College, Cambridge. MA (Economics). Sales and Marketing Dir, Royal Doulton, 1968–80; Man. Dir, 1980–83; Chairman: Royal Crown Derby, 1972–83; Lawleys Ltd, 1972–83. President: British Ceramic Manufacturers' Fedn, 1982–83; Fedn of European Porcelain and Earthenware Manufacturers, 1982–83. Chm., Water Services Assoc., 1991– (Vice-Chm., 1990–91). Mem., Grand Council, CBI, 1984–. Mem. Court, Keele Univ., 1984–. *Recreations:* ornithology, field sports, reading. *Address:* Tittensor Chase, Staffs ST12 9HH. *Club:* Carlton.

BELLAMY, Rear-Adm. Albert John, CB 1968; OBE 1956; FIMA; first Deputy Director, Polytechnic of the South Bank, 1970–80; *b* Upton-on-Severn, 26 Feb. 1915; *s* of late A. E. Bellamy and late Mrs A. E. Bellamy; *m* 1942, Dorothy Joan Lawson; one *s* one *d*. *Educ:* Hanley Castle Grammar Sch.; Downing Coll., Cambridge (Buchanan Exhibitioner). 1st cl. hons Pts I and II, Math. tripos. Asst master, Berkhamsted Sch., 1936–39. Joined RN, 1939, as Instructor Lieut; Fleet Instr and Meteorological Officer, America and WI, 1948–50 (HMS Glasgow); Instr Comdr, 1950; Headmaster, RN Schs, Malta, 1951–54; HMS Ark Royal, 1955–56; Dean of the College, RN Engineering Coll., Manadon, Plymouth, 1956–60; Instr Capt., 1958; staff of Dir, Naval Educn Service, 1960–63; Dir of Studies, RN Electrical, Weapons and Radio Engineering Sch., HMS Collingwood, 1963–65; Instr Rear-Adm., 1965; Dir, Naval Educn Service and Hd of Instructor Branch, MoD, 1965–70. Mem., Home Office Extended Interview non-Service Mems Panel, 1980–87. *Recreations:* gardening, show jumping (BSJA representative for Dorset), crosswords, parish council work, finance work with two charities. *Address:* The Cottage, Kington Magna, Gillingham, Dorset. *T:* East Stour (074785) 668.

BELLAMY, Alexander (William); retired; Senior Legal Assistant, Council on Tribunals, 1967–76 (temporary Legal Assistant, 1963–67); *b* Aug. 1909; *m* 1931, Lena Marie Lauga Massy. *Educ:* Mill Hill Sch.; Clare Coll., Cambridge. Called to Bar, Gray's Inn, 1934; practised at Bar, London, 1934–38; Magistrate, Straits Settlements and FMS, 1938; seconded as District Magistrate, Gold Coast, 1942; legal staff, Malaya Planning Unit, WO, 1944; Crown Counsel, Singapore, 1946; District Judge (Civil), Singapore, 1948; District Judge and 1st Magistrate, Singapore, 1952; actg Puisne Judge, Fed. of Malaya, 1953–54; Puisne Judge, Supreme Court, Nigeria, 1955; Actg Chief Justice, High Court of Lagos and Southern Cameroons, 1959, 1960; Actg Chief Justice, High Court of Lagos, 1961; a Judge of High Court of Lagos and Southern Cameroons, 1955–62.

BELLAMY, Christopher William; QC 1986; *b* 25 April 1946; *s* of late William Albert Bellamy, TD, MRCS, LRCP and of Vyvienne Hilda, *d* of Albert Meyrick, OBE; *m* 1975, Maria-Elizabeth (*née* Hoffmann) (marr. diss. 1982; she *d* 1986); *m* 1989, Deirdre Patricia (*née* Turner); one *s* one *d*. *Educ:* Tonbridge Sch.; Brasenose Coll., Oxford (MA). Called to the Bar, Middle Temple, 1968; taught in Africa, 1968–69; in practice at Bar, 1970–; Asst Recorder, 1989–. Gov., Ravensbourne Coll. of Design and Communication, 1988–. *Publications:* (with G. Child) Common Market Law of Competition, 1973, 3rd edn 1987, Supplement 1991; papers and articles on legal matters. *Recreations:* history, walking. *Address:* 4 Raymond Buildings, Gray's Inn, WC1R 5BP. *T:* 071–405 7211. *Club:* Athenæum.

BELLAMY, David James, PhD; FLS; FIBiol; botanist; writer and broadcaster; *b* 18 Jan. 1933; *s* of Thomas Bellamy and Winifred (*née* Green); *m* 1959, Rosemary Froy; two *s* three *d*. *Educ:* London University: Chelsea Coll. of Science and Technology (BSc); Bedford Coll. (PhD). Lectr, then Sen. Lectr, Dept of Botany, Univ. of Durham, 1960–80; Hon. Prof. of Adult and Continuing Educn, 1980–82; Special Prof., Nottingham Univ., 1987–; Vis. Prof. of Natural Heritage Studies, Massey Univ., NZ, 1988–89. Founder Dir, Conservation Foundn; Dir, David Bellamy Associates, envmtl consultants, 1988–; Trustee: WWF, 1985–89; Living Landscape Trust, 1985–; President: WATCH, 1982; YHA, 1983–; Population Concern, 1988–; Nat. Assoc. Envmtl Educn, 1989–; Governor, Repton Sch., 1983–89. Chief I Spy, 1983. Presenter and script writer for television and radio programmes, BBC and ITV; programmes include Longest Running Show on Earth, 1985; main series: Life in our Sea, 1970; Bellamy on Botany, 1973; Bellamy's Britain, 1975; Bellamy's Europe, 1977; Botanic Man, 1979; Up a Gum Tree, 1980; Backyard Safari, 1981; The Great Seasons, 1982; Bellamy's New World, 1983; You Can't See The Wood, 1984; Discovery, 1985; Seaside Safari, 1985; End of the Rainbow Show, 1985; Bellamy's Bugle, 1986; Turning the Tide, 1986; The End of the Rainbow Show, 1986; Bellamy's Bird's Eye View, 1988; Moa's Ark, 1990. DUniv Open 1984. Frances Ritchie Meml Prize, Rambler's Assoc., 1989. Order of the Golden Ark (Netherlands), 1989. *Publications:* Peatlands, 1974; Bellamy on Botany, 1974; Bellamy's Britain, 1975; Bellamy's Europe, 1977; Life Giving Sea, 1977; Botanic Man, 1978; Half of Paradise, 1979; The Great Seasons, 1981; Backyard Safari, 1981; Discovering the Countryside with David Bellamy: vols I and II, 1982, vols III and IV, 1983; The Mouse Book, 1983; Bellamy's New World, 1983; The Queen's Hidden Garden, 1984; Turning the Tide, 1986; The Vanishing Bogs of Ireland, 1986; Bellamy's Changing Countryside, 4 vols, 1989; (with Brendan Quayle) England's Last Wilderness, 1989; England's Lost Wilderness, 1990; (with Jane Gifford) Wilderness in Britain, 1991. *Recreations:* children, ballet. *Address:* Mill House, Bedburn, Bishop Auckland, Co. Durham DL13 3NW.

BELLAMY, Prof. Edmund Henry, MA, PhD; Professor of Physics in the University of London, Westfield College, 1960–84, now Emeritus; *b* 8 April 1923; *s* of Herbert Bellamy and Nellie (*née* Ablett); *m* 1946, Joan Roberts; three *s*. *Educ:* Quarry Bank Sch., Liverpool; King's Coll., Cambridge. Lectr in Natural Philosophy, Univ. of Glasgow, 1951–59, Sen. Lectr, 1959–60; Vis. Physicist, Univ. of Pisa, 1960. Mem., Nuclear Physics Board of Science Research Council, 1965–66. Visiting Professor: Univ. of Stanford, 1966–67; Univ. of Pisa, 1985–86; Emeritus Fellow, Leverhulme Trust, 1987–89; Consultant, Univ. of Florida, 1990. *Publications:* numerous scientific papers in Proc. Phys. Soc. and other journals. *Recreations:* skiing, squash, travel, football, golf. *Address:* 134 Main Road, Long Hanborough, Oxford OX7 2JY. *T:* Freeland (0993) 882227.

BELLAMY, (Kenneth) Rex; Tennis Correspondent, The Times, 1967–89; *b* 15 Sept. 1928; *s* of Sampson Bellamy and Kathleen May Bellamy; *m* 1951, Hilda O'Shea; one step *d*. *Educ:* Yeovil; Woodhouse Grammar Sch., Sheffield. National Service, RA and RASC, 1946–49. Sports and Feature Writer, Sheffield Telegraph, 1944–46 and 1949–53; Sports Writer: Birmingham Gazette, 1953–56; The Times, 1956–89. Mem., Inst. of Journalists. World Championship Tennis award for service to tennis, 1988; International Tennis-writing Awards: 5 from Assoc. of Tennis Professionals, 1975–79 (award discontinued); 2 from Women's Tennis Assoc., 1977–78. *Publications:* Teach Yourself Squash (jtly), 1968; The Tennis Set, 1972; The Story of Squash, 1978 rev. edn as Squash—A History, 1988; The Peak District Companion, 1981; Walking the Tops, 1984; Game, Set and Deadline, 1986; Love Thirty, 1990; Four Peaks, 1992. *Recreations:* hill-walking, golf. *Address:* 8

Guillards Oak, Midhurst, W Sussex GU29 9JZ. *Clubs:* Jesters (Hon. Mem.); Cowdray Park Golf.

BELLANY, Prof. Ian; Professor of Politics, University of Lancaster, since 1979; *b* 21 Feb. 1941; *s* of James Bellany and Jemima Bellany (*née* Emlay); *m* 1965, Wendy Ivey, *d* of Glyndwr and Bronwen Thomas; one *s* one *d*. *Educ:* Preston Lodge, Prestonpans; Firth Park Grammar Sch., Sheffield; Balliol Coll., Oxford (State Scholar, MA, DPhil). Foreign and Commonwealth Office, 1965–68; Res. Fellow in Internat. Relations, ANU, 1968–70; University of Lancaster: Lectr. later Sen. Lectr in Politics, 1970–79; Dir, Centre for Study of Arms Control and Internat. Security, 1979–90; Head, Dept of Politics, 1985–86. NATO Instl Fellow, 1989–90. Mem., Govt Adv. Panel on Disarmament, 1981–. Examr in Internat. Relations, LSE, 1985–88, in Internat. Studies, Birmingham Univ., 1990–. Founding Editor, Arms Control: Journal of Arms Control and Disarmament, 1980–91. *Publications:* Australia in the Nuclear Age, 1972; A Basis for Arms Control, 1991; edited jointly: Antiballistic Missile Defences in the 1980s, 1983; The Verification of Arms Control Agreements, 1983; The Nuclear Non-Proliferation Treaty, 1985; New Conventional Weapons and Western Defence, 1987; contribs to jls. *Recreations:* coarse carpentry, computing. *Address:* 42 Barton Road, Lancaster LA1 4ER. *T:* Lancaster (0524) 68157.

BELLANY, John, RA 1991 (ARA 1986); artist (painter); *b* Scotland, 18 June 1942; *s* of Richard Weatherhead Bellany and Agnes Craig Bellany; *m* 1st, 1964, Helen Margaret Percy (marr. diss. 1974); two *s* one *d*; 2nd, 1980, Juliet Gray (*née* Lister) (*d* 1985); 3rd, 1986 (for 2nd time), Helen Margaret Bellany. *Educ:* Cockenzie Public Sch., Scotland; Preston Lodge Sch., Scotland; Edinburgh Coll. of Art (DA); Royal Coll. of Art (MA Fine Art; ARCA). Lectr in Fine Art in various art colls and univs in Gt Britain, incl. Winchester Coll. of Art, Goldsmiths' Coll., London Univ., RCA; Artist in Residence, Victorian Coll. of the Arts, Melb., 1982. One man exhibitions: Nat. Portrait Gall., 1986; Fischer Fine Art, London, 1988–89; many others in Britain, USA, Australia, Europe; retrospective exhibitions: Scottish Nat. Gall. of Modern Art, Edin., and Serpentine Gall., London, 1986; Kunsthalle, Hamburg, 1988. Works represented in major museums and private collections throughout the world, incl. Tate Gall., V&A Mus., Mus. of Modern Art, NY; Metropolitan Mus., NY. Hon. Fellow Commoner, Trinity Hall, Cambridge, 1988. Hon. RSA 1987. Relevant publications: John Bellany, by Victor Musgrave and Philip Rawson, 1982; John Bellany, a Retrospective, by Douglas Hall, 1986; John Bellany (Portraits) (The Maxi Hudson Collection), by Robin Gibson, 1986; John Bellany, by Richard Cork, 1986; John Bellany, Retrospective, by Prof. D. Werner Hofmann and Keith Hartley, 1988. *Recreation:* climbing to and fro across Hadrian's Wall. *Address:* 59 Northside, Clapham Common, SW4 9SA. *T:* 071–228 0868; 19 Great Stuart Street, Edinburgh. *T:* 031–226 5183; c/o Fischer Fine Art, 30 King Street, SW1. *T:* 071–839 3942. *Club:* Scottish Arts (Edinburgh).

BELLENGER, Rev. Dr Dominic Terence Joseph, (Rev. Dom Aidan Bellenger), FRHistS; Head Master, Downside School, since 1991; *b* 21 July 1950; *s* of Gerald Bellenger and Kathleen Bellenger (*née* O'Donnell). *Educ:* Finchley Grammar Sch.; Jesus Coll., Cambridge (Scholar, MA, PhD); Angelicum Univ., Rome. Res. Student in History, 1972–78 and Lightfoot Schol. in Eccl. Hist., Cambridge, 1975–78; Assistant Master: St Mary's Sch., Cambridge, 1975–78; Downside Sch., 1978–82; Benedictine Monk, Downside Abbey, 1982; Priest, 1988; Housemaster, Downside Sch., 1989–91. Member: Cttee, Eccl. Hist. Soc., 1982–85; Cttee, English Benedictine Hist. Commn, 1987–; Council, Catholic Record Soc., 1990–; Trustee, Catholic Family Hist. Soc., 1990–. Leverhulme Res. Award, 1986. FRSA. Editor, South Western Catholic History, 1982–. *Publications:* English and Welsh Priests 1558–1800, 1984; The French Exiled Clergy, 1986; Opening the Scrolls, 1987; Letters of Bede Jarrett, 1989; (contrib.) Mélanges Charles Molette, 1989; articles in learned jls. *Recreations:* books, church architecture, talk, travel, writing. *Address:* Downside School, Stratton-on-the-Fosse, Bath BA3 4RJ, *T:* Stratton-on-the-Fosse (0761) 232206.

BELLEW, family name of **Baron Bellew.**

BELLEW; *see* Grattan-Bellew.

BELLEW, 7th Baron *cr* 1848; **James Bryan Bellew;** Bt 1688; *b* 5 Jan. 1920; *s* of 6th Baron Bellew, MC, and Jeanie Ellen Agnes (*d* 1973), *d* of late James Ormsby Jameson; *S* father, 1981; *m* 1st, 1942, Mary Elizabeth (*d* 1978), *d* of Rev. Edward Eustace Hill; two *s* one *d*; 2nd, 1978, Gwendoline, formerly wife of Major P. Hall and *d* of late Charles Redmond Clayton-Daubeny. Served War of 1939–45, Irish Guards (Captain). *Heir: s* Hon. Bryan Edward Bellew [*b* 19 March 1943; *m* 1968, Rosemary Sarah, *d* of Major Reginald Kilner Brasier Hitchcock; two *s*]. *Address:* Barmeath Castle, County Louth, S Ireland; Burgage House, Sheep Street, Stow on the Wold, Glos.

BELLEW, Hon. Sir George (Rothe), KCB 1961; KCVO 1953 (CVO 1950; MVO 1935); Kt 1950; FSA 1948; Secretary of the Order of the Garter, 1961–74, Garter Principal King of Arms, 1950–61; Genealogist of the Order of the Bath, 1950–61; Genealogist Order of St John, 1951–61; Knight Principal of Imperial Society of Knights Bachelor, 1957–62 (Deputy Knight Principal, 1962–71); Inspector of Regimental Colours, 1957–61; *b* 13 Dec. 1899; *s* of late Hon. Richard Bellew and Gwendoline, *d* of William R. J. Fitzherbert Herbert-Huddleston of Clytha; *m* 1935, Ursula Kennard, *e d* of late Anders Eric Knös Cull, Warfield House, Bracknell; one *s*. *Educ:* Wellington Coll.; Christ Church, Oxford. Served War of 1939–45: Squadron Leader RAFVR, 1940–45 (despatches). Formerly Portcullis Pursuivant of Arms; Somerset Herald, 1926–50, and Registrar of the Coll. of Arms, 1935–46. KStJ 1951 (Mem. Chapter Gen., 1951–). *Address:* The Grange, Old Park Lane, Farnham, Surrey GU9 0AH.

BELLINGER, Sir Robert (Ian), GBE 1967; Kt 1964; Chairman: Kinloch (PM) Ltd, 1946–75; National Savings Committee, 1970–75, and President, 1972–75; Director, Rank Organisation, 1971–83; *b* Tetbury, Glos, 10 March 1910; *s* of David Morgan Bellinger, Cardiganshire, and Jane Ballantine Deans, Edinburgh; *m* 1962, Christiane Marie Louise Janssens, Brussels; one *s* one *d*. *Educ:* Church of England sch. Elected Court of Common Council, 1953; Chm. City of London Freemen's Sch., 1957; Alderman for Ward of Cheap, 1958; Sheriff, City of London, 1962–63; Lord Mayor of London, 1966–67; one of HM Lieutenants, City of London, 1976–. Chairman: Panel for Civil Service Manpower Review, 1968–71; Adv. Cttee on Magistracy, City of London, 1968–76; Licensing Cttee, City of London; Finance Cttee, BBC; Governor, BBC, 1968–71; Trustee, St Paul's Cathedral Trust, 1977–; Dir, Arsenal Football Club. Chairman: Anglo-Danish Soc., 1976–83; Danish Trade Adv. Bd, 1979–82. Past Master, Broderers' Company; Liveryman, Fletchers' Company. Hon. DSc City Univ., 1966. Gentleman Usher of the Purple Rod, Order of the British Empire, 1969–85. KStJ 1966; Commandeur, Ordre de Léopold, cl. III (Belgium), 1963; Comdr, Royal Order of the Phoenix (Greece), 1963; Officier, Ordre de la Valeur Camerounaise (Cameroons), 1963; Knight Comdr of the Order of Dannebrog (Denmark), 1977. *Recreations:* tennis, football, music, motoring. *Address:* Penn Wood, Fulmer, Bucks. *T:* Fulmer (0753) 662029. *Club:* City Livery.

BELLINGHAM, Henry Campbell; MP (C) Norfolk North West, since 1983; *b* 29 March 1955; *s* of late Henry Bellingham. *Educ:* Eton; Magdalene Coll., Cambridge (BA 1977). Called to the Bar, Middle Temple, 1978. Partner in family farming and property co.; Underwriting Mem. of Lloyd's. Founder, W Norfolk Small Business Bureau, 1982; Founder-Mem. and sponsor, W Norfolk Local Enterprise Agency, 1986–; Mem. Exec., Nat. Small Business Bureau, 1982–. PPS to Sec. of State for Transport, 1990–. Mem., Select Cttee on the Environment, 1987–; Jt Vice Chm., Cons. Parly Smaller Businesses Cttee, 1987– (Sec., 1983–87); Jt Sec., Cons. NI Cttee, 1983–. Chm., Cons. Council on E Europe, 1989–. *Address:* House of Commons, SW1A 0AA. *Clubs:* White's, Pratt's.

BELLINGHAM, Sir Noel (Peter Roger), 7th Bt (2nd creation) *cr* 1796; accountant; *b* 4 Sept. 1943; *s* of Sir Roger Carroll Patrick Stephen Bellingham, 6th Bt, and of Mary, *d* of late William Norman; *S* father, 1973; *m* 1977, Jane, *d* of late Edwin William and of Joan Taylor, Sale, Cheshire. *Heir: b* Anthony Edward Norman Bellingham, *b* 24 March 1947. *Address:* 20 Davenport Park Road, Davenport, Stockport, Cheshire. *T:* 061–483 7168. *Club:* 64 Society (Cheshire).

BELLIS, Bertram Thomas; Headmaster, The Leys School, Cambridge, 1975–86; *b* 4 May 1927; *s* of Rev. Thomas J. Bellis and Mary A. Bellis; *m* 1952, Joan Healey; two *s*. *Educ:* Kingswood Sch., Bath; St John's Coll., Cambridge (Exhibr in Maths, MA). Rossall Sch., 1951–55; Highgate Sch., 1955–65; Headmaster, Daniel Stewart's Coll., 1965–72; Principal, Daniel Stewart's and Melville Coll., 1972–75. Chm., Scottish Educn Dept Cttee on Computers and the Schools (reports, 1969 and 1972); Member: Council, Inst. of Math., 1975–79; Educational Research Bd, SSRC, 1975–80. Governor: Queenswood Sch., 1980–; St John's Coll. Sch., 1981–86. Pres., Mathematical Assoc., 1971–72. Schoolmaster Fellow, Balliol Coll., Oxford, 1963; FIMA 1964; FRSE 1972. *Recreation:* fell walking. *Address:* 2 Eller Raise, Kendal, Cumbria LA9 6AB.

BELLIS, John Herbert; Chairman of Industrial Tribunals, Manchester Region, since 1984; *b* 11 April 1930; *s* of Thomas and Jane Bellis; *m* 1961, Sheila Helen McNeil Ford; two *s* one *d*. *Educ:* Friars Grammar Sch., Bangor; Liverpool Univ. (LLB). Admitted Solicitor, 1953. National Service, 1953–55. In practice as solicitor on own account, Penmaenmawr, N Wales, 1958–84. Parly Cand. (L) Conway, Caernarvonshire, 1959. *Recreations:* golf, walking, gardening. *Address:* 148 Grove Lane, Cheadle Hulme, Cheadle, Cheshire SK8 7NH. *T:* 061–439 7582.

BELLO, Mohammed; CON 1965; **Hon. Mr Justice Bello**; Chief Justice of Nigeria, since 1987; *b* 1930; *s* of Mallam Muhammadu Gidado; *m* 1962; many *c*. *Educ:* Harvard Law School. Called to the Bar, Lincoln's Inn. Northern Nigeria appointments: Crown Counsel, 1956; Magistrate, 1961; Dir of Public Prosecutions, 1964; Judge of the High Court, 1966; Senior Puisne Judge, North-Central and Kwara States, 1968; occasional Acting Chief Justice, Northern State, 1969–75; Justice of Supreme Court of Nigeria, 1975. Fellow, Nigerian Inst. of Advanced Legal Studies, 1984. Hon. LLD: Ibadan, 1987; Ahmadu Bello, 1990. *Recreation:* rambling. *Address:* (home) 15 Ikoyi Crescent, Lagos, Nigeria. *T:* 01–618847; Supreme Court of Nigeria, Lagos, Nigeria. *T:* 01–635426.

BELLOTTI, David Frank; MP (Lib Dem) Eastbourne, since Oct. 1990; *b* 13 Aug. 1943; *s* of Patrick Frank Bellotti and Elsie (*née* Venner); *m* 1st, 1965, Sheila (*née* Jones); one *s* one *d*; 2nd, 1973, Jennifer (*née* Compson) (separated); one *s*. *Educ:* Exeter Sch.; YMCA National Coll. (Diploma in Youth Service); Brighton Polytechnic (Diploma in Counselling). Civil Service, 1961–64; Young Men's Christian Association: student, Nat. Coll., 1964–65; Sec., St Helens, Llanelli, Norwich and Lewes, 1965–76; Regional Sec., South-East, 1977–81; Dir, Hove, 1981–90. *Recreations:* Association Football, politics, snooker. *Address:* House of Commons, SW1A 0AA. *T:* 071–219 5131; 45 Gildredge Road, Eastbourne BN21 4RY. *T:* Eastbourne (0323) 642499. *Club:* National Liberal.

BELLOW, family name of **Baron Bellwin**.

BELLOW, Saul; American writer; *b* 10 June 1915; *s* of Abraham and Liza Gordon Bellow; marr. diss.; three *s*. *Educ:* Univ. of Chicago; Northwestern Univ. Nobel Prize for Literature, 1976; Malaparté Prize for Literature, Italy, 1984. Hon. DLitt, Northwestern Univ., 1962. Commander, Legion of Honour (France), 1983; Commander, Order of Arts and Letters (France), 1985 (Croix de Chevalier, 1968). *Publications:* Dangling Man, 1944 (reissued 1972); The Victim, 1947; The Adventures of Augie March, 1953 (National Book Award, 1954); Seize the Day, 1956; Henderson the Rain King, 1959; Herzog, 1964 (National Book Award, Internat. Literary Prize, 1965); Mosby's Memoirs and Other Stories, 1969; Mr Sammler's Planet, 1970 (National Book Award, 1970); Humboldt's Gift, 1975 (Pulitzer Prize 1976); To Jerusalem and Back, 1976; The Dean's December, 1982; (short stories) Him with His Foot in His Mouth, 1984; More Die of Heartbreak, 1987; The Theft, 1989; The Bellarosa Connection, 1989. *Address:* University of Chicago, Chicago, Ill 60637, USA.

BELLOWS, James Gilbert; Senior Vice-President, News/MediaNews Group, since 1990; *b* 12 Nov. 1922; *s* of Lyman Hubbard Bellows and Dorothy Gilbert Bellows; *m* 1950, Marian Raines (decd); three *d*; *m* 1964, Maggie Savoy (decd); *m* 1971, Keven Ryan; one *d*. *Educ:* Kenyon Coll. (BA, LLB). Columbus (Ga) Ledger, 1947; News Editor Atlanta (Ga) Jl, 1950–57; Asst Editor, Detroit (Mich.) Free Press, 1957–58; Managing Editor Miami (Fla) News, 1958–61; Exec. Editor (News Ops), NY Herald Tribune, 1961–62; Editor, 1962–66; associate Editor, Los Angeles Times, 1966–75; Editor: Washington Star, 1975–78; Los Angeles Herald Examiner, 1979–82; Managing Editor, Entertainment Tonight (TV show), 1982–83; Exec. Producer, ABC-TV News, 1983–86; Dir of Editorial Develt, Prodigy, 1986–88; Managing Editor, USA Today on TV, 1988–89. Member: Kenyon Review Adv. Bd; Amer. Soc. of Newspaper Editors. *Address:* 1153 Rockingham, Los Angeles, Calif 90049, USA. *Club:* Bel-Air Country (Los Angeles).

BELLWIN, Baron *cr* 1979 (Life Peer), of the City of Leeds; **Irwin Norman Bellow**; JP; *b* 7 Feb. 1923; *s* of Abraham and Leah Bellow; *m* 1948, Doreen Barbara Saperia; one *s* two *d*. *Educ:* Lovell Road; Leeds Grammar School; Leeds Univ. LLB. Leader, Leeds City Council, 1975–79; Vice-Chm. Assoc. of Metropolitan Authorities, 1978–79. Parly Under Sec. of State, DoE, 1979–Jan. 1983; Minister of State, 1983–84. Mem., Commn for New Towns, 1985–; Vice-Pres., Internat. New Towns Assoc, 1985–. Non-executive Director: Taylor Woodrow, 1985–; Sinclair Goldsmith Holding, 1986–; Mountleigh Gp, 1987–; Trimoco plc, 1988–. JP Leeds, 1969. *Recreation:* golf. *Address:* Woodside Lodge, Ling Lane, Scarcroft, Leeds LS14 3HX. *T:* Leeds (0532) 892908. *Club:* Moor Allerton Golf (Club Pres.).

BELMORE, 8th Earl of, *cr* 1797; **John Armar Lowry-Corry**; Baron Belmore, 1781; Viscount Belmore, 1789; *b* 4 Sept. 1951; *s* of 7th Earl of Belmore and Gloria Anthea, *d* of late Herbert Bryant Harker, Melbourne, Australia; *S* father 1960; *m* 1984, Lady Mary Meade, *d* of 6th Earl of Clanwilliam; two *s*. *Educ:* Lancing; Royal Agricultural Coll., Cirencester. *Heir: s* Viscount Corry, *qv*. *Recreation:* fishing. *Address:* The Garden House, Castle Coole, Enniskillen, Co. Fermanagh, N Ireland BT74 6JX. *T:* Enniskillen (0365) 322463. *Club:* Kildare Street and University (Dublin).

BELOFF, family name of **Baron Beloff**.

BELOFF, Baron *cr* 1981 (Life Peer), of Wolvercote in the County of Oxfordshire; **Max Beloff**; Kt 1980; MA, DLitt (Oxon); FBA 1973; FRHistS; FRSA; *b* 2 July 1913; *er s* of late Simon and Mary Beloff; *m* 1938, Helen Dobrin; two *s*. *Educ:* St Paul's Sch.; Corpus Christi Coll., Oxford (Scholar). Gibbs Schol. in Mod. Hist., 1934; 1st Cl. Hons, School of Modern History, 1935; Senior Demy, Magdalen Coll., Oxford, 1935. Junior Research Fellow, Corpus Christi Coll., 1937; Asst Lecturer in History, Manchester Univ., 1939–46; Nuffield Reader in Comparative Study of Institutions, Oxford Univ., 1946–56; Fellow of Nuffield Coll., 1947–57; Gladstone Prof. of Govt and Public Admin, Oxford Univ., 1957–74, now Professor Emeritus, and Fellow, All Souls Coll., 1957–74, Emeritus Fellow, 1980–; Supernumerary Fellow, St Antony's Coll., Oxford, 1975–84; Principal, University Coll. at Buckingham, 1974–79. War of 1939–45, Royal Corps of Signals, 1940–41. Governor, Haifa Univ.; Ex-Trustee and Ex-Librarian, Oxford Union Soc. Hon. Fellow, Mansfield Coll., Oxford, 1989. Hon. LLD: Pittsburgh, USA, 1962; Manchester Univ., 1989; Hon. DCL, Bishop's Univ. Canada, 1976; Hon. DLitt Bowdoin Coll., USA, 1976; Hon. DrUniv. Aix-Marseille III, 1978. *Publications:* Public Order and Popular Disturbances, 1660–1714, 1938; The Foreign Policy of Soviet Russia, Vol. 1, 1947, Vol. 2, 1949; Thomas Jefferson and American Democracy, 1948; Soviet Policy in the Far East, 1944–51, 1953; The Age of Absolutism, 1660–1815, 1954; Foreign Policy and the Democratic Process, 1955; Europe and the Europeans, 1957; The Great Powers, 1959; The American Federal Government, 1959; New Dimensions in Foreign Policy, 1961; The United States and the Unity of Europe, 1963; The Balance of Power, 1967; The Future of British Foreign Policy, 1969; Imperial Sunset, vol. 1, 1969, 2nd edn 1988, vol. 2, Dream of Commonwealth 1921–42, 1989; The Intellectual in Politics, 1970; (with G. R. Peele) The Government of the United Kingdom, 1980, 2nd edn 1985; Wars and Welfare 1914–1945, 1984; edited: The Federalist 1948, 2nd edn 1987; Mankind and his Story, 1948; The Debate on the American Revolution, 1949, 2nd edn 1989; On the Track of Tyranny, 1959; (jtly) L'Europe du XIXe et XXe siècle, 1960–67; (with V. Vale) American Political Institutions in the 1970's, 1975; articles in English, French, Italian and American journals. *Recreation:* watching cricket. *Address:* c/o House of Lords, SW1. *T:* 071–219 6669. *Club:* Reform.
See also Hon. Michael Beloff.

BELOFF, Hon. Michael Jacob, MA; QC 1981; barrister and writer; a Recorder, since 1985; a Deputy High Court Judge, since 1989; *b* 19 April 1942; *s* of Baron Beloff, *qv*; *m* 1969, Judith Mary Arkinstall; one *s* one *d*. *Educ:* Dragon Sch., Oxford; Eton Coll. (King's Schol.; Captain of Sch. 1960); Magdalen Coll., Oxford (Demy; H. W. C. Davis Prizeman, 1962; BA Hist. (1st cl.) 1963, Law 1965; MA 1967). Pres., Oxford Union Soc., 1962; Oxford Union tour of USA, 1964. Called to the Bar, Gray's Inn, 1967 (Gerald Moody Schol., 1963; Atkin Schol., 1967), Bencher, 1988. Lectr in Law, Trinity Coll., Oxford, 1965–66. Legal Correspondent: New Society, 1969–79; The Observer, 1979–81. Vice-Pres., Administrative Law Bar Assoc., (first Chm., 1986–90); Mem., Bingham Law Reform Cttee on Discovery of Documents and Disclosure, 1982–; Chm., Oxford Univ. Tribunal into Alleged Plagiarism, 1990. Hon. Mem., Internat. Athletes' Club. *Publications:* A Short Walk on the Campus (with J. Aitken), 1966; The Plateglass Universities, 1968; The Sex Discrimination Act, 1976; Halsbury's Laws of England (contribution on Time), 1983; (contrib.) Judicial Safeguards in Administrative Proceedings, 1989; contrib. Encounter, Minerva, Irish Jurist, Political Qly, Current Legal Problems, Public Law, etc. *Recreation:* running. *Address:* 58 Park Town, Oxford OX2 6SJ; 41 Campden Hill Square, W8; 4–5 Gray's Inn Square, Gray's Inn, WC1R 5AY. *T:* 071–404 5252. *Clubs:* Reform; Vincent's (Oxford).

BELOFF, Nora; author and journalist; *b* 24 Jan. 1919; *m* 1977, Clifford Makins (*d* 1990). *Educ:* King Alfred Sch.; Lady Margaret Hall, Oxford. BA Hons History 1940. Polit. Intell. Dept, FO, 1941–44; British Embassy, Paris, 1944–45; reporter, Reuters News Agency, 1945–46; Paris corresp., The Economist, 1946–48; Observer corresp., Paris, Washington, Moscow, Brussels etc, 1948–78; political correspondent, 1964–76; roving correspondent, 1976–78. *Publications:* The General Says No, 1963; The Transit of Britain, 1973; Freedom under Foot, 1976; No Travel like Russian Travel, 1979 (US, as Inside the Soviet Empire: myth and reality, 1980); Tito's Flawed Legacy: Yugoslavia and the West 1939–1984, 1985 (US, as Tito's Flawed Legacy: Yugoslavia and the West 1939 till now, 1986; trans. Italian, 1987, Slovene, 1990, Serbo-Croat, 1991). *Address:* 11 Belsize Road, NW6 4RX. *T:* 071–586 0378.

BELPER, 4th Baron *cr* 1856; **Alexander Ronald George Strutt**; formerly Major, Coldstream Guards; *b* 23 April 1912; *s* of 3rd Baron and Hon. Eva Isabel Mary Bruce (*d* 1987), 2nd *d* of 2nd Baron Aberdare (she *m* 2nd, 6th Earl of Rosebery); *S* father 1956; *m* 1940, Zara Sophie Kathleen Mary (marr. diss. 1949), *y d* of Sir Harry Mainwaring, 5th Bt; one *s*. *Educ:* Harrow. Served War with Coldstream Guards, 1939–44 (wounded). *Heir: s* Hon. Richard Henry Strutt [*b* 24 Oct. 1941; *m* 1966, Jennifer Vivian, *d* of late Capt. Peter Winser and of Mrs James Whitaker; one *s* one *d*; *m* 1980, Judith Mary de Jonge, *d* of Mr and Mrs James Twynam, Kitemore House, Faringdon, Oxon]. *Address:* Kingston Hall, Nottingham.

BELSKY, Franta; sculptor; *b* Brno, 6 April 1921; *s* of Joseph Belsky, economist; *m* Margaret Owen (cartoonist Belsky) (*d* 1989). *Educ:* Acad. of Fine Arts, Prague; Royal Coll. of Art, London. ARCA, Hons Dip. 1950. Served War as gunner (France, 1940) Normandy, 1944; various decorations. Taught in art schs, 1950–55. FRBS (Mem. Council); Pres., Soc. of Portrait Sculptors, 1963–68; Governor, St Martin's Sch. of Art, 1967–88. Work in Nat. Portrait Gall. and collections in Europe and USA, for numerous co. councils, industrial, shipping and private cos and educn authorities: Paratroop Memorial, Prague, 1947; Lt-Col Peniakoff (Popski), Ravenna, 1952; statue of Cecil Rhodes, 8', Bulawayo, 1953; groups: Constellation, Colchester, 1953; Lesson, LCC housing develt, 1957–58; Triga, Knightsbridge, 1958; Joy-ride, Stevenage New Town Centre, 1958; Astronomer Herschel Memorial, 18', Slough, 1969; Oracle, 18', Temple Way House, Bristol, 1975 (RBS Sir Otto Beit Medal, 1976); Totem, 32', Manchester Arndale Centre, 1975 (RBS Sir Otto Beit Medal, 1978); fountains: European Shell Centre, 30', South Bank, 1961; Leap, 26', Blackwall Basin, 1988; reliefs: Epicentre, Doncaster City Centre, 1965; 1978 Jean Masson Davidson Award for Dist. in Portrait Sculpture; portraits include: Queen Mother, Birmingham Univ., 1962; Prince Philip, 1979 and HM the Queen, 1981, Nat. Portrait Gall.; Prince Andrew, 1963 and 1984; Prince William, 1985; statue of Sir Winston Churchill for Churchill Meml and Library in US, Fulton, Missouri, and bust in Churchill Archives, Cambridge, 1971 and Nat. Gall., Prague, 1990; Harry S. Truman, Presidential Library, Independence, Mo and H. S. T. Dam, Osage River, Mo; Adm. Cunningham, Trafalgar Square, 1969; Lord Cottesloe, Nat. Theatre; Mountbatten Meml, Horse Guards Parade, 1983, and bust, Queen Elizabeth II Conf. Centre, Westminster, 1986; Adm. Lord Lewin, HMS Dryad, 1985. Queen Mother 80th Birthday Crown coin. *Publications:* illus. and contrib. various books and jls. *Recreations:* ski-ing, gardening, amateur archaeology. *Address:* 4 The Green, Sutton Courtenay, Abingdon OX14 4AE.

BELSTEAD, 2nd Baron, *cr* 1938; **John Julian Ganzoni**; Bt 1929; PC 1983; JP; DL; HM Paymaster General, and Minister at the Northern Ireland Office, since 1990; *b* 30

Sept. 1932; *o s* of 1st Baron Belstead and Gwendolen Gertrude Turner (*d* 1962); *S* father, 1958. *Educ:* Eton; Christ Church, Oxford. MA 1961. Parliamentary Under-Secretary of State: DES, 1970–73; NI Office, 1973–74; Home Office, 1979–82; Minister of State: FCO, 1982–83; MAFF, 1983–87; DoE, 1987–88. Dep. Leader, H of L, 1983–87. Leader, H of L and Lord Privy Seal, 1988–90. Chm., Assoc. of Governing Bodies of Public Schools, 1974–79. JP Borough of Ipswich, 1962; DL Suffolk, 1979. *Heir:* none. *Address:* House of Lords, SW1A 0PW. *T:* 071-219 3000. *Clubs:* All England Lawn Tennis (Wimbledon); MCC.

BELTRAM, Geoffrey; Under-Secretary, Department of Health and Social Security, 1973–81; *b* 7 April 1921; *s* of George and Beatrice Dorothy Beltram; *m* 1945, Audrey Mary (*née* Harkett); one *s* one *d*. *Educ:* Dame Alice Owen's School. Tax Officer, Inland Revenue, 1938; served in RAF, 1941–46; Exec. Officer and Higher Exec. Officer, Min. of Town and Country Planning, 1947–51; Asst Principal, Nat. Assistance Bd, 1951–55; Principal 1955–63; Asst Sec. 1963–73 (NAB 1963–66, Min. of Social Security 1966–68, DHSS 1968–73). Vis. Res. Associate, LSE, 1981–84. *Publication:* Testing the Safety Net: a study of the Supplementary Benefit scheme, 1984. *Recreations:* literature, listening to music, opera, ballet, walking, tennis, swimming, writing.

BEN-TOVIM, Atarah, (Mrs Douglas Boyd), MBE 1980 (for services to children's music); Founder and Artistic Director, Children's Concert Centre, since 1975; *b* 1 Oct. 1940; *d* of Tsvi Ben-Tovim and Gladys Ben-Tovim; *m* 1976, Douglas Boyd; one *d*. *Educ:* Royal Acad. of Music, London. ARAM 1967. Principal Flautist, Royal Liverpool Philharmonic Orchestra, 1962–75; children's concerts with Atarah's Band, 1973–88. *Publications:* Atarah's Book (autobiog.), 1976, 2nd edn 1979; Atarah's Band Kits (14 published), 1978–; Children and Music, 1979; (jtly) The Right Instrument For Your Child, 1985; You Can Make Music!, 1986. *Recreations:* music, writing, France and the Mediterranean. *Address:* c/o Watson Little Ltd, 12 Egbert Street, NW1 8LJ. *T:* 071–722 9514.

BENABDELJALIL, Mohamed-Mehdi; Ambassador of the Kingdom of Morocco to the Court of St James's, 1981–86; *b* 12 Jan. 1930; *m* 1962, Mrs Kinza Abdelkhalek Torres; two *s* one *d*. *Educ:* Imperial Coll., Rabat, Morocco; Faculty of Law, Univ. of Paris; Inst. for Internat. Studies, and Inst. for Polit. Studies, Paris. Formerly: Head of Cabinet of Minister i/c Negotiations; Head of Cabinet of Minister of Interior; Head, Dept of Mines and Geology; Under-Sec. of State for Indust. Prodn and Mining; Gen. Sec., Min. of National Economy; Dir Gen., Bureau des Etudes et des Participations Industrielles; successively Ambassador in Bonn and Tehran (with accreditation to Turkey and Afghanistan); law practice, Casablanca, 1973–80. Grand Cross: West Germany; Lebanon; Iran. *Recreations:* sport, hunting. *Address:* c/o Ministry of Foreign Affairs and Co-operation, Casablanca, Morocco.

BENACERRAF, Prof. Baruj; Fabyan Professor of Comparative Pathology and Chairman of the Department of Pathology, Harvard Medical School, since 1970; President, Dana-Farber Cancer Institute, Boston, since 1980; *b* 29 Oct. 1920; *m* 1943, Annette Dreyfus; one *d*. *Educ:* Lycée Janson, Paris (BèsL 1940); Columbia Univ. (BS 1942); Medical Coll. of Virginia (MD 1945). Served US Army, 1946–48. Intern, Queens Gen. Hosp., NY, 1945–46; Res. Fellow, Dept of Micro-biol., Coll. of Physicians and Surgeons, Columbia Univ., 1948–49; Chargé de Recherches, CNRS, Hôpital Broussais, Paris, 1950–56; New York University School of Medicine: Asst Prof. of Pathol., 1956–58; Assoc. Prof. of Pathol., 1958–60; Prof. of Pathol., 1960–68; Chief, Lab. of Immunol., Nat. Inst. of Allergy and Infectious Diseases, NIH, Bethesda, 1968–70. Scientific Advr, WHO; Chm., Scientific Adv. Cttee, Centre d'Immunologie de Marseille, CNRS-INSERM; Member: Immunology A Study Sect., NIH, 1965–69; Adv. Council, National Inst. of Allergy and Infectious Disease, 1985–88; Scientific Adv. Cttee, Basel Inst. of Immunology, 1985–89; Member Scientific Advisory Board: Trudeau Foundn, 1970–76; Mass Gen. Hosp., 1971–74. President: Amer. Assoc. of Immunologists, 1973–74; Fedn of Amer. Socs for Exptl Biol., 1974–75; Internat. Union of Immunol Socs, 1980–83. Fellow, Amer. Acad. of Arts and Scis, 1972. Correspondent Emérite, Institut National de la Santé et de la Recherche Scientifique, 1988. Member: Nat. Acad. of Scis, 1973; Nat. Inst. of Med., 1981; Amer. Assoc. of Pathologists and Bacteriologists; Amer. Soc. for Exptl Pathol.; British Assoc. for Immunol.; French Soc. of Biol Chem.; Harvey Soc. Lectures: R. E. Dyer, NIH, 1969; Harvey, 1971, 1972; J. S. Blumenthal, Univ. of Minnesota, 1980. Hon. MD Geneva, 1980; Hon. DSc: Virginia Commonwealth Univ., 1981; NY Univ., 1981; Yeshiva Univ., 1982; Univ. Aix-Marseille, 1982; Columbia Univ., 1985; Adelphi Univ., 1988; Weizmann Inst., 1989. Rabbi Shai Shacknai Lectr and Prize, Hebrew Univ. of Jerusalem, 1974; T. Duckett Jones Meml Award, Helen Hay Whitney Foundn, 1976; Waterford Biomedical Science Award, 1980; (jtly) Nobel Prize for Physiology or Medicine, 1980; Rous-Whipple Award, Amer. Assoc. of Pathologists, 1985; Nat. Medal of Science, US, 1990. *Publications:* (with D. Katz) Immunological Tolerance, 1974; Immunogenetics and Immunodeficiency, 1975; (with D. Katz) The Role of Products of the Histocompatibility Gene Complex in Immune Responses, 1976; Textbook of Immunology, 1979; 650 articles in professional journals. *Recreations:* music, art collecting. *Address:* Department of Pathology, Harvard Medical School, 25 Shattuck Street, Boston, Mass 02115, USA. *T:* 617.732.1971.

BÉNARD, André Pierre Jacques, Hon. KBE 1991; French business executive; Member Supervisory Board, Royal Dutch Shell Group, since 1983; Chairman, Eurotunnel, since 1990 (Co-Chairman, 1986–90); *b* 19 Aug. 1922; *s* of Marcel Bénard and Lucie Thalmann; *m* 1946, Jacqueline Preiss; one *s*. *Educ:* Lycée Janson-de-Sailly; Lycée Georges Clémenceau, Nantes; Lycée Thiers, Marseilles; Ecole Polytechnique, Paris. Joined Royal Dutch Shell Group, 1946; with Société Anonyme des Pétroles Jupiter, 1946–49; Shell Petroleum Co., London, 1949–50; Société des Pétroles Shell Berre, 1950–59; Shell Française: Marketing Manager, 1964–67; Pres. Man. Dir, 1967–70; Regional Co-ordinator Europe, 1970; Man. Dir, Royal Dutch Shell Group, 1971–83. Senior Adviser, Lazard Frères, NY, 1983–90. Hon. Pres., French Chamber of Commerce and Industry, Netherlands, 1980–; Vice-Pres., French Chamber of Commerce, GB, 1985–. Médaille des Evadés; Médaille de la Résistance; Chevalier du Mérite Agricole; Chevalier de l'Ordre National du Mérite; Officier de la Légion d'Honneur; Comdr, Order of Orange Nassau. *Recreation:* golf. *Address:* Eurotunnel, Victoria Plaza, 111 Buckingham Palace Road, SW1W 0ST. *T:* 071–834 7575.

BENARROCH, Heather Mary, (Mrs E. J. Benarroch); *see* Harper, Heather.

BENAUD, Richard, OBE 1961; international sports consultant, journalist and media representative; BBC and Channel Nine Network television commentator, since 1960; *b* 6 Oct. 1930; *s* of Louis Richard Benaud and Irene Benaud; *m* 1967, Daphne Elizabeth Surfleet; two *s* by previous marr. *Educ:* Parramatta High Sch. Captain, Australian Cricket Team, 28 Tests, played for Australia 63 Tests, Tours to England, 1953, 1956, 1961; first cricketer to achieve double, 2000 runs, 200 wickets. *Publications:* Way of Cricket, 1960; Tale of Two Tests, 1962; Spin Me a Spinner, 1963; The New Champions, 1965; Willow Patterns, 1972; Benaud on Reflection, 1984. *Recreation:* golf. *Address:* (office) 19/178 Beach Street, Coogee, NSW 2034, Australia. *T:* Sydney 02 664 1124.

BENCE, Cyril Raymond; *b* 26 Nov. 1902; *s* of Harris Bryant Bence; *m* 1st, 1926, Florence Maud Bowler (*d* 1974); one *s* one *d*; 2nd, 1975, Mrs I. N. Hall (*née* Lewis). *Educ:* Pontywaen Sch.; Newport High Sch., Mon. Apprenticed to Ashworth Son & Co. Ltd of Dock Street, Newport, Mon, Weighing Machine Manufacturers; moved to Birmingham, 1937. Member of National Union of Scalemakers; Mem. of AEU; Mem. of Birmingham Trades Council, 1942–45; Pres. Witton Branch AEU. Contested (Lab) Handsworth Div. of Birmingham, at Gen. Elections of 1945 and 1950, and Bye-election Nov. 1950; MP (Lab) Dunbartonshire East, 1951–70. *Address:* Leda, Sweethay Close, Staplehay, Taunton, Som.

See also V. L. Pearl.

BENDALL, David Vere, CMG 1967; MBE 1945; HM Diplomatic Service, retired; Chairman: Banca Nazionale del Lavoro Investment Bank plc, since 1986; Banque Morgan Grenfell en Suisse, 1981–90 (Morgan Grenfell Switzerland SA, 1974–81); Morgan Grenfell Italia spa, 1982–90; *b* 27 Feb. 1920; *s* of John Manley Bendall; *m* 1941, Eve Stephanie Merrilees Galpin; one *d*. *Educ:* Winchester; King's Coll., Cambridge (BA). Served Grenadier Guards, 1940–46. Third Sec., Allied Force HQ, Caserta, 1946; Rome, 1947; FO, 1949; First Sec., Santiago, 1952; FO, 1955; seconded to NATO Secretariat, Paris 1957; FO, 1960; NATO Secretariat, Paris as Dep. Head, Economic and Finance Div. and Special Advisor on Defence Policy, 1962; Counsellor, 1962; Counsellor, Washington, 1965–69; Asst Under-Sec. of State for Western Europe, 1969–71. Chm., Morgan Grenfell Internat. Ltd, 1979–85; Director: Morgan Grenfell (Holdings) Ltd, 1971–85; Morgan Grenfell France, 1986–90; Dep. Chm., Avon Cosmetics, 1979–90; Member: Morgan Grenfell Internat. Adv. Council, 1986–87; London Adv. Bd, Banque de l'Indochine et de Suez, 1974–87. Chm., British Red Cross Soc., 1980–85 (Vice-Chm., 1979–80). CStJ 1985. *Recreations:* golf, tennis, shooting, languages. *Address:* 3 Eaton Terrace Mews, SW1. *T:* 071–730 4229; Ashbocking Hall, near Ipswich, Suffolk. *T:* Helmingham (047339) 262. *Club:* Boodle's.

BENDALL, Dr Eve Rosemarie Duffield; Chief Executive Officer, English National Board for Nursing, Midwifery and Health Visiting, 1981–86; *b* 7 Aug. 1927; *d* of Col F. W. D. Bendall, CMG, MA, and Mrs M. L. Bendall, LRAM, ARCM. *Educ:* Malvern Girls' Coll.; London Univ. (MA, PhD); Royal Free Hosp. (SRN). Ward Sister, Dorset County Hosp., 1953–55; Night Supt, Manchester Babies' Hosp., 1955–56; Nurse Tutor: United Sheffield Hosps Sch. of Nursing, 1958–61; St George's Hosp., London, 1961–63; Principal, Sch. of Nursing, Hosp. for Sick Children, Gt Ormond Street, 1963–69. Registrar, GNC, 1973–77. *Publications:* (jtly) Basic Nursing, 1963, 3rd edn 1970; (jtly) A Guide to Medical and Surgical Nursing, 1965, 2nd edn 1970; (jtly) A History of the General Nursing Council, 1969; So You Passed, Nurse (research), 1975. *Recreation:* gardening. *Address:* 31 Longhill Road, Ovingdean, Brighton, Sussex BN2 7BF.

BENDALL, Vivian Walter Hough; MP (C) Ilford North, since March 1978; surveyor and valuer; *b* 14 Dec. 1938; *s* of late Cecil Aubrey Bendall and Olive Alvina Bendall (*née* Hough); *m* 1969, Ann Rosalind (*née* Jarvis). *Educ:* Coombe Hill House, Croydon; Broad Green Coll., Croydon. LRVA 1976, MRSH 1965. Mem. Croydon Council, 1964–78; Mem. GLC, 1970–73; Chm., Greater London Young Conservatives, 1967–68. Backbench Committees: Vice-Chm., Transport Cttee, 1982–83; Sec., Foreign and Commonwealth Affairs Cttee, 1981–84; Vice-Chm., Employment Cttee, 1984–87 (Jt Sec. 1981–84); Former Member: Central Council for Care of the Elderly; South Eastern Area Reg. Assoc. for the Blind; Mem., Dr Barnardo's New Mossford Home Fund Raising Cttee. Contested (C) Hertford and Stevenage, Feb. and Oct. 1974. *Recreation:* cricket. *Address:* (business) 25 Brighton Road, South Croydon, Surrey CR2 6EA. *T:* 081–688 0341. *Clubs:* Carlton; Essex County Cricket.

BENDER, Prof. Arnold Eric; Emeritus Professor, University of London; Professor of Nutrition and Dietetics, University of London and Head of Department of Food Science and Nutrition, Queen Elizabeth College, 1978–83 (Professor of Nutrition, 1971–78); *b* 24 July 1918; *s* of Isadore and Rose Bender; *m* 1941, Deborah Swift; two *s*. *Educ:* Liverpool Inst. High Sch.; Univ. of Liverpool (BSc Hons); Univ. of Sheffield (PhD). FRSH, FIFST. Research, Pharmaceutical Industry, 1940–45 and 1950–54; Res. Fellow, National Inst. of Radiotherapy, Sheffield, 1945–47; Lectr, Univ. of Sheffield, 1947–49; Research, Food Industry, 1954–64; Teaching and Research, Univ. of London, 1965–83. Department of Health and Social Security: Gp Sec. of Working Party on Protein Requirements, 1963; Mem., Sub-cttee on Protein Requirements, 1967; Mem., Cttee on Toxic Chemicals in Food and the Environment, 1976–83; Mem., Cttee on Med. Aspects of Food Policy, 1978–85; Chm., Panel on Novel Foods, 1980–85. Ministry of Agriculture, Fisheries and Food: Mem., Cttee on Dietetic Foods, 1969–73 and on Composition of Foods, 1975–77; Mem., Adv. Cttee on Irradiated and Novel Foods, 1981–85 and on Naturally Occurring Toxic Substances in Foods, 1983–. Society of Chemical Industry: Mem. Council, 1982–85; Food Group: Hon. Sec., 1955–60; Chm., 1979–80; Vice-Chm., 1980–82; Chm., Nutrition Panel, 1960–63 and 1976–78. Royal Society of Health: Mem. Council, 1974–89; Chm. Council, 1987–88; Chm., Examinations Cttee, 1983–85; Chm., Conf. and Meetings Cttee, 1985–86; Chm., Food and Nutrition Gp, 1968–70 (Vice Chm., 1967–68). Member: Royal Soc. British Nat. Cttee for Biochem., 1963–69, for Nutritional Scis, 1976–85; Eur. Cttee for Co-operation in Sci. and Technol. (COST 91), 1980–83 (Chm., Nutrition Sub-cttee, 1982–83); Cttee on Protein Quality Evaluation, ARC, 1955–66; Sector D Res. Cttee, CNAA, 1982–; Pres., Inst. Food Sci. and Technol., 1989–91; Vice-Pres., Internat. Union of Food Sci. and Technol., 1983–87 (Mem. Exec., 1978–83). Hon. Treasurer, UK Nutrition Soc., 1962–67; Hon. Sec., UK Council for Food Sci. and Technol., 1964–77. Hon. DSc Univ. Complutense, Madrid, 1983. Mem. Editorial Board: Jl of Human Nutrition; Jl of Science of Food and Agriculture; Jl of Food Technol.; British Jl of Nutrition. *Publications:* Dictionary of Nutrition and Food Technology, 1960, 6th edn 1990, Japanese edn 1965, Arabic edn 1985; Nutrition and Dietetic Foods, 1967, 2nd edn 1973; Value of Food, 1970, 3rd edn 1979, Spanish edn 1972; Facts of Food, 1975, Polish edn 1979; Food Processing and Nutrition, 1978, Japanese edn 1978; The Pocket Guide to Calories and Nutrition, 1979, 2nd edn 1986, Dutch, US, Italian and Spanish edns, 1981; Nutrition for Medical Students, 1982; Health or Hoax?, 1985, Spanish edn 1987; Food Tables, 1986; research papers and review articles in Brit. Jl of Nutrition, Biochem. Jl, BMJ, Jl Human Nutrition, Jl Science Food and Agric., and other professional jls, and reports. *Recreations:* writing, gardening, lecturing. *Address:* 2 Willow Vale, Fetcham, Leatherhead, Surrey KT22 9TE. *T:* Bookham (0372) 454702.

See also B. G. Bender.

BENDER, Dr Brian Geoffrey; Under Secretary, Cabinet Office, since 1990; *b* 25 Feb. 1949; *s* of Arnold Eric Bender, *qv*; *m* 1974, Penelope Clark; one *s* one *d*. *Educ:* Greenford Grammar Sch.; Imperial Coll., London Univ. (BSc, PhD). Joined DTI, 1973; Private Sec. to Sec. of State for Trade, 1976–77; First Sec. (Trade Policy), Office of UK Permanent Rep. to EC, 1977–82; Principal (responsible for internat. steel issues), DTI, 1982–84; Counsellor (Industry), Office of UK Permanent Rep. to EC, 1985–89. *Recreations:* my children, theatre. *Address:* Cabinet Office, 70 Whitehall, SW1A 2AS. *T:* 071–270 0177.

BENDERSKY, Pamela May H.; *see* Hudson-Bendersky.

BENEDICTUS, David Henry; writer and director for stage, television and radio; *b* 16 Sept. 1938; *s* of late Henry Jules Benedictus and of Kathleen Constance (*née* Ricardo); *m* 1971, Yvonne Daphne Antrobus; one *s* one *d*. *Educ*: Stone House, Broadstairs; Eton College; Balliol College, Oxford (BA English); State Univ. of Iowa. News and current affairs, BBC Radio, 1961; Drama Director, BBC TV, 1962; Story Editor, Wednesday Play and Festival Series, BBC, 1965; Thames TV Trainee Director, at Bristol Old Vic, 1968; Asst Dir, RSC, Aldwych, 1970; Judith E. Wilson Vis. Fellow, Cambridge, and Fellow Commoner, Churchill Coll., Cambridge, 1981–82; Commissioning Editor, Drama Series, Channel 4 TV, 1984–86; Readings Editor, 1989–91, Editor, Readings, 1991–, BBC Radio. Writer in Residence: Sutton Library, Surrey, 1975; Kibbutz Gezer, Israel, 1978; Bitterne Library, Southampton, 1983–84. Antiques corresp., Standard, 1977–80; reviewer for books, stage, films, records, for major newspapers and magazines. Dir, Kingston Books, 1988–. Member: BAFTA; Amnesty International; Writers' Guild. *Publications*: The Fourth of June, 1962; You're a Big Boy Now, 1963; This Animal is Mischievous, 1965; Hump, or Bone by Bone Alive, 1967; The Guru and the Golf Club, 1969; A World of Windows, 1971; The Rabbi's Wife, 1976; Junk, how and where to buy beautiful things at next to nothing prices, 1976; A Twentieth Century Man, 1978; The Antique Collector's Guide, 1980; Lloyd George (from Elaine Morgan's screenplay), 1981; Whose Life is it Anyway? (from Brian Clarke's screenplay), 1981; Who Killed the Prince Consort?, 1982; Local Hero (from Bill Forsyth's screenplay), 1983; The Essential London Guide, 1984; Floating Down to Camelot, 1985; The Streets of London, 1986; The Absolutely Essential London Guide, 1986; Little Sir Nicholas, 1990; Transplant, 1991. *Recreations*: chess, tennis, squash, cricket, auctions, table tennis, piano playing, horse racing, eating. *Address*: 19 Oxford Road, Teddington, Middlesex TW11 0QA. *T*: 081–977 4715.

BENEDIKTSSON, Einar, MA; Knight Commander, Order of the Falcon, Iceland; Ambassador for Iceland to Norway, also accredited to Poland and Czechoslovakia, since 1991; *b* Reykjavik, 30 April 1931; *s* of Stefan M. Benediktsson and Sigridur Oddsdóttir; *m* 1956, Elsa Petursdóttir; three *s* two *d*. *Educ*: Colgate Univ., NY; Fletcher Sch. of Law and Diplomacy, Mass; London Sch. of Econs and Pol. Science; Inst. des Etudes Européennes, Turin. With OEEC, 1956–60; Head of Section, Mins of Econ. Affairs and Commerce, 1961–64, and Min. of For. Affairs, 1964; Counsellor, Paris, 1964–68; Head of Section, Min. of For. Affairs, 1968–70; Perm. Rep. to Internat. Orgns, Geneva, 1970–76; Chm., EFTA Council, 1975; Ambassador to France (also accredited to Spain and Portugal, and Perm. Rep. to OECD and UNESCO, 1976–82); Ambassador to UK and concurrently to The Netherlands, Nigeria and Ireland, 1982–86; Perm. Rep. to N Atlantic Council, 1986–90, and Ambassador to Belgium and Luxembourg, 1986–91. Holds foreign decorations. *Address*: Islands Ambassade, Stortingsgaten 30, 0161 Oslo 1, Norway. *T*: (02) 83-34-36; Langviksveien 6, Bygdoy, 0286 Oslo 2, Norway. *T*: (02) 43-84-84.

BENGOUGH, Sir Piers (Henry George), KCVO 1986; OBE 1973; DL; Her Majesty's Representative, Ascot, since 1982; *b* 24 May 1929; *s* of Nigel and Alice Bengough; *m* 1952, Bridget Shirley Adams; two *s*. *Educ*: Eton. Commnd 10th Royal Hussars (PWO), 1948; commanded Royal Hussars (PWO), 1971–73, retired. Formerly amateur rider; wins incl. Grand Military Gold Cup (4 times). Member: Jockey Club, 1965– (Steward, 1974–77, 1990–); Horserace Betting Levy Board, 1978–81; Director: Cheltenham Steeplechase Co., 1977–90; Hereford Racecourse Co., 1974–; Ludlow Race Club, 1979–; Chm., Compensation Fund for Jockeys, 1981–89. Hon. Col The Royal Hussars (PWO), 1983–90. DL Hereford and Worcester, 1987. *Recreations*: shooting, fishing. *Address*: Great House, Canon Pyon, Hereford HR4 8PD. *Clubs*: Cavalry and Guards, Pratt's.

BENJAMIN, Prof. Bernard; Professor of Actuarial Science, The City University, London, 1973–75, now Emeritus; *b* 8 March 1910; *s* of Joseph and Lucy Benjamin, London; *m* 1937, May Pate, Horham, Suffolk; two *d*. *Educ*: Colfe Grammar Sch.; Sir John Cass Coll. (London University). BSc (Hons); PhD London. LCC, 1928; statistician Public Health Dept, 1940; served War, 1943–46, RAF; statistician, General Register Office, 1952; Chief Statistician, 1954; Dir of Statistics, Ministry of Health, 1963–65; Dir of Research and Intelligence, GLC, 1965–70; Dir of Statistical Studies, CS College, 1970–73; Hon. Cons. in Med. Stats to Army, 1966. Chm., Statistics Users Council (formerly Standing Cttee of Statistics Users), 1971–90. Fellow: Inst. of Actuaries (a Vice-Pres. 1963; Pres., 1966–68; Gold Medal, 1975); Royal Statistical Soc. (Pres. 1970–71; Guy Medal in Gold, 1986); Galton Inst. (formerly Eugenics Soc.) (Pres., 1982–87; Galton Lectr, 1981). Hon. DSc: City Univ., London, 1981; Kent Univ. 1987. Internat. Insurance Prize of Italy, 1985. *Publications*: Social and Economic Factors in Mortality, 1965; Health and Vital Statistics, 1968; Demographic Analysis, 1969; The Population Census, 1970; (with H. W. Haycocks) The Analysis of Mortality and Other Actuarial Statistics, 1971; Statistics in Urban Administration, 1976; (ed) Medical Records, 1977; General Insurance, 1977; (with J. H. Pollard) The Analysis of Mortality and Other Actuarial Statistics, 1980; (jtly) Pensions: the problems of today and tomorrow, 1987; Population Statistics, 1989; numerous medical and population statistical papers and contribs to Jl of Royal Statistical Society and Jl of Inst. of Actuaries. *Recreations*: gardening, painting (both kinds). *Address*: 4 Mount Lodge, 53A Shepherds Hill, Highgate, N6 5QP. *Club*: Athenæum.

BENJAMIN, Brooke; see Benjamin, T. B.

BENJAMIN, George William John; composer, occasional conductor and pianist; *b* 31 Jan. 1960; *s* of William Benjamin and Susan Benjamin (*née* Bendon). *Educ*: Westminster School (private tuition with Peter Gellhorn); Paris Conservatoire (Olivier Messiaen); King's College, Cambridge (Alexander Goehr). MA, MusB. First London orchestral performance, BBC Proms, 1980; research at Institut de Recherche et Coordination Acoustique/Musique, Paris, 1984–87; Vis. Prof. of Composition, RCM, 1986–; performs, conducts and lectures on own and other contemp. music, GB, Europe, USA. Lili Boulanger Award, USA, 1985; Koussevitzky Internat. Record Award, 1987; Gramophone Contemp. Music Award, 1990. *Publications: orchestral*: Altitude, 1977; Ringed by the Flat Horizon, 1980; A Mind of Winter, 1981; At First Light, 1982; Jubilation, 1985; Antara, 1987; Cascade, 1990; *chamber music*: Piano Sonata, 1978; Octet, 1978; Flight, 1979; Sortilèges, 1981; Three Studies for Solo Piano, 1985; Upon Silence, 1990. *Address*: c/o Faber Music Ltd, 3 Queen Square, WC1N 3AU.

BENJAMIN, Louis; President, 1985–89, Managing Director, 1970–81, and Chief Executive, 1981–85, Stoll Moss Theatres Ltd (The London Palladium, Theatre Royal, Drury Lane, Victoria Palace, Apollo, Her Majesty's, Lyric, Globe, Queen's, Duchess, Garrick, Royalty and Cambridge Theatres); *b* 17 Oct. 1922; *s* of Benjamin and Harriet Benjamin; *m* 1954, Vera Doreen Ketteman; two *d*. *Educ*: Highbury County Sec. Sch. Served Second World War: RAC, India, Burma and Singapore. Joined Moss Empires Ltd, 1937; entered theatrical management as Second Asst Manager, London Palladium, 1945; Asst Man., then Box Office Man., Victoria Palace, 1948; Gen. Man., Winter Gardens, Morecambe, 1953; Pye Records: Sales Controller, 1959; Gen. Man., 1962; Man. Dir, 1963; Chm., Pye Records Gp, 1975–80; a Jt Man. Dir, ATV Corp., 1975; Mem., Exec. Bd, Associated Communications Corp., 1982–85; Director: ATV Music Ltd, 1962–85; Bermans & Nathans Ltd, 1973–84; Precision Records & Tapes Ltd, 1982–85; Precision Video Ltd, 1983–86. Entertainment Artistes Benevolent Fund: Vice-Pres., 1971–82; Life

Governor, 1982–; Presenter of Royal Variety Perf., annually, 1979–85, and of Children's Royal Variety Perf., 1981 and 1982; producer, HM Queen Mother's 90th Birthday Tribute, London Palladium, 1990. Companion, Grand Order of Water Rats; Mem., Exec. Cttee, Variety Club of GB; Hon. Council Mem., NSPCC, 1986–.

BENJAMIN, Pauline, (Mrs Joseph Benjamin); see Crabbe, Pauline.

BENJAMIN, Dr Ralph, CB 1980; DSc, PhD, BSc, FCGI, FEng, FIEE; Visiting Professor, University College and Imperial College of Science, Technology and Medicine, University of London, since 1988; *b* 17 Nov. 1922; *s* of Charles Benjamin and Claire Benjamin (*née* Stern); *m* 1951, Kathleen Ruth Bull, BA; one *s* (and one *s* decd). *Educ*: in Germany and Switzerland; St Oswald's Coll., Ellesmere; Imperial Coll. of Science and Technology, London. DSc(Eng) London, 1970; FEng 1983; FCGI 1982. Joined Royal Naval Scientific Service, 1944; Senior Scientific Officer, 1949; Principal Scientific Officer, 1952; Senior Principal Scientific Officer (Special Merit), 1955; Deputy Chief Scientific Officer (Special Merit), 1960; Head of Research and Deputy Chief Scientist, Admiralty Surface Weapons Establishment, 1961; Dir and Chief Scientist, Admiralty Underwater Weapons Estab., 1964–71, and Dir, Underwater Weapons R&D (Navy), 1965–71; Chief Scientist, GCHQ, 1971–82; Head of Communications Techniques, SHAPE Technical Centre, The Hague, 1982–87. Hon. consultant: Univ. of Illinois; US Office of Naval Research, 1956; IEE Marconi Premium, 1964; IERE Heinrich Hertz Premium, 1980, 1983; Council Mem., Brit. Acoustical Soc., 1971; Vis. Prof., Dept of Electrical and Electronic Engineering, Univ. of Surrey, 1973–80. FRSA 1984. *Publications*: Modulation, Resolution and Signal Processing for Radar Sonar and Related Systems, 1966; contribs to various advisory cttees, working parties, symposia, etc; articles in Jls of Inst. of Electrical and Electronic Engrs, Instn of Electrical Engineers and Inst. of Electronic and Radio Engineers, etc. *Recreations*: work, mountaineering, ski-ing, swimming, sub-aqua, canoeing, windsurfing. *Address*: 13 Bellhouse Walk, Rockwell Park, Bristol BS11 0UE. *Club*: Athenæum.

BENJAMIN, Prof. (Thomas) Brooke, MEng, MA, PhD; FRS 1966; Sedleian Professor of Natural Philosophy, and Fellow of The Queen's College, University of Oxford, since 1979; Adjunct Professor, Pennsylvania State University, since 1987; *b* 15 April 1929; *s* of Thomas Joseph Benjamin and Ethel Mary Benjamin (*née* Brooke); *m* 1st, 1956, Helen Gilda-Marie Rakower Ginsburg (marr. diss. 1974); one *s* two *d*; 2nd, 1978, Natalia Marie-Thérèse Court; one *d*. *Educ*: Wallasey Grammar Sch.; University of Liverpool; Yale Univ. (USA); University of Cambridge. BEng (Liverpool) 1950; MEng. (Yale) 1952; PhD (Cantab) 1955; MA (Oxon) 1979. Fellow of King's Coll., Cambridge, 1955–64; Asst Dir of Research, University of Cambridge, 1958–67; Reader in Hydrodynamics, Univ. of Cambridge, 1967–70; Prof. of Maths, and Dir, Fluid Mechanics Res. Inst., Essex Univ., 1970–78. Visiting Professor: Univ. of Wisconsin, 1980–81; Univ. of Houston, 1985; Univ. of Calif, Berkeley, 1986. Chairman: Mathematics Cttee, SRC, 1975–78; Jt Royal Soc./IMA Mathematical Educn Cttee, 1979–85; Nat. Conf. of Univ. Profs, 1989–; a Vice-Pres., Royal Soc., 1990–. Editor, Journal of Fluid Mechanics, 1960–65; Consultant to English Electric Co., 1956–67. Hon. DSc: Bath, 1989; Brunel, 1991. William Hopkins Prize, Cambridge Philosophical Soc., 1969. *Publications*: various papers on theoretical and experimental fluid mechanics. *Recreation*: music. *Address*: Mathematical Institute, 24–29 St Giles', Oxford OX1 3LB. *T*: Oxford (0865) 273525; *Fax*: Oxford (0865) 273583; 8 Hernes Road, Oxford OX2 7PU. *T*: Oxford (0865) 54439.

BENN, Anthony, OBE 1945; *b* 7 Oct. 1912; *s* of late Francis Hamilton Benn and Arta Clara Benn (*née* Boal); *m* 1943, Maureen Lillian Kathleen Benn (*née* Denbigh); two *s* four *d*. *Educ*: Harrow; Christ Church, Oxford (Scholar). Oxford Univ. Cricket XI, 1935. Price & Pierce Ltd, 1935 (Director, 1947, Chm., 1956–72). Joined Surrey and Sussex Yeomanry, 1936. Served War of 1939–45 (OBE): Staff Coll., 1942; Instructor, Middle East Staff Coll., 1943. Comdr, Order of the Lion of Finland, 1958. *Recreation*: travel.

BENN, Edward, CMG 1981; Minister (Defence Equipment), British Embassy, Washington, 1978–82, retired; *b* 8 May 1922; *s* of John Henry Benn and Alice (*née* Taylor); *m* 1947, Joan Taylor; one *d*. *Educ*: High Storrs Grammar Sch., Sheffield; Sheffield Univ. (BEng; 1st Cl. Hons Civil Engrg; Mappin Medal, 1943). Operational Research with Army, 1943–48; India and Burma, 1944–46 (Major); entered War Office, 1948; tank research, Supt Special Studies, and later Dep. Dir, Army Op. Res. Estabt, 1961; Asst Sci. Adviser to SACEUR, Paris, 1962–65; Dep. Chief Sci. Adviser, Home Office, 1966–68; Dir, Defence Policy, MoD, 1968–75; Under Sec. and Dep. Chief Scientist (RAF), MoD, 1975–78. *Recreation*: golf. *Address*: Pemberley, St Elizabeths, Eastcombe, Stroud, Glos GL6 7DR. *Club*: MCC.

BENN, Edward Glanvill; Life President, Benn Brothers plc, Publishers, since 1976, Chairman, 1945–75; *b* 1905; 2nd *s* of late Sir Ernest Benn, 2nd Bt, CBE; *m* 1931, Beatrice Catherine, MBE, *d* of Claude Newbald; one *s* one *d*. *Educ*: Harrow; Clare Coll., Cambridge. Served War of 1939–45, East Surrey Regt, 1940–45; Brigade Major, 138 Infantry Brigade, Italy, 1944 (despatches). Council Member: Nat. Advertising Benevolent Soc., 1937–61 (Trustee, 1951–80, and Pres. 1961–62); Advertising Assoc., 1951–67 (Hon. Treasurer 1960–65); Commonwealth Press Union, 1956– (Hon. Treasurer 1967–77, Hon. Life Mem. 1975; Astor Award, 1982); Vice Pres., Readers' Pension Cttee, 1950–; Life Vice Pres., Newspaper Press Fund, 1965– (Appeals Pres. 1971); Chm., Advertising Advisory Cttee, Independent Television Authority, 1959–64 (Mackintosh medal, 1967); Dir., Exchange Telegraph Co. Ltd, 1960–72 (Chm. 1969–72); Pres., Periodical Publishers Assoc., 1976–78. Master, Stationers' Company, 1977. *Address*: Crescent Cottage, Aldeburgh, Suffolk IP15 5HW. *Club*: Tandridge Golf (Hon. Life Mem.).

See also Sir J. J. Benn.

BENN, Sir (James) Jonathan, 4th Bt *cr* 1914; Chairman, Reedpack Paper Group, 1988–90; Chairman and Chief Executive, Reed Paper & Board (UK) Ltd, 1977–90; Director, Reedpack Ltd, 1988–90; *b* 27 July 1933; *s* of Sir John Andrews Benn, 3rd Bt, and of Hon. Ursula Lady Benn, *o d* of 1st Baron Hankey, PC, GCB, GCMG, GCVO, FRS; *S* father, 1984; *m* 1960, Jennifer Mary, *e d* of late Dr Wilfred Howells, OBE; one *s* one *d*. *Educ*: Harrow; Clare College, Cambridge (MA). Various positions with Reed International PLC (formerly A. E. Reed & Co.), 1957–; Director, Reed Paper & Board (UK) Ltd, 1971; Managing Dir 1976; Director, Reed Group Ltd, 1976. Pres., British Paper and Board Industries Fedn, 1985–87. *Recreations*: golf, skiing, music. *Heir*: *s* Robert Ernest Benn [*b* 17 Oct. 1963; *m* 1985, Sheila Margaret, 2nd *d* of Dr Alastair Blain]. *Address*: Fielden Lodge, Ightham, Kent TN15 9AN.

See also E. G. Benn, T. J. Benn.

BENN, John Meriton, CB 1969; Pro-Chancellor, Queen's University, Belfast, 1979–86 (Senator, 1973–86); *b* 16 July 1908; *s* of late Ernest and Emily Louise Benn, Burnley; *m* 1933, Valentine Rosemary, *d* of late William Seward, Hanwell; two *d*. *Educ*: Burnley Gram. Sch.; Christ's Coll., Cambridge (Scholar; Modern Languages Tripos, 1st Cl. Hons French, 2nd Cl. Hons German). Asst Master, Exeter Sch., 1931–34; Lektor, Halle Univ., Germany, 1934; Asst Master, Regent Street Polytechnic Secondary Sch., 1935; Inspector of Schs., Ministry of Education for Northern Ireland, 1935–44; Principal, 1944–51; Asst Sec., 1951–59; Senior Asst Sec., 1959–64; Permanent Sec., 1964–69; Comr for Complaints, NI, 1969–73; Parly Comr for Admin, NI, 1972–73. Chm., NI Schools

Exams Council, 1974–81. Chairman Board of Governors: Rupert Stanley Coll. of Further Educn, Belfast, 1986–; Sullivan Upper Sch., Holywood, 1987–89. Hon. LLD QUB, 1972. *Publication*: Practical French Proses, 1935. *Address*: 7 Tudor Oaks, Holywood, Co. Down BT18 0PA. *T*: Holywood (02317) 2817.

BENN, Sir Jonathan; *see* Benn, Sir (James) J.

BENN, Captain Sir Patrick (Ion Hamilton), 2nd Bt *cr* 1920; Captain, Reserve of Officers, late Duke of Cornwall's Light Infantry; Major, Norfolk Army Cadet Force, 1960; *b* 26 Feb. 1922; *o s* of late Col Ion Bridges Hamilton Benn, JP (*o s* of 1st Bt), Broad Farm, Rollesby, Gt Yarmouth, and late Theresa Dorothy, *d* of late Major F. H. Blacker, Johnstown, Co. Kildare; *S* grandfather, 1961; *m* 1959, Edel Jørgine, *d* of late Col W. S. Løbach, formerly of The Royal Norwegian Army, Andenes, Vesteraalen; one *s* one *d* (both adopted). *Educ*: Rugby. Served War of 1939–45 (despatches); North Africa, Italy, Greece, 1941–45; Capt. 1943; served Korea, 1951–52; retd, 1955. *Recreations*: shooting, fishing. *Address*: Rollesby Hall, Great Yarmouth, Norfolk NR29 5DT. *T*: Great Yarmouth (0493) 740313.

BENN, Timothy John; Chairman, Timothy Benn Publishing Ltd, since 1983, and other companies; *b* 27 Oct. 1936; *yr s* of Sir John Andrews Benn, 3rd Bt, and of Hon. Ursula Helen Alers Hankey; *m* 1982, Christine Grace Townsend. *Educ*: Harrow; Clare Coll., Cambridge (MA); Princeton Univ., USA; Harvard Business Sch., USA (National Marketing Council Course; Scholarship Award). FInstM. 2nd Lieut Scots Guards, 1956–57. Benn Brothers Ltd: Board Member, 1961–82; Managing Director, 1972–82; Dep. Chm., 1976–81; Chm., Benn Brothers plc, 1981–82; Ernest Benn: Board Member, 1967–82; Managing Director, 1973–82; Chairman and Managing Director, 1974–82. Chairman: Bouverie Publishing Co. (Publr, UK Press Gazette), 1983–; Buckley Press (Publr, Post Magazine and Insurance Monitor, Re-insurance, Insurance Directory), 1984–; Bouverie Data Services, 1986–; Henry Greenwood and Co. (Publr, British Jl of Photography), 1987–; Dalesman Publishing Co. (Publr, The Dalesman, Cumbria), 1989–; Stone & Cox (Publications), 1989–. Pres. Tonbridge Civic Soc., 1982–87. *Publication*: The (Almost) Compleat Angler, 1985. *Recreations*: writing, toymaking. *Address*: The Priory, Bordyke, Tonbridge, Kent TN9 1NN. *T*: Tonbridge (0732) 362038. *Club*: Flyfishers'.

See also Sir J. J. Benn.

BENN, Rt. Hon. Tony; PC 1964; MP (Lab) Chesterfield, since March 1984; *b* 3 April 1925; *er surv. s* of 1st Viscount Stansgate, DSO, DFC, PC, former Labour MP and Cabinet Minister (*d* 1960); having unsuccessfully attempted to renounce his right of succession, 1955 and 1960, won a bye-election in May 1961 only to be prevented from taking seat; instigated Act to make disclaimer possible, and disclaimed title for life, 1963; *m* 1949, Caroline Middleton De Camp, MA; three *s* one *d*. Served: RAFVR, 1943–45; RNVR, 1945–46. Joined Labour Party, 1943; Mem., NEC, 1959–60, 1962– (Chm., 1971–72); candidate for leadership of Labour Party, 1976, 1988, and for dep. leadership, 1971, 1981. MP (Lab) Bristol SE, Nov. 1950–1960 and Aug. 1963–1983; Postmaster-Gen., 1964–66, recommended establishment of GPO as public corp. and founded Giro; Minister of Technology, 1966–70, assumed responsibility for Min. of Aviation, 1967 and Min. of Power, 1969; opposition spokesman on Trade and Industry, 1970–74; Sec. of State for Industry and Minister for Posts and Telecommunications, 1974–75; Sec. of State for Energy, 1975–79. Pres., EEC Council of Energy Ministers, 1977. Chm., Campaign Gp, 1987–. Contested (Lab) Bristol East, 1983. *Publications*: The Privy Council as a Second Chamber, 1957; The Regeneration of Britain, 1964; The New Politics, 1970; Speeches, 1974; Arguments for Socialism, 1979; Arguments for Democracy, 1981; (ed) Writings on the Wall: a radical and socialist anthology 1215–1984, 1984; Out of the Wilderness, Diaries 1963–1967, 1987; Fighting Back: speaking out for Socialism in the Eighties, 1988; Office Without Power, Diaries 1968–72, 1988; Against the Tide, Diaries 1973–76, 1989; Conflicts of Interest, Diaries 1977–80, 1990; numerous pamphlets. *Address*: House of Commons, SW1A 0AA.

BENNER, Patrick, CB 1975; Deputy Secretary, Department of Health and Social Security, 1976–84; *b* 26 May 1923; *s* of Henry Grey and Gwendolen Benner; *m* 1952, Joan Christabel Draper; two *d*. *Educ*: Ipswich Sch.; University Coll., Oxford. Entered Min. of Health as Asst Princ., 1949; Princ., 1951; Princ. Private Sec. to Minister, 1955; Asst Sec., 1958; Under-Sec., Min. of Health, 1967–68, DHSS 1968–72; Dep. Sec., Cabinet Office, 1972–76. *Address*: 44 Ormond Crescent, Hampton, Mddx TW12 2TH. *T*: 081–979 1099. *Club*: Commonwealth Trust.

BENNET, family name of **Earl of Tankerville.**

BENNETT, Alan; dramatist and actor; *b* 9 May 1934; *s* of Walter Bennett and Lilian Mary Peel; unmarried. *Educ*: Leeds Modern Sch.; Exeter Coll., Oxford (BA Modern History, 1957; Hon. Fellow, 1987). Jun. Lectr, Modern History, Magdalen Coll., Oxford, 1960–62. Hon. DLitt Leeds, 1990. Co-author and actor, Beyond the Fringe, Royal Lyceum, Edinburgh, 1960, Fortune, London, 1961 and Golden, NY, 1962; author and actor: On the Margin (TV series), 1966; Forty Years On, Apollo, 1968; *stage plays*: Getting On, Queen's, 1971; Habeas Corpus, Lyric, 1973; The Old Country, Queen's, 1977; Enjoy, Vaudeville, 1980; Kafka's Dick, Royal Court, 1986; Single Spies (double bill: A Question of Attribution; An Englishman Abroad (also dir)), NT, 1988; The Wind in the Willows (adapted), Olivier, 1990; *BBC TV films*: A Day Out, 1972; Sunset Across the Bay, 1975; *TV Plays for LWT*, 1978–79: Doris and Doreen; The Old Crowd; Me! I'm Afraid of Virginia Woolf; All Day on the Sands; Afternoon Off; One Fine Day; *BBC TV plays*: A Little Outing, A Visit from Miss Prothero, 1977; Intensive Care, Say Something Happened, Our Winnie, Marks, A Woman of No Importance, Rolling Home; An Englishman Abroad, 1983; The Insurance Man, 1986; Talking Heads (series), 1988; 102 Boulevard Haussmann, 1991; *BBC TV documentary*: Dinner at Noon, 1988; *feature films*: A Private Function, 1984; Prick Up Your Ears, 1987. *Publications*: (with Cook, Miller and Moore) Beyond the Fringe, 1962; Forty Years On, 1969; Getting On, 1972; Habeas Corpus, 1973; The Old Country, 1978; Enjoy, 1980; Office Suite, 1981; Objects of Affection, 1982; A Private Function, 1984; The Writer in Disguise, 1985; Prick Up Your Ears (screenplay), 1987; Two Kafka Plays, 1987; Talking Heads, 1988; Single Spies, 1989; The Lady in the Van, 1990; The Wind in the Willows (adaptation), 1991. *Address*: c/o Peters Fraser & Dunlop, The Chambers, Chelsea Harbour, Lots Road, SW10 0XF. *T*: 071–376 7676.

BENNETT, (Albert) Edward; Director, Directorate of Nuclear Safety, Industry and the Environment, and Civil Protection, Commission of the European Communities; *b* 11 Sept. 1931; *s* of Albert Edward and Frances Ann Bennett; *m* 1957, Jean Louise Paston-Cooper; two *s*. *Educ*: University Coll. Sch., Hampstead; London Hosp. Med. Coll. MB BS London; FFCM 1972, FFOM 1984. Surgeon Lieut, RN, 1957–60; Senior Lectr, Dept of Clinical Epidemiology and Social Medicine, St. Thomas's Hosp. Med. Sch., 1964–70; Dir, Health Services Evaluation Gp, Univ. of Oxford, 1970–77; Prof. and Head of Dept of Clinical Epidemiology and Social Medicine, St George's Hosp. Med. Sch., Univ. of London, 1974–81; Director: Health and Safety Directorate, EEC, 1981–87; Directorate of Nuclear Safety and Control of Chemical Pollution, EEC, 1987. Hon. Editor, Internat. Jl of Epidemiology, 1977–81. *Publications*: Questionnaires in Medicine, 1975; (ed) Communications between Doctors and Patients, 1976; (ed) Recent Advances in Community Medicine, 1978; numerous sci. reports and contribs on epidemiology of chronic disease and evaluation of health services. *Recreations*: cinema, browsing. *Address*: Avenue des Pins 4, B1950 Kraainem, Brussels, Belgium. *T*: (02) 767 5947. *Club*: Athenæum.

BENNETT, Albert Joseph, CBE 1966; Secretary, National Health Service Staff Commission, 1972–75; Vice-Chairman, Paddington and North Kensington Health Authority, 1982–85; *b* 9 April 1913; *er s* of late Albert James Bennett and late Alice Bennett, Stourbridge, Worcs; unmarried. *Educ*: King Edward VI Sch., Stourbridge; St John's Coll., Cambridge (MA) Mathematical Tripos (Wrangler). Admin. Officer, LCC, 1936–39; Central Midwives Board: Asst Sec., 1939–45; Sec., 1945–47; Instructor Lieut, later Lt-Comdr, RN, 1940–45; Sec., NW Met. Regional Hosp. Bd, 1947–65; Principal Officer, NHS Nat. Staff Cttee, 1965–72; Under-Sec., DHSS, 1972–75, seconded as Sec., NHS Staff Commn. Member: Nat. Selection Cttee for Recruitment of Trainee Hospital Admin. Staff, 1955–64; Cttee of Inquiry into the Recruitment, Training and Promotion of Admin. and Clerical Staff in Hospital Service, 1962–63; Adv. Cttee on Hospital Engineers Training, 1967–72; Admin. Training Cttee, Cttee of Vice-Chancellors and Principals, 1970–72; Kensington and Chelsea and Westminster AHA(T), 1977–82, and Family Practitioner Cttee, 1977–85. *Recreations*: walking, gardening. *Address*: 19 Garson House, Gloucester Terrace, W2 3DG. *T*: 071–262 8311.

BENNETT, Alexander; *see* Bennett, F. O. A. G.

BENNETT, Andrew Francis; MP (Lab) Denton and Reddish, since 1983 (Stockport North, Feb. 1974–1983); Teacher; *b* Manchester, 9 March 1939; *m*; two *s* one *d*. *Educ*: Birmingham Univ. (BSocSc). Joined Labour Party, 1957; Member, Oldham Borough Council, 1964–74. Member, National Union of Teachers. Contested (Lab) Knutsford, 1970; an Opposition spokesperson on educn, 1983–88. Interested especially in social services and education. *Recreations*: photography, walking, climbing. *Address*: 28 Brownsville Road, Stockport SK4 4PF; House of Commons, SW1A 0AA.

BENNETT, Andrew John; Chief Natural Resources Adviser, Overseas Development Administration, Foreign and Commonwealth Office, since 1987; *b* 25 April 1942; *s* of Leonard Charles Bennett and Edna Mary Bennett (*née* Harding). *Educ*: St Edward's Sch., Oxford; University Coll. of N Wales (BSc Agr Scis 1965); Univ. of West Indies, Trinidad (DipTropAg 1967); Univ. of Reading (MSc Crop Protection 1970). VSO Kenya, 1965–66; Agricl Officer (Research), Govt of St Vincent, 1967–69; Maize Agronomist, Govt of Malawi, 1971–74; Crop Develt Manager, 1976–78, Chief Research Officer, 1978–79, S Region, Sudan; Asst Agricl Adviser, ODA, 1980–83; Natural Resources Adviser (ODA), SE Asia Develt Div., Bangkok, 1983–85; Head, British Develt Div. in Pacific (ODA), Fiji, 1985–87. *Recreations*: walking, boating. *Address*: Overseas Development Administration, Eland House, Stag Place, SW1E 5DH. *T*: 071-273 0619.

BENNETT, Charles John Michael, CBE 1974; FCA; Partner in Barton, Mayhew & Co., Chartered Accountants, 1937–71; *b* 29 June 1906; *e s* of late Hon. Sir Charles Alan Bennett and Constance Radeglance, *d* of Major John Nathaniel Still; *m* 1931, Audrey (*d* 1990), *d* of J. C. C. Thompson (killed in action, 1915); two *d*. *Educ*: Clifton Coll.; Trinity Coll., Cambridge. Served with HM Forces, 1939–45. Member: Electricity Supply Companies Commn, 1959, in Hong Kong; Fiji Sugar Inquiry Commn, 1961; Commn of Inquiry (Sugar Industry) 1962, in Mauritius; Commn of Inquiry into Banana Industry of St Lucia, 1963; Commn of Inquiry (Chm.) into Sugar Industry and Agriculture of Antigua, 1965; Commn of Enquiry into Sugar Industry of Guyana, 1967; Cttee of Enquiry into the pricing of certain contracts for the overhaul of aero-engines by Bristol Siddeley Engines Ltd. Mem. of Council, Institute of Chartered Accountants, 1963–69. Part-time Mem., Commonwealth Development Corp., 1965–73, Dep. Chm. 1970–71, 1972–73; Independent Mem., NEDC for Chemical Industry, and Chm., Pharmaceuticals Working Party, 1969. Mem., E Anglian Regional Cttee of Nat. Trust, 1971–81. *Recreations*: golf, fishing. *Address*: 15 St Olave's Court, St Petersburgh Place, W2 4JY. *T*: 071–229 9554. *Clubs*: Oriental; Royal West Norfolk Golf; Denham Golf.

See also R. H. Cooke.

BENNETT, Sir Charles (Moihi), Kt 1975; DSO 1943; company director, retired; President, New Zealand Labour Party, 1972–76; *b* 27 July 1913; *s* of Rt Rev. Frederick August Bennett, Bishop of Aotearoa, 1928–50, and Rangioue Bennett; *m* 1947, Elizabeth May Stewart. *Educ*: Univ. of New Zealand; Exeter Coll., Oxford. MA, DipSocSci, DipEd. Director of Maori Welfare, 1954–57; High Comr for New Zealand to Fedn of Malaya, 1959–63; Asst Sec., Dept of Maori Affairs, 1963–69. Mem., NZ Prisons Parole Bd, 1974–76. Hon. LLD Canterbury Univ. of NZ, 1973. Hon. Kt PMN (Malaysia), 1963. *Address*: 72 Boucher Avenue, Te Puke 3071, New Zealand.

See also Rt Rev. M. A. Bennett.

BENNETT, Edward; *see* Bennett, A. E.

BENNETT, Air Marshal Sir Erik Peter, KBE 1990; CB 1984; Commander, Sultan of Oman's Air Force, 1974–90; retired from RAF, 1991; *b* 3 Sept. 1928; *s* of Robert Francis and Anne Myra Bennett. *Educ*: The King's Hospital, Dublin. Air Adviser to King Hussein, 1961–62; RAF Staff College, 1963; Jt Services Staff Coll., 1968; RAF Coll. of Air Warfare, 1971. Order of Istiqlal (Jordan), 1960; Order of Oman, 1980; Order of Merit (Oman); Order of Sultan Qaboos (Oman), 1985; Medal of Honour (Oman), 1989. *Recreations*: reading, riding, sailing. *Address*: PO Box 2751, Seeb, Sultanate of Oman. *Clubs*: Royal Air Force, Beefsteak.

BENNETT, Rt. Hon. Sir Frederic (Mackarness), Kt 1964; PC 1985; DL; *b* 2 Dec. 1918; 2nd *s* of late Sir Ernest Bennett and of Lady (Marguerite) Bennett; *m* 1945, Marion Patricia, *e d* of Cecil Burnham, OBE, FRCSE. *Educ*: Westminster. Served War of 1939–45, enlisted Middx Yeo., 1939; commissioned RA, 1940; commended for gallantry, 1941; Military Experimental Officer in Petroleum Warfare Dept, 1943–46, when released with rank of Major. TA&VRA, 1973–83. Called to English Bar, Lincoln's Inn, 1946, Southern Rhodesian Bar, 1947. Observer, Greek Communist War, 1947–49; Diplomatic correspondent, Birmingham Post, 1950–52. Contested (C) Burslem, 1945, Ladywood Div. of Birmingham, 1950. MP (C): Reading N, 1951–55; Torquay, Dec. 1955–1974; Torbay, 1974–87. PPS: to Under-Sec. of State, Home Office, 1953–55, to Minister of Supply, 1956–57, to Paymaster-Gen., 1957–59, and to Pres. of Bd of Trade, 1959–61. Chm. Exec. Cttee, CPA Gen. Council, 1971–73; Leader, UK Delegation and Chm., Council of Europe and WEU Assemblies, 1979–87; Former Chm., Europ. Democratic Political Gp Council of Europe and CD, ED & RPR Federated Gp, WEU. Director: RHB Trust Co. Ltd; Squibb A/S; Commercial Union Assurance Co. Ltd, West End and Exeter Bds; Gibraltar Building Soc.; Gulf Banking and Trust Corp. Ltd (Caymans); Lord of the Manor of Mawddwy. Co-Pres., E-SU of Pakistan, 1988–. DL Greater London, 1990. Freeman, City of London, 1984. Hon. Dr of Law Istanbul, 1984. Comdr, Order of Phœnix, Greece, 1963; (Sithari) Star of Pakistan, 1st cl., 1964; Order of Al-Istiqlal, 1st cl., Jordan, 1980; Comdr, Order of Isabel la Católica, Spain, 1982; Order of Hilal-i-Quaid-i-

Azam, Pakistan, 1983; Commander's Cross, Order of Merit, FRG, 1989; Order (first class) of Polonia Restituta, Poland, 1990 (Comdr, 1977; Grand Comdr's Cross, 1984); Order of Knight of Vitezi, Hungary, 1990. *Publications:* Speaking Frankly, 1960; Detente and Security in Europe, 1976; China and European Security, 1978; The Near and Middle East and Western European Security, 1979, 2nd edn 1980; Impact of Individual and Corporate Incentives on Productivity and Standard of Living, 1980; Fear is the Key; Reds under the Bed, or the Enemy at the Gate—and Within, 1979, 3rd edn 1982. *Recreations:* shooting, fishing, yachting. *Address:* Cwmllecoediog, Aberangell, near Machynlleth, Powys SY20 9QP. *T:* Cemmaes Road (06502) 430; 2 Stone Buildings, Lincoln's Inn, WC2. *T:* 071–242 3900. *Club:* Carlton.

BENNETT, (Frederick Onslow) Alexander (Godwyn), TD; Chairman: Whitbread & Co. Ltd, 1972–77; Whitbread Investment Co. Ltd, 1977–88 (Director, since 1956); *b* 21 Dec. 1913; *s* of Alfred Bennett, banker and Marjorie Muir Bremner; *m* 1942, Rosemary, *d* of Sir Malcolm Perks, 2nd Bt, and of Neysa Gilbert (*née* Cheney); one *s* four *d*. *Educ:* Winchester Coll.; Trinity Coll., Cambridge (BA). Commnd 2nd Bn London Rifle Bde TA, 1938; Lt-Col 1944, GS01 SHAEF and 21 Army Gp (despatches twice). Joined Whitbread & Co. Ltd, 1935: Man. Dir, 1949; Dep. Chm., 1958; Chief Exec., 1967–75. Pres., Kent CCC, 1983–. Master, Brewers' Company, 1963–64; Chm., Brewers' Soc., 1972–74. US Bronze Star, 1944. *Recreations:* garden and countryside, music. *Address:* Grove House, Selling, Faversham, Kent ME13 9RN. *T:* Canterbury (0227) 752250. *Club:* MCC.

BENNETT, His Honour Harry Graham, QC 1968; a Circuit Judge, 1972–91; Designated Circuit Judge, Leeds, 1988–91; *b* 19 Sept. 1921; *s* of Ernest and Alice Mary Bennett, Cleckheaton, Yorks; *m* 1987, Elizabeth, *widow* of Judge Allister Lonsdale. *Educ:* Whitcliffe Mount Grammar Sch., Cleckheaton; King's Coll., London. Royal Artillery, 1943–47. Called to Bar, Gray's Inn, 1948. Recorder: Doncaster, 1966–68; York, 1968–71; Crown Court, 1972; Dep. Chm., ER of Yorks QS, 1964–71. Chm., Agricl Land Tribunal (N Area), 1967–72. *Address:* c/o Leeds Crown Court, Leeds LS2 7DG. *Club:* Leeds (Leeds).

BENNETT, Sir Hubert, Kt 1970; FRIBA; Architect in private practice; Architect to UNESCO Headquarters, Paris, since 1980; former Architect to the Greater London Council (formerly London County Council) and Superintending Architect of Metropolitan Buildings, 1956–71; *b* 4 Sept. 1909; *s* of late Arthur Bennett and Eleanor Bennett; *m* 1938, Louise F. C. Aldred; three *d*. *Educ:* Victoria University, Manchester, School of Architecture. Asst Lecturer, Leeds School of Architecture, 1933–35; Asst Lecturer, Regent Street Polytechnic Sch. of Architecture, 1935–40; Superintending Architect (Lands), War Dept, 1940–43; Borough Architect, Southampton, 1943–45; County Architect, W Riding of Yorks, 1945–56. Exec. Dir, English Property Corp. Ltd, 1971–79. Mem. of Council, RIBA, 1952–55, 1957–62, 1965–66, 1967–69; Hon. Treas., RIBA, 1959–62; Pres., W Yorks Soc. of Architects, 1954–66; Chm., Technical Panel, Standing Conf. on London Regional Planning, 1962–64; Member: Building Res. Bd, 1959–66; Timber Res. and Develt Assoc. Adv. Panel, 1965–68; Housing Study Mission from Britain to Canada, 1968. Dir, Help the Aged Housing Assoc. (UK) Ltd. Prof., Univ of NSW, 1973. Architect for the Hyde Park Corner-Marble Arch Improvement Scheme, Crystal Palace Recreational Centre and South Bank Arts Centre; Consulting Architect, Guest Palace for the Sultan of Oman, Muscat, 1982. RIBA Assessor, South Bank Competition, Vauxhall Cross, 1981; Assessor, City Polytechnic of Hong Kong, 1982–83. RIBA: Silver Medallist for Measured Drawings (Hon. Mention), 1932; Arthur Cates Prize, 1933; Sir John Soane Medallist, 1934; Neale Bursar, 1936; Godwin and Wimperis Bursar, 1948; RIBA London Architecture Bronze Medal, 1959; RIBA Bronze Medal, 1968. Royal Society of Arts Medal, 1934; Rome Scholarship Special Award, 1936; Min. of Housing and Local Govt Housing Medal, 1954, 1963, 1964, 1966, 1968; Civic Trust Awards; Sir Patrick Abercrombie Award (for planning project Thamesmead), Internat. Union of Architects, 1969; Fritz Schumacher Prize, 1970. Hon. Member: Architects in Industry Group; Inst. of Architects of Czechoslovakia; Soc. of Architects of Venezuela. *Address:* Broadfields, Liphook, Hants GU30 7JH. *T:* Liphook (0428) 724176.

BENNETT, Hugh Peter Derwyn; QC 1988; a Recorder, since 1990; *b* 8 Sept. 1943; *s* of Peter Ward Bennett, *qv* and Priscilla Ann Bennett; *m* 1969, Elizabeth (*née* Landon); one *s* three *d*. *Educ:* Haileybury and ISC; Churchill College, Cambridge (MA). Called to the Bar, Inner Temple, 1966; an Assistant Recorder, 1987. Mem., Supreme Court Rule Cttee, 1988–; a Chm. (part-time), Betting Levy Appeal Tribunal, 1989–. Hon. Legal Adv, Sussex County Playing Fields Assoc., 1988–. Fellow of Woodard Corp., 1987–; Mem. Council, Lancing Coll., 1981–. *Recreations:* cricket, tennis, shooting, fishing. *Address:* Queen Elizabeth Building, Temple, EC4. *T:* 071–583 7837. *Club:* MCC.

BENNETT, Hywel Thomas; actor; director; *b* 8 April 1944; *s* of Gordon Bennett and Sarah Gwen Bennett (*née* Lewis); *m* 1967, Cathy McGowan (marr. diss. 1988); one *d*. *Educ:* Henry Thornton Grammar School, Clapham; RADA (scholarship). *Stage:* Nat. Youth Theatre for 5 years; repertory, Salisbury and Leatherhead; first major roles in The Screwtape Letters and A Smashing Day, Arts Th., 1966; Edinburgh Festival, 1966, 1967; Shakespeare at Mermaid, Young Vic, Shaw Theatres, 1970–72; repertory and tours to 1977; Otherwise Engaged, Her Majesty's, 1977; She Stoops to Conquer, Nat. Theatre, 1985; Three Sisters, Albery, 1987; *directed:* plays at provincial theatres incl. Lincoln, Leatherhead, Birmingham, Coventry, Sheffield and Cardiff; *films:* All in Good Time, The Family Way, The Twisted Nerve, The Virgin Soldiers, Loot, The Buttercup Chain, Alice in Wonderland, Endless Night, Murder Elite, War Zone, The Twilight Zone, Checkpoint Chiswick, Frankie and Johnnie; *TV series:* Malice Aforethought; Pennies from Heaven; Tinker, Tailor, Soldier, Spy; Shelley (10 series); many radio plays, commercial voiceovers and film narrations. *Recreations:* fishing, golf, reading, walking. *Address:* c/o James Sharkey, Third Floor Suite, 15 Golden Square, W1R 3AG. *T:* 071–434 3801. *Clubs:* Savile, Wig and Pen (Hon. Mem.).

BENNETT, John, MBE 1945; HM Senior Chief Inspector of Schools for Scotland, 1969–73; *b* 14 Nov. 1912; *m* 1940, Johanne R. McAlpine, MA; two *s* one *d*. *Educ:* Edinburgh Univ. MA (first class hons) 1934. Schoolmaster until 1951. Served War of 1939–45: Capt. REME, 79 Armd Div., 1940–46. HM Inspector of Schools, 1951. *Recreations:* mathematics, golf, bridge. *Address:* 35 Cadzow Drive, Cambuslang, Glasgow G72 8NF. *T:* 041–641 1058.

BENNETT, Sir John (Mokonuiarangi), Kt 1988; QSO 1978; Chairman: Maori Education Foundation, since 1975; Te Kohanga Reo National Trust, since 1982; Nature Conservation Council, since 1984 (Member, since 1970); *b* 4 Sept. 1912; *e s* of Frederick Augustus Bennett and Arihia Rangioue Bennett; *m* 1939, Moana Hineiwaerea (*d* 1975); two *s* two *d* (and two *s* decd). *Educ:* Clive Sch.; Te Aute Coll.; Christchurch Teachers' Coll. Various teaching positions, 1934–74. Vice Pres., New Zealand Maori Council, 1982–. QSO awarded for Public Service, 1978; knighthood for services to education, 1988. *Address:* 70 Simla Avenue, PO Box 8486, Havelock North, Hawkes Bay, New Zealand. *T:* Hawkes Bay 8777.994.

See also Sir C. M. Bennett, Rt Rev. M. A. Bennett.

BENNETT, Rt. Rev. Manu Augustus, ONZ 1989; CMG 1981; DD; *b* 10 Feb. 1916; *s* of Rt Rev. F. A. Bennett, Bishop of Aotearoa, 1928–50, and Alice Rangioue Bennett; *m* 1944, Kathleen Clark; one *d*. *Educ:* Victoria Univ. Coll., Univ. of Hawaii. BSc 1954. Deacon, 1939; Priest, 1940; Vicar of Tauranga, Te Puke Maori District, Dio. Waiapu, 1940–44; Chaplain to 2 NZEF, 1944–46; Pastor of Rangitikei South-Manawatu Pastorate, Dio. Wellington, 1946–52; Asst Vicar of Church of Holy Nativity, Honolulu, 1953–54; Pastor of Wellington Pastorate, 1952–57; Vicar of Ohinemutu Pastorate, Waikato, 1964–68; Bishop of Aotearoa, 1968–81. Nat. Council of Churches Chaplain, Dept of Justice. Hon. DD Jackson Coll., 1964. *Address:* 8/2 Gemini Crescent, Rotorua, New Zealand.

See also Sir C. M. Bennett.

BENNETT, Mrs Mary Letitia Somerville, MA; Principal, St Hilda's College, Oxford, 1965–80, Hon. Fellow 1980; Pro-Vice-Chancellor, Oxford University, 1979–80; *b* 9 Jan. 1913; *o c* of Rt Hon. H. A. L. Fisher, OM, and Lettice Ilbert; *m* 1955, John Sloman Bennett, CMG (*d* 1990). *Educ:* Oxford High Sch.; Somerville Coll. (Schol.); 2nd Cl. Mods, 1st Cl. Lit. Hum.; Hon. Fellow, 1977. Jt Broadcasting Cttee, 1940–41; Transcription Service of BBC, 1941–45; Colonial Office, 1945–56. Mem., Hebdomodal Council, Oxford Univ., 1973–79. Hon. Sec., Society for the Promotion of Roman Studies, 1960–85. *Address:* Rock Cottage, Thursley, Surrey; 25A Alma Place, Oxford OX4 1JW. *Club:* University Women's.

BENNETT, Nicholas Jerome; MP (C) Pembroke, since 1987; Parliamentary Under Secretary of State, Welsh Office, since 1990; *b* 7 May 1949; *s* of Peter Ramsden Bennett and late Antonia Mary Flanagan; unmarried. *Educ:* Sedgehill Sch.; Polytechnic of North London (BA Hons Philosophy); Univ. of London Inst. of Educn (PGCE Distinction); Univ. of Sussex (MA). Educnl publishing, 1974; schoolmaster, 1976–85; educn officer, 1985–87. Chm., SE London Young Conservatives, 1972–73; Councillor, London Borough of Lewisham, 1974–82 (Leader of the Opposition, 1979–81); co-opted Mem., ILEA Educn Cttee, 1978–81. Contested (C): St Pancras N, 1973 and Greenwich, by-elec. 1974, GLC elections; Hackney Central, 1979. PPS to Minister of State, Department of Transport, 1990. Member: Select Cttee on Welsh Affairs, 1987–90; Select Cttee on Procedure, 1988–90; Vice-Chairman: (Wales), Cons. backbench Party Organisation Cttee; Assoc. of Cons. Clubs, 1990–. Member: British-Amer. Parly Gp; IPU; CPA; Catholic Union. Chm., Nat. Council for Civil Protection, 1990. *Publication:* (contrib.) Primary Headship in the 1990s, 1989. *Recreations:* swimming, history, transport, browsing in second-hand bookshops, cinema, small scale gardening. *Address:* House of Commons, SW1A 0AA. *T:* 071–219 4415.

BENNETT, Patrick, QC 1969; a Recorder of the Crown Court, since 1972; *b* 12 Jan. 1924; *s* of Michael Bennett; *m* 1951, Lyle Reta Pope; two *d*. *Educ:* Bablake Sch., Coventry; Magdalen Coll., Oxford. State Scholar, 1941, MA, BCL 1949. Served RNVR, 1943–46, Sub Lt. Called to Bar, Gray's Inn, 1949, Bencher 1976, Master of Students, 1980; Asst Recorder, Coventry, 1969–71; Dep. Chm., Lindsey QS, 1970–71. Mem., Mental Health Act Commn, 1984–86. Fellow: Internat. Soc. of Barristers, 1984; Nat. Inst. of Advocacy, 1980. *Publications:* Assessment of Damages in Personal Injury and Fatal Accidents, 1980; The Common Jury, 1986; Trial Techniques, 1986. *Recreations:* food, flying. *Address:* (home) 22 Wynnstay Gardens, W8. *T:* 071–937 2110; 233 rue Nationale, Boulogne sur Mer, France. *T:* 21 91 33 39; (professional) 2 Crown Office Row, Temple, EC4. *T:* 071–236 9337. *Clubs:* Hurlingham; Spartan Flying (Denham).

BENNETT, Peter Ward, OBE; Chairman, W. H. Smith & Son Holdings Ltd, 1977–82. *Address:* Dene House, Littledene, Glynde, Lewes, Sussex BN8 6LB.

See also H. P. D. Bennett.

BENNETT, Philip Hugh Penberthy, CBE 1972; FRIBA; FCIArb; Consultant, T. P. Bennett Partnership, architects, since 1980 (Partner, 1948–80, Senior Partner, 1967–80); *b* 14 April 1919; *o s* of late Sir Thomas Penberthy Bennett, KBE, FRIBA, and late Mary Langdon Edis; *m* 1943, Jeanne Heal; one *s* one *d*. *Educ:* Highgate Sch.; Emmanuel Coll., Cambridge (MA). Lieut (G) RNVR, 1940–46. Principal works: town centres at Bootle and Stratford (London); head offices for Norwich Union Insce Socs, Ford Motor Co. and other commercial cos; dept stores for United Africa Co. in Ghana and Nigeria, Bentalls (Kingston) and Fenwicks (Newcastle); extensions to Middlesex Hosp.; hostel for Internat. Students Trust; Cunard Internat. Hotel; flats for local authorities and private developers; buildings for airfield and dock develt. Chm., Building Regulations Adv. Cttee (DoE), 1965–77; former RIBA rep. on Jt Contracts Tribunal (Chm. 1973–78) and Nat. Jt Consultative Cttee (Chm. 1970); Mem. other cttees of RIBA and NEDO; Governor: Sch. of Building, 1952–72; Vauxhall Coll. of Further Educn, 1972–77; Member: Home Office Deptl Cttee enquiring into Fire Service, 1967–70; Adv. Council for Energy Conservation, 1974–76. Dir, BEC Building Trust Ltd, 1984–. *Publications:* Architectural Practice and Procedure, 1981; chapter on building, in Britain 1984, 1963; articles in Building, Financial Times, etc. *Recreations:* travel, drawing, theatre. *Address:* Grey Walls, Park Lane, Aldeburgh, Suffolk. *T:* Aldeburgh (0728) 452766.

BENNETT, Gen. Sir Phillip (Harvey), AC 1985 (AO 1981); KBE 1983; DSO 1969; Governor of Tasmania, since 1987; *b* 27 Dec. 1928; *m* 1955, Margaret Heywood; two *s* one *d*. *Educ:* Perth Modern Sch.; Royal Mil. Coll.; jssc, rcds, psc (Aust.). Served, 1950–56: 3rd Bn RAR, Korea (despatches), Sch. of Infantry (Instr), 25 Cdn Bde, Korea, Pacific Is Regt, PNG, and 16th Bn Cameron Highlanders of WA; Commando training, Royal Marines, England, Malta and Cyprus, 1957–58; OC 2 Commando Co., Melb., 1958–61; Aust. Staff Coll., 1961–62; Sen. Instr, then Chief Instr, Officer Cadet Sch., Portsea, 1962–65; AAG Directorate of Personal Services, AHQ, 1965–67; Co 1 RAR, 1967–69 (served Vietnam; DSO); Exchange Instr, Jt Services Staff Coll., England, 1969–71; COL Directorate of Co-ordination and Organization, AHQ, 1971–74; COS HQ Fd Force Comd, 1974–76; RCDS, England, 1976; Comdr 1st Div., 1977–79; Asst Chief of Def. Force Staff, 1979–82; Chief of General Staff, 1982–84; Chief of Defence Force, Australia, 1984–87. Hon. Col, Royal Tasmania Regt, 1987–. KStJ 1988. Hon. LLD New South Wales, 1987. *Recreations:* sailing, golf. *Address:* Government House, Hobart, Tas 7000, Australia. *T:* 002–342611. *Clubs:* Australian (Sydney); United Services (Brisbane); University House, Commonwealth (Canberra).

BENNETT, Ralph Featherstone; *b* 3 Dec. 1923; *o s* of late Mr and Mrs Ralph J. P. Bennett, Plymouth, Devon; *m* 1948, Delia Marie, *o d* of late Mr and Mrs J. E. Baxter, Franklyns, Plymouth; two *s* two *d*. *Educ:* Plympton Grammar Sch.; Plymouth Technical Coll. Articled pupil to City of Plymouth Transport Manager, 1940–43; Techn. Asst, Plymouth City Transp., 1943–54; Michelin Tyre Co., 1954–55; Dep. Gen. Man., City of Plymouth Transp. Dept, 1955–58; Gen. Manager: Gt Yarmouth Transp. Dept, 1958–60; Bolton Transp. Dept, 1960–65; Manchester City Transp., 1965–68; London Transport Executive (formerly London Transport Board): Mem., 1968–71; Dep. Chm., 1971–78; Chief Exec., 1975–78; Chairman: London Transport Executive, 1978–80; London Transport International, 1976–80. Pres., Confedn of Road Passenger Transport, 1977–78; Vice-President: Internat. Union of Public Transport, 1978–81; CIT, 1979–82. CEng;

FIMechE; FCIT; FRSA. *Address:* Buffers, Green Lane, Yelverton, South Devon PL20 6BW. *T:* Yelverton (0822) 852153. *Club:* National Liberal.

BENNETT, Raymond Clayton Watson; His Honour Judge Raymond Bennett; a Circuit Judge, since 1989; *b* 20 June 1939; *s* of Harold Watson and Doris Helena Bennett (previously Watson); *m* 1965, Elaine Margaret Haworth; one *s* one *d. Educ:* Bury Grammar Sch.; Manchester Univ. (LLB). Solicitor, 1964–72; called to the Bar, Middle Temple, 1972; practising barrister, 1972–89; an Asst Recorder, 1984; a Recorder, 1988. *Recreations:* sailing, cycling, tennis, squash, badminton, reading, painting, gardening. *Address:* c/o The Crown Court, Crown Square, Manchester.

BENNETT, Sir Reginald (Frederick Brittain), Kt 1979; VRD 1944; MA Oxon; BM, BCh, 1942; LMSSA 1937; DPM 1948; Grand Officer, Italian Order of Merit, 1977; company director and wine consultant; formerly psychiatrist and politician; *b* 22 July 1911; *e s* of late Samuel Robert Bennett and Gertrude (*née* Brittain); *m* 1947, Henrietta, *d* of Capt. H. B. Crane, CBE, RN; one *s* three *d. Educ:* Winchester Coll.; New College, Oxford. Oxford Univ. Air Squadron, 1931–34; RNVR, 1934–46; Fleet Air Arm, Medical Officer and Pilot; torpedoed twice. St George's Hosp., SW1, 1934–37; Maudsley Hosp., SE5, 1947–49. MP(C) Gosport and Fareham, 1950–74, Fareham, 1974–79; PPS to Rt Hon. Iain Macleod, MP, 1956–63; Chairman: House of Commons Catering Sub-Cttee, 1970–74, 1976–79; Anglo-Italian Parly Gp, 1971–79 (Hon. Sec. 1961–71); Parly and Scientific Cttee, 1959–62. Vice-Pres., Franco-British Parly Relations Cttee, 1973–79; Mem. Council, Internat. Inst. of Human Nutrition, 1975–. Helmsman: Shamrock V, 1934–35; Evaine, 1936–38; Olympic Games (reserve), 1936; in British-American Cup Team, 1949 and 1953 in USA; various trophies since. Chairman: Amateur Yacht Research Soc., 1972–90; World Sailing Speed Record Cttee, RYA/IYRU, 1980–. Hon. Lieut-Col, Georgia Militia, 1960; Hon. Citizen: of Atlanta, Ga, 1960; of Port-St Louis-du-Rhône, France, 1986. Commandeur du Bontemps-Médoc, 1959; Chevalier du Tastevin, 1970; Galant de la Verte Marennes; Chevalier de St Etienne, Alsace, 1971; Chevalier Bretvin (Muscadet), 1973; Legato del Chianti, 1983. *Publications:* articles on wine, medicine, psychiatry, politics and yacht racing. *Recreations:* sailing, painting, foreign travel, basking in the sun, avoiding exercise. *Address:* 30 Strand-on-the-Green, W4 3PH. *Clubs:* White's, London Corinthian Sailing; Imperial Poona Yacht (Cdre); Wykehamist Sailing (Cdre); Seaview Buffs, etc.

BENNETT, Richard Rodney, CBE 1977; composer; *b* 29 March 1936; *s* of H. Rodney and Joan Esther Bennett. *Educ:* Leighton Park Sch., Reading; Royal Academy of Music. Works performed, 1953–, at many Festivals in Europe, S Africa, USA, Canada, Australia, etc. Has written music for numerous films including: Indiscreet; The Devil's Disciple; Only Two Can Play; The Wrong Arm of the Law; Heavens Above; Billy Liar; One Way Pendulum; The Nanny; Far from the Madding Crowd; Billion Dollar Brain; Secret Ceremony; The Buttercup Chain; Figures in a Landscape; Nicholas and Alexandra; Lady Caroline Lamb; Voices; Murder on the Orient Express (SFTA award; Academy Award Nomination; Ivor Novello award, PRS); Permission to Kill; Equus (BAFTA Nomination); The Brinks Job; Yanks (BAFTA Nomination); Return of the Soldier; also the music for television series: The Christians; L. P. Hartley trilogy; The Ebony Tower; Tender is the Night; The Charmer; Poor Little Rich Girl; The Hiding Place; The Story of Anne Frank. Commissioned to write 2 full-length operas for Sadler's Wells: The Mines of Sulphur, 1965, A Penny for a Song, 1968; commnd to write opera for Covent Garden: Victory, 1970; (children's opera) All the King's Men, 1969; Guitar Concerto, 1970; Spells (choral work), 1975. *Publications include:* chamber music, orchestral music, educational music, song cycles, etc; articles for periodicals, about music. *Recreations:* cinema, modern jazz. *Address:* c/o Nigel Britten, Lemon Unna & Durbridge Ltd, 24 Pottery Lane, W11 4LZ.

BENNETT, Prof. Robert John, PhD; FBA 1991; Professor of Geography, London School of Economics, since 1985; *b* 23 March 1948; *s* of Thomas Edward Bennett and Kathleen Elizabeth Robson; *m* 1971, Elizabeth Anne Allen; two *s. Educ:* Taunton's Sch., Southampton; St Catharine's Coll., Cambridge (BA 1970; PhD 1974). Lecturer: University Coll. London, 1973–78; Univ. of Cambridge, 1978–85; Fellow and Dir of Studies, 1978–85, Tutor, 1981–85, Fitzwilliam Coll., Cambridge. Vis. Prof., Univ. California at Berkeley, 1978; Guest Schol., Brookings Instn, Washington DC, 1978, 1979, 1981; Hubert Humphrey Inst. Fellow, Univ. Minnesota, 1985; Univ. Fellow, Macquarie, 1987; Snyder Lectr, Toronto, 1988. Treas., IBG, 1990–; Mem. Council, RGS, 1990–. Murchison Award, RGS, 1982. Gen. Editor, Government and Policy, 1982–; European Co-Editor, Geographical Analysis, 1985–88. *Publications:* Environmental Systems (with R. J. Chorley), 1978; Spatial Time Series, 1979; Geography of Public Finance, 1980; (ed) European Progress in Spatial Analysis, 1981; (ed with N. Wrigley) Quantitative Geography, 1981; Central Grants to Local Government, 1982; (with K. C. Tan) Optimal Control of Spatial Systems, 1984; Intergovernmental Financial Relations in Austria, 1985; (with A. G. Wilson) Mathematical Methods in Human Geography and Planning, 1985; (ed with H. Zimmerman) Local Business Taxes in Britain and Germany, 1986; (with G. Krebs) Die Wirkung Kommunaler Steuern auf die Steuerliche Belastung der Kapitalbildung, 1987; (with G. Krebs) Local Business Taxes in Britain and Germany, 1988; (ed) Territory and Administration in Europe, 1989; (ed) Decentralisation, Local Governments and Markets, 1990; (with G. Krebs) Local Economic Development Initiatives in Britain and Germany, 1990. *Recreations:* the family, craftwork. *Address:* Department of Geography, London School of Economics, Houghton Street, WC2A 2AE.

BENNETT, Robin, Deputy Principal, Wandsworth Adult College, since 1989; *b* 6 Nov. 1934; *s* of Arthur James Bennett, Major RA, and Alice Edith Bennett, Kesgrave, Ipswich; *m* 1962, Patricia Ann Lloyd (separated 1986); one *s* one *d. Educ:* Northgate Grammar School, Ipswich; St. John's Coll., Univ. of Durham (BA); Queen's Coll., and Univ. of Birmingham (Dip Th). MEd Birmingham. Assistant Curate: Prittlewell, 1960–63; St Andrew with St Martin, Plaistow, 1963–65; Vicar, St Cedd, Canning Town, 1965–72; Rector of Loughton, 1972–75; Director, Oxford Inst. for Church and Society, 1975–77; Principal, Aston Training Scheme, 1977–82; Adult Education Officer, Gen. Synod Bd of Education, 1982–85; Archdeacon of Dudley and Dir of Lay Ministerial Develt and Training, Diocese of Worcester, 1985–86; Vice-Principal, Clapham Battersea Adult Educn Inst., 1986–89. Mem. Exec., Nat. Inst. of Adult Continuing Educn, 1982–89. Joined Society of Friends, 1988. *Recreations:* golf, travel, opera, League football.

BENNETT, Ronald Alistair, CBE 1986; QC (Scotland) 1959; Vice-President for Scotland, Value Added Tax Tribunals, since 1977; *b* 11 Dec. 1922; *s* of Arthur George Bennett, MC and Edythe Sutherland; *m* 1950, Margret Magnusson, *d* of Sigursteinn Magnusson, Icelandic Consul-Gen. for Scotland; three *s* three *d. Educ:* Edinburgh Academy; Edinburgh Univ.; Balliol Coll., Oxford. MA, LLB Univ. of Edinburgh, 1942; Muirhead and Dalgety Prizes for Civil Law, 1942. Lieut, 79th (Scottish Horse) Medium Regt RA, 1943–45; Capt. attached RAOC, India and Japan, 1945–46. Called to Scottish Bar, 1947; Vans Dunlop Schol. in Scots Law and Conveyancing, 1948; Standing Counsel to Min. of Labour and National Service, 1957–59; Sheriff-Principal: of Roxburgh, Berwick and Selkirk, 1971–74; of S Strathclyde, Dumfries and Galloway, 1981–82; of N Strathclyde, 1982–83. Lectr in Mercantile Law: Edinburgh Univ., 1956–68; Heriot-Watt

Univ., 1968–75. Chairman: Med. Appeal Tribunals (Scotland), 1971–; Agricultural Wages Bd for Scotland, 1973–; Local Govt Boundary Commn for Scotland, 1974–90; Northern Lighthouse Bd, April-Sept. 1974; Industrial Tribunals, (Scotland), 1977–; War Pension Tribunals, 1984–. Arbiter, Motor Insurers' Bureau appeals, 1975–; Mem., Scottish Medical Practices Cttee, 1976–88. *Publications:* Bennett's Company Law, 2nd edn, 1950; Fraser's Rent Acts in Scotland, 2nd edn 1952; Editor: Scottish Current Law and Scots Law Times Sheriff Court Reports, 1948–74; Court of Session Reports, 1976–88. *Recreations:* swimming, reading, music, gardening. *Address:* Laxamyri, 46 Cammo Road, Barnton, Edinburgh EH4 8AP. *T:* 031–339 6111. *Club:* New (Edinburgh).

BENNETT, Sir Ronald (Wilfred Murdoch), 3rd Bt, *cr* 1929; *b* 25 March 1930; *o s* of Sir Wilfred Bennett, 2nd Bt, and Marion Agnes, OBE (*d* 1985), *d* of late James Somervell, Sorn Castle, Ayrshire, and step *d* of late Edwin Sandys Dawes; *S* father 1952; *m* 1st, 1953, Rose-Marie Audrey Patricia, *o d* of Major A. L. J. H. Aubépin, France and Co. Mayo, Ireland; two *d*; 2nd, 1968, Anne, *d* of late Leslie George Tooker; *m* 3rd. *Educ:* Wellington Coll.; Trinity Coll., Oxford. *Heir:* cousin Mark Edward Francis Bennett, *b* 5 April 1960. *Clubs:* Kampala, Uganda (Kampala).

BENNETT, Roy Grissell, CMG 1971; TD 1947; Chairman, Maclaine Watson & Co. Ltd, London and Singapore, 1970–72 (Director, 1958–72), retired; Chairman, Beder International Singapore and Beder Malaysia, since 1972; *b* 21 Nov. 1917. *Educ:* privately and RMC Sandhurst. Served War of 1939–45, 17th/21st Lancers, seconded 24th Lancers, 1st Lothian and Border Horse, 1944–46; Major. Joined J. H. Vavasseur & Co. Ltd, Penang, 1946; Director, 1949; joined Maclaine, Watson & Co. Ltd, Singapore 1952, Dir London Board 1958–72, Man. Dir, Eastern interests, 1960; Chm. and Man. Dir, London and Singapore, 1970–72; Chm., Pilkington (SE Asia) Private Ltd and Fibreglass Pilkington Malaysia, 1972–89. Chairman: Singapore Internat. Chamber of Commerce, 1967–70; Singapore Chamber of Commerce Rubber Assoc., 1960–72; former Chm., Rubber Assoc. of Singapore (Dep. Chm. 1966–72); Chm. Council, Singapore Anti-Tuberculosis Assoc., 1962–; Founder Chm. and Governor, United World Coll., SE Asia, 1972– (Chm. Governors, 1972–79); Chm., Racehorse Spelling Station, Cameron Highlands, Malaysia, 1976–; Founder Chm., Riding for Disabled Assoc. of Singapore, 1982–85 (Mem. Cttee, 1982–; Life Hon. Mem., 1989); Patron, Nat. Kidney Foundn. MInstD. *Recreations:* economics, polo, racing, shooting, swimming, photography, motoring, safaris, camping, gardening, zoology, boating, reading, travelling, people especially of the East. *Address:* Beder International, PO Box 49, Bukit Panjang, Singapore 9168; 22 Jalan Perdana, Johore Bharu 80300, Malaysia. *T:* Johore Bharu (07) 234505, *Fax:* 60–7249006; Oak Tree House, South Holmwood, Surrey RH5 4NF. *T:* Dorking (0306) 889414. *Clubs:* Cavalry and Guards; Tanglin, British, Turf (Dep. Chm.), Polo (Patron; Past Chm.; Pres. 1958–70), AA Sports (Singapore); Turf, Polo, Town, Swimming (Penang); Victoria Racing (Melbourne).

BENNETT, William John, OBE 1946; LLD; retired 1977; Consultant, Iron Ore Company of Canada, Montreal; Chairman, C. D. Howe Institute; Director: Canadian Reynolds Metals Co. Ltd; Eldorado Nuclear Ltd; Peterson, Howell & Heather Canada Inc.; *b* 3 Nov. 1911; *s* of Carl Edward Bennett and Mary Agnes Downey; *m* 1936, Elizabeth Josephine Palleck; three *s* four *d. Educ:* University of Toronto (BA Hons). Private Sec., Minister of Transport, 1935–39; Chief Exec. Asst to Minister of Munitions and Supply, 1939–46; President: Atomic Energy of Canada Ltd, 1953–58; Canadian British Aluminium Co. Ltd, 1958–60. Eldorado Mining & Refining Ltd, 1946–58. Hon. LLD, Toronto Univ., 1955; Hon. Dr of Science, St Francis Xavier Univ., Antigonish, NS, 1956; Hon Dr of Laws, University of Ottawa, 1957. *Recreations:* ski-ing, music. *Address:* 1321 Sherbrooke Street West, Apt F41, Montreal, Quebec H3G 1J4, Canada. *Club:* Mount Royal (Montreal).

BENNETT, Hon. William Richards, PC (Can.); Premier of British Columbia, 1975–86; *b* 1932; *y s* of late Hon. William Andrew Cecil Bennett, PC (Can.) and of Annie Elizabeth May Richards; *m* Audrey; four *s.* Began a business career. Elected MP for Okanagan South (succeeding to a constituency which had been held by his father), 1973; Leader of Social Credit Group in Provincial House, 1973; formed Social Credit Govt after election of Dec. 1975. *Address:* RR1, Pritchard Drive, Westbank, BC V1Y 7P9, Canada.

BENNEY, (Adrian) Gerald (Sallis), RDI 1971; goldsmith and silversmith; Professor of Silversmithing and Jewellery, Royal College of Art, 1974–83; *b* 21 April 1930; *s* of late Ernest Alfred Benney and Aileen Mary Benney; *m* 1957, Janet Edwards; three *s* one *d. Educ:* Brighton Grammar Sch.; Brighton Coll. of Art (Nat. Dip. in Art); RCA (DesRCA). FSIAD 1975. Estabd 1st workshop, Whitfield Place, London, 1955; Consultant Designer, Viners Ltd, 1957–69; began designing and making Reading civic plate, 1963; discovered technique of texturing on silver, 1964; moved workshop to Bankside, London, 1969; began prodn of Beenham Enamels, 1970. Holds Royal Warrants of Appt to the Queen, the Duke of Edinburgh, Queen Elizabeth the Queen Mother and the Prince of Wales. Member: Govt's Craft Adv. Cttee, 1972–77; UK Atomic Energy Ceramics Centre Adv. Cttee, 1979–83; British Hallmarking Council, 1983–88. Metalwork Design Advisor to Indian Govt (UP State), 1977–78; Chm., Govt of India Hallmarking Survey, 1981; Export Advisor and Designer to Royal Selangor Pewter Co., Kuala Lumpur, 1986–. Major Exhibn, Worshipful Co. of Goldsmiths, 1973; Major one man exhibn of oil paintings, Solomon Gall., 1988. Liveryman, Goldsmiths' Co., 1964. Hon. MA Leicester, 1963. Freeman, Borough of Reading, 1984. *Recreations:* walking, oil painting, landscape gardening. *Address:* Beenham House, Beenham, Berks RG7 5LJ. *T:* Reading (0734) 744370. *Club:* Arts.

BENNION, Francis Alan Roscoe; barrister and writer; *b* 2 Jan. 1923; *o s* of Thomas Roscoe Bennion, Liverpool; *m* 1st, 1951, Barbara Elisabeth Braendle (separated 1971, marr. diss. 1975); three *d*; 2nd, 1977, Mary Field. *Educ:* John Lyon's, Harrow; Balliol Coll., Oxford. Pilot, RAFVR, 1941–46. Gibbs Law Scholar, Oxford, 1948. Called to Bar, Middle Temple, 1951 (Harmsworth Scholar); practised at Bar, 1951–53, 1985–88 and 1989–. Lectr and Tutor in Law, St Edmund Hall, Oxford, 1951–53; Office of Parly Counsel, 1953–65, and 1973–75; Dep. Parly Counsel, 1964; Parly Counsel, 1973–75; seconded to Govt of Pakistan to advise on drafting of new Constitution, 1956; seconded to Govt of Ghana to advise on legislation and drafting Constitution converting the country into a Republic, 1959–61. Sec., RICS, 1965–68; Governor, College of Estate Management, 1965–68. Co-founder and first Chm., Professional Assoc. of Teachers, 1968–72; Founder: Statute Law Soc., 1968 (Chm., 1978–79); Freedom Under Law, 1971; Dicey Trust, 1973; Towards One World, 1979; founder and first Chm., World of Property Housing Trust (later Sanctuary Housing Assoc.), 1968–72 (Vice-Pres., 1986–); Co-founder, Areopagitica Educnl Trust, 1979. *Publications:* Constitutional Law of Ghana, 1962; Professional Ethics: The Consultant Professions and their Code, 1969; Tangling with the Law, 1970; Consumer Credit Control, 1976–; Consumer Credit Act Manual, 1978, 3rd edn 1986; Statute Law, 1980, 3rd edn 1990; Statutory Interpretation, 1984, supplement 1989; Victorian Railway Days, 1989; The Sex Code: morals for moderns, 1991; articles and contribs to books on legal and other subjects. *Recreation:* creation. *Address:* 62 Thames Street, Oxford OX1 1SU. *T:* Oxford (0865) 251521. *Club:* MCC.

BENNITT, Mortimer Wilmot; Chairman, Islington Archaeology and History Society, since 1988; *b* 28 Aug. 1910; *s* of Rev. F. W. and Honoria Bennitt. *Educ:* Charterhouse; Trinity Coll., Oxford. Entered Office of Works, 1934. Served War of 1939–45: RAF, 1943–45. Under Sec., 1951; Dep. Dir, Land Commn, 1967–71; retired 1971. Chairman: Little Theatre Guild of Gt Britain, 1959–60; Tavistock Repertory Company, London, 1975–77. Patron of St Mary's, Bletchley. *Publication:* Guide to Canonbury Tower, 1980. *Recreation:* theatre. *Address:* 3/5 Highbury Grove, N5 1HH. *T:* 071–704 1335. *Clubs:* United Oxford & Cambridge University, Tower Theatre.

BENSON, family name of **Baron Benson.**

BENSON, Baron *cr* 1981 (Life Peer), of Drovers in the County of W Sussex; **Henry Alexander Benson,** GBE 1971 (CBE 1946); Kt 1964; FCA; Partner, Coopers and Lybrand (formerly Cooper Brothers & Co.), Chartered Accountants, 1934–75; Adviser to the Governor of the Bank of England, 1975–83; *b* 2 Aug. 1909; *s* of Alexander Stanley Benson and Florence Mary (*née* Cooper); *m* 1939, Anne Virginia Macleod; two *s* one *d.* *Educ:* Johannesburg, South Africa. ACA (Hons) 1932; FCA 1939. Commissioned Grenadier Guards, 1940–45; seconded from Army to Min. of Supply to advise on reorganisation of accounts of Royal Ordnance Factories, 1943–44, and in Dec. 1943 apptd Dir Ordnance Factories, to carry out reorganisation; apptd Controller of Building Materials, Min. of Works, 1945; Special appt to advise Minister of Health on housing production, 1945, and subseq. other appts, also Mem. Cttee (Wilson Cttee) to review work done on, and to make recommendations for further research into, processes for transformation of coal into oil, chemicals and gas, 1959–60. Mem., Crawley Development Corp., 1947–50; Mem., Royal Ordnance Factories Board, 1952–56; Dep. Chm. Advisory Cttee (Fleck Cttee) to consider organisation of National Coal Board, 1953–55. Dir Hudson's Bay Co., 1953–62 (Dep. Governor 1955–62); Director: Finance Corporation for Industry Ltd, 1953–79; Industrial and Commercial Finance Corp., 1974–79; Hawker Siddeley Gp, 1975–81; Council, Institute of Chartered Accountants, 1956–75 (Pres., 1966); Mem. Advisory Cttee on Legal Aid, 1956–60; Mem. Tribunal under Prevention of Fraud (Investments) Act 1939, 1957–75; Mem. Special Advisory Cttee to examine structure, finance and working of organisations controlled by British Transport Commission, 1960; apptd by Minister of Commerce, N Ireland, to investigate position of railways; to make recommendations about their future, and to report on effect which recommendations will have on transport system of Ulster Transport Authority, 1961; apptd Chm. of a Cttee to examine possible economies in the shipping and ancillary services engaged in meat, dairy products and fruit trades of New Zealand, 1962; Mem. Cttee apptd by Chancellor of the Exchequer to investigate practical effects of introduction of a turnover tax, 1963. Chm., Royal Commn on Legal Services, 1976–79. Joint Comr to advise on integration of Nat. Assoc. of Brit. Manufrs, FBI, Brit. Employers' Confed., and on formation of a Nat. Industrial Organisation (CBI), 1963; Joint Inspector, Bd of Trade, to investigate affairs of Rolls Razor Ltd, 1964; Indep. Chm. of British Iron & Steel Fedn Development Co-ordinating Cttee, 1966; Indep. Chm., Internat. Accounting Standards Cttee (IASC), 1973–76; Dir, Finance for Industry Ltd, 1974–79; Member: Permanent Jt Hops Cttee, 1967–74; Dockyard Policy Bd, 1970–75; NCB team of inquiry into Bd's purchasing procedures, 1973; CBI Company Affairs Cttee, 1972; City Liaison Cttee, 1974–75; Chm., Exec. Cttee of Accountants' Jt Disciplinary Scheme to review cases involving public concern, 1979–86; Vice-Pres., Union Européene des Experts Comptables économiques et financiers (UEC), 1969; Member: Cttee to enquire into admin and organisation of MoD; Cttee on Fraud Trials (Roskill Cttee), 1984–85; Council of Legal Educn, 1989–. Apptd by Nat. Trust as Chm. of adv. cttee to review management, organisation and responsibilities of Nat. Trust, 1967; apptd by Jt Turf Authorities as Chm. of The Racing Industry Cttee of Inquiry to make detailed study of financial structure and requirements of racing industry, 1967. Treasurer, Open Univ., 1975–79. Trustee, Times Trust, 1967–81. Hon. Bencher, Inner Temple, 1983; Freeman, City of London, 1986. Distinguished Service Award, Univ. of Hartford, 1977; Mem., Accounting Hall of Fame, Ohio State Univ., 1984; Founding Societies' Centenary Award, ICA, 1984. *Publication:* Accounting for Life (autobiog.), 1989. *Recreations:* shooting, golf, sailing. *Address:* 9 Durward House, 31 Kensington Court, W8 5BH. *T:* 071–937 4850. *Clubs:* Brooks's, Jockey; Royal Yacht Squadron.

BENSON, Sir Christopher (John), Kt 1988; FRICS; Chairman: MEPC plc, since 1988 (Managing Director, 1976–88); The Boots Company PLC, since 1990 (Director, since 1989); Housing Corporation, since 1990; *b* 20 July 1933; *s* of Charles Woodburn Benson and Catherine Clara (*née* Bishton); *m* 1960, Margaret Josephine, OBE, JP, *d* of Ernest Jefferies Bundy; two *s.* *Educ:* Worcester Cathedral King's Sch.; Thames Nautical Trng Coll., HMS Worcester. FRICS. Dir, House of Fraser plc, 1982–86; Chairman: LDDC, 1984–88; Reedpack Ltd, 1989–90; Vice-Chairman: Sun Alliance Gp, 1991–; Sun Alliance & London Insurance plc, 1991–. Underwriting Mem. of Lloyd's, 1979–. Pres., British Property Fedn, 1981–83; Chairman: Property Adv. Gp to DoE, 1988–90. Dir, Royal Opera House, 1984–. Chm., Civic Trust, 1985–90. Mem. Council, Marlborough Coll., 1982–90. Hon. Fellow, Wolfson Coll., Cambridge, 1990. Hon. Bencher, Middle Temple, 1984. Freeman: City of London, 1975; Co. of Watermen and Lightermen, 1985; Liveryman: Worshipful Co. of Gold and Silver Wyre Drawers, 1975; Guild of Air Pilots and Air Navigators, 1981. *Recreations:* farming, aviation, opera, ballet. *Clubs:* Garrick, Royal Automobile, MCC.

BENSON, David Holford; Vice Chairman, Kleinwort Benson Group Plc, since 1989; *b* 26 Feb. 1938; *s* of Sir Rex Benson, DSO, MVO, MC, and Lady Leslie Foster Benson; *m* 1964, Lady Elizabeth Mary Benson, *d* of 12th Earl of Wemyss and March, *qv*; one *s* two *d.* *Educ:* Eton Coll.; Madrid Univ. CIGasE 1989. Shell Transport & Trading, 1957–63; Kleinwort Benson Gp, 1963–. Non-Exec. Director: Rouse Co., 1986–; British Gas, 1988–. Trustee, Charities Official Investment Fund, 1985–. *Recreation:* painting. *Address:* (office) 20 Fenchurch Street, EC3P 3DB; 11 Brunswick Gardens, W8. *T:* 071–727 4949. *Clubs:* White's, English-Speaking Union.

BENSON, Prof. Frank Atkinson, OBE 1988; DL; BEng, MEng (Liverpool); PhD, DEng (Sheffield); FIEE, FIEEE; Professor and Head of Department of Electronic and Electrical Engineering, University of Sheffield, 1967–87; Pro-Vice Chancellor, 1972–76; *b* 21 Nov. 1921; *s* of late John and Selina Benson; *m* 1950, Kathleen May Paskell; two *s.* *Educ:* Ulverston Grammar Sch.; Univ. of Liverpool. Mem. research staff, Admty Signal Estab., Witley, 1943–46; Asst Lectr in Electrical Engrg, University of Liverpool, 1946–49; Lectr 1949–59, Sen. Lectr 1959–61, in Electrical Engrg, University of Sheffield; Reader in Electronics, University of Sheffield, 1961–67. DL South Yorks, 1979. *Publications:* Voltage Stabilizers, 1950; Electrical Engineering Problems with Solutions, 1954; Voltage Stabilized Supplies, 1957; Problems in Electronics with Solutions, 1958; Electric Circuit Theory, 1959; Voltage Stabilization, 1965; Electric Circuit Problems with Solutions, 1967; Millimetre and Submillimetre Waves, 1969; many papers on microwaves, gas discharges and voltage stabilization in learned jls. *Address:* 64 Grove Road, Sheffield S7 2GZ. *T:* Sheffield (0742) 363493.

BENSON, (Harry) Peter (Neville), CBE 1982; MC 1945; FCA; Chairman, Davy Corporation PLC, 1982–85; *b* 10 Feb. 1917; *s* of Harry Leedham Benson and Iolanthe Benson; *m* 1948, Margaret Young Brackenridge; two *s* one *d.* *Educ:* Cheltenham Coll. FCA 1946. Served War, S Staffs Regt, 1939–45 (Major; MC). Moore Stephens, 1946–48; John Mowlem, 1948–51; Dir, 1951–54, Man. Dir, 1954–57, Waring & Gillow; Dir, APV Co., 1957–66; Man. Dir, 1966–77, Chm., 1977–82, APV Holdings. Director: Rolls Royce Motors, 1971–80; Vickers Ltd, 1980–82. *Recreation:* golf. *Address:* The Gate House, Little Chesters, Nursery Road, Walton-on-the-Hill, Tadworth, Surrey KT20 7TX. *T:* Tadworth (0737) 813767. *Club:* Walton Heath Golf.

BENSON, Horace Burford; *b* 3 April 1904; *s* of Augustus W. Benson and Lucy M. (*née* Jarrett); *m* 1930, Marthe Lanier; one *s* one *d.* Called to Bar, Gray's Inn, 1936; practised as Barrister, Seychelles Islands, 1936–46; District Magistrate, Ghana, 1946; Puisne Judge, Ghana, 1952–57; retired, 1957. Temp. Magistrate, Basutoland, 1958–60; Puisne Judge, Basutoland, Bechuanaland Protectorate and Swaziland, 1960–61; Chief Justice, Basutoland (now Lesotho), 1965; Puisne Judge, Malawi, 1967–69. *Recreations:* bowls, bridge. *Address:* c/o Barclays Bank, West Norwood, SE27.

BENSON, James; President, James Benson Associates Inc., since 1987; Director: Duffy Design Group Inc., since 1988; Scali, McCabe, Sloves Inc., since 1989; *b* 17 July 1925; *s* of Henry Herbert Benson and Olive Benson (*née* Hutchinson); *m* 1950, Honoria Margaret Hurley; one *d.* *Educ:* Bromley Grammar Sch., Kent; Emmanuel Coll., Cambridge (MA). Manager, Res. and Promotion, Kemsley Newspapers, 1948–58; Dir, Mather & Crowther, 1959–65; Man. Dir, 1966–69, Chm., 1970–71 and 1975–78, Ogilvy & Mather Ltd; Vice-Chm., The Ogilvy Group (formerly Ogilvy & Mather Internat.) Inc., 1971–87. Chm., American Associates of the Royal Acad. Trust, 1983–. *Publications:* Above Us The Waves, 1953; The Admiralty Regrets, 1956; Will Not We Fear, 1961; The Broken Column, 1966. *Recreations:* swimming, walking, painting, reading. *Address:* 580 Park Avenue, New York, NY 10021, USA.

BENSON, Sir Jeffrey; *see* Benson, Sir W. J.

BENSON, Jeremy Henry, OBE 1984; architect in private practice, (Benson & Benson F/ARIBA), since 1954; *b* 25 June 1925; *s* of late Guy Holford Benson and Lady Violet Benson; *m* 1951, Patricia Stewart; two *s* three *d.* *Educ:* Eton; Architectural Assoc. (AADipl.); FRIBA. Royal Engineers, 1944–47. Pres., Georgian Gp, 1985– (Mem., Exec. Cttee, 1967–85; Chm., 1980–85); Chm., SPAB, 1989– (Vice-Chm., 1971–89; Mem. Exec. Cttee, 1959–); Vice-Chm., Joint Cttee of SPAB, GG, Victorian Soc., Civic Trust and Ancient Monuments Soc., 1972– (Mem., 1968–), and Chm. of its Tax Group; Member: Forestry Commn's Westonbirt Adv. Cttee, 1969–; Historic Buildings Council for England, 1974–84; Historic Buildings and Monuments Commn for England, 1983– (Chm., Gardens Cttee, 1985–); Adv. Cttee on Trees in the Royal Parks, 1977–80. *Recreation:* gardening. *Address:* Walpole House, Chiswick Mall, W4 2PS. *T:* 081–994 1611; Field Barn, Taddington, Temple Guiting, Cheltenham, Glos. *T:* Stanton (038673) 228. *Club:* Brooks's.

BENSON, Peter; *see* Benson, H. P. N.

BENSON, Maj.-Gen. Peter Herbert, CBE 1974 (MBE 1954); Member of Panel of Independent Inspectors, Planning Inspectorate, Departments of Environment and Transport, 1981–88; *b* 27 Oct. 1923; *s* of Herbert Kamerer Benson and Edith Doris Benson; *m* 1949, Diana Betty Ashmore; one *s* one *d.* Joined Army, 1944; commnd into S Wales Borderers, 1945; transf. to RASC, 1948, and Royal Corps of Transport, 1965; served, Palestine, Cyprus, Malaya and Singapore (three times), Borneo, Africa and Australia; Comdr, 15 Air Despatch Regt, 1966–68; GSO1 (DS) Staff Coll., Camberley, and Australian Staff Coll., 1968–70; Col Q (Movements), MoD (Army), 1971–72; Comdr, 2 Transport Gp RCT (Logistic Support Force), 1972–73. Comdr, ANZUK Support Gp Singapore, Sen. British Officer Singapore, and Leader, UK Jt Services Planning Team, 1973–74; Chief Transport and Movements Officer, BAOR, 1974–76; Dir Gen. of Transport and Movements (Army) (formerly Transport Officer in Chief (Army)), MoD, 1976–78. Chm., Grants Cttee, Army Benevolent Fund, 1980–. Col Comdt, RCT, 1978–90. Chm., Abbeyfield Soc., Beaminster, 1982–. Liveryman, Co. of Carmen, 1977. *Recreations:* golf, fly-fishing, photography. *Club:* Lyme Regis Golf.

BENSON, Sir (William) Jeffrey, Kt 1987; FCIB; Chairman, The 600 Group, since 1987 (Director, since 1983; Vice Chairman, 1985–87); *b* 15 July 1922; *s* of Herbert Benson and Lilian (*née* Goodson); *m* 1947, Audrey Winifred Parsons; two *s.* *Educ:* West Leeds High Sch. FCIB (FIB 1976). Served War, RAF, 1941–46. Joined National Provincial Bank Ltd, 1939; Asst Gen. Manager, 1965–68; National Westminster Bank: Reg. Exec. Dir, 1968–73; Gen. Man., Management Services Div., 1973–75; Dir, 1975–87; Dep. Chief Exec., 1975–77; Gp Chief Exec., 1978–82; a Dep. Chm., 1983–87. Chm., Export Guarantees Adv. Council, 1982–87; Pres., Inst. of Bankers, 1983–85. *Recreations:* golf, swimming. *Address:* Auben, Spencer Walk, The Drive, Rickmansworth, Herts. *T:* Rickmansworth (0923) 778260. *Clubs:* Clifton (Bristol); Phyllis Court (Henley).

BENTALL, Hugh Henry, MB; FRCS; Emeritus Professor of Cardiac Surgery, Royal Postgraduate Medical School, University of London, since 1985; Hon. Consulting Cardiac Surgeon, Hammersmith Hospital, since 1985; *b* 28 April 1920; *s* of late Henry Bentall and Lilian Alice Greeno; *m* 1944, Jean, *d* of late Hugh Cameron Wilson, MD, FRCS; three *s* one *d.* *Educ:* Seaford Coll., Sussex; Medical Sch. of St Bartholomew's Hospital, London. RNVR, Surg Lieut, 1945–47. Consultant Thoracic Surgeon, Hammersmith Hosp., 1955–85; Lecturer in Thoracic Surgery, Postgraduate Medical Sch., London, 1959; Reader, 1962–65; Prof., 1965–85. Order of Yugoslav Flag with Gold Leaves, 1984. *Publications:* books and papers on surgical subjects. *Recreations:* sailing, antique horology. *Address:* Royal Postgraduate Medical School of London, Ducane Road, W12 0NN. *T:* 081–743 2030. *Clubs:* Cruising Association; Royal Naval Sailing Association (Portsmouth); Royal Air Force Yacht (Hamble).

BENTALL, Leonard Edward; Chairman and Chief Executive, Bentalls, since 1990; *b* 26 May 1939; *s* of Leonard Edward Rowan Bentall, *qv*; *m* 1964, Wendy Ann Daniel; three *d.* *Educ:* Stowe School. FCA. Articled Clerk, Dixon Wilson Tubbs & Gillett, 1958–64. Bentalls, 1964–: Management Accountant, Merchandise Controller, Merchandise Dir, Man. Dir, Chm. and Man. Dir. Non-Exec. Dir, Associated Independent Stores, 1979–82. Pres., Roberts Marine (holiday home for mems of retail trade); Vice-Chm. and Chm., Finance Cttee of Governing Body, Brooklands Tech. Coll.; Trustee and Mem. Exec. Cttee, Steadfast Sea Cadet Corps, Kingston upon Thames. FInstD. *Address:* Bentalls PLC, Anstee House, Wood Street, Kingston upon Thames, Surrey KT1 1TS. *T:* 081–546 2002; Runnymede, Sandpit Hall Road, Chobham, Woking, Surrey GU24 8AN. *T:* Chobham (0276) 858256. *Clubs:* MCC, Surrey Cricket, Saints and Sinners.

BENTALL, (Leonard Edward) Rowan, DL; President, Bentalls PLC, since 1978 (Chairman, 1968–78 and Managing Director, 1963–78); *b* 27 Nov. 1911; *yr s* of late Leonard H. Bentall and Mrs Bentall; *m* 1st, 1937, Adelia Elizabeth (*d* 1986), *yr d* of late David Hawes and Mrs Hawes; three *s* two *d*; 2nd, 1987, Katherine Christina Allan, MCSP, SRP. *Educ:* Aldro Sch.; Eastbourne Coll. Joined family business, 1930. Served War of 1939–45: joined East Surrey Regt, 1940; commissioned, Royal Welch Fusiliers, 1941; served Middle East, N Africa, Sicily, Italy, France, Belgium, Holland, 231 (Malta)

Inf. Bde; now Hon. Captain, Royal Welch Fusiliers. Bentalls: Dep. Chm., 1950; Merchandise Dir, 1946–63. Pres., Surrey Br., Inst. of Directors, 1979–84. Mem. Nat. Exec. Cttee, Forces Help Soc. and Lord Roberts Workshops, 1984–88. Freeman of City of London, 1972. Pres., Steadfast Sea Cadet Corps; Gov., Horse Rangers, Hampton Court. FRSA. DL, Greater London 1977, Rep. for Kingston-upon-Thames 1979–84. Cavaliere, Order Al Merito della Repubblica Italiana, 1970. *Publication:* My Store of Memories, 1974. *Recreations:* gardening, ornithology. *Address:* Hill House, Broughton, near Stockbridge, Hants SO20 8DA. *Clubs:* Royal Automobile, Institute of Directors.
See also L. E. Bentall.

BENTHALL, Sir (Arthur) Paul, KBE 1950; FLS; Medal, Internationales Burgen Institut, 1978; *b* 25 Jan. 1902; *s* of Rev. Charles Francis Benthall and Annie Theodosia Benthall; *m* 1932, Mary Lucy (*d* 1988), *d* of John A. Pringle, Horam, Sussex; four *s*. *Educ:* Eton; Christ Church, Oxford. Joined Bird & Co. and F. W. Heilgers & Co., Calcutta, 1924; partner (later dir) of both firms, 1934–53; Pres., Bengal Chamber of Commerce, and of Assoc. Chambers of Commerce of India, 1948 and 1950; Mem. Central Board, Imperial Bank of India, 1948 and 1950–53; Chm. All India Board of Technical Studies in Commerce and Business Administration, 1950–53; Pres. Royal Agri-Horticultural Society of India, 1945–47; Pres., UK Citizens' Assoc. (India), 1952. Chairman: Bird & Co. (London) Ltd, 1953–73; Amalgamated Metal Corporation Ltd, 1959–72; Director: Chartered Bank, 1953–72; Royal Insurance Co. and Associated Cos, 1953–72. Trustee: Victoria Meml, Calcutta, 1950–53; Gandhi Meml Fund, India, 1948–63; Vice Chm., Indo-British Historical Soc., Madras, 1985–. Certified blind, 1985. *Publication:* The Trees of Calcutta, 1946. *Address:* Benthall Hall, Broseley, Salop. *T:* Telford (0952) 882254. *Club:* Oriental.
See also J. C. M. Benthall.

BENTHALL, Jonathan Charles Mackenzie; Director, Royal Anthropological Institute, since 1974; Editor, Anthropology Today, since 1985; *b* Calcutta, 12 Sept. 1941; *s* of Sir Arthur Paul Benthall, *qv*; *m* 1975, Zamira, *d* of Sir Yehudi Menuhin, *qv*; two *s* one step *s*. *Educ:* Eton (KS); King's Coll., Cambridge (MA). Sec., Inst. of Contemporary Arts, 1971–73. Member: UK Adv. Cttee, 1981–87, Overseas Adv. Cttee, 1985–86, 1990–, Council, 1987–90, Assembly, 1990–, SCF; Assoc. of Social Anthropologists, 1983. Chevalier de l'Ordre des Arts et des Lettres (France), 1973. *Publications:* Science and Technology in Art Today, 1972; The Body Electric: patterns of western industrial culture, 1976; (ed) Ecology: the Shaping Enquiry, 1972; (ed) The Limits of Human Nature, 1973; (ed jtly) The Body as a Medium of Expression, 1975. *Recreations:* listening to music, swimming, ski-ing. *Address:* 212 Hammersmith Grove, W6 7HG. *Club:* Athenæum.

BENTHALL, Sir Paul; *see* Benthall, Sir A. P.

BENTHAM, Prof. Richard Walker; Professor of Petroleum and Mineral Law, and Director of the Centre for Petroleum and Mineral Law Studies, University of Dundee, 1983–90; Professor Emeritus, since 1991; *b* 26 June 1930; *s* of Richard Hardy Bentham and Ellen Walker (*née* Fisher); *m* 1956, Stella Winifred Matthews; one *d*. *Educ:* Campbell Coll., Belfast; Trinity Coll., Dublin (BA, LLB). Called to the Bar, Middle Temple, 1955. Lecturer in Law: Univ. of Tasmania, 1955–57; Univ. of Sydney, 1957–61; Legal Dept, The British Petroleum Co. PLC, 1961–83 (Dep. Legal Advisor, 1979–83). Founder Mem., Scottish Council for Arbitration, 1988–; Mem. Council, Inst. of Internat. Business Law and Practice, ICC, 1988–; British nominated Mem., Panel of Arbitrators, Dispute Settlement Centre, IEA, 1989–. FRSA 1986. *Publications:* articles in learned jls in UK and overseas. *Recreations:* cricket, military history, military modelling. *Address:* West Bryans, 87 Dundee Road, West Ferry, Dundee DD5 1LZ. *T:* Dundee (0382) 77100.

BENTINCK, family name of **Earl of Portland**.

BENTLEY, (Anthony) Philip; QC 1991; Barrister, Stanbrook and Hooper, European Community Lawyers, Brussels, since 1980; *b* 5 Dec. 1948; *s* of Kenneth Bentley and Frances Elizabeth (*née* Scott); *m* 1980, Christine Anne-Marie Odile Bausier; two *s* two *d*. *Educ:* St George's Coll., Weybridge; St Catharine's Coll., Cambridge (MA). Called to the Bar, Lincoln's Inn, 1970. With ICI, 1973–77; Dilley & Custer, 1977–80. *Recreation:* oboist in amateur orchestras. *Address:* 42 rue du Taciturne, 1040 Brussels, Belgium. *T:* Brussels 230 50 59.

BENTLEY, Rt. Rev. David Edward; *see* Lynn, Bishop Suffragan of.

BENTLEY, David Jeffrey; Principal Assistant Legal Adviser, Home Office, since 1988; *b* 5 July 1935; *s* of late Harry Jeffrey Bentley and Katherine (*née* Barnett). *Educ:* Watford Grammar School; New College, Oxford (BCL, MA). Called to the Bar, Lincoln's Inn, 1963; University teaching, 1957–79; Asst Parly Counsel, 1965–67; Legal Adviser's Branch, Home Office, 1979–. *Recreations:* reading, listening to music, walking. *Address:* c/o Home Office, Queen Anne's Gate, SW1H 9AT. *Club:* United Oxford & Cambridge University.

BENTLEY, David Ronald; QC 1984; **His Honour Judge Bentley;** a Circuit Judge, since 1988; *b* 24 Feb. 1942; *s* of Edgar Norman and Hilda Bentley; *m* 1978, Christine Elizabeth Stewart; two *s*. *Educ:* King Edward VII Sch., Sheffield; University Coll. London. LLB (Hons) 1963; LLM and Brigid Cotter Prize, London Univ., 1979. Called to the Bar, Gray's Inn, 1969 (Macaskie Scholar). In practice at the bar, 1969–88; a Recorder, 1985–88. *Recreations:* legal history, wildlife, dogs, soccer, cinema.

BENTLEY, Ven. Frank William Henry; Archdeacon of Worcester and Canon Residentiary of Worcester Cathedral, since 1984; *b* 4 March 1934; *s* of Nowell and May Bentley; *m* 1st, 1957, Muriel Bland (*d* 1958); one *s*; 2nd, 1960, Yvonne Wilson; two *s* one *d*. *Educ:* Yeovil School; King's College London (AKC). Deacon 1958, priest 1959; Curate at Shepton Mallet, 1958–62; Rector of Kingsdon with Podymore Milton and Curate-in-charge, Yeovilton, 1962–66; Rector of Babcary, 1964–66; Vicar of Wiveliscombe, 1966–76; Rural Dean of Tone, 1973–76; Vicar of St John-in-Bedwardine, Worcester, 1976–84; Rural Dean of Martley and Worcester West, 1979–84. Hon. Canon of Worcester Cathedral, 1981. *Recreations:* gardening, countryside. *Address:* 7 College Yard, Worcester WR1 2LA. *T:* Worcester (0905) 25046.

BENTLEY, Rev. Canon Geoffrey Bryan; Hon. Canon of Windsor, since 1982; *b* 16 July 1909; *s* of late Henry Bentley; *m* 1938, Nina Mary, *d* of late George Coombe Williams, priest; two *s* two *d*. *Educ:* Uppingham Sch.; King's Coll., Cambridge (Scholar); Cuddesdon Coll., Oxford. BA and Carus Greek Testament Prize, 1932; MA 1935. Ordained, 1933; Asst Curate, St Cuthbert's, Copnor, 1933–35; Tutor of Scholae Cancellarii, Lincoln, 1935–38; Lecturer, 1938–52; Priest Vicar of Lincoln Cathedral and Chaplain of Lincoln County Hosp., 1938–52; Proctor in Convocation, 1945–55; Rector of Milton Abbot with Dunterton, Dio. Exeter, 1952–57; Examg Chap. to Bp of Exeter, 1952–74; Commissary of Bp of SW Tanganyika, 1952–61; Canon of Windsor, 1957–82, President, 1962, 1971 and 1976. Member: Archbp's Commns on Atomic Power, 1946, and Divine Healing, 1953; Archbp's Group on Reform of Divorce Law, 1964 (author of report, Putting Asunder). William Jones Golden Lectr, 1965; Scott Holland Lectr., 1966. *Publications:* The Resurrection of the Bible, 1940; Catholic Design for Living, 1940; Reform of the Ecclesiastical Law, 1944; God and Venus, 1964; Dominance or Dialogue?, 1965; (contrib.) Sexual Morality: three views, 1965; (contrib.) Abortion and the Sanctity of Human Life, 1985. *Address:* 5 The Cloisters, Windsor Castle, Berks SL4 1NJ. *T:* Windsor (0753) 863001.

BENTLEY, Prof. George, FRCS; Professor of Orthopaedic Surgery, University College and Middlesex School of Medicine (formerly at Institute of Orthopaedics), University of London, since 1982; *b* 19 Jan. 1936; *s* of George and Doris Bentley; *m* 1960, Ann Gillian Hutchings; two *s* one *d*. *Educ:* Rotherham Grammar Sch.; Sheffield Univ. (MB, ChB, ChM), FRCS 1964. House Surgeon, Sheffield Royal Infirmary, 1959–61; Lectr in Anatomy, Birmingham Univ., 1961–62; Surg. Registrar, Sheffield Royal Infirm., 1963–65; Sen. Registrar in Orthopaedics, Nuffield Orthopaedic Centre and Radcliffe Infirm., Oxford, 1967–69; Instructor in Orth., Univ. of Pittsburgh, USA, 1969–70; Lectr, 1970–71, Sen. Lectr and Reader in Orth., 1971–76, Univ. of Oxford; Prof. of Orth. and Accident Surgery, Univ. of Liverpool, 1976–82. *Publications:* (ed) 3rd edn vols I and II, Rob and Smith Operative Surgery—Orthopaedics, 1979; (ed) Mercer's Orthopaedic Surgery, 8th edn, 1983; papers on arthritis, accident surgery and scoliosis in leading med. and surg. jls. *Recreations:* tennis, music. *Address:* University Department of Orthopaedic Surgery, Royal National Orthopaedic Hospital, Stanmore, Middx HA7 4LP. *T:* 081–954 2300.

BENTLEY, John Ransome; Director, Wordnet International PLC, since 1983; *b* 19 Feb. 1940; *m* 1st, 1960 (marr. diss. 1969); one *s* one *d*; 2nd, 1982, Katherine Susan (marr. diss. 1986), *d* of Gerald Percy and the Marchioness of Bute. *Educ:* Harrow Sch. Chairman: Bardsey PLC, 1980–81; Intervision Video (Holdings) PLC, 1980–82. *Recreation:* living.

BENTLEY, Philip; *see* Bentley, A. P.

BENTLEY, Sir William, KCMG 1985 (CMG 1977); HM Diplomatic Service, retired; Chairman: Society of Pension Consultants, since 1987; Roehampton Institute, since 1988; Chairman: Coflexip UK Ltd, since 1988; DUCO Ltd, since 1990; *b* 15 Feb. 1927; *s* of Lawrence and Elsie Jane Bentley; *m* 1950, Karen Ellen Christensen; two *s* three *d*. *Educ:* Bury High Sch.; Manchester Univ.; Wadham Coll., Oxford (1st cl. Mod. Hist.); Coll. of Europe, Bruges. HM Foreign (later Diplomatic) Service, 1952; 3rd (later 2nd) Sec., Tokyo, 1952–57; United Nations Dept, Foreign Office, 1957–60; 1st Sec., UK Mission to United Nations, 1960–63; Far Eastern Dept, FO, 1963–65; Head of Chancery, Kuala Lumpur, 1965–69; Dep. Comr-Gen., British Pavilion, Expo 70, Osaka, 1969–70; Counsellor, Belgrade, 1970–73; Head of Permanent Under-Sec.'s Dept, FCO, 1973–74; Head of Far Eastern Dept, FCO, 1974–76; Ambassador to the Philippines, 1976–81; High Comr in Malaysia, 1981–83; Ambassador to Norway, 1983–87. Director: Dyno Industries UK, 1987–; Kenmore Refrigeration UK, 1987–. *Recreations:* golf, skiing, fishing, shooting. *Address:* 48 Bathgate Road, SW19 5PJ; Oak Cottage, Oak Lane, Crickhowell, Powys. *Clubs:* Brooks's; Roehampton.

BENTON, Joseph Edward; JP; MP (Lab) Bootle, since Nov. 1990; *b* 28 Sept. 1933; *s* of Thomas and Agnes Benton; *m* Doris; four *d*. *Educ:* St Monica's Primary and Secondary Sch.; Bootle Technical Coll. Nat. Service, RAF, 1955. Apprentice fitter and turner, 1949; former Personnel Manager, Pacific Steam Navigation Co.; Girobank, 1982–90. Councillor, Sefton Borough Council, 1970–90 (Leader, Labour Gp, 1985–90). Chm. of Govs, Hugh Baird Coll. of Technology. *Address:* c/o House of Commons, SW1A 0AA.

BENTON, Kenneth Carter, CMG 1966; *b* 4 March 1909; *s* of William Alfred Benton and Amy Adeline Benton (*née* Kirton); *m* 1938, Peggie, *d* of Maj.-Gen. C. E. Pollock, CB, CBE, DSO; one *s* one step *s* (and one step *s* decd). *Educ:* Wolverhampton Sch.; London Univ. Teaching and studying languages in Florence and Vienna, 1930–37; employed British Legation, Vienna, 1937–38; Vice-Consul, Riga, 1938–40; 2nd Sec., British Embassy, Madrid, 1941–43; 2nd, later 1st Sec., Rome, 1944–48; FO, 1948–50; 1st Sec., Rome, 1950–53; 1st Sec., Madrid, 1953–56; FO, 1956–62; 1st Sec. and Consul, Lima, 1963–64; FO, 1964–66; Counsellor, Rio de Janeiro, 1966–68; retd from Diplomatic Service, 1968. *Publications:* Twenty-fourth Level, 1969; Sole Agent, 1970; Spy in Chancery, 1972; Craig and the Jaguar, 1973; Craig and the Tunisian Tangle, 1974; Death on the Appian Way, 1974; Craig and the Midas Touch, 1975; A Single Monstrous Act, 1976; The Red Hen Conspiracy, 1977; Ward of Caesar, 1986; as James Kirton: Time for Murder, 1985; Greek Fire, 1985; The Plight of the Baltic States, 1986. *Recreations:* writing, painting. *Address:* 2 Jubilee Terrace, Chichester, West Sussex PO19 1XL. *T:* Chichester (0243) 787148. *Club:* Detection.

BENTON, Peter Faulkner, MA, CBIM; Director-General, British Institute of Management, since 1987; Director, The Turing Institute, since 1985; Chairman, Enfield District Health Authority, since 1986; *b* 6 Oct. 1934; *s* of late S. F. Benton and Mrs H. D. Benton; *m* 1959, Ruth, *d* of late R. S. Cobb, MC, and Mrs J. P. Cobb; two *s* three *d*. *Educ:* Oundle; Queens' Coll., Cambridge (MA Nat. Sciences). 2nd Lieut RE, 1953–55. Unilever Ltd, 1958–60; Shell Chemicals Ltd, 1960–63; Berger Jenson and Nicholson Ltd, 1963–64; McKinsey & Co. Inc., London and Chicago, 1964–71; Gallaher Ltd, 1971, Dir, 1973–77; Man. Dir, Post Office Telecommunications, 1978–81; Dep. Chm., British Telecom, 1981–83. Chairman: Saunders Valve Ltd, 1972–77; Mono Pumps Group, 1976–77; European Practice, Nolan, Norton & Co., 1984–87; Dir, Singer and Friedlander, 1983–89. Chm., Heating, Ventilating, Air Conditioning and Refrigerating Equipment Sector Working Party, NEDO, 1976–79; Member: Electronics Industry EDC, 1980–83; Econ. and Financial Policy Cttee, CBI, 1979–83; Special Adviser to EEC, 1983–84; Nat. Curriculum Science Wkg Gp, 1987–88; Indust. Develt Adv. Bd, DTI, 1988–; Ind. Mem., British Liby Adv. Council, 1988–. Vice-Pres., British Mech. Engrg Confedn, 1974–77. Chairman: Ditchley Conf. on Inf. Technol., 1982; Financial Times Conf., World Electronics, 1983; World Bank Conf. on Catastrophe Avoidance, Washington, 1988, Karlstad, 1989. Royal Signals Instn Lectr, London, 1980; ASLIB Lectr, 1988; Adam Smith Lectr, 1991. Pres., Highgate Literary and Scientific Instn, 1981–88. Chm., N London Hospice Gp, 1985–89. Governor, Molecule Club Theatre. *Publications:* Riding the Whirlwind, 1990; articles on management, science and IT. *Recreations:* reading, fishing, golf, gardening, looking at buildings. *Address:* Northgate House, Highgate Hill, N6 5HD. *T:* 081–341 1133. *Clubs:* Athenæum, United Oxford & Cambridge University, The Pilgrims; Blythe Sappers; Highgate Golf.

BENTON JONES, Sir Simon W. F.; *see* Jones.

BENTSEN, Lloyd Millard, Jr; Member for Texas, US Senate, since 1971; *b* 11 Feb. 1921; *s* of late Lloyd and of Edna Ruth Bentsen; *m* 1943, Beryl Ann Longino; two *s* one *d*. *Educ:* Univ. of Texas (LLB 1942). Served USAAF, 1942–45 (DFC; Air Medal). Admitted to Texas Bar, 1942; in private practice, 1945–48; Judge, Hidalgo County, Texas, 1946–48. Mem. of Congress, 1948–54. Pres., Lincoln Consolidated, Houston, 1955–70. Democratic running mate to Michael Dukakis, US Presidential election, 1988. *Address:* Office of the Senate, Washington, DC 20515, USA.

BENYON, Thomas Yates; Founder: Intelligence Technology Holdings, since 1985; Homecare Residential and Nursing Services PLC, since 1987; Director of various companies; *b* 13 Aug. 1942; *s* of late Thomas Yates Benyon and Joan Ida Walters; *m* 1968, Olivia Jane (*née* Scott Plummer); two *s* two *d*. *Educ:* Wellington Sch., Somerset; RMA

Sandhurst. Lieut, Scots Guards, 1963–67. Insurance Broker, 1967–71; Director of various companies, 1971–: commodity broking, leasing, banking. Chm., Milton Keynes HA, 1990–. Councillor, Aylesbury Vale DC, 1976–79. Contested (C): Huyton, Feb. 1974; Haringey (Wood Green), Oct. 1974; MP (C) Abingdon, 1979–83; Vice Chm., Health and Social Services Cttee, 1982–83; Mem., Social Services Select Cttee, 1980–83. Chm., Assoc. of Lloyd's Members, 1983–85. Vice-Pres., Guidepost Trust (charity for mentally sick), 1978–. *Recreation:* hunting. *Address:* Old Rectory, Adstock, Buckingham. *Club:* Pratt's.

BENYON, William Richard, DL; MP (C) Milton Keynes, since 1983 (Buckingham, 1970–83); *b* 17 Jan. 1930; *e s* of late Vice-Adm. R. Benyon, CB, CBE, and of Mrs. Benyon, The Lambdens, Beenham, Berkshire; *m* Elizabeth Ann Hallifax; two *s* three *d. Educ:* Royal Naval Coll., Dartmouth. Royal Navy, 1947–56; Courtaulds Ltd, 1956–64; Farmer, 1964–. PPS to Minister of Housing and Construction, 1972–74; Conservative Whip, 1974–76. Mem., Berks CC, 1964–74; JP 1962–78, DL 1970, Berks. *Address:* Englefield House, Englefield, near Reading, Berkshire RG7 5EN. *T:* Reading (0734) 302221. *Clubs:* Boodle's, Pratt's.

BÉRÉGOVOY, Pierre; Minister for the Economy, Finance and Budget, France, since 1988; *b* 23 Dec. 1925; *s* of Adrien Bérégovoy and Irène (*née* Baudelin); *m* 1948, Gilberte Bonnet; one *s* two *d. Educ:* Ecole primaire, supérieure, Elbeuf; Institut du travail, Faculté de Droit, Strasbourg. Head of Sub-div., subseq. Asst to Dir, Soc. pour le développement de l'industrie du gaz, 1958–78; Chargé de mission, Gaz de France, 1978–81. Sec. Gen. to Presidency, 1981–82; Minister: of Social Affairs and Nat. Solidarity, 1982; for Economy, Finance and Budget, 1984–86; Deputy for Nièvre, 1986. Mem., Econ. and Social Council, 1979–81. Founder mem., Parti Socialiste Autonome, 1958; Member: Secretariat, Parti Socialiste Unifié, 1963–67; Managing Cttee and Exec. Bd, Parti Socialiste, 1969; Nat. Sec. for Social Affairs, 1973–75, in charge of External Affairs, 1975–81 (responsible for party to Liaison Cttee of the Left). Founder, Socialisme moderne, 1967. *Publication:* contrib. Economy and Liberty periodical. *Recreations:* rural antiquities, football, cycling, cross-country running. *Address:* 139 rue de Bercy, 75012 Paris, France. *T:* 40 04 04 04.

BERESFORD, family name of **Baron Decies** and **Marquess of Waterford.**

BERESFORD, Sir (Alexander) Paul, Kt 1990; dental surgeon; Councillor (C), Wandsworth Borough Council, since 1978, Leader of the Council, since 1983; *b* 6 April 1946; *s* of Raymond and Joan Beresford; *m* Julie Haynes; three *s* one *d. Educ:* Richmond Primary Sch., Richmond, Nelson, NZ; Waimea Coll., Richmond; Otago Univ., Dunedin. *Address:* Flat 21, 140 Park Lane, W1Y 3AA.

BERESFORD, Prof. Maurice Warwick, FBA 1985; Professor of Economic History, University of Leeds, 1959–85, now Emeritus; *b* 6 Feb. 1920; *s* of late H. B. Beresford and Mrs N. E. Beresford. *Educ:* Boldmere and Green Lane Elementary Schs; Bishop Vesey's Grammar Sch., Sutton Coldfield; Jesus Coll., Cambridge. Historical Tripos, Pt I class I, 1940, Pt II class I, 1941; MA 1945. On Staff of Birmingham Univ. Settlement, 1941–42; Sub-warden, Percival Guildhouse, Rugby, 1942–43; Warden, 1943–48; University of Leeds: Lecturer, 1948–55; Reader, 1955–59; Dean, 1958–60; Chm., Sch. of Economic Studies, 1965–68, 1971–72, 1981–83; Chm. of Faculty Bd, 1968–70. Harrison Vis. Prof. of History, Coll. of William and Mary, Virginia, 1975–76; Vis. Prof. of History, Strathclyde Univ., 1987–90. Chairman: Yorks Citizens' Advice Bureaux Cttee, 1963–69; Parole Review Cttee, Leeds Prison, 1970–; Northern Area Inst. for Study and Treatment of Delinquency, 1973–78; Co-opted Mem., City of Leeds Probation Cttee, 1972–78; SSRC, Economic and Social History Cttee, 1972–75. Minister's nominee, Yorkshire Dales National Park Cttee, 1964–71; Member: Consumer Council, 1966–71; Hearing Aids Council, 1969–71; Royal Commn on Historical Monuments (England), 1979–90. Hon. Vice-Pres., Yorks Archaeolog. Soc., 1986 (Medallist, 1989); Hon. Patron, Thoresby Soc., 1985. Hon. DLitt: Loughborough, 1984; Hull, 1986. *Publications:* The Leeds Chambers of Commerce, 1951; The Lost Villages of England, 1954, rev. edn 1983; History on the Ground, 1957, rev. edn 1984; (with J. K. S. St Joseph) Medieval England: an Aerial Survey, 1958, rev. edn 1979; Time and Place, 1962; New Towns of the Middle Ages, 1967, rev. edn 1988; (Ed, with G. R. J. Jones) Leeds and Its Region, 1967; (with J. G. Hurst) Deserted Medieval Villages, 1971, rev. edn 1989; (with H. P. R. Finberg) English Medieval Boroughs, 1973; (with B. J. Barber) The West Riding County Council 1889–1974, 1979; Walks Round Red Brick, 1980; Time and Place: collected essays, 1985; East End, West End, 1988; (with J. G. Hurst) Wharram Percy — Deserted Medieval Village, 1990; contribs to Economic History Review, Agricultural History Review, Medieval Archaeology, etc. *Recreations:* music, theatre, maps, delinquency. *Address:* 6 Claremont Avenue, Leeds LS3 1AT. *T:* Leeds (0532) 454563.

BERESFORD, Meg; gardener, The Iona Community, since 1991; General Secretary, Campaign for Nuclear Disarmament, 1985–90; *b* 5 Sept. 1937; *d* of late John Tristram Beresford and of Anne Beresford; *m* 1959, William Tanner; two *s. Educ:* Sherborne School for Girls; Seale Hayne Agricultural Coll., Newton Abbot; Univ. of Warwick. Community worker, Leamington Spa; Organising Sec., European Nuclear Disarmament, 1981–83. *Publications:* Into the Twenty First Century; contributor to End Jl, Sanity. *Recreations:* walking, reading, camping, music. *Address:* 79a Mildmay Road, N1 4PU.

BERESFORD-PEIRSE, Sir Henry Grant de la Poer, 6th Bt *cr* 1814; *b* 7 Feb. 1933; *s* of Sir Henry Campbell de la Poer Beresford-Peirse, 5th Bt, CB, and of Margaret, *d* of Frank Morison Seafield Grant, Knockie, Inverness-shire; *S* father, 1972; *m* 1966, Jadranka, *d* of Ivan Njerš, Zagreb, Yugoslavia; two *s. Heir: s* Henry Njerš de la Poer Beresford-Peirse, *b* 25 March 1969.

BERESFORD-WEST, Michael Charles; QC 1975; a Recorder of the Crown Court, 1975–83; *b* 3 June 1928; *s* of late Arthur Charles, OBE, KPM and Ida Dagmar West; *m* 1st, 1956, Patricia Eileen Beresford (marr. diss.); two *s* one *d*; 2nd, 1986, Sheilagh Elizabeth Davies. *Educ:* St Peter's, Southbourne; Portsmouth Grammar Sch.; Brasenose Coll., Oxford (MA). Nat. Service, Intell. Corps, Middle East, SIME. Called to Bar, Lincoln's Inn, 1952, Inner Temple, 1980; Western Circuit, 1953–65; SE Circuit, 1965; a Chm., Independent Schools Tribunal and Tribunal (Children's Act 1948), 1974–80. *Recreations:* swimming, lawn tennis, music, golf. *Address:* 1 Gray's Inn Square, WC1R 5AG. *T:* 071–404 5416. *Clubs:* MCC (1951–80); Hampshire Hogs Cricket; Nomads; Aldeburgh Yacht, Bar Yacht; Aldeburgh Golf.

BERG, Rev. John J.; *see* Johansen-Berg.

BERG, Prof. Paul, PhD; Willson Professor of Biochemistry, since 1970, and Director, Beckman Center for Molecular and Genetic Medicine, since 1985, Stanford University School of Medicine; *b* New York, 30 June 1926; *m* Mildred Levy; one *s. Educ:* Pennsylvania State Univ. (BS); Western Reserve Univ. (PhD). Pre-doctoral and post-doctoral med. research, 1950–54; scholar in cancer research, American Cancer Soc., Washington Univ., 1954; Asst to Associate Prof. of Microbiology, Washington Univ., 1955–59; Stanford Univ. Sch. of Medicine: Associate Prof. of Biochem., 1959–60; Prof., Dept of Biochem., 1960, Chm. 1969–74; Non-resident Fellow, Salk Inst., 1973–83. Editor, Biochemical and Biophysical Res. Communications, 1959–68; Member: NIH Study, Sect. on Physiol Chem.; Editorial Bd, Jl of Molecular Biology, 1966–69; Bd of Sci. Advisors, Jane Coffin Childs Foundn for Med. Res.; Adv. Bds to Nat. Insts of Health, Amer. Cancer Soc., Nat. Sci. Foundn, MIT and Harvard, 1970–80; Council, Nat. Acad. of Scis, 1979. Former Pres., Amer. Soc. of Biological Chemists; Foreign Member: Japan Biochem. Soc., 1978–; French Acad. of Scis, 1981–. Lectures: Harvey, 1972; Lynen, 1977; Weizmann Inst., 1977; Univ. of Pittsburgh, 1978; Priestly, Pennsylvania State Univ., 1978; Shell, Univ. of California at Davis, 1978; Dreyfus, Northwestern Univ., 1979; Jesup, Columbian Univ., 1980; Karl-August-Förster, Univ. of Mainz, 1980; David Rivett Meml, CSIR, Melb., 1980. Hon. DSc: Rochester and Yale Univs, 1978; Washington Univ., St Louis, 1986; numerous awards include: Eli Lilly Award, 1959; Calif. Scientist of the Year, 1963; Nat. Acad. of Scis, 1966, 1974; Amer. Acad. of Arts and Scis, 1966; Henry J. Kaiser, Stanford Univ. Sch. of Med., 1969, 1972; Dist, Alumnus, Pennsylvania State Univ.; V. D. Mattia Prize of Roche Inst. for Molec. Biol., 1972; Gairdner Foundn Award, Nobel Prize in Chemistry, New York Acad. of Scis and Albert Lasker Med. Res. awards, 1980; National Medal of Science, 1983. *Publications:* many scientific articles and reviews. *Address:* Stanford University Medical Center, Stanford, California 94305, USA.

BERGANZA, Teresa; singer (mezzo-soprano); *b* Madrid, Spain; *d* of Guillermo and Maria Ascension Berganza; *m*; three *c*. Début in Aix-en-Provence, 1957; début in England, Glyndebourne, 1958; appeared at Glyndebourne, 1959; Royal Opera House, Covent Garden, 1959, 1960, 1963, 1964, 1976, 1977, 1979, 1981, 1984, 1985; Royal Festival Hall, 1960, 1961, 1962, 1967, 1971; appears regularly in Vienna, Milan, Aix-en-Provence, Holland, Japan, Edinburgh, Paris, Israel, America. Prizes: Lucretia Arana; Nacional Lírica, Spain; Lily Pons, 1976; Acad. Nat. du Disque Lyrique; USA record award; Harriet Cohen Internat. Music Award, 1974; Grand Prix Rossini; Médaille d'or, Ville Aix-en-Provence; International Critic Award, 1988. Charles Cross (6 times); Grand Cross, Isabel la Católica, Spain; Gran Cruz al Mérito en las Bellas Artes, Spain; Commandeur, l'Ordre des Arts et des Lettres, France. *Publication:* Flor de Soledad y Silencio, 1984. *Recreations:* music, books, the arts. *Address:* 28200 San Lorenzo del Escorial, Madrid, Spain. *T:* 34–1–890.48.06.

BERGER, John; author and art critic; *b* London, 5 Nov. 1926; *s* of late S. J. D. Berger, OBE, MC, and Mrs Miriam Berger (*née* Branson). *Educ:* Central Sch. of Art; Chelsea Sch. of Art. Began career as a painter and teacher of drawing; exhibited at Wildenstein, Redfern and Leicester Galls, London. Art Critic: Tribune; New Statesman. Vis. Fellow, BFI, 1990–. Numerous TV appearances, incl.: Monitor; two series for Granada TV. Scenario: (with Alain Tanner) La Salamandre; Le Milieu du Monde; Jonas (New York Critics Prize for Best Scenario of Year, 1976); Play me Something (also principal rôle) (Europa Prize, Barcelona Film Fest., 1989). George Orwell Meml Prize, 1977; State Prize for Artistic Achievement, Austria, 1990. *Publications: fiction:* A Painter of Our Time, 1958; The Foot of Clive, 1962; Corker's Freedom, 1964; G (Booker Prize, James Tait Black Meml Prize), 1972; Into their Labours (trilogy): Pig Earth, 1979; Once in Europa, 1989; Lilac and Flag, 1991; *theatre:* with Nella Bielski: Question of Geography, 1986 (staged Marseilles, 1984, Paris, 1986 and by RSC, Stratford, 1987); Francisco Goya's Last Portrait, 1989; *non-fiction:* Marcel Frishman, 1958; Permanent Red, 1960; The Success and Failure of Picasso, 1965; (with J. Mohr) A Fortunate Man: the story of a country doctor, 1967; Art and Revolution, Moments of Cubism and Other Essays, 1969; The Look of Things, Ways of Seeing, 1972; The Seventh Man, 1975 (Prize for Best Reportage, Union of Journalists and Writers, Paris, 1977); About Looking, 1980; (with J. Mohr) Another Way of Telling, 1982 (televised, 1989); And Our Faces, My Heart, Brief as Photos, 1984; The White Bird, 1985 (USA, as The Sense of Sight, 1985); *translations:* (with A. Bostock): Poems on the Theatre, by B. Brecht, 1960; Return to My Native Land, by Aime Cesaire, 1969; (with Lisa Appignanesi) Oranges for the Son of Alexander Levy, by Nella Bielski, 1982. *Address:* Quincy, Mieussy, 74440 Taninges, France.

BERGER, Vice-Adm. Sir Peter (Egerton Capel), KCB 1979; LVO 1960; DSC 1949; MA; Bursar, 1981–91, and Fellow, Selwyn College, Cambridge, since 1981; *b* 11 Feb. 1925; *s* of late Capel Colquhoun Berger and Winifred Violet Berger (*née* Levett-Scrivener); *m* 1956, June Kathleen Pigou; three *d. Educ:* Harrow Sch. MA Cantab 1984. Served War of 1939–45: entered RN as a Cadet, 1943; Normandy and South of France landings in HMS Ajax, 1944; Sub-Lt, 1945; Lieut, 1946; Yangtse Incident, HMS Amethyst, 1949; Lt-Comdr, 1953; Comdr, 1956; Fleet Navigating Officer, Home Fleet, 1956–58; Navigating Officer, HM Yacht Britannia, 1958–60; Commanded HMS Torquay, 1962–64; Captain, 1964; Defence, Naval and Military Attaché, The Hague, 1964–66; commanded HMS Phoebe, 1966–68; Commodore, Clyde, 1971–73; Rear-Adm., 1973; Asst Chief of Naval Staff (Policy), 1973–75; COS to C-in-C Fleet, 1976–78; Flag Officer Plymouth, Port Admiral Devonport, Comdr Central Sub Area Eastern Atlantic and Comdr Plymouth Sub Area Channel, 1979–81, retired 1981. *Recreations:* shooting, fishing, history. *Address:* Linton End House, Linton Road, Balsham, Cambs CB1 6HA. *T:* Cambridge (0223) 892959.

BERGERSEN, Dr Fraser John, FRS 1981; FAA 1985; Chief Research Scientist, Division of Plant Industry, CSIRO, Canberra, since 1972; *b* 26 May 1929; *s* of Victor E. and Arabel H. Bergersen; *m* 1952, Gladys Irene Heather; two *s* one *d. Educ:* Univ. of Otago, New Zealand (BSc, MSc (Hons)); Univ. of New Zealand (DSc 1962). Bacteriology Dept, Univ. of Otago, 1952–54; Div. of Plant Industry, CSIRO, Canberra, Aust., 1954–, currently engaged full-time in scientific research in microbiology, with special reference to symbiotic nitrogen fixation in legume root-nodules. Foreign Sec., Aust. Acad. of Science, 1989–. David Rivett Medal, CSIRO Officers' Assoc. 1968. *Publications:* Methods for Evaluating Biological Nitrogen Fixation, 1980; Root Nodules of Legumes: structure and functions, 1982; one hundred and fifty articles and chapters in scientific journals and books. *Recreations:* music, gardening. *Address:* CSIRO Division of Plant Industry, GPO Box 1600, Canberra City, ACT 2601, Australia. *T:* (06) 2465098, (home) (06) 2477413.

BERGHUSER, Sir Hugo (Erich), Kt 1989; MBE 1981; Member of Parliament, Papua New Guinea, since 1987; Minister for Civil Aviation, Tourism and Culture, since 1987; *b* Germany, 25 Oct. 1935. *Educ:* Volksschule, Stiepel; Trade School, Bochum. Cabinet-maker. Embarked on ship to emigrate to Australia, 1958; ship (Skaubryn) caught fire and sank in the Indian Ocean; arrived in Papua New Guinea in 1959; active in the building industries, meat trade and timber sawmilling trade, employing over 700. Independence Medal, PNG, 1975; Queen's Jubilee Medal, 1977; Service Medal, PNG, 1980; Long Service Medal, PNG, 1985. Distinctive Cross, 1st Cl. (Germany), 1986; Hon. Consulate Gen. (Turkey). *Address:* PO Box 1785, Boroko, NCD, Papua New Guinea. *Club:* Papua.

BERGMAN, (Ernst) Ingmar; Swedish film producer; Director, Royal Dramatic Theatre, Stockholm; director of productions on television; *b* Uppsala, 14 July 1918; *s* of a Chaplain to the Royal Court at Stockholm; *m* 1971, Mrs Ingrid von Rosen; (eight *c* by previous marriages). *Educ:*Stockholm Univ. Producer, Royal Theatre, Stockholm, 1940–42; Producer and script-writer, Swedish Film Co., 1940–44; Theatre Director: Helsingborg, 1944–46; Gothenburg, 1946–49; Malmo, 1952–1959. Produced: Hedda Gabler, Cambridge, 1970; Show, 1971; King Lear, 1985; Hamlet, 1986, Nat. Theatre, 1987; Miss Julie, Nat. Th., 1987; Lady from the Sea, Oslo, A Doll's House, Theatre Royal Glasgow, 1990. Films (British titles) produced include: Torment, 1943; Crisis, 1945; Port of Call, 1948; Summer Interlude, 1950; Waiting Women, 1952; Summer with Monika, 1952; Sawdust and Tinsel, 1953; A Lesson in Love, 1953; Journey into Autumn, 1954; Smiles of a Summer Night, 1955; The Seventh Seal, 1956–57; Wild Strawberries, 1957; So Close to Life, 1957; The Face, 1958; The Virgin Spring, 1960 (shown Edinburgh Fest., 1960); The Devil's Eye, 1961 (shown Edinburgh Fest., 1961); Through a Glass Darkly, 1961; Winter Light, 1962; The Silence, 1963; Now About all these Women, 1964 (first film in colour); Persona, 1967; Hour of the Wolf, 1968; Shame, 1968; The Rite, 1969; The Passion, 1970; The Fâro Document, 1970 (first documentary, shown Vienna Fest., 1980); The Touch, 1971; Cries and Whispers, 1972 (NY Film Critics Best Film Award, 1972); Scenes from a Marriage, 1974 (BBC TV Series, 1975; published, 1975; British première as play, Chichester, 1990); Face to Face, 1976 (BBC TV Series, 1979); The Serpent's Egg, 1977; Autumn Sonata, 1978; From the Life of the Marionettes, 1981; Fanny and Alexander, 1983 (published, 1989). Has gained several international awards and prizes for films; Goethe Prize, 1976; Great Gold Medal, Swedish Acad. of Letters, 1977. *Publications:* Four Stories, 1977; The Magic Lantern (autobiog.), 1988.

BERGMAN, Ingmar; *see* Bergman, E. I.

BERGONZI, Prof. Bernard, FRSL; Professor of English, University of Warwick, since 1971; *b* 13 April 1929; *s* of late Carlo and Louisa Bergonzi; *m* 1st, 1960, Gabriel Wall (*d* 1984); one *s* two *d*; 2nd, 1987, Anne Samson. *Educ:* Wadham Coll., Oxford (BLitt, MA). Asst Lectr in English, Manchester Univ., 1959–62, Lectr, 1962–66; Sen. Lectr, Univ. of Warwick, 1966–71, Pro-Vice-Chancellor, 1979–82. Vis. Lectr, Brandeis Univ., 1964–65; Vis. Professor: Stanford Univ., 1982; Univ. of Louisville, 1988; Vis. Fellow, New Coll., Oxford, 1987. FRSL 1984. *Publications:* Descartes and the Animals (verse), 1954; The Early H. G. Wells, 1961; Heroes' Twilight, 1965; The Situation of the Novel, 1970; Anthony Powell, 1971; T. S. Eliot, 1972; The Turn of a Century, 1973; Gerard Manley Hopkins, 1977; Reading the Thirties, 1978; Years (verse), 1979; The Roman Persuasion (novel), 1981; The Myth of Modernism and Twentieth Century Literature, 1986; Exploding English, 1990. *Recreations:* conversation, looking at pictures and buildings. *Address:* Department of English, University of Warwick, Coventry CV4 7AL. *T:* Coventry (0203) 523523.

BERGSTRÖM, Prof. Sune, MD; Swedish biochemist; *b* 10 Jan. 1916; *s* of Sverker Bergström and Wera (*née* Wistrand). *Educ:* Karolinska Inst (MD 1944, DMedSci 1944). Squibb Inst., USA, 1941–42; Med. Nobel Inst., Stockholm, 1942–46; Basle Univ., 1946–47; Prof. of Biochemistry, Lund Univ., 1947–58; Prof at Karolinska Inst, 1958–80, Dean of Med. Faculty, 1963–66, Rector, 1969–77. Consultant to WHO. Chm., Board, Nobel Foundn, 1975–87 (and Chm., Adv. Council, Med. Research, 1977–82). Member: Swedish Acad. of Scis; Swedish Acad. of Engineering; Amer. Acad. of Arts and Scis; Nat. Acad. of Scis, USA; Acad. of Sci., USSR; Acad. of Med. Scis, USSR; Papal Acad. of Sci.; Hon. Mem., Amer. Soc. of Biol. Chemists. Albert Lasker Basic Med. Research Award, 1977; (jtly) Nobel Prize for Physiology or Medicine, 1982. *Publications:* papers on heparin, autoxidation, bile acids and chlorestrol, prostaglandins. *Address:* Karolinska Institutet, Nobelkansli, PO Box 60250, 10401 Stockholm, Sweden.

BERIO, Luciano; composer; *b* 24 Oct. 1925; *s* of Ernesto Berio and Ada dal Fiume; *m* 1st, 1950, Cathy Berberian (marr. diss. 1964; she *d* 1983); one *d*; 2nd, 1964, Susan Oyama (marr. diss. 1971); one *s* one *d*; 3rd, 1977, Talia Pecker; two *s*. *Educ:* Liceo Classico, Oneglia; Conservatorio G. Verdi, Milan. Hon. degree in Composition, City Univ., London, 1979. Works include: Differences, 1958; Epifanie, 1959–63; Circles, 1960; Passaggio, 1962; Laborintus II, 1965; Sinfonia, 1968; Concerto for 2 pianos, 1972; Opera, 1969–74; Sequenzas I–XI for solo instruments, and for female voice, 1958–88; A-Ronne for five actors, 1974–75; Coro for chorus and orchestra, 1975–76; La Ritirata Notturna di Madrid, 1975; Ritorno degli Snovidenia, 1977; La Vera Storia, 1981; Un Re in Ascolto, 1983; Voci, 1984; Requies, 1985; Formazioni, 1986; Ricorrenze, 1987; Concerto II (Echoing Curves), 1988; Ofanim, 1988; Canticum Novissimi Testamenti, 1989; Rendering (Schubert), 1990. *Address:* Il Colombaio, Radicondoli (Siena), Italy.

BERIOZOVA, Svetlana; Ballerina; *b* 24 Sept. 1932; *d* of Nicolas and Maria Beriozoff (Russian); *m* 1959, Mohammed Masud Khan (marr. diss. 1974; he *d* 1989). *Educ:* New York, USA. Joined Grand Ballet de Monte Carlo, 1947; Metropolitan Ballet, 1948–49; Sadler's Wells Theatre Ballet, 1950–52; Sadler's Wells Ballet (now The Royal Ballet), 1952. Has created leading rôles in Designs for Strings (Taras), Fanciulla delle Rose (Staff), Trumpet Concerto (Balanchine), Pastorale (Cranko), The Shadow (Cranko), Rinaldo and Armida (Ashton), The Prince of the Pagodas (Cranko), Antigone (Cranko), Baiser de la Fée (MacMillan), Diversions (MacMillan), Persephone (Ashton), Images of Love (MacMillan). Classical Roles: Le Lac des Cygnes, The Sleeping Beauty, Giselle, Coppélia, Sylvia, Cinderella. Other rôles currently danced: Les Sylphides, The Firebird, The Lady and Fool, Checkmate, Fête Etrange, Ondine, Nutcracker. Has danced with The Royal Ballet in USA, France, Italy, Australia, S Africa, Russia, and as guest ballerina in Belgrade, Granada, Milan (La Scala), Stuttgart, Bombay, Nervi, Helsinki, Paris, Vienna, New Zealand, Zurich. Played the Princess in The Soldier's Tale (film), 1966. Has frequently appeared on television. *Relevant publications:* Svetlana Beriosova (by C. Swinson), 1956, Svetlana Beriosova (by A. H. Franks), 1958. *Recreation:* the arts. *Address:* 10 Palliser Court, Palliser Rd, W14.

BERISAVLJEVIĆ, Živan; Member of the Presidency of the Provincial Committee of the League of Communists of Vojvodina, since 1981; *b* 19 Sept. 1935; *s* of Rajko and Ljubica Prodanović; *m* 1963, Slobodanka Koledin; two *d*. *Educ:* Belgrade Univ. Held leading political functions in Youth League of Socialist Republic of Serbia, 1955–62; Editor-in-Chief, Gledista magazine, 1962–65; held scientific, cultural, educational and press positions, Central Cttee of League of Communists of Serbia, 1962–67; Sec. for Educn, Science and Culture, Serbia, 1967–71; Official of Assembly, Serbia, 1971–72; Advr to Fed. Sec., 1972–74, Asst Fed. Sec., i/c press, information and cultural affairs, 1974–77, Yugoslav Fed. Secretariat for Foreign Affairs. Mem., Commn for Information and Propaganda, Exec. Cttee of Presidency of League of Communists of Yugoslavia, 1972–77; Yugoslav Ambassador to London, 1977–81; Mem., Cttee for Internat. Relations of Central Cttee of League of Communists of Yugoslavia, 1982–. Formerly: Mem. Council, Museum of Contemporary Art, Belgrade; Mem. Federal Cttees for Information, and for Science and Culture. Pres., Univ. of Novi Sad, 1981–. Several decorations. *Publications:* Democratisation of Society and the League of Communists, 1967; Cultural Action, 1972; Education between the Past and Future, 1973; many articles and papers in journals and newspapers. *Recreations:* tennis, football, walking. *Address:* Bulevar Marsala Tita 20, Novi Sad, Yugoslavia.

BERKELEY, Baroness (17th in line); (*cr* 1421; called out of abeyance, 1967); **Mary Lalle Foley-Berkeley;** *b* 9 Oct. 1905; *e d* of Col Frank Wigram Foley, CBE, DSO (*d* 1949), Royal Berks Regt, and Eva Mary Fitzhardinge, Baroness Berkeley; *S* mother, Baroness Berkeley (16th in line) (*d* 1964). *Heiress presumptive:* *sister* Hon. Cynthia Ella [*b* 31 Jan. 1909; *m* 1937, Brig. Ernest Adolphus Leopold Gueterbock (*d* 1984); one *s*]. *Address:* Pickade Cottage, Great Kimble, Aylesbury, Bucks. *T:* Princes Risborough (08444) 3051.

BERKELEY, Frederic George; Chief Master of the Supreme Court Taxing Office, 1988–92 (Master, 1971–88); *b* 21 Dec. 1919; *s* of late Dr Augustus Frederic Millard Berkeley and Anna Louisa Berkeley; *m* 1988, Helen Kathleen Lucy; one step *s* one step *d*, and one *s* one *d* (and one *d* decd) of previous marriage. *Educ:* Elstree Sch.; Aldenham Sch.; Pembroke Coll., Cambridge (MA). Admitted Solicitor, 1948. Served War of 1939–45, Leics Regt, Normandy (wounded); Major; DADAWS Allied Land Forces SE Asia, 1945–46. Partner in Lewis & Lewis (from 1964 Penningtons and Lewis & Lewis), 1951–70. Mem. No 1 (London) Legal Aid Area Cttee (later No 14), 1954–70, Vice-Chm. 1964–70, Chm. 1970. General Editor and contributor, Butterworth's Costs Service, 1984–. *Recreations:* reading, travel. *Address:* 10 Dover House, Abbey Park, Beckenham, Kent BR3 1QB. *T:* 081–650 4634.

BERKELEY, Humphry John; writer and broadcaster; Director, Sharon Allen Leukaemia Trust, since 1984; *b* 21 Feb. 1926; *s* of late Reginald Berkeley, author and playwright, former MP (L), and Mrs Hildegarde Tinne. *Educ:* Dragon Sch., Oxford; Malvern; Pembroke Coll., Cambridge (Exhibitioner); BA 1947, MA 1963; Pres., Cambridge Union, 1948; Chm., Cambridge Univ. Conservative Assoc., 1948. Held various appointments at Conservative Political Centre, 1949–56; Dir Gen., UK Council of European Movement, 1956–57; Chairman of Coningsby Club, 1952–55; Hon. Sec., Carlton Club Political Cttee, 1954–59. MP (C) Lancaster, 1959–66; seconded Act of Parlt which abolished death penalty for murder, 1965; introduced Private Members Bill to make homosexual conduct between consenting male adults no longer a crime, which obtained second reading in H of C, 1966; Member, British Parly Delegn to Council of Europe and Council of WEU, 1963–66; personal representative of Colonial Secretary in constitutional talks in Seychelles, 1965; Hon. Sec., Cons. Parly West Africa Cttee, 1959–64; Hon. Sec., UN Parly Gp, 1962–64; joined Labour Party July 1970; contested (Lab) N Fylde, Oct. 1974; joined SDP, 1981; contested (SDP) Southend East, 1987; rejoined Labour Party, Dec. 1988. Director: Caspair Ltd; Island Developments Ltd. Mem., Prince Philip's Cttee on Overseas Volunteers, 1966–70; Chm., UNA of GB and NI, 1966–70; Vice-Chm, Nat. Coordinating Cttee for 25th Anniversary of UN, 1970; Mem., UK Nat. Commn for Unesco, 1966–71. Patron, Internat. Centre for Child Studies, 1984–. Hon. Treasurer, Howard League for Penal Reform, 1965–71; Mem. Governing Body, Inst. for Study of Internat. Relations, Sussex Univ., 1969–. *Publications:* The Power of the Prime Minister, 1968; Crossing the Floor, 1972; The Life and Death of Rochester Sneath, 1974; The Odyssey of Enoch: a political memoir, 1977; The Myth that will not Die: the formation of the National Government 1931, 1978; (with Jeffrey Archer) Faces of the Eighties, 1987. *Address:* 3 Pages Yard, Church Street, Chiswick, W4 2PA. *Club:* Savile.

BERKELEY, Michael Fitzhardinge; composer and broadcaster; *b* 29 May 1948; *s* of late Sir Lennox Randal Berkeley and of Elizabeth Freda (*née* Bernstein); *m* 1979, Deborah Jane Coltman-Rogers; one *d*. *Educ:* Westminster Cathedral Choir Sch.; The Oratory Sch.; Royal Acad. of Music (ARAM 1984). Studied privately with Richard Rodney Bennett; rock musician; phlebotomist, St Bartholomew's Hosp., 1969–71; Presentation Asst, LWT, 1973; Announcer, BBC Radio 3, 1974–79; Associate Composer to Scottish Chamber Orch., 1979; regular presenter of arts programmes for BBC (Kaleidoscope, Radio 4, Meridian, World Service, Mainly for Pleasure, Radio 3); introduces proms, concerts and festivals for BBC2 and Radio 3, and BBC television documentaries. Member: Exec. Cttee, Assoc. of Professional Composers, 1982–84; Central Music Adv. Cttee, BBC, 1986–90; Gen. Adv. Council, BBC, 1990–; New Music Sub-Cttee, Arts Council of GB, 1984–86; Music Panel Adviser to Arts Council, 1986–; acts as expert witness in cases of musical plagiarism. *Compositions: orchestral music:* Fanfare and National Anthem, 1979; Primavera, 1979; Flames, 1981; Gregorian Variations, 1982; Daybreak and a Candle End, 1985; Gethsemane Fragment, 1990; Entertaining Master Punch, 1991; *for chamber or small orchestra:* Meditations, 1977 (Guinness Prize for Composition); Fantasia Concertante, 1978; Uprising: Symphony in one movement, 1980; Suite; the Vision of Piers the Ploughman, 1981; The Romance of the Rose, 1982; Coronach, 1988; *concertos:* Concerto for Oboe and String Orch., 1977; Concerto for Cello and Small Orch., 1983; Concerto for Horn and String Orch., 1984; Organ Concerto, 1987; *chamber music:* String Trio, 1978; American Suite, 1980; Chamber Symphony, 1980; String Quartet No 1, 1981; Nocturne, 1982; Piano Trio, 1982; Music from Chaucer, 1983; Quintet for Clarinet and Strings, 1983; String Quartet No 2, 1984; The Mayfly, 1984; Pas de deux, 1985; For the Savage Messiah, 1985; Quartet Study, 1987; *strings:* Etude de Fleurs, 1979; Sonata for Violin and Piano, 1979; Iberian Notebook, 1980; Variations on Greek Folk-Songs, 1981; Funerals and Fandangos, 1984; A Mosaic for Father Popieluszko, 1985; *guitar:* Lament, 1980; Worry Beads, 1981; Sonata in One Movement, 1982; Impromptu, 1985; *keyboard:* Passacaglia, 1978; Strange Meeting, 1978; Organ Sonata, 1979; *woodwind:* Three Moods, 1979; American Suite, 1980; Fierce Tears, 1984; Flighting, 1985; Keening, 1987; *vocal music for solo voice:* The Wild Winds, 1978; Rain, 1979; Wessex Graves, 1981; Songs of Awakening Love, 1986; Speaking Silence, 1986; *choral music:* At the Round Earth's Imagin'd Corners, 1980; The Crocodile and Father William, 1982; Easter, 1982; As the Wind Doth Blow, 1983; Hereford Communion Service, 1985; Pasce Oves Meas, 1985; Verbum Caro Factum Est, 1987; The Red Macula, 1989; Night Song in the Jungle, 1990; *oratorio:* Or Shall We Die?, 1983 (text by Ian McEwan; filmed for Channel 4); *ballet:* Bastet, 1988; *film music:* Captive, 1986; Twenty-one, 1990. *Publications:* musical compositions; articles in The Observer, The Guardian, The Listener, The Sunday Telegraph, and Vogue. *Recreations:* looking at paintings, reading, walking and hill farming in mid-Wales. *Address:* 49 Blenheim Crescent, W11 2EF. *T:* 071–229 6945.

BERKELEY MILNE, Alexander; *see* Milne, A. B.

BERKHOUWER, Cornelis; Chevalier, Order of the Netherlands Lion 1966; Commander, Order of Orange–Nassau, 1979; Member, European Parliament, 1963–84, elected Member, 1979–84; *b* Alkmaar, Holland, 19 March 1919; *m* 1966, Michelle Martel; one *s*. *Educ:* Amsterdam Univ. Dr of Law 1946. Barrister, High Court of Amsterdam, 1942. Pres., European Parliament, 1973–75, Vice-Pres., 1975–79. Grand Cross of Merit (Italy), 1974; Grand Cross of Merit (Spain), 1981. *Publications:* Conversion of Void Legal Acts (thesis), 1946; Medical Responsibilities, 1951; Civil Responsibility for Illegal Publicity, 1954. *Recreations:* tennis, ancient literature, swimming, bibliothèque, vinothèque, chess. *Address:* 56 Stationsweg, Heiloo, Netherlands. *Clubs:* National Liberal; de Witte (The Hague); Cercle Gaulois (Brussels); Cercle Interallié (Paris).

BERKOFF, Steven; actor, director and writer; *b* 3 Aug. 1937; *s* of Polly and Al Berks (formerly Berkovitch); *m* (marr. diss). *Educ:* Raines Foundation Grammar School, Stepney; Grocers' Co. Sch., Hackney. *Plays acted,* 1965–: Zoo Story; Arturo Ui; *plays directed/acted/wrote,* 1969–: Metamorphosis (also directed on Broadway, 1989); Macbeth (directed and acted); Agamemnon; The Trial; The Fall of the House of Usher; East; Kvetch; season of 3 plays, NT; Hamlet (directed and acted); Decadence; Greek; West; *wrote and directed:* Sink the Belgrano, Mermaid, 1986; *directed:* Coriolanus, NY, 1988; Salomé, Edinburgh Festival, NT (and acted), 1989, Phoenix (and acted), 1990; The Trial, NT, 1991; *films acted:* Prisoner of Rio, 1988; The Krays, 1990. *Publications:* East and other plays, 1977; The Trial (play adaptation), 1978; Gross Intrusion (short stories), 1979; Decadence, 1982; Greek, 1982; West, 1985; Lunch, 1985; Harry's Xmas, 1985; Kvetch,

1987; Acapulco, 1987; Sink the Belgrano, 1987; Massage, 1987; America, 1988; I Am Hamlet, 1989; A Prisoner in Rio, 1989. *Recreation:* writing, photography, travel. *Address:* c/o Joanna Marston, 1 Clareville Grove Mews, SW7 5AN. *T:* 071–370 1080.

BERKSHIRE, Archdeacon of; *see* Griffiths, Ven. D. N.

BERKSON, David Mayer; a Recorder of the Crown Court, since 1978; an Assistant Judge Advocate General, since 1988; *b* 8 Sept. 1934; *s* of Louis Berkson and Regina Berkson (*née* Globe); *m* 1961, Pamela Anne (*née* Thwaite); one *d. Educ:* Birkenhead School. Called to the Bar, Gray's Inn, 1957. Dep. Judge Advocate, 1984–87. Legal Mem., Mental Health Review Tribunal for the Mersey Area, 1982–84. *Address:* c/o Office of the Judge Advocate General, 22 Kingsway, WC2B 6LE. *Clubs:* Athenæum (Liverpool); Border and County (Carlisle).

BERLIN, Sir Isaiah, OM 1971; Kt 1957; CBE 1946; FBA 1957; MA; President of the British Academy, 1974–78; Fellow of All Souls College, Oxford; *b* 6 June 1909; *s* of Mendel and Marie Berlin; *m* 1956, Aline, *d* of Pierre de Gunzbourg. *Educ:* St Paul's Sch.; Corpus Christi Coll., Oxford. Lectr in Philosophy, New Coll., Oxford, 1932; Fellow: All Souls, 1932–38; New Coll., 1938–50; war service with Min. of Information, in New York, 1941–42, at HM Embassy in Washington, 1942–46, HM Embassy, Moscow, Sept. 1945–Jan. 1946; Fellow, All Souls Coll., Oxford, 1950–66, 1975–; Chichele Prof. of Social and Pol Theory, Oxford Univ., 1957–67; Pres., Wolfson Coll., Oxford 1966–Mar. 1975, Hon. Fellow, 1975. Mem. Cttee of Awards: Commonwealth (Harkness) Fellowships, 1960–64; Kennedy Scholarships, 1967–79. Vice-Pres., British Academy, 1959–61; Pres. Aristotelian Soc., 1963–64. Mem., Academic Adv. Cttee., Univ. of Sussex, 1963–66. Visiting Professor: Harvard Univ., 1949, 1951, 1953, 1962; Bryn Mawr Coll., 1952; Chicago Univ., 1955; Princeton Univ., 1965; ANU, Canberra, 1975; Prof. of Humanities, City Univ. of NY, 1966–71. Lectures: Northcliffe, UCL, 1953; Mellon, Nat. Gall. of Art, Washington, DC, 1965; Danz, Washington Univ., 1971. Foreign Member: American Academy of Arts and Sciences; American Academy-Institute of Arts and Letters; American Philosophical Soc. Member, Board of Directors, Royal Opera House, Covent Garden, 1954–65, 1974–87; a Trustee, Nat. Gall., 1975–85. Hon. Pres., British Friends of the Univ. of Jerusalem. Hon. doctorates of the following universities: Hull, 1965; Glasgow, 1967; E Anglia, 1967; Brandeis (USA), 1967; Columbia, 1968; Cambridge, 1970; London, 1971; Jerusalem, 1971; Liverpool, 1972; Tel Aviv, 1973; Harvard, 1979; Sussex, 1979; Johns Hopkins, 1981; Northwestern, 1981; NY, 1982; Duke, 1983; City, NY, 1983; New Sch. of Social Research, NY, 1987; Oxford, 1987; Ben Gurion, 1988; Yale, 1989. Hon. Fellow: Corpus Christi Coll., Oxford; St Anthony's Coll., Oxford; Wolfson Coll., Cambridge. Erasmus Prize (jtly), 1983; Agnelli Internat. Prize for Ethics, 1987. *Publications:* Karl Marx, 1939, 4th edn 1978; Translation of First Love by I. S. Turgenev, 1950; The Hedgehog and the Fox, 1953, 4th edn 1979; Historical Inevitability, 1954; The Age of Enlightenment, 1956; Moses Hess, 1958; Two Concepts of Liberty, 1959; Mr Churchill in 1940, 1964; Four Essays on Liberty, 1969; Fathers and Children, 1972; Vico and Herder, 1976; Russian Thinkers, 1978; Concepts and Categories, 1978; Against the Current, 1979; Personal Impressions, 1980; translation of A Month in the Country by I. S. Turgenev, 1980; The Crooked Timber of Humanity, 1990. *Address:* All Souls College, Oxford. *Clubs:* Athenæum, Brooks's, Garrick; Century (New York).

BERLINS, Marcel Joseph; journalist and broadcaster; *b* 30 Oct. 1941; *s* of Jacques and Pearl Berlins. *Educ:* schools in France and South Africa; Univ. of Witwatersrand (BComm, LLB); LSE (LLM). Legal Asst, Lord Chancellor's Dept, 1969–71; Legal Corresp. and leader writer, The Times, 1971–82; freelance writer and TV presenter, 1982–86; Editor, Law Magazine, 1987–88; presenter, Radio 4 Law in Action, 1988–; columnist, The Guardian, 1988–. *Publications:* Barrister behind Bars, 1974; (with Geoffrey Wansell) Caught in the Act, 1974; (with Clare Dyer) Living Together, 1982; (with Clare Dyer) The Law Machine, 1982, 3rd edn 1989; (ed) The Law and You, 1986; numerous articles for newspapers, magazines and legal jls. *Recreations:* cinema, jazz. *Address:* 7 Leighton Crescent, NW5 2QY. *T:* 071–485 3965.

BERMAN, Edward David, (ED Berman), MBE 1979; social entrepreneur, playwright, theatre director and producer; educationalist; Founder, Chief Executive and Artistic Director, Inter-Action, since 1968; *b* 8 March 1941; 2nd *s* of Jack Berman and Ida (*née* Webber); naturalized British citizen, 1976. *Educ:* Harvard (BA Hons); Exeter Coll., Oxford (Rhodes Schol.); Dept of Educnl Studies, Oxford (1978–). *Plays:* 8 produced since 1966; *director: theatre:* (premières) *inter alia* Dirty Linen (London and Broadway), 1976, and The Dogg's Troupe (15 minute) Hamlet, (ed) by Tom Stoppard, 1976 (also filmed, 1976); The Irish Hebrew Lesson, 1976 and Samson and Delilah, 1978, by Wolf Mankowitz; Dogg's Hamlet, Cahoot's Macbeth, 1979, by Tom Stoppard; *producer: theatre:* 125 stage premières for adults and 170 new plays for children, London, 1967–89; *maker of films:* (educational) The Head, 1971; Two Weeler, 1972; Farm in the City, 1977; Marx for Beginners Cartoon (co-prod., voice dir), 1978; *actor:* over 1200 performances as Prof. Dogg, Otto Première Check, Super Santa. Editor: 18 community arts, action and constructive leisure handbooks, 1972–; 2 anthologies of plays, 1976–78. Trustee and Founder, Inter-Action Trust, 1968; Director and Founder: Ambiance Lunch-Hour Th. Club, 1968; Prof. Dogg's Troupe for Children, 1968; Labrys Trust, 1969; Inter-Action Advisory Service, 1970; Infilms, 1970; The Almost Free Th., 1971; Inprint Publishing Unit, 1972; City Farm 1, 1972; Alternative Education Project, 1973–84; Inter-Action Trust Ltd, 1974; Town and Country Inter-Action (Milton Keynes) Ltd, 1975; Ambiance Inter-Action Inc., 1976; Talacre Centre Ltd, 1977; Co-Founder: Inter-Action Housing Trust Ltd, 1970; NUBS, Neighbourhood Use of Bldgs and Space; Community Design Centre, 1974; Beginners Books Ltd, 1978; Inter-Action Housing Co-operative, 1978. Founder, Artistic Dir, BARC, British Amer. Rep. Co., 1978. Devised: Inter-Action Creative Game Method, 1967; Super Santa, Father Xmas Union, 1967–82; Chairman: Save Piccadilly Campaign, 1971–80; Talacre Action Gp, 1972; Nat. Assoc. of Arts Centres, 1975–79; Dir, Islington Bus Co., 1974–76; Treas., Fair Play for Children Campaign, 1975–77; Founder: City Farm Movement, 1976; WAC—Weekend Arts Coll., 1979; co-founder: Sport-Space, 1976; FUSION—London and Commonwealth Youth Ensemble, 1981. Founder and Co-Director: Internat. Inst. for Social Enterprise, 1980; Country Wings, 1981; OPS, Occupation Preparation Systems, 1982; Options Training Ltd, 1983; Social Property Developments Ltd; East London Radio Riverside Ltd; Founder and Trustee, Inter-Action Social Enterprise Trust Ltd, Social Enterprise Foundn of Inter-Action, 1984; Cdre, Ships-in-the-City, 1988; Founder and Director: Network Inter-Action; Youth-Tech; Starlab, 1989. Special Adviser on inner city matters to Sec. of State for the Environment, 1982–83, Youth Options Menu, 1984. As community artist: created 17 formats for participatory theatre, 1968–85; Community Media Van, 1983; Community Cameos, 1977–83; MIY—Make It Yourself, 1978; RIY—Raise It Yourself, 1981. *Publications:* Prof. R. L. Dogg's Zoo's Who I and II, 1975; Selecting Business Software, 1984; Make a Real Job of It, Breaks for Young Bands, 1985; How to Set Up a Small Business, 1987; Healthy Learning Songs & Activities, 1989; New Game Songs & Activities, 1989; Early Learning Maths Songs and Activities, 1991. *Recreations:* solitude, conversation, work, music. *Address:* Inter-Action Trust, HMS President (1918), Victoria Embankment, EC4Y 0HJ. *T:* 071–583 2652.

BERMAN, Franklin Delow, CMG 1986; Deputy Legal Adviser, Foreign and Commonwealth Office, since 1988; *b* 23 Dec. 1939; *s* of Joshua Zelic Berman and Gertrude (*née* Levin); *m* 1964, Christine Mary Lawler; two *s* three *d. Educ:* Rondebosch Boys' High Sch., Cape Town; Univ. of Cape Town; Wadham and Nuffield Colls, Oxford. BA, BSc Cape Town; MA Oxford. Rhodes Scholar, 1961; Martin Wronker Prizeman, 1963; called to Bar (Middle Temple), 1966. HM Diplomatic Service, 1965: Asst Legal Adviser, FO, 1965; Legal Adviser: British Military Govt, Berlin, 1971; British Embassy, Bonn, 1972; Legal Counsellor, FCO, 1974; Counsellor and Legal Adviser, UK Mission to UN, NY, 1982; FCO, 1985. Chairman: Diplomatic Service Assoc., 1979–82; Staff Tribunal, Internat. Oil Pollution Fund, 1986–. *Recreations:* walking, reading, music, choral singing. *Address:* c/o Foreign and Commonwealth Office, SW1. *T:* 071–270 3000. *Club:* United Oxford & Cambridge University.

BERMAN, Lawrence Sam, CB 1975; retired; *b* 15 May 1928; *yr s* of Jack and Violet Berman; *m* 1954, Kathleen D. Lewis; one *s* one *d. Educ:* St Clement Danes Grammar Sch.; London Sch. of Economics. BSc (Econ) 1st cl. hons 1947; MSc (Econ) 1950. Res. Asst, LSE, 1947; Nuffield Coll., Oxford, 1948; Econ. Commn for Europe, 1949; Central Statistical Office: Asst Statistician 1952; Statistician 1955; Chief Statistician 1964; Asst Dir 1968; Dir of Statistics, Depts of Industry and Trade, 1972–83. Statistical Advr, Caribbean Tourism R & D Centre, Barbados, 1984–85. Editor, National Income Blue Book, 1954–60; Member: Council, Royal Statistical Soc., 1970–74 (Vice-Pres., 1973–74); Council Internat. Assoc. for Research in Income and Wealth, 1980–85; ISI. *Publications:* Caribbean Tourism Statistical Reports; articles and papers in Jl of Royal Statistical Soc., Economica, Economic Trends, Statistical News, etc. *Recreations:* travel, theatre, collecting sugar tongs and bow ties. *Address:* 10 Carlton Close, Edgware, Mddx HA8 7PY. *T:* 081–958 6938.

BERMANT, Chaim Icyk; author, since 1966; *b* 26 Feb. 1929; *s* of Azriel Bermant and Feiga (*née* Daets); *m* 1962, Judy Weil; two *s* two *d. Educ:* Queen's Park Sch., Glasgow; Glasgow Yeshiva; Glasgow Univ. (MA Hons; MLitt); London School of Economics (MScEcon). School-master, 1955–57; Economist, 1957–58; Television script writer, 1958–61; Journalist, 1961–66. *Publications:* Jericho Sleep Alone, 1964; Berl Make Tea, 1965; Ben Preserve Us, 1965; Diary of an Old Man, 1966; Israel, 1967; Swinging in the Rain, 1967; Troubled Eden, 1969; The Cousinhood, 1971; Here Endeth the Lesson, 1969; Now Dowager, 1971; Roses are Blooming in Picardy, 1972; The Last Supper, 1973; The Walled Garden, 1974; Point of Arrival, 1975; The Second Mrs Whitberg, 1976; Coming Home, 1976 (Wingate-Jewish Chronicle Book Award); The Squire of Bor Shachor, 1977; The Jews, 1978; Now Newman was Old, 1978; Belshazzar, 1979; (with Dr M. Weitzman) Ebla, 1979; The Patriarch, 1981; On the Other Hand, 1982; The House of Women, 1983; Dancing Bear, 1984; What's the Joke, 1986; Titch, 1987; The Companion, 1987; Lord Jacobovits: the authorised biography of the Chief Rabbi, 1990; Murmurings of a Licensed Heretic, 1990. *Recreations:* walking, sermon-tasting. *Address:* c/o Gillon Aitken, 29 Fernshaw Road, SW10 0TG. *T:* 071–351 7651.

BERMINGHAM, Gerald Edward; MP (Lab) St Helens South, since 1983; *b* Dublin, 20 Aug. 1940; *s* of late Patrick Xavier Bermingham and Eva Terescena Bermingham; *m* 1st, 1964, Joan (marr. diss.); two *s;* 2nd, 1978, Judith. *Educ:* Cotton College, N Staffs; Wellingborough Grammar School; Sheffield University. LLB Hons. Admitted Solicitor, 1967; called to the Bar, Gray's Inn, 1985. Councillor, Sheffield City Council, 1975–79, 1980–82. Contested (Lab) SE Derbyshire, 1979. *Recreations:* sport, reading, TV. *Address:* 10 Devonshire Drive, Sheffield S17 3PJ; 51B Junction Lane, St Helens, Merseyside WA9 3JN. *T:* St Helens (0744) 810083.

BERMUDA, Bishop of, since 1990; **Rt. Rev. William John Denbigh Down;** *b* 15 July 1934; *s* of William Leonard Frederick Down and Beryl Mary Down (*née* Collett); *m* 1960, Sylvia Mary Aves; two *s* two *d. Educ:* Farnham Grammar School; St John's Coll., Cambridge (BA 1957; MA 1961); Ridley Hall, Cambridge. Deacon 1959, priest 1960, Salisbury; Asst Curate, St Paul's Church, Salisbury, 1959–63; Chaplain, Missions to Seamen, 1963–74: South Shields, 1963–65; Hull, 1965–71; Fremantle, WA, 1971–74; Dep. Gen. Secretary, Missions to Seamen, 1975, Gen. Sec. 1976–90; Chaplain, St Michael Paternoster Royal, 1976–90; Hon. Asst Curate, St John's, Stanmore, 1975–90. Hon. Canon of Gibraltar, 1985–90, of Kobe, 1987–. Chaplain RANR, 1972–74. Hon. Chaplain, Worshipful Co. of Carmen, 1977–90, (Hon. Chaplain Emeritus, 1990), of Farriers, 1983–90 (Hon. Chaplain Emeritus, 1990), of Innholders, 1983–90. Freeman, City of London, 1981. Hon. FNI 1991. *Publications:* On Course Together, 1989; contrib. to Internat. Christian Maritime Assoc. Bulletin. *Recreations:* sport (keen follower of soccer, cricket, golf), ships and the sea, travel, walking. *Address:* Bishop's Lodge, PO Box HM 769, Hamilton HM CX, Bermuda. *T:* Bermuda 2922967. *Clubs:* Commonwealth Trust; Royal Bermuda Yacht, Royal Hamilton Amateur Dinghy (Bermuda).

BERNAL-PEREIRA, Gen. Waldo; Bolivian Orders of: Merito Aeronautico; Guerrilleros Lanza; Merito Naval; Constancia Militar; Merito Aeronautico Civil; La Gran Orden de la Educación (Colombia); US Legion of Merit; Commander-in-Chief, Bolivian Air Force, since 1980; *b* 5 Dec. 1934; *s* of Romulo Bernal and Amalia Pereira; *m* Maria Antonieta Arze; three *s. Educ:* German Coll., Oruro, Bolivia; Military Aviation Coll.; Pilotage Course, USA; grad. as Pilot in Reese AFB, USA, 1958; Modern Meteorological Techniques Course at Chanute AFB, USA; Squadron Comd Course, Air Force Univ., Maxwell AFB, USA; Diploma, Comd and Mil. Staff, Buenos Aires, Argentina; Diploma Top Grade Nat. Studies, La Paz, Bolivia. Pilot Instructor, Air Force Mil. Coll., 1958; Pilot, Mil. Air Transport, 1959; Head of Operations, Aerial Fighter Gp, 1964; Head of Mil. Aeronaut. Polytechnic, 1966; Chief of Dept III, Aerial Comd Ops, 1970; Comdr, Air Transport Gp, 1972; Comdr, Mil. Aviation Coll., 1973; Head of Presidential COS, 1974; Minister of State for Education and Culture, Aug. 1974–Nov. 1976; Air Attaché, Bolivian Embassy, Washington, 1977; Comdr, Mil. Aviation Coll., 1978; Ambassador to Court of St James's, 1979–80. *Recreation:* tennis. *Address:* Avenida Julio C. Patiño No 665, Calacoto, Casilla No 345, La Paz, Bolivia; Comando General de la Fuerza Aérea Boliviana, Avenida Montes No 734, La Paz, Bolivia.

BERNARD, Sir Dallas (Edmund), 2nd Bt *cr* 1954; Chairman: National & Foreign Securities Trust Ltd, 1981–86; Thames Trust Ltd, 1983–86; Director: Dreyfus Intercontinental Investment Fund NV, since 1970; Dreyfus Dollar International Fund Inc., since 1982; *b* 14 Dec. 1926; *o s* of Sir Dallas Gerald Mercer Bernard, 1st Bt, and Betty (*d* 1980), *e d* of late Sir Charles Addis, KCMG; *S* father, 1975; *m* 1st, 1959 (marr. diss. 1979); three *d;* 2nd, 1979, Mrs Monica Montford, *d* of late James Edward Hudson; one *d. Educ:* Eton Coll.; Corpus Christi Coll., Oxford (MA). FCIS. Director: Morgan Grenfell (Holdings) Ltd, 1972–79; Morgan Grenfell & Co. Ltd, 1964–77; Dominion Securities Ltd, Toronto, 1968–79; Italian Internat. Bank Plc, 1978–89. Mem. Monopolies and Mergers Commn, 1973–79. Mem. Council, GPDST, 1988– (Finance Cttee, 1975–). *Heir:* none. *Address:* 8 Eaton Place, SW1X 8AD. *T:* 071–235 2318. *Clubs:* Brooks's, Lansdowne.

BERNARD, Jeffrey Joseph; columnist, The Spectator, since 1976; *b* 27 May 1932; *s* of Oliver P. Bernard and Fedora Roselli Bernard; *m* 1st, 1958, Jacki; 2nd, 1966, Jill; one *d;* 3rd, 1978, Susan (marr. diss. 1981). *Educ:* Nautical College, Pangbourne. Odd jobs until

1958; film editor, 1958–62; actor, 1963; journalist and columnist, 1964–, for Sunday Times, New Statesman, Sporting Life and Spectator. 'Jeffrey Bernard is Unwell', a play by Keith Waterhouse based on 10 Spectator columns, Low Life, 1989. *Publications:* High Life – Low Life, 1982; Low Life, 1986; Talking Horses, 1987; More Low Life, 1989. *Recreations:* cricket, racing, cooking, Mozart. *Address:* 29 Greek Street, Soho, W1V 5LL. *T:* 071–437 5920. *Clubs:* Groucho, Chelsea Arts.

BERNARD, Joan Constance, MA, BD; FKC; Principal of Trevelyan College, University of Durham, and Honorary Lecturer in Theology, 1966–79; *b* 6 April 1918; *d* of late Adm. Vivian Henry Gerald Bernard, CB, and Eileen Mary Bernard. *Educ:* Ascham Sch., Sydney, NSW; St Anne's Coll., Oxford Univ. (BA Lit. Hum. 1940, MA 1943); King's Coll., London (BD 1961). War Service, ATS, 1940–46; AA Comd, 1940–44; SO Air Def. Div., SHAEF, 1944–45 (mentioned in despatches 1945); Special Projectile Ops Gp, July-Nov. 1945. Dep. Admin. Officer, NCB, 1946–50; Asst Sec., Educn, Music and Drama, NFWI, 1950–57; full-time student, 1957–61; Warden, Canterbury Hall, Univ. of London, and part-time Lectr, Dept of Theol., KCL, 1962–65; FKC 1976. Mem., Ordination Candidates' Cttee, ACCM, 1972–91; Examining Chaplain to Bishop of Southwark, 1984–. Governor: Godolphin Sch., Salisbury, 1980–89; St Saviour's Sch., Southwark, 1981–85. FRSA 1984. *Recreations:* music (assisted John Tobin in Handel research for many years); mountaineering, photography. *Address:* 89 Rennie Court, Upper Ground, SE1 9NZ.

BERNERS, Baroness (15th in line) *cr* 1455; **Vera Ruby Williams;** *b* 25 Dec. 1901; *d* of late Hon. Rupert Tyrwhitt, Major RA (5th *s* of Emma Harriet, Baroness Berners) and of Louise I. F. (*née* Wells); *S* cousin, 1950; *m* 1927, Harold Williams, Colonial Civil Service; two *d*. *Educ:* Ladies' Coll., Eastbourne; St Agnes' Sch., East Grinstead. *Co-heiresses: d* Hon. Mrs Michael Kirkham [*b* (Pamela Vivian Williams) 30 Sept. 1929; *m* 1952; two *s* one *d*]; and *d* Hon. Mrs Kelvin Pollock [*b* (Rosemary Tyrwhitt Williams) 20 July 1931; *m* 1959; two *s*]. *Address:* Ashwellthorpe, Charlton Lane, Cheltenham, Glos. *T:* Cheltenham (0242) 519595.

BERNEY, Sir Julian (Reedham Stuart), 11th Bt *cr* 1620; *b* 26 Sept. 1952; *s* of Lieut John Reedham Erskine Berney (killed on active service in Korea, 1952), Royal Norfolk Regt, and of Hon. Jean Davina, *d* of 1st Viscount Stuart of Findhorn, PC, CH, MVO, MC; *S* grandfather, 1975; *m* 1976, Sheena Mary, *yr d* of Ralph Day and Ann Gordon Day; two *s* one *d*. *Educ:* Wellington Coll.; North-East London Polytechnic. ARICS. *Recreation:* sailing. *Heir: s* William Reedham John Berney, *b* 29 June 1980. *Address:* Reeds House, 40 London Road, Maldon, Essex CM9 6HE. *T:* Maldon (0621) 853420. *Club:* Royal Ocean Racing.

BERNSTEIN, family name of **Baron Bernstein.**

BERNSTEIN, Baron *cr* 1969 (Life Peer), of Leigh; **Sidney Lewis Bernstein,** LLD; President, Granada Group PLC, since 1979, Chairman, 1934–79 (Granada Television, Granada Theatres, Granada TV Rental, Granada Motorway Services, Novello & Co.); *b* 30 Jan. 1899; *s* of Alexander and Jane Bernstein; *m* Sandra, *d* of Charles and Charlotte Malone, Toronto; one *s* two *d*. A founder, Film Society, 1924. Mem., Mddx CC, 1925–31. Films Adviser, Min. of Inf., 1940–45; Liaison, British Embassy, Washington, 1942; Chief, Film Section, AFHQ N Africa, 1942–43; Chief, Film Section, SHAEF, 1943–45. Lectr on Film and Internat. Affairs, New York Univ. and Yale. Mem., Resources for Learning Cons. Cttee, Nuffield Foundn, 1965–72. Governor, Sevenoaks Sch., 1964–74. Fellow, BFI, 1984. *Address:* 36 Golden Square, W1R 4AH. *Club:* Garrick.

BERNSTEIN, Alexander; Chairman, Granada Group plc, since 1979 (Director, since 1964); *b* 15 March 1936; *s* of late Cecil Bernstein and of Myra Ella, *d* of Lesser and Rachel Lesser; *m* 1962, Vanessa Anne, *d* of Alwyn and Winifred Mills; one *s* one *d*. *Educ:* Stowe Sch.; St John's Coll., Cambridge. Man. Dir, 1964–68, Chm., 1977–86, Granada TV Rental Ltd; Jt Man. Dir, Granada Television Ltd, 1971–75; Dir, Waddington Galleries, 1966–. Trustee: Civic Trust for the North-West, 1964–86; Granada Foundn, 1968–. Chm., Royal Exchange Theatre, 1983– (Dep. Chm., 1980–83). Member of Court: Univ. of Salford, 1976–87; Univ. of Manchester, 1983–. Hon. DLitt Salford 1981. *Recreations:* modern art, ski-ing, gardening. *Address:* 36 Golden Square, W1R 4AH.

BERNSTEIN, Prof. Basil Bernard; Karl Mannheim Professor of Sociology of Education, since 1979, Head of Sociological Research Unit, since 1963, University of London; *b* 1 Nov. 1924; *s* of Percival and Julia Bernstein; *m* 1955, Marion Black; two *s*. *Educ:* LSE (BScEcon); UCL (PhD). Teacher, City Day Coll., Shoreditch, 1954–60; Hon. Research Asst, UCL, 1960–62; University of London Institute of Education: Sen. Lectr, Sociology of Educn, 1963; Reader in Sociology of Educn, 1965; Prof., 1967; Senior Pro-Director, 1983–89. Hon. DLitt: Leicester, 1974, Rochester, 1989; Fil H Dr Univ. of Lund, 1980; DUniv Open, 1983. *Publications:* Class Codes and Control, Vol. I, Theoretical Studies Towards a Sociology of Language, 1971, 2nd edn 1974, (ed) Vol. II, Applied Studies Towards a Sociology of Language, 1973, Vol. III, Towards a Theory of Educational Transmissions, 1975, revd edn 1977, Vol. IV, The Structuring of Pedagogic Discourse, 1990; (with W. Brandis) Selection and Control, 1974; (with U. Lundgren) Macht und Control, 1985; (with M. Diaz) Towards a Theory of Pedagogic Discourse, 1986; Poder, Educatión y Conciencia: sociología de la tranmisión cultural, 1988. *Recreations:* music, painting, conversation, etc. *Address:* 90 Farquhar Road, Dulwich, SE19 1LT. *T:* 081–670 6411.

BERNSTEIN, Ingeborg, (Inge); Her Honour Judge Bernstein; a Circuit Judge, since 1991; *b* 24 Feb. 1931; *d* of Sarah and Eli Bernstein; *m* 1967, Eric Geoffrey Goldrein; one *s* one *d*. *Educ:* Peterborough County School; St Edmund's College, Liverpool; Liverpool University. Called to the Bar, Inner Temple, 1952; practice on Northern Circuit; a Recorder, 1978–91. Chm., Mental Health Review Tribunal; Mem., Mental Health Act Commn, 1984–86. *Recreations:* children and domesticity. *Address:* 14 Castle Street, Liverpool L2 0NE. *T:* 051–236 4421.

BERNSTEIN, Ronald Harold, DFC 1944; QC 1969; FCIArb; a Recorder of the Crown Court, 1974–90; *b* 18 Aug. 1918; *s* of late Mark and Fanny Bernstein; *m* 1955, Judy, *d* of David Levi, MS, and Vera Levi; three *s* one *d*. *Educ:* Swansea Grammar Sch.; Balliol Coll., Oxford. BA (Jurisprudence) 1939; FCIArb 1982. Served in RA, 1939–46, and in 654 Air OP Sqdn, RAF, 1942–46. Commanded 661 Air OP Sqdn, RAuxAF, 1954–56. Called to the Bar, Middle Temple, 1948, Bencher, 1975–. Mem., Gen. Council of the Bar, 1965–69; Vice-Pres., CIArb, 1988–. Pres., Highgate Soc., 1983–. Hon. ARICS 1986; Hon. FSVA 1987. *Publications:* (jointly) The Restrictive Trade Practices Act, 1956; Handbook of Rent Review, 1981, and subseq. edns to 1989; Handbook of Arbitration Practice, 1987; (Joint Editor) Foa, Landlord and Tenant, 8th edn, 1957. *Address:* (professional) Falcon Chambers, Falcon Court, EC4Y 1AA. *T:* 071–353 2484; (home) 081–340 9933; *Fax:* 081–348 7676. *Club:* Athenæum.

BERRAGAN, Maj.-Gen. Gerald Brian, CB 1988; Chief Executive, Institute of Packaging, since 1988; *b* 2 May 1933; *s* of William James and Marion Beatrice Berragan; *m* 1956, Anne Helen Kelly; three *s*. Commissioned REME 1954; attached 7th Hussars, Hong Kong, 1954–55; transf. RAOC 1956; served UK, Belgium, Germany and with 44 Para Bde (TA); Staff College, 1966; Nat. Defence Coll., 1972–73; Comdr RAOC 3 Div., 1973–76; AQMG HQ N Ireland, 1976–78; HQ DGOS, 1978–80; Comdt Central Ordnance Depot, Chilwell, 1980–82; Sen. Management Course, Henley, 1982; Comdt COD Bicester, 1982–83; Dir, Supply Ops (Army), 1983–85; Sen. Internat. Defence Management Course, USA, 1985; Dir Gen. of Ordnance Services, 1985–88. Col Comdt, RAOC, 1988–. FInstPS. FBIM. *Recreations:* offshore sailing, tennis. *Clubs:* Athenæum, Army and Navy.

BERRIDGE, (Donald) Roy, CBE 1981; FEng; Chairman, South of Scotland Electricity Board, 1977–82 (Deputy Chairman, 1974–77); *b* 24 March 1922; *s* of Alfred Leonard Berridge and Pattie Annie Elizabeth (*née* Holloway); *m* 1945, Marie (*née* Kinder); one *d*. *Educ:* King's Sch., Peterborough; Leicester Coll. of Art and Technology. FEng 1979; FIMechE 1962. Taylor, Taylor & Hobson Ltd, Leicester, 1940; James Gordon & Co., 1946; British Electricity Authority, 1948; seconded to AERE, Harwell, 1952; Reactor Design Engr, CEGB, 1962; Chief Generation Design Engr, 1964–70; Dir-Gen., Gen. Develt Constr. Div., CEGB, 1970–72; Dir of Engrg, SSEB, 1972–74. Dir, Howden Gp, 1982–88. Member: N of Scotland Hydro-Electric Bd, 1977–82; Scottish Economic Council, 1977–83; CBI (Scottish Council), 1977–83. *Recreations:* golf, clockmaking. *Address:* East Gate, Chapel Square, Deddington, Oxford OX5 4SG.

BERRIDGE, Dr Michael John, FRS 1984; Deputy Chief Scientific Officer, Agricultural and Food Research Council, since 1987; Fellow of Trinity College, Cambridge, since 1972; *b* 22 Oct. 1938; *s* of George Kirton Berridge and Stella Elaine Hards; *m* 1965, Susan Graham Winter; one *s* one *d*. *Educ:* University Coll. of Rhodesia and Nyasaland (BSc); Univ. of Cambridge (PhD). Post-doctoral Fellow: Univ. of Virginia, 1965–66; Case Western Reserve Univ., Cleveland, Ohio, 1966–69. Mem., AFRC Lab. of Molecular Signalling (formerly Unit of Insect Neurophysiology and Pharmacology), Dept of Zoology, Univ. of Cambridge, 1969–; SPSO, AFRC, 1981–87. *Publications:* papers in Jl Exptl Biol., Biochem. Jl and Nature. *Recreations:* golf, gardening. *Address:* 13 Home Close, Histon, Cambridge CB4 4JL. *T:* Cambridge (0223) 232416.

BERRIEDALE, Lord; Alexander James Richard Sinclair; *b* 26 March 1981; *s* and *heir* of Earl of Caithness, *qv*.

BERRILL, Sir Kenneth, GBE 1988; KCB 1971; Chairman, Robert Horne Group, 1987–90 (Deputy Chairman, 1982–87); *b* 28 Aug. 1920; *m* 1st, 1941, Brenda West (marr. diss.); one *s*; 2nd, 1950, June Phillips (marr. diss.); one *s* one *d*; 3rd, 1977, Jane Marris. *Educ:* London Sch. of Economics; Trinity Coll., Cambridge. BSc(Econ) London; MA Cantab, 1949. Served War, 1939–45, REME. Economic Adviser to Turkey, Guyana, Cameroons, OECD, and World Bank. Univ. Lectr in Economics, Cambridge, 1949–69; Rockefeller Fellowship Stanford and Harvard Univs, 1951–52; Fellow and Bursar, St Catharine's Coll., Cambridge, 1949–62, Hon. Fellow, 1974; Prof., MIT, 1962; Fellow and First Bursar, King's Coll., Cambridge, 1962–69, Hon. Fellow, 1973; HM Treasury Special Adviser (Public Expenditure), 1967–69; Chm., UGC, 1969–73; Head of Govt Econ. Service and Chief Economic Advr, HM Treasury, 1973–74; Head of Central Policy Review Staff, Cabinet Office, 1974–80; Chm., Vickers da Costa Ltd and Vickers da Costa & Co. Hong Kong Ltd, 1981–85; Chm., SIB, 1985–88. Mem., Stock Exchange, London, 1981–85. Member: Council for Scientific Policy, 1969–72; Adv. Bd for Research Councils, 1972–77; Adv. Council for Applied R&D, 1977–80; Brit. Nat. Commn for UNESCO, 1967–70; UN Cttee for Develt Planning, 1984–87; Inter-Univ. Council, 1969–73; UGC, Univ. of S Pacific, 1972–85; Council, Royal Economic Soc., 1972– (Vice Pres., 1986–); Adv. Bd, RCDS, 1974–80; Review Bd for Govt Contracts, 1981–85; Chm. Exec. Cttee, NIESR, 1988–; (Nominated), Governing Council, Lloyd's, 1983–88. Dir, UK-Japan 2000 Gp, 1986–90. Advr, Nippon Credit Internat. Ltd, 1989–. Governor: Administrative Staff Coll., Henley, 1969–84; Overseas Develt Inst., 1969–73; Mem. Council, Salford Univ., 1981–84; Pro Chancellor, Open Univ., 1983–. Cambridge City Cllr, 1963–67. Chm., Commonwealth Equities Fund, 1990–; Dep. Chm., General Funds Investment Trust, 1982–85; Director: Investing in Success Investment Trust, 1965–67; Ionian Bank, 1969–73; Dep. Chm., Universities' Superannuation Scheme, 1981–85 (Chm., Jt Negotiating Cttee, 1990–). Trustee, London Philharmonic, 1987–. McDonnell Scholar, World Inst. for Develt Economic Res., 1988, 1990. CBIM 1987. FRSA 1988; Hon. Fellow: LSE, 1970; Chelsea Coll., London, 1973. Hon. LLD: Cambridge, 1974; Bath, 1974; East Anglia, 1975; Leicester, 1975; DUniv Open, 1974; Hon. DTech Loughborough, 1974; Hon DSc Aston, 1974. Jephcott Lectr and Medallist, 1978; Stamp Meml Lectr, 1980. *Recreations:* ski-ing, sailing. *Address:* Salt Hill, Bridle Way, Grantchester, Cambs CB3 9NY. *T:* Cambridge (0223) 840335, *Fax:* Cambridge (0223) 845939. *Clubs:* Climbers (Hon. Mem.); Himalayan; Cambridge Alpine.

BERRILL, Prof. Norman John, PhD, DSc; FRS 1952; FRSC; FAAAS; lately Strathcona Professor of Zoology, McGill University, Montreal; *b* 28 April 1903. *Educ:* Bristol Gram. Sch., Somerset, England; Bristol Univ.; London Univ. BSc Bristol; PhD, DSc London. FRSC 1936; FAAAS 1979. *Publications:* The Tunicata, 1951; The Living Tide, 1951; Journey into Wonder, 1953; Sex and the Nature of Things, 1954; The Origin of Vertebrates, 1955; Man's Emerging Mind, 1955; You and the Universe, 1958; Growth, Development and Pattern, 1962; Biology in Action, 1966; Worlds Apart, 1966; Life of the Oceans, 1967; The Person in the Womb, 1968; Developmental Biology, 1971; Development, 1976. *Address:* 410 Swarthmore Avenue, Swarthmore, Pa 19081, USA.

BERRIMAN, Sir David, Kt 1990; FCIB; CBIM; Chairman, North East Thames Regional Health Authority, 1984–90; Director (non-executive), Britannia Building Society, since 1983; *b* 20 May 1928; *s* of late Algernon Edward Berriman, OBE and late Enid Kathleen Berriman (*née* Sutcliffe); *m* 1st, 1955, Margaret Lloyd (*née* Owen) (marr. diss. 1970); two *s*; 2nd, 1971, Shirley Elizabeth (*née* Wright). *Educ:* Winchester; New Coll., Oxford (MA, Dip. Econ. and Pol. Sc.); Harvard Business Sch. PMD course, 1961. First National City Bank of New York, 1952–56; Ford Motor Co. Ltd, 1956–60; AEI Hotpoint, 1960–63; Gen. Manager, United Leasing Corporation Ltd, 1963–64; Morgan Grenfell & Co. Ltd: Manager, 1964; Exec. Dir, 1968–73; Dir, Guinness Mahon & Co. Ltd, 1973–87 (Exec. Dir, 1973–85). Chairman: Bunzl Textile Holdings Ltd, 1981–88 (Dep. Chm., 1980); Alban Communications Ltd, 1988–90 (Dir, 1983–; Dep. Chm., 1987–88); Director (non-exec.): Cable and Wireless, 1975–88; Sky Television (formerly Satellite Television), 1981–89 (Chm., 1981–85); Bahrein Telecommunications Corp., 1982–88; Ashenden Enterprises Ltd, 1983–; E European Develt Ltd, 1990–; Central European Property Develt, 1990–. Chm., Lewisham and N Southwark DHA, 1981–84. Member: Bd of Trade's Interim Action Cttee for the Film Industry, 1977–85; Govt review body on Harland and Wolff diversification, 1980; British Screen Adv. Council, 1985–. Director: British Screen Finance Ltd, 1985–91; Nat. Film Develt Fund, 1985–91; Videotron Corp., 1989–. Dep. Chm., Nat. Film and Television School, 1988– (Gov., 1977–). Chairman: MacIntyre (for mentally handicapped), 1978– (Governor, 1972); MacIntyre Foundn, 1986–; Member, Council: Internat. Hosp. Fedn, 1985–86; King Edward's Hosp. Fund for London, 1985–90. Trustee, Kent Community Housing Trust, 1990–. *Recreations:* golf, lawn tennis. *Address:* Ashenden, Plaxtol, Sevenoaks, Kent TN15 0QA. *Clubs:* Royal Automobile, International Lawn Tennis; Wildernesse Golf (Sevenoaks); Royal St George's Golf.

BERRY, family name of **Viscount Camrose, Baron Hartwell** and **Viscount Kemsley.**

BERRY, Anthony Arthur; Chairman, Berry Bros & Rudd Ltd, 1965–85; *b* 16 March 1915; *s* of Francis L. Berry and Amy Marie (*née* Freeman); *m* 1953, Sonia Alice, *d* of Sir Harold Graham-Hodgson, KCVO; one *s* one *d*. *Educ:* Charterhouse; Trinity Hall, Cambridge. Served War, RNVR, 1939–45, incl. 2¼ yrs in the Mediterranean. Joined the wine trade on leaving Cambridge, 1936; rejoined family firm of Berry Bros & Rudd on completion of war service; Dir, 1946–. Worshipful Co. of Vintners: Liveryman, 1946; Mem. Court, 1972–; Master, 1980–81. *Recreations:* golf, walking. *Address:* 4 Cavendish Crescent, Bath, Avon BA1 2UG. *T:* Bath (0225) 422669. *Clubs:* Boodle's, MCC; Saintsbury; Bath and County (Bath); Royal Wimbledon Golf; Royal St George's Golf (Sandwich).

BERRY, (Anthony) Scyld (Ivens); cricket correspondent, The Independent on Sunday, since 1991; *b* 28 April 1954; *s* of Prof. Francis Berry, *qv*; *m* 1984, Sunita Ghosh. *Educ:* Westbourne School, Sheffield; Ampleforth College; Christ's College, Cambridge (MA Oriental Studies). Cricket correspondent: The Observer, 1978–89; The Sunday Correspondent, 1989–90. *Publications:* Cricket Wallah, 1982; Train to Julia Creek, 1984; (ed) The Observer on Cricket, 1987; Cricket Odyssey, 1988; (with Phil Edmonds) 100 Great Bowlers, 1989. *Recreations:* playing village cricket, being at home or in North Yemen. *Address:* c/o The Independent on Sunday, 40 City Road, EC1Y 2DB. *Club:* Hinton Charterhouse Cricket.

BERRY, Cicely Frances, (Mrs H. D. Moore), OBE 1985; Voice Director, Royal Shakespeare Co., since 1969; *b* 17 May 1926; *d* of Cecil and Frances Berry; *m* 1951, Harry Dent Moore (*d* 1978); two *s* one *d*. *Educ:* Eothen Sch., Caterham, Surrey; Central Sch. of Speech and Drama, London. Teacher, Central Sch. of Speech and Drama, 1948–68; 4-week Voice Workshops: Nat. Repertory Co. of Delhi, 1980; Directors and Actors in Australia (org. by Aust. Council), 1983; Directors, Actors, Teachers in China, Chinese Min. of Culture, 1984. Plays directed: Hamlet, Educn Dept, NT, 1985; King Lear, The Other Place, Stratford and Almeida Theatre, 1989. Patron of Northumberland and Leicester Youth Theatres. FRSAMD 1987. *Publications:* Voice and the Actor, 1973, 6th edn 1986; Your Voice and How to Use it Successfully, 1975, 4th edn 1985; The Actor and His Text, 1987.

BERRY, Prof. Colin Leonard, FRCPath; Professor of Morbid Anatomy, University of London, at The London Hospital Medical College, since 1976; *b* 28 Sept. 1937; *s* of Ronald Leonard Berry and Peggy-Caroline (*née* Benson); *m* 1960, Yvonne Waters; two *s*. *Educ:* privately, and Beckenham Grammar Sch.; Charing Cross Hosp. Med. Sch. (MB, BS; Governors' Clinical Gold Medal, Llewellyn Schol., Pierera Prize in Clinical Subjects, Steadman Prize in Path.); trained in Histopath., Charing Cross Hosp., 1962–64. MD, PhD (London). Lectr and Sen. Lectr, Inst. of Child Health, London, 1964–70; Reader in Pathology, Guy's Hosp. Med. Sch., 1970–76. Gillson Scholar, Worshipful Soc. of Apothecaries, 1967–68 and 1970–72; Arris and Gail Lectr, RCS, 1973. Chairman: Cttee on Dental and Surgical Materials, 1982– (Vice-Chm., 1979–82); Scientific Sub-Cttee on Pesticides, MAFF, 1984–87; Adv. Cttee on Pesticides, MAFF/DHSS, 1988– (Mem., 1982–87); Member: Toxicology Review Panel, WHO, 1976–84, 1987–; Scientific Adv. Commn on Pesticides, EEC, 1981–88; Cttee on Toxicity of Chemicals in Food, Consumer Products and the Environment, 1982–88; Cttee on Safety of Medicines, Dept. of Health, 1990–; MRC, 1990–; Chm., Physiological Systems and Disorders Bd, MRC, 1990– (Mem., 1988–). President: Developmental Path. Soc., 1976–79; European Soc. of Pathology, 1989–91 (Pres. elect, 1987–89); Sec. Fedn of Assocs of Clinical Profs, 1987–; Hon. Sec., ACP, 1982–85 (Meetings Sec., 1979–82). Scientific Advr, BIBRA, 1987–90. Treasurer, RCPath, 1988– (Asst Registrar, 1981–84). Asst to Court, Apothecaries' Soc., 1990–. *Publications:* Teratology: trends and applications, 1975; Paediatric Pathology, 1981, 2nd edn 1989; Diseases of the Arterial Wall, 1988; contrib. Cardiac Pathology (Pomerance and Davies), 1975, and to other texts; numerous publns in LJl of Path., Circulation Res. and other path. jls. *Recreations:* sailing, fishing, pond building. *Address:* 1 College Gardens, Dulwich SE21 7BE. *T:* 081–299 0066. *Club:* Reform.

BERRY, Prof. Francis; Emeritus Professor of English Language and Literature, Royal Holloway College, University of London, since 1980; *b* 23 March 1915; *s* of James Berry and Mary Augusta Jane Berry (*née* Ivens); *m* 1st, 1947, Nancy Melloney (*d* 1967), *d* of Cecil Newton Graham; one *s* one *d*; 2nd, 1970, Patricia (marr. diss. 1975), *d* of John Gordon Thomson; 3rd, 1979, Eileen, *d* of Eric Charles Lear. *Educ:* Hereford Cathedral Sch.; Dean Close Sch.; University Coll., Exeter. BA London (1st cl. hons); MA Exeter. Solicitor's articled clerk, 1931; University Coll., Exeter, 1937. War Service, 1939–46. University Coll., Exeter, 1946; successively Asst Lectr, Lectr, Sen. Lectr, Reader in English Literature, and Prof. of English Literature, Univ. of Sheffield, 1947–70; Prof. of English Lang. and Lit., Royal Holloway Coll., Univ. of London, 1970–80. Visiting Lecturer: Carleton Coll., Minn, USA, 1951–52; University Coll. of the West Indies, Jamaica, 1957; W.P. Ker Lectr, Glasgow, 1979; Lectr for British Council: in India, 1966–67; tour of univs in Japan, 1983, of univs of New Zealand, 1988; Vis. Fellow, ANU, Canberra, 1979; Vis. Prof. of English, Univ. of Malawi, 1980–81. Pres. SW of England Shakespeare Trust, 1985. FRSL 1968. Hon. Fellow, RHBNC, London Univ., 1987. *Publications:* Gospel of Fire, 1933; Snake in the Moon, 1936; The Iron Christ, 1938; Fall of a Tower, 1942; Murdock and Other Poems, 1947; The Galloping Centaur, 1952, 2nd edn 1970; Herbert Read, 1953, 2nd edn 1961; An Anthology of Medieval Poems (ed), 1954; Poets' Grammar: time, tense and mood in poetry, 1958, 2nd edn, 1974; Morant Bay and other poems, 1961; Poetry and the Physical Voice, 1962; The Shakespeare Inset, 1965, 2nd edn 1971; Ghosts of Greenland, 1967; John Masefield: the Narrative Poet, 1968; (ed) Essays and Studies for the English Association, 1969; Thoughts on Poetic Time, 1972; I Tell of Greenland (novel), 1977; From the Red Fort: new and selected poems, 1984; contributor: Review of English Studies; Essays in Criticism; BBC Radio Three, ABC, etc. *Recreations:* following first-class cricket, chess, travel, gardening. *Address:* 4 Eastgate Street, Winchester, Hants SO23 8EB. *T:* Winchester 54439. *Club:* Hampshire (Winchester).
See also A. S. I. Berry.

BERRY, Rt. Rev. Fraser; *see* Berry, Rt Rev. R. E. F.

BERRY, Dr James William; Director General (formerly Director) of Scientific and Technical Intelligence, 1982–89; *b* 5 Oct. 1931; *s* of Arthur Harold Berry and Mary Margaret Berry; *m* 1960, Monica Joan Hill; three *d*. *Educ:* St Mary's Coll., Blackburn; Municipal Technical Coll., Blackburn; Manchester Univ. (BSc); Leeds Univ. (PhD); CEng, FIEE. Royal Signals and Radar Estab., Malvern, 1956–60; Admiralty Surface Weapons Estab., Portsdown, 1960–76 (Head of Computer Div., 1972–76); Dir of Long Range Surveillance and Comd and Control Projs, MoD (PE), 1976–79; Dir Gen. Strategic Electronic Systems, MoD (PE), 1979–82. Organist and choirmaster, St Michael's RC Church, Leigh Park, Havant; 'cellist mem. of Petersfield Orch., Fareham Phil. Orch., and Bowes Music Gp. *Recreations:* music (organ, 'cello, piano), walking, bird watching. *Club:* Civil Service.

BERRY, John, CBE 1968; MA (Cantab); PhD (St Andrews); FRSE 1936; DL; Consultant on Water Impoundment Biology, retired 1990; Conservation and Fisheries Adviser to: North of Scotland Hydro-Electric Board, 1968–89; South of Scotland Electricity Board, 1973–89; *b* Edinburgh, 5 Aug. 1907; *o s* of late William Berry, OBE, DL, Tayfield, Newport, Fife; *m* 1936, Hon. Bride Fremantle, MA (Cantab), 3rd *d* of 3rd Baron Cottesloe, CB; two *s* one *d*. *Educ:* Eton; Trinity Coll., Cambridge. BA 1929 (Zoo. Chem. Phys. Pt I and Law Pt II); MA 1933; PhD 1935; Salmon research, Fishery Bd for Scotland, 1930–31; Biological Research Station, University Coll., Southampton, Research Officer, 1932–36 and Dir, 1937–39. Press Censor for Scotland, 1940–44; Biologist and Information Officer, North of Scotland Hydro-Electric Bd, 1944–49; Dir of Nature Conservation in Scotland, 1949–67. Consultant Ecologist, Scottish Landowners' Fedn, 1984–87. Chm., Interdepartmental Salmon Res. Gp (UK and Ireland), 1971–82; Dir, British Pavilion, Expo '71, Budapest. Mem., Scottish Marine Biology Assoc., 1947–71 (RSE rep., Exec. Cttee, 1947; Mem Council, 1948–54, 1957–66). Pres. 1954–56, Vice-Pres. 1956–60, and Mem., 1966–72, Commn on Ecology, Internat. Union for Conservation of Natural Resources; UK rep., Exec. Bd, Internat. Wildfowl Research Bureau, 1963–72; Vice-President: RZS Scotland, 1959–82 (Hon. Life Fellow and Hon. Vice-Pres., 1982); Scottish Wildlife Trust; Vice-Pres. and Mem. Council, Wildfowl Trust, 1969– (Hon. Life Fellow, 1983). Mem. Court, Dundee Univ., and Delegate to Commonwealth Univs Congress, 1970–78. Hon. LLD Dundee, 1970; Hon. DSc St Andrews, 1991. DL Fife, 1969. *Publications:* The Status and Distribution of Wild Geese and Wild Duck in Scotland, 1939; various papers and articles on fresh-water fisheries, hydro-electric development and ornithology. *Recreations:* natural history (esp. wild geese and insects), music. *Address:* The Garden House, Tayfield, Newport-on-Tay, Fife DD6 8HA. *T:* Newport-on-Tay (0382) 543118. *Club:* New (Edinburgh).
See also P. F. Berry.

BERRY, Prof. Michael Victor, FRS 1982; Royal Society Research Professor, Bristol University, since 1988; *b* 14 March 1941; *s* of Jack and Marie Berry; *m* 1st, 1961, Eveline Ethel Fitt (marr. diss. 1969); two *s*; 2nd, 1971, Lesley Jane Allen (marr. diss. 1984); two *d*; 3rd, 1984, Monica Suzi Saiovici; one *s* one *d*. *Educ:* Univ. of Exeter (BSc); Univ. of St Andrews (PhD). Bristol University: Res. Fellow, 1965–67; Lectr, 1967–74; Reader, 1974–78; Prof. of Physics, 1978–88. Bakerian Lectr, Royal Soc., 1987. Mem., Royal Scientific Soc., Uppsala, 1988. Maxwell Medal and Prize, Inst. of Physics, 1978; Dirac Medal and Prize, Inst. of Physics, 1990; Lilienfeld Prize, Amer. Physical Soc., 1990; Royal Medal, Royal Soc., 1990. *Publications:* Diffraction of Light by Ultrasound, 1966; Principles of Cosmology and Gravitation, 1976; about 200 research papers, book reviews, etc, on physics. *Recreations:* cooking, walking. *Address:* H. H. Wills Physics Laboratory, Tyndall Avenue, Bristol BS8 1TL. *T:* Bristol (0272) 303911, 303603.

BERRY, Very Rev. Peter Austin; Provost of Birmingham, since 1986; *b* 27 April 1935; *s* of Austin James Berry and Phyllis Evelyn Berry. *Educ:* Solihull Sch.; Keble Coll., Oxford (MA, English and Theol.); St Stephen's House, Oxford. Intelligence Corps, 1954–56. Ordained deacon, 1962, priest, 1963; Chaplain to Bishop of Coventry, 1963–70; Midlands Regl Officer, Community Relations Commn, 1970–73; Canon Residentiary, Coventry Cathedral, 1973–77; Vice-Provost of Coventry, 1977–85. Mem., Gen. Synod of C of E, 1990–. Fellow, Lanchester Coll., Coventry, 1985. *Recreations:* music, theatre, architecture. *Address:* Birmingham Cathedral, Colmore Row, Birmingham B3 2QB. *T:* 021–236 6323; 16 Pebble Mill Road, Edgbaston, Birmingham B5 7SA; The Round House, Ilmington, Compton Scorpion, Warwicks.

BERRY, Peter Fremantle; Managing Director and Crown Agent, Crown Agents for Oversea Governments and Administrations, since 1988; *b* 17 May 1944; *s* of John Berry, *qv*; *m* 1972, Paola Padovani; one *s* two *d*. *Educ:* Eton Coll.; Lincoln Coll., Oxford (MA Hons Mod. History). Harrisons & Crosfield, London, 1966–73: Manager: Kuala Belait, Brunei, 1968; Indonesia, 1970; Anglo Indonesian Corp., London: Gen. Man., 1973; Dir, 1974–82; Crown Agents for Oversea Governments and Administrations, 1982–: Director: Asia and Pacific, based Singapore, 1982–84; ME, Asia and Pacific, based London, 1984–88. Dir, Thomas Tapling Ltd, 1987–; Mem., Management Bd, Resource, BSI, 1989–. Member: Rubber Growers Assoc., 1978–82; Council: Malaysia, Singapore and Brunei Assoc., 1982–87; Indonesia Assoc., 1974– (Chm., 1986–89). *Recreations:* wildlife and country pursuits, culture and people of SE Asia, travel and Third-World development. *Address:* St Nicholas House, St Nicholas Road, Sutton, Surrey SM1 1EL. *T:* 081–643 3311. *Clubs:* Royal Automobile, Commonwealth Trust.

BERRY, Rt. Rev. (Robert Edward) Fraser; Bishop of Kootenay, 1971–89; *b* Ottawa, Ont, 21 Jan. 1926; *s* of Samuel Berry and Claire Hartley; *m* 1951, Margaret Joan Trevorrow Baillie; one *s* one *d*. *Educ:* Sir George Williams Coll., Montreal; McGill Univ., Montreal; Montreal Diocesan Theological Coll. Assistant, Christ Church Cathedral, Victoria, BC, 1953–55; Rector: St Margaret's, Hamilton, Ont, 1955–61; St Mark's, Orangeville, Ont, 1961–63; St Luke's, Winnipeg, Manitoba, 1963–67; St Michael and All Angels, Kelowna, BC, 1967–71. Hon. DD, Montreal Diocesan Theol Coll., 1973. *Recreations:* reading, boating, angling, swimming, walking. *Address:* 1857 Maple Street, Kelowna, BC V1Y 1H4, Canada. *T:* (604) 762–2923. *Clubs:* Vancouver (Vancouver); Kelowna Yacht.

BERRY, Prof. Robert James, FRSE 1981; FIBiol; Professor of Genetics in the University of London, since 1974; *b* 26 Oct. 1934; *o s* of Albert Edward James Berry and Nellie (*née* Hodgson); *m* 1958, Anne Caroline Elliott, *d* of Charles Elliott and Evelyn Le Cornu; one *s* two *d*. *Educ:* Shrewsbury Sch.; Caius Coll., Cambridge (MA); University Coll. London (PhD; DSc 1976). Lectr, subseq. Reader, then Prof., in Genetics, at Royal Free Hospital Sch. of Medicine, 1962–78; Prof. of Genetics at University Coll. London, 1978–. Mem., Human Fertilization and Embryology Authy, 1990–. Member: Gen. Synod, 1970–90; Board of Social Responsibility of the General Synod, 1976–; Natural Environment Research Council, 1981–87; Council, Zoological Soc. of London, 1986– (Vice-Pres., 1988–90); President: Linnean Soc., 1982–85; British Ecological Soc., 1987–89; Chm., Research Scientists' Christian Fellowship, 1968–88. Trustee, Nat. Museums and Galleries, Merseyside, 1986–. Governor, Monkton Combe Sch., 1979–. *Publications:* Teach Yourself Genetics, 1965, 3rd edn 1977; Adam and the Ape, 1975; Inheritance and Natural History, 1977; (jtly) Natural History of Shetland, 1980; (ed) Biology of the House Mouse, 1981; Neo-Darwinism, 1982; (ed) Evolution in the Galapagos, 1984; (jtly) Free to be Different, 1984; Natural History of Orkney, 1985; (ed jtly) The People of Orkney, 1986; (ed jtly) Nature, Natural History and Ecology, 1987; (ed jtly) Changing Attitudes to Nature Conservation, 1987; God and Evolution, 1988; (ed jtly) Evolution, Ecology and Environmental Stress, 1989; (ed) Real Science, Real Faith, 1991. *Recreations:* hill-walking slowly (especially Munros), recovering. *Address:* Department of Biology, University College London, Gower Street, WC1E 6BT. *T:* 071–380 7170.

BERRY, Dr Robert Langley Page, CBE 1979; Chairman, 1968–78, Deputy Chairman, 1978–79, Alcoa of Great Britain Ltd; *b* 22 Nov. 1918; *s* of Wilfred Arthur and Mabel Grace Berry; *m* 1946, Eleanor Joyce (*née* Cramp); one *s* one *d*. *Educ:* Sir Thomas Rich's Sch., Gloucester; Birmingham Univ. (BSc (Hons), PhD). Served war, Royal Engrs, 1939–45. ICI Metals Div., 1951–66, Director, 1960–66; Man. Dir, Impalco, 1966–68. Non-Exec. Dir, Royal Mint, 1981–86. Dir, Nat. Anti-Waste Prog., 1976–80. President: Inst. of Metals, 1973; Aluminium Fedn, 1974. *Publications:* several, in scientific jls.

Recreations: fly-fishing, gardening. *Address:* Waterloo Cottage, Waterloo Lane, Fairford, Glos GL7 4BP. *T:* Cirencester (0285) 712038. *Club:* Army and Navy.

BERRY, Prof. Roger Julian, RD 1987; FRCP; FRCR; Director, Health, Safety and Environmental Protection, British Nuclear Fuels plc, since 1987; *b* 6 April 1935; *s* of Sidney Norton Berry and Beatrice (*née* Mendelson); *m* 1960, Joseline Valerie Joan (*née* Butler). *Educ:* Stuyvesant High Sch., New York; New York Univ. (BA); Duke Univ. (BSc, MD); Magdalen Coll., Oxford (MA, DPhil). MRC External Staff and Hd, Radiobiol. Lab., Churchill Hosp., Oxford, also Hon. Cons. Med. Radiobiologist, Oxford AHA, and Clin. Lectr, Univ. of Oxford, 1969–74; Hd, Neutrons and therapy-related effects gp, MRC Radiobiol. Unit, Harwell, 1974–76; Sir Brian Windeyer Prof. of Oncology, Mddx Hosp. Med. Sch., 1976–87. Member: Internat. Commn on Radiological Protection, 1985–89; Nat. Radiological Protection Bd, 1982–87; MRC Cttee on Effects of Ionizing Radiation, and Chm., Radiobiol. Sub-Cttee, 1983–87; Brit. Cttee on Radiation Units and Measurements, 1978–, Vice-Chm. 1984–; DoE Radioactive Waste Management Cttee, 1984–87; DHSS Cttee on Med. Aspects of Radiation in the Environment, 1985–87, Black Enquiry on Windscale; CBI Health and Safety Policy Cttee, 1988–; CIA Health, Safety and Envmt Council, 1990–. President: BIR, 1986–87; Radiology Sect., RSM, 1985–86; Chm., Sci. Adv. Cttee, Thames Cancer Registry, 1985–87. Surg. Captain, RNR, 1986, and PMO (Reserves), 1987–89. QHP 1987–89. Hon. Fellow, Amer. Coll. of Radiology, 1983. OStJ 1990. Editor, Cell and Tissue Kinetics, 1976–80. *Publications:* Manual on Radiation Dosimetry (jtly), 1970; contributor to Oxford Textbook of Medicine, Florey's Textbook of Pathology; over 160 sci. papers in Brit. Jl of Radiology, etc. *Recreations:* sailing, music, naval history. *Address:* Well Cottage, Parkgate Road, Mollington, Chester CH1 6NE. *T:* Chester (0244) 851367; (office) Padgate (0925) 835022. *Clubs:* Naval and Military; Royal Naval Sailing Association.

BERRY, (Roger) Simon; QC 1990; *b* 9 Sept. 1948; *e s* of Kingsland Jutsum Berry and Kathleen Margaret Berry (*née* Parker); *m* 1974, Jennifer Jane, *d* of Jonas Birtwistle Hall and Edith Emilé Hall (*née* Vester); three *s. Educ:* St Brendan's Coll., Bristol; Manchester Univ. (LLB). Admitted Solicitor, 1973; Partner, Stanley, Wasbrough & Co., Solicitors, Bristol (later Veale Wasbrough), 1975–77; removed from Roll, 1977, at own request, in order to seek call to the Bar; called to the Bar, Middle Temple, 1977; Mem., Middle Temple and Lincoln's Inn; Harmsworth Benefactor's Law Schol.; Mem., Western Circuit, 1978–; in practice at Chancery Bar, 1978–. Member: Chancery Bar Assoc., 1978– (Mem. Cttee, 1984, 1985); Professional Negligence Bar Assoc., 1991–. *Recreations:* family, cycling, ski-ing, keeping fit. *Address:* 9 Old Square, Lincoln's Inn, WC2A 3SR. *T:* 071–405 4682. *Clubs:* Ski of Great Britain, Riverside.

BERRY, Air Cdre Ronald, CBE 1965 (OBE 1946); DSO 1943; DFC 1940 and Bar, 1943; RAF retired; Director of Control Operations, Board of Trade, 1965–68; *b* 3 May 1917; *s* of W. Berry, Hull; *m* 1940, Nancy Watson, Hessle, near Hull; one *d. Educ:* Hull Technical Coll. VR Pilot, Brough Flying Sch., 1937–39; 603 F Sqdn, Turnhouse/Hornchurch, 1939–41 (Battle of Britain); Sqdn Ldr, and CO 81 F Sqdn, North Africa, 1942; Wing Comdr, and CO 322 F Wing, North Africa, 1942–43; Camberley Army Staff Coll., 1944; CO, RAF Acklington, 1945–46; jssc 1955; various operational appts in Fighter and Bomber Comd; V Sqdn, 1957–59; Group Capt., Air Min. and HQ Bomber Comd, 1959. *Recreations:* motoring, gardening, flying. *Address:* Aldrian, Mereview Avenue, Hornsea, N Humberside HU18 1RR.

BERRY, Scyld; *see* Berry, A. S. I.

BERRY, Simon; *see* Berry, Roger S.

BERTHOIN, Georges Paul; Chevalier, Légion d'Honneur, 1990; Médaille militaire, Croix de Guerre, Médaille de la Résistance avec Rosette, France, 1945; Executive Member of the Trilateral Commission (Japan, N America, W Europe), since 1973, Chairman, since 1975; Honorary International Chairman, the European Movement, since 1981 (Chairman, 1978–81); *b* Nérac, France, 17 May 1925; *s* of Jean Berthoin and Germaine Mourgnot; *m* 1st, 1950, Ann White Whittlesey; four *d*; 2nd, 1965, Pamela Jenkins; two *s. Educ:* Grenoble Univ.; École Sciences Politiques, Paris; Harvard Univ. Licencié ès Lettres (Philosophie), Licencié en Droit, Laureate for Economics (Grenoble). Lectr, McGill Univ., Montreal, 1948; Private Sec. to French Minister of Finance, 1948–50; Head of Staff of Superprefect of Alsace-Lorraine-Champagne, 1950–52. Joined High Authority of European Coal and Steel Community, and then Principal Private Sec. to its Pres. (Jean Monnet), 1952–53–55. Dep. Chief Rep. of ECSC in UK, 1956–67; Chargé d'Affaires for Commission of the European Communities (ECSC Euratom-Common Market), 1968; Principal Adviser to the Commission, and its Dep. Chief Rep. in London, 1969–70, Chief Representative, 1971–73. Member: Nine Wise Men Gp on Africa, 1988–89; Bd, Aspen Inst., Berlin; Friends of Jean Monnet; Adv. Bd, Johns Hopkins Univ. Bologna Center Sch. of Advanced Studies. Regular Lectr, RCDS, London. *Recreations:* art, theatre, walking, collecting objects. *Address:* 67 Avenue Niel, 75017 Paris, France.

BERTHON, Vice-Adm. Sir Stephen (Ferrier), KCB 1980; *b* 24 Aug. 1922; *s* of late Rear-Adm. C. P. Berthon, CBE and Mrs C. P. Berthon (*née* Ferrier); *m* 1948, Elizabeth Leigh-Bennett; two *s* two *d. Educ:* Old Malthouse, Swanage; RNC Dartmouth. Served War of 1939–45 at sea, Mediterranean, Atlantic, Russia; spec. communications, 1945–46; Flag Lieut Singapore, 1946–48; submarines, 1949–51; East Indies Flagship, 1951–52; HMS Mercury, 1952–54; Staff of Flag Officer Aircraft Carriers, 1954–56; Fleet Communications Officer Mediterranean, 1957–59; jssc 1959; Comdr HMS Mercury, 1959–61; Jt Planning Staff, 1961–64; Naval Attaché, Australia, 1964–66; Dir of Defence Policy, MoD, 1968–71; Cdre HMS Drake, 1971–73; Flag Officer Medway and Port Adm. Chatham, 1974–76; Asst Chief of Naval Staff (Op. Req.), 1976–78; Dep. Chief of Defence Staff (Operational Requirements), 1978–81; retired 1981. Jt MFH, Avon Vale Hunt, 1981–84. *Recreations:* hunting, riding, gardening, walking, painting. *Club:* Army and Navy.

BERTHOUD, Prof. Jacques Alexandre; Professor of English and Head, Department of English and Related Literature, University of York, since 1980; *b* 1 March 1935; *s* of Alexandre L. Berthoud and Madeleine (*née* Bourquin); *m* 1958, Astrid Irene (*née* Titlestad); one *s* two *d. Educ:* Univ. of the Witwatersrand, Johannesburg (BA and BA Hons). Lectr, English Dept, Univ. of Natal, Pietermaritzburg, 1960–67; Lectr, subseq. Sen. Lectr, English Dept, Univ. of Southampton, 1967–79. British Chm., Amnesty Internat., 1978–80. *Publications:* (with Dr C. van Heyningen) Uys Krige, 1966; Joseph Conrad, the Major Phase, 1978; (ed) books for OUP and Penguin Books. *Recreation:* sleeping. *Address:* 30 New Walk Terrace, Fishergate, York YO1 4BG. *T:* York (0904) 629212.

BERTHOUD, Sir Martin (Seymour), KCVO 1985; CMG 1985; HM Diplomatic Service, retired; *b* 20 Aug. 1931; *s* of Sir Eric Berthoud, KCMG and late Ruth Tilston, *d* of Sir Charles Bright, FRSE; *m* 1960, Marguerite Joan Richarda Phayre; three *s* one *d. Educ:* Rugby Sch.; Magdalen Coll., Oxford (BA). Served with British Embassies in: Tehran, 1956–58; Manila, 1961–64; Pretoria/Cape Town, 1967–71; Tehran, 1971–73; Counsellor, Helsinki, 1974–77; Inspector, HM Diplomatic Service, 1977–79; Head of N. American Dept, FCO, 1979–81; Consul-General, Sydney, 1982–85; High Comr, Trinidad and Tobago, 1985–91. Commander, Order of the Lion, Finland, 1976. *Recreations:* squash, tennis, food and wine, photography, bird-watching. *Address:* Gillyflower Cottage, Stoke by Nayland, Colchester CO6 4RD. *T:* Colchester (0206) 263237. *Club:* United Oxford & Cambridge University.

BERTIE, family name of **Earl of Lindsey and Abingdon.**

BERTRAM, Dr Brian Colin Ricardo; Director-General, Wildfowl and Wetlands Trust, since 1987; *b* 14 April 1944; *s* of Dr Colin Bertram and Dr (Cicely) Kate Bertram, *qv*; *m* 1975, Katharine Jean Gillie; one *s* two *d. Educ:* Perse School, Cambridge; St John's Coll., Cambridge (BA 1965; MA 1968); PhD Cambridge, 1969. FIBiol 1981. Research Fellow, Serengeti Res. Inst., Tanzania, 1969–73; Sen. Res. Fellow, King's Coll., Cambridge, 1976–79; Curator of Mammals, 1980–87, and Curator of Aquarium and Invertebrates, 1982–87, Zoological Society of London. *Publication:* Pride of Lions, 1978. *Recreations:* family, friends, zoology, garden, travel. *Address:* Fieldhead, Amberley, Stroud, Glos GL5 5AG. *T:* Amberley (0453) 872796. *Club:* Zoological.

BERTRAM, Dr Christoph; Diplomatic Correspondent, Die Zeit, since 1986; *b* 3 Sept. 1937; German national; *m* 1st, 1967, Renate Edith Bergemann (marr. diss. 1980); 2nd, 1980, Ragnhild Lindemann; two *s* two *d. Educ:* Free Univ. Berlin and Bonn Univ. (law); Institut d'Etudes Politiques, Paris (political science). Dr of Law 1967. Joined Internat. Inst. for Strategic Studies as Research Associate, 1967, Asst Dir, 1969–74, Dir, 1974–82; Mem. Planning Staff, West German Min. of Defence, 1969–70. Political and Foreign Editor, Die Zeit, 1982–85. *Publications:* (with Alastair Buchan *et al.*) Europe's Futures—Europe's Choices, 1969; Mutual Force Reductions in Europe: the political aspects, 1972; (ed, with Johan J. Holst) New Strategic Factors in the North Atlantic, 1977; Arms Control and Technological Change, 1979. *Recreations:* clocks, sailing. *Address:* Die Zeit, Pressehaus, Speersort 1, W-2000 Hamburg 1, Germany. *Club:* Garrick.

BERTRAM, (Cicely) Kate, MA; PhD; JP; President, Lucy Cavendish College, Cambridge, 1970–79 (Tutor, 1965–70; Hon. Fellow, 1982); *b* 8 July 1912; *d* of late Sir Harry Ralph Ricardo, FRS; *m* 1939, Dr George Colin Lawder Bertram (Fellow and formerly Senior Tutor of St John's Coll., Cambridge); four *s. Educ:* Hayes Court, Kent; Newnham Coll., Cambridge. MA, PhD (Cantab), 1940. Jarrow Research Studentship, Girton Coll., Cambridge, 1937–40. Mem. Colonial Office Nutrition Survey, in Nyasaland, 1939; Adviser on Freshwater Fisheries to Govt of Palestine, 1940–43. Mem. Council, New Hall, Cambridge, 1954–66; Associate of Newnham Coll. FLS. JP: Co. Cambridge, and Isle of Ely, 1959; W Sussex, 1981. *Publications:* Lucy Cavendish College, Cambridge: a history of the early years, 1989; 2 Crown Agents' Reports on African Fisheries, 1939 and 1942; papers on African Fish, in zoological jls; papers and articles on Sirenia (with G.C.L. Bertram). *Recreations:* foreign travel, gardening. *Address:* Ricardo's, Graffham, near Petworth, Sussex GU28 0PU. *T:* Graffham (07986) 205. *Club:* English-Speaking Union.
See also B. C. R. Bertram.

BERTRAM, Robert David Darney; Partner, Dundas & Wilson, Clerks to the Signet, Edinburgh, since 1969; *b* 6 Oct. 1941; *s* of late D. N. S. Bertram; *m* 1967, Patricia Joan Laithwaite; two *s. Educ:* Edinburgh Academy; Oxford Univ. (MA); Edinburgh Univ. (LLB (Hons), Berriedale Keith Prize). An Assistant Solicitor, Linklaters & Paines, London, 1968–69. Associate, Institute of Taxation, 1970 (Mem., Technical Cttee, 1986–); Examiner, Law Society of Scotland, 1972–75; Member: Scottish Law Commn, 1978–86; (part-time), VAT Tribunal, Scotland, 1984–. Non-exec. Dir, The Weir Group plc, 1983–. *Publications:* contribs to professional jls. *Address:* 25 Charlotte Square, Edinburgh EH2 4EZ. *T:* 031–225 1234. *Clubs:* Scottish Arts, Edinburgh University Staff.

BESCH, Anthony John Elwyn, FGSM; opera and theatre director, since 1950; Head of Opera Studies, Guildhall School of Music and Drama, 1986–89; *b* 5 Feb. 1924; *s* of Roy Cressy Frederick Besch and late Anne Gwendolen Besch. *Educ:* Rossall Sch., Lancs; Worcester Coll., Oxford (MA). FGSM 1989. Dir, opera and theatre, 1950–: Royal Opera House, Covent Garden; Glyndebourne Opera; English Nat. Opera, London Coliseum; Scottish Opera; Opera North; New Opera Co., London; Handel Opera Soc.; Edinburgh Festival; Wexford Festival; Deutsche Oper, Berlin; Royal Netherlands Opera; Théâtre de la Monnaie, Brussels; Teatro Colon, Buenos Aires; New York City Opera; San Francisco Opera; Canadian Opera Co.; Nat. Arts Centre, Canada; Australian Opera; State Opera, S Australia; Victoria State Opera. FRSA 1990. *Recreation:* gardening. *Address:* 19 Church Lane, Aston Rowant, Oxfordshire OX9 5SS. *Club:* Garrick.

BESLEY, Christopher; a Metropolitan Magistrate, 1964–88; *b* 18 April 1916; *s* of late C. A. Besley, Tiverton; *m* 1947, Pamela, *d* of Dr W. E. David, Sydney, Australia; four *s* two *d. Educ:* King's Coll., Wimbledon; King's Coll., London. Barrister, Gray's Inn, 1938; practised Western Circuit. Served War of 1939–45, Devon Regt (wounded, N Africa). *Address:* Queen Elizabeth Building, Temple, EC4; 15 Belvedere Avenue, SW19 7PP. *T:* 081–946 2184; Nanquidno House, St Just-in-Penwith, Cornwall.

BESSBOROUGH, 10th Earl of, *cr* 1739, Earl (UK), *cr* 1937; **Frederick Edward Neuflize Ponsonby;** DL; Baron of Bessborough; Viscount Duncannon, 1723; Baron Ponsonby, 1749; Baron Duncannon (UK), 1834; Chairman, Stansted Park Foundation, since 1984; *b* 29 March 1913; *s* of 9th Earl of Bessborough, PC, GCMG, and Roberte de Neuflize, GCStJ (*d* 1979), *d* of late Baron Jean de Neuflize; *S* father, 1956; *m* 1948, Mary, *d* of Charles A. Munn, USA; one *d. Educ:* Eton; Trinity Coll., Cambridge (MA). Performed many leading parts for Stansted Players, Marlowe Soc., Montreal Rep., Ottawa Little Theatre, 1931–35. Contested W Div. Islington (Nat. Govt), 1935. Joined Sussex Yeomanry (TA), 1936; Sec., League of Nations High Commission for Refugees, 1936–39. Served War of 1939–45, France, Flanders and Dunkirk; ADC to Comdr, Canadian Corps; Experimental Officer (Capt.) Tank Gunnery; GSO2 (liaison) in West and North Africa; Second and subsequently First Sec., British Embassy, Paris, 1944–49. Formerly: with Robert Benson, Lonsdale and Co. Ltd and Overseas Adviser to Pye Gp of Cos; Director: High Definition Films; Associated Broadcasting Development Co. Ltd; ATV; Planned Communications; Glyndebourne Arts Trust; Sherek Players, Ltd; English Stage Co. Ltd; Chm., Southdown Radio Ltd; Chm., Inst. for Educnl TV. Chm. of Governors, British Soc. for Internat. Understanding, 1951–71; Chm., International Atlantic Cttee, 1952–55, and 1989–; Chm. and Pres., European Atlantic Group, 1954–61, Co-Pres., 1988, Pres. 1989–; Vice-Pres., British Atlantic Cttee, 1957–. Mem. of UK Parly Delegn to USSR, 1960, and subseq. visits on trade, sci. and technol, incl. setting up London–Moscow TV link and visits to Siberian Res. Insts. Parly Sec. for Science, Oct. 1963; Jt Parly Under-Sec. of State for Educn and Science, 1964; Cons. front bench spokesman on Science, Technology, Power, Foreign and Commonwealth Affairs, 1964–70; Minister of State, Min. of Technology, June-Oct. 1970; led delegns to European space confs in Brussels and Washington, 1970. Dep. Chm., Metrication Board, 1969–70 (Chm., Agricl Cttee); Chm., Cttee of Inquiry into the Res. Assocs, 1972–73. Lectures throughout world on British sci. and ind.; Member: Parly and Scientific Cttee (Vice-Pres., twice); European Parliament, 1972–79 (Vice-Pres., 1973–76; Dep. Leader, European Cons. Gp, 1972–77; Chm., Euro–Arab dialogue, 1977–79; Chm., Cttee on Dual Mandate, 1977–79; Mem. Cttees on Budgets, Energy, Research and Technology); House of Lords Select Cttees on European

Communities and Science and Technology, 1979–85 (Sub-Cttees on Sci. and Govt, Energy Research, Remote Sensing by Satellite); Adv. Bd, Parly Office of Sci. and Technology, 1988–. Led missions to People's Republic of China, 1977, 1984. Member: Amer. Philosophical Soc.; Soc. of Dilettanti. President: SE Assoc. of Building Socs; Men of the Trees; Chichester Cons. Assoc.; Chichester Festival Theatre Trust; Chichester Operatic Soc.; British Theatre Assoc.; Emsworth Maritime and Historical Trust; Trustee, Shakespeare Globe Trust; Patron of British Art, Tate Gall. Chm. of Governors, Dulwich Coll., 1972–73. DL West Sussex, 1977. OStJ; Chevalier Legion of Honour; MRI; FRSA; FRGS. *Plays and publications:* Nebuchadnezzar (with Muriel Jenkins), 1939 (broadcast by BBC); The Four Men (after H. Belloc), for Fest. of Britain, 1951; Like Stars Appearing, 1953 (perf. Glyndebourne 1954); The Noon is Night, 1954; Darker the Sky, 1955; Triptych, 1957; A Place in the Forest, 1958; Return to the Forest, 1962; (with Clive Aslet) Enchanted Forest, 1984; articles, reviews. *Heir pres.: c* Arthur Mountifort Longfield Ponsonby [*b* 11 Dec. 1912; *m* 1939, Patricia (*d* 1952), *d* of Col Fitzhugh Lee Minnigerode, Va, USA; one *s* one *d*; *m* 1956, Princess Anne Marie Galitzine (marr. diss., 1963), *d* of late Baron Sir Rudolph Slatin Pasha; *m* 1963, Madeleine, *d* of Maj.-Gen. Laurence Grand, CB, CIE, CBE; two *s*]. *Address:* 4 Westminster Gardens, SW1P 4JA. *T:* 071–828 5959; Stansted Park, Rowland's Castle, Hants. *T:* Rowlands Castle (0705) 412223. *Clubs:* Turf, Garrick, Beefsteak, Roxburghe.

See also Lady M. B. M. Browne.

BESSEY, Gordon Scott, CBE 1968; *b* 20 Oct. 1910; *s* of late Edward Emerson and Mabel Bessey, Great Yarmouth; *m* 1937, Cynthia (JP 1966), *d* of late William and Mary Bird, Oxford; one *s* three *d*. *Educ:* Heath Sch., Halifax; St Edmund Hall, Oxford. BA 1932, Dip Ed 1933, MA 1937. Teaching: Keighley and Cheltenham, 1933–37; Admin. Asst, Surrey, 1937–39; Asst, later Dep. Educn Officer, Norfolk, 1939–45; Dep. Educn Officer, Somerset, 1945–49. Mem., Youth Service Development Council, 1960–67; Chm., Working Party on part-time training of Youth Leaders, 1961–62; Pres., Assoc. of Chief Educn Officers, 1963; Treas., Soc. of Educn Officers, 1971–74; Chairman: Educnl Adv. Council of IBA (formerly ITA), 1970–74; County Educn Officers' Soc., 1969–70; Dir of Educn, Cumberland, 1949–74, Cumbria, 1974–75. Chairman: East Cumbria Community Health Council, 1974–79; Assoc. of Community Health Councils in England and Wales, 1977–79; Voluntary Action, Cumbria, 1975–84. Hon. DCL Newcastle upon Tyne, 1970. *Recreations:* fishing, golf, fell-walking, ornithology. *Address:* 8 St George's Crescent, Carlisle. *T:* Carlisle (0228) 22253. *Club:* Border and County (Carlisle).

BEST, family name of **Baron Wynford.**

BEST, Alfred Charles, CBE 1962 (OBE 1953); DSc (Wales); Director of Services, Meteorological Office, 1960–66; *b* 7 March 1904; *s* of late Charles William Best, Barry, Glam; *m* 1932, Renée Margaret, *d* of late John Laughton Parry, Blaina, Mon; two *s*. *Educ:* Barry Grammar Sch.; University Coll., Cardiff. Professional Asst, Meteorological Office, 1926; appointments: Shoeburyness, 1926; Porton, 1928; Air Min., 1933; Malta, 1936; Larkhill, 1939; Air Min., 1940; Wing Comdr RAFVR, ACSEA, 1945; Air Min., 1945; Research, 1945–54; Meteorological Office Services, 1955–66. *Publications:* Physics in Meteorology, 1957; meteorological papers in jls. *Recreation:* photography. *Address:* 10 Flintgrove, Bracknell, Berks RG12 2JN. *T:* Bracknell (0344) 421772.

BEST, Edward Wallace, CMG 1971; JP; Deputy Chairman, Melbourne and Metropolitan Board of Works, 1975–79; *b* 11 Sept. 1917; *s* of Edward Lewis Best and Mary Best (*née* Wallace); *m* 1940, Joan Winifred Ramsay; three *d*. *Educ:* Trinity Grammar Sch. and Wesley Coll., Melbourne. Served War 6 years with AIF; 3½ years PoW (Lieut). Elected to Melbourne City Council, 1960; Lord Mayor of Melbourne, 1969–71; has served on numerous cttees: Electric Supply, Finance, Civic Square Bldg, Victoria Market Redevelopment Cttees; Melbourne and Metropolitan Bd of Works Finance and Publicity Cttee; Sidney Myer Music Bowl, 1967– (Chm. 1969); Victorian Olympic Park Cttee of Management, 1967–; Chm., Sports and Recreation Council to Victoria State Govt; Trustee for Olympic Park (Exec. Mem. on Vic. Olympic Cttee which applied for 1956 Melbourne Olympic Games); Mem. Publicity and Pentathlon Cttees at Melbourne Games); Chm., Exhibn Buildings, 1973–75; Melbourne Moomba Festival, 1969– (Pres. 1969–71); Lord Mayor's Holiday Camp, 1969– (Chm. 1969–71); associated 25 years with Lord Mayor's Fund, in an adv. capacity, for appeals; Mem. Cttee: Royal Agricultural Soc. Council, 1970–; Equestrian Fedn of Australia, 1965–75; Moonee Valley Racing Club, 1975–. Visited Edinburgh, Commonwealth Games, 1970 to present Melbourne's application for 1974 Commonwealth Games; Victorian Chm., 1972 Aust. Olympic Appeal, 1971–72, 1974 Commonwealth Games Appeal; Pres., XXth World Congress of Sports Medicine; Chm., Victorian Olympic Council, 1970–75. *Recreations:* racing, hunting, farming; athletics (rep. Australia at 1938 Empire Games; former Victorian champion sprinter). *Address:* Eildon Hills, Maddens Lane, Coldstream, Vic 3770, Australia. *Clubs:* Australian, Bendigo Jockey, Melbourne Cricket, Moonee Valley Racing, Victorian Amateur Turf, Victoria Racing, Royal Automobile Club of Victoria.

BEST, Prof. Ernest; Professor of Divinity and Biblical Criticism, University of Glasgow, 1974–82, now Professor Emeritus; Dean of the Faculty of Divinity, 1978–80; *b* 23 May 1917; *s* of John and Louisa Elizabeth Best; *m* 1949, Sarah Elizabeth Kingston; two *d*. *Educ:* Methodist Coll., Belfast; Queen's Univ., Belfast (BA, MA, BD, PhD); Presbyterian Coll., Belfast. Asst Minister, First Bangor Presbyterian Church, 1943–49; Minister, Caledon and Minterburn Presbyt. Churches, 1949–63; Lectr (temp.), Presbyt. Coll., Belfast, 1953–54; Guest Prof., Austin Presbyt. Theol Seminary, Texas, 1955–57; Lectr in Biblical Lit. and Theol., St Andrews Univ., 1963–74 (Sen. Lectr 1971–74). Lectures: Nils W. Lund, Chicago, 1978; Manson Meml, Manchester Univ., 1978; Sprunt, Richmond, Virginia, 1985; Ethel M. Wood, London Univ., 1986. Vis. Prof. of New Testament Studies, Knox Coll., Dunedin, NZ, 1983; Vis. Fellow, Univ. of Otago, 1983. Jt Editor, Biblical Theology, 1962–72; Associate Editor, Irish Biblical Studies, 1978–. *Publications:* One Body in Christ, 1955; The Temptation and the Passion, 1965, 2nd edn 1990; The Letter of Paul to the Romans, 1967; 1 Peter, 1971; 1 and 2 Thessalonians, 1972; From Text to Sermon, 1977, 2nd edn 1988; Text and Interpretation (ed jtly), 1979; Following Jesus, 1981; Mark: the Gospel as story, 1983; Disciples and Discipleship, 1986; 2 Corinthians, 1987; Paul and His Converts, 1988; contrib. Biblica, Ecumenical Review, Expository Times, Interpretation, Jl Theol Studies, New Testament Studies, Novum Testamentum, Scottish Jl Theology, Catholic Biblical Qly, Zeit. neu. test. Wiss. *Recreations:* vegetable growing, golf. *Address:* 13 Newmill Gardens, St Andrews, Fife KY16 8RY.

BEST, Dr Geoffrey Francis Andrew; Senior Associate Member, St Antony's College, Oxford, since 1988; *b* 20 Nov. 1928; *s* of Frederick Ebenezer Best and Catherine Sarah Vanderbrook (*née* Bultz); *m* 1955, Gwenllyan Marigold Davies; two *s* one *d*. *Educ:* St Paul's Sch.; Trinity Coll., Cambridge (MA, PhD). Army (RAEC), 1946–47; Choate Fellow, Harvard Univ., 1954–55; Fellow of Trinity Hall and Asst Lectr, Cambridge Univ., 1955–61; Lectr, Edinburgh Univ., 1961–66; Sir Richard Lodge Prof. of History, Edinburgh Univ., 1966–74; Prof. of History, Sch. of European Studies, 1974–85 (Hon. Prof., 1982–85), Dean, 1980–82, Univ. of Sussex; Academic Visitor, Dept of Internat. Relations, LSE, 1985–88. Vis. Prof., Chicago Univ., 1964; Visiting Fellow: All Souls Coll., Oxford, 1969–70; LSE, 1983–85; ANU, 1984; Fellow, Woodrow Wilson Internat.

Center, Washington, DC, 1978–79. Lees Knowles Lectr, Cambridge, 1970; Joanne Goodman Lectr, Univ. of Western Ontario, 1981. Mem. Council, British Red Cross Soc., 1981–84, Hon. Consultant, 1985–91. Jt Editor, Victorian Studies, 1958–68; Editor, War and Society Newsletter, 1973–82. FRHistS 1977–84. *Publications:* Temporal Pillars, 1964; Shaftesbury, 1964; Bishop Westcott and the Miners, 1968; Mid-Victorian Britain, 1971; (ed) Church's Oxford Movement, 1971; (jt ed) War, Economy and the Military Mind, 1976; Humanity in Warfare, 1980; War and Society in Revolutionary Europe, 1982; Honour Among Men and Nations, 1982; Nuremberg and After: the continuing history of war crimes and crimes against humanity, 1984; (ed jtly) History, Society and the Churches, 1985; (ed) The Permanent Revolution, 1988; contrib. various jls. *Address:* 19 Buckingham Street, Oxford OX1 4LH.

BEST, His Honour Giles Bernard; a Circuit Judge, 1975–91; *b* 19 Oct. 1925; *yr s* of late Hon. James William Best, OBE. *Educ:* Wellington Coll.; Jesus Coll., Oxford. Called to Bar, Inner Temple, 1951; Dep. Chm., Dorset QS, 1967–71; a Recorder, 1972–75. *Recreations:* walking, fishing. *Address:* Pitcombe, Little Bredy, Dorset.

BEST, Keith (Lander); Director, Prisoners Abroad, since 1989; *b* 10 June 1949; *s* of late Peter Edwin Wilson Best and of Margaret Louisa Best. *Educ:* Brighton Coll.; Keble Coll., Oxford (BA (Hons) Jurisprudence; MA). Assistant Master, Summerfields Sch., Oxford, 1967; called to the Bar, Inner Temple, 1971; Lectr in Law, 1973. Served: 289 Parachute Battery, RHA (V), 1970–76; with RM on HMS Bulwark, 1976; Naval Gunfire Liaison Officer with Commando Forces (Major). Councillor, Brighton Borough Council (Chm. Lands Cttee, Housing Cttee), 1976–80. MP (C): Anglesey, 1979–83; Ynys Môn, 1983–87. PPS to Sec. of State for Wales, 1981–84. Former Chm., All Party Alcohol Policy and Services Gp; former Mem., Select Cttee on Welsh Affairs. Chairman: Bow Gp Defence Cttee; British Cttee for Vietnamese Refugees; Internat. Council of Parliamentarians' Global Action; Member: UN Disarmament Cttee; Young Conservative Nat. Adv. Cttee, 1978. Mem. Cttee, Assoc. of Lloyd's Mems. Founder Member: Two Piers Housing Co-operative, 1977; Brighton Housing Trust, 1976; school manager, Downs County First Sch. and Downs Middle Sch., 1976. *Publications:* Write Your Own Will, 1978 (paperback); The Right Way to Prove a Will, 1980 (paperback); contrib. District Councils Rev. *Recreations:* parachuting, walking, photography, travel. *Address:* 15 St Stephen's Terrace, SW8 1DJ. *Clubs:* St Stephen's Constitutional; Royal Artillery Mess (Woolwich); Holyhead Conservative.

BEST, Sir Richard (Radford), KCVO 1990; CBE 1989 (MBE 1977); HM Diplomatic Service; Ambassador to Iceland, since 1989; *b* 28 July 1933; *s* of Charles and Frances Best (*née* Raymond); *m* 1st, 1957, Elizabeth Vera Wait (*d* 1968); two *d*; 2nd, 1969, Mary Hill (*née* Wait); one *s*. *Educ:* Worthing High Sch.; University Coll. London (BA Hons). Home Office, 1957–66; HM Diplomatic Service, 1966–: CO (formerly CRO), 1966–68; served Lusaka, 1969–72; Stockholm, 1972–76; FCO, 1976–79; served New Delhi, 1979–83; FCO, 1983–84; Dep. High Comr, Kaduna, 1984–88. BBC 'Brain of Britain', 1966. Life Mem., Kaduna Br., Nigeria–Britain Assoc. Grand Cross, Order of Icelandic Falcon. *Recreations:* cricket watching, gardening, reading. *Address:* c/o Foreign and Commonwealth Office, SW1A 2AH. *Club:* Royal Over-Seas League.

BEST, Richard Stuart, OBE 1988; Director, Joseph Rowntree Memorial Trust, since 1988; *b* 22 June 1945; *s* of Walter Stuart Best, DL, JP and Frances Mary Chignell; *m* 1st, 1970, Ima Akpan (marr. diss. 1976); one *s* one *d*; 2nd, 1978, Belinda Janie Tremayne Stemp; one *s* one *d*. *Educ:* Shrewsbury School; University of Nottingham (BA). British Churches Housing Trust, 1968–73 (Dir, 1971–73); Dir, Nat. Fedn of Housing Assocs, 1973–88. Trustee: Sutton Housing Trust, 1971–84 (Dep. Chm., 1983–84); Internat. Year of Shelter for the Homeless 1987 Trust; Chm., Omnium Central Housing Assoc., 1978–80; Committee Member: UK Housing Trust, 1976–88; Sutton Hastoe Housing Assoc., 1982–; Member: Social Policy Cttee, C of E Bd for Social Responsibility, 1986–; BBC/IBA Central Appeals Cttee, 1989–; Cttee, Assoc. of Charitable Foundns, 1989–; Comr, Rural Develt Commn, 1989–; Board Member: Anchor Housing Assoc., 1985–88. Sec., Duke of Edinburgh's Inquiry into British Housing, 1984–86. *Publication:* Rural Housing: problems and solutions, 1981. *Address:* West Wing, Grimston Park, near Tadcaster, N Yorks LS24 9DB. *Club:* Travellers'.

BEST-SHAW, Sir John (Michael Robert), 10th Bt *cr* 1665; retired; *b* 28 Sept. 1924; *s* of Sir John James Kenward Best-Shaw, 9th Bt, Commander RN, and Elizabeth Mary Theodora (*d* 1986), *e d* of Sir Robert Hughes, 12th Bt; *S* father, 1984; *m* 1960, Jane Gordon, *d* of A. G. Guthrie; two *s* one *d* (and one *s* decd). *Educ:* Lancing; Hertford Coll., Oxford (MA); Avery Hill Coll., London (Teachers' Cert.). Captain Royal West Kent Regt, 1943–47. Royal Fedn of Malaya Police, 1950–58; church work, 1958–71; teaching, 1972–82. *Recreations:* gardening, writing. *Heir: s* Thomas Joshua Best-Shaw, *b* 7 March 1965. *Address:* The Stone House, Boxley, Maidstone, Kent ME14 3DJ. *T:* Maidstone (0622) 57524. *Club:* Commonwealth Trust.

BESTERMAN, Edwin Melville Mack, MD, MA, Cantab; FRCP; FACC; Honorary Consultant Cardiologist: Department of Medicine, University of the West Indies (Mona Faculty, Jamaica), since 1985; St Mary's Hospital, London, since 1985; Paddington Green Children's Hospital, since 1985; Hon. Consultant Physician, Department of Medicine, Hammersmith Hospital, since 1981; *b* 4 May 1924; *s* of late Theodore Deodatus Nathaniel Besterman and Evelyn; *y d* of Arthur Mack, NY; *m* 1978, Perri Marjorie Burrowes, *d* of R. Burrowes, Kingston, Jamaica, WI; four *s* by previous marriage. *Educ:* Stowe Sch.; Trinity Coll., Cambridge; Guy's Hospital. BA (Cantab) 1943 (1st cl. hons Physiology), MA 1948; MB, BChir 1947; MRCP 1949; MD 1955 (Raymond Horton Smith Prize); FRCP 1967; FACC 1985. Out-patient Officer, Guy's Hosp., 1947; House Physician, Post-graduate Medical Sch., Hammersmith, 1948; Registrar, Special Unit for Juvenile Rheumatism, Canadian Red Cross Memorial Hosp., Taplow, Berks, 1949–52; First Asst (Lectr), Inst of Cardiology and Nat. Heart Hosp., 1953–56; Sen. Registrar, Middlesex Hosp., 1956–62; Consultant Cardiologist: St Mary's Hosp., London, 1962–85; Paddington Green Children's Hosp., 1972–85. Member: Brit. Cardiac Soc.; Faculty of History of Medicine and Pharmacy; British Pacing Group. *Publications:* contribs to Paul Wood, Diseases of the Heart and Circulation, 3rd edn, 1968; articles on phonocardiography, pulmonary hypertension, atherosclerosis, blood platelet function, lipid fractions and drug trials in angina and hypertension in Brit. Heart Jl, Brit. Med. Jl, Lancet, Circulation, Atherosclerosis Research, etc. *Recreations:* photography, gardening, fishing, tennis, dogs. *Address:* PO Box 340, Stony Hill, Kingston 9, Jamaica, West Indies. *Club:* Liguanea.

BESTOR, Arthur (Eugene); Professor of History, University of Washington, 1962–76, now Emeritus; *b* 20 Sept. 1908; *s* of Arthur Eugene and Jeanette Louise Lemon Bestor; *m* 1st, 1931, Dorothea Nolte (marr. diss.); 2nd, 1939, Anne Carr (*d* 1948); two *s*; 3rd, 1949, Dorothy Alden Koch; one *s*. *Educ:* Yale Univ. PhB 1930; PhD 1938. Yale University: Instructor in English, 1930–31; Instructor in History, 1934–36; Teachers Coll., Columbia University: Associate in History, 1936–37; Asst Prof. of History, 1937–42; Stanford University: Asst Prof. of Humanities, 1942–45; Associate Prof. of History, 1945–46; Lectr in American History, Univ. of Wisconsin, 1947; University of Illinois: Associate Prof. of History, 1947–51; Prof. of History, 1951–62. Harold Vyvyan Harmsworth Prof.

of American History, Oxford, 1956–57; Fulbright Vis. Prof., University of Tokyo, 1967. Editor-in-chief, Chautauquan Daily, Chautauqua, NY, 1931–33. Fellow, Newberry Library, Chicago, Ill., 1946; John Simon Guggenheim Memorial Fellow, 1953–54, 1961–62. President: Ill. State Historical Soc., 1954–55; Council for Basic Education, 1956–57; Pacific Coast Branch, Amer. Historical Assoc., 1976. MA (Oxon) by decree, 1956; LLD Lincoln Univ. (Pa), 1959; LittD Univ. of Southern Indiana, 1988. John Addison Porter Prize, Yale Univ., 1938; Albert J. Beveridge Award, Amer. Historical Assoc., 1946. *Publications:* Chautauqua Publications, 1934; David Jacks of Monterey, 1945; Education and Reform at New Harmony, 1948; Backwoods Utopias, 1950, 2nd edn 1970; Educational Wastelands, 1953, 2nd edn 1985; The Restoration of Learning, 1955; State Sovereignty and Slavery (in Jl Ill State Historical Soc.), 1961; The American Civil War as a Constitutional Crisis (in Amer. Historical Review), 1964; Separation of Powers in the Realm of Foreign Affairs (in Seton Hall Law Review), 1974; Respective Roles of Senate and President in the Making and Abrogation of Treaties (in Washington Law Review), 1979; jointly: Problems in American History, 1952, 3rd edn 1966; Three Presidents and Their Books, 1955; The Heritage of the Middle West, 1958; Education in the Age of Science, 1959; Interpreting and Teaching American History, 1961; The American Territorial System, 1973; contribs to Amer. Hist. Review, Jl of Hist. of Ideas, Amer. Jl of Internat. Law, William and Mary Quarterly, Encounter, Procs Amer. Philosophical Soc., American Scholar, Daedalus, Washington Law Review, New England Quarterly, Jl of Southern History, Harvard Educational Review, New Republic, Scientific Monthly, School and Society. *Recreations:* photography, walking. *Address:* Department of History, DP-20, Smith Hall, University of Washington, Seattle, Washington 98195, USA; (home) 4553 55th Avenue NE, Seattle, Washington, 98105, USA. *Club:* Elizabethan (New Haven).

BESWICK, John Reginald, CBE 1973; FCIArb; FBIM; *b* 16 Aug. 1919; *s* of Malcolm Holland Beswick and Edythe Beswick (*née* Bednall); *m* 1943, Nadine Caruth Moore Pryde; one *s* two *d*. *Educ:* Manchester Grammar Sch.; Rossall Sch.; Trinity College, Cambridge (MA). Sub-Lt RNVR, 1940–42: anti submarine trawlers, N and S Atlantic; Lt RNVR, 1942–46: submarines, home waters and Far East. Called to Bar, Lincoln's Inn, 1947. Practised at Chancery Bar, 1947–51. Sec., Mullard Ltd, 1951–62; Jt Sec., Philips Electrical Industries Ltd, 1953–62; Dir, Mullard Equipment Ltd, 1955–62; Dir, Soc. of Motor Manufrs & Traders Ltd, 1963–79; Dir-Gen., British Ports Assoc., 1980–83; Dir, Mersey Docks and Harbour Co., 1984–87. Member: CBI Council, 1965–79; Council, Inst. of Advanced Motorists, 1966–76. UK delegate, Bureau Permanent International des Constructeurs d'Automobiles, 1966–79. FCIArb 1978. FRSA 1954; FBIM 1982. Asst, Worshipful Co. of Coachmakers, 1973–79. *Recreations:* golf, fly-fishing, reading. *Address:* White House, Redhill, near Buntingford, Herts SG9 0TG. *T:* Broadfield (076388) 256. *Clubs:* Naval and Military; East Herts Golf.

BETHE, Prof. Hans Albrecht, PhD; Professor of Theoretical Physics, Cornell University, 1937–75, now Professor Emeritus; *b* Strassburg, Germany, 2 July 1906; *m* 1939, Rose Ewald; one *s* one *d*. *Educ:* Goethe Gymnasium, Frankfurt on Main; Univs of Frankfurt and Munich. PhD Munich, 1928. Instructor in Theoretical Physics, Univs of Frankfurt, Stuttgart, Munich and Tübingen, 1928–33; Lectr, Univs of Manchester and Bristol, England, 1933–35; Asst Prof., Cornell Univ., Ithaca, 1935–37. Dir, Theoretical Physics Div. of Los Alamos Atomic Scientific Laboratory, 1943–46. Sabbatic leave to Cambridge Univ., academic year, 1955–56. Mem., President's Science Adv. Cttee, 1956–59. Member: Nat. Acad. Sciences; Amer. Physical Soc.; Amer. Astron. Soc.; For. Mem., Royal Society. Holds hon. doctorates in Science. US Medal of Merit, 1946; Planck Medal, German Physical Soc., 1955; Eddington Medal, Royal Astronomical Soc., 1961; Enrico Fermi Award, US Atomic Energy Commn, 1961; Nobel Prize for Physics, 1967. *Publications:* (jt author) Elementary Nuclear Theory, 1947; Mesons and Fields, 1955; Quantum Mechanics of One- and Two-Electron Atoms, 1957; Intermediate Quantum Mechanics, 1964; contributions to: Handbuch der Physik, 1933, 1954; Reviews of Mod. Physics, 1936–37; Physical Review. *Address:* Laboratory of Nuclear Studies, Cornell University, Ithaca, NY 14853, USA.

BETHEL, David Percival, CBE 1983; Director, Leicester Polytechnic, 1973–87; *b* Bath, 7 Dec. 1923; *m* 1943, Margaret Elizabeth, *d* of late Alexander Wrigglesworth; one *s* one *d*. *Educ:* King Edward VI Sch., Bath; Crypt Grammar Sch., Glos; West of England Coll. of Art; Bristol Univ., 1946–51; NDD, ATD, FRSA, FSAE, FCSD, ARWA. Served with RN, Far East, 1943–45. Lectr, Stafford Coll. of Art, 1951–56; Deputy Principal, Coventry Coll. of Art, 1956–65; Principal, Coventry Coll. of Art, 1965–69; Dep. Dir, Leicester Polytechnic, 1969–73. Pres., Nat. Soc. for Art Educn, 1965–66; Member: Nat. Adv. Cttee for Art Educn, 1965–71; Jt Summerson Coldstream Cttee, 1968–70; The Design Council, 1980–88; Nat. Adv. Bd for Local Authority Higher Educn, 1983–87; OECD Directing Gp for Management of Higher Educn, 1984–87; Cttee for Internat. Co-operation in Higher Educn, British Council, 1981–88; Chairman: CNAA Cttee for Art and Design (and Research Degrees Sub-Cttee), 1975–81; Educn and Trng Bd, Chartered Soc. of Designers, 1987–; Study Team on Delivery of Primary Health Care Services, 1987–88; Cttee of Dirs of Polytechnics, 1978–80; Vice-Chm., Inter-Univs and Polytechnics Council for Higher Educn Overseas. Sometime Design Consultant to Massey Ferguson, Van Heusen, Monotype Corp., etc. British Council Adviser to Hong Kong Govt, 1971–; Chairman: UGC/NAB Town & Country Planning Courses Cttee, 1985–86; Hong Kong Planning Cttee for Academic Accreditation, 1986–; Hong Kong Council for Acad. Accreditation, 1989–; Member: Hong Kong UPGC, 1982–; World Council, INSEA; Council of Europe; Chairman: Cyril Wood Meml Trust; Leicester Haymarket Theatre, 1979–85. Paintings and prints in Glos. Libraries, Stafford Art Gallery, Coventry, RWA, private collections. Mem., Worshipful Co. of Frame-Work Knitters. Aust. Commonwealth Travelling Fellowship, 1979. Hon. LLD Leicester, 1982; Hon. DLitt Loughborough, 1987. *Publications:* A Case of Sorts, 1991; An Industrious People, 1991. *Recreations:* travel; study of art, design, architecture; archæology and music. *Address:* 48 Holmfield Road, Stoneygate, Leicester LE2 1SA. *Club:* Athenæum.

BETHEL, Martin; QC 1983; a Recorder of the Crown Court, since 1979; *b* 12 March 1943; *o s* of late Rev. Ralph Bethel and of Enid Bethel; *m* 1974, Kathryn Denby; two *s* one *d*. *Educ:* Kingswood Sch.; Fitzwilliam Coll., Cambridge (MA, LLM). Called to the Bar, Inner Temple, 1965; North-Eastern Circuit (Circuit Junior, 1969). *Recreations:* family, sailing, skiing. *Address:* (chambers) Pearl Chambers, 22 East Parade, Leeds LS1 5BU. *T:* Leeds (0532) 452702.

BETHELL, family name of **Barons Bethell** and **Westbury.**

BETHELL, 4th Baron *cr* 1922, of Romford; **Nicholas William Bethell;** Bt 1911; Member (C) European Parliament, since 1975, elected Member for London North-West, since 1979; free-lance writer; *b* 19 July 1938; *s* of Hon. William Gladstone Bethell (*d* 1964) (3rd *s* of 1st Baron), and of Ann Margaret Bethell (*née* Barlow, now Don); *S* kinsman, 1967; *m* 1964, Cecilia Mary (marr. diss. 1971, she *d* 1977), *er d* of Prof. A. M. Honeyman; two *s*. *Educ:* Harrow; Pembroke Coll., Cambridge (PhD 1987). On editorial staff of Times Literary Supplement, 1962–64; a Script Editor in BBC Radio Drama, 1964–67. A Lord in Waiting (Govt Whip, House of Lords), June 1970–Jan. 1971. Chm., Friends of Cyprus, 1981–. *Publications:* Gomulka: his Poland and his Communism, 1969; The War Hitler Won, 1972; The Last Secret, 1974; Russia Besieged, 1977; The Palestine Triangle, 1979; The Great Betrayal, 1984; *translations:* Six Plays, by Slawomir Mrozek, 1967; Elegy to John Donne, by Joseph Brodsky, 1967; Cancer Ward, by A. Solzhenitsyn, 1968; The Love Girl and the Innocent, by A. Solzhenitsyn, 1969; The Ascent of Mount Fuji, by Chingiz Aitmatov, 1975; dramatic works for radio and TV; occasional journalism. *Recreations:* poker, cricket. *Heir: s* Hon. James Nicholas Bethell [*b* 1 Oct. 1967. *Educ:* Harrow; Edinburgh Univ.]. *Address:* 73 Sussex Square, W2 2SS. *T:* 071–402 6877. *Clubs:* Garrick, Pratt's.

BETHELL, Prof. Leslie Michael; Professor of Latin American History, since 1986, and Director, Institute of Latin American Studies, since 1987, University of London; *b* 12 Feb. 1937; *s* of late Stanley Bethell and of Bessie Bethell (*née* Stoddart); *m* 1961 (marr. diss. 1983); two *s*. *Educ:* Cockburn High Sch., Leeds; University Coll. London (BA, PhD). Lectr in History, Univ. of Bristol, 1961–66; Lectr 1966–74, Reader 1974–86, in Hispanic Amer. and Brazilian History, UCL. *Publications:* The Abolition of the Brazilian Slave Trade, 1970; (ed) The Cambridge History of Latin America: vols I and II, Colonial Latin America, 1984, vol. III, From Independence to *c* 1870, 1985, vols IV and V, From *c* 1870 to 1930, 1986, vol. VII, Mexico, Central America and the Caribbean since 1930, 1990, vol. VIII, Spanish South America since 1930, 1991. *Address:* 2 Keats Grove, Hampstead, NW3 2RT. *T:* 071–435 5861.

BETHELL, Richard Anthony; Lord-Lieutenant of Humberside, since 1983; *b* 22 March 1922; *s* of late William Adrian Bethell and Cicely Bethell (*née* Cotterell); *m* 1945, Lady Jane Pleydell-Bouverie, *d* of 7th Earl of Radnor, KG, KCVO; two *s* two *d*. *Educ:* Eton. JP, ER Yorks, 1950; DL 1975, High Sheriff 1976–77, Vice Lord-Lieutenant 1980–83, Humberside. *Address:* Rise Park, Hull HU11 5BL. *T:* Hornsea (0964) 562241.

BETHUNE, Sir Alexander Maitland Sharp, 10th Bt (NS), *cr* 1683; retired; Director: Copytec Services Ltd, 1964–86; Contoura Photocopying Ltd, 1952–86; *b* 28 March 1909; *o s* of late Alexander Bethune, JP, DL, of Blebo, Cupar, Fife, 9th Bt of Scotscraig, and Elisabeth Constance Carnegie (*d* 1935), 3rd *d* of Frederick Lewis Maitland-Heriot of Ramornie, Fife; *S* father, 1917; *m* 1955, Ruth Mary, *d* of J. H. Hayes; one *d*. *Educ:* Eton; Magdalene Coll., Cambridge. *Recreations:* golf, nature. *Address:* 21 Victoria Grove, W8 5RW.

BETHUNE, Hon. Sir (Walter) Angus, Kt 1979; pastoralist; *b* 10 Sept. 1908; *s* of Frank Pogson Bethune and Laura Eileen Bethune; *m* 1936, Alexandra P., *d* of P. A. Pritchard; one *s* one *d*. *Educ:* Hutchin's Sch., Hobart; Launceston Church of England Grammar Sch. Served War, RAAF Air Crew, Middle East, 1940–43. Member, Hamilton Municipal Council, 1936–56, resigned (Dep. Warden, 1955–56). MHA, Wilmot, Tasmania, 1946–75, resigned; Leader of Opposition, 1960–69; Premier and Treasurer, Tasmania, 1969–72. Leader of Liberal Party, 1960–72, resigned. President: Clarendon Children's Homes, 1977–83; St John's Ambulance Brigade (Tasmania), 1979–86. OStJ 1982. *Address:* 553 Churchill Avenue, Sandy Bay, Tas 7005, Australia. *Clubs:* Tasmanian; Naval, Military and Air Force; Royal Autocar of Tasmania.

BETT, Michael, CBE 1990; MA; Vice-Chairman, British Telecommunications Plc, since 1990; *b* 18 Jan. 1935; *s* of Arthur Bett, OBE and Nina Daniells; *m* 1959, Christine Angela Reid; one *s* two *d*. *Educ:* St Michael's Coll.; Aldenham Sch.; Pembroke Coll., Cambridge. FIPM, CBIM. Dir, Industrial Relations, Engrg Employers' Fedn, 1970–72; Personnel Dir, General Electric Co. Ltd, 1972–77; Dir of Personnel, BBC, 1977–81; British Telecom: Bd Mem. for Personnel, 1981–84; Corporate Dir, Personnel and Corporate Services, 1984–85; Man. Dir Local (Inland) Communications Services, 1985–87; Man. Dir, UK Communications, 1987–88; Man. Dir, British Telecom UK, 1988–90. Member: Pay Bd, 1973–74; Training Levy Exemption Referee, 1975–82; Civil Service Arbitration Tribunal, 1977–83; Cttee of Inquiry into UK Prison Services, 1978–79; Cttee of Inquiry into Water Service Dispute, 1983; NHS Management Inquiry, 1983; Armed Forces Pay Review Body, 1983–87; Civil Service Coll. Adv. Council, 1983–88; Trng Commn (formerly MSC), 1985–89; Chm., Nurses Pay Rev. Body, 1990–. Council, Cranfield Inst. of Technology, 1982–87; Council, Inst. Manpower Studies; Council, Internat. Management Centre from Buckingham. Chm., Bromley CABx, 1985–; Governor, Forest Sch., Snaresbrook, 1984–. Dir, English Shakespeare Co., 1988–. Vice-Pres., Royal Television Soc. FRSA. Hon. Col, 81 Signal Sqn (Vols), RCS, 1990–. DBA (*hc*): IMCB, 1986; CNAA/Liverpool Poly., 1991. *Recreations:* television and radio, theatre, music, cooking, gardening. *Address:* A985 BT Centre, 81 Newgate Street, EC1A 7AJ.

BETTLEY, F(rancis) Ray, TD 1945; MD; FRCP; Physician for Diseases of the Skin, Middlesex Hospital, London, 1946–74, now Emeritus; Physician, St John's Hospital for Diseases of the Skin, London, 1947–74, now Emeritus; formerly Dean, Institute of Dermatology, British Postgraduate Medical Federation; Lieutenant-Colonel RAMC, TARO; *b* 18 Aug. 1909; *yr s* of late Francis James Bettley; *m* 1951, Jean Rogers, 2nd *d* of late Archibald Barnet McIntyre; one *s* (one *d* decd), and one adopted *d*. *Educ:* Whitgift Sch., Croydon; University Coll., London; University Coll. Hosp. Medically qualified, 1932; MD 1935; FRCP 1948. Gazetted RAMC TA, 1932; Resident House-appointments, 1932–33; Radcliffe-Crocker Student (Vienna, Strasbourg), 1936; Hon. Dermatologist to Cardiff Royal Infirmary, 1937; various military hosps in UK and Middle East, 1939–44; Dermatologist and Venereologist, E Africa Comd, 1944–45. Malcolm Morris Lectr, 1959 and 1970; Watson Smith Lectr (RCP), 1960; Emeritus Mem., and former Pres., Brit. Assoc. of Dermatologists; Hon. or Corresp. Mem. of dermatological assocs of: Belgium, Denmark, France, Netherlands, India, Israel, Poland, USA, Venezuela. *Publications:* Skin Diseases in General Practice, 1949; Editor, British Jl of Dermatology, 1949–59; medical papers in various medical jls. *Recreation:* painting. *Address:* The Dower House, Headbourne Worthy, Winchester, Hants SO23 7JG. *T:* Winchester (0962) 885423. *Club:* Athenæum.

BETTRIDGE, Brig. John Bryan, CBE 1983; Principal, Emergency Planning College (formerly Civil Defence College), since 1984; *b* 16 Aug. 1932; *s* of Henry George Bettridge and Dorothy Bettridge; *m* 1959, one *s* one *d*. *Educ:* Eastbourne Grammar School. Commissioned RA, 1951; regimental duty, 3 RHA and 52 Locating Regt, 1952–59; Instructor, RMA Sandhurst, 1959–61; Student, Staff Coll., Camberley, 1962; War Office, 1964–66; Bty Comd, 1 RHA, 1968–70; Comd, 3 RHA, 1973–75, Hong Kong; Chief Instructor, Tactics, RSA, 1976; Comd RA 2 Div., 1977–78; RCDS 1979; Dep. Comdt, Staff Coll., 1980–82; Comdt, RSA Larkhill, 1983–84. *Recreations:* golf, carpentry. *Address:* Cherry Garth, Main Street, Bishopthorpe, York YO2 1RB. *T:* York (0904) 704270.

BETTS, Prof. Alan Osborn, PhD, MA, BSc, MRCVS; academic management consultant, since 1989; Principal and Dean, The Royal Veterinary College, University of London, 1970–89, now Emeritus Professor; *b* 11 March 1927; *s* of late A. O. and D. S. A. Betts; *m* 1st, 1952, Joan M. Battersby; one *s* one *d*; 2nd, 1990, Jane M. Jones. *Educ:* Royal Veterinary Coll.; Magdalene Coll., Cambridge. Asst in Gen. Practice, 1949; Animal Health Trust Research Scholar, 1950–52; Demonstrator, Univ. of Cambridge, 1952–56; Commonwealth Fund Fellow, Cornell Univ., USA, 1955–56; University Lectr, Cambridge, 1956–64; Prof. of Veterinary Microbiology and Parasitology, Univ. of London, 1964–70. Leverhulme Vis. Fellow, Graduate Sch. of Admin, Univ. of Calif,

Davis, 1982. Vice-Chm., 1976–88, Acting Chm., 1989, Governing Body of Wye Coll.; University of London: Dep. Vice-Chancellor, 1984–88; Chairman: Collegiate Council, 1981–84; Cttee of Management, Audiovisual Centre, 1981–89; Working Party on Communication Technol., 1981–89; Member: Jt Planning Cttee, 1981–88; Univ. Court, 1983–88. Treasurer: BVA, 1967–70; RCVS, 1978–81; Pres., Vet. Res. Club, 1984–85. Member: Brit. Pharmacopoeia Commn, 1978– (Chairman: Cttee 'N', 1978–; Cttee 'J', 1988–); EC Adv. Cttee on Veterinary Trng, 1980–90 (Chm., Working Party, 1984–90). Governor, Imperial Cancer Research Fund (Mem. Council, 1988–); Sec./Treas., Foundn for Internat. Exchange of Scientific and Cultural Information by Telecommunications, 1988–89. Trustee, Hunterian Mus., RCSE, 1990–. Dalrymple-Champneys Cup and Medal of BVA, 1978; Faculty Medal, Vet. Faculty, Univ. of Munich, 1985. *Publications:* Viral and Rickettsial Infections of Animals, 1967; papers in microbiological and veterinary jls. *Recreations:* travel, gliding. *Address:* Lower Boycott, Stowe, Buckingham MK18 5JZ. *T:* Buckingham (0280) 813287. *Club:* Athenæum.

BETTS, Air Vice-Marshal (Charles) Stephen, CBE 1963; MA; Head of Control and Inspection Division, Agency for the Control of Armaments, WEU, Paris, 1974–84; *b* 8 April 1919; *s* of H. C. Betts, Nuneaton; *m* 1st, 1943, Pauline Mary (deceased), *d* of Lt-Col P. Heath; two *d*; 2nd, 1964, Margaret Doreen, *d* of Col W. H. Young, DSO. *Educ:* King Edward's Sch., Nuneaton; Sidney Sussex Coll., Cambridge. Joined RAF 1941; Air Cdre 1966; Asst Comdt (Eng.), RAF Coll., Cranwell, 1971–72; Air Vice-Marshal 1972; AOC No 24 Group, RAF, 1972–73, retired 1974. *Recreations:* travel, music. *Address:* Cranford, Weston Road, Bath BA1 2XX. *T:* Bath (0225) 310995; Le Moulin de Bourgeade, Bourg-du-Bost, 24600 Riberac, France. *T:* 53.90.96.93. *Club:* Royal Air Force.

BETTS, Clive James Charles; Leader, Sheffield City Council, since 1987; Deputy Chairman, Association of Metropolitan Authorities, since 1988; *b* 13 Jan. 1950; *s* of Harold and late Nellie Betts. *Educ:* Longley Sch., Sheffield; King Edward VII Sch., Sheffield; Pembroke Coll., Cambridge (BA Econ). Sheffield City Council: Councillor (Lab), 1976–; Chm., Housing Cttee, 1980–86; Chm., Finance Cttee, 1986–88; Dep. Leader, 1986–87. Chairman: S Yorks Pension Authority, 1989–; AMA Housing Cttee, 1985–89. Director: Universiade GB Ltd, 1987–; Hallamshire Investments, 1989–. *Recreations:* Sheffield Wednesday FC, cricket, squash, walking, real ale. *Address:* Town Hall, Sheffield S1 2HH. *T:* Sheffield (0742) 734701.

BETTS, Lily Edna Minerva, (Mrs John Betts); *see* Mackie, L. E. M.

BETTS, Rt. Rev. Stanley Woodley, CBE 1967; *b* 23 March 1912; *yr s* of Hubert Woodley and Lillian Esther Betts. *Educ:* Perse Sch.; Jesus Coll., Cambridge (MA 1937); Ridley Hall, Cambridge. Curate of St Paul's Cheltenham, 1935–38; Chaplain, RAF, 1938–47 (despatches); Sen. Chaplain of BAFO, Germany, 1946–47; Comdt, RAF Chaplains' Sch., Dowdeswell Court, 1947; Chaplain, Clare Coll., Cambridge, 1947–49; Chaplain, Cambridge Pastorate, 1947–56; Proctor in Convocation, 1952–59; Vicar of Holy Trinity Cambridge, 1949–56; Exam. Chaplain to Bishop of Southwell, 1947–56; Select Preacher to University of Cambridge, 1955; Suffragan Bishop of Maidstone, 1956–66; Archbishop of Canterbury's Episcopal Representative with the three Armed Forces, 1956–66; Dean of Rochester, 1966–77. Chm., Bd of the Church Army, 1970–80; Vice-President: Lee Abbey, 1977–; Wadhurst Coll., 1984– (Chm. Council 1976–84). *Address:* 2 King's Houses, Old Pevensey, Sussex BN24 5JR. *T:* Eastbourne (0323) 762421. *Club:* National.

BETTS, Stephen; *see* Betts, C. S.

BEVAN, (Andrew) David Gilroy; MP (C) Yardley (Birmingham), since 1979; Principal, A. Gilroy Bevan, Incorporated Valuers & Surveyors; *b* 10 April 1928; *s* of Rev. Thomas John Bevan and Norah Gilroy Bevan; *m* 1967, Cynthia Ann Villiers Boulstridge; one *s* three *d*. *Educ:* Woodrough's Sch., Moseley; King Edward VI Sch., Birmingham. Served on Birmingham City Council and later W Midlands County Council, 1959–81; past Mem., Finance and Gen. Purposes Cttee, and Policy and Priorities Cttee; past Chm., City Transport Cttee, W Midlands PTA and Transport and Highways Cttee; Jt Chm., Parly Road Passenger Transport Cttee, 1987–; Member, House of Commons Committees: Select Cttee on Transport, 1983–; All Party Leisure and Recreation Industry (Jt Chm., 1979–); Urban Affairs and New Towns (Jt Hon. Sec., 1980–87; Vice Chm., 1987–); Tourism (Chm., 1984–); Cdre, H of C Yacht Club, 1989. FIAA&S 1962 (Past Chm., W Midlands Br.); FRVA 1971; FSVA 1968 (Past Chm., W Midlands Br.); FFB 1972; FCIA 1954; MRSH 1957. *Recreations:* gardening, walking. *Address:* The Cottage, 12 Wentworth Road, Four Oaks Park, Sutton Coldfield, West Midlands B74 2SG. *T:* (home) 021–308 3292; (business) 021–308 6319. *Club:* Carlton.
See also P. G. Bevan.

BEVAN, Rear-Adm. Christopher Martin, CB 1978; Under Treasurer Gray's Inn, 1980–89; *b* London, 22 Jan. 1923; *s* of Humphrey C. Bevan and Mary F. Bevan (*née* Mackenzie); *m* 1948, Patricia C. Bedford; one *s* three *d*. *Educ:* Stowe Sch., Bucks; Victoria Univ., Wellington, NZ. Trooper in Canterbury Yeoman Cavalry (NZ Mounted Rifles), 1941; joined RN as Ord. Seaman, 1942; served remainder of 1939–45 war, Mediterranean and N Atlantic; commissioned 1943; Comdr 1958; Captain 1967; Supt Weapons and Radio, Dockyard Dept, MoD (Navy), 1967–70; Asst Dir, Weapons Equipment (Surface), later, Captain Surface Weapons Acceptance, Weapons Dept, MoD (Navy), 1970–73; Dir, Naval Officer Appts (Engrs), 1973–76; ADC to the Queen, 1976; Rear-Adm. 1976; Flag Officer Medway and Port Adm. Chatham, 1976–78. *Recreations:* photography, theatre, music, travel. *Address:* c/o Messrs C. Hoare and Co., 37 Fleet Street, EC4P 4DQ. *Clubs:* Boodle's, Hurlingham.

BEVAN, David Gilroy; *see* Bevan, A. D. G.

BEVAN, (Edward) Julian; QC 1991; *b* 23 Oct. 1940; *m* 1966, Bronwen Mary Windsor Lewis; two *s* two *d*. *Educ:* Eton. Called to the Bar, Gray's Inn, 1962, Bencher, 1989; Standing Counsel for the Inland Revenue, 1974; Jun. Treasury Counsel, 1977, Sen. Treasury Counsel, 1985, First Sen. Treasury Counsel, 1989–91, Central Criminal Court. *Address:* 30 Halsey Street, SW3 2PT. *T:* 071–584 1316. *Clubs:* White's, Garrick.

BEVAN, Prof. Hugh Keith; JP; Professor of Law, University of Hull, 1969–89; *b* 8 Oct. 1922; *s* of Thomas Edward Bevan and Marjorie Avril Bevan (*née* Trick); *m* 1950, Mary Harris; one *s* one *d*. *Educ:* Neath Grammar Sch.; University Coll. of Wales, Aberystwyth. LLB 1949, LLM 1966. Called to the Bar, Middle Temple, 1959. Served RA, 1943–46. University of Hull: Lectr in Law, 1950–61; Sen. Lectr in Law, 1961–69; Pro Vice-Chancellor, 1979–82; Vis. Fellow, Wolfson Coll., Cambridge, 1986 and 1989–90. Chm., Rent Assessment Cttees, 1982–. Pres., Soc. of Public Teachers of Law, 1987–88. JP Kingston-upon-Hull, 1972 (Chm. of Bench, 1984–89). *Publications:* Source Book of Family Law (with P. R. H. Webb), 1964; Law Relating to Children, 1973; (with M. L. Parry) The Children Act 1975, 1978; Child Law, 1988; numerous articles. *Recreations:* music, golf. *Address:* Faculty of Law, University of Hull, Cottingham Road, Hull HU6 7RX. *T:* Hull (0482) 46311 ext. 6237.

BEVAN, John Penry Vaughan; a Recorder, since 1988; *b* 7 Sept. 1947; *s* of late Llewellyn Vaughan Bevan and of Hilda Molly Bevan; *m* 1st, 1971, Dinah Nicholson; two *d*; 2nd, 1978, Veronica Aliaga-Kelly; one *s* one *d*. *Educ:* Radley Coll.; Magdalene Coll., Cambridge (BA). Called to the Bar, Middle Temple, 1970. 6th Sen. Prosecuting Counsel at Central Criminal Court, 1989–91. *Recreation:* sailing. *Clubs:* Leander (Henley-on-Thames); Aldeburgh Yacht; Orford Sailing.

BEVAN, John Stuart; Director of Education Services, London Residuary Body, since 1989; *b* 19 Nov. 1935; *s* of Frank Oakland and Ruth Mary Bevan; *m* 1960, Patricia Vera Beatrice (*née* Joyce); two *s* two *d*. *Educ:* Eggar's Grammar Sch.; Jesus Coll., Oxford; S Bartholomew's Hosp. Med. Coll. MA, MSc; FInstP. Health Physicist, UK Atomic Energy Authority, 1960–62; Lectr, then Sen. Lectr in Physics, Polytechnic of the South Bank (previously Borough Polytechnic), 1962–73; Inner London Education Authority: Asst Educn Officer, then Sen. Asst Educn Officer, 1973–76; Dep. Educn Officer, 1977–79; Dir of Educn, 1979–82; Sec., NAB, 1982–88. Former Member, National Executive Committees: Nat. Union of Teachers; Assoc. of Teachers in Technical Instns (Pres., 1972–73). Scout Association: Asst, later Dep. Comr, Kent, 1982–; Chm., Nat. Activities Bd, 1988–. Hon. Fellow: Polytechnic of the South Bank, 1987; Westminster Coll., Oxford, 1990. DUniv Surrey, 1990. *Publications:* occasional papers in the educnl press. *Recreations:* scouting, mountaineering. *Address:* 4 Woodland Way, Bidborough, Tunbridge Wells, Kent TN4 0UX. *T:* Tunbridge Wells (0892) 27461.

BEVAN, Julian; *see* Bevan, E. J.

BEVAN, Rt. Rev. Kenneth Graham; *b* 27 Sept. 1898; *s* of late Rev. James Alfred Bevan, MA; *m* 1927, Jocelyn Duncan Barber; three *d*. *Educ:* The Grammar Sch., Great Yarmouth; London Coll. of Divinity. Deacon, 1923; Priest, 1924; Curate of Holy Trinity, Tunbridge Wells, 1923–25; Missionary, Diocese of Western China, 1925–36, Diocese of Eastern Szechwan, 1936–40; Bishop of Eastern Szechwan, 1940–50; Vicar of Woolhope, 1951–66; Rural Dean, Hereford (South), 1955–66; Prebendary de Moreton et Whaddon, Hereford Cathedral, 1956–66; Master of Archbishop Holgate's Hosp., Wakefield, 1966–77; Asst Bp, dio. of Wakefield, 1968–77. *Address:* Grimston Court, Hull Road, York YO1 5LE.

BEVAN, Sir Martyn Evan E.; *see* Evans-Bevan.

BEVAN, Michael Guy Molesworth; Lord Lieutenant of Cambridgeshire, since 1985; *b* 23 Aug. 1926; *s* of late Temple Percy Molesworth Bevan and Amy Florence Bevan (*née* Briscoe); *m* 1948, Mary Brocklebank; three *s* one *d*. *Educ:* Eton College. Grenadier Guards, 1944–47. Joined City of London company, 1948; Director, Briscoes Ltd, Walford Maritime Hldgs Ltd, 1953–85; farmer, 1957–. Governor, Papworth Trust (formerly Papworth Village Settlement), 1962– (Chm., 1980–). Syndic, Fitzwilliam Mus. 1985–. KStJ 1986. *Recreations:* classical music, cricket, bridge. *Address:* Longstowe Hall, Longstowe, Cambridge CB3 7UH. *T:* Caxton (0954) 719203.

BEVAN, Nicolas, CB 1991; Assistant Under Secretary of State, Ministry of Defence, since 1985; *b* 8 March 1942; *s* of late Roger Bevan, BM, and Diana Mary Bevan (*née* Freeman); *m* 1982, Helen Christine, *d* of N. A. Berry. *Educ:* Westminster Sch.; Corpus Christi Coll., Oxford (MA LitHum). Ministry of Defence: Asst Principal, 1964; Principal, 1969; Private Sec. to Chief of Air Staff, 1970–73; Cabinet Office, 1973–75; Asst Sec., 1976; RCDS 1981. *Recreation:* gardening. *Address:* c/o Ministry of Defence, SW1. *Club:* Commonwealth Trust.

BEVAN, Prof. Peter Gilroy, CBE 1983; MB, ChB; FRCS; Consultant Surgeon, Dudley Road Hospital, Birmingham, 1958–87; Professor of Surgery and Postgraduate Medical Education, University of Birmingham, 1981–87, now Emeritus Professor; *b* 13 Dec. 1922; *s* of Rev. Thomas John Bevan and Norah (*née* Gilroy); *m* 1949, Patricia Joan (*née* Laurie) (*d* 1985); one *s* one *d*; *m* 1990, Beryl Margaret (*née* Perry). *Educ:* King Edward VI High Sch., Birmingham; Univ. of Birmingham Medical Sch. (MB, ChB 1946; ChM 1958). LRCP MRCS 1946, FRSC 1952; Hon. FRCSI 1984. Served RAMC, BAOR, 1947–49 (Captain). Demonstrator in Anatomy, Univ. of Birmingham, 1949–51; Resident Surgical Officer, Birmingham Children's Hosp., 1954–55; Lectr in Surgery and Sen. Surgical Registrar, Queen Elizabeth Hosp., Birmingham, 1954–58; WHO Vis. Prof. of Surgery to Burma, 1969; Director, Board of Graduate Clinical Studies, Univ. of Birmingham, 1978–87; Postgrad. Tutor, Birmingham Medical Inst., 1989–. Royal College of Surgeons: Mem. Council, 1971–83; Vice-Pres., 1980–82; Dir, Overseas Doctors Training Scheme Cttee, 1986–90. Founder Chm., W Midlands Oncology Assoc., 1974–79; Vice-Pres., Brit. Assoc. of Surgical Oncology, 1975–78; President: Pancreatic Soc. of GB, 1977; British Inst. of Surgical Technologists, 1980–; Assoc. of Surgeons of GB and Ireland, 1984–85 (Fellow, 1960–; Mem. Council, 1975–85); W Midlands Surgical Soc., 1986. EEC: UK representative: on Monospecialist Section of Surgery, 1975–84; on Adv. Cttee on Medical Trng, 1980–85. Civil Consultant Advr in Gen. Surgery to RN, 1983–84; Med. Adviser, Midlands Div., Ileostomy Assoc., 1976–87. Chm., Adv. Cttee of Deans, 1986–88. Chairman: Steering Gp on Operating Theatres, Dept of Health, 1988–89; Jt Planning Adv. Cttee, Dept of Health, 1990–; Medical Mem., Pensions Appeal Tribunals, 1987–89; Mem., Medical Appeals Tribunal, 1989–. Former Member: Jt Planning Adv. Cttee; Central Manpower Cttee; Jt Consultants Cttee; Council for Postgraduate Med. Educn. *Publications:* Reconstructive Procedures in Surgery, 1982; various surgical papers in BMJ, Brit. Jl Surgery, Lancet, Annals of RCS. *Recreations:* inland waterways, golf, photography, music, gardening. *Address:* 10 Russell Road, Moseley, Birmingham B13 8RD. *T:* 021–449 3055. *Club:* Edgbaston Golf (Birmingham).
See also A. D. G. Bevan.

BEVAN, Rev. Canon Richard Justin William, PhD, ThD; Chaplain to The Queen, since 1986; Canon Emeritus, Carlisle Cathedral, since 1989 (Canon Residentiary, Carlisle Cathedral, 1982–89, Treasurer and Librarian, 1982–89, Vice-Dean, 1987–89); *b* 21 April 1922; *s* of Rev. Richard Bevan, Vicar of St Harmon, Radnorshire and Margaret Bevan; *m* 1948, Sheila Rosemary Barrow, of Fazakerley, Liverpool; three *s* one *d* (and one *s* decd). *Educ:* St Edmund's Sch., Canterbury; St Augustine's Coll., Canterbury; Lichfield Theol Coll.; St Chad's Coll., Univ. of Durham (Theol. Prizeman; BA, LTh). ThD: Geneva Theol. Coll., 1972; Greenwich Univ., USA, 1990; PhD Columbia Pacific Univ., 1980. Ordained Deacon, Lichfield Cathedral, 1945, priest, 1946; Asst Curate, Stoke-on-Trent, 1945–49; Chaplain, Aberlour Orphanage and licence to officiate, dio. of Moray, Ross and Caithness, 1949–51; Asst Master, Burnley Tech. High Sch., 1951–60; Asst Curate, Church Kirk, 1951–56, Whalley, 1956–60; Rector, St Mary-le-Bow, Durham and Chaplain to Durham Univ., 1960; Vicar, St Oswald's United Benefice, 1964–74; Convener of Chaplains, Univ of Durham, 1964–74; Rector of Grasmere, 1974–82. Examg Chaplain to Bishop of Carlisle, 1970–; Chaplain, Durham Girls' High Sch., 1966–74; Vice-Pres., Friends of St Chad's Coll., 1990– (Governor, St Chad's Coll., 1969–89). First Pres., and Founder Mem., Grasmere Village Soc., 1976–78; Dove Cottage Local Cttee, 1974–82. *Publications:* (ed) Steps to Christian Understanding, 1959; (ed) The Churches and Christian Unity, 1964; (ed) Durham Sermons, 1964; Unfurl the Flame (poetry), 1980; A Twig of Evidence: does belief in God make sense?, 1986; articles on ethics and culture. *Recreations:* poetry reading, musical appreciation, train spotting. *Address:* Beck Cottage, West End,

Burgh-by-Sands, Carlisle CA5 6BT. *T:* Burgh-by-Sands (0228) 576781. *Club:* Victory Services.

BEVAN, Richard Thomas, MD; FRCP; Chief Medical Officer, Welsh Office, 1965–77, retired; *b* 13 Jan. 1914; *s* of T. Bevan, Bridgend; *m* 1940, Dr Beryl Bevan (*née* Badham) (*d* 1986); two *s* one *d*. *Educ:* Welsh Nat. Sch. of Medicine. MB, BCh 1939; DPH 1941; MD 1955; FRCP; FFCM. Resident Medical Officer, St David's Hosp., Cardiff; RAF, 1941–46; Lecturer, Welsh Nat. Sch. of Medicine, 1946–68; Deputy County MO, Glamorgan CC, 1948–62. QHP 1974–77. *Address:* 47 Chelveston Crescent, Solihull, W Midlands B91 3YH. *T:* 021–704 9890.

BEVAN, Sir Timothy (Hugh), Kt 1984; Director: Barclays Bank PLC, since 1966 (Chairman, 1981–87); Foreign & Colonial Investment Trust plc; BET plc, since 1987 (Chairman, 1988–91); *b* 24 May 1927; *y s* of late Hugh Bevan and Pleasance (*née* Scrutton); *m* 1952, Pamela, *e d* of late Norman Smith and late Margaret Smith; two *s* two *d*. *Educ:* Eton. Lieut Welsh Guards. Called to Bar, 1950. Joined Barclays Bank Ltd, 1950; Vice-Chm., 1968–73; Dep. Chm., 1973–81. Chm., Cttee of London Clearing Bankers, 1983–85. Mem., NEDC, 1986–87. *Recreations:* sailing, gardening. *Address:* c/o Barclays Bank, 54 Lombard Street, EC3V 9EX. *Clubs:* Cavalry and Guards, Royal Ocean Racing; Royal Yacht Squadron.

BEVAN, Rear-Adm. Timothy Michael, CB 1986; Assistant Chief of the Defence Staff (Intelligence), 1984–87, retired; *b* 7 April 1931; *s* of Thomas Richard and Margaret Richmond Bevan; *m* 1970, Sarah Knight; three *s*. *Educ:* Eton College. psc(n), jssc. Entered RN, 1949; commanded: HMS Decoy, 1966; HMS Caprice, 1967–68; HMS Minerva, 1971–72; HMS Ariadne, 1976–78; HMS Ariadne, and Captain of 8th Frigate Sqdn, 1980–82; Britannia Royal Naval Coll., 1982–84.

BEVAN, Walter Harold, CBE 1977; FCIS; Chairman, Gateshead District Health Authority (formerly of Gateshead Area Health Authority), 1977–84; *b* 22 May 1916; *s* of late Walter Bevan and Sarah (*née* Grainger); *m* 1958, Patricia Edna Sadler, *d* of late Sir Sadler Forster, CBE, DCL; twin *s* and *d*. *Educ:* Gateshead Sch. FCIS 1961. 5th Bn Royal Northumberland Fusiliers, TA, 1938–42; served War: commissioned RA; Arakan campaign, Burma, with 81st W African Div., 1942–46; 4/5 Bn Royal Northumberland Fusiliers, TA, 1947–52. Asst to Sec., North Eastern Trading Estates Ltd, 1937, Chief Accountant 1956; English Industrial Estates Corporation: Chief Accountant, 1960; Sec., 1966; Finance Dir and Sec., 1973; Chief Exec. and Chm., Management Bd, 1974–79. Governor, Gateshead Technical Coll., 1971–81. *Publications:* articles on industrial estates and distribution of industry. *Recreations:* public and voluntary services, bowling, reading. *Address:* Cornerways, Lyndhurst Grove, Low Fell, Gateshead NE9 6AX. *T:* 091–487 6827.

BEVERIDGE, Crawford William; Chief Executive, Scottish Enterprise, since 1991; *b* 3 Nov. 1945; *s* of William Wilson Beveridge and Catherine Crawford Beveridge; *m* 1977, Marguerite DeVoe; one *s* one *d*. *Educ:* Edinburgh Univ. (BSc); Bradford Univ. (MSc). Appts with Hewlett Packard in Scotland, Switzerland, USA, 1968–77; European Personnel Manager, Digital Equipment Corp., 1977–81; Vice-Pres., Human Resources, Analog Devices, 1982–85; Vice-Pres., Corporate Resources, Sun Microsystems, 1985–90. *Recreations:* music, cooking, paperweights. *Address:* 120 Bothwell Street, Glasgow G2 7JP.

BEVERIDGE, Dr Gordon Smith Grieve, FRSE; FEng 1984; FIChemE; FRSA; MRIA; President and Vice-Chancellor, The Queen's University of Belfast, since 1986; *b* 28 Nov. 1933; *s* of late Victor Beattie Beveridge and Elizabeth Fairbairn Beveridge (*née* Grieve); *m* 1963, Geertruida Hillegonda Johanna, (Trudy), Bruyn, *d* of late Gerrit Hendrik Brüjn and Johanna (*née* Breyaen); two *s* one *d*. *Educ:* Inverness Royal Academy; Univ. of Glasgow (BSc, 1st Cl. Hons Chem. Engrg); Royal College of Science and Technology, Glasgow (ARCST 1st Cl. Hons Chem. Engrg); Univ. of Edinburgh (PhD). Asst Lectr, Univ. of Edinburgh, 1956–60; post-doctoral Harkness Fellow of Commonwealth Fund, New York, at Univ. of Minnesota, 1960–62; Vis. Prof., Univ. of Texas, 1962–64; Lectr, Univ. of Edinburgh and Heriot-Watt Univ., 1962–67; Sen. Lectr/Reader, Heriot-Watt Univ., 1967–71; Prof. of Chem. Engrg and Head of Dept of Chem. and Process Engrg, Univ. of Strathclyde, Glasgow, 1971–86. Consultant to industry. Institution of Chemical Engineers: Fellow, 1969–; Vice-Pres., 1979–81, 1983–84, Pres., 1984–85; Exec. Cttee, 1981–86; Hon. Librarian, 1977–84; Mem., Council, 1975–76, 1977–; Scottish Branch: Sec., 1963–71; Vice-Chm., 1972–74; Chm., 1974–76. Society of Chemical Industry, London: Mem. Council, 1978–88; Vice-Pres., 1985–88; Chm. of W of Scotland Section, 1978–86. Council of Engineering Institutions (Scotland): Member, 1977–82; Vice-Chm., 1979–80; Chm., 1980–81; Organiser of 1981 Exhibn, Engineering in the '80s, Edinburgh. Council for National Academic Awards: Chemical, Instrumentation and Systems Engrg Bd, 1976–81: Vice-Chm., 1979–81; Engineering Bd, 1981–84. Science and Engineering Research Council (formerly Science Research Council), various committees: 1973–76, 1980–83; Mem., Engrg Bd; Chm., Process Engrg Cttee (formerly Chemical Engrg Cttee), 1983–86. Engineering Council: Mem., 1981–May 1992; Vice-Chm., 1984–85; Chm., Standing Cttee for Professional Instns, 1982–88; Chm., Standing Cttee for Regions and Assembly, 1989–May 1992. NEDO: Mem., Chemicals EDC, 1983–88; Chm., Petrochemicals Sector Wkg Gp, 1983–87. Chm., Local Organising Cttee, BAAS, Belfast, 1986–87; Dep. Chm., Armagh Observatory Bicentenary Cttee; Member: NI Econ. Res. Centre, 1986–; NI Partnership, 1987–; Engrg and Technol. Adv. Cttee, British Council, 1986–89; Educnl Adv. Cttee, Ulster TV, 1986–; Adv. Council, ESDU Internat. Ltd, 1983–88 (Chm. Adv. Council, 1983–86); Council, OU, 1988–; Newcomen Soc., 1989–; Smeatonian Soc. of Civil Engrs, 1991–. Chairman: Navan Fort Initiative Gp, 1987–89; Navan at Armagh, 1989–; Navan at Armagh Management Ltd, 1990–; Director: Queen's University Bookbinding Ltd, 1989– (Chm., 1989–); QUBIS Ltd, 1986–; The University Book Shop Ltd, 1986–; Cremer and Warner Ltd, 1984– (Chm., 1985–90). Pres., Retirement Assoc., NI, 1986–; Patron: Abercorn Trust, 1986–; Linenhall Liby Appeal, 1989; John Whyte Trust Fund, 1990–; Vice Patron, NI Business Achievement Award Trust, 1990–. CBIM 1990. FRSA 1987; MRIA 1989. Associate Editor, Computers and Chemical Engineering, 1974–87. *Publications:* Optimization - theory and practice (with R. S. Schechter), 1970; multiple pubns in learned jls. *Recreations:* Irish, Scottish and Dutch history, Marlburian war-games, family golf, walking. *Address:* The Office of the Vice-Chancellor, The Queen's University of Belfast, Belfast, Northern Ireland BT7 1NN. *T:* Belfast (0232) 245133. *Club:* Caledonian.

BEVERIDGE, John Caldwell, QC 1979; Recorder, Western Circuit, since 1975; *b* 26 Sept. 1937; *s* of William Ian Beardmore Beveridge, *qv*; *m* 1st, 1972, Frances Ann Clunes Grant Martineau (marr. diss. 1988); 2nd, 1989, Lilian Moira Weston Adamson. *Educ:* Jesus Coll., Cambridge (MA, LLB). Called to the Bar, Inner Temple, 1963, Bencher, 1985; Western Circuit; called to the Bar, NSW, 1975, QC (NSW), 1980. Partner, Beveridge & Forwood, Zurich. Conservative Mem., Westminster City Council, 1968–72. Freeman, City of London. Jt Master, Westmeath Foxhounds, 1976–79. *Recreations:* hunting, shooting, travelling. *Address:* Bathealton Court, Bathealton, Taunton, Somerset TA4 2AJ. *T:* Wiveliscombe (0984) 24611; 5 St James's Chambers, Ryder Street, SW1Y 6QA. *T:* 071–839 2660. *Clubs:* Brooks's, Turf, Beefsteak.

BEVERIDGE, William Ian Beardmore, MA, ScD Cantab; DVSc Sydney; Professor of Animal Pathology, Cambridge, 1947–75; Emeritus Fellow of Jesus College; *b* 1908; *s* of J. W. C. and Ada Beveridge; *m* 1935, Patricia, *d* of Rev. E. C. Thomson; one *s*. *Educ:* Cranbrook Sch., Sydney; St Paul's Coll., University of Sydney. ScD Cantab 1974. Research bacteriologist, McMaster Animal Health Laboratory, Sydney, 1931–37; Commonwealth Fund Service Fellow at Rockefeller Inst. and at Washington, 1938–39; Walter and Eliza Hall Inst. for Medical Research, Melbourne, 1941–46; Visiting Worker, Pasteur Inst., Paris, 1946–47; Vis. Prof., Ohio State Univ., 1953; Guest Lectr, Norwegian Veterinary Sch., 1955; first Wesley W. Spink Lectr on Comparative Medicine, Minnesota, 1971. Consultant: WHO, Geneva, 1964–79; Bureau of Animal Health, Canberra, 1979–84; Vis. Fellow, John Curtin Sch. of Med. Res., ANU, Canberra, 1979–84, Fellow, University House, 1980–85. Chm. Permanent Cttee of the World Veterinary Assoc., 1957–75. DVM (*hc*) Hanover, 1963; Hon. Associate RCVS, 1963; Life Fellow, Aust. Vet. Assoc., 1963; Hon. Member: British Veterinary Assoc., 1970; Amer. Vet. Med. Assoc., 1973; World Veterinary Congresses, 1975; Univ. House, Canberra, 1986; Hon. Foreign Mem., Académie Royale de Médicine de Belgique, 1970; Foundation Fellow, Aust. Coll. Vet. Scientists, 1971; Mem., German Acad. for Scientific Research, Leopoldina, 1974; Hon. Dip., Hungarian Microbiological Assoc., Budapest, 1976. Karl F. Meyer Goldheaded Cane Award, 1971; Gamgee Gold Medal, World Vet. Assoc., 1975; Medal of Honour, French Nat. Cttee of World Vet. Assoc., 1976. *Publications:* The Art of Scientific Investigation, 1950; Frontiers in Comparative Medicine, 1972; Influenza: the last great plague, 1977; Seeds of Discovery, 1980; Viral Diseases of Farm Livestock, 1981; Bacterial Diseases of Cattle, Sheep and Goats, 1983; articles on infectious diseases of man and domestic animals and comparative medicine, in scientific jls. *Recreations:* bush-walking, skiing. *Address:* 5 Bellevue Road, Wentworth Falls, Blue Mountains, NSW 2782, Australia. *T:* (047) 571606.

See also J C. Beveridge.

BEVERLEY, Lt-Gen. Sir Henry (York La Roche), KCB 1991; OBE 1979; Commandant General Royal Marines, since 1990; *b* 25 Oct. 1935; *s* of Vice-Adm. Sir York Beverley, KBE, CB, and Lady Beverley; *m* 1963, Sally Ann Maclean; two *d*. *Educ:* Wellington College. DS Staff Coll., 1976–78; CO 42 Cdo RM, 1978–80; Comdt CTC RM, 1980–82; Director RM Personnel, MoD, 1983–84; Comd 3 Cdo Bde RM, 1984–86; Maj.-Gen. Trng and Reserve Forces RM, 1986–88; CoS to CGRM, 1988–90. *Recreations:* cricket, golf, skiing. *Club:* Army and Navy.

BEVERTON, Prof. Raymond John Heaphy, CBE 1968; FRS 1975; FIBiol 1973; Emeritus Professor of Fisheries Science, University of Wales; *b* 29 Aug. 1922; *s* of Edgar John Beverton and Dorothy Sybil Mary Beverton; *m* 1947, Kathleen Edith Marner; three *d*. *Educ:* Forest Sch., Snaresbrook; Downing Coll., Cambridge (MA). Cambridge, 1940–42 and 1946–47. Joined Fisheries Research Lab. (MAFF), 1947; Dep. Dir, Fisheries Res., 1959–65; Sec., NERC, 1965–80; Sen. Res. Fellow, Univ. of Bristol, engaged on study of change and adaptation in scientific res. careers, 1981–82; Prog. Integrator, Internat. Fedn of Insts for Advanced Study, 1982–84; Hon. Professorial Fellow, UWIST, 1982–84; Prof. of Fisheries Science, 1984–89, Head of Sch. of Pure and Applied Biol., 1988–89, Univ. of Wales Coll. of Cardiff (formerly at UWIST); Chm., Management Cttee, Millport Biol. Lab., 1985–. Hon. posts during research career: Chm., Comparative Fishing Cttee of ICES, 1957–62; Chm., Res. and Statistics Cttee of Internat. Commn for Northwest Atlantic Fisheries, 1960–63. Member: MAFF Fisheries R & D Bd, 1972–79; NRPB, 1976–80. Head of UK delegn to Intergovernmental Oceanographic Commn, 1981–84; Vis. Lectr in fish population dynamics, Univ. of Southampton, 1982–86. Chm., Nat. Scis Adv. Cttee for UNESCO, 1984–85. Pres., Fisheries Soc. of British Isles, 1983–; Vice-Pres., Freshwater Biological Assoc., 1980–; Mem. Council, Scottish Marine Biol. Assoc., 1984–86; Trustee, World Wildlife Fund UK, 1983–85. Editor, Jl ICES, 1983–. Hon. DSc Wales, 1989. *Publications:* (with S. J. Holt) On the Dynamics of Exploited Fish Populations, 1957; (with G. W. D. Findlay) Funding and Policy for Research in the Natural Sciences (in The Future of Research, ed. Geoffrey Oldham), 1982; papers on mathematical basis of fish population dynamics, theory and practice of fisheries conservation and various fisheries research topics. *Recreations:* fishing, sailing, golf, music. *Address:* Montana, Old Roman Road, Langstone, Gwent NP6 2JU.

BEVINGTON, Eric Raymond, CMG 1961; *b* 23 Jan. 1914; *s* of late R. Bevington and N. E. Bevington (*née* Sutton); *m* 1939, Enid Mary Selina (*née* Homer); one *s* one *d*. *Educ:* Monkton Combe Sch.; Loughborough Coll.; Queens' Coll., Cambridge. CEng, MIMechE. Cadet, HM Overseas Service, Gilbert and Ellice Islands, 1937; District Officer, Fiji, 1942; Sec., Commn of Enquiry into Cost of Living Allowances, Nigeria, 1945–46; Admin. Officer Cl I, Fiji, 1950; Asst Col Sec. (Develt), Fiji, 1951; Develt Comr, Brunei, 1954; Financial Sec., Fiji, 1958–61, Development Commissioner, 1962–63; Mem., Executive Council, Fiji, 1958–63; Senior Project Engineer, Wrigh Rain Ltd, 1964–67; Appeals Inspector, Min. of Housing and Local Govt, 1967–70; Sen. Housing and Planning Inspector, DoE, 1970–78. Mem., New Forest DC, 1979–83. *Publication:* The Things We Do For England, 1990. *Recreations:* golf, sailing, zymurgy. *Address:* Holmans Cottage, Bisterne Close, Burley, Hants BH24 4AZ. *T:* Burley (04253) 3316.

BEVINS, Rt. Hon. John Reginald, PC 1959; *b* 20 Aug. 1908; *e s* of John Milton and Grace Eveline Bevins, Liverpool; *m* 1933, Mary Leonora Jones; three *s*. *Educ:* Dovedale Road and Liverpool Collegiate Schs. Served War of 1939–45; gunner, 1940; Major, RASC, 1944; MEF and Europe. Mem. Liverpool City Council, 1935–50. Contested West Toxteth Div., 1945, and Edge Hill (bye-election), 1947; MP (C) Toxteth Div. of Liverpool, 1950–64; PPS to the Minister of Housing and Local Government, 1951–53; Parliamentary Sec., Ministry of Works, 1953–57, Ministry of Housing and Local Govt, 1957–59; Postmaster-General, 1959–64. *Publication:* The Greasy Pole, 1965. *Address:* 37 Queen's Drive, Liverpool L18 2DT. *T:* 051–722 8484.

See also K. M. Bevins.

BEVINS, Kenneth Milton, CBE 1973; TD 1951; Director: Royal Insurance plc, 1970–88; Royal Insurance Holdings, 1988–89; *b* 2 Nov. 1918; *yr s* of late John Milton Bevins and Grace Eveline Bevins, Liverpool; *m* 1st, 1940, Joan Harding (*d* 1969); two *d*; 2nd, 1971, Diana B. Sellers, *y d* of late Godfrey J. Sellers, Keighley. *Educ:* Liverpool Collegiate Sch. Joined Royal Insurance Co. Ltd, 1937. Served War, 1939–46: 136 Field Regt, RA, incl. with 14th Army in Burma, 1943–46 (Major). Sec., Royal Insurance Co. Ltd, 1957; Gen. Manager, 1963; Dep. Chief Gen. Manager, 1966; Chief Gen. Manager, 1970–80; Director: Trade Indemnity Co. Ltd, 1970–80 (Chm., 1975–80); Mutual & Federal Insurance Co. Ltd, 1971–80; British Aerospace plc, 1981–87. Dir, Fire Protection Assoc., 1963–77 (Chm., 1966–68). Member: Jt Fire Research Organisation Steering Cttee, 1966–68; Home Secretary's Standing Cttee on Crime Prevention, 1967–73; Exec. Cttee, City Communications Centre, 1976–80; Bd, British Aerospace, 1980–81; Govt Cttee to review structure, functions and status of ECGD, 1983–84. Chm., British Insurance Assoc., 1971–73 (Dep. Chm., 1967–71). *Recreations:* travel, gardening, reading, painting. *Address:* Linton, The Drive, Sevenoaks, Kent TN13 3AF. *T:* Sevenoaks (0732) 456909. *Clubs:* Oriental, Army and Navy.

See also Rt Hon. J. R. Bevins.

BEWES, Rev. Preb. Richard Thomas; Rector, All Souls Church, Langham Place, since 1983; Prebendary of St Paul's Cathedral, since 1988; *b* 1 Dec. 1934; *s* of Cecil and Sylvia Bewes; *m* 1964, Elisabeth Ingrid Jaques; two *s* one *d. Educ:* Marlborough Sch.; Emmanuel Coll., Cambridge (MA); Ridley Hall, Cambridge. Deacon, 1959; priest, 1960; Curate of Christ Church, Beckenham, 1959–65; Vicar: St Peter's, Harold Wood, 1965–74; Emmanuel, Northwood, 1974–83. *Publications:* God in Ward 12, 1973; Advantage Mr Christian, 1975; Talking about Prayer, 1979; The Pocket Handbook of Christian Truth, 1981; John Wesley's England, 1981; The Church Reaches Out, 1981; The Church Overcomes, 1983; On The Way, 1984; Quest for Truth, 1985; Quest for Life, 1985; The Church Marches On, 1986; When God Surprises, 1986; The Resurrection, 1989; A New Beginning, 1989. *Recreations:* tennis, photography, audio-visual production. *Address:* 2 All Souls Place, W1N 3DB. *T:* 071–580 6029.

BEWICK, Herbert; retired barrister; *b* 4 April 1911; *s* of late James Dicker and Elizabeth Jane Bewick. *Educ:* Whitehill Secondary Sch., Glasgow; Royal Grammar Sch., Newcastle upon Tyne; St Catharine's Coll., Cambridge. Called to Bar, Gray's Inn, 1935; Recorder of Pontefract, 1961–67; Chm. of Industrial Tribunal (Newcastle upon Tyne), 1967–72; practised in common law, 1972–84. *Address:* Flat 33, Russell Court, Adderstone Crescent, Jesmond, Newcastle upon Tyne NE2 2HH. *T:* 091–281 1138.

BEWICKE-COPLEY, family name of **Baron Cromwell.**

BEWLEY, Edward de Beauvoir; Hon. Mr Justice Bewley; Judge of the High Court of Hong Kong, since 1980; *b* 12 March 1931; *s* of Harold de Beauvoir Bewley and Phyllis Frances Cowdy; *m* 1st, 1956, Sheelagh Alice Brown; one *s*; 2nd, 1968, Mary Gwenefer Jones; three *d. Educ:* Shrewsbury School; Trinity College, Dublin. BA, LLB; Barrister at Law. Administrative Officer, Northern Rhodesia, 1956–59; English Bar, 1960–61; Resident Magistrate, Nyasaland, 1961–64; Magistrate, Hong Kong, 1964–76, District Judge, 1976–80. *Recreations:* golf, skiing, squash, reading, music. *Address:* 76E Peak Road, The Peak, Hong Kong. *T:* 5–8496111. *Clubs:* Hong Kong; Royal Irish Yacht (Dun Laoghaire), Royal Hong Kong Golf.

BEWLEY, Thomas Henry, Hon. CBE 1988; MA; MD; FRCP, FRCPI; Hon. Senior Lecturer, St George's Hospital Medical School, University of London, since 1974; Consultant Psychiatrist, Tooting Bec and St Thomas' Hospitals, 1961–88; *b* 8 July 1926; *s* of Geoffrey Bewley and Victoria Jane Wilson; *m* 1955, Beulah Knox, MD, FFCM; one *s* four *d. Educ:* St Columba's College, Dublin; Trinity College, Dublin University (MA, MD 1958). FRCPsych 1984; Hon. FRCPsych. Hon. MD Dublin, 1987. Qualified TCD, 1950; trained St Patrick's Hosp., Dublin, Maudsley Hosp., Univ. of Cincinnati. Member: Standing Adv. Cttee on Drug Dependence, 1966–71; Adv. Council on Misuse of Drugs, 1972–84; Consultant Adviser on Drug Dependence to DHSS, 1972–81; Consultant, WHO, 1969–78. Pres., RCPsych, 1984–87 (Dean, 1977–82); Jt Co-founder and Mem. Council, Inst. for Study of Drug Dependence, 1967–. *Publications:* Handbook for Inceptors and Trainees in Psychiatry, 1976, 2nd edn 1980; papers on drug dependence, medical manpower and side effects of drugs. *Address:* 11 Garrads Road, SW16 1JU. *T:* 081–769 1703. *Club:* London Chapter of Irish Georgian Society.

BEXON, Roger, CBE 1985; Chairman, Laporte plc (formerly Laporte Industries (Holdings)), since 1986; Managing Director, British Petroleum Co., 1981–86, and Deputy Chairman, 1983–86; *b* 11 April 1926; *s* of late MacAlister Bexon, CBE, and Nora Hope Bexon (*née* Jenner); *m* 1951, Lois Loughran Walling; one *s* one *d. Educ:* Denstone Coll. (schol.); St John's Coll., Oxford (MA); Tulsa Univ. (MS). Geologist and petroleum engineer with Trinidad Petroleum Development Co. Ltd, 1946–57; management positions with British Petroleum Co., E Africa, 1958–59; Libya, 1959–60; Trinidad, 1961–64; London, 1964–66; Manager, North Sea Operations, 1966–68; General Manager, Libya, 1968–70; Regional Coordinator, Middle East, London, 1971–73; Gen. Manager, Exploration and Production, London, 1973–76; Managing Director, BP Exploration Co. Ltd, London, 1976–77; Chm., Goal Petroleum, 1990–; Director: Standard Oil Co., 1982–86 (Dir and Sen. Vice Pres., 1977–80); BP Canada Inc., 1983–87; BICC, 1985–; Lazard Bros, 1986–; Fenner plc (formerly J. H. Fenner (Hldgs)), 1986–89; Cameron Iron Works, 1987–89; Astec (BSR) PLC (formerly BSR International), 1989–. Mem. Council, British–N American Res. Assoc., 1986–. *Publications:* general and technical contribs to internat. jls on oil and energy matters. *Recreations:* reading, golf, Times crossword puzzles. *Address:* c/o Laporte plc, 3 Bedford Square, WC1B 3RA. *T:* 071–580 0223.

BEYFUS, Drusilla Norman; writer, editor, broadcaster; Lecturer, Central St Martin's College of Art, since 1989; *d* of Norman Beyfus and Florence Noel Barker; *m* 1956, Milton Shulman, *qv*; one *s* two *d. Educ:* Royal Naval Sch.; Channing Sch. Woman's Editor, Sunday Express, 1950; columnist, Daily Express, 1952–55; Associate Editor, Queen magazine, 1956; Home Editor, The Observer, 1963; Associate Editor, Daily Telegraph magazine, 1966; Editor, Brides and Setting Up Home magazine, 1972–79; Associate Editor, 1979–87, Contributing Editor, 1987–88, Vogue magazine; Editor, Harrods Magazine, 1987–88; columnist, Sunday Telegraph, 1990–. TV and radio appearances, incl. Call My Bluff and talks programmes. *Publications:* (with Anne Edwards) Lady Behave, 1956 (rev. edn 1969); The English Marriage, 1968; The Brides Book, 1981; The Art of Giving, 1987; contrib. to Sunday Times, Punch, New Statesman, Daily Telegraph. *Recreations:* walking, modern art, cooking. *Address:* 51G Eaton Square, SW1. *T:* 071–235 7162.

See also Earl of Mulgrave.

BEYNON, Ernest Geoffrey; Joint General Secretary, Assistant Masters and Mistresses Association, 1979–87; *b* 4 Oct. 1926; *s* of late Frank William George and Frances Alice Pretoria Beynon; *m* 1956, Denise Gwendoline Rees; two *s* one *d. Educ:* Borden Grammar Sch., Kent; Univ. of Bristol, 1944–47, 1949–50 (BSc (Hons Maths) 1947, CertEd 1950). National Service, Royal Artillery, 1947–49. Mathematics Master, Thornbury Grammar Sch., Glos, 1950–56; Mathematics Master and Sixth Form Master, St George Grammar Sch., Bristol, 1956–64; Asst Sec., Assistant Masters Assoc., 1964–78. Last Chm., Teachers' Panel, Burnham Primary and Secondary Cttee, 1985–87. Mem., Univ. of Bristol Court, 1986–; Trustee and Manager, Muntham House Sch., 1979–. Member, Committee: Welwyn Garden City Soc., 1988–; St Albans Dist, Hertford County Assoc. of Change-Ringers, 1989–. Hon. FCP, 1985. *Publications:* many reports/pamphlets for AMA, incl. The Middle School System, Mixed Ability Teaching, Selection for Admission to a University. *Recreations:* family, campanology, canal boating, walking, books. *Address:* 3 Templewood, Welwyn Garden City, Herts AL8 7HT. *T:* Welwyn Garden (0707) 321380.

BEYNON, Sir Granville; see Beynon, Sir W. J. G.

BEYNON, Ven. James Royston; Archdeacon of Winchester, 1962–73, now Emeritus; *b* 16 Sept. 1907; *s* of James Samuel and Catherine Beynon; *m* 1933, Mildred Maud Fromings (*d* 1986); four *d. Educ:* St Augustine's Coll., Canterbury. LTh Durham. Ordained, 1931; Chaplain, Indian Eccl. Estabt, 1933; Senior Chaplain: Peshawar, 1941; Quetta, 1943; Archdeacon of Lahore, 1946–48; Vicar of Twyford, Winchester, 1948–73;

Rural Dean of Winchester, 1958–62. Hon. CF, 1945. *Address:* 1511 Geary Avenue, London, Ontario N5X 1G6, Canada.

BEYNON, Dr John David Emrys, FEng 1988; FIEE; Principal, King's College London, since 1990; *b* 11 March 1939; *s* of John Emrys and Elvira Beynon; *m* 1964, Hazel Janet Hurley; two *s* one *d. Educ:* Univ. of Wales (BSc); Univ. of Southampton (MSc, PhD). FIERE 1977; FIEE 1978. Scientific Officer, Radio Res. Station, Slough, 1962–64; Univ. of Southampton: Lectr, Sen. Lectr and Reader, 1964–77; Prof. of Electronics, UWIST, Cardiff, 1977–79; University of Surrey: Prof. of Elec. Engrg, 1979–90; Head of Dept of Electronic and Elec. Engrg, 1979–83; Pro-Vice-Chancellor, 1983–87; Sen. Pro-Vice-Chancellor, 1987–90. Vis. Prof., Carleton Univ., Ottawa, 1975; Cons. to various cos, Govt estabts and Adviser to British Council, 1964–. Member: Accreditation Cttee, IEE, 1983–89; Adv. Cttee on Engrg and Technology, British Council, 1983–; Technology Sub-Cttee, UGC, 1984–89; Nat. Electronics Council, 1985–; Cttee 1, CICHE, 1990–; Adv. Cttee, Erasmus, 1990–. Engrg Professors' Conference: Hon. Sec., 1982–84; Vice-Chm., 1984–85 and 1987–88; Chm., 1985–87. FRSA 1982; FKC 1990. Hon. Fellow, UC Swansea, 1990. *Publications:* Charge-Coupled Devices and Their Applications (with D. R. Lamb), 1980; papers on plasma physics, semiconductor devices and integrated circuits, and engrg educn. *Recreations:* music, photography, travel. *Address:* King's College London, Strand, WC2R 2LS. *T:* 071–836 5454.

BEYNON, Prof. John Herbert, DSc; FRS 1971; Professor Emeritus, University of Wales, since 1991; *b* 29 Dec. 1923; British; *m* 1947, Yvonne Lilian (*née* Fryer); no *c. Educ:* UC Swansea, Univ. of Wales. BSc (1st cl. hons Physics); DSc; CPhys; FInstP; CChem; FRSC. Experimental Officer, Min. of Supply, Tank Armament Research, 1943–47; ICI Ltd (Organics Div.), 1947–74; Associate Research Man. i/c Physical Chemistry, 1962–70; Sen. Res. Associate, 1965–74. University College of Swansea, University of Wales: Hon. Professorial Fellow, and Lectr in Chemistry, 1967–74; Royal Soc. Res. Prof., 1974–86; Res. Prof., 1987–90. Prof. of Chemistry, Purdue Univ., Indiana, 1969–75; Associate Prof. of Molecular Sciences, Univ. of Warwick, 1972–74; Vis. Prof., Univ. of Essex, 1973–74, 1982–; Hon. Prof., Univ. of Warwick, 1977–. Chm., Science Curriculum Develt Cttee, Cttee for Wales, 1983–88. *Publications:* Mass Spectrometry and its Applications in Organic Chemistry, 1960; Mass and Abundance Tables for use in Mass Spectrometry, 1963; The Mass Spectra of Organic Molecules, 1968; Table of Ion Energies for metastable transitions in mass spectrometry, 1970; Metastable Ions, 1973; An Introduction to Mass Spectrometry, 1981; Current Topics in Mass Spectrometry and Chemical Kinetics, 1982; Application of Transition State Theory to Unimolecular Reactions, 1983; papers in Proc. Royal Soc., Nature, Jl Sci. Inst., Jl Applied Physics, Chem. Soc., JACS, Trans Faraday Soc., Int. Jl Mass Spectrom. and Ion Physics, Org. Mass Spectrom., Anal. Chem., etc. *Recreations:* photography, golf. *Address:* Chemistry Building, University College Swansea, Singleton Park, Swansea SA2 8PP. *T:* Swansea (0792) 295298; 17 Coltshill Drive, Mumbles, Swansea SA3 4SN. *T:* Swansea (0792) 368718. *Clubs:* Swansea Sports (Chm., 1988–); Bristol Channel Yacht.

BEYNON, Timothy George, MA; FRGS 1983; Headmaster, The Leys School, Cambridge, 1986–90; *b* 13 Jan. 1939; *s* of George Beynon and Fona I. Beynon; *m* 1973, Sally Jane Wilson; two *d. Educ:* Swansea Grammar Sch.; King's Coll., Cambridge (MA). City of London Sch., 1962–63; Merchant Taylors' Sch., 1963–78; Headmaster, Denstone Coll., 1978–86. *Recreations:* ornithology, fishing, shooting, sport, music, expeditions. *Address:* The Croft, College Road, Denstone, Uttoxeter, Staffs ST14 5HR.

BEYNON, Prof. Sir (William John) Granville, Kt 1976; CBE 1959; PhD, DSc; FRS 1973; Professor and Head of Department of Physics, University College of Wales, Aberystwyth, 1958–81, now Emeritus; *b* 24 May 1914; *s* of William and Mary Beynon; *m* 1942, Megan Medi, *d* of Arthur and Margaret James; two *s* one *d. Educ:* Gowerton Grammar Sch.; University Coll., Swansea. Scientific Officer, later Senior Scientific Officer, National Physical Laboratory, 1938–46; Lecturer, later Senior Lecturer in Physics, University Coll. of Swansea, 1946–58. Mem., SRC, 1976–80. Mem., Schools Council, 1965–76; Pres., 1972–75, Hon. Pres., 1981–, URSI; Hon. Professorial Fellow, UC Swansea, 1981–; Hon. DSc Leicester, 1981. *Publications:* (ed) Solar Eclipses and the Ionosphere, 1956; (ed) Proceedings Mixed Commission on the Ionosphere, 1948–58; numerous publications in scientific jls. *Recreations:* music, cricket, tennis, Rugby. *Address:* Caebryn, Caergôg, Aberystwyth, Dyfed SY23 1ET. *T:* Aberystwyth (0970) 3947.

BHASKAR, Prof. Krishan Nath; Director, Motor Industry Research Unit Ltd, Norwich, since 1988; *b* 9 Oct. 1945; *s* of late Dr Ragu Nath Bhaskar and Mrs Kamla Bhaskar (*née* Dora Skill); *m* 1977, Fenella Mary (*née* McCann); one *s* one *d. Educ:* St Paul's Sch., London; London Sch. of Econs and Pol. Science (BSc Econ 1st Cl. Hons, MSc Econ). Lectr, LSE, 1968–70; Lectr in Accounting, Univ. of Bristol, 1970–78; Prof. of Accountancy and Finance, UEA, 1978–88. *Publications:* (with D. Murray) Macroeconomic Systems, 1976; Building Financial Models: a simulation approach, 1978; Manual to Building Financial Models, 1978; The Future of the UK Motor Industry, 1979; The Future of the World Motor Industry, 1980; (with M. J. R. Shave) Computer Science Applied to Business Systems, 1982; The UK and European Motor Industry: analysis and future prospects, 1983; (jtly) Financial Modelling with a Microcomputer, 1984; (with R. J. Housden) Management Information Systems and Data Processing for the Management Accountant, 1985, new edn, as Information Technology Management, 1990; (with B. C. Williams) The Impact of Microprocessors on the Small Practice, 1985; A Fireside Chat on Databases for Accountants, 1985; *reports:* A Research Report on the Future of the UK and European Motor Industry, 1984; Jaguar: an investor's guide, 1984; Car Pricing in Europe, 1984; (with G. R. Kaye) Financial Planning with Personal Computers, Vol. 1, 1985, Vol. 2, 1986; State Aid to the European Motor Industry, 1985, updated edn 1987; Demand Growth: a boost for employment?, 1985; Japanese Automotive Strategies: a European and US perspective, 1986; Quality and the Japanese Motor Industry: lessons for the West?, 1986; The Future of Car Retailing in the UK, 1987; A Single European Market? an automotive perspective, 1988; Rover: profile, progress and prospects, 1988; Automotive Trade Restrictions in Western Europe, 1989; The Greek Vehicle Market: future opportunities, 1989; Into the 1990s: future strategies of the vehicle producers of South Korea and Malaysia, 1990. *Address:* Motor Industry Research Unit, 2 Dove Street, Norwich NR2 1DE. *T:* Norwich (0603) 614991.

BHATTACHARYYA, Prof. Sushantha Kumar, CEng; Lucas Professor of Manufacturing Systems Engineering, University of Warwick, since 1980; *b* 6 June 1940; *s* of Sudhir Bhattacharyya and Hemanalini (*née* Chakraborty); *m* 1981, Bridie Rabbite; three *d. Educ:* IIT, Kharagpur (BTech); Univ. of Birmingham (MSc, PhD). MIMechE, FIProdE; FBIM. CAV Ltd, 1960–63; Prodn Engr, Joseph Lucas Ltd, 1964–68; University of Birmingham: Lectr, Dept of Engrg Prodn, 1970; Hd of Manufacturing Systems Gp, 1972. Mem., Nat. Consumer Council, 1990–. *Publications:* numerous, on operational and technological change in manufacturing industry. *Recreations:* family, flying, cricket. *Address:* Engineering Department, University of Warwick, Coventry CV4 7AL. *T:* Coventry (0203) 523155. *Club:* Athenæum.

BHUTTO, Hon. Benazir; Prime Minister of Pakistan, 1988–90; *b* 21 June 1953; *d* of late Zulfikar Ali Bhutto and of Begum Nusrat Bhutto; *m* 1987, Asif Ali Zardari; one *s* one *d.*

Educ: Harvard Univ.; Lady Margaret Hall, Oxford. Under house arrest, 1977–84; leader in exile, Pakistan People's Party, with Begum Nusrat Bhutto; returned to Pakistan, 1986. *Publication:* Daughter of the East, 1988.

BIANCHERI, Boris, Hon. GCVO 1990; Italian Ambassador to the Court of St James's, since 1987; *b* 3 Nov. 1930; *s* of Augusto and Olga Wolff von Stomersee; *m* 1979, Flavia Arzeni; one *s* one *d*. *Educ:* Univ. of Rome (Law Degree). Joined Min. of Foreign Affairs, 1956; served Athens, 1959; Economic Dept, Min. of Foreign Affairs, 1964–67; Sec.-Gen., Commn for 1970 Osaka Exhibn, 1968; First Counsellor, Cultural Relations, Min. of Foreign Affairs, 1971; Political Counsellor, London, 1972–75; Chef de Cabinet, Sec. of State for Foreign Affairs, 1978; Minister, 1979; Ambassador, Tokyo, 1980–84; Dir.-Gen., Political Affairs, Min. of Foreign Affairs, 1985. Gran Croce, Ordine al Merito della Repubblica Italiana; numerous foreign orders. *Recreations:* gardening, boating, swimming, horse-riding. *Address:* 4 Grosvenor Square, W1X 9LA. *T:* 071–629 8200. *Clubs:* Brooks's; Circolo Della Caccia (Rome).

BIBBY, Benjamin; *see* Bibby, J. B.

BIBBY, Sir Derek (James), 2nd Bt *cr* 1959, of Tarporley, Co. Palatine of Chester; MC 1945; DL; Chairman, Bibby Line Group Ltd (formerly Bibby Line Ltd), 1969–June 1992; *b* 29 June 1922; *s* of Major Sir (Arthur) Harold Bibby, 1st Bt, DSO, DL, LLD, and of Marjorie, *d* of Charles J. Williamson; *S* father, 1986; *m* 1961, Christine Maud, *d* of late Rt Rev. F. J. Okell, MA, DD, Bishop of Stockport; four *s* one *d*. *Educ:* Rugby; Trinity Coll., Oxford (MA). Served War, Army, 1942–46. DL Cheshire, 1987. *Recreations:* shooting, gardening. *Heir:* *s* Michael James Bibby, *b* 2 Aug. 1963. *Address:* Willaston Grange, Willaston, South Wirral L64 2UN. *T:* 051–327 4913. *Club:* Commonwealth Trust.

BIBBY, (John) Benjamin; Director, since 1961, Chairman, 1970–78, J. Bibby & Sons PLC; *b* 19 April 1929; *s* of late J. P. and D. D. Bibby; *m* 1956, Susan Lindsay Paterson; two *s* one *d*. *Educ:* Oundle Sch.; St Catharine's Coll., Cambridge (MA). Called to the Bar, Gray's Inn, 1981. Has held various positions in J. Bibby & Sons PLC, 1953–. Mem. Council, Univ. of Liverpool, 1978–81; Mem. Exec. Cttee, West Kirby Residential Sch., 1978–87. Mem. Cttee, 1982–, Hon. Treas., 1987–, Nat. Squib Owners' Assoc. (Chm., 1983–87). JP Liverpool 1975–81. *Publication:* (with C. L. Bibby) A Miller's Tale, 1978. *Recreations:* sailing, gardening. *Address:* Kirby Mount, Warwick Drive, West Kirby, Wirral, Merseyside L48 2HT. *T:* 051–625 8071. *Clubs:* Royal Thames Yacht; West Kirby Sailing; Royal Mersey Yacht; Royal Anglesey Yacht.

BICESTER, 3rd Baron *cr* 1938, of Tusmore; **Angus Edward Vivian Smith;** *b* 20 Feb. 1932; *s* of Lt-Col Hon. Stephen Edward Vivian Smith (*d* 1952) (2nd *s* of 1st Baron) and Elenor Anderson, *d* of Edward S. Hewitt, New York City; *S* uncle, 1968. *Educ:* Eton. *Heir:* *b* Hugh Charles Vivian Smith, *b* 8 Nov. 1934.

BICK, Martin James M.; *see* Moore-Bick.

BICKERSTETH, Rt. Rev. John Monier, KCVO 1989; Clerk of the Closet to The Queen, 1979–89; *b* 6 Sept. 1921; *yr s* of late Rev. Canon Edward Monier Bickersteth, OBE; *m* 1955, Rosemary, *yr d* of late Edward and Muriel Cleveland-Stevens, Gaines, Oxted; three *s* one *d*. *Educ:* Rugby; Christ Church, Oxford; Wells Theol College. MA Oxon 1953. Captain, Buffs and Royal Artillery, 1941–46. Priest, 1951; Curate, St Matthew, Moorfields, Bristol, 1950–54; Vicar, St John's, Hurst Green, Oxted, 1954–62; St Stephen's, Chatham, 1962–70; Hon. Canon of Rochester, 1968–70; Bishop Suffragan of Warrington, 1970–75; Bishop of Bath and Wells, 1975–87. A C of E delegate to 4th Assembly, WCC, 1968. Chaplain and Sub-Prelate, OStJ, 1977. Chairman: Royal Sch. of Church Music, 1977–88; Bible Reading Fellowship, 1978–90; Vice Chm., Central Bd of Finance of Church of England, 1981–84. Mem., Marlborough Coll. Council, 1980–91. Freeman of the City of London, 1979. *Publication:* (jtly) Clerks of the Closet in the Royal Household, 1991. *Recreations:* country pursuits. *Address:* Beckfords, Newtown, Tisbury, Wilts SP3 6NY. *T:* Tisbury (0747) 870479. *Club:* Commonwealth Trust.

BICKERTON, Frank Donald, CBE 1966; Director General, Central Office of Information, 1971–74; *b* 22 June 1917; *s* of F. M. Bickerton and A. A. Hibbert; *m* 1945, Linda Russell; two *s*. *Educ:* Liverpool Collegiate Sch. Min. of Health, in Public Relations Div., 1935–40. Served War, RNVR, 1940–45. Min. of National Insurance (later Min. of Pensions and Nat. Insurance), 1946–61: initially Asst Press Officer and in charge of Information Div., 1952–61; Chief Information Officer, Min. of Transport, 1961–68; Controller (Home), COI, 1968–71. *Recreations:* walking, gardening. *Address:* 6 Diana Close, Granville Rise, Totland, Isle of Wight PO39 0EE.

BICKFORD, James David Prydeaux; HM Diplomatic Service; Under Secretary, Ministry of Defence, since 1987; *b* 28 July 1940; *s* of William A. J. P. Bickford and late Muriel Bickford (*née* Smythe); *m* 1965, Carolyn Jane, *d* of late Major W. A. R. Sumner, RHA; three *s*. *Educ:* Downside; Law Society's College of Law, London. Admitted to Roll of Solicitors, 1963; Solicitor of the Supreme Court. In practice, J. J. Newcombe, Solicitors, Okehampton, 1963–69; Crown Counsel and Legal Advr to Govt of Turks and Caicos Islands, BWI, 1969–71; Asst Legal Advr, FCO, 1971–79 and 1982–84; Legal Advr, British Mil. Govt, Berlin, 1979–82; Legal Counsellor, FCO, 1984–87. Mem., Panel of Legal Experts, Internat. Telecommunications Satellite Orgn, 1985–; Chm., Assembly of Internat. Maritime Satellite Orgn, 1985–87. *Publication:* Land Dealings Simplified in the Turks and Caicos Islands, 1971. *Recreations:* the family, sailing, fishing. *Address:* c/o National Westminster Bank, Torrington, Devon EX38 8HP.

BICKFORD SMITH, John Roger, CB 1988; TD 1950; *b* 31 Oct. 1915; *er s* of late Leonard W. Bickford Smith, Camborne, Cornwall, For. Man., ICI, and late Anny Grete (*née* Huth); *m* 1st, 1939, Cecilia Judge Heath (marr. diss.) (decd), *er d* of W. W. Heath, Leicester; two *s*; 2nd, 1972, Baronin Joaise Miranda et Omnes Sancti von Kirchberg-Hohenheim. *Educ:* Eton (King's Schol.); Hertford Coll., Oxford (Schol.). BA 1937; MA 1952. Commnd in Duke of Cornwall's LI (TA), 1939; served 1939–46: UK, India, Burma and Germany; AJAG (Major), 1942; Lieut-Col 1944. Called to Bar, Inner Temple, 1942, Bencher, 1985. Practised at Common Law Bar in London and on Midland Circuit, 1946–67; Master of Supreme Court, QBD, 1967–88, Sen. Master and Queen's Remembrancer, 1983–88. Master, Bowyers' Co., 1986–88. *Publications:* The Crown Proceedings Act 1947, 1948; various contribs to legal pubns. *Recreation:* foreign travel. *Address:* 65 Gibson Square, N1 0RA. *Club:* Garrick.

BICKNELL, Mrs Christine Betty, CBE 1986; MA (Oxon); retired; *b* 23 Dec. 1919; *er d* of Walter Edward and Olive Isabelle Reynolds; *m* 1960, Claud Bicknell, *qv*. *Educ:* St Martin-in-the-Fields High Sch. for Girls; Somerville Coll., Oxford (Exhibr). BA 1941. Board of Trade, 1941–60; Northern Regional Officer, Min. of Land and Natural Resources, 1965–67. Chairman: Prudhoe and Monkton HMC, 1966–70; Leavesden HMC, 1971–74; Kensington and Chelsea and Westminster AHA (T), 1973–77; Victoria HA, 1982–85; Member: Newcastle RHB, 1961–70, and NW Metrop. RHB, 1971–74; Nat. Whitley Council for Nurses and Midwives, 1962–70; Northern Econ. Planning Bd, 1965–67; Bd of Governors, Royal Vic. Infirm., Newcastle upon Tyne, 1965–70 and St Bartholomew's Hosp., 1971–74; Chm., CS Selection Bds, 1970–90; Member: Industrial Tribunals, 1977–88; Newspaper Panel, Monopolies Commn, 1973–83; British Library Board, 1979–82; Pres., Hosp. Domestic Administrators' Assoc., 1970–74. *Recreations:* gardening, mountains, travel, sailing. *Address:* Aikrigg End Cottage, Burneside Road, Kendal LA9 6DZ. *Clubs:* Alpine, United Oxford & Cambridge University.

BICKNELL, Claud, OBE 1946; a Law Commissioner, 1970–75; a part-time Chairman of Industrial Tribunals, 1975–83; *b* Rowlands Gill, near Newcastle upon Tyne, 15 June 1910; 2nd *s* of Raymond Bicknell and Phillis Bicknell (*née* Lovibond); *m* 1st, 1934, Esther Irene (*d* 1958), *e d* of Kenneth Bell; one *s* two *d* (one *d* decd); 2nd, 1960, Christine Betty Reynolds (*see* C. B. Bicknell). *Educ:* Oundle Sch.; Queens' Coll., Cambridge. MA 1935. Pres., Cambridge Univ. Mountaineering Club, 1930–31. Admitted as a solicitor, 1934; Asst Solicitor, 1934–39, and partner, 1939–70, in firm of Stanton, Atkinson & Bird, Newcastle upon Tyne. Dir, Northern Corporation Ltd, 1939–53. Auxiliary Fire Service, Newcastle upon Tyne, 1939–41; Nat. Fire Service, 1941–45; Sen. Fire Staff Officer, Home Office, 1943–45. Mem. Planning Bd, Lake District Nat. Park, 1951–70 (Chm., Development Control Cttee, 1957–70). Chm., Newcastle upon Tyne Housing Improvement Trust Ltd, 1966–70. Pres., Newcastle upon Tyne Incorp. Law Soc., 1969. *Recreation:* mountains. *Address:* Aikrigg End Cottage, Burneside Road, Kendal LA9 6DZ. *Clubs:* Garrick, Alpine.

See also Sir J. R. Shelley, Bt.

BICKNELL, Gioconda, (Mrs J. D. Bicknell); *see* De Vito, G.

BIDDLE, Martin, FBA 1985; FSA, FRHistS; Director, Winchester Research Unit, since 1968; Astor Senior Research Fellow in Medieval Archaeology, Hertford College, Oxford, since 1989; *b* 4 June 1937; *s* of Reginald Samuel Biddle and Gwladys Florence Biddle (*née* Baker); *m* 1966, Birthe, *d* of Landsretssagfører Axel Th. and Anni Kjølbye of Sønderborg, Denmark; two *d* (and two *d* by previous marr.). *Educ:* Merchant Taylors' Sch., Northwood; Pembroke Coll., Cambridge (MA 1965); MA Oxon 1967; MA Pennsylvania 1977. FSA 1964; FRHistS 1970; MIFA 1984. Second Lieut, 4 RTR, 1956; 1 Indep. Sqn, RTR, Berlin, 1956–57. Asst Inspector of Ancient Monuments, MPBW, 1961–63; Lectr in Medieval Archaeology, Univ. of Exeter, 1963–67; Vis. Fellow, All Souls Coll., Oxford, 1967–68; Dir, University Museum, and Prof. of Anthropology and of History of Art, Univ. of Pennsylvania, 1977–81; Lectr of The House, Christ Church, Oxford, 1983–86. Directed excavations and investigations: Nonsuch Palace, 1959–60; Winchester, 1961–71; Repton (with wife), 1974–88; St Alban's Abbey (with wife), 1978, 1982–84; Holy Sepulchre, Jerusalem (with wife), 1989–90. Archaeological Consultant: Canterbury Cathedral; St Alban's Abbey Church and Cathedral; Eurotunnel, etc. Chm., Rescue, Trust for British Archaeology, 1971–75. Mem., Royal Commn on Historical Monuments of England, 1984–. General Editor, Winchester Studies, 1976–. (With Birthe Biddle) Frend Medal, Soc. of Antiquaries, 1986. *Publications:* (with C. Heighway) The Future of London's Past, 1973; (with F. Barlow and others) Winchester in the Early Middle Ages, 1976; (with H.M. Colvin, J. Summerson and others) The History of the King's Works, vol. iv, pt 2, 1982; King Arthur's Round Table, 1990; Approaches in Urban Archaeology, 1990; papers on archaeological, historical and art-historical subjects in learned jls. *Recreations:* travel, esp. Hellenic travel, reading. *Address:* 19 Hamilton Road, Oxford OX2 7PY. *T:* Oxford (0865) 513056. *Club:* Athenæum.

BIDDULPH, family name of **Baron Biddulph.**

BIDDULPH, 5th Baron *cr* 1903; **Anthony Nicholas Colin Maitland Biddulph;** interior designer; sporting manager; *b* 8 April 1959; *s* of 4th Baron Biddulph and of Lady Mary, *d* of Viscount Maitland (killed in action, 1943) and *g d* of 15th Earl of Lauderdale; *S* father, 1988. *Educ:* Cheltenham; RAC, Cirencester. *Heir:* *b* Hon. William Ian Robert Maitland Biddulph, *b* 27 March 1963. *Recreations:* shooting, fishing, painting. *Address:* 8 Orbel Street, SW11 3NZ. *Club:* Raffles.

BIDDULPH, Constance; *see* Holt, C.

BIDDULPH, Sir Ian D'Olier, (Jack), 11th Bt *cr* 1664, of Westcombe, Kent; *b* 28 Feb. 1940; *s* of Sir Stuart Royden Biddulph, 10th Bt and of Muriel Margaret, *d* of Angus Harkness, Hamley Bridge, S Australia; *S* father, 1986; *m* 1967, Margaret Eleanor, *o d* of late John Gablonski, Oxley, Brisbane; one *s* two *d*. *Heir:* *s* Paul William Biddulph, *b* 30 Oct. 1967. *Address:* Christensens Road, Mount Walker, M/S 23, via Rosewood, Qld 4340, Australia.

BIDE, Sir Austin (Ernest), Kt 1980; Hon. President, Glaxo Holdings plc, since 1985 (Chief Executive, 1973–80; Chairman, 1973–85); non-executive Chairman, BL plc, 1982–86 (Deputy Chairman, 1980–82; Director, 1977–86); *b* 11 Sept. 1915; *o s* of late Ernest Arthur Bide and Eliza Bide (*née* Young); *m* 1941, Irene (*née* Ward); three *d*. *Educ:* County Sch., Acton; Univ. of London. 1st cl. hons BSc Chemistry; FRSC, CChem. Govt Chemist's Dept, 1932–40; Research Chemist, Glaxo, 1940: i/c Chemical Devlt and Intellectual Property, 1944–54; Dep. Sec., 1954–59; Sec., 1959–65; Dir, 1963–71; Dep. Chm., 1971–73; Dir, J. Lyons & Co. Ltd, 1977–78. Member: Review Body, UGC, 1985–87; Working Party on Biotechnology (under auspices of ACARD/ABRD and Royal Soc.) (Report 1980); Adv. Cttee on Industry to the Vice-Chancellors and Principals of UK Univs, 1984–87; Chm., Information Technology 1986 Cttee, 1986. Member: Adv. Council, Inst. of Biotechnological Studies, 1985–89; Council, Inst. of Manpower Studies, 1985–; Chairman: Visiting Cttee, Open Univ., 1982–89; Adam Smith Inst., 1986– (Mem., 1985–). Chairman: QCA Ltd, 1985–88; Micro-test Res. Ltd, 1987–90; United Environmental Systems, 1988–90; CGEA (UK) Ltd, 1991–; Dir, Oxford Consultancy Ltd, 1988–. Confederation of British Industry: Member: Council, 1974–85; President's Cttee, 1983–86; Chm., Res. and Technol. Cttee, 1977–86; British Institute of Management: CBIM (FBIM 1972); Mem. Council, 1976–; Chm., Finance Cttee, 1976–79; Dir, BIM Foundn, 1977–79. Medical Research Council: Mem., 1986–90; Chm., Investment Cttee, 1988–90; Chm., Pensions Trust, 1988–90; Mem., AIDS Cttee, 1987–90. Mem. Court, British Shippers Council, 1984– (Chm., 1989–); Trustee, British Motor Industry Heritage Trust, 1983–86. Chm., Salisbury Cathedral Spire Appeal Cttee, 1987–, and Trustee, Salisbury Cathedral Spire Trust, 1987–. Mem. Council, Imperial Soc. of Knights Bachelor, 1980–. CIEx 1987; FInstD 1989; Hon. FIChemE 1983; Hon. FIIM 1983 (Vice-Pres., 1983); Hon. Fellow: Inst. Biotechnological Studies 1985; St Catherine's Coll., Oxford, 1987. Hon. DSc: QUB, 1986; CNAA, 1990; DUniv OU, 1991. Gold Medal, BIM, 1983; Duncan Davies Medal, R&D Soc., 1990. *Publications:* papers in learned jls on organic chemical subjects. *Recreations:* fishing, handicrafts. *Club:* Hurlingham.

BIDGOOD, John Claude, MIEx; Chairman: Anglo-Dominion Finance Co. Ltd; Anglo-Dominion Construction Co. Ltd; Anglo-Dominion Trading Co. Ltd; *b* 12 May 1914; *s* of late Edward Charles Bidgood, Leeds; *m* 1945, Sheila Nancy Walker-Wood; one *s* two *d*. *Educ:* London Choir Sch.; Woodhouse Technical Sch. Served early part of War of 1939–45 as Pilot RAF. Mem. Leeds City Council, 1947–55 (late Chm. Works Cttee and City Architects Cttee); contested (C) N E Leeds, 1950, 1951; MP (C) Bury and Radcliffe, 1955–64; PPS to Joint Parly Secs, Min. of Pensions and Nat. Insurance, 1957–58; Mem. Parly Select Cttee on Estimates, 1958–64. Director: Bidgood Holdings Ltd; Edward

Bidgood & Co. Ltd; Bidgood Larsson Ltd; Wright & Summerhill Ltd; R. Horsfield & Co. Ltd; Constructional Erection Ltd; Bidgood Larsson (Iraq) Ltd; Chm., Yorks Assoc. for the Disabled, 1950–58; Member: Inst. of Export; Leeds and Bradford Joint Aerodrome Cttee, 1951–55; W Riding Rating Valuation Court, 1955. Mayor, Chapeltown Corporation, 1987–88. Governor, Bury Grammar Schs, 1955. Hon. Citizen, City of Atlanta, Georgia, 1960; Freeman, City of London; Liveryman and Mem., Worshipful Co. of Horners. *Recreations:* music, travel. *Address:* The Old Joinery, Walton, near Wetherby, W Yorks LS23 7DQ. *T:* Boston Spa (0937) 844028. *Clubs:* City Livery, Naval and Military; Leeds (Leeds).

BIDSTRUP, (Patricia) Lesley, MD, FRCP, FRACP; Member, Medical Appeals Tribunal, 1970–88; private consulting concerned mainly with industrial medicine, since 1958; *b* 24 Oct. 1916; *d* of Clarence Leslie Bidstrup, Chemical Works Manager, South Australia, and Kathleen Helena Bidstrup (*née* O'Brien); *m* 1952, Ronald Frank Guymer, TD, MD, FRCP, FRCS, DPH, DIH; one step *s* one step *d. Educ:* Kadina High Sch. and Walford House, Adelaide, SA. MB, BS (Adel.) 1939; MD (Adel.) 1958; FRACP 1954; FRCP (Lond.) 1964. Resident Ho. Phys. and Registrar, Royal Adelaide Hosp., SA, 1939–41. Hon. Capt., AAMC, 1942–45. MO, UNRRA, Glyn-Hughes Hosp., Belsen, 1945–46. General practice: Acting Hon. Asst Phys., Royal Adelaide Hosp.; Tutor in Med., St Mark's Coll., Adelaide, and in Univ. of Adelaide Med. Sch.; Lectr in Med., Univ. of Adelaide Dental Faculty, 1942–45; Asst, Dept for Research in Industrial Medicine, MRC, 1947–58; Clinical Asst (Hon.), Chest Dept, St Thomas' Hosp., 1958–78. Member: Scientific Sub-Cttee on Poisonous Substances used in Agriculture and Food Storage, 1956–58; Industrial Injuries Adv. Council, 1970–83. Visiting Lectr, TUC Centenary Inst. of Occupational Health; Examiner for Diploma in Industrial Health: Conjoint Bd, 1965–71, 1980–82; Society of Apothecaries, 1970–76; External Examiner for Diploma in Industrial Health, Dundee, 1980–82. Fellow, Amer. Coll. of Occupational Medicine. William P. Yant Award, Amer. Industrial Hygiene Assoc., 1989. Mayoress, Royal Borough of Kingston-upon-Thames, 1959, 1960. *Publications:* The Toxicity of Mercury and its Compounds, 1964; chapters in: Cancer Progress, 1960; The Prevention of Cancer, 1967; Clinical Aspects of Inhaled Particles, 1972; contribs to Brit. Jl Indust. Med., Lancet, BMJ, Proc. Royal Soc. Med., ILO Encyclopaedia on Industrial Diseases. *Recreations:* people, theatre, music. *Address:* 11 Sloane Terrace Mansions, Sloane Terrace, SW1X 9DG. *T:* 071–730 8720.

BIDWELL, Sir Hugh (Charles Philip), GBE 1989; Non-executive Chairman, Riggs AP Bank Ltd, since 1991 (non-executive Director, since 1989); Chief Executive, since 1988, and Vice Chairman, since 1990, Allied-Lyons Eastern Ltd; Director: Glendronach Distillery Co. Ltd, since 1989; Allied-Lyons International Brands Ltd, since 1991; Chairman, British Invisibles, since 1991; Lord Mayor of London, 1989–90; *b* 1 Nov. 1934; *s* of Edward and late Elisabeth Bidwell; *m* 1962, Jenifer Celia Webb; two *s* one *d. Educ:* Stonyhurst College. Nat. Service, 1953–55; commissioned E Surrey Regt, seconded to 1st Bn KAR, based Nyasaland. Viota Foods, 1957–70 (Dir, 1962–70); Dir, Robertson Foods, 1968–70; Chairman: Pearce Duff & Co. Ltd, 1970–85; Gill & Duffus Foods Ltd, 1984–85; Ellis, Son & Vidler, 1986–88; Dir, Argyll Gp, 1990–. Member: Council, London Chamber of Commerce & Industry, 1976–85; Exec. Council, British-Soviet Chamber of Commerce, 1989–; European Trade Cttee, BOTB, 1988–; Sino-British Trade Council, 1989–; Council, China-Britain Trade Gp, 1990–; Exec. Cttee, Food Manufacturers' Fedn, 1973–86; Food from Britain Council, 1983–89 (Chm., Export Bd, 1983–86); Pres., British Food Export Council, 1980–87; Dep. Pres., Food and Drink Fedn, 1985–86. Alderman, Billingsgate Ward, 1979–; Sheriff of the City of London, 1986–87. Master, Grocers' Co., 1984–85. President: Billingsgate Ward Club; Billingsgate Christian Mission & Dispensary; Fishmongers' & Poulterers' Instn. *Recreations:* golf, fishing, tennis, cricket. *Address:* Waterlane Farm, Bovingdon, Herts HP3 0NA. *T:* Hemel Hempstead (0442) 832179; 59 Eaton Mews North, SW1X 8LL. *T:* 071–235 7762; (office) 071–588 7575. *Clubs:* Boodle's, City of London, MCC; Denham Golf, Royal St George's.

BIDWELL, Sydney James; MP (Lab) Ealing, Southall, since 1974 (Southall, 1966–74); *b* Southall, 14 Jan. 1917; *s* of late Herbert Emmett Bidwell; *m* 1941; one *s* one *d. Educ:* Elementary sch., evening classes and trade union study. Railway worker (formerly NUR activist); Tutor and Organiser, Nat. Council of Labour Colls. Mem., TGWU (sponsored as MP by union). TUC Reg. Educn Officer, London, 1963–66. Mem., Southall Bor. Council, 1951–55. Contested (Lab): E Herts, 1959; Herts SW, 1964. Mem., Parly Select Cttee on Race Relations and Immigration, 1968–79; Mem., Select Cttee on Transport, 1979–. *Publications:* Red White and Black Book on Race-Relations, 1976; The Turban Victory, 1977; articles on TU and Labour history. *Recreations:* soccer, painting, cartooning. *Address:* House of Commons, SW1.

BIERICH, Marcus; Chairman, Board of Management, Robert Bosch GmbH, Stuttgart, since 1984; *b* 29 April 1926. *Educ:* Univs of Münster and Hamburg (PhD 1951; studies in mathematics, science and philosophy). Bankhaus Delbrück Schickler & Co., 1956–61; Director 1961–67, Mem. Bd of Management 1967–80, Mannesmann AG, Düsseldorf; Mem. Bd of Management, Allianz Versicherungs-AG, München, 1980–84. Hon. Dr.rer.oec Univ. of Bochum, 1977. *Address:* Robert Bosch GmbH, Postfach 10 60 50, 7000 Stuttgart 10, Federal Republic of Germany. *T:* 0711/811–6101.

BIFFEN, Rt. Hon. (William) John, PC 1979; MP (C) Shropshire North, since 1983 (Oswestry Division of Salop, Nov. 1961–1983); *b* 3 Nov. 1930; *s* of Victor W. Biffen; *m* 1979, Mrs Sarah Wood (*née* Drew); one step *s* one step *d. Educ:* Dr Morgan's Sch., Bridgwater; Jesus Coll., Cambridge (BA). Worked in Tube Investments Ltd, 1953–60; Economist Intelligence Unit, 1960–61. Chief Sec. to the Treasury, 1979–81; Sec. of State for Trade, 1981–82; Lord Pres. of the Council, 1982–83; Leader of House of Commons, 1982–87 and Lord Privy Seal, 1983–87. Director: Glynwed International, 1987–; J. Bibby & Sons, 1988–; Rockware Gp, 1988–. *Publication:* Inside the House of Commons, 1989. *Address:* c/o House of Commons, SW1A 0AA.

BIGGAM, Robin Adair; Chairman, BICC plc, since 1992 (Managing Director, 1986–87; Chief Executive, 1987–91); *b* 8 July 1938; *s* of Thomas and Eileen Biggam; *m* 1962, Elizabeth McArthur McDougall; one *s* two *d. Educ:* Lanark Grammar Sch. Chartered accountant. Peat Marwick Mitchell, 1960–63; ICI, 1964–81; Director: ICL, 1981–84; Dunlop Holdings plc, 1984–85; Non Executive Director: Chloride Group plc, 1985–87; Lloyds Abbey Life plc (formerly Abbey Life Gp), 1985–90. *Recreations:* golf, swimming, gardening. *Address:* Devonshire House, Mayfair Place, W1X 5FH. *T:* 071–629 6622. *Club:* Royal Automobile.

BIGGAR, (Walter) Andrew, CBE 1980 (OBE 1967); MC 1945; FRAgS; farming since 1956; *b* 6 March 1915; *s* of Walter Biggar and Margaret Sproat; *m* 1945, Patricia Mary Irving Elliot; one *s* one *d. Educ:* Sedbergh Sch., Cumbria; Edinburgh Univ. (BScAgric). FRAgS 1969. Commnd Royal Signals, 1938; War Service, 51st Highland Div., 1939–46; POW, Germany, 1940–45. Rowett Res. Inst., 1935–54. Director and Trustee: Scottish Soc. for Research in Plant Breeding, 1958–88; Animal Diseases Res. Assoc., 1966–. Member: Farm Animals Welfare Adv. Cttee, 1967–77; ARC, 1969–80; Scottish Agricultural Develt Council, 1971–82; JCO Consultative Bd, 1980–84; Chm., Animals Bd, JCO, 1973–80. Dir, Caledonian Investment & Finance Co., 1986–89. Chm., Moredun Animal Health Trust, 1988–. Governor: St Margaret's Sch., Edinburgh, 1960–81; Grassland Res. Inst., 1962–81 (Hon. Fellow, 1981); Scottish Crop Res. Inst., 1980–83. *Recreation:* photography. *Address:* Magdalenehall, St Boswells, Roxburghshire TD6 0EB. *T:* St Boswells (0835) 23741.

BIGGART, (Thomas) Norman, CBE 1984; WS; Partner, Biggart Baillie & Gifford, WS, Solicitors, Glasgow and Edinburgh, since 1959; *b* 24 Jan. 1930; *o s* of Andrew Stevenson Biggart, JP and Marjorie Scott Biggart; *m* 1956, Eileen Jean Anne Gemmell; one *s* one *d. Educ:* Morrisons Acad., Crieff; Glasgow Univ. (MA 1951, LLB 1954). Served RN, 1954–56 (Sub-Lt RNVR). Law Society of Scotland: Mem. Council, 1977–86; Vice-Pres., 1981–82; Pres., 1982–83. Chm., Scottish Cttee, Council on Tribunals, 1990–. Pres., Business Archives Council, Scotland, 1977–86. Member: Exec. Cttee, Scottish Council (Development and Industry), 1984–; Scottish Tertiary Educn Adv. Council, 1984–87; Scottish Records Adv. Council, 1985–. Director: Clydesdale Bank, 1985–; New Scotland Insurance Gp, 1986– (Chm., 1989–); Beechwood Glasgow, 1989– (Chm., 1989–). Trustee, Scottish Civic Trust, 1989–. Hon. Mem., American Bar Assoc., 1982. OStJ 1968. *Recreations:* golf, hill walking. *Address:* Gailes, Kilmacolm, Renfrewshire PA13 4LZ. *T:* Kilmacolm (050587) 2645. *Clubs:* Royal Scottish Automobile, The Western (Glasgow).

BIGGS; *see* Ewart-Biggs.

BIGGS, Dr John, FRSC; Moderator, Free Church Federal Council, March 1992–93; *b* 3 Jan. 1933; *s* of Horace James Biggs and Elsie Alice Biggs, Leicester; *m* 1965, Brenda Muriel Hicklenton. *Educ:* Wyggeston Grammar Sch. for Boys, Leicester; Downing Coll., Cambridge (Graystone Scholar). MA, PhD (Cantab). CChem; FRSC (FCS 1958). DSIR Res. Fellow, Cambridge, 1958–60; Lectr in Chemistry, Univ. of Hull, 1960–87. President: Baptist Students' Fedn, 1955–56; Yorkshire Baptist Assoc., 1973–74; Baptist Union of GB: Chm., Home Mission Working Gp, 1981–88; Mem. Council, 1978–, Chm., 1990–; Pres., 1989–90. Governor, Northern Baptist Coll., Manchester; Mem., Bd of Trustees, Baptist Theol Seminary, Rüschlikon, Zurich. *Recreations:* fell-walking, opera, photography. *Address:* 91 Southella Way, Kirkella, Hull HU10 7LZ. *T:* Hull (0482) 650888. *Club:* Penn.

BIGGS, Brig. Michael Worthington, CBE 1962 (OBE 1944); MA; CEng, MICE; *b* 16 Sept. 1911; *s* of late Lt-Col Charles William Biggs, OBE, Cheltenham and late Winifred Jesse Bell Biggs (*née* Dickinson); *m* 1940, Katharine Mary, *d* of late Sir Walter Harragin, CMG, QC, Colonial Legal Service, and Lady Harragin; two *d. Educ:* Cheltenham Coll.; RMA Woolwich; Pembroke Coll., Cambridge. MA (Cantab) 1966; MICE 1967. 2nd Lieut RE, 1931; served War of 1939–45, E Africa, Abyssinia (Bde Major), and Burma (GSO1 and CRE); Lt-Col 1942; Col 1954; Mil. Adviser to High Comr, Australia, 1954–57; Brig. 1960; Chief of Staff, E Africa Comd, 1960–62; Dir of Quartering (Army), MoD, 1963–66; retd, 1966. Group Building Exec., Forte's (Holdings) Ltd, 1966–67; Manager, Hatfield and Welwyn Garden City, Commn for New Towns, 1967–78. Member: Council, TCPA, 1978–86; Exec. Cttee, Hertfordshire Soc.; Chm., Herts Bldg Preservation Trust, 1978–86. Pres., KAR and EAF Officers' Dinner Club. Freeman, City of London, 1985. *Recreations:* golf, gardening. *Address:* Strawyards, High Street, Kimpton, Herts SG4 8PT. *T:* Kimpton (0438) 823498. *Club:* Army and Navy.

BIGGS, Sir Norman (Parris), Kt 1977; Director, Banco de Bilbao, 1981–87; *b* 23 Dec. 1907; *s* of John Gordon Biggs and Mary Sharpe Dickson; *m* 1936, Peggy Helena Stammwitz (*d* 1990); two *s* one *d. Educ:* John Watson's Sch., Edinburgh. Bank of England, 1927–46; Dir, Kleinwort Sons & Co. Ltd, 1946–52; Esso Petroleum Company, Ltd: Dir, 1952–66, Chm., 1968–72; Chairman: Williams & Glyn's Bank Ltd, 1972–76; United International Bank Ltd, 1970–79; Deputy Chairman: National and Commercial Banking Gp Ltd, 1974–76; Privatbanken Ltd, 1980–83; Director: Royal Bank of Scotland, 1974–76; Gillett Bros Discount Co. Ltd, 1963–77. Mem., Bullock Cttee on Industrial Democracy, 1976. *Address:* Northbrooks, Danworth Lane, Hurstpierpoint, Sussex BN6 9LW. *T:* Hurstpierpoint (0273) 832022.

BIGGS, Prof. Peter Martin, CBE 1987; PhD, DSc; FRS 1976; Director of Animal Health (formerly Animal Disease Research), Agricultural and Food Research Council, 1986–88, retired; Visiting Professor of Veterinary Microbiology, Royal Veterinary College, University of London, since 1982; Andrew D. White Professor-at-Large, Cornell University, since 1988; *b* 13 Aug. 1926; *s* of Ronald Biggs and Cécile Biggs (*née* Player); *m* 1950, Alison Janet Molteno; two *s* one *d. Educ:* Bedales Sch.; Cambridge Sch., USA; Queen's Univ., Belfast; Royal Veterinary Coll., Univ. of London (BSc 1953, DSc 1975); Univ. of Bristol (PhD 1958). FRCVS, FRCPath, FIBiol, CBiol. Served RAF, 1944–48; Research Asst, Univ. of Bristol, 1953–55, Lectr, 1955–59; Houghton Poultry Research Station: Head of Leukosis Experimental Unit, 1959–74; Dep. Dir, 1971–74; Dir, 1974–86. Sir William Dick Meml Lectr, Univ. of Edinburgh, 1974 and 1987; E.H.W. Wilmott Guest Lectr, Univ. of Bristol, 1977. Mem., Management Bd, AFRC, 1986–88. Hon. Life Pres., World Vet. Poultry Assoc., 1985; Pres., Inst. of Biol., 1990–. Hon. FRASE 1986. Hon. DVM Ludwig-Maximilians Univ., 1976; Dr *hc* Liège, 1991. Tom Newman Meml Award, 1964; Poultry Science Award, British Oil and Cake Mills, 1968; J. T. Edwards Meml Medal, 1969; Dalrymple-Champneys Cup and Medal, 1973; Bledisloe Veterinary Award, 1977; Wooldridge Meml Medal, 1978; Joszef Marek Meml Medal, Vet. Univ. of Budapest, 1979; Victory Medal, Central Vet. Soc., 1980; Gordon Meml Medal, Robert Fraser Gordon Meml Trust, 1989; Wolf Foundn Prize in Agric., 1989. *Publications:* scientific papers on viruses and infectious disease. *Recreations:* music making, boating. *Address:* Willows, London Road, St Ives, Huntingdon, Cambridgeshire PE17 4ES. *T:* St Ives (0480) 63471. *Club:* Farmers'.

BIGHAM, family name of **Viscount Mersey** and of **Lady Nairne.**

BIGNALL, John Reginald, FRCP; Physician, Brompton Hospital, 1957–79; *b* 14 Oct. 1913; *s* of Walter and Nellie Bignall; *m* 1939, Ruth Thirtle; one *s* three *d. Educ:* Nottingham High Sch.; St John's Coll. Cambridge; London Hospital. MA 1938; MD 1947; FRCP 1961. Served in RAMC, 1941–46, Middle East and Mediterranean (Major).

BIJUR, Peter Isaac; President, Texaco Europe, since 1990; *b* 14 Oct. 1942; *m* 1966, Anne Montgomery; two *s* one *d. Educ:* Univ. of Pittsburgh (BA Pol. Sci. 1964); Columbia Univ. (MBA 1966). Texaco, 1966–: Manager, Buffalo sales dist, 1971–73; Asst Manager to Vice-Pres. for public affairs, 1973–75; Staff Co-ordinator, dept of strategic planning, 1975–77; Asst to Exec. Vice-Pres., 1977–80; Manager, Rocky Mountain Refining and Marketing, 1980–81; Asst to Chm. of Bd, 1981–83; Pres., Texaco Oil Trading & Supply Co., 1984; Vice-Pres., special projects, 1984–86; Pres. and Chief Exec., Don Mills, Texaco Canada, 1987; Chm., Pres. and Chief Exec., Texaco Canada Resources, Calgary, 1988; Chm., Texaco Ltd, 1989–91. *Address:* Texaco Europe, 2000 Westchester Avenue, White Plains, NY 10650, USA.

BILBY, Prof. Bruce Alexander, BA, PhD; FRS 1977; Consultant; Professor of the Theory of Materials, University of Sheffield, 1966–84, now Emeritus; *b* 3 Sept. 1922; *e s* of late George Alexander Bilby and Dorothy Jean (*née* Telfer); *m* 1st, 1946, Hazel Joyce (*née* Casken); two *s* one *d*; 2nd, 1966, Lorette Wendela (*née* Thomas); two *s. Educ:* Dover

Grammar Sch.; Peterhouse, Cambridge (BA); Univ. of Birmingham (PhD). Admiralty, 1943–46. Research, Birmingham, 1946–51; Univ. of Sheffield: Royal Soc. Sorby Res. Fellow, 1951–57; J. H. Andrew Res. Fellow, 1957–58; Reader in Theoretical Metallurgy, 1958–62, Prof., 1962–66. Has made contributions to theory of dislocations and its application to the deformation, transformation and fracture of metallic crystals. Rosenhain Medal, 1963. *Publications:* contribs to learned jls. *Recreation:* sailing. *Address:* 32 Devonshire Road, Totley, Sheffield S17 3ND. *T:* Sheffield 361086; Department of Mechanical and Process Engineering, The University, Mappin Street, Sheffield S1 3JD. *T:* Sheffield (0742) 768555.

BILL, (Edward) Geoffrey (Watson), OBE 1991; FSA, FRHistS; Lambeth Librarian, 1958–91; Lecturer and Archivist, Christ Church, Oxford, 1950–91; *b* 19 Feb. 1924; *s* of Edward Richard Bill and Anne (*née* Greenwood); *m* Margaret Nancy Finch; one *s* one *d*. *Educ:* Kingston Grammar Sch.; Balliol Coll., Oxford (MA). FRHistS 1983; FSA 1984. Served Army, 1943–46 (Lieut). Dept of Western MSS, Bodleian Library, Oxford, 1954–58. DLitt Lambeth, 1983. *Publications:* Christ Church Meadow, 1965; (with Dr J. F. A. Mason) Christ Church and Reform 1850–1867, 1970; University Reform in Nineteenth Century Oxford, 1973; Education at Christ Church Oxford 1660–1800, 1988; Catalogue of MSS in Lambeth Palace Library, 1972–83. *Recreation:* avoiding gardening. *Address:* Moss Cottage West, Foxfield, Broughton-in-Furness, Cumbria LA20 6BT. *T:* Broughton-in-Furness (0229) 716315.

BILLETT, Paul Rodney, CB 1981; *b* 19 Feb. 1921; *s* of late Arthur William and Grace Hilda Billett; *m* 1st, 1945, Muriel Gwendoline Marsh (*d* 1977); one *s*; 2nd, 1985, Eileen May Nourse. *Educ:* Commonweal and College Grammar Schools, Swindon. Entered Exchequer and Audit Dept, 1939. Served RASC, 1941–46. Deputy Secretary, Exchequer and Audit Dept, 1975–81 (retired). *Address:* Wynthorpe, Cornsland, Brentwood, Essex CM14 4JL. *T:* Brentwood (0277) 224830.

BILLING, Melvin George, CMG 1961; retired as Provincial Commissioner, Provincial Administration, Northern Rhodesia (1951–62); *b* 24 June 1906; *s* of Stuart Morrison Billing and Gertrude Roswell Billing; *m* 1934, Kathleen Jane, *d* of late A. N. Brand; no *c*. *Educ:* Dulwich Coll.; Worcester Coll., Oxford. Provincial Administration, Northern Rhodesia: Cadet, 1930; District Officer, 1932; Grade II, 1942; Grade I, 1946; Senior, 1950. *Recreations:* bowls, photography. *Address:* Formosa Garden Village, Box 416, Plettenberg Bay, Cape 6600, S Africa. *Club:* Commonwealth Trust.

BILLINGHAM, Prof. Rupert Everett, MA, DPhil, DSc Oxon; FRS 1961; Professor and Chairman, Department of Cell Biology and Anatomy, Southwestern Medical School, University of Texas Health Science Center at Dallas, 1971–86; Professor Emeritus, 1990; *b* 15 Oct. 1921; *o s* of Albert Everett and Helen Louise Billingham, Oxford; *m* 1951, Jean Mary Morpeth; two *s* one *d*. *Educ:* City of Oxford High Sch.; Oriel Coll., Oxford. Served 1942–46, as Lieut RNVR. Asst Lectr, later Lectr in Zoology, University of Birmingham, 1947; Junior Research Fellow, British Empire Cancer Campaign, 1950; Intermediate Research Fellow, Brit. Emp. Cancer Campaign, 1953; Hon. Res. Asst, later Res. Associate, Dept of Zoology, University Coll., London, 1951; Wistar Prof. of Zoology, Univ. of Pennsylvania, USA, and Mem. of Wistar Institute of Anatomy and Biology, Philadelphia, 1957; Prof. and Chm., Dept of Medical Genetics, Univ. of Pennsylvania Med. Sch., Pa, 1965–71. Member: Allergy and Immunology Study Section, Nat. Insts of Health, US Public Health Service, 1958–62; Transplantation and Immunology Cttee, Nat. Insts of Health, 1968–70, 1971–73; Scientific Adv. Cttee, Massachusetts General Hospital, 1976–79; Nat. Allergy and Infectious Diseases Council, Nat. Insts of Health, 1980–83; Sigma Xi College of Nat. Lecturers, 1981–83; President: Transplantation Soc., 1974; Internat. Soc. for Immunology of Reproduction, 1983–86. Hon. Mem., British Transplantation Soc., 1988. Fellow, New York Acad. of Sciences, 1962; Fellow, Amer. Acad. of Arts and Sciences, 1965. Lectures: Herman Beerman, Soc. for Investigative Dermatology, 1963; I. S. Ravdin, Amer. College of Surgeons, 1964; *Sigma Xi*, Yale, 1965; Nat. Insts of Health, 1965; J. W. Jenkinson Meml, Oxford, 1965–66; Harvey, NY, 1966; Kinyoun, Nat. Inst. of Allergy and Infectious Diseases, 1979; Dist. Guest, Soc. for Gyn. Investigation, 1982. Hon. DSc Trinity Coll., Hartford, Conn, USA. Alvarenga Prize, Coll. Physicians, Philadelphia, 1963; Hon. Award Medal, Amer. Assoc. of Plastic Surgeons, 1964; Adair Award, Amer. Gynecological Soc., 1971; AOA Honor Med. Soc., 1974. *Publications:* The Immunobiology of Transplantation (with W. K. Silvers), 1971; The Immunobiology of Mammalian Reproduction (with A. E. Beer) 1976; contribs to scien. jls on biology of skin, immunology of tissue transplantation and immunology of manmalian reproduction. *Recreations:* woodwork, gardening. *Address:* Route 2, Box 102B, Vineyard Haven, Mass 02568, USA. *T:* (508) 693–7939.

BILLINGTON, Dr James Hadley; Librarian of Congress, USA, since 1987; *b* 1 June 1929; *s* of Nelson Billington and Jane Coolbaugh; *m* 1957, Marjorie Anne Brennan; two *s* two *d*. *Educ:* Princeton Univ.; Balliol College, Oxford (Rhodes Scholar; DPhil 1953). Served US Army, 1953–56. Harvard University: Instructor in History, 1957–58; Asst Prof. of History and Res. Fellow, Russian Res. Center, 1958–59; Asst Prof. of History, 1958–61; Associate Prof. of History, 1962–64, Prof., 1964–73, Princeton; Dir, Woodrow Wilson Internat. Center for Scholars, Washington, 1973–87. Visiting Research Professor: Inst. of History, Acad. of Scis, USSR, 1966–67; Univ. of Helsinki, 1960–61; Ecole des Hautes Etudes en Scis Sociales, Paris, 1985, 1988; Vis. Lectr, USA, Europe, Asia; Guggenheim Fellow, 1960–61. Member: Amer. Acad. of Arts and Scis; Council on Foreign Relations; numerous hon. degrees. Chevalier, Ordre des Arts et des Lettres. *Publications:* Mikhailovsky and Russian Populism, 1958; The Icon and the Axe: an interpretive history of Russian culture, 1966; The Arts of Russia, 1970; Fire in the Minds of Men: origins of the Revolutionary Faith, 1980; contribs to learned jls. *Address:* Library of Congress, Washington, DC 20540, USA. *T:* (202) 707–5205.

BILLINGTON, Kevin; film, theatre and television director; *b* 12 June 1934; *s* of Richard and Margaret Billington; *m* 1967, Lady Rachel Mary Pakenham (*see* Lady Rachel Billington); two *s* two *d*. *Educ:* Bryanston Sch.; Queens' Coll., Cambridge (BA). Film dir, BBC prog., Tonight, 1960–63; documentary film dir, BBC, 1963–67; films include: A Sort of Paradise; Many Mexicos; The Mexican Attitude; Twilight of Empire; Mary McCarthy's Paris; These Humble Shores; Matador; A Few Castles in Spain; The English Cardinal; A Socialist Childhood; Madison Avenue, USA; ATV documentary, All The Queen's Men. *Feature Film Director:* Interlude, 1967; The Rise and Rise of Michael Rimmer, 1969; The Light at the Edge of the World, 1970; Voices, 1974; Reflections, 1984. *Television Director:* And No One Can Save Her, 1973; Once Upon a Time is Now (documentary), 1978; The Music Will Never Stop (documentary), 1979; Henry VIII, 1979; The Jail Diary of Albie Sachs, 1980; The Good Soldier, 1981; Outside Edge, 1982; The Sonnets of William Shakespeare, 1984; Heartland, 1989; Small Doses, 1990. *Theatre Director:* Find Your Way Home, 1970; Me, 1973; The Birthday Party, 1974; The Caretaker, 1975; Bloody Neighbours, 1975; Emigrés, 1976; The Homecoming, 1978; Quartermaine's Terms, 1982; The Deliberate Death of a Polish Priest, 1985 (Channel Four, 1986); The Philanthropist, 1986; The Lover, and A Slight Ache (double bill), 1987; The Breadwinner, 1989; Veterans Day, 1989. Chm., BAFTA, 1989–90 and 1990–91. Screenwriters' Guild Award, 1966 and 1967; Guild of TV Producers and Directors Award, 1966 and 1967. *Recreation:* swimming. *Address:* 30 Addison Avenue, W11 4QR. *Club:* Garrick.

BILLINGTON, Michael; Drama Critic of The Guardian, since 1971; *b* 16 Nov. 1939; *s* of Alfred Billington and Patricia (*née* Bradshaw); *m* 1978, Jeanine Bradlaugh. *Educ:* Warwick Sch.; St Catherine's Coll., Oxford (BA). Trained as journalist with Liverpool Daily Post and Echo, 1961–62; Public Liaison Officer and Director for Lincoln Theatre Co., 1962–64; reviewed plays, films and television for The Times, 1965–71. Film Critic: Birmingham Post, 1968–78; Illustrated London News, 1968–81; London Arts Correspondent, New York Times, 1978–; Drama Critic, Country Life, 1987–. Contributor to numerous radio and television Arts programmes, incl. Kaleidoscope, Critics' Forum, The Book Programme, Arena. Presenter, The Billington Interview and Theatre Call, BBC World Service. Writer and Presenter, television profiles of Peggy Ashcroft, Peter Hall and Alan Ayckbourn. Prof. of Drama, Colorado Coll., 1981. IPC Critic of the Year, 1974. *Publications:* The Modern Actor, 1974; How Tickled I Am, 1977; (ed) The Performing Arts, 1980; The Guinness Book of Theatre Facts and Feats, 1982; Alan Ayckbourn, 1983; Tom Stoppard, 1987; Peggy Ashcroft, 1988; (ed) Twelfth Night, 1990. *Recreations:* work, travel, cricket. *Address:* 15 Hearne Road, W4 3NJ. *T:* 081–995 0455. *Club:* Garrick.

BILLINGTON, Lady Rachel (Mary); writer; *b* 11 May 1942; *d* of 7th Earl of Longford, *qv*, and Countess of Longford, *qv*; *m* 1967, Kevin Billington, *qv*; two *s* two *d*. *Educ:* London Univ. (BA English). Work includes: short stories; four BBC radio plays; two BBC TV plays, Don't be Silly, 1979, Life After Death, 1981. Reviewer; feature writer, Sunday Telegraph. *Publications:* All Things Nice, 1969; The Big Dipper, 1970; Lilacs out of the Dead Land, 1971; Cock Robin, 1973; Beautiful, 1974; A Painted Devil, 1975; A Woman's Age, 1979; Occasion of Sin, 1982; The Garish Day, 1985; Loving Attitudes, 1988; Theo and Matilda, 1990; *for children:* Rosanna and the Wizard-Robot, 1981; The First Christmas, 1983; Star-Time, 1984; The First Easter, 1987; Theo and Matilda, 1990; The First Miracles, 1990. *Recreation:* children. *Address:* 30 Addison Avenue, W11 4QR. *Clubs:* Society of Authors, PEN.

BILLOT, Barbara Kathleen; Deputy Director (Under-Secretary), Department for National Savings, 1974–80; *b* 26 May 1920; *d* of Alfred Billot and Agnes Billot (*née* Hiner). *Educ:* Petersfield County High Sch. for Girls. Post Office Savings Bank: Clerical Officer 1938; Exec. Off. 1939; Higher Exec. Off. 1946; Sen. Exec. Off. 1953; Chief Exec. Off. 1957; Principal, Post Office Headquarters, 1960; Sen. Chief Exec. Off., PO Savings Dept, 1961; Principal Exec. Off. (Estabt Off.), 1969; Asst Sec., Dept for Nat. Savings, 1971. *Recreations:* reading, theatre-going. *Address:* 6 Springbank, Chichester, W Sussex PO19 4BX. *T:* Chichester (0243) 776295.

bin YEOP, Tan Sri Abdul Aziz, Al-Haj; PSM (Malaysia); Hon. GCVO 1972; Member, Malaysian Parliament; Partner in legal firm, Aziz and Mazlan, Advocates and Solicitors, 1966–71, and since 1973; *b* 5 Oct. 1916; *m* 1942, Puan Sri Hamidah Aziz; six *s* three *d*. *Educ:* King Edward VII Sch., Perak, Malaysia. Malay Administrative Service, 1937; called to Bar, Lincoln's Inn, 1950; Malayan Civil Service, 1951; First Asst State Sec., Perak 1954; London Univ. (course in Community Development), 1955. Permanent Sec., Min. of Agriculture, 1958–62; Dep. Sec., Malaysian Affairs Div., Prime Minister's Dept, 1962–64; Permanent Sec., Min. of Education, 1964–66. Chm. and Dir of firms in Malaysia, 1966–71. High Comr for Malaysia in London, 1971–73. First Chm., Bd of Governors of BERNAMA (Malaysia's National News Agency), 1967–71; Chairman: Council, Universiti Teknologi, Malaysia, 1974– (Pro-chancellor, 1977–80); Majlis Amanah Raayat, Malaysia, 1975–. *Recreations:* walking, reading, fishing. *Address:* c/o Aziz and Mazlan, Advocates and Solicitors, Wisma Getah Asli, 1st Floor, 148 Jalan Ampang, Kuala Lumpur 50450, Malaysia. *T:* Kuala Lumpur 03–2439188 and 03–2439193, *Fax:* 03–2433525.

BING, Inigo Geoffrey; a Metropolitan Stipendiary Magistrate, since 1989; *b* 1 April 1944; *s* of late Geoffrey Henry Cecil Bing, QC and Christian Frances Bing; *m* 1980, Shirley-Anne Holmes (*née* Benka); three step *c*. *Educ:* St Olave's Grammar Sch., Southwark; Birmingham Univ. (LLB). Called to the Bar, Inner Temple, 1967; practised London and SE Circuit. Mem. (Lab) London Borough of Lambeth, 1971–78 (Chm., F and GP Cttee, 1974–78); Co-founder, Lambeth Community Law Centre. Contested (SDP) Braintree 1983 and 1987. *Publications:* (contrib.) The Radical Challenge, ed Kilmarnock, 1987; Criminal Procedure and Sentencing in the Magistrates' Court, 1990. *Recreations:* reading, writing, music, exploring France, the company of friends. *Address:* c/o Greenwich Magistrates' Court, Blackheath Road, SE10 8PG. *Club:* Reform.

BING, Sir Rudolf (Franz Joseph), KBE 1971 (CBE 1956); General Manager, Metropolitan Opera, New York, 1950–72; Distinguished Professor, Brooklyn College, City University of New York, 1972–75; Director Columbia Artists Management, since 1973; *b* Vienna, 9 Jan. 1902; *m* 1929, Nina (*née* Schelemskaja) (*d* 1983); *m* 1987, Carroll Lee Douglass (marr. annulled, 1989). *Educ:* Vienna. Hessian State Theatre, Darmstadt, 1928–30; Civic Opera, Berlin-Charlottenburg, 1930–33. Gen. Manager, Glyndebourne Opera, 1935–49; Artistic Director, Edinburgh Festival, 1947–49. Holds hon. doctorates in music and in letters, from the US. Légion d'Honneur, 1958; Comdr's Cross of Order of Merit, Federal Republic of Germany, 1958; Grand Silver Medal of Honour, Republic of Austria, 1959; Comdr, Order of Merit, Republic of Italy, 1959, Grand Officer, 1970. *Publication:* 5000 Nights at the Opera, 1972.

BINGHAM, family name of **Baron Clanmorris** and of **Earl of Lucan.**

BINGHAM, Lord; George Charles Bingham; *b* 21 Sept. 1967; *s* and *heir* of 7th Earl of Lucan, *qv*. *Educ:* Eton; Trinity Hall, Cambridge.

BINGHAM, Caroline Margery Conyers; professional writer; *b* 7 Feb. 1938; *o d* of Cedric and Muriel Worsdell; *m* 1958, Andrew Bingham (marr. diss. 1972); one *d*. *Educ:* Mount Sch., York; Convent de la Sagesse, Newcastle upon Tyne; Cheltenham Ladies' Coll.; Univ. of Bristol (BA Hons History). Res. Fellow, Dept of History, RHBNC, London Univ., 1985–87. *Publications:* The Making of a King: the early years of James VI and I, 1968 (USA 1969); James V, King of Scots, 1971; (contrib.) The Scottish Nation: a history of the Scots from Independence to Union, 1972; The Life and Times of Edward II, 1973; The Stewart Kingdom of Scotland, 1371–1603, 1974 (USA 1974); The Kings and Queens of Scotland, 1976 (USA 1976); The Crowned Lions: the Early Plantagenet Kings, 1978; James VI of Scotland, 1979; The Voice of the Lion (verse anthology), 1980; James I of England, 1981; Land of the Scots: a short history, 1983; History of Royal Holloway College 1886–1986, 1987. *Address:* 164 Regent's Park Road, NW1 8XN.

BINGHAM, Hon. Charlotte Mary Thérèse; playwright and novelist; *b* 29 June 1942; *d* of 7th Baron Clanmorris (John Bingham) and of Madeleine Mary, *d* of late Clement Ebel; *m* 1964, Terence Brady, *qv*; one *s* one *d*. *Educ:* The Priory, Haywards Heath; Sorbonne. *TV series* with Terence Brady: Boy Meets Girl; Take Three Girls; Upstairs Downstairs; Away From It All; Play for Today; No—Honestly; Yes—Honestly; Pig in the Middle; Thomas and Sarah; The Complete Lack of Charm of the Bourgeoisie; Nanny; Oh Madeline! (USA TV); Father Matthew's Daughter; Forever Green; The Upper Hand; *TV films:* Love With a Perfect Stranger, 1986; Losing Control, 1987; The

Seventh Raven, 1987; This Magic Moment, 1988; *stage*: (contrib.) The Sloane Ranger Revue, 1985; I Wish, I Wish, 1989. *Publications*: Coronet among the Weeds, 1963; Lucinda, 1965; Coronet among the Grass, 1972; Belgravia, 1983; Country Life, 1984; At Home, 1986; To Hear A Nightingale, 1988; The Business, 1989; In Sunshine or In Shadow, 1991; with Terence Brady: Victoria, 1972; Rose's Story, 1973; Victoria and Company, 1974; Yes—Honestly, 1977. *Recreations*: horses, watching others garden. *Address*: c/o Murray Pollinger, 222 Old Brompton Road, SW5 0BZ. *Club*: Society of Authors.

BINGHAM, Sir (Eardley) Max, Kt 1988; QC (Tas.) 1974; Chairman, Queensland Criminal Justice Commission, since 1989; *b* 18 March 1927; *s* of Thomas Eardley and Olive Bingham; *m* 1952, Margaret Garrett Jesson; three *s* one *d*. *Educ*: Univ. of Tasmania (LLB (Hons)); Lincoln Coll., Oxford (BCL; Rhodes Schol., 1950); Univ. of California at Berkley (Harkness Commonwealth Fund Fellow, 1963). RANR, 1945–46. Legal practice, and teaching, Univ. of Tasmania, 1953–69. MHA Tasmania, 1969–84; Attorney-General, 1969–72; Leader of the Opposition, 1972–79, Dep. Leader of the Opposition, 1982; Dep. Premier of Tas., 1982–84. Mem., Nat. Crime Authority, 1984–87. *Publications*: contribs to jls. *Recreations*: farming, reading, sailing. *Address*: 14 Musgrove Road, Geilston Bay, Tas 7015, Australia. *T*: 438331. *Clubs*: Tasmanian, Royal Yacht of Tasmania (Hobart).

BINGHAM, John, CBE 1991; FRS 1977; Deputy Chief Scientific Officer at Plant Breeding International, Cambridge, 1981–90; *b* 19 June 1930. SPSO, Plant Breeding Inst., Cambridge, to 1981. Has researched in plant breeding, culminating in production of improved, highly successful winter wheat varieties for British agriculture. Mullard Medal of Royal Society, 1975. *Address*: 25 Stansgate Avenue, Cambridge CB2 2QZ. *T*: Cambridge (0223) 247737.

BINGHAM, Sir Max; *see* Bingham, Sir E. M.

BINGHAM, His Honour Richard Martin, TD 1949; QC 1958; a Circuit Judge, 1972–88; *b* 26 Oct. 1915; *s* of late John and Dorothy Ann Bingham; *m* 1949, Elinor Stephenson; one *d*. *Educ*: Harrow; Clare Coll., Cambridge. Called to Bar, Inner Temple, 1940; Bencher, 1964; joined Northern Circuit, 1946; Recorder of Oldham, 1960–71; Judge of Appeal, IoM, 1965–72. Served with 59th Med. Regt, RA (TA), 1937–46 and 1947–49: Major from 1945; Campaigns, Dunkirk and NW Europe (despatches, 1944). Mem. of Liverpool City Council, 1946–49. MP (C) Garston Division of Liverpool, Dec. 1957–March 1966. Member: HO Departmental Cttee on Coroners, 1965; Royal Commn Assizes and Quarter Sessions, 1966. *Publications*: Cases on Negligence, 1st edn 1961, 3rd edn 1978; Cases and Statutes on Crime, 1980; Crown Court Law and Practice, 1987. *Address*: Hook End, Gayton, Merseyside L60 3SR. *T*: 051–342 5793. *Clubs*: Royal Automobile; Royal Liverpool Golf.

BINGHAM, Rt. Hon. Sir Thomas (Henry), Kt 1980; PC 1986; **Rt. Hon. Lord Justice Bingham;** a Lord Justice of Appeal, since 1986; *b* 13 Oct. 1933; *o s* of late Dr T. H. Bingham and Dr C. Bingham, Reigate; *m* 1963, Elizabeth, *o d* of late Peter Loxley; two *s* one *d*. *Educ*: Sedbergh; Balliol Coll., Oxford (MA; Hon. Fellow, 1989). Royal Ulster Rifles, 1952–54 (2nd Lt); London Irish Rifles (TA) 1954–59. Univ. of Oxford: Gibbs Schol. in Mod. Hist., 1956; 1st cl. Hons, Mod. Hist., 1957. Eldon Law Schol., 1957; Arden Schol., Gray's Inn, 1959; Cert. of Honour, Bar Finals, 1959; called to Bar, Gray's Inn, 1959; Bencher, 1979. Standing Jun. Counsel to Dept of Employment, 1968–72; QC 1972; a Recorder of the Crown Court, 1975–80; Judge of the High Court of Justice, Queen's Bench Div., and Judge of the Commercial Court, 1980–86. Leader, Investigation into the supply of petroleum and petroleum products to Rhodesia, 1977–78. Mem., Lord Chancellor's Law Reform Cttee; Chairman: Council of Legal Educn, 1982–86; Adv. Council, Centre for Commercial Law Studies, Queen Mary and Westfield Coll., London Univ., 1989–. Visitor, Balliol Coll., Oxford, 1986–. Governor: Sedbergh, 1978–88; Atlantic Coll., 1984–89. Special Trustee, St Mary's Hosp., 1985– (Chm., 1988–); Visitor, RPMS, 1989–; Member: St Mary's Med. Sch. Delegacy, 1988–; Council, KCL, 1989–. Fellow, Winchester, 1983–91. *Publication*: Chitty on Contracts, (Asst Editor) 22nd edn, 1961. *Address*: Royal Courts of Justice, Strand, WC2.

BINGLEY, Juliet Martin, (Lady Bingley), MBE 1991; Research Social Worker, City Corporation Social Services, based at St Mark's Hospital, EC1, since 1990 (Senior Social Worker, 1973–90); *b* 18 July 1925; *d* of Mary Kate Vick and Reginald Vick, OBE, MCh, FRCS; *m* 1948, Adm. Sir Alexander Noel Campbell Bingley, GCB, OBE (*d* 1972); one *s* two *d*. *Educ*: King Alfred School, Hampstead; London Sch. of Economics. Associated Mem., Inst. of Medical Social Workers. Social Worker, St Bartholomew's Hosp., 1945–48. Chairman: Nat. Assoc. of Mental Health, 1979–84; Good Practices in Mental Health, 1989. CStJ 1962. Companion of Honour, Republic of Malta, 1976. *Recreations*: music, gardening, reading, theatre, moving furniture, collecting Staffordshire figures, lawn mowing. *Address*: Hoddesdonbury Farm, Hoddesdon, Herts EN11 5LP. *T*: Hoddesdon (0992) 463238.

BINNEY, H(arry) A(ugustus) Roy, CB 1950; Director-General, 1951–70, Director-General, International, 1971–72, British Standards Institution; retired; *b* 18 May 1907; *s* of Harry Augustus Binney, Churston, Devon; *m* 1944, Barbara Poole (*d* 1975); three *s* one *d* (and one *d* decd). *Educ*: Royal Dockyard Sch., Devonport; London Univ. BSc(Eng). Entered Board of Trade, 1929, Under-Sec. 1947–51. Chairman: Standardization Cttee, European Productivity Agency, 1953–58; Cttee for European Standardization (CEN), 1963–65; Mem. Council, 1951–72, Vice-Pres., 1964–69, ISO. UN Advr on Standards to Govt of Cyprus, 1974–77. Hon. Life Fellow, Standards Engrg Soc. of America; Hon. Life Mem., American Soc. for Testing and Materials. FKC; FRSA. *Recreation*: gardening. *Address*: Hambutts Orchard, Edge Lane, Painswick, Glos GL6 6UW. *T*: Painswick (0452) 813718.

BINNEY, Marcus Hugh Crofton, OBE 1983; writer; President, SAVE Britain's Heritage, since 1984 (Chairman, 1975–84); *s* of late Lt-Col Francis Crofton Simms, MC and of Sonia, *d* of Rear-Adm. Sir William Marcus Charles Beresford-Whyte, KCB, CMG (she *m* 2nd, Sir George Binney, DSO); *m* 1st, 1966, Hon. Sara Anne Vanneck (marr. diss. 1976), *e d* of 6th Baron Huntingfield; 2nd, 1981, Anne Carolyn, *d* of Dr T. H. Hills, Merstham, Surrey; two *s*. *Educ*: Magdalene Coll., Cambridge (BA 1966). Architectural writer, 1968–77; Architectural Editor, 1977–84, Editor, 1984–86, Country Life; Ed., Landscape, 1987; architectural correspondent, The Times, 1991–. Sec., UK Cttee, Internat. Council on Monuments and Sites, 1972–81; Dir, Rly Heritage Trust, 1985–. *Publications*: (with Peter Burman): Change and Decay: the future of our churches, 1977; Chapels and Churches: who cares?, 1977; (with Max Hanna) Preservation Pays, 1978; (ed jtly) Railway Architecture, 1979; (ed jtly) Our Past Before Us, 1981; (with Kit Martin) The Country House: to be or not to be, 1982; (with Max Hanna) Preserve and Prosper, 1983; Sir Robert Taylor, 1984; Our Vanishing Heritage, 1984; contributor to: Satanic Mills, 1979; Elysian Gardens, 1979; Lost Houses of Scotland, 1980; Taking the Plunge, 1982; SAVE Gibraltar's Heritage, 1982; Vanishing Houses of England, 1983; (contrib.) Time Gentlemen Please, 1983. *Address*: c/o The Times, 1 Pennington Street, E1 9XN.

BINNIE, David Stark, OBE 1979; FCIT; FBIM; railway and rapid transport consultant; *b* 2 June 1922; *s* of Walter Archibald Binnie and Helen (*née* Baxter), Bonkle, Lanarkshire; *m* 1947, Leslie Archibald; one *s* one *d*. *Educ*: Wishaw High School. British Railways: Gen. and Signalling Asst to Gen. Manager Scottish Region, 1955; Asst District Operating Supt 1961, District Operating Supt 1963, Glasgow North; Divisional Movements Manager, Glasgow Div., 1965; Movements Manager, Scottish Region, 1967; Divisional Manager, SE Div., Southern Region, 1969; Asst Gen. Manager, Southern Region, 1970, Gen. Manager, 1972; Exec. Dir, Freight, BR Board, 1974–76; Gen. Manager, BR, London Midland Region, 1977–80. Lt-Col Engineer and Railway Staff Corps, RE (T&AVR). OStJ. *Recreation*: Dartmoor and Highland life. *Address*: Above Ways, Lower Knowle Road, Lustleigh, Devon TQ13 9SE. *T*: Lustleigh (06477) 386.

BINNIG, Prof. Dr Gerd Karl; IBM Fellow, since 1986; Honorary Professor of Physics, University of Munich, since 1987; *b* 20 July 1947; *m* 1969, Lore; one *s* one *d*. *Educ*: J. W. Goethe Univ., Frankfurt/M (DipPhys; PhD). Research staff mem., IBM Zurich Res. Lab., in fields of superconductivity of semiconductors and scanning tunneling microscopy, 1978–, Gp Leader 1984–; IBM Almaden Res. Center, San José, and collab. with Stanford Univ., 1985–86; Vis. Prof., Stanford Univ., 1985–86. Member: Technology Council, IBM Acad., 1989–; Supervisory Bd, Mercedes Automobil Holding AG, 1989–. For. Associate Mem., Acad. of Scis, Washington, 1987. Hon. FRMS 1988. Scanning Tunneling Microscopy awards: Physics Prize, German Phys. Soc., 1982; Otto Klung Prize, 1983; (jtly) King Faisal Internat. Prize for Science and Hewlett Packard Europhysics Prize, 1984; (jtly) Nobel Prize in Physics, 1986; Elliot Cresson Medal, Franklin Inst., Philadelphia, 1987; Minnie Rosen Award, Ross Univ., NY, 1988. Grosses Verdienstkreuz mit Stern und Schulterband des Verdienstordens (FRG), 1987. *Recreations*: music, tennis, soccer, golf. *Address*: IBM Research Division, Physics Group Munich, Schellingstrasse 4, 8000 München 40, Germany. *T*: (089) 28 86 77–8.

BINNING, Lord; George Edmund Baldred Baillie-Hamilton; *b* 27 Dec. 1985; *s* and heir of Earl of Haddington, *qv*.

BINNING, Kenneth George Henry, CMG 1976; Director of Government Relations, NEI plc (formerly NEI International), since 1983; *b* 5 Jan. 1928; *o s* of late Henry and Hilda Binning; *m* 1953, Pamela Dorothy, *o d* of A. E. and D. G. Pronger; three *s* one *d*. *Educ*: Bristol Grammar Sch.; Balliol Coll., Oxford. Joined Home Civil Service, 1950; Nat. Service, 1950–52; HM Treasury, 1952–58; Private Sec. to Financial Sec., 1956–57; AEA, 1958–65; seconded to Min. of Technology, 1965; rejoined Civil Service, 1968; Dir-Gen. Concorde, 1972–76 and Under-Sec., DTI later Dept of Industry, 1972–83. Mem., BSC, 1980–83. *Recreations*: music, gardening. *Address*: 12 Kemerton Road, Beckenham, Kent BR3 2NJ. *T*: 081–650 0273. *Club*: Reform.

BINNS, David John, CBE 1989; General Manager, Warrington and Runcorn Development Corporation, 1981–89; Member, Warrington District Health Authority, since 1990; *b* 12 April 1929; *s* of Henry Norman Binns, OBE and Ivy Mary Binns; *m* 1957, Jean Margaret Evans; one *s* (one *d* decd). *Educ*: Fleetwood Grammar Sch.; Rossall Sch.; Sheffield Univ. LLB 1951. Solicitor 1954. Articled Clerk, Sheffield City Council, 1949; Asst Solicitor, Warrington County Borough Council, 1954; Dep. Town Clerk, Warrington County Borough Council, 1958; Gen. Manager, Warrington Develt Corp., 1969–81. *Recreations*: walking, gardening, music. *Address*: 4 Cedarways, Appleton, Warrington, Cheshire WA4 5EW. *T*: Warrington (0925) 62169. *Club*: Warrington (Warrington).

BINNS, Geoffrey John; His Honour Judge Binns; a Circuit Judge, since 1980; *b* 12 Oct. 1930; *s* of Rev. Robert Arthur Geoffrey Binns and Elizabeth Marguerite Binns; *m* 1964, Elizabeth Anne Poole Askew. *Educ*: Perse Sch.; Jesus Coll., Cambridge (MA). Admitted solicitor, 1956; Partner, Fraser, Woodgate & Beall, Wisbech, 1958–80; a Recorder of the Crown Court, 1977–80. Chm., N Cambs Hosp. Management Cttee, 1970–74; Member: E Anglian Reg. Hosp. Bd, 1972–74; E Anglian RHA, 1974–76; Panel of Chairmen, Cambridge Univ. Ct of Discipline, 1976–80. Registrar, Archdeaconry of Wisbech, 1972–80. *Publication*: Contributing Ed., Butterworths' County Court Precedents and Pleadings, 1985. *Recreations*: golf, gardening. *Address*: c/o Combined Court Centre, Bishopgate, Norwich. *T*: Norwich (0603) 761776. *Club*: Norfolk (Norwich).

BINNS, Malcolm; concert pianist; *b* 29 Jan. 1936; *s* of Douglas and May Binns. *Educ*: Bradford Grammar Sch.; Royal Coll. of Music (ARCM, Chappell Gold Medal, Medal of Worshipful Co. of Musicians). London début, 1957; Henry Wood Proms début, 1960; Royal Festival Hall début, 1961; Festival Hall appearances in London Philharmonic Orchestra International series, 1969–; toured with Scottish Nat. Orch., 1989; concerts at Aldeburgh, Leeds, Three Choirs (1975), Bath and Canterbury Festivals; regular appearances at Promenade concerts and broadcasts for BBC Radio. First complete recording of Beethoven piano sonatas on original instruments, 1980; première recordings of Sir William Sterndale Bennett's piano concertos with London Philharmonic and Philharmonia Orchs, 1990. *Recreation*: collecting antique gramophone records. *Address*: 233 Court Road, Orpington, Kent BR6 9BY. *T*: Orpington (0689) 31056.

BINNS, St John, MBE 1977; JP; Member, West Yorkshire County Council, 1974–86 (Chairman, 1984–85); *b* 25 July 1914; *s* of John William and Lena Binns; *m* 1938, Gwendoline, *e d* of Fred and Minnie Clough; one *s*. *Educ*: Holbeck Junior Technical School. Amalgamated Union of Engineering Workers: Leeds District Pres., 1948, Sec., 1953; Divisional Organiser, 1970. Councillor, Leeds City Council, 1956 (Chm., Civic Catering, Plans, Licensing, Fire Cttees); Alderman, 1972; W Yorks Metropolitan County Council: Chm., Leeds Area Cttee, 1976; Chm., Personnel Cttee and Chief Whip, 1981–84. JP Leeds, 1959. *Recreation*: gardening. *Address*: 146 West Park Drive (West), Roundhay, Leeds LS8 2DA.

BINNY, John Anthony Francis; *b* 13 Dec. 1911. *Educ*: Wellington College. Supplementary Reserve of Officers, 15th/19th The King's Royal Hussars, 1936. Served War of 1939–45, France and Burma (despatches). Chm., Blue Circle Industries, 1975–78; formerly Chairman: Mercantile Investment Trust; Law Debenture Corp.; Dep. Chm., Nat. Westminster Bank plc, 1972–81; formerly Dep. Chm., TI Group. *Address*: Byways, Pound Lane, Burley, Ringwood, Hampshire BH24 4EF. *Clubs*: Cavalry and Guards, White's, MCC.

BINTLEY, David Julian; Resident Choreographer and Principal Dancer with the Royal Ballet, since 1986; *b* 17 Sept. 1957; *s* of David Bintley and Glenys Bintley (*née* Ellinthorpe); *m* 1981, Jennifer Catherine Ursula Mills; one *s*. *Educ*: Holme Valley Grammar School. Royal Ballet School, 1974; Sadler's Wells Royal Ballet, 1976; first professional choreography, The Outsider, 1978; youngest choreographer to work at the Royal Opera House, for production of Adieu, 1980; first three act ballet, The Swan of Tuonela, 1982; Company Choreographer, 1983–85, Resident Choreographer, 1985–86, Sadler's Wells Royal Ballet. Evening Standard Award for Ballet, for Choros and Consort Lessons, both 1983; Laurence Olivier Award for Petrushka, 1984; Manchester Evening News Award for Dance, for Still Life at the Penguin Café, 1987.

BIOBAKU, Dr Saburi Oladeni, CMG 1961; MA, PhD; Research historian and management consultant; Research Professor and Director, Institute of African Studies, University of Ibadan, 1976–83; *b* 16 June 1918; *s* of late Chief S. O. Biobaku, Aré of Iddo, Abeokuta; *m* 1949, Muhabat Folasade, *d* of Alhaji L. B. Agusto, barrister-at-law, Lagos; one *s. Educ:* Govt Coll., Ibadan; Higher Coll., Yaba; University Coll., Exeter; Trinity Coll., Cambridge. BA London, 1945; BA Cantab, 1947, MA 1951; PhD London, 1951. Education Officer, Nigeria, 1947–53; Registrar, University Coll., Ibadan, 1953–57; Dir, Yoruba Historical Research Scheme, 1956–; Sec. to Premier and Executive Council, Western Nigeria, 1957–61; Pro-Vice-Chancellor, Univ. of Ife, Nigeria, 1961–65; Vice-Chancellor, Univ. of Lagos, 1965–72; Chairman, Management Consultant Services Ltd, Lagos, 1972–76, 1983–. Hon. DLitt. Created: Aré of Iddo, Abeokuta, 1958; Agbakin of Igbore, 1972; Maye of Ife, 1980; Baapitan of Egbaland, 1980. *Publications:* The Origin of the Yoruba, 1955; The Egba and Their Neighbours, 1842–1872, 1957; Living Cultures of Nigeria, 1977; contribs to Africa, jl of Nigerian Historical Soc., Odu (Joint Ed.), etc. *Recreations:* soccer, tennis, badminton, swimming, walking. *Address:* PO Box 7741, Lagos, Nigeria. *T:* (home) 961430. *Clubs:* Metropolitan (Lagos); Dining (Ibadan).

BIRAN, Yoav; Ambassador of Israel to the Court of St James's, since 1988; *b* 17 July 1939; *s* of Michael and Rachel Barsky; *m* (separated); one *s* two *d. Educ:* Hebrew University of Jerusalem (post grad. studies, history, internat. relns). Joined Min. of For. Affairs, Jerusalem, 1963; ME and Afr. Depts, 1963–65; Second Sec., Ethiopia, 1965–67; First Sec., Uganda, 1967–70; Prin. Asst to Asst Dir-Gen. in charge of World Jewry and Inf., 1970–72, Dep. Dir of Dir-Gen.'s Cabinet, 1972–74, Min. of For. Affairs; Mem., Israel Delegn to Geneva Peace Conf., Dec. 1973; Dir of Dept, Center for Res. and Policy Planning, Min. of For. Affairs, 1975–77; Minister Plenipotentiary, 1977–82, Chargé d'Affaires, 1982–83, London; elected Distinguished Mem., Israel For. Service and of Israel Civil Service, 1983; Asst Dir Gen., Admin, 1984–87, N Amer. and Disarmament Affairs, 1987–88, FO, Jerusalem. *Recreations:* theatre, collecting antiquarian maps and books. *Address:* Embassy of Israel, 2 Palace Green, W8 4QB. *T:* 071–937 8050.

BIRCH, Alexander Hope, CMG 1970; OBE 1961; HM Diplomatic Service, retired; *b* 19 Jan. 1913; *s* of Denys Goldney and Lucy Helen Booth Birch; *m* 1st, 1940, Honor Pengelley (marr. diss., 1948); 2nd, 1953, Joan Hastings-Hungerford (*d* 1982); no *c. Educ:* St Catherine's and St Mark's Colls, Alexandria, and privately. Appointed to: HM Embassy, Cairo, 1937; Addis Ababa, 1942; Moscow, 1946; Budapest, 1947; Tel-Aviv, 1949; Second Sec. (Inf.), Baghdad, 1950, First Sec. and Consul, Seoul, 1951, and Djakarta, 1954; First Sec. (Commercial), Khartoum, 1956, and Paris, 1961; Counsellor (Commercial), Paris, 1962, and Baghdad, 1965; Counsellor (Economic and Commercial), Accra, 1967–70; Dep. High Comr, Perth, WA, 1970–73; Administrative Adviser to Premier of Antigua, 1973–75. *Recreations:* international affairs, reading, walking. *Address:* Woodrow, Edgehill Road, Clevedon, Avon BS21 7BZ.

BIRCH, Prof. Anthony Harold, PhD; FRSC 1988; Professor of Political Science, University of Victoria, British Columbia, 1977–89, now Emeritus; *b* 17 Feb. 1924; *o s* of late Frederick Harold Birch and Rosalind Dorothy Birch; *m* 1953, Dorothy Madeleine Overton, Bayport, New York; one *s* one *d. Educ:* The William Ellis Sch.; University Coll., Nottingham; London Sch. of Economics. BSc (Econ) London, with 1st cl. hons, 1945; PhD London, 1951. Asst Principal, Board of Trade, 1945–47; University of Manchester: Asst Lectr in Govt, 1947–51; Lectr, 1951–58; Senior Lectr in Government, 1958–61; Prof. of Political Studies, Univ. of Hull, 1961–70; Prof. of Political Sci., Exeter Univ., 1970–77. Commonwealth Fund Fellow at Harvard Univ. and University of Chicago, 1951–52. Consultant to Government of Western Region of Nigeria, 1956–58. Vis. Prof. Tufts Univ., 1968; Vis. Fellow, ANU, 1987. Vice-Pres., Internat. Political Sci. Assoc., 1976–79; Life Vice-Pres., UK Political Studies Assoc., 1976– (Chm., 1972–75). *Publications:* Federalism, Finance and Social Legislation, 1955; Small-Town Politics, 1959; Representative and Responsible Government, 1964; The British System of Government, 1967, 8th edn 1990; Representation, 1971; Political Integration and Disintegration in the British Isles, 1977; Nationalism and National Integration, 1989; articles in various journals. *Recreation:* sailing. *Address:* 1901 Fairfield Road, Victoria, BC V8S 1H2, Canada.

BIRCH, Prof. Arthur John, AC 1987; CMG 1979; DPhil (Oxon); FRS 1958; FAA, FRACI; Professor of Organic Chemistry, Australian National University, 1967–80, now Emeritus; Professorial Fellow, Lincoln College, Oxford, since 1980; *b* 3 Aug. 1915; *s* of Arthur Spencer and Lily Birch; *m* 1948, Jessie Williams; three *s* two *d. Educ:* Sydney Technical High Sch.; Sydney Univ. MA Oxon 1981; MSc: Sydney, 1939; Manchester, 1957. Scholar of the Royal Commission for the Exhibition of 1851, Oxford, 1938–41; Research Fellow, Oxford, 1941–45; ICI Research Fellow, Oxford, 1945–48; Smithson Fellow of the Royal Society, Cambridge, 1949–52; Prof. of Organic Chemistry, University of Sydney, 1952–55; Prof. of Organic Chemistry, Manchester Univ., 1955–67; Dean, Research Sch. of Chemistry, ANU, Canberra, 1967–70, 1973–76; Newton Abraham Prof., Univ. of Oxford, 1980–81. Treas., Australian Acad. Science, 1969–73, Pres., 1982–86; Pres., RACI, 1978. Chairman: Ind. Enquiry into CSIRO, 1976–; Aust. Marine Sciences and Technologies Adv. Cttee, 1978–81. UNDP Consultant, People's Republic of China, 1980, 1982, 1984, 1986; OECD Examiner, Denmark, 1987. Foreign Mem., USSR Acad. of Science, 1976; Foreign Fellow, Indian Nat. Sci. Acad., 1990; Hon. FRCS 1980. Hon. DSc: Sydney, 1977; Manchester, 1982; Monash, 1982. Davy Medal, Royal Soc., 1972; Tetrahedron Prize, Tetrahedron Jl, 1987; ANZAAS Medal, 1990. *Publications:* How Chemistry Works, 1950; 426 original scientific communications, chiefly in Journal of Chemical Soc. and Australian Journal of Chemistry. *Address:* Department of Chemistry, Australian National University, PO Box 4, Canberra, ACT 2601, Australia.

BIRCH, Prof. Bryan John, FRS 1972; Professor of Arithmetic, University of Oxford, since 1985; Professorial Fellow of Brasenose College, Oxford, since 1985 (Fellow since 1966); *b* 25 Sept. 1931; *s* of Arthur Jack and Mary Edith Birch; *m* 1961, Gina Margaret Christ; two *s* one *d. Educ:* Shrewsbury Sch.; Trinity Coll., Cambridge (MA, PhD). Harkness Fellow, Princeton, 1957–58; Fellow: Trinity Coll., Cambridge, 1956–60; Churchill Coll., Cambridge, 1960–62; Sen. Lectr, later Reader, Univ. of Manchester, 1962–65; Reader in Mathematics, Univ. of Oxford, 1966–85. *Publications:* articles in learned jls, mainly on number theory; various editorships. *Recreations:* gardening (theoretical), opera, watching marmots. *Address:* Green Cottage, Boars Hill, Oxford OX1 5DQ. *T:* Oxford (0865) 735367; Mathematical Institute, 25–29 St Giles, Oxford. *T:* Oxford (0865) 273525.

BIRCH, Dennis Arthur, CBE 1977; DL; Councillor, West Midlands County Council, 1974–77; *b* 11 Feb. 1925; *s* of George Howard and Leah Birch; *m* 1948, Mary Therese Lyons; one *d. Educ:* Wolverhampton Municipal Grammar Sch. Wolverhampton County Borough Council: elected, 1952; served, 1952–74; Alderman, 1970–73; Mayor, 1973–74; Leader, 1967–73. Elected (following Local Govt reorganisation) Chm. West Midlands CC, 1974–76. DL West Midlands, 1979. MInstM. *Address:* 3 Tern Close, Wolverhampton Road East, Wolverhampton WV4 6AU. *T:* Sedgley (0902) 883837.

BIRCH, Frank Stanley Heath; public sector consultant; Deputy Commander, 1990–92, Commander from April 1992, London District, St John Ambulance; *b* 8 Feb. 1939; *s* of late John Stanley Birch, CEng and Phyllis Edna Birch (*née* Heath), BA; *m* 1963, Diana Jacqueline Davies, BA; one *d. Educ:* Weston-super-Mare Grammar Sch. for Boys; Univ. of Wales (BA); Univ. of Birmingham (Inst. of Local Govt Studies). IPFA; MBIM. Entered local govt service, 1962; various appts, City Treasurer and Controller's Dept, Cardiff, 1962–69; Chief Internal Auditor, Dudley, 1969–73; Asst County Treasurer, 1973–74, Asst Chief Exec., 1974–76, W Midlands CC; Chief Exec., Lewisham, 1976–82; Town Clerk and Chief Exec., Croydon, 1982–90. Hon. Clerk, Gen. Purposes Cttee, 1982–90, Principal Grants Advr, 1983–86, London Boroughs Assoc.; Sec., London Co-ordinating Cttee, 1985–86. Dir, Croydon Business Venture Ltd, 1983–. Freeman, City of London, 1980. FRSA 1980. OStJ 1988 (Mem. Council, London Br., 1986–); Vice-Pres., London Br., SJAB, 1988–90. *Publications:* various articles on public admin and local govt management. *Recreations:* music, walking, caravanning, the countryside. *Address:* St John Ambulance, London (Prince of Wales's) District, Edwina Mountbatten House, 63 York Street, W1H 1PS.

BIRCH, John Allan, CMG 1987; HM Diplomatic Service; Ambassador to Hungary, since 1989; *b* 24 May 1935; *s* of late C. Allan Birch, MD, FRCP; *m* 1960, Primula Haselden; three *s* one *d. Educ:* Leighton Park Sch.; Corpus Christi Coll., Cambridge (MA). Served HM Forces, Middlesex Regt, 1954–56. Joined HM Foreign Service, 1959; served: Paris, 1960–63; Singapore, 1963–64; Bucharest, 1965–68; Geneva, 1968–70; Kabul, 1973–76; Royal Coll. of Defence Studies, 1977; Comprehensive Test Ban Treaty Negotiations, Geneva, 1977–80; Counsellor, Budapest, 1980–83; Hd of East European Dept, FCO, 1983–86; Ambassador and Dep. Perm. Rep. to UN, NY, 1986–89. *Recreations:* tennis, ski-ing. *Address:* c/o Foreign and Commonwealth Office, SW1. *Club:* Athenæum.

BIRCH, John Anthony, MA, DMus; FRCM, FRCO(CHM), LRAM; Organist and Director of the Choir, Temple Church, since 1982; University Organist, University of Sussex, since 1967; Professor, Royal College of Music, since 1959; Organist: to the Royal Choral Society, since 1966; of the Royal Philharmonic Orchestra, since 1983; Curator-Organist, Royal Albert Hall, since 1984; *b* 9 July 1929; *s* of late Charles Aylmer Birch and Mabel (*née* Greenwood), Leek, Staffs; unmarried. *Educ:* Trent Coll.; Royal Coll. of Music (ARCM); Royal Coll. of Organists (Pitcher Scholar). Organist and Choirmaster, St Thomas's Church, Regent Street, London, 1950–53; Accompanist to St Michael's Singers, 1952–58; Organist and Choirmaster, All Saints Church, Margaret Street, London, 1953–58; Sub-Organist, HM Chapels Royal, 1957–58; Organist and Master of the Choristers, Chichester Cathedral, 1958–80. With the Cathedral Organists of Salisbury and Winchester re-established the Southern Cathedrals Festival, 1960; Musical Advr, Chichester Festival Theatre, 1962–80; Choirmaster, Bishop Otter Coll., Chichester, 1963–69. Rep. 1950–66, and Man. Dir, 1966–73, C. A. Birch Ltd, Staffs. Accompanist, Royal Choral Soc., 1965–70; Examr to Associated Bd, Royal Schs of Music, 1958–77; Vis. Lectr in Music, Univ. of Sussex, 1971–83. Special Comr, Royal Sch. of Church Music; Royal College of Organists: Mem. Council, 1964–; Pres., 1984–86. Fellow, Corp. of SS Mary and Nicolas (Woodard Schs), 1973–; Governor: Hurstpierpoint Coll., 1974–; St Catherine's, Bramley, 1981–89. Has made concert appearances in France, Belgium, Germany, Switzerland, Netherlands, Spain, Portugal, Scandinavia and Far East; recital tours: Canada and US, 1966 and 1967, Australia and NZ, 1969, S Africa, 1978. DMus Lambeth, 1989; Hon. MA Sussex, 1971. *Address:* 13 King's Bench Walk, Temple, EC4Y 7EN. *T:* 071–353 5115; Fielding House, 14 The Close, Salisbury, Wilts SP1 2EB. *T:* Salisbury (0722) 412458. *Clubs:* Garrick; New (Edinburgh).

BIRCH, Peter Gibbs; Group Chief Executive, Abbey National plc (formerly Abbey National Building Society), since 1988 (Chief Executive, 1984–88); *b* 4 Dec. 1937; *m* 1962, Gillian (*née* Benge); three *s* one *d. Educ:* Allhallows Sch., Devon. Royal West Kent Regt, 1957–58 (2nd Lieut). Nestlé Co., 1958–65; Sales Manager, Gillette, 1965; Gen. Sales Manager, Gillette Australia, 1969; Man. Dir, Gillette, NZ, 1971; Gen. Manager, Gillette, SE Asia, 1973; Gp Gen. Manager, Gillette, Africa, ME, Eastern Europe, 1975; Man. Dir, Gillette UK, 1981. Director: Abbey National (formerly Abbey Nat. Building Soc.), 1984–; Hoskyns Gp, 1988–; Argos, 1990–. Chm., Council of Mortgage Lenders, 1991–. FCBSI. Pres., Middlesex Assoc. of Boys' Clubs, 1988–. *Recreations:* active holidays, swimming. *Address:* Abbey House, Baker Street, NW1 6XL.

BIRCH, Philip Thomas; Director, Piccadilly Radio, since 1973 (Founding Managing Director, 1973–83); *b* 23 April 1927; *s* of Thomas Stephen Birch and Ivy May Birch (*née* Bunyard); *m* 1979, Shiona Nelson Hawkins; four *s* one *d.* Commnd Queen's Own Royal W Kent Regt, BAOR, 1945–47. Space Buyer, Notley Advertising, 1948–49; Media and Account Dir, J. Walter Thompson Co., 1950–64; Founding Man. Dir, Radio London, 1964–68; Head of Broadcasting, Associated Newspapers Gp, 1969–73. Founding Chairman: Associated Indep. Radio Services, 1973–81; AIRC Pension Trust, 1974–83; Chm., Assoc. of Indep. Radio Contractors Ltd, 1976; Founding Chm., Indep. Radio Sales, 1981–86; Director: Associated Indep. Radio Gp, 1973–83; Indep. Radio News, 1983. *Recreations:* aviation, sailing, travel. *Address:* Piccadilly Radio, Piccadilly Plaza, Manchester M1 4AW. *T:* 061–236 9913. *Club:* St James (Manchester).

BIRCH, Reginald; Chairman, Communist Party of Britain (Marxist Leninist), since 1968; Member, General Council of the TUC, 1975–79; Member, Executive Council, AUEW, 1966–79; *b* 7 June 1914; *s* of Charles and Anne Birch; *m* 1942, Dorothy; three *s. Educ:* St Augustine's Elementary Sch., Kilburn. Apprentice toolmaker, 1929; at trade (toolmaker), until 1960. Divisional Organiser, AEU, 1960–66. Mem., Energy Commn, 1977–79. *Recreations:* swimming, growing herbs. *Address:* 29 Langley Park, NW7. *T:* 081–959 7058.

BIRCH, Robert Edward Thomas, CBE 1979; Director General, Federation Against Copyright Theft, 1982–85; *b* 9 May 1917; *s* of late Robert Birch and Edith Birch; *m* 1946, Laura Pia Busini; two *d. Educ:* Dulwich Coll. Served RA, 1940–46; Africa, Italy, NW Europe; Major. Admitted solicitor, 1942; joined Solicitors' Dept, New Scotland Yard, 1946; Dep. Solicitor, 1968; Solicitor, 1976–82. *Recreations:* swimming, travel.

BIRCH, Robin Arthur; Deputy Secretary (Policy), Department of Social Security, since 1990; *b* 12 Oct. 1939; *s* of Arthur and Olive Birch; *m* 1962, Jane Marion Irvine Sturdy; two *s. Educ:* King Henry VIII Sch., Coventry; Christ Church, Oxford (Marjoribanks Scholar, 1957; Craven Scholar, 1959; MA). Entered Min. of Health as Asst Principal, 1961; Private Sec. to Charles Loughlin, MP (Parly Sec.), 1965–66; Principal, 1966; seconded to: Interdeptl Social Work Gp, 1969–70; Home Office (Community Develt Project), 1970–72; Asst Sec., DHSS, 1973; Chm., Working Party on Manpower and Trng for Social Services, 1974–76 (Report, 1976); Principal Private Sec. to Rt Hon. Norman St John-Stevas, MP (Leader of the House of Commons), 1980–81; Under Sec., DHSS, 1982; Asst Auditor Gen., Nat. Audit Office, 1984–86, on secondment; Dir, Regl Orgn, Dept of Social Security, 1988–90. Hon. Sec., Friends of Christ Church Cathedral, Oxford, 1978–. *Recreations:* family and friends; travel by train and bicycle; music, mainly before 1809; byways of classical antiquity; model railway. *Address:* Department of Social Security, Richmond House, 79 Whitehall, SW1A 2NS.

BIRCH, Roger, CBE 1987; QPM 1980; CBIM; Chief Constable, Sussex Police, since 1983; *b* 27 Sept. 1930; *s* of John Edward Lawrence Birch and Ruby Birch; *m* 1954, Jeanne

Margaret Head; one *s*. *Educ:* King's Coll., Taunton. Cadet, Royal Naval Coll., Dartmouth, 1949–50; Pilot Officer, RAF, 1950–52. Devon Constabulary, 1954–72: Constable, uniform and CID; then through ranks to Chief Supt; Asst Chief Constable, Mid-Anglia Constab., 1972–74; Dep. Chief Constable, Kent Constab., 1974–78; Chief Constable, Warwickshire Constab., 1978–83. Dir, Police Extended Interviews, 1983–91; Pres., Assoc. of Chief Police Officers, 1987–88 (Vice-Pres., 1986–87; Chm., Traffic Cttee, 1983–86; Chm., Internat. Affairs Adv. Cttee, 1988–); Vice Chm., Internat. Cttee, Internat. Assoc. of Chiefs of Police, 1989–; Trustee: Police Dependants' Trust, 1981–; Police Gurney Fund, 1983–. Mem., St John Ambulance Council, Sussex, 1986–. UK Vice-Pres., Royal Life Saving Soc., 1985– (Chm., SE Region, 1983–). Mem. Council, IAM, 1984–. Hon. LLD Sussex, 1991. *Publications:* articles on criminal intelligence, breath measuring instruments and on the urban environment, in learned jls. *Recreations:* swimming, music. *Address:* Police Headquarters, Malling House, Lewes, East Sussex BN7 2DZ. *T:* Lewes (0273) 475432. *Club:* Royal Air Force.

BIRCH, Prof. William; Visiting Professor of Geography and Education, University of Bristol, since 1990; *b* 24 Nov. 1925; *s* of Frederick Arthur and Maude Olive Birch; *m* 1950, Mary Vine Stammers; one *s* one *d*. *Educ:* Ranelagh Sch.; Univ. of Reading. BA 1949, PhD 1957. Royal Navy, 1943–46, Sub-Lt RNVR. Lectr, Univ. of Bristol, 1950–60; Prof. of Geography, Grad. Sch. of Geog., Clark Univ., Worcester, Mass, USA, 1960–63; Prof., and Chm. of Dept of Geog., Univ. of Toronto, Canada, 1963–67; Prof., and Head of Dept of Geog., Univ. of Leeds, 1967–75; Dir, Bristol Polytechnic, 1975–86. Vis. Prof., Inst. of Educn, London Univ., 1986–88. Pres., Inst. of British Geographers, 1976–77; Chm., Cttee of Directors of Polytechnics, 1982–84. Mem., ESRC, 1985–88. *Publications:* The Isle of Man: a study in economic geography, 1964; The Challenge to Higher Education: reconciling responsibilities to scholarship and society, 1988; contribs on higher educn policy and on geography and planning, Trans Inst. Brit. Geographers, Geog. Jl, Economic Geog., Annals Assoc. Amer. Geographers, Jl Environmental Management, Studies in Higher Educn, etc. *Recreations:* yachting, badminton, travel, gardening, pottery, building. *Address:* 3 Rodney Place, Clifton, Bristol BS8 4HY. *T:* Bristol (0272) 739719.

BIRCHALL, Prof. (James) Derek, OBE 1990; FRS 1982; FRSC; ICI Senior Research Associate, Mond Division, since 1975; *b* 7 Oct. 1930; *s* of David Birchall and Dora Mary Birchall; *m* 1956, Pauline Mary Jones (*d* 1990); two *s*. Joined ICI, 1957; Research Leader, 1965; Research Associate, 1970. Visiting Professor: Univ. of Surrey, 1976–88; MIT, 1984–86; Univ. of Durham, 1987–; Professor Associate: Brunel Univ., 1983–; Sheffield Univ., 1989–; Industrial Fellow, Wolfson Coll., Oxford, 1977–79. Mem., Individual Merit Panel, HM Treasury, 1988–89. Lectures: John D. Rose Meml, SCI, 1983; Mellor Meml, Inst. of Ceramics, 1984; Hurter Meml, SCI, Univ. of Liverpool, 1986; Sir Eric Rideal Meml, SCI, 1989. Ambrose Congreve Energy Award, 1983. *Publications:* A Classification of Fire Hazards, 1952, 2nd edn 1961; contribs to various encyclopedias and to learned jls, *ie* Nature, on inorganic chemistry and materials science. *Recreations:* old books, new cars. *Address:* Braeside, Stable Lane, Mouldsworth, Chester CH3 8AN. *T:* Manley (09284) 320.

BIRCHENOUGH, (John) Michael, BSc, PhD; Visiting Professor, School of Education, Open University, 1986–89; *b* 17 Jan. 1923; *s* of John Buckley Birchenough and Elsie Birchenough; *m* 1945, Enid Humphries; two *s*. *Educ:* Ashford Grammar Sch., Kent; Chiswick County Sch.; London Univ. Chemist, May & Baker Ltd, 1943–45; teaching posts, 1946–60; HM Inspector of Schools, 1960; Staff Inspector, 1966; Chief Inspector, 1968–72; Chief Inspector, ILEA, 1973–83; Res. Fellow, Sch. of Educn, Univ. of Bristol, 1983–86. Pres., Educn Section, BAAS Annual Meeting, Stirling, 1974. *Publications:* contribs to Jl of Chem. Soc. and other scientific jls. *Address:* 28 London Lane, Great Paxton, Huntingdon, Cambs PE19 4RH.

BIRD, Prof. Adrian Peter, PhD; FRS 1989; Buchanan Professor of Genetics, Edinburgh University, since 1990; *b* 3 July 1947; *s* of Kenneth George Bird and Aileen Mary Bird; *m* 1976 (separated); one *s* one *d*. *Educ:* Queen Elizabeth's Grammar School, Hartlebury; Univ. of Sussex (BSc(Hons)); Univ. of Edinburgh (PhD 1971). Damon Runyan Fellow, Yale, 1972–73; postdoctoral fellowship, Univ. of Zurich, 1974–75; Medical Research Council, Edinburgh: scientific staff, Mammalian Genome Unit, 1975–85, actg Dir, 1986–87; Hd of Structural Studies Sect., Clin. and Population Cytogenetics Unit, 1987; Sen. Scientist, Inst. for Molecular Pathol., Vienna, 1988–90. *Publications:* articles in Nature, Cell and other jls. *Recreations:* hill running, ball games, music, food. *Address:* Institute of Cell and Molecular Biology, University of Edinburgh, King's Buildings, Mayfield Road, Edinburgh EH9 3JR. *T:* 031–667 1081.

BIRD, Rev. Dr Anthony Peter; General Medical Practitioner, since 1979; Principal of The Queen's College, Edgbaston, Birmingham, 1974–79; *b* 2 March 1931; *s* of late Albert Harry Bird and Noel Whitehouse Bird; *m* 1962, Sabine Boehmig; two *s* one *d*. *Educ:* St John's Coll., Oxford (BA LitHum, BA Theol, MA); Birmingham Univ. (MB, ChB, 1970). Deacon, 1957; Priest, 1958; Curate of St Mary's, Stafford, 1957–60; Chaplain, then Vice-Principal of Cuddesdon Theological Coll., 1960–64. General Medical Practitioner, 1972–73. Member: Home Office Policy Adv. Cttee on Sexual Offences, 1976–80; Parole Board, 1977–80. Freedom of Information Campaign Award, 1986. *Publication:* The Search for Health: a response from the inner city, 1981. *Recreations:* water, walking, music—J. S. Bach, innovation in primary health care. *Address:* 93 Bournbrook Road, Birmingham B29 7BX.

BIRD, Ven. (Colin) Richard (Bateman); Archdeacon of Lambeth, since 1988; *b* 31 March 1933; *s* of Paul James Bird and Marjorie Bird (*née* Bateman); *m* 1963, Valerie Wroughton van der Bijl; one *s* two *d*. *Educ:* privately; County Technical Coll., Guildford; Selwyn Coll., Cambridge (MA); Cuddesdon Theol Coll. Curate: St Mark's Cathedral, George, S Africa, 1958–61; St Saviour's Claremont, Cape Town, 1961–64; Rector, Parish of Northern Suburbs, Pretoria, 1964–66; Rector, Tzaneen with Duiwelskloof and Phalaborwa, N Transvaal, 1966–70; Curate, Limpsfield, Surrey, 1970–75; Vicar of St Catherine, Hatcham, 1975–88; RD, Deptford, 1980–85; Hon. Canon of Southwark, 1982–88. *Recreations:* theatre and concert going, walking, bird-watching. *Address:* 7 Hoadly Road, Streatham, SW16 1AE. *T:* 081–769 4384; 5 Croft Terrace, Hastings, East Sussex TN34 3HG. *T:* Hastings (0424) 430432.

BIRD, James Gurth, MBE 1945; TD 1951; *b* 30 Jan. 1909; *s* of Charles Harold Bird and Alice Jane Bird (*née* Kirtland); *m* 1940, Phyllis Ellis Pownall; one *s* two *d*. *Educ:* King William's Coll., Isle of Man (Scholar); St Catharine's Coll., Cambridge (exhibnr). Classical Tripos Pts I and II, BA 1931, MA 1933. Asst Master, Rossall Sch., 1931–33; Asst Master and House Master, Denstone Coll., 1933–47 (interrupted by War Service); Head Master, William Hulme's Grammar Sch., Manchester, 1947–74. FRSA. *Recreations:* golf, gardening. *Address:* Ty Deryn, Ravenspoint Road, Trearddur Bay, Holyhead, Gwynedd LL65 2AX.

BIRD, John Alfred William; Member (Lab) Midlands West, European Parliament, since March 1987; *m* Gwen Davies; two *s*. Member: Wolverhampton BC, 1962–73; Wolverhampton Metropolitan BC, 1973–88 (Chm., Educn Cttee, 1972–80; Leader, 1973–87); W Midlands CC, 1973–81; Vice-Chm., W Midlands Police Cttee, 1973–77. Chm., W Midlands DCs, 1986–87; Vice-Pres., AMA, 1987– (Mem. Council, 1974–87); Member: W Midlands EDC, 1973–81; W Midlands Regl Econ. Forum, 1986–87; Pres., Norwest Midlands Br., Chartered Inst. of Marketing, 1990–91. European Parliament: Chm., British Lab Gp, 1989–; Mem., Ext. Econ. Relations Cttee. Mem., AEU, 1950– (Shop Steward, 1953–63). Hon. Fellow, Faculty of Sci. and Technol., Wolverhampton Poly. *Address:* (office) Rooms 2/3 Gresham Chambers, 14 Lichfield Street, Wolverhampton WV1 1DP.

BIRD, Michael Gwynne, CBE 1985; Chairman, Varity Holdings Ltd (formerly Massey-Ferguson Holdings Ltd), since 1980; *b* 16 Aug. 1921; *s* of Edward Gwynne Bird, Chaplain, RN, and Brenda Bird (*née* Rumney); *m* 1944, Frances Yvonne Townley; one *s* two *d*. *Educ:* Harrow Sch.; St Catharine's Coll., Cambridge. Served war: commnd, Rifle Bde, 1941; demobilised (Major), 1946. Colonial Service (Administration), Malawi, 1948–54; called to the Bar, Inner Temple, 1955; joined Massey-Ferguson, 1955; Director: Legal Services, Massey-Ferguson Ltd, 1977; Varity Corp. (formerly Massey-Ferguson Ltd), 1988– (Chm., European Cos, 1982–90). *Address:* Broad Oak, Clive Road, Esher, Surrey KT10 8PS. *T:* Esher (0372) 466241. *Clubs:* Oriental, MCC.

BIRD, Michael James; Chairman of Industrial Tribunal, Cardiff, since 1987; *b* 11 Nov. 1935; *s* of Walter Garfield and Ireen Bird; *m* 1963, Susan Harris; three *d*. *Educ:* Lewis Sch., Pengam; King's Coll., Univ. of London (LLB Hons). Solicitor (Hons) 1961. Assistant solicitor, 1961–62; Partner, T. S. Edwards & Son, 1962–67, Sen. Partner, 1967–84. Deputy Registrar of County and High Court, 1976–77; Chairman of Industrial Tribunal, Cardiff (part-time), 1977–83; Chm. of Industrial Tribunal, Bristol, 1984–87. Chm., Gwent Italian Soc., 1978–86 (Sec., 1976–78); Member: Royal Life Saving Soc., 1976– (President's Commendation, 1984); Amateur Swimming Assoc. (Advanced Teacher, 1981–). *Recreations:* water sports, opera. *Address:* 17 Allt-yr-yn Avenue, Newport, Gwent NP9 5DA. *T:* Newport (0633) 52000.

BIRD, Ven. Richard; *see* Bird, Ven. C. R. B.

BIRD, Richard; Under Secretary, Department of Transport, since 1990; *b* 12 Feb. 1950; *s* of Desmond and Betty Bird; *m* 1973, Penelope Anne Frudd; one *s* one *d*. *Educ:* King's Sch., Canterbury; Magdalen Coll., Oxford (BA 1972; MA 1975). Admin Trainee, DoE, 1971–73; Asst Private Sec. to Minister for Planning and Local Govt, 1974–75; Principal, Dept of Transport, 1975–78; First Sec., UK Rep. to EC, Brussels, 1978–82; Principal Private Sec. to Sec. of State for Transport, 1982–83; Asst Sec., Dept of Transport, 1983–90. Mem., Oxford Univ. Fencing Club, 1969–71 (represented Britain at World Youth Fencing Championship, 1970). *Recreations:* choral singing, summer sports. *Address:* Department of Transport, 2 Marsham Street, SW1P 3EB.

BIRD, Sir Richard Dawnay M.; *see* Martin-Bird.

BIRD, Sir Richard (Geoffrey Chapman), 4th Bt *cr* 1922; *b* 3 Nov. 1935; *er* surv. *s* of Sir Donald Bird, 3rd Bt, and of Anne Rowena (*d* 1969), *d* of late Charles Chapman; *S* father, 1963; *m* 1st, 1957, Gillian Frances (*d* 1966), *d* of Bernard Haggett, Solihull; two *s* four *d*; 2nd, 1968, Helen Patricia, *d* of Frank Beaumont, Pontefract; two *d*. *Educ:* Beaumont. *Heir:* *s* John Andrew Bird, *b* 19 Jan. 1964. *Address:* 39 Ashleigh Road, Solihull, W Midlands B91 1AF.

BIRD, Richard Herries, CB 1983; Deputy Secretary, Department of Education and Science, 1980–90; *b* 8 June 1932; *s* of late Edgar Bird and Armorel (*née* Dudley-Scott); *m* 1963, Valerie, *d* of Edward and Mary Sanderson; two *d*. *Educ:* Winchester Coll.; Clare Coll., Cambridge. Min. of Transport and Civil Aviation, 1955; Principal Private Sec. to Minister of Transport, 1966–67; CSD 1969; DoE 1971; DES 1973. *Address:* 53 Kippington Road, Sevenoaks, Kent TN13 2LL.

BIRD, Rt. Hon. Vere Cornwall, PC 1982; Prime Minister of Antigua and Barbuda, since 1981; *b* 7 Dec. 1910. *Educ:* St John's Boys' School, Antigua; Salvation Army Training School, Trinidad. Founder Mem. Exec., Antigua Trades and Labour Union, 1939 (Pres., 1943–67); Member: Antigua Legislative Council, 1945; Antigua Exec. Council, 1946 (Cttee Chm., 1951–56, land reform); Ministry of Trade and Production, 1956–60; first Chief Minister, 1960–67, first Premier, 1967–71; re-elected to Parlt, 1976, 1980; Leader, Antigua Labour Party. *Address:* Office of the Prime Minister, St John's, Antigua, West Indies.

BIRD-WILSON, Air Vice-Marshal Harold Arthur Cooper, CBE 1962; DSO 1945; DFC 1940 and Bar 1943; AFC 1946 and Bar 1955; *b* 20 Nov. 1919; *m* 1942, Audrey Wallace; one *s* one *d*. *Educ:* Liverpool Coll. Joined RAF, Nov. 1937; No 17 Fighter Sqdn, Kenley, 1938. Served War of 1939–45 (France, Dunkirk, Battle of Britain): Flt Comdr No 234 Sqdn, 1941; Sqdn Comdr Nos 152 and 66, 1942 (despatches); Wing Leader, No 83 Gp, 1943; Comd and Gen. Staff Sch., Fort Leavenworth, Kansas, USA, 1944; Wing Leader, Harrowbeer, Spitfire Wing and then Bentwater Mustang Wing, 1944–45; CO, Jet Conversion Unit, 1945–46; CO, Air Fighting Development Sqdn, CFE, 1946–47; Op. Staff, HQ, MEAF, 1948; RAF Staff Coll., Bracknell, 1949; Personal Staff Officer to C-in-C, MEAF, 1949–50; RAF Flying Coll., Manby, 1951; OC Tactics, later CO AFDS, CFE, 1952–54; Staff, BJSM, Washington, USA, 1954–57; Staff, Air Sec. Dept., Air Min., 1957–59; CO, RAF Coltishall, 1959–61; Staff Intell., Air Min., 1961–63; AOC and Comdt, CFS, 1963–65; AOC Hong Kong, 1965–67; Dir of Flying (Research and Develt), Min. of Technology, 1967–70; AOC No 23 Gp, 1970–73; Comdr, S Maritime Air Region, RAF, 1973–74, retired. BAC, Saudi Arabia, then British Aerospace, 1974–84, retired. Czechoslovak Medal of Merit 1st class, 1945; Dutch DFC, 1945.

BIRDSALL, Derek Walter, RDI; AGI; FCSD; freelance graphic designer; *b* 1 Aug. 1934; *s* of Frederick Birdsall and Hilda Birdsall (*née* Smith); *m* 1954, Shirley Thompson; three *s* one *d*. *Educ:* King's Sch., Pontefract, Yorks; Wakefield Coll. of Art, Yorks; Central Sch. of Arts and Crafts, London (NDD). National Service, RAOC Printing Unit, Cyprus, 1955–57. Lectr in Typographical Design, London Coll. of Printing, 1959–61; freelance graphic designer, working from his studio in Covent Garden, later Islington, 1961–; Founding Partner, Omnific Studios Partnership, 1983. Vis. Prof. of Graphic Art and Design, RCA, 1987–88. Consultant designer, The Independent Magazine, 1989–. Has broadcast on TV and radio on design subjects and his work; catalogue designs for major museums in UK and USA have won many awards, incl. Gold Medal, New York Art Directors' Club, 1987. Mem., AGI, 1968–; FCSD (FSIAD 1964); RDI 1982; FRSA. *Publications:* (with C. H. O'D. Alexander) Fischer *v* Spassky, 1972; (with C. H. O'D. Alexander) A Book of Chess, 1974; (with Carlo M. Cippola) The Technology of Man—a visual history, 1978. *Recreations:* chess, poker. *Address:* 9 Compton Avenue, Islington, N1 2XD. *T:* 071–359 1201. *Club:* Chelsea Arts.

BIRDSALL, Mrs Doris, CBE 1985; Lord Mayor of Bradford Metropolitan District, 1975–76; *b* 20 July 1915; *d* of Fred and Violet Ratcliffe; *m* 1940, James Birdsall; one *s* one *d*. *Educ:* Hanson Girls' Grammar School. Mem. Bradford City Council, 1958, Chm. of Educn Cttee, 1972–74; Mem. Bradford Univ. Council, 1963–. Hon. MA Bradford, 1975; Hon. LHD Lesley Coll., Mass, 1976. *Address:* 24 Baildon Road, Baildon, Bradford, West Yorks. *T:* Bradford (0274) 596251.

BIRDWOOD, family name of **Baron Birdwood.**

BIRDWOOD, 3rd Baron *cr* 1938, of Anzac and of Totnes; **Mark William Ogilvie Birdwood;** Bt 1919; Chairman, Martlet Ltd, since 1986; *b* 23 Nov. 1938; *s* of 2nd Baron Birdwood, MVO, and of Vere Lady Birdwood, CVO; *S* father, 1962; *m* 1963, Judith Helen, *e d* of late R. G. Seymour Roberts; one *d. Educ:* Radley Coll.; Trinity Coll., Cambridge. Commnd RHG. Director: Wrightson Wood Ltd, 1979–86; Du Pont Pixel Systems (formerly Benchmark Technology); Comac, 1988–; Scientific Generics, 1989–. Liveryman, Glaziers' Co. *Address:* 5 Holbein Mews, SW1W 8NW; Russell House, Broadway, Worcs WR12 7BU. *Club:* Brooks's.

See also Earl of Woolton.

BIRK, family name of **Baroness Birk.**

BIRK, Baroness *cr* 1967 (Life Peer), of Regent's Park in Greater London; **Alma Birk,** JP; journalist; *d* of late Barnett and Alice Wilson; *m* Ellis Birk; one *s* one *d. Educ:* South Hampstead High Sch.; LSE. BSc Econ (Hons) London. Leader of Labour Group, Finchley Borough Council, 1950–53; contested (Lab): Ruislip-Northwood, 1950; Portsmouth West, 1951, 1955. Baroness in Waiting (Govt Whip), March-Oct. 1974; Parly Under-Sec. of State, DoE, 1974–79; Minister of State, Privy Council Office, 1979; Opposition frontbench spokesman H of L on arts, libraries, heritage and broadcasting, 1990–. Associate Editor, Nova, 1965–69. Dir, New Shakespeare Co. Ltd, 1979–. Formerly Lectr and Prison Visitor, Holloway Prison. Mem., Youth Service Develt Council, 1967–71; Chm., Health Educn Council, 1969–72; President: Assoc. of Art Instns, 1984–; Craft Arts Design Assoc., 1984–; Vice-President: AMA, 1982–; Council for Children's Welfare, 1968–75; H. G. Wells Soc., 1967–; Stamford Hill Associated Clubs, 1967–70; Redbridge Jewish Youth Centre, 1970–; Playboard, 1984–; Member: Fabian Soc., 1946– (Sec., Fabian Soc. Res. Cttee on Marriage and Divorce, 1951–52); Howard League for Penal Reform, 1948– (Exec., 1980–); Hendon Group Hosp. Management Cttee, 1951–59; Panel, London Pregnancy Adv. Service, 1968–; RCOG working party on the unplanned pregnancy, 1969–72; Exec., Council of Christians and Jews, 1971–77; Hon. Cttee, Albany Trust; Ct of Governors, LSE, 1971–; Council, British Museum Soc., 1979–; Council, RSA, 1981–87; Adv. Cttee on Service Candidates, 1984–; All-party Penal Affairs Gp, 1983–; Council, Georgian Gp, 1985–; Chm. Arts Sub-Cttee, Holocaust Meml Cttee, 1979–. Trustee: Yorkshire Sculpture Park, 1980–; Health Promotion Res. Trust, 1983–; Stress Syndrome Foundn, 1983–; Governor: BFI, 1981–87; Mander Mitchenson Theatre Collection, 1981–. FRSA 1980. JP Highgate, 1952. *Publications:* pamphlets, articles. *Recreations:* travelling, theatre, reading, talking. *Address:* 3 Wells Rise, NW8 7LH.

BIRKENHEAD, Bishop Suffragan of, since 1974; **Rt. Rev. Ronald Brown;** *b* 7 Aug. 1926; *s* of Fred and Ellen Brown; *m* 1951, Joyce Hymers (*d* 1987); one *s* one *d. Educ:* Kirkham Grammar Sch.; Durham Univ. (BA, DipTh). Vicar of Whittle-le-Woods, 1956; Vicar of St Thomas, Halliwell, Bolton, 1961; Rector and Rural Dean of Ashton-under-Lyne, 1970. *Recreations:* antiques and golf. *Address:* Trafford House, Queen's Park, Chester CH4 7AX. *T:* Chester (0244) 675895.

BIRKETT, family name of **Baron Birkett.**

BIRKETT, 2nd Baron *cr* 1958, of Ulverston; **Michael Birkett;** President, School for Performing Arts and Technology, British Record Industry Trust, since 1990; *b* 22 Oct. 1929; *s* of 1st Baron Birkett, PC and Ruth Birkett (*née* Nilsson, she *d* 1969); *S* father, 1962; *m* 1st, 1960, Junia Crawford (*d* 1973); 2nd, 1978, Gloria Taylor; one *s. Educ:* Stowe; Trinity Coll., Cambridge. Asst Dir at Ealing Studios and Ealing Films, 1953–59; Asst Dir, 1959–61, on films including: The Mark; The Innocents; Billy Budd; Associate Producer: Some People, 1961–62; Modesty Blaise, 1965; Producer: The Caretaker, 1962; Marat/Sade, 1966; A Midsummer Night's Dream, 1967; King Lear, 1968–69; Director: The Launching and The Soldier's Tale, 1963; Overture and Beginners, the More Man Understands, 1964; Outward Bound, 1971. Dep. Dir, National Theatre, 1975–77; Consultant to Nat. Theatre on films, TV and sponsorship, 1977–79; Dir for Recreation and Arts, GLC, 1979–86; Adviser to South Bank Bd, 1986–89; Exec. Dir, Royal Philharmonic Soc., 1989–90; Dir, Olympic Festival 1990, Manchester, 1990. A Vice-Pres., British Board of Film Classification, 1985–. Chairman: Children's Film & TV Foundn, 1981–; Theatres Adv. Council, 1986–. Master, Curriers' Co., 1975–76. *Recreations:* music, printing, horticulture. *Heir: s* Hon. Thomas Birkett, *b* 25 July 1982. *Address:* House of Lords, SW1.

BIRKETT, Peter Vidler; QC 1989; a Recorder, since 1989; *b* 13 July 1948; *s* of Neville Lawn Birkett, MA, MB BCh, FRES and Marjorie Joy Birkett; *m* 1976, Jane Elizabeth Fell; two *s. Educ:* Sedbergh School; Univ. of Leicester. Called to the Bar, Inner Temple, 1972; practice on SE Circuit, 1973–77, on N Circuit, 1977–. Asst Recorder, 1986–89. *Recreations:* golf, ski-ing, conversation, playing the piano. *Address:* 18 St John Street, Manchester M3 4EA. *T:* 061–834 9843. *Club:* Wilmslow Golf.

BIRKIN, Sir Derek; *see* Birkin, Sir J. D.

BIRKIN, Sir John (Christian William), 6th Bt *cr* 1905, of Ruddington Grange, Notts; Director, Compound Eye Productions, since 1987; *b* 2 July 1953; *s* of Sir Charles Lloyd Birkin, 5th Bt and Janet (*d* 1983), *d* of Peter Johnson; *S* father, 1985. *Educ:* Eton; Trinity Coll., Dublin; London Film School. *Heir: cousin* James Francis Richard Birkin, *b* 27 Feb. 1957. *Address:* 23 St Luke's Street, Chelsea, SW3 3RP. *T:* 071–351 4810.

BIRKIN, Sir (John) Derek, Kt 1990; TD 1965; Chairman, The RTZ Corporation PLC (formerly Rio Tinto-Zinc Corporation), since 1991 (Chief Executive and Deputy Chairman, 1985–91); *b* 30 Sept 1929; *s* of Noah and Rebecca Birkin; *m* 1952, Sadie Smith; one *s* one *d. Educ:* Hemsworth Grammar Sch. Managing Director: Velmar Ltd, 1966–67; Nairn Williamson Ltd, 1967–70; Dep. Chm. and Man. Dir, Tunnel Holdings Ltd, 1970–75; Chm. and Man. Dir, Tunnel Holdings, 1975–82; Dir, The RTZ Corporation (formerly Rio Tinto-Zinc Corp.), 1982–, Dep. Chief Exec., 1983–85. Director: Smiths Industries, 1977–84; British Gas Corp., 1982–85; George Wimpey, 1984–; CRA Ltd (Australia), 1985–; Rio Algom Ltd (Canada), 1985–; The Merchants Trust PLC, 1986–; British Steel plc (formerly BSC), 1986–; Barclays PLC, 1990–. Member: Review Body on Top Salaries, 1986–89; Council, Industrial Soc., 1985–. Trustee, Royal Opera House, 1990–. CBIM 1980; FRSA 1988. *Recreations:* opera, Rugby, cricket. *Address:* (office) 6 St James's Square, SW1Y 4LD.

BIRKINSHAW, Prof. John Howard, DSc; FRSC; retired as Professor of Biochemistry and Head of Department of Biochemistry, London School of Hygiene and Tropical Medicine, University of London (1956–62), now Emeritus; *b* 8 Oct. 1894; *s* of John Thomas and Madeline Birkinshaw, Garforth, near Leeds; *m* 1929, Elizabeth Goodwin Guthrie, Ardrossan, Ayrshire; one *s* one *d. Educ:* Leeds Modern Sch.; Leeds Univ. War service, 1915, West Yorks Regt and Machine Gun Corps (POW); demobilised, 1919. BSc Hons 1920, MSc 1921, DSc 1929, Leeds. Research Biochemist to Nobel's Explosives Co. (later ICI), 1920–30; Research Asst to Prof. Raistrick, London Sch. of Hygiene and Tropical Medicine, 1931; Senior Lecturer, 1938; Reader, 1945. *Publications:* about 60 scientific papers in Biochemical Journal, Philos. Trans. Royal Society, etc. *Recreation:* photography. *Address:* 87 Barrow Point Avenue, Pinner, Mddx HA5 3HE. *T:* 081–866 4784.

BIRKMYRE, Sir Henry, 2nd Bt *cr* 1921, of Dalmunzie; *b* 24 March 1898; *er s* of Sir Archibald Birkmyre, 1st Bt and Anne, *e d* of Capt. James Black; *S* father, 1935; *m* 1922, Doris Gertrude, *er d* of late Col H. Austen Smith, CIE; one *s* one *d. Educ:* Wellington. War Service in France with RFA, 1917. *Heir: s* Archibald Birkmyre [*b* 12 Feb. 1923; *m* 1953, Gillian Mary, *o d* of Eric Downes, OBE; one *s* two *d*]. *Recreation:* golf. *Address:* Tudor Rest, 2 Calverley Park Garden, Tunbridge Wells TN1 2DE.

See also Baron De Ramsey.

BIRKS, Dr Jack, CBE 1975; FEng 1978; Chairman: British Maritime Technology, since 1985; North American Gas Investment Trust plc, since 1989; *b* 1 Jan. 1920; *s* of late Herbert Horace Birks and of Ann Birks; *m* 1948, Vere Elizabeth Burrell-Davis; two *s* two *d. Educ:* Ecclesfield Grammar Sch.; Univ. of Leeds (BSc, PhD). Served with REME, Europe and India, 1941–46 (despatches, Captain). Exploration Research Div., Anglo Iranian Oil Co., 1948–57; Man., Petroleum Engrg Research, BP Research Centre, Sunbury, 1957–59; Vice-Pres. Exploration, BP North America, NY, 1959–62; various techn. and managerial appts, subseq. Dir and Gen. Man., Iranian Oil Exploration & Producing Co., Teheran and Masjid-i-Sulaiman, 1962–70; Gen. Man., Exploration and Production Dept, British Petroleum Co. Ltd, London, 1970–72; Technical Dir, BP Trading Ltd, and Dep. Chm., BP Trading Exec. Cttee, 1972–77; a Man. Dir, British Petroleum, 1978–82; Chairman: BP Coal, 1981–82; Selection Trust, 1981–82; BP Minerals International, 1981–82; NMI Ltd, 1982–85; Charterhouse Petroleum, 1982–86; Schroder Energy, subseq. LAE Energy Inc., 1981–88; London American Energy NV, 1986–88 (Dir, 1981–88); Mountain Petroleum, 1988–90 (Dir, 1986–90); Director: Jebsens Drilling, subseq. Midland and Scottish Resources, 1982–; George Wimpey, 1982–90; Petrofina (UK), 1986–89; Bellwether Exploration Co., 1988–. Member: SRC, 1976–80; Meteorological Cttee, 1977–82; Adv. Council on R&D, Dept of Energy, 1978–82; Offshore Energy Technology Bd, Dept of Energy, 1978–82. Mem. Council, Royal Instn of GB, 1988–. President: Soc. for Underwater Technology, 1974; Pipeline Industries Guild, 1979–81; Inst. of Petroleum, 1984–86. Hon. FIMechE 1987. Hon. LLD Aberdeen, 1981; DU Surrey, 1981. *Publications:* contribs to technical internat. oil jls, sci. papers on oilfields develts and North Sea oil. *Recreations:* tennis, cricket, golf. *Address:* 1A Alwyne Road, Canonbury, N1 2HH. *T:* 071–226 4905; High Silver, High Street, Holt, Norfolk NR25 6BN. *T:* Holt (0263) 712847. *Clubs:* Athenæum; Norfolk (Norwich).

BIRKS, Michael; His Honour Judge Birks; a Circuit Judge, since 1983; *b* 21 May 1920; *s* of late Falconer Moffat Birks, CBE, and Monica Katherine Lushington (*née* Mellor); *m* 1947, Ann Ethne, *d* of Captain Henry Stafford Morgan; one *d. Educ:* Oundle; Trinity Coll., Cambridge. Commissioned 22nd Dragoons, 1941; attached Indian Army, 1942, invalided out, 1943. Admitted Solicitor, 1946; Assistant Registrar: Chancery Div., High Court, 1953–60; Newcastle upon Tyne group of County Courts, 1960–61; Registrar: Birkenhead gp of County Courts, 1961–66; W London County Court, 1966–83; a Recorder of the Crown Court, 1979–83. Adv. Editor, Atkins Court Forms, 1966–; Jt Editor, County Court Practice, 1976–83. Mem. County Court Rule Cttee, 1980–83. *Publications:* Gentlemen of the Law, 1960; Small Claims in the County Court, 1973; Enforcing Money Judgments in the County Court, 1980; contributed titles: County Courts and Interpleader (part), 4th edn Halsbury's Laws of England; Judgments and Orders (part), References and Inquiries (part), Service (part), and Transfer (part), County Courts Atkins Court Forms; contribs to legal jls. *Recreation:* sailing. *Address:* c/o South Eastern Circuit Office, New Cavendish House, 18 Maltravers Street, WC2R 3EU.

BIRKS, Prof. Peter Brian Herrenden, FBA 1989; Regius Professor of Civil Law, University of Oxford, and Fellow of All Souls College, Oxford, since 1989; *b* 3 Oct. 1941; *e s* of Dr Peter Herrenden Birks and Mary (*née* Morgan); *m* 1984, Jacqueline S. Berrington (*née* Stimpson). *Educ:* Trinity Coll., Oxford (MA); University Coll., London (LLM). DCL Oxon; LLD Edin., 1991. Lectr in Laws, UCL, 1966–71; Law Fellow, Brasenose Coll., Oxford, 1971–81; Prof. of Civil Law, and Head of Dept of Civil Law, Edinburgh Univ., 1981–87; Prof. of Law, Southampton Univ., 1988–89. Hon. Sec., SPTL, 1989– (Mem. Council, 1988–); Member: Lord Chancellor's Adv. Cttee on Legal Educn, 1989–; Social Sciences Cttee, Schs Exams and Assessment Council, 1989– (Chm., Law Cttee, 1988–89). *Publications:* Introduction to the Law of Restitution, 1985; (ed with D. N. MacCormick) The Legal Mind, 1986; (with G. McLeod) The Institutes of Justinian, 1987; (ed) New Perspectives on the Roman Law of Property, 1989; articles on Roman law, legal history and restitution. *Address:* 8 Cobden Crescent, Oxford OX1 4LJ. *T:* Oxford (0865) 727170; All Souls College, Oxford OX1 4AL. *T:* Oxford (0865) 279338, *Fax:* Oxford (0865) 279299. *Club:* Athenæum.

BIRLEY, Anthony Addison, CB 1979; Clerk of Public Bills, House of Commons, 1973–82, retired; *b* 28 Nov. 1920; *s* of Charles Fair Birley and Eileen Mia Rouse; *m* 1951, Jane Mary Ruggles-Brise; two *d. Educ:* Winchester (exhibnr); Christ Church, Oxford (MA). Served War in RA (Ayrshire Yeomanry), 1940–45, in North Africa and Italian campaigns (wounded). Asst Clerk, House of Commons, 1948; Clerk of Standing Cttees, 1970. *Recreations:* gardening, walking, racing. *Address:* Holtom House, Paxford, Chipping Campden, Glos. GL55 6XH. *T:* Paxford (038678) 318. *Club:* Army and Navy.

BIRLEY, Sir Derek, Kt 1989; Vice-Chancellor, University of Ulster, 1984–91; *b* 31 May 1926; *s* of late Sydney John and late Margaret Birley; *m* 1990, Prof. Norma Reid. *Educ:* Hemsworth Grammar Sch.; Queens' Coll., Cambridge; Manchester Univ. BA 1950, MA 1954, Cantab. Royal Artillery, 1944–48; Schoolmaster, Queen Elizabeth Grammar Sch., Wakefield, 1952–55; Admin. Asst, Leeds Educn Cttee, 1955–59; Asst Educn Officer: Dorset, 1959–61; Lancs, 1961–64; Dep. Dir of Educn, Liverpool, 1964–70; Rector, Ulster Polytechnic, 1970–84. *Publications:* The Education Officer and his World, 1970; (with Anne Dufton) An Equal Chance, 1971; Planning and Education, 1972; The Willow Wand, 1979. *Recreations:* books, cricket, jazz. *Address:* Ferndown, Wall Hill Road, Coventry CV7 8AD.

BIRLEY, Prof. Eric, MBE 1943; FSA 1931; FBA 1969; Professor of Roman-British History and Archæology, University of Durham, 1956–71, now Professor Emeritus; *b* 12 Jan. 1906; *y s* of J. Harold Birley; *m* 1934, Margaret Isabel, *d* of Rev. James Goodlet; two *s. Educ:* Clifton Coll.; Brasenose Coll., Oxford (Hon. Fellow, 1987). Lecturer, University of Durham, 1931; Reader, 1943. War of 1939–45: Military Intelligence, Lt-Col, GSO1 Military Intelligence Research Section; Chief of German Military Document Section, War Dept. Vice-Master, Hatfield Coll., Durham, 1947–49, Master, 1949–56; first Dean of Faculty of Social Sciences, Univ. of Durham, 1968–70. President: Soc. of Antiquaries of Newcastle upon Tyne, 1957–59; Cumberland and Westmorland Antiquarian and Archaeological Soc., 1957–60; Architectural and Archæological Soc. of Durham and Northumberland, 1959–63; Member: German Archæological Inst.; Ancient Monuments Board for England, 1966–76; Hon. Member, Gesellschaft Pro Vindonissa (Switzerland); Hon. FSAScot, 1980; Chm., Vindolanda Trust, 1970–; Hon. Life Pres., Internat. Congress of Roman Frontier Studies, 1974. Hon. Dr Phil Freiburg i Br, 1970; Hon. DLitt Leicester, 1971; Dr *hc* Heidelberg, 1986. Polonia Restituta, 1944; Legion of Merit, 1947. *Publications:*

The Centenary Pilgrimage of Hadrian's Wall, 1949; Roman Britain and the Roman Army, 1953; (ed) The Congress of Roman Frontier Studies 1949, 1952; Research on Hadrian's Wall, 1961; (jt ed) Roman Frontier Studies 1969, 1974; Fifty-one Ballades, 1980; The Roman Army: papers 1929–1986, 1988; numerous papers on Roman Britain and on the Roman army, excavation reports, etc. *Recreation:* archæology. *Address:* Carvoran House, Greenhead, Carlisle CA6 7JB. *T:* Gilsland (06977) 47594.

BIRLEY, James Leatham Tennant, CBE 1990; FRCP, FRCPsych, DPM; Consultant Psychiatrist, Bethlem Royal and Maudsley Hospitals, 1969–90, Emeritus Psychiatrist, 1990; President, Royal College of Psychiatrists, 1987–90; *b* 31 May 1928; *s* of late Dr James Leatham Birley and Margaret Edith (*née* Tennant); *m* 1954, Julia Davies; one *s* three *d. Educ:* Winchester Coll.; University Coll., Oxford; St Thomas' Hosp., London. Maudsley Hospital: Registrar, 1960; Sen. Registrar, 1963; Mem. Scientific Staff, MRC Social Psychiatry Research Unit, 1965; Dean, Inst. of Psychiatry, 1971–82. Dean, RCPsych, 1982–87. *Publications:* contribs to scientific jls. *Recreations:* music, gardening. *Address:* 133 Sydenham Hill, SE26 6LW.

BIRLEY, Michael Pellew, MA (Oxon); Housemaster, 1970–80, Assistant Master, 1980–84, Marlborough College; *b* 7 Nov. 1920; *s* of late Norman Pellew Birley, DSO, MC, and of Eileen Alice Morgan; *m* 1949, Ann Grover (*née* Street); two *s* two *d. Educ:* Marlborough Coll.; Wadham Coll., Oxford. 1st class Classical Honour Moderations, 1940; 1st class *Litterae Humaniores,* 1947; MA 1946. Served War of 1939–45 with the Royal Fusiliers; joined up, Sept. 1940; commissioned, April 1941; abroad, 1942–45 (despatches); demobilised, Jan. 1946. Taught Classics: Shrewsbury Sch., 1948–50; Eton Coll., 1950–56; Headmaster, Eastbourne College, 1956–70. Member Council: Ardingly Coll., 1981–90; Marlborough Coll., 1985–89. Fellow, Woodard Corp., 1983–90. *Recreations:* sailing, gardening, wine-making. *Address:* Long Summers, Cross Lane, Marlborough, Wilts SN8 1LA. *T:* Marlborough (0672) 512830.

BIRLEY, Prof. Susan Joyce, (Mrs David Norburn); Professor of Management, The Management School, Imperial College, since 1990; *m* 1st, 1964, Arwyn Hopkins (marr. diss. 1970); 2nd, 1975, Prof. David Norburn, *qv. Educ:* Nelson Grammar Sch.; University College London (BSc 1964); PhD London 1974. FSS. Teacher, Dunsmore Sch., 1964–66; Lectr, Lanchester Polytechnic, 1966–68; Lectr and Sen. Lectr, Poly. of Central London, 1968–72; Sen. Res. Fellow, City Univ., 1972–74; London Business School: Sen. Res. Fellow, 1974–79; Lectr in Small Business, 1979–82; University of Notre Dame, USA: Adjunct Associate Prof., 1978–82; Associate Prof. of Strategy and Entrepreneurship, 1982–85; Philip and Pauline Harris Prof. of Entrepreneurship, Cranfield Inst. of Technol., 1985–90. Academic Dir, European Foundn for Entrepreneurship Res., 1988–. Member: CNAA, 1987–90; NI Economic Council, 1988–; PCFC, 1988–; Adv. Panel on Deregulation, DTI, 1989–. Founder Director and Shareholder: Guidehouse Group, 1980–85; Greyfriars Ltd, 1982–85; Newchurch & Co., 1986– (Chm.). Governor, Harris City Technol. Coll., 1990. Freeman, City of London, 1964. Mem. Editl Bds, various business jls. *Publications:* From Private to Public (jtly), 1977; The Small Business Casebook, 1979; The Small Business Casebook: teaching manual, 1980; New Enterprises, 1982; (contrib.) Small Business and Entrepreneurship, ed Burns and Dewhurst, 1989; (jtly) Exit Routes, 1989; (jtly) The British Entrepreneur, 1989; (ed) European Entrepreneurship: emerging growth companies, 1989; (contrib.) The Future of Leadership: developing managers for the 1990s, ed Syrett, 1990; numerous contribs to learned jls. *Recreation:* gardening. *Address:* 10 Ripplevale Grove, N1 1HU. *T:* 071–607 1566.

BIRMINGHAM, Archbishop of, (RC), since 1982; **Most Rev. Maurice Noël Léon Couve de Murville;** *b* 27 June 1929; *s* of Noël Couve de Murville and Marie, *d* of Sir Louis Souchon. *Educ:* Downside School; Trinity Coll., Cambridge (MA); STL (Institut Catholique, Paris); MPhil (Sch. of Oriental and African Studies, Univ. of London). Priest, 1957; Curate, St Anselm's, Dartford, 1957–60; Priest-in-Charge, St Francis, Moulsecoomb, 1961–64; Catholic Chaplain: Univ. of Sussex, 1961–77; Univ. of Cambridge, 1977–82. *Publications:* (with Philip Jenkins) Catholic Cambridge, 1983; John Milner 1752–1826, 1986. *Recreations:* walking, gardening, local history. *Address:* 57 Mearse Lane, Barnt Green, Birmingham B45 8HJ. *T:* 021–445 1467.

BIRMINGHAM, Bishop of, since 1987; **Rt. Rev. Mark Santer,** MA; *b* 29 Dec. 1936; *s* of late Rev. Canon Eric Arthur Robert Santer and Phyllis Clare Barlow; *m* 1964, Henriette Cornelia Weststrate; one *s* two *d. Educ:* Marlborough Coll.; Queens' Coll., Cambridge; Westcott House, Cambridge. Deacon, 1963; priest 1964; Asst Curate, Cuddesdon, 1963–67; Tutor, Cuddesdon Theological Coll., 1963–67; Fellow and Dean of Clare Coll., Cambridge, 1967–72 (and Tutor, 1968–72; Hon. Fellow, 1987); Univ. Asst Lectr in Divinity, 1968–72; Principal of Westcott House, Cambridge, 1973–81; Hon. Canon of Winchester Cathedral, 1978–81; Area Bishop of Kensington, 1981–87. Co-Chm., Anglican Roman Catholic Internat. Commn, 1983–. *Publications:* (contrib.) The Phenomenon of Christian Belief, 1970; (with M. F. Wiles) Documents in Early Christian Thought, 1975; Their Lord and Ours, 1982; (contrib.) The Church and the State, 1984; (contrib.) Dropping the Bomb, 1985; articles in: Jl of Theological Studies; New Testament Studies; Theology. *Address:* Bishop's Croft, Old Church Road, Harborne, Birmingham B17 0BG. *T:* 021–427 1163.

BIRMINGHAM, Auxiliary Bishop of, (RC); *see* Pargeter, Rt. Rev. P.

BIRMINGHAM, Provost of; *see* Berry, Very Rev. P. A.

BIRMINGHAM, Archdeacon of; *see* Duncan, Ven. J. F.

BIRRELL, James Drake, FCA; FCBSI; Chief Executive, Halifax Building Society, since 1988; *b* 18 Aug. 1933; *s* of James Russell Birrell, MA and Edith Marion Birrell, BSc (*née* Drake); *m* 1958, Margaret Anne Pattison; two *d. Educ:* Belle Vue Grammar School, Bradford. FCA 1955; FCBSI 1989. Boyce Welch & Co. (articled clerk), 1949–55; Pilot Officer, RAF, 1955–57; chartered accountant, Price Waterhouse, 1957–60; Accountant, ADA Halifax, 1960–61; Management Accountant, Empire Stores, 1961–64; Dir and Co. Sec., John Gladstone & Co., 1964–68; Halifax Building Society, 1968–. *Recreations:* golf, gardening, archaeology, local history. *Address:* Kinnesswood, Greenroyd Avenue, Skircoat Green, Halifax HX3 0JN.

BIRT, John; Deputy Director-General, BBC, since 1987; *b* 10 Dec. 1944; *s* of Leo Vincent Birt and Ida Birt; *m* 1965, Jane Frances (*née* Lake); one *s* one *d. Educ:* St Mary's Coll., Liverpool; St Catherine's Coll., Oxford (MA). Producer, Nice Time, 1968–69; Joint Editor, World in Action, 1969–70; Producer, The Frost Programme, 1971–72; Executive Producer, Weekend World, 1972–74; Head of Current Affairs, LWT, 1974–77; Co-Producer, The Nixon Interviews, 1977; Controller of Features and Current Affairs, LWT, 1977–81; Dir of Programmes, LWT, 1982–87. Member: Wilton Park Academic Council, 1980–83; Media Law Gp, 1983–; Broadcasting Research Unit: Mem., Working Party on the new Technologies, 1981–83; Mem., Exec. Cttee, 1983–87. FRTS 1989. *Publications:* various articles in newspapers and journals. *Recreation:* walking. *Address:* c/o BBC, Broadcasting House, W1A 1AA.

BIRT, Prof. (Lindsay) Michael, AO 1986; CBE 1980; Vice-Chancellor, University of New South Wales, since 1981; *b* 18 Jan. 1932; *s* of Robert Birt and Florence Elizabeth Chapman; *m* 1959, Jenny Tapfield; two *s. Educ:* Melbourne Boys' High Sch.; Univ. of Melbourne; Univ. of Oxford. BAgrSc, BSc and PhD (Melb), DPhil (Oxon). Univ. of Melbourne: Lectr in Biochemistry, 1960–63, Sen. Lectr in Biochem., 1964; Sen. Lectr in Biochem., Univ. of Sheffield, 1964–67; Foundn Prof. of Biochemistry, ANU, 1967–73; Vice-Chancellor designate, Wollongong Univ. Coll., Nov. 1973; Vice-Chancellor, Univ. of Wollongong, 1975–81; Emer. Prof., ANU, 1974. Hon. DLitt Wollongong, 1981; Hon. LLD Sheffield, 1988. *Publication:* Biochemistry of the Tissues (with W. Bartley and P. Banks), 1968 (London), 1970 (Germany, as Biochemie), 1972 (Japan). *Recreations:* music, reading. *Address:* University of New South Wales, PO Box 1, Kensington, NSW 2033, Australia. *T:* (02) 697–2884; *Fax:* (02) 662–7471. *Clubs:* Union (Sydney); Melbourne Cricket, Sydney Cricket.

BIRT, Ven. Canon William Raymond; Archdeacon of Berkshire, 1973–77; Archdeacon Emeritus, since 1985; Hon. Canon of Christ Church Cathedral, Oxford, 1980; *b* 25 Aug. 1911; *s* of Rev. Douglas Birt, Rector of Leconfield with Scorborough, and Dorothy Birt; *m* 1936, Marie Louise Jeaffreson (*d* 1990); one *s* two *d. Educ:* Christ's Hospital; Ely Theological Coll. Journalist until 1940. Major, 22nd Dragoons (RAC), 1941–46 (despatches). Publisher, 1946–55. Deacon, 1956; priest, 1957; Curate, Caversham, 1956–59; Vicar, St George, Newbury, 1959–71; Rector of West Woodhay, 1971–81, Asst Rector, 1981–91; Rural Dean of Newbury, 1969–73. *Recreations:* gardens and gardening. *Address:* 1 The Old Bakery, George Street, Kingsclere, Newbury, Berkshire RG15 8NQ. *T:* Kingsclere (0635) 297426.

BIRTS, Peter William; QC 1990; a Recorder, since 1989; *b* 9 Feb. 1946; *s* of John Claude Birts and Audrey Lavinia Birts; *m* 1971, Penelope Ann Eyre; two *d* one *s. Educ:* Lancing College; St John's College, Cambridge (choral scholarship; MA). Called to the Bar, Gray's Inn, 1968; Mem., Gen. Council of the Bar, 1989. Freeman, City of London, 1967. *Publications:* Trespass: summary procedure for possession of land (with Alan Willis), 1987; Remedies for Trespass, 1990. *Recreations:* music, shooting. *Address:* Farrar's Building, Temple, EC4Y 7BD. *T:* 071–583 9241. *Club:* Hurlingham.

BIRTWISTLE, Maj.-Gen. Archibald Cull, CB 1983; CBE 1976 (OBE 1971); DL; Signal Officer in Chief (Army), 1980–83, retired; Master of Signals, since 1990; *b* 19 Aug. 1927; *s* of Walter Edwin Birtwistle and Eila Louise Cull; *m* 1956, Sylvia Elleray; two *s* one *d. Educ:* Sir John Deane's Grammar School, Northwich; St John's Coll., Cambridge (MA Mech. Sciences). CEng, MIEE. Commissioned, Royal Signals, 1949; served: Korea (despatches, 1952); UK; BAOR; CCR Sigs 1 (Br) Corps, 1973–75; Dep. Comdt, RMCS, 1975–79; Chief Signal Officer, BAOR, 1979–80. Col Comdt, Royal Corps of Signals, 1983–89, and 1990–; Hon. Colonel: Durham and South Tyne ACF, 1983–88; 34 (Northern) Signal Regt (Vol.), TA, 1988–90. DL N Yorks, 1991. *Recreations:* all sports, especially Rugby (former Chairman, Army Rugby Union), soccer and cricket; gardening. *Address:* c/o National Westminster Bank PLC, 97 High Street, Northallerton, North Yorks DL7 8PS.

BIRTWISTLE, Sir Harrison, Kt 1988; composer; an Associate Director, National Theatre, since 1975; *b* 1934; *m* Sheila; three *s. Educ:* Royal Manchester Coll. of Music; RAM. Dir of Music, Cranborne Chase Sch., 1962–65. Vis. Fellow, Princeton Univ., 1966–68; Cornell Vis. Prof. of Music, Swarthmore Coll., 1973; Vis. Slee Prof., State Univ. of NY at Buffalo, 1974–75. Evening Standard Award for Opera, 1987. *Publications:* Refrains and Choruses, 1957; Monody for Corpus Christi, 1959; Précis, 1959; The World is Discovered, 1960; Chorales, 1962, 1963; Entre'actes and Sappho Fragments, 1964; Three Movements with Fanfares, 1964; Tragoedia, 1965; Ring a Dumb Carillon, 1965; Carmen Paschale, 1965; The Mark of the Goat, 1965, 1966; The Visions of Francesco Petrarca, 1966; Verses, 1966; Punch and Judy, 1966–67 (opera); Three Lessons in a Frame, 1967; Linoii, 1968; Nomos, 1968; Verses for Ensembles, 1969; Down by the Greenwood Side, 1969; Hoquetus David (arr. of Machaut), 1969; Cantata, 1969; Ut Hermita Solvs, 1969; Medusa, 1969–70; Prologue, 1970; Nenia on the Death of Orpheus, 1970; An Imaginary Landscape, 1971; Meridian, 1971; The Fields of Sorrow, 1971; Chronometer, 1971; Epilogue—Full Fathom Five, 1972; Tombeau, 1972; The Triumph of Time, 1972; La Plage: eight arias of remembrance, 1972; Dinah and Nick's Love Song, 1972; Chanson de Geste, 1973; The World is Discovered, 1973; Grimethorpe Aria, 1973; 5 Chorale Preludes from Bach, 1973; Chorales from a Toyshop, 1973; Interludes from a Tragedy, 1973; The Mask of Orpheus, 1973–84 (opera) (Grawemeyer Award, Univ. of Louisville, 1987); Melencolia I, 1975; Pulse Field, Bow Down, Silbury Air, 1977; For O, for O, the Hobby-horse is forgot, 1977; Carmen Arcardiae Mechanicae Perpetuum, 1978; agm, 1979; On the Sheer Threshold of the Night, 1980; Quintet, 1981; Pulse Sampler, 1981; Deowa, 1983; Yan Tan Tetherer, 1984; Still Movement, 1984; Secret Theatre, 1984; Songs by Myself, 1984; Earth Dances, 1986; Fanfare for Will, 1987; Endless Parade, 1987; Gawain, 1990 (opera); Four Poems by Jaan Kaplinski, 1991. *Address:* c/o Allied Artists Agency, 42 Montpelier Square, SW7 1JZ.

BISCHOFF, Winfried Franz Wilhelm, (Win); Group Chief Executive, Schroders plc, since 1984 (Director, since 1983); Chairman, J. Henry Schroder Wagg & Co. Ltd, since 1983 (Director, since 1978); *b* 10 May 1941; *s* of Paul Helmut Bischoff and Hildegard (*née* Kühne); *m* 1972, Rosemary Elizabeth, *d* of Hon. Leslie Leathers; two *s. Educ:* Marist Brothers, Inanda, Johannesburg, S Africa; Univ. of the Witwatersrand, Johannesburg (BCom). Man. Dir, Schroders & Chartered Ltd, Hong Kong, 1971–82. *Recreations:* opera, music, golf. *Address:* 28 Bloomfield Terrace, SW1W 8PQ. *Clubs:* Hurlingham; Frilford Heath Golf, Woking Golf.

BISCOE, Rear-Adm. Alec Julian T.; *see* Tyndale-Biscoe.

BISCOE, Prof. Timothy John; Jodrell Professor of Physiology, since 1979, and Vice Provost, since 1990, University College London; *b* 28 April 1932; *s* of late Rev. W. H. Biscoe and Mrs M. G. Biscoe; *m* 1955, Daphne Miriam (*née* Gurton); one *s* two *d. Educ:* Latymer Upper School; The London Hospital Medical College. BSc (Hons) Physiology, 1953; MB, BS 1957; FRCP 1983. London Hospital, 1957–58; RAMC Short Service Commission, 1958–62; Physiologist, CDEE, Porton Down, 1959–62; ARC Inst. of Animal Physiology, Babraham, 1962–65; Res. Fellow in Physiology, John Curtin Sch. of Med. Res., Canberra, 1965–66; Associate Res. Physiologist, Cardiovascular Res. Inst., UC Medical Center, San Francisco, 1966–68; University of Bristol: Res. Associate, Dept of Physiology, 1968–70; 2nd Chair of Physiology, 1970–79; Head of Dept of Physiology, 1975–79. McLaughlin Vis. Prof., McMaster Univ., Ont, 1986; Hooker Distinguished Vis. Prof., McMaster Univ., 1990. Hon. Sec., Physiological Soc., 1977–82; Member Council: Harveian Soc., 1983–86; Research Defence Soc., 1983–90 (Hon. Sec., 1983–86). *Publications:* papers on neurophysiology in Journal of Physiology, etc. *Recreations:* looking, listening, reading. *Address:* Department of Physiology, University College London, Gower Street, WC1E 6BT. *T:* 071–387 7050. *Club:* Garrick.

BISHOP, family name of **Baroness O'Cathain**.

BISHOP, Alan Henry, CB 1989; HM Chief Inspector of Prisons for Scotland, since 1989; *b* 12 Sept. 1929; *s* of Robert Bishop and May Watson; *m* 1959, Marjorie Anne Conlan; one *s* one *d*. *Educ:* George Heriot's Sch., Edinburgh; Edinburgh Univ. (MA 1st Cl. Hons Econ. Science, 1951, 2nd Cl. Hons History, 1952). Served RAF Educn Br., 1952–54. Asst Principal, Dept of Agric. for Scotland, 1954; Private Sec. to Parly Under-Secs of State, 1958–59; Principal, 1959; First Sec., Food and Agric., Copenhagen and The Hague, 1963–66; Asst Sec., Scottish Develt Dept, 1968; Asst Sec., Commn on the Constitution, 1969–73; Asst Under-Sec. of State, 1980–84, Principal Establishment Officer, 1984–89, Scottish Office. *Recreations:* contract bridge (Pres., Scottish Bridge Union, 1979–80), theatre, golf. *Address:* St Andrew's House, Edinburgh EH1 3DE. *T:* 031–244 2335. *Clubs:* New, Melville, Bridge (Edinburgh); Murrayfield Golf.

BISHOP, Dr Arthur Clive; Deputy Director, British Museum (Natural History), 1982–89, and Keeper of Mineralogy, 1975–89; *b* 9 July 1930; *s* of late Charles Henry Bishop and Hilda (*née* Clowes); *m* 1962, Helen (*née* Bennison); one *d*. *Educ:* Wolstanton County Grammar Sch., Newcastle, Staffs; King's Coll., Univ. of London (FKC 1985). BSc 1951, PhD 1954. Geologist, HM Geological Survey, 1954; served RAF Educn Br., 1955–57; Lectr in Geology, Queen Mary Coll., Univ. of London, 1958; Principal Sci. Officer, British Museum (Natural History), 1969, Deputy Keeper 1972. Geological Society: Daniel Pidgeon Fund, 1958; Murchison Fund, 1970; Vice-Pres., 1977–78; Mineralogical Society: Gen. Sec., 1965–72; Vice-Pres., 1973–74; Pres., 1986–87; Pres., Geologists' Assoc., 1978–80; Vice-Pres., Inst. of Science Technology, 1973–82. Mem. d'honneur, La Société Jersiaise, 1983. *Publications:* An Outline of Crystal Morphology, 1967; (with W. R. Hamilton and A. R. Woolley) Hamlyn Guide to Minerals, Rocks and Fossils, 1974; papers in various jls, mainly on geology of Channel Is and Brittany, and on dioritic rocks. *Recreations:* drawing and painting. *Address:* 4 Viewfield Road, Bexley, Kent DA5 3EE. *T:* 081–302 9602.

BISHOP, Rt. Rev. Clifford Leofric Purdy; *b* 1908; *s* of Rev. E. J. Bishop; *m* 1949, Ivy Winifred Adams. *Educ:* St John's, Leatherhead; Christ's Coll., Cambridge (MA); Lincoln Theological Coll. Deacon 1932; Priest, 1933; Curacies, 1932–41; Vicar, St Geo., Camberwell, 1941–49; Rural Dean, 1943–49; Curate-in-charge, All Saints, Newington, 1944–47; Rector of: Blakeney, 1949–53 (Rural Dean of Walsingham, 1951–53); Bishop Wearmouth, 1953–62 (Rural Dean of Wearmouth and Surrogate, 1953–62); Hon. Canon of Durham, 1958–62; Bishop Suffragan of Malmesbury, 1962–73; Canon of Bristol, 1962–73. *Address:* Rectory Cottage, Cley-next-Sea, Holt, Norfolk NR25 7BA. *T:* Cley (0263) 740250.

BISHOP, Prof. David Hugh Langler, PhD, DSc; FIBiol; Director, Natural Environment Research Council Institute of Virology, since 1984; Fellow, St Cross College, Oxford, since 1984; *b* 31 Dec. 1937; *s* of late Reginald Samuel Harold Bishop and of Violet Rose Mary Langler; *m* 1st, 1963, Margaret Duthie; one *s* one *d*; 2nd, 1971, Polly Roy; one *s*. *Educ:* Liverpool Univ. (BSc 1959, PhD 1962); MA 1984, DSc 1988, Oxon. FIBiol 1989. Postdoctoral Fellow, CNRS, Gif-sur-Yvette, 1962–63; Research Associate, Univ. of Edinburgh, 1963–66, Univ. of Illinois, 1966–69; Asst Prof., 1969–70, Associate Prof., 1970–71, Columbia Univ.; Associate Prof., 1971–75, Prof., 1975, Rutgers Univ.; Prof., Univ. of Alabama in Birmingham, 1975–84 (Sen. Scientist, Comprehensive Cancer Center, 1975–84; Chm., Dept of Microbiology, 1983–84). Vis. Fellow, Lincoln Coll., Oxford, 1981–82; Vis. Prof. of Virology, Oxford Univ., 1984–. Nathaniel A. Young Award in Virology, 1981. *Publications:* Rhabdoviruses, 1979; numerous contribs to books and jls. *Recreation:* hill walking. *Address:* 8 Carey Close, Off Five Mile Drive, Oxford OX2 8HX. *T:* Oxford (0865) 512361.

BISHOP, Sir Frederick (Arthur), Kt 1975; CB 1960; CVO 1957; Director-General of the National Trust, 1971–75; *b* 4 Dec. 1915; *o s* of A. J. Bishop, Bristol; *m* 1940, Elizabeth Finlay Stevenson; two *s* one *d*. *Educ:* Colston's Hospital, Bristol. LLB (London). Inland Revenue, 1934. Served in RAF and Air Transport Auxiliary, 1942–46. Ministry of Food, 1947, where Principal Private Secretary to Ministers, 1949–52; Asst Secretary, Cabinet Office, 1953–55; Principal Private Secretary to the Prime Minister, 1956–59; Deputy Secretary: of the Cabinet, 1959–61; Min. of Agriculture, Fisheries and Food, 1961–64; Perm. Sec., Min. of Land and Natural Resources, 1964–65, resigned. Chm., Home Grown Timber Advisory Cttee, 1966–73; Member: BBC Gen. Adv. Council, 1971–75; Crafts Adv. Council, 1973–75. Director: S. Pearson & Son Ltd, 1965–70; Pearson Longman, 1970–77; English China Clays Ltd, 1975–86; Devon and Cornwall Bd, Lloyds Bank, 1976–86. *Address:* Manor Barn, Church Road, Bramshott, Liphook GU30 7SH.

BISHOP, George Robert, DPhil; FRSE; CPhys, FInstP; Director General, Ispra Establishment, Joint Research Centre, European Commission, Ispra, Italy, 1983–92, retired (Director, 1982–83); *b* 16 Jan. 1927; *s* of George William Bishop and Lilian Elizabeth Garrod; *m* 1952, Adriana Giuseppina, *d* of Luigi Caberlotto and Giselda Mazzariol; two *s* one *d*. *Educ:* Christ Church, Oxford (MA, DPhil). ICI Research Fellow, Univ. of Oxford, 1951; Research Fellow, St Antony's Coll., Oxford, 1952; Chercheur, Ecole Normale Supérieure, Paris, 1954; Ingénieur-Physicien, Laboratoire de l'Accelerateur Linéaire, ENS, Orsay, 1958; Prof., Faculté des Sciences, Univ. de Paris, 1962; Kelvin Prof. of Natural Philosophy, Univ. of Glasgow, 1964–76; Dir, Dept of Natural and Physical Sciences, JRC, Ispra, 1974–82. Hon. DSc, Strathclyde, 1979. *Publications:* Handbuch der Physik, Band XLII, 1957; β and X-Ray Spectroscopy, 1960; Nuclear Structure and Electromagnetic Interactions, 1965; numerous papers in learned jls on nuclear and high energy physics. *Recreations:* literature, music, swimming, tennis, gardening, travel. *Address:* 3 Holly House, Sawyer's Hall Lane, Brentwood, Essex CM15 9BP. *T:* Brentwood (0277) 225530; via Irpinia 22, Mestre (VE), Italy. *T:* (041) 5440430.

BISHOP, Sir George (Sidney), Kt 1975; CB 1958; OBE 1947; Director, Booker McConnell Ltd, 1961–82 (Vice-Chairman, 1970–71, Chairman, 1972–79); Director: Barclays Bank International, 1972–83; Barclays Bank Ltd, 1974–83; Ranks Hovis McDougall, 1976–84; International Basic Economy Corporation, USA, 1980–83; *b* 15 Oct. 1913; *o s* of late J. and M. Bishop; *m* 1940, Marjorie Woodruff (marr. diss. 1961); one *d*; *m* 1961, Una Padel. *Educ:* Ashton-in-Makerfield Grammar Sch.; London Sch. of Economics. Social service work in distressed areas, 1935–38; SW Durham Survey, 1939; Ministry of Food, 1940; Private Secretary to Minister of Food, 1945–49; Under-Secretary, Ministry of Agriculture, Fisheries and Food, 1949–59, Dep. Secretary, 1959–61. Chm., Bookers Agricultural Holdings Ltd, 1964–70; Director: Nigerian Sugar Co. Ltd, 1966–70; Agricultural Mortgage Corp. Ltd, 1973–79. Chairman: Internat. Sugar Council, 1957; West India Cttee, 1969–71 (Pres., 1977–); Industry Co-operative Programme, 1976–78; Council, Overseas Develt Inst., 1977–84; Vice-Chm., Internat. Wheat Council, 1959; Member: Panel for Civil Service Manpower Review, 1968–70; Royal Commn on the Press, 1974–77; Council, CBI, 1973–80; Dir, Industry Council for Develt, USA (Chm., 1979); Governor, Nat. Inst. for Economic and Social Research, 1968–. President: RGS, 1983–87 (Mem. Council, 1980–; Hon. Fellow 1980; a Vice Pres., 1981); Britain-Nepal Soc., 1979–89; Mem., Management Cttee, Mount Everest Foundn, 1980– (Vice Chm. 1982; Chm. 1983). *Recreations:* mountaineering, motoring, photography. *Address:* Brenva, Eghams Wood Road, Beaconsfield, Bucks HP9 1JX. *T:* Beaconsfield (0494) 673096. *Clubs:* Reform, Travellers', Himalayan, Alpine, Royal Geographical Society, MCC.

BISHOP, James Drew; Editor-in-Chief, Illustrated London News Publications, since 1987; Director, Illustrated London News & Sketch Ltd, since 1973; Editorial Director, Natural World, since 1981; *b* 18 June 1929; *s* of late Sir Patrick Bishop, MBE, MP, and Vera Drew; *m* 1959, Brenda Pearson; two *s*. *Educ:* Haileybury; Corpus Christi Coll., Cambridge. Reporter, Northampton Chronicle & Echo, 1953; joined editorial staff of The Times, 1954; Foreign Correspondent, 1957–64; Foreign News Editor, 1964–66; Features Editor, 1966–70; Editor, Illustrated London News, 1971–87. Dir, International Thomson Publishing Ltd, 1980–85. Chm., Assoc. of British Editors, 1987–. Mem. Adv. Bd, Annual Register, 1970– (contributor, Amer. sect., 1960–88). *Publications:* A Social History of Edwardian Britain, 1977; Social History of the First World War, 1982; (with Oliver Woods) The Story of The Times, 1983; (ed) The Illustrated Counties of England, 1985. *Recreations:* reading, walking, looking and listening. *Address:* (home) 11 Willow Road, NW3 1TJ. *T:* 071–435 4403; (office) 20 Upper Ground, SE1 9PF. *T:* 071–928 2111. *Clubs:* United Oxford & Cambridge University, MCC.

BISHOP, Dr John Edward; freelance musician; Director of Music, Cotham Parish Church, Bristol, 1976–90; *b* 23 Feb. 1935; *s* of late Reginald John Bishop and of Eva Bishop (*née* Lucas). *Educ:* Cotham Sch., Bristol; St John's Coll., Cambridge (Exhibr); Reading and Edinburgh Univs. MA, MusB Cantab; DMus Edin.; FRCO (CHM); ADCM; Hon. FBSM. John Stewart of Rannoch Schol. (Univ. prize) 1954. Organist and Asst Dir of Music, Worksop Coll., Notts, 1958–69; Dir of Music, Worksop Coll., 1969–73; Birmingham School of Music: Dir of Studies, 1973–74; Sen. Lectr, 1974–79; Principal Lectr, Head of Organ Studies and Head of Admissions, 1979–87. Hon. Dir of Music, St Paul's Church, Birmingham, 1986; Dir, Bristol Highbury Singers, 1978–90; Consultant, Wells Cathedral Sch., 1986–. Organ recitalist (incl. many broadcasts) and choral conductor, pianist, coach and adjudicator, 1960–. Former Pres., Sheffield, Birmingham and Bristol Organists' Assocs. *Publications:* various articles on history and practice of church music and 19th century organ design. *Recreations:* walking, ecclesiology, savouring the countryside, cities and towns, railways, architecture. *Address:* 98 High Kingsdown, Bristol BS2 8ER. *T:* Bristol (0272) 423373.

BISHOP, Prof. (John) Michael, MD; Professor of Microbiology and Immunology, since 1972, and of Biochemistry and Biophysics, since 1982, and Director, G. W. Hooper Research Foundation, since 1981, University of California, San Francisco; *b* 22 Feb. 1936; *s* of John and Carrie Bishop; *m* 1959, Kathryn Putman; two *s*. *Educ:* Gettysburg Coll., Gettysburg (AB); Harvard Univ., Boston (MD). Intern/Asst Resident in Internal Med., Mass. Gen. Hosp., 1962–64; Res. Associate, NIAID, NIH, 1964–67; Vis. Scientist, Heinrich-Pette Inst., Hamburg, 1967–68; Asst Prof., Microbiology, 1968–70, Associate Prof., Microbiology, 1970–72, Univ. of California. Member: Nat. Acad. of Scis, 1980–; Amer. Acad. of Arts and Scis, 1984–. Hon. DSc Gettysburg, 1983. Albert Lasker Award for Basic Med. Res., 1982; Passano Foundn Award, 1983; Warren Triennial Prize, 1983; Armand Hammer Cancer Res. Award, 1984; Gen. Motors Cancer Res. Award, 1984; Gairdner Foundn Internat. Award, 1984; ACS Medal of Honor, 1985; (jtly) Nobel Prize in Physiology or Medicine, 1989. *Publications:* (ed jtly) Genes and Cancer, vol. 17, 1984; (ed jtly) Cancer Surveys — proteins encoded by oncogenes, vol. 5, 1986; over 200 pubns in refereed sci. jls. *Recreations:* music, reading, theatre. *Address:* 1542 HSW, University of California, San Francisco, Calif 94143, USA. *T:* 415–476–3211.

BISHOP, Dame (Margaret) Joyce, DBE 1963 (CBE 1953); MA Oxon; Head Mistress of The Godolphin and Latymer School, Hammersmith, W6, 1935–63, retired; *b* 28 July 1896; 2nd *d* of Charles Benjamin and Amy Bishop. *Educ:* Edgbaston High Sch., Birmingham; Lady Margaret Hall, Oxford. English Mistress, Hertfordshire and Essex High Sch., 1918–24; Head Mistress, Holly Lodge High Sch., Smethwick, Staffs, 1924–35. Member Working Party set up by Minister of Education to enquire into Recruitment of Women to Teaching Profession, 1947. President, Association of Head Mistresses, 1950–52. Member: Secondary School Examinations Council, 1950–62; University Grants Cttee, 1961–63; Council for Professions Supplementary to Medicine, 1961–70; TV Research Cttee set up by Home Secretary, 1963–69. Chairman, Joint Cttee of the Four Secondary Associations, 1956–58. FKC 1973. *Recreations:* listening to cassettes and radio, the theatre. *Address:* 22 Malbrook Road, Putney, SW15 6UF. *T:* 081–788 5862.

BISHOP, Michael; *see* Bishop, J. M.

BISHOP, Sir Michael David, Kt 1991; CBE 1986; Chairman: Airlines of Britain Holdings Plc; British Midland Airways, Manx Airlines and Loganair; *b* 10 Feb. 1942; *s* of Clive Leonard Bishop and Lilian Bishop (*née* Frost). *Educ:* Mill Hill School. Joined Mercury Airlines, Manchester, 1963; British Midland Airways Ltd, 1964–; Dir, Airtours plc. Member: E Midlands Electricity Bd, 1980–83; E Midlands Reg. Bd, Central Television, 1981–89; Chm., D'Oyly Carte Opera Trust Ltd, 1989–. Hon. Mem., Royal Soc. of Musicians of GB, 1989; CRAeS, 1989. Hon. DTech Loughborough Univ. of Technology, 1989. *Recreation:* music. *Address:* Donington Hall, Castle Donington, near Derby DE7 2SB. *T:* Derby (0332) 810741. *Club:* St James's (Manchester).

BISHOP, Michael William; Director of Social Services, Manchester City Council, since 1989; *b* 22 Oct. 1941; *s* of Ronald Lewis William and Gwendoline Mary Bishop; *m* Loraine Helen Jones; two *s* one *d*. *Educ:* Manchester Univ. (BA (Econs) Ili Hons); Leicester Univ. (CertAppSocStudies). Director of Social Services, Cleveland CC, 1981–89. *Recreations:* horse riding and competing. *Address:* Social Services Department, Town Hall, Manchester M60 2AF. *T:* 061–234 3804.

BISHOP, Prof. Peter Orlebar, AO 1986; DSc; FRS 1977; FAA; Professor Emeritus, Australian National University, since 1983; Visiting Scholar, Department of Anatomy, University of Sydney, since 1987; *b* 14 June 1917; *s* of Ernest John Hunter Bishop and Mildred Alice Havelock Bishop (*née* Vidal); *m* 1942, Hilare Louise Holmes; one *s* two *d*. *Educ:* Barker Coll., Hornsby; Univ. of Sydney (MB, BS, DSc). Neurol Registrar, Royal Prince Alfred Hosp., Sydney, 1941–42; Surgeon Lieut, RANR, 1942–46; Fellow, Postgrad. Cttee in Medicine (Sydney Univ.) at Nat. Hosp., Queen Square, London, 1946–47 and Dept Anatomy, UCL, 1947–50; Sydney University: Res. Fellow, Dept Surgery, 1950–51; Sen. Lectr, 1951–54, Reader, 1954–55, Prof. and Head, Dept Physiology, 1955–67; Prof. and Head of Dept of Physiology, John Curtin School of Medical Res., ANU, 1967–82; Vis. Fellow, ANU, 1983–87. Visiting Professor: Japan Soc. for Promotion of Science, 1974, 1982; Katholieke Universiteit Leuven, Belgium, 1984–85; Guest Prof., Zürich Univ., 1985; Vis. Fellow, St John's Coll., Cambridge, Jan.–Oct. 1986. FAA 1967; Fellow: Aust. Postgrad. Fedn in Medicine, 1969; Nat. Vision Res. Inst. of Australia, 1983. Hon. Member: Neurosurgical Soc. of Aust., 1970; Ophthalmol Soc. of NZ, 1973; Aust. Assoc. of Neurologists, 1977; Australian Neuroscience Soc., 1986; Aust. Physiol and Pharmacol Soc., 1987. Hon. MD Sydney, 1983. *Publications:* contribs on physiological optics and visual neurophysiology. *Recreation:* bushwalking. *Address:* Department of Anatomy, University of Sydney, NSW 2006, Australia; 139 Cape Three Points Road, Avoca Beach, NSW 2260.

BISHOP, Stanley Victor, MC 1944; management consultant; Director, Britarge Ltd, since 1979; *b* 11 May 1916; *s* of George Stanley Bishop, MA; *m* 1946, Dorothy Primrose Dodds, Berwick-upon-Tweed; two *s* one *d*. *Educ:* Leeds. Articled to Beevers & Adgie, Leeds; CA 1937. Served War of 1939–45: enlisted London Scottish (TA), 1938; commissioned, West Yorkshire Regt, 1940; served overseas, 1940–45, Middle East, India and Burma (MC) (Hon. Major). Joined Albert E. Reed and Co. Ltd, 1946; Brush Group, 1951; Massey Ferguson Ltd, 1959–79; Perkins Diesel Engine Group, 1963. Man. Dir, British Printing Corp., 1966–70; Chm. and Dir various cos, 1970–73 and 1979–; Dir, Massey-Ferguson Europe Ltd, 1973–79. Has lectured to British Institute of Management, Institute of Chartered Accountants, Oxford Business Summer School, etc. *Publication:* Business Planning and Control, 1966. *Recreations:* golf, swimming, pottering. *Address:* Halidon, Rogers Lane, Ettington, Stratford-upon-Avon, Warwicks CV37 7SX.

BISHOP, Stephen; *see* Bishop-Kovacevich.

BISHOP, Terence Alan Martyn, FBA 1971; *b* 10 Nov. 1907; *s* of Cosby Martyn Bishop. *Educ:* Christ's Hospital; Keble Coll., Oxford. 2nd Mods, 1928; 2nd Hist. 1930; BA 1931, MA 1947; MA Cantab 1947. Asst Master, Glenalmond Coll., 1930–31. Served War of 1939–45; 2nd Lieut, RA, 1940; Capt., 1944. Lectr in Medieval Hist., Balliol Coll., 1946–47; Reader in Palaeography and Diplomatic, Dept of History, Cambridge Univ., 1947–73. *Publications:* books and articles on palaeography, etc, incl.: Facsimiles of English Royal Writs to AD 1100 (with P. Chaplais), 1957; Scriptores Regis, 1961; (ed) Umbrae Codicum Occidentalium (Vol. 10), 1966 (Holland); English Caroline Minuscule, 1971. *Address:* 16 Highbury Road, Wimbledon, SW19 7PR.

BISHOP-KOVACEVICH, Stephen; pianist and conductor; *b* 17 Oct. 1940. *Educ:* studied under Lev Shorr and Myra Hess. Solo and orchestral debut, San Francisco, USA 1951; London debut, Nov. 1961. Concert tours: in England, Europe and USA, with many of the world's leading orchestras, incl. New York Philharmonic, Los Angeles Philharmonic, Israel Philharmonic, Amsterdam Concertgebouw, London Symphony, London Philharmonic, and BBC Symphony. Has appeared at Edinburgh, Bath, Berlin and San Sebastian Festivals. Gave 1st performance of Richard Rodney Bennett's Piano Concerto, 1969 (this work is dedicated to and has been recorded by him, under Alexander Gibson). Performed all Mozart Piano concertos, 1969–71. Principal Guest Conductor, Australian Chamber Orch., 1987–; Music Dir, Irish Chamber Orch. Edison Award for his recording of Bartok's 2nd Piano Concerto and Stravinsky's Piano Concerto, with BBC Symphony Orchestra, under Colin Davis. *Recreations:* snooker, chess, films, tennis. *Address:* c/o Terry Harrison Artists Management, 9a Penzance Place, W11 4PE. *T:* 071–221 7741.

BISSELL, Claude Thomas, CC 1969; MA, PhD; FRSC 1957; Professor, University of Toronto, since 1971 (President of the University, 1958–71); *b* 10 Feb. 1916; *m* 1945, Christina Flora Gray; one *d*. *Educ:* University of Toronto; Cornell Univ. BA 1936, MA 1937, Toronto; PhD Cornell, 1940. Instructor in English, Cornell, 1938–41; Lecturer in English, Cornell, 1938–41; Lecturer in English, Toronto, 1941–42. Canadian Army, 1942–46; demobilised as Capt. University of Toronto: Asst Prof. of English, 1947–51; Assoc. Prof. of English, 1951–56; Prof. of English, 1962; Asst to Pres., 1948–52; Vice-Pres., 1952–56; Dean in Residence, University Coll., 1946–56; Pres., Carleton Univ., Ottawa, 1956–58; Chm., The Canada Council, 1960–62. President, Nat. Conference of Canadian Universities and Colleges, 1962–; Chairman, Canadian Universities Foundation, 1962–; President, World University Service of Canada, 1962–63. Visiting Prof. of Canadian Studies, Harvard, 1967–68. Aggrey-Fraser-Guggisberg Meml Lectr, Ghana Univ., 1976. Hon. DLitt: Manitoba, 1958; W Ontario, 1971; Lethbridge, 1972; Leeds, 1976; Toronto, 1977; Hon. LLD: McGill, 1958; Queen's, 1959; New Brunswick, 1959; Carleton, 1960; Montreal, 1960; The St Lawrence, 1962; British Columbia, 1962; Michigan, 1963; Columbia, 1965; Laval, 1966; Prince of Wales Coll., 1967; Windsor, 1968; St Andrews, 1972. *Publications:* (ed) University College, A Portrait, 1853–1953, 1953; (ed) Canada's Crisis in Higher Education, 1957; (ed) Our Living Tradition, 1957; (ed) Great Canadian Writing, 1966; The Strength of the University, 1968; Halfway up Parnassus, 1974; The Humanities in the University, 1977; The Young Vincent Massey, 1981; The Imperial Canadian, 1986; number of articles on literary subjects in Canadian and American jls. *Address:* 229 Erskine Avenue, Toronto, Ontario M4P 1Z5, Canada. *Clubs:* Arts and Letters, York (Toronto); Cercle Universitaire (Ottawa).

BISSELL, Frances Mary; The Times Cook, since 1987; *b* 19 Aug. 1946; *d* of Robert Maloney and Mary Maloney (*née* Kelly); *m* 1970, Thomas Emery Bissell; one step *d*. *Educ:* Univ. of Leeds (BA Hons French). VSO Nigeria, 1965–66; Assistante, Ecole Normale, Albi, 1968–69; British Council, 1970– (leave of absence, 1987–); food and cookery writer, cook and consultant, 1983–. Guest cook: Mandarin Oriental, Hong Kong, 1987 and 1990; London Intercontinental, 1987 and 1988; Manila Peninsula, 1989; guest teacher: Bogotá Hilton, Colombia, 1988; Ballymaloe Cooking Sch., Ireland, 1990. Mem. judging panel: THF Hotels Chef of the Year, 1988 and 1990; Catey Award Function Menu, 1989 and 1990; A Fresh Taste of Britain, Women's Farming Union, 1989. Mem., Guild of Food Writers, 1985. *Publications:* A Cook's Calendar, 1985; The Pleasures of Cookery, 1986; Ten Dinner Parties for Two, 1988; Sainsbury's Book of Food, 1989; Oriental Flavours, 1990; contrib. to Caterer and Hotelkeeper, Sunday Times Mag., Homes and Gardens, House & Garden, Decanter, Forte Magazine, Food and Entertaining. *Recreations:* travelling and reading. *Address:* c/o The Times Features, 1 Pennington Street, E1 9XN. *T:* 071–782 5187.

BISSON, Rt. Hon. Sir Gordon (Ellis), Kt 1991; PC 1987; Judge of the Court of Appeal, New Zealand, 1986–90; *b* 23 Nov. 1918; *s* of Clarence Henry Bisson and Ada Ellis; *m* 1948, Myra Patricia Kemp; three *d*. *Educ:* Napier Boys High Sch.; Victoria Coll., Wellington; Univ. of NZ. LLB. Served War of 1939–45, RN and RNZN, 1940–45 (mentioned in despatches); Lt Comdr RNZNVR. Partner, Bisson Moss Robertshawe & Co., Barristers and Solicitors, Napier, NZ, 1946–78; Crown Solicitor, Napier, 1961; Judge, Courts Martial Appeal Ct, 1976; Judge of Supreme Ct, 1978. Vice-President: NZ Law Soc., 1974–77; NZ Sect., Internat. Commn of Jurists, 1979–. *Publication:* (jtly) Criminal Law and Practice in New Zealand, 1961. *Recreations:* tennis, fly-fishing. *Address:* 15 Golf Road, Heretaunga, Wellington 6402, New Zealand. *Clubs:* Wellington, Wellington Golf (Wellington, NZ).

BISZTYGA, Jan; Officer's Cross of the Order of Polonia Restituta 1970; Order of Merit 1973; Ideology Department, Polish United Workers' Party; expert in Office of President of the Polish Republic, since 1990; *b* 19 Jan. 1933; *s* of Kazimierz Biszytyga; *m* 1956, Otylia; one *s*. *Educ:* Jagiellonian Univ. (MSc Biochemistry). Asst Professor, Jagiellonian Univ., Cracow, 1954–57; political youth movement, 1956–59; Min. for Foreign Affairs, 1959–63; Attaché, New Delhi, 1963–64; Min. for Foreign Affairs, 1964–69; Head of Planning Dept, Min. for Foreign Affairs, 1969–71; Dep. Foreign Minister, 1972–75; Ambassador in Athens, 1975–78, to UK, 1978–81. *Recreations:* game shooting, fishing, history. *Address:* Jaworzyńska 11–18, Warsaw, Poland.

BJARNASON, Sigurdur; Commander with Star, Order of the Icelandic Falcon, 1950; Hon. Emblem, Foundation of the Icelandic Republic, 1944; Ambassador of Iceland (stationed in Reykjavik) to India and other West Asian countries, since 1982; *b* 18 Dec. 1915; *s* of Bjarni Sigurdsson and Björg Bjornsdóttir; *m* 1956, Ólöf Pálsdóttir, sculptress; one *s* one *d*. *Educ:* Univ. of Iceland (Law); Univ. of Cambridge (Internat. and Company Law). Editor of weekly newspaper, 1942–47; Political Editor, Morgunbladid, 1947–56, Editor in Chief, 1956–70. Mem. Icelandic Parlt (Althing), 1942–70; Pres. Lower House, 1949–56 and 1963–70; Chm. Cttee of Foreign Affairs, 1963–70. Mem. govt and municipal cttees, including Pres. Municipal Council of Isfajördur, 1946–50; Mem. Council of State Radio of Iceland, 1947–70, Chm. 1959 and Vice-Chm. 1960–70. Pres. Icelandic Sect. of Soc. for Inter-scandinavian Understanding, 1965–70. Member Nordic Council, 1952–59 and 1963–70; Vice-Pres., 1952–56 and 1959; Pres., 1965 and 1970. Delegate of Iceland to UN Gen. Assembly, 1960, 1961 and 1962; Mem. Cultural Cttee of Nordic Countries, 1954–70. Mem. Icelandic Cttee on territorial rights, 1957–58. Ambassador to: Denmark, Turkey, 1970–76; Ireland, 1970–82; China, 1973–76; UK, The Netherlands and Nigeria, 1976–82. Commander of the Finnish Lion, 1958; Commander, Order of the Vasa (Sweden), 1958; Grand Cross: Order of Dannebrog (Denmark), 1970; Order of Orange-Nassau (Netherlands), 1982. *Publications:* articles for foreign periodicals, especially within the field of culture and Scandinavian co-operation. *Recreations:* fishing, bird watching. *Address:* Útsalir, Seltjarnarnes, Iceland.

BJELKE-PETERSEN, Hon. Sir Johannes, KCMG 1984; Premier of Queensland, 1968–87; *b* Dannevirke, NZ, 13 Jan. 1911; *s* of late C. G. Bjelke-Petersen, Denmark; *m* 1952, Florence Isabel (elected as Senator for Queensland in Commonwealth Parliament, 1981), *d* of J. P. Gilmour; one *s* three *d*. *Educ:* Taabinga Valley Sch.; corresp. courses, and privately. MLA National Party (formerly Country Party): for Nanango, 1947–50; for Barambah, 1950–87; Minister for Works and Housing, Qld, 1963–68. *Address:* Bethany, Kingaroy, Queensland 4610, Australia.

BLACK, Alastair Kenneth Lamond, CBE 1989; DL; Under Sheriff of Greater London, since 1974; Clerk, Bowyers' Company, since 1985; *b* 14 Dec. 1929; *s* of Kenneth Black and Althea Joan Black; *m* 1955, Elizabeth Jane, *d* of Sir Henry Darlington, KCB, CMG, TD; one *s* two *d*. *Educ:* Sherborne Sch.; Law Soc. Coll. of Law. Admitted solicitor, 1953. Nat. Service, Intelligence Corps, 1953–55, Lieut. Partner in Messrs Burchell & Ruston, Solicitors, 1953–. Dep. Sheriff, Co. of London, then Greater London, 1953–74; DL Greater London, 1978. Mem. Council, Shrievalty Assoc., 1985–; Vice-Pres., Under Sheriffs Assoc., 1985–87, Pres., 1987–. Member: House of Laity, Gen. Synod, 1982–; (a Chm., Gen. Synod, 1991–); Dioceses Commn, 1986–; Ecclesiastical Fees Adv. Commn, 1986–. Lay Reader, 1983–. *Publications:* contributions to: Halsbury's Laws of England, 4th edn, vols 25, 1978, and 42, 1983; Atkin's Court Forms, 3rd edn, vols 19, 1972 (rev. edn 1985), 22, 1968, and 36, 1977 (rev. edn 1988); Enforcement of a Judgement, 7th edn, 1986. *Recreations:* horseracing, gardening, travel. *Address:* South Lodge, Effingham, Surrey KT24 5QE. *T:* Bookham (0372) 452862.

BLACK, Col Anthony Edward Norman, OBE 1981; Chief Executive Commissioner, Scout Association, since 1987; *b* 20 Jan. 1938; *s* of late Arthur Norman Black and Phyllis Margaret Ranicar; *m* 1963, Susan Frances Copeland; two *s*. *Educ:* Brighton College; RMA Sandhurst. Commissioned RE, 1957; served Kenya, Aden, Germany, Cyprus; Army Staff Course, Camberley, 1970; GSO1 Ghana Armed Forces Staff Coll., 1976–78; CO 36 Engr Regt, 1978–80; Col GS MGO Secretariat, 1980–82; Comd Engrs Falkland Islands, 1983; Comdt, Army Apprentices Coll., Chepstow, 1983–86; retired 1987. FBIM. *Recreations:* dinghy sailing, walking, gardening, bird watching. *Address:* c/o Scout Association, Baden-Powell House, Queen's Gate, SW7 5JS. *T:* 071–584 7030. *Club:* Commonwealth Trust.

BLACK, Archibald Niel; Professor of Engineering, University of Southampton, 1968–72, retired; *b* 10 June 1912; *s* of late Steuart Gladstone Black, Glenormiston, Victoria, Australia, and Isabella McCance (*née* Moat); *m* 1940, Cynthia Mary Stradling; one *s* two *d*. *Educ:* Farnborough Sch.; Eton Coll.; Trinity Coll., Cambridge. 1st cl. hons with distinction in Applied Mechanics in Mech. Sciences Tripos, Cambridge, 1934; MA 1938. Lectr and Demonstrator in Engrg Science, Oxford Univ., 1935; Donald Pollock Reader in Engrg Science, Oxford Univ., 1945–50; Prof. of Mech. Engrg, Southampton Univ., 1950–67. Dep. Chm., Universities Central Council on Admissions, 1964–72. Hon. DSc Southampton, 1975. *Publications:* (with K. Adlard Coles) North Biscay Pilot, 1970, revd edn 1977; papers in Proc. Royal Soc. and technical jls. *Recreation:* sailing. *Address:* Little Pensbury, Compton Street, Compton, Winchester, Hants SO21 2AS. *T:* Twyford (0962) 712360. *Club:* Royal Cruising.

BLACK, Barrington; a Metropolitan Stipendiary Magistrate, since 1984; an Assistant Recorder, since 1987; *b* 16 Aug. 1932; *s* of Louis and Millicent Black; *m* 1962, Diana Black (*née* Heller), JP; two *s* two *d*. *Educ:* Roundhay Sch.; Leeds Univ. (Pres. of Union, 1952; Vice-Pres., NUS, 1953–54; LLB). Admitted Solicitor, 1956. Served Army, 1956–58, commnd RASC. Partner, Walker, Morris & Coles, 1958–69; Sen. Partner, Barrington Black, Austin & Co., 1969–84. Chairman: Inner London Juvenile Court, 1985–; Family Court, 1991–. Mem. Court and Council, Leeds Univ., 1979–84. Councillor, Harrogate Bor. Council, 1964–67; contested (L) Harrogate, 1964. Member: Inner London Probation Cttee; British Acad. of Forensic Science, 1976–. *Recreations:* ski-bobbing, opera, music. *Address:* c/o Bow Street Magistrates' Court, WC2E 7AS.

BLACK, Colin Hyndmarsh; Chairman, Kleinwort Benson Investment Management Ltd, since 1988; *b* 4 Feb. 1930; *s* of Daisy Louise (*née* Morris) and Robert Black; *m* 1955, Christine Fleurette Browne; one *s* one *d*. *Educ:* Ayr Acad.; Fettes Coll.; St Andrews Univ. (MA); Edinburgh Univ. (LLB). Brander and Cruickshank, Aberdeen, 1957–71 (Partner in charge of investment management); Globe Investment Trust, 1971–90, Dep Chm., 1983–90. Chairman: Scottish Widows' Fund and Life Assurance Soc., 1987–; Assoc. of Investment Trust Cos, 1987–89; Non-Exec. Director: Kleinwort Benson Gp plc, 1988–; Scottish Power plc, 1990–; Temple Bar Investment Trust, 1963–; Clyde Petroleum, 1976–; Electra Investment Trust, 1975–. *Recreations:* golf, gardening, reading, watching cricket, walking Labradors. *Address:* 15 Tudor Close, Fairmile Park Road, Cobham, Surrey KT11 2PH. *T:* Cobham (0932) 65656. *Club:* New (Edinburgh).

BLACK, Conrad Moffat, OC 1990; Chairman, since 1979, Chief Executive, since 1985, Argus Corporation Ltd; Chairman, Daily Telegraph plc, since 1987 (Director, since 1985); *b* 25 Aug. 1944; *m* 1978, Shirley Gail Joanna Catherine Louise (name changed by deed poll from Hishon); two *s* one *d*. *Educ:* Carleton Univ. (BA); Laval Univ. (LLL); MA History McGill, 1973. Chairman and Chief Executive: Ravelston Corp., 1979–; Hollinger Inc., 1985–; Chm., Saturday Night Magazine Inc., 1987–; Dep. Chm., American Publishing Co., 1987–; Vice-Chm., Norcen Energy Resources, 1986–; Mem. Exec., 1979–, and Dir, 1977–, Canadian Imperial Bank of Commerce; Director: Algoma Central Railway, 1984–; Brascan, 1986–; Canadian Marconi Co., 1988–; Confederation Life Insurance Co., 1977–; Eaton's of Canada, 1976–; Hees International Bancorp. Inc., 1986–; Tridel Enterprises Inc., 1986–; The Financial Post Company Ltd, 1988–; Unimédia (1988) Inc.; Jerusalem Post Publications Ltd, 1989–; Henry Birks & Sons Ltd, 1990–; The Spectator (1828) Ltd, 1990–. Dir, Clarke Inst. of Psychiatry Foundn, 1989–. Hon LLD: St Francis Xavier, 1979; McMaster, 1979; Carleton, 1989; Hon. LittD Univ. of Windsor, 1979. KLJ. *Publication:* Duplessis, 1977. *Address:* c/o 10 Toronto Street,

Toronto, Ont M5C 2B7, Canada. *T:* 416–363–8721; The Daily Telegraph plc, Peterborough Court at South Quay, 181 Marsh Wall, E14 9SR. *Clubs:* Everglades (Palm Beach); Toronto, York, Toronto Golf (Toronto); University, Mount Royal (Montreal).

BLACK, Sir Cyril (Wilson), Kt 1959; JP; *b* 1902; *s* of Robert Wilson Black, JP, and Annie Louise Black (*née* North); *m* 1930, Dorothy Joyce, *d* of Thomas Birkett, Wigston Hall, Leicester; one *s* two *d*. *Educ:* King's College Sch. Chartered Surveyor, FRICS; Chairman: Temperance Permanent Building Soc., 1939–73; Beaumont Properties Ltd, 1933–80; London Shop Property Trust Ltd, 1951–79; M. F. North Ltd, 1948–81, and other companies. JP County of London, 1942; Member Wimbledon Borough Council, 1942–65; Mayor, 1945–46, 1946–47; Alderman, 1942–65; Member, London Borough of Merton Council, 1965–78; Mayor, 1965–66; Member Surrey County Council, 1943–65; County Alderman, 1952–65, and Chm., 1956–59; MP (C) Wimbledon, 1950–70. DL Surrey, 1957–66; DL Greater London, 1966–. Governor of King's College Sch., Wimbledon Coll., Ursuline Convent Sch., Wimbledon, and other Schools. Freedom of City of London, 1943; Freedom of Wimbledon, 1957. Hon. Mem., Houses of Parliament Christian Fellowship; Patron: Wimbledon Youth Cttee; Wimbledon Community Assoc.; Member: SW Metrop. Regional Hospital Board, 1959–62; Baptist Union Council (Pres., 1970–71); Free Church Federal Council; Vice-President: Girls' Bde, 1969– (Hon. Treasurer, 1939–69); Boys' Bde, (Hon. Treasurer, 1962–69). Pres., United Nations Association (London Region), 1964–65. *Recreations:* public work, music, reading. *Address:* Rosewall, Calonne Road, Wimbledon, SW19. *T:* 081–946 2588.

BLACK, Sir David; *see* Black, Sir R. D.

BLACK, Sir Douglas (Andrew Kilgour), Kt 1973; MD, FRCP; Professor of Medicine, Manchester University and Physician, Manchester Royal Infirmary, 1959–77, now Emeritus; Chief Scientist, Department of Health and Social Security, 1973–77; *b* 29 May 1913; *s* of late Rev. Walter Kilgour Black and Mary Jane Crichton; *m* 1948, Mollie Thorn; one *s* two *d*. *Educ:* Forfar Academy; St Andrews Univ. BSc 1933; MB, ChB 1936; MD 1940; MRCP 1939; FRCP 1952; FACP, FRACP, FRCPGlas, 1978; FRCPath, FRCPI, FRCPE, 1979; FRCPsych, 1982; FRCGP, FRCOG, FFCM, 1983; FFOM 1984. MRC Research Fellow, 1938–40; Beit Memorial Research Fellow, 1940–42. Major RAMC, 1942–46. Lecturer, then Reader, in Medicine, Manchester Univ., 1946–58. Horder Travelling Fellow, 1967; Sir Arthur Sims Commonwealth Travelling Prof., 1971; Rock Carling Fellow, 1984. Lectures: Goulstonian, RCP, 1953; Bradshaw, RCP, 1965; Lumleian, RCP, 1970; Harben, RIPH&H, 1973; Crookshank, RCR, 1976; Harveian Orator, RCP, 1977; Maurice Bloch, Glasgow, 1979; Linacre, St John's Coll., Cambridge, 1980; Lloyd Roberts, RSM, 1980; John Locke, Soc. of Apothecaries, 1990; Thomas Young, St George's Hosp. Med. Sch., 1990. Secretary, Manchester Medical Soc., 1957–59. Member: Medical Research Council, 1966–70 and 1971–77 (Chm., Clinical Res. Bd, 1971–73); Assoc. of Physicians; Medical Research Soc.; Renal Assoc., etc. President: RCP, 1977–83; Section X, British Assoc., 1977; Medical Protection Soc., 1982–85; BMA, 1984–85; Hon. Mem., Manchester Lit. and Phil. Soc., 1991. Trustee, 1968–77, Chm., 1977–83, Smith Kline & French Foundn. Chm., Research Working Group on Inequalities in Health, 1977–80. Hon. DSc: St Andrews, 1972; Manchester, 1978; Leicester, 1980; Hon. LLD Birmingham, 1984; Hon. MD Sheffield, 1984. KStJ 1989. *Publications:* Sodium Metabolism in Health and Disease, 1952; Essentials of Fluid Balance, 4th edn, 1967; The Logic of Medicine, 1968; (ed) Renal Disease, 4th edn, 1979; An Anthology of False Antitheses (Rock Carling Lecture), 1984; Invitation to Medicine, 1987; Recollections and Reflections, 1987; contributions to various medical journals. *Recreations:* reading and writing. *Address:* The Old Forge, Duchess Close, Whitchurch-on-Thames, near Reading, RG8 7EN. *T:* Pangbourne (0734) 844693. *Club:* Athenæum.

BLACK, Eugene R(obert); Banker, United States; Chairman: Blackwell Land Co. Inc.; Scandinavian Securities Corp.; Director, Warner Communications; *b* Atlanta, Ga, USA, 1 May 1898; *s* of Eugene R. Black and Gussie Grady; *m* 1st, 1918, Elizabeth Blalock (decd); one *s* one *d*; 2nd, 1930, Susette Heath; one *s*. *Educ:* Univ. of Georgia. Atlanta Office, Harris, Forbes & Co. (NY Investment Bankers), 1919; Manager, Atlanta Office, Chase-Harris, Forbes Corp., in charge of Atlanta, New Orleans, Houston and Dallas offices, 1933; Chase National Bank of the City of NY: 2nd Vice-Pres., 1933; Vice-Pres., 1937; Senior Vice-Pres., 1949, resigned. US Executive Director, Internat. Bank for Reconstruction and Development, 1947–49, President, 1949–53. Consultant and Dir, Chase Manhattan Bank, 1963–70; Consultant, American Express Co., 1970–78. Special Adviser to President Johnson on SE Asia development, 1965–69; Trustee, Corporate Property Investors, and other financial trusteeships. Medal of Freedom (US), 1969. Holds numerous hon. doctorates and has been decorated by many countries. *Publications:* The Diplomacy of Economic Development, 1963 (trans. other languages); Alternative in Southeast Asia, 1969. *Recreations:* golf, fishing; student of William Shakespeare. *Address:* PO Box 753, Southampton, NY 11969–0753, USA. *Clubs:* Athenæum (London, England); Lotos, River (New York); International (Washington, DC); National Golf Links of America (Southampton, NY), etc.

BLACK, Air Vice-Marshal George Philip, CB 1987; OBE 1967; AFC 1962 (Bar 1971); FBIM; Royal Air Force, retired 1987; Senior Defence Adviser, GEC–Marconi Ltd; *b* 10 July 1932; *s* of William and Elizabeth Black; *m* 1954, Ella Ruddiman (*née* Walker); two *s*. *Educ:* Hilton Acad., Aberdeen. Joined RAF, 1950; flying trng in Canada, 1951; served, 1952–64: fighter pilot; carrier pilot (on exchange to FAA); Flying Instr; HQ Fighter Comd; commanded No 111 (Fighter) Sqdn, 1964–66; Mem., Lightning Aerobatic Team, 1965; commanded Lightning Operational Conversion Unit, 1967–69; commanded No 5 (Fighter) Sqdn, 1969–70 (Huddleston Trophy); JSSC, 1970; Air Plans, MoD, 1971–72; Stn Comdr, RAF Wildenwrath, and Harrier Field Force Comdr, RAF Germany, 1972–74; Gp Captain Ops HQ 38 Gp, 1974–76; RCDS, 1977; Gp Captain Ops HQ 11 (Fighter) Gp, 1978–80; Comdr Allied Air Defence Sector One, 1980–83; Comdt ROC, 1983–84; DCS (Ops), HQ AAFCE, 1984–87. Air ADC to the Queen, 1981–83. FBIM 1977. *Recreations:* philately, military aviation history, railways. *Address:* GEC–Marconi Ltd, The Grove, Warren Lane, Stanmore, Middx HA7 4LY. *Club:* Royal Air Force.

BLACK, Iain James, QC 1971; **His Honour Judge Black;** a Circuit Judge, since 1986. Called to the Bar, Gray's Inn, 1947, Bencher, 1985–86; Dep. Chm., Staffs QS, 1965–71; a Recorder, 1972–86. Member: Criminal Injuries Compensation Bd, 1975–86; Mental Health Review Tribunal, 1984–. *Address:* 3 Fountain Court, Steelhouse Lane, Birmingham B4 6DR. *T:* 021–236 5854.

BLACK, James Walter, QC 1979; a Recorder of the Crown Court, since 1976; *b* 8 Feb. 1941; *s* of Dr James Black and Mrs Clementine M. Black (*née* Robb); *m* 1st, 1964, Jane Marie Keyden; two *s* one *d*; 2nd, 1985, Diana Marjorie Day (*née* Harris); one *d*. *Educ:* Harecroft Hall, Gosforth, Cumbria; Trinity Coll., Glenalmond, Perthshire; St Catharine's Coll., Cambridge (MA). Called to the Bar, Middle Temple, 1964; NSW Bar, 1986. *Recreations:* fishing, sailing, golf. *Address:* Guildhall Chambers, 23 Broad Street, Bristol BS1 2HG. *T:* Bristol (0272) 273366; 2 King's Bench Walk, Temple, EC4Y 7DE. *T:* 071–353 1746. *Clubs:* Royal Scottish Automobile (Glasgow); Royal Dornoch Golf.

BLACK, Sir James (Whyte), Kt 1981; FRCP; FRS 1976; Professor of Analytical Pharmacology, King's College Hospital Medical School, University of London, since 1984; *b* 14 June 1924. *Educ:* Beath High Sch., Cowdenbeath; Univ. of St Andrews (MB, ChB). Asst Lectr in Physiology, Univ. of St Andrews, 1946; Lectr in Physiology, Univ. of Malaya, 1947–50; Sen. Lectr, Univ. of Glasgow Vet. Sch., 1950–58; ICI Pharmaceuticals Ltd, 1958–64; Head of Biological Res. and Dep. Res. Dir, Smith, Kline & French, Welwyn Garden City, 1964–73; Prof. and Head of Dept of Pharmacology, University College, London, 1973–77; Dir of Therapeutic Research, Wellcome Res. Labs, 1978–84. Mem., British Pharmacological Soc., 1961–. Hon. FRSE 1986. Hon. Fellow, London Univ., 1990. Mullard Award, Royal Soc., 1978; (jtly) Nobel Prize for Physiology or Medicine, 1988. *Address:* Analytical Pharmacology Unit, Rayne Institute, 123 Coldharbour Lane, SE5 9NU. *T:* 071–274 7437.

BLACK, Adm. Sir (John) Jeremy, GBE 1991 (MBE 1963); KCB 1987; DSO 1982; Stia Negara Brunei 1963; Commander-in-Chief, Naval Home Command, 1989–91; Flag Aide-de-Camp to the Queen, 1989–91; *b* 1932; *s* of Alan H. Black and G. Black; *m* 1958, Alison Pamela Barber; two *s* one *d*. *Educ:* Royal Naval College, Dartmouth (entered 1946). Korean War and Malayan Emergency, 1951–52; qualified in gunnery, 1958; commanded HM Ships: Fiskerton, 1960–62 (Brunei Rebellion, 1962); Decoy, 1969 (Comdr 1969, Captain 1974); Fife, 1977; RCDS 1979; Director of Naval Operational Requirements, Naval Staff, 1980–81; commanded HMS Invincible (Falklands), 1982–83; Flag Officer, First Flotilla, 1983–84; ACNS (Policy), Oct-Dec. 1984; ACNS, 1985–86; Dep. CDS (Systems), 1986–89. Mem. Council, RUSI, 1987–89. Chm., Whitbread Round the World Race Cttee, 1990–; Governor, Ocean Youth Club, 1991–. Cdre, RNSA, 1989–; Pres., RN Clay Pigeon Assoc., 1990–. *Recreations:* sailing, history. *Clubs:* Commonwealth Trust; Royal Yacht Squadron.

BLACK, John Newman, CEng, FICE, FIMarE; FRGS; Consultant, Robert West and Partners, Chartered Consulting Engineers, since 1990; *b* 29 Sept. 1925; *s* of late John Black and late Janet Black (*née* Hamilton); *m* 1952, Euphemia Isabella Elizabeth Thomson; two *d*. *Educ:* Cumberland and Medway Technical Colls. Civil and marine engrg naval stations and dockyards, UK and abroad, incl. Singapore, Hong Kong, Colombo, Gibraltar and Orkney Isles, 1941–64; joined PLA as Civil Engr, 1964; Planning and Construction, Tilbury Docks, 1964–66; Planning Manager, 1967; seconded to Thames Estuary Develt Co. Ltd, for work on Maplin Airport/Seaport Scheme, 1969; Asst Dir Planning, PLA, 1970; Director: Maplin, 1972; Tilbury Docks, 1974; all London Docks, 1977; Man. Dir, 1978–81; Bd Mem., 1978–86, Chief Exec., 1982–86, and Dep. Chm., 1985–86, PLA. Dep. Chm., PLA (Met. Terminals) Ltd, 1974; Director: PLACON Ltd (PLA's cons. subsid. co.), 1972; Orsett Depot Ltd, 1974; Port Documentation Services Ltd (Chm.), 1978; Chairman: Thames Riparian Housing Assoc., 1974; PLA Group Property Holdings, 1984. Member: Exec. Council, British Ports Assoc., 1982–86; Exec. Cttee, Nat. Assoc. of Port Employers, 1982–86 (Vice-Chm., 1984–86); British Nat. Cttee, Permt Internat. Assoc. of Navigation Congresses, 1981–; London Maritime Assoc., 1975; Council, ICHCA Internat., 1985–86; Nat. Exec. Cttee, ICHCA (UK), 1985–. Co-Adviser to Indian Govt on port ops and potential, 1968; lectures: for UN, Alexandria, 1975; for ESCAP (UN), Bangkok, 1983. FInstPet. Freeman: City of London, 1977; Watermen and Lightermen of River Thames, 1977. *Publications:* numerous articles and papers in Geographical Jl, Civil Engr and other learned jls. *Recreations:* shooting, fishing. *Address:* Westdene Cottage, Tanyard Hill, Shorne, near Gravesend, Kent DA12 3EN.

BLACK, John Nicholson, MA, DPhil, DSc; FRSE; Principal, Bedford College, University of London, 1971–81; *b* 28 June 1922; *e s* of Harold Black, MD, FRCP, and Margaret Frances Black (*née* Nicholson); *m* 1st, 1952, Mary Denise Webb (*d* 1966); one *s* one *d*; 2nd, 1967, Wendy Marjorie Waterston; two *s*. *Educ:* Rugby Sch.; Exeter Coll., Oxford. MA 1952, DPhil 1952, Oxford; DSc 1965, Adelaide; FRSE 1965. Served War, RAF, 1942–46. Oxford Univ., 1946–49; BA Hons Cl. 1 (Agri.) 1949; Agricl Research Council Studentship, 1949–52; Lectr, Sen. Lectr, Reader, Univ. of Adelaide (Waite Agricl Research Inst.), 1952–63; André Mayer Fellowship (FAO), 1958; Prof. of Forestry and Natural Resources, Univ. of Edinburgh, 1963–71. Dir and Sec., The Wolfson Foundn, 1981–87; Dir, The Wolfson Family Charitable Trust, 1987–89. Mem., Nat. Environment Research Council, 1968–74; Mem. Council and Finance Cttee, RAF Benevolent Fund, 1989–. Chm., Donizetti Soc., 1984–87. *Publications:* The Dominion of Man, 1970; Donizetti's Operas in Naples, 1983; The Italian Romantic Libretto, 1984; (contrib. entries (26) on Italian librettists) The New Grove Dictionary of Opera; papers on: ecological subjects in scientific jls (70); Italian opera libretti (30). *Recreations:* music, repair and restoration of porcelain and pottery. *Address:* Paddock House, Pyrton, near Watlington, Oxon OX9 5AP. *T:* Watlington (049161) 2600.

BLACK, Prof. Joseph, CBE 1980; PhD; FEng, FIMechE, FRAeS; Professor of Engineering, University of Bath, 1960–85, Head of School of Engineering, 1960–70 and 1973–85; *b* 25 Jan. 1921; *s* of Alexander Black and Hettie Black; *m* 1946, Margaret Susan Hewitt; three *s* one *d*. *Educ:* Royal Belfast Academical Instn; QUB (BScEng, MSc). PhD Bristol; FRAeS 1961, FIMechE 1964, FEng 1981. Scientific Officer, RAE, 1941–44; Res. Fellow, QUB, 1944–45; Aerodynamicist, de Havilland Aircraft, 1945–46; Lectr/Sen. Lectr in Engrg, Univ. of Bristol, 1946–59. Gillette Fellow, USA, 1963. Pro-Vice-Chancellor, Univ. of Bath, 1970–73. Member: UGC, 1964–74 (Chm. Educnl Technol. Cttee); (founder) Council for Educnl Technol., 1974–; A/M Cttee, SRC, 1975–79; Design Council, 1977–82 (Chm. Engrg Components Awards 1976, Engrg Products Awards 1977); Mech. Engrg and Machine Tool Requirement Bd, DoI, 1979–81. SERC/Design Council Engrg Design Co-ordinator, 1985–89. Hon. DTech Loughborough, 1990. Silver Jubilee Medal, 1977. *Publications:* Introduction to Aerodynamic Compressibility, 1950; contrib. aeronaut. and mech. engrg jls (UK and Europe). *Recreations:* photography, antiquarian books, silversmithing. *Address:* 20 Summerhill Road, Bath BA1 2UR. *T:* Bath (0225) 23970. *Club:* Athenæum.

BLACK, Margaret McLeod; Head Mistress, Bradford Girls' Grammar School, 1955–75; *b* 1 May 1912; *d* of James Black and Elizabeth Malcolm. *Educ:* Kelso High Sch.; Edinburgh Univ. (MA). Classics Mistress, Lancaster Girls' Grammar Sch., 1936–44, and Manchester High Sch. for Girls, 1944–50; Head Mistress, Great Yarmouth Girls' High Sch., 1950–55. President: Leeds Branch of Classical Assoc., 1963–65; Joint Assoc. of Classical Teachers, 1967–69; Yorkshire Divl Union of Soroptimist Clubs, 1968–69. *Recreation:* music. *Club:* Royal Over-Seas League.

BLACK, Rev. Prof. Matthew, DD, DLitt, DTheol, LLD; FRSE; FBA 1955; Professor of Divinity and Biblical Criticism, and Principal of St Mary's College, University of St Andrews, 1954–78; now Emeritus Professor; Dean of the Faculty of Divinity, 1963–67; *b* 3 Sept. 1908; *s* of late James and Helen Black, Kilmarnock, Ayrshire; *m* 1938, Ethel M., *d* of late Lt-Comdr A. H. Hall, Royal Indian Navy; one *s* one *d*. *Educ:* Kilmarnock Academy; Glasgow Univ. Glasgow: 1st cl. hons MA Classics, 1930; 2nd cl. hons Mental Philosophy, 1931; BD with distinction in Old Testament, 1934; DLitt 1944; Dr Phil Bonn, 1937. Hon. DTheol Münster, 1960; Hon. LLD St Andrews, 1980; Hon. DD: Glasgow, 1954; Cambridge, 1965; Queen's, Ontario, 1967. Buchanan Prize, Moral Philosophy, 1929; Caird Scholar, Classics, 1930; Crombie Scholar, Biblical Criticism,

1933 (St Andrews award); Brown Downie Fellow, 1934; Maxwell Forsyth Fellow and Kerr Travelling Scholarship, Trinity Coll., Glasgow, 1934. Asst to Prof. of Hebrew, Glasgow, 1935–37; Warden of Church of Scotland Students' Residence, 1936–37; Asst Lecturer in Semitic Languages and Literatures, University of Manchester, 1937–39; Bruce Lectr, Trinity Coll., Glasgow, 1940; Lectr in Hebrew and Biblical Criticism, Univ. of Aberdeen, 1939–42; Minister of Dunbarney, Church of Scotland, 1942–47; Officiating CF, Bridge of Earn, 1943–47; Lecturer in New Testament Language and Literature, Leeds Univ., 1947–52; Prof. of Biblical Criticism and Biblical Antiquities, University of Edinburgh, 1952–54. Chm., Adv. Cttee of Peshitta Project of Univ. of Leiden, 1968–78. Morse Lectr, 1956 and De Hoyt Lectr, 1963, Union Theological Seminary, NY; Thomas Burns Lectr, Otago, 1967. Pres., Soc. for Old Testament Study, 1968. FRSE 1977. Pres., SNTS, 1970–71; Corresp. Mem., Göttingen Akademie der Wissenschaften, 1957; Mem., Royal Soc. of Scis, Uppsala, 1979; Hon. Member: Amer. Soc. of Biblical Exegesis, 1958; American Bible Soc., 1966. British Academy Burkitt Medal for Biblical Studies, 1962. *Publications:* Rituale Melchitarum (Stuttgart), 1938; An Aramaic Approach to the Gospels and Acts, 3rd edn, 1967 (Die Muttersprache Jesu, 1982); A Christian Palestinian Syriac Horologion, Texts and Studies, Contributions to Patristic Literature, New Series, Vol. I, 1954; The Scrolls and Christian Origins, 1961, repr. 1983; General and New Testament Editor, Peake's Commentary on the Bible (revised edn, 1962); Bible Societies' edn of the Greek New Testament (Stuttgart), 1966; (Jt Editor) In Memoriam Paul Kahle (Berlin), 1968; (Editor and contributor) The Scrolls and Christianity, 1968; (with A. M. Denis) Apocalypsis Henochi Graece Fragmenta Pseudepigraphorum, 1970; Commentary on Romans, 1973, 2nd edn 1989; (ed with William A. Smalley) On Language, Religion and Culture, in honor Eugene A. Nida, 1974; (organising Editor) The History of the Jewish People in the Age of Jesus Christ: vol. I, ed by G. Vermes and F. Millar, 1973; vol. II, ed jtly with G. Vermes and F. Millar, 1979; vol. III, ed by G. Vermes, F. Millar and M. Goodman, Part 1, 1986, Part 2, 1987; (jtly) The Book of Enoch or I Enoch, 1985; Editor, New Testament Studies, to 1977; articles in learned journals. *Address:* St Michael's, 40 Buchanan Gardens, St Andrews, Fife KY16 9LX. *Club:* Royal and Ancient.

BLACK, Neil Cathcart, OBE 1989; Principal Oboist, English Chamber Orchestra, since 1970; *b* 28 May 1932; *s* of Harold Black and Margaret Frances Black; *m* 1st, 1960, Jill (*née* Hemingsley); one *s* two *d*; 2nd, 1984, Janice Mary (*née* Knight). *Educ:* Rugby; Exeter College, Oxford (BA History). Entered musical profession, 1956; Principal Oboist: London Philharmonic Orch., 1959–61; in various chamber orchs, incl. London Mozart Players, Acad. of St Martin-in-the-Fields, 1965–72; oboe soloist internationally. Hon. RAM 1969. *Recreations:* wine, travel. *Address:* c/o English Chamber Orchestra, 2 Coningsby Road, W5 4HR. *T:* 081–840 6565.

BLACK, Prof. Paul Joseph, OBE 1983; PhD; FInstP; Professor of Science Education, University of London, since 1976; *b* 10 Sept. 1930; *s* of Walter and Susie Black; *m* 1957, Mary Elaine Weston; four *s* one *d*. *Educ:* Rhyl Grammar Sch.; Univ. of Manchester (BSc); Univ. of Cambridge (PhD). FInstP 1986. Royal Society John Jaffé Studentship, 1953–56. Univ. of Birmingham: Lectr in Physics, 1956–66; Reader in Crystal Physics, 1966–74; Prof. of Physics (Science Education), 1974–76; Dir, Centre for Science and Maths Educn, Chelsea Coll., Univ. of London, 1976–85; subseq., following merger of colls, Head, Centre for Educnl Studies, KCL, 1985–89 (FKC 1990); Dean, Faculty of Educn, Univ. of London, 1978–82. Educnl Consultant: to Nuffield Chelsea Curriculum Trust, 1978–; to OECD, 1988–. Vice-Pres., Royal Instn of Great Britain, 1983–85; Chairman: Council, Grubb Inst. for Behavioural Studies, 1985–90; National Curriculum Task Gp on Assessment and Testing, DES, 1987–88; Member: School Curriculum Develt Cttee, 1984–88; Nat. Curriculum Council, 1988– (Dep. Chm., 1989–); Exec., Univs Council for Educn of Teachers, 1982–86; Res. Grants Bd, ESRC, 1987–90; Internat. Commn on Physics Educn, 1987–; Pres., Groupe Internat. de la Recherche sur l'Enseignement de la Physique, 1984–; Hon. Pres., Assoc. for Science Educn, 1986; Hon. Life Mem., Assoc. for Science Educn, 1986; Hon. Member: Standing Conf. on Sch. Science and Technol., 1989; CGLI, 1989. Bragg Medal, Inst. of Physics, 1973. Kt of St Gregory, 1973. FRSA 1990. *Publications:* (jtly) Nuffield Advanced Physics Project, 1972; (contrib.) Higher Education Learning Project Books, 1977; papers on crystallography, and on physics and science, and technology education. *Address:* 16 Wilton Crescent, SW19 3QZ. *T:* 081–542 4178.

BLACK, Peter Blair, JP; Senior Partner, P. Blair Black & Partners, since 1948; *b* 22 April 1917; *s* of Peter Blair Black and Cissie Crawford Samuel; *m* 1952, Mary Madeleine Hilly, Philadelphia; one *s* three *d*. *Educ:* Sir Walter St John's, Battersea; Bearsden Acad.; Sch. of Building. CC 1949, Alderman 1961, Middlesex; Mem., GLC, 1963–86, Chm., 1970–71, Leader, Recreation and Community Services Policy Gp, 1977–81; motivator of Thames Barrier project; Chm., Cons. Group, GLC, 1982. Chm., Thames Water Authority, 1973–78; Pres., Pure Rivers Soc., 1976–. Leader: GLC group to Moscow and Leningrad, 1971; British delegn to Washington, Potomac/Thames River Conf., 1977; Mem. internat. team to Tokyo, Metropolitan Clean Air Conf., 1971. Mem. Exec. Cttee, Nat. Union of Cons. and Unionist Assocs, 1987–. Frequent performer on TV and radio. Former Member: Thames Conservancy Bd; Metrop. Water Bd; Jager Cttee on Sewage Disposal; PLA; Council, Nat. Fedn of Housing Socs; Founder Chm., Omnium Housing Assoc., 1962; Chm., 1972, Pres., 1983, Abbeyfield, London Region. JP Thames Div., 1961. Freeman: City of London; Tucson, Arizona. *Recreations:* small boats and fishing. *Address:* 101A Limmer Lane, Felpham, Sussex PO22 7LP. *T:* Middleton-on-Sea (024369) 2054. *Clubs:* Middleton Sports; Sewers Synonymous (Dir).

BLACK, Prof. Robert; QC (Scot.) 1987; Professor of Scots Law, University of Edinburgh, since 1981; *b* 12 June 1947; *s* of James Little Black and Jeannie Findlay Lyon. *Educ:* Lockerbie Acad.; Dumfries Acad.; Edinburgh Univ. (LLB); McGill Univ., Montreal (LLM); Lord Pres. Cooper Meml Prize, Univ. of Edinburgh, 1968; Vans Dunlop Scholarship, Univ. of Edinburgh, 1968; Commonwealth Scholarship, Commonwealth Scholarship Commn, 1968. Advocate, 1972; Lectr in Scots Law, Univ. of Edinburgh, 1972–75; Sen. Legal Officer, Scottish Law Commn, 1975–78; in practice at Scottish Bar, 1978–81; Temp. Sheriff, 1981–. Gen. Editor, The Laws of Scotland: Stair Memorial Encyclopaedia, 1988– (Dep., then Jt, Gen. Editor, 1981–88). *Publications:* An Introduction to Written Pleading, 1982; Civil Jurisdiction: the new rules, 1983; articles in UK and S African legal jls. *Recreation:* baiting sociologists. *Address:* 6/4 Glenogle Road, Edinburgh EH3 5HW. *T:* 031–557 3571. *Clubs:* Sloane; Scottish Arts (Edinburgh).

BLACK, Sir Robert (Brown), (Sir Robin Black), GCMG 1962 (KCMG 1955; CMG 1953); OBE 1949 (MBE (mil.) 1948); *b* 3 June 1906; *s* of late Robert and Catherine Black, formerly of Blair Lodge, Polmont, Stirlingshire; *m* 1937, (Elsie) Anne Stevenson, CStJ (*d* 1986); two *d*. *Educ:* George Watson's Coll.; Edinburgh Univ. Colonial Administrative Service, 1930; served in Malaya, Trinidad, N Borneo, Hong Kong. Served War of 1939–45, commissioned in Intelligence Corps, 1942; 43 Special Military Mission; POW Japan, 1942–45. Colonial Secretary, Hong Kong, 1952–55; Governor and C-in-C: Singapore, 1955–57; Hong Kong, 1958–64. Chancellor: Hong Kong Univ., 1958–64; Chinese University of Hong Kong, 1963–64. Mem., Commonwealth War Graves Commn, 1964–82. Chm., Clerical, Medical and General Life Assurance Soc., 1975–78. Chm., Internat. Social Service of GB, 1965–73, Pres., 1973–82. LLD (*hc*): Univ. of Hong Kong; Chinese Univ. of Hong Kong. KStJ. Grand Cross Order of Merit, Peru. *Recreations:* walking, fishing. *Address:* Mapletons House, Ashampstead Common, near Reading, Berks RG8 8QN. *Club:* East India, Devonshire, Sports and Public Schools.

BLACK, Sir (Robert) David, 3rd Bt *cr* 1922; DL; *b* 29 March 1929; *s* of Sir Robert Andrew Stransham Black, 2nd Bt, ED, and Ivy (*d* 1980), *d* of late Brig.-Gen. Sir Samuel Wilson, GCMG, KCB, KBE; *S* father, 1979; *m* 1st, 1953, Rosemary Diana (marr. diss. 1972), *d* of Sir Rupert John Hardy, 4th Bt; two *d* (and one *d* decd); 2nd, 1973, Dorothy Maureen, *d* of Major Charles R. Eustace Radclyffe and *widow* of A. R. D. Pilkington. *Educ:* Eton. Lieut, Royal Horse Guards, 1949; Captain 1953; Major 1960; retired, 1961. Served with Berkshire and Westminster Dragoons, TA, 1964–67, and Berkshire Territorials, TAVR III, 1967–69; Vice-Chm., Berkshire, Eastern Wessex TAVRA, 1985–. Joint Master, Garth and South Berks Foxhounds, 1965–73. Hon. Col, 94 (Berks Yeo.) Signal Sqn (TA), 1988–. DL Caithness, 1991. *Recreations:* hunting, shooting, stalking and fishing. *Heir:* none. *Address:* Elvendon Priory, Goring, near Reading, Berks RG8 0LS. *T:* Goring-on-Thames (0491) 872160; Shurrery Lodge, Shebster, Thurso, Caithness. *T:* Reay (084781) 252. *Club:* Cavalry and Guards.

BLACK, Prof. Robert Denis Collison, FBA 1974; Professor of Economics, and Head of Department of Economics, Queen's University Belfast, 1962–85, now Emeritus; *b* 11 June 1922; *s* of William Robert Black and Rose Anna Mary (*née* Reid), Dublin; *m* 1953, Frances Mary, *o d* of William F. and Mary Weatherup, Belfast; one *s* one *d*. *Educ:* Sandford Park Sch.; Trinity Coll., Dublin (Hon. Fellow, 1982). BA 1941, BComm 1941, PhD 1943, MA 1945. Dep. for Prof. of Polit. Economy, Trinity Coll., Dublin, 1943–45; Asst Lectr in Economics, Queen's Univ., Belfast, 1945–46, Lectr, 1946–58, Sen. Lectr, 1958–61, Reader, 1961–62. Rockefeller Post-doctoral Fellow, Princeton Univ., 1950–51; Visiting Prof. of Economics, Yale Univ., 1964–65; Dean of Faculty of Economics and Social Sciences, QUB, 1967–70; Pro-Vice-Chancellor, 1971–75. President: Statistical & Social Inquiry Soc. of Ireland, 1983–86; Section F, BAAS, 1984–85. Distinguished Fellow, History of Economics Soc., USA, 1987. MRIA 1974. Hon. DSc(Econ) QUB, 1988. *Publications:* Centenary History of the Statistical Society of Ireland, 1947; Economic Thought and the Irish Question 1817–1870, 1960; Catalogue of Economic Pamphlets 1750–1900, 1969; Papers and Correspondence of William Stanley Jevons, Vol. I, 1972, Vol. II, 1973, Vols III-VI, 1977, Vol. VII, 1981; Ideas in Economics, 1986; articles in Economic Jl, Economica, Oxford Econ. Papers, Econ. History Review, etc. *Recreations:* travel, music. *Address:* Queen's University, Belfast, Northern Ireland BT7 1NN. *T:* Belfast (0232) 245133.

BLACK, Sir Robin; *see* Black, Sir R. B.

BLACK, Sheila (Psyche), OBE 1986; feature writer; Director, MAI plc (formerly Mills and Allen International), since 1976; *b* 6 May 1920; *d* of Clement Johnston Black, CA, and Mildred Beryl Black; *m* 1st, 1939, Geoffrey Davien, Sculptor (marr. diss. 1951); one *d* (one *s* decd); 2nd, 1951, L. A. Lee Howard (marr. diss. 1973). *Educ:* Dorset; Switzerland; RADA. Actress, until outbreak of War of 1939–45; Asst to production manager of an electrical engineering factory. Post-war, in advertising; then in journalism, from the mid-fifties; Woman's Editor, Financial Times, 1959–72; specialist feature writer, The Times, 1972–79; Chm., Interflex Data Systems (UK) Ltd, 1975–83. Features writer for The Director, Financial Weekly, Punch, Mediaworld, and many newspapers and magazines. Chairman: Nat. Gas Consumers' Council, 1981–86; Gas Consumers Council, 1986–88; Dir, Money Management Council, 1985–90; Member: Furniture Develt Council, 1967–70; Liquor Licensing Laws Special Cttee, 1971–72; (part-time) Price Commn, 1973–77; Nat. Consumer Council, 1981–; Calcutt Cttee on Privacy and Related Matters, 1989–90. Dir, Countrywide Workshops Charitable Trust, 1982–88 and 1989–. Mem. Council, Inst. of Directors, 1975–90. Freeman, City of London, 1985. *Publications:* The Black Book, 1976; Mirabelle: cuisine de qualité et tradition, 1979; The Reluctant Money Minder, 1980; various others. *Recreations:* gardening, grandchildren, football. *Address:* c/o National Westminster Bank, 104 Tottenham Court Road, W1A 3AW.

BLACKBURN, Bishop of, since 1989; **Rt. Rev. Alan David Chesters;** *b* 26 Aug. 1937; *s* of Herbert and Catherine Rebecca Chesters; *m* 1975, Jennie Garrett; one *s*. *Educ:* Elland Grammar Sch., W Yorks; St Chad's Coll., Univ. of Durham (BA Mod. History); St Catherine's Coll., Oxford (BA Theol., MA); St Stephen's House, Oxford. Curate of St Anne, Wandsworth, 1962–66; Chaplain and Head of Religius Education, Tiffin School, Kingston-upon-Thames, 1966–72; Director of Education and Rector of Brancepeth, Diocese of Durham, 1972–84; Hon. Canon of Durham Cathedral, 1975–84; Archdeacon of Halifax, 1985–89. A Church Comr, 1982–89 (Mem., Bd of Governors, 1984–89). Mem., General Synod, 1975– (Mem., Standing Cttee, 1985–89, 1990–). *Recreations:* railways, hill walking, reading. *Address:* Bishop's House, Ribchester Road, Blackburn BB1 9EF.

BLACKBURN, Archdeacon of; *see* Robinson, Ven. W. D.

BLACKBURN, Provost of; *see* Jackson, Very Rev. Lawrence.

BLACKBURN, Captain (David) Anthony (James), LVO 1978; RN; Commodore, Clyde, since 1990; *b* 18 Jan. 1945; *s* of late Lieut J. Blackburn, DSC, RN, and late Mrs M. J. G. Pickering-Pick; *m* 1973, Elizabeth Barstow; three *d*. *Educ:* Taunton Sch. RNC Dartmouth, 1963; HMS Kirkliston (in comd), 1972–73; Equerry-in-Waiting to the Duke of Edinburgh, 1976–78; Exec. Officer, HMS Antrim, 1978–81; MoD (Navy), 1981–83; Comdr, HMS Birmingham, 1983–84; MoD (Navy), 1984–86; HMS York (in comd) and Captain Third Destroyer Sqn, 1987–88; Dir, Naval Manpower and Trng (Seamen), MoD, 1988–90. *Club:* Royal Cruising.

BLACKBURN, Guy, MBE (mil.) 1944; MChir, FRCS; Consultant Surgeon Emeritus, Guy's Hospital; *b* 20 Nov. 1911; *s* of Dr A. E. Blackburn, Beckenham; *m* 1953, Joan, *d* of Arthur Bowen, Pontycymmer, Wales; one *d* (and one *s* by a previous marriage). *Educ:* Rugby; Clare Coll., Cambridge (MA). MRCS, LRCP 1935; MB, BChir 1935; FRCS 1937; MChir 1941. House appointments, St Bartholomew's Hospital, 1935–37; Brackenbury Scholar in Surgery, 1935; Demonstrator of Anatomy and Chief Asst in Surgery, 1938–39; Military Service, 1942–46; Lt-Col i/c Surgical Div., 1945–46; served in N Africa and Italy. Hunterian Prof., RCS, 1946; late Examiner in Surgery, Univs of Cambridge and London; Member Court of Examiners, RCS, 1962–68. Hon. Visiting Surgeon, Johns Hopkins Hospital, Baltimore, USA, 1957; President, Medical Society of London, 1964–65. Hon. Consulting Surgeon, British Army at Home, 1967–76. Pres., Assoc. of Surgeons of GB and Ireland, 1976–77. Master, Soc. of Apothecaries, 1980–81. *Publications:* (co-ed) A Textbook of Surgery, 1958; (co-ed) Field Surgery Pocket Book, 1981; various publications in medical jls and books. *Address:* 4 Holly Lodge Gardens, N6 6AA. *T:* 081–340 9071. *Club:* Garrick.

BLACKBURN, (Jeffrey) Michael; Director and Chief Executive, Leeds Permanent Building Society, since 1987; *b* 16 Dec. 1941; *s* of Jeffrey and Renee Blackburn; *m* 1987, Louise Clair Vasquez; two *s*, and one *s* one *d* from a previous marriage. *Educ:* Northgate Grammar Sch., Ipswich. FCIB; CBIM. Chief Manager, Lloyds Bank Business Adv. Service, 1979–83; Dir and Chief Exec., Joint Credit Card Co. Ltd, 1983–87. Mem. Court and Council, Leeds Univ., 1989–. *Recreations:* music, theatre. *Address:* Leeds Permanent Building Society, Permanent House, The Headrow, Leeds LS1 1NS. *Club:* Oriental.

BLACKBURN, John; QC 1984; barrister; *b* 13 Nov. 1945; *s* of Harry and Violet Blackburn; *m* 1st, 1970, Alison Nield (marr. diss. 1978); 2nd, 1979, Elizabeth Parker; two *s*. *Educ:* Rugby Sch.; Worcester Coll., Oxford (Scholar, 1967; Gibbs Prize in Law, 1967). Called to the Bar, Middle Temple, 1969 (Astbury Law Scholar). Practising barrister, 1970–. *Recreations:* cricket, golf, paintings, wine. *Address:* 1 Atkin Building, Gray's Inn, WC1R 5BQ.

BLACKBURN, John Graham, PhD; MP (C) Dudley West, since May 1979; *b* 2 Sept. 1933; *s* of Charles Frederick Blackburn and Grace Blackburn; *m* 1958, Marjorie (*née* Thompson); one *s* one *d*. *Educ:* Liverpool Collegiate Sch.; Liverpool Univ.; Berlin Univ. (PhD). Staff/Sgt, Special Investigation Br., Royal Military Police, 1949–53; D/Sgt, Liverpool Police, 1953–65; National Sales Manager with an Internat. Public Engrg Gp, 1965–79; Sales Dir, Solway Engrg Co. Ltd, 1965–. Member, Wolverhampton Council, 1970–80; Member: Home Affairs Select Cttee, 1980–83; Select Cttee for Services, 1987–; Vice Chm., Cons. Parly Cttee for Arts and Heritage, 1986– (Sec., 1980–86). Chm., Cons. Friends of Israel, 1985–; Mem., Council of Europe, 1983–85. Member: POUNC, 1972–80; Ecclesiastical Council, 1979–. Freeman: City of London, 1980; City of Tel Aviv, 1981. FInstM 1979; FISE 1975; FInstMSM 1976; FRSA 1984. *Recreation:* keen yachtsman. *Address:* 129 Canterbury Road, Penn, Wolverhampton WV4 4EQ. *T:* Wolverhampton (0902) 36222. *Clubs:* Wolverhampton and Bilston Athletic (Vice-President); Traeth Coch Yacht (Executive Member).

BLACKBURN, Michael; *see* Blackburn, J. M.

BLACKBURN, Michael John, FCA; Chairman, Touche Ross & Co., since 1990 (Managing Partner, 1984–90); *b* 25 Oct. 1930; *s* of Francis and Ann Blackburn; *m* 1955, Maureen (*née* Dale); one *s* two *d*. *Educ:* Kingston Grammar Sch. Joined Touche Ross, 1954; Partner, 1960. Chm., GEI International, 1990–; Dir, Anglo–American Insce Co., 1991–. *Recreations:* horse racing, gardening. *Address:* (office) Peterborough Court, 133 Fleet Street, EC4A 2TR. *T:* 071–936 3000. *Club:* City of London.

BLACKBURN, Michael Scott; His Honour Judge Blackburn; a Circuit Judge, since 1986; *b* 16 Jan. 1936; *m* 1961, Vivienne (*née* Smith); one *s* one *d*. *Educ:* Dame Allan's Sch., Newcastle upon Tyne; William Hulme's Grammar Sch., Manchester; Keble Coll., Oxford (MA). Notary Public. Recorder, 1981–86. President: Manchester Law Society, 1979–80; Manchester Medico-Legal Soc., 1986–88; Chairman, North Western Legal Services Cttee, 1981–85; Mem., Parole Bd, 1985–88. *Recreations:* squash rackets, hill walking, fishing. *Club:* Northern Lawn Tennis (Manchester).

BLACKBURN, Peter Hugh, FCA; Chairman and Managing Director, Nestlé Holdings (UK) PLC, since 1991; *b* 17 Dec. 1940; *s* of Hugh Edward Blackburn and Sarah Blackburn (*née* Moffatt); *m* 1967, Gillian Mary Popple; three *d*. *Educ:* Douai Sch., Reading; Leeds Univ. (BA Hons Philosophy and French); Poitiers Univ. (Dipl. French); Inst. of Chartered Accts. R. S. Dawson & Co., Bradford (articles), 1962–66; John Mackintosh & Sons: Works Accountant, Halifax, 1966–67; Financial Controller, Norwich, 1967–72; Rowntree Mackintosh: Chief Accountant and Finance Dir, Overseas Div., 1972–75; Asst Man. Dir, later Man. Dir, European Div., 1975–84 (Advanced Management Prog., Harvard Business Sch., 1976); Group Board Dir, 1982; Jt Chm., later Chm., UK and Eire Region, 1985–88; Chm., Rowntree UK, 1989–91; Head, Nestlé Chocolate, Confectionery and Biscuit Strategy Group, 1989–90. Nat. Pres., Modern Languages Assoc., 1987–89; Chm., Council, Festival of Languages Young Linguist Competition, 1985–89. Mem., Council of Industry and Higher Educn, 1990–. Mem. Council, York Univ., 1989–. Hon. FIL 1989. *Recreations:* fell walking, swimming, photography. *Address:* Nestlé Holdings (UK), St George's House, Park Lane, Croydon CR9 1NR. *Club:* Yorkshire (York).

BLACKBURN, Ronald Henry Albert; a Planning Appeals Commissioner for Northern Ireland, 1980–89, retired; *b* 9 Feb. 1924; *s* of late Sidney James and Ellen Margaret Selina Blackburn; *m* 1950, Annabell Hunter; two *s*. *Educ:* Royal Belfast Academical Institution; Univ. of London (LLB (Hons)). Intelligence Service, 1943; Dept of the Foreign Office, 1944–46. Parly Reporting Staff (N Ire.), 1946–52; Second Clerk Asst, Parlt of N Ire., 1952–62; Clerk Asst, 1962–71; Clerk of the Parliaments, 1971–73; Clerk to NI Assembly, 1973–79; Clerk to NI Constitutional Convention, 1975–76. *Recreations:* golf, gardening. *Address:* Trelawn, Jordanstown Road, Newtownabbey, Co. Antrim, N Ireland BT37 0QD. *T:* Whiteabbey (0232) 862035.

BLACKBURNE, Rt. Rev. Hugh Charles; *b* 4 June 1912; *s* of late Very Rev. Harry William Blackburne; *m* 1944, Doris Freda, *widow* of Pilot Officer H. L. N. Davis; two *s* one *d*. *Educ:* Marlborough; Clare Coll., Cambridge (MA); Westcott House, Cambridge. Deacon, 1937; Priest, 1938; Curate of Almondbury, Yorks, 1937–39. Chaplain to the Forces, 1939–47; served with 1st Guards Bde, 11th Armoured Div., HQ Anti-Aircraft Comd, and as Chaplain, RMC, Sandhurst. Rector, Milton, Hants, 1947–53; Vicar, St Mary's, Harrow, 1953–61. Rector of the Hilborough Group, 1961–72; Vicar of Ranworth and Chaplain for the Norfolk Broads, 1972–77; Hon. Canon of Norwich, 1965–77; Chaplain to the Queen, 1962–77. Bishop Suffragan of Thetford, 1977–80. *Recreations:* sailing, bird-watching. *Address:* 39 Northgate, Beccles, Suffolk NR34 9AU.

BLACKER, Lt-Gen. Anthony Stephen Jeremy, CBE 1987 (OBE 1979); FIMechE; Master-General of the Ordnance, Ministry of Defence, since 1991; *b* 6 May 1939; *s* of Kenneth Anthony Blacker, CBE and late Louise Margaret Blacker (*née* Band); *m* 1973, Julia Mary (*née* Trew); two *d*. *Educ:* Sherborne School; RMA Sandhurst; Corpus Christi Coll., Cambridge (BA Hons). FIMechE 1990. Commissioned Royal Tank Regt, 1959; Staff Coll., 1971; MA to VCGS, 1976–79; Comd 1 RTR, 1979–81; Mil. Dir of Studies, RMCS, 1981–82; Comd 11 Armd Brigade, 1982–84; Principal Staff Officer to Chief of Defence Staff, 1985–87; Comdt, RMCS, 1987–89. Col Comdt, REME, 1987–; ACDS (Operational Requirements), Land Systems, MoD, 1989–91. Col Comdt, RTR, 1988–. *Recreations:* ski-ing, squash, tennis. *Address:* Ministry of Defence, Main Building, Whitehall, SW1A 2HB.

BLACKER, Dr Carmen Elizabeth, FBA 1989; Lecturer in Japanese, 1958–91, and Fellow of Clare Hall, since 1965, Cambridge University; *b* 13 July 1924; *d* of Carlos Paton Blacker, MC, GM, MA, MD, FRCP and Helen Maud Blacker (*née* Pilkington). *Educ:* Benenden School; School of Oriental Studies, London University; Somerville Coll., Oxford (Hon. Fellow, 1991). PhD London Univ., 1957. Visiting Professor: Columbia Univ., 1965; Princeton Univ., 1979; Vis. Fellow, Kyoto Univ., 1986. Pres., Folklore Soc., 1982–84 (Hon. Mem., 1988). Order of the Precious Crown (Japan), 1988. *Publications:* The Japanese Enlightenment: a study of the writing of Fukuzawa Yukichi, 1964; The Catalpa Bow: a study of Shamanistic practices in Japan, 1975, rev. edn 1986; articles in Monumenta Nipponica, Folklore, Trans of Asiatic Soc. of Japan, Asian Folklore Studies, etc. *Recreations:* walking, comparative mythology. *Address:* Willow House, Grantchester, Cambridge CB3 9NF. *T:* Cambridge (0223) 840196. *Clubs:* University Women's, Groucho.

BLACKER, Gen. Sir Cecil (Hugh), GCB 1975 (KCB 1969; CB 1967); OBE 1960; MC 1944; Adjutant-General, Ministry of Defence (Army), 1973–76, retired; ADC (General) to the Queen, 1974–76; *b* 4 June 1916; *s* of Col Norman Valentine Blacker and Olive Georgina (*née* Hope); *m* 1947, Felicity Mary, *widow* of Major J. Rew and *d* of Major I. Buxton, DSO; two *s*. *Educ:* Wellington Coll. Joined 5th Royal Inniskilling Dragoon Guards, 1936; Commanded 23rd Hussars, 1945; Instructor, Staff Coll., Camberley, 1951–54; Commanded 5th Royal Inniskilling Dragoon Guards, 1955–57; Military Asst to CIGS, 1958–60; Asst Commandant, RMA, Sandhurst, 1960–62; Commander, 39 Infantry Brigade Group, 1962–64; GOC 3rd Div., 1964–66; Dir, Army Staff Duties, MoD, 1966–69; GOC-in-C Northern Command, 1969–70; Vice-Chief of the General Staff, 1970–73. Colonel Commandant: RMP, 1971–76; APTC, 1971–76; Col, 5th Royal Inniskilling Dragoon Guards, 1972–81. Member: Jockey Club, 1954– (Dep. Sen. Steward, 1984–86); Horserace Betting Levy Bd, 1981–84; President: BSJA, 1976–80; BEF, 1980–84. *Publications:* The Story of Workboy, 1960; Soldier in the Saddle, 1963. *Recreations:* painting; amateur steeplechase rider, 1947–54; represented GB in World Modern Pentathlon Championships, 1951; represented GB in Showjumping, 1959–61.

BLACKER, Captain Derek Charles, RN; Director of Personnel, Orion Royal Bank Ltd, 1984–88; *b* 19 May 1929; *s* of Charles Edward Blacker and Alexandra May Farrant; *m* 1952, Brenda Mary Getgood; one *s* one *d*. *Educ:* County Sch., Isleworth; King's Coll., Univ. of London (BSc Hons 1950). Entered RN, 1950; specialisations: navigation, meteorology, oceanography; HMS Birmingham, HMS Albion, BRNC Dartmouth, HMS Hermes, 1956–69; Comdr 1965; NATO Commands: SACLANT, 1969; CINCHAN, 1972; SACEUR, 1974; Captain 1975; Dir of Public Relations (RN), 1977–79; Bd Pres., Admiralty Interview Bd, 1980; staff of C-in-C, Naval Home Comd, 1980–81; Dir of Naval Oceanography and Meteorology, MoD, 1981–84. Naval ADC to the Queen, 1983–84. *Recreations:* music, tennis, golf, country pursuits. *Address:* Altamura, Shaldon, Devon TQ14 0BH. *T:* Shaldon (0626) 872304. *Club:* Army and Navy.

BLACKER, Norman; Managing Director, Eastern Regions, British Gas, since 1989; *b* 22 May 1938; *s* of Cyril Norman Blacker and Agnes Margaret Blacker; *m* 1961, Jennifer Mary Anderson. *Educ:* Wolverton Grammar School. IPFA; CIGasE; CBIM. British Gas Corporation: Dir of Finance, Northern Reg., 1976–80; Dir of Finance, 1980–84; Chm., N Eastern Region, then British Gas N Eastern, 1985–89. *Address:* British Gas plc, Rivermill House, 152 Grosvenor Road, SW1V 3JL. *T:* 071–821 1444.

BLACKETT, Sir George (William), 10th Bt *cr* 1673; *b* 26 April 1906; *s* of Sir Hugh Douglas Blackett, 8th Bt, and Helen Katherine (*d* 1943), *d* of late George Lowther; *S* brother, 1968; *m* 1st, 1933, Euphemia Cicely (*d* 1960), *d* of late Major Nicholas Robinson; 2nd, 1964, Daphne Laing, *d* of late Major Guy Laing Bradley, TD, Hexham, Northumberland. Served with Shropshire Yeomanry and CMP, 1939–45. *Recreations:* hunting, forestry, farming. *Heir:* *b* Major Francis Hugh Blackett [*b* 16 Oct. 1907; *m* 1st, 1950, Elizabeth Eily Barrie (*d* 1982), 2nd *d* of late Howard Dennison; two *s* two *d*; 2nd, 1985, Mrs Joan Chowdry]. *Address:* Colwyn, Corbridge, Northumberland. *T:* Corbridge (043471) 2252. *Club:* English-Speaking Union.

BLACKETT-ORD, His Honour Andrew James, CVO 1988; a Circuit Judge, 1972–87; Vice-Chancellor, County Palatine of Lancaster, 1973–87; *b* 21 Aug. 1921; 2nd *s* of late John Reginald Blackett-Ord, Whitfield, Northumberland; *m* 1945, Rosemary Bovill; three *s* one *d*. *Educ:* Eton; New Coll., Oxford (MA). Scots Guards, 1943–46; called to Bar, 1947, Bencher, Lincoln's Inn, 1985; County Court Judge, 1971. Mem. Council, Duchy of Lancaster, 1973–87. Chancellor, dio. of Newcastle-upon-Tyne, 1971–. *Recreations:* reading, art, shooting, country life, travel. *Address:* Helbeck Hall, Brough, Kirkby Stephen, Cumbria CA17 4DD. *T:* Brough (07683) 41323. *Clubs:* Garrick, Lansdowne.

BLACKHAM, Rear-Adm. Joseph Leslie, CB 1965; DL; *b* 29 Feb. 1912; *s* of Dr Walter Charles Blackham, Birmingham, and Margaret Eva Blackham (*née* Bavin); *m* 1938, Coreen Shelford Skinner, *er d* of Paym. Captain W. S. Skinner, CBE, RN; one *s* one *d*. *Educ:* West House Sch., Edgbaston; RNC Dartmouth. Specialised in Navigation; served war of 1939–45; JSSC 1950; Comdr, RNC Greenwich, 1953–54; Captain 1954; Admty, 1955–57; Sen. Officer, Reserve Fleet at Plymouth, 1957–59; Admty Naval Staff, 1959–61; Cdre. Supt, HM Dockyard, Singapore, 1962–63; Rear-Adm. 1963; Admiral Supt, HM Dockyard, Portsmouth, 1964–66; retired. Mem., IoW Hosp. Management Cttee, 1968–74; Vice-Chm., IoW AHA 1974–82; Chm., Family Practitioners Cttee, IoW, 1974–85; Mem., Bd of Visitors, HM Prison, Parkhurst, 1967–82 (Chm., 1974–77). CC Isle of Wight, 1967–77 (Chm., 1975–77); DL Hants and IoW, 1970–87; High Sheriff, IoW, 1975. Mentioned in despatches for service in Korea, 1951. *Address:* Trinity Cottage, Love Lane, Bembridge, Isle of Wight PO35 5NH. *T:* Isle of Wight (0983) 874386.

BLACKLEY, Air Vice-Marshal Allan Baillie, CBE 1983; AFC; BSc; Deputy Chief of Staff (Operations), HQ Allied Air Forces Central Europe, 1989–91; *b* 28 Sept. 1937. Flight Lieut, 1961; Sqn Leader, 1968; Wing Comdr, 1974; Directorate of Air Staff Plans, Dept of CAS, Air Force Dept, 1977; Gp Capt., 1980; OC RAF Valley and ADC to the Queen, 1980–82; Gp Capt (Air Defence) RAF Strike Comd, 1982–83; Dir (Air Defence), MoD, 1984–85; Air Cdre, 1985; Comdt, RAF CFS, Scampton, 1985–87; SASO, No 11 Gp, 1987–89.

BLACKMAN, Sir Frank (Milton), KA 1985; KCVO 1985 (CVO 1975); OBE 1969 (MBE 1964); Ombudsman for Barbados, since 1987; *b* 31 July 1926; *s* of late A. Milton Blackman and Winnifred Blackman (*née* Pile); *m* 1958, Edith Mary Knight; one *s*. *Educ:* Wesley Hall Boys' Sch., Barbados; Harrison Coll., Barbados. Clerical Officer, Colonial Secretary's Office, 1944–56; Sec., Public Service Commn, 1956–57; Asst. Sec., Colonial Sec.'s Office, 1957; Cabinet Office/Premier's Office, 1958–66: Clerk of the Legislative Council, 1958–64; Perm. Sec./Cabinet Sec., 1966–86; Head of CS, 1981–86. *Recreation:* gardening. *Address:* Rendezvous Hill, Christ Church, Barbados. *T:* 427–3463.

BLACKMAN, Gilbert Albert Waller, CBE 1978 (OBE 1973); FEng; FIMechE; CBIM; Chairman, Central Electricity Generating Board, Jan.–March 1990, retired; Director, National Power, since 1990; *b* 28 July 1925; *s* of Ernest Albert Cecil Blackman and Amy Blackman; *m* 1948, Lilian Rosay. *Educ:* Wanstead County High Sch.; Wandsworth Tech. Coll. (CEng, FIMechE 1967). Hon. FInst E (FInstF 1964). Trainee Engr, London Div., Brit. Electricity Authority, 1948–50; various appts in power stns, 1950–63; Central Electricity Generating Board: Stn Supt, Belvedere, 1963–64; Asst Reg. Dir, E Midlands Div., 1964–67; Asst Reg. Dir, Midlands Reg., 1967–70; Dir of Generation, Midlands Reg., 1970–75; Dir Gen., N Eastern Reg., 1975–77; Mem., 1977–90; Dep. Chm. and Prodn Man. Dir, 1986–89; Chm., British Electricity Internat. Ltd, 1988–90. *Recreations:* music, photography, walking. *Address:* Gryphon Lodge, 15 Norton Park, St Mary's Hill, Sunninghill, Berks SL5 9BW. *T:* Ascot (0344) 24374.

See also L. C. F. Blackman.

BLACKMAN, Dr Lionel Cyril Francis; Director, British American Tobacco Co. Ltd, 1980–84 (General Manager, Group Research and Development, 1978–80); *b* 12 Sept. 1930; *s* of Ernest Albert Cecil Blackman and Amy McBain; *m* 1955, Susan Hazel Peachey (marr. diss. 1983); one *s* one *d*. *Educ:* Wanstead High Sch.; Queen Mary Coll., London.

BSc 1952; PhD 1955. Scientific Officer, then Senior Research Fellow, RN Scientific Service, 1954–57; ICI Research Fellow, then Lectr in Chemical Physics of Solids, Imperial Coll., London, 1957–60; Asst Dir (London), then Dir, Chemical Research Div., BR, 1961–64; Dir of Basic Research, then Dir Gen., British Coal Utilisation Research Assoc., 1964–71; Director: Fibreglass Ltd (subsid. of Pilkington Bros Ltd), 1971–78; Compocem Ltd, 1975–78; Cemfil Corp. (US), 1975–78; Vice-Pres., Cementos y Fibras SA (Spain), 1976–78. CEng; CChem; FRSC; DIC; SFInstE. *Publications:* (ed) Modern Aspects of Graphite Technology, 1970; Athletics World Records in the 20th Century, 1988; papers in various scientific and technical jls on dropwise condensation of steam, ferrites, sintering of oxides, graphite and its crystal compounds, glass surface coatings, glass reinforced cement. *Recreations:* gardening, music, wine. *Address:* Griffin House, Knowl Hill, The Hockering, Woking, Surrey GU22 7HL. *T:* Woking (0483) 766328.

See also G. A. W. Blackman.

BLACKMORE, Dr Stephen; Keeper of Botany, Natural History Museum, since 1990; *b* 30 July 1952; *s* of Edwin Arthur and Josephine Blackmore; *m* 1973, Patricia Jane Melrose Hawley; one *s* one *d*. *Educ:* Univ. of Reading (BSc 1973; PhD 1976). Botanist and Administrator, Royal Society Aldabra Research Station, Indian Ocean, 1976–77; Head of Nat. Herbarium and Lectr in Botany, Univ. of Malaŵi, 1977–80; Head of Palynology Section, Dept of Botany, BM (Natural Hist.), 1980–90. *Publications:* Bee Orchids, 1985; Buttercups, 1985; (ed jtly) Pollen and Spores: form and function, 1986; (ed jtly) Evolution, Systematics and Fossil History of the Hamamelidae, 2 vols, 1989; (ed jtly) Microspores: evolution and ontogeny, 1990; (ed jtly) Pollen and Spores: patterns of diversification, 1991; contribs to professional jls. *Recreations:* photography, blues guitar music. *Address:* Department of Botany, Natural History Museum, Cromwell Road, SW7 5BD. *T:* 071–938 8992.

BLACKMUN, Harry A(ndrew); Associate Justice, United States Supreme Court, since 1970; *b* Nashville, Illinois, 12 Nov. 1908; *s* of late Corwin Manning Blackmun and of Theo Huegely (*née* Reuter); *m* 1941, Dorothy E. Clark; three *d*. *Educ:* Harvard Univ.; Harvard Law Sch. AB, LLB. Admitted to Minnesota Bar, 1932; private legal practice with Dorsey, Colman, Barker, Scott & Barber, Minneapolis, 1934–50: Associate, 1934–38; Jun. Partner, 1939–42; General Partner, 1943–50; Instructor: St Paul Coll. of Law, 1935–41; Univ. of Minnesota Law Sch., 1945–47; Resident Counsel, Mayo Clinic, Rochester, 1950–59; Judge, US Ct of Appeals, 8th Circuit, 1959–70. Member: American Bar Assoc.; Amer. Judicature Soc.; Minnesota State Bar Assoc.; 3rd Judicial Dist (Minn) Bar Assoc.; Olmsted Co. (Minn) Bar Assoc.; Judicial Conf. Adv. Cttee on Judicial Activities, 1969–79; Rep. of Judicial Br., Nat. Historical Pubns and Records Commn, 1975–82 and 1986–; Mem., Bd of Mems, Mayo Assoc. Rochester, 1953–60; Bd of Dirs and Exec. Cttee, Rochester Methodist Hosp., 1954–70; Trustee: Hamline Univ., St Paul, 1964–70; William Mitchell Coll. of Law, St Paul, 1959–74. Mem. Faculty, Salzburg Seminar in Amer. Studies (Law), 1989 (Chm., 1977); Co-moderator: Seminar on Justice and Society, Aspen Inst., 1979–90; Seminar on Constitutional Justice and Society, Aspen Inst. Italia, Rome, 1986; participant, Franco-Amer. Colloquium on Human Rights, Paris, 1979; Vis. Instr on Constitutional Law, Louisiana State Univ. Law Sch's summer session, France, 1986. Hon. LLD: De Pauw Univ., Hamline Univ., and Ohio Wesleyan Univ., 1971; Morningside Coll., and Wilson Coll., 1972; Dickinson Sch. of Law, 1973; Drake Univ., 1975; Southern Illinois Univ., Pepperdine Univ., and Emory Univ., 1976; Rensselaer Polytech. Inst., 1979; Nebraska Univ., and New York Law Sch., 1983; McGeorge Sch. of Law, 1984; Vermont Law Sch., and Dartmouth Coll., 1985; Carleton Coll., and Luther Coll., 1986; Drury Coll., Tufts Univ., and Ill Inst. of Technol. Chicago-Kent Coll. of Law, 1987; Northern Ill Univ., and Brooklyn Law Sch., 1988; New York Univ., 1989; Hon. DLitt. Dickinson Sch. of Law, 1983; Hon. DPS Ohio Northern Univ., 1973; Hon. DHL: Oklahoma City, 1976; Massachusetts Sch. of Professional Psychology, 1984. *Publications:* contrib. legal and medical jls. *Recreations:* reading, music. *Address:* Supreme Court Building, 1 First Street NE, Washington, DC 20543, USA.

BLACKSHAW, Alan, VRD 1970; business consultant and author; Consultant Director, Strategy International Ltd, since 1980; Director, Alan Blackshaw Associates Ltd, since 1987; *b* 7 April 1933; *s* of late Frederick William and Elsie Blackshaw; *m* 1st, 1956, Jane Elizabeth Turner (marr. diss. 1983); one *d*; 2nd, 1984, Dr Elspeth Paterson Martin, *d* of late Rev. Gavin C. Martin and Agnes Martin; one *s* two *d*. *Educ:* Merchant Taylors' Sch., Crosby; Wadham Coll., Oxford (MA). Royal Marines (commnd), 1954–56, and RM Reserve, 1956–76. Entered Home Civil Service, Min. of Power, 1956; 1st Sec., UK Delegn to OECD, Paris, 1965–66; Principal Private Sec. to Minister of Power, 1967–69; with Charterhouse Gp on loan, 1972–73; Dept of Energy: Under Sec., 1974; Offshore Supplies Office, 1974–78 (Dir-Gen., 1977–78); Coal Div., 1978–79; Consultant, NCB, 1979–86. Member: Scottish Council for Develt and Industry, 1974–78; Offshore Energy Technol. Bd, 1977–78; Ship and Marine Technol. Requirements Bd, 1977–78; Scottish Sports Council, 1990–. Libel damages against Daily Telegraph (upheld in Ct of Appeal, 1983) and Daily Mail, 1981. Pres., Oxford Univ. Mountaineering Club, 1953–54; Alpine Club: Editor, Alpine Jl, 1968–70; Vice-Pres., 1979–81; Trustee, 1980–90; Chm., Publications Sub-Cttee, 1986–; British Mountaineering Council: Pres., 1973–76; Patron, 1979–; Chairman: Standing Adv. Cttee on Mountain Trng Policy, 1980–86 and 1990–; Ski Touring and Mountaineering Cttee, 1981–. Chairman: Sports Council's Nat. Mountain Centre (formerly Nat. Centre for Mountain Activities), Plas y Brenin, 1986–; Mountaineering Cttee, UIAA, 1990– (Mem., 1985–; Dep. Chm., 1989–90); Leader, British Alpine Ski Traverse, 1972; Ski Club of Great Britain: Vice-Pres., 1977–80, 1983–85; Pery Medal, 1977; Pres., Eagle Ski Club, 1979–81; British Ski Federation: Vice-Pres., 1983–84; Chm., 1984–86. Sec., Edinburgh Br., Oxford Soc., 1989–. Freeman, City of London. FRGS; FInstPet. *Publication:* Mountaineering, 1965, 3rd revision 1975. *Recreations:* mountaineering and ski-ing. *Address:* 2 Clark Road, Edinburgh EH5 3BD. *T:* 031–551 3153; Les Autannes, Le Tour, Chamonix-Mont Blanc 74440, France. *T:* (010 33) 50 54 12 20. *Club:* Royal Scottish Automobile.

BLACKSHAW, William Simon; Headmaster of Brighton College, 1971–87; *b* 28 Oct. 1930; *s* of late C. B. Blackshaw, sometime Housemaster, Cranleigh School and of Kathleen Mary (who *m* 1965, Sir Thomas McAlpine, 4th Bt); *m* 1956, Elizabeth Anne Evans; one *s* one *d* (and one *s* decd). *Educ:* Sherborne Sch.; Hertford Coll., Oxford. 2nd cl. hons Mod. Langs. Repton School: Asst Master, 1955–71; Head of Modern Languages Dept, 1961–66; Housemaster, 1966–71. *Publication:* Regardez! Racontez!, 1971. *Recreations:* philately, painting, cricket, golf. *Address:* Squash Court, The Green, Rottingdean, East Sussex BN2 7HA.

BLACKSTONE, Baroness *cr* 1987 (Life Peer), of Stoke Newington in Greater London; **Tessa Ann Vosper Blackstone,** PhD; Master, Birkbeck College, since 1987; Chairman, General Advisory Council of BBC, since 1987; *b* 27 Sept. 1942; *d* of late Geoffrey Vaughan Blackstone and of Joanna Blackstone; *m* 1963, Tom Evans (marr. diss.); one *s* one *d*. *Educ:* Ware Grammar Sch.; London School of Economics (BScSoc, PhD). Associate Lectr, Enfield Coll., 1965–66; Asst Lectr, then Lectr, Dept of Social Administration, LSE, 1966–75; Adviser, Central Policy Review Staff, Cabinet Office, 1975–78; Prof. of Educnl Admin, Univ. of London Inst. of Educn, 1978–83; Dep. Educn Officer (Resources), then Clerk and Dir of Education, ILEA, 1983–87. Fellow, Centre for Studies in Social Policy, 1972–74; Special Rowntree Visiting Fellow, Policy Studies Inst., 1987. First Chm., Inst. for Public Policy Research, 1988–. Director: Project Fullemploy, 1984–; Royal Opera House, 1987–; Member: Planning Bd, Arts Council of GB, 1986–90; Management Cttee, King Edward's Hosp. Fund for London, 1990–. Opposition spokesman on educn and science, H of L, 1990–. *Publications:* Students in Conflict (jtly), 1970; A Fair Start, 1971; Education and Day Care for Young Children in Need, 1973; The Academic Labour Market (jtly), 1974; Social Policy and Administration in Britain, 1975; Disadvantage and Education (jtly), 1982; Educational Policy and Educational Inequality (jtly), 1982; Response to Adversity (jtly), 1983; Testing Children (jtly), 1983; Inside the Think Tank (jtly), 1988; Prisons and Penal Reform, 1990. *Address:* 2 Gower Street, WC1E 6DP. *T:* 071-631 6274.

BLACKWELL, Sir Basil (Davenport), Kt 1983; FEng; Chief Executive, 1974–85, and Chairman, 1985, Westland PLC (formerly Westland Aircraft Ltd) (Vice-Chairman, 1974–84, Deputy Chairman, 1984); retired; *b* Whitkirk, Yorks, 8 Feb. 1922; *s* of late Alfred Blackwell and late Mrs H. Lloyd; *m* 1948, Betty Meggs, *d* of late Engr Captain Meggs, RN; one *d*. *Educ:* Leeds Grammar Sch.; St John's Coll., Cambridge (MA; Hughes Prize); London Univ. (BScEng). FIMechE; FRAeS (Gold Medal, 1982); CBIM. Sci. Officer, Admiralty, 1942; Rolls-Royce Ltd, 1945; Engine Div., Bristol Aeroplane Co. Ltd, 1949; Bristol Siddeley Engines Ltd: Dep. Chief Engr, 1959; Sales Dir, 1963; Man. Dir, Small Engine Div., 1965 (subseq. Small Engines Div. of Rolls-Royce Ltd). Commercial Dir, Westland Aircraft Ltd, 1970–72; Westland Helicopters Ltd: Man. Dir, 1972; Chm., 1976–85; Chairman: British Hovercraft Corp., 1979–85; Normalair-Garrett Ltd, 1979–85. Member Council: BIM; CBI; NDIC; SBAC (Vice-Pres., 1978; Pres., 1979 and 1980; Dep. Pres., 1980); EEF (Vice-Pres., 1983–85). Pres., AECMA, 1984–85 (Président d'honneur 1985). Hon. DSc, Bath Univ., 1984. *Publications:* contrib. professional jls. *Recreations:* gardens and gardening. *Address:* High Newland, Newland Garden, Sherborne, Dorset DT9 3AF. *T:* Sherborne (0935) 813516. *Club:* United Oxford & Cambridge University.

BLACKWELL, Prof. Donald Eustace, MA, PhD; Savilian Professor of Astronomy, University of Oxford, 1960–88, now Emeritus; Fellow of New College, Oxford, 1960–88, now Emeritus; *b* 27 May 1921; *s* of John Blackwell and Ethel Bowe; *m* 1951, Nora Louise Carlton; two *s* two *d*. *Educ:* Merchant Taylors' Sch.; Sandy Lodge; Sidney Sussex Coll., Cambridge. Isaac Newton Student, University of Cambridge, 1947; Stokes Student, Pembroke Coll., Cambridge, 1948; Asst Director, Solar Physics Observatory, Cambridge, 1950–60. Various Astronomical Expeditions: Sudan, 1952; Fiji, 1955; Bolivia, 1958 and 1961; Canada, 1963; Manuae Island, 1965. Pres., RAS, 1973–75. *Publications:* papers in astronomical journals. *Address:* 4 Pullens Field, Headington, Oxford OX3 0BU.

BLACKWELL, Rt. Rev. Douglas Charles; a Suffragan Bishop of Toronto (Area Bishop of Trent-Durham), since 1988; *b* 3 June 1938; *s* of late William John Blackwell and Ethel N. Blackwell (*née* Keates); *m* 1963, Sandra Dianne Griffiths; one *s* two *d*. *Educ:* Wycliffe Coll., Univ. of Toronto (DipTh, LTh). Deacon 1963, priest 1964; Asst Curate, St Stephen's, Calgary, 1964; Vicar, Cochrane Mission, Diocese of Calgary, 1966; Rector, St Paul's, North Battleford, Diocese of Saskatoon, 1969; Regional Dean of Battleford, 1970; Archdeacon of Battlefords–Lloydminster, 1973; Asst Director, Aurora Conf. Centre, Diocese of Toronto, 1974; Executive Asst to Archbishop of Toronto, 1977; Canon of St James's Cathedral, Toronto, 1978; Archdeacon of York, 1986. Hon. DD Wycliffe Coll., Toronto, 1990. *Address:* 135 Adelaide Street East, Toronto, Ontario M5C 1L8, Canada. *T:* 363–6021.

BLACKWELL, John Charles, CBE 1988; Director (formerly Controller), Science and Education Division, British Council, since 1989; *b* 4 Nov. 1935; *s* of Charles Arthur Blackwell and Louisa Amy Blackwell (*née* Sellers); *m* 1st, 1961, Julia Rose; one *s*; 2nd, 1978, Inger Beatrice Lewin; one step *s*. *Educ:* Glynn Grammar Sch., Ewell; Dudley Coll. of Educn (Cert. in Educn); Bristol Univ. (BA, MEd, PhD). Metropolitan Police Cadet, 1952–53; RAF, 1954–56; teacher, Dempsey Secondary Sch., London, 1958–60; joined British Council, 1966; Asst Rep., Tanzania, 1966–70; Educn Officer, Calcutta, 1971–72; Asst Educn Adviser, New Delhi, 1973–75; Head, Schools and Teacher Educn Unit, 1976–78; attached British Embassy, Washington, 1979; Dir, Educn Contrasts Dept, 1980–83; Rep., Indonesia, 1983–89. *Recreations:* boating, fishing, reading. *Address:* British Council, 10 Spring Gardens, SW1A 2AH. *T:* 071–930 8466.

BLACKWELL, Julian, (Toby); DL; Chairman, The Blackwell Group Ltd, since 1980; *b* 10 Jan. 1929; *s* of Sir Basil Henry Blackwell and late Marion Christine, *d* of John Soans; *m* 1953, Jennifer Jocelyn Darley Wykeham; two *s* one *d*. *Educ:* Winchester; Trinity Coll., Oxford. Served 5th RTR, 1947–49; 21st SAS (TA), 1950–59. Dir and Chm., various Blackwell companies, 1956–. Chm. Council, ASLIB, 1966–68 (Vice-Pres., 1982); Mem., Library and Inf. Services Council, 1981–84; Co-founder and Chm., Mail Users' Assoc., 1975–78 and 1987–; Pres., Booksellers' Assoc., 1980–82; Chairman: Thames Business Advice Centre, 1986–; Heart of England TEC, 1989–; Fox FM, 1989–; Cottontail Ltd, 1990–. Chm., Son White Meml Trust, 1991–. DL Oxon 1987, High Sheriff, 1991. *Recreations:* sawing firewood, sailing. *Address:* c/o 50 Broad Street, Oxford OX1 3BQ. *T:* Oxford (0865) 792111. *Clubs:* Athenæum, Special Forces; Royal Yacht Squadron; Leander (Henley); Royal Southern Yacht (Southampton).

BLACKWOOD, family name of **Baron Dufferin and Clandeboye.**

BLACKWOOD, Wing Comdr George Douglas; Chairman, William Blackwood & Sons Ltd, publishers and printers, 1948–83; Editor of Blackwood's Magazine, and Managing Director of William Blackwood & Sons Ltd, 1948–76; *b* 11 Oct. 1909; *e s* of late James H. Blackwood and *g g g s* of Wm Blackwood, founder of Blackwood's Magazine; *m* 1936, Phyllis Marion, *y d* of late Sir John Caulcutt, KCMG; one *s* one *d*. *Educ:* Eton; Clare Coll., Cambridge. Short Service Commission in RAF, 1932–38; re-joined 1939. Formed first Czech Fighter Squadron, 1940–41; Battle of Britain (despatches); commanded Czech Wing of Royal Air Force 2nd TAF, 1944 (despatches); retired 1945. Czech War Cross, 1940; Czech Military Medal 1st class, 1944. *Recreations:* countryside activities. *Address:* Airhouse, Oxton, Berwickshire TD2 6PX. *T:* Oxton (05785) 225.

BLAIKLEY, Robert Marcel; HM Diplomatic Service, retired; *b* 1 Oct. 1916; *s* of late Alexander John Blaikley and late Adelaide Blaikley (*née* Miller); *m* 1942, Alice Mary Duncan; one *s* one *d*. *Educ:* Christ's Coll., Finchley; St John's Coll., Cambridge. Served HM Forces, 1940–46. Inland Revenue, 1946–48; General Register Office, 1948–65, Asst Secretary, 1958; transferred to Diplomatic Service as Counsellor, 1965; on loan to Colonial Office, 1965–66; Head of Aviation and Telecommunications Dept, CO, 1966–68; Counsellor, Jamaica, 1968–71, Ghana, 1971–73. *Recreations:* walking, growing shrubs. *Address:* 17 Chestnut Grove, Upper Westwood, Bradford-on-Avon, Wilts BA15 2DQ.

BLAIR, Sir Alastair Campbell, KCVO 1969 (CVO 1953); TD 1950; WS; JP; *b* 16 Jan. 1908; 2nd *s* of late William Blair, WS, and late Emelia Mylne Campbell; *m* 1933,

Catriona Hatchard, *o d* of late Dr William Basil Orr; four *s*. *Educ:* Cargilfield; Charterhouse; Clare Coll., Cambridge (BA); Edinburgh Univ. (LLB). Writer to the Signet, 1932; retired 1977 as Partner, Dundas & Wilson, CS. RA (TA) 1939; served 1939–45 (despatches); Secretary, Queen's Body Guard for Scotland, Royal Company of Archers, 1946–59; appointed Captain 1982; retired 1984. Purse Bearer to The Lord High Commissioner to the General Assembly of the Church of Scotland, 1961–69. Chm., subseq. Vice-Pres., Edinburgh Area Scout Council, 1964– (Silver Wolf, 1990). JP Edinburgh, 1954. *Recreations:* curling, golf. *Address:* 7 Abbotsford Court, Colinton Road, Edinburgh EH10 5EH. *T:* 031-447 3095. *Club:* New (Edinburgh).

See also M. C. Blair.

BLAIR, Anthony Charles Lynton, (Tony); MP (Lab) Sedgefield, since 1983; *b* 6 May 1953; *s* of Leo Charles Lynton Blair and late Hazel Blair; *m* 1980, Cherie Booth; two *s* one *d*. *Educ:* Durham Choristers School; Fettes College, Edinburgh; St John's College, Oxford. Called to the Bar, Lincoln's Inn, 1976. *Address:* Myrobella, Trimdon Station, Co. Durham TS29 6DU. *T:* Hartlepool (0429) 882202; (office) 071–219 4456. *Clubs:* Trimdon Colliery and Deaf Hill Working Men's, Trimdon Village Working Men's, Fishburn Working Men's.

BLAIR, Bruce Graeme Donald; QC 1989; *b* 12 April 1946; *s* of late Dr Donald Alexander Sangster Blair, MA, MD, DPM and Eleanor Violet Blair (*née* Van Ryneveld); *m* 1970, Susanne Blair (*née* Hartung); three *d* (and one *s* decd). *Educ:* Harrow School; Magdalene College, Cambridge. Called to the Bar, Middle Temple, 1969. *Publication:* Practical Matrimonial Precedents (jtly), 1989. *Recreations:* bridge, tennis, turf. *Address:* 1 Mitre Court Buildings, Temple, EC4Y 7BS. *T:* 071–353 0434. *Club:* MCC.

BLAIR, Lt-Gen. Sir Chandos, KCVO 1972; OBE 1962; MC 1941 and bar, 1944; GOC Scotland and Governor of Edinburgh Castle, 1972–76; *b* 25 Feb. 1919; *s* of Brig.-Gen. Arthur Blair and Elizabeth Mary (*née* Hoskyns); *m* 1947, Audrey Mary Travers; one *s* one *d*. *Educ:* Harrow; Sandhurst. Commnd into Seaforth Highlanders, 1939; comd 4 KAR, Uganda, 1959–61; comd 39 Bde, Radfan and N. Ireland. GOC 2nd Division, BAOR, 1968–70; Defence Services Secretary, MoD, 1970–72. Col Comdt, Scottish Div., 1972–76; Col, Queen's Own Highlanders, 1975–83. *Recreations:* golf, fishing, shooting. *Club:* Naval and Military.

BLAIR, Claude; FSA 1956; Keeper, Department of Metalwork, Victoria and Albert Museum, 1972–82; *b* 30 Nov. 1922; *s* of William Henry Murray Blair and Lilian Wearing; *m* 1952, Joan Mary Greville Drinkwater; one *s*. *Educ:* William Hulme's Grammar Sch., Manchester; Manchester Univ. (MA). Served War, Army (Captain RA), 1942–46. Manchester Univ., 1946–51; Asst, Tower of London Armouries, 1951–56; Asst Keeper of Metalwork, V&A, 1956–66; Dep. Keeper, 1966–72. Hon. Editor, Jl of the Arms and Armour Soc., 1953–77. Consultant to Christie's, 1983–; Member: Redundant Churches Fund, 1982–; Exec. Cttee, Council for the Care of Churches, 1983–; Arch. Adv. Panel, Westminster Abbey, 1979–. Vice-Pres., Soc. of Antiquaries, 1990; Hon. Pres., Meyrick Soc.; Hon. Vice-President: Soc. for Study of Church Monuments, 1984– (Hon. Pres., 1978–84); Monumental Brass Soc. Hon. Freeman, Cutlers' Co. Liveryman: Goldsmiths' Co.; Armourers and Brasiers' Co. Medal of Museo Militar, Barcelona, 1969; Medal of Arms and Armour Soc., 1986. *Publications:* European Armour, 1958 (2nd edn, 1972); European and American Arms, 1962; The Silvered Armour of Henry VIII, 1965; Pistols of the World, 1968; Three Presentation Swords in the Victoria and Albert Museum, 1972; The James A. de Rothschild Collection: Arms, Armour and Miscellaneous Metalwork, 1974; (ed) Pollard's History of Firearms, 1983; (ed) The History of Silver, 1987; numerous articles and reviews in Archaeological Jl, Jl of Arms and Armour Soc., Connoisseur, Waffen-und Kostümkunde, etc. *Recreations:* travel, looking at churches, listening to music. *Address:* 90 Links Road, Ashtead, Surrey KT21 2HW. *T:* Ashtead (0372) 75532. *Club:* Anglo-Polish.

BLAIR, Sir Edward Thomas H.; *see* Hunter-Blair.

BLAIR, Prof. Gordon Purves, PhD, DSc; FEng 1982; FIMechE, FSAE; Professor of Mechanical Engineering since 1976, Head of the Department of Mechanical and Industrial Engineering since 1982, and of the Department of Mechanical and Manufacturing, Aeronautical and Chemical Engineering, since 1987, Pro-Vice-Chancellor, since 1989, Queen's University of Belfast; *b* 29 April 1937; *s* of Gordon Blair and Mary Helen Jones Blair; *m* 1964, Norma Margaret Millar; two *d*. *Educ:* Queen's Univ. of Belfast (BSc; PhD 1962; DSc 1978). CEng, FIMechE 1977; FSAE 1979. Asst Prof., New Mexico State Univ., 1962–64; Queen's Univ. of Belfast: Lectr, 1964–71; Sen. Lectr, 1971–73; Reader, 1973–76; Dean, Faculty of Engrg, 1985–88. Chm., Automobile Div., IMechE, 1991–. *Publications:* The Basic Design of Two-Stroke Engines, USA, 1990; wide pubn in IMechE and SAE Jls on design and develt of internal combustion engines. *Recreations:* golf, fishing. *Address:* 9 Ben Madigan Park South, Newtownabbey, N Ireland BT36 7PX. *T:* Belfast (0232) 773280. *Clubs:* Cairndhu Golf; Royal Portrush Golf.

BLAIR, Michael Campbell; General Counsel, Securities and Investments Board, since 1991; *b* 26 Aug. 1941; *s* of Sir Alastair Blair, *qv*; *m* 1966, Halldóra Isabel (*née* Tunnard); one *s*. *Educ:* Rugby Sch.; Clare Coll., Cambridge (MA, LLM); Yale Univ., USA (Mellon Fellow; MA). Called to the Bar, Middle Temple, 1965 (Harmsworth Law Scholar). Lord Chancellor's Dept, 1966–87: Private Sec. to the Lord Chancellor, 1968–71; Sec., Law Reform Cttee, 1977–79; Under Sec., 1982–87; Circuit Administrator, Midland and Oxford Circuit, 1982–86; Hd, Courts and Legal Services Gp, 1986–87. Attended Cabinet Office Top Management Programme, 1986. Dir of Legal Services, SIB, 1987–91. Chm., Bar Assoc. for Commerce, Finance and Industry, 1990–; Member: Gen. Council of the Bar, 1989–; Bar Cttee, 1989–. *Publications:* Sale of Goods Act 1979, 1980; Financial Services: the new core rules, 1991; legal articles in Modern Law Rev., Lancet, New Law Jl, Civil Justice Qly, Jl of Internat. Banking and Financial Law, etc. *Address:* 3 Burbage Road, SE24 9HJ. *T:* 071–274 7614. *Club:* Athenæum.

BLAIR, Thomas Alexander, QC (NI) 1958; Chief Social Security (formerly National Insurance) Commissioner (Northern Ireland), 1969–83; *b* 12 Dec. 1916; *s* of late John Blair and of Wilhelmina Whitla Blair (*née* Downey); *m* 1947, Ida Irvine Moore; two *s* one *d*. *Educ:* Royal Belfast Academical Instn; Queen's Univ. Belfast (BA, LLB). Served War, in Royal Navy, 1940–46 (commissioned, 1941). Called to Bar of N Ireland, 1946. Chairman: Wages Councils; War Pensions Appeal Tribunal. Sen. Crown Counsel for Co. Tyrone; Mem. Departmental Cttee on Legal Aid. Apptd Dep. Nat. Insurance Umpire, 1959; Pres., Industrial Tribunals (NI), 1967–69; Chief Nat. Insurance Commissioner (NI), 1969. *Recreation:* golf. *Address:* Lilac Cottage, Bowden, Melrose, Roxburghshire TD6 0SS. *T:* St Boswells (0835) 23680.

BLAIR, Tony; *see* Blair, A. C. L.

BLAIR-KERR, Sir William Alexander, (Sir Alastair Blair-Kerr), Kt 1973; President of the Court of Appeal for Bermuda, 1979–89; *b* 1 Dec. 1911; *s* of William Alexander Milne Kerr and Annie Kerr (*née* Blair), Dunblane, Perthshire, Scotland; *m* 1942, Esther Margaret Fowler Wright (*d* 1990); one *s* one *d*. *Educ:* McLaren High Sch., Callander; Edinburgh Univ. (MA, LLB). Solicitor in Scotland, 1939; Advocate (Scots Bar), 1951. Advocate and Solicitor, Singapore, 1939–41; Straits Settlements Volunteer Force, 1941–42; escaped from Singapore, 1942; Indian Army: Staff Capt. "A" Bombay Dist. HQ, 1942–43; DAAG 107 Line of Communication area HQ, Poona, 1943–44; British Army: GSO2, War Office, 1944–45; SO1 Judicial, BMA Malaya, 1945–46. Colonial Legal Service (HM Overseas Service): Hong Kong: Magistrate, 1946–48; Crown Counsel, 1949; Pres. Tenancy Tribunal, 1950; Crown Counsel, 1951–53; Sen. Crown Counsel, 1953–59; District Judge, 1959–61; Puisne Judge, Supreme Court, 1961–71; Sen. Puisne Judge, Supreme Court, 1971–73; President: Court of Appeal: for the Bahamas, 1978–80; for Belize, 1978–81; for Turks and Caicos Islands, 1978–81; Mem., Ct of Appeal for Gibraltar, 1982–87; sometime Actg Chief Justice of Hong Kong. Pres., various Commns of Inquiry. *Recreations:* golf, walking, music. *Address:* Gairn, Kinbuck, Dunblane, Perthshire FK15 0NQ. *T:* Dunblane (0786) 823377. *Club:* Royal Over-Seas League.

BLAIR-OLIPHANT, Air Vice-Marshal David Nigel Kington, CB 1966; OBE 1945; *b* 22 Dec. 1911; *y s* of Col P. L. K. Blair-Oliphant, DSO, Ardblair Castle, Blairgowrie, Perthshire, and Laura Geraldine Bodenham; *m* 1942, Helen Nathalie Donald (*d* 1983), *yr d* of Sir John Donald, KCIE; one *s* (and one *s* and one *d* decd). *Educ:* Harrow; Trinity Hall, Cambridge (BA). Joined RAF, 1934; Middle East and European Campaigns, 1939–45; RAF Staff Coll., 1945–48; Group Capt. 1949; Air Cdre 1958; Director, Weapons Engineering, Air Ministry, 1958–60; British Defence Staffs, Washington, 1960–63; Acting Air Vice-Marshal, 1963; Pres., Ordnance Board, 1965–66; Air Vice-Marshal, 1966. *Address:* 9 Northfield Road, Sherfield-on-Lodon, Basingstoke, Hants RG27 0DR. *T:* Basingstoke (0256) 882724. *Club:* Royal Air Force.

BLAIS, Hon. Jean Jacques, PC (Can.) 1976; QC (Can.) 1978; Member of Law Firm, Lette McTaggart Blais Martin, since 1988; *b* 27 June 1940; *m* 1968, Maureen Ahearn; two *s* one *d*. *Educ:* Secondary Sch., Sturgeon Falls; Univ. of Ottawa (BA, LLB). Professional lawyer. MP (L) Nipissing, Ontario, 1972, re-elected 1974, 1979, 1980; defeated Sept. 1984; Parliamentary Sec. to Pres. of Privy Council, 1975; Post Master General, 1976; Solicitor General, 1978; Minister of Supply and Services, and Receiver General, 1980; Minister of Nat. Defence, 1983–84. Lectr in Private Internat. Law, Ottawa Univ., 1986–88. Mem., Security and Intelligence Review Cttee, 1984–. Mem. Exec. Cttee, Bd of Govs, Univ. of Ottawa, 1988–. *Recreations:* squash, skiing, swimming. *Address:* (office) 10th Floor, 100 Sparks Street, Ottawa, Ontario K1P 5B7, Canada. *T:* 416–237 6430.

BLAKE, family name of **Baron Blake.**

BLAKE, Baron *cr* 1971 (Life Peer), of Braydeston, Norfolk; **Robert Norman William Blake,** FBA 1967; JP; Provost of The Queen's College, Oxford, 1968–87, Hon. Fellow, 1987; Pro-Vice-Chancellor, Oxford University, 1971–87; Joint Editor, Dictionary of National Biography, 1980–90; *b* 23 Dec. 1916; *er s* of William Joseph Blake and Norah Lindley Daynes, Brundall, Norfolk; *m* 1953, Patricia Mary, *e d* of Thomas Richard Waters, Great Plumstead, Norfolk; three *d*. *Educ:* King Edward VI Sch., Norwich; Magdalen Coll., Oxford (MA), 1st Cl. Final Honour Sch. of Modern Greats, 1938; Eldon Law Scholar, 1938. Served War of 1939–45; Royal Artillery; North African campaign, 1942; POW in Italy, 1942–44; escaped, 1944; despatches, 1944. Student and Tutor in Politics, Christ Church, Oxford, 1947–68; Censor, 1950–55; Senior Proctor, 1959–60; Ford's Lectr in English History for 1967–68; Mem., Hebdomadal Council, 1959–81. Member: Royal Commn on Historical Manuscripts, 1975– (Chm., 1982–89); Bd of Trustees, BM, 1978–88; Bd, Channel 4, 1983–86. Chm., Hansard Soc. Commn on Electoral Reform, 1975–76; Pres., Electoral Reform Soc., 1986–. Mem. (Conservative) Oxford City Council, 1957–64. Governor of Norwich Sch.; Rhodes Trustee, 1971–87 (Chm., 1983–87). Prime Warden, Dyers' Co., 1976–77. High Bailiff of Westminster Abbey and Searcher of the Sanctuary, 1988–89; High Steward of Westminster Abbey, 1989–. Hon. Student, Christ Church, Oxford, 1977. Hon. DLitt: Glasgow, 1972; East Anglia, 1983; Westminster Coll., Fulton, Mo, 1987; Buckingham, 1988. *Publications:* The Private Papers of Douglas Haig, 1952; The Unknown Prime Minister (Life of Andrew Bonar Law), 1955; Disraeli, 1966; The Conservative Party from Peel to Churchill, 1970, 2nd edn, The Conservative Party from Peel to Thatcher, 1985; The Office of Prime Minister, 1975; (ed with John Patten) The Conservative Opportunity, 1976; A History of Rhodesia, 1977; Disraeli's Grand Tour, 1982; (ed) The English World, 1982; The Decline of Power 1915–1964, 1985; (ed jtly) Salisbury: the man and his policies, 1987; (ed) Oxford Illustrated Encyclopaedia, Vol. 4, World History from 1800, 1989. *Address:* Riverview House, Brundall, Norfolk NR13 5LA. *T:* Norwich (0603) 712133. *Clubs:* Beefsteak, Brooks's, Pratt's, United Oxford & Cambridge University; Vincent's (Oxford); Norfolk County.

BLAKE, Sir Alfred (Lapthorn), KCVO 1979 (CVO 1975); MC 1945; DL; Director, The Duke of Edinburgh's Award Scheme, 1967–78; Consultant with Blake Lapthorn, Solicitors, Portsmouth and area, since 1985 (Partner, 1949–85, Senior Partner, 1983–85); *b* 6 Oct. 1915; *s* of late Leonard Nicholson Blake and Nora Woodfall Blake (*née* Lapthorn); *m* 1st, 1940, Beatrice Grace Nellthorp (*d* 1967); two *s*; 2nd, 1969, Alison Kelsey Dick, Boston, Mass, USA. *Educ:* Dauntsey's Sch. LLB (London), 1938. Qual. Solicitor and Notary Public, 1938. Royal Marines Officer, 1939–45: Bde Major 2 Commando Bde, 1944; Lieut-Col comdg 45 (RM) Commando and Holding Operational Commando, 1945 (despatches). Mem., Portsmouth CC, 1950–67 (Past Chm., Portsmouth Educn Cttee); Lord Mayor of Portsmouth, 1958–59. Mem., Youth Service Development Coun., 1960–66; Pres., Portsmouth Youth Activities Cttee, 1976–; Patron: Elizabeth Foundn, 1984–; Portsmouth Family Welfare, 1987–. Lay Canon, Portsmouth Cathedral, 1962–72. Hon. Fellow, Portsmouth Polytechnic, 1981. DL Hants, 1991. *Recreation:* golf. *Address:* 1 Kitnocks Cottages, Wickham Road, Curdridge, Southampton SO3 2HG. *T:* Botley (0489) 783660.

BLAKE, Charles Henry, CB 1966; a Commissioner of Customs and Excise, 1968–72; European Adviser, British American Tobacco Co., 1972–76; *b* 29 Nov. 1912; *s* of Henry and Lily Blake, Westbury on Trym, Bristol; *m* 1938, M. Jayne McKinney (*d* 1974), *d* of James and Ellen McKinney, Castle Finn, Co. Donegal; three *d*. *Educ:* Cotham Grammar Sch.; Jesus Coll., Cambridge (Major Scholar). Administrative Class, Home Civil Service, 1936; HM Customs and Excise: Princ., 1941; Asst Sec., 1948; Comr and Sec., 1957–64; Asst Under-Sec. of State, Air Force Dept, MoD, 1964–68. *Recreation:* gardens. *Address:* 33 Grenville Court, Chorleywood, Herts WD3 5PZ. *T:* Chorleywood (09278) 3795. *Clubs:* United Oxford & Cambridge University; Moor Park.

BLAKE, Prof. Christopher, CBE 1991; FRSE; Chairman, Glenrothes Development Corporation, since 1987; *b* 28 April 1926; *s* of George Blake and Eliza Blake; *m* 1951, Elizabeth McIntyre; two *s* two *d*. *Educ:* Dollar Academy; St Andrews Univ. MA St Andrews 1950, PhD St Andrews 1965. Served in Royal Navy, 1944–47. Teaching posts, Bowdoin Coll., Maine, and Princeton Univ., 1951–53; Asst, Edinburgh Univ., 1953–55; Stewarts & Lloyds Ltd, 1955–60; Lectr and Sen. Lectr, Univ. of St Andrews, 1960–67; Sen. Lectr and Prof. of Economics, 1967–74, Bonar Prof. of Applied Econs, 1974–88, Univ. of Dundee. Dir, Alliance Trust plc, 1974–; Chm., William Low & Co. plc, 1985–90 (Dir, 1980–90). Member: Council for Applied Science in Scotland, 1978–86; Royal Commn on Envtl Pollution, 1980–86. Treasurer, RSE, 1986–89. *Publications:* articles in economic and other jls. *Recreation:* golf. *Address:* Westlea, Wardlaw Gardens, St Andrews, Fife KY16 9DW. *T:* St Andrews (0334) 73840. *Clubs:* New (Edinburgh); Royal and Ancient (St Andrews).

BLAKE, David Charles; Managing Director, Kings Cross Project, British Rail Board, since 1991; *b* 23 Sept. 1936; *s* of Walter David John Blake and Ellen Charlotte Blake; *m* 1959, Della Victoria Stevenson; two *s*. *Educ:* South East Essex Technical Sch.; South East Essex Technical Coll. CEng, MIMechE. Engrg apprentice, Stratford Locomotive Works, 1953–57; Technical Management, BR Eastern Reg., 1957–69; Construction Engr, W Coast Main Line Electrification, 1969–74; Area Maintenance Engineer: Motherwell Scottish Reg., 1974–75; Shields Scottish Reg., 1975–76; Rolling Stock Engr, Scottish Reg., 1976–78; Electrical Engr, E Reg., 1978–80; Chief Mechanical and Electrical Engr, Southern Reg., 1980–82; Director: Manufacturing and Maintenance Policy, BRB, 1983–87; Mech. and Elec. Engrg, BRB, 1987–90. *Recreations:* gardening, hill walking. *Address:* Silverglade House, Oak Avenue, Thakeham Copse, Storrington, West Sussex RH20 3PW. *T:* Storrington (0903) 744671.

BLAKE, Prof. David Leonard; Professor of Music, University of York, since 1976; *b* 2 Sept. 1936; *s* of Leonard Blake and Dorothy Blake; *m* 1960, Rita Muir; two *s* one *d*. *Educ:* Latymer Upper School; Gonville and Caius College, Cambridge (BA 1960, MA 1963); Deutsche Akademie der Künste, Berlin, GDR. School teacher: Ealing Grammar Sch., 1961–62; Northwood Secondary Sch., 1962–63; University of York: Granada Arts Fellow, 1963–64; Lectr in Music, 1964; Sen. Lectr, 1971–76. *Recordings* (own compositions): Violin concerto: In Praise of Krishna; Variations for Piano; The Almanack. *Publications* include: It's a Small War (musical for schools), 1963; Chamber Symphony, 1981; Lumina (Ezra Pound) (cantata for soprano, baritone, chorus and orch.), 1969; Metamorphoses for large orch., 1978; Nonet for wind, 1979; The Bones of Chuang Tzu (cantata for baritone and piano), 1976; In Praise of Krishna: Bengali lyrics, 1976; String Quartet No 2, 1977; Violin Concerto, 1979; Toussaint (opera), 1977; From the Mattress Grave (song cycle), 1981; Arias for clarinet, 1981; Cassation for wind, 1982; Sonata alla marcia, 1982; Clarinet Quintet, 1983; Three choruses (Robert Frost), 1985; Capriccio for seven players, 1988; Fantasia for violin, 1989; The Plumber's Gift (opera), 1989; Seasonal Variants, 1991. *Recreations:* conservation (mills etc), political debate. *Address:* Mill Gill, Askrigg, near Leyburn, North Yorks DL8 3HR. *T:* Wensleydale (0969) 50364.

BLAKE, Sir Francis Michael, 3rd Bt *cr* 1907; *b* 11 July 1943; *o s* of Sir F. Edward C. Blake, 2nd Bt and Olive Mary (*d* 1946) *d* of Charles Liddell Simpson; *S* father, 1950; *m* 1968, Joan Ashbridge, *d* of F. C. A. Miller; two *s*. *Educ:* Rugby. *Heir:* *s* Francis Julian Blake, *b* 17 Feb. 1971. *Address:* The Dower House, Tillmouth Park, Cornhill-on-Tweed, Northumberland TD12 4UR. *T:* Coldstream (0890) 2443.

BLAKE, (Henry) Vincent; marketing consultant; Secretary, Glassfibre Reinforced Cement Association, 1977–86; *b* 7 Dec. 1912; *s* of Arthur Vincent Blake and Alice Mabel (*née* Kerr); *m* 1938, Marie Isobel Todd; one *s*. *Educ:* King Edward's High Sch., Birmingham. Pupil apprentice, Chance Brothers, Lighthouse Engineers, Birmingham, 1931–34; subseq. Asst Sales Manager, 1937 and Sales Manager there, of Austinlite Ltd, 1945; Textile Marketing Manager, Fibreglass Ltd, 1951; Commercial Manager: Glass Yarns and Deeside Fabrics Ltd, 1960; BTR Industries Ltd, Glass and Resin Div., 1962–63, Plastics Group, 1963–66; Gen. Manager, Indulex Engineering Co. Ltd, 1966–71. Mem. Council and Chm., Reinforced Plastics Gp, British Plastics Fedn, 1959. Mem. Council, Royal Yachting Assoc., 1980– (Vice-Chm., Thames Valley Region, 1979–). *Publications:* articles in technical jls on reinforced plastics. *Recreations:* sailing, motoring, reading, and waiting for my wife. *Address:* Little Orchard, Fern Lane, Little Marlow, Bucks SL7 3SD. *T:* Bourne End (06285) 20252. *Club:* Datchet Water Sailing (Hon. Life Mem.), Cookham Reach Sailing (Hon. Life Mem.), Pwllheli Sailing.

BLAKE, John Clifford, CB 1958; *b* 12 July 1901; *s* of late Alfred Harold and Ada Blake, Prestwich, Lancs; *m* 1928, Mary Lilian Rothwell; one *s* two *d*. *Educ:* Manchester Grammar Sch.; Queen's Coll., Oxford (MA). Admitted solicitor, 1927. Ministry of Health Solicitor's Dept, 1929; Solicitor and Legal Adviser to Ministries of Health and Housing and Local Government, and to Registrar Gen., 1957–65; Mem., Treasurer and Jt Exec. Sec., Anglican-Methodist Unity Commn, 1965–69; Vice-Pres., Methodist Conference, 1968. *Recreations:* music, especially organ and choral. *Address:* 3 Clifton Court, 297 Clifton Drive South, St Anne's on Sea, Lancs FY8 1HN. *T:* St Anne's (0253) 728365.

BLAKE, John Michael; Managing Director, Blake Publishing, since 1991; *b* 6 Nov. 1948; *s* of late Major Edwin Blake, MBE, and of Joyce Blake; *m* 1968, Diane Sutherland Campbell; one *s* two *d*. *Educ:* Westminster City Grammar Sch.; North-West London Polytechnic. Reporter: Hackney Gazette, 1966; Evening Post, Luton, 1969; Fleet Street News Agency, 1970; Columnist: London Evening News, 1971; London Evening Standard, 1980; The Sun, 1982; Asst Editor, Daily Mirror, 1985; Editor, The People, 1988–89; Asst Editor, Daily Mail, 1989–91; Pres., Mirror Group Newspapers (USA), 1989; Exec. Producer, Sky Television, 1990. *Publications:* Up and Down with The Rolling Stones, 1978; All You Needed Was Love, 1981. *Recreations:* sailing, scuba diving, distance running, travel. *Address:* Blake Publishing Ltd, Bishopsview House, 98 Great North Road, N2.

BLAKE, Marianne Teresa, (Mrs D. W. J. Blake); *see* Neville-Rolfe, M. T.

BLAKE, Mary Netterville, MA; Headmistress, Manchester High School for Girls, 1975–83; *b* 12 Sept. 1922; *d* of John Netterville Blake and Agnes Barr Blake. *Educ:* Howell's Sch., Denbigh; St Anne's Coll., Oxford (MA). Asst Mistress, The Mount Sch., York, 1945–48; Head of Geography Dept, King's High Sch., Warwick, 1948–56; Associate Gen. Sec., Student Christian Movement in Schools, 1956–60; Head Mistress, Selby Grammar Sch., 1960–75. Pres., Assoc. of Headmistresses, 1976–77; first Pres., Secondary Heads Assoc., 1978. *Address:* 70A Guarlford Road, Malvern, Worcs WR14 3QT. *T:* Malvern (0684) 564359.

BLAKE, Peter Thomas, CBE 1983; RA 1980 (ARA 1974); RDI 1987; ARCA; painter; *b* 25 June 1932; *s* of Kenneth William Blake; *m* 1963, Jann Haworth (marr. diss. 1982); two *d*; *m* 1987, Chrissy Wilson; one *d*. *Educ:* Gravesend Tech. Coll.; Gravesend Sch. of Art; RCA. Works exhibited: ICA, 1958, 1960; Guggenheim Competition, 1958; Cambridge, 1959; RA, 1960; Musée d'Art Moderne, Paris, 1968; Waddington Galls, 1970, 1972 and 1979; Stedlijk Mus., Amsterdam, 1973; Kunstverein, Hamburg, 1973; Gemeentemuseum, Arnhem, 1974; Palais des Beaux-Arts, Brussels, 1974; Galleria Documenta, Turin, 1982; retrospective exhibn, Tate Gall., 1983; works in public collections: Trinity Coll., Cambridge; Carlisle City Gall.; Tate Gall.; Arts Council of GB; Mus. of Modern Art, NY; V & A Mus.; Mus. Boymans-van Beuningen, Rotterdam; Calouste Gulbenkian Foundn, London; RCA; Whitworth Art Gall., Univ. of Manchester; Baltimore Mus. of Art, Md; *Publications:* illustrations for: Oxford Illustrated Old Testament, 1968; Roger McGough, Summer with Monica, 1978; cover illustration, Arden Shakespeare: Othello, 1980; Anthony and Cleopatra, 1980; Timon of Athens, 1980; contribs to: Times Educnl Supp.; Ark; Graphis 70; World of Art; Architectural Rev.; House and Garden; Painter and Sculptor. *Recreations:* sculpture, wining and dining, going to rock and roll concerts, boxing and wrestling matches; living well is the best revenge. *Address:* c/o Waddington Galleries Ltd, 11 Cork Street, W1X 1PD.

BLAKE, Quentin Saxby, OBE 1988; RDI; FCSD; freelance artist and illustrator, since 1957; Visiting Professor, Royal College of Art, since 1989; *b* 16 Dec. 1932; *s* of William Blake and Evelyn Blake. *Educ:* Downing Coll., Cambridge (MA). Royal College of Art: Tutor, 1965–77; Head, Dept of Illustration, 1978–86; Vis. Tutor, 1986–89; Sen. Fellow, 1988. Exhibns of watercolour drawings, Workshop Gallery: Invitation to the Dance, 1972; Runners and Riders, 1973; Creature Comforts, 1974; Water Music, 1976; Retrospective exhibn of illustration work, Nat. Theatre, 1984. *Publications:* (author and illustrator) for children: Patrick, 1968; Jack and Nancy, 1969; Angelo, 1970; Snuff, 1973; The Adventures of Lester, 1977; Mr Magnolia, 1980 (Fedn of Children's Bk Gps Award; Kate Greenaway Medal, 1981); Quentin Blake's Nursery Rhyme Book, 1983; The Story of the Dancing Frog, 1984; Mrs Armitage on Wheels, 1987; Quentin Blake's ABC, 1989; All Join In, 1990; Cockatoos, 1991; (ed and illus.) Custard and Company, by Ogden Nash, 1979; (illustrator) for children: Russell Hoban: How Tom Beat Captain Najork and his Hired Sportsmen, 1974 (Whitbread Lit. Award, 1975; Hans Andersen Honour Book, 1975); A Near Thing for Captain Najork, 1976; The Rain Door, 1986; Hilaire Belloc: Algernon and Other Cautionary Tales, 1991; Roald Dahl: The Enormous Crocodile, 1978; The Twits, 1980; George's Marvellous Medicine, 1981; Revolting Rhymes, 1982; The BFG, 1982; The Witches, 1983; Dirty Beasts, 1984; The Giraffe and the Pelly and Me, 1985; Matilda, 1988; Rhyme Stew, 1989; Esio Trot, 1990; books by John Yeoman, Joan Aiken, Clement Freud, Sid Fleischman, Michael Rosen, Sylvia Plath, Margaret Mahy and Dr Seuss; (illustrator) for adults: Aristophanes, The Birds, 1971; Lewis Caroll, The Hunting of the Snark, 1976; Stella Gibbons, Cold Comfort Farm, 1977; Evelyn Waugh, Black Mischief, 1980, Scoop, 1981; George Orwell, Animal Farm, 1984; Cyrano de Bergerac, Voyages to the Sun and Moon, 1991. *Address:* 30 Bramham Gardens, SW5 0HF. *T:* 071–373 7464.

BLAKE, Sir Richard; *see* Blake, Sir T. R. V.

BLAKE, Richard Frederick William; Editor, Whitaker's Almanack, 1981–86; *b* 9 April 1948; *s* of late Frederick William Blake and of Doris Margaret Blake; *m* 1973, Christine Vaughan; one *d*. *Educ:* Archbishop Tenison's Grammar School. Joined J. Whitaker & Sons, Ltd (Whitaker's Almanack Dept), 1966; apptd Asst Editor of Whitaker's Almanack, 1974. *Recreations:* music, sport. *Address:* 118 Warren Drive, Elm Park, Hornchurch, Essex RM12 4QX.

BLAKE, Sir (Thomas) Richard (Valentine), 17th Bt *cr* 1622, of Menlough; Director, Sir Richard Blake & Associates Ltd; *b* 7 Jan. 1942; *s* of Sir Ulick Temple Blake, 16th Bt, and late Elizabeth Gordon (she *m* 1965, Vice-Adm. E. Longley-Cook, CB, CBE, DSO); *S* father, 1963; *m* 1976, Mrs Jacqueline Hankey; *m* 1982, Bertice Reading (marr. diss. 1986; she *d* 1991). *Educ:* Bradfield Coll., Berks. Member, Standing Council of Baronets. *Recreations:* shooting; Royal Naval Reserve. *Heir:* *kinsman* Anthony Telio Bruce Blake [*b* 5 May 1951; *m* 1988, Geraldine, *d* of Cecil Shnaps]. *Address:* c/o 10 South Pallant, Chichester, Sussex. *T:* Chichester (0243) 787518. *Club:* Chequers (Bognor Regis).

BLAKE, Vincent; *see* Blake, H. V.

BLAKEMORE, Prof. Colin Brian; Waynflete Professor of Physiology, Oxford University, since 1979; Fellow of Magdalen College, since 1979; *b* 1 June 1944; *s* of Cedric Norman Blakemore and Beryl Ann Smith; *m* 1965, Andrée Elizabeth Washbourne; three *d*. *Educ:* King Henry VIII Sch., Coventry; Corpus Christi Coll., Cambridge (Smyth Scholar; BA 1965, MA 1969, ScD 1988); Univ. of Calif, Berkeley (PhD 1968); Magdalen Coll., Oxford (MA 1979; DSc 1989). Harkness Fellow, Neurosensory Lab., Univ. of Calif, Berkeley, 1965–68; Cambridge University: Fellow and Dir of Medical Studies, Downing Coll., 1971–79; Univ. Demonstr in Physiol., 1968–72; Univ. Lectr in Physiol., 1972–79; Leverhulme Fellow, 1974–75. Dir, McDonnell-Pew Centre for Cognitive Neuroscience, Oxford, 1989–; Associate Dir, MRC Oxford Res. Centre in Brain and Behaviour, 1991–. Royal Soc. Locke Res. Fellow, 1976–79. Chm., Neurobiology and Mental Health Bd Grants Cttee, MRC, 1977–79. Vis. Professor: NY Univ., 1970; MIT, 1971; Royal Soc. Study Visit, Keio Univ., Tokyo, 1974; Lethaby Prof., RCA, 1978; Storer Vis. Lectr, Univ. of Calif, Davis, 1980; Vis. Scientist, Salk Inst., 1982, 1983; Macallum Vis. Lectr, Univ. of Toronto, 1984. Vice-Pres., BAAS, 1990– (Pres., Gen. Section, 1989); Hon. Pres., World Cultural Council, 1983–. Member: Central Council, Internat. Brain Res. Org., 1973–; BBC Science Consultative Group, 1975–79; British Nat. Cttee for Physiol. Scis, 1988–90; Professional Adv. Cttee, Schizophrenia: A National Emergency, 1989–. Hon. Associate, Rationalist Press Assoc., 1986–. BBC Reith Lectr, 1976; Presenter, The Mind Machine, BBC2 series, 1988; Lectures: Aubrey Lewis, Inst. of Psych., 1979; Lord Charnwood, Amer. Acad. of Optometry, 1980; Vickers, Neonatal Soc., 1981; Kershman, Eastern Assoc. of Electroencephalographers, NY, 1981; Harveian, Harveian Soc. of London, 1982; Christmas, Royal Instn, 1982; Earl Grey Meml, Newcastle Univ., 1982; George Frederic Still, BPA, 1983; Edridge-Green, RCS, 1984; Cyril Leslie Oakley Meml, Leeds Univ., 1984; Plenary, European Neuroscience Assoc., 1984; Mac Keith Meml, Brit. Paediatric Neurology Assoc., 1985; Faculty of Science, RHC, 1985; Halliburton, KCL, 1986; Cairns Meml, Cambridge Univ., 1986; Bertram Louis Abrahams, RCP, 1986; Norman McAlister Gregg (also Medal), RACO, 1988; Dietrich Bodenstein, Univ. of Va, 1989; Charnock Bradley, Univ. of Edinburgh, 1989; Doyne, Oxford Ophthalmol Congress, 1989 (also Medal); G. L. Brown, Physiol Soc., 1990. Robert Bing Prize, Swiss Acad. of Med. Sciences, 1975; Richardson Cross Medal, S Western Opthalmol Soc., 1978; Copeman Medal, Corpus Christi Coll., Cambridge, 1976; Man of the Year, Royal Assoc. for Disability and Rehabilitation, 1978; Phi Beta Kappa Award in Sci., 1978; John Locke Medal, Apothecaries' Soc., 1983; Prix du Docteur Robert Netter, Acad. Nat. de Médecine, Paris, 1984; Cairns Medal, Cairns Meml Fund, 1986; Michael Faraday Award, Royal Soc., 1989. *Publications:* Handbook of Psychobiology (with M. S. Gazzaniga), 1975; Mechanics of the Mind, 1977; (with S. A. Greenfield) Mindwaves, 1987; The Mind Machine, 1988; (with H. B. Barlow and M. Weston-Smith) Images and Understanding, 1990; Vision: coding and efficiency, 1990; res. reports in Jl of Physiol., Jl of Neuroscience, Nature, etc. *Recreation:* wasting time. *Address:* University Laboratory of Physiology, Parks Road, Oxford OX1 3PT.

BLAKEMORE, Michael Howell; freelance director; *b* Sydney, NSW, 18 June 1928; *s* of late Conrad Blakemore and Una Mary Blakemore (*née* Litchfield); *m* 1st, 1960, Shirley (*née* Bush); one *s*; 2nd, 1986, Tanya McCallin; two *d*. *Educ:* The King's Sch., NSW; Sydney Univ.; Royal Academy of Dramatic Art. Actor with Birmingham Rep. Theatre, Shakespeare Memorial Theatre, etc, 1952–66; Co-dir, Glasgow Citizens Theatre (1st prod., The Investigation), 1966–68; Associate Artistic Dir, Nat. Theatre, 1971–76. Dir, Players, NY, 1978. Resident Dir, Lyric Theatre, Hammersmith, 1980. Best Dir, London Critics, 1972. *Productions include:* A Day in the Death of Joe Egg, 1967, Broadway 1968; Arturo Ui, 1969; Forget-me-not Lane, 1971; Design for Living, 1973; Knuckle, 1974; Separate Tables, 1976; Privates on Parade, 1977; Candida, 1977; All My Sons, 1981; Benefactors, 1984, NY, 1986; Made in Bangkok, 1986; Lettice and Lovage, 1987; Uncle Vanya, 1988; City of Angels, Broadway, 1989; *National Theatre:* The National Health,

1969; Long Day's Journey Into Night, 1971; The Front Page, Macbeth, 1972; The Cherry Orchard, 1973; Plunder, 1976; After the Fall, 1990; *Lyric Theatre, Hammersmith:* Make and Break, 1980 (his opening production); Travelling North, 1980; The Wild Duck, 1980; Noises off, 1982 (transf. to Savoy, 1982, NY, 1983 (Drama Desk Award, NY, 1983–84)). *Films:* A Personal History of the Australian Surf, 1981; Privates on Parade, 1983. *Publication:* Next Season, 1969 (novel). *Recreation:* surfing. *Address:* 11a St Martin's Almshouses, Bayham Street, NW1 0BD. *T:* 071–267 3952.

BLAKENEY, Hon. Allan Emrys; PC (Canada) 1982; Professor of Public Law, University of Saskatchewan, Saskatoon, since 1990; *b* Bridgewater, NS, 7 Sept. 1925; *m* 1st, 1950, Mary Elizabeth (Molly) Schwartz (*d* 1957), Halifax, NS; one *s* one *d*; 2nd, 1959, Anne Gorham, Halifax; one *s* one *d*. *Educ:* Dalhousie Univ. (BA, LLB); Queen's Coll., Oxford (MA). Univ. Medal for Achievement in Coll. of Law, Dalhousie; Rhodes Schol. Sec. and Legal Adviser, Saskatchewan Crown Corps, 1950; Chm., Saskatchewan Securities Commn, 1955–58; private law practice, 1958–60 and 1964–70. MLA, Saskatchewan, 1960–88; formerly Minister of Educn, Provincial Treas. and Health Minister; Chm., Wascana Centre Authority, 1962–64; Opposition Financial Critic, 1964–70; Dep. Leader, 1967–70; Federal New Democratic Party President, 1969–71; Saskatchewan NDP Leader and Leader of Opposition, 1970; Premier, 1971–82; Leader of Opposition, Sask, 1982–87. Prof. of Public Law, Osgoode Hall Law Sch., York Univ., Toronto, 1988–90. Formerly Dir and Vice-Pres., Sherwood Co-op. and Sherwood Credit Union. Hon. DCL Mount Allison, 1980; Hon. LLD Dalhousie, 1981. *Recreations:* reading, swimming, formerly ice hockey and badminton. *Address:* Box 4375, Regina, Sask S4P 3W7, Canada.

BLAKENHAM, 2nd Viscount *cr* 1963, of Little Blakenham; **Michael John Hare;** Chairman and Chief Executive, Pearson plc, since 1983; *b* 25 Jan. 1938; *s* of 1st Viscount Blakenham, PC, OBE, VMH, and of Hon. Beryl Nancy Pearson, *d* of 2nd Viscount Cowdray; *S* father, 1982; *m* 1965, Marcia Persephone, *d* of Hon. Alan Hare, *qv*; one *s* two *d*. *Educ:* Eton College; Harvard Univ. (AB Econ.). Life Guards, 1956–57; English Electric, 1958; Harvard, 1959–61; Lazard Brothers, 1961–63; Standard Industrial Group, 1963–71; Royal Doulton, 1972–77; Pearson, 1977– (Man. Dir, 1978–83). Chm., The Financial Times, 1983–; Partner, Lazard Partners, 1984–; Director: Lazard Bros, 1975–; Sotheby's Holdings Inc., 1987–; Elsevier NV, 1988–; MEPC plc, 1990–; UK-Japan 2000 Group, 1990–; Mem., Internat. Adv. Bd, Lafarge Coppee, 1979–. Member: H of L Select Cttee on Science and Technol., 1985–88; Nature Conservancy Council, 1986–90; Pres., Sussex Wildlife Trust (formerly Sussex Trust for Nature Conservation), 1983–; Chm., Royal Soc. for Protection of Birds, 1981–86, Vice-Pres., 1986–. *Address:* 17th Floor, Millbank Tower, SW1P 4QZ. *T:* 071–828 9020.

BLAKER, George Blaker, CMG 1963; Under-Secretary, HM Treasury, 1955–63, and Department of Education and Science, 1963–71 retired; *b* Simla, India, 30 Sept. 1912; *m* 1938, Richenda Dorothy Buxton (*d* 1987); one *d*. *Educ:* Eton; Trinity Coll., Cambridge. Private Sec. to Ministers of State in the Middle East, 1941–43; Cabinet Office, 1943; Private Sec. to Sec. of War Cabinet, 1944; Principal Private Sec. to Minister of Production and Presidents of the Board of Trade, 1945–47; accompanied Cabinet Mission to India, 1946; Sec. of UK Trade Mission to China, 1946; HM Treasury, 1947; UK Treasury Representative in India, Ceylon and Burma, 1957–63. President: Surrey Trust for Nature Conservation, 1969–80; Scientific and Medical Network, 1986– (Hon. Sec., 1973–86). Gold Medal, Royal Soc. for the Protection of Birds, 1934. *Address:* Lake House, Ockley, Surrey RH5 5NS.

BLAKER, Sir John, 3rd Bt *cr* 1919; *b* 22 March 1935; *s* of Sir Reginald Blaker, 2nd Bt, TD, and of Sheila Kellas, *d* of Dr Alexander Cran; *S* father, 1975; *m* 1st, 1960, Catherine Ann (marr. diss. 1965), *d* of late F. J. Thorold; 2nd, 1968, Elizabeth Katherine, *d* of late Col John Tinsley Russell, DSO. *Address:* Stantons Farm, East Chiltington, near Lewes, East Sussex BN7 3BB.

BLAKER, Rt. Hon. Sir Peter (Allan Renshaw), KCMG 1983; PC 1983; MA; MP (C) Blackpool South, since 1964; *b* Hong Kong, 4 Oct. 1922; *s* of late Cedric Blaker, CBE, MC; *m* 1953, Jennifer, *d* of late Sir Pierson Dixon, GCMG, CB; one *s* two *d*. *Educ:* Shrewsbury; Trinity Coll., Toronto (BA, 1st class, Classics); New Coll., Oxford (MA). Served 1942–46: Argyll and Sutherland Highlanders of Canada (Capt., wounded). Admitted a Solicitor, 1948. New Coll., Oxford, 1949–52; 1st Class, Jurisprudence, Pass degree in PPE. Pres. Oxford Union. Called to Bar, Lincoln's Inn, 1952. Admitted to HM Foreign Service, 1953; HM Embassy, Phnom Penh, 1955–57; UK High Commn, Ottawa, 1957–60; FO, 1960–62; Private Sec. to Minister of State for Foreign Affairs, 1962–64. Attended Disarmament Conf., Geneva; UN Gen. Assembly, 1962 and 1963; signing of Nuclear Test Ban Treaty, Moscow, 1963. An Opposition Whip, 1966–67; PPS to Chancellor of Exchequer, 1970–72; Parliamentary Under-Secretary of State: (Army), MoD, 1972–74; FCO, 1974; Minister of State: FCO, 1979–81; for the Armed Forces, MoD, 1981–83. Joint Secretary: Conservative Parly Foreign Affairs Cttee, 1965–66; Trade Cttee, 1967–70; Exec. Cttee of 1922 Cttee, 1967–70; Vice-Chm., All-Party Tourism Cttee, 1974–79; Member: Select Cttee on Conduct of Members, 1976–77; Public Accounts Commn, 1987–; Chairman: Hong Kong Parly Gp, 1970–72, 1983–; Cons. For. and Commonwealth Affairs Cttee, 1983– (Vice-Chm., 1974–79); Mem. Exec. Cttee, British-American Parly Gp, 1975–79; Hon. Sec., Franco-BritishParly Relations Cttee, 1975–79. Chm., Bd, Royal Ordnance Factories, 1972–74; Chm. Governors, Welbeck Coll., 1972–74; Mem. Council: Chatham House, 1977–79, 1986–90; Council for Arms Control, 1983–; Freedom Assoc., 1984–; Vice-Chairman: Peace Through NATO, 1983–; GB-USSR Assoc., 1983– (Mem. Council, 1974–79); Vice-Pres., Cons. Foreign and Commonwealth Council, 1983–; Governor, Atlantic Inst., 1978–79; Trustee, Inst. for Negotiation and Conciliation, 1984–. Chm., Maclean Hunter Cablevision Ltd; company director; Underwriting Mem. of Lloyd's; farmer. *Recreations:* sailing, opera, shooting. *Address:* c/o House of Commons, SW1A 0AA. *Club:* Garrick.

BLAKISTON, Sir Ferguson Arthur James, 9th Bt *cr* 1763; farmer; *b* 19 Feb. 1963; *er s* of Sir Arthur Norman Hunter Blakiston, 8th Bt, and Mary Ferguson (*d* 1982), *d* of late Alfred Ernest Gillingham, Cave, S Canterbury, NZ; *S* father, 1977. *Educ:* Lincoln Coll., NZ (Diploma in Agriculture 1983). *Heir: b* Norman John Balfour Blakiston, Stock and Station Agent, *b* 7 April 1964.

BLAKSTAD, Michael Björn; Chairman and Chief Executive, Chrysalis Television Ltd, since 1989; Chairman, Blackrod Interactive Services, since 1989; *b* 18 April 1940; *s* of late Clifford and Alice Blakstad; *m* 1965, Patricia Marilyn Wotherspoon; one *s* twin *d*. *Educ:* Ampleforth Coll.; Oriel Coll., Oxford (MA Lit. Hum.). General trainee, BBC, 1962–68; Producer, Yorkshire Television, 1968–71; freelance TV producer, 1971–74; Programme Editor, BBC, 1974–80; Dir of Programmes, TV South, 1980–84. Founder and Managing Director, Blackrod, 1980 (Chm., 1981–84); Chm. and Chief Exec., Workhouse Productions, 1984–88; Chairman: Filmscreen Internat. Ltd, 1984–86; Friday Productions, 1984–88; Jt Chief Exec., Videodisc Co., 1984–88; Dir, Chrysalis Gp. Director: IPPA, 1986–; Internat. Video Communications Assoc., 1988–; Winchester Theatre Royal, 1988–. Awards include: Radio Industries Club, 1975, 1977, 1979; RTS, 1976; BAFTA/Shell Prize, 1976; BIM/John Player, 1976; Nyon, 1978. Hon. MSc Salford, 1983; FRSA; MRI. *Publications:* The Risk Business, 1979; Tomorrow's World looks to the Eighties, 1979. *Recreations:* golf, writing. *Address:* The Tudor House, Workhouse Lane, East Meon, Hants. *Club:* Reform.

BLAMEY, Norman Charles, RA 1975 (ARA 1970); Senior Lecturer, Chelsea School of Art, London, 1963–79; *b* 16 Dec. 1914; *s* of Charles H. Blamey and Ada Blamey (*née* Beacham); *m* 1948, Margaret (*née* Kelly); one *s*. *Educ:* Holloway Sch., London; Sch. of Art, The Polytechnic, Regent Street, London. ROI 1952; Hon. ROI 1974. Exhibited at: RA, RHA, ROI, RBA, NEAC, and provincial galleries; *mural decorations in:* Anglican Church of St Luke, Leagrave, Beds, 1956; Lutheran Church of St Andrew, Ruislip Manor, Middx, 1964; *works in permanent collections:* Municipal Gall., Port Elizabeth, S Africa; Beaverbrook Gall., Fredericton, NB; Beecroft Art Gall., Southend-on-Sea; Towner Art Gall., Eastbourne; Preston Art Gall.; Pennsylvania State Univ. Mus of Art; La Salle Coll., Pa; V & A Museum; Tate Gall.; Chantry Bequest purchase, 1972, 1985; Govt Art Collection; *portraits include:* Mrs Alison Munro, Dr Harry Pitt, Rev. Dennis Nineham, Sir Cyril Clarke, Prof. Graham Higman, Rt Hon. Bernard Weatherill, Speaker of H of C, Sir Alec Merrison, FRS, William Golding, Sir William Rees-Mogg, Sir Christopher Ball. Works in private collections in UK and USA. RA Summer Exhibitions: Rowney Bicentenary Award, 1983; Charles Wollaston Award, 1984. *Recreation:* walking. *Address:* 39 Lyncroft Gardens, NW6 1LB. *T:* 071–435 9250.

BLAMIRE, Roger Victor; veterinary consultant; Director of Veterinary Field Services, Ministry of Agriculture, Fisheries and Food, 1979–83; *b* 9 July 1923; *s* of Thomas Victor Blamire and Anetta Elizabeth (*née* Lawson); *m* 1947, Catherine Maisie Ellis Davidson; two *d*. *Educ:* Kendal Sch.; Royal (Dick) Veterinary Coll., Edinburgh. MRCVS, DVSM. RAVC, 1945–48 (Captain); served India, Burma and Malaya. MAF, 1949; Asst Vet. Officer, City of London, 1949; Dep. Chief Advr on Meat Inspection, MOF, 1952; Dep. Dir, Vet. Field Services, MAFF, 1968. Hon. FRSH, 1979. *Recreations:* walking, gardening, listening to music. *Address:* 5 Atbara Road, Teddington, Middx TW11 9PA. *T:* 081–943 4225.

BLAMIRE-BROWN, John, DL; County Clerk and Chief Executive, Staffordshire County Council, 1973–78; *b* 16 April 1915; *s* of Rev. F. J. Blamire Brown, MA; *m* 1945, Joyce Olivia Pearson; two *s*. *Educ:* Cheam Sch.; St Edmund's Sch., Canterbury. Solicitor 1937. Served War of 1939–45, Royal Marines (Captain). Asst Solicitor, Wednesbury, 1937; West Bromwich, 1946; Staffs CC, 1948; Deputy Clerk of County Council and of Peace, 1962; Clerk, Staffs CC, 1972; Clerk to Lieutenancy, 1972–78; Sec., Staffs Probation and After Care Cttee; Hon. Sec., W Mids Planning Authorities Conf., 1972–78. Dep. Chm., Manpower Services Commn Area Board, Staffs, Salop, W Midlands (North), 1978–83. Mem. Council, Beth Johnson Foundn, 1978–83; Governor, Newcastle-under-Lyme Endowed Schools, 1978–83; Chm., St Giles Hospice Ltd, 1979–84. DL Staffs, 1974. *Recreations:* local history, gardening. *Address:* The Mount, Codsall Wood, Wolverhampton, West Midlands WV8 1QS. *T:* Codsall (09074) 2044.

BLANC, Raymond René; chef; Patron and Chairman, Blanc Restaurants Ltd, since 1984; *b* 19 Nov. 1949; *m* (marr. diss.); two *s*. *Educ:* CEG de Valdahon; Lycée technique de horlogerie, Besançon. Chef de rang, 1971; Manager and chef de cuisine, 1976; proprietor and chef, Les Quat' Saisons, Summertown, 1977; Dir and Chm., Maison Blanc, 1978–88; proprietor, Le Petit Blanc, 1984–88; Chef/patron and Chairman, Le Manoir aux Quat' Saisons, 1984–. Sen. Mem., Academie Culinaire de France. Master Chef Great Britain. Personalité de l'année, 1989. Commandeur de l'Assoc. Internat. des Maîtres Conseils en Gastronomie Française. *Publication:* Recipes from Le Manoir aux Quat' Saisons, 1988. *Recreations:* reading, tennis, riding, classical and rock music. *Address:* Manoir aux Quat' Saisons, Church Road, Great Milton, near Oxford OX9 7PD.

BLANCH, family name of **Baron Blanch.**

BLANCH, Baron *cr* 1983 (Life Peer), of Bishopthorpe in the county of North Yorkshire; **Rt. Rev. and Rt. Hon. Stuart Yarworth Blanch,** PC 1975; *b* 1918; *s* of late William Edwin and of Elizabeth Blanch; *m* 1943, Brenda Gertrude, *d* of late William Arthur Coyte; one *s* four *d*. *Educ:* Alleyns Sch., Dulwich; Oxford (BA 1st cl. Theo. 1948, MA 1952). Employee of Law Fire Insurance Soc. Ltd, 1936–40; Navigator in RAF, 1940–46; St Catherine's Coll., Oxford, 1946–49 (Hon. Fellow, 1975); Curate of Highfield, Oxford, 1949–52; Vicar of Eynsham, Oxon, 1952–57; Tutor and Vice-Principal of Wycliffe Hall, Oxford, 1957–60 (Chm. 1967–); Oriel Canon of Rochester and Warden of Rochester Theological Coll., 1960–66; Bishop of Liverpool, 1966–75; Archbishop of York, 1975–83. Sub-Prelate, OStJ, 1975–88. Chm., Sandford St Martin Trust, 1988–. Hon. Fellow, St Peter's Coll., Oxford, 1983. Hon. LLD Liverpool, 1975; Hon. DD: Hull, 1977; Wycliffe Coll., Toronto, 1979; Manchester, 1984; DUniv York, 1979. *Publications:* The World Our Orphanage, 1972; For All Mankind, 1976; The Christian Militant, 1978; The Burning Bush, 1978; The Trumpet in the Morning, 1979; The Ten Commandments, 1981; Living by Faith, 1983; Way of Blessedness, 1985; Encounters with Christ, 1988. *Recreations:* sport, meteorology, walking, music. *Address:* Bryn Celyn, The Level, Shenington, near Banbury, Oxfordshire OX15 6NA. *Club:* Commonwealth Trust.

BLANCH, Mrs Lesley, (Madame Gary); FRSL; author; *b* 1907; *m* 2nd, 1945, Romain Kacew (Romain Gary) (marr. diss. 1962; he *d* 1980). *Educ:* by reading, and listening to conversation of elders and betters. FRSL 1969. *Publications:* The Wilder Shores of Love (biog.), 1954; Round the World in Eighty Dishes (cookery), 1956; The Game of Hearts (biog.), 1956; The Sabres of Paradise (biog.), 1960; Under a Lilac Bleeding Star (travels), 1963; The Nine Tiger Man (fict.), 1965; Journey into the Mind's Eye (autobiog.), 1968; Pavilions of the Heart (biog.), 1974; Pierre Loti: portrait of an escapist (biog.), 1983; From Wilder Shores: the tables of my travels (travel/autobiog.), 1989. *Recreations:* travel, opera, acquiring useless objects, animal welfare, gardening. *Address:* Roquebrune Village, 06190 Roquebrune-Cap-Martin, France. *Club:* Taharir (formerly Mahommed Ali) (Cairo).

BLANCHARD, Francis; Chevalier de la Légion d'Honneur; Member, French Economic and Social Council, since 1989; *b* Paris, 21 July 1916; *m* 1940, Marie-Claire Boué; two *s*. *Educ:* Univ. of Paris. French Home Office; Internat. Organisation for Refugees, Geneva, 1947–51; Internat. Labour Office, Geneva, 1951–89: Asst Dir-Gen., 1956–68; Dep. Dir-Gen., 1968–74; Dir-Gen., 1974–89. Dr *hc* Brussels, Cairo and Manila. *Recreations:* ski-ing, hunting, riding. *Address:* Prébailly, 01170 Gex, France. *T:* 50–41–51–70 Gex.

BLANCO WHITE, Thomas Anthony, QC 1969; *b* 19 Jan. 1915; *s* of late G. R. Blanco White, QC, and Amber Blanco White, OBE; *m* 1950, Anne Katherine Ironside-Smith; two *s* one *d*. *Educ:* Gresham's Sch.; Trinity Coll., Cambridge. Called to Bar, Lincoln's Inn, 1937, Bencher 1977. Served RAFVR, 1940–46. *Publications:* Patents for Inventions, 1950, 1955, 1962, 1974, 1983, etc. *Recreations:* gardening, photography. *Address:* Francis Taylor Building, EC4Y 7BY.

BLAND, (Francis) Christopher (Buchan); Chairman: LWT (Holdings), since 1984; Life Sciences International plc, since 1987; *b* 29 May 1938; *e s* of James Franklin MacMahon Bland and Jess Buchan Bland (*née* Brodie); *m* 1981, Jennifer Mary, Viscountess Enfield, *er d* of late Rt Hon. W. M. May, PC, FCA, MP, and of Mrs May, Mertoun Hall,

Holywood, Co. Down; one *s* and two step *s* two step *d*. *Educ:* Sedbergh; The Queen's Coll., Oxford (Hastings Exhibnr). 2nd Lieut, 5th Royal Inniskilling Dragoon Guards, 1956–58; Lieut, North Irish Horse (TA), 1958–69. Dir, NI Finance Corp., 1972–76; Dep. Chm., IBA, 1972–80; Chairman: Sir Joseph Causton & Sons, 1977–85; Century Hutchinson Group, 1984–89; Director: Nat. Provident Instn, 1978–88; Storehouse plc, 1988–. Mem. GLC, for Lewisham, 1967–70; Chm., ILEA Schs Sub-Cttee, 1970; Mem. Burnham Cttee, 1970; Chm., Bow Group, 1969–70; Editor, Crossbow, 1971–72; Chairman: NHS Rev. Gp on Nat. Trng Council and Nat. Staff Cttees, 1982; Hammersmith Special Health Authority, 1982–. Governor, Prendergast Girls Grammar Sch. and Woolwich Polytechnic, 1968–70; Mem. Council: RPMS, 1982–; St Mary's Med Sch., 1984–88. *Publications:* Bow Group pamphlet on Commonwealth Immigration; (with Linda Kelly) Feasts, 1987. *Recreations:* fishing, skiing; formerly: Captain, OU Fencing Team, 1961; Captain, OU Modern Pentathlon Team, 1959–60; Mem. Irish Olympic Fencing Team, 1960. *Address:* Abbots Worthy House, Abbots Worthy, Winchester, Hants SO21 1DR. *T:* Winchester (0962) 881333; 10 Catherine Place, SW1E 6HF. *T:* 071–834 0021. *Club:* Beefsteak.

BLAND, Sir Henry (Armand), Kt 1965; CBE 1957; FRSA; *b* 28 Dec. 1909; *s* of Emeritus Prof. F. A. Bland, CMG, and Elizabeth Bates Jacobs; *m* 1933, Rosamund, *d* of John Nickal; two *d* (and one *d* decd). *Educ:* Sydney High Sch.; Univ. of Sydney. LLB (Hons) 1932. Admitted Solicitor Supreme Court of NSW, 1935. Entered NSW Public Service, 1927; Alderman, Ryde (NSW) Municipal Council, 1937–39; Acting Agent-Gen. for NSW in London, 1940–41; Adviser on Civil Defence to NSW and Commonwealth Govts, 1941; Princ. Asst to Dir-Gen. of Manpower, 1941–45; Asst Sec., First Asst Sec., 1946–51, Sec. 1952–67, Dept of Labour and National Service; Sec., Dept of Defence, Australia, 1967–70. Leader, Austr. Govt Delegns to Confs: 1948, 1953, 1957, 1960, 1962, 1963, 1964, 1966; Austr. Govt Rep. on the Governing Body of ILO, 1963–67; Adviser on industrial relations to Singapore Govt, 1958. Bd of Inquiry into Victorian Land Transport System, 1971; Chairman: Cttee on Administrative Discretions, 1972–73; Bd of Inquiry into Victorian Public Service, 1973–75; Commonwealth Admin. Rev. Cttee, 1976; ABC, 1976; Arbitrator between Aust. Nat. Railways and Tasmanian Govt, 1978. Chm. and Dir of numerous cos, 1970–. *Address:* 54 Kenilworth Gardens, Kangaloon Road, Bowral, NSW 2576, Australia. *T:* (048) 613320. *Clubs:* Athenæum (Melbourne); Bowral Golf.

BLAND, Louise Sarah, (Mrs S. Bland); *see* Godfrey, L. S.

BLAND, Lt-Col Sir Simon (Claud Michael), KCVO 1982 (CVO 1973; MVO 1967); Extra Equerry to Princess Alice Duchess of Gloucester and the Duke and Duchess of Gloucester, since 1989 (Comptroller, Private Secretary and Equerry, 1972–89); *b* 4 Dec. 1923; *s* of late Sir Nevile Bland, KCMG, KCVO; *m* 1954, Olivia, *d* of late Major William Blackett, Arbigland, Dumfries; one *s* three *d*. *Educ:* Eton College. Served War of 1939–45, Scots Guards, in Italy; BJSM, Washington, 1948–49; 2nd Bn, Scots Guards, Malaya, 1949–51; Asst Mil. Adviser at UK High Commn, Karachi, 1959–60; Comptroller and Asst Private Sec. to late Duke of Gloucester, 1961–74 and Private Sec. to late Prince William, 1968–72. Dir, West End Bd, Commercial Union, 1964–; Consultant: Industrial Metal Services, 1989–; Operation Raleigh, 1989–. Member Council: Distressed Gentlefolk Aid Assoc., 1990–; Order of St John for Kent, 1990–; Coll. of St Barnabas, 1990–; President: Friends of Edenbridge Hosp., 1990–; Lingfield Br., Riding for the Disabled, 1990–; Trustee, Grant Maintained Sch. Trust, 1990–. Freeman, City of London, 1988. KStJ 1988. *Recreation:* shooting. *Address:* Gabriels Manor, Edenbridge, Kent TN8 5PP. *T:* Edenbridge (0732) 862340. *Club:* Buck's.

BLANDFORD, Marquess of; Charles James Spencer-Churchill; formerly on agricultural course at Royal Agricultural College, Cirencester and at Royal Berkshire College of Agriculture; *b* 24 Nov. 1955; *e s* and *heir* of 11th Duke of Marlborough, *qv*; *m* 1990, Rebecca Mary, *d* of Peter Few Brown. *Educ:* Pinewood; Harrow. *Address:* Blenheim Palace, Woodstock, Oxon. *Clubs:* Turf, Tramp's, Annabel's; Racquet and Tennis (New York).

BLANDFORD, Eric George, CBE 1967; formerly a Judge of the Supreme Court of Aden; *b* 10 March 1916; *s* of George and Eva Blanche Blandford; *m* 1940, Marjorie Georgina Crane; one *s*. *Educ:* Bristol Grammar Sch. Admitted Solicitor Supreme Court, England, 1939; LLB (London) 1939. War Service, 1939–46 (despatches): India, Burma, Malaya; rank on release Temp. Major RA. Solicitor in London, 1946–51; Asst Comr of Lands, Gold Coast, 1951; Dist Magistrate, Gold Coast, 1952; called to the Bar, Inner Temple, 1955; Chief Registrar, Supreme Court, Gold Coast, 1956; Registrar of High Court of Northern Rhodesia, 1958; Judge, Supreme Court of Aden, 1961–68; Dep. Asst Registrar of Criminal Appeals, 1968–78; Asst Registrar of Criminal Appeals, Royal Courts of Justice, 1978–81. Chm. Aden Municipality Inquiry Commn, 1962. *Publication:* Civil Procedure Rules of Court, Aden, 1967. *Recreations:* country pursuits. *Address:* Trelindy, Porthilly, Rock, Cornwall PL27 6JX.

BLANDFORD, Heinz Hermann, CBE 1981; Fellow, Royal Postgraduate Medical School, Hammersmith Hospital, 1973 (Member Council, 1964–89; Treasurer, 1964–82; Vice Chairman, 1982–89); Chairman of Trustees, Blandford Trust for advancement of medical research and teaching, since 1964; Director, LSP Innovations Ltd, since 1987; *b* Berlin, Germany, 28 Aug. 1908; *s* of late Judge Richard Blumenfeld and Hedwig Kersten; *m* 1933, Hilde Kleczewer; one *s* one *d*. *Educ:* Augusta Gymnasium; Univs of Berlin and Hamburg. Controller of continental cos in ceramic, pharmaceutical, iron and steel industries, 1933–39; Chm., Ulvir Ltd and various cos, 1936–76. Pioneered synthesis, manufacture and use of Liquid Fertilisers in the UK, 1945–60. School of Pharmacy, London University: Mem. Council, 1975–89; Treas., 1976–87; Vice-Chm., 1979–86; Hon. Fellow, 1988; British Postgraduate Medical Federation: Mem. Governing Body, 1969–86; Hon. Treas., 1969–84; Chm., 1977–79, Dep. Chm., 1980–85; Member: Management Cttee, Inst. of Ophthalmology, Moorfields, 1974–86; Court of Governors, LSHTM, 1982–; Governor, London House for Overseas Graduates, 1977–80. Member: Org. Cttee, 6th World Congress of Cardiology, London, 1971; Board of Governors: Hammersmith and St Mark's Hospitals, 1972–74. *Recreations:* farming, gardening, walking. *Address:* Holtsmere Manor, Holtsmere End, Redbourn, Herts AL3 7AW. *T:* Redbourn (0582) 792206. *Club:* Farmers'.

BLANDFORD, Prof. Roger David, FRS 1989; Richard Chace Tolman Professor of Theoretical Astrophysics, California Institute of Technology, since 1989; *b* 28 Aug. 1949; *s* of Jack George and Janet Margaret Blandford; *m* 1972, Elizabeth Denise Kellett; two *s*. *Educ:* King Edward's Sch., Birmingham; Magdalene Coll., Cambridge Univ. (BA, MA, PhD; Bye Fellow 1973). Res. Fellow, St John's Coll., Cambridge, 1973–76; Inst. for Advanced Study, Princeton, 1974–75; CIT, 1976–. *Address:* 130–33 Caltech, Pasadena, Calif 91125, USA. *T:* 818–356 4200.

BLANDY, Prof. John Peter, MA, DM, MCh, FRCS, FACS; Consultant Surgeon: The Royal London (formerly London) Hospital, since 1964; St Peter's Hospital for the Stone, since 1969; Professor of Urology, University of London, since 1969; *b* 11 Sept. 1927; *s* of late Sir E. Nicolas Blandy, KCIE, CSI, ICS and Dorothy Kathleen (*née* Marshall); *m* 1953, Anne, *d* of Hugh Mathias, FRCS, Tenby; four *d*. *Educ:* Clifton Coll.; Balliol Coll., Oxford; London Hosp. Med. Coll. BM, BCh 1951; MA 1953; FRCS 1956; DM 1963; MCh 1963; FACS 1980. House Phys. and House Surg., London Hosp., 1952; RAMC, 1953–55; Surgical Registrar and Lectr in Surgery, London Hosp., 1956–60; exchange Fellow, Presbyterian St Luke's Hosp., Chicago, 1960–61; Sen. Lectr, London Hosp., 1961; Resident Surgical Officer, St Paul's Hosp., 1963–64. McLaughlin-Gallie Vis. Prof., Royal Coll. of Physicians and Surgeons of Canada, 1988. Member: BMA; RSM; Council, RCS, 1982– (Hunterian Prof., 1964); Internat. Soc. Pædiatric Urol. Surg.; Internat. Soc. of Urological Surgeons; British Assoc. Urological Surgeons (Pres., 1984); President: European Assoc. of Urology, 1986–88; European Bd of Urology, 1991–92; Fellow, Assoc. of Surgeons. Hon. Fellow, Urological Society: of Australasia, 1973; of Canada, 1986; of Denmark, 1986; of Germany, 1987; Hon. Fellow: Mexican Coll. of Urology, 1974; Amer. Urol Assoc., 1989. Maurice Davidson Award, Fellowship of Postgrad. Med., 1980; St Peter's Medal, British Assoc. of Urol Surgs, 1982; Francisco Diaz Medal, Spanish Urol Assoc., 1988. *Publications:* (with A. D. Dayan and H. F. Hope-Stone) Tumours of the Testicle, 1970; Transurethral Resection, 1971; (ed) Urology, 1976; Lecture Notes on Urology, 1976; Operative Urology, 1978; (ed with B. Lytton) The Prostate, 1986; (with J. Moors) Urology for Nurses, 1989; (ed with R. T. D. Oliver and H. F. Hope-Stone) Urological and Genital Cancer, 1989; papers in surgical and urological jls. *Recreation:* painting. *Address:* The Royal London Hospital, Whitechapel, E1 1BB. *T:* 071–377 7000.

BLANK, Maurice Victor; Chairman, since 1991, and Chief Executive, since 1985, Charterhouse plc; Chairman and Chief Executive, Charterhouse Bank Ltd, since 1985; *b* 9 Nov. 1942; *s* of Joseph Blank and Ruth Blank (*née* Levey); *m* 1977, Sylvia Helen (*née* Richford); two *s* one *d*. *Educ:* Stockport Grammar Sch.; St Catherine's Coll., Oxford (MA). Solicitor of the Supreme Court. Joined Clifford-Turner as articled clerk, 1964: Solicitor, 1966; Partner, 1969; Dir, and Head of Corporate Finance, Charterhouse Bank, 1981. *Publication:* (jtly) Weinberg and Blank on Take-Overs and Mergers, 3rd edn 1971 to 5th edn 1989. *Recreations:* family, cricket, tennis, theatre. *Address:* 1 Paternoster Row, St Paul's, EC4M 7DH. *T:* 071–248 4000.

BLANKS, Howard John; Under-Secretary, Highways Policy and Programme, Department of Transport, 1985–88; *b* 16 June 1932; *s* of Lionel and Hilda Blanks; *m* 1958, Judith Ann (*née* Hughes). *Educ:* Barking Abbey Sch.; Keble Coll., Oxford (BA 1st Cl. Hons Music). National Service, RAF (Pilot), 1956–58. Air Traffic Control Officer, Min. of Aviation, 1958–64; Principal, Min. of Aviation (later Min. of Technology and Aviation Supply), 1964–71; Private Sec. to Chief Executive, Min. of Defence (Procurement Executive), 1972; Assistant Secretary: MoD, 1972–75; Cabinet Office, 1975–77; Dept of Trade, 1977–79; Under-Secretary, Head of Civil Aviation Policy Div., Dept of Trade (subseq. Transport), 1980–85. *Recreations:* music, travel. *Address:* Withinlee, Hedgehog Lane, Haslemere, Surrey GU27 2PJ. *T:* Haslemere (0428) 652468.

BLANNING, Dr Timothy Charles William, FBA 1990; Reader in Modern European History, University of Cambridge, since 1987; Fellow, Sidney Sussex College, Cambridge, since 1968; *b* 21 April 1942; *s* of Thomas Walter Blanning and Gwendolyn Marchant (*née* Jones); *m* 1988, Nicky Susan Jones. *Educ:* King's Sch., Bruton, Somerset; Sidney Sussex Coll., Cambridge (BA, MA; PhD 1967). Res. Fellow, Sidney Sussex Coll., Cambridge, 1965–68; Asst Lectr in History, 1972–76, Lectr in History, 1976–87, Univ. of Cambridge. *Publications:* Joseph II and Enlightened Despotism, 1970; Reform and Revolution in Mainz 1740–1803, 1974; The French Revolution in Germany, 1983; The Origins of the French Revolutionary Wars, 1986; The French Revolution: aristocrats versus bourgeois?, 1987. *Recreations:* music, gardening. *Address:* Sidney Sussex College, Cambridge CB2 3HU. *T:* Cambridge (0223) 338800.

BLANTYRE, Archbishop of, (RC), since 1968; **Most Rev. James Chiona;** *b* 1924. *Educ:* Nankhunda Minor Seminary, Malaŵi; Kachebere Major Seminary, Malaŵi. Priest, 1954; Asst Parish Priest, 1954–57; Prof., Nankhunda Minor Seminary, 1957–60; study of Pastoral Sociology, Rome, 1961–62; Asst Parish Priest, 1962–65; Auxiliary Bishop of Blantyre and Titular Bishop of Bacanaria, 1965; Vicar Capitular of Archdiocese of Blantyre, 1967. *Recreation:* music. *Address:* Archbishop's House, PO Box 385, Blantyre, Malaŵi. *T:* (10)633516.

BLASCHKO, Hermann Karl Felix, MD; FRS 1962; Emeritus Reader in Biochemical Pharmacology, Oxford University, and Emeritus Fellow, Linacre College, Oxford, since 1967 (Hon. Fellow, 1990); *b* Berlin, 4 Jan. 1900; *o s* of late Prof. Alfred Blaschko, MD and late Johanna Litthauer; *m* 1944, Mary Douglas Black, *d* of late John Robert Black, Yelverton, S Devon; no *c*. *Educ:* Universities of Berlin, Freiburg im Breisgau and Göttingen. MD Freiburg; PhD Cambridge; MA Oxon. Research Asst to late Prof. O. Meyerhof at Berlin-Dahlem and Heidelberg at various periods, 1925–32; University Asst in Physiology, Univ. of Jena, 1928–29; worked at UCL, 1929–30 and 1933–34; Physiological Lab., Cambridge Univ., 1934–44; came to Oxford, 1944. Visiting Professor: Yale Univ., 1967–68; Upstate Medical Center, Syracuse, NY, 1968; RCS, 1968–73; Univ. of Pennsylvania, 1969; Univ. of Bergen, Norway, 1969–70. Hon. Prof., Faculty of Medicine, Heidelberg, 1966. Member of Editorial Board of: Pharmacological Reviews, 1957–64; British Journal of Pharmacology and Chemotherapy, 1959–65; Journal of Physiology, 1965–72; Neuropharmacology, 1962–72; Naunyn-Schmiedebergs Arch. Exp. Pharmak., 1966–85; Molecular Pharmacol., 1966–77. Mem. Neuropharmacology Panel, International Brain Research Organisation (IBRO). Hon. FRSocMed, 1978; Hon. Member: British Pharmacological Soc., 1979; Hungarian Pharm. Soc., 1979; Physiological Soc., 1980; Berliner Medizinische Ges., 1980; Corresp. Mem., German Pharmacolog. Soc. Schmiedeberg Plakette, 1972; Hon. Pres., Internat. Catecholamine Symposium, Göteborg, 1983. First Thudichum Lectr and Medallist, London, 1974; Aschoff Lectr, Freiburg, 1974; Wellcome Gold Medal in Pharmacology, 1990. Hon. MD: Berlin (Free Univ.), 1966; Bern, 1984; Freiburg im Breisgau, 1990. *Publications:* numerous papers in scientific publications. *Address:* Department of Pharmacology, South Parks Road, Oxford OX1 3QT; 24 Park Town, Oxford OX2 6SH.

BLASHFORD-SNELL, Col John Nicholas, MBE 1969; on staff of Ministry of Defence, since 1983; *b* 22 Oct. 1936; *s* of late Rev. Prebendary Leland John Blashford Snell and Gwendolen Ives Sadler; *m* 1960, Judith Frances (*née* Sherman); two *d*. *Educ:* Victoria Coll., Jersey, CI; RMA, Sandhurst. Commissioned Royal Engineers, 1957; 33 Indep. Fd Sqdn RE Cyprus, 1958–61; comd Operation Aphrodite (Expedition) Cyprus, 1959–61; Instructor: Junior Leaders Regt RE, 1962–63; RMA Sandhurst, 1963–66; Adjt 3rd Div. Engineers, 1966–67; comd Great Abbai Expedn (Blue Nile), 1968; sc RMCS Shrivenham and Camberley, 1968–69; comd Dahlak Quest Expedn, 1969–70; GSO2 MoD, 1970–72; comd British Trans-Americas Expedn, 1971–72; OC 48 Fd Sqdn RE, service in Belize, Oman, Ulster, 1972–74; comd Zaire River Expedn, 1974–75; CO Junior Leaders Regt RE, 1976–78; Dir of Operations, Operation Drake, 1977–81; on staff (GSO1), MoD, 1978–82; in command, The Fort George Volunteers, 1982–83. Operation Raleigh: Operations Dir, 1982–88; Dir Gen., 1989–. Hon. Chm., Scientific Exploration Soc., 1969–. Freeman, City of Hereford, 1984. Hon. DSc Durham, 1986. Darien Medal (Colombia), 1972. *Publications:* Weapons and Tactics (with Tom Wintringham), 1970; (with Richard Snailham) The Expedition Organiser's Guide, 1970, 2nd edn 1976; Where the Trails Run Out, 1974; In the Steps of Stanley, 1975, 2nd edn 1975; (with A. Ballantine) Expeditions the Experts' Way, 1977, 2nd edn 1978; A Taste for Adventure, 1978; (with Michael Cable) Operation Drake, 1981; Mysteries: Encounters with the Unexplained, 1983; Operation Raleigh, the Start of an Adventure, 1987; (with Ann Tweedy) Operation Raleigh, Adventure Challenge, 1988; (with Ann Tweedy) Operation Raleigh, Adventure Unlimited, 1990. *Recreations:* motoring, shooting, underwater diving, stamp collecting. *Address:* c/o CHQ, Operation Raleigh, Alpha Place, Flood Street, SW3 5SZ. *Clubs:* Royal Automobile, Wig and Pen; Explorers' (New York) (Chm., British Chapter).

BLATCH, family name of **Baroness Blatch**.

BLATCH, Baroness *cr* 1987 (Life Peer), of Hinchingbrooke in the county of Cambridgeshire; **Emily May Blatch,** CBE 1983; Minister of State, Department of the Environment, since 1991; *b* 24 July 1937; *d* of Stephen Joseph and Sarah Triggs; *m* 1963, John Richard Blatch, AFC; two *s* one *d* (of whom one *s* one *d* are twins) (and one *s* decd). *Educ:* Prenton, Birkenhead; Huntingdonshire College. WRAF, 1955–59; Ministry of Aviation, 1959–63. Member: Bd, Peterborough Develt Corp., 1984–89; Cambs CC, 1977–89 (Leader, 1981–85); ACC, 1981–85; European Econ. and Social Cttee, 1986–87; Cons. Nat. Local Govt Adv. Cttee, 1988–. Baroness in Waiting (Govt Whip), H of L, 1990; Parly Under-Sec. of State for the Envmt, 1990–91. Chm., Anglo-American Community Relations Cttee, RAF Alconbury, 1985–91. Pres., Nat. Benevolent Inst., 1989–. FRSA 1985. *Recreations:* music, theatre. *Address:* House of Lords, SW1A 0PW. *Clubs:* Royal Air Force, University Women's.

BLATCHLEY, Geraldine; *see* James, G.

BLATCHLY, John Marcus, MA, PhD; FSA 1975; Headmaster, Ipswich School, since 1972; *b* 7 Oct. 1932; *s* of late Alfred Ernest Blatchly and of Edith Selina Blatchly (*née* Giddings); *m* 1955, Pamela Winifred, JP, *d* of late Major and Mrs L. J. Smith; one *s* one *d*. *Educ:* Sutton Grammar Sch., Surrey; Christ's Coll., Cambridge (Natural Scis Triposes; BA, MA, PhD). Instr Lieut RN, 1954–57. Asst Master and Head of Science Dept: King's Sch., Bruton, 1957–62; Eastbourne Coll., 1962–66; Charterhouse, 1966–72 (PhD awarded 1967 publication of work carried out with Royal Society grants at these three schools). Pres., Suffolk Inst. of Archaeology and History, 1975–; Chm., Suffolk Records Soc., 1988–; Trustee, five county and town conservation trusts in Suffolk; Hon. Custodian, Ipswich Old Town Library, 1982–. Editor, Conference and Common Room (Journal of HMC Schools), 1987–; Hon. Treas., HMC, 1990–. *Publications:* Organic Reactions, vol. 19, 1972 (jtly, with J. F. W. McOmie); The Topographers of Suffolk, 1976, 5th edn 1988; (with Peter Eden) Isaac Johnson of Woodbridge, 1979; Eighty Ipswich Portraits, 1980; (ed) Davy's Suffolk Journal, 1983; The Town Library of Ipswich: a history and catalogue, 1989; many papers in chemical, educnl, archaeological and antiquarian jls. *Recreations:* opera, chamber music, books. *Address:* Headmaster's House, Ipswich School, Suffolk IP1 3QY. *T:* Ipswich (0473) 259941.

BLATHERWICK, David Elliott Spiby, CMG 1990; OBE 1973; HM Diplomatic Service; Ambassador in Dublin, since 1991; *b* 13 July 1941; *s* of Edward S. Blatherwick; *m* 1964, (Margaret) Clare Crompton; one *s* one *d*. *Educ:* Lincoln Sch.; Wadham Coll., Oxford. Entered FO, 1964; Second Sec., Kuwait, 1968; First Sec., Dublin, 1970; FCO, 1973; Head of Chancery, Cairo, 1977; seconded to Home Civil Service, 1981; Hd Energy, Science and Space Dept, FCO, 1983; sabbatical leave at Stanford Univ., Calif, 1985–86; Counsellor and Hd of Chancery, UK Mission to UN, NY, 1986–89; Prin. Finance Officer and Chief Inspector, FCO, 1989–91. *Publication:* The International Politics of Telecommunications, 1987. *Recreations:* music, sailing, walking. *Address:* c/o Foreign and Commonwealth Office, King Charles Street, SW1A 2AH. *Club:* Athenæum.

BLAUG, Prof. Mark, PhD; FBA 1989; Consultant Professor, University of Buckingham, since 1984; Professor of the Economics of Education, University of London Institute of Education, 1967–84, now Professor Emeritus; *b* 3 April 1927; *s* of Bernard Blaug and Sarah (*née* Toeman); *m* 1st, 1946, Rose Lapone (marr. diss.); 2nd, 1954, Brenda Ellis (marr. diss.); one *s*; 3rd, 1969, Ruth M. Towse; one *s*. *Educ:* Queen's Coll., NY (BA); Columbia Univ. (MA, PhD). Asst Prof., Yale Univ., 1954–62; Sen. Lectr, then Reader, Univ. of London Inst. of Educn, 1963–67; Lectr, LSE, 1963–78. Vis. Prof., Exeter Univ., 1989–. Guggenheim Foundn Fellow, 1958–59. Dist. Fellow, Hist. of Econs Soc., 1988. Foreign Hon. Mem., Royal Netherlands Acad. of Arts and Scis, 1984. *Publications:* Ricardian Economics, 1958; Economic Theory in Retrospect, 1962, 4th edn 1985; (jtly) The Causes of Graduate Unemployment in India, 1969; Introduction to the Economics of Education, 1970; Education and the Employment Problem in Developing Countries, 1973; (jtly) The Practice of Manpower Forecasting, 1973; The Cambridge Revolution?, 1974; The Methodology of Economics, 1980; Who's Who in Economics, 1983, 2nd edn 1986; Great Economists Since Keynes, 1984; Great Economists Before Keynes, 1985; Economic History and the History of Economics, 1986; The Economics of Education and the Education of an Economist, 1987; Economic Theories: true or false?, 1990; Keynes: Life, Ideas and Legacy, 1990. *Recreations:* talking, walking, sailing. *Address:* Langsford Barn, Peter Tavy, Tavistock, Devon PL19 9LY. *T:* Tavistock (0822) 810562.

BLAYNEY, Elizabeth Carmel, (Eily Blayney); Head of Library and Records Department and Departmental Record Officer (Assistant Secretary), Foreign and Commonwealth Office, 1977–85, retired; *b* 19 July 1925; *d* of William Blayney, MRCS, LRCP, Medical Practitioner (previously County Inspector, RIC) of Harrold, Beds, and Mary Henrietta *d* of John Beveridge, sometime Town Clerk of Dublin. *Educ:* St Mary's Convent, Shaftesbury; The Triangle, S Molton Street. Chartered Librarian. Served War, WTS(FANY) in UK, India and Ceylon (Force 136), 1944–46. Library Asst, Hampstead Borough Libraries, 1947–50; Assistant Librarian: RSA, 1950–52; CO/CRO Jt Library, CRO, 1953; Head of Printed Library, FO, 1959–68; Librarian i/c, ODM, 1968–69; Librarian, FCO, 1969–77. *Address:* 6 Bamville Wood, East Common, Harpenden, Herts AL5 1AP. *T:* Harpenden (0582) 715067.

BLEACKLEY, David, CMG 1979; DPhil; Head, Overseas Division, and Assistant Director, Institute of Geological Sciences, 1975–80; *b* 1 Feb. 1919; *s* of Alfred Mason and Hilda Gertrude Bleackley; *m* 1st, 1945, Peggy Florence Chill (*d* 1966); one *s* one *d*; 2nd, 1973, Patricia Clavell Strakosch (*née* Hore); two step *s* one step *d*. *Educ:* City of Oxford Sch.; The Queen's Coll., Oxford (BA 1939, MA 1942, DPhil 1960). Served War, Royal Engineers, 1939–45. Geologist: Shell Oil Co., 1946–50; Geological Survey, British Guiana, 1954–57, Dep. Dir, 1957–60; Overseas Geological Surveys, 1960–65; Dep. Head, Overseas Div., Inst. of Geological Sciences, 1965–75. FIMM 1969; FGS 1943. *Publications:* papers in various jls. *Recreations:* walking, shooting. *Address:* Well Farm, Dagnall, near Berkhamsted, Herts HP4 1QU. *T:* Little Gaddesden (044284) 3232.

BLEAKLEY, Rt. Hon. David Wylie, CBE 1984; PC (NI) 1971; Chief Executive, Irish Council of Churches, since 1980; *b* 11 Jan. 1925; *s* of John Wesley Bleakley and Sarah Bleakley (*née* Wylie); *m* 1949, Winifred Wason; three *s*. *Educ:* Ruskin Coll., Oxford; Queen's Univ., Belfast. MA, DipEconPolSci (Oxon). Belfast Shipyard, 1940–46; Oxford and Queen's Univ., 1946–51; Tutor in Social Studies, 1951–55; Principal, Belfast Further Educn Centre, 1955–58; Lectr in Industrial Relations, Kivukoni Coll., Dar-es-Salaam, 1967–69; Head of Dept of Economics and Political Studies, Methodist Coll., Belfast, 1969–79. MP (Lab) Victoria, Belfast, Parliament of N Ireland, 1958–65; contested: (Lab) East Belfast, General Elections, 1970, Feb. and Oct. 1974. Minister of Community Relations, Govt of NI, March-Sept. 1971; Member (NILP), E Belfast: NI Assembly, 1973–75; NI Constitutional Convention, 1975–76. Mem., Cttee of Inquiry on Police, 1978. Chm., NI Standing Adv. Commn on Human Rights, 1980–84. Irish Deleg. to Anglican Consultative Council, 1976; Deleg. to World Council of Churches; Pres., Church Missionary Soc., 1983–; WEA and Open Univ. tutor; Vis. Sen. Lectr in Peace Studies, Univ. of Bradford, 1974–. Mem., Press Council, 1987–90. Hon. MA Open, 1975. *Publications:* Ulster since 1800: regional history symposium, 1958; Young Ulster and Religion in the Sixties, 1964; Peace in Ulster, 1972; Faulkner: a biography, 1974; Saidie Patterson, Irish Peacemaker, 1980; In Place of Work, 1981; The Shadow and Substance, 1983; Beyond Work—Free to Be, 1985; Will the Future Work, 1986; regular contribs to BBC and to press on community relations and industrial studies. *Address:* 8 Thornhill, Bangor, Co. Down, Northern Ireland BT19 1RD. *T:* Bangor (0247) 454898.

BLEANEY, Prof. Brebis, CBE 1965; FRS 1950; MA, DPhil; Warren Research Fellow, Royal Society, 1977–80, Leverhulme Emeritus Fellow, 1980–82; Fellow, 1957–77, Senior Research Fellow, 1977–82, Wadham College, Oxford, now Emeritus Fellow; Dr Lee's Professor of Experimental Philosophy, University of Oxford, 1957–77, now Emeritus Professor; *b* 6 June 1915; *m* 1949, Betty Isabelle Plumpton; one *s* one *d*. *Educ:* Westminster City Sch.; St John's Coll., Oxford. Lecturer in Physics at Balliol Coll., Oxford, 1947–50. Research Fellow, Harvard Univ. and Mass Institute of Technology, 1949. University Demonstrator and Lectr in Physics, Univ. of Oxford, 1945–57; Fellow and Lectr in Physics, St John's Coll., Oxford, 1947–57; Tutor, 1950–57; Hon. Fellow, 1968. Visiting Prof. in Physics in Columbia Univ., 1956–57; Harkins Lectr, Chicago Univ., 1957; Kelvin Lectr, Instn Electrical Engineers, 1962; Morris Loeb Lectr, Harvard Univ., 1981; Cherwell Simon Meml Lectr, Oxford Univ., 1981–82; John and Abigail Van Vleck Lectr, Univ. of Minnesota, 1985; Visiting Professor: Univ. of California, Berkeley, 1961; Univ. of Pittsburgh, 1962–63; Manitoba, 1968; La Plata, Argentina, 1971; Amer. Univ. in Cairo, 1978; Univ. of NSW, 1981. Mem. Council for Scientific and Industrial Res., 1960–62; Chm., British Radiofrequency Spectroscopy Gp, 1983–85. FRSA 1971. Corr. Mem. Acad. of Sciences, Inst. of France, 1974, Associé Etranger, 1978; For. Hon. Mem., Amer. Acad. of Arts and Scis, 1978; DSc *hc* Porto, Portugal, 1987. Charles Vernon Boys Prize, Physical Soc., 1952; Hughes Medal, Royal Society, 1962; ISMAR Prize, Internat. Soc. for Magnetic Resonance, 1983; Holweck Medal and Prize, Inst. of Physics and Société Française de Physique, 1984. *Publications:* (with B. I. Bleaney) Electricity and Magnetism, 1957, 3rd edn, 1976, revd edn in 2 vols, 1989; (with A. Abragam) Electron Paramagnetic Resonance, 1970, revd edn 1986; over 200 papers in Proceedings of the Royal Society and Proceedings of the Physical Society, etc. *Recreations:* music and tennis. *Address:* Clarendon Laboratory, Parks Road, Oxford OX1 3PU.

BLEASDALE, Alan; playwright and novelist, since 1975; *b* 23 March 1946; *s* of George and Margaret Bleasdale; *m* 1970, Julia Moses; two *s* one *d*. *Educ:* St Aloysius RC Jun. Sch., Huyton; Wade Deacon Grammar Sch., Widnes; Padgate Teachers Trng Coll. (Teacher's Cert.). Schoolteacher, 1967–75. Hon. DLitt Liverpool Poly., 1991. BAFTA Writers Award, 1982; RTS Writer of the Year, 1982. *Publications:* Scully, 1975; Who's been sleeping in my bed, 1977; No more sitting on the Old School Bench, 1979; Boys from the Blackstuff, 1982 (televised; Broadcasting Press Guild Television Award for Best Series, 1982; Best British TV Drama of the Decade, ITV Achievement of the Decade Awards, 1989); Are you lonesome tonight?, 1985 (Best Musical, London Standard Drama Awards, 1985); No Surrender (film script), 1986; Having a Ball, 1986; It's a Madhouse, 1986; The Monocled Mutineer, 1986 (televised 1986); GBH (TV series), 1991. *Recreation:* rowing. *Address:* c/o Harvey Unna & Stephen Durbridge Ltd, 24 Pottery Lane, Holland Park, W11 4LZ. *T:* 071–727 1346.

BLEASDALE, Cyril, OBE 1988; FCIT; MBIM; FRSA; Director, Scotrail, since 1990; *b* 8 July 1934; *s* of Frederick and Alice Bleasdale; *m* 1970, Catherine; two *d*. *Educ:* Evered High Sch., Liverpool; Stanford Univ., Calif (Sen. Exec. Program). Man. Dir, Freightliner Ltd, 1975–82; Dir, Inter City British Rail, 1982–86; Gen. Manager, BR London Midland Region, 1986–90. *Recreations:* music, fitness. *Address:* Scotrail House, 58 Port Dundas Road, Glasgow G4 0HG.

BLEASE, family name of **Baron Blease.**

BLEASE, Baron *cr* 1978 (Life Peer), of Cromac in the City of Belfast; **William John Blease,** JP; *b* 28 May 1914; *e s* of late William and Sarah Blease; *m* 1939, Sarah Evelyn Caldwell; three *s* one *d*. *Educ:* elementary and technical schs; Nat. Council of Labour Colls; WEA. Retail Provision Trade (apprentice), 1929; Retail Grocery Asst (Branch Manager), 1938–40; Clerk, Belfast Shipyard, 1940–45; Branch Manager, Co-operative Soc., Belfast, 1945–59; Divl Councillor, Union of Shop Distributive Workers, 1948–59; NI Officer, 1959–75, Exec. Consultant, 1975–76, Irish Congress of Trade Unions; Divl Chm. and Nat. Exec. Mem., Nat. Council of Labour Colls, 1948–61; Exec. Mem., NI Labour Party, 1949–59 (Dep. Chm., 1957–58); Trustee, LPNI, 1986–. Labour Party Spokesman in House of Lords, on N Ireland, 1979–82; Trade Union Side Sec., NI CS Industrial Jt Council, 1975–77. Member: NI Co-operative Develt Agency, 1987–; NI Economic Council, 1964–75; Review Body on Local Govt, NI, 1970–71; Review Body on Ind. Relations, NI, 1970–73; Working Party on Discrimination in Employment, NI, 1972–73; NI Trng Res. Cttee, 1966–80; NI Regional Adv. Bd, BIM, 1971–80; NUU Vocational Guidance Council, 1974–83; Ind. Appeals Tribunals, 1974–76; Local Govt Appeals Tribunal, 1974–83; Irish Council of Churches Working Party, 1974–; IBA, 1974–79; Standing Adv. Commn on Human Rights, NI, 1977–79; Police Complaints Bd, 1977–80; Conciliation Panel, Ind. Relations Agency, 1978–89; Security Appeal Bd, NI SC Commn, 1979–88; Chm., Community Service Order Cttee, 1979–80; Rapporteur, EEC Cross Border Communications Study on Londonderry/Donegal, 1978; President: NI Assoc., NACRO, 1982–85; NI Hospice, 1981–85; E Belfast Access Council for Disabled, 1982–88; NI Widows Assoc., 1985–89; Belfast Housing Aid, 1989–. Trustee: Belfast Charitable Trust for Integrated Educn, 1984–88; TSB Foundn, NI, 1986–. Mem., Management Bd, Rathgael Young People's Centre, 1989–. Mem., Bd of Govs, St Mae Nissis Coll., 1981–90. Ford Foundn Travel Award, USA, 1959. Hon. Res. Fellow, Univ. of Ulster, 1976–83; Jt Hon. Res. Fellow, TCD, 1976–79. Hon. FBIM 1981 (MBIM 1970). JP Belfast, 1976–. Hon. DLitt New Univ. of Ulster, 1972; Hon. LLD QUB, 1982. *Publication:* Encyclopaedia of Labour Law, vol. 1: The Trade Union Movement in Northern Ireland, 1983. *Recreations:* gardening, reading. *Address:* 30 Clonaver Crescent North, Belfast BT4 2FD.

BLECH, Harry, CBE 1984 (OBE 1962); Hon. RAM, 1963; Musical Director, Haydn-Mozart Society, and Founder and Conductor, London Mozart Players, 1949–84; *b* 2 March 1910; British; *m* 1935, Enid Marion Lessing (*d* 1977); one *s* two *d*; *m* 1957, Marion Manley, pianist; one *s* three *d*. *Educ:* Central London Foundation; Trinity Coll. of Music (Fellow); Manchester Coll. of Music (Fellow). Joined BBC Symphony Orchestra, 1930–36. Responsible for formation of: Blech Quartet, 1933–50; London Wind Players, 1942 (conductor); London Mozart Players, 1949 (Conductor Laureate); Haydn-Mozart

Soc., 1949; London Mozart Choir, 1952. Dir of Chamber Orchestra, RAM, 1961–65. FRSA. *Address:* The Owls, 70 Leopold Road, Wimbledon, SW19 7JQ.

BLEDISLOE, 3rd Viscount *cr* 1935; **Christopher Hiley Ludlow Bathurst,** QC 1978; *b* 24 June 1934; *s* of 2nd Viscount Bledisloe, QC, and of Joan Isobel Krishaber; *S* father, 1979; *m* (marr. diss. 1986); two *s* one *d. Educ:* Eton; Trinity Coll., Oxford. Called to the Bar, Gray's Inn, 1959; Bencher, 1986. *Heir: s* Hon. Rupert Edward Ludlow Bathurst, *b* 13 March 1964. *Address:* Lydney Park, Glos GL15 6BT. *T:* Dean (0594) 842566; Fountain Court, Temple, EC4Y 9DH. *T:* 071–583 3335.

BLEEHEN, Prof. Norman Montague; Cancer Research Campaign Professor of Clinical Oncology and Hon. Director of MRC Unit of Clinical Oncology and Radiotherapeutics, since 1975, and Director, Radiotherapeutics, and Oncology Centre, since 1984, University of Cambridge; Fellow of St John's College, Cambridge, since 1976; *b* 24 Feb. 1930; *s* of Solomon and Lena Bleehen; *m* 1969, Tirza, *d* of Alex and Jenny Loeb. *Educ:* Manchester Grammar Sch.; Haberdashers' Aske's Sch.; Exeter Coll., Oxford (Francis Gotch medal, 1953); Middlesex Hosp. Med. School. BA 1951, BSc 1953, MA 1954, BM, BCh 1955, Oxon; MRCP 1957, FRCP 1973; FRCR 1964; DMRT 1962. MRC Res. Student, Biochem. Dept, Oxford, 1951; house appts: Middlesex Hosp., 1955–56; Hammersmith Hosp., 1957; Asst Med. Specialist Army, Hanover, 1957; Med. Specialist Army, Berlin, 1959 (Captain); Jun. Lectr in Medicine, Dept of Regius Prof. of Medicine, Oxford, 1959–60; Registrar and Sen. Registrar in Radiotherapy, Middlesex Hosp. Med. Sch., 1961–66; Lilly Res. Fellow, Stanford Univ., 1966–67; Locum Consultant, Middlesex Hosp., 1967–69; Prof. of Radiotherapy, Middlesex Hosp. Med. Sch., 1969–75. Consultant advr to CMO, DHSS, for radiation oncology, 1986–. Simon Lectr, RCR, 1986. Member: Jt MRC/CRC Cttee for jtly supported insts, 1971–74; Coordinating Cttee for Cancer Res., 1973–79, 1987–; Council, Imperial Cancer Res. Fund, 1973–76; Council, Brit. Inst. of Radiology, 1974–77; Sci. Cttee, Cancer Res. Campaign, 1976–; MRC Cell Bd, 1980–84; UICC Fellowships Cttee, 1983–87; Council, European Organisation for Treatment of Cancer, 1983–88; Council, RCR, 1987–; Vice-President: Bd of Dirs, Internat. Assoc. for Study of Lung Cancer, 1980–82; EEC Cancer Experts Cttee, 1987–; Pres., Internat. Soc. of Radiation Oncology, 1985–89; Chairman: MRC Lung Cancer Wkg Party, 1973–89; MRC Brain Tumour Wkg Party, 1978–89; MRC Cancer Therapy Cttee, 1972–88; British Assoc. for Cancer Res., 1976–79; Soc. for Comparative Oncology, 1983–86. Hon. FACR 1984. Hon. doctorate Bologna, 1990. Roentgen Prize, British Inst. of Radiology, 1986. *Publications:* (ed jtly) Radiation Therapy Planning, 1983; (Scientific Editor) British Medical Bulletin 24/1, The Scientific Basis of Radiotherapy, 1973; various on medicine, biochemistry cancer and radiotherapy. *Recreations:* gardening, television. *Address:* 21 Bentley Road, Cambridge CB2 2AW. *T:* Cambridge (0223) 354320. *Club:* Athenæum.

BLELLOCH, Sir John Niall Henderson, KCB 1987 (CB 1983); Permanent Under-Secretary of State, Northern Ireland Office, 1988–90, retired; *b* 24 Oct. 1930; *s* of late Ian William Blelloch CMG and Leila Mary Henderson; *m* 1958, Pamela, *d* of late James B. and E. M. Blair; one *s* (and one *s* decd). *Educ:* Fettes Coll.; Gonville and Caius Coll., Cambridge (BA). Nat. Service, RA, 1949–51 (commnd 1950). Asst Principal, War Office, 1954; Private Sec. to successive Parly Under Secs of State, 1956–58; Principal, 1958; MoD, 1964–80; London Business Sch. (EDP 3), 1967; Asst Sec., 1968; RCDS, 1974; Asst Under-Sec. of State (Air), Procurement Exec., 1976; Asst Under-Sec. of State, Defence Staff, 1979; Dep. Sec., NI Office, 1980–82; Dep. Under-Sec of State (Policy and Programmes), MoD, 1982–84; Second Permanent Under-Sec. of State, MoD, 1984–88. Comr, Royal Hosp. Chelsea, 1988–. *Recreations:* golf, squash, skiing, learning the piano. *Address:* c/o Bank of Scotland, 57/60 Haymarket, SW1. *Clubs:* Roehampton; Royal Mid-Surrey Golf.

BLENKINSOP, Dorothy, CBE 1990; Regional Nursing Officer, Northern Regional Health Authority, 1973–89, retired; *b* 15 Nov. 1931; *d* of late Joseph Henry Blenkinsop, BEM, and Thelma Irene (*née* Bishop). *Educ:* South Shields Grammar Sch. for Girls. MA (Dunelm) 1978. SRN 1953; SCM 1954; Health Visitors Cert. 1962. Ward Sister, Royal Victoria Infirmary, Newcastle upon Tyne, 1955–61; Health Visitor, S Shields, 1962–64; Dep. Matron, Gen. Hosp., S Shields, 1964–67; Durham Hospital Management Committee: Prin. Nurse, Durham City Hosps, 1967–69; Prin. Nursing Officer (Top), 1969–71; Chief Nursing Officer, 1971–73. Mem. Methodist Church. Vice-Chm., BBC North Regl Adv. Council, 1990–. Gov., Newcastle upon Tyne Poly., 1989–. Hon. MSc CNAA, 1990. *Publications:* (with E. G. Nelson): Changing the System, 1972; Managing the System, 1976; articles in nursing press. *Recreation:* gardening. *Address:* 143 Temple Park Road, South Shields, Tyne and Wear NE34 0EN. *T:* South Shields (091) 4561429.

BLENNERHASSETT, His Honour Francis Alfred, (Frank), QC 1965; a Circuit Judge, 1978–89; *b* 7 July 1916; 2nd *s* of John and Annie Elizabeth Blennerhassett; *m* 1948, Betty Muriel Bray; two *d. Educ:* Solihull Sch. Served War of 1939–45 RA and Royal Warwicks Regt, Britain and East Africa (Captain). Called to Bar, Middle Temple, 1946; Bencher, 1971; Oxford Circuit. Dep. Chm., Staffordshire QS, 1963–71; Recorder of New Windsor, 1965–71; a Recorder of the Crown Court, 1972–78; Hon. Recorder of New Windsor, 1972–76; Hon. Recorder of Windsor and Maidenhead, 1976–89. Legal Assessor to GMC and Dental Council, 1971–78; Chm., Govt Cttee on Drinking and Driving, 1975–76; Member: Parole Bd, 1981–83; Home Office Cttee on Magistrates' Courts Procedure, 1989–. *Recreation:* golf. *Address:* Manor Cottage, Hampton in Arden, Warwickshire BG2 0AE. *T:* Hampton in Arden (06755) 2660. *Club:* Copt Heath Golf.

BLENNERHASSETT, Sir (Marmaduke) Adrian (Francis William), 7th Bt, *cr* 1809; *b* 25 May 1940; *s* of Lieut Sir Marmaduke Blennerhassett, 6th Bt, RNVR (killed in action, 1940), and Gwenfra (*d* 1956), *d* of Judge Harrington-Morgan, Churchtown, Co. Kerry, and of Mrs Douglas Campbell; *S* father 1940; *m* 1972, Carolyn Margaret, *yr d* of late Gilbert Brown; one *s* one *d. Educ:* Michael Hall, Forest Row; McGill Univ.; Imperial Coll., Univ. of London (MSc); Cranfield Business Sch. (MBA). *Recreations:* flying (private pilot's licence), ocean racing (sailing), ski-ing. *Heir: s* Charles Henry Marmaduke Blennerhassett, *b* 18 July 1975. *Address:* 54 Staveley Road, Chiswick, W4 3ES. *Club:* Royal Ocean Racing.

BLESSLEY, Kenneth Harry, CBE 1974 (MBE 1945); ED; Valuer and Estates Surveyor, Greater London Council, 1964–77; *b* 28 Feb. 1914; *s* of Victor Henry le Blond Blessley and Ellen Mary Blessley; *m* 1946, Gwendeline MacRae; two *s. Educ:* Haberdashers' Aske's Hampstead Sch.; St Catharine's Coll., Cambridge (MA); Coll. of Estate Management. FRICS. Private practice, West End and London suburbs. Served War of 1939–45, TA Royal Engrs, Persia, Middle East, Sicily, Italy (despatches 1942 and 1944). Sen. Property Adviser, Public Trustee, 1946–50; Dep. County Valuer, Mddx CC, 1950–53; County Valuer, Mddx CC, 1953–65. Mem. Urban Motorways Cttee, 1970–72; Chm., Covent Garden Officers' Steering Gp, 1970–77; Chm., Thamesmead Officers' Steering Gp, 1971–76; Pres., Assoc. of Local Authority Valuers and Estate Surveyors, 1962 and 1972; Mem. Gen. Council, RICS, 1972–78, Pres., Gen. Practice Div., 1976–77. Pres., Old Haberdashers' Assoc., 1963 (Pres. RFC, 1966–68). *Publications:* numerous articles and papers on compensation, property valuation and development. *Recreations:* music, drama, sport, motoring. *Address:* 99 Maplehurst Road, Summersdale, Chichester, West Sussex PO19 4RP. *T:* Chichester (0243) 528188.

BLEWITT, Major Sir Shane (Gabriel Basil), KCVO 1989 (CVO 1987; LVO 1981); Keeper of the Privy Purse and Treasurer to the Queen, since 1988; Receiver-General, Duchy of Lancaster, since 1988; *b* 25 March 1935; *s* of late Col Basil Blewitt; *m* 1969, Julia Morrogh-Bernard, *widow* of Major John Morrogh-Bernard, Irish Guards, and *d* of late Mr Robert Calvert; one *s* one *d* (and one step *s* one step *d*). *Educ:* Ampleforth Coll.; Christ Church, Oxford (MA Hons Mod. Languages). Served Irish Guards, 1956–74; Antony Gibbs and Sons, 1974; Asst Keeper, 1975–85, Dep. Keeper, 1985–88, of the Privy Purse. *Recreations:* gardening, shooting. *Club:* White's.

BLIGH, family name of **Earl of Darnley.**

BLIN-STOYLE, Prof. Roger John, FRS 1976; Professor of Theoretical Physics, University of Sussex, 1962–90, now Emeritus; *b* 24 Dec. 1924; *s* of Cuthbert Basil St John Blin-Stoyle and Ada Mary (*née* Nash); *m* 1949, Audrey Elizabeth Balmford; one *s* one *d. Educ:* Alderman Newton's Boys' Sch., Leicester; Wadham Coll., Oxford (Scholar). MA, DPhil Oxon; FInstP; ARCM. Served Royal Signals, 1943–46 (Lieut). Pressed Steel Co. Res. Fellow, Oxford Univ., 1951–53; Lectr in Math. Physics, Birmingham Univ., 1953–54; Sen. Res. Officer in Theoret. Physics, Oxford Univ., 1952–62; Fellow and Lectr in Physics, Wadham Coll., Oxford, 1956–62, Hon. Fellow, 1987; Vis. Associate Prof. of Physics, MIT, 1959–60; Vis. Prof. of Physics, Univ. of Calif, La Jolla, 1960; Sussex University: Dean, Sch. of Math. and Phys. Sciences, 1962–68; Pro-Vice-Chancellor, 1965–67; Dep. Vice-Chancellor, 1970–72; Pro-Vice-Chancellor (Science), 1977–79. Chm., School Curriculum Develt Cttee, 1983–88. Member: Royal Greenwich Observatory Cttee, 1966–70; Nuclear Physics Bd, SRC, later SERC, 1967–70, 1982–84; Council, Royal Soc., 1982–83. Pres., Inst. of Physics, 1990–92. Hon. DSc Sussex, 1990. Rutherford Medal and Prize, IPPS, 1976. Editor: Reports on Progress in Physics, 1977–82; Student Physics Series, 1983–87. *Publications:* Theories of Nuclear Moments, 1957; Fundamental Interactions and the Nucleus, 1973; Nuclear and Particle Physics, 1991; papers on nuclear and elementary particle physics in scientific jls. *Recreation:* making music. *Address:* 14 Hill Road, Lewes, E Sussex BN7 1DB. *T:* Lewes (0273) 473640.

BLISHEN, Anthony Owen, OBE 1968; HM Diplomatic Service; Counsellor, Foreign and Commonwealth Office, since 1981; *b* 16 April 1932; *s* of Henry Charles Adolphus Blishen and Joan Cecile Blishen (*née* Blakeney); *m* 1963, Sarah Anne Joscelyne; three *s* one *d. Educ:* Clayesmore Sch., Dorset; SOAS, London Univ. Commnd Royal Hampshire Regt, 1951; Lt 1st Bn: BAOR, 1953; Malaya, 1953–55; Captain, GSO3 HQ 18 Inf. Bde, Malaya, 1955–56; attached HQ Land Forces, Hong Kong (language trng), 1957–59; GSO3 HQ Far East Land Forces, Singapore, 1960–62; FO, 1963–65; First Sec. and Consul, Peking, 1965–67; First Sec., FCO, 1968–70; Chargé d'Affaires (ad interim), Ulan Bator, 1970; Trade Comr (China trade), Hong Kong, 1971–73; First Sec., FCO, 1973–77; First Sec., 1977–78, Counsellor, 1978–81, Tokyo. *Recreations:* Renaissance music, oriental languages. *Address:* c/o Foreign and Commonwealth Office, SW1A 2AH.

BLISHEN, Edward; author; *b* 29 April 1920; *s* of William George Blishen and Elizabeth Anne (*née* Pye); *m* 1948, Nancy Smith; two *s. Educ:* Queen Elizabeth's Grammar Sch., Barnet. Weekly Newspaper reporter, 1937–40; agricultural worker, 1941–46. Teaching: Prep. Schoolmaster, 1946–49; Secondary Modern School Teacher, 1950–59. Carnegie Medal, 1970; Soc. of Authors Travelling Scholarship, 1979. FRSL 1989. *Publications:* Roaring Boys, 1955; This Right Soft Lot, 1969; (with Leon Garfield) The God Beneath the Sea, 1970; (with Leon Garfield) The Golden Shadow, 1972; *autobiography:* A Cackhanded War, 1972; Uncommon Entrance, 1974; Sorry, Dad, 1978; A Nest of Teachers, 1980; Shaky Relations, 1981 (J. R. Ackerley Prize); Lizzie Pye, 1982; Donkey Work, 1983; A Second Skin, 1984; The Outside Contributor, 1986; The Disturbance Fee, 1988; The Penny World, 1990; *edited:* Junior Pears Encyclopaedia, 1961–; Oxford Miscellanies, 1964–69; Blond Encyclopaedia of Education, 1969; The School that I'd Like, 1969; The Thorny Paradise, 1975; *compiled:* Oxford Book of Poetry for Children, 1964; Come Reading, 1967; (with Nancy Blishen) A Treasury of Stories for Five Year Olds, 1989. *Recreations:* ambling, broadcasting, listening to music. *Address:* 12 Bartrams Lane, Hadley Wood, Barnet EN4 0EH. *T:* 081–449 3252.

BLISS, Christopher John Emile, PhD; FBA 1988; Nuffield Reader in International Economics, Oxford University, and Fellow of Nuffield College, since 1977; *b* 17 Feb. 1940; *s* of John Llewlyn Bliss and Patricia Paula (*née* Dubern); *m* 1983, Ghada (*née* Saqf El Hait); one *s* two *d* by previous marr. *Educ:* Finchley Catholic Grammar Sch.; King's Coll., Cambridge (BA 1962, MA 1964, PhD 1966). Fellow of Christ's Coll., Cambridge, 1965–71; Asst Lectr, 1965–67, and Lectr, 1967–71, Cambridge Univ.; Prof. of Econs, Univ. of Essex, 1971–77. Dir, General Funds Investment Trust Ltd, 1980–87. Fellow, Econometric Soc., 1978. Editor or Asst Editor, Rev. of Econ. Studies, 1967–71; Man. Editor, Oxford Economic Papers, 1989–. *Publications:* Capital Theory and the Distribution of Income, 1975; (with N. H. Stern) Palanpur: the economy of an Indian village, 1982; papers and reviews in learned jls. *Recreation:* music. *Address:* Nuffield College, Oxford OX1 1NF. *T:* Oxford (0865) 278573.

BLISS, John Cordeux, QPM; retired as Deputy Assistant Commissioner, Metropolitan Police, 1971 (seconded as National Co-ordinator of Regional Crime Squads of England and Wales from inception, 1964–71); *b* 16 March 1914; *s* of late Herbert Francis Bliss and Ida Muriel (*née* Hays); *m* 1947, Elizabeth Mary, *d* of Charles Gordon Howard; one *s* two *d. Educ:* Haileybury Coll. Metropolitan Police Coll., Hendon, 1936–37. Served in RAF, 1941–45, Flt Lt, 227 Sqdn, MEF. Various ranks of Criminal Investigation Dept of Metropolitan Police, 1946–62; seconded as Dir of Criminal Law at Police Coll., Bramshill, 1962–63; Dep. Comdr, 1963–64. Barrister, Middle Temple, 1954. Mem., Parole Bd, 1973–76 and 1978–81. Liveryman, Merchant Taylors' Company. Churchill Memorial Trust Fellowship, 1967; Queen's Police Medal, 1969. *Recreations:* gardening; formerly: Rugby football, tennis. *Address:* Foxhanger Down, Hurtmore, Godalming, Surrey GU7 2RG. *T:* Guildford (0483) 422487. *Club:* Royal Air Force.

BLISSETT, Alfreda Rose; *see* Hodgson, A. R.

BLIX, Hans, PhD, LLD; Director General, International Atomic Energy Agency, since 1981; *b* 28 June 1928; *s* of Gunnar Blix and Hertha Blix (*née* Wiberg); *m* 1962, Eva Margareta Kettis; two *s. Educ:* Univ. of Uppsala; Columbia Univ.; Univ. of Cambridge (PhD); Stockholm Univ. (LLD). Associate Prof. in International Law, 1960; Ministry of Foreign Affairs, Stockholm: Legal Adviser, 1963–76; Under-Secretary of State, in charge of internat. development co-operation, 1976; Minister for Foreign Affairs, 1978; Under-Secretary of State, in charge of internat. development co-operation, 1979. Member: Sweden's delegn to UN General Assembly, 1961–81; Swedish delegn to Conference on Disarmament in Geneva, 1962–78. Hon. doctorate, Moscow State Univ., 1987. *Publications:* Treaty Making Power, 1959; Statsmyndigheternas Internationella Förbindelser, 1964; Sovereignty, Aggression and Neutrality, 1970; The Treaty-Maker's Handbook, 1974. *Recreations:* skiing, hiking. *Address:* International Atomic Energy Agency, POB 100, A-1400 Vienna, Austria. *T:* 2360, ext. 1111.

BLOCH, Prof. Konrad E.; Higgins Professor of Biochemistry, Harvard University, since 1954; *b* 21 Jan. 1912; *s* of Frederick D. Bloch and Hedwig (*née* Striemer); *m* 1941, Lore Teutsch; one *s* one *d*. *Educ:* Technische Hochschule, Munich; Columbia Univ., New York. MA Oxon 1982. Instructor and Research Associate, Columbia Univ., 1939–46; Univ. of Chicago: Asst Prof., 1946–48; Associate Prof., 1948–50; Prof., 1950–54. Newton-Abraham Vis. Prof., and Fellow of Lincoln Coll., Oxford, 1982. Foreign Mem., Royal Soc., 1982. Nobel Prize for Medicine (jointly), 1964; US Nat. Medal of Science, 1988. *Publications:* Lipide Metabolism, 1961; numerous papers in biochemical journals. *Address:* 16 Moon Hill Road, Lexington, Mass 02173, USA. *T:* (617) 862–9076; Department of Chemistry, Harvard University, 12 Oxford Street, Cambridge, Mass 02138, USA.

BLOCH, Prof. Maurice Émile Félix, PhD; FBA 1990; Professor of Anthropology, University of London at London School of Economics, since 1984; *b* 21 Oct. 1939; *s* of late Pierre Bloch and of Claude Kennedy; step *s* of John Stodart Kennedy, *qv*; *m* 1963, Jean Helen Medlicott; one *s* one *d*. *Educ:* Lycée Carnot, Paris; Perse Sch., Cambridge; LSE (BA 1962); Fitzwilliam Coll., Cambridge (PhD 1968). Asst Lectr, Univ. of Wales, Swansea, 1968; Lectr, LSE, 1969; Reader, London Univ., 1977. Corresp. Mem., Académie Malgache, Madagascar, 1965. *Publications:* Placing the Dead, 1971; Marxism and Anthropology, 1983; From Blessing to Violence, 1986; Ritual, History and Power, 1989. *Recreation:* book binding. *Address:* Department of Anthropology, London School of Economics, Houghton Street, WC2A 2AE. *T:* 071–405 7686.

BLOCH, Dame Merle Florence; *see* Park, Dame Merle F.

BLOCK, Maj.-Gen. Adam Johnstone Cheyne, CB 1962; CBE 1959 (OBE 1951); DSO 1945; *b* 13 June 1908; *s* of late Col Arthur Hugh Block, RA; *m* 1945, Pauline Bingham, *d* of late Col Norman Kennedy, CBE, DSO, TD, DL, Doonholm, Ayr; two *d* (and one *d* decd). *Educ:* Blundell's; RMA Woolwich. 2nd Lieut RA 1928; served War of 1939–45 (France, UK, N Africa and Italy); CO 24th Field Regt, RA, 1943–45. GSO1, RA and AMS, GHQ, 1945–47; AQMG and GSO1 Trg AA Comd, 1947–50; Lieut-Col, 1950; Senior Directing Staff (Army). Joint Services Staff College, 1950–53; Col, 1953; CRA 6 Armd Div., 1953; Comdt, School of Artillery, Larkhill, 1956; Maj.-Gen. 1959; GOC Troops, Malta, 1959–62; retd. Chief Information Officer to General Synod (formerly Church Assembly), 1965–72. Mem. Basingstoke DC, 1973–75. Col Comdt, Royal Regt of Artillery, 1965–73. *Recreations:* all country pursuits. *Address:* St Cross House, Whitchurch, Hants RG28 7AS. *T:* Whitchurch (0256) 892344.

BLOCK, Brig. David Arthur Kennedy William, CBE 1961; DSO 1945; MC 1943; retired; *b* 13 June 1908; *s* of late Col Arthur Hugh Block; *m* 1949, Elizabeth Grace (*d* 1975), *e d* of late Lieut-Col E. G. Troyte-Bullock, CMG, Zeals House, Wiltshire, and *widow* of Major G. E. Sebag-Montefiore, D'Anvers House, Culworth, near Banbury; no *c*. *Educ:* Blundell's; RMA, Woolwich. Served War of 1939–45 (despatches, MC, DSO); CO 152nd (Ayrshire Yeomanry) Field Regt, RA, 1943–45; Coll. Comdr, RMA Sandhurst, 1947–50. CO 2nd Regt RHA, 1950–53; GSO1 Secretariat, SHAPE, 1953–54; CRA, 7th Armoured Div., 1954–57; Comd 18th Trg Bde, RA, 1958–61; retired, 1961. ADC to the Queen, 1959. *Recreations:* hunting, shooting, golf. *Address:* Benville Manor Lodge, Corscombe, Dorchester, Dorset DT2 0NW. *T:* Corscombe (093589) 205. *Club:* Army and Navy.

BLOCK, David Greenberg, AC 1988 (AO 1983); adviser and company director; *b* 21 March 1936; *s* of Emanuel Block and Hannah Greenberg; *m* 1959, Naomi Denfield; one *s* three *d*. *Educ:* King Edward VII Sch., Johannesburg; Univ. of Witwatersrand (BJuris cum laude). Joined Schroder-Darling & Co., 1964, Dir, 1967–72; Chairman: David Block & Associates, 1972–81; Trinity Properties, 1984–90; George Ward Group, 1986–89; Dep. Chm., Concrete Constructions, 1990; Director: CSR, 1977–88; Kalamazoo Holdings, 1986–; Dir, Lloyds Bank NZA, Chm., Lloyds Internat., Dir, Lloyds Merchant Bank (UK) and Adviser, Lloyds Merchant Bank Holdings, 1981–86; Consultant, Coudert Brothers, 1986–; Adviser: Coopers & Lybrand, 1986–; S. G. Warburg Group, 1987–. Consultant: to Prime Minister and Cabinet, 1986–89; to govts, cos and instns, 1986–; to Premier's Dept, NSW, 1987–88; Mem., Cttee of Enquiry into inflation and taxation, 1975; Chm., Efficiency Scrutiny Unit and Admin. Reform Unit, 1986–88. Comr, Aust. Film Commn, 1978–81; Chm., Sydney Opera House Trust, 1981–89. Dir, Univ. of NSW Foundn, 1989–. Fellow, Senate of Univ. of Sydney, 1983–87. *Recreations:* swimming, squash, music, theatre. *Address:* (home) 30 Clarke Street, Vaucluse, NSW 2030, Australia. *T:* 337 6211; (office) Box 2650, GPO, Sydney, NSW 2001, Australia. *T:* 285 7822, *Fax:* 264 6990. *Clubs:* American, University (Sydney).

BLOEMBERGEN, Prof. Nicolaas; Gerhard Gade University Professor, Harvard University, 1980–90; *b* 11 March 1920; *m* 1950, Huberta Deliana Brink; one *s* two *d*. *Educ:* Univ. of Utrecht (BA, MA); Univ. of Leiden (PhD). Research Associate, Leiden, 1947–48; Harvard University: Associate Prof., 1951; Gordon McKay Prof. of Applied Physics, 1957; Rumford Prof. of Physics, 1974. Hon. DSc: Laval Univ., 1987; Connecticut Univ., 1988. Stuart Ballantine Medal, Franklin Inst., 1961; Nat. Medal of Science, 1974; Lorentz Medal, Royal Dutch Acad. of Science, 1978; Alexander von Humboldt Senior US Scientist Award, Munich, 1980; (jtly) Nobel Prize in Physics, 1981; IEEE Medal of Honor, 1983; Dirac Medal, Univ. of NSW, 1983. Commander, Order of Orange Nassau (Netherlands), 1983. *Publications:* Nuclear Magnetic Relaxation, 1948 (New York 1961); Nonlinear Optics, 1965, 4th printing, 1982; over 300 papers in scientific jls. *Address:* Pierce Hall, Harvard University, Cambridge, Mass 02138, USA. *T:* (617) 495–3336.

BLOEMFONTEIN, Bishop of, since 1982; **Rt. Rev. Thomas Shaun Stanage;** *b* 6 April 1932; *s* of Robert and Edith Clarice Stanage. *Educ:* King James I Grammar Sch., Bishop Auckland; Univ. of Oxford (MA, Hons Theology, 1956). Curate, St Faith, Great Crosby, 1958–61; Minister of Conventional District of St Andrews, Orford, 1961–63; Vicar, St Andrew, Orford, 1963–70; Rector, All Saints, Somerset West, 1970–75; Dean of Kimberley, 1975–78; Bishop Suffragan of Johannesburg, 1978–82. Liaison Bishop to Missions to Seamen, Southern Africa. Hon. DD, Nashotah Theol Sem., Wisconsin, 1986. *Recreations:* flying (private pilot); music (organ, violin and piano). *Address:* Bishop's House, 16 York Road, Bloemfontein, 9301, S Africa. *T:* (051) 314351. *Clubs:* Bloemfontein; Good Hope Flying, Cape Aero (Cape Town).

BLOFELD, Hon. Sir John Christopher Calthorpe, Kt 1990; DL; **Hon. Mr Justice Blofeld;** a Judge of the High Court of Justice, Queen's Bench Division, since 1990; *b* 11 July 1932; *s* of late T. R. C. Blofeld, CBE; *m* 1961, Judith Anne, *er d* of Alan Mohun and Mrs James Mitchell; two *s* one *d*. *Educ:* Eton; King's Coll., Cambridge. Called to Bar, Lincoln's Inn, 1956, Bencher, 1990; QC 1975; a Recorder of the Crown Court, 1975–82; a Circuit Judge, 1982–90. Inspector, Dept of Trade, 1979–81. Chancellor, Dio. St Edmundsbury and Ipswich, 1973. DL Norfolk, 1991. *Recreations:* cricket, gardening. *Address:* Royal Courts of Justice, Strand, WC2A 2LL. *Club:* Boodle's.

BLOIS, Sir Charles (Nicholas Gervase), 11th Bt, *cr* 1686; farming since 1965; *b* 25 Dec. 1939; *s* of Sir Gervase Ralph Edmund Blois, 10th Bt and Mrs Audrey Winifred Blois (*née* Johnson); *S* father, 1968; *m* 1967, Celia Helen Mary Pritchett; one *s* one *d*. *Educ:* Harrow; Trinity Coll., Dublin; Royal Agricultural Coll., Cirencester. Australia, 1963–65. *Recreations:* yachting, shooting. *Heir:* *s* Andrew Charles David Blois, *b* 7 Feb. 1971. *Address:* Red House, Westleton, Saxmundham, Suffolk. *T:* Westleton (072873) 200. *Clubs:* Cruising Association; Ocean Cruising.

BLOKH, Alexandre, PhD, (pen-name **Jean Blot**); writer, since 1956; International Secretary, PEN Club, since 1982; *b* Moscow, 31 March 1923; *s* of Arnold Blokh, man of letters, and Anne (*née* Berlinrote); *m* 1956, Nadia Ermolaiev. *Educ:* Bromsgrove Public Sch., Worcester; Univ. of Paris (PhD Law, PhD Letters). International Civil Servant, United Nations, 1947–62: New York, until 1956; Geneva, 1958–62; Director, Arts and Letters, UNESCO, Paris, 1962–81. Critic, arts and letters, in reviews: Arche, Preuves, NRF. Prix des Critiques, 1972; Prix Valéry Larbaud, 1977; Prix Cazes, 1982; Grand Prix de la Critique, 1986; Prix International de la Paix, 1990. *Publications: novels:* Le Soleil de Cavouri, 1956; Les Enfants de New York, 1959; Obscur Ennemi, 1961; Les Illusions Nocturnes, 1964; La Jeune Géante, 1969; La Difficulté d'aimer, 1971; Les Cosmopolites, 1976; Gris du Ciel, 1981; Tout l'été, 1985; Sainte Imposture, 1988; *essays:* Marguerite Yourcenar; Ossip Mandelstan; Là où tu iras; Sporade; Ivan Gontcharov; La Montagne Sainte; Albert Cohen; Si loin de Dieu et autres voyages. *Address:* 34 Square Montsouris, 75014 Paris. *T:* 589 34 16; 38 King Street, WC2. *T:* 071–379 7939.

BLOM-COOPER, Louis Jacques, QC 1970; a Judge of the Courts of Appeal, Jersey and Guernsey, since 1989; Chairman, Mental Health Act Commission, since 1988; *b* 27 March 1926; *s* of Alfred Blom-Cooper and Ella Flesseman, Rotterdam; *m* 1952 (marr. diss. 1970); two *s* one *d*; *m* 1970, Jane Elizabeth, *e d* of Maurice and Helen Smither, Woodbridge, Suffolk; one *s* two *d*. *Educ:* Port Regis Prep. Sch.; Seaford Coll.; King's Coll., London; Municipal Univ. of Amsterdam; Fitzwilliam Coll., Cambridge. LLB London, 1952; Dr Juris Amsterdam, 1954. HM Army, 1944–47: Capt., E Yorks Regt. Called to Bar, Middle Temple, 1952; Bencher, 1978. Mem., Home Secretary's Adv. Council on the Penal System, 1966–78. Chm., Panel of Inquiry into circumstances surrounding the death of Jasmine Beckford, 1985; Commissioner of Inquiry: into allegations of arson and political corruption in the Turks and Caicos Is, 1986 (report published, 1986); into the N Creek Develt Project, Turks and Caicos Is, 1986–87. Chairman: Indep. Cttee for the Supervision of Standards of Telephone Information Services, 1986–; Commn on the future of Occupational Therapy, 1988–89; Press Council, 1989–90. Vice-Pres., Howard League for Penal Reform, 1984– (Chm., 1973–84). Chm., BBC London Local Radio Adv. Council, 1970–73. Jt Dir, Legal Res. Unit, Bedford Coll., Univ. of London, 1967–82; Vis. Prof., QMC, London Univ., 1983–88. Trustee, Scott Trust (The Guardian Newspaper), 1982–88. Joint Editor, Common Market Law Reports. JP Inner London, 1966–79 (transf. City of London, 1969). FRSA 1984. *Publications:* Bankruptcy in Private International Law, 1954; The Law as Literature, 1962; The A6 Murder (A Semblance of Truth), 1963; (with T. P. Morris) A Calendar of Murder, 1964; Language of the Law, 1965; (with O. R. McGregor and Colin Gibson) Separated Spouses, 1970; (with G. Drewry) Final Appeal: a study of the House of Lords in its judicial capacity, 1972; (ed) Progress in Penal Reform, 1975; (ed with G. Drewry) Law and Morality, 1976; Penalty of Imprisonment, 1989; Guns for Antigua, 1990; contrib. to Modern Law Review, Brit. Jl of Criminology, Brit. Jl of Sociology. *Recreations:* watching and reporting on Association football, reading, music, writing, broadcasting. *Address:* 2 Ripplevale Grove, N1 1HU. *T:* 071–607 8045; Glebe House, Montgomery, Powys. *T:* Montgomery (0686) 668458. *Clubs:* Athenæum, MCC.

BLOMEFIELD, Sir (Thomas) Charles (Peregrine), 6th Bt *cr* 1807; Fine Art Dealer; *b* 24 July 1948; *s* of Sir Thomas Edward Peregrine Blomefield, 5th Bt, and of Ginette, Lady Blomefield; *S* father, 1984; *m* 1975, Georgina Geraldine, *d* of Commander C. E. Over, Lugger End, Portscatho, Cornwall; one *s* two *d*. *Educ:* Wellington Coll., Berks; Mansfield Coll., Oxford. Christie's, 1970–75; Wildenstein and Co., 1975–76; Director, Lidchi Art Gallery, Johannesburg, 1976–78; Man. Director, Charles Blomefield and Co., 1980–; Dir, Thomas Heneage and Co. Ltd, 1982–; Dir, Fleetwood-Hesketh Ltd, 1982–. *Recreations:* travel, listening to music. *Heir:* *s* Thomas William Peregrine Blomefield, *b* 16 July 1983. *Address:* Clapton Manor, Cheltenham, Glos GL54 2LG. *T:* Cotswold (0451) 20255.

BLOMFIELD, Brig. John Reginald, OBE 1957; MC 1944; *b* 10 Jan. 1916; *s* of late Douglas John Blomfield, CIE, and Coralie, *d* of F. H. Tucker, Indian Police; *m* 1939, Patricia Mary McKim; two *d*. *Educ:* Clifton Coll.; RMA, Woolwich; Peterhouse, Cambridge (MA). Commissioned Royal Engineers, 1936; Lt-Col 1955; Col 1961; Brig. 1965. Retired as Dep. Director, Military Engineering Experimental Establishment, 1969. New Towns Commn Manager, Hemel Hempstead, 1969–78. MBIM 1966. *Recreations:* cruising, ocean racing. *Address:* 9 Armstrong Close, Brockenhurst, Hants. *Clubs:* Royal Ocean Racing; Royal Lymington Yacht.

BLONDEL, Prof. Jean Fernand Pierre; Professor of Political Science, European University Institute, Florence, since 1985; *b* Toulon, France, 26 Oct. 1929; *s* of Fernand Blondel and Marie Blondel (*née* Santelli); *m* 1st, 1954, Michèle (*née* Hadet) (marr. diss. 1979); two *d*; 2nd, 1982, Mrs Theresa Martineau. *Educ:* Collège Saint Louis de Gonzague and Lycée Henri IV, Paris; Institut d'Etudes Politiques and Faculté de Droit, Paris; St Antony's Coll., Oxford. Asst Lectr, then Lectr in Govt, Univ. of Keele, 1958–63; Vis. ACLS Fellow, Yale Univ., 1963–64; Prof. of Government, 1964–84, and Dean, Sch. of Comparative Studies, 1967–69, Univ. of Essex; Vis. Prof., Carleton Univ., Canada, 1969–70; Vis. Schol., Russell Sage Foundn, NY, 1984–85. Exec. Dir, European Consortium for Political Res., 1970–79. Mem., Royal Swedish Acad. of Scis, 1990. Hon. DLitt Salford, 1990. *Publications:* Voters, Parties and Leaders, 1963; (jtly) Constituency Politics, 1964; (jtly) Public Administration in France, 1965; An Introduction to Comparative Government, 1969; (jtly) Workbook for Comparative Government, 1972; Comparing Political Systems, 1972; Comparative Legislatures, 1973; The Government of France, 1974; Thinking Politically, 1976; Political Parties, 1978; World Leaders, 1980; The Discipline of Politics, 1981; The Organisation of Governments, 1982; (jtly) Comparative Politics, 1984; Government Ministers in the Contemporary World, 1985; Political Leadership, 1987; (ed jtly) Western European Cabinets, 1988; Comparative Government, 1990; articles in: Political Studies, Parliamentary Affairs, Public Administration, Revue Française de Science Politique, European Jl of Political Research, etc. *Recreation:* holidays in Provence. *Address:* 15 Marloes Road, W8 6LQ. *T:* 071–370 6008; c/o European University Institute, S Domenico di Fiesole, I-50016 Florence, Italy; 9 rue Général de Partouneaux, Mourillon, Toulon, France.

BLOOD, Bindon, (Peter); Director, Western Marketing Consultants Ltd, since 1987; Senior Industrialist and Enterprise Counsellor for Department of Trade and Industry, since 1986; *b* 24 Sept. 1920; *o s* of Brig. William Edmunds Robarts Blood, CBE, MC, Croix de Guerre, and Eva Gwendoline (*née* Harrison); *m* 1953, Elizabeth Ann, *d* of Harold Drummond Hillier, MC; one *s* one *d*. *Educ:* Imperial Service Coll., Windsor. Family public works and civil engineering business, 1938–41; served Royal Engineers, 1941–46 (despatches 1944); Engineering Div., Forestry Commn, 1946–48; regular commn, RE, 1948; Second i/c, RE Officer Training Unit, 1948–51; Staff Coll., Camberley, 1951; Sec., Army Bd, NATO Mil. Agency for Standardisation, 1952–53; invalided from service, 1953; Intelligence Co-ordination Staff, FO, 1953–58; Founder and formerly Managing

Director: Isora Integrated Ceilings Ltd; Clean Room Construction Ltd; Mitchel and King (Sales) Ltd; Dep. Chm. and Group Marketing Dir, King Group. Institute of Marketing: Dir of Marketing Services, 1971; Dir-Gen., 1972–84. Chm., Industrial Market Research Ltd, 1984–87. Gov., Berks Coll. of Art and Design, 1975–89 (Chm. of Govs, 1981–86). FRSA, FInstM. *Recreations:* photography, furniture restoration, travel, music, local community activities. *Address:* The Malt Cottage, School Lane, Cookham Village, Berks SL6 9QN. *T:* Bourne End (06285) 25319.

BLOOM, André Borisovich; *see* Anthony, Metropolitan.

BLOOM, Charles, QC 1987; a Recorder of the Crown Court, since 1983; *b* 6 Nov. 1940; *s* of Abraham Barnett Bloom and Freda Bloom (*née* Craft); *m* 1967, Janice Rachelle Goldberg; one *s* one *d. Educ:* Manchester Central Grammar School; Manchester University. LLB Hons 1962. Called to the Bar, Gray's Inn, 1963; practised on Northern Circuit, 1963–. Chm., Medical Appeal Tribunals, 1979–. *Recreations:* tennis, theatre. *Address:* 28 St John Street, Manchester. *T:* 061–834 8418. *Club:* Friedland Postmusaf Tennis (Cheadle).

BLOOM, Claire; *b* London, 15 Feb. 1931; *d* of late Edward Bloom and of Elizabeth Bloom; *m* 1st, 1959, Rod Steiger (marr. diss. 1969); one *d*; 2nd, 1969; 3rd, 1990, Philip Roth, *q.v. Educ:* Badminton, Bristol; America and privately. First work in England, BBC, 1946. Stratford: Ophelia, Lady Blanche (King John), Perdita, 1948; The Damask Cheek, Lyric, Hammersmith, 1949; The Lady's Not For Burning, Globe, 1949; Ring Round the Moon, Globe, 1949–50. Old Vic: 1952–53: Romeo and Juliet; 1953: Merchant of Venice; 1954: Hamlet, All's Well, Coriolanus, Twelfth Night, Tempest; 1956: Romeo and Juliet (London, and N American tour). Cordelia, in Stratford Festival Company, 1955 (London, provinces and continental tour); Duel of Angels, Apollo, 1958; Rashomon, NY, 1959; Altona, Royal Court, 1961; The Trojan Women, Spoleto Festival, 1963; Ivanov, Phoenix, 1965; A Doll's House, NY, 1971; Hedda Gabler, 1971; Vivat! Vivat Regina!, NY, 1971; A Doll's House, Criterion, 1973 (filmed 1973); A Streetcar Named Desire, Piccadilly, 1974; Rosmersholm, Haymarket, 1977; The Cherry Orchard, Chichester Fest., 1981; These are Women, a portrait of Shakespeare's heroines, own one-woman perfs, 1981– (US tour, 1981–82); When We Dead Waken, Almeida, 1990. First film, Blind Goddess, 1947; *films include:* Limelight; The Man Between; Richard III; Alexander the Great; The Brothers Karamazov; The Buccaneers; Look Back in Anger; Three Moves to Freedom; The Brothers Grimm; The Chapman Report; The Haunting; 80,000 Suspects; Alta Infedelta; Il Maestro di Vigevano; The Outrage; The Spy Who Came in From The Cold; Charly; Three into Two won't go; A Severed Head; Red Sky at Morning; Islands In The Stream; The Clash of the Titans, 1979; Always, 1984; Sammy and Rosie Get Laid, 1987; Crimes and Misdemeanors, 1989. *Television:* first appearance on television programmes, 1952, since when she has had frequent successes on TV in the US: In Praise of Love, 1975; Anastasia, 1986; Queenie, 1986; BBC: A Legacy, 1975; The Ghost Writer, 1983; Shadowlands, 1985 (BAFTA award Best TV Actress); Time and the Conways, 1985; Oedipus the King, 1986; BBC Shakespeare: Katharine in Henry VIII, 1979; Gertrude in Hamlet, 1980; the Queen in Cymbeline, Lady Constance in King John, 1983; ITV: series: Brideshead Revisited, 1981; Intimate Contact, 1987; Shadow on the Sun, 1988; play, The Belle of Amherst, 1986. Distinguished Vis. Prof., Hunter Coll., NY, 1989. *Publication:* Limelight and After (autobiog.), 1982. *Recreations:* opera, music. *Address:* c/o Jeremy Conway, 18–21 Jermyn Street, SW1Y 6HB

BLOOM, G(eorge) Cromarty, CBE 1974; General Manager and Chief Executive, The Press Association Ltd, 1961–75; *b* 8 June 1910; *s* of late George Highfield Bloom and Jessie Bloom (*née* Cromarty); *m* 1st, 1940, Patricia Suzanne Ramplin (*d* 1957); two *s*; 2nd, 1961, Sheila Louise Curran; one *s. Educ:* Australia and China, privately; Keble Coll., Oxford. With Reuters Ltd, 1933–60. Dep. Chm., London Broadcasting Co., 1976–81. Vice-Chm., Internat. Press Telecommunications Council, 1971–75; Vice-Pres., Alliance Européenne des Agences de Presse, 1971–75; Chm., CPU Telecommunications Cttee, 1973–77. *Address:* 1 Tivoli Court, Tivoli Road, Cheltenham GL50 2TD. *T:* Cheltenham (0242) 239413.

BLOOM, Ronald; HM Diplomatic Service, retired; free-lance political/commercial consultant; Director: Trefoil Partnership Ltd, since 1982; Eastasia Technology Inc. (Hong Kong), since 1984; Partner, RFP Associates Ltd Partnership, since 1986; Chairman, Chely Plan Co. (Hong Kong), since 1986; *b* 21 Jan. 1926; *s* of John Bloom and Marjorie Bloom (*née* Barker); *m* 1956, Shirley Evelyn Edge; one *s* two *d. Educ:* inadequately. HM Forces, DLI, E Yorks Regt, 1943–57. Joined HM Diplomatic Service, 1958; Hong Kong, 1958–61; Singapore, 1961–63; FO, 1963–65; Zomba, 1965–67; FO, 1967–69; Kuala Lumpur, 1969–71; Singapore, 1971–74; Counsellor, FO, 1974–81. UK Representative: The Parvus Co., USA; Internat. Trade & Communications Inc., USA. *Publications:* reviews in Man (Royal Anthropol Inst.), occasional articles on uniforms and model soldiers. *Address:* The Old House, Deep Street, Prestbury, Glos. *T:* Cheltenham (0242) 44141; Trefoil Partnership Ltd, 50 Pall Mall, SW1. *T:* 071–839 1030. *Clubs:* Brooks's, Special Forces.

BLOOMFIELD, Barry Cambray, MA, FLA; Director, Collection Development, Humanities and Social Sciences, British Library, 1985–90; *b* 1 June 1931; *s* of Clifford Wilson Bloomfield and Eileen Elizabeth (*née* Cambray); *m* 1958, Valerie Jean Philpot. *Educ:* East Ham Grammar Sch.; University College of the South-West, Exeter; University Coll. London; Birkbeck Coll., London. Served in Intelligence Corps, Malaya, 1952–54. Assistant, National Central Library, 1955; Librarian, College of S Mark and S John, Chelsea, 1956–61; Asst Librarian, London Sch. of Economics, 1961–63; Dep. Librarian, 1963–72, Librarian, 1972–78, School of Oriental and African Studies; Dir, India Office Library and Records, British Library (formerly FCO), 1978–85 and concurrently Keeper, Dept of Oriental MSS and Printed Bks, British Library, 1983–85. Chm., SCONUL Group of Orientalist Libraries, 1975–80; Pres., Bibliographical Soc., 1990– (Vice-Pres., 1979–90); Member: Council, Royal Asiatic Soc., 1980–84; British Assoc. for Cemeteries in S Asia, 1980–90; Britain-Burma Soc., 1980–90; Exec. Cttee, Friends of the Nat. Libraries, 1981–; Chm., Rare Books Gp, LA, 1991–; International Federation of Library Associations: Chairman: Sect. on Bibliography, 1985–89; Div. of Bibliographic Control, 1985–89; Mem., Professional Bd, 1987–89. Trustee, Shakespeare Birthplace Trust, 1987–91. Vis. Professor, Univ. of Florida, 1963; Vis. Fellow, Univ. of Hawaii, 1977. *Publications:* New Verse in the '30s, 1960; W. H. Auden: a bibliography, 1964, 2nd edn 1972; ed, Autobiography of Sir J. P. Kay Shuttleworth, 1964; ed, (with V. J. Bloomfield, J. D. Pearson) Theses on Africa, 1964; ed, Theses on Asia, 1967; ed, The Acquisition and Provision of Foreign Books by National and University Libraries in the UK, 1972; An Author Index to Selected British 'Little' Magazines, 1976; Philip Larkin: a bibliography 1933–1976, 1979; (ed) Middle East Studies and Libraries, 1980; numerous articles in library and bibliog. jls. *Recreations:* reading, music. *Address:* Brambling, 24 Oxenturn Road, Wye, Kent TN25 5BE. *T:* Wye (0233) 813038. *Clubs:* Commonwealth Trust, Civil Service.

BLOOMFIELD, Sir Kenneth Percy, KCB 1987 (CB 1982); National Governor for Northern Ireland, BBC, since 1991; Head of Northern Ireland Civil Service, and Second Permanent Under Secretary of State, Northern Ireland Office, 1984–91; *b* 15 April 1931; *o c* of Harry Percy Bloomfield and Doris Bloomfield, Belfast; *m* 1960, Mary Elizabeth Ramsey; one *s* one *d. Educ:* Royal Belfast Academical Instn; St Peter's Coll., Oxford (MA; Hon. Fellow, 1991). Min. of Finance, N Ireland, 1952–56; Private Sec. to Ministers of Finance, 1956–60; Dep. Dir, British Industrial Develt Office, NY, 1960–63; Asst and later Dep. Sec. to Cabinet, NI, 1963–72; Under-Sec., Northern Ireland Office, 1972–73; Sec. to Northern Ireland Executive, Jan.-May 1974; Permanent Secretary: Office of the Executive, NI, 1974–75; Dept of Housing, Local Govt and Planning, NI, 1975–76; Dept of the Environment, NI, 1976–81; Dept of Commerce, NI, 1981–82; Dept of Economic Develt, 1982–84. Chm., Chief Officers' Management Forum, NI Public Services. Governor, Royal Belfast Academical Instn. Bass Ireland Lectr, Univ. of Ulster, 1991. Hon. LLD QUB, 1991. Dr Ben Wilson Trophy for Individual or Corporate Excellence, NI Chamber of Commerce and Industry, 1990. *Recreations:* reading history and biography, swimming. *Address:* c/o Stormont Castle, Belfast BT4 3ST. *T:* Belfast (0232) 63011.

BLOOR, Prof. David; Professor of Applied Physics, University of Durham, since 1989; *b* 25 July 1937; *s* of Alfred Edwin Bloor and Gladys Ellen Bloor (*née* Collins); *m* 1960, Margaret E. A. Avery; four *s* (and one *s* decd). *Educ:* Queen Mary College London (BSc, PhD). CPhys, FInstP. Lectr, Dept of Physics, Univ. of Canterbury, NZ, 1961–64; Queen Mary College London: Lectr, Dept of Physics, 1964; Reader, 1980–84; Prof. of Polymer Physics, 1984–89. Humboldt Fellow, Univ. of Stuttgart, 1975–76; Erskine Fellow, Univ. of Canterbury, NZ, 1983; Royal Society SERC Indust. Fellow, GEC Marconi Res. Centre, 1985–86. *Publications:* contribs to professional jls. *Recreations:* cycling, gardening. *Address:* Applied Physics Group, School of Engineering and Applied Science, University of Durham, South Road, Durham DH1 3LE. *T:* 091–374 2393.

BLOSSE, Sir Richard Hely L.; *see* Lynch-Blosse.

BLOT, Jean; *see* Blokh, A.

BLOUNT, Bertie Kennedy, CB 1957; DrPhilNat; CChem, FRSC; *b* 1 April 1907; *s* of late Col G. P. C. Blount, DSO, and late Bridget Constance, *d* of Maj.-Gen. J. F. Bally, CVO; unmarried. *Educ:* Malvern Coll.; Trinity Coll., Oxford (MA 1932, BSc 1929); Univ. of Frankfurt (DrPhilNat 1931). Ramsay Memorial Fellow, 1931; 1851 Senior Student, 1933; Dean of St Peter's Hall, Oxford, 1933–37; Messrs Glaxo Laboratories Ltd: Head of Chemical Research Laboratory, 1937; Principal Technical Executive, 1938–40. Served Army (Intelligence Corps), War of 1939–45; Capt. 1940; Major 1942; Col 1945. Asst Director of Research, The Wellcome Foundation, 1947; Director of Research Branch, Control Commission for Germany, 1948, and subsequently also Chief of Research Div. of Military Security Board; Director of Scientific Intelligence, Min. of Defence, 1950–52; Dep. Secretary, DSIR, 1952; Min. of Technology, 1964; retired 1966. Member Exec. Cttee, British Council, 1957–66. Royal Society of Arts: Armstrong Lecturer, 1955; Cantor Lecturer, 1963. Member Parry Cttee to review Latin American Studies in British Universities, 1962; Pres., Exec. Cttee, Internat. Inst. of Refrigeration, 1963–71, Hon. Pres. 1971; Hon. Member: (British) Inst. of Refrigeration, 1971; Max-Planck-Ges. zur Förderung der Wissenschaften, 1984. Hon. Fellow, St Peter's Coll., Oxford, 1988. Golden doctorate, Frankfurt Univ., 1982. *Publications:* papers in scientific and other journals. *Recreations:* travel, walking, gardening. *Address:* Tarrant Rushton House, Blandford, Dorset. *T:* Blandford (0258) 52256. *Club:* Athenæum.

BLOUNT, Sir Walter (Edward Alpin), 12th Bt *cr* 1642; DSC 1943 and two Bars 1945; farmer; *b* 31 Oct. 1917; *s* of Sir Edward Robert Blount, 11th Bt, and Violet Ellen (*d* 1969), *d* of Alpin Grant Fowler; *S* father, 1978; *m* 1954, Eileen Audrey, *d* of late Hugh B. Carritt; one *d. Educ:* Beaumont College; Sidney Sussex Coll., Cambridge (MA). Served RN, 1939–47. Qualified as Solicitor, 1950; practised Gold Coast, West Africa, 1950–52; London and Cambridge, 1952–76; Consultant, London, 1976. Farmer, Tilkhurst, East Grinstead, Sussex, 1978–. Lloyd's Underwriter. *Recreation:* sailing. *Heir:* none. *Address:* 19 St Anns Terrace, St John's Wood, NW8. *T:* 071–722 0802; Regent House, Seaview, IoW. *Clubs:* Bembridge Sailing, Seaview Yacht, Cambridge Cruising, RNVR Sailing, Law Society Yacht, Island Sailing.

BLOW, Prof. David Mervyn, FRS 1972; Professor of Biophysics, since 1977, and Head of the Department of Physics, since 1991 at Imperial College, University of London (Dean of the Royal College of Science, 1981–84); *b* 27 June 1931; *s* of Rev. Edward Mervyn and Dorothy Laura Blow; *m* 1955, Mavis Sears; one *s* one *d. Educ:* Kingswood Sch.; Corpus Christi Coll., Cambridge (MA, PhD). FInstP. Fulbright Scholar, Nat. Inst. of Health, Bethesda, Md, and MIT, 1957–59; MRC Unit for Study of Molecular Biological Systems, Cambridge, 1959–62; MRC Lab. of Molecular Biology, Cambridge, 1962–77; College Lectr and Fellow, Trinity Coll., Cambridge, 1968–77. Pres., British Crystallographic Assoc., 1984–87. Mem. Governing Body, Imperial Coll., London, 1987–. Biochem. Soc. CIBA Medal, 1967; (jtly) Charles Léopold Meyer Prize, 1979; (jtly) Wolf Foundn Prize for Chemistry, 1987. *Publications:* papers and reviews in scientific jls. *Recreations:* walking, sailing. *Address:* Blackett Laboratory, Imperial College of Science, Technology and Medicine, University of London, SW7 2BZ.

BLOW, Joyce, (Mrs Anthony Darlington), FIPR; FBIM; Chairman, Mail Order Publishers' Authority, since 1985; *b* 4 May 1929; *d* of late Walter Blow and Phyllis (*née* Grainger); *m* 1974, Lt-Col J. A. B. Darlington, RE retd. *Educ:* Bell Baxter Sch., Cupar, Fife; Edinburgh Univ. (MA Hons). FIPR 1964. John Lewis Partnership, 1951–52; FBI, 1952–53; Press Officer, Council of Indust. Design, 1953–63; Publicity and Advertising Manager, Heal & Son Ltd, 1963–65; entered Civil Service on first regular recruitment of direct entry Principals from business and industry: BoT, 1965–67; Monopolies Commn (gen. enquiry into restrictive practices in supply of prof. services), 1967–70; DTI, 1970, Asst Sec. 1972; Dept of Prices and Consumer Protection, 1974–77; Under-Secretary: OFT, 1977–80; DTI, 1980–84. Chm., E Sussex FHSA, 1990–. Vice-Pres., Inst. of Trading Standards Admin, 1985–; Mem., Council, Money Management Council, 1986–; Bd Mem. and Chm., Consumer Policy Cttee, BSI, 1987–90. Founder Mem. and Past Pres. Assoc. of Women in Public Relations. Trustee, Univ. of Edinburgh Develt Trust, 1990–. Freeman, City of London. *Publication:* Consumers and International Trade: a handbook, 1987. *Recreations:* music, particularly opera; travel. *Address:* 17 Fentiman Road, SW8 1LD. *T:* 071–735 4023; 9 Crouchfield Close, Seaford, E Sussex. *Clubs:* Arts, Reform.

BLOW, Sandra, RA 1978 (ARA 1971); *b* 14 Sept. 1925; *d* of Jack and Lily Blow. *Educ:* St Martin's School of Art; Royal Academy Sch.; Accademia di Belle Arti, Rome. Tutor, Painting School, Royal Coll. of Art, 1960–75. *One-man Exhibitions:* Gimpel Fils, 1952, 1954, 1960, 1962; Saidenburg Gallery, NY, 1957; New Art Centre, London, 1966, 1968, 1971, 1973; Francis Graham-Dixon, 1991. Represented in group exhibitions in Britain (including British Painting 74, Hayward Gall.), USA, Italy, Denmark, France. Won British Section of Internat. Guggenheim Award, 1960; 2nd prize, John Moore's Liverpool Exhibition, 1961; Arts Council Purchase Award, 1965–66. *Official Purchases:* Peter Stuyvesant Foundation; Nuffield Foundation; Arts Council of Great Britain; Arts Council of N Ireland; Walker Art Gallery, Liverpool; Allbright Knox Art Gallery, Buffalo, NY; Museum of Modern Art, NY; Tate Gallery; Gulbenkian Foundation; Min. of Public Building and Works; Contemp. Art Society; silk screen prints: Victoria and Albert

…itzwilliam Museum, Cambridge; City of Leeds Art Gall.; Graves Art Gall., …; painting purchased for liner Queen Elizabeth II. *Address:* 12 Sydney Close, SW3. …1–589 8610.

…OWERS, Dr Anthony John, CBE 1985; JP, DL; CBiol; FIMLS; Director-General, St John Ambulance, since 1991; Commissioner, Mental Health Act Commission, since 1987; Director of Corporate Affairs, Magellan Medical Communications, since 1990; *b* 11 Aug. 1926; *s* of Geoffrey Hathaway and Louise Blowers; *m* 1948, Yvonne Boiteux-Buchanan; two *s* one *d*. *Educ:* Sloane Sch., Chelsea; Sir John Case Coll.; Univ. of London; Univ. of Surrey (PhD 1982). FIMLS 1983; CBiol 1984. Served War, RCS, 1944–45; served: RAMC, 1945–46; RWAFF, 1946–48. Min. of Agriculture, 1948–59, Exptl Officer, 1953–54; Sandoz Pharmaceuticals, 1959–91; Sen. Res. Officer, 1973–87; Psychopharmacology Consultant, 1987–91; Consultant in Bacteriology, Mansi Labs, 1973–90. Chm., W Surrey and NE Hants HA, 1981–86; Member: Surrey AHA, 1973–80 (Vice Chm., 1976–77); SW Thames RHA, 1980–81; Mental Health Review Tribunal, 1975–. Member: Chertsey UDC, 1964–74 (Chm., 1969–70, 1973–74); Runnymede BC, 1973–84 (Chm., 1973–74); Surrey CC, 1970–85 (Vice Chm., Social Services Cttee, 1973–77); Surrey Police Authority, 1973–90 (Chm., 1981–85); Chm., Runnymede and Elmbridge Police Community Liaison Cttee, 1983–91. Chairman: SE Region, Duke of Edinburgh's Award, 1990–; Surrey Magistrates' Soc., 1988–; Member: Council, Magistrates' Assoc., 1986–91; Bd of Visitors, Coldingley Prison, 1978–; Court, Surrey Univ., 1986–; Surrey Scout Council, 1991–; Pres., Runnymede Scout Council, 1970–84. Governor: Fullbrook Sch., 1967–85 (Chm., 1981–85); Ottershaw Sch., 1975–81 (Chm., 1979–81). Liveryman, Worshipful Soc. of Apothecaries, 1988 (Yeoman, 1983–88); Freeman, City of London, 1983; Hon. Freeman, Bor. of Runnymede, 1985. JP 1970, DL 1986, High Sheriff, 1990–91, Surrey. KStJ 1991. *Publications:* contribs to med. and scientific books and jls. *Recreations:* fund-raising, gardening. *Address:* St John Ambulance, 1 Grosvenor Crescent, SW1X 7EF; Westward, 12 Birch Close, Boundstone, Farnham, Surrey GU10 4TJ. *T:* Frensham (025125) 2769.

BLOY, Rt. Rev. Francis Eric Irving, DD, STD; *b* Birchington, Isle of Thanet, Kent, England, 17 Dec. 1904; *s* of Rev. Francis Joseph Field Bloy and Alice Mary (*née* Poynter); *m* 1929, Frances Forbes Cox, Alexandria, Va; no *c*. *Educ:* University of Missouri (BA); Georgetown Univ. of Foreign Service; Virginia Theological Seminary (BD). Rector, All Saints Ch., Reisterstown, Maryland, 1929–33; Assoc. Rector, St James-by-the-Sea, La Jolla, Calif, 1933–35, Rector, 1935–37; Dean, St Paul's Cathedral, Los Angeles, Calif, 1937–48; Bishop of Los Angeles, 1948–73. DD: Ch. Divinity Sch. of the Pacific, Berkeley, Calif, 1942; Occidental Coll., Los Angeles, 1953; Va Theol Sem., 1953; STD: Ch. Divinity Sch. of the Pacific, 1948; Univ. of S Calif, 1955. Pres., Church Federation of Los Angeles, 1946–47; Pres., Univ. Religious Conf., 1956; Hon. Chm. Bd of Trustees, Good Samaritan Hosp.; Mem. Town Hall. *Address:* 3919 Starland Drive, Flintridge, Calif 91011, USA. *Club:* California (Los Angeles).

BLUCK, Duncan Robert Yorke, CBE 1990 (OBE 1984); Chairman: British Tourist Authority, 1984–90; English Tourist Board, 1984–90; Director, John Swire & Sons, since 1984; *b* 19 March 1927; *s* of Thomas Edward Bluck and Ida Bluck; *m* 1952, Stella Wardlaw Murdoch; one *s* three *d*. *Educ:* Taunton Sch. RNVR, 1944–47. Joined John Swire & Sons, 1948; Dir, 1964–, Chief Exec., 1971–84, Chm., 1980–84, Cathay Pacific Airways; Chairman: John Swire & Sons (HK) Ltd, 1980–84; Swire Pacific Ltd, 1980–84; Swire Properties Ltd, 1980–84. Dir, Hongkong and Shanghai Banking Corp., 1981–84. Chairman: English Schools Foundn (Hongkong), 1978–84; Hongkong Tourist Assoc., 1981–84; Kent Economic Develt Bd, 1986–. Governor, Marlborough House Sch., 1986–; Mem. Ct, Univ. of Kent. JP Hong Kong, 1981–84. *Recreations:* sailing, tennis. *Address:* Elfords, Hawkhurst, Kent TN18 4RP. *T:* Hawkhurst (05805) 2153. *Clubs:* Brooks's; Hongkong, Sheko (Hongkong).

BLUE, Rabbi Lionel; Lecturer, Leo Baeck College, since 1967; Convener of the Beth Din (Ecclesiastical Court) of the Reform Synagogues of Great Britain, 1971–88; *b* 6 Feb. 1930; *s* of Harry and Hetty Blue. *Educ:* Balliol Coll., Oxford (MA History); University Coll. London (BA Semitics); Leo Baeck Coll., London (Rabbinical Dip). Ordained Rabbi, 1960; Minister to Settlement Synagogue and Middlesex New Synagogue, 1960–63; European Dir, World Union for Progressive Judaism, 1963–66; Co-Editor, Forms of Prayer, 1967–; broadcaster, 1967–; Feature Writer: The Universe, 1979–; The Standard, 1985–86. *Publications:* To Heaven with Scribes and Pharisees, 1975; (jtly) A Taste of Heaven, 1977; (ed jtly) Forms of Prayer (Sabbath and Daily), 1977; A Backdoor to Heaven, 1979, revd edn 1985; (ed jtly) Forms of Prayer (Days of Awe), 1985; Bright Blue, 1985; (jtly) Simply Divine, 1985; Kitchen Blues, 1985; Bolts from the Blue, 1986; Blue Heaven, 1987; (jtly) Daytrips to Eternity, 1987; (jtly) The Guide to the Here and Hereafter, 1988; Blue Horizons, 1989. *Recreations:* window shopping, package holidays, monasteries, cooking. *Address:* Leo Baeck College, 80 East End Road, N3 2SY. *T:* 081–349 4525.

BLUGLASS, Prof. Robert Saul, MD, FRCPsych; Professor of Forensic Psychiatry, University of Birmingham, since 1979 (Regional Postgraduate Clinical Tutor in Forensic Psychiatry, since 1967); Clinical Director, Reaside Clinic, Birmingham, since 1987; *b* 22 Sept. 1930; *s* of Henry Bluglass and Fay (*née* Griew); *m* 1962, Jean Margaret Kerry (*née* Montgomery); one *s* one *d*. *Educ:* Warwick Sch., Warwick; Univ. of St Andrews (MB, ChB 1957, MD 1967). DPM 1962; FRCPsych 1976 (MRCPsych 1971). Formerly, Sen. Registrar in Psych., Royal Dundee Liff Hosp. and Maryfield Hosp., Dundee; Consultant in For. Psych., W Midlands RHA and the Home Office, 1967–; Consultant i/c Midland Centre for For. Psych., All Saints Hosp., Birmingham, 1967–; Hon. Lectr in For. Psych., Univ. of Birmingham, 1968–75, Sen. Clin. Lectr in For. Psych., 1975–79; Jt Dir, Midland Inst. of For. Medicine, 1975–87. Dep. Regional Advr in Psychiatry, W Midlands RHA, 1985–87, Regional Advr, 1987–; Specialist Advr, H of C Select Cttee on Social Services, 1985–87. Member: Adv. Cttee on Alcoholism, DHSS, 1975–80; Adv. Council on Probation, Home Office, 1974–77; Mental Health Act Commn, 1983–85; Forensic Psych. Res. Liaison Gp, DHSS. Royal College of Psychiatrists: Mem., Ct of Electors, 1976–79; Mem. Council, 1973–76, 1976–78, 1980–86, 1986–; Vice-Pres., 1983–85; Chm., For. Psych. Specialist Section, 1978–82; Chm., Midlands Div., 1986–. FRSocMed 1975; Past Pres., Sect. of Psych., Birmingham Med. Inst.; Mem., Brit. Acad. of For. Sciences. Baron ver Heyden de Lancey Law Prize, RSocMed, 1983; Highly Commended, Glaxo Prize, 1990. *Publications:* Psychiatry, The Law and The Offender, 1980; A Guide to the Mental Health Act 1983, 1983; (ed with Prof. Sir Martin Roth) Psychiatry, Human Rights and the Law, 1985; (ed with Dr Paul Bowden) The Principles and Practice of Forensic Psychiatry, 1990; articles in Brit. Jl of Hosp. Med., BMJ, and Med., Science and the Law. *Recreations:* water-colour painting, cooking, gardening, swimming. *Address:* Reaside Clinic, Bristol Road South, Rubery, Rednal, Birmingham B45 9BE.

BLUMBERG, Prof. Baruch Samuel, MD, PhD; Master of Balliol College, Oxford, since 1989; University Professor of Medicine and Anthropology, University of Pennsylvania, since 1970; Fox Chase Distinguished Scientist, Senior Adviser to the President, Fox Chase Cancer Center, since 1989; *b* 28 July 1925; *s* of Meyer Blumberg and Ida Blumberg; *m* 1954, Jean Liebesman Blumberg; two *s* two *d*. *Educ:* Union Coll. (BS Physics, 1946); Columbia University Coll. of Physicians and Surgeons (MD 1951); Balliol Coll., Oxford Univ. (PhD Biochemistry, 1957); FRCP 1984. US Navy, 1943–46 (Lieut JG). US Public Health Service (rank of med. dir, col), and Chief, Geographic Medicine and Genetics Sect., Nat. Insts. of Health, Bethesda, Md, 1957–64; Associate Dir for Clinical Res., then Vice-Pres. for Population Oncology, Fox Chase Cancer Center, 1964–89; Clin. Prof., Dept of Epidemiology, Univ. of Washington Sch. of Public Health, 1983–89. George Eastman Vis. Prof., Oxford Univ., 1983–84. Mem. Nat. Acad. of Sciences, Washington, DC. Hon. Fellow: Balliol Coll., Oxford, 1977; Indian Acad. of Scis. Hon. DSc: Univ. of Pittsburgh, 1977; Union Coll., Schenectady, NY, 1977; Med. Coll. of Pa, 1977; Dickinson Coll., Carlisle, Pa, 1977; Hahnemann Med. Coll., Philadelphia, Pa, 1977; Elizabethtown Coll., Pa, 1988; Ball State Univ., Muncie, 1989; Dr *hc* Univ. of Paris VII, 1978. (Jt) Nobel Prize in Physiology or Medicine, 1976. *Publications:* (ed) Genetic Polymorphisms and Geographic Variations in Disease, 1961; (ed jtly) Medical Clinics of North America: new developments in medicine, 1970; (ed jtly) Hepatitis B: the virus, the disease and the vaccine, 1984; *chapters in:* McGraw-Hill Encyclopedia of Science and Technology Yearbook, 1962; The Genetics of Migrant and Isolate Populations, ed E. Goldschmidt, 1963; Hemoglobin: its precursors and metabolites, ed F. W. Sunderman and F. W. Sunderman, Jr, 1964; McGraw-Hill Yearbook of Science and Technology, 1970; (also co-author chapter) Viral Hepatitis and Blood Transfusion, ed G. N. Vyas and others, 1972; Hematology, ed W. J. Williams and others, 1972; Progress in Liver Disease, Vol. IV, ed H. Popper and F. Schaffner, 1972; Australia Antigen, ed J. E. Prier and H. Friedman, 1973; Drugs and the Liver, ed. W. Gerok and K. Sickinger, 1975 (Germany); (*jtly*) *chapters in:* Progress in Medical Genetics, ed A. G. Steinberg and A. G. Bearn, 1965 (also London); Viruses Affecting Man and Animals, ed M. Sanders and M. Schaeffer, 1971; Perspectives in Virology, 1971; Transmissible Disease and Blood Transfusion, ed T. J. Greenwalt and G. A. Jamieson, 1975; Physiological Anthropology, ed A. Damon, 1975; Hepatite a Virus B et Hemodialyse, 1975 (Paris); Onco-Developmental Gene Expression, 1976; contrib. symposia; over 390 articles in scientific jls. *Recreations:* squash, canoeing, middle distance running, cattle raising. *Address:* Fox Chase Cancer Center, Philadelphia, Pa 19111, USA. *T:* 215–728–2203; Balliol College, Oxford OX1 3BJ. *Clubs:* Athenæum; Explorers (NY).

BLUMENTHAL, W(erner) Michael, PhD; Limited Partner, Lazard Frères & Co., since 1990; *b* Germany, 3 Jan. 1926. *Educ:* Univ. of California at Berkeley; Princeton Univ. Research Associate, Princeton Univ., 1954–57; Vice-Pres., Dir, Crown Cork Internat. Corp., 1957–61; Dep. Asst Sec. of State for Econ. Affairs, Dept of State, 1961–63; Dep. Special Rep. of the President (with rank Ambassador) for Trade Negotiations, 1963–67; Pres., Bendix Internat., 1967–70; Bendix Corp.: Dir, 1967–77; Vice-Chm., 1970–71; Pres. and Chief Operating Officer, 1971–72; Chm. and Chief Exec. Officer, 1972–77; US Secretary of the Treasury, 1977–79; Burroughs Corp. subseq. Unisys: Chief Exec. Officer, 1980–90; Vice-Chm., 1980; Chm., 1981–90. Director: Tenneco, Inc.; Daimler-Benz InterServices; Internat. Adv. Bd, Chemical Bank; Mem., Business Council. *Address:* (office) One Rockefeller Plaza, New York, NY 10020, USA.

BLUMER, Rodney Milnes, (Rodney Milnes); Editor, Opera magazine, since 1986; *b* 26 July 1936; *s* of Charles Eric Milnes Blumer and Kathleen Bertha Croft. *Educ:* Rugby School; Christ Church, Oxford (BA Hons Hist.). Editorial Dir, Rupert Hart-Davis Ltd, 1966–68; Music Critic, Queen magazine, later Harpers and Queen, 1968–87; Opera Critic: The Spectator, 1970–90; Evening Standard, 1990–; contribs to Opera, 1971–; Editl Bd, 1973; Associate Editor, 1976. Pres., Critics' Circle, 1988–90. Kt, Order of White Rose (Finland). *Publications:* numerous opera translations. *Recreation:* European travel. *Address:* 3/23 Northwood Hall, N6 5PH.

BLUMFIELD, Clifford William, OBE 1976; Director, Dounreay Nuclear Power Development Establishment, 1975–87, and Deputy Managing Director, Northern Division, UKAEA, 1985–87; *b* 18 May 1922; *m* 1944, Jeanne Mary; three *c*. *Educ:* Ipswich Boys' Central Sch. CEng, FIMechE, FINucE. With Reavell & Co. Ltd, 1938–44; served REME, 1944–47 (Major); Min. of Supply, Harwell, 1947–54; UKAEA, Harwell, 1954–58; Atomic Energy Estabt, Winfrith, 1958–68 (Group Leader, Design Gp, and Head of Gen. Ops and Tech. Div.); Asst Dir, Ops and Engineering, later Dep. Dir, Dounreay, 1968–75. *Address:* Rosebank, Janet Street, Thurso, Caithness KW14 7EG.

BLUMGART, Prof. Leslie Harold, MD; FRCS, FRCSE, FRCSGlas; Professor of Surgery, University of Bern, Switzerland, since 1986; *b* 7 Dec. 1931, of S African parentage; *m* 1955, Pearl Marie Navias (decd); *m* 1968, Sarah Raybould Bowen; two *s* two *d*. *Educ:* Jeppe High Sch., Johannesburg, SA; Univ. of Witwatersrand (BDS); Univ. of Sheffield (MB, ChB Hons; MD 1969). Prize Medal, Clin. Med. and Surg.; Ashby-de-la-Zouche Prize, Surg., Med., Obst. and Gynaecol. FRCS 1966, FRCSGlas 1973, FRCSE 1976. General dental practice, Durban, SA, 1954–59; Sen. Surgical Registrar, Nottingham Gen. Hosp. and Sheffield Royal Infirmary, 1966–70; Sen. Lectr and Dep. Dir, Dept of Surgery, Welsh Nat. Sch. of Med., also Hon. Cons. Surg., Cardiff Royal Inf., 1970–72; St Mungo Prof. of Surgery, Univ. of Glasgow, and Hon. Cons. Surg., Glasgow Royal Inf., 1972–79; Prof. of Surgery, Royal Postgrad. Sch. of London and Dir of Surgery, Hammersmith Hosp., 1979–86. Moynihan Fellow, Assoc. of Surgs of Gt Brit. and Ire., 1972; Mayne Vis. Prof., Univ. of Queensland, Brisbane, 1976; Vis. Prof., Univ. of Lund, Sweden, 1977; Nimmo Vis. Prof., Adelaide Univ., 1982; Purvis Oration, 1974; President's Oration, Soc. for Surgery of Aliment. Tract, Toronto, 1977; Lectures: Honyman Gillespie, Univ. of Edinburgh, 1978; Walton, RCPGlas, 1984; Monsarrat, Univ. of Liverpool, 1985; Legg Meml, KCH, 1985; Philip Sandblom, Lund Univ., Sweden, 1986; T. E. Jones Meml, Cleveland Clinic, USA, 1986; L. W. Edwards, Vanderbilt Univ., USA, 1987. One time examiner in Surgery: Univs of: Cambridge; Hong Kong; Edinburgh. Member: BMA, 1963–; Assoc. of Surgs of Gt Brit. and Ire., 1971–; Surgical Research Soc., 1971–; Brit. Assoc. of Surgical Oncology, 1976–; Brit. Soc. of Gastroenterology, 1972–; Swiss Surg. Soc., 1987; Swiss Soc. of Gastroenterology, 1987; Editorial Cttee, Brit. Jl of Surgery, 1973–87. Hon. Member: Soc. for Surgery of Aliment. Tract, USA, 1977; Danish Surg. Soc., 1988; Yugoslavian Surg. Soc., 1988; French Surg. Soc., 1990; Pres., Internat. Biliary Assoc., 1987. Acral Medal, Swedish Soc. Surgery, 1990. Order of Prasidda, Prabala-Gorkha-Dakshin Bahu, Nepal, 1984. *Publications:* (ed with A. C. Kennedy), Essentials of Medicine and Surgery for Dental Students, 3rd edn 1977, 4th edn 1982; (ed) The Biliary Tract, 1982; (ed) Surgery of the Liver and Biliary Tract, vols 1 and 2, 1987; The Management of Benign and Malignant Strictures of the Biliary Tract (Current Problems in Surgery), 1987; chapters in: Recent Advances in Surgery, 1973, 1980, 1988; Abdominal Operations, 1974, 1980; Textbook of Surgical Physiology, 1977, 1987; Surgical Gastroenterology, 1978, 1983, 1987; Hepatotrophic Factors, 1978; Liver and Biliary Disease, 1979, 1985; Operative Surgery—Abdomen, 4th edn 1983; Gastrointestinal and Hepatobiliary Cancer, 1983; Gastrointestinal Surgery, 1985; Hepatic and Biliary Cancer, 1986; Atlas of General Surgery, 1987; Surgery of the Gallbladder and Bile Ducts, 1987; Difficult Problems in General Surgery, 1989; numerous publications concerned with medical educn, gastrointestinal surgery and aspects of oncology with particular interests in surgery of the liver, pancreas and biliary tract and hepatic pathophysiology in med. and surgical jls. *Recreations:* water colour painting, wood carving. *Address:* Universitätsklinik für Viszerale und Transplantations Chirurgie, Inselspital, 3011 Berne, Switzerland. *T:* 031–64 24 12; Thorackerstrasse 10, 3074 Muri, Switzerland.

BLUNDELL, Commandant Daphne Mary, CB 1972; Director, WRNS, 1970–73; *b* 19 Aug. 1916. *Educ:* St Helen's Sch., Northwood; Bedford Coll., London. Worked for LCC as Child Care Organiser. Joined WRNS, Nov. 1942; commnd 1943; served in Orkneys, Ceylon, E Africa; Malta, 1954–56; Staff of Flag Officer Naval Air Comd, 1964–67; Staff of C-in-C Portsmouth, 1967–69; Supt WRNS Training and Drafting, 1969–70. Supt 1967; Comdt 1970, retd 1973; Hon. ADC to the Queen, 1970–73. Governor, St Helen's Sch., Northwood. *Address:* 15 Northbrook Drive, Northwood, Mddx HA6 2YU.

BLUNDELL, Prof. Derek John; Professor of Environmental Geology, University of London, since 1975; *b* 30 June 1933; *s* of Frank and Mollie Blundell; *m* 1960, Mary Patricia Leonard. *Educ:* Univ. of Birmingham (BSc); Imperial Coll., London (DIC, PhD). Res. Fellow 1957, Lectr 1959, in Geology, Univ. of Birmingham; Sen. Lectr 1970, Reader 1972, in Geophysics, Univ. of Lancaster; Royal Soc. Vis. Prof., Univ. of Ghana, 1974; Prof. of Environmental Geol., Univ. of London, first at Chelsea Coll. (Hd of Geol. Dept), 1975, then at Royal Holloway and Bedford New Coll., 1985–. Pres., Geological Soc., 1988–90. Mem., Academia Europaea. *Publications:* contribs to learned jls mainly relating to seismic exploration of the earth's crust, to earthquake hazards and, early on, to palæomagnetism. *Recreations:* travel, ski-ing. *Address:* Springwood, Tite Hill, Englefield Green, Surrey TW20 0NF. *T:* Egham (0784) 433170. *Club:* Athenæum.

BLUNDELL, Sir Michael, KBE 1962 (MBE 1943); *b* 7 April 1907; *s* of Alfred Herbert Blundell and Amelia Woodward Blundell (*née* Richardson); *m* 1946, Geraldine Lötte Robarts (*d* 1983); one *d. Educ:* Wellington Coll. Settled in Kenya as farmer, 1925. 2nd Lieut, RE, 1940; Major, 1940; Lieut-Col, 1941; Col, 1944; served Abyssinian campaign and SEAC. Commissioner, European Settlement, 1946–47; MLC, Rift Valley Constituency, Kenya, 1948–63; Leader European Members, 1952–54; Minister on Emergency War Council, Kenya, 1954–55; Minister of Agriculture, Kenya, 1955–59 and April 1961–June 1963; Leader of New Kenya Group, 1959–63. Chairman: Pyrethrum Board of Kenya, 1949–54; Egerton Agricultural Coll., 1962–72; EA Breweries Ltd, 1964–77; Uganda Breweries Ltd, 1965–76; Dir, Barclays Bank of Kenya Ltd, 1968–82. Chm., Kenya Soc. for the Blind, 1977–81. Freeman, Goldsmiths' Co., 1950; Hon. Col, 3rd KAR, 1955–61; Judge, Guernsey cattle, RASE, 1977. *Publications:* So Rough a Wind, 1964; The Wild Flowers of Kenya, 1982; Collins Guide to The Wild Flowers of East Africa, 1987. *Recreations:* gardening, music, 18th century English porcelain. *Address:* Box 30181, Nairobi, Kenya. *T:* Nairobi 512278. *Clubs:* Lansdowne; Muthaiga (Nairobi).

BLUNDELL, Prof. Thomas Leon, FRS 1984; Deputy Chairman and Secretary, Agricultural and Food Research Council, since 1991; *b* 7 July 1942; *s* of Horace Leon Blundell and Marjorie Blundell; one *s*; *m* 1987, Bancinyane Lynn Sibanda; two *d. Educ:* Steyning Grammar Sch.; Brasenose Coll., Oxford (BA, DPhil). Postdoctoral Res. Fellow, Laboratory of Molecular Biophysics, Oxford Univ., 1967–72; Jun. Res. Fellow, Linacre Coll., Oxford, 1968–70; Lectr, Biological Scis, Sussex Univ., 1973–76; Prof. of Crystallography, Birkbeck Coll., Univ. of London, 1976–90. Director, International Sch. of Crystallography, 1981–. Member Council: SERC, 1989–90 (Mem., 1979–82, Chm., 1983–87, Biological Scis Cttee; Mem., Science Bd, 1983–87); Council, AFRC, 1985–90 (Member: Soils Res. Grants Cttee, 1986–90; Food Res. Cttee, 1987–90); MRC AIDS Res. Steering Cttee, 1987–90; ACOST, 1988–90. Hon. Dir, ICRF Unit of Structural Molecular Biology, 1989–. Lectures: Plenary, Internat. Congress of Crystallography, 1969 and 1978; Gerhardt Schmidt, Weizman Inst., Israel, 1983; Plenary, Europ. Cryst. Meeting, 1983; Ferdinand Springer, Fedn of Europ. Biochemical Socs, 1984; Plenary, Asian and Ocean Biochemical Soc., 1986; Plenary, Fedn of European Biochemical Socs, 1987; Plenary, Internat. Juvenile Diabetes Congress, 1988. Councillor, Oxford CBC, 1970–73 (Chm. Planning Cttee, 1972–73). Industrial Consultant: CellTech, 1981–86; Pfizer Central Res., Groton, USA and Sandwich, UK, 1984–90; Abingworth Management Ltd, 1988–90. Governor, Birkbeck Coll., 1985–89 (Hon. Fellow, 1989). Hon. Fellow, Linacre Coll., Oxford, 1991. Alcon Award for Dist. Work in Vision Research, 1985; Gold Medal, Inst. of Biotechnological Studies, 1987; Sir Hans Krebs Medal, Fedn of European Biochemical Socs, 1987; Ciba Medal, UK Biochemical Soc., 1988; Feldberg Prize for Biology and Medicine, 1988. Jt Editor, Progress in Biophysics and Molecular Biology, 1979–; Member Editorial Advisory Board: Biochemistry, 1986–89; Protein Engineering, 1986–. *Publications:* Protein Crystallography, 1976; papers in Jl of Molecular Biology, Nature, European Jl of Biochemistry, etc. *Recreations:* playing jazz, listening to opera, walking. *Address:* 1 Asmara Road, NW2 3SS. *T:* 071–794 6085.

BLUNDEN, Sir George, Kt 1987; Deputy Governor, Bank of England, 1986–90 (Executive Director, 1976–84, Non-Executive Director, 1984–85); Chairman, London Pensions Fund Authority, since 1989; *b* 31 Dec. 1922; *s* of late George Blunden and Florence Holder; *m* 1949, Anne, *d* of late G. J. E. and Phyllis Bulford; two *s* one *d. Educ:* City of London Sch.; University Coll., Oxford (MA). Royal Sussex Regt, 1941–45. Bank of England, 1947–55; IMF, 1955–58; Bank of England: rejoined 1958; Dep. Chief Cashier, 1968–73; Chief of Management Services, 1973–74; Head of Banking Supervision, 1974–76. Jt Dep. Chm., Leopold Joseph Hldgs, 1984–85 and 1990–; Director: Eagle Star Hldgs, 1984–85; Portals Hldgs, 1984–86; Grindlays Hldgs, 1984–85. Advr, Union Bank of Switzerland in London, 1990–. Chm., Group of Ten Cttees, BIS, Basle, on Banking Regulations and Supervisory Practices, 1974–77, on Payments Systems, 1981–83; Chm., cttee to oversee estabt and operation of Code of Banking Practice, 1990–. Chm. Governors, St Peter's Gp of Hosps, 1978–82; Chm., St Peter's Hosps Special Trustees, 1982–; Chm., Inst. of Urology, 1982–88 (Hon. Treasurer, 1975–78); Mem. Council, Imperial Cancer Res. Fund, 1981– (Treas., 1988–91; Chm., 1991–). Chairman: Samuel Lewis Housing Trust, 1985 (Trustee, 1980–85); St Peter's Trust for Kidney Res., 1988–90 (Trustee, 1971–); Vice-Pres., Opportunities for the Disabled, 1980–90. Member: Court, Mermaid Theatre Trust, 1979–84; Council, RCM, 1983– (Dep. Chm., 1990–). Mem., Livery, Goldsmiths' Co., 1987. *Address:* Crossfield Farmhouse, Hindringham, Fakenham, Norfolk NR21 0PS. *T:* Fakenham (0328) 878509. *Clubs:* Reform, MCC.

BLUNDEN, Sir Philip (Overington), 7th Bt *cr* 1766, of Castle Blunden, Kilkenny; artist and art restorer; *b* 27 Jan. 1922; *s* of Sir John Blunden, 5th Bt and Phyllis Dorothy (*d* 1967), *d* of Philip Crampton Creaghe; *S* brother, 1985; *m* 1945, Jeannette Francesca Alexandra, *e d* of Captain D. Macdonald, RNR; two *s* one *d. Educ:* Repton. Served RN, 1941–46 (1939–45 Star, Atlantic Star, Defence Medal). Estate Manager, Castle Blunden, 1947–60; engaged in marketing of industrial protective coatings, 1962–83; in art and art restoration, 1976–. *Recreations:* fishing, field sports, swimming, tennis, reading. *Heir: s* Hubert Chisholm Blunden [*b* 9 Aug. 1948; *m* 1975, Ellish O'Brien; one *s* one *d*]. *Address:* 66 Lucan Heights, Lucan, Co. Dublin; 19 Kingswood Drive, Clondalkin, Co. Dublin. *T:* Dublin 520435. *Club:* Royal Dublin Society (Life Mem.).

BLUNKETT, David; MP (Lab) Sheffield, Brightside, since 1987; *b* 6 June 1947; *m* (marr. diss.); three *s. Educ:* night sch. and day release, Shrewsbury Coll. of Technol. and Richmond Coll. of Further Educn, Sheffield; Nat. Cert. in Business Studies, E Midlands Gas Bd; Sheffield Univ. (BA Hons Pol Theory and Instns); Huddersfield Holly Bank Coll. of Educn (Tech.) (PGCFE). Tutor in Industrial Relns, Barnsley Coll. of Technol., 1974–87. Elected to Sheffield City Council (at age of 22), 1970; Chm., Family and Community Services Cttee, 1976–80; Leader, 1980–87; Dep. Chm., AMA, 1984–87. Joined Labour Party at age of 16; Mem., Labour Party NEC, 1983–; Chm., Labour Party Cttee on Local govt, 1984–. Front bench spokesman on the environment, with special responsibility for local govt and poll tax, 1988–. *Publications:* (jtly) Local Enterprise and Workers' Plans, 1981; (jtly) Building from the Bottom: the Sheffield Experience, 1983; (jtly) Democracy in Crisis: the town halls respond, 1987. *Address:* House of Commons, SW1A 0AA.

BLUNT, Charles William; Chief Executive Officer, American Chamber of Commerce in Australia; *b* Sydney, 19 Jan. 1951; *s* of R. S. G. Blunt; *m* Gail; two *s. Educ:* Sydney Univ. (BEcon). AASA; CPA. Exec. appts in mining, finance and agricultural industries. *Recreations:* tennis, reading. *Address:* PO Box 66, Wahroonga, NSW 2076, Australia. *Clubs:* Union, American (Sydney).

BLUNT, David John; QC 1991; a Recorder of the Crown Court, since 1990; writer; *b* 25 Oct. 1944; *s* of late Vernon Egerton Rowland Blunt and of Catherine Vera Blunt; *m* 1976, Zaibonessa Ebrahim; one *s* one *d. Educ:* Farnham Grammar Sch.; Trinity Hall, Cambridge (MA Hons). Called to the Bar, Middle Temple, 1967. Asst Recorder, 1985–90. Contested (L): Lambeth Central, 1978, 1979; Cornwall SE, 1983. First TV play broadcast, 1976. *Recreations:* walking, running, cycling, reading, writing, old cars. *Address:* 4 Pump Court, Temple, EC4Y 7AN. *T:* 071–353 2656.

BLUNT, Sir David Richard Reginald Harvey, 12th Bt *cr* 1720; *b* 8 Nov. 1938; *s* of Sir Richard David Harvey Blunt, 11th Bt and Elisabeth Malvine Ernestine, *d* of Comdr F. M. Fransen Van de Putte, Royal Netherlands Navy (retd); *S* father, 1975; *m* 1969, Sonia Tudor Rosemary (*née* Day); one *d. Heir: kinsman:* Robin Anthony Blunt, CEng, MIMechE [*b* 23 Nov. 1926; *m* 1st, 1949, Sheila Stuart (marr. diss. 1962), *d* of C. Stuart Brindley; one *s*; 2nd, 1962, June Elizabeth, *d* of Charles Wigginton; one *s*].

BLUNT, Maj.-Gen. Peter, CB 1978; MBE 1955; GM 1959; *b* 18 Aug. 1923; *s* of A. G. Blunt and M. Blunt; *m* 1949, Adrienne, *o d* of Gen. T. W. Richardson; three *s.* Joined Army aged 14 yrs, 1937; commnd Royal Fusiliers; served Duke of Cornwall's LI and Royal Scots Fusiliers, until 1946; foreign service, 1946–49; Staff Coll., 1957; Jt Services Staff Coll., 1963; RCDS, 1972; comd 26 Regt, Bridging, 1965; GSO 1 Def. Plans, FARELF, 1968; Comdr RCT 1 Corps, 1970; Dep. Transport Officer-in-Chief (Army), later Transp. Off.-in-Chief, 1973; Asst Chief of Personnel and Logistics (Army), MoD, 1977–78; Asst Chief of Defence Staff (Personnel and Logistics), MoD, 1978–79. Man. Dir, Earls Court Ltd, 1979–80; Exec. Vice-Chm., Brompton and Kensington Special Catering Co. Ltd, 1979–80; Jt Man. Dir, Angex-Watson, 1980–83; Dir, Associated Newspapers, 1984–90; Chm. and Man. Dir, Market Sensors, 1986–88; Man. Dir, 1980–88, non-exec. Chm., 1988–90, Angex Ltd; Chm., Argus Shield Ltd, 1988–89. Rep. Col Comdt, RCT, 1987–89 (Col Comdt, 1974–89). Specially apptd Comr, Royal Hosp., Chelsea, 1979–85. Exec. Mem., Caravan Club, 1989–. Liveryman, Co. of Carmen, 1973. *Recreation:* fishing. *Address:* Harefield House, Crowood Lane, Ramsbury, Marlborough, Wilts SN8 2PT. *T:* Marlborough (0672) 20296. *Club:* RCT Luncheon (Pres.).

BLYE, Douglas William Alfred, CMG 1979; OBE 1973; company director and financial consultant; *b* 15 Dec. 1924; *s* of William Blye and Ethel Attwood; *m* 1955, Juanita, (June), Buckley. *Educ:* King's Road Sch., Herne Bay; Maidstone Polytechnic. ACMA. Served War, RAF, 1941–46. Various commercial and industrial appts in UK, 1947–55; Govt of Fedn of Malaya, 1955–58; Hong Kong Govt, 1958–85, Sec. for Monetary Affairs, 1977–85; Econ. and Financial Advr, Govt of Dubai, 1986–87. *Recreations:* squash, tennis. *Address:* 21 Mountbatten Way, Brabourne Lees, Ashford, Kent TN25 6PZ. *T:* Sellindge (0303) 812705.

BLYTH, family name of **Baron Blyth.**

BLYTH, 4th Baron *cr* 1907; **Anthony Audley Rupert Blyth;** Bt 1895; *b* 3 June 1931; *er s* of 3rd Baron Blyth and Edna Myrtle (*d* 1952), *d* of Ernest Lewis, Wellington, NZ; *S* father, 1977; *m* 1st, 1954, Elizabeth Dorothea (marr. diss., 1962), *d* of R. T. Sparrow, Vancouver, BC; one *s* two *d*; 2nd, 1963, Oonagh Elizabeth Ann, *yr d* of late William Henry Conway, Dublin; one *s* one *d. Educ:* St Columba's College, Dublin. *Heir: s* Hon. Riley Audley John Blyth, *b* 4 March 1955. *Address:* Blythwood Estate, Athenry, Co. Galway.

BLYTH, Charles, (Chay Blyth), CBE 1972; BEM; Managing Director: Crownfields Ltd, since 1989; British Steel Challenge, Round World Yacht Race 1992–93, since 1989; *b* 14 May 1940; *s* of Robert and Jessie Blyth; *m* 1962, Maureen Margaret Morris; one *d. Educ:* Hawick High School. HM Forces, Para. Regt, 1958–67. Cadbury Schweppes, 1968–69; Dir, Sailing Ventures (Hampshire) Ltd, 1969–73. Rowed North Atlantic with Captain John Ridgway, June-Sept. 1966; circumnavigated the world westwards solo in yacht British Steel, 1970–71; circumnavigated the world eastwards with crew of paratroopers in yacht Great Britain II, and Winner, Elapsed Time Prize Whitbread Round the World Yacht Race, 1973–74; Atlantic sailing record, Cape Verde to Antigua, 1977; won Round Britain Race in yacht Great Britain IV, 1978 (crew Robert James); won The Observer/Europe 1 doublehanded transatlantic race in record time, 1981 (crew Robert James); Number One to Virgin Atlantic Challenge II successful attempt on the Blue Riband, 1986. Yachtsman of the Year, Yachting Journalists Accos., 1971; Chichester Trophy, RYS, 1971. *Publications:* A Fighting Chance, 1966; Innocent Aboard, 1968; The Impossible Voyage, 1971; Theirs is the Glory, 1974. *Recreations:* sailing, horse-riding, hunting. *Address:* Hill Farm Cottage, 18 Highlands Road, Fareham, Hants PO16 7XN. *Clubs:* Caledonian, Special Forces, Royal Ocean Racing; Royal Southern Yacht, Royal Western Yacht.

BLYTH, Sir James, Kt 1985; Director and Chief Executive, The Boots Company PLC, since 1987; *b* 8 May 1940; *s* of Daniel Blyth and Jane Power Carlton; *m* 1967, Pamela Anne Campbell Dixon; one *d* (one *s* decd). *Educ:* Spiers Sch.; Glasgow Univ. (MA Hons). Mobil Oil Co., 1963–69; General Foods Ltd, 1969–71; Mars Ltd, 1971–74; Director and General Manager: Lucas Batteries Ltd, 1974–77; Lucas Aerospace Ltd, 1977–81; Dir, Joseph Lucas Ltd, 1977–81; Head of Defence Sales, MoD, 1981–85; Managing Director: Plessey Electronic Systems, 1985–86; The Plessey Co plc, 1986–87. Non-exec. Director: Imperial Gp PLC, 1984–86; Cadbury-Schweppes PLC, 1986–90; British Aerospace, 1990–. Mem. Council, SBAC, 1977–81; Pres., ME Assoc., 1988–. Gov., London Business Sch., 1987–. FRSA. Liveryman, Coachmakers' and Coach Harness Makers' Co. *Recreations:* ski-ing, tennis, paintings, theatre. *Address:* The Boots Company PLC, Nottingham NG2 3AA. *Clubs:* East India, Queen's, Royal Automobile.

BLYTH, John Douglas Morrison, CMG 1981; HM Diplomatic Service, retired; *b* 23 July 1924; *s* of late William Naismith Blyth and Jean (*née* Morrison); *m* 1st, 1949, Gabrielle Elodie (*née* Belloc) (*d* 1971); three *s* two *d*; 2nd, 1973, Lucy Anne (*née* Alcock); one *s* one *d. Educ:* Christ's Coll.; Lincoln Coll., Oxford (MA); Downing Coll., Cambridge (MA). Served War, RNVR, 1942–46. Editor, The Polar Record (publd by Scott Polar Res. Inst., Cambridge), 1949–54; joined FO, 1954; served: Geneva, 1955; Athens, 1959; Leopoldville, 1963; Accra, 1964; FO, 1966; Athens, 1968; FCO, 1972; Vienna, 1974; FCO, 1977. Pres., Hélène Heroys Literary Foundn, 1975–. Hon. Sec., Suffolk Preservation Soc., 1985–. *Publications:* articles in The Polar Record. *Recreations:* gardening, military history, enjoying wine. *Address:* Crownland Hall, Walsham-le-Willows, Suffolk IP31 3BU. *T:* Walsham-le-Willows (03598) 369. *Club:* Naval and Military.

BLYTHE, James Forbes, TD 1946; **His Honour Judge Blythe;** a Circuit Judge, since 1978; Solicitor; *b* Coventry, 11 July 1917; *s* of J. F. Blythe and Dorothy Alice (*née* Hazlewood); *m* 1949, Margaret, *d* of P. D. Kinsey; two *d. Educ:* Wrekin Coll.; Birmingham Univ. (LLB). Commissioned TA, Royal Warwickshire Regt, 1936–53 (Major); served War of 1939–45 with BEF in France (Dunkirk), 1939–40; Central Mediterranean Force (Tunisia, Sicily, Corsica, S France and Austria), 1942–45; Air Liaison Officer GSO II (Ops) with RAF (Despatches). Admitted solicitor, 1947; private practitioner in partnership in Coventry and Leamington Spa, 1948. HM Deputy Coroner for City of Coventry and Northern Dist of Warwickshire, 1954–64; HM Coroner for City of Coventry, 1964–78; a Recorder of the Crown Court, 1972–78. Pres., Warwicks Law Soc., 1978–79. *Recreations:* shooting, sailing; past player and Sec. Coventry Football Club (RU). *Address:* Hazlewood, Upper Ladyes' Hill, Kenilworth, Warwickshire CV8 2FB. *Clubs:* Army and Navy; Drapers (Coventry); Tennis Court (Leamington Spa).

BLYTHE, Mark Andrew; Principal Assistant Solicitor, Treasury Solicitor's Department, since 1989; *b* 4 Sept. 1943; *s* of John Jarratt Blythe and Dorothy Kathleen Blythe (*née* Brooks); *m* 1972, Brigid Helen Frazer (*née* Skemp); two *s* one *d. Educ:* King Edward VII Grammar Sch., Sheffield; University Coll., Oxford (BCL, MA; Gibbs Prize in Law, 1963). Called to the Bar, Inner Temple, 1966; Attorney, NY Bar, 1980. Teaching Associate, Univ. of Pennsylvania Law Sch., 1965–66; Chambers of John Mills, QC, Chancery Bar, 1967–77; Legal Consultant, NY, 1978–80; Treasury Solicitor's Dept, 1981–; Assistant Solicitor, European Div., 1986–89. *Publications:* contrib. various legal jls. *Recreations:* 'cello (badly), escaping to Northumberland. *Address:* Queen Anne's Chambers, 28 Broadway, SW1H 9JS.

BLYTHE, Rex Arnold; Under-Secretary, Board of Inland Revenue, 1981–86, retired; *b* 11 Nov. 1928; *s* of late Sydney Arnold Blythe and Florence Blythe (*née* Jones); *m* 1953, Rachel Ann Best; one *s* two *d. Educ:* Bradford Grammar Sch.; Trinity Coll., Cambridge (BA Classics). Entered Inland Revenue as Inspector of Taxes, 1953; Sen. Inspector, 1962; Principal Inspector, 1968; Asst Sec., 1974. *Recreations:* golf, photography, walking. *Address:* 32 Townsend Lane, Harpenden, Herts AL5 2QS. *T:* Harpenden (0582) 715833. *Club:* MCC.

BOAG, Prof. John Wilson; Professor of Physics as Applied to Medicine, University of London, Institute of Cancer Research, 1965–76, now Emeritus; *b* Elgin, Scotland, 20 June 1911; *s* of John and Margaret A. Boag; *m* 1938, Isabel Petrie; no *c. Educ:* Universities of Glasgow, Cambridge and Braunschweig. Engineer, British Thomson Houston Co., Rugby, 1936–41; Physicist, Medical Research Council, 1941–52; Visiting Scientist, National Bureau of Standards, Washington, DC, 1953–54; Physicist, British Empire Cancer Campaign, Mount Vernon Hospital, 1954–64; Royal Society (Leverhulme) Visiting Prof. to Poland, 1964. President: Hosp. Physicists' Assoc., 1959; Assoc. for Radiation Res. (UK), 1972–74; Internat. Assoc. for Radiation Res., 1970–74; British Inst. of Radiology, 1975–76. L. H. Gray Medal, ICRU, 1973; Barclay Medal, BIR, 1975. *Publications:* papers on radiation dosimetry, statistics, radiation chemistry, radiodiagnosis. *Address:* Flat 1, 40 Overton Road, Sutton, Surrey SM2 6QR.

BOAL, (John) Graham; a Recorder of the Crown Court, since 1985; First senior Treasury Counsel at the Central Criminal Court, since 1991; *b* 24 Oct. 1943; *s* of late Surg. Captain Jackson Graham Boal, RN, and late Dorothy Kenley Boal; *m* 1978, Elizabeth Mary East; one *s. Educ:* Eastbourne Coll.; King's Coll. London (LLB). Called to the Bar, Gray's Inn, 1966; Junior Treasury Counsel, 1977–85; Sen. Prosecuting Counsel to the Crown, Central Criminal Court, 1985–91. Vice Chm., Criminal Bar Assoc., 1991–. *Recreations:* theatre, watching sport. *Address:* Queen Elizabeth Building, Temple, EC4Y 9BS. *Clubs:* Garrick, MCC; Royal Wimbledon Golf.

BOAM, Maj.-Gen. Thomas Anthony, CB 1987; CBE 1978 (OBE 1973); Director, British Consultants Bureau, since 1988; *b* 14 Feb. 1932; *s* of late Lt-Col T. S. Boam, OBE, and of Mrs Boam; *m* 1961, Penelope Christine Mary Roberts; one *s* two *d. Educ:* Bradfield Coll.; RMA Sandhurst. Commissioned Scots Guards, 1952; Canal Zone, Egypt (with 1SG), 1952–54; GSO3, MO4 War Office, 1959–61; psc 1962; Kenya (with 2 Scots Guards), 1963–64; DAA&QMG 4 Guards Bde, 1964–65; Malaysia (with 1SG), 1966–67; BM 4 Guards Bde, 1967–69; GSO1 (DS) Staff Coll., Camberley, 1970–71; CO 2SG, 1972–74; RCDS 1974–75; Comd BAAT Nigeria, 1976–78; BGS (Trg) HQ UKLF, 1978; Dep. Comdr and COS Hong Kong, 1979–81; Hd of British Defence Staff Washington, and Defence Attaché, 1981–84, Mil. Attaché, 1981–83; Comdr, British Forces Hong Kong, and Maj.-Gen., Brigade of Gurkhas, 1985–87. Mem., Exec. Council, Hong Kong, 1985–87. *Recreations:* shooting, fishing, gardening, sport. *Address:* c/o Barclays Bank, 23 Euston Road, NW1 2SB. *Clubs:* St Stephen's Constitutional, MCC.

BOARDMAN, family name of **Baron Boardman.**

BOARDMAN, Baron *cr* 1980 (Life Peer), of Welford in the County of Northamptonshire; **Thomas Gray Boardman,** MC 1944; TD 1952; DL; Chairman, National Westminster Bank, 1983–89 (Director, 1979–89; Chairman, Eastern Region, 1979–83); *b* 12 Jan. 1919; *s* of John Clayton Boardman, late of Daventry, and Janet Boardman, formerly Houston; *m* 1948, (Norah Mary) Deirdre, *widow* of John Henry Chaworth-Musters, Annesley Park, Nottingham, and *d* of late Hubert Vincent Gough; two *s* one *d. Educ:* Bromsgrove. Served Northants Yeomanry, 1939–45 and subsequently; Commanding Northants Yeomanry, 1956. Qualified as a Solicitor, 1947. MP (C) Leicester SW, Nov. 1967–74, Leicester South Feb.-Sept. 1974; Minister for Industry, DTI, 1972–74; Chief Sec. to Treasury, 1974. Jt Hon. Treas., Cons. Party, 1981–82. Chairman: Chamberlain Phipps Ltd, 1958–72; The Steetley Co. Ltd, 1978–83 (Dir, 1975–83); Director: Allied Breweries Ltd, 1968–72 and 1974–77 (Vice-Chm., 1975–76); MEPC, 1980–89; Adv. Bd, LEK Partnership, 1990–. Pres., Assoc. of British Chambers of Commerce, 1977–80. Chm., Cttee of London and Scottish Bankers, 1987–89. Mem., Exec. Assoc. of Cons. Peers, 1981–84. DL Northants, 1977–, High Sheriff, Northants, 1979. *Recreation:* riding. *Address:* 29 Tufton Court, Tufton Street, SW1P 3QH. *T:* 071–222 6793; The Manor House, Welford, Northampton. *T:* Welford (0858) 575235. *Club:* Cavalry and Guards.
See also Baron Ellenborough.

BOARDMAN, Harold; *b* 12 June 1907; *m* 1936, Winifred May, *d* of Jesse Thorlby, Derbys; one *d. Educ:* Bolton and Derby. Formerly Trade Union Official. For 3 yrs Mem. Derby Town Council. MP (Lab) Leigh, 1945–79; PPS to Ministry of Labour, 1947–51. ILO Confs in Geneva, 1947, 1949, 1950, and San Francisco, 1948; Delegate to Council of Europe, 1960, 1961. Former Exec. Mem., NW Industrial Develt Assoc., from 1946.

BOARDMAN, Sir John, Kt 1989; FSA 1957; FBA 1969; Lincoln Professor of Classical Archaeology and Art, and Fellow of Lincoln College, University of Oxford, since 1978; *b* 20 Aug. 1927; *s* of Frederick Archibald Boardman; *m* 1952, Sheila Joan Lyndon Stanford; one *s* one *d. Educ:* Chigwell Sch.; Magdalene Coll., Cambridge (BA 1948, MA 1951, Walston Student, 1948–50; Hon. Fellow 1984). 2nd Lt, Intell. Corps, 1950–52. Asst Dir, British Sch. at Athens, 1952–55; Asst Keeper, Ashmolean Museum, Oxford, 1955–59; Reader in Classical Archaeology, Univ. of Oxford, 1959–78; Fellow of Merton Coll., Oxford, 1963–78, Hon. Fellow, 1978. Geddes-Harrower Prof., Aberdeen Univ., 1974; Vis. Prof., Australian Inst. of Archaeology, 1987; Prof. of Ancient History, Royal Acad., 1989–. Editor: Journal of Hellenic Studies, 1958–65; Lexicon Iconographicum, 1972–. Conducted excavations on Chios, 1953–55, and at Tocra in Libya, 1964–65. Delegate, OUP, 1979–89. Corr. Fellow, Bavarian Acad. of Scis, 1969; Fellow, Inst. of Etruscan Studies, Florence, 1983; Hon. Fellow, Archael Soc. of Athens, 1989; Foreign Mem., Royal Danish Acad., 1979; Mem. associé, Acad. des Inscriptions et Belles Lettres, Institut de France, 1991 (Correspondant, 1985). Hon. MRIA, 1986. Hon. Dr, Dept of Archaeology and History, Univ. of Athens, 1991. Cromer Greek Prize, British Acad., 1959. *Publications:* Cretan Collection in Oxford, 1961; Date of the Knossos Tablets, 1963; Island Gems, 1963; Greek Overseas, 1964, rev. edn 1980; Greek Art, 1964, rev. edns 1973, 1984; Excavations at Tocra, vol. I 1966, vol. II 1973; Pre-Classical, 1967, repr. 1978; Greek Emporio, 1967; Engraved Gems, 1968; Archaic Greek Gems, 1968; Greek Gems and Finger Rings, 1970; (with D. Kurtz) Greek Burial Customs, 1971; Athenian Black Figure Vases, 1974; Athenian Red Figure Vases, Archaic Period, 1975; Intaglios and Rings, 1975; Corpus Vasorum, Oxford, vol. 3, 1975; Greek Sculpture, Archaic Period, 1978; (with M. Robertson) Corpus Vasorum, Castle Ashby, 1978; (with M. L. Vollenweider) Catalogue of Engraved Gems, Ashmolean Museum, 1978; (with D. Scarisbrick) Harari Collection of Finger Rings, 1978; (with E. La Rocca) Eros in Greece, 1978; Escarabeos de Piedra de Ibiza, 1984; La Ceramica Antica, 1984; Greek Sculpture, Classical Period, 1985; (with D. Finn) The Parthenon and its Sculptures, 1985; (jtly) The Oxford History of the Classical World, 1986; Athenian Red Figure Vases, Classical Period, 1989; articles in jls. *Address:* 11 Park Street, Woodstock, Oxford OX7 1SJ. *T:* Woodstock (0993) 811259. *Club:* Athenæum.

BOARDMAN, Sir Kenneth (Ormrod), Kt 1981; DL; Chairman, Boardman Securities Ltd, since 1952; Founder Chairman, Planned Giving Ltd, since 1959; *b* 18 May 1914; *s* of Edgar Nicholas Boardman and Emily Boardman; *m* 1939, Lucy Stafford; one *s* two *d. Educ:* St Peter's Sch., Swinton, Lancs. Trooper, Duke of Lancaster's Own Yeomanry, 1932–33; served War 1939–45, Major RA, 1942–46. Chm., K. O. Boardman Internat. Ltd, 1954–78. Hon. Treasurer, NW Area of Conservative Party, 1977–84; Member: Nat. Union of Cons. and Unionist Assocs, 1975–84 (Patron NW Area, 1984–); NW Industrial Council, 1967–84; several Cons. constituency offices 1984. Pres., Manchester E Euro Constituency, 1984–. Dist Chm., NSPCC 100th Anniv. Appeal, 1984; President: Stockport & Dist NSPCC, 1985–; Stockport Cancer Res. Campaign, 1990; Appeals Chm., John Charnley Trust, 1985–; Patron, Hallé 125th Anniv. Appeal, 1984. Chm., Stockport Parish Church Restoration Fund, 1974–. Liveryman, Farriers Co., 1965–. *Recreations:* gardening, reading and writing, horse racing.

BOARDMAN, Norman Keith, PhD, ScD; FRS 1978; FAA; FTS; post-retirement Fellow, Commonwealth Scientific and Industrial Research Organization, since 1990 (Chief Executive, 1986–90); *b* 16 Aug. 1926; *s* of William Robert Boardman and Margaret Boardman; *m* 1952, Mary Clayton Shepherd; two *s* five *d. Educ:* Melbourne Univ. (BSc 1946, MSc 1949); St John's Coll., Cambridge (PhD 1954, ScD 1974). FAA 1972; FTS 1986. ICI Fellow, Cambridge, 1953–55; Fulbright Scholar, Univ. of Calif, LA, 1964–66. Res. Officer, Wool Res. Section, CSIRO, 1949–51; CSIRO Div. of Plant Industry: Sen. Res. Scientist, 1956; Principal Res. Scientist, 1961; Sen. Prin. Res. Scientist, 1966; Chief Res. Scientist, 1968; Mem. Exec., 1977–85, Chm. and Chief Exec., 1985–86, CSIRO. Member: Aust. Res. Grants Cttee, 1971–75; Council, ANU, 1979–89 and 1990–; Bd, Aust. Centre for Internat. Agricl Research, 1982–88; Nat. Water Research Council, 1982–85; Prime Minister's Science Council, 1989–90. Member Board: Sirotech Ltd, 1986–90; Landcare Aust. Ltd, 1990–. Pres., Aust. Biochem. Soc., 1976–78; Treas., Aust. Acad. of Sci, 1978–81. Corresp. Mem., Amer. Soc. of Plant Physiologists. Hon. DSc Newcastle, NSW. David Syme Res. Prize, Melbourne Univ., 1967; Lemberg Medal, Aust. Biochem. Soc., 1969. *Publications:* scientific papers on plant biochemistry, partic. photosynthesis and structure, function and biogenesis of chloroplasts; papers on science and technology policy. *Recreations:* reading, tennis, listening to music. *Address:* 6 Somers Crescent, Forrest, ACT 2603, Australia. *T:* (06) 2951746. *Club:* Commonwealth (Canberra).

BOASE, Martin; Chairman: Omnicom UK plc, since 1989; Predator Three PLC, since 1990; Director, Omnicom Group Inc., since 1989; *b* 14 July 1932; *s* of Prof. Alan Martin Boase and Elizabeth Grizelle Boase; *m* 1st, 1960, Terry Ann Moir (marr. diss. 1971); one *s* one *d*; 2nd, 1974, Pauline Valerie Brownrigg; one *s* one *d. Educ:* Bedales Sch.; Rendcomb Coll.; New Coll., Oxford. MA; FIPA 1976. Executive, The London Press Exchange, Ltd, 1958–60; Pritchard Wood and Partners, Ltd: Manager, 1961–65; Dir, then Dep. Man. Dir, 1965–68; Founding Partner, The Boase Massimi Pollitt Partnership, Ltd, 1968; Chm., Boase Massimi Pollitt plc, 1977–89 (Jt Chm., 1977–79). Chm., Advertising Assoc., 1987–. Dir, Oxford Playhouse Trust, 1991–. *Recreation:* the Turf. *Address:* c/o Omnicom UK plc, 54 Baker Street, W1.

BOATENG, Prof. Ernest Amano, GM 1968; Environmental and Educational Consultant; Emeritus Professor of Geography, University of Ghana, since 1989; *b* 30 Nov. 1920; 2nd *s* of late Rev. Christian Robert and Adelaide Akonobea Boateng, Aburi, Ghana; *m* 1955, Evelyn Kensema Danso, *e d* of late Rev. Robert Opong Danso and of Victoria Danso, Aburi; four *d. Educ:* Achimota Coll.; St Peter's Hall, Oxford (Gold Coast Govt Schol.). Henry Oliver Beckit Meml Prize, 1949; BA (Geog.) 1949, MA 1953, MLitt 1954. UC Ghana: Lectr in Geography, 1950–57; Sen. Lectr, 1958–61; University of Ghana: Prof. of Geography, 1961–73; Dean, Faculty of Social Studies, 1962–69; Principal, 1969–71, Vice-Chancellor, 1971–73, Univ. Coll., Cape Coast, later Univ. of Cape Coast, Ghana. Vis. Asst Prof., Univ. of Pittsburgh and UCLA, 1960–61. Pres., Ghana Geographical Assoc., 1959–69; Foundn Fellow, Ghana Acad. of Arts and Sciences (Sec. 1959–62, Pres., 1973–76); Mem., Unesco Internat. Adv. Cttee on Humid Tropics Research, 1961–63; Mem., Scientific Council for Africa, 1963–; Mem., Nat. Planning Commn of Ghana, 1961–64; Smuts Vis. Fellow, Univ. of Cambridge, 1965–66; Vis. Prof., Univ. of Pittsburgh, 1966; Deleg., UN Conf. on geographical names, Geneva, 1967; Mem., Council for Scientific and Industrial Research, Ghana, 1967–75; Dir, Ghana Nat. Atlas Project, 1965–77; Chm., Geographical Cttee, Ghana 1970 population census; Chm., Environmental Protection Council, Ghana, 1973–81; Member: Nat. Economic Planning Council of Ghana, 1974–78; Chm., Land Use Planning Cttee of Ghana, 1978–79; Pres., Governing Council of UNEP, 1979, Senior Consultant, 1980–; Member: Constituent Assembly for drafting constitution for third Republic of Ghana, 1978–79; Presidential Task Force on Investments, Ghana, 1980; Nat. Council for Higher Educn, 1975–82; Chm., W African Exams Council, 1977–85. Pres., Ghana Wildlife Soc., 1974–87. Alternate Leader, Ghana Delegn to UN Conf., Vancouver, 1976. Hon. Mem., Ghana Inst. of Planners, 1984. FRSA 1973. Hon. DLitt Ghana, 1979. Nat. Book Award, Ghana, 1978. *Publications:* A Geography of Ghana, 1959; (contrib.) Developing Countries of the World, 1968; (contrib.) Population Growth and Economic Development in Africa, 1972; Independence and Nation Building in Africa, 1973; A Political Geography of Africa, 1978; African Unity: the dream and the reality (J. B. Danquah Memorial Lectures 1978), 1979; various pamphlets, Britannica and other encyclopaedia articles and articles in geographical and other jls and reference works. *Recreations:* photography, gardening. *Address:* Environmental Consultancy Services, PO Box 84, Trade Fair Site, Accra, Ghana. *T:* Accra 777875; (home) 3 Aviation Road, Airport Residential Area, Accra, Ghana.

BOATENG, Paul Yaw; MP (Lab) Brent South, since 1987; barrister-at-law; *b* 14 June 1951; *s* of Eleanor and Kwaku Boateng; *m* 1980, Janet Alleyne; two *s* three *d*. *Educ:* Ghana Internat. Sch.; Accra Acad.; Apsley Grammar Sch.; Bristol Univ. (LLB Hons); Coll. of Law. Admitted Solicitor, 1976; Solicitor, Paddington Law Centre, 1976–79; Solicitor and Partner, B. M. Birnberg and Co., 1979–87; called to the Bar, Gray's Inn, 1989. Legal Advr, Scrap Sus Campaign, 1977–81. Greater London Council: Mem. (Lab) for Walthamstow, 1981–86; Chm., Police Cttee, 1981–86; Vice-Chm., Ethnic Minorities Cttee, GLC, 1981–86. Contested (Lab) Hertfordshire W, 1983. Chairman: Afro-Caribbean Educn Resource Project, 1978–86; Westminster CRC, 1979–81; Vice-Pres., Waltham Forest CRC, 1981–. Opposition frontbench spokesman on treasury and economic affairs, 1989–. Mem., H of C Environment Cttee, 1987–89. Member: NEC Lab. Party Sub-Cttee on Human Rights, 1979–83; Lab. Party Jt Cttee on Crime and Policing, 1984–85; Home Sec.'s Adv. Council on Race Relations, 1981–86; WCC Commn on prog. to combat racism, 1984–; Police Training Council, 1981–85; Exec., NCCL, 1980–86. Chm. Governors, Priory Park Sch., 1978–84; Governor, Police Staff Coll., Bramshill, 1981–84. Mem. Bd, ENO, 1984–. Broadcaster. *Recreations:* escapist. *Address:* House of Commons, SW1A 0AA. *Clubs:* Mangrove; Black and White Café (Bristol).

BOBROW, Prof. Martin, FRCP, FRCPath; Prince Philip Professor of Paediatric Research, United Medical and Dental Schools of Guy's and St Thomas' Hospitals, University of London, since 1982; *b* 6 Feb. 1938; *s* of Joe and Bessie Bobrow; *m* 1963, Lynda Geraldine Strauss; three *d*. *Educ:* Univ. of the Witwatersrand (BSc Hons 1958; MB BCh 1963; DSc Med 1979). MRCPath 1978, FRCPath 1990; FRCP 1986. Clin. Sci. Officer MRC Population Genetics Res. Unit, 1965–72; Consultant in Clin. Genetics, Oxford, and Mem., MRC Ext. Sci. Staff, Genetics Lab., Oxford Univ., 1974–81; Prof. of Human Genetics, Univ. of Amsterdam, 1981–82; Dir, SE Thames Regl Genetics Centre, Guy's Hosp., 1982–. Member, MRC, 1988–; Chairman: Cttee on Med. Aspects of Radiation in the Envt, 1985–; Unrelated Live Donor Transplant Regulatory Authy, 1990–; Member: Res. and Med. Soc. Serv. Cttees, Muscular Dystrophy Gp, 1980–; Internat. Standing Cttee on Human Cytogenetic Nomenclature, 1981–; Black Adv. Gp on Possible Increased Incidence of Cancer in West Cumbria, 1983–84; Med. Adv. and Res. Cttees, Spastics Soc., 1983–89; Human Genome Orgn, 1989–; Cttee to examine the ethical implications of gene therapy, 1989–. *Publications:* papers in sci. books and jls. *Address:* Paediatric Research Unit, 8th Floor, Guy's Hospital, SE1 9RT. *T:* 071–955 4456.

BOCK, Prof. Claus Victor, MA, DrPhil; Professor of German Language and Literature, Westfield College, University of London, 1969–84, now Emeritus; Hon. Research Fellow, Westfield College (now Queen Mary and Westfield College), 1984; *b* Hamburg, 7 May 1926; *o s* of Frederick Bock, merchant and manufacturer, and Margot (*née* Meyerhof). *Educ:* Quaker Sch., Eerde, Holland; Univs of Amsterdam, Manchester, Basle. DrPhil (insigni cum laude) Basle 1955. Asst Lectr in German, Univ. of Manchester, 1956–58; University of London: Lectr, Queen Mary Coll., 1958–69; Reader in German Lang. and Lit., 1964; Chm., Bd of Studies in Germanic Langs and Lit., 1970–73; Hon. Dir, Inst. of Germanic Studies, 1973–81 (Hon. Fellow, 1989); Dean, Fac. of Arts, 1980–84; Mem., Senate, 1981–83; Mem., Acad. Council, 1981–83; Mem., Central Research Fund (A), 1981–84. Mem. Council, English Goethe Soc., 1965–; Chm., Stichting Castum Peregrini, 1984– (Mem., 1971–). Hon. Pres., Assoc. of Teachers of German, 1973–75. Mem., Maatschappij der Nederlandse Letteren, 1977. Mem. Editl Bd, Bithell Series of Dissertations, 1978–84. Officer, Order of Merit (FRG), 1984. *Publications:* Deutsche erfahren Holland 1725–1925, 1956; Q. Kuhlmann als Dichter, 1957; ed (with Margot Ruben) K. Wolfskehl Ges. Werke, 1960; ed (with G. F. Senior) Goethe the Critic, 1960; Pente Pigadia und die Tagebücher des Clement Harris, 1962; ed (with L. Helbing) Fr. Gundolf Briefwechsel mit H. Steiner und E. R. Curtius, 1963; Wort-Konkordanz zur Dichtung Stefan Georges, 1964; ed (with L. Helbing) Fr. Gundolf Briefe Neue Folge, 1965; A Tower of Ivory?, 1970; (with L. Helbing and K. Kluncker) Stefan George: Dokumente seiner Wirkung, 1974; (ed) London German Studies, 1980; (with K. Kluncker) Wolfgang Cordan: Jahre der Freundschaft, 1982; Untergetaucht unter Freunden, 1985, 3rd edn 1989; Besuch im Elfenbeinturm (selected essays), 1990; articles in English and foreign jls and collections. *Recreation:* foreign travel. *Address:* Queen Mary and Westfield College, Kidderpore Avenue, NW3 7ST. *T:* 071–435 7141; 8 Heath Drive, NW3 7SN. *T:* 071–435 8598.

BODDINGTON, Ewart Agnew, JP; Chairman, Boddington Group PLC (formerly Boddington's Breweries), 1970–88, President and non-executive Director, since 1989; *b* 7 April 1927; *m* 1954, Vine Anne Clayton (*d* 1989); two *s* one *d*. *Educ:* Stowe Sch., Buckingham; Trinity Coll., Cambridge (MA). Jt Man. Dir, Boddingtons', 1957, Man. Dir, 1980. Dir, Northern Bd, National Westminster Bank, 1977–. Pres., Inst. of Brewing, 1972–74; Chm., Brewers' Soc., 1984–85; Mem., Brewers' Co., 1980–. JP Macclesfield, 1959; High Sheriff of Cheshire, 1978–79. Hon. MA Manchester, 1977. *Recreations:* shooting, golf, fishing, music. *Address:* Fanshawe Brook Farm, Henbury, Macclesfield. *T:* Marton Heath (0260) 244387.

BODDINGTON, Lewis, CBE 1956; *b* 13 Nov. 1907; *s* of James and Anne Boddington; *m* 1936, Morfydd, *d* of William Murray; no *c*. *Educ:* Lewis' Sch., Pengam; City of Cardiff Technical Coll.; University Coll. of S Wales and Monmouthshire. Pupil Engineer, Fraser & Chalmers Engineering Works, Erith, 1928–31; Asst to Major H. N. Wylie, 1931–36; Royal Aircraft Establishment, 1936; Head of Catapult Section, 1938; Supt of Design Offices, 1942–45; Head of Naval Aircraft Dept, 1945–51; Asst Dir (R&D) Naval, Min. of Supply, 1951–53; Dir Aircraft R&D (RN), 1953–59; Dir-Gen., Aircraft R&D, 1959–60; Dir and Consultant, Westland Aircraft, 1961–72. Medal of Freedom of USA (Bronze Palm), 1958. *Address:* Flat 6, Penarth House, Stanwell Road, Penarth CF6 2EY.

BODDY, Jack Richard, MBE 1973; JP; Group Secretary, Agricultural and Allied Workers Trade Group, Transport and General Workers Union, 1982–87 (General Secretary, National Union of Agricultural and Allied Workers, 1978–82); *b* 23 Aug. 1922; *s* of Percy James Boddy and Lucy May Boddy, JP; *m* 1943, Muriel Lilian (*née* Webb) (*d* 1987); three *s* one *d*; *m* 1990, (Margaret) Joan Laws. *Educ:* City of Norwich Sch. Agricultural worker, 1939; farm foreman, 1943. District Organiser: Lincolnshire NUAAW, 1953; Norfolk NUAAW, 1960. Mem., TUC Gen. Council, 1978–83. Leader, Workers' side, Agricl Wages Bd, 1978–87. Member: Agricl Cttee, EDC, 1978–88; Economic and Social Cttee, EEC, 1980–90; Food and Drink Cttee, EDC, 1984–87; Industrial Injuries Adv. Cttee, DHSS, 1983–87. Member: Swaffham Town Council, 1987– (Dep. Mayor, 1990–91; Mayor, 1991–92); Breckland District Council, 1987–. Pres., Mid Norfolk Mencap, 1988–. Freeman, City of Norwich. JP Swaffham, 1947. *Recreations:* caravanning, gardening. *Address:* The Brambles, 2b Spinners Lane, Swaffham, Norfolk PE37 7ND. *T:* Swaffham (0760) 22916.

BODEN, Edward Arthur; retired; Agent-General for Saskatchewan, Canada, 1973–77; *b* 13 Nov. 1911; *s* of English and Welsh parents; *m* 1939, Helen Harriet Saunders; one *s* one *d*. *Educ:* Cutknife, Saskatchewan, Canada. Born and raised on a Saskatchewan farm and actively farmed until 1949, retaining interest in farm until 1973. Royal Canadian Mounted Police, 1937–39. Saskatchewan Wheat Pool and Canadian Fedn of Agriculture, 1939–73; held several active positions in these organisations and retired, as 1st Vice-Pres., 1973; in this field acted on various provincial and national govtl bds and cttees; Advr to Saskatchewan Dept of Industry and Commerce, 1977–78; policy Advr, Dept of Agriculture, and Co-ordinator of Sask's 75th Anniv. Celebration for Agricl features 1980, 1979–81; with others, rep. Canada at internat. agricultural confs in different parts of the world. Sen. Counsellor, Provincial Sen. Citizens' Council, 1982–. *Recreations:* boxing, hunting. *Address:* Box 988, Battleford, Saskatchewan S0M 0E0, Canada.

BODEN, Leonard, RP; FRSA; portrait painter; *b* Greenock, Scotland, 1911; *s* of John Boden; *m* Margaret Tulloch (portrait painter, as Margaret Boden, PS, FRSA); one *d*. *Educ:* Sedbergh; Sch. of Art, Glasgow; Heatherley Sch. of Art, London. *Official portraits* include: HM Queen Elizabeth II; HRH The Prince Philip, Duke of Edinburgh; HM Queen Elizabeth the Queen Mother; HRH The Prince of Wales; The Princess Royal; HH Pope Pius XII; Field Marshals Lord Milne and Lord Slim, Margaret Thatcher, and many others. Vice-President: Artists' Gen. Benevolent Instn; St Ives Soc. of Artists; Governor, Christ's Hospital. Freeman, City of London; Liveryman, Painter-Stainers Co. Gold Medal, Paris Salon, 1957. *Work reproduced in:* The Connoisseur, The Artist, Fine Art Prints. *Address:* 36 Arden Road, N3 3AN. *T:* 081–346 5706. *Clubs:* Savage, Chelsea Arts.

BODEN, Prof. Margaret Ann, ScD, PhD; FBA 1983; Professor of Philosophy and Psychology, University of Sussex, since 1980; *b* 26 Nov. 1936; *d* of late Leonard Forbes Boden, OBE, LLB and Violet Dorothy Dawson; *m* 1967, John Raymond Spiers (marr. diss. 1981); one *s* one *d*. *Educ:* City of London Sch. for Girls; Newnham Coll., Cambridge (Major schol. in Med. Scis; Sarah Smithson Scholar in Moral Scis; MA; Associate, 1981; ScD 1990); Harvard Grad. Sch. (Harkness Fellow; AM; PhD in Cognitive and Social Psychology). Asst Lectr, then Lectr, in Philosophy, Birmingham Univ., 1959–65; Sussex University: Lectr, 1965–72; Reader, 1972–80; Founding Dean, Sch. of Cognitive Sciences, later Cognitive and Computing Sciences, 1987. Vis. Scientist, Yale Univ., 1979. Co-founder, Dir, 1968–85, Sec., 1968–79, Harvester Press. Founding Chm., Hist. and Philosophy of Psychology Sect., BPsS, 1983. Member: Council for Science and Society, 1986– (Trustee, 1990–91); ABRC, 1989–90 (Chm., Working Gp on Peer-Review, 1989–90); Council, Royal Inst. of Philosophy, 1987–; Council, British Acad., 1988– (Vice-Pres., 1989–91). Patron, British Trust, 1991–. Leslie McMichael Premium, IERE, 1977. *Publications:* Purposive Explanation in Psychology, 1972; Artificial Intelligence and Natural Man, 1977; Piaget, 1979; Minds and Mechanisms, 1981; Computer Models of Mind, 1988; Artificial Intelligence in Psychology, 1989; The Philosophy of Artificial Intelligence, 1990; The Creative Mind: myths and mechanisms, 1990; General Editor: Explorations in Cognitive Science; Harvester Studies in Cognitive Science; Harvester Studies in Philosophy; contribs to philosophical and psychological jls. *Recreations:* dress-making, dreaming about the South Pacific. *Address:* School of Cognitive and Computing Sciences, University of Sussex, Brighton BN1 9QH. *T:* Brighton (0273) 678386. *Club:* Reform.

BODEN, Thomas Bennion, OBE 1978; Deputy President, National Farmers' Union of England and Wales, 1979; Chairman, European Economic Community Advisory Committee on Questions of Agricultural Structure Policy, 1985–89; *b* 23 Oct. 1915; *s* of late Harry Bertram Boden and Florence Nellie Mosley; *m* 1939, Dorothy Eileen Ball; one *s* two *d*. *Educ:* Alleynes Grammar Sch., Uttoxeter; Nottingham Univ. BSc course up to final year, when moved into farming on death of father, 1937; became involved in agricultural politics through NFU, 1948; office holder of NFU, 1977. JP Staffs 1957–85. *Publications:* articles on agricultural taxation, farm structures in EEC, farm finance, young new entrants into farming. *Recreations:* cricket, tennis, swimming, hockey. *Address:* Denstone Hall, Denstone, Uttoxeter, Staffs. *T:* Rocester (0889) 590243. *Clubs:* Farmers', NFU.

BODEY, David Roderick Lessiter; QC 1991; *b* 14 Oct. 1947; *s* of late Reginald Augustus Bodey, FIA and Betty Francis Bodey; *m* 1976, Ruth (*née* MacAdorey); one *s* one *d*. *Educ:* King's Sch., Canterbury; Univ. of Bristol (LLB Hons 1969). Called to the Bar, Middle Temple, 1970 (Harmsworth Scholar, 1970). An Asst Recorder, 1989. Legal Assessor to UK Central Council for Nursing, Midwifery and Health Visiting, 1983. *Recreations:* music, marathon running. *Address:* Queen Elizabeth Building, Temple, EC4Y 9BS. *T:* 071–583 7837. *Club:* Lansdowne.

BODGER; *see* Steele-Bodger.

BODILLY, Sir Jocelyn, Kt 1969; VRD; Chairman, Industrial Tribunals for London (South), 1976–86, retired; Chief Justice of the Western Pacific, 1965–75; *b* 1913; *m* 1st, 1936, Phyllis Maureen (*d* 1963), *d* of Thomas Cooper Gotch, ARA; 2nd, 1964, Marjorie, *d* of Walter Fogg. *Educ:* Munro Coll., Jamaica; Schloss Schule, Salem, Baden; Wadham Coll., Oxford. Called to Bar, Inner Temple, 1937; engaged in private practice until War; Royal Navy until 1946; RNVR, 1937–56 (Lt-Comdr (S)); Lt-Comdr, RNR, Hong Kong, 1961–65. High Court Judge, Sudan, 1946–55; Crown Counsel, Hong Kong, 1955, Principal Crown Counsel, 1961–65. *Address:* Myrtle Cottage, St Peters Hill, Newlyn, Penzance, Cornwall TR18 5EQ. *Club:* Royal Ocean Racing.

BODMER, Sir Walter (Fred), Kt 1986; FRCPath; FRS 1974; CBiol, FIBiol; Director General, Imperial Cancer Research Fund, since 1991 (Director of Research, 1979–91); *b* 10 Jan. 1936; *s* of late Dr Ernest Julius and Sylvia Emily Bodmer; *m* 1956, Julia Gwynaeth Pilkington; two *s* one *d*. *Educ:* Manchester Grammar Sch.; Clare Coll., Cambridge. BA 1956, MA, PhD 1959, Cambridge. FRCPath 1984; FIBiol 1990. Research Fellow 1958–61, Official Fellow 1961, Hon. Fellow 1989, Clare Coll., Cambridge; Demonstrator in Genetics, Univ. of Cambridge, 1960–62; Asst Prof. 1962–66, Associate Prof. 1966–68, Prof. 1968–70, Dept of Genetics, Stanford Univ.; Prof. of Genetics, Univ. of Oxford, 1970–79. Non-exec. Dir, Fisons plc, 1990–. Chairman: BBC Sci. Consultative Gp, 1981–87; Bd of Trustees, BM (Natural History), 1989– (Trustee, 1983–); Member: BBC Gen. Adv. Council, 1981– (Chm., 1987); Council, Internat. Union Against Cancer, 1982–; Adv. Bd for Res. Councils, 1983–88; Chairman: Cttee on Public Understanding of Science, 1990–; Orgn of European Cancer Insts, 1990–; President: Royal Statistical Soc., 1984–85 (Vice-Pres., 1983–84); BAAS, 1987–88 (Vice-Pres., 1989–); Assoc. for Science Educn, 1989–90; Human Genome Orgn, 1990–; British Soc. for Histocompatibility and Immunogenetics, 1990–91; Vice-President: Royal Instn, 1981–82; Parly and Scientific Cttee, 1990–; Hon. Vice-Pres., Res. Defence Soc., 1990–. Trustee, Sir John Soane's Mus., 1983–. Hon. Member: British Soc. of Gastroenterology, 1989; Amer. Assoc. of Immunologists, 1985; For. Associate, US Nat. Acad. of Scis, 1981; Foreign Member: Czechoslovak Acad. of Scis, 1988–; Amer. Philosophical Soc., 1989; For. Hon. Mem., Amer. Acad. Arts and Scis, 1972; Fellow, Internat. Inst. of Biotechnology, 1989; Hon. Fellow, Keble Coll., Oxford, 1982; Hon. FRCP 1985; Hon. FRCS 1986. Hon. DSc: Bath, 1988; Oxford, 1988; Hull, 1990; Edinburgh, 1990; DUniv Surrey, 1990; Laurea *hc* in Medicine and Surgery, Univ. of Bologna, 1987. William Allan Meml Award, Amer. Soc. Human Genetics, 1980; Conway Evans Prize, RCP/Royal Soc., 1982; Rabbi Shai

Shacknai Meml Prize Lectr, 1983; John Alexander Meml Prize and Lectureship, Univ. of Pennsylvania Med. Sch., 1984; Rose Payne Dist. Scientists Lectureship, Amer. Soc. for Histocompatibility and Immunogenetics, 1985; Bernal Lectr, Royal Soc., 1986; Neil Hamilton-Fairley Medal, 1990. *Publications:* The Genetics of Human Populations (with L. L. Cavalli-Sforza), 1971; (with A. Jones) Our Future Inheritance: choice or chance?, 1974; (with L. L. Cavalli-Sforza) Genetics, Evolution and Man, 1976; research papers in genetical, statistical and mathematical jls, etc. *Recreations:* playing the piano, riding, swimming. *Address:* Imperial Cancer Research Fund, Lincoln's Inn Fields, WC2A 3PX. *T:* 071–242 0200. *Club:* Athenæum.

BODMIN, Archdeacon of; *see* Whiteman, Ven. R. D. C.

BODY, Sir Richard (Bernard Frank Stewart), Kt 1986; MP (C) Holland with Boston, since 1966; *b* 18 May 1927; *s* of Lieut-Col Bernard Richard Body, formerly of Hyde End, Shinfield, Berks; *m* 1959, Marion, *d* of late Major H. Graham, OBE; one *s* one *d*. Called to the Bar, Middle Temple, 1949. Underwriting Mem. of Lloyd's. Contested (C) Rotherham, 1950; Abertillery bye-election, 1950; Leek, 1951; MP (C) Billericay Div., Essex, 1955–Sept. 1959. Member: Jt Select Cttee on Consolidation of Law, 1975–; Commons Select Cttee on Agric., 1979–87 (Chm., 1986–87). Chm., Open Seas Forum, 1971–. Jt Chm., Council, Get Britain Out referendum campaign, 1975. Dir, New European Publications Ltd, 1986–. *Publications:* The Architect and the Law, 1954; (contrib.) Destiny or Delusion, 1971; (ed jtly) Freedom and Stability in the World Economy, 1976; Agriculture: The Triumph and the Shame, 1982; Farming in the Clouds, 1984; Red or Green for Farmers, 1987; Europe of Many Circles, 1990; Our Food, Our Land, 1991. *Address:* Jewell's Farm, Stanford Dingley, near Reading, Berks RG7 6LX. *T:* Reading (0734) 744295. *Clubs:* Carlton, Reform, Farmers'.

BOE, Norman Wallace; Deputy Solicitor to Secretary of State for Scotland, since 1987; *b* 30 Aug. 1943; *s* of Alexander Thomson Boe and Margaret Wallace Revans; *m* 1968, Margaret Irene McKenzie; one *s* one *d*. *Educ:* George Heriot's Sch., Edinburgh; Edinburgh Univ. LLB Hons 1965. Admitted Solicitor, 1967. Legal apprentice, Lindsays, WS, 1965–67; Legal Asst, Menzies & White, WS, 1967–70; Office of Solicitor to Sec. of State for Scotland, 1970–. *Recreations:* golf, gardening, dog-walking. *Address:* c/o Solicitor's Office, Scottish Office, New St Andrew's House, Edinburgh. *T:* 031–244 4884. *Club:* Edinburgh University Staff.

BOEGNER, Jean-Marc; Grand Officier, Légion d'Honneur; Commandeur, Ordre National du Mérite; Ambassadeur de France, 1973; *b* 3 July 1913; *s* of Marc and Jeanne Boegner; *m* 1945, Odilie de Moustier; three *d*. *Educ:* Lycée Janson-de-Sailly; Ecole Libre des Sciences Politiques; Paris University (LèsL). Joined French diplomatic service, 1939; Attaché: Berlin, 1939; Ankara, 1940; Beirut, 1941; Counsellor: Stockholm, 1945; The Hague, 1947; Ministry of Foreign Affairs, Paris, 1952–58; Counsellor to Charles de Gaulle, 1958–59; Ambassador to Tunisia, 1959–60; Permanent Representative of France: to EEC, 1961–72; to OECD, 1975–78. *Publication:* Le Marché commun de Six à Neuf, 1974. *Address:* 19 rue de Lille, 75007 Paris, France.

BOERMA, Addeke Hendrik; Director-General, Food and Agriculture Organisation of the United Nations, 1968–75; *b* 3 April 1912; *m* 1953, Dinah Johnston; five *d*. *Educ:* Agricultural Univ., Wageningen. Netherlands Farmers' Organisation, 1935–38; Ministry of Agriculture of the Netherlands, 1938–45; Commissioner for Foreign Agricultural Relations, 1946; FAO positions: Regional Representative for Europe, 1948–51; Dir, Economics Div., 1951–58; Head of Programme and Budgetary Service, 1958–62; Asst Dir-Gen., 1960; Exec. Dir, World Food Programme, 1962–67. Holds Hon. Degrees from Univs in USA, Netherlands, Belgium, Hungary, Canada, Italy and Greece. Wateler Peace Prize, Carnegie Foundn, The Hague, 1976. Comdr, Netherlands Order of Lion; Commander, Order of Leopold II, Belgium; Officer, Ordre Mérite Agricole, France; Cavaliere di Gran Croce (Italy). *Address:* Prinz Eugenstrasse 44/10, 1040 Vienna, Austria.

BOEVEY, Sir Thomas (Michael Blake) C.; *see* Crawley-Boevey.

BOGARDE, Dirk; *see* Van den Bogaerde, D. N.

BOGDANOV, Michael; Joint Artistic Director, English Shakespeare Company, since 1986; Artistic Director/Executive Producer, Deutsche Schauspielhaus, Hamburg, since 1989; *b* 15 Dec. 1938; *s* of Francis Benzion Bogdin and Rhoda Rees Bogdin; *m* 1966, Patsy Ann Warwick; two *s* one *d*. *Educ:* Lower School of John Lyon, Harrow; Univ. of Dublin Trinity Coll. (MA); Univs of the Sorbonne, and Munich. Writer, with Terence Brady, ATV series, Broad and Narrow, 1965; Producer/Director with Telefis Eireann, 1966–68; opening production of Theatre Upstairs, Royal Court, A Comedy of the Changing Years, 1969; The Bourgeois Gentilhomme, Oxford Playhouse, 1969; Asst Dir, Royal Shakespeare Theatre Co., 1970–71; Associate Dir, Peter Brook's A Midsummer Night's Dream, Stratford 1970, New York 1971, World Tour 1972; Dir, Two Gentlemen of Verona, São Paulo, Brazil, 1971; Associate to Jean Louis Barrault, Rabelais, 1971; Associate Director: Tyneside Th. Co., 1971–73; Haymarket Th., Leicester; Director: Phoenix Th., Leicester, 1973–77; Young Vic Th., London, 1978–80; an Associate Dir, Nat. Theatre, 1980–88. Directed: The Taming of the Shrew, RSC, Stratford 1978, London 1979 (SWET Dir of the Year award, 1979); The Seagull, Toho Th. Co., Tokyo, 1980; Shadow of a Gunman, RSC, 1980; The Knight of the Burning Pestle, RSC, 1981; Hamlet, Dublin, 1983; Romeo and Juliet, Tokyo, 1983, RSC, 1986; The Mayor of Zalamea, Washington, 1984; Measure for Measure, Stratford, Ont., 1985; Mutiny (musical), 1985; Donnerstag aus Licht, Royal Opera House, 1985; Julius Caesar, Schauspielhaus, Hamburg, 1986 (also filmed by ZDF TV); Reineke Fuchs, Schauspielhaus, Hamburg, 1987; The Canterbury Tales, Prince of Wales, 1987; Montag, Stockhausen Opera, La Scala, Milan, 1988 (world première); Hamlet, Hamburg, 1989; National Theatre productions: Sir Gawain and the Green Knight, The Hunchback of Notre Dame, 1977–78; The Romans in Britain, Hiawatha, 1980; One Woman Plays, The Mayor of Zalamea, The Hypochondriac, 1981; Uncle Vanya, The Spanish Tragedy, 1982; Lorenzaccio, 1983; You Can't Take it With You, 1983; Strider, 1984; English Shakespeare Co. productions: Henry IV (Parts I and II), Henry V, UK tour, European tour, Old Vic, and Canada, 1986–87; The Wars of the Roses (7 play history cycle), UK, Europe and world tour, 1987–89 (Laurence Olivier Award, Dir of the Year, 1989); Coriolanus, The Winter's Tale, UK and world tour, 1990–91. Deviser and Presenter, Shakespeare Lives, TV series, 1983. Co-author, plays, adaptations and children's theatre pieces. *Recreations:* cricket, wine, music, sheep. *Address:* English Shakespeare Company, 369 St John Street, EC1V 4LB.

BOGDANOVICH, Peter; film director, writer, producer, actor; *b* Kingston, NY, 30 July 1939; *s* of Borislav Bogdanovich and Herma (*née* Robinson); *m* 1962, Polly Platt (marr. diss. 1970); two *d*; *m* 1988, L. B. Straten. Owner, Crescent Moon Productions, Inc., LA, 1986–. Member: Dirs Guild of America; Writers' Guild of America; Acad. of Motion Picture Arts and Sciences. *Theatre:* Actor, Amer. Shakespeare Fest., Stratford, Conn, 1956, NY Shakespeare Fest., 1958; Dir and producer, off-Broadway: The Big Knife, 1959; Camino Real, Ten Little Indians, Rocket to the Moon, 1961; Once in a Lifetime, 1964. *Films include:* The Wild Angels (2nd-Unit Dir, co-writer, actor), 1966; Targets (dir, co-writer, prod., actor), 1968; The Last Picture Show (dir, co-writer), 1971 (NY Film Critics' Award for Best Screenplay, British Acad. Award for Best Screenplay); Directed by John Ford (dir, writer, interviewer), 1971; What's Up, Doc? (dir, co-writer, prod.), 1972 (Writers' Guild of America Award for Best Screenplay); Paper Moon (dir, prod.), 1973 (Silver Shell Award, Spain); Daisy Miller (dir, prod.), 1974 (Brussels Festival Award for Best Director); At Long Last Love (dir, writer, prod.), 1975; Nickelodeon (dir, co-writer), 1976; Saint Jack (dir, co-writer, actor), 1979 (Pasinetti Award, Critics' Prize, Venice Festival); They All Laughed (dir, writer), 1981; Mask (dir), 1985; Illegally Yours (dir, prod., co-writer), 1988; Texasville (dir, prod., writer), 1990. *TV:* CBS This Morning (weekly commentary), 1987–89. *Publications:* The Cinema of Orson Welles, 1961; The Cinema of Howard Hawks, 1962; The Cinema of Alfred Hitchcock, 1963; John Ford, 1968; Fritz Lang in America, 1969; Allan Dwan: the last pioneer, 1971; Pieces of Time: Peter Bogdanovich on the Movies (Picture Shows in the UK) 1961–85, 1973, enlarged 1985; The Killing of the Unicorn: Dorothy Stratten, 1960–1980, a Memoir, 1984; (ed with introd.) A Year and a Day Calendar 1991, 1990; features on films in Esquire, New York Times, Village Voice, Cahiers du Cinema, Los Angeles Times, New York Magazine, Vogue, Variety etc., 1961–. *Address:* c/o William Peiffer, 2040 Avenue of the Stars, Century City, Calif 90067, USA; Martin Baum, Rick Nicita, CAA, 9830 Wilshire Boulevard, Beverly Hills, Calif 90212, USA.

BOGGIS-ROLFE, Hume, CB 1971; CBE 1962; farmer; *b* 20 Oct. 1911; *s* of Douglass Horace Boggis-Rolfe and Maria Maud (*née* Bailey); *m* 1941, Anne Dorothea, *e d* of Capt. Eric Noble, Henley-on-Thames; two *s* one *d*. *Educ:* Westminster Sch.; Freiburg Univ.; Trinity Coll., Cambridge. Called to Bar, Middle Temple, 1935. Army, Intelligence Corps, 1939–46 (Lieut-Col). Private Sec. to Lord Chancellor, 1949–50; Asst Solicitor in Lord Chancellor's Office, 1951–65; Sec. to Law Commn, 1965–68; Deputy Clerk of the Crown in Chancery, and Asst Perm. Sec. to Lord Chancellor, 1968–75, and Deputy Secretary, Lord Chancellor's Office, 1970–75. Master, Merchant Taylors' Co., 1971–72. Chm., Friends of the Elderly and Gentlefolks' Help, 1977–84. *Recreations:* gardening, travelling. *Address:* 22 Victoria Square, SW1W 0RB. *T:* 071–834 2676; The Grange, Wormingford, Colchester, Essex. *T:* Bures (0787) 227303. *Club:* Athenæum.

BOGIE, David Wilson; Sheriff of Grampian, Highland and Islands at Aberdeen and Stonehaven, since 1985; *b* 17 July 1946; *o s* of late Robert T. Bogie, Edinburgh; *m* 1983, Lady Lucinda Mackay, *o d* of Earl of Inchcape, *qv*. *Educ:* George Watson's Coll.; Edinburgh Univ. (LLB); Balliol Coll., Oxford (MA). FSAScot. Admitted to Faculty of Advocates, 1972; Temp. Sheriff, 1981. *Recreations:* architecture, heraldry, antiquities. *Address:* 50 Whitehall Road, Aberdeen AB2 4PR. *Clubs:* Brooks's; New (Edinburgh); Royal Northern and University (Aberdeen).

BOGLE, David Blyth, CBE 1967; WS; formerly Senior Partner, Lindsays, WS, Edinburgh; Member of Council on Tribunals, 1958–70, and Chairman of Scottish Committee, 1962–70; *b* 22 Jan. 1903; *s* of late Very Rev. Andrew Nisbet Bogle, DD and Helen Milne Bogle; *m* 1955, Ruth Agnes Thorley. *Educ:* George Watson's Coll., Edinburgh; Edinburgh Univ. (LLB). Writer to the Signet, 1927. Commissioned in the Queen's Own Cameron Highlanders, 1940, and served in UK and Middle East, 1942–45; demobilised, with rank of Major, 1945. *Recreation:* RNIB talking books. *Address:* 3 Belgrave Crescent, Edinburgh EH4 3AQ. *T:* 031–332 0047. *Club:* New (Edinburgh).

BOGLE, Ellen Gray, CD 1987, High Commissioner for Jamaica in London, since 1989; also Ambassador to Denmark, Finland, Norway, Sweden and Spain, since 1990; *b* 9 Oct. 1941; *d* of late Victor Grey Williams and Eileen Avril Williams; *m* (marr. diss.); one *s* one *d*. *Educ:* St Andrew High Sch., Jamaica; Univ. of the West Indies, Jamaica (BA). Dir of For. Trade, Min. of For. Affairs, Jamaica, 1978–81; Dir, Jamaica Nat. Export Corp., 1978–81; High Comr to Trinidad and Tobago, Barbados, E Caribbean and Guyana, and Ambassador to Suriname, 1982–89. *Recreations:* gardening, reading, cooking, table tennis. *Address:* 1 Prince Consort Road, SW7 2BZ. *T:* 071–823 9911.

BOGSCH, Arpad, Dr jur; Director General, World Intellectual Property Organization, since 1973 (Deputy Director General, 1963–73); *b* 24 Feb. 1919; *s* of Arpad Bogsch and Emilia Taborsky; *m*; one *s* one *d*. *Educ:* Univ. of Budapest (Dr jur); Univ. of Paris (Dr jur); George Washington Univ. (LLM). Called to the Budapest Bar, 1940, to the Washington DC Bar, 1952. Private law practice, Budapest, 1940–48; Legal Officer, Unesco, Paris, 1948–54; Legal Adviser, Library of Congress, Washington DC, 1954–63. LLD *hc* George Washington Univ., 1985. Decorations from: Sweden, 1967; Austria, 1977; Spain, 1980; Senegal and Republic of Korea, 1981; Bulgaria, 1985; France, Japan and Thailand, 1986. *Address:* 34 chemin des Colombettes, 1211 Geneva, Switzerland. *T:* 022.99.91.11.

BOHAN, William Joseph, CB 1988; Assistant Under Secretary of State, Home Office, 1979–89, retired; *b* 10 April 1929; *s* of John and Josephine Bohan; *m* 1955, Brenda Skevington; one *s* (one *d* decd). *Educ:* Finchley Catholic Grammar Sch.; Cardinal Vaughan Sch., Kensington; King's Coll., Cambridge (Chancellor's Classical Medallist, 1952). Home Office: Asst Principal, 1952; Principal, 1958; Sec., Cttee on Immigration Appeals, 1966–67; Asst Sec., 1967. Chm., European Cttee on Crime Problems, 1987–89. *Recreations:* languages and literature, walking. *Address:* 16 Mostyn Road, SW19 3LJ. *T:* 081–542 1127.

BOHM, Prof. David (Joseph), PhD; FRS 1990; Professor of Theoretical Physics, Birkbeck College, University of London, 1961–83, now Emeritus; *b* 20 Dec. 1917; *s* of Samuel and Freda Bohm; *m* 1956, Sarah Woolfson; no *c*. *Educ:* Pennsylvania State Coll. (BS); University of Calif (PhD). Research Physicist, University of Calif, Radiation Laboratory, 1943–47; Asst Prof., Princeton Univ., 1947–51; Prof., University de São Paulo, Brazil, 1951–55; Prof., Technion, Haifa, Israel, 1955–57; Research Fellow, Bristol Univ., 1957–61. Elliot Cresson Medal, Franklin Inst., 1991. *Publications:* Quantum Theory, 1951; Causality and Chance in Modern Physics, 1957; Special Theory of Relativity, 1965; Fragmentation and Wholeness, 1976; Wholeness and Order: cosmos and consciousness, 1979; Wholeness and the Implicate Order, 1980; various papers in Physical Review, Nuovo Cimento, Progress of Theoretical Physics, British Jl for Philosophy of Science, etc, inc. papers on Implicate Order and A New Mode of Description in Physics. *Recreations:* walking, conversation, music (listener), art (viewer). *Address:* c/o Physics Department, Birkbeck College, Malet Street, WC1.

BOHR, Prof. Aage Niels, DSc, DrPhil; physicist, Denmark; Professor of Physics, University of Copenhagen, since 1956; *b* Copenhagen, 19 June 1922; *s* of late Prof. Niels Bohr and Margrethe Nørlund; *m* 1st, Marietta Bettina (*née* Soffer) (*d* 1978); two *s* one *d*; 2nd, 1981, Bente, *d* of late Chief Physician Johannes Meyer and Lone (*née* Rubow) and *widow* of Morten Scharff. *Educ:* Univ. of Copenhagen. Jun. Scientific Officer, Dept of Scientific and Industrial Research, London, 1943–45; Research Asst, Inst. for Theoretical Physics, Univ. of Copenhagen, 1946; Dir, Niels Bohr Inst. (formerly Inst. for Theoretical Physics), 1963–70. Bd Mem., Nordita, 1958–74, Dir, 1975–81. Member: Royal Danish Acad. of Science, 1955–; Royal Physiolog. Soc., Sweden, 1959–; Royal Norwegian Acad. of Sciences, 1962–; Acad. of Tech. Sciences, Copenhagen, 1963–; Amer. Phil. Soc., 1965–; Amer. Acad. of Arts and Sciences, 1965–; Nat. Acad. of Sciences, USA, 1971–; Royal

Swedish Acad. of Sciences, 1974–; Yugoslavia Acad. of Sciences, 1976–; Pontificia Academia Scientiarum, 1978–; Norwegian Acad. of Sciences, 1979–; Polish Acad. of Sciences, 1980–; Finska Vetenskups-Societeten, 1980–; Deutsche Akademie der Naturforscher Leopoldina, 1981–. Awards: Dannie Heineman Prize, 1960; Pius XI Medal, 1963; Atoms for Peace Award, 1969; H. C. Ørsted Medal, 1970; Rutherford Medal, 1972; John Price Wetherill Medal, 1974; (jointly) Nobel Prize for Physics, 1975; Ole Rømer Medal, 1976. Dr *hc*: Manchester, 1961; Oslo, 1969; Heidelberg, 1971; Trondheim, 1972; Uppsala, 1975. *Publications*: Rotational States of Atomic Nuclei, 1954; (with Ben R. Mottelson) Nuclear Structure, vol. I, 1969, vol. II 1975. *Address*: Strandgade 34, 1st Floor, 1401 Copenhagen K, Denmark.

BOHUSZ-SZYSZKO, Dame Cicely (Mary Strode); *see* Saunders, Dame C. M. S.

BOILEAU, Sir Guy (Francis), 8th Bt *cr* 1838; sports administrator; *b* 23 Feb. 1935; *s* of Sir Edmond Charles Boileau, 7th Bt, and of Marjorie Lyle, *d* of Claude Monteath D'Arcy; *S* father, 1980; *m* 1962, Judith Frances, *d* of George Conrad Hannan; two *s* three *d*. *Educ:* Xavier College, Melbourne; Royal Military Coll., Duntroon, Australia. Lieut, Aust. Staff Corps, 1956; Platoon Comdr, 3rd Bn, Royal Aust. Regt, Malaysia, 1957–58; Observer, UN Mil. Observer Gp in India and Pakistan, 1959–60; Instructor, Aust. Army Training Team, Vietnam, 1963–64; attached US Dept of Defence, Washington, DC, 1966–68; Security Adviser, Dept of the Administrator, Territory of Papua-New Guinea, 1970–71; CO, Army Intelligence Centre, 1972–74; Directing Staff (Instructor), Aust. Staff Coll., 1975–76; SO1 Personnel, HQ Third Mil. Dist, 1979. *Recreations*: tennis, boating, fishing. *Heir: s* Nicolas Edmond George Boileau, *b* 17 Nov. 1964. *Address*: 14 Faircroft Avenue, Glen Iris, Victoria 3146, Australia. *T:* (03) 822 8273. *Club:* The Heroes (Toorak, Victoria).

BOISSIER, Roger Humphrey; Chairman, Pressac Holdings PLC, since 1990; *b* 30 June 1930; *y s* of late Ernest Boissier, DSC, FIEE and Doris Boissier (*née* Bingham), of Bingham's Melcombe; *m* 1965, Elizabeth (Bridget) Rhoda, *e d* of Sir Gerald Ley, Bt, TD and Rosemary, Lady Ley; one *s* one *d*. *Educ:* Harrow School. International Combustion, 1950–52; Cooper-Parry, Hall, Doughty & Co, 1952–53; Merz & McLellan, 1953–55; Aiton & Co, 1955–83, Man. Dir, 1975–83; Exec Dir, Whessoe, 1975–83; Non-Exec. Director: Pressac Holdings, 1984 (Dep. Chm., 1989); British Gas, 1986–; T & N, 1987–; Edward Lumley Holdings, 1988–; Severn Trent, 1989–; Consultant, Allott & Lomax, 1984–; former dir or mem. other cos and public bodies. Mem. Exec., Brit. Nat. Cttee, World Energy Council, 1975– (Chm., 1977–80). Mem. Court and Council, Loughborough Univ. of Technol., 1991–; Gov., Harrow Sch., 1976– (Dep. Chm., 1988). High Sheriff of Derbyshire, 1987–88. Master, Tin Plate Workers' Co, 1988–89. CIGasE 1983; Companion, Inst. of Energy, 1991; FInstD; FRSA. *Recreations:* cars, foreign travel, reading. *Address:* Easton House, The Pastures, Repton, Derby DE6 6GG. *T:* Burton-on-Trent (0283) 702274, *Fax:* Burton-on-Trent (0283) 701489. *Clubs:* City Livery, MCC; Surrey County Cricket; County (Derby).

BOIZOT, Peter James, MBE 1986; Chairman and Managing Director, PizzaExpress Ltd, since 1965; *b* 16 Nov. 1929; *s* of Gaston Charles and Susannah Boizot. *Educ:* King's Sch., Peterborough (chorister, Peterborough Cathedral); St Catharine's Coll., Cambridge. MA (BA (Hons) History). Various jobs, predominantly in sales field, 1953–64; founded PizzaExpress Ltd, 1965; Dir, Connoisseur Casino, 1970–82. Publisher Jazz Express, monthly magazine, 1983–. Founder and Chm., Soho Restaurateurs Assoc., 1980–. Dir, CENTEC. Vice Chm., Westminster Chamber of Commerce. Contested (L) Peterborough, Feb. and Oct. 1974. Pres., Hampstead and Westminster Hockey Club, 1986–; a Vice-Pres., Hockey Assoc., 1990–. FHCIMA 1989. Bolla Award, 1983; Hotel and Caterer Food Service Award, 1989. Cavaliere Ufficiale, Al Merito della Repubblica Italiana, 1983. *Publication:* PizzaExpress Cook Book, 1976, 2nd edn 1976. *Recreations:* hockey, presenting jazz, opening new restaurants. *Address:* 10 Lowndes Square, SW1X 9HA. *T:* 071–235 9100. *Clubs:* National Liberal, Royal Automobile.

BOJAXHIU, Agnes Gonxha; *see* Teresa, Mother.

BOK, Derek; Professor of Law, since 1961 and President, 1971–91, Harvard University; *b* Bryn Mawr, Pa, 22 March 1930; *s* of late Curtis and of Margaret Plummer Bok (now Mrs William S. Kiskadden); *m* 1955, Sissela Ann Myrdal, *d* of Karl Gunnar and Alva Myrdal, *qqv*; one *s* two *d*. *Educ:* Stanford Univ., BA; Harvard Univ., JD; Inst. of Political Science, Univ. of Paris (Fulbright Scholar); George Washington Univ., MA in Economics. Served AUS, 1956–58. Asst Prof. of Law, Harvard Univ., 1958–61, Dean of Law Sch., 1968–71. *Publications:* The First Three Years of the Schuman Plan, 1955; (ed with Archibald Cox) Cases and Materials on Labor Law, 5th edn 1962, 6th edn 1965, 7th edn 1969, 8th edn 1977; (with John Dunlop) Labor and the American Community, 1970; Beyond the Ivory Tower, 1982; Higher Learning, 1986; Universities and the future of America, 1990. *Recreations:* gardening, tennis, skiing. *Address:* c/o Harvard University, Cambridge, Mass 02138, USA.

BOKSENBERG, Prof. Alexander, PhD; FRS 1978; FRAS; Director, Royal Greenwich Observatory, since 1981; *b* 18 March 1936; *s* of Julius Boksenberg and Ernestina Steinberg; *m* 1960, Adella Coren; one *s* one *d*. *Educ:* Stationers' Co.'s Sch.; Univ. of London (BSc, PhD). Dept of Physics and Astronomy, University Coll. London: SRC Res. Asst, 1960–65; Lectr in Physics, 1965–75; Head of Optical and Ultraviolet Astronomy Res. Group, 1969–81; Reader in Physics, 1975–78; SRC Sen. Fellow, 1976–81; Prof. of Physics, 1978–81. Sherman Fairchild Dist. Schol., CIT, 1981–82; Visiting Professor: Dept of Physics and Astronomy, UCL, 1981–; Astronomy Centre, Univ. of Sussex, 1981–89; Hon. Prof. of Experimental Astronomy, Univ. of Cambridge, 1991–. Pres., West London Astronomical Soc., 1978–; Mem. and Pres., Internat. Scientific Cttee, Canary Is Observatories, 1981–; Mem., Anglo-Australian Telescope Bd, 1989–. Mem., Academia Europaea, 1989. Fellow, UCL, 1991. FRAS 1965; FRSA 1984. Freeman, 1984, Liveryman, 1989, Clockmakers' Co. Asteroid (3205) Boksenberg, named 1988. Dr *hc*, l'Observatoire de Paris, 1982; Hon. DSc Sussex, 1991. *Publications:* (ed jtly) Modern Technology and its Influence on Astronomy, 1990; contrib. learned jls. *Recreation:* ski-ing. *Address:* Royal Greenwich Observatory, Madingley Road, Cambridge CB3 0EZ. *T:* Cambridge (0223) 374886. *Club:* Athenæum.

BOLAM, James; actor; *b* Sunderland, 16 June 1938; *s* of Robert Alfred Bolam and Marion Alice Bolam (*née* Drury). *Educ:* Bede Grammar Sch., Sunderland; Bemrose Sch., Derby. First stage appearance, The Kitchen, Royal Court, 1959; later plays include: Events While Guarding the Bofors Gun, Hampstead, 1966; In Celebration, Royal Court, 1969; Veterans, Royal Court, 1972; Treats, Royal Court, 1976; Who Killed 'Agatha' Christie?, Ambassadors, 1978; King Lear (title rôle), Young Vic, 1981; Run for Your Wife!, Criterion, 1983; Arms and the Man, Cambridge; Who's Afraid of Virginia Woolf?, Birmingham, 1989; Victory, Chichester, 1989; Jeffrey Bernard is Unwell, Apollo, 1990. *Films:* Straight on till Morning, Crucible of Terror, Otley, A Kind of Loving, Half a Sixpence, Murder Most Foul, The Likely Lads, In Celebration, Whatever Happened to the Likely Lads?, The Great Question. *Television series:* The Likely Lads; Whatever Happened to the Likely Lads?; When the Boat Comes In; The Limbo Connection (Armchair Thriller Series); Only When I Laugh; The Beiderbecke Affair; Room at the Bottom; Andy Capp; The Beiderbecke Tapes; The Beiderbecke Connection; also As You Like It, Macbeth, in BBC Shakespeare. *Address:* c/o Barry Burnett Organisation Ltd, Suite 42–43, Grafton House, 2–3 Golden Square, W1.

BOLAND, John Anthony; Public Trustee and Accountant General, 1987–91 (Public Trustee, 1980–87); *b* 23 Jan. 1931; *s* of late Daniel Boland, MBE, and Hannah Boland (*née* Barton), Dublin; *m* 1972, Ann, *d* of James C. Doyle and Maureen Doyle. *Educ:* Castleknock Coll.; Xavier Sch.; Christian Brothers, Synge Street; Trinity Coll., Dublin (MA, LLB). Called to the Bar, Middle Temple, 1956; called to Irish Bar, 1967. Joined Public Trustee Office, 1956; Chief Administrative Officer, 1974–79; Asst Public Trustee, 1979–80. Hon. Member, College Historical Soc., TCD; Trustee of Trinity College Dublin (Univ. of Dublin) Trust. Asst Editor, The Supreme Court Practice, 1984–91. *Recreations:* walking, foreign travel, trying to catch up on life. *Address:* c/o Lloyds Bank, 67 Kingsway, WC2B 6SX. *Club:* Kildare Street and University (Dublin).

BOLEAT, Mark John; Director-General, The Building Societies Association, since 1987; *b* 21 Jan. 1949; *s* of Paul Boleat and Peggy Boleat (*née* Still). *Educ:* Victoria College, Jersey; Lanchester Polytechnic and Univ. of Reading (BA Econ, MA Contemp. European Studies). FCBSI. Asst Master, Dulwich College, 1972; Economist, Indust. Policy Group, 1973; The Building Societies Association: Asst Sec., 1974; Under Sec., 1976; Dep. Sec., 1979; Dep. Sec.-Gen., 1981; Sec.-Gen., 1986. Sec.-Gen., Internat. Union of Housing Finance Instns (formerly Internat. Union of Building Socs and Savings Assocs), 1986–89; Mem. Bd, Housing Corp., 1988–; Chm., Circle 33 Housing Trust, 1990–. Chm. Governors, Eastbury Farm Sch., 1989–. *Publications:* The Building Society Industry, 1982; National Housing Finance Systems: a comparative study, 1985; Housing in Britain, 1986; (with Adrian Coles) The Mortgage Market, 1987; Building Societies: the regulatory framework, 1988; articles on housing and housing finance. *Recreations:* reading, writing, squash, golf. *Address:* 26 Westbury Road, Northwood, Mddx HA6 3BU. *T:* Northwood (09274) 23684. *Club:* Carlton.

BOLES, Sir Jeremy John Fortescue, 3rd Bt, *cr* 1922; *b* 9 Jan. 1932; *s* of Sir Gerald Fortescue Boles, 2nd Bt, and Violet Blanche (*d* 1974), *er d* of late Major Hall Parlby, Manadon, Crown Hill, S Devon; *S* father 1945; *m* 1st, 1955, Dorothy Jane (marr. diss. 1970), *yr d* of James Alexander Worswick; two *s* one *d*; 2nd, 1970, Elisabeth Gildroy, *yr d* of Edward Phillip Shaw; one *d*; 3rd, 1982, Marigold Aspey (*née* Seckington). *Heir: s* Richard Fortescue Boles, *b* 12 Dec. 1958.

BOLES, Sir John Dennis, (Sir Jack), Kt 1983; MBE 1960; DL; Director General of the National Trust, 1975–83; *b* 25 June 1925; *s* of late Comdr Geoffrey Coleridge Boles and Hilda Frances (*née* Crofton); *m* 1st, 1953, Benita (*née* Wormald) (*d* 1969); two *s* three *d*; 2nd, 1971, Lady Anne Hermione, *d* of 12th Earl Waldegrave, *qv*. *Educ:* Winchester Coll. Rifle Brigade, 1943–46. Colonial Administrative Service (later Overseas Civil Service), North Borneo (now Sabah), 1948–64; Asst Sec., National Trust, 1965, Sec., 1968; Mem., Devon and Cornwall Regl Cttee, Nat. Trust, 1985–. Dir, SW Region Bd, Lloyds Bank plc, 1984–91. Trustee, Ernest Cook Trust. DL Devon, 1991. *Address:* Rydon House, Talaton, near Exeter, Devon EX5 2RP. *Club:* Army and Navy.

BOLGER, Hon. James B., (Hon. Jim Bolger); Prime Minister of New Zealand, since 1990; MP (Nat. Party) King Country, since 1972; Leader of National Party, New Zealand, since 1986; *b* 1935; *m* Joan Bolger; nine *c*. Sheep and cattle farmer, Te Kuiti. Parly Under-Sec., Min. of Agric. and Fisheries, Min. of Maori Affairs and Min. of Rural Banking and Finance, 1975; Minister of Fisheries and Associate Minister of Agric., 1977; Minister of Labour, 1978–84; Minister of Immigration, 1978–81; Leader of the Opposition, 1986–90. Pres., ILO, 1983. *Recreations:* fishing, reading. *Address:* Parliament Buildings, Wellington, New Zealand.

BOLINGBROKE, 7th Viscount *cr* 1712, **AND ST JOHN,** 8th Viscount *cr* 1716; **Kenneth Oliver Musgrave St John;** Bt 1611; Baron St John of Lydiard Tregoze, 1712; Baron St John of Battersea, 1716; *b* 22 March 1927; *s* of Geoffrey Robert St John, MC (*d* 1972) and Katherine Mary (*d* 1958), *d* of late A. S. J. Musgrave; *S* cousin, 1974; *m* 1st, 1953, Patricia Mary McKenna (marr. diss. 1972); one *s*; 2nd, 1972, Jainey Anne McRae (marr. diss. 1987); two *s*. *Educ:* Eton; Geneva Univ. Chairman, A&P Gp of Cos, 1958–75; Director: Shaw Savill Holidays Pty Ltd; Bolingbroke and Partners Ltd; Wata Investment Inc., Panama. Pres., Travel Agents Assoc. of NZ, 1966–68; Dir, World Assoc. of Travel Agencies, 1966–75; Chm., Aust. Council of Tour Wholesalers, 1972–75. Fellow, Aust. Inst. of Travel; Mem., NZ Inst. of Travel. *Recreations:* golf, cricket, tennis, history. *Heir: s* Hon. Henry Fitzroy St John, *b* 18 May 1957. *Address:* 15 Tonbridge Mews, Shrewsbury Street, Merivale, Christchurch, New Zealand. *Club:* Christchurch (Christchurch, NZ).

BOLLAND, (David) Michael; Managing Director, Channel X Ltd, since 1990; Project Director, Channel X Broadcasting (Scotland) Ltd, 1991; *b* 27 Feb. 1947; *s* of Allan Bolland and Eileen Lindsay; *m* 1987, Katie Lander; one *s*, one *d*, and one *s* two *d* by former marrs. *Educ:* Hillhead High School, Glasgow. Film editor, BBC Scotland, 1965–73; TV Producer, BBC TV, 1973–81; Channel Four Television: Commissioning Editor, Youth, 1981–83; Senior Commissioning Editor, Entertainment, 1983–87; Asst Dir of Programmes, and Head of Art and Entertainment Gp, 1987–88; Controller Arts and Entertainment, and Dep. Dir of Progs, 1988–90; Man. Dir, Initial Films and Television, 1990. Chm., Edinburgh Internat. TV Fest., 1990. Member: RTS; BAFTA. *Recreation:* catching up with the world. *Address:* 2c Belsize Park Gardens, NW3 4LD. *T:* 071–586 9518.

BOLLAND, Sir Edwin, KCMG 1981 (CMG 1971); HM Diplomatic Service, retired; Ambassador to Yugoslavia, 1980–82; *b* 20 Oct. 1922; *m* 1948, Winifred Mellor; one *s* three *d* (and one *s* decd). *Educ:* Morley Grammar Sch.; University Coll., Oxford. Served in Armed Forces, 1942–45. Foreign Office, 1947; Head of Far Eastern Dept, FO, 1965–67; Counsellor, Washington, 1967–71; St Antony's Coll., Oxford, 1971–72; Ambassador to Bulgaria, 1973–76; Head of British delegn to Negotiations on MBFR, 1976–80. *Recreations:* walking, gardening. *Address:* Lord's Spring Cottage, Godden Green, Sevenoaks, Kent TN15 0JS. *T:* Sevenoaks (0732) 61105.

BOLLAND, Group Captain Guy Alfred, CBE 1943; Chief Intelligence Officer, BJSM (AFS), Washington, USA, 1956–59, retired; *b* 5 Nov. 1909; 3rd *s* of late Capt. L. W. Bolland; *m* 1935, Sylvia Marguerite, 2nd *d* of late Oswald Duke, Cambridge; one *s* three *d*. *Educ:* Gilbert Hannam Sch., Sussex. Commissioned RAF, 1930. Served in Iraq and Home Squadrons. Served War of 1939–45: commanded 217 Squadron during attacks on French ports, 1940; North African Operations, 1943 (despatches, CBE). *Recreation:* golf. *Address:* The Oaks, Shaftesbury Road, Woking, Surrey GU22 7DU. *T:* Woking (0483) 760548.

BOLLAND, John; His Honour Judge Bolland; a Circuit Judge since 1974; *b* 30 March 1920; *s* of late Dominic Gerald Bolland and Gladys Bolland; *m* 1947, Audrey Jean Toyne (*née* Pearson) (*d* 1989); one *s* one step *s* one step *d*. *Educ:* Malvern Coll.; Trinity Hall, Cambridge (BA). Commnd Royal Warwicks Regt, 1939; 2nd Bn 6th Gurkha Rifles,

1941–46. Called to Bar, Middle Temple, 1948. *Recreations:* cricket, Rugby, golf, theatre. *Address:* 11 Firle Road, North Lancing, Sussex BN15 0NY. *T:* Lancing (0903) 755337.

BOLLAND, Michael; *see* Bolland, D. M.

BOLLERS, Hon. Sir Harold (Brodie Smith), Kt 1969; CCH 1982; Chairman, Elections Commission, since 1982; Chief Justice of Guyana, 1966–80; *b* 5 Feb. 1915; *s* of late John Bollers; *m* 1st, 1951, Irene Mahadeo (*d* 1965); two *s* one *d*; 2nd, 1968, Eileen Hanoman; one *s*. *Educ:* Queen's Coll., Guyana; King's Coll., London; Middle Temple. Called to the Bar, Feb. 1938; Magistrate, Guyana, 1946, Senior Magistrate, 1959; Puisne Judge, Guyana, 1960. *Recreations:* reading, walking. *Address:* 252 South Road, Bourda, Georgetown, Guyana.

BOLT, Rear-Adm. Arthur Seymour, CB 1958; DSO 1951; DSC 1940 and bar 1941; *b* 26 Nov. 1907; *s* of Charles W. Bolt, Alverstoke, Hants; *m* 1933, Evelyn Mary June, *d* of Robert Ellis, Wakefield, Yorks; four *d*. *Educ:* Nautical Coll., Pangbourne; RN Coll. Dartmouth. Joined RN, 1923. Served War of 1939–45; HMS Glorious and Warspite (DSC and Bar), and at Admiralty. Capt. HMS Theseus (Korea), 1949–51; Dir Naval Air Warfare, Admty, 1951–53; Chief of Staff to Flag Officer Air (Home), 1954–56; Dep. Controller of Military Aircraft, Min. of Supply, 1957–60; retd. Capt. 1947; Rear-Adm. 1956. *Recreations:* tennis, squash, sailing. *Address:* 12 Mount Boone Way, Dartmouth, Devon TQ6 6PL. *T:* Dartmouth (08043) 3448. *Clubs:* Royal Naval and Royal Albert Yacht (Portsmouth); Royal Naval Sailing Association; Dartmouth Yacht.

BOLT, David Ernest, CBE 1984; FRCS; President, British Medical Association, 1987–88; *b* 21 Sept. 1921; *s* of Rev. E. A. J. Bolt and Hilda I. Bolt; *m* 1955, Phyllis Margaret, (Peggy), Fudge; two *d*. *Educ:* Queen Elizabeth's Hosp., Bristol; Univ. of Bristol. MB ChB 1945; FRCS 1950. Senior Surgical Registrar, W Middx Hosp. and St Mary's Hosp., Paddington, 1955–60; Consultant Surgeon, W Middx Hosp., 1960–82; Hon. Lectr, Charing Cross Hosp., 1972–82. British Medical Association: Mem., Central Cttee for Hosp. Med. Service (Dep. Chm., 1975–79; Chm., 1979–83); Dep. Chm.; Jt Consultants' Cttee, 1979–83; Mem. Council, 1975–83. Mem., GMC, 1979–89 (Chm., Professional Conduct Cttee). *Publications:* articles on surgical subjects in professional jls. *Recreations:* motor boat cruising, tree planting, reading, walking. *Address:* Feniton House, Feniton, Honiton, Devon EX14 0BE. *T:* Honiton (0404) 850921. *Clubs:* Athenæum, Royal Society of Medicine.

BOLT, Air Marshal Sir Richard (Bruce), KBE 1979 (CBE 1973); CB 1977; DFC 1945; AFC 1959; Chairman, Pacific Aerospace Corp. of New Zealand, since 1982; *b* 16 July 1923; *s* of George Bruce Bolt and Mary (*née* Best); *m* 1st, 1946, June Catherine South (*d* 1984); one *s* one *d*; 2nd, 1987, Janice Caroline Tucker. *Educ:* Nelson Coll., NZ. Began service with RNZAF in mid 1942; served during 2nd World War in RAF Bomber Command (Pathfinder Force); Chief of Air Staff, NZ, 1974–76; Chief of Defence Staff, NZ, 1976–80. *Recreations:* fly fishing, golf, horse racing. *Address:* 14b Nikau Grove, Lower Hutt, Wellington, NZ. *Club:* Wellington (Wellington, NZ).

BOLT, Robert Oxton, CBE 1972; playwright; *b* 15 Aug. 1924; *s* of Ralph Bolt and Leah Binnion; *m* 1st, 1949, Celia Ann Roberts (marr. diss., 1967); one *s* two *d*; 2nd, 1967, Sarah Miles (marr. diss. 1976); one *s*; 3rd, 1980, Ann Zane (marr. diss. 1985); remarried, 1988, Sarah Miles. *Educ:* Manchester Grammar Sch. Left sch., 1941; Sun Life Assurance Office, Manchester, 1942; Manchester Univ., 1943; RAF and Army, 1943–46; Manchester Univ., 1946–49; Exeter Univ., 1949–50; teaching, 1950–58; English teacher, Millfield Sch., 1952–58. Hon. LLD Exeter, 1977. *Plays:* The Critic and the Heart, Oxford Playhouse, 1957; Flowering Cherry, Haymarket, 1958; A Man for All Seasons, Globe, 1960 (filmed 1967); The Tiger and The Horse, Queen's, 1960; Gentle Jack, Queen's, 1963; The Thwarting of Baron Bolligrew, 1966; Vivat! Vivat Regina!, Piccadilly, 1970; State of Revolution, Nat. Theatre, 1977; *screenplays:* Lawrence of Arabia, 1962; Dr Zhivago, 1965 (Academy Award); Man for all Seasons, 1967 (Academy Award); Ryan's Daughter, 1970; Lady Caroline Lamb, 1972 (also dir.); The Bounty, 1984; The Mission, 1986; TV and radio plays. *Address:* c/o Margaret Ramsay Ltd, 14a Goodwins Court, St Martin's Lane, WC2. *Club:* The Spares (Somerset) (Hon. Life Mem.).

BOLTON, 7th Baron, *cr* 1797; **Richard William Algar Orde-Powlett;** *b* 11 July 1929; *s* of 6th Baron Bolton; *S* father, 1963; *m* 1st, 1951, Hon. Christine Helena Weld Forester (marr. diss.), *e d* of 7th Baron Forester, and of Marie Louise Priscilla, CStJ, *d* of Sir Herbert Perrott, 6th Bt, CH, CB; two *s* one *d*; 2nd, 1981, Masha Anne, *d* of Major F. E. Hudson, Winterfield House, Hornby, Bedale, Yorks; *m* 1991, Mrs Lavinia Fenton. *Educ:* Eton; Trinity Coll., Cambridge (BA). Chairman, Richmond Div., Conservative Assoc., 1957–60; Chairman Yorkshire Div., Royal Forestry Soc., 1962–64; Member Council, Timber Growers' Organization. Director: Yorkshire Insurance Co., 1964–70; General Accident Life Assurance Ltd, 1970–. JP, North Riding of Yorkshire, 1957–80. FRICS. *Recreations:* shooting, fishing. *Heir: s* Hon. Harry Algar Nigel Orde-Powlett [*b* 14 Feb. 1954; *m* 1977, Philippa, *d* of Major P. L. Tapply; three *s*]. *Address:* Park House, Wensley, Leyburn, North Yorkshire. *T:* Wensleydale (0969) 22464. *Clubs:* White's; Central African Deep Sea Fishing.

BOLTON, Bishop Suffragan of, since 1991; **Rt. Rev. David Bonser;** *b* 1 Feb. 1934; *s* of George Frederick and Alice Bonser; *m* 1960, Shirley Wilkinson; one *s* two *d*. *Educ:* Hillhouse Secondary Sch., Huddersfield; King's Coll., London Univ. (AKC); Manchester Univ. (MA). Curate: St James's, Heckmondwike, 1962–65; St George's, Sheffield, 1965–68; Rector of St Clement's, Chorlton-cum-Hardy, 1968–82; Hon. Canon of Manchester Cathedral, 1980–82; Area Dean of Hulme, 1981–82; Archdeacon of Rochdale, 1982–91; Team Rector, Rochdale Team Ministry, 1982–91 (Vicar of St Chad's, 1982–86). *Recreations:* theatre, reading, walking, skiing, music. *Address:* 4 Sandfield Drive, Lostock, Bolton, Lancs BL6 4DU. *T:* Bolton (0204) 43400. *Club:* Commonwealth Trust.

BOLTON, Archdeacon of; *no new appointment at time of going to press.*

BOLTON, Group Captain David; Director, Royal United Services Institute for Defence Studies, since 1981; *b* 15 April 1932; *o s* of late George Edward and Florence May Bolton; *m* 1955, Betty Patricia Simmonds; three *d*. *Educ:* Bede Grammar Sch., Sunderland. Entered RAF as National Serviceman; commnd RAF Regt, 1953; subsequent service in Egypt, Jordan, Singapore, Aden, Cyprus, Malta and Germany; RAF Staff Coll., 1969; National Def. Coll., 1972; Central Planning Staff, MoD, 1973–75; OC 33 Wing RAF Regt, 1975–77; Comdt RAF Regt Depot, Catterick, 1977–80; retd 1980; Dep. Dir and Dir of Studies, RUSI, 1980–81. Member: RUSI Council, 1973–79; IISS, 1964–; RIIA, 1975–; Council, British Atlantic Cttee, 1981–. Hon. Steward, Westminster Abbey, 1981–. Mem. Editl Bd, Brassey's Yearbook, 1982–; Gen. Editor, RUSI-Macmillan Defence Studies, 1983–. Trench Gascoigne Essay Prize, RUSI, 1972. *Publications:* contrib. learned jls. *Recreations:* music, theatre, jogging, work. *Address:* Royal United Services Institute for Defence Studies, Whitehall, SW1A 2ET. *T:* 071–930 5854. *Club:* Royal Air Force.

BOLTON, Eric James, CB 1987; Senior Chief Inspector of Schools, Department of Education and Science, 1983–91; *b* 11 Jan. 1935; *s* of late James and Lilian Bolton; *m* 1960, Ann Gregory; one *s* twin *d*. *Educ:* Wigan Grammar Sch.; Chester Coll.; Lancaster Univ. MA. English teacher at secondary schs, 1957–68; Lectr, Chorley Teacher Training Coll., 1968–70; Inspector of Schs, Croydon, 1970–73; HM Inspector of Schs, 1973–79; Staff Inspector (Educnl Disadvantage), 1979–81; Chief Inspector of Schools, DES, 1981–83. *Publications:* Verse Writing in Schools, 1964; various articles in educnl jls. *Recreations:* reading, music and opera, fly fishing.

BOLTON, Sir Frederic (Bernard), Kt 1976; MC; FIMarE; Chairman: The Bolton Group, since 1953; Dover Harbour Board, 1983–88 (Member, 1957–62 and 1980–88); *b* 9 March 1921; *s* of late Louis Hamilton Bolton and late Beryl Dyer; *m* 1st, 1950, Valerie Margaret Barwick (*d* 1970); two *s*; 2nd, 1971, Vanessa Mary Anne Robarts; two *s* two *d*. *Educ:* Rugby. Served War, with Welsh Guards, 1940–46 (MC 1945, Italy); Northants Yeomanry, 1952–56. Member: Lloyd's, 1945–; Baltic Exchange, 1946–. Chm., Atlantic Steam Nav. Co. & Subs, 1960–71; Dir, B.P. Tanker Co., 1968–82; Mem., Brit. Rail Shipping & Int. Services Bd, 1970–82 (now Sealink UK Ltd). Pres., Chamber of Shipping of UK, 1966; Mem., Lloyd's Register of Shipping Gen. Cttee, 1961–86; Chairman: Ship & Marine Technol. Requirements Bd, 1977–81; British Ports Assoc., 1985–88; Member: PLA, 1964–71; Nat. Ports Council, 1967–74; President: Inst. of Marine Engineers, 1968–69 and 1969–70; British Shipping Fedn, 1972–75; Internat. Shipping Fedn, 1973–82; Gen. Council of British Shipping, 1975–76; British Maritime League, 1985–. Hon. FNI. Grafton Hunt: Jt Master, 1956–67, Chm., 1967–72. *Recreations:* country sports. *Address:* Pudlicote, near Charlbury, Oxon OX7 3HX. *Clubs:* City of London, Cavalry and Guards.

BOLTON, Prof. Geoffrey Curgenven, DPhil; Professor of Australian History, University of Queensland, since 1989; *b* 5 Nov. 1931; *s* of Frank and Winifred Bolton, Perth, W Australia; *m* 1958, (Ann) Carol Grattan; two *s*. *Educ:* North Perth State Sch.; Wesley Coll., Perth; Univ. of Western Australia; Balliol Coll., Oxford, (DPhil). FRHistS 1967; FAHA 1974; FASSA 1976. Res. Fellow, ANU, 1957–62; Sen. Lectr, Monash Univ., 1962–65; Prof. of Modern Hist., Univ. of Western Australia, 1966–73; Prof. of History, 1973–82 and 1985–89, and Pro-Vice-Chancellor, 1973–76, Murdoch Univ.; Prof. of Australian Studies, Univ. of London, 1982–85. Mem. Council, Australian Nat. Maritime Museum, Sydney, 1985–91. Deleg., Constitutional Convention, Sydney, 1991–. FRSA. General Editor, Oxford History of Australia, 1987–91. *Publications:* Alexander Forrest, 1958; A Thousand Miles Away, 1963; The Passing of the Irish Act of Union, 1966; Dick Boyer, 1967; A Fine Country to Starve In, 1972; Spoils and Spoilers: Australians Make Their Environment, 1981; Oxford History of Australia, vol. 5, 1990; articles in learned jls. *Recreation:* sleep. *Address:* Department of History, University of Queensland, St Lucia, Qld 4072, Australia. *Clubs:* Athenæum; Queensland Cricketers.

BOLTON, John Eveleigh, CBE 1972; DSC 1945; DL; Chairman and Managing Director, Growth Capital Ltd, since 1968; Chairman: Hall Bolton Estates Ltd; Atesmo Ltd; Riverview Investments Ltd; *b* 17 Oct. 1920; *s* of late Ernest and Edith Mary Bolton; *m* 1948, Gabrielle Healey Hall (*d* 1989), *d* of late Joseph and Minnie Hall; one *s* one *d*. *Educ:* Ilkley Sch.; Wolverhampton Sch.; Trinity Coll., Cambridge (Cassel Travelling Schol., 1948; BA Hons Econs 1948, MA 1953); Harvard Business School (Baker Schol., 1949; MBA with dist., 1950). Articled pupil to Chartered Acct, 1937–40; intermed. exam. of Inst. of Chartered Accts, 1940. Served War of 1939–45 (DSC): Destroyers, Lt RNVR, 1940–46. Research for Harvard in British Industry, 1950–51; Finance Dir, Solartron Laboratory Instruments Ltd, Kingston-upon-Thames, 1951–53 (Chm., 1953); Chm. and Man. Dir: Solartron Engineering Ltd, 1952; The Solartron Electronic Group Ltd, Thames Ditton and subseq. Farnborough, Hants, 1954–63 (Dep. Chm., 1963–65). Director: NCR Co. Ltd; Alphameric PLC; Black & Decker Group Inc.; Black & Decker Holdings Inc.; Black & Decker Investment Co.; Black & Decker Corp.; Plasmec PLC; Dawson International plc; Johnson Wax Ltd; Redland plc; Hoskyns plc; Business Advisers Ltd; Camperdowne Investment Holdings Ltd; Pres., Develt Capital Gp Ltd, 1984–88. A Gen. Comr of Income Tax, 1964–. British Institute of Management: Chm. Council, 1964–66; Bowie Medal 1969; CBIM; Life Vice-Pres.; Pres., Engrg Industries Assoc., 1981–84; Chm. and Founder Subscriber: Advanced Management Programmes Internat. Trust; Foundn for Management Educn; Business Grads Assoc.; Dir, Management Publications Ltd, 1966–73 (Chm., 1969); Mem. Exec. Cttee, AA; Hon. Treasurer, Surrey Univ., 1975–82 (Past Chm.); Member: Sub-Cttee on Business Management Studies, UGC; Council of Industry for Management Educn; Harvard Business Sch. Vis. Cttee, 1962–75; Adv. Cttee on Industry, Cttee of Vice-Chancellors, 1984–; Business Educn Forum, 1969–74. Mem. Org. Cttee, World Research Hospital. Member: UK Automation Council, 1964–65; Adv. Cttee for Management Efficiency in NHS, 1964–65; Cttee for Exports to New Zealand, 1965–68; Adv. Cttee, Queen's Award to Industry, 1972–; Council, Inst. of Dirs; Chm., Economic Develt Cttee for the Rubber Industry, 1965–68; Vice-Chm., Royal Commn on Local Govt in England, 1966–69; Chm., Committee of Inquiry on Small Firms, 1969–71. Trustee, Small Business Research Trust. Life FRSA. DL Surrey, 1974; High Sheriff of Surrey, 1980–81. DUniv Surrey, 1982; Hon. DSc Bath, 1986. *Publications:* articles in newspapers and journals; various radio and TV broadcasts on industrial topics. *Recreations:* shooting, swimming, gardening, opera, antiques. *Address:* Sunnymead, Tite Hill, Englefield Green, Surrey TW20 0NH. *T:* Egham (0784) 35172. *Clubs:* Harvard Club of London, Institute of Directors.

BOMBAY, Archbishop of, (RC), since 1978; **His Eminence Simon Ignatius Cardinal Pimenta;** *b* 1 March 1920; *s* of late Joseph Anthony Pimenta and Rosie E. Pimenta. *Educ:* St Xavier's Coll., Bombay (BA with Maths); Propaganda Univ., Rome (Degree in Canon Law). Secretary at Archbishop's House, Bombay, 1954; also Vice-Chancellor and Defensor Vinculi; Vice Rector of Cathedral, 1960; Visiting Prof. of Liturgy, Bombay Seminary, 1960–65; Rector of Cathedral and Episcopal Vicar for Liturgy and Pastoral Formation of Junior Clergy, 1967; Rector of Seminary, 1971; Auxiliary Bishop, 1971; Coadjutor Archbishop with right of succession, 1977. Pres., Catholic Bishops' Conf. of India, 1982–88. Cardinal, 1988. *Publications:* (edited) The Catholic Directory of Bombay, 1960 and 1964 edns; Circulars and Officials of the Archdiocese of Bombay, 3 vols; booklet on the Cathedral of the Holy Name. *Address:* Archbishop's House, 21 Nathalal Parekh Marg, Bombay 400 039, India. *T:* 2021093, 2021193, 2021293.

BOMFORD, Nicholas Raymond, MA; Head Master of Harrow, since 1991; *b* 27 Jan. 1939; *s* of late Ernest Raymond Bomford and of Patricia Clive Bomford (*née* Brooke), JP; *m* 1966, Gillian Mary Reynolds; two *d*. *Educ:* Kelly Coll.; Trinity Coll., Oxford (MA, Mod. History). Teaching appts, 1960–64; Lectr in History and Contemp. Affairs, BRNC, Dartmouth, 1964–66, Sen. Lectr, 1966–68; Wellington Coll., 1968–76 (Housemaster, 1973–76); Headmaster: Monmouth Sch., 1977–82; Uppingham Sch., 1982–91. Chm., Jt Standing Cttee, HMC/IAPS, 1986–89; Nat. Rep., HMC Cttee, 1990–. Mem. Navy Records Soc. (Councillor, 1967–70, 1973–76, 1984–88). FRSA 1989. *Publications:* Documents in World History, 1914–70, 1973; (contrib.) Dictionary of World History, 1973. *Recreations:* shooting (Captain OURC, 1959–60; England VIII (Elcho match), 1960), fishing, gardening, music, enjoying Welsh border country and Southern France. *Address:* Harrow School, Harrow-on-the-Hill, Middlesex HA1 3HW.

BOMPAS, Donald George, CMG 1966; Managing Executive, Philip and Pauline Harris Charitable Trust, since 1986; *b* 20 Nov. 1920; *yr s* of Rev. E. Anstie Bompas; *m* 1946,

Freda Vice, *y d* of F. M. Smithyman, Malawi; one *s* one *d*. *Educ*: Merchant Taylors' Sch., Northwood; Oriel Coll. Oxford. MA Oxon, 1947. Overseas Audit Service, 1942–66, retired; Nyasaland, 1942–47; Singapore, 1947–48; Malaya (now Malaysia), 1948–66; Deputy Auditor-General, 1957–60; Auditor-General, Malaysia (formerly Malaya), 1960–66. Dep. Sec., Guy's Hosp. Med. and Dental Schools, 1966–69, Sec., 1969–82; Dep. Sec., 1982–83, Sec., 1984–86, UMDS of Guy's and St Thomas's Hosps. Chm., Univ. of London Purchasing Gp, 1976–82. Mem. Exec., Federated Pension Schemes, 1979–86. Liveryman, Merchant Taylors' Co., 1951. JMN (Hon.) Malaya, 1961. *Address*: 8 Birchwood Road, Petts Wood, Kent BR5 1NY. *T*: Orpington (0689) 821661. *Club*: Commonwealth Trust.

BON, Christoph Rudolf; Partner, Chamberlin Powell & Bon, since 1952; *b* 1 Sept. 1921; *s* of Rudolf Bon and Nelly Fischbacher. *Educ*: Cantonal Gymnasium, Zürich; Swiss Federal Inst. of Technology, Zürich (DipArch ETH 1946). Prof. Holford's Office—Master Plan for City of London, 1946; Studio BBPR, Milan, 1949–50; teaching at Kingston Sch. of Art, 1950–52; Founder Partner, Chamberlin Powell & Bon, 1952. Work includes: Golden Lane Estate; Expansion of Leeds Univ.; schools, housing and commercial buildings; New Hall, Cambridge; Barbican. *Address*: 60 South Edwardes Square, W8 6HL. *T*: 071–602 6462.

BONALLACK, Michael Francis, OBE 1971; Secretary, Royal and Ancient Golf Club of St Andrews, since 1983; *b* 31 Dec. 1934; *s* of Sir Richard (Frank) Bonallack, *qv*; *m* 1958, Angela Ward; one *s* three *d*. *Educ*: Chigwell; Haileybury. National Service, 1953–55 (1st Lieut, RASC). Joined family business, Bonallack and Sons Ltd, later Freight Bonallack Ltd, 1955; Director, 1962–74; Dir, Buckley Investments, 1976–84. Chairman: Golf Foundn, 1977–83; Professional Golfers' Assoc., 1976–82; Pres., English Golf Union, 1982. *Recreation*: golf (British Amateur Champion, 1961, 1965, 1968, 1969, 1970; English Amateur Champion, 1962–63, 1965–67 and 1968; Captain, British Walker Cup Team, 1971; Bobby Jones Award for distinguished sportsmanship in golf, 1972). *Address*: Clatto Lodge, Blebo Craigs, Cupar, Fife. *T*: Strathkinness (033485) 600. *Clubs*: Chantilly (France); Pine Valley (USA); and 20 others.

BONALLACK, Sir Richard (Frank), Kt 1963; CBE 1955 (OBE (mil.) 1945); MIMechE; *b* 2 June 1904; *s* of Francis and Ada Bonallack; *m* 1930, Winifred Evelyn Mary Esplen (*d* 1986); two *s* one *d*. *Educ*: Haileybury. War service in TA, 1939–45; transferred to TA Reserve, 1946, with rank of Colonel. Bonallack and Sons Ltd, subseq. Freight Bonallack Ltd: Chm., 1953–74; Dir, 1971–87; Pres., 1974–87; Dir, Alcan Transport Products, 1979–85. Chm., Freight Container Section, SMMT, 1967–83; Mem., Basildon Development Corporation, 1962–77. Chm., Working Party, Anglo-Soviet Cttee for Jt Technical Collaboration, 1961–65. *Recreation*: golf. *Address*: 4 The Willows, Thorpe Bay, Southend on Sea, Essex SS1 3SH. *T*: Southend (0702) 588180.

See also M. F. Bonallack.

BONAR, Sir Herbert (Vernon), Kt 1967; CBE 1946; Chairman, 1949–74, and Managing Director, 1938–73, The Low & Bonar Group Ltd; retired 1974; *b* 26 Feb. 1907; *s* of George Bonar and Julia (*née* Seehusen); *m* 1935, Marjory (*née* East) (*d* 1990); two *s*. *Educ*: Fettes Coll.; Brasenose Coll., Oxford (BA). Joined Low & Bonar Ltd, 1929; Director, 1934; Managing Director, 1938; Chairman and Managing Director, 1949. Jute Control, 1939–46; Jute Controller, 1942–46. Trustee, WWF, UK, 1974–80 (Vice Pres. 1981). Hon. LLD: St Andrews, 1955; Birmingham, 1974; Dundee, 1985. Comdr, Order of the Golden Ark, Netherlands, 1974. *Recreations*: golf, fishing, photography, wild life preservation. *Address*: St Kitts, 24A Albany Road, Broughty Ferry, Dundee, Angus DD5 1NT. *T*: Dundee (0382) 79947. *Clubs*: Blairgowrie Golf; Panmure Golf.

BOND, Alan, AO 1984; Chairman, Dallhold Investments Pty Ltd, since 1987; *b* 22 April 1938; *s* of Frank and Kathleen Bond; *m* 1956, Eileen Teresa Hughes; two *s* two *d*. *Educ*: Perivale Sch., Ealing, UK; Fremantle Boys' Sch., W Australia. Chairman, Bond Corporation Holdings Ltd, 1969–90 (interests in property, brewing, electronic media, oil and gas, minerals, airships); Chairman: North Kalgurli Mines Ltd, 1985–89; Gold Mines of Kalgoorlie Ltd, 1987–89; Director: Dallhold Nickel Management Pty; MEQ Nickel Pty; Mid-East Minerals Ltd; Metals Exploration Ltd; Bond University Ltd. Syndicate Head, America's Cup Challenge 1983 Ltd; Australia II Winners of 1983 America's Cup Challenge, following three previous attempts: 1974 Southern Cross, 1977 Australia, 1980 Australia. Australian of the Year, 1977. *Recreation*: yachting. *Address*: Dalkeith, Western Australia. *Clubs*: Royal Ocean Racing; Young Presidents Organisation, Royal Perth Yacht, Cruising Yacht, Claremont Yacht, Western Australian Turf (WA).

BOND, Rt. Rev. (Charles) Derek; see Bradwell, Area Bishop of.

BOND, Edward; playwright and director; *b* 18 July 1934; *m* 1971, Elisabeth Pablé. Northern Arts Literary Fellow, 1977–79. Hon. DLitt Yale, 1977. George Devine Award, 1968; John Whiting Award, 1968. *Opera Libretti*: We Come to the River (music by Hans Werner Henze), 1976; The English Cat (music by Hans Werner Henze), 1983; *ballet libretto*: Orpheus, 1982; *translations*: Chekhov, The Three Sisters, 1967; Wedekind, Spring Awakening, 1974. *Publications*: (plays): Saved, 1965; Narrow Road to the Deep North, 1968; Early Morning, 1968; The Pope's Wedding, 1971; Passion, 1971; Black Mass, 1971; Lear, 1972; The Sea, 1973; Bingo, 1974; The Fool, 1976; A-A-merica! (Grandma Faust, and The Swing), 1976; Stone, 1976; The Woman, 1978; The Bundle, 1978; Theatre Poems and Songs, 1978; The Worlds and The Activist Papers, 1980; Restoration, 1981; Summer: a play for Europe, 1982; Derek, 1983; Human Cannon, 1984; The War Plays (part 1, Red Black and Ignorant; part 2, The Tin Can People; part 3, Great Peace), 1985; Jackets, 1989; The Company of Men, 1990; September, 1990; Olly's Prison (TV), 1990; Collected Poems 1978–1985, 1987; Notes of Post-Modernism, 1990. *Recreation*: the study of physics, because in physics the problems of human motives do not have to be considered (for the benefit of newspaper reporters: this is a joke, as anyone who had attended a rehearsal with actors would know). *Address*: c/o Margaret Ramsay, 14A Goodwins Court, St Martin's Lane, WC2N 4LL.

BOND, Godfrey William; Public Orator, Oxford University, since 1980; Senior Fellow, Pembroke College, and Dean, since 1979; *b* 24 July 1925; *o s* of William Niblock Bond, MC of Newry and Janet Bond (*née* Godfrey) of Dublin; *m* 1959, Alison, *d* of Mr Justice T. C. Kingsmill Moore, Dublin; one *s* two *d*. *Educ*: Campbell Coll.; Royal Belfast Acad. Inst.; Trinity Coll. Dublin (Scholar 1946; Berkeley Medal 1948; BA 1st Cl. Classics (gold medal); 1st Cl. Mental and Moral Sci. 1949); St John's Coll., Oxford (MA). Served War Office and Foreign Office (GCHQ), 1943–45; Fellow and Classical Tutor, Pembroke Coll., Oxford, 1950–; Senior Tutor, 1962–72; Oxford University: Lectr in Classics, 1952–; Senior Proctor, 1964–65; Gen. Bd of Faculties, 1970–76; Visitor, Ashmolean Museum, 1972–81. Mem., Inst. for Advanced Study, Princeton, 1969–70. *Publications*: editions of Euripides, Hypsipyle, 1963, Heracles, 1981; orations (mostly Latin) in OU Gazette, 1980–; memorial addresses, articles and reviews. *Recreations*: people and places in Greece, France and Ireland; opera, dining, swimming. *Address*: Masefield House, Boars Hill, Oxford OX1 5EY. *T*: Oxford (0865) 735373. *Clubs*: Athenæum; Kildare Street and University (Dublin).

BOND, Maj.-Gen. Henry Mark Garneys, JP; Vice Lord-Lieutenant of Dorset, since 1984; *b* 1 June 1922; *s* of W. R. G. Bond, Tyneham, Dorset; unmarried. *Educ*: Eton. Enlisted as Rifleman, 1940; commnd in Rifle Bde, 1941; served Middle East and Italy; seconded to Parachute Regt, 1947–50; ADC to Field Marshal Viscount Montgomery of Alamein, 1950–52; psc 1953; served in Kenya, Malaya, Cyprus and Borneo; Comd Rifle Bde in Cyprus and Borneo, 1964–66; Comd 12th Inf. Bde, 1967–68; idc 1969; Dir of Defence Operational Plans and Asst Chief of Defence Staff (Ops), 1970–72; retd 1972. Pres., Dorset Natural History and Archaeological Soc., 1972–75; Chairman: Dorset Br., CPRE, 1975–78; Dorset Community Council, 1978–81; Dorset Police Authy, 1980–. Mem., Dorset CC, 1973–85 (Vice-Chm., 1981–85). JP Dorset, 1972 (Chm., Wareham Bench, 1984–89). High Sheriff of Dorset, 1977, DL Dorset, 1977. Chm., Governors of Milton Abbey Sch., 1979–. *Recreations*: forestry, reading. *Address*: Moigne Combe, Dorchester, Dorset DT2 8JH. *T*: Warmwell (0305) 852265. *Club*: Boodle's.

BOND, Sir Kenneth (Raymond Boyden), Kt 1977; Vice-Chairman, The General Electric Company plc, 1985–90 (Financial Director, 1962–66; Deputy Managing Director, 1966–85), retired; *b* 1 Feb. 1920; *s* of late James Edwin and Gertrude Deplidge Bond; *m* 1958, Jennifer Margaret, *d* of late Sir Cecil and Lady Crabbe; three *s* three *d*. *Educ*: Selhurst Grammar School. Served TA, Europe and Middle East, 1939–46. FCA 1960 (Mem. 1949). Partner, Cooper & Cooper, Chartered Accountants, 1954–57; Dir, Radio & Allied Industries Ltd, 1957–62. Member: Industrial Develt Adv. Bd, 1972–77; Cttee to Review the Functioning of Financial Instns, 1977–80; Audit Commn, 1983–86; Civil Justice Rev. Adv. Cttee, 1985–88. *Recreation*: golf. *Address*: Woodstock, Wayside Gardens, Gerrards Cross, Bucks. *T*: Gerrards Cross (0753) 883513. *Club*: Addington Golf.

BOND, Michael; author; *b* 13 Jan. 1926; *s* of Norman Robert and Frances Mary Bond; *m* 1950, Brenda Mary Johnson (marr. diss. 1981); one *s* one *d*; *m* 1981, Susan Marfrey Rogers. *Educ*: Presentation College, Reading. RAF and Army, 1943–47; BBC Cameraman, 1947–66; full-time author from 1966. Paddington TV series, 1976. *Publications*: *for children*: A Bear Called Paddington, 1958; More About Paddington, 1959; Paddington Helps Out, 1960; Paddington Abroad, 1961; Paddington at Large, 1962; Paddington Marches On, 1964; Paddington at Work, 1966; Here Comes Thursday, 1966; Thursday Rides Again, 1968; Paddington Goes to Town, 1968; Thursday Ahoy, 1969; Parsley's Tail, 1969; Parsley's Good Deed, 1969; Parsley's Problem Present, 1970; Parsley's Last Stand, 1970; Paddington Takes the Air, 1970; Thursday in Paris, 1970; Michael Bond's Book of Bears, 1971; Michael Bond's Book of Mice, 1972; The Day the Animals Went on Strike, 1972; Paddington Bear, 1972; Paddington's Garden, 1972; Parsley the Lion, 1972; Parsley Parade, 1972; The Tales of Olga da Polga, 1972; Olga Meets her Match, 1973; Paddington's Blue Peter Story Book, 1973; Paddington at the Circus, 1973; Paddington Goes Shopping, 1973; Paddington at the Sea-side, 1974; Paddington at the Tower, 1974; Paddington on Top, 1974; Windmill, 1975; How to make Flying Things, 1975; Eight Olga Readers, 1975; Paddington's Loose End Book, 1976; Paddington's Party Book, 1976; Olga Carries On, 1976; Paddington's Pop-up Book, 1977; Paddington Takes the Test, 1979; Paddington's Cartoon Book, 1979; J. D. Polson and the Liberty-Head Dime, 1980; J. D. Polson and the Dillogate Affair, 1981; Paddington on Screen, 1981; Olga Takes Charge, 1982; The Caravan Puppets, 1983; Paddington at the Zoo, 1984; Paddington and the Knickerbocker Rainbow, 1984; Paddington's Painting Exhibition, 1985; Paddington at the Fair, 1985; Oliver the Greedy Elephant, 1985; Paddington at the Palace, 1986; Paddington Minds the House, 1986; Paddington's Busy Day, 1987; Paddington and the Marmalade Maze, 1987; Paddington's Magical Christmas, 1988; with Karen Bond: Paddington Posts a Letter, 1986; Paddington at the Airport, 1986; Paddington's London, 1986; *for adults*: Monsieur Pamplemousse, 1983; Monsieur Pamplemousse and the Secret Mission, 1984; Monsieur Pamplemousse on the Spot, 1986; Monsieur Pamplemousse Takes the Cure, 1987; The Pleasures of Paris, 1987; Monsieur Pamplemousse Aloft, 1989; Monsieur Pamplemousse Investigates, 1990; Monsieur Pamplemousse Rests His Case, 1991. *Recreations*: photography, travel, cars, wine. *Address*: 22 Maida Avenue, W2 1SR. *T*: 071–262 4280. *Club*: Wig and Pen.

BOND, Prof. Michael Richard, FRCPsych, FRCPGlas, FRCSE; Professor of Psychological Medicine, since 1973, Vice Principal, since 1986, Administrative Dean, Faculty of Medicine, since 1991, University of Glasgow; *b* 15 April 1936; *s* of Frederick Richard Bond and Dorothy Bond (*née* Gardner); *m* 1961, Jane Issitt; one *s* one *d*. *Educ*: Magnus Grammar Sch., Newark, Notts; Univ. of Sheffield (MD, PhD). Ho. Surg./Ho. Phys., Royal Inf., Sheffield, 1961–62; Asst Lectr/Res. Registrar, Univ. Dept of Surgery, Sheffield, 1962–64; Res. Registrar/Lectr, Univ. Dept of Psychiatry, Sheffield, 1964–67; Sen. Ho. Officer/Res. Registrar, Registrar/Sen. Registrar, Inst. of Neurological Scis, Glasgow, 1968–71; Lectr in Neurosurgery, Univ. Dept of Neurosurgery, Glasgow, 1971–73. Locum Cons. Neurosurgeon, Oxford, 1972; Hon. Cons. Psychiatrist, Greater Glasgow Health Bd, 1973–. Mem., UFC, 1991–. *Publications*: Pain, its nature, analysis and treatment, 1979, 2nd edn 1984; (co-ed) Rehabilitation of the Head Injured Adult, 1983, 2nd edn 1989; papers on psychological and social consequences of severe brain injury, psychological aspects of chronic pain and cancer pain, 1963–, and others on similar topics. *Recreations*: painting, collecting antique books, forest walking, ornithological preservation, gardening. *Address*: 33 Ralston Road, Bearsden, Glasgow G61 3BA. *T*: (home) 041–942 4391; (work) 041–334 9826. *Club*: Athenæum.

BOND-WILLIAMS, Noel Ignace, CBE 1979; Director, National Exhibition Centre Ltd, 1970–89; *b* 7 Nov. 1914; *s* of late W. H. Williams, Birmingham; *m* 1939, Mary Gwendoline Tomey (*d* 1989); one *s* two *d*. *Educ*: Oundle Sch.; Birmingham Univ. (BSc). FIM, FBIM. Pres. Guild of Undergrads 1936–37, Pres. Guild of Grads 1947, Birmingham Univ. Various appts in metal industry; Director: Enfield Rolling Mills Ltd, 1957–65; Delta Metal Co. Ltd, 1967–77; Vice-Chm., 1978–79, Chm., 1979–83, Remploy Ltd; Dir, 1972–85, and Vice-Chm., 1979–85, Lucas (Industries) Ltd. Industrial Adviser, DEA, 1965–67. Pres., Birmingham Chamber of Commerce, 1969. Member: Commn on Industrial Relations, 1971–74; Price Commn, 1977–79. Mem. Council, Industrial Soc., 1947–78; Pres., Brit. Non-ferrous Metals Fedn, 1974–75. Pro-Chancellor, Univ. of Aston in Birmingham, 1970–81. Hon. DSc Aston, 1975. *Publications*: papers and articles on relationships between people in industry. *Recreation*: sailing. *Address*: Courtyard House, High Street, Lymington, Hants SO41 9AH. *T*: Lymington (0590) 672593. *Clubs*: Metallics; Royal Ocean Racing, Royal Cruising, Royal Lymington Yacht.

BONDI, Prof. Sir Hermann, KCB 1973; FRS 1959; FRAS; Master of Churchill College, Cambridge, 1983–90, Fellow, since 1990; Professor of Mathematics, King's College, London, since 1954 (titular since 1971, emeritus since 1985); *b* Vienna, 1 Nov. 1919; *s* of late Samuel and Helene Bondi, New York; *m* 1947, Christine M. Stockman, *d* of late H. W. Stockman, CBE; two *s* three *d*. *Educ*: Realgymnasium, Vienna; Trinity Coll., Cambridge (MA). Temporary Experimental Officer, Admiralty, 1942–45; Fellow Trinity Coll., Cambridge, 1943–49, and 1952–54; Asst Lecturer, Mathematics, Cambridge, 1945–48; University Lecturer, Mathematics, Cambridge, 1948–54. Dir-Gen., ESRO, 1967–71; Chief Scientific Advr, MoD, 1971–77; Chief Scientist, Dept of Energy, 1977–80; Chm. and Chief Exec., NERC, 1980–84. Research Associate, Cornell Univ.,

1951; Lecturer, Harvard Coll. Observatory, 1953; Lowell Lecturer, Boston, Mass, 1953; Visiting Prof. Cornell Univ., 1960; Halley Lecturer, Oxford, 1962; Tarner Lectr, Cambridge, 1965; Lees-Knowles Lectr, Cambridge, 1974. Chairman: Space Cttee, MoD, 1964–65; Nat. Cttee for Astronomy, 1963–67; Adv. Council on Energy Conservation, 1980–82; IFIAS 1984–. Secretary, Royal Astronomical Soc., 1956–64; Mem., SRC, 1973–80. President: Inst. of Mathematics and its Applications, 1974–75; British Humanist Assoc.; Assoc. of British Science Writers, 1981–85; Soc. for Res. into Higher Educn, 1981–; Assoc. for Science Educn, 1982; Hydrographic Soc., 1985–87; Rationalist Press Assoc., 1982–. Member: Science Policy Foundn; Mem., Ct, London Univ., 1963–67. FKC 1968. Hon. DSc: Sussex 1974; Bath 1974; Surrey 1974; York 1980; Southampton 1981; Salford, 1982; Birmingham, 1984; St Andrews, 1985. Hon. FIEE 1979. Einstein Soc. gold medal, 1983; Gold Medal, Inst. of Mathematics and its Applications, 1988; G. D. Birla Internat. Award for Humanism, 1990. *Publications:* Cosmology, 1952 (2nd edn 1960); The Universe at Large, 1961; Relativity and Commonsense, 1964; Assumption and Myth in Physical Theory, 1968; (with Dame Kathleen Ollerenshaw) Magic Squares of Order Four, 1982; papers on astrophysics, etc, in Proc. Royal Society, Monthly Notices, Royal Astronomical Society, Proc. Cam. Phil. Society, etc. *Recreations:* walking, skiing, travelling. *Address:* Churchill College, Cambridge CB3 0DS; 60 Mill Road, Impington, Cambs CB4 4XN.

BONE, Charles, RI, ARCA, FRSA; President, Royal Institute of Painters in Water Colours, 1979–89; Governor, Federation of British Artists, 1976–81 and since 1983 (Member, Executive Council, 1983–84 and 1986–88); *b* 15 Sept. 1926; *s* of William Stanley and Elizabeth Bone; *m* Sheila Mitchell, FRBS, ARCA, sculptor; two *s. Educ:* Farnham Coll. of Art; Royal Coll. of Art (ARCA). FBI Award for Design. Consultant, COSIRA, 1952–70; Craft Adviser, Malta Inds Assoc., Malta, 1952–78; Lecturer, Brighton Coll. of Art, 1950–86; Director, RI Galleries, Piccadilly, 1965–70. Many mural paintings completed, including those in Eaton Square and Meretea, Italy; oils and water colours in exhibns of RA, London Group, NEAC and RBA, 1950–; 29 one-man shows, 1950–; works in private collections in France, Italy, Malta, America, Canada, Japan, Australia, Norway, Sweden, Germany. Designer of Stourhead Ball, 1959–69; produced Ceramic Mural on the History of Aerial Photography. Critic for Arts Review. Mem. Council, RI, 1964– (Vice-Pres. 1974). Hon. Member: Medical Art Soc.; Soc. Botanical Artists. Hon. FCA (Can.). Hunting Gp Prize for a British Watercolour, 1984. *Film:* Watercolour Painting: a practical guide, 1990. *Publication:* Waverley (author and illust.), 1991. *Address:* Winters Farm, Puttenham, Guildford, Surrey GU3 1AR. *T:* Guildford (0483) 810226.

BONE, Rt. Rev. John Frank Ewan; see Reading, Area Bishop of.

BONE, Quentin, JP; MA, DPhil; FRS 1984; Zoologist, Marine Biological Association UK, since 1959 (Deputy Chief Scientific Officer); *b* 17 Aug. 1931; *s* of late Stephen Bone and of Mary Adshead, *qv; m* 1958, Susan Elizabeth Smith; four *s. Educ:* Warwick Sch.; St John's Coll., Oxon. Naples Scholarship, 1954; Fellow by examination, Magdalen Coll., Oxford, 1956. Zoologist at Plymouth Laboratory, 1959. *Publications:* Biology of Fishes (with N. B. Marshall), 1983; papers on fish and invertebrates, mainly in Jl of Mar. Biol Assoc. UK. *Address:* Marchant House, 98 Church Road, Plymstock, Plymouth, Devon.

BONE, Roger Bridgland; HM Diplomatic Service; Counsellor, Foreign and Commonwealth Office, since 1989; *b* 29 July 1944; *s* of late Horace Bridgland Bone and of Dora R. Bone (*née* Tring); *m* 1970, Lena M. Bergman; one *s* one *d. Educ:* William Palmer's Sch., Grays; St Peter's Coll., Oxford (MA). Entered HM Diplomatic Service, 1966; UK Mission to UN, 1966; FCO, 1967; 3rd Sec., Stockholm, 1968–70; 2nd Sec., FCO, 1970–73; 1st Secretary: Moscow, 1973–75; FCO, 1975–78; UK Perm. Rep. to European Communities, Brussels, 1978–82; Asst Private Sec. to Sec. of State for Foreign and Commonwealth Affairs, 1982–84; Vis. Fellow, Harvard Univ. Center for Internat. Affairs, 1984–85; Counsellor, 1985–89, and Head of Chancery, 1987–89, Washington. *Recreations:* music, wine. *Address:* c/o Foreign and Commonwealth Office, SW1A 2AH.

BONE, Mrs Stephen; see Adshead, Mary.

BONE, Dr Thomas Renfrew, CBE 1987; Principal, Jordanhill College of Education, since 1972; *b* 1935; *s* of James Renfrew Bone and Mary Williams; *m* 1959, Elizabeth Stewart; one *s* one *d. Educ:* Greenock High Sch.; Glasgow Univ. MA 1st cl. English 1956, MEd 1st cl. 1962, PhD 1967. Teacher, Paisley Grammar Sch., 1957–62; Lecturer: Jordanhill Coll., 1962–63; Glasgow Univ., 1963–67; Hd of Educn Dept, Jordanhill Coll., 1967–71. Vice-Chm., Gen. Teaching Council for Scotland, 1987– (Mem., 1974–). FCCEA 1984. *Publications:* Studies in History of Scottish Education, 1967; School Inspection in Scotland, 1968; chapters in: Whither Scotland, 1971; Education Administration in Australia and Abroad, 1975; Administering Education: international challenge, 1975; European Perspectives in Teacher Education, 1976; Education for Development, 1977; Practice of Teaching, 1978; World Yearbook of Education, 1980; The Management of Educational Institutions, 1982; The Effective Teacher, 1983; Strathclyde: changing horizons, 1985; The Changing Role of the Teacher, 1987; Teacher Education in Europe, 1990. *Recreation:* golf. *Address:* Jordanhill College of Education, Southbrae Drive, Glasgow G13 1PP. *T:* 041–950 3200. *Clubs:* Western Gailes Golf; Paisley Burns.

BONEY, Guy Thomas Knowles; QC 1990; a Recorder, since 1985; *b* 28 Dec. 1944; *o c* of Thomas Knowles Boney, MD and Muriel Hilary Eileen Long, FRCS; *m* 1976, Jean Harris Ritchie; two *s. Educ:* Winchester College; New College, Oxford (BA 1966; MA 1987). Called to the Bar, Middle Temple, 1968 (Harmsworth Scholar); in practice on Western Circuit, 1969–. *Publications:* The Road Safety Act 1967, 1971; contribs to: Halsbury's Laws of England, 4th edn (Road Traffic); horological jls. *Recreations:* horology, music (Organist, King's Somborne Parish Church, 1980–), amateur theatre. *Address:* 3 Pump Court, Temple, EC4Y 7AJ. *Clubs:* Reform; Hampshire (Winchester).

BONFIELD, Peter Leahy, CBE 1989; Chairman and Chief Executive, ICL plc, since 1990; *b* 3 June 1944; *s* of George and Patricia Bonfield; *m* 1968, Josephine Houghton. *Educ:* Hitchin Boys Grammar School, Loughborough Univ. (BTech Hons; Hon. DTech, 1988). FIEE 1990, FBCS 1990, FCIM 1990. Texas Instruments Inc., Dallas, USA, 1966–81; Group Exec. Dir, ICL, 1981–84; Chm. and Man. Dir, STC Internat. Computers Ltd, 1984–90; Dir, 1985–90, and Dep. Chief Exec., 1987–90, STC plc. *Recreations:* music, sailing, jogging. *Address:* ICL plc, ICL House, 1 High Street, Putney, SW15 1SW. *T:* 081–788 7272. *Club:* Royal Automobile.

BONGERS, Paul Nicholas; Director, Local Government International Bureau, since 1988; *b* 25 Oct. 1943; *s* of Henry Bongers and late Marjorie Bongers (*née* Luxton); *m* 1968, Margaret Collins; two *s* two *d. Educ:* Bradfield Coll.; New Coll., Oxford (MA); DPA Univ. of London (external), 1968. Administrative Trainee, City of Southampton, 1965–68; Personal Asst to Chief Exec., City of Nottingham, 1968–69; Administrator, Council of Europe, 1969–71; Assistant Secretary: AMC, 1971–74; AMA, 1974–78; Exec. Sec., British Sections, IULA/CEMR, 1978–88. Founder and Dir, European Information Service, monthly bulletin, 1978–. *Publications:* Local Government and 1992, 1990; articles in local govt jls. *Recreations:* family, music, countryside, travel, the arts. *Address:* Local Government International Bureau, 35 Great Smith Street, SW1P 3BJ.

BONHAM, Major Sir Antony Lionel Thomas, 4th Bt, *cr* 1852; DL; late Royal Scots Greys; *b* 21 Oct. 1916; *o s* of Maj. Sir Eric H. Bonham, 3rd Bt, and Ethel (*d* 1962), *y d* of Col Leopold Seymour; *S* father 1937; *m* 1944, Felicity, *o d* of late Col. Frank L. Pardoe, DSO, Bartonbury, Cirencester; three *s. Educ:* Eton; RMC. Served Royal Scots Greys, 1937–49; retired with rank of Major, 1949. DL Glos 1983. *Heir: s* (George) Martin (Antony) Bonham [*b* 18 Feb. 1945; *m* 1979, Nenon Baillieu, *e d* of R. R. Wilson and Hon. Mrs Wilson, Durford Knoll, Upper Durford Wood, Petersfield, Hants; one *s* three *d*]. *Address:* Ash House, Ampney Crucis, Cirencester, Glos. *T:* Poulton (028585) 391.

BONHAM, Nicholas; Deputy Chairman, W. & F. C. Bonham & Sons Ltd, since 1987; *b* 7 Sept. 1948; *s* of Leonard Charles Bonham and Diana Maureen (*née* Magwood); *m* 1977, Kaye Eleanor (*née* Ivett); two *d. Educ:* Trent College. Joined W. & F. C. Bonham & Sons Ltd, Fine Art Auctioneers, 1966; Dir, 1970; Man. Dir, 1975–87. Dir, Montpelier Properties, 1970–. *Recreations:* sailing, tobogganing, ski-ing, golf, swimming. *Address:* Montpelier Galleries, Montpelier Street, SW7 1HH. *T:* 071–584 9161. *Clubs:* Kennel; Royal Thames Yacht, South West Shingles Yacht, Seaview Yacht; Berkshire Golf; St Moritz Tobogganing, St Moritz Sporting.

BONHAM CARTER, family name of **Baron Bonham-Carter.**

BONHAM-CARTER, Baron *cr* 1986 (Life Peer), of Yarnbury in the county of Wiltshire; **Mark Raymond Bonham Carter;** Editorial Consultant, William Collins Publishers, since 1981; Chairman, Governors of The Royal Ballet, since 1985 (Governor, since 1960); *b* 11 Feb. 1922; *e s* of late Sir Maurice Bonham Carter, KCB, KCVO, and Violet, *d* of 1st Earl of Oxford and Asquith, KG, PC (Baroness Asquith of Yarnbury, DBE); *m* 1955, Leslie, *d* of Condé Nast, NY; three *d* and one step-*d. Educ:* Winchester; Balliol Coll., Oxford (Scholar); University of Chicago (Commonwealth Fund Fellowship). Served Grenadier Guards, 1941–45; 8th Army (Africa) and 21st Army Group (NW Europe); captured, 1943; escaped; (despatches). Contested (L) Barnstaple, 1945; MP (L), Torrington Div. of Devonshire, March 1958–59; Mem., UK Delegn to the Council of Europe, 1958–59; contested (L) Torrington, 1964. Director, Wm Collins & Co. Ltd, 1955–58. First Chm., Race Relations Bd, 1966–70; Chm., Community Relations Commn, 1971–77; Vice-Pres., Consumers' Assoc., 1972– (Mem. Council, 1966–71); Jt Chm., Anglo-Polish Round Table Conf., 1971–; Mem. Council, Inst. of Race Relations, 1966–72. Chm., Writers and Scholars Educnl Trust, 1977–89. A Dir, Royal Opera House, Covent Garden, 1958–82; Vice Chm. and a Governor, BBC, 1975–81. Chm., Outer Circle Policy Unit, 1976–80. Mem. Court of Governors, LSE, 1970–81. Hon. Fellow: Manchester Polytechnic; Wolfson Coll., Oxford, 1990. Hon. LLD Dundee, 1978. *Publications:* (ed) The Autobiography of Margot Asquith, 1962; contributor to: Radical Alternative (essays), 1962; articles, reviews in various jls. *Address:* 13 Clarendon Road, W11 4JB. *T:* 071–229 5200. *Clubs:* Brooks's, MCC.
See also Hon. R. H. Bonham Carter.

BONHAM-CARTER, John Arkwright, CVO 1975; DSO 1942; OBE 1967; ERD 1952; Chairman and General Manager, British Railways London Midland Region, 1971–75; *b* 27 March 1915; *s* of late Capt. Guy Bonham-Carter, 19th Hussars, and Kathleen Rebecca (*née* Arkwright); *m* 1939, Anne Louisa Charteris; two *s. Educ:* Winchester Coll.; King's Coll., Cambridge (Exhibitioner). 1st class hons Mech. Scis, Cantab, 1936; MA 1970. Joined LNER Co. as Traffic Apprentice, 1936; served in Royal Tank Regt, 1939–46 (despatches, 1940 and 1942); subsequently rejoined LNER; held various appointments; Asst General Manager, BR London Midland Region, 1963–65; Chief Operating Officer, BR Board, 1966–68; Chm. and Gen. Manager, BR Western Region, 1968–71. Lieut-Col, Engr and Transport (formerly Engr and Rly) Staff Corps RE (TA), 1966–71, Col 1971–. FCIT. KStJ 1984; Comdr, St John Ambulance, Dorset, 1984–87. *Recreations:* theatre, foreign travel, cabinet making and carpentry. *Address:* Redbridge House, Crossways, Dorchester, Dorset DT2 8DY. *T:* Warmwell (0305) 852669. *Club:* Army and Navy.

BONHAM CARTER, Hon. Raymond Henry; Executive Director, S. G. Warburg & Co. Ltd, 1967–77; retired in 1979 following disability; *b* 19 June 1929; *s* of Sir Maurice Bonham Carter, KCB, KCVO, and Lady Violet Bonham Carter, DBE (later Baroness Asquith of Yarnbury); *m* 1958, Elena Propper de Callejon; two *s* one *d. Educ:* Winchester Coll.; Magdalen Coll., Oxford (BA 1952); Harvard Business Sch. (MBA 1954). Irish Guards, 1947–49. With J. Henry Schröder & Co., 1954–58; acting Advr, Bank of England, 1958–63; Alternate Exec. Dir for UK, IMF, and Mem., UK Treasury and Supply Delegn, Washington, 1961–63; S. G. Warburg & Co. Ltd, 1964; Director: Transport Development Group Ltd, 1969–77; Banque de Paris et des Pays Bas NV, 1973–77; Mercury Securities Ltd, 1974–77; seconded as Dir, Industrial Develt Unit, DoI, 1977–79. Mem. Council, Internat. Inst. for Strategic Studies (Hon. Treasurer, 1974–84). *Address:* 7 West Heath Avenue, NW11 7QS.
See also Baron Bonham-Carter.

BONHAM CARTER, Richard Erskine; Physician to the Hospital for Sick Children, Great Ormond Street, 1947–75, to University College Hospital, 1948–66; *b* 27 Aug. 1910; *s* of late Capt. A. E. Bonham-Carter and late M. E. Bonham-Carter (*née* Malcolm); *m* 1946, Margaret (*née* Stace); three *d. Educ:* Clifton Coll.; Peterhouse, Cambridge; St Thomas' Hospital. Resident Asst Physician, Hospital for Sick Children, Great Ormond Street, 1938. Served War of 1939–45 in RAMC; DADMS 1 Airborne Div., 1942–45; despatches, 1944. *Publications:* contributions to Text-Books of Pædiatrics and to medical journals. *Recreations:* gardening, fishing. *Address:* Castle Sweyn Cottage, Achnamara, Argyll.

BONHAM-CARTER, Victor; Joint Secretary, Society of Authors, 1971–78, Consultant, 1978–82; Secretary, Royal Literary Fund, 1966–82; *b* 13 Dec. 1913; *s* of Gen. Sir Charles Bonham-Carter, GCB, CMG, DSO, and Gabrielle Madge Jeanette (*née* Fisher); *m* 1st, 1938, Audrey Edith Stogdon (marr. diss. 1979); two *s*; 2nd, 1979, Cynthia Claire Sanford. *Educ:* Winchester Coll.; Magdalene Coll., Cambridge (MA); Hamburg and Paris. Worked on The Countryman, 1936–37; Dir, School Prints Ltd, 1937–39, 1945–60; Army, R Berks Regt and Intell. Corps, 1939–45; farmed in W Somerset, 1947–59; historian of Dartington Hall Estate, Devon, 1951–66; on staff of Soc. of Authors, 1963–82. Active in Exmoor National Park affairs, 1955–; Pres., Exmoor Soc., 1975–; Partner, Exmoor Press, 1969–89. *Publications:* The English Village, 1952; (with W. B. Curry) Dartington Hall, 1958; Exploring Parish Churches, 1959; Farming the Land, 1959; In a Liberal Tradition, 1960; Soldier True, 1965; Surgeon in the Crimea, 1969; The Survival of the English Countryside, 1971; Authors by Profession, vol. 1 1978, vol. 2 1984; Exmoor Writers, 1987; The Essence of Exmoor, 1991; many contribs to jls, radio, etc on country life and work; also on authorship matters, esp. Public Lending Right. *Recreations:* music, conversation. *Address:* The Mount, Milverton, Taunton TA4 1QZ. *Club:* Authors'.

BONINGTON, Christian John Storey, CBE 1976; mountaineer, writer and photographer; *b* 6 Aug. 1934; *s* of Charles Bonington, journalist, and Helen Anne Bonington (*née* Storey); *m* 1962, Muriel Wendy Marchant; two *s* (and one *s* decd). *Educ:* University Coll. Sch., London. RMA Sandhurst, 1955–56; commnd Royal Tank Regt, 1956–61. Unilever Management Trainee, 1961–62; writer and photographer, 1962–.

Climbs: Annapurna II, 26,041 ft (1st ascent) 1960; Central Pillar Freney, Mont Blanc (1st ascent), 1961; Nuptse, 25,850 ft (1st ascent), 1961; North Wall of Eiger (1st British ascent), 1962; Central Tower of Paine, Patagonia (1st ascent), 1963; Mem. of team, first descent of Blue Nile, 1968; Leader: successful Annapurna South Face Expedition, 1970; British Everest Expedition, 1972; Brammah, Himalayas (1st ascent), 1973; co-leader, Changabang, Himalayas (1st ascent), 1974; British Everest Expedition (1st ascent SW face), 1975; Ogre (1st ascent), 1977; jt leader, Kongur, NW China (1st ascent), 1981; Shivling West (1st ascent), 1983; Mt Vinson, highest point of Antarctica (1st British ascent), 1983; reached Everest summit, 1985. President: British Mountaineering Council, 1988– (Vice-Pres., 1976–79, 1985–88); British Orienteering Fedn, 1985–; Vice-Pres., Army Mountaineering Assoc., 1980–. Pres., LEPRA, 1983. FRGS (Founders' Medal, 1974). Hon. Fellow, UMIST, 1976; Hon. MA Salford, 1973; Hon. DSc: Sheffield, 1976; Lancaster, 1983. Lawrence of Arabia Medal, RSAA, 1986. *Publications:* I Chose to Climb (autobiog.), 1966; Annapurna South Face, 1971; The Next Horizon (autobiog.), 1973; Everest, South West Face, 1973; Everest the Hard Way, 1976; Quest for Adventure, 1981; Kongur: China's elusive summit, 1982; (jtly) Everest: the unclimbed ridge, 1983; The Everest Years, 1986; Mountaineer (autobiog.), 1989. *Recreations:* mountaineering, ski-ing, orienteering. *Address:* Badger Hill, Nether Row, Hesket Newmarket, Wigton, Cumbria. *T:* Caldbeck (06998) 286. *Clubs:* Alpine, Alpine Ski, Army and Navy, Climbers, Fell and Rock Climbing, Border Liners.

BONNER, Frederick Ernest, CBE 1974; Deputy Chairman, Central Electricity Generating Board, 1975–86; Member (part-time), Monopolies and Mergers Commission, since 1987; Director (non-executive), Nuclear Electric plc, since 1990; *b* 16 Sept. 1923; *s* of late George Frederick Bonner and Mrs Bonner, Hammersmith; *m* 1st, 1957, Phyllis (*d* 1976), *d* of late Mr and Mrs H. Holder; 2nd, 1977, Mary, *widow* of Ellis Walter Aries, AFC, ARICS. *Educ:* St Clement Danes Holborn Estate Grammar Sch. BSc(Econ) London; DPA, JDipMA. Local Govt (Fulham and Ealing Borough Councils), 1940–49. Central Electricity Authority: Sen. Accountant, 1949–50; Asst Finance Officer, 1950–58; Central Electricity Generating Board: Asst Chief Financial Officer, 1958–61; Dep. Chief Financial Officer, 1961–65; Chief Financial Officer, 1965–69; Member, 1969–75; Mem., UKAEA, 1977–86; Chairman: British Airways Helicopters, 1983–85; Uranium Inst., 1985–87. FCA, IPFA, CBIM. *Recreations:* music, gardening, reading. *Address:* Joya, 20 Craigweil Manor, Aldwick, Bognor Regis, W Sussex PO21 4DJ.

BONNER, Paul Max; Director, Programme Planning Secretariat, Independent Television Association, since 1987; *b* 30 Nov. 1934; *s* of Jill and late Frank Bonner; *m* 1956, Jenifer Hubbard; two *s* one *d.* *Educ:* Felsted Sch., Essex. National Service commission, 1953–55. Local journalism, 1955; Radio production, BBC Bristol, 1955–57; Television production, BBC Bristol, 1957–59; BBC Lime Grove, 1959–62; Television Documentary prodn and direction, BBC Lime Grove and Kensington House, 1962–74; Editor, Community Programmes for BBC, 1974–77; Head of Science and Features Programmes for BBC, 1977–80; Channel Controller, Channel Four TV, 1980–83; Exec. Dir and Programme Controller, Channel Four TV, 1983–87. A Manager, Royal Instn, 1982–85; Governor, Nat. Film and TV School, 1983–88; Director: Broadcasting Support Services, 1982–; House of Commons Broadcasting Unit Ltd, 1989–; Member: Bd, Children's Film Unit, 1989–; Cttee for Public Understanding of Science, 1986–. FRTS 1989. *Publications:* documentaries include: Strange Excellency, 1964; Climb up to Hell, 1967; Lost: Four H Bombs, 1967; Search for the Real Che Guevara, 1971; Who Sank the Lusitania?, 1972. *Recreations:* photography, the theatre, sailing, walking, listening to good conversation. *Address:* North View, Wimbledon Common, SW19 4UJ. *Club:* Reform.

BONNET, C. M.; *see* Melchior-Bonnet.

BONNET, Maj.-Gen. Peter Robert Frank, CB 1991; MBE 1975; General Officer Commanding, Western District, since 1989; *b* 12 Dec. 1936; *s* of James Robert and Phyllis Elsie Bonnet; *m* 1961, Sylvia Mary Coy; two *s.* *Educ:* Royal Military Coll. of Science, Shrivenham. BSc (Engrg). Commnd from RMA Sandhurst, 1958; RMCS Shrivenham, 1959–62; apptd to RHA, 1962; Staff trng, RMCS and Staff Coll., Camberley, 1969–70; Comd (Lt-Col), 26 Field Regt, RA, 1978–81; Comd RA (Brig.) 2nd Div., 1982–84; attendance at Indian Nat. Defence Coll., New Delhi, 1985; Dir RA, 1986–89. *Recreations:* tennis, sculpture, painting. *Address:* Headquarters Western District, Shrewsbury SY3 7LT. *T:* Shrewsbury (0743) 236060. *Club:* Army and Navy.

BONNETT, Prof. Raymond, CChem, FRSC; Professor of Organic Chemistry, Queen Mary and Westfield (formerly Queen Mary) College, London, since 1976; *b* 13 July 1931; *s* of Harry and Maud Bonnett; *m* 1956, Shirley Rowe; two *s* one *d.* *Educ:* County Grammar Sch., Bury St Edmunds; Imperial Coll. (BSc, ARCS); Cambridge Univ. (PhD); DSc London 1972. Salters' Fellow, Cambridge, 1957–58; Res. Fellow, Harvard, 1958–59; Asst Prof., Dept of Chemistry, Univ. of British Columbia, 1959–61; Lectr in Organic Chem., 1961–66, Reader in Organic Chem., 1966–74, Prof. 1974–76, Hd of Dept of Chemistry, 1982–87, QMC, London Univ. *Publications:* sci. papers, esp. in Jls of Royal Soc. of Chemistry and Biochemical Soc. *Recreations:* theatre, private press books, gardening. *Address:* Elmbank, 19 Station Road, Epping, Essex CM16 4HG. *T:* Epping (0378) 73203.

BONNEY, George Louis William, MS, FRCS; Consulting Orthopædic Surgeon, St Mary's Hospital, London, since 1984; *b* 10 Jan. 1920; *s* of late Dr Ernest Bonney and Gertrude Mary Williams; *m* 1950, Margaret Morgan; two *d.* *Educ:* Eton (Scholar); St Mary's Hospital Medical Sch. MB, BS, MRCS, LRCP 1943; FRCS 1945; MS (London) 1947. Formerly: Surg.-Lieut RNVR; Research Assistant and Senior Registrar, Royal National Orthopædic Hospital; Consultant Orthopædic Surgeon: Southend Group of Hospitals; St Mary's Hosp., London, 1954–84 (Sen. Consultant, 1979–84). Travelling Fellowship of British Postgraduate Med. Fedn, Univ. of London, 1950. Watson-Jones Lectr, RCS, 1976. Hon. Fellow, Medical Defence Union; Mem., SICOT. *Publications:* chapters in Operative Surgery, 1957; Clinical Surgery, 1966; Clinical Orthopædics, 1983; Micro-reconstruction of Nerve Injuries, 1987; Current Therapy in Neurologic Disease, 1987; Medical Negligence, 1990; Clinical Neurology, 1991; papers in medical journals on visceral pain, circulatory mechanisms, nerve injuries and on various aspects of orthopædic surgery. *Recreations:* fishing, shooting, photography, music. *Address:* 71 Porchester Terrace, W2 3TT. *T:* 071–262 4236; Wyeside Cottage, Fawley, Hereford HR1 4SP. *T:* Hereford (0432) 840219. *Club:* Leander.

BONNICI, Carmelo M.; *see* Mifsud Bonnici.

BONSALL, Sir Arthur (Wilfred), KCMG 1977; CBE 1957; *b* 25 June 1917; *s* of late Wilfred Bonsall and Sarah Bonsall; *m* 1941, Joan Isabel Wingfield (*d* 1990); four *s* three *d.* *Educ:* Bishop's Stortford Coll.; St Catharine's Coll., Cambridge. 2nd Cl. Hons Mod. Langs. Joined Air Ministry, 1940; transf. to FO 1942; IDC, 1962; Dir, Govt Communications HQ, 1975–78. *Recreation:* coarse gardening. *Address:* 1 Coxwell Court, Coxwell Street, Cirencester, Glos GL7 2BQ.

    See also F. F. Bonsall.

BONSALL, Prof. Frank Featherstone, FRS 1970; Professor of Mathematics, University of Edinburgh, 1965–84, now Emeritus; *b* 1920; *s* of late Wilfred Bonsall and Sarah

Bonsall; *m* 1947, Gillian Patrick. *Educ:* Bishop's Stortford Coll.; Merton Coll., Oxford. *Publications* (all with J. Duncan): Numerical Ranges of Operators on Normed Spaces and of Elements of Normed Algebras, 1971; Numerical Ranges II, 1973; Complete Normed Algebras, 1973. *Recreation:* walking. *Address:* 18 Rossett Park Road, Harrogate HG2 9NP.

    See also Sir A. W. Bonsall.

BONSER, Rt. Rev. David, *see* Bolton, Bishop Suffragan of.

BONSER, Air Vice-Marshal Stanley Haslam, CB 1969; MBE 1942; CEng, FRAeS; Director, Easams Ltd, 1972–81; *b* 17 May 1916; *s* of late Sam Bonser and late Phoebe Ellen Bonser; *m* 1941, Margaret Betty Howard; two *s.* *Educ:* Sheffield University. BSc 1938; DipEd 1939. Armament Officer, Appts, 1939–44; British Air Commn, Washington, DC, 1944–46; Coll. of Aeronautics, 1946–47; RAE, Guided Weapons, 1947–51; Chief Instr (Armament Wing) RAF Techn. Coll., 1951–52; Staff Coll., Bracknell, 1953, psa 1953; Project Officer, Blue Streak, Min. of Technology, 1954–57; Asst Dir, GW Engineering, 1957–60; Senior RAF Officer, Skybolt Development Team, USA, 1960–62; Dir, Aircraft Mechanical Engineering, 1963–64; Dir, RAF Aircraft Development (mainly Nimrod), 1964–69; Dep. Controller of Equipment, Min. of Technology and MoD, 1969–71; Aircraft C, MoD, 1971–72. *Recreations:* scout movement, gardening. *Address:* Chalfont, Waverley Avenue, Fleet, Hants GU13 8NW. *T:* Fleet (0252) 615835.

BONSEY, Mary, (Mrs Lionel Bonsey); *see* Norton, M.

BONSOR, Sir Nicholas (Cosmo), 4th Bt *cr* 1925; MP (C) Upminster, since 1983 (Nantwich, 1979–83); *b* 9 Dec. 1942; *s* of Sir Bryan Cosmo Bonsor, 3rd Bt, MC, TD, and of Elizabeth, *d* of late Captain Angus Valdimar Hambro; *S* father, 1977; *m* 1969, Hon. Nadine Marisa Lampson, *d* of 2nd Baron Killearn, *qv*; two *s* three *d* (including twin *d*). *Educ:* Eton; Keble College, Oxford (MA). Barrister-at-law, Inner Temple. Served Royal Buckinghamshire Yeomanry, 1964–69. Practised at the Bar, 1967–75. CLA Legal and Parly Sub-Cttee, 1978–82; Sec., Cons. Africa Sub-Cttee, 1979–80; Vice-Chairman: Cons. Foreign Affairs Cttee, 1981–83; Cons. Defence Cttee, 1987–. Chairman: Cyclotron Trust for Cancer Treatment, 1984–; Food Hygiene Bureau, 1987–; British Field Sports Soc., 1988–; Chm., Standing Council of the Baronetage, 1990– (Vice-Chm., 1987–90); Trustee: Baronets' Trust, 1986–; Verdin Trust for Mentally Handicapped, 1983–. Mem., Council of Lloyd's, 1987–. FRSA 1970. *Publications:* political pamphlets on law and trades unions and defence. *Recreations:* sailing, shooting, military history. *Heir:* *s* Alexander Cosmo Walrond Bonsor, *b* 8 Sept. 1976. *Address:* Liscombe Park, Leighton Buzzard, Beds LU7 0JN. *Clubs:* White's, Pratt's; Royal Yacht Squadron.

BONY, Prof. Jean V., MA; Professor of the History of Art, University of California at Berkeley, 1962–80, now Emeritus; *b* Le Mans, France, 1 Nov. 1908; *s* of Henri Bony and Marie Normand; *m* 1st, 1936, Clotilde Roure (*d* 1942); one *d;* 2nd, 1953, Mary England. *Educ:* Lycée Louis-le-Grand, Paris; Sorbonne. Agrégé d'Histoire Paris; MA Cantab; Hon. FSA; Corres. Fellow, British Academy. Bulteau-Lavisse Research Scholarship, 1935–37; Asst Master, Eton Coll., 1937–39 and 1945–46. Served War of 1939–45; 1st Lieut, French Infantry, 1939–44; POW, Germany, June 1940–Dec. 1943. Research Scholar, Centre Nat. de la Recherche Scientifique, 1944–45; Lecturer in History of Art at the French Inst. in London, 1946–61. Focillon Fellow and Vis. Lectr, Yale Univ., 1949; Slade Prof. of Fine Art, University of Cambridge, and Fellow of St John's Coll., Cambridge, 1958–61; Vis. Prof. and Mathews Lectr, Columbia Univ., 1961; Lecturer in History of Art at the University of Lille, France, 1961–62; Wrightsman Lectr, New York Univ., 1969; Vis. Fellow, Humanities Res. Centre, ANU, 1978; John Simon Guggenheim Meml Fellow, 1981; Kress Prof., Nat. Gall. of Art, Washington, 1982; Vis. Andrew W. Mellon Prof. of Fine Arts, Univ. of Pittsburgh, 1983; Algur H. Meadows Prof. of Art Hist., Southern Methodist Univ., Dallas, 1984–87; Getty Lectr in Art, Univ. of Southern California, LA, 1988. *Publications:* Notre-Dame de Mantes, 1946; French Cathedrals (with M. Hürlimann and P. Meyer), 1951 (revised edn, 1967); (ed) H. Focillon: The Art of the West in the Middle Ages, English edn 1963, new edn 1969; The English Decorated Style, 1979; French Gothic Architecture of the 12th and 13th Centuries, 1983; articles in Bulletin Monumental, Congrès Archéologiques de France, Journal of Warburg and Courtauld Institutes, Journal of British Archæological Assoc., etc. *Address:* Department of History of Art, University of California, Berkeley, California 94720, USA.

BONYNGE, Dame Joan; *see* Sutherland, Dame Joan.

BONYNGE, Richard, AO 1983; CBE 1977; opera conductor; *b* Sydney, 29 Sept. 1930; *s* of C. A. Bonynge, Epping, NSW; *m* 1954, Dame Joan Sutherland, *qv*; one *s.* *Educ:* Sydney Conservatorium (pianist). Official debut, as Conductor, with Santa Cecilia Orch. in Rome, 1962; conducted first opera, Faust, Vancouver, 1963. Has conducted in most leading opera houses in world, and in Edinburgh, Vienna and Florence Fests. Has been Princ. Conductor and Artistic/Musical Dir of cos, incl. Sutherland/Williamson Internat. Grand Opera Co., Aust., 1965; Vancouver Opera, 1974–78; Australian Opera, 1975–85. Many opera and ballet recordings; also recital discs with Sutherland, Tebaldi, Tourangeau and Pavarotti, and many orchestral and ballet anthologies. *Publication:* (with Dame Joan Sutherland) The Joan Sutherland Album, 1986. *Address:* c/o Ingpen and Williams, 14 Kensington Court, W8.

BOOKER, Christopher John Penrice; journalist and author; *b* 7 Oct. 1937; *s* of late John Booker and Margaret Booker; *m* 1979, Valerie, *d* of late Dr M. S. Patrick, OBE; two *s.* *Educ:* Dragon Sch., Oxford; Shrewsbury Sch.; Corpus Christi Coll., Cambridge (History). Liberal News, 1960; jazz critic, Sunday Telegraph, 1961; Editor, Private Eye, 1961–63, and regular contributor, 1965–; resident scriptwriter, That Was The Week That Was, 1962–63, and Not So Much A Programme, 1963–64; contributor to Spectator, 1962–, Daily Telegraph, 1972– (Way of the World column, as Peter Simple II, 1987–90), and to many other newspapers and jls. Wrote extensively on property develt, planning and housing, 1972–77 (with Bennie Gray, Campaigning Journalist of the Year, 1973); City of Towers—the Rise and Fall of a Twentieth Century Dream (TV prog.), 1979. Mem., Cowgill enquiry into post-war repatriations from Austria, 1986–90. *Publications:* The Neophiliacs: a study of the revolution in English life in the 50s and 60s, 1969; (with Candida Lycett-Green) Goodbye London, 1973; The Booker Quiz, 1976; The Seventies, 1980; The Games War: a Moscow journal, 1981; contrib. Private Eye anthologies. *Recreations:* the psychology of storytelling, nature, music, following Somerset cricket team. *Address:* The Old Rectory, Litton, Bath BA3 4PW. *T:* Chewton Mendip (076121) 263.

BOOKER-MILBURN, Donald; Sheriff of Grampian, Highland and Islands, since 1983; *b* Dornoch, 20 May 1940; *s* of late Captain Booker Milburn, DSO, MC, Coldstream Guards, and late Betty Calthrop Calthrop; *m* 1963, Marjorie Lilian Elizabeth Burns; one *s* one *d.* *Educ:* Trinity College, Glenalmond; Grenoble Univ.; Jesus Coll., Cambridge (BA); Edinburgh Univ. (LLB). Admitted to Faculty of Advocates, 1968; Standing Junior Counsel to RAF, 1977–80; Sheriff of Lothian and Borders, 1980–83. *Recreations:* golf, skiing. *Address:* Clashmore House, Clashmore, Dornoch, Sutherland. *Clubs:* New (Edinburgh); Royal & Ancient Golf (St Andrews); Royal Dornoch Golf.

BOOLELL, Sir Satcam, Kt 1977; Attorney General, Minister of Justice and Minister of External Affairs and Emigration, Mauritius, since 1986; *b* New Grove, Mauritius, 11 Sept. 1920; *m* 1948, Inderjeet Kissoodaye (*d* 1986); two *s* one *d*; *m* 1987, Myrtha Poblete. *Educ:* primary and secondary schs in New Grove, Mare d'Albert, Rose Belle, and Port-Louis; LSE (LLB Hons 1951). Called to the Bar, Lincoln's Inn, 1952. Civil servant, Mauritius, 1944–48. Minister of Agric. and Natural Resources, 1959–82; Minister of Economic Planning, 1983–85. Mem. Central Exec., Mauritius Labour Party, 1955–. Rep. Mauritius, internat. confs. Founder, French daily newspaper, The Nation. Comdr, Légion d'Honneur (France), 1990. *Recreations:* reading travel books, gardening, walking in the countryside. *Address:* Ministry of Justice, Port Louis, Mauritius; 4bis Bancilhon Street, Port-Louis. *T:* 2–0079.

BOON, George Counsell, FSA; FRHistS; FRNS; Hon. Research Associate, National Museum of Wales, since 1989 (Keeper of Archaeology and Numismatics, 1976–86, Senior Keeper and Curator, 1987–89); *b* 20 Sept. 1927; *s* of Ronald Hudson Boon and Eveline Counsell; *m* 1956, Diana Margaret Martyn; two *s* one *d*. *Educ:* Bristol Univ. BA Hons (Latin). FRNS 1954; FSA 1955; FRHistS 1978. Archaeological Assistant, Reading Museum and Art Gallery, 1950–56; Asst Keeper, Dept of Archaeology, 1957–76. Member: Ancient Monuments Bd for Wales, 1979–90; Royal Commn on Ancient and Historical Monuments (Wales), 1979–90. Pres., Cambrian Archaeol Assoc., 1986–87. Vice-President: Soc. for Promotion of Roman Studies, 1977–; Soc. of Antiquaries, 1979–83. Corresp. Mem., German Archaeological Inst., 1968. *Publications:* Roman Silchester, 1957, 2nd edn 1974; Isca, the Roman Legionary Fortress at Caerleon, Mon., 1972; Welsh Tokens of the Seventeenth Century, 1973; Cardiganshire Silver and the Aberystwyth Mint in Peace and War, 1981; Welsh Hoards 1979–1981, 1986; contribs to learned journals. *Recreations:* none worth mention. *Address:* 43 Westbourne Road, Penarth, South Glam CF6 2HA. *T:* Penarth (0222) 709588. *Clubs:* unclubbable.

BOON, John Trevor, CBE 1968; Chairman, Mills & Boon Ltd, since 1972; *b* 21 Dec. 1916; 3rd *s* of Charles Boon and Mary Boon (*née* Cowpe); *m* 1943, Felicity Ann, *d* of Stewart and Clemence Logan; four *s*. *Educ:* Felsted Sch.; Trinity Hall, Cambridge (scholar). 1st Cl. Pts I and II History Tripos. Served War, 1939–45: with Royal Norfolk Regt and S Wales Borderers (despatches). Historical Section of War Cabinet, 1945–46. Joined Mills & Boon Ltd, 1938, Man. Dir, 1963, Chm., 1972–. Dir, Wood Bros Glass Works Ltd, 1968, Chm., 1973–75, Dep. Chm., 1975–78. Vice Chm., Harlequin Enterprises Ltd, Toronto, 1972–83. Chairman: Harlequin Overseas, 1978–; Marshall Editions, 1977–; Director: Harmex, 1978–82; Harlequin France, 1980–82 (Chm., 1978–80); Torstar Corp., Toronto, 1981–85; Open University Educational Enterprises, 1977–79. President: Soc. of Bookmen, 1981; Internat. Publishers Assoc., 1972–76 (Hon. Mem., 1982); Chairman: Publishers Adv. Panel of British Council, 1977–81; Book Trade Res. Cttee, 1978–82; Director: Book Tokens Ltd, 1964–84; Book Trade Improvements Ltd, 1966–84; Publishers Association: Mem. Council, 1953, Treas., 1959–61, Pres., 1961–63, Vice-Pres., 1963–65. Over-seas missions: for British Council, to SE Asia, USSR (twice), Czechoslovakia; for Book Development Council, to Malaysia, Singapore, and New Zealand. Mem. Management Cttee, Wine Soc., 1971–77. Hon. MA, Open Univ., 1983. *Recreations:* walking, swimming, wine, books, friends. *Address:* Mills & Boon Ltd, Eton House, 18–24 Paradise Road, Richmond, Surrey TW9 1SR. *Clubs:* Beefsteak, Garrick, Royal Automobile, Savile; Hawks (Cambridge).

BOON, Sir Peter Coleman, Kt 1979; Goodyear Professor of Business Administration, Kent State University, USA, 1983–86; *b* 2 Sept. 1916; *s* of Frank Boon and Evelyn Boon; *m* 1940, Pamela; one *s* one *d*. *Educ:* Felsted. Stock Exchange, 1933–34; Lloyds & National Provincial Foreign Bank, 1934–35; Dennison Mfg Co., USA, 1936–39; Armed Services, War of 1939–45, 1939–46; Dennison Mfg, 1946; graduate trainee, Hoover Ltd, 1946, Managing Dir (Australia), 1955–65; Managing Dir, Hoover Ltd, 1965–75, Chm., 1975–78. Dir, Belden & Blake UK Inc., 1985–. FBIM; FRSA 1980. Hon. LLD Strathclyde, 1978. Chevalier de l'Ordre de la Couronne, Belgium. *Recreations:* horses, swimming, golf, theatre, economics, National Trust for Scotland, boys clubs, education. *Clubs:* Royal Wimbledon Golf; Western Racing, Australian, Imperial Services, American National, Royal Sydney Yacht Squadron, Australian Jockey, Sydney Turf (Australia).

BOON, Dr William Robert, FRS 1974; retired; *b* 20 March 1911; *s* of Walter and Ellen Boon; *m* 1938, Marjorie Betty Oury; one *s* two *d*. *Educ:* St Dunstan's Coll., Catford; King's Coll., London. BSc, PhD, FRSC, FKC 1976. Research, Chemotherapy and Crop Protection, ICI, 1936–69; Dir, Jealott's Hill Res. Station, 1964–69; Man. Dir, Plant Protection Ltd, 1969–73. Vis. Prof., Reading Univ., 1968. Member: Adv. Bd for the Research Councils, 1972–76; NERC, 1976–79. Hon. DSc Cranfield, 1981. Mullard Medal of Royal Society, 1972; Medal, British Crop Protection Council, 1987. *Publications:* papers in Jl Chem. Soc., Jl Soc. Chem. Ind., etc. *Recreation:* reading. *Address:* The Gables, Sid Road, Sidmouth, Devon EX10 9AQ. *T:* Sidmouth (0395) 514069. *Club:* Farmers'.

BOORD, Sir Nicolas (John Charles), 4th Bt *cr* 1896; scientific translator; English training specialist; *b* 10 June 1936; *s* of Sir Richard William Boord, 3rd Bt, and of Yvonne, Lady Boord, *d* of late J. A. Hubert Bird; *S* father, 1975; *m* 1965, Françoise Renée Louise Mouret. *Educ:* Eton (Harmsworth Lit. Prize, 1952); Sorbonne, France; Societa Dante Alighieri, Italy; Univ. of Santander, Spain. *Publications:* (trans. jtly) The History of Physics and the Philosophy of Science—Selected Essays (Armin Teske), 1972; numerous translations of scientific papers for English and American scientific and technical jls. *Recreations:* English and French literature and linguistics. *Heir:* *b* Antony Andrew Boord [*b* 21 May 1938; *m* 1960, Anna Christina von Krogh; one *s* one *d*]. *Address:* 61 Traverse Le Mée, 13009 Marseille, France. *T:* 73.13.95.

BOORMAN, Lt-Gen. Sir Derek, KCB 1986 (CB 1982); Lieutenant of the Tower of London, since 1989; *b* 13 Sept. 1930; *s* of late N. R. Boorman, MBE, and of Mrs A. L. Boorman (*née* Patman); *m* 1956, Jennifer Jane Skinner; one *s* two *d*. *Educ:* Wolstanton; RMA Sandhurst. Commnd N Staffords, 1950; Adjt 1 Staffords, 1958–59; Staff Coll., 1961; HQ 48 Gurkha Inf. Bde, 1962–64; Jt Services Staff Coll., 1968; CO 1 Staffords, 1969–71; Instr, Staff Coll., 1972–73; Comdr 51 Inf. Bde, 1975–76; RCDS, 1977; Dir, Public Relations (Army), 1978–79; Director of Military Operations, 1980–82; Comdr, British Forces Hong Kong, and Maj.-Gen. Bde of Gurkhas, 1982–85; Chief of Defence Intelligence, 1985–88. Colonel: 6th Queen Elizabeth's Own Gurkha Rifles, 1983–88; Staffordshire Regt (Prince of Wales's), 1985–90. Director: Tarmac Construction, 1988–; Crown House Engineering, 1989–; Thai Holdings Ltd, 1989–. Chm., Camberwell HA, 1989–. *Recreations:* shooting, gardening, music. *Address:* c/o Lloyds Bank (Cox's & King's Branch), Pall Mall, SW1. *Club:* Naval and Military.

BOORMAN, Edwin Roy Pratt; Chairman and Chief Executive, Kent Messenger Group, since 1986 (Managing Director, 1965–86); Chairman, Messenger Print Ltd; *b* 7 Nov. 1935; *s* of H. R. P. Boorman, *qv*; *m* 1st, Merrilyn Ruth Pettit (marr. diss. 1982); four *d*; 2nd, 1983, Janine Craske; one *s*. *Educ:* Rydal; Queens' Coll., Cambridge (MA Econ. History). National Service, 1954–56. Cambridge Univ., 1956–59; Kent Messenger, 1959; Editor: South Eastern Gazette, 1960–62; Kent Messenger, 1962–65. Dep. Councillor, Newspaper Soc. Court Assistant, Livery, Worshipful Co. of Stationers and Newspapermakers; President: Dickens Area Newsagents' Benevolent Assoc.; Maidstone Surgical Aid; Finance Dir, Royal British Legion Industries. Gov., Sutton Valence Sch. Vice-Pres., Age Concern, Kent; Chm., Kent Assoc. of Boys' Clubs, 1988–. Tax Comr, Maidstone District 1. *Recreation:* sailing. *Address:* Redhill Farm, 339 Redhill, Wateringbury, Kent ME18 5LB. *Clubs:* Veteran Car, Kent CCC; Royal Yachting Association, Medway Yacht, Ocean Cruising.

BOORMAN, Henry Roy Pratt, CBE 1966 (MBE 1945); President, Kent Messenger Group, since 1982 (Chairman, 1970–82); *b* 21 Sept. 1900; *s* of Barham Pratt Boorman and Elizabeth Rogers; *m* 1st, 1933, Enid Starke; one *s*; 2nd, 1947, Evelyn Clinch; one *d*. *Educ:* Leys Sch., Cambridge; Queens' Coll., Cambridge (MA). FJI 1936. Entered journalism, 1922; Proprietor and Editor, Kent Messenger, 1928; Chairman, South Eastern Gazette, 1929. Chairman, Kent Newspaper Proprietors' Assoc., 1931, 1932 and 1951; Mem. Council, Newspaper Soc., 1958, President, 1960. War Service: Regional Information Officer, SE Region, Tunbridge Wells, 1939; Dep. Welfare Officer for Kent, 1941; Major 1944; War Correspondent in Europe, 1939–40 and 1944, Berlin, 1949. Association of Men of Kent and Kentish Men: Editor, Journal Kent, 1931–62 (Chm. Council, 1949–51); Association's Sir Edward Hardy Gold Medal, 1964; in 1981, tenor bell in renewed peal in Canterbury Cathedral presented in his name by Kent Messenger staff. Maidstone Town Council: Councillor, 1934–46 and 1961–70; Mayor of Maidstone, 1962, Alderman, 1964. Liveryman, Worshipful Co. of Stationers and Newspaper Makers, 1933 (Mem. Ct of Assts, 1966–72). JP Maidstone Div. of Kent 1962; DL Kent, 1968–82. SBStJ 1946 (Mem. Council, StJ, 1960–66). *Publications:* Merry America (Royal Tour of Canada and United States), 1939; Hell's Corner, 1940; Kent—Our Glorious Heritage, 1951; Kentish Pride, 1952; Kent and the Cinque Ports, 1958; Kent Messenger Centenary, 1959; Kent—a Royal County, 1966; Spirit of Kent—Lord Cornwallis, 1968; Kent Our County, 1979. *Recreation:* world travel. *Address:* St Augustine's Priory, Bilsington, Ashford, Kent TN25 7AU. *T:* Aldington (0233) 720252. *Club:* Commonwealth Trust.

BOORSTIN, Dr Daniel J.; FRHistS; (12th) Librarian of Congress, 1975–87, now Emeritus; *b* 1 Oct. 1914; *s* of Samuel Boorstin and Dora (*née* Olsan); *m* 1941, Ruth Carolyn Frankel; three *s*. *Educ:* schs in Tulsa, Okla; Harvard Univ. (AB, summa cum Laude); Balliol Coll., Oxford (Rhodes Schol., BA Juris. 1st Cl. Hons, BCL 1st Cl. Hons); Yale Univ. Law Sch. (Sterling Fellow, JSD). Called to Bar, Inner Temple, 1937; admitted Mass Bar, 1942. Instr, tutor in history and lit., Harvard Univ. and Radcliffe Coll., 1938–42; Lectr, legal history, Law Sch., Harvard, 1939–42; Sen. Attorney, Office of Lend Lease Admin, Washington, DC, 1942–43; Office of Asst SG, USA, 1942–43; Asst Prof. of History, Swarthmore Coll., 1942–44; Univ. of Chicago, 1944–69: Asst Prof., 1944–49; Associate Prof., Preston and Sterling Morton Distinguished Prof. of Amer. History, 1956–69. During his 25 years tenure at Chicago, Visiting Lectr at Rome and Kyoto Univs, Sorbonne and Cambridge (Fellow, Trinity Coll., and Pitt Prof. of Amer. History and Instns; LittD 1968). Smithsonian Institution: Dir, Nat. Museum History and Techn., 1969–73; Sen. Historian, 1973–75. Many public service membership assignments, trusteeships, and active concern with a number of Amer. Assocs, esp. those relating to Amer. history, educn and cultural affairs. Past Pres., American Studies Assoc. Hon. FAGS. Hon. LittD Sheffield, 1979; Hon. DLitt: Cambridge, 1968; East Anglia, 1980; Sussex, 1983; numerous other hon. degrees. Watson-Davis Prize of the History of Science, Soc. for Discoverers, 1986; Charles Frankel Prize, Nat. Endowment for the Humanities, 1989; Nat. Book Award Medal for Distinguished Contribution to American Letters, 1989. Officier de L'Ordre de la Couronne, Belgium, 1980; Chevalier, Légion d'Honneur, France, 1984; Grand Officer, Order of Prince Henry the Navigator, Portugal, 1985; First Class Order of the Sacred Treasure, Japan, 1986. *Publications: include:* The Mysterious Science of the Law, 1941; The Lost World of Thomas Jefferson, 1948; The Genius of American Politics, 1953; The Americans: The Colonial Experience, 1958 (Bancroft Prize); America and the Image of Europe, 1960; The Image, 1962; The Americans: The National Experience, 1965 (Parkman Prize); The Decline of Radicalism, 1969; The Sociology of the Absurd, 1970; The Americans: The Democratic Experience, 1973 (Pulitzer Prize for History and Dexter Prize, 1974); Democracy and Its Discontents, 1974; The Exploring Spirit (BBC 1975 Reith Lectures), 1976; The Republic of Technology, 1978; (with Brooks M. Kelley) A History of the United States, 1980; The Discoverers, 1984 (Watson-Davis Prize); Hidden History, 1987; (for young readers) Landmark History of the American People, vol. I, From Plymouth to Appomattox, 1968; vol. II, From Appomattox to the Moon, 1970; New Landmark History of the American People, 1987; (ed) Delaware Cases 1792–1830, 1943; (ed) An American Primer, 1966; (ed) American Civilization, 1971; (ed) The Chicago History of American Civilization (30 vols). *Address:* (home) 3541 Ordway Street, NW, Washington, DC 20016, USA; (office) Library of Congress, Washington, DC 20540. *T:* (202) 955–2652. *Clubs:* Cosmos, National Press (Washington); Elizabethan (Yale); International House (Japan).

BOOTE, Col Charles Geoffrey Michael, MBE 1945; TD 1943; DL; Vice Lord-Lieutenant of Staffordshire, 1969–76; *b* 29 Sept. 1909; *s* of Lt-Col Charles Edmund Boote, TD, The North Staffordshire Regt (killed in action, 1916); *m* 1937, Elizabeth Gertrude (*d* 1980), *er d* of Evan Richard Davies, Market Drayton, Salop; three *s*. *Educ:* Bedford Sch. 2nd Lt 5th Bn North Staffordshire Regt, 1927. Served 1939–45, UK and NW Europe; despatches, 1945; Lt-Col, 1947. Director, H. Clarkson (Midlands) Ltd, 1969–75. Dir, Brit. Pottery Manufacturers' Fedn (Trustee) Ltd, 1955, retd Dec. 1969; Pres., Brit. Pottery Manufacturers' Fedn, 1957–58; Vice-Chm., Glazed and Floor Tile Manufacturers' Assoc., 1953–57. Hon. Col 5/6 Bn North Staffordshire Regt, 1963–67; Mem. Staffs TAVR Cttee, retd 1976. JP, Stoke-on-Trent, 1955–65; DL, 1958, JP 1959, High Sheriff, 1967–68, Staffordshire. Chm., Eccleshall PSD, 1971–76; Mem. Court of Governors, Keele Univ., 1957. *Recreations:* salmon fishing; British Racing Drivers' Club (Life Mem.); North Staffordshire Hunt (Hon. Sec. 1948–59). *Address:* Morile Mhor, Tomatin, Inverness-shire IV13 7YN. *T:* Tomatin (08082) 319. *Club:* Army and Navy.

BOOTE, Robert Edward, CVO 1971; first Director General, Nature Conservancy Council, 1973–80; *b* 6 Feb. 1920; *s* of Ernest Haydn Boote and Helen Rose Boote; *m* 1948, Vera (*née* Badian); one *s* one *d*. *Educ:* London Univ. (BSc Econ). DPA; FREconS 1953–61; AIPR 1957–61; FCIS 1960–81. War service, 1939–46, Actg Lt-Col, Hon. Major. Admin. Officer, City of Stoke-on-Trent, 1946–48; Chief Admin. Officer, Staffs County Planning and Develt Dept, 1948–54; Principal, 1954–64, Dep. Dir, 1964–73, Nature Conservancy. Sec. 1965–71, formerly Dep. Sec., Countryside in 1970 Confs, 1963, 1965, 1970 and numerous study groups; Mem., Pesticides Cttee, 1958–73; Chm., Broadland Report, 1963–65; UK Deleg. to Council of Europe Cttee for Conservation of Nature and Natural Resources, 1963–71; Mem., Countryside Review Cttee, 1977–79; a Chief Marshal to the Queen, 1970; various posts in meetings of UN, UNESCO, EEC and OECD, 1968–81; Chm. Preparatory Gp for Conservation Year 1970; Chm. Organising Cttee for European Conservation Conf. 1970 (Conf. Vice-Pres.); Chm. European Cttee, 1969–71; Consultant for European Architectural Heritage Year 1975; Advr, H of L Select Cttee on Europ. Communities, 1980–81. International Union for Conservation of Nature and Natural Resources: Treas., 1975–78; Mem., Governing Council and Bureau, 1975–81; a Vice-Pres., 1978–81; Rep., Internat. Conf. on Antarctic Marine Living Resources, 1980; Chm., Antarctica Resolution, 1981; Election Officer, 1984; Founder and

Chm., 1974–80, Mem., 1980–85, UK Cttee. Council Member: FFPS, 1979–83; RGS, 1983–86; BTCV (Vice-Pres.) 1980–; RSNC (Vice-Pres.) 1980–; RSNC Wildlife Appeal, 1983–87; WWF, 1980–86; Ecological Parks Trust, 1980–85; YPTES (Chm.), 1982–87; Friends of ENO, 1980–87; Common Ground Internat., 1981–85; Cttees for UK Conservation and Develt Prog., 1980–83; HGTAC, Forestry Commn, 1981–87; Conservator, Wimbledon and Putney Commons, 1981–; Patron, CSV, 1978–85; Chairman: Instn of Environmental Sciences, 1981–84; Seychelles Appeal Cttee, Royal Soc., 1980–87; Chm., Gp A, Ditchley Foundn Anglo/Amer. Conf. on Environment, 1970; Lead Speaker, Eurogespracht, Vienna, 1970; Mem., Entretiens Ecologiques de Dijon, 1981; UK Officer Rep., Eur. Environment Ministers Conf., 1976; Judge, Berlin world agro/environ films and TV competitions, 1970, 1972, 1974 and 1980. Initiator and Chm., Age Resource, 1988–; a Vice-Pres., Age Concern, 1990–. FRSA 1971. Hon. Associate, Landscape Inst., 1971; Hon. MRTPI, 1978. Greek Distinguished Service Medal, 1946; van Tienhoven European Prize, 1980; Merit Award, IUCN, 1984. Adviser: Macmillan Guide to Britain's Nature Reserves, 1980–; Shell Better Britain Campaign, 1980–91. Member Editorial Boards: Internat. Jl of Environmental Studies, 1975–; Town Planning Review, 1979–85; Internat. Jl Environmental Educn and Information, 1981–83. Helped to prepare, and appeared in films, Pacemaker, 1970, Man of Action (BBC), 1977. *Publications:* (as Robert Arvill) Man and Environment, 1967 (5th edn 1984); numerous papers, articles, addresses, TV and radio broadcasts, over 3 decades in UK and internat. professional confs in 40 countries. *Recreations:* travel, theatre, music. *Address:* 3 Leeward Gardens, SW19 7QR. *T:* 081–946 1551.

BOOTH; *see* Gore-Booth.

BOOTH; *see* Sclater-Booth, family name of Baron Basing.

BOOTH, Alan Shore, QC 1975; **His Honour Judge Alan Booth;** a Circuit Judge, since 1976; *b* Aug. 1922; 4th *s* of Parkin Stanley Booth and Ethel Mary Shore; *m* 1954, Mary Gwendoline Hilton; one *s* one *d. Educ:* Shrewsbury Sch.; Liverpool Univ. (LLB). Served War of 1939–45, RNVR, Fleet Air Arm (despatches 1944): Sub-Lt 1942; HMS Illustrious, 1943–45; Lieut 1944. Called to Bar, Gray's Inn, 1949. A Recorder of the Crown Court, 1972–76. Governor, Shrewsbury Sch., 1969. *Recreation:* golf. *Address:* 18 Abbey Road, West Kirby, Wirral L48 7EW. *T:* 051–625 5796. *Clubs:* Royal Liverpool Golf; Royal and Ancient (St Andrews).

BOOTH, Rt. Hon. Albert Edward, PC 1976; CIMechE 1985; Public Transport Officer, Hounslow Council, since 1988; *b* 28 May 1928; *e s* of Albert Henry Booth and Janet Mathieson; *m* 1957, Joan Amis; three *s. Educ:* St Thomas's Sch., Winchester; S Shields Marine Sch.; Rutherford Coll. of Technology. Engineering Draughtsman. Election Agent, 1951 and 1955. County Borough Councillor, 1962–65. Exec. Dir, S Yorks Passenger Transport Exec., 1983–87. MP (Lab) Barrow-in-Furness, 1966–83; Minister of State, Dept of Employment, 1974–76; Sec. of State for Employment, 1976–79; Opposition spokesman on transport, 1979–83. Chm., Select Cttee on Statutory Instruments, 1970–74. Treasurer, Labour Party, 1984. Contested (Lab): Tynemouth, 1964; Barrow and Furness, 1983; Warrington South, 1987. *Address:* Hounslow Council, Civic Centre, Lampton Road, Hounslow TW3 4DN.

BOOTH, Anthony John, CEng, FIEE; Corporate Director, British Telecommunications PLC, since 1984; Managing Director, Worldwide Networks, since 1991; *b* 18 March 1939; *s* of Benjamin and Una Lavinia Booth; *m* 1965, Elspeth Marjorie (*née* Fraser); one *s* one *d. Educ:* Bungay Grammar Sch.; London Univ. (BScEng, DMS). Joined Post Office Res. Dept, 1957; Exec. Engr and Sen. Exec. Engr, Telecom HQ, 1965–71; Asst Staff Engr, Central HQ Appointments, 1971–74; Head of Section and Div., External Telecom Exec., 1974–78; Head of Div., THQ, 1978–79; Dir, Internat. Networks, 1979–80; Regional Dir, London Region, 1980–83; Man. Dir, BT International, 1983–91. Gov., Ealing Coll., 1989. Member, Guild of Freemen of City of London, 1982–. MInstD 1985; CBIM 1986. *Recreations:* philately, golf, silversmithing, synchronised swimming official. *Address:* British Telecom Centre, 81 Newgate Street, EC1A 7AJ.

BOOTH, Brian George, JP; FSS; Rector and Chief Executive, Lancashire Polytechnic, since 1989; *b* 6 Sept. 1942; *s* of George and Ada Booth; *m* 1965, Barbara Ann (*née* Wright); two *d. Educ:* Univ. of Manchester (BA Econ 1964); Brunel Univ. (MTech 1972). FSS 1968. Asst Lectr in Statistics, High Wycombe Coll. of Technology, 1965–68; Lectr, Sen. Lectr, and Principal Lectr, Kingston Polytechnic, 1968–73; Head, Dept of Business and Admin, 1974–78, Dean, Faculty of Business and Management, 1978–82, Preston Polytechnic; Dep. Dir, Preston Polytechnic, later Lancashire Polytechnic, 1982–89. Chair of Bd, Preston Business Venture, 1983–. JP Preston, 1987. FRSA 1990. *Recreations:* golf, watching Preston North End. *Address:* 9 Moorfield Close, Fulwood, Preston, Lancs PR2 4SW. *T:* Preston (0772) 864243.

BOOTH, Charles Leonard, CMG 1979; LVO 1961; HM Diplomatic Service, retired; re-employed in Foreign and Commonwealth Office, 1985–90; *b* 7 March 1925; *s* of Charles Leonard and Marion Booth; *m* 1958, Mary Gillian Emms; two *s* two *d. Educ:* Heywood Grammar Sch.; Pembroke Coll., Oxford Univ., 1942–43 and 1947–50. Served RA (Capt.), 1943–47. Joined HM Foreign Service, 1950; Foreign Office, 1950–51; Third and Second Secretary, Rangoon, 1951–55; FO, 1955–60 (Private Sec. to Parly Under-Sec. of State, 1958–60); First Sec., Rome, 1960–63; Head of Chancery, Rangoon, 1963–64, and Bangkok, 1964–67; FO, 1967–69. Counsellor, 1968; Deputy High Comr, Kampala, 1969–71; Consul-General and Counsellor (Administration), Washington, 1971–73; Counsellor, Belgrade, 1973–77; Ambassador to Burma, 1978–82; High Comr, Malta, 1982–85. Officer of Order of Merit of Italian Republic, 1961. *Recreations:* opera, gardening, walking. *Address:* 7 Queen Street, Southwold, Suffolk IP18 6EQ. *Club:* Travellers'.

BOOTH, Sir Christopher (Charles), Kt 1983; Director, Clinical Research Centre, Medical Research Council, 1978–88; *b* 22 June 1924; *s* of Lionel Barton Booth and Phyllis Petley Duncan; *m* 1st, 1959, Lavinia Loughridge, Belfast; one *s* one *d*; 2nd, 1970, Soad Tabaqchali; one *d. Educ:* Sedbergh Sch., Yorks; University of St Andrews; MB 1951, MD 1958 (Rutherford Gold Medal). Junior appointments at Dundee Royal Infirmary, Hammersmith Hosp. and Addenbrooke's Hosp., Cambridge; successively Medical Tutor, Lecturer in Medicine and Senior Lecturer, Postgraduate Medical School of London; Prof. and Dir of Dept of Medicine, RPMS, London Univ., 1966–77. Member: Adv. Bd to Res. Councils, 1976–78; MRC, 1981–84; Chm., Medical Adv. Cttee, British Council, 1979–85; President: British Soc. of Gastroenterology, 1978–79; BMA, 1986–87; RSocMed, 1988; Johnson Soc., 1987–88; Chm., Royal Naval Personnel Cttee, 1985–. FRCP 1964; FRCPEd 1967; Hon. FACP 1973; Hon. FRSM 1991. For. Mem., Amer. Philosophical Soc., 1981. Docteur (*hc*): Paris, 1975; Poitiers, 1981; Hon. LLD Dundee, 1982. Dicke Gold Medal, Dutch Soc. of Gastroenterology, 1973; Ludwig Heilmeyer Gold Medal, German Soc. for Advances in Internal Medicine, 1982. Chevalier de l'Ordre National du Mérite (France), 1977. *Publications:* (with Betsy C. Corner) Chain of Friendship: Letters of Dr John Fothergill of London, 1735–1780, 1971; (with G. Neale) Disorders of the Small Intestine, 1985; Doctors in Science and Society, 1987; papers in med. jls on relationship of nutritional disorders to disease of the alimentary tract, and on medical history. *Recreations:* fishing, history. *Address:* 9 Kent Terrace, NW1 4RP. *T:* 071–724 3379.

BOOTH, Dr Clive; Director, Oxford Polytechnic, since 1986; *b* 18 April 1943; *s* of Henry Booth and Freda Frankland; *m* 1969, Margaret Sardeson. *Educ:* King's Sch., Macclesfield; Trinity Coll., Cambridge (MA 1969); Univ. of California, Berkeley (Harkness Fellow, 1973; MA 1974; PhD 1976). Joined DES, 1965; Prin. Pvte Sec. to Sec. of State for Educn and Science, 1975–77; Asst Sec., 1977–81; Dep. Dir, Plymouth Polytechnic, 1981–84; Mem., HM Inspectorate, DES, 1984–86. Member: Governing Council, SRHE, 1981–; Adv. Cttee, Brunel Univ. Educn Policy Centre, 1986–; Computer Bd for Univs and Res. Councils, 1987–; CNAA Cttee for Information and Develt Services, 1987–; Fulbright Academic Administrators Selection Cttee, 1988–; Council for Industry and Higher Educn, 1990–; Chm., PCFC Steering Gp on Statistical Information, 1989–. Director: Thames Action Resource Gp for Educn and Trng, 1986–; Thames Valley Technology Centre, 1989–. Leverhulme Res. Fellow, 1983. Gov., Headington and Wheatley Park Schs. Jt Ed., Higher Educn Qly, 1986–; Mem., Editorial Bd, Oxford Review of Educn, 1990–. *Recreations:* circuit training, walking, bridge, opera. *Address:* Oxford Polytechnic, Gipsy Lane, Headington, Oxford OX3 0BP. *T:* Oxford (0865) 819002.

BOOTH, Rev. Canon David Herbert, MBE 1944; Provost, Shoreham College (formerly Shoreham Grammar School), Sussex, since 1977 (Headmaster, 1972–77); Chaplain to the Queen, 1957–77; *b* 26 Jan. 1907; *s* of Robert and Clara Booth; *m* 1942, Diana Mary Chard; two *s* one *d. Educ:* Bedford Sch.; Pembroke Coll., Cambridge; Ely Theological Coll. BA (3rd cl. Hist. Trip. part II), 1931; MA 1936; deacon, 1932; priest, 1933; Curate, All Saints', Hampton, 1932–34; Chaplain, Tonbridge Sch., 1935–40; Chaplain, RNVR, 1940–45; Rector of Stepney, 1945–53; Vicar of Brighton, 1953–59; Prebendary of Waltham in Chichester Cathedral, 1953–59; Archdeacon of Lewes, 1959–71; Prebendary of Bury in Chichester Cathedral, 1972–76; Canon Emeritus of Chichester, 1976. Select Preacher, University of Cambridge, 1947. Mem. of Archbishop's Commission on South East, 1965. Pres., Nat. Schs Jumping Championship, 1963–. *Recreations:* horses, gardening and family life. *Address:* Courtyard Cottage, School Road, Charing, near Ashford, Kent TN27 0HX. *T:* Charing (023371) 3349.

BOOTH, Sir Douglas Allen, 3rd Bt, *cr* 1916; writer and producer for television; *b* 2 Dec. 1949; *s* of Sir Philip Booth, 2nd Bt, and Ethel, *d* of Joseph Greenfield, NY, USA; *S* father 1960. *Educ:* Beverly Hills High Sch.; Harvard Univ. (Harvard Nat. Scholarship, Nat. Merit Scholarship, 1967); BA (*magna cum laude*) 1975. *Recreations:* music, back-packing. *Heir: b* Derek Blake Booth, *b* 7 April 1953. *Address:* 1626 Sycamore Drive, Topanga, Calif 90290, USA.

BOOTH, Eric Stuart, CBE 1971; FRS 1967; FEng 1976; Chairman, Yorkshire Electricity Board, 1972–79; *b* 14 Oct. 1914; *s* of Henry and Annie Booth; *m* 1945, Mary Elizabeth Melton (*d* 1987); two *d*; *m* 1988, Pauline Margaret Ford. *Educ:* Batley Grammar Sch.; Liverpool Univ. Apprentice, Metropolitan Vickers Electrical Co. Ltd, 1936–38; Technical Engineer, Yorks Electric Power Co., 1938–46; Dep., later City Electrical Engineer and Manager, Salford Corporation, 1946–48; various posts associated with construction of Power Stations with British, later Central Electricity Authority, 1948–57, Dep. Chief Engineer (Generation Design and Construction), 1957; Chief Design and Construction Engineer, 1958–59, Bd Mem. for Engrg, 1959–71, CEGB. Part-time Mem., UKAEA, 1965–72; Pres., IEE, 1976–77. Dir, British Electricity Internat., 1979–84; Consultant to Electricity Council, 1979–84; Advisor to Coll. of Power Technology, 1982–. Hon. FIEE 1986. Hon. DTech Bradford, 1980. *Address:* Pinecroft, Upper Dunsforth, York YO5 9RU. *T:* Boroughbridge (0423) 322821.

BOOTH, Sir Gordon, KCMG 1980 (CMG 1969); CVO 1976; HM Diplomatic Service, retired; adviser on international trade and investment; Adviser: Hanson PLC, since 1989; Bechtel Group, since 1983; Vice Chairman, Bechtel Ltd, since 1986; *b* 22 Nov. 1921; *s* of Walter and Grace Booth, Bolton, Lancs; *m* 1944, Jeanne Mary Kirkham; one *s* one *d. Educ:* Canon Slade Sch.; London Univ. (BCom). Served War of 1939–45: Capt. RAC and 13/18th Royal Hussars, 1941–46. Min. of Labour and Bd of Trade, 1946–55; Trade Comr, Canada and West Indies, 1955–65; Mem. HM Diplomatic Service, 1965–80; Counsellor (Commercial), British Embassy in Copenhagen, 1966–69; Dir, Coordination of Export Services, DTI, 1969–71; Consul-General, Sydney, 1971–74; HBM Consul-Gen., NY, and Dir-Gen. of Trade Develt in USA, 1975–80; Chm., SITPRO Bd, 1980–86. Director: Hanson PLC (formerly Hanson Trust), 1981–89; City of London Heliport Ltd, 1989–. *Recreations:* golf, bridge. *Address:* Pilgrims Corner, Ebbisham Lane, Walton on the Hill, Surrey KT20 5BT. *T:* Tadworth (0737) 3788. *Clubs:* Brooks's; Walton Heath Golf.

BOOTH, His Honour James; a Circuit Judge (formerly a County Court Judge), 1969–84; *b* 3 May 1914; *s* of James and Agnes Booth; *m* 1954, Joyce Doreen Mather; two *s* one *d. Educ:* Bolton Sch.; Manchester Univ. Called to Bar, Gray's Inn, 1936 (Arden Scholar, Gray's Inn). Town Clerk, Ossett, Yorks, 1939–41. RAFVR, 1941–46 (Flt-Lieut). Contested (L): West Leeds, 1945; Darwen, 1950. Recorder of Barrow-in-Furness, 1967–69. *Recreation:* fell walking. *Address:* Spinney End, Worsley, Lancs M28 4QN. *T:* 061–790 2003.

BOOTH, John Antony W.; *see* Ward-Booth.

BOOTH, John Barton, FRCS; Consultant Otolaryngologist, Royal London Hospital (formerly London Hospital), since 1972; Hon. Consultant, St Luke's Hospital for the Clergy, since 1983; Civil Consultant (Otology), Royal Air Force, since 1983; *b* 19 Nov. 1937; *s* of (Percy) Leonard Booth and Mildred Amy (*née* Wilson); *m* 1966, Carroll Griffiths; one *s. Educ:* Canford Sch., Dorset; King's Coll., London (AKC 1963); King's Coll. Hosp. Med. Sch. (MB, BS 1963). FRCS 1963. House Surgeon: Birmingham Accident Hosp., 1964; Hosp. for Sick Children, Gt Ormond St, 1965; House Surgeon, Registrar, Sen. Registrar, RNTNEH, 1966–70; Sen. Registrar, Royal Free Hosp., 1970–72; Clin. Assistant, Neuro-Otology, Nat. Hosp. for Nervous Diseases, 1968, 1971; Consultant Surgeon, RNTNEH, 1973–78; Hon. Consultant Laryngologist: Musicians Benevolent Fund, 1974–; Royal Coll. of Music, 1974–; Newspaper Press Fund, 1982–; Royal Opera House, Covent Gdn, 1983–; Royal Soc. of Musicians of GB, 1987–; Concert Artistes Assoc., 1987–; Webber-Douglas Acad. of Dramatic Art, 1987–. Hunterian Prof., RCS, 1980–81. Vice-Chm., 1960–61, Chm., 1961–62, Vice-Pres., 1962–63, Fedn of Univ. Conservatives; Mem., Gen. Purposes and Exec. Cttees, Cons. Party, 1961–62. FRSM 1967 (Mem. Council, 1980–88). MRAeS 1990. Howell Meml Prize (jtly), Univ. of London, 1988. Editor, Jl of Laryngology and Otology, 1987– (Asst Editor, 1979–87). *Publications:* (ed) Vol. 3, The Ear, of 5th edn of Scott-Brown's Otolaryngology, 1987; chapters in: Rob and Smith, Operative Surgery, 3rd edn 1976; Audiology and Audiological Medicine, vol. I, 1981; Otologic Medicine and Surgery, 1988. *Recreations:* golf, the arts. *Address:* 18 Upper Wimpole Street, W1M 7TB. *T:* 071–935 5631. *Clubs:* Royal Automobile, United and Cecil, MCC.

BOOTH, John Dick L.; *see* Livingston Booth.

BOOTH, John Wells; *b* 19 May 1903; *s* of late Charles and Grace Wells Booth, Liverpool; *m* 1929, Margaret, *d* of late Mr and Mrs S. J. Lawry; two *s* one *d*. *Educ:* Royal Naval Colls Osborne and Dartmouth. Royal Navy, 1917–25 (Lieut Comdr). Booth Steamship Co. Ltd., 1926–45 (Chm., 1939–45); Dir, Alfred Booth & Co. Ltd, 1935–79 (Chm., 1952–74). Civil Aviation, 1945–50. Chm., British South American Airways Corporation, 1946–49; Dep. Chm., BOAC, 1949–50; Bd Mem., BOAC, 1950–65; Dir, Phoenix Assurance Co. Ltd, 1945–73. Former Chairman: Liverpool Seamens' Welfare Cttee (Mem. Seamens' Welfare Bd); Liverpool Steamship Owners' Assoc.; former JP for Co. of Cheshire. *Address:* Hilary Lodge, Somerton Road, Hartest, Bury St Edmunds IP29 4NA. *T:* Bury St Edmunds (0284) 830426. *Club:* Flyfishers'.

BOOTH, Hon. Dame Margaret (Myfanwy Wood), DBE 1979; **Hon. Mrs Justice Booth;** a Judge of the High Court, Family Division, since 1979; *b* 1933; *d* of late Alec Wood Booth and of Lilian May Booth; *m* 1982, Joseph Jackson, QC (*d* 1987). *Educ:* Northwood Coll.; University Coll., London (LLM; Fellow, 1982). Called to the Bar, Middle Temple, 1956; Bencher, 1979. QC 1976. Chairman: Family Law Bar Assoc., 1976–78; Matrimonial Causes Procedure Cttee, 1982–85; Children Act Procedure Adv. Cttee, 1990. Governor, Northwood Coll., 1975–; Mem. Council, Univ. Coll. London, 1980–84. *Publications:* (co-ed) Rayden on Divorce, 10th-15th edns; (co-ed) Clarke Hall and Morrison on Children, 9th edn 1977, (cons. ed.) 10th edn 1985. *Address:* c/o Royal Courts of Justice, Strand, WC2A 2LL. *Club:* Reform.

BOOTH, Michael Addison John W.; *see* Wheeler-Booth.

BOOTH, Peter John Richard; Textile National Trade Group Secretary, Transport and General Workers Union, since 1986; *b* 27 March 1949; *s* of Eric Albert and Edith Booth; *m* 1970, Edwina Ivy; three *s*. *Educ:* Little London Infant Sch.; Rawdon Littlemore Junior Sch., Rawdon; Benton Park Secondary Modern School. Dyers' Operative, 1964; National Union of Dyers, Bleachers and Textile Workers: District Officer, 1973; Nat. Research Officer, 1975; Nat. Organiser, 1980; transf. to TGWU, 1982; Nat. Trade Group Organiser, 1982. Director: Man-Made Fibres Industry Trng Adv. Bd, 1986–; Apparel, Knitting & Textiles Alliance, 1989–; Vice Pres., British Textile Confedn, 1989–; Member: TUC Textiles, Clothing and Footwear Industries Cttee, 1976–; Confedn of British Wool Textiles Trng Bd, 1986–; Carpet Industry Trng Council, 1986–; Nat. Textile Trng Gp, 1989–; Presidium, European TU Cttee, 1990–; Health and Safety Cttee, Cotton & Allied Textiles Industry Adv. Cttee. *Publication:* The Old Dog Strike, 1985. *Recreations:* walking, gardening, dominoes, chess. *Address:* Dye House, St John's Court, Yeadon, Leeds. *T:* Leeds (0532) 502182. *Club:* Yeadon Trades Hall.

BOOTH, Richard George William Pitt; Chairman, Richard Booth (Bookshops) Ltd, Bookseller, since 1961; Chairman, Welsh Booksellers Association, since 1987; *b* 12 Sept. 1938; *m* 1987, Hope Estcourt Stuart (*née* Barrie). *Educ:* Rugby; Univ. of Oxford. *Publications:* Country Life Book of Book Collecting, 1976; Independence for Hay, 1977. *Recreations:* creating a monarchy in Hay (began home rule movement, 1 April 1977); gardening. *Address:* Hay Castle, Hay-on-Wye, via Hereford HR3.

BOOTH, Sir Robert (Camm), Kt 1977; CBE 1967; TD; Chairman, National Exhibition Centre Ltd, 1975–82 (Founder Director, 1970–82; Chief Executive, 1977–78); *b* 9 May 1916; *s* of late Robert Wainhouse Booth; *m* 1939, Veronica Courtenay, *d* of late F. C. Lamb; one *s* three *d*. *Educ:* Altrincham Grammar Sch.; Manchester Univ. (LLB). Called to Bar, Gray's Inn. War Service 8th (A) Bn Manchester Regt, France, Malta, Middle East, Italy, 1939–46. Manchester Chamber of Commerce, 1946–58; Sec., Birmingham Chamber of Industry and Commerce, 1958–65, Dir, 1965–78, Pres., 1978–79. Local non-exec. dir, Barclays Bank, 1977–84; Member: W Midlands Econ. Planning Council, 1974–77; BOTB Adv. Council, 1975–82; Midlands Adv. Bd, Legal and General Assurance Soc., 1979–86; Midlands and NW Bd, BR, 1979–85; Bd, Inst. of Occupational Health, 1980–90. Trustee, Nuffield Trust for the Forces of the Crown, 1977–. Life Mem., Court of Governors, 1969, Birmingham Univ. (Mem. Council, 1973–78); Governor, Sixth Form Coll., Solihull, 1974–77; Hon. Mem., British Exhbns Promotions Council, 1982. Overseas travel with 20 trade missions and author of marketing and economic publications. Marketor and Freeman, City of London, 1978. Hon. DSc Aston, 1975; Hon. FInstM; FRSA 1975. Midland Man of the Year Press Radio and TV Award, 1970. Officier de la Légion d'Honneur, 1982. *Address:* White House, 7 Sandal Rise, Solihull B91 3ET. *T:* 021–705 5311.

BOOTH, Rev. William James; Sub-Dean of Her Majesty's Chapels Royal, Deputy Clerk of the Closet, Sub-Almoner and Domestic Chaplain to The Queen, since 1991; Priest-Vicar of Westminster Abbey, since 1987; *b* 3 Feb. 1939; *s* of William James Booth and Elizabeth Ethel Booth. *Educ:* Ballymena Acad., Co. Antrim; TCD (MA). Curate, St Luke's Parish, Belfast, 1962–64; Chaplain, Cranleigh Sch., Surrey, 1965–74. Priest-in-Ordinary to The Queen, 1976–91. Chaplain, Westminster School, London, 1974–91. Organiser, PHAB annual residential courses at Westminster (and formerly at Cranleigh). *Recreations:* music, hi-fi, cooking. *Address:* Marlborough Gate, St James's Palace, SW1. *T:* 071–930 6609.

BOOTH-CLIBBORN, Rt. Rev. Stanley Eric Francis; *see* Manchester, Bishop of.

BOOTHBY, Sir Brooke (Charles), 16th Bt *cr* 1660, of Broadlow Ash, Derbyshire; *b* 6 April 1949; *s* of Sir Hugo Robert Brooke Boothby, 15th Bt and of (Evelyn) Ann, *d* of Late H. C. R. Homfray; *S* father, 1986; *m* 1976, Georgiana Alexandra, *o d* of late Sir John Wriothesley Russell, GCVO, CMG; two *d*. *Educ:* Eton; Trinity Coll., Cambridge (BA Econs). Man. Dir, Fontygary Leisure, 1979–; Chm., Tourism Quality Services Ltd, 1990–. Chairman: Historic Houses Assoc. Inheritance Cttee, 1984–86; Nat. Caravan Council Parks Div., 1987–90. High Sheriff, South Glamorgan, 1986–87. *Recreation:* shooting. *Heir: kinsman* George William Boothby [*b* 18 June 1948; *m* 1977, Sally Louisa Thomas; three *d*]. *Address:* Fonmon Castle, Barry, South Glamorgan CF6 9ZN. *T:* Rhoose (0446) 710206.

BOOTHMAN, Campbell Lester; His Honour Judge Boothman; a Circuit Judge, since 1988; *b* 3 Sept. 1942; *s* of Gerald and Ann Boothman; *m* 1966, Penelope Evelyn Pepe; three *s*. *Educ:* Oundle; King's College, London. Called to the Bar, Inner Temple, 1965. A Recorder, 1985–88. *Recreations:* skiing, squash. *Address:* The Glen, Tower House Lane, Wraxall, Bristol.

BOOTHMAN, Derek Arnold, FCA; Chairman: First Manchester Properties Plc, since 1988; Burns Anderson Group Plc, since 1991; Deputy Chairman, Central Manchester Development Corporation, since 1988; *b* 5 June 1932; *s* of Eric Randolph Boothman and Doris Mary Boothman; *m* 1958, Brenda Margaret; one *s* one *d*. *Educ:* William Hulme's Grammar Sch., Manchester. Articled to J. Needham & Co., 1948; Mem., ICA, 1954; National Service, RAF, 1954–56; Partner: J. Needham & Co. (now part of Binder Hamlyn), 1957; Binder Hamlyn, Chartered Accts, 1974–88; Chm., Piccadilly Radio Plc, 1988–90 (Dir, 1985–90); Director (non-executive): Remploy Ltd, 1987–; Mynshul Bank Plc, 1988–; BCMB Ltd, 1990–. President: Manchester Chartered Accountants Students Soc., 1967–68; Manchester Soc. of Chartered Accountants, 1968–69; Institute of Chartered Accountants in England and Wales: Council Member, 1969–; Treasurer, 1981–83; Vice-Pres., 1983–85; Dep. Pres., 1985–86; Pres., 1986–87. Member, Accounting Standards Cttee, 1974–82. Chm. of Governors, William Hulme's Grammar Sch., 1988–; Mem. Ct, Univ. of Manchester, 1990–. Liveryman, Worshipful Company of Chartered Accountants, 1976–. *Publications:* contribs to professional press and lectures on professional topics, internationally. *Recreations:* cricket, skiing, gardening, travel. *Address:* Ashworth Dene, Wilmslow Road, Mottram St Andrew, Cheshire SK10 4QH. *T:* Prestbury (0625) 829101. *Clubs:* St James's (Manchester); Withington Golf (Manchester) (past Captain).

BOOTHROYD, Betty; MP (Lab) West Bromwich West, since 1974 (West Bromwich, May 1973–1974); Deputy Chairman of Ways and Means and Deputy Speaker, House of Commons, since 1987; *b* Yorkshire, 8 Oct. 1929; *d* of Archibald and Mary Boothroyd. *Educ:* Dewsbury Coll. of Commerce and Art. Personal/Political Asst to Labour Ministers. Accompanied Parly delegns to: European Confs, 1955–60; Soviet Union, China and Vietnam, 1957; delegate to N Atlantic Assembly, 1974. An Asst Govt Whip, Oct. 1974–Nov. 1975; Member: Select Cttee on Foreign Affairs, 1979–81; Speaker's Panel of Chairmen, 1979–87; House of Commons Commn, 1983–87. Mem., European Parlt, 1975–77. Mem., Labour Party NEC, 1981–87. Councillor, Hammersmith Borough Council, 1965–68. Contested (Lab): SE Leicester (by-elec.), 1957; Peterborough (gen. elec.), 1959; Nelson and Colne (by-elec.), 1968; Rossendale (gen. elec.), 1970. Mem. Ct, Birmingham Univ., 1982–. *Recreations:* dominoes, scrabble. *Address:* House of Commons, SW1A 0AA.

BOOTLE-WILBRAHAM, family name of **Baron Skelmersdale.**

BOR, Walter George, CBE 1975; FRIBA, DistTP; FRTPI; FRSA; Consultant: Llewelyn-Davies Weeks, since 1976; Llewelyn-Davies Planning, since 1984; Partner, Llewelyn-Davies Weeks Forestier-Walker & Bor, London, 1966–76; *b* 1916, Czech parentage; father chemical engineer; *m* Dr Muriel Blackburn; two *s* one *d*. *Educ:* Prague Univ. (degree of Arch.); Bartlett Sch. of Architecture and Sch. of Planning and Regional Research, London (Dip.). Private architectural practice, London, 1946–47; London County Council, 1947–62 (in charge of planning of London's East End, 1958; Dep. Planning Officer with special responsibility for civic design, 1960–62); Liverpool City Planning Officer, 1962–66. Mem. Minister's Planning Advisory Gp, 1964–65. In private practice as architect and planning consultant, 1966–. Pres., Town Planning Inst., 1970–71; Vice-Pres., Housing Centre Trust, 1971–88. Visiting Professor: Princeton Univ., 1977–79; Rice Univ., Houston, 1980–81. Mem., Severn Barrage Cttee, 1978–81; Consultant, UNDP, Cyprus, 1982–83; Advr, Shenzhen City Planning Commn, China, 1987–; Pres., London Forum of Amenity Socs, 1989–. *Publications:* Liverpool Interim Planning Policy, 1965; Liverpool City Centre Plan (jt), 1966; Two New Cities in Venezuela (jt), 1967–69; The Milton Keynes Plan (jt), 1970; Airport City (Third London Airport urbanisation studies) (jt), 1970; The Making of Cities, 1972; SE London and the Fleet Line for LTE (jt), 1973; Bogota Urban Development for UNDP (jt), 1974; Concept Plan for Tehran new city centre, 1974; Shetland Draft Structure Plan, 1975; (jtly) Unequal City: Birmingham Inner Area Study, 1977; (jtly) Shenzhen, China: airport and urban design reports, 1987; articles for jls of RTPI, RIBA, TCPA, ICE, RICS, Amer. Inst. of Planners, Princeton Univ., Hong Kong Inst. of Planners; Urbanistica, Habitat Internat.; Ekistics. *Recreations:* music, theatre, sketching, sculpting, pottery. *Address:* 99 Swains Lane, Highgate, N6 6PJ. *T:* 081–340 6540. *Club:* Reform.

BOREEL, Sir Francis (David), 13th Bt, *cr* 1645; Counsellor, Netherlands Foreign Service, 1966–87 (Attaché, 1956), retired; *b* 14 June 1926; *s* of Sir Alfred Boreel, 12th Bt and Countess Reiniera Adriana (*d* 1957), *d* of Count Francis David Schimmelpenninck; *S* father 1964; *m* 1964, Suzanne Campagne; three *d*. *Educ:* Utrecht Univ. *Recreations:* tennis, sailing. *Heir: kinsman* Stephen Gerard Boreel [*b* 9 Feb. 1945; *m* Francien P. Kooyman; one *s*]. *Address:* Kapellstraat 25, 4351 A. L. Veere, Netherlands.

BOREHAM, Sir (Arthur) John, KCB 1980 (CB 1974); Director, Central Statistical Office, and Head of the Government Statistical Service, 1978–85, retired; *b* 30 July 1925; 3rd *s* of late Ven. Frederick Boreham, Archdeacon of Cornwall and Chaplain to the Queen, and late Caroline Mildred Boreham; *m* 1948, Heather, *o d* of Harold Edwin Horth, FRIBA, and Muriel Horth; three *s* one *d*. *Educ:* Marlborough; Trinity Coll., Oxford. Agricultural Economics Research Inst., Oxford, 1950; Min. of Food, 1951; Min. of Agric., 1952; Gen. Register Office, 1955; Central Statistical Office, 1958; Chief Statistician, Gen. Register Office, 1963; Dir of Economics and Statistics, Min. of Technology, 1967–71; Central Statistical Office: Asst Dir, 1971–72; Dep. Dir, 1972–78. Vis. Fellow, Nuffield Coll., Oxford, 1981–88. President: Inst. of Statisticians, 1984–; Assoc. of Social Res. Orgns, 1990–. *Recreations:* music, golf. *Address:* Piperscroft, Brittain's Lane, Sevenoaks, Kent TN13 2NG. *T:* Sevenoaks (0732) 454678.

BOREHAM, Hon. Sir Leslie Kenneth Edward, Kt 1972; **Hon. Mr Justice Boreham;** a Judge of the High Court, Queen's Bench Division, since 1972; Presiding Judge, North Eastern Circuit, 1974–79; Deputy Chairman, Agricultural Lands Tribunal; *m*; one *s* one *d*. Served War of 1939–45, RAF. Called to the Bar at Lincoln's Inn, Nov. 1947; Bencher 1972. QC 1965. Recorder of Margate, 1968–71. Joined South-Eastern Circuit. Dep. Chm. 1962–65, Chm. 1965–71, East Suffolk QS. *Recreations:* gardening, golf. *Address:* 1 Paper Buildings, Temple, EC4.

BORG, Alan Charles Nelson, CBE 1991; PhD; FSA; Director General, Imperial War Museum, since 1982; *b* 21 Jan. 1942; *s* of late Charles John Nelson Borg and Frances Mary Olive Hughes; *m* 1st, 1964, Anne (marr. diss.), *d* of late Dr William Blackmore; one *s* one *d*; 2nd, 1976, Caroline, *d* of late Captain Lord Francis Hill; two *d*. *Educ:* Westminster Sch.; Brasenose Coll., Oxford (MA); Courtauld Inst. of Art (PhD). Lecteur d'anglais, Université d'Aix-Marseille, 1964–65; Lectr, History of Art, Indiana Univ., 1967–69; Asst Prof. of History of Art, Princeton Univ., 1969–70; Asst Keeper of the Royal Armouries, HM Tower of London, 1970–78; Keeper, Sainsbury Centre for Visual Arts, Univ. of E Anglia, 1978–82. *Publications:* Architectural Sculpture in Romanesque Provence, 1972; European Swords and Daggers in the Tower of London, 1974; Torture and Punishment, 1975; Heads and Horses, 1976; Arms and Armour in Britain, 1979; (ed with A. R. Martindale) The Vanishing Past: studies presented to Christopher Hohler, 1981; War Memorials, 1991; articles in learned jls. *Recreations:* fencing (Oxford blue, 1962, 1963), music, travel. *Address:* Telegraph House, 36 West Square, SE11 4SP.

BORG, Björn Rune; tennis player; *b* 6 June 1956; *s* of Rune and Margaretha Borg; *m* 1980, Mariana Simionescu (marr. diss. 1984); one *s* by Jannike Bjorling; *m* 1989, Loredana Berte. *Educ:* Blombacka Sch., Södertälje. Started to play tennis at age of 9; won Wimbledon junior title, 1972; became professional player in 1972. Mem., Swedish Davis Cup team, annually 1972–80 (youngest player ever in a winning Davis Cup team, 1975). Championship titles: Italian, 1974, 1978; French, 1974, 1975, 1978, 1979, 1980, 1981; Wimbledon, record of 5 consecutive singles titles, 1976–80; World Champion, 1978, 1979, 1980; Masters, 1980, 1981. *Publication:* (with Eugene Scott) Björn Borg: my life and game, 1980. *Address:* c/o International Management Group, The Pier House, Strand on the Green, Chiswick, W4 3NN.

BORG COSTANZI, Prof. Edwin J.; Rector, University of Malta, 1964–80 and since 1988; Consultant to Government of Malta, since 1987; *b* 8 Sept. 1925; 2nd *s* of late Michael Borg Costanzi and M. Stella (*née* Camilleri); *m* 1948, Lucy Valentino; two *s* one *d*. *Educ:* Lyceum, Malta; Royal University of Malta (BSc, BE&A); Balliol College, Oxford (BA 1946, MA 1952); Malta Rhodes Scholar, 1945. Professor of Mathematics, Royal University of Malta, 1950–64; Vis. Fellow, Univ. of Southampton, 1980–82; Professorial Res. Fellow, 1982–85, Hd of Dept of Computer Sci., 1985–87, Brunel Univ. Chm., 1976–77, Mem., 1965–66, 1968–69, 1972–74, 1977–78, Council of ACU. *Recreations:* fishing, photography. *Address:* University of Malta, Msida, Malta. *Club:* Casino (Valletta Malta).

BORGES, Thomas William Alfred; Managing Director, Thomas Borges & Partners Ltd, since 1949; Deputy Chairman, Phoenix Timber Group PLC, 1986–91; *b* 1 April 1923; *s* of Arthur Borges, Prague, and Paula Borges; *m* 1st (marr. diss.); 2nd, 1966, Serena Katherine Stewart (*née* Jamieson); two *s*. *Educ:* Dunstable Grammar Sch.; Luton Technical Coll. Served War, 1941–45. Trained in banking, shipping and industry, 1945–49; Dir, Borges Law & Co., Sydney and Melbourne, 1951; Chm., Smith Whitworth Ltd, 1974–80. Governor, Royal National Orth. Hosp., 1968– (Dep. Chm., 1978–80, Chm., 1980–82); Dir, Inst. of Orths, Univ. of London, 1968– (Dep. Chm., 1978–80, Chm., 1980–82); Member: Grants Cttee, King Edward VII Hosp. Fund, 1975–80; Council, Professions Supp. to Medicine, 1980–88 (Dep. Chm., 1982–88); Treasurer, Riding for Disabled Assoc., 1977–84. Chm., Australian Art Foundn, 1984–. Exec. Mem., Sir Robert Menzies Meml Trust, 1981–. *Publication:* Two Expeditions of Discovery in North West and Western Australia by George Grey, 1969. *Recreations:* collecting Australiana, riding, swimming. *Address:* Porchester Lodge, 70 Westbourne Park Road, W2 5PJ. *T:* 071–229 5220. *Club:* Garrick.

BORINGDON, Viscount; Mark Lionel Parker; *b* 22 Aug. 1956; *s* and *heir* of 6th Earl of Morley, *qv*; *m* 1983, Carolyn Jill, *d* of Donald McVicar, Meols, Wirral, Cheshire; two *d*. *Educ:* Eton. Commissioned, Royal Green Jackets, 1976. *Address:* Pound House, Yelverton, Devon.

BORLAND, David Morton; former Chairman, Cadbury Ltd; Director, Cadbury Schweppes Ltd; *b* 17 Jan. 1911; *s* of David and Annie J. Borland; *m* 1947, Nessa Claire Helwig; one *s* one *d*. *Educ:* Glasgow Academy; Brasenose Coll., Oxford (BA). Management Trainee, etc., Cadbury Bros Ltd, Bournville, Birmingham, 1933. War service, Royal Marines (Lieut-Col), 1940–46. Sales Manager, J. S. Fry & Sons Ltd, Somerdale, Bristol, 1946; Sales Dir and a Man. Dir, J. S. Fry & Sons Ltd, 1948; a Man. Dir, British Cocoa & Chocolate Co. Ltd, 1959, and of Cadbury Bros Ltd, 1963. Mem. Govt Cttee of Inquiry into Fatstock and Meat Marketing and Distribution, 1962. Bristol University: Mem. Council, 1962–88; Pro-Chancellor, 1983–89; Hon. Fellow, 1989. Hon. LLD Bristol, 1980. *Recreation:* golf. *Address:* Garden Cottage, 3 Hollymead Lane, Stoke Bishop, Bristol BS9 1LN. *T:* Bristol (0272) 683978. *Clubs:* Achilles; Vincent's (Oxford).

BORLAUG, Norman Ernest, PhD; Consultant, International Center for Maize and Wheat Improvement; *b* 25 March 1914; *s* of Henry O. and Clara Vaala Borlaug; *m* 1937, Margaret Gibson; one *s* one *d*. *Educ:* Univ. of Minnesota; BS 1937; MS 1940; PhD 1942. US Forest Service (USDA), 1935–1937–1938; Biologist, Dupont de Nemours & Co, 1942–44; Plant Pathologist and Genetist, Wheat Improvement, employed by Rockefeller Foundn (Associate Dir of Agricultural Sciences) and Dir of Wheat Program, International Center for Maize and Wheat Improvement (CIMMYT), 1944–79. Dir, Population Crisis Cttee, 1971; Asesor Especial, Fundación para Estudios de la Población (Mexico), 1971–; Member: Adv. Council, Renewable Natural Resources Foundn, 1973–; Citizens' Commn on Science, Law and Food Supply, 1973–; Council for Agricl Science and Tech., 1973–; Commn on Critical Choices for Americans 1973–. Mem., Nat. Acad. of Scis (USA), 1968; Foreign Mem., Royal Soc., 1987. Outstanding Achievement Award, Univ. of Minnesota, 1959; Sitara-Imtiaz (Star of Distinction) (Pakistan), 1968, Hilal-I-Imtiaz 1978. Nobel Peace Prize, 1970. Holds numerous hon. doctorates in Science, both from USA and abroad; and more than 30 Service Awards by govts and organizations, including US Medal of Freedom, 1977. *Publications:* more than 70 scientific and semi-popular articles. *Recreations:* hunting, fishing, baseball, wrestling, football, golf. *Address:* c/o International Center for Maize and Wheat Improvement (CIMMYT), Apartado Postal 6–641, Lisboa 27, 06600 Mexico DF, Mexico. *T:* 761–33–11.

BORLEY, Lester; Director, National Trust for Scotland, since 1983; *b* 7 April 1931; *er s* of Edwin Richard Borley and Mary Dorena Davies; *m* Mary Alison, *e d* of Edward John Pearce and Kathleen Florence Barratt; three *d*. *Educ:* Dover Grammar Sch.; Queen Mary Coll. and Birkbeck Coll., London Univ. Pres. of Union, QMC, 1953; Dep. Pres., Univ. of London Union, 1954; ESU debating team tour of USA, 1955. Joined British Travel Assoc., 1955; Asst to Gen. Manager, USA, 1957–61; Manager: Chicago Office, 1961–64; Australia, 1964–67; West Germany, 1967–69; Chief Executive: Scottish Tourist Bd, 1970–75; English Tourist Bd, 1975–83. Member: Exec. Cttee, Scotland's Garden Scheme, 1970–75, 1983–; Council, Nat. Gardens Scheme, 1975–83; Park and Gardens Cttee, Zool Soc. of London, 1979–83. Governor, Edinburgh Film House, 1987–. Founder Fellow, Tourism Soc., 1978. FRSA 1982. Hon. FRSGS 1989. Honorable Kentucky Col, 1963. *Recreations:* listening to music, looking at pictures, gardening. *Address:* 4 Belford Place, Edinburgh EH4 3DH. *T:* 031–332 2364; The Old Schoolhouse, Wester Elchies, Morayshire. *Club:* New (Edinburgh).

BORN, Gustav Victor Rudolf, FRCP 1976; FRS 1972; FKC; Professor of Pharmacology, King's College, University of London, 1978–86, now Emeritus; Director, The William Harvey Research Institute, St Bartholomew's Hospital Medical College; *b* 29 July 1921; *s* of late Prof. Max Born, FRS; *m* 1st, 1950, Wilfrida Ann Plowden-Wardlaw (marr. diss., 1961); two *s* one *d*; 2nd, 1962, Dr Faith Elizabeth Maurice-Williams; one *s* one *d*. *Educ:* Oberrealschule, Göttingen; Perse Sch., Cambridge; Edinburgh Academy; University of Edinburgh. Vans Dunlop Scholar; MB, ChB, 1943; DPhil (Oxford), 1951, MA 1956. Med. Officer, RAMC, 1943–47; Mem. Scientific Staff, MRC, 1952–53; Research Officer, Nuffield Inst. for Med. Research, 1953–60 and Deptl Demonstrator in Pharmacology, 1956–60, University of Oxford; Vandervell Prof. of Pharmacology, RCS and Univ. of London, 1960–73; Sheild Prof. of Pharmacology, Univ. of Cambridge, and Fellow, Gonville and Caius Coll., Cambridge, 1973–78. Vis. Prof. in Chem., NW Univ., Illinois, 1970–; William S. Creasy Vis. Prof. in Clin. Pharmacol., Brown Univ., 1977; Prof. of Fondation de France, Paris, 1982–84. Hon. Dir, MRC Thrombosis Res. Gp, 1964–73. Scientific Advr, Vandervell Foundn, 1967–; Pres., Internat. Soc. on Thrombosis and Haemostasis, 1977–79; Trustee, Heineman Med. Res. Center, Charlotte, NC, 1981–. Member: Ed. Board, Heffters' Handbook of Experimental Pharmacology; Cttee of Enquiry into Relationship of Pharmaceut. Industry with Nat. Health Service (Sainsbury Cttee), 1965–67; Kuratorium, Lipid Liga, Munich; Kuratorium, Ernst Jung Foundn, Hamburg; Forensic Science Adv. Gp, Home Office. Hon. Life Mem., New York Acad. of Scis. Lectures: Beyer, Wisconsin Univ., 1969; Sharpey-Schäfer, Edinburgh Univ., 1973; Cross, RCS, 1974; Wander, Bern Univ., 1974; Johnson Meml, Paris, 1975; Lo Yuk Tong Foundn, Hong Kong Univ., and Heineman Meml, Charlotte, NC, 1978; Carlo Erba Foundn, Milan, 1979; Sir Henry Dale, RCS, 1981; Rokitansky, Vienna, and Oration to Med. Soc., London, 1983. Mem., Akad. Leopoldina; Corresp. Member: German Pharmacological Soc.; Royal Belgian Acad. of Medicine; Rheinisch-Westfälische Akad. der Wissenschaften, Düsseldorf. Hon. Fellow, St Peter's Coll., Oxford, 1972; FKC 1988. Hon. D de l'Univ.: Bordeaux, 1978; Paris, 1987; Hon. MD: Münster, 1980; Leuven, 1981; Edinburgh, 1982; Munich, 1989; Hon. DSc Brown Univ., 1987. Albrecht von Haller Medal, Göttingen Univ., 1979; Ratschow Medal, Internat. Kur. of Angiology, 1980; Auenbrugger Medal, Graz Univ., 1984; Royal Medal, Royal Soc., 1987; Morawitz Prize, 1990; Pfleger Prize, 1990. Chevalier de l'Ordre National de Mérite, France, 1980. *Publications:* articles in scientific jls and books. *Recreations:* music, rough gardening. *Address:* William Harvey Research Institute, St Bartholomew's Hospital Medical College, Charterhouse Square, EC1M 6BQ. *T:* 071–982 6070; 10 Woodland Gardens, N10. *Club:* Garrick.

BORODALE, Viscount; Sean David Beatty; *b* 12 June 1973; *s* and *heir* of 3rd Earl Beatty, *qv*.

BORODIN, George; *see* Sava, George.

BORRADAILE, Maj.-Gen. Hugh Alastair, CB 1959; DSO 1946; Vice Adjutant-General, War Office, 1960–63, retired; *b* 22 June 1907; *s* of late Lt-Col B. Borradaile, RE, Walnut Cottage, Wylye, Wilts; *m* 1936, Elizabeth Barbara, *d* of late R. Powell-Williams, Woodcroft, Yelverton, Devon; one *s* one *d*. *Educ:* Wellington Coll.; RMC Sandhurst. Commissioned Devon Regt 1926; King's African Rifles, 1931–37; Staff Coll., Camberley, 1939; GSO1, GHQ West Africa, 1942–43; CO 5, E Lancs Regt, 1944; CO 7 Somrset LI, 1944–45; GSO1, 30 Corps 1945; Asst Chief of Staff (Exec.), CCG, 1945–46; CO 1 Devon, 1946–48; Dep. Chief Intelligence Div., CCG, 1948–50; National Defence Coll., Canada, 1950–51; Brig. A/Q AA Command 1951–53; Comd 24 Inf. Bde, 1953–55; Dept Military Sec. (A), War Office, 1955–57; Gen. Officer Commanding South-West District and 43rd (Wessex) Infantry Div., TA, 1957–60. Col, Devon and Dorset Regt, 1962–67. Master, Worshipful Co. of Drapers', 1971–72 (Liveryman 1956–). *Recreations:* reading, watching TV. *Address:* Waterstreet Farm, Curry Rivel, Langport, Somerset TA10 0HH. *T:* Langport (0458) 251268. *Club:* Army and Navy.

BORRETT, Ven. Charles Walter; Archdeacon of Stoke-upon-Trent and Hon. Canon of Lichfield Cathedral, 1971–82, now Archdeacon Emeritus; Priest-in-charge of Sandon, Diocese of Lichfield, 1975–82; a Chaplain to the Queen, 1980–86; *b* 15 Sept. 1916; *s* of Walter George Borrett, farmer, and Alice Frances (*née* Mecrow); *m* 1941, Jean Constable, *d* of Charles Henry and Lilian Constable Pinson, Wolverhampton; one *s* two *d*. *Educ:* Framlingham Coll., Suffolk; Emmanuel Coll., Cambridge (MA); Ridley Hall, Cambridge. Deacon, 1941; Priest, 1943; Curate: of All Saints, Newmarket, 1941–45; of St Paul, Wolverhampton, 1945–48; of Tettenhall Regis, 1948–49; Vicar of Tettenhall Regis, 1949–71; Rural Dean of Trysull, 1958–71; Prebendary of Flixton in Lichfield Cathedral, 1964–71. Chm., C of E Council for Deaf, 1976–86. Fellow, Woodard Schs, 1972–86. *Address:* 34 Queensway, Mildenhall, Bury St Edmunds IP28 7JL. *T:* Mildenhall (0638) 712718. *Club:* Hawks (Cambridge).

BORRETT, Louis Albert Frank; a Chairman, Police Disciplinary Appeals, since 1987; *b* 8 Aug. 1924; *e s* of late Albert B. Borrett and Louise Alfreda Eudoxie Forrestier; *m* 1946, Barbara Betty, *er d* of late Frederick Charles Bamsey and of Lily Gertrude Thompson. *Educ:* France and England; Folkestone Teachers' Trng Coll.; King's Coll., Univ. of London (LLB 1954). Called to the Bar, Gray's Inn, 1955. Served War, Army: volunteered, 1940; RASC, London Dist and South Eastern Comd; commnd Royal Sussex Regt, 1944; served India and Burma Border; Intell. Officer, 9th Royal Sussex, during invasion of Malaya, 1945; GSO III (Ops), ALFSEA, 1946 (Burma Star, Defence Medal, Victory Medal); demob., 1946 (Captain). Schoolmaster, 1947–53; barrister, in practice on South-Eastern circuit, 1955–86; a Recorder, 1980–89. Assist Comr, Boundary Commn, 1964–67. *Recreations:* hunting, horse riding, music, the French language. *Address:* Queen Elizabeth Building, Temple, EC4Y 9BS. *T:* 071–353 7181; 54 Farm Close, East Grinstead, West Sussex RH19 3QG. *T:* East Grinstead (0342) 312350; Chantry Cottage, Tunstall, Woodbridge, Suffolk IP12 2JW.

BORRIE, Sir Gordon (Johnson), Kt 1982; QC 1986; Director General of Fair Trading, 1976–June 1992; *b* 13 March 1931; *s* of Stanley Borrie, Solicitor; *m* 1960, Dorene, *d* of Herbert Toland, Toronto, Canada; no *c*. *Educ:* John Bright Grammar Sch., Llandudno; Univ. of Manchester (LLB, LLM). Barrister-at-Law and Harmsworth Scholar of the Middle Temple; called to Bar, Middle Temple, 1952; Bencher, 1980. Nat. Service: Army Legal Services, HQ Brit. Commonwealth Forces in Korea, 1952–54. Practice as a barrister, London, 1954–57. Lectr and later Sen. Lectr, Coll. of Law, 1957–64; University of Birmingham: Sen. Lectr in Law, 1965–68; Prof. of English Law and Dir, Inst. of Judicial Admin, 1969–76; Dean of Faculty of Law, 1974–76; Hon. Prof. of Law, 1989–. Member: Parole Bd for England and Wales, 1971–74; CNAA Legal Studies Bd, 1971–76; Circuit Adv. Cttee, Birmingham Gp of Courts, 1972–74; Council, Consumers' Assoc., 1972–75; Consumer Protection Adv. Cttee, 1973–76; Equal Opportunities Commn, 1975–76. Vice-Pres., Inst. of Trading Standards Admin, 1985–. Sen. Treasurer, Nat. Union of Students, 1955–58. Hon. Mem., SPTL, 1989. Contested (Lab): Croydon, NE, 1955; Ilford, S, 1959. Gov., Birmingham Coll. of Commerce, 1966–70. FRSA 1982. Hon. LLD: City of London Polytechnic, 1989; Manchester Univ., 1990; Hull Univ., 1991. *Publications:* Commercial Law, 1962, 6th edn 1988; The Consumer, Society and the Law (with Prof. A. L. Diamond), 1963, 4th edn 1981; Law of Contempt (with N. V. Lowe), 1973, 2nd edn 1983; The Development of Consumer Law and Policy (Hamlyn Lectures), 1984. *Recreations:* gastronomy, piano playing, travel. *Address:* Manor Farm, Abbots Morton, Worcestershire WR7 4NA. *T:* Inkberrow (0386) 792330; 1 Plowden Buildings, Temple, EC4Y 9BU. *T:* 071–353 4434. *Clubs:* Garrick, Reform (Chm., 1990–).

BORTHWICK, family name of **Baron Borthwick**.

BORTHWICK, 23rd Lord *cr* c 1450 (Scot.); **John Henry Stuart Borthwick of That Ilk,** TD 1943; DL, JP; Baron of Heriotmuir and Laird of Crookston, Midlothian; Hereditary Falconer of Scotland to the Queen; Chairman: Heriotmuir Properties Ltd, since 1965; Heriotmuir Exporters Ltd, since 1972; Director, Ronald Morrison & Co. Ltd, since 1972; *b* 13 Sept. 1905; *s* of Henry, 22nd Lord Borthwick (*d* 1937); claim to Lordship admitted by Lord Lyon, 1986; *m* 1938, Margaret Frances (*d* 1976), *d* of Alexander Campbell Cormack, Edinburgh; twin *s*. *Educ:* Fettes Coll., Edinburgh; King's Coll., Newcastle (DipAgric 1926). Formerly RATA, re-employed 1939; served NW Europe, Allied Mil. Govt Staff (Junior Staff Coll., SO 2), 1944; CCG (CO 1, Lt-Col), 1946. Dept of Agriculture for Scotland, 1948–50; farming own farms, 1950–71; Partner in Crookston Farms, 1971–79. National Farmers Union of Scotland: Mid and West Lothian Area Cttee, 1967–73 (Pres. 1970–72); Mem. Council, 1968–72; Member: Lothians Area Cttee, NFU Mutual Insurance Soc., 1969; Scottish Southern Regional Cttee, Wool Marketing Bd, 1966–87. Mem., Scottish Landowners' Fedn, 1937– (Mem., Land Use Cttee, 1972–83; Mem., Scottish Livestock Export Gp, 1972–83). Chm., Area Cttee, South of Scotland Electricity Bd Consultative Council, 1972–76. Chm., Monitoring Cttee for Scottish Tartans, 1976; Dir, Castles of Scotland Preservation Trust, 1985–. County Councillor, Midlothian, 1937–48; JP 1938; DL Midlothian (later Lothian Region), 1965; Member:

Local Appeal Tribunal (Edinburgh and the Lothians), 1963–75; Midlothian Valuation Cttee, 1966–78. Member: Standing Council of Scottish Chiefs; The Committee of the Baronage of Scotland (International Delegate); Mem. Corresp., Istituto Italiano di Genealogia e Araldica, Rome and Madrid, 1964; Hon. Mem., Council of Scottish Clans Assoc., USA, 1975. Hon. Mem., Royal Military Inst. of Canada, 1976. Patron, Normandy Veterans Assoc., 1985–. KLJ, GCLJ 1975; Comdr, Rose of Lippe, 1971; Niadh Nask, 1982. *Recreations:* shooting, travel, history. *Heir: s* Master of Borthwick, *qv*. *Address:* Crookston, Heriot, Midlothian EH38 5YS. *Clubs:* New, Puffins (Edinburgh).

BORTHWICK, Master of; Hon. John Hugh Borthwick; farmer and landowner; *b* 14 Nov. 1940; *er twin s* and *heir* of Lord Borthwick, *qv*; *m* 1974, Adelaide, *d* of A. Birkmyre; two *d*. *Educ:* Gordonstoun; Edinburgh School of Agriculture (SDA, NDA). *Recreations:* wild trout fishing, stalking. *Address:* The Neuk, Heriot, Midlothian EH38 5YS. *T:* Heriot (087535) 236. *Club:* New (Edinburgh).

BORTHWICK, Jason; *see* Borthwick, W. J. M.

BORTHWICK, Sir John Thomas, 3rd Bt *cr* 1908; MBE 1945; *b* 5 Dec. 1917; *S* to Btcy of uncle (1st and last Baron Whitburgh), 1967; *m* 1st, 1939; three *s*; 2nd, 1962; two *s*. *Heir: s* Antony Thomas Borthwick, *b* 12 Feb. 1941.

BORTHWICK, Kenneth W., CBE 1980; JP; DL; Rt Hon. Lord Provost of the City of Edinburgh, 1977–80; Lord Lieutenant of the City and County of Edinburgh, 1977–80; *b* 4 Nov. 1915; *s* of Andrew Graham Borthwick; *m* 1942, Irene Margaret Wilson, *d* of John Graham Wilson, Aberdeen; two *s* one *d*. *Educ:* George Heriot Sch., Edinburgh. Served War of 1939–45: Flying Officer, RAF. Elected Edinburgh Town Council, 1963; Lothian Regional Council, 1974–77; Edinburgh District Council, 1976. Judge of Police, 1972–75. Member: Lothians River Bd, 1969–73; Organising Cttee, Commonwealth Games, Edinburgh, 1970; Edinburgh and Lothian Theatre Trust, 1975–76; Lothian and Borders Police Bd, 1975–77; British Airports Authorities Consultative Cttee, 1977–80; Convention of Scottish Local Authorities, 1977; Scottish Council Develt and Industry, 1977; Chairman: Edinburgh Dist. Licensing Court, 1975–77; Edinburgh Internat. Festival Soc., 1977–80; Edinburgh Military Tattoo Policy Cttee, 1977–80; Queen's Silver Jubilee Edinburgh Appeal Fund, 1977; Organising Cttee, XIII Commonwealth Games, Scotland 1986, 1983–86. Curator of Patronage, Univ. of Edinburgh, 1977–80. Governor, George Heriot Sch., 1965–73. Vice-President (ex officio): RZS of Scotland, 1977–80; Lowland TA&VRA, 1977–80. DL City of Edinburgh, 1980. Hon. Consul for Malaŵi, 1982. OStJ. *Recreations:* golf, gardening. *Address:* 17 York Road, Edinburgh EH5 3EJ. *Club:* Caledonian (Hon. Mem.).

BORTHWICK, (William) Jason (Maxwell), DSC 1942; *b* 1 Nov. 1910; *er s* of late Hon. William Borthwick and Ruth (*née* Rigby); *m* 1937, Elizabeth Elworthy (*d* 1978), Timaru, NZ; one *s* three *d*. *Educ:* Winchester; Trinity Coll., Cambridge (BA). Called to Bar, Inner Temple, 1933. Commnd RNVR, 1940, Comdr (QO) 1945. Joined Thomas Borthwick & Sons Ltd, 1934, Dir 1946–76; Dir, International Commodities Clearing House Ltd and subsids, 1954–84; Dir, Commonwealth Develt Corp., 1972–78; Mem., Central Council of Physical Recreation, 1955–; Chm., Nat. Sailing Centre, 1965–79. *Recreations:* yachting, shooting. *Address:* North House, Brancaster Staithe, King's Lynn, Norfolk PE31 8BY. *T:* Brancaster (0485) 210475. *Clubs:* United Oxford & Cambridge University, Royal Thames Yacht.

BORWICK, family name of **Baron Borwick.**

BORWICK, 4th Baron, *cr* 1922; **James Hugh Myles Borwick;** Bt *cr* 1916; MC 1944; Major HLI retired; *b* 12 Dec. 1917; *s* of 3rd Baron and Irene Phyllis, *d* of late Thomas Main Paterson, Littlebourne, Canterbury; *S* father 1961; *m* 1954, Hyllarie Adalia Mary, *y d* of late Lieut-Col William Hamilton Hall Johnston, DSO, MC, DL, Bryn-y-Groes, Bala, N Wales; four *d*. *Educ:* Eton; RMC, Sandhurst. Commissioned as 2nd Lieut HLI, 1937; Capt. 1939; Major 1941; retired, 1947. *Recreations:* field sports, sailing. *Heir: half b* Hon. George Sandbach Borwick [*b* 18 Oct. 1922; *m* 1981, Esther, Lady Ellerman (*d* 1985)]. *Address:* Lower Minchingdown, Black Dog, Crediton, Devon EX17 4QX. *T:* Tiverton (0884) 860735. *Club:* Royal Ocean Racing.

BOSCAWEN, family name of **Viscount Falmouth.**

BOSCAWEN, Hon. Robert Thomas, MC 1944; MP (C) Somerton and Frome, since 1983 (Wells, 1970–83); *b* 17 March 1923; 4th *s* of 8th Viscount Falmouth and Dowager Viscountess Falmouth, CBE; *m* 1949, Mary Alice, JP London 1961, *e d* of Col Sir Geoffrey Ronald Codrington, KCVO, CB, CMG, DSO, OBE, TD; one *s* two *d*. *Educ:* Eton; Trinity College, Cambridge. Served Coldstream Guards, 1941–50 (with 1st (armoured) Bn Coldstream Guards, Normandy to N Germany, wounded 1945); NW Europe, 1944–45; attached to British Red Cross Civilian Relief Orgn in occupied Europe, 1946–47. Mem., London Exec. Council, Nat. Health Service, 1954–65; Underwriting Mem. of Lloyd's, 1952–. Contested Falmouth and Camborne (C), 1964, 1966. Asst Govt Whip, 1979–81; a Lord Comr of HM Treasury, 1981–83; Vice-Chamberlain of HM Household, 1983–86, Comptroller, 1986–88. Mem., Select Cttee on Expenditure, 1974; Vice-Chm., Conservative Parly Health and Social Security Cttee, 1974–79. Mem. Parly Delegns, USSR 1977, Nepal 1981; led Parly Delegn to UN Assembly, 1987. *Recreation:* sailing. *Address:* House of Commons, SW1A 0AA. *Clubs:* Pratt's; Royal Yacht Squadron.

BOSE, Mihir, FICA; freelance author and journalist, since 1987; *b* 12 Jan. 1947; *s* of Kiran Chandra Bose and Sova Rani Bose; *m* 1986, Kalpana; one *d*. *Educ:* St Xavier's High Sch.; St Xavier's Coll., Bombay (BSc Physics and Maths). Cricket Corresp., LBC, 1974–75; For. Corresp., Sunday Times, Spectator, New Society, 1975–78; freelance writer, 1979; Editor: International Fund Guide, 1980–81; Pensions, 1981–83; Financial Planning Ed. 1983–84, City Ed. 1984–86, Dep. Ed. 1985–86, Financial Weekly; City Features Ed., London Daily News, 1986–87; freelance writer, mainly on regular contract basis, specialising in finance, sports and feature writing for Sunday Times, Spectator, Mail on Sunday, Daily Telegraph, Independent, The Times, Guardian, 1987–. *Publications:* Keith Miller, 1979, 2nd edn 1980; The Lost Hero, 1982; All in a Day's Work, 1983; The Aga Khan, 1984; A Maidan View, 1986; The Crash, 1988, 3rd edn 1989, incl. Jap. edn; Insurance: are you covered?, 1988, 2nd edn 1991; Crash – a new money crisis, 1989; (jtly) Fraud, 1989; Cricket Voices and History of Indian Cricket, 1990; Michael Grade, 1991. *Recreations:* running his own cricket team, reading, films, travelling. *Clubs:* Reform; Saturday (Calcutta).

BOSONNET, Paul Graham; Deputy Chairman, BOC Group, since 1985; *b* 12 Sept. 1932; *s* of Edgar Raymond Bosonnet and Sylvia Gladys Cradock; *m* 1958, Joan Colet Cunningham; one *s* two *d*. *Educ:* St John's College, Southsea. FCA. Accountant, British Oxygen Co., 1957; Dir, BOC International, 1976. Chm., Logica, 1990–. *Recreations:* genealogy, walking. *Address:* 7 Oakcroft Close, West Byfleet, Surrey KT14 6JQ. *T:* Byfleet (0932) 342991.

BOSSANO, Hon. Joseph; Chief Minister, Gibraltar, since 1988; MP (Gibraltar Socialist Labour Party); *b* 10 June 1939; *s* of Maria Teresa and Oscar Bossano; *m* (marr. diss.); three *s* one *d*; *m* 1988, Rose Torrilla. *Educ:* Gibraltar Grammar School; Univ. of London (BScEcon); Univ. of Birmingham (BA). Factory worker, 1958–60; Seaman, 1960–64; Health Inspector, 1964–68; student, 1968–72; building worker, 1972–74; Union leader, 1974–88; MP 1972–; Leader of Opposition, 1984–88. *Recreations:* thinking, cooking, gardening. *Address:* 6 Convent Place, Gibraltar. *T:* 70071.

BOSSOM, Hon. Sir Clive, 2nd Bt, *cr* 1953; *b* 4 Feb. 1918; *s* of late Baron Bossom (Life Peer); *S* to father's Baronetcy, 1965; *m* 1951, Lady Barbara North, *sister* of 9th Earl of Guilford, *qv*; three *s* one *d*. *Educ:* Eton. Regular Army, The Buffs, 1939–48; served Europe and Far East. Kent County Council, 1949–52; Chm. Council Order of St John for Kent, 1951–56; Mem. Chapter General, Order of St John (Mem., Jt Cttee, 1961–; Chm., Ex-Services War Disabled Help and Homes Dept, 1973–87, Vice Chm., 1987–; Almoner, 1987–). Contested (C) Faversham Div., 1951 and 1955. MP (C) Leominster Div., Herefordshire, 1959–Feb. 1974; Parliamentary Private Secretary: to Jt Parly Secs, Min. of Pensions and Nat. Insce, 1960–62; to Sec. of State for Air, 1962–64; to Minister of Defence for RAF, 1964; to Home Secretary, 1970–72. Chm., Europ Assistance Ltd, 1973–88. President: Anglo-Belgian Union, 1970–73, 1983–85 (Chm., 1967–70; Vice-Pres., 1974–82, 1985–); Anglo-Netherlands Soc., 1978–89; BARC, 1985–; Vice-President: Industrial Fire Protection Assoc., 1981–88; Fédération Internationale de L'Automobile, 1975–81 (Vice-Pres. d'Honneur, 1982–); Internat. Social Service, 1989– (Internat. Pres., 1984–89); Chairman: RAC, 1975–78; RAC Motor Sports Council, 1975–81; RAC Motor Sports Assoc. Ltd, 1979–82; Iran Soc. 1973–76 (Vice-Pres., 1977–); Mem. Council, RGS, 1982–86. Trustee, Brooklands Museum Trust, 1987–. Liveryman of Worshipful Company of Grocers (Master, 1979). FRSA. KStJ 1961. Comdr, Order of Leopold II; Order of Homayoun III (Iran), 1977; Comdr, Order of the Crown (Belgium), 1977; Kt Comdr, Order of Orange Nassau (Netherlands), 1980. *Recreation:* travel. *Heir: s* Bruce Charles Bossom, [*b* 22 Aug. 1952; *m* 1985, Penelope Jane, *d* of late Edward Holland-Martin and of Mrs Holland-Martin, Overbury Court, Glos; two *d*]. *Address:* 97 Cadogan Lane, SW1X 9DU. *T:* 071–245 6531. *Clubs:* Royal Automobile, Carlton.

BOSSY, Rev. Michael Joseph Frederick, SJ; Rector and Parish Priest in the Parish of St Aloysius, Glasgow, since 1988 (Assistant Priest, 1986–88); *b* 22 Nov. 1929; *s* of F. J. Bossy and K. Bossy (*née* White). *Educ:* St Ignatius Coll., Stamford Hill; Heythrop Coll., Oxon (STL); Oxford Univ. (MA). Taught at: St Ignatius Coll., Stamford Hill, 1956–59; St Francis Xavier's Coll., Liverpool, 1963–64; Stonyhurst Coll., 1965–85 (Headmaster, 1972–85). *Recreation:* watching games. *Address:* St Aloysius Residence, 56 Hill Street, Glasgow G3 6RH. *T:* 041–332 3039.

BOSTOCK, David John; Under Secretary and Head of European Community Group, HM Treasury, since 1990; *b* 11 April 1948; *s* of John C. Bostock and Gwendoline G. (*née* Lee); *m* 1975, Beth Ann O'Byrne; one *s* one *d*. *Educ:* Cheltenham Grammar Sch.; Balliol Coll., Oxford (BA Mod. Hist. 1969); University Coll. London (MSc Econs of Public Policy 1978). VSO, Indonesia, 1970. Joined HM Treasury, 1971; Second Sec., Office of UK Permanent Rep. to EC, 1973–75; Principal: HM Treasury, 1975–81; Cabinet Office (Economic Secretariat), 1981–83; Asst Sec., HM Treasury, 1983–85; Financial and Econ. Counsellor, Office of UK Permanent Rep. to EC, 1985–90. *Recreations:* choral singing, walking, looking at old buildings, drinking beer. *Address:* HM Treasury, Parliament Street, SW1P 3AG.

BOSTOCK, James Edward, RE 1961 (ARE 1947); ARCA London; painter and engraver; *b* Hanley, Staffs, 11 June 1917; *s* of William George Bostock, pottery and glass-worker, and Amy (*née* Titley); *m* 1939, Gwladys Irene (*née* Griffiths); three *s*. *Educ:* Borden Grammar Sch., Sittingbourne; Medway Sch. of Art, Rochester; Royal College of Art. War Service as Sgt in Durham LI and Royal Corps of Signals. Full-time Teacher, 1946–78; Vice-Principal, West of England Coll. of Art, 1965–70; Academic Develt Officer, Bristol Polytechnic, 1970–78. Elected Mem. of Soc. of Wood Engravers, 1950. Mem. Council. Soc. of Staffs Artists, 1963. Mem., E Kent Art Soc., 1980. Exhibited water-colours, etchings, wood engravings and drawings at RA, NEAC, RBA, RE, RI and other group exhibitions and in travelling exhibitions to Poland, Czechoslovakia, South Africa, Far East, New Zealand, USA, Sweden, Russia and Baltic States, and the provinces. One-man shows: Mignon Gall., Bath; Univ. of Bristol; Bristol Polytechnic; Margate Library Gall.; Deal Lib. Gall.; Broadstairs Lib. Gall.; Folkestone Lib. Gall.; Phillip Maslen Gall., Canterbury. Works bought by V & A Museum, British Museum, British Council, Hull, Swindon, Stoke-on-Trent and Bristol Education Cttees, Hunt Botanical Library, Pittsburgh, Hereford Mus., and private collectors. Commissioned work for: ICI Ltd, British Museum (Nat. Hist.), Odhams Press, and other firms and public authorities. *Publications:* Roman Lettering for Students, 1959; wood engraved illustrations to Poems of Edward Thomas, 1988; articles in: Times, Guardian, Staffordshire Sentinel, Studio, Artist; reproductions in Garrett, History of British Wood Engraving, 1978. *Address:* White Lodge, 80 Lindenthorpe Road, Broadstairs, Kent CT10 1DB. *T:* Thanet (0843) 69782.

BOSTOCK, Rev. Canon Peter Geoffrey, MA; Clergy Appointments Adviser, 1973–76; Deputy Secretary, Board for Mission and Unity, General Synod of Church of England, 1971–73; Canon Emeritus, Diocese of Mombasa, 1958; *b* 24 Dec. 1911; *s* of Geoffrey Bostock; *m* 1937, Elizabeth Rose; two *s* two *d*. *Educ:* Charterhouse; The Queen's Coll., Oxon; Wycliffe Hall, Oxon. Deacon, 1935; Priest, 1937; CMS Kenya, 1935–58; became Canon of Diocese of Mombasa, 1952; Archdeacon, 1953–58; Vicar-Gen., 1955–58. Examining Chaplain to Bishop of Mombasa, 1950–58; Chm., Christian Council of Kenya, 1957–58; Archdeacon of Doncaster and Vicar, High Melton, 1959–67; Asst Sec., Missionary and Ecumenical Council of Church Assembly, 1967–71. *Recreations:* home and family. *Address:* 6 Moreton Road, Oxford OX2 7AX. *T:* Oxford (0865) 515460. *Club:* Commonwealth Trust.

BOSTON, family name of **Baron Boston of Faversham.**

BOSTON, 10th Baron *cr* 1761; **Timothy George Frank Boteler Irby;** Bt 1704; *b* 27 March 1939; *s* of 9th Baron Boston, MBE, and Erica N. (*d* 1990), *d* of T. H. Hill; *S* father, 1978; *m* 1967, Rhonda Anne, *d* of R. A. Bate; two *s* one *d*. *Educ:* Clayesmore School, Dorset; Southampton Univ. (BSc Econ.). *Heir: s* Hon. George William Eustace Boteler Irby, *b* 1 Aug. 1971. *Address:* 135 Bishop's Mansions, Stevenage Road, Fulham, SW6. *T:* 071–731 1936.

BOSTON OF FAVERSHAM, Baron *cr* 1976 (Life Peer), of Faversham, Kent; **Terence George Boston;** QC 1981; barrister; Chairman, TVS Entertainment plc (formerly TVS), 1980–90; *b* 21 March 1930; *yr* surv. *s* of late George T. Boston and of Kate (*née* Bellati); *m* 1962, Margaret Joyce (Member: SE Metropolitan Regional Hospital Board, 1970–74; Mental Health Review Appeals Tribunal (SE Metropolitan area), 1970–74; market research consultant), *er d* of late R. H. J. Head and of Mrs H. F. Winters, and step *d* of late H. F. Winters, Melbourne, Australia. *Educ:* Woolwich Polytechnic Sch.; King's Coll., University of London. Dep. President, University of London Union, 1955–56. Commnd in RAF during Nat. Service, 1950–52; later trained as pilot with University of London Air Sqdn. Called to the Bar: Inner Temple, 1960; Gray's Inn, 1973; BBC News Sub-Editor, External Services, 1957–60; Senior BBC Producer (Current Affairs),

1960–64; also Producer of Law in Action series (Third Programme), 1962–64. Joined Labour Party, 1946; contested (Lab) Wokingham, 1955 and 1959; MP (Lab) Faversham, Kent, June 1964–70; PPS to: Minister of Public Building and Works, 1964–66; Minister of Power, 1966–68; Minister of Transport, 1968–69; Asst Govt Whip, 1969–70; Minister of State, Home Office, 1979; opp. front bench spokesman on home affairs, 1979–84, on defence, 1984–86. UK Deleg. to UN Gen. Assembly,, XXXIst, XXXIInd and XXXIIIrd Sessions, 1976–78. Member: Executive Cttee, International Union of Socialist Youth, 1950; Select Cttee on Broadcasting Proceedings of Parliament, 1966; Speaker's Conference on Electoral Law, 1965–68. Trustee, Parly Lab. Party Benevolent Fund, 1967–70. Founder Vice-Chm., Great Britain—East Europe Centre, 1967–69; Chm., The Sheppey Gp, 1967–. *Recreations:* opera (going, not singing), fell-walking. *Address:* House of Lords, SW1A 0PW.

BOSTON, David Merrick, OBE 1976; MA; Director (formerly Curator), Horniman Public Museum and Public Park Trust (formerly Horniman Museum and Library), London, since 1965; *b* 15 May 1931; *s* of late Dr H. M. Boston, Salisbury; *m* 1961, Catharine, *d* of Rev. Prof. E. G. S. Parrinder, *qv*; one *s* two *d*. *Educ:* Rondebosch, Cape Town; Bishop Wordsworth's, Salisbury; Selwyn Coll., Cambridge; Univ. of Cape Town. BA History Cantab 1954; MA 1958. RAF, 1950–51; Adjt, Marine Craft Trng School. Field survey, S African Inst. of Race Relations, 1955; Keeper of Ethnology, Liverpool Museums, 1956–62; Assist Keeper, British Museum, New World archaeology and ethnography, 1962–65. Chm., British Nat. Cttee of Internat. Council of Museums, 1976–80; Vice-Chm., Internat. Cttee for Museums of Ethnography, 1989–; Mem. Council: Museums Assoc., 1969; Royal Anthropological Inst., 1969 (Vice-Pres., 1972–75, 1977–80, Hon. Sec., 1985–88). Visiting Scientist: National Museum of Man, Ottawa, 1970; Japan Foundation, Tokyo, 1986. FMA; FRAS; FRGS. Ordenom Jugoslavenske Zastave sa zlatnom zvezdom na ogrlici (Yugoslavia), 1981. *Publications:* Pre-Columbian Pottery of the Americas, 1980; contribs to learned jls and encyclopaedias and on Pre-European America, in World Ceramics (ed R. J. Charleston). *Address:* 10 Oakleigh Park Avenue, Chislehurst, Kent. *T:* 081–467 1049.

BOSTON, Richard; writer; *b* 29 Dec. 1938. *Educ:* Stowe; Regent Street Polytechnic School of Art; King's Coll., Cambridge (MA). Taught English in Sicily, Sweden and Paris; acted in Jacques Tati's Playtime. Editorial staff of Peace News, TLS, New Society; columnist and feature writer, The Guardian, at intervals, 1972–. Editor: The Vole, 1977–80; Quarto, 1979–82. *Publications:* The Press We Deserve (ed), 1969; An Anatomy of Laughter, 1974; The Admirable Urquhart, 1975; Beer and Skittles, 1976; Baldness Be My Friend, 1977; The Little Green Book, 1979; C. O. Jones's Compendium of Practical Jokes, 1982; Osbert: a portrait of Osbert Lancaster, 1989. *Recreation:* shelling peas. *Address:* The Old School, Aldworth, Reading, Berks. *T:* Compton (0635) 578587.

BOSVILLE MACDONALD OF SLEAT, Sir Ian Godfrey, 17th Bt, *cr* 1625; FRICS, MRSH; 25th Chief of Sleat; *b* 18 July 1947; *er s* of Sir (Alexander) Somerled Angus Bosville Macdonald of Sleat, 16th Bt, MC, 24th Chief of Sleat and of Mary, Lady Bosville Macdonald of Sleat; *S* father 1958; *m* 1970, Juliet Fleury, *o d* of late Maj.-Gen. J. M. D. Ward-Harrison, OBE, MC; one *s* two *d*. *Educ:* Pinewood Sch.; Eton Coll.; Royal Agricultural Coll. ARICS 1972; FRICS 1986. Member (for Bridlington South), Humberside CC, 1981–84. MRSH 1972; Mem., Econ. Res. Council, 1979–. Chm., Rural Develt Commn, Humberside, 1988–; President: British Food and Farming in Humberside, 1989; Humberside Br., British Red Cross, 1988–; Humberside Young Farmers. High Sheriff, Humberside, 1988–89. *Heir: s* Somerled Alexander Bosville Macdonald, younger of Sleat, *b* 30 Jan. 1976. *Recreation:* ornithology. *Address:* Thorpe Hall, Rudston, Driffield, North Humberside. *T:* Kilham (026282) 239; Upper Duntulm, By Portree, Isle of Skye. *T:* Duntulm (047052) 206. *Clubs:* Lansdowne, Brooks's, White's.

BOSWALL, Sir (Thomas) Alford H.; *see* Houstoun-Boswall.

BOSWELL, Lt-Gen. Sir Alexander (Crawford Simpson), KCB 1982; CBE 1974 (OBE 1971; MBE 1962); Lieutenant-Governor and Commander-in-Chief, Guernsey, 1985–90; *b* 3 Aug. 1928; *s* of Alexander Boswell Simpson Boswell and Elizabeth Burns Simpson Boswell (*née* Park); *m* 1956, Jocelyn Leslie Blundstone Pomfret, *d* of Surg. Rear-Adm. A. A. Pomfret, CB, OBE; five *s*. *Educ:* Merchiston Castle Sch.; RMA, Sandhurst. Enlisted in Army, 1947; Commnd, Argyll and Sutherland Highlanders, Dec. 1948; regimental appts, Hong Kong, Korea, UK, Suez, Guyana, 1949–58; sc Camberley, 1959; Mil. Asst (GS02) to GOC Berlin, 1960–62; Co. Comdr, then Second in Comd, 1 A and SH, Malaya and Borneo, 1963–65 (despatches 1965); Directing Staff, Staff Coll., Camberley, 1965–68; CO, 1 A and SH, 1968–71; Col GS Trng Army Strategic Comd, 1971; Brig. Comdg 39 Inf. Bde, 1972–74; COS, 1st British Corps, 1974–76; NDC (Canada), 1976–77; GOC 2nd Armd Div., 1978–80; Dir, TA and Cadets, 1980–82; GOC Scotland and Governor of Edinburgh Castle, 1982–85. Col, Argyll and Sutherland Highlanders, 1972–82; Hon. Col, Tayforth Univs OTC, 1982–86; Col Comdt, Scottish Div., 1982–86. Captain of Tarbet, 1974–82. KStJ 1985. *Address:* c/o Bank of Scotland, Palmerston Place Branch, 32 West Maitland Street, Edinburgh EH12 5DZ. *Clubs:* Army and Navy; New (Edinburgh).

BOSWELL, Timothy Eric; MP (C) Daventry, since 1987; an Assistant Government Whip, since 1990; *b* 2 Dec. 1942; *s* of late Eric New Boswell and of Joan Winifred Caroline Boswell; *m* 1969, Helen Delahay, *d* of Rev. Arthur Rees; three *d*. *Educ:* Marlborough Coll.; New Coll., Oxford (MA; Dip. Agricl Econs). Conservative Res. Dept, 1966–73 (Head of Econ. Section, 1970–73); managed family farming business, 1974–87; part-time Special Adviser to Minister of Agriculture, Fisheries and Food, 1984–86. Chm., Leics, Northants and Rutland Counties Br., NFU, 1983; Mem. Council, 1966–90, Pres., 1984–90, Perry Foundn (for Agricl Res.); Mem., AFRC, 1988–90. PPS to Financial Sec. to the Treasury, 1989–90. Member: Select Cttee for Agriculture, 1987–89; Sec., Cons. Backbench Cttee on Agriculture, 1987–89; Chm., All-Party Charity Law Review Panel, 1988–90. Treas., 1976–79, Chm., 1979–83, Daventry Constituency Cons. Assoc. Contested (C) Rugby, Feb. 1974. *Recreations:* the countryside, shooting, snooker, poetry. *Address:* House of Commons, SW1A 0AA. *T:* 071–219 3520. *Club:* Farmers'.

BOSWOOD, Anthony Richard; QC 1986; *b* 1 Oct. 1947; *s* of Noel Gordon Paul Boswood and Cicily Ann Watson; *m* 1973, Sarah Bridget Alexander; three *d*. *Educ:* St Paul's Sch.; New Coll., Oxford (BCL, MA). Called to Bar, Middle Temple, 1970. *Recreations:* opera, riding, tennis. *Address:* Fountain Court, Temple, EC4 9DH. *T:* 071–583 3335; Podere Casanuova, Pieveasciata, Castelnuovo Berardenga (SI), Italy. *Club:* Hurlingham.

BOSWORTH, (John) Michael (Worthington), CBE 1972; FCA; Deputy Chairman, British Railways Board, 1972–83 (Vice-Chairman, 1968–72); *b* 22 June 1921; *s* of Humphrey Worthington Bosworth and Vera Hope Bosworth; *m* 1955, Patricia Mary Edith Wheelock; one *s* one *d*. *Educ:* Bishop's Stortford Coll. Served Royal Artillery, 1939–46. Peat, Marwick, Mitchell & Co., 1949–68, Partner, 1960. Chairman: British Rail Engineering Ltd, 1969–71; British Rail Property Bd, 1971–72; British Rail Shipping and International Services Ltd, now Sealink UK Ltd, 1976–84; BR Hovercraft Ltd, 1976–81; British Transport Hotels, 1978–83; British Rail Investments Ltd, 1981–84; British Rail Trustee Co., 1984–86; Director: Hoverspeed (UK) Ltd, 1981–89; British Ferries, 1984–90. Vice Pres., Société Belgo-Anglaise des Ferry-Boats, 1979–87. Dir, Compass Hotels Ltd, 1988–. *Recreations:* ski-ing, vintage cars. *Address:* Cross Farm, Yetminster, Sherborne, Dorset DT9 6LG. *Club:* Royal Automobile.

BOSWORTH, Sir Neville (Bruce Alfred), Kt 1987; CBE 1982; Consultant, Grove Tompkins Bosworth, Solicitors, Birmingham, since 1989; *b* 18 April 1918; *s* of W. C. N. Bosworth; *m* 1945, Charlotte Marian Davis; one *s* two *d*. *Educ:* King Edward's Sch., Birmingham; Birmingham Univ. LLB. Admitted Solicitor, 1941; Sen. Partner, Bosworth, Bailey Cox & Co., Birmingham, until 1989. Birmingham City Council, 1950–; County Bor. Councillor (Erdington Ward), 1950–61; Alderman, 1961–74; Dist Councillor (Edgbaston Ward), 1973–; Lord Mayor of Birmingham, 1969–70; Dep. Mayor, 1970–71; Leader of Birmingham City Council, 1976–80, 1982–84; Leader of Opposition, 1972–76, 1980–82 and 1984–87; Cons. Gp Leader, 1972–87 (Dep. Gp Leader, 1971–72); Chairman: Gen. Purposes Cttee, 1966–69; Finance Cttee, 1976–80, 1982–84; National Exhibn Centre Cttee, 1976–80. Chm., W Midlands Police Bd, 1985–86. County Councillor (Edgbaston Ward), W Midlands CC, 1973–86; Chm., Legal and Property Cttee, 1977–79; Vice-Chm., Finance Cttee, 1980–81. Chm., Sutton Coldfield Cons. Assoc., 1963–66; Vice-Chm., Birmingham Cons. Assoc., 1972–87; Mem., Local Govt Adv. Cttee, National Union of Cons. and Unionist Assocs, 1973–. Vice Chm., Assoc. of Metropolitan Authorities, 1978–80, and Mem. Policy Cttee, 1976–80; Vice-Pres., Birmingham and Dist Property Owners Assoc.; Dir, Nat. Exhibn Centre Ltd, 1970–72, 1974–; Mem., W Midlands Econ. Council, 1978–79. Trustee, several charitable trusts; Mem. Council, Birmingham Univ.; former Governor, King Edward VI Schs, Birmingham (Dep. Bailiff, 1979–80). Hon. Freeman, City of Birmingham, 1982. *Recreations:* politics, football, bridge. *Address:* Hollington, Luttrell Road, Four Oaks, Sutton Coldfield, Birmingham B74 2SR. *T:* 021–308 0647; 54 Newhall Street, Birmingham B3 3QG. *T:* 021–236 8091.

BOTHA, Matthys (Izak); South African Diplomat, retired; *b* 31 Oct. 1913; *s* of Johan Hendrik Jacobus Botha and Anna Botha (*née* Joubert); *m* 1940, Hester le Roux (*née* Bosman); two *s* *Educ:* Selborne Coll.; Pretoria Univ. BA, LLB. Called to the Transvaal Bar, Dept of Finance, Pretoria, 1931–44; S African Embassy, Washington, 1944–51; S African Permanent Mission to UN, NY, 1951–54; Head, Political Div., Dept Foreign Affairs, Pretoria, 1955–59; Envoy Extraordinary and Minister Plenipoteniary, Switzerland, 1959–60; Minister, London, 1960–62; Ambassador and Permanent Rep., UN, NY, 1962–70; Ambassador to: Canada, 1970–73; Italy, 1973–77 (also to Costa Rica and El Salvador, 1973–74, and to Panama, 1973–76); Court of St James's, 1977–78; Ciskei, 1983–85. Member: Simon Vanderstel Foundn; South African Foundn; Huguenot Soc. Knight of Grand Cross, Order of Merit (Italy), 1977. *Recreations:* swimming, golfing, cycling. *Address:* 7 de Jongh Street, The Strand, Cape Province, 7140, South Africa. *Club:* Stellenbosch Golf.

BOTHA, Pieter Willem, DMS 1976; Star of South Africa, 1979; State President, Republic of South Africa, 1984–89 (Prime Minister, and Minister of National Intelligence Service, 1978–84); *b* 12 Jan. 1916; *s* of Pieter Willem and Hendriena Christina Botha; *m* 1943, Anna Elizabeth Rossouw; two *s* three *d*. *Educ:* Paul Roux; Bethlehem, Orange Free State; Univ. of Orange Free State, Bloemfontein. MP for George, 1948–84; Deputy Minister of the Interior, 1958; Minister of Community Development and of Coloured Affairs, 1961; Minister of Public Works, 1964; Minister of Defence, 1966–80. Leader of the National Party in the Cape Province, 1966–86; Chief Leader of Nat. Party, 1978–89. Hon. Doctorate in: Military Science, Stellenbosch Univ., 1976; Philosophy, Orange Free State Univ., 1981; DAdmin *hc* Pretoria Univ., 1985. Grand Cross of Military Order of Christ, Portugal, 1967; Order of Propitious Clouds with Special Grand Cordon, Taiwan, 1980; Grand Collar, Order of Good Hope, Republic of S Africa, 1985. *Recreations:* horseriding, walking, reading, small game hunting. *Address:* Die Anker, Wilderness 6560, South Africa.

BOTHA, Roelof Frederik, (Pik Botha), DMS 1981; Minister of Foreign Affairs, South Africa, since 1977; Minister of Information, since 1978; MP (National Party) for Westdene, since 1977; *b* 27 April 1932; *m* 1953, Helena Susanna Bosman; two *s* two *d*. *Educ:* Volkskool, Potchefstroom; Univ. of Pretoria (BA, LLB). Dept of Foreign Affairs, 1953; diplomatic missions, Europe, 1956–62; Mem. team from S Africa, in SW Africa case, Internat. Court of Justice, The Hague, 1963–66, 1970–71; Agent for S African Govt, Internat. Court of Justice, 1965–66; Legal Adviser, Dept of Foreign Affairs, 1966–68; Under-Sec. and Head of SW Africa and UN Sections, 1968–70. National Party, MP for Wonderboom, 1970–74. Mem., SA Delegn to UN Gen. Assembly, 1967–69, 1971, 1973–74. Served on select Parly Cttees, 1970–74. South African Permanent Representative to the UN, NY, 1974–77; South African Ambassador to the USA, 1975–77. Grand Cross, Order of Good Hope, 1980; Order of the Brilliant Star with Grand Cordon, 1980. *Address:* House of Assembly, Cape Town, South Africa; c/o Department of Foreign Affairs, Pretoria, South Africa.

BOTHWELL, Most Rev. John Charles, DD; Archbishop of Niagara and Metropolitan of Ontario, 1985–91; Bishop of Niagara, 1973–91; *b* 29 June 1926; *s* of William Alexander Bothwell and Anne Bothwell (*née* Campbell); *m* 1951, Joan Cowan; three *s* two *d*. *Educ:* Runnymede Public School; Humberside Coll. Inst., Toronto; Trinity Coll., Univ. of Toronto (BA 1948, LTh 1951, BD 1952; DD 1972). Asst Priest, St James' Cathedral, Toronto, 1951–53; Sen. Assistant at Christ Church Cathedral, Vancouver, 1953–56; Rector: St Aidan's, Oakville, Ont, 1956–60; St James' Church, Dundas, Ont, 1960–65; Canon of Christ Church Cathedral, Hamilton, Ont, 1963; Dir of Programs for Niagara Diocese, 1965–69; Exec. Dir of Program, Nat. HQ of Anglican Church of Canada, Toronto, 1969–71; Bishop Coadjutor of Niagara, 1971–73. Chancellor, Trinity Coll., Univ. of Toronto, 1991–. Hon. Sen. Fellow, Renison Coll., Univ. of Waterloo, 1988. Hon. DD: Huron Coll., Univ. of Western Ont, 1989; Wycliffe Coll., Univ. of Toronto, 1989. *Publications:* Taking Risks and Keeping Faith, 1985; An Open View: keeping faith day by day, 1990. *Recreations:* golf, cross-country ski-ing, swimming. *Address:* 838 Glenwood Avenue, Burlington, Ont L7T 2J9, Canada. *T:* 416/634–8649. *Clubs:* Dundas Valley Golf and Country (Dundas, Ont); Hamilton Chamber of Commerce (Hamilton, Ont).

BOTT, Ian Bernard, FEng 1985; Director, Admiralty Research Establishment, Ministry of Defence, 1984–88, retired; consultant engineer, since 1989; *b* 1 April 1932; *s* of late Edwin Bernard and Agnes Bott; *m* 1955, Kathleen Mary (*née* Broadbent); one *s* one *d*. *Educ:* Nottingham High Sch.; Southwell Minster Grammar Sch.; Stafford Technical Coll.; Manchester Univ. BSc Hon. Physics; FIEE, FInstP. Nottingham Lace Industry, 1949–53. Royal Air Force, 1953–55. English Electric, Stafford, 1955–57; Royal Radar Estabt, 1960–75 (Head of Electronics Group, 1973–75); Counsellor, Defence Research and Development, British Embassy, Washington DC, 1975–77; Ministry of Defence: Dep. Dir Underwater Weapons Projects (S/M), 1977–79; Asst Chief Scientific Advr (Projects), 1979–81; Dir Gen., Guided Weapons and Electronics, 1981–82; Principal Dep. Dir, AWRE, MoD, 1982–84. Mem. Council, Fellowship of Engrg, 1987–90. Chm., Portsmouth Area Hospice, 1989–. Freeman, City of London, 1985; Liveryman, Co. of

Engineers, 1985. *Publications:* papers on physics and electronics subjects in jls of learned socs. *Recreations:* building, horology, music. *Club:* Royal Automobile.

BOTT, Prof. Martin Harold Phillips, FRS 1977; Professor, 1966–88, Research Professor, since 1988, in Geophysics, University of Durham; *b* 12 July 1926; *s* of Harold Bott and Dorothy (*née* Phillips); *m* 1961, Joyce Cynthia Hughes; two *s* one *d*. *Educ:* Clayesmore Sch. Dorset; Magdalene Coll., Cambridge (Scholar). MA, PhD. Nat. Service, 1945–48 (Lieut, Royal Signals). Durham University: Turner and Newall Fellow, 1954–56; Lectr, 1956–63; Reader, 1963–66. Anglican Lay Reader. Mem. Council, Royal Soc., 1982–84. Murchison Medallist, Geological Soc. of London, 1977; Clough Medal, Geol Soc. of Edinburgh, 1979; Sorby Medal, Yorkshire Geol Soc., 1981. *Publications:* The Interior of the Earth, 1971, 2nd edn 1982; papers in learned jls. *Recreations:* walking, mountains. *Address:* 11 St Mary's Close, Shincliffe, Durham DH1 2ND. *T:* Durham (091) 3864021.

BOTTAI, Bruno; Secretary General, Ministry of Foreign Affairs, Italy, since 1987; *b* 10 July 1930; *s* of Giuseppe Bottai and Cornelia Ciocca. *Educ:* Univ. of Rome (law degree). Joined Min. for For. Affairs, 1954; Vice Consul, Tunis, 1956; Second Sec., Perm. Representation to EC, Brussels, 1958; Gen. Secretariat, Co-ord. Service, Min. for For. Affairs, 1961; Counsellor, London, 1966; Dep. Chef de Cabinet, Min. for For. Affairs, 1968; Minister-Counsellor, Holy See, 1969; Diplomatic Advr to Pres., Council of Ministers, 1970; Hd of Press and Inf. Dept 1972, Dep. Dir-Gen. of Political Affairs 1976, Min. for For. Affairs; Ambassador to Holy See and Sovereign Mil. Order of Malta, 1979; Dir-Gen. Pol. Affairs, Min. for For. Affairs, 1981; Ambassador to UK, 1985–87. Numerous decorations from Europe, Africa, Latin Amer. countries, Holy See, Malta. *Publications:* political essays and articles. *Recreations:* modern paintings and modern sculpture, theatre, reading, walking. *Address:* Ministry of Foreign Affairs, Piazzale della Farnesina, 00194 Rome, Italy. *Clubs:* Hurlingham, Les Ambassadeurs.

BOTTING, Maj.-Gen. David Francis Edmund, CBE 1986; Director General of Ordnance Services, Ministry of Defence, since 1990; *b* 15 Dec. 1937; *s* of Leonard Edmund Botting and Elizabeth Mildred Botting (*née* Stacey); *m* 1962, Anne Outhwaite; two *s*. *Educ:* St Paul's School, London. National Service, RAOC, 1956; commissioned Eaton Hall, 1957; Regular Commission, 1958; regtl appts, Kineton, Deepcut, Borneo, Singapore and Malaya, 1957–67; sc 1968; BAOR, 1972–74; 1 Div., 1974–75; 3rd Div., 1981–82; Col AQ 1 Div., 1982–85; Comd Sup. 1 (BR) Corps, 1987; ACOS HQ UKLF, 1987–90. *Recreations:* sport, esp. golf, philately, furniture restoration. *Address:* c/o Lloyds Bank, 10 Sheep Street, Bicester, Oxon OX6 7JZ. *Club:* Army and Navy.

BOTTING, Louise; broadcaster and financial journalist; Chairman, Douglas Deakin Young, since 1988 (Managing Director, 1982–88); *b* 19 Sept. 1939; *d* of Robert and Edith Young; marr. diss.; two *d*; *m* 1989, L. A. Carpenter, *qv*. *Educ:* Sutton Coldfield High School; London Sch. of Economics (BSc Econ.). Kleinwort Benson, 1961–65; Daily Mail, 1970–75; British Forces Broadcasting, 1971–83; Douglas Deakin Young, financial consultancy, 1975–. BBC Moneybox, 1977–. Mem. Top Salaries Review Body, 1987–. *Address:* Douglas Deakin Young Ltd, Empire House, 175 Piccadilly, W1V 9DB. *T:* 071–499 1206.

See also J. R. C. Young.

BOTTINI, Reginald Norman, CBE 1974; General-Secretary, National Union of Agricultural and Allied Workers, 1970–78; Member, General Council of TUC, 1970–78; *b* 14 Oct. 1916; *s* of Reginald and Helena Teresa Bottini; *m* 1946, Doris Mary Balcomb; no *c*. *Educ:* Bec Grammar School. Apptd Asst in Legal Dept of Nat. Union of Agricultural Workers, 1945; Head of Negotiating Dept, 1954; elected Gen.-Sec., Dec. 1969. Member: Agricultural Wages Bd, 1963–78; Agricultural Economic Development Cttee, 1970–78; (part-time) SE Electricity Bd, 1974–83; Food Hygiene Adv. Council, 1973–83; BBC Agric. Adv. Cttee, 1973–78; Econ. and Soc. Cttee, EEC, 1975–78; Clean Air Council, 1975–80; Adv. Cttee on Toxic Substances, 1977–80; Meat and Livestock Commn, 1977–86 (and Chm. of its Consumers Cttee); Panel Mem., Central Arbitration Cttee, 1977–86; Commn on Energy and the Environment, 1978–81; Waste Management Adv. Council, 1978–81; Employees' Panel, Industrial Tribunals, 1984–85. Formerly: Secretary: Trade Union Side, Forestry Commn Ind. and Trades Council; Trade Union Side, British Sugar Beet Nat. Negotiating Cttee; Chairman: Trade Union Side, Nat. Jt Ind. Council for River Authorities; Market Harborough Volunteer Bureau, 1987– (Vice-Chm., 1986–87); formerly Member: Central Council for Agric. and Hort. Co-operation; Nat. Jt Ind. Council for County Roadmen. *Recreations:* gardening, driving. *Address:* 43 Knights End Road, Great Bowden, Market Harborough, Leics LE16 7EY. *T:* Market Harborough (0858) 464229. *Clubs:* Farmers'; Probus (Market Harborough).

BOTTO DE BARROS, Adwaldo Cardoso; Director-General, International Bureau of Universal Postal Union, since 1985; *b* 19 Jan. 1925; *s* of Julio Botto de Barros and Maria Cardoso Botto de Barros; *m* 1951, Neida de Moura; one *s* two *d*. *Educ:* Military Coll., Military Engineering Inst. and Higher Military Engineering Inst., Brazil. Railway construction, 1952–54; Dir, industries in São Paulo and Curitiba, 1955–64; Dir, Handling Sector, São Paulo Prefecture, Financial Adviser to São Paulo Engrg Faculty and Adviser to Suzano Prefecture, 1965–71; Regional Dir, São Paulo, 1972–74, Pres., 1974–84, Brazilian Telegraph and Post Office, Brasília-DF. Mem. and Head, numerous delegns to UPU and other postal assocs overseas, 1976–84. Numerous Brazilian and foreign hons and decorations. *Recreations:* philately, sports. *Address:* International Bureau of the UPU, Weltpoststrasse 4, 3000 Berne 15, Switzerland. *T:* 031/43 22 11.

BOTTOMLEY, Baron *cr* 1984 (Life Peer), of Middlesbrough in the County of Cleveland; **Arthur George Bottomley,** OBE 1941; PC 1951; *b* 7 Feb. 1907; *s* of late George Howard Bottomley and Alice Bottomley; *m* 1936, Bessie Ellen Wiles (*see* Lady Bottomley); no *c*. *Educ:* Gamuel Road Council Sch.; Extension Classes at Toynbee Hall. London Organiser of National Union of Public Employees, 1935–45, 1959–62. Walthamstow Borough Council, 1929–49; Mayor of Walthamstow, 1945–46; Chairman of Emergency Cttee and ARP Controller, 1939–41. Dep. Regional Commissioner for S-E England, 1941–45. MP (Lab): Chatham Division of Rochester, 1945–50, Rochester and Chatham 1950–59; Middlesbrough East, 1962–74, Teesside, Middlesbrough, 1974–83. Parliamentary Under-Secretary of State for Dominions, 1946–47; Sec. for Overseas Trade, Board of Trade, 1947–51; Sec. of State for Commonwealth Affairs, 1964–66; Minister of Overseas Develt, 1966–67. Land Tax Comr, Becontree Div. of Essex; Special Govt Mission to Burma, 1947; Deleg. to UN, New York, 1946, 1947 and 1949; Leader: UK delegation to World Trade and Employment Conference, Havana, 1947; UK Delegn to Commonwealth Conference, Delhi, 1949; Trade Mission to Pakistan, 1950; Special Mission to West Indies, 1951; Member: Consultative Assembly, Council of Europe, 1952, 1953 and 1954; Leader: Parliamentary Labour Party Mission to Burma, 1962, to Malaysia, 1963; UK Delegation to CPA Conferences, Australia, Canada, Malawi, Malaysia, Mauritius; Member, Parliamentary Missions to: India, 1946; Kenya, 1954; Ghana, 1959; Cyprus, 1963; Hong Kong, 1964; China, 1983. Chairman: Commonwealth Relations and Colonies Group, Parly Labour Party, 1963; Select Parly Cttee on Race Relations and Immigration, 1969; Select Cttee on Cyprus, 1975; Special Parly Cttee on Admin and Orgn of House of Commons Services, 1976; House of Commons Commn, 1980–83; Treasurer, Commonwealth Parly Assoc., 1974 (Vice-Chm., UK Branch, 1968 and 1974–77). Chm., Attlee Foundn, 1978–; President: Britain-India Forum, 1981–; Britain-Burma Soc., 1981–. Hon. Fellow, Hunterian Soc., 1985. Hon. Freeman of Chatham, 1959; Freeman: City of London, 1975; Middlesbrough, 1976. Awarded title of Aung San Tagun, Burma, 1981. *Publications:* Why Britain should Join the Common Market, 1959; Two Roads to Colonialism, 1960; The Use and Abuse of Trade Unions, 1961; Commonwealth Comrades and Friends, 1986. *Recreations:* walking and theatre-going. *Address:* 19 Lichfield Road, Woodford Green, Essex IG8 9SU.

BOTTOMLEY, Lady; Bessie Ellen Bottomley, DBE 1970; *b* 28 Nov. 1906; *d* of Edward Charles Wiles and Ellen (*née* Estall); *m* 1936, Baron Bottomley, *qv*; no *c*. *Educ:* Maynard Road Girls' Sch.; North Walthamstow Central Sch. On staff of NUT, 1925–36. Member: Walthamstow Borough Council, 1945–48; Essex CC, 1962–65; Chm., Labour Party Women's Section, E Walthamstow, 1946–71, Chingford, 1973–. Mem., Forest Group Hosp. Man. Cttee, 1949–73; Mem., W Roding Community Health Council, 1973–76. Chm., Walthamstow Nat. Savings Cttee, 1949–65; Vice-Pres., Waltham Forest Nat. Savings Cttee, 1965– (Chm., 1975–). Mayoress of Walthamstow, 1945–46. Mem., WVS Regional Staff (SE England), 1941–45. Past Mem., Home Office Adv. Cttee on Child Care. Chm. of Govs of two Secondary Modern Schools, 1948–68, also group of Primary and Infant Schools; Chm. of Governors of High Schools. Mem., Whitefield Trust. JP 1955–76 and on Juvenile Bench, 1955–71; Dep. Chm., Waltham Forest Bench. *Recreations:* theatre, gardening. *Address:* 19 Lichfield Road, Woodford Green, Essex IG8 9SU.

BOTTOMLEY, Sir James (Reginald Alfred), KCMG 1973 (CMG 1965); HM Diplomatic Service, retired; *b* 12 Jan. 1920; *s* of Sir (William) Cecil Bottomley, KCMG, and Alice Thistle Bottomley (*née* Robinson), JP; *m* 1941, Barbara Evelyn (Vardon); two *s* two *d* (and one *s* decd). *Educ:* King's College Sch., Wimbledon; Trinity Coll., Cambridge. Served with Inns of Court Regt, RAC, 1940–46. Dominions Office, 1946; Pretoria, 1948–50; Karachi, 1953–55; Washington, 1955–59; UK Mission to United Nations, 1959; Dep. High Commissioner, Kuala Lumpur 1963–67; Assst Under-Sec. of State, Commonwealth Office (later FCO), 1967–70; Dep. Under-Sec. of State, FCO, 1970–72; Ambassador to South Africa, 1973–76; Perm. UK Rep. to UN and other Internat. Organisations at Geneva, 1976–78; Dir, Johnson Matthey plc, 1979–85. Mem., British Overseas Trade Bd, 1972. *Recreation:* golf. *Address:* 22 Beaufort Place, Thompson's Lane, Cambridge CB5 8AG. *T:* Cambridge (0223) 328760.

BOTTOMLEY, Peter James; MP (C) Eltham, since 1983 (Greenwich, Woolwich West, June 1975–1983); *b* 30 July 1944; *er s* of Sir James Bottomley, *qv*; *m* 1967, Virginia Garnett (*see* V. H. B. M. Bottomley); one *s* two *d*. *Educ:* comprehensive sch.; Westminster Sch.; Trinity Coll., Cambridge (MA). Driving, industrial sales, industrial relations, industrial economics. Contested (C) GLC elect., Vauxhall, 1973; (C) Woolwich West, Gen. Elecs, 1974. PPS to Minister of State, FCO, 1982–83, to Sec. of State for Social Services, 1983–84, to Sec. of State for NI, 1990; Parly Under Sec. of State, Dept of Employment, 1984–86, Dept of Transport, 1986–89, NI Office, 1989–90. Secretary: Cons. Parly Social Services Cttee, 1977–79; Cons. Parly For. and Commonwealth Cttee, 1979–81. Mem., Transport House Br., T&GWU, 1971–; Pres., Cons. Trade Unionists, 1978–80; Vice-Pres., Fedn of Cons. Students, 1980–82. Chairman: British Union of Family Orgns, 1973–80; Family Forum, 1980–82; Church of England Children's Soc., 1983–84. Mem. Council, MIND, 1981–82; Trustee, Christian Aid, 1978–84. Parly Swimming Champion, 1980–81, 1984–86; Captain, Parly Football Team. Castrol/Inst. of Motor Industry Road Safety Gold Medal, 1988. *Recreation:* children. *Address:* House of Commons, SW1A 0AA.

BOTTOMLEY, Virginia Hilda Brunette Maxwell, JP; MP (C) Surrey South-West, since May 1984; Minister for Health, since 1989; Co-Chairman, Women's National Commission, since 1991; *b* 12 March 1948; *d* of W. John Garnett, *qv*; *m* Peter Bottomley, *qv*; one *s* two *d*. *Educ:* Putney High Sch.; Univ. of Essex (BA); London Sch. of Econs and Pol Science (MSc). Research for Child Poverty Action Gp, and Lectr in a Further Educn Coll., 1971–73; Psychiatric Social Worker, Brixton and Camberwell Child Guidance Units, 1973–84. Vice Chm., National Council of Carers and their Elderly Dependants, 1982–88. Dir, Mid Southern Water Co., 1987–88. Mem., MRC, 1987–88. Contested (C) IoW, 1983. PPS to: Minister of State for Educn and Science, 1985–86; Minister for Overseas Develt, 1986–87; Sec. of State for Foreign and Commonwealth Affairs, 1987–88; Parly Under-Sec. of State, DoE, 1988–89. Sec., Cons. Backbench Employment Cttee, 1985; Fellow, Industry Parlt Trust, 1987. Mem., Court of Govs, LSE, 1985–. JP Inner London, 1975 (Chm., Lambeth Juvenile Court, 1981–84). *Recreation:* family. *Address:* House of Commons, SW1A 0AA. *T:* 071–219 6499. *Club:* Seaview Yacht.

BOTTOMS, Prof. Anthony Edward; Wolfson Professor of Criminology and Director of the Institute of Criminology, University of Cambridge, since 1984; Fellow of Fitzwilliam College, Cambridge, since 1984; *b* 29 Aug. 1939; *yr s* of James William Bottoms, medical missionary, and Dorothy Ethel Bottoms (*née* Barnes); *m* 1962, Janet Freda Wenger; one *s* two *d*. *Educ:* Eltham Coll.; Corpus Christi Coll., Oxford (MA); Corpus Christi Coll., Cambridge (MA); Univ. of Sheffield (PhD). Probation Officer, 1962–64; Research Officer, Inst. of Criminology, Univ. of Cambridge, 1964–68; Univ. of Sheffield: Lecturer, 1968–72; Sen. Lectr, 1972–76; Prof. of Criminology, 1976–84; Dean of Faculty of Law, 1981–84. Canadian Commonwealth Vis. Fellow, Simon Fraser Univ., BC, 1982. Member: Parole Bd for England and Wales, 1974–76; Home Office Res. and Adv. Gp on Long-Term Prison System, 1984–90. Trustee, Police Foundn, 1990–. Editor, Howard Journal of Penology and Crime Prevention, 1975–81. *Publications:* (jtly) Criminals Coming of Age, 1973; (jtly) The Urban Criminal, 1976; (jtly) Defendants in the Criminal Process, 1976; The Suspended Sentence after Ten Years (Frank Dawtry Lecture), 1980; (ed jtly) The Coming Penal Crisis, 1980; (ed jtly) Problems of Long-Term Imprisonment, 1987; (jtly) Social Inquiry Reports, 1988; (jtly) Intermediate Treatment and Juvenile Justice, 1990; Crime Prevention facing the 1990s (James Smart Lecture), 1990; various articles and reviews. *Address:* Institute of Criminology, 7 West Road, Cambridge CB3 9DT. *T:* Cambridge (0223) 335360.

BOTVINNIK, Mikhail Moisseyevich; Order of Lenin, 1957; Order of the Badge of Honour, 1936 and 1945; Order of the Red Banner of Labour, 1961; Order of the October Revolution, 1981; Senior Scientist, USSR Research Institute for Electroenergetics, since 1955; *b* Petersburg, 17 Aug. 1911; *s* of a dental technician; *m* 1935, Gayane Ananova; one *d*. *Educ:* Leningrad Polytechnical Institute (Grad.). Thesis for degree of: Candidate of Technical Sciences, 1937; Doctor of Technical Sciences, 1952; Professor, 1972. Chess master title, 1927; Chess grandmaster title, 1935. Won Soviet chess championship in 1931, 1933, 1939, 1941, 1944, 1945, 1952; World chess title, 1948–57, 1958–60 and 1961–63. Honoured Master of Sport of the USSR, 1945. *Publications:* Flohr-Botvinnik Match, 1934; Alekhin-Euwe Return Match, 1938; Selected Games, 1937, 1945, 1960; Tournament Match for the Absolute Champion Title, 1945; Botvinnik-Smyslov Match, 1955; Eleventh Soviet Chess Championship, 1939; Smyslov-Botvinnik Return Match, 1960; Regulation of Excitation and Static Stability of Syndronous Machines, 1950; Asynchronized Synchronous Machines, 1960; Algorithm Play of Chess, 1968; Controlled

AC Machines (with Y. Shakarian), 1969; Computers, Chess and Long-Range Planning, 1971; Botvinnik's Best Games 1947–70, 1972; Three matches of Anatoly Karpov, 1975; On Cybernetic Goal of Game, 1975; A Half Century in Chess, 1979; On Solving of Inexact Search, 1979; Fifteen Games and their History, 1981; Selected Games 1967–70, 1981; Achieving the Aim, 1981; Analytical and critical works 1923–41, 1984, 1942–56, 1985, 1957–70, 1986; Chess Method of Solution Search Problems, 1989. *Address:* 3 Frunsenskaja 7 (flat 154), Moscow, USSR. *T:* 242.15,86.

BOTWOOD, Richard Price; Director-General, Chartered Institute of Transport, since 1989; *b* 1 June 1932; *s* of Allan Bertram and Hilda Amelia Botwood; *m* 1964, Victoria Sanderson; one *s* one *d*. *Educ:* Oundle School. Sec., Tozer Kemsley & Millbourn, 1952–56; Dir, International Factors, 1956–61; Asst Man. Dir, Melbray Group, 1961–73; Chm. and Man. Dir, W. S. Sanderson (Morpeth), wine and spirit merchants, 1973–85; Dir-Gen., Air Transport Users' Cttee, 1986–89. *Recreations:* opera, gardening, squash, golf. *Address:* 34 Brook Green, W6 7BL. *T:* 071–603 5277.

BOUCHIER, Prof. Ian Arthur Dennis, CBE 1990; Professor of Medicine, University of Edinburgh, since 1986; *b* 7 Sept. 1932; *s* of E. A. and M. Bouchier; *m* 1959, Patricia Norma Henshilwood; two *s*. *Educ:* Rondebosch Boys' High Sch., Cape Town; Univ. of Cape Town. MB, ChB, MD, FRCP, FRCPE, FRSE, FIBiol. Groote Schuur Hospital: House Officer, 1955–58; Registrar, 1958–61; Asst Lectr, Royal Free Hosp., 1962–63; Instructor in Medicine, Boston Univ. Sch. of Medicine, 1964–65; Sen. Lectr 1965–70, Reader in Medicine 1970–73, Univ. of London; Prof. of Medicine, 1973–86, and Dean, Faculty of Medicine and Dentistry, 1982–86, Univ. of Dundee. Pres., World Organisation of Gastroenterology, 1990– (Sec. Gen., 1982–90). Member: Chief Scientist Cttee, Scotland, 1980–; MRC, 1982–86; Council, RCPE, 1984–90; Council, British Soc. of Gastroenterology, 1987–90 (Chm., Educn Cttee, 1987–90). Goulstonian Lectr, RCP, 1971. Visiting Professor of Medicine: Michigan Univ., 1979; McGill Univ., 1983; RPMS, 1984; Shenyang Univ., Hong Kong Univ., 1988. Chm., Editl Bd, Current Opinion in Gastroenterology, 1987–91; Member, Editorial Board: Baillière's Clinical Gastroenterology, 1987–; Hellenic Jl of Gastroenterology, 1988–; Internat. Gastroenterology, 1988–. *Publications:* (ed) Clinical Investigation of Gastrointestinal Function, 1969, 2nd edn 1981; Gastroenterology, 1973, 3rd edn 1982; (ed) Clinical Skills, 1976, 2nd edn 1981; (ed) Recent Advances in Gastroenterology 5, 1983; (ed) Textbook of Gastroenterology, 1984; (ed) Clinical Investigations in Gastroenterology, 1988; 400 scientific papers and communications. *Recreations:* history of whaling, music of Berlioz, cooking. *Address:* Department of Medicine, The Royal Infirmary, Edinburgh EH3 9YW. *T:* 031–229 2477. *Club:* New (Edinburgh).

BOUGH, Francis Joseph; broadcaster; Presenter, Sky News Channel, since 1989; *b* 15 Jan. 1933; *m*; three *s*. *Educ:* Oswestry; Merton College, Oxford (MA). With ICI, 1957–62; joined BBC, 1962; presenter of Sportsview, 1964–67, of Grandstand, 1967–82, of Nationwide, 1972–83, of breakfast television, 1983–87, of Holiday, 1987–88, of 6 o'clock Live, LWT, 1989–. Former Oxford soccer blue, Shropshire sprint champion. *Publications:* Cue Frank! (autobiog.), 1980; Frank Bough's Breakfast Book, 1984. *Address:* c/o Jon Roseman Associates Ltd, 103 Charing Cross Road, WC2.

BOUGHEY, John Fenton C.; *see* Coplestone-Boughey.

BOUGHEY, Sir John (George Fletcher), 11th Bt *cr* 1798; *b* 12 Aug. 1959; *s* of Sir Richard James Boughey, 10th Bt, and of Davina Julia (now the Lady Loch), *d* of FitzHerbert Wright; *S* father, 1978. *Heir: b* James Richard Boughey [*b* 29 Aug. 1960; *m* 1989, Katy Fenwick-Clennell; one *d*]. *Address:* Bratton House, Westbury, Wilts.

BOULET, Gilles, OC 1985; Assistant to the President, University of Quebec, since 1988 (President, 1978–88); *b* 5 June 1926; *s* of Georges-A. Boulet and Yvonne Hamel; *m* 1971, Florence Lemire; one *s* one *d*. *Educ:* Coll. St Gabriel de St Tite; Séminaire St Joseph de Trois-Rivières; Laval Univ. (LTh 1951, DèsL 1954); Université Catholique de Paris (LPh, MA 1953). Prof. of Literature and History, Séminaire Ste Marie, Shawinigan, 1953–61; Centre d'Etudes Universitaires de Trois-Rivières: Founder, 1960; Dir, 1960–69; Prof. of Lit. and Hist., 1961–66; Laval University: Prof. of French, Faculty of Lit., 1955–62; Aggregate Prof., Fac. of Arts, 1959; Rector, Univ. du Québec à Trois-Rivières, 1969–78, Rector-Founder, 1979. Founder and Pres., Inter-Amer. Orgn for Higher Educn, 1981–. Dr *hc* Universidade Federal de Rio Grande do Norte, Brazil, 1983; Hon. Master of Administration, Univ. Autonoma de Guerrero, Mexico, 1984. Comdr, Assoc. Belgo-Hispanique, 1980; Comdr, Mérite et Dévouement Français, 1980; Officier de la Légion d'Honneur (France), 1988. Duvernay Award, Soc. St-Jean-Baptiste de Trois-Rivières (literature award), 1978; Gold Medal, Univ. Federal da Bahia, Brazil, 1983; Gold Medal of Merit (Sousandrade), Universidade Federal do Maranhâo, Brazil, 1986; Medal, Gloire de l'Escolle, Laval Univ., 1988. Personality of the Year, CKTM/TV, 1988 . *Publications:* (with Lucien Gagné) Le Français Parlé au Cours Secondaire, vols I and II, 1962, vols III and IV, 1963; Textes et Préceptes Littéraires, vol. I, 2nd edn, 1967, vol. II, 1964; (with others) Le Boréal Express, Album no 1, 1965, Album no 2, 1967; De la philosophie comme passion de la liberté, 1984; Going Global, 1988. *Recreations:* reading, skiing, skating. *Address:* 3021 de la Promenade, Ste Foy, Quebec G1W 2J5, Canada. *T:* (418) 657–2147. *Clubs:* Quebec Garrison, Saint-Maurice Hunting and Fishing (Quebec).

BOULEZ, Pierre; composer; Director, Institut de Recherche et de Coordination Acoustique/Musique, since 1976; *b* Montbrison, Loire, France, 26 March 1925. *Educ:* Saint-Etienne and Lyon (music and higher mathematics); Paris Conservatoire. Studied with Messiaen and René Leibowitz. Theatre conductor, Jean-Louis Barrault Company, Paris, 1948; visited USA with French Ballet Company, 1952. Has conducted major orchestras in his own and standard classical works in Great Britain, Europe and USA, including Edinburgh Festival, 1965; also conducted Wozzeck in Paris and Frankfurt; Parsifal at Bayreuth, 1966; Chief Conductor, BBC Symphony Orchestra, 1971–75; Chief Conductor and Music Dir, NY Philharmonic, 1971–77; Dir, Bayreuth Festival, 1976–80. Hon. DMus: Cantab, 1980; Oxon, 1987. Charles Heidsieck Award for Outstanding Contribution to Franco-British Music, 1989. Interested in poetry and aesthetics of Baudelaire, Mallarmé and René Char. *Compositions include:* Trois Psalmodies (Piano solo), 1945; Sonata No 1 (piano), 1946; Sonatine for flute and piano, 1946; Sonata No 2 (piano), 1948; Polyphonie X for 18 solo instruments, 1951; Visage nuptial (2nd version), 1951; Structures for 2 pianos, 1952; Le Marteau sans Maître (voice and 6 instruments), 1954; Sonata No 3 (piano), 1956; Deux Improvisations sur Mallarmé for voice and 9 instruments, 1957; Doubles for orchestra, 1958; Poésie pour Pouvoir for voices and orchestra, 1958; Soleil des Eaux (text by René Char) for chorus and orchestra, 1958; Pli selon Pli: Hommage à Mallarmé, for voice and orchestra, 1960; Eclat, 1965; Domaines for solo clarinet, 1968; Cummings ist der Dichter (16 solo voices and instruments), 1970; Eclat/Multiples, 1970; Explosante Fixe (8 solo instruments), 1972; Rituel, for orchestra, 1975; Messagesquisses (7 celli), 1977; Notations, for orch., 1980; Répons, for orch. and live electronics, 1981–86; Dérive, 1985; Dialogue de l'Ombre Double, 1986. *Publications:* Penser la musique d'aujourd'hui, 1966 (Boulez on Music Today, 1971); Relevés d'apprenti, 1967; Par volonté et par hasard, 1976; Points de Repère, 1981; Orientations, 1986; Jalons, 1989; Le pays fertile—Paul Klee, 1989. *Address:* IRCAM, 31 rue St Merri, 75004 Paris, France. *T:* 4277 1233.

BOULIND, Mrs (Olive) Joan, CBE 1975; Fellow, 1973–79, and Tutor, 1974–79, Hughes Hall, Cambridge; *b* 24 Sept. 1912; *e d* of Douglas Siddall and Olive Raby; *m* 1936, Henry F. Boulind (decd), MA, PhD; one *s* (and one *s* one *d* decd). *Educ:* Wallasey High Sch., Cheshire; Univ. of Liverpool (BA 1st class Hons History, Medieval and Modern; DipEd); MA Cantab 1974. Teacher: Wirral Co. Sch. for Girls, 1934–36; Cambridgeshire High Sch. for Girls, 1963. Nat. Pres., Nat. Council of Women, 1966–68 (Sen. Vice-Pres., 1964–66); Co-Chm., Women's Consultative Council, 1966–68; Leader, British delegn to conf. of Internat. Council of Women, Bangkok, 1970; Co-Chm., Women's Nat. Commn, 1973–75; Co-Chm., UK Co-ordinating Cttee for Internat. Women's Year, 1975; Chm., Westminster College Management Cttee, 1980–88. Member: Commn on the Church in the Seventies, Congregational Church in England and Wales, 1970–72 (Vice-Chm., 1971–72); Ministerial Trng Cttee, United Reformed Church, 1972–79 and 1982–86 (Chm., 1982–86); East Adv. Council, BBC, 1976–84 (Chm. 1981–84). Deacon, Emmanuel Congregational Ch., Cambridge, 1958–66. Trustee, Homerton Coll. of Educn, 1955–. *Recreations:* reading, travel, music. *Address:* 28 Rathmore Road, Cambridge CB1 4AD.

BOULTER, Prof. Donald, CBE 1991; FIBiol; Head of Department of Biological Sciences, University of Durham, 1988–91 (Professor of Botany and Head of Department of Botany, 1966–88); Director of Durham University Botanic Garden, 1966–91; *b* 25 Aug. 1926; *s* of late George Boulter and of Vera Boulter; *m* 1956, Margaret Eileen Kennedy; four *d*. *Educ:* Portsmouth Grammar Sch.; Christ Church, Oxford (BA, MA, DPhil). FIBiol 1970. Served RAF, 1945–48. Sessel Fellow, Yale Univ., 1953–54; Asst Lectr in Botany, King's Coll., London, 1955–57; Lectr 1957–64, Sen. Lectr 1964–66, Liverpool Univ. Vis. Prof., Univ. of Texas, Austin, 1967. Member: AFRC, 1985–; Biological Scis Sub-Cttee, UFC (formerly UGC), 1988–89; Chm., Plants & Soils Res. Grant Bd, 1986–89; Pres., Sect. K, BAAS, 1981. Dep. Chm. Governing Body, AFRC Inst. of Horticultural Res., 1987–90; Member, Governing Body: Scottish Crop Res. Inst., 1986–; AFRC Inst. of Plant Sci. Res., 1989–92. Exec. Cttee, Horticultural Res. Internat., 1990–92. FRSA 1972. Tate & Lyle Award for Phytochem., 1975. *Publications:* (ed) Chemotaxonomy of the Leguminosae, 1971; (associate ed) Qualitas Plantarum: Plant Foods for Human Nutrition, 1980; (ed) Encyclopedia of Plant Physiology, vol. 14B: Nucleic Acids and Proteins, 1982; papers in sci. jls on molecular evolution, genetic engrg of crops, biochem. and molecular biol of seed develt. *Recreation:* travel. *Address:* 5 Crossgate, Durham DH1 4PS. *T:* Durham (091) 3861199.

BOULTER, Patrick Stewart, FRCSE, FRCS; Consultant Surgeon, Royal Surrey County Hospital and Regional Radiotherapy Centre, since 1962; President, Royal College of Surgeons of Edinburgh, since 1991; *b* 28 May 1927; *s* of Frederick Charles Boulter, MC and Flora Victoria Boulter of Annan, Dumfriesshire; *m* 1946, Patricia Mary Eckersley Barlow, *d* of S. G. Barlow of Lowton, Lancs; two *d*. *Educ:* King's Coll. Sch.; Carlisle GS; Guy's Hosp. Med. Sch., Univ. of London (MB BS Hons and Gold Medal, 1955). Guy's Hospital and Medical School, University of London: House Surgeon, 1955–56; Res. Fellow, Dept of Surgery, 1956–57; Lectr in Anatomy, 1956–57; Sen. Surgical Registrar, 1959–62; Hon. Consultant Surgeon, 1963; Surgical Registrar, Middlesex Hosp., 1957–59; Consultant Surgeon, St Luke's Hosp., 1962–91; Vis. Surgeon, Cranleigh and Cobham Hosps, 1962–91. Visiting Professor: Surrey Univ., 1986– (Hon. Reader, 1968–80); univs in USA, Australia, NZ, Pakistan and India. Examnr, Univs of Edinburgh, London, Nottingham and Newcastle. Royal College of Surgeons: Surgical Tutor, 1964; Regl Advr, 1975; Penrose May teacher, 1985–; Royal College of Surgeons of Edinburgh: Examnr, 1979; Mem. Council, 1984–; Vice-Pres., 1989–91. Hon. FRACS 1985. *Publications:* articles and book chapters on surgical subjects, esp. breast disease, surgical oncology and endocrine surgery. *Recreations:* mountaineering, ski-ing, fly-fishing. *Address:* Cairnsmore, Fairway, Merrow, Guildford, Surrey GU1 2XN. *T:* Guildford (0483) 504977; Quarry Cottage, Salkeld Dykes, Penrith, Cumbria CA11 9LL. *T:* Lazenby (076883) 8822. *Clubs:* Alpine, Caledonian; New (Edinburgh); Yorkshire Fly Fishers; Swiss Alpine.

BOULTING, Roy; Producer and Joint Managing Director, Charter Film Productions Ltd, since 1973; *b* 21 Nov. 1913; *s* of Arthur Boulting and Rose Bennett. *Educ:* HMS Worcester; Reading Sch. Formed independent film production company with twin brother John, 1937. Served War of 1939–45, RAC, finishing as Capt.; films for Army included Desert Victory and Burma Victory. Producer: Brighton Rock, 1947; Seven Days to Noon, 1950; Private's Progress, 1955; Lucky Jim (Edinburgh Festival), 1957; I'm All Right Jack, 1959; Heavens Above!, 1962. Director: Pastor Hall, 1939; Thunder Rock, 1942; Fame is the Spur, 1947; The Guinea Pig, 1948; High Treason, 1951; Singlehanded, 1952; Seagulls over Sorrento, Crest of the Wave, 1953; Josephine and Men, 1955; Run for the Sun, 1955; Brothers in Law, 1956; Happy is the Bride, 1958; Carlton-Browne of the FO, 1958–59; I'm All Right Jack, 1959; The Risk, 1960; The French Mistress, 1960; Suspect, 1960; The Family Way, 1966; Twisted Nerve, 1968; There's a Girl in My Soup, 1970; Soft Beds, Hard Battles, 1974; Danny Travis, 1978; The Last Word, 1979; The Moving Finger, 1984. *Play:* (with Leo Marks) Favourites, 1977. Dir, British Lion Films Ltd, 1958–72. Mem. Adv. Council, Dirs' and Producers' Rights Soc., 1988–. Hon. Dr RCA, 1990. *Address:* Charter Film Productions Ltd, Twickenham Film Studios, St Margarets, Twickenham, Middlesex. *Club:* Lord's Taverners.

BOULTING, S. A.; *see* Cotes, Peter.

BOULTON, Sir Christian; *see* Boulton, Sir H. H. C.

BOULTON, Sir Clifford (John), KCB 1990 (CB 1985); Clerk of the House of Commons, since 1987; *b* 25 July 1930; *s* of Stanley Boulton and Evelyn (*née* Hey), Cocknage, Staffs; *m* 1955, Anne, *d* of Rev. E. E. Raven, Cambridge; one adopted *s* one adopted *d*. *Educ:* Newcastle-under-Lyme High School; St John's Coll., Oxford (exhibnr). MA (Modern History). National Service, RAC, 1949–50; Lt Staffs Yeomanry (TA). A Clerk in the House of Commons, 1953–; Clerk of Select Cttees on Procedure, 1964–68 and 1976–77; Public Accounts, 1968–70; Parliamentary Questions, 1971–72; Privileges, 1972–77; Clerk of the Overseas Office, 1977–79; Principal Clerk, Table Office, 1979–83; Clerk Asst, 1983–87. A school Governor and subsequently board mem., Church Schools Company, 1965–79. *Publications:* (ed) Erskine May's Parliamentary Practice, 21st edn, 1989; contribs to Halsbury's Laws of England, 4th edn, and Parliamentary journals. *Address:* House of Commons, SW1A 0AA. *T:* 071–219 3300; 2 Main Street, Lyddington, Oakham LE15 9LT. *T:* Uppingham (0572) 823487.

BOULTON, Prof. Geoffrey Stewart; Regius Professor of Geology, University of Edinburgh, since 1986; *b* 28 Nov. 1940; *s* of George Stewart and Rose Boulton; *m* 1964, Denise Bryers Lawns; two *d*. *Educ:* Longton High Sch.; Birmingham Univ. BSc, PhD, DSc; FGS. British Geol Survey, 1962–64; Demonstrator, Univ. of Keele, 1964–65; Fellow, Univ. of Birmingham, 1965–68; Hydrogeologist, Kenya, 1968; Lectr, then Reader, Univ. of E Anglia, 1968–86. Prof., Amsterdam Univ., 1982–86. FGS 1961; FRSE 1989. *Publications:* numerous articles in learned jls on polar, quaternary, glacial and marine geology and glaciology. *Recreations:* music, mountaineering. *Address:* 19 Lygon Road, Edinburgh EH16 5QD.

BOULTON, Sir (Harold Hugh) Christian, 4th Bt *cr* 1905; *b* 29 Oct. 1918; *s* of Sir (Denis Duncan) Harold (Owen) Boulton, 3rd Bt, and Louise McGowan (*d* 1978), USA; *S* father, 1968. *Educ:* Ampleforth College, Yorks. Late Captain, Irish Guards (Supplementary Reserve). *Address:* c/o Bank of Montreal, City View Branch, 1491 Merivale Road, Nepean, Ontario K2C 3H3, Canada.

BOULTON, Prof. James Thompson; Director, Institute for Advanced Research in the Humanities, University of Birmingham, since 1987 (Fellow, 1984); *b* 17 Feb. 1924; *e s* of Harry and Annie M. P. Boulton; *m* 1949, Margaret Helen Leary; one *s* one *d*. *Educ:* University College, Univ. of Durham; Lincoln Coll., Oxford. BA Dunelm 1948; BLitt Oxon 1952; PhD Nottingham 1960. FRSL 1968. Served in RAF, 1943–46 (Flt-Lt). Lectr, subseq. Sen. Lectr and Reader in English, Univ. of Nottingham, 1951–64; John Cranford Adams Prof. of English, Hofstra Univ., NY, 1967; Prof. of English Lit., Univ. of Nottingham, 1964–75, Dean, Faculty of Arts, 1970–73; University of Birmingham: Prof. of English Studies and Head of Dept of English Lang. and Lit., 1975–88, Prof. Emeritus, 1989; Dean of Faculty of Arts, 1981–84; Public Orator, 1984–88. Chm. of Govs, Fircroft Coll., Selly Oak, 1985–. Mem. Exec. Cttee, Anglo-American Associates (NY), 1968–75. Editor, Renaissance and Modern Studies, 1969–75, 1985. General Editor: The Letters of D. H. Lawrence, 1973–; The Works of D. H. Lawrence, 1975–. Hon. DLitt Durham, 1991. *Publications:* (ed) Edmund Burke: A Philosophical Enquiry into . . . the Sublime and Beautiful, 1958, rev. edn 1987; (ed) C. F. G. Masterman: The Condition of England, 1960; The Language of Politics in the Age of Wilkes and Burke, 1963, 2nd edn 1975; (ed) Dryden: Of Dramatick Poesy etc, 1964; (ed) Defoe: Prose and Verse, 1965, 2nd edn 1975; (with James Kinsley) English Satiric Poetry: Dryden to Byron, 1966; (ed) Lawrence in Love: Letters from D. H. Lawrence to Louie Burrows, 1968; (ed) Samuel Johnson: The Critical Heritage, 1971; (with S. T. Bindoff) Research in Progress in English and Historical Studies in the Universities of the British Isles, vol. 1, 1971, vol. 2, 1976; (ed) Defoe: Memoirs of a Cavalier, 1972; (ed) The Letters of D. H. Lawrence, vol. 1, 1979, vol. 2 (jtly), 1982, vol. 3 (jtly), 1984, vol. 4 (jtly), 1987, vol. 5 (jtly), 1989, vol. 6 (jtly), 1991; (contrib.) Renaissance and Modern Essays (ed G. R. Hibbard), 1966; (contrib.) The Familiar Letter in the 18th Century (ed H. Anderson), 1966; papers in Durham Univ. Jl, Essays in Criticism, Renaissance and Modern Studies, Modern Drama, etc. *Recreation:* gardening. *Address:* Institute for Advanced Research in the Humanities, University of Birmingham, PO Box 363, Birmingham B15 2TT.

See also P. H. Boulton.

BOULTON, Rev. Canon Peter Henry; Canon Residentiary of Southwell Minster, since 1987; Diocesan Director of Education, Southwell, since 1987; Chaplain to the Queen, since 1991; *b* 12 Dec. 1925; *s* of Harry Boulton and Annie Mary Penty Boulton; *m* 1955, Barbara Ethelinda Davies, SRN, SCM; three *s*. *Educ:* Lady Lumley's Grammar Sch., Pickering, N Yorks; St Chad's Coll., Univ. of Durham (BA Hons Theology); Ely Theol Coll., Cambs. Served War, RNVR, 1943–46. Ordained deacon, 1950, priest, 1951 (Chester). Asst Curate: Coppenhall S Michael, Crewe, 1950–54; S Mark, Mansfield, 1954–55; Vicar: Clipstone Colliery Village, Notts, 1955–60; St John the Baptist, Carlton, Nottingham, 1960–67; Worksop, 1967–87; Hon. Canon of Southwell, 1975–87. Proctor in Convocation and Mem., Gen. Synod of C of E, 1959–; Prolocutor of York Convocation and Jt Chm., House of Clergy, Gen. Synod, 1980–90; Member: Howick Commn on Crown Appts, 1962–64; Standing Cttee of Gen. Synod, 1974–90; Churches' Council for Covenanting, 1978–82; Corp. of Church House, 1980–90; Crown Appts Commn, 1982–87 and 1988–; Legal Adv. Commn of Gen. Synod, 1985–91; Gen. Synod Bd of Educn, 1991–. Chaplain Convenor, Bassetlaw Dist Hosps, 1967–87. Mem., Notts County Educn Cttee, 1987–. C of E Delegate: ACC, 1972–80; WCC Assembly, Nairobi, 1975. *Publications:* articles in learned and ecclesiastical jls. *Recreations:* crosswords, bridge, local history, pruning, swimming. *Address:* Dunham House, Westgate, Southwell, Notts NG25 0JL. *T:* Southwell 814504.

See also J. T. Boulton.

BOULTON, Sir William (Whytehead), 3rd Bt *cr* 1944; Kt 1975; CBE 1958; TD 1949; Secretary, Senate of the Inns of Court and the Bar, 1974–75; *b* 21 June 1912; *s* of Sir William Boulton, 1st Bt, and Rosalind Mary (*d* 1969), *d* of Sir John Davison Milburn, 1st Bt, of Guyzance, Northumberland; *S* brother, 1982; *m* 1944, Margaret Elizabeth, *o d* of late Brig. H. N. A. Hunter, DSO; one *s* two *d*. *Educ:* Eton; Trinity Coll., Cambridge. Called to Bar, Inner Temple, 1936; practised at the Bar, 1937–39. Secretary, General Council of the Bar, 1950–74. Served War of 1939–45: with 104th Regt RHA (Essex Yeo.) and 14th Regt RHA, in the Middle East, 1940–44; Staff Coll., Camberley, 1944. Control Commission for Germany (Legal Div.), 1945–50. Gazetted 2nd Lieut TA (Essex Yeo.), 1934; retired with rank of Hon. Lieut-Col. *Publications:* A Guide to Conduct and Etiquette at the Bar of England and Wales, 1st edn 1953, 6th edn, 1975. *Heir:* *s* John Gibson Boulton, *b* 18 Dec. 1946. *Address:* The Quarters House, Alresford, near Colchester, Essex CO7 8AY. *T:* Wivenhoe (0206) 822450.

BOUNDS, (Kenneth) Peter; Chief Executive, Liverpool City Council, since 1991; *b* 7 Nov. 1943; *s* of Rev. Kenneth Bounds and Doris Bounds; *m* 1965, Geraldine Amy Slee; two *s*. *Educ:* Ashville College, Harrogate. Admitted Solicitor, 1971. Dir of Admin, Stockport MBC, 1973–82; Chief Exec., Bolton MBC, 1982–91. Pres., Assoc. of Dist Secs, 1980–81; Company Secretary: Greater Manchester Econ. Develt Ltd, 1986–91; NW Tourist Bd, 1986–91. Mem., President's Council, Methodist Church, 1981–84. Hon. Fellow, Bolton Inst. of Higher Educn, 1991. *Recreations:* music, walking. *Address:* Municipal Buildings, Dale Street, Liverpool.

BOURASSA, Robert; Leader, Quebec Liberal Party, 1970–77 and since 1983; Prime Minister of Québec, 1970–76 and since 1985; Member of Québec National Assembly for St Laurent, since 1986 (for Mercier, 1966–76 and for Bertrand, 1985); *b* 14 July 1933; *s* of Aubert Bourassa and Adrienne Courville; *m* 1958, Andrée Simard; one *s* one *d*. *Educ:* Jean-de-Brébeuf Coll.; Univs of Montreal, Oxford and Harvard. Gov.-Gen.'s Medal Montreal 1956. MA Oxford 1959. Admitted Quebec Bar 1957. Fiscal Adviser to Dept of Nat. Revenue and Prof. in Econs and Public Finance, Ottawa Univ., 1960–63; Sec. and Dir of Research of Bélanger Commn on Public Finance, 1963–65; Special Adviser to Fed. Dept of Finance on fiscal and econ. matters, 1965–66; Prof. of Public Finance, Univs of Montreal and Laval, 1966–69; financial critic for Quebec Liberal Party, Pres. Polit. Commn and Mem. Liberal Party's Strategy Cttee; Minister of Finance, May-Nov. 1970; Minister of Inter-govtl Affairs, 1971–72. Lectr, Institut d'Etudes Européennes, Brussels, 1977–78; Prof., Center of Advanced Internat. Studies, Johns Hopkins Univ., 1978; Prof., Univ. de Laval, Univ. de Montréal, 1979; Visiting Professor: INSEAD, Fontainebleau, 1976; Univ. of Southern Calif., 1981; Yale Univ., 1982. Hon. DPhil Univ. of Tel-Aviv, 1987. *Publications:* Bourassa/Québec!, 1970; La Baie James, 1973 (James Bay, 1973); Les années Bourassa: l'intégrae des entretiens Bourassa–St Pierre, 1977; Deux fois la Baie James, 1981; Power from the North, 1985; L'Energie du Nord: la force du Québec, 1985; Le défi technologique, 1985. *Address:* 885 Grande-Allée Est, Edifice "J", Québec, Québec G1A 1A2, Canada.

BOURDEAUX, Rev. Canon Michael Alan; General Director, Keston Research, Oxford (formerly Keston College, Kent), since 1969; *b* 19 March 1934; *s* of Richard Edward and Lillian Myra Bourdeaux; *m* 1st, 1960, Gillian Mary Davies (*d* 1978); one *s* one *d*; 2nd, 1979, Lorna Elizabeth Waterton; one *s* one *d*. *Educ:* Truro Sch.; St Edmund Hall, Oxford (MA Hons Mod. Langs); Wycliffe Hall, Oxford (Hons Theology). Moscow State Univ., 1959–60; Deacon, 1960; Asst Curate, Enfield Parish Church, Mddx, 1960–64; researching at Chislehurst, Kent, on the Church in the Soviet Union, with grant from Centre de Recherches, Geneva, 1965–68. Vis. Prof., St Bernard's Seminary, Rochester, NY, 1969; Vis. Fellow, LSE, 1969–71; Research Fellow, RIIA, Chatham House, 1971–73; Dawson Lectr on Church and State, Baylor Univ., Waco, Texas, 1972; Chavasse Meml Lectr, Oxford Univ., 1976; Kathryn W. Davis Prof. in Slavic Studies, Wellesley Coll., Wellesley, Mass, 1981; Vis. Fellow, St Edmund Hall, Oxford, 1989–90. Hon. Canon, Rochester Cathedral, 1990–. Founded Keston College, a research centre on religion in the Communist countries, 1969. Founder of journal, Religion in Communist Lands, 1973–. Templeton Prize for Progress in Religion, 1984. *Publications:* Opium of the People, 1965, 2nd edn 1977; Religious Ferment in Russia, 1968; Patriarch and Prophets, 1970, 2nd edn 1975; Faith on Trial in Russia, 1971; Land of Crosses, 1979; Risen Indeed, 1983; (with Lorna Bourdeaux) Ten Growing Soviet Churches, 1987; Gorbachev, Glasnost and the Gospel, 1990. *Recreations:* singing in the Philharmonia Chorus; officiating, as Member British Tennis Umpires Assoc., at Wimbledon and abroad. *Address:* Keston Research, 33a Canal Street, Oxford OX2 6BQ. *Club:* Athenæum.

BOURDILLON, Mervyn Leigh, JP; Lord-Lieutenant of Powys, since 1986; *b* 9 Aug. 1924; *s* of late Prebendary G. L. Bourdillon; *m* 1961, Penelope, *d* of late P. W. Kemp-Welch, OBE; one *s* three *d*. *Educ:* Haileybury. Served RNVR, 1943–46. Forestry Comr, 1973–76. Mem. Brecon County Council, 1962–73; DL 1962, JP 1970, High Sheriff 1970, Brecon; Vice Lord-Lieutenant, Powys, 1978–86. *Address:* Llwyn Madoc, Beulah, Llanwrtyd Wells, Powys LD5 4TU.

BOURDON, Derek Conway, FIA; Director, 1981–84, and General Manager, 1979–84, Prudential Assurance Co. Ltd; Director, London and Manchester Group PLC, since 1986; *b* 3 Nov. 1932; *s* of Walter Alphonse Bourdon and late Winifred Gladys Vera Bourdon; *m* 1st, Camilla Rose Bourdon (marr. diss.); one *s* one *d*; 2nd, Jean Elizabeth Bourdon. *Educ:* Bancroft's School. FIA 1957. RAF Operations Research (Pilot Officer), 1956–58. Joined Prudential, 1950; South Africa, 1962–65; Dep. General Manager, 1976–79. Chairman, Vanbrugh Life, 1974–79. Member, Policyholders Protection Board, 1980–84; Chm., Industrial Life Offices Assoc., 1982–84 (Vice-Chm., 1980–82). *Recreations:* golf, bowls. *Club:* Crowborough Beacon Golf.

BOURKE, family name of **Earl of Mayo.**

BOURKE, Christopher John; Metropolitan Stipendiary Magistrate, since 1974; *b* 31 March 1926; *e s* of late John Francis Bourke of the Oxford Circuit and late Eileen Winifred Bourke (*née* Beddoes); *m* 1956, Maureen, *y d* of late G A. Barron-Boshell; two *s* one *d*. *Educ:* Stonyhurst; Oriel Coll., Oxford. Served Army, 1944–48: commnd Glos Regt; served BAOR and Jamaica (ADC to Governor). Called to Bar, Gray's Inn, 1953; Oxford Circuit, 1954–55; Dir of Public Prosecutions Dept, 1955–74. *Recreations:* history of art, water colour painting, music. *Address:* 61 Kingsmead Road, SW2 3HY. *T:* 081–671 3977.

BOURKE, Ven. Michael; Archdeacon of Bedford, since 1986; *b* 28 Nov. 1941; *s* of Gordon and Hilda Bourke; *m* 1968, Elizabeth Bieler; one *s* one *d*. *Educ:* Hamond's Grammar Sch., Swaffham, Norfolk; Corpus Christi Coll., Cambridge (Mod. Langs, MA); Univ. of Tübingen (Theology); Cuddesdon Theological Coll. Curate, St James', Grimsby, 1967–71; Priest-in-charge, Panshanger Conventional Dist (Local Ecumenical Project), Welwyn Garden City, 1971–78; Vicar, All Saints', Southill, Beds, 1978–86; Course Dir, St Albans Diocese Ministerial Trng Scheme, 1975–87. *Recreations:* astronomy, railways, European history. *Address:* 84 Bury Road, Shillington, Hitchin, Herts SG5 3NZ. *T:* Hitchin (0462) 711958.

BOURN, James; HM Diplomatic Service, retired; *b* 30 Aug. 1917; *s* of James and Sarah Gertrude Bourn; *m* 1st, 1944, Isobel Mackenzie (*d* 1977); one *s*; 2nd, 1981, Moya Livesey. *Educ:* Queen Elizabeth's Grammar Sch., Darlington; Univ. of Edinburgh (MA Hons 1979). Executive Officer, Ministry of Health, 1936. War of 1939–45; served (Royal Signals), in India, North Africa and Italy; POW; Captain. Higher Exec. Officer, Ministry of National Insurance, 1947; Asst Principal, Colonial Office, 1947; Principal, 1949; Secretary to the Salaries Commission, Bahamas, 1948–49; Private Sec. to Perm. Under-Sec., 1949; seconded to Tanganyika, 1953–55; UK Liaison Officer to Commn for Technical Co-operation in Africa (CCTA), 1955–57; Commonwealth Relations Office, 1961; seconded to Central African Office, 1962; Dar es Salaam, 1963; Deputy High Commissioner in Zanzibar, Tanzania, 1964–65; Counsellor and Dep. High Comr, Malawi, 1966–70; Ambassador to Somalia, 1970–73; Consul-General, Istanbul, 1973–75. *Address:* c/o National Westminster Bank, 20 Market Place, Richmond, North Yorks DL10 4QF. *Club:* Commonwealth Trust.

BOURN, Sir John Bryant, KCB 1991 (CB 1986); Comptroller and Auditor General, since 1988; *b* 21 Feb. 1934; *s* of Henry Thomas Bryant Bourn and late Beatrice Grace Bourn; *m* 1959, Ardita Ann Fleming; one *s* one *d*. *Educ:* Southgate County Grammar Sch.; LSE. 1st cl. hons BScEcon 1954, PhD 1958. Air Min. 1956–63; HM Treasury, 1963–64; Private Sec. to Perm. Under-Sec., MoD, 1964–69; Asst Sec. and Dir of Programmes, Civil Service Coll., 1969–72; Asst Sec., MoD, 1972–74; Under-Sec., Northern Ireland Office, 1974–77; Asst Under-Sec. of State, MoD, 1977–82; Dep. Sec., Northern Ireland Office, 1982–84; Dep. Under Sec. of State (Defence Procurement), MoD, 1985–88. Vis. Prof., LSE, 1983–. *Publications:* articles and reviews in professional jls. *Recreations:* swimming, squash rackets. *Address:* National Audit Office, 159–197 Buckingham Palace Road, Victoria, SW1W 9SP.

BOURNE, Prof. Frederick John; Director, Agricultural and Food Research Council Institute for Animal Health, and Professor of Animal Health, University of Bristol, since 1988; *b* 3 Jan. 1937; *s* of Sidney John Bourne and Florence Beatrice Bourne; *m* 1959, Mary Angela Minter; two *s*. *Educ:* Univ. of London (BVetMed); Univ. of Bristol (PhD). MRCVS 1961. Gen. vet. practice, 1961–67; University of Bristol: Lectr in Animal Husbandry, 1967–76; Reader in Animal Husbandry, 1976–80; Prof. and Hd of Dept of Verterinary Medicine, 1980–88. Vis. Prof., Univ. of Reading, 1990–. *Publications:* over 100 contribs to variety of jls, incl. Immunology, Vet. Immunology and Immunopath., Res. in Vet. Sci., Infection and Immunity. *Recreations:* gardening, fishing, golf, cricket, music. *Address:* AFRC Institute for Animal Health, Compton, near Newbury, Berks RG16 0NN. *T:* Newbury (0635) 578411.

BOURNE, Gordon Lionel, FRCS, FRCOG; Hon. Consultant, Department of Obstetrics and Gynæcology, St Bartholomew's Hospital, London; Consultant Gynæcologist to Royal Masonic Hospital since 1973; *b* 3 June 1921; *s* of Thomas Holland Bourne and Lily Anne (*née* Clewlow); *m* 1948, Barbara Eileen Anderson; three *s* one *d*. *Educ:* Queen Elizabeth Grammar Sch., Ashbourne; St Bartholomew's Hosp.; Harvard Univ. MRCS, LRCP

1945, FRCS 1954; MRCOG 1956, FRCOG 1962; FRSocMed. Highlands Hosp., 1948; Derbs Royal Infirm., 1949; City of London Mat. Hosp., 1952; Hosp. for Women, Soho, 1954; Gynæcol Registrar, Middlesex Hosp., 1956; Sen. Registrar, Obsts and Gynae., St Bartholomew's Hosp., 1958; Nuffield Trav. Fellow, 1959; Res. Fellow, Harvard, 1959; Cons. Gynæcol., St Luke's Hosp., 1963. Arris and Gale Lectr, RCS, 1964; Mem. Bd of Professions Suppl. to Medicine, 1964; Regional Assessor in Maternal Deaths, 1974; Examr in Obsts and Gynae., Univs of London, Oxford and Riyadh, Jt Conjt Bd and RCOG, Central Midwives Bd; Mem. Ct of Assts, Haberdashers' Co., 1968, Master, 1984; Mem. Bd of Governors, 1971–83, Chm., 1980–83, Haberdashers' Aske's Schs, Hatcham; Mem., 1983–, Chm., 1987–, Bd of Governors, Haberdashers' Aske's Schs, Elstree. *Publications:* The Human Amnion and Chorion, 1962; Shaw's Textbook of Gynæcology, 9th edn, 1970; Recent Advances in Obstetrics and Gynæcology, 11th edn, 1966—13th edn, 1979; Modern Gynæcology with Obstetrics for Nurses, 4th edn, 1969 and 5th edn, 1973; Pregnancy, 1972, 5th edn 1989; numerous articles in sci. and professional jls. *Recreations:* ski-ing, water-ski-ing, shooting, swimming, writing, golf. *Address:* 147 Harley Street, W1N 1DL. *T:* 071–935 4444; Oldways, Bishop's Avenue, N2 0BN. *T:* 081–458 4788. *Club:* Carlton.

BOURNE, James Gerald, MA, MD (Cantab), FFARCS, FDSRCS; Consulting Anæsthetist: St Thomas' Hospital, London; Salisbury Hospital Group; *b* 6 March 1906; *y s* of late W. W. Bourne, Garston Manor, Herts and of late Clara (*née* Hollingsworth); *m* 1957, Jenny Liddell (*d* 1967); one *s*; *m* 1968, Susan Clarke; two *s*. *Educ:* Rugby; Corpus Christi Coll., Cambridge; St Thomas' Hospital. 1st class Geographical Tripos Part I, 1925; 1st class Geographical Tripos Part II, 1926; Exhibition and Prizes; MRCS, LRCP 1937; MB, BChir Cantab 1939; DA England 1945; FFARCS 1953; MD (Cantab), 1960; FDSRCS 1986. Major RAMC, 1939–45. *Publications:* Nitrous Oxide in Dentistry: Its Danger and Alternatives, 1960; Studies in Anæsthetics, 1967; contributions to medical literature. *Recreations:* fishing, walking, music. *Address:* Melstock, Nunton, Salisbury, Wilts SP5 4HN. *T:* Salisbury (0722) 329734.

BOURNE, Sir (John) Wilfrid, KCB 1979 (CB 1975); QC 1981; Clerk of the Crown in Chancery, and Permanent Secretary, Lord Chancellor's Office, 1977–82; Barrister-at-Law; *b* 27 Jan. 1922; *s* of late Captain Rt Hon. R. C. Bourne, MP, and Lady Hester Bourne; *m* 1958, Elizabeth Juliet, *d* of late G. R. Fox, of Trewardreva, Constantine, Cornwall; two *s*. *Educ:* Eton; New Coll., Oxford (MA). Served War, Rifle Brigade, 1941–45. Called to Bar, Middle Temple, 1948, Bencher 1977; practised at Bar, 1949–56; Lord Chancellor's Office, 1956–82, Principal Assistant Solicitor, 1970–72, Deputy Sec., 1972–77. *Recreation:* gardening. *Address:* Povey's Farm, Ramsdell, Basingstoke, Hants. *Club:* Leander (Henley-on-Thames).

BOURNE, Prof. Kenneth, FRHistS; FBA 1984; Professor of International History, London School of Economics and Political Science, University of London, since 1976 (Vice-Chairman, Academic Board, 1985–88); *b* 17 March 1930; *s* of Clarence Arthur Bourne and Doris (*née* English); *m* 1955, Eleanor Anne (*née* Wells); one *s* one *d*. *Educ:* Southend High Sch.; University College of South West; LSE. BA Exeter and London; PhD London. Research Fellow: Inst. of Hist. Research, Univ. of London, 1955–56; Reading Univ., 1956; Asst Lectr, then Lectr, LSE, 1957–69; Reader in Internat. History, Univ. of London, 1969–76; Chm., Bd of Studies in History, London Univ., 1983–84. Fulbright Fellow and Sen. Research Fellow, British Assoc. for American Studies, 1961–62; Vis. Lectr, Univ. of California, Davis, 1966–67; Scaife Distinguished Vis. Lectr, Kenyon Coll., 1971; Kratter Prof., Stanford Univ., 1979; Vis. Prof., Univ. of S Mississippi, 1981; Griffin Lectr, Stanford Univ., 1983; Vis. Prof., Univ. of S Alabama, 1983; Albert Biever Meml Lectr, Loyola Univ., 1983; James Pinckney Harrison Prof., Coll. of William and Mary, 1984–85; Distinguished Vis. Prof. in Humanities, Univ. of Colorado, 1988; J. Richardson Dilworth Fellow, Inst. for Advanced Study, Princeton, 1989; Nuffield Foundn Social Scis Res. Fellow, 1991. Member: Council, List and Index Soc., 1986–; British Nat. Cttee, Internat. Congress of Hist. Scis, 1987–88; Archives and Manuscripts Cttee, Univ. of Southampton, 1988–. Member: Senate, Univ. of London, 1987–91; Council, SSEES, 1987–. Governor: Wilson's Grammar Sch., Camberwell, 1964–74; Wilson's Sch., Sutton, 1972–84; LSE, 1986–90. *Publications:* Britain and the Balance of Power in North America, 1967 (Albert B. Corey Prize); (with D. C. Watt) Studies in International History, 1967; The Foreign Policy of Victorian England, 1970; The Blackmailing of the Chancellor, 1975; Letters of Viscount Palmerston, 1979; Palmerston: the early years, 1982; (ed, with D. C. Watt) British Documents on Foreign Affairs, 1983–. *Recreation:* book-collecting. *Address:* 15 Oakcroft Road, SE13 7ED. *T:* 081–852 6116.

BOURNE, Margaret Janet, OBE 1982; Assistant Chief Scientific Adviser (Capabilities), Ministry of Defence, since 1987; *b* 18 Aug. 1931; *d* of Thomas William Southcott and Nora Annie Southcott (*née* Pelling); *m* 1960, George Brian Bourne. *Educ:* Twickenham Grammar Sch.; Royal Holloway Coll. (BSc). MRAeS. Fairey Engineering, 1953–62; Army Operational Res. Estabt, 1962–65; Defence Operational Analysis Estabt, 1965–76; Asst Dir, Scientific Adv. Gp Army, 1976–80; Hd of Assessments Div., ASWE, 1980–82; Hd of Weapon Dept, ASWE, 1982–84; Dep. Dir, Admiralty Res. Estabt, 1984–87. *Recreations:* playing early music, gardening, natural history. *Address:* c/o Ministry of Defence, SW1A 2HB.

BOURNE, (Rowland) Richard; Director, Commonwealth Human Rights Initiative, since 1990; Deputy Director, The Commonwealth Institute, 1983–89; *s* of late Arthur Brittan and Edith Mary Bourne; *m* 1966, Juliet Mary, *d* of John Attenborough, CBE; two *s* one *d*. *Educ:* Uppingham Sch., Rutland; Brasenose Coll., Oxford (BA Mod. Hist.). Journalist, The Guardian, 1962–72 (Education correspondent, 1968–72); Asst Editor, New Society, 1972–77; Evening Standard: Dep. Editor, 1977–78; London Columnist, 1978–79; Founder Editor, Learn Magazine, 1979. Consultant: Internat. Broadcasting Trust, 1980–81; Adv. Council for Adult and Continuing Educn, 1982. Chm., Survival Internat. 1983–. Treas., Anglo-Portuguese Foundn, 1985–87. *Publications:* Political Leaders of Latin America, 1969; (with Brian MacArthur) The Struggle for Education, 1970; Getulio Vargas of Brazil, 1974; Assault on the Amazon, 1978; Londoners, 1981; (with Jessica Gould) Self-Sufficiency, 16–25, 1983; Lords of Fleet Street, 1990. *Recreations:* theatre, fishing, supporting Charlton Athletic. *Address:* 36 Burney Street, SE10 8EX. *T:* 081–853 0642. *Club:* Royal Automobile.

BOURNE, Sir Wilfrid; *see* Bourne, Sir J. W.

BOURNE-ARTON, Major Anthony Temple, MBE 1944; *b* 1 March 1913; 2nd *s* of W. R. Temple Bourne, Walker Hall, Winston, Co. Durham, and Evelyn Rose, 3rd *d* of Sir Frank Wills, Bristol; assumed surname of Bourne-Arton, 1950; *m* 1938, Margaret Elaine, *er d* of W. Denby Arton, Sleningford Park, Ripon, Yorks; two *s* two *d*. *Educ:* Clifton. Served Royal Artillery, 1933–48; active service, 1936, Palestine; 1939–45: France, N Africa, Sicily and Italy (despatches, MBE); Malaya, 1947–48. Gen. Commissioner Income Tax, 1952–80; has served on Bedale RDC, and N Riding County Agric. Cttee; County Councillor, N Riding of Yorks, 1949–61; CC, W Riding of Yorks, 1967–70; Chm., Yorkshire Regional Land Drainage Cttee, 1973–80. MP (C) Darlington, 1959–64; PPS to the Home Sec., 1962–64. JP N Riding of Yorks, 1950–80. *Recreations:* fishing and shooting. *Address:* The Old Rectory, West Tanfield, Ripon, N Yorks HG4 5JH. *T:* Bedale (0677) 70333.

BOURNS, Prof. Arthur Newcombe, OC 1982; FRSC 1964; President and Vice-Chancellor, 1972–80, Professor of Chemistry 1953–81, now Emeritus, McMaster University; *b* 8 Dec. 1919; *s* of Evans Clement Bourns and Kathleen Jones; *m* 1943, Marion Harriet Blakney; two *s* two *d*. *Educ:* schs in Petitcodiac, NB; Acadia Univ. (BSc); McGill Univ. (PhD). Research Chemist, Dominion Rubber Co., 1944–45; Lectr, Acadia Univ., 1945–46; Asst Prof. of Chemistry, Saskatchewan Univ., 1946–47; McMaster Univ.: Asst Prof., 1947–49; Associate Prof., 1949–53; Dean, Faculty of Grad. Studies, 1957–61; Chm., Chemistry Dept, 1965–67; Vice-Pres., Science and Engrg Div., 1967–72; Actg Pres., 1970. Nuffield Trav. Fellow in Science, University Coll., London, 1955–56. Chm., Gordon Res. Conf. on Chem. and Physics of Isotopes (Vice-Chm. 1959–60; Chm., 1961–62); Nat. Res. Council of Canada: Mem. Grant Selection Cttee in Chem., 1966–69 (Chm. 1968–69); Mem. Council, 1969–75; Mem. Exec. Cttee, 1969–75; Mem. or Chm. various other cttees; Natural Scis and Engrg Res. Council: Member: Council, 1978–85; Exec. Cttee, 1978–; Allocations Cttee, 1978–86; Cttee on Strategic Grants, 1978–83; Chm., Grants and Scholarships Cttee, 1978–83; Mem., Adv. Cttee on University/Industry Interface, 1979–83; Vis. Res. Officer, 1983–84. Member: Ancaster Public Sch. Bd, 1963–64; Bd, Royal Botanic Gdns, 1972–80 (Vice-Chm.); Cttee on Univ. Affairs, Prov. Ontario; Canadian Cttee for Financing Univ. Res., 1978–80; Council of Ontario Univs, 1972–80; Bd of Dirs and Exec. Cttee, Assoc. of Univs and Colleges of Canada, 1974–77; Mohawk Coll. Bd of Dirs, 1975–82; Council, Canadian Inst. for Advanced Research, 1983–89; Chm., Internat. Adv. Cttee, Chinese Univ. Develt Project, 1985–; Pres. and Chm. Exec. Cttee, Canadian Bureau for Internat. Educn, 1973–76. McMaster Univ. Med. Centre: Member: Bd of Trustees, 1972–80; Exec. Cttee, 1972–80. Director: Nuclear Activation Services, 1978–80; Slater Steel Industries Ltd, 1975–79. British Council Lectr, 1963. Assoc. Editor, Canadian Jl Chemistry, 1966–69; Mem. Editorial Bd, Science Forum, 1967–73. FCIC 1954 (Chm. Hamilton Section, 1952–53; Mem. Educn Cttee, 1953–59; Mem. Council, 1966–69; Montreal Medal, 1976). Hon. Prof., Jiangxi Univ., China, 1989. Hon. DSc: Acadia, 1968; McGill, 1977; New Brunswick, McMaster, 1981; Hon. LLD Brock, 1980. *Address:* Unit 10, 2407 Woodward Avenue, Burlington, Ont L7R 1V2, Canada.

BOURTON, Cyril Leonard, CB 1977; Deputy Secretary (Finance), and Accountant General, Department of Health and Social Security, 1974–76; *b* 28 Dec. 1916; *s* of late Leonard Victor Bourton; *m* 1940, Elizabeth Iris Savage; two *s* one *d*. *Educ:* St Dunstan's Coll., Catford. Nat. Debt Office, 1933–37; Min. of Health, later DHSS: Dep. Accountant-Gen., 1958; Asst Sec., Exec. Councils Div., 1964; Under-Sec. for Finance and Accountant Gen., 1967. *Recreations:* fishing, photography, genealogy. *Address:* 19 Mytten Close, Cuckfield, Haywards Heath, West Sussex RH17 5LN. *T:* Haywards Heath (0444) 456030.

BOUVERIE; *see* Pleydell-Bouverie, family name of Earl of Radnor.

BOVELL, Hon. Sir (William) Stewart, Kt 1976; JP; Agent-General for Western Australia, in London, 1971–74; *b* 19 Dec. 1906; *s* of A. R. Bovell and Ethel (*née* Williams), Busselton, Western Australia. *Educ:* Busselton, WA. Banking, 1923–40. Served War, RAAF, 1941–45, Flt Lt. MLA: for Sussex, WA, 1947–50; for Vasse, WA, 1950–71. Minister: for Labour, WA, 1961–62; for Lands, Forests and Immigration, WA, 1959–71. Govt Whip, WA, 1950–53; Opposition Whip, WA, 1953–57. Rep., Australian States Gen. Council, at British Commonwealth Parly Assoc., in Nairobi, Kenya, and Victoria Falls, S Rhodesia, 1954. Mem. Bd of Governors, Bunbury CofE Cathedral Grammar Sch., 1974 (Vice-Chm.). Hon. Lay Canon, St Boniface CofE Cathedral, Bunbury, WA, 1975. JP 1949, WA. Patron: Polocrosse Assoc. of WA; Geographe Bay Yacht Club. *Recreations:* swimming, tennis, walking. *Address:* 24 West Street, Busselton, WA 6280, Australia.

BOVENIZER, Vernon Gordon Fitzell, CMG 1948; Assistant Under-Secretary of State, Ministry of Defence, 1964–68, retired; *b* 22 July 1908; *s* of Rev. Michael Fitzell Bovenizer and Mary Gordon; *m* 1937, Lillian Cherry (*d* 1970), *d* of John Henry Rowe, Cork; two *s* two *d*. *Educ:* Liverpool Coll.; Sidney Sussex Coll., Cambridge (Scholar). War Office, 1931–45; Control Commission for Germany, 1945, until return to War Office, 1948; Asst Private Sec. to Secretaries of State for War, 1936, and 1940–42; Resident Clerk, 1934–37; Asst Sec., 1942, civilian liaison with US Armies in the UK; Establishment Officer and Dir of Organisation, CCG, 1945–47; Asst Sec. and Dep. Comptroller of Claims, War Office, 1948–58; Counsellor, UK Delegation to NATO, 1958–60; Asst Under-Sec. of State, War Office, 1960–68. US Medal of Freedom, 1945. *Recreations:* tennis and squash. *Address:* 6 Cambanks, Union Lane, Cambridge; 9 The Square, Annalong, Co. Down. *Club:* Reform.

BOVET, Prof. Daniel; Hon. Professor, University of Rome, Italy; *b* Neuchatel, Switzerland, 23 March 1907; *s* of Pierre Bovet and Amy Babut; *m* Filomena Nitti; three *s*. Institut Pasteur, Paris, 1929–47 (first as an asst and afterwards Chief of the Laboratory of Therapeutic Chemistry); Chief of the Laboratory of Therapeutic Chemistry, Istituto Superiore di Sanità, Rome, 1947–64; Prof. of Pharmacology, Fac. of Medicine, Univ. of Sassari, Italy, 1964–71; Prof. of Psychobiol., Faculty of Sci., Rome Univ., 1971–77. Mem. of the Accademia Nazionale dei XL, 1949; Mem. of Accademia naz. dei Lincei, 1958; Foreign Mem., Royal Soc., 1962. Nobel Prize for Physiology or Medicine, 1957. Grande Ufficiale dell' Ordine della Repubblica Italiana, 1959; Comdr, Légion d'Honneur, 1980. *Publications:* (in collaboration with F. Bovet-Nitti) Structure chimique et activité pharmacodynamique du système nerveux végétatif, 1948 (Bale, Switzerland); (in collaboration with F. Bovet-Nitti and G. B. Marini-Bettolo) Curare and Curare-like Agents, 1957 (Amsterdam, Holland); (in collaboration with R. Blum and others) Controlling Drugs, 1974 (San Francisco); Une chimie qui guérit—histoire des sulfamides, 1989 (Paris). *Recreation:* wandering in Amazonia. *Address:* 33 Piazza S Apollinare, 00186 Rome, Italy. *T:* 6865297.

BOVEY, Dr Leonard; Editor, Materials & Design, since 1985; Head of Technological Requirements Branch, Department of Industry, 1977–84; *b* 9 May 1924; *s* of late Alfred and Gladys Bovey; *m* 1943, Constance Hudson (*d* 1987); one *s* one *d*. *Educ:* Heles Sch., Exeter; Emmanuel Coll., Cambridge (BA, PhD). FInstP; CPhys. Dunlop Rubber, 1943–46; Post-doctoral Fellow, Nat. Res. Council, Ottawa, 1950–52; AERE Harwell, 1952–65; Head W Mids Regional Office, Birmingham, Min. of Technology, 1966–70; Regional Dir, Yorks and Humberside, DTI, 1970–73; Counsellor (Scientific and Technological Affairs), High Commn, Ottawa, 1974–77. Foreign correspondent, Soc. for Advancement of Materials and Processes Engineering (USA) Jl, 1987–. *Publications:* Spectroscopy in the Metallurgical Industry, 1963; papers on spectroscopy in Jl Optical Soc. Amer., Spectrochimica Acta, Jl Phys. Soc. London. *Recreations:* repairing neglected household equipment, work, reading (particularly crime novels), walking, theatre, music. *Address:* 32 Radnor Walk, Chelsea SW3 4BN. *T:* 071–352 4142. *Club:* Civil Service.

BOVEY, Philip Henry; Under Secretary, Department of Trade and Industry, since 1985; *b* 11 July 1948; *s* of Norman Henry Bovey and Dorothy Yvonne Kent Bovey; *m* 1974, Jenet Alison, *d* of late Rev. Canon J. M. McTear and Margaret McTear; one *s* one *d*. Educ:

Rugby; Peterhouse, Cambridge (schol.; MA). Solicitor. 3rd Sec., FCO, 1970–71; with Slaughter and May, 1972–75; Legal Assistant, 1976; Sen. Legal Assistant, 1976; Depts of Trade and Industry, 1976–77; Cabinet Office, 1977–78; Depts of Trade, Industry, Prices and Consumer Protection, then DTI, 1978–85; Asst Solicitor, 1982. Companies Act Inspector, 1984–88 (report published 1988). *Recreation:* photography. *Address:* 102 Cleveland Gardens, Barnes, SW13 0AH. *T:* 081–876 3710.

BOWATER, Sir Euan David Vansittart, 3rd Bt *cr* 1939, of Friston, Suffolk; *b* 9 Sept. 1935; *s* of Sir Noël Vansittart Bowater, 2nd Bt, GBE, MC, and of Constance Heiton, *d* of David Gordon Bett; *S* father, 1984; *m* 1964, Susan Mary Humphrey, *d* of late A. R. O. Slater, FCA; two *s* two *d. Educ:* Eton; Trinity Coll., Cambridge (BA). *Recreations:* travel, golf. *Heir: s* Moray David Vansittart Bowater, *b* 24 April 1967.

BOWATER, Sir J(ohn) Vansittart, 4th Bt *cr* 1914; *b* 6 April 1918; *s* of Captain Victor Spencer Bowater (*d* 1967) (3rd *s* of 1st Bt) and Hilda Mary (*d* 1918), *d* of W. Henry Potter; *S* uncle, Sir Thomas Dudley Blennerhassett Bowater, 3rd Bt, 1972; *m* 1943, Joan Kathleen, (*d* 1982), *d* of late Wilfrid Scullard; one *s* one *d. Educ:* Branksome School, Godalming, Surrey. Served Royal Artillery, 1939–46. *Heir: s* Michael Patrick Bowater [*b* 18 July 1949; *m* 1968, Alison, *d* of Edward Wall; four *d*]. *Address:* 214 Runnymede Avenue, Bournemouth, Dorset BH11 9SP. *T:* Bournemouth (0202) 571782.

BOWDEN, family name of **Baron Aylestone.**

BOWDEN, Andrew, MBE 1961; MP (C) Kemptown Division of Brighton since 1970; *b* 8 April 1930; *s* of William Victor Bowden, Solicitor, and Francesca Wilson; *m* Benita Napier; one *s* one *d. Educ:* Ardingly College. Paint industry, 1955–68; Man. Dir, Personnel Assessments Ltd, 1969–71; Man. Dir, Haymarket Personnel Selection Ltd, 1970–71; Director: Sales Education & Leadership Ltd, 1970–71; Jenkin and Purser (Holdings) Ltd, 1973–77. Mem., Wandsworth Borough Council, 1956–62. Contested (C): N Hammersmith, 1955; N Kensington, 1964; Kemp Town, Brighton, 1966. Jt Chm., All Party Old Age Pensioners Parly Gp, 1972–; Chm., All Party BLESMA Gp; Mem. Select Cttee on Expenditure, 1973–74, on Abortion, 1975, on Employment, 1979–. Mem., Council of Europe, 1987–. Nat. Chm., Young Conservatives, 1960–61. Internat. Chm., People to People, 1981–. Nat. Pres., Captive Animals Protection Soc., 1978–. Mem. School Council, Ardingly Coll., 1982–. *Recreations:* fishing, chess, golf. *Address:* House of Commons, SW1. *T:* 071–219 5047. *Club:* Carlton.

BOWDEN, Sir Frank Houston, 3rd Bt *cr* 1915; MA Oxon; retired industrialist and landowner; *b* 10 Aug. 1909; *o s* of Sir Harold Bowden, 2nd Bt, GBE, and of Vera, *d* of Joseph Whitaker, JP, FZS; *S* father 1960; *m* 1st, 1934, Marie-José, *d* of Charles Stiénon and Comtesse Laure de Messey; one *s*; 2nd, 1937, Lydia Eveline (*d* 1981), *d* of Jean Manolovici, Bucharest; three *s*; 3rd, 1989, Oriol Annette Mary, *d* of Charles Hooper Bath. *Educ:* Rugby; Merton Coll., Oxford. Served with RNVR, 1939–44. President: University Hall, Buckland, 1967–71; British Kendo Association, 1969. Hon. Vice-Pres., 3rd World Kendo Championships, 1976. *Recreation:* collecting weapons and armour, particularly Japanese (Vice-Chm. Japan Soc. of London, 1970–75, 1979–82, 1984–87, Vice-Pres., 1987–). *Heir: s* Nicholas Richard Bowden, *b* 13 Aug. 1935. *Address:* The Old Vicarage, Winkfield, Windsor, Berks SL4 4SE. *Clubs:* White's, Hurlingham, Royal Thames Yacht.

BOWDEN, Gerald Francis, TD 1971; MP (C) Dulwich, since 1983; barrister and chartered surveyor; *b* 26 Aug. 1935; *s* of Frank Albert Bowden and Elsie Bowden (*née* Burrill); *m* 1967, Heather Elizabeth Hill (*née* Hall) (*d* 1984); two *d*, and one step *s* one step *d. Educ:* Battersea Grammar School; Magdalen College, Oxford. MA; FRICS 1984 (ARICS 1971). Called to the Bar, Gray's Inn, 1963. Worked in advertising industry, 1964–68; property marketing and investment, 1968–72; Principal Lecturer in Law, Dept of Estate Management, Polytechnic of the South Bank, 1972–. Mem. GLC for Dulwich, 1977–81; a co-opted Mem., ILEA, 1981–84. PPS to Minister for Arts, 1990–. Mem., Select Cttee on Educn, Sci. and Arts, 1990–. Vice-Chairman: Cons. Backbench Educn Cttee, 1987–89; Cons. Backbench Arts and Heritage Cttee, 1987–. Pres., Greater London Conservative Trade Unionists, 1985–88. Pres., Southwark Chamber of Commerce, 1986–. After Nat. Service, continued to serve in TA until 1984 (Lt-Col). *Publications:* An Introduction to the Law of Contract and Tort (with Alan S. Morris), 1977; The Housing Act, 1988. *Recreations:* gardening, renovating old houses, books, pictures. *Address:* House of Commons, SW1A 0AA. *T:* 071–219 6374. *Clubs:* United Oxford & Cambridge University, Chelsea Arts.

BOWDEN, Logan S.; *see* Scott Bowden.

BOWDEN, Prof. Ruth Elizabeth Mary, OBE 1980; DSc London, MB, BS, FRCS; Professor of Anatomy: Royal Free Hospital School of Medicine, University of London, 1951–80, now Emeritus; Royal College of Surgeons of England, 1984–89; Hon. Research Fellow, Institute of Neurology, since 1980; *b* 21 Feb. 1915; *o c* of late Frank Harold and Louise Ellen Bowden. *Educ:* Westlands Sch.; St Paul's Girls' Sch.; London (Royal Free Hospital) Sch. of Medicine for Women, University of London. House Surg. and later House Physician, Elizabeth Garrett Anderson Hosp. (Oster House branch), 1940–42; House Surg., Royal Cancer Hosp., 1942; Grad. Asst in Nuffield Dept of Orthopædic Surgery, Peripheral Nerve Injury Unit, Oxford, 1942–45; Asst Lecturer in Anatomy, Royal Free Hospital Sch. of Medicine, 1945; later Lecturer, then University Reader in Human Anatomy, 1949; Rockefeller Travelling Fellowship, 1949–50; Hunterian Prof., RCS, 1950; part-time Lectr, Dept of Anatomy, St Thomas's Hosp. Med. Sch., 1980–83. WHO Consultant in anatomy, Khartoum Univ., 1972, 1974, 1977. President: Anat. Soc. of Gt Brit. and Ireland, 1970; Medical Women's Fedn, 1981. Member: Exec. Cttee, Women's Nat. Commn, 1984–89; Council and Exec. Cttee, N London Hospice Gp, 1986– (Chm., Professional Sub-Cttee, 1986–). FRSM; Fellow: Brit. Orthopædic Assoc.; Linnean Soc. Vice-President: Chartered Soc. of Physiotherapy (Chm., 1960–70); Inst. of Science Technology (Pres., 1960–65); Riding for the Disabled Assoc. DCLJ 1988, DMLJ 1984. Jubilee Medal, 1977; Wood Jones Medal, RCS, 1988. *Publications:* Peripheral Nerve Injuries, 1958; contribs to Peripheral Nerve Injuries Report of Medical Research Council; contrib. to Oxford Companion to Medicine; contribs to medical and scientific jls. *Recreations:* reading, music, painting, walking, gardening, carpentry. *Address:* 6 Hartham Close, Hartham Road, N7 9JH. *T:* 071–607 3464.

BOWE, David Robert; Member (Lab) Cleveland and Yorkshire North, European Parliament, since 1989; *b* Gateshead, 19 July 1953; *m*; one *s. Educ:* Sunderland Polytechnic; Bath Univ. BSc; PGCE. Former science teacher. Mem., Middlesbrough Borough Council, 1983– (Chm., Monitoring and Review Cttee). N Regl Sec., Socialist Educnl Assoc. Mem., NUPE. *Address:* 14 Thornfield Grove, Middlesbrough, Cleveland TS1 4RH.

BOWEN, Maj.-Gen. Bryan Morris, CB 1988; Paymaster-in-Chief and Inspector of Army Pay Services, 1986–89, retired; *b* 8 March 1932; *s* of Frederick Bowen and Gwendoline Bowen (*née* Morris); *m* 1955, Suzanne Rowena (*née* Howell); two *d. Educ:* Newport High Sch.; Exeter Univ. FCCA, FCMA; ndc, psc†, sq, pfc. Joined RE, 1953, served UK and BAOR; transf. RAPC, 1958; Paymaster 1/6 QEO Gurkha Rifles, Malaya and UK, 1960–63; Army Cost and Management Accounting Services, 1963–68; DAAG, MoD, 1968–70; Exchange Officer, US Army, Washington, DC, 1970–72; Nat. Defence Coll., 1972–73; DS, RMCS Shrivenham, 1973–76; AAG, MOD, 1976–79; Col (Principal), MoD F4(AD), 1979–81; Chief Paymaster, Army Pay Office (Officers Accounts), 1981–82; Dep. Paymaster-in-Chief, 1982–85. Col Comdt, RAPC, 1990–. Mem. Council, CIMA, 1990–; Chm., Oxfordshire Cttee, Army Benevolent Fund, 1990–; Special Comr, Duke of York's Royal Mil. Sch., Dover, 1990–; Dir, United Services Trustee, 1990–. Freeman, City of London, 1987. *Recreations:* golf, church affairs, gardening. *Address:* Yew Tree House, Claypits Lane, Shrivenham, Swindon, Wilts SN6 8AH. *Clubs:* Lansdowne; Frilford Heath Golf.

BOWEN, Prof. David Aubrey Llewellyn, FRCP, FRCPE, FRCPath; Professor of Forensic Medicine, University of London, 1977–89, now Emeritus; Head of Department of Forensic Medicine and Toxicology, Charing Cross Hospital Medical School, 1973–89 (Charing Cross and Westminster Medical School, 1985–89); Hon. Consultant Pathologist, Charing Cross Hospital, 1973–89; *b* 31 Jan. 1924; *s* of late Dr Thomas Rufus Bowen and Catherine (*née* Llewellyn); *m* 1st, 1950, Joan Rosemary Davis (*d* 1973); two *s* one *d*; 2nd, 1975, Helen Rosamund Landcastle. *Educ:* Caterham Sch.; Garw Secondary Sch., Pontycymmer; University College of Wales, Cardiff; Corpus Christi Coll., Cambridge (MA); Middlesex Hosp. Med. Sch. (MB BChir 1947); DipPath 1955; DMJ Soc. of Apoth. of London 1962. FRCPE 1971; FRCPath 1975; FRCP 1982. Ho. posts at W Middlesex Hosp. and London Chest Hosp., 1947 and 1950; RAMC, 1947–49; Jun. Resident Pathologist, Bristol Royal Inf., 1950–51; Registrar in Path., London Chest Hosp., 1951–52; Registrar and Sen. Registrar in Clin. Path., National Hosp. for Nervous Diseases, 1952–56; Asst Pathologist and Sen. Registrar, Royal Marsden Hosp., 1956–57; Demonstr 1957–63, Lectr 1963–66, in Forensic Medicine, St George's Hosp. Med. Sch.; Sen. Lectr 1966–73, Reader 1973–77, in Forensic Medicine, Vice-Dean 1974–78, Charing Cross Hosp. Med. Sch.; Lectr in Forensic Medicine, Oxford Univ., 1974–89. Chairman: Div. of Pathology, Charing Cross Hosp., 1976–78; Apptd and Recog. Teachers in Path., Charing Cross Hosp. Med. Sch., 1980–82; Examiner: Univ. of Riyadh, Saudi Arabia, 1978–81; on Forensic Med., RCPath, 1976–; for Diploma of Med. Jurisprudence, Soc. of Apothecaries of London, 1970–; for MD (Forensic Medicine) and Diploma in Legal Medicine, Univ. of Sri Lanka, 1985. Lectr, Metropolitan Police Trng Coll., Hendon, 1976–84; W. D. L. Fernando Oration to Medical Legal Soc. of Sri Lanka, 1985. Vice-President: Medico-Legal Soc., 1977–; Medical Defence Union, 1979–; President: British Assoc. in Forensic Med., 1977–79; W London Medico-Chirurgical Soc., 1987–88; Member: British Academy in Forensic Sci. and Forensic Sci. Soc., 1960– (Mem. Council, 1965–67); British Div. of Internat. Acad. of Path., 1974–; Acad. Internat. de Médicine Légale et de Méd. Sociale, 1976–; RCPath Adv. Cttee on Forensic Path., 1973–76 and 1980–82. Vice-Pres., Old Caterhamians Assoc., 1987–88. *Publications:* sci. papers in numerous med., forensic med. and path. jls. *Recreations:* hockey, jogging. *Address:* 19 Letchmore Road, Radlett, Herts WD7 8HU. *T:* Radlett (0923) 856936. *Club:* West Herts Hockey (Watford).

BOWEN, Edward Farquharson, TD 1976; Partner, Thorntons, WS, since 1990; *b* 1 May 1945; *s* of Stanley Bowen, *qv*; *m* 1975, Patricia Margaret Brown, *y d* of Rev. R. Russell Brown, Perth; two *s* two *d. Educ:* Melville Coll., Edinburgh; Edinburgh Univ. (LLB 1966). Enrolled as Solicitor in Scotland, 1968; admitted to Faculty of Advocates, 1970. Standing Jun. Counsel: to Scottish Educn Dept, 1977–79; to Home Office in Scotland, 1979; Advocate-Depute, 1979–83; Sheriff of Tayside Central and Fife, 1983–90. Served RAOC (TA and T&AVR), 1964–80. *Recreation:* golf. *Address:* Westgate, Glamis Drive, Dundee DD2 1QL. *Clubs:* New (Edinburgh); Hon. Company of Edinburgh Golfers; Panmure Golf.

BOWEN, Maj.-Gen. Esmond John, CB 1982; Director, Army Dental Service, 1978–82; *b* 6 Dec. 1922; *s* of Major Leslie Arthur George Bowen, MC, and Edna Grace Bowen; *m* 1948, Elsie (*née* Midgley); two *s* two *d* (and one *d* decd). *Educ:* Clayesmore Sch.; Univ. of Birmingham. LDS Birmingham 1946. Commd Lieut, RADC, 1947; Captain 1948; Major 1955; Lt-Col 1962; Chief Instructor, Depot and Training Establishment RADC, 1966–69; CO Nos 2 and 3 Dental Groups, 1969–74; Asst Dir, Army Dental Service, 1974–76; Comdt, HQ and Training Centre, RADC, 1976–77; Brig. 1977; Dep. Dir, Dental Service, HQ BAOR, 1977–78. QHDS, 1977–82. Col Comdt, RADC, 1982–87. OStJ 1975. *Recreations:* target rifle and muzzle loading shooting. *Address:* 72 Winchester Road, Andover, Hants. *T:* Andover (0264) 23252. *Club:* Lansdowne.

BOWEN, (Evan) Roderic, QC 1952; MA, LLD; Master Emeritus of the Middle Temple; *b* 6 Aug. 1913; 2nd *s* of late Evan Bowen, JP, and late Margaret Ellen Twiss, The Elms, Cardigan. *Educ:* Cardigan Schs; University Coll., Aberystwyth; St John's Coll., Cambridge. Practised at the bar with chambers in Cardiff until 1940; served in HM Forces, 1940–45, in the ranks and subsequently as an officer on staff of Judge Advocate-Gen. MP (L) County of Cardigan, 1945–66; Dep. Chm. of Ways and Means, House of Commons, 1965–66. Recorder of: Carmarthen, 1950; Merthyr Tydfil, 1953–60; Swansea, 1960–64; Cardiff, 1964–67; Chm., Montgomeryshire QS, 1959–71; Social Security (formerly Nat. Insurance) Comr, 1967–86. Chm. Welsh Parliamentary Party, 1955. Pres., St David's UC, Lampeter, 1977–. Hon. LLD Wales, 1972. *Address:* 3 Maynard Court, Fairwater Road, Llandaff, Cardiff. *T:* Cardiff (0222) 563207. *Club:* County (Cardiff).

BOWEN, Rear-Adm. Frank; defence industry consultant, since 1985; *b* 25 Jan. 1930; *s* of Alfred and Lily Bowen; *m* 1954, Elizabeth Lilian Richards; one *s* two *d. Educ:* Cowley Sch., St Helen's; Royal Naval Engineering Coll. CEng; MIMechE; FBIM. RNC Dartmouth, 1948; served various ships and RN establishments incl. HMS Eagle and Excellent, 1956–60, and Scylla, 1971–73; served in Washington, 1968–70 and 1976–78; i/c HMS Collingwood, 1981–82; Special Project Dir, MoD, PE; Captain 1974; Rear-Adm., 1982–84. Dir, Dowty-Cap Ltd, 1985–89. Chm. and Man. Dir, Naval Systems Exchange Ltd; Chm., SALS Ltd, 1990–. MInstD. *Recreations:* amateur stage, social golf. *Address:* c/o Midland Bank plc, 102 High Street, Lymington, Hants SO4 9ZP.

BOWEN, Sir Geoffrey Fraser, Kt 1977; Managing Director, Commercial Banking Company of Sydney Ltd, Australia, 1973–76, retired (General Manager, 1970–73); *m* 1st, Ruth (decd), *d* of H. E. Horsburgh; two *s* one *d*; 2nd, Isabel, *d* of H. T. Underwood. *Address:* Cavendish, 16/562 Pacific Highway, Killara, NSW 2071, Australia. *Clubs:* Union (Sydney); Warrawee Bowling; Killara Golf.

BOWEN, John Griffith; playwright and novelist; freelance drama producer for television; *b* 5 Nov. 1924; *s* of Hugh Griffith Bowen and Ethel May Cook; unmarried. *Educ:* Queen Elizabeth's Grammar Sch., Crediton; Pembroke Coll., Oxford; St Antony's Coll., Oxford. Frere Exhibition for Indian Studies, Oxford, 1951–52 and 1952–53. Asst Editor, The Sketch, 1954–57; Advertising Copywriter and Copy Chief, 1957–60; Consultant on TV Drama, Associated TV, 1960–67; productions for Thames TV, LWT, BBC. *Publications:* The Truth Will Not Help Us, 1956; After the Rain, 1958; The Centre of the Green, 1959; Storyboard, 1960; The Birdcage, 1962; A World Elsewhere, 1965; The Essay Prize, 1965; Squeak, 1983; The McGuffin, 1984 (filmed for TV, 1986); The Girls, 1986; Fighting Back, 1989; *plays:* I Love You, Mrs Patterson, 1964; After the Rain, 1967; Fall and Redemption, 1967; Little Boxes, 1968; The Disorderly Women, 1968; The Corsican

Brothers, 1970; The Waiting Room, 1970; Robin Redbreast, 1972; Heil Caesar, 1973; Florence Nightingale, 1975; Which Way Are You Facing?, 1976; Singles, 1977; Bondage, 1978; The Inconstant Couple (adaptation of Marivaux, L'Heureux Stratagème), 1978; Uncle Jeremy, 1981; The Geordie Gentleman (adaptation of Molière's Le Bourgeois Gentilhomme), 1987. *Address:* Old Lodge Farm, Sugarswell Lane, Edgehill, Banbury, Oxon OX15 6HP. *T:* Tysoe (029588) 401.

BOWEN, Very Rev. Lawrence; Dean of St Davids Cathedral, 1972–84; *b* 9 Sept. 1914; *s* of William and Elizabeth Ann Bowen; *m* 1941, Hilary Myrtle Bowen; two *d. Educ:* Llanelli Gram. Sch.; Univ. Coll. of Wales, Aberystwyth (BA 1st Cl.); St Michael's Coll., Llandaff (Crossley Exhibnr and Sen. Student). Ordained in St Davids Cathedral, 1938; Curate of Pembrey, 1938–40; Minor Canon, St Davids Cathedral, 1940–46; Vicar of St Clears with Llanginning, 1946–64; Rector of Tenby, 1964–72; Rector of Rectorial Benefice of Tenby with Gumfreston and Penally, 1970–72; Canon of St Davids Cathedral (Mathry), 1972. Surrogate. *Recreations:* golf, cricket, writing Welsh poetry. *Address:* Saddle Point, Slade Way, Fishguard, Dyfed SA65 9NY.

BOWEN, Hon. Lionel Frost, AC 1991; MHR (Lab) Kingsford-Smith, NSW, 1969–90; Attorney-General of Australia, 1984–90; Chairman, National Gallery, Canberra, since 1990; *b* 28 Dec. 1922; *m* 1953, Claire Clement; five *s* three *d. Educ:* Sydney Univ. (LLB). Alderman, 1947, Mayor, 1949–50, Randwick Council; MLA, NSW, 1962–69; Postmaster Gen., 1972–74; Special Minister of State, 1974–75; Minister for Manufg Industry, 1975; Minister for Trade, 1983–84; Dep. Prime Minister, 1983–90. Dep. Leader, ALP, 1977–83. *Recreations:* surfing, reading. *Address:* 24 Mooramie Avenue, Kensington, NSW 2033, Australia.

BOWEN, Sir Mark Edward Mortimer, 5th Bt *cr* 1921, of Colworth, Co. Bedford; *b* 17 Oct. 1958; *s* of Sir Thomas Frederic Charles Bowen, 4th Bt and of Jill, *d* of Lloyd Evans; *S* father, 1989; *m* 1983, Kerry Tessa, *d* of Michael Moriarty; one *s* one *d. Heir: s* George Edward Michael Bowen, *b* 27 Dec. 1987. *Address:* 14 Pendarves Road, West Wimbledon, SW20 8TS.

BOWEN, Most Rev. Michael George; *see* Southwark, Archbishop and Metropolitan of, (RC).

BOWEN, Hon. Sir Nigel (Hubert), AC 1988; KBE 1976; Chief Justice (formerly Chief Judge), Federal Court of Australia, 1976–90; *b* Summerland, BC, Canada, 26 May 1911; *s* of late O. P. Bowen, Ludlow, England; *m* 1st, 1947, Eileen Cecily (*d* 1983), *d* of F. J. Mullens; three *d*; 2nd, 1984, Ermyn Krippner. *Educ:* King's Sch., Sydney; St Paul's Coll., Sydney Univ. (BA, LLB). Served 2nd AIF, 1942–46 (Captain). Admitted NSW Bar 1936, Victorian Bar 1954; QC (Austr.) 1953; Vice-Pres., Law Council of Australia, 1957–60; Pres., NSW Bar Council, 1959–61. Editor, Australian Law Jl, 1946–58. MHR (L) Australia for Parramatta, NSW, 1964–73, retired; Attorney-General, Australia, 1966–69 and March-Aug. 1971; Minister for Educn and Science, 1969–71; Minister for Foreign Affairs, Aug. 1971–Dec. 1972. Judge of Court of Appeal of NSW, 1973–76; Chief Judge in Equity, 1974–76. Head of Austr. Delegn and Vice-Pres. of UN Internat. Conf. on Human Rights, 1968; Leader of Austr. Delegations: to Unesco Inter-Govtl Conf. of Ministers on Cultural Policies, 1970; to UN, 1971 and 1972. *Recreations:* swimming, music. *Club:* Union (Sydney).

BOWEN, Roderic; *see* Bowen, (Evan) Roderic.

BOWEN, Stanley, CBE 1972; Hon. Sheriff, Lothian and Borders, since 1975; *b* Carnoustie, Angus, 4 Aug. 1910; *s* of late Edward Bowen and Ellen Esther Bowen (*née* Powles), Birmingham; *m* 1943, Mary Shepherd Greig, *d* of late Alexander Greig and Mary Shand Greig (*née* Shepherd), Carnoustie; two *s* one *d. Educ:* Barry Sch., Angus; Grove Academy, Dundee; University Coll., Dundee. Enrolled Solicitor, in Scotland, 1932; entered Procurator Fiscal Service, in Scotland, 1933; Procurator Fiscal Depute at Hamilton, Lanarkshire, 1937; Interim Procurator Fiscal at Airdrie, Lanarkshire, 1938; Crown Office, Edinburgh: Legal Asst, 1941; Principal Asst, 1945; Crown Agent for Scotland, 1967–74. Chm., Sec. of State for Scotland's working party on forensic pathology services, 1975; Member: Sec. of State for the Environment's working party on drinking and driving offences, 1975; Sub-Cttee for legislation on transplantation of human tissues, Council of Europe, 1975–76; Police Adv. Bd for Scotland, 1976–83 (sub-cttee on police discipline, 1976, and working party on Cadet entry, 1979); Sec. of State for Scotland's working group on identification evidence in criminal cases, 1977; Council, Scottish Assoc. for Care and Resettlement of Offenders, 1978–83; Council, Corstorphine Trust, 1978–90 (Chm., 1982–90; Hon. Vice-Pres., 1990). *Recreations:* golf, gardening. *Address:* Achray, 20 Dovecot Road, Corstorphine, Edinburgh EH12 7LE. *T:* 031–334 4096. *Clubs:* New, Press (Edinburgh); Carnoustie Golf.
See also E. F. Bowen.

BOWEN, Thomas Edward Ifor L.; *see* Lewis-Bowen.

BOWEN, Prof. William G(ordon), PhD; President, The Andrew W. Mellon Foundation, since 1988; Senior Fellow, Woodrow Wilson School of Public and International Affairs, Princeton University, since 1988 (President Emeritus of the University, 1988); *b* 6 Oct. 1933; *s* of Albert A. and Bernice C. Bowen; *m* 1956, Mary Ellen Maxwell; one *s* one *d. Educ:* Denison Univ. (AB); Princeton Univ. (PhD). Princeton University: Asst Prof. of Economics, Associate Prof. of Economics; Prof. of Econs, 1958–88; Provost, 1967–72; Pres., 1972–88. Director: NCR, 1975–; Reader's Digest, 1985–; Merck, 1986–; American Express, 1988–. Trustee, Center for Advanced Study in the Behavioral Sciences, 1986–; Regent, Smithsonian Instn, 1980–. Hon. LLD: Denison, Rutgers, Pennsylvania and Yale, 1972; Harvard, 1973; Jewish Theol Seminary, 1974; Seton Hall Univ., 1975; Dartmouth and Princeton, 1987; Brown, 1988. *Publications:* Economic Aspects of Education, 1964; (with W. J. Baumol) Performing Arts: the Economic Dilemma, 1966; (with T. A. Finegan) Economics of Labor Force Participation, 1969; Ever the Teacher, 1987; (with Julie Ann Sosa) Prospects for Faculty in the Arts & Sciences, 1989, etc; contribs to Amer. Econ. Review, Economica, Quarterly Jl of Economics, etc. *Address:* 140 E 62 Street, New York, NY 10021, USA. *T:* 212–838–8400.

BOWER, Michael Douglas; Organiser, Sheffield Co-operative Development Group, since 1981; *b* 25 Aug. 1942; *s* of Stanley Arthur Bower and Rachael Farmer; *m* 1966, Susan Millington; two *d. Educ:* Colwyn Bay Grammar Sch.; Royal Coll. of Advanced Technol., Salford. Civil engr, 1961–64; journalist, 1965–77; with The Star, Sheffield, 1968–77; Regional Organiser, NUJ, 1977–81. Mem., Press Council, 1976–77. Mem., Sheffield Metropolitan DC, 1976– (Chm., Educn Cttee, 1983–). Contested (Lab) Hallam Div. of Sheffield, 1979. *Recreations:* walking, golf. *Address:* 146 Scott Road, Sheffield S4 7BJ. *T:* Sheffield (0742) 443462. *Club:* Carlton Working Men's (Gleadless, Sheffield).

BOWER, Stephen Ernest D.; *see* Dykes Bower.

BOWERING, Christine, MA; Headmistress, Nottingham High School for Girls (GPDST), since 1984; *b* 30 June 1936; *d* of Kenneth Soper and Florence E. W. Soper; *m* 1960, Rev. John Anthony Bowering; one *s* one *d. Educ:* St Bernard's Convent, Westcliff-on-Sea; Newnham Coll., Cambridge (MA). Assistant Teacher: St Bernard's Convent; Ursuline Convent, Brentwood; Sheffield High Sch. (GPDST). Chm., Educn. sub-cttee, GSA, 1989–. Mem., Engineering Council, 1988–. Gov., Nottingham Poly., 1989–. *Address:* The Vicarage, 2 Sunderland Street, Tickhill DN11 9QJ. *T:* Doncaster (0302) 742224. *Club:* University Women's.

BOWERING, Ven. Michael Ernest; Archdeacon of Lindisfarne, since 1987; *b* 25 June 1935; *s* of Hubert James and Mary Elizabeth Bowering; *m* 1962, Aileen (*née* Fox); one *s* two *d. Educ:* Barnstaple Grammar School; Kelham Theological Coll. Curate: St Oswald, Middlesbrough, 1959–62; Huntington with New Earswick, York, 1962–64; Vicar, Brayton with Barlow, 1964–72; RD of Selby, 1971–72; Vicar, Saltburn by the Sea, 1972–81; Canon Residentiary of York Minster and Secretary for Mission and Evengelism, 1981–87. *Recreations:* crosswords, walking the dog. *Address:* 12 Rectory Park, Morpeth, Northumberland NE61 2SZ. *T:* Morpeth (0670) 513207.

BOWERMAN, David Alexander; retired; *b* 19 April 1903; *s* of Frederick and Millicent Bowerman; *m* 1925, Constance Lilian Hosegood (*d* 1959); four *s* one *d*; *m* 1962, June Patricia Ruth Day. *Educ:* Queen's Coll., Taunton. Farmer, 1923–36; Wholesale Fruit and Potato Merchant (Director), 1936–60. Chairman, Horticultural Marketing Council, 1960–63. Director, 1963–75: Jamaica Producers Marketing Co. Ltd; JP Fruit Distributors Ltd; Horticultural Exports (GB) Ltd. *Recreations:* sailing, golf, gardens. *Address:* The Spinney, Brenchley, Kent. *T:* Brenchley (089272) 2149. *Clubs:* Lamberhurst Golf; Isle of Purbeck Golf.

BOWERS, Michael John; Managing Director, TW Oil (UK) Ltd, since 1985; *b* 1 Oct. 1933; *s* of Arthur Patrick and Lena Frances Bowers; *m* 1959, Caroline (*née* Clifford); two *d. Educ:* Cardinal Vaughan Sch., Kensington. BP Group: various appts in Supply, Distribution Planning and Trading, 1951–73; Vice-Pres. and Dir, BP North America Inc. (NY), 1973–76; Man. Dir and Chief Exec. Officer, BP Gas, 1976–81; Dir, BP Shipping/BP Exploration, 1980–81; Regional Co-ordinator, Western Hemisphere, 1981–83; Chief Exec., International Petroleum Exchange of London Ltd, 1983–85. *Recreations:* gardening, tennis, bridge, chess. *Address:* Wood End, Warren Drive, Kingswood, Surrey KT20 6PZ. *T:* Mogador (0737) 832629.

BOWERS, Roger George, OBE 1984; PhD; Director (formerly Controller), English Language and Literature Division, British Council, since 1989; *b* 23 May 1942; *s* of George Albert Bowers and Hilda Mary Bowers (*née* Wells); *m* 1963, Gweneth Iris Pither (marr. diss.); one *s* one *d. Educ:* Royal Grammar Sch., Guildford; Wadham Coll., Oxford (BA); Reading Univ. (MPhil; PhD). Joined British Council, 1964; Tutor to Overseas Students, Univ. of Birmingham, 1965; Asst Regl Dir, Cape Coast, Ghana, 1965–69; seconded to Eng. Lang. Trng Inst., Allahabad, 1971–73; Asst Regl Educ. Advr, Calcutta, 1973–76; Eng. Lang. Consultancies Dept, 1978–80; seconded to Ain Shams Univ., Cairo, 1980–84; Dir, Eng. Lang. Services Dept, 1984–85; Dep. Controller, Eng. Lang. and Lit. Div., 1985–89. Jt Editor, Cambridge Handbooks for Language Teachers, 1985–; Member: Editorial Cttee, ELT Documents, 1984–; Bd of Management, ELT Jl, 1985–. *Publications:* In Passing, 1976; Talking About Grammar, 1987; Word Play, 1990. *Recreations:* gardening, cooking, eating. *Address:* 25 Hillbrow, Richmond Hill, Surrey TW10 6BH. *T:* 081–948 6342.

BOWERY, Prof. Norman George, PhD, DSc; Wellcome Professor of Pharmacology, The School of Pharmacy, University of London, since 1987; *b* 23 June 1944; *s* of George Bowery and Olga (*née* Beevers); *m* 1970, Barbara Joyce (*née* Westcott); one *s* two *d. Educ:* Christ's Coll., Finchley; NESCOT; St Bartholomew's Med. Coll., Univ. of London (PhD 1974; DSc 1987). MIBiol 1970. Res. Asst, CIBA Labs, 1963–70; Res. Student, St Bart's Med. Coll., London, 1970–73; Postdoctoral Res. Fellow, Sch. of Pharmacy, London Univ., 1973–75; Lectr in Pharmacology, 1975–82, Sen. Lectr in Pharm., 1982–84, St Thomas's Hosp. Med. Sch.; Section Leader, Neuroscience Res. Centre, Merck, Sharp & Dohme, Harlow, 1984–87. *Publications:* Actions and Interactions of GABA and Benzodiazepines, 1984; GABAergic Mechanisms in the Mammalian Periphery, 1986; GABA: basic mechanisms to clinical applications, 1989; $GABA_B$ Receptors in Mammalian Function, 1990. *Recreations:* gardening, socializing, walking, family life. *Address:* Department of Pharmacology, The School of Pharmacy, 29/39 Brunswick Square, WC1N 1AX. *T:* 071–753 5899.

BOWES, Richard Noel; Deputy Chairman, Willis Faber plc and Chairman, Willis Faber and Dumas, 1985–88, retired; *b* 17 Dec. 1928; *m* 1961, Elizabeth Lyle; one *s* two *d. Educ:* Epsom College; Worcester Coll., Oxford (MA). Called to the Bar, Gray's Inn, 1950. RN, 1950–53. Willis Faber and Dumas, 1953–88. *Address:* Fairacre, Enton, Godalming, Surrey. *T:* Godalming (0483) 416544.

BOWES, Roger Norman; Chief Executive, Association for Information Management (Aslib), since 1989; *b* 28 Jan. 1943; *s* of late Russell Ernest Bowes and Sybil Caroline Rose Bowes (*née* Bell); *m* 1st, 1961, Denise Hume Windsor (marr. diss. 1974); one *d*; 2nd, 1977, Ann Rosemary O'Connor (*née* Hamstead) (marr. diss. 1988). *Educ:* Chiswick and Dorking Grammar Schools. Advertisement Executive: Associated Newspapers, 1962–67; IPC/Mirror Gp Newspapers, 1967–70; Marketing Exec./Sales Manager, Mirror Gp, 1970–75; Media Dir, McCann Erickson Advertising, 1976–78; Mirror Gp Newspapers: Adv. Dir, 1978–81; Dep. Chief Exec., 1982–83; Chief Exec., 1984; Man. Dir, Guinness Enterprises, 1985; Chief Exec., Express Gp Newspapers, 1985–86; Chm., Citybridge, 1987–. Member: Library and Information Services Council; Advertising Assoc. Council; PIRA Council. *Recreations:* political and military history, cookery, architectural restoration, classic cars. *Address:* Aslib, Information House, 20–24 Old Street, EC1V 9AP. *T:* 071–253 4488, *Fax:* 071–430 0514.

BOWES LYON, family name of **Earl of Strathmore.**

BOWES LYON, Simon Alexander, FCA; director of insurance and manufacturing companies; Lord-Lieutenant of Hertfordshire, since 1986; *b* 17 June 1932; *s* of Hon. Sir David Bowes Lyon, KCVO, and of Rachel Bowes Lyon (*née* Spender Clay); *m* 1966, Caroline, *d* of Rt Rev. Victor Pike, CB, CBE, DD, and of Dorothea Pike; three *s* one *d. Educ:* Eton; Magdalen Coll., Oxford (BA). *Recreations:* botany, gardening, shooting, music. *Address:* St Paul's Walden Bury, Hitchin, Herts. *T:* Whitwell (043887) 1218. *Clubs:* White's, Brooks's.

BOWETT, Prof. Derek William, CBE 1983; QC 1978; LLD; FBA 1983; Whewell Professor of International Law, Cambridge University, 1981–91; a Professorial Fellow of Queens' College, Cambridge; *b* 20 April 1927; *s* of Arnold William Bowett and Marion Wood; *m* 1953, Betty Northall; two *s* one *d. Educ:* William Hulme's Sch., Manchester; Downing Coll., Cambridge. MA, LLB, LLD (Cantab), PhD (Manchester). Called to the Bar, Middle Temple, 1953, Hon. Bencher, 1975. Lectr, Law Faculty, Manchester Univ. 1951–59; Legal Officer, United Nations, New York, 1957–59; Lectr, Law Faculty, Cambridge Univ., 1960–76, Reader, 1976–81; Fellow of Queens' Coll., 1960–69, President 1969–82. Gen. Counsel, UNRWA, Beirut, 1966–68. Mem., Royal Commn on Environmental Pollution, 1973–77. *Publications:* Self-defence in International Law, 1958; Law of International Institutions, 1964; United Nations Forces, 1964; Law of the Sea,

1967; Search for Peace, 1972; Legal Régime of Islands in International Law, 1978. *Recreations:* music, cricket, tennis. *Address:* Queens' College, Cambridge CB3 9ET. *T:* Cambridge (0223) 335555.

BOWEY, Prof. Angela Marilyn, PhD; Director, Pay Advice and Research Centre, Glasgow, since 1986; Professor of Business Administration, Strathclyde Business School, University of Strathclyde, Glasgow, 1976–87; *b* 20 Oct. 1940; *d* of Jack Nicholas Peterson and Kathleen (*née* Griffin); *m* 1st, 1960, Miklos Papp; two *s* one *d*; 2nd, 1965, Gregory Bowey (marr. diss. 1980); one *s* one *d*. *Educ:* Withington Girls Sch., Manchester; Univ. of Manchester (BA Econ, PhD). Technical Asst, Nuclear Power Gp, 1961–62; Asst Lectr, Elizabeth Gaskell Coll. of Educn, 1967–68; Manchester Business School: Res. Associate, 1968–69; Res. Fellow, 1969–72; Lectr, 1972–76. Vis. Professor: Admin. Staff Coll. of India, 1975; Western Australian Inst. of Technology, 1976; Univ. of WA, 1977; Prahran Coll. of Advanced Educn, Australia, 1978; Massey Univ., NZ, 1978. ACAS Arbitrator, 1977–; Dir, Pay and Rewards Res. Centre, 1978–85; Comr, Equal Opportunities Commn, 1980–86; Member: Scottish Econ. Council, 1980–83; Police Adv. Bd (Scotland) (formerly Adv. Panel on Police), 1983–88. Gov., Scottish Police Coll., 1985–88. Editor, Management Decision, 1979–82. *Publications:* Job and Pay Comparisons (with Tom Lupton), 1973, 2nd edn 1974; A Guide to Manpower Planning, 1974, 2nd edn 1977; (with Tom Lupton) Wages and Salaries, 1974, 2nd edn 1982; Handbook of Salary and Wage Systems, 1975, 2nd edn 1982; The Sociology of Organisations, 1976; (with Richard Thorpe and Phil Hellier) Payment Systems and Productivity, 1986; Managing Salary and Wage Systems, 1987; articles in Brit. Jl of Indust. Relations, Jl of Management Studies, and Management Decision. *Address:* Pay Advice and Research Centre, PO Box, Neptune House, Marina Bay, Gibraltar.

BOWEY, Olwyn, RA 1975 (ARA 1970); practising artist (painter); *b* 10 Feb. 1936; *o d* of James and Olive Bowey. *Educ:* William Newton Sch., Stockton; West Hartlepool Sch. of Art; Royal Coll. of Art. One-man shows: Zwemmer Gall., 1961; New Grafton Gall., 1969; also exhibited at Leicester Gall., Royal Academy; work purchased through Chantrey Bequest for Tate Gall., Royal Academy, Min. of Works, etc.

BOWICK, David Marshall, CBE 1977; Member, British Railways Board, 1976–80; retired; *b* 30 June 1923; *s* of George Bowick, Corstorphine, Edinburgh; *m* Gladys May (*née* Jeffries) (*d* 1988); one *d*. *Educ:* Boroughmuir Sch., Edinburgh; Heriot-Watt Coll., Edinburgh. Served with Fleet Air Arm, 1942–46. Movements Supt, Kings Cross, 1962; Planning Officer, British Railways Board Headquarters, 1963; Asst Gen. Man., London Midland Region, BR, 1965; Exec. Dir, Personnel, BRB Headquarters, 1969; Gen. Manager, London Midland Region, BR, 1971; Chief Exec. (Railways), BR, 1971–78; Vice-Chm. (Rail), BRB, 1978–80. Pres., Group of Nine EEC Railways, 1978–80. Mem. Council, Manchester Business Sch. Col RE, T&AVR. FREconS; FCIT; CBIM; FRSA. *Recreations:* sailing, swimming, golf, travel, theatre. *Address:* Villa Tuffolina, Shipwreck Promenade, Xemxija, St Paul's Bay, Malta. *Club:* Union (Sliema, Malta).

BOWIE, Rev. (Alexander) Glen, CBE 1984; Principal Chaplain (Church of Scotland and Free Churches), Royal Air Force, 1980–84, retired; *b* 10 May 1928; *s* of Alexander Bowie and Annie (*née* McGhie); *m* 1952, Mary McKillop; two *d*. *Educ:* Stevenston High Sch.; Irvine Royal Acad.; Glasgow Univ. (BSc 1951; Dip Theol 1954); BA Open Univ., 1977. Assistant, Beith High Church, 1952–54; ordained, 1954; entered RAF Chaplains' Br., 1955; served: RAF Padgate, 1955–56; Akrotiri, 1956–59; Stafford, 1959–61; Butzweilerhof, 1961–64; Halton, 1964–67; Akrotiri, 1967–70; RAF Coll., Cranwell, 1970–75; Asst Principal Chaplain, 1975; HQ Germany, 1975–76; HQ Support Comd, 1976–80. QHC 1980–84; Hon. Chaplain, Royal Scottish Corp., 1981–. Editor, Scottish Forces Bulletin, 1985–. Moderator of Presbytery of England, 1988–89. *Recreations:* oil painting, travel, leading Holy Land tours. *Address:* 16 Weir Road, Hemingford Grey, Huntingdon, Cambs PE18 9EH. *T:* Huntingdon (0480) 63269. *Club:* Royal Air Force.

BOWIE, David; international recording artist and performer; film and stage actor; video and film producer; graphic designer; *b* 8 Jan. 1947; *s* of Hayward Stenton Jones and Margaret Mary Burns; *m* (marr. diss.); one *s*. *Educ:* Stansfield Road Sch., Brixton. Artiste from age of 16; many major recordings, 1970–, and video productions, 1979–; numerous live musical stage performances; guest appearances on television shows. Actor: *films:* The Man who Fell to Earth, 1976; Just a Gigolo, 1978; The Hunger, 1982; Merry Christmas, Mr Lawrence, 1983; Ziggy Stardust and the Spiders from Mars, 1983; Absolute Beginners, 1986; Labyrinth, 1986; Into the Night; The Last Temptation of Christ; *stage:* The Elephant Man, New York 1980; *television:* Baal, 1982. Recipient of internat. music and entertainment awards. *Recreations:* painting, skiing. *Address:* c/o Duncan Heath Associates, 162 Wardour Street, W1V 3AT.

BOWIE, Rev. Glen; *see* Bowie, Rev. A. G.

BOWIE, Graham Maitland; Chief Executive, Lothian Regional Council, since 1986; *b* 11 Nov. 1931; *s* of John Graham Bowie and Agnes Bowie; *m* 1962, Maureen Jennifer O'Sullivan; one *s* two *d*. *Educ:* Alloa Academy; Univ. of St Andrews (MA); Univ. of Glasgow (LLB). National Service, 1956–58. Asst Sec., Glasgow Chamber of Commerce, 1958–60; Product Planner, Ford Motor Co., 1960–64; Edinburgh Corp. Educn Dept, 1964–69; ILEA, 1969–75; Dir of Policy Planning, Lothian Regional Council, 1975–86. *Recreations:* walking, travel, the arts. *Address:* 8 Keith Crescent, Edinburgh.

BOWIE, Stanley Hay Umphray, DSc; FRS 1975; FEng 1976; FRSE, FIMM, FMSA; Consultant Geologist; Assistant Director, Chief Geochemist, Institute of Geological Sciences, 1968–77; *b* 24 March 1917; *s* of Dr James Cameron and Mary Bowie; *m* 1948, Helen Elizabeth, *d* of Dr Roy Woodhouse and Florence Elizabeth Pocock; two *s*. *Educ:* Grammar Sch. and Univ. of Aberdeen (BSc, DSc). Meteorological Office, 1942; commissioned RAF, 1943; HM Geological Survey of Gt Britain: Geologist, Sen. Geologist and Principal Geologist, 1946–55; Chief Geologist, Atomic Energy Div., 1955–67; Chief Consultant Geologist to UKAEA, 1955–77. Visiting Prof. of Applied Geology, Univ. of Strathclyde, 1968–85; Vis. Prof., Imperial Coll., London, 1985–. Principal Investigator, Apollo 11 and 12 lunar samples, 1969–71; Chairman: Internat. Mineralogical Assoc., Commn on Ore Microscopy, 1970–78; Royal Soc. Working Party on Envtl Geochem. and Health, 1979–81; DoE Res. Adv. Gp, Radioactive Waste Management, 1984–85; Mem., Radioactive Waste Management Adv. Cttee, 1978–82. Chm., Shetland Sheep Breeders Gp, 1989–; Vice-Pres., Geological Soc., 1972–74; Mem. Council, Mineralogical Soc., 1954–57, 1962–65 (Chairman: Applied Mineralogy Gp, 1969–72; Geochem. Gp, 1972–75). FGS 1959; FMSA 1963; FRSE 1970; FIMM 1972 (Pres. 1976–77); Hon. FIMM 1987. Silver Medal, RSA, 1959. *Publications:* (ed jtly) Uranium Prospecting Handbook, 1972; (ed jtly) Mineral Deposits of Europe, Vol. 1: North-West Europe, 1978; (with P. R. Simpson) The Bowie-Simpson System for the Microscopic Determination of Ore Minerals, 1980; (ed jtly) Environmental Geochemistry and Health, 1985; contributions to: Nuclear Geology, 1954; Physical Methods in Determinative Mineralogy, 1967, 2nd edn 1977; Uranium Exploration Geology, 1970; Proceedings of the Apollo Lunar Science Conference, 1970; Proceedings of the Second Lunar Science Conference, 1971; Uranium Exploration Methods, 1973; Recognition and Evaluation of Uraniferous Areas, 1977; Theoretical and Practical Aspects of Uranium Geology, 1979; Nuclear Power Technology, 1983; Applied Environmental Geochemistry, 1983; numerous papers in scientific and technical jls on uranium geology and economics, mineralogy, geophysics and geochemistry, and articles on rare breeds of domesticated animals. *Recreations:* farming, preservation of rare breeds, gardening, photography. *Address:* Tanyard Farm, Clapton, Crewkerne, Somerset TA18 8PS. *T:* Crewkerne (0460) 72093.

BOWIS, John Crocket, OBE 1981; MP (C) Battersea, since 1987; *b* 2 Aug. 1945; *s* of Thomas Palin Bowis and Georgiana Joyce (*née* Crocket); *m* 1968, Caroline May (*née* Taylor); two *s* one *d*. *Educ:* Tonbridge Sch.; Brasenose Coll., Oxford (MA). Tutor, Cumberland Lodge, Windsor Great Park Student Conference Centre, 1966–67; Cons. Party Agent, Peterborough, Derby, Harborough and Blaby, 1968–72; Conservative Central Office: National Organiser, Fedn of Cons. Students, 1972–75; Nat. Organiser, Cons. Trade Unionists, 1975–79; Dir of Community Affairs, 1979–81; Campaign Dir, 1981–82, Public Affairs Dir, 1983–87, British Insurance Brokers Assoc.; Press and Parly Consultant, Nat. Fedn of Self-employed and Small Firms, 1982–83. Councillor (C) Royal Bor. of Kingston upon Thames, 1982–86 (Chm. of Educn, 1985–86). PPS to Minister for Local Govt and Inner Cities, DoE, 1989–90, to Sec. of State for Wales, 1990–. Mem., Select Cttee on Members' Interests, 1987–90; Sec., All Party Gp on Social Sci., 1988–. Secretary: Cons. Inner Cities Cttee, 1987–89; Cons. Educn Cttee, 1988–89; Cons. Arts and Heritage Cttee, 1988–89; Parly Adviser to ACFHE, 1987–. Vice-Pres., Internat. Soc. for Human Rights, 1988–. Hon, Jt Pres., British Youth Council, 1987–. *Recreations:* theatre, music, art, sport. *Address:* House of Commons, SW1A 0AA. *T:* 071–219 6214, 081–949 2555.

BOWKER, Alfred Johnstone, (John), MC 1944; Regional Chairman of Industrial Tribunals, Southampton, 1978–87; *b* 9 April 1922; *s* of Alfred Bowker and Isabel Florence (*née* Brett); *m* 1947, Ann, *er d* of late John Christopher Fairweather and Gunhild Fairweather; one *s* one *d*. *Educ:* Winchester Coll.; Christ Church, Oxford (MA). Served War, Coldstream Guards, 1941–47: Italian Campaign; Captain. Solicitor in private practice, Winchester, 1949–57; Resident Magistrate, Northern Rhodesia, 1957–65; solicitor in private practice, Salisbury, Wilts, 1965–71; Chm. of Indust. Tribunals, Newcastle upon Tyne, 1972–75. Winchester City Councillor (C), 1954–57; Hants County Councillor (C), 1989–. Liveryman, Skinners' Co., 1943. Master, Meon Valley Beagles, 1954–56; Jt Master, Hursley Foxhounds, 1968–69 and 1970–71. *Recreations:* hunting, reading history.

BOWKER, Prof. John Westerdale; Fellow, Trinity College, Cambridge, since 1984 (Dean, 1984–91); Hon. Canon of Canterbury Cathedral, since 1985; Adjunct Professor of Religion, North Carolina State University, since 1986; Adjunct Professor of Religious Studies, University of Pennsylvania, since 1986; *b* 30 July 1935; *s* of Gordon Westerdale Bowker and Marguerite (*née* Burdick); *m* 1963, Margaret Roper; one *s*. *Educ:* St John's Sch., Leatherhead; Worcester Coll., Oxford (MA); Ripon Hall, Oxford. National Service, RWAFF, N Nigeria, 1953–55. Henry Stephenson Fellow, Sheffield Univ., 1961; Deacon, St Augustine's, Brocco Bank, Sheffield, 1961; Priest and Dean of Chapel, Corpus Christi Coll., Cambridge, 1962; Asst Lectr, 1965, Lectr, 1970, Univ. of Cambridge; Prof. of Religious Studies, Univ. of Lancaster, 1974–85. Lectures: Wilde, Univ. of Oxford, 1972–75; Staley, Rollins Coll., Florida, 1978–79; Public, Univ. of Cardiff, 1984; Riddell, Newcastle Univ., 1985; Boutwood, Univ. of Cambridge, 1985; Harris Meml, Toronto, 1986; Boardman, Univ. of Pa, 1988; Montefiore, Univ. of Southampton, 1989; Scott Holland, London Univ., 1989; Bicentary, Univ. of Georgetown, Washington, 1989. Member: Durham Commn on Religious Educn, 1967–70; Root Commn on Marriage and Divorce, 1967–71; Archbps' Commn on Doctrine, 1977–86; Patron, Marriage Research Inst.; Hon. Pres., Stauros; Vice-President: Inst. on Religion in an Age of Science, 1980; Culture and Animals Foundn, 1984–; Pres., Christian Action on AIDS, 1987–. Editor, Oxford Companion to Religions of the World, 1977–. *Publications:* The Targums and Rabbinic Literature, 1969, 2nd edn 1979; Problems of Suffering in Religions of the World, 1970, 3rd edn 1987; Jesus and the Pharisees, 1973; The Sense of God, 1973; The Religious Imagination and the Sense of God, 1978; Uncle Bolpenny Tries Things Out, 1973; Worlds of Faith, 1983; (ed) Violence and Aggression, 1983; Licensed Insanities: religions and belief in God in the contemporary world, 1987; The Meanings of Death, 1991; A Year to Live, 1991. *Recreations:* walking, books, gardening, cooking, painting, poetry. *Address:* 14 Bowers Croft, Cambridge CB1 4RP. *T:* (college) Cambridge (0223) 338400.

BOWLBY, Sir Anthony Hugh Mostyn, 2nd Bt, *cr* 1923; *b* 13 Jan. 1906; *e s* of Sir Anthony Bowlby, 1st Bt and Maria Bridget (*d* 1957), *d* of Rev. Canon Hon. Hugh W. Mostyn; *S* father, 1929; *m* 1930, Dora Evelyn, *d* of John Charles Allen; two *d*. *Educ:* Wellington Coll.; New Coll., Oxford. *Heir: nephew* Richard Peregrine Longstaff Bowlby [*b* 11 Aug. 1941; *m* 1963, Xenia, *o d* of R. P. A. Garrett; one *s* one *d*]. *Address:* The Old Rectory, Ozleworth, near Wotton-under-Edge, Glos.

See also Sir E. H. P. Brown, J. Dromgoole.

BOWLBY, Rt. Rev. Ronald Oliver; Assistant Bishop, Diocese of Lichfield, since 1991; *b* 16 August 1926; *s* of Oliver and Helena Bowlby; *m* 1956, Elizabeth Trevelyan Monro; three *s* two *d*. *Educ:* Eton Coll.; Trinity College, Oxford (MA; Hon. Fellow, 1989); Westcott House, Cambridge. Curate of St Luke's, Pallion, Sunderland, 1952–56; Priest-in-charge and Vicar of St Aidan, Billingham, 1956–66; Vicar of Croydon, 1966–72; Bishop of: Newcastle, 1973–80; Southwark, 1980–91. Chairman: Hospital Chaplaincies Council, 1975–82; Social Policy Cttee, Bd for Social Responsibility, 1986–90; Mem., Anglican Consultative Caouncil, 1977–85. Pres., Nat. Fedn of Housing Assocs, 1988–. Hon. Fellow, Newcastle upon Tyne Polytechnic, 1980. *Publications:* contrib. Church without Walls, ed Lindars, 1969; contrib. Church and Politics Today, ed Moyser, 1985. *Recreations:* walking, gardening, music. *Address:* 4 Uppington Avenue, Bellevue, Shrewsbury SY3 7JL.

BOWLER, Geoffrey, FCIS; Chief General Manager, Sun Alliance & London Insurance Group, 1977–87; *b* 11 July 1924; *s* of James Henry Bowler and Hilda May Bowler. *Educ:* Sloane Sch., Chelsea. FCIS 1952. Dir, British Aviation Insurance Co., 1976–87 (Chm., 1977–83). Dep. Chm., British Insurance Assoc., 1977, Chm. 1979–80. *Address:* 13 Green Lane, Purley, Surrey CR8 3PP. *T:* 081–660 0756.

BOWLER, Ian John, CBE 1971 (OBE 1957); President, Iranian Management & Engineering Group Ltd, since 1965; Chairman: International Management & Engineering Group Ltd, since 1973 (Managing Director, 1964–68); Wilmeg, Tehran, since 1979; ICE, Moscow/London; *b* 1920; *s* of Major John Arthur Bowler; *m* 1963, Hamideh, *d* of Prince Yadollah Azodi, GCMG; two *d*, and one step *s* one step *d*. *Educ:* King's Sch., Worcester; privately; Oxford Univ. Director of Constructors, John Brown, 1961–64. Director: IMEG (Offshore) Ltd, 1974–; MMC Gas, Kuala Lumpur. Mem., RNLI, 1983–. MInstPet. *Publication:* Predator Birds of Iran, 1973. *Recreations:* ornithology, yachting. *Address:* 6 rue Bonaparte, 75006 Paris, France; 28 Mallord Street, SW3. *T:* 071–352 9795. *Clubs:* Royal Thames Yacht, Ocean Cruising; S.R.R. (La Rochelle, France).

BOWLES, Rt. Rev. Cyril William Johnston; Hon. Assistant Bishop, diocese of Gloucester, since 1987; *b* Scotstoun, Glasgow, 9 May 1916; *s* of William Cullen Allen Bowles, West Ham, and Jeanie Edwards Kilgour, Glasgow; *m* 1965, Florence Joan, *d* of late John Eastaugh, Windlesham. *Educ:* Brentwood Sch.; Emmanuel Coll., Jesus Coll. (Lady Kay Scholar) and Ridley Hall, Cambridge. 2nd cl., Moral Sciences Tripos, Pt. I, 1936; 1st cl., Theological Tripos, Pt. I, and BA, 1938; 2nd cl., Theological Tripos, Pt. II, 1939; MA 1941. Deacon 1939, Priest 1940, Chelmsford; Curate of Barking Parish Church, 1939–41; Chaplain of Ridley Hall, Cambridge, 1942–44; Vice-Principal, 1944–51; Principal, 1951–63; Hon. Canon of Ely Cathedral, 1959–63; Archdeacon of Swindon, 1963–69; Bishop of Derby, 1969–87. Mem. of House of Lords, 1973–87. Select Preacher: Cambridge, 1945, 1953, 1958, 1963; Oxford, 1961; Dublin, 1961. Exam. Chaplain to Bishop of Carlisle, 1950–63; to Bishops of Rochester, Ely and Chelmsford, 1951–63; to Bishop of Bradford, 1956–61; to Bishop of Bristol, 1963–69. Hon. Canon, Bristol Cathedral, 1963–69; Surrogate, 1963–69; Commissary to Bishop of the Argentine, 1963–69. Mem., Archbishops' Liturgical Commn, 1955–75. Pres., St John's Coll., Durham, 1970–84 (Hon. Fellow, 1991); Visitor of Ridley Hall, 1979–87. *Publications:* contributor: The Roads Converge, 1963; A Manual for Holy Week, 1967; The Eucharist Today, 1974. *Address:* Rose Lodge, Tewkesbury Road, Stow-on-the-Wold, Cheltenham, Glos GL54 1EN. *T:* Cotswold (0451) 31965.

BOWLES, Godfrey Edward; Managing Director, Pearl Group, since 1989; *b* 21 Dec. 1935; *s* of Llewellyn Crowley Bowles and Florence Jane Edwards; *m* 1958, Elizabeth Madge Dunning; two *s* two *d*. *Educ:* Commonweal Grammar Sch., Swindon; Exeter Coll., Oxford (MA). Emigrated to Australia, 1959; joined Australian Mutual Provident Society: Dep. Manager, Wellington, NZ, 1976; Manager, WA Br., Perth, 1980; Manager, Victoria Br., Melbourne, 1983; Chief Manager, Corporate Services, Sydney, 1986; Gen. Manager, AMP Corporate, Sydney, 1988; returned to UK after acquisition of Pearl Gp by AMP Soc., 1989. *Recreations:* running, including marathons, reading, music, theatre, cinema. *Address:* Pearl Assurance House, Thorpe Wood, Peterborough PE3 6SA. *T:* Peterborough (0733) 63212.

BOWLES, Peter; actor; *b* 16 Oct. 1936; *s* of Herbert Reginald Bowles and Sarah Jane (*née* Harrison); *m* 1961, Susan Alexandra Bennett; two *s* one *d*. *Educ:* High Pavement Grammar Sch., Nottingham; RADA (schol.; Kendal Prize 1955). London début in Romeo and Juliet, Old Vic, 1956; *theatre* includes: Happy Haven, Platonov, Royal Court, 1960; Afternoon Men, Arts, 1961; Absent Friends, Garrick, 1975; Dirty Linen, Arts, 1976; Born in the Gardens, Globe, 1980; Some of My Best Friends Are Husbands, nat. tour, 1985; The Entertainer, Shaftesbury, 1986; Canaries Sometimes Sing, Albery, 1987; Man of the Moment, Globe, 1990; *films* include: Blow Up, 1966; The Charge of the Light Brigade, 1967; Laughter in the Dark, 1968; A Day in the Death of Joe Egg, 1970; *television series* include: Rumpole of the Bailey, 1976–91; To the Manor Born, 1979–82; Only when I Laugh, 1979–82; The Bounder, 1982–83; The Irish RM, 1983–85; Lytton's Diary, 1984–86 (also co-created series); Executive Stress, 1987–88; Shadow on the Sun, 1988; Perfect Scoundrels, 1990–91 (also co-created series). Comedy Actor of the Year, Pye Awards, 1984; ITV Personality of the Year, Variety Club of GB, 1984. *Recreations:* motoring, physical jerks. *Address:* c/o London Management, 235–241 Regent Street, W1. *T:* 071–493 1610. *Clubs:* Garrick, Chelsea Arts, Groucho.

BOWLEY, Martin Richard; QC 1981; a Recorder of the Crown Court, 1979–88; *b* 29 Dec. 1936; *s* of late Charles Colin Stuart Bowley and Mary Evelyn Bowley. *Educ:* Magdalen Coll. Sch., Oxford; Queen's Coll., Oxford (Styring Exhibnr, 1955; MA; BCL 1961). National Service, 1955–57: commnd Pilot Officer as a Fighter Controller; served 2nd Tactical Air Force, 1956–57. Called to the Bar, Inner Temple, 1962; Midland and Oxford Circuit; Member: Senate and Bar Council, 1985–86; Gen. Council of Bar, 1987–88, 1989–; Chm., Bar Cttee, 1987. Member: Lord Chancellor's Standing Commn on Efficiency, 1986–87; Marre Cttee on Future of Legal Profession, 1987–88. Chm., Questors Theatre, 1972–84 and 1988– (Sec., 1963–72); Mem. Standing Cttee, Little Theatre Guild of GB, 1974–84 (Vice-Chm., 1979–81, Chm., 1981–84). *Recreations:* playing at theatre, watching cricket, island hopping. *Address:* Flat E, 23/24 Great James Street, WC1N 3EL. *T:* 071–831 1674; 1 King's Bench Walk, Temple, EC4Y 7DB. *T:* 071–353 8436. *Clubs:* MCC, Questors.

BOWMAN; *see* Kellett-Bowman.

BOWMAN, (Edwin) Geoffrey, CB 1991; Parliamentary Counsel, since 1984; *b* Blackpool, Lancs, 27 Jan. 1946; *er s* of John Edwin Bowman and Lillian Joan Bowman (*née* Nield); *m* 1969, Carol Margaret, *er d* of late Alexander Ogilvie and of Ethel Ogilvie; two *s* one *d*. *Educ:* Roundhay Sch., Leeds; Trinity Coll., Cambridge (Senior Scholar; MA (1st cl.), LLM (1st cl.)). Called to Bar, Lincoln's Inn (Cassel Scholar), 1968; in practice, Chancery Bar, 1969–71; joined Parliamentary Counsel Office, 1971 (with Law Commission, 1977–79); Dep. Parly Counsel, 1981–84. *Publication:* The Elements of Conveyancing (with E. L. G. Tyler), 1972. *Recreations:* music (bassoon), English medieval history. *Address:* Parliamentary Counsel Office, 36 Whitehall, SW1A 2AY. *T:* 071–210 6629. *Club:* Les Amis du Basson Français (Paris).

BOWMAN, Eric Joseph; consultant, since 1986; *b* 1 June 1929; *s* of late Joseph John Bowman and Lilley Bowman; *m* 1951, Esther Kay; one *d*. *Educ:* Stationers' Company's School; College of Estate Management. FRICS. Private practice, 1945–51; Royal Engineers, 1951–53; private practice, 1953–54; Min. of Works, 1954–63; Min. of Housing and Local Govt, 1963–73; Directorate of Diplomatic and Post Office Services, MPBW, later DoE, 1973–80; Directorate of Quantity Surveying Services, DoE, 1980–83; Dir of Building and Quantity Surveying Services, PSA, DoE, 1983–86. *Recreations:* fly fishing, walking, swimming, gardening, reading. *Address:* Mearsons Farm, Hubbersty Head, Crosthwaite, near Kendal, Cumbria LA8 8JB. *T:* Crosthwaite (04488) 400.

BOWMAN, Geoffrey; *see* Bowman, E. G.

BOWMAN, Sir George, 2nd Bt *cr* 1961, of Killingworth, Northumberland; *b* 2 July 1923; *s* of Sir James Bowman, 1st Bt, KBE, and of Jean, *d* of Henry Brook, Ashington, Northumberland; *S* father, 1978; *m* 1960, Olive (*née* Case); three *d*. *Heir:* none. *Address:* Parkside, Killingworth Drive, Newcastle upon Tyne NE12 0ES.

BOWMAN, James Thomas; counter-tenor; Teacher of Voice, Guildhall School of Music, since 1983; *b* Oxford, 6 Nov. 1941; *s* of Benjamin and Cecilia Bowman. *Educ:* Ely Cathedral Choir Sch.; King's Sch., Ely; New Coll., Oxford. MA (History) 1967; DipEd 1964. Schoolmaster, 1965–67. Many concert performances with Early Music Consort, 1967–76; operatic performances with: English Opera Gp, 1967; Sadler's Wells Opera, 1970–; Glyndebourne Festival Opera, 1970–; Royal Opera, Covent Gdn, 1972; Sydney Opera, Australia, 1978; Opéra Comique, Paris, 1979; Le Châtelet, Paris, 1982; Geneva, 1983; Scottish Opera, 1985; La Scala, Milan, 1988, 1991; La Fenice, Venice, 1991; Paris Opera, 1991; Badisches Staatsteater, Karlsruhe, 1984; in USA at Santa Fe and Wolf Trap Festivals, Dallas and San Francisco Operas; at Aix-en-Provence Fest., 1979; operatic roles include: Oberon, in A Midsummer Night's Dream; Endymion, in La Calisto; the Priest, in Taverner; Polinesso, in Ariodante; Apollo, in Death in Venice; Astron, in Ice Break; Ruggiero in Alcina; title rôles: Gulio Cesare; Tamerlano; Xerxes; Scipione; Giustino; Orlando. Has made recordings of oratorio and Medieval and Renaissance vocal music. Lay Vicar, Westminster Abbey, 1969. *Recreations:* ecclesiastical architecture; collecting records. *Address:* 4 Brownlow Road, Redhill RH1 6AW.

BOWMAN, Sir Jeffery (Haverstock), Kt 1991; FCA; Chairman, Price Waterhouse Europe, since 1988; *b* 3 April 1935; *s* of Alfred Haverstock Bowman and Doris Gertrude Bowman; *m* 1963, Susan Claudia Bostock; one *s* two *d*. *Educ:* Winchester Coll. (schol.); Trinity Hall, Cambridge (major schol.; BA Hons 1st cl. in Law). Served RHG, 1953–55 (commnd, 1954). Price Waterhouse: articled in London, 1958; NY, 1963–64; admitted to partnership, 1966; Mem., Policy Cttee, 1972–; Dir of Tech. Services, 1973–76; Dir, London Office, 1979–81; Sen. Partner, 1982–91. Auditor, Duchy of Cornwall, 1971–. Vice-Pres., Union of Indep. Cos, 1983–; Member: Council, ICAEW, 1986– (Mem., Accounting Standards Cttee, 1982–87); Council, Industrial Soc., 1985–; Economic and Financial Policy Cttee, CBI, 1987–; City Capital Markets Cttee, 1989–; Council, Business in the Community, 1985–. Gov., Brentwood Sch., 1985–. FRSA 1989. *Recreations:* golf, opera, gardening, sailing. *Address:* The Old Rectory, Boreham, Chelmsford, Essex CM3 3EP. *T:* Chelmsford (0245) 467233. *Club:* Garrick.

BOWMAN, Dr John Christopher, CBE 1986; PhD; FIBiol; Chief Executive, National Rivers Authority, 1989–91; *b* 13 Aug. 1933; *s* of M. C. Bowman and C. V. Simister; *m* 1961, S. J. Lorimer; three *d*. *Educ:* Manchester Grammar Sch.; Univ. of Reading (BSc); Univ. of Edinburgh (PhD). Geneticist, later Chief Geneticist, Thornbers, Mytholmroyd, Yorks, 1958–66. Post-doctoral Fellow, North Carolina State Univ., Raleigh, NC, USA, 1964–65; University of Reading: Prof. of Animal Production, 1966–81; Head of Dept of Agric., 1967–71; Dir, Univ. Farms, 1967–78; Dir, Centre for Agricl Strategy, 1975–81; Sec., NERC, 1981–89. Hon. DSc Cranfield, 1990. *Publications:* An Introduction to Animal Breeding, 1974; Animals for Man, 1977; (with P. Susmel) The Future of Beef Production in the European Community, 1979; (jtly) Hammond's Farm Animals, 1983. *Recreations:* golf, tennis, gardening. *Address:* Farm House, Sonning, Reading, Berks RG4 0TH.

BOWMAN, Maj-Gen. John Francis, CB 1986; Director of Army Legal Services, 1984–86; Member Council, British Red Cross Society, since 1988; *b* 5 Feb. 1927; *s* of Frank and Gladys Bowman; *m* 1956, Laura Moore; one *s* one *d*. *Educ:* Queen Elizabeth Grammar Sch., Penrith; Hertford Coll., Oxford (MA Hons). Called to the Bar, Gray's Inn, 1955. Served RN, 1945–48. Journalist and barrister, 1951–56; Directorate of Army Legal Services, 1956–86. Life Vice-Pres., Army Boxing Assoc., 1986. *Recreations:* sailing, mountain walking. *Address:* c/o Midland Bank, Sloane Square Branch, 145 Sloane Street, SW1X 9BN. *Club:* Royal Naval and Royal Albert Yacht.

BOWMAN, Sir John Paget, 4th Bt, *cr* 1884; *b* 12 Feb. 1904; *s* of Rev. Sir Paget Mervyn Bowman, 3rd Bt, and Rachel Katherine (*d* 1936), *d* of late James Hanning, Kilcrone, Co. Cork; *S* father 1955; *m* 1st, 1931, Countess Cajetana Hoyos (*d* 1948), *d* of Count Edgar Hoyos, Schloss Soos, Lower Austria; one *d* (one *s* decd); 2nd, 1948, Frances Edith Marian, *d* of Sir Beethom Whitehead, KCMG (*d* 1928), Efford Park, Lymington. *Educ:* Eton. Formerly 2nd Lieut 98th (Surrey and Sussex Yeomanry) Field Brigade RA. *Heir:* *cousin* Paul Humphrey Armytage Bowman [*b* 10 Aug. 1921; *m* 1st, 1943, Felicité Anne Araminta MacMichael (marr. diss.); 2nd, 1947, Gabrielle May Currie (marr. diss.); one *d*; 3rd, 1974, Elizabeth Deirdre Churchill]. *Address:* Bishops Green House, Newbury, Berks.

BOWMAN, Dr Sheridan Gail Esther, FSA; Keeper, Department of Scientific Research, British Museum, since 1989; *b* Westlock, Alta, Canada, 11 March 1950; *o d* of late Otto Michael Bowman and of Eva (*née* McKnight). *Educ:* Whitehaven County Grammar Sch., Cumbria; St Anne's Coll., Oxford (Open Scholar; MA; DPhil Physics, 1976); Chelsea Coll., London (MSc Maths, 1981); (extramural) London Univ. (Dip. in Archaeol., 1985). FSA 1986. Scientific Officer, BM, 1976. *Publications:* Radiocarbon Dating, 1990; (ed) Science and the Past, 1991; papers on scientific techniques, particularly dating, applied to archaeology. *Recreations:* heath and fell walking, gardening. *Address:* Department of Scientific Research, British Museum, WC1B 3DG. *T:* 071–323 8669.

BOWMAN, William Powell, OBE 1972; Chairman, Covent Garden Market Authority, since 1988; *b* 22 Oct. 1932; *s* of George Edward and Isabel Conyers Bowman; *m* 1956, Patricia Elizabeth McCoskrie; two *s*. *Educ:* Uppingham School. MInstM 1964. Nat. Service, RAF, 1951–53; RAuxAF, 1953–57. Sales Manager: Goodall Backhouse & Co. Ltd, 1953–59; Cheeseboro Ponds Ltd, 1959–61; Marketing Manager, Dorland Advertising Ltd, 1961–63; United Biscuits UK Ltd: Marketing Manager, 1963–66; Man. Dir, Internat. Div., 1966–77; Gp Personnel Dir, 1977–84; Dir, The Extel Group PLC and Chm., Royds Advertising Gp, 1984–86; Chm., Royds McCann Ltd, 1986–87. Chairman: Trident Trust, 1985–; Forum for Occupational Counselling and Unemployment Services Ltd, 1986–89; Van der Hass BV, 1987–89; Gibbson Blackthorn, 1989; Director: Harvey Bergenroth & Partners Ltd, 1987–89; Right Associates, 1989. Chairman: British Food Export Council, 1971–73; Cake and Biscuit Alliance, 1975–77; London Enterprise Agency, 1983–84; Industry and Parliament Trust, 1983–84; Flowers and Plants Assoc., 1989–; St Peters Res. Trust, 1990–; Dir, Nat. Assoc. of Fresh Produce, 1989–; Mem., Develt Trust, Zool Soc. of London, 1987–. Freeman: City of London, 1989; Fruiterers' Co., 1990; Mem., Guild of Freemen, 1989–. FIPM 1980; FBIM 1984; FInstD 1984; FZS 1986. *Recreations:* gardening, music. *Address:* The Coach House, Shardeloes, Old Amersham, Bucks HP7 0RL. *T:* Amersham (0494) 724187. *Clubs:* Royal Air Force, White Elephant.

BOWMAN-SHAW, Sir (George) Neville, Kt 1984; Chairman: Boss Trucks Ltd, since 1959; Lancer Boss Group Ltd, since 1966; Steinbock GmbH, since 1983; Boss France SA, since 1967; Lancer Boss Fördergeräte Vertriebsgesellschaft, mbH (Austria), since 1966; Lancer Boss Ireland Ltd, since 1966; Boss Trucks España SA, since 1987; *b* 4 Oct. 1930; *s* of George Bowman-Shaw and Hazel Bowman-Shaw (*née* Smyth); *m* 1962, Georgina Mary Blundell; three *s* one *d*. *Educ:* Caldicott Preparatory Sch.; then private tutor. Farming Trainee, 1947; Management Trainee in Engineering Co., 1948. Commissioned in 5th Royal Inniskilling Dragoon Guards, 1950. Sales Manager: Matling Ltd, Wolverhampton, 1953; Materials Handling Equipment (GB) Ltd, London, and Matbro Ltd, London, 1955. Member: Development Commn, 1970–77; Design Council, 1979–84; BOTB, 1982–85. President: Bedfordshire Rural Community Council; SW Beds and N Luton Conservative Assocs. Chm. of Governors, Hawtreys School. High Sheriff, Bedfordshire, 1987–88. *Recreations:* shooting, wildfowl collection. *Address:* Toddington Manor, Toddington, Bedfordshire. *T:* Toddington (05255) 2576. *Clubs:* Carlton, St Stephen's Constitutional, Cavalry and Guards.

BOWMAR, Sir (Charles) Erskine, Kt 1984; QSO 1977; JP; *b* 6 May 1913; *s* of Erskine Bowmar and Agnes Julia (*née* Fletcher); *m* 1938, Kathleen Muriel Isobel McLeod; two *s* four *d*. *Educ:* Gore Public Sch.; Gore High Sch.; Southland Tech Coll. Member: West Gore Sch. Cttee, 1952–; Bd of Governors, Gore High Sch., 1961–; Exec., NZ Counties Assoc. (former Vice-Pres.; PP, Otago and Southland Counties Assoc.); Nat. Roads Board; Chm., Southland County Council (Mem., 1953–); Chm., Southland United Council, 1979–; Mem., Gore Agricl and Pastoral Assoc., 1940, Life Mem., 1964. Mem., Southland Harbour, 1957–65; Vice-Pres., Southland Progress League; former Mem., NZ Territorial

Local Govt Council. JP 1964. *Recreations:* mountaineering (Mem., NZ Alpine Club, 1933), trout fishing, golf, gardening. *Address:* Waikaia Plains Station, N6 Rural Delivery, Gore, Southland, New Zealand. *T:* 101M Balfour.

BOWMONT AND CESSFORD, Marquis of; Charles Robert George Innes-Ker; *b* 18 Feb. 1981; *s* and *heir* of Duke of Roxburghe, *qv*.

BOWN, Jane Hope, (Mrs M. G. Moss), MBE 1985; Photographer for The Observer, since 1950; *b* 13 March 1925; *d* of Charles Wentworth Bell and Daisy Bown; *m* 1954, Martin Grenville Moss, *qv*; two *s* one *d*. *Educ:* William Gibbs Sch., Faversham. Chart corrector, WRNS, 1944–46; student photographer, Guildford School of Art, 1946–50. Hon. DLitt Bradford, 1986. *Publications:* The Gentle Eye: a book of photographs, 1980; Women of Consequence, 1986; Men of Consequence, 1987; The Singular Cat, 1988. *Recreations:* restoring old houses; chickens. *Address:* Parsonage Farm, Bentworth, near Alton, Hants. *T:* Alton (0420) 62175.

BOWN, Prof. Lalage Jean, OBE 1977; FRSE; Director, Department of Adult and Continuing Education, University of Glasgow, since 1981; *b* 1 April 1927; *d* of Arthur Mervyn Bown, MC and Dorothy Ethel (*née* Watson); two foster *d*. *Educ:* Wycombe Abbey Sch.; Cheltenham Ladies' Coll.; Somerville Coll., Oxford (MA); Oxford Post-grad. Internship in Adult Education. FRSE 1991. Resident Tutor: University Coll. of Gold Coast, 1949–55; Makerere University Coll., Uganda, 1955–59; Asst Dir, then Dep. Dir, Extramural Studies, Univ. of Ibadan, Nigeria, 1960–66; Dir, Extramural Studies and Prof. (*ad personam*), Univ., of Zambia, 1966–70; Prof. of Adult Educn, Ahmadu Bello Univ., Nigeria, 1971–76, Univ. of Lagos, Nigeria, 1977–79; Dean of Educn, Univ. of Lagos, 1979–80; Vis. Fellow, Inst. of Development Studies, 1980–81. Member: Bd, British Council, 1981–89; Scottish Community Educn Council, 1982–88; Exec. Cttee, Scottish Inst. of Adult and Continuing Educn, 1982–88; Bd, Network Scotland, 1983–88; Bd of Trustees, Nat. Museums of Scotland, 1987–; Council, Insite Trust, 1987–; Bd of Trustees, Womankind, 1988–; Interim Trustee, Books for Develt, 1987–90; British Mem., Commonwealth Standing Cttee on Student Mobility and Higher Educn Co-operation, 1989–. Governor, Inst. of Develt Studies, 1982–; President: Develt Studies Assoc., 1984–86; British Comparative and Internat. Educn Soc., 1985–86; Vice-President: WEA, 1989–91 (Hon. Vice-Pres., 1984–88); Commonwealth Assoc. for Educn and Trng of Adults, 1990–. Hon. Vice-Pres., Townswomen's Guilds, 1984–. Hon. Life Member: People's Educnl Assoc., Ghana, 1973; African Adult Educn Assoc., 1976. DUniv Open, 1975. William Pearson Tolley Medal, Syracuse Univ., USA, 1975; Meritorious Service Award, Nigerian Nat. Council for Adult Educn, 1979. *Publications:* (ed with Michael Crowder) Proceedings of First International Congress of Africanists, 1964; Two Centuries of African English, 1973; (ed) Adult Education in Nigeria: the next 10 years, 1975; A Rusty Person is Worse than Rusty Iron, 1976; Lifelong Learning: prescription for progress, 1979; (ed with S. H. O. Tomori) A Handbook of Adult Education for West Africa, 1980; (ed with J. T. Okedara) An Introduction to Adult Education: a multi-disciplinary and cross-cultural approach for developing countries, 1980; numerous articles in learned jls. *Recreations:* travel, reading, entertaining friends. *Address:* 37 Partickhill Road, Glasgow G11 5BP. *T:* (office) 041–339 8855. *Club:* Royal Over-Seas League.

BOWNESS, Sir Alan, Kt 1988; CBE 1976; Director of the Tate Gallery, 1980–88; Director, Henry Moore Foundation, since 1988 (Member, Committee of Management, 1984–88); *b* 11 Jan. 1928; *er s* of George Bowness and Kathleen (*née* Benton); *m* 1957, Sarah Hepworth-Nicholson, *d* of Ben Nicholson, OM, and Dame Barbara Hepworth, DBE; one *s* one *d*. *Educ:* University Coll. Sch.; Downing Coll., Cambridge (Hon. Fellow 1980); Courtauld Inst. of Art, Univ. of London (Hon. Fellow 1986). Worked with Friends' Ambulance Unit and Friends' Service Council, 1946–50; Reg. Art Officer, Arts Council of GB, 1955–57; Courtauld Inst., 1957–79, Dep. Dir, 1978–79; Reader, 1967–78, Prof. of Hist. of Art, 1978–79, Univ. of London. Vis. Prof., Humanities Seminar, Johns Hopkins Univ., Baltimore, 1969. Mem. Internat. Juries: Premio Di Tella, Buenos Aires, 1965; São Paulo Bienal, 1967; Venice Biennale, 1986; Lehmbruck Prize, Duisburg, 1970; Rembrandt Prize, 1979–. Arts Council: Mem., 1973–75 and 1978–80; Mem., Art Panel, 1960–80 (Vice-Chm., 1973–75, Chm., 1978–80); Mem., Arts Film Cttee, 1968–77 (Chm., 1972–75). Member: Fine Arts Cttee, Brit. Council, 1960–69 and 1970– (Chm., 1981–); Exec. Cttee, Contemp. Art Soc., 1961–69 and 1970–86; Cultural Adv. Cttee, UK National Commn for UNESCO, 1973–82. Governor, Chelsea Sch. of Art, 1965–; Hon. Sec., Assoc. of Art Historians, 1973–76; Dir, Barbara Hepworth Museum, St Ives, Cornwall, 1976–. Mem. Council, RCA, 1978– (Hon. Fellow 1984). Hon. Fellow, Bristol Polytechnic, 1980. Exhibitions arranged and catalogued include: 54:64 Painting and Sculpture of a Decade (with L. Gowing), 1964; Dubuffet, 1966; Sculpture in Battersea Park, 1966; Van Gogh, 1968; Rodin, 1970; William Scott, 1972; French Symbolist Painters (with G. Lacambre), 1972; Ceri Richards, 1975; Courbet (with M. Laclotte), 1977. Chevalier, l'Ordre des Arts et des Lettres, France, 1973. *Publications:* William Scott Paintings, 1964; Impressionists and Post Impressionists, 1965; (ed) Henry Moore: complete sculpture 1955–64 (vol. 3) 1965, 1964–73 (vol. 5) 1977, 1974–80 (vol. 4) 1983, 1949–54 (vol. 2) 1987; Modern Sculpture, 1965; Barbara Hepworth Drawings, 1966; Alan Davie, 1967; Recent British Painting, 1968; Gauguin, 1971; Barbara Hepworth: complete sculpture 1960–70, 1971; Modern European Art, 1972; Ivon Hitchens, 1973; (contrib.) Picasso 1881–1973, ed R. Penrose, 1973; (contrib.) The Genius of British Painting, ed D. Piper, 1975; articles in Burlington Magazine, TLS, Observer, and Annual Register. *Recreations:* listening to music; reading, especially poetry and 19th century fiction. *Address:* 91 Castelnau, SW13 9EL. *T:* 081–748 9696; 16 Piazza, St Ives, Cornwall. *T:* Penzance (0736) 795444. *Club:* Athenæum.

BOWNESS, Sir Peter (Spencer), Kt 1987; CBE 1981; DL; Partner, Weightman, Sadler (formerly Horsley, Weightman, Richardson and Sadler), Solicitors, Purley, since 1970; Leader of Croydon Council, since 1976; *b* 19 May 1943; *s* of Hubert Spencer Bowness and Doreen (Peggy) Bowness; *m* 1969, Marianne Hall (marr. diss.); one *d*; *m* 1984, Mrs Patricia Jane Cook. *Educ:* Whitgift Sch., Croydon. Admitted Solicitor, 1966. Elected (C) Croydon Council, 1968; Mayor of Croydon, 1979–80; Chm., London Boroughs Assoc., 1978–; Dep. Chm., Assoc. of Metropolitan Authorities, 1978–80. Member: Audit Commn, 1983–; London Residuary Body, 1985–; Nat. Training Task Force, 1989–. Hon. Col, 151 (Greater London) Transport Regt RCT (V), 1988–. DL Greater London, 1981; Freeman, City of London, 1984. *Recreations:* travel, theatre. *Address:* 1/2 The Exchange, Purley Road, Purley, Surrey CR2 2YY. *T:* 081–660 6455. *Club:* Carlton.

BOWRING, Edgar Rennie Harvey, MC 1945; Chairman, C. T. Bowring & Co. Ltd, 1973–78; Director, Marsh & McLennan Cos Inc., New York, 1980–88, Advisory Director, since 1988; *b* 5 Nov. 1915; *y s* of Arthur Bowring; *m* 1940, Margaret Grace (*née* Brook); two *s* one *d*. *Educ:* Eastbourne Coll.; Clare Coll., Cambridge (MA); Berkeley Coll., Yale, USA (Mellon Fellow). War of 1939–45: commissioned Kent Yeomanry, RA, 1939; served in Iceland, France and Germany (despatches, 1944); demobilised, 1946. Solicitor, 1949; Partner in Cripps Harries Hall & Co., 1950–55. Member of Lloyd's, 1962. Joined C. T. Bowring & Co. (Insurance) Ltd, 1956 (Dir, 1960); Dep. Chm., 1966, Chief Exec., 1970, Chm., 1973–77, C. T. Bowring (Insurance) Holdings Ltd. Chairman: English & American Insurance Co. Ltd, 1965–71; Crusader Insurance Co. Ltd, 1973–77; Bowmaker Ltd, 1973–77. Pres., Insurance Inst. of London, 1971–72 (Dep. Pres., 1970–71); Vice-Pres., Corporation of Insurance Brokers, 1970–77; Mem., Insurance Brokers Registration Council, 1979–81. Chm., City Cttee for Electoral Reform, 1978–82. Comdt, West Kent Special Constab., 1965–71. Trustee, Meml Univ. of Newfoundland Harlow Campus, 1979–. CBIM. *Recreations:* gardening, golf. *Address:* Leopards Mill, Horam, Sussex. *T:* Horam Road (04353) 2687. *Clubs:* City University; Rye Golf; Piltdown Golf.

BOWRING, Maj.-Gen. John Humphrey Stephen, CB 1968; OBE 1958; MC 1941; FICE; *b* 13 Feb. 1913; *s* of late Major Francis Stephen Bowring and late Mrs Maurice Stonor; *m* 1956, Iona Margaret (*née* Murray); two *s* two *d*. *Educ:* Downside; RMA Woolwich; Trinity Coll., Cambridge. MA 1936. Commissioned, 1933; Palestine, 1936; India, 1937–40; Middle East, 1940–42; India and Burma, 1942–46; British Military Mission to Greece, 1947–50; UK, 1951–55; CRE, 17 Gurkha Div., Malaya, 1955–58; Col GS, War Office, 1958–61; Brig., Chief Engineer, Far East, 1961–64; Brig. GS, Ministry of Defence, 1964–65; Engineer-in-Chief, 1965–68. Col, The Gurkha Engineers, 1966–71; Col Comdt, RE, 1968–73. Dir, Consolidated Gold Fields, 1969–82. High Sheriff, Wiltshire, 1984. Kt SMO Malta, 1986. *Address:* The Manor, Coln St Aldwyns, Cirencester, Glos GL7 5AG. *T:* Coln St Aldwyns (028575) 492. *Clubs:* Army and Navy, Royal Ocean Racing.

BOWRING, Air Vice-Marshal John Ivan Roy, CB 1977; CBE 1971; CEng, FRAeS; FBIM; management consultant, aircraft maintenance; Head of Technical Training and Maintenance, British Aerospace (formerly British Aircraft Corporation), Riyadh, Saudi Arabia, 1978–88, retired; *b* 28 March 1923; *s* of Hugh Passmore Bowring and Ethel Grace Bowring; *m* 1945, Irene Mary Rance; two *d*. *Educ:* Great Yarmouth Grammar Sch., Norfolk; Aircraft Apprentice, RAF Halton-Cosford, 1938–40; Leicester Tech. Coll.; commissioned, RAF, 1944; NW Europe, 1944–47; RAF, Horsham St Faith's, Engrg duties, 1947–48; RAF South Cerney, Pilot trng, 1949; Engr Officer: RAF Finningly, 1950–51; RAF Kai-Tak, 1951–53; Staff Officer, AHQ Hong Kong, ADC to Governor, Hong Kong, 1953–54; Sen. Engr Officer, RAF Coltishall, 1954–56; exchange duties with US Air Force, Research and Develt, Wright Patterson Air Force Base, Ohio, 1956–60; RAF Staff Coll., Bracknell, 1960; Air Min. Opl Requirements, 1961–64; OC Engrg Wing, RAF St Mawgan, 1964–67; Head of F111 Procurement Team, USA, 1967–68; OC RAF Aldergrove, NI, 1968–70; RCDS, 1971; Dir of Engrg Policy, MoD, 1972–73; AO Engrg, RAF Germany, 1973–74; SASO, RAF Support Comd, 1974–77; AO Maintenance, 1977. FBIM. *Recreations:* sailing, golf. *Club:* Royal Air Force.

BOWRING, Peter; Chairman, C. T. Bowring & Co. Ltd, 1978–82; Director, Marsh & McLennan Cos Inc., New York, 1980–85 (Vice-Chairman, 1982–84); *b* 22 April 1923; *e s* of Frederick Clive Bowring and Agnes Walker (*née* Cairns); *m* 1946, Barbara Ekaterina Brewis (marr. diss.); one *s* one *d*; *m* 1986, Mrs Carole Dear. *Educ:* Shrewsbury Sch. Served War, 1939–45: commnd Rifle Bde, 1942; served in Egypt, N Africa, Italy, Austria (mentioned in despatches, 1945); demobilised 1946. Joined Bowring Group of Cos, 1947: Dir, C. T. Bowring & Co. Ltd, 1956–84, Dep. Chm. 1973–78; Chairman: C. T. Bowring Trading (Holdings) Ltd, 1967–84; Bowmaker (Plant) Ltd, 1972–83; Bowring Steamship Co. Ltd, 1974–82; Bowmaker Ltd, 1978–82; C. T. Bowring (UK) Ltd, 1980–84. Director: City Arts Trust Ltd, 1984– (Chm., 1987–); Independent Primary and Secondary Educn Trust, 1986–. Mem. of Lloyd's, 1968–. Chm., Help the Aged Ltd, 1977–87, Pres., 1988–. Dir, Centre for Policy Studies, 1983–88. Chm., Aldeburgh Foundn, 1982–89. Chairman: Inter-Action Social Enterprise Trust, 1989–91; Bd of Governors, St Dunstan's Educnl Foundn, 1977–91; Mem. Bd of Governors, Shrewsbury Sch. Trustee: Ironbridge Gorge Mus. Develt Trust, 1989–; Upper Severn Navigation Trust, 1989–; Zoological Soc. Develt Trust. Member: Guild of Freemen of City of London; Worshipful Co. of Insurers; Guild of World Traders (Master, 1989–90). FRSA. *Recreations:* sailing, motoring, listening to music, photography, cooking. *Address:* Flat 79, New Concordia Wharf, Mill Street, SE1 2BA. *T:* 071-237 0818. *Clubs:* Royal Thames Yacht; Royal Green Jackets.

BOWRING, Prof. Richard John; Professor of Modern Japanese Studies, and Fellow of Downing College, University of Cambridge, since 1985; *b* 6 Feb. 1947; *s* of late Richard Arthur Bowring and of Mabel Bowring (*née* Eddy); *m* 1970, Susan (*née* Povey); one *d*. *Educ:* Blundell's Sch.; Downing Coll., Cambridge (PhD 1973). Lectr in Japanese, Monash Univ., 1973–75; Asst Prof. of Japanese, Columbia Univ., NY, 1978–79; Associate Prof. of Japanese, Princeton Univ., NJ, 1979–84; Cambridge University: Lectr in Japanese, 1984; Chm, Faculty Bd of Oriental Studies, 1987–89. Trustee, Cambridge Foundn, 1989–. *Publications:* Mori Ogai and the Modernization of Japanese Culture, 1979; trans., Murasaki Shikibu: her diary and poetic memoirs, 1982; Murasaki Shikibu: The Tale of Genji, 1988. *Address:* Downing College, Cambridge CB2 1DQ.

BOWRON, John Lewis, CBE 1986; solicitor; Legal Assessor to Insurance Brokers Registration Council Disciplinary Committee, since 1987; Secretary-General, The Law Society, 1974–87; *b* 1 Feb. 1924; *e s* of John Henry and Lavinia Bowron; *m* 1950, Patricia, *d* of Arthur Cobby; two *d*. *Educ:* Grangefield Grammar Sch., Stockton-on-Tees; King's Coll., London (LLB, FKC 1976). Principal in Malcolm Wilson & Cobby, Solicitors, Worthing, 1952–74. Member of the Council of the Law Society, 1969–74. Mem., Disciplinary Appeals Cttee, Stock Exchange, 1987–; Chm. (part-time), Social Security Appeal Tribunals, 1988–. *Recreations:* golf, music. *Address:* Wellington Cottage, Albourne, Hassocks, W Sussex. *T:* Hurstpierpoint (0273) 833345.

BOWSER of Argaty and the King's Lundies, David Stewart, JP; a Forestry Commissioner, 1974–82; landowner since 1947; *b* 11 March 1926; *s* of late David Charles Bowser, CBE and Maysie Murray Bowser (*née* Henderson); *m* 1951, Judith Crabbe; one *s* four *d*. *Educ:* Harrow; Trinity Coll., Cambridge (BA Agric). Captain, Scots Guards, 1944–47. Member: Nat. Bd of Timber Growers Scotland Ltd (formerly Scottish Woodland Owners' Assoc.), 1960–82 (Chm. 1972–74); Regional Adv. Cttee, West Scotland Conservancy, Forestry Commn, 1964–74 (Chm. 1970–74). Chm., Scottish Council, British Deer Soc., 1989–; Mem., Blackface Sheep Breeders' Assoc. (Vice-Pres., 1981–83; Pres., 1983–84); Pres., Highland Cattle Soc., 1970–72. Trustee, Scottish Forestry Trust, 1983–89. Mem. Perth CC, 1954–61; JP Co. Perth, 1956. *Recreations:* shooting, fishing, stalking. *Address:* Auchlyne, Killin, Perthshire FK21 8RG.

BOWSHER, Peter Charles, QC 1978; FCIArb; **His Honour Judge Bowsher;** an Official Referee and Circuit Judge, since 1987; *b* 9 Feb. 1935; *s* of Charles and Ellen Bowsher; *m* 1960, Deborah, *d* of Frederick Wilkins and Isobel Wilkins (*née* Copp), Vancouver; two *s*. *Educ:* Ardingly; Oriel Coll., Oxford (MA). FCIArb 1990. Commnd Royal Artillery, 1954; Territorial Army XX Rifle Team, 1957. Called to the Bar, Middle Temple, 1959, Bencher, 1985. A Recorder, 1983–87. Harmsworth Scholar; Blackstone Entrance Scholar. A Legal Assessor to GMC and GDC, 1979–87. Indep. Review Body, Modified Colliery Review Procedure, 1986–87; Adjudicator, Crown Prosecution Service (Transfer of Staff) Regulations, 1985, 1986–87. Mem. Council, Soc. for Computers and Law, 1990–. *Recreations:* photography, music. *Address:* Royal Courts of Justice, Strand, WC2A 2LL. *Clubs:* Brooks's, Royal Automobile.

BOWTELL, Ann Elizabeth, CB 1989; Principal Establishment and Finance Officer, Department of Health, since 1990 (on secondment); *b* 25 April 1938; *d* of John Albert and Olive Rose Kewell; *m* 1961, Michael John Bowtell; two *s* two *d*. *Educ:* Kendrick Girls' Sch., Reading; Girton Coll., Cambridge (BA). Asst Principal, Nat. Assistance Board, 1960; Principal: Nat. Assistance Board, 1964; Min. of Social Security, 1966; DHSS, 1968; Asst Sec., 1973, Under Sec., 1980, DHSS; Dep. Sec., DHSS, later Dept of Social Security, 1986. *Recreations:* children, cooking, walking. *Address:* Department of Health, 79 Whitehall, SW1.

BOWYER, family name of **Baron Denham.**

BOWYER, Gordon Arthur, OBE 1970; RIBA; FCSD; Partner, Bowyer Langlands Batchelor, Chartered Architects, since 1948; *b* 21 March 1923; *s* of Arthur Bowyer and Kathleen Mary Bowyer; *m* 1950, Ursula Meyer; one *s* one *d*. *Educ:* Dauntsey's Sch.; Polytechnic of Central London. Architect and designer in private practice, in partnership with Ursula Bowyer, Iain Langlands and Stephen Batchelor, 1948–. Practice started with design of Sports Section, South Bank Exhibn, Fest. of Britain, 1951; schs and hostel for handicapped children in Peckham, Bermondsey and Dulwich, 1966–75; housing for Southwark, GLC, Family Housing Assoc., London & Quadrant Housing Assoc. and Greenwich Housing Soc., 1969–83; numerous office conversions for IBM (UK), 1969–89; Peckham Methodist Church, 1975; new offices and shops for Rank City Wall at Brighton, 1975 and Folkestone, 1976; Treasury at Gloucester Cathedral, 1976; conservation at Vanbrugh Castle, Greenwich, 1973, Charlton Assembly Rooms, 1980, Hill Hall, Essex, 1982; lecture theatre, library and accommodation, Jt Services Defence Coll., RNC, Greenwich, 1983; Cabinet War Rooms Museum, Whitehall (with Alan Irvine), 1984; refurbishment of Barry Rooms at Nat. Gall., Stuart & Georgian Galls at Nat. Portrait Gall. and East Hall of Science Museum; new Prints & Drawings and Japanese Gall. at BM. At present working on gall. plan for Science Museum and Jane Austen Study Centre. Hon. Sec., SIAD, 1957–58. Dir, NMM Enterprises Ltd, 1985–. Mem. Council, Friends of the Nat. Maritime Mus., 1985–; Trustee, Nat. Maritime Museum, 1977–. *Address:* 111 Maze Hill, SE10 8XQ. *T:* (office) 071–836 1452. *Club:* Arts.

BOWYER, William, RA 1981 (ARA 1974); RP, RBA, RWS; Head of Fine Art, Maidstone College of Art, 1971–82; *b* 25 May 1926; *m* 1951, Vera Mary Small; two *s* one *d*. *Educ:* Burslem School of Art; Royal College of Art (ARCA). Hon. Sec., New English Art Club. *Recreations:* cricket (Chiswick and Old Meadonians Cricket Clubs), snooker. *Address:* 12 Cleveland Avenue, Chiswick, W4 1SN. *T:* 081–994 0346. *Club:* Dover Street Arts.

BOWYER-SMYTH, Sir T. W.; *see* Smyth.

BOX, Betty Evelyn, (Mrs P. E. Rogers), OBE 1958; Film Producer; *b* 25 Sept.; *m* 1949, Peter Edward Rogers; no *c*. *Educ:* home. Director: Welbeck Film Distributors Ltd, 1958–; Ulster Television, 1955–85. *Films include:* Dear Murderer; When the Bough Breaks; Miranda; Blind Goddess; Huggett Family series; It's Not Cricket; Marry Me; Don't Ever Leave Me; So Long at the Fair; Appointment with Venus; Venetian Bird; A Day to Remember; The Clouded Yellow; Doctor in the House; Mad About Men; Doctor at Sea; The Iron Petticoat; Checkpoint; Doctor at Large; Campbell's Kingdom; A Tale of Two Cities; The Wind Cannot Read; The 39 Steps; Upstairs and Downstairs; Conspiracy of Hearts; Doctor in Love; No Love for Johnnie; No, My Darling Daughter; A Pair of Briefs; The Wild and the Willing; Doctor in Distress; Hot Enough for June; The High Bright Sun; Doctor in Clover; Deadlier than the Male; Nobody Runs Forever; Some Girls Do; Doctor in Trouble; Percy; The Love Ban; Percy's Progress. *Address:* Pinewood Studios, Iver, Bucks.

BOX, Donald Stewart; Member, The Stock Exchange, since 1945; Senior Partner, Lyddon, Stockbrokers, 1978–86 (Partner, 1966–86); *b* 22 Nov. 1917; *s* of late Stanley Carter Box and Elizabeth Mary Stewart Box; *m* 1st, 1940, Margaret Kennington Bates (marr. diss. 1947); 2nd, 1948, Peggy Farr, *née* Gooding (marr. diss. 1973); 3rd, 1973, Margaret Rose Davies; one *d*. *Educ:* Llandaff Cathedral Sch.; St John's Sch., Pinner; County Sch., Harrow. RAF ranks, 1939, commissioned, 1941; overseas service Egypt, Palestine, Transjordan, 1941–44; demobbed with rank of Flt-Lieut, 1945. Partner, Henry J. Thomas & Co., stockbrokers, 1945–66. MP (C) Cardiff North, 1959–66. Non-exec. dir, N. M. Rothschild & Sons (Wales) Ltd, 1988–. *Recreations:* indifferent tennis, studying race form, doodling and doggerel. *Address:* Laburnum Cottage, Sully Road, Penarth, S Glam CF6 2TX. *T:* Penarth (0222) 707966; (office) 14 Douglas Buildings, Royal Stuart Lane, Cardiff CF1 6EL. *T:* Cardiff (0222) 494822. *Club:* Cardiff and County (Cardiff).

BOX, Prof. George Edward Pelham, BEM 1946; FRS 1985; Professor of Statistics, since 1960, and Vilas Research Professor, Department of Statistics, since 1980, University of Wisconsin-Madison; *b* 18 Oct. 1919; *s* of Harry and Helen (Martin) Box; *m* 1st, 1945, Jessie Ward; 2nd, 1959, Joan G. Fisher; one *s* one *d*; 3rd, 1985, Claire Louise Quist. *Educ:* London University (BSc Maths and Statistics 1947, PhD 1952, DSc 1961). Served War of 1939–45 in Army; res. at Chemical Defence Exptl Station, Porton. Statistician and Head Statn, Statistical Res. Section, ICI, Blackley, 1948–56; Dir, Stats Tech. Res. Group, Princeton Univ., 1956–60. Res. Prof., Univ. of N Carolina, 1952–53; Ford Foundn Vis. Prof., Harvard Business Sch., 1965–66; Vis. Prof., Univ. of Essex, 1970–71. President: Amer. Statistical Assoc., 1978; Inst. of Mathematical Statistics, 1979. Trustee, Biometrika Trust, 1985–. Fellow, Amer. Acad. of Arts and Scis, 1974; FAAAS, 1974. Hon. DSc: Univ. of Rochester, NY, 1975; Carnegie Mellon Univ., 1989. Numerous medals and awards. *Publications:* Statistical Methods in Research and Production, 1957; Design and Analysis of Industrial Experiments, 1959; Evolutionary Operation: a statistical method for process improvement, 1969; Time Series Analysis Forecasting and Control, 1970; Bayesian Inference in Statistical Analysis, 1973; Statistics for Experimenters, 1977; Empirical Model Building and Response Surfaces, 1986. *Address:* Department of Statistics, University of Wisconsin-Madison, 1210 West Dayton Street, Madison, Wis 53706, USA. *T:* (608) 263–2520.

BOXALL, Bernard, CBE 1963; Deputy Chairman, Lancer Boss Group Ltd; *b* 17 Aug. 1906; *s* of late Arthur Boxall and of Mrs Maud Mary Boxall (*née* Mills); *m* 1931, Marjorie Lilian, *d* of late William George Emery and Mrs Emery; one *s* one *d*. *Educ:* King's Coll. Sch., Wimbledon; Imperial Coll., London Univ. (BSc (Hons), FCGI), Fellow 1971. James Howden & Co. Ltd, 1928–33; J. A. King & Co. Ltd, 1934–42; Production-Engineering Ltd, 1942–59; Management Consultant, 1959–. Chm., British United Trawlers Ltd, 1969–71. Dir, Lindustries Ltd, and Chm. of its engineering cos, 1960–71. Member: Highland Trnspt Bd, 1963–66; IRC, 1966–71; Scottish Economic Planning Council, 1967–71; Monopolies Commn, 1969–74. Mem., Company of Coachmakers and Coach Harness Makers (Master, 1977–78). FIMechE, FIProdE. *Recreation:* golf. *T:* Cranleigh (0483) 274340. *Club:* Walton Heath Golf.

BOXALL, Mrs Lewis; *see* Buss, Barbara Ann.

BOXER, Air Vice-Marshal Sir Alan (Hunter Cachemaille), KCVO 1970; CB 1968; DSO 1944; DFC 1943; *b* 1 Dec. 1916; *s* of late Dr E. A. Boxer, CMG, Hastings, Hawkes Bay, NZ; *m* 1941, Pamela Sword; two *s* one *d*. *Educ:* Nelson Coll., New Zealand. Commissioned in RAF, 1939; Trng Comd until 1942; flying and staff appts, Bomber Comd, 1942–45. RAF Staff Coll., 1945; Jt Staff, Cabinet Offices, 1946–47; Staff Coll., Camberley, 1948; Strategic Air Comd, USAF and Korea, 1949–51; Central Fighter Estabt, 1952–53; Mem. Directing Staff, RAF Staff Coll., 1954–56; CO No 7 Sqdn, RAF, 1957; Group Capt. and CO, RAF Wittering, 1958–59; Plans, HQ Bomber Comd, 1960–61; Air Cdre, idc, 1962; SASO: HQ No 1 Gp, RAF, 1963–65; HQ Bomber Comd, 1965–67; Defence Services Sec., MoD, 1967–70. Virtuti Militari (Polish), Bronze Star (US), Air Medal (US).

BOXER, Charles Ian; writer; *b* 11 Feb. 1926; *s* of Rev. William Neville Gordon Boxer and Margaret Boxer; *m* 1968, Hilary Fabienne Boxer. *Educ:* Glasgow High Sch.; Edinburgh Univ. (BL). Church of England ministry, 1950–54; apprentice to solicitors, 1954–58; Mem., Dominican Order (RC), 1958–67; Sen. Community Relations Officer for Wandsworth, 1967–77; Dir, Community Affairs and Liaison Div., Commn for Racial Equality, 1977–81. Communicator of the Year, BAIE Awards, 1976. *Recreation:* music. *Address:* Parish Farmhouse, Hassell Street, Hastingleigh, near Ashford, Kent TN25 5JE. *T:* Elmsted (023375) 219.

BOXER, Prof. Charles Ralph, FBA 1957; Emeritus Professor of Portuguese, University of London, since 1968; Fellow, King's Coll., 1967; *b* 8 March 1904; *s* of Col Hugh Boxer and Jane Boxer (*née* Patterson); *m* 1945, Emily Hahn; two *d*. *Educ:* Wellington Coll.; Royal Military Coll., Sandhurst. Commissioned Lincs Regt, 1923. Served War of 1939–45 (wounded, POW in Japanese hands, 1941–45). Retired with rank of Major, 1947. Camoens Prof. of Portuguese, London Univ., 1947–51; Prof. of the History of the Far East, London Univ., 1951–53; resigned latter post and re-apptd Camoens Prof., 1953–67; Prof. of History of Expansion of Europe Overseas, Yale, 1969–72. Visiting Research Prof., Indiana Univ., 1967–79; Emeritus Prof. of History, Yale, 1972–. Hon. Fellow, SOAS, 1974. A Trustee of National Maritime Museum, 1961–68. For. Mem., Royal Netherlands Acad. of Scis, 1976. Dr *hc* Universities of Utrecht (1950), Lisbon (1952), Bahia (1959), Liverpool (1966), Hong Kong (1971), Peradeniya (1980). Gold Medal, Institute Historico e Geografico Brasileiro, 1986. Order of Santiago da Espada (Portugal); Grand Cross of the Order of the Infante Dom Henrique (Portugal); Kt Order of St Gregory the Great, 1969. *Publications:* The Commentaries of Ruy Freyre de Andrade, 1929; The Journal of M. H. Tromp, *Anno* 1639, 1930; Jan Compagnie in Japan, 1600–1817, 1936 (2nd edn 1950); Fidalgos in the Far East, 1550–1770, 1948; The Christian Century in Japan, 1549–1640, 1951, 2nd edn 1967; Salvador de Sá and the Struggle for Brazil and Angola, 1952; South China in the 16th Century, 1953; The Dutch in Brazil, 1624–1654, 1957; The Tragic History of the Sea, 1589–1622, 1959; The Great Ship from Amacon, 1959; Fort Jesus and the Portuguese in Mombasa, 1960; The Golden Age of Brazil, 1695–1750, 1962; Race Relations in the Portuguese Colonial Empire, 1415–1825, 1963; The Dutch Seaborne Empire, 1600–1800, 1965; Portuguese Society in the Tropics, 1966; Further Selections from the Tragic History of the Sea, 1969; The Portuguese Seaborne Empire, 1415–1825, 1969; Anglo-Dutch Wars of the 17th Century, 1974; Mary and Misogyny, 1975; João de Barros: Portuguese humanist and historian of Asia, 1981; From Lisbon to Goa 1500–1750, 1984; Portuguese Conquest and Commerce in Southern Asia 1500–1750, 1985; Portuguese Merchants and Missionaries in Feudal Japan 1543–1640, 1986; Dutch Merchants and Mariners in Asia 1602–1795, 1988; numerous articles in learned periodicals. *Address:* Ringshall End, Little Gaddesden, Herts HP4 1NF. *Clubs:* Athenæum; Yale (New York).

BOXER, Air Cdre Henry Everard Crichton, CB 1965; OBE 1948; idc, ndc, psc; *b* 28 July 1914; *s* of late Rear-Adm. Henry P. Boxer; *m* 1938, Enid Anne Louise, *d* of late Dr John Moore Collyns; two *s* two *d*. *Educ:* Shrewsbury Sch.; RAF Coll., Cranwell. Commissioned RAF, 1935; No 1 Fighter Squadron, 1935–37; No 1 Flying Training Sch., 1937–39; Specialist Navigator, 1939. Served War of 1939–45, in UK, S Africa and Europe. BJSM, Washington, DC, 1945–48; directing Staff, RAF Staff Coll., 1949–50; Coastal Command, 1951–52; Nat. Defence Coll., Canada, 1952–53; Air Ministry, 1953–56; OC, RAF Thorney Island, 1956–58. ADC to the Queen, 1957–59; IDC, 1959; Sen. Air Liaison Officer and Air Adviser to British High Comr in Canada, 1960–62; AO i/c Admin, HQ Coastal Comd, 1962–65; Dir of Personnel (Air), MoD (RAF), 1965–67; retd, 1967. Counsellor (Defence Equipment), British High Commn, Ottawa, 1967–74; retd, 1975. *Address:* 42 Courtenay Place, Lymington, Hants SO41 9NQ. *T:* Lymington (0590) 672584. *Club:* Royal Air Force.

BOYCE, Graham Hugh, CMG 1991; HM Diplomatic Service; Ambassador and Consul-General, Doha, since 1990; *b* 6 Oct. 1945; *s* of Hugh Boyce and Madeleine Boyce (*née* Manley); *m* 1970, Janet Elizabeth Spencer; one *s* three *d*. *Educ:* Hurstpierpoint Coll.; Jesus Coll., Cambridge (MA). VSO, Antigua, 1967; HM Diplomatic Service, 1968; Ottawa, 1971; MECAS, 1972–74; 1st Sec., Tripoli, Libya, 1974–77; FCO, 1977–81; Kuwait, 1981–85; Asst Hd of ME Dept, FCO, 1985–86; Counsellor and Consul-Gen., Stockholm, 1987–90. *Recreations:* tennis, squash, reading. *Address:* c/o Foreign and Commonwealth Office, King Charles Street, SW1A 2AH.

BOYCE, Joseph Frederick, JP; FRICS; General Manager, Telford Development Corporation, 1980–86; *b* 10 Aug. 1926; *s* of Frederick Arthur and Rosalie Mary Boyce; *m* 1953, Nina Margaret, *o d* of A. F. Tebb, Leeds; two *s*. *Educ:* Roundhay Sch., Leeds; Leeds Coll. of Technology. Pupil and Asst Quantity Surveyor, Rex Procter & Miller, Chartered Quantity Surveyors, 1942–53; Sen. Quantity Surveyor, Bedford Corp., 1953–55; Group Quantity Surveyor, Somerset CC, 1955–60; Principal Asst Quantity Surveyor, Salop CC, 1960–64; Telford Development Corporation: Chief Quantity Surveyor, 1964–71; Technical Dir, 1971–76; Dep. Gen. Manager, 1976–80. JP Shrewsbury, 1975. *Publications:* technical articles and publications on new towns, in learned journals. *Recreations:* reading, travel, hill walking, France. *Address:* The Uplands, 5 Port Hill Gardens, Shrewsbury, Shropshire SY3 8SH.

BOYCE, Rear-Adm. Michael Cecil, OBE 1982; Flag Officer Sea Training, since 1991; *b* 2 April 1943; *s* of Comdr Hugh Boyce, DSC, RN and Madeleine Boyce (*née* Manley); *m* 1971, Harriette Gail, *d* of late Surg. Capt. (D) Kenneth Fletcher, RN and Georgina Fletcher; one *s* one *d*. *Educ:* Hurstpierpoint Coll.; BRNC, Dartmouth. Joined RN, 1961; qualified Submarines, 1965 and TAS, 1970; served in HM Submarines Anchorite, Valiant, and Conqueror, 1965–72; commanded: HM Submarines: Oberon, 1973–74; Opossum, 1974–75; Superb, 1979–81; HMS Brilliant, 1983–84; Captain (SM), Submarine Sea Training, 1984–86; RCDS, 1988; Sen. Naval Officer, ME, 1989; Dir Naval Staff Duties, 1989–91. *Recreations:* squash, tennis, photography. *Address:* c/o Naval Secretary, Old Admiralty Building, Spring Gardens, SW1A 2BE.

See also G. H. Boyce.

BOYCE, Michael David; Chief Executive, South Glamorgan County Council, and Clerk to the Lieutenancy, since 1987; *b* 27 May 1937; *s* of Clifford and Vera Boyce; *m* 1962, Audrey May Gregory; one *s* one *d*. *Educ:* Queen Elizabeth's Sch., Crediton. DMA 1962; Dip. in French, UC Cardiff, 1984. Admitted Solicitor, 1968. Asst Solicitor, 1968–69, Sen. Asst Solicitor, and Asst Clerk of the Peace, 1969–71, Exeter CC; Dep. Town Clerk, 1971–73, Dep. Chief Exec., 1973–74, Newport, Gwent; County Solicitor, S Glam, 1974–87. Sec., Lord Chancellor's Adv. Cttee, 1987–. *Recreations:* France and French,

Association Football, badminton, music, railways, travel. *Address:* 1 White Oaks Drive, St Mellons, Cardiff CF3 9EX. *T:* Cardiff (0222) 791927.

BOYCE, Peter John, PhD; Vice-Chancellor, Murdoch University, Western Australia, since 1985; *b* 20 Feb. 1935; *s* of Oswald and Marjorie Boyce; *m* 1962, Lorinne Peet; one *s* two *d. Educ:* Wesley Coll., Perth, WA; Univ. of Western Australia (MA); Duke Univ., USA (PhD). Res. Fellow, then Fellow, Dept of Internat. Relns, ANU, 1964–66; Nuffield Fellow, St Antony's Coll., Oxford, 1966–67; Sen. Lectr, then Reader, in Political Science, Tasmania Univ., 1967–75; Prof. of Pol. Science and Hd, Dept of Govt, Queensland Univ., 1976–79; Prof. of Politics and Hd of Dept, Univ. of W Australia, 1980–84. Vis. Fellow, Corpus Christi Coll., Cambridge, 1989. Exec. Mem., Aust.-NZ Foundn, 1979–83; Member: Aust. Human Rights Commn, 1981–86; Consultative Cttee on Relns with Japan, 1983–85. Lay Canon of St George's Cath., Perth. Editor, Australian Outlook, 1973–77. *Publications:* Malaysia and Singapore in International Diplomacy, 1968; Foreign Affairs for New States, 1977; (co-ord. ed.) Dictionary of Australian Politics, 1980; (co-ord. ed.) Politics in Queensland, 1980; (co-ord. ed.) The Torres Strait Treaty, 1981; (ed) Independence and Alliance, 1983; Diplomacy in the Market Place, 1991. *Recreations:* gardening, walking, church music. *Address:* 38 Clanmel Road, Floreat Park, WA 6014, Australia. *T:* 387 1992.

BOYCE, Sir Robert (Charles) Leslie, 3rd Bt *cr* 1952; *b* 2 May 1962; *s* of Sir Richard (Leslie) Boyce, 2nd Bt, and of Jacqueline Anne (who *m* 2nd, 1974, Christopher Boyce-Dennis), *o d* of Roland A. Hill; *S* father, 1968; *m* 1985, Fiona, second *d* of John Savage, Whitmore Park, Coventry. *Educ:* Cheltenham Coll; Salford Univ. (BSc 1984, 1st cl. hons). Medical student, Queen's Med. Centre, Nottingham. *Heir: uncle* John Leslie Boyce [*b* 16 Nov. 1934; *m* 1st, 1957, Finola Mary (marr. diss. 1975). *d* of late James Patrick Maxwell; one *s* three *d*; 2nd, 1980, Fusako, *d* of Yoneseku Ishibashi; two *d*].

BOYCE, Walter Edwin, OBE 1970; Director of Social Services, Essex County Council, 1970–78; *b* 30 July 1918; *s* of Rev. Joseph Edwin Boyce and Alice Elizabeth Boyce; *m* 1942, Edna Lane (*née* Gargett); two *d. Educ:* High Sch. for Boys, Trowbridge, Wilts. Admin. Officer, Warwickshire CC, 1938–49. Served war, commnd RA; Gunnery sc, 1943; demob. rank Major, 1946. Dep. County Welfare Officer: Shropshire, 1949–52; Cheshire, 1952–57; Co. Welfare Officer, Essex, 1957–70. Adviser to Assoc. of County Councils, 1965–78; Mem., Sec. of State's Adv. Personal Social Services Council, 1973 until disbanded, 1980 (Chm., People with handicaps Gp); Mem., nat. working parties on: Health Service collaboration, 1972–74; residential accommodation for elderly and mentally handicapped, 1974–78; boarding houses, 1981. Pres., County Welfare Officers Soc., 1967–68. Governor, Queen Elizabeth's Foundn for the Disabled, 1980–. *Recreations:* sailing, golf, in sports, particularly Rugby and athletics, voluntary services, travel. *Address:* Highlanders Barn, Newmans Green, Long Melford, Suffolk CO10 0AD.

BOYCOTT, Prof. Brian Blundell, FRS 1971; Director, Medical Research Council Cell Biophysics Unit, 1980–89; Senior Research Fellow, Anatomy Department, Guy's Hospital, since 1990; Emeritus Professor of Biology, London University, 1990; *b* 10 Dec. 1924; *s* of Percy Blundell Boycott and Doris Eyton Lewis; *m* 1950, Marjorie Mabel Burchell; one *s* (and one *s* decd). *Educ:* Royal Masonic Sch. Technician, Nat. Inst. Medical Research, and undergraduate (BSc), Birkbeck Coll., London, 1942–46; University Coll., London: Asst Lectr, Zoology, 1946–47; Hon. Res. Asst, Anatomy, 1947–52; Lectr, Zoology, 1952–62; Reader in Zoology, Univ. of London, 1962, Prof. of Zoology, 1968–70, Prof. of Biology by title, 1971–89. Vis. Lectr, Harvard Univ., 1963. Dep. Chm., Neuroscis and Mental Health Bd, MRC, 1989–91. Member: Adv. Council, British Library Board, 1976–80; Council, 1975–87, Acad. Consultative Cttee, 1989–, Open Univ.; Council, Royal Soc., 1976–78; Univ. of London Cttee on Academic Organization, 1980–82; Comr, 1851 Exhibition, 1974–84. FKC 1990. DUniv Open, 1988. Scientific medal, Zoological Soc. London, 1965. *Publications:* various articles in learned jls on structure and function of nervous systems. *Recreations:* nothing of special notability. *Address:* c/o Department of Anatomy, UMDS of Guy's and St Thomas's, Guy's Hospital, London Bridge, SE1 9RT. *T:* 071–955 5000.

BOYCOTT, Geoffrey; cricketer; *b* 21 Oct. 1940; *s* of late Thomas Wilfred Boycott and Jane Boycott. *Educ:* Kinsley Modern Sch.; Hemsworth Grammar Sch. Played cricket for Yorkshire, 1962–86, received County Cap, 1963, Captain of Yorkshire, 1970–78. Played for England, 1964–74, 1977–82; scored 100th first-class hundred, England v Australia, 1977, 150th hundred, 1986; passed former world record no of runs scored in Test Matches, Delhi, Dec. 1981. Mem., General Cttee, Yorks CCC, 1984–. *Publications:* Geoff Boycott's Book for Young Cricketers, 1976; Put to the Test: England in Australia 1978–79, 1979; Geoff Boycott's Cricket Quiz, 1979; On Batting, 1980; Opening Up, 1980; In the Fast Lane, 1981; Master Class, 1982; Boycott, The Autobiography, 1987; Boycott on Cricket, 1990. *Recreations:* golf, tennis. *Address:* c/o Yorkshire County Cricket Club, Headingley Cricket Ground, Leeds, Yorks LS6 3BY.

BOYD, family name of **Baron Kilmarnock.**

BOYD OF MERTON, 2nd Viscount *cr* 1960, of Merton-in-Penninghame, Co. Wigtown; **Simon Donald Rupert Neville Lennox-Boyd;** Chairman, Save the Children Fund, since 1987; *b* 7 Dec. 1939; *e s* of 1st Viscount Boyd of Merton, CH, PC, and of Lady Patricia Guinness, *d* of 2nd Earl of Iveagh, KG, CB, CMG, FRS; *S* father, 1983; *m* 1962, Alice Mary (JP, High Sheriff of Cornwall, 1987–88), *d* of late Major M. G. D. Clive and of Lady Mary Clive; two *s* two *d. Educ:* Eton; Christ Church, Oxford. Dep. Chm., Arthur Guinness & Sons, 1981–86. Pres. Council, British Exec. Service Overseas, 1985–. Trustee, Guinness Trust, 1974–. *Heir: s* Hon. Benjamin Alan Lennox-Boyd, *b* 21 Oct. 1964. *Address:* Wivelscombe, Saltash, Cornwall PL12 4QY. *T:* Saltash (0752) 842672; 9 Warwick Square, SW1V 2AA. *T:* 071–821 1618. *Clubs:* White's; Royal Yacht Squadron.

BOYD, Sir Alexander Walter, 3rd Bt, *cr* 1916; *b* 16 June 1934; *s* of late Cecil Anderson Boyd, MC, MD, and Marjorie Catharine, *e d* of late Francis Kinloch, JP, Shipka Lodge, North Berwick; *S* uncle, 1948; *m* 1958, Molly Madeline, *d* of late Ernest Arthur Rendell; two *s* three *d. Heir: s* Ian Walter Rendell Boyd [*b* 14 March 1964; *m* 1986, LeeAnn Dillon; one *s*]. *Address:* Box 261, Whistler, BC, Canada.

BOYD, Arthur Merric Bloomfield, AO 1979; OBE 1970; painter; *b* Melbourne, 24 July 1920; *s* of William Merric Boyd and Doris Lucy Eleanor Gough; *m* 1945, Yvonne Hartland Lennie; one *s* two *d. Educ:* State Sch., Murrumbeena, Vic, Australia. Was taught painting and sculpture by parents and grandfather, Arthur Merric Boyd; served in Australian Army, 1940–43. Exhibited first in Australia, 1937; has lived and exhibited in Europe and Australia since 1959; first one-man exhibn painting, London, 1960; retrospective exhibn, Whitechapel Gall., 1962; designed for ballet at Edinburgh Festival and Sadler's Wells Theatre, 1961, and at Covent Garden Royal Opera House, 1963; tapestry 30′ × 60′ designed for new Parliament House, Canberra, installed 1988. *Publications:* include (illus.) Mars, by Peter Porter, 1988; *relevant publications:* Arthur Boyd, by Franz Philipp, 1967; Arthur Boyd Drawings, by Christopher Tadgell, 1973; Artist and River, by Sandra McGrath, 1983; Arthur Boyd—Seven Persistent Images, by Grazia Gunn, 1985; The Art of Arthur Boyd, by Ursula Hoff, 1986.

BOYD, Atarah, (Mrs Douglas Boyd); *see* Ben-Tovim, A.

BOYD, Christopher; *see* Boyd, T. C.

BOYD, David John; QC 1982; Director: Legal Services, Digital Equipment Co. Ltd, since 1986; Digital Equipment Scotland Ltd, since 1987; *b* 11 Feb. 1935; *s* of David Boyd and Ellen Jane Boyd (*née* Gruer); *m* 1960, Raija Sinikka Lindholm, Finland; one *s* one *d. Educ:* Eastbourne Coll.; St George's Sch., Newport, USA (British-Amer. schoolboy schol.); Gonville and Caius Coll., Cambridge (MA). FCIArb 1979. Various secretarial posts, ICI, 1957–62; Legal Asst, Pfizer, 1962–66; called to the Bar, Gray's Inn, 1963, Bencher 1988; Sec. and Legal Officer, Henry Wiggin & Co., 1966; Asst Sec. and Sen. Legal Officer (UK), Internat. Nickel, 1968; Dir, Impala Platinum, 1972–78; Sec. and Chief Legal Officer, 1972–86, and Dir, 1984–86, Inco Europe; practising barrister, 1986. Gen. Comr of Income Tax, 1978–83. Chm., Bar Assoc. for Commerce, Finance and Industry, 1980–81; Mem., Senate of Inns of Court and Bar, 1978–81. Sec. Gen., Assoc. des Juristes d'Entreprise Européens (European Company Lawyers Assoc.), 1983–84. Legal Advisor to Review Bd for Govt Contracts, 1984–. Chm., CBI Competition Panel, 1988–. *Recreations:* theatre-going, holidaying in France. *Address:* 44 Riverine, Grosvenor Drive, Maidenhead, Berks SL6 8PF. *T:* Maidenhead (0628) 75412; Beeches, Upton Bishop, Ross-on-Wye, Herefordshire. *T:* Upton Bishop (098985) 214.

BOYD, Dennis Galt, CBE 1988; Chief Conciliation Officer, Advisory, Conciliation and Arbitration Service, since 1980; *b* 3 Feb. 1931; *s* of late Thomas Ayre Boyd and Minnie (*née* Galt); *m* 1953, Pamela Mary McLean; one *s* one *d. Educ:* South Shields High School for Boys. National Service, 1949–51; Executive Officer, Civil Service: Min. of Supply/Min. of Defence, 1951–66; Board of Trade, 1966–69; Personnel Officer, Forestry Commission, 1969–75; Director of Corporate Services Health and Safety Executive, Dept of Employment, 1975–79; Director of Conciliation (ACAS), 1979–80. Hon. FIPM 1985. *Recreations:* golf, compulsory gardening. *Address:* Dunelm, Silchester Road, Little London, near Basingstoke. *Club:* Civil Service.

BOYD, Sir Francis; *see* Boyd, Sir J. F.

BOYD, Gavin, CBE 1977; Consultant, Boyds, solicitors, since 1978; Director, Scottish Opera Theatre Royal Ltd, since 1973 (Chairman, 1973–88); *b* 4 Aug. 1928; *s* of Gavin and Margaret Boyd; *m* 1954, Kathleen Elizabeth Skinner; one *s. Educ:* Glasgow Acad.; Univ. of Glasgow. MA (Hons); LLB. Partner, Boyds, solicitors, Glasgow, 1955–77. Director: Stenhouse Holdings Ltd, 1970–79 (Chm., 1971–78); Scottish Opera, 1970–88; North Sea Assets plc, 1972–88 (Dep. Chm., 1981–88); Paterson Jenks plc, 1972–81; Scottish Television plc, 1973–; Ferranti plc, 1975–88; British Carpets plc, 1977–81; Merchant House of Glasgow, 1982–. Trustee, Scottish Hosps Endowment Res. Trust, 1978–. Mem. Court, Univ. of Strathclyde, 1973– (Convener, Finance Cttee, 1979–83; Chm. Court, 1983–88); Mem., Law Soc. of Scotland. Hon. LLD Strathclyde, 1982. *Recreations:* music and the performing arts, particularly opera, hill walking. *Address:* Tigh Geal, 6 Milton Hill, Dumbarton G82 2TS.

BOYD, Ian Robertson; HM Stipendiary Magistrate, West Yorkshire, 1982–89; a Recorder of the Crown Court, 1983–88; *b* 18 Oct. 1922; *s* of Arthur Robertson Boyd, Edinburgh, and Florence May Boyd (*née* Kinghorn), Leeds; *m* 1952, Joyce Mary Boyd (*née* Crabtree); one *s* one *d. Educ:* Roundhay Sch.; Leeds Univ. (LLB (Hons)). Served Army, 1942–47: Captain Green Howards; Royal Lincolnshire Regt in India, Burma, Malaya, Dutch East Indies. Leeds Univ., 1947; called to Bar, Middle Temple, 1952; practised North Eastern Circuit, 1952–72; HM Stipendiary Magistrate, sitting at Hull, 1972–82. Sometime Asst/Dep. Recorder of Doncaster, Newcastle, Hull and York. *Recreation:* gardener manqué.

BOYD, James Edward, CA; Director and Financial Adviser, Denholm group of companies, since 1968; *b* 14 Sept. 1928; *s* of Robert Edward Boyd and Elizabeth Reid Sinclair; *m* 1956, Judy Ann Christey Scott; two *s* two *d. Educ:* Kelvinside Academy; The Leys Sch., Cambridge. CA Scot. (dist.) 1951. Director: Lithgows (Hldgs), 1962–87; Ayrshire Metal Products plc, 1965– (Dep. Chm., 1989–); Invergordon Distillers (Holdings) plc, 1966–88; GB Papers plc, 1977–87; Jebsens Drilling plc, 1978–85; Scottish Widows' Fund & Life Assurance Soc., 1981– (Dep. Chm., 1988–); Shanks & McEwan Gp Ltd, 1983–; Scottish Exhibn Centre Ltd, 1983–89; British Linen Bank Ltd, 1983– (Gov., 1986–); Bank of Scotland, 1984–; Yarrow PLC, 1984–86 (Chm., 1985–86); Bank of Wales, 1986–88; Save and Prosper Gp Ltd, 1987–89; James River UK Hldgs Ltd, 1987–90; Chairman: London & Gartmore Investment Trust plc, 1978–; English & Caledonian Investment plc, 1981–. Partner, McClelland Ker & Co. CA (subseq. McClelland Moores & Co.), 1953–61; Finance Director: Lithgows Ltd, 1962–69; Scott Lithgow Ltd, 1970–78; Chm., Fairfield Shipbuilding & Engrg Co. Ltd, 1964–65; Man. Dir, Invergordon Distillers (Holdings) Ltd, 1966–67; Director: Nairn & Williamson (Holdings) Ltd, 1968–75; Carlton Industries plc, 1978–84. Dep. Chm., BAA plc (formerly British Airports Authority), 1985–; Member: CAA (part-time), 1984–85; Clyde Port Authority, 1974–80; Working Party on Scope and Aims of Financial Accounts (the Corporate Report), 1974–75; Exec. Cttee, Accountants Jt Disciplinary Scheme, 1979–81; Mem. Council, Inst. of Chartered Accountants of Scotland, 1977–83 (Vice-Pres., 1980–82, Pres., 1982–83). Mem. Council, Glenalmond Coll., 1983–. *Recreations:* tennis, golf, gardening. *Address:* Dunard, Station Road, Rhu, Dunbartonshire, Scotland G84 8LW. *T:* Rhu (0436) 820441.

BOYD, James Fleming, CB 1980; Member, Civil Service Appeal Board, 1984–90; *b* 28 April 1920; *s* of late Walter and late Mary Boyd; *m* 1949, Daphne Steer, Hendon; one *s* one *d. Educ:* Whitehill Sch., Glasgow. Tax Officer, Inland Revenue, 1937; served with HM Forces, RAF, 1940–46; Inspector of Taxes, 1950; Principal Inspector, 1964; Senior Principal Inspector, 1970; Dep. Chief Inspector of Taxes, 1973; Dir of Operations, Inland Revenue, 1975–77, Dir Gen. (Management), 1978–81. Financial Advr, B. & C. E. Holiday Management Scheme, 1981–86. *Recreations:* history, gardening. *Address:* 2A The Avenue, Potters Bar, Herts EN6 1EB.

BOYD, John Dixon Iklé, CMG 1985; HM Diplomatic Service; Chief Clerk, Foreign and Commonwealth Office, since 1989; *b* 17 Jan. 1936; *s* of Prof. James Dixon Boyd and Amélie Lowenthal; *m* 1st, 1968, Gunilla Kristina Ingegerd Rönngren; one *s* one *d*; 2nd, 1977, Julia Daphne Raynsford; three *d. Educ:* Westminster Sch.; Clare Coll., Cambridge (BA); Yale Univ. (MA). Joined HM Foreign Service, 1962; Hong Kong, 1962–64; Peking, 1965–67; Foreign Office, 1967–69; Washington, 1969–73; 1st Sec., Peking, 1973–75; secondment to HM Treasury, 1976; Counsellor: (Economic), Bonn, 1977–81; (Economic and Soc. Affairs), UK Mission to UN, 1981–84; Asst Under-Sec. of State, FCO, 1984; Political Advr, Hong Kong, 1985–87; Dep. Under-Sec. of State, FCO, 1987–89. *Recreations:* music, fly fishing. *Address:* c/o Foreign and Commonwealth Office, SW1.

BOYD, Sir (John) Francis, Kt 1976; a Vice-President, Open Spaces Society, since 1982; *b* 11 July 1910; *s* of John Crichton Dick Boyd and Kate Boyd, Ilkley, Yorks; *m* 1946, Margaret, *d* of George Dobson and Agnes Dobson, Scarborough, Yorks; one *s* two *d. Educ:* Ilkley Grammar Sch.; Silcoates Sch., near Wakefield, Yorks. Reporter: Leeds

Mercury, 1928–34; Manchester Guardian, 1934–37; Parly Correspondent, Manchester Guardian, 1937–39. Aux. Fire Service, London, 1939; Monitoring Unit, BBC, 1940; Army, 1940–45. Political Correspondent, Manchester Guardian and Guardian, 1945–72; Political Editor, 1972–75. Chm., Lobby Journalists, 1949–50. Hon. LLD Leeds, 1973. *Publications:* Richard Austen Butler, 1956; (ed) The Glory of Parliament, by Harry Boardman, 1960; British Politics in Transition, 1964. *Recreations:* reading, walking, gardening. *Address:* 7 Summerlee Avenue, N2 9QP. *T:* 081–444 8601.

BOYD, Dr John Morton, CBE 1987; FRSE; ecologist; Consultant: Forestry Commission, since 1985; North of Scotland Hydro-Electric Board, since 1985; National Trust for Scotland, since 1985; Mirror Publishing, since 1989; Director, Scotland, Nature Conservancy Council, 1971–85; *b* Darvel, Ayrshire, 31 Jan. 1925; *s* of Thomas Pollock Boyd and Jeanie Reid Morton; *m* 1954, Winifred Isobel Rome; four *s. Educ:* Kilmarnock Acad.; Glasgow Univ. (BSc, PhD, DSc). FRSE 1968. Served War, 1943–47: Flt Lieut RAF. Nature Conservancy Council: Reg. Officer, 1957–68; Asst Dir, 1969–70. Nuffield Trav. Fellow, ME and E Africa, 1964–65; Leader, British Jordan Expedn, 1966; Mem., Royal Soc. Aldabra Expedn, 1967. Member: Council, Royal Scottish Zool Soc., 1963–69, 1980–85, 1986–89; Council, Azraq Internat. Biol Stn, Jordan, 1967–69; Council, National Trust for Scotland, 1971–85; Seals Adv. Cttee, NERC, 1973–79; BBC Scottish Agr. Adv. Cttee, 1973–76; Exec. Bd, Internat. Waterfowl Res. Bureau, 1976–78; Council, Royal Soc. of Edinburgh, 1978–81; Consultative Panel on Conservation of the Line and Phoenix Islands (Central Pacific), 1981–86. Internat. Union for Conservation of Nature and Natural Resources: British Rep., Kinshasa, 1975, Geneva, 1977, Ashkhabad, 1978, Christchurch, 1981, and Madrid, 1985; Mem. Commn on Ecology, 1976–; Confs, Senegal/Gambia and Switzerland, 1980, Holland, 1981, Catalonia and Indonesia, 1982, Malaysia, 1983, Bavaria, 1985. Co-Chm., Area VI Anglo-Soviet Environmental Protection Agreement, 1977–85; Chm., UK Internat. Conservation Cttee, 1980; Member: Council, Scottish Wildlife Trust, 1985–; Cttee, Centre for Human Ecology, Edinburgh Univ., 1985–; Panel on Scottish Popular Mountain Areas, CCS, 1989; Vice-Pres., Scottish Conservation Projects Trust, 1985–. Church of Scotland Rep., WCC Convocation Justice, Peace and Integrity of Creation, Seoul, 1990. Lectures: Keith Entwistle Meml, Cambridge, 1968; British Council, Amman, Nicosia and Ankara, 1972; East African Tours, Swan (Hellenic) Ltd, 1972–; Meml in Agr. Zool., W of Scotland Agr. Coll., 1976; Sir William Weipers Meml, Glasgow Univ. Vet. Sch., 1980; Nat. Trust for Scotland Jubilee, 1981; British Council, Jakarta, 1982, Delhi and Kuala Lumpur, 1983. Gen. Editor, Island Biology Series, Edinburgh Univ. Press, 1985–. FRSA 1985; FRZSScot 1985; FRSGS 1987; CBiol 1987, FiBiol 1987. Neill Prize, Royal Soc. of Edinburgh, 1985. *Publications:* (with K. Williamson) St Kilda Summer, 1960; (with K. Williamson) Mosaic of Islands, 1963; (with F. F. Darling) The Highlands and Islands, 1964; Travels in the Middle East and East Africa, 1966; (with P. A. Jewell and C. Milner) Island Survivors, 1974; (ed) The Natural Environment of the Outer Hebrides, 1979; (ed with D. R. Bowes) The Natural Environment of the Inner Hebrides, 1983; Fraser Darling's Islands, 1986; (with I. L. Boyd) The Hebrides: a natural history, 1990; scientific papers on nature conservation and animal ecology. *Recreations:* hill-walking, painting, photography. *Address:* 57 Hailes Gardens, Edinburgh EH13 0JH. *T:* 031–441 3220; Balephuil, Tiree, Argyll PA77 6UE. *Club:* New (Edinburgh).

BOYD, Leslie Balfour, CBE 1977; Courts Administrator, Central Criminal Court, 1972–77; *b* 25 Nov. 1914; *e s* of late Henry Leslie Boyd, Mem. of Lloyds, of Crowborough, Sussex, and Beatrix Boyd, *d* of Henry Chapman, for many years British Consul at Dieppe; *m* 1936, Wendy Marie, *d* of George and Nancy Blake, Oswestry, Salop; one *s* one *d. Educ:* Evelyn's; Royal Naval College, Dartmouth. Invalided out of Royal Navy, 1931. Called to the Bar, Gray's Inn, 1939; joined staff of Central Criminal Court, 1941; Dep. Clerk of Court, 1948; Clerk of the Court, 1955–71; Dep. Clerk of Peace, 1949–55, Clerk of the Peace, 1955–71, City of London and Town and Borough of Southwark. Master, Worshipful Company of Gold and Silver Wyre Drawers, 1969. *Publications:* contributor to Criminal Law and Juries titles, 3rd edn, Juries title, 4th edn, of Halsbury's Laws of England. *Recreations:* gardening and travel. *Address:* Flat G, Mulberry Court, 2 Highbury Hill, Islington, N5 1BA.

BOYD, Morgan Alistair, CMG 1990; Deputy General Manager, Commonwealth Development Corporation, since 1991; *b* 1 May 1934; *s* of Norman Robert Boyd and Kathleen Muriel Boyd; *m* 1959, Judith Mary Martin. *Educ:* Marlborough College; Wadham College, Oxford (BA, MA 1955). FRGS 1957. Management trainee, CDC, 1957; Exec., Malaysia, 1958–66; Manager, East Caribbean Housing, Barbados, 1967–70; Gen. Manager, Tanganyika Develt Finance Co., 1970–74; Advr, Industrial Develt Bank, Kenya, 1975; Regl Controller, Central Africa, 1976–80, East Africa, 1981–82; Dep. Gen. Manager, Investigations, London, 1983–84; Dir of Ops, Commonwealth Develt Corp., 1985. RSA 1990. *Publication:* Royal Challenge Accepted, 1962. *Recreations:* music, sailing, travel. *Address:* 7 South Hill Mansions, South Hill Park, NW3 2SL. *T:* 071–435 1082. *Clubs:* Naval, English-Speaking Union.

BOYD, Sir Robert (Lewis Fullarton), Kt 1983; CBE 1972; FRS 1969; Professor of Physics in the University of London, 1962–83, now Emeritus; Director, Mullard Space Science Laboratory of Department of Physics and Astronomy of University College, London, 1965–83; *b* 1922; *s* of late William John Boyd, PhD, BSc; *m* 1949, Mary, *d* of late John Higgins; two *s* one *d. Educ:* Whitgift Sch.; Imperial Coll., London (BSc (Eng) 1943); University Coll., London (PhD 1949; Fellow 1988). FIEE 1967; FInstP 1972. Exp. Officer at Admty Mining Estabt, 1943–46; DSIR Res. Asst, 1946–49; ICI Res. Fellow, 1949–50, Maths Dept, UCL; ICI Res. Fellow, Physics Dept, UCL, 1950–52; Lectr in Physics, UCL, 1952–58, Reader in Physics, UCL, 1959–62. Prof. of Astronomy (part-time), Royal Institution, 1961–67; IEE Appleton Lectr, 1976; Bakerian Lectr, Royal Soc., 1978; Halley Lectr, Univ. of Oxford, 1981. Chairman: Meteorol Res. Cttee, MoD, 1972–75; Astronautics Cttee, MoD, 1972–77; Member: BBC Science Cons. Gp, 1970–79; SRC, 1977–81 (Chm., Astronomy, Space and Radio Bd, 1977–80); Council, Physical Soc., 1958–60; Council, RAS, 1962–66 (Vice-Pres., 1964–66); British Nat. Cttee on Space Res., 1976–87. Pres., Victoria Inst., 1965–76. Trustee, Nat. Maritime Museum, 1980–89. Governor: St Lawrence Coll., 1965–76; Croydon Coll., 1966–80; Southlands Coll., 1976–; Chm., London Bible Coll., 1983–90. Hon. DSc Heriot-Watt, 1979. *Publications:* The Upper Atmosphere (with H. S. W. Massey), 1958; Space Research by Rocket and Satellite, 1960; Space Physics, 1975; papers in sci. jls on space sci. and other topics. *Recreation:* elderly Rolls Royce motor cars. *Address:* Roseneath, 41 Church Street, Littlehampton, West Sussex BN17 5PU. *T:* Littlehampton (0903) 714438.

BOYD, Robert Stanley, CB 1982; Solicitor of Inland Revenue, 1979–86; *b* 6 March 1927; *s* of Robert Reginald Boyd (formerly Indian Police) and Agnes Maria Dorothea, *d* of Lt-Col Charles H. Harrison; *m* 1965, Ann, *d* of Daniel Hopkin. *Educ:* Wellington; Trinity Coll., Dublin (BA, LLB). Served RN, 1945–48. Called to Bar, Inner Temple, 1954. Joined Inland Revenue, 1959; Prin. Asst Solicitor, 1971–79. *Address:* Great Beere, North Tawton, Devon EX20 2BR.

BOYD, Stewart Craufurd, QC 1981; *b* 25 Oct. 1943; *s* of Leslie Balfour Boyd and Wendy Marie Boyd; *m* 1970, Catherine Jay; one *s* three *d. Educ:* Winchester Coll.; Trinity Coll., Cambridge (MA). Called to the Bar, Middle Temple, 1967, Bencher, 1989. *Publications:* (ed) Scrutton, Charterparties, 18th edn 1972, 19th edn 1984; (with Sir Michael Mustill) The Law and Practice of Commercial Arbitration, 1982, 1989; contrib. Civil Justice Rev., Arbitration Internat., Lloyd's Commercial and Maritime Law Qly. *Recreations:* boats, pianos, gardens. *Address:* 1 Gayton Crescent, NW3 1TT. *T:* 071–431 1581.

BOYD, (Thomas) Christopher; farmer; *b* 1916; *m*; one *s* two *d.* Army, 1940–44; civil servant, 1939 and 1944–48; MP (Lab) Bristol NW, 1955–59; Chelsea Borough Councillor, 1953–59. *Address:* Middlegill, Moffat, Dumfriesshire. *T:* Beattock (06833) 415.

BOYD, Dame Vivienne (Myra), DBE 1986 (CBE 1983); Chairman, Taita Home and Hospital for the Elderly, since 1989; Member: Advertising Standards Complaints Board (formerly Advertising Standards Council), since 1988; Environmental Choice Management Advisory Committee, since 1990; *b* 11 April 1926; *d* of Hugh France Lowe and Winifred May Lowe (*née* Shearer); *m* 1948, Robert Macdonald Boyd; one *s* three *d. Educ:* Eastern Hutt Sch.; Hutt Valley High Sch.; Victoria Coll., Univ. of New Zealand (MSc (Hons)). President: Dunedin Free Kindergarten Assoc., 1965; NZ Baptist Women's League, 1966; Nat. Council of Women of NZ, 1978–82; NZ Baptist Union of Churches and Missionary Soc., 1984–85. Member: Royal Commn on Nuclear Power Generation, 1976–78; Equal Opportunities Tribunal, 1979–89; chaired: Abortion Supervisory Cttee, 1979–80; Women and Recreation Conf., 1981; Review of Preparation and Initial Employment of Nurses, 1986; Consumer Council, NZ, 1983–88 (Mem., 1975–88); Consumers' Inst. of NZ Inc., 1988–89 (Mem. Bd, 1989–90); Convener, Internat. Council of Women Standing Cttee on Social Welfare, 1982–88. Silver Jubilee Medal, 1977. *Recreations:* reading, gardening. *Address:* 202 Waiwhetu Road, Lower Hutt, New Zealand. *T:* 00644 695028.

BOYD, William Andrew Murray, FRSL; author; *b* 7 March 1952; *s* of Dr Alexander Murray Boyd and Evelyn Boyd; *m* 1975, Susan Anne (*née* Wilson). *Educ:* Gordonstoun Sch.; Glasgow Univ. (MA Hons English and Philosophy); Jesus Coll., Oxford. Lecturer in English, St Hilda's Coll., Oxford, 1980–83; Television Critic, New Statesman, 1981–83. FRSL 1983. Chevalier de l'Ordre des Arts et des Lettres (France), 1991. *Publications:* A Good Man in Africa, 1981 (Whitbread Prize 1981, Somerset Maugham Award 1982); On the Yankee Station, 1981; An Ice-Cream War, 1982 (John Llewellyn Rhys Prize, 1982); Stars and Bars, 1984; School Ties, 1985; The New Confessions, 1987; Brazzaville Beach, 1990 (James Tait Black Meml Prize, 1990). *Screenplays:* Good and Bad at Games (TV), 1983; Dutch Girls (TV), 1985; Scoop (TV), 1987; Stars and Bars, 1988; Aunt Julia and the Scriptwriter, 1990; Mr Johnson, 1990. *Recreations:* tennis, strolling. *Address:* c/o Harvey Unna and Stephen Durbridge Ltd, 24 Pottery Lane, Holland Park, W11 4LZ.

BOYD-CARPENTER, family name of **Baron Boyd-Carpenter.**

BOYD-CARPENTER, Baron *cr* 1972 (Life Peer), of Crux Easton in the County of Southampton; **John Archibald Boyd-Carpenter,** PC 1954; *b* 2 June 1908; *s* of late Sir Archibald Boyd-Carpenter, MP; *m* 1937, Margaret, *e d* of Lieut-Col G. L. Hall, OBE; one *s* two *d. Educ:* Stowe; Balliol Coll., Oxford. Pres. Oxford Union, 1930; BA (History, 1930); Diploma in Economics, 1931; toured USA with Oxford Union Debating Team, 1931; Harmsworth Law Scholar, Middle Temple, 1933; Council of Legal Education's Prize for Constitutional Law, 1934; called to Bar, Middle Temple, 1934, and practised in London and SE Circuit. Contested (MR) Limehouse for LCC, 1934. Joined Scots Guards, 1940; held various staff appointments and served with AMG in Italy, retired with rank of Major. MP (C) for Kingston-upon-Thames, 1945–72; Financial Sec., to the Treasury, 1951–54; Minister of Transport and Civil Aviation, 1954–Dec. 1955; Minister of Pensions and National Insurance, Dec. 1955–July 1962; Chief Sec. to the Treasury and Paymaster-Gen., 1962–64; Opposition Front Bench Spokesman on Housing, Local Government and Land, 1964–66; Chm., Public Accounts Cttee, 1964–70. Chairman: Greater London Area Local Govt Cttee, Conservative Party, 1968; London Members Cttee, 1966–72; Pres. Wessex Area, Nat. Union of Conservative and Unionist Assocs, 1977–80. Chairman: CAA, 1972–77; Rugby Portland Cement, 1976–84 (Dir, 1970–76); Orion Insurance Co., 1969–72; CLRP Investment Trust, 1970–72; Dir, TR Far East Income (formerly Australia Investment) Trust, 1977–, and other cos; Mem. Council, Trust House Forte Ltd, 1977–. Governor, Stowe School; Chairman: Carlton Club, 1979–86; Assoc. of Cons. Peers, 1990; Mail Users' Assoc., 1986–90; Sort Out Sunday Cttee, 1986–. High Steward, Royal Borough of Kingston-upon-Thames, 1973–. DL Greater London, 1973–83. *Publications:* Way of Life, 1980; newspaper articles. *Recreations:* tennis and swimming. *Address:* 12 Eaton Terrace, SW1. *T:* 071–730 7765; Crux Easton House, Crux Easton, near Newbury, Berks. *T:* Highclere (0635) 253037. *Club:* Carlton.

See also Hon. T. P. J. Boyd-Carpenter, S. E. M. Hogg.

BOYD-CARPENTER, Maj.-Gen. Hon. Thomas Patrick John, MBE 1973; Assistant Chief of Defence Staff (Programmes), since 1989; *b* 16 June 1938; *s* of Baron Boyd-Carpenter, *qv*; *m* 1972, Mary-Jean (*née* Duffield); one *s* two *d. Educ:* Stowe. Commnd 1957; served UK, Oman, Malaya, Borneo and Germany; Instr, Staff Coll., 1975–77; Defence Fellowship, Aberdeen Univ., 1977–78; CO 1st Bn Scots Guards, 1979–81; Comdr 24 Inf. Brigade, 1983–84; Dir, Defence Policy, 1985–87; COS, HQ BAOR, 1988–89. *Publication:* Conventional Deterrence: into the 1990s, 1989. *Recreations:* reading, gardening. *Address:* c/o Barclays Bank, 6 Market Place, Newbury, Berks.

See also S. E. M. Hogg.

BOYDE, Prof. Patrick, PhD; FBA 1987; Serena Professor of Italian, since 1981, and Fellow of St John's College, since 1965, University of Cambridge; *b* 30 Nov. 1934; *s* of Harry Caine Boyde and Florence Colonna Boyde; *m* 1956, Catherine Mavis Taylor; four *s. Educ:* Braintree County High Sch.; Wanstead County High Sch.; St John's Coll., Cambridge. BA 1956, MA 1960, PhD 1963. Nat. service, commnd RA, 1956–58. Research, St John's Coll., Cambridge, 1958–61; Asst Lectr in Italian, Univ. of Leeds, 1961–62; Asst Lectr, later Lectr, Univ. of Cambridge, 1962–81. Corresp. Fellow, Accademia Nazionale dei Lincei, 1986. *Publications:* Dante's Lyric Poetry (with K. Foster), 1967; Dante's Style in his Lyric Poetry, 1971; Dante Philomythes and Philosopher: Man in the Cosmos, 1981. *Recreations:* walking, backpacking, music.

BOYDELL, (The Worshipful Chancellor) Peter Thomas Sherrington, QC 1965; Leader, Parliamentary Bar, since 1975; Chancellor of Dioceses of Truro since 1957, Oxford since 1958 and Worcester since 1959; *b* 20 Sept. 1920; *s* of late Frank Richard Boydell, JP, and late Frances Barton Boydell, Blenheim Lodge, Whitegate Drive, Blackpool; unmarried. *Educ:* Arnold Sch., Blackpool; Manchester Univ. LLB Manchester 1940. Served War of 1939–45; Adjt, 17th Field Regt, RA, 1943; Bde Major, RA, 1st Armoured Div., 1944; Bde Major, RA, 10th Indian Div., 1945. Qualified as Solicitor, 1947. Called to Bar, Middle Temple, 1948, Bencher, 1970, Dep. Treas., 1988, Treas., 1989. Chm., Planning and Local Govt Cttee of the Bar, 1973–86; Founder Chm., Local Govt and Planning, Bar Assoc., 1986–90. Mem., Legal Board of Church Assembly, 1958–71. Contested (C) Carlisle, 1964. Associate (by invitation and election) RICS, 1982; Mem., CIArb, 1985. *Recreations:* mountaineering, music, travel. *Address:* 45 Wilton

Crescent, SW1X 8RX. *T:* 071–235 5505; 2 Harcourt Buildings, Temple, EC4. *T:* 071–353 8415. *Clubs:* Garrick, Royal Automobile; Climbers.

BOYDEN, (Harold) James; *b* 19 Oct. 1910; *s* of late Claude James and late Frances Mary Boyden; *m* 1st, 1935, Emily Pemberton (*d* 1988); 2nd, 1990, Mrs Sue Hay. *Educ:* Elementary Sch., Tiffin Boys, Kingston; King's Coll., London. BA (History), 1932; BSc (Econ), London External, 1943; Barrister-at-law, Lincoln's Inn, 1947. Pres., King's Coll. Union Soc., 1931–32. Master: Henry Mellish Grammar Sch., 1933–35; Tiffin Boys Sch., 1935–40; Lectr, Extra-Mural Depts of London, Nottingham and Southampton Univs, 1934–47. RAF, 1940–45; Sqdn-Ldr, 1944–45; Chief Training Officer, Admiralty, 1945–47; Dir Extra-Mural Studies, Durham Univ., 1947–59. Durham City and County Magistrate, 1951–; CC for Durham City, 1952–59; Chm. Durham County Education Cttee, 1959 (Vice-Chm. 1957–59); Chm., Exec. Cttee Nat. Inst. for Adult Education, 1958–61; Mem. Newcastle Regional Hospital Board, 1958–64; Fabian Soc. Executive, 1961–65. MP (Lab) Bishop Auckland, 1959–79; Jt Parly Under-Sec. of State, Dept of Education and Science, 1964–65; Parliamentary Sec., Ministry of Public Building and Works, 1965–67; Parly Under-Sec. (Army), MoD, 1967–69. Chm., Select Cttee of Expenditure, 1974–79; Sec., Anglo-French Parly Cttee, 1974–79. Overseas Lecture Tours: for Foreign Office, Germany, 1955 and 1957; for British Council, Ghana, Sierra Leone, 1956; Sierra Leone, 1961; for Admiralty, Malta, 1959. Member: WEA; Fabian Soc.; Nat. Union of General and Municipal Workers; National Trust; Council of Europe, 1970–73, WEU, 1970–73. FKC 1969. *Recreations:* walking, gardening, foreign travel, swimming. *Address:* 18 Salisbury Crescent, Oxford OX2 7TL. *T:* Oxford (0865) 58408. *Clubs:* South Church Workman's, Eldon Lane Workman's (Bishop Auckland); Southerne (Newton Aycliffe).

BOYER, John Leslie, OBE 1982; Chief Executive, Zoological Society of London, 1984–88; *b* 13 Nov. 1926; *s* of Albert and Gladys Boyer; *m* 1953, Joyce Enid Thomasson; one *s* two *d*. *Educ:* Nantwich; Acton Grammar Sch. Served Army, 1944–48: commnd into South Lancashire Regt, 1946, and attached to Baluch Regt, then Indian Army. Joined Hongkong and Shanghai Banking Corp., 1948: served Hong Kong, Burma, Japan, India, Malaysia, Singapore; General Manager, Hong Kong, 1973; Director, March 1977; Dep. Chm., Sept. 1977–81; Chm., Antony Gibbs Hldgs Ltd, 1981–83. Director: Anglo and Overseas Trust (formerly Anglo and American Securities) PLC, 1981–; Overseas Investment Trust (formerly North Atlantic Securities), 1981–. Chm., Adv. Bd, Wright Seligman & Co., 1988–. *Recreations:* walking, swimming, bridge, reading. *Address:* Friars Lawn, Norwood Green Road, Norwood Green, Mddx UB2 4LA. *T:* 081–574 8489. *Clubs:* Oriental; Shek O (Hong Kong); Tanglin (Singapore).

BOYERS, (Raphael) Howard, DFC 1945; Regional Chairman of Industrial Tribunals, Sheffield, 1984–87, retired 1988; *b* 20 Oct. 1915; *yr s* of late Bernard Boyers and Jennie Boyers; *m* 1st, 1949, Anna Moyra Cowan (*d* 1984); three *d*; 2nd, 1985, Estelle Wolman (*née* Davidson), JP; two step *s* one step *d*. *Educ:* King Edward VI Grammar School, Retford. Admitted Solicitor, 1939. Served War, RAF, 1940–45; 130 Sqdn, 10 Gp Fighter Comd, 1941; 51 Sqdn, 4 Gp Bomber Comd, 1944–45. Sen. Partner, Boyers Howson & Co., 1946–72. Clerk of the Peace, City of Sheffield, 1964–71; Chairman: VAT Tribunals, 1972–75; Industrial Tribunals, 1975–80; acting Regional Chm., 1980–84. *Recreations:* theatre, music, watching football. *Address:* 49 Cortworth Road, Sheffield S11 9LN. *T:* Sheffield (0742) 362041. *Clubs:* Royal Air Force; Sheffield (Sheffield).

BOYES, Sir Brian Gerald B.; *see* Barratt-Boyes.

BOYES, James Ashley; Headmaster of City of London School, 1965–84; *b* 27 Aug. 1924; *s* of late Alfred Simeon Boyes and of Edith May Boyes; *m* 1st, 1949, Diana Fay (*née* Rothera), MA Cantab; two *d*; 2nd, 1973, April Tanner (*née* Rothery). *Educ:* Rugby Sch.; Clare Coll., Cambridge. Lieut RNVR; N Russian convoys and Brit. Pacific Fleet, 1942–46. Cambridge Univ., 1942, 1946–48; 1st class Hons Mod. Hist., 1948; Mellon Fellowship, Yale Univ., 1948–50; MA Yale, 1950. Asst Master, Rugby Sch., 1950–55; Headmaster, Kendal Grammar Sch., Westmorland, 1955–60; Dir of Studies, Royal Air Force Coll., Cranwell, 1960–65. *Recreations:* squash racquets, sailing. *Address:* 12 Linver Road, SW6 3RB. *Clubs:* Royal Automobile, Hurlingham; Harlequins RUFC (Hon. Mem.); Hawks (Cambridge); Royal Windermere Yacht.

BOYES, Kate Emily Tyrrell, (Mrs C. W. Sanders); Chairman, Civil Service Selection Boards, since 1978; *b* 22 April 1918; *e d* of S. F. Boyes, Sandiacre, Derbyshire; *m* 1944, Cyril Woods Sanders, *qv*; one *s* three *d*. *Educ:* Long Eaton Grammar Sch.; (Scholar) Newnham Coll., Cambridge. Economics Tripos, 1939; MA (Cantab). Administrative Class, Home Civil Service, 1939; Private Sec. to Parly Sec., 1942–45; Principal, 1945; Sec. to Council on Prices, Productivity and Incomes, 1958–60; Asst Sec., 1961; Speechwriter to President of Bd of Trade, 1963–64; Under-Sec., Europe, Industry and Technology Div., DTI, later Dept of Trade, 1972–78. Member: Council, National Trust, 1967–79; Exec., Keep Britain Tidy Gp, 1980–. *Recreations:* climbing, sailing, ski-ing, archæology. *Address:* 41 Smith Street, SW3 4EP. *T:* 071–352 8053; Giles Point, Winchelsea, Sussex. *T:* Rye (0797) 226431; Canower, Cashel, Connemara, Ireland. *Clubs:* Ski Club of Gt Britain; Island Cruising (Salcombe).

BOYES, Roland; MP (Lab) Houghton and Washington, since 1983; *m* Patricia; two *s*. Member (Lab) Durham, European Parliament, 1979–84. An opposition frontbench spokesman on: Parly environment team, 1985–88; Parly defence team, 1988–. Founder Chm., All Party Photography Gp, 1987–. Member GMB. Chm., Tribune Gp, 1985–86. Dir, Hartlepool United AFC, 1987–. *Publication:* People in Parliament, 1990. *Address:* (home) 12 Spire Hollin, Peterlee, Co. Durham. *T:* 091–586 3917; (office) 5A Grangewood Close, Shiney Row, Houghton-le-Spring, Tyne & Wear. *T:* 091–385 7825, *Fax:* 091–385 4785; (House of Commons) 071–219 3587, *Fax:* 071–219 5657. *Clubs:* Peterlee Labour, Peterlee Cricket (Pres.); Peterlee Football; Houghton Buffs; Easington Lane, North Biddick, Westward, Celtic, Stella Maris, Gardeners, Usworth, and Glendale Working Men's.

BOYLAN, Prof. Patrick John, PhD; FMA; FGS; Professor of Arts Policy and Management, City University, since 1990; *b* 17 Aug. 1939; *s* of Francis Boylan and Mary Doreen (*née* Haxby), Hull, Yorks. *Educ:* Marist Coll., Hull; Univ. of Hull (BSc 1960; PGCE 1961); Univ. of Leicester (PhD 1985). Museums Diploma (with Distinction), Museums Assoc., 1966. FGS 1973. Asst Master, Marist Coll., Hull, 1961–63; Keeper of Geology and Natural History, Kingston upon Hull Museums, 1964–68; Dir of Museums and Art Gallery, Exeter City Council, 1968–72; Dir of Museums and Art Gall., 1972–74; Dir of Museums and Arts, Leics County Council, 1974–90. International Council of Museums: Chm., Internat. Cttee for Training of Personnel, 1983–89; Chm., UK Nat. Cttee, 1987–; Mem., Adv. Cttee, 1983–; Mem., Exec. Council, 1989–. Councillor, Museums Assoc., 1970–71 and 1986– (Centenary Pres., 1988–90); Chm., Library Cttee, Geol Soc., 1984–87. FBIM 1990 (MBIM 1975); FRSA 1990. *Publications:* Ice Age in Yorkshire and Humberside, 1983; The Changing World of Museums and Art Galleries, 1986; Museums 2000: politics, people, professionals and profits, 1991; over 80 papers in learned jls and chapters in books on museums, prof. training, geology, natural history and history of science. *Recreations:* the arts (especially opera and contemporary arts and crafts), history of science research, avoiding gardening. *Address:* Department of Arts Policy and Management, City University, Frobisher Crescent, Barbican, EC2Y 8HB. *T:* 071–628 5641, *Fax:* 071–588 2756; 40 Guilford Road, Stoneygate, Leicester LE2 2RB. *T:* Leicester (0533) 707265. *Club:* Leicester Rotary.

BOYLAND, Prof. Eric, (Dick), PhD London, DSc Manchester; Professor of Biochemistry, University of London, at Chester Beatty Research Institute, Institute of Cancer Research, Royal Marsden Hospital, 1948–70, now Emeritus Professor; Visiting Professor in Environmental Toxicology, London School of Hygiene and Tropical Medicine, 1970–76; *b* Manchester, 24 Feb. 1905; *s* of Alfred E. and Helen Boyland; *m* 1931, Margaret Esther (*d* 1985), *d* of late Maj.-Gen. Sir Frederick Maurice, KCMG, CB; two *s* one *d*. *Educ:* Manchester Central High Sch.; Manchester Univ. BSc Tech. 1926; MSc 1928; DSc 1936. Research Asst in Physiology, Manchester Univ., 1926–28; Grocers' Company Scholar and Beit Memorial Fellow for Med. Research at Lister Institute for Preventive Medicine, 1928–30, and Kaiser Wilhelm Institut für Medizinische Forschung, Heidelberg, 1930–31; Physiological Chemist to Royal Cancer Hosp., London, 1931; Reader in Biochemistry, University of London, 1935–47. Research Officer in Ministry of Supply, 1941–44; Ministry of Agriculture, 1944–45. Consultant to Internat. Agency for Research on Cancer, Lyon, 1970–72; Member WHO Panel on Food Additives. Hon. FFOM, RCP, 1982. Hon. PhD Frankfurt, 1982; Hon. MD Malta, 1985. Judd Award for Cancer Research, New York, 1948. *Publications:* The Biochemistry of Bladder Cancer, 1963; Modern Trends in Toxicology, vol. I, 1962, vol. II, 1974; scientific papers in biochemistry and pharmacology. *Recreations:* walking, painting and looking at paintings. *Address:* King's College London, Chelsea Campus, Manresa Road, SW3 6LX; 42 Bramerton Street, SW3 5LA. *T:* 071–352 2601. *Clubs:* Athenæum; Rucksack (Manchester).

BOYLE, family name of **Earls of Cork, Glasgow,** and **Shannon.**

BOYLE, Viscount; Richard Henry John Boyle; in catering trade; *b* 19 Jan. 1960; *s* and *heir* of 9th Earl of Shannon, *qv*. *Educ:* Northease Manor School, Lewes. *Recreations:* motocross and trials.

BOYLE, Alan Gordon; QC 1991; *b* 31 March 1949; *s* of Dr Michael Morris Boyle and Hazel Irene Boyle; *m* 1981, Claudine-Aimée Minne-Vercruysse; two *d*. *Educ:* Royal Shrewsbury Sch.; St Catherine's Coll., Oxford (BA). Called to the Bar, Lincoln's Inn, 1972. *Recreations:* walking, music. *Address:* 13 Old Square, Lincoln's Inn, WC2A 3UA. *T:* 071–242 6105.

BOYLE, Archibald Cabbourn, MD; FRCP; Hon. Consultant Physician, King Edward VII, Midhurst, 1984–87; Director, Department of Rheumatology, Middlesex Hospital, 1954–83; Hon. Consultant Rheumatologist, King Edward VII Hospital for Officers, 1980–83; Hon. Clinical Adviser, Department of Rheumatological Research, Middlesex Hospital Medical School; *b* 14 March 1918; *s* of late Arthur Hislop Boyle and of Flora Ellen Boyle; *m* 1st, Patricia Evelyn Tallack (*d* 1944); one *d*; 2nd, Dorothy Evelyn (marr. diss. 1982), *widow* of Lieut G. B. Jones; one *s*; 3rd, 1983, June Rosemary Gautrey (*née* Pickett). *Educ:* Dulwich Coll.; St Bartholomew's Hospital. DPhysMed 1947; MD 1949; FRCP 1959. House Physician, St Bartholomew's Hosp., 1941–42. Served War of 1939–45 in Far East, and later as Command Specialist in Physical Medicine. Registrar and Sen. Asst, 1946–49, and Asst Physician, 1949–54, Mddx Hosp.; Consultant in Physical Medicine, Bromley Gp of Hosps, 1950–54; Physician, Arthur Stanley Inst. for Rheumatic Diseases, 1950–65. Member: Bd of Governors, Mddx Hosp.; Bd of Governors, Charterhouse Rheumatism Clinic; Bd of Studies in Medicine, Univ. of London; Council, British Assoc. for Rheumatology and Rehabilitation (Pres., 1973–74); British League against Rheumatism (Vice-Pres., 1972–77; Pres., 1977–81); Council, Section of Physical Medicine, RSM, 1950– (Pres., 1956–58; Vice-Pres., 1970–); Heberden Soc.; Cttee on Rheumatology and Rehabilitation, RCP. Ernest Fletcher Meml Lectr, RSM, 1971. Formerly: Examnr in Physical Medicine, RCP; Examnr to Chartered Soc. of Physiotherapy; Editor, Annals of Physical Medicine, 1956–63; Sec., Internat. Fedn of Physical Medicine, 1960–64; Chm., Physical Medicine Gp, BMA, 1956–58; Pres., London Br., Chartered Soc. of Physiotherapy. Former Member: Council, British Assoc. of Physical Medicine and Rheumatology, 1949–72 (Vice-Pres., 1965–68; Pres., 1970–72); Cttee on Chronic Rheumatic Diseases, RCP; Regional Scientific, and Educn, Sub-Cttees, Arthritis and Rheumatism Council; Physiotherapists Bd, Council for Professions Supplementary to Medicine; Central Consultants and Specialists Cttee, BMA; Med. Adv. Cttee, British Rheumatism and Arthritis Assoc. *Publications:* A Colour Atlas of Rheumatology, 1974; contribs to medical jls, mainly on rheumatic disease. *Recreation:* gardening. *Address:* Iping Barn, Iping, near Midhurst, West Sussex GU29 0PE. *T:* Midhurst (0730) 816467.

BOYLE, Marshal of the Royal Air Force Sir Dermot (Alexander), GCB 1957 (CB 1946); KCVO 1953; KBE 1953 (CBE 1945); AFC 1939; Vice-Chairman, British Aircraft Corporation, 1962–71; *b* 2 Oct. 1904; 2nd and *e* surv. *s* of A. F. Boyle, Belmont House, Queen's Co., Ire.; *m* 1931, Una Carey; two *s* one *d* (and one *s* decd). *Educ:* St Columba's Coll., Ireland; RAF (Cadet) Coll., Cranwell. Commissioned RAF 1924; Air ADC to the King, 1943; Air Commodore, 1944; Air Vice-Marshal, 1949; Air Marshal, 1954; Air Chief Marshal, 1956; Marshal of the Royal Air Force, 1958; Dir-Gen. of Personnel, Air Ministry, 1948–49; Dir-Gen. of Manning, Air Ministry, 1949–51; AOC No. 1 Group Bomber Command, 1951–53; AOC-in-C, Fighter Command, 1953–55; Chief of Air Staff, 1956–59. Master, Guild of Air Pilots and Air Navigators, 1965–66. Chairman: Bd of Trustees, RAF Museum, 1965–74; Ct of Governors, Mill Hill Sch., 1969–76; Dep. Chm., RAF Benevolent Fund, 1971–80. J. P. Robertson Meml Trophy, Air Public Relations Assoc., 1973. *Address:* Fair Gallop, Brighton Road, Sway, Hants SO41 6EA. *Club:* Royal Air Force.

BOYLE, Kay, (Baroness Joseph von Franckenstein); writer; Professor in English Department, San Francisco State University, 1963–80, now Emeritus; *b* St Paul, Minn, USA, 19 Feb. 1902; *d* of Howard Peterson Boyle; *m* 1921, 1931 and 1943; one *s* five *d*. Member: National Institute of Arts and Letters, 1958; Amer. Acad. and Inst. of Arts and Letters, 1978. O. Henry Memorial Prize for best short story of the year, 1936, 1941; Guggenheim Fellowship, 1934, 1961; Center for Advanced Studies Wesleyan Univ. Fellowship, 1963; Radcliffe Inst. for Independent Study, 1964, 1965. Writer-in-residence: Hollins Coll., Virginia, 1970–71; Bowling Green State Univ., 1986. Hon. DLitt: Columbia Coll., Chicago, 1971; Southern Illinois, 1982; Bowling Green State Univ., 1986; Hon. DHL Skidmore Coll., 1977. San Francisco Art Commn Award of Honor, 1978; Amer. Book Award, 1983; Lannan Foundn Award, 1989. *Publications: novels:* Plagued by the Nightingale; Year Before Last; Gentlemen, I Address You Privately; My Next Bride; Death of a Man; The Crazy Hunter, 1938; Monday Night; Primer for Combat; Avalanche; A Frenchman Must Die; "1939"; His Human Majesty; The Seagull on the Step, 1955; Three Short Novels, 1958; Generation Without Farewell, 1959; The Underground Woman, 1975; *volumes of short stories:* Wedding Day; The First Lover; The White Horses of Vienna; The Crazy Hunter; Thirty Stories; The Smoking Mountain; Nothing Ever Breaks Except the Heart, 1966; Fifty Stories, 1980; Life Being the Best, 1988; *essays:* Breaking the Silence, 1962; The Long Walk at San Francisco State and other essays, 1970; Words That Must Somehow Be Said, 1985; *memoirs:* The Autobiography of Emanuel Carnevali, 1967; Being Geniuses Together, 1968; *poetry:* A Glad Day; American Citizen; Collected Poems, 1962; Testament for my Students and other poems, 1970; This is Not a Letter, 1985. *For Children:* The Youngest Camel; Pinky, the Cat Who Liked to Sleep, 1966; Pinky in Persia, 1968. *Recreations:* ski-ing, mountain climbing. *Address:* c/o Watkins/Loomis Agency Inc., 150 East 35th Street, New York, NY 10016, USA.

BOYLE, Leonard Butler, CBE 1977; Director and General Manager, Principality Building Society, Cardiff, 1956–78; *b* 13 Jan. 1913; *s* of Harold and Edith Boyle; *m* 1938, Alice Baldwin Yarborough (*d* 1989); two *s*. *Educ:* Roundhay Sch., Leeds. FCBSI. Chief of Investment Dept, Leeds Permanent Building Soc., 1937; Asst Man., Isle of Thanet Bldg Soc., 1949; Jt Asst Gen. Man., Hastings and Thanet Bldg Soc., 1951, Sec. 1954. Building Socs Assoc.: Mem. Council, 1956–78 (Chm. Gen. Purposes Cttee, 1958–60; Chm. Develt Cttee, 1967–71); Chm. of Council, 1973–75 (Dep. Chm. 1971–73); Vice-Pres., 1978); Vice-Pres., CBSI, 1982–. Consultant, Manchester Exchange Trust. *Recreations:* gardening, walking, golf. *Address:* Northwick Cottage, Marlpit Lane, Seaton, Devon EX12 2HH. *T:* Seaton (0297) 22194.

BOYLE, Sir Stephen Gurney, 5th Bt *cr* 1904; *b* 15 Jan. 1962; *s* of Sir Richard Gurney Boyle, 4th Bt, and of Elizabeth Ann, *yr d* of Norman Dennes; *S* father, 1983. *Heir: b* Michael Desmond Boyle, *b* 16 Sept. 1963.

BOYLES, Edgar William; Under Secretary, Inland Revenue, 1975–81; *b* 24 March 1921; *s* of William John Boyles and Jessie Louisa Boyles; *m* 1950, Heather Iris Hobart, SRN; three *s* one *d*. *Educ:* Bedford Modern Sch. RAF, 1940–46. Tax Officer, Inland Revenue, 1939; Principal Inspector of Taxes, 1962; Sen. Principal Inspector, 1967. *Recreations:* chess, gardening, watching cricket. *Address:* The Keeley, 155 Bedford Road, Wootton, Bedford MK43 9BA. *T:* Bedford (0234) 851875.

BOYNE, 10th Viscount *cr* 1717; **Gustavus Michael George Hamilton-Russell,** DL; JP; Baron Hamilton, 1715; Baron Brancepeth, 1866; a Lord in Waiting, since 1981; *b* 10 Dec. 1931; *s* of late Hon. Gustavus Lascelles Hamilton-Russell and *g s* of 9th Viscount; *S* grandfather, 1942; *m* 1956, Rosemary Anne, 2nd *d* of Major Sir Dennis Stucley, 5th Bt; one *s* two *d* (and one *d* decd). *Educ:* Eton; Sandhurst; Royal Agricl Coll., Cirencester. Commissioned Grenadier Guards, 1952. Director: Nat. Westminster Bank, 1976–90 (Chm., W Midlands and Wales Regional Bd, 1976–90); Private Patients Plan Ltd, 1986–; Priplan Investments, 1987–; Chairman: Ludlow Race Club Ltd, 1987–; Harper Adams, 1990–. Mem., 1963–83, Dep. Chm., 1975–82, Telford Develt Corp. Governor, Wrekin Coll., Telford, 1965–86. CStJ. JP 1961, DL 1965, Salop. *Heir: s* Hon. Gustavus Michael Stucley Hamilton-Russell, *b* 27 May 1965. *Address:* Burwarton House, Bridgnorth, Salop. *T:* Burwarton (074633) 203. *Club:* White's.
See also Lord Forbes.

BOYNE, Donald Arthur Colin Aydon, CBE 1977; Director, 1974–85, Consultant, 1984–86, The Architectural Press; *b* 15 Feb. 1921; 2nd *s* of late Lytton Leonard Boyne and Millicent (*née* Nisbet); *m* 1947, Rosemary Pater; two *s* one *d*. *Educ:* Tonbridge Sch.; Architectural Assoc. School of Architecture, 1943–47. Indian Army, 8/13 FF Rifles, 1940–43. Editor, Architects' Jl, 1953–70; Chm., Editorial Bd, Architectural Review and Architects' Jl, 1971–74. Hon. FRIBA 1969. *Address:* Kentlands, Hildenborough, Kent TN11 8NR. *T:* Hildenborough (0732) 833539.

BOYNE, Sir Henry Brian, (Sir Harry Boyne), Kt 1976; CBE 1969; Political Correspondent, The Daily Telegraph, London, 1956–76; *b* 29 July 1910; 2nd *s* of late Lockhart Alexander Boyne, Journalist, Inverness, and late Elizabeth Jane Mactavish; *m* 1935, Margaret Little Templeton, Dundee; one *d*. *Educ:* High Sch. and Royal Academy, Inverness. Reporter, Inverness Courier, 1927; Dundee Courier and Advertiser, 1929. On active service, 1939–45, retiring with rank of Major, The Black Watch (RHR). Staff Correspondent, Glasgow Herald, at Dundee, 1945, and Edinburgh, 1949; Political Correspondent, Glasgow Herald, 1950. Dir of Communications, Conservative Central Office, 1980–82. Chairman: Parly Lobby Journalists, 1958–59 (Hon. Sec., 1968–71); Parly Press Gallery, 1961–62. Political Writer of Year, 1972. Mem., Police Complaints Bd, 1977–80; Chm., Bd of Visitors, HM Prison, Pentonville, 1980. Mem. Council, Savers' Union, 1982–86. *Publications:* The Houses of Parliament, 1981; Scotland Rediscovered, 1986. *Recreations:* reading, walking, watching cricket. *Address:* 122 Harefield Road, Uxbridge UB8 1PN. *T:* Uxbridge (0895) 55211.

BOYNE, Maj.-Gen. John, CB 1987; MBE 1965; CEng, FIMechE; FBIM; company director, since 1988; *b* 7 Nov. 1932; *s* of John Grant Boyne and Agnes Crawford (*née* Forrester); *m* 1956, Norma Beech; two *s*. *Educ:* King's Sch., Chester; Royal Military Coll. of Science, Shrivenham (BScEng 1st Cl. Hons). CEng, FIMechE 1975; FBIM 1975. Served in Egypt, Cyprus, Libya and UK, 1951–62; Staff Coll., Camberley, 1963; DAQMG(Ops) HQ MEC, Aden, 1964–66; OC 11 Infantry Workshop, REME, BAOR, 1966–67; Jt Services Staff Coll., 1968; GSO2 MoD, 1968–70; GSO1 (DS), Staff Coll., 1970–72; Comdr REME, 2nd Div., BAOR, 1972–73; AAG MoD, 1973–75; CSO (Personnel) to CPL, MoD, 1975–76; Dep. Dir Elec. and Mech. Engrg, 1st British Corps, 1976–78; RCDS, 1979; Dep. Dir Personal Services (Army), MoD, 1980–82; Vice Adjutant Gen. and Dir of Manning (Army), MoD, 1982–85; Dir Gen., Electrical and Mechanical Engrg, Logistic Executive (Army), MoD, 1985–88. Col Comdt, REME, 1988– (Rep. Col Comdt, 1989–90). Trustee, Army Benevolent Fund, 1986–. *Recreations:* music, philately, football. *Address:* c/o Midland Bank, 48 High Street, Runcorn, Cheshire WA7 1AN.

BOYNTON, Sir John (Keyworth), Kt 1979; MC 1944; LLB; MRTPI; DL; Chief Executive, Cheshire County Council, 1974–79; Solicitor; *b* 14 Feb. 1918; *s* of late Ernest Boynton, Hull; *m* 1st, 1947, Gabrielle Stanglmaier, Munich (*d* 1978); two *d*; 2nd, 1979, Edith Laane, The Hague. *Educ:* Dulwich Coll. Served War, 15th Scottish Reconnaissance Regt, 1940–46 (despatches, MC). Dep. Clerk, Berks CC, 1951–64; Clerk, Cheshire CC, 1964–74. Member: Planning Law Cttee of Law Soc., 1964–88; Economic Planning Council for NW, 1965; Exec. Council of Royal Inst. of Public Admin., 1970; Council of Industrial Soc., 1974–; Council, PSI, 1978–83. Pres., RTPI, 1976. Election Commissioner, Southern Rhodesia, 1979–80. DL Cheshire 1975. *Publications:* Compulsory Purchase and Compensation, 1964 (6th edn 1990); Job at the Top, 1986. *Recreation:* golf. *Address:* 1B Oakhill Avenue, NW3 7RD. *T:* 071–435 0012. *Club:* Army and Navy.

BOYS, Penelope Ann, (Mrs D. C. H. Wright); Deputy Director General, Office of Electricity Regulation, since 1989; *b* 11 June 1947; *d* of late Hubert John Boys and of Mollie Blackman Boys; *m* 1977, David Charles Henshaw Wright. *Educ:* Guildford County Sch. for Girls. Exec. Officer, DES, 1966–69; Asst Principal, Min. of Power, 1969–72; Private Sec., Minister without Portfolio, 1972–73; Principal, Dept of Energy, 1973–78; seconded to BNOC, 1978–80; Head of Internat. Unit, Dept of Energy, 1981–85; seconded to HM Treasury as Head, ST2 Div., 1985–87; Dir of Personnel, Dept of Energy, 1987–89. *Recreations:* entertaining, racing, walking. *Address:* Office of Electricity Regulation, Hagley House, Hagley Road, Birmingham B16 8QG. *T:* 021–456 6207.

BOYS-SMITH, Captain Humphry Gilbert, DSO 1940; DSC 1943; RD; RNR, retired; *b* 20 Dec. 1904; *s* of late Rev. Edward Percy Boys-Smith, MA, Rural Dean of Lyndhurst, Hants, and Charlotte Cecilia, *d* of late Thomas Backhouse Sandwith, CB, HM Consular Service; *m* 1935, Marjorie Helen (*d* 1981), *d* of Capt. Matthew John Miles Vicars-Miles, JP; no *c*. *Educ:* Pangbourne Nautical Coll. Joined Royal Naval Reserve, 1921; Merchant Navy, 1922–35; Extra Master's Certificate, 1930; HM Colonial Service, 1935–40 (Palestine) and 1946–50 (Western Pacific High Commission as Marine Supt); Addnl Mem. RNR Advisory Cttee, 1949–51; War Course, Royal Naval Coll., Greenwich, 1950–51. Courtaulds Ltd, Central Staff Dept, 1951–68. Placed on Retired List of RNR, 1952; Younger Brother of Trinity House, 1944; Mem. of Hon Company of Master Mariners, 1946; Assoc. Instn Naval Architects, 1948; served War of 1939–45 (DSO and Bar, DSC, despatches and American despatches). *Address:* Dibben's, Semley, Shaftesbury, Dorset SP7 9BW. *T:* East Knoyle (0747) 830358.
See also Rev. J. S. Boys Smith.

BOYS SMITH, Rev. John Sandwith, MA; Master of St John's College, Cambridge, 1959–69 (Fellow, 1927–59 and since 1969; Senior Bursar, 1944–59); Vice-Chancellor, University of Cambridge, 1963–65; Canon Emeritus of Ely Cathedral since 1948; *b* 8 Jan. 1901; *e s* of late Rev. E. P. Boys Smith, formerly Vicar of Hordle, Hants, and Charlotte Cecilia, *e d* of late T. B. Sandwith, CB; *m* 1942, Gwendolen Sara, *o d* of late W. J. Wynn; two *s*. *Educ:* Sherborne Sch.; St John's Coll., Cambridge. Economics Tripos Part I, Class II, division 2, 1921; BA, Theological Tripos, Part I, Sec. B, Class I, 1922; Scholar and Naden Student in Divinity, St John's Coll., 1922; Theological Tripos Part II, Sec. V, Class 1, 1924; Burney Student, 1924; Marburg University, 1924–25; Deacon, 1926; Curate of Sutton Coldfield, Birmingham, 1926–27; Priest, 1927; Chaplain of St John's Coll., Cambridge, 1927–34, and Director of Theological Studies, 1927–40, and 1944–52; Assistant Tutor, 1931–34; Tutor, 1934–39; Junior Bursar, 1939–40; University Lecturer in Divinity, Cambridge, 1931–40; Stanton Lecturer in the Philosophy of Religion, Cambridge Univ., 1934–37; Ely Professor of Divinity in the University of Cambridge and Canon of Ely Cathedral, 1940–43. Hon. Fellow: Trinity Coll., Dublin, 1968; Darwin Coll., Cambridge, 1969; New Hall, Cambridge, 1987. Hon. LLD, Cambridge, 1970. *Publications:* Religious Thought in the Eighteenth Century (with late J. M. Creed), 1934; Memories of St John's College Cambridge 1919–1969, 1983. *Address:* 1 Dulwich Mead, Half Moon Lane, SE24 9HS. *T:* 071–274 9334; St John's College, Cambridge.
See also Capt. H. G. Boys-Smith, S. W. Boys Smith.

BOYS SMITH, Stephen Wynn; Assistant Under Secretary of State, Home Office, since 1989; *b* 4 May 1946; *s* of Rev. Dr John Sandwith Boys Smith, *qv*; *m* 1971, Linda Elaine Price; one *s* one *d*. *Educ:* Sherborne Sch.; St John's Coll., Cambridge (MA); Univ. of British Columbia (MA). Home Office, 1968; Asst Private Sec. to Home Sec., 1971–73; Central Policy Review Staff, Cabinet Office, 1977; Home Office, 1979; Private Sec. to Home Sec., 1980–81; NI Office, 1981; Principal Private Sec. to Sec. of State for NI, 1981–82; Home Office, 1984; Principal Private Sec. to Home Sec., 1985–87. *Recreations:* gardening, reading. *Address:* Home Office, Queen Anne's Gate, SW1H 9AT. *T:* 071–273 2746.

BOYSE, Prof. Edward Arthur, MD; FRS 1977; Distinguished Professor, University of Arizona, Tucson, since 1989; Member, Sloan-Kettering Institute for Cancer Research, New York, 1967–89; Professor of Biology, Cornell University, 1969–89; *b* 11 Aug. 1923; *s* of late Arthur Boyse, FRCO, and Dorothy Vera Boyse (*née* Mellersh); *m* 1951, Jeanette (*née* Grimwood) (marr. diss. 1987); two *s* one *d*; *m* 1987, Judith Bard. *Educ:* St Bartholomew's Hosp. Med. Sch., Univ. of London. MB BS 1952; MD 1957. Aircrew, RAF, 1941–46, commnd 1943. Various hospital appts, 1952–57; research at Guy's Hosp., 1957–60; research appts at NY Univ. and Sloan-Kettering Inst., 1960–89. Amer. Cancer Soc. Res. Prof., 1977. Member: Amer. Acad. of Arts and Scis, 1977; Nat. Acad. of Scis, USA, 1979. Cancer Research Institute Award in Tumor Immunology, 1975; Isaac Adler Award, Rockefeller and Harvard Univs, 1976. *Publications:* papers relating genetics and immunology to development and cancer. *Address:* Department of Microbiology and Immunology, University of Arizona Health Sciences Center, 1501 N Campbell Avenue, Tucson, Arizona 85724, USA.

BOYSON, Rt. Hon. Sir Rhodes, Kt 1987; PC 1987; MP (C) Brent North, since Feb. 1974; *b* 11 May 1925; *s* of Alderman William Boyson, MBE, JP and Mrs Bertha Boyson, Haslingden, Rossendale, Lancs; *m* 1st, 1946, Violet Burletson (marr. diss.); two *d*; 2nd, 1971, Florette MacFarlane. *Educ:* Haslingden Grammar Sch.; UC Cardiff; Manchester Univ. (BA, MA); LSE (PhD); Corpus Christi Coll., Cambridge. Served with Royal Navy. Headmaster: Lea Bank Secondary Modern Sch., Rossendale, 1955–61; Robert Montefiore Secondary Sch., Stepney, 1961–66; Highbury Grammar Sch., 1966–67; Highbury Grove Sch., 1967–74. Chm., Nat. Council for Educnl Standards, 1974–79. Chm., Churchill Press and Constitutional Book Club, 1969–79. Councillor: Haslingden, 1957–61; Waltham Forest, 1968–74 (Chm. Establishment Cttee, 1968–71); Chm., London Boroughs Management Services Unit, 1968–70. Formerly Youth Warden, Lancs Youth Clubs. Contested (C) Eccles, 1970. Vice-Chm., Cons Parly Educn Cttee, 1975–76; Hon. Sec. Cons. Adv. Cttee on Educn, 1975–78; Opposition spokesman on educn, 1976–79; Parly Under-Sec. of State, DES, 1979–83; Minister of State: for Social Security, DHSS, 1983–84; NI Office, 1984–86; for Local Govt, DoE, 1986–87. Mem. Exec., 1922 Cttee, 1987–. Educnl columnist, Spectator, 1969. *Publications:* The North-East Lancashire Poor Law 1838–1871, 1965; The Ashworth Cotton Enterprise, 1970; (ed) Right Turn, 1970; (ed) Down with the Poor, 1971; (ed) Goodbye to Nationalisation, 1972; (ed) Education: Threatened Standards, 1972; (ed) The Accountability of Schools, 1973; Oversubscribed: the story of Highbury Grove, 1974; Crisis in Education, 1975; (jt ed) Black Papers on Education, 1969–77; (ed) 1985: An Escape from Orwell's 1984, 1975; Centre Forward, 1978. *Recreations:* reading, writing, talk, hard work, meeting friends, inciting the millenialistic Left in education and politics. *Address:* House of Commons, SW1. *T:* 071-219 4507; 71 Paines Lane, Pinner, Middx. *T:* 081–866 2071. *Clubs:* Carlton, St Stephen's; Churchill (N Wembley), Wembley Conservative.

BOZZOLI, Guerino Renzo, DSc(Eng); Chairman, New Era (non-racial) Schools Trust, since 1981; Vice-Chancellor and Principal, University of the Witwatersrand, Johannesburg, 1969–77; *b* Pretoria, 24 April 1911; *s* of late B. Bozzoli, *m* 1936, Cora Collins, *d* of late L. N. B. Collins; one *s* three *d*. *Educ:* Sunnyside Sch. and Boys' High Sch., Pretoria; Witwatersrand Univ. BSc(Eng) 1933, DSc(Eng) 1948; PrEng. Major, SA Corps of Signals, 1940–45 (commendation 1944). Asst Engr, African Broadcasting Co., 1934–36; Jun. Lectr, Dept of Electrical Engrg, Witwatersrand Univ., Lectr, 1939, Sen. Lectr, 1942; apptd Prof. and Head of Dept of Electrical Engineering, 1948. Dean, Univ. Residence, Cottesloe, 1948–56; Dean, Faculty of Engrg, 1954–57 and 1962–65; Senate Mem., Council of the Univ., 1957–68; Deputy Vice-Chancellor, 1965–68. Chm. Council, Mangosuthu Technikon, Kwa Zulu, 1978–85. Member: Straszacker Commn of Enquiry into Univ. Educn of Engineers, 1957–68; de Vries Commn of Enquiry into SA Univs, 1968–75; Nat. Educn Council, 1975–. President: SAIEE, 1955; AS&TS of SA, 1969–70; SA Assoc. for Advancement of Science, 1972. Hon. FSAIEE; Hon. FRSSAf 1976. Hon. LLD: Univ. of Cape Town, 1977; Univ. of Witwatersrand, 1978. *Publications:* numerous articles and papers on engineering education. *Recreations:* swimming, woodwork, electronics. *Address:* 121 Dundalk Avenue, Parkview, Johannesburg, 2193, South Africa. *T:* Johannesburg 646–1015. *Clubs:* 1926, Scientific and Technical (Johannesburg).

BRABAZON, family name of **Earl of Meath.**

BRABAZON OF TARA, 3rd Baron *cr* 1942; **Ivon Anthony Moore-Brabazon;** Minister of State, Department of Transport, since 1990; *b* 20 Dec. 1946; *s* of 2nd Baron Brabazon of Tara, CBE, and Henriette Mary (*d* 1985), *d* of late Sir Rowland Clegg; *S* father, 1974; *m* 1979, Harriet Frances, *o d* of Mervyn P. de Courcy Hamilton, Salisbury, Zimbabwe; one *s* one *d. Educ:* Harrow. Mem., Stock Exchange, 1972–84. A Lord in Waiting (Govt Whip), 1984–86; Parly Under-Sec. of State, Dept of Transport, 1986–89; Minister of State, FCO, 1989–90. *Recreations:* sailing, Cresta Run. *Heir: s* Hon. Benjamin Ralph Moore-Brabazon, *b* 15 March 1983. *Address:* House of Lords, SW1. *Clubs:* White's; Royal Yacht Squadron; Bembridge Sailing, St Moritz Tobogganing.

BRABHAM, Sir John Arthur, (Sir Jack Brabham), Kt 1979; OBE 1966; retired, 1970, as Professional Racing Driver; Managing Director: Jack Brabham (Motors) Ltd; Jack Brabham (Worcester Park) Ltd; Engine Developments Ltd; *b* Sydney, Australia, 2 April 1926; *m* 1951, Betty Evelyn; three *s. Educ:* Hurstville Technical Coll., Sydney. Served in RAAF, 1944–46. Started own engineering business, 1946; Midget Speedway racing, 1946–52; several championships (Australian, NSW, South Australian); numerous wins driving a Cooper-Bristol, Australia, 1953–54; to Europe, 1955; Australian Grand Prix, 1955 and 1963 (debut of Repco Brabham); World Champion Formula II, 1958, also many firsts including Casablanca, Goodwood, Brands Hatch, NZ Grand Prix, Belgian Grand Prix; Formula II Champion of France, 1964. World Champion Driver: (after first full Formula I Season with 2½-litre car), 1959–60, 1960–61, 1966. First in Monaco and British Grandes Epreuves, 1959; won Grand Prix of: Holland, Belgium, France, Britain, Portugal, Denmark, 1960; Belgium, 1961. Elected Driver of the Year by Guild of Motoring Writers, 1959, 1966 and 1970, Sportsman of the Year by Australian Broadcasting Co., 1959; left Cooper to take up building own Grand Prix cars, 1961; debut, 1962; first ever constructor/driver to score world championship points, 1963; cars finished first: French GP; Mexican GP, 1964; Formula II and Formula III cars world-wide success, 1963; awarded Ferodo Trophy, 1964 and again, 1966; won French Grand Prix and British Grand Prix, 1966; won French Grand Prix, 1967. RAC Gold Medal, 1966; BARC Gold Medal, 1959, 1966, 1967; Formula I Manufacturers' Championship, 1966, 1967. *Publications:* Jack Brabham's Book of Motor Racing, 1960; When the Flag Drops, 1971; contribs to British journals. *Recreations:* photography, water ski-ing, under-water swimming, flying. *Address:* c/o 33 Central Road, Worcester Park, Surrey KT4 8EG. *Clubs:* Royal Automobile, British Racing and Sports Car, British Racing Drivers'; Australian Racing Drivers'.

BRABOURNE, 7th Baron, *cr* 1880; **John Ulick Knatchbull,** 16th Bt, *cr* 1641; film and television producer; Chairman, Thames Television, since 1990 (Director, since 1978); *b* 9 Nov. 1924; *s* of 5th Baron and Lady Doreen Geraldine Browne (Order of the Crown of India; DStJ) (*d* 1979), *y d* of 6th Marquess of Sligo; *S* brother, 1943; *m* 1946, Lady Patricia Edwina Victoria Mountbatten (*see* Countess Mountbatten of Burma); four *s* two *d* (and one *s* decd). *Educ:* Eton; Oxford. *Films Produced:* Harry Black, 1958; Sink the Bismarck!, 1959; HMS Defiant, 1961; Othello, 1965; The Mikado, 1966; Romeo and Juliet; Up the Junction, 1967; Dance of Death, 1968; Tales of Beatrix Potter, 1971; Murder on the Orient Express, 1974; Death on the Nile, 1978; Stories from a Flying Trunk, 1979; The Mirror Crack'd, 1980; Evil Under the Sun, 1982; A Passage to India, 1984; Little Dorrit, 1987. TV Series: National Gallery, 1974; A Much-Maligned Monarch, 1976; Leontyne, 1987. Chairman: Copyright Promotions Gp, 1974–; North Downs Cable, 1990–; Dir, Thorn EMI, 1981–86. Governor: BFI, 1979– (Fellow, 1985); National Film Sch., 1980–; Mem., British Screen Adv. Council, 1985–; Trustee: BAFTA, 1975–; Science Museum, 1984–; Nat. Mus. of Photography, Film and Television, 1984–. Pres., Kent Trust for Nature Conservation; Chairman: Council, Caldecott Community; Governors, Norton Knatchbull Sch.; Governor: Wye Coll.; Gordonstoun Sch.; United World Colleges; Dep. Pro-Chancellor, Univ. of Kent. *Heir: s* Lord Romsey, *qv. Address:* Newhouse, Mersham, Ashford, Kent TN25 6NQ. *T:* Ashford (0233) 623466; Mersham Productions Ltd, 41 Montpelier Walk, SW7 1JH. *T:* 071–589 8829, *Fax:* 071–584 0024.

BRACEGIRDLE, Dr Brian, FSA, FRPS, FIBiol; research consultant in microscopy, and Fellow, Science Museum, since 1990; *b* 31 May 1933; *o c* of Alfred Bracegirdle; *m* 1st, 1958, Margaret Lucy Merrett (marr. diss. 1974); one *d*; 2nd, 1975, Patricia Helen Miles; no *c. Educ:* King's Sch., Macclesfield; Univ. of London (BSc, PhD). DipRMS. FRPS 1969; FIBiol 1976; FSA 1981. Technician in industry, 1950–57; Biology Master, Erith Grammar Sch., 1958–61; Sen. Lectr in Biol., S Katharine's Coll., London, 1961–64; Head, Depts of Nat. Science and Learning Resources, Coll. of All Saints, London, 1964–77; Science Museum: Keeper, Wellcome Mus. of Hist. of Medicine, 1977; Head of Dept of Med. Scis, Asst Dir and Head of Collections, Management Div., 1987–89. Hon. Lectr in History of Medicine, UCL; Hon. Res. Fellow in Hist. of Sci., Imperial Coll., 1990–. Hon. Treasurer, ICOM (UK); Pres., Assoc. Européenne de Musées de l'Histoire des Sciences Médicales. Chm., Inst. of Medical and Biological Illustrations, 1983–84; President: Assoc. Européenne de Musées de l'Histoire des Sciences Medicales, 1984–; Quekett Microscopical Club, 1985–88; Vice-Pres., Royal Microscopical Soc., 1988–; Hon. Treas., ICOM (UK), 1982–. *Publications:* Photography for Books and Reports, 1970; The Archaeology of the Industrial Revolution, 1973; The Evolution of Microtechnique, 1978, 1987; (ed) Beads of Glass: Leeuwenhoek and the early microscope, 1984; (with W. H. Freeman): An Atlas of Embryology, 1963, 1978; An Atlas of Histology, 1966; An Atlas of Invertebrate Structure, 1971; An Advanced Atlas of Histology, 1976; (with P. H. Miles): An Atlas of Plant Structure, vol. I, 1971; An Atlas of Plant Structure, Vol. II, 1973; Thomas Telford, 1973; The Darbys and the Ironbridge Gorge, 1974; An Atlas of Chordate Structure, 1977; papers on photography for life sciences, on scientific topics, and on history of science/medicine. *Recreations:* walking, music, travel. *Address:* Cold Aston Lodge, Cold Aston, Cheltenham, Glos GL54 3BN. *T:* Cotswold (0451) 20181. *Club:* Athenæum.

BRACEWELL, Hon. Dame Joyanne (Winifred), (Hon. Dame Joyanne Copeland), DBE 1990; **Hon. Mrs Justice Bracewell;** a Judge of the High Court of Justice, Family Division, since 1990; *b* 5 July 1934; *d* of Jack and Lilian Bracewell; *m* 1963, Roy Copeland; one *s* one *d. Educ:* Manchester Univ. (LLB, LLM). Called to Bar, Gray's Inn, 1955; pupillage at the Bar, 1955–56; Mem., Northern Circuit, 1956–90; a Recorder of the Crown Court, 1975–83; QC 1978; a Circuit Judge, 1983–90. Family Div. Liaison Judge for London, 1990–. Consulting Ed., Butterworth's Family Law Service, 1989–. Hon. LLD Manchester, 1991. *Recreations:* antiques, cooking, reading, walking, bridge, wildlife conservation. *Address:* Royal Courts of Justice, Strand, WC2A 2LL.

BRACEWELL-SMITH, Sir Charles, 4th Bt *cr* 1947, of Keighley; *b* 13 Oct. 1955; *s* of Sir George Bracewell Smith, 2nd Bt, MBE, and Helene Marie (*d* 1975), *d* of late John Frederick Hydock, Philadelphia, USA; *S* brother, 1983; *m* 1977, Carol Vivien, *d* of Norman Hough, Cookham, Berks. *Heir:* none. *Address:* Park Lane Hotel, Piccadilly, W1Y 8BX.

BRACKENBURY, Ven. Michael Palmer; Archdeacon of Lincoln, since 1988; *b* 6 July 1930; *s* of Frank Brackenbury and Constance Mary (*née* Palmer); *m* 1953, Jean Margaret, *d* of Oscar Arnold Harrison and May (*née* Norton). *Educ:* Norwich School; Lincoln Theological Coll. ACII 1956. RAF, 1948–50. Asst Curate, South Ormsby Group, 1966–69; Rector of Sudbrooke with Scothern, 1969–77; RD of Lawres, 1973–78; Diocesan Dir of Ordinands, Lincoln, 1977–87; Personal Assistant to Bishop of Lincoln, 1977–88; Canon and Prebendary of Lincoln, 1979–; Diocesan Lay Ministry Adviser, Lincoln, 1986–87. Mem., Gen. Synod of C of E, 1989–. *Recreations:* music, reading, cricket, travel. *Address:* 2 Ashfield Road, Sleaford, Lincs NG34 7DZ. *T:* Sleaford (0529) 307149.

BRADBEER, Sir (John) Derek (Richardson), Kt 1988; OBE 1973; TD 1965; DL; Partner, Wilkinson Maughan (formerly Wilkinson Marshall Clayton & Gibson), since 1961; President of the Law Society, 1987–88; *b* 29 Oct. 1931; *s* of William Bertram Bradbeer and Winifred (*née* Richardson); *m* 1962, Margaret Elizabeth Chantler; one *s* one *d. Educ:* Canford Sch.; Sidney Sussex Coll., Cambridge (MA). Nat. Service, 2nd Lieut RA, 1951–52; TA, 1952–77: Lt-Col Comdg 101 (N) Med. Regt RA(V), 1970–73; Col, Dep. Comdr 21 and 23 Artillery Bdes, 1973–76; Hon. Col, 101 (N) Field Regt, RA(V), 1986–. Admitted Solicitor, 1959. Mem., Criminal Injuries Compensation Bd, 1988–. Mem. Council, 1973–, Vice-Pres., 1986–87, Law Soc.; Pres., Newcastle upon Tyne Incorp. Law Soc., 1982–83; Gov., Coll. of Law, 1983–. Dir, Newcastle and Gateshead Water Co., 1978–. Vice-Chm., N of England TA&VRA, 1988–. DL Tyne and Wear, 1988. *Recreations:* reading, gardening, sport. *Address:* Forge Cottage, Shilvington, Ponteland, Newcastle upon Tyne NE20 0AP. *T:* Whalton (067075) 214. *Clubs:* Army and Navy; Northern Counties (Newcastle upon Tyne).

BRADBROOK, Prof. Muriel Clara, MA, PhD, 1933; LittD Cantab 1955; FBA 1990; *b* 27 April 1909; *d* of Samuel Bradbrook, Supt HM Waterguard at Liverpool and Glasgow. *Educ:* Hutchesons' Sch., Glasgow; Oldershaw Sch., Wallasey; Girton Coll., Cambridge. English Tripos, Class I, 1929, 1930; Harness Prize, 1931, Allen Scholar, 1935–36; in residence, Somerville Coll., Oxford, 1935–36. Cambridge University: Univ. Lecturer, 1945–62; Reader, 1962–65; Professor of English, 1965–76; Mistress of Girton College, 1968–76 (Vice-Mistress, 1962–66; Fellow, 1932–35, 1936–68, and 1976–). Board of Trade, Industries and Manufactures Depts 2 and 3, 1941–45; in residence at Folger Library, Washington, and Huntington Library, California, 1958–59; Fellow, Nat. Humanities Center, N Carolina, 1979. Tour of the Far East for Shakespeare's Fourth Centenary, 1964; Trustee, Shakespeare's Birthplace, 1967–82, 1985–. Visiting Professor: Santa Cruz, California, 1966; Kuwait, 1969; Tokyo, 1975; Kenyon Coll., USA, 1977; Rhodes Univ., SA, 1979; Clark Lecturer, Trinity Coll., Cambridge, 1968. Hon. Prof., Graduate Sch. of Renaissance Studies, Warwick Univ., 1987–90. Foreign Mem., Norwegian Acad. of Arts and Scis, 1966; Hon. Mem., Mod. Lang. Assoc. of America, 1974. FRSL 1947. Hon. LittD: Liverpool, 1964; Sussex, 1972; London, 1973; Hon. LLD Smith Coll., USA, 1965; Hon. PhD, Gothenburg, 1975; Hon. LHD Kenyon Coll., USA, 1977. Freedom, City of Hiroshima. *Publications:* Elizabethan Stage Conditions, 1932; Themes and Conventions of Elizabethan Tragedy, 1934; The School of Night, 1936; Andrew Marvell (with M. G. Lloyd Thomas), 1940; Joseph Conrad, 1941; Ibsen the Norwegian, 1947; T. S. Eliot, 1950; Shakespeare and Elizabethan Poetry, 1951; The Queen's Garland, 1953; The Growth and Structure of Elizabethan Comedy, 1955; Sir Thomas Malory, 1957; The Rise of the Common Player, 1962; English Dramatic Form, 1965; That Infidel Place, 1969; Shakespeare the Craftsman, 1969; Literature in Action, 1972; Malcolm Lowry: his art and early life, 1974; The Living Monument, 1976; Shakespeare: the poet in his world, 1978; John Webster, Citizen and Dramatist, 1980; Collected Papers, 4 vols, 1982–89; Muriel Bradbrook on Shakespeare, 1984; numerous articles and reviews. *Recreations:* travel, theatre. *Address:* 91 Chesterton Road, Cambridge CB4 3AP. *T:* Cambridge (0223) 352765. *Clubs:* University Women's; ADC (Cambridge).

BRADBURN, John; Chief Registrar of the High Court of Justice in Bankruptcy, 1984–88; Registrar of the Companies Court and Clerk of the Restrictive Practices Court, 1980–88; *b* 4 April 1915; *s* of Harold and Fanny Louise Bradburn; *m* 1948, Irène Elizabeth Norman, JP, *yr d* of Denham Grindley and Bertha Norman; two *s. Educ:* Repton; Trinity Coll., Oxford (MA). Served War, 1939–46; Oxfordshire and Bucks LI; Major. Called to the Bar, Inner Temple, 1939; practised at Chancery Bar, Lincoln's Inn, 1946–79 (Bencher, 1972–); a Conveyancing Counsel of the Supreme Court, 1977–80; Lord Chancellor's Legal Visitor, Ct of Protection, 1980–83. Mem., Gen. Council of the Bar, 1962–66. *Recreation:* freemasonry. *Address:* West Mews, 11 Calcot Court, Calcot Park, Reading, Berks RG3 5RW. *T:* Reading (0734) 425418. *Club:* MCC.

BRADBURY, family name of **Baron Bradbury.**

BRADBURY, 2nd Baron, *cr* 1925, of Winsford; **John Bradbury;** *b* 7 Jan. 1914; *s* of 1st Baron Bradbury, GCB, and Hilda (*d* 1949), 2nd *d* of W. A. Kirby; *S* father 1950; *m* 1st, 1939, Joan, *o d* of W. D. Knight, Darley, Addlestone, Surrey; one *s* one *d*; 2nd, 1946, Gwerfyl, *d* of late E. S. Roberts, Gellifor, Ruthin; one *d. Educ:* Westminster; Brasenose Coll., Oxford. *Heir: s* Hon. John Bradbury [*b* 17 March 1940; *m* 1968, Susan, *d* of late W. Liddiard, East Shefford, Berks; two *s*]. *Address:* Wingham, Summerhays, Leigh Hill Road, Cobham, Surrey. *T:* Cobham (0932) 7757.

BRADBURY, Anita Jean, (Mrs Philip Bradbury); *see* Pollack, A. J.

BRADBURY, Edgar; Managing Director, Skelmersdale Development Corporation, 1976–85; *b* 5 June 1927; *s* of Edgar Furniss Bradbury and Mary Bradbury; *m* 1954, Janet Mary Bouchier Lisle; two *s* one *d. Educ:* Grove Park Sch., Wrexham; The High Sch., Newcastle, Staffs; King's Coll., Durham Univ. LLB (Hons). Solicitor. Asst Solicitor: Scarborough BC, 1952–54; St Helens CBC, 1954–57; Dep. Town Clerk, Loughborough, 1957–59; Town Clerk and Clerk of the Peace, Deal, 1960–63; Legal Dir, Skelmersdale Develt Corp., 1963–76. Vice-Chm., W Lancs Health Authority, 1984– (Mem., 1982–). *Recreations:* tennis, bridge. *Address:* Overdale, Granville Park, Aughton, Ormskirk. *T:* Aughton Green (0695) 422308.

BRADBURY, Surgeon Vice-Adm. Sir Eric (Blackburn), KBE 1971; CB 1968; FRCS 1972; Medical Director-General of the Navy, 1969–72; Chairman, Tunbridge Wells District Health Authority, 1981–84; *b* 2 March 1911; *s* of late A. B. Bradbury, Maze, Co. Antrim; *m* 1939, Elizabeth Constance Austin (*d* 1991); three *d. Educ:* Royal Belfast Academical Instn; Queen's Univ., Belfast; MB, BCh 1934; DMRD (London) 1949; Hon. LLD 1973. Joined RN (Medical Service), 1934; served at sea in HMS Barham, HMS Endeavour, HMS Cumberland, 1935–38 and in HMS Charybdis and HMHS Oxfordshire, 1941–45; served in RN Hospitals: Haslar, Chatham, Plymouth and Malta; Med. Officer-in-Charge, RN Hosp., Haslar, and Comd MO, Portsmouth, 1966–69. QHP 1966–72. *Address:* The Gate House, Nevill Park, Tunbridge Wells, Kent TN4 8NN. *T:* Tunbridge Wells (0892) 27661.

BRADBURY, Prof. Malcolm Stanley, CBE 1991; FRSL; Professor of American Studies, University of East Anglia, since 1970; *b* 7 Sept. 1932; *s* of Arthur Bradbury and Doris Ethel (*née* Marshall); *m* 1959, Elizabeth Salt; two *s. Educ:* University Coll. of Leicester

(BA); Queen Mary Coll., Univ. of London (MA; Hon. Fellow, 1984); Univ. of Manchester (PhD). Staff Tutor in Literature and Drama, Dept of Adult Education, Univ. of Hull, 1959–61; Lectr in English Language and Literature, Dept of English, Univ. of Birmingham, 1961–65; Lectr (later Sen. Lectr and Reader) in English and American Literature, Sch. of English and American Studies, Univ. of East Anglia, 1965–70. Visiting Professor: Univ. of Zürich, 1972; Washington Univ., St Louis, 1982; Univ. of Queensland, 1983. Chm. of Judges, Booker McConnell Prize for Fiction, 1981. Hon. DLitt: Leicester, 1986; Birmingham, 1989. Editor: Arnold Stratford-upon-Avon Studies series; Methuen Contemporary Writers series. Adapted for television: Tom Sharpe, Blott on the Landscape, 1985; Tom Sharpe, Porterhouse Blue, 1987 (Internat. Emmy Award); Alison Lurie, Imaginary Friends, 1987; Kingsley Amis, The Green Man, 1990; television serials: Anything More Would Be Greedy, 1989; The Gravy Train, 1990, 1991. *Publications: non-fiction:* Evelyn Waugh, 1962; E. M. Forster: a collection of critical essays (ed), 1965; What is a Novel?, 1969; A Passage to India: a casebook, 1970; (ed) Penguin Companion to Literature, vol. 3: American (with E. Mottram), 1971; The Social Context of Modern English Literature, 1972; Possibilities: essays on the state of the novel, 1973; (with J. W. McFarlane) Modernism, 1976; (ed) The Novel Today, 1977; (ed) An Introduction to American Studies (with H. Temperley), 1981; Saul Bellow, 1982; All Dressed Up And Nowhere To Go (humour), 1982; The Modern American Novel, 1983; Why Come to Slaka? (humour), 1986; No, Not Bloomsbury (essays), 1987; (ed) Penguin Book of Modern British Short Stories, 1987; Mensonge (humour), 1987; The Modern World: ten great writers, 1987; Unsent Letters (humour), 1988; (with R. Ruland) From Puritanism to Postmodernism: a history of American literature, 1991; *fiction:* Eating People is Wrong, 1959; Stepping Westward, 1965; The History Man, 1975; Who Do You Think You Are? (short stories), 1976; The After Dinner Game (television plays), 1982; Rates of Exchange, 1982 (shortlisted, Booker Prize); Cuts: a very short novel, 1987. *Recreations:* none. *Address:* School of English and American Studies, University of East Anglia, Norwich NR4 7TJ. *T:* Norwich (0603) 56161. *Club:* Royal Over-Seas League.

BRADBURY, Ray Douglas; author; *b* Waukegan, Ill, USA, 22 Aug. 1920; *s* of Leonard S. Bradbury and Esther Moberg; *m* 1947, Marguerite Susan McClure; four *d*. *Educ:* Los Angeles High Sch. First Science-Fiction stories, 1941–44; stories sold to Harpers', Mademoiselle, The New Yorker, etc., 1945–56. Stories selected for: Best American Short Stories, 1946, 1948, 1952, 1958; O. Henry Prize Stories, 1947, 1948; and for inclusion in numerous anthologies. *Screenplays:* Moby Dick, 1954; Icarus Montgolfier Wright, 1961; The Martian Chronicles, 1964; The Picasso Summer, 1968; The Halloween Tree, 1968; The Dreamers; And The Rock Cried Out. Benjamin Franklin Award for Best Story Published in an Amer. Magazine of General Circulation, 1954; 1000 dollar Grant from Inst. of Arts and Letters, 1954. *Publications: novels:* Dark Carnival, 1947; Fahrenheit 451, 1953 (filmed); (for children) Switch on the Night, 1955; Dandelion Wine, 1957; Something Wicked This Way Comes, 1962 (filmed 1983; adapted for stage, 1986); The Small Assassin, 1973; Mars and the Minds of Man, 1973; The Mummies of Guanajuato, 1978; The Ghosts of Forever, 1981; Death is a Lonely Business, 1986; The Toynbee Convector, 1989; A Graveyard for Lunatics, 1990; *short stories:* The Martian Chronicles, 1950 (English edn, The Silver Locusts, 1957); The Illustrated Man, 1951 (filmed with The Day It Rained Forever); The Golden Apples of the Sun, 1953; The October Country, 1955; A Medicine for Melancholy (English edn, The Day It Rained Forever), 1959; (for children) R Is For Rocket, 1962; (for children) S Is For Space, 1962; The Machineries of Joy, 1964; The Autumn People, 1965; The Vintage Bradbury, 1965; Tomorrow Midnight, 1966; Twice Twenty-Two, 1966; I Sing the Body Electric!, 1969; Long After Midnight, 1976; *general:* Zen and the Art of Writing, 1973; *poems:* When Elephants Last in the Dooryard Bloomed, 1973; Where Robot Mice and Robot Men Run Round in Robot Towns, 1977; This Attic where the Meadow Greens, 1980; The Haunted Computer and the Android Pope, 1981; *plays:* The Meadow, 1947; The Anthem Sprinters (one-act), 1963; The World of Ray Bradbury (one-act), 1964; The Wonderful Ice Cream Suit and Other Plays (one-act), 1965; Any Friend of Nicholas Nickleby's is a Friend of Mine, 1968; Pillar of Fire, 1975. *Recreations:* oil painting, ceramics, collecting native masks. *Address:* 10265 Cheviot Drive, Los Angeles, Calif 90064, USA.

BRADBURY, Rear-Adm. Thomas Henry, CB 1979; Group Personnel Executive, Davy Corporation, since 1987; *b* 4 Dec. 1922; *s* of Thomas Henry Bradbury and Violet Buckingham; *m* 1st, 1945, Beryl Doreen Evans (marr. diss. 1979); one *s* one *d*; 2nd, 1979, Sarah Catherine, *d* of Harley Hillier and Mrs Susan Hillier. *Educ:* Christ's Hosp. CO HMS Jufair, 1960–62; Supply Officer, HMS Hermes, 1965–67; Sec. to Controller of Navy, MoD, 1967–70; CO HMS Terror, 1970–71; RCDS, 1972; Dir, Naval Admin. Planning, MoD, 1974–76; Flag Officer, Admiralty Interview Bd, 1977–79. Gp Personnel Dir, Inchcape Gp of Cos, 1979–86. *Recreations:* sailing, gardening. *Address:* Padgham Down, Dallington, Heathfield, E Sussex TN21 9NS. *T:* Rushlake Green (0435) 830208.

BRADBY, Prof. David Henry, PhD; Professor of Drama and Theatre Studies, University of London, at Royal Holloway and Bedford New College, since 1988; *b* 27 Feb. 1942; *s* of Edward Lawrence Bradby, *qv*; *m* 1965, Rachel Anderson, writer; three *s* one *d*. *Educ:* Rugby Sch.; Trinity College, Oxford (MA); PhD Glasgow; CertEd Bristol. Lectr, Glasgow Univ., 1966–70; University of Kent at Canterbury: Lectr, 1971; Sen. Lectr, 1979–85; Reader in French Theatre Studies, 1985–88; Prof. of Theatre Studies, Univ. of Caen, 1983–84. FRSA. *Publications:* People's Theatre (with John McCormick), 1978; The Theatre of Roger Planchon, 1984; Modern French Drama 1940–1980, 1984; (with David Williams) Directors' Theatre, 1988; Le Théâtre Français Contemporain, 1990. *Recreation:* forestry. *Address:* Department of Drama and Theatre Studies, Royal Holloway and Bedford New College, Egham, Surrey TW20 0EX.

BRADBY, Edward Lawrence; Principal, St Paul's College, Cheltenham, 1949–72; *b* 15 March 1907; *y s* of late H. C. Bradby, Ringshall End, near Berkhamsted, Herts; *m* 1939, Bertha Woodall, *y d* of late Henry Woodall, Yotes Court, Mereworth, Maidstone; three *s* one *d*. *Educ:* Rugby Sch.; New College, Oxford (MA). Asst Master, Merchant Taylors' Sch., 1930–34; International Student Service, 1934–39; Secretary to Cttee for England and Wales, 1934–36; Asst General Secretary, Geneva, 1936–37; General Secretary, Geneva, 1937–39; Principal, Royal Coll., Colombo, Ceylon, 1939–46; Principal, Eastbourne Emergency Training Coll., 1946–49. Hon. MEd Bristol, 1972. *Publications:* Editor, The University Outside Europe, a collection of essays on university institutions in 14 countries, 1939; Seend, a Wiltshire Village Past and Present, 1981; The Book of Devizes, 1985; Seend Heritage, 1985. *Address:* 13 Hansford Square, Combe Down, Bath, Avon BA2 5LH. *T:* Bath (0225) 834092. *Club:* Commonwealth Trust.

See also D. H. Bradby.

BRADDON, Russell Reading; author; *b* 25 Jan. 1921; *s* of Henry Russell Braddon and Thelma Doris Braddon (*née* Reading). *Educ:* Sydney Church of England Grammar Sch.; Sydney Univ. (BA). Failed Law finals; began writing, by chance, 1949; been writing ever since. Has scripted, narrated and presented television documentaries, 1984–, inc. contrib. to Great Rivers of the World series, BBC, 1985. *Publications:* The Piddingtons, 1950; The Naked Island, 1951; Those in Peril, 1954; Cheshire, VC, 1954; Out of the Storm, 1956; Nancy Wake, 1956; End of a Hate, 1958; Gabriel Comes to 24, 1958; Proud American Boy, 1960; Joan Sutherland, 1962; The Year of the Angry Rabbit, 1964; Roy Thomson of Fleet Street, 1965; Committal Chamber, 1966; When the Enemy is Tired, 1968; The Inseparables, 1968; Will You Walk a Little Faster, 1969; The Siege, 1969; Prelude and Fugue for Lovers, 1971; The Progress of Private Lilyworth, 1971; End Play, 1972; Suez: splitting of a nation, 1973; The Hundred Days of Darien, 1974; All the Queen's Men, 1977; The Finalists, 1977; The Shepherd's Bush Case, 1978; The Predator, 1980; The Other Hundred Years War, 1983; Thomas Baines, 1986; Images of Australia, 1988; Funnelweb, 1990. *Recreation:* not writing. *Address:* c/o John Farquharson Ltd, 162–168 Regent Street, W1R 5TB.

BRADEN, Bernard; free-lance performer and dabbler; *b* 16 May 1916; *s* of Rev. Dr Edwin Donald Braden and Mary Evelyn Chastey; *m* 1942, Barbara Kelly; one *s* two *d*. *Educ:* Maple Grove Public Sch., Point Grey Junior High Sch., Magee High Sch., Vancouver, Canada. Radio engineer, announcer, singer, actor in Vancouver, Canada, 1937–43; wrote and performed in plays for Canadian Broadcasting Corporation, 1940–43, in Vancouver and Toronto, 1943–49. Moved to England, 1949. London plays include: Street-Car Named Desire; Biggest Thief in Town; The Man; No News From Father; Anniversary Waltz; The Gimmick; Period of Adjustment; Spoon River Anthology; Apple Cart. BBC radio programmes include: Breakfast with Braden; Bedtime with Braden; Braden Beside Himself. TV includes: inauguration of BBC School's broadcasts; The Brains Trust; Early to Braden; On the Braden Beat; Braden's Week; All Our Yesterdays. Man. Dir, Adanac Productions Ltd; Dir, Prime Performers Ltd. Hon. Chancellor, London School of Economics, 1955. BAFTA Features Personality Award; British Variety Club Light Entertainment Personality; RTS Award for artistry in front of the camera. *Publications:* These English, 1948; The Kindness of Strangers, 1990. *Recreations:* family, tennis, and finding time. *Address:* 2 Ovington Square, SW3 1LN.

BRADEN, Hugh Reginald, CMG 1980; Mayor of Worthing, May 1991–92; *b* 1923; *s* of late Reginald Henry Braden and Mabel Braden (*née* Selby); *m* 1946, Phyllis Grace Barnes; one *d*. *Educ:* Worthing High School for Boys; Brighton College of Technology. Joined War Office, 1939; served War, Royal Navy, 1942–45; Far East Land Forces, 1946–50; British Army of the Rhine, 1953–56; War Office and Min. of Defence, 1956–66; jssc 1967; British Embassy, Washington, 1968–70; Min. of Defence, 1971–80 (Asst Under Sec. of State, 1978–80). Dir, A. B. Jay, 1981–90. Borough Councillor, Worthing, 1983–. *Address:* Field House, Honeysuckle Lane, High Salvington, Worthing, West Sussex BN13 3BT. *T:* Worthing (0903) 60203.

BRADFIELD, John Richard Grenfell, CBE 1986; PhD; Senior Bursar, Trinity College, Cambridge, 1956–Dec. 1992; Founder, and Manager, Cambridge Science Park, 1970–Dec. 1992; *b* 20 May 1925; *s* of Horace and Ada Bradfield; *m* 1951, Jane Wood; one *s*. *Educ:* Trinity Coll., Cambridge (schol. 1942; MA, PhD). Research Fellow in Cell Biology, Trinity Coll., Cambridge, 1947; Commonwealth (Harkness) Fellow, Chicago, 1948; Jun. Bursar, Trinity Coll., Cambridge, 1951. Director: Cambridge Water Co., 1965–. Cambridge Building Soc., 1968–; Biotechnology Investments, 1989–; Anglian Water, 1989– (Bd Mem., 1975–89); Chm., Abbotstone Agricl Property Unit Trust, 1975–. Darwin College, Cambridge: proposed foundn, 1963; Hon. Fellow, 1973. FRSA. *Publications:* scientific papers on cell biology. *Recreations:* walking, arboretum-visiting. *Address:* Trinity College, Cambridge CB2 1TQ. *T:* Cambridge (0223) 338400.

BRADFORD, 7th Earl of, *cr* 1815; **Richard Thomas Orlando Bridgeman;** Bt 1660; Baron Bradford, 1794; Viscount Newport, 1815; *b* 3 Oct. 1947; *s* of 6th Earl of Bradford, TD, and Mary Willoughby (*d* 1986), *er d* of Lt-Col T. H. Montgomery, DSO; *S* father, 1981; *m* 1979, Joanne Elizabeth, *d* of B. Miller; three *s* one *d*. *Educ:* Harrow; Trinity College, Cambridge. Owner of Porters Restaurant of Covent Garden. *Publications:* (compiled) My Private Parts and the Stuffed Parrot, 1984; The Eccentric Cookbook, 1985. *Heir: s* Viscount Newport, *qv*. *Address:* Woodlands House, Weston-under-Lizard, Shifnal, Salop. *T:* (office) Weston-under-Lizard (095276) 201.

BRADFORD, Bishop of; *no new appointment at time of going to press.*

BRADFORD, Archdeacon of; *see* Shreeve, Ven. D. H.

BRADFORD, Provost of; *see* Richardson, Very Rev. J. S.

BRADFORD, (Sir) Edward Alexander Slade, 5th Bt, *cr* 1902 (but does not use the title); *b* 18 June 1952; *s* of Major Sir Edward Montagu Andrew Bradford, 3rd Bt (*d* 1952) and his 2nd wife, Marjorie Edith (*née* Bere); *S* half-brother, Sir John Ridley Evelyn Bradford, 4th Bt, 1954. *Heir: uncle* Donald Clifton Bradford [*b* 22 May 1914; *m* 1949, Constance Mary Morgan; three *d*].

BRADFORD, Prof. Eric Watts, MDS (Sheffield); DDSc (St Andrews); Professor of Dental Surgery, 1959–85, now Emeritus, and Pro-Vice-Chancellor, 1983–85, University of Bristol; *b* 4 Nov. 1919; *e s* of E. J. G. and C. M. Bradford; *m* 1946, Norah Mary Longmuir; two *s* three *d*. *Educ:* King Edward VII Sch., Sheffield; High Storrs Grammar Sch., Sheffield; Univ. of Sheffield (Robert Styring Scholar). LDS, Sheffield, 1943; BDS, Sheffield, 1944; MDS, Sheffield, 1950; DDSc St Andrews, 1954. Lieut, Army Dental Corps, Nov. 1944; Capt. Nov. 1945. Lectr, Univ. of Sheffield, 1947–52; Senior Lectr, Univ. of St Andrews, 1952–59; Dean, Faculty of Medicine, Bristol University, 1975–79. Mem., Gen. Dental Council, 1979–85. *Publications:* many papers on dental anatomy in British and other journals. *Address:* 9 Cedar Court, Glenavon Park, Sneyd Park, Bristol BS9 1RL. *T:* Bristol (0272) 681849.

BRADFORD, Rt. Hon. Roy Hamilton, PC (NI) 1969; Member (U) for East Belfast, Northern Ireland Assembly, 1973–75; Minister for the Environment, Northern Ireland Executive, 1974; *b* 7 July 1921; *s* of Joseph Hamilton Bradford, Rockcorry, Co. Monaghan, and Isabel Mary (*née* McNamee), Donemana, Co. Tyrone; *m* 1946, Hazel Elizabeth, *d* of Capt. W. Lindsay, Belfast; two *s*. *Educ:* Royal Belfast Academical Institution; Trinity Coll., Dublin. Foundation Schol. 1940; First Class Hons (BA) German and French (with Gold Medal) 1942 (TCD). Army Intelligence, 1943–47 (France, Belgium, Germany). BBC and ITV Producer and Writer, 1950–. Dir, Geoffrey Sharp Ltd, 1962–. MP (U) for Victoria, Parlt of NI, 1965–73; Asst Whip (Unionist Party), 1966; Parly Sec., Min. of Educn, 1967; Chief Whip, Sept. 1968–April 1969; Minister of Commerce, NI, 1969–71; Minister of Develt, NI, 1971–72. Contested (Off U) North Down, 1974. Pres., NI European Movt, 1987–. *Publications:* Excelsior (novel), 1960; The Last Ditch (novel), 1981; Rogue Warrior of the SAS: the Life of Lt-Col R. B. "Paddy" Mayne, DSO, 1987. *Recreations:* golf, architecture. *Address:* Ardkeen, Carnalea, Bangor, Co. Down, N Ireland. *T:* Bangor (0247) 465012. *Club:* Royal and Ancient Golf (St Andrews).

BRADING, Keith, CB 1974; MBE 1944; Chief Registrar of Friendly Societies and Industrial Assurance Commissioner, 1972–81; *b* 23 Aug. 1917; *s* of late Frederick C. Brading and late Lilian P. Brading (*née* Courtney); *m* 1949, Mary Blanche Robinson, *d* of late William C. and Blanche Robinson. *Educ:* Portsmouth Grammar Sch. Called to Bar, Gray's Inn, 1950. Entered Inland Revenue (Estate Duty Office), 1936. Served War, Royal Navy, 1941–46 (Lieut RNVR); Solicitor's Office, Inland Revenue, 1950; Asst Solicitor, 1962; Asst Registrar of Friendly Societies and Dep. Industrial Assurance Commissioner,

1969. Vice-President: CBSI, 1981–; Bldg Socs Assoc., 1982–. Pres., Soc. of Co-operative Studies, 1983–. Chairman: Kensington Housing Trust, 1987–; UK Co-operative Council, 1991–. *Publications:* contrib. Halsbury's Laws of England and Atkins Court Forms and Precedents. *Address:* 35 Chiswick Staithe, W4 3TP. *T:* 081–995 0517. *Club:* Savile.

BRADLAW, Prof. Sir Robert (Vivian), Kt 1965; CBE 1950; Hon. Professor of Oral Pathology, Royal College of Surgeons of England, since 1948; Emeritus Professor of Oral Medicine, University of London; Emeritus Consultant, Royal Navy; *b* 14 April 1905; *s* of Philip Archibald Bradlaw, Blackrock, Co. Dublin; unmarried. *Educ:* Cranleigh; Guy's Hosp.; University of London. Hilton Prize, etc, Guy's Hosp.; Hon. Degrees, Univs of Belfast, Birmingham, Boston, Durham, Leeds, Malta, Melbourne, Meshed, Montreal and Newcastle upon Tyne; Fellow, Royal Colleges of Surgeons of England, Edinburgh, Glasgow, Ireland, etc; Hon. Fellow, RSM, 1975. Tomes Prize for Research, RCS 1939–41; Howard Mummery Prize for Research, BDA, 1948–53; Colyer Gold Medal, RCS; Hunterian Prof., RCS 1955; Hon. Gold Medal, RCS, 1972; Chevalier de la Santé Publique (France), 1950; Knight, Order of St Olaf, Norway; Commander, Order of Homayoun, Iran. *Recreations:* fishing, golf, orchids, oriental ceramics. *Address:* The Manse, Stoke Goldington, Newport Pagnell, Bucks.

BRADLEY, Anthony Wilfred; barrister and legal author; Editor, Public Law, since 1986; *b* 6 Feb. 1934; *s* of David and Olive Bradley (*née* Bonsey); *m* 1959, Kathleen Bryce; one *s* three *d*. *Educ:* Dover Grammar Sch.; Emmanuel Coll., Cambridge (BA 1957, LLB 1958, MA 1961). Solicitor of the Supreme Court, 1960 (Clifford's Inn Prize); called to the Bar, Inner Temple, 1989. Asst Lectr, 1960–64, Lectr, 1964–68, Cambridge, and Fellow of Trinity Hall, 1960–68; Prof. of Constitutional Law, 1968–89, Dean, Faculty of Law, 1979–82, Prof. Emeritus, 1990, Univ. of Edinburgh. Vis. Reader in Law, UC, Dar es Salaam, 1966–67; Vis. Prof. of Public Law, Univ. of Florence, 1984. Chairman: Edinburgh Council for Single Homeless, 1984–88; Social Security Appeal Tribunal, 1984–89; Sub-Cttee on Police Powers, ESRC, 1985–; Member Wolfenden Cttee on Voluntary Orgns, 1974–78; Social Scis and Law Cttee, SSRC, 1975–79; Social Studies Sub-Cttee, UGC, 1985–89; Cttee of Inquiry into Local Govt in Scotland, 1980; Cttee to review local govt in Islands of Scotland, 1983–84. *Publications:* (with M. Adler) Justice, Discretion and Poverty, 1976; (with D. J. Christie) The Scotland Act 1978, 1979; (ed) Wade and Bradley, Constitutional and Administrative Law, 10th edn, 1985; Administrative Law (in Stair Meml Encyc. of the Laws of Scotland), 1987; articles in legal jls. *Recreation:* music. *Address:* Cloisters, 1 Pump Court, Temple, EC4Y 7AA. *T:* 071–583 0303; 19 Grosvenor Road, Richmond, Surrey TW10 6PE. *T:* 081–948 3127.

BRADLEY, Sir Burton Gyrth B.; *see* Burton-Bradley.

BRADLEY, Dr Charles Clive; Managing Director, Sharp Laboratories of Europe Ltd, since 1990; *b* 11 April 1937; *s* of Charles William Bradley and late Winifred Smith; *m* 1965, Vivien Audrey Godley; one *s* one *d*. *Educ:* Longton High Sch.; Birmingham Univ. (BSc Hons in Physics, 1958); Emmanuel Coll., Cambridge (PhD 1962). Nat. Phys. Lab., 1961–67; MIT, USA, 1967, 1969; Nat. Bureau of Standards, USA, 1968; Nat. Phys. Lab., 1969–75; DoI, 1975–82, SPSO and Head of Energy Unit, 1978–82; Counsellor (Science and Technology), British Embassy, Tokyo, 1982–88; Head of Secretariat, ACOST, Cabinet Office, 1988–90. Dep. Comr Gen. for Britain, Sci. Expo Tokyo, 1985. A. F. Bulgin Prize, IERE, 1972. *Publications:* High Pressure Methods in Solid State Research, 1969; contribs to jls on lasers, metals and semiconductors. *Recreations:* tennis, gardening. *Address:* Sharp Laboratories of Europe Ltd, Neave House, Winsmore Lane, Abingdon, Oxon OX14 5UD.

BRADLEY, (Charles) Stuart, CBE 1990; Managing Director, Associated British Ports, since 1988; *b* 11 Jan. 1936; *s* of Charles and Amelia Jane Bradley; *m* 1959, Kathleen Marina (*née* Loraine); one *s* one *d* (and one *s* decd). *Educ:* Penarth County Sch.; University Coll. Southampton (Warsash). Master Mariner, 1961; FCIT 1978. Deck Officer, P&OSN Co., 1952–64; joined British Transport Docks Bd, subseq. Associated British Ports, 1964; Dock and Harbour Master, Silloth, 1968–70; Dock Master, 1970–74, Dock and Marine Superintendent, 1974–76, Plymouth; Docks Manager, Lowestoft, 1976–78; Port Manager, Barry, 1978–80; Dep. Port Manager, 1980–85, Port Manager, 1985–87, Hull; Asst Man. Dir (Resources), 1987–88. *Recreations:* Welsh Rugby football, cycling, walking, theatre. *Address:* c/o 150 Holborn, EC1N 2LR. *T:* 071–430 1177. *Clubs:* Honourable Company of Master Mariners; Cardiff Athletic.

BRADLEY, Clive; Chief Executive, The Publishers Association (incorporating Book Development Council, Educational Publishers Council and University, College and Professional Publishers Council), since 1976; Director, Confederation of Information Communication Industries, since 1984; *b* 25 July 1934; *s* of late Alfred and Kathleen Bradley. *Educ:* Felsted Sch., Essex; Clare Coll., Cambridge (Scholar; MA); Yale Univ. (Mellon Fellow). Called to the Bar, Middle Temple. Current Affairs Producer, BBC, 1961–63; Broadcasting Officer, Labour Party, 1963–64; Political Editor, The Statist, 1965–67; Gp Labour Adviser, IPC, 1967–69; Dep. Gen. Man., Daily and Sunday Mirror, 1969–71; Controller of Admin, IPC Newspapers, 1971–72; i/c IPC local radio applications, 1972–73; Dir i/c new prodn arrangements, The Observer, 1973–75. Dep. Chairman: Central London Valuation Tribunal; Member: Gen. Assembly, Organising Cttee, World Congress on Books, London, 1982; PA delegns to USSR, China, Australia/NZ, Southern Africa and Canada; IPA Congresses, Stockholm, 1980, Mexico City, 1984, London (also host), 1988. Governor, Felsted Sch. Contested (Lab) S Kensington, by-election, March 1968. *Publications:* Which Way?, 1970; (ed) The Future of the Book, 1982; articles on politics, economics, the press, television, industrial relations. *Recreations:* reading, travel. *Address:* 8 Northumberland Place, Richmond, Surrey TW10 6TS. *T:* 081–940 7172; 19 Bedford Square, WC1B 3HJ. *T:* 071–580 6321. *Clubs:* Reform, Groucho; Elizabethan (Yale).

BRADLEY, Prof. Daniel Joseph, PhD; FRS 1976; FInstP; Professor of Optical Electronics, Trinity College Dublin, since 1980; Emeritus Professor of Optics, London University, 1980; *b* 18 Jan. 1928; *s* of late John Columba Bradley and Margaret Mary Bradley; *m* 1958, Winefride Marie Therese O'Connor; four *s* one *d*. *Educ:* St Columb's Coll., Derry; St Mary's Trng Coll., Belfast; Birkbeck and Royal Holloway Colls, London (BSc Maths, BSc Physics, PhD). Primary Sch. Teacher, Derry, 1947–53; Secondary Sch. Teacher, London area, 1953–57; Asst Lectr, Royal Holloway Coll., 1957–60; Lectr, Imperial Coll. of Science and Technol., 1960–64; Reader, Royal Holloway Coll., 1964–66; Prof. and Head of Dept of Pure and Applied Physics, QUB, 1966–73; Prof. of Optics, 1973–80, and Head of Physics Dept, 1976–80, Imperial Coll., London. Vis. Scientist, MIT, 1965; Consultant, Harvard Observatory, 1966. Lectures: Scott, Cambridge, 1977; Tolansky Meml, RSA, 1977. Chairman: Laser Facility Cttee, SRC, 1976–79; British Nat. Cttee for Physics, 1979–80; Quantum Electronics Commn, IUPAP, 1982–85; Member: Rutherford Lab. Estab. Cttee, SRC, 1977–79; Science Bd, SRC, 1977–80; Council, Royal Soc., 1979–80. Gov., Sch. of Cosmic Physics, DIAS, 1981–. MRIA 1969; Fellow, Optical Soc. of America, 1975. Hon. DSc: NUU, 1983; QUB, 1986. Thomas Young Medal, Inst. of Physics, 1975; Royal Medal, Royal Soc., 1983; C. H. Townes Award, Optical Soc. of America, 1989. *Publications:* papers on optics, lasers, spectroscopy, chronoscopy and astronomy in Proc. Roy. Soc., Phil. Mag., Phys. Rev., J. Opt. Soc. Amer., Proc. IEEE, Chem. Phys. Letts, Optics Communications. *Recreations:* television, walking, DIY. *Address:* Trinity College, Dublin 2, Ireland. *T:* Dublin 772941.

BRADLEY, Prof. David John, DM; FRCP; FRCPath; FFCM; Professor of Tropical Hygiene, University of London and Director, Ross Institute, since 1974; *b* 12 Jan. 1937; *s* of Harold Robert and Mona Bradley; *m* 1961, Lorne Marie, *d* of late Major L. G. Farquhar and Marie Farquhar; two *s* two *d*. *Educ:* Wyggeston Sch., Leicester; Selwyn Coll., Cambridge (Scholar); University Coll. Hosp. Med. Sch. (Atchison Schol., Magrath Schol., Trotter Medal in Surgery, Liston Gold Medal in Surgery, BA Nat. Scis Tripos, Med. Scis and Zoology, 1st cl. Hons, Frank Smart Prize Zool.; MB, BChir, MA 1960); DM Oxon 1972. FIBiol 1974; FFCM 1979; FRCPath 1981; FRCP 1985. Med. Res. Officer, Ross Inst. Bilharzia Res. Unit, Tanzania, 1961–64; Lectr, 1964–66, Sen. Lectr, 1966–69, Makerere Univ. of East Africa, Uganda; Trop. Res. Fellow of Royal Soc., Sir William Dunn Sch. of Pathology, Oxford, 1969–73; Sen. Res. Fellow, Staines Med. Fellow, Exeter Coll., Oxford, 1971–74; Clinical Reader in Path., Oxford Clinical Med. Sch., 1973–74; Chm., Div. of Communicable and Tropical Diseases, LSHTM, 1982–88. Co-Director, Malaria Ref. Lab., PHLS, 1974–; Hon. Specialist Community Physician, NW Thames RHA, 1974–, NE Thames RHA, 1984–; Hon. Consultant in Trop. and Communicable Diseases, Bloomsbury DHA, 1983–; Dir, WHO Collaborating Centre Envtl Control of Vectors, 1983–; Mem., Bd of Trustees, Internat. Centre for Diarrhoeal Disease Res., Bangladesh, 1979–85 (Chm., 1982–83); Consultant Advisor to Dir, Royal Tropical Inst., Amsterdam; Advr, Indep. Internat. Commn on Health Res.; Member: WHO Expert Adv. Panel on Parasitic Diseases, 1972–; Tech. Adv. Gp, Diarrhoea Programme, 1979–85; Panel of Experts on Envtl Management, 1981–; External Review Gp on Trop. Diseases Programme, 1987. For. Corresp. Mem., Royal Belgian Acad. of Medicine, 1984; Corresp. Mem., German Tropenmedizingesellschaft, 1980; Hon. FIPHE, 1981. Editor, Jl of Trop. Med. and Hygiene, 1981–. Chalmers Medal, RSTM&H, 1980. *Publications:* (with G. F. and A. U. White) Drawers of Water, 1972; (with O. V. Baroyan) Problems and Perspectives in Tropical Diseases (in Russian), 1979; (with E. E. Sabben-Clare and B. Kirkwood) Health in Tropical Africa during the Colonial Period, 1980; (with R. G. Feachem, D. D. Mara and H. Garelick) Sanitation and Disease, 1983; papers in learned jls. *Recreations:* natural history, landscape gardens, travel. *Address:* Ross Institute, London School of Hygiene and Tropical Medicine, Keppel Street, WC1E 7HT. *T:* 071–636 8636; 11 Selwyn House, Lansdowne Terrace, WC1N 1DJ. *T:* 071–278 3918.

BRADLEY, David Rice; Chief Executive, London Borough of Havering, since 1990; *b* 9 Jan. 1938; *s* of George Leonard Bradley and Evelyn Annie Bradley; *m* 1962, Josephine Elizabeth Turnbull Fricker (*née* Harries); two *s*. *Educ:* Christ Coll., Brecon; St Catharine's Coll., Cambridge (Exhibnr; MA English); Edinburgh Univ. (Dip. in Applied Linguistics). British Council: served: Dacca, 1962–65; Allahabad, 1966–69; New Delhi, 1969–70; Dir of Studies, British Inst., Madrid, 1970–73; Department of the Environment: Principal, Res. Admin, 1973–76; Planning, Develt Control, 1976–78; Inner Cities, 1978–79; Rayner Study (develt of Management Inf. System for Ministers), 1979–80; Central Policy Planning Unit, 1980–81; Study of Local Govt Finance (Grade 5), 1981–82; on special leave, Gwilym Gibbon Res. Fellow, Nuffield Coll., Oxford, 1982–83; Finance, Envmtl Servs, 1983–86; London Urban Develt, sponsorship of LDDC, 1986–88; Dir (G3) Merseyside Task Force, DoE, 1988–90. *Recreation:* gardening. *Address:* 27 Clare Lawn Avenue, SW14 8BE. *T:* 081–876 2232.

BRADLEY, Prof. Donald Charlton, CChem, FRSC; FRS 1980; Professor of Inorganic Chemistry, 1965–87, and Head of Chemistry Department, 1978–82, Fellow, 1988, Queen Mary College, University of London; Emeritus Professor, University of London, since 1988; *b* 7 Nov. 1924; *m* 1st, 1948, Constance Joy Hazeldean (*d* 1985); one *s*; 2nd, 1990, Ann Levy (*née* MacDonald). *Educ:* Hove County School for Boys; Birkbeck Coll., Univ. of London (BSc 1st Cl. Hons Chemistry, PhD, DSc). Research Asst, British Electrical and Allied Industries Research Assoc., 1941–47; Asst Lectr in Chemistry, 1949–52, Lectr in Chemistry, 1952–59, Birkbeck Coll.; Prof. of Chemistry, Univ. of Western Ontario, Canada, 1959–64. Univ. of London: Chm., Bd of Studies in Chemistry and Chemical Industries, 1977–79; Mem. Senate, 1981–87. Mem., Soc. of Chem. Industry; MRI 1979 (Mem. Council, 1987–; Hon. Sec., 1988–); Royal Society of Chemistry: Pres. Dalton Div., 1983–85; Ludwig Mond Lectr. Exec. Editor, Polyhedron, 1982–. FRSA 1982. *Publications:* (jtly) Metal Alkoxides, 1978; numerous pubns on synthesis and structure of metallo-organic compounds, co-ordination chemistry and inorganic polymers, mainly in Jl of Chemical Soc. *Recreations:* travelling, listening to music; amateur interest in archaeology. *Address:* Department of Chemistry, Queen Mary and Westfield College, Mile End Road, E1 4NS. *T:* 081–980 4811.

BRADLEY, Edgar Leonard, OBE 1979; Metropolitan Stipendiary Magistrate, 1967–83; *b* 17 Nov. 1917; 2nd *s* of Ernest Henry and Letitia Bradley, W Felton, Oswestry; *m* 1942, Elsa, *o d* of Colin and Elizabeth Matheson, Edinburgh; two *s* three *d*. *Educ:* Malvern Coll.; Trinity Hall, Cambridge. BA 1939; MA 1944. Called to Bar, Middle Temple, 1940. Served 1940–46, RA; Capt. and Adjt, 1943–45; Major, GSO2, Mil. Govt of Germany, 1946. Practised at Bar, 1946–51, SE Circuit, Central Criminal Ct, S London and Surrey Sessions. Legal Dept of Home Office, 1951–54. Sec., Departmental Cttee on Magistrates' Courts Bill, 1952; Sec. of Magistrates' Courts Rule Cttee, 1952–54; Clerk to Justices: Wrexham and Bromfield, 1954–57; Poole, 1957–67. Justices' Clerks Society: Mem. Council, 1957–67; Hon. Sec., 1963–67. Mem., Nat. Adv. Council on Trng of Magistrates, 1965–67; Magistrates' Association: Vice Pres., 1984–; Mem. Council, 1968–84; Chm. Legal Cttee, 1973–82. Adv. tour of Magistrates' Courts in Ghana, 1970. *Publications:* (with J. J. Senior) Bail in Magistrates' Courts, 1977; articles in legal jls. *Recreations:* golf, music. *Address:* 55 St Germains, Bearsden, Glasgow G61 2RS. *T:* 041-942 5831. *Clubs:* Army and Navy; Buchanan Castle Golf (Glasgow).

BRADLEY, Keith John Charles; MP (Lab) Manchester, Withington, since 1987; *b* 17 May 1950; *m*; one *s* one *d*. *Educ:* Manchester Polytechnic (BA Hons); York Univ. (MPhil). Former health service administrator, North West RHA. Mem., Manchester City Council, 1983–88. Joined Labour Party, 1973; Mem., Manchester Withington Co-op Party. Member: MSF; COHSE. *Address:* House of Commons, SW1A 0AA. *T:* 071-219 5124; 83 Claude Road, Chorlton, Manchester M21 2DE. *T:* (constituency office) 061-446 2047.

BRADLEY, Michael John, CMG 1990; QC (Cayman Islands) 1983; Governor of Turks and Caicos Islands, West Indies, since 1987; *b* 11 June 1933; *s* of late Joseph Bradley and Catherine Bradley (*née* Cleary); *m* 1965, Patricia Elizabeth Macauley; one *s*. *Educ:* St Malachy's Coll., Belfast; Queen's Univ., Belfast (LLB Hons). Solicitor, Law Soc. of NI, 1964; Attorney, Supreme Ct, Turks and Caicos Is, 1980; Barrister-at-law, Eastern Caribbean Supreme Ct, 1982. Solicitor, NI, 1964–67; State Counsel, Malawi, 1967–69; Volume Editor, Halsbury's Laws, 1970; Sen., later Chief, Parly Draftsman, Botswana, 1970–72; UN Legal Advr to Govt of Antigua, 1973–76; Reg. Legal Draftsman to Govts of E Caribbean, British Develt Div. in the Caribbean, FCO, 1976–82; Attorney General: British Virgin Is, 1977–78; Turks and Caicos Is, 1980; Montserrat, 1981; Cayman Is, 1982–87. *Recreations:* reading, philately, travel, good wine. *Address:* c/o Foreign and

Commonwealth Office, SW1A 2AH; Waterloo, Government House, Grand Turk, Turks and Caicos Islands, West Indies. *T:* 809.946.2309. *Clubs:* Commonwealth Trust; Mill Reef (Antigua); Meridian (Turks and Caicos Islands).

BRADLEY, Maj.-Gen. Peter Edward Moore, CB 1968; CBE 1964 (OBE 1955); DSO 1946; Trustee, Vindolanda Trust, 1982–85 (Secretary, 1975–82); *b* 12 Dec. 1914; *s* of late Col Edward de Winton Herbert Bradley, CBE, DSO, MC, DL; *m* Margaret, *d* of late Norman Wardhaugh of Haydon Bridge, Northumberland; three *s. Educ:* Marlborough; Royal Military Academy, Woolwich. 2nd Lieut, Royal Signals, 1934. Served War of 1939–45; India, Middle East, Italy and North West Europe (DSO 6th Airborne Div.). Lieut-Col 1954; Col 1957; Brig. 1962; Maj.-Gen. 1965; Signal Officer in Chief (Army), Ministry of Defence, 1965–67; Chief of Staff to C-in-C Allied Forces Northern Europe, Oslo, 1968–70, retired. Dunlop Ltd, 1970–75. Col Comdt, Royal Signals, 1967–82, Master of Signals, 1970–82; Col Gurkha Signals, 1967–74. CEng, FIEE, 1966; FBIM, 1970. *Address:* c/o RHQ Royal Signals, 56 Regency Street, SW1P 4AD.

BRADLEY, Richard Alan; Headmaster, Rivers Country Day School, Massachusetts, USA, since 1981; *b* 6 Oct. 1925; *s* of late Reginald Livingstone Bradley, CBE, MC, and of Phyllis Mary Richardson; *m* 1971, Mary Ann Vicary; one *s* two *d* by previous marriage. *Educ:* Marlborough Coll.; Trinity Coll., Oxford (Scholar). 2nd cl. hons Mod. History. Royal Marines, 1944–46; Oxford, 1946–48; Club Manager, Oxford and Bermondsey Club, 1949. Asst Master: Dulwich Coll., 1949–50; Tonbridge Sch., 1950–66 (Head of History Dept, 1957–66; Housemaster of Ferox Hall, 1961–66); Warden of St Edward's Sch., Oxford, 1966–71; Headmaster, Ridley Coll., Canada, 1971–81. *Recreations:* games, dramatics, mountains. *Address:* Rivers Country Day School, 333 Winter Street, Weston, Mass 02193, USA. *Club:* Vincent's (Oxford).

BRADLEY, Prof. Richard John, FSA; Professor of Archaeology, Reading University, since 1987; *b* 18 Nov. 1946; *s* of John Newsum Bradley and Margaret Bradley (*née* Saul); *m* 1976, Katherine Bowden. *Educ:* Portsmouth Grammar Sch.; Magdalen Coll., Oxford (MA). MIFA. Lectr in Archaeology, 1971–84, Reader, 1984–87, Reading Univ. Mem., Royal Commn on Historical Monuments of England, 1987–. *Publications:* (with A. Ellison) Rams Hill: a Bronze Age Defended Enclosure and its Landscape, 1975; The Prehistoric Settlement of Britain, 1978; (ed with J. Barrett) Settlement and Society in the British Later Bronze Age, 1980; The Social Foundations of Prehistoric Britain, 1984; (ed with J. Gardiner) Neolithic Studies, 1984; (with J. Barrett) Landscape, Monuments and Society, 1990; The Passage of Arms: an archæological analysis of prehistoric hoards and votive deposits, 1990; (ed with J. Barrett and M. Hall) Papers on the Prehistoric Archaeology of Cranborne Chase, 1991; contribs to learned jls. *Recreations:* literature, twentieth century music, watercolours, secondhand bookshops. *Address:* Department of Archaeology, The University, Whiteknights, Reading RG6 2AA. *T:* Reading (0734) 318130.

BRADLEY, Roger Thubron, FICFor; FIWSc; Commissioner, Private Forestry and Development, Forestry Commission, since 1985; *b* 5 July 1936; *s* of Ivor Lewis Bradley and Elizabeth Thubron; *m* 1959, Ailsa Mary Walkden; one *s* one *d. Educ:* Lancaster Royal Grammar Sch.; St Peter's Coll., Oxford (MA). FICFor 1980; FIWSc 1985. Asst District Officer, Kendal, 1960; Mensuration Officer, Alice Holt, 1961; Working Plans Officer, 1967; District Officer, North Argyll, 1970; Asst Conservator, South Wales, 1974; Conservator, North Wales, 1977; Forestry Commission: Dir, and Sen. Officer for Wales, 1982–83; Dir, Harvesting and Marketing, Edinburgh, 1983–85. Chm., Commonwealth Forestry Assoc., 1988–. *Publications:* Forest Management Tables, 1966, 2nd edn 1971; Forest Planning, 1967; Thinning Control in British Forestry, 1967, 2nd edn 1971; various articles in Forestry, etc. *Recreation:* sailing. *Clubs:* Commonwealth Trust, Royal Over-Seas League.

BRADLEY, Stanley Walter; Director, Harman Group Ltd, since 1988; Director General, British Printing Industries Federation, 1983–88; *b* 9 Sept. 1927; *s* of Walter Bradley; *m* 1955, Jean Brewster; three *s* one *d. Educ:* Boys' British Sch., Saffron Walden. Joined Spicers Ltd, 1948: held posts in prodn, marketing and gen. management; Personnel Dir, 1973–83; Dir, Capital Spicers Ltd, Eire, 1971–83. Chm., BPIF Manufg Stationery Industry Gp, 1977–81; Pres., E Anglian Printing Industries Alliance, 1978–79; Mem., Printing Industries Sector Working Party, 1979–87; Chm., Communications Action Team, 1980–85. *Recreations:* painting, golf, fishing. *Address:* Dale House, Hogs Lane, Chrishall, Royston, Herts SG8 8RB. *T:* Royston (0763) 838820.

BRADLEY, Stuart; *see* Bradley, C. S.

BRADLEY, Thomas George; Director, British Section, European League for Economic Co-operation, since 1979; *b* 13 April 1926; *s* of George Henry Bradley, Kettering; *m* 1953, Joy, *d* of George Starmer, Kettering; two *s. Educ:* Kettering Central Sch., Northants. Elected to Northants County Council, 1952, County Alderman, 1961; Mem., Kettering Borough Council, 1957–61. Transport Salaried Staffs' Association: Branch Officer, 1946–58; Mem. Exec. Cttee, 1958–77; Treasurer, 1961–64; Pres., 1964–77; Acting Gen. Sec., 1976–77. MP Leicester NE, July 1962–1974, Leicester E, 1974–83 (Lab, 1962–81, SDP, 1981–83); PPS: to Minister of Aviation, 1964–65; to Home Secretary, 1966–67; to Chancellor of the Exchequer, 1967–70; Chm., Select Cttee on Transport, 1979–83. Vice-Chm., Labour Party, 1974–75, Chm., 1975–76; Mem., Labour Party NEC, 1966–81. Contested: (Lab) Rutland and Stamford, 1950, 1951 and 1955; (Lab) Preston S, 1959; (SDP) Leicester E, 1983. *Address:* The Orchard, 111 London Road, Kettering, Northants. *T:* Kettering (0536) 513019. *Club:* Savile.

BRADLEY, William Ewart; Special Commissioner of Income Tax, 1950–75; *b* 5 Sept. 1910; *s* of W. E. Bradley, Durham City; *m* 1949, Mary Campbell Tyre; two *s. Educ:* Johnston Sch., Durham; LSE, London Univ. Inland Revenue, 1929–50. *Address:* 45 Spottiswoode Gardens, St Andrews, Fife KY16 8SB. *T:* St Andrews (0334) 76907.

BRADLEY GOODMAN, Michael; *see* Goodman, M. B.

BRADMAN, Sir Donald (George), AC 1979; Kt 1949; President of South Australian Cricket Association, 1965–73; Chairman, Australian Cricket Board, 1960–63 and 1969–72; *b* Cootamundra, NSW, 27 Aug. 1908; *s* of George and Emily Bradman; *m* 1932, Jessie, *d* of James Menzies, Mittagong, NSW; one *s* one *d. Educ:* Bowral Intermediate High Sch. Played for NSW 1927–34; for S Australia, 1935–49; for Australia 1928–48, Capt. 1936–48; records include: highest aggregate and greatest number of centuries in England *v* Australia test matches; highest score for Australia *v* England in test matches (334 at Leeds, 1930). Formerly stock and share broker and Mem. Stock Exchange of Adelaide Ltd. *Publications:* Don Bradman's Book, 1930; How to Play Cricket, 1935; My Cricketing Life, 1938; Farewell to Cricket, 1950, repr. 1988; The Art of Cricket, 1958; The Bradman Albums, 1988; *relevant publications:* Bradman: The Great, by B. J. Wakley, 1959; Sir Donald Bradman, by Irving Rosenwater, 1978; Bradman—The Illustrated Biography, by Michael Page, 1983. *Recreations:* cricket, golf, tennis, billiards, squash. *Address:* 2 Holden Street, Kensington Park, SA 5068, Australia. *Clubs:* MCC (Hon. Life Mem. and Hon. Life Vice-Pres.); Commerce (Adelaide).

BRADMAN, Godfrey Michael; Chairman and Joint Chief Executive, Rosehaugh PLC, since 1979; *b* 9 Sept. 1936; *s* of William Isadore Bradman and Anne Brenda Bradman (*née* Goldsweig); *m* 1975, Susan Clayton Bennett; two *s* three *d.* FCA 1961. Principal and Sen. Partner, Godfrey Bradman and Co. (Chartered Accountants), 1961; Chm. and Chief Exec., London Mercantile Corp. (Bankers), 1969; Chairman: Rosehaugh Estates PLC (formerly Copartnership Property Develts Ltd), 1973–; Pelham Homes Ltd, 1980–; Shearwater Property Holdings PLC, 1984–; Rosehaugh Heritage PLC, 1986–; Home for Life PLC, 1986–; Joint Chairman: Rosehaugh Stanhope Develts (Hldgs) PLC, 1983–; Rosehaugh Associated Ports Develts PLC, 1985–; Dir, London Regeneration Consortium PLC, 1987–. Founder, CLEAR (Campaign for Lead-Free Air) Ltd, 1981–; Jt Founder and Council Mem., Campaign for Freedom of Information, 1983–; Citizen Action, 1983– (Dir, AIDS Policy Unit, 1987–); Chm., Friends of the Earth Trust, 1983–; Council Mem., UN Internat. Year of Shelter for the Homeless, 1987; Pres., Soc. for the Protection of Unborn Children Educnl Res. Trust, 1987–. Founder of self-build housing schemes for unemployed and people on low incomes, 1987–. Mem. governing body, LSHTM, 1988–. *Recreations:* his children, reading, horseriding. *Address:* 53 Queen Anne Street, W1M 0LJ.

BRADNEY, John Robert; HM Diplomatic Service, retired; Oman Government Service, 1986–89; *b* 24 July 1931; *s* of Rev. Samuel Bradney, Canon Emeritus of St Alban's Abbey, and Constance Bradney (*née* Partington); *m* 1st, Jean Marion Halls (marr. diss. 1971); one *s* two *d*; 2nd, 1974, Sandra Cherry Smith, *d* of Richard Arthur Amyus Smith, MC. *Educ:* Christ's Hospital. HM Forces, 1949–51, Herts Regt and RWAFF; Colonial Police, Nigeria, 1953–65 (Chief Superintendent); HM Diplomatic Service, 1965; First Sec., Lagos, 1974; FCO, 1977–86 (Counsellor, 1985). DSM Oman, 1989. *Recreations:* salmon and trout fishing, gardening, ornithology. *Address:* Barclays Bank PLC, Penrith, Cumbria CA11 7YB. *Club:* Royal Over-Seas League.

BRADSHAW, Prof. Anthony David, PhD; FRS 1982; FIBiol; Holbrook Gaskell Professor of Botany, University of Liverpool, 1968–88, now Emeritus; *b* 17 Jan. 1926; *m* Betty Margaret Bradshaw; three *d. Educ:* St Paul's Sch., Hammersmith; Jesus Coll., Cambridge (BA 1947; MA 1951); PhD Wales 1959. FIBiol 1971. Lectr, 1952–63, Sen. Lectr, 1963–64, Reader in Agricl Botany, 1964–68, UCNW, Bangor. Member: Nature Conservancy Council, 1969–78; Natural Environment Res. Council, 1969–74; Bd of Management, Sports Turf Res. Inst., 1976–. Pres., British Ecological Soc., 1981–83. Fellow, Indian Nat. Acad. Sci., 1990. Trustee, Nat. Museums and Galls on Merseyside, 1986–. *Publications:* (ed jtly) Teaching Genetics, 1963; (with M. J. Chadwick) The Restoration of Land, 1980; (with others) Quarry Reclamation, 1982; (with others) Mine Wastes Reclamation, 1982; (with R. A. Dutton) Land Reclamation in Cities, 1982; (with Alison Burt) Transforming our Waste Land: the way forward, 1986; (ed jtly) Ecology and Design in Landscape, 1986; contribs to symposia and learned jls. *Recreations:* sailing, gardening, appreciating land. *Address:* Department of Environmental and Evolutionary Biology, The University, Liverpool L69 3BX.

BRADSHAW, Sir Kenneth (Anthony), KCB 1986 (CB 1982); Administrator, Compton Verney Opera Project, since 1988; *b* 1 Sept. 1922; *s* of late Herbert and Gladys Bradshaw. *Educ:* Ampleforth Coll.; St Catharine's Coll., Cambridge (1st Cl. Hons History); MA 1947. War Service, 1942–45; served with Royal Ulster Rifles (2nd Bn), NW Europe (despatches). Temp. Asst Principal, Min. of Supply, Oct.-Dec. 1946; a Clerk in the House of Commons, 1947–87; seconded as Clerk of the Saskatchewan Legislature, 1966 session; Clerk of Overseas Office, 1972–76; Clerk, House of Commons, 1983–87. Pres., Assoc. of Secs Gen. of Parlts, IPU, 1986–87 (Jt Sec., 1955–71; Vice-Pres., 1984–86). *Publication:* (with David Pring) Parliament and Congress, 1972, new edn 1982. *Club:* Garrick.

BRADSHAW, Martin Clark; Director, Civic Trust, since 1987; *b* 25 Aug. 1935; *s* of late Cyril Bradshaw and Nina Isabel Bradshaw; *m* 1st, 1959, Patricia Anne Leggatt (*d* 1981); two *s* one *d*; 2nd, 1986, Gillian Rosemary Payne; three step *s* one step *d. Educ:* King's Sch., Macclesfield; St John's Coll., Cambridge (MA); Univ. of Manchester (DipTP); MRTPI. Staff Surveyor, Lands and Surveys Dept, Uganda Protectorate, 1958–63; Asst Planning Officer, Planning Dept, City of Manchester, 1963–67; Asst Dir, City of Toronto Planning Bd, 1967–70; Asst Chief Planner, Cheshire CC, 1970–72; Asst County Planning Officer, Leics CC, 1972–73; Exec. Dir, Planning and Transport, 1973–81, Dir of Planning, 1981–86, W Yorks MCC; DoE Local Plans Inspectorate, 1986–87. Council Mem. and Jun. Vice-Pres., RTPI, 1989–. Gen. Comr for Income Tax, Bedford, 1988–. FRSA 1985. *Recreations:* theatre, music, art, travel, cooking, golf. *Address:* 38 Beverley Crescent, Bedford MK40 4BY. *T:* Bedford (0234) 340744.

BRADSHAW, Maurice Bernard, OBE 1978; Secretary-General, 1958–79, Governor, 1979–81, a Director, 1981–83, Federation of British Artists; Hon. Member Extraordinary, Royal Society of Portrait Painters, 1983; *b* 7 Feb. 1903; 7th *s* of John Bradshaw; *m* 1927, Gladys (*d* 1983), 2nd *d* of Henry Harvey Frost; one *d. Educ:* Christ's Coll., Finchley. Jun. Clerk, Furness Withy & Co., 1918. Dir, Art Exhibns Bureau, 1926–; Asst Sec., British Artists Exhibns, 1927–35; Organising Sec., Floating Art Gall. aboard Berengaria, 1928; Sec., Empire Art Loan Exhibn Soc., 1932; Sec., Modern Architectural Res. Gp, 1938. Commissioned RAFVR, 1941–45. Sec. following art socs: Royal Inst. Oil Painters, 1966–74, Royal Inst. Painters in Watercolours, 1969–79, Royal Soc. British Artists, 1958–74, Royal Soc. Marine Artists, 1938–72, Royal Soc. Portrait Painters, 1955–83, Royal Soc. Miniature Painters, Sculptors and Gravers, 1959–72, Royal British Colonial Soc. of Artists (temp. known as Commonwealth Soc. of Artists), 1930–83, Artists of Chelsea, 1949–72, National Soc., 1968–74, New English Art Club, 1955–74, Pastel Soc., 1968–77, Soc. Aviation Artists, 1954–83, Soc. Graphic Artists, 1968–75, Soc. Mural Painters, 1968–, Soc. Portrait Sculptors, 1969–83, Soc. Wildlife Artists, 1963–80, Soc. Women Artists, 1968–79, Senefelder Gp, 1968–83. *Recreations:* woodwork, philately. *Address:* Holbrook Park House, Holbrook, near Horsham, W Sussex RH12 4PW.

BRADSHAW, Prof. Peter, FRS 1981; Thomas V. Jones Professor of Engineering, Department of Mechanical Engineering, Stanford University, since 1988; *b* 26 Dec. 1935; *s* of Joseph W. N. Bradshaw and Frances W. G. Bradshaw; *m* 1968, Sheila Dorothy (*née* Brown). *Educ:* Torquay Grammar Sch.; St John's Coll., Cambridge (BA). Scientific Officer, Aerodynamics Div., National Physical Lab., 1957–69; Imperial College, London: Sen. Lectr, Dept of Aeronautics, 1969–71; Reader, 1971–78; Prof. of Experimental Aerodynamics, 1978–88. *Publications:* Experimental Fluid Mechanics, 1964, 2nd edn 1971; An Introduction to Turbulence and its Measurement, 1971, 2nd edn 1975; (with T. Cebeci) Momentum Transfer in Boundary Layers, 1977; (ed) Topics in Applied Physics: Turbulence, 1978; (with T. Cebeci and J. H. Whitelaw) Engineering Calculation Methods for Turbulent Flow, 1981; (with T. Cebeci) Convective Heat Transfer, 1984; author or co-author of over 100 papers in Jl of Fluid Mechanics, AIAA Jl, etc. *Recreations:* ancient history, walking. *Address:* Department of Mechanical Engineering, Stanford University, Palo Alto, Calif 94305–3030, USA.

BRADSHAW, Lt-Gen. Sir Richard (Phillip), KBE 1977; Director General, Army Medical Services, 1977–81; *b* 1 Aug. 1920; *s* of late John Henderson Bradshaw and late May Bradshaw (*née* Phillips); *m* 1946, Estelle, *d* of late Emile Meyer; one *d. Educ:* Newport

High Sch.; London Univ.; Westminster Hosp. MRCS, LRCP 1945; FRCPath 1967; FFCM 1977; DTM&H 1953; FRSocMed, FRSTM&H, Mem. BMA. House appts Westminster and Kent and Canterbury Hosps. Commnd RAMC, 1946; appts as Hosp. Pathologist, Mil. Hosps in UK and Ceylon; Staff appts in Path., WO, 1950–52; Comd Cons. Pathologist, E Africa, 1954–57; Exch. Officer, Armed Forces Inst. of Path., Washington, 1959–60; Demonstr in Path., Royal Army Med. Coll., Millbank, 1961–63; Asst Dir of Path., BAOR, 1966–69; Prof. of Path., Royal Army Med. Coll., Millbank, 1969–71; CO, Cambridge Mil. Hosp., Aldershot, 1971–73; Comdt RAMC Trng Centre, 1973–75; DMS, BAOR, 1975–77. QHP 1975–81. Member: Council, Sir Oswald Stoll Foundn, Fulham, 1977– (Chm., Management Cttee, 1983–); Council and Cttee, Phyllis Tuckwell Meml Hospice, Farnham, 1981–; formerly HM Comr, Royal Hosp., Chelsea. CStJ 1977. *Publications:* articles and reports in professional jls. *Recreations:* bird-watching, gardening, working with wood. *Address:* Pennys, 88B West Street, Farnham, Surrey GU9 7EN.

BRADSHAW, Prof. William Peter; Professor of Transport Management, University of Salford, since 1986; Senior Visiting Research Fellow, Centre for Socio-Legal Studies, Wolfson College, Oxford, since 1985; Chairman, Ulsterbus and Citybus Ltd, since 1987; *b* 9 Sept. 1936; *s* of Leonard Charles Bradshaw and Ivy Doris Bradshaw; *m* 1957, Jill Hayward; one *s* one *d. Educ:* Univ. of Reading (BA Pol. Economy, 1957; MA 1960). FCIT 1987 (MCIT 1966). Joined Western Region of British Railways as Management Trainee, 1959; various appts, London and W of England Divs; Divl Manager, Liverpool, 1973; Chief Operating Man., LMR, 1976, Dep. Gen. Man. 1977; Chief Ops Man., BR HQ, 1978; Dir, Policy Unit, 1980; Gen. Man., Western Region, BR, 1983–85. *Recreations:* growing hardy plants; playing member of a brass band. *Address:* Centre for Socio-Legal Studies, Wolfson College, Oxford OX2 6UD. *T:* Oxford (0865) 52967; Ulsterbus Ltd, Milewater Road, Belfast BT9 3BG. *Club:* National Liberal.

BRADWELL, Area Bishop of; Rt. Rev. (Charles) Derek Bond; appointed Bishop Suffragan of Bradwell, 1976, Area Bishop, 1984; *b* 4 July 1927; *s* of Charles Norman Bond and Doris Bond; *m* 1951, Joan Valerie Meikle; two *s* two *d. Educ:* Bournemouth Sch.; King's Coll., London. AKC (2nd hons). Curate of Friern Barnet, 1952; Midlands Area Sec. of SCM in Schools and Public Preacher, dio. Birmingham, 1956; Vicar: of Harringay, 1958; of Harrow Weald, 1962; Archdeacon of Colchester, 1972–76. Nat. Chm., CEMS, 1983–86. *Recreation:* travel. *Address:* Bishop's House, 21 Elmhurst Avenue, Benfleet, Essex SS7 5RY. *T:* Basildon (0268) 755175.

BRADY, Rev. Canon Ernest William; Dean of Edinburgh, 1976–82 and 1985–86; *b* 10 Nov. 1917; *s* of Ernest and Malinda Elizabeth Brady; *m* 1948, Violet Jeanne Louise Aldworth; one *s* one *d. Educ:* Harris Academy, Dundee (Dux and Classics Medallist, 1936); Univ. of St Andrews; Edinburgh Theological Coll. (Luscombe Schol. 1942). LTh (Dunelm) 1942. Deacon 1942, Priest 1943; Asst Curate, Christ Church, Glasgow, 1942; Asst Curate, St Alphage, Hendon, 1946; Rector, All Saints, Buckie, 1949; Rector, All Saints, Edinburgh, 1957; Chaplain, Royal Infirmary of Edinburgh, 1959–74; Priest-in-Charge, Priory Church of St Mary of Mount Carmel, South Queensferry, 1974–82; Canon of St Mary's Cathedral, Edinburgh, 1967, Hon. Canon, 1983; Synod Clerk, Diocese of Edinburgh, 1969. Sub-dean, Collegiate Church of St Vincent, Edinburgh (Order of St Lazarus of Jerusalem), 1982–89. Kt of Holy Sepulchre of Jerusalem (Golden Cross with Crown), 1984. *Recreations:* Holy Land pilgrimage; choral music; ecclesiastical vestments and embroidery. *Address:* 44 Glendevon Place, Edinburgh EH12 5UJ. *T:* 031–337 9528.

BRADY, Prof. (John) Michael; BP Professor of Information Engineering, Oxford University, since 1985; *b* 30 April 1945; *s* of John and Priscilla Mansfield; *m* 1967, Naomi Friedlander; two *d. Educ:* Manchester Univ. (BSc (1st Cl. Hons Mathematics) 1966; Renold Prize 1967; MSc 1968); Australian National Univ. (PhD 1970). Lectr, Computer Science, 1970, Sen. Lectr 1979, Essex Univ.; Sen. Res. Scientist, MIT, 1980. Mem., ACOST, 1990–. *Publications:* Theory of Computer Science, 1975; Computer Vision, 1981; Robot Motion, 1982; Computational Theory of Discourse, 1982; Robotics Research, 1984; Artificial Intelligence and Robotics, 1984; Robotics Science, 1989; contribs to jls on computer vision, robotics, artificial intelligence, computer science. *Recreations:* squash, windsurfing, music, winetasting.

BRADY, Nicholas Frederick; Secretary of the US Treasury, since 1988; *b* 11 April 1930; *s* of James Brady and Eliot Brady; *m* 1952, Katherine Douglas; three *s* one *d. Educ:* Yale Univ. (BA 1952); Harvard Univ. (MBA 1954). Joined Dillon Read & Co. Inc., 1954; Vice-Pres., 1961; Pres. and Chief Exec. Officer, 1971; Chm. and Chief Exec. Officer, 1982–88. Mem., US Senate, Apr.–Dec. 1982. Posts on federal commns include: Chairman: Commn on Executive, Legislative and Judicial Salaries, 1985; Task Force on Market Mechanisms, 1987–88; Mem., Central Amer. Study Commn, 1983. *Address:* Department of the Treasury, 1500 Pennsylvania Avenue, NW, Washington, DC 20220, USA.

BRADY, Terence Joseph; playwright, novelist and actor, since 1962; *b* 13 March 1939; *s* of late Frederick Arthur Noel and Elizabeth Mary Brady; *m* Charlotte Mary Thérèse Bingham, *qv*; one *s* one *d. Educ:* Merchant Taylors', Northwood; TCD (BA Moderatorship, History and Polit. Science). Actor: Would Anyone who saw the Accident?, The Dumb Waiter, Room at the Top, 1962; Beyond the Fringe, 1962–64; Present from the Corporation, In the Picture, 1967; Quick One 'Ere, 1968; films include: Baby Love; Foreign Exchange; TV appearances include plays, comedy series and shows, incl. Nanny, 1981, and Pig in the Middle, 1981, 1982, 1983. Writer for *radio:* Lines from my Grandfather's Forehead (BBC Radio Writers' Guild Award, Best Radio Entertainment, 1972); *television:* Broad and Narrow; TWTWTW; with Charlotte Bingham: TV series: Boy Meets Girl; Take Three Girls; Upstairs Downstairs; Away From It All; Play for Today; Plays of Marriage; No—Honestly; Yes—Honestly; Thomas and Sarah; Pig in the Middle; The Complete Lack of Charm of the Bourgeoisie; Nanny; Oh Madeline! (USA TV); Father Matthew's Daughter; A View of Meadows Green; TV Films: Love with a Perfect Stranger; Losing Control, 1987; The Seventh Raven, 1987; This Magic Moment, 1988; Riders, 1990; *stage:* (contrib.) The Sloane Ranger Revue, 1985; I wish I wish, 1989. Mem., Point to Point Owners Assoc., 1988–. *Publications:* Rehearsal, 1972; The Fight Against Slavery, 1976; with Charlotte Bingham: Victoria, 1972; Rose's Story, 1973; Victoria and Company, 1974; Yes—Honestly, 1977; (with Michael Felton) Point-to-Point, 1990; regular contribs to Daily Mail, Living, Country Homes and Interiors, Punch. *Recreations:* painting, music, horse racing, avoiding dinner parties. *Address:* c/o Murray Pollinger, 222 Old Brompton Road, SW5 0BZ. *Clubs:* PEN, Society of Authors.

BRAGG, Melvyn; writer; Presenter and Editor, The South Bank Show, for ITV, since 1978; Controller of Arts, London Weekend Television, since 1990 (Head of Arts, 1982–90); Chairman, Border Television, since 1990 (Deputy Chairman, 1985–90); *b* 6 Oct. 1939; *s* of Stanley Bragg and Mary Ethel (*née* Parks); *m* 1st, 1961, Marie-Elisabeth Roche (decd); one *d*; 2nd, 1973, Catherine Mary Haste; one *s* one *d. Educ:* Nelson-Thomlinson Grammar Sch., Wigton; Wadham Coll., Oxford (MA). BBC Radio and TV Producer, 1961–67; writer and broadcaster, 1967–. Novelist, 1964–. Mem. ACTT. Presenter: BBC TV series: 2nd House, 1973–77; Read all About It (also editor), 1976–77; Start the Week, Radio 4, 1988–. Mem. Arts Council, and Chm. Literature Panel of Arts

Council, 1977–80. President: Cumbrians for Peace, 1982–; Northern Arts, 1983–87; Nat. Campaign for the Arts, 1986–. Domus Fellow, St Catherine's Coll., Oxford, 1990. FRSL; FRTS. Hon. Fellow, Lancashire Polytechnic, 1987. DUniv; Hon. DLitt Liverpool, 1986. *Plays:* Mardi Gras, 1976 (musical); Orion (TV), 1977; The Hired Man, 1984 (musical); *screenplays:* Isadora; Jesus Christ Superstar; (with Ken Russell) Clouds of Glory. *Publications:* Speak for England, 1976; Land of the Lakes, 1983 (televised); Laurence Olivier, 1984; Rich: the life of Richard Burton, 1988; *novels:* For Want of a Nail, 1965; The Second Inheritance, 1966; Without a City Wall, 1968; The Hired Man, 1969; A Place in England, 1970; The Nerve, 1971; Josh Lawton, 1972; The Silken Net, 1974; A Christmas Child, 1976; Autumn Manoeuvres, 1978; Kingdom Come, 1980; Love and Glory, 1983; The Maid of Buttermere, 1987; A Time to Dance, 1990; articles for various English jls. *Recreations:* walking, books. *Address:* 12 Hampstead Hill Gardens, NW3. *T:* 071–435 7215. *Clubs:* Garrick, Groucho, PEN.

BRAGG, Stephen Lawrence, MA, SM; FEng; FIMechE; FRAeS; Administrator, Cambridge Office, American Friends of Cambridge University, since 1988; *b* 17 Nov. 1923; *e s* of Sir Lawrence Bragg, CH, OBE, MC, FRS and Lady Bragg, CBE; *m* 1951, Maureen Ann (*née* Roberts); three *s. Educ:* Rugby Sch.; Cambridge Univ.; Massachusetts Inst. of Technology. BA 1945, MA 1949 (Cambridge); SM 1949 (MIT). FEng 1981. Rolls-Royce Ltd, 1944–48; Commonwealth Fund Fellow, 1948–49; Wm Jessop Ltd, Steelmakers, 1949–51; Rolls-Royce Ltd, 1951–71: Chief Scientist, 1960–63; Chief Research Engineer, 1964–68; Dir, Aero Div., 1969–71. Vice-Chancellor, Brunel Univ., 1971–81; Fellow, Wolfson Coll., Cambridge, 1982–91. Eastern Region Broker, SERC, 1981–83. Dir in Industrial Co-operation, Cambridge Univ., 1984–88. Chm., Cambridge DHA, 1982–86. Member: Univ. Grants Cttee, 1966–71; Aeronautical Research Council, 1970–73; Court of ASC, Henley, 1972–81; SRC Engineering Bd, 1976–79; Airworthiness Requirements Bd, 1979–81; Chm., Adv. Cttee on Falsework, 1973–75. Corres. Mem. Venezuelan Acad. Sci., 1975. Hon. DEng Sheffield, 1969; Hon. DTech Brunel, 1982. *Publications:* Rocket Engines, 1962; articles on Jet Engines, Research Management, University/Industry Collaboration, etc. *Recreation:* railway history. *Address:* 22 Brookside, Cambridge CB2 1JQ. *T:* Cambridge (0223) 62208. *Club:* Athenæum.

See also Sir Mark Heath, D. P. Thomson.

BRAGGINS, Maj.-Gen. Derek Henry, CB 1986; Director General, Transport and Movements, Army, 1983–86; *b* 19 April 1931; *s* of late Albert Edward Braggins and of Hilda Braggins; *m* 1953, Sheila St Clair (*née* Stuart); three *s. Educ:* Rothesay Academy; Hendon Technical College. FBIM 1979, FCIT 1983. Commissioned RASC, 1950; RCT, 1965; regtl and staff appts, Korea, Malaya, Singapore, Ghana, Aden, Germany and UK; student, Staff Coll., Camberley, 1962, JSSC, Latimer, 1970; CO 7 Regt RCT, 1973–75; Col AQ Commando Forces RM, 1977–80; Comd Transport and Movements, BAOR, 1981–83. Col Comdt, RCT, 1986–; Pres., RASC/RCT Assoc., 1987–. Freeman, City of London, 1983; Hon. Liveryman, Worshipful Co. of Carmen, 1983. *Recreations:* hashing, shooting, fishing, gardening.

BRAHAM, Allan John Witney, PhD; Keeper and Deputy Director, the National Gallery, since 1978; *b* 19 Aug. 1937; *s* of Dudley Braham and Florence Mears; *m* 1963, Helen Clare Butterworth; two *d. Educ:* Dulwich Coll.; Courtauld Inst. of Art, Univ. of London (BA 1960, PhD 1967). Asst Keeper, National Gall., 1962, Dep. Keeper, 1973. Arts Council Exhibn (with Peter Smith), François Mansart, 1970–71; National Gall. Exhibitions: (co-ordinator and editor) The Working of the National Gallery, 1974; Velázquez, The Rokeby Venus, 1976; Giovanni Battista Moroni, 1978; Italian Renaissance Portraits, 1979; El Greco to Goya, 1981; Wright of Derby "Mr and Mrs Coltman", 1986. *Publications:* Dürer, 1965; Murillo (The Masters), 1966; The National Gallery in London: Italian Painting of the High Renaissance, 1971; (with Peter Smith) François Mansart, 1973; Funeral Decorations in Early Eighteenth Century Rome, 1975; (with Hellmut Hager) Carlo Fontana: The Drawings at Windsor Castle, 1977; The Architecture of the French Enlightenment, 1980 (Hitchcock Medal, Banister Fletcher Prize); National Gall. catalogues: The Spanish School (revised edn), 1970, and booklets: Velázquez, 1972; Rubens, 1972; Architecture, 1976; Italian Paintings of the Sixteenth Century, 1985; contrib. prof. jls, etc. *Recreation:* history of architecture. *Address:* 15A Acol Road, NW6 3AA.

BRAHAM, Harold, CBE 1960; HM Diplomatic Service, retired; *b* Constantinople, 11 Oct. 1907; *er s* of late D. D. Braham, of The Times; *m* 1941, Cicely Edith Norton Webber (*d* 1990); one *s* one *d. Educ:* St Peter's Coll., Adelaide; New College, Oxford. Entered HM Consular Service, China, 1931. Retired as HM Consul-Gen., Paris, 1966. *Address:* Caserio Torret 19, San Luis, 07710 Prov. Baleares, Spain.

BRAHIMI, Lakhdar; Assistant Secretary-General, League of Arab States, Tunis, since 1984; *b* 1934; *m* 1964; two *s* one *d. Educ:* Faculté de Droit and Institut des Sciences Politiques, Algiers; then Paris. Permanent Rep. of FLN and later of Provisional Govt of Algeria, in SE Asia, 1956–61; Gen. Secretariat, Min. of External Affairs, 1961–63; Ambassador to Egypt and Sudan, and Permanent Rep. to Arab League, 1963–70; Ambassador to Court of St James's, 1971–79; Mem., Central Cttee, National Liberation Front, Algeria, 1979–84; Pol Advr to President Chadli, 1982–84. *Address:* The League of Arab States, Tunis, Tunisia.

BRAIN, family name of **Baron Brain.**

BRAIN, 2nd Baron *cr* 1962, of Eynsham; **Christopher Langdon Brain;** Bt 1954; *b* 30 Aug. 1926; *s* of 1st Baron Brain, MA, DM, FRS, FRCP and Stella, *er d* of late Reginald L. Langdon-Down; *S* father 1966; *m* 1953, Susan Mary, *d* of George P. and Ethelbertha Morris; three *d. Educ:* Leighton Park Sch., Reading; New College, Oxford. MA 1956. Royal Navy, 1946–48. Liveryman, 1955, Upper Warden, 1974–75, Asst, 1980, Renter Bailiff, 1983–84, Upper Bailiff, 1984–85, Worshipful Co. of Weavers. Chm., Rhone-Alps Regional Council, British Chamber of Commerce, France, 1967. ARPS 1970. *Recreations:* bird watching, sailing, fly-fishing. *Heir: b* Hon. Michael Cottrell Brain, MA, DM, FRCP, FRCP Canada, Prof. of Medicine, McMaster Univ. [*b* 6 Aug. 1928; *m* 1960, Dr the Hon. Elizabeth Ann Herbert, *e d* of Baron Tangley, KBE; one *s* two *d*]. *Address:* The Old Rectory, 34 Cross Street, Moretonhampstead, Devon TQ13 8NL. *Club:* Oxford and Cambridge Sailing Society.

BRAIN, Albert Edward Arnold; Regional Director (East Midlands), Department of the Environment, and Chairman of Regional Economic Planning Board, 1972–77; *b* 31 Dec. 1917; *s* of Walter Henry and Henrietta Mabel Brain; *m* 1947, Patricia Grace Gallop; two *s* one *d. Educ:* Rendcomb Coll., Cirencester; Loughborough College. BSc (Eng) London, external; DLC hons Loughborough; CEng, MICE, MIMunE. Royal Engineers, 1940–46; Bristol City Corp., 1946–48; Min. of Transport: Asst Engr, London, 1948–54; Civil Engr, Wales, 1954–63; Sen. Engr, HQ, 1963–67; Asst Chief Engr, HQ, 1967–69; Divl Road Engr, W Mids, now Regional Controller (Roads and Transportation), 1969–72. Pres., Old Rendcombian Soc., 1986–. *Recreations:* gardening, bridge, golf. *Address:* Withyholt Lodge, Moorend Road, Charlton Kings, Cheltenham GL53 9BW. *T:* Cheltenham (0242) 576264.

BRAIN, Sir (Henry) Norman, KBE 1963 (OBE 1947); CMG 1953; *b* 19 July 1907; *s* of late B. Brain, Rushall, Staffs; *m* 1939, Nuala Mary, *d* of late Capt. A. W. Butterworth; one *s* (and one *s* decd). *Educ:* King Edward's Sch., Birmingham; The Queen's Coll., Oxford (MA). Entered the Consular Service, 1930, and served at Tokyo, Kobe, Osaka, Tamsui, Manila, Mukden, Shanghai and Dairen; interned by Japanese, 1941–42; repatriated and served in Foreign Office, 1943; appointed to Staff of Supreme Allied Comdr, South-East Asia, 1944–46; Political Adviser to Saigon Control Commission, 1945; served with Special Commissioner in South-East Asia, at Singapore, 1946–48; Counsellor in Foreign Office, 1949; Inspector of HM Foreign Service Estabts, 1950–53; Minister, Tokyo, 1953–55; Ambassador to Cambodia, 1956–58; Asst Under-Sec. of State, FO, 1958–61; Ambassador to Uruguay, 1961–66, retired, 1966. Chairman: Royal Central Asian Soc., 1970–74; Japan Soc. of London, 1970–73; Pres., British Uruguayan Soc., 1974–. *Recreations:* music, golf. *Address:* St Andrews, Abney Court, Bourne End, Bucks SL8 5DL. *Club:* Canning.

BRAINE, Rt. Hon. Sir Bernard (Richard), Kt 1972; PC 1985; DL; MP (C) Castle Point, since 1983 (Billericay Division of Essex, 1950–55; South East Essex, 1955–83); Father of the House of Commons, since 1987; *b* Ealing, Middx, 24 June 1914; *s* of Arthur Ernest Braine; *m* 1935, Kathleen Mary Faun (*d* 1982); three *s*. *Educ:* Hendon County Grammar Sch. Served North Staffs Regt in War of 1939–45: West Africa, SE Asia, NW Europe; Staff Coll., Camberley, 1944 (sc); Lt-Col. Chm., British Commonwealth Producers' Organisation, 1958–60; Parly Sec., Min. of Pensions and National Insurance, 1960–61; Parly Under-Sec. of State for Commonwealth Relations, 1961–62; Parly Sec., Min. of Health, 1962–64; Conservative front bench spokesman on Commonwealth Affairs and Overseas Aid, 1967–70; Chm., Select Cttees on Overseas Aid, 1970–71, on Overseas Develt, 1973–74; Treasurer, UK Branch of Commonwealth Parly Assoc., 1974–77 (Dep. Chm., 1964 and 1970–74). Chairman: British-German Parly Group, 1970–; British-Greek Parly Group, 1979–; All-party Pro Life Cttee; Founder and Chm., All-party Misuse of Drugs Cttee, 1984–88; Nat. Council on Alcoholism, 1973–82; UK Chapter, Soc. of Internat. Develt, 1976–83; Vice-Chm., Parly Human Rights Gp, 1979–. President: UK Cttee for Defence of the Unjustly Prosecuted, 1980–88; River Thames Soc., 1981–87; Greater London Alcohol Adv. Service, 1983–. President, Cons. Clubs of Benfleet, Hadleigh and Canvey Is. Associate Mem., Inst. of Develt Studies, Univ. of Sussex, 1971–; Vis. Prof., Baylor Univ., Texas, 1987–. A Governor, Commonwealth Inst., 1968–81, Trustee, 1981–. FRSA 1971. DL Essex, 1978. KStJ 1985; KCSG 1987; GCLJ 1987; GCMLJ 1988. Europe Peace Cross, 1979; Knight Comdr's Cross with Star, German Order of Merit, 1984 (Comdr's Cross, 1974); Grand Comdr, Order of Honour (Greece), 1987; Grand Cross, Order of Polonia Restituta, 1990 (Comdr's Cross with Star, 1983). *Address:* King's Wood, Rayleigh, Essex SS6 7AW. *Club:* Beefsteak.

BRAINE, Rear-Adm. Richard Allix, CB 1956; retired; *b* 18 Nov. 1900; *m* 1922, Lilian Violet (*d* 1985); one *s*. *Educ:* Dean Close Memorial Sch., Cheltenham. Joined RN as asst clerk, 1918; Comdr (S), Dec. 1938; Capt. (S), Dec. 1948; Rear-Adm. 1954. Command Supply Officer, Staff of Flag Officer Air (Home), 1954–56, Portsmouth, 1956–57. *Address:* The Old Cottage, Littlewick Green, near Maidenhead, Berks SL6 3RA. *T:* Littlewick Green (062882) 4484.

BRAININ, Norbert, OBE 1960; concert violinist; formed Amadeus Ensemble, incorporating Amadeus Trio, 1988; Professor of Chamber Music, Hochschule für Musik, Cologne, since 1976; Professor for Chamber Music, Royal Academy of Music, since 1986; *b* Vienna, 12 March 1923; *s* of Adolph and Sophie Brainin; *m* 1948, Kathe Kottow; one *d*. *Educ:* High Sch., Vienna. Commenced musical training in Vienna at age of seven and continued studies there until 1938; emigrated to London in 1938 and studied with Carl Flesch and Max Rostal; won Carl Flesch prize for solo violinists at the Guildhall Sch. of Music, London, 1946. Formed Amadeus String Quartet, 1947, Leader until disbanded in 1987. DUniv York, 1968. Grand Cross of Merit, 1st cl. Fed. Republic of Germany, 1972; Cross of Honour for Arts and Science (Austria), 1972. *Address:* 19 Prowse Avenue, Bushey Heath, Herts. *T:* 081–950 7379.

BRAITHWAITE, His Honour Bernard Richard; a Circuit Judge (formerly County Court Judge), 1971–88; *b* 20 Aug. 1917; *s* of Bernard Leigh Braithwaite and Emily Dora Ballard Braithwaite (*née* Thomas); unmarried. *Educ:* Clifton; Peterhouse, Cambridge. BA (Hons), Law. Served War: 7th Bn Somerset LI, 1939–43; Parachute Regt, 1943–46; Captain, Temp. Major. Called to Bar, Inner Temple, 1946. *Recreations:* hunting, sailing. *Address:* Summerfield House, Uley, Gloucestershire. *Club:* Boodle's.

BRAITHWAITE, Eustace Edward Adolph Ricardo; writer; Ambassador of Guyana to Venezuela, 1968–69; *b* 27 June 1922. *Educ:* New York Univ.; Cambridge Univ. Served War of 1939–45, RAF. Schoolteacher, London, 1950–57; Welfare Officer, LCC, 1958–60; Human Rights Officer, World Veterans Foundation, Paris, 1960–63; Lecturer and Education Consultant, Unesco, Paris, 1963–66; Permanent Rep. of Guyana to UN, 1967–68. Ainsfield-Wolff Literary Award, 1961; Franklin Prize. *Publications:* To Sir With Love, 1959; Paid Servant, 1962; A Kind of Homecoming, 1962; Choice of Straws, 1965; Reluctant Neighbours, 1972; Honorary White, 1976. *Recreations:* dancing and tennis.

BRAITHWAITE, Sir (Joseph) Franklin (Madders), Kt 1980; DL; CBIM; Chairman: Baker Perkins Holdings plc, 1980–84; Peterborough Independent Hospital plc, 1981–87; *b* 6 April 1917; *s* of late Sir John Braithwaite and Martha Janette (*née* Baker); *m* 1939, Charlotte Isabel, *d* of late Robert Elmer Baker, New York; one *s* one *d*. *Educ:* Bootham Sch.; King's Coll., Cambridge, 1936–39 (BA 1939, MA 1955). Served Army, 1940–46 (Captain). Joined Baker Perkins Ltd, 1946, Director 1950, Vice-Chm. 1956; Chairman, Baker Perkins Exports Ltd, 1966; Man. Dir, Baker Perkins Holdings Ltd, 1971. Director, Lloyds Bank Ltd, Eastern Counties Regional Board, 1979–87. Member: Mech. Engrg Industry Economic Development Cttee, 1974–79; Management Board, 1978–82, Commercial and Econ. Cttee, 1977–84, Engrg Employers' Fedn; Board of Fellows, 1974–79, Economic and Social Affairs Cttee, 1979–84, BIM. Mem., Peterborough Develt Corp., 1981–88, Dep. Chm. 1982–88. President, Process Plant Assoc., 1977–79, Hon. life Vice-Pres., 1981. DL Cambs, 1983. *Recreations:* music, golf. *Address:* 7 Rutland Terrace, Stamford, Lincs PE9 2QD. *T:* Stamford (0780) 51244. *Club:* Army and Navy.

BRAITHWAITE, Sir Rodric (Quentin), KCMG 1988 (CMG 1981); HM Diplomatic Service; Ambassador to the Soviet Union, 1988–May 1992; *b* 17 May 1932; *s* of Henry Warwick Braithwaite and Lorna Constance Davies; *m* 1961, Gillian Mary Robinson; three *s* one *d* (and one *s* decd). *Educ:* Bedales Sch.; Christ's Coll., Cambridge. 1st cl. Mod. Langs, Pts I and II. Mil. Service, 1950–52. Joined Foreign (subseq. Diplomatic) Service, 1955; 3rd Sec., Djakarta, 1957–58; 2nd Sec., Warsaw, 1959–61; FO, 1961–63; 1st Sec. (Commercial), Moscow, 1963–66; 1st Sec., Rome, 1966–69; FCO, 1969–72; Vis. Fellow, All Souls Coll., Oxford, 1972–73; Head of European Integration Dept (External), FCO, 1973–75; Head of Chancery, Office of Permanent Rep. to EEC, Brussels, 1975–78; Head of Planning Staff, FCO, 1979–80; Asst Under Sec. of State, FCO, 1981; Minister Commercial, Washington, 1982–84; Dep. Under-Sec. of State, FCO, 1984–88. *Recreations:* chamber music (viola); sailing; Russia. *Address:* c/o Foreign and Commonwealth Office, SW1A 2AL.

BRAMALL, family name of **Baron Bramall.**

BRAMALL, Baron *cr* 1987 (Life Peer), of Bushfield in the County of Hampshire; **Field Marshal Edwin Noel Westby Bramall,** KG 1990; GCB 1979 (KCB 1974); OBE 1965; MC 1945; JP; HM Lord-Lieutenant of Greater London, since 1986; Chief of the Defence Staff, 1982–85; *b* 18 Dec. 1923; *s* of late Major Edmund Haselden Bramall and Mrs Katherine Bridget Bramall (*née* Westby); *m* 1949, Dorothy Avril Wentworth Vernon; one *s* one *d*. *Educ:* Eton College. Commnd into KRRC, 1943; served in NW Europe, 1944–45; occupation of Japan, 1946–47; Instructor, Sch. of Infantry, 1949–51; psc 1952; Middle East, 1953–58; Instructor, Army Staff Coll., 1958–61; on staff of Lord Mountbatten at MoD, 1963–64; CO, 2 Green Jackets, KRRC, Malaysia during Indonesian confrontation, 1965–66; comd 5th Airportable Bde, 1967–69; idc 1970; GOC 1st Div. BAOR, 1971–73; Lt-Gen., 1973; Comdr, British Forces, Hong Kong, 1973–76; Gen., 1976; C-in-C, UK Land Forces, 1976–78; Vice-Chief of Defence Staff (Personnel and Logistics), 1978–79; Chief of the General Staff, 1979–82; Field Marshal 1982. ADC (Gen.), 1979–82. Col Comdt, 3rd Bn Royal Green Jackets, 1973–84; Col, 2nd Goorkhas, 1976–86; President: Greater London TAVRA, 1986–; Gurkha Bde Assoc., 1987–. A Trustee, Imperial War Museum, 1983– (Chm., 1989–). JP London 1986. KStJ 1986. *Recreations:* cricket, painting, travel. *Address:* Lieutenancy Office, Westminster City Hall, PO Box 240, Victoria Street, SW1E 6QP. *Clubs:* Travellers', Army and Navy, Pratt's, MCC (Pres., 1988–89), I Zingari, Free Foresters.

See also Sir E. A. Bramall.

BRAMALL, Sir (Ernest) Ashley, Kt 1975; DL; Member (Lab), Greater London Council, Bethnal Green and Bow, 1973–86 (Tower Hamlets, 1964–73); Chairman: GLC, 1982–83; ILEA, 1965–67 and 1984–86 (Leader, 1970–81); *b* 6 Jan. 1916; *er s* of late Major E. H. Bramall and Mrs K. B. Bramall (*née* Westby); *m*; three *s*. *Educ:* Westminster and Canford Schs; Magdalen Coll., Oxford. Served in Army, 1940–46; Major; psc 1945. Contested Fareham Div. of Hants, 1945; MP (Lab) for Bexley, 1946–50; contested Bexley, 1950, 1951, 1959; Watford, 1955. Barrister, Inner Temple. Member: LCC (Lab) Bethnal Green, 1961; Westminster CC, 1959–68; Chm., Council of LEAs, 1975–76, 1977–78, Vice-Chm., 1976–77; Leader, Management Panel, Burnham Cttee (Primary and Secondary), 1973–78; Chm., Nat. Council for Drama Trng, 1981–89; Mem. Council, City Univ., 1984–90. Hon. Sec., Theatres Adv. Council, 1987–. Governor, Museum of London, 1981–. DL Greater London, 1981. Grand Officer, Order of Orange Nassau, 1982. *Address:* 2 Egerton House, 59–63 Belgrave Road, SW1V 2BE. *T:* 071–828 0973.

See also Field Marshal Baron Bramall.

BRAMALL, Margaret Elaine, OBE 1969; MA; JP; Vice-President, National Council for One Parent Families (formerly National Council for the Unmarried Mother and her Child) (Director, 1962–79); Lecturer, Applied Social Studies Course, University of Surrey, since 1979; *b* 1 Oct. 1916; *d* of Raymond Taylor, MA and Nettie Kate Taylor, BA; *m* 1939, Sir Ashley Bramall (marr. diss.); two *s*. *Educ:* St Paul's Girls' Sch., Hammersmith; Somerville Coll., Oxford (BA 1939, MA 1942); LSE (Social Science Hon. Certif. 1950); Inst. of Almoners (Certif. 1951). JP Richmond 1965. Member: Probation Case Cttee; Management Cttee, Humming Bird Housing Assoc. *Publications:* contrib., One Parent Families, ed Dulan Barber, 1975; contrib. social work jls. *Recreations:* gardening, family. *Address:* 74 Fifth Cross Road, Twickenham, Mddx TW2 5LE. *T:* 081–894 3998.

BRAMLEY, Prof. Sir Paul (Anthony), Kt 1984; FRCS, FDSRCS; Professor of Dental Surgery, University of Sheffield, 1969–88, now Emeritus; *b* 24 May 1923; *s* of Charles and Constance Bramley; *m* 1952, Hazel Morag Boyd, MA, MB ChB; one *s* three *d*. *Educ:* Wyggeston Grammar Sch., Leicester; Univ. of Birmingham. MB ChB, BDS. HS, Queen Elizabeth Hosp., Birmingham, 1945; Capt., RADC, 224 Para Fd Amb., 1946–48; MO, Church of Scotland, Kenya, 1952; Registrar, Rooksdown House, 1953–54; Consultant Oral Surgeon, SW Region Hosp. Bd, 1954–69; Dir, Dept of Oral Surgery and Orthodontics, Plymouth Gen. Hosp. and Truro Royal Infirmary, 1954–69; Civilian Consultant, RN, 1959–88, now Emeritus; Dean, Sch. of Clinical Dentistry, Univ. of Sheffield, 1972–75. Consultant Oral Surgeon, Trent Region, 1969–88. Member: General Dental Council, 1973–89; Council, Medical Protection Soc., 1970–; Council, RCS, 1975–83 (Tomes Lectr, 1980; Dean of Faculty of Dental Surgery, 1980–83; Colyer Gold Medal, 1988); Royal Commission on NHS; Dental Strategy Review Group; Chm., Standing Dental Adv. Cttee; Consultant Adviser, DHSS; Hon. Sec., British Assoc. of Oral Surgeons, 1968–72, Pres., 1975; President: S Yorks Br., British Dental Assoc., 1975; Oral Surgery Club of GB, 1985–86; Inst. of Maxillofacial Technol., 1987–89; Pres., BDA, 1988–89. Chm., Dental Protection Ltd, 1989–. Adviser, Prince of Songkla Univ., Thailand, 1982–; External Examiner to RCS, RCSI, RCSG, RACDS, Univs of Birmingham, Baghdad, Hong Kong, London, Singapore, Trinity College Dublin, Cardiff, NUI. Former Lay Reader, dios of Winchester and Exeter. Hon. FRACDS. Hon. DDS: Birmingham, 1987; Prince of Songkla Univ., 1989. Fellow, Internat. Assoc. of Oral and Maxillofacial Surgeons. Bronze Medal, Helsinki Univ., 1989. *Publications:* (with J. Norman) The Temporomandibular Joint: disease, disorders, surgery, 1989; scientific articles in British and foreign medical and dental jls. *Address:* Greenhills, Back Lane, Hathersage S30 1AR.

BRAMMA, Harry Wakefield, FRCO; Director, Royal School of Church Music, since 1989; Organist and Director of Music, All Saints', Margaret Street, since 1989; *b* 11 Nov. 1936; *s* of Fred and Christine Bramma. *Educ:* Bradford Grammar Sch.; Pembroke Coll., Oxford (MA). FRCO 1958. Dir of Music, King Edward VI Grammar Sch., Retford, Notts, 1961; Asst Organist, Worcester Cathedral, 1963; Dir of Music, The King's Sch., Worcester, 1965; Organist, Southwark Cathedral, 1976. Conductor, Kidderminster Choral Soc., 1972–79. Examnr, Associated Bd of Royal Schs of Music, 1978–89. Mem. Council, RCO, 1979, Hon. Treas., 1987–. *Recreations:* travel, walking. *Address:* Addington Palace, Croydon, Surrey CR9 5AD. *T:* 081-654 7676.

BRAMMER, Leonard Griffith, RE 1956 (ARE 1932); painter and etcher; Supervisor of Art and Crafts, Stoke-on-Trent Education Authority, 1952–69; retired; *b* 4 July 1906; *s* of Frederick William Brammer and Minnie Griffith; *m* 1934, Florence May, *d* of William and Mary Barnett, Hanley; one *d*. *Educ:* Burslem Sch. of Art; Royal College of Art (Diploma Associate); awarded Travelling Scholarship, School of Engraving, Royal College of Art, 1930; represented in Tate Gallery, British Museum, Victoria & Albert Museum, Ashmolean, Oxford, City of Stoke-on-Trent Art Gallery, City of Carlisle Art Gallery, Wedgwood Museum, Barlaston, Keele Univ., Gladstone Pottery Museum, Collection of Contemporary Art Soc., The Collections of The British Council, etc; was exhibitor at Royal Academy and all leading English and American exhibitions. *Address:* Sŵn-y-Wylan, Beach Road, Morfa Bychan, Porthmadog, Gwynedd LL49 9YA.

BRAMPTON, Sally Jane, (Mrs Jonathan Powell); freelance journalist; *b* 15 July 1955; *d* of Roy and Pamela Brampton; *m* 1981, Nigel Cole (marr. diss.); *m* 1990, Jonathan Powell. *Educ:* Ashford Sch., Ashford, Kent; St Clare's Hall, Oxford; St Martin's School of

Art, London. Fashion Writer, Vogue, 1978; Fashion Editor, Observer, 1981; Editor, Elle (UK), 1985–89; Associate Editor, Mirabella, 1990–91. *Publication:* Good Grief (novel), 1992. *Address:* 10a Wedderburn Road, NW3. *Club:* Groucho.

BRAMWELL, Richard Mervyn; QC 1989; *b* 29 Sept. 1944; *s* of Clifford and Dorothy Bramwell; *m* 1968, Susan Green; one *d. Educ:* Stretford Grammar Sch.; LSE (LLB, LLM). Called to the Bar, Middle Temple, 1967. *Publications:* Taxation of Companies and Company Reconstructions, 1973, 5th edn 1991; Inheritance Tax on Lifetime Gifts, 1987. *Recreations:* hunting, tennis. *Address:* 3 Temple Gardens, Temple, EC4Y 9AU. *T:* 071–353 7884.

BRANAGH, Kenneth Charles; actor and director; *b* 10 Dec. 1960; *s* of William and Frances Branagh; *m* 1989, Emma Thompson. *Educ:* Meadway Comprehensive Sch., Reading; Royal Academy of Dramatic Art (Bancroft Gold Medalist). *Theatre:* Another Country, Queen's, 1982 (SWET Award, Most Promising Newcomer; Plays and Players Award); The Madness; Francis; Henry V, Golden Girls, Hamlet, Love's Labours Lost, 1984–85; Tell Me Honestly (also author); Across the Roaring Hill; The Glass Maze; formed Renaissance Theatre Company, 1987: Romeo and Juliet; Public Enemy (also author); Much Ado About Nothing; As You Like It; Hamlet; Look Back in Anger (also televised); A Midsummer Night's Dream (also dir); King Lear (also dir); *directed:* Romeo and Juliet; Twelfth Night (also televised); The Life of Napoleon; (with Peter Egan) Uncle Vanya; *films include:* A Month in the Country; High Season; Henry V (also dir) (Evening Standard Best Film of the Year, 1989; Oscar, Best Costume Design, 1990; BFI Award, Best Film and Technical Achievement, 1990; Young European Film of the Year, 1990; NY Critics Circle Award, Best New Dir); Dead Again (also dir), 1991; *television includes:* Fortunes of War; Boy in the Bush; Billy Trilogy; To the Lighthouse; Strange Interlude; Ghosts; The Lady's Not for Burning. European Actor of the Year, 1990. *Publications:* Public Enemy (play), 1988; Beginning (autobiog.), 1989. *Recreations:* reading, playing guitar. *Address:* 83 Berwick Street, W1V 3PJ. *T:* 071–287 6672.

BRANCH, Prof. Michael Arthur, PhD; Director, School of Slavonic and East European Studies, since 1980, and Professor of Finnish, since 1986, University of London; *b* 24 March 1940; *s* of Arthur Frederick Branch and Mahala Parker; *m* 1963, Ritva-Riitta Hannele, *d* of Erkki Kari, Heinola, Finland; three *d. Educ:* Shene Grammar Sch.; Sch. of Slavonic and East European Studies, Univ. of London (BA 1963; PhD 1967). School of Slavonic and East European Studies: Asst Lectr and Lectr in Finno-Ugrian Studies, 1967–72; Lectr, 1972–77, and Reader in Finnish, 1977; Chm., Dept of East European Language and Literature, 1979–80. Corresponding Member: Finno-Ugrian Soc., 1977; Finnish Literature Soc. (Helsinki), 1980. Hon. PhD Oulu (Finland), 1983. Comdr, Lion of Finland, 1980. *Publications:* A. J. Sjögren, 1973; (jtly) Finnish Folk Poetry: Epic, 1977; (jtly) A Student's Glossary of Finnish, 1980; (jtly) Edith Södergran, 1991; (jtly) The Great Bear, 1992. *Recreations:* gardening, walking. *Address:* 33 St Donatt's Road, SE14 6NU. *T:* 071–637 4934. *Club:* Athenæum.

BRANCH, Sir William Allan Patrick, Kt 1977; Managing Director and Grenada Representative on the Windward Islands Banana Association (Mirabeau, Capitol, Hope Development and Dougaldston Estates); *b* 17 Feb. 1915; *m* Thelma (*née* Rapier); one *s. Educ:* Grenada Boys' Secondary Sch. Dep. Manager, Mt Horne Agricl Estate, 1936; Manager Mt Horne, Boulogne, Colombier, Industry and Grand Bras Agricl Estates, 1941. Chairman, Eastern Dist Agricl Rehabilitation Cttee; Dep. Chm. Bd of Dirs, Grenada Banana Co-op Soc.; Director: Grenada Cocoa Industry; Parochial and Island Anglican Church Council; Managing Cttee: Grenada Boy Scouts Assoc.; St Andrew's Anglican Secondary Sch; Member, Central Agricl Rehabilitation Cttee. Knighthood awarded for services to agriculture, Grenada, Windward Islands. *Address:* Dougaldston, Gouyave, St John's, Grenada.

BRANCKER, Sir (John Eustace) Theodore, Kt 1969; President of the Senate, Barbados, 1971–76; *b* 9 Feb. 1909; *s* of Jabel Eustace and Myra Enid Vivienne Brancker; *m* 1967, Esme Gwendolyn Walcott (OBE 1987). *Educ:* Harrison Coll., Barbados; Grad., Inst. of Political Secretaries; LSE (Certificate in Colonial Admin, 1933). Called to Bar, Middle Temple, 1933; in private practice; QC (Barbados) 1961. Mem., House of Assembly, Barbados, 1937–71 (Leader of Opposition, 1956–61; Speaker, 1961–71). Mem., Medico-Legal Soc. Mem., CPA. Life Fellow, Royal Commonwealth Soc.; Life Mem., Barbados Mus. and Historical Soc. Chm., 1973, Hon. Awards Liaison Officer, 1978, Duke of Edinburgh Award Scheme. Mem., Soc. of Friends of Westminster Cathedral. Charter Pres., Rotary Club, Barbados. Mem. Adv. Bd, St Joseph Hosp. of Sisters of the Sorrowful Mother. Hon. LLD, Soochow Univ., 1973. FZS; FRSA (Life Fellow). Queen's Coronation Medal, 1953; Silver Jubilee Medal, 1977. *Recreations:* classical music, chess, drama. *Address:* Valencia, Holetown, St James's, Barbados. *T:* 432-0775. *Clubs:* Royal Over-Seas League (Life Mem.), Challoner (London); Empire, Bridgetown, Sunset Crest (Barbados); Rotary International.

BRAND, family name of **Viscount Hampden.**

BRAND, Hon. Lord; David William Robert Brand; a Senator of the College of Justice in Scotland, 1972–89; *b* 21 Oct. 1923; *s* of late James Gordon Brand, Huntingdon, Dumfries, and Frances (*née* Bull); *m* 1st, 1948, Rose Josephine Devlin (*d* 1968); four *d*; 2nd, Bridget Veronica Lynch (*née* Russell), *widow* of Thomas Patrick Lynch, Beechmount, Mallow, Co. Cork. *Educ:* Stonyhurst Coll.; Edinburgh Univ. Served War of 1939–45; Commissioned Argyll and Sutherland Highlanders, 1942; Capt. 1945. Admitted to Faculty of Advocates, 1948; Standing Junior Counsel to Dept of Education for Scotland, 1951; Advocate-Depute for Sheriff Court, 1953; Extra Advocate-Depute for Glasgow Circuit, 1955; Advocate-Depute, 1957–59; QC Scot. 1959; Senior Advocate-Depute, 1964; Sheriff of Dumfries and Galloway, 1968; Sheriff of Roxburgh, Berwick and Selkirk, 1970; Solicitor-General for Scotland, 1970–72. Chm., Medical Appeal Tribunal, 1959–70. Kt, SMO Malta. *Publications:* Joint Editor, Scottish Edn of Current Law, 1948–61; Scottish Editor, Encyclopedia of Road Traffic Law and Practice, 1960–64; contributor to Scots Law Times. *Recreation:* golf. *Address:* Ardgarten, Marmion Road, N Berwick, E Lothian EH39 4PG. *T:* North Berwick (0620) 3208. *Clubs:* New (Edinburgh); Honourable Company of Edinburgh Golfers.

BRAND, Alexander George, MBE 1945; *b* 23 March 1918; *s* of David Wilson Brand and Janet Ramsay Brand (*née* Paton); *m* 1947, Helen Constance Campbell; one *s* one *d. Educ:* Ayr Academy; Univ. of Glasgow. MA 1940, LLB 1948. Admitted Solicitor, 1948. Served in Royal Air Force, 1940–46 (Flt Lt). Legal Asst: Dumbarton CC, 1948; in Office of Solicitor to the Secretary of State for Scotland, 1949; Sen. Legal Asst, 1955; Asst Solicitor, 1964; Dep. Solicitor, 1972–79. Sec. of Scottish Law Commn, 1965–72. *Recreations:* golf, theatre, music, reading. *Address:* 16 Queen's Avenue, Edinburgh EH4 2DF. *T:* 031–332 4472. *Club:* Bruntsfield Links Golfing Society (Edinburgh).

BRAND, Prof. Charles Peter, FBA 1990; Professor of Italian, 1966–88, and Vice-Principal, 1984–88, University of Edinburgh; *b* 7 Feb. 1923; *er s* of Charles Frank Brand and Dorothy (*née* Tapping); *m* 1948, Gunvor, *yr d* of Col I. Hellgren, Stockholm; one *s* three *d. Educ:* Cambridge High Sch.; Trinity Hall, Cambridge. War Service, Intelligence Corps, 1943–46. Open Maj. Scholar, Trinity Hall, 1940; 1st Class Hons. Mod. Languages, Cantab, 1948; PhD Cantab, 1951. Asst Lecturer, Edinburgh Univ., 1952; Cambridge University: Asst Lecturer, subsequently Lecturer, 1952–66; Fellow and Tutor, Trinity Hall, 1958–66. Cavaliere Ufficiale, 1975, Commendatore, 1988, al Merito della Repubblica Italiana. General Editor, Modern Language Review, 1971–77; Editor, Italian Studies, 1977–. *Publications:* Italy and the English Romantics, 1957; Torquato Tasso, 1965; Ariosto: a preface to the Orlando Furioso, 1974; contributions to learned journals. *Recreations:* sport, travel, gardening. *Address:* 21 Succoth Park, Edinburgh EH12 6BX. *T:* 031–337 1980.

BRAND, David William Robert; *see* Brand, Hon. Lord.

BRAND, Geoffrey Arthur; Under-Secretary, Department of Employment, 1972–85; *b* 13 June 1930; *s* of late Arthur William Charles Brand and Muriel Ada Brand; *m* 1954, Joy Trotman; two *d. Educ:* Andover Grammar Sch.; University Coll., London. Entered Min. of Labour, 1953; Private Sec. to Parly Sec., 1956–57; Colonial Office, 1957–58; Private Sec. to Minister of Labour, 1965–66; Asst. Sec., Industrial Relations and Research and Planning Divisions, 1966–72. Mem., Archbishop of Canterbury's Adv. Gp on Urban Priority Areas, 1986–. *Address:* Cedarwood, Seer Green, Beaconsfield, Bucks HP9 2UH. *T:* Beaconsfield (0494) 676637.

BRANDES, Lawrence Henry, CB 1982; Under Secretary and Head of the Office of Arts and Libraries, 1978–82; *b* 16 Dec. 1924; *m* 1950, Dorothea Stanyon; one *s* one *d. Educ:* Beltane Sch.; London Sch. of Economics. Min. of Health, 1950; Principal Private Sec. to Minister, 1959; Nat. Bd for Prices and Incomes, 1966; Dept of Employment and Productivity, 1969; Under-Sec., DHSS, 1970; HM Treasury, 1975. Mem., Museums and Galls Commn, 1987– (Chm., Conservation Cttee, 1987–). Director: Dance Umbrella; London Internat. Fest. of Theatre. Mem., Dulwich Picture Gall. Management Cttee (Vice-Chm., 1988–); Trustee, SS Great Britain Project. *Address:* 4 Hogarth Hill, NW11 6AX.

BRANDO, Marlon; American actor, stage and screen; *b* Omaha, Nebraska, 3 April 1924; *s* of Marlon Brando; *m* 1957, Anna Kashfi (marr. diss., 1959); one *s. Educ:* Libertyville High Sch., Illinois; Shattuck Military Academy, Minnesota. Entered Dramatic Workshop of New School for Social Research, New York, 1943; has studied with Elia Kazan and Stella Adler. *Plays include:* I Remember Mama, Broadway, 1944; Truckline Café, 1946; Candida, 1946; A Flag is Born, 1946; The Eagle Has Two Heads, 1946; A Streetcar Named Desire, 1947. *Films include:* The Men, 1950; A Streetcar Named Desire, 1951; Viva Zapata!, 1952; Julius Cæsar, 1953; The Wild Ones, 1953; Désirée, 1954; On the Waterfront, 1954; Guys and Dolls, 1955; Tea House of the August Moon, 1956; Sayonara, 1957; The Young Lions, 1958; The Fugitive Kind, 1960; Mutiny on the Bounty, 1962; The Ugly American, 1963; Bedtime Story, 1964; The Satoteur, Code Name-Morituri, 1965; The Chase, 1966; Appaloosa, 1966; Southwest to Sonora, 1966; A Countess from Hong Kong, 1967; Reflections in a Golden Eye, 1967; Candy, 1968; The Night of the Following Day, 1969; Quiemad!, 1970; The Nightcomers, 1971; The Godfather, 1972; Last Tango in Paris, 1972; The Missouri Breaks, 1975; Apocalypse Now, 1977; Superman, 1978; The Formula, 1981; A Dry White Season, 1990; The Freshman, 1990. Directed, produced and appeared in One-Eyed Jacks, 1959. Academy Award, best actor of year, 1954, 1972.

BRANDON, family name of **Baron Brandon of Oakbrook.**

BRANDON OF OAKBROOK, Baron *cr* 1981 (Life Peer), of Hammersmith in Greater London; **Henry Vivian Brandon;** Kt 1966; MC 1942; PC 1978; a Lord of Appeal in Ordinary, since 1981; *b* 3 June 1920; *y s* of late Captain V. R. Brandon, CBE, RN, and late Joan Elizabeth Maud Simpson; *m* 1955, Jeanette Rosemary, *e d* of late J. V. B. Janvrin; three *s* one *d. Educ:* Winchester Coll. (Scholar); King's Coll., Cambridge (Scholar 1938, Stewart of Rannoch Scholar 1939). Commnd 2nd Lieut RA 1939; Major 1944; served Madagascar, 1942, India and Burma, 1942–45. BA 1946. Barrister, Inner Temple, 1946 (Entrance and Yarborough Anderson Scholar); Member Bar Council, 1951–53; QC 1961; Judge of the High Court of Justice, Probate, Divorce and Admiralty Division, 1966–71, Family Division, 1971–78; Judge of the Admiralty Court, 1971–78; Judge of the Commercial Court, 1977–78; a Lord Justice of Appeal, 1978–81. Member panel of Lloyd's arbitrators in salvage cases, 1961–66; Member panel from which Wreck Commissioners chosen, 1963–66. Hon. LLD Southampton, 1984. *Recreations:* cricket, bridge, travelling. *Address:* 6 Thackeray Close, SW19. *T:* 081–947 6344; House of Lords, SW1A 0PW. *Club:* MCC.

BRANDON, (Oscar) Henry, CBE 1985; Columnist, New York Times World Syndicate, since 1987; Associate Editor and Chief American correspondent of the Sunday Times, retired 1983; *b* 9 March 1916; *m* 1970, Mabel Hobart Wentworth; one *d. Educ:* Univ. of Prague and Lausanne. Joined Sunday Times, 1939; War Correspondent, N Africa and W Europe, 1943–45; Paris Correspondent, 1945–46; Roving Diplomatic Correspondent, 1947–49; Washington Correspondent, 1950–83; Syndicated Columnist for Washington Star, 1979–81. Guest scholar, The Brookings Instn, Washington, DC, 1983–. Hon. LittD Williams Coll., 1979. Foreign corresp. award, Univ. of California, Los Angeles, 1957; award, Lincoln Univ., Jefferson City, Missouri, 1962; Hannen Swaffer award, 1964; Sigma Delta Chi Soc. Award, 1983. *Publications:* As We Are, 1961; In The Red, 1966; Conversations with Henry Brandon, 1966; The Anatomy of Error, 1970; The Retreat of American Power, 1973; Special Relationships, 1989. *Recreations:* ski-ing, tennis, swimming, photography. *Address:* 3604 Winfield Lane NW, Washington, DC 20007, USA. *T:* (202) 338–8506.

BRANDON, Prof. Percy Samuel, (Prof. Peter Brandon); Professor of Electrical Engineering, 1971–84, Head of Electrical Division, 1981–84, University of Cambridge, now Professor Emeritus; *b* 9 Nov. 1916; *s* of P. S. Brandon, OBE; *m* 1942, Joan Edith Marriage, GRSM (London), LRAM; two *s. Educ:* Chigwell Sch.; Jesus Coll., Cambridge (MA). Joined The Marconi Company, 1939; Research Div., 1940–71. Frequency Measurement, 1940–44: Aerial Section, 1944–45. FM Radar, 1945–53; Chief of Guidance Systems, 1953–57; Chief of Mathematics and Systems Analysis Gp, 1957–65; Manager of Theoretical Sciences Laboratory, 1965–68; Asst Dir of Research, 1965–68; Manager of Research Div. of GEC-Marconi Electronics, 1968–71. Part-time lecturing at Mid-Essex Technical Coll., and others, 1945–66. FInstP, FIEE. *Publications:* contribs to Marconi Review, IEE Proc., Agardograph, Electronic Engineering, etc. *Recreations:* colour photography, hi-fi, using computers. *Address:* New Courts, 8 Bridge Lane, Little Shelford, Cambridge CB2 5HE. *T:* Cambridge (0223) 842541.

BRANDON-BRAVO, Martin Maurice, FBIM; MP (C) Nottingham South, since 1983; *b* 25 March 1932; *s* of late Issac, (Alfred), and Phoebe Brandon-Bravo; *m* 1964, Sally Anne Wallwin; two *s. Educ:* Latymer Sch. FBIM 1980. Joined Richard Stump Ltd, later Richard Stump (1979), 1952; successively Floor Manager, Factory Manager, Production Dir and Asst Man. Dir; Man. Dir., 1979–83; non-exec. Dir, 1983–; Dir, Hall & Earl Ltd, 1970–83. Mem., Nottingham City Council, 1968–70 and 1976–87; Chm., 1970–73, Pres., 1975–83, Nottingham West Cons. Party Orgn; Dep. Chm., City of Nottingham Cons. Fedn. Contested (C) Nottingham East, 1979. PPS to Minister of State for Housing and Urban Affairs, 1985–87, to Minister of State, Home Office, 1987–89, to Home Sec., 1989–90, to Lord Privy Seal and Leader of the House of Lords, 1990–. Mem., Nat. Water Sport Centre Management Cttee, 1972–83; Pres., Nottingham and Union Rowing Club. *Recreation:* rowing (Mem., Internat. Umpires' Commn; holder of Internat. Licence). *Address:* The Old Farmhouse, 27 Rectory Place, Barton-in-Fabis, Nottingham NG11 0AL. *T:* Nottingham (0602) 830459. *Clubs:* Carlton; Leander.

BRANDRETH, Gyles Daubeney; author, broadcaster; Chairman: Victorama Ltd, since 1974; Complete Editions Ltd, since 1988; Director, Newarke Wools Ltd, since 1988; Chairman, National Playing Fields Association, since 1989; *b* 8 March 1948; *s* of late Charles Brandreth and of Alice Addison; *m* 1973, Michèle Brown; one *s* two *d. Educ:* Lycée Français de Londres; Betteshanger Sch., Kent; Bedales Sch., Hants; New Coll., Oxford (Scholar). Pres. Oxford Union, Editor of Isis. Chm., Archway Productions Ltd, 1971–74; Dir, Colin Smythe Ltd, 1971–73; Dep. Chm., Unicorn Heritage, 1987–90. Freelance journalist, 1968–: contrib. Observer, Guardian, Daily Mail, Daily Mirror, Evening Standard, Spectator, Punch, Homes & Gardens, She, Woman's Own; Columnist: Honey, 1968–69; Manchester Evening News, 1971–72; Woman, 1972–73, 1986–88; TV Times, 1989–; Press Assoc. weekly syndicated column in USA, 1981–85; Ed., Puzzle World, 1989–. Broadcaster, 1969–: TV series incl.: Child of the Sixties, 1969; Puzzle Party, 1977; Chatterbox, 1977–78; Memories, 1982; Countdown, 1983–; TV-am, 1983–90; Railway Carriage Game, 1985; Catchword, 1986; (with Hinge and Bracket) Dear Ladies (TV script); (with Julian Slade) Now We Are Sixty (play); Theatrical producer, 1971–: Through the Looking-Glass, 1972; Oxford Theatre Fest., 1974, 1976; The Dame of Sark, Wyndham's, 1974; The Little Hut, Duke of York's, 1974; Dear Daddy, Ambassador's, 1976; also Son et Lumière. Founder: National Scrabble Championships, 1971; British Pantomime Assoc., 1971; Teddy Bear Mus., Stratford-upon-Avon, 1988. Dir, Europ. Movement's People for Europe campaign, 1975. Prospective Parly Cand. (C) Chester, 1991–. Appeals Chm., NPFA, 1983–89. Three times holder, world record for longest-ever after-dinner speech (4 hrs 19 mins, 1976; 11 hrs, 1978; 12 hrs 30 mins, 1982). *Publications: general:* Created in Captivity, 1972; Brandreth's Party Games, 1972; Discovering Pantomime, 1973; Brandreth's Bedroom, 1973; I Scream for Ice Cream, 1974; A Royal Scrapbook, 1976; Yarooh!, 1976; The Funniest Man on Earth, 1977; The Magic of Houdini, 1978; The Complete Husband, 1978; Pears Book of Words, 1979; The Last Word, 1979; The Joy of Lex, 1980; More Joy of Lex, 1982; Great Theatrical Disasters, 1982; The Books of Mistaikes, 1982; The Complete Public Speaker, 1983; John Gielgud: a celebration, 1984; Great Sexual Disasters, 1984; (with George Hostler) Wit Knits, 1985; Cats' Tales, 1986; (with Linda O'Brien) Knitability, 1987; Even Greater Sexual Disasters, 1987; (ed) Everyman's Modern Phrase and Fable, 1990; over thirty books on games, puzzles, pastimes, family entertainment; over seventy books for children of stories, jokes, riddles, games, puzzles, magic and fun. *Address:* Britannia House, Glenthorne Road, W6 0LF. *T:* 081–741 2228.

BRANDRICK, David Guy, CBE 1981; Secretary, British Coal Corporation (formerly National Coal Board), 1972–89, retired; Director, British Coal Enterprise, since 1985; *b* 17 April 1932; *s* of Harry and Minnie Brandrick; *m* 1956, Eunice Fisher; one *s* one *d. Educ:* Newcastle-under-Lyme High Sch.; St John's Coll., Oxford (MA). Joined National Coal Board, 1955; Chairman's Office, 1957; Principal Private Secretary to Chairman, 1961; Departmental Sec., Production Dept, 1963; Dep. Sec. to the Bd, 1967. *Recreation:* walking.

BRANDT, Paul Nicholas; His Honour Judge Brandt; a Circuit Judge, since 1987; *b* 21 Nov. 1937; *s* of late Paul Francis and of Barbara Brandt. *Educ:* St Andrew's Sch., Eastbourne; Marlborough Coll.; New Coll., Oxford (BA 2nd Cl. Hons Sch. of Jurisprudence). Called to the Bar, Gray's Inn, 1963; a Recorder, 1983–87. *Recreations:* sailing, shooting, Rugby football. *Address:* Colchester & Clacton County Court, Falkland House, 25 Southway, Colchester, Essex CO3 3EG. *Clubs:* Royal Harwich Yacht (Woolverstone, Suffolk), Bar Yacht.

BRANDT, Peter Augustus; Chairman, Atkins Fulford Ltd, since 1977; *b* 2 July 1931; *s* of late Walter Augustus Brandt and late Dorothy Gray Brandt (*née* Crane); *m* 1962, Elisabeth Margaret (*née* ten Bos); two *s* one *d. Educ:* Eton Coll.; Trinity Coll., Cambridge (MA). Joined Wm Brandt's Sons & Co. Ltd, Merchant Bankers, 1954; Mem. Bd, 1960; Chief Executive, 1966; resigned, 1972. Director: London Life Assoc., 1962–89; Corp. of Argentine Meat Producers (CAP) Ltd and affiliates, 1970; Edward Bates (Holdings) Ltd, 1972–77; Edward Bates & Sons Ltd, 1972–77 (Chm., 1974–77). Mem., Nat. Rivers Authy (formerly Nat. Rivers Adv. Cttee), 1988–. *Recreations:* sailing, rowing, steam engines, wild fowl. *Address:* Spout Farm, Boxford, Colchester, Essex CO6 5HA. *Clubs:* Carlton; Leander (Henley-on-Thames).

BRANDT, Willy; Chairman, Social Democratic Party (SPD), Federal Republic of Germany, 1964–87, Hon. Chairman since 1987; Member, German Federal Parliament, 1949–57, and since 1969; *b* 18 Dec. 1913; *m* 1948, Rut Hansen (marr. diss.); three *s* one *d*; *m* 1983, Brigitte Seebacher. *Educ:* Johanneum, Lübeck; University of Oslo. Fled from Lübeck to Norway, 1933. Chief Editor, Berliner Stadtblatt, 1950–51. Mem., Social Democratic Party (SPD), 1931–; Rep. Federal Board of SPD (German Social Democratic Party) in Berlin, 1948–49, Deputy Chairman of SPD, 1962–63. President Berlin House of Representatives, 1955–57; Governing Mayor of W Berlin, 1957–66; President German Conference of Mayors, 1958–63; President German Federal Council, 1957–58; Vice-Chancellor and Foreign Minister, 1966–69, Chancellor 1969–74, Federal Republic of Germany; Mem., European Parlt, 1979–83. Pres., Socialist International, 1976–. Chm., Commn on Develt Issues, (which produced Brandt reports, North-South: a programme for survival, 1980, and Common Crisis: North-South: cooperation for world recovery, 1983), 1977–79. Dr (*hc*): Pennsylvania Univ., 1959; Maryland Univ., 1960; Harvard Univ., 1963; Hon. DCL: Oxford Univ., 1969; Leeds, 1982, etc. Nobel Prize for Peace, 1971. Grosskreuz des Verdienstordens der Bundesrepublik Deutschland, 1959. *Publications:* Efter segern, 1944; Forbrytere og andre Tyskere, 1946; (with Richard Löwenthal) Ernst Reuter: Ein Leben für die Freiheit, 1957; Von Bonn nach Berlin, 1957; Mein Weg nach Berlin (recorded by Leo Lania), 1960; Plädoyer für die Zukunft, 1961; The Ordeal of Co-existence, 1963; Begegnungen mit Kennedy, 1964; (with Günter Struve) Draussen, 1966 (UK, as In Exile, 1971); Friedenspolitik in Europa, 1968; Essays, Reflections and Letters 1933–47, 1971; Der Wille zum Frieden, 1971; Über den Tag hinaus, 1974; Begegnungen und Einsichten, 1976 (UK as People and Politics, 1978); Frauen heute, 1978; Links und frei, 1982; World Armament and World Hunger, 1986; Menschenrechte misshandelt und missbraucht, 1987; Erinnerungen, 1989; many publications on topical questions in Sweden and Norway; articles in home and foreign journals. *Address:* (office) Bundeshaus, 5300 Bonn 1, Germany. *T:* 162758.

BRANIGAN, Sir Patrick (Francis), Kt 1954; QC; *b* 30 Aug. 1906; *e s* of late D. Branigan and Teresa, *d* of Thomas Clinton, Annagassan, Co. Louth; *m* 1935, Prudence, *yr d* of late Dr A. Avent, Seaton, Devon; one *s* one *d. Educ:* Newbridge Coll., Co. Kildare; Trinity Coll., Dublin. BA 1st Class Hons in Law and Political Science and gold medallist, 1928; called to Irish Bar, Certificate of Honour, 1928 (1st Victoria Prize, 1927); called to Bar, Gray's Inn, 1935. Practised at Irish Bar, 1928–30; Downing Coll., Cambridge, 1930–31; Colonial Administrative Service, Kenya, 1931; Crown Counsel, Tanganyika, 1934; Solicitor-General, N. Rhodesia, 1938; Chairman NR Man-power Cttee, 1939–41; Chairman Conciliation Board, Copperbelt Strike, 1940; Member NR Nat. Arbitration Tribunal, 1940–46; Member Strauss Arbitration Tribunal, Bulawayo, 1944; Chairman, Road Transport Services Board and Electricity Board of N. Rhodesia, 1939–46; Legal Secretary to Govt of Malta and Chairman Malta War Damage Commission, 1946–48; periodically acting Lieut-Governor of Malta, 1947–48. Minister of Justice and Attorney-General, Gold Coast, 1948–54; QC Gold Coast, 1949; retired, 1955. Chairman of Commission of inquiry into Copperbelt industrial unrest, 1956. Chm., Suflex Ltd, 1955–83. Dep. Chm. Devon QS, 1958–71; a Recorder of the Crown Court, 1972–75. Chairman: Pensions Appeal Tribunal, 1955–81; Agricultural Land Tribunal for SW Area of England, 1955–79; Nat. Insurance Med. Appeal Tribunal, SW Reg., 1960–78; Mental Health Review Tribunal, SW England, 1960–78; Mem., Industrial Disputes Tribunal, 1955–59. Knight Commander of Order of St Gregory, 1956. *Address:* C'an San Juan, La Font, Pollensa, Majorca. *T:* 3471 530767.

BRANN, Col William Norman, OBE 1967; ERD; JP; Lord Lieutenant for County Down, 1979–90, retired; *b* 16 Aug. 1915; *s* of Rev. William Brann, BA, LLB, and Francesca Brann; *m* 1950, Anne Elizabeth Hughes; one *s* two *d. Educ:* Campbell Coll., Belfast. With Beck & Scott Ltd, Food Importers, Belfast, 1934–80, Chm., 1984–. Served War of 1939–45, Army, France and Far East; TA, 1947–53. Hon. ADC to HE the Governor of N Ireland, 1952–72. Belfast Harbour Comr, 1960–79. Chm., UVF Hosp. for Ex Service Men and Women; Pres., Burma Star Assoc., NI. County Down: DL 1974–79; JP 1980; High Sheriff, 1982. KStJ 1991. *Recreations:* farming, gardening, hunting. *Address:* Drumavaddy, Craigantlet, Newtownards, Co. Down, BT23 4TG. *T:* Holywood 2224. *Club:* Ulster Reform (Belfast).

BRANNAN, Charles Franklin; lawyer; *b* 23 Aug. 1903; *s* of John Brannan and Ella Louise Street; *m* 1932, Eda Seltzer; no *c. Educ:* Regis Coll., and University of Denver Law Sch., Denver, Colorado, USA. Private law practice, Denver, Colorado, 1929–35; Asst Regional Attorney: Resettlement Administration, Denver, 1935–37; Regional Attorney, Office of the Solicitor, US Dept of Agriculture, Denver, 1937–41; Regional Director of Farm Security Administration, US Dept of Agriculture, Denver, 1941–44; Asst Administrator, Farm Security Administration, US Dept of Agriculture, Washington, DC, April-June 1944; Asst Secretary of Agriculture, Washington, DC, June 1944–48; Secretary of Agriculture, USA, 1948–Jan. 1953. Pres., Bd of Water Commissioners, Denver, 1976. Hon. Degrees: Doctor of Laws from the University of Denver and Doctor of Science from the Colorado Agricultural and Mechanical Coll. Hon. Phi Beta Kappa. *Address:* (home) 3131 East Alameda, Denver, Colorado 80209, USA; (office) 3773 Cherry Creek North Drive, Denver, Colo 80239. *Club:* Denver Athletic (Denver, Colorado).

BRANSON, Rear Adm. Cecil Robert Peter Charles, CBE 1975; *b* 30 March 1924; *s* of Cecil Branson and Marcelle Branson; *m* 1946, Sonia Moss; one *d. Educ:* RNC, Dartmouth. Served, HMS Dragon, W Africa, S Atlantic, Indian Ocean and Far East (present during time of fall of Singapore and Java), 1941–42; Sub-Lieut's Courses, 1942–43; qual. as submarine specialist, served in HM S/M Sea Rover, Far East, 1944–45; various appts in S/Ms, 1945–53; First Lieut, HMS Defender, 1953–55; jssc; CO, HMS Roebuck, Dartmouth Trng Sqdn, 1957; Staff, Flag Officer Flotillas Mediterranean, 1959–60; Jt Planning Staff, MoD, 1960–62; Exec. Officer, HMS Victorious, Far East, 1962–64; CO, HMS Rooke, Gibraltar, 1965; NATO Def. Coll., 1965; Defence Planning Staff, MoD, 1966–68; CO, HMS Phoebe, and Captain (D) Londonderry Sqdn, 1968–70; Naval Attaché, Paris, 1970–73; CO, HMS Hermes, 1973–74 (Hermes headed RN task force evacuating Brit. and foreign subjects from Cyprus beaches after Turkish invasion, 1973); Asst Chief of Naval Staff (Ops), MoD, 1975–77; retired. *Club:* Army and Navy.

BRANSON, Edward James, MA; financial consultant; a Metropolitan Stipendiary Magistrate, 1971–87; barrister-at-law; *b* 10 March 1918; *s* of late Rt Hon. Sir George Branson, PC, sometime Judge of High Court, and late Lady (Mona) Branson; *m* 1949, Evette Huntley, *e d* of late Rupert Huntley Flindt; one *s* two *d. Educ:* Bootham Sch., York; Trinity Coll., Cambridge. Served War, 1939–46, Staffordshire Yeomanry: Palestine, Egypt, and Western Desert 1941–42; GSO 3 (Ops) attd 2 NZ Div. for Alamein, 1942; GS02 (Ops), attd 6 (US) Corps for Salerno and Anzio landings, 1943–44; subseq. GSO2 (Ops) 53 (W) Div. in Germany. Called to the Bar, Inner Temple, 1950; practised London and SE Circuit. *Recreations:* shooting, fishing, archaeology. *Address:* 8 Craven Cottages, Hofland Road, W14 0LN. *T:* 071–602 2700; Humble Pie, Binixim, Puerto de Mahon, Menorca. *T:* 3471 369134.

See also R. Branson.

BRANSON, Richard Charles Nicholas; Founder and Chairman, Virgin Group; *b* 18 July 1950; *s* of Edward James Branson, *qv*; *m* 1st, 1969 (marr. diss.); 2nd, 1989, Joan Templeman; one *s* one *d. Educ:* Stowe. Editor, Student magazine, 1968–69; set up Student Advisory Centre (now Help), 1970. Founded Virgin Mail-Order Co., 1969, followed by Virgin Retail, Virgin Record Label, Virgin Music Publishing, Virgin Recording Studios; estabd Virgin Record subsids in 25 countries, 1980–86; founded Virgin Atlantic Airways, 1984; Voyager Gp Ltd formed 1986, encompassing interests in travel, clubs and hotels; Virgin Records launched in US, 1987. Pres., UK 2000, 1988– (Chm., 1986–88); Dir, Intourist Moscow Ltd, 1988–. Launched charity, The Healthcare Foundn, 1987. Captain, Atlantic Challenger II, winner Blue Riband for fastest crossing of Atlantic by a ship, 1986; with Per Lindstrand, first to cross Atlantic in hot air balloon, 1987, and Pacific, 1991 (longest flight in hot air balloon, 6700 miles, and fastest speed, 200 mph, 1991). *Address:* c/o Virgin Group Ltd, 120 Campden Hill Road, W8 7AR.

BRANSON, William Rainforth, CBE 1969; retired; *b* 2 Jan. 1905; *s* of late A. W. Branson, JP; *m* 1932, Dorothy Iris Green (*d* 1982); no *c. Educ:* Rydal Sch.; University of Leeds. BSc, 1st Class Hons (Fuel and Gas Engrg), 1927; MSc 1930. Asst Engineer, Gas Light & Coke Co., London, 1927–37; Asst Engineer, later Dep. Engineer, Cardiff Gas Light & Coke Co., 1937–45; Dep. Controller, later Controller, Public Utilities Br., Control Commn for Germany, 1945–49; Planning Engineer, Wales Gas Board, 1949–51; Technical Officer, E Midlands Gas Board, 1952–54; Dep. Chairman, W. Midlands Gas Board, 1954–65; Chm., Scottish Gas Bd, 1965–68; Dir, Woodall-Duckham Group Ltd, 1969–73. President, Instn of Gas Engineers, 1964–65. *Recreation:* music. *Address:* Sidmouth House West, Cotmaton Road, Sidmouth EX10 8ST.

BRANT, Colin Trevor, CMG 1981; CVO 1979; HM Diplomatic Service, retired; *b* 2 June 1929; *m* 1954, Jean Faith Walker; one *s* two *d. Educ:* Christ's Hospital, Horsham; Sidney Sussex Coll., Cambridge (MA). Served Army, 4th Hussars (now Queen's Royal Irish Hussars), active service, Malaya, 1948–49; Pilot, Cambridge Univ. Air Squadron, 1951–52. Joined Sen. Br., Foreign Office, 1952; MECAS, Lebanon, 1953–54; Bahrain, 1954; Amman, 1954–56; FO, 1956–59; Stockholm, 1959–61; Cairo, 1961–64; Joint Services Staff Coll., Latimer, Bucks, 1964–65 (jssc); FO, 1965–67; Head of Chancery and Consul, Tunis, 1967–68; Asst Head, Oil Dept, FCO, 1969–71; Counsellor (Commercial), Caracas, 1971–73; Counsellor (Energy), Washington, 1973–78; Ambassador to Qatar, 1978–81; FCO Fellow, St Antony's Coll., Oxford, 1981–82; Consul Gen., and Dir Trade

Promotion, Johannesburg, 1982–87. Consultant, Carmichael & Sweet, Portsmouth, 1990–. Donation Governor, Christ's Hosp., 1980, Almoner 1989. *Recreations:* music, painting, history. *Address:* The Old School House, Horcott, Fairford, Glos GL7 4BX. *Clubs:* Travellers', Royal Over-Seas League.

BRASH, Rev. Alan Anderson, OBE 1962; Moderator, Presbyterian Church of New Zealand, 1978–79; *b* 5 June 1913; *s* of Thomas C. Brash, CBE, New Zealand, and Margaret Brash (*née* Allan); *m* 1938, Eljean Ivory Hill; one *s* one *d. Educ:* Dunedin Univ., NZ (MA); Edinburgh Univ. (BD). Parish Minister in NZ, 1938–46 and 1952–56; Gen. Sec., NZ Nat. Council of Churches, 1947–52 and 1957–64, East Asia Christian Conf., 1958–68; Dir, Christian Aid, London, 1968–70; Dir, Commn on Inter-Church Aid, Refuge and World Service, WCC, 1970–73; Dep. Gen. Sec., WCC, 1974–78. Hon. DD Toronto, 1971. *Address:* 13 Knightsbridge Drive, Forrest Hill, Auckland 10, New Zealand.

BRASH, Robert, CMG 1980; HM Diplomatic Service, retired; Ambassador to Indonesia, 1981–84; *b* 30 May 1924; *s* of Frank and Ida Brash; *m* 1954, Barbara Enid Clarke; three *s* one *d. Educ:* Trinity Coll., Cambridge (Exhbnr). War Service, 1943–46. Entered Foreign Service, 1949; Djakarta, 1951–55; FO, 1955–58; First Sec., 1956; Jerusalem, 1958–61; Bonn, 1961–64; Bucharest, 1964–66; FCO, 1966–70; Counsellor, 1968; Canadian Nat. Defence Coll., 1970–71; Counsellor and Consul-Gen., Saigon, 1971–73; Counsellor, Vienna, 1974–78; Consul-Gen., Düsseldorf, 1978–81. Chm., Guildford Rambling Club, 1986–89. *Recreations:* walking, gardening, stained glass, golf. *Address:* Woodbrow, Woodham Lane, Woking, Surrey G21 5SR.

BRASHER, Christopher William; Columnist, The Observer, since 1961 (Olympic Correspondent, 1961–89); Race Director, London Marathon 1980–91; Chairman, Reebok UK Ltd, since 1990; Managing Director: Brasher Leisure Ltd, since 1977; Fleetfoot Ltd, since 1979; *b* 21 Aug. 1928; *s* of William Kenneth Brasher and Katie Howe Brasher; *m* 1959, Shirley Bloomer; one *s* two *d. Educ:* Rugby Sch.; St John's Coll., Cambridge. MA. Pres., Mountaineering Club and Athletic Club, Cambridge Univ. Management Trainee and Jun. Executive, Mobil Oil Co., 1951–57; Sports Editor, The Observer, 1957–61; BBC Television: Reporter, Tonight, 1961–65; Editor, Time Out, and Man Alive, 1964–65; Head of Gen. Features, 1969–72; reporter/producer, 1972–81. Co-Founder and Chm., British Orienteering Fedn (formerly English Orienteering Assoc.), 1966–69. Rep. GB, Olympic Games, 1952 and 1956; Gold Medal for 3,000 metres Steeplechase, 1956. National Medal of Honour, Finland, 1975; Sports Writer of the Year (British Press Awards), 1968, 1976. *Publications:* The Red Snows (with Sir John Hunt), 1960; Sportsmen of our Time, 1962; Tokyo 1964: a diary of the XVIIIth Olympiad, 1964; Mexico 1968: a diary of the XIXth Olympics, 1968; Munich 72, 1972; (ed) The London Marathon: the first ten years, 1991. *Recreations:* mountains, fishing, orienteering, social running. *Address:* The Navigator's House, River Lane, Richmond, Surrey. *T:* 081–940 8822. *Clubs:* Alpine, Hurlingham; Ranelagh Harriers (Petersham); Thames Hare and Hounds (Kingston Vale).

BRASNETT, John, CMG 1987; HM Diplomatic Service, retired; Deputy High Commissioner, Bombay, 1985–89; *b* 30 Oct. 1929; *s* of late Norman Vincent Brasnett and of Frances May Brasnett (*née* Hewlett); *m* 1956, Jennifer Ann Reid; one *s* one *d. Educ:* Blundells Sch.; Selwyn Coll., Cambridge (BA). Served Royal Artillery, 1948–49. Colonial Administrative Service, Uganda, 1953–65; retired from HM Overseas CS as Dep. Administrator, Karamoja District, 1965; entered HM Diplomatic Service, 1965; 1st Sec., OECD Delegn, 1968; Dep. High Comr, Freetown, 1970; FCO, 1973; Olympic Attaché, Montreal, 1975–76; Dep. High Comr, Accra, 1977–80; Counsellor (Econ. and Commercial), Ottawa, 1980–85). *Recreations:* reading, photography. *Address:* 8 Croft Way, Sevenoaks, Kent TN13 2JX. *Club:* Commonwealth Trust.

BRASS, John, CBE 1968; BSc, FEng, FIMinE; FRSA; Member, National Coal Board, 1971–73; *b* 22 Oct. 1908; 2nd *s* of late John Brass, Mining Engineer, and late Mary Brass (*née* Swainston); *m* 1934, Jocelyn Constance Cape, Stroud, Glos; three *s* (one *d* decd). *Educ:* Oundle Sch.; Birmingham Univ. (BSc Hons). Various appointments, all in mining; Chm., W Midlands Division, NCB, 1961–67; Regional Chm., Yorks and NW Areas, NCB, 1967–71. Chm., Amalgamated Construction Co., 1976–86. *Address:* 2 Fledborough Road, Wetherby, W Yorks LS22 4AB.

BRASS, Prof. William, CBE 1981; FBA 1979; Professor of Medical Demography, 1978–88, now Emeritus, and Director of Centre for Population Studies, 1978–88, London School of Hygiene and Tropical Medicine; *b* 5 Sept. 1921; *s* of John Brass and Margaret Tait (*née* Haigh); *m* 1948, Betty Ellen Agnes Topp; two *d. Educ:* Royal High Sch., Edinburgh; Edinburgh Univ. (MA Hons Maths and Nat. Phil., 1943). Scientific Officer, Royal Naval Scientific Service, 1943–46; E African Statistical Dept, Colonial Service, 1948–55; Lectr in Statistics, 1955–64, Sen. Lectr 1964, Aberdeen Univ.; London Sch. of Hygiene and Trop. Medicine: Reader in Med. Demography, 1965–72; Dir, Centre for Overseas Population Studies, 1974–78; Head, Dept of Med. Stats and Epidemiology, 1977–82. Pres., Internat. Union for the Scientific Study of Population, 1985–89. For. Associate, US Nat. Acad. of Scis, 1984. Mindel Sheps Award for distinguished contribn to demography, Population Assoc. of America, 1978. *Publications:* The Demography of Tropical Africa, 1968; Metodos para estimar la fecundidad y la mortalidad en poblaciones con datos Limitados: selección de trabajos, 1974; Methods of Estimating Fertility and Mortality from Limited and Defective Data, 1975; Advances in Methods for Estimating Fertility and Mortality from Limited and Defective Data, 1985; about 100 papers in learned jls. *Recreations:* travel, observing art and archaeology. *Address:* 3 Holt Close, N10 3HW. *T:* 081–883 1195.

BRASSEY, family name of **Baron Brassey of Apethorpe.**

BRASSEY OF APETHORPE, 3rd Baron, *cr* 1938, of Apethorpe; **David Henry Brassey;** Bt 1922; JP; DL; *b* 16 Sept. 1932; *er s* of 2nd Baron Brassey of Apethorpe, MC, TD, and late Lady Brassey of Apethorpe; *S* father, 1967; *m* 1st, 1958, Myrna Elizabeth (*d* 1974), *o d* of late Lt-Col John Baskervyle-Glegg; one *s*; 2nd, 1978, Caroline, *y d* of late Lt-Col G. A. Evill; two *d.* Commissioned, Grenadier Guards, 1951; Major, 1966, retired, 1967. JP 1970, DL 1972, Northants. *Heir:* *s* Hon. Edward Brassey, *b* 9 March 1964. *Address:* The Manor House, Apethorpe, Peterborough. *T:* Stamford (0780) 470231. *Club:* White's.

BRASSEY, Lt-Col Hon. Peter (Esmé); Lord-Lieutenant of Cambridgeshire, 1975–81; *b* 5 Dec. 1907; *o surv. s* of 1st Baron Brassey of Apethorpe; *m* 1944, Lady Romayne Cecil (OBE 1986), 2nd *d* of 5th Marquess of Exeter, KG, CMG; two *s* one *d. Educ:* Eton; Magdalene Coll., Cambridge. Barrister-at-Law, Inner Temple, Midland Circuit, 1931. Northamptonshire Yeomanry, Lieut-Col, 1945; served NW Europe (wounded). Dir, The Essex Water Co. Ltd, 1970–85 (Chm., 1981–85). DL 1961, High Sheriff, 1966, and Vice-Lieutenant, 1966–74, County of Huntingdon and Peterborough. KStJ 1976. *Recreations:* shooting, fishing. *Address:* Pond House, Barnack, Stamford, Lincs PE9 3DN. *T:* Stamford (0780) 740238. *Club:* Carlton.

BRATBY, Jean Esme Oregon; *see* Cooke, J. E. O.

BRATBY, John Randall, RA 1971 (ARA 1959); ARCA; FIAL; RBA; FRSA; Painter and Writer; Member of London Group; Editor in Chief, Art Quarterly, since 1987; *b* 19 July 1928; *s* of George Alfred Bratby and Lily Beryl Randall; *m* 1953, Jean Esme Oregon Cooke, RA (*see* Jean E. Cooke) (marr. diss. 1977); three *s* one *d*; *m* 1977, Patti Prime. *Educ:* Tiffin Boys' Sch.; Kingston School of Art; Royal College of Art. Teacher: Carlisle College of Art, 1956; Royal College of Art, 1957–58. Gained prizes and scholarships, 1954–57. Numerous one-man exhibitions at Beaux Arts Gallery from 1954; Zwemmer Gallery from 1959; Thackeray Gallery; Furneaux Gallery; Nat. Theatre (twice); Phoenix Gall., London and Lavenham; Albemarle Gall.; also in galleries abroad. Exhibited: Royal Academy (yearly) from 1955; Nat. Portrait Gall. (retrospective); has also shown pictures in various international exhibitions and festivals; Venice Biennale, 1956. Guggenheim Award for Great Britain, 1956 and 1958; won junior section of John Moores Liverpool Exhibn, 1957; Paintings for film The Horse's Mouth, 1958. Works in public collections: Tate Gallery; Arts Council of Great Britain; British Council; Contemporary Arts Society. National Galleries: Canada; New Zealand; NSW and Victoria; galleries in many cities and towns of Great Britain; Victoria and Albert Museum; Ashmolean Museum; Museum of Modern Art, New York; also in many other public and private art collections, in Great Britain, the Commonwealth and USA. Paintings for film, Mistral's Daughter, 1984. Has made television appearances and sound broadcasts. *Publications: fiction:* Breakdown, 1960; Breakfast and Elevenses, 1961; Break-Pedal Down, 1962 (also TV play); Break 50 Kill, 1963; *non-fiction:* studio publication of colour reproductions of own work, 1961; Stanley Spencer, 1969; *illustrator:* Horse's Mouth, 1965; (contrib.) Oxford Illustrated Old Testament, 1968; The Devils, 1984; Apocryphal Letters, by Edward Lowerby, 1985. *Recreations:* watching TV, cider, buying clothes for my wife. *Address:* Les Ateliers, The Cupola, Belmont Road, Hastings, Sussex TN35 5NR. *T:* Hastings (0424) 434037.

BRATT, Guy Maurice, CMG 1977; MBE 1945; HM Diplomatic Service; Counsellor, Foreign and Commonwealth Office, 1977–80 (retired); *b* 4 April 1920; *s* of late Ernst Lars Gustaf Bratt and late Alice Maud Mary Bratt (*née* Raper); *m* 1945, Françoise Nelly Roberte Girardet; two *s* one *d. Educ:* Merchant Taylors' Sch.; London Univ. (BA). Served Army, 1939–46 (MBE): Major, Royal Signals. Solicitor 1947. Asst Sec., Colonial Develt Corp.; joined HM Foreign (subseq. Diplomatic) Service, 1952; served FO, 1952–54; Berlin, 1954–56; Brussels, 1956–58; FO, 1958–62; Vienna, 1962–66; FCO, 1966–70; Geneva, 1970–72; FCO, 1972–74; Washington, 1974–77. *Recreations:* music, railways, mountaineering. *Address:* 2 Orchehill Rise, Gerrards Cross, Bucks SL9 8PR. *T:* Gerrards Cross (0753) 883106. *Club:* Travellers'.

BRATZA, Nicolas Dušan; QC 1988; *b* 3 March 1945; *s* of late Milan Bratza, concert violinist, and Hon. Margaret Bratza (*née* Russell). *Educ:* Wimbledon Coll.; Brasenose Coll., Oxford (BA 1st Cl. Hons, MA). Instructor, Univ. of Pennsylvania Law Sch., 1967–68; called to Bar, Lincoln's Inn, 1969 (Hardwicke and Droop Schol.); Jun. Counsel to the Crown, Common Law, 1979–88. Vice-Chm., British Inst. of Human Rights, 1990–. *Publications:* (jtly) Contempt of Court, and Crown Proceedings, in Halsbury's Laws of England, 4th edn. *Recreations:* music, cricket. *Address:* 1 Hare Court, Temple, EC4Y 7BE. *T:* 071–353 3171. *Clubs:* Garrick, MCC.

BRAVO, Martin Maurice B.; *see* Brandon-Bravo.

BRAY, Denis Campbell, CMG 1977; CVO 1975; JP; Chairman, Denis Bray Consultants Ltd, Hong Kong, since 1985; *b* 24 Jan. 1926; *s* of Rev. Arthur Henry Bray and Edith Muriel Bray; *m* 1952, Marjorie Elizabeth Bottomley; four *d* (one *s* decd). *Educ:* Kingswood Sch.; Jesus Coll., Cambridge (MA). BScEcon London. RN, 1947–49. Colonial Service Devonshire Course, 1949–50; Admin. Officer, Hong Kong, 1950; Dist Comr, New Territories, 1971; Hong Kong Comr in London, 1977–80; Sec. for Home Affairs, Hong Kong, 1973–77 and 1980–84, retd. Chairman: English Schools Foundn, Hong Kong, 1985–; Jubilee Sports Centre, Hong Kong, 1985–89. Director: First Pacific Davies (Hldgs), 1986–; First Pacific Bancshares Hldgs 1987–; Herald (Hong Kong) Ltd, 1987–; Leighton Asia Ltd, 1990–; Exec. Dir, Community Chest of Hong Kong, 1985–. Pres., Hong Kong Yachting Assoc., 1989–. JP 1960–85, and 1987. *Recreations:* ocean racing and cruising. *Address:* 8A-7 Borrett Mansions, 8–9 Bowen Road, Hong Kong. *T:* 526 3630. *Clubs:* Travellers', London Rowing, Royal Ocean Racing; Leander (Henley-on-Thames); Hong Kong, Royal Hong Kong Jockey, Royal Hong Kong Yacht; Tai Po Boat.
See also J. W. Bray.

BRAY, Jeremy William; MP (Lab) Motherwell South, since 1983 (Motherwell and Wishaw, Oct. 1974–1983); *b* 29 June 1930; *s* of Rev. Arthur Henry Bray and Mrs Edith Muriel Bray; *m* 1953, Elizabeth (*née* Trowell); four *d. Educ:* Aberystwyth Grammar Sch.; Kingswood Sch.; Jesus Coll., Cambridge (PhD 1956). Researched in pure mathematics at Cambridge, 1953–55; Choate Fellow, Harvard Univ., USA, 1955–56; Technical Officer, Wilton Works of ICI, 1956–62. Contested (Lab) Thirsk and Malton, General Election, 1959; MP (Lab) Middlesbrough West, 1962–70. Opposition spokesman on science and technology, 1983–. Member: Select Cttee on Nationalised Industries, 1962–64; Estimates Cttee, 1964–66; Expenditure Cttee, 1978–79; Select Cttee on Treasury and Civil Service, 1979–83 (Chm., Sub-cttee, 1981–82); Chairman: Labour, Science and Technol Group, 1964–66; Economic Affairs Estimates Sub-Cttee, 1964–66; Parly Sec., Min. of Power, 1966–67; Jt Parly Sec., Min. of Technology, 1967–69. Dir, Mullard Ltd, 1970–73; Consultant, Battelle Res. Centre, Geneva, 1973; Sen. Res. Fellow, 1974, Vis. Prof., 1975–79, Univ. of Strathclyde; Vis. Res. Fellow, Imperial Coll., 1989–. Dep. Chm., Christian Aid, 1972–84; Co-Dir, Programme of Res. into Econometric Methods, Imperial Coll., 1971–74. Chm., Fabian Soc., 1971–72. *Publications:* Decision in Government, 1970; Production Purpose and Structure, 1982; Fabian pamphlets and articles in jls. *Recreation:* sailing. *Address:* House of Commons, SW1A 0AA.
See also D. C. Bray.

BRAY, Hon. Dr John Jefferson, AC 1979; Chancellor of the University of Adelaide, 1968–83; *b* 16 Sept. 1912; *s* of Harry Midwinter Bray and Gertrude Eleonore Bray (*née* Stow). *Educ:* St Peter's Coll., Adelaide; Univ. of Adelaide. LLB 1932, LLB Hons 1933, LLD 1937. Admitted to South Australian Bar, 1933; QC 1957. Univ. of Adelaide: Actg Lectr in Jurisprudence, 1941, 1943, 1945, 1951; Actg Lectr in Legal History, 1957–58; Lectr in Roman Law, 1959–66; Chief Justice of Supreme Court of SA, 1967–78. DUniv Adelaide, 1983. *Publications:* Poems, 1962; Poems 1961–1971, 1972; Poems 1972–1979, 1979; (ed jtly) No 7 Friendly Street Poetry Reader, 1983; The Bay of Salamis and Other Poems, 1986; Satura: selected poetry and prose, 1988; The Emperor's Doorkeeper, 1988; Seventy Seven (poems), 1990; contribs to: Well and Truly Tried, 1982 (Festschrift for Sir Richard Eggleston); Adelaide Law School Centenary Essays, 1983; Australian Law Jl. *Address:* 39 Hurtle Square, Adelaide, South Australia 5000. *Club:* University of Adelaide.

BRAY, Prof. Kenneth Noel Corbett, PhD; FRS 1991; CEng; Hopkinson and Imperial Chemical Industries Professor of Applied Thermodynamics, Cambridge University, since 1985; *b* 19 Nov. 1929; *s* of Harold H. Bray and Effie E. Bray; *m* 1958, Shirley Maureen Culver; two *s* one *d. Educ:* Univ. of Cambridge (BA); Univ. of Southampton (PhD); MSE Princeton; CEng; MRAeS; MAIAA. Engr in Research Dept, Handley Page Aircraft, 1955–56; University of Southampton, 1956–85: Dean, Faculty of Engrg and Applied

Science, 1975–78; Head, Dept of Aeronautics and Astronautics, 1982–85. Vis. appt, Avco–Everett Res. Lab., Mass, USA, 1961–62; Vis. Prof., MIT, 1966–67; Vis. Res. Engr, Univ. of California, San Diego, 1975, 1983. *Publications:* on topics in gas dynamics, chemically reacting flows, molecular energy transfer processes and combustion. *Recreations:* walking, wood carving, gardening. *Address:* 23 De Freville Avenue, Cambridge CB4 1HW.

BRAY, Maj.-Gen. Paul Sheldon, CB 1991; Paymaster-in-Chief and Inspector of Army Pay Services, since 1989; *b* 31 Jan. 1936; *s* of Gerald Bray and Doris (*née* Holt); *m* 1958, Marion Diana Naden; one *s* two *d*. *Educ:* Purbrook Park County High Sch.; RMA Sandhurst. FCIS, ndc, psc†, sq, pfc. Commissioned RA 1956; served BAOR, Cyprus, UK; transf. RAPC 1965; served Malaya, N Wales, MoD, HQ UKLF, HQ Scotland, HQ NE District; OC RAPC Training Centre, 1976–77; NDC 1978; DS RMCS Shrivenham, 1979–82; MoD 1982; Chief Paymaster, Army Pay Office (Officers' Accounts), 1982–83; Comdt, Defence ADP Training Centre, 1983–85; Chief Paymaster ADP, RAPC Computer Centre, 1985–89. Trustee, Winchester Children's Holiday Trust, 1989. *Recreations:* music, theatre, travel, oenology, rearranging the garden. *Address:* c/o Corps HQ, RAPC Worthy Down, Winchester, Hants SO21 2RG. *Club:* Hampshire (Winchester).

BRAY, Sir Theodor (Charles), Kt 1975; CBE 1964; Chancellor, Griffith University, Brisbane, 1975–85; *b* 11 Feb. 1905; *s* of Horace and Maude Bray; *m* 1931, Rosalie (*d* 1988), *d* of Rev. A. M. Trengove; three *s* two *d* (and one *s* one *d* decd). *Educ:* state schs; Adelaide Univ. Apprentice Printer, Reporter, Register, Adelaide; Sub-editor, Chief Sub-editor, The Argus, Melbourne; Editor (26 yrs), Editor-in-Chief, Jt Man. Dir, Queensland Newspapers Pty Ltd, 1936–70, Dir, 1956–80; Chm., Australian Associated Press, 1968–70; Mem., Austr. Council for the Arts, 1969–73; Austr. Chm., Internat. Press Inst., 1962–70; Chm., Griffith Univ. Council, 1970–75. *Recreations:* bowls, travel. *Address:* 10/64 Macquarie Street, St Lucia, Qld 4067, Australia. *T:* 8707442. *Clubs:* Queensland, Johnsonian (Brisbane).

BRAY, William John, CBE 1975; FEng 1978; Director of Research, Post Office, 1966–75 (Dep. Director, 1965); *b* 10 Sept. 1911; British; *m* 1936, Margaret Earp; one *d* (and one *d* decd). *Educ:* Imperial Coll., London Univ. Electrical engineering apprenticeship, Portsmouth Naval Dockyard, 1928–32; Royal and Kitchener Scholarships, Imperial Coll., 1932–34; entered PO Engineering Dept as Asst Engineer, 1934; Commonwealth Fund Fellowship (Harkness Foundation) for study in USA, 1956–57; Staff Engineer, Inland Radio Br., PO Engineering Dept, 1958. Vis. Prof., UCL, 1974–78. External Examr, MSc (Communications), Imperial Coll., London, 1976–80. Participation in work of International Radio Consultative Cttee of International Telecommunication Union and European Postal and Telecommunication Conferences; Consultant to UK Council for Educnl Technology, 1976–78. MSc(Eng), FCGI, DIC, FIEE; DUniv Essex, 1976. J. J. Thomson Medal, IEE, 1978. *Publications:* Memoirs of a Telecommunications Engineer, 1983; papers in Proc. IEE (IEE Ambrose Fleming Radio Sect. and Electronics Div. Premium Awards). *Recreation:* writing a book on pioneers of telecommunications. *Address:* The Pump House, Bredfield, Woodbridge, Suffolk IP13 6AH. *T:* Woodbridge (0672) 385838.

BRAY, Winston, CBE 1970; Deputy Chairman and Deputy Chief Executive, BOAC, 1972–74; Member Board, BOAC, 1971–74; Member Board, BAAC Ltd (formerly BOAC (AC Ltd), 1969–74; *b* 29 April 1910; *s* of late Edward Bray and Alice Walker; *m* 1937, Betty Atterton Miller; one *s* one *d* (and one *d* decd). *Educ:* Highgate Sch.; London Univ. (BCom). Missouri Pacific Railroad, USA, 1932; Asst to Traffic Manager, British Airways, 1938; Traffic Dept, BOAC, 1940; Sales Promotion Supt, 1946; Sales Manager, 1950; Sales Planning Manager, 1954; Dir of Planning, 1964; Planning Dir, 1969; Dep. Managing Dir, 1972. FCIT. *Recreations:* sailing, gardening. *Address:* Altenburg, Trafford Road, Great Missenden, Bucks HP16 0BT. *Club:* Royal Automobile.

BRAYBROOK, Edward John, CB 1972; *b* 25 Oct. 1911; *s* of late Prior Wormsley Braybrook and Kate Braybrook; *m* 1937, Eva Rosalin Thomas; one *s* two *d*. *Educ:* Edmonton Latymer Secondary Sch. Asst Naval Store Officer, Admty, Chatham, Malta and Devonport, 1930–37; Deputy Naval Store Officer, Admty, 1938–39; Naval Store Officer, Admty and Haslemere, 1940–43; Suptg Naval Store Officer, Levant, 1943; Comdr/Captain (SP) RNVR Suptg Naval Store Officer, Ceylon and Southern India, 1944–46; Supt, Perth, Scotland, 1946–47; Asst Director of Stores, Admty, 1947–53; Suptg Naval Store Officer, Chatham, 1953–55; Deputy Director of Stores, Admty, 1955–64; Director of Stores (Naval), MoD, 1964–70; Dir-Gen. Supplies and Transport (Naval), MoD, 1970–73. *Recreations:* gardening, photography, painting, handicrafts. *Address:* 22 Church Drive, North Harrow, Middlesex HA2 7NW. *T:* 081–427 0838.

BRAYBROOKE, 10th Baron *cr* 1788; **Robin Henry Charles Neville;** DL; Hereditary Visitor of Magdalene College, Cambridge; Patron of three livings; farmer and landowner; *b* 29 Jan. 1932; *s* of 9th Baron Braybrooke and Muriel Evelyn (*d* 1962), *d* of William C. Manning; *S* father, 1990; *m* 1st, 1955, Robin Helen Brockhoff (marr. diss. 1974); four *d* (inc. twins) (and one *d* decd); 2nd, 1974, Linda Norman; three *d*. *Educ:* Eton; Magdalene Coll., Cambridge (MA); RAC Cirencester. Commnd Rifle Bde, 1951; served 3rd Bn King's African Rifles in Kenya and Malaya, 1951–52. Dir of Essex and Suffolk Insurance Co. until amalgamation with Guardian Royal Exchange. Member: Saffron Walden RDC, 1959–69; for Stansted, Essex CC, 1969–72; Council of CLA, 1965–83; Agricl Land Tribunal, Eastern Area, 1975–. Chairman: Price Trust, 1983–; Rural Develt Commn for Essex, 1984–90. Pres., Essex Show, 1990. DL Essex, 1980. *Recreations:* railway and airfield operating, flying, motorcycling. *Heir: kinsman* George Neville, *b* 23 March 1943. *Address:* Abbey House, Audley End, Saffron Walden, Essex CB11 4JB. *T:* Saffron Walden (0799) 22484. *Clubs:* Boodle's, Farmers'.

BRAYBROOKE, Rev. Marcus Christopher Rossi; Hon. Priest-in-charge, Christ Church, Bath, since 1984; Prebendary, Wells Cathedral, since 1990; *b* 16 Nov. 1938; *s* of late Lt-Col Arthur Rossi Braybrooke and of Marcia Nona Braybrooke; *m* 1964, Mary Elizabeth Walker, JP, BSc, CQSW; one *s* one *d*. *Educ:* Cranleigh School; Magdalene College, Cambridge (BA, MA); Madras Christian College; Wells Theological College; King's College, London (MPhil). Curate, St Michael's, Highgate, 1964–67; Team Vicar, Strood Clergy Team, 1967–73; Rector, Swainswick, Langridge, Woolley, 1973–79; Dir of Training, Dio. of Bath and Wells, 1979–84. A Vice-Pres., World Congress of Faiths, 1986– (Chm., 1978–83; Chm., Internat. Cttee, 1988–); Exec. Director, Council of Christians and Jews, 1984–87. Chm., Internat. Interfaith Orgns Co-ordinating Cttee, 1990–. Examng Chaplain to Bishop of Bath and Wells, 1984–88. Editor: World Faiths Insight, 1976–; Common Ground, 1987–. *Publications:* Together to the Truth, 1971; The Undiscovered Christ of Hinduism, 1973; Interfaith Worship, 1974; Interfaith Organizations: a historical directory, 1980; Time to Meet, 1990; contrib. to various theol books and jls incl. Theology, The Modern Churchman, The Tablet. *Recreations:* gardening, home decorating, tennis, swimming, travel, photography. *Address:* 2 The Bassetts, Box, Corsham, Wilts SN14 9ER. *T:* Bath (0225) 742827, *Fax:* 0225 742954.

BRAYBROOKE, Neville Patrick Bellairs; writer; *b* 30 May 1925; *s* of Patrick Philip William Braybrooke and Lettice Marjorie Bellairs; *m* 1953, June Guesdon Jolliffe; one step *d*. *Educ:* Ampleforth. *Publications:* This is London, 1953; London Green: The Story of Kensington Gardens, Hyde Park, Green Park and St James's Park, 1959; London, 1961; The Idler: novel, 1961; The Delicate Investigation (play for BBC), 1969; Four Poems for Christmas, 1986; Dialogue with Judas (long poem), 1989; *edited:* The Wind and the Rain: quarterly, 1941–1951; T. S. Eliot: a symposium for his 70th birthday, 1958, 7th edn 1986; A Partridge in a Pear Tree: a celebration for Christmas, 1960; Pilgrim of the Future: a Teilhard de Chardin symposium, 1966, 2nd edn, 1968; The Letters of J. R. Ackerley, 1975, 2nd edn 1977; Seeds in the Wind: 20th century juvenilia from W. B. Yeats to Ted Hughes, 1989, 3rd edn 1991; contrib. Independent, Guardian, New Statesman, New Yorker, Observer, Saturday Review, Sunday Times, The Times, Times Lit. Suppl., Sunday Telegraph, Spectator, Tablet. *Recreations:* animals, walking, reading little reviews, hats. *Address:* Grove House, Castle Road, Cowes, IoW PO31 7QZ. *T:* Cowes (0983) 293950; 10 Gardnor Road, NW3 1HA. *T:* 071–435 1851. *Clubs:* Island Sailing; PEN.

BRAYE, Baroness (8th in line) *cr* 1529, of Eaton Braye, Co. Bedford; **Penelope Mary Aubrey-Fletcher;** *b* 28 Sept. 1941; *d* of 7th Baron Braye and of Dorothea, *yr d* of late Daniel C. Donoghue, Philadelphia; *S* father, 1985; *m* 1981, Lt-Col Edward Henry Lancelot Aubrey-Fletcher, Grenadier Guards. *Educ:* Assumption Convent, Hengrave Hall; Univ. of Warwick. Pres., Blaby Cons. Assoc., 1986–; Dep. Pres., Northants Red Cross, 1983–; Chm. School Cttee, St Andrew's Occupational Therapy School, 1988–. Governor: St Andrew's Hosp., Northampton, 1978–; Three Shires Hosp., Northampton, 1983–. High Sheriff of Northants, 1983; JP South Northants, 1981–86. *Co-heiresses: cousins* Linda Kathleen Fothergill [*b* 2 May 1930, *née* Browne; *m* 1965, Comdr Christopher Henry Fothergill, RN; two *s*; Theresa Beatrice Browne, *b* 9 Aug. 1934]. *Address:* Stanford Hall, Lutterworth, Leics LE17 6DH.

BRAYNE, Richard Bolding, MBE 1957; Clerk of the Worshipful Company of Ironmongers, 1973–90; *b* 28 Oct. 1924; 3rd *s* of late Brig. Frank Lugard Brayne, MC, CSI, CIE, ICS, and late Iris Goodeve Brayne, K-i-H; *m* 1947, Anne Stoddart Forrest; one *s* two *d*. *Educ:* Sherborne Sch.; Pembroke Coll., Cambridge. Indian Army, 3rd (Peshawar) Indian Mountain Battery, FF, India, Burma and Far East, 1942–46. Entered Colonial Service as DO, Tanganyika, 1948; Staff Officer to HRH The Princess Margaret's tour of Tanganyika, 1956; Dist Comr, 1957; Principal, Admin. Trng Centre and Local Govt Trng Centre, 1960. Prin. Asst Sec., Min. of Educn, 1963; Mem., E African UGC and Makerere Univ. College Council, 1963; retd from Colonial Service, 1964. Sec., Brit. Paper and Board Makers' Assoc., 1964; Trng Adviser and Develt Manager, Construction Industry Trng Bd, 1966. Asst Clerk of Worshipful Co. of Ironmongers, 1971. Member: Exec. Cttee, Nat. Assoc. of Almshouses, 1972– (Chm., 1981–87); Council, Royal Surgical Aid Soc., 1972– (Chm., 1982–87). *Recreations:* shooting, golf, D-I-Y. *Address:* Thriftwood Cottage, Broomlands Lane, Limpsfield, Surrey RH8 0SP. *T:* Oxted (0883) 722300.

BRAYNE-BAKER, John, CMG 1957; Colonial Administrative Service, Nigeria (retired); *b* 13 Aug. 1905; *s* of Francis Brayne-Baker and Dorothea Mary Brayne-Baker (*née* Porcher); *m* 1947, Ruth Hancock; no *c*. *Educ:* Marlborough Coll.; Worcester Coll., Oxford. Nigeria: Asst District Officer, 1928; District Officer, 1938; Senior District Officer, 1948; Resident, 1953. Senior Resident and Deputy Commissioner of the Cameroons, 1954–56; retired 1956. Member, Tiverton RDC, 1959–74, Tiverton DC, 1973–76. *Recreations:* gardening and golf. *Address:* 48 Markers, Uffculme, Cullompton, Devon EX15 3DZ. *T:* Craddock (0884) 840236. *Club:* Tiverton Golf (Tiverton).

BRAYNE-NICHOLLS, Rear-Adm. (Francis) Brian (Price), CB 1965; DSC 1942; General Secretary, Officers Pensions Society, 1966–79; *b* 1 Dec. 1914; *s* of late Dr G. E. E. Brayne-Nicholls and *g s* of Sir Francis W. T. Brain; *m* 1st, 1939, Wendy (*née* Donnelly) (*d* 1983); one *d*; 2nd, 1986, Mimi M. Scott. *Educ:* RNC, Dartmouth. Sub-Lieut and Lieut, HMS Bee on Yangtse River, 1936–39; specialised in Navigation, 1939; Navigating Officer of: HM Ships Nelson, Rodney, Cardiff, 1939–41, Manxman (during many mining ops, Malta convoys and Madagascar op.), 1941–42; Combined Ops, taking part in Sicily (despatches), Salerno, and Normandy landings. Navigating Officer: HMS Glory, 1944–46; HMS Vanguard, 1948; Comdr 1948; Comdg Officer: HMS Gravelines, 1952–53; HMS St Kitts, 1953–54; Capt 1954; Naval Asst to First Sea Lord, 1954–55; Comdg Officer, HMS Apollo, 1955–57; NATO Standing Group, Washington, 1957–59; Captain of Navigation Direction Sch., HMS Dryad, 1959–61; Admiralty, 1961–63; Rear-Adm. 1963; Chief of Staff to Commander, Far East Fleet, 1963–65. Younger Brother, Trinity House. Mem., Nautical Inst. *Recreation:* golf. *Address:* 3 Tedworth Square, SW3 4DU. *T:* 071–352 1681. *Club:* Naval and Military.

BRAYNEN, Sir Alvin (Rudolph), Kt 1975; JP; Consultant to Shell, Bahamas, 1969–82; High Commissioner for the Commonwealth of the Bahamas in London, 1973–77; *b* 6 Dec. 1904; *s* of William Rudolph Braynen and Lulu Isabelle Braynen (*née* Griffin); *m* 1969, Ena Estelle (*née* Elden); (one *s* one *d* by a previous marriage). *Educ:* Public Sch., The Current, Eleuthera, Bahamas; Boys' Central Sch., Nassau, Bahamas (teacher trng). Public Sch. Headmaster, 1923–25. Entered commercial world, 1925, as clerk; founded his own petroleum commn firm, 1930, disposing of it in 1965. MP for Cat Island, 1935–42 and constituency for what is now known as St John, 1942–72; Dep. Speaker of House of Assembly, 1949–53, and 1963–66; MEC, 1953–58; Speaker of House of Assembly, 1967–72. During years 1952–58 he was Chairman of several Boards, incl. those responsible for Educn, Public Works, Prisons and Traffic; past Member: Bds of Agriculture, Health, Tourism, Out Island Develt and Educn; Mem., both Constitutional Confs from the Bahamas to London in 1963 and 1968; Chm., Exec. Cttee of Conf. of Commonwealth Caribbean Parliamentary Heads and Clerks; also served as either Chm. or Dep. Chm. of important Nat. Festivities for many years, such as Coronation of the Queen, visit of Princess Margaret, First Constitutional Day, 1964, and supervised arrangements for Conf. of Delegates of Commonwealth Parliamentary Conf. held at Nassau, 1968. Organised Bahamas Chamber of Commerce (first Exec. Sec.); Founder and first Pres., Nassau Mutual Aid Assoc.; first Pres., Kiwanis Club (Montague Branch). JP Bahamas 1952. *Recreations:* swimming; collects books on the Bahamas; collects coins and stamps. *Address:* PO Box N42, Nassau, Bahamas.

BRAYSHAW, (Alfred) Joseph, CBE 1975 (OBE 1964); JP; DL; Secretary, The Magistrates' Association, 1965–77; *b* Manchester, 20 Dec. 1912; *er s* of late Shipley Neave Brayshaw and late Ruth Cotterell (*née* Holmes), JP; *m* 1st, Joan Hawkes (*d* 1940); 2nd, 1943, Marion Spencer, *y d* of late Spencer Johnson, Bury St Edmunds; three *s*. *Educ:* Sidcot Sch., Somerset; engineering factories; Dalton Hall, Univ. of Manchester. Brayshaw Furnaces & Tools Ltd, 1934–40; CBCO, 1941–46; Asst Sec., then Gen. Sec., Friends' Relief Service, 1946–48; Gen. Sec., Nat. Marriage Guidance Council, 1949–64 (a Vice-Pres., 1964–); Pres., Guildford and District Marriage Guidance Council, 1983–87. JP Surrey, 1958; DL Surrey, 1983; Chairman: Farnham Bench, 1979–82; Surrey Magistrates' Soc., 1979–83. *Publication:* Public Policy and Family Life, 1980. *Recreation:* gardening. *Address:* Apple Trees, Beech Road, Haslemere, Surrey GU27 2BX. *T:* Haslemere (0428) 642677.

BRAZIER, Julian William Hendy; MP (C) Canterbury, since 1987; *b* 24 July 1953; *s* of Lt-Col P. H. Brazier; *m* 1984, Katharine Elizabeth, *d* of Brig. P. M. Blagden; twin *s*. *Educ*: Wellington Coll.; Brasenose Coll., Oxford (schol. in maths; MA); London Business Sch. Pres., Oxford Univ. Cons. Assoc., 1974. Former Capt., TA. Management consultant to industry, H. B. Maynard, internat. management consultants. Contested (C) Berwick-upon-Tweed, 1983. PPS to Minister of State, HM Treasury, 1990–. Sec., subseq. Vice Chm., Cons. Backbench Defence Cttee, 1988–90. *Publications*: pamphlets on defence and economic policy. *Address*: House of Commons, SW1A 0AA.

BRAZIER-CREAGH, Maj.-Gen. Sir (Kilner) Rupert, KBE 1962 (CBE 1947); CB 1954; DSO 1944; Secretary of the Horse Race Betting Levy Board, 1961–65; Director of Staff Duties, War Office, 1959–61, retired; *b* 12 Dec. 1909; 2nd *s* of late Lt-Col K. C. Brazier-Creagh; *m* 1st, 1938, Elizabeth Mary (*d* 1967), *d* of late E. M. Magor; one *s* two *d*; 2nd, 1968, Mrs Marie Nelson. *Educ*: Rugby; RMA, Woolwich. 2nd Lieut, 1929; served War of 1939–45 (despatches, DSO); Bde Major, 9th Armoured Div., 1941; GSO1 12th Corps, 1943; Commanded 25th Field Regt, 1944; BGS 21st Army Group and BAOR, 1945–48 (CBE); idc 1949; DDRA, War Office, 1950; CRA 11th Armoured Div., 1951–52; Chief of Staff Malaya Command, 1952–55 (despatches, CB); Asst Comdt, Staff Coll., 1955–57; Chief of Staff, Eastern Command, 1957–59. Officer, American Legion of Merit, 1945. *Recreation*: racing. *Address*: Travis Corners Road, Garrison, New York, USA.

BREACH, Gerald Ernest John; Director, Project Group, Export Credits Guarantee Department, 1988–90; *b* 14 March 1932; *s* of Ernest Albert Breach and Jane Breach; *m* 1st, 1958, Joan Elizabeth Eckford; one *s* one *d*; 2nd, 1988, Sylvia Eileen Harding. *Educ*: Roan Sch., Greenwich. Nat. Service, Royal Signals, 1950–52. Joined: ECGD, 1952; ECGD Management Bd, 1988. *Recreations*: boating, rambling. *Address*: Bourne End, Bucks. *Club*: Overseas Bankers'.

BREADALBANE AND HOLLAND, 10th Earl of, *cr* 1677; **John Romer Boreland Campbell;** Mac Chailein Mhic Dhonnachaidh (celtic designation); Viscount of Tay and Paintland; Lord Glenorchy, Benederaloch, Ormelie and Weik, 1677; Bt of Glenorchy; Bt of Nova Scotia, 1625; *b* 28 April 1919; *o s* of 9th Earl of Breadalbane and Holland, MC; *S* father, 1959; *m* 1949, Coralie (marr. diss.), *o d* of Charles Archer. *Educ*: Eton; RMC, Sandhurst; Basil Patterson Tutors; Edinburgh Univ. Entered Black Watch (Royal Highlanders), 1939; served France, 1939–41 (despatches); invalided, 1942. *Recreations*: piobaireachd, Scottish highland culture. *Heir*: none. *Address*: House of Lords, SW1; 29 Mackeson Road, Hampstead, NW3.

BREADEN, Very Rev. Robert William; Dean of Brechin since 1984; Rector of St Mary's, Broughty Ferry, since 1972; *b* 7 Nov. 1937; *s* of Moses and Martha Breaden; *m* 1970, Glenice Sutton Martin; one *s* four *d*. *Educ*: The King's Hospital, Dublin; Edinburgh Theological Coll. Deacon 1961, priest 1962; Asst Curate: St Mary's, Broughty Ferry, 1961–65; Rector, Church of the Holy Rood, Carnoustie, 1965–72; Canon of St Paul's Cathedral, Dundee, 1977. *Recreations*: gardening, horse riding; Rugby enthusiast. *Address*: St Mary's Rectory, 46 Seafield Road, Broughty Ferry, Dundee DD5 3AN. *T*: Dundee (0382) 77477.

BREALEY, Prof. Richard Arthur; Midland Bank Professor of Corporate Finance, London Business School, since 1982; *b* 9 June 1936; *s* of late Albert Brealey and of Irene Brealey; *m* 1967, Diana Cecily Brown Kelly; two *s*. *Educ*: Queen Elizabeth's, Barnet; Exeter Coll., Oxford (MA, 1st Cl. Hons PPE). Sun Life Assce Co. of Canada, 1959–66; Keystone Custodian Funds of Boston, 1966–68; London Business School: Prudential Res. Fellow, 1968–74; Sen. Lectr, 1972–74; Barclaytrust Prof. of Investment, 1974–82; Dep. Prin., 1984–88; Governor, 1984–88. Dir, Swiss Helvetia Fund Inc., 1987–. Pres., European Finance Assoc., 1975; Dir, Amer. Finance Assoc., 1979–81. *Publications*: An Introduction to Risk and Return from Common Stocks, 1969, 2nd edn 1983; Security Prices in a Competitive Market, 1971; (with J. Lorie) Modern Developments in Investment Management, 1972, 2nd edn 1978; (with S. C. Myers) Principles of Corporate Finance, 1981, 4th edn 1991; articles in professional jls. *Recreations*: ski-ing, rock climbing, pottery. *Address*: Haydens Cottage, The Pound, Cookham, Berks SL6 9QE. *T*: Bourne End (06285) 20143.

BREAM, Julian, CBE 1985 (OBE 1964); guitarist and lutenist; *b* 15 July 1933; *e s* of Henry G. Bream; *m* 1st, Margaret Williamson; one adopted *s*; 2nd, 1980, Isobel Sanchez. *Educ*: Royal College of Music (Junior Exhibition Award, 1945 and Scholarship, 1948). Began professional career at Cheltenham, 1947; London début, Wigmore Hall, 1950; subsequently has appeared in leading world festivals in Europe, USA, Australia and Far East. A leader in revival of interest in Elizabethan Lute music, on which he has done much research; has encouraged contemporary English compositions for the guitar. Formed Julian Bream Consort, 1960; inaugurated Semley Festival of Music and Poetry, 1971. DUniv Surrey, 1968. *Recreations*: playing the guitar; cricket, table tennis, gardening, backgammon. *Address*: c/o Harold Holt Ltd, 31 Sinclair Road, W14 0NS.

BREARE, William Robert Ackrill; Chairman and Managing Director: R. Ackrill Ltd, 1955–82; Lawrence & Hall Ltd, 1963–81; *b* 5 July 1916; *s* of late Robert Ackrill Breare and late Emily Breare (*née* Waddington); *m* 1942, Sybella Jessie Macduff Roddick, *d* of late John Roddick, Annan; one *s* two *d*. *Educ*: Old College, Windermere; Charterhouse; Wadham Coll., Oxford (MA). BCL Oxon 1938. Sub-Lt RNVSR, 1935–39; Comdr RNVR, 1942–44. Dir, R. Ackrill Ltd, newspaper publishers, 1938. Pres., Yorks Newspaper Soc., 1953 and 1972; Mem. Council, Newspaper Soc., 1967–81; Mem. Press Council, 1972–81. Contested (C) Rother Valley, 1950. *Recreations*: music, sailing. *Address*: Harrison Hill House, Starbeck, Harrogate, N Yorks. *T*: Harrogate (0423) 883302.

BREARLEY, Christopher John Scott; Deputy Secretary, Local Government, Department of the Environment, since 1990; *b* 25 May 1943; *s* of Geoffrey Brearley and Winifred (*née* Scott); *m* 1971, Rosemary Stockbridge; two *s*. *Educ*: King Edward VII Sch., Sheffield; Trinity Coll., Oxford. MA 1964, BPhil 1966. Entered Ministry of Transport, 1966; Private Sec. to Perm. Sec., 1969–70; Principal, DoE, 1970; Sec. to Review of Develt Control Procedures (Dobry), DoE, 1973–74; Private Sec. to the Secretary of the Cabinet, Cabinet Office, 1974–76; Asst Sec., 1977; Under Sec., 1981; Dir of Scottish Services, PSA, 1981–83; Cabinet Office, 1983–85; DoE, 1985–. Governor, Watford Grammar Sch. for Boys, 1988–. *Recreations*: crosswords, walking. *Address*: Department of the Environment, 2 Marsham Street, SW1. *T*: 071–276 3479. *Club*: New (Edinburgh).

BREARLEY, (John) Michael, OBE 1978; psycho-analyst; *b* 28 April 1942; *s* of Horace and late Midge Brearley; lives with Mana Sarabhai; two *c*. *Educ*: City of London Sch.; St John's Coll., Cambridge (MA). Lectr in Philosophy, Univ. of Newcastle-upon-Tyne, 1968–71. Middlesex County Cricketer, intermittently, 1961–82, capped 1964, Captain, 1971–82; played first Test Match, 1976; Captain of England XI, 1977–80, 1981. *Publications*: (with Dudley Doust) The Return of the Ashes, 1978; (with Dudley Doust) The Ashes Retained, 1979; Phoenix: the series that rose from the ashes, 1982; The Art of Captaincy, 1985; (with John Arlott) Arlott in Conversation with Mike Brearley, 1986; articles for the Sunday Times and Observer. *Club*: MCC (Hon. Life Mem.).

BREARS, Peter Charles David, FMA, FSA; Director, Leeds City Museums, since 1979; *b* 30 Aug. 1944; *s* of Charles Brears and Mary (*née* Fett). *Educ*: Castleford Technical High Sch.; Leeds Coll. of Art (DipAD 1967). FMA 1980; FSA 1980. Hon. Asst, Wakefield City Museum, 1957–66; Keeper of Folk Life, Hampshire CC, 1967–69; Curator: Shibden Hall, Halifax, 1969–72; Clarke Hall, Wakefield, 1972–75; Castle Museum, York, 1975–79. Chm., Leeds Symposium for Food History, 1986–; Founder, 1975, and Mem., 1975–, Group for Regional Studies in Museums, subseq. Social Hist. Curators Gp, 1975; Mem., Social History and Industrial Classification Wkg Party, 1978–; Sec., Soc. for Folk Life Studies, 1984–. *Publications*: The English Country Pottery, 1971; Yorkshire Probate Inventories, 1972; The Collectors' Book of English Country Pottery, 1974; Horse Brasses, 1981; The Gentlewoman's Kitchen, 1984; Traditional Food in Yorkshire, 1987; North Country Folk Art, 1989; Of Curiosities and Rare Things, 1989; Treasures for the People, 1989; articles in Folk Life, Post-Medieval Archaeology, etc; museum guides and catalogues. *Recreations*: hill walking, drawing, cookery. *Address*: c/o Leeds City Museum, Calverley Street, Leeds LS1 3AA. *T*: Leeds (0532) 462632.

BRECHIN, Bishop of, since 1990; **Rt. Rev. Robert Taylor Halliday;** *b* 7 May 1932; *s* of James Halliday and Agnes Logan Halliday (*née* Scott); *m* 1960, Georgina Mabel, (Gena) (*née* Chadwin); one *d*. *Educ*: High Sch. of Glasgow; Univ. of Glasgow (MA, BD); Episcopal Theol Coll., Edinburgh. Deacon 1957; priest 1958. Assistant Curate: St Andrew's, St Andrews, 1957–60; St Margaret's, Newlands, Glasgow, 1960–63; Rector, Church of the Holy Cross, Davidson's Mains, Edinburgh, 1963–83; External Lectr in New Testament, Episcopal Theol Coll., Edin., 1963–74; Canon of St Mary's Cathedral, Edinburgh, 1973–83; Rector of St Andrew's, St Andrews, 1983–90; Tutor in Biblical Studies, Univ. of St Andrews, 1984–90. Hon. Canon, Trinity Cathedral, Davenport, Iowa, 1990. *Recreations*: walking, reading. *Address*: The Bishop's Room, St Paul's Cathedral, Castlehill, Dundee DD1 1TD. *T*: Dundee (0382) 29230/24486; Bishop's House, 35 Carlogie Road, Carnoustie DD7 6ER. *T*: Carnoustie (0241) 55781.

BRECHIN, Dean of; *see* Breaden, Very Rev. R. W.

BRECKENRIDGE, Prof. Alasdair Muir, MD; FRCP; FRSE; Professor of Clinical Pharmacology, University of Liverpool, since 1974; *b* 7 May 1937; *s* of Thomas and Jane Breckenridge; *m* 1967, Jean Margaret Boyle; two *s*. *Educ*: Bell Baxter Sch., Cupar, Fife; Univ. of St Andrews (MB, ChB Hons 1961); Univ. of London (MSc 1968); Univ. of Dundee (MD Hons 1974). FRCP 1974; FRSE 1991; House Phys. and Surg., Dundee Royal Infirm., 1961–62; Asst, Dept of Medicine, Univ. of St Andrews, 1962–63; successively House Phys., Registrar, Sen. Registrar, Tutor, Lectr and Sen. Lectr, Hammersmith Hosp. and RPMS, 1964–74. Non-exec. Dir, Mersey RHA, 1990– (Chm., Res. Cttee, 1987–). NHS Advr in Clin. Pharm. to CMO, 1982–; Mem., NHS Adv. Cttee on Drugs, 1985– (Vice Chm., 1986–). Committee on Safety of Medicines: Mem., 1982–; Chm., Adverse Reactions Subgroup, 1987–; Chm., Adverse Reactions to Vaccination and Immunisation Subcttee, 1989–. Medical Research Council: Mem., Clin. Trials Cttee, 1983–; Mem., Physiol Systems and Disorders Bd, 1987– (Vice Chm., 1990–91); Mem., AIDS Therapeutic Cttee, 1989–. Royal College of Physicians: Mem. Council, 1983–86; Mem., Res. Cttee, 1983–88; Mem., Clin. Pharm. Cttee, 1990–; Goulstonian Lectr, 1975. British Pharmacological Society: Mem., 1972–; Foreign Sec., 1984–; Chm., Clin. Section, 1988–; Chm. Editl Bd, British Jl of Clin. Pharmacol., 1983–87. Member: Panel on Tropical and Infectious Disease, Wellcome Trust, 1984–87; Res. Cttee, British Heart Foundn, 1977–82; Steering Cttee for Chemotherapy of Malaria, WHO, 1987–; Exec. Cttee, Internat. Union of Pharm., 1981–87. Mem., Assoc. of Physicians, 1975–. Paul Martini Prize in Clin. Pharm., 1974; Poulson Medal, Norwegian Pharmacol Soc., 1988. Exec. Editor, Pharmacology and Therapeutics, 1982–. *Publications*: papers on clinical pharmacology in various jls. *Recreations*: hill-walking, golf, music. *Address*: Cree Cottage, Feather Lane, Heswall, Wirral L60 4RL. *T*: 051–342 1096.

BRECKNOCK, Earl of; James William John Pratt; *b* 11 Dec. 1965; *s* and *heir* of Marquess Camden, *qv. Educ*: Eton.

BREDIN, Maj.-Gen. Humphrey Edgar Nicholson, CB 1969; DSO 1944 (and bars, 1945 and 1957); MC 1938 (and bar, 1939); DL; Appeals Secretary, Cancer Research Campaign, Essex and Suffolk, 1971–83; *b* 28 March 1916; *s* of Lieut-Colonel A. Bredin, late Indian Army, and Ethel Bredin (*née* Homan); *m* 1st, 1947, Jacqueline Geare (marr. diss., 1961); one *d*; 2nd, 1965, Anne Hardie; two *d*. *Educ*: King's School, Canterbury; RMC, Sandhurst. Commissioned Royal Ulster Rifles, 1936; Commanded: 6th Royal Inniskilling Fusiliers, 1944; 2nd London Irish Rifles, 1945; Eastern Arab Corps, Sudan Defence Force, 1949–53; 2nd Parachute Regt, 1956–57; 99th Gurkha Infty Bde Group, 1959–62. Campaigns: Dunkirk, 1940; N Africa, 1943; Italy, 1943–45; Palestine, 1937–39 and 1946–47; Suez, 1956; Cyprus, 1956–57; Singapore-Malaya Internal Security, 1959–62; Chief of British Commander-in-Chief's Mission to Soviet Forces in Germany, 1963–65; Commanded 42nd Div. (TA), 1965–68. Brig. 1964; Maj.-Gen. 1965; Dir, Volunteers, Territorials and Cadets, 1968–71; retired 1971. Col Comdt, The King's Division, 1968–71; Col of the Regt, Royal Irish Rangers, 1979–85; Hon. Col D (London Irish Rifles) Co., 4th (V) Bn, The Royal Irish Rangers, 1980–86. Chm. Essex Co. Cttee, Army Benevolent Fund, 1983–. DL Essex, 1984. *Recreations*: shooting, fishing, gardening. *Address*: Bovills Hall, Ardleigh, Essex CO7 7RT. *T*: Colchester (0206) 230217. *Club*: Army and Navy.

BREDIN, James John; Specialist in television archives; *b* 18 Feb. 1924; *s* of late John Francis and Margaret Bredin; *m* 1958, Virginia Meddowes, *d* of John Meddowes and Mrs K. Thomas; one *s* two *d*. *Educ*: Finchley Catholic Grammar Sch.; London University. Served Fleet Air Arm, RNVR, S/Lieut, 1943–46. Scriptwriter, This Modern Age Film Unit, 1946–50; Producer, current affairs programmes, BBC TV, 1950–55; Sen. Producer, Independent Television News, 1955–59; Smith-Mundt Fellowship, USA, 1957; Producer of Documentaries, Associated Television, 1959–64; Man. Dir, Border TV Ltd, 1964–82. Chm., Guild of Television Producers and Directors, 1961–64. Director: Independent Television News Ltd, 1970–72; Independent Television Publications Ltd, 1965–82. FRTS 1983. Press Fellow, Wolfson Coll., Cambridge, 1987. *Address*: 25 Stack House, Cundy Street, SW1W 9JS. *T*: 071–730 2689. *Club*: Beefsteak.

BREEN, Geoffrey Brian; Metropolitan Stipendiary Magistrate, since 1986; Chairman of Juvenile Courts, since 1989; an Assistant Recorder, since 1989; *b* 3 June 1944; *s* of Ivor James Breen and Doreen Odessa Breen; *m* 1976, Lucy Bolaños; one *s* one *d*. *Educ*: Harrow High School. Articled to Stiles Wood & Co., Harrow, 1962–67; admitted Solicitor, 1967; Partner, Stiles, Wood, Head & Co, 1970–75; Sen. Partner, Stiles, Breen & Partners, 1976–86; Partner, Blaser Mills & Newman, Bucks and Herts, 1976–86. Mem., British Acad. of Forensic Scis, 1989–. *Recreations*: classical guitar, reading, do-it-yourself, aviculture. *Address*: Highbury Corner Magistrates' Court, 51 Holloway Road, N7 8JA.

BREEN, Dame Marie (Freda), DBE 1979 (OBE 1958); *b* 3 Nov. 1902; *d* of Frederick and Jeanne Chamberlin; *m* 1928, Robert Tweeddale Breen (*d* 1968); three *d*. *Educ*: St Michael's C of E Girls' Grammar Sch. Senator for Victoria, 1962–68, retired. Hon. Internat. Sec., Nat. Council of Women of Victoria, 1948–52, Pres., 1954–58, now Hon. Member; Vice-Pres., Australian/Asian Assoc. of Victoria, 1956–74; Chm., UNICEF

Victorian Cttee, 1969–73; President: Victorian Family Council, 1958–78; Victorian Assoc. of Citizens' Advice Bureaux, 1970–78; Australian Assoc. of Citizens' Advice Bureaux, 1973–75, 1977–79; Victorian Family Planning Assoc., 1970–71; Patron, FPA of Victoria, 1985–; Executive Mem. and Vice-Pres., Queen Elizabeth Hosp. for Mothers and Babies, 1943–78; Chm., Victorian Consultative Cttee on Social Develt, 1980–82. Mayoress of Brighton, Vic., 1941–42; JP 1948. *Recreations:* music, reading. *Address:* 51 Carpenter Street, Brighton, Victoria 3186, Australia. *T:* 592 2314. *Club:* Lyceum (Melbourne).

BREEZE, Alastair Jon, CMG 1990; HM Diplomatic Service; Counsellor, Foreign and Commonwealth Office, since 1987; *b* 1 June 1934; *s* of Samuel Wilfred Breeze and Gladys Elizabeth Breeze; *m* 1960, Helen Burns Shaw; two *s* one *d*. *Educ:* Mill Hill School; Christ's College, Cambridge (Scholar; MA 1959). Served Royal Marines, 1953–55. Foreign Office, 1958; 3rd Sec., Jakarta, 1960–62; FO, 1962–64; 2nd Sec., seconded to Colonial Office for service in Georgetown, 1964–66; 1st Sec., Tehran, 1967–71; FCO, 1971–72; 1st Sec., Islamabad, 1972–75, Lagos, 1976–79; FCO, 1979–83; Counsellor, UK Mission to UN, NY, 1983–87. *Recreations:* sailing, ornithology. *Address:* c/o Foreign and Commonwealth Office, SW1A 2AH.

BREHONY, Dr John Albert Noel, CMG 1991; HM Diplomatic Service; Counsellor, Foreign and Commonwealth Office, since 1984; *b* 11 Dec. 1936; *s* of Patrick Paul Brehony and Agnes Maher; *m* 1961, Jennifer Ann (*née* Cox); one *s* one *d*. *Educ:* London Oratory Sch.; Univ. of Durham (BA, PhD). Tutor, Durham Univ., 1960; Economist Intell. Unit, 1961; Res. Fellow, Jerusalem (Jordan), 1962; Lectr, Univ. of Libya, 1965–66; FO, 1966; Kuwait, 1967–69; Aden, 1970–71; Amman, 1973–77; Cairo, 1981–84. *Recreations:* Middle Eastern history, tennis, golf, opera. *Address:* c/o Foreign and Commonwealth Office, King Charles Street, SW1A 2AH. *Club:* Athenæum.

BREMRIDGE, Sir John (Henry), KBE 1983 (OBE 1976); *b* 12 July 1925; *m* 1956, Jacqueline Everard (MBE 1987); two *s* two *d*. *Educ:* Dragon Sch.; Cheltenham Coll.; St John's Coll., Oxford (MA). Army service: The Rifle Brigade, 1943–47. Joined John Swire & Sons, 1949; retired as Chm., John Swire & Sons (HK) Ltd, Swire Pacific Ltd, and Cathay Pacific Airways Ltd, 1980. Financial Sec., Hong Kong, 1981–86. Director: John Swire and Sons, 1987–89; Orient Express Hotels, 1986–89; Schroders, 1987–89. Hon. DSocSc Chinese Univ., 1980; Hon. DCL Hong Kong Univ., 1982. *Recreation:* bad golf. *Address:* Church House, Bradford-on-Avon, Wilts BA15 1LN. *T:* Bradford-on-Avon (02216) 6136. *Clubs:* Oriental; Hong Kong.

BRENCHLEY, Thomas Frank, CMG 1964; HM Diplomatic Service, retired; *b* 9 April 1918; *m* 1946, Edith Helen Helfand (*d* 1980); three *d*. *Educ:* privately and at Sir William Turner's Sch., Coatham; Merton Coll., Oxford (Modern History post-mastership; Classical Hon. Mods, 1938; MA Philos. and Ancient Hist., 1946; Mem., Sen. Common Room, 1987; Hon. Fellow 1991); Open Univ. (BA in Science and Technol., 1986). CS quals in Arabic, Norwegian and Polish. Served with Royal Corps of Signals, 1939–46; Major on Staff of Military Attaché, Ankara, 1943–45; Director, Telecommunications Liaison Directorate, Syria and Lebanon, 1945–46. Civil Servant, GCHQ, 1947; transferred to Foreign Office, 1949; First Secretary: Singapore, 1950–53; Cairo, 1953–56; FO, 1956–58; MECAS, 1958–60; Counsellor, Khartoum, 1960–63; Chargé d'Affaires, Jedda, 1963; Head of Arabian Department, Foreign Office, 1963–67; Assistant Under-Secretary of State, Foreign Office, 1967–68; Ambassador to: Norway, 1968–72; Poland, 1972–74; Vis. Fellow, Inst. for Study of Conflict, 1974–75; Dep. Sec., Cabinet Office, 1975–76. Dep. Sec. Gen. and Chief Exec., Arab-British Chamber of Commerce, 1976–83; Chairman: Institute for Study of Conflict, 1983–89; Res. Inst. for Study of Conflict and Terrorism, 1989–; Pres., Internat. Inst. for Study of Conflict, Geneva, 1989–. Dir, Center for Security Studies, Washington DC, 1988–. *Publications:* New Dimensions of European Security (ed), 1975; Norway and her Soviet Neighbour: NATO's Arctic Frontier, 1982; Diplomatic Immunities and State-sponsored Terrorism, 1984; Living With Terrorism: the problem of air piracy, 1986; Britain and the Middle East: an economic history 1945–87, 1989; Aegean Conflict and the Law of the Sea, 1990. *Recreation:* collecting (and sometimes reading) books. *Address:* 19 Ennismore Gardens, SW7 1AA. *Club:* Travellers'.

BRENDEL, Alfred, Hon. KBE 1989; concert pianist since 1948; *b* 5 Jan. 1931; *s* of Albert Brendel and Ida Brendel (*née* Wieltschnig); *m* 1960, Iris Heymann-Gonzala (marr. diss. 1972); one *d*; *m* 1975, Irene Semler; one *s* two *d*. Studied piano with: S. Deželić, 1937–43; L. V. Kaan, 1943–47; also under Edwin Fischer, P. Baumgartner and E. Steuermann; composition with Artur Michl. Vienna State Diploma, 1947; Premio Bolzano Concorso Busoni, 1949. Hon. RAM; Hon. Mem., Amer. Acad. of Arts and Sciences, 1984; Hon. Fellow, Exeter Coll., Oxford, 1987; Hon. DMus: London, 1978; Sussex, 1980; Oxford, 1983. Busoni Foundn Award, 1990. Commandeur des Arts et des Lettres, 1985. Concerts: most European countries, North and Latin America, Australia and New Zealand, also N and S Africa and Near and Far East. Many appearances Vienna and Salzburg Festivals, 1960–. Other Festivals: Athens, Granada, Bregenz, Würzburg, Aldeburgh, York, Cheltenham, Edinburgh, Bath, Puerto Rico, Barcelona, Prague, Lucerne, Dubrovnik, etc. Many long playing records (Bach to Schoenberg) incl. first complete recording of Beethoven's piano works (Grand Prix du Disque, 1965). Cycle of Beethoven Sonatas: London, 1962, 1977, 1982–83; Copenhagen, 1964; Vienna, 1965, 1982–83; Puerto Rico, 1968; BBC and Rome, 1970; Munich and Stuttgart, 1977; Amsterdam, Paris and Berlin, 1982–83; New York, 1983; Cycle of Schubert piano works 1822–28 in 19 cities, incl. London, Paris, Amsterdam, Berlin, Vienna, New York, Los Angeles, 1987–88. *Television (series):* Schubert Piano Music (13 films), Bremen, 1978; Alfred Brendel Masterclass, BBC, 1983; Liszt Années de Pèlerinage, BBC, 1986; Schubert Last Three Sonatas, BBC, 1988. *Publications:* Musical Thoughts and Afterthoughts (Essays), 1976; Music Sounded Out, 1990; essays on music, in: HiFi Stereophonie, Music and Musicians, Phono, Fono Forum, Osterreichische Musikzeitschrift, Gramophone, Die Zeit, New York Rev. of Books, etc. *Recreations:* literature, art galleries, architecture, unintentional humour, "kitsch". *Address:* Ingpen & Williams, 14 Kensington Court, W8.

BRENIKOV, Prof. Paul, FRTPI; Professor and Head of Department of Town and Country Planning, University of Newcastle upon Tyne, 1964–86, now Professor Emeritus; *b* 13 July 1921; *o s* of Pavel Brenikov and Joyce Mildred Jackson, Liverpool; *m* 1943, Margaret, *e d* of Albert McLevy, Burnley, Lancs; two *s* one *d*. *Educ:* St Peter's Sch., York; Liverpool Coll.; Univ. of Liverpool (BA (Hons Geog.), MA, DipCD). War service with RNAS, 1941–46. Sen. Planning Officer, Lancs CC, 1950–55; Lectr, Dept of Civic Design, Univ. of Liverpool, 1955–64; Planning Corresp., Architect's Jl, 1957–63; Environmental Planning Consultant: in UK, for former Bootle CB, 1957–64; Govt of Ireland, 1963–67; overseas, for UN; Chile, 1960–61; E Africa, 1964; OECD; Turkey, 1968. Royal Town Planning Institute: Mem. Council, 1967–78; Chm., Northern Br., 1973–74. Member: Subject Cttee of UGC, 1975–86; DoE Local Plans Inspector's Panel, 1985–. *Publications:* contrib. Social Aspects of a Town Development Plan, 1951; contrib. Land Use in an Urban Environment, 1961; (jtly) The Dublin Region: preliminary and final reports, 1965 and 1967; other technical pubns in architectural, geographical, planning and sociological jls. *Recreations:* drawing, painting, listening to music, walking, reading. *Address:* 46 Mitchell Avenue, Jesmond, Newcastle upon Tyne NE2 3LA. *T:* 091–281 2773.

BRENNAN, Anthony John Edward, CB 1981; Deputy Secretary, Northern Ireland Office, 1982–87; *b* 24 Jan. 1927; 2nd *s* of late Edward Joseph Brennan and Mabel Brennan (*née* West); *m* 1958, Pauline Margery, *d* of late Percy Clegg Lees; two *s* one *d*. *Educ:* St Joseph's; London Sch. of Economics (Leverhulme Schol.). BSc Econ 1946. Served Army, RA, RAEC, 1946–49; Asst Principal, Home Office, 1949; Private Sec. to Parly Under-Sec. of State, 1953–54; Principal, 1954; Principal Private Sec. to Home Sec., 1963; Asst Sec., 1963; Asst Under Sec. of State, Criminal Dept, 1971–75, Immigration Dept, 1975–77; Dep. Under-Sec. of State, Home Office, 1977–82. Sec., Royal Commn on Penal System, 1964–66; Mem., UN Cttee on Crime Prevention and Control, 1979–84. *Recreations:* bridge, theatre, athletics. *Address:* c/o Northern Ireland Office, Whitehall, SW1. *Club:* Athenæum.

BRENNAN, Archibald Orr, (Archie Brennan), OBE 1981; Director, Edinburgh Tapestry Co., since 1962; Visiting Artist, Papua New Guinea, since 1978; *s* of James and Jessie Brennan; *m* 1956, Elizabeth Hewitt Carmichael; three *d*. *Educ:* Boroughmuir Sch., Edinburgh; Edinburgh College of Art (DA). Training as tapestry weaver/student, 1947–62; Lectr, Edinburgh College of Art, 1962–78. Pres., Society of Scottish Artists, 1977–78; Chm., British Craft Centre, 1977–78; travelling lectr, UK, USA, Canada, Australia, Papua New Guinea, 1962–78. Fellow, ANU, 1974–75. *Publications:* articles in various jls. *Address:* 8 Bridge Place, Edinburgh EH3 5JJ. *T:* 031–332 2897.

BRENNAN, Brian John, MC 1944; Chairman, Lloyd's of London Press Ltd, 1985–88; Deputy Chairman of Lloyd's, 1981–83 (Underwriting Member, since 1951); *b* 17 May 1918; *s* of Alfred Eric Brennan and Jean (*née* Wallace); *m* 1950, Mary Patricia Newbould; one *s* two *d*. *Educ:* Dulwich College. Joined E. W. Payne, Lloyd's Brokers, 1936. Member, HAC, 1938; commnd Cameronians (Scottish Rifles), 1939; India, 1/Cameronians, 1940–45; Burma, 1942; Burma, 1944; commanded 26 Column 1/Cameronians 111 Bde Special Force; Lt-Col 1/Cameronians, 1944–45. Director, E. W. Payne, 1947, Chm., 1966–74; Director, Montagu Trust, 1967–74; Dep. Chm., Bland Payne Holdings, 1974–78; Chm., Bland Payne Reinsurance Brokers, 1974–78; Dir, Sedgwick Forbes Bland Payne Holdings, 1979; Chm., Sedgwick Payne, 1979; Dir, Sedgwick Gp Ltd, 1980. Mem., Cttee of Lloyd's, 1975–80, 1981–84. *Recreations:* Rugby (Old Alleynians, Kent, London, Barbarians); sailing, tennis, gardening. *Address:* Weybank House, Meadrow, Godalming, Surrey GU7 3BZ. *Clubs:* Lloyd's Yacht, British Sportsman's.

BRENNAN, Daniel Joseph; QC 1985; a Recorder of the Crown Court, since 1982; *b* 19 March 1942; *s* of late Daniel Brennan and Mary Brennan; *m* 1968, Pilar, *d* of late Luis Sanchez Hernandez; four *s*. *Educ:* St Bede's Grammar Sch., Bradford; Victoria University of Manchester (LLB Hons). President, University Union, 1964–65. Called to the Bar: Gray's Inn, 1967; King's Inns, Dublin, 1990. Legal Assessor, UK Nursing Council. Mem., Criminal Injuries Compensation Bd, 1989–. *Publications:* Provisional Damages, 1986; (contrib.) Bullen and Leake, Precedents of Pleading, 13th edn, 1990. *Address:* Brook House, Brook Lane, Alderley Edge SK9 7RU. *T:* Alderley Edge (0625) 585552; (chambers) 39 Essex Street, WC1R 3AT. *T:* 071–583 1111.

BRENNAN, Edward A.; Chairman and Chief Executive Officer, since 1986, and President, since 1989, Sears, Roebuck & Co.; *b* 16 Jan. 1934; *s* of Edward Brennan and Margaret (*née* Bourget); *m* 1955, Lois Lyon; three *s* three *d*. *Educ:* Marquette Univ., Wisconsin (BA). Joined Sears as salesman in Madison, Wisconsin, 1956; asst store manager, asst buyer, store manager, other positions in diff. locations, to 1969; Asst Manager, NY group, 1969–72; Gen. Manager, Sears Western NY group, 1972–75; Admin. Asst to Vice-Pres., Sears Eastern Territory, 1975; Gen. Manager, Boston group, 1976; Exec. Vice Pres., Southern Territory, 1978; Pres., Sears, Roebuck, 1980; Chm. and Chief Exec., Sears Merchandise Group, 1981; Pres. and chief operating officer, Sears, Roebuck & Co., 1984; dir of other cos. Member: President's Export Council; Business Roundtable; Conference Bd; business adv. council, Chicago Urban League; Civic Cttee, Commercial Club; Chm., Board of Governors, United Way of America; Member, Boards of Trustees: Savings and Profit Sharing Fund of Sears Employees; Univs of DePaul and Marquette; Chicago Museum of Science and Industry. *Address:* Sears, Roebuck and Co., Sears Tower, Chicago, Ill 60684, USA. *T:* (312) 875–1902.

BRENNAN, Hon. Sir (Francis) Gerard, AC 1988; KBE 1981; **Hon. Justice Brennan;** Justice of the High Court of Australia, since 1981; *b* 22 May 1928; *s* of Hon. Mr Justice (Frank Tenison) Brennan and Mrs Gertrude Brennan; *m* 1953, Patricia (*née* O'Hara); three *s* four *d*. *Educ:* Christian Brothers Coll., Rockhampton, Qld; Downlands Coll., Toowoomba, Qld; Univ. of Qld (BA, LLB). Called to the Queensland Bar, 1951; QC (Australia) 1965. Judge, Aust. Indust. Court, and Additional Judge of Supreme Court of ACT, 1976–81; Judge, Fed. Court of Australia, 1977–81. President: Admin. Appeals Tribunal, 1976–79; Admin. Review Council, 1976–79; Bar Assoc. of Qld, 1974–76; Aust. Bar Assoc., 1975–76; National Union of Aust. Univ. Students, 1949. Member: Exec. Law Council of Australia, 1974–76; Aust. Law Reform Commn, 1975–77. Hon. LLD TCD, 1988. *Recreation:* gardening. *Address:* 10 Kurundi Place, Hawker, ACT 2614, Australia. *T:* (062) 546794. *Club:* Commonwealth (Canberra).

BRENNAN, William Joseph, Jr; Legion of Merit, 1945; Associate Justice, Supreme Court of the US, 1956–90; *b* 25 April 1906; *s* of William J. Brennan and Agnes McDermott; *m* 1st, 1928, Marjorie Leonard (*d* 1982); two *s* one *d*; 2nd, 1983, Mary Fowler. *Educ:* University of Pennsylvania; Harvard. BS Univ. of Pennsylvania, 1928; LLB Harvard, 1931. Admitted to New Jersey Bar, 1931; practised in Newark, New Jersey, 1931–49, Member Pitney, Hardin, Ward & Brennan; Superior Court Judge, 1949–50; Appellate Division Judge, 1950–52; Supreme Court of New Jersey Justice, 1952–56; served War of 1939–45 as Colonel, General Staff Corps, United States Army. Hon. LLD: Pennsylvania, Wesleyan, St John's, 1957; Rutgers, 1958; Notre Dame, Harvard, 1968; Princeton, Columbia, Brandeis, NY Law Sch., John Marshall Law Sch., 1986; Ohio State, Yale 1987; Glasgow, 1989; UC Dublin, 1990; Hon. DCL: New York Univ., Colgate, 1957; Hon. SJD Suffolk Univ., 1956. Hon. Bencher, Lincoln's Inn, 1985. *Address:* c/o US Supreme Court, 1 First Street NE, Washington, DC 20543, USA.

BRENNER, Sydney, CH 1987; DPhil; FRCP; FRS 1965; Director, MRC Molecular Genetics Unit, Cambridge, since 1986 (Member of Scientific Staff, MRC Laboratory of Molecular Biology, since 1957); Fellow of King's College, Cambridge, since 1959; *b* Germiston, South Africa, 13 Jan. 1927; *s* of Morris Brenner and Lena (*née* Blacher); *m* 1952, May Woolf Balkind; one *s* two *d* (and one step *s*). *Educ:* Germiston High School; University of the Witwatersrand, S Africa; Oxford University (Hon. Fellow, Exeter Coll., 1985). MSc 1947, MB, BCh 1951, Univ. of the Witwatersrand; DPhil Oxon, 1954; FRCP 1979; Hon. FRCPath 1990. Dir, MRC Lab. of Molecular Biology, 1979–86. Mem., MRC, 1978–82, 1986–. Hon. Prof. of Genetic Medicine, Cambridge Univ., 1989–. Carter-Wallace Lectr, Princeton, 1966, 1971; Gifford Lectr, Glasgow, 1978–79; Dunham Lectr, Harvard, 1984; Croonian Lectr, Royal Soc., 1986. External Scientific Mem., Max-Planck Soc., 1988; Mem., Academia Europaea, 1989; Foreign Hon. Member, American Academy of Arts and Sciences, 1965; Foreign Associate, Nat. Acad. of Sciences, USA,

1977; Mem., Deutsche Akademie der Naturforscher, Leopoldina, 1975 (Gregor Mendel Medal, 1970); Foreign Member: Amer. Philosophical Soc., 1979; Real Academia de Ciencias, Spain, 1985; Foreign Associate, Royal Soc. of S Africa, 1983; Hon. Mem., Chinese Soc. of Genetics, 1989. Hon. FRSE 1979. Hon. FIASc 1989. Hon. DSc: Dublin, 1967; Witwatersrand, 1972; Chicago, 1976; London, 1982; Leicester, 1983; Oxford, 1985; Hon. LLD Glasgow, 1981. Warren Triennial Prize, 1968; William Bate Hardy Prize, Cambridge Philosophical Soc., 1969; (jtly) Lasker Award for Basic Medical Research, 1971; Royal Medal, Royal Soc., 1974; (jtly) Prix Charles Leopold Mayer, French Acad. of Science, 1975; Gairdner Foundn Annual Award, 1978; Krebs Medal, FEBS, 1980; CIBA Medal, Biochem. Soc., 1981; Feldberg Foundn Prize, 1983; Neil Hamilton Fairley Medal, RCP, 1985; Rosenstiel Award, Brandeis Univ., 1986; Prix Louis Jeantet de Medecine, Switzerland, 1987; Genetics Soc. of America Medal, 1987; Harvey Prize, Technion-Israel Inst. of Technol., 1987; Hughlings Jackson Medal, RSocMed, 1987; Waterford Bio-Medical Sci. Award, Res. Inst. of Scripps Clinic, USA, 1988; Kyoto Prize, 1990. *Publications:* papers in scientific journals. *Recreation:* rumination. *Address:* MRC Molecular Genetics Unit, Hills Road, Cambridge CB2 2QH. *T:* Cambridge (0223) 248011.

BRENT, Prof. Leslie, FIBiol; Professor Emeritus, University of London; *b* 5 July 1925; *s* of Charlotte and Arthur Baruch; *m* 1954, Joanne Elisabeth Manley (marr. diss. 1991); one *s* two *d. Educ:* Bunce Court Sch., Kent; Birmingham Central Technical Coll.; Univ. of Birmingham; UCL. BSc Birmingham, PhD London; FIBiol 1964. Laboratory technician, 1941–43; Army service, 1943–47, Captain; Lectr, Dept of Zoology, UCL, 1954–62; Rockefeller Res. Fellow, Calif Inst. of Technology, 1956–57; Res. scientist, Nat. Inst. for Med. Res., 1962–65; Prof. of Zoology, Univ. of Southampton, 1965–69; Prof. of Immunology, St Mary's Hosp. Med. Sch., London, 1969–90. European Editor, Transplantation, 1963–68; Gen. Sec., British Transplantation Soc., 1971–75 (Hon. Mem., 1988); Pres., The Transplantation Society, 1976–78; Chairman: Organising Cttee, 9th Internat. Congress of The Transplantation Soc., 1978–82; Fellowships Ctte, Inst. of Biol., 1982–85. Pres., Guild of Undergrads, Birmingham Univ., 1950–51. Chairman: Haringey Community Relations Council, 1979–80; Haringey SDP, 1981–83. Hon. MRCP 1986. Hon. mem. of several foreign scientific socs. Vice-Chancellor's Prize, Birmingham Univ., 1951; Scientific Medal, Zool Soc., 1963. Played hockey for UAU and Staffs, 1949–51. Co-editor, Immunology Letters, 1983–90. *Publications:* (ed jtly) Organ Transplantation: current clinical and immunological concepts, 1989; articles in scientific and med. jls on transplantation immunology. *Recreations:* music, singing (Crouch End Festival Chorus), fell-walking, chess, novels, coarse cricket. *Address:* 30 Hugo Road, N19 5EU.

BRENT, Michael Leon; QC 1983; a Recorder, since 1990; *b* 8 June 1936; *m* 1965, Rosalind Keller; two *d. Educ:* Manchester Grammar Sch.; Manchester Univ. (LLB Hons). Called to the Bar, Gray's Inn, 1961; practised on: Northern Circuit, 1961–67 (Circuit Junior, 1964); Midland and Oxford Circuit, 1967–. *Address:* 2 Dr Johnson's Buildings, Temple, EC4Y 7AY. *T:* 071–353 5371.

BRENTFORD, 4th Viscount *cr* 1929, of Newick; **Crispin William Joynson-Hicks;** Bt of Holmbury, 1919; Bt of Newick, 1956; Partner, Taylor Joynson Garrett (formerly Joynson-Hicks), since 1961; *b* 7 April 1933; *s* of 3rd Viscount Brentford and Phyllis (*d* 1979), *o d* of late Major Herbert Allfrey, Tetbury, Glos; *S* father, 1983; *m* 1964, Gillian Evelyn, *er d* of Gerald Edward Schluter, OBE; one *s* three *d. Educ:* Eton; New College, Oxford. Admitted solicitor, 1960. Master, Girdlers' Co., 1983–84. *Heir: s* Hon. Paul William Joynson-Hicks, *b* 18 April 1971. *Address:* Cousley Place, Wadhurst, East Sussex TN5 6HF. *T:* Wadhurst (098288) 3737.

BRENTON, Howard; playwright; *b* 13 Dec. 1942; *s* of Donald Henry Brenton and Rose Lilian (*née* Lewis); *m* 1970, Jane Fry; two *s. Educ:* Chichester High Sch. for Boys; St Catharine's Coll., Cambridge (BA Hons English). *Full-length stage plays:* Revenge, 1969; Hitler Dances, and Measure for Measure (after Shakespeare), 1972; Magnificence, 1973; The Churchill Play, 1974; Government Property, 1975; Weapons of Happiness, 1976 (Evening Standard Award); Epsom Downs, 1977; Sore Throats, 1979; The Romans in Britain, 1980; Thirteenth Night, 1981; The Genius, 1983; Bloody Poetry, 1984; Greenland, 1988; H. I. D. (Hess is Dead), 1989; *one-act stage plays:* Gum and Goo, Heads, The Education of Skinny Spew, and Christie in Love, 1969; Wesley, 1970; Scott of the Antartic, and A Sky-blue Life, 1971; How Beautiful with Badges, 1972; Mug, 1973; The Thing (for children), 1982; *collaborations:* (with six others) Lay-By, 1970; (with six others) England's Ireland, 1971; (with David Hare) Brassneck, 1973; (with Trevor Griffiths, David Hare and Ken Campbell), Deeds, 1978; (with Tony Howard) A Short Sharp Shock, 1980; (with Tunde Ikoli) Sleeping Policemen, 1983; (with David Hare) Pravda, 1985 (London Standard Award); (with Tariq Ali) Iranian Nights, 1989; (with Tariq Ali) Moscow Gold, 1990; *television plays:* Lushly, 1971; Brassneck (adaptation of stage play), 1974; The Saliva Milkshake, 1975 (also perf. theatre); The Paradise Run, 1976; Desert of Lies, 1984; *television series:* Dead Head, 1986; *translations:* Bertolt Brecht, The Life of Galileo, 1980; Georg Buchner, Danton's Death, 1982; Bertolt Brecht, Conversations in Exile, 1982. *Publications:* Diving for Pearls (novel), 1989; many plays published. *Recreation:* painting. *Address:* c/o Margaret Ramsay Ltd, 14A Goodwin's Court, St Martin's Lane, WC2N 4LL. *T:* 071–240 0691.

BRENTWOOD, Bishop of, (RC), since 1980; **Rt. Rev. Thomas McMahon;** *b* 17 June 1936. *Address:* Bishop's House, Stock, Ingatestone, Essex CM4 9BU. *T:* Stock (0277) 840268.

BRERETON, Donald; Under Secretary, Head of Prime Minister's Efficiency Unit, since 1989; *b* 18 July 1945; *s* of Clarence Vivian and Alice Gwendolin Brereton; *m* 1969, Mary Frances Turley; one *s* two *d. Educ:* Plymouth Coll.; Univ. of Newcastle upon Tyne (BA Hons Pol. and Soc. Admin). VSO, Malaysia, 1963–64. Asst Principal, Min. of Health, 1968; Asst Private Sec. to Sec. of State for Social Services, 1971; Private Sec. to Perm. Sec., DHSS, 1972; Prin., Health Services Planning, 1973; Private Sec. to Sec. of State for Social Services, 1979–82; Asst Sec., 1980; Hd of DHSS Policy Strategy Unit, 1982–83; Sec. to Housing Benefit Rev. Team, 1984. *Recreations:* squash, holidays, books, bridge. *Address:* 70 Whitehall, SW1A 2AS. *T:* 071–270 0257.

BRESSON, Robert, Officier, Légion d'Honneur, 1971; Grand Croix, Ordre National du Mérite, 1990; Commandeur, Arts et Lettres, 1974; film producer since 1934; *b* 25 Sept. 1901; *s* of Léon Bresson and Marie-Elisabeth Clausels; *m* 1926, Leidia van der Zee. *Educ:* Lycée Lakanal, Sceaux. Started as painter; then producer of short films, Affaires Publiques. Full-length films produced include: Les Anges du Péché, 1943; Les Dames du Bois de Boulogne, 1948; Journal d'un Curé de Campagne, 1951 (Internat. Grand Prix, Venice); Un Condamné à Mort s'est Echappé, 1956; Pickpocket, 1960; Procès de Jeanne d'Arc, 1962 (Jury's special prize, Cannes); Au Hasard Balthazar, 1966; Mouchette, 1967; Une Femme Douce, 1969; Quatre nuits d'un rêveur, 1971; Lancelot du Lac, 1974; Le diable, probablement, 1977; L'Argent, 1983. *Publication:* Notes sur le cinématographe, 1976. *Address:* 49 quai de Bourbon, 75004 Paris, France.

BRETSCHER, Barbara Mary Frances, (Mrs M. S. Bretscher); *see* Pearse, B. M. F.

BRETSCHER, Mark Steven, PhD; FRS 1985; Head, Division of Cell Biology, Medical Research Council Laboratory of Molecular Biology, Cambridge, since 1984; *b* 8 Jan. 1940; *s* of late Egon Bretscher, CBE and of Hanni (*née* Greminger); *m* 1978, Barbara Mary Frances Pearse, *qv*; one *s* one *d. Educ:* Abingdon Sch., Berks; Gonville and Caius Coll., Cambridge (MA, PhD). Res. Fellow, Gonville and Caius Coll., Cambridge, 1964–70; Mem., Scientific Staff, MRC Lab. of Molecular Biology, Cambridge, 1965–. Vis. Professor: Harvard Univ., 1975; Stanford Univ., 1984. Friedrich Miescher Prize, Swiss Biochemical Soc., 1979. *Publications:* papers in scientific jls on protein biosynthesis, membrane structure and cell locomotion. *Recreation:* gardening. *Address:* Ram Cottage, Commercial End, Swaffham Bulbeck, Cambridge CB5 0ND. *T:* Cambridge (0223) 811276.

BRETT, family name of **Viscount Esher.**

BRETT, Sir Charles (Edward Bainbridge), Kt 1990; CBE 1981; Partner, L'Estrange & Brett, Solicitors, Belfast, since 1954; *b* 30 Oct. 1928; *s* of Charles Anthony Brett and Elizabeth Joyce (*née* Carter); *m* 1953, Joyce Patricia Worley; three *s. Educ:* Rugby Sch.; New Coll., Oxford (Schol.; MA History). Solicitor, 1953. Journalist, Radiodiffusion Française and Continental Daily Mail, 1949–50. Member: Child Welfare Council of Northern Ireland, 1958–61; Northern Ireland Cttee, National Trust, 1956–83 and 1985– (Mem. Council, 1975–89); Arts Council of N Ireland, 1970–76; Chairman: N Ireland Labour Party, 1962; Ulster Architectural Heritage Soc., 1968–78 (Pres., 1979–); HEARTH Housing Assoc., 1978 and 1985–; NI Housing Exec., 1979–84 (Mem. Bd, 1971–77, Vice-Chm., 1977–78); Internat. Fund for Ireland, 1986–89. Mem. Bd, Irish Architectural Archive, Dublin, 1985–88. Hon. Mem., Royal Society of Ulster Architects, 1973; Hon. MRIAI 1988; Hon. FRIBA 1987. Hon. LLD QUB, 1989. *Publications:* Buildings of Belfast 1700–1914, 1967, rev. edn 1985; Court Houses and Market Houses of Ulster, 1973; Long Shadows Cast Before, 1978; Housing a Divided Community, 1986; lists and surveys for Ulster Architectural Heritage Soc., National Trusts of Guernsey and Jersey, and Alderney Soc. *Address:* 9 Chichester Street, Belfast BT1 4JG. *Club:* United Oxford & Cambridge University.

BRETT, Jeremy, (Peter Jeremy William Huggins); actor; *b* 3 Nov. 1935; *s* of Lt-Col H. W. Huggins, DSO, MC, DL, and late Elizabeth Huggins; *m* 1958 (marr. diss.); one *s*; *m* 1978; one *s. Educ:* Eton; Central Sch. of Drama. National Theatre, 1967–71: Orlando, in As You Like It; Berowne, in Love's Labour's Lost; Tesman, in Hedda Gabler; Bassanio, in The Merchant of Venice; Che Guevara, in Macrune's Guevara; The Son, in Voyage round my Father, Haymarket, 1972; Otto, in Design for Living, Phoenix, 1973–74; The Way of the World, Stratford, Ont, 1976; Prospero, in The Tempest, Toronto, 1982; narrator, Martha Graham ballet, Song, New York, 1985; Willie, in Aren't We All, Broadway, 1985; title rôle in The Secret of Sherlock Holmes, Wyndham's, 1988. Films include: Nicholas, in War and Peace, 1955; Freddie, in My Fair Lady, 1965; also TV appearances, including: Max de Winter in Rebecca, 1978; George, Duke of Bristol, in On Approval, 1980; Edward Ashburnham in The Good Soldier, 1981; title rôle in Macbeth The Last Visitor, 1982; Robert Browning in The Barretts of Wimpole Street, 1982; title rôle in William Pitt the Younger, 1983; title rôle in The Adventures of Sherlock Holmes, 1984, The Return of Sherlock Holmes, 1986, The Casebook of Sherlock Holmes, 1991; Mr Nightingale, in Florence Nightingale; Brian Foxworth, in Deceptions, 1986; Sherlock Holmes, in The Sign of Four, 1987. *Recreation:* archery. *Address:* 9538 Brighton Way, Suite 322, Beverly Hills, Calif 90210, USA. *Club:* Woodmen of Arden (Meriden).

BRETT, John Alfred, MA; Headmaster, Durham School, Durham, 1958–67; retired; *b* 26 Oct. 1915; *s* of Alfred Brett, Harrogate, Yorks; *m* 1939, Margaret Coode; one *s* three *d. Educ:* Durham School; St Edmund Hall, Oxford. MA (Hons Modern History). Temp. teacher, Stowe School, 1938; Teacher, Diocesan College, Rondebosch, South Africa, 1939; restarted Silver Tree Youth Club for non-Europeans, Cape Town. Army: Gunner to Major, RA, 1940–44; Instructor 123 OCTU Catterick; invasion of Normandy, 1944 (lost right eye); Military testing officer, WOSBs, finally Senior Military Testing Officer, War Office Selection Centre. Returned to post at Diocesan College, Rondebosch, 1946; Housemaster, 1948; Temp. teacher, Canford School, Wimborne, Dorset, 1954; Headmaster, Shaftesbury Grammar School, 1954. Diocesan Lay Reader. Member Council: Brathay Hall Centre; McAlpine Educnl Endowments Ltd. Governor, Bernard Gilpin Society. *Recreations:* sport (Captain Oxford University Rugby Football Club, 1937, and Member British Touring XV to Argentina, 1936); travel; reading. *Address:* 32 Homefarris House, Bleke Street, Shaftesbury, Dorset SP7 8AU.

BRETT, Lionel; *see* Esher, 4th Viscount.

BRETT, Michael John Lee; Editor, Investors Chronicle, 1977–82; *b* 23 May 1939; *s* of John Brett and Margaret Brett (*née* Lee). *Educ:* King's Coll. Sch., Wimbledon; Wadham Coll., Oxford (BA Modern Langs). Investors Review, 1962–64; Fire Protection Assoc., 1964–68; Investors Chronicle, 1968–82, Dep. Editor, 1973–77. Past Director: Throgmorton Publications; Financial Times Business Publishing Div. *Recreations:* travelling, reading. *Address:* 134 Offord Road, N1. *T:* 071–609 2362.

BRETT, Prof. Raymond Laurence; G. F. Grant Professor of English, University of Hull, 1952–82; *b* 10 January 1917; *s* of late Leonard and Ellen Brett; *m* 1947, Kathleen Tegwen, *d* of late Rev. C. D. Cranmer; two *s. Educ:* Bristol Cathedral School; University of Bristol (1st Class Hons BA, English and Philosophy, 1937; Taylor Prizeman, Hannam-Clark Prizeman, Haldane of Cloan Post-Grad. Studentship); University College, Oxford (BLitt 1940). Service in Admiralty, 1940–46; on Staff of First Lord; Lectr in English, Univ. of Bristol, 1946–52; Dean, Faculty of Arts, Hull Univ., 1960–62. Visiting Professor: Univ. of Rochester, USA, 1958–59; Kiel Univ., Osnabrück Univ., 1977; Baroda Univ., Jadavpur Univ., 1978; Univ. of Ottawa, 1981. Hon. DLitt Hull, 1983. *Publications:* The Third Earl of Shaftesbury: A Study in 18th Century Literary Theory, 1951; Coleridge's Theory of Imagination (English Essays), 1949; George Crabbe, 1956; Reason and Imagination, 1961; (with A. R. Jones) a critical edition of Lyrical Ballads by Wordsworth and Coleridge, 1963, rev. edn 1991; Thomas Hobbes (The English Mind), 1964; (ed) Poems of Faith and Doubt, 1965; An Introduction to English Studies, 1965; Fancy and Imagination, 1969; (ed) S. T. Coleridge, 1971, 2nd edn 1978; William Hazlitt, 1978; (ed) Barclay Fox's Journal, 1979; (ed) Andrew Marvell, 1979; articles in: The Times, Time and Tide, Essays and Studies, Review of English Studies, Modern Language Review, Philosophy, English, South Atlantic Qly, Critical Qly, etc. *Address:* 19 Mill Walk, Cottingham, North Humberside HU16 4RP. *T:* Hull (0482) 847115.

BRETT, William Henry; General Secretary, Institution of Professionals, Managers and Specialists, since 1989; *b* 6 March 1942; *s* of William Joseph Brett and Mary Brett (*née* Murphy); *m* 1961, Jean Valerie (marr. diss. 1986); one *s* one *d*; lives with Janet Winters; two *d. Educ:* Radcliffe Secondary Technical College, Manchester. British Railways, 1958–64; TSSA, 1964–66; NW Organiser, NUBE (now BIFU), 1966–68; E Midlands Divl Officer, ASTMS, 1968–74; Asst Sec., IPCS later IPMS, Asst Gen. Sec., 1980, elected Gen. Sec., 1988. Mem., Gen. Council, TUC, 1989–. Exec. Sec., Internat. Fedn of Air Traffic Electronic Assocs, 1984–; Mem. Public Services Internat. Exec. Cttee, 1981–.

Recreations: travelling, reading. *Address:* 36 Bassant Road, Plumstead, SE18. *T:* 081–855 0596. *Clubs:* Plumstead Working Men's, Lydd War Memorial.

BRETTEN, George Rex, QC 1980; barrister-at-law; *b* 21 Feb. 1942; *s* of Horace Victor Bretten and Kathleen Edna Betty Bretten; *m* 1965, Maureen Gillian Crowhurst; one *d. Educ:* King Edward VII Sch., King's Lynn; Sidney Sussex Coll., Cambridge (MA, LLB). Lectr, Nottingham Univ., 1964–68; Asst Director, Inst. of Law Research and Reform, Alberta, Canada, 1968–70; called to the Bar, Lincoln's Inn, 1965, a Bencher 1989; in practice, 1971–. *Publication:* Special Reasons, 1977. *Recreations:* hobby farming, tennis, riding. *Address:* Church Farm, Great Eversden, Cambridgeshire CB3 7HN. *T:* Cambridge (0223) 263538.

BREW, Richard Maddock, CBE 1982; DL; Chairman, Budget Boilers Ltd, since 1984; *b* 13 Dec. 1930; *s* of late Leslie Maddock Brew and Phyllis Evelyn Huntsman; *m* 1953, Judith Anne Thompson Hancock; two *s* two *d. Educ:* Rugby Sch.; Magdalene Coll., Cambridge (BA). Called to the Bar, Inner Temple, 1955. After practising for short time at the Bar, joined family business, Brew Brothers Ltd, SW7, 1955, and remained until takeover, 1972. Chm., Monks Dormitory Ltd, 1979–; Regl Dir, Lloyds Bank, 1988–. Mem., NE Thames RHA, 1982–90 (Vice-Chm., 1982–86); Chm., Tower Hamlets DHA, 1990–. Farms in Essex. Member: Royal Borough of Kensington Council, 1959–65; Royal Borough of Kensington and Chelsea Council, 1964–70; Greater London Council: Mem., 1968–86; Alderman, 1968–73; Vice-Chm., Strategic Planning Cttee, 1969–71; Chm., Covent Garden Jt Development Cttee, 1970–71 and Environmental Planning Cttee, 1971–73; Mem. for Chingford, 1973–86; Dep. Leader of Council and Leader, Policy and Resources Cttee, 1977–81; Dep. Leader, Cons. Party and Opposition Spokesman on Finance, 1981–82; Leader of the Opposition, 1982–83. Mem., Nat. Theatre Bd, 1982–86. Mem., Pony Club Council, 1975–. High Sheriff, Greater London, 1988–89. DL Greater London, 1989. *Recreations:* hunting, gardening. *Address:* The Abbey, Coggeshall, Essex CO6 1RD. *T:* Coggeshall (0376) 561246. *Clubs:* Carlton, MCC.

BREWER, Prof. Derek Stanley, LittD; FSA; Master of Emmanuel College, Cambridge, 1977–90; Professor of English, University of Cambridge, 1983–90, now Professor Emeritus; *b* 13 July 1923; *s* of Stanley Leonard Brewer and Winifred Helen Forbes; *m* 1951, Lucie Elisabeth Hoole; three *s* two *d. Educ:* elementary school; The Crypt Grammar Sch.; Magdalen Coll., Oxford (Matthew Arnold Essay Prize, 1948; BA, MA 1948); Birmingham Univ. (PhD 1956). LittD Cantab 1980. Commnd 2nd Lieut, Worcestershire Regt, 1942; Captain and Adjt, 1st Bn Royal Fusiliers, 1944–45. Asst Lectr and Lectr in English, Univ. of Birmingham, 1949–56; Prof. of English, Internat. Christian Univ., Tokyo, 1956–58; Lectr and Sen. Lectr, Univ. of Birmingham, 1958–64; Lectr in English, Univ. of Cambridge, 1965–76, Reader in Medieval English, 1976–83; Fellow of Emmanuel Coll., Cambridge, 1965–77. Founder, D. S. Brewer Ltd, for the publication of academic books, 1972; now part of Boydell and Brewer Ltd (Dir, 1979–). Mem., Council of the Senate, Cambridge, 1978–83; Chairman: Fitzwilliam Museum Enterprises Ltd, 1978–90; Univ. Library Synd., 1980–; English Faculty Bd, Cambridge, 1984–86, 1989. Sir Israel Gollancz Meml Lectr, British Academy, 1974; first William Matthews Lectr, Univ. of London, 1982; first Geoffrey Shepherd Meml Lectr, Univ. of Birmingham, 1983; Sandars Reader, Univ. of Cambridge, 1991. First British Council Vis. Prof. of English to Japan, 1987; Vis. Prof., Japan Soc. for Promotion of Science, 1988. President: The English Assoc., 1982–83, 1987–; Internat. Chaucer Soc., 1982–84. Chm. Trustees, British Taiwan Cultural Inst., 1990–; Trustee (Treas.), SOS Villages (UK), 1990–; Hon. Trustee, Osaka Univ. of Arts, 1987–. FSA 1977. Hon. Mem., Japan Acad., 1981; Corresp. Fellow, Medieval Soc. of America, 1987. Hon. LLD: Keio Univ., Tokyo, 1982; Harvard Univ., 1984; Hon. DLitt: Birmingham, 1985; Williams coll., USA, 1990; DUniv: York, 1985; Sorbonne, 1988. Univ. of Liège, 1990. Seatonian prize, Univ. of Cambridge, 1969, 1972, 1983, 1986 and 1988, (jtly) 1979 and 1980, (*prox. acc.*) 1985 and 1990. Editor, The Cambridge Review, 1981–86. *Publications:* Chaucer, 1953, 3rd edn 1973; Proteus, 1958 (Tokyo); (ed) The Parlement of Foulys, 1960; Chaucer in his Time, 1963; (ed and contrib.) Chaucer and Chaucerians, 1966; (ed) Malory's Morte Darthur: Parts Seven and Eight, 1968; (ed and contrib.) Writers and their Backgrounds: Chaucer, 1974; (ed) Chaucer: the Critical Heritage, 1978; Chaucer and his World, 1978; Symbolic Stories, 1980, 2nd edn 1988; (ed jtly) Aspects of Malory, 1981; English Gothic Literature, 1983; Tradition and Innovation in Chaucer, 1983; Chaucer: the Poet as Storyteller, 1984; Chaucer: an introduction, 1984; (ed) Beardsley's Le Morte Darthur, 1985; (with E. Frankl) Arthur's Britain: the land and the legend, 1985; (ed) Studies in Medieval English Romances, 1988; numerous articles in learned jls, reviews, etc. *Recreations:* reading, walking, looking at paintings and antiquities, travelling, publishing other people's books. *Address:* 240 Hills Road, Cambridge; Emmanuel College, Cambridge CB2 3AP. *T:* Cambridge (0223) 334200.

BREWER, Rear-Adm. George Maxted Kenneth, CB 1982; Flag Officer Medway and Port Admiral Chatham, 1980–82; *b* Dover, 4 March 1930; *s* of Captain George Maxted Brewer and Cecilia Victoria (*née* Clark); *m* 1989, Betty Mary, *o d* of Comdr C. H. Welton, RN and Elsie Gwendoline (*née* Harris). *Educ:* Pangbourne College. In Command: HMS Carysfort, Far East and Mediterranean, 1964–65; HMS Agincourt, Home, 1967; HMS Grenville, Far East and Mediterranean, 1967–69; HMS Juno, and Captain Fourth Frigate Sqdn, Home and Mediterranean, 1973–74; rcds 1975; In Command: HMS Tiger, and Flag Captain to Flag Officer Second Flotilla, Far East, 1978; HMS Bulwark, NATO area, 1979–80. ADC to HM the Queen, 1980. *Recreation:* watercolour painting. *Address:* c/o National Westminster Bank, 2 West Street, Portchester, Fareham, Hants. *Clubs:* Royal Navy of 1765 and 1785, Naval and Military.

BREWER, Rt. Rev. John; *see* Lancaster, Bishop of, (RC).

BRIANT, Bernard Christian, CVO 1977 (MVO 1974); MBE 1945; FRICS; Consultant, Messrs Daniel Smith, Chartered Surveyors, since 1982; Church Commissioner, 1981–89; *b* 11 April 1917; *s* of Bernard Briant and Cecily (*née* Christian); *m* 1942, Margaret Emslie, *d* of A. S. Rawle; one *s* two *d. Educ:* Stowe Sch.; Trinity Coll., Oxford (MA). FRICS 1948. Served War, 1939–45: Tunisia, Italy and Austria; Major, Intell. Corps. Joined Briant & Son, Chartered Surveyors, 1938, Partner 1948; Partner, Daniel Smith, 1970, Sen. Partner, 1976–82. Mem. various cttees, RICS, 1948–70 (Mem. Council, 1962–70); Clerk, Co. of Chartered Surveyors, 1980–85. Director: C of E Bldg Soc., 1953–67; S of England Building Soc., 1967–80; London and S of England Bldg Soc., 1980–83; Anglia Bldg Soc., 1983–87; Nationwide Anglia Bldg Soc., 1987–88; Mem., Cttee of Management, Lambeth and Southwark Housing Soc., 1971–89 (Vice-Chm., 1983–86). Land Steward, Manor of Kennington of Duchy of Cornwall, 1963–76; Agent, All Souls Coll., Oxford, 1966–79. Governor, Polytechnic of South Bank, 1980–88. *Recreations:* golf, walking, reading. *Address:* 33 The Terrace, Aldeburgh, Suffolk IP15 5HJ. *Clubs:* United Oxford & Cambridge University; Aldeburgh Golf, Rye Golf.

BRIAULT, Dr Eric William Henry, CBE 1976; Education Officer, Inner London Education Authority, 1971–76; Visiting Professor of Education, University of Sussex, 1977–81 and 1984–85; *b* 24 Dec. 1911; *s* of H. G. Briault; *m* 1935, Marie Alice (*née* Knight); two *s* one *d. Educ:* Brighton, Hove and Sussex Grammar Sch.; Peterhouse, Cambridge (Robert Slade Schol.). 1st cl. hons Geography, 1933; MA Cantab 1937; PhD London 1939. School teaching, 1933–47; Inspector of Schools, LCC, 1948–56; Dep. Educn Officer, ILEA, 1956–71. Dir, res. project on falling rolls in secondary schs, 1978–80. Hon. Sec., RGS, 1953–63. Hon. DLitt Sussex, 1975. *Publications:* Sussex, East and West (Land Utilisation Survey report), 1942; (jtly) Introduction to Advanced Geography, 1957; (jtly) Geography In and Out of School, 1960; (jtly) Falling Rolls in Secondary Schools, Parts I and II, 1980; (ed jtly) Primary School Management, 1990. *Recreations:* travel, gardening, music, theatre and ballet; formerly athletics (Cambridge blue) and cross-country running (Cambridge half-blue). *Address:* Woodedge, Hampers Lane, Storrington, W Sussex RH20 3HZ. *T:* Storrington (0903) 743919.

BRICE, (Ann) Nuala, PhD; Assistant Secretary-General, The Law Society, since 1987; *b* 22 Dec. 1937; *d* of William Connor and Rosaleen Gertrude Connor (*née* Gilmartin); *m* 1963, Geoffrey James Barrington Groves Brice, *qv*; one *s. Educ:* Loreto Convent, Manchester; University Coll. London. LLB (Hons), LLM 1976, PhD 1982, London. Admitted Solicitor of the Supreme Court, 1963 (Stephen Heelis Gold Medal and John Peacock Conveyancing Prize, 1963). The Law Society: Asst Solicitor, 1963; Asst Sec., 1964; Sen. Asst Sec., 1973; Deptl Sec., 1982. Sec., Revenue Law Cttee, 1972–82. Vis. Associate Prof. of Law, Tulane Univ., New Orleans, USA, 1990–. *Recreations:* reading, music, gardening. *Address:* Yew Tree House, Spring Coppice, Lane End, Bucks HP14 3NU. *T:* High Wycombe (0494) 881810; 15 Gayfere Street, Smith Square, SW1P 3HP. *T:* 071–799 3807. *Club:* University Women's.

BRICE, Air Cdre Eric John, CBE 1971 (OBE 1957); CEng; AFRAeS; MBIM; RAF retd; stockbroker; *b* 12 Feb. 1917; *s* of Courtenay Percy Please Brice and Lilie Alice Louise Brice (*née* Grey); *m* 1942, Janet Parks, Roundhay, Leeds, Yorks; two *s* one *d. Educ:* Loughborough Coll. (DLC). Joined RAF, 1939; served War, MEAF, 1943–46 (Sqdn Ldr). Air Ministry, 1946–50; Parachute Trg Sch., 1950–52; Wing Comdr, 1952; RAE, Farnborough, 1952–58; Comd, Parachute Trg Sch., 1958–60; RAF Coll., Cranwell, 1960–61; Gp Capt., 1961; RAF Halton, 1961–64; Comd, RAF Innsworth, Glos, 1964–66; Dir, Physical Educn, RAF, MoD, 1966–68; Air Cdre, 1968; Dep. AOA, RAF Headqrs, Maintenance Comd, 1968–71; April 1971, retd prematurely. *Recreations:* athletics (Combined Services and RAF athletic blues); Rugby football (RAF trialist and Blackheath Rugby Club); captained Loughborough Coll. in three sports. *Address:* Durns, Boldre, Hampshire. *T:* Lymington (0590) 672196. *Clubs:* Royal Air Force; Royal Lymington Yacht.

BRICE, Geoffrey James Barrington Groves, QC 1979; barrister; a Recorder of the Crown Court, since 1980; *b* 21 April 1938; *s* of late Lt-Cdr John Edgar Leonard Brice, MBE and Winifred Ivy Brice; *m* 1963, Ann Nuala Brice, *qv*; one *s. Educ:* Magdalen Coll. Sch., Brackley; University Coll., London (LLB). Called to the Bar, Middle Temple, 1960, Bencher, 1986; Harmsworth Scholar and Robert Garraway Rice Prize, 1960. Vis. Prof. of Maritime Law, Tulane Univ., 1989–. Lloyd's Arbitrator, 1978–; Wreck Commissioner, 1979–. Chairman: London Bar Arbitration Scheme, 1986–; London Common Law and Commercial Bar Assoc., 1988–89; Member: UK Govt Delegn to IMO Legal Cttee, 1984–89; Gen. Council of the Bar, 1988–89. *Publications:* Maritime Law of Salvage, 1983; (contrib.) Limitation of Shipowners' Liability, 1986; articles in legal jls. *Recreations:* music, opera. *Address:* Yew Tree House, Spring Coppice, Newmer Common, Lane End, Bucks. *T:* High Wycombe (0494) 881810; 15 Gayfere Street, Smith Square, SW1. *T:* 071–799 3807; Queen Elizabeth Building, Temple, EC4Y 9BS. *T:* 071–353 9153. *Club:* Athenæum.

BRICE, Nuala; *see* Brice, A. N.

BRICKELL, Christopher David, CBE 1991; VMH 1976; Director General, Royal Horticultural Society, since 1985; *b* 29 June 1932; *s* of Bertram Tom Brickell and Kathleen Alice Brickell; *m* 1963, Jeanette Scargill Flecknoe; two *d. Educ:* Queen's College, Taunton; Reading Univ. (BSc Horticulture). Joined Royal Horticultural Society Garden, Wisley, 1958: Asst Botanist, 1958; Botanist, 1960; Sen. Scientific Officer, 1964; Dep.Dir, 1968; Dir, 1969–85. George Robert White Medal of Honor, Mass Hort. Soc., 1988. *Publications:* Daphne: the genus in cultivation, 1976; Pruning, 1979; The Vanishing Garden, 1986; An English Florilegium, 1987; (ed) The Gardener's Encyclopaedia of Plants and Flowers, 1989; botanical papers in Flora Europaea and Flora of Turkey; horticultural papers in RHS Jl and Alpine Garden Soc. Bulletin. *Recreations:* gardening, sailing, squash, tennis. *Address:* Royal Horticultural Society, Vincent Square, SW1P 2PE.

BRICKWOOD, Sir Basil (Greame), 3rd Bt *cr* 1927; *b* 21 May 1923; *s* of Sir John Brickwood, 1st Bt and Isabella Janet Gibson (*d* 1967), *d* of James Gordon; *S* half-brother, 1974; *m* 1956, Shirley Anne Brown; two *d. Educ:* King Edward's Grammar Sch., Stratford-upon-Avon; Clifton. Served War, RAF, 1940–46. *Club:* Royal Air Force.

BRIDEN, Prof. James Christopher, PhD; FGS, FRAS; Director of Earth Sciences, Natural Environment Research Council, since 1986; Hon. Professor, University of Leeds, since 1986; *b* 30 Dec. 1938; *s* of Henry Charles Briden and Gladys Elizabeth (*née* Jefkins); *m* 1968, Caroline Mary (*née* Gillmore); one *s* one *d. Educ:* Royal Grammar Sch., High Wycombe; St Catherine's Coll., Oxford (MA); ANU (PhD 1965). FGS 1962; FRAS 1962. Research Fellow: Univ. of Rhodesia, 1965–66; Univ. of Oxford, 1966–67; Univ. of Birmingham, 1967–68; University of Leeds: Lectr, 1968–73; Reader, 1973–75; Prof. of Geophysics, 1975–86; Head, Dept of Earth Sciences, 1976–79 and 1982–85. Canadian Commonwealth Fellow and Vis. Prof., Univ. of Western Ontario, 1979–80. Mem., NERC, 1981–86; Chm., Jt Assoc. for Geophysics, 1981–84 (Chm., Founding Cttee, 1978–79); Member: Science Adv. Cttee, British Council, 1990–; Governing Council, Internat. Seismol Centre, 1978–83; Council, Eur. Geophysical Soc., 1976–84; Council, RAS, 1978–79. Murchison Medal, Geol Soc., 1984. Editor, Earth and Planetary Science Letters, 1971–. *Publications:* (with A. G. Smith) Mesozoic and Cenozoic Palaeocontinental World Maps, 1977; (with A. G. Smith and A. M. Hurley) Phanerozoic Palaeocontinental World Maps, 1981; over 80 papers on palaeomagnetism, palaeoclimates, tectonics and aspects of geophysics. *Recreations:* opera, music, theatre, sport. *Address:* Natural Environment Research Council, Polaris House, North Star Avenue, Swindon, Wilts SN2 1EU. *T:* Swindon (0793) 411730.

BRIDGE, family name of **Baron Bridge of Harwich.**

BRIDGE OF HARWICH, Baron *cr* 1980 (Life Peer), of Harwich in the County of Essex; **Nigel Cyprian Bridge;** Kt 1968; PC 1975; a Lord of Appeal in Ordinary, since 1980; *b* 26 Feb. 1917; *s* of late Comdr C. D. C. Bridge, RN; *m* 1944, Margaret Swinbank; one *s* two *d. Educ:* Marlborough College. Army Service, 1940–46; commnd into KRRC, 1941. Called to the Bar, Inner Temple, 1947; Bencher, 1964, Reader, 1985, Treasurer, 1986; Junior Counsel to Treasury (Common Law), 1964–68; a Judge of High Court, Queen's Bench Div., 1968–75; Presiding Judge, Western Circuit, 1972–74; a Lord Justice of Appeal, 1975–80. Mem., Security Commn, 1977–85 (Chm. 1982–85). Hon. Fellow, Wolfson Coll., Cambridge, 1989. *Address:* House of Lords, SW1.

See also Very Rev. A. C. Bridge.

BRIDGE, Very Rev. Antony Cyprian; Dean of Guildford, 1968–86; *b* 5 Sept. 1914; *s* of late Comdr C. D. C. Bridge, RN; *m* 1937, Brenda Lois Streatfeild; one *s* two *d. Educ:* Marlborough College. Scholarship to Royal Academy School of Art, 1932. Professional painter thereafter. War of 1939–45: joined Army, Sept. 1939; commissioned Buffs, 1940; demobilised as Major, 1945. Ordained, 1955; Curate, Hythe Parish Church till 1958; Vicar of Christ Church, Lancaster Gate, London, 1958–68. Mem., Adv. Council V&A Museum, 1976–79. FSA 1987. *Publications:* Images of God, 1960; Theodora: portrait in a Byzantine landscape, 1978; The Crusades, 1980; Suleiman The Magnificent, 1983; One Man's Advent, 1985; Richard the Lionheart, 1989. *Recreations:* bird-watching, reading. *Address:* 34 London Road, Deal, Kent CT14 9TE.
See also Baron Bridge of Harwich.

BRIDGE, John, GC 1944; GM 1940 and Bar 1941; Director of Education for Sunderland Borough Council (formerly Sunderland County Borough Council), 1963–76, retired; *b* 5 Feb. 1915; *s* of late Joseph Edward Bridge, Culcheth, Warrington; *m* 1945, F. J. Patterson; three *d. Educ:* London Univ. BSc Gen. Hons, 1936 and BSc Special Hons (Physics), 1937; Teacher's Dip., 1938. Schoolmaster: Lancs CC, Sept.-Dec. 1938; Leighton Park, Reading, Jan.-Aug. 1939; Firth Park Grammar Sch., Sheffield, Sept. 1939–Aug. 1946 (interrupted by war service). Served War: RNVR June 1940–Feb. 1946, engaged on bomb and mine disposal; demobilised as Lt Comdr RNVR. *Recreations:* gardening, travel, fell walking, photography, fishing. *Address:* 37 Park Avenue, Roker, Sunderland SR6 9NJ. *T:* 091–548 6356.

BRIDGE, Keith James; consultant; *b* 21 Aug. 1929; *s* of late James Henry Bridge and Lilian Elizabeth (*née* Nichols); *m* 1960, Thelma Ruby (*née* Hubble); three *d* (and one *s* decd). *Educ:* Sir George Monoux Grammar Sch., Walthamstow; Corpus Christi Coll., Oxford (MA). CIPFA 1959; CBIM 1978. Local govt service, 1953; Dep. City Treasurer, York, 1965; Borough Treas., Bolton, 1967; City Treas., Manchester, 1971; County Treasurer, Greater Manchester Council, 1973; Chief Exec., Humberside CC, 1978–83. Mem., W Yorks Residuary Body, 1985–91. Financial Adviser to Assoc. of Metrop. Authorities, 1971–78; Mem. Council, 1972–84, Pres., 1982–83, Chartered Inst. of Public Finance and Accountancy; Pres., Soc. of Metropolitan Treasurers, 1977–78. Member: Audit Commn for Local Authorities in Eng. and Wales, 1983–86; Exec. Council, Business in the Community, 1982–84; Bd, Public Finance Foundn, 1984–90; Educn Assets Bd, 1988–; Football Licensing Authy, 1990–. Dir, Phillips & Drew, 1987–89. Chm., York Diocesan Pastoral Cttee, 1989–. Freeman, City of London, 1986. *Publications:* papers in professional jls. *Recreations:* gardening, literature, music. *Address:* Conifers, 11 Eastgate, Lund, Driffield, N Humberside YO25 9TQ. *T:* Driffield (0377) 81627.

BRIDGE, Ronald George Blacker, CBE 1990 (OBE 1985); Hong Kong Civil Service, retired; *b* 7 Sept. 1932; *s* of Blacker Frank Bridge and Aileen Georgina Edith (*née* Shaw); *m* 1956, Olive Tyrrell Brown; two *s* two *d. Educ:* Charterhouse; Lincoln Coll., Oxford (MA). National Service, 1954–56. Colonial Office Devonshire Course, 1956–57; Hong Kong Civil Service, 1957–89; language study, 1957–58; Resettlement Officer, 1958–61; Asst Sec. (Lands and Buildings), 1961–69; Asst Comr for Resettlement, 1969–72; Asst Colonial Sec. (Estabt), 1971–72; Dep. Sec. for the Civil Service, 1972–76; Dep. Sec. for Security, 1976–77; Sec. for the Civil Service, 1977–78; Dir of Immigration, 1978–83; Comr for Labour, 1983–86; Sec. for Educn and Manpower, 1986–89. *Recreations:* walking, reading. *Address:* 15 Lincoln Street, SW3 2TP. *T:* 071–581 8090.

BRIDGEMAN, family name of **Earl of Bradford** and **Viscount Bridgeman.**

BRIDGEMAN, 3rd Viscount *cr* 1929, of Leigh; **Robin John Orlando Bridgeman,** CA; *b* 5 Dec. 1930; *s* of Hon. Geoffrey John Orlando Bridgeman, MC, FRCS (*d* 1974) (2nd *s* of 1st Viscount) and Mary Meriel Gertrude Bridgeman (*d* 1974), *d* of Rt Hon. Sir George John Talbot; *S* uncle, 1982; *m* 1966, (Victoria) Harriet Lucy, *d* of Ralph Meredyth Turton; four *s. Educ:* Eton. CA 1958. Partner: Fenn & Crosthwaite, 1973; Henderson Crosthwaite & Co., 1975–86; Director: Guinness Mahon & Co. Ltd, 1988–90; Nestor-BNA, 1988–. Special Trustee, Hammersmith Hosp. *Recreations:* shooting, ski-ing, gardening, music. *Heir: s* Hon. William Orlando Caspar Bridgeman, *b* 15 Aug. 1968. *Address:* 19 Chepstow Road, W2 5BP. *T:* 071-727 4065; Watley House, Sparsholt, Winchester SO21 2LU. *T:* Sparsholt (096272) 297. *Clubs:* Beefsteak, MCC; Pitt.

BRIDGEMAN, (John) Michael, CB 1988; Chief Registrar of Friendly Societies and Industrial Assurance Commissioner, 1982–91; First Commisioner (Chairman), Building Societies Commission, 1986–91; *b* 26 April 1931; *s* of John Wilfred Bridgeman, *qv*, and Mary Bridgeman (*née* Wallace); *m* 1958, June Bridgeman, *qv*; one *s* four *d. Educ:* Marlborough Coll.; Trinity Coll., Cambridge. Asst Principal, BoT, 1954; HM Treasury, 1956–81, Under Sec., 1975–81. *Address:* c/o National Westminster Bank, 1 St James's Square, SW1Y 4JX. *Club:* Reform.

BRIDGEMAN, John Wilfred, CBE 1960; BSc London, AKC; retired as Principal, Loughborough Training College, 1950–63; Principal, Loughborough Summer School, 1931–63; *b* 25 Jan. 1895; *s* of late John Edward Bridgeman and Alice Bridgeman, Bournemouth; *m* 1st, 1928, Mary Jane Wallace (*d* 1961); one *s*; 2nd, 1963, Helen Ida Mary Wallace. *Educ:* King's College, University of London; London Day Training College. Industry, 1910–15; taught at technical colleges, Bournemouth, Bath and Weymouth, 1915–20; Asst Master, Lyme Regis Grammar School, 1923; Senior Maths Master, Wolverhampton Secondary Gram. Sch., 1926; Head of Dept for Training of Teachers, Loughborough Coll., 1930. Chm., Assoc. of Teachers in Colls and Depts of Education, 1952; Leader of Staff Panel, Pelham Cttee, 1955–63. Hon. MA Nottingham, 1961; Hon. DLitt Loughborough, 1978. *Recreations:* chess, reading. *Address:* Flat 3, Laleham Court, Woking, Surrey GU21 4AX. *T:* Woking (0483) 721523.
See also J. M. Bridgeman.

BRIDGEMAN, Mrs June, CB 1990; Deputy Chair, Equal Opportunities Commission, since 1991; *b* 26 June 1932; *d* of Gordon and Elsie Forbes; *m* 1958, John Michael Bridgeman, *qv*; one *s* four *d. Educ:* variously, England and Scotland; Westfield Coll., London Univ. (BA). Asst Principal, BoT, 1954; subseq. served in DEA, NBPI, Min. of Housing and Local Govt, DoE; Under Secretary: DoE 1974–76; Central Policy Review Staff, Cabinet Office, 1976–79; Dept of Transport, 1979–90. Mem., Central Bd of Finance, C of E, 1979–83; Bishops Selector for ACCM, 1974–89. Mem. Council, PSI, 1984–90; Foundn Gov., Skinners' Sch., 1985–. *Recreations:* family, gardening, local history, opera. *Address:* c/o National Westminster Bank, 1 St James's Square, SW1Y 4JX.

BRIDGEMAN, Michael; *see* Bridgeman, J. M.

BRIDGER, Rev. Canon Gordon Frederick; Principal, Oak Hill Theological College, since 1987; *b* 5 Feb. 1932; *s* of late Dr John Dell Bridger and Hilda Bridger; *m* 1962, Elizabeth Doris Bewes; three *d. Educ:* Christ's Hospital, Horsham; Selwyn Coll., Cambridge (MA Hons Theology); Ridley Hall, Cambridge. Curate, Islington Parish Church, 1956–59; Curate, Holy Sepulchre Church, Cambridge, 1959–62; Vicar, St Mary, North End, Fulham, 1962–69; Chaplain, St Thomas's Episcopal Church, Edinburgh, 1969–76; Rector, Holy Trinity Church, Heigham, Norwich, 1976–87; RD Norwich (South), 1981–86; Exam. Chaplain to Bishop of Norwich, 1981–86; Hon. Canon,

Norwich Cathedral, 1984–87, now Hon. Canon Emeritus. *Publications:* The Man from Outside, 1969, rev. edn 1978; A Day that Changed the World, 1975; A Bible Study Commentary (I Corinthians—Galatians), 1985; reviews in The Churchman and other Christian papers and magazines. *Recreations:* music, sport, reading. *Address:* 10 Farm Lane, Oak Hill Theological College, Chase Side, Southgate, N14 4PP.

BRIDGER, Pearl, MBE 1947; Director, Central Personnel, Post Office, 1968–72, retired; *b* 9 Dec. 1912; *d* of Samuel and Lottie Bridger. *Educ:* Godolphin and Latymer Girls' Sch., London, W6. BA (Hons) Open Univ., 1978. Entered Post Office as Executive Officer, 1931; Asst Telecommunications Controller, 1938; Principal, 1947; Asst Sec., 1954; Director, 1968. *Address:* 95 Deanhill Court, SW14. *T:* 081–876 8877. *Club:* Civil Service.

BRIDGES, family name of **Baron Bridges.**

BRIDGES, 2nd Baron *cr* 1957; **Thomas Edward Bridges,** GCMG 1988 (KCMG 1983; CMG 1975); HM Diplomatic Service, retired; *b* 27 Nov. 1927; *s* of 1st Baron Bridges, KG, PC, GCB, GCVO, MC, FRS, and late Hon. Katharine Dianthe, *d* of 2nd Baron Farrer; *S* father, 1969; *m* 1953, Rachel Mary, *y d* of late Sir Henry Bunbury, KCB; two *s* one *d. Educ:* Eton; New Coll., Oxford. Entered Foreign Service, 1951; served in Bonn, Berlin, Rio de Janeiro and at FO (Asst Private Sec. to Foreign Secretary, 1963–66); Head of Chancery, Athens, 1966–68; Counsellor, Moscow, 1969–71; Private Sec. (Overseas Affairs) to Prime Minister, 1972–74; RCDS 1975; Minister (Commercial), Washington, 1976–79; Dep. Under Sec. of State, FCO, 1979–82; Ambassador to Italy, 1983–87. Mem., Select Cttee on Eur. Communities, H of L, 1988–. Dir, Consolidated Gold Fields, 1988–89; Mem., Anglian Bd, BR. Indep. Bd Mem., Securities and Futures Authority (formerly Securities Assoc.), 1989–. Chm., UK Nat. Cttee for UNICEF, 1989–. Member: Council, Aldeburgh Foundn; E Anglian Regl Cttee, NT. Pres., Dolmetsch Foundn. *Heir: s* Hon. Mark Thomas Bridges [*b* 25 July 1954; *m* 1978, Angela Margaret, *er d* of J. L. Collinson, Mansfield, Notts; three *d*]. *Address:* 57 Church Street, Orford, Woodbridge, Suffolk IP12 2NT.

BRIDGES, Brian; Under Secretary, Family Practitioner Services Division 2, Department of Health, since 1988; *b* 30 June 1937; *s* of late William Ernest Bridges; *m* 1970, Jennifer Mary Rogers. *Educ:* Harrow Weald County Grammar Sch.; Univ. of Keele (BA 1961). Joined Civil Service, 1961; Principal, 1967; Asst Sec. 1975; Under Sec., DHSS, 1985; Dir of Estabts and Personnel, DHSS, 1985–88. *Recreations:* Antiquarian. *Address:* 36 Chiltern Road, Wendover, Bucks.

BRIDGES, Rt. Rev. Dewi Morris; *see* Swansea and Brecon, Bishop of.

BRIDGES, Prof. James Wilfrid; Director, Robens Institute of Industrial and Environmental Health and Safety, since 1978, Professor of Toxicology, since 1979, and Dean, Faculty of Science, since 1988, University of Surrey; *b* 9 Aug. 1938; *s* of Wilfrid Edward Seymour Bridges and Mary Winifred Cameron; *m* 1963, Daphne (*née* Hammond) (separated); one *s* one *d. Educ:* Bromley Grammar Sch.; Queen Elizabeth Coll., London Univ.; St Mary's Hosp. Med. Sch., London Univ. BSc, PhD; MRCPath, FRSC, CChem; FIBiol; FIOSH; MInstEnvSci. Lectr, St Mary's Hosp. Med. Sch., 1962–68; Senior Lectr then Reader, Dept of Biochemistry, Univ. of Surrey, 1968–78. Visiting Professor: Univ. of Texas at Dallas, 1973, 1979; Univ. of Rochester, NY, 1974; Sen. Scientist, Nat. Inst. of Envtl Health Scis, N Carolina, 1976. Chm., British Toxicology Soc., 1980–81; First Pres., Fedn of European Toxicology Socs, 1985–88. Mem. Council, Inst. of Biology. FRSA. *Publications:* (ed jtly) Progress in Drug Metabolism, 10 vols, 1976–88; over 250 research papers and reviews in scientific jls. *Recreations:* theatre going, various sports. *Address:* Liddington Lodge, Liddington Hall Drive, Guildford GU3 3AE.

BRIDGES, Dame Mary (Patricia), DBE 1981; *b* 6 June 1930; *d* of Austin Edward and Lena Mabel Fawkes; *m* 1951, Bertram Marsdin Bridges; one step *s.* Chm., Honiton Div. Cons. Assoc., 1968–71; Chm., Western Area, covering 29 constituencies from Cornwall to Glos, 1976–79; past Chm., Cons. Western Area Women's Adv. Cttee and CPC Cttee; Mem. Cttee, Littleham Urban Ward, Exmouth (Pres., 1981); Pres., Western Provincial Area, Nat. Union of Cons. and Unionist Assocs, 1987–. Women's Section of Royal British Legion: Pres., Exmouth Br., 1965–; Chm., Devon County Women's Section, 1979–91; County Vice Pres., 1991; SW Area Rep. to Central Cttee, 1985–; Nat. Vice-Chm., 1989–. Former Mem., Exe Vale HMC; Founder Chm., Exmouth Council of Voluntary Service. Member: Exec., Resthaven, Exmouth, 1970– (Chm., League of Friends, 1971–90); Devon FPC, 1985–91; Political Cttee, Television South West; President: Exmouth and Budleigh Salterton Br., CRUSE, 1980–88; Exmouth Campaign Cttee, Cancer Research, 1981– (Chm., 1975–81); Founder Pres., Exmouth Br., British Heart Foundn, 1984; Mem., SW Electricity Consultative Council, 1982–90 (Chm., Devon Cttee, 1986–90); Mem., Exmouth Cttee, LEPRA, 1962– (Hon. Sec., 1964–87); Dir, Home Care Trust, 1988–; Co-optative Trustee, Exmouth Welfare Trust, 1979–; Co-founder, and Trustee 1988–, Exmouth and Lympstone Hospiscare, 1988–; Trustee, Exmouth Adventure Trust for Girls, 1988–; Exec. Mem., St Loye's Coll. for Trng the Disabled for Commerce and Industry, 1988–; Governor, Rolle Coll., Exmouth, 1982–88. Hon. Life Mem., Retford Cricket Club, 1951; Hon. Vice-Pres., Exmouth Cricket Club, 1981. *Recreations:* cricket, reading. *Address:* Walton House, Fairfield Close, Exmouth, Devon EX8 2BN. *T:* Exmouth (0395) 265317.

BRIDGES, Ven. Peter Sydney Godfrey; Archdeacon of Warwick, 1983–90, now Emeritus; Canon-Theologian of Coventry Cathedral, 1977–90, now Emeritus; *b* 30 Jan. 1925; *s* of Sidney Clifford Bridges and Winifred (*née* Livette); *m* 1952, Joan Penlerick (*née* Madge); two *s. Educ:* Raynes Park Grammar Sch.; Kingston upon Thames Sch. of Architecture; Lincoln Theol College. ARIBA 1950, Dip. Liturgy and Architecture 1967. Gen. and ecclesiastical practice, 1950–54; Lectr, Nottingham Sch. of Architecture, 1954–56. Deacon, 1958; Priest, 1959. Asst Curate, Hemel Hempstead, 1958–64; Res. Fellow, Inst. for Study of Worship and Religious Architecture, Univ. of Birmingham, 1964–67 (Hon. Fellow, 1967–72 and 1978); Warden, Anglican Chaplaincy and Chaplain to Univ. of Birmingham, 1965–68; Lectr, Birmingham Sch. of Arch., 1967–72; eccles. architect and planning consultant, 1968–75; Chm., New Town Ministers Assoc., 1968–72; Co-Dir, Midlands Socio-Religious Res. Gp, 1968–75; Dir, Chelmsford Diocesan R&D Unit, 1972–77; Archdeacon of Southend, 1972–77; Archdeacon of Coventry, 1977–83. Advr for Christian Spirituality, Dio. of Coventry, 1990–. Mem., Cathedrals Advisory Commn for England, 1981–86. Chm., Painting and Prayer, 1989–. *Publications:* Socio-Religious Institutes, Lay Academies, etc, 1967; contrib. Church Building, res. bulletins (Inst. for Study of Worship and Relig. Arch.), Clergy Review, Prism, Christian Ministry in New Towns, Cathedral and Mission, Church Architecture and Social Responsibility. *Recreations:* architecture, singing, painting. *Address:* Saint Clare, 1 Bell Court, The Maltings, Royal Leamington Spa CV32 5FH. *T:* Leamington Spa (0926) 335491. *Club:* Commonwealth Trust.

BRIDGES, Sir Phillip (Rodney), Kt 1973; CMG 1967; *b* 9 July 1922; *e s* of late Captain Sir Ernest Bridges and Lady Bridges; *m* 1st, 1951, Rosemary Ann Streeten (marr. diss. 1961); two *s* one *d*; 2nd, 1962, Angela Mary (*née* Dearden), *widow* of James Huyton. *Educ:* Bedford School. Military Service (Capt., RA) with Royal W African Frontier Force in W

Africa, India and Burma, 1941–47; Beds Yeo., 1947–54. Admitted Solicitor (England), 1951; Colonial Legal Service, 1954; Barrister and Solicitor, Supreme Court of The Gambia, 1954; Solicitor-General of The Gambia, 1963; QC (Gambia) 1964; Attorney-General of The Gambia, 1964–68; Chief Justice of The Gambia, 1968–83. *Address:* Weavers, Coney Weston, Bury St Edmunds, Suffolk IP31 1HG. *T:* Coney Weston (035921) 316. *Club:* Travellers'.

BRIDGES-ADAMS, John Nicholas William; a Recorder of the Crown Court, since 1972; *b* 16 Sept. 1930; *s* of late William Bridges-Adams, CBE; *m* 1962, Jenifer Celia Emily, *d* of David Sandell, FRCS. *Educ:* Stowe; Oriel Coll., Oxford (Scholar; MA, DipEd). Commnd Royal Artillery, 1949, transf. to RAFVR 1951 and served with Oxford and London Univ. Air Sqdn; Flying Officer, 2623 Sqdn RAuxAF Regt, 1980–82. Called to Bar, Lincoln's Inn, 1958 (Gray's Inn *ad eundem* 1979); Head of Chambers, 1979; Mem., Young Barristers Cttee, Bar Council, 1960–61; Actg Junior, Mddx Sessions Bar Mess, 1965–67. Mem., Exec. Cttee, Soc. of Cons. Lawyers, 1967–69 (Chairman: Rates of Exchange sub-cttee, 1967–70; Criminal Law sub-cttee, 1983–87; Criminal Justice and Sentencing sub-cttee, 1987–); Mem., House of Lords Reform Cttee, CAER, 1982. Chm., panel from which Representations Cttees under Dumping at Sea Act 1974 drawn, 1976–85, and under Food and Environment Protection Act 1985, 1985–. Contested (C) West Bromwich West, Oct. 1974. Governor, St Benedict's Upper Sch., 1980–83. Member: RIIA; IISS; FCIArb. *Publication:* contrib. on collisions at sea, 3rd edn of Halsbury's Laws of England, Vol. 35. *Recreation:* throwing my weight about. *Address:* 4 Verulam Buildings, Gray's Inn, WC1R 5LW. *T:* 071–405 6114; Fornham Cottage, Fornham St Martin, Bury St Edmunds, Suffolk. *T:* Bury St Edmunds (0284) 755307. *Clubs:* Savile, Garrick.

BRIDGEWATER, Allan; Group Chief Executive, Norwich Union Insurance Group, since 1989; *b* 26 Aug. 1936; *m* 1960, Janet Bridgewater; three *d*. *Educ:* Wyggeston Grammar Sch., Leicester. ACII, FIPM, CBIM. Asst Gen. Man., Norwich Union Insce Gp, 1979; Dep. Gen. Man. 1983, Gen. Man. 1984, Norwich Union Fire Insce Soc. Ltd; Norwich Union Insurance Group: Dir, 1985; Dep. Chief Gen. Man., 1988. Pres., Chartered Insurance Inst., 1989–90. FRSA. *Address:* Norwich Union Insurance Group, 8 Surrey Street, Norwich, Norfolk NR1 3NG. *T:* Norwich (0603) 622200.

BRIDGEWATER, Bentley Powell Conyers; Secretary of the British Museum, 1948–73; *b* 6 Sept. 1911; *s* of Conyers Bridgewater, OBE, Clerk to Commissioners of Taxes for City of London, and Violet Irene, *d* of Dr I. W. Powell, Victoria, BC. *Educ:* Westminster School (King's Schol.); Christ Church, Oxford (Westminster Schol., BA 1933, MA 1965). Asst Keeper, British Museum, 1937; Asst Sec., 1940. Seconded to Dominions Office, 1941–42, and to Foreign Office, 1942–45; returned to British Museum, 1946; Deputy Keeper, 1950; Keeper, 1961; retired, 1973. *Recreation:* music. *Address:* 4 Doughty Street, WC1N 2PH. *Club:* Athenæum.

BRIDGLAND, Milton Deane, AO 1987; FTS, FRACI, FAIM; Chairman: ICI Australia Ltd, since 1980; ANZ Banking Group Ltd, since 1989 (Director, since 1982; Deputy Chairman, 1987–89); *b* 8 July 1922; *s* of late Frederick H. and Muriel E. Bridgland, Adelaide; *m* 1945, Christine L. Cowell; three *d*. *Educ:* St Peter's Coll., Adelaide; Adelaide Univ. (BSc). Joined ICI Australia Ltd, 1945; Technical Manager, Plastics Gp, 1955–62; Ops Dir, 1962–67, Man. Dir, 1967–71, Dulux Australia Ltd; Exec. Dir 1971, Man. Dir, 1978–84, ICI Australia Ltd. Chm., Jennings Properties Ltd, 1985–; Director: Jennings Group (formerly Industries) Ltd, 1984–; Freeport–McMoRan Australia Ltd, 1987–89. President: Aust. Chemical Industry Council, 1977; Aust. Industry Develt Assoc., 1982–83. Vice President: Aust. Business Roundtable, 1983; Business Council of Australia, 1983–84; Dir, Aust. Inst. of Petroleum, 1980–84; Mem., National Energy Adv. Cttee, 1977–80. Member, Board of Management: Univ. of Melbourne Grad. Sch. of Management, 1983–86; Crawford Fund for Internat. Agricl Res. Chm. Adv. Bd, Salvation Army, Southern Territory, 1986–90. Mem., Cook Soc. *Recreation:* tennis. *Address:* 178 Barkers Road, Hawthorn, Vic 3122, Australia. *T:* (03) 819 3939. *Clubs:* Athenæum, Australian (Melbourne).

BRIDGWATER, Prof. John, FEng 1987; FIChemE; Professor since 1980, Dean, Faculty of Engineering since 1989, and Head of Inter-Disciplinary Research Centre in Materials for High Performance Applications since 1989, University of Birmingham; *b* 10 Jan. 1938; *s* of Eric and Mary Bridgwater; *m* 1962, Diane Louise Tucker; one *s* one *d*. *Educ:* Solihull Sch.; St Catharine's Coll., Cambridge (Major Scholar; MA, PhD, ScD); Princeton Univ. (MSE). Chemical Engineer, Courtaulds, 1961–64; University of Cambridge: Demonstrator in Chem. Engrg, 1964–69; Univ. Lectr in Chem. Engrg and Fellow, St Catharine's Coll., 1969–71; Esso Res. Fellow in Chem. Engrg, Hertford Coll., Oxford, 1971–73; Univ. Lectr in Engrg Sci., Univ. of Oxford and Lubbock Fellow in Engrg, Balliol Coll., 1973–80; Head, Sch. of Chem. Engrg, Univ. of Birmingham, 1983–89. Vis. Associate Prof., Univ. of British Columbia, 1970–71. Mem., Engrg Bd, SERC, 1986–89; Chm., Process Engrg Cttee, SERC, 1986–89. Exec. Editor, Chem. Engrg Science, 1983–. *Publications:* papers on chem. and process engineering in professional jls. *Recreations:* long distance running, India, France, Relate (marriage guidance). *Address:* School of Chemical Engineering, University of Birmingham, Edgbaston, Birmingham B15 2TT. *T:* 021–414 5322.

BRIDLE, Rear-Adm. Gordon Walter, CB 1977; MBE 1952; *b* 14 May 1923; *s* of Percy Gordon Bridle and Dorothy Agnes Bridle; *m* 1944, Phyllis Audrey Page; three *s*. *Educ:* King Edward's Grammar Sch., Aston, Birmingham; Northern Grammar Sch., Portsmouth; Royal Dockyard Sch., Portsmouth (Whitworth Scholar); Imperial Coll., London (ACGI). CEng, FIEE. jssc. Loan Service, Pakistan, 1950–52; served HM Ships: Implacable, St James, Gambia, Newfoundland, Devonshire; Proj. Manager, Sea Slug and Sea Dart, Mins of Aviation/Technol.; comd HMS Collingwood, 1969–71; Dir, Surface Weapons Projects, ASWE; Asst Controller of the Navy, 1974–77. Mem. Council, C of E Soldiers', Sailors' and Airmen's Clubs, 1982. *Address:* 25 Heatherwood, Midhurst, Sussex GU29 9LH. *T:* Midhurst (0730) 812838.

BRIDLE, Ronald Jarman, FEng 1979; private consultant and inventor, Cardiff University Industry Centre, since 1989; Director, Key Resources International, since 1984; *b* 27 Jan. 1930; *s* of Raymond Bridle and Dorothy (*née* Jarman); *m* Beryl Eunice (*née* Doe); two *d*. *Educ:* West Monmouth Grammar Sch.; Bristol Univ. (BSc). FEng, FICE, FIHE. Graduate Asst, Monmouthshire CC, 1953–55; Exec. Engr, Gold Coast Govt, 1955–57; Sen. Engr, Cwmbran Develt Corp., 1957–60; Principal Designer, Cardiff City, 1960–62; Project Engr, Sheffield-Leeds Motorway, West Riding CC, 1962–65; Dep. County Surveyor II, Cheshire CC, 1965–67; Dir, Midland RCU, DoE, 1967–71; Dep. Chief Highway Engr, 1971–73, Under-Sec., Highways 1, 1973–75, Chief Highway Engr, 1975–76, DoE; Chief Highway Engr, Dept of Transport, 1976–80; Controller of R&D, Dept of Transport, and Dir, Transport and Road Res. Lab., 1980–84. Dir (Technology and Develt), Mitchell Cotts PLC, 1984–86; Chm., Permanent Formwork Ltd, 1987–89. FRSA. Former Member: Council, ICE; EDC for Civil Engrg; Past Pres., IHE; Mem. Bd., BSI, 1979–85; Chm., Building and Civil Engineering Council, BSI, 1979–85. *Publications:* papers in jls of ICE, IHE and internat. confs. *Recreations:* golf, painting. *Address:* Parsonage Farm, Kemeys Commander, Usk, Gwent NP5 1SU. *T:* Nantyderry (0873) 880929. *Club:* Royal Automobile.

BRIDPORT, 4th Viscount, *cr* 1868; **Alexander Nelson Hood;** Baron Bridport, 1794; 7th Duke of Bronte in Sicily (*cr* 1799); Managing Director, Shearson Lehman Hutton Finance SA, since 1986; *b* 17 March 1948; *s* of 3rd Viscount Bridport and Sheila Jeanne Agatha, *d* of Johann van Meurs; *S* father, 1969; *m* 1st, 1972, Linda Jacqueline Paravicini (marr. diss.), *d* of Lt-Col and Mrs V. R. Paravicini; one *s*; 2nd, 1979, Mrs Nina Rindt-Martyn; one *s*. *Educ:* Eton; Sorbonne. *Heir:* *s* Hon. Peregrine Alexander Nelson Hood, *b* 30 Aug. 1974. *Address:* Villa Jonin, 1261 Le Muids, Vaud, Switzerland. *T:* 022–661705, *Fax:* 022–661898. *Club:* Brooks's.

BRIEGEL, Geoffrey Michael Olver; Legacy Officer, The Institute of Cancer Research: Royal Cancer Hospital, since 1983; *b* 13 July 1923; *s* of late Roy C. Briegel, TD, and Veria Lindsey Briegel; *m* 1947, Barbara Mary Richardson; three *s* one *d*. *Educ:* Highgate Sch. Served War, RAF, 1942–46 (514 Sqdn Bomber Command). Called to Bar, Lincoln's Inn, 1950; Public Trustee Office, 1954; Clerk of the Lists, Queen's Bench Div., and Legal Sec. to Lord Chief Justice of England, 1963; Dep. Circuit Administrator, South Eastern Circuit, 1971; Dep. Master of the Court of Protection, 1977–83. *Recreations:* target rifle and pistol shooting, swimming, cricket, theatre. *Club:* Royal Air Force.

BRIEN, Alan; novelist and journalist; *b* 12 March 1925; *s* of late Ernest Brien and Isabella Brien (*née* Patterson); *m* 1st, 1947, Pamela Mary Jones; three *d*; 2nd, 1961, Nancy Newbold Ryan; one *s* one *d*; 3rd, 1973, Jill Sheila Tweedie, *qv*. *Educ:* Bede Grammar Sch., Sunderland; Jesus Coll., Oxford. BA (Eng Lit). Served war RAF (air-gunner), 1943–46. Associate Editor: Mini-Cinema, 1950–52; Courier, 1952–53; Film Critic and Columnist, Truth, 1953–54; TV Critic, Observer, 1954–55; Film Critic, 1954–56, New York Correspondent, 1956–58, Evening Standard; Drama Critic and Features Editor, Spectator, 1958–61; Columnist, Daily Mail, 1958–62; Columnist, Sunday Dispatch, 1962–63; Political Columnist, Sunday Pictorial, 1963–64; Drama Critic, Sunday Telegraph, 1961–67; Columnist: Spectator, 1963–65; New Statesman, 1966–72; Punch, 1972–84; Diarist, 1967–75, Film Critic, 1976–84, Sunday Times. Regular broadcaster on radio, 1952–, and television, 1955–. Hannen Swaffer (now IPC) Critic of Year, 1966, 1967. *Publications:* Domes of Fortune (essays), 1979; Lenin: the novel (novel), 1987; And When Rome Falls (novel), 1991. *Recreations:* procrastination, empyromancy. *Address:* 15 Marlborough Yard, Holloway Road, N19 4ND. *T:* 071–281 9640; Blaen-y-Glyn, Pont Hyndwr, Llandrillo, Clwyd. *T:* Llandrillo (049084) 291. *Club:* Garrick.

BRIERLEY, Christopher Wadsworth, CBE 1987; Senior Adviser, Natural Gas Development Unit, World Bank, Washington, USA, since 1990; Managing Director, Resources and New Business, 1987–89, and Member of the Board, 1985–89, British Gas plc (formerly British Gas Corporation); *b* 1 June 1929; *s* of Eric Brierley and Edna Mary Lister; *m* 1st, Dorothy Scott (marr. diss. 1980); two *d*; 2nd, 1984, Dilwen Marie Srobat (*née* Morgan). *Educ:* Whitgift Middle School, Croydon. FCMA, ACIS. Branch Accountant, Hubert Davies & Co., Rhodesia, 1953–56; private business, N Rhodesia, 1956–59; Accountant, EMI, 1960; Chief Accountant, EMI Records, 1965; Dir of Finance, Long & Hambly, 1968; Chief Accountant, E Midlands Gas Bd, 1970; Director of Finance: Eastern Gas Bd, 1974; British Gas, 1977; Dir, 1980, Man. Dir, 1982, Economic Planning, British Gas. *Recreations:* golf, music, sailing. *Address:* 6 Stobarts Close, Knebworth, Herts SG3 6ND. *T:* Stevenage (0438) 814988. *Club:* Royal Automobile.

BRIERLEY, John David, CB 1978; retired Civil Servant; *b* 16 March 1918; *s* of late Walter George Brierley and late Doris Brierley (*née* Paterson); *m* 1956, Frances Elizabeth Davis; one (adopted) *s* one (adopted) *d*. *Educ:* elementary schools, London and Croydon; Whitgift Sch., Croydon; Lincoln Coll., Oxford. *Lit. Hum.*, BA Hons, 1940. Served War: Army, RASC, 1940–46. Ministry of Education: Asst Principal, 1946; Principal, 1949; Dept of Education and Science: Asst Sec., 1960; Under-Sec., 1969; Principal Finance Officer, 1969–75; Under Sec., DES, 1969–77. Dean of Studies, Working Mens' Coll., NW1, 1978–81 (Mem. Corp., 1980–); Governor, Croydon High Sch. (GPDST), 1980–. *Recreations:* fell-walking, cycling, photography, music. *Address:* Little Trees, Winterbourne, near Newbury, Berks RG16 8AS. *T:* Chieveley (0635) 248870.

BRIERLEY, Sir Ronald (Alfred), Kt 1988; Chairman: Tozer Kemsley & Millbourn (Holdings) PLC, since 1986; GPG plc, 1990; *b* Wellington, 2 Aug. 1937; *s* of J. R. Brierley. *Educ:* Wellington Coll. Editor, New Zealand Stocks and Shares, 1957–63; Chairman: Brierley Investments Ltd, 1961–89 (Founder, 1961, Pres. 1989–); Industrial Equity Ltd, 1966–89; Chm., Bank of New Zealand, 1987–88 (Dir, 1985–88; Dep. Chm., 1986). *Address:* Tozer Kemsley & Millbourn, 40 Church Street, Staines, Middlesex TW18 4EP; Brierley Investments Ltd, 10 Eastcheap, EC3M 1DJ. *Clubs:* American National, City Tattersall's (NSW).

BRIERLEY, Sir Zachry, Kt 1987; CBE 1978 (MBE 1969); Chairman, Z. Brierley Ltd, 1957–90 (Chairman and Managing Director, 1957–73); *b* 16 April 1920; *s* of late Zachry Brierley and of Nellie (*née* Ashworth); *m* 1946, Iris Macara; one *d*. *Educ:* Rydal Sch., Colwyn Bay. Served War: commnd RAF, 1941. Joined family business, Z. Brierley Ltd, 1938: Dir, 1952; Chm. and Man. Dir, 1957. Dir, Develt Corp. for Wales, 1974–77. Chairman: Small and Medium Firms Commn, Union des Industries de la Communauté Européenne, Brussels, 1975–77; Wales Adv. Cttee, Design Council, 1977–86 (Mem. Design Council, 1976–86). Member: Welsh Indust. Develt Bd, Welsh Office, 1972–82; Welsh Develt Agency, 1975–86; Bd, Civic Trust for Wales, 1976–; Cttee to Review Functioning of Financial Instns, 1977–80; Council, Machine Tool Trade Assoc., 1977–80; Bd of Governors, Llandrillo Tech. Coll., 1975–82; Bd of Governors, Penrhos Coll., 1980–. Chairman: Conservative Polit. Centre (Wales), 1975–79; Conwy Cons. and Unionist Assoc., 1980–82 (also past Chm. and Vice Pres.); Wales Area Cons. Council, 1982–86 (Pres., 1986–); N Wales Business Club, 1984–. Vice Chm., North Wales Medical Centre, 1979–87. Liveryman, Basketmakers' Co., 1978–; Freeman, City of London, 1977. CBIM 1990. *Recreations:* philately, travel, reading, sketching. *Address:* West Point, Gloddaeth Avenue, Llandudno, Gwynedd, N Wales LL30 2AN. *T:* Llandudno (0492) 76970. *Club:* Carlton.

BRIERS, Richard David, OBE 1989; actor since 1955; *b* 14 Jan. 1934; *s* of Joseph Briers and Morna Richardson; *m* 1957, Ann Davies; two *d*. *Educ:* Rokeby Prep. Sch., Wimbledon; Ridgeway Sch., Wimbledon. RADA, 1954–56 (silver medal). First appearance in London in Gilt and Gingerbread, Duke of York's, 1959. *Plays:* (major parts in): Arsenic and Old Lace, 1965; Relatively Speaking, 1966; The Real Inspector Hound, 1968; Cat Among the Pigeons, 1969; The Two of Us, 1970; Butley, 1972; Absurd Person Singular, 1973; Absent Friends, 1975; Middle Age Spread, 1979; The Wild Duck, 1980; Arms and the Man, 1981; Run for Your Wife, 1983; Why Me?, 1985; The Relapse, 1986; Twelfth Night, 1987 (televised 1988); Midsummer Night's Dream, King Lear, 1990; Wind in the Willows, Uncle Vanya, 1991. *Television series:* Brothers-in-Law; Marriage Lines; The Good Life; OneUpManShip; The Other One; Norman Conquests; Ever-Decreasing Circles; All In Good Faith. *Films:* Chorus of Disapproval, 1989; Henry V, 1989. *Publications:* Natter Natter, 1981; Coward and Company, 1987. *Recreations:* reading, gardening. *Address:* c/o ICM Ltd, 388–396 Oxford Street, W1N 9HE.

BRIGDEN, Wallace, MA, MD, FRCP; Consulting Physician: London Hospital, and Cardiac Department, London Hospital; National Heart Hospital; Consulting Cardiologist to the Royal Navy, now Emeritus; *b* 8 June 1916; *s* of Wallis Brigden and Louise Brigden (*née* Clarke). *Educ:* Latymer School; University of Cambridge; King's College Hospital; Yale University. Senior Scholar, King's College, Cambridge; First Class Natural Sciences Tripos, Parts I and II, 1936, 1937; Henry Fund Fellowship, Yale University, USA, 1937–38; Burney Yeo Schol., King's College Hospital, 1938. RAMC, 1943–47, Med. Specialist and O/C Medical Division. Lecturer in Medicine, Post-Grad. Med. School of London; Physician, Hammersmith Hospital, 1948–49; Asst Physician, later Consultant Physician, London Hospital and Cardiac Dept of London Hosp., 1949–81; Asst Physician, later Consultant Physician, National Heart Hospital, 1949–81; Cons. Cardiologist, Special Unit for Juvenile Rheumatism, Taplow, 1955–59; Director Inst. of Cardiology, 1962–66. Cons. Physician to Munich Re-Insurance Co., 1974–. Pres., Assurance Medical Society, 1987–89. St Cyres Lectr, 1956; R. T. Hall Lectr, Australia and New Zealand, 1961; Hugh Morgan Vis. Prof., Vanderbilt Univ., 1963. Late Assistant Editor, British Heart Journal. Mem. British Cardiac Society and Assoc. of Physicians. *Publications:* Section on Cardiovascular disease in Price's Textbook of Medicine; Myocardial Disease, Cecil-Loeb Textbook of Medicine; contributor to the Lancet, British Heart Jl, British Medical Jl. *Recreation:* painting. *Address:* 45 Wimpole Street, W1. *T:* 071–935 1201; Willow House, 38 Totteridge Common, N20 8NE. *T:* 081–959 6616.

BRIGGS, family name of **Baron Briggs.**

BRIGGS, Baron *cr* 1976 (Life Peer), of Lewes, E Sussex; **Asa Briggs,** MA, BSc (Econ); FBA 1980; Provost, Worcester College, Oxford, 1976–91; Chancellor, Open University, since 1978; *b* 7 May 1921; *o s* of William Walker Briggs and Jane Briggs, Keighley, Yorks; *m* 1955, Susan Anne Banwell, *o d* of late Donald I. Banwell, Keevil, Wiltshire; two *s* two *d*. *Educ:* Keighley Grammar School; Sidney Sussex College, Cambridge (1st cl. History Tripos, Pts I and II, 1940, 1941; 1st cl. BSc (Econ.), Lond., 1941). Gerstenberg studentship in Economics, London, 1941. Served in Intelligence Corps, 1942–45. Fellow of Worcester College, Oxford, 1945–55; Reader in Recent Social and Economic History, Oxford, 1950–55; Member, Institute for Advanced Study, Princeton, USA, 1953–54; Faculty Fellow of Nuffield College, Oxford, 1953–55; Professor of Modern History, Leeds Univ., 1955–61; University of Sussex: Professor of History, 1961–76; Dean, School of Social Studies, 1961–65; Pro Vice-Chancellor, 1961–67; Vice-Chancellor, 1967–76. Chm. Bd of Governors, Inst. of Develt Studies, 1967–76, Mem., 1976–. Visiting Professor: ANU, 1960; Chicago Univ., 1966, 1972. Sen. Gannett Fellow, Columbia Univ. 1988. Dep. Pres., WEA, 1954–58, Pres., 1958–67. Mem., UGC, 1959–67; Chm., Cttee on Nursing, 1970–72 (Cmnd 5115, 1972). Trustee: Glyndebourne Arts Trust, 1966–; Internat. Broadcasting Inst., 1968–87; (Chm.) Heritage Educn Gp, 1976–86; Civic Trust, 1976–86; Chairman: Standing Conf. for Study of Local History, 1969–76; Council, European Inst. of Education, 1975–; Adv. Bd for Redundant Churches, 1983–89; Vice-Chm. of Council, UN Univ., 1974–80; Governor, British Film Institute, 1970–77; President: Social History Soc., 1976–; The Ephemera Soc., 1984–; British Assoc. for Local History, 1984–86; Assoc. of Research Associations, 1986–88; Vice-Pres., Historical Assoc., 1986–. Mem., Ct of Governors, Administrative Staff Coll., 1971–. Mem., Amer. Acad. of Arts and Sciences, 1970. Hon. Fellow: Sidney Sussex Coll., Cambridge, 1968; Worcester Coll., Oxford, 1969; St Catharine's Coll., Cambridge, 1977. Hon. DLitt: East Anglia, 1966; Strathclyde, 1973; Leeds, 1974; Cincinnati, 1977; Liverpool, 1977; Open Univ., 1979; Birmingham, 1989; Hon. DSc Florida Presbyterian, 1966; Hon. LLD: York, Canada, 1968; New England, 1972; Sussex, 1976; Bradford, 1978; Rochester, NY, 1980; Ball State, 1985; E Asia, 1987; George Washington, 1988. Marconi Medal for Communications History, 1975; Médaille de Vermeil de la Formation, Fondation de l'Académie d'Architecture, 1979. *Publications:* Patterns of Peace-making (with D. Thomson and E. Meyer), 1945; History of Birmingham (1865–1938), 1952; Victorian People, 1954; Friends of the People, 1956; The Age of Improvement, 1959; (ed) Chartist Studies, 1959; (ed with John Saville) Essays in Labour History, Vol. I, 1960, Vol. II, 1971, Vol. III, 1977; (ed) They Saw it Happen, 1897–1940, 1961; A Study of the Work of Seebohm Rowntree, 1871–1954, 1961; History of Broadcasting in the United Kingdom: vol. I, The Birth of Broadcasting, 1961; vol. II, The Golden Age of Wireless, 1965; vol. III, The War of Words, 1970; Vol. IV, Sound and Vision, 1979; Victorian Cities, 1963; William Cobbett, 1967; How They Lived, 1700–1815, 1969; (ed) The Nineteenth Century, 1970; (ed with Susan Briggs) Cap and Bell: Punch's Chronicle of English History in the Making 1841–1861, 1973; (ed) Essays in the History of Publishing, 1974; Iron Bridge to Crystal Palace: impact and images of the Industrial Revolution, 1979; Governing the BBC, 1979; The Power of Steam, 1982; Marx in London, 1982; A Social History of England, 1983; Toynbee Hall, 1984; Collected Essays, 2 vols, 1985; The BBC: the first fifty years, 1985; (with Joanna Spicer) The Franchise Affair, 1986; Victorian Things, 1988. *Recreation:* travelling. *Address:* The Caprons, Keere Street, Lewes, Sussex. *Clubs:* Beefsteak, United Oxford & Cambridge University.

BRIGGS, Sir Geoffrey (Gould), Kt 1974; President, Pensions Appeal Tribunals for England and Wales, 1980–87; Justice of Appeal, Court of Appeal of Gibraltar, 1983–88; *b* 6 May 1914; 2nd *s* of late Reverend C. E. and Mrs Briggs, Amersham, Buckinghamshire; unmarried. *Educ:* Sherborne; Christ Church, Oxford (BA, BCL; MA 1984). Called to Bar (Gray's Inn), 1938; served War of 1939–45, County of London Yeomanry (Major). Attorney-General, E Region, Nigeria, 1954–58; QC (Nigeria), 1955; Puisne Judge, Sarawak, N Borneo and Brunei, 1958–62; Chief Justice of the Western Pacific, 1962–65; a Puisne Judge, Hong Kong, 1965–73; Chief Justice: Hong Kong, 1973–79; Brunei, 1973–79; Pres., Brunei Court of Appeal, 1979–88. DSNB 1974. FRSA 1984. *Address:* 1 Farley Court, Melbury Road, Kensington, W14 8LJ. *Club:* Wig and Pen.

BRIGGS, Rt. Rev. George Cardell, CMG 1980; *b* Latchford, Warrington, Cheshire, 6 Sept. 1910; *s* of George Cecil and Mary Theodora Briggs; unmarried. *Educ:* Worksop Coll., Notts; Sidney Sussex Coll., Cambridge (MA); Cuddesdon Theological Coll. Deacon 1934; priest 1935; Curate of St Alban's, Stockport, 1934–37; Missionary priest, Diocese of Masasi, Tanzania, 1937; Archdeacon of Newala and Canon of Masasi, 1955–64; Rector of St Alban's, Dar-es-Salaam, 1964–69; Warden of St Cyprian's Theological Coll., Masasi, 1969–73; Bishop of Seychelles, 1973–79; Asst Bishop, Diocese of Derby, and Assistant Priest, parish of St Giles, Matlock, 1979–80. *Recreations:* walking, reading, music. *Address:* 1 Lygon Lodge, Newland, Malvern WR13 5AX. *T:* Malvern (0684) 572941. *Club:* Commonwealth Trust.

BRIGGS, Isabel Diana, (Mrs Michael Briggs); *see* Colegate, I. D.

BRIGGS, John; *see* Briggs, Peter J.

BRIGGS, Dr (Michael) Peter; Executive Secretary, British Association for the Advancement of Science, since 1990; *b* 3 Dec. 1944; *s* of Hewieson Briggs and Doris (*née* Habberley); *m* 1969, Jennifer Elizabeth Watts; one *s* one *d*. *Educ:* Abbeydale Boys' Grammar Sch., Sheffield; Univ. of Sussex (BSc, DPhil). Jun. Res. Fellow in Theoretical Chem., Univ. of Sheffield, 1969–71; Res. Assistant, Dept of Architecture, Univ. of Bristol, 1971–73; Deputation Sec., Methodist Church Overseas Div., 1973–77; Area Sec. (Herts

and Essex), Christian Aid, BCC, 1977–80; British Association for the Advancement of Science: Educn Manager, 1980–86; Public Affairs Man., 1986–88; Dep. Sec., 1988–90. Sec., Assoc. of British Science Writers, 1986–. Chairman: Management Cttee, Methodist Church Div. of Social Responsibility, 1983–86; Methodist Youth World Affairs Management Cttee, 1984–. Methodist Local Preacher, 1974–. FRSA 1990. *Recreation:* walking. *Address:* British Association for the Advancement of Science, Fortress House, 23 Savile Row, W1X 1AB. *T:* 071–494 3326.

BRIGGS, Patrick David, MA; Head Master, William Hulme's Grammar School, since 1987; *b* 24 Aug. 1940; *s* of late Denis Patrick Briggs and of Nancy Sylvester (*née* Jackson); *m* 1968, Alicia Dorothy O'Donnell; two *s* one *d*. *Educ:* Pocklington Sch.; Christ's Coll., Cambridge (MA). Bedford Sch., 1965–87 (Sen. Housemaster, 1983–87). Rugby Blue, Cambridge, 1962; England Rugby trialist, 1968 and 1969; Mem. Barbarians, 1968–69; RFU staff coach, 1973–; England Under-23 Rugby coach, 1975–80; Team Manager, England Students Rugby, 1988–. Mem., Manchester Lit. and Phil Soc. *Publication:* The Parents' Guide to Independent Schools, 1979. *Recreations:* cricket, Rugby, squash, golf, fell walking, poetry, theatre. *Address:* Dunoon, 254 Wilbraham Road, Manchester M16 8PR. *T:* 061–226 2058. *Clubs:* East India, Devonshire, Sports and Public Schools, XL; Hawks (Cambridge); Quidnuncs, Cheshire County Cricket, Lancashire County Cricket.

BRIGGS, Peter; *see* Briggs, M. P.

BRIGGS, (Peter) John; a Recorder of the Crown Court, since 1978; *b* 15 May 1928; *s* of late Percy Briggs and of Annie M. Folker; *m* 1956, Sheila Phyllis Walton; one *s* three *d*. *Educ:* King's Sch., Peterborough; Balliol Coll., Oxford. MA, BCL. Called to the Bar, Inner Temple, 1953. Legal Member, Mersey Mental Health Review Tribunal, 1969 (Dep. Chm., 1971, Chm., 1981); Pres., Merseyside Medico-Legal Soc., 1982–84. *Recreation:* music, particularly amateur operatics. *Address:* Third Floor, Peel House, Harrington Street, Liverpool L2 9XN. *T:* 051–236 0718.

BRIGGS, Raymond Redvers, DFA; FCSD; freelance illustrator, since 1957; author, since 1961; *b* 18 Jan. 1934; *s* of Ernest Redvers Briggs and Ethel Bowyer; *m* 1963, Jean Taprell Clark (*d* 1973). *Educ:* Rutlish Sch., Merton; Wimbledon School of Art; Slade School of Fine Art. NDD; DFA London. Part-time Lecturer in Illustration, Faculty of Art, Brighton Polytechnic, 1961–87. *Publications:* The Strange House, 1961; Midnight Adventure, 1961; Ring-A-Ring O'Roses, 1962; Sledges to the Rescue, 1963; The White Land, 1963; Fee Fi Fo Fum, 1964; The Mother Goose Treasury, 1966 (Kate Greenaway Medal, 1966); Jim and the Beanstalk, 1970; The Fairy Tale Treasury, 1972; Father Christmas, 1973 (Kate Greenaway Medal, 1973); Father Christmas Goes On Holiday, 1975; Fungus The Bogeyman, 1977; The Snowman, 1978 (animated film, 1982); Gentleman Jim, 1980 (play, Nottingham Playhouse, 1985); When the Wind Blows, 1982 (play, BBC Radio and Whitehall Th., 1983; text publd 1983; cassette 1984; animated film, 1987); Fungus the Bogeyman Plop-Up Book, 1982; The Tin-Pot Foreign General and the Old Iron Woman, 1984; The Snowman Pop-Up, 1986; Unlucky Wally, 1987; Unlucky Wally Twenty Years On, 1989. *Recreations:* gardening, reading, walking, second-hand bookshops. *Address:* Weston, Underhill Lane, Westmeston, Hassocks, Sussex BN6 8XG. *Club:* Groucho.

BRIGGS, Rear-Admiral Thomas Vallack, CB 1958; OBE (mil.) 1945; DL (Retd); a Vice-Patron, Royal Naval Association (President, 1971–76); *b* 6 April 1906; *e s* of late Admiral Sir Charles John Briggs, and Lady Briggs (*née* Wilson); *m* 1947, Estelle Burland Willing, Boston, USA; one step *s*. *Educ:* The Grange, Stevenage, Herts; Imperial Service College, Windsor. Joined Royal Navy 1924; served HMS Thunderer, Hood, Wishart, Antelope, Wolsey, Nelson, Excellent, and Faulkner, 1924–37; Advanced Gunnery Specialist; served War of 1939–45: HMS Ark Royal, 1939–40; AA Comdr HMS Excellent, 1941–42; HMS Newcastle, 1943–44; staff of Flag Officer 2nd in Command, Eastern Fleet, 1944–45 (OBE and despatches twice); HMS Renown, Queen Elizabeth and Nelson; HMS Comus, 1945–46; US Naval War Coll., Newport, RI, 1946–47; Dep. Dir. of Naval Ordnance (G), 1947–49; commanded 5th Destroyer Flotilla, HMS Solebay, 1949–50, and HMS Cumberland, 1953–54; IDC, 1951; Chief of Staff: Plymouth, 1952–53, Home Fleet and Eastern Atlantic, 1956–57; Rear-Adm. 1956; Asst Controller of the Navy, 1958, retired. Director: Hugh Stevenson & Sons Ltd, 1958–69; Hugh Stevenson & Sons (North East) Ltd, 1964; Bowater-Stevenson Containers Ltd, 1969–71; Free-Stay Holidays Ltd, 1971; Internat. Consumer Incentives Ltd, 1974–83; Meru Group Ltd, 1978–83. Vice-Chm., City of Westminster Soc. for Mentally Handicapped Children, 1969; Mem., Management Cttee, Haileybury and ISC Junior Sch., Windsor, 1959–80 (Chm., 1978–80); Life Governor, Haileybury and Imperial Service Coll., 1959 (Mem. Council, 1959–80); Pres., Haileybury Soc., 1973–74. Fellow, Inst. of Marketing, 1970–83. Chm., Aldeburgh Festival Club, 1979–80. DL Greater London, 1970–82 (Representative DL, Kingston upon Thames, 1970–79). *Recreations:* golf, shooting. *Address:* 29 Twin Bridge Road, Madison, Conn 06443, USA. *Clubs:* White's; RN Golfing Society, Aldeburgh Golf (Captain, 1981–82); RN Sailing Association; RN Ski; Madison Winter, Madison Art.

BRIGHOUSE, Prof. Timothy Robert Peter; Professor of Education and Head of Department, University of Keele, since 1989; *b* 15 Jan. 1940; *s* of Denison Brighouse and Mary Howard Brighouse; *m* 1st, 1962, Mary Elizabeth Demers (marr. diss. 1988); one *s* one *d*; 2nd, 1989, Elizabeth Ann (formerly Kearney). *Educ:* St Catherine's College, Oxford (MA Modern History); DipEd; DEd (CNAA) Oxford Poly, 1989. Head of History Dept, Cavendish Grammar Sch., Buxton, 1962–64; Dep. Head and Warden, Chepstow Comm. Coll., 1964–66; Asst Educn Officer, Monmouthshire Educn Dept, 1966–69; Sen. Asst Educn Officer, Bucks Educn Dept, 1969–74; Under-Sec., Educn, ACC, 1974–76; Dep. Educn Officer, ILEA, 1976–78; Chief Educn Officer, Oxon, 1978–89. *Publications:* Revolution in Education and Training (jt editor and author), 1986; Managing the National Curriculum (jt editor and author), 1990. *Recreations:* gardening, politics. *Address:* Willowbank, Old Road, Headington, Oxford OX3 8ZA. *T:* Oxford (0865) 66995.

BRIGHT, Colin Charles; HM Diplomatic Service; Deputy Head of Mission, Berne, since 1989; *b* 2 Jan. 1948; *s* of William Charles John Bright and Doris (*née* Sutton); *m* 1st, 1978, Helen-Anne Michie; 2nd, 1990, Jane Elizabeth Gurney Pease; one *d* decd. *Educ:* Christ's Hospital; St Andrews Univ. (MA Hons 1971). FCO, 1975–77; Bonn, 1977–79; FCO, 1979–83; seconded to Cabinet Office, 1983–85; British Trade Develt Office, NY, 1985–88. *Address:* c/o Foreign and Commonwealth Office, SW1A 2AH.

BRIGHT, Graham Frank James; MP (C) Luton South, since 1983 (Luton East, 1979–83); *b* 2 April 1942; *s* of late Robert Frank Bright and Agnes Mary (*née* Graham); *m* 1972, Valerie, *d* of late E. H. Woolliams; one *s*. *Educ:* Hassenbrook County Sch.; Thurrock Technical Coll. Marketing Exec., Pauls & White Ltd, 1958–70; Man. Dir, 1970–, and Chm., 1977–, Dietary Foods Ltd. PPS to Ministers of State, Home Office, 1984–87, DoE, 1988–89, to Paymaster Gen., 1989–90, to Prime Minister, 1990–. Mem. Select Cttee on House of Commons Services, 1982–84. Jt Sec. to Parly Aviation Gp, 1984–; Chm., Cons. Backbench Smaller Businesses Cttee, 1983–84, 1987–88 (Vice-Chm., 1980–83; Sec., 1979–80); Vice-Chairman: Cons. Backbench Food and Drink Sub-Cttee, 1983 (Sec., 1983–85); Backbench Aviation Cttee, 1987–88; former Sec., Space Sub-Cttee;

Introduced Private Member's Bill (Video Recordings Act), 1984. Member: Thurrock Bor. Council, 1966–79; Essex CC, 1967–70. Contested: Thurrock, 1970 and Feb. 1974; Dartford, Oct. 1974; Chm., Eastern Area CPC, 1977–79; Mem., Nat. CPC, 1980–; Vice Chm., YC Org., 1970–72; Pres., Eastern Area YCs, 1981–. Dir, Smaller Businesses Bureau, 1989– (Vice Chm., 1980–89). *Publications:* pamphlets on airports, small businesses, education. *Recreations:* golf, gardening. *Address:* House of Commons, SW1A 0AA. *T:* 071–219 5156. *Club:* Carlton.

BRIGHT, Sir Keith, Kt 1987; PhD, CChem, FRSC, FCIT; Chairman, Electrocomponents plc, since 1990 (Chief Executive, 1989–90; Director, since 1986); *b* 30 Aug. 1931; *s* of Ernest William Bright and Lilian Mary Bright; *m* 1st, 1959, Patricia Anne Harrison (marr. diss.); one *s* one *d*; 2nd, 1985, Margot Joan Norman; one *d*. *Educ:* University of London (BSc, PhD). Chief of Research, Passfield Research Laboratories; Man. Dir, Formica International Ltd, 1967–73; Group Chief Exec., Sime Darby (Holdings) Ltd, 1974–77; Group Chief Exec., Associated Biscuit Manufacturers Ltd, 1977–82; Chm. and Chief Exec., LTE, subseq. LRT, 1982–88. Mem., British Airports Authy, 1982–85; Director: Extel Group, 1979–87; London & Continental Advertising, 1979–87; Chm., Thomas Goode & Co., 1988–. *Publications:* numerous papers in technical and scientific jls. *Recreations:* music, golf. *Address:* (office) 21 Knightsbridge, SW1X 7LY.

BRIGHTLING, Peter Henry Miller; Assistant Under Secretary of State, Ministry of Defence, 1973–81; *b* 12 Sept. 1921; *o s* of late Henry Miller Brightling and Eva Emily Brightling (*née* Fry); *m* 1951, Pamela Cheeseright; two *s* two *d*. *Educ:* City of London Sch.; BSc(Econ), London. War of 1939–45: Air Ministry, 1939–40; MAP, 1940–41; served in RAF, 1941–46. Ministry of: Supply, 1946–59; Aviation, 1959–67; Technology, 1967–70; Aviation Supply, 1970–71; MoD (Procurement Executive), 1971. *Address:* 5 Selwyn Road, New Malden, Surrey KT3 5AU. *T:* 081–942 8014.

BRIGHTMAN, family name of **Baron Brightman.**

BRIGHTMAN, Baron *cr* 1982 (Life Peer), of Ibthorpe in the County of Hampshire; **John Anson Brightman;** Kt 1970; PC 1979; a Lord of Appeal in Ordinary, 1982–86; *b* 20 June 1911; 2nd *s* of William Henry Brightman, St Albans, Herts; *m* 1945, Roxane Ambatielo; one *s*. *Educ:* Marlborough College; St John's College, Cambridge (Hon. Fellow, 1982). Called to the Bar, Lincoln's Inn, 1932; Bencher 1966. QC 1961. Able Seaman, Merchant Navy, 1939–40; RNVR (Lieut-Commander), 1940–46; Assistant Naval Attaché, Ankara, 1944. Attorney-General of the Duchy of Lancaster, and Attorney and Serjeant within the County Palatine of Lancaster, 1969–70; Judge of the High Court of Justice, Chancery Div., 1970–79; a Lord Justice of Appeal, 1979–82; Judge, Nat. Industrial Relns Court, 1971–74. Chairman, House of Lords Select Committee: on Charities, 1983–84; on Abortion Law, 1987–88; on City of Bristol Develt, 1988; on Spitalfields Market, 1989. Member, General Council of the Bar, 1956–60, 1966–70. *Recreations:* sailing, ski-ing, mountain walking. *Address:* House of Lords, SW1A 0PW. *T:* 071–219 6262.

BRIGHTON, Peter, BSc, CEng, FIEE, FRAeS, CBIM; Director General, Engineering Employers' Federation, since 1989; *b* 26 March 1933; *s* of late Henry Charles Brighton and Ivy Irene Brighton (*née* Crane); *m* 1959, Anne Maureen Lewis Jones; one *d* (one *s* decd). *Educ:* Wisbech Grammar Sch.; Reading Univ. (BSc); RAF Technical Coll. and Staff Coll. Pilot, Engr and Attaché, RAF, 1955–71, retd as Wing Comdr. Man. Dir, Rockwell-Collins UK, 1974–77; Regional Man. Dir, Plessey Co., 1977–78; Man. Dir, Cossor Electronics Ltd, 1978–85; British Aerospace PLC: Divl Man. Dir, 1985–87; Co. Dir of Operations, 1988. Pres., Electronic Engineering Assoc., 1984–85. Mem. Ct, Cranfield Inst. of Technology, 1989–. Liveryman, Coachmakers and Coach Harness Makers Co., 1989; Freeman of City of London, 1989. *Publications:* articles on aviation topics in learned jls. *Recreations:* flying (current pilot's licence), bridge, golf. *Address:* St Andrew's Cottage, Church Lane, Much Hadham, Herts SG10 6DH. *T:* Much Hadham (027984) 2309. *Clubs:* Athenæum, Royal Air Force.

BRIGHTY, Anthony David, CMG 1984; CVO 1985; HM Diplomatic Service; Ambassador to Czech and Slovak Federal Republic, since 1991; *b* 7 Feb. 1939; *s* of C. P. J. Brighty and Winifred (*née* Turner); *m* 1st, 1963, Diana Porteous (marr. diss. 1979); two *s* two *d*; 2nd, 1982, Jane Docherty. *Educ:* Northgate Grammar Sch., Ipswich; Clare Coll., Cambridge (BA). Entered FO, 1961; Brussels, 1962–63; Havana, 1964–66; FO, 1967–69, resigned; joined S. G. Warburg & Co., 1969; reinstated in FCO, 1971; Saigon, 1973–74; UK Mission to UN, NY, 1975–78; RCDS, 1979; Head of Personnel Operations Dept, FCO, 1980–83; Counsellor, Lisbon, 1983–86; Dir, Cabinet of Sec.-Gen. of NATO, 1986–87; Resident Chm., CSSB, 1988; Ambassador to Cuba, 1989–91. *Address:* c/o Foreign and Commonwealth Office, SW1A 2AH.

BRIGINSHAW, family name of **Baron Briginshaw.**

BRIGINSHAW, Baron *cr* 1974 (Life Peer), of Southwark; **Richard William Briginshaw;** General Secretary, National Society of Operative Printers, Graphical and Media Personnel, 1951–75; Member, Council, Advisory, Conciliation and Arbitration Service, 1974–76; *b* Lambeth; married. *Educ:* Stuart School, London. Later studied economics, trade union and industrial law, and physical anthropology (UCL diploma course). Elected Asst Secretary, London Machine Branch of Union, 1938. Joined Services, 1940; subseq. in Army, saw service overseas in India, Iraq, Persia, Palestine, Egypt, France, etc; left Army, 1946. Returned to printing trade; re-elected to full-time trade union position, 1949. Vice-Pres. 1961–72, Mem. Exec. Council 1951–72, Printing and Kindred Trades Fedn; TUC: Mem. Gen. Council, 1965–75; Member of Finance and General Purposes, Economic, Organisation, and International Cttees; Member: BOTB, 1975–77; British Nat. Oil Corp., 1976–79. Pres. of two London Confs on World Trade Development, 1963. Member: Joint Committee on Manpower, 1965–70; Parly and Scientific Cttee, 1985–; Parly Gp for Energy Studies, 1979–. Patron, Coll. of Osteopaths, 1975–. Member: Bd of Govs, Dulwich Coll., 1967–72; Court, Cranfield Inst. of Technology. Hon. LLD New Brunswick, 1968. *Publications:* (four booklets): Britain's World Rating, 1962; Britain and the World Trade Conference, 1963; Britain's World Rating, 1964; Britain's Oil, the Big Sell Out?, 1979. *Recreations:* swimming, painting, music.

BRIGSTOCKE, family name of **Baroness Brigstocke.**

BRIGSTOCKE, Baroness *cr* 1990 (Life Peer), of Kensington in the Royal Borough of Kensington and Chelsea; **Heather Renwick Brigstocke;** consultant and company director; High Mistress of St Paul's Girls' School, 1974–89; *b* 2 Sept. 1929; *d* of late Sqdn-Ldr J. R. Brown, DFC and Mrs M. J. C. Brown, MA; *m* 1952, Geoffrey Brigstocke (*d* 1974); three *s* one *d*. *Educ:* Abbey Sch., Reading; Girton Coll., Cambridge (MA, Pt I Classics, Pt II Archaeolog. and Anthropol.); Univ. Winchester Reading Prize, 1950. Classics Mistress, Francis Holland Sch., London, SW1, 1951–53; part-time Classics Mistress, Godolphin and Latymer Sch., 1954–60; part-time Latin Teacher, National Cathedral Sch., Washington, DC, 1962–64; Headmistress, Francis Holland Sch., London, NW1, 1965–74. Member: Council, London House for Overseas Graduates, 1965– (Vice-Chm., 1975–80); Council, Middlesex Hosp. Med. Sch., 1971–80; Trustee, Nat. Gall., 1975–82; Mem., Cttee, AA, 1975–90; Governor, Wellington Coll., 1975–87; Pres., Bishop Creighton House Settlement, Fulham, 1977–; Governor, The Royal Ballet Sch., 1977–; Member Council: RHC, 1977–85; The City Univ., 1978–83; Pres., Girls' Schools Assoc., 1980–81; Trustee: Kennedy Meml Trust, 1980–85; City Technology Colleges Trust, 1987–; Governor, United World College of the Atlantic, 1980–85; Non-exec. Dir, LWT, 1982–90; Ind. Dir., The Times, 1990–; Mem. Council, RSA, 1983–87; Governor, Forest Sch., 1983–90; Mem. Council, St George's House, Windsor, 1984–90; Chairman: Autistic Care and Trng Develt Appeal, 1990–; Thames LWT Telethon Trust, 1990; Chm. of Trustees, Geffrye Mus., 1990–; Mem., HEA, 1989–; Mem., Modern Foreign Langs Wkg Gp, 1989–90. *Address:* House of Lords, SW1A 0PW. *T:* 071–219 3000.

BRIGSTOCKE, Rear-Adm. John Richard; Flag Officer, Flotilla Two, since 1991, re-titled Commander, UK Task Force Group, from April 1992; *b* 30 July 1945; *s* of late Rev. Canon George Edward Brigstocke and Mollie (*née* Sandford); *m* 1979, Heather Day; two *s*. *Educ:* Marlborough Coll.; BRNC, Dartmouth; RCDS. Joined RN, 1962; commands: HMS Upton; HMS Bacchante; HMS York; Capt. (D) 3rd Destroyer Squadron; BRNC Dartmouth; HMS Ark Royal. Younger Brother, Trinity House, 1981. *Recreations:* family, ski-ing, riding. *Address:* c/o Naval Secretary, Old Admiralty Building, Spring Gardens, SW1A 2BE.

BRILLIANT, Fredda, (Mrs Herbert Marshall); sculptor; *m* 1935, Herbert P. J. Marshall (*d* 1991). *Educ:* The Gymnasium (High Sch.), Lodz, Poland; Chelsea Art Sch. (drawing). Sculptor, 1934–; actress and singer, USA, 1930–33; actress and script writer in England, 1937–50. Sculptures include: Nehru, Krishna Menon, Indira Gandhi, Paul Robeson, Herbert Marshall, Mahatma Gandhi (in Tavistock Square; Gandhi model now in the Queen's Collection in Reading Room of St George's, Windsor Castle, 1983), Buckminster Fuller, Carl Albert, Sir Maurice Bowra, Lord Elwyn-Jones, Sir Isaac Hayward, Tom Mann, Dr Delyte Morris, Elie Wiesel, Pope John Paul II (work in progress). Exhibns in London include: Royal Academy, Leicester Galls, Royal Watercolour Soc., Whitechapel Gall., St Paul's Cathedral; other exhibns in Melbourne, Moscow, Bombay and Washington. Work in permanent collections: Nat. Art Gall., New Delhi; Mayakovsky Mus. and Shevchenko Mus., USSR; Southern Illinois Univ. FRSA; FIAL. Mem. Soc. of Portrait Sculptors. *Publications:* Biographies in Bronze (The Sculpture of Fredda Brilliant), 1986; The Black Virgin, 1986; Women in Power, 1987; *short stories:* Truth in Fiction, 1986. *Recreations:* writing lyrics, composing songs and singing, attending classical concerts. *Address:* c/o Center for Soviet Studies, Southern Illinois University, Carbondale, Illinois 62901, USA.

BRIMACOMBE, Prof. John Stuart, FRSE, FRSC; Roscoe Professor of Chemistry, University of Dundee, since 1969; *b* Falmouth, Cornwall, 18 Aug. 1935; *s* of Stanley Poole Brimacombe and Lillian May Kathleen Brimacombe (*née* Candy); *m* 1959, Eileen (*née* Gibson); four *d*. *Educ:* Falmouth Grammar Sch.; Birmingham Univ. (DSc). DSc Dundee Univ. Lectr in Chemistry, Birmingham Univ., 1961–69. Meldola Medallist, 1964. *Publications:* (co-author) Mucopolysaccharides, 1964; numerous papers, reviews, etc, in: Jl Chem. Soc., Carbohydrate Research, etc. *Recreations:* sport, swimming. *Address:* 29 Dalhousie Road, Barnhill, Dundee. *T:* Dundee (0382) 79214.

BRIMELOW, family name of **Baron Brimelow.**

BRIMELOW, Baron *cr* 1976 (Life Peer), of Tyldesley, Lancs; **Thomas Brimelow,** GCMG 1975 (KCMG 1968; CMG 1959); OBE 1954; Chairman, Occupational Pensions Board, 1978–82; *b* 25 Oct. 1915; *s* of late William Brimelow and Hannah Smith; *m* 1945, Jean E. Cull; two *d*. *Educ:* New Mills Grammar School; Oriel College, Oxford; Hon. Fellow, 1973. Laming Travelling Fellow of the Queen's College, Oxford, 1937, Hon. Fellow, 1974. Probationer Vice-Consul, Danzig, 1938; served in Consulate, Riga, 1939 and Consulate-Gen., New York, 1940; in charge of Consular Section of Embassy, Moscow, 1942–45; Foreign Office, 1945; Foreign Service Officer, Grade 7, 1946; First Sec. (Commercial), and Consul, Havana, 1948; trans. to Moscow, 1951; Counsellor (Commercial), Ankara, 1954; Head of Northern Department of the Foreign Office, 1956; Counsellor, Washington, 1960–63; Minister, British Embassy, Moscow, 1963–66; Ambassador to Poland, 1966–69; Dep. Under-Sec. of State, FCO, 1969–73; Permanent Under-Sec. of State, FCO, and Head of the Diplomatic Service, 1973–75. Mem., European Parlt, 1977–78. *Address:* 12 West Hill Court, Millfield Lane, N6 6JJ. *Club:* Athenæum.

BRINCKMAN, Sir Theodore (George Roderick), 6th Bt *cr* 1831; publisher and antiquarian bookseller; *b* 20 March 1932; *s* of Sir Roderick Napoleon Brinckman, 5th Bt, DSO, MC, and Margaret Wilson Southam; *S* father, 1985; *m* 1st, 1958, Helen Mary Anne Cook (marr. diss. 1983); two *s* one *d*; 2nd, 1983, Hon. Greta Sheira Bernadette Murray, formerly wife of Christopher Murray, and *d* of Baron Harvington, *qv*. *Educ:* Trinity College School, Port Hope, Ontario; Millfield; Christ Church, Oxford; Trinity Coll., Toronto (BA). *Heir:* *s* Theodore Jonathan Brinckman, *b* 19 Feb. 1960. *Address:* Somerford Keynes House, Cirencester, Glos GL7 6DN. *T:* Cirencester (0285) 861526, 860554. *Clubs:* White's; University (Toronto).

BRIND, (Arthur) Henry, CMG 1973; HM Diplomatic Service, retired; *b* 4 July 1927; *o s* of late T. H. Brind and late N. W. B. Brind; *m* 1954, Barbara Harrison; one *s* one *d*. *Educ:* Barry; St John's Coll., Cambridge. HM Forces, 1947–49. Colonial Administrative Service: Gold Coast/Ghana, 1950–60; Regional Sec., Trans-Volta Togoland, 1959. HM Diplomatic Service, 1960–87: Acting High Comr, Uganda, 1972–73; High Comr, Mauritius, 1974–77; Ambassador to Somali Democratic Republic, 1977–80; Vis. Research Fellow, RIIA, 1981–82; High Comr, Malaŵi, 1983–87. Grand Comdr, Order of Lion of Malaŵi, 1985. *Recreations:* walking, swimming, books. *Address:* 20 Grove Terrace, NW5 1PH. *T:* 071–267 1190. *Club:* Reform.

BRIND, Maj.-Gen. Peter Holmes Walter; CBE 1962 (OBE 1948); DSO 1945; DL; Vice President, Surrey Branch, British Red Cross Society, since 1984 (Deputy President, 1977–84); *b* 16 Feb. 1912; *yr s* of late General Sir John Brind, KCB, KBE, CMG, DSO; *m* 1942, Patricia Stewart Walker, *er d* of late Comdr S. M. Walker, DSC, RN, Horsalls, Harrietsham, Kent; three *s*. *Educ:* Wellington College; RMC, Sandhurst. Commissioned Dorset Regt, 1932. ADC to Governor of Bengal, 1936–39; Adjt, NW Europe, 1940; GSO 3 War Office, 1940–41; DAAG, HQ 12 Corps and Canadian Corps, 1941–42; Bde Major 1942; GSO 2 (MO) War Office, 1942; Comdt, Battle School, 1944, Comdg 2 Devons, NW Europe, 1944–45, GSO 1 (MT) War Office, 1946; GSO 1 (Ops), Palestine, 1948; GSO 1 (Plans), Egypt, 1949; GSO 1 (SD), War Office, 1950–54; Bt Lt-Col, 1952; Comdg 5th KAR (Kenya), 1954; Lt-Col, 1954; Col, 1955; Comdg 5 Inf. Bde Gp (BAOR), 1956; IDC 1959; Brig., 1960; Brig., AQ Middle East, 1960; BGS Eastern Comd, 1962; ADC to the Queen, 1964; Maj.-Gen., 1965; COS, Northern Comd, 1965–67. Dir, BRCS (Surrey Branch), 1968–77. DL Surrey, 1970. *Recreations:* gardening, music. *Address:* Milestones, Hill Road, Haslemere, Surrey GU27 2JN.

BRINDLEY, Prof. Giles Skey, MA, MD; FRS 1965; FRCP; Professor of Physiology in the University of London at the Institute of Psychiatry, 1968–Sept. 1992; Hon. Director, Medical Research Council Neurological Prostheses Unit, 1968–Sept. 1992; Hon.

Consultant Physician, Maudsley Hospital, since 1971; *b* 30 April 1926; *s* of late Arthur James Benet Skey and Dr Margaret Beatrice Marion Skey (*née* Dewhurst), later Brindley; *m* 1st, 1959, Lucy Dunk Bennell (marr. diss.); 2nd, 1964, Dr Hilary Richards; one *s* one *d*. *Educ*: Leyton County High School; Downing College, Cambridge (Hon. Fellow, 1969); London Hospital Medical College. Various jun. clin. and res. posts, 1950–54; Russian lang. abstractor, British Abstracts of Medical Sciences, 1953–56; successively Demonstrator, Lectr and Reader in physiology, Univ. of Cambridge, 1954–68; Fellow: King's Coll., Cambridge, 1959–62; Trinity Coll., Cambridge, 1963–68. Chm. of Editorial Board, Journal of Physiology, 1964–66 (Member 1959–64). Visiting Prof., Univ. of California, Berkeley, 1968. Hon. FRCS 1988. Liebrecht-Franceschetti Prize, German Ophthalmological Soc., 1971; Feldberg Prize, Feldberg Foundn, 1974; St Peter's Medal, British Assoc. of Urological Surgeons, 1987. *Publications*: Physiology of the Retina and Visual Pathway, 1960, 2nd edn 1970; papers in scientific, musicological and medical journals. *Recreations*: ski-ing, orienteering, cross-country and track running (UK over-55 and over-60 record holder, 3000m steeplechase), designing, making and playing various musical instruments (inventor of the logical bassoon). *Address*: 102 Ferndene Road, SE24 0AA. *T*: 071–274 2598. *Club*: Thames Hare and Hounds.

BRINK, Prof. André Philippus, DLitt; Professor of English, University of Cape Town, since 1991; *b* 29 May 1935; *s* of Daniel Brink and Aletta Wilhelmina Wolmarans; three *s* one *d*. *Educ*: Potchefstroom Univ. (MA Eng. Lit. 1958, MA Afr. Lit. 1959); Rhodes Univ. (DLitt 1975). Rhodes University: Lectr, 1961; Sen. Lectr, 1975; Associate Prof., 1977; Prof. of Afrikaans and Dutch Literature, 1980–91. Hon. DLitt Witwatersrand, 1985. Prix Médicis étranger, 1981; Martin Luther King Meml Prize, 1981. Chevalier de la Légion d'honneur, 1982; Officier, l'Ordre des Arts et des Lettres, 1987. *Publications*: in Afrikaans: Die meul teen die hang, 1958; over 40 titles (novels, plays, travel books, literary criticism, humour); in English: Looking on Darkness, 1974; An Instant in the Wind, 1976; Rumours of Rain, 1978; A Dry White Season, 1979; A Chain of Voices, 1982; Mapmakers (essays), 1983; The Wall of the Plague, 1984; The Ambassador, 1985; (ed with J. M. Coetzee) A Land Apart, 1986; States of Emergency, 1988; An Act of Terror, 1991. *Address*: University of Cape Town, Rondebosch, 7700, South Africa.

BRINK, Prof. Charles Oscar, LittD Cambridge; PhD Berlin; FBA; Kennedy Professor of Latin in the University of Cambridge, 1954–74, now Kennedy Professor Emeritus; Fellow of Gonville and Caius College, since 1955; *b* 13 March 1907; *m* 1942, Daphne Hope Harvey; three *s*. *Educ*: School and University, Berlin; Travelling Scholarship, Oxford. Member of editorial staff, Thesaurus linguæ Latinæ, 1933–38; Member of editorial staff, Oxford Latin Dictionary, 1938–41; Acting Classical Tutor, Magdalen College, Oxford, 1941–45; Member of Faculty of Literæ Humaniores, Oxford, 1941–48; MA Oxford (decree, 1944); Senior Classics Master, Magdalen College School, Oxford, 1943–48; Senior Lecturer in Humanity, University of St Andrews, 1948–51; Professor of Latin, University of Liverpool, 1951–54; MA Cambridge (BIII 6), 1954. Member Inst. for Advanced Study, Princeton, US, 1960–61, 1966. De Carle Lecturer, University of Otago, NZ, 1965; Vis. Prof., Univ. of Bonn, 1970; Professore Ospite Linceo, Scuola Normale Superiore, Pisa, 1977; James C. Loeb Lectr, Harvard Univ., 1978; Woodward Lectr, Yale Univ., 1989. Hon. Member, Jt Assoc. of Classical Teachers (Pres. 1969–71). Chm., Classics Committee, Schools Council, 1965–69; Trustee, Robinson Coll., Cambridge, 1973–85 (Chm., 1975–85; Hon. Fellow, 1985–). Pres., Internat. Commn, Thesaurus Linguæ Latinæ, 1988– (Vice-Pres., 1979–88). Corresp. Mem., Bayerische Akad. der Wissenschaften, Munich, 1972–. Founding Jt Editor, Cambridge Classical Texts and Commentaries, 1963–87. *Publications*: Imagination and Imitation (Inaug. Lect., Liverpool, 1952), 1953; Latin Studies and the Humanities (Inaug. Lect., Cambridge, 1956), 1957; On reading a Horatian Satire, 1965; Horace on Poetry: vol. I, Prolegomena, 1963; vol. II, The Ars Poetica, 1971; vol III, Epistles Book II, 1982; Studi classici e critica testuale in Inghilterra (Pisa), 1978; English Classical Scholarship: historical reflections on Bentley, Porson, and Housman, 1986; papers on Latin and Greek subjects. *Address*: Gonville and Caius College, Cambridge CB2 1TA.

BRINK, David Maurice, DPhil; FRS 1981; Fellow and Tutor, Balliol College, Oxford, since 1958; H. J. G. Moseley Reader in Physics, Oxford University, since 1989; *b* 20 July 1930; *s* of Maurice Ossian Brink and Victoria May Finlayson; *m* 1958, Verena Wehrli; one *s* two *d*. *Educ*: Friends' Sch., Hobart; Univ. of Tasmania (BSc); Univ. of Oxford (DPhil). Rhodes Scholar, 1951–54; Rutherford Scholar, 1954–58; Lecturer, Balliol Coll., Oxford, 1954–58; Univ. Lectr, Oxford, 1958–89. Instructor, MIT, 1956–57. Rutherford Medal and Prize, Inst. of Physics, 1982. *Publications*: Angular Momentum, 1962, 2nd edn 1968; Nuclear Forces, 1965; Semi-classical Methods in Nucleus–Nucleus Scattering, 1985. *Recreations*: birdwatching, mountaineering. *Address*: 34 Minster Road, Oxford OX4 1LY. *T*: Oxford (0865) 246127.

BRINLEY JONES, Robert; *see* Jones.

BRINTON, Timothy Denis; self-employed broadcasting consultant, presentation tutor and communications adviser; *b* 24 Dec. 1929; *s* of late Dr Denis Hubert Brinton; *m* 1st, 1954, Jane-Mari Coningham; one *s* three *d*; 2nd, 1965, Jeanne Frances Wedge; two *d*. *Educ*: Summer Fields, Oxford; Eton Coll., Windsor; Geneva Univ.; Central Sch. of Speech and Drama. BBC staff, 1951–59; ITN, 1959–62; freelance, 1962–. Mem., Kent CC, 1974–81. Chm., Dartford Gravesham HA, 1988–90. MP (C): Gravesend, 1979–83; Gravesham, 1983–87. Court, Univ. of London, 1978–; Med. Sch. Council, St Mary's Hosp., Paddington, 1983–88. Member: BAFTA; RTS. Gov., Wye Coll., London Univ., 1989–. *Address*: 78 Lupus Street, SW1V 3EL. *T*: 071-834 1181; Westwell House, Tenterden, Kent TN30 6TT. *T*: Tenterden (05806) 3030. *Club*: Reform.

BRISBANE, Archbishop of, and Metropolitan of the Province of Queensland, since 1990; **Most Rev. Peter John Hollingworth**, AO 1988; OBE 1976; *b* 10 April 1935; *m* 1960, Kathleen Ann Turner; three *d*. *Educ*: Murrumbeena and Lloyd Street State Schools; Scotch Coll., Melbourne; Trinity Coll., Univ. of Melbourne (BA 1958; MA 1981); Australian Coll. of Theol. (ThL 1960); Univ. of Melbourne (Dip. Social Studies, 1969). Commercial Cadet, Broken Hill Pty, 1952–53. Priest in charge, St Mary's, N Melbourne, 1960–64; Brotherhood of St Laurence: Chaplain and Dir of Youth Work, 1964–70; Assoc. Dir, 1970–79; Exec. Dir, 1980–90; Canon, St Paul's Cathedral, Melbourne, 1980; Bishop in the Inner City, dio. of Melbourne, 1985–90. Mem., Australian Assoc. of Social Workers, 1970–78. Hon. LLD: Monash, 1986; Melbourne, 1990. *Publications*: Australians in Poverty, 1978; The Powerless Poor, 1972; The Poor: victims of affluence, 1974. *Recreations*: writing, reading, swimming. *Address*: Bishopsbourne, 39 Elderwell Avenue, Hamilton, Qld 4007, Australia.

BRISBANE, Archbishop of, (RC), since 1973; **Most Rev. Francis Roberts Rush**, DD; *b* 11 Sept. 1916; *s* of T. J. Rush. *Educ*: Christian Brothers' Coll., Townsville; Mt Carmel, Charters Towers; St Columba's Coll., Springwood; Coll. de Propaganda Fide, Rome. Assistant Priest, Townsville, Mundingburra and Ingham; Parish Priest, Abergowrie and Ingham; Bishop of Rockhampton, 1960–73. *Address*: Wynberg, 790 Brunswick Street, New Farm, Queensland 4005, Australia.

BRISBANE, Assistant Bishops of; *see* Browning, Rt Rev. G. V., Charles, Rt Rev. A. O.

BRISCO, Sir Donald Gilfrid, 8th Bt *cr* 1782; JP; *b* 15 Sept. 1920; *s* of Sir Hylton (Musgrave Campbell) Brisco, 7th Bt and Kathleen (*d* 1982), *d* of W. Fenwick McAllum, New Zealand; *S* father, 1968; *m* 1945, Irene, *o d* of Henry John Gage, Ermine Park, Brockworth, Gloucestershire; three *d*. Served War of 1939–45 with Royal New Zealand Air Force and Royal Air Force (prisoner of war in Germany and Italy). Retired Farmer. JP Hawke's Bay, 1967. *Heir: cousin* Campbell Howard Brisco [*b* 1944; *m* 1969, Kay Janette, *d* of Ewan W. McFadzien; two *s* one *d*]. *Address*: 27a Chambers Street, PO Box 8165, Havelock North, Hawke's Bay, New Zealand.

BRISCOE, Brian Anthony; Chief Executive, Hertfordshire County Council, since 1990; *b* 29 July 1945; *s* of Anthony Brown Briscoe and Lily Briscoe; *m* 1969, Sheila Mary Cheyne; three *s*. *Educ*: Newcastle Royal Grammar Sch.; St Catharine's Coll., Cambridge (MA, DipTP). MRTPI, ARICS. Asst Planner, Derbyshire CC, 1967–71; Section Head, Herefordshire CC, 1971–74; Asst Chief Planner, W Yorks CC, 1974–79; Dep. County Planning Officer, Herts, 1979–88; County Planning Officer, Kent, 1988–90. FRSA. *Publications*: contribs to planning and property jls; chapter in English Structure Planning, 1982. *Recreations*: family, golf, Newcastle United FC. *Address*: County Hall, Hertford SG13 8DE. *T*: Hertford (0992) 555601.

BRISCOE, Sir John (Leigh Charlton), 4th Bt *cr* 1910; DFC 1945; *b* 3 Dec. 1911; *er s* of Sir Charlton Briscoe, 3rd Bt, MD, FRCP, and Grace Maud (*d* 1973) *d* of late Rev. W. S. Stagg; *S* father 1960; *m* 1948, Teresa Mary Violet, OBE 1972, *d* of late Brig.-Gen. Sir Archibald Home, KCVO, CB, CMG, DSO; two *s* one *d*. *Educ*: Harrow; Magdalen College, Oxford, BA 1933; ACA 1937; MA 1949. Served War of 1939–45 (DFC); RAFVR, 1942–46; Director of Aerodromes, Ministry of Aviation, 1961–66; Dir of Operations, British Airports Authy, 1966–72. *Recreations*: old cars, castles, and carpets. *Heir: s* John James Briscoe, [*b* 15 July 1951; *m* 1985, Felicity M., *e d* of D. M. Watkinson]. *Address*: Little Acres, Grays Park Road, Stoke Poges, Bucks. *T*: Farnham Common (02814) 2394. *Club*: Royal Air Force.

BRISE; *see* Ruggles-Brise.

BRISON, Ven. William Stanley; CMS Missionary, Nigeria, since 1992; *b* 20 Nov. 1929; *s* of William P. Brison and Marion A. Wilber; *m* 1951, Marguerite Adelia Nettleton; two *s* two *d*. *Educ*: Alfred Univ., New York (BS Eng); Berkeley Divinity School, New Haven, Conn (STM, MDiv). United States Marine Corps, Captain (Reserve), 1951–53. Engineer, Norton Co., Worcester, Mass, 1953–54. Vicar, then Rector, Christ Church, Bethany, Conn, 1957–69; Archdeacon of New Haven, Conn, 1967–69; Rector, Emmanuel Episcopal Church, Stamford, Conn, 1969–72; Vicar, Christ Church, Davyhulme, Manchester, 1972–81; Rector, All Saints', Newton Heath, Manchester, 1981–85; Area Dean of North Manchester, 1981–85; Archdeacon of Bolton, 1985–91; Archdeacon Emeritus, 1991. *Recreations*: squash, jogging, hiking. *Address*: c/o Hulme, 1 College Road, Oldham OL8 4HU.

BRISTER, William Arthur Francis, CB 1984; Deputy Director General of Prison Service, 1982–85; *b* 10 Feb. 1925; *s* of Arthur John Brister and Velda Mirandoli; *m* 1949, Mary Speakman; one *s* one *d* (and one *s* decd). *Educ*: Douai Sch.; Brasenose Coll., Oxford (MA 1949). Asst Governor Cl. II, HM Borstal, Lowdham Grange, 1949–52; Asst Principal, Imperial Trng Sch., Wakefield, 1952–55; Asst Governor II, HM Prison, Parkhurst, 1955–57; Dep. Governor, HM Prison: Camp Hill, 1957–60; Manchester, 1960–62; Governor, HM Borstal: Morton Hall, 1962–67; Dover, 1967–69; Governor II, Prison Dept HQ, 1969–71; Governor, HM Remand Centre, Ashford, 1971–73; Governor I, Prison Dept HQ, 1973–75, Asst Controller, 1975–79; Chief Inspector of the Prison Service, 1979–81; HM Dep. Chief Inspector of Prisons, 1981–82. Mem., Parole Board, 1986–89. Nuffield Travelling Fellow, Canada and Mexico, 1966–67. *Recreations*: shooting, music, Venetian history. *Clubs*: United Oxford & Cambridge University, English-Speaking Union.

BRISTOL, 7th Marquess of, *cr* 1826; **Frederick William John Augustus Hervey;** Baron Hervey of Ickworth, 1703; Earl of Bristol, 1714; Earl Jermyn, 1826; Hereditary High Steward of the Liberty of St Edmund; Governing Partner, Jermyn Shipping; Director, Bristol Estates Ltd; *b* 15 Sept. 1954; *s* of 6th Marquess of Bristol and Pauline Mary, *d* of Herbert Coxon Bolton; *S* father, 1985; *m* 1984, Francesca (marr. diss.), *d* of Douglas Fisher. *Educ*: Harrow; Neuchâtel Univ. MInstD. *Heir*: half-*b* Lord Frederick William Charles Nicholas Wentworth Hervey, *b* 26 Nov. 1961. *Address*: Ickworth, Bury St Edmunds, Suffolk. *Clubs*: House of Lords Yacht, Royal Thames Yacht; Travellers' (Paris); Monte Carlo Country.

BRISTOL, Bishop of, since 1985; **Rt. Rev. Barry Rogerson;** *b* 25 July 1936; *s* of Eric and Olive Rogerson; *m* 1961, Olga May Gibson; two *d*. *Educ*: Magnus Grammar School; Leeds Univ. (BA Theology). Midland Bank Ltd, 1952–57; Leeds Univ. and Wells Theol Coll., 1957–62; Curate: St Hilda's, South Shields, 1962–65; St Nicholas', Bishopwearmouth,. Sunderland, 1965–67; Lecturer, Lichfield Theological Coll., 1967–71, Vice-Principal, 1971–72; Lectr, Salisbury and Wells Theol Coll., 1972–75; Vicar, St Thomas', Wednesfield, 1975–79; Team Rector, Wednesfield Team Ministry, 1979; Bishop Suffragan of Wolverhampton, 1979–85. Chm., ACCM, 1987–. *Recreations*: cinema and stained glass windows. *Address*: Bishop's House, Clifton Hill, Bristol BS8 1BW.

BRISTOL, Dean of; *see* Carr, Very Rev. A. W.

BRISTOL, Archdeacon of; *see* Banfield, Ven. D. J.

BRISTOW, Alan Edgar, OBE 1966; Chairman: Briway Transit Systems, since 1985; Air & Ocean Aids Ltd, since 1985; *b* 3 Sept. 1923; *m* 1945; one *s* one *d*. *Educ*: Portsmouth Grammar School. Cadet, British India Steam Navigation Co., 1939–43; Pilot, Fleet Air Arm, 1943–46; Test Pilot, Westland Aircraft Ltd, 1946–49; Helicopair, Paris/Indo-China, 1949–51; Man. Dir, Air Whaling Ltd (Antarctic Whaling Expedns), 1951–54; Man. Dir, then Chm., Bristow Helicopters Ltd, 1954–85; Dir, British United Airways Ltd, 1960–70, Man. Dir 1967–70. Cierva Memorial Lectr, RAeS, 1967. FRAeS 1967. Croix de Guerre (France), 1950. *Publications*: papers to RAeS. *Recreations*: flying, shooting, sailing, farming, four-in-hand driving. *Address*: Baynards Park Estate, Cranleigh, Surrey GU6 8EE. *T*: Cranleigh (0483) 277170.

BRISTOW, Hon. Sir Peter (Henry Rowley), Kt 1970; a Judge of the High Court, Queen's Bench Division, 1970–85; *b* 1 June 1913; *s* of Walter Rowley Bristow, FRCS and Florence (*née* White); *m* 1st, 1940, Josephine Noel Leney (*d* 1969); one *s* one *d*; 2nd, 1975, Elsa, *widow* of H. B. Leney. *Educ*: Eton; Trinity College, Cambridge. Pilot, RAFVR, 1936–45. Called to the Bar, Middle Temple, 1936, Bencher 1961, Treasurer 1977; QC 1964; Mem., Inns of Court Senate, 1966–70 (Hon. Treas., 1967–70); Judge, Court of Appeal, Guernsey, and Court of Appeal, Jersey, 1965–70; Dep. Chm., Hants QS, 1964–71; Judge of the Commercial Court and Employment Appeals Tribunal, 1976–78; Vice-Chm., Parole Bd, 1977–78 (Mem. 1976); Presiding Judge, Western Circuit, 1979–82. *Publication*: Judge for Yourself, 1986. *Recreations*: fishing, gardening. *Address*: The Folly, Membury, Axminster, Devon EX13 7AG.

BRITISH COLUMBIA, Metropolitan of Ecclesiastical Province of; *see* New Westminster, Archbishop of.

BRITISH COLUMBIA, Bishop of, since 1985; **Rt. Rev. Ronald Francis Shepherd;** *b* 15 July 1926; *s* of Herbert George Shepherd and Muriel Shepherd (*née* Grant); *m* 1952, Ann Alayne Dundas, *d* of Rt Hon. R. S. Dundas; four *s* two *d*. *Educ:* Univ. of British Columbia (BA Hons 1948); King's Coll., London (AKC 1952). Fellow, Coll. of Preachers, Washington, DC, 1972. Curate, St Stephen's, Rochester Row, London SW, 1952–57; Rector: St Paul's, Glanford, Ont, 1957–59; All Saints, Winnipeg, 1959–65; Dean and Rector: All Saints Cathedral, Edmonton, 1965–69; Christ Church Cathedral, Montreal, 1970–83; Rector, St Matthias, Victoria, 1983–84. Hon. DDiv. St John's Coll., Winnipeg, 1988. *Recreations:* reading, gardening, walking. *Address:* 1256 Beach Drive, Victoria, BC V8S 2N3, Canada. *T:* 604-598 7882. *Club:* Union of British Columbia (Victoria).

BRITTAN, Rt. Hon. Sir Leon, Kt 1989; PC 1981; QC 1978; a Vice-President, Commission of the European Communities, since 1989; *b* 25 Sept. 1939; *s* of late Dr Joseph Brittan and Mrs Rebecca Brittan; *m* 1980, Diana Peterson. *Educ:* Haberdashers' Aske's Sch.; Trinity Coll., Cambridge (MA); Yale Univ. (Henry Fellow). Chm., Cambridge Univ. Conservative Assoc., 1960; Pres., Cambridge Union, 1960; debating tour of USA for Cambridge Union, 1961. Called to Bar, Inner Temple, 1962; Bencher, 1983. Chm., Bow Group, 1964–65; contested (C) North Kensington, 1966 and 1970. MP (C): Cleveland and Whitby, Feb. 1974–1983; Richmond, Yorks, 1983–88. Editor, Crossbow, 1966–68; formerly Mem. Political Cttee, Carlton Club; Vice-Chm. of Governors, Isaac Newton Sch., 1968–71; Mem. European North American Cttee, 1970–78; Vice-Chm., Nat. Assoc. of School Governors and Managers, 1970–78; Vice-Chm., Parly Cons. Party Employment Cttee, 1974–76; opposition front bench spokesman on Devolution, 1976–79, on employment, 1978–79; Minister of State, Home Office, 1979–81; Chief Sec. to the Treasury, 1981–83; Sec. of State for Home Dept, 1983–85; Sec. of State for Trade and Industry, 1985–86. Chm., Soc. of Cons. Lawyers, 1986–88. Hersch Lauterpacht Meml Lectr, Cambridge, 1990. Hon. DCL Newcastle, 1990; Hon. LLD Hull, 1990. *Publications:* (contrib.) The Conservative Opportunity; pamphlets: Millstones for the Sixties (jtly), Rough Justice, Infancy and the Law, How to Save Your Schools, To spur, not to mould, A New Deal for Health Care, Discussions on Policy, Monetary Union. *Recreations:* opera, art, cricket, walking. *Address:* Commission of the European Communities, 200 rue de la Loi, 1049 Brussels, Belgium. *Clubs:* Carlton, MCC.
See also Samuel Brittan.

BRITTAN, Samuel; Principal Economic Commentator, since 1966, and Assistant Editor, since 1978, Financial Times; *b* 29 Dec. 1933; *s* of late Joseph Brittan, MD, and of Rebecca Brittan (*née* Lipetz). *Educ:* Kilburn Grammar Sch.; Jesus Coll., Cambridge (Hon. Fellow, 1988). 1st Class in Economics, 1955; MA Cantab. Various posts in Financial Times, 1955–61; Economics Editor, Observer, 1961–64; Adviser, DEA, 1965. Fellow, Nuffield Coll., Oxford, 1973–74, Vis. Fellow, 1974–82; Vis. Prof. of Economics, Chicago Law Sch., 1978; Hon. Prof. of Politics, Warwick Univ., 1987–. Mem., Peacock Cttee on Financing the BBC, 1985–86. Hon. DLitt Heriot-Watt, 1985. Financial Journalist of the Year Award 1971; George Orwell Prize (for political journalism), 1980; Ludwig Erhard Prize (for economic writing), 1988. *Publications:* The Treasury under the Tories, 1964, rev. edn, Steering the Economy, 1969, 1971; Left or Right: The Bogus Dilemma, 1968; The Price of Economic Freedom, 1970; Capitalism and the Permissive Society, 1973, rev. edn as A Restatement of Economic Liberalism, 1988; Is There an Economic Consensus?, 1973; (with P. Lilley) The Delusion of Incomes Policy, 1977; The Economic Consequences of Democracy, 1977; How to End the Monetarist Controversy, 1981; The Role and Limits of Government, 1983; articles in various jls. *Address:* c/o Financial Times, Number One Southwark Bridge, SE1 9HL.
See also Rt Hon. Sir Leon Brittan.

BRITTEN, Alan Edward Marsh; Regional Vice-President, Mobil Europe, since 1991; *b* 26 Feb. 1938; *s* of Robert Harry Marsh Britten and Helen Marjorie (*née* Goldson); *m* 1967, Judith Clare Akerman; two *d*. *Educ:* Radley; Emmanuel Coll., Cambridge (MA English); Williams Coll., Mass (American Studies). Mobil Oil Co.: joined 1961; marketing and planning, UK, USA, Italy; Chief Exec., Mobil Cos in E Africa, 1975–77, Denmark, 1980–81, Portugal, 1982–84, Benelux, 1984–86; Managing Dir, Mobil Oil Co., 1987–89; Manager, Internat. Planning, Mobil Oil Corp., 1989–91. Member: Council for Aldeburgh Foundn; Council, Royal Warrant Holders' Assoc.; Adv. Board, Ten Days at Princeton. *Recreations:* music, tourism, gardening, letter writing. *Address:* c/o Mobil Oil Co., 54–60 Victoria Street, SW1E 6QB. *T:* 071–828 9777. *Club:* Garrick.

BRITTEN, Brig. George Vallette, CBE 1947 (OBE 1942, MBE 1940); HM Diplomatic Service, retired; *b* 19 March 1909; *s* of John Britten, Bozeat Manor, Northamptonshire, and Elizabeth Franziska Britten (*née* Vallette); *m* 1937, Shirley Jean Stewart Wink; three *s*. *Educ:* Wellingborough; RMC Sandhurst. Regtl duty in UK, 1929–38; Staff Coll., Camberley, 1938–39. Served War: HQ 2 Corps, France and Belgium, 1939–40; Staff appts in UK, 1940–41; with 1st Airborne Div. in UK, N Africa and Sicily, 1942–43; DCS, 5(US) Army, N Africa and Italy, 1943–44; HQ, 21st Army Gp, NW Europe, 1944–45. DCS, Brit. Military Govt, Germany, 1945–47. Regtl Duty, Berlin and Austria, 1947–49; WO, 1949–51; Comdt, Sch. of Infty, Hythe, 1952–54; Instr, US Army Staff Coll., Kansas, 1954–56; Planning Staff, NATO, Fontainebleau, 1956–58; Mil. Attaché, Brit. Embassy, Bonn, 1958–61; retired from Army, 1961; Ghana Desk, Commonwealth Office, 1961–62; with British High Commissions, Enugu, Kaduna, and Bathurst, 1962–66; Head of Chancery, British Embassy, Berne, 1967–71. American Legion of Merit, 1946; W German Grosses Verdienst Kreuz, 1959. *Recreation:* gardening. *Address:* 41 Bosville Drive, Sevenoaks, Kent TN13 3JA.

BRITTEN, Rae Gordon, CMG 1972; HM Diplomatic Service, retired; *b* 27 Sept. 1920; *s* of Leonard Arthur Britten and Elizabeth Percival Taylor; *m* 1952, Valentine Alms (marr. diss. 1974); one *s* three *d*; *m* 1977, Mrs Joan Dorothy Bull. *Educ:* Liverpool Institute High School; Magdalen College, Oxford. Served War 1941–45 (artillery and infantry). Research Assistant with Common Ground Ltd, 1947; apptd Commonwealth Relations Office, 1948; 2nd Sec., Brit. High Commn in India (Calcutta, 1948–49, Delhi, 1949–50): 1st Sec. Brit. High Commn., Bombay, 1955–58, Karachi, 1961–62; Deputy High Commissioner: Peshawar, March 1962; Lahore, June 1962–July 1964; Kingston, Jamaica, 1964–68; Head of Trade Policy Dept, FCO, 1968–71; Dep. High Comr, Dacca, and British Rep. to Bangladesh, 1971–72; Counsellor and Head of Chancery, Oslo, 1973–76; Head of SW Pacific Dept, FCO, 1976–78; Counsellor on Special Duties, FCO, 1978–80. *Club:* Commonwealth Trust.

BRITTEN, Maj.-Gen. Robert Wallace Tudor, CB 1977; MC; *b* 28 Feb. 1922; *s* of Lt-Col Wallace Ernest Britten, OBE; *m* 1947, Elizabeth Mary, *d* of Edward H. Davies, Pentre, Rhondda; one *s* one *d*. *Educ:* Wellington Coll.; Trinity Coll., Cambridge. CBIM; CompICE. 2nd Lieut RE, 1941; served War of 1939–45, Madras Sappers and Miners, 19th Indian Div., India and Burma; Comdr 21 Fd Pk Sqn and 5 Fd Sqn RE, 1947–50; on staff WO, 1951–53; British Liaison Officer to US Corps of Engrs, 1953–56; comd 50 Fd Sqn RE, 1956–58; on staff WO, 1958–61; on staff of 1 (BR) Corps BAOR, 1961–64; Lt-Col in comd 1 Trg Regt RE, 1964–65; GSO1 (DS), Jt Services Staff Coll., 1965–67; Comd 30 Engr Bde (V) and Chief Engr Western Comd, 1967; idc 1969; Dir of Equipment Management, MoD (Army), 1970–71; DQMG, 1971–73; GOC West Midland Dist, 1973–76, retired. Brig. 1967; Maj.-Gen. 1971. Col Comdt, RE, 1977–82. Chm., RE Assoc., 1978–83. Hon. Col, Birmingham Univ. OTC, 1978–87. Dir, R and E Co-ordination Ltd. *Recreations:* bridge building, fishing, dowsing (Vice Pres., Brit. Soc. Dowsers). *T:* Haslemere (0428) 642261. *Club:* Army and Navy

BRITTENDEN, (Charles) Arthur; Senior Consultant, Lowe Bell Communications Ltd, since 1988; Director of Corporate Relations, News International, 1981–87; General Manager (Editorial), Times Newspapers, 1982–87; Director, Times Newspapers Ltd, 1982–87; *b* 23 Oct. 1924; *o s* of late Tom Edwin Brittenden and Caroline (*née* Scrivener); *m* 1st, 1953, Sylvia Penelope Cadman (marr. diss., 1960); 2nd, 1966, Ann Patricia Kenny (marr. diss. 1972); 3rd, 1975, Valerie Arnison. *Educ:* Leeds Grammar School. Served in Reconnaissance Corps, 1943–46. Yorkshire Post, 1940–43, 1946–49; News Chronicle, 1949–55; joined Sunday Express, 1955: Foreign Editor, 1959–62; Northern Editor, Daily Express, 1962–63; Dep. Editor, Sunday Express, 1963–64; Exec. Editor, 1964–66, Editor, 1966–71, Daily Mail; Dep. Editor, The Sun, 1972–81. Dir, Harmsworth Publications Ltd, 1967–71; Man. Dir, Wigmore Cassettes, 1971–72. Dir, Dowson-Shurman Associates Ltd, 1990–. Mem., 1982–86, Jt Vice-Chm., 1983–86, Press Council. *Address:* 22 Park Street, Woodstock, Oxon OX7 1SP.

BRITTON, Andrew James Christie; Director, National Institute of Economic and Social Research, since 1982; *b* 1 Dec. 1940; *s* of late Prof. Karl William Britton and Sheila Margaret Christie; *m* 1963, Pamela Anne, *d* of His Honour Edward Sutcliffe, *qv*; three *d*. *Educ:* Royal Grammar Sch., Newcastle upon Tyne; Oriel Coll., Oxford (BA); LSE (MSc). Joined HM Treasury as Cadet Economist, 1966; Econ. Asst, 1968; Econ. Adviser, 1970; Sen. Econ. Adviser: DHSS, 1973; HM Treasury, 1975; London Business Sch., 1978–79; Under Sec., HM Treasury, 1980–82. Licensed Reader, Dio. of Southwark, 1986–. Mem., Industry and Econ. Affairs Cttee, Gen. Synod, 1989–. *Publications:* (ed) Employment, Output and Inflation, 1983; The Trade Cycle in Britain, 1986; (ed) Policymaking with Macroeconomic Models, 1989; Macroeconomic Policy in Britain 1974–87, 1991. *Address:* 15 Hawthorn Road, Wallington, Surrey SM6 0SY. *Club:* United Oxford & Cambridge University.

BRITTON, Prof. Denis King, CBE 1978; Professor of Agricultural Economics at Wye College, 1970–83, now Emeritus Professor; Hon. Fellow, Wye College, 1986; *b* 25 March 1920; *s* of Rev. George Charles Britton and Harriet Rosa (*née* Swinstead); *m* 1942, Margaret Alice Smith; one *s* two *d*. *Educ:* Caterham School; London School of Economics, London University (BSc (Econ.)). Asst Statistician, Ministry of Agriculture and Fisheries, 1943–47; Lecturing and Research at University of Oxford, Agricultural Economics Res. Inst., 1947–52; MA Oxon 1948 (by decree); Economist, United Nations Food and Agriculture Organisation, Geneva, 1952–59; Gen. Manager, Marketing and Economic Res., Massey-Ferguson (UK) Ltd, 1959–61; Prof. of Agricultural Economics, Univ. of Nottingham, 1961–70; Dean, Faculty of Agriculture and Horticulture, Univ. of Nottingham, 1967–70. Member: EDC for Agriculture, 1966–83; Home Grown Cereals Authority, 1969–87; Adv. Council for Agriculture and Horticulture, 1973–80; Adv. Cttee, Nuffield Centre for Agric. Strategy, 1975–80; MAFF Gp to review Eggs Authority, 1985; Chairman: Council, Centre for European Agricl Studies, Wye Coll., 1974–79; Forestry Commn Rev. Gp on Integration of Farming and Forestry, 1983–84; President: Internat. Assoc. of Agric. Economists, 1976–79; British Agric. Economics Soc., 1977–78; Special Adviser, House of Commons Select Cttee on Agric., 1980–83. Vis. Prof., Uppsala, 1973; Winegarten Lecture, NFU, 1981. Farmers' Club Cup, 1966. FSS 1943; FRAgS 1970; FRASE 1980. Hon. DAgric, Univ. of Bonn, 1975; Hon. DEcon, Univ. of Padua, 1982. *Publications:* Cereals in the United Kingdom, 1969; (with Berkeley Hill) Size and Efficiency in Farming, 1975; (with H. F. Marks) A Hundred Years of British Food and Farming: a statistical survey, 1989; (ed) Agriculture in Britain: changing pressures and policies, 1990; articles in Jl of Royal Statistical Society, Jl of Agricultural Economics, Jl of RSA, Farm Economist, etc. *Recreations:* music, golf, micro-computing. *Address:* 29 Chequers Park, Wye, Ashford, Kent TN25 5BB.

BRITTON, Sir Edward (Louis), Kt 1975; CBE 1967; General Secretary, National Union of Teachers, 1970–75; retired; *b* 4 Dec. 1909; *s* of George Edwin and Ellen Alice Britton; *m* 1936, Nora Arnald; no *c*. *Educ:* Bromley Grammar School, Kent; Trinity College, Cambridge. Teacher in various Surrey schools until 1951; Headmaster, Warlingham County Secondary School, Surrey, 1951–60; General Secretary, Association of Teachers in Technical Institutions, 1960–68. Pres., National Union of Teachers, 1956–57. Sen. Res. Fellow, Educn Div., Sheffield Univ., 1975–79; Mem. of staff, Christ Church Coll., Canterbury, 1979–86. Vice-Pres., NFER, 1979–; Member: TUC General Council, 1970–74; Beloe Cttee on Secondary Schs Exams, 1960; Schools Council, 1964–75; Adv. Cttee for Supply and Trng of Teachers, 1973–75; Burnham Primary and Secondary Cttee, 1956–75 (Jt Sec. and Leader of Teachers' Panel, 1970–75); Burnham Further Educn Cttee, 1959–69 (Jt Sec. and Leader of Teachers' Panel, 1961–69); Officers' Panel, Soulbury Cttee (and Leader), 1970–75; Staff Panel, Jt Negotiating Cttee Youth Leaders (and Leader), 1970–75; Warnock Cttee on Special Educn, 1974–78; Council and Exec., CGLI, 1974–77; Central Arbitration Cttee, 1977–83. Chm., Nat. Centre for Cued Speech for the Deaf, 1986–88. FCP, 1967; Hon. FEIS, 1974. Hon. DEd CNAA, 1969. *Publications:* many articles in educational journals. *Address:* 40 Nightingale Road, Guildford, Surrey GU1 1ER.

BRITTON, John William; Assistant Chief Scientific Advisor (Projects and Research), Ministry of Defence, since 1990; *b* 13 Dec. 1936; *s* of John Ferguson and Dinah Britton; *m* 1961, Maisie (*née* Rubython); one *s* one *d*. *Educ:* Bedlington Grammar Sch.; Bristol Univ. (BScEng 1st Cl. Hons). Royal Aircraft Establishment, Bedford, 1959–83: Hd, Flight Res. Div., 1978–80; Chief Supt and Hd, Flight Systems Bedford Dept, 1981–83; RCDS 1984; Dir, Avionic Equipment and Systems, MoD PE, 1985–86; Science and Technology Assessment Office, Cabinet Office, 1987; Dir Gen. Aircraft 3, MoD PE, 1987–90. *Recreations:* wine making, oil painting, motor racing (watching), gardening (especially dahlias and fuchsias). *Address:* Assistant Chief Scientific Advisor (Projects and Research), Ministry of Defence, Main Building, Whitehall, SW1A 2HB.

BRITZ, Jack; General Secretary, Clearing Bank Union, 1980–83; independent human resources consultant, since 1983; *b* 6 Nov. 1930; *s* of Alfred and Hetty Britz; *m* 1955, Thelma Salaver; one *s* two *d*. *Educ:* Luton Grammar School. Entered electrical contracting industry, 1944; various posts in industry; Director, Rolfe Electrical Ltd, 1964–65. National Recruitment Officer, EETPU, 1969–74; short period with Commission on Industrial Relations as sen. industrial relations officer, 1974; Personnel Manager, Courage Eastern Ltd, 1974–77; Gp Personnel Director, Bowthorpe Group Ltd, 1977–80. *Recreations:* walking, history, wargaming, etc. *Address:* West Wing, Longdown Hollow, Hindhead Road, Hindhead, Surrey GU26 6AY.
See also L. Britz.

BRITZ, Lewis; Executive Councillor, Electrical, Electronic, Telecommunication & Plumbing Union, since 1983; Member: Monopolies and Mergers Commission, since

1986; Industrial Tribunals, since 1990; *b* 7 Jan. 1933; *s* of Alfred and Hetty Britz; *m* 1960, Hadassah Rosenberg; four *d*. *Educ:* Hackney Downs Grammar Sch.; Acton Technical Coll. (OND Elec. Engrg); Nottingham Univ. (BSc (Hons) Engrg). Head of Research, 1967–71, Nat. Officer, 1971–83, EETPU. Director: LEB, 1977–87; British Internat. Helicopters, 1987–; Esca Services, 1990–. *Recreation:* philately. *Address:* 30 Braemar Gardens, West Wickham, Kent BR4 0JW. *T:* 081–777 5986.

See also J. Britz.

BRIXWORTH, Bishop Suffragan of, since 1989; **Rt. Rev. Paul Everard Barber;** *b* 16 Sept. 1935; *s* of Cecil Arthur and Mollie Barber; *m* 1959, Patricia Jayne Walford; two *s* two *d* (and one *s* decd). *Educ:* Sherborne School; St John's Coll., Cambridge (BA 1958, MA 1966); Wells Theological College. Deacon 1960, priest 1961, dio. Guildford; Curate of St Francis, Westborough, 1960–66; Vicar: Camberley with Yorktown, 1966–73; St Thomas-on-The Bourne, Farnham, 1973–80; Rural Dean of Farnham, 1974–79; Archdeacon of Surrey, 1980–89; Hon. Canon of Guildford, 1980–89. General synod, 1979–85; Member, Council of College of Preachers, 1969–. *Recreations:* diocesan clergy cricket, theatre. *Address:* 4 The Avenue, Dallington, Northampton NN5 7AN. *T:* Northampton (0604) 759423.

BROACKES, Sir Nigel, Kt 1984; Chairman, Trafalgar House PLC; *b* Wakefield, 21 July 1934; *s* of late Donald Broackes and Nan Alford; *m* 1956, Joyce Edith Horne; two *s* one *d*. *Educ:* Stowe. Nat. Service, commnd 3rd Hussars, 1953–54. Stewart & Hughman Ltd, Lloyds Underwriting agents, 1952–55; various property developments, etc, 1955–57; Trafalgar House Ltd: Man. Dir 1958; Dep. Chm. and Jt Man. Dir 1968; Chm. 1969. Chm., Ship and Marine Technology Requirements Bd, 1972–77; Dep. Chm., Offshore Energy Technology Bd, 1975–77; Chm. Designate, then Chm., London Docklands Develt Corp., 1979–84; British Chm., EuroRoute, 1984–86; non-exec. Director: Distillers Co., 1985–86; Eurotunnel plc, 1986–87; Channel Tunnel Gp Ltd, 1986–87. Mem. Council, Nat. Assoc. of Property Owners, 1967–73. Governor, Stowe Sch., 1974–81. Trustee: Royal Opera House Trust, 1976–81; National Maritime Museum, 1987–; Mem. Advisory Council, Victoria and Albert Museum, 1980–83. Dir, Horserace Totalisator Bd, 1976–81. Chm., Crafts Council, 1991–. Mem., European Round Table, 1990–. Freeman, City of London; Liveryman, Worshipful Co. of Goldsmiths (Mem., Court of Assts, 1987–). Guardian Young Businessman of the Year, 1978. *Publication:* A Growing Concern, 1979. *Recreation:* silversmith. *Address:* 41 Chelsea Square, SW3 6LH; Checkendon Court, Checkendon, Oxon RG8 0SR.

BROADBENT, Donald Eric, CBE 1974; MA, ScD; FRS 1968; External Staff, Medical Research Council, 1974–91, retired; *b* 6 May 1926; *m* 1st, 1949, Margaret Elizabeth Wright; two *d*; 2nd, 1972, Margaret Hope Pattison Gregory. *Educ:* Winchester College; Pembroke College, Cambridge. RAF Engrg short course, 1st cl., 1944; Moral Science Tripos (Psychology), 1st cl., 1949. Scientific Staff, Applied Psychology Res. Unit, 1949–58 (Dir, 1958–74). Fellow, Pembroke College, Cambridge, 1965–74. Pres., British Psychol. Society, 1965; Pres., Sect. J. Brit. Assoc. for Advancement of Science, 1967; Vis. Fellow, All Souls College, Oxford, 1967–68; Fellow, Wolfson Coll., Oxford, 1974–91. Mem., SSRC, 1973–75; Chm., ESRC/MRC/SERC Initiative on Cognitive Science, 1987–91; Mem., Adv. Cttee on Safety of Nuclear Installations, 1987–. Fellow, Acoustical Soc. of Amer.; past or present Council Member: Royal Soc.; British Acoustical Soc.; British Psychol Soc.; Ergonomics Res. Soc.; Experimental Psychology Soc.; Fellow, Human Factors Soc.; For. Associate, US Nat. Acad. Sci., 1971; Hon. FFOM 1982; Hon. FRCPsych 1985. Hon. DSc: Southampton, 1974; York, 1979; Loughborough, 1982; City, 1983; Brussels, 1985; Cranfield, 1991; Wales, 1991. APA Dist. Scientist Award, 1975. *Publications:* Perception and Communication, 1958; Behaviour, 1961; Decision and Stress, 1971; In Defence of Empirical Psychology, 1973; many papers in jls of above societies and of Amer. Psychol Assoc. *Recreations:* reading, camping, photography. *Address:* c/o Department of Experimental Psychology, South Parks Road, Oxford OX1 3UD.

BROADBENT, Dr Edward Granville, FRS 1977; FEng, FRAeS, FIMA; Visiting Professor, Imperial College of Science and Technology (Mathematics Department), London University, since 1983; *b* 27 June 1923; *s* of Joseph Charles Fletcher Broadbent and Lucetta (*née* Riley); *m* 1949, Elizabeth Barbara (*née* Puttick). *Educ:* Huddersfield Coll.; St Catharine's Coll., Cambridge (State Scholarship, 1941; Eng Scholar; MA, ScD). FRAeS 1959; FIMA 1965. Joined RAE (Structures Dept), 1943; worked on aero-elasticity (Wakefield Gold Medal, RAeS, 1960); transf. to Aerodynamics Dept, 1960; worked on various aspects of fluid mechanics and acoustics; DCSO (IM), RAE, 1969–83, retired. FRSA 1984. *Publication:* The Elementary Theory of Aero-elasticity, 1954. *Recreations:* duplicate bridge, chess, music, theatre. *Address:* 11 Three Stiles Road, Farnham, Surrey GU9 7DE. *T:* Farnham (0252) 714621.

BROADBENT, Sir Ewen, KCB 1984 (CB 1973); CMG 1965; Director, Carroll Industries Corp., since 1988; Vice-Chairman, Farnborough Aerospace Development Corporation, since 1986; *b* 9 Aug. 1924; *s* of late Rev. W. Broadbent and of Mrs Mary Broadbent; *m* 1951, Squadron Officer Barbara David, *d* of F. A. David, Weston-super-Mare; one *s*. *Educ:* King Edward VI School, Nuneaton; St John's College, Cambridge. Served with Gordon Highlanders, 1943–47 (Captain); Cambridge, 1942–43 and 1947–49; Air Ministry, 1949; Private Sec. to Secretary of State for Air, 1955–59; Asst Secretary, 1959; Dep. Chief Officer, Sovereign Base Areas, Cyprus, 1961, Chief Officer, 1964; Ministry of Defence, 1965–84: Private Sec. to Sec. of State for Defence, 1967–68; Asst Under-Sec. of State, 1969–72; Dep. Under-Sec. of State (Air), 1972–75; Dep. Under-Sec. of State (Civilian Management), 1975–82; Second Perm. Under-Sec. of State, 1982–84. Trustee, RAF Mus., 1985–. Chairman: Look Ahead Housing Assoc., 1988–; Council for Voluntary Welfare Work, 1989–. Vice-Chm. Council, RUSI, 1990–. *Publication:* The Military and Government, from Macmillan to Heseltine, 1988. *Recreation:* golf. *Address:* 18 Park Hill, Ealing, W5. *T:* 081–997 1978. *Clubs:* Commonwealth Trust, Army and Navy.

BROADBENT, Sir George (Walter), 4th Bt *cr* 1893, of Brook Street, Co. London and Longwood, Yorkshire; AFC 1979; Squadron Leader, RAF; *b* 23 April 1935; *s* of John Graham Monroe Broadbent (*d* 1967) (*g s* of 1st Bt) and Elizabeth Mary Beatrice Broadbent (*née* Dendy) (*d* 1976); *S* cousin, 1987; *m* 1962, Valerie Anne, *o d* of Cecil Frank Ward; one *s* one *d*. *Educ:* Stamford School. Joined RAF, 1954. *Recreations:* walking, music. *Heir:* *s* Andrew George Broadbent, Captain 1 PWO, *b* 26 Jan. 1963. *Address:* 98 Heworth Green, York YO3 7TQ.

BROADBENT, (John) Michael; Director, Christie Manson & Woods, since 1967, and Head, Wine Department, since 1966; *b* 2 May 1927; *s* of late John Fred Broadbent and of Hilary Louise Broadbent; *m* 1954, Daphne Joste; one *s* one *d*. *Educ:* Rishworth Sch., Yorks; Bartlett Sch. of Architecture, UCL (Cert. in Architecture 1952). Commissioned RA, 1945–48 (Nat. Service). Trainee, Laytons Wine Merchants, 1952–53; Saccone & Speed, 1953–55; John Harvey & Sons, Bristol, 1955–66: local Dir, 1962; Dir and UK Sales Manager, 1963; Christie's, 1966–; Chm., Christie's South Kensington, 1978–79. Wine Trade Art Society: Founder Mem., 1955; Chm., 1972–; Institute of Masters of Wine: Educn Cttee, 1962–66; Mem. Council, 1966–78; Chm., 1971–72; Chm., Central Panel MW Examn Bd, 1982–85; Pres., Northern Wine Soc., 1962–67; Distillers' Company: Liveryman, 1964–80; Mem. Council, 1981–; Master, 1990–91; International Wine and Food Society: Life Mem.; Mem. Council, 1969–; Internat. Pres., 1985–91; Gold Medal, 1989; Chm., Wine and Spirit Benevolent Soc., 1991–. Numerous awards from wine socs and other instns. Chevalier, Ordre National du Mérite, 1979; La Médaille de la Ville de Paris (gold medal), 1989. Editor: Christie's Wine Review annual, 1972–80; Christie's Price Index of Vintage Wines, 1982–84 and 1989. *Publications:* Wine Tasting, 1st edn 1968 (numerous foreign edns); The Great Vintage Wine Book, 1980 (foreign edns); Pocket Guide to Wine Tasting, 1988; contribs to Wine Magazine, Decanter and other jls. *Recreations:* playing the piano, painting. *Address:* Chippenham Lodge, Old Sodbury, Avon BS17 6RQ; 87 Rosebank, SW6 6LJ. *Clubs:* Brooks's, Saintsbury.

BROADBENT, Simon Hope; Chief Economic Adviser (formerly Head of Economic Advisers), Foreign and Commonwealth Office, since 1984; *b* 4 June 1942; *s* of Edmund Urquhart Broadbent, CBE and Doris Hope; *m* 1966, Margaret Ann Taylor; two *s* one *d*. *Educ:* University College School; Hatfield College, Durham (BA); Magdalen College, Oxford (BPhil). Malawi Civil Service, 1964; Economic Adviser, FCO, 1971; First Sec., UK Treasury and Supply delegn, Washington, 1974; seconded to Bank of England, 1977; Senior Economic Adviser and Joint Head, Economists Dept, FCO, 1978; Institut Universitaire de Hautes Etudes Internationales, Geneva, 1984. *Address:* c/o Foreign and Commonwealth Office, SW1A 2AH. *T:* 071–270 2721.

BROADBRIDGE, family name of **Baron Broadbridge.**

BROADBRIDGE, 3rd Baron *cr* 1945, of Brighton; **Peter Hewett Broadbridge;** Bt 1937; Director, The London Venture Capital Market Ltd, since 1980; *b* 19 Aug. 1938; *s* of 2nd Baron Broadbridge and Mabel Daisy (*d* 1966), *o d* of Arthur Edward Clarke; *S* father, 1972; *m* 1st, 1967, Mary (marr. diss. 1980), *o d* of W. O. Busch; two *d*; 2nd, 1989, Sally Finn. *Educ:* Hurstpierpoint Coll., Sussex; St Catherine's Coll., Oxford (MA, BSc). Unilever Ltd, 1963–65; Colgate Palmolive Ltd, 1966; Gallaher Ltd, 1967–70; Peat, Marwick Mitchell & Co., EC2, 1970–78; Management Consultant, Coopers and Lybrand and Associates Ltd, 1979–80. Pres., Nat. Assoc. of Leisure Gardeners, 1978–81. Freeman, City of London, 1980; Liveryman, Worshipful Co. of Goldsmiths, 1983. *Recreations:* tennis, squash, antiques, silversmithing. *Heir:* *cousin* Martin Hugh Broadbridge [*b* 29 Nov 1929; *m* 1st 1954, Norma, *d* of late Major Herbert Sheffield, MC; one *s* one *d*; 2nd, 1968, Elizabeth, *d* of J. E. Trotman]. *Address:* House of Lords, SW1A 0PW.

BROADHURST, Air Chief Marshal (retd) Sir Harry, GCB 1960 (KCB 1955; CB 1944); KBE 1945; DSO and Bar, 1941; DFC 1940, and Bar, 1942; AFC 1937; Managing Director, A. V. Roe & Co. Ltd, 1961–66; Director, 1961–76, Deputy Managing Director 1965–76, Hawker Siddeley Aviation Ltd; Director, Hawker Siddeley Group Ltd, 1968–76; *b* 1905; *m* 1st, 1929, Doris Kathleen French; one *d*; 2nd, 1946, Jean Elizabeth Townley; one *d*. Joined RAF, 1926; served with: No 11 (B) Sqdn, UK, 1926–28, India, 1928–31; 41 (F) Sqdn, 1932–33; 19 (F) Sqdn, 1933–36; Chief Instr, No 4 FTS, Egypt, 1937; RAF Staff Coll., 1938; served War: OC No 111 (F) Sqdn, 1939–40; Wing Comdr Trng No 11 (F) Gp, Jan.–May 1940; OC No 60 (F) Wing, France, May 1940; OC Fighter Sector, Wittering, June–Dec. 1940, Hornchurch, 1940–42; Dep. SASO No 11 (F) Gp, May–Oct. 1942; SASO and AOC Western Desert, 1942–43; 83 Group Commander Allied Expeditionary Air Force, 1944–45; AO i/c Admin. Fighter Command, 1945–46; AOC 61 Group, 1947–48; idc 1949; SASO, BAFO (now 2nd TAF), Germany, 1950–51; ACAS (Ops), 1952–53; C-in-C 2nd Tactical Air Force, Germany, 1954–56; Air Officer Commanding-in-Chief, Bomber Command, Jan. 1956–May 1959; Cmdr Allied Air Forces, Central Europe, 1959–61. Vice-Pres., 1973–74, Pres., 1974–75, Dep. Pres., 1975–76, SBAC. Kt Grand Cross of Order of Orange Nassau, 1948; Legion of Merit (US). *Address:* Lock's End House, Birdham, Chichester, W Sussex PO20 7BB. *T:* Birdham (0243) 512717. *Club:* Royal Air Force.

BROADLEY, John Kenneth Elliott, CMG 1988; HM Diplomatic Service; Ambassador to the Holy See, 1988–91; *b* 10 June 1936; *s* of late Kenneth Broadley and late Rosamund Venn (*née* Elliott); *m* 1961, Jane Alice Rachel (*née* Gee); one *s* two *d*. *Educ:* Winchester Coll.; Balliol Coll., Oxford (Exhibnr, MA). Served Army, 1st RHA, 1954–56. Entered HM Diplomatic Service, 1960; Washington, 1963–65; La Paz, 1965–68; FCO, 1968–73; UK Mission to UN, Geneva, 1973–76; Counsellor, Amman, 1976–79; FCO, 1979–84; Dep. Governor, Gibraltar, 1984–88. Mem., Exec. Council for Anglican Centre, Rome, 1988–91. *Recreations:* windsurfing, hill walking, tennis, family. *Address:* c/o Foreign and Commonwealth Office, SW1A 2AH. *Club:* Royal Automobile.

BROCAS, Viscount; Patrick John Bernard Jellicoe; *b* 29 Aug. 1950; *s* and *heir* of 2nd Earl Jellicoe, *qv*; *m* 1971, separated 1971, marr. diss. 1980; two *s* (*b* 1970, 1977). *Educ:* Eton. Profession, engineer.

BROCK; *see* Clutton-Brock.

BROCK, Michael George, CBE 1981; Warden of St George's House, Windsor Castle, since 1988; *b* 9 March 1920; *s* of late Sir Laurence George Brock and Ellen Margery Brock (*née* Williams); *m* 1949, Eleanor Hope Morrison; three *s*. *Educ:* Wellington Coll. (Schol.); Corpus Christi Coll., Oxford (Open Schol.; First Cl. Hons Mod. Hist. 1948; MA 1948). FRHistS 1965; FRSL 1983. War service (Middlesex Regt), 1940–45. Corpus Christi Coll., Oxford: Jun. Res. Fellow, 1948–50; Fellow and Tutor in Modern History and Politics, 1950–66, Fellow Emeritus, 1977; Hon. Fellow, 1982; Oxford University: Jun. Proctor, 1956–57; Univ. Lectr, 1951–70; Mem., Hebdomadal Council, 1965–76, 1978–86; Vice Pres. and Bursar, Wolfson Coll., Oxford, 1967–76; Prof. of Educn and Dir, Sch. of Educn, Exeter Univ., 1977–78; Warden of Nuffield Coll., Oxford, 1978–88; Pro-Vice-Chancellor, Oxford Univ., 1980–88. Church Comr, 1990–. FRSA 1987. Hon. Fellow: Wolfson Coll., Oxford, 1977; Nuffield Coll., Oxford, 1988; Hon FSRHE 1986. Hon. DLitt Exeter, 1982. *Publications:* The Great Reform Act, 1973; (ed with Eleanor Brock) H. H. Asquith: Letters to Venetia Stanley, 1982; many articles on historical topics and on higher education. *Address:* 24 The Cloisters, Windsor Castle, Berks SL4 1NJ. *T:* Windsor (0753) 866444. *Clubs:* Athenæum, Oxford Union.

BROCK, Dr Sebastian Paul, FBA 1977; Reader in Syriac Studies, University of Oxford, since 1991; Fellow of Wolfson College, Oxford, since 1974; *b* 1938; *m* 1966, Helen M. C. (*née* Hughes). *Educ:* Eton College; Univ. of Cambridge (BA 1962, MA 1965); MA and DPhil Oxon 1966. Asst Lectr, 1964–66, Lectr, 1966–67, Dept of Theology, Univ. of Birmingham; Lectr, Hebrew and Aramaic, Univ. of Cambridge, 1967–74; Lectr in Aramaic and Syriac, Univ. of Oxford, 1974–90. Corres. Mem., Syriac Section, Iraqi Acad., 1979. Editor, JSS, 1987–90. *Publications:* Pseudepigrapha Veteris Testamenti Graece II; Testamentum Iobi, 1967; The Syriac Version of the Pseudo-Nonnos Mythological Scholia, 1971; (with C. T. Fritsch and S. Jellicoe) A Classified Bibliography of the Septuagint, 1973; The Harp of the Spirit: Poems of St Ephrem, 1975, 2nd edn 1983; The Holy Spirit in Syrian Baptismal Tradition, 1979; Sughyotho Mgabyotho, 1982; Syriac Perspectives on Late Antiquity, 1984; Turgome d'Mor Ya'qub da-Srug, 1984; The Luminous Eye: the spiritual world vision of St Ephrem, 1985; (with S. A. Harvey) Holy Women of the Syrian Orient, 1987; Vetus Testamentum Syriace III. 1: Liber Isaiae, 1987;

The Syriac Fathers on Prayer and the Spiritual Life, 1987; St Ephrem: Hymns on Paradise, 1990; contrib. Jl of Semitic Studies, JTS, Le Muséon, Oriens Christianus, Orientalia Christiana Periodica, Parole de l'Orient, Revue des études arméniennes. *Address:* Wolfson College, Oxford OX2 6UD; Oriental Institute, Pusey Lane, Oxford OX1 2LE.

BROCK, Prof. William Ranulf, FBA 1990; Fellow of Selwyn College, Cambridge, since 1947; Professor of Modern History, University of Glasgow, 1967–81, now Emeritus; *b* 16 May 1916; *s* of Stewart Ernst Brock and Katherine Helen (*née* Temple Roberts); *m* 1950, Constance Helen (*née* Brown); one *s* one *d. Educ:* Christ's Hosp.; Trinity Coll., Cambridge (MA, PhD). Prize Fellow 1940 (in absentia). Military service (Army), 1939–45; Asst Master, Eton Coll., 1946–47. Commonwealth Fund Fellow, Berkeley, Calif, Yale and Johns Hopkins, 1952–53, 1958; Vis. Professor: Michigan Univ., 1968; Washington Univ., 1970; Maryland Univ., 1980; Charles Warren Fellow, Harvard Univ., 1976; Leverhulme Emeritus Fellow, 1981. *Publications:* Lord Liverpool and Liberal Toryism, 1941; The Character of American History, 1960; An American Crisis, 1963; The Evolution of American Democracy, 1970; Conflict and Transformation 1844–1877, 1973; The Sources of History: the United States 1790–1890, 1975; Parties and Political Conscience, 1979; Scotus Americanus, 1982; Investigation and Responsibility, 1985; Welfare, Democracy and the New Deal, 1988; contrib. New Cambridge Mod. History, Vols VII and XI; articles and reviews in History, Jl Amer. Studies, Jl Amer. Hist., etc. *Recreation:* antiques. *Address:* 49 Barton Road, Cambridge CB3 9LG. *T:* Cambridge (0223) 313606.

BROCKBANK, (James) Tyrrell; solicitor; Vice Lord-Lieutenant of Durham, since 1990; *b* 14 Dec. 1920; *y s* of late James Lindow Brockbank; *m* 1950, Pamela, *yr d* of late Lt-Col J. Oxley Parker, TD, and Mary Monica (*née* Hills); four *s. Educ:* St Peter's Sch., York; St John's Coll., Cambridge (MA). Served War of 1939–45 with Sherwood Foresters and Inns of Court Regt. Asst Solicitor, Wolverhampton, 1949–51; Asst Clerk, Hertfordshire, 1951–54; Dep. Clerk, Nottinghamshire, 1954–61; Clerk of the Peace, Durham, 1961–71; Clerk of Durham CC, 1961–74; Clerk to the Lieutenancy, 1964–88; DL 1970, High Sheriff, 1989, Durham. Member, Local Govt Boundary Commn for England, 1976–85. *Recreations:* fishing, shooting, golf. *Address:* The Orange Tree, Shincliffe Village, Durham DH1 2NN. *T:* 091–386 5569. *Clubs:* Travellers'; Durham County (Durham).

BROCKBANK, Maj.-Gen. John Myles, (Robin), CBE 1972; MC 1943; Vice Lord-Lieutenant of Wiltshire, since 1990; *b* 19 Sept. 1921; *s* of Col J. G. Brockbank, CBE, DSO, and Eireine Marguerite Robinson; *m* 1953, Gillian Findlay, *yr d* of Sir Edmund Findlay, 2nd Bt of Aberlour; three *s* one *d. Educ:* Eton Coll.; Oxford Univ. Commissioned into 12 Royal Lancers, 1941. Served War, North Africa, Italy, 1941–45. Served Germany: 1955–58, 1964–68 and 1970–72; Cyprus, 1959; USA, 1961–64; Staff Coll., 1950; IDC 1969; CO, 9/12 Royal Lancers; Comdr, RAC, HQ 1 Corps; Chief of Staff, 1 Corps; Dir, RAC, 1972–74; Vice-Adjutant General, MoD, 1974–76, retd. Col, 9/12 Lancers, 1982–85. Dir, British Field Sports Soc., 1976–84. DL Wilts 1982. *Recreations:* field sports, gardening, bird watching. *Address:* Manor House, Steeple Langford, Salisbury, Wilts SP3 4NQ. *T:* Salisbury (0722) 790353. *Club:* Cavalry and Guards.

BROCKBANK, Tyrrell; see Brockbank, J. T.

BROCKET, 3rd Baron, *cr* 1933; **Charles Ronald George Nall-Cain**, Bt 1921; *b* 12 Feb. 1952; *s* of Hon. Ronald Charles Manus Nall-Cain (*d* 1961), and of Elizabeth Mary (who *m* 2nd, 1964, Colin John Richard Trotter), *d* of R. J. Stallard; *S* grandfather, 1967; *m* 1982, Isabell Maria Lorenzo, *o d* of Gustavo Lorenzo, Whaleneck Drive, Merrick, Long Island, NY; one *s. Educ:* Eton. 14/20 Hussars, 1970–75 (Lieut). *Heir:* *s* Hon. Alexander Christopher Charles Nall-Cain, *b* 30 Sept. 1984. *Address:* Brocket Hall, Welwyn, Herts.

BROCKHOFF, Sir Jack (Stuart), Kt 1979; company director; *b* 1908; *s* of Mr and Mrs Frederick Douglas Brockhoff. *Educ:* Wesley coll., Vic. Chairman and Managing Director: Brockhoff's Biscuits Pty Ltd; Arnott-Brockhoff-Guest Pty Ltd; Dir, Arnotts Ltd; Chm. of Dirs, Jack Brockhoff Foundn. *Recreations:* golf, bowls, fishing. *Address:* 113 Beach Road, Sandringham, Vic 3191, Australia. *T:* 598 9227. *Clubs:* Woodlands Golf, Victoria Golf, Sandringham, Sandringham Yacht, Royal Automobile of Victoria, Victoria Racing, Victoria Amateur Turf.

BROCKHOLES, Michael John F.; see Fitzherbert-Brockholes.

BROCKHOUSE, Dr Bertram Neville, OC 1982; FRS 1965; Professor of Physics, McMaster University, Canada, 1962–84, now Emeritus; *b* 15 July 1918; *s* of Israel Bertram Brockhouse and Mable Emily Brockhouse (*née* Neville); *m* 1948, Doris Isobel Mary (*née* Miller); four *s* two *d. Educ:* University of British Columbia (BA); University of Toronto (PhD). Served War of 1939–45 with Royal Canadian Navy. Lectr, University of Toronto, 1949–50; Research Officer, Atomic Energy of Canada Ltd, 1950–59; Branch Head, Neutron Physics Br., 1960–62. Foreign Member: Royal Swedish Acad. of Sciences, 1984; Amer. Acad. of Arts and Sciences, 1990. Hon. DSc: Waterloo, 1969; McMaster, 1984. *Publications:* some 75 papers in learned journals. *Address:* PO Box 7338, Ancaster, Ontario L9G 3N6, Canada. *T:* (416) 648 6329.

BROCKINGTON, Prof. Colin Fraser; Professor of Social and Preventive Medicine, Manchester University, 1951–64, Emeritus, 1964; *b* 8 Jan. 1903; *s* of late Sir William Brockington; *m* 1933, Dr Joyce Margaret Furze; three *s* one *d. Educ:* Oakham Sch.; Gonville and Caius Coll., Cambridge; Guy's Hosp., London. MD, MA, DPH, BChir Cantab, MSc Manchester, MRCS, MRCP; barrister-at-law, Middle Temple. Medical Superintendent, Brighton Infectious Diseases Hosp. and Sanatorium, 1929; Asst County Medical Officer, Worcs CC, 1930–33; general medical practice, Kingsbridge, Devon, 1933–36; Medical Officer of Health, Horsham and Petworth, 1936–38; Dep. County Medical Officer of Health, Warwickshire CC, 1938–42; County Medical Officer of Health: Warwickshire CC, 1942–46; West Riding CC, 1946–51. Member: Central Adv. Council for Educn (Eng.), 1945–56; Central Training Council in Child Care (Home Office), 1947–53; Adv. Council for Welfare of Handicapped (Min. of Health), 1949–54; Nursing Cttee of Central Health Services Council (Min. of Health), 1949–51; Council of Soc. of Med. Officers of Health, 1944–66; Public Health Cttee of County Councils Assoc., 1945–49. Chairman: WHO Expert Cttee on School Health, 1950; Symposium on "Mental Health-Public Health Partnership," 5th Internat. Congress on Mental Health, Toronto, 1954; WHO Research Study Group on Juvenile Epilepsy, 1955; UK Cttee of WHO, 1958–61. Took part as Expert in Technical Discussions on Rural Health at World Health Assembly, 1954; Far Eastern Lecture Tour for British Council, 1956–57; visited India, 1959, 1962, S America 1960, Jordan 1966–67, Spain 1967, Arabia 1968, Turkey 1955, 1969, 1970, 1972, Greece 1970, for WHO. Lecture Tour: S Africa and Middle East, 1964. *Publications:* Principles of Nutrition, 1952; The People's Health, 1955; A Short History of Public Health, 1956 (2nd edn 1966); World Health, 1958 (3rd edn 1975); The Health of the Community, 1955, 1960, 1965; Public Health in the Nineteenth Century, 1965; The Social Needs of the Over-Eighties, 1966; The Health of the Developing World, 1985; wide range of contribs to learned jls. *Recreations:* bookbinding, travel. *Address:* Werneth, Silverburn, Ballasalla, Isle of Man. *T:* Castletown (Isle of Man) (0624) 3465.

BROCKLEBANK, Sir Aubrey (Thomas), 6th Bt *cr* 1885; ACA; *b* 29 Jan. 1952; *s* of Sir John Montague Brocklebank, 5th Bt, TD, and of Pamela Sue, *d* of late William Harold Pierce, OBE; *S* father, 1974; *m* 1979, Dr Anna-Marie Dunnet (marr. diss. 1989); two *s. Educ:* Eton; University Coll., Durham (BSc Psychology). *Recreations:* deep sea tadpole wrestling, shooting, motor racing. *Heir:* *s* Aubrey William Thomas Brocklebank, *b* 15 Dec. 1980. *Address:* 18 Montagu Mews South, W1H 1TE.

BROCKLEBANK-FOWLER, Christopher; management consultant; *b* 13 Jan. 1934; 2nd *s* of Sidney Straton Brocklebank Fowler, MA, LLB; *m* 1st, 1957, Joan Nowland (marr. diss. 1975); two *s;* 2nd, 1975, Mrs Mary Berry (marr. diss. 1986). *Educ:* Perse Sch., Cambridge. Farm pupil on farms in Suffolk, Cambridgeshire and Norfolk, 1950–55. National service (submarines), Sub-Lt, RNVR, 1952–54. Farm Manager, Kenya, 1955–57; Lever Bros Ltd (Unilever Cos Management Trainee), 1957–59; advertising and marketing consultant, 1959–79; Chm., Overseas Trade and Develt Agency Ltd, 1979–83; Man. Dir, Cambridge Corporate Consultants Ltd, 1985–87. Mem. Bow Group, 1961–81 (Chm., 1968–69; Dir, Bow Publications, 1968–71). Mem. London Conciliation Cttee, 1966–67; Vice-Chm. Information Panel, Nat. Cttee for Commonwealth Immigrants, 1966–67; Mem. Exec. Cttee, Africa Bureau, 1970–74; Chm., SOS Childrens Villages, 1978–84. MP King's Lynn, 1970–74, Norfolk North West, 1974–83 (C, 1970–81, SDP, 1981–83); Chm., Conservative Parly Sub-Cttee on Horticulture, 1972–74; Vice-Chairman: Cons. Parly Cttee on Agriculture, 1974–75; Cons. Parly Foreign and Commonwealth Affairs Cttee, 1979 (Jt Sec., 1974–75, 1976–77); Cons. Parly Trade Cttee, 1979–80; SDP Agriculture Policy Cttee, 1982–83; Chairman: UN Parly Gp, 1979–83 (Jt Sec., 1971–78); Cons. Parly Overseas Develt Sub-Cttee, 1979–81; SDP Third World Policy Cttee, 1981–87; Member: Select Cttee for Overseas Develt, 1973–79; Select Cttee on Foreign Affairs, 1979–81; SDP Nat. Steering Cttee, 1981–82; SDP Nat. Cttee, 1982; SDP Parly spokesman on Agriculture, 1981–82, on Overseas Develt, 1981–83, on Foreign Affairs, 1982–83. Contested: (C) West Ham (North), 1964; (SDP) 1983, (SDP/Alliance) 1987, Norfolk North West. Vice Chm., Centre for World Develt Educn, 1980–83; Governor, Inst. of Develt Studies, 1978–81. FRGS; MCIM; M CAM; FInstD; Hon. Fellow IDS. *Publications:* pamphlets and articles on race relations, African affairs, overseas development. *Recreations:* painting, fishing, shooting, swimming. *Address:* The Long Cottage, Flitcham, near King's Lynn, Norfolk. *T:* Hillington (0485) 600255. *Club:* Commonwealth Trust.

BROCKLEHURST, Major-General Arthur Evers, CB 1956; DSO 1945; late RA; *b* 20 July 1905; *m* 1940, Joan Beryl Parry-Crooke; twin *d. Educ:* King's School, Canterbury; RMA Woolwich. 2nd Lieut, RA, 1925; CRA 6th Armoured Div., 1951; IDC 1954; DDPS (B) 1955; Chief of Staff, Malaya Comd, 1956–57; GOC, Rhine Dist, BAOR, 1958–59; Dep. Comdr BAOR, 1959–61; retired 1961. Chm., Devizes Constituency Cons. Assoc., 1963–65. *Recreation:* painting watercolours. *Address:* Downland Cottage, Bottlesford, Pewsey, Wilts SN9 6LU. *Club:* Army and Navy.

BROCKLEHURST, Prof. John Charles, CBE 1988; FRCP, FRCPE, FRCPGlas; Professor of Geriatric Medicine, University of Manchester, 1970–89, now Emeritus; *b* 31 May 1924; *s* of late Harold John Brocklehurst and of Dorothy Brocklehurst; *m* 1956, Susan Engle; two *s* one *d. Educ:* Glasgow High Sch.; Ayr Academy; Univ. of Glasgow (MB ChB 1947; MD Hons 1950). Christine Hansen Research Fellow, Glasgow Univ., 1948–49; RAMC (to rank of Major), 1949–51; Medical Registrar, Stobhill Hosp., and Asst Lectr, Dept of Materia Medica and Therapeutics, Glasgow Univ., 1952–53 and 1958–59; MO, Grenfell Mission, Northern Newfoundland and Labrador, 1955–57; Cons. Geriatrician, Bromley Hosp. Gp and Cray Valley and Sevenoaks Hosp. Gp, 1960–69; Cons. in Geriatric and Gen. Med., Guy's Hosp., London, 1969–70. Dir, Univ. of Manchester Unit for Biological Aging Research (formerly Geigy Unit for Res. in Aging), 1974–89; Chm., Age Concern England, 1973–77, Hon. Vice-Pres., 1980–; Governor, Research into Ageing (formerly British Foundn for Age Research), 1980–; President: Soc. of Chiropodists, 1977–83; British Geriatrics Soc., 1984–86. Vis. Professor of Geriatric Med. and Chm., Div. of Geriatric Med., Univ. of Saskatchewan, Canada, 1978–79. Hon. MSc Manchester 1974. Bellahouston Gold Medal, Univ. of Glasgow, 1950; Willard Thomson Gold Medal, Amer. Geriatrics Soc., 1978; Sandoz Prize, Internat. Assoc. of Gerontology, 1989; Founder's Medal, British Geriatrics Soc., 1990. *Publications:* Incontinence in Old People, 1951; The Geriatric Day Hospital, 1971; ed and part author, Textbook of Geriatric Medicine and Gerontology, 1973, 3rd edn 1985; Geriatric Care in Advanced Societies, 1975; (jtly) Geriatric Medicine for Students, 1976, 3rd edn, 1986; (jtly) Progress in Geriatric Day Care, 1980; (jtly) Colour Atlas of Geriatric Medicine, 1983; (ed and part author) Urology: the elderly, 1985; Geriatric Pharmacology and Therapeutics, 1985; (jtly) British Geriatric Medicine in the 1980s, 1987. *Recreations:* water colour painting, the mandoline. *Address:* 59 Stanneylands Road, Wilmslow, Cheshire SK9 4EX. *Clubs:* East India and Devonshire, Royal Society of Medicine.

BROCKLEHURST, Robert James, DM; Emeritus Professor of Physiology, University of Bristol, since 1965; *b* Liverpool, 16 Sept. 1899; *e s* of George and Sarah Huger Brocklehurst, Liverpool; *m* 1st, 1928, Sybille (*d* 1968), *y d* of Captain R. H. L. Risk, CBE, RN; two *s* one *d*; 2nd, 1970, Dora Millicent (*d* 1986), *y d* of late Alexander Watts. *Educ:* Harrow Sch.; University College, Oxford (Scholar; 1st Class Honours in Physiology); St Bartholomew's Hospital. BA 1921; MA, BM, BCh, 1924; DM, 1928; MRCS, LRCP, 1925; Demonstrator of Physiology, St Bartholomew's Hosp. Medical Coll., 1925–26; Radcliffe Travelling Fellow, 1926–28; Lecturer, 1928–29, and Senior Lecturer, 1929–30, in Dept of Physiology and Biochemistry, Univ. Coll., London; Prof. of Physiology, 1930–65, and Dean of Med. Fac., 1934–47, Univ. of Bristol, and Univ. Rep. on GMC, 1935–65 (Jt Treas., 1962–65); Long Fox Meml Lectr, 1952; Mem. Inter-departmental Cttee on Dentistry, 1943; Mem. Dental Bd of UK, 1945–56; Additional Mem., GDC, 1956–65; Pres., Bath, Bristol and Somerset Branch, BMA 1959; Fellow BMA, 1967; Pres. Bristol Medico-Chirurgical Society, 1960; Member Council, 1958–63, and President Sect. I (Physiology), 1950, British Association; Mem., S-W Regional Hosp. Bd, and Bd of Govs of United Bristol Hosps, 1947–66; Chm, Moorhaven Hosp. Management Cttee, 1966–71; a representative of Diocese of Bristol in the Church Assembly, 1945–65; Member, Central Board of Finance, 1957–65; Chm., Bristol Diocesan Bd of Finance, 1951–65. Mem., Council Westonbirt School, 1955–75 (Chm., 1956–68); Member Council, Christ Church College, Canterbury, 1961–73; Churchwarden, St Mary's, Stoke Bishop, 1939–60; a Vice-President Gloucester and Bristol Diocesan Association of Church Bell Ringers. Chm., Glos, Somerset and N Devon Regional Group, YHA, 1934–45. Served in Tank Corps, 1918–19. *Publications:* Papers on physiological, biochemical and educational subjects in medical and scientific jls. *Recreation:* gardening. *Address:* Cleeve, Court Road, Newton Ferrers, Plymouth, Devon PL8 1DE. *T:* Plymouth (0752) 872397. *Clubs:* Alpine, Commonwealth Trust, Royal Over-Seas League.

BROCKLESBY, Prof. David William, CMG 1991; FRCVS; Professor of Tropical Animal Health and Director of Centre for Tropical Veterinary Medicine, Royal (Dick) School of Veterinary Studies, University of Edinburgh, 1978–90; *b* 12 Feb. 1929; *s* of late David Layton Brocklesby, AFC, and Katherine Jessie (*née* Mudd); *m* 1957, Jennifer Mary Hubble, MB, BS; one *s* three *d. Educ:* Terrington Hall Sch.; Sedbergh Sch.; Royal Vet. Coll., Univ. of London; London Sch. of Hygiene and Tropical Med. MRCVS 1954;

FRCVS (by election) 1984; MRCPath 1964, FRCPath 1982; DrMedVet Zürich 1965. Nat. Service, 4th Queen's Own Hussars (RAC), 1947–49. Vet. Res. Officer (Protozoologist), E Afr. Vet. Res. Org., Muguga, Kenya, 1955–66; Hd of Animal Health Res. Dept, Fisons Pest Control, 1966–67; joined ARC Inst. for Res. on Animal Diseases, Compton, as Parasitologist, 1967; Hd of Parasitology Dept, IRAD, 1969–78. Member: Senatus Academicus, Univ. of Edinburgh, 1978–90; Governing Body, Animal Virus Res. Inst., Pirbright, 1979–86; Bd, Edinburgh Centre of Rural Economy, 1981–88; Council, RCVS, 1985–89. Mem. Editorial Board: Research in Veterinary Science, 1970–88; Tropical Animal Health and Production, 1978–90; British Vet. Jl, 1982–90. *Publications:* papers in sci. jls and chapters in review books, mainly on tropical and veterinary protozoa. *Recreations:* formerly squash and golf, now TV and The Times. *Address:* 3 Broomieknowe, Lasswade, Midlothian EH18 1LN. *T:* 031–663 7743.

BROCKMAN, Rev. John St Leger, CB 1988; Permanent Deacon, St Joseph's RC Church, Epsom, since 1988; *b* 24 March 1928; *s* of late Prof. Ralph St Leger Brockman and Estelle Wilson; *m* 1954, Sheila Elizabeth Jordan; one *s* two *d* (and one *d* decd). *Educ:* Ampleforth; Gonville and Caius Coll., Cambridge. MA, LLB. Called to the Bar, Gray's Inn, 1952. Legal Asst, Min. of National Insurance, 1953; Sen. Legal Asst, Min. of Pensions and National Insurance, 1964; Asst Solicitor, DHSS, 1973; Under Sec. and Principal Asst Solicitor, DHSS, 1978; Solicitor to DHSS, to Registrar General and to OPCS, 1985–89. *Publications:* compiled and edited: The Law relating to Family Allowances and National Insurance, 1961; The Law relating to National Insurance (Industrial Injuries), 1961. *Address:* 304 The Greenway, Epsom, Surrey KT18 7JF. *T:* Epsom (0372) 720242.

BROCKMAN, Vice-Admiral Sir Ronald, KCB 1965; CSI 1947; CIE 1946; CVO 1979; CBE 1943; Extra Gentleman Usher to the Queen, since 1979 (Gentleman Usher, 1967–79); *b* 8 March 1909; *er s* of late Rear-Adm. H. S. Brockman, CB; *m* 1932, Marjorie Jean Butt; one *s* three *d*. *Educ:* Weymouth Coll., Dorset. Entered Navy, 1927; Assistant Secretary to First Sea Lord, Admiral of the Fleet Sir Roger Backhouse, 1938–39; Lieut-Commander 1939; Admiral's Secretary to First Sea Lord, Admiral of the Fleet Sir Dudley Pound, 1939–43; Commander 1943; Admiral's Secretary to Admiral of the Fleet Lord Mountbatten in all appointments, 1943–59; Private Secretary to Governor-General of India, 1947–48. Principal Staff Officer to the Chief of Defence Staff, Min. of Defence, 1959–65. Captain, 1953; Rear-Admiral, 1959; Vice-Admiral, 1963; retired list, 1965. Mem., Rugby Football Union Cttee, 1956–. Asst in Court of Tin Plate Workers alias Wireworkers' Company. DL Devon. KStJ 1985; Mem. Chapter-Gen., Order of St John. Special Rosette of Cloud and Banner (China), 1946; Chevalier Legion of Honour and Croix de Guerre, 1946; Bronze Star Medal (USA), 1947. *Address:* 3 Court House, Basil Street, SW3 1AJ. *T:* 071–584 1023. *Clubs:* White's, Naval, MCC; Royal Western Yacht Club of England.

BROCKMAN, Hon. Sir Thomas Charles D.; *see* Drake-Brockman.

BRÖDER, Ernst-Günther, DEcon; German economist and financial executive; President, and Chairman of the Board of Directors, European Investment Bank, since 1984 (a Director, 1980–84); *b* Cologne, 6 Jan. 1927. *Educ:* Univs of Cologne, Mayence, Freiburg and Paris. Corporate staff, Bayer AG Leverkusen, 1956–61; Projects Dept, World Bank, 1961–64; Kreditanstalt für Wiederaufbau, 1964–84: Manager, 1969–75; Mem., Bd of Management, 1975–84; Bd of Management Spokesman, 1980–84. Member: Special Adv. Gp, Asian Develt Bank, 1981–82; Panel of Conciliators, Internat. Centre for Settlement of Investment Disputes, 1976–. *Address:* European Investment Bank, 100 boulevard Konrad Adenauer, L-2950 Luxembourg. *T:* 43 79–1.

BRODIE, Sir Benjamin David Ross, 5th Bt *cr* 1834; *b* 29 May 1925; *s* of Sir Benjamin Collins Brodie, 4th Bt, MC, and Mary Charlotte (*d* 1940), *e d* of R. E. Palmer, Ballyheigue, Co. Kerry; *S* father, 1971; *m*; one *s* one *d*. *Educ:* Eton. Formerly Royal Corps of Signals. *Heir:* *s* Alan Brodie.

BRODIE, Colin Alexander, QC 1980; *b* 19 April 1929; *s* of Sir Benjamin Collins Brodie, 4th Bt, MC, and late Mary Charlotte, *e d* of R. E. Palmer, Ballyheigue, Co. Kerry; *m* 1955, Julia Anne Irene, *yr d* of Norman Edward Wates; two *s*. *Educ:* Eton; Magdalen Coll., Oxford. 2/Lieut 8th KRI Hussars, 1949–50. Called to the Bar, Middle Temple, 1954. Bencher, Lincoln's Inn, 1988. *Recreations:* polo, hunting. *Address:* 24 Old Buildings, Lincoln's Inn, WC2. *T:* 071–404 0946.

BRODIE, Elizabeth, (Mrs S. E. Brodie); *see* Gloster, E.

BRODIE OF BRODIE, (Montagu) Ninian (Alexander), DL; JP; Chief of Clan Brodie; landowner since 1953; *b* 12 June 1912; *s* of I. A. M. Brodie of Brodie (*d* 1943) and C. V. M. Brodie of Brodie (*née* Hope) (*d* 1958); *m* 1939, Helena Penelope Mills Budgen (*d* 1972); one *s* one *d*. *Educ:* Eton. Stage, films, TV, 1933–40 and 1945–49. Served Royal Artillery, 1940–45. JP Morayshire, 1958; Hon. Sheriff-Substitute, 1958; DL Nairn, 1970. *Recreations:* shooting, collecting pictures. *Heir:* *s* Alastair Ian Ninian Brodie, Younger of Brodie [*b* 7 Sept. 1943; *m* 1968, Mary Louise Johnson; two *s* one *d*]. *Address:* Brodie Castle, Forres, Moray IV36 0TE, Scotland. *T:* Brodie (03094) 202.

BRODIE, Philip Hope; QC (Scot) 1987; *b* 14 July 1950; *s* of Very Rev. Peter Philip Brodie; *m* 1983, Carol Dora McLeish; two *s* one *d*. *Educ:* Dollar Academy; Edinburgh Univ. (LLB Hons); Univ. of Virginia (LLM). Admitted Faculty of Advocates, 1976; Standing Junior Counsel, MOD (Scotland) PE, and HSE, 1983. Mem., Mental Welfare Commn for Scotland, 1985–. Part-time Chm., Industrial Tribunals, 1987–. *Recreations:* walking, ski-ing, reading. *Address:* 2 Cobden Crescent, Edinburgh EH9 2BG. *T:* 031–667 2651.

BRODIE, Robert, CB 1990; Solicitor to the Secretary of State for Scotland, since 1987; *b* 9 April 1938; *s* of Robert Brodie, MBE and Helen Ford Bayne Grieve; *m* 1970, Jean Margaret McDonald; two *s* two *d*. *Educ:* Morgan Acad., Dundee; St Andrews Univ. (MA 1959, LLB 1962). Admitted Solicitor, 1962. Office of Solicitor to the Sec. of State for Scotland: Legal Asst, 1965; Sen. Legal Asst, 1970; Asst Solicitor, 1975; Dep. Dir, Scottish Courts Admin, 1975–82; Dep. Solicitor to Sec. of State for Scotland, 1984–1987. *Recreations:* music, hill-walking. *Address:* 45 Stirling Road, Edinburgh EH5 3JB. *T:* 031–552 2028.

BRODIE, Stanley Eric, QC 1975; a Recorder of the Crown Court, since 1975; *b* 2 July 1930; *s* of Abraham Brodie, MB, BS and Cissie Rachel Brodie; *m* 1956, Gillian Rosemary Joseph; two *d*; *m* 1973, Elizabeth Gloster, *qv*; one *s* one *d*. *Educ:* Bradford Grammar Sch.; Balliol Coll., Oxford (MA). Pres., Oxford Univ. Law Soc., 1952. Called to Bar, Inner Temple, 1954; Bencher, 1984; Mem. NE Circuit, 1954; Lectr in Law, Univ. of Southampton, 1954–55. Mem., Bar Council, 1987–89. *Recreations:* opera, boating, winter sports, fishing. *Address:* Skeldon House, Dalrymple, Ayrshire KA6 6ED. *T:* Dalrymple (029256) 223; 39 Clarendon Street, SW1V 4RE. *T:* 071–821 0975. *Club:* Flyfishers'.

BRODIE, Maj.-Gen. Thomas, CB 1954; CBE 1949; DSO 1951; late The Cheshire Regt; *b* 20 Oct. 1903; *s* of Thomas Brodie, Bellingham, Northumberland; *m* 1938, Jane Margaret Chapman-Walker; three *s* one *d*. *Educ:* Durham Univ. (BA 1924). Adjutant, The Cheshire Regt, 1935–37; Instructor, RMA Sandhurst, 1938–39; commanded: 2 Manchester Regt, 1942–43; 14th Infantry Brigade in Wingate Expedition, Burma, 1944; 1 Cheshire Regt, 1946–47; Palestine, 1947–48 (CBE and despatches); commanded 29 Inf. Bde, Korea, 1951 (DSO, US Silver Star Medal, US Legion of Merit); GOC 1 Infantry Div., MELF, 1952–55; Colonel, The Cheshire Regiment, 1955–61; retired 1957. Economic League, 1957–84. *Address:* Greenball, Crawley Ridge, Camberley, Surrey GU15 2AJ. *Club:* Army and Navy.

BRODIE-HALL, Sir Laurence Charles, Kt 1982; CMG 1976; Director, 1962–82, Consultant, 1975–82, Western Mining Corporation; Chairman: Board of Management, Western Australian School of Mines; West Australian Foundation for the Museum of Science and Technology; *b* 10 June 1910; *m* 1st, 1940, Dorothy Jolly (decd); three *s* two *d*; 2nd, 1978, Jean Verschuer. *Educ:* Sch. of Mines, Kalgoorlie (Dip. Metallurgy 1947, DipME 1948). Served War, RAE. Geologist, Central Norseman Gold Corp., 1948–49; Tech. Asst to Man. Dir, Western Mining Corp., 1950–51; Gen. Supt, Gt Western Consolidated, 1951–58; Gen. Supt, 1958–68, Exec. Dir, WA, 1967–75, Western Mining Corp.; Chairman: Gold Mines of Kalgoorlie (Aust.) Ltd, 1974–82; Central Norseman Gold Corp. NL, 1974–82; Westintech Innovation Corp. Ltd, 1984–88; Director: Ansett WA (formerly Airlines WA), 1983–; Coolgardie Gold NL, 1985–; former Chm. or Dir of many subsidiaries, and Dir, Alcoa of Australia Ltd, 1971–83. Pres., WA Chamber of Mines, 1970–75 (Life Mem.); Past Pres., Australasian Inst. of Mining and Metallurgy (Institute Medal, 1977, Hon. Life Mem., 1987); Chm., WA State Cttee, CSIRO, 1971–81. Hon. DTech, WA Inst. Technology, 1978. *Address:* (office) 2 Cliff Street, Perth, WA 6000, Australia. *Club:* Weld (Perth).

BRODRICK, family name of **Viscount Midleton.**

BRODRICK, Michael John Lee; His Honour Judge Brodrick; a Circuit Judge, since 1987; *b* 12 Oct. 1941; *s* of His Honour Norman John Lee Brodrick, *qv*; *m* 1969, Valerie Lois Stroud; one *s* one *d*. *Educ:* Charterhouse; Merton Coll., Oxford (2nd Jurisp.). Called to the Bar, Lincoln's Inn, 1965; Western Circuit; a Recorder, 1981–87. Judicial Mem., Transport Tribunal, 1986. Mem., Senate of Inns of Court and Bar, 1979, served 1979–82; Mem., Wine Cttee, Western Circuit, 1982–86. *Recreation:* gardening. *Club:* Hampshire (Winchester).

BRODRICK, His Honour Norman John Lee, QC 1960; JP; MA; a Circuit Judge (formerly a Judge of the Central Criminal Court), 1967–82; *b* 4 Feb. 1912; 4th *s* of late William John Henry Brodrick, OBE; *m* 1940, Ruth Severn, *d* of late Sir Stanley Unwin, KCMG; three *s* one *d*. *Educ:* Charterhouse; Merton College, Oxford. Called to the Bar, Lincoln's Inn, 1935, Bencher, 1965; Mem. Senate of Four Inns of Court, 1970–71. Western Circuit, 1935. Temporary civil servant (Ministry of Economic Warfare and Admiralty), 1939–45. Bar Council, 1950–54 and 1962–66. Recorder: of Penzance, 1957–59; of Bridgwater, 1959–62; of Plymouth, 1962–64. Chairman, Mental Health Review Tribunal, Wessex Region, 1960–63; Deputy Chairman, Middlesex Quarter Sessions, 1961–65; Recorder of Portsmouth, 1964–67; Chm., IoW QS, 1964–67, Dep. Chm. 1967–71. Chm., Deptl Cttee on Death Certification and Coroners, 1965–71. JP Hants, 1967. *Recreations:* gardening, model railways. *Address:* Slade Lane Cottage, Rogate, near Petersfield, Hants GU31 5BL. *T:* Rogate (073080) 605.

See also M. J. L. Brodrick.

BRODSKY, Joseph Alexandrovich; poet; *b* Leningrad, 24 May 1940; *s* of Alexander I. Brodsky and Maria M. Brodsky (*née* Volpert); one *s*. *Educ:* Leningrad. Began writing poetry 1955; imprisoned as dissident, Arkhangelsk region, 1964–65; left for Vienna, 1972; went on to London and USA; poet in residence, Univ. of Michigan, 1972–73 and 1974–80; John and Catherine MacArthur Foundn Grant, 1981; teaching poetry and literature: Columbia Univ. (Russian Inst.); NY Univ. (Fellow, Inst. of Humanities); Mt Holyoke, Smith, Amherst and Hampshire Colls; Queen's Coll., City Univ. of NY. Hon. DLitt Yale, 1978 and other awards. Nobel Prize for Literature, 1987. *Publications:* Elegy for John Donne and other poems, 1967; Selected Poems, 1973; A Part of Speech, 1980; Less Than One, 1981 (Nat. Book Critics' Award, USA); To Urania, 1988. *Address:* c/o Farrar, Straus & Giroux Inc., 19 Union Square West, New York, NY 10003, USA.

BROERS, Prof. Alec Nigel, PhD; FRS 1986; FEng 1985; FIEE; Professor of Electrical Engineering and Head of Electrical Division, Cambridge University, since 1984; Master of Churchill College, Cambridge, since 1990; *b* 17 Sept. 1938; *s* of late Alec William Broers and of Constance Amy (*née* Cox); *m* 1964, Mary Therese Phelan; two *s*. *Educ:* Geelong Grammar School; Melbourne Univ. (BSc Physics 1958, Electronics 1959); Caius College, Cambridge Univ. (BA Mech Scis 1962, PhD Mech Scis 1965). IBM Thomas Watson Research Center: Research Staff Mem., 1965–67; Manager, Electron Beam Technology, 1967–72; Manager, Photon and Electron Optics, 1972–80; IBM East Fishkill Laboratory: Manager, Lithography Systems and Technology Tools, 1981–82; Manager, Semiconductor Lithography and Process Develt, 1982–83; Manager, Advanced Develt, 1983–84; Mem., Corporate Tech. Cttee, IBM Corporate HQ, 1984; Fellow, Trinity Coll., Cambridge, 1985–90. IBM Fellow, 1977. Prize for Industrial Applications of Physics, Amer. Inst. of Physics, 1982; Cledo Brunetti Award, IEEE, 1985. *Publications:* patents, papers and book chapters on electron microscopy, electron beam lithography, integrated circuit fabrication. *Recreations:* music, small-boat sailing, skiing, tennis. *Address:* The Master's Lodge, Churchill College, Cambridge CB3 0DS.

BROGAN, Lt-Gen. Sir Mervyn (Francis), KBE 1972 (CBE 1964; OBE 1944); CB 1970; Chief of the General Staff, Australia, 1971–73, retired; *b* 10 Jan. 1915; *s* of Bernard Brogan, Dubbo, NSW; *m* 1941, Sheila, *d* of David S. Jones, Canberra; two *s*. *Educ:* RMC Duntroon (Sword of Honour, 1935); Wesley Coll., Univ. of Sydney. Commnd 1935; BEng Sydney, 1938. Served War of 1939–45: New Guinea, 1942–45 (despatches 1943); trng UK and BAOR, 1946–47; Chief Instructor, Sch. of Mil. Engrg, 1947–49; trng UK and USA, 1950–52; jssc 1952; Chief Engr, Southern Comd, 1953–54; Dir of Mil. Trng, 1954–55; BGS: Army HQ, 1956; FARELF, 1956–58; idc 1959; Comdt Australian Staff Coll., 1960–62; GOC Northern Comd, 1962–64; Dir Jt Service Plans, Dept of Defence, 1965–66; QMG 1966–68; GOC Eastern Comd, 1968–71. Director: Copperfield Gold NL; Laverton Gold NL. Hon. FIEAust; CPEng; FAIM. JP. *Recreations:* surfing, tennis. *Address:* 71/53 Ocean Avenue, Double Bay, NSW 2028, Australia. *T:* 32–9509. *Clubs:* Union, Australian Jockey, Tattersall's, Royal Sydney Golf, City Tattersall's, Australasian Pioneers (Sydney).

BROINOWSKI, John Herbert, CMG 1969; FCA; finance and investment consultant; Senior Partner, J. H. Broinowski & Storey, Chartered Accountants, 1944–54; Founder/Chairman and Managing Director, Consolidated Metal Products Ltd, 1954–70; Chairman: Utilux Ltd, since 1977; Vielun Poll Hereford Stud, since 1955; Allied-Lyons Australia, since 1982; Zip Heaters Ltd, since 1986; Photographic Index of Australian Wildlife, since 1980; *b* 19 May 1911; *s* of late Dr G. H. Broinowski and late Mrs Ethel Broinowski (*née* Hungerford); *m* 1939, Jean Gaerloch Broinowski, *d* of Sir Norman and Lady Kater; one *s* one step *s*. *Educ:* Sydney Church of England Grammar Sch. Served Australian Imperial Forces (Captain), 1940–44, New Guinea. Chief Exec. and Dep. Chm., Schroder Darling and Co. Ltd, 1963–73; Exec. Chm., Sims Consolidated Ltd, 1970–83; Director: Electrical

Equipment Ltd, 1954–77; Readers Digest Aust., 1955–77; Mount Morgan Ltd, 1962–67 (Chm.); Peko-Wallsend Ltd, 1962–83; South British United Insurance Gp, 1965–73; Hoyts Theatres Ltd, 1968–79 (Chm.); Compunet Ltd, 1969–77 (Chm.); Orient Lloyd Gp, Singapore, 1970–87 (Chm.): Doulton Aust. Ltd, 1972–77; Robe River Ltd, 1972–73; Aquila Steel Co. Ltd, 1973–81 (Chm.), Formfit Ltd, 1974–79 (Chm.); John Sands Ltd, 1974–77; Clive Hall Ltd, 1974–84 (Chm.); Castlemaine Tooheys Ltd, 1977–83 (Dep. Chm.); Hin Kong Ltd, 1977–86 (Chm.); Judson Steel Corp., San Francisco, 1979–83 (Chm.). Chm. Cttee, Photographic Index of Australian Wildlife, 1980–. Hon. Life Member: Aust. Council for Rehabilitation of the Disabled (Pres., 1964–68); NSW Soc. for Crippled Children (Pres., 1970–77); Vice-Pres., Internat. Soc. for Rehabilitation of the Disabled, 1966–72. *Address:* 1c Wentworth Place, Point Piper, Sydney, NSW 2027, Australia. *T:* 02/3287534. *Clubs:* Australian, Royal Sydney Golf (Sydney).

BROKE; *see* Willoughby de Broke.

BROKE, Col George Robin Straton, LVO 1977; Equerry-in-Waiting to the Queen, 1974–77; *b* 31 March 1946; *s* of Maj.-Gen. R. S. Broke, *qv*; *m* 1978, Patricia Thornhill Shann, *d* of Thomas Thornhill Shann; one *s*. *Educ:* Eton. Commissioned into Royal Artillery, 1965; CO 3 RHA, 1987–89. *Recreation:* country sports. *Address:* Ivy Farm, Holme Hale, Thetford, Norfolk. *T:* Holme Hale (0760) 440225. *Club:* Lansdowne.

BROKE, Maj.-Gen. Robert Straton, CB 1967; OBE 1946; MC 1940; Director, Wellman plc (formerly Wellman Engineering Corporation), and Chairman of six companies within the Group, 1968–88; *b* 15 March 1913; *s* of Rev. Horatio George Broke and Mary Campbell Broke (*née* Adlington); *m* 1939, Ernine Susan Margaret Bonsey; two *s*. *Educ:* Eton College (KS); Magdalene College, Cambridge (BA). Commissioned Royal Artillery, 1933. Commander Royal Artillery: 5th Division, 1959; 1st Division, 1960; 1st (British) Corps 1961; Northern Army Group, 1964–66, retired. Col Comdt, RA, 1968–78; Representative Col Comdt, 1974–75. Chm., Iron and Steel Plant Contractors Assoc., 1972, 1977. Pres., Metallurgical Plantmakers' Fedn, 1977–79. *Recreations:* country sports. *Address:* Ivy Farm, Holme Hale, Thetford, Norfolk IP25 7DJ. *T:* Holme Hale (0760) 440225. *Club:* Army and Navy.

See also G. R. S. Broke.

BROME, Vincent; author; *s* of Nathaniel Gregory and Emily Brome. *Educ:* Streatham Grammar School; Elleston School; privately. Formerly: Feature Writer; Editor, Menu Magazines; Min. of Information; Asst Editor, Medical World. Since then author biographies, novels, plays and essays; broadcaster. Mem., British Library Adv. Cttee, 1975–82. *Plays:* The Sleepless One (prod. Edin), 1962; BBC plays. *Publications:* Anthology, 1936; Clement Attlee, 1947; H. G. Wells, 1951; Aneurin Bevan, 1953; The Last Surrender, 1954; The Way Back, 1956; Six Studies in Quarrelling, 1958; Sometimes at Night, 1959; Frank Harris, 1959; Acquaintance With Grief, 1961; We Have Come a Long Way, 1962; The Problem of Progress, 1963; Love in Our Time, 1964; Four Realist Novelists, 1964; The International Brigades, 1965; The World of Luke Jympson, 1966; Freud and His Early Circle, 1967; The Surgeon, 1967; Diary of A Revolution, 1968; The Revolution, 1969; The Imaginary Crime, 1969; Confessions of a Writer, 1970; The Brain Operators, 1970; Private Prosecutions, 1971; Reverse Your Verdict, 1971; London Consequences, 1972; The Embassy, 1972; The Day of Destruction, 1975; The Happy Hostage, 1976; Jung—Man and Myth, 1978; Havelock Ellis—philosopher of sex, 1981; Ernest Jones: Freud's alter ego, 1983; The Day of the Fifth Moon, 1984; J. B. Priestley, 1988; contrib. The Times, Sunday Times, Observer, Manchester Guardian, New Statesman, New Society, Encounter, Spectator, TLS etc. *Recreations:* writing plays and talking. *Address:* 45 Great Ormond Street, WC1. *T:* 071–405 0550. *Club:* Savile.

BROMET, Air Comdt Dame Jean (Lena Annette), (Lady Bromet); *see* Conan Doyle, Air Comdt Dame J. L. A.

BROMHEAD, (Sir) John Desmond Gonville, (6th Bt *cr* 1806); *S* father, 1981, but does not use title. *Heir: cousin* John Edmund de Gonville Bromhead [*b* 10 Oct. 1939; *m* 1965, Janet Frances, *e d* of Harry Vernon Brotherton, Moreton-in-Marsh, Glos; one *s* one *d*].

BROMLEY, Archdeacon of; *see* Francis, Ven. E. R.

BROMLEY, Lance Lee, MA; MChir; FRCS; Director of Medical and Health Services, Gibraltar, 1982–85; Honorary Consultant Cardiothoracic Surgeon, St Mary's Hospital, W2; *b* 16 Feb. 1920; *s* of late Lancelot Bromley, MChir, FRCS, of London and Seaford, Sussex, and Dora Ridgway Bromley, Dewsbury, Yorks; *m* 1952, Rosemary Anne Holbrook; three *d*. *Educ:* St Paul's School; Caius Coll., Cambridge. Late Capt. RAMC. Late Travelling Fell. Amer. Assoc. for Thoracic Surgery. Consultant Thoracic Surgeon, St Mary's Hosp., 1953–80; Consultant Gen. Surgeon, Teddington Hosp., 1953–80. *Publications:* various contributions to medical journals. *Recreations:* sailing, golf. *Address:* 26 Molyneux Street, W1. *T:* 071–262 7175. *Club:* Royal Ocean Racing.

See also Sir Charles Knowles, Bt.

BROMLEY, Leonard John, QC 1971; **His Honour Judge Bromley;** a Circuit Judge, since 1984; *b* 21 Feb. 1929; 2nd *s* of George Ernest and Winifred Dora Bromley; *m* 1962, Anne (*née* Bacon); three *d*. *Educ:* City of Leicester Boys' Sch.; Selwyn Coll., Cambridge (exhibnr). MA, LLM (Cantab). National Service: 2nd Lt, RA, Hong Kong, 1947–49. Selwyn Coll., Cambridge, 1949–53; called to Bar, Lincoln's Inn, 1954; Bencher, 1978; Greenland Scholar, Lincoln's Inn. In practice, Chancery Bar, 1954–84; a Recorder, 1980–84. Chief Social Security Comr, 1984–90. Gen. Council of the Bar: Mem., 1970–74; Chm., Law Reform Cttee, 1972–74; Mem., Exec. Cttee, 1972–74. Chm., Performing Right Tribunal, 1980–83. A Legal Assessor to: GMC, 1977–84; GDC, 1977–84; Governor, Latymer Sch., Edmonton, 1978–84. Vice Cdre, Bar Yacht Club, 1971–75. *Recreations:* sailing, walking. *Address:* c/o South Eastern Circuit Office, Lord Chancellor's Department, 18 Maltravers Street, WC2R 3EU. *Club:* Athenæum.

BROMLEY, Prof. Peter Mann; Professor of English Law, University of Manchester, 1985–86 (Professor of Law, 1965–85), now Professor Emeritus; *b* 20 Nov. 1922; *s* of Frank Bromley and Marion Maud (*née* Moy); *m* 1963, Beatrice Mary, *d* of Eric Charles Cassels Hunter and Amy Madeleine (*née* Renold). *Educ:* Ealing Grammar Sch.; The Queen's College, Oxford (MA 1948). Called to the Bar, Middle Temple, 1951. Served War, Royal Artillery, 1942–45. University of Manchester: Asst Lectr 1947–50, Lectr 1950–61, Sen. Lectr 1961–65; Dean, Faculty of Law, 1966–68, 1972–74 and 1981–83; Pro-Vice-Chancellor, 1977–81; Principal, Dalton Hall, 1958–65. Vis. Prof. of Law, Univ. of Buckingham, 1987–88. Chm., Cttee on Professional Legal Educn in NI, 1983–85; Member: Adv. Cttee on Legal Educn, 1972–75; University Grants Cttee, 1978–85 (Chm., Social Studies Sub-cttee, 1979–85); Commonwealth Scholarship Commn, 1986–. Editor, Butterworths Family Law Service, 1983–. *Publications:* Family Law, 1957, 7th edn (with N. V. Lowe) 1987; (contrib.) Parental Custody and Matrimonial Maintenance, 1966; (contrib.) Das Erbrecht von Familienangehörigen, 1971; (contrib.) The Child and the Courts, 1978; (contrib.) Adoption, 1984; (contrib.) Children and the Law, 1990; articles in various legal jls. *Recreations:* walking, listening to music. *Address:* Paddock Brow, Faulkners Lane, Mobberley, Cheshire WA16 7AL. *T:* Mobberley (0565) 872183. *Club:* United Oxford & Cambridge University.

BROMLEY, Sir Rupert Charles, 10th Bt, *cr* 1757; *b* 2 April 1936; *s* of Major Sir Rupert Howe Bromley, MC, 9th Bt, and Dorothy Vera (*d* 1982), *d* of late Sir Walford Selby, KCMG, CB, CVO; *S* father, 1966; *m* 1962, Priscilla Hazel, *d* of late Maj. Howard Bourne, HAC; three *s*. *Educ:* Michaelhouse, Natal; Rhodes Univ.; Christ Church, Oxford. *Recreations:* equestrian. *Heir: s* Charles Howard Bromley, *b* 31 July 1963. *Address:* PO Box 249, Rivonia, Transvaal, 2128, South Africa.

BROMLEY-DAVENPORT, William Arthur; landowner; chartered accountant; Lord-Lieutenant of Cheshire, since 1990; *b* 7 March 1935; *o s* of Lt-Col Sir Walter Bromley-Davenport, TD, DL and Lenette, *d* of Joseph Y. Jeanes, Philadelphia; *m* 1962, Elizabeth Watts, Oldwick, NJ; one *s* one *d*. *Educ:* Eton; Cornell Univ., NY. Mem. ICA, 1966. National Service, 2nd Batt. Grenadier Guards, 1953–54; Hon. Col 3rd (Vol.) Batt. 22nd (Cheshire) Regt, 1985. Owns land in UK and Norway. Dir, Macclesfield and Vale Royal Groundwork Trust Ltd, 1987–91; Mem. Cttee (past Chm.) Cheshire Br., CLA, 1962–. Pres., Cheshire Scout Council, 1990– (Chm., 1981–90). Chm. of Govs, King's Sch., Macclesfield, 1986–. JP 1975, DL 1982, High Sheriff 1983–84, Cheshire. *Address:* The Kennels, Capesthorne, Macclesfield; Fiva, Aandalsnes, Norway.

BROMWICH, Prof. Michael; CIMA Professor of Accounting and Financial Management, London School of Economics and Political Science, since 1985; *b* 29 Jan. 1941; *s* of William James Bromwich and Margery (*née* Townley); *m* 1972, Christine Margaret Elizabeth Whitehead (OBE 1991). *Educ:* Wentworth High Sch., Southend; London School of Economics (BScEcon 1965); FCMA. Ford Motor Co., 1958–62 and 1965–66; Lectr, LSE, 1966–70; Professor: UWIST, 1971–77; Univ. of Reading, 1977–85. Mem. Council, ICMA, 1980–85; Vice Pres., ICMA, later CIMA, 1985–87, Pres., CIMA, 1987–88. Mem., Accounting Standards Cttee, 1981–84. *Publications:* Economics of Capital Budgeting, 1976; Economics of Accounting Standard Setting, 1985; (jtly) Management Accounting: evolution not revolution, 1989; co-ed others, incl. Essays in British Accounting Research; several articles. *Recreations:* working and eating in restaurants. *Address:* 14 Thornhill Road, N1 1HW. *T:* 071–607 9323.

BRON, Prof. Anthony John, FRCS, FCOphth; Professor and Head of Department of Ophthalmology, Director, Nuffield Laboratory of Ophthalmology, and Fellow of Linacre College, Oxford; *b* 3 Feb. 1936. *Educ:* London Univ. (BSc 1957; MB BS 1961); Guy's Hosp. (DO 1964); MA Oxon 1973. LRCP 1960; MRCS 1960, FRCS 1968. Guy's Hosp., 1961–63; Clin. Fellow in Ophthalmol., Johns Hopkins Univ., 1964–65; Res. Assistant, Inst. of Ophthalmol., 1964–65; Moorfields Eye Hospital: Chief Clin. Assistant, 1965; Resident Surg. Officer, 1965–68; Lectr, 1968–70; Sen. Lectr and Hon. Consultant, 1970–73; Margaret Ogilvie's Reader in Ophthalmol., Oxford Univ., 1973–89; Hon. Consultant, Oxford Eye Hosp., 1989–. *Publications:* (contrib.) The Inborn Errors of Metabolism; The Unquiet Eye, 1983, 2nd edn 1987. *Address:* Nuffield Laboratory of Ophthalmology, Walton Street, Oxford OX2 6AW. *T:* Oxford (0865) 248996.

BRON, Eleanor; actress and writer; *d* of Sydney and late Fagah Bron. *Educ:* North London Collegiate Sch., Canons, Edgware; Newnham Coll., Cambridge (BA Hons Mod. Langs). De La Rue Co., 1961. Appearances include: revue, Establishment Nightclub, Soho, 1962, and New York, 1963; Not so much a Programme, More a Way of Life, BBC TV, 1964; several TV series written with John Fortune, and TV series: Making Faces, written by Michael Frayn, 1976; Pinkerton's Progress, 1983; *TV plays and films include:* Nina, 1978; My Dear Palestrina, 1980; A Month in the Country, 1985; Quartermaine's Terms, 1987; Changing Step, 1989; The Hour of the Lynx, 1990. *Stage roles include:* Jennifer Dubedat, The Doctor's Dilemma, 1966; Jean Brodie, The Prime of Miss Jean Brodie, 1967, 1984; title role, Hedda Gabler, 1969; Portia, The Merchant of Venice, 1975; Amanda, Private Lives, 1976; Elena, Uncle Vanya, 1977; Charlotte, The Cherry Orchard, 1978; Margaret, A Family, 1978; On Her Own, 1980; Goody Biddy Bean; The Amusing Spectacle of Cinderella and her Naughty, Naughty Sisters, 1980; Betrayal, 1981; Heartbreak House, 1981; Duet for One, 1982; The Duchess of Malfi, 1985; The Real Inspector Hound, and The Critic (double bill), 1985; Jocasta and Ismene, Oedipus and Oedipus at Colonus, 1987; Infidelities, 1987; The Madwoman of Chaillot, 1988; The Chalk Garden, 1989; The Miser, and The White Devil, 1991; opera, Die Glückliche Hana, Nederlandse Oper, Amsterdam, 1991. *Films include:* Help!; Alfie; Two for the Road; Bedazzled; Women in Love; The National Health; The Day that Christ Died, 1980; Turtle Diary, 1985; Little Dorrit, 1987; The Attic, 1988. Author: song-cycle with John Dankworth, 1973; verses for Saint-Saens' Carnival of the Animals, 1975 (recorded). A Dir, Actors Centre, 1982–. *Publications:* Is Your Marriage Really Necessary (with John Fortune), 1972; (contrib.) My Cambridge, 1976; (contrib.) More Words, 1977; Life and Other Punctures, 1978; The Pillow Book of Eleanor Bron, 1985.*Address:* c/o Jeremy Conway Ltd, 18–21 Jermyn Street, SW1. *Club:* Actors Centre.

BRONFMAN, Edgar Miles; Chairman and Chief Executive Officer: The Seagram Company Ltd, since 1975; Joseph E. Seagram & Sons Inc.; *b* 20 June 1929; *s* of late Samuel Bronfman and of Saidye Rosner. *Educ:* Trinity College Sch., Port Hope, Ont., Canada; Williams Coll., Williamstown, Mass, US; McGill Univ., Montreal (BA 1951). President: Joseph E. Seagram & Sons, Inc, 1957; The Seagram Company Ltd, 1971; Dir, E. I. duPont de Nemours & Co. Pres., World Jewish Congress, 1980–. Hon. LHD Pace Univ., NY, 1982; Hon. Dr Laws Williams Coll., Williamstown, 1986. *Address:* 375 Park Avenue, New York, NY 10152, USA. *T:* (212) 572–7000.

BROOK, Anthony Donald, FCA; Managing Director Broadcasting, TVS Entertainment plc, since 1989; *b* 24 Sept. 1936; *s* of Donald Charles Brook and Doris Ellen (*née* Emmett); *m* 1965, Ann Mary Reeves; two *d*. *Educ:* Eastbourne Coll. FCA 1970 (ACA 1960). Joined Associated Television Ltd, 1966; Financial Controller, ATV Network Ltd, 1969; Dir of External Finance, IBA, 1974; Finance Dir/Gen. Man., ITC Entertainment Ltd, 1978; Dep. Man. Dir, Television South plc, 1981; Man. Dir (Television), Television South, then TVS Entertainment, 1984–89. Man. Dir, TVS Television Ltd, 1986. *Recreations:* sailing, travel. *Address:* 18 Brookvale Road, Highfield, Southampton SO2 1QP. *Clubs:* Tamesis (Teddington, Mddx); Royal Southern Yacht (Hamble, Hants).

BROOK, Air Vice-Marshal David Conway Grant, CB 1990; CBE 1983; Civil Emergencies Adviser, Home Office, since 1989; *b* 23 Dec. 1935; *s* of late Air Vice-Marshal William Arthur Darville Brook, CB, CBE and of Jean Brook (now Jean Hamilton); *m* 1961, Jessica (*née* Lubbock); one *s* one *d*. *Educ:* Marlborough Coll.; RAF Coll. Pilot, Nos 263, 1 (Fighter) and 14 Sqdns, 1957–62 (Hunter aircraft; fighter combat leader); ADC to AOC-in-C Near East Air Force, 1962–64; CO No 1 (Fighter) Sqdn, 1964–66 (Hunter Mk 9); RN Staff Course, 1967 (psc); RAF Adviser to Dir Land/Air Warfare (MoD Army), 1968–69; Wing Comdr Offensive Support, Jt Warfare Estab., 1970–72; CO No 20 (Army Cooperation) Sqdn, 1974–76 (Harrier); Station Comdr, RAF Wittering, 1976–78 (Harrier); rcds, 1979; Principal Staff Officer to Chief of Defence Staff, 1980–82; SASO, HQ RAF Germany, 1982–85; Air Officer Scotland and NI, 1986–89; rcds, 1989. *Publications:* contrib. to Brasseys Annual. *Recreations:* golf, music, canal boating, walking, fishing. *Address:* c/o Lloyds Bank, Cranbrook, Kent TN17 3DJ.

BROOK, (Gerald) Robert, CBE 1981; Chief Executive, 1977–86, and Chairman, 1985–86, National Bus Company (Deputy Chairman, 1978–85); *b* 19 Dec. 1928; *s* of

Charles Pollard Brook and Doris Brook (*née* Senior); *m* 1957, Joan Marjorie Oldfield; two *s* one *d*. *Educ:* King James Grammar Sch., Knaresborough. FCIS, FCIT. Served Duke of Wellington's Regt, 1947–49. Appointments in bus companies, from 1950; Company Secretary: Cumberland Motor Services Ltd, 1960; Thames Valley Traction Co. Ltd, 1963; General Manager: North Western Road Car Co. Ltd, 1968; Midland Red Omnibus Co. Ltd, 1972; Regional Director, National Bus Company, 1974; Director: Scottish Transport Gp; United Transport Internat. Plc; United Transport Buses Ltd; S Yorks Transport Ltd; Midland Fox Holdings Ltd. Pres., CIT, 1987–88. *Publications:* papers for professional instns and learned socs. *Recreation:* reading military history. *Address:* Hallow Cottage, Crimple Lane, Follifoot, near Harrogate, N Yorks HG3 1DF. *Club:* Army and Navy.

BROOK, Helen, (Lady Brook); Founder, 1963, and President, Brook Advisory Centre for Young People (Chairman, 1964–74); *b* 12 Oct. 1907; *d* of John and Helen Knewstub; *m* 1937, Sir Robin Brook, *qv*; two *d* (and one *d* of previous marriage). *Educ:* Convent of Holy Child Jesus, Mark Cross, Sussex. Voluntary Worker: Family Planning Association, 1949–; Family Planning Sales, 1972– (Chm., 1974–81); Vice President: Nat. Assoc. of Family Planning Nurses, 1980–; FPA, 1982. *Recreations:* painting, gardening. *Address:* 31 Acacia Road, NW8 6AS. *T:* 071–722 5844; Claydene Garden Cottage, Cowden, Kent.

BROOK, Leopold, BScEng, FICE, FIMechE; Director, Renishaw plc, since 1980; *b* 2 Jan. 1912; *s* of Albert and Kate Brook, Hampstead; *m* 1st, 1940, Susan (*d* 1970), *d* of David Rose, Hampstead; two *s*; 2nd, 1974, Mrs Elly Rhodes; two step *s* one step *d*. *Educ:* Central Foundation School, London; University College, London. L. G. Mouchel & Partners, Cons. Engineers, 1935–44; Simon Engineering Ltd, 1944–77 (Chief Exec., 1967–70; Chm., 1970–77); Chairman: Associated Nuclear Services Ltd, 1977–90; Brown & Sharpe Group (UK), 1979–88. Fellow, UCL, 1970–. CBIM; FRSA 1973. *Recreations:* music, theatre, walking. *Address:* 55 Kingston House North, Prince's Gate, SW7 1LW. *T:* 071–584 2041. *Clubs:* Athenæum, Hurlingham.
See also R. E. Rhodes.

BROOK, Peter Stephen Paul, CBE 1965; Producer; Co-Director, The Royal Shakespeare Theatre; *b* 21 March 1925; 2nd *s* of Simon Brook; *m* 1951, Natasha Parry, stage and film star; one *s* one *d*. *Educ:* Westminster; Greshams; Magdalen College, Oxford (Hon. Fellow, 1991). Productions include: The Tragedy of Dr Faustus, 1942; The Infernal Machine, 1945; Birmingham Repertory Theatre: Man and Superman, King John, The Lady from the Sea, 1945–46; Stratford: Romeo and Juliet, Love's Labour's Lost, 1947; London: Vicious Circle, Men Without Shadows, Respectable Prostitute, The Brothers Karamazov, 1946; Director of Productions, Royal Opera House, Covent Garden, 1947–50: Boris Godunov, La Bohème, 1948; Marriage of Figaro, The Olympians, Salome, 1949. Dark of the Moon, 1949; Ring Round the Moon, 1950; Measure for Measure, Stratford, 1950, Paris, 1978; The Little Hut, 1950; The Winter's Tale, 1951; Venice Preserved, 1953; The Little Hut, New York, Faust, Metropolitan Opera House, 1953; The Dark is Light Enough; Both Ends Meet, 1954; House of Flowers, New York, 1954; The Lark, 1955; Titus Andronicus, Stratford, 1955; Hamlet, 1955; The Power and the Glory, 1956; Family Reunion, 1956; The Tempest, Stratford, 1957; Cat on a Hot Tin Roof, Paris, 1957; View from the Bridge, Paris, 1958; Irma la Douce, London, 1958; The Fighting Cock, New York, 1959; Le Balcon, Paris, 1960; The Visit, Royalty, 1960; King Lear, Stratford and Aldwych, 1962; The Physicists, Aldwych, 1963; Sergeant Musgrave's Dance, Paris, 1963; The Persecution and Assassination of Marat..., Aldwych, 1964 (New York, 1966); The Investigation, Aldwych, 1965; US, Aldwych, 1966; Oedipus, National Theatre, 1968; A Midsummer Night's Dream, Stratford, 1970, NY, 1971; Timon of Athens, Paris, 1974 (Grand Prix Dominique, 1975; Brigadier Prize, 1975); The Ik, Paris, 1975, London, 1976; Ubu Roi, Paris, 1977; Antony and Cleopatra, Stratford, 1978, Aldwych, 1979; Ubu, Young Vic, 1978; Conference of the Birds, France, Australia, NY, 1980; The Cherry Orchard, Paris, 1981, NY, 1988; La tragédie de Carmen, Paris, 1981, NY, 1983 (Emmy Award, and Prix Italia, 1984); The Mahabharata, Avignon and Paris, 1985, Glasgow, 1988, televised, 1989 (Internat. Emmy Award 1990); Woza Albert, Paris, 1988; Carmen, Glasgow, 1989; The Tempest, Glasgow and Paris, 1990; work with Internat. Centre of Theatre Research, Paris, Iran, W Africa, and USA, 1971, Sahara, Niger and Nigeria, 1972–73. *Directed films:* The Beggar's Opera, 1952; Moderato Cantabile, 1960; Lord of the Flies, 1962; The Marat/Sade, 1967; Tell Me Lies, 1968; King Lear, 1969; Meetings with Remarkable Men, 1979; The Tragedy of Carmen, 1983. Hon. DLitt: Birmingham; Strathclyde, 1990. SWET award, for outstanding contribn by UK theatre artist to US theatre season, 1983. Freiherr von Stein Foundn Shakespeare Award, 1973. Officier de l'Ordre des Arts et des Lettres; Legion of Honour (France), 1987. *Publications:* The Empty Space, 1968; The Shifting Point (autobiog.), 1988. *Recreations:* painting, piano playing and travelling by air. *Address:* c/o CICT, 56 rue de l'Université, 75007 Paris, France.

BROOK, Sir Ralph Ellis; *see* Brook, Sir Robin.

BROOK, Prof. Richard John, OBE 1988; ScD; Cookson Professor of Materials Science, University of Oxford, since 1991; Professorial Fellow, St Cross College, Oxford, since 1991; *b* 12 March 1938; *s* of Frank Brook and Emily Sarah (*née* Lytle); *m* 1961, Elizabeth Christine Aldred; one *s* one *d*. *Educ:* Univ. of Leeds (BSc 1st class Hons Ceramics); MIT (ScD Ceramics). Res. Asst, MIT, 1962–66; Asst Prof. of Materials Science, Univ. of S California, 1966–70; Gp Leader, AERE, 1970–74; Prof. and Head of Dept of Ceramics, Univ. of Leeds, 1974–88; Scientific Mem., Max Planck Soc. and Dir, Max Planck Inst. Metallforschung, Stuttgart, 1988–91. Fellow: Inst. of Cermics, 1978 (Pres., 1984–86); American Ceramic Soc., 1979. Hon. Prof., Univ. of Stuttgart, 1990–. Mellor Meml Lectr, 1989; Stuijts Meml Lectr, 1989. Editor, Jl of European Ceramic Soc., 1989–. *Publications:* Encyclopedia of Advanced Ceramic Materials, 1991; papers in publications of Inst. of Ceramics, American Ceramic Soc. *Recreation:* Europe. *Address:* Department of Materials, University of Oxford, Parks Road, Oxford OX1 3PH; 15 Rawlinson Road, Oxford OX2 6UE. *T:* Oxford (0865) 53394; Forststrasse 180, D-7000 Stuttgart 1, Germany. *T:* 711 6364112.

BROOK, Robert; *see* Brook, G. R.

BROOK, Sir Robin, Kt 1974; CMG 1954; OBE 1945; Member: City and E London Area Health Authority, 1974–82 (Vice Chairman, 1974–79); City and Hackney District Health Authority, 1982–86; *b* 19 June 1908; *s* of Francis Brook, Harley Street, and Mrs E. I. Brook; *m* 1937, Helen (*see* Helen Brook), *e d* of John Knewstub; two *d*. *Educ:* Eton; King's College, Cambridge. Served 1941–46; Brig., 1945 (OBE, despatches, Legion of Merit (Commander), Legion of Honour, Croix de Guerre and Bars, Order of Leopold (Officer), Belgian Croix de Guerre). Director, Bank of England, 1946–49. Formerly Chairman: Augustine Investments; Ionian Bank; Leda Inv. Trust; Jove Inv. Trust; W. E. Sykes; Carclo; Sir Joseph Cawston; Gordon Woodroffe; Vice-Chm., United City Merchants. Chm., 1966–68, Pres., 1968–72, London Chamber of Commerce and Industry; Pres., Assoc. of British Chambers of Commerce, 1972–74; Pres., Assoc. of Chambers of Commerce of EEC, 1974–76; Leader of Trade Missions: for HM Govt to Libya and Romania; for London or British Chambers of Commerce to France, Iran, China, Greece, Finland and Hungary; HM Govt Dir, BP Co., 1970–73; Deputy Chairman: British Tourist and Holidays Board, 1946–50; Colonial Development Corp., 1949–53. Mem., Foundn for Management Educn, 1975–82. Sports Council: Mem., 1971–78; Vice-Chm., 1974; Chm., 1975–78; Chm., Sports Devlt Cttee, 1971–74. Mem., Cttee on Invisible Exports, 1969–74; Mem. Court, Council, Finance and Hon. Degrees Cttees, City Univ.; Hon. Treasurer: Amateur Fencing Assoc., 1946–61; CCPR, 1961–77 (also Mem. Exec.); Family Planning Association, 1966–75. High Sheriff of County of London, 1950; Mem. Council, Festival of Britain. Mem. Council and Exec. Cttee, King Edward's Fund; Pres., London Homes for the Elderly, 1980– (Chm., 1973–80). St Bartholomew's Hospital: Governor, 1962–74; Treasurer and Chm., 1969–74; Chm., Special Trustees, 1974–88; Pres., St Bartholomew's Med. Coll., 1969–88; Governor, Royal Free Hosp., 1962–74; Mem. Governors and Exec. Cttee, Sports Aid Foundn, 1975–. Past Master, Wine Warden, Haberdashers' Co.; Governor of schools. Hon. DSc City, 1989. *Recreation:* British Sabre Champion, 1936; Olympic Games, 1936, 1948; Capt. British Team, 1933 (3rd in European Championship), etc. *Address:* 31 Acacia Road, NW8 6AS.

BROOK, William Edward; British Council Officer, retired; *b* 18 Jan. 1922; *s* of William Stafford Brook and Dorothy Mary (*née* Thompson); *m* 1950, Rene Dorothy Drew; two *s* one *d*. *Educ:* Highgate Sch.; St Edmund Hall, Oxford (BA Mod. Langs, 1949; MA 1953). Served RAF, 1940–46: Africa, ME and Italy. Apptd to British Council, 1949; Lectr, Salonika, 1949–51; Asst Dir, Northern Provinces, Nigeria, 1951–56; Lecturer: Kuwait, 1956–59; Tripoli, Libya, 1959–62; Regional Director: Moshi, Tanganyika, 1962–67; Frankfurt, W Germany, 1967–72; Rep., Bahrain (with Qatar, UAE and Oman), 1972–76; Dir, Overseas Educnl Appts Dept, 1976; Controller, Appts Div., 1977–79; Representative, Canada, and Counsellor (Cultural), Ottawa, 1979; retd 1982. *Recreations:* music, gardening, bird-watching. *Address:* Clarke's Cottage, Rimpton, near Yeovil, Somerset BA22 8AD. *T:* Marston Magna (0935) 850828.

BROOK-PARTRIDGE, Bernard; Director: Edmund Nuttall Ltd, since 1986; Kyle Stewart, since 1989; Partner, Carsons, Brook-Partridge & Co. (Planning Consultants), since 1972; *b* Croydon, 1927; *o s* of late Leslie Brook-Partridge and late Gladys Vere Burchell (*née* Brooks), Sanderstead; *m* 1st, 1951, Enid Elizabeth (marr. diss. 1965), 2nd *d* of late Frederick Edmund Hatfield and late Enid Hatfield (*née* Lucas), Sanderstead; two *d*; 2nd, 1967, Carol Devonald, *o d* of late Arnold Devonald Francis Lewis and late Patricia (*née* Thomas), Gower, S Wales; two *s*. *Educ:* Selsdon County Grammar Sch.; Cambridgeshire Tech. Coll.; Cambridge Univ.; London Univ.; Gray's Inn. Military Service, 1945–48. Studies, 1948–50. Cashier/Accountant, Dominion Rubber Co. Ltd, 1950–51; Asst Export Manager, British & General Tube Co. Ltd, 1951–52; Asst Sec., Assoc. of Internat. Accountants, 1952–59; Sec.-Gen., Institute of Linguists, 1959–62; various teaching posts, Federal Republic of Germany, 1962–66; Special Asst to Man. Dir, M. G. Scott Ltd, 1966–68. Business consultancy work on own account, incl. various dirships with several client cos, 1968–72; Dir and Sec., Roban Engineering Ltd and predecessor company, 1971–; Chm., Brompton Troika Ltd, 1985–; Director: Alan Wooff Associates Ltd, 1985–; Pugh, Carmichael (Consultants) Ltd, 1988–; PEG Management Consultants plc, 1989–; MKL Consulting Engrs Ltd, 1988–; Local Govt and Pol Advisor to Transmanche-Link UK, 1988 and 1989. Contested (C) St Pancras North, LCC, 1958; Mem. (C) St Pancras Metropolitan Borough Council, 1959–62. Prospective Parly Cand. (C), Shoreditch and Finsbury, 1960–62; contested (C) Nottingham Central, 1970. Greater London Council: Mem. for Havering, 1967–73, for Havering (Romford), 1973–85; Chm., 1980–81; Chairman: Planning and Transportation (NE) Area Bd, 1967–71; Town Develt Cttee, 1971–73; Arts Cttee, 1977–78; Public Services and Safety Cttee, 1978–79; Opposition spokesman: for Arts and Recreation, 1973–77; for Police Matters, 1983–85; Member: Exec. Cttee, Greater London Arts Assoc., 1973–78; Exec. Council, Area Museums Service for SE England, 1977–78; Council and Exec., Greater London and SE Council for Sport and Recreation, 1977–78; GLC Leaders' Cttee with special responsibility for Law and Order and Police Liaison matters, 1977–79; Dep. Leader, Recreation and Community Services Policy Cttee, 1977–79. Member: Exec. Cttee, Exmoor Soc., 1974–79; BBC Radio London Adv. Council, 1974–79; Gen. Council, Poetry Soc., 1977–86 (Treas., 1982–84); Board Member: Peterborough Develt Corp., 1972–88 (Chm., Queensgate Management Services); London Festival Ballet (and Trustee), 1977–79; Young Vic Theatre Ltd, 1977–88 (Chm., 1983–87); London Orchestral Concert Bd Ltd, 1977–78; ENO, 1977–78; London Contemp. Dance Trust, 1979–84; Governor and Trustee: SPCK, 1976–; Sadler's Wells Foundn, 1977–79; Chm., London Music Hall Trust, 1983–; Vice-Chm., London Music Hall Protection Soc. Ltd (Wilton's Music Hall), 1983–88 (Mem. Bd, 1978–; Chm., 1981–83); Chairman: London Symphony Chorus Develt Cttee, 1981–88; Samuel Lewis Housing Trust, 1985– (Trustee, 1976–); St George's Housing Assoc., 1985– (Mem., Management Cttee, 1976–); Pres., British Sch. of Osteopathy Appeal Fund, 1980–84. President: Witan (GLC Staff) Rifle Club, 1979–; City of London Rifle League, 1980–; Gtr London Horse Show, 1982–85; Gtr London (County Hall) Br., Royal British Legion, 1988– . FCIS (Mem. Council, 1981–, Treas., 1984, Vice-Pres. 1985, Pres., 1986); MBIM. Hon. FIET. Hon. PhD Columbia Pacific, 1982. Order of Gorkha Dakshina Bahu (2nd cl.), Nepal, 1981. *Publications:* Europe—Power and Responsibility: Direct Elections to the European Parliament (with David Baker), 1972; innumerable contribs to learned jls and periodicals on linguistics and translation, the use of language, political science and contemporary politics. *Recreations:* conversation, opera, ballet, classical music and being difficult. *Address:* 14 Redcliffe Street, SW10 9DT. *T:* 071–373 1223. *Clubs:* Athenæum, United and Cecil, Nikaean, Sette of Odd Volumes; Surrey County Cricket.

BROOKE, family name of **Viscount Alanbrooke,** of **Baroness Brooke of Ystradfellte** and of **Viscount Brookeborough.**

BROOKE, Lord; Guy David Greville; *b* 30 Jan. 1957; *s* and *heir* of 8th Earl of Warwick, *qv* and of Mrs Harry Thomson Jones; *m* 1981, Susan McKinley Cobbold; one *s*. *Educ:* Summerfields, Eton and Ecole des Roches. *Recreations:* golf, surfing. *Heir:* *s* Hon. Charles Fulke Chester Greville, *b* 27 July 1982. *Address:* 4 Walter Street, Claremont, Western Australia 6010. *T:* 384 9940. *Club:* White's.

BROOKE OF YSTRADFELLTE, Baroness *cr* 1964 (Life Peer); **Barbara Brooke,** DBE 1960; *b* 14 Jan. 1908; *y d* of late Canon A. A. Mathews; *m* 1933, Henry Brooke, PC, CH (later Baron Brooke of Cumnor) (*d* 1984); two *s* two *d*. *Educ:* Queen Anne's School, Caversham. Joint Vice-Chm., Conservative Party Organisation, 1954–64. Member: Hampstead Borough Council, 1948–65; North-West Metropolitan Regional Hospital Board, 1954–66; Management Cttee, King Edward's Hospital Fund for London, 1966–71; Chairman: Exec. Cttee Queen's Institute of District Nursing, 1961–71; Governing Body of Godolphin and Latymer School, Hammersmith, 1960–78. Hon. Fellow, Queen Mary and Westfield College. *Address:* Romans Halt, Mildenhall, Marlborough, Wilts SN8 2LX.
See also Hon. Sir H. Brooke, Rt Hon. P. L. Brooke, Rev. A. K. Mathews.

BROOKE, Sir Alistair Weston, 4th Bt *cr* 1919, of Almondbury; *b* 12 Sept. 1947; *s* of Major Sir John Weston Brooke, 3rd Bt, TD, and Rosemary (*d* 1979), *d* of late Percy Nevill, Birling House, West Malling, Kent; *S* father, 1983; *m* 1982, Susan Mary, *d* of

Barry Charles Roger Griffiths, MRCVS, Church House, Norton, Powys; one *d. Educ:* Repton; Royal Agricultural Coll., Cirencester. *Recreations:* shooting, farming, racehorse training. *Heir: b* Charles Weston Brooke [*b* 27 Jan. 1951; *m* 1984, Tanya Elizabeth, *d* of Antony Thelwell Maurice; two *d*]. *Address:* Wootton Farm, Pencombe, Hereford. *T:* Pencombe (08855) 615.

BROOKE, Arthur Caffin, CB 1972; Chairman, Arts Council of Northern Ireland, 1982–86 (Member, 1979–86); *b* 11 March 1919; *s* of late Rev. James M. Wilmot Brooke and Constance Brooke; *m* 1942, Margaret Florence Thompson; two *s. Educ:* Abbotsholme Sch.; Peterhouse, Cambridge (MA). Served War, Royal Corps of Signals, 1939–46. Northern Ireland Civil Service, 1946–79; Ministry of Commerce, 1946–73: Asst Sec., Head of Industrial Development Div., 1955; Sen. Asst Sec., Industrial Development, 1963; Second Sec., 1968; Permanent Sec., 1969; Permanent Sec., Dept of Educn, 1973–79. *Address:* 4 Camden Court, Brecon, Powys LD3 7RP. *T:* Brecon (0874) 5617.

BROOKE, Prof. Bryan Nicholas, MD, MChir, FRCS; Emeritus Professor (Professor of Surgery, University of London, at St George's Hospital 1963–80); lately consultant surgeon, St George's Hospital; *b* 21 Feb. 1915; *s* of George Cyril Brooke, LitD, FSA (numismatist) and Margaret Florence Brooke; *m* 1940, Naomi Winefride Mills; three *d. Educ:* Bradfield College, Berkshire; Corpus Christi College, Cambridge; St Bartholomew's Hospital, London. FRCSEng 1942; MChir (Cantab.) 1944; MD (Birm.) with hons 1954. Lieut-Colonel, RAMC, 1945–46. Lecturer in Surgery, Aberdeen Univ., 1946–47; Reader in Surgery, Birmingham Univ., 1947–63; Hunterian Prof. RCS, 1951 and 1979. Examiner in Surgery, Universities of: Birmingham, 1951–63; Cambridge, 1958–; Bristol, 1961–; London, 1962–; Glasgow, 1969; Oxford, 1970; Hong Kong, 1972; Nigeria, 1975; RCS, 1973; Chm., Ct of Examnrs, RCS, 1978. Member, Medical Appeals Tribunal, 1948–87. Founder Pres., Ileostomy Assoc. of GB, 1957–82. Chm., Malvern Girls' Coll., 1972–82. Copeman Medal for Scientific Research, 1960; Graham Award (Amer. Proctologic Soc.), 1961; Award of NY Soc., Colon and Rectal Surgeons, 1967. Hon. FRACS, 1977; Hon. Mem., British Soc. of Gastroenterology, 1979. Consultant Editor, World Medicine, 1980–82. *Publications:* Ulcerative Colitis and its Surgical Treatment, 1954; You and Your Operation, 1957; United Birmingham Cancer Reports, 1953, 1954, 1957; (co-editor) Recent Advances in Gastroenterology, 1965; (co-author) Metabolic Derangements in Gastrointestinal Surgery, 1966; Understanding Cancer, 1971; Crohn's Disease, 1977; The Troubled Gut, 1986; (jtly) A Garden of Roses, 1987; Editor, Jl Clinics in Gastroenterology; contrib. to various surgical works. Numerous articles on large bowel disorder, medical education, steroid therapy. *Recreation:* painting. *Address:* 112 Balham Park Road, SW12 8EA. *Club:* Athenæum.

BROOKE, Prof. Christopher Nugent Lawrence, MA; LittD; FSA; FRHistS; FBA 1970; Dixie Professor of Ecclesiastical History, since 1977, and Fellow, Gonville and Caius College, 1949–56 and since 1977, University of Cambridge; *b* 1927; *y s* of late Professor Zachary Nugent Brooke and Rosa Grace Brooke; *m* 1951, Rosalind Beckford, *d* of Dr and Mrs L. H. S. Clark; three *s. Educ:* Winchester College (Scholar); Gonville and Caius College, Cambridge (Major Scholar). BA 1948; MA 1952; LittD 1973. Army service in RAEC, Temp. Captain 1949. Cambridge University: College Lecturer in History, 1953–56; Praelector Rhetoricus, 1955–56; Asst Lectr in History, 1953–54; Lectr, 1954–56; Prof. of Mediæval History, University of Liverpool, 1956–67; Prof. of History, Westfield Coll., Univ. of London, 1967–77. Member: Royal Commn on Historical Monuments (England), 1977–83; Reviewing Cttee on Export of Works of Art, 1979–82. Vice-Pres., Soc. of Antiquaries, 1975–79, Pres., 1981–84. Corresp. Fellow, Medieval Acad. of America, 1981; Corresp. Mem., Monumenta Germaniae Historica, 1988. DUniv York, 1984. Lord Mayor's Midsummer Prize, City of London, 1981. *Publications:* The Dullness of the Past, 1957; From Alfred to Henry III, 1961; The Saxon and Norman Kings, 1963; Europe in the Central Middle Ages, 1964, 2nd edn 1987; Time the Archsatirist, 1968; The Twelfth Century Renaissance, 1970; Structure of Medieval Society, 1971; Medieval Church and Society (sel. papers), 1971; (with W. Swaan) The Monastic World, 1974; (with G. Keir) London, 800–1216, 1975; Marriage in Christian History, 1977; (with R. B. Brooke) Popular Religion in the Middle Ages, 1000–1300, 1984; A History of Gonville and Caius College, 1985; The Church and the Welsh Border, 1986; (with J. R. L. Highfield and W. Swaan) Oxford and Cambridge, 1988; The Medieval Idea of Marriage, 1989; part Editor: The Book of William Morton, 1954; The Letters of John of Salisbury, vol. I, 1955, vol. II, 1979; Carte Nativorum, 1960; (with A. Morey) Gilbert Foliot and his letters, 1965 and (ed jtly) The Letters and Charters of Gilbert Foliot, 1967; (with D. Knowles and V. London) Heads of Religious Houses, England and Wales 940–1216, 1972; (with D. Whitelock and M. Brett) Councils and Synods, vol. I, 1981; (with Sir Roger Mynors) Walter Map, De Nugis Curialium (revision of M. R. James edn), 1983; (with M. Brett and M. Winterbottom) Hugh the Chanter, History of the Church of York (revision of C. Johnson edn), 1990; contributed to: A History of St Paul's Cathedral, 1957; A History of York Minster, 1977; general editor: Oxford (formerly Nelson's) Medieval Texts, 1959–87; Nelson's History of England, etc; articles and reviews in English Historical Review, Cambridge Historical Journal, Studies in Church History, Bulletin of Inst. of Historical Research, Downside Review, Traditio, Bulletin of John Rylands Library, Jl of Soc. of Archivists, etc. *Address:* Gonville and Caius College, Cambridge CB2 1TA.

BROOKE, (Christopher) Roger (Ettrick); Chairman, Candover Investments plc, since 1991; *b* 2 Feb. 1931; *s* of Ralph Brooke and Marjorie (*née* Lee); *m* 1958, Nancy Belle Lowenthal; three *s* one *d. Educ:* Tonbridge; Trinity Coll., Oxford (MA). Served HM Diplomatic Service: Bonn, 1955–57; Southern Dept, FO, 1958–60; Washington, 1960–63; Tel Aviv, 1963–66. Dep. Man. Dir, IRC, 1966–69; Man. Dir, Scienta SA, 1969–71; Dir, Pearson Gp, 1971–79; Gp Man. Dir, EMI, 1979–80; Chief Exec., Candover Investments plc, 1980–90; Dir, Slough Estates plc, 1980–, and various other cos. *Publication:* Santa's Christmas Journey, 1985. *Recreations:* golf, tennis, theatre, reading, travel. *Address:* c/o Candover Investments plc, 20 Old Bailey, EC4M 7LN; Water Meadow, Swarraton, near Alresford, Hants. *T:* Alresford (0962) 732259. *Clubs:* Brooks's; Woking Golf.

BROOKE, Clive; General Secretary, Inland Revenue Staff Federation, since 1988; Member, TUC General Council, since 1989; *b* 21 June 1942; *s* of Mary Brooke (*née* Colbeck) and John Brooke; *m* 1967, Lorna Hopkin Roberts. *Educ:* Thornes House School, Wakefield. Asst Sec., 1964–82, Dep. Gen. Sec., 1982–88, Inland Revenue Staff Fedn. Member: TUC Employment Policy Cttee, 1989–; TUC Youth Forum, 1989–; TUC Financial Services Cttee, 1989–; Council of Civil Service Unions (Mem., Major Policy Cttee); Inland Revenue Deptl Whitley Council, TUS, 1976–88 (Chm., 1986–88); H of C Speaker's Commn on Citizenship, 1988–; Chm., Duke of Edinburgh UK Study Conf., 1989 (Mem., Canada Conf., 1980); Trustee, Community Services Volunteers, 1989–. Labour Party mem. and activist. *Recreations:* opera, ballet, church affairs, speedway. *Address:* Inland Revenue Staff Federation, Douglas Houghton House, 231 Vauxhall Bridge Road, SW1V 1EH. *T:* 071–834 8254.

BROOKE, Sir Francis (George Windham), 4th Bt *cr* 1903; *b* 15 Oct. 1963; *s* of Sir George Cecil Francis Brooke, 3rd Bt, MBE, and of Lady Melissa Brooke, *er d* of 6th Earl of Dunraven and Mount-Earl, CB, CBE, MC; *S* father, 1982; *m* 1989, Katharine Elizabeth, *o d* of Marmaduke Hussey, *qv* and Lady Susan Hussey, *qv. Educ:* Eton; Edinburgh University (MA Hons). *Heir: cousin* Lt-Comdr Geoffrey Arthur George Brooke, DSC, RN retd [*b* 25 April 1920; *m* 1956, Venetia Mabel, *o d* of late Captain the Hon. Oswald Wykeham Cornwallis, OBE, RN; three *d*]. *Address:* 49 Masbro Road, W14 0LU; Glenbevan, Croom, Co. Limerick, Ireland. *Clubs:* Turf; Kildare Street and University (Dublin).

BROOKE, Hon. Sir Henry, Kt 1988; **Hon. Mr Justice Brooke;** Judge of the High Court of Justice, Queen's Bench Division, since 1988; *b* 19 July 1936; *s* of Lord Brooke of Cumnor, PC, CH and of Lady Brooke of Ystradfellte, *qv*; *m* 1966, Bridget Mary Kalaugher; three *s* one *d. Educ:* Marlborough College; Balliol Coll., Oxford. MA (1st Cl. Classical Hon. Mods, 1st Cl. Lit. Hum.). Called to the Bar, Inner Temple, 1963, Bencher, 1987; Junior Counsel to the Crown, Common Law, 1978–81; QC 1981; a Recorder, 1983–88; Counsel to the Inquiry, Sizewell 'B' Nuclear Reactor Inquiry, 1983–85; DTI Inspector, House of Fraser Hldgs plc, 1987–88. Mem., Bar Council, 1987–88 (Chairman: Professional Standards Cttee, 1987–88; Race Relations Cttee, 1989–); Chairman: Computer Cttee, Senate of the Inns of Court and the Bar, 1985–86; London Common Law and Commercial Bar Assoc., 1988 (Vice-Chm., 1986–87); Mem., Information Technology and the Courts Cttee, 1986–87, 1990–. *Publications:* Institute Cargo Clauses (Air), 1986; (contrib.) Halsbury's Laws of England, 4th edn. *Address:* Royal Courts of Justice, Strand, WC2. *Club:* Brooks's.

See also Rt Hon. P. L. Brooke.

BROOKE, Rt. Hon. Peter Leonard, PC 1988; MP (C) City of London and Westminster South, since Feb. 1977; Secretary of State for Northern Ireland, since 1989; *b* 3 March 1934; *s* of Lord Brooke of Cumnor, PC, CH and of Lady Brooke of Ystradfellte, *qv*; *m* 1st, 1964, Joan Margaret Smith (*d* 1985); three *s* (and one *s* decd); 2nd, 1991, Lindsay Allinson. *Educ:* Marlborough; Balliol College, Oxford (MA); Harvard Business School (MBA). Vice-Pres., Nat. Union of Students, 1955–56; Chm., Nat. Conf., Student Christian Movement, 1956; Pres., Oxford Union, 1957; Commonwealth Fund Fellow, 1957–59. Research Assistant, IMEDE, Lausanne, 1960–61. Spencer Stuart & Associates, Management Consultants, 1961–79 (Director of parent company, 1965–79, Chairman 1974–79); lived in NY and Brussels, 1969–73. Mem., Camden Borough Council, 1968–69. Chm., St Pancras N Cons. Assoc., 1976–77. Contested (C) Bedwellty, Oct. 1974; an Asst Govt Whip, 1979–81; a Lord Comr of HM Treasury, 1981–83; Parly Under Sec. of State, DES, 1983–85; Minister of State, HM Treasury, 1985–87; Paymaster Gen., HM Treasury, 1987–89; Chm., Conservative Party, 1987–89. Pres., Incorp. Assoc. of Prep. Schs, 1980–83; Trustee: Wordsworth Trust (formerly Dove Cottage), 1976–; Cusichaca Project, 1978–. Lay Adviser, St Paul's Cathedral, 1980–. Sen. Fellow, RCA, 1987; Presentation Fellow, KCL, 1989. *Recreations:* churches, conservation, cricket, pictures, planting things. *Address:* c/o House of Commons, SW1. *Clubs:* Brooks's, City Livery, MCC, I Zingari, St George's (Hanover Square) Conservative.

See also Hon. Sir H. Brooke.

BROOKE, Sir Richard (Neville), 10th Bt *cr* 1662; *b* 1 May 1915; *s* of Sir Richard Christopher Brooke, 9th Bt, and Marian Dorothea (*d* 1965), *d* of late Arthur Charles Innes, MP, of Dromantine, Co. Down; *S* father, 1981; *m* 1st, 1937, Lady Mabel Kathleen Jocelyn (marr. diss. 1959; she *d* 1985), *d* of 8th Earl of Roden; two *s*; 2nd, 1960, Jean Evison, *d* of late Lt-Col A. C. Corfe, DSO. *Educ:* Eton. Served as Lieutenant, Scots Guards, 1939–46; prisoner of war (escaped). Chartered Accountant (FCA), 1946; Senior Partner, Price Waterhouse & Co., European Firms, 1969–75; retired, 1975. *Recreations:* racing, fishing. *Heir: s* Richard David Christopher Brooke [*b* 23 Oct. 1938; *m* 1st, 1963, Carola Marion (marr. diss. 1978), *d* of Sir Robert Erskine-Hill, 2nd Bt; two *s*; 2nd, 1979, Lucinda Barlow, *o d* of late J. F. Voelcker and of Jean Constance Voelcker, Lidgetton, Natal]. *Address:* Pond Cottage, Crawley, near Winchester, Hants. *T:* Sparsholt (096272) 272. *Club:* Boodle's.

BROOKE, Rodney George; DL; Secretary, Association of Metropolitan Authorities, since 1990; Visiting Research Fellow, Royal Institute of Public Administration, since 1989; Visiting Fellow, Nuffield Institute for Health Service Studies, University of Leeds, since 1989; *b* 22 Oct. 1939; *s* of George Sidney Brooke and Amy Brooke; *m* 1967, Dr Clare Margaret Cox; one *s* one *d. Educ:* Queen Elizabeth's Grammar Sch., Wakefield. Admitted solicitor (hons), 1962. Rochdale County Bor. Council, 1962–63; Leicester CC, 1963–65; Stockport County Bor. Council, 1965–73; West Yorkshire Metropolitan County Council: Dir of Admin, 1973–81; Chief Exec. and Clerk, 1981–84; Clerk to W Yorks Lieutenancy, 1981–84; Chief Exec., Westminster City Council, 1984–89; Clerk to Gtr London Lieutenancy, 1987–89; Chm., Bradford HA, 1989–90. Secretary: Yorks and Humberside Tourist Board, 1974–84; Yorks and Humberside Develt Assoc., 1974–84; Hon. Sec., London Boroughs Assoc., 1984–90; Dir, Foundn for IT in Local Govt, 1988–; Member: Action London, 1988–90. Exec., SOLACE, 1981–84, 1987–89; CS Final Selection Bd. Dir, Dolphin Square Trust, 1987–; Chm., London NE, Royal Jubilee and Prince's Trusts, 1984–. Associate, Ernst & Young, 1989–90. Editl Advr, Longman Gp, 1989–90. Hon. Fellow, Inst. of Govt Studies, Birmingham Univ. FRSA. DL Greater London, 1989. National Order of Merit (France), 1984; Nat. Order of Aztec Eagle (Mexico), 1985; Medal of Merit (Qatar), 1985; Order of Merit (Germany), 1986; Legion of Merit (Senegal), 1988. *Publications:* Managing the Enabling Authority, 1989; The Environmental Role of Local Government, 1990; articles on local govt. *Recreations:* skiing, opera, Byzantium. *Address:* Stubham Lodge, Clifford Road, Middleton, Ilkley, West Yorks LS29 0AX. *T:* Ilkley (0943) 601869; 706 Grenville House, Dolphin Square, SW1V 3LX. *T:* 071–798 8086. *Clubs:* Athenæum, Ski Club of Great Britain.

BROOKE, Roger; *see* Brooke, C. R. E.

BROOKE-LITTLE, John Philip Brooke, CVO 1984 (MVO 1969); Norroy and Ulster King of Arms, and King of Arms, Registrar and Knight Attendant on the Most Illustrious Order of St Patrick, since 1980; Librarian, since 1974, and Treasurer, since 1978, College of Arms; *b* 6 April 1927; *s* of late Raymond Brooke-Little, Unicorns House, Swalcliffe; *m* 1960, Mary Lee, *o c* of late John Raymond Pierce; three *s* one *d. Educ:* Clayesmore Sch; New Coll., Oxford (MA). Earl Marshal's staff, 1952–53; Gold Staff Officer, Coronation, 1953; Bluemantle Pursuivant of Arms, 1956–67; Richmond Herald, 1967–80; Registrar, Coll. of Arms, 1974–82. Asst Dir, Heralds' Museum, Tower of London, 1983–; Adviser on heraldry: Nat. Trust, 1983–; Shrievalty Assoc., 1983–. Founder of Heraldry Soc. and Chm., 1947; Hon. Editor, The Coat of Arms, 1950; Fellow, Soc. of Genealogists, 1969; Hon. Fellow, Inst. of Heraldic and Genealogical Studies, 1979. Chm., Harleian Soc., 1984–; Pres., English Language Literary Trust, 1985–. Governor Emeritus, Clayesmore Sch. (Chm., 1971–83). Freeman and Liveryman, Scriveners' Co. of London (Master, 1985–86). FSA 1961. KStJ 1975; Knight of Malta, 1955, Knight Grand Cross of Grace and Devotion, Order of Malta, 1974 (Chancellor, British Assoc., 1973–77); Comdr Cross of Merit of Order of Malta, 1964; Cruz Distinguida (1st cl.) de San Raimundo de Peñafort, 1955; Grand Cross of Grace, Constantinian Order of St George, 1975. *Publications:* Royal London, 1953; Pictorial History of Oxford, 1954; Boutell's Heraldry, 1970, 1973, 1978 and 1983 (1963 and 1966 edns with C. W. Scott-Giles); Knights of the Middle Ages,

1966; Prince of Wales, 1969; Fox-Davies' Complete Guide to Heraldry, annotated edn, 1969; (with Don Pottinger and Anne Tauté) Kings and Queens of Great Britain, 1970; An Heraldic Alphabet, 1973; (with Marie Angell) Beasts in Heraldry, 1974; The British Monarchy in Colour, 1976; Royal Arms, Beasts and Badges, 1977; Royal Ceremonies of State, 1979; genealogical and heraldic articles. *Recreations:* cooking, humming. *Address:* Heyford House, Lower Heyford, near Oxford OX5 3NZ. *T:* Steeple Aston (0869) 40337; College of Arms, EC4V 4BT. *T:* 071–248 1310. *Clubs:* City Livery, Chelsea Arts (Hon. Member).

BROOKE-ROSE, Prof. Christine; novelist and critic; Professor of English Language and Literature, University of Paris, 1975–88 (Lecturer, 1969–75). *Educ:* Oxford and London Univs. MA Oxon 1953, PhD London 1954. Research and criticism, 1955–. Reviewer for: The Times Literary Supplement, The Times, The Observer, The Sunday Times, The Listener, The Spectator, and The London Magazine, 1956–68; took up post at Univ. of Paris VIII, Vincennes, 1969. Has broadcast in book programmes on BBC, and on 'The Critics', and ABC Television. Hon. LittD East Anglia, 1988. Travelling Prize of Society of Authors, 1964; James Tait Black Memorial Prize, 1966; Arts Council Translation Prize, 1969. *Publications: novels:* The Languages of Love, 1957; The Sycamore Tree, 1958; The Dear Deceit, 1960; The Middlemen, 1961; Out, 1964; Such, 1965; Between, 1968; Thru, 1975; Amalgamemnon, 1984; Xorandor, 1986; Verbivore, 1990; Textermination, 1991; *criticism:* A Grammar of Metaphor, 1958; A ZBC of Ezra Pound, 1971; A Rhetoric of the Unreal, 1981; Stories, Theories and Things, 1991; *short stories:* Go when you see the Green Man Walking, 1969; short stories and essays in various magazines, etc. *Recreations:* people, travel. *Address:* c/o Cambridge University Press, PO Box 110, Cambridge CB2 3RL.

BROOKE TURNER, Alan, CMG 1980; HM Diplomatic Service, retired; Director, Great Britain/East Europe Centre, since 1987; *b* 4 Jan. 1926; *s* of late Arthur Brooke Turner, MC; *m* 1954, Hazel Alexandra Rowan Henderson; two *s* two *d*. *Educ:* Marlborough; Balliol Coll., Oxford (Sen. Schol.). 1st cl Hon. Mods 1949; 1st cl. Lit. Hum. 1951. Served in RAF, 1944–48. Entered HM Foreign (subseq. Diplomatic) Service, 1951; FO, 1951; Warsaw, 1953; 3rd, later 2nd Sec. (Commercial), Jedda, 1954; Lisbon, 1957; 1st Sec., FO, 1959 (UK Delegn to Nuclear Tests Conf., Geneva, 1962); Cultural Attaché, Moscow, 1962; FO, 1965; Fellow, Center for Internat. Affairs, Harvard Univ., 1968; Counsellor, Rio de Janeiro, 1969–71; Head of Southern European Dept, FCO, 1972–73; Counsellor and Head of Chancery, British Embassy, Rome, 1973–76; Civil Dep. Comdt and Dir of Studies, NATO Defense Coll., Rome, 1976–78; Internat. Inst. for Strategic Studies, 1978–79; Minister, Moscow, 1979–82; Ambassador to Finland, 1983–85. Member: Council, Anglican Centre, Rome, 1976–77; Anglican Synod Wkg Gp on Peacemaking, 1986–88; Council, SSEES, 1987– (Chm., 1989–). *Recreations:* sailing, skiing. *Address:* Poultons, Moor Lane, Dormansland, Lingfield, Surrey RH7 6NX; 11 Marsham Court, Marsham Street, SW1P 4JY. *Club:* Travellers'.

BROOKEBOROUGH, 3rd Viscount *cr* 1952, of Colebrooke; **Alan Henry Brooke;** Bt 1822; DL; farmer; Major UDR (Company Commander since 1988); *b* 30 June 1952; *s* of 2nd Viscount Brookeborough, PC and of Rosemary Hilda (*née* Chichester); *S* father, 1987; *m* 1980, Janet Elizabeth, *d* of J. P. Cooke, Doagh, Ballyclare. *Educ:* Harrow; Millfield. Commissioned 17th/21st Lancers, 1971; transferred 4th (County Fermanagh) Bn, UDR, 1977; Company Commander, 1981–83. Now farms and runs an estate with a shooting/fishing tourist enterprise. Mem., EEC Agricl Sub-Cttee, House of Lords, 1988–. DL Co. Fermanagh. *Recreations:* shooting, fishing. *Heir: b* Hon. Christopher Arthur Brooke, *b* 16 May 1954. *Address:* Colebrooke, Brookeborough, Co. Fermanagh, N Ireland. *T:* Brookeborough (036553) 402. *Club:* Cavalry and Guards.

BROOKER, Alan Bernard; JP, DL; FCA; Chairman: Kode International, since 1988; Serif Cowells, since 1990; *b* 24 Aug. 1931; *s* of late Bernard John Brooker and of Gwendoline Ada (*née* Launchbury); *m* 1957, Diana (*née* Coles); one *s* two *d*. *Educ:* Chigwell School, Essex. FCA 1954. Served 2nd RHA (2nd Lieut), 1954–56. Articled, Cole, Dickin & Hills, Chartered Accountants, 1949–54, qualified 1954; Manager, Cole, Dickin & Hills, 1956–58; Accountant, Independent Dairies, 1958–59; Asst Accountant, Exchange Telegraph Co., 1959–64; Dir, 1964–87, Chm. and Chief Exec., 1980–87, Extel Group. Vice-Chairman: Provident Financial Group, 1983–; James Martin Associates, 1987–89; Non-exec. Director: Pauls plc, 1984–85; Aukett Associates, 1988–; Plysu, 1988–; PNA Holdings, 1988–89; Addison Worldwide, 1990–. Member: Council, CBI London Region, 1980–83; Companies Cttee, CBI, 1979–83; Council, CPU, 1975–88. Appeal Chm., Newspaper Press Fund, 1985–86. Governor: Chigwell School, 1968– (Chm., 1978–); Felixstowe Coll., 1986–. Freeman, City of London; Liveryman, Stationers and Newspapermakers' Co. (Court Asst, 1985–). Churchwarden, St Bride's, Fleet Street, 1986–. JP Essex 1972, DL Essex 1982. FInstD; FRSA 1980. *Recreations:* cricket, golf. *Address:* Plowlands, Laundry Lane, Little Easton, Dunmow, Essex CM6 2JW. *Clubs:* East India, MCC; Royal Worlington and Newmarket Golf.

BROOKES, family name of **Baron Brookes.**

BROOKES, Baron *cr* 1975 (Life Peer), of West Bromwich; **Raymond Percival Brookes,** Kt 1971; Life President, GKN plc (formerly Guest, Keen & Nettlefolds Ltd) (Group Chairman and Chief Executive, 1965–74); *b* 10 April 1909; *s* of William and Ursula Brookes; *m* 1937, Florence Edna Sharman; one *s*. Part-time Mem., BSC, 1967–68. First Pres., British Mechanical Engrg Confedn, 1968–70; a Vice-Pres., Engrg Employers' Fedn, 1967–75. Member: Council, UK S Africa Trade Assoc. Ltd, 1967–74; Council, CBI, 1968–75; BNEC, 1969–71; Wilberforce Ct of Inquiry into electricity supply industry dispute, Jan. 1971; Industrial Develt Adv. Bd, 1972–75. Member: Exec. Cttee, 1970–, Council, 1969–, Pres., 1974–75, Soc. of Motor Manufacturers & Traders Ltd; Court of Governors, Univ. of Birmingham, 1966–75; Council, Univ. of Birmingham, 1968–75. Pres., Motor Ind. Res. Assoc., 1973–75. Chm., Rea Bros (IoM) Ltd, 1976–89; Director: Plessey Co. Ltd, 1974–89; AMF Inc., 1975–78. *Recreations:* golf, fly-fishing. *Address:* GKN plc, PO Box 55, Redditch, Worcs B98 0TL; (private) Mallards, Santon, Isle of Man.

BROOKES, Beata; *b* 1931. *Educ:* Lowther College, Abergele; Univ. of Wales, Bangor; studied politics in USA (US State Dept Scholarship). Former social worker, Denbighshire CC; company secretary and farmer. Contested (C) Widnes, 1955, Warrington, 1963, Manchester Exchange, 1964. Contested (C) N Wales, European Parly Elecn, 1989. MEP (C) N Wales, 1979–89; Mem., Educn and Agricl Cttees. Member: Clwyd AHA, 1973–80 (Mem., Welsh Hosp. Bd, 1963–74); Clwyd Family Practitioner Cttee; Clwyd CC Social Services Cttee, 1973–81; Flintshire Soc. for Mentally Handicapped; N Wales Council for Mentally Handicapped; Council for Professions Supplementary to Medicine; Exec. Cttee, N Wales Cons. Group. Pres., N Wales Assoc. for the Disabled. *Address:* The Cottage, Wayside Acres, Bodelwyddan, near Rhyl, North Wales.

BROOKES, James Robert; Consultant, British Computer Society, since 1991 (Chief Executive, 1987–91); *b* 2 Sept. 1941; *s* of James Brookes and Hettie Brookes (*née* Colley); *m* 1964, Patricia Gaskell; three *d*. *Educ:* Manchester Grammar Sch.; Corpus Christi Coll., Oxford (MA Maths). FBCS. Various posts as systems and applications programmer in develt, tech. support and sales; Northern Branch Manager, Univs and Nat. Research Region, Ferranti/Internat. Computers, 1962–67; Computer Services Manager, Queen's Univ. Belfast, 1967–69; Operations Manager, Univ. of Manchester Regional Computer Centre, 1969–75; Director: SW Univs Regional Computer Centre, 1975–87; Bath Univ. Computer Service, 1983–87. FRSA 1988. Mem., Co. of Information Technologists, 1988. Freeman, City of London, 1989. *Recreations:* sailing, fellwalking, cycling, bridge, squash, badminton. *Address:* 29 High Street, Marshfield, Chippenham, Wilts SN14 8LR. *T:* (home) Bath (0225) 891294; (office) 071–637 0471. *Clubs:* United Oxford & Cambridge University; Cannons Country (Bath).

BROOKES, John; landscape designer; *b* 11 Oct. 1933; *s* of Edward Percy Brookes and Margaret Alexandra Brookes. *Educ:* Durham; Dip. Landscape, UCL. Asst to Brenda Colvin, 1957, to Dame Sylvia Crowe, 1958–61; private practice, 1964–; Director: Inchbald Sch. of Garden Design, 1970–78; Inchbald Sch. of Interior Design, Tehran, 1978–80; founded Clock House Sch. of Garden Design, Sussex, 1980; gardening corresp., Evening Standard, 1988–89; Principal Lectr, Kew Sch. of Garden Design, 1990–91. Design workshops and lectures, UK and overseas, incl. annually at Henry Clewes Foundn, La Napoule; design and construction of gardens, and consultancies, UK, Europe, Japan, USA. *Publications:* Room Outside, 1969; Gardens for Small Spaces, 1970; Garden Design and Layout, 1970; Living in the Garden, 1971; Financial Times Book of Garden Design, 1975; Improve Your Lot, 1977; The Small Garden, 1977; The Garden Book, 1984; A Place in the Country, 1984; The Indoor Garden Book, 1986; Gardens of Paradise, 1987; The Country Garden, 1987; The New Small Garden Book, 1989. *Recreations:* reading, pottering, entertaining. *Address:* Clock House, Denmans, Fontwell, near Arundel, West Sussex BN18 0SU. *T:* Eastergate (0243) 542808; *Fax:* Eastergate (0243) 544064.

BROOKES, Peter C.; *see* Cannon-Brookes, P.

BROOKES, Sir Wilfred (Deakin), Kt 1979; CBE 1972; DSO 1944; AEA 1945; Chairman, Deakin University Foundation, 1982–87; *b* 17 April 1906; *s* of Herbert Robinson Brookes and Ivy Deakin; *m* 1928, Betty (*d* 1968), *d* of A. H. Heal; one *s*. *Educ:* Melbourne Grammar Sch.; Melbourne Univ. Exec., later Alternate Dir, Aust. Paper Manufacturers Ltd, 1924–38; Exec. Dir, Box and Container Syndicate, 1938–39. War Service, 1939–45: Sqdn Officer, RAAF, 1939–41 (despatches); CO 24 Sqdn, 1942 (despatches); CO 22 Sqdn, 1942; CO 7 Fighter Section HQ; Comdr, 78th Fighter Wing, New Guinea Offensive, 1943–45; Dir of Postings, RAAF HQ, rank of Gp Captain, 1945. Chairman (retired): Associated Pulp and Paper Mills, 1952–78 (Dir, 1945–78); Colonial Mutual Life Soc., 1965–78 (Dir, 1955–78); Electrolytic Refining & Smelting Co. of Australia Ltd, 1956–80; Apsonor Pty Ltd, to 1983 (Dir, 1960–83); Collins Wales Pty Ltd, 1978–82 (Dir, 1974–82); Director: BH South Group, 1956–82; North Broken Hill, 1970–82; Alcoa of Australia, 1961–83. Past Pres., Inst. of Public Affairs; Chm., Edward Wilson Charitable Trust (Trustee, 1960–); Patron, Deakin Foundn, 1988–. Hon. Dr of Letters Deakin, 1982. Dep. Chm., Corps of Commissionaires, 1979–88 (Governor, 1975–90). *Recreations:* swimming, walking. *Address:* 20 Heyington Place, Toorak, Victoria 3142, Australia. *T:* 8224553. *Clubs:* Melbourne, Australian (Melbourne).

BROOKING, Maj.-Gen. Patrick Guy, CB 1988; MBE 1975; Chief Executive, Worldwide Subsidiaries, KRONE AG (Berlin), since 1990; *b* 4 April 1937; *s* of late Captain C. A. H. Brooking, CBE, RN, and G. M. J. White (*née* Coleridge); *m* 1964, Pamela Mary Walford; one *s* one *d*. *Educ:* Charterhouse Sch. Dip. (French Lang.); Alliance Française, Paris, 1955. Commnd 5th Royal Inniskilling Dragoon Guards, 1956; early career served in England, W Germany, NI, Cyprus, with UN; sc 1969; Mil. Asst to Comdr 1st British Corps, 1970–71; Bde Major 39 Bde, Belfast, 1974–75; comd his regt, 1975–77; Instr Army Staff Coll., 1978; RCDS 1981; Comdr 33 Armd Bde, Paderborn Garrison, 1982–83; Commandant and GOC Berlin (British Sector), 1985–89; Dir Gen., Army Manning and Recruiting, 1989–90, retd. *Recreations:* ski-ing, tennis, golf, music (esp. choral singing). *Address:* c/o National Westminster Bank, 26 Haymarket, SW1. *Club:* Cavalry and Guards.

BROOKING, Trevor David, MBE 1981; football broadcaster, since 1984; *b* 2 Oct. 1948; *s* of Henry and Margaret Brooking; *m* 1970, Hilkka Helina Helakorpi; one *s* one *d*. *Educ:* Ilford County High Sch. Professional footballer with West Ham United, 1965–84: played 642 games; scored 111 goals; FA Cup winner, 1975, *v* Fulham, 1980, *v* Arsenal (scoring only goal); won Football League Div. 2, 1980–81; 47 appearances for England, 1974–82. Chm., Eastern Council for Sport and Recreation, 1986–; Mem., Sports Council, 1989–. *Publications:* Trevor Brooking (autobiog.), 1981; Trevor Brooking's 100 Great British Footballers, 1988. *Recreations:* golf, tennis.

BROOKNER, Dr Anita, CBE 1990; Reader, Courtauld Institute of Art, 1977–88; *o c* of Newson and Maude Brookner. *Educ:* James Allen's Girls' Sch.; King's Coll., Univ. of London (FKC 1990); Courtauld Inst.; Paris. Vis. Lectr, Univ. of Reading, 1959–64; Slade Professor, Univ. of Cambridge, 1967–68; Lectr, Courtauld Inst. of Art, 1964. Fellow, New Hall, Cambridge. *Publications:* Watteau, 1968; The Genius of the Future, 1971; Greuze: the rise and fall of an Eighteenth Century Phenomenon, 1972; Jacques-Louis David, 1980; (ed) The Stories of Edith Wharton, Vol. 1, 1988, Vol. 2, 1989; *novels:* A Start in Life, 1981; Providence, 1982; Look at Me, 1983; Hotel du Lac, 1984 (Booker McConnell Prize; filmed for TV, 1986); Family and Friends, 1985; A Misalliance, 1986; A Friend from England, 1987; Latecomers, 1988; Lewis Percy, 1989; Brief Lives, 1990; A Closed Eye, 1991; articles in Burlington Magazine, etc. *Address:* 68 Elm Park Gardens, SW10. *T:* 071–352 6894.

BROOKS, family name of **Barons Brooks of Tremorfa** and **Crawshaw.**

BROOKS OF TREMORFA, Baron *cr* 1979 (Life Peer), of Tremorfa in the County of South Glamorgan; **John Edward Brooks;** *b* 12 April 1927; *s* of Edward George Brooks and Rachel Brooks (*née* White); *m* 1948 (marr. diss. 1956); one *s* one *d*; *m* 1958, Margaret Pringle; two *s*. *Educ:* elementary schools; Coleg Harlech. Secretary, Cardiff South East Labour Party, 1966–84; Member, South Glamorgan CC, 1973– (Leader, 1973–77, 1986–; Chm., 1981–82). Contested (Lab) Barry, Feb. and Oct. 1974; Parliamentary Agent to Rt Hon. James Callaghan, MP, Gen. Elections, 1970, 1979. Chm., Labour Party, Wales, 1978–79. Opposition defence spokesman, 1980–81. Steward, British Boxing Bd of Control, 1986–. President: Welsh ABA; Cardiff City FC. *Recreations:* reading, most sports. *Address:* 46 Kennerleigh Road, Rumney, Cardiff, S Glam CF3 9BJ.

BROOKS, Alan; Group Managing Director, BPB Gypsum Industries (formerly Gypsum Products, BPB Industries), since 1988; *b* 30 Dec. 1935; *s* of Charles and Annie Brooks; *m* 1959, Marie Curtis; one *s* two *d*. *Educ:* Leeds Univ. (BSc 1st Cl. Mining Engineering; 1st Cl. Cert. of Competency, Mines and Quarries). Asst Mine Manager, Winsford Salt Mine, ICI, 1961–66; British Gypsum: Dep. Mines Agent, 1966–71; Dir, Midland Region, 1971–74; Production Dir, 1974–77; Dep. Man. Dir, 1977–85; Man. Dir, 1985–88; Chairman: British Gypsum, 1988–; Westroc Industries, Canada, 1988–. *Recreation:* fell walking. *Address:* Langley Park House, Uxbridge Road, Slough SL3 6DU. *T:* Slough (0753) 73273.

BROOKS, Prof. Cleanth; Gray Professor of Rhetoric, Yale University, USA, 1947–75, now Emeritus Professor; *b* 16 Oct. 1906; *s* of Rev. Cleanth and Bessie Lee Witherspoon

Brooks; *m* 1934, Edith Amy Blanchard (*d* 1986); no *c*. *Educ:* The McTyeire School; Vanderbilt, Tulane and Oxford Universities. Rhodes Scholar, Louisiana and Exeter, 1929; Lecturer, later Prof., Louisiana State Univ., 1932–47; Prof. of English, later Gray Prof. of Rhetoric, Yale Univ., 1947–75. Visiting Professor: Univ. of Texas; Univ. of Michigan; Univ. of Chicago; Univ. of Southern California; Bread Loaf School of English; Univ. of South Carolina, 1975; Tulane Univ., 1976; Univ. of North Carolina, 1977; Univ. of Tennessee, 1978. Cultural Attaché at the American Embassy, London, 1964–66. Managing Editor and Editor (with Robert Penn Warren), The Southern Review, 1935–42. Fellow, Library of Congress, 1953–63; Guggenheim Fellow, 1953 and 1960; Sen. Fellow, Nat. Endowment for the Humanities, 1975; Mellon Fellow, Nat. Humanities Center, 1980–81. Mem. Council of Scholars, Library of Congress, 1986–88. Member: Amer. Acad. of Arts and Scis; Amer. Acad. Inst. of Arts and Letters; Amer. Philos. Soc.; RSL. Lamar Lectr, 1984; Jefferson Lectr, Nat. Endowment for the Humanities, 1985. Hon. DLitt: Upsala Coll., 1963; Kentucky, 1963; Exeter, 1966; Washington and Lee, 1968; Tulane, 1969; Univ. of the South, 1974; Newberry Coll., 1979; Hon. LHD: St Louis, 1968; Centenary Coll., 1972; Oglethorpe Univ., 1976; St Peter's Coll., 1978; Lehigh Univ., 1980; Millsaps Coll., 1983; Univ. of New Haven, 1984; Univ. of S Carolina, 1984. *Publications:* Modern Poetry and the Tradition, 1939; (ed) Thomas Percy and Richard Farmer, 1946; The Well Wrought Urn, 1947; (with R. P. Warren) Understanding Poetry, 1938; (with R. P. Warren) Modern Rhetoric, 1950; (with W. K. Wimsatt, Jr) Literary Criticism: A Short History, 1957; The Hidden God, 1963; William Faulkner: The Yoknapatawpha Country, 1963; A Shaping Joy, 1971; (with R. W. B. Lewis and R. P. Warren) American Literature: the Makers and the Making, 1973; (ed) Thomas Percy and William Shenstone, 1977; William Faulkner: Toward Yoknapatawpha and Beyond, 1978; William Faulkner: First Encounters, 1983; The Language of the American South, 1985; On the Prejudices, Predilections, and Firm Beliefs of William Faulkner, 1987; Historical Evidence and the Reading of Seventeenth-Century Poetry, 1991; (Gen. Editor, with David N. Smith and A. F. Falconer) The Percy Letters, 1942–; contrib. articles, reviews to literary magazines, journals. *Address:* 70 Ogden Street, New Haven, Conn 06511, USA. *Club:* Athenæum.

BROOKS, Douglas; Director: Walker Brooks and Partners Ltd, since 1980; Flexello Castors & Wheels plc, since 1987; *b* 3 Sept. 1928; *s* of Oliver Brooks and Olive Brooks; *m* 1952, June Anne (*née* Branch); one *s* one *d*. *Educ:* Newbridge Grammar Sch.; University Coll., Cardiff (Dip. Soc. Sc.). CIPM. Girling Ltd: factory operative, 1951–53; Employment Officer, 1953–56; Hoover Ltd: Personnel Off., 1956–60; Sen. Personnel Off., 1960–63; Dep. Personnel Man., 1963–66; Indust. Relations Advr, 1966–69; Gp Personnel Man., 1969–73; Personnel Dir, 1973–78; Group Personnel Manager, Tarmac Ltd, 1979–80. Member: Council, SSRC, later ESRC, 1976–82; BBC Consultative Gp on social effects of television, 1978–80; Hon. Soc. Cymmrodorion, 1981–. Vis. Fellow, PSI, 1982–84. Vice-Pres., IPM, 1972–74. Chm., Wooburn Fest. Soc. Ltd, 1978–86. *Publications:* various articles in professional jls. *Recreations:* talking, music, reading, gardening, cooking. *Address:* Old Court, Winforton, Hereford HR3 6EA. *T:* Eardisley (05446) 8425. *Club:* Reform.

BROOKS, Edwin, PhD; FAIM, FCIM; Deputy Principal, Charles Sturt University (formerly Riverina-Murray Institute of Higher Education, Wagga Wagga, New South Wales), 1988–89; Dean Emeritus; *b* Barry, Glamorgan, 1 Dec. 1929; *s* of Edwin Brooks and Agnes Elizabeth (*née* Campbell); *m* 1956, Winifred Hazel Soundie; four *s* one *d*. *Educ:* Barry Grammar Sch.; St John's Coll., Cambridge. PhD (Camb) 1958. National Service, Singapore, 1948–49. MP (Lab) Bebington, 1966–70. Univ. of Liverpool: Lectr, Dept of Geography, 1954–66 and 1970–72; Sen. Lectr, 1972–77; Dean, College Studies, 1975–77; Riverina College of Advanced Education, later Riverina-Murray Institute of Higher Education: Dean of Business and Liberal Studies, 1977–82; Dean of Commerce, 1982–88; Dir, Albury-Wodonga Campus, 1982. Councillor, Birkenhead, 1958–67. Mem., Courses Cttee, Higher Educn Bd of NSW, 1978–82; Dir, Australian Business Educn Council, 1986–89. Dir and Dep. Chm., Wagga Wagga Base Hosp., 1989–. Pres., Wagga Wagga Chamber of Commerce, 1988–90. FAIM 1983; FCIM 1989. *Publications:* This Crowded Kingdom, 1973; (ed) Tribes of the Amazon Basin in Brazil, 1973. *Recreations:* gardening, listening to music. *Address:* Inchnadamph, Gregadoo Road, Wagga Wagga, NSW 2650, Australia. *T:* (069) 226798.

BROOKS, Eric Arthur Swatton, MA; Head of Claims Department, Foreign Office, 1960 until retirement, 1967; *b* 9 Oct. 1907; *yr s* of late A. E. Brooks, MA, Maidenhead; *m* 1947, Daphne Joyce, *yr d* of late George McMullan, MD, FRCSE, Wallingford; one *s* one *d*. *Educ:* Reading Sch.; New Coll., Oxford (MA). 2nd cl. hons Jurisprudence, 1929. Solicitor, 1932; practised in London, 1932–39. Mem. Law Soc., 1934– (Mem. Overseas Relations Cttee, 1949–). Served War of 1939–45 in Admty and Min. of Aircraft Production, and in Operational Research as Hon. Ft-Lieut RAFVR until 1944; Disposal of Govt Factories of Min. of Aircraft Production, 1944–Dec. 1945. Foreign Office, 1946–. Served on Brit. Delegns in negotiations with: Polish and Hungarian Governments, 1953, 1954; Bulgarian Government, 1955; Rumanian Government, 1955, 1956, 1960; USSR, 1964, 1965, 1966, 1967. British Representative on Anglo-Italian Conciliation Commn, until 1967. Councillor: Borough of Maidenhead, 1972–74; Royal Borough of Windsor and Maidenhead, 1973–87. Pres., Maidenhead and Dist Civic Soc., 1989–. *Publications:* The Foreign Office Claims Manual, 1968; Maidenhead and its Name, 1985; Earlier Days of Maidenhead Golf Club, 1985; articles, on Compensation in International Law, in legal jls, and on local history, town planning, and flood prevention. *Recreations:* golf (Oxford Univ. team *v* Cambridge Univ., 1929; various later Amateur European Championships); gardening. *Address:* Kitoha, 116b Grenfell Road, Maidenhead, Berks SL6 1HB. *T:* Maidenhead (0628) 21621.

BROOKS, Most Rev. Francis Gerard; *see* Dromore, Bishop of, (RC).

BROOKS, John Ashton, CBE 1989; FCIB; Director: Midland Bank plc, 1981–91; Hongkong and Shanghai Banking Corp., 1989–91; Chairman, Thomas Cook Group Ltd, since 1988; *b* 24 Oct. 1928; *s* of Victor Brooks and Annie (*née* Ashton); *m* 1959, Sheila (*née* Hulse); one *s* one *d*. *Educ:* Merchant Taylors' Sch., Northwood. Joined Midland Bank, 1949; Manager: 22 Victoria Street Br., 1970; Threadneedle Street Br., 1972; Gen. Man., Computer Operations, 1975; Dep. Gp Chief Exec., Midland Group, 1981–89. President: Chartered Inst. of Bankers, 1987–88; Assoc. of Banking Teachers, 1990–. *Recreations:* reading, walking. *Clubs:* Overseas Bankers', Institute of Directors.

BROOKS, Leslie James, CEng, FRINA; RCNC; Deputy Director of Engineering (Constructive), Ship Department, Ministry of Defence (Procurement Executive), 1973–76, retired; *b* 3 Aug. 1916; *yr s* of late C. J. D. Brooks and Lucy A. Brooks, Milton Regis, Sittingbourne, Kent; *m* 1941, Ruth Elizabeth Olver, Saltash, Cornwall; two *s*. *Educ:* Borden Grammar Sch., Sittingbourne, Kent; HM Dockyard Schs, Sheerness and Chatham; Royal Naval Engrg Coll., Keyham; RNC, Greenwich. War of 1939–45: Asst Constructor, Naval Construction Dept, Admty, Bath, 1941–44; Constr Lt-Comdr on Staff of Allied Naval Comdr, Exped. Force, and Flag Officer, Brit. Assault Area, 1944. Constr in charge Welding, Naval Constrn Dept, Admty, Bath, 1945–47; Constr Comdr, Staff of Comdr-in-Chief, Brit. Pacific Fleet, 1947–49; Constr in charge, No 2 Ship Tank, Admty Experiment Works, Haslar, Gosport, 1949–54. Naval Constrn Dept, Admty, Bath: Constr, Merchant Shipping Liaison, 1954–56; Chief Constr in charge of Conversion of First Commando Ships, and of Operating Aircraft Carriers, 1956–62; Dep. Supt, Admty Exper. Works, Haslar, 1962–64; Senior Officers War Course, RNC Greenwich, 1964–65; Ship Dept, Bath: Asst Dir of Naval Constrn, Naval Constrn Div., MoD(N), 1965–68; Asst Dir of Engrg (Ships), MoD(PE), 1968–73; Dep. Dir of Engrg/Constr., MoD(PE), 1973. Mem., Royal Corps of Naval Constructors. *Recreations:* walking, photography, natural history. *Address:* Merrymeet, Perrymead, Bath BA2 5AY. *T:* Bath (0225) 832856.

BROOKS, Mel; writer, director, actor; *b* Brooklyn, 1926; *m* Florence Baum; two *s* one *d*; *m* 1964, Anne Bancroft; one *s*. TV script writer for series: Your Show of Shows, 1950–54; Caesar's Hour, 1954–57; Get Smart, 1965–70. Films: (cartoon) The Critic (Academy Award), 1963; writer and director: The Producers (Academy Award), 1968; Young Frankenstein, 1974; writer, director and actor: The Twelve Chairs, 1970; Blazing Saddles, 1973; Silent Movie, 1976; writer, director, actor and producer: High Anxiety, 1977; History of the World Part 1, 1981; Spaceballs, 1987; actor, producer: To Be Or Not To Be, 1983. Film productions include The Elephant Man, 1980. Several album recordings. *Address:* c/o Twentieth Century-Fox Film Corporation, Box 900, Beverly Hills, Calif 90213, USA.

BROOKS, Prof. Nicholas Peter, DPhil; FSA, FRHistS; FBA 1989; Professor and Head of Department of Medieval History, University of Birmingham, since 1985; *b* 14 Jan. 1941; *s* of W. D. W. Brooks, *qv*; *m* 1967, Chloë Carolyn Willis; one *s* one *d*. *Educ:* Winchester Coll.; Magdalen Coll., Oxford (Demy; MA DPhil). FRHistS 1970; FSAScot 1970–85; FSA 1974. Lectr in Medieval Hist., 1964–78, Sen. Lectr, 1978–85, St Andrews Univ.; Birmingham University: Chm., Sch. of History, 1987–89; Chm., Jun. Year Abroad prog., 1988–. Gen. Ed., Studies in the Early Hist. of Britain, 1978–. *Publications:* (ed) Latin and the Vernacular Languages in Early Medieval Britain, 1981; The Early History of the Church of Canterbury, 1984; numerous articles in festschriften, Medieval Archaeology, Anglo-Saxon England, Trans of RHistS, etc. *Recreations:* gardening, bridge, swimming, walking. *Address:* School of History, University of Birmingham, PO Box 363, Birmingham B15 2TT. *T:* 021–414 5736.

BROOKS, Timothy Gerald Martin; JP; farmer; Lord-Lieutenant of Leicestershire, since 1989; *b* 20 March 1929; *s* of late Hon. Herbert William Brooks, *s* of 2nd Baron Crawshaw, and of Hilda Muriel (*née* Steel); *m* 1951, Hon. Ann Fremantle, *d* of Baron Cottesloe, *qv* and late Lady Elizabeth Harris; three *s* two *d*. *Educ:* Eton; RAC, Cirencester (NDA). Set up farm and market garden, Wistow, 1953; now farms 1100 acres; Director: Wistow Hall Gardens Ltd; Thomas Tapling & Co. Ltd. Mem., Harborough DC, 1975–89 (Chm., 1983–84). Mem., Leics Co. Cttee, CLA (Chm., 1978–80). Chairman of Governors: Brooksby Agricl Coll., 1986–; Wyggeston's Hosp., Leicester, 1988–. Churchwarden, St Wistan's, Wistow. JP 1960, High Sheriff, 1979–80, Leics. *Recreations:* arts, shooting, tennis. *Address:* Wistow Hall, near Great Glen, Leicester LE8 0QF.

BROOKS, William Donald Wykeham, CBE 1956; MA, DM (Oxon); FRCP; retired; Consulting Physician: St Mary's Hospital; Brompton Hospital; to the Royal Navy; to the King Edward VII Convalescent Home for Officers, Osborne; Chief Medical Officer, Eagle Star Insurance Co.; *b* 3 Aug. 1905; *er s* of A. E. Brooks, MA (Oxon), Maidenhead, Berks; *m* 1934, Phyllis Kathleen, *e d* of late F. A. Juler, CVO; two *s* two *d*. *Educ:* Reading School; St John's College, Oxford (White Scholar); St Mary's Hospital, London (University Scholar); Strong Memorial Hospital, Rochester, New York. First Class Honours, Final Honour School of Physiology, 1928; Cheadle Gold Medallist, 1931; Fereday Fellow St John's College, Oxford, 1931–34; Rockefeller Travelling Fellow, 1932–33; Goulstonian Lecturer, 1940; Marc Daniels Lecturer, RCP, 1957. Asst Registrar, 1946–50, RCP; Censor, RCP, 1961– (Council, 1959–61, Senior Vice-President and Senior Censor, 1965); Member Association of Physicians of Great Britain and Ireland. Served War 1940–45 as Surgeon Captain, RNVR. Editor, Quarterly Jl of Medicine, 1946–67. *Publications:* numerous articles on general medical topics and on chest diseases in various medical journals; Sections on Chest Wounds, Respiratory Diseases and Tuberculosis, Conybeare's Textbook of Medicine; Respiratory Diseases section in the Official Naval Medical History of the War. *Recreations:* golf, shooting, gardening, bridge. *Address:* Two Acres, Fryern Road, Storrington, W Sussex RH20 4NT. *T:* Storrington (0903) 742159.

See also E. A. S. Brooks, N. P. Brooks.

BROOKSBANK, Sir (Edward) Nicholas, 3rd Bt *cr* 1919; with Christie's, since 1974; *b* 4 Oct. 1944; *s* of Sir Edward William Brooksbank, 2nd Bt, TD, and of Ann, 2nd *d* of Col T. Clitherow; *S* father, 1983; *m* 1970, Emma, *d* of Baron Holderness, *qv*; one *s* one *d*. *Educ:* Eton. Royal Dragoons, 1963–69; Blues and Royals, 1969–73; Adjutant, 1971–73. *Heir:* *s* (Florian) Tom (Charles) Brooksbank, *b* 9 Aug. 1982. *Address:* Ryton Grange, Malton, North Yorks.

BROOKSBANK, Sir Nicholas; *see* Brooksbank, Sir E. N.

BROOKSBY, John Burns, CBE 1973; FRS 1980; Director, Animal Virus Research Institute, Pirbright, 1964–79; *b* 25 Dec. 1914; *s* of George B. Brooksby, Glasgow; *m* 1940, Muriel Weir; one *s* one *d*. *Educ:* Hyndland Sch., Glasgow; Glasgow Veterinary Coll.; London University. MRCVS 1935; FRCVS 1978; BSc (VetSc) 1936; PhD 1947; DSc 1957; FRSE 1968; Hon. DSc Edinburgh, 1981. Research Officer, Pirbright, 1939; Dep. Dir, 1957; Dir, 1964. *Publications:* papers on virus diseases of animals in scientific jls. *Address:* The Burlings, 48 High Street, Swaffham Bulbeck, Cambridge CB5 0LX. *T:* Cambridge (0223) 812607.

BROOM, Prof. Donald Maurice, FIBiol; Colleen Macleod Professor of Animal Welfare, since 1986, Fellow, St Catharine's College, since 1987, University of Cambridge; *b* 14 July 1942; *s* of late Donald Edward Broom and of Mavis Edith Rose Broom; *m* 1971, Sally Elizabeth Mary Riordan; three *s*. *Educ:* Whitgift Sch.; St Catharine's Coll., Cambridge (MA, PhD); FIBiol 1986. Lectr, 1967, Sen. Lectr, 1979, Reader, 1982, Dept of Pure and Applied Zoology, Univ. of Reading. Vis. Asst Prof., Univ. of California, Berkeley, 1969; Vis. Lectr, Univ. of W Indies, Trinidad, 1972; Vis. Scientist, CSIRO Div. of Animal Prodn, Perth, WA, 1983. Invited Expert: EEC Farm Animal Welfare Expert Gp, 1981–; Council of Europe Standing Cttee of Eur. Convention for Protection of Animals kept for Farming Purposes, 1987–; Hon. Res. Associate, AFRC Inst. for Grassland and Animal Production, 1985–. Member: Council, Assoc. for Study of Animal Behaviour, 1980–83 (Hon. Treas., 1971–80); Internat. Ethological Cttee, 1976–79; Council, Soc. for Vet. Ethology, 1981–84 (Vice-Pres., 1986–87, 1989–91; Pres., 1987–89); NERC Special Cttee on Seals, 1986–. Trustee, Farm Animal Care Trust, 1986–. George Fleming Prize, British Vet. Jl, 1990. *Publications:* Birds and their Behaviour, 1977; Biology of Behaviour, 1981; (ed jtly) The Encyclopaedia of Domestic Animals, 1986; (ed) Farmed Animals, 1986; (with A. F. Fraser) Farm Animal Behaviour and Welfare, 1990; numerous papers in behaviour, psychol, zool, ornithol, agricl and vet. jls. *Recreations:* squash, water-polo, modern pentathlon, ornithology. *Address:* Department of Clinical Veterinary Medicine, Madingley Road, Cambridge CB3 0ES. *T:* Cambridge (0223) 337697. *Club:* Hawks (Cambridge).

BROOM, Air Marshal Sir Ivor (Gordon), KCB 1975 (CB 1972); CBE 1969; DSO 1945; DFC 1942 (Bar to DFC 1944, 2nd Bar 1945); AFC 1956; international aerospace consultant, since 1977; Chairman: Gatwick Handling Ltd, since 1982; Farnborough Aerospace Development Corporation, since 1985; *b* Cardiff, 2 June 1920; *s* of Alfred Godfrey Broom and Janet Broom; *m* 1942, Jess Irene Broom (*née* Cooper); two *s* one *d*. *Educ:* West Monmouth Grammar Sch.; Pontypridd County Sch., Glam. Joined RAF, 1940; commissioned, 1941; 114 Sqdn, 107 Sqdn, 1941; CFS Course, 1942; Instr on: 1655 Mosquito Trg Unit; 571 Sqdn, 128 Sqdn, and 163 Sqdn, 1943–45; HQ, ACSEA, 1945–46. Commanded 28 (FR) Sqdn, 1946–48; RAF Staff Coll. Course, Bracknell, 1949; Sqdn Comdr, No 1 ITS, 1950–52; No 3 Flying Coll. Course, Manby, 1952–53; commanded 57 Sqdn, 1953–54; Syndicate Leader, Flying Coll., Manby, 1954–56; commanded Bomber Command Development Unit, Wittering, 1956–59; Air Secretary's Dept, 1959–62; commanded RAF Bruggen, 1962–64; IDC, 1965–66; Dir of Organisation (Establishments), 1966–68; Commandant, Central Flying School, 1968–70; AOC No 11 (Fighter) Gp, Strike Comd, 1970–72. Dep. Controller, 1972–74, Controller, 1974–77, Nat. Air Traffic Services; Mem., CAA Bd, 1974–77. Dir, Plessey Airports Ltd, 1982–86. Vice-Pres., RAFA, 1981–. *Recreations:* golf, skiing. *Address:* Cherry Lawn, Bridle Lane, Loudwater, Rickmansworth, Herts WD3 4JB. *Club:* Royal Air Force.

BROOME, David, OBE 1970; farmer; British professional show jumper; *b* Cardiff, 1 March 1940; *s* of Fred and Amelia Broome, Chepstow, Gwent; *m* 1976, Elizabeth, *d* of K. W. Fletcher, Thirsk, N Yorkshire; three *s*. *Educ:* Monmouth Grammar Sch. for Boys. European Show Jumping Champion (3 times); World Show Jumping Champion, La Baule, 1970; Olympic Medallist (Bronze) twice, 1960, 1968; King George V Gold Cup 5 times (a record, in 1981). Mounts include: Sunsalve, Aachen, 1961; Mr Softee, Rotterdam, 1967, and Hickstead, 1969; Beethoven, La Baule, France, 1970, as (1st British) World Champion; Sportsman and Philco, Cardiff, 1974; Professional Champion of the World. *Publications:* Jump-Off, 1971; (with S. Hadley) Horsemanship, 1983. *Recreations:* hunting (MFH), shooting, golf. *Address:* Mount Ballan Manor, Crick, Chepstow, Gwent, Wales. *T:* Caldicot (0291) 420778.

BROOME, John Lawson, CBE 1987; Founder and Chairman, Alton Towers Theme Park, since 1980 (Chief Executive, 1980–90); Chairman and Chief Executive, Battersea Leisure; *b* 2 Aug. 1943; *s* of late Albert Henry and Mary Elizabeth Broome; *m* 1972, Jane Myott Bagshaw; one *s* two *d*. *Educ:* Rossall School. School master, 1960–65; Dir, JLB Investment Property Group, 1961–, and numerous other companies. Member: BTA; Internat. Assoc. of Amusement Parks and Attractions, USA (Chm., Internat. Cttee; Chm., Internat. Council). Vice-Pres., Ironbridge Gorge Museum Trust. Governor, N Staffs Polytechnic. President: Staffs Moorlands Talking Newspaper for the Blind; Staffs Moorlands Athletic Club. *Recreations:* ski-ing, travelling, antiques, old paintings, objects d'art, fine gardens. *Address:* Stretton Hall, Malpas, Cheshire SY14 7JA. *T:* (office) Oakamoor (0538) 702200. *Clubs:* Grosvenor (Chester); Eaton Golf, Deeside Ramblers Hockey.

BROOMFIELD, Nigel Hugh Robert Allen, CMG 1986; HM Diplomatic Service; Deputy Under-Secretary of State (Defence), Foreign and Commonwealth Office, since 1990; *b* 19 March 1937; *s* of Arthur Allen Broomfield and Ruth Sheilagh Broomfield; *m* 1963, Valerie Fenton; two *s*. *Educ:* Haileybury Coll.; Trinity Coll., Cambridge (BA (Hons) English Lit.). Commnd 17/21 Lancers, 1959, retired as Major, 1968. Joined FCO as First Sec., 1969; First Secretary: British Embassy, Bonn, 1970–72; British Embassy, Moscow, 1972–74; European Communities Dept, London, 1975–77; RCDS, 1978; Political Advr and Head of Chancery, British Mil. Govt, Berlin, 1979–81; Head of Eastern European and Soviet Dept, 1981–83, and Head of Soviet Dept, 1983–85, FCO; Dep. High Comr and Minister, New Delhi, 1985–88; Ambassador to GDR, 1988–90. Captain, Cambridge Squash Rackets and Real Tennis, 1957–58; British Amateur Squash Champion, 1958–59 (played for England, 1957–60). *Recreations:* tennis, squash, cricket, gardening, reading, music. *Address:* c/o Foreign and Commonwealth Office, SW1A 2AH. *Clubs:* Royal Automobile, MCC; Hawks (Cambridge).

BROOMHALL, Maj.-Gen. William Maurice, CB 1950; DSO 1945; OBE 1932; *b* 16 July 1897; *o s* of late Alfred Edward Broomhall, London. *Educ:* St Paul's School; Royal Military Academy, Woolwich. Commissioned Royal Engineers, 1915; France and Belgium, 1914–21 (wounded twice); Waziristan, 1921–24 (medal and clasp); NW Frontier of India, 1929–31 (despatches, clasp, OBE); Staff College, Camberley, 1932–33. Served North-West Europe, 1939–45 (Despatches, DSO); Chief Engineer, Allied Forces, Italy, 1946; Chief Engineer, British Army of the Rhine, 1947–48; Chief Engineer, Middle East Land Forces, 1948–51; retired, 1951. *Address:* The Cottage, Park Lane, Beaconsfield, Bucks HP9 2HR. *Club:* Army and Navy.

BROPHY, Brigid (Antonia), (Lady Levey), FRSL; author and playwright; *b* 12 June 1929; *o c* of late John Brophy; *m* 1954, Sir Michael Levey, *qv*; one *d*. *Educ:* St Paul's Girls' Sch.; St Hugh's Coll., Oxford. Awarded Jubilee Scholarship at St Hugh's Coll., Oxford, 1947 and read classics. Co-organiser, Writers Action Gp campaign for Public Lending Right, 1972–82; Exec. Councillor, Writers' Guild of GB, 1975–78; a Vice-Chm., British Copyright Council, 1976–80. A Vice-Pres., Nat. Anti-Vivisection Soc., 1974–. Awarded Cheltenham Literary Festival First Prize for a first novel, 1954; London Magazine Prize for Prose, 1962. *Publications:* Hackenfeller's Ape, 1953; The King of a Rainy Country, 1956; Black Ship to Hell, 1962; Flesh, 1962; The Finishing Touch, 1963; The Snow Ball, 1964; Mozart the Dramatist, 1964, 2nd edn 1988; Don't Never Forget, 1966; (in collaboration with Michael Levey and Charles Osborne) Fifty Works of English Literature We Could Do Without, 1967; Black and White: a portrait of Aubrey Beardsley, 1968; In Transit, 1969; Prancing Novelist, 1973; The Adventures of God in his Search for the Black Girl, and other fables, 1973; Pussy Owl, 1976; Beardsley and his World, 1976; Palace Without Chairs, 1978; The Prince and the Wild Geese, 1983; A Guide to Public Lending Right, 1983; Baroque 'n' Roll, 1987; Reads, 1989. *Plays:* The Burglar, Vaudeville, 1967 (published with preface, 1968); The Waste Disposal Unit, Radio (published 1968). *Visual Art:* (with Maureen Duffy, *qv*) Prop Art, exhibn, London, 1969. *Address:* Flat 3, 185 Old Brompton Road, SW5 0AN. *T:* 071–373 9335.

BROPHY, Michael John Mary; Director, Charities Aid Foundation, since 1982; *b* 24 June 1937; *s* of Gerald and Mary Brophy; *m* 1962, Sarah Rowe; three *s* one *d*. *Educ:* Ampleforth Coll.; Royal Naval Coll., Dartmouth. Entered Royal Navy, 1955; retired as Lt-Comdr, 1966. Associate Dir, J. Walter Thompson, 1967–74; Appeals Dir, Spastics Soc., 1974–82; Sec., Council for Charitable Support, 1986–. FRSA 1986. *Recreations:* travel, walking. *Address:* Chalk Croft, Cuilfail, Lewes, E Sussex. *Club:* Athenæum.

BROSAN, Dr George Stephen, CBE 1982; TD 1960; consulting engineer; Director, North East London Polytechnic, 1970–82; *b* 8 Aug. 1921; *o s* of Rudolph and Margaret Brosan; *m* 1952, Maureen Dorothy Foscoe; three *d*. *Educ:* Kilburn Grammar Sch.; Faraday House; The Polytechnic; Birkbeck Coll., London. Faraday Scholar, 1939. PhD 1951; DFH 1957; FIEE 1964; FIMA 1966; FIMechE 1971; CEng 1976; Hon. FIProdE 1980; MRIN 1983; CBIM (formerly FBIM) 1975. Teaching staff, Regent Street Polytechnic, 1950–58; Head of Dept, Willesden Coll. of Technology, 1958–60; Further Educn Officer, Middlesex CC, 1960–62; Principal, Enfield Coll. of Technology, 1962–70. Pres., Tensor Club of GB, 1973–82; Pres., IProdE, 1975–77; Mem. Council, BIM, 1975–79; Chairman: CEI Educn Cttee, 1978–79; Accountancy Educn Consultative Bd, 1979–82. Life Mem., ASME, 1977. Hon. MIED 1968; Hon. Mem., Council for Educn in the Commonwealth, 1983; CNI 1983. Chevalier du Tastevin, 1976; Yachtmaster Ocean, 1986. *Publications:* (jtly) Advanced Electrical Power and Machines, 1966; (jtly) Patterns and Policies in Higher Education, 1971; numerous articles and papers in academic and professional press. *Recreation:* yachting. *Address:* High Orchard, Mark Way, Godalming, Surrey GU7 2BB; Tartagli Alti, Paciano 06060, Province of Perugia, Italy. *Club:* Reform.

BROTHERHOOD, Air Cdre William Rowland, CBE 1952; retired as Director, Guided Weapons (Trials), Ministry of Aviation (formerly Supply), 1959–61; *b* 22 Jan. 1912; *s* of late James Brotherhood, Tintern, Mon.; *m* 1939, Margaret (*d* 1981), *d* of late Ernest Sutcliffe, Louth, Lincs; one *s* one *d*. *Educ:* Monmouth School; RAF College, Cranwell. Joined RAF, 1930; Group Captain, 1943; Air Commodore, 1955; Director, Operational Requirements, Air Ministry, 1955–58. *Address:* Inglewood, Llandogo, Monmouth, Gwent. *T:* Dean (0594) 530333.

BROTHERS, Air Cdre Peter Malam, CBE 1964; DSO 1944; DFC 1940, and Bar, 1943; Managing Director, Peter Brothers Consultants Ltd, 1973–86; *b* 30 Sept. 1917; *s* of late John Malam Brothers; *m* 1939, Annette, *d* of late James Wilson; three *d*. *Educ:* N. Manchester Sch. (Br. of Manchester Grammar). Joined RAF, 1936; Flt-Lieut 1939; RAF Biggin Hill, Battle of Britain, 1940; Sqdn-Ldr 1941; Wing Comdr 1942; Tangmere Fighter Wing Ldr, 1942–43; Staff HQ No. 10 Gp, 1943; Exeter Wing Ldr, 1944; US Comd and Gen. Staff Sch., 1944–45; Central Fighter Estab., 1945–46; Colonial Service, Kenya, 1947–49; RAF Bomber Sqdn, 1949–52; HQ No. 3 Gp, 1952–54; RAF Staff Coll., 1954; HQ Fighter Comd, 1955–57; Bomber Stn, 1957–59; Gp Capt., and Staff Officer, SHAPE, 1959–62; Dir of Ops (Overseas), 1962–65; Air Cdre, and AOC Mil. Air Traffic Ops, 1965–68; Dir of Public Relations (RAF), MoD (Air), 1968–73; retired 1973. Freeman, Guild Air Pilots and Air Navigators, 1966 (Liveryman, 1968; Warden, 1971; Master, 1974–75); Freeman, City of London, 1967. Editorial Adviser, Defence and Foreign Affairs publications, 1973–76. Patron, Spitfire Assoc., Australia, 1971–; Vice-President: Spitfire Soc., 1984–; Devon Emergency Volunteers, 1986– (Chm., 1981–86). *Recreations:* golf, sailing, fishing, swimming, flying. *Address:* c/o National Westminster Bank, Topsham, Devon. *Clubs:* Royal Air Force; Honiton Golf.

BROTHERTON, Ven. John Michael; Archdeacon of Chichester and Canon Residentiary of Chichester Cathedral, since 1991; *b* 7 Dec. 1935; *s* of late Clifford and Minnie Brotherton; *m* 1963, Daphne Margaret Yvonne, *d* of Sir Geoffrey Meade, *qv*; three *s* one *d*. *Educ:* St John's Coll., Cambridge (MA); Cuddesdon Coll., Oxford; Univ. of London Inst. of Educn (PGCE). Ordained: deacon, 1961; priest, 1962; Asst Curate, St Nicolas, Chiswick, 1961–64; Chaplain, Trinity Coll., Port of Spain, Trinidad, 1965–69; Rector of St Michael's, Diego Martin, Trinidad, 1969–75; Vicar, St Mary and St John, Oxford, and Chaplain, St Hilda's Coll., Oxford, 1976–81; Rural Dean of Cowley, 1978–81; Vicar, St Mary, Portsea, 1981–91. Hon. Canon, St Michael's Cathedral, Kobe, Japan, 1986. *Recreations:* travel, walking. *Address:* 4 Canon Lane, Chichester, West Sussex PO19 1PX. *T:* Chichester (0243) 779134.

BROTHERTON, Michael Lewis; formed Michael Brotherton Associates, Parliamentary and Financial Consultants, 1986; *b* 26 May 1931; *s* of late John Basil Brotherton and Maud Brotherton; *m* 1968, Julia, *d* of Austin Gerald Comyn King and Katherine Elizabeth King, Bath; three *s* one *d*. *Educ:* Prior Park; RNC Dartmouth. Served RN, 1949–64: qual. Observer 1955; Cyprus, 1957 (despatches); Lt-Comdr 1964, retd. Times Newspapers, 1967–74. Chm., Beckenham Conservative Political Cttee, 1967–68; contested (C) Deptford, 1970; MP (C) Louth, Oct. 1974–1983. Pres., Hyde Park Tories, 1975. Mem., Select Cttee on violence in the family, 1975–76. *Recreations:* cricket, cooking, gardening, talking. *Address:* The Old Vicarage, Wrangle, Boston, Lincs PE22 9EP. *T:* Boston (0205) 870688. *Clubs:* Army and Navy, MCC; Conservative Working Men's, Louth (Louth); Castaways; Cleethorpes Conservative; Immingham Conservative.

BROTHWOOD, John, MRCP, FFCM, FRCPsych, FFOM; Chief Medical Officer, Esso Petroleum (UK), and Exxon (formerly Esso) Chemicals, 1979–90, retired; *b* 23 Feb. 1931; *s* of Wilfred Cyril Vernon Brothwood and late Emma Bailey; *m* 1957, Dr Margaret Stirling Meyer; one *s* one *d*. *Educ:* Marlborough Coll.; Peterhouse, Cambridge (Schol.); Middlesex Hosp. MB BChir (Cantab) 1955; MRCP 1960, DPM (London) 1964, FFCM 1972, FRCPsych 1976, FFOM 1988. Various posts in clinical medicine (incl. Registrar, Maudsley Hosp. and military service as Captain RAMC), 1955–64; joined DHSS (then Min. of Health) as MO, 1964; posts held in mental health, regional liaison, chronic disease policy and medical manpower and educn; SPMO and Under Secretary, DHSS, 1975–78. Lay Reader, Parish of St Barnabas, Dulwich, 1982–. *Publications:* various, on NHS matters, especially mental health policy and related topics. *Recreations:* diverse. *Address:* 81 Calton Avenue, SE21 7DF. *T:* 081–693 8273.

BROUCHER, David Stuart; HM Diplomatic Service; Counsellor Economic, Bonn, since 1989; *b* 5 Oct. 1944; *s* of Clifford Broucher and Betty Broucher (*née* Jordan); *m* 1971, Marion Monika Blackwell; one *s*. *Educ:* Manchester Grammar School; Trinity Hall, Cambridge (MA Modern Languages). Foreign Office, 1966; British Military Govt, Berlin, 1968; Cabinet Office, 1972; Prague, 1975; FCO, 1978; UK Perm. Rep. to EC, 1983; Counsellor, Jakarta, 1985–89. *Recreations:* music, golf, sailing. *Address:* c/o Foreign and Commonwealth Office, SW1.

BROUGH, Dr Colin, FRCPE; FFCM; Chief Administrative Medical Officer, Lothian Health Board, 1980–88; *b* 4 Jan. 1932; *s* of Peter Brough and Elizabeth C. C. Chalmers; *m* 1957, Maureen Jennings; four *s* one *d*. *Educ:* Bell Baxter Sch., Cupar; Univ. of Edinburgh (MB ChB). DPH 1965; DIH 1965; FFCM 1978; MRCPE 1981; FRCPE 1982. House Officer, Leicester General Hosp. and Royal Infirmary of Edinburgh, 1956–57; Surg.-Lieut, Royal Navy, 1957–60; General Practitioner, Leith and Fife, 1960–64; Dep. Medical Supt, Royal Inf. of Edinburgh, 1965–67; ASMO, PASMO, Dep. SAMO, South-Eastern Regional Hosp. Board, Scotland, 1967–74; Community Medicine Specialist, Lothian Health Board, 1974–80. *Recreations:* golf, shooting, fishing, first aid. *Address:* The Saughs, Gullane, East Lothian EH31 2AL. *T:* Gullane (0620) 842179.

BROUGH, Edward; Chairman, Volker Stevin (UK) Ltd, 1980–82; *b* 28 May 1918; *s* of late Hugh and Jane Brough; *m* 1941, Peggy Jennings; two *s*. *Educ:* Berwick Grammar School; Edinburgh University (MA). Joined Unilever Ltd, 1938. War service, KOSB, 1939–46 (Captain). Rejoined Unilever, 1946; Commercial Dir, 1951, Man. Dir, 1954, Lever's Cattle Foods Ltd; Chairman, Crosfields (CWG) Ltd, 1957; Lever Bros & Associates Ltd: Development Dir, 1960; Marketing Dir, 1962; Chm., 1965; Hd of Unilever's Marketing Div., 1968–71; Dir of Unilever Ltd and Unilever NV, 1968–74, and Chm. of UK Cttee, 1971–74. Chm., Adriaan Volker (UK) Ltd, 1974–80. Mem., NBPI, 1967–70. FBIM 1967. *Recreations:* flyfishing, golf. *Address:* Far End, The Great Quarry, Guildford, Surrey GU1 3XN. *T:* Guildford (0483) 504064; St John's, Chagford, Devon. *Club:* Farmers'.

BROUGH, Michael David, FRCS; Consultant Plastic Surgeon, University College Hospital, Royal Free, Whittington and Royal Northern Hospitals, since 1982; *b* 4 July

1942; *s* of late Kenneth David Brough and of Frances Elizabeth Brough (*née* Davies); *m* 1974, Dr Geraldine Moira Sleigh; two *s* two *d*. *Educ:* Westminster Sch.; Christ's Coll., Cambridge (MA); Middlesex Hosp. Med. Sch. (MB, BChir). Med. posts at Middlesex and Central Middlesex Hosps, 1968–71; Surgical trng posts, Birmingham Hosps, 1971–74; Plastic Surgery trng posts, Mount Vernon Hosp., London, Odstock Hosp., Salisbury, Whithington Hosp., Manchester, 1975–80; Cons. Plastic Surg., St Andrews Hosp., Billericay, Queen Elizabeth Hosp., Hackney, Whipps Cross Hosp., 1980–82. *Publications:* chapters in: Rob and Smith, Operative Surgery, 3rd edn 1976–79 and 4th edn 1988; Kirk and Williamson, General Surgical Operations, 2nd edn 1987; contribs to med. jls on plastic and reconstructive surgery. *Recreations:* family, ski-ing, Modern Pentathlon Half-Blue, 1964. *Address:* The Consulting Suite, 82 Portland Place, W1N 3DH. *T:* 071–935 8910. *Club:* Hawks (Cambridge).

BROUGHAM, family name of **Baron Brougham and Vaux.**

BROUGHAM AND VAUX, 5th Baron *cr* 1860; **Michael John Brougham;** *b* 2 Aug. 1938; *s* of 4th Baron and Jean, *d* of late Brig.-Gen. G. B. S. Follett, DSO, MVO; *S* father, 1967; *m* 1st, 1963, Olivia Susan (marr. diss. 1968), *d* of Rear-Admiral Gordon Thomas Seccombe Gray; one *d*; 2nd, 1969, Catherine Gulliver (marr. diss. 1981), *d* of W. Gulliver; one *s*. *Educ:* Lycée Jaccard, Lausanne; Millfield School. Pres., RoSPA, 1986–89. *Heir:* *s* Hon. Charles William Brougham, *b* 9 Nov. 1971. *Address:* 11 Westminster Gardens, Marsham Street, SW1P 4JA.

BROUGHAM, Christopher John; QC 1988; *b* 11 Jan. 1947; *s* of late Lt-Comdr Patrick Brougham and of Elizabeth Anne (*née* Vestey); *m* 1974, Mary Olwen (*née* Corker); one *s* three *d*. *Educ:* Radley Coll.; Worcester Coll., Oxford (BA Hons). Called to the Bar, Inner Temple, 1969; Dep. High Court Bankruptcy Registrar, 1984. Dep. Churchwarden, Christ Church, Kensington, 1980–. *Recreations:* music, crossword puzzles. *Address:* 3/4 South Square, Gray's Inn, WC1R 5HP. *T:* 071–696 9900.

BROUGHSHANE, 2nd Baron (UK), *cr* 1945; **Patrick Owen Alexander Davison;** *b* 18 June 1903; *er s* of 1st Baron and Beatrice Mary, *d* of Sir Owen Roberts; *S* father, 1953; *m* 1929, Bettine, *d* of Sir Arthur Russell, 6th Bt; (one *s* decd). *Educ:* Winchester; Magdalen College, Oxford. Barrister, Inner Temple, 1926. Served War of 1939–45: with Irish Guards, 1939–41; Assistant Secretary (Military), War Cabinet, 1942–45. Has US Legion of Merit. *Heir:* *b* Hon. (William) Kensington Davison, DSO, DFC, *b* 25 Nov. 1914. *Address:* 21 Eaton Square, SW1; 28 Fisher Street, Sandwich, Kent. *Club:* White's.

BROUGHTON, family name of **Baron Fairhaven.**

BROUGHTON, Air Marshal Sir Charles, KBE 1965 (CBE 1952); CB 1961; RAF retired; Air Member for Supply and Organization, Ministry of Defence, 1966–68; *b* 27 April 1911; *s* of Charles and Florence Gertrude Broughton; *m* 1939, Sylvia Dorothy Mary Bunbury; one *d* (and one *d* decd). *Educ:* New Zealand; RAF College, Cranwell. Commissioned, 1932; India, 1933–37; Flying Instructor, 1937–40. Served War of 1939–45 in Coastal Command and Middle East (despatches four times). Flying Training Command, 1947–49; Air Ministry, 1949–51; Imperial Defence College, 1952; NATO, Washington DC, 1953–55; Far East, 1955–58; Transport Command, 1958–61; Dir-General of Organization, Air Min. (subseq. Min. of Defence), 1961–64; UK Representative in Ankara on Permanent Military Deputies Group of Central Treaty Organization (Cento), 1965–66. *Address:* c/o Royal Bank of Scotland (Jersey) Ltd, PO Box 678, St Helier, Jersey, Channel Islands. *Club:* Royal Air Force.

BROUGHTON, Major Sir Evelyn Delves, 12th Bt, *cr* 1660; *b* 2 Oct. 1915; *s* of Major Sir Henry Delves Broughton, 11th Bt, and Vera Edyth Boscawen (*d* 1968); *S* father, 1942; *m* 1st, 1947, Hon. Elizabeth Florence Marion Cholmondeley (marr. diss., 1953; she *d* 1988), *er d* of 4th Baron Delamere; 2nd, 1955, Helen Mary (marr. diss. 1974), *d* of J. Shore, Wilmslow, Cheshire; three *d* (one *s* decd); 3rd, 1974, Mrs Rona Crammond. *Educ:* Eton; Trinity Coll., Cambridge. Formerly 2nd Lieut Irish Guards and Major RASC. *Heir presumptive: kinsman* David Delves Broughton, *b* 7 May 1942. *Address:* 37 Kensington Square, W8 5HP. *T:* 071–937 8883; Doddington, Nantwich, Cheshire. *T:* Nantwich (0270) 841258. *Clubs:* Brooks's; White's; Tarporley Hunt.

See also Baron Lovat.

BROUGHTON, Leonard, DL; Member, Lancashire County Council, 1974–89 (Chairman and Leader, 1974–81); *b* 21 March 1924; *s* of Charles Cecil Broughton and Florence (*née* Sunman); *m* 1949, Kathleen Gibson; one *d*. *Educ:* Kingston-upon-Hull. Served RASC, 1942–47. Estates Manager, Bedford Borough Council, 1957; business man. Member: Blackpool County Borough Council, 1961–74 (Leader, 1968–73); Blackpool Bor. Council, 1974–79; NW Co. Boroughs' Assoc., 1968–74; NW Economic Planning Council, 1970–72; Assoc. of Co. Councils, 1973–77; Board, Central Lancs Develt Corp., 1976–84. Mem. Courts, Lancaster and Salford Univs, 1974–81; Vice-President: Lancs Youth Clubs Assoc., 1974–81; NW Arts Assoc., 1974–81; Blackpool Social Service Council, 1974–84; Chm., Blackpool and Fylde Civilian Disabled Soc., 1964–84. Freeman, Co. Borough of Blackpool, 1973. DL Lancs, 1975; High Sheriff of Lancashire, 1983–84. *Recreations:* gardening, overseas travel. *Address:* 14 The Grove, Cleveleys, Blackpool, Lancs FY5 2JD.

BROUMAS, Nikolaos; retired General; Hon. Deputy Chief, Hellenic Armed Forces; Ambassador of Greece to the Court of St James's, 1972–74; *b* 22 Aug. 1916; *s* of Taxiarches and Kostia Broumas; *m* 1945, Claire Pendelis; two *d*. *Educ:* Greek Military Academy. US Infantry Coll., 1947–48; Greek Staff Coll., 1952; Greek Nat. Defence Coll., 1954. Co. Comdr, Greece, 1940–41, Western Desert, 1942–43 and Italy, 1944; Co. and Bn Comdr, Greek Guerrilla War, 1946–49; Liaison Officer, Allied Comd Far East, Korean War, 1951; Dep. Nat. Rep. to NATO Mil. Cttee, 1959–61; Dep. Chief of Greek Armed Forces, 1969–72. Kt Comdr, Orders of George I and of the Phoenix. (Greek) Gold Medal for Valour (4 times); Military Cross (twice); Medal for Distinguished Services (twice); Medal of Greek Italian War; Medal of Middle East War; UN Medal of Korean War, 1951; US Bronze Star Medal with oak leaf cluster, 1951. *Recreation:* hunting. *Address:* 5 Argyrokastrou Street, Papagos, Athens, Greece.

BROUN, Sir Lionel John Law, 12th Bt, *cr* 1686; *b* 25 April 1927; *s* of 11th Bt and Georgie, *y d* of late Henry Law, Sydney, NSW; *S* father 1962. *Heir:* *c* William Windsor Broun [*b* 1917; *m* 1952, D'Hrie King, NSW; two *d*]. *Address:* 23 Clanalpine Street, Mosman, NSW 2088, Australia.

BROWALDH, Tore; Grand Cross, Order of Star of the North, 1974; Kt Comdr's Cross, Order of Vasa, 1963; Hon. Chairman, Svenska Handelsbanken, since 1988; Deputy Chairman, Nobel Foundation, since 1966; *b* 23 Aug. 1917; *s* of Knut Ernfrid Browaldh and Ingrid Gezelius; *m* 1942, Gunnel Eva Ericson; three *s* one *d*. *Educ:* Stockholm Univ. (MA Politics, Economics and Law, 1941). Financial Attaché, Washington, 1943; Asst Sec., Royal Cttee of Post-War Econ. Planning, and Admin. Sec., Industrial Inst. for Econ. and Social Res., 1944–45; Sec. to Bd of Management, Svenska Handelsbanken, 1946–49; Dir of Econ., Social, Cultural and Refugee Dept, Secretariat Gen., Council of Europe, Strasbourg, 1949–51; Exec. Vice Pres., Confedn of Swedish Employers, 1951–54; Chief Gen. Man., Svenska Handelsbanken, 1955–66, Chm., 1966–78, Vice-Chm., 1978–88. Chairman: Svenska Cellulosa AB, 1965–88; Sandrew theater and movie AB, 1963–; Swedish IBM, 1978–; Swedish Unilever AB, 1977–; Industrivärden, 1976–88; Deputy Chairman: Beijerinvest AB, 1975–88; AB Volvo, 1977–81; Director: Volvo Internat. Adv. Bd, 1980–88; IBM World Trade Corp., Europe/ME/Africa, New York, 1979–88; Unilever Adv. Bd, Rotterdam and London, 1976–88. Member: Swedish Govt's Econ. Planning Commn, 1962–73 and Res. Adv. Bd, 1966–70; Consultative Cttee, Internat. Fedn of Insts for Advanced Study, 1972–; UN Gp of Eminent Persons on Multinational Corporations, 1973–74; Royal Swedish Acad. of Sciences; Hudson Inst., USA; Soc. of Scientists and Members of Parlt, Sweden; Royal Swedish Acad. of Engrg Sciences; Royal Acad. of Arts and Sciences, Uppsala. Dr of Technol. *hc* Royal Inst. of Technol., 1967; Dr of Econs *hc* Gothenburg, 1980. St Erik's Medal, Sweden, 1961; Gold Medal for public service, Sweden, 1981. *Publications:* Management and Society, 1961; (autobiography): vol. I, The Pilgrimage of a Journeyman, 1976; vol. II, The Long Road, 1980; vol. III, Against the Wind, 1984. *Recreations:* jazz, piano, golf, chess. *Address:* (office) Svenska Handelsbanken, Kungsträdgårdsgatan 2, 106 70 Stockholm, Sweden. *T:* 46–08–22 92 20; (home) Sturegatan 14, 114 36 Stockholm. *T:* 46–08–61 96 43. *Club:* Sällskapet (Stockholm).

BROWN, Alan James; HM Diplomatic Service, retired; Deputy Commissioner-General, UN Relief and Works Agency for Palestine Refugees, 1977–84; *b* 28 Aug. 1921; *s* of W. Y. Brown and Mrs E. I. Brown; *m* 1966, Joy Aileen Key Stone (*née* McIntyre); one *s*, and two step *d*. *Educ:* Magdalene College, Cambridge (MA). Served with HM Forces, 1941–47; CRO 1948; 2nd Sec., Calcutta, 1948–50; CRO, 1951; Private Sec. to Parly Under-Secretary of State, 1951–52; 1st Secretary, Dacca, Karachi, 1952–55; CRO, 1955–57; Kuala Lumpur, 1957–62; CRO, 1962–63; Head of Information Policy Dept, 1963–64; Dep. High Comr, Nicosia, 1964; Head of Far East and Pacific Dept, CRO, 1964–66; Dep. High Comr, Malta, 1966–70; Dep High Comr, later Consul-Gen., Karachi, 1971–72; Ambassador to Togo and Benin, 1973–75; Head of Nationality and Treaty Dept, FCO, 1975–77. *Recreation:* sailing. *Address:* Prospect House, 53 Lodge Hill Road, Lower Bourne, Farnham GU10 3RD. *Club:* United Oxford & Cambridge University.

BROWN, Alan Thomas, CBE 1978; DL; Chief Executive, Oxfordshire County Council, 1973–88; *b* 18 April 1928; *s* of Thomas Henry Brown and Lucy Lilian (*née* Betts); *m* 1962, Marie Christine East; two *d*. *Educ:* Wyggeston Grammar Sch., Leicester; Sidney Sussex Coll., Cambridge (Wrangler, Maths Tripos 1950, MA 1953). Fellow CIPFA, 1961. Asst, Bor. Treasurer's Dept, Wolverhampton, 1950–56; Asst Sec., IMTA, 1956–58; Dep. Co. Treas., Berks CC, 1958–61; Co. Treas., Cumberland CC, 1961–66; Town Clerk and Chief Exec., Oxford City Council, 1966–73. Member: SE Econ. Planning Council, 1975–79; Audit Commn, 1989–. DL Oxon 1978. *Recreations:* chess, horticulture, music, reading. *Address:* 7 Field House Drive, Oxford OX2 7NT. *T:* Oxford (0865) 515809.

BROWN, Alan Winthrop; Director, Resources and Planning, Health and Safety Executive, since 1989; *b* 14 March 1934; *s* of James Brown and Evelyn V. Brown (*née* Winthrop); *m* 1959, Rut Berit (*née* Ohlson); two *s* one *d*. *Educ:* Bedford Sch.; Pembroke Coll., Cambridge (BA Hons); Cornell Univ., NY (MSc). Joined Min. of Labour, 1959; Private Sec. to Minister, 1961–62; Principal, 1963; Asst Sec., 1969. Dir of Planning, Employment Service Agency, 1973–74; Under-Sec. and Head of Incomes Div., DoE, 1975; Chief Exec., Employment Service Div., 1976–79, Trng Services Div., 1979–82, MSC; Hd Electricity Div., Dept of Energy, 1983–85; Dir. Personnel and Management Services Div., Dept of Employment, 1985–89. *Publications:* papers on occupational psychology and industrial training. *Recreations:* reading history and poetry, gardening. *Address:* Health and Safety Executive, Baynards House, Chepstow Place, W2 4TF.

BROWN, (Albert) Peter (Graeme); Consultant in Press and Public Relations to the Imperial Cancer Research Fund, 1978–83; Press Officer to Royal Commission on National Health Service, 1979; *b* 5 April 1913; *s* of William Edward Graeme Brown, accountant, and Amy Powell Brown; unmarried. *Educ:* Queen Elizabeth's Sch., Darlington. Reporter, Sub-Editor, Dep.-Chief Sub-Editor, Westminster Press, 1932–40. Served War of 1939–45: Royal Navy, Officer, Western Approaches; Normandy; Far East; destroyers and assault ships. Information Divs, Ministries of Health, Local Govt and Planning, also Housing and Local Govt, 1946; Chief Press and Inf. Officer, Min. of Housing and Local Govt, 1958; Dir of Information, DHSS, and Advr to Sec. of State for Social Services, 1968–77. *Recreations:* cricket, opera (Mem. Friends of Covent Garden), classical music, art (Mem., Friends of RA). *Address:* 107 Hamilton Terrace, St John's Wood, NW8. *T:* 071–286 9192. *Club:* MCC.

BROWN, Alexander Cosens Lindsay, CB 1980; Chief Veterinary Officer, Ministry of Agriculture, Fisheries and Food, 1973–80; *b* Glasgow, 30 Jan. 1920; *s* of William Tait Brown and Margaret Rae; *m* 1945, Mary McDougal Hutchison; two *s*. *Educ:* Hutchesons' Grammar Sch., Glasgow; Glasgow Veterinary Coll. Diploma of RCVS; FRCVS 1980. Ministry of Agriculture, Fisheries and Food: appointed Vet. Officer to Dorset, 1943; Divisional Vet. Officer, HQ Tolworth, 1955; Divisional Vet. Officer, Essex, 1958–62; Dep. Regional Vet. Officer, W Midland Region, Wolverhampton, 1962–63; Regional Vet. Officer, Eastern Region, Cambridge, 1963; HQ Tolworth, 1967; Dep. Dir, Veterinary Field Services, 1969–70, Dir, 1970–73. Mem. ARC, 1975–80. *Publications:* contribs to Jl of Royal Soc. of Medicine, Veterinary Record, State Veterinary Jl. *Recreations:* gardening, swimming, reading. *Address:* 29 Ashwood Park, Fetcham, Leatherhead, Surrey KT22 9NT. *T:* Bookham (0372) 457997.

BROWN, Alexander Douglas G.; *see* Gordon-Brown.

BROWN, Sir Allen (Stanley), Kt 1956; CBE 1953; MA; LLM; Australian Commissioner for British Phosphate Commissioners and Christmas Island Phosphate Commission, 1970–76; *b* 3 July 1911; *m* 1936, Hilda May Wilke; one *s* two *d*. Dir-Gen. of Post-War Reconstruction, 1948. Sec., PM's Dept and Sec. to Cabinet, Commonwealth Govt, 1949–58; Deputy Australian High Commissioner to UK, 1959–65; Australian Ambassador to Japan, 1965–70. *Address:* 2/28 Ridgeway Avenue, Kew, Victoria 3101, Australia. *Club:* Melbourne (Melbourne).

BROWN, Prof. Archibald Haworth, FBA 1991; Professor of Politics, University of Oxford, since 1989; Fellow, St Antony's College, Oxford, since 1971; *b* 10 May 1938; *s* of late Rev. Alexander Douglas Brown and of Mary Brown (*née* Yates); *m* 1963, Patricia Susan Cornwall; one *s* one *d*. *Educ:* Annan Acad.; Dumfries Acad.; City of Westminster Coll.; LSE (BSc Econ, 1st Cl. Hons 1962). MA Oxon 1972. Reporter, Annandale Herald and Annandale Observer, 1954–56. National Service, 1956–58. Lectr in Politics, Glasgow Univ., 1964–71; British Council exchange scholar, Moscow Univ., 1967–68; Lectr in Soviet Instns, Univ. of Oxford, 1971–89. Visiting Professor: of Political Science, Yale Univ. and Univ. of Connecticut, 1980; Columbia Univ., NY, 1985; Univ. of Texas, Austin, 1990–91; INSEAD, 1991; Henry L. Stimson Lectures, Yale Univ., 1980. *Publications:* Soviet Politics and Political Science, 1974; (ed with M. C. Kaser) The Soviet Union since the Fall of Khrushchev, 1975, 2nd edn 1978; (ed with J. Gray) Political Culture and Political Change in Communist States, 1977, 2nd edn 1979; (ed with T. H.

Rigby and P. B. Reddaway) Authority, Power and Policy in the USSR: essays dedicated to Leonard Schapiro, 1980; (ed jtly) The Cambridge Encyclopedia of Russia and the Soviet Union, 1982, 2nd edn 1992; (ed with M. C. Kaser) Soviet Policy for the 1980s, 1982; (ed) Political Culture and Communist Studies, 1984; (ed) Political Leadership in the Soviet Union, 1989; (ed) The Soviet Union: a biographical dictionary, 1990; (ed) New Thinking in Soviet Politics, 1992; The Gorbachev Factor in Soviet Politics, 1992; papers in academic jls and symposia. *Recreations:* novels and political memoirs, opera, ballet, cricket (now as spectator). *Address:* St Antony's College, Oxford OX2 6JF. *T:* Oxford (0865) 59651.

BROWN, Gen. Arnold, OC 1982; International Leader, and General, Salvation Army, 1977–81; *b* 13 Dec. 1913; *s* of Arnold Rees Brown and Annie Brown; *m* 1939, Jean Catherine Barclay; two *d. Educ:* Belleville Collegiate, Canada. Commnd Salvation Army Officer, 1935; Editor, Canadian War Cry, 1937–47; Nat. Publicity Officer, Canada, 1947–62; Nat. Youth Officer, Canada, 1962–64; Head of Internat. Public Relations, Internat. HQ, London, 1964–69; Chief of Staff, 1969–74; Territorial Comdr, Canada and Bermuda, 1974–77. Freeman, City of London, 1978. Hon. LHD Asbury Coll., USA, 1972; Hon. DD Olivet Coll., USA, 1981. *Publications:* What Hath God Wrought?, 1952; The Gate and the Light, 1984; Fighting for His Glory, 1988; Yin: the mountain the wind blew here, 1988. *Recreations:* reading, writing, music. *Address:* 117 Bannatyne Drive, Willowdale, Ontario M2L 2P5, Canada. *Club:* Rotary of London and Toronto.

BROWN, Rt. Rev. Arthur Durrant; a Suffragan Bishop of Toronto, since 1981 (Bishop of York–Scarborough); *b* 7 March 1926; *s* of Edward S. Brown and Laura A. Durrant; *m* 1949, Norma Inez Rafuse; three *d. Educ:* Univ. of Western Ontario (BA 1949); Huron College (LTh 1949). Ordained deacon, 1949; priest, 1950, Huron. Rector: of Paisley with Cargill and Pinkerton, 1948–50; of Glenworth and St Stephen, London, Ont., 1950–53; of St John, Sandwich, Windsor, Ont., 1953–63; of St Michael and All Angels, Toronto, 1963–80; Canon of Toronto, 1972–74; Archdeacon of York, Toronto, 1974–80. Member: Nat. Exec. Council, Anglican Church of Canada, 1969–81; Judicial Council of Ontario, 1978–85; Multi-Cultural Council of Ontario, 1985–87; Special Adv. Cttee, Ontario Assoc. of Homes for the Aged, 1985–; Press Council of Ontario, 1986. Chm. Adv. Bd, Cdn Foundn on Compulsive Gambling (Ontario), 1983–. Patron and Mem. Adv. Cttee, Cdn Diabetes Assoc., 1984–. Chairman: Canadian Friends to West Indian Christians, 1982–; Royal Visit Children's Fund, 1984–. Columnist, Toronto Sunday Sun, 1974–86. Mem., Corp. of Huron Coll., 1961–. City of Toronto Civic Award, 1981. Hon. DD: Huron Coll., 1979; Wycliffe Coll., 1981. *Address:* 5 Gossamer Avenue, Willowdale, Ontario M2M 2X1, Canada; Bishop's Room, St Paul L'Amoreaux, 3333 Finch Avenue East, Agincourt, Ontario M1W 2R9, Canada. *T:* (416) 497–7550.

BROWN, Arthur Godfrey Kilner, MA; Headmaster, Worcester Royal Grammar School, 1950–78; *b* 21 Feb. 1915; *s* of Rev. Arthur E. Brown, CIE, MA, BSc, and Mrs E. G. Brown, MA, formerly of Bankura, India; *m* 1939, Mary Denholm Armstrong; one *s* three *d. Educ:* Warwick Sch.; Peterhouse, Cambridge. BA Cantab 1938; MA 1950. Assistant Master, Bedford School, 1938–39; King's School, Rochester, 1939–43; Cheltenham College, 1943–50. Elected to Headmasters' Conference, 1950. Founder Mem., Worcester Civic Soc. (Chm., 1960–66); Foundn Trustee, Swan Theatre, Worcester (Chm., 1965–70 and 1977–82); Pres., Worcester Rotary Club, 1975. *Recreations:* athletics (Silver Medal, 400 metres, and Gold Medal, 1,600 metres relay, Olympic Games, 1936; Gold Medal, 400 metres, World Student Games, 1937, and European Championships, 1938); music, gardening, house maintenance, following sport. *Address:* Palmer's Cottage, Coneyhurst, near Billingshurst, West Sussex RH14 9DN. *Clubs:* Achilles; Hawks (Cambridge) (Pres., 1937); Probus (Horsham Weald).
See also Hon. Sir R. K. Brown.

BROWN, A(rthur) I(vor) Parry, FFARCS; Anæsthetist: London Hospital, 1936–73; London Chest Hospital, 1946–73; Harefield Hospital, 1940–73; Royal Masonic Hospital, 1950–73; retired; *b* 23 July 1908; *s* of A. T. J. Brown; *m* Joyce Marion Bash. *Educ:* Tollington Sch., London; London Hospital. MRCS, LRCP, 1931; MB, BS London, 1933; DA, 1935; FFARCS, 1951. Member of the Board of the Faculty of Anæsthetists, RCS; Pres., Sect. of Anæsthetics, RSM, 1972–73; Fellow, Assoc. of Anæsthetists; Member, Thoracic Soc. *Publications:* chapter in Diseases of the Chest, 1952; contributions to: Thorax, Anæsthesia. *Address:* Long Thatch, Church Lane, Balsham, Cambridge CB1 6DS. *T:* Cambridge (0223) 893012.

BROWN, Sir (Arthur James) Stephen, KBE 1967; CEng, MIMechE; Director, Porvair Ltd, 1971–87; Chairman: Stone-Platt Industries Ltd, 1968–73 (Deputy Chairman, 1965–67); Molins Ltd, 1971–78; Deputy Chairman, Chloride Group, 1965–73; *b* 15 Feb. 1906; *s* of Arthur Mogg Brown, and Ada Kelk (*née* Upton); *m* 1935, Margaret Alexandra McArthur; one *s* one *d. Educ:* Taunton School; Bristol University (BSc(Eng.)). Apprenticed British Thomson-Houston Co. Ltd, 1928–32; joined J. Stone & Co. Ltd, 1932, Dir, 1945; Man. Dir J. Stone & Co. (Deptford) Ltd (on formation), 1951; Divisional Dir, Stone-Platt Industries Ltd (on formation), 1958; Dir, Fairey Co., 1971–76. Pres., Engineering Employers' Fedn, 1964–65; Pres., Confedn of British Industry, 1966–68; Founder Mem., Export Council for Europe, 1960 (Dep. Chm., 1962–63); Mem., NEDC, 1966–71. Hon. DSc Aston Univ., 1967. *Recreations:* fishing, golf. *Address:* Flat 20, Danny House, Hurstpierpoint, Sussex BN6 9BB. *T:* Hurstpierpoint (0273) 833755.

BROWN, Prof. Arthur Joseph, CBE 1974; FBA 1972; Professor of Economics, University of Leeds, 1947–79, now Emeritus; Pro-Vice-Chancellor, Leeds University, 1975–77; *b* 8 Aug. 1914; *s* of J. Brown, Alderley Edge, Cheshire; *m* 1938, Joan H. M., *d* of Rev. Canon B. E. Taylor, Holy Trinity, Walton Breck, Liverpool; two *s* (and one *s* decd). *Educ:* Bradford Grammar School; Queen's College, Oxford (Hon. Fellow, 1985). First Class Hons in Philosophy, Politics and Economics, 1936, MA, DPhil 1939. Fellow of All Souls College, Oxford, 1937–46; Lectr in Economics, Hertford College, Oxford, 1937–40; on staff of: Foreign Research and Press Service, 1940–43; Foreign Office Research Dept, 1943–45; Economic Section, Offices of the Cabinet, 1945–47. Head of Dept of Economics and Commerce, University of Leeds, 1947–65. Visiting Professor of Economics, Columbia University, City of New York, Jan.-June 1950. President Section F, British Assoc. for the Advancement of Science, 1958; Member: East African Economic and Fiscal Commn, 1960; UN Consultative Group on Economic and Social Consequences of Disarmament, 1961–62; First Secretary of State's Advisory Group on Central Africa, 1962; Hunt Cttee on Intermediate Areas, 1967–69; UGC, 1969–78 (Vice-Chm., 1977–78). Pres., Royal Economic Soc., 1976–78, Vice-Pres., 1978–. Chairman, Adv. Panel on Student Maintenance Grants, 1967–68. Vis. Prof. ANU, 1963; directing Regional Economics project, National Institute of Economic and Social Research, 1966–72. Hon. DLitt: Bradford, 1975; Kent, 1979; Hon. LLD Aberdeen, 1978; Hon. LittD Sheffield, 1979. *Publications:* Industrialisation and Trade, 1943; Applied Economics-Aspects of the World Economy in War and Peace, 1948; The Great Inflation, 1939–51, 1955; Introduction to the World Economy, 1959; The Framework of Regional Economics in the United Kingdom, 1972; (with E. M. Burrows) Regional Economic Problems, 1977; (with J. Darby) World Inflation since 1950: a comparative international study, 1985; articles in various journals. *Recreations:* gardening and walking. *Address:* 24 Moor Drive, Leeds LS6 4BY. *T:* Leeds (0532) 755799. *Club:* Athenæum.
See also W. A. Brown.

BROWN, Brig. Athol Earle McDonald, CMG 1964; OBE 1956; *b* 2 Jan. 1905; *s* of W. J. C. G. and Alice Catherine Brown, Armidale, NSW; *m* 1929, Millicent Alice Heesh, Sydney; two *s* one *d. Educ:* The Armidale Sch., NSW; Royal Australian Naval Coll.; Sydney Univ. Served War of 1939–45: Royal Australian Artillery, AIF, Middle East and New Guinea; Director, War Graves Services, AIF, 1944–46; Lt-Col, 1944; Brigadier, 1946. Secretary-General: Imperial War Graves Commn, 1946–60; Commonwealth-Japanese Jt Cttee, 1956–69; Dir and Sec.-Gen., Commonwealth War Graves Commn, Pacific Region, 1960–69. *Recreations:* golf, bowls, motoring. *Address:* 351 Belmore Road, North Balwyn, Victoria 3104, Australia. *T:* 857 7544. *Club:* Royal Automobile of Victoria, Masonic (Melbourne).

BROWN, (Austen) Patrick; Permanent Secretary, Department of Transport, since 1991; *b* 14 April 1940; *s* of late Austen K. and of Dorothy Mary Brown; *m* 1966, Mary (*née* Bulger); one *d. Educ:* Royal Grammar School, Newcastle upon Tyne; School of Slavonic and East European Studies, Univ. of London. Carreras Ltd, 1961–69 (Cyprus, 1965–66, Belgium, 1967–68); Management Consultant, Urwick Orr & Partners, UK, France, Portugal, Sweden, 1969–72; DoE, 1972; Asst. Sec., Property Services Agency, 1976–80, Dept of Transport, 1980–83; Under Sec., Dept of Transport, 1983–88; Dep. Sec., DoE, 1988–90; Second Perm. Sec., and Chief Exec., PSA, DoE, 1990–91. *Address:* c/o Department of Transport, 2 Marsham Street, SW1P 3EB.

BROWN, Barry; *see* Brown, James B. C.

BROWN, Dame Beryl P.; *see* Paston Brown.

BROWN, Adm. Sir Brian (Thomas), KCB 1989; CBE 1983; Chief of Naval Personnel, Second Sea Lord and Admiral President, Royal Naval College, Greenwich, 1988–91, retired; *b* 31 Aug. 1934; *s* of Walter Brown and Gladys (*née* Baddeley); *m* 1959, Veronica, *d* of late Wing Comdr and Mrs J. D. Bird; two *s. Educ:* Peter Symonds School. Pilot in 898 and 848 Sqdns, 1959–62; Dep. Supply Officer, HMY Britannia, 1966–68; Supply Officer, HMS Tiger, 1973–75; Secretary to: VCNS, 1975–78; First Sea Lord, 1979–82; rcds 1983; CO HMS Raleigh, 1984–85; DGNPS, 1986; Dir Gen., Naval Manpower and Trng, 1986–88, and Chief Naval Supply and Secretariat Officer, 1987–88. CBIM 1989. Hon. DEd CNAA, 1990. Freeman, City of London, 1989; Liveryman, Gardeners' Co.. *Recreations:* cricket, gardening. *Address:* c/o Lloyds Bank, High Street, Winchester, Hants SO23 9BU. *Club:* Army and Navy.

BROWN, Bruce Macdonald; High Commissioner of New Zealand to Canada, since 1988; *b* 1930; *s* of John Albert Brown and Caroline Dorothea Brown (*née* Jorgenson); *m* 1953, Edith Irene (*née* Raynor) (*d* 1989); two *s* one *d*; *m* 1990, Françoise Rousseau. *Educ:* Victoria University of Wellington (MA Hons). Private Secretary to Prime Minister, 1957–59; Second Sec., Kuala Lumpur, 1960–62; First Sec. (later Counsellor), New Zealand Mission to UN, New York, 1963–67; Head of Administration, Min. of Foreign Affairs, Wellington, 1967–68; Director, NZ Inst. of International Affairs, 1969–71; NZ Dep. High Commissioner, Canberra, 1972–75; Ambassador to Iran, 1975–78, and Pakistan, 1976–78; Asst Sec., Min. of Foreign Affairs, 1978–81; Dep. High Comr in London, 1981–85; Ambassador to Thailand, Vietnam and Laos, 1985–88, to Burma, 1986–88. *Publications:* The Rise of New Zealand Labour, 1962; ed, Asia and the Pacific in the 1970s, 1971. *Recreations:* reading, golf. *Address:* c/o New Zealand High Commission, Metropolitan House, Suite 727, 99 Bank Street, Ottawa, Ont K1P 6G3, Canada. *Club:* Reform.

BROWN, Carter; *see* Brown, John C.

BROWN, Cedric Harold, FEng 1990; FIGasE; FICE; Senior Managing Director, British Gas plc, since 1991; *b* 7 March 1935; *s* of late William Herbert Brown and Constance Dorothy Brown (*née* Frances); *m* 1956, Joan Hendry; one *s* three *d. Educ:* Sheffield, Rotherham and Derby Colleges of Technology. Pupil Gas Distribution Engineer, E Midlands Gas Bd, 1953–58, Tech. Asst, 1958–59; Engineering Asst, Tunbridge Wells Borough Council, 1959–60; engineering posts, E Midlands Gas Bd, 1960–75 (Chief Engineer, 1973–75); Dir of Engineering, E Midlands Gas, 1975–78; British Gas Corp., subseq. British Gas plc: Asst Dir (Ops) and Dir (Construction), 1978–79; Dir, Morecambe Bay Project, 1980–87; Regl Chm., British Gas W Midlands, 1987–89; Dir, Man. Dir, Exploration and Production, 1989; Man. Dir, Regl Services, 1989–91. Dir, Bow Valley Industries, 1988–. Vice-Pres., IGasE, 1991–. Liveryman, Engineers' Co., 1988–. *Publications:* tech. papers to professional bodies. *Recreations:* sport, countryside, places of historic interest. *Address:* British Gas plc, Rivermill House, 152 Grosvenor Road, SW1V 3JL. *T:* 071–821 1444.

BROWN, (Cedric Wilfred) George E.; *see* Edmonds-Brown.

BROWN, Charles Dargie, FEng 1981; consulting engineer, retired; Joint Chairman, Mott, Hay & Anderson, Consulting Engineers, 1981–89; *b* 13 April 1927; *s* of William Henry Brown and Jean Dargie; *m* 1952, Sylvia Margaret Vallis; one *s* one *d. Educ:* Harris Acad., Dundee; St Andrews Univ. (BScEng, 1st Cl. Hons.). FICE. Joined staff of Mott, Hay & Anderson, 1947; engaged on highways, tunnels and bridge works, incl. Tamar Bridge, Forth Road Bridge, George Street Bridge, Newport, Kingsferry and Queensferry Bridges, 1947–65; Partner and Director, 1965. Principally concerned with planning, design and supervision of major works, incl. Mersey Queensway tunnels and new London Bridge, and projects in Hong Kong, Malaysia, Singapore, Indonesia, Australia and USA, 1965–89. Member, Smeatonian Soc. of Civil Engrs, 1984–. Hon. LLD Dundee, 1982. *Publications:* papers to Instn of Civil Engrs, on Kingsferry Bridge, George St Bridge, London Bridge and Mersey tunnels; also various papers to engrg confs. *Recreations:* golf, gardening, bird watching, reading. *Address:* Mallards Mere, Russell Way, Petersfield, Hants GU31 4LD. *T:* Petersfield (0730) 67820. *Club:* Royal Automobile.

BROWN, Lt-Col Sir Charles Frederick Richmond, 4th Bt, *cr* 1863; TD; DL; *b* 6 Dec. 1902; *er s* of Frederick Richmond Brown (*d* 1933; 2nd *s* of 2nd Bt); *S* uncle, 1944; *m* 1st, 1933, Audrey (marr. diss., 1948), 2nd *d* of late Col Hon. Everard Baring, CVO, CBE, and late Lady Ulrica Baring; one *s* two *d*; 2nd, 1951, Hon. Gwendolen Carlis Meysey-Thomson (marr. diss. 1969; she *d* 1989), *y d* of 1st (and last) Baron Knaresborough; 3rd, 1969, Pauline, *widow* of Edward Hildyard, Middleton Hall, Pickering, Yorks. *Educ:* Eton. Joined Welsh Guards, 1921; Captain 1932; retired with a gratuity, 1936; joined 5th Bn Green Howards, Territorial Army, as a Major, March 1939; Lieut-Colonel comdg 7th Bn Green Howards, July 1939, and proceeded to France with 7th Bn, April 1940. DL, North Riding of County of York, 1962. Hon. Alderman, after 27 years' service, of N Riding and N Yorks CC. *Heir: s* George Francis Richmond Brown [*b* 3 Feb. 1938; *m* 1978, Philippa Jane, *d* of late E. J. Wilcox; two *s*]. *Recreations:* ornithology, growing species rhododendrons, country pursuits. *Address:* Middleton Hall, Pickering, N Yorks YO18 8NX. *Clubs:* Cavalry and Guards, Pratt's; Yorkshire (York).

BROWN, Christina Hambley; *see* Brown, Tina.

BROWN, Christopher; Director, National Society for Prevention of Cruelty to Children, since 1989; *b* 21 June 1938; *s* of Reginald Frank Greenwood Brown and Margaret Eleanor Brown; *m* 1968, Helen Margaret, *d* of George A. Woolsey and Hilda M. Woolsey; three *s* one *d*. *Educ:* Hertford Grammar Sch.; KCL. AKC; Home Office Cert. in Probation. Ordained Deacon, 1963, Priest, 1964; Assistant Curate, Diocese of Southwark: St Hilda's, Crofton Park, 1963; St Michael's, Wallington, 1964–67. Probation Officer, Nottingham, 1968–72; Sen. Probation Officer, W Midlands, 1972–74; Asst Dir, Social Services, Solihull, 1974–76; Asst Chief Probation Officer, Hereford and Worcester, 1976–79; Chief Probation Officer: Oxfordshire, 1979–86; Essex, 1986–89. Member: Parole Bd, 1985–87; Trng Cttee, Inst. for Study and Treatment of Delinquency, 1986–89; Professional Adv. Cttee, NSPCC, 1986–89; Chm., Social Issues Cttee, Assoc. of Chief Officers of Probation, 1985–87. Mem., Green Coll., Oxford, 1981–86. Licensed to officiate, Dio. Chelmsford, 1986–. *Publications:* contribs to various jls on social work practice and community issues, 1971–. *Recreations:* walking, architecture, music, conversation, gardening. *Address:* (office) 67 Saffron Hill, EC1N 8RS. *T:* 071–242 1626.

BROWN, Christopher David, MA; Headmaster, Norwich School, since 1984; *b* 8 July 1944; *s* of E. K. Brown; *m* 1972, Caroline Dunkerley; two *d*. *Educ:* Plymouth College; Fitzwilliam College, Cambridge. MA. Assistant Master: The Leys School, Cambridge, 1967–71; Pangbourne College, 1971–73; Radley College, 1973–84 (Head of English, 1975–84). *Address:* 16 The Close, Norwich NR1 4DZ.

BROWN, Rev. Cyril James, OBE 1956; Rector of Warbleton, 1970–77; Chaplain to the Queen, 1956–74; *b* 12 Jan. 1904; *s* of late James Brown, Clifton, Bristol; *m* 1931, Myrtle Aufrère, *d* of late Mark Montague Ford, London; no *c*. *Educ:* Westminster Abbey Choir School; Clifton College; Keble College, Oxford; St Stephen's House, Oxford. Curate of St Gabriel's, Warwick Square, 1927–31; Chaplain, Missions to Seamen, Singapore, 1931–34, Hong Kong, 1934–41; Chaplain, Hong Kong RNVR, 1941–46; Youth Secretary, Missions to Seamen, 1946–47, Superintendent, 1947–51, General Superintendent, 1951–59, General Secretary, 1959–69; Prebendary of St Paul's, 1958–69. *Publications:* contributions to East and West Review, World Dominion, etc. *Recreation:* choral music. *Address:* 16 Merlynn, Devonshire Place, Eastbourne, Sussex. *Club:* Devonshire (Eastbourne).

BROWN, Sir (Cyril) Maxwell Palmer, (Sir Max), KCB 1969 (CB 1965); CMG 1957; Permanent Secretary, Department of Trade, March–June 1974; *b* 30 June 1914; *s* of late Cyril Palmer Brown; *m* 1940, Margaret May Gillhespy; three *s* one *d*. *Educ:* Wanganui College; Victoria University College, NZ; Clare College, Cambridge. Princ. Private Secretary to Pres. Board of Trade, 1946–49; Monopolies Commn, 1951–55; Counsellor (Commercial) Washington, 1955–57; returned to Board of Trade; Second Permanent Sec., 1968–70; Sec. (Trade), DTI, 1970–74; Mem., 1975–81, Dep. Chm., 1976–81, Monopolies and Mergers Commn. Director: John Brown & Co., 1975–82; ERA Technology Ltd, 1974–86; RHP Gp plc (formerly Ransome Hoffmann Pollard Ltd), 1975–88. *Address:* 20 Cottenham Park Road, Wimbledon, SW20 0RZ. *T:* 081–946 7237.

BROWN, Dr Daniel McGillivray, BSc, PhD, ScD; FRS 1982; ARSC; Emeritus Reader in Organic Chemistry, Cambridge University, since 1983; Fellow of King's College, Cambridge, since 1953; Attached Fellow, Laboratory of Molecular Biology, Cambridge; *b* 3 Feb. 1923; *s* of David Cunninghame Brown and Catherine Stewart (*née* McGillivray); *m* 1953, Margaret Joyce Herbert; one *s* three *d*. *Educ:* Glasgow Acad.; Glasgow Univ. (BSc); London Univ. (PhD); Cambridge Univ. (PhD, ScD). Res. Chemist, Chester Beatty Res. Inst., 1945–53; Asst Dir of Res., 1953–58, Lectr, 1959–67, Reader in Org. Chem., 1967–83, Cambridge Univ.; Vice-Provost, King's Coll., Cambridge, 1974–81. Vis. Professor: Univ. of Calif, LA, 1959–60; Brandeis Univ., 1966–67. *Publications:* scientific papers, mainly in chemical jls. *Recreations:* modern art, gardening, spasmodic fly-fishing. *Address:* 60 Hartington Grove, Cambridge CB1 4UE. *T:* Cambridge (0223) 245304.

BROWN, Sir David, Kt 1968; Chairman, David Brown Holdings Ltd, and Vosper Ltd, until going to live abroad in 1978; *b* 10 May 1904; *s* of Francis Edwin (Frank) and Caroline Brown; *m* 1st, 1926, Daisie Muriel Firth (marr. diss. 1955); one *s* one *d*; 2nd, 1955, Marjorie Deans (marr. diss. 1980); 3rd, 1980, Paula Benton Stone. *Educ:* Rossall School; Private Tutor in Engineering; Huddersfield Technical Coll. FIMechE. Apprentice, David Brown and Sons (Hudd.), Ltd, 1921; Dir, 1929; Man. Dir, 1932. Founded David Brown Tractors Ltd (first company to manufacture an all-British tractor in England), 1935; Chm., Aston Martin Lagonda Ltd, 1946–72; formed, 1951, The David Brown Corp. Ltd (Chm.), embracing gears, machine tools, castings, etc. Pres., Vosper Ltd, and Chm., Vosper Private Ltd, Singapore, 1978–86; Director: David Brown Corp. of Australia Ltd, 1965–; David Brown Gear Industries Pty Ltd (Australia), 1963–; David Brown Gear Industries (Pty) Ltd (South Africa), 1969–. Past Member: Board of Governors of Huddersfield Royal Infirmary; Council of Huddersfield Chamber of Commerce. Life Governor, RASE. First Englishman to open Canadian Farm and Industrial Equipment Trade Show, Toronto, 1959; inaugurated Chief Flying Sun of Iroquois Tribe of Mohawk Nation, Toronto, 1959. Hon. Dato SPMJ (Johore), 1978. *Address:* L'Estoril, 31 Avenue Princesse Grace, Monte Carlo, MC 98000, Monaco. *Clubs:* Guards Polo (Life Mem.); International des Anciens Pilotes de Grand Prix (Bergamo); Monte Carlo Country (Roquebrune-Cap-Martin); Monaco Yacht, Monaco Automobile.

BROWN, Prof. David Anthony, PhD; FRS 1990; FIBiol; Professor of Pharmacology, Middlesex Hospital Medical School and University College London, since 1987; *b* 10 Feb. 1936; *s* of Alfred William and Florence Brown; two *s* one *d*. *Educ:* Univ. of London (BSc, BSc, PhD). Asst Lectr 1961–65, Lectr 1965–73, Dept of Pharmacology, St Bart's Hosp. Med. Coll.; Dept of Pharmacology, School of Pharmacy, Univ. of London: Sen. Lectr, 1973–74; Reader, 1974–77; Professor, 1977–79; Wellcome Professor, 1979–87. Visiting Professor: Univ. of Chicago, 1970; Univ. of Iowa, 1971, 1973; Univ. of Texas, 1979, 1980, 1981; Vis. Scientist, Armed Forces Radiobiology Res. Inst., Bethesda, Md, 1976; Fogarty Schol.-in-Residence, NIH, Bethesda, 1985–86. Member: Physiological Soc., 1970; British Pharmacological Soc., 1965–; Biochemical Soc., 1969–; Academia Europaea, 1990. *Publications:* contribs to Jl of Physiology, British Jl of Pharmacology. *Recreation:* filling in forms. *Address:* Department of Pharmacology, University College London, Gower Street, WC1E 6BT.

BROWN, Prof. David Clifford; writer on music; Professor of Musicology, Southampton University, 1983–89, now Professor Emeritus; *b* 8 July 1929; *s* of Bertram and Constance Brown; *m* 1953, Elizabeth (*née* Valentine); two *d*. *Educ:* Sheffield Univ. (BA, MA, BMus); PhD Southampton Univ. LTCL. RAF 1952–54. Schoolmaster, 1954–59; Music Librarian, London Univ., 1959–62; Southampton University: Lectr in Music, 1962; Sen. Lectr, 1970; Reader, 1975. Many broadcast talks and scripts incl. Tchaikovsky and his World, 1980, Tchaikovsky: a fateful gift, 1984, and A Sympathetic Person, 1989–90. *Publications:* Thomas Weelkes, 1969; Mikhail Glinka, 1974; John Wilbye, 1974; Tchaikovsky, vol. 1, 1978, vol. 2, 1982, vol. 3, 1986, vol. 4, 1991; contribs to jls and periodicals. *Recreation:* walking. *Address:* Braishfield Lodge West, Braishfield, Romsey, Hants SO51 0PS. *T:* Braishfield (0794) 68163.

BROWN, David John Bowes, CBE 1982; FCSD; Chairman: Artix Ltd (formerly DJB Engineering Ltd), since 1973; AWD Ltd (formerly Bedford Truck & Bus), since 1987; Automotive Development Centre Ltd, since 1988; *b* 2 Aug. 1925; *s* of Matthew and Helene Brown; *m* 1st, 1954, Patricia Robson (marr. diss. 1982); two *s* two *d*; 2nd, 1986, Eve Watkinson. *Educ:* King James Grammar Sch., Knaresborough; Leeds College of Technology. Logging Contractor, UK and W Africa, 1946–60; joined Hunslet Engine Co. as Designer/Draughtsman, 1960–62; designed and patented transmission and exhaust gas conditioning systems for underground mines tractors; joined Chaseside as Chief Designer, 1962–65; designed and patented 4 wheel drive loading shovels; became Director and Chief Executive; joined Muir-Hill Ltd as Man. Dir, 1965–73; designed and patented 4 wheel drive tractors, cranes, steering systems, transmissions, axles; started DJB Engineering Ltd, 1973; designed, manufactured and sold a range of off-highway articulated dump trucks in Peterlee, Co. Durham. The company has gained 4 Queen's Awards and 1 Design Council Award. Artix has exclusive design and manufg contracts with Caterpillar Inc.; AWD Ltd, formed when Bedford Truck and Bus business was purchased from General Motors, produces on-highway and military trucks from 7·5 to 120 tonnes; ADC Ltd, also purchased from General Motors, is an independent vehicle design and develt co. *Address:* Ravensthorpe Manor, Boltby, Thirsk, North Yorks YO7 2DX; Artix Ltd, Peterlee, Co Durham SR8 2HX. *T:* 091–586 3333; AWD Ltd, Boscombe Road, Dunstable, Beds LU5 4SE. *T:* Dunstable (0582) 472244; ADC Ltd, Windmill Road, Luton, Beds LU1 3HL. *T:* Luton (0582) 446000.

BROWN, David K.; *see* Kennett Brown.

BROWN, Rev. Canon Prof. David William, PhD; Van Mildert Professor of Divinity, University of Durham and Canon of Durham Cathedral, since 1990; *b* 1 July 1948; *s* of David William Brown and Catherine Smith. *Educ:* Keil Sch., Dumbarton; Edinburgh Univ. (MA 1st cl. Classics 1970); Oriel Coll., Oxford (BA 1st cl. Phil. and Theol. 1972); Clare Coll., Cambridge (PhD 1976); Westcott House, Cambridge. Fellow, Chaplain and Tutor in Theol. and Phil., Oriel Coll., Oxford and Univ. Lectr in Theol., 1976–90. *Publications:* Choices: ethics and the Christian, 1983; The Divine Trinity, 1985; Continental Philosophy and Modern Theology, 1987; Invitation to Theology, 1989; (ed) Newman: a man for our time, 1990. *Recreations:* gardening, reading, listening to music. *Address:* 14 The College, Durham DH1 3EQ. *T:* 091–386 4657; Theology Department, Abbey House, Palace Green, Durham DH1 3RS. *T:* 091–374 2064.

BROWN, Vice-Adm. Sir David (Worthington), KCB 1984; Chairman, Broadmoor Special Hospital, since 1987; self-employed management consultant; *b* 28 Nov. 1927; *s* of late Captain J. R. S. Brown, RN and of Mrs D. M. E. Brown; *m* 1958, Etienne Hester Boileau; three *d*. *Educ:* HMS Conway. Joined RN, 1945; commanded HM Ships MGB 5036, MTB 5020, Dalswinton, Chailey, Cavendish, Falmouth, Hermione, Bristol; Dir, Naval Ops and Trade, 1971–72; Dir of Officers Appointments (Exec.), 1976–78; Asst Chief of Defence Staff (Ops), 1980–82; Flag Officer Plymouth, Port Adm. Devonport, Comdr Central Sub Area Eastern Atlantic, Comdr Plymouth Sub Area Channel, 1982–85. Younger Brother of Trinity House. FIPM. *Recreations:* sailing, fishing. *Address:* c/o Barclays Bank, 107 Commercial Road, Portsmouth, Hants PO1 1BT. *Club:* Army and Navy.

BROWN, Denise Lebreton, (Mrs Frank Waters), RE 1959 (ARE 1941); RWA 1986 (ARWA 1980); artist; *d* of Frederick Peter Brown and Jeanne Lebreton; *m* 1938, Frank William Eric Waters (*d* 1986); one *s*. *Educ:* Lyzeum Nonnenwerth im Rhein; Royal College of Art. British Instn Schol. in Engraving, 1932; ARCA 1935; RCA Travelling Schol., 1936; *prox. acc.* Rome Scholarship in Engraving, 1936. Has exhibited at: Royal Academy regularly since 1934; Royal Society of Painter-Etchers and Engravers; Royal West of England Acad.; also in Canada, USA and S Africa. Work represented in British, V&A, and Ashmolean Museums. *Publications:* books illustrated include: several on gardening; children's books, etc. *Recreations:* music, gardening. *Address:* 7 Priory Lodge, Nightingale Place, Rickmansworth, Herts WD3 2DG. *Club:* Royal Air Force.

BROWN, Denys Downing, CMG 1966; MM 1945; HM Diplomatic Service, retired; *b* 16 Dec. 1918; *s* of A. W. Brown, Belfast, and Marjorie Downing; *m* 1954, Patricia Marjorie, *e d* of Sir Charles Bartley; one *s* one *d*. *Educ:* Hereford Cathedral School; Brasenose College, Oxford (Scholar). Oxf. and Bucks LI, 1939–45 (prisoner-of-war, 1940; escaped, 1945). Entered Foreign Service, 1946; served in Poland, Germany, Egypt, Yugoslavia, Sweden, and FO; Minister (Economic), Bonn, retired 1971; Dir, P&O Steam Navigation Co., 1971–80. *Recreations:* reading, travel. *Address:* Step Cottage, Shadyhanger, Godalming, Surrey GU7 2HR. *T:* Godalming (0483) 416635.

BROWN, Sir Derrick H.; *see* Holden-Brown.

BROWN, Sir Douglas (Denison), Kt 1983; Chairman, 1981–87 and Managing Director, 1954–87, James Corson & Co. Ltd; *b* 8 July 1917; *s* of Robert and Alice Mary Brown; *m* 1941, Marion Cruickshanks Emmerson; one *s* one *d*. *Educ:* Bablake Sch., Coventry. Served Army, 1940–46: RE, 1940–41; commnd RA, 1941; India, ME, N Africa, Italy; mentioned in despatches; retd in rank of Major. Mem. Exec. Cttee, Clothing Manufrs of GB, 1967–82; Chm., Leeds and Northern Clothing Assoc., 1975–77; Vice Chm., Wooltac, 1982–, Mem. Cttee, 1988–; Chm., Clothing Initiative, 1988–90; Mem., Exec. BCIA, 1988–90; Hon. Mem., Yorks Humberside BCIA, 1990. Chairman: NW Leeds Cons. Assoc., 1961–74 (Pres. 1974); Yorks Area Cons. Assoc., 1978–83 (Treasurer, 1971–78); Mem., Nat. Exec. Cttee, Cons. and Unionist Assoc., 1971–90; Mem., Cons. Bd of Finance, 1971–78. Mem., Gas Consumer Council, NE Area, 1981–86; Bd Mem., Yorkshire Water Authority, 1983–86. Pres., Water Aid Yorkshire, 1988; Vice-Chm., St Edmund's PCC, Roundhay, 1981–. Chm., Bd of Governors, Jacob Kramer Coll. of Further Educn, 1978–. *Recreations:* gardening, Rugby, cricket, golf. *Address:* Bankfield, 6 North Park Road, Leeds LS8 1JD. *T:* Leeds (0532) 662151.

BROWN, Hon. Sir Douglas (Dunlop), Kt 1989; **Hon. Mr Justice Douglas Brown;** a Judge of the High Court of Justice, Family Division, since 1989; *b* 22 Dec. 1931; *s* of late Robert Dunlop Brown, MICE, and Anne Cameron Brown; *m* 1960, June Margaret Elizabeth McNamara; one *s*. *Educ:* Ryleys Sch., Alderley Edge; Manchester Grammar Sch.; Manchester Univ. (LLB). Served in RN, 1953–55; Lieut, RNR. Called to Bar, Gray's Inn, 1953; practised Northern Circuit from 1955; Mem. General Council of Bar, 1967–71; Asst Recorder, Salford City QS, 1971; a Recorder of the Crown Court, 1972–80; QC 1976; a Circuit Judge, 1980–88; Family Div. Liaison Judge, Northern Circuit, 1990–. Mem., Parole Bd for England and Wales, 1985–87. *Recreations:* cricket, golf, music. *Address:* Royal Courts of Justice, Strand, WC2A 2LL. *Club:* Wilmslow Golf.

BROWN, Edmund Gerald, Jr, (Jerry Brown); lawyer, writer and politician; Attorney with Fulbright Jaworski, 1986–91; *b* 7 April 1938; *s* of Edmund Gerald Brown and Bernice (*née* Layne). *Educ:* Univ. of California at Berkeley (BA 1961); Yale Law School (JD 1964). Admitted to California Bar, 1965; Research Attorney, Calif. Supreme Court, 1964–65; with Tuttle & Taylor, LA, 1966–70; Sec. of State, Calif., 1971–74; Governor of California, 1975–83; Democratic Candidate for US Senator from California, 1982.

Trustee, Los Angeles Community Colls, 1969–70. *Address:* 3022 Washington Street, San Francisco, Calif 94115, USA. *T:* 415–928–5073.

BROWN, Prof. Edwin Thomas, PhD, DSc Eng; FTS; FIEAust; FIMM; Deputy Vice-Chancellor, University of Queensland, Australia, since 1990 (Dean of Engineering, 1987–90); *b* 4 Dec. 1938; *s* of George O. and Bessie M. Brown. *Educ:* Castlemaine High Sch.; Univ. of Melbourne (BE 1960, MEngSc 1964); Univ. of Queensland (PhD 1969); Univ. of London (DSc Eng 1985). MICE 1976; MASCE 1965; FIMM 1980; FIEAust 1987 (MIEAust 1965); FTS 1990. Engr, State Electricity Commn of Victoria, 1960–64; James Cook Univ. of North Queensland (formerly UC of Townsville): Lectr, 1965–69; Sen. Lectr, 1969–72; Associate Prof. of Civil Engrg, 1972–75; Imperial College, Univ. of London: Reader in Rock Mechanics, 1975–79; Prof. of Rock Mechanics, 1979–87; Dean, RSM, 1983–86; Hd, Dept of Mineral Resources Engrg, 1985–87. Res. Associate, Dept of Civil and Mineral Engrg, Univ. of Minnesota, 1970; Sen. Visitor, Dept of Engrg, Univ. of Cambridge, 1974; Vis. Prof., Dept of Mining and Fuels Engrg, Univ. of Utah, 1979. Chm., British Geotechnical Soc., 1982–83; Pres., Internat. Soc. for Rock Mechanics, 1983–87. Foreign Mem., Fellowship of Engrg, 1989. Instn of Mining and Metallurgy: Consolidated Gold Fields Gold Medal, 1984; Sir Julius Wernher Meml Lecture, 1985. Editor-in-Chief, Internat. Jl of Rock Mechanics and Mining Sciences, 1975–82. *Publications:* (with E. Hoek) Underground Excavations in Rock, 1980; (ed) Rock Characterization, Testing and Monitoring, 1981; (with B. H. G. Brady) Rock Mechanics for Underground Mining, 1985; (ed) Analytical and Computational Methods in Engineering Rock Mechanics, 1987; papers on rock mechanics in civil engrg and mining jls. *Recreations:* cricket, jazz. *Address:* J. D. Storey Building, University of Queensland, St Lucia, Qld 4072, Australia. *T:* 07–365 1316.

BROWN, Prof. Eric Herbert, PhD; Professor of Geography, University College London, 1966–88, Honorary Research Fellow, since 1988; *b* 8 Dec. 1922; *s* of Samuel Brown and Ada Brown, Melton Mowbray, Leics; *m* 1945, Eileen (*née* Reynolds) (*d* 1984), Llanhowell, Dyfed; two *d*. *Educ:* King Edward VII Grammar Sch., Melton Mowbray; King's Coll., London (BSc 1st Cl. Hons). MSc Wales, PhD London. Served War: RAF Pilot, Coastal Comd, 1941–45. Asst Lectr, then Lectr in Geography, University Coll. of Wales, Aberystwyth, 1947–49; University College London: Lectr, then Reader in Geog., 1950–66; Dean of Students, 1972–75; Alumnus Dir, 1989–91; Mem. Senate, Univ. of London, 1981–86. Vis. Lectr, Indiana Univ., USA, 1953–54; Vis. Prof., Monash Univ., Melbourne, 1971. Mem., NERC, 1981–84. Geographical Adviser, Govt of Argentina, 1965–68; Hon. Mem., Geograph. Soc. of Argentina, 1968. Chairman: British Geomorphol Res. Group, 1971–72; British Nat. Cttee for Geog., 1985–90. Royal Geographical Society: Back Grant, 1961; Hon. Sec., 1977–87; Vice-Pres., 1988–89, Hon. Vice-Pres., 1989; Hon. Fellow, 1989; Pres., Inst. of British Geographers, 1978. *Publications:* The Relief and Drainage of Wales, 1961; (with W. R. Mead) The USA and Canada, 1962; (ed) Geography Yesterday and Tomorrow, 1980; contrib. Geog. Jl, Phil. Trans Royal Soc., Proc. Geologists' Assoc., Trans Inst. of British Geographers, and Geography. *Recreations:* watching Rugby football, wine. *Address:* Monterey, Castle Hill, Berkhamsted, Herts HP4 1HE. *T:* Hemel Hempstead (0442) 864077. *Clubs:* Athenæum, Geographical.

BROWN, Captain Eric Melrose, CBE 1970 (OBE 1945; MBE 1944); DSC 1942; AFC 1947; RN; Chief Executive, European Helicopter Association, since 1980; *b* 21 Jan. 1919; *s* of Robert John Brown and Euphemia (*née* Melrose); *m* 1942, Evelyn Jean Margaret Macrory; one *s*. *Educ:* Royal High Sch., Edinburgh; Edinburgh University. MA 1947. Joined Fleet Air Arm as Pilot, 1939; Chief Naval Test Pilot, 1944–49; Resident British Test Pilot at USN Air Test Center, Patuxent River, 1951–52; CO No 804 Sqdn, 1953–54; Comdr (Air), RN Air Stn, Brawdy, 1954–56; Head of British Naval Air Mission to Germany, 1958–60; Dep. Dir (Air), Gunnery Div., Admty, 1961; Dep. Dir, Naval Air Warfare and Adviser on Aircraft Accidents, Admty, 1962–64; Naval Attaché, Bonn, 1965–67; CO, RN Air Stn, Lossiemouth, 1967–70. Chief Exec., British Helicopter Adv. Bd, 1970–87, Vice-Pres., 1988–. Chm., British Aviation Bicentenary Exec. Cttee, 1984. FRAeS 1964 (Pres., 1982–83; Chm., RAeS Rotorcraft Sect., 1973–76). Hon. FEng (Pakistan) 1984; Hon. Fellow, Soc. of Experimental Test Pilots, 1984. Liveryman, GAPAN, 1978. British Silver Medal for Practical Achievement in Aeronautics, 1949; Anglo-French Breguet Trophy, 1983; Bronze Medal, Fédération Aéronautique Internationale, 1986. *Publications:* Wings on My Sleeve, 1961; (jtly) Aircraft Carriers, 1969; Wings of the Luftwaffe, 1977; Wings of the Navy, 1980; The Helicopter in Civil Operations, 1981; Wings of the Weird and the Wonderful, vol. 1, 1982, vol. 2, 1985; Duels in the Sky, 1989. *Recreations:* golf, ski-ing, bridge. *Address:* Carousel, New Domewood, Copthorne, Sussex RH10 3HF. *T:* Copthorne (0342) 712610. *Clubs:* Naval and Military, City Livery; Explorers' (NY).

BROWN, Sir (Ernest) Henry Phelps, Kt 1976; MBE 1945; FBA 1960; Professor of Economics of Labour, University of London, 1947–68, now Emeritus Professor; *b* 10 Feb. 1906; *s* of E. W. Brown, Calne, Wiltshire; *m* 1932, Dorothy Evelyn Mostyn, *d* of Sir Anthony Bowlby, 1st Bt, KCB; two *s* one *d*. *Educ:* Taunton School; Wadham College, Oxford (Scholar). Secretary of Oxford Union, 1928; 1st Class Hons Modern History, 1927; Philosophy, Politics and Economics, 1929. Fellow of New College, Oxford, 1930–47 (Hon. Fellow, 1987); Hon. Fellow, Wadham College, Oxford, 1969–; Rockefeller Travelling Fellow in USA, 1930–31. Served War of 1939–45, with Royal Artillery; BEF; ADGB; First Army; Eighth Army (MBE). Member: Council on Prices, Productivity and Incomes, 1959; Nat. Economic Development Council, 1962; Royal Commn on Distribn of Income and Wealth, 1974–78. Chairman, Tavistock Inst. of Human Relations, 1966–68. Pres., Royal Economic Soc., 1970–72. Hon. DLitt Heriot-Watt, 1972; Hon. DCL Durham, 1981. *Publications:* The Framework of the Pricing System, 1936; A Course in Applied Economics, 1951; The Balloon (novel), 1953; The Growth of British Industrial Relations, 1959; The Economics of Labor, 1963; A Century of Pay, 1968; The Inequality of Pay, 1977; The Origins of Trade Union Power, 1983; Egalitarianism and the Generation of Inequality, 1988. *Recreations:* walking; represented Oxford *v* Cambridge cross-country running, 1926. *Address:* 16 Bradmore Road, Oxford OX2 6QP. *T:* Oxford (0865) 56320.

See also M. K. Hopkins.

BROWN, Prof. Fred, FRS 1981; Adjunct Professor, School of Epidemiology and Public Health, Yale University, since 1990; Professorial Fellow, Queen's University, Belfast, since 1986; *b* 31 Jan. 1925; *m* 1948, Audrey Alice Doherty; two *s*. *Educ:* Burnley Grammar Sch.; Manchester Univ. BSc 1944, MSc 1946, PhD 1948. Asst Lectr, Manchester Univ., 1946–48; Lectr, Bristol Univ. Food Preservation Res. Station, 1948–50; Senior Scientific Officer: Hannah Dairy Res. Inst., Ayr, 1950–53; Christie Hosp. and Holt Radium Inst., Manchester, 1953–55; Head, Biochemistry Dept, 1955–83, and Dep. Dir, 1980–83, Animal Virus Res. Inst., Pirbright, Surrey; Hd of Virology Div., Wellcome Res. Labs, Beckenham, Kent, 1983–90; Prof. of Microbiology, Univ. of Surrey, 1989–90. *Publications:* papers on viruses causing animal diseases, in scientific journals. *Recreations:* cricket, Association football, listening to classical music, fell walking. *Address:* Syndal, Glaziers Lane, Normandy, Surrey GU3 2DF. *T:* Guildford (0483) 811107.

BROWN, Sir (Frederick Herbert) Stanley, Kt 1967; CBE 1959; BSc; FEng, FIMechE, FIEE; retired; Chairman, Central Electricity Generating Board, 1965–72 (Deputy-Chairman, 1959–64); *b* 9 Dec. 1910; *s* of Clement and Annie S. Brown; *m* 1937, Marjorie Nancy Brown; two *d*. *Educ:* King Edward's School, Birmingham; Birmingham University. Corp. of Birmingham Electric Supply Dept, 1932–46; West Midlands Joint Electricity Authority, 1946–47; Liverpool Corporation Electricity Supply Department, 1947–48; Merseyside and N Wales Division of British Electricity Authority; Generation Engineer (Construction), 1948–49; Chief Generation Engineer (Construction), 1949–51; Deputy Generation Design Engineer of British Electricity Authority, 1951–54; Generation Design Engineer, 1954–57, Chief Engineer, 1957, of Central Electricity Authority; Member for Engineering, Central Elec. Generating Board, 1957–59. President: Instn of Electrical Engineers, 1967–68; EEIBA, 1969–70. Member: Council, City and Guilds of London Inst., 1969–; Court of Govs, Univ. of Birmingham, 1969–. Hon. DSc: Aston, 1971; Salford, 1972. *Publications:* various papers to technical institutions. *Recreation:* gardening. *Address:* Cobbler's Hill, Compton Abdale, Glos. *T:* Withington (024289) 233.

BROWN, Hon. Geoffrey E.; *see* Ellman-Brown.

BROWN, Rev. Canon Geoffrey Harold; Vicar of St Martin-in-the-Fields, since 1985; *b* 1 April 1930; *s* of Harry and Ada Brown; *m* 1963, Elizabeth Jane Williams; two *d*. *Educ:* Monmouth Sch.; Trinity Hall, Cambridge. MA. Asst Curate, St Andrew's, Plaistow, 1954–60; Asst Curate, St Peter's, Birmingham and Sub-Warden of Pre-Ordination Training Scheme, 1960–63; Rector: St George's, Newtown, Birmingham, 1963–73; Grimsby, 1973–85. Hon. Canon Lincoln Cathedral, 1978; Canon Emeritus, 1985. *Recreations:* the countryside, photography, theatre. *Address:* 6 St Martin's Place, WC2N 4JJ. *T:* 071–930 1862.

BROWN, Hon. George Arthur, CMG; Governor, Bank of Jamaica, 1967–78 and since 1989; *b* 25 July 1922; *s* of Samuel Austin Brown and Gertrude Brown; *m* 1964, Leila Leonie Gill; two *d* (and one *s* one *d* by previous marriage). *Educ:* St Simon's College, Jamaica; London School of Economics. Jamaica Civil Service: Income Tax Dept, 1941; Colonial Secretary's Office, 1951; Asst Secretary, Min. of Finance, 1954; Director, General Planning Unit, 1957; Financial Secretary, 1962; Dep. Administrator, 1978–84, Associate Administrator, 1984–89, UNDP. *Publications:* contrib. Social and Economic Studies (University College of the West Indies). *Recreations:* hiking, boating, fishing. *Address:* Bank of Jamaica, PO Box 621, Kingston, Jamaica. *Club:* Jamaica (Jamaica).

BROWN, George Frederick William, CMG 1974; Member, Melbourne Underground Railway Loop Authority, since 1971; *b* 12 April 1908; *s* of late G. Brown; *m* 1933, Catherine Mills; one *d* (and one *d* decd). *Educ:* Christian Brothers' Coll., Essendon; Phahran Techn. Coll.; Royal Melbourne Inst. Technology. FIE (Aust.), AMIME (Aust.), FCIT. Victorian Railways, 1923; Asst Engr 1929; Country Roads Bd, 1934; Plant Engr Newport Workshops, 1939–43; Supt Loco. Maintenance, 1943–53; Chief Mech. Engr, 1953–58; Comr, 1958–61; Dep. Chm., 1961–67; Chm., 1967–73; Mem., Victorian Railway Bd, 1973–77. Mem. Council, Royal Melb. Inst. Technology, 1958–74, Pres. 1970. *Publications:* articles in techn. jls on rail transport. *Recreation:* golf. *Address:* Unit 1, 10 Lucas Street, East Brighton, Victoria 3187, Australia. *Clubs:* Kelvin Victoria, Victoria Golf, MCC (Victoria).

BROWN, George Mackay, OBE 1974; FRSL 1977; author; *b* 17 Oct. 1921; *s* of John Brown and Mary Jane Mackay. *Educ:* Stromness Acad.; Newbattle Abbey Coll.; Edinburgh Univ. (MA). Hon. MA Open Univ., 1976; Hon. LLD Dundee, 1977; Hon. DLitt Glasgow, 1985. *Publications: fiction:* A Calendar of Love, 1967; A Time to Keep, 1969; Greenvoe, 1972; Magnus, 1973; Hawkfall, 1974; The Two Fiddlers, 1975; The Sun's Net, 1976; Pictures in the Cave, 1977; Six Lives of Frankle the Cat, 1980; Andrina, 1983; Time in a Red Coat, 1984; Christmas Stories, 1985; The Golden Bird, 1987; The Masked Fisherman, 1989; *plays:* A Spell for Green Corn, 1970; Three Plays, 1984; The Loom of Light, 1986; A Celebration for Magnus (son et lumière), 1987; *poetry:* Fishermen with Ploughs, 1971; Winterfold, 1976; Selected Poems, 1977; Voyages, 1983; Christmas Poems, 1984; Tryst in Egilsay, 1989; The Wreck of the Archangel, 1989; Selected Poems 1954–1983, 1991; *essays, etc:* An Orkney Tapestry, 1969; Letters from Hamnavoe, 1975; Under Brinkie's Brae, 1979; Portrait of Orkney, 1981; (ed) Selected Prose of Edwin Muir, 1987. *Recreation:* reading. *Address:* 3 Mayburn Court, Stromness, Orkney KW16 3DH.

BROWN, Prof. Sir (George) Malcolm, Kt 1985; FRS 1975; consultant geologist; Director: British Geological Survey (formerly Institute of Geological Sciences), 1979–85; Geological Museum, 1979–85; Geological Survey of Northern Ireland, 1979–85; *b* 5 Oct. 1925; *s* of late George Arthur Brown and Anne Brown; *m* 1st, 1963 (marr. diss. 1977); 2nd, 1985, Sally Jane Marston, *e d* of A. D. Spencer, *qv*; two step *d*. *Educ:* Coatham Sch., Redcar; Durham Univ. (BSc, DSc); Oxford Univ. (MA, DPhil). RAF, 1944–47. FGS. Commonwealth Fund (Harkness) Fellow, Princeton Univ., 1954–55; Lectr in Petrology, Oxford Univ., 1955–66; Fellow, St Cross Coll., Oxford, 1965–67; Carnegie Instn Res. Fellow, Geophysical Lab., Washington DC, 1966–67; Prof. of Geology, 1967–79 (now Emeritus), Dean of Faculty of Science, 1978–79, and Pro-Vice-Chancellor, 1979, Durham Univ. Vis. Prof., Univ. of Berne, 1977–78; Adrian Vis. Fellow, Univ. of Leicester, 1983. NASA Principal Investigator, Apollo Moon Programme, 1967–75; Geol Advr to ODA, 1979–85. Member: Natural Environment Res. Council, 1972–75; Council, Royal Soc., 1980–81. Pres., Section C (Geology), British Assoc., 1987–88. Mem. Council, RHBNC, Univ. of London, 1987–89. UK Editor, Physics and Chemistry of the Earth, 1977–79. Hon. DSc Leicester, 1984; DUniv Open, 1990. Daniel Pidgeon Fund Award, 1952, Wollaston Fund Award, 1963, Murchison Medal, 1981, Geol Soc. of London. *Publications:* (with L. R. Wager) Layered Igneous Rocks, 1968; (contrib.) Methods in Geochemistry, 1960; (contrib.) Basalts, 1967; (contrib.) Planet Earth, 1977; (contrib.) Origin of the Solar System, 1978; papers in several sci. jls. *Recreations:* travel and exploration, classical guitar playing. *Address:* Rose Dene, Shipton Road, Milton-under-Wychwood, Oxford OX7 6JT. *T:* Shipton (0993) 830812. *Club:* Royal Over-Seas League.

BROWN, Sir George (Noel), Kt 1991; **Hon. Chief Justice Brown;** Chief Justice, Belize, since 1990; Deputy Governor-General, since 1985; *b* 13 June 1942; *s* of late Noel Todd Brown and Elma Priscilla Brown; *m* 1974, Magdalene Elizabeth Bucknor; one *d*, and one *s* two *d* from previous marriage. *Educ:* St Michael's Coll., Belize City; Carlton Univ., Ottawa (Cert. in Public Admin); Univ. of WI (LLB Hons); Norman Manley Law Sch., Council of Legal Educn, Univ. of WI (Legal Educn Cert.); Nairobi Law Sch., Kenya (Cert. in Legislative Drafting). Customs Examiner, Customs and Excise Dept, 1960–67; Clerk of Courts, Magistracy Dept, 1967–69; Admin. Asst, Min. of Trade and Ind., 1970–72; Actg Magistrate, Belize Judicial Dist and Itinerant countrywide, 1972–73; Crown Counsel, Attorney General's Ministry, 1978–81; Solicitor General, 1981–84; Puisne Judge, Supreme Court Justice, 1984–85 and 1986–90; Actg Chief Justice, 1985–86. *Publication:* Consumer Society and the Law, 1976. *Recreations:* yachting, football (soccer), especially coaching and managing primary and secondary schools teams. *Address:* c/o Supreme Court, Belize City, PO Box 170, Belize, Central America. *T:* 02–77256; PO Box 236, Belize City, Belize. *T:* 02–77055. *Club:* Belize Yacht (Belize City).

BROWN, Prof. George William, FBA 1986; Member, External Scientific Staff, Medical Research Council, since 1980; Hon. Professor of Sociology, Royal Holloway and Bedford

New College, London University, since 1980; *b* 15 Nov. 1930; *s* of late William G. Brown and of Lily Jane (*née* Hillier); *m* 1st, 1954, Gillian M. Hole (marr. diss. 1970); one *s* one *d*; 2nd, 1978, Seija T. Sandberg (marr. diss. 1987); one *d*; 3rd, 1990, Elizabeth A. Davies. *Educ:* Kilburn Grammar Sch.; University Coll. London (BA Anthropol. 1954); LSE (PhD 1961). Scientific Staff, DSIR, 1955–56; MRC Social Psychiatry Res. Unit, Inst. of Psychiatry, 1956–67; joined Social Res. Unit, Bedford Coll., London Univ., 1967; Prof. of Sociology, London Univ. and Jt Dir, Social Res. Unit, Bedford Coll., 1973–80. Mem., Academia Europaea, 1990. Hon.FRCPsych, 1987 *Publications:* (jtly) Schizophrenia and Social Care, 1966; (with J. K. Wing) Institutionalism and Schizophrenia, 1970; (with T. O. Harris) Social Origins of Depression, 1978; Life Events and Illness, 1989; numerous contribs to jls. *Address:* 40 Addington Square, SE5. *T:* 071–703 2124.

BROWN, Prof. Gillian; Professor of English as an International Language, University of Cambridge, since 1988; Fellow of Clare College, Cambridge, since 1988; *b* 23 Jan. 1937; *d* of Geoffrey Rencher Read and Elsie Olive Chapman; *m* 1959, Edward Keith Brown; three *d*. *Educ:* Perse Sch. for Girls; Girton Coll., Cambridge (MA); Univ. of Edinburgh (PhD 1971). Lectr, University Coll. of Cape Coast, Ghana, 1962–64; Lectr, 1965–81, Reader, 1981–83, Univ. of Edinburgh; Prof., Univ. of Essex, 1983–88 (Dean of Social Scis, 1985–88). Mem., ESRC Educn and Human Devlt Cttee, 1983–87; Chm., Research Grants Board, ESRC, 1987–; Member: Kingman Cttee, 1987–88; UGC, subseq. UFC, 1988–; Council, Philological Soc., 1988–; British Council English Teaching Adv. Cttee, 1989–. Gov., Bell Educnl Trust, 1987–. Dr *hc* Univ. of Lyon, 1987. Member, Editorial Boards: Jl of Semantics; Jl of Applied Linguistics; Second Language Acquisition Res. *Publications:* Phonological Rules and Dialect Variation, 1972; Listening to Spoken English, 1977; (with George Yule) Discourse Analysis, 1983; articles in learned jls. *Address:* Clare College, Cambridge CB2 1TL.

BROWN, Dame Gillian (Gerda), DCVO 1981; CMG 1971; HM Diplomatic Service, retired; *b* 10 Aug. 1923; *er d* of late Walter Brown and late Gerda Brown (*née* Grenside). *Educ:* The Spinney, Gt Bookham; Stoatley Hall, Haslemere; Somerville Coll., Oxford (Hon. Fellow 1981). FO, 1944–52; 2nd Sec., Budapest, 1952–54; FO, 1954–59; 1st Sec., Washington, 1959–62; 1st Sec., UK Delegn to OECD, Paris, 1962–65; FO, 1965–66; Counsellor and Head of Gen. Dept, FO, subseq. Head of Aviation, Marine and Telecommunications Dept, later Marine and Transport Dept, FCO, 1967–70; Counsellor, Berne, 1970–74; Under Sec., Dept of Energy, 1975–78; Asst Under Sec. of State, FCO, 1978–80; Ambassador to Norway, 1981–83. Mem., Panel of Chairmen, CSSB, 1984–88. Council Mem., Greenwich Forum, 1985–. Chm., Anglo-Norse Soc., 1988–. Hon. LLD Bath, 1981. Grand Cross, Order of St Olav, 1981. *Address:* c/o Midland Bank plc, Central Hall, Westminster, SW1P 3AS.

BROWN, Prof. Godfrey Norman; Professor of Education, University of Keele, 1967–80, now Emeritus; Director, Betley Court Gallery, since 1980; *b* 13 July 1926; *s* of Percy Charles and Margaret Elizabeth Brown; *m* 1960, Dr Freda Bowyer; three *s*. *Educ:* Whitgift Sch.; School of Oriental and African Studies, London; Merton Coll., Oxford (MA, DPhil). Army service, RAC and Intelligence Corps, 1944–48. Social Affairs Officer, UN Headquarters, NY, 1953–54; Sen. History Master, Barking Abbey Sch., Essex, 1954–57; Lectr in Educn, University Coll. of Ghana, 1958–61; Sen. Lectr, 1961, Prof., 1963, Univ. of Ibadan, Nigeria; Dir, Univ. of Keele Inst. of Educn, 1967–80. Visiting Prof., Univ. of Rhodesia and Nyasaland, 1963; Chm., Assoc. for Recurrent Educn, 1976–77; Mem., Exec. Cttee and Bd of Dirs, World Council for Curriculum and Instruction, 1974–77. OECD Consultant on teacher education, Portugal, 1980. Vice-Pres., Community Council of Staffs, 1984–. Collector of the Year Award, Art and Antiques, 1981; Newcastle-under-Lyme Civic Award for Conservation, 1990. *Publications:* An Active History of Ghana, 2 vols, 1961 and 1964; Living History, 1967; Apartheid, a Teacher's Guide, 1981; Betley Through the Centuries, 1985; This Old House: a domestic biography, 1987; ed (with J. C. Anene) Africa in the Nineteenth and Twentieth Centuries, 1966; ed, Towards a Learning Community, 1971; ed (with M. Hiskett) Conflict and Harmony in Education in Tropical Africa, 1975; contrib. educnl and cultural jls. *Recreations:* family life; art history, conservation. *Address:* Betley Court, Betley, near Crewe, Cheshire CW3 9BH. *T:* Crewe (0270) 820652.

BROWN, Gordon; *see* Brown, James G.

BROWN, Harold, PhD; Chairman, The Johns Hopkins Foreign Policy Institute, School of Advanced International Studies, since 1984 (Visiting Professor, 1981–84); *b* 19 Sept. 1927; *s* of A. H. Brown and Gertrude Cohen Brown; *m* 1953, Colene McDowell; two *d*. *Educ:* Columbia Univ. (AB 1945, AM 1946, PhD in Physics 1949). Res. Scientist, Columbia Univ., 1945–50, Lectr in Physics, 1947–48; Lectr in Physics, Stevens Inst. of Technol., 1949–50; Res. Scientist, Radiation Lab., Univ. of Calif, Berkeley, 1951–52; Gp Leader, Radiation Lab., Livermore, 1952–61; Dir, Def. Res. and Engrg, Dept of Def., 1961–65; Sec. of Air Force, 1965–69; Pres., Calif Inst. of Technol., Pasadena, 1969–77; Sec. of Defense, USA, 1977–81. Sen. Sci. Adviser, Conf. on Discontinuance of Nuclear Tests, 1958–59; Delegate, Strategic Arms Limitations Talks, Helsinki, Vienna and Geneva, 1969–77. Member: Polaris Steering Cttee, 1956–58; Air Force Sci. Adv. Bd, 1956–61; (also Consultant) President's Sci. Adv. Cttee, 1958–61. Hon. DEng Stevens Inst. of Technol., 1964; Hon. LLD: Long Island Univ., 1966; Gettysburg Coll., 1967; Occidental Coll., 1969; Univ. of Calif, 1969; Hon. ScD: Univ. of Rochester, 1975; Brown Univ., 1977; Univ. of the Pacific, 1978; Univ. of S Carolina, 1979; Franklin and Marshall Coll., 1982; Chung Ang Univ. (Seoul, Korea), 1983. Member: Amer. Phys. Soc., 1946; Nat. Acad. of Engrg, 1967; Amer. Acad. of Arts and Scis, 1969; Nat. Acad. of Scis, 1977. One of Ten Outstanding Young Men of Year, US Jun. Chamber of Commerce, 1961; Columbia Univ. Medal of Excellence, 1963; Air Force Exceptl Civil. Service Award, 1969; Dept of Def. Award for Exceptionally Meritorious Service, 1969; Joseph C. Wilson Award, 1976; Presidential Medal of Freedom, 1981. *Publication:* Thinking About National Security: defense and foreign policy in a dangerous world, 1983. *Address:* School of Advanced International Studies, The Johns Hopkins Foreign Policy Institute, 1619 Massachusetts Avenue, NW, Washington, DC 20036, USA. *Clubs:* Athenæum; Bohemian (San Francisco); California (Los Angeles); City Tavern (Washington, DC).

BROWN, Harold Arthur Neville, CMG 1963; CVO 1961; HM Diplomatic Service, retired; *b* 13 Dec. 1914; *s* of Stanley Raymond and Gladys Maud Brown; *m* 1939, Mary McBeath Urquhart; one *s* one *d*. *Educ:* Cardiff High School; University College, Cardiff. Entered Ministry of Labour as 3rd Class Officer, 1939; Asst Principal, 1943; Private Sec. to Permanent Sec. of Min. of Labour and Nat. Service, 1944–46; Principal, 1946; Labour Attaché, Mexico City (and other countries in Central America and the Caribbean), 1950–54; transferred to Foreign Office, 1955; Head of Chancery, Rangoon, 1958 and 1959; British Ambassador in Liberia, 1960–63; Corps of Inspectors, Foreign Office, 1963–66; Ambassador to Cambodia, 1966–70; Consul-General, Johannesburg, 1970–73; Minister, Pretoria, Cape Town, 1973–74. Knight Great Band of the Humane Order of African Redemption, 1962. *Address:* 14 Embassy Court, King's Road, Brighton BN1 2PX.

BROWN, Harold James, AM 1979; BSc, ME; Hon. DSc; FIE(Australia); FIREE; retired; management consultant, Adelaide, South Australia, 1976–85; Technical Director, Philips Industries Holdings Ltd, Sydney, 1961–76; *b* 10 July 1911; *s* of Allison James and Hilda Emmy Brown; *m* 1936, Hazel Merlyn Dahl Helm; two *s* two *d*. *Educ:* Fort Street Boys' High Sch.; Univ. of Sydney, NSW, Australia. BSc 1933; BE (Univ. Medal) 1935; ME (Univ. Medal) 1945; Hon. DSc 1976. Research Engineer, Amalgamated Wireless Australasia Ltd, 1935–37; Electrical Engineer, Hydro-electric Commission of Tasmania, 1937–39; Research Officer and Principal Research Officer, Council for Scientific and Industrial Research, 1939–45; Chief Communications Engineer, Australian Nat. Airways Pty Ltd, 1945–47; Prof. of Electrical Engineering, Dean of Faculty of Engineering and Asst Director, NSW Univ. of Technology, 1947–52; Controller R&D, Dept of Supply, Melbourne, 1952–54; Controller, Weapons Research Establishment, Department of Supply, Commonwealth Government of Australia, 1955–58; Technical Director, Rola Co. Pty Ltd, Melbourne, 1958–61. Awarded Queen's Silver Jubilee Medal, 1977. *Publications:* numerous technical articles in scientific journals. *Recreations:* gardening, bowling. *Address:* 20 Woodbridge, Island Drive, Delfin Island, South Australia 5021.

BROWN, (Harold) Vivian (Bigley); Head of Competition Policy Division, Department of Trade and Industry, since 1989; *b* 20 Aug. 1945; *s* of Alec Sidney Brown and Joyce Brown (*née* Bigley); *m* 1970, Jean Josephine Bowyer, *yr d* of late Sir Eric Bowyer, KCB, KBE and Lady Bowyer (now Lady Caine); two *s*. *Educ:* Leeds Grammar Sch.; St John's Coll., Oxford (BA); St Cross Coll., Oxford (BPhil Islamic Philosophy). Min. of Technology, 1970; DTI, 1972–74 (Private Sec. to Permanent Sec., 1972–73); FCO, 1975–79 (First Sec. Commercial Jeddah); DTI, 1979–86; Hd of Sci. and Technol. Assessment Office, Cabinet Office, 1986–89. *Publication:* Islamic Philosophy and the Classical Tradition (with S. M. Stern and A. Hourani), 1972. *Recreations:* playing piano, cycling, cooking. *Address:* Department of Trade and Industry, 1–19 Victoria Street, SW1H 0ET.

BROWN, Sir Henry Phelps; *see* Brown, Sir E. H. P.

BROWN, Henry Thomas C.; *see* Cadbury-Brown.

BROWN, Prof. Herbert Charles, PhD; R. B. Wetherill Research Professor Emeritus, Purdue University, 1978 (Professor, 1947–60, R. B. Wetherill Research Professor, 1960–78); *b* 22 May 1912; *s* of Charles Brown and Pearl (*née* Gorinstein); *m* 1937, Sarah Baylen; one *s*. *Educ:* Wright Jun. Coll., Chicago (Assoc. Sci. 1935); Univ. of Chicago (BS 1936; PhD 1938). Univ. of Chicago: Eli Lilly Postdoctoral Res. Fellow, 1938–39; Instr, 1939–43; Wayne University: Asst Prof., 1943–46; Associate Prof., 1946–47. Member: Nat. Acad. of Sciences, USA, 1957–; Amer. Acad. of Arts and Sciences, 1966–; Hon. Mem., Phi Lambda Upsilon, 1961–; Hon. Fellow, Chem. Soc., London, 1978– (Centenary Lectr, 1955; C. K. Ingold Medal, 1978); Foreign Fellow, Indian Nat. Science Acad., 1978–. Hon. Dr of Science: Univ. of Chicago, 1968; Wayne State Univ., 1980; Hebrew Univ. Jerusalem, 1980; Pontifica Univ. Catolica de Chile, 1980; Wales, 1982; Purdue, 1982, etc. (Jtly) Nobel Prize in Chemistry, 1979. Amer. Chemical Society: Harrison Howe Award, Rochester Sect., 1953; Nichols Medal, NY Sect., 1959; Linus Pauling Medal, Oregon and Puget Sound Sects, 1968; Roger Adams Medal, Organic Div., 1971; Priestley Medal, 1981. Award for Creative Res. in Org. Chem., Soc. of Organic Chem. Mfg Assoc., 1960; Herbert Newby McCoy Award, Purdue Univ., 1965 (1st co-recipient); Nat. Medal of Science, US Govt, 1969; Madison Marshall Award, 1975; Allied Chemical Award for Grad. Trng and Innovative Chem., 1978 (1st recipient); Perkins Medal, Amer. Sect., Soc. of Chemical Industry, 1982; Gold Medal, Amer. Inst. Chem., 1985; Chem. Sci. Award, Nat. Acad. of Scis, 1987; G. M. Kossolopoff Medal, Auburn Sect., Amer. Chem. Soc., 1987. Order of the Rising Sun, Gold and Silver Star (Japan), 1989. *Publications:* Hydroboration, 1962; Boranes in Organic Chemistry, 1972; Organic Syntheses via Boranes, 1975; The Non-classical Ion Problem, 1977; (with A. Pelter, K. Smith) Borane Reagents, 1988; over 1070 scientific articles in Jl Amer. Chem. Soc., Jl Org. Chem., Jl Organometal. Chem., and Synthesis. *Recreations:* travel, photography. *Address:* Department of Chemistry, Purdue University, West Lafayette, Ind 47907, USA. *T:* (317) 494–5316.

BROWN, Prof. H(oward) Mayer; Ferdinand Schevill Distinguished Service Professor of Music, University of Chicago, since 1976; *b* 13 April 1930; *s* of Alfred R. and Florence Mayer Brown; unmarried. *Educ:* Harvard Univ. AB 1951, AM 1954, PhD 1959. Walter Naumburg Trav. Fellow, Harvard, 1951–53; Instructor in Music, Wellesley Coll., Mass, 1958–60; Univ. of Chicago: Asst Prof., 1960–63; Assoc. Prof., 1963–66; Prof., 1967–72; Chm., 1970–72; Dir of Collegium Musicum, 1960–83; King Edward Prof. of Music, KCL, 1972–74. Guggenheim Fellow, Florence, 1963–64; Villa I Tatti Fellow, Florence, 1969–70; Andrew D. White Prof.-at-large, Cornell Univ., 1972–76; Prof. of Music, Univ. of Chicago, 1974–. Pres., Amer. Musicological Soc., 1978–80; Vice-Pres., Internat. Musicological Soc., 1982–87. Fellow, Amer. Acad. of Arts and Scis, 1983–. Hon. DMus Bates Coll., Maine, 1989. Galileo Galilei Prize, Univ. of Pisa, 1987. *Publications:* Music in the French Secular Theater, 1963; Theatrical Chansons, 1963; Instrumental Music Printed Before 1600, 1965; (with Joan Lascelle) Musical Iconography, 1972; Sixteenth-Century Instrumentation, 1972; Music in the Renaissance, 1976; Embellishing Sixteenth-Century Music, 1976; Chansonnier from the Time of Lorenzo the Magnificent, 2 vols, 1983. contrib. Jl Amer. Musicological Soc., Acta musicologica, Musical Quarterly, etc. *Address:* 5000 East End Avenue, Chicago, Ill 60615, USA. *Club:* Reform.

BROWN, Hugh Dunbar; *b* 18 May 1919; *s* of Neil Brown and Grace (*née* Hargrave); *m* 1947, Mary Glen Carmichael; one *d*. *Educ:* Allan Glen's School and Whitehill Secondary School, Glasgow. Formerly Civil Servant, Ministry of Pensions and National Insurance. Member of Glasgow Corporation, 1954; Magistrate, Glasgow, 1961. MP (Lab) Provan Div. of Glasgow, 1964–87. Parly Under-Sec. of State, Scottish Office, 1974–79. *Recreation:* golf. *Address:* 29 Blackwood Road, Milngavie, Glasgow G62 7LB.

BROWN, Ian James Morris; playwright; Drama Director, Arts Council, since 1986; *b* 28 Feb. 1945; *s* of Bruce Beveridge Brown and Eileen Frances Scott Carnegie; *m* 1968, Judith Ellen Sidaway; one *s* one *d*. *Educ:* Dollar Academy; Edinburgh Univ. MA Hons, MLitt, DipEd. Playwright, 1969–; Schoolmaster, 1967–69, 1970–71; Lectr in Drama, Dunfermline Coll., 1971–76; British Council: Asst Rep., Scotland, 1976–77; Asst Regional Dir, Istanbul, 1977–78; Crewe and Alsager College: Head of Drama, 1978–79; Head of Performance Arts, 1979–82; Programme Leader, BA Hons Drama Studies, 1982–86; Programme Dir, Alsager Arts Centre, 1980–86. Chm., Scottish Soc. of Playwrights, 1973–75, 1984–87; convenor, NW Playwrights' Workshop, 1982–85; British Theatre Institute: Vice-Chm., 1983–85; Chm., 1985–87. Productions: Mother Earth, 1970; The Bacchae, 1972; Positively the Last Final Farewell Performance (ballet), 1972; Rune (choral work), 1973; Carnegie, 1973; The Knife, 1973; The Fork, 1976; New Reekie, 1977; Mary, 1977; Runners, 1978; Mary Queen and the Loch Tower, 1979; Joker in the Pack, 1983; Beatrice, 1989; (jtly) First Strike, 1990; The Scotch Play, 1991; Bondagers, 1991. *Publications:* articles on drama, theatre and arts policy. *Recreations:* theatre, sport, travel. *Address:* Arts Council, 14 Great Peter Street, SW1P 3NQ.

BROWN, Jack, MBE 1985; JP; General Secretary, Amalgamated Textile Workers Union, 1976–86; *b* 10 Nov. 1929; *s* of Maurice Brown and Edith (*née* Horrocks); *m* 1952, Alice (*née* Brown); one *s*. *Educ:* Pennington CofE Primary Sch., Leigh, Lancs; Leigh CofE Secondary Sch., Leigh. Commenced employment in cotton industry as operative, Dec.

1943; Royal Artillery, 1949–51; full time Trade Union Official (Organiser), 1954; District Sec., 1961–72; Asst Gen. Sec., 1972–76. Non-exec. Mem., NW Electricity Bd, 1984–90. JP Greater Manchester, 1967. *Recreations:* reading, Rugby League football. *Address:* 11 Thomas Street, Atherton, Manchester M29 9DP. *T:* Atherton (0942) 870218. *Club:* Soldiers and Sailors (Atherton).

BROWN, Col James, CVO 1985; RNZAC (retd); General Secretary to the Duke of Edinburgh's Award Scheme in New Zealand, since 1986; *b* 15 Aug. 1925; *y s* of late John Brown and Eveline Bertha (*née* Cooper), Russells Flat, North Canterbury, NZ; *m* 1952, Patricia Sutton; two *d. Educ:* Christchurch Boys' High Sch., NZ; Royal Military Coll., Duntroon, Australia (grad 1947). NZ Regular Army, 1947–71: active service, Korea, 1951–52; Reg. Comr of Civil Defence, Dept of Internal Affairs, NZ, 1971–77. Official Sec. to Governor-Gen. of NZ, 1977–85. Col Comdt, RNZAC, 1982–86; Pres., NZ Army Assoc., 1986–. *Recreations:* fishing, shooting. *Address:* PO Box 11–467, Wellington, New Zealand. *Clubs:* Wellington, Wellesley (Wellington).

BROWN, Maj.-Gen. James, CB 1982; Director of Management Information Services Division, University of London, since 1986; *b* 12 Nov. 1928; *s* of late James Brown; *m* 1952, Lilian May Johnson; two *s. Educ:* Methodist Coll., Belfast; RMA Sandhurst; psc, jssc, rcds. Commissioned RAOC 1948; served UK (attached 1 DWR), Egypt, Cyprus, War Office, 1948–58; Staff Coll., Camberley, 1959; BAOR, UK, 1960–64; JSSC, Latimer, 1964–65; HQ Gurkha Inf. Bde Borneo, 1965–66 (despatches); MoD, 1966–67; Comdr RAOC, 4 Div., 1967–70; AA&QMG (Ops/Plans), HQ 1 (BR) Corps, 1970–72; Central Ordnance Depots, Donnington and Bicester, 1972–75; Dep. Dir, Ordnance Services, MoD, 1975; RCDS, 1976; Dep. Dir, Personal Services, MoD, 1977–80; Dir Gen. of Ordnance Services, 1980–83. Col Comdt, RAOC, 1983–85. Sec., Univ. of London Computer Centre, 1983–86. *Address:* c/o Royal Bank of Scotland, Holt's Branch, Kirkland House, Whitehall, SW1.

BROWN, James Alexander, TD 1948; QC 1956; Recorder of Belfast, 1978–82; *b* 13 June 1914; *s* of Rt Hon. Mr Justice (Thomas Watters) Brown and Mary Elizabeth Brown; *m* 1950, Shirley Wallace Sproule; one *s* two *d. Educ:* Campbell College, Belfast; Balliol College, Oxford (BA; Pres., Oxford Union Soc., 1936). Served 1/Royal Ulster Rifles, 1939–45 (wounded; Captain). Called Bar of NI, 1946; called English Bar (GI), 1950. County Court Judge, Co. Down, 1967–78.

BROWN, Dr (James) Barry (Conway), OBE 1978; Director, British Council, Poland, since 1992; *b* 3 July 1937; *s* of Frederick Clarence and Alys Brown; *m* 1963, Anne Rosemary Clough; two *s* one *d. Educ:* Cambridge Univ. (BA Nat. Sci 1959; MA 1963); Birmingham Univ. (MSc 1960; PhD 1963). Research Officer, CEGB, Berkeley Nuclear Labs, 1963–67; British Council: Sen. Sci. Officer, Sci. Dept, 1967–69; Sci. Officer, Madrid, 1969–72, Paris, 1972–78; Head, Sci. and Technology Group, 1978–81; Rep. and Cultural Counsellor, Mexico, 1981–85; Dep. Controller (Higher Educn Div.), 1985–89; Dir, EC Liaison Unit (Higher Education), Brussels, 1989–91. *Recreations:* music, travel in (and study of) countries of posting, singing, reading. *Address:* c/o British Council, 10 Spring Gardens, SW1A 2BN; 42 Hazel Road, Purley-on-Thames, Reading RG8 8BB. *T:* Reading (0734) 417581.

BROWN, (James) Gordon; MP (Lab) Dunfermline East, since 1983; *b* 20 Feb. 1951; *s* of Rev. Dr John Brown and J. Elizabeth Brown. *Educ:* Kirkcaldy High Sch.; Edinburgh Univ. MA 1972; PhD 1982. Rector, Edinburgh Univ., 1972–75; Temp. Lectr, Edinburgh Univ., 1976; Lectr, Glasgow Coll. of Technology, 1976–80; Journalist and Current Affairs Editor, Scottish TV, 1980–83. Member: NUJ; TGWU. Chm., Labour Party Scottish Council, 1983–84; Opposition Chief Sec. to the Treasury, 1987–89; Opposition Trade and Industry Sec., 1989–. Contested (Lab) S Edinburgh, 1979. *Publications:* (ed) The Red Paper on Scotland, 1975; (with H. M. Drucker) The Politics of Nationalism and Devolution, 1980; (ed) Scotland: the real divide, 1983; Maxton, 1986; Where There is Greed, 1989. *Recreations:* reading and writing, football and tennis. *Address:* 48 Marchmont Road, Edinburgh.

BROWN, Jerry; *see* Brown, E. G.

BROWN, Joe, MBE 1975; freelance guide and climber, and film maker for television and cinema; *b* 26 Sept. 1930; *s* of J. Brown, Longsight, Manchester; *m* 1957, Valerie Gray; two *d. Educ:* Stanley Grove, Manchester. Started climbing while working as plumber in Manchester; pioneered new climbs in Wales in early 1950's; gained internat. reputation after climbing West Face of Petit Dru, 1954; climbed Kanchenjunga, 1955; Mustagh Tower, 1956; Mt Communism, USSR, 1962; Trango Tower, 1976; Cotaphxi, 1979; Mt Kenya, 1984; Mt McInley, 1986; other expdns: El Torro, 1970; Bramah 2, 1978; Thalaysagar, 1982; Everest NE Ridge, 1986 and 1988. Climbing Instructor, Whitehall, Derbs, 1961–65; opened climbing equipment shops, Llanberis, 1965, Capel Curig, 1970; Leader of United Newspapers Andean Expedn, 1970; Roraima Expedn, 1973. Hon. Fellow, Manchester Polytechnic, 1970. *Publication:* (autobiog.) The Hard Years, 1967. *Recreations:* mountaineering, ski-ing, fishing. *Address:* Menai Hall, Llanberis, Gwynedd. *T:* Llanberis (0286) 870327. *Club:* Climbers'.

BROWN, John, CBE 1982; FEng 1984; FIEE; Part-time Dean of Technology, Brunel University, 1988–91; *b* 17 July 1923; *s* of George Brown and Margaret Ditchburn Brown; *m* 1947, Maureen Dorothy Moore; one *d. Educ:* Edinburgh University. Radar Research and Development Estab., 1944–51; Lectr, Imperial Coll., 1951–54; University Coll., London: Lectr, 1954–56; Reader, 1956–64; Prof., 1964–67; seconded to Indian Inst. of Technology as Prof. of Electrical Engrg, 1962–65; Prof. of Elect. Engineering, Imperial Coll. of Science and Technology, 1967–81 (Head of Dept, 1967–79); Tech. Dir, Marconi Electrical Devices Ltd, 1981–83; Dir, Univ. and Schs Liaison, GEC, 1983–88. Mem., SRC, 1977–81 (Chm., Engrg Bd, 1977–81); Chm., Joint ESRC-SERC Cttee, 1988–; Member: Engrg Group, Nat. Advisory Bd, 1983–84; Engrg Cttee, CNAA, 1985–87; Accreditation Cttee, CNAA, 1987–89. Pres., IEE, 1979–80 (Vice-Pres., 1975–78; Dep. Pres., 1978–79); Pres., IEEIE, 1981–85 (Treasurer, 1989–). Governor: S Bank Polytechnic, 1985–90; Willesden Coll. of Technology, 1985–86. Hon. FIElecIE 1986. *Publications:* Microwave Lenses, 1953; (with H. M. Barlow) Radio Surface Waves, 1962; Telecommunications, 1964; (with R. H. Clarke) Diffraction Theory and Antennas, 1980; papers in Proc. IEE, etc. *Recreation:* gardening. *Address:* 18 Green Tiles, Green Tiles Lane, Denham, Uxbridge UB9 5HX.

BROWN, John, CMG 1989; HM Diplomatic Service; Consul-General, Toronto, and Director, Trade Promotion and Investment, 1989–91; *b* 13 July 1931; *s* of John Coultas Scofield Brown and Sarah Ellen Brown (*née* Brown); *m* 1955, Christine Ann Batchelor; one *d. Educ:* South Shields High School. Export Credits Guarantee Dept, 1949; Grenadier Guards, 1949–51; Board of Trade, 1967; seconded to HM Diplomatic Service, 1969; Diplomatic Service, 1975; First Secretary and Head of Chancery, Accra, 1977; FCO, 1979, Counsellor, 1981; Counsellor (Commercial) and Dir of Trade Promotion, Brtitish Trade Develt Office, NY, 1984. *Recreation:* walking. *Club:* Royal Over-Seas League.

BROWN, John B.; *see* Blamire-Brown.

BROWN, (John) Carter; Director, National Gallery of Art, Washington, DC, since 1969; Chairman, Commission of Fine Arts, since 1971; *b* 8 Oct. 1934; *s* of John Nicholas Brown and Anne Kinsolving Brown; *m* 1976, Pamela Braga Drexel; one *s* one *d. Educ:* Harvard (AB *summa cum laude* 1956; MBA 1958); Inst. of Fine Arts, NY Univ. (Museum Trng Prog., Metropol. Museum of Art; MA 1961). Studied: with Bernard Berenson, Florence, 1958; Ecole du Louvre, Paris, 1958–59; Rijksbureau voor Kunsthistorische Documentatie, The Hague, 1960. National Gallery of Art: Asst to Dir, 1961–63; Asst Dir, 1964–68; Dep. Dir, 1968–69. Mem. Bd of Govs, John Carter Brown Liby, Brown Univ. Trustee: Amer. Acad. in Rome; Amer. Fedn of Arts; Corning Mus. of Glass; Inst. of Fine Arts, NY Univ.; John F. Kennedy Center for Performing Arts; Nat. Geographic Soc.; Nat. Trust for Historic Preservation; Storm King Art Center; Winterthur Mus. Hon. Mem., Amer. Inst. of Architects, 1975. Holds twelve hon. degrees. Gold Medal of Honor, National Arts Soc., 1972; Gold Medal of Honor, Nat. Inst. of Social Sciences, 1987. Commandeur, l'Ordre des Arts et des Lettres, France, 1975; Chevalier de la Légion d'Honneur, France, 1976; Knight, Order of St Olav, Norway, 1979; Comdr, Order of the Republic, Egypt, 1979; Comdr, Order of Orange-Nassau, Netherlands, 1982; Commendatore, Order of Merit of Italian Republic, 1984; Kt Comdr, Order of Isabel la Católica, Spain, 1985; Austrian Cross of Honor for Arts and Letters, 1986; Comdr, Royal Order of the Polar Star, Sweden, 1988. Phi Beta Kappa, 1956. Author/Dir, (film), The American Vision, 1966. *Publications:* contrib. professional jls and exhibn catalogues. *Recreations:* sailing, riding, photography. *Address:* National Gallery of Art, Constitution Avenue at 4th Street NW, Washington, DC 20565, USA. *T:* (office) (202) 842–6001. *Clubs:* Knickerbocker, Century Association, New York Yacht (New York).

BROWN, Sir John (Douglas Keith), Kt 1960; Chairman, McLeod Russel plc, London, 1972–79 (Director, 1963–83), retired; Director of other companies; *b* 8 Sept. 1913; *s* of late Ralph Douglas Brown and Rhoda Miller Keith; *m* 1940, Margaret Eleanor, *d* of late William Alexander Burnet; two *s. Educ:* Glasgow Acad. CA 1937. Joined Messrs. Lovelock & Lewes, Chartered Accountants, Calcutta, October 1937 (Partnership, 1946; retired 1948); joined Jardine Henderson Ltd as a Managing Director, 1949; Chairman, 1957–63. Pres. Bengal Chamber of Commerce and Industry and Associated Chambers of Commerce of India, 1958–60; Pres. UK Citizens' Assoc. (India), 1961. Mem. Eastern Area Local Bd, Reserve Bank of India, 1959–63; Mem. Advisory Cttee on Capital Issues, Govt of India, 1958–63; Mem. Technical Advisory Cttee on Company Law, 1958–63; Mem. Companies Act Amendment Cttee, 1957; Mem. Central Excise Reorganisation Cttee, 1960. *Recreations:* gardening, walking. *Address:* Glenyra, 60 Kingswood Firs, Grayshott, Hindhead, Surrey GU26 6ER. *T:* Hindhead (042873) 4173. *Clubs:* Oriental; Bengal (Calcutta).

BROWN, Rt. Rev. John Edward; *see* Cyprus and the Gulf, Bishop in.

BROWN, Sir John (Gilbert Newton), Kt 1974; CBE 1966; MA; Vice President, Blackwell Group Ltd, since 1987 (Director, 1980–87); *b* 7 July 1916; *s* of John and Molly Brown, Chilham, Kent; *m* 1946, Virginia, *d* of late Darcy Braddell and Dorothy Braddell; one *s* two *d. Educ:* Lancing Coll.; Hertford Coll., Oxford (MA Zoology). Bombay Branch Oxford University Press, 1937–40; commissioned Royal Artillery, 1941; served with 5th Field Regiment, 1941–46; captured by the Japanese at Fall of Singapore, 1942; prisoner of war, Malaya, Formosa and Japan, 1942–45; returned Oxford University Press, 1946; Sales Manager, 1949; Publisher, 1956–80; Chm., University Bookshops (Oxford) Ltd; Chm., 1980–83, Dep. Chm., 1983–87, Dir, 1980–87, B. H. Blackwell Ltd; Chm., 1983–85, Dir, 1983–87, Basil Blackwell Ltd (formerly Basil Blackwell Publisher Ltd); Director: Willshaw Booksellers Ltd, Manchester, 1966–89; Book Tokens Ltd, 1973–89; Archival Facsimiles Ltd, 1986–89; John Brown Publishing Ltd, 1989–. President, Publishers' Association, 1963–65. Member: Nat. Libraries Cttee; EDC for Newspapers, Printing and Publishing Industry, 1967–70; Adv. Cttee on Scientific and Technical Information, 1969–73; Communication Adv. Cttee for UK Nat. Cttee for UNESCO; Royal Literary Fund (Asst Treasurer); Bd of British Library, 1973–79; Royal Soc. Cttee on Scientific Information; Mem. Bd, British Council, 1968–81; Open Univ. Visiting Cttee. Professorial Fellow, Hertford Coll., Oxford, 1974–80. FRSA 1964. *Address:* Milton Lodge, Great Milton, Oxford OX9 7NJ. *T:* Great Milton (0844) 279217. *Club:* Garrick.

BROWN, (John) Michael, CBE 1986; HM Diplomatic Service, retired; *b* 16 Nov. 1929; *m* 1955, Elizabeth Fitton; one *s* one *d.* Served at: Cairo, 1954–55; Doha, 1956–57; FO, 1957–60; Havana, 1960–62; FO, 1962–64; Jedda, 1965–66; Maseru, 1966–67; Bogotá, 1967–69; FCO, 1969–71; Ankara, 1971–73; Tripoli, 1973–75; FCO, 1976–79; Ambassador to Costa Rica and Nicaragua, 1979–82; Consul-Gen., Geneva, 1983–85.

BROWN, Prof. John Russell; Professor of Theatre, University of Michigan, Ann Arbor, since 1985; *b* 15 Sept. 1923; *yr s* of Russell Alan and Olive Helen Brown, Coombe Wood, Somerset; *m* 1961, Hilary Sue Baker; one *s* two *d. Educ:* Monkton Combe Sch.; Keble Coll., Oxford. Sub-Lieut (AE) RNVR, 1944–46. Fellow, Shakespeare Inst., Stratford-upon-Avon, 1951–55; Lectr and Sen. Lectr, Dept of English, Birmingham Univ., 1955–63; Hd of Dept of Drama and Theatre Arts, Univ. of Birmingham, 1964–71; Prof. of English, Sussex Univ., 1971–82; Prof. of Theatre Arts, State Univ. of NY at Stony Brook, 1982–85; Artistic Dir, Project Theatre, Michigan Univ., 1985–89. Reynolds Lectr, Colorado Univ., 1957; Vis. Prof. Graduate Sch., New York Univ., 1959; Mellon Prof. of Drama, Carnegie Inst., Pittsburgh, 1964; Vis. Prof., Zürich Univ., 1969–70; Univ. Lectr in Drama, Univ. of Toronto, 1970. Robb Lectr, Univ. of Auckland, 1976; Lansdowne Visitor, Univ. of Victoria, BC, 1990. Associate, NT, 1973–88. Member: Adv. Council of Victoria and Albert Museum, 1980–83; Adv. Council of Theatre Museum, 1974–83 (Chm., 1979–83); Arts Council of GB, 1980–83, and Chm. Drama Panel, 1980–83 (formerly Dep. Chm.). *Theatre productions include:* Twelfth Night, Playhouse, Pittsburgh, 1964; Macbeth, Everyman, Liverpool, 1965; The White Devil, Everyman, 1969; Crossing Niagara, Nat. Theatre at the ICA, 1975; They Are Dying Out, Young Vic, 1976; Old Times, British Council tour of Poland, 1976; Judgement, Nat. Theatre, 1977; Hamlet (tour), 1978; Macbeth, Nat. Theatre (co-director), 1978; The Vienna Notes and The Nest, Crucible, Sheffield, 1979; Company, Nat. Theatre, 1980; Faith Healer, Nat. Theatre and Santa Fe, 1982, and, with Candida, British Council tour of India, 1983; The Double Bass, Nat. Theatre, 1984; The Daughter-in-Law, Antique Pink, Oedipus, Waiting for Godot, Don Juan, Every Good Boy, Project Theater, Ann Arbor, Mich, USA, 1985–89; Richard II, Nat. Theatre, Educn Project Tour, 1987; Much Ado About Nothing, Playhouse, Cincinnati, 1989; Burn This, Dunedin, NZ, 1989. Gen. Editor: Stratford-upon-Avon Studies, 1960–67; Stratford-upon-Avon Library, 1964–; Theatre Production Studies, 1981–. *Publications:* (ed) The Merchant of Venice, 1955; Shakespeare and his Comedies, 1957; (ed) The White Devil, 1960; Shakespeare: The Tragedy of Macbeth, 1963; (ed) The Duchess of Malfi, 1965; (ed) Henry V, 1965; Shakespeare's Plays in Performance, 1966; Effective Theatre, 1969; Shakespeare's The Tempest, 1969; Shakespeare's Dramatic Style, 1970; Theatre Language, 1972; Free Shakespeare, 1974; Discovering Shakespeare, 1981; Shakespeare and his Theatre, 1982; A Short Guide to Modern British Drama, 1983; Shakescenes, 1991; articles in Shakespeare Survey, Critical Quarterly, Tulane Drama Review, Studies in Bibliography, etc. *Recreations:* gardening, travel. *Address:* Court Lodge, Hooe, Battle, Sussex TN33 9HT. *Club:* Overseas.

BROWN, Joseph Lawler, CBE 1978; TD 1953; FMIC; CBIM; DL; Chairman and Managing Director, The Birmingham Post & Mail Ltd, 1973–77; *b* 22 March 1921; *s* of late Neil Brown; *m* 1950, Mabel Smith, SRN, SCM; one *s* one *d*. *Educ:* Peebles; Heriot-Watt Coll., Edinburgh. BA Open Univ. FCIM (FInstM 1976); CBIM (formerly FBIM) 1978. Served War, The Royal Scots, 1939–46 (Major). The Scotsman Publications Ltd, 1947–60; Coventry Newspapers Ltd: Gen. Man., 1960; Jt Man. Dir, 1961; Man. Dir, 1964–69; The Birmingham Post & Mail Ltd: Dep. Man. Dir, 1970; Man. Dir, 1971. Director: Cambridge Newspapers Ltd, 1965–69; Press Assoc., 1968–75 (Chm. 1972); Reuters Ltd, 1972–75; BPM (Holdings) Ltd, 1973–81. Pres., Birmingham Chamber of Industry and Commerce, 1979–80. Exec. Chm., Birmingham Venture, 1981–85. Mem., Bromsgrove and Redditch DHA, 1982–84; Mem., Hereford and Worcester Family Practitioner Cttee, 1982–83. Mem. Council, Regular Forces Employment Assoc., 1983–87; Warden, Neidpath Castle, Peebles, 1983–84. Mem., Peebles Guildry Corp., 1991–. Life Mem., Court, Birmingham Univ., 1980; Bailiff, Schs of King Edward the Sixth in Birmingham, 1987–88. DL County of W Midlands, 1976. Kt, Mark Twain Soc., 1979. Commendatore, Order Al Merito Della Repubblica Italiana, 1973. *Publication:* (with J. C. Lawson) History of Peebles 1850–1990, 1990. *Recreations:* gardening, fishing, Japanese woodcuts. *Address:* Westerly, 37 Mearse Lane, Barnt Green, Birmingham B45 8HH. *T:* 021–445 1234.

BROWN, June P.; *see* Paterson-Brown.

BROWN, Rt. Rev. Laurence Ambrose, MA; *b* 1 Nov. 1907; 2nd *s* of Frederick James Brown; *m* 1935, Florence Blanche, *d* of late William Gordon Marshall; three *d*. *Educ:* Luton Grammar School; Queens' College, Cambridge (MA); Cuddesdon Theological College, Oxford. Asst Curate, St John-the-Divine, Kennington, 1932–35; Curate-in-Charge, St Peter, Luton, Beds, 1935–40; Vicar, Hatfield Hyde, Welwyn Garden City, 1940–46; Sec. Southwark Dio. Reorganisation Cttee, 1946–60; Sec. S London Church Fund and Southwark Dio. Bd of Finance, 1952–60; Canon Residentiary, Southwark, 1950–60; Archdeacon of Lewisham and Vice-Provost of Southwark, 1955–60; Suffragan Bishop of Warrington, 1960–69; Bishop of Birmingham, 1969–77; Priest-in-Charge of Odstock with Nunton and Bodenham, dio. Salisbury, 1977–84. Mem. Church Assembly, later General Synod, and Proctor in Convocation, 1954–77; Chairman: Advisory Council for Church's Ministry, 1966–71; Industrial Christian Fellowship, 1971–77; Mem., Religious Adv. Bd, Scout Assoc., 1953–83. Mem., House of Lords, 1973–77. *Publications:* pamphlets on church building in post-war period. *Address:* 7 St Nicholas Road, Salisbury, Wilts SP1 2SN. *T:* Salisbury (0722) 333138.

BROWN, Prof. Lawrence Michael, PhD; FRS 1982; Professor of Physics, University of Cambridge, since 1990; Founding Fellow, Robinson College, Cambridge, since 1977; *b* 18 March 1936; *s* of Bertson Waterworth Brown and Edith Waghorne; *m* 1965, Susan Drucker; one *s* two *d*. *Educ:* Univ. of Toronto (BASc); Univ. of Birmingham (PhD). Athlone Fellow, Univ. of Birmingham, 1957; W. M. Tapp Research Fellow, Gonville and Caius Coll., Cambridge, 1963; University Demonstrator, Cavendish Laboratory, 1965; Lectr, 1970–83, Reader, 1983–90, Cambridge Univ.; Lectr, Robinson Coll., Cambridge, 1977–90. *Publications:* many papers on structure and properties of materials and electron microscopy in Acta Metallurgica and Philosophical Magazine. *Address:* 74 Alpha Road, Cambridge CB4 3DG. *T:* Cambridge (0223) 62987.

BROWN, Leslie; Deputy Chairman, Prudential Assurance Co. Ltd, 1970–74 (a Director, 1965–77); *b* 29 Oct. 1902; *s* of late W. H. Brown and late Eliza J. Fiveash; *m* 1930, Frances V., *d* of T. B. Lever; two *s* one *d*. *Educ:* Selhurst Grammar School. Joined Prudential Assurance Co. Ltd, 1919; Secretary and Chief Investment Manager, Prudential Assurance Co. Ltd, 1955–64 (Joint Secretary 1942); Chairman: Prudential Unit Trust Managers Ltd, 1968–75; Prudential Pensions Ltd, 1970–75. Member, Jenkins Committee on Company Law Amendment, 1960. Deputy-Chairman, Insurance Export Finance Co. Ltd, 1962–65. Inst. of Actuaries: FIA 1929; Vice-Pres., 1949–51. *Recreation:* bowls. *Address:* 12 Park View, Christchurch Road, Purley, Surrey CR8 2NL.

BROWN, Leslie F.; *see* Farrer-Brown.

BROWN, Rt. Rev. Leslie Wilfrid, CBE 1965; *b* 10 June 1912; *s* of Harry and Maud Brown; *m* 1939, Annie Winifred, *d* of Hon. R. D. Megaw, Belfast; one *d*. *Educ:* Enfield Gram. School; London College of Divinity (London Univ.). BD 1936, MTh 1944, DD 1957. MA Cantab. hon. causa, 1953. Deacon, Curate St James' Milton, Portsmouth, 1935; priest, 1936. Missionary, CMS, 1938 to Cambridge Nicholson Instn, Kottayam, Travancore, S India. Fellow Commoner and Chaplain, Downing College, Cambridge, 1943; Kerala United Theological Seminary, Trivandrum: tutor, 1945, Principal, 1946, and from 1951. Chaplain, Jesus Coll., Cambridge and Select Preacher before Univ. of Cambridge, 1950, 1967, 1979, Oxford, 1967. Archbishop of Uganda, Rwanda and Burundi, 1961–65; Bishop of Namirembe, 1960–65 (of Uganda, 1953–60; name of diocese changed); Bishop of St Edmundsbury and Ipswich, 1966–78. Chm., ACCM, 1972–76. Hon. Fellow, Downing Coll., Cambridge, 1966. DD (*hc*) Trinity Coll., Toronto, 1963. Chaplain and Sub-Prelate, Order of St John, 1968. *Publications:* The Indian Christians of St Thomas, 1956, 2nd edn 1982; The Christian Family, 1959; God as Christians see Him, 1961; Relevant Liturgy, 1965; Three Worlds, One Word, 1981; The King and the Kingdom, 1988. *Address:* 47 New Square, Cambridge CB1 1EZ. *Club:* Commonwealth Trust.

BROWN, Prof. Lionel Neville, OBE 1988; Professor of Comparative Law, University of Birmingham, 1966–90, Emeritus Professor, since 1990; Leverhulme Fellow, 1990–Aug. 1992; *b* 29 July 1923; *s* of Reginald P. N. Brown and Fanny Brown (*née* Carver); *m* 1957, Mary Patricia Vowles; three *s* one *d*. *Educ:* Wolverhampton Grammar Sch.; Pembroke Coll., Cambridge (Scholar; MA, LLM); Lyons Univ. (Dr en Droit). RAF, 1942–45; Cambridge, 1945–48; articled to Wolverhampton solicitor, 1948–50; Rotary Foundn Fellow, Lyons Univ., 1951–52; Lectr in Law, Sheffield Univ., 1953–55; Lectr in Comparative Law, Birmingham Univ., 1956, Sen. Lectr, 1957; Sen. Res. Fellow, Univ. of Michigan, 1960. Mem., Council on Tribunals, 1982–88; Chm., Birmingham Social Security Appeal Tribunal, 1988–. Visiting Professor: Univ. of Tulane, New Orleans, 1968; Univ. of Nairobi, 1974; Laval, 1975, 1979, 1983, 1990; Limoges, 1986; Mauritius, 1988, 1989; Aix-en-Provence, 1991. Commonwealth Foundn Lectr (Caribbean), 1975–76. Dr *hc* Limoges, 1989. Officier dans l'Ordre des Palmes Académiques, 1987. *Publications:* (with F. H. Lawson and A. E. Anton) Amos and Walton's Introduction to French Law, 2nd edn 1963 and 3rd edn 1967; (with J. F. Garner) French Administrative Law, 1967, 3rd edn 1983; (with F. G. Jacobs) Court of Justice of the European Communities, 1977, 3rd edn 1989. *Recreations:* landscape gardening, country walking, music. *Address:* Willow Rise, Waterdale, Compton, Wolverhampton, West Midlands WV3 9DY. *T:* Wolverhampton (0902) 26666. *Club:* United Oxford & Cambridge University.

BROWN, Sir Malcolm; *see* Brown, Sir G. M.

BROWN, (Marion) Patricia; Under-Secretary (Economics), Treasury, 1972–85; *b* 2 Feb. 1927; *d* of late Henry Oswald Brown and Elsie Elizabeth (*née* Thompson). *Educ:* Norwich High Sch. for Girls; Newnham Coll., Cambridge. Central Economic Planning Staff, Cabinet Office, 1947; Treasury, 1948–54; United States Embassy, London, 1956–59; Treasury, 1959–85. Mem. Council, Royal Holloway and Bedford New Coll., London Univ., 1985–. Godmother of Lucy Harland and Benjamin Watts. *Recreations:* bird watching, gardening, walking. *Address:* 28 The Plantation, SE3 0AB. *T:* 081–852 9011.

BROWN, Sir Max; *see* Brown, Sir C. M. P.

BROWN, Sir Mervyn, KCMG 1981 (CMG 1975); OBE 1963; HM Diplomatic Service, retired; *b* 24 Sept. 1923; *m* 1949, Elizabeth Gittings. *Educ:* Ryhope Gram. Sch., Sunderland; St John's Coll., Oxford. Served in RA, 1942–45. Entered HM Foreign Service, 1949; Third Secretary, Buenos Aires, 1950; Second Secretary, UK Mission to UN, New York, 1953; First Secretary, Foreign Office, 1956; Singapore, 1959; Vientiane, 1960; again in Foreign Office, 1963–67; Ambassador to Madagascar, 1967–70; Inspector, FCO, 1970–72; Head of Communications Operations Dept, FCO, 1973–74; Asst Under-Sec. of State (Dir of Communications), 1974; High Comr in Tanzania, 1975–78, and concurrently Ambassador to Madagascar; Minister and Dep. Perm. Representative to UN, 1978; High Comr in Nigeria, 1979–83, and concurrently Ambassador to Benin. Chairman: Visiting Arts Unit of GB, 1983–89; Anglo-Malagasy Soc., 1986–; Vice-Pres., Commonwealth Youth Exchange Council, 1984–87. *Publications:* Madagascar Rediscovered, 1978; articles and reviews on the history of Madagascar in Jl of African History, Tanzania Notes and Records, and Bulletin de l'Académie Malgache. *Recreations:* music, tennis, history. *Address:* 195 Queen's Gate, SW7 5EU. *Clubs:* Commonwealth Trust, Hurlingham, All England Lawn Tennis.

BROWN, Michael; *see* Brown, J. M.

BROWN, Maj.-Gen. Michael, FRCP, FRCPE; Director of Army Medicine, 1988–90, retired; *b* 17 Jan. 1931; *s* of Eric Charles Brown and Winifred Ethel Brown (*née* Kemp); *m* 1955, Jill Evelyn; two *s*. *Educ:* Bedford Sch.; University Coll. Hosp. London (MB BS; BSc Physiol.). DTM&H. House posts, UCH, 1954–55; RAMC 1956; Consultant Physician, 1966; Jt Prof. of Military Medicine, RCP and RAMC Coll., 1981–85; Consultant Physician, BAOR, 1985–88. QHP, 1988–90. Fellow, UCL, 1991. OStJ 1990. *Recreations:* golf, photography. *Address:* c/o Royal Bank of Scotland, Farnborough, Hants GU14 7NR.

BROWN, Air Vice-Marshal Michael John Douglas; retired; consulting engineer; *b* 9 May 1936; *s* of late N. H. B. Brown, AMIERE; *m* 1961, Audrey, *d* of late L. J. Woodward, Gidea Park, Essex; one *s*. *Educ:* Drayton Manor, W7; RAF Technical Coll., Henlow; Trinity Hall, Cambridge (MA); CEng; MRAeS; MRIN; AFIMA. Commnd RAF Technical Br., 1954; Cambridge Univ. Air Sqdn, 1954–57; RAF pilot trng, 1958–59; served in Bomber Comd, 1959–61; signals duties in Kenya (also assisted with formation of Kenya Air Force), 1961–64; advanced weapons course, 1965–66; Defence Operational Analysis Estabt, 1966–69; RAF Staff Coll., 1970; MoD Operational Requirements Staff, 1971–73; RAF Boulmer, 1973–75; USAF Air War Coll., 1975–76; HQ RAF Strike Comd, 1976–78; Comdr, RAF N Luffenham, 1978–80; rcds 1981; Dir, Air Guided Weapons, MoD (PE), 1983–86; Dir Gen., Strategic Electronic Systems, MoD (PE), 1986–91. *Address:* c/o Lloyds Bank, 7 Pall Mall, SW1Y 5NA. *Club:* Royal Air Force.

BROWN, Ven. Michael René Warneford; Archdeacon of Nottingham, 1960–77, now Archdeacon Emeritus; *b* 7 June 1915; *s* of late George and Irene Brown; *m* 1978, Marie Joyce Chaloner, *d* of late Walter Dawson, and of Sarah Dawson, Burbage, Leics; three step *s*. *Educ:* King's School, Rochester; St Peter's College, Oxford; St Stephen's House, Oxford (MA). Deacon 1941; priest, 1942; Asst Master, Christ's Hospital, 1939–43; Curate of West Grinstead, 1941–43. Chap. RNVR, 1943–46; chaplain and Dean of St Peter's College and Curate of St Mary the Virgin, Oxford, 1946; Lecturer, RN College, Greenwich, 1946–47; Librarian, 1948–50 and Fellow, 1948–52, of St Augustine's Coll., Canterbury; Priest-in-charge of Bekesbourne, 1948–50; Asst Secretary, CACTM, 1950–60. Examining Chaplain: to Bishop of Southwell, 1954–77; to Archbishop of Canterbury, 1959–60; Commissary to Bishop of Waikato, 1958–70; Hon. Officiating Chaplain, RM, Deal, Kent, 1987–. Member: Church of England Pensions Board, 1966–84; Church Commissioners' Redundant Churches Cttee, 1978–88; Chm., Redundant Churches' Uses Cttee in Canterbury Dio., 1980–89; Vice-Chm., Diocesan Adv. Cttee for the Care of Churches, 1980–; Church Commissioner, 1968–78. *Recreations:* antiquarian and aesthetic, especially English paintings and silver. *Address:* Faygate, 72 Liverpool Road, Walmer, Deal, Kent CT14 7LR. *T:* Deal (0304) 361326. *Club:* Athenæum.

BROWN, Michael Russell; MP (C) Brigg and Cleethorpes, since 1983 (Brigg and Scunthorpe, 1979–83); *b* 3 July 1951; *s* of Frederick Alfred Brown and Greta Mary Brown, OBE (*née* Russell). *Educ:* Andrew Cairns Sch., Sussex; Univ. of York (BA (Hons) Economics and Politics). Graduate Management Trainee, Barclays Bank Ltd, 1972–74; Lecturer and Tutor, Swinton Conservative Coll., 1974–75; part-time Asst to Michael Marshall, MP, 1975–76; Law Student, 1976–77, Member of Middle Temple; Personal Asst to Nicholas Winterton, MP, 1976–79. PPS to Hon. Douglas Hogg, Minister of State, DTI, 1989–90, FCO, 1990–. Mem., Energy Select Cttee, 1986–89; Sec., 1981–87, Vice-Chm., 1987–89, Conservative Parly N Ireland Cttee. *Recreations:* cricket, walking. *Address:* House of Commons, SW1. *Clubs:* Reform; Scunthorpe Conservative, Immingham Conservative (Pres.), Cleethorpes Conservative.

BROWN, Prof. Michael Stuart, MD; Regental Professor, University of Texas; Professor of Internal Medicine and Genetics, University of Texas Southwestern Medical School at Dallas, since 1974; *b* 13 April 1941; *s* of Harvey and Evelyn Brown; *m* 1964, Alice Lapin; two *d*. *Educ:* Univ. of Pennsylvania (AB 1962, MD 1966). Resident in Internal Medicine, Mass. Gen. Hosp., Boston, 1966–68; Research Scientist, NIH, Bethesda, 1968–71; Asst Prof., Univ. of Texas Southwestern Med. Sch. at Dallas, 1971–74; Associate Prof., 1974–76. For. Mem., Royal Soc., 1991. Lounsbery Award, 1979; Albert D. Lasker Award, 1985; (jtly) Nobel Prize in Medicine or Physiology for the discovery of receptors for Low Density Lipoproteins, a fundamental advance in the understanding of cholesterol metabolism, 1985. *Publications:* numerous papers to learned jls. *Address:* Department of Molecular Genetics, University of Texas Southwestern Medical School, 5323 Harry Hines Boulevard, Dallas, Texas 75235, USA.

BROWN, Prof. Morris Jonathan, FRCP; Professor of Clinical Pharmacology, Cambridge University, since 1985; Fellow of Gonville and Caius College, Cambridge, since 1989; *b* 18 Jan. 1951; *s* of Arnold and Irene Brown; *m* 1977, Diana Phylactou; three *d*. *Educ:* Harrow; Trinity College, Cambridge (MA, MD); MSc London. FRCP 1987. Lectr, Royal Postgraduate Medical School, 1979–82; Senior Fellow, MRC, 1982–85. *Publications:* Advanced Medicine 21, 1985; articles on adrenaline and cardiovascular disease. *Recreations:* violin playing, tennis. *Address:* 104 Grange Road, Cambridge CB3 9AA.

BROWN, Nicholas Hugh; MP (Lab) Newcastle upon Tyne East, since 1983; *b* 13 June 1950; *s* of late R. C. Brown and of G. K. Brown (*née* Tester). *Educ:* Swatenden Secondary Modern Sch.; Tunbridge Wells Tech. High Sch.; Manchester Univ. (BA 1971). Trade Union Officer, GMWU Northern Region, 1978–83. Mem., Newcastle upon Tyne City Council, 1980–. Opposition front-bench dep. spokesman on legal affairs, 1985–87; opposition front-bench treasury spokesman, 1987–. *Address:* 43 Cardigan Terrace, Heaton,

Newcastle upon Tyne. *T:* 091–265 4353. *Clubs:* Shieldfield Workingmen's, West Walker Social, Newcastle Labour (Newcastle).

BROWN, Patricia; *see* Brown, M. P.

BROWN, Patrick; *see* Brown, A. P.

BROWN, Peter; *see* Brown, A. P. G.

BROWN, Prof. Peter Robert Lamont, FBA 1971; FRHistS; Rollins Professor of History, Princeton University since 1986 (Visiting Professor, 1983–86); *b* 26 July 1935; *s* of James Lamont and Sheila Brown, Dublin; *m* 1st, 1959, Friedl Esther (*née* Löw-Beer); two *d*; 2nd, 1980, Patricia Ann Fortini; 3rd, 1989, Elizabeth Gilliam. *Educ:* Aravon Sch., Bray, Co. Wicklow, Ireland; Shrewsbury Sch.; New Coll., Oxford (MA). Harmsworth Senior Scholar, Merton Coll., Oxford and Prize Fellow, All Souls Coll., Oxford, 1956; Junior Research Fellow, 1963, Sen. Res. Fellow, 1970–73, All Souls Coll.; Fellow, All Souls Coll., 1956–75; Lectr in Medieval History, Merton Coll. Oxford, 1970–75; Special Lectr in late Roman and early Byzantine History, 1970–73, Reader, 1973–75, Univ. of Oxford; Prof. of History, Royal Holloway Coll., London Univ., 1975–78; Prof. of History and Classics, Univ. of Calif. at Berkeley, 1978–86. Fellow, Amer. Acad. of Arts and Scis, 1978. Hon. DTheol Fribourg, 1975; Hon. DHL Chicago, 1978. *Publications:* Augustine of Hippo: a biography, 1967; The World of Late Antiquity, 1971; Religion and Society in the Age of St Augustine, 1971; The Making of Late Antiquity, 1978; The Cult of the Saints: its rise and function in Latin Christianity, 1980; Society and the Holy in Late Antiquity, 1982; The Body and Society: men, women and sexual renunciation in Early Christianity, 1989. *Address:* Department of History, Princeton University, Princeton, NJ 08544, USA.

BROWN, Peter Wilfred Henry; Secretary of the British Academy, since 1983; *b* 4 June 1941; *s* of late Rev. Wilfred George Brown and Joan Margaret (*née* Adams); *m* 1968, Kathleen Clarke (marr. diss.); one *d*. *Educ:* Marlborough Coll.; Jesus Coll., Cambridge (Rustat Schol.). Assistant Master in Classics, Birkenhead Sch., 1963–66; Lectr in Classics, Fourah Bay Coll., Univ. of Sierra Leone, 1966–68; Asst Sec., School of Oriental and African Studies, Univ. of London, 1968–75; Dep. Sec., British Academy, 1975–83 (Actg Sec., 1976–77). Member: British Library Adv. Council, 1983–; Governing Body, GB/E Europe Centre, 1983–; Council: GB/USSR Assoc., 1983–; SSEES, Univ. of London, 1984–; Committee of Management: Inst. of Archaeol., Univ. of London, 1984–86; Inst. of Classical Studies, Univ. of London, 1984–; Warburg Inst., Univ. of London, 1987–; CNAA Cttee for Arts and Humanities, 1985–87; Cttee for Research, 1987–. Fellow, National Humanities Center, N Carolina, 1978. *Recreations:* travel on business, reading, listening to classical music, photography. *Address:* The British Academy, 20–21 Cornwall Terrace, NW1 4QP. *T:* 071–487 5966; 34 Victoria Road, NW6 6PX.

BROWN, Philip Anthony Russell, CB 1977; Director, National Provident Institution, 1985–90; *b* 18 May 1924; *e s* of late Sir William Brown, KCB, KCMG, CBE, and of Elizabeth Mabel (*née* Scott); *m* 1954, Eileen (*d* 1976), *d* of late J. Brennan; *m* 1976, Sarah Elizabeth Dean (*see* S. E. Brown). *Educ:* Malvern; King's Coll., Cambridge. Entered Home Civil Service, Board of Trade, 1947; Private Sec. to Perm. Sec., 1949; Principal, 1952; Private Sec. to Minister of State, 1953; Observer, Civil Service Selection Board, 1957; returned to BoT, 1959; Asst Sec., 1963; Head of Overseas Information Co-ordination Office, 1963; BoT, 1964; Under-Sec., 1969; Head of Establishments Div. 1, BoT, later DTI, 1969; Head of Cos Div., DTI, 1971; Dep. Sec., Dept of Trade, 1974–83. Head of External Relations, Lloyd's of London, 1983–85; Dir of Policy, IMRO, 1985–. Mem., Disciplinary Cttee, ICA, 1985–. Mem., London Adv. Bd, Salvation Army, 1982–. *Publication:* contrib. to Multinational Approaches: corporate insiders, 1976; articles in various jls. *Recreations:* reading, gardening, music. *Club:* United Oxford & Cambridge University.

BROWN, Ralph, RA 1972 (ARA 1968); ARCA 1955; sculptor; *b* 24 April 1928; *m* 1st, 1952, M. E. Taylor (marr. diss. 1963); one *s* one *d*; 2nd, 1964, Caroline Ann Clifton-Trigg; one *s*. *Educ:* Leeds Grammar School. Studied Royal College of Art, 1948–56; in Paris with Zadkine, 1954; travel scholarships to Greece 1955, Italy 1957. Tutor, RCA, 1958–64. Sculpture Prof., Salzburg Festival, Summer 1972. Work exhibited: John Moores, Liverpool (prizewinner 1957), Tate Gallery, Religious Theme 1958, Arnhem Internat. Open Air Sculpture, 1958; Middelheim Open Air Sculpture, 1959; Battersea Park Open Air Sculpture, 1960, 1963, 1966, 1977; Tokyo Biennale, 1963; British Sculptors '72, RA, 1972; Holland Park Open Air, 1975. One man Shows: Leicester Galls, 1961, 1963; Archer Gall., 1972; Salzburg 1972; Munich 1973; Montpellier 1974; Marseilles 1975; Oxford 1975; Taranman Gall., 1979; Browse & Darby Gall., 1979; Beaux Arts, Bath, 1983, 1987; Charles Foley Gall., Columbus, US, 1984; Lloyd Shine Gall., Chicago, 1984; Retrospective, Leeds City Art Gall. and Warwick Arts Centre, 1988. Work in Collections: Tate Gallery, Arts Council, Contemp. Art Society, Kröller-Müller, Gallery of NSW, Stuyvesant Foundation, City of Salzburg, Nat. Gallery of Wales, Allbright-Knox Gall., and at Leeds, Bristol, Norwich, Aberdeen, etc. *Address:* c/o Royal Academy of Arts, Piccadilly, W1V 0DS.

BROWN, Rt. Rev. Mgr Ralph, JCD; Vicar General, Diocese of Westminster, since 1976; *b* 30 June 1931; *s* of John William and Elizabeth Josephine Brown. *Educ:* Highgate Sch.; St Edmund's Coll., Old Hall Green, Herts; Pontifical Gregorian Univ., Rome. Licence in Canon Law, 1961, Doctorate, 1963. Commnd Middlesex Regt, 1949; Korea, 1950. Ordained priest, Westminster Cathedral, 1959; Vice-Chancellor, Vice Officialis, dio. of Westminster, 1964–69; Officialis, Westminster, 1969–76; Canonical Advr to British Mil. Ordinariate, 1987–. Pres., Canon Law Soc. of GB and Ireland, 1980–86, Sec., 1986–89. Apptd Papal Chamberlain, 1972; National Co-ordinator for Papal Visit to England and Wales, 1982; Prelate of Honour to HH the Pope, 1987; elected to Old Brotherhood of English Secular Clergy, 1987. Hon. Member: Canon Law Soc. of Aust. and NZ, 1975; Canadian Canon Law Soc., 1979; Canon Law Soc. of Amer., 1979. KHS 1985; KCHS 1991. *Publications:* Marriage Annulment, 1969, rev. edn 1990; (ed) Matrimonial Decisions of Great Britain and Ireland, 1969–; co-translator, The Code of Canon Law in English Translation, 1983; articles in Heythrop Jl, Studia Canonica, Theological Digest, The Jurist. *Address:* 42 Francis Street, SW1P 1QW. *T:* (office) 071–828 3255/5380. *Club:* Anglo-Belgian.

BROWN, Hon. Sir Ralph Kilner, Kt 1970; OBE (mil.) 1945; TD 1952; DL; a Judge of the High Court, Queen's Bench Division, 1970–84; a Judge of Employment Appeal Tribunal, 1976–84; *b* 28 Aug. 1909; *s* of Rev. A. E. Brown, CIE, MA, BSc; *m* 1943, Cynthia Rosemary Breffit; one *s* two *d*. *Educ:* Kingswood School; Trinity Hall, Cambridge (Squire Law Scholar; MA). Barrister, Middle Temple (Harmsworth Scholar; Bencher, 1964; Master Reader, 1982); Midland Circuit, 1934 and Northern Circuit, 1975. TA 1938; War Service, 1939–46; DAQMG NW Europe Plans; DAAG HQ53 (Welsh) Div.; AQMG (Planning), COSSAC; Col Q (Ops) and Brig. Q Staff HQ 21 Army Group (despatches, OBE); Hon. Col, TARO, 1952. QC 1958; Recorder of Lincoln, 1960–64; Recorder of Birmingham, 1964–65; Chairman, Warwicks QS, 1964–67 (Dep. Chm., 1954–64); a Judge of the Central Criminal Court, 1965–67; Recorder of Liverpool, and Judge of the Crown Court at Liverpool, 1967–69; Presiding Judge, N Circuit, 1970–75. Chairman, Mental Health Review Tribunal, Birmingham RHB Area, 1962–65. Contested (L) Oldbury and Halesowen, 1945 and 1950; South Bucks, 1959 and 1964; Pres., Birmingham Liberal Organisation, 1946–56; Pres., and Chm., W Midland Liberal Fedn, 1950–56; Mem., Liberal Party Exec., 1950–56. Pres., Birmingham Bn, Boys Bde, 1946–56; Mem., Exec., Boys Bde, 1950–55; Former Member: CCPR; Cttee of RNIB; Cttee of RNID. Former Mem., Governing Body, Kingswood Sch. DL Warwickshire, 1956. Guild of Freemen, City of London. *Publication:* The Office of Reader in the Middle Temple, 1982. *Recreations:* watching athletics (represented Cambridge University and Great Britain; British AAA Champion 440 yds hurdles, 1934); cricket, Rugby football. *Address:* 174 Defoe House, Barbican, EC2Y 8DN. *Clubs:* Naval and Military; Hawks (Cambridge).

See also A. G. K. Brown.

BROWN, Mrs Ray; *see* Vaughan, Elizabeth.

BROWN, Rev. Raymond; *see* Brown, Rev. Robert R.

BROWN, Rev. Raymond; Senior Minister, Victoria Baptist Church, Eastbourne, since 1987; *b* 3 March 1928; *s* of Frank Stevenson Brown and Florence Mansfield; *m* 1966, Christine Mary Smallman; one *s* one *d*. *Educ:* Spurgeon's Coll., London (BD, MTh); Fitzwilliam Coll., Cambridge (MA, BD, PhD). Minister: Zion Baptist Church, Cambridge, 1956–62; Upton Vale Baptist Church, Torquay, 1964–71; Tutor in Church History, Spurgeon's Coll., London, 1971–73, Principal 1973–86. Pres., Evangelical Alliance, 1975–76; Trustee, Dr Daniel Williams's Charity, 1980–; Nat. Chaplain, Girls' Brigade, 1986–90. *Publications:* Their Problems and Ours, 1969; Let's Read the Old Testament, 1971; Skilful Hands, 1972; Christ Above All: the message of Hebrews, 1982; Bible Study Commentary: 1 Timothy-James, 1983; The English Baptists of the Eighteenth Century, 1986; The Bible Book by Book, 1987; contribs to: What the Bible Says, 1974; Dictionary of Christian Spirituality, 1983; My Call to Preach, 1986; Encyclopedia of World Faiths, 1987; New Dictionary of Theology, 1988; The Empty Cross, 1989. *Recreations:* music, fell walking. *Address:* 35 Baldwin Avenue, Eastbourne, East Sussex BN21 1UL. *T:* Eastbourne (0323) 648291. *Club:* Penn.

BROWN, Prof. Robert, DSc London; FRS 1956; Regius Professor of Botany, Edinburgh University, 1958–77, now Emeritus Professor; *b* 29 July 1908; *s* of Thomas William and Ethel Minnie Brown; *m* 1940, Morna Doris Mactaggart. *Educ:* English School, Cairo; University of London. Assistant Lecturer in Botany, Manchester University, 1940–44; Lecturer in Botany, Bedford College, London, 1944–46; Reader in Plant Physiology, Leeds University, 1946–52; Professor of Botany, Cornell University, 1952–53; Director, Agricultural Research Council Unit of Plant Cell Physiology, 1953–58. *Publications:* various papers on plant physiology in the Annals of Botany, Proceedings of Royal Society and Journal of Experimental Botany. *Recreation:* gardening. *Address:* 5 Treble House Terrace, Blewbury, Didcot, Oxfordshire OX11 9NZ. *T:* Blewbury (0235) 850415.

BROWN, Robert; His Honour Judge Robert Brown; a Circuit Judge, since 1988; *b* 21 June 1943; *s* of Robert and Mary Brown; *m* 1st, 1964, Susan (marr. diss. 1971); one *s* one *d*; 2nd, 1973, Carole; two step *s*. *Educ:* Arnold Sch., Blackpool; Downing Coll., Cambridge (Exhibnr; BA, LLB). Called to Bar, Inner Temple, 1968 (Major Schol.); a Recorder, 1983–88. *Recreation:* golf. *Address:* (chambers) 2 Old Bank Street, Manchester. *T:* 061–832 3781. *Club:* Royal Lytham St Annes Golf.

BROWN, Robert Burnett; Under Secretary, Corporate Management Division, Department of Social Security, since 1989; *b* 10 Aug. 1942; *s* of late David Brown and of Isabella Dow; *m* 1972, Anne Boschetti. *Educ:* Kirkcaldy High Sch.; Edinburgh Univ. (1st cl. Hons BSc Chemistry). Min. of Social Security, 1967; DHSS, 1971–83; Cabinet Office and HM Treasury, 1983–87; DHSS and DSS, 1987–89. *Recreations:* jazz, rock and roll, football, Greece. *Address:* Department of Social Security, The Adelphi, 1–11 John Adam Street, WC1N 6NT.

BROWN, Sir Robert C.; *see* Crichton-Brown.

BROWN, Robert Crofton; DL; Member, Newcastle City Council, since 1988; *b* 16 May 1921; *m* 1945, Marjorie Hogg, Slaithwaite, Yorks; one *s* one *d*. *Educ:* Denton Road Elementary School; Atkinson Road Technical School; Rutherford Coll. Apprenticed plumber and gasfitter, Newcastle & Gateshead Gas Co., 1937. War Service, 1942–46. Plumber from 1946; Inspector, 1949; in service of Northern Gas Board until 1966. Secretary of Constituency Labour Party and Agent to MP for 16 years. MP (Lab): Newcastle upon Tyne West, 1966–83; Newcastle upon Tyne North, 1983–87. Parly Sec., Ministry of Transport, 1968–70; Parly Under-Sec., Social Security, March-Sept. 1974; Parly Under-Sec. of State for Defence for the Army, 1974–79. Vice-Chairman: Trade Union Gp of MPs, 1970–74; PLP Transport Gp, 1970–74; PLP Defence Gp, 1981–83; Member: Select Cttee on Nationalised Inds, 1966–68; Speakers Conf., 1966–68. Member Newcastle Co. Borough Council (Chief Whip, Lab. Gp), retd 1968. DL Tyne and Wear 1988. *Recreations:* walking, reading, gardening, watching Association football. *Address:* 1 Newsham Close, The Boltons, North Walbottle, Newcastle upon Tyne NE5 1QD. *T:* 091–267 2199.

BROWN, Robert Glencairn; Director (formerly Deputy Chief Officer), Housing Corporation, since 1986; *b* 19 July 1930; *s* of William and Marion Brown (*née* Cockburn); *m* 1957, Florence May Stalker; two *s*. *Educ:* Hillhead High Sch., Glasgow. Commnd, RCS, 1949–51. Forestry Commn, 1947–68; seconded to CS Pay Res. Unit, 1963–64 and to Min. of Land and Natural Resources, 1964–68; Min. of Housing and Local Govt, later DoE, 1968–71; seconded to Nat. Whitley Council, Staff Side, 1969; Asst Dir, Countryside Commn, 1971–77; Department of the Environment: Asst Sec., 1977–83; Under Sec., 1983–86. *Recreations:* gardening, ski-ing, reading. *Address:* 2 The Squirrels, Pinner, Middx HA5 3BD. *T:* 081–866 8713. *Club:* Ski Club of Great Britain.

BROWN, Prof. Robert Hanbury, AC 1986; FRS 1960; Professor of Physics (Astronomy), in the University of Sydney, 1964–81, now Emeritus Professor; *b* 31 Aug. 1916; *s* of Colonel Basil Hanbury Brown and Joyce Blaker; *m* 1952, Hilda Heather Chesterman; two *s* one *d*. *Educ:* Tonbridge School; Brighton Technical College; City and Guilds College, London. BSc (Eng), London (external), 1935; DIC, 1936; DSc Manchester, 1960. MIEE, 1938. Air Ministry, Bawdsey Research Station, working on radar, 1936–42; British Air Commission, Washington, DC, 1942–45; Principal Scientific Officer, Ministry of Supply, 1945–47; ICI Research Fellow of Manchester University, 1949; Professor of Radio-Astronomy in the University of Manchester, 1960–63. Pres., Internat. Astronomical Union, 1982–85. ARAS 1986; FAA 1967. Hon. Mem., Aust. Optical Soc., 1987; Hon. FNA 1975; Hon. FASc 1975; Hon. Fellow, Royal Astronomical Soc. of Canada, Astronomical Soc. of India, 1987. Hon. DSc: Sydney, 1984; Monash, 1984. Holweck Prize, 1959; Eddington Medal, 1968; Lyle Medal, 1971; Britannica Australia Award, 1971; Hughes Medal, 1971; Michelson Medal, Franklin Inst., 1982; ANZAAS Medal, 1987. *Publications:* The Exploration of Space by Radio, 1957; The Intensity Interferometer, 1974; Man and the Stars, 1978; Photons, Galaxies and Stars, 1985; Wisdom of Science,

1986; publications in Physical and Astronomical Journals. *Address:* White Cottage, Penton Mewsey, Andover, Hants SP11 0RQ.

BROWN, Rev. (Robert) Raymond; QHC 1990; Principal Chaplain, Church of Scotland and Free Churches, Royal Air Force, since 1990 (Assistant Principal Chaplain, 1987–90); *b* 24 March 1936; *s* of Robert Brown and Elsie (*née* Dudson); *m* 1959, Barbara (*née* Johnson); three *s* one *d. Educ:* Stockport Sch.; Univ. of Leeds (BA Hons Philosophy); Univ. of Manchester (BD Hons Theology). Ordained Methodist minister, 1959; Minister: Luton Industrial Coll. and Mission, 1959–64; Heald Green and Handforth, 1964–67; commnd RAF Chaplain, 1967; Vice Principal, RAF Chaplains' Sch., 1978–83; Comd Chaplain, RAF Germany, 1983–87. *Recreations:* music and drama (amateur singer and actor), writing for pleasure. *Address:* Trinity Cottage, 6 Church Terrace, Melton Mowbray, Leics LE13 0PW. *T:* Melton Mowbray (0664) 61179. *Club:* Royal Air Force.

BROWN, Robert Ross Buchanan, CBE 1968; CEng, FIEE; Chairman, Southern Electricity Board, 1954–74; *b* 15 July 1909; 2nd *s* of Robert and Rhoda Brown, Sydney, Australia; *m* 1940, Ruth Sarah Aird; one *s* two *d. Educ:* The King's School, Sydney; Sydney University; Cambridge University. BA (Cantab.), BSc. Deputy Gen. Manager, Wessex Electricity Co., 1938. Captain 4th County of London Yeomanry, 1940–45. Gen. Manager, Wessex Electricity Co., 1945; Deputy Chairman, Southern Electricity Board, 1948. *Recreations:* gardening, golf. *Address:* Mumbery Lodge, School Hill, Wargrave, Reading, Berks RG10 8DY.

BROWN, Ven. Robert Saville; Archdeacon of Bedford, 1974–79, Archdeacon Emeritus since 1979; *b* 12 Sept. 1914; *s* of John Harold Brown and Frances May Brown; *m* 1947, Charlotte, *d* of late Percy John and Edith Furber; one *s. Educ:* Bedford Modern Sch.; Selwyn Coll., Cambridge (MA). Curate: Gt Berkhamsted, 1940–44; St Mary's, Hitchin, 1944–47; Vicar, Wonersh, 1947–53; Rector, Gt Berkhamsted, 1953–69; Canon of St Albans Cath., 1965; Vicar of St Paul's, Bedford, 1969–74; Priest-in-Charge of Old Warden, 1974–79. *Recreations:* reading, travel, chess. *Address:* The Rowans, 29 The Rise, Amersham, Bucks HP7 9AG. *T:* Amersham (0494) 728376.

See also F. R. Furber.

BROWN, Roland George MacCormack; Legal Adviser, Technical Assistance Group, Commonwealth Secretariat, 1975–87; *b* 27 Dec. 1924; 2nd *s* of late Oliver and of Mona Brown; *m* 1964, Irene Constance, *d* of Rev. Claude Coltman; two *s* one *d. Educ:* Ampleforth College; Trinity College, Cambridge. Called to the Bar, Gray's Inn, Nov. 1949. Practised at the Bar, Nov. 1949–May 1961; Attorney-Gen., Tanganyika, later Tanzania, 1961–65; Legal Consultant to Govt of Tanzania, 1965–72; Fellow, Inst. of Develt Studies, Sussex Univ., 1973–75; on secondment as Special Adviser to Sec. of State for Trade, 1974. *Publication:* (with Richard O'Sullivan, QC) The Law of Defamation. *Recreation:* swimming.

BROWN, Rt. Rev. Ronald; *see* Birkenhead, Bishop Suffragan of.

BROWN, Ronald, (Ron); MP (Lab) Edinburgh Leith, since 1979; *b* Edinburgh, 1940; *s* of James Brown and Margaret McLaren; *m* 1963, May Smart; two *s. Educ:* Pennywell Primary Sch., Edinburgh; Ainslie Park High Sch., Edinburgh; Bristo Technical Inst., Edinburgh. National Service, Royal Signals. Five yrs engrg apprenticeship with Bruce Peebles and Co. Ltd, East Pilton, Edinburgh. Chm., Pilton Br., AUEW; formerly: Chm. Works Cttee, Edinburgh Dist of SSEB; Convenor of Shop Stewards, Parsons Peebles Ltd, Edinburgh. Formerly Councillor for Central Leith, Edinburgh Town Council; Regional Councillor for Royston/Granton, Lothian Reg. Council, 1974–79. Member: Lothian and Borders Fire Bd, 1974–79; Central Scotland Water Develt Bd, 1974–79. *Address:* c/o House of Commons, SW1A 0AA.

BROWN, Ronald William; JP; Deputy Director General, Federation of Master Builders, since 1987 (Director of Industrial Relations, 1984); *b* 7 Sept. 1921; *s* of George Brown; *m* 1944, Mary Munn; one *s* two *d. Educ:* Elementary School, South London; Borough Polytechnic. Sen. Lectr in Electrical Engineering, Principal of Industrial Training Sch. Leader, Camberwell Borough Council, 1956; Alderman and Leader, London Bor. of Southwark, 1964. MP Shoreditch and Finsbury, 1964–74, Hackney South and Shoreditch, 1974–83 (Lab, 1964–81, SDP, 1981–83); Asst Govt Whip, 1966–67; contested (SDP) Hackney South and Shoreditch, 1983. Member: Council of Europe Assembly and WEU, 1965–76; European Parlt, 1977–79. Chm., Energy Commn, Rapporteur on Science, Technology and Aerospace questions; Parly Advr to Furniture, Timber and Allied Trades Union, 1967–81. Member: Council of Europe, 1979–83; WEU, 1979–83. Mem. Bldg Cttee, Construction ITB, 1985–. FBIM. Assoc. Mem., Inst. of Engineering Designers. JP Co. London, 1961. *Address:* 45 Innings Drive, Pevensey Bay, E Sussex BN24 6BH.

BROWN, Ronald William; Deputy Legal Adviser and Solicitor to Ministry of Agriculture, Fisheries and Food, to Forestry Commission and to (EEC) Intervention Board for Agricultural Produce, 1974–82; *b* 21 April 1917; *o s* of late William Nicol Brown and Eleanor Brown (*née* Dobson); *m* 1958, Elsie Joyce (*d* 1983), *er d* of late Sir Norman Guttery, KBE, CB and Lady Guttery (*née* Crankshaw); two *s. Educ:* Dover Coll.; Corpus Christi Coll., Cambridge (MA). War service, 1939–45, King's Own Royal Regt (Lancaster), France, W Desert, Burma (Chindits) (Major). Called to Bar, Gray's Inn, 1946. Entered Legal Dept, Min. of Agric. and Fisheries, 1948; Asst Solicitor, MAFF, 1970. *Address:* 18 Tracery, Park Road, Banstead, Surrey SM7 3DD. *T:* Burgh Heath (0737) 358569. *Club:* Royal Automobile.

BROWN, Roy Dudley; Director, Association of West European Shipbuilders, 1977–83; *b* 5 Aug. 1916; *y s* of late Alexander and Jessie Brown; *m* 1941, Maria Margaret Barry McGhee; one *s* one *d. Educ:* Robert Gordon's Coll., Aberdeen; Aberdeen Univ. (MA 1935, LLB 1937). In private law practice, Glasgow, 1937–38; joined Shipbldg Conf., London, 1938; War Service, RN; Jt Sec. on amalgamation of Shipbldg Conf., Shipbldg Employers Fedn, and Dry Dock Owners and Repairers Central Council into Shipbuilders and Repairers National Assoc., 1967; Dep. Dir, 1973, until dissolution of Assoc. on nationalization, 1977. Sec., Shipbldg Corp. Ltd, 1943–77. Liveryman, Worshipful Co. of Shipwrights. *Recreations:* golf, wine, gardening. *Address:* 109 Upper Selsdon Road, Sanderstead, Surrey CR2 0DP. *T:* 081–657 7144.

BROWN, Rear-Adm. Roy S. F.; *see* Foster-Brown.

BROWN, Russell; *see* Brown, J. R.

BROWN, Sarah Elizabeth; Head of Companies Division, Department of Trade and Industry, since 1986; *b* 30 Dec. 1943; *d* of Sir Maurice Dean, KCB, KCMG and Anne (*née* Gibson); *m* 1976, Philip A. R. Brown, *qv. Educ:* St Paul's Girls' Sch.; Newnham Coll., Cambridge (BA Nat. Sci.). Joined BoT as Asst Principal, 1965; Private Sec. to Second Perm. Sec., 1968; Principal, 1970; Asst. Sec., 1978; Sec. to Crown Agents Tribunal, 1978–82; Personnel Management Div., 1982–84; Head of Financial Services Bill team, 1984–86; Under Sec., 1986. *Recreations:* travel, theatre, gardening. *Address:* c/o Department of Trade and Industry, 10–18 Victoria Street, SW1H 0NN.

BROWN, Hon. Sir Simon Denis, Kt 1984; **Hon. Mr Justice Simon Brown;** a Judge of the High Court of Justice, Queen's Bench Division, since 1984; *b* 9 April 1937; *s* of late Denis Baer Brown and of Edna Elizabeth (*née* Abrahams); *m* 1963, Jennifer Buddicom; two *s* one *d. Educ:* Stowe Sch.; Worcester Coll., Oxford (law degree). Commnd 2nd Lt RA, 1955–57. Called to the Bar, Middle Temple, 1961 (Harmsworth Schol.); Master of the Bench, Hon. Soc. of Middle Temple, 1980–; a Recorder, 1979–84; First Jun. Treasury Counsel, Common Law, 1979–84. Pres., Security Service (Complaints) Tribunal, 1989–. *Recreations:* golf, skiing, theatre, fishing, reading. *Address:* Royal Courts of Justice, Strand, WC2. *Clubs:* Denham Golf; Lindrick Golf.

BROWN, Sir Stanley; *see* Brown, Sir F. H. S.

BROWN, Sir Stephen; *see* Brown, Sir A. J. S.

BROWN, Rt. Hon. Sir Stephen, Kt 1975; PC 1983; a Lord Justice of Appeal, 1983–88; President of the Family Division, since 1988; *b* 3 Oct. 1924; *s* of Wilfrid Brown and Nora Elizabeth Brown, Longdon Green, Staffordshire; *m* 1951, Patricia Ann, *d* of Richard Good, Tenbury Wells, Worcs; two *s* (twins) three *d. Educ:* Malvern College; Queens' College, Cambridge (Hon. Fellow, 1984). Served RNVR (Lieut), 1943–46. Barrister, Inner Temple, 1949; Bencher, 1974. Dep. Chairman, Staffs QS, 1963–71; Recorder of West Bromwich, 1965–71; QC 1966; a Recorder, and Honorary Recorder of West Bromwich, 1972–75; a Judge of the High Court, Family Div., 1975–77, QBD, 1977–83; Presiding Judge, Midland and Oxford Circuit, 1977–81. Member: Parole Board, England and Wales, 1967–71; Butler Cttee on mentally abnormal offenders, 1972–75; Adv. Council on Penal System, 1977; Chairman: Adv. Cttee on Conscientious Objectors, 1971–75; Council of Malvern Coll., 1976–. Hon. LLD Birmingham, 1985. *Recreation:* sailing. *Address:* Royal Courts of Justice, Strand, WC2A 2LL. *Clubs:* Garrick; Birmingham (Birmingham).

BROWN, Stephen David Reid; HM Diplomatic Service; Consul-General, Melbourne, since 1989; *b* 26 Dec. 1945; *s* of Albert Senior Brown and Edna Brown; *m* 1965, Pamela Gaunt; one *s* one *d. Educ:* RMA Sandhurst; Univ. of Sussex (BA Hons). Served HM Forces, RA, 1966–76; FCO, 1976–77; 1st Sec., Nicosia, 1977–80; 1st Sec. (Commercial), Paris, 1980–85; FCO, 1985–89; DTI, 1989. *Recreations:* reading, swimming, ski-ing, sailing. *Address:* c/o Foreign and Commonwealth Office, King Charles Street, SW1A 2AH. *Clubs:* Melbourne, Royal Melbourne Yacht Squadron (Melbourne).

BROWN, Stuart Christopher; QC 1991; *b* 4 Sept. 1950; *s* of late Geoffrey Howard Brown and of Olive Baum; *m* 1973, Imogen Lucas; two *d. Educ:* Acklam High Sch., Middlesbrough; Worcester Coll., Oxford (BA, BCL). Called to the Bar, Inner Temple, 1974. Practises on NE Circuit; an Asst Recorder, 1988–. *Recreations:* family, wind-surfing. *Address:* Midwood, 25 Hodgson Crescent, Leeds LS17 8PG; Pearl Chambers, 22 East Parade, Leeds LS1 5BY.

BROWN, Sir Thomas, Kt 1974; Chairman, Eastern Health and Social Services Board, Northern Ireland (formerly NI Hospitals Authority), 1967–84, retired; *b* 11 Oct. 1915; *s* of Ephraim Hugh and Elizabeth Brown; *m* 1988, Dr Eleanor A. Thompson. *Educ:* Royal Belfast Academical Institution. Admitted Solicitor, 1938. Mem., Royal Commn on NHS, 1976–79. *Recreation:* boating. *Address:* Westgate, Portaferry, Co. Down, Northern Ireland BT22 1PF. *T:* Portaferry (02477) 28309.

BROWN, Thomas Walter Falconer, CBE 1958; Consultant in Marine Engineering; *b* 10 May 1901; *s* of Walter Falconer Brown, MB, ChB, DPH, and Catherine Edith (*née* McGhie); *m* 1947, Lucy Mason (*née* Dickie); one *s* one *d. Educ:* Ayr Academy; Glasgow University; Harvard University. BSc (special dist. in Nat. Philos.), 1921; DSc (Glas.), 1927; SM (Harvard), 1928; Assoc. of Royal Technical College, Glasgow, 1922. Asst General Manager, Alex Stephen & Sons Ltd, Linthouse, 1928–35; Technical Manager, R. & W. Hawthorn Leslie & Co. Ltd, Newcastle upon Tyne, 1935–44; Director of Parsons and Marine Engineering Turbine Research and Development Assoc., Wallsend, 1944–62; Director of Marine Engineering Research (BSRA), Wallsend Research Station, 1962–66. Liveryman, Worshipful Co. of Shipwrights, Freedom City of London, 1946. Eng Lieut, and Eng Lt-Comdr RNVR, Clyde Div., 1924–36. De Laval Gold Medal, Sweden, 1957. *Publications:* various technical papers in: Trans Instn Mech. Engineers, Inst. Marine Engineers, NE Coast Instn of Engineers & Shipbuilders, etc. *Recreations:* model-making and gardening. *Address:* 12 The Dene, Wylam, Northumberland NE41 8JB. *T:* Wylam (0661) 2228.

BROWN, Tina, (Christina Hambley Brown); Editor in Chief, Vanity Fair Magazine, since 1984; *b* 21 Nov. 1953; *d* of Bettina Iris Mary Kohr Brown and George Hamley Brown; *m* 1981, Harold Matthew Evans, *qv*; one *s* one *d. Educ:* Univ. of Oxford (MA). Columnist for Punch, 1978; Editor, Tatler, 1979–83. Catherine Pakenham Prize, Most Promising Female Journalist (Sunday Times), 1973; Young Journalist of the Year, 1978. *Plays:* Under the Bamboo Tree (Sunday Times Drama Award), 1973; Happy Yellow, 1977. *Publications:* Loose Talk, 1979; Life as a Party, 1983. *Address:* Vanity Fair Magazine, 350 Madison Avenue, New York, NY 10017, USA. *T:* (212) 880–7204.

BROWN, Vivian; *see* Brown, H. V. B.

BROWN, William, CBE 1971; Chairman, Scottish Television plc, since 1991; *b* 24 June 1929; *s* of Robert C. Brown, Ayr; *m* 1955, Nancy Jennifer, 3rd *d* of Prof. George Hunter, Edmonton, Alta; one *s* three *d. Educ:* Ayr Academy; Edinburgh University. Lieut, RA, 1950–52. Scottish Television Ltd: London Sales Manager, 1958; Sales Dir, 1961; Dep. Man. Dir, 1963; Man. Dir, 1966–90; Dep. Chm., 1974–91. Chm., Scottish Amicable Life Assurance Soc., 1989– (Dir, 1981–); Director: ITN, 1972–77, 1987–; Radio Clyde Ltd, 1973–90; Channel Four Co. Ltd, 1980–84. Dir, Scottish Opera Theatre Royal Ltd, 1974–91. Mem., Royal Commn on Legal Services in Scotland, 1976–80. Chm., Council, Independent Television Cos Assoc., 1978–80. Trustee, Nat. Museums of Scotland, 1991–. Dr *hc* Edinburgh. Ted Willis Award, (special award given in conjunction with Pye TV Awards), 1982; Gold Medal, RTS, 1984. *Recreations:* gardening, golf, films. *Address:* Scottish Television plc, Cowcaddens, Glasgow G2 3PR. *T:* 041–332 9999. *Clubs:* Caledonian; Prestwick Golf, Royal and Ancient Golf (St Andrews).

BROWN, Prof. William Arthur; Montague Burton Professor of Industrial Relations, University of Cambridge, since 1985; Fellow, Wolfson College, Cambridge, since 1985; *b* 22 April 1945; *s* of Prof. Arthur Joseph Brown, *qv. Educ:* Leeds Grammar Sch.; Wadham Coll., Oxford (BA Hons). Economic Asst, NBPI, 1966–68; Res. Associate, Univ. of Warwick, 1968–70; SSRC's Industrial Relations Research Unit, University of Warwick: Res. Fellow, 1970–79; Dep. Dir, 1979–81; Dir, 1981–85. *Publications:* Piecework Bargaining, 1973; The Changing Contours of British Industrial Relations, 1981; articles in industrial relations jls, etc. *Recreations:* walking, gardening. *Address:* Wolfson College, Cambridge CB3 9BB.

BROWN, Sir William B. P.; *see* Pigott-Brown.

BROWN, William Charles Langdon, OBE 1982; Deputy Group Chief Executive, Standard Chartered PLC, since 1988 (Director, since 1987); Deputy Chairman, Standard

Chartered Bank, since 1989; *b* 9 Sept. 1931; *s* of Charles Leonard Brown and Kathleen May Tizzard; *m* 1959, Nachiko Sagawa; one *s* two *d*. *Educ:* John Ruskin Sch., Croydon; Ashbourne Grammar Sch., Derbyshire. Joined Westminster Bank, 1947; transf. to Standard Chartered Bank (formerly Chartered Bank of India, Australia and China, the predecessor of Chartered Bank), 1954; Standard Chartered Bank: Tokyo, 1954–59; Bangkok, 1959–62; Hong Kong, 1962–69; Man., Singapore, 1969–72; Country Man., Bangkok, 1972–75; Area Gen. Man., Hong Kong, 1975–87. Various additional positions in Hong Kong, 1975–87, include: MLC Hong Kong; Chm., Hong Kong Export Credit Insce Corp. Adv. Bd; Mem. Council, Hong Kong Trade Develt Council; Chm., Hong Kong Assoc. of Banks; Director: Mass Railway Corp.; Wing Lung Bank Ltd. FCIB 1984; FInstD 1988. Hon. DSSc Chinese Univ. of Hong Kong, 1987. *Recreations:* mountain walking, snow ski-ing, yoga, philately, photography, caligraphy, classical music. *Address:* Appleshaw, 11 Central Avenue, Findon Valley, Worthing, Sussex BN14 0DA. *T:* Worthing (0903) 873175; Flat 4, 19 Inverness Terrace, Kensington Gardens, W2 3TJ. *T:* 071–243 1332. *Clubs:* Oriental, Royal Automobile; Hong Kong, Shek-O, Ladies Recreation (Hong Kong).

BROWN, Dr William Christopher, OBE 1966; RDI 1977; Founder, Brown Beech & Associates, 1987; *b* 16 Sept. 1928; *s* of William Edward Brown and Margaret Eliza Brown; *m* 1964, Celia Hermione Emmett. *Educ:* Monmouth Sch.; University Coll., Southampton (BScEng); Imperial Coll. of Science and Technol., London (DIC); FIC 1987. Partner, Freeman, Fox & Partners, 1970–85. Principal designer for major bridges, incl.: Volta River, 1956; Forth Road, 1964; Severn and Wye, 1966; Auckland Harbour, 1969; Erskine, 1971; Bosporus, 1973; Avonmouth, 1975; Humber, 1981; Bosporus 2, 1988. Holds patents on new concepts for long-span bridges. Designer for radio telescopes in Australia and Canada, and for other special structures. Master, Faculty of RDI, 1983–85. Hon. FRIBA 1978. McRobert Award, 1970; UK and European steel design awards, 1968, 1971, 1976. *Publications:* technical papers for engrg instns in UK and abroad. *Recreations:* archaeology, photography, motoring. *Address:* 1 Allen Mansions, Allen Street, W8 6UY. *T:* 071–937 6550. *Club:* Royal Over-Seas League.

BROWN, William Eden T.; *see* Tatton Brown.

BROWN, W(illiam) Glanville, TD; Barrister-at-Law; *b* 19 July 1907; *s* of late Cecil George Brown, formerly Town Clerk of Cardiff, and late Edith Tyndale Brown; *m* 1st, 1935, Theresa Margaret Mary Harrison (decd); one *s*; 2nd, 1948, Margaret Isabel Dilks, JP (*d* 1988), *o d* of late Thomas Bruce Dilks, Bridgwater. *Educ:* Llandaff Cathedral School; Magdalen College School and Magdalen College, Oxford; in France, Germany and Italy. Called to Bar, Middle Temple, 1932. Contested (L) Cardiff Central, 1935, St Albans, 1964. Served War of 1939–45, in Army (TA), Aug. 1939–Dec. 1945; attached to Intelligence Corps; served overseas 3½ years in E Africa Command, Middle East and North-West Europe. Junior Prosecutor for UK Internat. Military Tribunal for the Far East, Tokyo, 1946–48; Member: the National Arbitration Tribunal, 1949–51; Industrial Disputes Tribunal, 1959; Deputy-Chairman of various Wages Councils, 1950–64; Joint Legal Editor of English Translation of Common Market Documents for Foreign Office, 1962–63; Lectr in Germany on behalf of HM Embassy, Bonn, 1965–73. Mem., Mental Health Review Tribunal for NE Metropolitan RHB Area, 1960–79. Life Mem., RIIA. Fellow, Inst. of Linguists. *Publication:* Translation of Brunschweig's French Colonialism, 1871–1914, Myths and Realities. *Recreations:* walking, reading, watching cricket, travel. *Address:* 55 Laurel Way, Totteridge, N20. *T:* 081–445 5312. *Club:* National Liberal.

BROWN, Rev. William Martyn; *b* 12 July 1914; *s* of Edward Brown, artist; *m* 1939, Elizabeth Lucy Hill; one adopted *s*. *Educ:* Bedford School; Pembroke College, Cambridge (Scholar). 1st Class Honours in Modern Languages, 1936, MA 1947. Assistant Master, Wellington College, 1936–47; Housemaster 1943–47; Headmaster: The King's School, Ely, 1947–55; Bedford School, 1955–75. Commissioner of the Peace, 1954. Ordained 1976; Priest-in-charge, Field Dalling and Saxlingham, 1977–84; RD of Holt, 1984–88. *Recreation:* watercolour painting. *Address:* Lodge Cottage, Field Dalling, Holt, Norfolk NR25 7AS. *T:* Binham (0328) 830403.

BROWNE, family name of **Baron Craigton, Baron Kilmaine, Baron Oranmore, Marquess of Sligo.**

BROWNE, Andrew Harold; full-time Chairman of Industrial Tribunals, Nottingham Region, since 1983; *b* 2 Dec. 1923; *s* of late Harold and Ada Caroline Browne; *m* 1951, Jocelyn Mary Vade Ashmead; two *s* one *d*. *Educ:* Repton; Trinity Hall, Cambridge (MA). ACIArb 1983. Served Royal Navy, 1942–46; Lieut RNVR. Admitted Solicitor, 1950; Partner in firm of Wells & Hind, Nottingham, 1952–83. Dep. Clerk of the Peace, Nottingham City Sessions, 1951–55. Chairman, National Insurance Local Tribunal, Nottingham, 1965–83; Member, E Midland Rent Assessment Panel, 1966–83 (Vice-Pres., 1972–83). Part-time Chm. of Industrial Tribunals, 1975. Lay Chm., Bingham Deanery Synod, 1987. Chm., Reserve Forces Reinstatement Cttee, 1991. *Recreations:* rural England, organ music. *Address:* The House in the Garden, Elton, near Nottingham NG13 9LA. *T:* Whatton (0949) 50419. *Club:* Aula.

BROWNE, Anthony Arthur Duncan M.; *see* Montague Browne.

BROWNE, Bernard Peter Francis K.; *see* Kenworthy-Browne.

BROWNE, Air Cdre Charles Duncan Alfred, CB 1971; DFC 1944; FBIM; RAF, retired; *b* 8 July 1922; *m* 1946, Una Felicité Leader; one *s*. War of 1939–45: served Western Desert, Italy, Corsica and S France in Hurricane and Spitfire Sqdns; post war service in Home, Flying Training, Bomber and Strike Commands; MoD; CO, RAF Brüggen, Germany, 1966–68; Comdt, Aeroplane and Armament Exp. Estab., 1968–71; Air Officer i/c Central Tactics and Trials Orgn, 1971–72. *Club:* Royal Air Force.

BROWNE, Rt. Rev. Denis George; *see* Auckland (NZ), Bishop of, (RC).

BROWNE, Desmond John Michael; QC 1990; *b* 5 April 1947; *s* of Sir Denis John Browne, KCVO, FRCS and of Lady Moyra Browne, *qv*; *m* 1973, Jennifer Mary Wilmore; two *d*. *Educ:* Eton College; New College, Oxford (Scholar). Called to the Bar, Gray's Inn, 1969. *Recreations:* Australiana, 20th-century British prints, Sussex Downs. *Address:* 10 South Square, Gray's Inn, WC1R 5EU. *T:* 071–242 2902. *Clubs:* Brooks's, Beefsteak.

BROWNE, (Edward) Michael (Andrew); QC 1970; *b* 29 Nov. 1910; *yr s* of Edward Granville Browne, Fellow of Pembroke Coll., Cambridge, and Alice Caroline Browne (*née* Blackburne Daniell); *m* 1937, Anna Florence Augusta, *d* of James Little Luddington; two *d*. *Educ:* Eton; Pembroke Coll., Cambridge (Scholar); 1st class History Tripos, 1932; MA. Barrister, Inner Temple, 1934, *ad eundem* Lincoln's Inn. Bencher, Inner Temple, 1964. Practiced (mainly in Chancery Div.) until retirement in 1984. FCIArb. Served War of 1939–45: RA (anti aircraft) and GS, War Office (finally GSO3, Capt.). *Address:* 19 Wallgrave Road, SW5 0RF. *T:* 071–373 3055. *Club:* Athenæum.

BROWNE, Gillian Brenda B.; *see* Babington-Browne.

BROWNE, John Ernest Douglas Delavalette; MP (C) Winchester, since 1979; Managing Director, Falcon Finance Management Ltd, since 1978; *b* Hampshire, 17 Oct. 1938; *s* of Col Ernest Coigny Delavalette Browne, OBE, and late Victoria Mary Eugene (*née* Douglas); *m* 1st, 1965, Elizabeth Jeannette Marguerite Garthwaite (marr. diss.); 2nd, 1986, Elaine Boylen (*née* Schmid). *Educ:* Malvern; RMA Sandhurst (Gwynn-Jones Schol.); Cranfield Inst. of Technology (MSc); Harvard Business Sch. (MBA). Served Grenadier Guards, British Guiana (Battalion Pilot), Cyprus, BAOR, 1959–67; Captain 1963; TA, Grenadier Guards (Volunteers), 1981–, Major 1985. Associate, Morgan Stanley & Co., New York, 1969–72; Pember & Boyle, 1972–74; Director: Middle East Operations, European Banking Co., 1974–78; Worms Investments, 1981–83; Scansat (Broadcasting) Ltd, 1988–; Internat. Bd, World Paper (Boston), 1988–; Tijari Finance Ltd, 1989–; Adviser: Barclays Bank Ltd, 1978–84; Trustees Household Div., 1979–83. Dir, Churchill Private Clinic, 1980–. Mem., H of C Treasury Select Cttee, 1982–87; Secretary: Conservative Finance Cttee, 1982–84; Conservative Defence Cttee, 1982–83; Chm., Conservative Smaller Business Cttee, 1984–87; UK deleg. to N Atlantic Assembly, 1986– (rapporteur on human rights, 1989–). Councillor (C), Westminster Council, 1974–78; Mem., NFU. Patron: Winchester Preservation Trust, 1980–; Winchester Cadets Assoc., 1980–. Trustee, Winnall Community Assoc., 1981–. Pres., Winchester Gp for Disabled People, 1982–. Mem. Court, Univ. of Southampton, 1979–; Governor, Malvern Coll. Liveryman, Goldsmiths' Co., 1982–; OStJ. Interests include: economics, gold and internat. monetary affairs, defence, broadcasting. *Publications:* various articles on finance, gold (A New European Currency—The Karl, ₭, 1972), defence, Middle East, Soviet leadership. *Recreations:* riding, skiing, sailing, shooting, golf, tennis. *Address:* House of Commons, SW1A 0AA. *Clubs:* Boodle's, Turf.

BROWNE, Air Vice-Marshal John Philip Ravenscroft, CBE 1985; Director General Support Services (RAF), Ministry of Defence, since 1989; *b* 27 April 1937; *s* of late Charles Harold Browne and Lorna Browne (*née* Bailey); *m* 1962, Gillian Dorothy Smith; two *s*. *Educ:* Brockenhurst County High Sch.; Southampton Univ. (BSc(Eng)). CEng, MICE, MRAeS. Commissioned Airfield Construction Branch, RAF, 1958; appts in NEAF and UK, 1959–66; transf. to Engineer Branch, 1966; RAF Coll., Cranwell, 1966–67; aircraft engineering appts, RAF Valley and MoD, 1967–71; RAF Staff Coll., 1972; OC Engrg Wing, RAF Valley, 1973–75; staff appts, MoD and HQ RAF Germany, 1975–82; Asst Dir, Harrier Projects, 1982–85, Dir, Electronics Radar Airborne, 1985–86, Dir, Airborne Early Warning, 1986–89, MoD (PE). MBIM. *Recreations:* reading, walking, photography, music. *Address:* c/o Lloyds Bank, New Milton, Hants. *Club:* Royal Air Force.

BROWNE, Mervyn Ernest, CBE 1976; ERD 1954; HM Diplomatic Service, retired 1976; *b* 3 June 1916; *s* of late Ernest Edmond Browne and of Florence Mary Browne; *m* 1942, Constance (*née* Jarvis) (*d* 1988); three *s*. *Educ:* Stockport Sec. Sch.; St Luke's Coll., Exeter; University Coll., Exeter. BScEcon London; BA Exeter. RA, 1940–46; TA, 1947–53; AER, RASC, 1953–60. Distribution of industry res., BoT, 1948–56; HM Trade Comr Service: Trade Comr, Wellington, NZ, 1957–61 and Adelaide, 1961–64; Principal Trade Comr, Kingston, Jamaica, 1964–68; HM Diplomatic Service: Counsellor (Commercial), Canberra, 1968–70; Dir, Brit. Trade in S Africa, Johannesburg, 1970–73; Consul-Gen., 1974–76 and Chargé d'Affaires, 1974 and 1976, Brit. Embassy, Manila. *Recreations:* militaria, lepidoptery, squash rackets. *Address:* 21 Dartmouth Hill, Greenwich, SE10 8AJ. *T:* 081–691 2993.

BROWNE, Michael; *see* Browne, E. M. A.

BROWNE, Lady Moyra (Blanche Madeleine), DBE 1977 (OBE 1962); National Chairman, Support Groups, and Governor, Research into Ageing (formerly British Foundation for Age Research), since 1987; *b* 2 March 1918; *d* of 9th Earl of Bessborough, PC, GCMG; *m* 1945, Sir Denis John Browne, KCVO, FRCS (*d* 1967); one *s* one *d*. *Educ:* privately. State Enrolled Nurse, 1946. Dep. Supt-in-Chief, 1964, Supt-in-Chief, 1970–83, St John Amb. Bde. Vice-Chm. Central Council, Victoria League, 1961–65; Vice-Pres., Royal Coll. of Nursing, 1970–85. Hon. Mem., British Assoc. of Paediatric Surgeons, 1990. GCStJ 1984. *Recreations:* music, fishing, travel. *Address:* 16 Wilton Street, SW1. *T:* 071–235 1419.

See also D. J. M. Browne.

BROWNE, Rt. Hon. Sir Patrick (Reginald Evelyn), PC 1974; Kt 1965; OBE (mil.) 1945; TD 1945; a Lord Justice of Appeal, 1974–80, retired; *b* 28 May 1907; *er s* of Edward Granville Browne, Sir Thomas Adams's Prof. of Arabic, Fellow of Pembroke Coll., Cambridge, and Alice Caroline (*née* Blackburne-Daniell); *m* 1st, 1931, Evelyn Sophie Alexandra (*d* 1966), *o d* of Sir Charles and Lady Walston; two *d*; 2nd, 1977, Lena, *y d* of late Mr and Mrs James Atkinson. *Educ:* Eton; Pembroke Coll., Cambridge (Hon. Fellow, 1975). Barrister-at-law, Inner Temple, 1931; QC 1960; Bencher, 1962. Deputy Chairman of Quarter Sessions, Essex, Co. Cambridge and Isle of Ely, 1963–65; a Judge of the High Court of Justice, Queen's Bench Div., 1965–74. Pres., Cambs Branch, Magistrates' Assoc., 1972–85. A Controller, Royal Opera House Development Land Trust, 1981–84. Served Army, 1939–45; GSO 1, Lt-Col. *Publication:* Judicial Reflections, in Current Legal Problems 1982. *Address:* Thriplow Bury, Thriplow, Royston, Herts SG8 7RN. *T:* Fowlmere (0763) 208234. *Clubs:* Garrick; Cambridge County.

See also Prof. Sir H. P. F. Swinnerton-Dyer, Bt.

BROWNE, Percy Basil; DL; Chairman, Devon & Exeter Steeplechases Ltd, since 1990; *b* 2 May 1923; *s* of late Captain W. P. Browne, MC. *Educ:* The Downs, Colwall; Eton College. Served War of 1939–45 with Royal Dragoons in Italy and NW Europe. Rode in Grand National, 1953. MP (C) Torrington Division of Devon, 1959–64. Dir, Appledore Shipbuilders Ltd, 1965–72 (former Chm.); Chairman: N Devon Meat Ltd, 1982–86; Western Counties Bldg Soc., 1983–85; West of England Bldg Soc., 1987–89 (Vice-Chm., 1985–87); Vice-Chm., Regency & West of England Bldg Soc., 1989–90. Mem., SW Reg. Hosp. Bd, 1967–70. Chm., Minister of Agriculture's SW Regl Panel, 1985–88. High Sheriff, Devon, 1978; DL Devon, 1984. *Address:* Ford, Silverton, Exeter EX5 4DQ. *T:* Exeter (0392) 881496.

BROWNE, Peter K.; *see* Kenworthy-Browne.

BROWNE, Robert William M.; *see* Moxon Browne.

BROWNE, Sheila Jeanne, CB 1977; Principal, Newnham College, Cambridge, 1983–Aug. 1992; *b* 25 Dec. 1924; *d* of Edward Elliott Browne. *Educ:* Lady Margaret Hall, Oxford (MA; Hon. Fellow 1978); Ecole des Chartes, Paris. Asst Lectr, Royal Holloway Coll., Univ. of London, 1947–51; Tutor and Fellow of St Hilda's Coll., Oxford and Univ. Lectr in French, Oxford, 1951–61, Hon. Fellow, St Hilda's Coll., 1978; HM Inspector of Schools, 1961–70; Staff Inspector, Secondary Educn, 1970–72; Chief Inspector, Secondary Educn, 1972; Dep. Sen. Chief Inspector, DES, 1972–74, Senior Chief Inspector, 1974–83. Hon. Fellow: Lancashire Polytechnic, 1989; Polytechnic of N London, 1989.Hon. DLitt Warwick, 1981; Hon. LLD: Exeter, 1984; Birmingham, 1987. *Recreations:* medieval France, language, mountains. *Address:* Newnham College, Cambridge CB3 9DF. *T:* Cambridge (0223) 335700.

BROWNE-CAVE, Sir Robert C.; *see* Cave-Browne-Cave.

BROWNE-WILKINSON, Rt. Hon. Sir Nicolas Christopher Henry, Kt 1977; PC 1983; Vice-Chancellor of the Supreme Court, since 1985; *b* 30 March 1930; *s* of late Canon A. R. Browne-Wilkinson and Molly Browne-Wilkinson; *m* 1st, 1955, Ursula de Lacy Bacon (*d* 1987); three *s* two *d*; 2nd, 1990, Mrs Hilary Tuckwell. *Educ:* Lancing; Magdalen Coll., Oxford (BA). Called to Bar, Lincoln's Inn, 1953 (Bencher, 1977); QC 1972. Junior Counsel: to Registrar of Restrictive Trading Agreements, 1964–66; to Attorney-General in Charity Matters, 1966–72; in bankruptcy, to Dept of Trade and Industry, 1966–72; a Judge of the Courts of Appeal of Jersey and Guernsey, 1976–77; a Judge of the High Court, Chancery Div., 1977–83; a Lord Justice of Appeal, 1983–85. Pres., Employment Appeal Tribunal, 1981–83. Pres., Senate of the Inns of Court and the Bar, 1984–86. *Recreations:* farming, gardening. *Address:* Royal Courts of Justice, Strand, WC2A 2LL.

BROWNING, (David) Peter (James); CBE 1984; MA; Chief Education Officer of Bedfordshire, 1973–89; *b* 29 May 1927; *s* of late Frank Browning and Lucie A. (*née* Hiscock); *m* 1953, Eleanor Berry, *d* of late J. H. Forshaw, CB, FRIBA; three *s*. *Educ:* Christ's Coll., Cambridge (Engl. and Mod. Langs Tripos); Sorbonne; Univs of Strasbourg and Perugia. Personal Asst to Vice-Chancellor, Liverpool Univ., 1952–56; Teacher, Willenhall Comprehensive Sch., 1956–59; Sen. Admin. Asst, Somerset LEA, 1959–62; Asst Dir of Educn, Cumberland LEA, 1962–66; Dep. Chief Educn Officer, Southampton LEA, 1966–69; Chief Educn Officer of Southampton, 1969–73. Member: Schools Council Governing Council and 5–13 Steering Cttee, 1969–75; Council, Univ. of Southampton, 1970–73; CofE Bd of Educn Schools Cttee, 1970–75; Council, Nat. Youth Orch., 1972–77; Merchant Navy Trng Bd, 1973–77; British Educnl Administration Soc. (Chm., 1974–78; Founder Mem., Council of Management); UGC, 1974–79; Taylor Cttee of Enquiry into Management and Govt of Schs, 1975–77; Governing Body, Centre for Inf. on Language Teaching and Research, 1975–80; European Forum for Educational Admin (Founder Chm., 1977–84); Library Adv. Council (England), 1978–81; Bd of Governors, Camb. Inst. of Educn (Vice-Chm., 1980–89); Univ. of Cambridge Faculty Bd of Educn, 1983–; Council of Management, British Sch. Tech., 1984–87, Trust Dir, 1987–; Lancaster Univ. Council, 1988–; Dir, Nat. Educnl Resources Inf. Service, 1988–. Governor: Gordonstoun Sch., 1985–; Lakes Sch., Windermere, 1988–; Charlotte Mason Coll. of Higher Educn, Ambleside, 1988–; London Coll. of Dance, 1990–. Consultant, Ministry of Education: Sudan, 1976; Cyprus, 1977; Italy, 1981. Sir James Matthews Meml Lecture, Univ. of Southampton, 1983. FRSA 1981. Cavaliere, Order of Merit (Republic of Italy), 1985; Médaille d'honneur de l'Oise, 1988; Commandeur, Ordre des Palmes Académiques (Republic of France), 1989 (Officier, 1985). *Publications:* Editor: Julius Caesar for German Students, 1957; Macbeth for German Students, 1959; contrib. London Educn Rev., Educnl Administration jl, and other educnl jls. *Recreations:* gardening, music, travel. *Address:* Park Fell, Skelwith, near Ambleside, LA22 9NP. *T:* Ambleside (05394) 33978; 43/45 Chilkwell Street, Glastonbury BA6 8DE. *T:* Glastonbury (0458) 32514.

BROWNING, Most Rev. Edmond Lee; Presiding Bishop of the Episcopal Church in the United States, since 1986; *b* 11 March 1929; *s* of Edmond Lucian Browning and Cora Mae Lee; *m* 1953, Patricia A. Sparks; four *s* one *d*. *Educ:* Univ. of the South (BA 1952); School of Theology, Sewanee, Tenn (BD 1954). Curate, Good Shepherd, Corpus Christi, Texas, 1954–56; Rector, Redeemer, Eagle Pass, Texas, 1956–59; Rector, All Souls, Okinawa, 1959–63; Japanese Lang. School, Kobe, Japan, 1963–65; Rector, St Matthews, Okinawa, 1965–67; Archdeacon of Episcopal Church, Okinawa, 1965–67; first Bishop of Okinawa, 1967–71; Bishop of American Convocation, 1971–73; Executive for National and World Mission, on Presiding Bishop's Staff, United States Episcopal Church, 1974–76; Bishop of Hawaii, 1976–85. Chm., Standing Commn on World Mission, 1979–82. Member: Exec. Council, Episcopal Church, 1982–85; Anglican Consultative Council, 1982–. Hon. DD: Univ. of the South, Sewanee, Tenn, 1970; Gen. Theol Seminary, 1986; Church Divinity Sch. of the Pacific, 1987; Seabury Western Seminary, 1987; Hon. DHL: Chaminade Univ., Honolulu, 1985; St Paul's Coll., Lawrenceville, Va, 1987. *Publication:* Essay on World Mission, 1977. *Address:* c/o Episcopal Church Center, 815 Second Avenue, New York, NY 10017, USA. *T:* 212–867–8400.

BROWNING, Rt. Rev. George Victor; Bishop of the Northern Region, Brisbane, since 1985 (Assistant Bishop, Diocese of Brisbane); Principal of St Francis' Theological College, Brisbane, since 1987; *b* 28 Sept. 1942; *s* of John and Barbara Browning; *m* 1964, Margaret; three *s*. *Educ:* Ardingly Coll.; Lewes County Grammar Sch., Sussex; St John's Coll., Morpeth, Qld (ThL 1st cl. Hons 1965). Curate: Inverell, 1966–68; Armidale, 1968–69; Vicar, Warialda, 1969–73; Vice Warden and Lectr in Old Testament Studies and Pastoral Theol., St John's Coll., Morpeth, 1973–75 (Acting Warden, 1974); Rector of Singleton, Rural Dean and Archdeacon of the Upper Hunter, 1976–84; Rector of Woy Woy and Archdeacon of the Central Coast, 1984–85. *Recreations:* reading, running (anything that presents a challenge). *Address:* St Francis' Theological College, 233 Milton Road, Milton, Qld 4064, Australia. *T:* (07) 3694286.

BROWNING, Ian Andrew; Chief Executive, Wiltshire County Council, since 1984; *b* 28 Aug. 1941; *m* 1967, Ann Carter; two *s*. *Educ:* Liverpool Univ. (BA Hons Pol Theory and Instns). Solicitor. Swindon BC, 1964–70; WR, Yorks, 1970–73; S Yorks CC, 1973–76; Wilts CC, 1976–. *Recreations:* golf, travel, ornithology. *Address:* Wiltshire County Council, County Hall, Trowbridge, Wilts BA14 8JN. *T:* Trowbridge (0225) 753641.

BROWNING, Dr Keith Anthony, FRS 1978; Director of Research, Meteorological Office, Bracknell, since 1989; *b* 31 July 1938; *s* of late Sqdn Ldr James Anthony Browning and Amy Hilda (*née* Greenwood); *m* 1962, Ann Muriel (*née* Baish), BSc, MSc; one *s* two *d*. *Educ:* Commonweal Grammar Sch., Swindon, Wilts; Imperial Coll. of Science and Technology, Univ. of London. BSc, ARCS, PhD, DIC. Research atmospheric physicist, Air Force Cambridge Research Laboratories, Mass, USA, 1962–66; in charge of Meteorological Office Radar Research Lab., RSRE, Malvern, 1966–85; Dep. Dir (Phys. Res.), Met. Office, Bracknell, 1985–89; Principal Research Fellow, 1966–69; Principal Scientific Officer, 1969–72; Sen. Principal Scientific Officer, 1972–79; Dep. Chief Scientific Officer, 1979–89, Chief Scientific Officer, 1989–. Ch. Scientist, Nat. Hail Res. Experiment, USA, 1974–75; Vis. Prof., Dept of Meteorology, Univ. of Reading, 1988–. Member: Council, Royal Met. Soc., 1971–74 (Vice-Pres., 1979–81, 1987–88 and 1990–91; Pres., 1988–90); Editing Cttee, Qly Jl RMetS, 1975–78; Inter-Union Commn on Radio Meteorology, 1975–78; Internat. Commn on Cloud Physics, 1976–84; British Nat. Cttee for Physics, 1979–84; British Nat. Cttee for Geodesy and Geophysics, 1983–89 (Chm., Met. and Atmos. Phys. Sub-Cttee, 1985–89, Vice-Chm., 1979–84); NERC, 1984–87; British Nat. Cttee for Space Res., 1986–89 (Remote Sensing Sub-Cttee, 1986–89); British Nat. Cttee, 1988–89, Scientific Steering Gp, Global Energy and Water Cycle Experiment, 1988–, WMO/ICSU Scientific Cttee, 1990–, World Climate Res. Prog.; Royal Soc. Interdisciplinary Sci. Cttee for Space Res., 1990–; Academia Europaea. L. F. Richardson Prize, 1968, Buchan Prize, 1972, William Gaskell Meml Medal, 1982, RMetS; L. G. Groves Meml Prize for Meteorology, Met. Office, 1969; Meisinger Award, 1974, Jule Charney Award, 1985, Amer. Met. Soc. (Fellow of the Society, 1975); Charles Chree Medal and Prize, Inst. of Physics, 1981. *Publications:* (ed) Nowcasting, 1982; meteorological papers in learned jls, mainly in Britain and USA. *Recreations:* home and garden.

BROWNING, Peter; *see* Browning, D. P. J.

BROWNING, Rex Alan, CB 1984; Deputy Secretary, Overseas Development Administration, 1981–86, retired; *b* 22 July 1930; *s* of Gilbert H. W. Browning and Gladys (*née* Smith) *m* 1961, Paula McKain; three *d*. *Educ:* Bristol Grammar Sch.; Merton Coll., Oxford (Postmaster) (MA). HM Inspector of Taxes, 1952; Asst Principal, Colonial Office, 1957; Private Sec. to Parly Under-Sec. for the Colonies, 1960; Principal, Dept of Techn. Co-operation, 1961; transf. ODM, 1964; seconded to Diplomatic Service as First Sec. (Aid), British High Commn, Singapore, 1969; Asst Sec., 1971; Counsellor, Overseas Develt, Washington, and Alternate UK Exec. Dir, IBRD, 1973–76; Under-Secretary: ODM, 1976–78; Dept of Trade, 1978–80; ODA, 1980–81. *Address:* Taranaki House, Trusham, near Newton Abbot, Devon TQ13 0NR.

BROWNING, Prof. Robert, MA; FBA 1978; Professor Emeritus, University of London; *b* 15 Jan. 1914; *s* of Alexander M. Browning and Jean M. Browning (*née* Miller); *m* 1st, 1946, Galina Chichekova; two *d*; 2nd, 1972, Ruth Gresh. *Educ:* Kelvinside Academy, Glasgow; Glasgow Univ. (MA); Balliol Coll., Oxford. Served Army, Middle East, Italy, Balkans, 1939–46. Harmsworth Sen. Scholar, Merton Coll., Oxford, 1946; Lectr, University Coll. London, 1947, Reader, 1955; Prof. of Classics and Ancient History, Birkbeck Coll., Univ. of London, 1965–81. Fellow, Dumbarton Oaks, Washington, DC, 1973–74, 1982, Long-Term Fellow 1983. President, Soc. for Promotion of Hellenic Studies, 1974–77; Life Vice-Pres., Assoc. Internat. des Etudes Byzantines, 1981; Chm., National Trust for Greece, 1985–. Corresponding Mem., Athens Acad., 1981. Hon. DLitt Birmingham, 1980; Hon. DPhil Athens, 1988. Gold Medal for Excellence in Hellenic Studies, Onassis Center for Hellenic Studies, NY Univ., 1990. Comdr of the Order of the Phoenix, Greece, 1984. *Publications:* Medieval and Modern Greek, 1969, rev. edn 1983; Justinian and Theodora, 1971, rev. edn 1987; Byzantium and Bulgaria, 1975; The Emperor Julian, 1976; Studies in Byzantine History, Literature and Education, 1977; The Byzantine Empire, 1980; (ed) The Greek World, Classical, Byzantine and Modern, 1985; History, Language and Literacy in the Byzantine World, 1989; articles in learned jls of many countries. *Address:* 17 Belsize Park Gardens, NW3 4JG.

BROWNING, Rev. Canon Wilfrid Robert Francis; Canon Residentiary of Christ Church Cathedral, Oxford, 1965–87, Hon. Canon since 1987; *b* 29 May 1918; *s* of Charles Robert and Mabel Elizabeth Browning; *m* 1948, Elizabeth Beeston; two *s* two *d*. *Educ:* Westminster School; Christ Church, Oxford; Cuddesdon Coll., Oxford. MA, BD Oxon. Deacon 1941, priest 1942, dio. of Peterborough; on staff of St Deiniol's Library, Hawarden, 1946–48; Vicar of St Richard's, Hove, 1948–51; Rector of Great Haseley, 1951–59; Lectr, Cuddesdon Coll., Oxford, 1951–59 and 1965–70; Canon Residentiary of Blackburn Cath. and Warden of Whalley Abbey, Lancs, 1959–65; Director of Ordinands and Post-Ordination Trng (Oxford dio.), 1965–85; Dir of Trng for Non-Stipendiary Ordinands and Clergy, 1972–88; Examining Chaplain: Blackburn, 1960–70; Manchester, 1970–78; Oxford, 1965–89. Member of General Synod, 1973–85; Select Preacher, Oxford Univ., 1972, 1981. *Publications:* Commentary on St Luke's Gospel, 1960, 6th edn 1981; Meet the New Testament, 1964; ed, The Anglican Synthesis, 1965; Handbook of the Ministry, 1985. *Address:* 33 Dunstone Road, Plymstock, Plymouth PL9 8RJ. *T:* Plymouth (0752) 403039; 42 Alexandra Road, Oxford OX2 0DB. *T:* Oxford (0865) 723464.

BROWNLEE, Prof. George; Professor of Pharmacology, King's College, University of London, 1958–78, retired; now Emeritus Professor; *b* 1911; *s* of late George R. Brownlee and of Mary C. C. Gow, Edinburgh; *m* 1940, Margaret P. M. Cochrane (*d* 1970), 2nd *d* of Thomas W. P. Cochrane and Margaret P. M. S. Milne, Bo'ness, Scotland; three *s*; 2nd, 1977, Betty Jean Gaydon (marr. diss. 1981), *o d* of Stanley H. Clutterham and Margaret M. Fox, Sidney, Australia. *Educ:* Tynecastle Sch.; Heriot Watt Coll., Edinburgh, BSc 1936, DSc 1950, Glasgow; PhD 1939, London. Rammell Schol., Biological Standardization Labs of Pharmaceutical Soc., London; subseq. Head of Chemotherapeutic Div., Wellcome Res. Labs, Beckenham; Reader in Pharmacology, King's Coll., Univ. of London, 1949. Editor, Jl of Pharmacy and Pharmacology, 1955–72. FKC, 1971. *Publications:* (with Prof. J. P. Quilliam) Experimental Pharmacology, 1952; papers on: chemotherapy of tuberculosis and leprosy; structure and pharmacology of the polymyxins; endocrinology; toxicity of drugs; neurohumoral transmitters in smooth muscle, etc., in: Brit. Jl Pharmacology; Jl Physiology; Biochem. Jl; Nature; Lancet; Annals NY Acad. of Science; Pharmacological Reviews, etc. *Recreations:* collecting books, making things. *Address:* 602 Gilbert House, Barbican, EC2Y 8BD. *T:* 071–638 9543. *Club:* Athenæum.
See also G. G. Brownlee.

BROWNLEE, Prof. George Gow, PhD; FRS 1987; E. P. Abraham Professor of Chemical Pathology, Sir William Dunn School of Pathology, University of Oxford, since 1980; Fellow of Lincoln College, Oxford, since 1980; *b* 13 Jan. 1942; *s* of Prof. George Brownlee, *qv*; *m* 1966, Margaret Susan Kemp; one *s* one *d*. *Educ:* Dulwich College; Emmanuel Coll., Cambridge (MA, PhD). Scientific staff of MRC at Laboratory of Molecular Biology, Cambridge, 1966–80. Fellow, Emmanuel Coll., Cambridge, 1967–71. Colworth Medal, 1977, Wellcome Trust Award, 1985, Biochemical Soc. *Publications:* Determination of Sequences in RNA (Vol. 3, Part I of Laboratory Techniques in Biochemistry and Molecular Biology), 1972; scientific papers in Jl of Molecular Biology, Nature, Cell, Nucleic Acids Research, etc. *Recreations:* gardening, cricket. *Address:* Sir William Dunn School of Pathology, South Parks Road, Oxford OX1 3RE. *T:* Oxford (0865) 275559.

BROWNLIE, Albert Dempster; Vice-Chancellor, University of Canterbury, Christchurch, New Zealand, since 1977; *b* 3 Sept. 1932; *s* of Albert Newman and Netia Brownlie; *m* 1955, Noelene Eunice (*née* Meyer); two *d*. *Educ:* Univ. of Auckland, NZ (MCom). Economist, NZ Treasury, 1954–55. Lecturer, Sen. Lectr, Associate Prof. in Economics, Univ. of Auckland, 1956–64; Prof. and Head of Dept of Economics, Univ. of Canterbury, Christchurch, 1965–77. Chairman: Monetary and Economic Council, 1972–78; Australia-NZ Foundn, 1979–83; UGC Cttee to Review NZ Univ. Educn, 1980–82; NZ Vice-Chancellors' Cttee, 1983–84; Member: Commonwealth Experts Group on New Internat. Economic Order, 1975–77; Commonwealth Experts Gp on Econ. Growth, 1980; Wage Hearing Tribunal, 1976. Silver Jubilee Medal, 1977. *Publications:* articles in learned jls. *Address:* University of Canterbury, Christchurch 1, New Zealand. *T:* 667–001.

BROWNLIE, Prof. Ian, QC; DCL; FBA; International Law practitioner; Chichele Professor of Public International Law, and Fellow of All Souls College, University of Oxford, since 1980; *b* 19 Sept. 1932; *s* of John Nason Brownlie and Amy Isabella (*née* Atherton); *m* 1st, 1957, Jocelyn Gale; one *s* two *d*; 2nd, 1978, Christine Apperley. *Educ:* Alsop High Sch., Liverpool; Hertford Coll., Oxford (Gibbs Scholar, 1952; BA 1953); King's Coll., Cambridge (Humanitarian Trust Student, 1955). DPhil Oxford, 1961; DCL Oxford, 1976. Called to the Bar, Gray's Inn, 1958, Bencher, 1987; QC 1979. Lectr,

Nottingham Univ., 1957–63; Fellow and Tutor in Law, Wadham Coll., Oxford, 1963–76 and Lectr, Oxford Univ., 1964–76; Prof. of Internat. Law, LSE, Univ. of London, 1976–80. Reader in Public Internat. Law, Inns of Ct Sch. of Law, 1973–76. Dir of Studies, Internat. Law Assoc., 1982–91. Delegate, OUP, 1984–. Lectr, Hague Acad. of Internat. Law, 1979. Editor, British Year Book of International Law, 1974–. Mem., Inst. of Internat. Law, 1985 (Associate Mem., 1977). FBA 1979. Japan Foundn Award, 1978. *Publications*: International Law and the Use of Force by States, 1963; Principles of Public International Law, 1966 (4th edn 1990; Russian edn, ed G. I. Tunkin, 1977; Japanese edn, 1989; Certif. of Merit, Amer. Soc. of Internat. Law, 1976); Basic Documents in International Law, 1967 (3rd edn 1983); The Law Relating to Public Order, 1968; Basic Documents on Human Rights, 1971 (2nd edn 1981); Basic Documents on African Affairs, 1971; African Boundaries, a legal and diplomatic encyclopaedia, 1979; State Responsibility, part 1, 1983; (ed jtly) Liber Amicorum for Lord Wilberforce, 1987. *Recreation*: travel. *Address*: 2 Hare Court, Temple, EC4Y 7BH. *T*: 071–583 1770; All Souls College, Oxford OX1 4AL. *T*: Oxford (0865) 279342; 43 Fairfax Road, Chiswick, W4 1EN. *T*: 081–995 3647.

BROWNLOW, family name of **Baron Lurgan.**

BROWNLOW, 7th Baron *cr* 1776; **Edward John Peregrine Cust;** Bt 1677; Chairman and Managing Director of Harris & Dixon (Underwriting Agencies) Ltd, 1976–82; *b* 25 March 1936; *o s* of 6th Baron Brownlow and Katherine Hariot (*d* 1952), 2nd *d* of Sir David Alexander Kinloch, 11th Bt, CB, MVO; *S* father, 1978; *m* 1964, Shirlie Edith, 2nd *d* of late John Yeomans, The Manor Farm, Hill Croome, Upton-on-Severn, Worcs; one *s*. *Educ*: Eton. Member of Lloyd's, 1961–88; Director, Hand-in-Hand Fire and Life Insurance Soc. (branch office of Commercial Union Assurance Co. Ltd), 1962–82. High Sheriff of Lincolnshire, 1978–79. *Heir*: *s* Hon. Peregrine Edward Quintin Cust, *b* 9 July 1974. *Address*: La Maison des Prés, St Peter, Jersey JE3 7EL. *Clubs*: White's, Pratt's; United (Jersey).

BROWNLOW, Air Vice-Marshal Bertrand, CB 1982; OBE 1967; AFC 1962; Executive Director, Marshall of Cambridge (Engineering) Ltd, since 1987; *b* 13 Jan. 1929; *s* of Robert John Brownlow and Helen Louise Brownlow; *m* 1958, Kathleen Shannon; two *s* one *d*. *Educ*: Beaufort Lodge Sch. Joined RAF, 1947; 12 and 101 Sqdns, ADC to AOC 1 Gp, 103 Sqdn, 213 Sqdn, Empire Test Pilots' Sch., OC Structures and Mech. Eng Flt RAE Farnborough, RAF Staff Coll., Air Min. Op. Requirements, 1949–64; Wing Comdr Ops, RAF Lyneham, 1964–66; Jt Services Staff Coll., 1966–67; DS RAF Staff Coll., 1967–68; Def. and Air Attaché, Stockholm, 1969–71; CO Experimental Flying, RAE Farnborough, 1971–73; Asst Comdt, Office and Flying Trng, RAF Coll., Cranwell, 1973–74; Dir of Flying (R&D), MoD, 1974–77; Comdt, A&AEE, 1977–80; Comdt, RAF Coll., Cranwell, 1980–82; Dir Gen., Trng, RAF, 1982–83, retired 1984. Silver Medal, Royal Aero Club, 1983, for servs to RAF gliding. *Recreations*: squash, tennis, golf, gliding (Gold C with two diamonds). *Address*: Woodside, Abbotsley Road, Croxton, Huntingdon, Cambs PE19 4SZ. *T*: Croxton (048087) 663. *Club*: Royal Air Force.

BROWNLOW, James Hilton, CBE 1984; QPM 1978; HM Inspector of Constabulary for North Eastern England, 1983–89; *b* 19 Oct. 1925; *s* of late Ernest Cuthbert Brownlow and Beatrice Annie Elizabeth Brownlow; *m* 1947, Joyce Key; two *d*. *Educ*: Worksop Central School. Solicitor's Clerk, 1941–43; served war, RAF, Flt/Sgt (Air Gunner), 1943–47. Police Constable, Leicester City Police, 1947; Police Constable to Det. Chief Supt, Kent County Constabulary, 1947–69; Asst Chief Constable, Hertfordshire Constabulary, 1969–75; Asst to HM Chief Inspector of Constabulary, Home Office, 1975–76; Dep. Chief Constable, Greater Manchester Police, 1976–79; Chief Constable, S Yorks Police, 1979–82. Queen's Commendation for Brave Conduct, 1972. Officer Brother OStJ 1981. *Recreations*: golf, gardening.

BROWNLOW, Kevin; author; film director; *b* 2 June 1938; *s* of Thomas and Niña Brownlow; *m* 1969, Virginia Keane; one *d*. *Educ*: University College School. Entered documentaries, 1955; became film editor, 1958, and edited many documentaries; with Andrew Mollo dir. feature films: It Happened Here, 1964; Winstanley, 1975; dir. Charm of Dynamite, 1967, about Abel Gance, and restored his classic film Napoleon (first shown London, Nov. 1980, NY, Jan. 1981). With David Gill produced and directed TV series: Hollywood, 1980; Thames Silents, 1981– (incl. The Big Parade); Unknown Chaplin, 1983; British Cinema—Personal View, 1986; Buster Keaton: a hard act to follow, 1987; Harold Lloyd—The Third Genius, 1990; Supervising Editor, No Surrender, 1986. *Publications*: The Parade's Gone By . . ., 1968; How it Happened Here, 1968; The War, the West and the Wilderness, 1978; Hollywood: the pioneers, 1979; Napoleon: Abel Gance's classic film, 1983; Behind The Mask of Innocence, 1991; many articles on film history. *Recreation*: motion pictures. *Address*: Photoplay Productions, 21 Princess Road, NW1 8JR.

BROWNLOW, Col William Stephen; Lord-Lieutenant of Co. Down, since 1990; *b* 9 Oct. 1921; *s* of late Col Guy J. Brownlow, DSO, DL, and Elinor H. G. Brownlow, *d* of Col George J. Scott, DSO; *m* 1961, Eveleigh, *d* of Col George Panter, MBE; one *s* two *d*. *Educ*: Eton; Staff Coll., Camberley (psc). Major, Rifle Bde, 1940–54 (wounded, despatches); Hon. Col 4 Bn Royal Irish Rangers, 1973–78. Member: Down CC, 1969–72; NI Assembly, 1973–75. Member: Irish Nat. Hunt Cttee, 1956–; Irish Turf Club, 1982–; Chairman: Downpatrick Race Club, 1960–90; NI Reg., British Field Sports Soc., 1971–90; Master, East Down Foxhounds, 1956–62. JP 1956, DL 1961, High Sheriff 1959, Co. Down. *Recreation*: field sports. *Address*: Ballywhite House, Portaferry, Co. Down BT22 1PB. *T*: Portaferry (02477) 28325. *Club*: Army and Navy.

BROWNRIGG, Sir Nicholas (Gawen), 5th Bt, *cr* 1816; *b* 22 Dec. 1932; *s* of late Gawen Egremont Brownrigg and Baroness Lucia von Borosini, *o d* of Baron Victor von Borosini, California; *S* grandfather, 1939; *m* 1959, Linda Louise Lovelace (marr. diss. 1965), Beverly Hills, California; one *s* one *d*; *m* 1971, Valerie Ann, *d* of Julian A. Arden, Livonia, Michigan, USA. *Educ*: Midland Sch.; Stanford Univ. *Heir*: *s* Michael Gawen Brownrigg, *b* Oct. 1961. *Address*: PO Box 548, Ukiah, Calif 95482, USA.

BROWNRIGG, Philip Henry Akerman, CMG 1964; DSO 1945; OBE 1953; TD 1945; *b* 3 June 1911; *s* of late Charles E. Brownrigg, Master of Magdalen Coll. Sch., Oxford; *m* 1936, Marguerite Doreen Ottley; three *d*. *Educ*: Eton; Magdalen Coll., Oxford (BA). Journalist, 1934–52; Editor, Sunday Graphic, 1952. Joined Anglo American Corp. of S Africa, 1953: London Agent, 1956; Dir in Rhodesia, 1961–63; Dir in Zambia, 1964–65; retd, 1969. Director (apptd by Govt of Zambia): Nchanga Consolidated Copper Mines Ltd, 1969–80; Roan Consolidated Mines Ltd, 1969–80. Joined TA, 1938; served War of 1939–45 with 6 R Berks, and 61st Reconnaissance Regt (RAC); Lieut-Col 1944; CO 4/6 R Berks (TA) 1949–52. Insignia of Honour, Zambia, 1981. *Publication*: Kenneth Kaunda, 1989. *Recreations*: golf, sport on TV. *Address*: Wheeler's, Checkendon, near Reading, Berks RG8 0NJ. *T*: Checkendon (0491) 680328.

BROWSE, Lillian Gertrude; author; private archivist; *d* of Michael Browse and Gladys Browse (*née* Meredith); *m* 1st, 1934, Ivan H. Joseph; 2nd, 1964, Sidney H. Lines. *Educ*: Barnato Park, Johannesburg. Studied with Margaret Craske at Cecchetti Ballet Sch., London, 1928–30; joined Dolin-Nemtchinova ballet co., 1930; gave up ballet and worked at Leger Galls, London, 1931–39; organised war-time exhibns at Nat. Gall. and travelling exhibns for CEMA, 1940–45, also exhibns for Inst. of Adult Educn; Organising Sec., Red Cross picture sale, Christie's, 1942; founder partner, Roland, Browse & Delbanco, 1945; Founder Dir, Browse & Darby, 1977–81. Ballet Critic, Spectator, 1950–54. Organised: Sickert exhibn, Edinburgh, 1953; Sickert centenary exhibn, Tate Gall., 1960; exhibited own private collection at Courtauld Inst. Galls, 1983. Hon. Fellow, Courtauld Inst., 1986. *Publications*: Augustus John Drawings, 1941; Sickert, 1943; Degas Dancers, 1949; William Nicholson: Catalogue Raisonné, 1955; Sickert, 1960; Forain, the Painter, 1978; (ed) Ariel Books on the Arts, 1946; contribs to Apollo, Sunday Times, Country Life, Burlington Magazine. *Recreation*: gardening. *Address*: Little Wassell, Ebernoe, near Petworth, West Sussex GU28 9LD.

BROWSE, Prof. Norman Leslie, MD, FRCS; Professor of Surgery, St Thomas's Hospital Medical School, since 1981, and Consultant Surgeon, St Thomas' Hospital, since 1965; *b* 1 Dec. 1931; *s* of Reginald and Margaret Browse; *m* 1957, Dr Jeanne Menage; one *s* one *d*. *Educ*: St Bartholomew's Hosp. Med. Coll. (MB BS 1955); Bristol Univ. (MD 1961). FRCS 1959. Lectr in Surgery, Westminster Hosp., 1962–64; Harkness Fellow, Res. Associate, Mayo Clinic, Rochester, Minn, 1964–65. St Thomas's Hospital Medical School: Reader in Surgery, 1965–72; Prof. of Vascular Surgery, 1972–81. Hon. Consultant (Vascular Surgery) to: Army, 1980–; RAF, 1982–. Mem. Council, RCS, 1986–. President: European Soc. for Cardiovascular Surgery, 1982–84; Assoc. of Profs of Surgery, 1985–87; Surgical Res. Soc., 1990–92; Venous Forum, RSM, 1990–; Vascular Surgical Soc. of GB and Ireland, 1991–92. *Publications*: Physiology and Pathology of Bed Rest, 1964; Symptoms and Signs of Surgical Disease, 1978; Reducing Operations for Lymphoedema, 1986; Diseases of the Veins, 1988; papers on all aspects of vascular disease. *Recreations*: marine art, mediaeval history, sailing. *Address*: Blaye House, Home Farm Close, Esher, Surrey KT10 9HA. *T*: Esher (0372) 65058.

BROXBOURNE, Baron *cr* 1983 (Life Peer), of Broxbourne in the County of Hertfordshire; **Derek Colclough Walker-Smith;** 1st Bt *cr* 1960; PC 1957; QC 1955; TD; Director, William Weston Gallery Ltd; *b* April 1910; *y s* of late Sir Jonah Walker-Smith; *m* 1938, Dorothy, *d* of late L. J. W. Etherton, Rowlands Castle, Hants; one *s* two *d*. *Educ*: Rossall; Christ Church, Oxford. 1st Class Hons Modern History, Oxford Univ., 1931. Called to Bar, Middle Temple, 1934, Bencher 1963. MP (C) Hertford, 1945–55, Herts East, 1955–83; Parly Sec. to the Board of Trade, 1955–Nov. 1956; Economic Secretary to the Treasury, Nov. 1956–Jan. 1957; Minister of State, Board of Trade, 1957; Minister of Health, 1957–60. Chairman: Cons. Adv. Cttee on Local Govt, 1954–55; 1922 Cttee, 1951–55. Mem., European Parlt, 1973–79 (Chm. of Legal Cttee, 1975–79). Chm., Soc. of Conservative Lawyers, 1969–75; Chm., Nat. House Building Council, 1973–78. ARICS; FCIArb; FIQS. *Publication*: (jtly) Walker-Smith on the Standard Forms of Building Contracts, 1987. *Heir* (to baronetcy only): *s* John Jonah Walker-Smith, *qv*. *Address*: 7 Kepplestone, The Meads, Eastbourne; 20 Albany Court, Palmer Street, SW1. *Club*: Garrick.

BRUBECK, David Warren; jazz musician, composer; *b* Concord, Calif, 6 Dec. 1920; *s* of Howard Brubeck and Elizabeth Ivey; *m* 1942, Iola Whitlock; five *s* one *d*. *Educ*: Pacific Univ. (BA); Mills Coll. (postgrad.). Pianist with dance bands and jazz trio, 1946–49; leader, Dave Brubeck Octet, Trio and Quartet, 1946–; formed Dave Brubeck Quartet, 1951; tours to festivals and colls, incl. tour of Europe and Middle East (for US State Dept) and tours in Aust., Japan and USSR; Europe, Australia, Canada, S America, with 3 sons, as Two Generations of Brubeck. Fellow, Internat. Inst. of Arts and Sciences; Duke Ellington Fellow, Yale Univ. Exponent of progressive Jazz; many awards from trade magazines; numerous recordings. Has composed: over 250 songs; *ballet*: Points on Jazz, 1962; Glances, 1976; *orchestral*: Elementals, 1963; They All Sang Yankee Doodle, 1975; *flute and guitar*: Tritonis, 1979; *piano*: Reminiscences of the Cattle Country, 1946; Four by Four; *oratorios*: The Light in the Wilderness, 1968; Beloved Son, 1978; The Voice of the Holy Spirit, 1985; *cantatas*: Gates of Justice, 1969; Truth is Fallen, 1971; La Fiesta de la Posada, 1975; In Praise of Many, 1989; *chorus and orchestra*: 6 Variations of Pange Lingua, 1983; Upon This Rock Chorale and Fugue, 1987; I See Satie, 1987; Lenten Triptych, 1988; Four New England Pieces, 1988; *mass*: To Hope, a celebration, 1980; *jazz* incl. Blue Rondo à la Turk; In Your Own Sweet Way; The Duke. Duke Ellington Fellow, Yale Univ. Hon. PhD: Univ. of Pacific; Fairfield Univ.; Bridgeport Univ., 1982; Mills Coll., 1982; Niagara Univ. Broadcast Music Inc. Jazz Pioneer Award, 1985; Compostela Humanitarian award, 1986; Connecticut Arts award, 1987; American Eagle award, Nat. Music Council, 1988. Officier de l'Ordre des Arts et des Lettres (France), 1990. *Address*: Derry Music, 601 Montgomery Street, Suite 800, San Francisco, Calif 94111, USA; c/o Sutton Artists Corporation, 119 West 57th Street, Suite 512, New York, NY 10019, USA; Box 216, Wilton, Connecticut 06897, USA.

BRUCE, family name of **Barons Aberdare,** and **Bruce of Donington,** of **Lord Balfour of Burleigh,** and of **Earl of Elgin.**

BRUCE; *see* Cumming-Bruce and Hovell-Thurlow-Cumming-Bruce.

BRUCE, Lord; Charles Edward Bruce; *b* 19 Oct. 1961; *s* and *heir* of 11th Earl of Elgin, *qv*; *m* 1990, Amanda, *yr d* of James Movius; one *d*. *Educ*: Eton College; Univ. of St Andrews (MA Hons). A Page of Honour to HM the Queen Mother, 1975–77. *Address*: 11 Muschamp Road, SE15 4EG. *T*: 071–639 9509. *Club*: Brooks's.

BRUCE OF DONINGTON, Baron *cr* 1974 (Life Peer), of Rickmansworth; **Donald William Trevor Bruce;** economist; Chartered Accountant, Halpern & Woolf; writer; Member of European Parliament, 1975–79; *b* 3 Oct. 1912; *s* of late W. T. Bruce, Norbury, Surrey; *m* 1st, 1939, Joan Letitia Butcher (marr. diss.); one *s* two *d* (and one *d* decd); 2nd, 1981, Cyrena Shaw Heard. *Educ*: Grammar School, Donington, Lincs; FCA 1947. Re-joined Territorial Army, March 1939; commissioned, Nov. 1939; Major, 1942; served at home and in France until May 1945 (despatches). MP (Lab) for North Portsmouth, 1945–50; Parliamentary Private Sec. to Minister of Health, 1945–50; Member Min. of Health delegn to Sweden and Denmark, 1946, and of House of Commons Select Cttee on Public Accounts, 1948–50. Opposition spokesman on Treasury, economic and industrial questions, House of Lords, 1979–83, on trade and industry, 1983–86, on Treasury and economic questions, 1986–90. *Publications*: miscellaneous contributions on political science and economics to newspapers and periodicals. *Address*: 301–305 Euston Road, NW1.

BRUCE, Alexander Robson, CMG 1961; OBE 1948; Assistant Secretary, Board of Trade, 1963–67, retired; *b* 17 April 1907; *m* 1936, Isobel Mary Goldie (*d* 1988); four *d*. *Educ*: Rutherford Coll., Newcastle upon Tyne; Durham Univ. Asst Trade Comr, 1933–42, Trade Commissioner, 1942–43, Montreal; Commercial Sec., British Embassy, Madrid, 1943–46; Trade Comr, Ottawa, 1946–50; Asst Sec., Bd of Trade, 1950–54 and 1963–; Principal British Trade Commissioner in NSW, 1955–63. *Recreation*: golf. *Address*: 37 North Road, Highgate, N6 4BE. *Club*: Highgate Golf.

BRUCE, Sir Arthur Atkinson, KBE 1943; MC 1917; Director: Wallace Brothers & Co. Ltd, 1947–65; Chartered Bank of India, 1949–70; *b* 26 March 1895; *s* of late John Davidson Bruce, Jarrow-on-Tyne; *m* 1928, Kathleen Frances (*d* 1952), *d* of John Emeris

Houldey, ICS (retd), Penn, Bucks; three *d*. *Educ:* Cambridge. Director Reserve Bank of India, 1935–46; Chairman Burma Chamber of Commerce, 1936, 1942, 1946. Member of Council, London Chamber of Commerce, 1960–65. *Address:* Silverthorne, 5 Grenfell Road, Beaconsfield, Bucks. *Club:* Oriental.

BRUCE, Christopher; dancer, choreographer, opera producer; Resident Choreographer, Houston Ballet, since 1989; Associate Choreographer, English National Ballet (formerly London Festival Ballet), since 1986; *b* Leicester, 3 Oct. 1945; *m* Marian Bruce; two *s* one *d*. *Educ:* Ballet Rambert Sch. Joined Ballet Rambert Company, 1963; leading dancer with co. when re-formed as modern dance co., 1966; Associate Dir, 1975–79; Associate Choreographer, 1979; leading roles include: Pierrot Lunaire, The Tempest ((Tetley); L'Apres-Midi d'un Faune (Nijinsky); Cruel Garden (also choreographed with Lindsay Kemp); choreographed: for Ballet Rambert: George Frideric (1st work), 1969; Wings, 1970; For Those Who Die as Cattle, 1971; There Was a Time, 1972; Weekend, 1974; Ancient Voices of Children, 1975; Black Angels, 1976; Cruel Garden, 1977; Night with Waning Moon, 1977; Dancing Day, 1981; Ghost Dances, 1981; Berlin Requiem, 1982; Concertino, 1983; Intimate Pages, 1984; Sergeant Early's Dream, 1984; Ceremonies, 1986; for London Festival Ballet, later English National Ballet: Land, 1985; The World Again, 1986; The Dream is Over, 1987; Swansong, 1988; Symphony in Three Movements, 1990; for Tanz Forum, Cologne: Cantata, 1981; for Nederlands Dans Theater: Village Songs, 1981; Curses and Blessings, 1983; for Houston Ballet, Gautama Buddha, 1989; works for Royal Ballet, Batsheva Dance Co., Munich Opera Ballet, Gulbenkian Ballet Co., Australian Dance Theatre, Royal Danish Ballet, Royal Swedish Ballet. Kent Opera: choreographed and produced Monteverdi's Il Ballo delle Ingrate, and Combattimento di Tancredi e Clorinda, 1980; chor. John Blow's Venus and Adonis, 1980; co-prod Handel's Agrippina, 1982. Choreographed Mutiny (musical), Piccadilly, 1985. TV productions: Ancient Voices of Children, BBC, 1977; Cruel Garden, BBC, 1981–82; Ghost Dances, Channel 4, 1982; Requiem, Danish-German co-prodn, 1982; Silence is the end of our Song, Danish TV, 1984; The Dream is Over (to John Lennon songs), Danish–German co-prodn, 1985. Evening Standard's inaugural Dance Award, 1974. *Address:* c/o Houston Ballet, 1916 West Gray, PO 13150, Houston, Tex 77219-3150, USA.

BRUCE, David, CA; Partner, Deloitte Haskins & Sells, 1974–87; *b* 21 Jan. 1927; *s* of David Bruce and Margaret (*née* Gregson); *m* 1955, Joy Robertson McAslan; four *d*. *Educ:* High School of Glasgow. Commissioned, Royal Corps of Signals, 1947–49. Qualified as Chartered Accountant, 1955; Partner, Kerr McLeod & Co., Chartered Accountants, 1961 (merged with Deloitte Haskins & Sells, 1974); retired 1987. Vice-Pres., Inst. of Chartered Accountants of Scotland, 1978–79 and 1979–80, Pres. 1980–81. Mem., Council on Tribunals, 1984–90 (Mem., Scottish Cttee, 1984–90). *Recreations:* angling, curling, cooking. *Address:* 8 Beechwood Court, Bearsden, Glasgow G62 2RY.

BRUCE, Sir (Francis) Michael Ian; *see* Bruce, Sir Michael Ian.

BRUCE, George John Done, RP 1959; painter of portraits, landscapes, still life, flowers; *b* 28 March 1930; *s* of 11th Lord Balfour of Burleigh, Brucefield, Clackmannan, Scotland and Violet Dorothy, *d* of Richard Henry Done, Tarporley, Cheshire; *b* of 12th Lord Balfour of Burleigh, *qv*. *Educ:* Westminster Sch.; Byam Shaw Sch. of Drawing and Painting. Hon. Sec., Royal Soc. of Portrait Painters, 1970–84, Vice-Pres., 1984–90. *Recreations:* hang-gliding, ski-ing, windsurfing. *Address:* 6 Pembroke Walk, W8 6PQ. *T:* 071–937 1493. *Club:* Athenæum.

BRUCE, Sir Hervey (James Hugh), 7th Bt *cr* 1804; Major, The Grenadier Guards; *b* 3 Sept. 1952; *s* of Sir Hervey John William Bruce, 6th Bt, and Crista, (*d* 1984), *y d* of late Lt-Col Chandos De Paravicini, OBE; *S* father, 1971; *m* 1979, Charlotte, *e d* of Jack Gore, Flood Street, SW3; one *s* one *d*. *Educ:* Eton; Officer Cadet School, Mons. *Recreations:* polo, tapestry. *Heir:* *s* Hervey Hamish Peter Bruce, *b* 20 Nov. 1986. *Address:* Middlefield House, School Lane, Colsterworth, near Grantham, Lincs NG33 5NW. *Club:* Cavalry and Guards.

BRUCE, Ian Cameron; MP (C) Dorset South, since 1987; Chairman, Ian Bruce Associates Ltd, since 1975; *b* 14 March 1947; *s* of Henry Bruce and Ellen Flora Bruce (*née* Bingham); *m* 1969, Hazel Bruce (*née* Roberts); one *s* three *d*. *Educ:* Chelmsford Tech. High Sch.; Bradford Univ.; Mid-Essex Tech. Coll. Mem., Inst. of Management Services. Student apprentice, Marconi, 1965–67; Work Study Engineer: Marconi, 1967–69; Pye Unicam, 1969–70; Haverhill Meat Products, 1970–71; Factory Manager and Work Study Manager, BEPI (Pye), 1971–74; Factory Manager, Sinclair Electronics, 1974–75; Chm. and Founder, gp of Employment Agencies and Management Consultants, 1975–. Mem., Employment Select Cttee, 1990–. Parly Consultant to Telecommunication Managers Assoc., 1989–. *Publications:* numerous articles in press and magazines, both technical and political. *Recreations:* scouting, badminton, writing, sailing, camping. *Address:* House of Commons, SW1A 0AA. *T:* (home) Weymouth (0305) 833320; (office) 071–219 5086.

BRUCE, Ian Waugh; Director-General, Royal National Institute for the Blind, since 1983; Visiting Professor, City University Business School, since 1990; *b* 21 April 1945; *s* of Thomas Waugh Bruce and Una (*née* Eagle); *m* 1971, Anthea Christine, (Tina), *d* of Dr P. R. Rowland, FRSC; one *s* one *d*. *Educ:* King Edward VI Sch., Southampton; Central High Sch., Arizona; Univ. of Birmingham (BSocSc Hons 1968). CBIM 1991 (FBIM 1981; MBIM 1975). Apprentice Chem. Engr, Courtaulds, 1964–65; Marketing Trainee, then Manager, Unilever, 1968–70; Appeals and PR Officer, then Asst Dir, Age Concern England, 1970–74; Dir, National Volunteer Centre, 1975–81; Controller of Secretariat, then Asst Chief Exec., Bor. of Hammersmith and Fulham, 1981–83. Consultant, UN Div. of Social Affairs, 1970–72; Sec., Volunteurope, Brussels, 1979–81; Adviser, BBC Community Progs Unit, 1979–81; Member: Educn Adv. Council, IBA, 1981–83; Exec. Cttee, NCVO, 1978–81, 1990–; National Good Neighbour Campaign, 1977–79; Council, Retired Executives Action Clearing House, 1978–83; Adv. Council, Centre for Policies on Ageing, 1979–83; Disability Alliance Steering Cttee, 1985–; Exec. Cttee, Age Concern England, 1986–; Nat. Adv. Council on Employment of Disabled People, 1987–; DHSS Cttee on Inter-Agency Collaboration on Visual Handicap, 1987–88; Bd, Central London TEC, 1990–; Co-Chair, Disability Benefits Consortium, 1988–. Mem., Art Panel, Art Film Cttee and New Activities Cttee, Arts Council of GB, 1967–71; Spokesman, Artists Now, 1973–77. Chm., Coventry Internat. Centre, 1964. FRSA 1991. Sir Raymond Priestley Expeditionary Award, Univ. of Birmingham, 1968. *Publications:* Public Relations and the Social Services, 1972; (jtly) Patronage of the Creative Artist, 1974, 2nd edn 1975; Blind and Partially Sighted People in Britain, 1991; papers on visual handicap, voluntary and community work, old people, contemporary art and marketing. *Recreations:* the arts, the countryside. *Address:* 54 Mall Road, W6 9DG. *Club:* ICA.

BRUCE, Malcolm Gray; MP Gordon, since 1983 (L 1983–88, Lib Dem since 1988); *b* 17 Nov. 1944; *s* of David Stewart Bruce and Kathleen Elmslie (*née* Delf); *m* 1969, Veronica Jane Wilson; one *s* one *d*. *Educ:* Wrekin Coll., Shropshire; St Andrews Univ. (MA 1966); Strathclyde Univ. (MSc 1970). Liverpool Daily Post, 1966–67; Buyer, Boots Pure Drug Co., 1967–68; A. Goldberg & Son, 1968–69; Res. Information Officer, NE Scotland Develt Authority, 1971–75; Marketing Dir, Noroil Publishing House (UK), 1975–81; Jt Editor/Publisher/ Dir, Aberdeen Petroleum Publishing, 1981–84. Dep. Chm., Scottish Liberal Party, 1975–84 (Energy Spokesman, 1975–83); Liberal Parly Spokesman on Scottish Affairs, 1983–85, on Energy, 1985–87, on Trade and Industry, 1987–88; Alliance Parly Spokesman on Employment, 1987; Lib Dem Natural Resources (energy and conservation) Spokesman, 1988–90. Leader, Scottish Liberal Democrats, 1988–. Rector of Dundee Univ., 1986–89. Vice-Pres., Nat. Deaf Children's Soc., 1990– (Pres., Grampian Br., 1985–). *Publications:* A New Life for the Country: a rural development programme for West Aberdeenshire, 1978; Putting Energy to Work, 1981; (with others) A New Deal for Rural Scotland, 1983; (with Paddy Ashdown) Growth from the Grassroots, 1985. *Recreations:* theatre, music, travel, fresh Scottish air. *Address:* Grove Cottage, Grove Lane, Torphins AB31 4HJ. *T:* Torphins (03398) 82386. *Club:* National Liberal.

BRUCE, Sir Michael Ian, 12th Bt, *cr* 1629; partner, Gossard-Bruce Co., from 1953; President, Newport Sailing Club Inc., since 1978; Director, Lenders Indemnity Corp., since 1985; *b* 3 April 1926; *s* of Sir Michael William Selby Bruce, 11th Bt and Doreen Dalziel, *d* of late W. F. Greenwell; *S* father 1957; holds dual UK and US citizenship; has discontinued first forename, Francis; *m* 1st, 1947, Barbara Stevens (marr. diss., 1957), *d* of Frank J. Lynch; two *s*; 2nd, 1961, Frances Keegan (marr. diss., 1963); 3rd, 1966, Marilyn Ann (marr. diss., 1975), *d* of Carter Mulally. *Educ:* Forman School, Litchfield, Conn; Pomfret, Conn. Served United States Marine Corps, 1943–46 (Letter of Commendation); S Pacific area two years, Bismarck Archipelago, Bougainville, Philippines. Owner, Latitude 57° Marine Shipping Co., 1966; Master Mariner's Ticket, 1968; Pres., Newport Academy of Sail, Inc., 1979–; Owner, American Maritime Co. Chm., Yacht Masters and Marine Assoc. Liaison Cttee, US Coast Guard. *Recreations:* sailing, spear-fishing. *Heir:* *s* Michael Ian Richard Bruce, *b* 10 Dec. 1950. *Address:* 3432 Via Oporto #204, Newport Beach, Calif 92663, USA. *T:* 714–675–7100. *Clubs:* Rockaway Hunt; Lawrence Beach; Balboa Bay (Newport Beach); Vikings of Scandia (Los Angeles).

BRUCE, Michael Stewart Rae; *see* Marnoch, Hon. Lord.

BRUCE, Robert Nigel (Beresford Dalrymple), CBE 1972 (OBE (mil.) 1946); TD; CEng, Hon. FIGasE; *b* 21 May 1907; *s* of Major R. N. D. Bruce, late of Hampstead; *m* 1945, Elizabeth Brogden, *d* of J. G. Moore; twin *s* two *d*. *Educ:* Harrow School (Entrance and Leaving Scholar); Magdalen College, Oxford (Exhibitioner). BA (Hons Chem.) and BSc. Joined Territorial Army Rangers (KRRC), 1931; Major, 1939; served Greece, Egypt, Western Desert, 1940–42; Lt-Col Comdg Regt, 1942; GHQ, MEF, Middle East Supply Centre, 1943–45; Col, Dir. of Materials, 1944. Joined Gas, Light and Coke Co., as Research Chemist, 1929; Asst to Gen. Manager, 1937, Controller of Industrial Relations, 1946; Staff Controller, 1949, Dep. Chm., 1956, North Thames Gas Bd; Chm., S Eastern Gas Bd, 1960–72. President: British Road Tar Assoc., 1964 and 1965; Coal Tar Research Assoc., 1966; Institution of Gas Engineers, 1968; Mem. Bd, CEI, 1968–80. Chm. Governing Body, Westminster Technical Coll., 1958–76. Sec., Tennis and Rackets Assoc., 1974–81. *Publications:* Chronicles of the 1st Battalion the Rangers (KRRC), 1939–45; contribs to Proc. Royal Society, Jl Soc. Chemical Industry, Jl Chemical Society. *Recreations:* travel, golf, fishing, military history. *Address:* Fairway, 57 Woodland Grove, Weybridge, Surrey KT13 9EQ. *T:* Weybridge (0932) 852372. *Club:* Queen's (Hon. Mem.).

BRUCE-GARDNER, Sir Douglas (Bruce), 2nd Bt, *cr* 1945; Director, Guest, Keen & Nettlefolds Ltd, 1960–82; *b* 27 Jan. 1917; *s* of Sir Charles Bruce-Gardner, 1st Bt; *S* father, 1960; *m* 1st, 1940, Monica Flumerfelt (marr. diss. 1964), *d* of late Sir Geoffrey Jefferson, CBE, FRS; one *s* two *d*; 2nd, 1964, Sheila Jane, *d* of late Roger and Barbara Stilliard, Seer Green, Bucks; one *s* one *d*. *Educ:* Uppingham; Trinity College, Cambridge. Lancashire Steel, 1938–51; Control Commn, Germany, 1945–46; joined GKN, 1951. Dir, GKN Ltd, 1960, Dep. Chm., 1974–77; Dep. Chm., GKN Steel Co. Ltd, 1962, Gen. Man. Dir, 1963–65, Chm., 1965–67; Chairman: GKN Rolled & Bright Steel Ltd, 1968–72; GKN (South Wales) Ltd, 1968–72; Exors of James Mills Ltd, 1968–72; Parson Ltd, 1968–72; Brymbo Steel Works Ltd, 1974–77; Miles Druce & Co. Ltd, 1974–77; Exec. Vice-Chm., UK Ops, Gen. Products, GKN Ltd, 1972–74; Dep. Chm., GKN (UK) Ltd, 1972–75; Director: Henry Gardner & Co. Ltd, 1952–68; Firth Cleveland Ltd, 1972–75; BHP-GKN Holdings Ltd, 1977–78; Dep.-Chm., Iron Trades Employers' Insurance Assoc., 1984–87 (Dir, 1977–87). President: Iron and Steel Inst., 1966–67; British Indep. Steel Producers' Assoc., 1972; Iron and Steel Employers' Assoc., 1963–64. Prime Warden, Blacksmiths' Co., 1983–4. *Recreations:* fishing, photography. *Heir:* *s* Robert Henry Bruce-Gardner [*b* 10 June 1943; *m* 1979, Veronica Ann Hand-Oxborrow, *d* of late Rev. W. E. Hand and of Mrs R. G. Oxborrow, Caterham; two *s*]. *Address:* Stocklands, Lewstone, Ganarew, near Monmouth NP5 3SS. *T:* Symonds Yat (0600) 890216.

BRUCE LOCKHART, Logie, MA; Headmaster of Gresham's School, Holt, 1955–82; *b* 12 Oct. 1921; *s* of late John Harold Bruce Lockhart; *m* 1944, Josephine Agnew; two *s* two *d* (and one *d* decd). *Educ:* Sedbergh School; St John's College, Cambridge (Schol. and Choral Studentship). RMC Sandhurst, 1941; served War of 1939–45; 9th Sherwood Foresters, 1942; 2nd Household Cavalry (Life Guards), 1944–45. Larmor Award, 1947; Asst Master, Tonbridge School, 1947–55. Sponsor, Nat. Council for Educnl Standards. *Publication:* The Pleasures of Fishing, 1981. *Recreations:* fishing, writing, music, natural history, games; Blue for Rugby football, 1945, 1946, Scottish International, 1948, 1950, 1953; squash for Cambridge, 1946. *Address:* Church Farm House, Lower Bodham, near Holt, Norfolk NR25 6PS. *T:* Holt (0263) 712137. *Club:* East India, Devonshire, Sports and Public Schools.

BRUCE-MITFORD, Rupert Leo Scott, FBA 1976; Research Keeper in the British Museum, 1975–77 (Keeper of British and Mediæval Antiquities, 1954–69, of Mediæval and Later Antiquities, 1969–75); *b* 14 June 1914; 4th *s* of C. E. Bruce-Mitford, Madras, and Beatrice (Allison), *e d* of John Fall, British Columbia; *m* 1st, 1941, Kathleen Dent (marr. diss. 1972); one *s* two *d*; 2nd, 1975, Marilyn Roberta (marr. diss. 1984), *o d* of Robert J. Luscombe, Walton on the Hill, Staffs; 3rd, 1988, Margaret Edna, *o d* of Charles A. Adams, Trowbridge, Wilts. *Educ:* Christ's Hospital; Hertford College, Oxford (Baring Scholar; Hon. Fellow, 1984); DLitt Oxon 1987. Temp. Asst Keeper, Ashmolean Museum, 1937; Asst Keeper, Dept of British and Mediæval Antiquities, British Museum, 1938; Royal Signals, 1939–45; Deputy Keeper, British Museum, 1954. FSA 1947 (Sec., Soc. of Antiquaries, 1950–54, Vice-Pres., 1972–76); FSA Scot. Slade Professor of Fine Art, Univ. of Cambridge, 1978–79. Vis. Fellow, All Souls Coll., Oxford, 1978–79; Professorial Fellow, Emmanuel Coll., Cambridge, 1978–79; Faculty Visitor, Dept of English, ANU, Canberra, 1981. Excavations: Seacourt, Berks, 1938–39; Mawgan Porth, Cornwall, 1949–54; Chapter House graves, Lincoln Cathedral, 1955; Sutton Hoo, Suffolk, 1965–68. Pres., Soc. for Mediæval Archæol., 1957–59; Vice-Pres., UISPP World Archaeol Congress, 1986 (resigned, S African non-participation issue). Member: Ancient Monuments Bd, England, 1954–77; Perm. Council, UISPP, 1957–79; German Archæological Inst.; Italian Inst. of Prehistory and Protohistory; Corresp. Member, Jutland Archæological Society; Hon. Mem., Suffolk Inst. of Archaeology; For. Corresp. Mem., Acad. du Var. For. Trustee, Instituto de Valencia de Don Juan, Madrid, 1954–75. Lectures: Dalrymple, Glasgow, 1961; Thomas Davis Radio, Dublin, 1964; Jarrow, 1967; O'Donnell, Wales, 1971; Garmonsway, York, 1973; Crake, Mount Allison Univ., NB, 1980. Liveryman,

Worshipful Co. of Clockmakers. Hon. LittD Dublin 1966. *Publications:* The Society of Antiquaries of London; Notes on its History and Possessions (with others), 1952; Editor and contributor, Recent Archæological Excavations in Britain, 1956; (with T. J. Brown, A. S. C. Ross and others), Codex Lindisfarnensis (Swiss facsimile edn), 1957–61; (trans. from Danish) The Bog People, by P. V. Glob, 1969; The Sutton Hoo Ship-burial, a handbook, 1972, revd edn 1979; Aspects of Anglo-Saxon Archaeology, 1974; The Sutton Hoo Ship-burial, Vol. I, 1975, Vol. II, 1978, Vol. III, 1983; (ed) Recent Archaeological Excavations in Europe, 1975; papers and reviews in learned journals. *Recreations:* reading, chess, watching sport, travel. *Address:* Eton House, Broad Street, Bampton, Oxford OX8 2LX. *Clubs:* Athenæum, Garrick, MCC.

BRÜCK, Prof. Hermann Alexander, CBE 1966; DPhil (Munich); PhD (Cantab); Astronomer Royal for Scotland and Regius Professor of Astronomy in the University of Edinburgh, 1957–75; now Professor Emeritus; Dean of the Faculty of Science, 1968–70; *b* 15 Aug. 1905; *s* of late H. H. Brück; *m* 1st, 1936, Irma Waitzfelder (*d* 1950); one *s* one *d*; 2nd, 1951, Dr Mary T. Conway; one *s* two *d*. *Educ:* Augusta Gymnasium, Charlottenburg; Universities of Bonn, Kiel, Munich, and Cambridge. Astronomer, Potsdam Astrophysical Observatory, 1928; Lectr, Berlin University, 1935; Research Associate, Vatican Observatory, Castel Gandolfo, 1936; Asst Observer, Solar Physics Observatory, Cambridge, 1937; John Couch Adams Astronomer, Cambridge University, 1943; Asst Director, Cambridge Observatory, 1946; Director, Dunsink Observatory and Professor of Astronomy, Dublin Institute for Advanced Studies, 1947–57. Mem., Bd of Governors, Armagh Observatory, NI, 1971–84. MRIA, 1948; FRSE, 1958; Member Pontif. Academy of Sciences, Rome, 1955, Mem. Council, 1964–86; Corr. Member Academy of Sciences, Mainz, 1955. Hon. DSc: NUI, 1972; St Andrews, 1973. *Publications* (ed jtly) Astrophysical Cosmology, 1982; The Story of Astronomy in Edinburgh, 1983; (with Mary T. Brück) The Peripatetic Astronomer: a biography of Charles Piazzi Smyth, 1988; scientific papers in journals and observatory publications. *Recreation:* music. *Address:* Craigower, Penicuik, Midlothian EH26 9LA. *T:* Penicuik (0968) 75918.

BRUDENELL-BRUCE, family name of **Marquess of Ailesbury.**

BRÜGGEN, Frans; recorder player and conductor; *b* Amsterdam, 1934. *Educ:* Univ. of Amsterdam. Prof., Royal Hague Conservatoire, 1955; formerly: Erasmus Prof., Harvard Univ.; Regents Prof., Univ. of Calif, Berkeley. Former Dir, Mozart Ensemble, Amsterdam; founder, Orch. of The Eighteenth Century, 1981; guest conductor: Minnesota Orch.; Concertgebouw Orch., Amsterdam; San Francisco SO. Gives regular concert tours and master classes, and has made many recordings. Researches and edits music for the recorder and is actively interested in design and manufacture of the instrument. *Address:* c/o Artist Management International, 12/13 Richmond Buildings, W1V 5AF; Amstelveld 4, NL-1017 JD, Amsterdam, The Netherlands.

BRUINVELS, Peter Nigel Edward; news broadcaster, political commentator and freelance journalist; Principal, Peter Bruinvels Associates, media management and public affairs consultants, founded 1986; *b* 30 March 1950; *er s* of Stanley and Ninette Maud Bruinvels; *m* 1980, Alison Margaret, *o d* of Major David Gilmore Bacon, RA retd; two *d*. *Educ:* St John's Sch., Leatherhead; London Univ. (LLB Hons). Bar Exams, Council of Legal Educn. Co. Sec., BPC Publishing, 1978–81; Sec./Lawyer, Amari PLC, 1981–82; Management Consultant and company director, 1982–. Chairman: Law Students Cons. Assoc. of GB, 1974–76; SE Area Young Conservatives, 1977–79; Dorking CPC, 1979–83; Mem., Cons. Nat. Union Exec., 1976–81. Contested (C) Leicester E, 1987. MP (C) Leicester E, 1983–87. Jt Chm., British Parly Lighting Gp; Vice-Chairman: Cons. Backbench Cttee on Urban Affairs and New Towns, 1984–87; Cons. Backbench Cttee on Education, 1986–87; Sec., Anglo-Netherlands Parly Gp, 1983–87; Chm., British-Malta Parly Gp, 1984–87; Member: Cons. Backbench Cttee on Home Affairs, 1983–87; Cons. Backbench Cttee on NI, 1983–87; Life Mem., British-Amer. Parly Gp, 1983. Promoter, Crossbows Act, 1987. Sponsor, Cons. Family Campaign, 1986–. Dir, Aalco Nottingham Ltd, 1983–88. Member: Guildford Dio. Synod 1979–; Gen. Synod, 1985–; MIPR 1981; FRSA 1986; Hon. MCIM 1987; MJI 1988; Fellow, Industry and Parliament Trust. Granted Freedom, City of London, 1980. *Publications:* Zoning in on Enterprise, 1982; Light up the Roads, 1984; Sharing in Britain's Success—a Study in Widening Share Ownership, Through Privatisation, 1987; Investing in Enterprise—a Comprehensive Guide to Inner City Regeneration and Urban Renewal, 1989. *Recreations:* political campaigning, the media, Church of England. *Address:* 14 High Meadow Close, Dorking, Surrey. *Clubs:* Carlton, Inner Temple, Corporation of Church House.

BRUMFIT, Prof. Christopher John; Professor of Education, since 1984, Director, Centre for Language in Education, since 1986, University of Southampton; *b* 25 Oct. 1940; *s* of late John Raymond Brumfit and of Margaret May Brumfit (*née* Warner; she *m* 2nd, 1942, Frank Greenaway, *qv*); *m* 1st, 1965, Elizabeth Ann Sandars (marr. diss.); one *s*; 2nd, 1986, Rosamond Frances Mitchell; one *s*. *Educ:* Glyn Grammar Sch., Epsom; Brasenose Coll., Oxford (BA English Lang. and Lit.); Univ. of Essex (MA Applied Linguistics); PhD London 1983; Makerere Coll., Univ. of East Africa (DipEd). Head of English, Tabora Govt Sch., Tanzania, 1964–68; Lectr in Educn, Univ. of Dar es Salaam, 1968–71; Lectr in English and Linguistics, City of Birmingham Coll. of Educn, 1972–74; Lectr in Educn with ref. to English for Speakers of Other Languages, Univ. of London Inst. of Educn, 1974–80; Reader in Educn, Univ. of London, 1980–84; Head, Sch. of Educn, 1986–90, Dean, Faculty of Educnl Studies, 1990–, Univ. of Southampton. Chm., BAAL, 1982–85; Vice-Pres., Assoc. Internat. de Linguistique Appliquée, 1984–87. Editor: ELT Documents, 1982–90; Review of English Language Teaching, 1990–. *Publications:* (jtly) Teaching English as a Foreign Language, 1978; (with K. Johnson) The Communicative Approach to Language Teaching, 1979; Problems and Principles in English Teaching, 1980; English for International Communication, 1982; (with J. Roberts) An Introduction to Language and Language Teaching, 1983; (with M. Finocchiaro) The Functional-Notional Approach, 1983; Teaching Literature Overseas, 1983; Language Teaching Projects for the Third World, 1983; Communicative Methodology in Language Teaching, 1984; General English Syllabus Design, 1984; Language and Literature Teaching, 1985; (jtly) English as a Second Language in the UK, 1985; The Practice of Communicative Teaching, 1986; (with R. A. Carter) Literature and Language Teaching, 1986; Language in Teacher Education, 1988; (with R. Mitchell) Research in the Language Classroom, 1990; The Language Learner's Bedside Book, 1991; Assessment in Literature Teaching, 1991; Applied Linguistics and English Language Teaching, 1992. *Recreations:* Russian literature, academic cricket, opera, walking. *Address:* 43 Church Lane, Highfield, Southampton SO2 1SY. *T:* Southampton (0703) 557346. *Club:* Athenæum.

BRUNA, Dick; graphic designer; writer and illustrator of children's books; *b* 23 Aug. 1927; *s* of A. W. Bruna and J. C. C. Erdbrink; *m* 1953, Irene de Jongh; two *s* one *d*. *Educ:* Primary Sch. and Gymnasium, Utrecht, Holland; autodidact. Designer of book jackets, 1945–, and of posters, 1947– (many prizes); writer and illustrator of children's books, 1953– (1st book, The Apple); also designer of postage stamps, murals, greeting cards and picture postcards. Exhibn based on Miffy (best-known character in children's books), Gemeentemuseum, Arnhem, 1977. Member: Netherlands Graphic Designers; Authors League of America Inc.; PEN Internat.; Alliance Graphique Internat. *Publications:* 67 titles

published and 60 million copies printed by 1987; children's books translated into 28 languages. *Address:* (studio) 3 Jeruzalemstraat, 3512 KW, Utrecht. *T:* 030–316042. *Club:* Art Directors (Netherlands).

BRUNDIN, Clark Lannerdahl; PhD; Vice Chancellor, University of Warwick, since 1985; *b* 21 March 1931; *s* of late Ernest Walfrid Brundin and of Elinor Brundin (*née* Clark); *m* 1959, Judith Anne (*née* Maloney); two *s* two *d*. *Educ:* Whittier High Sch., California; California Inst. of Technology; Univ. of California, Berkeley (BSc, PhD); MA Oxford. Electronics Petty Officer, US Navy, 1951–55. Associate in Mech. Engrg, UC Berkeley, 1956–57; Demonstr. Dept of Engrg Science, Univ. of Oxford, 1957–58; Res. Engr, Inst. of Engrg Res., UC Berkeley, 1959–63; Univ. Lectr, Dept of Engrg Sci., Univ. of Oxford, 1963–85, Vice-Chm., Gen. Bd of the Faculties, 1984–85; Jesus College, Oxford: Fellow and Tutor in Engrg, 1964–85; Sen. Tutor, 1974–77; Estates Bursar, 1978–84; Hon. Fellow, 1985. Vis. Prof., Univ. of Calif Santa Barbara, 1978. Mem., CICHE, 1987–. Director: Cokethorpe Sch. Educnl Trust, 1983–; Heritage Projects (Oxford) Ltd, 1985–; Blackwell Scientific Publications Ltd, 1990–; Chairman: Anchor Housing Assoc., 1985–; Cloister Homes, 1989–90. Governor, Magdalen College Sch., 1987–. *Publications:* articles on rarefied gas dynamics in sci. lit. *Recreations:* sailing, mending old machinery, music of all sorts. *Address:* University of Warwick, Coventry CV4 7AL. *T:* Coventry (0203) 523630. *Clubs:* Athenæum, Royal Fowey Yacht, Fowey Gallants Sailing (Fowey, Cornwall).

BRUNEI, HM Sultan of; *see* Negara Brunei Darussalam.

BRUNER, Jerome Seymour, MA, PhD; Watts Professor of Psychology, University of Oxford, 1972–80; G. H. Mead University Professor, New School for Social Research, New York, 1980–88; Research Professor of Psychology, New York University, since 1987; Fellow, New York Institute for the Humanities; *b* New York, 1 Oct. 1915; *s* of Herman and Rose Bruner; *m* 1st, 1940, Katherine Frost (marr. diss. 1956); one *s* one *d*; 2nd, 1960, Blanche Marshall McLane (marr. diss. 1984); 3rd, 1987, Carol Fleisher Feldman. *Educ:* Duke Univ. (AB 1937): Harvard Univ. (AM 1939, PhD 1941). US Intelligence, 1941; Assoc. Dir, Office Public Opinion Research, Princeton, 1942–44; govt public opinion surveys on war problems, 1942–43; political intelligence, France, 1943; Harvard University: research, 1945–72; Prof. of Psychology, 1952–72; Dir, Centre for Cognitive Studies, 1961–72. Lectr, Salzburg Seminar, 1952; Bacon Prof., Univ. of Aix-en-Provence, 1965. Editor, Public Opinion Quarterly, 1943–44; Syndic, Harvard Univ. Press, 1962–63. Member: Inst. Advanced Study, 1951; White House Panel on Educnl Research and Develt. Guggenheim Fellow, Cambridge Univ., 1955; Fellow: Amer. Psychol Assoc. (Pres., 1964–65; Distinguished Scientific Contrib. award, 1962); Amer. Acad. Arts and Sciences; Swiss Psychol Soc. (hon.); Soc. Psychol Study Social Issues (past Pres.); Amer. Assoc. Univ. Profs; Puerto Rican Acad. Arts and Sciences (hon.). Hon. DHL Lesley Coll., 1964; Hon. DSc: Northwestern Univ., 1965; Sheffield, 1970; Bristol, 1975; Hon. MA, Oxford, 1972; Hon. DSocSci, Yale, 1975; Hon. LLD: Temple Univ., 1965; Univ. of Cincinnati, 1966; Univ. of New Brunswick, 1969; Hon. DLitt: North Michigan Univ., 1969; Duke Univ., 1969; Dr *hc*: Sorbonne, 1974; Leuven, 1976; Ghent, 1977; Madrid, 1987; Free Univ., Berlin, 1988; Columbia, 1988. *Publications:* Mandate from the People, 1944; (with Krech) Perception and Personality: A Symposium, 1950; (with Goodnow and Austin) A Study of Thinking, 1956; (with Smith and White) Opinions and Personality, 1956; (with Bresson, Morf and Piaget) Logique et Perception, 1958; The Process of Education, 1960; On Knowing: Essays for the Left Hand, 1962; (ed) Learning about Learning: A conference report, 1966; (with Olver, Greenfield, and others) Studies in Cognitive Growth, 1966; Toward a Theory of Instruction, 1966; Processes of Cognitive Growth: Infancy, Vol III, 1968; The Relevance of Education, 1971; (ed Anglin) Beyond the Information Given: selected papers of Jerome S. Bruner, 1973; (with Connolly) The Growth of Competence, 1974; (with Jolly and Sylva) Play: its role in evolution and development, 1976; Under Five in Britain, 1980; Communication as Language, 1982; In Search of Mind: essays in autobiography, 1983; Child's Talk, 1983; Actual Minds, Possible Worlds, 1986; Acts of Meaning, 1990; contribs technical and professional jls. *Recreation:* sailing. *Address:* 200 Mercer Street, New York, NY 10012, USA. *Clubs:* Royal Cruising; Century (New York); Cruising Club of America.

BRUNNER, Dr Guido; Grand Cross, Order of Federal Republic of Germany; German diplomat and politician; Ambassador of the Federal Republic of Germany in Madrid, since 1982; *b* Madrid, 27 May 1930; *m* 1958, Christa (*née* Speidel). *Educ:* Bergzabern, Munich; German Sch., Madrid; Univs of Munich, Heidelberg and Madrid (law and econs). LLD Munich; Licentiate of Law Madrid. Diplomatic service, 1955–74, 1981–; Private Office of the Foreign Minister, 1956; Office, Sec. of State for For. Affairs, 1958–60; German Observer Mission to the UN, New York, 1960–68; Min. for Foreign Affairs: Dept of scientific and technol relns, 1968–70; Spokesman, 1970–72; Head of Planning Staff, Ambassador and Head of Delegn of Fed. Rep. of Germany, Conf. for Security and Coop. in Europe, Helsinki/Geneva, 1972–74; Mem., Commn of the European Communities, (responsible for Energy, Research, Science and Educn), 1974–80; Mem., Bundestag, 1980–81; Mayor of Berlin and Minister of Economics and Transport, Jan.-May 1981; Ambassador, Min. of Foreign Affairs, Bonn, 1981–82. Corresp. Mem., Spanish Acad. of History, 1986–. Hon. DLitt Heriot-Watt, 1977; Dr *hc*; Technical Faculty, Patras Univ., Greece: City Univ., London, 1980. Melchett Medal, Inst. of Energy, 1978. Grand Cross, Order of Civil Merit, Spain, 1978; Grand Cross, Order of Leopold, Belgium, 1981; Grand Cross, Order of Merit, FRG, 1981; Grand Cross, Order of Isabel la Católica, Spain, 1986. *Publications:* Bipolarität und Sicherheit, 1965; Friedenssicherungsaktionen der Vereinten Nationen, 1968; Stolz wie Don Rodrigo, 1982; El Poder y la Unión, 1989; contrib. Vierteljahreshefte für Zeitgeschichte, Aussenpolitik, Europa-Archiv. *Address:* Embajada de la República Federal de Alemania, C/Fortuny 8, 28010 Madrid, Spain.

BRUNNER, Sir John Henry Kilian, 4th Bt *cr* 1895; *b* 1 June 1927; *s* of Sir Felix John Morgan Brunner, 3rd Bt, and of Dorothea Elizabeth, OBE, *d* of late Henry Brodribb Irving; *S* father, 1982; *m* 1955, Jasmine Cecily, *d* of late John Wardrop Moore; two *s* one *d*. *Educ:* Eton; Trinity Coll., Oxford (BA 1950). Served as Lieut RA. On staff, PEP, 1950–53; Talks producer, 1953; Economic Adviser, Treasury, 1958–61; Asst Manager, Observer, 1961. *Heir:* *s* Nicholas Felix Minturn Brunner, *b* 16 Jan. 1960. *Address:* 13 Glyndon Avenue, Brighton, Vic 3186, Australia.

BRUNNING, David Wilfrid; His Honour Judge Brunning; a Circuit Judge, since 1988; *b* 10 April 1943; *s* of Wilfred and Marion Brunning; *m* 1967, Deirdre Ann Shotton; three *s*. *Educ:* Burton upon Trent Grammar Sch.; Worcester Coll., Oxford (BA 1965, DPA 1966). Articled Clerk, Leics CC, 1966–67; Lectr, Loughborough Technical College, 1968; Mem. of Chambers, King Street, Leicester, and of Midland and Oxford Circuit, 1970–88. Chairman: Kirk Lodge Probation Hostel, 1973–89; Leicester Anchor Club, 1983–89. *Recreations:* campanology, squash, walking, wine, music. *Address:* Bushby House, Main Street, Bushby, Leics LE7 9PL.

BRUNSDEN, Prof. Denys, PhD; Professor of Geography, Department of Geography, King's College, University of London, since 1983; *b* 14 March 1936; *s* of Francis Stephen Brunsden and Mabel Florence (*née* Martin); *m* 1961, Elizabeth Mary Philippa (*née*

Wright); one *s* one *d*. *Educ*: Torquay Grammar Sch. for Boys; King's Coll., Univ. of London (BSc Hons Geography; PhD 1963). King's College, London: Tutorial Student, 1959–60; Asst Lectr, 1960–63; Lectr, 1963–75; Reader, 1975–83. Vis. Lectr, 1964–65, Erskine Fellow, 1988, Univ. of Canterbury, NZ; Vis. Associate Prof., Louisiana State Univ., 1971. Chairman: British Geomorphol Res. Gp, 1985–86; Wkg Pty for Collaboration in Internat. Geomorphology, 1985–; President: Geographical Assoc., 1986–87; Internat. Assoc. of Geomorphologists, 1989–; Vice-Pres., RGS, 1984–87. Gill Meml Award, RGS (for contribs to study of mass movement and fieldwork), 1977; Republic of China Award Lectr, 1988–89; Assoc. of American Geographers Honours, 1991. *Publications*: Dartmoor, 1968; Slopes, Forms and Process, 1970; (with J. C. Doornkamp) The Unquiet Landscape, 1971 (USA 1976, Australia 1976, Germany 1977); (with J. B. Thornes) Geomorphology and Time, 1977; (with C. Embleton and D. K. C. Jones) Geomorphology: present problems, future prospects, 1978; (with J. C. Doornkamp and D. K. C. Jones) The Geology, Geomorphology and Pedology of Bahrain, 1980; (with R. U. Cooke, J. C. Doornkamp and D. K. C. Jones) The Urban Geomorphology of Drylands, 1982; (with D. B. Prior) Slope Instability, 1984; (with R. Gardner, A. S. Goudie and D. K. C. Jones) Landshapes, 1989; Natural Disasters, 1990. *Recreations*: making walking sticks and shepherd's-crooks, painting, reading thrillers, watching TV, enjoying dinner parties and fine wine, talking, travelling to exotic places, eating, drinking and relaxing in the Drôme. *Address*: Department of Geography, King's College London, Strand, WC2R 2LS. *Club*: Geographical.

BRUNSDON, Norman Keith; Agent General for New South Wales in London, since 1989; *b* 11 Jan. 1930; *s* of late G. A. Brunsdon; *m* 1953, Ruth, *d* of late W. Legg; one *s* one *d*. *Educ*: Wagga Wagga High Sch., NSW. FCA. Price Waterhouse, Australia: joined, 1951; Partner, 1963; Mem. Policy Cttee (Bd), 1970–86; Partner-in-Charge, Sydney, 1975–81; Chm. and Sen. Partner, Australia, 1982–86; World Firm Policy Cttee (Bd) and Council of Firms, 1979–86. Chm., Aust. Govt's Taxation Adv. Cttee, 1979–83; Trustee, Econ. Develt of Aust. Cttee, 1977–86. Vice-Pres., Thai-Aust. Chamber of Commerce & Industry, 1982–85; Member: Pacific Basin Econ. Council, 1982–86; Aust. Japan Business Co-op. Cttee, 1982–86; Standing Cttee, C of E Dio. Sydney, 1969–74; C of E Children's Homes Cttee, 1974–84 (Treasurer, 1969–75); Acting Chm., 1972–73); Governor, King's Sch., Parramatta, 1977–86. Hon. Mem., Cook Soc. Freeman, City of London, 1989. FRSA. *Recreations*: music, opera, theatre, reading, sailing, golf. *Address*: New South Wales Government, 75 King William Street (Level 7), EC4N 7HA. *T*: 071–283 2166; 71 Coolawin Road, Northbridge, NSW 2063, Australia. *Clubs*: Royal Automobile, East India; Australian (Sydney); Royal Sydney Yacht Squadron.

BRUNSKILL, Ronald William, OBE 1990; MA, PhD; FSA; architect, lecturer and author; Hon. Fellow, School of Architecture, University of Manchester, since 1989 (Lecturer, 1960–73, Senior Lecturer, 1973–84, Reader in Architecture, 1984–89); *b* 3 Jan. 1929; *s* of William Brunskill and Elizabeth Hannah Brunskill; *m* 1960, Miriam Allsopp; two *d*. *Educ*: Bury High Sch.; Univ. of Manchester (BA Hons Arch. 1951, MA 1952, PhD 1963). Registered Architect and ARIBA, 1951; FSA 1975. National Service, 2nd Lieut RE, 1953–55. Studio Asst in Arch., Univ. of Manchester, 1951–53; Architectural Asst, LCC, 1955; Asst in Arch., Univ. of Manchester, 1955–56; Commonwealth Fund Fellow (arch. and town planning), MIT, 1956–57; Architect to Williams Deacon's Bank, 1957–60; Architect in private practice, 1960–66; Partner, Carter, Brunskill & Associates, chartered architects, 1966–69, Consultant, 1969–73. Vis. Prof., Univ. of Florida, Gainesville, 1969–70. President: Vernacular Arch. Gp, 1974–77; Cumberland and Westmorland Antiquarian and Archaeol Soc., 1990– (Vice-Pres., 1975–90); Vice-Pres., Weald and Downland Museum Trust, 1980–; Chairman: Ancient Monuments Soc., 1990– (Hon. Architect, 1983–88; Vice-Chm., 1988–90); Friends of Friendless Churches, 1990–; Member: Historic Bldgs Council for England, 1978–84; Royal Commn on Ancient and Historical Monuments of Wales, 1983–; Historic Buildings and Monuments Commn (English Heritage), 1989– (Mem., Historic Buildings Adv. Cttee and Ancient Monuments Adv. Cttee of Historic Buildings and Monuments Commn, 1984–90); Cathedrals Adv. Commn for England, 1981–; Manchester Diocesan Adv. Cttee for Care of Churches, 1973–79 and 1987–; Manchester Cathedral Fabric Cttee, 1987–; Blackburn Cathedral Fabric Cttee, 1989–; Chester Cathedral Fabric Cttee, 1989–; Council, Soc. for Folk Life Studies, 1969–72 and 1980–83. Trustee, British Historic Buildings Trust, 1985–. Neale Bursar, RIBA, 1962; President's Award, Manchester Soc. of Architects, 1977. *Publications*: Illustrated Handbook of Vernacular Architecture, 1971, 3rd edn (enlarged) 1987; Vernacular Architecture of the Lake Counties, 1974; (with Alec Clifton-Taylor) English Brickwork, 1977; Traditional Buildings of Britain, 1981; Houses (in series, Collins Archaeology), 1982; Traditional Farm Buildings of Britain, 1982, 2nd edn (enlarged) 1987; Timber Building in Britain, 1985; Brick Building in Britain, 1990; articles and reviews in archaeol and architectural jls. *Recreation*: enjoying the countryside. *Address*: Three Trees, 8 Overhill Road, Wilmslow SK9 2BE. *T*: Wilmslow (0625) 522099; 159 Glan Gors, Harlech, Gwynedd LL46 2SA. *Club*: Athenæum.

BRUNT, Peter Astbury, FBA 1969; Camden Professor of Ancient History, Oxford University, and Fellow of Brasenose College, 1970–82; *b* 23 June 1917; *s* of Rev. Samuel Brunt, Methodist Minister, and Gladys Eileen Brunt. *Educ*: Ipswich Sch.; Oriel Coll., Oxford. Open Schol. in History, Oriel Coll., Oxford, 1935; first classes in Class. Mods, 1937, and Lit. Hum., 1939; Craven Fellowship, 1939. Temp. Asst Principal and (later) Temp. Principal, Min. of Shipping (later War Transport), 1940–45. Sen. Demy, Magdalen Coll., Oxford, 1946; Lectr in Ancient History, St Andrews Univ., 1947–51; Fellow and Tutor of Oriel Coll., Oxford, 1951–67, Dean, 1959–64, Hon. Fellow, 1973; Fellow and Sen. Bursar, Gonville and Caius Coll., Cambridge, 1968–70. Editor of Oxford Magazine, 1963–64; Chm., Cttee on Ashmolean Museum, 1967; Deleg., Clarendon Press, 1971–79; Mem. Council, British Sch. at Rome, 1972–87; Pres., Soc. for Promotion of Roman Studies, 1980–83. *Publications*: Thucydides (selections in trans. with introd.), 1963; Res Gestae Divi Augusti (with Dr J. M. Moore), 1967; Social Conflicts in the Roman Republic, 1971; Italian Manpower 225 BC–AD 14, 1971, rev. edn 1987; (ed) Arrian's Anabasis (Loeb Classical Library), vol. I, 1976, vol. II, 1983; The Fall of the Roman Republic and related essays, 1988; Roman Imperial Themes, 1990; articles in classical and historical jls. *Address*: 37 Woodstock Close, Woodstock Road, Oxford. *T*: Oxford (0865) 53024.

BRUNT, Peter William, MD, FRCP, FRCPE; Physician to the Queen in Scotland, since 1983; Consultant Physician and Gastroenterologist, Grampian Health Board, Aberdeen, since 1970; Clinical Senior Lecturer in Medicine, University of Aberdeen, since 1970; *b* 18 Jan. 1936; *s* of late Harry Brunt and Florence J. J. Airey; *m* 1961, Dr Anne Lewis, *d* of Rev. R. H. Lewis; three *d*. *Educ*: Manchester Grammar Sch.; Cheadle Hulme Sch.; King George V Sch.; Univ. of Liverpool. MB, ChB 1959. Gen. Med. training, Liverpool Royal Infirmary and Liverpool Hosps, 1959–64; Research Fellow, Johns Hopkins Univ. Sch. of Medicine, 1965–67; Lectr in Medicine, Edinburgh Univ., 1967–68; Senior Registrar, Gastrointestinal Unit, Western Gen. Hosp., Edinburgh, 1968–69. Hon. Lectr in Medicine, Royal Free Hosp. Sch. of Medicine, Univ. of London, 1969–70. Mem., Assoc. of Physicians of GB and Ireland. *Publications*: (with M. Losowsky and A. E. Read) Diseases of the Liver and Biliary System, 1984; (with P. F. Jones and N. A. G. Mowat) Gastroenterology, 1984. *Recreations*: mountaineering, music, operatics, Crusaders' Union. *Address*: 17 Kingshill Road, Aberdeen AB2 4JY. *T*: Aberdeen (0224) 314204.

BRUNTISFIELD, 1st Baron, *cr* 1942, of Boroughmuir; **Victor Alexander George Anthony Warrender,** MC 1918; 8th Bt of Lochend, East Lothian, *cr* 1715; late Grenadier Guards; *b* 23 June 1899; *s* of 7th Bt and Lady Maud Warrender (*d* 1945), *y d* of 8th Earl of Shaftesbury; *S* to father's Baronetcy, 1917; *m* 1920, Dorothy (marr. diss. 1945), *y d* of late Colonel R. H. Rawson, MP, and Lady Beatrice Rawson; three *s*; *m* 1948, Tania, *y r d* of late Dr Kolin, St Jacob, Dubrovnik, Jugoslavia; one *s* one *d*. *Educ*: Eton. Served European War, 1917–18 (MC, Russian Order of St Stanislas, Star of Roumania, St Ann of Russia with sword); MP (U) Grantham Division of Kesteven and Rutland, 1923–42; an assistant Whip, 1928–31; Junior Lord of the Treasury, 1931–32; Vice-Chamberlain of HM Household, 1932–35; Comptroller of HM Household, 1935; Parliamentary and Financial Secretary to Admiralty, 1935; Financial Secretary, War Office, 1935–40; Parliamentary and Financial Secretary, Admiralty, 1940–42; Parliamentary Secretary, Admiralty, 1942–45. Heir: *s* Col Hon. John Robert Warrender, *qv*. *Address*: Résidence Le Village, CH-1837 Château-d 'Oex, Switzerland. *Club*: Turf.
See also Lord Reay, Hon. R. H. Warrender.

BRUNTON, Sir (Edward Francis) Lauder, 3rd Bt, *cr* 1908; Physician; *b* 10 Nov. 1916; *s* of Sir Stopford Brunton, 2nd Bt, and Elizabeth, *o d* of late Professor J. Bonsall Porter; *S* father 1943; *m* 1946, Marjorie, *o d* of David Sclater Lewis, MSc, MD, CM, FRCP (C); one *s* one *d*. *Educ*: Trinity College School, Port Hope; Bryanston School; McGill Univ. BSc 1940; MD, CM 1942; served as Captain, RCAMC. Hon. attending Physician, Royal Victoria Hosp., Montreal. Fellow: American Coll. of Physicians; Internat. Soc. of Hematology; Life Member: Montreal Mus. of Fine Arts; Art Gall. of Nova Scotia. Heir: *s* James Lauder Brunton, MD, FRCP(C) [*b* 24 Sept. 1947; *m* 1967, Susan, *o d* of Charles Hons; one *s* one *d*]. *Address*: PO Box 140, Guysborough, Nova Scotia B0H 1N0, Canada. *Club*: Royal Nova Scotia Yacht Squadron.

BRUNTON, Sir Gordon (Charles), Kt 1985; Chairman: Bemrose Corporation plc, since 1978; Martin Currie Pacific Trust plc, since 1985; The Racing Post plc, since 1985; Community Industry Ltd, since 1985; Ingersoll Publications Ltd, since 1988; *b* 27 Dec. 1921; *s* of late Charles Arthur Brunton and late Hylda Pritchard; *m* 1st, 1946, Nadine Lucile Paula Sohr (marr. diss. 1965); one *s* two *d* (and one *s* decd); 2nd, 1966, Gillian Agnes Kirk; one *s* one *d*. *Educ*: Cranleigh Sch.; London Sch. of Economics. Commnd into RA, 1942; served Indian Army, Far East; Mil. Govt, Germany, 1946. Joined Tothill Press, 1947; Exec. Dir, Tothill, 1956; Man. Dir, Tower Press Gp of Cos, 1958; Exec. Dir, Odhams Press, 1961; joined Thomson Organisation, 1961; Man. Dir, Thomson Publications, 1961; Dir, Thomson Organisation, 1963; Chm., Thomson Travel, 1965–68; Man. Dir and Chief Exec., Internat. Thomson Orgn plc (formerly Thomson British Hldgs) and The Thomson Orgn Ltd, 1968–84; Pres., Internat. Thomson Orgn Ltd, 1978–84. Director: Times Newspapers Ltd, 1967–81; Sotheby Parke Bernet Group, 1978–83 (Chm., 1982–83, Chm. Emeritus, Sotheby's Holding Inc., 1983); Cable and Wireless plc, 1981–; Yattendon Investment Trust Ltd, 1985–; Sports Bureau Internat. Ltd, 1985–86; Chairman: John Silver (Hldgs), 1985–86; Euram Consulting, 1985–; Communications and General Consultants, 1985–; Cavendish Shops, 1985–; Mercury Communications, 1986–90; Cavendish Retail, 1987–; Focus Investments, 1987–; Racing Internat., 1989–. President: Periodical Publishers Assoc., 1972–74, 1981–83; Nat. Advertising Benevolent Soc., 1973–75 (Trustee, 1980–); History of Advertising Trust, 1981–84; Chm., EDC for Civil Engrg, 1978–84; Member: Printing and Publishing Ind. Trng Bd, 1974–78; Supervisory Bd, CBI Special Programmes Unit, 1980–84; Business in the Community Council, 1981–84; Chm., Independent Adoption Service, 1986–. Mem., South Bank Bd, Arts Council, 1985–. Governor: LSE (Fellow, 1978); Ashridge Management Coll., 1983–86; Ct of Governors, Henley—The Management Coll., 1983–85; Mem. Council, Templeton College (formerly Oxford Centre for Management Studies), 1976–; Mem., Finance Cttee, OUP, 1985–. *Recreations*: books, breeding horses. *Address*: North Munstead, Godalming, Surrey GU8 4AX. *T*: Godalming (0483) 416313. *Club*: Garrick.

BRUNTON, Sir Lauder; *see* Brunton, Sir E. F. L.

BRUS, Prof. Wlodzimierz, PhD; Professor of Modern Russian and East European Studies, University of Oxford, 1985–88, now Emeritus Professor; Professorial Fellow, Wolfson College, 1985–88, now Emeritus Fellow; Senior Research Fellow, St Antony's College, Oxford, since 1989; *b* 23 Aug. 1921; *s* of Abram Brus and Helena (*née* Askanas); *m* 1st, 1940, Helena Wolińska; 2nd, 1945, Irena Stergień; two *d*; 3rd, 1956, Helena Wolińska; one *s*. *Educ*: Saratov, USSR (MA Economic Planning); Warsaw, Poland (PhD Pol. Econ.). Polish Army, 1944–46. Junior Editor, Nowe Drogi (theoretical journal of Polish Workers' (later United Workers') Party), 1946–49; Asst (later Associate) Prof. of Political Economy, Central Sch. of Planning & Statistics, Warsaw, 1949–54; Hd of Dept of Political Economy, Inst. of Social Sciences attached to Central Cttee, Polish United Workers' Party, 1950–56; Prof. of Political Econ., Univ. of Warsaw, 1954–68; Dir, Research Bureau, Polish Planning Commn, 1956–68; Vice-Chm., Econ. Adv. Council of Poland, 1957–63; research worker, Inst. of Housing, Warsaw, 1968–72; Vis. Sen. Res. Fellow, Univ. of Glasgow, 1972–73; Sen. Res. Fellow, St Antony's Coll., Oxford, 1973–76; Univ. Lectr and Fellow, Wolfson Coll., Oxford, 1976–85. Visiting Professor (or Senior Fellow): Rome, 1971; Catholic Univ. of Louvain, 1973; Columbia, 1982; Johns Hopkins Bologna Centre, 1983. Consultant to World Bank, 1980–82, 1984. Officers' Cross, Order of Polonia Restituta, Poland, 1954; Polish and Soviet war medals, 1944, 1945. *Publications*: The Law of Value and Economic Incentives, 1956 (trans Hungarian, 1957); General Problems of Functioning of the Socialist Economy, 1961 (published in 10 langs); Economics and Politics of Socialism, 1973 (published in 6 langs); Socialist Ownership and Political Systems, 1975 (published in 8 langs); Economic History of Eastern Europe, 1983 (published in 6 langs); (with K. Laski) From Marx to the Market: socialism in search of an economic system, 1989; contribs to Soviet Studies, Jl of Comparative Economics, Cambridge Jl of Economics. *Recreations*: walking, swimming. *Address*: 21 Bardwell Court, Bardwell Road, Oxford OX2 6SX. *T*: Oxford (0865) 53790.

BRUTON, John (Gerard); TD (Fine Gael), Meath, Dáil Eireann (Parliament of Ireland), since 1969; Leader of Fine Gael, since 1990 (Deputy Leader, 1989–90); *b* 18 May 1947; *s* of Matthew Joseph Bruton and Doris Bruton (*née* Delany); *m* 1981, Finola Gill; one *s* three *d*. *Educ*: St Dominic's Coll., Dublin; Clongowes Wood Coll., Co. Kildare; University Coll., Dublin (BA, BL); King's Inns, Dublin; called to the Bar, 1972. National Secretary, Fine Gael Youth Group, 1966–69. Mem., Dáil Committee of Procedure and Privileges, 1969–73, 1982–; Fine Gael Spokesman on Agriculture, 1972–73; Parliamentary Secretary: to Minister for Education, 1973–77; to Minister for Industry and Commerce, 1975–77; Fine Gael Spokesman: on Agriculture, 1977–81; on Finance, Jan.–June 1981; Minister: for Finance, 1981–82, for Industry and Energy, 1982–83, for Industry, Trade, Commerce and Tourism, 1983–86, for Finance, 1986–87; Fine Gael Spokesman on Industry and Commerce, 1987–89, on education, 1989; Leader of the House, 1982–86. Pres., EEC Industry, Research and Internal Market Councils, July–Dec. 1984. Mem., Parly Assembly, Council of Europe, 1989–. Hon. Citizen of Sioux City, Iowa, USA, 1970; Ambassador of Good Will, Hon. Dist. Citizen and Washington General, State of Washington, 1983; Calif. Legislature Assembly Rules Cttee and Calif. Senate Rules Cttee Commendations,

1983. *Publications:* Reform of the Dail, 1980; A Better Way to Plan the Nation's Finances, 1981; Industrial Policy—White Paper, 1984; Tourism Policy—White Paper, 1985; Fine Gael policy documents on 1992 and on televising of parliament; contrib. Furrow magazine. *Recreation:* reading history. *Address:* Cornelstown, Dunboyne, Co. Meath. *T:* 255573.

BRYAN, Sir Arthur, Kt 1976; Lord-Lieutenant of Staffordshire, since 1968; President, Waterford Wedgwood Holdings plc and a Director, Waterford Glass Group plc, 1986–88 (Managing Director, 1963–85, Chairman, 1968–86, Wedgwood); *b* 4 March 1923; *s* of William Woodall Bryan and Isobel Alan (*née* Tweedie); *m* 1947, Betty Ratford; one *s* one *d*. *Educ:* Longton High Sch., Stoke-on-Trent. Served with RAFVR, 1941–45. Joined Josiah Wedgwood & Sons Ltd, 1947; London Man., 1953–57; General Sales Man., 1959–60; Director and President, Josiah Wedgwood & Sons Inc. of America, 1960–62; Director: Josiah Wedgwood & Sons Ltd, Barlaston, 1962; Josiah Wedgwood & Sons (Canada) Ltd; Josiah Wedgwood & Sons (Australia) Pty Ltd; Phoenix Assurance Co., 1976–85; Friends' Provident Life Office, 1985–; Rank Organisation, 1985–; United Kingdom Fund Inc., 1987–. Member: BOTB, 1978–82 (Chm., N American Adv. Gp, 1973–82); British-American Associates, 1988–; Marshall Aid Commem. Cttee, 1988–; Chm., Consumer Market Adv. Cttee, DTI, 1988–. Pres., British Ceramic Manufacturers' Fedn, 1970–71; Mem., Design Council, 1977–82. Mem. Ct, Univ. of Keele. FRSA 1964 (Mem. Council, 1980–82); Fellow, Inst. of Marketing (grad. 1950); CBIM (FBIM 1968); Comp. Inst. Ceramics. KStJ 1972. Hon. MUniv. Keele, 1978. *Recreations:* walking, swimming and reading. *Address:* Parkfields Cottage, Tittensor, Stoke-on-Trent, Staffs ST12 9HQ. *T:* Barlaston (078139) 2686.

BRYAN, Dora, (Mrs William Lawton); actress; *b* 7 Feb. 1924; *d* of Albert Broadbent and Georgina (*née* Hill); *m* 1954, William Lawton; one *s* (and one *s* one *d* adopted). *Educ:* Hathershaw Council Sch., Lancs. Pantomimes: London Hippodrome, 1936; Manchester Palace, 1937; Alhambra, Glasgow, 1938; Oldham Repertory, 1939–44; followed by Peterborough, Colchester, Westcliff-on-Sea. ENSA, Italy, during War of 1939–45. Came to London, 1945, and appeared in West End Theatres: Peace in our Time; Travellers' Joy; Accolade; Lyric Revue; Globe Revue; Simon and Laura; The Water Gypsies; Gentlemen Prefer Blondes; Six of One; Too True to be Good; Hello, Dolly!; They Don't Grow on Trees; Rookery Nook, Her Majesty's, 1979; The Merry Wives of Windsor, Regent's Park, 1984; She Stoops to Conquer, Nat. Theatre, 1985; The Apple Cart, Haymarket, 1986; Charlie Girl, Victoria Palace, 1986, Birmingham, 1988; Pygmalion, Plymouth, New York, 1987; 70, Girls, 70, Vaudeville, 1991. Chichester Festival seasons, 1971–74; London Palladium season, 1971; London Palladium Pantomime season, 1973–74. Has also taken parts in farces televised from Whitehall Theatre. *Films include:* The Fallen Idol, 1949; A Taste of Honey, 1961 (British Acad. Award); Two a Penny, 1968; Great St Trinian's Train Robbery, 1970; Apartment Zero, 1989. *TV series:* appearances on A to Z; Sunday Night at the London Palladium; According to Dora, 1968; Both Ends Meet, 1972. Cabaret in Canada, Hong Kong and Britain. Has made recordings. *Publication:* According to Dora (autobiog.), 1987. *Recreations:* reading, patchwork quilts. *Address:* 118 Marine Parade, Brighton, East Sussex. *T:* Brighton (0273) 603235.

BRYAN, Gerald Jackson, CMG 1964; CVO 1966; OBE 1960; MC 1941; Member, Lord Chancellor's Panel of Independent Inquiry Inspectors, since 1982; *b* 2 April 1921; *yr s* of late George Bryan, OBE, LLD, and Ruby Evelyn (*née* Jackson), Belfast; *m* 1947, Georgiana Wendy Cockburn, OStJ, *d* of late William Barraud and Winnifred Hull; one *s* two *d*. *Educ:* Wrekin Coll.; RMA, Woolwich; New Coll., Oxford. Regular Commn, RE, 1940; served Middle East with No 11 (Scottish) Commando, 1941; retd 1944, Capt. (temp. Maj.). Apptd Colonial Service, 1944; Asst District Comr, Swaziland, 1944; Asst Colonial Sec., Barbados, 1950; Estabt Sec., Mauritius, 1954; Administrator, Brit. Virgin Is, 1959; Administrator of St Lucia, 1962–67, retired; Govt Sec. and Head of Isle of Man Civil Service, 1967–69; General Manager: Londonderry Develt Commn, NI, 1969–73; Bracknell Develt Corp., 1973–82. Director: Lovaux Engrg Co. Ltd, 1982–88; MDSL, 1988–. Sec. Gen., Assoc. of Contact Lens Manufacturers, 1983–88. Mem. (C), Berks CC, 1983–85. Treasurer, Gordon Boys' Sch., Woking, 1979–. Chm., St John Council for Berks, 1981–88. KStJ 1985, Mem., Chapter Gen., 1987–. FBIM. *Recreations:* swimming, walking. *Address:* Whitehouse, Murrell Hill Lane, Binfield, Berks RG12 5BY. *T:* Bracknell (0344) 425447.

BRYAN, Margaret, CMG 1988; HM Diplomatic Service, retired; Ambassador to Panama, 1986–89; *b* 26 Sept. 1929; *d* of late James Grant and Dorothy Rebecca Galloway; *m* 1952, Peter Bernard Bryan (marr. diss. 1981). *Educ:* Cathedral Sch., Shanghai; Croydon High Sch.; Girton Coll., Cambridge (MA Modern Languages). Second, later First, Secretary, FCO, 1962–80; Head of Chancery and Consul, Kinshasa, 1980–83; Counsellor, Havana, 1983–86. *Recreations:* theatre, travel, cookery, embroidery. *Address:* 10 Park Road, Blockley, Moreton-in-Marsh, Glos GL56 8BZ. *Club:* Royal Over-Seas League.

BRYAN, Sir Paul (Elmore Oliver), Kt 1972; DSO 1943; MC 1943; *b* 3 Aug. 1913; *s* of Rev. Dr J. I. Bryan, PhD; *m* 1st, 1939, Betty Mary (*née* Hoyle) (*d* 1968); three *d*; 2nd, 1971, Cynthia Duncan (*née* Ashley Cooper), *d* of late Sir Patrick Ashley Cooper and of Lady Ashley Cooper, Hexton Manor, Herts. *Educ:* St John's School, Leatherhead (Scholar); Caius College, Cambridge (MA). War of 1939–45; 6th Royal West Kent Regt; enlisted, 1939; commissioned, 1940; Lieut-Col, 1943; served in France, N Africa, Sicily, Italy; Comdt 164th Inf. OCTU (Eaton Hall), 1944. Sowerby Bridge UDC, 1947; contested Sowerby, By-Election, 1948, and General Elections, 1950 and 1951. MP (C): Howden Div. of ER Yorks, 1955–83; Boothferry, 1983–87. Member Parliamentary Delegation: to Peru, 1955, to Algeria, 1956, to Germany, 1960, to USA and Canada, 1961, to India, 1966, to Uganda and Kenya, 1967, to Hong Kong, 1969, to Japan and Indonesia, 1969, to China, 1972, to Mexico, 1981. Assistant Government Whip, 1956–58; Parliamentary Private Secretary to Minister of Defence, 1956; a Lord Commissioner of the Treasury, 1958–61; Vice-Chairman, Conservative Party Organisation, 1961–65; Conservative Front Bench Spokesman on Post Office and broadcasting, 1965; Minister of State, Dept of Employment, 1970–72. Chm., All Party Hong Kong Parly Gp, 1974–87; Vice-Chm., Conservative 1922 Cttee, 1977–87. Chairman: Croydon Cable Television, subseq. United Artists Cables Internat. (London South), 1985–; Scottish Eagle Insce Co., 1990–; Director: Granada TV Rental Ltd, 1966–70; Granada Television, 1972–83; Granada Theatres, 1973–83; Greater Manchester Independent Radio Ltd, 1972–84; Maritime Union Assurance Co. (Bermuda) Ltd, 1980–88; Scottish Lion Insurance Co. Ltd, 1981–; Hewetson Holdings Ltd, 1983–; Dep. Chm., Furness Withy and Co. Ltd, 1984–89 (Dir, 1983–). *Address:* Park Farm, Sawdon, near Scarborough, North Yorks. *T:* Scarborough (0723) 859370; 5 Westminster Gardens, Marsham Street, SW1. *T:* 071–834 2050.

BRYAN, Robert Patrick, OBE 1980; security consultant; Police Adviser to Foreign and Commonwealth Office, and Inspector General of Dependent Territories Police, 1980–85, retired; *b* 29 June 1926; *s* of Maurice Bryan and Elizabeth (*née* Waite); *m* 1948, Hazel Audrey (*née* Braine) (*d* 1990); three *s*. *Educ:* Plaistow Secondary Sch.; Wanstead County High Sch. Indian Army (Mahratta LI), 1944–47. Bank of Nova Scotia, 1948–49; Metropolitan Police: Constable, 1950; Dep. Asst Commissioner, 1977, retired 1980. National Police College: Intermediate Comd Course, 1965; Sen. Comd Course, 1969; occasional lecturer. RCDS 1974. Chm., Food Distribn Security Assoc., 1988– Governor, Hampton Sch., 1978–. *Publications:* contribs to police and related pubns, particularly on community relations and juvenile delinquency. *Address:* c/o National Westminster Bank, High Street, Teddington, Mddx TW11 8EP.

BRYANS, Dame Anne (Margaret), DBE 1957 (CBE 1945); DStJ; Chairman, Order of St John of Jerusalem and BRCS Service Hospitals Welfare and VAD Committee, 1960–89; Vice-Chairman, Joint Committee, Order of St John and BRCS, 1976–81; *b* 29 Oct. 1909; *e d* of late Col Rt Hon. Sir John Gilmour, 2nd Bt, GCVO, DSO, MP of Montrave and late Mary Louise Lambert; *m* 1932, Lieut-Comdr J. R. Bryans, RN, retired (*d* 1990); one *s*. *Educ:* privately. Joined HQ Staff British Red Cross Society, 1938; Deputy Commissioner British Red Cross and St John War Organisation, Middle East Commission, 1943; Commissioner Jan.-June 1945. Dep. Chm., 1953–64, Vice-Chm., 1964–76, Exec. Cttee, BRCS; Lay Mem., Council for Professions Supplementary to Med., 1973–79; Chm., Relief Cttee, Nations Fund for Nurses, 1980–. Member: Ethical practices Sub-Cttee, Royal Free Hosp., 1974–; Royal Free Hosp. Sch. Council, 1968–; Bd of Governors, Eastman Dental Hosp., 1973–79; Camden and Islington AHA, 1974–79; Vice-Pres., Open Sect., RSocMed, 1975, Pres. 1980–82; former Member: ITA, later IBA; Govt Anglo-Egyptian Resettlement Bd; BBC/ITA Appeals Cttee; Med. Sch. St George's Hosp.; Special Trustee and former Chm., Royal Free Hosp. and Friends of Royal Free Hosp.; former Chairman: Bd of Governors, Royal Free Hosp.; Council, Florence Nightingale Hosp.; Trustee, Florence Nightingale Aid in Sickness Trust, 1979–; Vice-Pres., Royal Coll. of Nursing; former Governor, Westminster Hosp. FRSM 1976. *Address:* 57 Elm Park House, Elm Park Gardens, SW10. *Clubs:* New Cavendish; Royal Lymington Yacht.

BRYANS, Tom, OBE 1983 (MBE 1975); Chief General Manager, Trustee Savings Bank Central Board (formerly TSB Association Ltd), 1975–82; *b* 16 Sept. 1920; *s* of Thomas and Martha Bryans; *m* 1947, Peggy Irene Snelling; two *s*. *Educ:* Royal Belfast Academical Instn. AIB 1950; FSBI 1972. Served War, 1939–46. Joined Belfast Savings Bank, 1938; Asst Gen. Man., 1969; Gen. Man., 1971. *Recreations:* sailing, golfing, gardening and music.

BRYANT, (Alan) Christopher; Chairman, Bryant Group plc (formerly Bryant Holdings Ltd), since 1962 (Managing Director, 1960–88); *b* 28 July 1923; *s* of Ebenezer John Bryant and Ivy Maud Bryant (*née* Seymour); *m* 1951, Jean Mary Nock; four *d*. *Educ:* West House School, Birmingham; Malvern Coll.; Birmingham Univ. (BSc (Hons)). FCIOB 1958. Engineer Officer, Fleet Air Arm, 1944–47 (Sub-Lieut, RNVR); Project Manager, 1946–48, Director, 1948–86, C. Bryant & Son Ltd. Non-exec. Dir, BSG International plc, 1985–. Chm., 1969–, Pres. and Chm., 1987–, Birmingham YMCA; Chm., Finance Cttee, Nat. Council of YMCAs, 1977–. *Recreations:* sailing, shooting, walking. *Address:* (office) Cranmore House, Cranmore Boulevard, Solihull B90 4SD. *T:* 021–711 1212. *Clubs:* Naval; South Caernarvonshire Yacht.

BRYANT, Rear-Adm. Benjamin, CB 1956; DSO 1942 (two bars, 1943); DSC 1940; *b* 16 Sept. 1905; *s* of J. F. Bryant, MA, FRGS, ICS (retd); *m* 1929, Marjorie Dagmar Mynors (*née* Symonds) (*d* 1965); one *s* one *d*; *m* 1966, Heather Elizabeth Williams (*née* Hance) (*d* 1989). *Educ:* Oundle; RN Colls Osborne and Dartmouth. Entered submarine branch of RN, 1927; Commanded: HMS/M Sea Lion, 1939–41; HMS/M Safari, 1941–43; comd 7th and 3rd Submarine Flotillas, 1943–44; comd 4th s/m Flotilla, British Pacific Fleet, 1945–47; comd HMS Dolphin Submarine School, and 5th Submarine Flotilla, 1947–49; Commodore (submarines), 1948; idc 1950; Commodore, RN Barracks, Devonport, 1951–53; Flag Captain to C-in-C Mediterranean, 1953–54; Rear-Admiral, 1954. Deputy Chief of Naval Personnel (Training and Manning), 1954–57; retired, 1957. Staff Personnel Manager, Rolls Royce Scottish Factories, 1957–68. *Recreations:* fishing, golf, shooting. *Address:* Quarry Cottage, Kithurst Lane, Storrington, West Sussex RH20 4LP.

BRYANT, Christopher; *see* Bryant, A. C.

BRYANT, David John, CBE 1980 (MBE 1969); Director, Drakelite Ltd (International Bowls Consultants), since 1978; international bowler; *b* 27 Oct. 1931; *s* of Reginald Samuel Harold Bryant and Evelyn Claire (*née* Weaver); *m* 1960, Ruth Georgina (*née* Roberts); two *d*. *Educ:* Weston Grammar Sch.; St Paul's Coll., Cheltenham; Redland Coll., Bristol (teacher training colls). National Service, RAF, 1950–52; teacher trng, 1953–55; schoolmaster, 1955–71; company director, sports business, 1971–78. World Singles Champion, 1966, 1980 and 1988; World Indoor Singles Champion, 1979, 1980 and 1981; World Indoor Pairs Champion, 1986, 1987, 1989 and 1990; Kodak Masters International Singles Champion, 1978, 1979 and 1982; Gateway International Masters Singles Champion, 1984, 1985, 1986, 1987; Woolwich International Singles Champion, 1988, 1989; World Triples Champion, 1980; Commonwealth Games Gold Medallist: Singles: 1962, 1970, 1974 and 1978; Fours: 1962. Numerous national and British Isles titles, both indoor and outdoor. *Publications:* Bryant on Bowls, 1966; Bowl with Bryant, 1984; Bryant on Bowls, 1985; The Game of Bowls, 1990. *Recreations:* angling, gardening. *Address:* 47 Esmond Grove, Clevedon, Avon BS21 7HP. *T:* Clevedon (0272) 875423. *Clubs:* Clevedon Bowling, Clevedon Conservative.

BRYANT, David Michael Arton; His Honour Judge Bryant; a Circuit Judge, since 1989; *b* 27 Jan. 1942; *s* of Lt-Col and Mrs A. D. Bryant; *m* 1969, Diana Caroline, *d* of Brig. and Mrs W. C. W. Sloan; two *s* one *d*. *Educ:* Wellington Coll.; Oriel Coll., Oxford (Open Scholar; BA). Called to the Bar, Inner Temple, 1964; practised North Eastern Circuit, 1965–89. A Recorder, 1985–89. *Recreations:* gardening, shooting, dining. *Address:* Sleningford Park, Ripon, N Yorks HG4 3JA. *Club:* Carlton.

BRYANT, Rt. Rev. Denis William, DFC 1942; retired; *b* 31 Jan. 1918; *s* of Thomas and Beatrice Maud Bryant; *m* 1940, Dorothy Linda (*née* Lewis); one *d*. *Educ:* Clark's Coll., Ealing; Cardiff Techn. Coll. Joined RAF; Wireless Operator/Air Gunner, 1936; Navigator, 1939; France, 1940 (despatches); Pilot, 1943; commn in Secretarial Br., 1948; Adjt, RAF Hereford, 1950; Sqdn-Ldr i/c Overseas Postings Record Office, Gloucester, 1951; Sqdn-Ldr DP7, Air Min., 1953. Ordinand, Queen's Coll., Birmingham, 1956; Deacon, 1958; Priest, 1959; Rector of Esperance, 1961–67; Archdeacon of Goldfields, 1966–67; Bishop of Kalgoorlie, 1967 until 1973 when Kalgoorlie became part of Diocese of Perth; Asst Bishop of Perth, and Archdeacon and Rector of Northam, 1973–75; Rector of Dalkeith, WA, 1975–85. Hon. Chaplain, Anglican Homes, 1985–. *Recreations:* squash, tennis, oil painting. *Address:* Sundowner Centre, 416 Stirling Highway, Cottesloe, WA 6011, Australia. *T:* (090) 384 1178.

BRYANT, Air Vice-Marshal Derek Thomas, CB 1987; OBE 1974; Air Officer Commanding, Headquarters Command and Staff Training and Commandant, Royal Air Force Staff College, 1987–89, retired; *b* 1 Nov. 1933; *s* of Thomas Bryant and Mary (*née* Thurley); *m* 1956, Patricia Dodge; one *s* one *d*. *Educ:* Latymer Upper Grammar Sch., Hammersmith. Fighter pilot, 1953; Qualified Flying Instructor, 1957; Sqdn Comdr, 1968–74; OC RAF Coningsby, 1976–78; SASO HQ 38 Gp, 1982–84; Dep. Comdr, RAF Germany, 1984–87; various courses and staff appts. *Recreations:* gardening, golf. *Address:* Manor Stables, Lower Swell, Fivehead, Taunton, Somerset TA3 6PH. *Club:* Royal Air Force.

BRYANT, Prof. Greyham Frank, PhD; FEng 1988; FIEE; FIMA; Professor of Control, Imperial College, London University, since 1982; *b* 3 June 1931; *s* of Ernest Noel Bryant and Florence Ivy (*née* Russell); *m* 1955, Iris Sybil Jardine; two *s*. *Educ:* Reading Univ.; Imperial Coll. (PhD). FIMA 1973; FIEE 1987. Sen. Scientific Officer, Iron and Steel Res., London, 1959–64; Imperial College: Res. Fellow, 1964–67; Reader in Industrial Control, 1975–82. Chm., Broner Consultants, 1979–88; Director: Greycon Consultants, 1985–; Circulation Research, 1989–. *Publications:* Automation of Tandem Mills (jtly), 1973; papers on design of management control schemes, multivariable control and modelling, in learned jls. *Recreation:* music. *Address:* 18 Wimborne Avenue, Norwood Green, Middlesex UB2 4HB. *T:* 081–574 5648.

BRYANT, Judith Marie, (Mrs H. M. Hodkinson), SRN; Fellow, King's Fund College (on secondment from North East Thames Regional Health Authority), since 1990 (part-time Fellow, 1986–90); *b* 31 Dec. 1942; *d* of Frederic John Bryant and Joan Marion (*née* Summerfield); *m* 1986, Prof. Henry Malcolm Hodkinson, *qv*. *Educ:* City of London Sch. for Girls; The London Hosp. (SRN 1964); Brunel Univ. (MPhil 1983). Ward Sister, UCH, 1965–69; Nursing Officer, subseq. Sen. Nursing Officer, Northwick Park Hosp., Harrow, 1969–75; Divl Nursing Officer, Harrow, 1975–78; Dist Nursing Officer, Enfield, 1978–82, Victoria, 1982–85; Chief Nursing Officer and Dir of Quality Assurance, Riverside HA, 1985–86; Regl Nursing Officer, NE Thames RHA, 1986–90. Florence Nightingale Meml Scholar, USA and Canada, 1970. Adviser, DHSS Res. Liaison Cttee for the Elderly, 1977–83; Member: SW Herts DHA, 1981–86; NHS Training Authority, Nurses and Midwives Staff Training Cttee, 1986–89; 1930 Fund for Dist Nurses, 1985–. *Recreations:* opera, gardening, early English pottery, 18th century glass. *Address:* 8 Chiswick Square, Burlington Lane, W4 2QG. *T:* 081–747 0239.

BRYANT, Michael Dennis, CBE 1988; actor; National Theatre player, since 1977; an Associate of the National Theatre, since 1984; *b* 5 April 1928; *s* of William and Ann Bryant; *m* 1958, Josephine Martin (marr. diss. 1980); two *s* two *d*; *m* 1990, Judith Mary Coke. *Educ:* Battersea Grammar Sch. Merchant Navy, 1945; Army, 1946–49; drama sch., 1949–51; theatre and television, 1957–77; RSC, 1964–65. Rôles with NT include: Hieronimo, in Spanish Tragedy; Iago, in Othello; Lenin, in State of Revolution (Best Actor, SWET awards, 1977); title rôle, in Mayor of Zalamea (Best Actor, British Theatrical Assoc. awards, 1981); Enobarbus, in Antony and Cleopatra, and Gloucester, in King Lear (Best Supporting Actor: Olivier awards, 1987; (for Enobarbus) London Critics awards, 1987); Prospero, in The Tempest, 1988; Polonius, in Hamlet, 1989. Council Mem., RADA, 1982–; Mem., NT Foundn, 1990–. *Recreation:* rambling. *Address:* Willow Cottage, Kington Magna, Dorset SP8 5EW.

BRYANT, Prof. Peter Elwood, FRS 1991; Watts Professor of Psychology, Oxford University, since 1980; Fellow of Wolfson College, Oxford, since 1980. *Educ:* Clare College, Cambridge (BA 1963, MA 1967). University Lecturer in Human Experimental Psychology, Oxford, 1967–80; Fellow, St John's Coll., Oxford, 1967–80. Editor, British Jl of Developmental Psychol., 1982–88. President's award, BPsS, 1984. *Publications:* Perception and Understanding in Young Children, 1974; (with L. Bradley) Children's Reading Problems, 1985; (with U. Goswami) Phonological Skills and Learning to Read, 1990. *Address:* Wolfson College, Oxford OX2 6UD.

BRYANT, Peter George Francis; Under Secretary, Overseas Trade Division 3, Department of Trade and Industry, since 1989; *b* 10 May 1932; *s* of late George Bryant, CBE and Margaret Bryant; *m* 1961, Jean (*née* Morriss); one *s* one *d*. *Educ:* Sutton Valence Sch.; Birkbeck Coll., London Univ. (BA). Joined Civil Service as Exec. Officer, Min. of Supply, 1953; Higher Exec. Officer, BoT, 1960; Principal, 1967; 1st Sec. (Commercial), Vienna (on secondment), 1970; Dir of British Trade Drive in S Germany, 1973; Department of Trade (later Department of Trade and Industry): Asst Sec., 1974 (Head, Overseas Projs Gp); Civil Aviation Internat. Relations Div., 1978; Under Sec., Chemicals, Textiles and Paper Div., 1981; seconded to HM Diplomatic Service as Consul-Gen., Düsseldorf, 1985–88, and Dir-Gen. of Trade and Investment Promotion, FRG, 1988.

BRYANT, Richard Charles, CB 1960; Under-Secretary, Board of Trade, 1955–68; *b* 20 Aug. 1908; *s* of Charles James and Constance Byron Bryant, The Bounds, Faversham, Kent; *m* 1938, Elisabeth Ellington, *d* of Dr. A. E. Stansfeld, FRCP; two *s* two *d*. *Educ:* Rugby; Oriel College, Oxford. Entered Board of Trade, 1932; Ministry of Supply, 1939–44. *Address:* Marsh Farm House, Brancaster, Norfolk. *T:* Brancaster (0485) 210206. *Club:* Travellers'.

BRYANT, Thomas; HM Diplomatic Service; Consul General, Zürich, since 1991; *b* 1 Nov. 1938; *s* of George Edward Bryant and Ethel May Bryant (*née* Rogers); *m* 1961, Vivien Mary Theresa Hill; twin *s* one *d*. *Educ:* William Ellis Sch., London; Polytechnic of Central London (DMS). Nat. service, Army, 1957–59. Entered FO, 1957; Hong Kong, 1963; Peking, 1963–65; Vice Consul, Frankfurt, 1966–68; Second Sec., Tel Aviv, 1968–72; First Sec., FCO, 1973–76; Vienna, 1976–80; FCO, 1980–84, Counsellor, 1982; Hd of Finance Dept, 1982–84; Consul-Gen., Munich, 1984–88; Dep. High Comr, Nairobi, 1988–91. *Recreations:* cricket, soccer, tennis, classical music, laughter. *Address:* c/o Foreign and Commonwealth Office, SW1A 2AH.

BRYARS, Donald Leonard; Commissioner of Customs and Excise, 1978–84 and Director, Personnel, 1979–84, retired; *b* 31 March 1929; *s* of late Leonard and Marie Bryars; *m* 1953, Joan (*née* Yealand); one *d*. *Educ:* Goole Grammar Sch.; Leeds Univ. Joined Customs and Excise as Executive Officer, 1953, Principal, 1964, Asst Sec., 1971; on loan to Cabinet Office, 1976–78; Director, General Customs, 1978–79. *Address:* 15 Ellwood Rise, Chalfont St Giles, Bucks HP8 4SU. *T:* Chalfont St Giles (02407) 5466. *Club:* Civil Service (Chm., 1981–85).

BRYARS, John Desmond, CB 1982; Deputy Under Secretary of State (Finance and Budget), Ministry of Defence, 1979–84, retired; *b* 31 Oct. 1928; *s* of William Bryars, MD and Sarah (*née* McMeekin); *m* 1964, Faith, *d* of Frederick Momber, ARCM and Anne Momber. *Educ:* St Edward's Sch., Oxford; Trinity Coll., Oxford (schol.; MA). Army, 1946–48. Entered Civil Service, Air Ministry, 1952; HM Treasury, 1960–62; Private Sec. to Sec. of State for Air, 1963–64, to Minister of Defence, RAF, 1964–65; Asst Sec., MoD, 1965–73; RCDS 1973; Asst Under-Sec. of State, MoD, 1973–75 and 1977–79; Under Sec., Cabinet Office, 1975–77. *Address:* 42 Osterley Road, Osterley, Isleworth, Middlesex TW7 4PN. *Club:* Commonwealth Trust.

BRYCE; *see* Graham Bryce and Graham-Bryce.

BRYCE, Gabe Robb, OBE 1959; Sales Manager (Operations) British Aircraft Corporation, 1965–75; occupied in breeding dogs and boarding cats, until retirement from animal world, 1987; *b* 27 April 1921; *m* 1943, Agnes Lindsay; one *s* one *d*. *Educ:* Glasgow High School. Served in RAF, 1939–46. Vickers-Armstrongs (Aircraft) Ltd, 1946–60 (Chief Test Pilot, 1951–60). Participated as First or Second Pilot, in Maiden Flights of following British Aircraft: Varsity; Nene Viking; Viscount 630, 700 and 800; Tay Viscount; Valiant; Pathfinder; Vanguard; VC-10; BAC 1–11; Chief Test Pilot, British Aircraft Corporation, 1960–64. Fellow Soc. of Experimental Test Pilots (USA), 1967. Sir Barnes Wallis Meml Medal, GAPAN, 1980. *Recreations:* squash, tennis. *Address:* 8 Rowan Green, Rosslyn Park, Weybridge, Surrey KT13 9NF. *T:* Weybridge (0932) 858996.

BRYCE, Sir Gordon; *see* Bryce, Sir W. G.

BRYCE, Rt. Rev. Jabez Leslie; *see* Polynesia, Bishop in.

BRYCE, Sir (William) Gordon, Kt 1971; CBE 1963; Chief Justice of the Bahamas, 1970–73; *b* 2 Feb. 1913; *s* of James Chisholm Bryce and Emily Susan (*née* Lees); *m* 1940, Molly Mary, *d* of Arthur Cranch Drake; two *d*. *Educ:* Bromsgrove Sch.; Hertford Coll., Oxford (MA). Called to Bar, Middle Temple. War Service, 1940–46 (Major). Colonial Service: Crown Counsel, Fiji, 1949; Solicitor General, Fiji, 1953; Attorney General: Gibraltar, 1956; Aden, 1959; Legal Adviser, S Arabian High Commn, 1963; Attorney General, Bahamas, 1966. Comr, revised edn of Laws: of Gilbert and Ellice Islands, 1952; of Fiji, 1955; Comr, Bahamas Law Reform and Revision Commn, 1976. *Recreations:* riding, gardening. *Address:* Broom Croft, Lydeard St Lawrence, Taunton, Somerset TA4 3QZ.

BRYCE-SMITH, Prof. Derek, PhD, DSc; CChem, FRSC; Professor of Organic Chemistry, University of Reading, 1965–89, part-time, since 1989; *b* 29 April 1926; *s* of Charles Philip and Amelia Smith; *m* 1st, 1956, Marjorie Mary Anne Stewart (*d* 1966); two *s* two *d*; 2nd, 1969, Pamela Joyce Morgan; two step *d*. *Educ:* Bancrofts Sch., Woodford Wells; SW Essex Tech. Coll.; West Ham Municipal Coll.; Bedford Coll., London. Research Chemist: Powell Duffryn Res. Ltd, 1945–46; Dufay-Chromex Ltd, 1946–48; Inst. of Petroleum Student, Bedford Coll., 1948–51; ICI Post-doctoral Fellow, KCL, 1951–55; Asst Lectr in Chem., KCL, 1955–56; Lectr in Chem., 1956–63, Reader, 1963–65, Reading Univ. Founding Chm., European Photochem. Assoc., 1970–72; Founding Vice-Chm., UK Br., Internat. Solar Energy Soc., 1973–74; Chm., RSC Photochemistry Gp, 1981–. John Jeyes Endowed Lectureship and Silver Medal, RSC, 1984–85. *Publications:* (with R. Stephens) Lead or Health, 1980, 2nd edn 1981; (with E. Hodgkinson) The Zinc Solution, 1986; (RSC Senior Reporter and contrib.) Photochemistry: a review of chemical literature, vols 1–22, 1970–; contribs to learned jls in the fields of photochem., organometallic chem., environmental chem. and philosophy of sci. *Recreations:* gardening, making music. *Address:* Highland Wood House, Mill Lane, Kidmore End, Reading, Berks RG4 9HB. *T:* Kidmore End (0734) 723132.

BRYDEN, David John; Keeper, Department of Science, Technology and Working Life, National Museums of Scotland, since 1988; *b* 23 Nov. 1943; *s* of George Bryden and Marion (*née* Bellingham); *m* 1964, Helen Margaret Willison; two *s*. *Educ:* Univ. of Leicester (BSc(Engrg)); Linacre Coll., Oxford (Dip. in Hist. and Philos. of Sci.). Asst Keeper II, Royal Scottish Mus., 1966–70; Curator, Whipple Mus. of Hist. of Sci., Univ. of Cambridge, 1970–78; Fellow and Steward, St Edmund's House, 1977–78; Asst Keeper I, Science Mus. Library, 1979–87; Academic Administrator, Gresham Coll., 1987–88. *Publications:* Scottish Scientific Instrument Makers 1600–1900, 1972; articles on early scientific instruments. *Address:* Royal Museum of Scotland, Chambers Street, Edinburgh EH1 1JF. *T:* 031–225 7534.

BRYDEN, William Campbell Rough, (Bill Bryden); Associate Director, The Royal National Theatre, since 1975; Head of Drama Television, BBC Scotland, since 1984; *b* 12 April 1942; *s* of late George Bryden and of Catherine Bryden; *m* 1971, Hon. Deborah Morris, *d* of Baron Killanin, *qv*; one *s* one *d*. *Educ:* Hillend Public Sch.; Greenock High Sch. Documentary writer, Scottish Television, 1963–64; Assistant Director: Belgrade Theatre, Coventry, 1965–67; Royal Court Th., London, 1967–69; Associate Dir, Royal Lyceum Th., Edinburgh, 1971–74; Dir, Cottesloe Theatre (Nat. Theatre), 1978–80. Director, Royal Opera House, Covent Garden: Parsifal, 1988; The Cunning Little Vixen, 1990. Director: Bernstein's Mass, GSMD, 1987; A Life in the Theatre, Haymarket, 1989; The Ship, Harland and Wolff Shipyard, Glasgow, 1990; Cops, Greenwich, 1991. BBC Television: Exec. Producer: Tutti Frutti, by John Byrne, 1987 (Best Series, BAFTA awards); The Play on 1 (series), 1989; Dir, The Shawl, by David Mamet, 1989. Member Board, Scottish Television, 1979–85. Dir of the Year, Laurence Olivier Awards, 1985, Best Dir, Brit. Th. Assoc. and Drama Magazine Awards, 1986, and Evening Standard Best Dir Award, 1985 (for The Mysteries, NT, 1985). *Publications: plays:* Willie Rough, 1972; Benny Lynch, 1974; Old Movies, 1977; *screenplay:* The Long Riders, 1980; *films:* (writer and director) Ill Fares The Land, 1982; The Holy City (for TV), 1985; Aria, 1987. *Recreation:* music. *Address:* The Royal National Theatre, South Bank, SE1 9PX. *T:* 071–928 2033.

BRYER, Prof. Anthony Applemore Mornington, FSA 1972; Director, Centre for Byzantine, Ottoman and Modern Greek Studies, since 1976; Professor of Byzantine Studies, University of Birmingham, since 1980; *b* 31 Oct. 1937; *e s* of Group Captain Gerald Mornington Bryer, OBE and Joan Evelyn (*née* Grigsby); *m* 1961, Elizabeth Lipscomb; three *d*. *Educ:* Canford Sch.; Sorbonne Univ.; Balliol Coll., Oxford (Scholar; BA, MA; DPhil 1967); Athens Univ. Nat. Service, RAF (Adjutant), 1956–58. University of Birmingham: Research Fellow, 1964–65, Lectr, 1965–73, Sen. Lectr, 1973–76, in Medieval History; Reader in Byzantine Studies, 1976–79; Dir of Byzantine Studies, 1969–76. Visiting Fellow: Dumbarton Oaks, Harvard, 1971–; Merton Coll., Oxford, 1985. Founder and Dir, annual British Byzantine Symposia, 1966–; Chm., British Nat. Cttee, Internat. Byzantine Assoc., 1989– (Sec., 1976–89); former Vice-Pres., Nat. Trust for Greece; Mem., Managing Cttees, British Sch. at Athens and British Inst. of Archaeology, Ankara; Trustee, Uppingham Sch.; Consultant to Cyprus Govt on res. in humanities, 1988–89; field trips to Trebizond and Pontos, 1959–; Hellenic Cruise lectr, 1967–; British Council specialist lectr, Greece, Turkey and Australia; Loeb Lectr, Harvard, 1979; Vis. Byzantinist, Medieval Acad. of America, 1987; Wiles Lectr, QUB, 1990. Co-founder and publisher, Byzantine and Modern Greek Studies, 1975–. *Publications:* Byzantium and the Ancient East, 1970; Iconoclasm, 1977; The Empire of Trebizond and the Pontos, 1980; (with David Winfield) The Byzantine Monuments and Topography of the Pontos, 2 vols, 1985; (with Heath Lowry) Continuity and Change in late Byzantine and Early Ottoman Society, 1986; Peoples and Settlement in Anatolia and the Caucasus 800–1900, 1988; articles in learned jls. *Recreations:* travel, trying to find BBC Third Programme. *Address:* Centre for Byzantine, Ottoman and Modern Greek Studies, University of Birmingham, PO Box 363, Birmingham B15 2TT. *T:* 021–414 5777. *Clubs:* Buckland (Birmingham); Lochaline Social (Morvern); Black Sea (Trabzon).

BRYMER, Jack, OBE 1960; Hon. RAM; Principal Clarinettist, London Symphony Orchestra, since 1972; *b* 27 Jan. 1915; *s* of J. and Mrs M. Brymer, South Shields, Co. Durham; *m* 1939, Joan Richardson, Lancaster; one *s*. *Educ:* Goldsmiths' College, London University. Schoolmaster, Croydon, general subjects, 1935–40. RAF, 1940–45. Principal Clarinettist: Royal Philharmonic Orchestra, 1946–63; BBC Symphony Orchestra, 1963–72; Prof., Royal Acad. of Music, 1950–58; Prof., Royal Military Sch. of Music, Kneller Hall, 1969–73; Prof., Guildhall Sch. of Music and Drama, 1981–; Member of Wigmore, Prometheus and London Baroque ensembles; Director of London Wind Soloists. Has directed recordings of the complete wind chamber music of Mozart, Beethoven, Haydn and J. C. Bach. Presenter of several BBC music series, inc. At Home (nightly). Has taken a life-long interest in mainstream jazz, and in later life has toured and performed as soloist with many of finest British and American players in that field. Hon. RAM 1955; FGSM 1986; Hon. MA Newcastle upon Tyne, 1973. Cobbett Medal, Worshipful Co. of Musicians, 1989. *Publications:* The Clarinet (Menuhin Guides), 1976; From Where I Sit (autobiog.), 1979; In the Orchestra, 1987. *Recreations:* golf, tennis, swimming, carpentry, gardening, music. *Address:* Underwood, Ballards Farm Road, South Croydon, Surrey. *T:* 081–657 1698. *Club:* Croham Hurst Golf.

BRYSON, Col (James) Graeme, OBE 1954; TD 1949; JP; Vice-Lord-Lieutenant of Merseyside, 1979–89; *b* 4 Feb. 1913; 3rd *s* of John Conway Bryson and Oletta Bryson; *m* Jean (*d* 1981), *d* of Walter Glendinning; two *s* four *d* (and one *s* decd). *Educ:* St Edward's Coll.; Liverpool Univ. (LLM). Admitted solicitor, 1935. Commnd 89th Field Bde RA (TA), 1936; served War, RA, 1939–45 (Lt-Col 1944); comd 470 (3W/Lancs) HAA Regt, 1947–52, and 626 HAA Regt, 1952–55; Bt-Col 1955; Hon. Col 33 Signal Regt (V), 1975–81. Sen. Jt Dist Registrar and Liverpool Admiralty Registrar, High Court of Justice, Liverpool, and Registrar of Liverpool County Court, 1947–78; Dep. Circuit Judge, Northern Circuit, 1978–82. President: Assoc. of County Court Registrars, 1969; Liverpool Law Soc., 1969; City of Liverpool, 1965–, NW Area, 1979–90, Royal British Legion. Chm., Med. Appeal Tribunal, 1978–85; Member: Lord Chancellor's Cttee for enforcement of debts (Payne), 1965–69; IOM Commn to reform enforcement laws, 1972–74; Vice-Patron, Nat. Assoc. for Employment of Regular Sailors, Soldiers and Airmen, 1989– (Mem. Council, 1952–89). FRSA 1989. JP Liverpool, 1956; DL Lancs, 1965, later Merseyside. The Queen's Commendation for Brave Conduct, 1961. KHS 1974; KCHS 1990. *Publication:* (jtly) Execution, in Halsbury's Laws of England, 3rd edn 1976. *Recreations:* local history, boating. *Address:* Sunwards, Thirlmere Road, Hightown, Liverpool L38 3RQ. *T:* 051–929 2652. *Clubs:* Athenæum (Liverpool; Pres., 1969); Lancashire County Cricket.

BRYSON, Adm. Sir Lindsay (Sutherland), KCB 1981; FRSE 1984; FEng; Chairman: Marine Technology Directorate, since 1986; ERA Technology, since 1990 (Director, since 1985); Lord Lieutenant of East Sussex, since 1989; *b* 22 Jan. 1925; *s* of James McAuslan Bryson and Margaret Bryson (*née* Whyte); *m* 1951, Averil Curtis-Willson; one *s* two *d*. *Educ:* Allan Glen's Sch., Glasgow; London Univ. (External) (BSc (Eng)); FIEE (Hon. FIEE 1991), FRAeS. Engrg Cadet, 1942; Electrical Mechanic, RN, 1944; Midshipman 1946; Lieut 1948; Comdr 1960; Captain 1967; comd HMS Daedalus, RNAS Lee-on-Solent, 1970–71; RCDS 1972; Dir, Naval Guided Weapons, 1973; Dir, Surface Weapons Project (Navy), 1974–76; Dir-Gen. Weapons (Naval), 1977–81; and Chief Naval Engr Officer, 1979–81; Controller of the Navy, 1981–84. Dep. Chm., GEC-Marconi (formerly The Marconi Co. and GEC Avionics), 1987–90; Dir (non-exec.), Molins, 1988–. Institution of Electrical Engineers: Vice-Pres., 1982–84; Dep. Pres., 1984–85; Pres., 1985–86; Faraday Lectr, 1976–77. President: Soc. of Underwater Technol., 1989–91; Assoc. of Project Managers, 1991–. Worshipful Co. of Cooks: Liveryman, 1964; Assistant, 1980; Warden, 1985; Second Master, 1986; Master, 1987; Liveryman, Worshipful Co. of Engrs, 1988. Chairman of Council: Sussex Univ., 1989– (Vice-Chm., 1988–89); Brighton Coll., 1990– (Governor, 1986–). Hon. Fellow, Paisley Coll. of Technology, 1986; Hon. DSc Strathclyde, 1987; Hon DSc(Eng) Bristol, 1988. KStJ 1990. *Publications:* contrib. Jl RAeS, Jl IEE, Trans RINA, Seaford Papers, Control Engineering. *Recreations:* opera, fair weather sailing, gardening, badminton. *Address:* 74 Dyke Road Avenue, Brighton BN1 5LE. *T:* Brighton (0273) 553638. *Club:* Army and Navy.

BUCCLEUCH, 9th Duke of, *cr* 1663, **AND QUEENSBERRY,** 11th Duke of, *cr* 1684; **Walter Francis John Montagu Douglas Scott,** KT 1978; VRD; JP; Baron Scott of Buccleuch, 1606; Earl of Buccleuch, Baron Scott of Whitchester and Eskdaill, 1619; Earl of Doncaster and Baron Tynedale (Eng.), 1662; Earl of Dalkeith, 1663; Marquis of Dumfriesshire, Earl of Drumlanrig and Sanquhar, Viscount of Nith, Torthorwold, and Ross, Baron Douglas, 1684; Hon. Captain RNR; Captain, the Queen's Body Guard for Scotland, Royal Company of Archers; Lord-Lieutenant of Roxburgh, since 1974, of Ettrick and Lauderdale, since 1975; *b* 28 Sept. 1923; *o s* of 8th Duke of Buccleuch, KT, PC, GCVO, and of Vreda Esther Mary, *er d* of late Major W. F. Lascelles and Lady Sybil Lascelles, *d* of 10th Duke of St Albans; *S* father, 1973; *m* 1953, Jane, *d* of John McNeill, QC, Appin, Argyll; three *s* one *d*. *Educ:* Eton; Christ Church, Oxford. Served War of 1939–45, RNVR. MP (C) Edinburgh North, 1960–73; PPS to the Sec. of State for Scotland, 1962–64. Chairman: Royal Assoc. for Disability and Rehabilitation; Buccleuch Heritage Trust, 1985–; Living Landscape Trust, 1986–; President: Royal Highland & Agricultural Soc. of Scotland, 1969; St. Andrew's Ambulance Assoc.; Royal Scottish Agricultural Benevolent Inst.; Scottish Nat. Inst. for War Blinded; Royal Blind Asylum & School; Galloway Cattle Soc.; East of England Agricultural Soc., 1976; Commonwealth Forestry Assoc.; Vice-Pres., RSSPCC; Hon. President: Animal Diseases Research Assoc.; Scottish Agricultural Organisation Soc. DL, Selkirk 1955, Midlothian 1960, Roxburgh 1962, Dumfries 1974; JP Roxburgh 1975. Countryside Award, Countryside Commn and CLA, 1983. *Heir:* *s* Earl of Dalkeith, *qv*. *Address:* Bowhill, Selkirk. *T:* Selkirk (0750) 20732.

BUCHAN, family name of **Baron Tweedsmuir.**

BUCHAN, 17th Earl of, *cr* 1469; **Malcolm Harry Erskine;** JP; Lord Auchterhouse, 1469; Lord Cardross, 1610; Baron Erskine, 1806; *b* 4 July 1930; *s* of 16th Earl of Buchan and of Christina, Dowager Countess of Buchan, *d* of late Hugh Woolner and adopted *d* of late Lloyd Baxendale; *S* father, 1984; *m* 1957, Hilary Diana Cecil, *d* of late Sir Ivan McLannahan Power, 2nd Bt; two *s* two *d*. *Educ:* Eton. JP Westminster. *Heir:* *s* Lord Cardross, *qv*. *Address:* Newnham House, Newnham, Basingstoke, Hants. *Club:* Carlton.

BUCHAN OF AUCHMACOY, Captain David William Sinclair, JP; Chief of the Name of Buchan; *b* 18 Sept. 1929; *o s* of late Captain S. L. Trevor, late of Lathbury Park, Bucks, and late Lady Olivia Trevor, *e d* of 18th Earl of Caithness; *m* 1961, Susan Blanche Fionodbhar Scott-Ellis, *d* of Baron Howard de Walden and Seaford, *qv*; four *s* one *d*. *Educ:* Eton; RMA Sandhurst. Commissioned 1949 into Gordon Highlanders; served Berlin, BAOR and Malaya; ADC to GOC, Singapore, 1951–53; retired 1955. Member of London Stock Exchange. Sen. Partner, Messrs Gow and Parsons, 1963–72. Changed name from Trevor through Court of Lord Lyon King of Arms, 1949, succeeding 18th Earl of Caithness as Chief of Buchan Clan. Member: Queen's Body Guard for Scotland; The Pilgrims; Canada Club; Friends of Malta GC; Alexandra Rose Day Council; Council, Royal Sch. of Needlework, 1987–; Cons. Industrial Fund Cttee, 1988–. Governor, London Clinic, 1988–. Mem., Worshipful Company of Broderers (Warden, 1991). Vice-President: Aberdeenshire CCC, 1962–; Bucks CCC, 1984–. JP Aberdeenshire, 1959–; JP London, 1972–. KStJ 1987 (OStJ 1981); Mem. Council for London, Order of St John. *Recreations:* cricket, tennis, squash. *Address:* 28 The Little Boltons, SW10. *T:* 071–373 0654; Auchmacoy House, Ellon, Aberdeenshire. *T:* Ellon (0358) 20229; Appt. D-310, Puente Romano, Marbella, Spain. *Clubs:* White's, Royal Automobile, Turf, MCC, City of London, Pratt's, Pitt; Puffin's (Edinburgh).

BUCHAN, Ven. Eric Ancrum; Archdeacon of Coventry, 1965–77, Archdeacon Emeritus, since 1977; *b* 6 Nov. 1907; *s* of late Frederick Samuel and Florence Buchan. *Educ:* Bristol Grammar School; St Chad's College, University of Durham (BA). Curate of Holy Nativity, Knowle, Bristol, 1933–40. Chaplain RAFVR, 1940–45. Vicar of St Mark's with St Barnabas, Coventry, 1945–59; Hon. Canon of Coventry Cathedral, 1953; Chaplain Coventry and Warwickshire Hospital, 1945–59; Sec. Laymen's Appeal, Dio. of Coventry, 1951–53; Rural Dean of Coventry, 1954–63; Rector of Baginton, 1963–70. Member Central Board of Finance, 1953–80 (Chm., Develt and Stewardship Cttee, 1976–80; Mem., Church Commrs and CBF Joint Liaison Cttee, 1976–80); Mem. Schools Council, 1958–65; Chm. Dio. Board of Finance, 1958–77; Organiser of Bishop's Appeal, 1958–61; Dio. Director of Christian Stewardship, 1959–65; Domestic Chaplain to Bishop of Coventry, 1961–65; Church Commissioner, 1964–78; Member, Governing Body, St Chad's College, Durham University, 1966–83. Awarded Silver Acorn for outstanding services to the Scout Movement, 1974. *Address:* 6B Millers Green, The Cathedral, Gloucester GL1 2BN. *T:* Gloucester (0452) 415944.

BUCHAN, Janey, (Jane O'Neil Buchan); Member (Lab) Glasgow, European Parliament, since 1979; *b* 30 April 1926; *d* of Joseph and Christina Kent; *m* 1945, Norman Findlay Buchan, MP (*d* 1990); one *s*. *Educ:* secondary sch.; commercial coll. Housewife; Socialist; occasional scriptwriting and journalism. Mem., Strathclyde Regl Council, 1974 (Vice-Chm., Educn Cttee); Chm., local consumer gp; formerly Chm., Scottish Gas Consumers' Council. *Recreations:* books, music, theatre, television. *Address:* 72 Peel Street, Glasgow G11 5LR. *T:* 041–339 2583.

BUCHAN, Sir John, (Sir Thomas Johnston Buchan), Kt 1971; CMG 1961; Chairman, Buchan Laird International Planners, since 1982; Chairman and Chief Executive, Buchan, Laird and Buchan, Architects, 1957–82; *b* 3 June 1912; *s* of Thomas Johnston Buchan; *m* 1948, Virginia, *d* of William Ashley Anderson, Penn., USA; one *s* two *d*. *Educ:* Geelong Grammar School. Served Royal Aust. Engineers (AIF), 1940–44 (Capt.). Member Melbourne City Council, 1954–60. Member Federal Exec., Liberal Party, 1959–62; President, Liberal Party, Victorian Division, Australia, 1959–62, Treasurer, 1963–67; Pres., Australian American Assoc., Victoria, 1964–68, Federal Pres., Australian American Assoc., 1968–70, Vice-Pres., 1971–82. Member: Council, Latrobe University, 1964–72; Cttee of Management, Royal Melbourne Hosp., 1968–78. Founding Mem. and Dep. Chm., Nat. Cttee for Youth Employment, 1983–86; Co-Founder Apex Association of Australia. *Recreations:* golf, reading. *Address:* 11 Fairlie Court, South Yarra, Vic 3141, Australia. *Club:* Melbourne (Melbourne).

BUCHAN, Dr Stevenson, CBE 1971; Chief Scientific Officer, Deputy Director, Institute of Geological Sciences, 1968–71; *b* 4 March 1907; *s* of late James Buchan and Christian Ewen Buchan (*née* Stevenson), Peterhead; *m* 1937, Barbara, *yr d* of late Reginald Hadfield, Droylsden, Lancs; one *s* one *d*. *Educ:* Peterhead Acad.; Aberdeen Univ. BSc 1st cl. hons Geology, James H. Hunter Meml Prize, Senior Kilgour Scholar, PhD; FRSE, FGS. Geological Survey of Great Britain: Geologist, 1931; Head of Water Dept, 1946; Asst Dir responsible for specialist depts in GB and NI, 1960; Chief Geologist, Inst. of Geological Sciences, 1967. Mem. various hydrological cttees; Founder Mem., Internat. Assoc. of Hydrogeologists (Pres., 1972–77; Advr, 1980–; Hon. Mem., 1985–); Pres., Internat. Ground-Water Commn of Internat. Assoc. of Hydrological Sciences, 1963–67; British Deleg. to Internat. Hydrological Decade; Scientific Editor, Hydrogeological Map of Europe; Vis. Internat. Scientist, Amer. Geol Inst.; Pres. Section C (Geology), Brit. Assoc., Dundee, 1968. Hon. FIWEM. Awarded Geol Soc.'s Lyell Fund, and J. B. Tyrell Fund for travel in Canada. *Publications:* Water Supply of County of London from Underground Sources; papers on hydrogeology and hydrochemistry. *Recreation:* oenology. *Address:* Southside Place, 122 The Street, Rockland St Mary, Norwich NR14 7HQ. *T:* Surlingham (05088) 8092.

BUCHAN, Sir Thomas Johnston; *see* Buchan, Sir John.

BUCHAN-HEPBURN, Sir Ninian (Buchan Archibald John), 6th Bt, *cr* 1815, of Smeaton-Hepburn; is a painter; Member, Queen's Body Guard for Scotland, Royal Company of Archers; *b* 8 Oct. 1922; *s* of Sir John Buchan-Hepburn, 5th Bt; *S* father 1961; *m* 1958, Bridget (*d* 1976), *er d* of late Sir Louis Greig, KBE, CVO. *Educ:* St Aubyn's, Rottingdean, Sussex; Canford School, Wimborne, Dorset. Served QO Cameron Hldrs, India and Burma, 1939–45 (wounded, 1944). Studied painting, Byam Shaw School of Art. Exhibited at: Royal Academy, Royal Scottish Academy, London galleries. Work in many public and private collections. *Recreations:* music, gardening, shooting. *Heir:* *kinsman* John Alastair Trant Kidd Buchan-Hepburn [*b* 27 June 1931; *m* 1957, Georgina Elizabeth Turner; one *s* three *d*]. *Address:* Logan, Port Logan, Wigtownshire DG9 9ND. *T:* Ardwell (077686) 239. *Club:* New (Edinburgh).

BUCHANAN, Sir Andrew George, 5th Bt *cr* 1878; farmer; chartered surveyor in private practice; Lord-Lieutenant and Keeper of the Rolls for Nottinghamshire, since 1991; *b* 21 July 1937; *s* of Major Sir Charles Buchanan, 4th Bt, and Barbara Helen (*d* 1986), *o d* of late Lt-Col Rt Hon. Sir George Stanley, PC, GCSI, GCIE; *S* father, 1984; *m* 1966, Belinda Jane Virginia (*née* Maclean), JP, *widow* of Gresham Neilus Vaughan; one *s* one *d*, and one step *s* one step *d*. *Educ:* Eton; Trinity Coll., Cambridge; Wye Coll., Univ. of London. Nat. Service, 2nd Lieut, Coldstream Guards, 1956–58. Chartered Surveyor with Smith-Woolley & Co, 1965–70. Chm., Bd of Visitors, HM Prison Ranby, 1983 (Vice-Chm. 1982). Commanded A Squadron (SRY), 3rd Bn Worcs and Sherwood Foresters (TA), 1971–74; Hon. Col, B Sqn (SRY), Royal Yeo., 1989–. High Sheriff, Notts, 1976–77; DL Notts, 1985. *Recreations:* skiing, shooting. *Heir:* *s* George Charles Mellish Buchanan, *b* 27 Jan. 1975. *Address:* Hodsock Priory, Blyth, Worksop, Notts S81 0TY. *T:* Blyth (Notts) (0909) 591204. *Club:* Boodle's.

BUCHANAN, Sir Charles Alexander James L.; *see* Leith-Buchanan.

BUCHANAN, Prof. Sir Colin (Douglas), Kt 1972; CBE 1964; Lieut-Colonel; consultant with Colin Buchanan & Partners, 47 Princes Gate, London; *b* 22 Aug. 1907; *s* of William Ernest and Laura Kate Buchanan; *m* 1933, Elsie Alice Mitchell (*d* 1984); two *s* one *d*. *Educ:* Berkhamsted School; Imperial College, London. Sudan Govt Public Works Dept, 1930–32; Regional planning studies with F. Longstreth Thompson, 1932–35; Ministry of Transport, 1935–39. War Service in Royal Engineers, 1939–46 (despatches). Ministry of Town and Country Planning (later Ministry of Housing and Local Govt), 1946–61; Urban Planning Adviser, Ministry of Transport, 1961–63; Prof. of Transport, Imperial Coll., London, 1963–72; Prof. of Urban Studies and Dir, Sch. for Advanced Urban Studies, Bristol Univ., 1973–75. Vis. Prof., Imperial Coll., London, 1975–78. Member: Commn on Third London Airport, 1968–70; Royal Fine Art Commn, 1972–74. Pres., CPRE, 1980–85. Pres., Friends of the Vale of Aylesbury, 1985–. Hon. DCL Oxon, 1972; Hon. DSc: Leeds, 1972; City, 1972. *Publications:* Mixed Blessing, The Motor in Britain, 1958; Traffic in Towns (Ministry of Transport report), 1963, (paperback edn), 1964; The State of Britain, 1972; No Way to the Airport, 1981; numerous papers on town planning and allied subjects. *Recreations:* photography, carpentry, caravan touring. *Address:* Appletree House, Lincombe Lane, Boars Hill, Oxford OX1 5DU. *T:* Oxford (0865) 739458.

See also L. D. Reynolds.

BUCHANAN, Rt. Rev. Colin Ogilvie; Vicar of St Mark's, Gillingham, Kent, since 1991; Hon. Assistant Bishop, Diocese of Rochester, since 1989; *b* 9 Aug. 1934; *s* of late Prof. Robert Ogilvie Buchanan and of Kathleen Mary (*née* Parnell); *m* 1963, Diana Stephenie Gregory; two *d. Educ:* Whitgift Sch., S Croydon; Lincoln Coll., Oxford (BA, 2nd Cl. Lit. Hum., MA). Theological training at Tyndale Hall, Bristol, 1959–61; deacon, 1961; priest, 1962; Curate, Cheadle, Cheshire, 1961–64; joined staff of London Coll. of Divinity (now St John's Coll., Nottingham), 1964; posts held: Librarian, 1964–69; Registrar, 1969–74; Director of Studies, 1974–75; Vice-Principal, 1975–78; Principal, 1979–85; Hon. Canon of Southwell Minster, 1982–85; Bishop Suffragan of Aston, 1985–89. Member: Church of England Liturgical Commn, 1964–86; Doctrinal Commn, 1986–91; General Synod of C of E, 1970–85, 1990–; Assembly of British Council of Churches, 1971–80. Proprietor, Grove Books, 1970–85, Hon. Manager, 1985–. *Publications:* (ed) Modern Anglican Liturgies 1958–1968, 1968; (ed) Further Anglican Liturgies 1968–1975, 1975; (jtly) Growing into Union, 1970; (ed jtly) Anglican Worship Today, 1980; (ed) Latest Anglican Liturgies 1976–1984, 1985; (jtly) Reforming Infant Baptism, 1990; editor: Grove Booklets on Ministry and Worship, 1972–; Grove Liturgical Studies, 1975–86; Alcuin/Grove Joint Liturgical Studies, 1987– (regular author in these series); News of Liturgy, 1975–; contrib. learned jls. *Recreations:* interested in electoral reform, sport, etc. *Address:* St Mark's Vicarage, 173 Canterbury Street, Gillingham, Kent ME7 5UA. *T:* Medway (0634) 51818, *Fax:* Medway (0634) 573549.

BUCHANAN, Sir Dennis; *see* Buchanan, Sir R. D.

BUCHANAN, Rt. Rev. George Duncan; *see* Johannesburg, Bishop of.

BUCHANAN, Isobel Wilson, (Mrs Jonathan King); soprano; *b* 15 March 1954; *d* of Stewart and Mary Buchanan; *m* 1980, Jonathan Stephen Geoffrey King (otherwise Jonathan Hyde, actor); two *d. Educ:* Cumbernauld High Sch.; Royal Scottish Academy of Music and Drama (DRSAMD 1974). Australian Opera principal singer, 1975–78; freelance singer, 1978–; British debut, Glyndebourne, 1978; Vienna Staatsoper debut, 1978; American debut: Santa Fé, 1979; Chicago, 1979; New York, 1979; German debut, Cologne, 1979; French debut, Aix-en-Provence, 1981; ENO debut, 1985; Paris Opera debut, 1986. Performances also with Scottish Opera, Covent Garden, Munich Radio, Belgium, Norway, etc. Various operatic recordings. *Recreations:* reading, gardening, cooking, dressmaking, knitting, yoga. *Address:* c/o Sandor Gorlinsky, 36 Dover Street, W1.

BUCHANAN, Prof. James McGill; Distinguished Professor of Economics, George Mason University, since 1983; *b* 2 Oct. 1919; *s* of James Buchanan and Lila Scott; *m* 1945, Anne Bakke. *Educ:* Middle Tennessee State Coll. (BS 1940); Univ. of Tennessee (MA 1941); Univ. of Chicago (PhD 1948). Lieut, USNR, 1941–46. Professor of Economics: Univ. of Tennessee, 1950–51; Florida State Univ., 1951–56; Univ. of Virginia, 1956–62, 1962–68 (Paul G. McIntyre Prof.); UCLA, 1968–69; Virginia Polytechnic Inst., 1969–83 (Univ. Dist. Prof.). Fulbright Res. Scholar, Italy, 1955–56; Ford Faculty Res. Fellow, 1959–60; Fulbright Vis. Prof., Univ. of Cambridge, 1961–62. Fellow, Amer. Acad. of Arts and Scis; Dist. Fellow, Amer. Econ. Assoc. (Seidman Award, 1984). Hon. Dr, US and overseas Univs. Nobel Prize for Economics, 1986. *Publications:* Prices, Incomes and Public Policy (jtly), 1954; Public Principles of Public Debt, 1958; The Public Finances, 1960; Fiscal Theory and Political Economy, 1960; (with G. Tullock) The Calculus of Consent, 1962; Public Finance in Democratic Process, 1966; The Demand and Supply of Public Goods, 1968; Cost and Choice, 1969; (with N. Devletoglou) Academia in Anarchy, 1970; (ed jtly) Theory of Public Choice, 1972; (with G. F. Thirlby) LSE Essays on Cost, 1973; The Limits of Liberty, 1975; (with R. Wagner) Democracy in Deficit, 1977; Freedom in Constitutional Contract, 1978; What Should Economists Do?, 1979; (with G. Brennan) The Power to Tax, 1980; (with G. Brennan) The Reason of Rules, 1985; Liberty Market and State, 1985; (jtly) El Analisis Economico de la Politico, 1985; (ed jtly) Deficits, 1987; Economics: between predictive science and moral philosophy, 1987; Economica y Politicia, 1987; Marktens Graenser, 1988; (ed) Explorations into Constitutional Economics, 1989; Essays on the Political Economy, 1989. *Address:* Center for the Study of Public Choice, George's Hall, George Mason University, Fairfax, Va 22030, USA; PO Box G, Blacksburg, Va 24060, USA.

BUCHANAN, John David, MBE 1944; ERD 1989; DL; Headmaster of Oakham School, Rutland, 1958–77; *b* 26 Oct. 1916; *e s* of late John Nevile Buchanan and Nancy Isabel (*née* Bevan); *m* 1946, Janet Marjorie (*d* 1990), *d* of late Brig. J. A. C. Pennycuick, DSO; three *s* four *d* (and one *s* decd). *Educ:* Stowe; Trinity College, Cambridge. Served with Grenadier Guards, 1939–46; Adjutant, 3rd Bn Grenadier Guards, 1941–43 (despatches, 1943); Brigade Major, 1st Guards Bde, 1944–45; Private Secretary to Sir Alexander Cadogan, Security Council for the UN, 1946. Assistant Master, Westminster Under School, 1948; Assistant Master, Sherborne School, 1948–57. Administrator, Inchcape Educational Scholarship Scheme, 1978–; Educnl Consultant to Jerwood Foundn, 1978–. DL Leics, 1980. *Publications:* Operation Oakham, 1984; Oakham Overture to Poetry, 1985. *Recreation:* gardening. *Address:* Rose Cottage, Owston, Leics.

BUCHANAN, Vice-Adm. Sir Peter (William), KBE 1980; *b* 14 May 1925; *s* of Lt-Col Francis Henry Theodore Buchanan and Gwendolen May Isobel (*née* Hunt); *m* 1953, Audrey Rowena Mary (*née* Edmondson); three *s* one *d. Educ:* Malvern Coll. Joined RN, 1943; served in HM Ships King George V, Birmingham, destroyers and frigates; comd HMS Scarborough 1961–63; Far East, 1963–65 (despatches); HMS Victorious, 1965–67; British Antarctic Survey, 1967–68; comd HMS Endurance, 1968–70; MoD, 1970–72; comd HMS Devonshire, 1972–74; MoD, 1974–76; Rear-Adm. 1976; Naval Sec., 1976–78; Vice-Adm., 1979; Chief of Staff, Allied Naval Forces Southern Europe, 1979–82. Younger Brother of Trinity House. Mem. Council, Malvern Coll. Liveryman, Shipwrights' Co., 1984; Mem. Court of Assts, Guild of Freemen of City of London, 1985. FNI. *Recreation:* sailing. *Clubs:* Caledonian; Royal Yacht Squadron.

BUCHANAN, Sir (Ranald) Dennis, Kt 1991; MBE 1976; Chairman and Managing Director, Talair Pty Ltd, since 1958; *b* Sydney, 6 Nov. 1932; *s* of Stanley Brisbane Buchanan and Jessica (*née* Hall); *m* 1956, Della Agnes Brown; four *s* five *d* (and one *s* decd). *Educ:* All Saints Coll., Bathurst, NSW. Joined Gibbes Sepik Airways Ltd, Wewak, PNG, 1949; purchased Territory Airlines Ltd, 1957 (renamed Talair Pty Ltd, 1975). *Recreation:* farming. *Address:* PO Box 108, Goroka, Eastern Highlands Province, Papua New Guinea. *T:* (office) (675) 721408; (home) (675) 721984. *Clubs:* Royal Automobile (Sydney); Aero (Goroka, PNG).

BUCHANAN, Richard, JP; *b* 3 May 1912; *s* of late Richard Buchanan and late Helen Henderson; *m* 1st, 1938, Margaret McManus (*d* 1963); six *s* two *d*; 2nd, 1971, Helen Duggan, MA, DipEd. *Educ:* St Mungo's Boys' School; St Mungo's Academy; Royal Technical Coll. Councillor, City of Glasgow, 1949–64 (Past Chm. Libraries, Schools and Standing Orders Cttees); Hon. City Treasurer, 1960–63. MP (Lab) Springburn, Glasgow, 1964–79; PPS to Treasury Ministers, 1967–70; Mem. Select Cttees: Public Accounts; Services. Chm., West Day School Management, 1958–64; Governor, Notre Dame College of Education, 1959–64, etc. Chm., Belvidere Hospital; Member Board of Managers, Glasgow Royal Infirmary; Hon. Pres., Scottish Library Assoc. (Pres., 1963); Life Mem., Scottish Secondary Teachers' Assoc., 1979; Chairman: Scottish Central Library; Adv. Cttee, Nat. Library of Scotland; Cttee on Burrell Collection; H of C Library Cttee; St Mungo's Old Folks' Day Centre, 1979–85; Director, Glasgow Citizens Theatre. Pres., (Clan) Buchanan Soc., 1989–. JP Glasgow, 1954. Hon. FLA, 1979. *Recreations:* theatre, walking, reading. *Address:* 18 Gargrave Avenue, Garrowhill, Glasgow G69 7LP. *T:* 041–771 7234. *Club:* St Mungo's Centenary (Glasgow).

BUCHANAN, Prof. Robert Angus, PhD; FSA; FRHistS; Founder and Director, Centre for the History of Technology, Science and Society, University of Bath, since 1964; Head of Humanities Group, School of Humanities and Social Sciences, since 1970; Professor of the History of Technology, since 1990; Director, National Cataloguing Unit for the Archives of Contemporary Scientists, since 1987; *b* 5 June 1930; *s* of Roy Graham Buchanan and Bertha (*née* Davis); *m* 1955, Brenda June Wade; two *s. Educ:* High Storrs Grammar Sch. for Boys, Sheffield; St Catharine's Coll., Cambridge (MA, PhD). FRHistS 1978; FSA 1990. Educn Officer to Royal Foundn of St Katharine, Stepney, 1956–60 (Co-opted Mem., LCC Educn Cttee, 1958–60); Asst Lectr, Dept of Gen. Studies, Bristol Coll. of Science and Technol. (now Univ. of Bath), 1960; Lectr, 1961; Sen. Lectr, 1966; Reader in Hist. of Technol., Univ. of Bath, 1981–90. Vis. Lectr, Univ. of Delaware, USA, 1969; Vis. Fellow, ANU, Canberra, 1981; Vis. Lectr, Huazhong (Central China) Univ. of Science and Tech., Wuhan, People's Repub. of China, 1983; Jubilee Chair in History of Technol., Chalmers Univ., Göteborg, Sweden, Autumn term, 1984. Royal Comr, Royal Commn on Historical Monuments (England), 1979–; Sec.-Gen., Internat. Cttee for History of Technol., 1981–; Sec., Res. Cttee on Indust. Archaeology, Council for British Archaeology, 1972–79; President: (Founding), Bristol Indust. Archaeology Soc., 1967–70; Assoc. for Indust. Archaeology, 1974–77; Newcomen Soc. for History of Engrg and Technol., 1981–83; Chm., Water Space Amenity Commn's Working Party on Indust. Archaeology, 1982–83; Member: Properties Cttee, National Trust, 1974–; Technol Preservation Awards Cttee, Science Museum, 1973–81. Hon. DSc (Engrg) Chalmers Univ., Göteborg, Sweden, 1986. Leonardo da Vinci Medal, Soc. for Hist. of Technol., 1989. *Publications:* Technology and Social Progress, 1965; (with Neil Cossons) Industrial Archaeology of the Bristol Region, 1969; Industrial Archaeology in Britain, 1972, 2nd edn 1982; (with George Watkins) Industrial Archaeology of the Stationary Steam Engine, 1976; History and Industrial Civilization, 1979; (with C. A. Buchanan) Industrial Archaeology of Central Southern England, 1980; (with Michael Williams) Brunel's Bristol, 1982; The Engineers: a history of the engineering profession in Britain, 1989. *Recreations:* Cambridge Judo half-blue, 1955; rambling, travelling, exploring. *Address:* Centre for the History of Technology, Science and Society, University of Bath, Claverton Down, Bath BA2 7AY. *T:* Bath (0225) 826826, ext. 5833.

BUCHANAN, Sir Robert Wilson, (Sir Robin), Kt 1991; CA; Chairman, Wessex Regional Health Authority, since 1988; *b* 28 Sept. 1930; *s* of Robert Downie and Mary Hobson Buchanan; *m* Naomi Pauline (*née* Lewis); three *d. Educ:* Dumbarton Acad.; Glasgow Acad. Mem., Inst. of Chartered Accts of Scotland, 1953. CA, Bath, 1965–; Lloyd's Underwriter, 1977–. Chairman: Buchanan Read Group, 1978–87; Micro Biological Holdings; Bath Securities; Cuningham Supplies; Avonbest; Court Engineering; Millfield Enterprises. Chm., Bath DHA, 1982–88; Vice-Chm., NHS Training Authy, 1983–88; Mem., Bath City Council, 1978–86; Mem., Wessex Med. Trust, 1988–. Mem. Council, Bath Internat. Fest., 1970–88 (Chm., 1982–86, 1988; Chm., Visual Arts Trust, 1988); Trustee, Robin Buchanan Charitable Trust, 1985–. Mem., Court, 1984–, and Council, 1985–, Bath Univ.; Treas., Millfield Sch., 1963–. *Recreations:* golf, beach walking. *Address:* Belmont House, Belmont Road, Bath, Avon BA2 5JR. *T:* Bath (0225) 833768; Settlers Beach, St James, Barbados. *T:* 422 3025.

BUCHANAN-DUNLOP, Richard, QC 1966; *b* 19 April 1919; *s* of late Canon W. R. Buchanan-Dunlop and Mrs R. E. Buchanan-Dunlop (*née* Mead); *m* 1948, Helen Murray Dunlop; three *d. Educ:* Marlborough College; Magdalene College, Cambridge. Served in Royal Corps of Signals, 1939–46 (Hon. Major). BA (Hons) Law, Cambridge, 1949; Harmsworth Scholar, 1950. Called to the Bar, 1951. *Publications:* Skiathos and other Poems, 1984; Old Olive Men, 1986; Hie Paeeon: songs from the Greek Isles, 1989. *Recreations:* painting, writing. *Address:* Skiathos, Greece.

BUCHANAN-JARDINE, Sir A. R. J.; *see* Jardine.

BUCHTHAL, Hugo, FBA 1959; PhD; Ailsa Mellon Bruce Professor, 1970–75, Professor of Fine Arts, 1965–70, New York University Institute of Fine Arts; now Emeritus Professor; *b* Berlin, 11 Aug. 1909; *m* 1939, Amalia Serkin; one *d. Educ:* Universities of Berlin, Heidelberg, Paris and Hamburg. PhD, Hamburg, 1933; Resident in London from 1934; Lord Plumer Fellowship, Hebrew University, 1938; Librarian, Warburg Institute, 1941; Lecturer in History of Art, University of London, 1944; Reader in the History of Art, with special reference to the Near East, 1949; Professor of the History of Byzantine Art in the University of London, 1960. Visiting Scholarship, Dumbarton Oaks, Harvard University, 1950–51, 1965, 1974, 1978; Temp. Member Inst. for Advanced Study, Princeton, NJ, 1959–60, 1968, 1975–76; Visiting Professor Columbia University, New York, 1963. Prix Schlumberger, Académie des Inscriptions et Belles Lettres, 1958, 1981; Guggenheim Fellow, 1971–72; Corres. Mem., Oesterreichische Akad. der Wissenschaften, 1975; Hon. Fellow, Warburg Inst., 1975. *Publications:* The Miniatures of the Paris Psalter, 1938; (with Otto Kurz) A Handlist of illuminated Oriental Christian Manuscripts, 1942; The Western Aspects of Gandhara Sculpture, 1944; Miniature Painting in the Latin Kingdom of Jerusalem, 1957; Historia Trojana, studies in the history of mediaeval secular illustration, 1971; (jtly) The Place of Book Illumination in Byzantine Art, 1976; (with Hans Belting) Patronage in Thirteenth Century Constantinople: an atelier of late Byzantine illumination and calligraphy, 1978; The Musterbuch of Wolfenbüttel and its position in the art of the thirteenth century, 1979; Art of the Mediterranean World, AD 100 to AD 1400, 1983 (collected essays); numerous articles in learned journals. *Address:* 22 Priory Gardens, N6. *T:* 081–348 1664.

BUCHWALD, Art, (Arthur); American journalist, author, lecturer and columnist; *b* Mount Vernon, New York, 20 Oct. 1925; *s* of Joseph Buchwald and Helen (*née* Kleinberger); *m* 1952, Ann McGarry, Warren, Pa; one *s* two *d. Educ:* University of Southern California. Sergeant, US Marine Corps, 1942–45. Columnist, New York Herald Tribune: in Paris, 1949–62; in Washington, 1962–. Syndicated columnist whose articles appear in 550 newspapers throughout the world. Mem., AAIL, 1986–. Pulitzer Prize for outstanding commentary, 1982. *Publications:* (mostly published later in England) Paris After Dark, 1950; Art Buchwald's Paris, 1954; The Brave Coward, 1957; I Chose Caviar, 1957; More Caviar, 1958; A Gift from the Boys, 1958; Don't Forget to Write, 1960; Art Buchwald's Secret List to Paris, 1961; How Much is That in Dollars?, 1961; Is it Safe to Drink the Water?, 1962; I Chose Capitol Punishment, 1963; . . . and Then I told the President, 1965; Son of the Great Society, 1966; Have I Ever Lied to You?, 1968; The Establishment is Alive and Well in Washington, 1969; Sheep on the Runway (Play), 1970; Oh, to be a Swinger, 1970; Getting High in Government Circles, 1971; I Never Danced at the White House, 1973; I Am not a Crook, 1974; Bollo Caper, 1974; Irving's Delight, 1975; Washington is Leaking, 1976; Down the Seine and up the Potomac, 1977; The Buchwald Stops Here, 1978; Laid Back in Washington, 1981; While Reagan Slept,

1984; You Can Fool All of the People All the Time, 1985; I Think I Don't Remember, 1987; Whose Rose Garden is it Anyway?, 1989. *Recreations:* tennis, chess, marathon running. *Address:* 2000 Pennsylvania Avenue NW, Washington, DC 20006, USA. *T:* Washington 393–6680.

BUCK, Albert Charles; business consultant; *b* 1 March 1910; *y s* of William and Mary Buck; *m* 1st, 1937, Margaret Court Hartley; one *d*; 2nd, 1951, Joan McIntyre; one *d*; 3rd, 1970, Mrs Aileen Ogilvy. *Educ:* Alderman Newton's Sch., Leicester; Selwyn Coll., Cambridge (MA). Joined J. J. Colman Ltd, as management trainee, 1931; Export Manager, 1939; Director: Reckitt & Sons Ltd, 1941; Joseph Farrow & Co. Ltd, 1947–69; Thomas Green & Son, 1950–60; Reckitt & Colman (Household) Div.; Industrial Adviser to HM Govt (Dep. Sec.), 1969–73. Member: Incorporated Soc. of British Advertisers (Pres., 1961–63); Internat. Union of Advertiser Societies (Pres. 1963–65); Advertising Standards Authority, 1962–71; Internat. Foundation for Research in Advertising (Pres., 1965–71). Mackintosh medal for personal and public services to Advertising, 1965. *Publications:* sundry articles to jls and newspapers. *Recreations:* winter sports, shooting, fishing. *Address:* 46 Pearson Park, Hull HU5 2TG. *T:* Hull (0482) 470828.

BUCK, Sir (Philip) Antony (Fyson), Kt 1983; QC 1974; MP (C) Colchester North, since 1983 (Colchester, 1961–83); Barrister-at-Law; *b* 19 Dec. 1928; *yr s* of late A. F. Buck, Ely, Cambs; *m* 1st, 1955, Judy Elaine (marr. diss. 1989), *o d* of late Dr C. A. Grant, Cottesloe, Perth, W Australia, and late Mrs Grant; one *d*; 2nd, 1990, Bienvenida Perez-Blanco. *Educ:* King's School, Ely; Trinity Hall, Cambridge. BA History and Law, 1951, MA 1954. Chm. Cambridge Univ. Cons. Assoc. and Chm. Fedn of Univ. Conservative and Unionist Associations, 1951–52. Called to the Bar, Inner Temple, 1954; Legal Adviser, Nat. Association of Parish Councils, 1957–59, Vice-Pres., 1970–74; sponsored and piloted through the Limitation Act, 1963. PPS to Attorney-General, 1963–64; Parly Under-Sec. of State for Defence (Navy), MoD, 1972–74. Sec., Conservative Party Home Affairs Cttee, 1964–70, Vice-Chm., 1970–72, Chm. Oct./Nov. 1972; Chm., Cons. Parly Defence Cttee, 1979–89; Mem. Exec., 1922 Cttee, Oct./Nov. 1972, 1977–; Chm., Select Cttee on Parly Comr for Administration (Ombudsman), 1977–. *Recreations:* most sports, reading. *Address:* House of Commons, SW1A 0AA. *T:* 071–219 4011. *Club:* United Oxford & Cambridge University.

BUCKHURST, Lord; William Herbrand Thomas Sackville; *b* 13 June 1979; *s* and *heir* of Earl De La Warr, *qv*.

BUCKINGHAM, Area Bishop of; Rt. Rev. Simon Hedley Burrows; appointed Bishop Suffragan of Buckingham, 1974, Area Bishop, 1985; *b* 8 Nov. 1928; *s* of late Very Rev. H. R. Burrows, and Joan Lumsden, *d* of Rt Rev. E. N. Lovett, CBE; *m* 1960, Janet Woodd; two *s* three *d*. *Educ:* Eton; King's Coll., Cambridge (MA); Westcott House, Cambridge. Curate of St John's Wood, 1954–57; Chaplain of Jesus Coll., Cambridge, 1957–60; Vicar of Wyken, Coventry, 1960–67; Vicar of Holy Trinity, Fareham, 1967–74, and Rector of Team Ministry, 1971–74. *Address:* Sheridan, Grimms Hill, Great Missenden, Bucks HP16 9BD. *T:* Great Missenden (02406) 2173.

BUCKINGHAM, Archdeacon of; *see* Morrison, Ven. J. A.

BUCKINGHAM, Amyand David, FRS 1975; Professor of Chemistry, University of Cambridge, since 1969, Fellow of Pembroke College, since 1970; *b* 28 Jan. 1930; 2nd *s* of late Reginald Joslin Buckingham and late Florence Grace Buckingham (formerly Elliot); *m* 1965, Jillian Bowles; one *s* two *d*. *Educ:* Barker Coll., Hornsby, NSW; Univ. of Sydney; Corpus Christi Coll., Cambridge (Shell Postgraduate Schol.). Univ. Medal 1952, MSc 1953, Sydney; PhD 1956, ScD 1985, Cantab. 1851 Exhibn Sen. Studentship, Oxford Univ., 1955–57; Lectr and subseq. Student and Tutor, Christ Church, Oxford, 1955–65; Univ. Lectr in Inorganic Chem. Lab., Oxford, 1958–65; Prof. of Theoretical Chem., Univ. of Bristol, 1965–69. Vis. Lectr, Harvard, 1961; Visiting Professor: Princeton, 1965; Univ. of California (Los Angeles), 1975; Univ. of Illinois, 1976; Univ. of Wisconsin, 1978; Vis. Fellow, ANU, 1979 and 1982; Vis. Erskine Fellow, Univ. of Canterbury, NZ, 1990. FRACI 1961 (Masson Meml Schol. 1952; Rennie Meml Medal, 1958); FRSC (formerly FCS) (Harrison Meml Prize, 1959; Tilden Lectr 1964; Theoretical Chemistry and Spectroscopy Prize, 1970; Member Faraday Div. (Pres., 1987–89; Mem. Council, 1965–67, 1975–83, 1987–); FInstP; Fellow: Optical Soc. of America; Amer. Phys. Soc.; Mem., Amer. Chem. Soc. Editor: Molecular Physics, 1968–72; Chemical Physics Letters, 1978–. Member: Chemistry Cttee, SRC, 1967–70; Adv. Council, Royal Mil. Coll. of Science, Shrivenham, 1973–87. Senior Treasurer: Oxford Univ. Cricket Club, 1959–64; Cambridge Univ. Cricket Club, 1977–90 (Pres., 1990–). Hon. Dr, Univ. de Nancy I, 1979. *Publications:* The Laws and Applications of Thermodynamics, 1964; Organic Liquids, 1978; papers in scientific jls. *Recreations:* walking, woodwork, cricket, tennis, travel. *Address:* 37 Millington Road, Cambridge CB3 9HW.

BUCKINGHAM, Ven. Hugh Fletcher; Archdeacon of the East Riding, since 1988; *b* 13 Sept. 1932; *s* of Rev. Christopher Leigh Buckingham and Gladys Margaret Buckingham; *m* 1967, Alison Mary Cock; one *s* one *d*. *Educ:* Lancing College; Hertford Coll., Oxford (MA Hons). Curate: St Thomas', Halliwell, Bolton, 1957–60; St Silas', Sheffield, 1960–65; Vicar of Hindolveston and Guestwick, dio. Norwich, 1965–70; Rector of Fakenham, 1970–88. Hon. Canon of Norwich Cathedral, 1985–88. *Publications:* How To Be A Christian In Trying Circumstances, 1985; Feeling Good, 1989. *Recreations:* pottery, gardening. *Address:* Brimley Lodge, 27 Molescroft Road, Beverley, North Humberside HU17 7DX. *T:* Hull (0482) 881659.

BUCKINGHAM, Prof. Richard Arthur; Professor of Computer Education, Birkbeck College, University of London, 1974–78, now Professor Emeritus; *b* 17 July 1911; *s* of George Herbert Buckingham and Alice Mary Watson (*née* King); *m* 1939 Christina O'Brien; one *s* two *d*. *Educ:* Gresham's Sch., Holt; St John's Coll., Cambridge. Asst Lecturer in Mathematical Physics, Queen's University, Belfast, 1935–38; Senior 1851 Exhibitioner, University College, London and MIT, 1938–40. At Admiralty Research Laboratory, Teddington, and Mine Design Dept, Havant, 1940–45. University Coll., London: Lecturer in Mathematics, 1945–50; Lecturer in Physics, 1950–51; Reader in Physics, 1951–57; Dir, Univ. of London Computer Unit, later Inst. of Computer Science, 1957–73, and Prof. of Computing Science, 1963–74. FBCS; FRSA. *Publications:* Numerical Methods, 1957; (jtly) Information Systems Education, 1987; papers in Proc. Royal Soc., Proc. Phys. Soc., London, Jl Chem. Physics, Trans. Faraday Soc., Computer Journal, etc. *Address:* Challens, Heather Way, Sullington, West Sussex RH20 4DD.

BUCKINGHAMSHIRE, 10th Earl of, *cr* 1746; **George Miles Hobart-Hampden;** Bt 1611; Baron Hobart 1728; company director; *b* 15 Dec. 1944; *s* of Cyril Langel Hobart-Hampden (*d* 1972) (*g g s* of 6th Earl), and Margaret Moncrieff Hilborne Hobart-Hampden (*née* Jolliffe) (*d* 1985); *S* cousin, 1983; *m* 2nd, 1975, Alison Wightman (*née* Forrest); two step *s*. *Educ:* Clifton College; Exeter Univ. (BA Hons History); Birkbeck Coll. and Inst. of Commonwealth Studies, Univ. of London (MA Area Studies). With Noble Lowndes and Partners Ltd, 1970–81; Dir, Scottish Pension Trustees Ltd, 1979–81, resigned; Director: Antony Gibbs Pension Services Ltd, 1981–86; The Angel Trust Co., 1982–86; Wardley Investment Services (UK) Ltd, 1986–; Wardley Investment Services International Ltd (Man. Dir, 1988–); Wardley Investment Services Ltd, 1988–; Wardley Unit Trust Managers Ltd (Chm.), 1988–; Wardley Fund Managers (Jersey) Ltd (Chm.), 1988–; Gota Global Selection, 1988–; Wardley Investment Services (Luxembourg) SA, 1988–; Wardley Asia Investment Services (Luxembourg) SA (Chm.), 1989–; Wardley Global Selection, 1989–; Korea Asia Fund, 1990–. Member: H of L Select Cttee on European Affairs, Sub-Cttee A, 1985–; H of L Sub-Cttee on Staffing of Community Instns, 1987–88. FInstD. Patron, Hobart Town (1804) First Settlers Assoc. *Recreations:* music, squash, fishing, rugby football. *Heir:* Sir John Vere Hobart, Bt, *qv*. *Address:* House of Lords, SW1. *Clubs:* Western (Glasgow); West of Scotland Football.

BUCKLAND, Maj.-Gen. Ronald John Denys Eden, CB 1974; MBE 1956; DL; Chief Executive, Adur District Council, 1975–85; *b* 27 July 1920; *s* of late Geoffrey Ronald Aubert Buckland, CB and Lelgarde Edith Eleanor (*née* Eden); *m* 1968, Judith Margaret Coxhead; two *d*. *Educ:* Winchester; New College, Oxford (MA). Commissioned into Coldstream Gds, Dec. 1940. Served War of 1939–45: NW Europe, with 4th Coldstream Gds, 1944–45 (wounded twice). GSO3, Gds Div., BAOR, 1946; Adjt, 1st Bn Coldstream Gds, Palestine and Libya, 1948; DAA&QMG, 2nd Guards Bde and 18th Inf. Bde, Malaya, 1950–52 (Dispatches); DAAG, 3rd Div., Egypt, 1954; jssc 1956; Bde Major, 1st Gds Bde, Cyprus, 1958; Bt Lt-Col 1959; Bde Major, 51st Inf. Bde, 1960; commanded 1st Bn, Coldstream Gds, 1961, British Guiana, 1962; GSO1, 4th Div., BAOR, 1963; Brig. 1966; Comdr, 133 Inf. Bde (TA), 1966; ACOS, Joint Exercises Div., HQ AFCENT, Holland, 1967; idc 1968; DA&QMG, 1st British Corps, BAOR, 1969; Maj.-Gen. 1969; Chief of Staff, HQ Strategic Command, 1970; Maj.-Gen. i/c Admin, UKLF, 1972–75. DL W Sussex, 1986. *Recreations:* travel, watching cricket, bricklaying. *Clubs:* Pratt's, Leander; Sussex.

BUCKLAND, Ross; Chief Executive and Director, Unigate plc, since 1990; *b* 19 Dec. 1942; *s* of William Arthur Haverfield Buckland and Elizabeth Buckland; *m* 1966, Patricia Ann Bubb; two *s*. *Educ:* Sydney Boys' High Sch. Various positions in cos engaged in banking, engrg and food ind., 1958–66; Dir, Finance and Admin, Elizabeth Arden Pty Ltd, 1966–73; Kellogg (Australia) Pty Ltd, 1973–77, Man. Dir, 1978; Pres. and Chief Exec., Kellogg Salada Canada Inc., 1979–80; Chm., Kellogg Co. of GB Ltd and Dir, European Ops and Vice-Pres., Kellogg Co., USA, 1981–90. Fellow, Australian Soc. Certified Practising Accountants; FCIS; FIGD. *Recreation:* walking. *Address:* Unigate plc, Unigate House, Wood Lane, W12 7RP. *T:* 081–749 8888. *Clubs:* Roehampton; Sydney Cricket.

BUCKLE, (Christopher) Richard (Sandford), CBE 1979; writer; critic; exhibition designer; Director, Theatre Museum Association, since 1978; *b* 6 Aug. 1916; *s* of late Lieut-Col C. G. Buckle, DSO, MC, Northamptonshire Regt, and Mrs R. E. Buckle (*née* Sandford). *Educ:* Marlborough; Balliol. Founded "Ballet", 1939. Served Scots Guards, 1940–46; in action in Italy (despatches, 1944). Started "Ballet" again, 1946; it continued for seven years. Ballet critic of the Observer, 1948–55: ballet critic of the Sunday Times, 1959–75; advised Canada Council on state of ballet in Canada, 1962; advised Sotheby & Co. on their sales of Diaghilev Ballet material, 1967–69. First play, Gossip Column, prod Q Theatre, 1953; Family Tree (comedy), prod Connaught Theatre, Worthing, 1956. *Organised:* Diaghilev Exhibition, Edinburgh Festival, 1954, and Forbes House, London, 1954–55; The Observer Film Exhibition, London, 1956; Telford Bicentenary Exhibition, 1957; Epstein Memorial Exhibition, Edinburgh Festival, 1961; Shakespeare Exhibition, Stratford-upon-Avon, 1964–65; a smaller version of Shakespeare Exhibition, Edinburgh, 1964; Treasures from the Shakespeare Exhibition, National Portrait Gallery, London, 1964–65; The Communities on the March area in the Man in the Community theme pavilion, Universal and Internat. Exhibition of 1967, Montreal; Exhibition of Beaton Portraits, 1928–68, National Portrait Gallery, 1968; Gala of ballet, Coliseum, 1971; exhibn of Ursula Tyrwhitt, Ashmolean Mus., Oxford, 1974; exhibn Omaggio ai Disegnatori di Diaghilev, Palazzo Grassi, Venice, 1975; exhibn of ballet, opera and theatre costumes, Salisbury Fest., 1975; exhibn Happy and Glorious, 130 years of Royal photographs, Nat. Portrait Gallery, 1977; presented Kama Dev in recital of Indian dancing, St Paul's Church, Covent Garden, 1970; *designed:* (temporary) Haldane Library for Imperial College, South Kensington; new Exhibition Rooms, Harewood House, Yorks, 1959; redesigned interior of Dundee Repertory Theatre, 1963 (burnt down 3 months later). *Publications:* John Innocent at Oxford (novel), 1939; The Adventures of a Ballet Critic, 1953; In Search of Diaghilev, 1955; Modern Ballet Design, 1955; The Prettiest Girl in England, 1958; Harewood (a guide-book), 1959 and (re-written and re-designed), 1966; Dancing for Diaghilev (the memoirs of Lydia Sokolova), 1960; Epstein Drawings (introd. only), 1962; Epstein: An Autobiography (introd. to new edn only), 1963; Jacob Epstein: Sculptor, 1963; Monsters at Midnight: the French Romantic Movement as a background to the ballet Giselle (limited edn), 1966; Nijinsky, 1971; Nijinsky on Stage: commentary on drawings of Valentine Gross, 1971; (ed) U and Non-U revisited, 1978; Diaghilev, 1979; (ed) Self Portrait with Friends, selected diaries of Cecil Beaton, 1979; Buckle at the Ballet, 1980; (with Roy Strong and others) Designing for the Dancer, 1981; (contrib.) The Englishman's Room, ed A. Lees-Milne, 1986; (contrib.) Sir Iain Moncreiffe of that Ilk, ed J. Jolliffe, 1986; L'Après-midi d'un faune, Vaslav Nijinski (introd. only), 1983; (with John Taras) George Balanchine, Ballet Master, 1988; *autobiography:* 1, The Most Upsetting Woman, 1981; 2, In the Wake of Diaghilev, 1982. *Recreations:* caricature, light verse. *Address:* Roman Road, Gutch Common, Semley, Shaftesbury, Dorset SP7 9BE.

BUCKLE, Maj.-Gen. (Retd) Denys Herbert Vintcent, CB 1955; CBE 1948 (OBE 1945); Legion of Merit (USA) 1944; FCIT; Trustee, South Africa Foundation, since 1969; Director, Prince Vintcent & Co. (Pty) Ltd, Mossel Bay; *b* Cape, South Africa, 16 July 1902; *s* of Major H. S. Buckle, RMLI and ASC and of Agnes Buckle (*née* Vintcent), Cape Town; *m* 1928, Frances Margaret Butterworth (*d* 1990); one *d*. *Educ:* Boxgrove School, Guildford; Charterhouse, Godalming; RMC Sandhurst. 2nd Lieut, E Surrey Regt, 1923; transf. to RASC, 1926; Shanghai Def. Force, 1927–28; Asst Adjt, RASC Trg Centre, 1929–32; Adjt 44th (Home Counties) Divnl RASC, TA, 1932–36; Student Staff Coll., Camberley, 1936–37; Adjt Ceylon ASC, 1938; Bde Maj., Malaya Inf Bde, 1938–40; GSO 2, Trg Directorate, WO, 1940; AA & QMG, 8th Armd Div., 1940–41; GSO 1, Staff Coll., Camberley, 1941–42; Brig. Admin. Plans, GHQ Home Forces, "Cossac" and SHAEF, 1942–44; Brig. Q Ops, WO, 1944; DDST and Brig. Q, 21 Army Gp and BAOR, 1945–46; DQMG, FARELF, 1946–48; DDST, S Comd, 1948–49; Spec. Appts (Brig.), USA, 1949–50; Dir of Equipment, WO, 1950–51, and special appt, Paris, 1951; Comdt RASC Trg Centre, 1952–53; DST, MELF, 1953–56; Maj.-Gen. i/c Admin, GHQ, MELF, 1956–58; despatches, 1956 (Suez); retd 1958; ADC to King George VI 1951, to the Queen, 1952–54. FCIT 1971. Bursar, Church of England Training Colleges, Cheltenham, 1958–59. Divisional Manager SE Division, British Waterways, 1961–63; Director of Reorganisation, British Waterways, 1963–65. Dir, UK-S Africa Trade Assoc., 1965–68; Administrative Mem., Southern Africa Cttee, BNEC, 1967–68. Col Comdt RASC, 1959–64; Representative Col Comdt, RASC, 1961; Hon. Col 44th (Home Counties) RASC, 1962–65, Regt, RCT, 1965–67. Legion of Merit (USA), 1944. *Publications:* History of 44th Division, RASC, TA, 1932; The Vintcents of Mossel Bay, 1986. *Recreations:* reading, broadcasting, writing, walking, swimming, travel. *Address:* Flat A,

636 St Martini Gardens, Queen Victoria Street, Cape Town, 8001, South Africa. *T:* 246745. *Clubs:* Army and Navy; Western Province Sports (Cape Town).

BUCKLE, Rt. Rev. Edward Gilbert; Bishop in the Northern Region, Diocese of Auckland, New Zealand, since 1981; *b* 20 July 1926; *s* of Douglas Gordon Buckle and Claire Ettie Wellman; *m* 1949, Mona Ann Cain; one *s* three *d. Educ:* Hurstville Central Coll.; Moore Theological Coll., Univ. of Sydney (LTh); St Augustine's College, Canterbury, Eng. (DipCC). Served War, RAAF, 1944–45. Rector of Koorawatha, 1950–51; Chaplain, Snowy Mountains Hydro-Electric Authority, 1952–54; Rector, All Saints, Canberra, 1955–62; Canon, St Saviour's Cathedral, Goulburn, 1959; Dir of Adult Education for Gen. Bd of Religious Education, Melbourne, 1962–65. New Zealand: Vicar, St Matthew's-in-the-City, Auckland, 1966–67; Bishop's Executive Officer, 1967–70; Diocesan and Ecumenical Develt Officer, 1970–81; Archdeacon of Auckland, 1970–81. *Publications:* The Disturber: The Episcopacy of Ernest Henry Burgmann, Bishop of Canberra and Goulburn, 1957; A Station of the Cross, 1959; Cost of Living, study material on MRI; Family Affair, 1966; Urban Development, 1968; Interview 69, 1969; The Churches and East Coast Bays, 1970; The Isthmus and Redevelopment, 1973; Inner City Churches, 1973; Otara and the Churches, 1974; The Churches East of the Tamaki, 1974; Paroikia—the house alongside, 1978. *Recreations:* reading, sailing, squash. *Address:* 14 Kiwi Avenue, Maunu, Whangarei, Northland, New Zealand. *T:* 089 485 922. *Club:* Wellesley (Wellington, NZ).

BUCKLE, Richard; *see* Buckle, C. R. S.

BUCKLEY, family name of **Baron Wrenbury.**

BUCKLEY, Anthony James Henthorne; consultant; *b* 22 May 1934; *s* of late William Buckley, FRCS; *m* 1964, Celia Rosamund Sanderson, *d* of late C. R. Sanderson; one *s* two *d. Educ:* Haileybury and ISC; St John's Coll., Cambridge. MA, LLB, FCA. Peat Marwick Mitchell & Co., 1959–62; Rank Organisation Ltd, 1962–66; Slater Walker Securities Ltd, 1966–75, Man. Dir, 1972–75. *Address:* 2 St Mary's Grove, SW13 0JA.

BUCKLEY, Rt. Hon. Sir Denys (Burton), PC 1970; Kt 1960; MBE 1945; a Lord Justice of Appeal, 1970–81; *b* 6 Feb. 1906; 4th *s* of 1st Baron Wrenbury; *m* 1932, Gwendolen Jane (*d* 1985), *yr d* of late Sir Robert Armstrong-Jones, CBE, FRCS, FRCP; three *d. Educ:* Eton; Trinity College, Oxford. Called to the Bar, Lincoln's Inn, 1928, Bencher, 1949, Pro-Treasurer, 1967, Treasurer, 1969, Pres., Senate of the Inns of Court, 1970–72. Served War of 1939–45, in RAOC, 1940–45; Temporary Major; GSO II (Sigs Directorate), War Office. Treasury Junior Counsel (Chancery), 1949–60; Judge of High Court of Justice, Chancery Div., 1960–70. Member, Restrictive Practices Ct, 1962–70, President, 1968–70; Member: Law Reform Cttee, 1963–73; Cttee on Departmental Records, 1952–54; Advisory Council on Public Records, 1958–79. Hon. Fellow: Trinity Coll., Oxford, 1969; Amer. Coll. of Trial Lawyers, 1970. Master, Merchant Taylors' Co., 1972, First Upper Warden, 1986–87. CStJ 1966. Medal of Freedom (USA), 1945. *Address:* Flat 6, 105 Onslow Square, SW7 3LU. *T:* 071–584 4735; Stream Farm, Dallington, Sussex. *T:* Rushlake Green (0435) 830223. *Clubs:* Brooks's, Beefsteak.

BUCKLEY, Eric Joseph, MA; FIOP; Printer to the University of Oxford, 1978–83; Emeritus Fellow of Linacre College, Oxford, 1983 (Fellow, 1979–83); *b* 26 June 1920; *s* of Joseph William Buckley and Lillian Elizabeth Major (*née* Drake); *m* 1st, 1945, Joan Alice Kirby (*d* 1973); one *s* one *d*; 2nd, 1978, Harriett, *d* of Judge and Mrs Robert Williams Hawkins, Caruthersville, Mo, USA. *Educ:* St Bartholomew's, Dover. MA Oxon 1979 (by special resolution; Linacre College). Served War, RAOC and REME, ME and UK, 1939–45. Apprentice, Amalgamated Press, London, 1935; Dir, Pergamon Press Ltd, 1956–74; joined Oxford Univ. Press as Dir, UK Publishing Services, 1974. Liveryman, Stationers and Newspaper Makers Co., 1981; Freeman, City of London, 1980. *Recreations:* reading, theatre, cats. *Address:* 43 Sandfield Road, Oxford OX3 7RN. *T:* Oxford (0865) 60588.

BUCKLEY, George Eric; Counsellor, Atomic Energy, British Embassy, Tokyo, 1976–81; *b* 4 Feb. 1916; *s* of John and Florence Buckley; *m* 1941, Mary Theresa Terry; one *s* one *d. Educ:* Oldham High Sch.; Manchester Univ. BSc (Hons) Physics; MInstP. Lectr in Physics, Rugby Coll. of Technol., 1938. War service, Sqdn Ldr, RAF, 1940–46. Manager, Health Physics and Safety, Windscale Works, 1949; Works Manager, Capenhurst Works, 1952; Chief Ops Physicist, Risley, 1956; Chief Tech. Manager, Windscale and Calder Works, 1959; Superintendent: Calder Hall and Windscale Advanced Gas Cooled Reactors, 1964; Reactors, and Head of Management Services, 1974. *Recreations:* travel, good food, golf. *Address:* 12 Wast Water Rise, Seascale, Cumbria CA20 1LB. *T:* Seascale (09467) 28405.

BUCKLEY, James; Deputy Director General, General Council of British Shipping, since 1987; *b* 5 April 1944; *s* of late Harold Buckley and of Mabel Buckley; *m* 1972, Valerie Elizabeth Powles; one *d. Educ:* Sheffield City Grammar Sch.; Imperial College of Science and Technology (BSc, ARCS). RAF Operational Res., 1965. Principal Scientific Officer, 1971; Asst Sec., CSD; Private Secretary: to Lord Privy Seal, Lord Peart, 1979; to Lord President of Council, Lord Soames, 1979; to Chancellor of Duchy of Lancaster, Baroness Young, 1981; Sec., Civil Service Coll., 1982; Chief Exec., BVA, 1985–87. *Recreations:* photography, squash, tennis. *Address:* 29 Spenser Avenue, Weybridge, Surrey KT13 0ST. *T:* Weybridge (0932) 843893.

BUCKLEY, James Arthur, CBE 1975; Senior Energy Consultant and Director, CIRS Ltd, Newmarket, since 1976; *b* 3 April 1917; *s* of late James Buckley and of Elizabeth Buckley; *m* 1939, Irene May Hicks; two *s. Educ:* Christ's Hosp., Horsham, Sussex; Westminster Technical Coll.; Bradford Technical Coll. RAFVR, 1940–46. Gas Light & Coke Co.; Gas Supply Pupil, 1934; Actg Service Supervisor, 1939; Service Supervisor, 1946; North Thames Gas Board: Divisional Man., 1954; Commercial Man., 1962; Commercial Man. and Bd Mem., 1964; East Midlands Gas Board: Dep. Chm., 1966–67; Chm., 1967–68; Mem., Gas Council, later British Gas Corp., 1968–76. Pres., IGasE, 1971–72. *Address:* Grosvenor House, High Street, Newmarket. *T:* Newmarket (0638) 663030.

BUCKLEY, Sir John (William), Kt 1977; FRSA 1978; Hon. FIChemE; FIProdE; chairman and director of companies; Chairman, Davy Corporation (formerly Davy International Ltd), 1973–82, retired; *b* 9 Jan. 1913; *s* of John William and Florence Buckley; *m* 1st, 1935, Bertha Bagnall (marr. diss. 1967); two *s*; 2nd, 1967, Molly Neville-Clarke; one step *s* (and one step *s* decd). *Educ:* techn. coll. (Dipl. Engrg). George Kent Ltd, 1934–50 (Gen. Man. 1945–50); Man. Dir, Emmco Pty Ltd, 1950–55; Man. Dir, British Motor Corp. Pty Ltd, 1956–60; Vice Chm. and Dep. Chm., Winget, Gloucester Ltd, 1961–68; Man. Dir and Dep. Chm., Davy International Ltd, 1968–73; Chm., Alfred Herbert Ltd, 1975–79; Chairman: Oppenheimer International, 1983–; Engelhard Industries, 1979–85; John Buckley Associates Ltd, 1983–; Harman Ltd, 1985–; Alexanders Laing & Cruickshank Mergers and Acquisitions Ltd, 1986–; Amchem Ltd, 1989–; Director: Engelhard Corp. Inc., USA, 1982–86; Fuerst Day Lawson, 1981–. Dir, British Overseas Trade Bd, 1973–76. Mem., BSC, 1978–81. Hon. FIChemE 1975. Order of the Southern Cross (Brazil), 1977. *Recreations:* gardening, music, photography, fishing, painting. *Address:* 49 Drayton Gardens, SW10 9RX. *T:* 071–244 6486. *Club:* Boodle's.

BUCKLEY, Rear-Adm. Sir Kenneth (Robertson), KBE 1961; *b* 24 May 1904; 2nd *s* of late L. E. Buckley, CSI, TD; *m* 1937, Bettie Helen Radclyffe Dugmore; one *s* two *d. Educ:* RN Colleges Osborne and Dartmouth. Joined Navy Jan. 1918. Served War of 1939–45 (despatches). Comdr 1942; Capt. 1949; Rear-Adm. 1958. ADC to the Queen, 1956–58. Director of Engineering and Electrical Training of the Navy, and Senior Naval Electrical Officer, 1959–62. *Recreations:* golf, gardening. *Address:* Meadow Cottage, Cherque Lane, Lee-on-Solent, Hants. *T:* Lee-on-Solent (0705) 550646.

BUCKLEY, Martin Christopher Burton; Registrar in Bankruptcy, Companies Court, High Court of Justice, and Clerk of Restrictive Practices Court, since 1988; *b* 5 Oct. 1936; *s* of late Hon. Dr Colin Burton Buckley and Evelyn Joyce Buckley (*née* Webster); *m* 1964, Victoria Gay, *d* of Dr Stanhope Furber; two *s* three *d. Educ:* Rugby School; Trinity College, Oxford (MA). Called to the Bar, Lincoln's Inn, 1961; practised at Chancery Bar, 1962–88. *Publication:* (ed jtly) Buckley on the Companies Acts, 14th edn 1981 (1st edn 1873—9th edn 1909 by grandfather, Henry Burton Buckley, later 1st Baron Wrenbury). *Recreations:* amateur theatre, choral singing. *Address:* Crouchers, Rudgwick, Sussex RH12 3DD. *T:* Rudgwick (040372) 2255.

BUCKLEY, Michael Sydney; Under Secretary, Department of Energy, 1985–91; *b* 20 June 1939; *s* of Sydney Dowsett Buckley and Grace Bew Buckley; *m* 1972, Shirley Stordy (*d* 1991); one *s* one *d. Educ:* Eltham College; Christ Church, Oxford (MA; Cert. of Stats). Asst Principal, Treasury, 1962; Asst Private Sec. to Chancellor of Exchequer, 1965–66; Principal: Treasury, 1966–68 and 1971–74; CSD, 1968–71; Assistant Secretary: Treasury, 1974–77 and 1980–82; DoI, 1977–80; Under Sec., Cabinet Office, 1982–85. *Recreations:* photography, listening to music, reading. *Address:* 53 Bexley Road, SE9 2PE.

BUCKLEY, Lt-Comdr Sir (Peter) Richard, KCVO 1982 (CVO 1973; MVO 1968); Director, Malcolm McIntyre Consultancy, since 1989; *b* 31 Jan. 1928; 2nd *s* of late Alfred Buckley and Mrs E. G. Buckley, Crowthorne, Berks; *m* 1958, Theresa Mary Neve; two *s* one *d. Educ:* Wellington Coll. Cadet, RN, 1945. Served in HM Ships: Mauritius, Ulster, Contest, Defender, and BRNC, Dartmouth. Specialised in TA/S. Invalided from RN (Lt-Comdr), 1961. Private Sec. to the Duke and Duchess of Kent, 1961–89; Extra Equerry to the Duke of Kent, 1989–. Dir, Vickers Internat., 1981–89. Governor: Wellington Coll., 1989–; Eagle House Sch. *Recreations:* fishing, sailing, bee keeping. *Address:* Coppins Cottages, Iver, Bucks SL0 0AT. *T:* Iver (0753) 653004. *Clubs:* Army and Navy; All England Lawn Tennis and Croquet; Royal Yacht Squadron; Royal Dart Yacht.

BUCKLEY, Hon. Sir Roger (John), Kt 1989; **Hon. Mr Justice Buckley;** a Judge of the High Court of Justice, Queen's Bench Division, since 1989; *b* 26 April 1939; *s* of Harold and Marjorie Buckley; *m* 1965, Margaret Gillian, *d* of Robert and Joan Cowan; one *s* one *d. Educ:* Mill Hill Sch.; Manchester Univ. (LLB (Hons)). Called to the Bar, Middle Temple, 1962 (Harmsworth Schol.); Bencher, Middle Temple, 1987; QC 1979; a Recorder, 1986–89. *Recreations:* golf, theatre. *Address:* Royal Courts of Justice, WC2A 2LL. *Club:* Old Mill Hillians.

BUCKLEY, Dr Trevor, CEng, FIEE; Assistant Chief Scientific Adviser (Research), Ministry of Defence, since 1991; *b* 4 Feb. 1938; *s* of Harold Buckley and Selina (*née* Follos); *m* 1960, Mary Pauline Stubbs; one *s* one *d. Educ:* Barmouth Grammar Sch.; UCNW Bangor (BSc Hons Electronic Engrg, PhD). RRE, 1962–76 (Head of ATC Res. Div., 1972–76); Admiralty Underwater Weapons Estabt, 1976–82 (Head of Sonar Data Processing Res. Div., 1976–80, Dep. Dir Underwater Weapons Projects (SM), 1980–82); RCDS, 1983; Dir Gen., Air Weapons and Electronic Systems, 1984–86, Dep. Controller Res., 1986–91, MoD (PE). *Recreations:* photography, musical appreciation, fixing things. *Address:* 46 Moreland Drive, Gerrards Cross, Bucks SL9 8BD. *T:* Gerrards Cross (0753) 885920.

BUCKLEY, Major William Kemmis, MBE 1959; Vice Lord-Lieutenant of Dyfed, since 1989; President, Buckley's Brewery Ltd, 1983–86 (Director, 1960, Vice-Chairman, 1963–72, Chairman, 1972–83); *b* 18 Oct. 1921; *o s* of late Lt-Col William Howell Buckley, DL, and Karolie Kathleen Kemmis. *Educ:* Radley Coll.; New Coll., Oxford (MA). Commnd into Welsh Guards, 1941; served N Africa, Italy (despatches, 1945); ADC, 1946–47, Mil. Sec., 1948, to Governor of Madras; Staff Coll., Camberley, 1950; GSO2, HQ London Dist, 1952–53; OC Guards Indep. Para. Co., 1954–57; Cyprus, 1956; Suez, 1956; War Office, 1957; Mil. Asst to Vice-Chief of Imp. Gen. Staff, 1958–59; US Armed Forces Staff Coll., Norfolk, Va., 1959–60. Director: Rhymney Breweries Ltd, 1962–69; Whitbread (Wales) Ltd, 1969–81; Felinfoel Brewery Co., 1975–; Guardian Assurance Co. (S Wales), 1966–83 (Dep. Chm., 1967–83). Mem. Council, Brewers' Soc., 1967; Chm., S Wales Brewers' Assoc., 1971–74; Dep. Chm. and Treas., Nat. Trade Develt Assoc., 1966 (Chm., S Wales Panel, 1965); Lay Mem., Press Council, 1967–73. Chm., Council of St John of Jerusalem for Carms, 1966; Pres., Carms Antiquarian Soc., 1971– (Chm., 1968); Mem., Nat. Trust Cttee for Wales, 1962–70; Mem., T&AFA (Carms), 1962–82 and T&AFA (S Wales and Mon.), 1967–83; Jt Master and Hon. Sec., Pembrokeshire and Carms Otter Hounds, 1962. High Sheriff of Carms, 1967–68, DL Dyfed (formerly Carms) 1969. KStJ 1984 (CStJ 1966). *Publications:* contributions in local history journals. *Recreations:* gardening, bee-keeping, tapestry work. *Address:* Briar Cottage, Ferryside, Dyfed, S Wales. *T:* Ferryside (0267) 267359. *Clubs:* Brooks's; Cardiff and County (Cardiff).

BUCKMASTER, family name of **Viscount Buckmaster.**

BUCKMASTER, 3rd Viscount *cr* 1933, of Cheddington; **Martin Stanley Buckmaster,** OBE 1979; Baron 1915; HM Diplomatic Service, retired; *b* 11 April 1921; *s* of 2nd Viscount Buckmaster and Joan, Viscountess Buckmaster (*d* 1976), *d* of Dr Garry Simpson; *S* father, 1974. *Educ:* Stowe. Joined TA, 1939; served Royal Sussex Regt (Captain) in UK and Middle East, 1940–46. Foreign Office, 1946; Middle East Centre for Arab Studies, Lebanon, 1950–51; qualified in Arabic (Higher Standard); served in Trucial States, Sharjah (1951–53) and Abu Dhabi (Political Officer, 1955–58) and subsequently in Libya, Bahrain, FO, Uganda, Lebanon and Saudi Arabia, 1958–73; First Sec., FCO, 1973–77; Head of Chancery and Chargé d'Affaires, Yemen Arab Republic, 1977–81. Deputy Chairman: Council for the Advancement of Arab-British Studies; Christian Broadcasting Council. FRGS 1954. *Recreations:* walking, music, railways; Arab and African studies. *Heir: b* Hon. Colin John Buckmaster [*b* 17 April 1923; *m* 1946, May, *o d* of late Charles Henry Gibbon; three *s* two *d*]. *Address:* 90 Cornwall Gardens, SW7 4AX. *Club:* Travellers'.

BUCKMASTER, Rev. Cuthbert Harold Septimus; *b* 15 July 1903; *s* of Charles John and Evelyn Jean Buckmaster; *m* 1942, Katharine Mary Zoë (*d* 1974), 3rd *d* of Rev. Canon T. N. R. Prentice, Stratford-on-Avon; two *d. Educ:* RN Colls, Osborne and Dartmouth. Asst Curate St John's, Middlesbrough, 1927–30; Curate of Wigan, 1930–33; Chaplain of Denstone Coll., 1933–35; Warden of St Michael's Coll., Tenbury, Worcs, 1935–46; Rector of: Ashprington, with Cornworthy, 1957–59; Chagford, 1959–71. Chaplain RNVR, 1940; RN 1947. *Address:* 47 Carlyle Street, Byron Bay, NSW 2481, Australia.

BUCKMASTER, Colonel Maurice James, OBE 1943; Independent Public Relations Consultant, 1960–89, retired; *b* 11 Jan. 1902; *s* of Henry James Buckmaster and Eva Matilda (*née* Nason); *m* 1st, 1927, May Dorothy (*née* Steed); one *s* two *d*; 2nd, 1941, Anna Cecilia (*née* Reinstein) (*d* 1988). *Educ:* Eton College. J. Henry Schroder & Co., Merchant Bankers, 1923–29; Asst to Chairman, Ford Motor Co. Ltd, 1929–32; Manager, Ford Motor Co. (France), 1932–36; Head of European Dept, Ford Motor Co. Ltd, 1936–39 and 1945–50; Dir of Public Relations, 1950–60. Served War of 1939–45: 50th Div., G3I, Intelligence, 1939–40 (despatches); Intelligence Officer (Captain), Dakar expedition; Special Operations Executive, Head of French Section, 1941–45. Chevalier de la Légion d'Honneur, 1945, Officier 1978 (France); Croix de Guerre with Palms, Médaille de la Résistance (France), 1945; Legion of Merit (US), 1945. *Publications:* Specially Employed, 1961; They Fought Alone, 1964. *Recreation:* family life.

BUCKTON, Raymond William, FCIT; General Secretary, Associated Society of Locomotive Engineers and Firemen, 1970–87, retired; *b* 20 Oct. 1922; *s* of W. E. and H. Buckton; *m* 1954, Barbara Langfield; two *s*. *Educ:* Appleton Roebuck School. FCIT 1982. Employed in Motive Power Department, British Railways, 1940–60. Elected Irish Officer of ASLEF, 1960 (Dublin); District Organiser, York, Jan. 1963; Assistant General Secretary, July 1963; General Secretary, 1970. Member: Gen. Council, TUC, 1973–86 (Chm., 1983–84); IBA Gen. Adv. Council, 1976–81; Occupational Pensions Bd, 1976–82; Health Services Bd, 1977–80; Health and Safety Commn, 1982–86. Member: Council, Industrial Soc., 1973–; Standing Adv. Cttee, TUC Centenary Inst. of Occupational Health, 1974–; Nat. Adv. Council on Employment of Disabled People, 1975–; Industrial Injuries Adv. Council, 1976–; Dangerous Substances Adv. Cttee, 1976–; Adv. Cttee on Alcoholism, 1977–; Railway Industry Adv. Cttee, 1977–82; TUC Internat. Cttee, 1978–86; EEC Economic and Social Cttee, 1978–82; Exec., ETUC, 1982–; Commonwealth TUC, 1982–. Director: Transport 2000, 1985; Nirex, 1986–. Mem., Adv. Council for Transport of Radioactive Materials, 1986–89. Councillor, York City Council, 1952–55, Alderman, 1955–57. *Address:* 86 Hillside Gardens, Edgware, Middlesex HA8 8HD.

BUCKWELL, Prof. Allan Edgar; Professor of Agricultural Economics, Wye College, University of London, since 1984; *b* 10 April 1947; *s* of George Alfred Donald Buckwell and Jessie Ethel Buckwell (*née* Neave); *m* 1967, Susan Margaret Hopwood; two *s*. *Educ:* Wye Coll., Univ. of London (BSc Agric.); Manchester Univ. (MA Econ.). Research Associate, Agricl Adjustment Unit, Newcastle Univ., 1970–73; Lectr in Agricl Economics, Newcastle Univ., 1973–84. Kellogg Res. Fellow, Univ. of Wisconsin, Madison, 1974–75; Vis. Prof., Cornell Univ., 1983. *Publications:* (jtly) The Cost of the Common Agricultural Policy, 1982; articles in Jl Agricl Economics. *Recreations:* walking, gardening, making boomerangs. *Address:* 57 Oxenturn Road, Wye, Ashford, Kent TN25 5AY. *T:* Ashford (0233) 813106.

BUDD, Alan Peter; Chief Economic Adviser to the Treasury and Head of Government Economic Service, since 1991; *b* 16 Nov. 1937; *s* of late Ernest and Elsie Budd; *m* 1964, Susan (*née* Millott); three *s*. *Educ:* Oundle Sch. (Grocers' Co. Schol.); London School of Economics (Leverhulme Schol.; BScEcon); Churchill Coll., Cambridge (PhD). Lectr, Southampton Univ., 1966–69; Ford Foundn Vis. Prof., Carnegie-Mellon Univ., Pittsburgh, 1969–70; Sen. Economic Advr, HM Treasury, 1970–74; Williams & Glyn's Sen. Res. Fellow, London Business Sch., 1974–78; High Level Cons., OECD, 1976–77; Special Advr, Treasury and CS Cttee, 1979–81; Dir, Centre for Economic Forecasting, 1980–88, Prof. of Econs, 1981–91, London Business Sch.; Gp Economic Advr, Barclays Bank, 1988–91. Reserve Bank of Aust. Vis. Prof., Univ. of New South Wales, 1983. Member: Securities and Investments Board, 1987–88; ABRC, 1991–. Member: UK-Japan 2000 Gp, 1984–; Council, Inst. for Fiscal Studies, 1988–; Council, REconS, 1988–. Econs columnist, The Independent, 1991. *Publications:* The Politics of Economic Planning, 1978; articles in professional jls. *Recreations:* music, gardening. *Address:* c/o HM Treasury, Parliament Street, SW1P 3AG. *T:* 071–270 5203. *Club:* Reform.

BUDD, Bernard Wilfred, MA; QC 1969; *b* 18 Dec. 1912; *s* of late Rev. W. R. A. Budd; *m* 1944, Margaret Alison, MBE, *d* of late Rt Hon. E. Leslie Burgin, PC, LLD, MP; two *s*. *Educ:* Cardiff High Sch.; W Leeds High Sch.; Pembroke Coll., Cambridge (schol. in natural sciences). Joined ICS, 1935; various Dist appts incl. Dep. Comr, Upper Sind Frontier, 1942–43; Collector and Dist Magistrate, Karachi, 1945–46; cont. in Pakistan Admin. Service, 1947; Dep. Sec., Min. of Commerce and Works, Govt of Pakistan, 1947; Anti-corruption Officer and Inspector-Gen. of Prisons, Govt of Sind, 1949. Called to Bar, Gray's Inn, 1952; ceased English practice, 1982. Contested (L), Dover, 1964 and 1966, Folkestone and Hythe, Feb. and Oct. 1974 and 1979. Chm., Assoc. of Liberal Lawyers, 1978–82. Vice-Pres., Internat. Assoc. for the Protection of Industrial Property (British Group), 1978–. Methodist Local (lay) Preacher, 1933–. *Recreations:* birds, hill walking. *Address* Highlands, Elham, Canterbury, Kent CT4 6UG. *T:* Elham (030384) 350. *Clubs:* United Oxford & Cambridge University, National Liberal.

See also C. R. Budd.

BUDD, Colin Richard, CMG 1991; HM Diplomatic Service; Counsellor (Political), Bonn, since 1989; *b* 31 Aug. 1945; *s* of Bernard Wilfred Budd, *qv*; *m* 1971, Agnes Smit; one *s* one *d*. *Educ:* Kingswood Sch., Bath; Pembroke Coll., Cambridge. Entered HM Diplomatic Service, 1967; CO, 1967–68; Asst Private Sec. to Minister without Portfolio, 1968–69; Third Sec., Warsaw, 1969–72; Second Sec., Islamabad, 1972–75; FCO, 1976–80; First Sec., The Hague, 1980–84; Asst Private Sec. to Sec. of State for Foreign and Commonwealth Affairs, 1984–87; European Secretariat, Cabinet Office, 1988–89. *Recreations:* running, mountains, music (Mozart, chansons, Don McLean). *Address:* c/o Foreign and Commonwealth Office, King Charles Street, SW1.

BUDD, Rt. Rev. Mgr. Hugh Christopher; *see* Plymouth, Bishop of, (RC).

BUDDEN, Julian Medforth, OBE 1991; FBA 1987; *b* 9 April 1924; *s* of Prof. Lionel Bailey Budden and Dora Magdalene (*née* Fraser). *Educ:* Stowe Sch.; Queen's Coll., Oxford (MA); Royal Coll. of Music (BMus). Joined BBC Music Dept, 1951, as clerk; Music Producer, 1956–70; Chief Producer, Opera (Radio), 1970–76; External Services Music Organiser, 1976–83. *Publications:* The Operas of Verdi, vol. I 1973, vol. II 1978, vol. III 1981; Verdi, 1985; contribs to various musicological periodicals. *Address:* (March, April, July–Sept.) 94 Station Road, N3 2SG. *T:* 01–349 2954; (Oct.–Feb., May, June) Via Fratelli Bandiera, 9, 50137 Firenze, Italy. *T:* Florence 678471.

BUDDEN, Kenneth George, FRS 1966; MA, PhD; Reader in Physics, University of Cambridge, 1965–82, now Emeritus; Fellow of St John's College, Cambridge, since 1947; *b* 23 June 1915; *s* of late George Easthope Budden and Gertrude Homer Rea; *m* 1947, Nicolette Ann Lydia de Longesdon Longsdon; no *c*. *Educ:* Portsmouth Grammar Sch.; St John's College, Cambridge (MA, PhD). Telecommunications Research Establishment, 1939–41; British Air Commn., Washington, DC, 1941–44; Air Command, SE Asia, 1945. Research at Cambridge, 1936–39 and from 1947. *Publications:* Radio Waves in the Ionosphere, 1961; The Wave-Guide Mode Theory of Wave Propagation, 1961; Lectures on Magnetoionic Theory, 1964; The Propagation of Radio Waves, 1985; numerous papers in scientific jls, on the propagation of radio waves. *Recreation:* gardening. *Address:* 15 Adams Road, Cambridge CB3 9AD. *T:* Cambridge (0223) 354752.

BUDGEN, Nicholas William; MP (C) Wolverhampton South-West, since Feb. 1974; *b* 3 Nov. 1937; *s* of Captain G. N. Budgen; *m* 1964, Madeleine E. Kittoe; one *s* one *d*. *Educ:* St Edward's Sch., Oxford; Corpus Christi Coll., Cambridge. Called to Bar, Gray's Inn, 1962; practised Midland and Oxford Circuit. An Asst Govt Whip, 1981–82. *Recreations:* hunting, racing. *Address:* Malt House Farm, Colton, near Rugeley, Staffs. *T:* Rugeley (08894) 77059.

BUENO, Antonio De Padua Jose Maria; QC 1989; a Recorder, since 1989; *b* 28 June 1942; *s* of Antonio and Teresita Bueno; *m* 1966, Christine Mary Lees; three *d*. *Educ:* Downside School; Salamanca Univ. Called to the Bar, Middle Temple, 1964, and Gibraltar. An Asst Recorder, 1984–89. *Publications:* (ed jtly) Banking section, Atkin's Encyclopaedia of Court Forms, 2nd edn 1976; (Asst Editor, 24th edn 1979 and 25th edn 1983, Jt Editor, 26th edn 1988) Byles on Bills of Exchange; (Asst Editor) Paget's Law of Banking, 9th edn 1982. *Recreations:* fishing, shooting, flying. *Address:* 7 Pitt Street, W8 4NX. *T:* 071–937 0403. *Clubs:* East India, Flyfishers'.

BUERK, Michael Duncan; foreign correspondent and newscaster, television; *b* 18 Feb. 1946; *s* of Betty Mary Buerk and Gordon Charles Buerk; *m* 1968, Christine Lilley; two *s*. *Educ:* Solihull School. Thomson Newspapers, Cardiff, 1967–69; reporter, Daily Mail, 1969–70; producer, BBC radio, 1970–71; reporter: HTV (West), 1971–72; BBC TV (South), 1972–73; BBC TV London, 1973–76; correspondent, BBC TV: industrial, 1976–77; energy, 1977–79; Scotland, 1979–81; special corresp. and newscaster, 1981–83; Southern Africa, 1983–87; presenter, BBC TV News, 1988–. RTS TV Journalist of the Year and RTS News Award, 1984; UN Hunger Award, 1984; numerous other awards, UK and overseas, 1984, 1985; BAFTA News Award, 1985; James Cameron Meml Award, 1988; Science Writer of the Year Award, 1989. *Recreations:* travel, oenophily. *Address:* c/o BBC Television, W12 7RJ. *T:* 081–576 7771.

BUFFET, Bernard; Chevalier de la Légion d'Honneur; painter; *b* Paris, 10 July 1928; *m* 1958, Annabel May Schwob de Lure; one *s* two *d*. *Educ:* Lycée Carnot; Ecole Nat. Supérieure des Beaux-Arts. Annual exhibitions: Galerie Drouant-David, 1949–56; Galerie David et Garnier, 1957–67; Galerie Maurice Garnier, 1968–. Retrospective exhibitions: Paris, 1958; Berlin, 1958; Belgium, 1959; Tokyo and Kyoto, 1963, Musée d'Unterlinden, Colmar, 1969; Wieger Deurne, Holland, 1977; Musée postal, Paris, 1978; Zurich, 1983; Toulouse, 1985; Moscow and Leningrad, 1991. Buffet Museum founded in Japan, 1973; large room of his mystic works in Vatican Museum. Illustrator of books, engraver, lithographer and state designer. Grand Prix de la Critique, 1948. Officier des Arts et des Lettres; Mem., Acad. des Beaux-Arts, 1974. *Address:* c/o Galerie Maurice Garnier, 6 avenue Matignon, 75008 Paris, France; Domaine de la Baume, Tourtour, 83690 Salernes, France.

BUFORD, William Holmes; Editor, Granta, since 1979; Chairman, Granta Publications Ltd; *b* 6 Oct. 1954; *s* of William H. Buford and Helen Shiel; *m* 1991, Alicja Kobiernicka. *Educ:* Univ. of California, Berkeley (BA); King's College, Cambridge (MA). *Publications:* Among the Thugs, 1991; (ed) The Best of Granta Travel, 1991. *Address:* Granta Publications, 2–3 Hanover Yard, Noel Road, N1 8BE.

BUFTON, Air Vice-Marshal Sydney Osborne, CB 1945; DFC 1940; FRAeS; *b* 12 Jan. 1908; 2nd *s* of late J. O. Bufton, JP, Llandrindod Wells, Radnor; *m* 1943, Susan Maureen, *d* of Colonel E. M. Browne, DSO, Chelsea; two *d*. *Educ:* Dean Close School, Cheltenham. Commissioned RAF 1927; psa, 1939; idc, 1946. Served War of 1939–45, Bomber Comd, Nos 10 and 76 Sqdns, RAF Station, Pocklington, 1940–41; Dep. Dir Bomber Ops, 1941–43; Dir of Bomber Ops, Air Min., 1943–45; AOC Egypt, 1945–46; Central Bomber Establishment, RAF, Marham, Norfolk, 1947–48; Dep. Chief of Staff (Ops/Plans), Air Forces Western Europe, 1948–51; Dir of Weapons, Air Min., 1951–52; AOA Bomber Command, 1952–53; AOC Brit. Forces, Aden, 1953–55; Senior Air Staff Officer, Bomber Comd, 1955–58; Assistant Chief of Air Staff (Intelligence), 1958–61; retired Oct. 1961. Temp. Gp Capt. 1941; Temp. Air Cdre 1943; Subst. Gp Capt. 1946; Air Cdre 1948; Actg Air Vice-Marshal, 1952; Air Vice-Marshal, 1953. Invented radio and electronic construction system (Radionic), 1961–62; Man. Dir, Radionic Products Ltd, 1962–70. FRAeS 1970. High Sheriff of Radnorshire, 1967. Comdr Legion of Merit (US); Comdr Order of Orange Nassau (with swords), Netherlands. *Recreations:* hockey (Welsh International 1931–37, Combined Services, RAF), golf, squash. *Address:* 1 Castle Keep, London Road, Reigate, Surrey RH2 9PU. *T:* Reigate (0737) 243707. *Club:* Royal Air Force.

BUGOTU, Francis, CBE 1979; Cross of Solomon Islands, 1988; Permanent Representative of Solomon Islands to United Nations, since 1990; *b* 27 June 1937; *s* of Tione Kalapalua Bugotu and Rachael Samoa; *m* 1962, Ella Vehe; one *s* one *d*. *Educ:* NZ, Australia, Scotland, England and Solomon Is. Teacher and Inspector of Mission Schs for Ch. of Melanesia (Anglican), 1959–60; Mem., 1st Legislative Council, 1960–62; Lectr, Solomon Is Teachers Coll., 1964–68; Chief Educn Officer and Perm. Sec., Min. of Educn, 1968–75; Perm. Sec. to Chief Minister and Council of Ministers, and titular Head of Civil Service, 1976–78; Sec. for For. Affairs and Roving Ambassador/High Comr of Solomon Is, 1978–82; Sec.-Gen., S Pacific Commn, 1982–86. Chairman: Review Cttee on Educn, 1974–75; Solomon Is Tourist Authority, 1970–73; Solomon Is Scholarship Cttee, 1969–75. Consultant, esp. for S Pacific Commn; Founder Mem. and Chief Adviser, Kakamora Youth Club, 1968–75; Chief Comr of Scouts for Solomon Is, 1970–77. Chm., Solomon Is S Pacific Fest. of Arts Cttee; Dep. Chm., Solomon Is Airlines. Lay Rep., Ch. of Melanesia. *Publications:* (with A. V. Hughes) This Man (play), 1970 (also award winning film); papers on: impact of Western culture on Solomon Is; politics, economics and social aspects in Solomons; recolonising and decolonising; Solomon Is Pidgin. *Recreations:* interested in most ball games (soccer, cricket, basketball, Rugby, tennis, table-tennis, softball, snooker), swimming, music, dancing. *Address:* PO Box 528, Honiara, Solomon Islands.

BUIST, John Latto Farquharson, (Ian), CB 1990; Under Secretary, International Division, Foreign and Commonwealth Office (Overseas Development Administration), retired; *b* 30 May 1930; *s* of late Lt-Col Thomas Powrie Buist, RAMC, and of Christian Mary (*née* Robertson). *Educ:* Dalhousie Castle Sch.; Winchester Coll.; New Coll., Oxford (MA). Asst Principal, CO, 1952–54; Sec., Kenya Police Commn, 1953; seconded Kenya Govt, 1954–56; Principal, CO, 1956–61; Dept of Tech. Cooperation, 1961–62; Brit. High Commn, Dar-es-Salaam, 1962–64; Consultant on Admin, E African Common Services Org./Community, 1964–69; Sec., Commn on E African Cooperation and related bodies, 1966–69; Asst Sec., Min. of Overseas Develt, 1966–76; Under Sec., FCO (ODA), 1976–90. Mem. Bd, PLAN International (UK). Co-founder and several times Pres., Classical Assoc. of Kenya; Member: John Bate Choir; United Reformed Church. *Recreations:* singing and other music-making, walking. *Address:* 9 West Hill Road, SW18 1LH.

BUITER, Prof. Willem Hendrik, PhD; Juan T. Trippe Professor of International Economics, Yale University, since 1985; *b* 26 Sept. 1949; *s* of Harm Geert Buiter and

Hendrien Buiter, *née* van Schooten; *m* 1973, Jean Archer; one *s*. *Educ:* Cambridge Univ. (BA 1971); Yale Univ. (PhD 1975). Asst Prof., Princeton Univ., 1975–76; Lectr, LSE, 1976–77; Asst Prof., Princeton Univ., 1977–79; Prof. of Economics, Univ. of Bristol, 1980–82; Cassel Prof. of Economics, LSE, Univ. of London, 1982–85. Consultant: IMF, 1979–80; World Bank, 1986–; Specialist Adviser, House of Commons Select Cttee on the Treasury and CS, 1980–84; Adviser, Netherlands Min. of Educn and Science, 1985–86. Associate Editor, Econ. Jl, 1980–84. *Publications:* Temporary and Long Run Equilibrium, 1979; Budgetary Policy, International and Intertemporal Trade in the Global Economy, 1989; Macroeconomic Theory and Stabilization Policy, 1989; Principles of Budgetary and Financial Policy, 1990; International Macroeconomics, 1990; articles in learned jls. *Recreations:* tennis, poetry, music. *Address:* 42 East Pearl Street, New Haven, Conn 06513, USA.

BULFIELD, Peter William, CA; Deputy Chairman, Yamaichi Bank (UK) PLC, since 1991 (Managing Director and Chief Executive, 1988–91); *b* 14 June 1930; *s* of Wilfred Bulfield and Doris (*née* Bedford); *m* 1958, Pamela June Beckett; two *d*. *Educ:* Beaumont Coll., Old Windsor. Peat Marwick Mitchell & Co., 1947–59; J. Henry Schroder Wagg & Co., 1959–86, Dir, 1967–86; Director: Schroder Finance, 1966–73; Schroder Darling Hldgs, Sydney, 1973–80; Vice-Chm., Mitsubishi Trust & Banking Corporation (Europe) SA, 1973–84; Jt Dep. Chm., Schroder Internat., 1977–86; Dep. Chm., Crown Agents for Oversea Govts and Admin, 1982–85; Director: Yamaichi PLC, 1986–87; London Italian Bank, 1989–91. Member: Overseas Projects Board, 1983–86; Overseas Promotions Cttee, BIEC, 1984–86; Export Guarantees Adv. Council, 1985–88. *Recreations:* sailing, music, painting. *Address:* The Mill House, Merrieweathers, Mayfield, Sussex TN20 6RJ. *T:* Mayfield (0435) 872177. *Club:* Royal Thames Yacht.

BULGER, His Honour Anthony Clare, BA, BCL; a Circuit Judge (formerly County Court Judge), 1963–86; *b* 1912; *s* of Daniel Bulger; *m* Una Patricia Banks; one *s* one *d*. *Educ:* Rugby; Oriel Coll., Oxford. Called to the Bar, Inner Temple, 1936. Oxford Circuit; Dep Chm., 1958–70, Chm. 1970–71, Glos QS; Dep. Chm. Worcs QS, 1962–71; Recorder of Abingdon, 1962–63. *Address:* The Dower House, Forthampton, Glos. *T:* Tewkesbury (0684) 293257.

BULKELEY, Sir Richard H. D. W.; *see* Williams-Bulkeley.

BULL, Anthony, CBE 1968 (OBE 1944); Transport Consultant: Kennedy and Donkin, 1971–85; Freeman Fox and Partners, 1971–87; *b* 18 July 1908; 3rd *s* of Rt Hon. Sir William Bull, 1st Bt, PC, MP, JP, FSA (*d* 1931), and late Lilian, 2nd *d* of G. S. Brandon, Oakbrook, Ravenscourt Park; *m* 1946, Barbara (*d* 1947), *er d* of late Peter Donovan, Yonder, Rye, Sussex; one *d*. *Educ:* Gresham's Sch., Holt; Magdalene Coll., Cambridge (Exhibitioner; MA). Joined Underground Group of Cos, 1929; served in Staff, Publicity and Public Relations Depts and Chairman's Office. Sec. to Vice-Chm. London Passenger Transport Board, 1936–39. Served War, 1939–45; RE; Transportation Br., War Office, 1939–42; GHQ, Middle East, 1943; Staff of Supreme Allied Comdr, SE Asia (end of 1943); Col 1944; Transp. Div., CCG, 1945–46. Returned to London Transport as Chief Staff and Welfare Officer, 1946; Member: LTE, 1955–62; LTB, 1962–65; Vice-Chm., LTE (formerly LTB), 1965–71. Advr to House of Commons Transport Cttee, 1981–82. Inst. of Transport: served on Council, 1956–59; Vice-Pres., 1964–66; Hon. Librarian, 1966–69; Pres., 1969–70. Mem. Regional Advisory Council for Technological Educn, 1958–62 (Transp. Adv. Cttee, 1950–62; Chm. Cttee, 1953–62). CStJ 1969. Bronze Star (USA), 1946. *Publications:* contrib. to transport journals. *Recreation:* travel. *Address:* 35 Clareville Grove, SW7 5AU. *T:* 071–373 5647. *Club:* United Oxford & Cambridge University.

See also Sir S. G. Bull, Bt, Sir Robin Chichester-Clark.

BULL, George Anthony, OBE 1990; FRSL 1982; writer, translator and consultant; Director, Anglo-Japanese Economic Institute, since 1986; Editor, International Minds, since 1989; President, Central Banking Publications, since 1990; *b* 23 Aug. 1929; *s* of George Thomas Bull and Bridget Philomena (*née* Nugent); *m* 1957, Doreen Marjorie Griffin; two *s* two *d*. *Educ:* Wimbledon Coll.; Brasenose Coll., Oxford (MA). National Service, Royal Fusiliers, 1947–49. Reporter, Financial Times, 1952–56, Foreign News Editor, 1956–59; News Editor, London Bureau, McGraw-Hill World News, 1959–60; The Director, 1960–84: successively Dep. Editor, Editor, Editor-in-Chief. Dir 1971–, and Trustee 1976–, The Tablet; Trustee, The Universe, 1970–86; Consultant Editor, Penguin Business Library, 1985–. Director: Anvil Prodns (Oxford Playhouse) Ltd, 1980–87; Westminster & Overseas Trade Services, 1985–; Hugo Publications Ltd, 1986–. Chm., Commn for Internat. Justice and Peace, Episcopal Conf. of England and Wales, 1971–74; Mem. Council, RSL, 1986–; Mem., UK Cttee, European Cultural Foundn, 1987–; Hon. Treasurer, Soc. for Renaissance Studies, 1967–88; a Governor, St Mary's Coll., Strawberry Hill, 1976–87; Foundation Governor, St Thomas More Sch., 1980–87. *Publications:* (with A. Vice) Bid for Power, 1958, 2nd edn 1960; Vatican Politics, 1966; The Renaissance, 1968, new edn 1973; (ed) The Director's Handbook, 1969, 2nd edn 1978; (with E. D. Foster) The Director, his Money and his Job, 1970; (with Peter Hobday and John Hamway) Industrial Relations: the boardroom viewpoint, 1972; Venice: the most triumphant city, 1982, Folio Society 1980, USA 1982; Inside the Vatican, 1982, USA 1983, Italy 1983 (as Dentro il Vaticano), Germany and Japan 1987; Hungary, 1989; translations: Artists of the Renaissance, 1979–; (with Peter Porter) Life, Letters and Poetry of Michelangelo, 1987; The Travels of Pietro della Valle, 1989; translations for Penguin Classics: Life of Cellini, 1956; Machiavelli, The Prince, 1961; Vasari, Lives of the Artists, Vol. I, 1965, vol II, 1987; Castiglione, The Book of the Courtier, 1967; Aretino, Selected Letters, 1976. *Recreations:* book collecting, travelling. *Address:* 19 Hugh Street, SW1V 1QJ. *Clubs:* Garrick, Savile, Beefsteak.

BULL, John Michael; QC 1983; **His Honour Judge John Bull;** a Circuit Judge, since 1991; *b* 31 Jan. 1934; *s* of John Godfrey Bull and Eleanor Bull (*née* Nicholson); *m* 1959, Sonia Maureen, *d* of Frank William Woodcock; one *s* three *d*. *Educ:* Norwich Sch.; Corpus Christi Coll., Cambridge (Parker Exhibnr in Modern History; BA 1958; LLM 1959; MA 1963). Called to the Bar, Gray's Inn, 1960; Dep. Circuit Judge, 1972; Standing Counsel to the Board of Inland Revenue, Western Circuit, 1972–83; a Recorder, 1980–91.

BULL, Dr John Prince, CBE 1973; Director of MRC Industrial Injuries and Burns Unit, 1952–82; *b* 4 Jan. 1917; *s* of Robert James Bull and Ida Mary Bull; *m* 1939, Irmgard Bross; four *d*. *Educ:* Burton-on-Trent Grammar Sch.; Cambridge Univ.; Guy's Hospital. MA, MD, BCh Cantab; MRCS, FRCP; MFOM. Casualty Res. Officer, Min. of Home Security, 1941; RAMC, 1942–46; Mem. Research Staff 1947, Asst Dir 1948, MRC Unit, Birmingham Accident Hosp. Member: MRC, 1971–75; Med. Commn on Accident Prevention, 1975– (Chm., Transport Cttee, 1981–); Chairman: Regional Res. Cttee, West Midlands RHA, 1966–82; Inst. of Accident Surgery, 1980–83. Mem., Med. Res. Soc. FRSocMed. *Publications:* contrib. scientific and med. jls. *Recreation:* bricolage. *Address:* 73 Reddings Road, Moseley, Birmingham B13 8LP. *T:* 021–449 0474.

BULL, Megan Patricia, (Lady Bull), OBE 1982; Governor, Holloway Prison, 1973–82; *b* Naauwpoort, S Africa, 17 March 1922; *d* of Dr Thomas and Letitia Jones; *m* 1947, Sir Graham MacGregor Bull (*d* 1987); three *s* one *d*. *Educ:* Good Hope Seminary, Cape Town; Univ. of Cape Town. MB, ChB Cape Town 1944, DCH London 1947, MSc QUB 1961, DPM London 1970, MRCP 1974. Lectr in Physiology, Belfast Coll. of Technology, 1954–61; Med. Officer Student Health Dept, QUB, 1961–66; Prison Med. Officer, Holloway Prison, 1967–73. *Publications:* papers in various medical jls. *Address:* 29 Heath Drive, NW3 7SB.

BULL, Oliver Richard Silvester; Headmaster, Rugby School, 1985–90; *b* 30 June 1930; *s* of Walter Haverson Bull and Margaret Bridget Bull; *m* 1956, Anne Hay Fife; two *s* four *d*. *Educ:* Rugby Sch.; Brasenose Coll. Oxford (MA). Mil. Service (1st Beds and Herts), 1949–51. Asst Master, Eton Coll., 1955–77 (Housemaster, 1968–77); Headmaster, Oakham Sch., Rutland, 1977–84. *Recreations:* music, walking, reading, ball games. *Address:* Cwm Farm, Gladestry, Kington, Herefords.

BULL, Richard; *see* Bull, O. R. S.

BULL, Roger John; Director and Chief Executive, Polytechnic South West, Plymouth, since 1989; *b* 31 March 1940; *s* of William Leonard Bull and Marjorie Bull (*née* Slade); *m* 1964, Margaret Evelyn Clifton; one *s* one *d*. *Educ:* Churchers' Coll.; LSE (BSc Econ). FCCA. Research Fellow, DES/ICA, 1967–68; Principal Lectr in Accounting, Nottingham Poly., 1968–72; Head, Sch. of Accounting and Applied Econs, Leeds Poly., 1972–85; Dep. Dir (Academic), Plymouth Poly., 1986–89. Mem. and non exec. Dir, Plymouth HA, 1990–. Mem., Council, CNAA, 1981–87. *Publications:* Accounting in Business, 1969, 6th edn 1990; articles in professional jls. *Recreations:* tennis, music. *Address:* Polytechnic South West, Drake Circus, Plymouth PL4 8AA. *T:* Plymouth (0752) 232000; 3 Westmoor Park, Tavistock, Devon PL19 9AA. *Club:* Commonwealth Trust.

BULL, Sir Simeon (George), 4th Bt *cr* 1922, of Hammersmith; Senior Partner in legal firm of Bull & Bull; *b* 1 Aug. 1934; *s* of Sir George Bull, 3rd Bt and of Gabrielle, *d* of late Bramwell Jackson, MC; *S* father, 1986; *m* 1961, Annick Elizabeth Renée Geneviève, *d* of late Louis Bresson and of Mme Bresson, Chandai, France; one *s* two *d*. *Educ:* Eton; Innsbruck; Paris. Admitted solicitor, 1959. *Heir:* *s* Stephen Louis Bull, *b* 5 April 1966. *Address:* Beech Hanger, Beech Road, Shepherd's Hill, Merstham, Surrey RH1 3AE; Pen Enez, Pont l'Abbé, France. *Clubs:* MCC; Royal Thames Yacht.

BULL, Tony Raymond, FRCS; Consultant Surgeon: Charing Cross Hospital; Royal National Throat Nose and Ear Hospital; King Edward VII's Hospital for Officers; *b* 21 Dec. 1934; *m* 1958, Jill Rosemary Beresford Cook; one *s* two *d*. *Educ:* Monkton Coombe School; London Hosp. (MB BS 1958). FRCS 1962. Yearsley Lectr, RSocMed, 1982. Editor, Facial Plastic Surgery (Quarterly Monographs), 1983. *Publications:* Atlas of Ear, Nose and Throat Diagnosis, 1974, 2nd edn 1987; Recent Advances in Otolaryngology, 1978; Plastic Reconstruction in the Head and Neck, 1986; Diagnostic Picture Test, Ear, Nose and Throat, 1990. *Recreations:* tennis, golf. *Address:* 107 Harley Street, W1N 1DG. *T:* 071–935 3171; 26 Scarsdale Villas, W8 6PR. *T:* 071–937 3411. *Clubs:* MCC, Hurlingham, Queen's.

BULL, Sir Walter (Edward Avenon), KCVO 1977 (CVO 1964); FRICS; Consultant, Walter Bull & Co., chartered surveyors, since 1987; *b* 17 March 1902; *s* of Walter Bull, FRICS, and Florence Bull; *m* 1933, Moira Christian, *d* of William John Irwin and Margaret Irwin, Dungannon, N Ireland; one *s*. *Educ:* Gresham's Sch.; Aldenham. Sen. Partner, Vigers, 1942–74, Consultant, 1974–87. Dir, City of London Building Soc., 1957–74. Mem. Council, Duchy of Lancaster, 1957–74. Pres., RICS, 1956. Dep. Comr, War Damage Commn, 1952–75. Liveryman, Merchant Taylors' Co. Silver Jubilee Medal, 1977. *Publications:* papers to RICS on Landlord and Tenant Acts. *Recreations:* music, golf, bowls. *Address:* The Garden House, 1 Park Crescent, Brighton BN2 3HA. *T:* Brighton (0273) 681196. *Clubs:* Naval and Military, Gresham.

BULLARD, Denys Gradwell; Member, Anglian Water Authority and Chairman, Broads Committee, 1974–83; *b* 15 Aug. 1912; *s* of John Henry Bullard; *m* 1970, Diana Patricia Cox; one *s* one *d*. *Educ:* Wisbech Grammar Sch.; Cambridge Univ. Farmer. Broadcaster on agricultural matters both at home and overseas. MP (C) SW Div. of Norfolk, 1951–55; MP (C) King's Lynn, 1959–64. PPS: to Financial Sec., Treasury, 1955; to Min. of Housing and Local Govt, 1959–64. *Recreation:* gardening. *Address:* Elm House, Elm, Wisbech, Cambs PE14 0AB. *T:* Wisbech (0945) 583021.

BULLARD, Sir Giles (Lionel), KCVO 1985; CMG 1981; HM Diplomatic Service, retired; *b* 24 Aug. 1926; 2nd *s* of late Sir Reader Bullard and late Miriam (*née* Smith); *m* 1st, 1952, Hilary Chadwick Brooks (*d* 1978); two *s* two *d*; 2nd, 1982, Linda Rannells Lewis. *Educ:* Blundell's Sch.; Balliol Coll., Oxford. Army service, 1944–48; Oxford Univ., 1948–51 (Capt. OURFC); H. Clarkson & Co. Ltd, 1952–55; HM Foreign (later Diplomatic) Service, 1955; 3rd Sec., Bucharest, 1957; 2nd Sec., Brussels, 1958; 1st Sec., Panama City, 1960; FO, 1964; DSAO, 1965; Head of Chancery, Bangkok, 1967; Counsellor and Head of Chancery, Islamabad, 1969; FCO Fellow, Centre of South Asian Studies, Cambridge, 1973; Inspectorate, FCO, 1974; Consul-Gen., Boston, 1977; Ambassador, Sofia, 1980; High Comr, Bridgetown, 1983–86. *Recreation:* village life. *Address:* Manor House, West Hendred, Wantage, Oxon OX12 8RP. *Club:* Huntercombe Golf.

See also Sir J. L. Bullard.

BULLARD, Sir Julian (Leonard), GCMG 1987 (KCMG 1982; CMG 1975); HM Diplomatic Service, retired; Fellow of All Souls College, Oxford, 1950–57 and since 1988; *b* 8 March 1928; *s* of late Sir Reader Bullard, KCB, KCMG, CIE, and late Miriam, *d* of late A. L. Smith, Master of Balliol Coll., Oxford; *m* 1954, Margaret Stephens; two *s* two *d*. *Educ:* Rugby; Magdalen Coll., Oxford. Army, 1950–52; HM Diplomatic Service, 1953–88: served at: FO, 1953–54; Vienna, 1954–56; Amman, 1956–59; FO, 1960–63; Bonn, 1963–66; Moscow, 1966–68; Dubai, 1968–70; Head of E European and Soviet Dept, FCO, 1971–75; Minister, Bonn, 1975–79; Dep. Under-Sec. of State, 1979–84 and Dep. to Perm. Under Sec. of State and Political Dir, 1982–84, FCO; Ambassador, Bonn, 1984–88. Birmingham University: Mem. Council, 1988–; Chm. Council and Pro-Chancellor, 1989–. *Address:* 18 Northmoor Road, Oxford OX2 6UR. *T:* Oxford (0865) 512981.

See also Sir G. L. Bullard.

BULLEN, Air Vice-Marshal Reginald, CB 1975; GM 1945; MA; Senior Bursar and Fellow, Gonville and Caius College, Cambridge, 1976–87, Life Fellow and Property Developments Consultant, since 1988; *b* 19 Oct. 1920; *s* of Henry Arthur Bullen and Alice May Bullen; *m* 1952, Christiane (*née* Phillips); one *s* one *d*. *Educ:* Grocers' Company School. 39 Sqdn RAF, 458 Sqdn RAAF, 1942–44; Air Min., 1945–50; RAF Coll. Cranwell, 1952–54; psa 1955; Exchange USAF, Washington, DC, 1956–58; RAF Staff Coll., Bracknell, 1959–61; Admin. Staff Coll., Henley, 1962; PSO to Chief of Air Staff, 1962–64; NATO Defence Coll., 1965; Adjutant General, HQ Allied Forces Central Europe, 1965–68; Dir of Personnel, MoD, 1968–69; idc 1970; Dep. AO i/c Admin, HQ Maintenance Comd, 1971; AOA Training Comd, 1972–75. Chm., Huntingdon DHA, 1981–. MA Cantab, 1975. FBIM 1979 (MBIM 1971). *Publications:* various articles. *Address:* Gonville and Caius College, Cambridge CB2 1TA. *Club:* Royal Air Force.

BULLEN, Dr William Alexander; *s* of Francis Lisle Bullen and Amelia Morgan; *m* 1st, 1943, Phyllis, *d* of George Leeson; three *d*; 2nd, 1956, Mary (marr. diss. 1983), *d* of Leigh Crutchley; 3rd, 1983, Rosalind, *d* of Lawrence Gates. *Educ:* Merchant Taylors' Sch., Crosby; London Hosp. Med. Coll. MRCS, LRCP, MRCGP. Royal Tank Regt, UK and Middle East, 1939–45 (Hon. Major). Med. Dir, Boehringer Pfizer, 1957, Sales Man. 1958; Pres., Pfizer Canada, 1962; Gen. Man., Pfizer Consumer Opns UK, 1964–66; Chm., Coty (England), 1965; Man. Dir, Scribbans Kemp, 1966; Man. Dir, 1967–77, Dep. Chm., 1974, Chm., 1975–81, Thomas Borthwick & Sons plc; Chm., Whitburgh Investments, 1976–80. Président-Directeur Général, Boucheries Bernard, 1977–81. FBIM 1975. Liveryman, Butchers' Co.; Freeman, City of London. *Publication:* paper on acute heart failure in London Hosp. Gazette. *Recreations:* sailing, viticulture, music. *Club:* Royal Thames Yacht.

BULLER; *see* Manningham-Buller, family name of Viscount Dilhorne.

BULLER; *see* Yarde-Buller, family name of Baron Churston.

BULLER, Prof. Arthur John, ERD 1969; FRCP; Director of Research and Support Services (formerly Research Development Director), Muscular Dystrophy Group of GB, since 1982; Emeritus Professor of Physiology, University of Bristol; *b* 16 Oct. 1923; *s* of Thomas Alfred Buller, MBE, and Edith May Buller (*née* Wager); *m* 1946, Helena Joan (*née* Pearson); one *s* one *d* (and one *d* decd). *Educ:* Duke of York's Royal Military Sch., Dover; St Thomas's Hosp. Med. Sch. (MB, BS); BSc; FRCP 1976; FIBiol 1978; FRSA 1979. Kitchener Scholar, 1941–45; Lectr in Physiology, St Thomas' Hosp., 1946–49. Major, RAMC (Specialist in Physiology; Jt Sec., Military Personnel Research Cttee), 1949–53. Lectr in Medicine, St Thomas' Hosp., 1953–57. Royal Society Commonwealth Fellow, Canberra, Aust., 1958–59. Reader in Physiology, King's Coll., London, 1961–65; Gresham Prof. of Physic 1963–65; Prof. of Physiology, Univ. of Bristol, 1965–82, Dean, Fac. of Medicine, 1976–78, on secondment as Chief Scientist, DHSS, 1978–81. Hon. Consultant in Clinical Physiology, Bristol Dist Hosp. (T), 1970–85. Visiting Prof., Monash Univ., Aust., 1972; Long Fox Meml Lectr, Bristol, 1978; Milroy Lectr, RCP, 1983. Member: Bd of Governors, Bristol Royal Infirmary, 1968–74; Avon Health Authority (T), 1974–78; MRC, 1975–81; BBC, IBA Central Appeals Adv. Cttee, 1983–88; Chm., Neurosciences and Mental Health Bd, MRC, 1975–77; Dep. Chm., Health Promotion Res. Trust, 1983–. External Scientific Advisor, Rayne Inst., St Thomas' Hosp., 1979–85. *Publications:* contribs to books and various jls on normal and abnormal physiology. *Recreations:* clarets and conversation. *Address:* Lockhall, Cow Lane, Steeple Aston, Oxon OX5 3SG. *T:* Steeple Aston (0869) 47502. *Clubs:* Athenæum, Army and Navy.

BULLERS, Ronald Alfred, CBE 1988; QFSM 1974; FIFireE, FBIM; consultant fire prevention engineer; Chief Executive Officer, London Fire and Civil Defence Authority, 1986–87; *b* 17 March 1931; *m* 1954, Mary M. Bullers. *Educ:* Queen Mary's Grammar Sch., Walsall. Deputy Asst Chief Officer, Lancashire Fire Brigade, 1971; Dep. Chief Officer, Greater Manchester Fire Brigade, 1974, Chief Officer, 1977; Chief Officer, London Fire Bde, 1981–86. Adviser: Nat. Jt Council for Local Authority Fire Brigades, 1977–; Assoc. of Metropolitan Authorities, 1977–. OStJ. *Recreations:* gardening, travel. *Address:* 31 Pavillion Close, Aldridge, Walsall WA9 8LS.

BULLIMORE, John Wallace MacGregor; His Honour Judge Bullimore; a Circuit Judge, since 1991; *b* 4 Dec. 1945; *s* of late James Wallace Bullimore and of Phyllis Violet Emily Bullimore (*née* Brandt); *m* 1975, Christine Elizabeth Kinch; two *s* (one *d* decd). *Educ:* Queen Elizabeth Grammar School, Wakefield; Univ. of Bristol (LLB). Called to the Bar, Inner Temple, 1968; Chancellor, Diocese of Derby, 1980, of Blackburn, 1990. Mem., Gen. Synod of the Church of England, 1970–. *Address:* c/o North Eastern Circuit Administrator, West Riding House, Albion Street, Leeds LS1 5AA.

BULLMORE, (John) Jeremy David, CBE 1985; Chairman, J. Walter Thompson Co. Ltd, 1976–87; Director: The Guardian and Manchester Evening News plc, since 1988; WPP Group plc, since 1988; *b* 21 Nov. 1929; *s* of Francis Edward Bullmore and Adeline Gabrielle Bullmore (*née* Roscow); *m* 1958, Pamela Audrey Green; two *s* one *d*. *Educ:* Harrow; Christ Church, Oxford. Military service, 1949–50. Joined J. Walter Thompson Co. Ltd, 1954: Dir, 1964; Dep. Chm., 1975; Dir, J. Walter Thompson Co. (USA), 1980–87. Mem., Nat. Cttee for Electoral Reform, 1978–. Chm., Advertising Assoc., 1981–87. *Address:* 20 Embankment Gardens, SW3. *T:* 071–351 2197. *Club:* Arts.

BULLOCK, family name of **Baron Bullock.**

BULLOCK, Baron *cr* 1976 (Life Peer), of Leafield, Oxon; **Alan Louis Charles Bullock,** Kt 1972; FBA 1967; Founding Master, 1960, and Fellow, since 1980, St Catherine's College, Oxford (Master, 1960–80); Vice-Chancellor, Oxford University, 1969–73; *b* 13 Dec. 1914; *s* of Frank Allen Bullock; *m* 1940, Hilda Yates, *d* of Edwin Handy, Bradford; three *s* one *d* (and one *d* decd). *Educ:* Bradford Grammar Sch.; Wadham Coll., Oxford (Scholar). MA; 1st Class Lit Hum, 1936; 1st Class, Modern Hist., 1938. DLitt Oxon, 1969. Fellow, Dean and Tutor in Modern Hist., New Coll., 1945–52; Censor of St Catherine's Soc., Oxford, 1952–62; Chairman: Research Cttee of RIIA, 1954–78; Nat. Advisory Council on the Training and Supply of Teachers, 1963–65; Schools Council, 1966–69; Cttee on Reading and Other Uses of English Language, 1972–74 (Report, A Language for Life, published 1975); Trustees, Tate Gallery, 1973–80; Friends of Ashmolean Museum; Cttee of Enquiry on Industrial Democracy, 1976 (Report publ. 1977); Member: Arts Council of Great Britain, 1961–64; SSRC, 1966; Adv. Council on Public Records, 1965–77; Organising Cttee for the British Library, 1971–72. Joined Social Democratic Party, 1981. Sen. Fellow, Aspen Inst., USA; Trustee: Aspen Inst., Berlin; The Observer, 1957–69; Dir, The Observer, 1977–81. Raleigh Lectr, British Acad., 1967; Stevenson Meml Lectr, LSE, 1970; Leslie Stephen Lectr, Cambridge, 1976. Hon. Fellow: Merton Coll.; Wadham Coll.; Linacre Coll.; Wolfson Coll. For. Mem., Amer. Acad. Arts and Sciences, 1972; Mem., Academia Europaea, 1990. Hon. Dr Univ. Aix-Marseilles; Hon. DLitt: Bradford; Reading; Newfoundland; Leicester; Sussex; DUniv Open. Hon. FRIBA. Chevalier Légion d'Honneur, 1970. *Publications:* Hitler, A Study in Tyranny, 1952 (rev. edn 1964); The Liberal Tradition, 1956; The Life and Times of Ernest Bevin, Vol. I, 1960, Vol. II, 1967, Vol III (Ernest Bevin, Foreign Secretary), 1983; (ed) The Twentieth Century, 1971; (ed with Oliver Stallybrass) Dictionary of Modern Thought, 1977, new edn (with S. Trombley), 1988; (ed) The Faces of Europe, 1980; (ed with B. R. Woodings) Fontana Dictionary of Modern Thinkers, 1983; The Humanist Tradition in the West, 1985; Hitler and Stalin: Parallel Lives, 1991; Gen. Editor (with Sir William Deakin) of The Oxford History of Modern Europe. *Address:* St Catherine's College, Oxford OX1 3UJ; Gable End, 30 Godstow Road, Oxford OX2 8AJ. *T:* Oxford (0865) 513380.

BULLOCK, Edward Anthony Watson; HM Diplomatic Service, retired; *b* 27 Aug. 1926; *yr s* of late Sir Christopher Bullock, KCB, CBE, and late Lady Bullock (*née* Barbara May Lupton); *m* 1953, Jenifer Myrtle, *er d* of late Sir Richmond Palmer, KCMG, and late Lady Palmer (*née* Margaret Isabel Abel Smith); two *s* one *d*. *Educ:* Rugby Sch. (Scholar; Running VIII); Trinity Coll., Cambridge (Exhibitioner; MA). Chm., Cambridge Univ. Cons. Assoc. Served Life Guards, 1944–47. Joined Foreign Service, 1950; served: FO, 1950–52; Bucharest, 1952–54; Brussels, 1955–58; FO, 1958–61; La Paz, 1961–65; ODM, 1965–67; FCO, 1967–69; Havana, 1969–72; HM Treasury, 1972–74; Head of Pacific Dependent Territories Dept, FCO, 1974–77; Consul-Gen., Marseilles, 1978–83; Counsellor, FCO, 1983–85. *Recreations:* walking, gardening, tree-planting, reading. *Address:* c/o National Westminster Bank, 36 St James's Street, SW1. *Clubs:* United Oxford & Cambridge University; Union (Cambridge).

See also R. H. W. Bullock.

BULLOCK, Hugh, Hon. GBE 1976 (Hon. KBE 1957; Hon. OBE 1946); FRSA 1958; President, Pilgrims of the United States, since 1955; Chairman and Chief Executive Officer, Calvin Bullock Ltd; retired 1984; Head of Bullock Investment Advisory Co., since 1984; *b* 2 June 1898; *s* of Calvin Bullock and Alice Katherine (*née* Mallory); *m* 1933, Marie Leontine Graves (*d* 1986); two *d*. *Educ:* Hotchkiss Sch.; Williams Coll. (BA). Investment banker since 1921; President and Director: Calvin Bullock, Ltd, 1944–66; Bullock Fund, Ltd; Canadian Fund, Inc.; Canadian Investment Fund, Ltd; Dividend Shares, Inc.; Chairman and Director: Carriers & General Corp.; Nation-Wide Securities Co.; US Electric Light & Power Shares, Inc.; High Income Shares Inc.; Money Shares Inc.; Pres., Calvin Bullock Forum. Civilian Aide to Sec. of the Army, for First Army Area, United States, 1952–53 (US Army Certificate of Appreciation). Trustee: Roosevelt Hospital, 1949–69; Estate and Property of Diocesan Convention of New York; Williams Coll., 1960–68. Member Exec. Cttee, Marshall Scholarship Regional Cttee, 1955–58. Member: Amer. Legion; Academy of Political Science; Amer. Museum of Nat. History; Acad. of Amer. Poets (Dir.); Assoc. Ex-mems Squadron A (Gov. 1945–50); Council on Foreign Relations; Ends of the Earth; English-Speaking Union; Foreign Policy Assoc.; Investment Bankers Assoc. of Amer. (Gov. 1953–55); New England Soc.; Nat. Inst. of Social Sciences (Pres. 1950–53; Gold Medal, 1985); Newcomen Soc.; St George's Soc.; France America Assoc. Benjamin Franklyn Fellow, RSA. Hon. LLD; Hamilton Coll., 1954; Williams Coll., 1957. 2nd Lieut Infantry, European War, 1914–18; Lieut-Col, War of 1939–45 (US Army Commendation Ribbon). Distinguished Citizens' Award, Denver, 1958; Exceptional Service Award, Dept of Air Force, 1961; US Navy Distinguished Public Service Award, 1972. Assoc. KStJ 1961, and Vice-Pres. Amer. Society. Knight Comdr, Royal Order of George I (Greece), 1964. Is an Episcopalian. *Publication:* The Story of Investment Companies, 1959. *Address:* (office) 40th Floor, 1 Wall Street, New York, NY 10005, USA. *T:* 809 1920; (home) 1030 Fifth Avenue, New York, NY 10028. *T:* Trafalgar 9–5858. *Clubs:* White's (London); Bond (former Gov.), Century, Racquet and Tennis, Down Town Association, City Midday, River, Union, Williams, Church, New York Yacht (New York); Sleepy Hollow Country (Scarborough, NY); Denver County (Denver, Colo.); Chevy Chase, Metropolitan (Washington); Edgartown Yacht (Cdre), Edgartown Reading Room (Mass); West Side Tennis (Forest Hills, NY); Mount Royal (Montreal).

BULLOCK, John; Joint Senior Partner and Deputy Chairman, Coopers & Lybrand Deloitte; Chairman, Coopers & Lybrand Europe; *b* 12 July 1933; *s* of Robert and Doris Bullock; *m* 1960, Ruth Jennifer (*née* Bullock); two *s* (and one *s* decd). *Educ:* Latymer Upper School. FCA; FCMA; FIMC. Smallfield Fitzhugh Tillet & Co., 1949–56 and 1958–61; RAF Commission, 1956–58; Robson Morrow, 1961, Partner, 1965–70; Robson Morrow merged with Deloitte Haskins & Sells; Partner in charge, Deloitte Haskins & Sells Management Consultants, 1971–79; Deloitte Haskins & Sells: Managing Partner, 1979–85; Dep. Senior Partner, 1984–85; Sen. Partner, 1985–90; Vice Chm., Deloitte Haskins & Sells Internat., 1985–89; Chm., Deloitte Europe, 1985–89. Mem., UKAEA, 1981–. Mem., Co. of Chartered Accountants' of England and Wales, 1989–. *Recreations:* sailing, ski-ing, opera, ballet. *Address:* Coopers & Lybrand Deloitte, 128 Queen Victoria Street, EC4P 4JX.

BULLOCK, Richard Henry Watson, CB 1971; Consultant, Faulkbourn Consultancy Services; Director, Grosvenor Place Amalgamations Ltd; Director-General, Electronic Components Industry Federation, 1984–90 (Consultant Director, 1981–84); retired Civil Servant; *b* 12 Nov. 1920; *er s* of late Sir Christopher Bullock, KCB, CBE and late Lady Bullock (*née* Barbara May Lupton); *m* 1946, Beryl Haddan, *o d* of late Haddan J. Markes, formerly Malay Civil Service; one *s* one *d*. *Educ:* Rugby Sch. (Scholar); Trinity Coll., Cambridge (Scholar). Joined 102 OCTU (Westminster Dragoons), Nov. 1940; Commnd Westminster Dragoons (2nd County of London Yeo.), 1941; served in England, NW Europe (D-day), Italy, Germany, 1941–45; Instructor, Armoured Corps Officers' Training Sch., India, 1945–46; demobilized 1947, rank of Major. Established in Home Civil Service by Reconstruction Competition; joined Min. of Supply as Asst Principal, 1947; Principal, 1949; Asst Sec., 1956; on loan to War Office, 1960–61; Ministry of Aviation, 1961–64; Under-Sec., 1963; Min. of Technology, 1964–70, Head of Space Div., 1969–70, Dep. Sec., 1970; DTI, 1970–74; Dept of Industry, 1974–80; retired Nov. 1980. Mem., BOTB, 1975–78. Dir, Berkeley Seventh Round Ltd, 1981–87. Vice-Pres. (and Chm. 1978–82), Westminster Dragoons Assoc.; Pres., Old Rugbeian Soc., 1984–86; Dir, Rugby Sch. Develt Campaign, 1981–86. *Recreations:* fly-fishing, hockey (President: Dulwich Hockey Club, 1962–; Rugby Alternatives HC, 1976–; Civil Service Hockey Cttee/Assoc., 1978–84), lawn tennis, watching cricket. *Address:* 12 Peterborough Villas, SW6 2AT. *T:* 071–736 5132. *Clubs:* Army and Navy, MCC, Hurlingham; Union (Cambridge).

See also E. A. W. Bullock.

BULLOUGH, Prof. Donald Auberon, FSA, FRHistS; Professor of Mediaeval History, University of St Andrews, 1973–91, now Emeritus; *b* 13 June 1928; *s* of late William Bullough and of Edith Shirley (*née* Norman); *m* 1963, Belinda Jane Turland; two *d*. *Educ:* Newcastle-under-Lyme High Sch.; St John's Coll., Oxford (BA 1950, MA 1952). FRHistS 1958; FSA 1968. National Service, 1946–48: commnd RA (attached RHA). Harmsworth Scholar, Merton Coll., Oxford, 1951; Medieval Scholar, British Sch. at Rome, 1951; Fereday Fellow, St John's Coll., Oxford, 1952–55; Lectr, Univ. of Edinburgh, 1955–66; Prof. of Med. History, Univ. of Nottingham, 1966–73; Dean, Faculty of Arts, Univ. of St Andrews, 1984–88. Vis. Prof., Southern Methodist Univ., Dallas, Tex, 1965–66; British Acad. Overseas Vis. Fellow, Max-Planck-Inst. für Gesch., 1972–73; Lilly Endowment Fellow, Pennsylvania Univ., 1980–81; Vis. Prof., Rutgers Univ., NJ, 1991–92. Lectures: Ford's, in English Hist., Univ. of Oxford, 1979–80; Scott-Hawkins, Southern Methodist Univ., Dallas, 1980; Andrew Mellon, Catholic Univ., Washington, 1980; Raleigh, British Acad., 1985; (Inaugural) Hector Munro Chadwick, Univ. of Cambridge, 1990. Corresponding Fellow, Monumenta Germaniae Historica, 1983–. Mem. Council, Exec., Finance Cttee, British School at Rome, 1975– (Chm., Faculty of Hist., Archeol., and Letters, 1975–79, Acting Dir, 1984). Senate Mem., Nottingham Univ. Council, 1970–73; Mem., Nottingham Univ. Hosp. Management Cttee, 1971–74; Senatus Assessor, St Andrews Univ. Ct, 1977–81. Dir, Paul Elek Ltd, 1968–79. Major RA (TA); seconded OTC, 1957–67. *Publications:* The Age of Charlemagne, 1965 (2nd edn 1974; also foreign trans); (ed with R. L. Storey) The Study of Medieval Records, 1971; Carolingian Renewal: sources and heritage, 1991; contrib. XIX, XX, XXI, Settimana di Studi del Centro ital. di St. sull'Alto Medioevo; contrib. TLS, British and continental hist. jls, philatelic jls. *Recreations:* talk, looking at buildings, postal history, cooking. *Address:* 23 South Street, St Andrews, Fife KY16 9QS. *T:* St Andrews (0334) 72932. *Club:* Athenæum.

BULLOUGH, Dr Ronald, FRS 1985; Chief Scientist, UK Atomic Energy Authority, since 1988, and Director for Corporate Research, Harwell, since 1990; *b* 6 April 1931; *s* of Ronald Bullough and Edna Bullough (*née* Morrow); *m* 1954, Ruth Corbett; four *s*. *Educ:* Univ. of Sheffield. BSc, PhD, DSc. FIM 1964; FInstP 1962. Res. Scientist, AEI Fundamental Res. Lab., Aldermaston Court, Aldermaston, 1956–63; Theoretical Physicist and Group Leader, Harwell Res. Lab., Didcot, Berks, 1963–84; Hd, Materials Develt Div., Harwell, 1984–88; Dir for Underlying Res., Harwell, 1988–90. Visiting Professor: Univ. of Illinois, USA, 1964, 1973, 1979; Univ. of Wisconsin, USA, 1978; Rensselaer Polytechnical Inst., USA, 1968; Visiting Scientist: Nat. Bureau of Standards, USA, 1965; Oak Ridge Nat. Lab., USA, 1969, 1979; Comisión Nacional de Energía Atómica, Buenos Aires, Argentina, 1977. Hon. Citizen of Tennessee, 1967. *Publications:* articles in learned jls such as Proc. Roy. Soc., Phil. Mag., Jl of Nucl. Materials etc., on defect properties in crystalline solids, particularly in relation to the irradiation and mechanical response of materials. *Recreations:* walking, reading, music. *Address:* 4 Long Meadow, Manor Road, Goring-on-Thames, Reading, Berkshire RG8 9EQ. *T:* Goring (0491) 873266.

BULLOUGH, Prof. William Sydney, PhD, DSc Leeds; Professor of Zoology, Birkbeck College, University of London, 1952–81, now Emeritus; *b* 6 April 1914; *o s* of Rev. Frederick Sydney Bullough and Letitia Anne Cooper, both of Leeds; *m* 1942, Dr Helena F. Gibbs (*d* 1975), Wellington, NZ; one *s* one *d*. *Educ:* William Hulme Grammar Sch., Manchester; Grammar Sch., Leeds; Univ. of Leeds. Lecturer in Zoology, Univ. of Leeds, 1937–44, McGill Univ., Montreal, 1944–46; Sorby Fellow of Royal Society of London, 1946–51; Research Fellow of British Empire Cancer Campaign, 1951–52; Hon. Fellow: Soc. for Investigative Dermatology (US); AAAS, 1981. Vice-Pres., Zoological Soc., 1983–84. *Publications:* Practical Invertebrate Anatomy, 1950; Vertebrate Sexual Cycles, 1951; (for children) Introducing Animals, 1953; Introducing Animals-with-Backbones, 1954; Introducing Man, 1958; The Evolution of Differentiation, 1967; The Dynamic Body Tissues, 1983; scientific papers on vertebrate reproductive cycles, hormones, and chalones published in a variety of journals. *Recreation:* gardening. *Address:* 75 Hillfield Court, Belsize Avenue, NW3 4BG. *T:* 071–435 4558.

BULLUS, Wing Comdr Sir Eric (Edward), Kt 1964; journalist; *b* 20 Nov. 1906; 2nd *s* of Thomas Bullus, Leeds; *m* 1949, Joan Evelyn, *er d* of H. M. Denny; two *d*. *Educ:* Leeds Modern Sch.; Univ. of Leeds. Commnd RAFVR Aug. 1940; served War of 1939–45; Air Min. War Room, 1940–43; joined Lord Louis Mountbatten's staff in SE Asia, 1943; Wing Comdr, 1944; served India, Burma and Ceylon; demobilized, 1945. Journalist Yorkshire Post, Leeds and London, 1923–46. Mem. Leeds City Council, 1930–40; Sec., London Municipal Soc., 1947–50; Mem., Harrow UDC, 1947–50; Vice-Pres. Assoc. of Municipal Corps, 1953. MP (C) Wembley N, 1950–Feb. 1974; PPS to Secretary for Overseas Trade, and to Minister of State, 1953–56, to Minister of Aviation, 1960–62, to Secretary of State for Defence, 1962–64. FRGS, 1947; Fellow Royal Statistical Society, 1949. Foundation Mem. of Brotherton Collection Cttee of Univ. of Leeds, 1935; Member: Archdeaconry Council of Delhi, 1944; Management Board, Cambridge Mission to Delhi, 1954; House of Laity, Church Assembly, 1960. Ripon Diocesan Reader, 1929; London Diocesan Reader, 1947; St Alban's Diocesan Reader, 1960; Canterbury Diocesan Reader, 1967; Central Readers' Board, 1960; London Readers' Board, 1954; Council Westfield Coll., Univ. of London. Pres., Soc. of Yorkshiremen in London, 1969–70. *Publications:* History of Leeds Modern School, 1931; History of Church in Delhi, 1944; History of Lords and Commons Cricket, 1959. *Recreations:* played Headingley RU Football Club 15 years and Yorkshire Amateurs Assoc. Football Club; cricket and swimming (bronze and silver medallions). *Address:* Westway, Herne Bay, Kent CT6 8RL. *Clubs:* St Stephen's Constitutional, MCC.

BULMER, Esmond; *see* Bulmer, J. E.

BULMER, Dr Gerald; Rector of Liverpool Polytechnic, 1970–85 (sabbatical leave, 1984–85), retired; *b* 17 Nov. 1920; *s* of Edward and Alice Bulmer; *m* 1943, Greta Lucy Parkes, MA; two *d*. *Educ:* Nunthorpe Sch., York; Selwyn Coll., Cambridge. BA 1941; PhD 1944; MA 1945. Asst Master, King's Sch., Canterbury, 1945–49; Sen. Lecturer, Woolwich Polytechnic, 1949–53; Head of Dept of Science and Metallurgy, Constantine Technical Coll., Middlesbrough, 1954–57; Vice-Principal, Bolton Technical Coll., 1958–59; Principal, West Ham Coll. of Technology, 1959–64; Dir, Robert Gordon's Inst. of Technology, Aberdeen, 1965–70. Mem. Council CNAA, 1967–78. Freeman City of York, 1952. Hon. DSc CNAA, 1986. *Publications:* papers on organic sulphur compounds in Jl Chem. Soc. and Nature. *Address:* 11 Capilano Park, Winifred Lane, Aughton, Ormskirk, Lancs.

BULMER, (James) Esmond; Chairman, H. P. Bulmer Holdings, since 1982 (Director, since 1962, Deputy Chairman, 1980); *b* 19 May 1935; *e s* of late Edward Bulmer and Margaret Rye; *m* 1st, 1959, Morella Kearton; three *s* one *d*; 2nd, 1990, Susan Elizabeth Bower (*née* Murray). *Educ:* Rugby; King's Coll., Cambridge (BA); and abroad. Commissioned Scots Guards, 1954. Dir (non-exec.), Wales and W Midlands Regional Bd, National Westminster Bank PLC, 1982–. Chm., Hereford DHA, 1987–. MP (C): Kidderminster, Feb. 1974–1983; Wyre Forest, 1983–87. Mem. Exec. Cttee, Nat. Trust, 1977–87. *Recreations:* gardening, fishing. *Club:* Boodle's.

BULMER-THOMAS, Ivor, CBE 1984; FSA 1970; writer; Hon. Director, Friends of Friendless Churches; Vice-President, Church Union; *b* 30 Nov. 1905; *s* of late A. E. Thomas, Cwmbran, Newport, Mon.; *m* 1st, 1932, Dilys (*d* 1938), *d* of late Dr W. Llewelyn Jones, Merthyr Tydfil; one *s*; 2nd, 1940, Margaret Joan, *d* of late E. F. Bulmer, Adam's Hill, Hereford; one *s* two *d*. Assumed additional surname Bulmer by deed poll, 1952. *Educ:* West Monmouth Sch., Pontypool; Scholar of St John's (Hon. Fellow, 1985) and Senior Demy of Magdalen Coll., Oxford. 1st Class Math. Mods, 1925; 1st Class Lit. Hum., 1928; Liddon Student, 1928; Ellerton Essayist, 1929; Junior Denyer and Johnson Scholar, 1930; MA 1937; represented Oxford against Cambridge at Cross-country Running, 1925–27, and Athletics, 1926–28, winning Three Miles in 1927; Welsh International Cross-country Runner, 1926; Gladstone Research Student at St Deiniol's Library, Hawarden, 1929–30; on editorial staff of Times, 1930–37; chief leader writer to News Chronicle, 1937–39; acting deputy editor, Daily Telegraph, 1953–54. Served War of 1939–45 with Royal Fusiliers (Fusilier), 1939–40, and Royal Norfolk Regt (Captain, 1941), 1940–42, 1945. Contested (Lab) Spen Valley div., 1935; MP Keighley, 1942–50 (Lab 1942–48; C 1949–50); contested Newport, Mon (C), 1950. Parliamentary Secretary, Ministry of Civil Aviation, 1945–46; Parliamentary Under-Sec. of State for the Colonies, 1946–47. Delegate to Gen. Assembly, UN, 1946; first UK Mem., Trusteeship Council, 1947. Mem. of the House of Laity of the Church Assembly, 1950–70, of General Synod, 1970–85. Lately Chairman: Faith Press; Executive Cttee, Historic Churches Preservation Trust; Chairman: Redundant Churches Fund, 1969–76; Ancient Monuments Soc., 1975–90. Hon. DSc Warwick, 1979. Stella della Solidarietà Italiana, 1948. *Publications:* Coal in the New Era, 1934; Gladstone of Hawarden, 1936; Top Sawyer, a biography of David Davies of Llandinam, 1938; Greek Mathematics (Loeb Library), 1939–42; Warfare by Words, 1942; The Problem of Italy, 1946; The Socialist Tragedy, 1949; (ed) E. J. Webb, The Names of the Stars, 1952; The Party System in Great Britain, 1953; The Growth of the British Party System, 1965; (ed) St Paul, Teacher and Traveller, 1975; East Shefford Church, 1978; Dilysia: a threnody, 1987; contrib. to Dictionary of Scientific Biography, vol. 35 of Aufstieg und Niedergang der Römischen Welt, Classical Review, Classical Qly, Isis. *Address:* 12 Edwardes Square, W8 6HG. *T:* 071–602 6267; Old School House, Farnborough, Berks; Ty'n Mynydd, Rhoscolyn, Anglesey. *Clubs:* Athenæum; Vincent's (Oxford).

BULPITT, Cecil Arthur Charles, (Philip Bulpitt); Director, BIM Foundation Ltd, 1977–84 (Chairman, 1979–82); *b* 6 Feb. 1919; *s* of A. E. Bulpitt; *m* 1943, Joyce Mary Bloomfield; one *s* one *d*. *Educ:* Spring Grove Sch., London; Regent Street Polytechnic. Territorial Army, to rank of Staff Capt., RA, 1937–45. Carreras Ltd: joined firm, 1935; Gen. Manager, 1960; Asst Managing Dir, 1962; Dep. Chm. and Chief Exec., 1968; Chm. 1969–70. Dir, Thomas Tilling, 1973–81; Chairman: Tilling Construction Services Ltd, 1978–81; InterMed Ltd, 1978–81; Graham Building Services Ltd, 1979–81; Newey & Eyre Gp Ltd, 1979–81. Member: London Reg. Council, CBI, 1978–81; BBC Consultative Gp on Industrial and Business Affairs, 1980–84. MIPM 1955; FBIM 1963 (Vice-Chm. Council, and Dir, Bd of Companions, BIM, 1979–83). Freeman, City of London, 1969. *Publication:* The Chief Executive, 1971. *Recreations:* fishing, climbing, reading, travelling. *Address:* Apartment 308, Casa 3, Block 1, Andalucia del Mar, Nueva Andalucia, Málaga, Spain. *Clubs:* El Madronal Country; Las Brisas Golf (Nueva Andalucia, Spain).

BULTEEL, Christopher Harris, MC 1943; Director, GAP Activity Projects (GAP) Ltd, 1982–88; *b* 29 July 1921; *er s* of late Major Walter Bulteel and Constance (*née* Gaunt), Charlestown, Cornwall; *m* 1958, Jennifer Anne, *d* of late Col K. E. Previté, OBE and of Frances (*née* Capper), Hindgaston, Marnhull, Dorset; one *s* two *d*. *Educ:* Wellington Coll.; Merton Coll., Oxford. Served War with Coldstream Guards, 1940–46 (MC). Assistant Master at Wellington Coll., 1949–61; Head of history dept, 1959–61; Hon. Sec., Wellington Coll. Mission, 1959–61; Headmaster, Ardingly Coll., 1962–80. *Recreations:* natural history, sailing. *Address:* 3 Coastguard Cottages, Mevagissey, St Austell, Cornwall PL26 6QP. *T:* St Austell (0726) 843928; Street Farm Cottage, Park Street, Charlton, near Malmesbury, Wilts SN16 9DF. *T:* Tetbury (0666) 823764.

BUMBRY, Grace; opera singer and concert singer; *b* St Louis, Mo, 4 Jan. 1937. *Educ:* Boston Univ.; Northwestern Univ.; Music Academy of the West (under Lotte Lehmann). Debut: Paris Opera, 1960; Vienna State Opera, 1963; Salzburg Festival, 1964; Metropolitan Opera, 1965; La Scala, 1966. Appearances also include: Bayreuth Festival, 1961–; Royal Opera Covent Garden, London, 1963–, and in opera houses in Europe, S America and USA. Film, Carmen, 1968. Richard Wagner Medal, 1963. Hon. Dr of Humanities, St Louis Univ., 1968; Hon. doctorates: Rust Coll., Holly Spring, Miss; Rockhurst Coll., Kansas City; Univ. of Missouri at St Louis. Has made numerous recordings. *Recreations:* psychology, entertaining. *Address:* c/o Columbia Artists Management, attention Zemsky-Green, 165 West 57th Street, New York, NY 10019, USA.

BUNBURY; *see* McClintock-Bunbury, family name of Baron Rathdonnell.

BUNBURY, Bishop of, since 1984; **Rt. Rev. Hamish Thomas Umphelby Jamieson;** *b* 15 Feb. 1932; *s* of Robert Marshall Jamieson and Constance Marzetti Jamieson (*née* Umphelby); *m* 1962, Ellice Anne McPherson; one *s* two *d*. *Educ:* Sydney C of E Grammar Sch.; St Michael's House, Crafers (ThL); Univ. of New England (BA). Deacon 1955; Priest 1956. Mem. Bush Brotherhood of Good Shepherd, 1955–62. Parish of Gilgandra, 1957; Priest-in-Charge, Katherine, NT, 1957–62; Rector, Darwin, 1962–67; Canon of All Souls Cathedral, Thursday Island, 1963–67; Royal Australian Navy Chaplain, 1967–74; HMAS Sydney, 1967–68; HMAS Albatross, 1969–71; Small Ships Chaplain, 1972; HMAS Cerberus, 1972–74; Bishop of Carpentaria, 1974–84. *Recreations:* reading, music, gardening. *Address:* Bishopscourt, PO Box 15, Bunbury, WA 6230, Australia.

BUNBURY, Sir Michael; *see* Bunbury, Sir R. D. M. R.

BUNBURY, Sir Michael (William), 13th Bt *cr* 1681, of Stanney Hall, Cheshire; Partner, Smith & Williamson; *b* 29 Dec. 1946; *s* of Sir John William Napier Bunbury, 12th Bt, and of Pamela, *er d* of late Thomas Alexander Sutton; *S* father, 1985; *m* 1976, Caroline Anne, *d* of Col A. D. S. Mangnall, OBE; two *s* one *d*. *Educ:* Eton; Trinity College, Cambridge (MA). *Heir:* *s* Henry Michael Napier Bunbury, *b* 4 March 1980. *Address:* Naunton Hall, Rendlesham, Woodbridge, Suffolk IP12 2RD. *T:* Eyke (0394) 460235. *Club:* Boodle's.

BUNBURY, Lt-Comdr Sir (Richard David) Michael (Richardson-), 5th Bt, *cr* 1787; RN; *b* 27 Oct. 1927; *er s* of Richard Richardson-Bunbury (*d* 1951) and Florence Margaret Gordon, *d* of late Col Roger Gordon Thomson, CMG, DSO, late RA; *S* kinsman 1953; *m* 1961, Jane Louise, *d* of late Col Alfred William Pulverman, IA; two *s*. *Educ:* Royal Naval College, Dartmouth. Midshipman (S), 1945; Sub-Lieut (S), 1947; Lieut (S), 1948; Lieut-Comdr, 1956; retd 1967. Dir, Sandy Laird Ltd, 1988–. *Heir:* *s* Roger Michael Richardson-Bunbury, *b* 2 Nov. 1962. *Address:* Woodlands, Mays Hill, Worplesdon, Guildford, Surrey GU3 3RJ. *T:* Guildford (0483) 232034.

BUNCE, Michael John; Executive Director, Royal Television Society, since 1991; *b* 24 April 1935; *s* of late Roland Bunce, ARIBA, and of Dorie Bunce (*née* Woods); *m* 1961, Tina Sims; two *s* two *d*. *Educ:* St Paul's Sch; Kingston Coll. Nat. Service, RAF. Joined BBC as engineer; subseq. Studio Manager; Producer, People and Politics (World Service); Dir, Gallery; Producer: A Man Apart; The Murderer, 1965; Minorities in Britain; The Younger Generation; Italy and the Italians; Editor: Money Programme, 1968–70; Nationwide, 1970–75; Chief Asst, Current Affairs, TV and Editor, Tonight, 1975–78; Head: Information Services TV, 1978–82; Information Div., 1982–83; Controller, Information Services, 1983–91. Member: Francis Cttee, 1977; EBU Working Party on Direct Elections, 1978; Chm., Nat. Industries PR Officers, 1991–. Marshall Fund Vis. Fellow, USA, 1975. FRTS 1989 (Mem. Council and Chm. PR Cttee). Shell Internat. Television Award, 1969. *Recreations:* gardening, visiting fine buildings, fishing. *Address:* Royal Television Society, Tavistock House East, Tavistock Square, WC1H 9HR. *Clubs:* Reform, Groucho.

BUNCH, Sir Austin (Wyeth), Kt 1983; CBE 1978 (MBE 1974); National President, British Limbless Ex-Servicemen's Association, since 1983; *b* 1918; *s* of Horace William and Winifred Ada Bunch; *m* 1944, Joan Mary Peryer; four *d*. *Educ:* Christ's Hospital. FCA. Deloitte, Plender, Griffiths, 1935–48; Southern Electricity Board, 1949–76: Area Man., Newbury, 1962; Area Man., Portsmouth, 1966; Dep. Chm., 1967; Chm., 1974; Dep. Chm., Electricity Council, 1976–81, Chm., 1981–83; Chm., British Electricity Internat. Ltd, 1977–83; retd. Chm., Queen Mary's Roehampton Hosp. Trust, 1983–89. *Recreation:* sports for the disabled. *Address:* Sumner, School Lane, Cookham, Berks SL6 9QJ.

BUNDY, McGeorge; Professor of History, New York University, 1979–89, now Emeritus; *b* 30 March 1919; *s* of Harvey Hollister Bundy and Katharine Lawrence Bundy (*née* Putnam); *m* 1950, Mary Buckminster Lothrop; four *s*. *Educ:* Yale Univ. AB 1940. Political analyst, Council on Foreign Relations, 1948–49. Harvard University: Vis. Lectr, 1949–51; Associate Prof. of Government, 1951–54; Prof., 1954–61; Dean, Faculty of Arts and Sciences, 1953–61. Special Asst to the Pres. for National Security Affairs, 1961–66; President of the Ford Foundation, 1966–79. *Publications:* (with H. L. Stimson)

On Active Service in Peace and War, 1948; (ed) Pattern of Responsibility, 1952; The Strength of Government, 1968; Danger and Survival, 1988. *Address:* 133 East 80th Street, New York, NY 10021, USA.

BUNFORD, John Farrant, MA, FIA; Hon.FFA; Director, National Provident Institution for Mutual Life Assurance, 1964–85, retired (Manager and Actuary 1946–64); *b* 4 June 1901; *s* of late John Henry Bunford and Ethel Farrant Bunford; *m* 1929, Florence Louise, *d* of late John and Annie Pearson, Mayfield, Cork; two *s* one *d*. *Educ:* Christ's Hosp.; St Catharine's Coll., Cambridge. (MA). Scottish Amicable Life Assurance Soc., 1923–29. Royal Exchange Assurance, 1929–32; National Provident Institution: Dep. Asst Actuary, 1932; Asst Sec., 1933; Asst Manager, 1937. Institute of Actuaries: Fellow, 1930; Hon. Sec., 1944–45; Vice-Pres., 1948–50; Treas., 1952–53; Pres., 1954–56. Hon. Fellow the Faculty of Actuaries, 1956. *Recreation:* gardening. *Address:* 14 Shepherds Way, Liphook, Hants. *T:* Liphook (0428) 722594.

BUNGEY, Michael; Chairman and Chief Executive Officer, BSB Dorland Advertising Ltd (formerly Dorland Advertising), since 1987; Chairman, Backer Spielvogel Bates Europe, since 1988; *b* 18 Jan. 1940; *s* of William Frederick George and Irene Edith Bungey; *m* 1976, Darleen Penelope Cecilia Brooks; one *s* two *d*. *Educ:* St Clement Danes Grammar Sch.; LSE (BSc Econ). Marketing with Nestlé, 1961–65; Associate Dir, Crawfords Advertising, 1965–68; Account Dir, S. H. Benson Advertising, 1968–71; Chm., Michael Bungey DFS Ltd (Advertising Agency), 1972–84; Dep. Chm., Dorland Advertising, 1984–87. *Address:* BSB Dorland Advertising Ltd, 121–141 Westbourne Terrace, W2 6JR. *Club:* Hurlingham.

BUNKER, Albert Rowland, CB 1966; Deputy Under-Secretary of State, Home Office, 1972–75; *b* 5 Nov. 1913; *er* and *o* surv. *s* of late Alfred Francis Bunker and late Ethel Trudgian, Lanjeth, St Austell, Cornwall; *m* 1939, Irene Ruth Ella, 2nd *d* of late Walter and late Ella Lacey, Ealing; two *s*. *Educ:* Ealing Gram. Sch. Served in Royal Air Force, 1943–45. Service in Cabinet Office, HM Treasury, Ministry of Home Security and Home Office. *Recreation:* golf. *Address:* 35 Park Avenue, Ruislip HA4 7UQ. *T:* Ruislip (0895) 635331. *Clubs:* Royal Air Force; Denham Golf.

BUNN, Douglas Henry David; Chairman: All England Jumping Course, Hickstead; White Horse Caravan Co. Ltd; *b* 1 March 1928; *s* of late George Henry Charles Bunn and Alice Ann Bunn; *m* 1st, 1952, Rosemary Pares Wilson; three *d*; 2nd, 1960, Susan Dennis-Smith; two *s* one *d*; 3rd, 1979, Lorna Kirk; one *s* two *d*. *Educ:* Chichester High Sch.; Trinity Coll., Cambridge (MA). Called to Bar, Lincoln's Inn; practised at Bar, 1953–59; founded Hickstead, 1960; British Show Jumping Team, 1957–68; Vice-Chm., British Show Jumping Assoc. (Chm. 1969); Mem. British Equestrian Fedn; founded White Horse Caravan Co. Ltd, 1958; Chm., Southern Aero Club, 1968–72. Jt Master, Mid Surrey Drag Hounds, 1976–. *Recreations:* horses, flying, books, wine. *Address:* Hickstead Place, Sussex RH17 5NU. *T:* Hurstpierpoint (0273) 834666. *Clubs:* Buck's, Saints and Sinners (Chm., 1989–90), Turf.

BUNSTER, Don Alvaro; Fellow, Institute of Development Studies, University of Sussex, 1977; *b* 25 May 1920; *m* 1965, Raquel de Bunster (*née* Parot); three *s*. *Educ:* National Institute, Santiago; School of Law, Univ. of Chile; Faculty of Law, Central Univ. of Brazil, Rio de Janeiro; Faculty of Jurisprudence, Univ. of Rome, Italy. Judge Advocate of the Army, Chile, 1950–57; Prof. of Penal Law, Univ. of Chile, 1953–73; Gen. Sec., Univ. of Chile, 1957–69. Vis. Prof., Univ. of Calif., Berkeley, 1966–67. Vice-Pres., Inst. of Penal Sciences, 1969–70; Dir, Enciclopedia Chilena, 1970; Chilean Ambassador to Court of St James's, 1971–73; lecturing at Univs of Oxford and Liverpool, 1973–74; Senior Vis. Fellow, Centre of Latin-American Studies, Univ. of Cambridge, 1974–77. *Publications:* La malversación de caudales públicos, 1948; La voluntad del acto delictivo, 1950; articles, descriptive commentaries, etc, in various nat. and foreign magazines. *Recreations:* music, theatre.

BUNTING, Prof. Arthur Hugh, CMG 1971; consultant in tropical agricultural research and development; Professor of Agricultural Development Overseas, Reading University, 1974–82, now Emeritus; *b* 7 Sept. 1917; *e s* of S. P. and R. Bunting; *m* 1941, Elsie Muriel Reynard; three *s*. *Educ:* Athlone High Sch., Johannesburg, S Africa; Univ. of the Witwatersrand, Johannesburg; Oriel Coll., University of Oxford. BSc 1937. BSc (Hons Botany), MSc 1938, Witwatersrand; Rhodes Scholar for the Transvaal, 1938; DPhil Oxford, 1941; CBiol, FIBiol. Asst Chemist, Rothamsted Experimental Station, 1941–45; Member Human Nutrition Research Unit, Medical Research Council, 1945–47; Chief Scientific Officer, Overseas Food Corporation, 1947–51; Senior Research Officer, Sudan Min. of Agriculture, 1951–56; Prof. of Agricultural Botany, 1956–73, Dean, Faculty of Agriculture, 1965–71, Univ. of Reading. Pres., Assoc. of Applied Biologists, 1963–64, Hon. Mem., 1979–; Jt Editor, Journal of Applied Ecology, 1964–68. Foundn Mem., 1968–72, and Mem., 1974–80, Vice-Chm. 1975–77, and Chm. 1977–80, Board of Trustees, Internat. Inst. of Tropical Agriculture, Ibadan, Nigeria; Member: UK Council for Scientific Policy, 1970–72; UN Adv. Cttee on the Applications of Science and Technology to Develt (ACAST), 1972–75; Governing Bodies, Grassland Res. Inst., Hurley, 1959–77, Plant Breeding Inst., Cambridge, 1960–76; Consultant and then Mem., Scientific Cttee, Cotton Res. Corp., 1958–76 (Chm., 1972–76); Member: Panel of Scientific Advisers, CDC, 1967–; Meteorological Cttee, MoD, 1973–88; Foundn Mem., Internat. Bd for Plant Genetic Resources, 1974–78. LLD *hc* Ahmadu Bello Univ., 1968. *Publications:* (ed) Change in Agriculture, 1970; (ed jtly) Policy and Practice in Rural Development, 1976; (ed jtly) Advances in Legume Science, 1980; (ed) Agricultural Environments, 1987; numerous papers in scientific and agricultural journals. *Recreation:* music. *Address:* 27 The Mount, Caversham, Reading, Berks RG4 7RU. *T:* Reading (0734) 472487; 4 Earley Gate, University of Reading, Berks RG6 2AR. *T:* Reading (0734) 318320/1.

BUNTING, Sir (Edward) John, AC 1982; KBE 1977 (CBE 1960); Kt 1964; BA; Australian civil servant (retired); Chairman, Official Establishments Trust, since 1983; National Co-ordinator, Sir Robert Menzies Memorial Foundation, since 1978; *b* Ballarat, Vic, 13 Aug. 1918; *s* of late G. B. Bunting; *m* 1942, (Pauline) Peggy, *d* of late D. C. MacGruer; three *s*. *Educ:* Trinity Grammar School, Melbourne; Trinity Coll., Univ. of Melbourne (BA Hons; Hon. Fellow 1981). Asst Sec., Prime Minister's Dept, Canberra, 1949–53; Official Sec., Office of the High Commissioner for Australia, London, 1953–55; Deputy Sec., Prime Minister's Dept, Canberra, 1955–58; Secretary: Australian Cabinet, 1959–75; Prime Minister's Dept, 1959–68; Dept of the Cabinet Office, 1968–71; Dept of the Prime Minister and Cabinet, 1971–75; High Comr for Australia in UK, 1975–77. Chm., Roche-Maag Ltd, 1978–83. Mem., Australia Council, 1978–82. *Publication:* R. G. Menzies: a portrait, 1988. *Recreations:* cricket, music, reading. *Address:* 3 Wickham Crescent, Red Hill, ACT 2603, Australia. *Clubs:* Commonwealth (Canberra); Athenæum (Melbourne); Melbourne Cricket.

BUNTING, John Reginald, CBE 1965; author and educational consultant, retired; *b* 12 Nov. 1916; *s* of John Henry and Jane Bunting, Mansfield; *m* 1940, May Hope Sturdy, Malvern, Jamaica; no *c*. *Educ:* Queen Elizabeth's Grammar Sch., Mansfield; Queen's Coll., Oxford (MA, DipEd). Sen. English Master and Housemaster, Munro Coll., Jamaica, 1939–42; Headmaster, Wolmer's Sch., Jamaica, 1943–49; Principal, King's Coll., Lagos, 1949–54; Actg Dir of Broadcasting, Nigeria, June-Oct. 1952; Actg Inspector of Educn, Western Region, Nigeria, April-Oct. 1954; Dep. Chief Federal Adviser on Educn, Nigeria, 1954–58; Chief Federal Adviser on Educn, Nigeria, 1958–61; Educn Adviser, W Africa, Brit. Council, 1961 and Head, Graduate VSO Unit, 1962; Asst Controller, Educn Div., 1964; Evans Bros Ltd: Editorial Consultant, 1965–68; Dir, Overseas Sales and Publications, 1969; Dir-Gen., Centre for Educnl Develt Overseas, 1970–74; Adviser on Educn to British Council, 1974–76. Hon. Jt Editor, W African Jl of Educn, 1956–61. *Publications:* Civics for Self-Government, 1956; New African English Course (Book 5), 1960; (jtly) Caribbean Civics, 1960; (jtly) Civics for East Africa, 1961; Primary English Course (Book 6): for Ghana, 1962, for Sierra Leone, 1969, for West Cameroon, 1971; Civics: a course in citizenship and character training, 1973; To Light a Candle, 1976. *Recreations:* golf, fishing, painting, bowls. *Address:* 8 Springhill Gardens, Lyme Regis, Dorset DT7 3HL. *T:* Lyme Regis (02974) 3726. *Clubs:* MCC; Lyme Regis Golf.

BUNTING, Martin Brian, FCA; company director; Chief Executive, Clifford Foods PLC, since 1990; *b* 28 Feb. 1934; *s* of late Brian and Renee Bunting; *m* 1959, Veronica Mary Cope; two *s* one *d*. *Educ:* Rugby School. Director, Courage Ltd, 1972, Man. Dir, later Dep. Chm., 1974–84; Director: Imperial Group plc, 1975–84; Bluebird Toys, 1991–; non-executive Director: George Gale & Co. Ltd, 1984–; Longman Cartermill Ltd, 1985–90; Norcros plc, 1986–; Shepherd Neame Ltd, 1986–. Member, Monopolies and Mergers Commission, 1982–88. *Address:* The Lodge, Basingstoke Road, Riseley, near Reading RG7 1QD. *T:* Reading (0734) 883234, 885414. *Club:* Travellers'.
See also Earl of Macduff.

BUNTON, George Louis, MChir (Cantab), FRCS; Consultant Surgeon to University College Hospital, London, 1955–84, to Metropolitan Hospital, 1957–70, and to Northwood Hospital, 1958–84, retired; Emeritus Consulting Surgeon to University College and Middlesex Hospitals, 1986; *b* 23 April 1920; *s* of late Surg. Capt. C. L. W. Bunton, RN, and Marjorie Denman; *m* 1948, Margaret Betty Edwards (*d* 1988); one *d*. *Educ:* Epsom; Selwyn Coll., Cambridge; UCH. MB, BChir Cantab 1951; MRCS, LRCP 1944; FRCS 1951; MChir Cantab 1955. Served in RNVR 1944–47. University of London: Examr in Surgery, 1974–78; Mem., Academic Council, 1975–77; University College Hospital, London: Chm., Med. Cttee, 1977–80; Mem., Academic Bd, Med. Sch., 1970–78; Mem., Sch. Council, Med. Sch., 1976–81; Mem., Bd of Governors, 1972–74; Mem., Bd of Trustees, UC Gp of Hosps, 1978–82. Chairman: Health Gp, Centre for Policy Studies, 1980–84; S Camden Dist Med. Cttee, 1980–83; Member: Exec., University Hosps Assoc. (England and Wales), 1975–89 (Treasurer, 1980–89); Court of Examiners, RCS, 1977–84 (Chm., 1984). Fellow, Assoc. of Surgeons; Fellow, British Assoc. of Pædiatric Surgeons. *Publications:* contribs. to journals and books on surgical subjects. *Recreations:* gardening, music. *Address:* Smarkham Orchard, Madgehole Lane, Shamley Green, Guildford, Surrey GU5 0SS. *T:* Guildford (0483) 892187.

BUNYAN, Dr Peter John; Director General, Agricultural Development and Advisory Service and Regional Organisation, and Chief Scientific Adviser to Ministry of Agriculture, Fisheries and Food, since 1990; *b* London, 13 Jan. 1936; *o s* of Charles and Jenny Bunyan; *m* 1961, June Rose Child; two *s*. *Educ:* Raynes Park County Grammar Sch.; University Coll., Durham Univ. (BSc, DSc); King's Coll., Univ. of London (PhD). FRSC; CChem; FIBiol; FIFST. Research at KCL, 1960–62, at UCL, 1962–63; Ministry of Agriculture, Fisheries and Food: Sen. Scientific Officer, Infestation Control Lab., 1963–69; PSO, Pest Infestation Control Lab., 1969–73, Head of Pest Control Chemistry Dept, 1973–80; Head of Food Science Div., 1980–84; Head of Agricl Sci. Service, ADAS, 1984–87; Dir of R & D Service, ADAS, 1987–90. *Publications:* numerous scientific papers in wide variety of scientific jls. *Recreations:* gardening, jogging. *Address:* c/o Ministry of Agriculture, Fisheries and Food, Nobel House, 17 Smith Square, SW1P 3JR. *T:* 071–238 5958. *Club:* Farmers'.

BUNYARD, Sir Robert Sidney, Kt 1991; CBE 1986; QPM 1980; Commandant, Police Staff College, Bramshill and HM Inspector of Constabulary, since 1987; *b* 20 May 1930; *s* of Albert Percy Bunyard and Nellie Maria Bunyard; *m* 1948, Ruth Martin; two *d*. *Educ:* Queen Elizabeth Grammar Sch., Faversham; Regent Street Polytechnic Management Sch. (Dip. in Man. Studies). BA (Hons) Open Univ. MIPM; CBIM. Metropolitan Police, 1952; Asst Chief Constable, Leics, 1972; Dep. Chief Constable, 1977, Chief Constable, 1978–87, Essex Police. Man. Editor, Police Jl, 1981–88. *Publications:* Police: organization and command, 1978; Police Management Handbook, 1979; contrib. police jls. *Recreations:* music, opera, painting. *Address:* Police Staff College, Bramshill House, near Hartley Wintney, Hants RG27 0JW.

BURBIDGE, (Eleanor) Margaret, (Mrs Geoffrey Burbidge), FRS 1964; Professor of Astronomy, 1964–90, University Professor, 1984–90, now Emeritus, and Research Physicist, Department of Physics, since 1990, University of California at San Diego; *d* of late Stanley John Peachey, Lectr in Chemistry and Research Chemist, and of Marjorie Peachey; *m* 1948, Geoffrey Burbidge, *qv*; one *d*. *Educ:* Francis Holland Sch., London; University Coll., London (BSc); Univ. of London Observatory (PhD). Asst Director, 1948–50, Actg Director, 1950–51, Univ. of London Observatory; fellowship from Internat. Astron. Union, held at Yerkes Observatory, Univ. of Chicago, 1951–53; Research Fellow, California Inst. of Technology, 1955–57; Shirley Farr Fellow, later Associate Prof., Yerkes Observatory, Univ. of Chicago, 1957–62; Research Astronomer, 1962–64, Dir, Center for Astrophysics and Space Scis, 1979–88, Univ. of California at San Diego; Dir, Royal Greenwich Observatory, 1972–73. Abby Rockefeller Mauzé Vis. Prof., MIT, 1968. Member: American Acad. of Arts and Scis, 1969; US Nat. Acad. of Scis, 1978; Nat. Acad. of Scis Cttee on Science and Public Policy, 1979–81; Pres., Amer. Astronomical Soc., 1976–78; Chairwoman Bd of Dirs, Amer. Assoc. for Advancement of Science, 1983 (Pres., 1982). Fellow University Coll., London, 1967; Hon. Fellow, Lucy Cavendish Collegiate Soc., 1971. Hon. DSc: Smith Coll., Massachusetts, USA, 1963; Sussex, 1970; Bristol, 1972; Leicester, 1972; City, 1974; Michigan, 1978; Massachusetts, 1978; Williams Coll., 1979; State Univ. of NY at Stony Brook, 1984; Rensselaer Poly. Inst., 1986; Notre Dame Univ., 1986. Catherine Wolfe Bruce Medal, Astr. Soc. of the Pacific, 1982; Nat. Medal of Science (awarded by President of USA), 1984; Sesquicentennial Medal, Mt Holyoke Coll., 1987; Einstein Medal, World Cultural Council, 1988. *Publications:* Quasi-Stellar Objects (with Geoffrey Burbidge), 1967 (also USA, 1967); contribs to learned jls (mostly USA), Handbuch der Physik, etc. *Address:* Center for Astrophysics and Space Sciences, 0111, University of California, San Diego, La Jolla, California 92093, USA. *T:* 619–534–4477. *Club:* University Women's.

BURBIDGE, Prof. Geoffrey, FRS 1968; Professor of Physics, University of California, San Diego, 1963–84 and since 1988 (Associate Professor, 1962–63, Emeritus Professor, 1984–88); *b* 24 Sept. 1925; *s* of Leslie and Eveline Burbidge, Chipping Norton, Oxon; *m* 1948, Margaret Peachey (*see* E. M. Burbidge); one *d*. *Educ:* Chipping Norton Grammar Sch.; Bristol University; Univ. Coll., London. BSc (Special Hons Physics) Bristol, 1946; PhD London, 1951. Asst Lectr, UCL, 1950–51; Agassiz Fellow, Harvard Univ., 1951–52; Research Fellow, Univ. of Chicago, 1952–53; Research Fellow, Cavendish Lab., Cambridge, 1953–55; Carnegie Fellow, Mount Wilson and Palomar Observatories,

Caltech, 1955–57; Asst Prof., Dept of Astronomy, Univ. of Chicago, 1957–58; Assoc. Prof., 1958–62. Dir, Kitt Peak Nat. Observatory, Arizona, 1978–84. Phillips Vis. Prof., Harvard Univ., 1968. Elected Fellow, UCL, 1970. Pres., Astronomical Soc. of the Pacific, 1974–76; Trustee, Assoc. Universities Inc., 1973–82; Editor, Annual Review Astronomy and Astrophysics, 1973–. *Publications:* (with Margaret Burbidge) Quasi-Stellar Objects, 1967; scientific papers in Astrophysical Jl, Nature, Rev. Mod. Phys, Handbuch der Physik, etc. *Address:* Center for Astrophysics and Space Sciences, 0111, University of California, San Diego, La Jolla, Calif 92093, USA. *T:* (619) 534–6626.

BURBIDGE, Sir Herbert (Dudley), 5th Bt *cr* 1916; *b* 13 Nov. 1904; *s* of Herbert Edward Burbidge (*d* 1945) 2nd *s* of 1st Bt, and Harriet Georgina (*d* 1952), *d* of Henry Stuart Hamilton, Londonderry; *S* cousin, 1974; *m* 1933, Ruby Bly, *d* of Charles Ethelbert Taylor; one *s. Educ:* University Sch., Victoria, BC, Canada. Harrods Ltd, Knightsbridge, 1923–28; R. P. Clarke (Stock Brokers), Vancouver, BC, 1929–31; Merchandising Manager, Silverwood Industries of Vancouver, BC, 1931–70; retired 1970. President: Vancouver Executive Club, 1942; Vancouver Sales Executive Club, 1948. Mem. Bd of Referees, Workmen's Compensation Bd, 1943–61. *Recreation:* landscape gardening. *Heir: s* Peter Dudley Burbidge [*b* 20 June 1942; *m* 1967, Peggy Marilyn, *d* of Kenneth Anderson, Ladner, BC; one *s* one *d*]. *Club:* Vancouver Executive.

BURBIDGE, Mrs Margaret; *see* Burbidge, E. M.

BURBRIDGE, Very Rev. (John) Paul, MA Oxon and Cantab; FSA; Dean of Norwich, since 1983; *b* 21 May 1932; *e s* of late John Henry Gray Burbridge and Dorothy Vera Burbridge; *m* 1956, Olive Denise Grenfell; four *d. Educ:* King's Sch., Canterbury; King's Coll., Cambridge; New Coll., Oxford; Wells Theolog. Coll. Nat. Service Commn in RA, 1957. Jun. Curate, 1959, Sen. Curate, 1961, Eastbourne Parish Church; Vicar Choral of York Minster, 1962–66; Chamberlain, 1962–76; Canon Residentiary, 1966–76; Succentor Canonicorum, 1966; Precentor, 1969–76; Archdeacon of Richmond and Canon Residentiary of Ripon Cathedral, 1976–83. *Recreation:* model engineering. *Address:* The Deanery, Norwich, Norfolk NR1 4EG. *T:* Norwich (0603) 760140 and 626290.

See also S. N. Burbridge.

BURBRIDGE, Stephen Nigel, MA; Secretary, Monopolies and Mergers Commission, since 1986; *b* 18 July 1934; *s* of late John Henry Gray Burbridge and late Dorothy Vera (*née* Pratt). *Educ:* King's Sch., Canterbury; Christ Church, Oxford. National Service, 2 Lieut, RA, 1953–55. Asst Principal, Bd of Trade, 1958–62; Trade Commissioner, Karachi, 1963–65; 1st Secretary (Economic), Rawalpindi, 1965–67; Principal, BoT (marine), 1967–71; CS Selection Bd, 1971; Department of Trade and Industry: Asst Sec. (finance, research, marine, industrial policy), 1971–80; Under Sec. (export promotion, consumer affairs), 1980–86. *Recreations:* sports, reading, collecting. *Address:* Monopolies and Mergers Commission, New Court, 48 Carey Street, WC2A 2JT. *Clubs:* Rye Golf; West Sussex Golf.

See also J. P. Burbridge.

BURBURY, Hon. Sir Stanley Charles, KCMG 1981; KCVO 1977; KBE 1958; Governor of Tasmania, 1973–82; *b* 2 Dec. 1909; *s* of Daniel Charles Burbury and Mary Burbury (*née* Cunningham); *m* 1934, Pearl Christine Barren; no *c. Educ:* Hutchins Sch., Hobart; The Univ. of Tasmania. LLB 1933; Hon. LLD 1970. Admitted to Bar, 1934; QC 1950; Solicitor-Gen. for Tasmania, 1952; Chief Justice, Supreme Court of Tasmania, 1956–73. Pres., Nat. Heart Foundn of Australia, 1967–73; Nat. Pres., Winston Churchill Memorial Trust, 1980–85. KStJ 1974. Hon. Col, Royal Tasmanian Regt, 1974–82. *Recreations:* music and lawn bowls. *Address:* 3 Mona Street, Kingston, Tasmania 7150, Australia. *Clubs:* Tasmanian, Athenæum, Royal Hobart Bowls (Hobart).

BURCH, Maj.-Gen. Keith, CB 1985; CBE 1977 (MBE 1965); Director Personnel, Defence Staff, Ministry of Defence, 1985, retired; Chapter Clerk, York Minster, since 1985; *b* 31 May 1931; *s* of Christopher Burch and Gwendoline Ada (*née* James); *m* 1957, Sara Vivette Hales; one *s* two *d. Educ:* Bedford Modern Sch.; Royal Military Acad., Sandhurst. Commnd Essex Regt, 1951; DS Staff Coll., Camberley, 1968–69; Comd 3rd Bn Royal Anglian Regt, 1969–71; Asst Sec., Chiefs of Staff Cttee, MoD, 1972–75; Col GS HQ 2nd Armoured Div., 1975–78; Dir, Admin. Planning (Army), MoD, 1978–80; Indian National Defence Coll., New Delhi, 1981; Dep. Dir, Army Staff Duties, MoD, 1981–83; ACDS (Personnel and Logistics), 1984. *Recreations:* country pursuits. *Address:* Church House, Ogleforth, York YO1 2JN. *Club:* Yorkshire (York).

BURCH, Rt. Rev. William Gerald, DD; *b* Winnipeg, Manitoba, 5 March 1911; *m* 1942, Carroll Borrowman; four *d. Educ:* University of Toronto (BA); Wycliffe Coll., Toronto. Deacon, 1936; Priest, 1938. Curate, Christ Church, Toronto, 1936–40; Incumbent, Scarborough Junction with Sandown Park, 1940–42; Rector: St Luke, Winnipeg, 1942–52; All Saints, Windsor, 1952–56; Exam. Chaplain to Bishop of Huron, 1955–56; Canon of Huron, 1956; Dean and Rector, All Saints Cathedral, Edmonton, 1956–60; Suffragan Bishop of Edmonton, 1960–61; Bishop of Edmonton, 1961–76. *Address:* 901 Richmond Avenue, Victoria, BC V8S 3Z4, Canada. *T:* (604) 598 4369.

BURCHAM, Prof. William Ernest, CBE 1980; FRS 1957; Emeritus Professor of Physics, Birmingham University, since 1981; *b* 1 Aug. 1913; *er s* of Ernest Barnard and Edith Ellen Burcham; *m* 1st, 1942, Isabella Mary (*d* 1981), *d* of George Richard Todd and of Alice Louisa Todd; two *d*; 2nd, 1985, Patricia Newton, *er d* of Frank Harold Newton Marson and Miriam Eliza Marson. *Educ:* City of Norwich Sch.; Trinity Hall, Cambridge. Stokes Student, Pembroke Coll., Cambridge, 1937; Scientific Officer, Ministry of Aircraft Production, 1940, and Directorate of Atomic Energy, 1944; Fellow of Selwyn Coll., Cambridge, 1944; Univ. Demonstrator in Physics, Cambridge, 1945; Univ. Lecturer in Physics, Cambridge, 1946; Oliver Lodge Prof. of Physics, Univ. of Birmingham, 1951–80. Member: SRC, 1974–78; Council, Royal Soc., 1977–79. Hon. Life Fellow, Coventry Polytechnic, 1984. *Publications:* Nuclear Physics: an Introduction, 1963; Elements of Nuclear Physics, 1979; papers in Nuclear Physics A, Phys. Letters B, Phys. Rev. Letters. *Address:* 95 Witherford Way, Birmingham B29 4AN. *T:* 021–472 1226.

BURCHFIELD, Dr Robert William, CBE 1975; Editor, A Supplement to the Oxford English Dictionary, 1957–86; Chief Editor, The Oxford English Dictionaries, 1971–84; Senior Research Fellow, St Peter's College, Oxford, 1979–90, now Emeritus Fellow (Tutorial Fellow, 1963–79); *b* Wanganui, NZ, 27 Jan. 1923; *s* of Frederick Burchfield and Mary Burchfield (*née* Blair); *m* 1949, Ethel May Yates (marr. diss. 1976); one *s* two *d*; *m* 1976, Elizabeth Austen Knight. *Educ:* Wanganui Technical Coll., New Zealand, 1934–39; Victoria University Coll., Wellington, NZ, 1940–41, 1946–48; MA (NZ) 1948; Magdalen Coll., Oxford, 1949–53; BA (Oxon) 1951, MA 1955. Served War, Royal NZ Artillery, NZ and Italy, 1941–46. NZ Rhodes Scholar, 1949. Junior Lectr in English Lang., Magdalen Coll., Oxford, 1952–53; Lectr in English Lang., Christ Church, Oxford, 1953–57; Lectr, St Peter's Coll., Oxford, 1955–63. Hon. Sec., Early English Text Society, 1955–68 (Mem. Council, 1968–80); Editor, Notes and Queries, 1959–62; Pres., English Assoc., 1978–79. Hon. For. Mem., American Acad. of Arts and Scis, 1977–; Hon. Fellow, Inst. of Linguists, 1984–. Hon. DLitt, Liverpool, 1978; Hon. LitD Victoria Univ. of Wellington, NZ, 1983. Freedom of City of Wanganui, 1986. *Publications:* (with C. T. Onions and G. W. S. Friedrichsen) The Oxford Dictionary of English Etymology, 1966; A Supplement to the Oxford English Dictionary, vol. I (A-G), 1972, vol. II (H-N), 1976, vol. III (O-Scz), 1982, vol. IV (Se–Z), 1986; (with D. Donoghue and A. Timothy) The Quality of Spoken English on BBC Radio, 1979; The Spoken Language as an Art Form, 1981; The Spoken Word, 1981; The English Language, 1985; The New Zealand Pocket Oxford Dictionary, 1986; (ed) Studies in Lexicography, 1987; Unlocking the English Language, 1989; contribs to: Times Lit. Supp., Trans Philological Soc., Encounter, etc. *Recreations:* investigating English grammar, travelling, gardening. *Address:* The Barn, 14 The Green, Sutton Courtenay, Oxon OX14 4AE. *T:* Abingdon (0235) 848645. *Club:* Athenæum.

BURCHMORE, Air Cdre Eric, CBE 1972 (OBE 1963; MBE 1945); JP; RAF retired; *b* 18 June 1920; *s* of Percy William Burchmore and Olive Eva Ingledew; *m* 1941, Margaret Ovendale; one *d. Educ:* Robert Atkinson Sch., Thornaby; RAF Halton; Heriot-Watt Coll., Edinburgh. CEng, MRAeS. Royal Air Force: Aircraft Apprentice, 1936–39; Fitter 2, 1939–41; Engr Officer, 1941: served in Fighter Comd; Air Comd SE Asia, 1943–45; Air Min. and various home postings; Far East, 1952–55; London and Staff Coll.; Near East, 1960–62; comd RAF Sealand, 1963–66; Far East, 1967–68; Dir RAF Project (subseq. Dir Harrier Projects), MoD(PE), 1969–75; retired 1975. Dep. Dir of Housing, London Borough of Camden, 1975–80; Manager, Defence Support Services, Technicare Internat., 1981–84. JP Godstone, Surrey, 1979. *Address:* 28 Dorin Court, Landscape Road, Warlingham, Surrey CR3 9JT. *Club:* Royal Air Force.

BURDEKIN, Prof. Frederick Michael, FEng; Professor of Civil and Structural Engineering, University of Manchester Institute of Science and Technology, since 1977; *b* 5 Feb. 1938; *s* of Leslie and Gwendoline Burdekin; *m* 1965, Jennifer Meadley; two *s. Educ:* King's School, Chester; Trinity Hall, Cambridge (MA, PhD). MSc Manchester. FICE, FIMechE, FIStructE, FWeldI, FInstNDT. Welding Inst., 1961–68; Associate, Sandberg, Consulting Engineers, 1968–77. Vice-Principal External Affairs, UMIST, 1983–85. Chm., Manchester Science Park Ltd, 1988–. Mem., Engrg Council, 1990–. *Publications:* numerous papers on fracture, fatigue and welded structures. *Recreations:* music, sport, countryside. *Address:* 27 Springbank, Bollington, Macclesfield, Cheshire SK10 5LQ.

BURDEN, family name of **Baron Burden.**

BURDEN, 2nd Baron *cr* 1950, of Hazlebarrow, Derby; **Philip William Burden;** *b* 21 June 1916; *s* of 1st Baron Burden, CBE, and of Augusta, *d* of David Sime, Aberdeen; *S* father, 1970; *m* 1951, Audrey Elsworth, *d* of Major W. E. Sykes; three *s* three *d. Educ:* Raines Foundation School. *Heir: s* Hon. Andrew Philip Burden, *b* 20 July 1959.

BURDEN, Derrick Frank; HM Diplomatic Service, retired; Counsellor and Head of Claims Department, Foreign and Commonwealth Office, 1973–78; *b* 4 June 1918; *s* of late Alfred Burden and Louisa Burden (*née* Dean); *m* 1942, Marjorie Adeline Beckley; two *d. Educ:* Bec Sch., London. Crown Agents, 1936. Served War, King's Royal Rifle Corps, 1939–41. Joined Foreign Office, 1945; Comr-Gen.'s Office, Singapore, 1950–53; 2nd Sec., Moscow, 1954–56; 2nd Sec., Tokyo, 1957–59; HM Consul, Lourenço Marques, 1959–61; FO, 1962–67 (Asst Head of Protocol Dept, 1965); HM Consul, Khorramshahr (Iran), 1967–69; 1st Sec., Nairobi, 1969–71; HM Consul, Luanda (Angola), 1972–73. *Recreations:* golf, gardening. *Address:* 12 Strathmore Drive, Charvil, Reading, Berks RG10 9QT. *T:* Twyford (Berks) (0734) 340564. *Clubs:* Travellers'; Nairobi (Nairobi); Phyllis Court (Henley-on-Thames).

BURDETT, Sir Savile (Aylmer), 11th Bt, *cr* 1665; Managing Director: Rapaway Energy Ltd; Rydraulic Compressors Ltd; *b* 24 Sept. 1931; *s* of Sir Aylmer Burdett, 10th Bt; *S* father, 1943; *m* 1962, June E. C. Rutherford; one *s* one *d. Educ:* Wellington Coll.; Imperial Coll., London. *Heir: s* Crispin Peter Burdett, *b* 8 Feb. 1967. *Address:* Farthings, 35 Park Avenue, Solihull, West Midlands B91 3EJ. *T:* 021–711 1454.

BURDUS, (Julia) Ann; Director of Communications and Marketing, Olympia & York Canary Wharf, since 1989; *b* 4 Sept. 1933; *d* of Gladstone Beaty and Julia W. C. Booth; *m* 1981, Ian B. Robertson. *Educ:* Durham Univ. (BA Psychology). Clinical psychologist, 1956–60; Res. Exec., Ogilvy, Benson & Mather, 1961–67; Res. Dir, McCann Erickson, 1971–75, Vice Chm., 1975–77; Senior Vice-Pres., McCann Internat., 1977–79; Chm., McCann & Co., 1979–81; Director: Strategic Planning and Development, Interpublic, 1981–83; Audits of Great Britain Ltd, 1983–86; AGB Research, 1986–89. Chairman: Advertising Assoc., 1980–81; EDC for Distributive Trades, 1983–87. Jt Dep. Chm. and Mem., Health Educn Authority, 1987–. *Recreation:* home building. *Address:* (office) 10 Great George Street, SW1P 3AE.

BURFORD, Earl of; Charles Francis Topham de Vere Beauclerk; *b* 22 Feb. 1965; *s* and *heir* of Duke of St Albans, *qv. Educ:* Sherborne and Oxford. Created Brigadier-General of Louisiana, USA, on staff of Governor Edwin Edwards, 1986. Trustee, Shakespearean Authorship Trust; Chm., De Vere Soc.; Vice-Pres., Royal Stuart Soc., 1989–. Freeman, City of London 1986; Liveryman, Drapers' Co., 1990. *Address:* Canonteign, near Exeter, Devon. *Club:* Brooks's.

BURFORD, Eleanor; *see* Hibbert, Eleanor.

BURFORD, Jeremy Michael Joseph; QC 1987; a Recorder, since 1991; *b* 3 June 1942; *s* of Alexander Joseph Burford and Arlene Burford. *Educ:* Diocesan Coll., Cape Town; BA Cape Town; MA, LLB Cantab; LLM Harvard. Called to the Bar, Inner Temple, 1968. *Address:* 2 Mitre Court Buildings, Temple, EC4.

BURG, Gisela Elisabeth, Hon. CBE 1987 (for services to exports); Managing Director, Expotus Ltd, since 1968; *b* 12 Oct. 1939; *d* of Friedrich and Gerda Schlüsselburg. *Educ:* Gymnasium Philippinum, Weilburg, Germany; Ladies Coll., Wetzlar, Germany; Polytechnic of Central London. Founded Expotus Ltd, 1968. Vice-Pres., Fedn of British Audio, 1979–85 (Chm., 1976); Member: NEDO, 1979–84 (Mem. Electronic Sector Working Party); BOTB, 1982–. The Times/Veuve Clicquot Business Woman of the Year, 1981. *Recreations:* golf, horseracing. *Address:* 82 Kensington Heights, Campden Hill Road, W8 7BD. *T:* 071–727 8884. *Club:* Woburn Golf and Country (Beds).

BURGE, Prof. Ronald Edgar, CPhys; FInstP; Wheatstone Professor of Physics, since 1989, and Head of Department of Physics, since 1984, King's College, London; *b* 3 Oct. 1932; *s* of John Henry Burge and Edith Beatrice Burge (*née* Thompson); *m* 1953, Janet Mary (*née* Pitts); two *s. Educ:* Canton High Sch., Cardiff; King's Coll. London (BSc, PhD; FKC 1989); DSc London 1975. FInstP 1963. King's College London: Asst Lectr in Physics, 1954–58; Lectr in Physics, 1958–62; Reader in Biophysics, 1962–63; Prof. and Head of Dept of Physics, Queen Elizabeth Coll., Univ. of London, 1963–84; Prof. of Physics, KCL, 1984–89. Member: Swinnerton-Dyer Cttee concerning Academic Governance of Univ. of London, 1979–82; Computer Bd for Univs and Res. Councils (responsible for computer develt in univs in Scotland and, latterly, SW England), 1978–82. MRI 1988. *Publications:* papers in sci. jls on theory of scattering (electrons, x-rays and radar) and develts in electron microscopy and x-ray microscopy. *Recreations:* gardening, music. *Address:* 60 Sutherland Avenue, Orpington, Kent BR5 1RB. *T:* Orpington (0689) 821030.

BURGE, Stuart, CBE 1974; freelance director and actor; *b* 15 Jan. 1918; *s* of late H. O. Burge and K. M. Haig; *m* 1949, Josephine Parker; three *s* two *d*. *Educ:* Eagle House, Sandhurst; Felsted Sch., Essex. Served War of 1939–45, Intell. Corps. Actor; trained Old Vic, 1936–37; Oxford Rep., 1937–38; Old Vic and West End, 1938–39; Bristol Old Vic, Young Vic, Commercial Theatre, 1946–49; 1st Dir, Hornchurch, 1951–53; productions for theatre and TV, 1953–; Dir., Nottingham Playhouse, 1968–74; Artistic Dir., Royal Court Theatre, 1977–80. *Theatre:* Lulu, 1970; Measure for Measure, The Devil is an Ass, Edinburgh Fest. and Nat. Theatre, 1977; Another Country, Greenwich 1981 and Queen's 1982; (actor) The Seagull, Royal Court, 1981; The London Cuckolds, Lyric Hammersmith, 1985; Curtains, Hampstead, 1987, Whitehall, 1988; The Black Prince, Aldwych, 1989; *Opera:* La Colombe, Buxton and Sadler's Wells, 1983. *Television:* Bill Brand, Sons and Lovers, The Old Men at the Zoo, Much Ado About Nothing (BBC Shakespeare), Breaking Up, Naming the Names, The Rainbow, Chinese Whispers, Circles of Deceit, etc. Vis. Prof., UC Davis, USA; Hon. Prof. of Drama, Nottingham Univ. *Publication:* (ed) King John (Folio Society), 1973. *Address:* c/o Harriet Cruickshank, 97 Old South Lambeth Road, SW8 1XU.

BURGEN, Sir Arnold (Stanley Vincent), Kt 1976; FRCP 1969; FRS 1964; President, Academia Europaea, since 1988; Master of Darwin College, Cambridge, 1982–89; Deputy Vice-Chancellor, Cambridge University, 1985–89; *b* 20 March 1922; *s* of late Peter Burgen and Elizabeth Wolfers; *m* 1946, Judith Browne; two *s* one *d*. *Educ:* Christ's Coll., Finchley. Student, Middlesex Hospital Med. Sch., 1939–45; MRCP 1946. Ho. Phys., Middlesex Hospital, 1945; Demonstrator, 1945–48, Asst Lectr, 1948–49, in Pharmacology, Middlesex Hospital Med. Sch. Prof. of Physiology, McGill Univ., Montreal, 1949–62; Dep. Dir, Univ. Clinic, Montreal Gen. Hospital, 1957–62; Sheild Prof. of Pharmacology, Univ. of Cambridge, 1962–71; Fellow of Downing Coll., Cambridge, 1962–71, Hon. Fellow 1972; Dir, Nat. Inst. for Med. Res., 1971–82. Medical Research Council: Member, 1969–71, 1973–77; Hon. Dir, Molecular Pharmacology Unit, 1967–72; Chm., Tropical Medicine Res. Bd, 1977–81; Assessor, 1985–86. Pres., Internat. Union of Pharmacology, 1972–75; Member: Council, Royal Soc., 1972–73, 1980–86 (Vice Pres., 1980–86; Foreign Sec., 1981–86); Nat. Biol. Standards Bd, 1975–78; Med. Cttee, British Council, 1973–77; Gen. Cttee, ICSU, 1982–88; Exec. Cttee, Eur. Science Foundn, 1985–90; Chm., Adv. Cttee on Irradiated and Novel Foods, 1982–87. Dir, Amersham Internat., 1985–. Trustee, CIBA Foundn, 1985–. Academico Correspondiente, Royal Acad. of Spain, 1983; Mem., Deutsche Akad. der Naturforscher Leopoldina, 1984. Hon. Fellow, Wolfson Coll., Oxford, 1990. Hon. DSc: Leeds, 1973; McGill, 1973; Liverpool, 1989; Hon. MD: Utrecht, 1983; Zürich, 1983. DUniv. Surrey, 1983. Hon. FRCP (C); Hon. Mem., Amer. Assoc. of Physicians; Academician of Finland, 1990. *Publications:* Physiology of Salivary Glands, 1961; papers in Journals of Physiology and Pharmacology. *Recreation:* sculpture. *Address:* 2 Stukeley Close, Cambridge CB3 9LT.

BURGER, Warren Earl; Chief Justice of the United States, 1969–86; Chairman, Commission on the Bicentennial of the United States Constitution, since 1985; *b* St Paul, Minn, 17 Sept. 1907; *s* of Charles Joseph Burger and Katharine Schnittger; *m* 1933, Elvera Stromberg; one *s* one *d*. *Educ:* Univ. of Minnesota; St Paul Coll. of Law, later Mitchell Coll. of Law (LLB *magna cum laude*, LLD). Admitted to Bar of Minnesota, 1931; Mem. Faculty, Mitchell Coll. of Law, 1931–46. Partner in Faricy, Burger, Moore & Costello until 1953. Asst Attorney-Gen. of US, 1953–56; Judge, US Court of Appeals, Washington, DC, 1956–69. Chm., ABA Proj. Standards for Criminal Justice. Past Lectr, Law Schools in US and Europe. Hon. Master of the Bench of the Middle Temple, 1969. Pres. Bentham Club, UCL, 1972–73. Chancellor and Regent, Smithsonian Instn, Washington, DC; Hon. Chm., Inst. of Judicial Admin; Trustee: Nat. Gall. of Art, Washington, DC; Nat. Geographic Soc.; Trustee Emeritus: Mitchell Coll. of Law, St Paul, Minn; Macalester Coll., St Paul, Minn; Mayo Foundn, Rochester, Minn. *Publications:* articles in legal and professional jls. *Address:* c/o Supreme Court, Washington, DC 20543, USA.

BURGES, Alan; *see* Burges, N. A.

BURGES, Mrs (Margaret) Betty (Pierpoint), MBE 1937; Headmistress, Staines Preparatory School, 1973–88; Chairman, Surrey County Council Conservative Group, 1981–84; *d* of Frederick Eales Hanson and Margaret Pierpoint Hanson (*née* Hurst); *m* 1937, Cyril Travers Burges, MA (*d* 1975). *Educ:* Edgbaston High Sch., Birmingham. Civil Service, 1929–37 and 1940–45. Councillor, Surrey County Council, 1967–85; Chairman, General Purposes Cttee, 1974–84. *Recreations:* walking, travel. *Address:* 7 Gresham Road, Staines, Mddx TW18 2BT. *T:* Staines (0784) 452852.

BURGES, (Norman) Alan, CBE 1980; MSc, PhD; FIBiol; FLS; Vice-Chancellor, New University of Ulster, Coleraine, Northern Ireland, 1966–76; *b* 5 Aug. 1911; *s* of late Lieut J. C. Burges, East Maitland, NSW; *m* 1940, Florence Evelyn (*née* Moulton); three *d*. *Educ:* Sydney Univ., Australia (represented Sydney and Combined Australian Univs at athletics, 1932); Emmanuel Coll., Cambridge. Graduated, Sydney, BSc Hons., 1931; MSc, 1932; PhD Cambridge, 1937. Senior 1851 Scholar, 1937. Research Fellow, Emmanuel Coll., 1938; Prof. of Botany, Sydney Univ., 1947–52; Dean of Faculty of Science and Fellow of Senate, 1949–52; Holbrook Gaskell Prof. of Botany, Univ. of Liverpool, 1952–66, Acting Vice-Chancellor, 1964–65; Pro-Vice-Chancellor, 1965–66. Hon. Gen. Sec., ANZAAS, 1947–52; President: British Ecological Soc., 1958, 1959; British Mycological Soc., 1962; Mem. Cttee, Nature Conservancy, England, 1959–66; Mem., Waste Management Adv. Council; Joint Editor, Flora Europæa Project, 1956–. Chm., NI Adv. Council for Education, 1966–75; Chairman: Ulster American Folk Park, 1975–; NI American Bicentennial Cttee, 1975–77; Scots Irish Trust, 1977–; Chm., Nat. Trust NI Cttee, 1978–81. Mem., Acad. Adv. Cttee, Loughborough Univ., 1967–71. Served War of 1939–45, RAF Bomber Command (despatches). Hon. LLD QUB, 1973; Hon. DTech Loughborough, 1975; Hon. DSc Ulster, 1977. *Publications:* Micro-organisms in the Soil, 1958; (with F. Raw) Soil Biology, 1967; reports: Primary Educn in Northern Ireland, 1968; Existing Selection Procedure for Secondary Educn in Northern Ireland, 1971; Reorganisation of Secondary Educn in Northern Ireland, 1973; various in scientific journals on plant diseases and fungi. *Recreation:* sailing. *Address:* Beechcroft, Glenkeen Road, Aghadowey, Coleraine, Co. LondonderryBT51 4BN. *T:* Aghadowey (0265) 868224. *Club:* Royal Air Force.

BURGES, Maj.-Gen. Rodney Lyon Travers, CBE 1963; DSO 1946; *b* 19 March 1914; *s* of Richard Burges and Hilda Christine Burges (*née* Lyon); *m* 1946, Sheila Marion Lyster Goldby (*d* 1991), *d* of H. L. Goldby; one *d* (one *s* decd). *Educ:* Wellington; RMA, Woolwich. 2nd Lieut RA, 1934; war service in Burma, 1942 and 1944–45; CO The Berkshire Yeomanry (145 Fd Regt, RA), 1945; Comdr, E Battery, RHA, 1949–51; Bt Lt-Col 1953; 2nd in comd, 1 RHA, 1954–55; CO 3 RHA, 1955–57; CRA 3 Div., 1958–59; IDC, 1960; Brig. Q (Ops) WO, 1961–63; CCRA, 1 Corps, BAOR, 1963–64; Maj.-Gen. 1964; GOC, Cyprus District, 1964–66; VQMG, MoD, 1966–67. Joined Grieveson, Grant & Co., 1968, Partner 1971, retd 1978; Consultant to Pat Simon Wines Ltd, 1978–85; Dir, Caroline Fine Wines Ltd, 1982–85. Freeman and Liveryman, Fishmongers' Co., 1974. *Recreations:* racing, drinking wine in the sun. *Address:* Freemantle, Over Wallop, Hants SO20 8JE. *Clubs:* Buck's, Army and Navy.

BURGES WATSON, Richard Eagleson Gordon; *see* Watson, R. E. G. B.

BURGESS, Anthony, BA; Hon. DLitt; novelist and critic; *b* 25 Feb. 1917; *s* of Joseph Wilson and Elizabeth Burgess; *m* 1942, Llewela Isherwood Jones, BA (*d* 1968); *m* 1968, Liliana Macellari, *d* of Contessa Maria Lucrezia Pasi della Pergola; one *s*. *Educ:* Xaverian Coll., Manchester; Manchester Univ. Served Army, 1940–46. Lecturer: Birmingham Univ. Extra-Mural Dept., 1946–48; Ministry of Education, 1948–50; English Master, Banbury Grammar Sch., 1950–54; Education Officer, Malaya and Brunei, 1954–59. Vis. Fellow, Princeton Univ., 1970–71; Distinguished Prof., City Coll., NY, 1972–73. Hon. DLitt Manchester, 1982. Commandeur: de Mérite Culturel, Monaco, 1986; des Arts et des Lettres, France, 1986. TV scripts: Moses the Lawgiver and Jesus of Nazareth (series), 1977; Blooms of Dublin, 1982 (a musical for radio). *Publications:* Time for a Tiger, 1956; The Enemy in the Blanket, 1958; Beds in the East, 1959 (these three, as The Malayan Trilogy, 1972, and as The Long Day Wanes, 1982); The Right to an Answer, 1960; The Doctor is Sick, 1960; The Worm and the Ring, 1961; Devil of a State, 1961; A Clockwork Orange, 1962 (filmed, 1971, adapted for stage, 1990); The Wanting Seed, 1962; Honey for the Bears, 1963; The Novel Today, 1963; Language Made Plain, 1964; Nothing like the Sun, 1964; The Eve of Saint Venus, 1964; A Vision of Battlements, 1965; Here Comes Everybody—an introduction to James Joyce, 1965; Tremor of Intent, 1966; A Shorter Finnegans Wake, 1966; The Novel Now, 1967; Enderby Outside, 1968; Urgent Copy, 1968; Shakespeare, 1970; MF, 1971; Joysprick, 1973; Napoleon Symphony, 1974; The Clockwork Testament, 1974; Moses, 1976; A Long Trip to Teatime, 1976; Beard's Roman Women, 1976; ABBA ABBA, 1977; New York, 1977; L'Homme de Nazareth, 1977 (Man of Nazareth, 1979); Ernest Hemingway and His World, 1978; 1985, 1978; They Wrote in English (Italy), 1979; The Land Where the Ice Cream Grows, 1979; Earthly Powers, 1980; On Going to Bed, 1982; This Man and Music, 1982; The End of the World News, 1982; Enderby's Dark Lady, 1984; Ninety-Nine Novels, 1984; The Kingdom of the Wicked, 1985; Flame into Being, 1985; The Pianoplayers, 1986; Homage to Qwert Yuiop, (essays), 1986; Little Wilson and Big God, (autobiog.), 1987; Any Old Iron, 1989; The Devil's Mode, 1989; You've Had Your Time (autobiog.), 1990; *translations of stage plays:* (trans. Rostand) Cyrano de Bergerac, 1971; (trans. Sophocles) Oedipus the King, 1973; *translation of libretto:* Carmen, 1986; as *Joseph Kell:* One Hand Clapping, 1961; Inside Mr Enderby, 1963; as *John Burgess Wilson:* English Literature: A Survey for Students, 1958; contributor to Observer, Spectator, Listener, Encounter, Queen, Times Literary Supplement, Hudson Review, Holiday, Playboy, American Scholar, Corriere della Sera, Le Monde, etc. *Recreations:* music composition, piano-playing, cooking, language-learning. *Address:* 44 rue Grimaldi, MC 98000, Monaco; 1 and 2 Piazza Padella, Bracciano, Italy; 168 Triq Il-Kbira, Lija, Malta.

BURGESS, Anthony Reginald Frank, (Tony), CVO 1983; HM Diplomatic Service, retired; Counsellor and Head of Chancery, Havana, 1986–89; *b* 27 Jan. 1932; *s* of Beatrice Burgess; *m* 1960, Carlyn Shawyer; one *s*. *Educ:* Ealing Grammar Sch.; University College London (BScEcon). National Service, 1953–55; TA, 16 Airborne Div., 1955–57. Journalism, 1955–62; European Community Civil Service, 1962–65; HM Diplomatic Service, 1966–: 1st Sec., European Economic Organisations Dept, FCO, 1966–67; 1st Sec. (Political), Dhaka, 1967–69; 1st Sec., SE Asia Dept, FCO, 1970–72; 1st Sec. (Economic), Ottawa, 1972–76; Head of Chancery and HM Consul, Bogota, 1976–79; 1st Sec., Rhodesia Dept, FCO, 1979–80; Asst Head of Information Dept, FCO, 1980–82; Dep. High Comr, Dhaka, 1982–86. *Publication:* (jtly) The Common Market and the Treaty of Rome Explained, 1967. *Recreations:* travel, photography, shooting, riding. *Address:* c/o Barclays Bank, 23 St James's Street, SW1A 1HE. *Club:* Brooks's.

BURGESS, Averil; Headmistress, South Hampstead High School, GPDST, since 1975; *b* 8 July 1938; *d* of David and Dorothy Evans (*née* Owen); *m* 1959, Clifford Burgess (marr. diss. 1973). *Educ:* Ashby-de-la-Zouch Girls' Grammar Sch.; Queen Mary Coll., Univ. of London. BA Hons History. Assistant Mistress: Langleybury Secondary Modern Sch., 1959–60; Ensham Sch., 1960–62; Hatfield Sch., 1963–65; Fulham County Sch., 1965–69; Wimbledon High Sch., GPDST, 1969–74 (Head of History and Second Mistress). Chm., Policy Gp, ISJC, 1990–; Member: Bursaries Management Cttee, GPDST, 1979–86; Council for Accreditation of Teacher Educn, 1990–; Girls' Schools Association: Chm., Educn Sub-Cttee, 1984–88 (Mem., 1983–88); Mem., Exec. Cttee, 1984–91; Pres., 1988–89. Governor, Central Sch. of Speech and Drama, 1981–. *Recreations:* visiting France, listening to music (especially opera), mountain walking in Wales and other forms of non-competitive exercise. *Address:* South Hampstead High School, 3 Maresfield Gardens, NW3 5SS. *T:* 071–435 2899.

BURGESS, Claude Bramall, CMG 1958; OBE 1954; Minister for Hong Kong Commercial Relations with the European Communities and the Member States, 1974–82; *b* 25 Feb. 1910; *s* of late George Herbert Burgess, Weaverham, Cheshire, and Martha Elizabeth Burgess; *m* 1952, Margaret Joan Webb (marr. diss. 1965); one *s*; *m* 1969, Linda Nettleton, *e d* of William Grothier Beilby, New York. *Educ:* Epworth Coll.; Christ Church, Oxford. Eastern Cadetship in HM Colonial Administrative Service, 1932. Commissioned in RA, 1940; POW, 1941–45; demobilized with rank of Lieut-Col, RA, 1946. Colonial Office, 1946–48. Attended Imperial Defence Coll., London, 1951. Various Government posts in Hong Kong; Colonial Secretary (and Actg Governor on various occasions), Hong Kong, 1958–63, retd; Head of Co-ordination and Develt Dept, EFTA, 1964–73. *Address:* 75 Chester Row, SW1. *T:* 071–730 8758.

BURGESS, Cyril Duncan, CB 1989; ERD 1970; Chairman, Council for Registered Gas Installers, since 1991; *b* 18 Oct. 1929; *s* of John Arthur Burgess and Doris (*née* Sedgwick); *m* 1954, Jean Kathleen Whitney; one *s* one *d*. *Educ:* Southgate County Grammar Sch.; Univ. of London (BSc). CChem; MRSC. National Service, Royal Signals, 1950. Asst Engineer, English Electric Co., 1952; HM Factory Inspectorate, 1953; served in London and Huddersfield; Sup. Inspector, Scotland, 1974; Sec., Adv. Cttee on Asbestos, 1976; Dir, Hazardous Substances Div., HSE, 1978–89. Chm., Adv. Cttees on Dangerous Substances, 1982, on Toxic Substances, 1985. *Address:* 108 Gravel Lane, Hemel Hempstead, Herts HP1 1SB. *T:* Hemel Hempstead (0442) 253054.

BURGESS, Rev. David John; Guild Vicar of St Lawrence Jewry Next Guildhall, The Church of the Corporation of London, since 1987; a Chaplain to The Queen, since 1987; *b* 4 Aug. 1939; *e s* of Albert Burgess and Mary Burgess (*née* Kelsey); *m* 1976, Dr Kathleen Louise, *d* of Philip Lindsay Costeloe; one *s* one *d*. *Educ:* King's School, Peterborough; Trinity Hall, Cambridge; Cuddesdon Theological Coll. Orthodox Studentship, Halki, Istanbul, 1963–64. Curate, All Saints, Maidstone, 1965; Assistant Chaplain, University Coll., Oxford, 1966; Fellow, 1969; Chaplain, 1970; Domestic Bursar, 1971; Canon of St George's Chapel, Windsor, 1978–87. Hon. Fellow, Inst. of Clerks of Works, 1978; Churchill Hon. Fellow, Westminster Coll., Fulton, Miss, 1989. *Publications:* articles and reviews. *Recreations:* opera, art, cooking. *Address:* The Vicarage, St Lawrence Jewry Next Guildhall, EC2V 5AA. *T:* 071–600 9478.

BURGESS, Dilys Averil; *see* Burgess, A.

BURGESS, Gen. Sir Edward (Arthur), KCB 1982; OBE 1972; Deputy Supreme Allied Commander, Europe, 1984–87; Aide-de-Camp General to the Queen, 1985–87; *b* 30 Sept. 1927; *s* of Edward Burgess and Alice Burgess; *m* 1954, Jean Angelique Leslie Henderson; one *s* one *d*. *Educ:* All Saints Sch., Bloxham; Lincoln Coll., Oxford; RMA, Sandhurst. Commnd RA 1948; served Germany and ME, 1949–59; psc 1960; GSO 2 WO, 1961–63; served Germany and Far East, 1963–65; jssc 1966; Mil. Asst to C-in-C BAOR, 1966–67; GSO I (DS) Staff Coll., 1968–70; CO 25 Light Regt, RA, 1970–72; CRA 4th Div., 1972–74; Dir of Army Recruiting, 1975–77; Dir, Combat Development (Army), 1977–79; GOC Artillery Div., 1979–82; Comdr, UK Field Army, and Inspector Gen. TA, 1982–84. Gentleman Usher to the Sword of State, 1988–. Col Comdt, RA, 1982–. President: Royal British Legion, 1987–; Army Football Assoc., 1982–88; Hon. Vice Pres., FA, 1982–88. *Publications:* articles in military jls. *Recreations:* sailing, fishing, music, reading, gardening. *Address:* c/o Lloyds Bank, Haslemere, Surrey. *Club:* Army and Navy.

BURGESS, Geoffrey Harold Orchard; Chief Scientist (Agriculture and Horticulture), Ministry of Agriculture, Fisheries and Food, 1982–86; *b* 28 March 1926; *s* of late Harold Frank and Eva M. F. Burgess, Reading; *m* 1952, Barbara Vernon, *y d* of late Rev. Gilbert Vernon Yonge; two *s*. *Educ:* Reading Sch.; Univ. of Reading; UC Hull. BSc Reading, 1951 (Colin Morley Prizewinner 1950); PhD London, 1955. Special research appt, Univ. of Hull, 1951; Sen. Scientific Officer, DSIR, Humber Lab., Hull, 1954; PSO, Torry Res. Stn, Aberdeen, 1960; Officer i/c, Humber Lab., Hull, 1962; Director, Torry Res. Station, 1969–79; Head of Biology Div., Agrictl Science Service, and Officer i/c Slough Lab., MAFF, 1979–82. Hon. Res. Lectr in Fish Technology, Univ. of Aberdeen, 1969–79; Buckland Lectr, 1964; Hon. Lectr in Fish Technology, Univ. of Leeds, 1966–69; Mem. Adv. Cttee on Food Science, Univ. of Leeds, 1970–86; Mem., Panel of Fish Technology Experts, FAO, 1962–79. *Publications:* Developments in the Handling and Processing of Fish, 1965; (with Lovern, Waterman and Cutting) Fish Handling and Processing, 1965; The Curious World of Frank Buckland, 1967; scientific and technical papers, reviews, reports etc concerning handling, processing, transport and preservation for food, of fish, from catching to consumption. *Recreations:* music, book collecting, walking. *Address:* Stoneleghe, Croxton, Stafford ST21 6NL. *T:* Wetwood (063082) 202.

BURGESS, Geoffrey Kelsen; Chief Executive and Clerk, Cornwall County Council, since 1982 (Deputy Clerk, 1969–82); *b* 4 June 1935; *s* of Murray and Edith Burgess; *m* 1959, Brenda (*née* Martin); three *s*. *Educ:* Central Foundn Boys' Grammar Sch.; London Sch. of Econs and Pol Science (LLB). Admitted solicitor, 1959. Articled with Simon, Haynes, Barlas & Cassels, London, 1956–59; Assistant Solicitor: East Ham CBC, 1960–62; Worcs CC, 1962–63; Northumberland CC, 1963–65; Asst Clerk, Berks CC, 1965–69; Clerk: Devon and Cornwall Police Authy; Cornwall Magistrates' Courts Cttee; Cornwall Sea Fisheries Cttee; Secretary: Adv. Cttee on appt of Magistrates; Cornwall Probation Cttee. *Recreations:* music, walking. *Address:* c/o Cornwall County Council, County Hall, Truro TR1 3AY. *T:* Truro (0872) 74282.

BURGESS, Rear-Adm. John, CB 1987; LVO 1975; CEng; Director, Rolls-Royce and Associates, since 1987; *b* 13 July 1929; *s* of Albert Burgess and Winifred (*née* Evans); *m* 1952, Avis (*née* Morgan); two *d*. *Educ:* RN Engineering College; Advanced Engineering RN College, Greenwich; nuclear courses, RN College. HM Ships Aisne, Maidstone, Theseus, Implacable, Cumberland, Caprice; Lectr in Thermodynamics, RNEC, 1962–65; HMS Victorious; nuclear reactor design and manufacture at Rolls Royce, 1968–70; Naval Staff, Washington, DC, 1970–72; Royal Yacht Britannia, 1972–75; Head, Forward Design Group, Ship Dept, 1975–77; Naval Asst to Controller of the Navy, 1977–79; in Command, HMS Defiance, 1979–81; in Command, HMS Sultan, 1981–83; Man. Dir, HM Dockyard, Rosyth, 1984–87. *Publications:* papers to professional bodies. *Recreations:* golf, sailing.

BURGESS, Ven. John Edward; Archdeacon of Bath, since 1975; *b* 9 Dec. 1930; *s* of Herbert and Dorothy May Burgess; *m* 1958, Jonquil Marion Bailey; one *s* one *d*. *Educ:* Surbiton County Gram. Sch.; London Univ. (St John's Hall). BD (2nd Cl.), ALCD (1st Cl.). Shell Chemicals Ltd, 1947–53. Asst Curate, St Mary Magdalen, Bermondsey, 1957–60; Asst Curate, St Mary, Southampton, 1960–62; Vicar of Dunston with Coppenhall, Staffs, 1962–67; Chaplain, Staffordshire Coll. of Technology, 1963–67; Vicar of Keynsham with Queen Charlton and Burnett, Somerset, 1967–75; Rural Dean of Keynsham, 1971–74. *Recreation:* history of railways. *Address:* Birnfels, 56 Grange Road, Saltford, Bristol BS18 3AG. *T:* Saltford (0225) 873609, *Fax:* 0225 874110.

BURGESS, (Joseph) Stuart, CBE 1984; PhD; FRSC; Chairman, Oxford Regional Health Authority, since 1990; Advisor, Immuno International AG, since 1990; *b* 20 March 1929; *s* of late Joseph and Emma Burgess (*née* Wollerton); *m* 1955, Valerie Ann Street; one *s* one *d*. *Educ:* Barnsley Holgate Grammar School; University College London (1st Class Hons BSc Chem, PhD). Amersham International plc (formerly The Radiochemical Centre), 1953–89: Gp Marketing Controller, 1977–79; Chief Exec., 1979–89; Pres., Amersham Corp. USA, 1975–77. Dir, American Chamber of Commerce (UK), 1988–90. Mem., Innovation Adv. Bd, DTI, 1988–; Chm., Res. and Manufacturing Cttee, CBI, 1990–. CBIM 1986. *Recreations:* golf, music. *Address:* Barrington, Hearn Close, Penn, Bucks HP10 8JT. *T:* Penn (049481) 6387.

BURGESS, Sally, (Mrs N. S. Thornton); classical singer; *b* 9 Oct. 1953; *d* of Edna Rushton (formerly Burgess; *née* Sharman) and Douglas Burgess; *m* 1988, Neal Scott Thornton; one *s*. *Educ:* Royal College of Music. ARCM. Joined ENO 1977; for ENO as a soprano, rôles incl. Zerlina, Cherubino, Pamina, Mimi, Micaela; for ENO as a mezzo, rôles incl. Composer (Ariadne), Octavian, Sextus (Julius Caesar), Charlotte (Werther), Carmen, Fennimore (Fennimore and Gerda), 1990, Judith (Duke Bluebeard's Castle), 1991; for Opera North, Amneris (Aida), Dido (Trojans), Julie (Showboat), 1989–90, Orfeo (Glück), 1990; Smeraldina in Love for Three Oranges, Glyndebourne; Siebel (Faust), Maddalena (Rigoletto), Covent Garden, 1989; Amneris, Strasbourg, Wiesbaden, Lausanne and Nancy; numerous recordings. *Recreations:* family, cooking, walking, reading, singing jazz, theatre. Address: c/o Harrison/Parrott, 12 Penzance Place, W11 4PA.

BURGESS, Stuart; *see* Burgess, J. S.

BURGESS, Tony; *see* Burgess, A. R. F.

BURGH, 7th Baron, *cr* 1529 (title called out of abeyance, 1916; by some reckonings he is 9th Baron (from a *cr* 1487) and his father was 8th and grandfather 7th); **Alexander Peter Willoughby Leith;** *b* 20 March 1935; *s* of 6th (or 8th) Baron Burgh; *S* father 1959; *m* 1957, Anita Lorna Eldridge; two *s* one *d*. *Educ:* Harrow; Magdalene Coll., Cambridge (BA). *Heir:* *s* Hon. Alexander Gregory Disney Leith [*b* 16 March 1958; *m* 1984, Catherine Mary, *d* of David Parkes; one *s*].

BURGH, Sir John (Charles), KCMG 1982; CB 1975; President, Trinity College, University of Oxford, since 1987; Chairman, Associated Board of the Royal Schools of Music, since 1987; Director-General, British Council, 1980–87; *b* 9 Dec. 1925; *m* 1957, Ann Sturge; two *d*. *Educ:* Friends' Sch., Sibford; London Sch. of Economics (BSc Econ.; Leverhulme post-intermediate Schol.; Pres. of Union, 1949; Hon. Fellow, 1983). Asst Principal, BoT, 1950; Private Sec. to successive Ministers of State, BoT, 1954–57; Colonial Office, 1959–62; Mem., UK Delegation to UN Conf. on Trade and Develt, 1964; Asst Sec., DEA, 1964; Principal Private Sec. to successive First Secretaries of State and Secretaries of State for Econ. Affairs, 1965–68; Under-Sec., Dept of Employment, 1968–71; Dep.-Chm., Community Relations Commn, 1971–72; Deputy Secretary: Cabinet Office (Central Policy Rev. Staff), 1972–74; Dept of Prices and Consumer Protection, 1974–79; Dept of Trade, 1979–80. Member: Executive, PEP, 1972–78; Council, Policy Studies Inst., 1978–85; Council, RSA, 1982–85; Council, VSO, 1980–87; Acad. Council, Wilton Park, 1984–87; Exec. Cttee, Anglo-Austrian Soc., 1987–. Chairman: Nat. Opera Co-ordinating Cttee, 1991– (Sec., 1972–91); Oxford Educnl Trust for Develt of the Arts, 1991–; Dir, English Shakespeare Co., 1988–. Chm. Ct of Governors, LSE, 1985–87 (Gov., 1980–). Hon. RNCM 1986. Hon. LLD Bath, 1987. *Recreations:* friends, music, the arts generally. *Address:* Trinity College, Oxford OX1 3BH. *Club:* United Oxford & Cambridge University.

BURGHERSH, Lord; Anthony David Francis Henry Fane; *b* 1 Aug. 1951; *s* and *heir* of 15th Earl of Westmorland, *qv*; *m* 1985, Caroline Eldred, *d* of Keon Hughes; one *d*. *Educ:* Eton. Mem., Orbitex North Pole Expedn, 1990. Life Pres., St Moritz Sporting Club. Governor, Guild of Veteran Pilots and Racing Drivers. *Address:* London SW6 2AT.

BURGHLEY, Lord; Anthony John Cecil; *b* 9 Aug. 1970; *s* and *heir* of Marquess of Exeter, *qv*. *Educ:* Eton.

BURGNER, Thomas Ulric; Secretary, Committee of Vice Chancellors and Principals, since 1989; *b* 6 March 1932; *s* of John Henry Burgner and Clara Doerte Burgner (*née* Wolff); *m* 1958, Marion (*née* Chasik); two *s*. *Educ:* Haberdashers' Aske's, Hampstead; St Catharine's Coll., Cambridge (BA (Hons), MA); Dip. Personnel Management. Flying Officer, RAF, 1954–55. National Coal Board, 1955–61; Assoc. of Chemical and Allied Employers, 1961–65; Principal, Dept of Economic Affairs, 1965–69; HM Treasury: Principal, 1969–72; Asst Secretary, 1972–76; Head of Exchange Control Div., 1972–74; Head of General Aid Div., 1974–76; Under Secretary, 1976; on secondment as Sec., NEDC, 1976–80; Head of Public Enterprises Gp, 1980–85; Head, Industry, Agric. and Employment Gp, 1985–89. Mem., BSC, 1980–83. *Address:* CVCP, 29 Tavistock Square, WC1H 9EZ.

BURGON, Geoffrey; composer; *b* 15 July 1941; *s* of Alan Wybert Burgon and Ada Vera Isom; *m* 1963, Janice Elizabeth Garwood (marr. diss.); one *s* one *d*. *Educ:* Pewley Sch., Guildford; Guildhall School of Music and Drama; studied composition with Peter Wishart, trumpet with Bernard Brown. Freelance trumpeter, 1964–71: Royal Opera House (stage band), Philomusica, London Mozart Players, Northern Sinfonia, Jacques and Capriol Orchestras, also session work, theatres and jazz bands. Full time composer and conductor, 1971–; work in almost every musical genre, particularly orchestral, choral, and music for dance, film & TV; commissions from many Festivals, incl. Bath, Edinburgh, Cheltenham, Southern Cathedrals, Three Choirs, and Camden; also many works for Dance, incl. Ballet Rambert and London Contemporary Dance Theatre; work performed internationally. *Major works:* Gending; Alleluia Nativitas; The World Again; Acquainted with Night; Think on Dreadful Domesday; Canciones del Alma; Requiem; Revelations; Title Divine; Short Mass; The Golden Eternity; The Fire of Heaven, Dos Coros; A Hymn to the Creatures; The Golden Fish; The Calm; Running Figures; Goldbergs Dream; Songs, Lamentations and Praises; Mass; The Trials of Prometheus; Hymn to Venus; Five Sonnets of John Donne; Four Guitars; Six Studies for Solo Cello; Worldes Blisse; *film scores:* Life of Brian; Dogs of War; Turtle Diary; *television scores:* Tinker, Tailor, Soldier, Spy; Brideshead Revisited; Bleak House; Happy Valley; Chronicles of Narnia; Children of the North. Prince Pierre of Monaco Award, 1969; Ivor Novello Award, 1979, 1981; Gold Disc for Brideshead record, 1986. *Recreations:* playing jazz, cricket, Bristol motor cars, sleeping. *Address:* c/o Chester Music, 8/9 Frith Street, W1V 5TZ. *T:* 071–434 0066.

BURGOYNE, Rear-Adm. Robert Michael, CB 1982; Director, Royal Institute of Navigation, since 1983; *b* 20 March 1927; *s* of Robert and Elizabeth Burgoyne; *m* 1951, Margaret (Hilda) McCook; one *s* one *d*. *Educ:* Bradfield College; Magdalene College, Cambridge. Joined RN 1945; CO HMS Cleopatra, 1967–68; Captain 2nd Frigate Sqdn and CO HMS Undaunted, 1972–73; Dir, Maritime Tactical Sch., 1974–75; CO HMS Antrim, 1975–77; Comdr, British Navy Staff, Washington and UK Rep. to SACLANT, 1977–80; Senior Naval Member, Directing Staff, RCDS, 1980–82. *Address:* c/o Midland Bank, Gerrards Cross, Bucks SL9 8PH.

BURKE, Adm. Arleigh Albert; Navy Cross; DSM (3 Gold Stars); Legion of Merit (with 2 Gold Stars and Army Oak Leaf Cluster). Silver Star Medal, Purple Heart, Presidential Unit Citation Ribbon (with 3 stars), Navy Unit Commendation Ribbon; retired as Chief of Naval Operations, US Navy and Member of Joint Chiefs of Staff (1955–61); Member of Board of Directors, Freedoms Foundation, at Valley Forge; *b* 19 Oct. 1901; *s* of Oscar A. and Claire Burke; *m* 1923, Roberta Gorsuch; no *c*. *Educ:* United States Naval Academy; Univ. of Michigan (MSE). Commnd ensign, USN, 1923, advancing through grades to Admiral, 1955. USS Arizona, 1923–28; Gunnery Dept, US Base Force, 1928; Post-graduate course (explosives), 1929–31; USS Chester, 1932; Battle Force Camera Party, 1933–35; Bureau of Ordnance, 1935–37; USS Craven, 1937–39; USS Mugford, Captain, 1939–40; Naval Gun Factory, 1940–43; Destroyer Divs 43 and 44, Squadron 12 Comdg, 1943; Destroyer Squadron 23 Comdg, 1943–44; Chief of Staff to Commander Task Force 58 (Carriers), 1944–45; Head of Research and Development Bureau of Ordnance, 1945–46; Chief of Staff, Comdr Eighth Fleet and Atlantic Fleet, 1947–48; USS Huntington, Captain, 1949; Asst Chief of Naval Ops, 1949–50; Cruiser Div. 5, Comdr, 1951; Dep. Chief of Staff, Commander Naval Forces, Far East, 1951; Director Strategic Plans Div., Office of the Chief of Naval Operations, 1952–53; Cruiser Division 6, Commanding, 1954; Commander Destroyer Force, Atlantic, 1955. Member: American Legion; American Soc. of Naval Engineers and numerous other naval assocs, etc.; National Geographic Society; also foreign societies, etc. Holds several hon. degrees. Ul Chi Medal (Korea), 1954; Korean Presidential Unit Citation, 1954. *Recreations:* reading, gardening. *Address:* The Virginian, Apt 323, 9229 Arlington Boulevard, Fairfax, Va 22031, USA. *Clubs:* Army-Navy Town, Metropolitan, Chevy Chase, Alfalfa, Circus Saints and Sinners, Ends of the Earth, etc (Washington, DC); Quindecum (Newport, US); The Brook, Lotos, Salmagundi, Inner Wheel, Seawanhaka Corinthian Yacht (New York); Bohemian (San Francisco).

BURKE, Hon. Brian Thomas, AC 1988; JP; Australian Ambassador to Republic of Ireland and to the Holy See, since 1988; *b* 25 Feb. 1947; *s* of late Thomas Burke (Federal ALP Member for Perth, 1942–53), and Madeline Burke; *m* 1965, Susanne May Nevill; four *s* two *d*. *Educ:* Brigidine Convent; Marist Brothers' Coll.; Univ. of Western Australia. FAMI. Former journalist. MLA (Lab) Balga, WA, 1973–88; Opposition Shadow Minister, 1976–81; Leader of the Opposition, 1981–83; Premier and Treasurer of WA, 1983–88; Minister for: Women's Interests, 1983–87; Public Sector Management, 1987. Mem., numerous community and sporting orgns; former No 1 ticket holder, Perth FC; former Patron, Soccer Fedn of WA. Jaycees Outstanding Young W Australian Award, 1982. *Recreations:* reading, stamp-collecting, writing poetry, swimming, fishing. *Address:* Australian Embassy, FitzWilton House, Wilton Terrace, Dublin 2, Eire; PO Box 1242, West Perth, WA 6005, Australia.

BURKE, Prof. Derek Clissold; Vice-Chancellor, University of East Anglia, since 1987; *b* 13 Feb. 1930; *s* of late Harold Burke and Ivy Ruby (*née* Clissold); *m* 1955, Mary Elizabeth Dukeshire, New York; one *s* three *d. Educ:* Univ. of Birmingham (BSc, PhD, Chemistry). Res. Fellow, Yale Univ., 1953–55; Scientist, Nat. Inst. for Med. Res., London, 1955–60; Lectr and Sen. Lectr, Dept of Biochemistry, Univ. of Aberdeen, 1960–69; Prof. of Biol Scis, 1969–82, Pro-Vice-Chancellor, 1971–73, Univ. of Warwick; Vice-Pres. and Scientific Dir, Allelix Inc., Toronto, 1982–86. Member: MRC Cell Bd, 1976–79; Scientific Cttee, Cancer Res. Campaign, 1979–82 and of Cancer Res. Campaign Bd, 1987–; Europ. Molecular Biol Org., 1980–; Adv. Bd, AFRC Inst. of Food Res., 1989–; Adv. Cttee on Genetic Modification, HSE, 1987–; Chm., Adv. Cttee on Novel Foods and Processes, Dept of Health and MAFF, 1989–; Pres., Soc. for Gen. Microbiology, 1987–90. Editor and Editor in Chief, Journal of General Virology, 1976–87. Trustee, Norfolk and Norwich Fest., 1988–. Hon. LLD Aberdeen 1982. *Publications:* Creation and Evolution (ed and contrib.), 1985; numerous sci. papers on interferon and animal viruses. *Recreations:* music, walking. *Address:* University of East Anglia, Norwich NR4 7TJ. *T:* Norwich (0603) 56161. *Club:* Commonwealth Trust.

BURKE, Rt. Rev. Geoffrey; Titular Bishop of Vagrauta; Auxiliary Bishop of Salford (RC), 1967–88; *b* 31 July 1913; *s* of Dr Peter Joseph Burke and Margaret Mary (*née* Coman). *Educ:* St Bede's Coll., Manchester; Stonyhurst Coll.; Oscott Coll., Birmingham; Downing Coll., Cambridge (MA). Taught History, St Bede's Coll., 1940–66; Prefect of Studies, 1950; Rector, 1966. Consecrated Bishop 29 June 1967. *Address:* St John's Cathedral, 250 Chapel Street, Salford, Lancashire M3 5LL. *T:* 061–834 0333.

BURKE, Sir James (Stanley Gilbert), 9th Bt *cr* 1797 (Ire.), of Marble Hill, Galway; *b* 1 July 1956; *s* of Sir Thomas Stanley Burke, 8th Bt and Susanne Margaretha (*d* 1983), *er d* of Otto Salvisberg, Thun, Switzerland; *S* father, 1989; *m* 1980, Laura, *d* of Domingo Branzuela; one *s* one *d. Heir: s* Martin James Burke, *b* 22 July 1980. *Address:* Lindenbergstrasse 231, CH-5618 Bettwil, Switzerland.

BURKE, Jeffrey Peter, QC 1984; a Recorder of the Crown Court, since 1983; *b* 15 Dec. 1941; *s* of Samuel and Gertrude Burke; *m* 1966, Tessa Rachel Marks; two *s* one *d. Educ:* Shrewsbury Sch.; Brasenose Coll., Oxford (BA 1963). Called to the Bar, Inner Temple, 1964. *Recreations:* football, cricket, wine, books, music. *Address:* 12 Reynolds Close, NW11 7EA. *T:* 081–455 7825. *Clubs:* Economicals AFC; Caledon Cricket.

BURKE, John Kenneth; QC 1985; a Recorder of the Crown Court, since 1980; *b* 4 Aug. 1939; *s* of Kenneth Burke and Madeline Burke; *m* 1962, Margaret Anne (*née* Scattergood); three *d. Educ:* Stockport Grammar Sch. Served Cheshire Regt, 1958–60; TA Parachute Regt, 1962–67. Called to the Bar, Middle Temple, 1965. *Recreations:* painting and drawing, walking. *Address:* 1 Hawthorn View Cottage, Knutsford Road, Mobberley, Cheshire WA16 7BA. *T:* Mobberley (0565) 872627; (chambers) 18 St John Street, Manchester M3 4EA. *T:* 061–834 9843; (chambers) 14 Gray's Inn Square, WC1R 5JD. *T:* 071–242 0858.

BURKE, Sir Joseph (Terence Anthony), KBE 1980 (CBE 1973; OBE 1946); MA; Professor of Fine Arts, University of Melbourne, 1946–78, now Emeritus Professor; Fellow, Trinity College Melbourne, since 1973; Consultant in Art; *b* 14 July 1913; *s* of late R. M. J. Burke; *m* 1940, Agnes, *d* of late Rev. James Middleton, New Brunswick, Canada; one *s. Educ:* Ealing Priory Sch.; King's Coll., Univ. of London; Courtauld Institute of Art; Yale Univ., USA (Henry Fellow, 1936–37). Entered Victoria and Albert Museum, 1938; lent to Home Office and Min. of Home Security, Sept. 1939; private sec. to successive Lord Presidents of the Council (Rt Hon. Sir John Anderson, Rt Hon. C. R. Attlee, Rt Hon. Lord Woolton), 1942–45; and to the Prime Minister (Rt Hon. C. R. Attlee), 1945–46; Trustee of Felton Bequest; Fellow, Australian Acad. of the Humanities, Pres., 1971–73. Hon. DLitt Monash, 1977; Hon. DCL Melbourne. *Publications:* Hogarth and Reynolds: A Contrast in English Art Theory, 1943; ed William Hogarth's Analysis of Beauty and Autobiographical Notes, 1955; (with Colin Caldwell) Hogarth: The Complete Engravings, 1968; vol. IX, Oxford History of English Art, 1714–1800, 1976; articles in Burlington Magazine, Warburg Journal and elsewhere. *Recreations:* reading, nature study. *Address:* Dormers, Falls Road, Mount Dandenong, Victoria 3767, Australia. *Clubs:* Athenæum; Melbourne (Melbourne).

BURKE, Hon. Sir Kerry; *see* Burke, Hon. Sir T. K.

BURKE, Prof. Philip George, PhD; FRS 1978; MRIA 1974; Professor of Mathematical Physics, Queen's University of Belfast, since 1967 (Director, School of Mathematics and Physics, 1988–90); *b* 18 Oct. 1932; *s* of Henry Burke and Frances Mary Sprague; *m* 1959, Valerie Mona Martin; four *d. Educ:* Wanstead County High Sch.; Univ. of Exeter (BSc 1953); University Coll. London (PhD 1956, Fellow 1985). Res. Fellow, UCL, 1956–57; Asst Lectr, Univ. of London Inst. for Computer Science, 1957–59; Res. Fellow, Lawrence Berkeley Lab., Calif, 1959–62; Res. Fellow, then Principal Scientific Officer, later SPSO, Atomic Energy Res. Estabt, Harwell, 1962–67. Science Research Council: Mem., Physics Cttee, 1967–71; Mem., Atlas Comp. Cttee, 1973–76; Hd, Div. of Theory and Computational Sci., SRC (later SERC) Daresbury Lab., 1977–82; Chm., Science Bd Computer Cttee, SERC, 1976–77 and 1984–86; Chm., Scientific Computers Adv. Panel, SERC, 1988–; Mem., SERC, 1989–; Chm., Allocations and Resources Panel, Jt Res. Councils Supercomputer Cttee, 1988–. Mem., Council, Royal Soc., 1990–. Hon. DSc Exeter, 1981. *Publications:* (with H. Kleinpoppen) series editor, Physics of Atoms and Molecules; hon. editor, Computer Physics Communications; many papers in learned journals. *Recreations:* walking, swimming, reading. *Address:* Department of Applied Mathematics and Theoretical Physics, Queen's University of Belfast, Belfast BT7 1NN. *T:* Belfast (0232) 245133, *Fax:* Belfast (0232) 247895; 33 Leverogue Road, Lisburn, N Ireland BT27 5PP. *T:* Drumbo (0232) 826416; Brook House, Norley Lane, Crowton, near Northwich, Cheshire CW8 2RR. *T:* Kingsley (0928) 88301.

BURKE, Richard; President, Canon Foundation in Europe, since 1988; Special Advisor, Ernst and Young, European Community Office, Brussels, since 1985; *b* 29 March 1932; *s* of David Burke and Elisabeth Burke; *m* 1961, Mary Freeley; two *s* three *d. Educ:* University Coll., Dublin (MA). Called to the Bar, King's Inns. Mem., Dublin Co. Council, 1967–73 (Chm., 1972–73); Mem. Dail Eirann, for South County Dublin, 1969–77, for Dublin West, 1981–82; Fine Gael Chief Whip and spokesman on Posts and Telegraphs, 1969–73; Minister for Education, 1973–76. Commission of the European Communities: Member with special responsibility for Transport, Taxation, Consumer Protection, Relations with European Parlt, Research, Educ. and Sci., 1977–81, for Greenland, Greek Memorandum, Personnel and Admin, Jt Interpretation and Conf. Service, Statistical Office and Office of Publications, 1982–85; Vice Pres., 1984–85. Associate Fellow, Center for Internat. Affairs, Harvard Univ., 1980–81. *Recreations:* music, golf, travel. *Address:* 67 Ailesbury Road, Dublin 4, Ireland. *T:* Dublin 692520; (office) 204 Avenue Marcel Thiry, 1200 Brussels, Belgium.

BURKE, Hon. Sir (Thomas) Kerry, Kt 1990; MP (Lab) West Coast, New Zealand, since 1978; Speaker, New Zealand House of Representatives, since 1987; *b* 24 March 1942; *m* 1968, Jennifer Shiel; two *s*; 2nd, 1984, Helen Paske; one *s. Educ:* Linwood High Sch.; Univ. of Canterbury (BA); Christchurch Teachers' Coll. (Dip. Teaching). General labourer, Auckland, 1965–66; factory deleg., Auckland Labourers' Union; teacher: Rangiora High Sch., 1967–72; Greymouth High Sch., 1975–78. Chm., Rangiora Post-Primary Teachers' Assoc., 1969–71. MP (Lab) Rangiora, 1972–75; Minister of Regional Develt, and of Employment and Immigration, 1984–87. *Recreations:* ski-ing, swimming. *Address:* Parliament Buildings, Wellington, New Zealand.

BURKE, Tom; Director, The Green Alliance, since 1982; Special Adviser to Secretary of State for the Environment, since 1991; *b* 5 Jan. 1947; *s* of J. V. Burke, DSM, and Mary (*née* Bradley). *Educ:* St Boniface's, Plymouth; Liverpool Univ. (BA (Hons) Philosophy). Great George's Community Arts Project, 1969–70; Lecturer: West Cheshire Coll., 1970–71; Old Swan Technical Coll., 1971–73; Friends of the Earth: Local Groups Co-ordinator, 1973–75; Executive Director, 1975–79; Dir of Special Projects, 1979–80; Vice-Chm., 1980–81. Press Officer, European Environment Bureau, 1979–87; Sec., Ecological Studies Inst., 1987–. Member: Bd of Dirs, Earth Resources Research, 1975–87; Waste Management Adv. Council, 1976–81; Packaging Council, 1978–82; Exec. Cttee, NCVO, 1984–89; UK Nat. Cttee, European Year of the Environment, 1986–88; Exec. Cttee, European Environment Bureau, 1987–. Royal Humane Society Testimonials: on Vellum, 1966; on Parchment, 1968. Contested (SDP): Brighton Kemptown, 1983; Surbiton, 1987. Hon. Vis. Fellow, Manchester Business Sch., 1984. FRSA (Mem. Council, 1990). *Publications:* Europe: environment, 1981; (jtly) Pressure Groups in the Global System, 1982; (jtly) Ecology 2000, 1984; (jtly) The Green Capitalists, 1987; (jtly) Green Pages, 1988. *Recreations:* photography, birdwatching. *Address:* 36 Crewdson Road, SW9. *T:* 071–735 9019. *Club:* Reform.

BURKE-GAFFNEY, John Campion; Director-General, The British Red Cross Society, 1985–90; *b* 27 Feb. 1932; *s* of late Dr Henry Joseph O'Donnell Burke-Gaffney, OBE and Constance May (*née* Bishop); *m* 1956, Margaret Mary Jennifer (*née* Stacpoole); two *s* two *d. Educ:* Douai School. Called to the Bar, Gray's Inn, 1956. Served: RAC, 1950–52; E Riding of Yorks Imperial Yeomanry (Wenlock's Horse), 1952–56. Shell-Mex and BP Ltd, 1956–75; Shell UK Ltd, 1976–77; Man. Dir, Shell and BP Zambia Ltd, 1977–81; Gp Public Affairs, Shell Internat. Petroleum Co. Ltd, 1981–85. *Address:* c/o Coutts & Co., Park Lane Branch, 1 Old Park Lane, W1A 4AL.
See also M. A. B. Burke-Gaffney.

BURKE-GAFFNEY, Michael Anthony Bowes, QC 1977; a Recorder, since 1986; *b* Dar-es-Salaam, Tanzania, 1 Aug. 1928; *s* of late Henry Joseph O'Donnell Burke-Gaffney, OBE and Constance May (*née* Bishop); *m* 1961, Constance Caroline (*née* Murdoch); two *s* one *d. Educ:* Douai Sch.; RMA, Sandhurst. ACIArb. Commissioned Royal Irish Fusiliers, 1948; served with 1st Bn, Suez Canal Zone, Akaba, Gibraltar, BAOR and Berlin; served with Royal Ulster Rifles, Korean War, 1951, and in Hong Kong; qual. as interpreter in Turkish (studied at London Univ. and in Istanbul), 1955; Staff Captain, HQ 44 Div., 1956–58, when resigned commn and read for the Bar; joined Gray's Inn, 1956 (Lord Justice Holker Sen. Scholar); called to the Bar, 1959; Bencher, 1986. Jun. Counsel to HM Treasury in certain planning matters, 1974–77; a Legal Assessor to GMC and GDC, 1985–. Author, Three Lakes Inquiry Report, 1976; contrib. various articles in legal publications. *Recreations:* family, cricket, wildlife, viniculture. *Address:* Lamb Building, Temple, EC4Y 7AS. *T:* 071–353 6701. *Club:* Naval and Military.
See also J. C. Burke-Gaffney.

BURKETT, Mary Elizabeth, OBE 1978; FRGS; FMA; Director of Abbot Hall Art Gallery, and Museum of Lakeland Life and Industry, 1967–86, and Borough Museum, Kendal, 1977–86; retired; *d* of Ridley Burkett and Mary Alice Gaussen. *Educ:* Univ. of Durham (BA, Teachers' Cert.). FRGS 1978; FMA 1980. Taught art, craft, maths, etc, at Wroxall Abbey, 1948–54; Art and Craft Lectr, Charlotte Mason Coll., Ambleside, 1954–62; seven months in Turkey and Iran, 1962; Asst Dir, Abbot Hall, 1963–66. Formerly part-time Teacher of Art, Bela River Prison. Member: numerous cttees including National Trust (NW Region), 1978–85; Carlisle Diocesan Adv. Cttee, 1980–. Dir, Border Television, 1982–. Round the World trip, lecturing in Hong Kong, Perth (WA), NY as well as seeing the Great Wall of China, 1986. FRSA 1983; Fellow, Huguenot Soc., 1986. Leverhulme Award (to continue research on Lake District portraits), 1986–88. *Publications:* The Art of the Felt Maker, 1979; Kurt Schwitters (in the Lake District), 1979; (with David Sloss) William Green of Ambleside, 1984; contrib. art and archaeol jls, and gall. and museum catalogues. *Recreations:* travel, bird watching, photography, writing, doing research into more Cumbrian artists, lecturing, picking up stones. *Address:* Isel Hall, Cockermouth, Cumbria.

BURKILL, John Charles, ScD; FRS 1953; Honorary Fellow, Peterhouse, Cambridge; Emeritus Reader in Mathematical Analysis; *b* 1 Feb. 1900; *s* of Hugh Roberson Burkill and Bertha Burkill (nee Bourne); *m* 1928, Margareta, (*d* 1984), *d* of Dr Braun; one *s* (two *d* decd). *Educ:* St Paul's; Trinity Coll., Cambridge (Fellow 1922–28). Smith's Prize, 1923; Professor of Pure Mathematics in the University of Liverpool, 1924–29; Fellow of Peterhouse, 1929–67; Master of Peterhouse, 1968–73. Adams Prize, 1949. *Address:* 2 Archway Court, Barton Road, Cambridge CB3 9LW.

BURKITT, Denis Parsons, CMG 1974; MD, FRCSE; FRS 1972; Medical Research Council External Scientific Staff, 1964–76; Hon. Senior Research Fellow, St Thomas's Hospital Medical School, 1976–84; *b* Enniskillen, NI, 28 Feb. 1911; *s* of James Parsons Burkitt and Gwendoline (*née* Hill); *m* 1943, Olive Mary (*née* Rogers); three *d. Educ:* Dean Close Sch., Cheltenham; Dublin Univ. BA 1933; MB, BCh, BAO 1935; FRCSE 1938; MD 1946. Surgeon, RAMC, 1941–46. Joined HM Colonial Service: Govt Surgeon, in Uganda, 1946–64, and Lectr in Surgery, Makerere University Coll. Med. Sch.; final appt: Sen. consultant surgeon to Min. of Health, Uganda, 1961. First described a form of cancer common in children in Africa, now named Burkitt's Lymphoma. Foundn and Hon. Fellow, E Africa Assoc. of Surgeons; Hon. Fellow, Sudan Assoc. of Surgeons; Foreign Associate Mem., Académie des Sciences, France. Former Pres., Christian Medical Fellowship; a Vice-Pres., CMS. Hon. FRCSI, 1973; Hon. FRCPI, 1977. Harrison Prize, ENT Section of RSM, 1966; Stuart Prize, 1966, Gold Medal, 1978, BMA. Arnott Gold Medal, Irish Hosps and Med. Schs Assoc., 1968; Katharine Berkan Judd Award, Sloan-Kettering Inst., New York, 1969; Robert de Villiers Award, Amer. Leukaemia Soc., 1970; Walker Prize for 1966–70, RCS, 1971; Paul Ehrlich-Ludwig Darmstaedter Prize, Paul Ehrlich Foundn, Frankfurt, 1972; Soc. of Apothecaries' Medal, 1972; Albert Lasker Clinical Chemotherapy Award, 1972; Gairdner Foundn Award, 1973; (jtly) Bristol-Myers Award for Cancer Research, 1982; Charles S. Mott Prize, Gen. Motors Cancer Res. Foundn, 1982; Diplôme de Médaille d'Or, Académie de Médecine, France, 1982; Beaumont Bonelli Award for Cancer Research, Beaumont Foundn, Italy, 1983. Hon. FTCD; Hon. MD Bristol, 1979; Hon. DSc: E Africa, 1970; Leeds, 1982; Ulster, 1989;

Hon. DSc (Med) London, 1984. Le Prix Mondiale Cino del Duca, France, 1987. Co-editor, Fibre-depleted Foods and Disease (dietary film), 1985. *Publications:* Co-editor: Treatment of Burkitt's Lymphoma (UICC Monograph 8), 1967; Burkitt's Lymphoma, 1970; Refined Carbohydrate Foods and Disease, 1975; Don't Forget the Fibre in your Diet, 1979; Western Diseases, their emergence and prevention, 1981; over 300 contribs to scientific jls. *Address:* Hartwell Cottage, Bisley, Glos GL6 7AG. *T:* Gloucester (0452) 770245.

BURLAND, Prof. John Boscawen, FEng; Professor of Soil Mechanics in the University of London, at Imperial College of Science, Technology and Medicine (formerly Imperial College of Science and Technology), since 1980; *b* 4 March 1936; *s* of John Whitmore Burland and Margaret Irene Burland (*née* Boscawen); *m* 1963, Gillian Margaret, *d* of J. K. Miller; two *s* one *d*. *Educ:* Parktown Boys' High Sch., Johannesburg; Univ. of the Witwatersrand (BSc Eng, MSc Eng, DSc Eng); Univ. of Cambridge (PhD). MSAICE; FICE; MIStructE; FEng 1981. Res. Asst, Univ. of the Witwatersrand, 1960; Engineer, Ove Arup and Partners, London, 1961–63; Res. Student, Cambridge Univ., 63–66; Building Research Station: SSO and PSO, 1966–72; Head of Geotechnics Div., 1972–79; Asst Dir and Head of Materials and Structures Dept, 1979–80. Visiting Prof., Dept of Civil Engineering, Univ. of Strathclyde, 1973–82. Mem. Council, CIRIA, 1987–; Instn of Structural Engineers: Mem. of Council, 1979–82; Murray Buxton Silver Medal, 1977; Oscar Faber Bronze Medal, 1979; named in Special Award to DoE for Underground Car Park at Palace of Westminster, 1975; Oscar Faber Diploma, 1982; Instn of Civil Engineers: Telford Premium, 1972, 1985, 1987; Coopers Hill War Meml Medal, 1985; Baker Medal, 1986; Kelvin Medal, for outstanding contribn to engrg, 1989; Brit. Geotechnical Soc. Prize, 1968, 1971, 1974 and 1986. *Publications:* numerous papers on soil mechanics and civil engineering. *Recreations:* sailing, golf, painting, classical guitar.

BURLEIGH, Thomas Haydon, CBE 1977; Director, John Brown & Co. Ltd, 1965–77; *b* 23 April 1911; *s* of late J. H. W. Burleigh, Great Chesterford; *m* 1933, Kathleen Mary Lenthall, *d* of late Dr Gurth Eager, Hertford; two *s*. *Educ:* Saffron Walden Sch. RAF, short service commission, No 19 (F) Sqdn, 1930–35; Westland Aircraft Ltd, 1936–45; Thos. Firth & John Brown Ltd, 1945–48; Firth Brown Tools Ltd, 1948–77. Pres., Sheffield Chamber of Commerce, 1963–64; Pres. Nat. Fedn of Engineers' Tool Manufacturers, 1968–70; Master of Company of Cutlers in Hallamshire in the County of York, 1970–71. *Recreations:* golf, gardening. *Address:* Kirkgate, Holme next Sea, Hunstanton, Norfolk PE36 6LH. *T:* Holme (048525) 387. *Clubs:* Royal Air Force; Royal and Ancient Golf (St Andrews).

BURLEY, Dr Jeffery, CBE 1991; Director, Oxford Forestry Institute, Oxford University, since 1985; Professorial Fellow, Green College, Oxford, since 1981; *b* 16 Oct. 1936; *s* of Jack Burley and Eliza Burley (*née* Creese); *m* 1961, Jean Shirley (*née* Palmer); two *s*. *Educ:* Portsmouth Grammar Sch.; New College, Oxford (BA 1961); Yale (MF 1962; PhD 1965). Lieut, Royal Signals, 1954–57. O i/c and Unesco Expert, Forest Genetics Res. Lab., ARC of Central Africa, 1965–69; Sen. Res. Officer, Commonwealth Forestry Inst., Oxford, 1969–76; Univ. Lectr, 1976–83, Head of Dept of Forestry, 1983–85, Oxford. *Publications:* (ed jtly) Multipurpose tree germplasm, 1984; (ed jtly) Increasing productivity of multipurpose species, 1985; many book chapters resulting from conference papers; many contribs to periodicals and learned jls on forestry, agroforestry and forest tree breeding. *Recreations:* cricket, gardening. *Address:* Oxford Forestry Institute, South Parks Road, Oxford OX1 3RB. *T:* Oxford (0865) 275050.

BURLEY, Sir Victor (George), Kt 1980; CBE 1969; FIE(Aust); FIMechE, FIProdE; Chairman, Advisory Council of Commonwealth Scientific and Research Organization (CSIRO), 1979–81; Chairman, Allied Industries Pty Ltd, since 1984; *b* 4 Dec. 1914; *s* of G. H. Burley and M. A. Luby; *m* 1941, Alpha Loyal Lord; one *s* three *d*. *Educ:* High Sch., Tasmania; Univ. of Tasmania (BE). MIEE, FIFST; FInstD, FAIM. Cadbury-Fry-Pascall Pty Ltd, Australia, 1938–71: Chief Engr, Director and Vice-Chm.; Director, Cadbury Schweppes Aust Ltd, 1971–78; Cons. Dir, Cadbury Fry Hudson NZ; Technical Cons., Cadbury Schweppes UK, 1978–82. Member, Adv. Council, CSIRO, 1961–78; Chm., State Cttee, Tas. CSIRO, 1964–78; Foundn Mem., Commonwealth Adv. Cttee on Advanced Educn, 1965–71; Foundn Chm., Council of Advanced Educn, Tasmania, 1968–76; Mem., Sci. and Industry Forum, Aust. Acad. of Science, 1967–81. Director: Productivity Promotion Council, Australia, 1983–88; University Research Co., 1985–. University of Tasmania: Warden of Convocation, 1964–74; Mem., Faculty of Engrg, 1968–; Mem. Council, 1982–84. *Recreations:* music, reading. *Address:* Montaigne, 553 Sandy Bay Road, Hobart, Tasmania 7005. *T:* Hobart (002) 252–583. *Clubs:* Melbourne (Melbourne); Tasmanian (Hobart).

BURLIN, Prof. Terence Eric; Rector, Polytechnic of Central London, since 1984; *b* 24 Sept. 1931; *s* of Eric Jonas Burlin and Winifred Kate (*née* Thomas); *m* 1957, Plessey Pamela Carpenter; one *s* one *d*. *Educ:* Acton County School; University of Southampton (BSc); Univ. of London (DSc, PhD). CEng, FIEE 1976; CPhys, FInstP 1969. Physicist, Mount Vernon Hosp. and Radium Inst., 1953–57; Sen. Physicist, Hammersmith Hosp., 1957–62; Principal Physicist, St John's Hosp. for Diseases of the Skin, 1960–; Polytechnic of Central London: Sen. Lectr, 1962; Reader, 1969; Pro-Director, 1971; Sen. Pro-Rector, 1974; Acting Rector, 1982. British Cttee on Radiation Units and Measurements: Mem., 1966–74 and 1979–; Vice-Chm., 1983–84; Chm., 1984–; Member: Council, Inst. for Study of Drug Dependence, 1974–86; various Boards, CNAA; Cttee on Practical Determination of Dose Equivalent, Internat. Commn on Radiation Units and Measurements (Chm.), 1979–; Adv. Council on Adult and Continuing Educn, DES, 1980–83; Cttee on Effects of Ionising Radiation, Physics and Dosimetry Sub-Cttee, MRC, 1983–; Science Bd, SERC, 1986–. Mem. Council, BTEC, 1984–86. Hon. FCP. *Publications:* chapters in Radiation Dosimetry, 1968, 2nd edn 1972; papers on radiation dosimetry, radiological protection, biomechanical properties of skin, radiobiology. *Recreations:* music, tennis. *Address:* Polytechnic of Central London, 309 Regent Street, W1R 8AL. *T:* 071–580 2020. *Club:* Athenæum.

BURLINGTON, Earl of; William Cavendish; *b* 6 June 1969; *s* and *heir* of Marquess of Hartington, *qv*. *Address:* Beamsley Hall, Skipton, North Yorks BD23 6HD.

BURMAN, Sir (John) Charles, Kt 1961; DL; JP; *b* 30 Aug. 1908; *o s* of Sir John Burman, JP; *m* 1936, Ursula Hesketh-Wright, JP; two *s* two *d*. *Educ:* Rugby Sch. City Council, 1934–66 (Lord Mayor of Birmingham, 1947–49); General Commissioner of Income Tax, 1941–73; Indep. Chm., Licensing Planning Cttee, 1949–60; Chm. Birmingham Conservative and Unionist Assoc., 1963–72; County Pres. St John Ambulance Brigade, 1950–63; Member, Govt Cttee on Administrative Tribunals, 1955; Member Royal Commission on the Police, 1960. Director: Tarmac Ltd, 1955–71 (Chm., 1961–71); S Staffs Waterworks Co., 1949–82 (Chm. 1959–79). Life Governor, Barber Institute, at University of Birmingham (Trustee, 1936–90; Chm. Trustees, 1979–90). JP 1942; High Sheriff, Warwickshire, 1958, DL 1967. KStJ, 1961. Hon. LLD Birmingham, 1986. *Address:* Little Bickerscourt, Danzey Green, Tanworth-in-Arden, Warwickshire B94 5BL. *T:* Tanworth-in-Arden (05644) 2711.

BURMAN, Sir Stephen (France), Kt 1973; CBE 1954 (MBE 1943); MA; Chairman, Serck Ltd, Birmingham, 1962–70; Director: Averys, Ltd, 1951–73; Imperial Chemical Industries Ltd, 1953–75; Imperial Metal Industries Ltd, 1962–75; J. Lucas Industries Ltd, 1952–75, and of other industrial companies; *b* 27 Dec. 1904; *s* of Henry Burman; *m* 1931, Joan Margaret Rogers; one *s* (and one *s* decd). *Educ:* Oundle. Pres. Birmingham Chamber of Commerce, 1950–51 (Vice-Pres. 1949); Chm. United Birmingham Hosps., 1948–53; Dep. Chm. 1953–56. Dir, Midland Bank Ltd, 1959–76. Governor Birmingham Children's Hosp., 1944–48; Dep. Chm. Teaching Hosps. Assoc., 1949–53; Member, Midlands Electricity Board, 1948–65; Chm. Birmingham and District Advisory Cttee for Industry, 1947–49; Member Midland Regional Board for Industry, 1949–65, Vice-Chm. 1951–65; Member of Council and Governor, Univ. of Birmingham, 1949–76, Pro-Chancellor, 1955–66; General Commissioner for Income Tax, 1950–68. Member Royal Commission on Civil Service, 1953–56. Hon. LLD Birmingham, 1972. *Recreation:* gardening. *Address:* 12 Cherry Hill Road, Barnt Green, Birmingham B45 8LJ. *T:* 021–445 1529.

BURN, Adrian; *see* Burn, B. A. F.

BURN, Angus Maitland P.; *see* Pelham Burn.

BURN, (Bryan) Adrian (Falconer); London Managing Partner, BDO Binder Hamlyn, since 1988; *b* 23 May 1945; *s* of Peter and Ruth Burn; *m* 1968, Jeanette Carol; one *s* three *d*. *Educ:* Abingdon Sch. FCA. Whinney Murray, 1963–72; joined BDO Binder Hamlyn, 1972; seconded to DTI, 1975–77; Partner, BDO Binder Hamlyn, 1977, Managing Partner, 1988. Dir, Sinclair-Stevenson Ltd, 1990–. Mem., Financial Adjudication Panel, Second Severn Crossing, 1991–. *Recreations:* theatre, walking, sailing. *Address:* BDO Binder Hamlyn, 20 Old Bailey, EC4M 7BH; 13 Woodthorpe Road, Putney, SW15 6UQ. *T:* 081–788 6383. *Club:* Roehampton.

BURN, Michael Clive, MC 1945; writer; *b* 11 Dec. 1912; *s* of late Sir Clive Burn and Phyllis Stoneham; *m* 1947, Mary Booker (*née* Walter) (*d* 1974); no *c*. *Educ:* Winchester; New Coll., Oxford (open scholar); Hons Degree in Soc. Scis, Oxford, 1945, with distinction in all subjects (awarded whilst POW at Colditz). Journalist, The Times, 1936–39; Lieut 1st Bn Queens Westminsters, KRRC, 1939–40; Officer in Independent Companies, Norwegian Campaign, 1940, subseq. Captain No. 2 Commando; taken prisoner in raid on St Nazaire, 1942; prisoner in Germany, 1942–45. Foreign Correspondent for The Times in Vienna, Jugoslavia and Hungary, 1946–49. Keats Poetry First Prize, 1973. *Plays:* The Modern Everyman (prod. Birmingham Rep., 1947); Beyond the Storm (Midlands Arts Co., and Vienna, 1947); The Night of the Ball (prod. New Theatre, 1956). *Publications: novels:* Yes, Farewell, 1946, repr. 1975; Childhood at Oriol, 1951; The Midnight Diary, 1952; The Trouble with Jake, 1967; *sociological:* Mr Lyward's Answer, 1956; The Debatable Land, 1970; *poems:* Poems to Mary, 1953; The Flying Castle, 1954; Out On A Limb, 1973; Open Day and Night, 1978; *play:* The Modern Everyman, 1948; *non-fiction:* Mary and Richard, 1988. *Address:* Beudy Gwyn, Minffordd, Gwynedd, N Wales.

BURN, Rear Adm. Richard Hardy, AFC 1969; CEng; FRAeS; Director General Aircraft (Navy), Ministry of Defence, since 1990; *b* 26 May 1938; *s* of Margaret (*née* Hardy) and Douglas Burn; *m* 1967, Judith Sanderson (*née* Tigg); one *s* one *d* and one step *s* one step *d*. *Educ:* Berkhamsted; BRNC Dartmouth; RNEC Manadon. MIMechE. HMS Broadsword 1958, fighter pilot, 890 Naval Air Sqdn, HMS Ark Royal, 1961–62; test flying work (incl. 3 years exchange, US Navy), NDC Latimer, to 1975; develt of Sea Harrier, MoD (PE), 1975–78; Ops Officer, A&AEE, 1978–79; Air Eng. Officer, RNAS Yeovilton, 1980; Asst Dir Eng. (N), MoD, 1981–84; RCDS 1985; Dir, Aircraft Maint. and Repair, MoD (N), 1986–87; Dir, Helicopter Projects, MoD (PE), and ADC, 1988–90. Mem., Soc. of Experimental Test Pilots. FBIM. Commendation, US Navy, 1974; Médaille d'Honneur, Soc. d'Encouragement au Progrès, 1989. *Recreations:* skiing, golf, listening to music. *Address:* c/o Naval Secretary, Old Admiralty Building, Whitehall, SW1.

BURNELL, (Susan) Jocelyn B.; *see* Bell Burnell.

BURNET, Sir James William Alexander, (Sir Alastair Burnet), Kt 1984; broadcaster with Independent Television News, 1976–91; Associate Editor, News at Ten, 1982–91; *b* 12 July 1928; *s* of late Alexander and Schonaid Burnet, Edinburgh; *m* 1958, Maureen Campbell Sinclair. *Educ:* The Leys Sch., Cambridge; Worcester Coll., Oxford. Sub-editor and leader writer, Glasgow Herald, 1951–58; Commonwealth Fund Fellow, 1956–57; Leader writer, The Economist, 1958–62; Political editor, Independent Television News, 1963–64; Editor, The Economist, 1965–74; Editor, Daily Express, 1974–76. Ind. Dir, Times Newspapers Hldgs Ltd, 1982–; Director: ITN, 1982–90; United Racecourses Hldgs Ltd, 1985–. Has appeared regularly on TV progs, News at Ten, Panorama, This Week, TV Eye. Member: Cttee of Award, Commonwealth Fund, 1969–76; Cttee on Reading and Other Uses of English Language, 1972–75; Monopolies Commn specialist panel on newspaper mergers, 1973–; Council, Banking Ombudsman, 1985–; Hon. Vice-Pres., Inst. of Journalists, 1990. Richard Dimbleby Award, BAFTA, 1966, 1970, 1979; Judges' Award, RTS, 1981. *Address:* 43 Hornton Court, Campden Hill Road, W8 7NT. *T:* 071–937 7563; 33 Westbourne Gardens, Glasgow G12 9PF. *T:* 041–339 8073.

BURNET, Mrs Pauline Ruth, CBE 1970; JP; President, Cambridgeshire Mental Welfare Association, since 1977 (Chairman, 1964–76); Chairman, Cambridge Society for Mentally Handicapped Children, since 1982; *b* 23 Aug. 1920; *d* of Rev. Edmund Willis and Constance Marjorie Willis (*née* Bostock); *m* 1940, John Forbes Burnet (*d* 1989), Fellow of Magdalene Coll., Cambridge; one *s* one *d* (and one *s* decd). *Educ:* St Stephen's Coll., Folkestone (now at Broadstairs), Kent. Chm., Cambridgeshire AHA(T), 1973–82. Member: Windsor and Eton Hosp. Management Cttee, 1948–50; Fulbourn and Ida Darwin HMC, 1951–74 (Chm., 1969–74); E Anglian Regional Hosp. Bd, 1968–74; Bd of Governors of United Cambridge Hosps, 1966–74; Council, Assoc. of Hosp. Management Cttees until 1974 (Chm., 1966–68); Cambs FPC, 1985–87. Mem., Farleigh Hosp. Cttee of Inquiry, 1970. JP City of Cambridge, 1957; Chm., Cambs Magistrates' Courts Cttee, 1978–80. *Recreations:* walking, swimming. *Address:* Grange House, Selwyn Gardens, Cambridge CB3 9AZ. *T:* Cambridge (0223) 350726.

BURNETT, of Leys, Baronetcy of (unclaimed); *see under* Ramsay, Sir Alexander William Burnett, 7th Bt.

BURNETT, Most Rev. Bill Bendyshe, MA; LTh; *b* 31 May 1917; *s* of Richard Evelyn Burnett and Louisa Dobinson; *m* 1945, Sheila Fulton Trollip; two *s* one *d*. *Educ:* Bishop's College (Rondebosch); Michaelhouse (Natal); Rhodes University College; St Paul's Theological College, Grahamstown and Queen's College, Birmingham. Schoolmaster, St John's College, Umtata, 1940; Army, 1940–45; Deacon, St Thomas', Durban, 1946; Priest, 1947; Assistant priest, St Thomas', Durban, 1946–50; Chaplain, Michaelhouse, 1950–54; Vicar of Ladysmith, 1954–57; Bishop of Bloemfontein, 1957–67; Gen. Secretary, S African Council of Churches, 1967–69; Asst Bishop of Johannesburg, 1967–69; Bishop of Grahamstown, 1969–74; Archbishop of Cape Town and Metropolitan of S Africa, 1974–81. ChStJ 1975. Hon. DD Rhodes, 1980. *Publications:* Anglicans in Natal, 1953; (contrib.) Bishop's Move, 1978; (ed) By My Spirit: Renewal in the

Worldwide Anglican Church, 1988. *Recreation:* gardening. *Address:* 20 Milner Street, Grahamstown, 6140, South Africa.

BURNETT, Air Chief Marshal Sir Brian (Kenyon), GCB 1970 (KCB 1965; CB 1961); DFC 1942; AFC 1939; RAF, retired; Chairman, All England Lawn Tennis Club, Wimbledon, 1974–83; *b* 10 March 1913; *s* of late Kenneth Burnett and Anita Catherine Burnett (*née* Evans); *m* 1944, Valerie Mary (*née* St Ludger); two *s*. *Educ:* Charterhouse; Wadham Coll., Oxford (BA 1934; Hon. Fellow, 1974); Joined RAFO 1932; RAF 1934; Long Distance Record Flight of 7,158 miles from Egypt to Australia, Nov. 1938. Served War of 1939–45, in Bomber and Flying Training Commands; RAF Staff Coll. Course, 1944; Directing Staff, RAF Staff Coll., 1945–47; UN Military Staff Cttee, New York, 1947–48; Joint Planning Staff, 1949–50; SASO HQ No. 3 (Bomber) Group, 1951–53; CORAF Gaydon, 1954–55; ADC to the Queen, 1953–57; Director of Bomber and Reconnaissance Ops, Air Ministry, 1956–57; Imperial Defence Coll., 1958; Air Officer Administration, HQ Bomber Command, 1959–61; AOC No 3 Gp, Bomber Command, 1961–64; Vice-Chief of the Air Staff, 1964–67; Air Secretary, MoD, 1967–70; C-in-C, Far East Command, Singapore, 1970–71; retired 1972. Air ADC to the Queen, 1969–72. Pres., Squash Rackets Assoc., 1972–75. *Recreations:* tennis, squash rackets, golf, ski-ing. *Address:* Heather Hill, Littleworth Cross, Seale, Farnham, Surrey GU10 1JN. *Clubs:* Royal Air Force; Vincent's (Oxford); All England Lawn Tennis; Jesters Squash; International Lawn Tennis Club of Great Britain; Hankley Common Golf.

BURNETT, Charles John, FSAScot; Ross Herald, since 1988 (Dingwall Pursuivant, 1983); *b* 6 Nov. 1940; *s* of Charles Alexander Urquhart Burnett and Agnes Watt; *m* 1967, Aileen Elizabeth McIntyre; two *s* one *d*. *Educ:* Fraserburgh Academy; Gray's Sch. of Art, Aberdeen (DA); Aberdeen Coll. of Education (Teaching Cert.). PhD 1991. AMA; FHS Scot. House of Fraser, 1963–64; COI, 1964–68; Asst Dir, Letchworth Mus., 1968–71; Head of Design, Nat. Mus. of Antiquities of Scotland, 1971–85; Curator of Fine Art, Scottish United Services Mus., Edinburgh Castle, 1985–. Heraldic Adviser, Girl Guide Assoc. in Scotland, 1978–; Vice-Patron, Geneal. Soc. of Queensland, 1986–; Vice-Pres., Heraldry Soc. of Scotland, 1987–. KStJ 1991; Librarian, Priory of Order of St John in Scotland, 1987–. Hon. Citizen, Oklahoma, 1989. *Publications:* articles on Scottish heraldry. *Recreations:* reading, visiting places of historical interest. *Address:* 3 Hermitage Terrace, Edinburgh EH10 4RP. *T:* 031–447 5472.

BURNETT, Sir David Humphery, 3rd Bt, *cr* 1913; MBE 1945; TD; one of HM Lieutenants of the City of London; *b* 27 Jan. 1918; *s* of Sir Leslie Trew Burnett, 2nd Bt, CBE, TD, DL, and Joan, *d* of late Sir John Humphery; *S* father 1955; *m* 1948, Geraldine Elizabeth Mortimer, *d* of Sir Godfrey Arthur Fisher, KCMG; two *s* (and one *s* decd). *Educ:* Harrow; St John's Coll., Cambridge, MA. Served War of 1939–45 (despatches, MBE), in France, N Africa, Sicily and Italy; Temp. Lt-Col GSO1, 1945. Partner, David Burnett & Son, Chartered Surveyors, 1947–50; Director: Proprietors of Hay's Wharf Ltd, 1950–80 (Chm., 1965–80); Guardian Royal Exchange Assurance, 1967–88. Chairman: South London Botanical Institute, 1976–81 (Pres., 1985); London Assoc. of Public Wharfingers, 1964–71. Mem. PLA, 1962–75. Mem. Council, Brighton Coll. Master: Company of Watermen and Lightermen of the River Thames, 1964; Girdlers Company, 1970. FRICS 1970 (ARICS 1948); FBIM 1968; FLS 1979. *Heir:* *s* Charles David Burnett; [*b* 18 May 1951. *m* 1989, Victoria Joan, *d* of James Simpson].*Address:* Tandridge Hall, near Oxted, Surrey RH8 9NJ; Tillmouth Park, Cornhill-on-Tweed, Northumberland TD12 4UT. *Clubs:* Turf, United Oxford & Cambridge University.

BURNETT, Sir John (Harrison), Kt 1987; Chairman, Co-ordinating Commission for Biological Recording, 1989; *b* 21 Jan. 1922; *s* of Rev. T. Harrison Burnett, Paisley; *m* 1945, E. Margaret, *er d* of Rev. Dr E. W. Bishop; two *s*. *Educ:* Kingswood Sch., Bath; Merton Coll., Oxford. BA, MA 1947; DPhil 1953; Christopher Welch Scholar, 1947. FRSE 1957; FIBiol 1969. Lecturer, Lincoln Coll., 1948–49; Fellow (by Exam.) Magdalen Coll., 1949–53; Univ. Lecturer and Demonstrator, Oxford, 1949–53; Lecturer, Liverpool Univ., 1954–55; Prof. of Botany: Univ. of St Andrews, 1955–60; King's Coll., Newcastle, Univ. of Durham, 1961–63, Univ. of Newcastle, 1963–68; Dean of Faculty of Science, St Andrews, 1958–60, Newcastle, 1966–68; Public Orator, Newcastle, 1966–68; Regius Prof. of Botany, Univ. of Glasgow, 1968–70; Oxford University: Sibthorpian Prof. of Rural Economy and Fellow, St John's Coll., 1970–79; Member: Gen. Bd of Faculties, 1972–77 (Vice-Chm, 1974–76); Hebdomodal Council, 1974–79; Prin. and Vice-Chancellor, Univ. of Edinburgh, 1979–87. Exec. Sec., World Council for the Biosphere, 1987–. Lectures: Delgarno, Univ. of Manitoba, 1979–80; Bewley Meml, 1982; Peacock Meml, Dundee Univ., 1982; St Leonard's, Univ. of St Andrews, 1988. Chm. Scottish Horticultural Research Inst., 1959–74; Member: Nature Conservancy Scottish Cttee, 1961–66, English Cttee, 1966–69; Nature Conservancy Council, 1987–89 (Dep. Chm. and Acting Chm., 1988–89; Mem. Scottish Cttee, 1980–87); Nuffield Foundn Biol. Project, 1962–68 (Chm., 1965–68); British Mycological Soc. (Pres., 1982–83); Trustee, The New Phytologist, 1962–85, Advr, 1985–; Member: Academic Adv. Council, Univs of St Andrews and Dundee, 1964–66; Council, Univ. of Buckingham, 1989–. Member: Newcastle Reg. Hosp. Bd, 1964–68; Kingswood Assoc. (Pres., 1989). Served 1942–46 as Lieut RNVR (despatches). Hon. Fellow: RCSE, 1983; Green Coll., Oxford, 1988. Hon. DSc: Buckingham, 1981; Pennsylvania, 1983; Hon. LLD: Dundee, 1982; Strathclyde, 1983; Glasgow, 1987; Dr *hc* Edinburgh, 1988. Commendatore, Order of Merit (Italy), 1990. *Publications:* Vegetation of Scotland, ed and contrib., 1964; Fundamentals of Mycology, 1968, 2nd edn 1976; Mycogenetics, 1975; Fungal Walls and Hyphal Growth, ed and contrib., 1979; Edinburgh University Portraits II, 1986; Speciation and Evolution in Fungi, 1989; (jt ed. and contrib.) The Maintenance of the Biosphere, 1989; papers in various books and scientific journals. *Recreations:* walking, writing, gardens. *Address:* c/o Department of Plant Sciences, South Parks Road, Oxford. *Clubs:* Athenæum, Royal Over-Seas League.

BURNETT, Rev. Canon Philip Stephen; Church of England Board of Education, 1970–80; *b* 8 Jan. 1914; *s* of late Philip Burnett and Mrs Burnett, Salton, York; *m* 1954, Joan Hardy, *e d* of C. F. Hardy, Sheffield; one *s* one *d*. *Educ:* Scarborough Coll.; Balliol Coll., Oxford; Westcott House, Cambridge. Admitted Solicitor, 1936; Lay Missionary, Dio. Saskatchewan, Canada, 1939–41. Intelligence Corps, 1942–44; Staff Capt., GHQ, New Delhi, 1944–45, Deacon, 1947, Priest, 1948; Curate of St Andrew's, Chesterton, Cambridge, and Staff Sec., Student Christian Movement, 1947–49; Asst Gen. Sec., SCM, 1949–52; Vicar of St Mary, Bramall Lane, Sheffield, 1952–61; Rural Dean of Ecclesall, 1959–65; Canon Residentiary of Sheffield Cathedral, and Educn Secretary, Diocese of Sheffield, 1961–70, Canon Emeritus 1970–. Hon. Sec., Fellowship of the Maple Leaf, 1965–. *Address:* 91 Chelverton Road, Putney, SW15 1RW. *T:* 081–789 9934.

BURNETT, Rear-Adm. Philip Whitworth, CB 1957; DSO 1945; DSC 1943, and Bar, 1944; *b* 10 Sept. 1908; *s* of Henry Ridley Burnett; *m* 1947, Molly, *widow* of Brig. H. C. Partridge, DSO, and *d* of H. M. Trouncer; one *s* two *d*. *Educ:* Preparatory Sch., Seascale; Royal Naval Coll., Dartmouth. Served War of 1939–45; HMS Kelly, 1939–41; HMS Osprey, 1941–43; Western Approaches Escort Groups, 1943–45. Chief of Staff to Comdr-in-Chief, Portsmouth, 1955–57; retd list 1958. Lieut 1930; Comdr 1940; Capt. 1945; Rear-Adm. 1955.

BURNETT, Sir Walter (John), Kt 1988; President, Royal National Agricultural and Industrial Association of Queensland, since 1983; *b* 15 Jan. 1921; *s* of William Henry and Minna Anna Burnett; *m* 1945, Mabel Nestor Dalton; two *d*. *Educ:* Maleny Primary School; Church of England Grammar School; Pharmacy College, Queensland. Conducted own pharmacy business in Maleny for 32 years. Director: Geriatric Med. Foundn of Qld (also Founder Mem.); Sunshine Coast Hosps Bd, 1958–. Past Chm., Maleny Br., Qld Ambulance Transport Bde; Vice Patron, Schizophrenia Fellowship of S Qld, 1987. Mem., Electoral Re-distribution Commn, Brisbane City Council, 1984–85. Grand Master, United Grand Lodge of Qld, 1983–86. Past Pres., Maroochy Dist Bowls Assoc. *Recreation:* lawn bowls. *Address:* 28 Tamarind Street, Maleny, Qld 4552, Australia. *T:* 071 942290. *Clubs:* Tattersall's, Masonic (Brisbane).

BURNETT-STUART, Joseph; *b* 11 April 1930; *s* of late George Eustace Burnett-Stuart, CBE and Etheldreda Cecily (*née* Edge); *m* 1954, Mary Hermione, *d* of late John A. M. Stewart of Ardvorlich, TD; three *s* one *d*. *Educ:* Eton Coll.; Trinity Coll., Cambridge (BA). Bankers Trust Co., 1953–62; Dir, 1963–90, Chm., 1981–90, Robert Fleming Holdings Ltd. A Church Commissioner, 1984–. *Recreations:* gardening, shooting, fishing. *Clubs:* Boodle's; New (Edinburgh).

BURNEY, Sir Cecil (Denniston), 3rd Bt *cr* 1921; Chairman, JMD Group plc, since 1988; *b* 8 Jan. 1923; *s* of Sir Charles Dennistoun Burney, 2nd Bt, CMG, and Gladys (*d* 1982), *d* of George Henry High; *S* father, 1968; *m* 1957, Hazel Marguerite de Hamel, *yr d* of late Thurman Coleman; two *s*. *Educ:* Eton; Trinity Coll., Cambridge. Man. Dir, 1951–68, Chm., 1968–78, Northern Motors Ltd; Chm., Hampton Trust PLC, 1975–87; Director: Security Building Soc., 1959–71; Mount Martin Gold Mines NL, 1985–87. Member of Legislative Council, N Rhodesia, 1959–64; MP Zambia, 1964–68; Chairman, Public Accounts Cttee, Zambia, 1963–67. *Recreations:* tennis, skiing. *Heir:* *s* Nigel Dennistoun Burney, *b* 6 Sept. 1959. *Address:* PO Box 32037, Lusaka, Zambia; 5 Lyall Street, SW1X 8DW. *T:* 071–235 4014. *Clubs:* White's, Carlton, Turf, Buck's; Leander; Harare, Bulawayo (Zimbabwe); Ndola (Zambia).

BURNHAM, 5th Baron, *cr* 1903; **William Edward Harry Lawson,** Bt 1892; JP; DL; Lieutenant-Colonel; Scots Guards, retired 1968; *b* 22 Oct. 1920; *er s* of 4th Baron Burnham, CB, DSO, MC, TD, and (Marie) Enid, Lady Burnham, CBE (*d* 1979), *d* of Hugh Scott Robson, Buenos Aires; *S* father, 1963; *m* 1942, Anne, *yr d* of late Major Gerald Petherick, The Mill House, St Cross, Winchester; three *d* (one *s* decd). *Educ:* Eton. Royal Bucks Yeomanry, 1939–41; Scots Guards, 1941–68; commanded 1st Bn, 1959–62. Chairman: Sail Training Assoc.; Masonic Housing Assoc., 1980–. JP Bucks 1970, DL Bucks 1977. *Recreations:* sailing, shooting, ski-ing. *Heir:* *b* Hon. Hugh John Frederick Lawson [*b* 15 Aug. 1931; *m* 1955, Hilary Mary, *d* of Alan Hunter; one *s* two *d*]. *Address:* Hall Barn, Beaconsfield, Bucks HP9 2SG. *T:* Beaconsfield (0494) 673315. *Clubs:* Garrick, Turf; Royal Yacht Squadron.

BURNHAM, Rev. Anthony Gerald; General Secretary, United Reformed Church, from July 1992; Provincial Moderator, North Western Province, United Reformed Church, 1981–June 1992; *b* 2 March 1936; *s* of Selwyn and Sarah Burnham; *m* 1961, Valerie Florence Cleaver; one *s* two *d*. *Educ:* Silcoates Sch.; Manchester Univ. (BA Admin); Northern Coll., Manchester. Minister: Brownhill Congregational Church, Blackburn, 1961–66; Poulton-le-Fylde and Hambleton Congregational Churches, 1966–69; Lectr, Northern Coll., Manchester, 1969–77; Minister, SW Manchester United Reformed Churches, 1973–81. *Publications:* In The Quietness, 1981; Say One For Me, 1990; scripts for radio and TV. *Recreations:* theatre, cinema, jazz. *Address:* (until June 1992) 4 Marlowe Drive, Didsbury, Manchester M20 0DE. *T:* 061–445 9608; (from July 1992) 86 Tavistock Place, WC1H 9RT.

BURNINGHAM, John Mackintosh; free-lance author-designer; *b* 27 April 1936; *s* of Charles Burningham and Jessie Mackintosh; *m* 1964, Helen Gillian Oxenbury; one *s* two *d*. *Educ:* Summerhill School, Leiston, Suffolk; Central School of Art, Holborn, 1956–59 (Diploma). Now free-lance: illustration, poster design, exhibition, animated film puppets, and writing for children. *Publications:* Borka, 1963 (Kate Greenaway Medal, 1963); Trubloff, 1964; Humbert, 1965; Cannonball Simp, 1966; Harquin, 1967; Seasons, 1969; Mr Gumpy's Outing, 1970 (Kate Greenaway Award, 1971); Around the World in Eighty Days, 1972; Mr Gumpy's Motor Car, 1973; "Little Books" series: The Baby, The Rabbit, The School, The Snow, 1974; The Blanket, The Cupboard, The Dog, The Friend, 1975; The Adventures of Humbert, Simp and Harquin, 1976; Come Away jfrom the Water, Shirley, 1977; Time to Get Out of the Bath, Shirley, 1978; Would You Rather, 1978; The Shopping Basket, 1980; Play and Learn Books: abc, 123, Opposites, Colours, 1985; John Patrick Norman McHennessy—the Boy who is Always Late, 1987; Oi! Get off our Train, 1989. *Address:* c/o Jonathan Cape Ltd, 20 Vauxhall Bridge Road, SW1V 2FA.

BURNISTON, George Garrett, CMG 1972; OBE 1968; Consultant Physician in Rehabilitation Medicine; Senior Consultant in Rehabilitation Medicine, Prince Henry and Prince of Wales Hospitals, Sydney; Life Consultant in Rehabilitation Medicine, St George Hospital, Sydney, and Emeritus Consultant in Rehabilitation Medicine, Sutherland Hospital; *b* Sydney, NSW, 23 Nov. 1914; *s* of George Benjamin Burniston, Melbourne, Vic.; unmarried. *Educ:* Sydney High Sch.; Sydney Univ. (MB, BS). Served in RAAF Medical Service, 1940–47 (RAF Orthopaedic Service, UK, 1941–43); Gp Captain, RAAF Med. Reserve (retired). Dep. Co-ordinator of Rehabilitation, Min. of Post-War Reconstruction (Aust.), 1946–48. SMO, Dept of Social Services, 1948–53; Fulbright Fellow, USA and UK, 1953–54; PMO, Dept of Social Services, 1954–62; Chairman and Director, Division of Rehabilitation Medicine, Department of Medicine, Prince Henry, Prince of Wales and Eastern Suburbs Hospitals, Sydney, 1963–79; Sen. Lectr, 1963–77, Associate Prof., 1977–79, Sch. of Community Medicine, Univ. of NSW. Member: WHO Expert Advisory Panel on Medical Rehabilitation, 1958–84; Council, Cumberland Coll. of Health Sciences, Sydney, 1970–85 (Chm., 1980–85); Bd of Trustees, Cumberland Coll. Foundn, 1979–; Nat. Adv. Council for the Handicapped, Aust., 1977–83; Advanced Educn Council, Tertiary Educn Commn, 1979–86; Vice-Pres., Internat. Rehabilitation Med. Assoc., 1978–82; Pres., Aust. Coll. of Rehabilitation Med., 1980–82. Foundation Fellow, Aust. Coll. of Med. Administrators, 1968; Foundn Diplomate, Physical and Rehabilitation Medicine, 1971; FRSH 1973; FRACP 1976; Hon. Fellow, Cumberland Coll. of Health Scis, Sydney, 1987. *Recreations:* golf, swimming, painting, reading. *Address:* 701 Tradewinds, Boorima Place, Cronulla, NSW 2230, Australia. *T:* (02) 523–8383; Suite 804, 135 Macquarie Street, Sydney, NSW 2000, Australia. *T:* (02) 247 1951. *Club:* University (Sydney).

BURNLEY, Bishop Suffragan of, since 1988; **Rt. Rev. Ronald James Milner;** *b* 16 May 1927; *s* of Maurice and Muriel Milner; *m* 1950, Audrey Cynthia Howard; two *s* two *d* (and one *d* decd). *Educ:* Hull Grammar School; Pembroke Coll., Cambridge (MA); Wycliffe Hall, Oxford. Succentor, Sheffield Cathedral, 1953–58; Vicar: Westwood, Coventry, 1958–64; St James, Fletchamstead, Coventry, 1964–70; Rector of St Mary's, Southampton, 1970–73; Rector of the Southampton Team Ministry, 1973–83; Archdeacon of Lincoln, 1983–88. *Recreations:* ornithology, walking, music. *Address:* Dean House, 449 Padiham Road, Burnley, Lancs BB12 6TE. *T:* Burnley (0282) 23564.

BURNLEY, Christopher John; Burnley and Evans, Chartered Accountants, Halesowen, since 1989; *b* 1 May 1936; *s* of John Fox Burnley and Helena Burnley; *m* 1960, Carol Joan Quirk; two *d. Educ:* King William's College, Isle of Man. Chartered Accountant. Articled Clerk, 1953–59; Military service, 1959–62; Computer Systems Analyst, IBM, 1962–66; Management Consultant, Peat Marwick, 1966–67; Systems Planning Manager, Castrol, 1967–68; Sen. Planner, IBM, 1969–72; Financial Dir, Foseco FS, 1972–74; Group Treasurer, Foseco Minsep, 1974–75; Financial Dir, BAA, 1975–86; Finance Dir, Dan Air Engrg, 1987–88. *Recreation:* railway enthusiast. *Address:* Thirlmere, 173 Worcester Road, West Hagley, West Midlands DY9 0PB. *T:* Hagley (0562) 883592.

BURNS, Andrew; *see* Burns, R. A.

BURNS, Mrs Anne, (Mrs D. O. Burns); British Gliding Champion, 1966; Principal Scientific Officer, Royal Aircraft Establishment, Farnborough, Hants, 1953–77; *b* 23 Nov. 1915; *d* of late Major Fleetwood Hugo Pellew, W Yorks Regt, and of late Violet Pellew (*née* Du Pré); *m* 1947, Denis Owen Burns; no *c. Educ:* The Abbey Sch., Reading; St Hugh's Coll., Oxford (BA). Joined Min. of Supply, 1940. Engaged in aircraft research at RAE, Farnborough, Hants, under various ministries, 1940–. Feminine International Records: 4 gliding records in S Africa, 1961; records, S Africa, 1963, 1965; Colorado USA, 1967. Queen's Commendation for Valuable Services in the Air, 1955 and 1963. (With Denis Burns) Britannia Trophy, Royal Aero Club, 1961; Lilienthal Medal, Fédération Aéronautique Internationale, 1966. *Publications:* contrib. scientific jls. *Recreations:* snooker, fishing. *Address:* Clumps End, Lower Bourne, Farnham, Surrey GU10 3HF.

BURNS, Dr B(enedict) Delisle, FRS 1968; Visitor, Divison of Neurobiology, University of Newcastle upon Tyne; *b* 22 Feb. 1915; *s* of C. Delisle Burns and Margaret Hannay; *m* 1st, 1938, Angela Ricardo; four *s*; 2nd, 1954, Monika Kasputis; one *d. Educ:* University Coll. Sch.; Tübingen Univ.; King's Coll., Cambridge; University Coll. Hospital. MRCS, LRCP 1939. Univ. extension lecturing for WEA, 1936–38; operational research, 1939–45; Research Asst, Nat. Inst. for Med. Research, 1945–49; Assoc. Prof of Physiology, McGill Univ., Canada, 1950–58; Scientific Advisor to Dept of Veterans' Affairs, 1950–67; Prof. of Physiology, 1958–67, Chm., Dept of Physiology, 1965–67, McGill Univ., Canada; Head, Div. of Physiology and Pharmacology, Nat. Inst. of Medical Research, 1967–76; MRC External Staff, Anatomy Dept, 1976–80, Hon. Prof. of Neurobiology, 1977–80, Univ. of Bristol. *Publications:* The Mammalian Cerebral Cortex, 1958; The Uncertain Nervous System, 1968; about 80 articles on neurophysiology in scientific jls. *Recreations:* painting, interior decoration. *Address:* Division of Neurobiology, University of Newcastle upon Tyne, NE2 4HH. *T:* 091–222 6000, ext. 6948.

BURNS, David Allan; HM Diplomatic Service; Head of North America Department, Foreign and Commonwealth Office, since 1988; *b* 20 Sept. 1937; *s* of Allan Robert Desmond Burns, GM, and Gladys Frances Dine; *m* 1971, Inger Ellen Kristiansson; one *s* one *d. Educ:* Sir Anthony Browne's Sch., Brentwood, Essex. Served HM Forces, 1956–58. Language student and Third Secretary, British Embassy, Belgrade, 1962–65; Second Secretary, Bangkok, 1966–68; First Secretary, Washington, 1969–72; Head of Chancery, Belgrade, 1973–76; Asst Head of Arms Control Dept, FCO, 1976–79; Counsellor, Bangkok, 1979–83; Consul General, Boston, 1983–87. Mem., Marshall Scholarships Selection Cttee for New England, 1983–87. *Recreation:* walking. *Address:* c/o Foreign and Commonwealth Office, SW1A 2AH. *Clubs:* Travellers'; Royal Bangkok Sports.

BURNS, Maj.-Gen. Sir George; *see* Burns, Maj.-Gen. Sir W. A. G.

BURNS, Ian Morgan, CB 1990; Deputy Under Secretary of State, Home Office, since 1990; *b* 3 June 1939; *s* of Donald George Burns and late Margaret Brenda Burns; *m* 1965, Susan Rebecca (*née* Wheeler); two *d. Educ:* Bootham, York. LLB, LLM London. HM Forces, 1957–59. Examiner, Estate Duty Office, 1960; Asst Principal, 1965, Principal, 1969, Home Office; Principal, 1972, Asst Sec., 1974, NI Office; Asst Sec., Home Office, 1977; Under Sec., NI Office, 1979–84; Under Sec. (Finance), 1985, and Gen. Manager, Disablement Services, 1986, DHSS; Dep. Under Sec. of State, NI Office, 1987–90. *Recreations:* listening to music, adventurous gardening, collecting siurells. *Address:* c/o Home Office, 50 Queen Anne's Gate, SW1H 9AT. *Club:* Commonwealth Trust.

BURNS, James, CBE 1967; GM 1941; Chairman, Southern Gas Board, 1967–69, retired; *b* 27 Feb. 1902; *s* of William Wilson Burns and Isobella MacDonald; *m* 1934, Kathleen Ida Holt (*d* 1976); one *d* (one *s* decd). *Educ:* Inverness Royal Academy; Aberdeen Univ.; Cambridge Univ. BSc 1st cl. Hons 1925, PhD 1928, Aberdeen. Entered Research Dept, Gas Light & Coke Co., 1929; worked as Chem. Engr with Chemical Reactions Ltd, in Germany, 1930–32; Production Engr, Gas Light & Coke Co., 1941, dep. Chief Engr, 1945; Chief Engr, North Thames Gas Board, 1949, Dep-Chm. 1960–62; Chm, Northern Gas Board, 1962–67. President: Instn Gas Engrs, 1957–58; Inst. Fuel, 1961–62, etc. *Publications:* contrib. Jls Instn Gas Engrs, Inst. Fuel, etc. *Recreations:* golf, shooting, country pursuits. *Address:* 4 Corfu, Chaddesley Glen, Canford Cliffs, Dorset BH13 7PG. *T:* Canford Cliffs (0202) 707370.

BURNS, James; JP; DL; Convener, Strathclyde Regional Council, 1982–86; *b* 8 Feb. 1931; *s* of late James Burns and of Mary Burns (*née* Magee); *m* 1959, Jean Ward; two *s. Educ:* St Patrick's Sch., Shotts; Coatbridge Tech. Coll. Engineer with NCB, 1966–71. Member: Lanark CC, 1967–75; Lanarks Health Bd, 1973–77; Strathclyde Regional Council, 1974–; Chm., Gen. Purposes Cttee, 1975–82; Vice-Convener, 1978–82. Chm. Vis. Cttee, HM Prison, Shotts, 1980–; Member: Commonwealth Games Council for Scotland, 1982–86; Main Organising Cttee, Commonwealth Games 1986, 1982–86. Vice President: Glasgow Western St Andrew's Youth Club, 1982–86; St Andrew's Ambulance Assoc., 1984–86. Hon. President: Strathclyde CRC, 1982–86; Princess Louise Scottish Hosp. (Erskine Hosp.), 1982–86; Strathclyde Charities Band Assoc., 1982–86; Scottish Retirement Council, 1984–86; Hon. Vice Pres., SNO Chorus, 1982–86; Patron: Strathclyde Youth Club Assoc., 1982–86; YMCA Sports Centre, 1982–86; Scottish Pakistani Assoc., 1984–86. Trustee, The Pearce Institute, 1983–86. JP Motherwell, 1972. DL Monklands, Motherwell, Hamilton, E Kilbride and Clydesdale, 1989. *Recreations:* fishing, golf. *Address:* 57 Springhill Road, Shotts ML7 5JA. *T:* Shotts (0501) 20187. *Club:* Royal Scottish Automobile (Glasgow).

BURNS, Prof. James Henderson; Professor of the History of Political Thought, University College London, 1966–86, now Emeritus; *b* 10 Nov. 1921; *yr s* of late William Burns and Helen Craig Tait Henderson; *m* 1947, Yvonne Mary Zéla Birnie, *er d* of late Arthur Birnie, MA, and of Yvonne Marie Aline Louis; two *s* (and one *d* decd). *Educ:* George Watson's Boys' Coll., Edinburgh; Univ. of Edinburgh; Balliol Coll., Oxford. MA (Edinburgh and Oxon), PhD (Aberdeen). Sub-Editor, Home News Dept, BBC, 1944–45; Lectr in Polit. Theory, Univ. of Aberdeen, 1947–60; Head of Dept of Politics, 1952–60; Reader in the History of Political Thought, University Coll. London, 1961–66; Head of History Dept, UCL, 1970–75. John Hinkley Vis. Prof., Dept of History, Johns Hopkins Univ., Baltimore, 1987; Lectures: Creighton, London Univ., 1986; Carlyle, Oxford Univ., 1988. Gen. Editor, The Collected Works of Jeremy Bentham, 1961–79; Vice-Chm., Bentham Cttee, 1983– (Sec., 1966–78); Pres., Internat. Bentham Soc., 1986–. FRHistS 1962; Hon. Vice-Pres., RHistS, 1986– (Hon. Sec., 1965–70; Vice-Pres., 1978–82). *Publications:* Scottish University (with D. Sutherland Graeme), 1944; Scottish Churchmen and the Council of Basle, 1962; contributor to: (with S. Rose) The British General Election of 1951, by D. E. Butler, 1952; Essays on the Scottish Reformation, ed D. McRoberts, 1962; Mill: a collection of critical essays, ed J. B. Schneewind, 1968; Bentham on Legal Theory, ed M. H. James, 1973; Jeremy Bentham: ten critical essays, ed B. Parekh, 1974; Absolutism in Seventeenth Century Europe, ed J. Miller, 1990; edited (with H. L. A. Hart): Jeremy Bentham, An Introduction in the Principles of Morals and Legislation, 1970; Jeremy Bentham, A Comment on the Commentaries and A Fragment on Government, 1977; (with F. Rosen) Jeremy Bentham, Constitutional Code, vol. I, 1983; (ed) The Cambridge History of Medieval Political Thought c350–c1450, 1988; (ed) The Cambridge History of Political Thought 1450–1700, 1991; articles and reviews in: English Historical Review, Scottish Historical Review, Innes Review, Political Studies, History, Trans of RHistSoc, Historical Jl, Jl of Eccles. History, etc. *Address:* 6 Chiltern House, Hillcrest Road, Ealing, W5 1HL. *T:* 081–998 9515.

BURNS, Kevin Francis Xavier, CMG 1984; HM Diplomatic Service, retired; *b* 18 Dec. 1930; *m* 1963, Nan Pinto (*d* 1984); one *s* two *d. Educ:* Finchley Grammar Sch.; Trinity Coll., Cambridge (BA 1953). CRO, 1956–58; Asst Private Sec. to Sec. of State, 1958; 2nd Sec., 1959, 1st Sec., 1960–63, Colombo; CRO/FO, 1963–67; 1st Sec., Head of Chancery and Consul, Montevideo, 1967–70; FCO, 1970–73; Counsellor, UK Mission, Geneva, 1973–79; RCDS, 1979–80; Head of SE Asian Dept, FCO, 1980–83; High Commissioner: Ghana, 1983–86; Barbados, 1986–90. *Address:* c/o Lloyds Bank, 40 Rosslyn Hill, NW3 1NL.

BURNS, Michael; Chairman: Hatfield and Dunscroft Labour Party, 1965–86; South Yorkshire County Association, since 1986; *b* 21 Dec. 1917; *s* of Hugh Burns and Jane Ellin Burns; *m* 1939, Vera Williams (*d* 1984); two *d. Educ:* Thorne Grammar Sch. Served War, 1940–46: 1939–45 Star, France and Germany Star, War Medal, Defence Medal. Miner, Hatfield Main Colliery, 1934–40 and 1946–66; Thorpe Marsh Power Stn, 1966–70; Sch. Caretaker, Hatfield Travis Sch., 1970–81 (due to wife's illness); retd 1981. Mem., Nat. Cttee, NUPE, 1979–81; Chm., Health and Safety Local Govt Nat. Cttee, NUPE, 1979–81. Chairman: Goole CLP, 1977–83; Doncaster CVS, 1984–90 (Mem., 1977–); Doncaster Victim Support Scheme, 1985–; Member: S Yorks CC, 1973–86 (Chm., 1982–83); S Yorks Valuation Panel, 1974–89; S Yorks Charity Information Service, 1983–; Nat. Exec., CVSNA, 1985–87; Doncaster FPC, 1985–86; Doncaster Jt Consultative Cttee, 1985–89; Trustee, S Yorks Foundn Charity, 1986–; Chm., Friends of S Yorks Training Trust, 1988–. Pres., Hatfield Br., Arthritic Care, 1980–86. Governor, Hatfield High Sch., 1974–88; Chairman: Hatfield Ash Hill Sch. Bd of Governors, 1974–88 and 1989– (Vice-Chm., 1988–89); Govs, Hatfield Sheepdip Lane Sch., 1974–; Hatfield Chase Sch. (ESNS), 1984–. Church Warden, Christ Church, Dunscroft, 1964–79. *Recreations:* DIY, oil painting, politics. *Address:* 15 Manor Road, Hatfield, Doncaster, South Yorks DN7 6SA. *T:* Doncaster (0302) 846666.

BURNS, (Robert) Andrew; HM Diplomatic Service; Assistant Under-Secretary of State (Asia), Foreign and Commonwealth Office, since 1990; *b* 21 July 1943; *e s* of late Robert Burns, CB, CMG and Mary Burns (*née* Goodland); *m* 1973, Sarah Cadogan; two *s* one *d. Educ:* Highgate Sch.; Trinity Coll., Cambridge. BA (Classics), MA. Entered Diplomatic Service, 1965; UK Mission to UN, NY, 1965; FO 1966; Sch. of Oriental and African Studies, 1966–67; Univ. of Delhi, 1967; served New Delhi, FCO, and UK Delegation to CSCE, 1967–76; First Secretary and Head of Chancery, Bucharest, 1976–78; Private Sec. to Perm. Under Sec. and Head of Diplomatic Service, FCO, 1979–82; Fellow, Center for Internat. Affairs, Harvard Univ., 1982–83; Counsellor (Information), Washington, and Head of British Information Services, NY, 1983–86; Head of S Asian Dept, FCO, 1986–88; Head of News Dept, FCO, 1988–90. *Publication:* Diplomacy, War and Parliamentary Democracy, 1985. *Recreations:* music, theatre, country pursuits. *Address:* c/o Foreign and Commonwealth Office, SW1A 2AH. *Clubs:* Garrick, Royal Automobile.

BURNS, Sandra Pauline, CB 1989; Parliamentary Counsel, since 1980; *b* 19 June 1938; *d* of John Burns and Edith Maud Burns. *Educ:* Manchester Central High Sch.; Somerville Coll., Oxford (BCL, MA). Called to the Bar, Middle Temple, 1964. *Recreation:* computer programming. *Address:* 997 Finchley Road, Golders Green, NW11 7HB.

BURNS, Simon Hugh McGuigan; MP (C) Chelmsford, since 1987; *b* 6 Sept. 1952; *s* of Brian Stanley Burns, MC, and Shelagh Mary Nash; *m* 1982, Emma Mary Clifford; one *d. Educ:* Christ the King Sch., Accra, Ghana; Stamford Sch.; Worcester Coll., Oxford (BA Hons Modern History). Political Adviser to Rt Hon. Sally Oppenheim, 1975–81; Dir, What to Buy Ltd, 1981–83; Policy Exec., Inst. of Dirs, 1983–87. PPS to Minister of State: Dept of Employment, 1989–90; Dept of Educn, 1990–. *Recreations:* American politics, reading, swimming, travelling. *Address:* House of Commons, SW1A 0AA. *T:* 071–219 3000. *Club:* Chelmsford Conservative (Patron).

BURNS, Sir Terence, Kt 1983; Permanent Secretary, HM Treasury, since 1991; *b* 13 March 1944; *s* of Patrick Owen and Doris Burns; *m* 1969, Anne Elizabeth Powell; one *s* two *d. Educ:* Houghton-Le-Spring Grammar Sch.; Univ. of Manchester (BAEcon Hons). London Business School: Research posts, 1965–70; Lecturer in Economics, 1970–74; Sen. Lectr in Economics, 1974–79; Prof. of Economics, 1979; Director, LBS Centre for Economic Forecasting, 1976–79, Fellow, 1989; Chief Econ. Advr to the Treasury and Hd of Govt Econ. Service, 1980–91. Member, HM Treasury Academic Panel, 1976–79. Vice-Pres., Soc. of Business Economists, 1985–; Mem. Council, REconS, 1986–. *Publications:* various articles in economic jls. *Recreations:* soccer spectator, music, golf. *Address:* c/o HM Treasury, Parliament Street, SW1P 3AG. *T:* 071–270 5203. *Clubs:* Reform; Ealing Golf.

BURNS, Thomas Ferrier, OBE 1983; Editor of The Tablet, 1967–82; Chairman of Burns & Oates Ltd, 1948–67; Director, The Tablet Publishing Company, 1935–85; *b* 21 April 1906; *s* of late David Burns and late Clara (*née* Swinburne); *m* 1944, Mabel Marañon; three *s* one *d. Educ:* Stonyhurst. Press Attaché, British Embassy, Madrid, 1940–45. *Recreations:* painting and gardening. *Address:* Flat 7, 36 Buckingham Gate, SW1E 6PB. *T:* 071–834 1385. *Club:* Garrick.

BURNS, Prof. Tom, FBA 1982; Professor of Sociology, University of Edinburgh, 1965–81; *b* 16 Jan. 1913; *s* of John and Hannah Burns; *m* 1944, Mary Elizabeth Nora Clark; one *s* four *d. Educ:* Hague Street LCC Elementary Sch.; Parmiters Foundation Sch.; Univ. of Bristol (BA). Teaching in private schools in Tunbridge Wells and Norwich, 1935–39. Friends' Ambulance Unit, 1939–45 (PoW, Germany, 1941–43). Research Asst, W Midland Gp on Post-war Reconstruction and Planning, 1945–49; Lectr, Sen. Lectr and Reader, Univ. of Edinburgh, 1949–65. Vis. Prof., Harvard, 1973–74. Mem., SSRC, 1969–70. *Publications:* Local Government and Central Control, 1954; The Management of Innovation (with G. M. Stalker), 1961; (ed) Industrial Man, 1969; (ed with E. Burns) Sociology of Literature and Drama, 1973; The BBC: Public Institution and Private World, 1977; Erving Goffman, 1991; articles in a number of jls in Britain, USA, France, etc. *Recreations:* music, gardening. *Address:* Inchgarvie Lodge, South Queensferry, West Lothian EH30 9JS.

BURNS, Maj.-Gen. Sir (Walter Arthur) George, GCVO 1991 (KCVO 1962); CB 1961; DSO 1944; OBE 1953; MC 1940; retired; Lord-Lieutenant of Hertfordshire, 1961–86; *b* 29 Jan. 1911; *s* of late Walter Spencer Morgan and Evelyn Ruth Burns. *Educ:* Eton; Trinity Coll., Cambridge. BA Hons History. Commissioned Coldstream Guards 1932; ADC to Viceroy of India, 1938–40; Adjt 1st Bn, 1940–41 (MC); Brigade Major: 9 Inf. Bde, 1941–42; Sp. Gp Gds Armd Div., 1942; 32 Gds Bde, 1942–43; CO 3rd Bn Coldstream Gds, Italy, 1943–44 (DSO); Staff Coll., Camberley, 1945. Brigade Major, Household Bde, 1945–47; CO 3rd Bn Coldstream Gds, Palestine, 1947–50; AAG, HQ London Dist, 1951, 1952; Regimental Lt-Col Coldstream Gds, 1952–55; Comdg 4th Gds Bde, 1955–59. GOC London District and The Household Brigade, 1959–62; Col, Coldstream Guards, 1966–. Steward, The Jockey Club, 1964–. KStJ 1972. *Recreations:* shooting and racing. *Address:* Home Farm, North Mymms Park, Hatfield, Hertfordshire. *T:* Potters Bar (0707) 45117. *Clubs:* Jockey, Pratt's, Buck's.

BURNS, Prof. William, CBE 1966; Emeritus Professor of Physiology, University of London; Professor of Physiology, Charing Cross Hospital Medical School, 1947–77; Hon. Consultant Otologist, Charing Cross Group of Hospitals; *b* 15 Oct. 1909; *e s* of late Charles Burns, MB, ChB, JP and Mary Sillars, lately of Stonehaven, Scotland; *m* 1936, Margaret, *o d* of late W. A. Morgan, Glasgow; one *s* one *d*. *Educ:* Mackie Acad., Stonehaven; Aberdeen Univ. BSc 1932, MB ChB 1935, DSc 1943 Aberdeen. FRCP 1973. Asst in Physiology, Aberdeen, 1935; Lectr in Physiology, Aberdeen, 1936; Wartime duty with Admiralty, 1942; established in RN Scientific Service, 1946; Supt RN Physiological Laboratory, 1947; Chm., Flying Personnel Res. Cttee, RAF, 1978–80; Emeritus Civil Consultant to RN in Audiology; Hon. Consultant to RAF in Acoustic Science; pt-time activity for MRC, 1977–84. Member: Council, British Association for the Advancement of Science, 1956–61; Noise Adv. Council, 1977–81; BMA; formerly Mem., British Inst. of Acoustics; Hon. Life Mem., British Soc. Audiology. *Publications:* Noise and Man, 1968, 2nd edn 1973; (with D. W. Robinson) Hearing and Noise in Industry, 1970; articles on various aspects of hearing, in Journal of the Acoustical Soc. of America, Annals of Occupational Hygiene, Proc. Assoc. of Industrial Med. Officers, etc. *Recreations:* working in wood and metal; interested in engineering in general.

BURNSIDE, Dame Edith, DBE 1976 (OBE 1957); *m* W. K. Burnside; one *s* one *d*. *Educ:* St Michael's C of E Girls' Grammar Sch. President: Prince Henry's Hosp. Central Council of Auxiliary, from 1952 (now retired); Royal Melbourne Hosp. Almoner Ambulance, from 1952. Member of a number of cttees and socs for charities, the arts, and internat. friendship. *Address:* Grevisfield RSD, Wildwood Road, Sunbury, Vic 3429, Australia.

BURNSTOCK, Prof. Geoffrey, FRS 1986; FAA 1971; Professor of Anatomy, University of London, and Head of Department of Anatomy and Developmental Biology (formerly Anatomy and Embryology), University College London, since 1975; Convener, Centre for Neuroscience, University College London, since 1979; *b* 10 May 1929; *s* of James Burnstock and Nancy Green; *m* 1957, Nomi Hirschfeld; three *d*. *Educ:* King's Coll., London; Melbourne Univ. BSc 1953, PhD 1957 London; DSc Melbourne 1971. National Inst. for Medical Res., Mill Hill, 1956–57; Dept of Pharmacology, Oxford Univ., 1957–59; Rockefeller Travelling Fellowship, Univ. of Ill, 1959; Dept of Zoology, Univ. of Melbourne: Sen. Lectr, 1959–62; Reader, 1962–64; Prof. of Zoology and Chm. of Dept, 1964–75; Associate Dean (Biological Sciences), 1969–72. Vis. Prof., Dept of Pharmacology, Univ. of Calif, LA, 1970. Vice-Pres., Anatomical Soc. of GB and Ireland, 1990. Hon. MRCP 1987. Hon. MSc Melbourne 1962. Silver Medal, Royal Soc. of Victoria, 1970; Special Award, NIH Conf., Bethesda, USA, 1989. *Publications:* (with M. Costa) Adrenergic Neurons: their Organisation, Function and Development in the Peripheral Nervous System, 1975; (with Y. Uehara and G. R. Campbell) An Atlas of the Fine Structure of Muscle and its Innervation, 1976; (ed) Purinergic Receptors, 1981; (ed with G. Vrbová and R. O'Brien) Somatic and Autonomic Nerve-Muscle Interactions, 1983; (ed with S. G. Griffith) Nonadrenergic Innervation of Blood Vessels, 1988; (ed with S. Bloom) Peptides: a target for new drug development, 1991; (ed) The Autonomic Nervous System, vol. I: Autonomic Neuroeffector Mechanisms, 1991; papers on smooth muscle and autonomic nervous system, incl. purinergic nerves, in sci. jls. *Recreations:* tennis, wood sculpture. *Address:* Department of Anatomy and Developmental Biology, University College London, Gower Street, WC1E 6BT. *T:* 071–387 7050.

BURNTON, Stanley Jeffrey; QC 1982; *b* 25 Oct. 1942; *s* of Harry and Fay Burnton; *m* 1971, Gwenyth Frances Castle; one *s* two *d*. *Educ:* Hackney Downs Grammar Sch.; St Edmund Hall, Oxford. MA. Called to the Bar, Middle Temple, 1965, Bencher, 1991. *Recreations:* music, wine, travel, theatre. *Address:* 1 Essex Court, Temple, EC4Y 9AR. *T:* 071–583 2000.

BURNYEAT, Prof. Myles Fredric, FBA 1984; Laurence Professor of Ancient Philosophy, Cambridge, since 1984; *b* 1 Jan. 1939; *s* of Peter James Anthony Burnyeat and Cynthia Cherry Warburg; *m* 1st, 1971, Jane Elizabeth Buckley (marr. diss. 1982); one *s* one *d*; 2nd, 1984, Ruth Sophia Padel; one *d*. *Educ:* Bryanston Sch.; King's Coll., Cambridge (BA). Assistant Lecturer in Philosophy 1964, Lecturer in Philosophy 1965, University Coll. London; Lectr in Classics, Cambridge Univ., 1978; Fellow and Lectr in Philosophy, Robinson Coll., Cambridge, 1978. *Publications:* The Theaetetus of Plato, 1990; co-editor: Philosophy As It Is, 1979; Doubt and Dogmatism, 1980; Science and Speculation, 1982; (ed) The Skeptical Tradition, 1983; contribs to classical and philosophical jls. *Recreation:* travel. *Address:* Robinson College, Cambridge CB3 9AN.

BURRELL, Derek William; Headmaster, Truro School, 1959–86; Chairman, Methodist Day Schools' Committee, since 1988; *b* 4 Nov. 1925; *s* of late Thomas Richard Burrell and of Flora Frances Burrell (*née* Nash). *Educ:* Tottenham Grammar Sch.; Queens' Coll., Cambridge. Assistant Master at Solihull Sch. (English, History, Religious Instruction, Music Appreciation), 1948–52. Senior English Master, Dollar Academy, 1952–59. Vice-Pres., Methodist Conf., 1987–88. *Recreations:* music of any kind, theatre, wandering about London. *Address:* Flat 5, 2 Strangways Terrace, Truro, Cornwall TR1 2NY. *T:* Truro (0872) 77733. *Club:* East India, Devonshire, Sports and Public Schools.

BURRELL, Sir (John) Raymond, 9th Bt *cr* 1774; *b* 20 Feb. 1934; *s* of Sir Walter Raymond Burrell, 8th Bt, CBE, TD, and Hon. Anne Judith (OBE) (*d* 1987), *o d* of 3rd Baron Denman, PC, GCMG, KCVO; *S* father, 1985; *m* 1st, 1959, Rowena Frances (marr. diss. 1971), *d* of late M. H. Pearce; one *s*; 2nd, 1971, Margot Lucy, *d* of F. E. Thatcher, Sydney, NSW; one *s* one *d*. *Educ:* Eton; Royal Agricultural Coll., Cirencester. *Heir:* *s* Charles Raymond Burrell, *b* 27 Aug. 1962. *Address:* Rosemont, 14 Rosemont Avenue, Woollahra, NSW 2025, Australia. *Club:* Boodle's.

BURRELL, Peter, CBE 1957; Director, The National Stud, 1937–71; *b* 9 May 1905; *s* of Sir Merrik R. Burrell, 7th Bt; *m* 1st, 1929, Pamela Pollen (marr. diss., 1940); two *s*; 2nd, 1971, Mrs Constance P. Mellon (*d* 1980). *Educ:* Eton; Royal Agricultural Coll., Cirencester. *Recreations:* shooting, stalking. *Address:* Long Hill, Moulton Road, Newmarket, Suffolk CB8 8QQ. *T:* Newmarket (0638) 662280.

BURRELL, Sir Raymond; *see* Burrell, Sir J. R.

BURRENCHOBAY, Sir Dayendranath, KBE 1978; CMG 1977; CVO 1972; Governor-General of Mauritius, 1978–84; *b* 24 March 1919; *s* of Mohabeer Burrenchobay, MBE, and Anant Kumari Burrenchobay; *m* 1957, Oomawatee Ramphul; one *s* two *d*. *Educ:* Royal Coll., Curepipe, Mauritius; Imperial Coll., London (BScEng Hons); Inst. of Education, London (Postgrad. CertEd). Education Officer, Govt of Mauritius, 1951–60, Sen. Educn Officer, 1960–64, Chief Educn Officer, 1964; Permanent Secretary: Min. of Education and Cultural Affairs, 1964–68; Min. of External Affairs, Tourism and Emigration, also Prime Minister's Office, 1968–76; Secretary to Cabinet and Head of Civil Service, 1976–78. Attended various confs and seminars as Govt rep.; Chm., Central Electricity Bd, 1968–78. Hon. DCL, Univ. of Mauritius, 1978. Chevalier, Légion d'Honneur, 1975; Grand Cross, 1st Cl., Order of Merit, Fed. Republic of Germany, 1978. *Recreations:* swimming, walking. *Address:* S. Ramphul Street, Curepipe Road, Mauritius.

BURRETT, (Frederick) Gordon, CB 1974; Deputy Secretary, Civil Service Department, 1972–81; Chairman, Redundant Churches Fund, since 1982; Member, Executive Committee, First Division Pensioners Group, since 1984; *b* 31 Oct. 1921; *s* of Frederick Burrett and Marion Knowles; *m* 1943, Margaret Joan Giddins; one *s* two *d*. *Educ:* Emanuel Sch.; St Catharine's Coll., Cambridge. Served in Royal Engrs, N Africa, Italy, Yugoslavia, Greece, 1942–45 (despatches). HM Foreign, subseq. Diplomatic, Service, 1946; 3rd Sec., Budapest, 1946–49; FO, 1949–51; Vice-Consul, New York, 1951–54; FO, 1954–57; 1st Sec., Rome, 1957–60; transf. to HM Treasury, 1960; Private Sec. to Chief Sec., Treasury, 1963–64; Asst Secretary: HM Treasury, 1964; Cabinet Office, 1967–68; Secretary: Kindersley Review Body on Doctors' and Dentists' Remuneration; Plowden Cttee on Pay of Higher Civil Service, 1967–68; Civil Service Dept, 1968, Under-Sec. 1969. Mem., Civil Service Pay Res. Unit Bd, 1978–81; conducted govt scrutiny of V&A and Sci. Museums, 1982; Adviser to Govt of Oman on CS reorganisation, 1984; led govt review of policies and operations of Commonwealth Inst., 1986; leader of review team to examine responsibilities and grading of dirs of nat. museums and galls, 1987; conducted review of sen. posts of Arts Council and BFI, 1987–88; Chm., Cttee of Inquiry into CS Pay, Hong Kong, 1988–89. Chm., Wagner Soc., 1984–88. FSA 1985. *Publication:* article on the watercolours of John Massey Wright (1777–1866) in vol. 54 of the Old Water-Colour Society's Club Annual. *Recreations:* music, books, walking, reading. *Address:* Trinity Cottage, Church Road, Claygate, Surrey KT10 0JP. *T:* Esher (0372) 462783. *Club:* Athenæum.

BURRIDGE, Alan; Certification Officer for Trade Unions and Employers' Associations, 1981–85; *b* 15 Feb. 1921; *m* 1961, Joan Edith Neale; one *s*. *Educ:* William Ellis Sch.; Bristol Univ. (BA 1st Cl. Hons 1950). Served War, Army, 1939–46. Northern Assurance Co., 1936–39; Bristol Univ., 1947–50; Swinton Coll., 1950–53; London Municipal Soc., 1953–56; General Electric Co., 1956–67; Dept of Employment, 1967–81. *Address:* 1 Castle Hill Avenue, Berkhamsted, Herts HP4 1HJ. *T:* Berkhamsted (0442) 865276.

BURRILL, Timothy; Managing Director, Burrill Productions, since 1966; Chairman, Film Asset Developments Plc, since 1987; *b* 8 June 1931; *yr s* of L. Peckover Burrill, OBE and Marjorie S. Burrill; *m* 1st, 1959, Philippa (marr. diss. 1966), *o d* of Maurice and Margot Hare; one *d*; 2nd, 1968, Santa, *e d* of John and Betty Raymond; one *s* two *d*. *Educ:* Eton Coll.; Sorbonne Univ. Served Grenadier Guards, 1949–52: commnd 1950; served 2nd Bn, 1950–52. Jun. management, Cayzer Irvine & Co., 1952–56; entered film industry, 1956; joined Brookfield Prodns, 1965; Dir, World Film Services, 1967–69; first Prodn Administrator, National Film Sch., 1972; Man. Dir, Allied Stars (resp. for Chariots of Fire), 1979–80; Dir, Artistry Ltd, 1982–87 (resp. for Superman and Supergirl films); Consultant, National Film Develt Fund, 1980–81. Chairman: BAFTA, 1981–83 (Vice-Chm., 1979–81); First Film Foundn, 1989–; Producer Mem., Cinematograph Films Council, 1980–85; Member: Gen. Council, ACTT, 1975–76; Exec. Council, British Film and Television Producers Assoc., 1981–89; Exec. Council, The Producers Assoc., 1989–; Director: Fourth Protocol Films Ltd, 1985–; Central Casting Ltd, 1988–. Governor: National Film and Television Sch., 1981–; National Theatre, 1982–88. *Recreations:* theatre. *Address:* 19 Cranbury Road, SW6 2NS. *T:* 071–736 8673, *Fax:* 071–731 3921.

BURRINGTON, Ernest; Director, since 1986, Deputy Chairman and Assistant Publisher, since 1988, and Managing Director, since 1990, Mirror Group Newspapers; *b* 13 Dec. 1926; *s* of late Harold Burrington and of Laura Burrington; *m* 1950, Nancy Crossley; one *s* one *d*. Self-educated. Reporter, Oldham Chronicle, 1941–43; Army service, 1943–47; reporter and sub-editor, Oldham Chronicle, 1947–49; sub-editor, Bristol Evening World, 1950; Daily Herald: sub-editor, Manchester, 1950, night editor, 1955; London night editor, 1957; IPC Sun: night editor, 1964; Asst Editor, 1965; Asst Editor and night editor, News International Sun, 1969; dep. night editor, Daily Mirror, 1970; Dep. Editor, 1971, Associate Editor, 1972, Sunday People; Editor, The People, 1985–88 and 1989–90; Chm., Syndication Internat., 1989; Dep. Chm., Mirror Publishing Co., 1989; Director: Mirror Group Magazine and Newsday Ltd, 1990; (non-exec.) Sunday Correspondent, 1990; The European, 1990; IQ Newsgraphics, 1990; Sygma Picture Agency, Paris, 1990. Member: IPI; Foreign Press Assoc.; Trustee, Internat. Centre for Child Studies. *Recreations:* travel, tennis, bridge. *Address:* c/o Mirror Group Newspapers, 33 Holborn, EC1 8DQ.

BURROUGH, Alan, CBE 1970; Director, 1946–87, President, 1983–87, James Burrough plc (Chairman, 1968–82); Chairman, London Tideway Harbour Co. Ltd, since 1988; *b* 22 Feb. 1917; *s* of Ernest James Burrough and Sophie (*née* Burston); *m* 1939, Rosemary June Bruce; two *s* one *d*. *Educ:* St Paul's Sch., London; Jesus Coll., Cambridge Univ. (MA). Joined James Burrough Ltd, 1935. War of 1939–45: 91st Field Regt, RA, and 5th RHA (Captain). Rejoined James Burrough Ltd, 1945: Director, 1946; Deputy Chairman, 1967; Chairman, 1968; Director: Corby Distilleries Ltd, Montreal, 1968–82; Hawks Co. Ltd, 1989–. Dep. Pres., Oxon Br., British Red Cross, 1982–86. *Clubs:* Naval and Military; Hawks (Cambridge); Royal Channel Islands Yacht, Royal Lymington Yacht.

BURROUGH, John Outhit Harold, CB 1975; CBE 1963; *b* 31 Jan. 1916; *s* of Adm. Sir Harold M. Burrough, GCB, KBE, DSO, and late Nellie Wills Outhit; *m* 1944, Suzanne Cecile Jourdan; one *s* one *d*. *Educ:* Manor House, Horsham; RNC Dartmouth. Midshipman, 1934; Sub-Lt 1936; Lieut 1938; Lt-Comdr 1944; retd 1947. Foreign Office (GCHQ), 1946–65; IDC 1964; British Embassy, Washington, 1965–67; Under-Sec., Cabinet Office, 1967–69; an Under Sec., FCO (Govt Communications HQ), 1969–76. Director: Racal Communications Systems Ltd, 1976–79; Racal Communications Ltd, 1979–82. *Address:* The Old Vicarage, Guiting Power, Glos. *T:* Guiting Power (0451) 850596. *Club:* Naval and Military (Chm., 1969–72).

BURROUGH, Rt. Rev. John Paul, MBE 1946; MA Oxon; *b* 5 May 1916; *s* of Canon E. G. Burrough; *m* 1962, Elizabeth (Bess), *widow* of Stephen John White; one step-*d*. *Educ:* St Edward's Sch.; St Edmund Hall, Oxford; Ely Theol. College. Coach, Tigre Boat Club, Buenos Aires, 1938–39. Captain, Royal Signals, Malaya Campaign (POW), 1940–45. Asst, Aldershot Parish Church, 1946–51; Mission Priest, Dio. of Korea, 1951–59; Anglican Chaplain to Overseas Peoples in Birmingham, 1959–68; Canon Residentiary of Birmingham, 1967–68; Bishop of Mashonaland, 1968–81; Rector of Empingham and Hon. Asst Bishop, Diocese of Peterborough, 1981–85. Chaplain and Sub-Prelate, Order of St John of Jerusalem, 1969–. *Publications:* Lodeleigh, 1946; God and Human Chance, 1984; Angels Unawares, 1988. *Recreation:* rowing (Oxford crews, 1937 and 1938). *Address:* 6 Mill Green Close, Bampton, Oxon OX8 2HF. *T:* Bampton Castle (0993) 850952. *Clubs:* Leander (Henley); Vincent's (Oxford).

BURROW, Prof. John Anthony, FBA 1986; Winterstoke Professor of English, University of Bristol, since 1976; *b* 3 Aug. 1932; *s* of William and Ada Burrow; *m* 1956, Diana Wynne Jones; three *s. Educ:* Buckhurst Hill County High Sch., Essex; Christ Church, Oxford (BA, MA). Asst Lectr, King's Coll., London, 1955–57; Lectr in English, Christ Church, 1957–61, and Brasenose Coll., 1957–59, Oxford; Fellow in English, Jesus Coll., Oxford, 1961–75. Vis. Prof., Yale Univ., 1968–69. Hon. Dir, EETS, 1983–. *Publications:* A Reading of Sir Gawain and the Green Knight, 1965; Geoffrey Chaucer (critical anthology), 1969; Ricardian Poetry, 1971; (ed) English Verse 1300–1500, 1977; Medieval Writers and their Work, 1982; Essays on Medieval Literature, 1984; The Ages of Man, 1986; articles and reviews in learned jls. *Recreation:* music. *Address:* 9 The Polygon, Clifton, Bristol BS8 4PW. *T:* Bristol (0272) 277845.

BURROW, John Halcrow, OBE 1987; Chief Constable of Essex Police, since 1988; *b* 1935; *s* of John and Florence Burrow; *m* 1958, Ruth (*née* Taylor); two *s* one *d. Educ:* Ulverston Grammar School; University College London (LLB Hons). Lieut, 3rd Kenya Bn, King's African Rifles, 1953–55. Metropolitan Police, 1958–77; Asst/Dep. Chief Constable, Merseyside Police, 1977–88. Chairman: Technical and Res. Cttee, ACPO, 1990–; ACPO No 5 (SE) Region Cttee, 1991–; Shotley Training Centre Cttee, 1990–. *Recreation:* walking. *Address:* Essex Police HQ, PO Box 2, Springfield, Chelmsford, Essex CM2 6DA. *T:* Chelmsford (0245) 491491.

BURROW, Prof. John Wyon, FBA 1986; FRHistS 1971; Professor of Intellectual History, University of Sussex, since 1982; *b* 4 June 1935; *s* of Charles and Alice Burrow; *m* 1958, Diane Dunnington; one *s* one *d. Educ:* Exeter School; Christ's College, Cambridge (MA, PhD). Research Fellow, Christ's College, Cambridge, 1959–62; Fellow, Downing Coll., Cambridge, 1962–65; Lectr, Sch. of European Studies, Univ. of East Anglia, 1965–69; Reader in History, Univ. of Sussex, 1969–82. Vis. Prof., Univ. of California, Berkeley, 1981 and 1989; Vis. Fellow, History of Ideas Unit, ANU, 1983; Carlyle Lectr, Oxford, 1985; Christian Gauss Seminars, Princeton Univ., 1988. Hon. Dr Scienze Politiche, Bologna, 1988. *Publications:* Evolution and Society, 1966; A Liberal Descent, 1981 (Wolfson Prize); (with S. Collini and D. Winch) That Noble Science of Politics, 1983; Gibbon, 1985; Whigs and Liberals, 1988. *Recreation:* cooking. *Address:* 7 Ranelagh Villas, Hove, East Sussex BN3 6HE. *T:* Brighton (0273) 731296.

BURROWES, Edmund Stanley Spencer, CMG 1959; Financial Secretary, Barbados, 1951–66; *b* 16 Dec. 1906; *m* 1st, 1934, Mildred B. Jackson (decd); one *s* three *d*; 2nd, 1965, Gwen Searson. *Educ:* Queen's Coll., British Guiana. British Guiana Colonial Secretariat, 1924; Inspector of Labour, 1940; Deputy Commissioner, 1945; Labour Commissioner, Barbados, 1947. *Publication:* Occupational Terms on Sugar Estates in British Guiana, 1945. *Recreations:* diving, gardening. *Address:* 66 Meadow Mount, Churchtown, Dublin.

BURROWES, Norma Elizabeth; opera and concert singer; *d* of Henry and Caroline Burrowes; *m* 1969, Steuart Bedford, *qv* (marr. diss.); *m* 1987, Emile Belcourt; one *s* one *d. Educ:* Sullivan Upper Sch., Holywood, Co. Down; Queen's Univ., Belfast (BA); Royal Academy of Music (ARAM). Operas include: Zerlina in Don Giovanni, Glyndebourne Touring Opera (début); Blöndchen in Die Entführung aus dem Serail, Salzburg Festival, and again Blöndchen, Paris Opera, 1976 (début); Fiakermili, Royal Opera House (début), also Oscar, Despina, Nanetta, Woodbird; Entführung aus dem Serail, Ballo in Maschera, Der Rosenkavalier, Metropolitan, NY; Daughter of the Regiment, Midsummer Night's Dream, Elisir d'Amore, Canada; Cosi Fan Tutte, Romeo and Juliet, France; Marriage of Figaro, Germany; Gianni Schicchi, Switzerland; Marriage of Figaro, La Scala. Television operas include: Nanetta in Falstaff; Susanna in Marriage of Figaro and Lauretta in Gianni Schicchi. Sings regularly with major opera companies, gives concerts and recitals, GB and abroad; many recordings. Hon. DMus Queen's Univ. Belfast, 1979. *Recreations:* swimming, gardening, needlework. *Address:* 56 Rochester Road, NW1 9JG. *T:* 071–485 7322.

BURROWS, Sir Bernard (Alexander Brocas), GCMG 1970 (KCMG 1955; CMG 1950); *b* 3 July 1910; *s* of Edward Henry Burrows and Ione, *d* of Alexander Macdonald; *m* 1944, Ines, *d* of late John Walter; one *s* one *d. Educ:* Eton; Trinity Coll., Oxford. Entered HM Foreign Service (later Diplomatic Service), 1934; served at HM Embassy, Cairo, 1938–45; Foreign Office, 1945–50; Counsellor HM Embassy, Washington, 1950–53; Political Resident in the Persian Gulf, 1953–58; Ambassador to Turkey, 1958–62; Dep. Under-Secretary of State, FO, 1963–66; Permanent British Representative to N Atlantic Council, 1966–70, retired 1970. Dir-Gen., Federal Trust for Educn and Res., 1973–76. *Publications:* (with C. Irwin) Security of Western Europe, 1972; Devolution or Federalism, 1980; (with G. Edwards) The Defence of Western Europe, 1982; Footnotes in the Sand, 1990; contributed to: A Nation Writ Large, 1973; Federal Solutions to European Issues, 1978; The Third World War 1985, 1978; The Third World War: the untold story, 1982; articles and reviews in New Europe, etc. *Address:* Rubens West, East Dean, Chichester, West Sussex. *Club:* Travellers'.

BURROWS, General Eva, AO 1986; General of the Salvation Army, since 1986; *b* 15 Sept. 1929; *d* of Robert John Burrows and Ella Maria Burrows (*née* Watson). *Educ:* Brisbane State High School; Queensland Univ. (BA); London Univ. (PGCE); Sydney Univ. (MEd). Salvation Army: Missionary Educator, Howard Inst., Zimbabwe, 1952–67; Principal, Usher Inst., Zimbabwe, 1967–69; Vice-Principal 1970–73, Principal 1974–75; Internat. Coll. for Officers, London; Leader, Women's Social Services in GB and Ireland, 1975–77; Territorial Commander: Sri Lanka, 1977–79; Scotland, 1979–82; Australia, 1982–86. Hon. Dr of Liberal Arts, Ewha Woman's Univ., Seoul, S. Korea, 1988; Hon. LLD, Asbury Coll., USA, 1988. *Recreations:* classical music, reading, travel. *Address:* Salvation Army International Headquarters, 101 Queen Victoria Street, EC4P 4EP. *T:* 071–236 5222, *Fax:* 071–236 4981.

BURROWS, Fred, CMG 1981; PhD; Consultant to Hong Kong Government, 1990; *b* 10 Aug. 1925; *s* of late Charles Burrows; *m* 1955, (Jennifer) Winsome Munt; two *s. Educ:* Altrincham Grammar Sch.; Trinity Hall, Cambridge (MA). PhD Cantab, 1988. Served in RAF, 1944–47. Called to Bar, Gray's Inn, 1950; Asst Legal Adviser, Foreign Office, 1956–65; Legal Adviser, British Embassy, Bonn, 1965–67; returned to FO, 1967; Legal Counsellor, FCO, 1968–77; Counsellor (Legal Adviser), Office of UK Perm. Rep. to European Communities, 1977–80; Legal Counsellor, FCO, 1980–85; Law Officer (Special Duties), then (International Law), Hong Kong, 1985–90. JP Hong Kong, 1986–90. *Publication:* Free Movement in European Community Law, 1985. *Recreations:* sailing, trombone. *Address:* c/o Foreign and Commonwealth Office, SW1A 2AL.

BURROWS, (George) Richard (William); Chief Executive since 1977, and Chairman, since 1991, Irish Distillers Group; *b* 16 Jan. 1946; *m* 1970, Sherril Dix; one *s* three *d. Educ:* Wesley College, Dublin; Rathmines College of Commerce. FICA. Articled Stokes Bros & Pim, 1963–70; Asst to Man. Dir, Edward Dillon & Co., 1970; Man. Dir, Old Bushmills Distillery Co., 1972; Gen. Manager, Irish Distillers, 1976; Man. Dir, Irish Distillers Group, 1978. *Recreations:* sailing, Rugby. *Address:* Irish Distillers Group, Bow Street Distillery, Smithfield, Dublin 7, Ireland.

BURROWS, Lionel John, CBE 1974; Chief Inspector of Schools, Department of Education and Science, 1966–73; Educational Adviser, Methodist Residential Schools, 1974–84; *b* 9 March 1912; *s* of H. L. Burrows, HM Inspector of Schools, and Mrs C. J. Burrows; *m* 1939, Enid Patricia Carter; one *s* one *d. Educ:* King Edward VI Sch., Southampton; Gonville and Caius Coll., Cambridge. BA Cantab (1st cl. hons Mod. Langs Tripos) 1933. West Buckland Sch., Devon, Tiffin Sch., Kingston-upon-Thames and primary schools in London and Surrey, 1934–41; HM Forces (RASC and Intell. Corps), 1941–46; Commendation from US Army Chief of Staff, 1945; HM Inspector of Schools, 1946; Divisional Inspector, Metropolitan Div., 1960. Vice-Pres., Nat. Assoc. for Gifted Children, 1975–88. *Publication:* The Middle School: high road or dead end?, 1978. *Recreations:* natural history, fell-walking. *Address:* 34 Groby Road, Ratby, Leicester LE6 0LJ. *Club:* English-Speaking Union.

BURROWS, Prof. Malcolm, FRS 1985; Professor of Neuroscience, University of Cambridge, since 1986; *b* 28 May 1943; *s* of William Roy Burrows and Jean Jones Burrows; *m* 1966, Christine Joan Ellis; one *s* one *d. Educ:* Cambridge Univ. (MA, ScD 1983); St Andrews Univ. (PhD 1967). Reader in Neurobiology, Univ. of Cambridge, 1983–86. *Address:* 6 Cherry Bounds Road, Girton, Cambridge CB3 0JT.

BURROWS, Reginald Arthur, CMG 1964; HM Diplomatic Service, retired; *b* 31 Aug. 1918; *s* of late Arthur Richard Burrows; *m* 1952, Jenny Louisa Henriette Campiche (*d* 1985); one *s* one *d. Educ:* Mill Hill Sch.; St Catharine's Coll., Cambridge. Served with Royal Air Force during War; comd No. 13 (bomber) Sqdn, 1945. Entered the Foreign Service (now the Diplomatic Service), 1947; served in: Paris; Karachi; Tehran; Saigon; The Hague; Istanbul; Foreign Office; Minister, Islamabad, 1970–72; Univ. of Leeds, 1972–73; on secondment as Under-Sec., Civil Service Selection Bd, 1974–75; Asst Under-Sec. of State, 1975–78. *Recreations:* walking, studying Roman history. *Address:* Flat 9, Summer Court, Summer Hill, Harbledown, near Canterbury, Kent CT2 8NP. *T:* Canterbury (0227) 457394.

BURROWS, Richard; *see* Burrows, G. R. W.

BURROWS, Rt. Rev. Simon Hedley; *see* Buckingham, Area Bishop of.

BURSELL, Rev. Rupert David Hingston; QC 1986; **His Honour Judge Bursell;** a Circuit Judge, since 1988; *b* 10 Nov. 1942; *s* of Henry and Cicely Mary Bursell; *m* 1967, Joanna Ruth Gibb; two *s* one *d. Educ:* St John's School, Leatherhead; Univ. of Exeter (LLB); St Edmund Hall, Oxford (MA, DPhil). Called to the Bar, Lincoln's Inn, 1968; a Recorder, 1985–88. Chancellor, Vicar-General and Official Principal, Diocese of Durham, 1989–. Deacon, 1968; Priest, 1969; Hon. Curate: St Marylebone, 1968–69; St Mary the Virgin, Almondsbury, 1969–71; St Francis, Bedminster, 1971–83; Christ Church, and St Stephen, Bristol, 1983–88. *Publications:* (contrib.) Atkin's Court Forms, 1972, 2nd edn 1985; (contrib.) Halsbury's Laws of England, 1975; (jtly) Crown Court Practice, 1978; (contrib.) Principles of Dermatitis Litigation, 1985. *Recreations:* Church music, military history, archaeology of Greece and Holy Land. *Address:* The Crown Court, The Guildhall, Bristol BS1 2HL. *Club:* MCC.

BURSTALL, Dr Clare, FBPsS; Director, National Foundation for Educational Research in England and Wales, since 1983 (Deputy Director, 1972–83); *b* 3 Sept. 1931; *d* of Alfred and Lily Wells; *m* 1955, Michael Lyle Burstall (marr. diss. 1977); one *s* one *d. Educ:* King's Coll. and Birkbeck Coll., Univ. of London (BA Hons French, BA Hons Psychology, PhD Psychology); La Sorbonne, Paris. FBPsS 1975. Project Leader of team evaluating teaching of French in British primary schs, NFER, 1964–72. Charter Fellow, Coll. of Preceptors, 1988; FRSA 1990; Hon. Mem., CGLI, 1987. Hon. DSc Hull, 1988. *Publications:* French from Eight: a national experiment, 1968; French in the Primary School: attitudes and achievement, 1970; Primary French in the Balance, 1974; French from Age Eight or Eleven?, 1975; jl articles on various aspects of educnl research (eg, second language learning, large-scale assessment of achievement, class size, and management of educnl res.). *Recreations:* sailing, art collection, music, needlework. *Address:* Flat 2, 26 Lennox Gardens, SW1X 0DQ. *T:* 071–584 3127. *Club:* Royal Over-Seas League.

BURSTEIN, Hon. Dame Rose; *see* Heilbron, Hon. Dame R.

BURSTON, Sir Samuel (Gerald Wood), Kt 1977; OBE 1966; Grazier at Noss Estate, Casterton, Victoria, since 1945; President, Australian Woolgrowers and Graziers Council, 1976–79; *b* 24 April 1915; *s* of Maj.-Gen. Sir Samuel Burston, KBE, CB, DSO, VD, late RAAMC, and late Lady Burston; *m* 1940, Verna Helen Peebles (*d* 1980); one *s* one *d. Educ:* St Peter's Coll., Adelaide (Sch. Captain, 1933). Major, AIF, 1939–45 (despatches). Chm., Country Fire Authority, Vic, 1964–65; Pres., Graziers Assoc. of Vic, 1973–76; Councillor, Nat. Farmers Fedn, 1979–82; Vice-Pres., Confedn of Aust. Industry, 1978–82; Member: Nat. Employers Policy Cttee, 1970–78; Australian Wool Industry Policy Cttee, 1976–78; Aust. Sci. and Technol. Council, 1976–85 (acting Chm., 1982); Aust. Stats Adv. Council, 1976–80; Aust. Govt Econ. Consultative Gp, 1976–82; Nat. Labour Consultative Council, 1976–82; Reserve Bank Bd, 1977–87. Aust. Trade Develt Council, 1979–85; Trade Practices Cons. Council, 1979–82; Aust. Manufacturing Council, 1979–84; Chm., Perpetual Executors & Trustee Co. of Australia, 1981–87. Mem., Victorian Selection Cttee, Winston Churchill Meml Trust, 1967–81; Chm., Aust. Pastoral Res. Trust, 1988–. *Recreations:* golf, swimming. *Address:* 43/52 Brougham Place, North Adelaide, SA 5006, Australia. *T:* 08 267 3783. *Clubs:* Melbourne (Melbourne); Adelaide, Naval, Military and Air Force of South Australia (Adelaide); Royal Adelaide Golf.

BURT, Alistair James Hendrie; MP (C) Bury North, since 1983; Solicitor, Vallance Lickfolds (formerly Watts, Vallance & Vallance), London, since 1980; *b* 25 May 1955; *s* of James Hendrie Burt, med. practitioner and Mina Christie Robertson; *m* 1983, Eve Alexandra Twite; one *s* one *d. Educ:* Bury Grammar Sch.; St John's Coll., Oxford (BA Hons Jurisprudence, 1977). Pres., OU Law Soc., Michaelmas term, 1976. Articled Slater Heelis & Co., Manchester, 1978–80. Councillor, Archway Ward, London Bor. of Haringey, 1982–84. Parliamentary Private Secretary: to Sec. of State for the Environment, 1985–86; to Sec. of State for Educn and Science, 1986–89; to Chancellor of Duchy of Lancaster and Chm. of Cons. Party, 1989–90. Secretary: NW Cons. MPs Group, 1984–88; Parly Christian Fellowship, 1984–. *Recreations:* reading left-wing publications, sport, modern art, astronomy. *Address:* House of Commons, SW1A 0AA. *T:* 071–219 3000.

BURT, Hon. Sir Francis (Theodore Page), AC 1988; KCMG 1977; Governor of Western Australia, since 1990 (Lieutenant-Governor, 1977–90); *b* Perth, WA, 14 June 1918; *s* of A. F. G. Burt; *m* 1943, Margaret, *d* of Brig. J. E. Lloyd; two *s* two *d. Educ:* Guildford Grammar Sch.; Univ. of Western Australia (LLB, LLM); Hackett Schol., 1941; admitted to Bar of WA, 1941. Served War, RAN and RAAF, 1940–45. QC 1960; a Judge of Supreme Ct, WA, 1969–88; Chief Justice, WA, 1977–88. President: Law Soc. of WA, 1960–62; WA Bar Assoc., 1963–65. Visiting Lectr in Law, Univ. of WA, 1945–65. Chairman: Inst. of Radiotherapy, WA, 1960–62; Bd of Management, Sir Charles Gairdner

Hosp., Hollywood, WA, 1962–72; Queen Elizabeth II Medical Centre Trust, 1966–85; Mem., Senate of Univ. of WA, 1968–76. Hon. LLD Univ. of WA, 1987. *Recreations:* tennis, fishing. *Address:* 64 Leake Street, Peppermint Grove WA 6011, Australia. *Club:* Weld (Perth).

BURT, Gerald Raymond, OBE 1984; BEM 1947; FCIT; Chief Secretary, British Railways Board, 1976–84; *b* 15 Feb. 1926; *s* of Reginald George Burt and Lilian May Burt; *m* 1948, Edna Ivy Elizabeth Sizeland; two *s.* *Educ:* Latymer Upper Sch. FCIT 1971. Joined GWR as Booking Clerk, 1942: RE (Movement Control), 1944–47; BR Management Trainee, 1951–54; Gen. Staff, British Transport Commn, 1956–59; Divl Planning Officer, Bristol, 1959–62; Planning Officer, LMR, 1962–64; Divl Man., St Pancras, 1965; Traffic Man., Freightliners, 1967–70; Principal Corporate Planning Officer, British Railways Bd, 1970–76. Member: Council, Chartered Inst. of Transport, 1967–70, 1981–84; British Transport Police Cttee, 1984–88. Governor, British Transport Staff Coll., 1976–82. FRSA 1983. Scouting Medal of Merit, 1978. *Recreations:* gardening, the countryside. *Address:* Sizelands, Mill Lane, Wingrave, Aylesbury, Bucks HP22 4PL. *T:* Aylesbury (0296) 681458.

BURT, Maurice Edward; Deputy Director, Building Research Establishment, 1975–81, retired; *b* 17 Nov. 1921; *s* of Reginald Edward Burt and Bertha Winifred Burt; *m* 1947, Monica Evelyn Amy; one *s* three *d.* *Educ:* Victoria Coll., Jersey; Taunton's Sch., Southampton; BA Hons London, 1948. CEng, MICE; FRAeS. Aircraft industry, 1938–48; RAE, 1948–66 (Supt, Airworthiness, 1961–66); Head of Structures Dept, Transport and Road Res. Lab., 1966–73; Head of Res. Management, Dept of Environment, 1973–75. *Publications:* technical reports and articles. *Recreations:* golf, walking, gardening. *Address:* Roselle, Rue de Haut, St Lawrence, Jersey, CI JE3 1JQ. *T:* Jersey (0534) 35933.

BURT, Peter Alexander; Treasurer and Chief General Manager, Bank of Scotland, since 1988; *b* 6 March 1944; *s* of Robert W. Burt and May H. Rodger; *m* 1971, Alison Mackintosh Turner; three *s.* *Educ:* Merchiston Castle Sch., Edinburgh; Univ. of St Andrews (MA); Univ. of Pennsylvania (MBA). FIB (Scot.) 1987. Hewlett Packard Co., Palo Alto, 1968–70; CSL, Edinburgh, 1970–74; Edward Bates & Sons Ltd, Edinburgh, 1974; joined Bank of Scotland, 1975: Internat. Div., 1975–88; Asst Gen. Manager, 1979–84; Divisional Gen. Manager, 1984–85; Jt Gen. Manager, 1985–88. Mem., High Constables and Guard of Honour of Holyrood House, Edinburgh. *Recreations:* golf, skiing, gardening, reading. *Address:* Auldhame House, North Berwick EH39 5PW. *T:* North Berwick (0620) 3424. *Clubs:* Hon. Co. of Edinburgh Golfers (Muirfield); Gullane Golf (Gullane).

BURT-ANDREWS, Air Commodore Charles Beresford Eaton, CB 1962; CBE 1959; RAF retired; *b* 21 March 1913; *s* of late Major C. Burt-Andrews, RE; *m* 1st, 1941, Elizabeth Alsina Helen, *d* of late Sir Maurice Linford Gwyer, GCIE, KCB, KCSI; one *s* one *d*; 2nd, 1977, Joan Trésor (*née* Cayzer-Evans). *Educ:* Lindisfarne Coll.; Collège des Frères Chrétiens Sophia. Commnd RAF, 1935; served NWF India, 1937–42; S Waziristan ops, 1937; Burma, 1942; comd Army Co-op. Sqdn RAF, 1943; special ops, 1943–44; Air Attaché, British Embassy, Warsaw, 1945–47; Staff Coll., 1948; Sec. Gen. Allied Air Forces Central Europe, Fontainebleau, 1950–52; directing Staff RAF Staff Coll., 1953–55; Head of Far East Defence Secretariat, Singapore, 1955–58; First Comdt, Pakistan Air Force Staff Coll., 1959–61; UK Nat. Mil. Rep., SHAPE, Paris, 1962–65; Asst Comdt, RAF Staff Coll., Bracknell, 1965–68; retd, 1968. *Recreations:* painting, glass engraving. *Address:* 9 Erimi Close, Erimi Village, Limassol District, Cyprus. *Club:* Royal Air Force.

BURTON, family name of **Baroness Burton of Coventry.**

BURTON, 3rd Baron, *cr* 1897; **Michael Evan Victor Baillie;** *b* 27 June 1924; *er s* of Brig. Hon. George Evan Michael Baillie, MC, TD (*d* 1941) and *g s* of Baroness Burton (2nd in line); *S* grandmother, 1962; *m* 1st, 1948, Elizabeth Ursula Forster (marr. diss. 1977), *er d* of late Capt. A. F. Wise; two *s* four *d*; 2nd, 1978, Coralie Denise, 2nd *d* of late Claud R. Cliffe. *Educ:* Eton. Lieut, Scots Guards, 1944. Mem. Exec., Scottish Landowners Fedn. Mem., CC, 1948–75, JP 1961–75, DL 1963–65, Inverness-shire; Mem., Inverness Dist Council, 1984–. *Heir:* *s* Hon. Evan Michael Ronald Baillie [*b* 19 March 1949; *m* 1970, Lucinda (marr. diss.), *e d* of Robert Law, Newmarket; two *s* one *d*]. *Address:* Dochfour, Inverness IV3 6JY. *T:* Dochgarroch (046386) 252. *Clubs:* Cavalry and Guards; New (Edinburgh).

BURTON OF COVENTRY, Baroness, *cr* 1962, of Coventry (Life Peer); **Elaine Frances Burton;** Chairman, Mail Order Publishers' Authority, and President, Association of Mail Order Publishers, 1970–84; President, Institute of Travel Managers in Industry and Commerce, 1977–86; *b* Scarborough, 2 March 1904; *d* of Leslie and Frances Burton. *Educ:* Leeds Girls' Modern Sch.; City of Leeds Training Coll. Leeds elementary schools and evening institutes, 1924–35; South Wales Council of Social Service and educational settlements, 1935–37; National Fitness Council, 1938–39; John Lewis Partnership, 1940–45. Writer, lecturer, broadcaster, public relations consultant, 1945–50. MP (Lab) Coventry South, 1950–59. Member of parliamentary delegation to Netherlands, 1952 and to Soviet Union, 1954; Siam, 1956; South America, 1958; deleg. to Council of Europe; first woman Chm., Select Cttee on Estimates (sub-Cttee); Mem., Select Cttee on Practice and Procedure (House of Lords). Chairman: Domestic Coal Consumers' Council, 1962–65; Council on Tribunals, 1967–73; Member: Council Industrial Design, 1963–68; ITA, 1964–69; Sports Council, 1965–71; Air Transport Users Cttee, 1973–79. Founder Mem., Social Democratic Party, 1981–. Consultant to: John Waddington Ltd, 1959–61; The Reader's Digest, 1969–70; Courtaulds Ltd, 1960–73; Hon. Consultant, Air Transport Users Cttee, 1979– (Mem., 1973–79); Director: Consultancy Ltd, 1949–73; Imperial Domestic Appliances Ltd, 1963–66. *Publications:* What of the Women, 1941; And Your Verdict?, 1943; articles for press, magazines and political journals. *Recreations:* reading, ballet, opera; World's Sprint Champion, 1920; Yorkshire 1st XI (hockey), 1924–32. *Address:* 18 Vincent Court, Seymour Place, W1H 5WR. *T:* 071–262 0864.

BURTON, (Anthony) David; Chairman: London International Financial Futures Exchange, since 1988; Marshalls Finance Ltd; Director, S. G. Warburg & Co., Ltd; *b* 2 April 1937; *s* of Leslie Mitchell Burton and Marion Burton (*née* Marsh); *m* 1964, Valerie (*née* Swire); one *s* two *d.* *Educ:* Arnold Sch., Blackpool. FCIB; FCT. Bank of America National Trust and Savings Assoc., 1966–72; S. G. Warburg & Co. Ltd, 1972–. *Recreations:* antique glass, German pottery, music, opera, sport (participating and spectator). *Address:* c/o S. G. Warburg & Co. Ltd, 2 Finsbury Avenue, EC2M 2PA *T:* 071–606 1066, 071–860 0499. *Club:* MCC.

BURTON, Anthony George Graham; author and broadcaster, since 1968; *b* 24 Dec. 1934; *s* of Donald Graham Burton and Irene Burton; *m* 1959, Pip Sharman; two *s* one *d.* *Educ:* King James's Grammar Sch., Knaresborough; Leeds Univ. National Service, RAF, 1955–57. Research chemist, 1958–60; publishing, 1960–68. *Publications:* A Programmed Guide to Office Warfare, 1969; The Jones Report, 1970; The Canal Builders, 1972, 2nd edn 1981; Canals in Colour, 1974; Remains of a Revolution, 1975; Josiah Wedgwood, 1976; (jtly) Canal, 1976; The Miners, 1976; Back Door Britain, 1977; Industrial Archaeological Sites of Britain, 1977; (jtly) The Green Bag Travellers, 1978; The Past At Work, 1980; The Rainhill Story, 1980; The Past Afloat, 1982; The Changing River, 1982; The Shell Book of Curious Britain, 1982; National Trust Guide to Our Industrial Past, 1983; The Waterways of Britain, 1983; The Rise and Fall of King Cotton, 1984; (ed jtly) Canals: a new look, 1984; Walking the Line, 1985; Wilderness Britain, 1985; (jtly) Britain's Light Railways, 1985; The Shell Book of Undiscovered Britain and Ireland, 1986; (jtly) Landscape Detective, 1986; Britain Revisited, 1986; Opening Time, 1987; Steaming Through Britain, 1987; Walking Through History, 1988; Walk the South Downs, 1988; The Great Days of the Canals, 1989; Cityscapes, 1990; Astonishing Britain, 1990; *novels:* The Reluctant Musketeer, 1973; The Master Idol, 1975; The Navigators, 1976; A Place to Stand, 1977. *Recreations:* walking and travelling in search of steam engines and good beer; cinema. *Address:* 7A Belgrave Road, Clifton, Bristol BS8 2AA.

BURTON, Sir Carlisle (Archibald), Kt 1979; OBE 1968; Barbados High Commissioner to the Bahamas, since 1978; *b* 29 July 1921; *m* 1946, Hyacinth Marjorie Adelle Barker. *Educ:* Harrison Coll., Barbados, WI; Univ. of London (BA); School of Librarianship, Leeds (ALA); Univ. of Pittsburgh (MS). Assistant Master, Harrison Coll., Barbados, 1943–50; Sen. Asst Master, Bishop's High Sch., Tobago, 1950–51; Public Librarian, Barbados, 1953–58; Permanent Secretary: Min. of Educn, 1958–63; Min. of Health, 1963–71; Perm. Sec., Prime Minister's Office, and Head of Civil Service, 1972–81; Chm., Public Services Commn, Barbados, 1981–87, Turks and Caicos Islands, 1988–90. Member: Commonwealth Observer Gp at elections in Southern Rhodesia (Zimbabwe), 1980 and in Malaysia, 1990; Caribbean Community Review Team, 1989–91. Director: Barbados National Bank, 1978–86 (Dep. Chm., 1982–86); Insurance Corp. of Barbados, 1978–86 (Chm., 1981–86); Chm., Cave Hill Campus Council, Univ. of the WI, Barbados, 1984–. FRSA 1953. *Recreations:* (active) table tennis, swimming, bridge, reading; (spectator) cricket (Life Member, Barbados Cricket Assoc.), athletics (Life Member, Barbados Amateur Athletic Assoc.), soccer. *Address:* Caradelle, Mountjoy Avenue, Pine Gardens, St Michael, Barbados, West Indies. *T:* 429 3724.

BURTON, David; *see* Burton, A. D.

BURTON, David Harold; Group Director North, Network SouthEast, since 1991; *b* 28 Jan. 1947; *s* of George and Helen Burton; *m* 1973, Patricia Burton; one *s.* *Educ:* Bridlington Sch.; Leeds Univ. (BA (Hons) Geography). British Rail: Network Man., S Central Network SE, 1986; Dep. Gen. Man., Southern Region, 1988; Gen. Man., Anglia Region, 1989–91. *Recreations:* spectator sport, lousy golf. *Address:* Network House, 1 Eversholt Street, NW1 1DN. *T:* 071–922 4099.

BURTON, Sir George (Vernon Kennedy), Kt 1977; CBE 1972 (MBE (mil.) 1945); DL; Chairman, Fisons plc, 1973–84 (Chief Executive, 1966–76, Senior Vice-Chairman, 1966–71, Deputy Chairman, 1971–72); *b* 21 April 1916; *s* of late George Ethelbert Earnshaw Burton and Francesca (*née* Holden-White); *g s* of Sir Bunnell Burton, Ipswich; *m* 1st, 1945, Sarah Katherine Tcherniavsky (marr. diss.); two *s*; 2nd, 1975, Priscilla Margaret Gore, *d* of late Cecil H. King. *Educ:* Charterhouse; Germany. Served RA, 1939–45, N Africa, Sicily, Italy, Austria. Director: Barclays Bank Internat. plc, 1976–82; Thomas Tilling, 1976–83; Rolls-Royce Ltd, 1976–84. Member: Export Council for Europe, 1965–71 (Dep. Chm., 1967–71); Council, CBI, 1970–84 (Chm., CBI Overseas Cttee, 1975–81); BOTB, 1972–73 (BOTB European Trade Cttee, 1972–81; British Overseas Trade Adv. Council, 1975–79); Investment Insce Adv. Cttee, ECGD, 1971–76; Council on Internat. Develt of ODM, 1977–79; Council, BIM, 1968–70 (FBIM); NEDC, 1975–79; Whitford Cttee to Consider Law on Copyright and Designs, 1974–77; Ipswich County Borough Council, 1947–51; Ipswich Gp HMC; Assoc. for Business Sponsorship of the Arts, 1978–84; Governing Body, British National Cttee of Internat. Chamber of Commerce, 1979–86; Governor, Sutton's Hosp. in Charterhouse, 1979–; Chm., Ipswich Conservative Assoc., 1982–84. FRSA 1978. DL Suffolk, 1980. Commander: Order of Ouissam Alaouite, Morocco, 1968; Order of Léopold II, Belgium, 1974. *Recreation:* music. *Address:* Aldham Mill, Hadleigh, Suffolk IP7 6LE.

BURTON, Graham Stuart, CMG 1987; HM Diplomatic Service; Ambassador to the United Arab Emirates, since 1990; *b* 8 April 1941; *s* of late Cyril Stanley Richard Burton and of Jessie Blythe Burton; *m* 1965, Julia Margaret Lappin; one *s* one *d.* *Educ:* Sir William Borlase's Sch., Marlow. Foreign Office, 1961; Abu Dhabi, 1964; Middle East Centre for Arabic Studies, 1967; Kuwait, 1969; FCO, 1972; Tunis, 1975; UK Mission to United Nations, 1978; Counsellor, Tripoli, 1981; Head, Security Co-ordination Dept, FCO, 1984; Consul General, San Francisco, 1987. *Recreations:* golf, watching all sport, opera. *Address:* c/o Foreign and Commonwealth Office, SW1A 2AH. *Club:* MCC.

BURTON, Air Marshal Sir Harry, KCB 1971 (CB 1970); CBE 1963 (MBE 1943); DSO 1941; Air Officer Commanding-in-Chief, Air Support Command, 1970–73, retired; *b* 2 May 1919; *s* of Robert Reid Burton, Rutherglen; *m* 1st, 1945, Jean (*d* 1987), *d* of Tom Dobie; one *s* one *d*; 2nd, 1988, Sandra Robertson, *d* of Thomas McGlashan. *Educ:* Glasgow High Sch. Joined RAF 1937; served War of 1939–45, Europe, India, and Pacific (POW, 1940, escaped 1941; despatches, 1942); CO, RAF Scampton, 1960–62; SASO 3 (Bomber) Group, RAF, 1963–65; Air Executive to Deputy for Nuclear Affairs, SHAPE, 1965–67; AOC 23 Group, RAF, 1967–70. Group Captain 1958; Air Cdre 1963; Air Vice-Marshal 1965; Air Marshal 1971. *Address:* Mayfield, West Drive, Middleton-on-Sea, Sussex PO22 7TS. *Club:* Royal Air Force.

BURTON, Humphrey McGuire; Artistic Adviser, The Barbican Centre, since 1990 (Artistic Director, 1988–90); *b* 25 March 1931; *s* of Harry (Philip) and Kathleen Burton; *m* 1st, 1957, Gretel (*née* Davis); one *s* one *d*; 2nd, 1970, Christina (*née* Hellstedt); one *s* one *d.* *Educ:* Long Dene Sch., Chiddingstone; Judd Sch., Tonbridge; Fitzwilliam House, Cambridge (BA). BBC Radio, 1955–58; BBC TV, 1958–67: Editor, Monitor, 1962; Exec. Producer Music Programmes, 1963; Head of Music and Arts Programmes, 1965–67, productions inc. Workshop, Master Class, In Rehearsal, Britten at 50, Conversations with Glenn Gould; Head of Music and Arts, 1975–81; Exec. Producer opera relays from Covent Garden and Glyndebourne (Capriccio, Così fan tutte); Producer: Omnibus at Santa Fe Opera; West Side Story (Omnibus documentary), 1985; Producer/Director: TV Proms with Giulini and Solti, 1981, and with others, 1982–88; Walton 80th Birthday Concert (Previn), Verdi Requiem (Abbado), and Call me Kiri (Te Kanawa), 1982; Candide, Scottish Opera, Glasgow, 1988 and Barbican (conducted by Leonard Bernstein), 1989; Covent Garden opera relays: Manon Lescaut, Die Fledermaus, 1983; Andrea Chénier, 1985; Turandot, 1987; Die Entführung aus dem Serail, 1988; Così fan tutte, Prince Igor, 1990; Die Fledermaus (Joan Sutherland farewell), 1990. *Host of BBC series:* Omnibus, 1976–78, 1984–85; Young Musician of the Year, biennially 1978–90; Wagner's Ring, 1982; In Performance, 1978–82; Opera Month, 1979; other arts and music programmes; *London Weekend TV:* Head of Drama, Arts and Music, 1967–69; Editor/Introducer, Aquarius, 1970–75, programmes incl. Mahler Festival, Verdi Requiem, Trouble in Tahiti, The Great Gondola Race, Anatomy of a Record, etc; *other ITV companies:* 5 Glyndebourne operas, adapted and produced, Southern, 1972–74; The Beach at Falesa, World Premiere, Harlech, 1974; UN Day Concert with Pablo Casals, 1971; *French TV:* Berlioz' Requiem at Les Invalides, 1975; many free-lance prodns in Austria, Czechoslovakia, Germany, Hungary, Italy, Israel, Poland and USA, including Mahler,

Brahms, Schumann and Beethoven Cycles with Bernstein and Vienna Philharmonic; concerts with von Karajan and Berlin and Vienna Philharmonic, Giulini with LA Philharmonic, Mehta and NY Philharmonic, and Solti and Chicago SO; world première, Epitaph, by Charles Mingus, NY, 1989; Dir, Boris Godounov, Kirov, 1990. Producer: Leonard Bernstein's 70th Birthday Gala Season, Tanglewood, Mass, 1988; Bernstein Meml Concert, Carnegie Hall, 1990. Guest Dir, Hollywood Bowl 1983 Summer Music Fest. Chairman: EBU Music Experts Gp, 1976–82; EBU TV Music Working Party, 1982–86; Mem., New Music Sub-Cttee, Arts Council, 1981–83; Advr, Manchester Olympic Fest., 1990; Administrator, Royal Philharmonic Soc.'s Music Awards, 1989–. Hon. Professorial Fellow, University Coll., Cardiff, 1983–87. Hon. FCSD 1990. Desmond Davis Award, SFTA, 1966; Royal TV Soc. Silver Medal, 1971; Emmy, 1971 for 'Beethoven's Birthday' (CBS TV); Peabody Award, 1972; SFTA Best Specialised Series, 1974; Christopher Award, 1979; RAI Prize, Prix Italia and Robert Flaherty best documentary award, BAFTA (all for West Side Story), 1985; Emmy, 1988, for 'Celebrating Gershwin' (BBC TV). Chevalier de l'Ordre des Arts et des Lettres, 1975. *Publications:* contrib. Opera Now, Sunday Times, RSA Jl and Listener. *Recreations:* music-making, tennis, swimming, travel. *Address:* 123 Oakwood Court, W14 8LA. *Club:* Garrick.

BURTON, Iris Grace; Editorial Director, G+J of the UK publications, since 1988, including Prima, Best, and Let's Cook!; *d* of Arthur Burton and late Alice Burton; *m*; one *s* one *d. Educ:* Roan Girls' Grammar Sch., Greenwich; City of London Coll. Local newspaper, SE London Mercury, until 1966; Writer, then Features Editor, Woman's Own, 1966–78; Asst Editor, TV Times, 1978–80; Editor, Woman's Own, 1980–86. Editor-in-Chief: Prima magazine, 1986–87; Best magazine, 1987–88. *Address:* G+J of the UK, Portland House, Stag Place, SW1E 5AU; (home) Anerley, SE20.

BURTON, Rev. John Harold Stanley, MA Oxon; General Secretary, Church Lads' Brigade, 1954–64 and 1973–Jan. 1977; Member, Church of England Youth Council, 1954–64; *b* 6 Feb. 1913; *o s* of late John Stanley Burton, Grenadier Guards (killed in action 1916), and Lilian Bostock; *m* 1st, 1943, Susan Lella (*d* 1960), *o d* of Sir John Crisp, 3rd Bt; two *d*; 2nd, 1960, Jacqueline Mary Margaret, *o d* of P. L. Forte, Clifton, Bristol; one *d. Educ:* Marlborough; University Coll., Oxford; Westcott House, Cambridge. BA 2nd Class Hons. in Theology, Oxford, 1935; MA 1937; Deacon, 1936; Priest, 1938; Curate of Christ Church, Woburn Square, WC1, 1936–39; Cranleigh, Surrey, 1939–40; Head of Cambridge Univ. Settlement, Camberwell, 1940–43; Chaplain RAFVR, 1943; Fighter Command, 1943–44; 2nd Tactical Air Force, 1944; Bomber Command, 1945; Ordination Secretary, Air Command, SE Asia, and Chaplain 9 RAF General Hospital, Calcutta, 1945–46; demobilised Aug. 1946. Chaplain of Middlesex Hospital, W1, 1946–50; Chaplain of the Royal Free Hospital, 1950–54; Chairman of Hospital Chaplains Fellowship, 1953–54. *Publications:* (contrib.) A Priest's Work in Hospital, 1955; (contrib.) Trends in Youth Work, 1967. *Recreations:* Beagling, fishing, shooting, most games. *Address:* 45 Westbourne Terrace, W2 3UR. *T:* 071–262 8470. *Club:* Royal Air Force.

BURTON, Prof. Kenneth, FRS 1974; Professor of Biochemistry, 1966–88, now Emeritus, and Dean of Faculty of Science, 1983–86, University of Newcastle upon Tyne; *b* 26 June 1926; *s* of Arthur and Gladys Burton; *m* 1955, Hilda Marsden; one *s* one *d. Educ:* High Pavement Sch., Nottingham; Wath-upon-Dearne Grammar Sch.; King's Coll., Cambridge (MA, PhD). Asst Lectr in Biochem., Univ. of Sheffield, 1949, Lectr 1952; Res. Associate, Univ. of Chicago, 1952–54; MRC Unit for Research in Cell Metabolism, Oxford, 1954–66. Vis. Lectr in Medicine, Harvard, 1964; William Evans Vis. Prof., Univ. of Otago, 1977–78. *Publications:* scientific articles, especially on nucleic acids. *Recreations:* music, hill-walking. *Address:* 42 Cade Hill Road, Stocksfield, Northumberland NE43 7PU.

BURTON, Maurice, DSc; retired 1958; now free-lance author and journalist; *b* 28 March 1898; *s* of William Francis and Jane Burton; *m* 1929, Margaret Rosalie Maclean; two *s* one *d. Educ:* Holloway County Sch.; London Univ. Biology Master, Latymer Foundation, Hammersmith, 1924–27; Zoology Dept, British Museum (Natural History), SW7, 1927–58. Science Editor, Illustrated London News, 1946–64; Nature Correspondent, Daily Telegraph, 1949–90. FZS. Kt of Mark Twain, 1980. *Publications:* The Story of Animal Life, 1949; Animal Courtship, 1953; Living Fossils, 1954; Margins of the Sea, 1954; Animal Legends, 1955; Infancy in Animals, 1956; More Animal Legends, 1959; Phœnix Re-born, 1959; Under the Sea, 1960; Animal Senses, 1961; The Elusive Monster, 1961; Systematic Dictionary of Mammals, 1962; (jtly) Purnell's Encyclopedia of Animal Life, 1968–70; Wild Animals of the British Isles, 1968; The Hedgehog, 1969; Encyclopaedia of Animals, 1972; Introduction to Nature (for children), 1972; Prehistoric Animals, 1974; Deserts, 1974; The Colourful World of Animals, 1974; How Mammals Live, 1975; Just Like an Animal, 1978; A Zoo at Home, 1979; *juveniles:* When Dumb Animals Talk, 1955; British Mammals, 1958; Life in the Deep, 1958; In their Element, 1960; The Life of Birds, 1974; upwards of 100 non-technical books on natural history; numerous publications on Sponges in a variety of scientific journals. *Recreation:* gardening. *Address:* Weston House, Albury, Guildford, Surrey GU5 9AE. *T:* Shere (048641) 2369.

BURTON, Michael John; QC 1984; a Recorder, since 1989; *b* 12 Nov. 1946; *s* of late Henry Burton, QC, and Hilda Burton; *m* 1972, Corinne Ruth, *d* of Dr Jack Cowan, MC, and late Dorothy Cowan; four *d. Educ:* Eton Coll. (KS, Captain of the School); Balliol Coll., Oxford (MA). President, Balliol JCR, 1967; First President, Oxford Univ. SRC, 1968. Called to Bar, Gray's Inn, 1970; Law Lectr, Balliol Coll., Oxford, 1972–74. Contested: (Lab) RBK&C (local elections), 1971; (Lab) Stratford upon Avon, Feb. 1974; (SDP) Putney, GLC, 1981. *Recreations:* amateur theatricals, lyric writing, singing, bridge, watching Wimbledon Football Club. *Address:* 2 Crown Office Row, Temple, EC4Y 7HJ. *T:* 071–583 2681; High Trees, 63 Murray Road, Wimbledon, SW19 4PF.

BURTON, Michael St Edmund, CMG 1987; CVO 1979; HM Diplomatic Service; Minister, since 1985, and Head of Office, since 1990, Berlin; *b* 18 Oct. 1937; *s* of late Brig. G. W. S. Burton, DSO (and two Bars), and of Barbara Burton (*née* Kemmis Betty); *m* 1967, Henrietta Jindra Hones; one *s* one *d* (and one *d* decd). *Educ:* Bedford Sch.; Magdalen Coll., Oxford. MA. 2nd Lt, Rifle Brigade, 1955–57. Foreign Office, 1960; Asst Political Agent, Dubai, Trucial States, 1962–64; Private Sec. to Minister of State, FO, 1964–67; Second (later First) Sec. (Information), Khartoum, 1967–69; First Sec. (Inf.), Paris, 1969–72; Asst, Science and Technology Dept, FCO, 1972–75; First Sec. and Head of Chancery, Amman, 1975–77; Counsellor, Kuwait, 1977–79; Head of Maritime, Aviation and Environment Dept, FCO, 1979–81; Head of S Asian Dept, FCO, 1981–84; on secondment to BP as Head of Policy Rev. Unit, 1984–85; Dep. Comdt, Berlin, 1985–90. *Recreations:* tennis, opera, theatre, music. *Address:* c/o Foreign and Commonwealth Office, SW1A 2AH. *Clubs:* United Oxford & Cambridge University, Hurlingham.

BURTON, Richard Hilary; Chairman, Cable Authority, 1984–90; *b* 28 Dec. 1923; *s* of Robert Claud and Theodora Constance Helen Burton; *m* 1962, Priscilla Jane Coode-Adams; one *s* one *d. Educ:* Lancing; Brasenose Coll., Oxford (MA 2nd Cl. Hons Jurisprudence). Served War, 1942–46, 60th Rifles, Captain (mentioned in despatches); Mem., Military Courts, Palestine, 1946. Called to the Bar, Inner Temple, 1951; practised

at Bar, 1951–54. Gillette Industries Ltd: Manager, Legal Dept, 1954–65; Legal Dir, 1965–78; Chm., 1978–84; Dep. to the Chm., The Gillette Company (USA), 1984–88; Chm., Nestor-BNA plc, 1986–89. Chm., W Mddx Arts Develt Trust, 1978–86. Freeman: City of London, 1974; Co. of Information Technologists, 1988. FRSA. *Recreations:* cricket, real tennis, shooting, ornithology, lepidoptery. *Address:* Danmoor House, Heckfield, near Basingstoke, Hants RG27 0JY. *T:* Heckfield (0734) 326233. *Clubs:* Boodle's, MCC (Mem. Cttee, 1989–).

BURTON, Roger; City Treasurer, Birmingham City Council, since 1990; *b* 12 Oct. 1946; *s* of Norman Burton and Marjorie Rose (*née* Burgin); *m* 1st, 1968, Dorothy May Hey (marr. diss.); one *s* one *d*; 2nd, 1984, Susan Jane Griffiths; 3rd, 1991, Janet Elizabeth Mauchlen (*née* Davies); two step *s* one step *d. Educ:* Doncaster Grammar Sch.; Lanchester Polytechnic (BSc Econs 1968). CIPFA 1972; IRRV 1990. Coventry CC, 1968–79; Birmingham CC, 1979–. *Recreations:* sport, walking, photography, Real Ale. *Address:* Council House, PO Box 50, Birmingham B3 3AB. *T:* 021–235 3803.

BURTON, Sydney Harold, JP; FCBSI; Director, Gateway Building Society, 1981–88 (Managing Director, 1975–81); *b* 6 April 1916; *s* of Sydney Collard Burton and Maud Burton; *m* 1st, 1941, Jean Cowling (*d* 1985); one *d*; 2nd, 1986, Irene Robertson. *Educ:* Belle Vue High Sch., Bradford. Various appts with Bradford Equitable Building Soc. (excl. war years), 1932–63; joined Temperance Permanent Building Soc., 1963; Jt Gen. Manager, 1965; Gen. Man. and Sec., 1972; following merger of Temperance Permanent and Bedfordshire Bldg Socs became Chief Gen. Man. and Sec. of Gateway Bldg Soc., 1974. Pres., Building Societies Inst., 1976–77; Mem. Council, Building Societies Assoc., 1971–81. JP Worthing, 1974. *Recreations:* music and theatre, social and religious work. *Address:* Cherry Trees, 52 Beehive Lane, Ferring, Sussex BN12 5NR. *T:* Worthing (0903) 44704.

BURTON-BRADLEY, Sir Burton (Gyrth), Kt 1990; OBE 1982; MD; FRCPsych; Professor of Psychiatry, University of Papua New Guinea, since 1978; *b* 18 Nov. 1914; *s* of Alan Godfrey and Ruby Malvina Burton-Bradley; *m* 1950, Ingeborg Roeser (*d* 1972). *Educ:* Univs of Sydney, Melbourne, NSW; RCPsych. MD (NSW), BS. FRANZCP, FRACMA, DPM, DTM&H, DipAnth. MO, Western Suburbs Hosp., Sydney, 1945–46; GP, NSW, 1946–48; MO, Aust. Mil. Mission in Germany, 1949–50; Psychiatrist, Brisbane Mental Hosp., 1950–57; Colombo Plan Psychiatrist, Singapore, 1957–59; Lectr in Psychol Med., Univ. of Malaya, 1957–59; Chief, Mental Health, Papua New Guinea, 1959–77. Vice Pres., Asian Chapter, Internat. Coll. of Psychosomatic Medicine, 1991. Fellowships, awards, hon. appts, Canada, Europe, Japan, USA; Benjamin Rush Gold Medal, APA, 1974. Papua New Guinea Independence Medal, 1975. *Publications:* Longlong, 1973; South Pacific Ethnopsychiatry, 1967; l'Examen Psychiatrique de Autochtone de Papuasie et Nouvelle Guinée, 1967; Mixed-race Society in Port Moresby, 1968; Psychiatry and the Law in the Developing Country, 1970; Stone Age Crisis, 1975; Crisis en la edad de piedra, 1988; (ed) History of Medicine in Papua New Guinea, 1990; numerous sci. papers in learned jls. *Recreations:* patrolling, historical research in PNG. *Address:* PO Box 111, Port Moresby, Papua New Guinea. *T:* Port Moresby 255245.

BURTON-CHADWICK, Sir Joshua (Kenneth), 3rd Bt *cr* 1935; Sales Manager/Trainer, Joshua Chadwick Marketing Developers; *b* 1 Feb. 1954; *s* of Sir Robert Burton-Chadwick, (Sir Peter), 2nd Bt, and of Beryl Joan, *d* of Stanley Frederick J. Brailsford; *S* father, 1983. *Heir:* none.

BURY, John, OBE 1979; designer for theatre, opera and film; *b* 27 Jan. 1925; *s* of C. R. Bury; *m* 1st, 1947, Margaret Leila Greenwood (marr. diss.); one *s*; 2nd, 1966, Elizabeth Rebecca Blackborrow Duffield; two *s* one *d. Educ:* Cathedral Sch., Hereford; University Coll., London. Served with Fleet Air Arm (RN), 1942–46. Theatre Workshop, Stratford, E15, 1946–63; Assoc. Designer, Royal Shakespeare Theatre, 1963–73; Head of Design: RSC, 1965–68; NT, 1973–85. Arts Council: Designers' Working Gp, 1962–78; Mem., Drama Panel, 1960–68 and 1975–77; Chm., Soc. of British Theatre Designers, 1975–85. FRSA 1970. Hon. FRCA 1990. Co-winner, Gold Medal for Scene Design, Prague Quadrienale, 1975 and 1979; Antoinette Perry Awards (Best Set Design and Best Lighting), for Broadway prodn of Amadeus, 1981. *Address:* Burleigh House, Burleigh, Glos GL5 2PQ.

BURY, Lindsay Claude Neils; Chairman, Sharp Technology Fund, since 1985; Director, Apricot Computers, since 1968 (Chairman, 1972–89); *b* 13 Feb. 1939; *s* of Frank James Lindsay Bury and Diana Mary Lewis; *m* 1968, Sarah Ann Bury; one *s* one *d. Educ:* Eton; Trinity College, Cambridge (BA History). J. Henry Schroder Wragg, 1960–66; Singer & Friedlander, 1966–73; Dunbar & Co., 1973–83; Chairman: Jack Knight Group, 1985–; Sapphire International, 1990–; Director: Portals Holdings, 1973–; South Staffordshire Waterworks Co., 1981–; Electra Risk Capital, 1983–; Marwin Production Machines, 1986–; Christie Group, 1989–; Planning Consultancy, 1990–; IXI, 1990–. Chm. of Govs, Moor Park Sch.; Trustee, Millichope Foundn; WWF UK. *Recreations:* music, country pursuits. *Address:* Millichope Park, Munslow, Craven Arms, Shropshire. *T:* Munslow (058476) 234. *Club:* Turf.

BURY, Michael Oswell, OBE 1968; Consultant, Education and Training, Confederation of British Industry, 1986–87; *b* 20 Dec. 1922; *o s* of Lt-Col Thomas Oswell Bury, TD, and Constance Evelyn Bury; *m* 1954, Jean Threlkeld Wood, *d* of late William Threlkeld Wood; two *s* one *d. Educ:* Charterhouse; London Sch. of Economics. Served War of 1939–45: The Rifle Brigade (ranks of Rifleman to Captain), 1941–47. Steel Company of Wales, 1947–49; British Iron and Steel Fedn, 1949–64 (Dep. Dir, Labour and Trng, 1962–64); Dir, Iron and Steel Industry Trng Bd, 1964–70; Confederation of British Industry: Director, Educn, Trng and Technol., 1970–81; Dir, Corporate Affairs, 1981–84; Dir, Educn, Trng and Technol., 1985–86. Mem., Manpower Services Commn, 1974–81, 1985–87. *Recreations:* gardening, fishing, travel. *Address:* Springfield, Fingrith Hall Lane, Blackmore, Ingatestone, Essex CM4 0RU. *T:* Brentwood (0277) 821347. *Club:* Reform.

BURY, Shirley Joan, FSA; Keeper of Metalwork, Victoria and Albert Museum, 1982–85; *b* 1925; *d* of Ernest Leslie Saxton Watkin and Florence Keen; *m* 1947, John Morley Bury; one *s. Educ:* University of Reading. BA Fine Arts 1946, MA 1960; FSA 1972. Joined V & A 1948: Research Asst, 1948, Senior Research Asst, 1961, Circulation Dept; Asst Keeper, Library, 1962–68, Metalwork Dept, 1968–72; Dep. Keeper, Dept of Metalwork, 1972–82. Mem., British Hallmarking Council, 1974–85. Liveryman, Goldsmiths' Co., 1982–. *Publications:* Victorian Electroplate, 1972; V & A Jewellery Gallery Summary Catalogue, 1982; An Introduction to Rings, 1984; Sentimental Jewellery, 1985; Jewellery 1790–1910, 1988; (compiled and ed) Catalogue, Copy or Creation, Goldsmiths' Hall, 1967; (ed) Catalogue, Liberty's 1875–1975, V & A 1975; introd. to C. R. Ashbee, Modern English Silver, new edn 1974; contribs to Burlington Magazine, Connoisseur, Apollo, V & A Bulletin, Yearbook and Album. *Recreations:* theatre, walking, gardening.

BURY, Air Cdre Thomas Malcolm Grahame, CB 1972; OBE 1962; retired as Head of Technical Training and Maintenance, British Aircraft Corporation, Saudi Arabia; *b* 11 Sept. 1918; *s* of late Ernest Bury, OBE; *m* 1951, Dillys Elaine Jenkins, MBE, *d* of Dr Aneurin Jenkins, Swansea; two *s* one *d. Educ:* Forest Sch., E17. Served War, 1939–45,

NW Europe, Arabia. Joined RAF, 1935; STSO, HQ, 1 Gp, 1961–64; DDME, MoD, 1965–66; Senior Engr Officer, Air Forces Gulf, 1967–68; Command Mech. Engr, HQ Strike Command, 1968–73; retired 1973. *Address:* Las Bayas, 2 Benimeit, Buzón 124, Moraira, Alicante 03724, Spain.

BUSBY, Sir Matthew, Kt 1968; CBE 1958; President, Manchester United Football Club, since 1980; *b* 26 May 1909; *m* 1931, Jean Busby (*d* 1988); one *s* one *d* (and four *s* decd). *Educ:* St Brides, Bothwell. Footballer: Manchester City, 1929–36; Liverpool, 1936–39. Served Army, 1939–45. Manchester United Football Club: Manager, 1945–69; Gen. Manager, 1969–71; Dir, 1971–82. Mem., Football League Management Cttee, 1981–82. Freeman of Manchester, 1967. KCSG. *Publication:* My Story, 1957. *Recreations:* golf, theatre. *Address:* 6 Harboro Road, Sale, Cheshire M33 5AB.

BUSCH, Constantinus Albertus Maria; Corporate Finance Director, Philips International BV, since 1991; *b* 17 Aug. 1937; *m* 1963, Ingrid (*née* Haaksma); two *s* two *d*. *Educ:* in The Netherlands; Amsterdam Univ. (Economics degree). 1st Lieut, Dutch Army, 1962–64; Corporate Finance Dept, NV Philips Eindhoven, 1964–66; Manager, Philips Internat. Finance, Luxembourg, 1966–70; Naarden International NV: Treasurer, 1970–72; Dir of Finance and Mem. Bd of Management, 1973–80; Financial Dir, Philips Electronics UK, 1981–85; Corporate Finance Dir, NV Philips Eindhoven, 1985–87; UK Vice-Chm. and Financial Dir, Philips Electronics, 1988; Chm. and Man. Dir, Philips Electronics and Associated Industries, 1989–90. *Recreations:* music, particularly piano, clarinet and saxophone; tennis, golf, ski-ing. *Address:* Philips International BV, Groenewoudseweg 1, 5621 BA Eindhoven, Netherlands. *Club:* Foxhills (Addlestone).

BUSCH, Rolf Trygve; Comdr, Order of St Olav; Hon. GCVO 1988; Norwegian Ambassador to the Court of St James's, 1982–88; *b* 15 Nov. 1920; *s* of Aksel Busch and Alette (*née* Tunby); *m* 1950, Solveig Helle; one *s*. *Educ:* Oslo Univ. (degree in Law); National Defence Coll. Dep. Judge, 1946–47; entered Norwegian Foreign Service, 1947; Min. of For. Affairs, 1947–50; Sec., Cairo, 1950–52; Vice-Consul, New York, 1952–54; Min. of For. Affairs, 1954–56; National Def. Coll., 1956–57; First Sec., Norwegian Delegn to NATO, Paris, 1957–60; Min. of For. Affairs, 1960–65; Counsellor and Dep. Perm. Rep., Norwegian Delegn to NATO, Paris and Brussels, 1965–70; Dir-Gen., Min. of For. Affairs, 1970–71; Perm. Rep. to N Atlantic Council, 1971–77; Ambassador to Fed. Republic of Germany, 1977–82. Officer, Order of the Nile, Egypt; Comdr with Star, Order of the Falcon, Iceland; Grand Cross, Order of Merit, Fed. Republic of Germany. *Address:* 2 Hafrsfjords Gt, 0273 Oslo 2, Norway. *T:* 02 43 17 91.

BUSH, Alan; Composer; Conductor; Pianist; Professor of Composition, Royal Academy of Music, 1925–78; *b* 22 Dec. 1900; *s* of Alfred Walter Bush and Alice Maud (*née* Brinsley); *m* 1931, Nancy Rachel Head; two *d* (and one *d* decd). *Educ:* Highgate Sch.; Royal Academy of Music; Univ. of Berlin. ARAM 1922; Carnegie Award 1924; FRAM 1938; BMus London, 1940; DMus London, 1968. Arts Council Opera Award, 1951; Händel Prize, City Council of Halle (Saale), 1962; Corresp. Member, Deutsche Akademie der Künste, 1955. FRSA 1966. Hon. DMus Dunelm, 1970. Appeared as piano-recitalist, London, Berlin, etc., 1927–33; played solo part in own Piano Concerto, BBC, 1938, with Sir Adrian Boult conducting. Toured Ceylon, India, Australia as Examiner for Assoc. Board of Royal Schools of Music, London, 1932–33; concert tours as orchestral conductor, introducing British Music and own compositions, to USSR, 1938, 1939, 1963, 1967, 1969, 1973, Czechoslovakia, Yugoslavia, Poland, Bulgaria, 1947, Czechoslovakia and Bulgaria again, 1949, Holland, 1950, Vienna, 1951, Berlin (German Democratic Republic) and Hungary, 1952, and Berlin again, 1958; Première of opera "Wat Tyler" at the Leipzig Opera House, 1953 (British première, 1974); Première of opera "Men of Blackmoor" at the German National Theatre, Weimar, 1956; Première of opera "The Sugar Reapers" at the Leipzig Opera House, 1966; Première of opera "Joe Hill (The Man Who Never Died)", German State Opera, Berlin, 1970. Musical Adviser, London Labour Choral Union, 1929–40; Chairman Workers' Music Assoc., 1936–41 (President 1941–). Chairman Composers' Guild of Great Britain, 1947–48. *Publications:* In My Eighth Decade and Other Essays, 1980; *operas:* Wat Tyler; Men of Blackmoor; The Sugar Reapers; Joe Hill (The Man Who Never Died); and children's operettas; *choral works:* The Winter Journey, Op. 29; Song of Friendship, Op. 34; The Ballad of Freedom's Soldier, Op. 44 (mixed voices); The Dream of Llewelyn ap Gruffydd, Op. 35 (male voices); The Alps and Andes of the Living World, Op. 66 (mixed chorus); Song for Angela Davis; Africa is my Name, Op. 85; Turkish Workers' Marching Song (chorus and piano), Op. 101; The Earth in Shadow (mixed chorus and orch.), Op. 102; Mandela Speaking, to text by Nelson Mandela (baritone solo, mixed chorus and orch.), Op. 110; Folksong arrangements; *song cycles:* Voices of the Prophets, for tenor and piano, Op. 41; Seafarers' Songs for baritone and piano, Op. 57; The Freight of Harvest, for tenor and piano, Op. 69; Life's Span, for mezzo-soprano and piano, Op. 77; Three Songs for baritone and piano, Op. 86; Woman's Life, for soprano and piano, Op. 87; Two Shakespeare Sonnets, Op. 91; *orchestral works:* Dance Overture, Op. 12; Piano Concerto, Op. 18; Symphony No 1 in C, Op. 21; Overture "Resolution", Op. 25; English Suite for strings, Op. 28; Piers Plowman's Day Suite, Op. 30; Violin Concerto, Op. 32; Symphony No 2 "The Nottingham", op. 33; Concert Suite for 'cello and orchestra, Op. 37; Dorian Passacaglia and Fugue, Op. 52; Symphony No 3 "The Byron Symphony", op. 53; Variations, Nocturne and Finale on an English Sea Song for piano and orchestra, Op. 60; Partita Concertante, Op. 63; Time Remembered for Chamber Orchestra, Op. 67; Scherzo for Wind Orchestra with Percussion, Op. 68; Africa: Symphonic Movement for piano and orchestra, Op. 73; Concert Overture for an Occasion, Op. 74; The Liverpool Overture, Op. 76; Lascaux Symphony, Op. 98; Meditation in Memory of Anna Ambrose, Op. 107; Song Poem and Dance Poem for string orch. and piano, Op. 109; Serenade and Duet for string orch. and piano, Op. 111; *chamber music:* String Quartet, Op. 4; Piano Quartet, Op. 5; Five Pieces for Violin, Viola, Cello, Clarinet and Horn, Op. 6; Dialectic for string quartet, Op. 15; Three Concert Studies for piano trio, Op. 31; Suite for Two Pianos, Op. 65; Serenade for String Quartet, Op. 70; Suite of six for String Quartet, Op. 81; Compass Points, Suite for Pipes, Op. 83; Trio for clarinet, cello and piano, Op. 91; Concertino for two violins and piano, Op. 94; Piano Quintet, Op. 104; Octet for flute, clarinet, horn, string quartet and piano, Op. 105; Canzona for flute, clarinet, violin, cello and piano, Op. 106; *instrumental solos and duos:* Prelude and Fugue for piano, Op. 9; Relinquishment for piano, Op. 11; Concert Piece for 'cello and piano, Op. 17; Meditation on a German song of 1848 for violin and String Orchestra or piano, Op. 22; Lyric Interlude for violin and piano, Op. 26; Le Quatorze Juillet for piano, Op. 38; Trent's Broad Reaches for horn and piano, Op. 36; Three English Song Preludes for organ, Op. 40; Northumbrian Impressions for oboe and piano, Op. 42a; Autumn Poem for horn and piano, Op. 45; Two Ballads of the Sea for piano, Op. 50; Two Melodies for viola with piano accompaniment, Op. 47; Suite for harpsichord or piano, Op. 54; Three African Sketches for flute with piano accompaniment, Op. 55; Two Occasional Pieces for organ, Op. 56; For a Festal Occasion for organ, Op. 58A; Prelude, Air and Dance for violin with accompaniment for string quartet and percussion, Op. 61; Two Dances for Cimbalom, Op. 64; Pianoforte Sonata in A flat, Op. 71; Corentyne Kwe-Kwe for piano, Op. 75; Sonatina for recorders and piano, Op. 82; Twenty-four Preludes for Piano, Op. 84; Sonatina for viola and piano, Op. 88; Rhapsody for cello and piano, Op. 89; Meditation and Scherzo for double-bass and piano, Op. 93; Scots Jigganspiel for piano, Op. 95; Six Short Pieces for piano, Op. 99; Summer Fields and Hedgerows, Two Impressions for clarinet and piano, Op.100; Serenade and Duet for violin and piano, Op. 111; Distant Fields for piano, Op. 112; Piano Sonata in G, Op. 114; Two Pieces for Nancy for piano solo, Op. 115; Prelude and Concert Piece for organ, Op. 116; Suite for organ, Op. 117; Three Five Beat First Year Pieces for piano, Op. 118; Sonata for Piano, Op. 119; Sonata for cello and piano, Op. 120; Two Preludes and Fugues for piano, Op. 121; The Six Modes for piano duet, Op. 122; A Heart's Expression for piano, Op. 123; *textbook:* Strict Counterpoint in Palestrina Style; *essays:* In My Eighth Decade and other essays, 1980. *Recreations:* walking, foreign travel. *Address:* 25 Christchurch Crescent, Radlett, Herts WD7 8AQ. *T:* Radlett (0923) 856422.

BUSH, Bryan; His Honour Judge Bush; a Circuit Judge, since 1983; *b* 28 Nov. 1936; *s* of Maurice and Hetty Bush; *m* 1963, Jacqueline (*née* Rayman); two *s* one *d*. *Educ:* Leeds Grammar Sch.; Keble Coll., Oxford (MA). Called to the Bar, Gray's Inn, 1961; practising on NE Circuit, 1961–83; a Recorder of the Crown Court, 1978–83. *Recreations:* theatre, lawn tennis. *Address:* c/o Leeds Crown Court, Leeds LS1 3BE.

BUSH, Geoffrey Hubert; Under Secretary, Board of Inland Revenue, since 1988; *b* 5 April 1942; *s* of Sidney Arthur Bush and late Dorothy Elizabeth Bush; *m* 1965, Sylvia Mary Squibb; one *s* one *d*. *Educ:* Cotham Grammar Sch., Bristol. Tax Officer, 1959; Inspector of Taxes, 1968; Dist Inspector of Taxes, 1973; Principal Inspector of Taxes, 1981. *Recreation:* country week-ends. *Address:* (home) London and Devon; (office) c/o Board of Inland Revenue, Somerset House, WC2R 1LB. *Clubs:* Topsham Sailing (Devon); Knowle Lawn Tennis (Bristol).

BUSH, George Herbert Walker; President of the United States of America, since 1989; *b* Milton, Mass, 12 June 1924; *s* of late Prescott Sheldon Bush and of Dorothy (*née* Walker); *m* 1945, Barbara, *d* of Marvin Pierce, NY; four *s* one *d*. *Educ:* Phillips Acad., Andover, Mass; Yale Univ. (BA Econs 1948). Served War, USNR, Lieut, pilot (DFC, three Air Medals). Co-founder and Dir, Zapata Petroleum Corp., 1953–59; Founder, Zapata Offshore Co., Houston, 1954, Pres., 1956–64, Chm. Bd, 1964–66. Chm., Republican Party, Harris Co., Texas, 1963–64; Delegate, Republican Nat. Convention, 1964, 1968; Republican cand. US Senator from Texas, 1964, 1970; Mem., 90th and 91st Congresses, 7th District of Texas, 1967–70; US Perm. Rep. to UN, 1971–73; Chm., Republican Party Nat. Cttee, 1973–74; Chief, US Liaison Office, Peking, 1974–75; Dir, US Central Intelligence Agency, 1976–77; Vice-President of the USA, 1981–89. Cand. for Republican Presidential nomination, 1980. Hon. degrees from many colleges and univs incl. Beaver Coll., Adelphi Univ., Austin Coll., N Michigan Univ. *Publication:* (with Victor Gold) Looking Foward: an autobiography, 1988. *Recreations:* tennis, jogging, boating, fishing. *Address:* The White House, Washington, DC 20500, USA.

BUSH, Adm. Sir John (Fitzroy Duyland), GCB 1970 (KCB 1965; CB 1963); DSC 1941, and Bars, 1941, 1944; Vice-Admiral of the United Kingdom and Lieutenant of the Admiralty, 1979–84; *b* 1 Nov. 1914; *s* of late Fitzroy Bush, Beach, Glos; *m* 1938, Ruth Kennedy Horsey; three *s* two *d*. *Educ:* Clifton Coll. Entered Navy, 1933; served in Destroyers throughout War. Commanded HM Ships: Belvoir, 1942–44; Zephyr, 1944; Chevron, 1945–46. Comdr Dec. 1946; Plans Div., Admiralty, 1946–48; graduated Armed Forces Staff Coll., USA, 1949; Comd, HMS Cadiz, 1950–51; Capt. June 1952; Dep. Sec. Chiefs of Staff Cttee, 1953–55; Capt. (F) Sixth Frigate Sqdn, 1955–56; Cdre, RN Barracks, Chatham, 1957–59; Dir. of Plans, Admiralty, 1959–60; Rear-Adm. 1961; Flag Officer Flotillas (Mediterranean), 1961–62; Vice-Adm. 1963; Comdr, British Naval Staff and Naval Attaché, Washington, 1963–65; Vice-Chief of the Naval Staff, Ministry of Defence, 1965–67; C-in-C Western Fleet, C-in-C Eastern Atlantic, and C-in-C Channel (NATO), 1967–70; Admiral 1968; retd, 1970. Rear-Admiral of the UK, 1976–79. Dir, Gordon A. Friesen International Inc., Washington, DC, 1970–73. Adm., Texas (USA) Navy. Governor, Clifton Coll., 1973– (Chm. Council, 1978–81; Pres., 1982–87). Pres., Old Cliftonians Soc., 1967–69; Vice-Pres., Eighth Army Veterans Assoc., 1984–. Mem., E Hants District Council, 1974–76. *Recreations:* fishing, gardening. *Address:* Becksteddle House, Colemore, near Alton, Hants GU34 3PS. *T:* Tisted (042058) 367.

BUSH, Maj.-Gen. Peter John, OBE 1968; Controller, Army Benevolent Fund, 1980–87; *b* 31 May 1924; *s* of Clement Charles Victor Bush and Kathleen Mabel Peirce; *m* 1948, Jean Mary Hamilton; two *s* one *d*. *Educ:* Maidenhead County Sch. Commnd Somerset LI, 1944; comd LI Volunteers, 1966; GSO 1 HQ 14 Div./Malaya Dist, 1968; Comdr 3 Inf. Bde, 1971 (mentioned in despatches, 1973); Asst Comdt RMA Sandhurst, 1974; Chief of Staff and Head of UK Delegn to Live Oak, SHAPE, 1977–79, retd. Col, The Light Infantry, 1977–82. *Recreations:* natural history, walking, reading. *Address:* c/o Barclays Bank, High Street, Maidenhead, Berks SL6 1PX.

BUSHBY, Frederick Henry; Director of Services, Meteorological Office, 1978–84; *b* 10 Jan. 1924; *s* of Mr and Mrs Frederick George Bushby; *m* 1945, Joan Janet (*née* Gates); one *s*. *Educ:* Portsmouth Southern Secondary Sch.; Imperial Coll. of Science and Technol. (BSc 1st Cl. Hons Special Maths). ARCS. Meteorol Br., RAF, 1944–48; Meteorol Office, 1948–84; Asst Dir (Forecasting Res.), 1965–74; Dep. Dir (Dynamical Res.), 1974–77, (Forecasting), 1977–78. *Recreations:* bridge, bowls. *Address:* 25 Holmes Crescent, Wokingham, Berks RG11 2SE. *T:* Wokingham (0734) 784930.

BUSHE, Frederick Joseph William, RSA 1987 (ARSA 1977); Director and Founder, Scottish Sculpture Workshop, since 1979; *b* 1 March 1939; *s* of Frederick M. C. Bushe and Kathleen Welch; *m* 1st, 1956, Rosemary R. Beattie; three *s* one *d*; 2nd, 1984, Fiona M. S. Marr; one *d*. *Educ:* Out Lady's High Sch., Motherwell; Glasgow Sch. of Art (DA). Temp. Captain RAEC, 1954–58. Art teacher, Midlothian, 1958–60, Berwickshire, 1960–62; Lectr in Art Educn, Notre Dame, Liverpool, 1962–69, Aberdeen Coll. of Educn, 1969–79. Governor, Edinburgh Coll. of Art, 1983–88. Invited Artist: Formaviva Internat. Symposium of Sculptors, Yugoslavia, 1988; Terra Internat. Symposium, Kikinda, Yugoslavia, 1990. Work in numerous public collections; one man exhibitions: Edinburgh, 1962, 1971, 1982; Liverpool, 1966; Glasgow, 1974; Manchester, 1975; Stirling, 1978; group exhibns. *Recreation:* listening to music. *Address:* Rose Cottage, Lumsden, Huntly, Aberdeenshire AB54 4JJ. *T:* Rhynie (04646) 394.

BUSHELL, John Christopher Wyndowe, CMG 1971; HM Diplomatic Service, retired; Ambassador to Pakistan, 1976–79; *b* 27 Sept. 1919; *s* of late Colonel C. W. Bushell, RE, and Mrs Bushell, Netherbury, Dorset; *m* 1964, Mrs Theodora Todd, *d* of late Mr and Mrs Senior; one *s* (and one step *s* one step *d*). *Educ:* Winchester; Clare Coll., Cambridge. Served War of 1939–45, RAF. Entered FO, 1945; served in Moscow, Rome, FO; 1st Sec., 1950; NATO Defence Coll., Paris, 1953–54; Deputy Sec.-Gen., CENTO, 1957–59; Counsellor, 1961; Political Adviser to the Commander-in-Chief, Middle East, 1961–64; UK Delegn to NATO, Brussels, 1964–68; seconded to Cabinet Office, 1968–70; Minister and Deputy Commandant, British Mil. Govt, Berlin, 1970–74; Ambassador to Vietnam, 1974–75; FCO 1975–76. *Recreations:* varied. *Address:* 19 Bradbourne Street, SW6 3TF. *Club:* Travellers'.

BUSHNELL, Alexander Lynn, CBE 1962; County Clerk and Treasurer, Perth County Council, 1946–75, retired; *b* 13 Aug. 1911; *s* of William and Margaret Bushnell; *m* 1939, Janet Braithwaite Porteous; two *d*. *Educ:* Dalziel High Sch., Motherwell; Glasgow University. *Recreation:* golf. *Address:* 18 Fairies Road, Perth, Scotland. *T:* Perth (0738) 22675.

BUSK, Maj.-Gen. Leslie Francis Harry, CB 1990; Director General, British Heart Foundation, since 1990; *b* 12 Sept. 1937; *s* of late Lt-Col Charles William Francis Busk and Alice (*née* van Bergen); *m* 1960, Jennifer Helen Ring; three *s*. *Educ:* Wellington Coll.; RMA, Sandhurst; RMCS, Shrivenham (BSc (Eng) London Univ.). Commnd RE, 1957; served in UK, NI, BAOR, India and Singapore; Defence Services Staff Coll., India, 1969; OC 25 Field Sqn, 1971–73; Instr, Staff Coll., Camberley, 1975–77; CO 35 Engr Regt, 1977–79; C of S 2nd Armoured Div., 1979–81; Bde Comd 11 Engr Bde, 1981–83; RCDS, 1984; DMO, MoD, 1985–86; Army Pilots Course, 1986–87; Dir, AAC, 1987–89, retd. Hon. Col, RE Volunteers (Sponsored Units), 1986–; Col Comdt, RE, 1990–. President: Army Gliding Assoc., 1987–; Army Hockey Assoc., 1988–. *Recreations:* golf, tennis, mounting and framing pictures. *Address:* British Heart Foundation, 14 Fitzhardinge Street, W1H 4DH. *Club:* Naval and Military.

BUSS, Barbara Ann, (Mrs Lewis Boxall); freelance journalist, since 1976; Editor-in-Chief, Woman magazine, 1974–75; Consultant, IPC Magazines Ltd, 1975–76; *b* 14 Aug. 1932; *d* of late Cecil Edward Buss and Victoria Lilian (*née* Vickers); *m* 1966, Lewis Albert Boxall (*d* 1983); no *c*. *Educ:* Lady Margaret Sch., London. Sec., Conservative Central Office, 1949–52; Sec./journalist, Good Taste magazine, 1952–56; Journalist: Woman and Beauty, 1956–57; Woman, 1957–59; Asst Editor, Woman's Illustrated, 1959–60; Editor, Woman's Illustrated, 1960–61; Journalist, Daily Herald, 1961; Associate Editor, Woman's Realm, 1961–62; Editor: Woman's Realm, 1962–64; Woman, 1964–74. *Recreations:* reading, theatre, cinema. *Address:* 1 Arlington Avenue, N1 7BE. *T:* 071–226 3265.

BUSVINE, Prof. James Ronald; Professor of Entomology as applied to Hygiene in the University of London, 1964–76, Emeritus Professor 1977; *b* 15 April 1912; *s* of William Robert and Pleasance Dorothy Busvine; *m* 1960, Joan Arnfield; one *s* one *d*. *Educ:* Eastbourne Coll.; Imperial Coll. of Science and Technology, London Univ. BSc Special (1st Class Hons) 1933; PhD 1938; DSc 1948, London. Imperial Chemical Industries, 1936–39; MRC Grants, 1940–42; Entomological Adviser, Min. of Health, 1943–45; London Sch. of Hygiene and Tropical Medicine: Lecturer 1946; Reader 1954; Professor 1964. Member: WHO Panel of Experts on Insecticides, 1956– (Cttee Chm. 1959 and 1968); FAO Panel of Experts on Pest Resistance, 1967– (Cttee Rapporteur). Has travelled professionally in Malaya, Ceylon, Africa, USA, India, etc. *Publications:* Insects and Hygiene, 1951 (3rd edn 1980); A Critical Review of the Techniques for Testing Insecticides, 1957, 2nd edn 1971; Anthropod Vectors of Disease, 1975; Insects, Hygiene and History, 1976; I warmed both Hands, 1986; numerous scientific articles. *Recreations:* painting, golf. *Address:* Musca, 26 Braywick Road, Maidenhead, Berks SL6 1DA. *T:* Maidenhead (0628) 22888.

BUTCHER, Anthony John; QC 1977; a Recorder, since 1985; *b* 6 April 1934; *s* of late F. W. Butcher and of O. M. Butcher (*née* Ansell); *m* 1959, Maureen Workman (*d* 1982); one *s* two *d*. *Educ:* Cranleigh Sch.; Sidney Sussex Coll., Cambridge (MA, LLB). Called to the Bar, Gray's Inn, 1957, Bencher, 1986; in practice at English Bar, 1957–. Chm., Official Referees Bar Assoc., 1986–. *Recreations:* enjoying the arts and acquiring useless information. *Address:* Anthony Cottage, Polecat Valley, Hindhead, Surrey. *T:* Hindhead (042873) 4155; 1 Atkin Building, Gray's Inn, WC1R 5BQ. *T:* 071–404 0102. *Clubs:* Garrick, Beefsteak.

BUTCHER, John Patrick; MP (C) Coventry South West, since 1979. *Educ:* Huntingdon Grammar Sch.; Birmingham Univ. (BSocSc). Marketing exec. and Product Manager, computer industry, 1968–79. Mem., Birmingham City Council, 1972–78 (Vice-Chm., Educn Cttee). Parly Under Sec. of State, DoI, 1982–83, DTI, 1983–88, DES, 1988–89. *Address:* c/o House of Commons, SW1A 0AA.

BUTCHER, Richard James; Under Secretary (Legal), Department of Health and Social Security, 1983–87, retired; *b* 5 Dec. 1926; *s* of late James Butcher, MBE and Kathleen Butcher; *m* 1954, Sheila Joan Windridge; one *s* two *d*. *Educ:* City of London Sch.; Peterhouse, Cambridge (BA 1948, MA 1961). Called to the Bar, Lincoln's Inn, 1950. Served Educn Br., RAF, 1948–50 (Flying Officer). Entered Legal Civil Service as Legal Asst, 1951; Sen. Legal Asst, 1960; Asst Solicitor, 1971. *Recreation:* gardening. *Address:* The Knoll, Park View Road, Woldingham, Surrey CR3 7DN. *T:*Woldingham (0883) 652275.

BUTCHER, Willard Carlisle; Chairman, Executive Committee, Chase Manhattan Bank (formerly Chase National Bank), New York City, since 1990 (Chairman and Chief Executive, 1981–90); *b* Bronxville, NY, 25 Oct. 1926; *s* of Willard F. Butcher and Helen Calhoun; *m* 1st, 1949, Sarah C. Payne (*d* 1955); two *d*; 2nd, 1956, Elizabeth Allen (*d* 1978); one *s* one *d*; 3rd, 1979, Carole E. McMahon; one *s*. *Educ:* Scarsdale High School, New York; Middlebury Coll., Vermont; Brown Univ., Rhode Island (BA; Fellow, 1981). Served with USNR, 1944–45. Joined Chase National Bank, 1947; Asst Vice-Pres., 1956; Vice-Pres., 1958; Sen. Vice-Pres., 1961; assigned Internat. Dept, 1968; Exec. Vice-Pres. in charge of Dept, 1969; Vice-Chm. 1972; Pres. 1972–81; Chief Exec. Officer, 1979. Trustee, Amer. Enterprise Inst. (Chm., 1986–90). Director: Texaco Inc., 1981–; Asarco Inc., 1974–; Lincoln Center for the Performing Arts, 1981– (Vice Chm., 1986–); International Paper, 1989–. Hon. LLD: Pepperdine Univ.; Tulane Univ.; Hon. HLD Pace Univ. *Address:* 101 Park Avenue, NY 10178, USA.

BUTE, 6th Marquess of, *cr* 1796; **John Crichton-Stuart,** JP; Viscount Ayr, 1622; Bt 1627; Earl of Dumfries, Lord Crichton of Sanquhar and Cumnock, 1633; Earl of Bute, Viscount Kingarth, Lord Mountstuart, Cumrae, and Inchmarnock, 1703; Baron Mountstuart, 1761; Baron Cardiff, 1776; Earl of Windsor; Viscount Mountjoy, 1796; Hereditary Sheriff of Bute; Hereditary Keeper of Rothesay Castle; Lieutenant (RARO) Scots Guards, 1953; Lord-Lieutenant of Argyll and Bute, since 1990; *b* 27 Feb. 1933; *er s* (twin) of 5th Marquess of Bute and of Eileen, Marchioness of Bute, *yr d* of 8th Earl of Granard; *S* father, 1956; *m* 1st, 1955, Nicola (marr. diss. 1977), *o d* of late Lt-Comdr W. B. C. Weld-Forester, CBE; two *s* one *d* (and one *d* decd); 2nd, 1978, Mrs Jennifer Percy. *Educ:* Ampleforth Coll.; Trinity Coll., Cambridge. Pres., Scottish Standing Cttee for Voluntary Internat. Aid, 1968–75 (Chm., 1964–68); Chairman: Council and Exec. Cttee, National Trust for Scotland, 1969–84 (Vice-Pres., 1984–); Scottish Cttee, National Fund for Res. into Crippling Diseases, 1966–; Historic Bldgs Council for Scotland, 1983–88; Museums Adv. Bd (Scotland), 1984–85; Member: Countryside Commission for Scotland, 1970–78; Design Council, Scottish Cttee, 1972–76; Development Commission, 1973–78; Oil Develt Council for Scotland, 1973–78; Bd, British Council, 1987– (Chm., Scottish Adv. Cttee, 1987–); Council, RSA, 1990–. Trustee, Nat. Galleries of Scotland, 1980–87; Chm. Trustees, Nat. Museums of Scotland, 1985–. Hon. Sheriff-Substitute, County of Bute, 1976. Fellow, Inst. of Marketing, 1967; Hon. FIStructE, 1976; Hon. FRIAS, 1985. Pres., Scottish Veterans' Garden City Assoc. (Inc.), 1971–. Buteshire CC, 1956–75; Convener, 1967–70; DL Bute, 1961, Lord Lieutenant, 1967–75; JP Bute 1967. Hon. LLD Glasgow, 1970. *Heir:* *s* Earl of Dumfries, *qv*. *Address:* Mount Stuart, Rothesay, Isle of Bute PA20 9LR. *T:* Rothesay (0700) 502730. *Clubs:* Turf, White's; New, Puffin's (Edinburgh); Cardiff and County (Cardiff).

BUTENANDT, Prof. Adolf; Dr phil.; Dr med. hc; Dr med. vet. hc; Dr rer. nat. hc; Dr phil. hc; Dr sci. hc; Dr ing. eh; President, Max Planck Society, 1960–72, Hon. President since 1972; Director, Max Planck Institute for Biochemistry, München (formerly Kaiser Wilhelm Institute for Biochemistry, Berlin-Dahlem), 1936–72; Professor Ord. of Physiological Chemistry, München, 1956–71; Nobel Prize for Chemistry, 1939; *b* Bremerhaven-Lehe, 24 March 1903; *m* 1931, Erika von Ziegner; two *s* five *d*. *Educ:* Universities of Marburg and Göttingen. Privatdozent, Univ. of Göttingen, 1931; Prof. Ord. of Organic Chemistry, Technische Hochschule, Danzig, 1933; Honorarprofessor, Univ. Berlin, 1938; Prof. Ord. of Physiological Chemistry, Tübingen, 1945. Foreign Member: Royal Society, 1968; Académie des Sciences, Paris, 1974. *Publications:* numerous contribs to Hoppe-Seyler, Liebigs Annalen, Berichte der deutschen chemischen Gesellschaft, Zeitschrift für Naturforschung, etc. *Address:* München 60, Marsop Str. 5, Germany. *T:* (089) 885490.

BUTLER, family name of **Earl of Carrick,** of **Baron Dunboyne,** of **Earl of Lanesborough,** of **Viscount Mountgarret,** and of **Marquess of Ormonde.**

BUTLER, Rt. Hon. Sir Adam (Courtauld), Kt 1986; PC 1984; Director, H. P. Bulmer Holdings plc, since 1988; Deputy Chairman, CMW Group plc, since 1989; *b* 11 Oct. 1931; *s* of late Baron Butler of Saffron Walden, KG, CH, PC and late Sydney, *o c* of late Samuel Courtauld; *m* 1955, Felicity Molesworth-St Aubyn; two *s* one *d*. *Educ:* Eton; Pembroke College, Cambridge. National Service, 2nd Lieut KRRC, 1949–51. Cambridge (BA History/Economics), 1951–54. ADC to Governor-General of Canada, 1954–55; Courtaulds Ltd, 1955–73; Director: Aristoc Ltd, 1966–73; Kayser Bondor Ltd, 1971–73; Capital and Counties Property Co., 1973–79. MP (C) Bosworth, 1970–87. PPS to: Minister of State for Foreign Affairs, 1971–72; Minister of Agriculture, Fisheries and Food, 1972–74; PPS to Leader of the Opposition, 1975–79; an Asst Govt Whip, 1974; an Opposition Whip, 1974–75; Minister of State: DoI, 1979–81; NI Office, 1981–84; Defence Procurement, 1984–85. Mem. NFU. Mem. Court of Assistants, Goldsmiths' Co. 1987–. Chairman: Samuel Courtauld Trustees, 1989–; Airey Neave Trust, 1989–. Mem. Council, RSA, 1986–. Pres., BHS, 1989–. *Recreations:* field sports, music, pictures. *Address:* The Old Rectory, Lighthorne, Warwick. *T:* Leamington Spa (0926) 651214.

See also Hon. Sir R. C. Butler.

BUTLER, Allan Geoffrey Roy; HM Diplomatic Service, retired; Director, Saatchi & Saatchi Strategy; *b* 25 Aug. 1933; *s* of Frederick William Butler and Florence May Butler; *m* 1965, Pauline Rosalind Birch, SRN; three *d*. *Educ:* Chatham House School, Ramsgate. RAF, 1952–54. Colonial Office, 1954–66; served in Aden and Washington; Asst Private Sec. to Colonial Sec., 1965–66; HM Diplomatic Service, 1966; Birmingham University, 1966; Consul, Athens, 1967; First Sec., Athens, 1969, Georgetown, 1972, FCO, 1975; Head of Chancery, Dakar, 1977; Nat. Defence Coll., Latimer, 1981; Head of Parly Relations Unit, FCO, 1981; Ambassador to Mongolian People's Republic, 1984; Dep. Perm. Rep., UK Delegn to the Council of Europe, 1987–89. *Recreations:* walking, listening to music. *Address:* 123 Jay Court, Austin Road, Battersea, SW11 4LE.

BUTLER, Anthony John; Director of Personnel and Finance, HM Prison Service, since 1990; *b* 30 Jan. 1945; *s* of Martin Edward and Freda Alice Butler; *m* 1967, Margaret Ann, *d* of George and Margaret Randon; one *s* one *d*. *Educ:* Maidstone Grammar Sch.; University Coll., Oxford (Exhibnr, Mod. Hist.; MA); Inst. of Criminology and Trinity Hall, Cambridge (Dip. Crim.); Cambridge–Columbia Fellow, Columbia Law Sch., NY. Joined Home Office as Asst Principal, 1969; Police and Criminal Depts, 1969–72; Private Sec. to Minister of State, Home Office, 1972–74; Principal, Gen. Dept, Sex Discrimination and Race Relations Legislation Units and Broadcasting Dept, 1974–79; Private Sec. to Sec. of State for the Home Dept, 1979–80; Asst Sec., Broadcasting, Finance and Prisons Depts, 1980–88; Asst Under-Sec. of State, seconded to DoE, 1988 as Dir, Inner Cities; Principal Finance Officer, Home Office, 1990. Trustee, University Coll. Oxford Old Members' Trust, 1988–. *Recreations:* music, walking. *Address:* Home Office, Cleland House, Page Street, SW1P 4LN.

BUTLER, Arthur William, ERD 1964; Consultant on Parliamentary Relations to McAvoy Wreford Bayley, since 1989; Secretary, Parliamentary & Scientific Committee, since 1979; *b* 20 Jan. 1929; *s* of late F. Butler and of E. Butler; *m* 1958, Evelyn Mary Luetchford; one *d*. *Educ:* Wanstead High Sch.; LSE (BSc (Econ)). Universities' Prize Essayist, RAS, 1950. Nat. Service, India Cadet Co., Queen's Royal Regt, RAOC, 1946–48, 2nd Lt; Lt, AER, RAOC, 1953, Capt., 1957–64. Trainee, Kemsley Newspapers Graduate Trng Course, Middlesbrough Evening Gazette, 1951–55; Political Correspondent, News Chronicle, 1956–60; Political Ed., Reynolds News, 1960–62; Political Correspondent, Daily Express, 1963–69; Political Ed., Daily Sketch, 1969–71; Man. Dir, Partnerplan Public Affairs, 1971–74; Dir, Public Affairs Div., John Addey Associates, 1974–77; Vice-Chm., Charles Barker Watney & Powell, 1988–89 (Jt. Man. Dir, 1978–87). Secretary: Roads Campaign Council, 1974–86; All-Party Roads Study Gp, 1974–86; Founder Secretary: Parly All-Party Motor Industry Gp, 1978–90; Parly IT Cttee, 1981–84. Jt Managing Editor, Science in Parliament, 1989–; Editor, Free Romanian (English edn), 1985–. MRI. Freeman, City of London, 1976; Liveryman, Co. of Tobacco Pipe Makers, 1977. *Publications:* No Feet to Drag (with Alfred Morris, MP), 1972; (with C. Powell) The First Forty Years: a history of the Parliamentary & Scientific Committee, 1980; (with D. Smith) Lobbying in the British Parliament, 1986; articles in newspapers and various pubns. *Recreations:* travel, collecting books and militaria, gardening. *Address:* 30 Chester Way, Kennington, SE11 4UR. *T:* 071–587 5170.

BUTLER, Mrs Audrey Maude Beman, MA; Headmistress, Queenswood (GSA), Hatfield, Herts, since 1981; *b* 31 May 1936; *d* of Robert Beman Minchin and Vivien Florence Fraser Scott; *m* 1959, Anthony Michael Butler (marr. diss. 1981); two *d*. *Educ:* Queenswood, Hatfield; St Andrews Univ., Scotland (1st Cl. MA Hons, Geography and Polit. Economy; Scottish Univs Medal, RSGS, 1957–58). Asst Geography Teacher, Queenswood, 1958–59; part-time teacher, Raines Foundn Sch. for Girls, Stepney, 1959–61; Head of Geography, S Michael's, Burton Park, 1970–73, VI Form Tutor/Geography asst, 1974–78; first House Mistress of Manor House, Lancing Coll., 1978–81. Chm., Boarding Schs Assoc., 1989–91; Mem. Exec. Cttee, GSA, 1987–. Governor: Duncombe Sch., 1982–; Tockington Manor Sch., 1984–; Aldenham Sch., 1987–; Maltman's Green Sch., 1988–. Hon. Vice-Pres., Sussex County Ladies Golf Assoc., 1981–83; Vice-Pres., Herts LTA, 1986–. FRGS; Mem. Geographical Assoc.; MInstD 1986. *Recreations:* tennis and hockey (Blues, St Andrews Univ., 1956–57), golf (Sussex County Colours, 1970), travel. *Address:* Queenswood, Shepherd's Way, Brookmans Park, Hatfield, Herts AL9 6NS. *T:* Potters Bar (0707) 52262.

BUTLER, Basil Richard Ryland, OBE 1976; FEng; FIMM; Director: Brown and Root (UK) Ltd, since 1991; Murphy Oil Corp., Arkansas, since 1991; Chairman, BP Solar International, since 1991; *b* 1 March 1930; *s* of Hugh Montagu Butler and Annie Isabelle (*née* Wiltshire); *m* 1954, Lilian Joyce Haswell; one *s* two *d*. *Educ:* Denstone Coll., Staffs;

St John's Coll., Cambridge (MA). Reservoir Engr, Trinidad Leaseholds Ltd, 1954; Petroleum Engr to Chief Petroleum Engr and Supt Prodn Planning Div., Kuwait Oil Co., 1958–68; transf. to BP, Operations Man., Colombia, 1968; Ops Man., BP Alaska Inc., Anchorage, 1970; seconded to Kuwait Oil Co. as Gen. Man. Ops, 1972; Manager: Ninian Develts, BP Petroleum Development Co. Ltd, London, 1975; Sullom Voe Terminal, Shetland Is, 1976; BP Petroleum Development Ltd: Gen. Man., Exploration and Prodn, Aberdeen, 1978; Chief Exec., London, 1980; Dir, BP Internat. Ltd; Chm., BP Exploration Co. Ltd, 1986–89 (Man. Dir and Chief Exec., 1986); Man. Dir, British Petroleum Co. plc, 1986–91. Mem., Cttee for ME Trade. Pres., Inst. of Petroleum, 1990–June 1992. Liveryman, Shipwrights' Co., 1988. *Recreations:* sailing, music. *Address:* Brown and Root (UK) Ltd, 150 The Broadway, Wimbledon, SW19 1RX. *T:* 081–544 6616.

BUTLER, (Christopher) David; Deputy Director, Department for National Savings, since 1989; *b* 27 May 1942; *s* of Major B. D. Butler, MC (killed in action, 1944) and H. W. Butler (*née* Briggs); *m* 1967, Helen Christine, *d* of J. J. Cornwell and G. Cornwell (*née* Veysey); two *d*. *Educ:* Christ's Hospital; Jesus College, Oxford (MA). Joined HM Treasury, 1964; Asst Private Sec. to Chancellor of Exchequer, 1967–69; Sec., Cttee to Review Nat. Savings (Page Cttee), 1970–72; Head of public expenditure divs, HM Treasury, 1978–82; Head of corporate planning div., Central Computer and Telecoms Agency, 1982–85; HM Treasury: Under-Sec., 1985–89; Head of running costs, manpower and superannuation group, 1985–86; Principal Estabt and Finance Officer, 1987–89. Governor, Sadler's Wells Foundn, 1989–; Dir, Sadler's Wells Trust Ltd, 1989–. *Recreations:* ballet, opera, reading, family activities. *Address:* c/o Department for National Savings, Charles House, 375 Kensington High Street, W14 8SD.

BUTLER, Christopher John; MP (C) Warrington South, since 1987; *b* 12 Aug. 1950; *s* of Dr John Lynn Butler and late Eileen Patricia Butler; *m* 1989, Jacqueline Clair, *d* of Mr and Mrs R. O. F. Harper, Lymm, Cheshire. *Educ:* Emmanuel Coll., Cambridge (MA). Market Research Consultant, 1975–77; Cons. Res. Dept, 1977–80; Political Office, 10 Downing Street, 1980–83; Special Advr, Sec. of State for Wales, 1983–85; Market Res. Consultant, 1985–86; Special Advr, Minister for the Arts, and of the Civil Service, 1986–87. Mem., Select Cttee on Employment, 1990–. Vice Chm., All Party Leasehold Reform Gp, 1989–; Secretary: All Party Drugs Misuse Cttee, 1989–; All Party Penal Affairs Cttee, 1990–. *Recreations:* writing, tennis. *Address:* Flat 2, 48 Clifton Gardens, W9 1AU.

BUTLER, Sir Clifford (Charles), Kt 1983; FRS 1961; BSc, PhD; Vice-Chancellor of Loughborough University of Technology, 1975–85; *b* 20 May 1922; *s* of C. H. J. and O. Butler, Earley, Reading; *m* 1947, Kathleen Betty Collins; two *d*. *Educ:* Reading Sch.; Reading Univ. BSc 1942, PhD 1946, Reading. Demonstrator in Physics, Reading Univ., 1942–45; Asst Lecturer in Physics, Manchester Univ., 1945–47, Lecturer in Physics, 1947–53; Imperial College of Science and Technology, London: Reader in Physics, 1953–57; Professor of Physics, 1957–63; Asst Dir, Physics Dept, 1955–62; Prof. of Physics and Head of Physics Dept, 1963–70; Dean, Royal Coll. of Science, 1966–69; Dir, Nuffield Foundn, 1970–75. Charles Vernon Boys Prizeman, London Physical Soc., 1956. Member: Academic Planning Board, Univ. of Kent, 1963–71; Schools Council, 1965–84; Nuclear Physics Board of SRC, 1965–68; University Grants Cttee, 1966–71; Council, Charing Cross Hosp. Med. Sch., 1970–73; Council, Open Univ., 1971–85 (Vice-Chm., 1986–); Science Adv. Cttee, British Council, 1980–85; Chairman: Track Chamber Cttee, CERN, 1962–65; Standing Education Cttee, Royal Society, 1970–80; Council for the Educn and Training of Health Visitors, 1977–83; Adv. Council for Supply and Educn of Teachers, 1980–85; Steering Cttee, DES Educnl Counselling and Credit Transfer Information Service Project, 1983–89; ABRC/NERC Study Gp into Geol Surveying, 1985–87; Working Party on Res. Selectivity, Dept of Educn, NI, QUB and Univ. of Ulster, 1986–87. Pres., Internat. Union of Pure and Applied Physics, 1975–78 (Sec.-Gen., 1963–72; first Vice-Pres., 1972–75). Hon. DSc Reading, 1976; DUniv Open, 1986; Hon. DTech Loughborough, 1987. *Publications:* scientific papers on electron diffraction, cosmic rays and elementary particle physics in Proc. Royal Society and Physical Society, Philosophical Magazine, Nature, and Journal of Scientific Instruments, etc. *Address:* Low Woods Farm House, Belton, Loughborough, Leics LE12 9TR. *T:* Coalville (0530) 223125. *Club:* Athenæum.

BUTLER, Dr Colin Gasking, OBE 1970; FRS 1970; retired as Head of Entomology Department, Rothamsted Experimental Station, Harpenden, 1972–76 (Head of Bee Department, 1943–72); *b* 26 Oct. 1913; *s* of Rev. Walter Gasking Butler and Phyllis Pearce; *m* 1937, Jean March Innes; one *s* one *d*. *Educ:* Monkton Combe Sch., Bath; Queens' Coll., Cambridge. MA 1937, PhD 1938, Cantab. Min. of Agric. and Fisheries Research Schol., Cambridge, 1935–37; Supt Cambridge Univ. Entomological Field Stn, 1937–39; Asst Entomologist, Rothamsted Exper. Stn, 1939–43. Hon. Treas., Royal Entomological Soc., 1961–69, Pres., 1971–72, Hon. FRES, 1984; Pres., Internat. Union for Study of Social Insects, 1969–73; Mem., NT Regional Cttee for Devon and Cornwall, 1982–89. FRPS 1957; FIBiol. Hon. Fellow, British Beekeepers' Assoc., 1983. Silver Medal, RSA, 1945. *Publications:* The Honeybee: an introduction to her sense physiology and behaviour, 1949; The World of the Honeybee, 1954; (with J. B. Free) Bumblebees, 1959; scientific papers. *Recreations:* nature photography, fishing. *Address:* Silver Birches, Porthpean, St Austell, Cornwall PL26 6AU. *T:* St Austell (0726) 72480.

BUTLER, David; *see* Butler, C. D.

BUTLER, David; Chairman, Butler Cox & Partners, since 1977; *b* 1 Feb. 1936; *s* of James Charles Butler and Ethel Violet (*née* Newell); *m* 1st, 1956, Catherine Anita Harry (marr. diss. 1974); one *s* two *d*; 2nd, 1975, Frances Mary McMahon; one *d*. *Educ:* Mill Hill Sch.; Keble Coll., Oxford (BA Lit. Hum.). Management Trainee, Herts CC, 1960–64; Computer Manager, NW Metropolitan Hosp. Bd, 1964–65; Management Consultant, Urwick Gp, 1965–72; Dir, Diebold Europe, 1972–76; Chm., Butler Cox Foundn, 1977–. Director: Istel, 1983–; Octagon Services, 1986–; JMI Advisory Services, 1986–; Investment Advr, United Bank of Kuwait, 1985–. Mem., Fraud Trials Cttee, 1984–85; Vice Pres., BCS, 1981–83; Chm., Humanitec Foundn for the disabled, 1986–. *Publications:* The Convergence of Technologies, 1977; Britain and the Information Society, 1981; A Director's Guide to Information Technology, 1982; Trends in Information Technology, 1984; Information Technology and Realpolitik, 1986; The Men who Mastered Time (novel), 1986; Senior Management IT Education, 1987; numerous press articles. *Recreations:* cricket, Rugby, ancient history. *Address:* 12 Laurel Road, SW13 0EE. *T:* 081–876 1810. *Clubs:* United Oxford & Cambridge University, Real Time.

BUTLER, David Edgeworth, CBE 1991; Fellow of Nuffield College, Oxford, since 1954; *b* 1924; *yr s* of late Professor Harold Edgeworth Butler and Margaret, *d* of Prof. A. F. Pollard; *m* 1962, Marilyn Speers Evans (*see* M. S. Butler); three *s*. *Educ:* St Paul's; New Coll., Oxford (MA, DPhil). J. E. Procter Visiting Fellow, Princeton Univ., 1947–48; Student, Nuffield Coll., 1949–51; Research Fellow, 1951–54; Dean and Senior Tutor, 1956–64. Served as Personal Assistant to HM Ambassador in Washington, 1955–56. Hon. DUniv Paris, 1978; Hon. DSSc QUB, 1985. Co-editor, Electoral Studies, 1982–. *Publications:* The British General Election of 1951, 1952; The Electoral System in Britain 1918–51, 1953; The British General Election of 1955, 1955; The Study of Political Behaviour, 1958; (ed) Elections Abroad, 1959; (with R. Rose) The British General Election of 1959, 1960; (with J. Freeman) British Political Facts, 1900–1960, 1963; (with A. King) The British General Election of 1964, 1965; The British General Election of 1966, 1966; (with D. Stokes) Political Change in Britain, 1969; (with M. Pinto-Duschinsky) The British General Election of 1970, 1971; The Canberra Model, 1973; (with D. Kavanagh) The British General Election of February 1974, 1974; (with D. Kavanagh) The British General Election of October 1974, 1975; (with U. Kitzinger) The 1975 Referendum, 1976; (ed) Coalitions in British Politics, 1978; (ed with A. H. Halsey) Policy and Politics, 1978; (with A. Ranney), Referendums, 1978; (with A. Sloman) British Political Facts 1900–79, 1980; (with D. Kavanagh) The British General Election of 1979, 1980; (with D. Marquand) European Elections and British Politics, 1981; (with A. Ranney) Democracy at the Polls, 1981; (with V. Bogdanor) Democracy and Elections, 1983; Governing without a Majority, 1983; (with D. Kavanagh) The British General Election of 1983, 1984; A Compendium of Indian Elections, 1984; (with P. Jowett) Party Strategies in Britain, 1985; (with G. Butler) British Political Facts 1900–85, 1986; (with D. Kavanagh) The British General Election of 1987, 1988; British Elections since 1945, 1989; (with A. Low) Sovereigns and Surrogates, 1991; (with P. Roy) India Decides 1952–1989, 1991; (with B. Cain) Congressional Redistricting, 1991. *Address:* Nuffield College, Oxford. *T:* Oxford (0865) 278591. *Club:* United Oxford & Cambridge University.

BUTLER, Denis William Langford; Comptroller and City Solicitor to the City of London, 1981–89; *b* 26 Oct. 1926; *s* of late William H. Butler, Shrewsbury and Kitty Butler; *m* 1953, Marna (*née* Taylor); three *d*. *Educ:* Repton. RM, 1945–47. Admitted Solicitor, 1951. Assistant Solicitor: Norfolk CC, 1953–54; Shropshire CC, 1954–57; Sen. Asst Solicitor, Lindsey (Lincs) CC, 1957–60; Dep. Clerk, 1960–74, County Solicitor and Clerk, 1974–81, Wilts CC. Chm., County Secs Soc., 1974–76. Freeman, City of London, 1981; Liveryman, City of London Solicitors' Co., 1983–. *Recreations:* travel, gardening. *Address:* Pipers Croft, 18 Riverside Close, Laverstock, Salisbury, Wilts SP1 1QW. *T:* Salisbury (0722) 339035. *Clubs:* City Livery, Guildhall.

BUTLER, Edward Clive Barber, FRCS; Surgeon: The London Hospital, E1, 1937–69; Haroldwood Hospital, Essex, 1946–69; retired; *b* 8 April 1904; *s* of Dr Butler, Hereford; *m* 1939, Nancy Hamilton Harrison, Minneapolis, USA; two *s* one *d*. *Educ:* Shrewsbury Sch.; London Hospital. MRCS, LRCP 1928; MB, BS London, 1929; FRCS 1931. Resident posts London Hosp., 1928–32; Surgical Registrar, London Hosp., 1933–36; Surgeon, RMS Queen Mary, Cunard White Star Line, 1936. Hunterian Prof., RCS, 1939; examinerships at various times to London Univ. and Coll. of Surgeons. Pres. section of Proctology, Royal Soc. of Medicine, 1951–52; Member: Medical Soc. London; Royal Soc. Medicine. *Publications:* chapter on bacteraemia, in British Surgical Practice, 1948; on hand infections, in Penicillin (by Fleming), 1950; (jointly) on combined excision of rectum, in Treatment of Cancer and Allied Diseases (New York), 1952; articles on various surgical subjects in Lancet, BMJ, Proc. Royal Soc. Med., British Journal Surgery. *Recreations:* golf, gardening and yachting. *Address:* Flat 304, Enterprise House, Chingford, E4. *Club:* United Hospitals Sailing.

BUTLER, Air Vice-Marshal Eric Scott, CB 1957; OBE 1941; RAF; AOA HQ Fighter Command, 1957–61; *b* 4 Nov. 1907; *s* of Archibald Butler, Maze Hill, St Leonards-on-Sea, Sussex; *m* 1936, Alice Evelyn Tempest Meates (*d* 1985); three *s* one *d*. *Educ:* Belfast Academy. Commissioned RAF 1933; Bomber Command European War, 1939–45; idc 1952; Director of Organisation, Air Ministry, 1953–56. *Address:* Camden Cottage, High Street, Pevensey, Sussex BN24 5JP. *T:* Eastbourne (0323) 762353. *Club:* Royal Air Force.

BUTLER, Sir (Frederick Edward) Robin, KCB 1988; CVO 1986; Secretary of the Cabinet and Head of the Home Civil Service, since 1988; *b* 3 Jan. 1938; *s* of late Bernard Butler and of Nora Butler; *m* 1962, Gillian Lois Galley; one *s* two *d*. *Educ:* Harrow Sch.; University Coll., Oxford (BA Lit. Hum., 1961). Joined HM Treasury, 1961; Private Sec. to Financial Sec. to Treasury, 1964–65; Sec., Budget Cttee, 1965–69; seconded to Cabinet Office as Mem., Central Policy Rev. Staff, 1971–72; Private Secretary: to Rt Hon. Edward Heath, 1972–74; to Rt Hon. Harold Wilson, 1974–75; returned to HM Treasury as Asst Sec. i/c Gen. Expenditure Intell. Div., 1975; Under Sec., Gen. Expenditure Policy Gp, 1977–80; Prin. Establishments Officer, 1980–82; Principal Private Sec. to Prime Minister, 1982–85; Second Perm. Sec., Public Expenditure, HM Treasury, 1985–87. Governor, Harrow Sch., 1975– (Chm. of Govs, 1988–91). *Recreation:* competitive games. *Address:* Cabinet Office, SW1. *Clubs:* Athenæum, Brooks's, United Oxford & Cambridge University, Anglo-Belgian.

BUTLER, George, RWS 1958; RBA; NEAC; painter, principally in water-colour, in England and Provence; *b* 17 Oct. 1904; *s* of John George Butler; *m* 1933, Kcenia Kotliarevskaya; one *s* one *d*. *Educ:* King Edward VII School, Sheffield; Central School of Art. Director and Head of Art Dept, J. Walter Thompson Co. Ltd, 1933–60. Hon. Treas., Artists General Benevolent Institution, 1957–77. Mem., Société des Artistes Indépendants Aixois. *Address:* Riversdale, Castle Street, Bakewell, Derbyshire DE4 1DU. *T:* Bakewell (0629) 813133. *Club:* Arts.

BUTLER, George William P.; *see* Payne-Butler.

BUTLER, Gerald Norman, QC 1975; **His Honour Judge Butler;** a Circuit Judge, since 1982; Senior Judge at Southwark Crown Court, since 1984; *b* 15 Sept. 1930; *s* of Joshua Butler and Esther Butler (*née* Lampel); *m* 1959, Stella, *d* of Harris and Leah Isaacs; one *s* two *d*. *Educ:* Ilford County High Sch.; London Sch. of Economics; Magdalen Coll., Oxford. LLB London 1952, BCL Oxon 1954. 2nd Lieut, RASC, 1956–57. Called to Bar, Middle Temple, 1955. A Recorder of the Crown Court, 1977–82. *Recreations:* Rugby, opera, Japanese pottery. *Address:* Southwark Crown Court, SE1 2HU. *Club:* MCC.

BUTLER, Maj.-Gen. Hew Dacres George, CB 1975; DL; Secretary, Beit Trust, since 1978; *b* 12 March 1922; *s* of late Maj.-Gen. S. S. Butler, CB, CMG, DSO; *m* 1954, Joanna, *d* of late G. M. Puckridge, CMG, ED; two *s* one *d*. *Educ:* Winchester. Commnd Rifle Bde, 1941; Western Desert, 1942–43; POW, 1943–45; psc 1951; BM 7th Armd Bde, 1951–53; Kenya, 1954–55; Instructor, Staff Coll., 1957–60; CO 1 RB, 1962–64; Cyprus (despatches, 1965); comd 24 Inf. Bde, Aden, 1966–67; idc 1969; ACOS G3 Northag, 1970–72; GOC Near East Land Forces, 1972–74. Chief of Staff (Contingencies Planning), SHAPE, 1975–76; retired 1977. Underwriting Mem. of Lloyds. DL 1980, High Sheriff 1983, Hants. *Recreations:* shooting, racing, horticulture. *Address:* Bury Lodge, Hambledon, Hants PO7 6QL. *Clubs:* Boodle's, MCC.

BUTLER, Ian Geoffrey, CBE 1990; FCA; Chairman, Cookson Group, 1976–90 and since Nov. 1990; Director, Barclays Bank, since 1985; *b* 12 April 1925; *s* of Hubert Desramaux Butler and Nita Butler (*née* Blake); *m* 1973, Anne Robertson; two *d*. *Educ:* Huyton Hill, Liverpool; Stowe Sch.; Trinity Coll., Oxford (MA). Commissioned Coldstream Guards, 1943–47. Tansley Witt & Co., 1948–55, Partner, 1951–55; Goodlass Wall & Lead Industries, 1956– (subseq. named Cookson Group): Finance Dir, 1965; Managing Dir, 1973. Chm., Tioxide Gp, 1987–90. Treasurer and Mem. Exec. Cttee,

Internat. Yacht Racing Union; Mem. Council, Royal Yachting Assoc. (former Hon. Treasurer). *Recreations:* sailing, ski-ing, fell walking. *Address:* 105 Abingdon Road, W8 6QU. *T:* 071–937 5220. *Clubs:* Royal Thames Yacht; Royal Yacht Squadron, Itchenor Sailing.

BUTLER, James; *see* Butler, P. J.

BUTLER, James Walter, RA 1972 (ARA 1964); RWA; FRBS; *b* 25 July 1931; *m* (marr. diss.); one *d*; *m* 1975, Angela, *d* of Col Roger Berry, Johannesburg, South Africa; four *d*. *Educ:* Maidstone Grammar Sch.; Maidstone Coll. of Art; St Martin's Art Sch.; Royal Coll. of Art. National Diploma in Sculpture, 1950. Worked as Architectural Carver, 1950–53, 1955–60. Tutor, Sculpture and Drawing, City and Guilds of London Art School, 1960–75. Major commissions include: Portrait statue of Pres. Kenyatta, Nairobi, 1973; Monument to Freedom Fighters of Zambia, Lusaka, 1974; Statue, The Burton Cooper, Burton-on-Trent, 1977; Memorial Statue, Richard III, Leicester, 1980; Memorial Statue, Field Marshal Earl Alexander of Tunis, Wellington Barracks, London, 1985; Portrait Statue of Sir John Moore, Sir John Moore Barracks, Winchester, 1987; Portrait Statue of John Wilkes, New Fetter Lane, 1988; Dolphin Fountain, Dolphin Square, London, 1988; Skipping Girl, Harrow, 1988; The Leicester Seamstress, Leicester, 1990. Silver Medal, RBS, 1988. *Recreations:* interested in astronomy, golf. *Address:* Valley Farm, Radway, Warwick CV35 0UJ. *T:* Warwick (0926) 641938. *Club:* Arts.

BUTLER, John Manton, MSc; *b* 9 Oct. 1909; *m* 1940, Marjorie Smith, Melbourne; one *s* one *d*. *Educ:* Southland, NZ; Univ. of Otago (Sen. Schol., NZ, Physics; BSc 1929; Smeaton Schol. Chemistry, 1930, John Edmond Fellow, 1930; MSc 1st class Hons). Pres., Students' Union; Graduate Rep. Univ. Council. Joined Shell, NZ, 1934; served various Shell cos in UK, Australia and S Africa until 1957; Man. Dir, Lewis Berger (GB) Ltd, 1957; Dir, Berger, Jenson & Nicholson Ltd, 1969–74. Chm., BNEC Cttee for Exports to NZ, 1967 (Dep. Chm., 1965). Pres., NZ Soc., 1971. Member: Cttee, Spastics Soc.; St David's Cttee, Conservative Assoc., 1979–80; Aust. Inst. of Internat. Affairs, 1981–. Consultant. *Recreations:* travel, golf, photography. *Address:* Osborne, 28 Ranfurlie Crescent, Glen Iris, Victoria 3146, Australia. *T:* 259 9458. *Club:* Royal Melbourne Golf.

BUTLER, Prof. (John) Nicholas, (Nick), OBE 1988; RDI 1981; FCSD; industrial designer; Professor of Industrial Design, Royal College of Art, since 1987; Chairman and Joint Managing Director, BIB Design Consultants, since 1989; *b* 21 March 1942; *s* of William and Mabel Butler; *m* 1967, Kari Ann Morrison; two *s*. *Educ:* Leeds Coll. of Art (NDD); Royal Coll. of Art (DesRCA, 1st Cl. Hons). FCSD (FSIAD 1975). Founded BIB Design Consultants, 1967; Sen. Partner, 1967–89. Chm., British Design Export Gp, 1980–81; Member: Design Bd, RSA, 1987–; Design Council, 1988–. Hon. Sec., SIAD, 1978–81, Treasurer 1981–84. FRSA 1983. *Recreations:* reading, music, country pursuits, watching Rugby, drawing. *Address:* Burnham House, 45 Paradise Road, Richmond, Surrey TW9 1SA. *T:* 081–940 1849.

BUTLER, Mrs Joyce Shore; Chairman, Hornsey Housing Trust, 1980–88; *m*; one *s* one *d*. *Educ:* King Edward's High Sch., Birmingham. Member: Wood Green Council, 1947–64 (Leader, 1954–55; Deputy Mayor, 1962–63); First Chm., London Borough of Haringey, 1964–65; First Mayoress, 1965–66. MP (Lab & Co-op) Wood Green, 1955–74, Haringey, Wood Green, 1974–79; Vice-Chm., Labour Parly Housing and Local Govt Gp, 1959–64; Member: Estimates Cttee, 1959–60; Chairman's Panel, House of Commons, 1964–79; Jt Chm., Parly Cttee on Pollution, 1970–79; PPS to Minister for Land and Natural Resources, 1965. A Vice-Chm., Parly Labour Party, 1968–70. Exec. Mem., Housing and Town Planning Council; Founder and First Pres., Women's Nat. Cancer Control Campaign; Vice-Chm., Wood Green Age Concern; President: London Passenger Action Confern; Buller Road Over-60 Club, Wood Green. *Address:* 8 Blenheim Close, N21 2HQ. *Club:* University Women's.

BUTLER, Keith Stephenson, CMG 1977; HM Diplomatic Service, retired; Appeal Director for various charities, since 1978; *b* 3 Sept. 1917; *s* of late Raymond R. Butler and Gertrude Stephenson; *m* 1st, 1952, Geraldine Marjorie Clark (*d* 1979); 2nd, 1979, Mrs Priscilla Wittels; no *c*. *Educ:* King Edward's Sch., Birmingham; Liverpool Coll.; St Peter's Coll., Oxford (MA). HM Forces, 1939–47 (despatches): served, RA, in Egypt, Greece and Crete; POW, Germany, 1941–45. Foreign Correspondent for Sunday Times and Kemsley Newspapers, 1947–50. Joined HM Foreign Service, 1950; served: First Sec., Ankara and Caracas; Canadian Nat. Defence Coll.; Paris; Montreal. HM Consul-General: Seville, 1968; Bordeaux, 1969; Naples, 1974–77. *Publications:* contrib. historical and political reviews. *Recreation:* historical research. *Address:* Easter Cottage, Westbrook, Boxford, near Newbury, Berks RG16 8DN. *T:* Boxford (048838) 557.

BUTLER, Prof. Marilyn Speers, DPhil; King Edward VII Professor of English Literature, since 1986, and Fellow of King's College, since 1988, University of Cambridge; *b* 11 Feb. 1937; *d* of Sir Trevor Evans, CBE and Margaret (*née* Gribbin); *m* 1962, David Edgeworth Butler, *qv*; three *s*. *Educ:* Wimbledon High Sch.; St Hilda's Coll., Oxford (MA; DPhil). Trainee and talks producer, BBC, 1960–62; Oxford University: full-time res. and teaching, 1962–70, Jun. Res. Fellow, 1970–73, St Hilda's Coll.; Fellow and Tutor, St Hugh's Coll., 1973–85; Lectr, 1985–86. Pt-time Lectr, ANU, 1967; British Academy Reader, 1982–85. *Publications:* Maria Edgeworth: a literary biography, 1972; Jane Austen and the War of Ideas, 1975; Peacock Displayed, 1979; Romantics, Rebels and Reactionaries, 1981, 2nd edn 1985; (ed) Burke, Paine, Godwin and the Revolution Controversy, 1984; (ed with J. Todd) Works of Mary Wollstonecraft, 1989. *Address:* King's College, Cambridge.

BUTLER, Sir Michael; *see* Butler, Sir R. M. T.

BUTLER, Sir Michael (Dacres), GCMG 1984 (KCMG 1980; CMG 1975); HM Diplomatic Service, retired; Director: Hambros PLC, since 1986; Hambros Bank Ltd, since 1986; Wellcome Foundation, since 1986; Eurosynergies (France), since 1990; Incofina (Portugal), since 1990; Chairman: European Strategy Board, ICL, since 1988; European Unification Board, Hercules Europe, since 1989; Oriental Art Magazine, since 1988; *b* 27 Feb. 1927; *s* of T. D. Butler, Almer, Blandford, and Beryl May (*née* Lambert); *m* 1951, Ann, *d* of Rt Hon. Lord Clyde; two *s* two *d*. *Educ:* Winchester; Trinity Coll., Oxford. Joined HM Foreign Service, 1950; served in: UK Mission to UN, New York, 1952–56; Baghdad, 1956–58; FO, 1958–61 and 1965–68; Paris, 1961–65; Counsellor, UK Mission in Geneva, 1968–70; Fellow, Center for Internat. Affairs, Harvard, 1970–71; Counsellor, Washington, 1971–72; Head of European Integration Dept, FCO, 1972–74; Asst Under-Sec. in charge of European Community Affairs, FCO, 1974–76; Dep. Under-Sec. of State, FCO, 1976–79; Ambassador and Perm. UK Rep. to EC, Brussels, 1979–85. Chm., City European Cttee, British Invisibles (formerly BIEC), 1988–; Member: Standing Cttee on Internat. Relations, ACOST, 1987–; Panel of Conciliators, Internat. Centre for the Settlement of Investment. Disputes, 1987–. Mem. Council, Oriental Ceramic Soc., 1977–80 and 1985–88; Dep. Chm., Bd of Trustees, V&A Museum, 1985–. *Publications:* Chinese Porcelain, The Transitional Period 1620–82: a selection from the Michael Butler Collection, 1986; Europe: More than a Continent, 1986; The Butler Family Collection, 17th Century Chinese Porcelain, 1990; contribs to Trans Oriental Ceramic Soc. *Recreations:* collecting Chinese porcelain, ski-ing, tennis. *Address:* 36A Elm Park Road, SW3. *Club:* Brooks's.

BUTLER, Michael Howard, FCA; Finance Director, British Coal (formerly National Coal Board), since 1985, Member of the Board, since 1986; *b* 13 Feb. 1936; *s* of Howard Butler and Constance Gertrude Butler; *m* 1961, Christine Elizabeth Killer; two *s* one *d*. *Educ:* Nottingham High School. Articled pupil, H. G. Ellis Kennewell & Co., Nottingham, 1952–58; Stewarts & Lloyds Gp, 1960–62; National Coal Board: various posts, NCB HQ, W Midlands Div. and NE Area, 1962–68; Chief Accountant, Coal Products Div., 1968; Dep. Treas., NCB HQ, 1970; Treas. and Dep. Dir Gen. of Finance, 1978; Dir Gen. of Finance, 1981. *Recreations:* gardening, listening to music, playing tennis. *Address:* Banstead Down, Chorleywood Road, Rickmansworth, Herts WD3 4EH. *T:* Rickmansworth (0923) 778001; (office) 071–235 2020.

BUTLER, Prof. Neville Roy, MD; FRCP; FRCOG; Director, International Centre for Child Studies, since 1983; Professor of Child Health, Bristol University, 1965–85, Emeritus Professor, since 1985; Hon. Consultant Paediatrician, Bristol & Weston Teaching District and Southmead District, 1965–85; *b* Harrow, 6 July 1920; *o s* of late Dr C. J. Butler, MRCS, LRCP and Ida Margaret Butler; *m* 1954, Jean Ogilvie (marr. diss.), *d* of late John McCormack; two *d*. *Educ:* Epsom Coll.; Charing Cross Hosp. Med. Sch. MB BS 1942, MD 1949; MRCP 1946, FRCP 1965; DCH 1949; FRCOG 1979. Served RAMC, 1942–44, temp. Captain. First Assistant to Paediatric Unit, UCH, 1950; Med. Registrar and Pathologist, Hosp. for Sick Children, Gt Ormond St, 1953; Consultant Paediatrician, Oxford and Wessex RHB, 1957–63; Dir, Perinatal Mortality Survey, Birthday Trust Fund, 1958; Consultant Physician, Hosp. for Sick Children, Gt Ormond St and Sen. Lectr, Inst. of Child Health, London Univ., 1963–65. Co-Dir, Nat. Child Develt Study (1958 cohort), 1965–69; Dir, Child Health and Educn Study (1970 cohort), and Youthscan UK, 1975–89. Harding Meml Lect., RIBA, 1983. Member: BPA, 1958–; Neonatal Soc., 1961–; Cuban Paediatric Soc., 1973–; Hungarian Paediatric Soc., 1979–. *Publications:* jointly: Perinatal Mortality, 1963; 11,000 Seven Year Olds, 1966; Perinatal Problems, 1969; From Birth to Seven, 1972; ABO Haemolytic Diseases of the Newborn, 1972; The Social Life of Britain's Five Year Olds, 1984; Ethnic Minority Children, 1985; The Health of Britain's Five Year Olds, 1986; papers in scientific and med. jls. *Address:* Vine Cottage, Seagry Road, Sutton Benger, Chippenham, Wilts SN15 4RX. *T:* Chippenham (0249) 720688; International Centre for Child Studies, 310 Finchley Road, NW3 7AG. *T:* 071–435 4543. *Club:* Savage.

BUTLER, Nick; *see* Butler, J. N.

BUTLER, Norman John Terence; Director of Social Services, Hampshire, since 1988; *b* 18 Feb. 1946; *s* of Arthur Reginald Butler and Lucy Mary Butler; *m* 1978, Bethan Mary Lewis; two *d*. *Educ:* Peveril Bilateral Sch., Nottingham; Trent Polytechnic, Nottingham (Cert. in Social Work); Nat. Inst. of Social Work, London; Brunel Univ. (MA Public and Social Admin). Mental Welfare Officer, Nottingham, 1965–71; Sen. Social Worker, Nottingham, 1971–73; Area Man., Haringey, 1974–81; Asst Dir of Social Services, Royal Bor. of Kingston upon Thames, 1981–83; Dep. Dir of Social Services, E. Sussex, 1983–88. *Publications:* articles in various jls, incl. Social Work Today, Insight and Community Care. *Recreations:* squash, tennis, soccer, entertaining, being entertained. *Address:* (office) Trafalgar House, The Castle, Winchester, Hants SO23 8UQ. *T:* Winchester (0962) 841841; Westwood, New Farm Road, New Alresford, Hants SO24 9QH. *T:* Alresford (0962) 2572. *Club:* Winchester Squash and Tennis.

BUTLER, (Percy) James, CBE 1981; FCA; Senior Partner, KPMG Peat Marwick McLintock, since 1986; Chairman, KPMG, since 1991; farmer, since 1974; *b* 15 March 1929; *s* of late Percy Ernest Butler and Phyllis Mary Butler (*née* Bartholomew); *m* 1954, Margaret Prudence Copland; one *s* two *d*. *Educ:* Marlborough Coll.; Clare Coll., Cambridge (MA). Joined Peat, Marwick, Mitchell & Co., 1952; qualified, 1955; Partner, 1965; Gen. Partner, 1971; Managing Partner, London Reg., 1981–85; Dep. Sen. Partner, 1985–86; Sen. Partner, 1986; Mem. of KPMG Exec. Cttee and Council, 1987–. Mem. of Lloyd's. Dir, Mersey Docks and Harbour Co., 1972– (Dep. Chm., 1987–90); Business Advr to Treasury and CS Cttee, 1980–82; Member: Cttee on review of Railway Finance, 1982; Council, Business in the Community, 1988–90; Governing Body, City Res. Project. Treasurer, Pilgrims Soc., 1982–. Mem., Marlborough Coll. Council, 1975–. Mem. Council, CBI, 1989–. Liveryman: Worshipful Co. of Cutlers, 1965– (Mem. Court, 1985–); Worshipful Co. of Chartered Accountants in England and Wales, 1977–. *Recreations:* bridge, shooting. *Address:* Littleton House, Crawley, near Winchester SO21 2QF. *T:* Winchester (0962) 200806; Flat 8, Lennox Gardens, SW1 0DA. *T:* 071–581 8759. *Club:* Carlton.

BUTLER, Sir (Reginald) Michael (Thomas), 3rd Bt *cr* 1922; QC (Canada); Barrister and Solicitor, retired; sometime Partner of Butler, Angus, Victoria, BC; Director: Place Resources Corp.; Quinterra Resources Ltd; Teck Corporation; *b* 22 April 1928; *s* of Sir Reginald Thomas, 2nd Bt, and Marjorie Brown Butler; *S* father, 1959; *m* Marja McLean (marr. diss.); three *s*; one *s* adopted. *Educ:* Brentwood Coll., Victoria, BC; Univ. of British Columbia (BA). Called to Bar (Hons) from Osgoode Hall Sch. of Law, Toronto, Canada, 1954. *Heir: s* (Reginald) Richard (Michael) Butler [*b* 3 Oct. 1953; *m* 1982, Dale Karen, *d* of Frederick William Piner, Vancouver; one *s*]. *Address:* Old Park Cottage, 634 Avalon Street, Victoria, BC, Canada. *Club:* Vancouver (Vancouver).

BUTLER, Hon. Sir Richard (Clive), Kt 1981; DL; Chairman: Agricola (UK) Ltd, since 1986; Ferruzzi Trading (UK) Ltd, since 1986; Barton Bendish Farms Ltd, since 1986; County Natwest Investment Management, since 1989; Life Member, Council, National Farmers' Union, since 1962 (President, 1979–86); farmer since 1953; *b* 12 Jan. 1929; *e s* of late Baron Butler of Saffron Walden, KG, CH, PC and late Sydney, *o c* of late Samuel Courtauld; *m* 1952, Susan Anne Maud Walker; twin *s* one *d*. *Educ:* Eton Coll.; Pembroke Coll., Cambridge (MA). 2nd Lieut, Royal Horse Guards, 1947–49. Vice-Pres. 1970–71, Dep. Pres., 1971–79, NFU. Member: Agricultural Adv. Council, 1968–72; Central Council for Agricultural and Horticultural Co-operation, 1970–79. Director: National Westminster Bank, 1986–; Natwest Investment Bank, 1989–; National Farmers' Union Mutual Insurance Soc. Ltd, 1985–. Mem. Ct of Assts, Farmers' Co.; Third Warden, Skinners' Co., 1991–92. DL Essex, 1972. *Recreations:* hunting, shooting, tennis. *Address:* Penny Pot, Halstead, Essex CO9 1RY. *T:* Halstead (0787) 472828. *Club:* Farmers'.

See also Rt Hon. Sir A. C. Butler.

BUTLER, Richard Edmund, AM 1988; telecommunication adviser; Secretary-General, International Telecommunication Union, United Nations, Geneva, 1983–89 (Deputy Secretary-General, 1968–82); *b* 25 March 1926; *m* 1951, Patricia Carmel Kelly; three *s* two *d*. *Educ:* A, DPA; AASA; CPA; FRIPA. Posts in Australian Post Office, incl. Chief Industrial Officer, 1955–60; Exec. Officer, Dep. Asst Dir-Gen., 1960–68 (Ministerial and External Relations), 1960–68; apptd (in absentia) Sec., Aust. Telecommunications Commn, 1975 and later Dir, Corporate Planning Directorate. Formerly Member Australian delegations: for Internat. Telecommunication Satellite Consortium, Plenipotentiary Conf. 1965 (Dep. Leader; Mem. Administrative Council and Plan Cttees, 1962–68); to UN Conf. on Peaceful Uses of Outer Space, Vienna, 1968 (Dep. Leader); Advr and ITU Rep.,

Ind. Commn of ULCRA (Latin Amer. and Caribbean Broadcasting Union), 1990–. Mem., Admin. Cttee of Co-ordination for UN and Heads of Specialized Agencies; Chairman: Ad-Hoc UN Common System subsid. gps; ITU (Tripartite) Staff Pension Cttee, 1968–83; Member: Bd of Management, Centre for IT Res., Univ. of Wollongong, NSW; Adv. Cttee, Implementation of Australian Telecommns Reform decisions; (part-time) AUSTEL (Australian Regulatory Authority). Governor, Internat. Computer Commns Conf., 1975–85; UN System co-ordinator, Develt of Commns Infrastructure prog., world commns year, 1983. Hon. Mem., Greek Soc. of Air and Space Law, 1984. FRIPA; Hon. Fellow, Instn of Electronic and Telecommunications Engrs, New Delhi, 1988. Philipp Reis Medal, 1987. Grand Insignia, Order of Merit for Telecommunications, Spain, 1983. *Recreations:* golf, reading. *Address:* 40 Barrington Avenue, Kew, Vic 3101, Australia. *Clubs:* Commonwealth Trust, Royal Over-Seas League; CTA Commerce (Vic); Melbourne Cricket.

BUTLER, Sir Robin; *see* Butler, Sir F. E. R.

BUTLER, Dr Rohan D'Olier, CMG; MA; DLitt; FRHistS; Laureate, Institute of France; Fellow Emeritus of All Souls, Oxford, since 1984 (Fellow, 1938–84; Sub-Warden, 1961–63; representative at 12th International Historical Congress at Vienna, 1965, at 11th Anglo-American Conference of Historians, 1982); Member, Court, University of Essex, since 1971; *b* St John's Wood, 21 Jan. 1917; surv. *s* of late Sir Harold Butler, KCMG, CB, MA, and Olive, Lady Butler, *y c* of late Asst Inspector-General S. A. W. Waters, RIC, JP; *m* Lucy Rosemary, FRHS (Lady of the Manor of White Notley, Essex), *y c* of late Eric Byron, Lord of the Manor. *Educ:* Eton; abroad and privately; Balliol Coll., Oxford (Hall Prizeman, 1938). BA (1st Class Hons in Modern History), 1938; on International Propaganda and Broadcasting Enquiry, 1939; on staff of MOI, 1939–41 and 1942–44, of Special Operations Executive, 1941; served with RAPC, 1941–42, with HG, 1942–44 (Defence Medal, War Medal); on staff of FO, 1944–45; Editor of Documents on British Foreign Policy (1919–39), 1945–65 (with late Sir Llewellyn Woodward, FBA, 1945–54; Senior Editor, 1955–65); Sen. Editor, Documents on British Policy Overseas, 1973–82. Leverhulme Res. Fellow, 1955–57, Emeritus Fellow, 1984–86. Governor, Felsted Sch., 1959–77, representative on GBA, 1964–77; Trustee, Felsted Almshouses, 1961–77; Noel Buxton Trustee, 1961–67. Historical Adviser to Sec. of State for Foreign Affairs, 1963–68, for Foreign and Commonwealth Affairs, 1968–82 (from 14th Earl of Home to 6th Baron Carrington). On management of Inst. of Hist. Research, Univ. of London, 1967–77; Mem., Lord Chancellor's Adv. Council on Public Records, 1982–86. *Publications:* The Roots of National Socialism (1783–1933); Documents on British Foreign Policy, 1st series, vols i-ix, 2nd series, vol. ix; The Peace Settlement of Versailles, 1918–33 (in New Cambridge Modern History); Paradiplomacy (in Studies in Diplomatic History in honour of Dr G. P. Gooch, OM, CH, FBA); Introduction to Anglo-Soviet historical exhibition of 1967; Choiseul (special award, Prix Jean Debrousse, Acad. des Sciences Morales et Politiques, 1982); Documents on British Policy Overseas, series I, vol. i. *Recreation:* idling. *Address:* White Notley Hall, near Witham, Essex. *Clubs:* Beefsteak, The Lunch.

BUTLER, Rt. Rev. Thomas Frederick; *see* Leicester, Bishop of.

BUTLER, Col Sir Thomas Pierce, 12th Bt *cr* 1628; CVO 1970; DSO 1944; OBE 1954; Resident Governor and Major, HM Tower of London, 1961–71, Keeper of the Jewel House, 1968–71; *b* 18 Sept. 1910; *o s* of Sir Richard Pierce Butler, 11th Bt, OBE, DL, and Alice Dudley (*d* 1965), *d* of Very Rev. Hon. James Wentworth Leigh, DD; *S* father, 1955; *m* 1937, Rosemary Liège Woodgate Davidson-Houston, *d* of late Major J. H. Davidson-Houston, Pembury Hall, Kent; one *s* two *d*. *Educ:* Harrow; Trinity Coll., Cambridge. BA (Hons) Cantab, 1933. Grenadier Guards, 1933; served War of 1939–45 (wounded, POW, escaped); BEF France; 6th Bn, Egypt, Syria, Tripoli, N Africa; Staff Coll., 1944 (psc); Comd Guards Composite Bn, Norway, 1945–46; Comd 2nd Bn Grenadier Guards, BAOR, 1949–52; AQMG, London District, 1952–55; Col, Lt-Col Comdg the Grenadier Guards, 1955–58; Military Adviser to UK High Comr in New Zealand, 1959–61. Pres., London (Prince of Wales's) District, St John Ambulance Brigade. JP Co. of London 1961–71. CStJ. *Recreations:* fishing, travelling. *Heir:* *s* Richard Pierce Butler [*b* 22 July 1940; *m* 1965, Diana, *yr d* of Col S. J. Borg; three *s* one *d*]. *Address:* 6 Thurloe Square, SW7 2TA. *T:* 071–584 1225; Ballin Temple, Co. Carlow. *Club:* Cavalry and Guards.
See also Maj.-Gen. R. C. Keightley.

BUTLER, Vincent Frederick, RSA 1977; RGI 1989; figurative sculptor; works in bronze; *b* Manchester, 1933; *m* 1961, Camilla Luisa Meazza; two *s*. *Educ:* Acad. of Fine Art, Milan. Regular exhibitor at major exhibitions in Scotland; work in RA and several private galleries in Edinburgh, Glasgow and London. *Address:* 17 Deanpark Crescent, Edinburgh EH4 1PH. *T:* 031–332 5884.

BUTLER, Prof. William Elliott; Professor of Comparative Law in the University of London, since 1976; Director, Centre for the Study of Socialist Legal Systems, University College London, since 1982; *b* 20 Oct. 1939; *s* of William Elliott Butler and Maxine Swan Elmberg; *m* 1961, Darlene Mae Johnson (*d* 1989); two *s*. *Educ:* The American Univ. (BA); Harvard Law School (JD); The Johns Hopkins Univ. (MA, PhD); London Univ. (LLD). FSA 1989. Res. Asst, Washington Centre of Foreign Policy Res., Sch. of Advanced Internat. Studies, The Johns Hopkins Univ., 1966–68; Res. Associate in Law, and Associate, Russian Res. Centre, Harvard Univ., 1968–70; University of London: Reader in Comparative Law, 1970–76; Mem., SSEES, 1973– (Vice-Chm., 1983–88); Dean of Faculty of Laws, UCL, 1977–79; Vice Dean, 1986–88, Dean, 1988–90, Faculty of Laws, London Univ; Mem., Cttee of Management, Inst. of Advanced Legal Studies, 1985–88. Visiting Scholar: Faculty of Law, Moscow State Univ., 1972, 1980; Inst. of State and Law, USSR Acad. of Scis, 1976, 1981, 1983, 1984, 1988; Mongolian State Univ., 1979; Harvard Law Sch., 1982; Visiting Professor: NY Univ. Law Sch., 1978; Ritsumeikan Univ., 1985; Harvard Law Sch., 1986–87; Lectr, Hague Acad. of Internat. Law, 1985. Associé, Internat. Acad. of Comparative Law, 1982–; Member, Bar: Dist of Columbia (Dist Court and Court of Appeals); US Supreme Court; Union of Jurists of the USSR, 1990. Chm., Civil Rights in Russia Adv. Panel, Univ. of London, 1983–87; Co-ordinator, UCL-USSR Acad. of Sciences Protocol on Co-operation, 1981–; Special Counsel, Commn on Econ. Reform, USSR Council of Ministers, 1989–; Mem., Secretariat, Internat. Assoc. of Mongolists (Ulan Bator), 1987–; Hon. Member: All-Union Soc. of Bibliophiles, USSR, 1989; Soviet Assoc. of Maritime Law, 1990. Mem., Court of Governors, City of London Polytechnic, 1985–89. Sec., The Bookplate Soc., 1978–86 (Foreign Sec., 1988–); Exec. Sec., Féd. Internat. des Sociétés d'Amateurs d'Ex-Libris, 1988– (Vice-Pres., 1984–86). Editor, Year Book on Socialist Legal Systems, 1985–; Co-editor, The Bookplate Jl, 1989– (Editor, 1983–86); Mem., editorial bds of learned jls, incl. Marine Policy, 1988–; editor of looseleaf services and microfiche projects. FRSA 1986. *Publications:* more than 500 books, articles, translations, and reviews, including: The Soviet Union and the Law of the Sea, 1971; Russian Law, 1977; (with others) The Soviet Legal System, 3rd and 4th edns, 1977–84; A Source Book on Socialist International Organizations, 1978; Northeast Arctic Passage, 1978; International Law in Comparative Perspective, 1980; Basic Documents on Soviet Legal System, 1983, 2nd edn 1991; Chinese Soviet Republic 1931–1934, 1983; Soviet Law, 1983, 2nd edn 1988; Comparative Law and Legal System, 1985; The Law of the Sea and International Shipping, 1985; The Golden Era of American Bookplate Design, 1986; Justice and Comparative Law, 1987; International Law and the International System, 1987; The Non-Use of Force and International Law, 1989; Perestroika and International Law, 1990; The History of International Law in Russia 1647–1917, 1990; (with D. J. Butler) Modern British Bookplate Design, 1990; *translations of:* G. I. Tunkin, Theory of International Law, 1974; A. Kuznetsov, The Journey, 1984. *Recreations:* book collecting, bookplate collecting. *Address:* 20 Ainger Road, NW3 3AS. *T:* 071–586 2454. *Club:* Cosmos (Washington, DC).

BUTLER-SLOSS, Rt. Hon. Dame (Ann) Elizabeth (Oldfield), DBE 1979; PC 1988; **Rt. Hon. Lord Justice Butler-Sloss;** a Lord Justice of Appeal, since 1988; *b* 10 Aug. 1933; *d* of late Sir Cecil Havers, QC, and late Enid Snelling; *m* 1958, Joseph William Alexander Butler-Sloss, *qv*; two *s* one *d*. *Educ:* Wycombe Abbey Sch. Called to Bar, Inner Temple, Feb. 1955, Bencher, 1979; practice at Bar, 1955–70; Registrar, Principal Registry of Probate, later Family, Division, 1970–79; a Judge of the High Court, Family Div., 1979–88. Chm., Cleveland Child Abuse Inquiry, 1987–88. Contested (C), Lambeth, Vauxhall, 1959. A Vice Pres., Medico-Legal Soc.; Mem., Judicial Studies Bd, 1985–89. Pres., Honiton Agricultural Show, 1985–86. Hon. Fellow, St Hilda's Coll., Oxford, 1988. Hon. LLD Hull, 1988. *Publications:* Joint Editor: Phipson on Evidence (10th edn); Corpe on Road Haulage (2nd edn); a former Editor, Supreme Court Practice, 1976 and 1979. *Address:* c/o Royal Courts of Justice, Strand, WC2. *Club:* Lansdowne.
See also Baron Havers.

BUTLER-SLOSS, Joseph William Alexander; Hon. Mr Justice Butler-Sloss; a Judge of the High Court of Kenya, since 1984; *b* 16 Nov. 1926; 2nd and *o* surv. *s* of late Francis Alexander Sloss and Alice Mary Frances Violet Sloss (*née* Patchell); *m* 1958, Ann Elizabeth Oldfield Havers (*see* Rt. Hon. Dame (Ann) Elizabeth (Oldfield) Butler-Sloss); two *s* one *d*. *Educ:* Bangor Grammar Sch., Co. Down; Hertford Coll., Oxford. Ordinary Seaman, RN, 1944; Midshipman 1945, Sub-Lieut 1946, RNVR. MA (Jurisprudence) Hertford Coll., Oxford, 1951. Called to Bar, Gray's Inn, 1952; joined Western Circuit, 1954; joined Inner Temple; a Recorder, 1972–84. Joint Master, East Devon Foxhounds, 1970–76. *Recreations:* racing, the violin. *Address:* High Court of Kenya, PO Box 61, Nakuru, Kenya. *T:* Nakuru 41199; Higher Marsh Farm, Marsh Green, Rockbeare, Exeter, Devon. *T:* Whimple (0404) 822663. *Clubs:* Carlton; Muthaiga; Nairobi.

BUTLIN, Martin Richard Fletcher, CBE 1990; FBA 1984; Keeper of Historic British Collection, Tate Gallery, 1967–89; *b* 7 June 1929; *s* of Kenneth Rupert Butlin and Helen Mary (*née* Fletcher); *m* 1969, Frances Caroline Chodzko. *Educ:* Rendcomb Coll.; Trinity Coll., Cambridge (MA); Courtauld Inst. of Art, London Univ. (BA). DLit London 1984. Asst Keeper, Tate Gall., 1955–67. *Publications:* A Catalogue of the Works of William Blake in the Tate Gallery, 1957, 3rd edn 1990; Samuel Palmer's Sketchbook of 1824, 1962; Turner Watercolours, 1962; (with Sir John Rothenstein) Turner, 1964; (with Mary Chamot and Dennis Farr) Tate Gallery Catalogues: The Modern British Paintings, Drawings and Sculpture, 1964; The Later Works of J. M. W. Turner, 1965; William Blake, 1966; The Blake-Varley Sketchbook of 1819, 1969; (with E. Joll) The Paintings of J. M. W. Turner, 1977, 2nd edn 1984 (jtly, Mitchell Prize for the History of Art, 1978); The Paintings and Drawings of William Blake, 1981; Aspects of British Painting 1550–1800, from the Collection of the Sarah Campbell Blaffer Foundation, 1988; (with Mollie Luther and Ian Warrell) Turner at Petworth, 1989; (with Ted Gott and Irena Zdanowicz) William Blake in the Collection of the National Gallery of Victoria, 1989; selected paintings and prepared catalogues for following exhibitions: (with Andrew Wilton and John Gage) Turner 1775–1851, 1974; William Blake, 1978; (with Gert Schiff) William Blake, 1990; articles and reviews in Burlington Mag., Connoisseur, Master Drawings, Blake Qly, Blake Studies, Turner Studies. *Recreations:* music, travel. *Address:* 74c Eccleston Square, SW1V 1PJ.

BUTLIN, Prof. Robin Alan, DLitt; Professor of Geography, Loughborough University of Technology, since 1979 (Head of Department, 1979–91); *b* 31 May 1938; *s* of Rowland Henry Butlin and late Mona Butlin; *m* 1961, Norma Coroneo; two *s* one *d*. *Educ:* Liverpool Univ. (BA, MA); DLitt Loughborough, 1987. FRGS 1972. Demonstrator, University Coll. of N Staffordshire, 1961–62; Lectr in Geography, UC Dublin, 1962–71; Queen Mary College, University of London: Lectr in Geography, 1971; Sen. Lectr, 1975; Reader in Historical Geography, 1977–79; Dean, Sch. of Human and Environmental Studies, Loughborough Univ., 1983–86. Vis. Associate Prof. of Geography, Univ. of Nebraska, 1969–70; Vis. Professorial Fellow and Leverhulme Res. Fellow, Wolfson Coll., Cambridge, 1986–87. *Publications:* (ed with A. R. H. Baker) Studies of Field Systems in the British Isles, 1973; (ed) The Development of the Irish Town, 1977; (ed with R. A. Dodgshon) An Historical Geography of England and Wales, 1978, 2nd edn 1990; (ed with H. S. A. Fox) Change in the Countryside: essays on rural England 1500–1900, 1979; The Transformation of Rural England c. 1580–1800, 1982. *Recreations:* music, swimming, reading. *Address:* 30 Fairmount Drive, Loughborough, Leics LE11 3JR. *T:* Loughborough (0509) 268635.

BUTROS, Dr Albert Jamil; Istiqlal Order First Class, Jordan, 1987; Ambassador of Hashemite Kingdom of Jordan to the Court of St James's, 1987–91 and non-resident Ambassador to Ireland, 1988–91, and to Iceland, 1990–91; *b* 25 March 1934; *s* of Jamil Issa and Virginie Antoine (Albina); *m* 1962, Ida Maria Albina; four *d*. *Educ:* Univ. of London (BA Hons English 1958); Univ. of Exeter (BA *ad eundem* 1958); Columbia Univ. (PhD English 1963). Teacher, Amman, 1950–55; Instructor in English, Teacher's Coll., Amman, 1958–60; Lectr, Hunter Coll., City Univ., NY, 1961; Instructor, Miami Univ., Oxford, Ohio, 1962–63; University of Jordan: Asst Prof., English, 1963–65; Associate Prof., 1965–67; Acting Chm., Dept of English, 1964–67; Prof. of English, 1967–79 and 1985–; Chm., Dept of English, 1967–73, 1974–76; Dean, Research and Graduate Studies, 1973–76. Special Advr to HRH Crown Prince Hassan of Jordan, 1984–85. Dir Gen./Pres., Royal Sci. Soc., Amman, 1976–84. Vis. Prof., Ohio Wesleyan Univ., 1971–72; Sen. Res. Fellow, Internat. Develt Res. Centre, Canada, 1983–84. Member: Arab Thought Forum; World Affairs Council, Amman. Gov., Internat. Develt Res. Centre, Canada, 1986–. Fellow, World Acad. of Art and Sci., 1986. KStJ. Order of Merit, Italy, 1983. *Publications:* Tales of the Caliphs, 1965; Leaders of Arab Thought, 1969; articles and translations. *Recreations:* reading, writing, translation, art, world affairs, application of science and technology to development, walking. *Address:* PO Box 309, Jubeiha, Jordan.

BUTT, Sir (Alfred) Kenneth (Dudley), 2nd Bt *cr* 1929; Underwriting Member of Lloyd's, 1931–74; farmer and bloodstock breeder; *b* 7 July 1908; *o s* of Sir Alfred Butt, 1st Bt and Lady Georgina Mary Butt (*née* Say); *S* father, 1962; *m* 1st, 1938, Kathleen Farmar (marr. diss., 1948); 2nd, 1948, Mrs Ivor Birts (*née* Bain), BA Oxon, *widow* of Lt-Col Ivor Birts, RA (killed on active service). *Educ:* Rugby; Brasenose Coll., Oxford. Lloyd's, 1929–39. Royal Artillery, 1939–45, Major RA. Chairman, Parker Wakeling & Co. Ltd, 1946–54; Managing Director, Brook Stud Co., 1962–81. Pres., Aberdeen-Angus Cattle Soc., 1968–69; Chm., Thoroughbred Breeders Assoc., 1973. *Recreations:* shooting, horse-racing, travelling, paintings. *Address:* Wheat Hill, Sandon, Buntingford, Herts SG9 0RB. *T:* Kelshall (076387) 203; Flat 29, 1 Hyde Park Square, W2. *T:* 071–262 3988. *Clubs:* Carlton, etc.

BUTT, Geoffrey Frank; Principal Assistant Solicitor, HM Customs and Excise, since 1986; *b* 5 May 1943; *s* of late Frank Thomas Woodman Butt and Dorothy Rosamond Butt; *m* 1972, Lee Anne Davey; two *s* one *d*. *Educ:* Royal Masonic Sch., Bushey; Univ. of Reading (BA). Solicitor 1970. Joined Solicitor's Office, HM Customs and Excise as Legal Asst, 1971; Sen. Legal Asst, 1974; Asst Solicitor, 1982. *Recreations:* family life, classical music, literature and art, gardening.

BUTT, Sir Kenneth; *see* Butt, Sir A. K. D.

BUTT, Michael Acton; Director, BAT Industries PLC, since 1987; Chairman and Chief Executive: Eagle Star Holdings PLC, since 1987; Eagle Star Insurance Company, since 1987; *b* Thruxton, 25 May 1942; *s* of Leslie Acton Kingsford Butt and Mina Gascoigne Butt; *m* 1st, 1964, Diana Lorraine Brook; two *s*; 2nd, 1986, Zoe Benson. *Educ:* Rugby; Magdalen Coll., Oxford (MA History); INSEAD, France (MBA 1967). Bland Welch Gp, 1964; Dir, Bland Payne Holdings, 1970; Chm., Sedgwick Ltd, 1983–87; Dep. Chm., Sedgwick Gp plc, 1985–87; Dir, Farmers Group. Mem. European Cttee, Council for Invisible Exports; Board Member: INSEAD (Chm., Internat. Council); Assoc. of British Insurers (Mem., Gen. Insce Council); Vice Pres., Insurance Inst. of London. Trustee, Monteverdi Soc. *Recreations:* travel, tennis, opera, reading, family, the European movement. *Address:* 4 Maida Avenue, Little Venice, W2. *T:* 071–723 9657.

BUTT, Richard Bevan; Chief Executive, Rural Development Commission, since 1989; *b* 27 Feb. 1943; *s* of Roger William Bevan and Jean Mary (*née* Carter); *m* 1975, Amanda Jane Finlay; two *s*. *Educ:* Magdalen Coll., Oxford (BA Hist.); Lancaster Univ. (MA Regional Econs). Asst Principal, Min. of Housing, 1965–68; Sen. Res. Associate, Birmingham Univ., 1969–72; Consultant, 1972; HM Treasury: Principal, 1973–78; Asst Sec., 1978–86; seconded as Financial Counsellor, UK Perm. Repn to EC, 1981–84; Head of Conservation, English Heritage, 1986–89. *Recreations:* ceramics, architecture, travel. *Address:* 35 Gloucester Circus, SE10 8RY.

BUTTER, Major Sir David Henry, KCVO 1991; MC 1941; JP; landowner and farmer; company director; HM Lord-Lieutenant of Perth and Kinross, since 1975; *b* 18 March 1920; *s* of late Col Charles Butter, OBE, DL, JP, Pitlochry, and Agnes Marguerite (Madge), *d* of late William Clark, Newark, NJ, USA; *m* 1946, Myra Alice, *d* of Hon. Maj.-Gen. Sir Harold Wernher, 3rd Bt, GCVO, TD; one *s* four *d*. *Educ:* Eton; Oxford. Served War of 1939–45: 2nd Lieut Scots Guards, 1940, Western Desert and North Africa, Sicily (Staff), 1941–43; Italy (ADC to GOC 8th Army, Gen. Sir Oliver Leese, 1944); Temp. Major, 1946; retd Army, 1948. Brig., Queen's Body Guard for Scotland (Royal Company of Archers); Pres., Highland T&AVR, 1979–84. County Councillor, Perth, 1955–74; DL Perthshire, 1956, Vice-Lieutenant of Perth, 1960–71; HM Lieutenant of County of Perth, 1971–75, and County of Kinross, 1974–75. *Recreations:* shooting, golf, ski-ing, travel. *Address:* Cluniemore, Pitlochry, Scotland PH16 5NE. *T:* Pitlochry (0796) 2006; 64 Rutland Gate, SW7. *T:* 071–589 6731. *Clubs:* Turf; Royal and Ancient (St Andrews).

See also Lord Ramsay.

BUTTER, John Henry, CMG 1962; MBE 1946; Financial Director to Government of Abu Dhabi, 1970–83; *b* 20 April 1916; *s* of late Captain A. E. Butter, CMG, and late Mrs Baird; *m* 1950, Joyce Platt; three *s*. *Educ:* Charterhouse; Christ Church, Oxford. Indian Civil Service, 1939–47; Pakistan Admin. Service, 1947–50 (served in Punjab, except for period 1942–46 when was Asst to Political Agent, Imphal, Manipur State). HM Overseas Civil Service, Kenya, 1950–65 (Perm. Sec. to the Treasury, 1959–65); Financial Adviser, Kenya Treasury, 1965–69. *Publication:* Uncivil Servant, 1989. *Recreations:* golf, bridge. *Address:* PO Box 30181, Nairobi, Kenya; Whitehill, Gordon, Berwickshire. *Club:* East India.

See also Prof. P. H. Butter.

BUTTER, Neil (McLaren), QC 1976; **His Honour Judge Butter;** a Circuit Judge, since 1982; a Judge of Bow County Court, since 1986; *b* 10 May 1933; *y s* of late Andrew Butter, MA, MD and late Ena Butter, MB, ChB; *m* 1974, Claire Marianne Miskin. *Educ:* The Leys Sch.; Queens' Coll., Cambridge (MA). Called to Bar, Inner Temple, 1955. An Asst and Dep. Recorder of Bournemouth, 1971; Recorder of the Crown Court, 1972–82. Mem., Senate of the Inns of Court and the Bar, 1976–79. Inspector, for Dept of Trade, Ozalid Gp Hldgs Ltd, 1977–79. A Legal Assessor to GMC and GDC, 1979–82; Mem., Mental Health Review Tribunal, 1983–. Trustee, Kingdon-Ward Speech Therapy Trust, 1980–87. *Recreations:* motoring, holidays, browsing through Who's Who. *Address:* c/o 3 Serjeants' Inn, EC4Y 1BQ. *Clubs:* United Oxford & Cambridge University; Hampshire (Winchester).

BUTTER, Prof. Peter Herbert; Regius Professor of English, Glasgow University, 1965–86; *b* 7 April 1921; *s* of Archibald Butter, CMG, and Helen Cicely (*née* Kerr); *m* 1958, Bridget Younger; one *s* two *d*. *Educ:* Charterhouse; Balliol Coll., Oxford. Served in RA, 1941–46. Assistant, 1948, Lecturer, 1951, in English, Univ. of Edinburgh; Professor of English, Queen's Univ., Belfast, 1958–65. *Publications:* Shelley's Idols of the Cave, 1954; Francis Thompson, 1961; Edwin Muir, 1962; Edwin Muir: Man and Poet, 1966; (ed) Shelley's Alastor and Other Poems, 1971; (ed) Selected Letters of Edwin Muir, 1974; (ed) Selected Poems of William Blake, 1982; (ed) The Truth of Imagination: uncollected prose of Edwin Muir, 1988; (ed) Complete Poems of Edwin Muir, 1991; articles in periodicals. *Address:* Ashfield, Bridge of Weir, Renfrewshire. *T:* Bridge of Weir (0505) 613139. *Club:* New (Edinburgh).

See also J. H. Butter.

BUTTER, Peter Joseph Michael; Director of Operations, Property Services Agency, Building Management, Department of the Environment, since 1990; *b* 9 Dec. 1932; *s* of Joseph Butter and Kathleen (*née* Woodward); *m* 1956, Pamela Frances Roberts; three *s*. *Educ:* Brighton, Hove and Sussex Grammar School. Served Royal Signals, 1951–53. BR, 1953–67; Principal, Min. of Transport, 1967–73; Private Sec. to Minister of Transport, 1973; joined PSA, 1974: Hd, Defence Secretariat (Navy), 1974–79; Asst Dir, Estate Surveying Services, 1979–84; Dir, SE Region, 1984–88; Dir, Home Regional Services, 1988–90. *Recreations:* cricket umpiring, listening to music, exploring Britain. *Address:* PSA Services/BM, Whitgift Centre, Wellesley Road, Croydon CR9 3LY. *T:* 081–760 4378.

BUTTERFIELD, family name of **Baron Butterfield.**

BUTTERFIELD, Baron *cr* 1988 (Life Peer), of Stechford in the County of West Midlands; **William John Hughes Butterfield;** Kt 1978; OBE 1953; DM; FRCP; Regius Professor of Physic, University of Cambridge, 1976–87 (Deputy, since 1987); Master of Downing College, Cambridge, 1978–87; *b* 28 March 1920; *s* of late William Hughes Butterfield and of Mrs Doris North; *m* 1st, 1946, Ann Sanders (decd); one *s*; 2nd, 1950, Isabel-Ann Foster Kennedy; two *s* one *d*. *Educ:* Solihull Sch.; Exeter Coll., Oxford (DM 1968; Hon. Fellow, 1978); Johns Hopkins Univ. (MD 1951); MA, MD Cantab 1975. Repr. Oxford Univ.: Rugby football, *v* Cambridge, 1940–41; hockey, 1940–42 (Captain); cricket, 1942 (Captain). Member, Scientific Staff, Medical Research Council, 1946–58: Major RAMC, Army Operational Research Group, 1947–50; Research Fellow, Medical Coll. of Virginia, Richmond, Va, USA, 1950–52; seconded to Min. of Supply, 1952; seconded to AEA, 1956; Prof. of Experimental Medicine, Guy's Hospital, 1958–63; Prof. of Medicine, Guy's Hosp. Med. Sch., and Additional Physician, Guy's Hosp., 1963–71; Vice-Chancellor, Nottingham Univ., 1971–75; Professorial Fellow, Downing Coll., Cambridge, 1975–78; Vice-Chancellor, Cambridge Univ., 1983–85. Chairman: Bedford Diabetic Survey, 1962; Woolwich/Erith New Town Medical Liaison Cttee, 1965–71; SE Met. Reg. Hospital Board's Clinical Research Cttee, 1960–71; Scientific Advisory Panel, Army Personnel Research Cttee, 1970–76; Council for the Education and Training of Health Visitors, 1971–76; East Midlands Economic Planning Council, 1974–75; Medicines Commn, 1976–81; Member: UGC Medical Sub-Cttee, 1966–71; Council, British Diabetic Assoc., 1963–74 (Chm. 1967–74, Vice-Pres. 1974–); DHSS Cttee on Medical Aspects of Food Policy, 1964–80; DHSS Panel on Medical Research, 1974–76; MRC Cttee on General Epidemiology, 1965–74; MRC Clinical Res. Grants Bd, 1969–71; MRC, 1976–80; Anglo-Soviet Consultative Cttee; Minister of Health's Long Term Study Group; Health Educn Council, DHSS, 1973–77; Trent RHA, 1973–75; IUC Council and Exec. Cttee, 1973–; British Council Med. Adv. Cttee, 1971–80; Northwick Park Adv. Cttee, 1971–76; Council, European Assoc. for Study of Diabetes, 1968–71 (Vice-Pres.); Hong Kong Univ. and Polytechnic Grants Cttee, 1975–83; House of Lords Sci. of Technology Cttee, 1987–88; St George's House Council, 1987–. Chairman: Jardine Educnl Trust, 1982–; Health Promotion Res. Trust, 1983–; Croucher Foundn, Hong Kong, 1989– (Trustee, 1979–89); Trustee: GB-Sasakawa Foundn, 1985–; Ely Cathedral, 1986. Consultant, WHO Expert Cttee on Diabetes, 1964–80; Visitor, King Edward's Hospital Fund, 1964–71; Examiner in Medicine: Oxford Univ., 1960–66; Univ. of E Africa, 1966; Cambridge Univ., 1967–75; Pfizer Vis. Professor, NZ and Australia, 1965; Visiting Professor: Yale, 1966; Harvard, 1978. Rock Carling Fellow, RCP, 1968; Lectures: Oliver-Sharpey, RCP, 1967; Banting, BDA, 1970; Linacre, Cambridge, 1979; Roberts, Med. Soc. of London, 1981; Clayesmore, Blandford Forum, 1983; Northcott, Exeter, 1984; Cohen, Hebrew Univ. of Jerusalem, 1985. Dir, Prudential Corp., 1981–. Member: Editorial Board, Diabetaloga, 1964–69; Jl Chronic Diseases, 1968–. Hon. Fellow: NY Acad. Science, 1962; NY Acad. of Medicine, 1987; Hughes Hall, Cambridge, 1988; Corres. FACP, 1973. Hon. Med. Adviser, Leeds Castle. Patron, Richmond Soc., 1968–71. FRSA 1971. Hon. LLD Nottingham, 1977; Hon. DMedSci Keio Univ., Tokyo, 1983. Hon. DSc, Florida Internat. Univ., Miami, 1985; Hon. MD Chinese Univ., Hong Kong, 1989. *Publications:* (jointly) On Burns, 1953; Tolbutamide after 10 years, 1967; Priorities in Medicine, 1968; Health and Sickness: the choice of treatment, 1971; (ed) International Dictionary of Medicine and Biology, 1986; over 100 contribs to med. and allied literature incl. books, chapters, official reports and articles on diabetes, health care and educnl topics. *Recreations:* tennis (not lawn), cricket (village) and talking (too much). *Address:* 39 Clarendon Street, Cambridge CB1 1JX. *T:* Cambridge (0223) 328854. *Clubs:* Athenæum, MCC, Queen's; CURUFC (Pres., 1984–); CUCC (Pres., 1979–90).

BUTTERFIELD, Charles Harris, QC (Singapore) 1952; HMOCS, retired; *b* 28 June 1911; 2nd *s* of William Arthur Butterfield, OBE, and Rebecca Butterfield; *m* 1st, 1938, Monica, *d* of Austin Harrison, London; one *d*; 2nd, by special permission of the Holy See, Ellen, *d* of Ernest John Bennett, Singapore and *widow* of J. E. King, Kuala Lumpur, Singapore and Hooe. *Educ:* Downside; Trinity Coll., Cambridge. Barrister-at-law, Middle Temple, 1934. Entered Colonial Legal Service, 1938; Crown Counsel, Straits Settlements, 1938. Served Singapore RA (Volunteer) and RA, 1941–46; POW, 1942–45. Solicitor-General, Singapore, 1948–55, Attorney-General, 1955–57; Legal Adviser's Dept CRO and FCO, 1959–69; DoE and Sec. of State's Panel of Inspectors (Planning), 1969–74. *Recreations:* beagling, swimming, walking. *Address:* 18 Kewhurst Avenue, Cooden, Bexhill on Sea, E Sussex TN39 3BJ.

BUTTERFIELD, John Michael; Chief Executive, National Association of Youth Clubs, 1975–86; *b* 2 July 1926; *s* of late John Leslie Butterfield and Hilda Mary Butterfield (*née* Judson); *m* 1955, Mary Maureen, *d* of John Martin; one *s* twin *d* (and one *s* decd). *Educ:* Leeds Modern Sch.; Leeds Univ. John Butterfield & Son, Leeds, 1949–60; John Atkinson & Sons (Sowerby Bridge) Ltd, 1960–61. Youth Officer, Coventry Cathedral, 1961–68; Liverpool Council of Social Service: Head of Youth and Community Dept, 1968–72; Operations Dir, 1972–75. Mem., BCC, 1954–73 (Mem., 1952–68; Chm., Exec. Cttee, 1962–67, Youth Dept); Vice-Chairman: Nat. Council for Voluntary Youth Services, 1977–83; UK Adv. Cttee, SCF, 1990–; Chairman: Leics Council of Voluntary Youth Services, 1985–; Youthaid, 1986–90. Merseyside Advr, Baring Foundn, 1987–; UK Rep., Amer. Youth Work Center, 1987–. *Recreations:* music, reading, walking, railways. *Address:* 4 Church Farm Court, Aston Flamville, near Hinckley, Leics LE10 3AF. *T:* Hinckley (0455) 611027.

BUTTERFILL, John Valentine; MP (C) Bournemouth West, since 1983; *b* 14 Feb. 1941; *s* of George Thomas Butterfill and Elsie Amelia (*née* Watts); *m* 1965, Pamela Ross Ross-Symons; one *s* three *d*. *Educ:* Caterham Sch.; Coll. of Estate Management. FRICS 1974. Valuer, Jones, Lang, Wootton, 1961–64; Sen. Exec., Hammerson Gp, 1964–69; Dir, Audley Properties Ltd (Bovis Gp), 1969–71; Man. Dir, St Paul's Securities Gp, 1971–76; Sen. Partner, Curchod & Co., chartered surveyors, 1977–; Pres., European Property Associates, 1979–. PPS to Sec. of State for Energy, 1988–89, to Sec. of State for Transport, 1989–90. Vice-Chm., Backbench Tourism Cttee, 1986–88 (Jt Sec., 1984–85); Sec., Backbench Trade and Industry Cttee, 1987–88, 1991–. Chm., Cons. Gp for Europe, 1989–. *Publications:* contribs to Estates Gazette. *Recreations:* ski-ing, riding, tennis, bridge, music. *Address:* House of Commons, SW1A 0AA. *Club:* Carlton.

BUTTERSS, Rt. Rev. Robert Leopold, Bishop of the Central Region (Assistant Bishop of the Diocese of Melbourne), since 1985; *b* 17 Jan. 1931; *s* of A. L. Butterss; *m* 1956, Margaret (*née* Hayman); two *s* one *d*. *Educ:* Haileybury; Brighton and Ridley Coll., Melbourne. Curate, St Andrew's, Brighton, 1955–56; Vicar, Holy Trinity, Lara, 1956–60; Priest in charge, Popondetta, PNG, 1960–64; Vicar: Holy Trinity, Pascoe Vale, 1964–66; St Stephen's, Mt Waverley, 1970–76; Canon, St Peter and St Paul's Cathedral, PNG, 1976–83; Dean, St John's Cathedral, Brisbane, 1983–85. Chm., Australian Bd of Missions, Sydney, 1976–83. *Recreation:* music. *Address:* c/o St Paul's Cathedral, Flinders Lane, Melbourne, Vic 3000, Australia.

BUTTERWORTH, family name of **Baron Butterworth.**

BUTTERWORTH, Baron *cr* 1985 (Life Peer), of Warwick in the County of Warwickshire; **John Blackstock Butterworth,** CBE 1982; JP; DL; Vice-Chancellor, University of Warwick, 1963–85; Chairman, Metapraxis Ltd, since 1990 (Director, since 1986); *b* 13 March 1918; *o s* of John William and Florence Butterworth; *m* 1948, Doris Crawford Elder; one *s* two *d*. *Educ:* Queen Elizabeth's Grammar Sch., Mansfield; The Queen's Coll., Oxford. Royal Artillery, 1939–46. MA 1946. Called to Bar, Lincoln's Inn, 1947, Hon. Bencher, 1989. New Coll., Oxford: Fellow, 1946–63; Dean, 1952–56; Bursar, 1956–63; Sub Warden, 1957–58. Junior Proctor, 1950–51; Faculty Fellow of Nuffield Coll., 1953–58; Member of Hebdomadal Council, Oxford Univ., 1953–63. Managing Trustee 1964–85, Trustee, 1985–, Nuffield Foundation; Chairman: Inter-Univ. Council for Higher Educn Overseas, 1968–77; Universities Cttee for Non-teaching Staffs, 1970–85; Inquiry into work of Probation Officers and Social Workers in Local Authorities and Nat. Service, 1971–73; Standing Cttee on Internat. Co-operation in Higher Educn, British Council, 1981–85; Inter-Univ. and Polytechnic Council, 1981–85; Council, Foundn for Sci. and Technol., 1990–. Univ. Comr (Under Educn Reform Act 1988), 1988–; Member: Royal Commn on the Working of the Tribunals of Inquiry (Act), 1921, 1966; Intergovernmental Cttee on Law of Contempt in relation to Tribunals of Inquiry, 1968; Jarratt Cttee on University Efficiency, 1986; Cttee on the review of UGC, 1987; Fulbright Commn, 1988–; Noise Advisory Council, 1974–81; Bd, British Council 1981–85; British delegn to Commonwealth Educn Conferences in Lagos, 1968, Canberra, 1971, Kingston, 1974, Accra, 1977, Colombo, 1980. Governor, Royal Shakespeare Theatre, 1964–. DL Warwickshire, 1967–74, DL West Midlands 1974–; JP City of Oxford, 1962, Coventry, 1963–. Hon. DCL Univ. of Sierra Leone, 1976; Hon. DSc Univ. of Aston, 1985; Hon. LLD Warwick, 1986. *Address:* The Barn, Barton, Guiting Power, Glos GL54 5US. *T:* Guiting Power (0451) 850297. *Club:* Athenæum.

BUTTERWORTH, Sir (George) Neville, Kt 1973; DL; Chairman, Tootal Ltd (formerly English Calico Ltd), 1968–74; *b* 27 Dec. 1911; *s* of Richard Butterworth and Hannah (*née* Wright); *m* 1947, Barbara Mary Briggs; two *s*. *Educ:* Malvern; St John's Coll., Cambridge. Served with Royal Artillery, at home and overseas, 1939–45. Joined English Sewing Cotton Co. Ltd, 1933; Man. Dir, 1966; Dep. Chm., 1967; Chm., 1968, on merger with The Calico Printers' Assoc. Ltd. Dir, National Westminster Bank (North Regional Board), 1969–82; Mem., Royal Commn on Distribution of Income and Wealth, 1974–79. Chm., NW Regional Council of CBI, 1968–70; Former Mem., Grand Council of CBI; Trustee, Civic Trust for the North-West, 1967; Mem., Textile Council, 1970; CompTI 1973. Member: Court of Governors, Manchester Univ., 1973–79; Council, UMIST, 1973–79. FBIM 1968. High Sheriff 1974, DL 1974, Greater Manchester. *Address:* Oak Farm, Ollerton, Knutsford, Cheshire. *T:* Knutsford (0565) 3150.

BUTTERWORTH, Henry, CEng, MIMechE; retired; Managing Director, Ammunition Division, (formerly Director General (Ammunition)), Royal Ordnance plc (formerly Royal Ordnance Factories), 1979–88; Chairman, Royal Ordnance (Speciality Metals) Ltd, 1986–88; *b* 21 Jan. 1926; *s* of late Henry and Wilhemena Butterworth; *m* 1948, Ann Smith; two *s*. *Educ:* St Mary's, Leyland, Lancs. DipProd Birmingham. Apprenticeship, 1940–47; Draughtsman, 1947–52; Technical Asst, 1952–53; progressively, Shop Manager, Asst Manager, Manager, 1953–71; Director ROF: Cardiff, Burghfield, Glascoed, 1971–79. *Recreation:* coarse fishing. *Address:* 5 Vicarsfield Road, Worden Park, Leyland, Lancs PR5 2BH. *T:* Leyland (0772) 436073.

BUTTERWORTH, Prof. Ian, CBE 1984; FRS 1981; Senior Research Fellow, Imperial College, since 1991; Professor of Physics, University of London, 1971–91, now Emeritus; *b* 3 Dec. 1930; *s* of Harry and Beatrice Butterworth; *m* 1964, Mary Therese (*née* Gough); one *d*. *Educ:* Bolton County Grammar Sch.; Univ. of Manchester. BSc 1951; PhD 1954. Sen. Scientific Officer, UK Atomic Energy Authority, 1954–58; Lectr, Imperial Coll., 1958–64; Vis. Physicist, Lawrence Radiation Laboratory, Univ. of California, 1964–65; Sen. Lectr, Imperial Coll., 1965–68; Group Leader, Bubble Chamber Research Gp, Rutherford High Energy Laboratory, 1968–71; Professor, 1971–86, Head of Dept, 1980–83, Dept of Physics, Imperial Coll.; on leave of absence as Res. Dir, CERN, 1983–86; Principal, QMC, then QMW, 1986–91; Pro Vice-Chancellor for Eur. Affairs, London Univ., 1989–91. Science and Engineering Research Council (formerly Science Research Council): Mem., 1979–83 (Mem., Nuclear Physics Bd, 1972–75 and 1978–83, Chm., 1979–83; Mem., Particle Physics Cttee, 1978–79; Chm., Film Analysis Grants Cttee, 1972–75); UK deleg. on Council, CERN, 1979–82 (Mem., Research Bd, 1976–82; Chm., Super Proton Synchroton Cttee, 1976–79). Member: Physics Res. Cttee, Deutsches Elektronen Synchroton, Hamburg, 1981–85; Sci. Policy Cttee, Stanford Linear Accelerator Center, Calif, 1984–88; Sci. Adv. Cttee, British Council, 1986–; Academia Europaea, 1989; Council Member: Royal Soc., 1989–90; Inst. of Physics, 1989–; Hon. Mem., Manchester Lit. and Phil. Soc., 1987. Fellow, Imperial Coll., 1988. Dr *hc* Soka Univ., 1989. *Publications:* numerous papers in learned jls (on Hadron Spectroscopy and Application of Bubble Chamber to Strong and Weak Interaction Physics). *Recreations:* reading, history of art. *Address:* Blackett Laboratory, Imperial College, Prince Consort Road, SW7 2AZ; 1 The Pierhead, Wapping High Street, E1 9PN. *Club:* Athenæum.

BUTTERWORTH, Sir Neville; *see* Butterworth, Sir G. N.

BUTTFIELD, Dame Nancy (Eileen), DBE 1972; formerly Senator for South Australia; *b* 12 Nov. 1912; *d* of Sir Edward Wheewall Holden and Hilda May Lavis; *m* 1936, Frank Charles Buttfield; two *s*. *Educ:* Woodlands Church of England Girls' Grammar Sch., Adelaide; Composenea; Paris; Univ. of Adelaide, SA. Senator for South Australia, Oct. 1955–June 1965, re-elected July 1968–74. Exec. Mem., Commonwealth Immigration Adv. Council, 1955–; Vice-President: Good Neighbour Council of SA, 1956–62; Phoenix Soc. for the Physically Handicapped, 1959–. Dir, Co-operative Building Soc. of SA, 1959–. Mem. Council, Bedford Industries, 1965–. Mem., Nat. Council of Women of SA. *Recreations:* farming, dress-making, gourmet cooking, music. *Address:* 52 Strangeways Terrace, North Adelaide, SA 5006, Australia. *Clubs:* Queen Adelaide, Lyceum, Royal Adelaide Golf (all SA).

BUTTLE, Eileen, PhD; FIBiol; Secretary, Natural Environment Research Council, since 1989; *b* 19 Oct. 1937; *d* of late George Ernest Linford and of Mary Stewart Linford; *m* 1970, Hugh Langley Buttle. *Educ:* Harrow Weald County Grammar Sch.; Univ. of Southampton (BSc (Hons); PhD). FIBiol 1990. Post-doctoral Res. Fellow, Univ. of Southampton, 1963–65; Research Scientist: Nat. Inst. of Res. in Dairying, 1965–71; Cattle Breeding Centre, MAFF, 1971–76; Policy Administrator, MAFF, 1976–89. *Recreations:* golf, fly fishing. *Address:* 61 Baker Street, Reading, Berks RG1 7XY. *T:* Reading (0734) 590590. *Club:* Farmers'.

BUTTON, Henry George; author; *b* 11 Aug. 1913; *e s* of late Rev. Frank S. and Bertha B. Button; *m* 1938, Edith Margaret Heslop (*d* 1972); two *d*. *Educ:* Manchester Grammar Sch.; Christ's Coll., Cambridge (Scholar). Mod. and Medieval Langs Tripos, Part II, 1st Class (with dist.) 1934; MLitt 1977; Tiarks German Scholar (research at Univ. of Bonn), 1934–35; Sen. Studentship of Goldsmiths' Company, 1935–36. Entered Civil Service, 1937; Board of Trade, 1937–57 (served in Min. of Production, 1942; Counsellor, UK Delegn to OEEC, Paris, 1952–55; on staff of Monopolies Commn, 1955–56); transf. Min. of Agriculture, Fisheries and Food, 1957; Under-Sec., Min. of Agriculture, Fisheries and Food, 1960–73 (Principal Finance Officer, 1965–73). Res. Student, 1974–76, Fellow-Commoner, 1982–, Christ's Coll., Cambridge. Mem. Agricultural Research Council, 1960–62. Leader of various UK Delegns to FAO in Rome. BBC Brain of Britain for 1962; rep. Great Britain in radio quiz in Johannesburg, 1966; Bob Dyer's TV show, Sydney, 1967. *Publications:* The Guinness Book of the Business World (with A. Lampert), 1976; contribs to various jls both learned and unlearned, and to newspapers. *Recreations:* reading, writing, studying old businesses (hon. review ed., Business Archives Council, 1966–75; Hon. Sec., Tercentenarians' Club, 1969–), showing visitors round the colleges. *Address:* 7 Amhurst Court, Grange Road, Cambridge CB3 9BH. *T:* Cambridge (0223) 355698. *Club:* Civil Service.

BUTTRESS, Donald Reeve, FSA; ecclesiastical architect and surveyor; Partner, Buttress Fuller Alsop, Manchester, since 1974; Surveyor of the Fabric of Westminster Abbey, since 1988; *b* 27 April 1932; *s* of Edward Crossley Buttress and Evelyn Edna Reeve-Whaley; *m* 1956, Elsa Mary Bardsley; two *s* three *d*. *Educ:* Stockport Sch.; Univ. of Manchester (MA, DipArch). ARIBA. Flying Officer, RAF, 1958–61. Lectr, Manchester Univ., 1964–78; Vis. Prof. and Fulbright Travelling Scholar, Univ. of Florida, 1967–68. Architect to: Bangor and Sheffield Cathedrals, 1978–88; Leeds (RC) Cathedral, 1983–; Llandaff Cathedral, 1986–; Surveyor to the Fabric, Chichester Cathedral, 1985–. Member: Churches Sub-Cttee, English Heritage (HBMC), 1988–; Council for the Care of Churches, 1976–86, 1991–; Chester Dio. Adv. Cttee, 1970–88. Mem., Editl Bd, Church Building magazine, 1982–. *Publications:* Manchester Buildings, 1967; Gawthorpe Hall (NT guide), 1971; articles in learned jls. *Recreations:* ecclesiology, 18th Century furniture, stained glass, conservation of the countryside, heraldry. *Address:* Little Cloister, Westminster Abbey, SW1. *T:* 071–799 6893. *Club:* Royal Air Force.

BUTTREY, Prof. Theodore Vern, PhD; Keeper, Department of Coins, Fitzwilliam Museum, Cambridge, 1988–91; *b* 29 Dec. 1929; *s* of Theodore Vern Buttrey and Ruth Jeanette Scoutt; *m* 1st, 1954, Marisa Macina (marr. diss. 1967); three *s* one *d*; 2nd, 1967, Ann Elizabeth Johnston. *Educ:* Phillips Exeter Acad.; Princeton Univ. (BA 1950; PhD 1953). Instr, 1954–58, Asst Prof., 1958–64, Yale Univ.; University of Michigan: Associate Professor, 1964–67; Prof. of Greek and Latin, 1967–85; Prof. Emeritus, 1985–; Chm., Dept of Classical Studies, 1968–71, 1983–84; Dir, Kelsey Mus. of Archaeology, 1969–71. Member: Clare Hall, Cambridge, 1971–; Faculty of Classics, Cambridge Univ., 1975–. Pres., RNS, 1989–; Trustee, UK Numismatic Trust, 1989–. Medal, RNS, 1985. *Publications:* (jtly) Greek, Roman and Islamic Coins from Sardis, 1981; (jtly) Morgantina Studies: the coins, 1989; numerous publications in ancient and modern numismatics. *Recreations:* Ernest Bramah, P. G. Wodehouse, travel. *Address:* 6 de Freville Avenue, Cambridge CB4 1HR. *T:* Cambridge (0223) 351156.

BUXTON, family name of **Barons Buxton of Alsa** and **Noel-Buxton.**

BUXTON OF ALSA, Baron *cr* 1978 (Life Peer), of Stiffkey in the County of Norfolk; **Aubrey Leland Oakes Buxton,** MC 1943; DL; Director, Anglia Television, since 1958 (Chairman, 1986–88); Director, Survival Anglia Ltd; *b* 15 July 1918; *s* of Leland Wilberforce Buxton and Mary, *d* of Rev. Thomas Henry Oakes; *m* 1st, 1946, Pamela Mary (*d* 1983), *d* of Sir Henry Birkin, 3rd Bt; two *s* four *d*; 2nd, 1988, Mrs Kathleen Peterson, Maine, USA. *Educ:* Ampleforth; Trinity Coll., Cambridge. Served 1939–45, RA; combined ops in Arakan, 1942–45 (despatches, 1944). Extra Equerry to Duke of Edinburgh. A Trustee of the British Museum (Natural History), 1971–73. Member: Countryside Commn, 1968–72; Royal Commission on Environmental Pollution, 1970–74; British Vice Pres., World Wildlife Fund; Trustee, Wildfowl Trust; Treasurer, London Zoological Soc., 1978–83; Former Pres., Royal Television Soc.; Chairman: Independent Television Cos Assoc., 1972–75; UPITN Inc., USA, 1981–83; ITN, 1981–86. Wildlife Film Producer, Anglia TV. Golden Awards, Internat. TV Festival, 1963 and 1968; Silver Medal, Zoological Society of London, 1967; Silver Medal, Royal TV Society, 1968; Queen's Award to Industry, 1974; Gold Medal, Royal TV Soc., 1977. High Sheriff of Essex 1972; DL Essex, 1975–85. *Publications:* (with Sir Philip Christison) The Birds of Arakan, 1946; The King in his Country, 1955. *Recreations:* travel, natural history, painting, sport. *Address:* Old Hall Farm, Stiffkey, Norfolk. *Club:* White's.

BUXTON, Adrian Clarence, CMG 1978; HM Diplomatic Service, retired; Ambassador to Bolivia, 1977–81, and to Ecuador, 1981–85; *b* 12 June 1925; *s* of Clarence Buxton and Dorothy (*née* Lintott); *m* 1st, 1958, Leonora Mary Cherkas (*d* 1984); three *s*; 2nd, 1985, June Samson. *Educ:* Christ's Hosp., Horsham; Trinity Coll., Cambridge. RNVR, 1944–46; FO, 1947; 3rd Sec., Bangkok, 1948–52; FO, 1952–53; 2nd Sec., Khartoum, 1953–55; 2nd later 1st Sec., Bonn, 1955–58; 1st Sec. (Commercial) and Consul, Bogota, 1958–62; FO, 1962–64; 1st Sec., Saigon, 1964–67; 1st Sec. (Commercial), Havana, 1967–69; UK Dep. Permanent Rep. to UN and other internat. organisations at Geneva, 1969–73; Univ. of Surrey, 1973–74; Head of Training Dept and Dir Language Centre, FCO, 1974–75; Head of Maritime and Gen. Dept, FCO, 1975–77. *Recreations:* golf, choral singing. *Address:* 7 Grove Road, Merrow, Guildford, Surrey GU1 2HR.

BUXTON, Andrew Robert Fowell; Managing Director, since 1988, Deputy Chairman, since 1991, Barclays Bank PLC; *b* 5 April 1939; *m* 1965, Jane Margery Grant; two *d*. *Educ:* Winchester Coll.; Pembroke Coll., Oxford. Joined Barclays Bank Ltd, 1963; Dir, Barclays Bank UK Ltd, 1978; Barclays Bank PLC: Gen. Manager, 1980; Vice-Chm., 1984; Dep. Man. Dir, 1987; Vice-Chm., 1988–91. *Club:* Royal Automobile.

BUXTON, Prof. John Noel, FBCS; CEng; Professor of Information Technology, King's College, London, since 1984; *b* 25 Dec. 1933; *s* of John William Buxton and Laura Frances Buxton; *m* 1958, Moira Jean O'Brien; two *s* two *d*. *Educ:* Bradford Grammar Sch.; Trinity Coll., Cambridge (BA 1955, MA 1959). FBCS 1968. Flight Trials Engr, De Havilland Propellers, 1955–59; Ops Res. Scientist, British Iron and Steel Res. Assoc., 1959–60; Applied Science Rep., IBM UK, 1960–62; Lectr, Inst. of Computer Science, Univ. of London, 1962–66; Chief Software Consultant, CEIR (now Scicon Ltd) 1966–68; Prof. of Computer Science, Univ. of Warwick, 1968–84. UNDP Proj. Manager, Internat. Computing Educn Centre, Budapest, 1975–77; Vis. Scholar, Harvard Univ., 1979–80; Dir of Systems Engrng, DTI, 1989–91. *Publications:* (ed) Simulation Programming Languages, 1968; (ed jtly) Software Engineering Concepts and Techniques (Procs of NATO Confs 1968 and 1969), 1976; (jtly) The Craft of Software Engineering, 1987; three computer programming languages; papers in professional jls. *Recreations:* mountaineering, music, ancient houses. *Address:* Bull's Hall, Yaxley, near Eye, Suffolk IP23 8BZ.

BUXTON, Prof. Neil Keith; Director, Hatfield Polytechnic, since 1987; *b* 2 May 1940; *s* of William F. A. Buxton and Janet A. Buxton; *m* 1962, Margaret G. Buxton (*née* Miller); two *s* one *d*. *Educ:* Aberdeen Univ. (MA Hons Political Econs); PhD Heriot-Watt. Asst Lectr, Dept of Political Econ., Aberdeen Univ., 1962–64; Lectr, Dept of Econ., Univ. of Hull, 1964–69; Lectr and Sen. Lectr, 1969–78, Prof., 1979–83, Heriot-Watt Univ.; Depute Dir, Glasgow Coll. of Technology, 1983–87. Vis. Prof. in Econs and Public Admin, Lewis and Clark Coll., Oregon, 1982. *Publications:* (with T. L. Johnston and D. Mair) Structure and Growth of the Scottish Economy, 1971; (with D. I. Mackay) British Employment Statistics, 1977; Economic Development of the British Coal Industry, 1978; (ed) British Industry Between the Wars, 1979; articles in professional jls. *Recreations:* hockey, swimming, bridge. *Address:* Hatfield Polytechnic, College Lane, Hatfield, Herts. *T:* Hatfield (07072) 79000.

BUXTON, Paul William Jex; Northern Ireland Office, 1974–85 (Under Secretary, 1981–85); *b* 20 Sept. 1925; *s* of of late Denis Buxton and Emily Buxton (*née* Hollins); *m* 1st, 1950, Katharine Hull (marr. diss. 1971, she *d* 1977); two *s* one *d*; 2nd, 1971, Hon. Margaret Aston (*née* Bridges), PhD, FSA; two *d*. *Educ:* Rugby Sch.; Balliol Coll., Oxford (MA). Coldstream Guards, 1944–47. HM Foreign, later Diplomatic, Service, 1950–71; served Delhi, UN, Guatemala and Washington, latterly as Counsellor. Investment banking, 1972–74. Treasurer, Anti-Slavery International, 1986–; Mem. Council, Howard

League for Penal Reform, 1985–. *Address:* Castle House, Chipping Ongar, Essex CM5 9JT. *T:* Ongar (0277) 362642. *Club:* Brooks's.

BUXTON, Raymond Naylor, OBE 1975; BEM 1957; QPM 1971; *b* 16 Sept. 1915; *s* of late Tom Bird Buxton and Ethel Buxton, Rushall, Walsall; *m* 1939, Agatha, *d* of late Enoch and Elizabeth Price, Essington, Wolverhampton; three *s*. *Educ:* King Edward VI Grammar Sch., Stafford. Constable to Chief Supt in Staffordshire Co. Police. Served War, RAF, Navigator, 1943–45 (FO). Police Coll. Staff, 1958–61; Asst Chief Constable, then Dep. Chief Constable of Herts, 1963–69, Chief Constable, 1969–77; HM Inspector of Constabulary, 1977–79. *Address:* Mannicotts, Radford Rise, Weeping Cross, Stafford.

BUXTON, Richard Joseph, QC 1983; a Recorder, since 1987; a Law Commissioner, since 1989; *b* 13 July 1938; *o s* of Bernard Buxton, DSO, chartered mechanical engineer, and Sybil (*née* Hurley), formerly of Burton-upon-Trent; *m* 1987, Mary, *y d* of late Donald Tyerman, CBE and of Margaret Tyerman. *Educ:* Brighton Coll. (Schol.); Exeter Coll., Oxford (Schol.; First Cl. Final Hon. Sch. of Jurisprudence 1961, First Cl. BCL 1962; Vinerian Schol. 1962; MA). Lectr, Christ Church, 1962–63; Lectr 1963–64, Fellow and Tutor 1964–73, also Sub-Rector 1966–71, Exeter Coll., Oxford. Called to the Bar, Inner Temple, 1969; in practice, 1972–. Second Lieut RAOC, 1957–58. Councillor, Oxford CC, 1966–69. Chm. of Governors, Penton I and JM Sch., 1986–. *Publications:* Local Government, 1970, 2nd edn 1973; articles in legal periodicals. *Recreations:* walking, squash, EEC law. *Address:* 37 John Street, WC1. *Clubs:* United Oxford & Cambridge University; Hornsey Squash.

BUXTON, Ronald Carlile; MA Cantab; *b* 20 Aug. 1923; *s* of Murray Barclay Buxton and Janet Mary Muriel Carlile; *m* 1959, Phyllida Dorothy Roden Buxton; two *s* two *d*. *Educ:* Eton; Trinity Coll., Cambridge. Chartered Structural Engineer (FIStructE). Director of H. Young & Co., London and associated companies. MP (C) Leyton, 1965–66. *Recreations:* travel, music, riding. *Address:* Kimberley Hall, Wymondham, Norfolk; 67 Ashley Gardens, SW1. *Club:* Carlton.

BUXTON, Sir Thomas Fowell Victor, 6th Bt *cr* 1840; *b* 18 Aug. 1925; *s* of Sir Thomas Fowell Buxton, 5th Bt, and Hon. Dorothy Cochrane (*d* 1927), *yr d* of 1st Baron Cochrane of Cults; *S* father, 1945; *m* 1955, Mrs D. M. Chisenhale-Marsh (*d* 1965). *Educ:* Eton; Trinity Coll., Cambridge. *Heir: cousin* Jocelyn Charles Roden Buxton [*b* 8 Aug. 1924; *m* 1960, Ann Frances, *d* of Frank Smitherman, *qv*; three *d*].

BUYERS, Thomas Bartlett, OBE 1975; HM Chief Inspector of Prisons for Scotland, 1985–89, retired; *b* 21 March 1926; *s* of Charles Stuart Buyers and Bessie Heywood Buyers; *m* 1951, Agnes Lodge Alexander; three *d*. *Educ:* Glasgow Acad., Glasgow; Glasgow Univ. (BSc). MIChemE. Res. Chemist, Shell, 1947–50; professional and management posts, BP Chemicals, Grangemouth and Baglan Bay, 1951–73; Dir, Scottish Petroleum Office, 1973–74; Dir of Engrg, Offshore Supplies Office, Dept of Energy, 1974–75; BP Rep./Commissioning Man., Sullom Voe Terminal, Shetland, 1975–80; Special Projects Man., BP Chemicals, London, 1980–84. *Recreations:* gardening, hill walking, travel. *Address:* 9 Bishop Terrace, Kinnesswood, Kinross KY13 7JW.

BUZZARD, Sir Anthony (Farquhar), 3rd Bt *cr* 1929; Lecturer in Theology, Oregon Bible College, Illinois, since 1982; *b* 28 June 1935; *s* of Rear-Admiral Sir Anthony Wass Buzzard, 2nd Bt, CB, DSO, OBE, and Margaret Elfreda (*d* 1989), *d* of Sir Arthur Knapp, KCIE, CSI, CBE; *S* father, 1972; *m* 1970, Barbara Jean Arnold, Mendon, Michigan, USA; three *d*. *Educ:* Charterhouse; Christ Church, Oxford (MA 1960); Ambassador Coll., Pasadena, USA (BA); MA Th Bethany Theol Seminary, 1990. ARCM. Lecturer in French, Ambassador Coll., Pasadena, 1962–65; Peripatetic Music Teacher for Surrey County Council, 1966–68; Lectr in French and Hebrew, Ambassador Coll., Bricket Wood, Herts, 1969–74; teacher of mod. langs, American Sch. in London, 1974–81. Founded Restoration Fellowship, 1981. *Publications:* The Coming Kingdom of the Messiah: a Solution to the Riddle of the New Testament, 1988; articles on eschatology and Christology in various jls. *Recreations:* tennis, squash, music. *Heir: b* Timothy Macdonnell Buzzard [*b* 28 Jan. 1939; *m* 1970, Jennifer Mary, *d* of late Peter Patching; one *s* one *d*]. *Address:* (home) 1194 Mud Creek Road, Oregon, Ill 61061, USA; (office) Box 100, Oregon, Ill 61061, USA. *T:* (815) 734 4344.

BYAM SHAW, (John) James, CBE 1972; *b* 12 Jan. 1903; *o* surv. *s* of John Byam Shaw and Evelyn Pyke-Nott; *m* 1st, 1929, Eveline (marr. diss., 1938), *d* of Capt. Arthur Dodgson, RN; 2nd, 1945, Margaret (*d* 1965), *d* of Arthur Saunders, MRCVS; one *s*; 3rd, 1967, Christina, *d* of Francis Ogilvy and *widow* of W. P. Gibson. *Educ:* Westminster; Christ Church, Oxford. Scholar of Westminster and Christ Church; MA 1925; Hon. DLitt Oxford 1977. Worked independently in principal museums of Europe, 1925–33; Lecturer and Assistant to the Director, Courtauld Institute of Art, Univ. of London, 1933–34; joined P. & D. Colnaghi & Co., 1934; Director, 1937–68. Served in Royal Scots, UK, India and Burma, 1940–46 (wounded); Major, 1944. Lectr, Christ Church, Oxford, 1964–73; Associate Curator of pictures, Christ Church, Oxford, 1973–74; Hon. Student of Christ Church, 1976. Member: Council of the Byam Shaw Sch. of Art, 1957–77; Exec. Cttee, Nat. Art Collections Fund, 1968–85; Council, British Museum Soc., 1969–74; Gulbenkian Cttee on conservation of paintings and drawings, 1970–72; Conservation Cttee, Council for Places of Worship, 1970–77; Adv. Cttee, London Diocesan Council for Care of Churches, 1974–76. Mem., Cons. Cttee, Burlington Magazine, 1984–; Chm., Adv. Cttee, Master Drawings (NY), 1981 (Chm. Emeritus, 1987). Trustee, Watts Gall., 1957–88. FSA; FRSA. Hon. Fellow: Pierpont Morgan Library, NY; Ateneo Veneto. Grande Ufficiale, Ordine al Merito, Republic of Italy, 1982. Nat. Art Collections Fund Award, 1987. *Publications:* The Drawings of Francesco Guardi, 1951; The Drawings of Domenico Tiepolo, 1962; Catalogue of Paintings by Old Masters at Christ Church Oxford, 1967; Catalogue of Drawings by Old Masters at Christ Church, Oxford, 1976; Catalogue of exhibition, Disegni Veneti della Collezione Lugt, Venice, 1981; Catalogue of Italian Drawings at the Fondation Custodia (Lugt Collection), Institut Néerlandais, Paris, 1983 (Premio Salimbeni, 1984); (with George Knox) Italian 18th Century Drawings in the Robert Lehman Collection, Metropolitan Museum, New York, 1987; publications in Old Master Drawings (1926–39), Print Collectors' Quarterly, Burlington Magazine, Apollo, Master Drawings (New York), Art Quarterly (Detroit), Arte Veneta, etc. *Address:* 4 Abingdon Villas, Kensington, W8 6BX. *T:* 071–937 6128. *Club:* Athenæum.

BYAM SHAW, Nicholas Glencairn; Chairman, Macmillan Publishers Ltd, since 1990; *b* 28 March 1934; *s* of Lieut. Comdr David Byam Shaw, RN, OBE (killed in action, 19 Dec. 1941) and Clarita Pamela Clarke; *m* 1st, 1956, Joan Elliott; two *s* one *d*; 2nd, 1974, Suzanne Filer (*née* Rastello); 3rd, 1987, Constance Wilson (*née* Clarke). *Educ:* Royal Naval Coll., Dartmouth. Commnd RN, 1955 (Lieut). Joined William Collins Sons & Co. Ltd, Glasgow, as salesman, 1956; Sales Manager, 1960; Macmillan and Co., subseq. Macmillan Publishers Ltd: Sales Manager, 1964; Sales Dir, 1965; Dep. Man. Dir, 1967; Man. Dir, 1969–90. Director: St Martins Press, 1980–; Pan Books, 1983– (Chm., 1986–). *Recreations:* gardening, travel. *Address:* 9 Kensington Park Gardens, W11 3HB. *T:* 071–221 4547.

BYATT, Antonia Susan, (Mrs P. J. Duffy), CBE 1990; FRSL 1983; writer; *b* 24 Aug. 1936; *d* of His Honour John Frederick Drabble, QC and late Kathleen Marie Bloor; *m* 1st, 1959, Ian Charles Rayner Byatt, *qv* (marr. diss. 1969); one *d* (one *s* decd); 2nd, 1969, Peter John Duffy; two *d*. *Educ:* Sheffield High Sch.; The Mount Sch., York; Newnham Coll., Cambridge (BA Hons); Bryn Mawr Coll., Pa, USA; Somerville Coll., Oxford. Extra-Mural Lectr, Univ. of London, 1962–71; Lectr in Literature, Central Sch. of Art and Design, 1965–69; Lectr in English, 1972–81, Sen. Lectr, 1981–83, UCL. Associate of Newnham Coll., Cambridge, 1977–. Member: Social Effects of Television Adv. Gp, BBC, 1974–77; Bd of Communications and Cultural Studies, CNAA, 1978–84; Bd of Creative and Performing Arts, CNAA, 1985–87; Kingman Cttee on English Language, 1987–88; PEN (Macmillan Silver Pen of Fiction, 1986); Management Cttee, Soc. of Authors, 1984–88 (Dep. Chm., 1986; Chm., 1986–88). Broadcaster, reviewer; judge of literary prizes (Hawthornden, Booker, David Higham, Betty Trask). FRSL. Hon. DLitt Bradford, 1987. *Publications:* Shadow of a Sun, 1964; Degrees of Freedom, 1965; The Game, 1967; Wordsworth and Coleridge in their Time, 1970 (reprinted as Unruly Times: Wordsworth and Coleridge, Poetry and life, 1989); Iris Murdoch, 1976; The Virgin in the Garden, 1978; (ed) George Eliot, The Mill on the Floss, 1979; Still Life, 1985; Sugar and Other Stories, 1987; Possession: a romance, 1990 (Booker Prize, 1990; Irish Times/Aer Lingus Internat. Fiction Prize, 1990); (ed) George Eliot: Selected Essays, 1990; Passions of the Mind (essays), 1991. *Address:* 37 Rusholme Road, SW15 3LF. *T:* 081–789 3109.

BYATT, Sir Hugh Campbell, KCVO 1985; CMG 1979; HM Diplomatic Service, retired; Director, EFM Dragon Trust PLC, since 1987; Chairman, EFM Java Trust, since 1990; *b* 27 Aug. 1927; *e s* of late Sir Horace Byatt, GCMG, and Lady Byatt (*née* Olga Margaret Campbell), MBE; *m* 1954, Fiona, *d* of Ian P. Coats, DL, and May Coats, MBE; two *s* one *d*. *Educ:* Gordonstoun; New College, Oxford (MA 1951). Served in Royal Navy, 1945–48; HMOCS Nigeria, 1952–57; Commonwealth Relations Office, 1958; Bombay, 1961–63; CRO, 1964–65; seconded to Cabinet Office, 1965–67; Head of Chancery, Lisbon, 1967–70; Asst Head, South Asian Dept, FCO, 1970–71; Consul-General, Mozambique, 1971–73; Inspector, HM Diplomatic Service, 1973–75; RCDS, 1976; Dep. High Comr, Nairobi, 1977–78; Ambassador to Angola, 1978–81, to São Tomé, 1980–81, to Portugal, 1981–86. Advr, RTZ, 1986–. Mem., Parole Bd for Scotland, 1991–. Chm. of Govs, Centre for Inf. on Lang. Teaching and Res., 1986–90. FSAScot 1989. Knight Grand Cross, Mil. Order of Christ (Portugal), 1985. *Recreations:* sailing, fishing, gardening. *Address:* Leargnahension, Tarbert, Argyll PA29 6YB. *T:* Tarbert (08802) 820644. *Clubs:* Royal Ocean Racing; New (Edinburgh); Royal Highland Yacht (Oban).

See also R. A. C. Byatt.

BYATT, Ian Charles Rayner; Director General of Water Services, since 1989; *b* 11 March 1932; *s* of Charles Rayner Byatt and Enid Marjorie Annie Byatt (*née* Howat); *m* 1959, A. S. Byatt, *qv* (marr. diss. 1969); one *d* (one *s* decd). *Educ:* Kirkham Grammar Sch.; Oxford University. Commonwealth Fund Fellow, Harvard, 1957–58; Lectr in Economics, Durham Univ., 1958–62; Economic Consultant, HM Treasury, 1962–64; Lectr in Economics, LSE, 1964–67; Sen. Economic Adviser, Dept of Educn and Science, 1967–69; Dir of Econs and Stats, Min. of Housing and Local Govt, 1969–70; Dir Economics, DoE, 1970–72; Under Sec., 1972–78, Dep. Chief Econ. Advr, 1978–89, HM Treasury. Chm., Economic Policy Cttee of the European Communities, 1982–85 (Mem., 1978–89); Member: Central Council of Educn (England), 1965–66; Economics Cttee, CNAA, 1968–70; ESRC, 1983–89; Urban Motorways Cttee, 1970; Cttee on Water Services: Econ. and Financial Objectives, 1970–73; Chm., Adv. Cttee to HM Treasury on Accounting for Econ. Costs and Changing Prices, 1986. Member: Bd, Public Finance Foundn, 1984–89; Bd of Management, Internat. Inst. of Public Finance, 1987–90; Council, REconS, 1983– (Mem. Exec. Cttee, 1987–89). Sec., Holy Cross Centre Trust, 1988–. FRSA 1989. *Publications:* The British Electrical Industry 1875–1914, 1979; articles on economics in books and learned jls; official reports. *Recreation:* painting. *Address:* Office of Water Services, 7 Hill Street, Birmingham B5 4UA. *T:* 021–625 1350. *Club:* United Oxford & Cambridge University.

BYATT, Ronald Archer Campbell, (Robin), CMG 1980; HM Diplomatic Service, retired; High Commissioner in New Zealand and concurrently to Western Samoa, and Governor (non-resident), Pitcairn Islands, 1987–90; *b* 14 Nov. 1930; *s* of late Sir Horace Byatt, GCMG and late Olga Margaret Campbell, MBE; *m* 1954, Ann Brereton Sharpe, *d* of C. B. Sharpe; one *s* one *d*. *Educ:* Gordonstoun; New Coll., Oxford; King's Coll., Cambridge. Served in RNVR, 1949–50. Colonial Admin. Service, Nyasaland, 1955–58; joined HM Foreign (now Diplomatic) Service, 1959; FO, 1959; Havana, 1961; FO, 1963; UK Mission to UN, NY, 1966; Kampala, 1970; Head of Rhodesia Dept, FCO, 1972–75; Vis. Fellow, Glasgow Univ., 1975–76; Counsellor and Head of Chancery, UK Mission to UN, NY, 1977–79; Asst Under Sec. of State, FCO, 1979–80; High Comr in Zimbabwe, 1980–83; Mem, Directing Staff, RCDS, 1983–84; Ambassador to Morocco, 1985–87. Trustee, Beit Trust, 1987–. *Recreations:* sailing, boating (OUBC 1953), bird-watching, gardening. *Address:* Drim-na-Vullin, Lochgilphead, Argyll. *T:* Lochgilphead (0546) 2615. *Club:* United Oxford & Cambridge University.

See also Sir H. C. Byatt.

BYERS, Sir Maurice (Hearne), Kt 1982; CBE 1978; QC 1960; barrister; Solicitor-General of Australia, 1973–83; Chairman, Australian Constitutional Commission, 1986–88; *b* 10 Nov. 1917; *s* of Arthur Tolhurst Byers and Mabel Florence Byers (*née* Hearne); *m* 1949, Patricia Therese Davis; two *s* one *d*. *Educ:* St Aloysius Coll., Milson's Point, Sydney; Sydney Univ. LLB. Called to the Bar, 1944. Mem., Exec. Council, Law Council of Australia, 1966–68; Vice-Pres., NSW Bar Assoc., 1964–65, Pres., 1965–67. Leader, Australian delegations to: UN Commn on Internat. Trade Law, 1974, 1976–82; Diplomatic Conf. on Sea Carriage of Goods, Hamburg, 1979. Chm., Police Bd of NSW, 1984–88. Member: Council, ANU, 1975–78; Australian Law Reform Commn, 1984–85. *Address:* 14 Morella Road, Clifton Gardens, NSW 2088, Australia. *T:* 969 8257. *Clubs:* Commonwealth (Canberra); Union (Sydney).

BYERS, Dr Paul Duncan; Reader Emeritus in Morbid Anatomy, University of London; Head of Department of Morbid Anatomy, Institute of Orthopaedics, University of London, 1980–87, retired (Dean of Institute, 1971–79); *b* Montreal, 1922; *s* of A. F. Byers and Marion Taber; *m* 1959, Valery Garden. *Educ:* Bishops College Sch., PQ, Canada; McGill Univ. (BSc, MD, CM); Univ. of London (DCP, PhD). FRCPath. Alan Blair Memorial Fellow, Canadian Cancer Soc., 1955–57. Asst Morbid Anatomist, Inst. of Orthopaedics, 1960; Reader in Morbid Anatomy, Univ. of London, 1974. Hon. Consultant, Royal National Orthopaedic Hosp., 1965; Hon. Senior Lectr, Royal Postgrad. Med. Sch., 1969. Chm., Osteosarcoma Histopathol. Panel, MRC/EORTC, 1983–86; Member: Osteosarcoma Wkg Party, MRC, 1982–86; Soft Tissue Sarcoma Wkg Party, MRC, 1983–84. Mem., Management Cttee, Courtauld Inst. of Art, Univ. of London, 1979–82. *Publications:* articles in medical press on arthritis, metabolic bone disease, bone tumours, medical education. *Recreation:* arts. *Address:* 18 Wimpole Street, W1M 7AD. *T:* 071–580 5206.

BYFORD, Sir Lawrence, Kt 1984; CBE 1979; QPM 1973; DL; management consultant, since 1987; HM Chief Inspector of Constabulary, 1983–87; *b* 10 Aug. 1925; *s* of George Byford and Monica Irene Byford; *m* 1950, Muriel Campbell Massey; two *s* one *d. Educ:* Univ. of Leeds (LLB Hons). Barrister-at-Law. Joined W Riding Police, 1947; served on Directing Staff of Wakefield Detective Sch., 1959–62, and Police Staff Coll., Bramshill, 1964–66; Divl Comdr, Huddersfield, 1966–68; Asst Chief Constable of Lincs, 1968, Dep. Chief Constable 1970, Chief Constable, 1973–77; HM Inspector of Constabulary for: SE Region, 1977–78; NE Region, 1978–82. Lecture tour of univs, USA and Canada, 1976; Headed: British Police Mission to Turkey, 1978–79; official review into Yorkshire Ripper case, 1981. DL Lincs, 1987. Hon. LLD Leeds, 1987. *Recreations:* cricket, Pennine walking and travel. *Clubs:* Royal Over-Seas League (Chm., 1989–), MCC; Yorks CC (Pres., 1991–).

BYGRAVES, Max Walter, OBE 1983; entertainer; *b* 16 Oct. 1922; *s* of Henry and Lilian Bygraves, Rotherhithe, SE16; *m* 1942, Gladys Blossom Murray; one *s* two *d. Educ:* St Joseph's, Rotherhithe. Began in advertising agency, carrying copy to Fleet Street, 1936. Volunteered for RAF, 1940; served 5 years as fitter. Performed many shows for troops; became professional, 1946; has appeared in venues all over English-speaking world, incl. 18 Royal Command Performances; best selling record artist. Host, Family Fortunes, TV, 1983–85. *Publications:* I Wanna Tell You a Story (autobiog.), 1976; The Milkman's on his Way (novel), 1977; After Thoughts (autobiog.), 1988. *Recreations:* golf, painting, reading, writing. *Address:* Roebuck House, Victoria, SW1E 5BE. *T:* 071–828 4595. *Clubs:* St James's, East India.

BYNG, family name of **Earl of Strafford,** and of **Viscount Torrington.**

BYNOE, Dame Hilda Louisa, DBE 1969; in General Medical Practice, Port of Spain, Trinidad, 1974–89, retired; *b* Grenada, 18 Nov. 1921; *d* of late Thomas Joseph Gibbs, CBE, JP, Estate Proprietor, and Louisa Gibbs (*née* La Touche); *m* 1947, Peter Cecil Alexander Bynoe, ARIBA, Dip. Arch., former RAF Flying Officer; two *s. Educ:* St Joseph's Convent, St George's, Grenada; Royal Free Hospital Medical Sch., Univ. of London. MB, BS (London), 1951, MRCS, LRCP, 1951. Teacher, St Joseph's Convents, Trinidad and Grenada, 1939–44; hospital and private practice, London, 1951–53; public service with Govt of Trinidad and Tobago, 1954–55, with Govt of Guyana (then British Guiana), 1955–58, with Govt of Trinidad and Tobago, 1958–65; private practice, Trinidad, 1961–68; Governor of Associated State of Grenada, WI, 1968–74. Mem. YWCA. Patron: Caribbean Women's Assoc., 1970–; John Hayes Meml Kidney Foundn, 1979–; Music Foundn of Trinidad and Tobago, 1986–; African Assoc. of Trinidad and Tobago. *Recreations:* swimming, music, reading, poetry-writing. *Address:* 5A Barcant Avenue, Maraval, Trinidad. *Club:* Soroptimist (Port of Spain).

BYRNE, Sir Clarence (Askew), Kt 1969; OBE 1964; DSC 1945; Company Director, Mining, Insurance and Construction, Queensland; *b* 17 Jan. 1903; *s* of George Patrick Byrne, Brisbane, Qld, and Elizabeth Emma Askew, Dalby, Qld; *m* 1928, Nellie Ann Millicent Jones; one *s* one *d. Educ:* Brisbane Technical Coll. Mining Develt and Exploration, 1925–30; Oil Exploration, Roma, Qld, 1930–40. Served War, 1940–46 (DSC, Amer. Bronze Star Medal): Lt-Comdr; CO, HMAS Warrego, 1944–45. Pres., Qld Chamber of Mines, 1961–70; Exec. Dir, Conzinc Riotinto of Australia Ltd (Resident, Qld, 1957–68); Formerly: Chm., Qld Alumina Ltd; Director: Thiess Holdings Ltd; Walkers Ltd. Former Mem. Aust. Mining Industries Council, Canberra. *Recreations:* fishing, ocean cruising. *Address:* Culverston, Dingle Avenue, Caloundra, Qld 4551, Australia. *T:* Caloundra 91–1228. *Clubs:* United Service, Queensland (Brisbane).

BYRNE, Douglas Norman; Head of Marine Directorate, Department of Transport (formerly Marine Division, Department of Trade), 1980–84; *b* 30 Jan. 1924; *s* of Leonard William Byrne and Clarice Evelyn Byrne; *m* 1949, Noreen Thurlby Giles; one *s* one *d. Educ:* Portsmouth Grammar Sch.; St John's Coll., Cambridge (MA). RAF, 1942–46. Asst Principal, Min. of Supply, 1949; BoT, 1956; Cabinet Office, 1961–64; Asst Sec., 1964; on staff of Monopolies Commn, 1966–68; Under-Sec., Dept of Industry, 1974–77; Hd of Fair Trading Div., Dept of Prices and Consumer Protection, 1977–79; Under-Sec., Dept of Trade, 1979–83, Dept of Transport, 1983–84. *Recreations:* hill walking, natural history. *Club:* Royal Air Force.

BYRNE, John Keyes; *see* Leonard, Hugh.

BYRNE, Rev. Father Paul Laurence, OMI; OBE 1976; Provincial Superior, Anglo Irish Province of the Missionary Oblates of Mary Immaculate, since 1988; *b* 8 Aug. 1932; *s* of late John Byrne and Lavinia Byrne. *Educ:* Synge Street Christian Brothers' Sch. and Belcamp Coll., Dublin; University Coll., Dublin (BA, Hons Phil.); Oblate Coll., Piltown. Teacher, Belcamp Coll., 1959–65; Dean of Belcamp Coll., 1961–65; Dir, Irish Centre, Birmingham, 1965–68; Dir, Catholic Housing Aid Soc. (Birmingham) and Family Housing Assoc., Birmingham, 1965–69; Nat. Dir, Catholic Housing Aid Soc., and Dir, Family Housing Assoc., London, 1969–70; Dir, SHAC (a housing aid centre), 1969–76. Sec. Gen., Conf. of Major Religious Superiors of Ire., 1980–87. Board Member: Threshold Centre; Servite Houses; SHAC; Housing Corp., 1974–77. Hon. Mem., Inst. of Housing, 1972. *Recreations:* golf, theatre-going. *Address:* 170 Merrion Road, Ballsbridge, Dublin 4. *T:* Dublin 839857. *Club:* Foxrock Golf.

BYRNE, Terence Niall; HM Diplomatic Service; Deputy High Commissioner, Lusaka, since 1990; *b* 28 April 1942; *e s* of late Denis Patrick Byrne and of Kathleen Byrne (*née*

Carley); *m* 1st, 1966, Andrea Dennison (marr. diss. 1977); one *s* one *d*; 2nd, 1981, Susan Haddow Neill; two *d. Educ:* Finchley Catholic Grammar Sch.; Open Univ. (BA). Min. of Housing and Local Govt, 1964–68; Prime Minister's Office, 1968–70; MAFF, 1971–78 (Private Sec. to Parly Sec., MAFF, 1974–75); First Sec. (Agriculture), The Hague, 1978–82; Commonwealth Co-ordination Dept, FCO, 1982–84; Asst Head, UN Dept, FCO, 1984–85; Head of Chancery and Consul, Quito, 1986–89. *Recreations:* running, golf, cinema. *Address:* c/o Foreign and Commonwealth Office, King Charles Street, SW1A 2AH.

BYROM, Peter Craig, OBE 1987; self-employed textile consultant, since 1985; *b* 4 Dec. 1927; *s* of Robert Hunter Byrom, Master Cotton Spinner and Winifred Agnes Byrom (*née* Godwin); *m* 1st, 1952, Norma Frances Mawdesley Harris (marr. diss. 1984); three *s* three *d*; 2nd, 1984, Gillian Elizabeth Hoyte. *Educ:* Virginia Episcopal Sch., Lynchburg, USA; St Edward's Sch., Oxford; Univ. of Liverpool, Sch. of Architecture; Salford Royal Tech. Coll.; Admin. Staff Coll., Henley; Open Univ. (BA). CText, FTI. RNVR, 1945–48. Asst Gen. Manager, Robert Byrom (Stalybridge), cotton spinners, 1951–59; Merchandising Manager, British Nylon Spinners, 1959–64; Marketing Manager and Adv. and Promotions Manager, ICI Fibres, 1964–71; Dir, Deryck Healey Internat., 1972–74; Man. Dir, Dartington Hall Tweeds, 1975–85. Consultant to: ODA, Nepal, 1980; Intermediate Tech. Gp, India, 1986; Chm., British Colour Council, 1971–73; Mem., Textile and Fashion Bd, CNAA, 1974–77; Governor, Dartington Coll. of Arts, 1979–89; Chm. Council, RCA, 1981–86 (Mem., 1979–86; Sen. Fellow, 1983); Mem. Council, Textile Inst., 1986–. FRSA 1970 (Mem. Council, 1987–; Mem. Design Bd, 1986–, Chm., Textiles, Young Designers into Industry, 1985–90). *Publications:* Textiles: product design and marketing, 1987; contrib. to Young Designers into the Textile Industry. *Recreations:* hill farming on Dartmoor, walking, cycling, swimming, theatre, music, books. *Address:* Barton House, Woodland, Ashburton, Devon TQ13 7LN. *T:* Ashburton (0364) 53926.

BYRON, 13th Baron *cr* 1643, of Rochdale, Co. Lancaster; **Robert James Byron;** Partner, Holman Fenwick & Willan, since 1984; *b* 5 April 1950; *o surv. s* of 12th Baron Byron, DSO and Dorigen Margaret (*d* 1985); *o d* of Percival Kennedy Esdaile; *S* father, 1989; *m* 1979, Robyn Margaret, *d* of John McLean, Hamilton, NZ; one *s* three *d. Educ:* Wellington Coll.; Trinity Coll., Cambridge (MA). Called to the Bar, Inner Temple, 1974; admitted solicitor, 1978. *Heir: s* Hon. Charles Richard Gordon Byron, *b* 28 July 1990. *Address:* 19 Spencer Park, SW18 2SZ; Marlow House, Lloyds Avenue, EC3N 3AL.

BYRT, (Henry) John, QC 1976; **His Honour Judge Byrt;** a Circuit Judge, since 1983; *b* 5 March 1929; *s* of Dorothy Muriel Byrt and Albert Henry Byrt, CBE; *m* 1957, Eve Hermione Bartlett; one *s* two *d. Educ:* Charterhouse; Merton Coll., Oxford (BA, MA). Called to the Bar, Middle Temple, 1953; called within the Bar, 1976; a Recorder of the Crown Court, 1976–83. Pres., Social Security Appeal Tribunals and Medical Appeal Tribunals, 1983–89. Vice-Principal, Working Mens' Coll., London, 1978–82, Principal, 1982–87; Mem. Council, Queen's Coll., London, 1982–. *Recreations:* building, gardening, sailing, music. *Address:* 65 Gloucester Crescent, NW1 7EG. *T:* 071–485 0341. *Club:* Leander.

BYWATER, Air Cdre David Llewellyn, FRAeS, FBIM; Commandant, Aeroplane and Armament Experimental Establishment, Boscombe Down, since 1988; *b* 16 July 1937; *s* of Stanley and Gertrude Bywater; *m* 1960, Shelagh May Gowling; one *s* one *d. Educ:* Liverpool Inst. High Sch.; RAF Coll., Cranwell. No XV Sqdn, 1958–63; Empire Test Pilots Sch., 1964; A&AEE Test Pilot, 1965–68; RAF Staff Coll., 1969; HQ Germany, 1970–73; Wing Comdr Flying, RAE Farnborough, 1974–78; MoD Operational Requirements, 1979–81; Gp Captain, Superintendent of Flying, A&AEE, 1982–85; RAF Staff Coll., Bracknell, 1985–88. *Recreations:* sailing, ski-ing. *Club:* Royal Air Force.

BYWATERS, Eric George Lapthorne, CBE 1975; MB (London); FRCP; Professor of Rheumatology, Royal Postgraduate Medical School, University of London, 1958–75, now Emeritus; Hon. Consultant Physician, Hammersmith Hospital and Canadian Red Cross Memorial Hospital, Taplow, Bucks; Hon. Librarian, Heberden Library, Royal College of Physicians, since 1970; *b* 1 June 1910; *s* of George Ernest Bywaters and Ethel Penney; *m* 1935, Betty Euan-Thomas; three *d. Educ:* Sutton Valence Sch., Kent; Middx Hosp. (Sen. Broderip Schol., Lyell Gold Medallist). McKenzie McKinnon Fellow, RCP, 1935; Asst Clin. Pathologist, Bland Sutton Inst., 1936; Rockefeller Travelling Fellow and Harvard Univ. Research Fellow in Med., 1937–39; Beit Memorial Fellow, 1939; Actg Dir, MRC Clin. Res. Unit (Shock), 1943; Lectr in Med., Postgrad. Med. Sch., 1945; Dir, MRC Rheumatism Res. Unit, Taplow, 1958–75; Sen. MRC Res. Fellow, Bone and Joint Unit, London Hosp., 1977–. Pres., European League against Rheumatism, 1977 (Hon. Mem. 1981); Councillor, Internat. League against Rheumatism. Hon. Mem., Heberden Soc., 1977; Hon. FACP, 1973; Hon. FRCP&S (Canada), 1977; Hon. FRSM, 1983. Hon. MD Liège, 1973. Gairdner Foundation Medical Award, 1963; Heberden Orator and Medallist, 1966; Croonian Lectr, RCP, 1968; Bunim Lectr and Medallist, 1973; Ewart Angus Lectr, Toronto, 1974; Samuel Hyde Lectr, RSocMed, 1986. Hon. Mem. Dutch, French, Amer., German, Czech, Spanish, Portuguese, Aust., Indian, Canadian, Chilean, Peruvian, Jugoslav and Argentine Rheumatism Assocs. *Publications:* papers on rheumatism, Crush Syndrome, etc. *Recreations:* painting, gardening, tennis. *Address:* Long Acre, 53 Burkes Road, Beaconsfield, Bucks HP9 1PW.

C

CABALLÉ, Montserrat; Cross of Lazo de Dama of Order of Isabel the Catholic, Spain; opera and concert singer; *b* Barcelona, 12 April 1933; *d* of Carlos and Ana Caballé; *m* 1964, Bernabé Marti, tenor; one *s* one *d*. *Educ:* Conservatorio del Liceo, Barcelona. Continued to study singing under Mme Eugenia Kemeny. Carnegie Hall début as Lucrezia Borgia, 1965. London début in this role, with the London Opera Society, at the Royal Festival Hall, 1968. Has sung at Covent Garden, Glyndebourne, La Scala, Vienna, Metropolitan Opera, San Francisco and most major opera venues. Major roles include Maria Stuarda, Luisa Miller, Queen Elizabeth in Roberto Devereux, Imogene in Il Pirata, Violetta in La Traviata, Marguerite in Faust, Desdemona in Otello, Norma, Tosca, Turandot, Leonora in La Forza del Destino, Semiramide and also those of contemporary opera. Over 120 roles sung and recorded. Numerous hon. degrees, awards and medals. *Address:* c/o Carlos Caballé, Via Augusta 59, 08006 Barcelona, Spain.

CABLE, Sir James (Eric), KCVO 1976; CMG 1967; HM Diplomatic Service, retired; writer; *b* 15 Nov. 1920; *s* of late Eric Grant Cable, CMG; *m* 1954, Viveca Hollmerus; one *s*. *Educ:* Stowe; CCC, Cambridge. PhD 1973. Served Royal Signals, 1941–46, Major. Entered Foreign (now Diplomatic) Service, 1947; 2nd Sec., 1948; Vice-Consul, Batavia, 1949; 2nd Sec., Djakarta, 1949; acted as Chargé d'Affaires, 1951 and 1952; Helsinki, 1952; FO, 1953; 1st Sec., 1953; Mem. of British Delegn to Geneva Conf. on Indo-China, 1954; 1st Sec. (Commercial), Budapest, 1956; Head of Chancery and Consul, Quito, 1959; acted as Chargé d'Affaires, 1959 and 1960; FO, 1961 and Head of SE Asia Dept, Dec. 1963; Counsellor, Beirut, 1966; acted as Chargé d'Affaires at Beirut, 1967, 1968 and 1969; Research Associate, Institute for Strategic Studies, 1969–70; Head of Western Organisations Dept, FCO, 1970–71; Counsellor, Contingency Studies, FCO, 1971; Head of Planning Staff, 1971–75, and Asst Under-Sec. of State, 1972–75, FCO; Ambassador to Finland, 1975–80; Leverhulme Res. Fellow, 1981–82. *Publications:* Britain in Tomorrow's World, 1969 (as Grant Hugo); Appearance and Reality in International Relations, 1970 (as Grant Hugo); Gunboat Diplomacy, 1971, 3rd edn 1986; The Royal Navy and the Siege of Bilbao, 1979; Britain's Naval Future, 1983; Diplomacy at Sea, 1985; The Geneva Conference of 1954 on Indochina, 1986; Political Institutions and Issues in Britain, 1987; Navies in Violent Peace, 1989; Intervention at Abadan, 1991; articles in various jls. *Address:* 8 Essex Close, Cambridge CB4 2DW.

CABLE-ALEXANDER, Lt-Col Sir Patrick (Desmond William), 8th Bt *cr* 1809, of the City of Dublin; Secretary to the Council and Bursar, Lancing College, since 1984; *b* 19 April 1936; *s* of Sir Desmond William Lionel Cable-Alexander, 7th Bt and of Mary Jane, *d* of James O'Brien, Enniskillen; *S* father, 1988; *m* 1st, 1961, Diana Frances Rogers (marr. diss. 1976); two *d*; 2nd, 1976, Jane Mary Weekes (*née* Lewis); one *s*. *Educ:* Downside School; RMA Sandhurst. Commnd 3rd Carabiniers (POWDG), 1956; Lt-Col Royal Scots Dragoon Guards, 1976; comd Duke of Lancaster's Own Yeomanry, 1978–80; Chief of Staff, HQ North West District, 1980–83; retd, 1984. *Recreations:* cricket, gardening, visiting France, art. *Heir: s* Fergus William Antony Cable-Alexander, *b* 19 June 1981. *Address:* Windrush House, Hoe Court, Lancing, West Sussex BN15 0QX. *T:* Lancing (0903) 754772.

CABORN, Richard George; MP (Lab) Sheffield, Central, since 1983; *b* 6 Oct. 1943; *s* of George and Mary Caborn; *m* 1966, Margaret Caborn; one *s* one *d*. *Educ:* Hurlfield Comprehensive Sch.; Granville Coll. of Further Educn; Sheffield Polytechnic. Engrg apprentice, 1959–64; Convenor of Shop Stewards, Firth Brown Ltd, 1967–79. Mem. (Lab) Sheffield, European Parlt, 1979–84. *Recreation:* amateur football. *Address:* 29 Quarry Vale Road, Sheffield S12 3EB. *T:* Sheffield (0742) 393802. *Club:* Carlton Working Men's (Sheffield).

CACHELIN, Commissioner Francy; International Evangelist, The Salvation Army, 1987–89, retired; *b* 4 Aug. 1923; *s* of Maurice Cachelin and France Hauswirth; *m* 1951, Geneviève Irène Catherine Booth; two *s* two *d*. *Educ:* Lausanne School of Arts. Commissioned Salvation Army Officer, 1944; served in Switzerland as Corps Officer; Editor, The War Cry, in Belgium, 1951; responsible for youth work, France, 1957; Field Secretary, Switzerland, 1966; Chief Secretary, France, 1975, British Territory, 1977; Territorial Commander, Germany, 1979; British Comr, 1984. Federal Cross of Merit (FRG), 1984. *Recreation:* reading.

CACOYANNIS, Michael; director, stage and screen, since 1954; *b* 11 June 1922; *s* of late Sir Panayotis Cacoyannis and Angeliki, *d* of George M. Efthyvoulos and Zoe Constantinides, Limassol, Cyprus. *Educ:* Greek Gymnasium; Gray's Inn and Old Vic Sch., London. Radio Producer, BBC, Greek Service, 1941–50. Actor on English stage, 1946–51; parts included: Herod, in Salome, 1946; Caligula, in Caligula, 1949, etc. *Directed films:* Windfall in Athens, 1953; Stella, 1954; Girl in Black, 1956; A Matter of Dignity, 1958; Our Last Spring, 1960; The Wastrel, 1961; Electra, 1962; Zorba the Greek, 1964; The Day the Fish Came Out, 1967; The Trojan Women, 1971; Attila '74, 1975; Iphigenia, 1977; Sweet Country, 1986; directed *plays:* produced several of these in Athens for Ellie Lambetti's Company, 1955–61; The Trojan Women, New York, 1963–65, Paris, 1965; Things That Go Bump in the Night, and The Devils, New York, 1965; Iphigenia in Aulis, New York, 1968; King Oedipus, Abbey Theatre, Dublin, 1973; Miss Margarita, Athens, 1975; The Bacchae, Comédie Française, 1977, New York, 1980; The Glass Menagerie, Nat. Theatre, Athens, 1978; Antony and Cleopatra, Athens, 1979; Zorba (musical), USA, 1983; Electra, Epidaurus, 1984; Naked, Athens, 1989; Henceforward, Athens, 1990; directed *operas:* Mourning Becomes Electra, Metropolitan Opera, NY, 1967; La Bohème, Juillard, NY, 1972; La Traviata, Athens, 1983; Iphigenia in Aulis and in Tauris, Frankfurt State Opera, 1987; La Clemenza di Tito, Aix-en-Provence, 1988. Hon. DH Columbia Coll., Chicago, 1981. Order of the Phœnix (Greece), 1965; Commandeur des Arts et des Lettres, 1987. *Publications:* Collected Writings, 1990; *translations:* (into English) The Bacchae, 1982; (into Greek) Antony and Cleopatra, 1980; Hamlet, 1985; Coriolanus, 1990. *Recreations:* walking, swimming. *Address:* 15 Mouson Street, Athens 117–41, Greece.

CADBURY, Sir Adrian; *see* Cadbury, Sir G. A. H.

CADBURY, Dominic; *see* Cadbury, N. D.

CADBURY, Sir (George) Adrian (Hayhurst), Kt 1977; a Director of the Bank of England, since 1970; *b* 15 April 1929; *s* of late Laurence John Cadbury, OBE and Joyce, *d* of Lewis O. Mathews, Birmingham; *m* 1956, Gillian Mary, *d* of late E. D. Skepper, Neuilly-sur-Seine; two *s* one *d*. *Educ:* Eton Coll.; King's Coll., Cambridge (MA Economics). Coldstream Guards, 1948–49; Cambridge, 1949–52. Cadbury Schweppes: Dep. Chm. and Man. Dir, 1969–74; Chm., 1975–89; Director: Cadbury Bros Ltd, 1958; IBM UK Ltd, 1975–; Nat. Exhibition Centre, 1989–. Mem. Supervisory Bd, DAF NV, 1988–. Mem., Panel on Takeovers and Mergers, 1990–. Chancellor, Univ. of Aston in Birmingham, 1979–. Chairman: West Midlands Economic Planning Council, 1967–70; CBI Econ. & Financial Policy Cttee, 1974–80; Food & Drink Industries Council, 1981–83; Promotion of Non-Exec. Dirs, 1984–; Cttee on Financial Aspects of Corporate Governance, 1991–; Pres., Birmingham Chamber of Industry and Commerce, 1988–89. Freeman, City of Birmingham, 1982. Hon. DSc: Aston, 1973; Cranfield, 1985; Hon. LLD: Bristol, 1986; Birmingham, 1989. *Publication:* The Company Chairman, 1990. *Address:* Rising Sun House, Baker's Lane, Knowle, Solihull, W Midlands B93 8PT. *Clubs:* Athenæum, Boodle's; Hawks (Cambridge); Leander (Henley).
See also N. D. Cadbury.

CADBURY, George Woodall, OC 1990; Chairman Emeritus, Governing Body of International Planned Parenthood Federation, since 1975 (Chairman, 1969–75, Vice-Chairman, and Chairman of the Executive, 1963–69, and Special Representative, since 1960); *b* 19 Jan. 1907; *s* of George Cadbury and Edith Caroline Cadbury (*née* Woodall); *m* 1935, Mary Barbara Pearce; two *d*. *Educ:* Leighton Park Sch., Reading; King's Coll., Cambridge (personal pupil of J. M. Keynes); MA (Economics Tripos); Wharton Sch. of Finance and Commerce, Univ. of Pennsylvania. Man. Dir, British Canners Ltd, 1929–35; Marketing Controller and Man. Dir, Alfred Bird & Sons Ltd, 1935–45; Auxiliary, later Nat., Fire Service, 1939–41; Dep. Dir Material Production, Min. of Aircraft Production and British Air Commn (USA), 1941–45; Chm. Economic Advisory and Planning Bd, and Chief Industrial Executive, Prov. of Saskatchewan, 1945–51; Dir, Technical Assistance Administration, UN, 1951–60 (Dir of Ops, 1951–54; Adviser to Govts of Ceylon, Burma, Indonesia and Barbados, 1954–60; Advr to Govt of Jamaica, 1955–60). New Democratic Party of Canada: Pres., Ont, 1961–66; Fed. Treasurer, 1965–69; Mem., Fed. Exec., 1961–71; Life Mem., 1980. Chm., 1972–74 and 1976–78, Pres., 1978–82, Conservation Council of Ontario. Trustee: Bournville Village Trust, 1928–85; Youth Hostels Trust, 1931–; Sponsor and Council Mem., Minority Rights Group, 1967–; Hon. Director, 1961–: Planned Parenthood Fedn of Canada; Planned Parenthood, Toronto; Planned Parenthood Soc., Hamilton, Ont. Member: TGWU, 1925, Life Mem., 1973; League for Industrial Democracy, NY, 1928, Bd Mem., 1951–. Mem. Meetings Cttee, RIIA, 1931–35; Sec., W Midland Group for Post-War Reconstruction and Planning, 1939–41; Resident, Toynbee Hall, 1929–35, 1941–43. *Publications:* (jointly) When We Build Again, 1940; English County, 1942; Conurbation, 1942; Essays on the Left, 1971; A Population Policy for Canada, 1973. *Recreation:* railway practice and history. *Address:* 35 Brentwood Road, Oakville, Ont L6J 4B7, Canada. *T:* 416–845 3171.

CADBURY, (Nicholas) Dominic; Chief Executive, Cadbury Schweppes plc, since 1984; *b* 12 May 1940; *s* of late Laurence John Cadbury, OBE and Joyce Cadbury; *m* 1972, Cecilia Sarah Symes; three *d*. *Educ:* Eton Coll.; Trinity Coll., Cambridge; Stanford Univ. (MBA). Dir, Economist Gp, 1990–. Member: Royal Mint Adv. Cttee, 1986–; President's Cttee, CBI, 1989–; Stanford Adv. Council, 1989–; Food Assoc., 1989–. Vice Pres., Edgbaston High Sch. for Girls, Birmingham, 1987–. CBIM 1984. *Recreations:* tennis, golf, shooting.
See also Sir G. A. H. Cadbury.

CADBURY, Peter (Egbert); Chairman, Preston Publications Ltd, since 1985; *b* Great Yarmouth, Norfolk, 6 Feb. 1918; *s* of late Sir Egbert Cadbury, DSC, DFC; *m* 1st, 1947, Eugenie Benedicta (marr. diss. 1968), *d* of late Major Ewen Bruce, DSO, MC and of Mrs Bruce; one *s* one *d*; 2nd, 1970, Mrs Jennifer Morgan-Jones (*see* J. M. V. d'Abo) (marr. diss. 1976), *d* of Major Michael Hammond Maude, Ramsden, Oxon; one *s*; 3rd, 1976, Mrs Jane Mead; two *s*. *Educ:* Leighton Park Sch.; Trinity Coll., Cambridge (BA, MA 1939). Called to Bar, Inner Temple, 1946; practised at Bar, 1946–54. Served Fleet Air Arm, 1940, until released to Ministry of Aircraft Production, 1942, as Prodn, Research and Experimental Test Pilot. Contested (L) Stroud (Glos), 1945. Member, London Travel Cttee, 1958–60; Chm. and Man. Dir, Keith Prowse Group, 1954–71; Chairman: Alfred Hays Ltd, 1955–71; Ashton & Mitchell Ltd and Ashton & Mitchell Travel Co. Ltd, 1959–71; Air Westward Ltd, 1977–79; Air West Ltd, 1977–79; Educational Video Index Ltd, 1981–83; Westward Travel Ltd, 1982–84; Exec. Chm., Westward Television Ltd, 1960–80; Chm., Preston Estates, 1973–90; Director: Independent Television News Ltd, 1972–79; Willett Investments Ltd, 1955–. Chm., George Cadbury Trust, 1979–; Trustee: Help the Aged, 1986–; Mus. of Army Flying, 1986–; Winchester Cathedral Trust, 1986–. Freeman of City of London, 1948. *Recreations:* theatre, racing, flying, golf, tennis, sailing. *Address:* Armsworth Hill, Alresford, Hants SO24 9RJ. *T:* Alresford (0962) 734656, *Fax:* Alresford (0962) 734757; Flat 4, 42 Cadogan Square, SW1. *T:* 071–589 8755; (car) 0836 220214. *Clubs:* Buck's, XL (Forty), MCC, Lord's Taverners; Hawks (Cambridge); Island Sailing, Royal Motor Yacht, RAF Yacht.

CADBURY-BROWN, Henry Thomas, OBE 1967; TD; RA 1975 (ARA 1971); FRIBA; Professor of Architecture, Royal Academy, 1975–88; architect, in partnership with John F. Metcalfe, 1962–84; Hon. Fellow RCA; *b* 20 May 1913; *s* of Henry William Cadbury-Brown and Marion Ethel Sewell; *m* 1953, Elizabeth Romeyn, *d* of Prof. A. Elwyn, Croton on Hudson, NY. *Educ:* Westminster Sch.; AA Sch. of Architecture (Hons Diploma). Architect in private practice since winning competition for British Railways Branch Offices, 1937. Work includes pavilions for "The Origins of the People", main concourse and fountain display at Festival of Britain; schools, housing, display and interiors. Architect for new civic centre at Gravesend and halls for residence for Birmingham Univ. and, with Sir Hugh Casson and Prof. Robert Goodden, for new premises for Royal College of Art; awarded London Architecture Bronze Medal, 1963; lecture halls for Univ. of Essex; for RBK & C: Tavistock Cres. housing; World's End redevelt (in gp partnership Eric Lyons, Cadbury-Brown, Metcalfe & Cunningham). Taught at Architectural Association Sch., 1946–49; Tutor at Royal Coll. of Art, 1952–61. Invited as Visiting Critic to Sch. of Architecture, Harvard Univ., 1956. Member: RIBA Council, 1951–53; MARS (Modern Architectural Research) group. Pres. Architectural Assoc., 1959–60. TA and military service, 1931–45; Major RA (TD). DU Essex, 1989. *Recreations:* numerous, including work. *Address:* 18 Fentiman Road, SW8. *T:* 071–582 5630; 3 Church Walk, Aldeburgh, Suffolk. *T:* Aldeburgh (072885) 2591.

CADELL, Colin Simson, CBE 1944; Air Cdre RAF, retired; Vice Lieutenant for West Lothian, 1972–88; *b* 7 Aug. 1905; *s* of late Lt-Col J. M. Cadell, DL, Foxhall, Kirkliston, W Lothian; *m* 1939, Rosemary Elizabeth, *d* of Thomas Edward Pooley; two *s* one *d*. *Educ:* Merchiston; Edinburgh Univ.; Ecole Supérieur d'électricité, Paris. MA; AMIEE; Ingénieur ESE. Commnd RAF, 1926; Dir of Signals, Air Min., 1944; retd 1947. Man. Dir, International Aeradio, 1947–58; Director: Carron Company, 1958–71; Royal Bank of Scotland, 1963–69. Mem., Edinburgh Airport Consultative Cttee, 1972– (Chm., 1972–82). Mem. Queen's Body Guard for Scotland (Royal Company of Archers). DL: Linlithgowshire, 1963–72. Officer, US Legion of Merit, 1945. *Address:* 2 Upper Coltbridge Terrace, Edinburgh EH12 6AD. *Club:* New (Edinburgh).

CADELL, Vice-Adm. Sir John (Frederick), KBE 1983; District General Manager, Canterbury and Thanet Health Authority, since 1986; *b* 6 Dec. 1929; *s* of Henry Dunlop Mallock Cadell and Violet Elizabeth (*née* Van Dyke); *m* 1958, Jaquetta Bridget Nolan; one *s* two *d*. *Educ:* Britannia Royal Naval Coll., Dartmouth. Served in HMS Frobisher, 1946, then Mediterranean, Persian Gulf, North and Baltic Seas; 2 years with RNZN, to 1960; served in HMS Ashton, Dartmouth, HMS Leopard, 9th Minesweeping Sqdn, SACLANT, HMS Bulwark, 1960–70; Naval Asst to First Sea Lord, 1970–72; HMS Diomede, 1972–74; RCDS 1974–75; RN Presentation Team, 1975–76; Comd, Sch. of Maritime Ops, 1976–79; Dir Gen. Naval Personal Services, 1979–81; COS to Comdr, Allied Forces Southern Europe, 1982–85. *Recreations:* tennis, skiing, wind surfing.

CADELL, Patrick Moubray, FSAScot; Keeper of the Records of Scotland, since 1991; *b* 17 March 1941; *s* of Col H. M. Cadell of Grange, OBE and Christina Rose Nimmo; *m* 1968, Sarah Margaret Florence King; two *s* one *d*. *Educ:* Merchiston Castle Sch.; Trinity Coll., Cambridge (BA 1962); Toulouse Univ. FSAScot 1985. British Museum: guide lectr, Dept of Admin, 1964–66; Asst Keeper, Dept of Manuscripts, 1966–68; National Library of Scotland: Asst Keeper, Dept of Manuscripts, 1968–83; Keeper, Dept of Manuscripts, 1983–90. *Publications:* The Iron Mills at Cramond, 1973; (contrib.) The Water of Leith, 1984; The Abbey Court and High Constables of Holyrood, 1985; (contrib.) A Sense of Place: studies in Scottish Local history, 1988; (contrib.) For the Encouragement of Learning: Scotland's National Library 1689–1989, 1989; The Third Statistical Account of Scotland, Vol. for West Lothian, 1992; contribs on historical subjects to books and jls. *Recreations:* walking, the French language. *Address:* 11A Tipperlinn Road, Edinburgh EH10 5ET. *T:* 031–447 6630. *Club:* University Staff (Edinburgh).

CADIEUX, Hon. Léo, PC 1965; OC 1975; Ambassador of Canada to France, 1970–75; *b* 28 May 1908; *s* of Joseph E. Cadieux and Rosa Paquette, both French Canadian; *m* 1962, Monique, *d* of Placide Plante; one *s*. *Educ:* Commercial Coll. of St Jerome and Seminary of Ste Thérèse de Blainville, Quebec. Editorial staff of La Presse, Montreal, Quebec, 1930–41; Associate Dir of Public Relations, Can. Army, 1941–44; War Corresp. for La Presse, Montreal, 1944; Mayor of St Antoine des Laurentides, Que., 1948. First elected to House of Commons, gen. elec., 1962; re-elected gen. elec., 1963, 1965, 1968; apptd Associate Minister of Nat. Defence, 1965; Minister of National Defence, Canada, 1967–70. *Address:* 20 Driveway, Appt 1106, Ottawa K2P 1C8, Canada.

CADMAN, family name of **Baron Cadman.**

CADMAN, 3rd Baron *cr* 1937, of Silverdale; **John Anthony Cadman;** farmer, 1964–85; *b* 3 July 1938; *s* of 2nd Baron Cadman and Marjorie Elizabeth Bunnis; *S* father, 1966; *m* 1975, Janet Hayes; two *s*. *Educ:* Harrow; Selwyn Coll., Cambridge; Royal Agricultural Coll., Cirencester. *Heir: s* Hon. Nicholas Anthony James Cadman, *b* 18 Nov. 1977. *Address:* Heathcourt House, Ironmould Lane, Brislington, Bristol BS4 5RS. *T:* Bristol (0272) 775706.

CADMAN, Surg. Rear-Adm. (D) (Albert) Edward; CB 1977; Director of Naval Dental Services, 1974–77; *b* 14 Oct. 1918; *m* 1st, 1946, Margaret Henrietta Tomkins-Russell (*d* 1974); one *s* one *d*; 2nd, 1975, Mary Croil Macdonald (*d* 1987), Superintendent, WRNS; 3rd, 1988, Irene Davies (*née* Lowther). *Educ:* Dover Grammar Sch.; Guy's Hosp. Dental Sch. LDS RCS 1941. Surg. Lieut (D) RNVR, 1942; transf. to RN, 1947; served as Asst to Dir, Naval Dental Services, 1967–70; Comd Dental Surgeon on staff of Flag Officer, Naval Air Comd, 1970–74. QHDS 1974–77. *Recreations:* music, gardening, golf. *Address:* Solent House, 2 Solent Way, Alverstoke, Hants PO12 2NS. *T:* Gosport (0705) 586648.

CADOGAN, family name of **Earl Cadogan.**

CADOGAN, 7th Earl, *cr* 1800; **William Gerald Charles Cadogan,** MC 1943; DL; Baron Cadogan, 1718; Viscount Chelsea, 1800; Baron Oakley, 1831; Lieut-Colonel Royal Wiltshire Yeomanry, RAC; Captain Coldstream Guards R of O until 1964 (retaining hon. rank of Lieut-Colonel); *b* 13 Feb. 1914; *s* of 6th Earl and Lilian Eleanora Marie (who *m* 2nd, 1941, Lt-Col H. E. Hambro, CBE; she *d* 1973), *d* of George Coxon, Craigleith, Cheltenham; *S* father, 1933; *m* 1st, 1936, Hon. Primrose Lillian Yarde-Buller (from whom he obtained a divorce, 1959), *y d* of 3rd Baron Churston; one *s* three *d*; 2nd, 1961, Cecilia, *y d* of Lt-Col H. K. Hamilton-Wedderburn, OBE. *Educ:* Eton; RMC Sandhurst. Served war of 1939–45 (MC). Mem. Chelsea Borough Council, 1953–59; Mayor of Chelsea, 1964. DL County of London, 1958. *Heir: s* Viscount Chelsea, *qv*. *Address:* 28 Cadogan Square, SW1. *T:* 071–584 2335; Snaigow, Dunkeld, Perthshire. *T:* Caputh (073871) 223. *Club:* White's.

See also Baron Rockley.

CADOGAN, Prof. Sir John (Ivan George), Kt 1991; CBE 1985; PhD, DSc London; FRS 1976; FRSE, CChem, FRSC; Director of Research, British Petroleum, since 1981; Director: BP Chemicals Ltd, since 1983; BP Venezuela, since 1984; BP Solar International, since 1988; Visiting Professor of Chemistry, Imperial College of Science and Technology, since 1979; Professorial Fellow, University College of Swansea, University of Wales, since 1979; *b* Pembrey, Carmarthenshire, 8 Oct. 1930; *er s* of Alfred and Dilys Cadogan; *m* 1955, Margaret Jeanne, *d* of late William Evans, iron founder, Swansea; one *s* one *d*. *Educ:* Grammar Sch., Swansea; King's Coll., London (1st cl. Hons Chem. 1951). Research at KCL, 1951–54. Civil Service Research Fellow, 1954–56; Lectr in Chemistry, King's Coll., London, 1956–63; Purdie Prof. of Chemistry and Head of Dept, St Salvator's Coll., Univ. of St Andrews, 1963–69; Forbes Prof. of Organic Chemistry, Edinburgh Univ., 1969–79; Chief Scientist, BP Res. Centre, 1979–81. Director: BP Gas International, 1983–87; BP Ventures, 1981–90 (Chief Exec., 1988–90); Chm., Kaldair Internat., 1988–90. Mem., Royal Commn on Criminal Justice, 1991–. Member: Chemistry Cttee, SRC, 1967–71 (Chm. 1972–75); Council, SERC, 1981–85 (Chm., Science Bd, 1981–85; Mem., Science Bd, SRC, 1972–75); ACORD, Dept of Energy, 1987–89. Member: Council, Chem. Soc., 1966–69, 1973–76; Council, RIC, 1979–80; Chem. Soc.-RIC Unification Cttee, 1975–80; First Council, RSC, 1980–85 (Pres. RSC, 1982–84, 1989–); Council of Management, Macaulay Inst. for Soil Res., Aberdeen, 1969–79; Council, St George's Sch. for Girls, 1974–79; Council, RSE, 1975–80 (Vice-Pres., 1978–80); Council, Royal Soc., 1989–91 (Mem., Royal Soc. Sci. Inquiry, 1990–); Vice-Pres., Royal Instn, 1986–87 (Mem. Council, 1984–87). Member: Bd of Trustees, Royal Observatory Trust, Edinburgh, 1979–86; Adv. Bd, RCDS, 1989–; Adv. Bd, Eur. Business Management Sch., UC Swansea, 1990–; Trustee, Overseas Students Trust, UC Swansea, 1989–. Pres., Chem. Sect., BAAS, 1981. Chemistry Advr, Carnegie Trust Univ. of Scotland, 1985–. Fellow, KCL, 1976 (Mem. Council, 1980–; Vice-Chm., 1990–). First RSE Schs Christmas Lectures, 1980; Lectures: Tilden, Chem. Soc., 1971; David Martin Royal Soc. BAYS, 1981; Humphry Davy, Royal Instn, 1982; Holroyd Meml, Soc. Chem. Ind., 1984; Salters' Co., Royal Instn, 1984; Philips, Royal Soc., 1985; Pedler, RSC, 1986; Dalton, RSC, 1989. Hon. DSc: St Andrews, 1983; Wales, 1984; Edinburgh, 1986; Aberdeen, 1991; DUniv Stirling, 1984; Hon. Dr l'Univ Aix-Marseille, 1984. Samuel Smiles Prize, KCL, 1950; Millar Thomson Medallist, KCL, 1951; Meldola Medallist, Soc. of Maccabaeans and Royal Inst. of Chemistry, 1959; Corday-Morgan Medallist, Chem. Soc., 1965. *Publications:* Principles of Free Radical Chemistry, 1971; Organophosphorus Reagents in Organic Synthesis, 1979; about 230 scientific papers, mainly in Jl Chem. Soc. *Recreations:* gardening, supporting Rugby football (Vice-Pres., Crawshay's Welsh RFC, London Welsh RFC; Patron, Swansea RFCC). *Address:* British Petroleum Company plc, 1 Finsbury Circus, EC2M 7BA. *T:* 071–496 4025. *Club:* Athenæum.

CADOGAN, Peter William; lecturer, writer and campaigner; Secretary, East-West Peace People, since 1978; Co-Chairman, Anglo-Afghan Circle, since 1987; Co-ordinator, Northern Ireland Project, Gandhi Foundation, since 1988; *b* 26 Jan. 1921; *s* of Archibald Douglas Cadogan and Audrey Cadogan (*née* Wannop); *m* 1949, Joyce (marr. diss. 1969), *d* of William Stones, MP; one *d*. *Educ:* Tynemouth Sch., Tynemouth; Univ. of Newcastle, 1946–51 (BA (Hons) History, DipEd; Joseph Cowen Meml Prize, 1951). Served War, Air Sea Rescue Service, RAF, 1941–46. Teaching, Kettering and Cambridge, 1951–65. Committed to the Far Left, 1945–60; broke with Marxism, 1960. Founding Secretary, East Anglian Committee of 100: exploring theory and practice of non-violent direct action, 1961; Sec., Internat. Sub-Cttee of Cttee of 100, 1962; Sec. (full-time), National Cttee of 100, 1965–68. Mem., Nat. Council of CND, mix-sixties; Founding Sec., Save Biafra Campaign, 1968–70; Gen. Sec., South Place Ethical Soc., 1970–81; Co-Founder: Turning Point, 1975; Peace Anonymous, Action '84 and Summit '84, 1983–84. Chm., Blake Soc. of St James', 1990–. *Publications:* Extra-Parliamentary Democracy, 1968; Direct Democracy, 1974, rev. 1975; Early Radical Newcastle, 1975; Six Ballads for the Seventies, 1976; many articles in learned jls, periodicals and elsewhere. *Recreations:* reading, gardening, walking, social invention. *Address:* 3 Hinchinbrook House, Greville Road, NW6. *T:* 071–328 3709.

CADWALLADER, Air Vice-Marshal Howard George, CB 1974; RAF retd; Director of Purchasing, Post Office, 1978–79; *b* 16 March 1919; British; *m* 1950, Betty Ethel Samuels; no *c*. *Educ:* Hampton Sch., Mddx. Sen. Equipment Staff Officer: HQ Transport Comd, 1963–65; HQ FEAF Singapore, 1965–68; Dep. Dir of Equipment 14 MoD (Air), 1968–69; Comdt of RAF Supply Control Centre, Hendon, 1969–72; Dir of Movts (RAF), MoD (Air), 1972–73; SASO HQ Support Comd, RAF, 1973–74. Controller of Contracts, PO, 1974–78. *Recreations:* golf, sailing. *Address:* Spain.

CADWALLADER, Sir John, Kt 1967; Chairman and Managing Director of Allied Mills Ltd and subsidiaries, 1949–78; President, Bank of New South Wales, 1959–78, retired; *b* 25 Aug. 1902; *m* 1935, Helen Sheila Moxham; two *s* one *d*. *Educ:* Sydney Church of England Grammar Sch., NSW. *Recreations:* reading, golf. *Address:* 27 Marian Street, Killara, NSW 2071, Australia. *T:* 498 1974. *Clubs:* Commonwealth (Canberra, ACT); Australian, Union, Royal Sydney Golf (all Sydney, NSW); Elanora Country (NSW).

CÆSAR, Rev. Canon Anthony Douglass, CVO 1991 (LVO 1987); Sub-Dean of Her Majesty's Chapels Royal, Deputy Clerk of the Closet, Sub-Almoner and Domestic Chaplain to the Queen, 1979–91; Chaplain, St Cross Hospital, Winchester, since 1991; an Extra Chaplain to the Queen, since 1991; *b* 3 April 1924; *s* of Harold Douglass and Winifred Kathleen Cæsar. *Educ:* Cranleigh School; Magdalene Coll., Cambridge; St Stephen's House, Oxford. MA, MusB, FRCO. Served War with RAF, 1943–46. Assistant Music Master, Eton Coll., 1948–51; Precentor, Radley Coll., 1952–59; Asst Curate, St Mary Abbots, Kensington, 1961–65; Asst Sec., ACCM, 1965–70; Chaplain, Royal School of Church Music, 1965–70; Deputy Priest-in-Ordinary to the Queen, 1967–68, Priest-in-Ordinary, 1968–70; Resident Priest, St Stephen's Church, Bournemouth, 1970–73; Precentor and Sacrist, Winchester Cathedral, 1974–79; Hon. Canon of Winchester Cathedral, 1975–76 and 1979–, Residentiary Canon, 1976–79. *Publications:* (jt ed.) The New English Hymnal, 1986; part songs, church music. *Recreation:* other people. *Address:* Chaplain's Lodge, St Cross Hospital, Winchester, Hants SO23 9SD. *T:* Winchester (0962) 853525.

CÆSAR, Irving; author-lyrist; Past President of Songwriters' Protective Association; Member Board of Directors, American Society of Composers, Authors and Publishers; *b* New York, 4 July 1895; *s* of Rumanian Jews. *Educ:* public school; Chappaqua Quaker Inst.; City Coll. of New York. Protégé of Ella Wheeler Wilcox, who, when he was a boy of nine, became interested in bits of verse he wrote and published at the time; at twenty became attached to the Henry Ford Peace Expedition, and spent nine months travelling through neutral Europe (during the War) as one of the secretaries of the Ford Peace Conference; returned to America, and became interested in writing for the musical comedy stage. *Publications:* most important work up to present time, No, No, Nanette; has written hundreds of songs and collaborated in many other musical comedies; writer and publisher of Sing a Song of Safety, a vol. of children's songs in use throughout the public and parochial schools of USA; also Sing a Song of Friendship, a series of songs based on human rights; in England: The Bamboula, Swanee, Tea for Two (successive awards for being among the most performed ASCAP standards), I Want to be Happy, I Was So Young; author of "Peace by Wireless" proposal for freedom of international exchange of radio privilege between governments. *Recreations:* reading, theatre, swimming. *Address:* 850 Seventh Avenue, New York, NY 10019, USA. *Clubs:* Friars, Green Room, City (New York).

CAFFERTY, Michael Angelo; HM Diplomatic Service; Consul-General, Melbourne, Australia, 1983–87; *b* 3 March 1927; *m* 1950, Eileen E. Geer; two *s* three *d*. *Educ:* Univ.

of London. BoT, 1951; Asst Trade Comr, Johannesburg, 1955, Pretoria, 1957; seconded to FO, Buenos Aires, 1958; Trade Comr, Singapore, 1964; FCO, 1968; Consul (Commercial), Milan, 1974; First Sec. and Head of Chancery, Rome (Holy See), 1977; Ambassador and Consul-Gen., Santo Domingo, 1979–83. *Address:* 24 Phoenix Lodge Mansions, Brook Green, W6.

CAFFIN, Albert Edward, CIE 1947; OBE 1946; Indian Police (retired); *b* 16 June 1902; *s* of Claud Carter and Lilian Edith Caffin, Southsea; *m* 1929, Hilda Elizabeth Wheeler, Bournemouth; no *c. Educ:* Portsmouth. Joined Indian Police as Asst Supt, Bombay Province, 1922; Asst Inspector General, Poona, 1939; Dep. Comr, Bombay, 1944, Comr of Police, Bombay, 1947. *Recreation:* bowls. *Address:* C22 San Remo Towers, Sea Road, Boscombe, Bournemouth, Dorset BH5 1JT. *Club:* Royal Bombay Yacht.

CAFFIN, A(rthur) Crawford; a Recorder of the Crown Court, 1972–82; solicitor since 1932; *b* 10 June 1910; *s* of Charles Crawford Caffin and Annie Rosila Caffin; *m* 1933, Mala Pocock; one *d. Educ:* King's Sch., Rochester. Asst Solicitor: to Norfolk CC, 1933–37; to Bristol Corporation, 1937–46. Partner in firm of R. L. Frank & Caffin, Solicitors, Truro, 1946–72; Consultant with that firm, 1972–84. Pres., Cornwall Law Soc., 1960; Mem. Council, the Law Society, 1966–76; Dep. Chm., Traffic Commissioners for Western Traffic Area, 1964–84. *Recreation:* swimming. *Address:* Cove Cottage, Portloe, Truro, Cornwall TR2 5QY. *Club:* Farmers' (Truro).

CAGIATI, Dr Andrea; Grand Cross, Italian Order of Merit, 1979; Hon. GCVO; Ambassador, retired 1988; Vice Chairman, Alitalia, since 1989 (Director, since 1987); *b* Rome, 11 July 1922; *m* 1968, Sigrid von Morgen; one *s* one *d. Educ:* University of Siena (Dr of Law). Entered Foreign Service, 1948. Served: Secretary, Paris, 1950; Principal Private Sec. to Minister of State, 1951; Vice-Consul-General, New York, 1953; Prin. Private Sec. to Minister of State and subsequently Dept of Political Affairs, 1955; Counsellor, Athens, 1957; Counsellor, Mexico City, 1960; Delegate, Disarmament Cttee, Geneva, March–Dec. 1962; Italian Delegation, UN, June 1962; Head, NATO Dept, Dec. 1962; Minister-Counsellor, Madrid, 1966; Ambassador, Bogotá, 1968; Inst for Diplomatic Studies, 1971; Diplomatic Adviser to Prime Minister, 1972; Ambassador, Vienna, 1973; Ambassador, Court of St James's, 1980; Ambassador to the Holy See and to the Order of Malta, 1985. Hon. GCVO during State Visit to Italy of HM The Queen, Oct. 1980; KM, 1953; Grand Cross: Order of Merit, Austria, 1980; Order of Merit, Malta, 1987; Order of Pius IX, Holy See, 1988. *Publications:* La Diplomazia dalle origini al XVII secolo, 1944; Verso quale avvenire?, 1958; articles in quarterlies on foreign and defence affairs. *Recreations:* sculpture, golf, shooting. *Address:* Largo Olgiata, 15 (49D)–00123 Rome, Italy. *Club:* Nuovo Circolo Scacchi (Rome).

CAHILL, John Conway; non-executive Chairman, BTR Inc., since 1991; Chief Executive, BTR plc, 1987–90; *b* 8 Jan. 1930; *m* 1955; three *d.* Joined BTR Industries, 1955; Dep. Overseas Gen. Manager, 1963; Board of Directors, 1968; Dep. Managing Dir, 1976; Vice-Pres., BTR Inc., USA, 1978; Pres. and Chief Exec., BTR Inc., and Chm., BTR Pan American operations, 1979–87. *Recreations:* reading, gardening, music. *Address:* BTR Inc., 1000, 1 Main Place, 750 Main Street, Stamford, Conn 06901, USA.

CAHILL, Michael Leo; Head of Central and Southern Africa Department, Overseas Development Administration, 1983–88, retired; *b* 4 April 1928; *s* of John and Josephine Cahill; *m* 1961, Harriette Emma Clemency, *e d* of late Christopher Gilbert Eastwood, CMG and Catherine Eastwood; two *d. Educ:* Beaumont Coll.; Magdalen Coll., Oxford (Demy). National Service, Intelligence Corps, Trieste, 1950–52, Lieut. FO, 1953; CO, 1955; Asst Private Sec. to Sec. of State, 1956–57; Private Sec. to Parly Under-Sec., 1957–58; Dept of Technical Co-operation, 1961; Asst Sec., ODM, 1969; UK Perm. Deleg. to Unesco, 1972–74. Chm., Woldingham Sch. Parents Assoc., 1981–83. *Recreations:* history of the arts, pianism. *Address:* 9 Murray Road, SW19 4PD. *T:* 081–947 0568.
See also B. S. T. Eastwood.

CAHILL, Teresa Mary; opera and concert singer; *b* 30 July 1944; *d* of Florence and Henry Cahill; *m* 1971, John Anthony Kiernander (marr. diss. 1978). *Educ:* Notre Dame High Sch., Southwark; Guildhall School of Music and Drama; London Opera Centre (LRAM Singing, AGSM Piano). Glyndebourne début, 1969; Covent Garden début, 1970; La Scala Milan, 1976, Philadelphia Opera, 1981, specialising in Mozart and Strauss; concerts: all London orchestras, Boston Symphony Orch., Chicago Symphony Orch., Rotterdam Philharmonic Orch., West Deutscher Rundfunk, Warsaw Philharmonic, RAI Turin, Frankfurt Radio Orch., Vienna Fest., 1983, Berlin Fest., 1987, Promenade concerts; BBC radio and TV; recordings, incl. Strauss, Elgar and Mahler, for all major companies; master classes, Dartington Fest., 1984, 1986; recitals and concerts throughout Europe, USA, Far East. Silver Medal, Worshipful Co. of Musicians, 1966; John Christie Award 1970. *Recreations:* cinema, theatre, travel, reading, collecting antique furniture, photography. *Address:* 65 Leyland Road, SE12 8DW. *Club:* Royal Over-Seas League (Hon. Mem.).

CAHN, Sir Albert Jonas, 2nd Bt, *cr* 1934; company director; marital, sexual and family therapist; Director, Elm Therapy Centre, New Malden, since 1983; *b* 27 June 1924; *s* of Sir Julien Cahn, 1st Bt and Phyllis Muriel, *d* of A. Wolfe, Bournemouth; *S* father, 1944; *m* 1948, Malka, *d* of late R. Bluestone; two *s* two *d. Educ:* Headmaster's House, Harrow. *Recreations:* cricket, horse riding, photography. *Heir: s* Julien Michael Cahn, [*b* 15 Jan. 1951; *m* 1987, Marilynne Janelle, *d* of Frank Owen Blyth; one *s* one *d*]. *Address:* 10 Edgecoombe Close, Warren Road, Kingston upon Thames, Surrey KT2 7HP. *T:* 081–942 6956; Elm Therapy Centre, 70 Elm Road, New Malden, Surrey.

CAHN, Prof. Robert Wolfgang, PhD, DSc; FRS 1991; FIM; FInstP; Hon. Senior Associate, Department of Materials Science and Metallurgy, Cambridge University, since 1986; *b* 9 Sept. 1924; *s* of Martin and Else Cahn; *m* 1947, Patricia Lois Hanson; two *s* two *d. Educ:* Cambridge Univ. (BA 1945; PhD 1950; ScD 1963). FIM 1962; FInstP 1959. SO, later SSO, Harwell, 1947–51; Lectr, then Sen. Lectr, Physical Metallurgy Dept, Birmingham Univ., 1951–62; Professor of Materials Science: UCNW, 1962–64; Sussex Univ., 1965–81 (Dean of Engrg, 1973–78); Prof. of Physical Metallurgy, Université de Paris–Sud, 1981–83; Fairchild Distinguished Scholar, CIT, 1985–86. Vis. Prof., Univ. of Surrey, 1986–. Editor, several scientific jls. Foreign Mem., Göttingen Acad. Arts and Scis, 1987; Mem., Academia Europaea, 1989. FRSA. Ste Claire Deville Medal, Société Française de Métallurgie, 1978; A. A. Griffith Medal, Materials Science Club, 1984. *Publications:* (ed) Physical Metallurgy, 1965, 3rd edn 1983; (ed) Processing of Metals and Alloys, 1991; Artifice and Artefacts—100 Essays in Materials Science, 1991; contrib. scientific jls incl. Nature. *Recreations:* composing English prose, looking at paintings, mountains and alpine flowers, music. *Address:* Department of Materials Science and Metallurgy, Pembroke Street, Cambridge CB2 3QZ. *T:* and *Fax:* Cambridge (0223) 334381; 6 Storey's Way, Cambridge CB3 0DT. *T:* Cambridge (0223) 60143. *Club:* Fell and Rock Climbing (Lake District).

CAHN, Sammy; lyric writer; *b* New York, 18 June 1913; *s* of Abraham and Alice Cohen; *m* 1st, 1945, Gloria Delson (marr. diss. 1964); one *s* one *d*; 2nd, 1970, Tita Curtis. *Educ:* NY public schools. Violinist. Early songs (with Saul Chaplin): Rhythm is our Business;

Bei Mir Bist Du Schon; songs with Jule Styne include: Let it Snow; I'll Walk Alone; It's Magic; Academy Award songs: Three Coins in the Fountain, 1954; All the Way, 1957; High Hopes, 1959; Call Me Irresponsible, 1963; Emmy Award song: Love and Marriage; numerous songs for Frank Sinatra, for cinema, for US and UK productions. Pres., Songwriters' Hall of Fame; Mem., Bd of Dirs, ASCAP. *Publications:* I Should Care (autobiog.), 1974; The Songwriter's Rhyming Dictionary, 1984. *Address:* c/o ASCAP, 1 Lincoln Plaza, New York, NY 10023, USA.

CAILLARD, Air Vice-Marshal (Hugh) Anthony, CB 1981; retired 1982; Director General, Britain-Australia Society, and Hon. Secretary, Cook Society, 1982–89; Specialist Air Adviser, House of Commons Defence Committee, since 1985; *b* 16 April 1927; *s* of late Col F. Caillard, MC, and Mrs M. Y. Caillard; *m* 1957, Margaret-Ann Crawford, Holbrook, NSW, Australia; four *s. Educ:* Downside; Oriel Coll., Oxford. Cranwell, 1947–49; served, 1949–65: 13 Sqdn, Egypt; ADC to C-in-C MEAF, and to AOC-in-C Tech. Trng Comd; 101 Sqdn, Binbrook; RAAF No 2 Sqdn; 49 Sqdn (Sqdn Ldr) and 90 Sqdn; RN Staff Coll.; HQ Bomber Comd (Wg Cdr); OC 39 Sqdn, Malta, 1965–67; Jt Services Staff Coll., 1967; Planning Staffs, MoD, 1967–70; Asst Air Attaché, Washington (Gp Captain), 1970–73; OC Marham, 1974–75; Def. Intell. Staff (Air Cdre), 1975–79; Dep. Chief of Staff, Ops and Intelligence, HQ Allied Air Forces, Central Europe, 1979–82. Chairman: Ex Forces Fellowship Centre, 1987–; Ex Services Mental Welfare Soc., 1990–; Member: Grants and Appeals Cttee, RAF Benevolent Fund, 1987–; Britain-Australia Bicentennial Cttee, 1984–88; Council, British Atlantic Cttee, 1988–; Trustee, Australian Arts Foundn, 1985–89. *Address:* 114 Ashley Road, Walton-on-Thames, Surrey KT12 1HW. *Club:* Royal Air Force.

CAILLAT, Claude; Swiss Ambassador to the Court of St James's, 1980–83; retired; *b* 24 Sept. 1918; *s* of Aymon Caillat and Isabelle Caillat (*née* Bordier); *m* 1948, Béatrice de Blonay; two *s* one *d. Educ:* Univ. of Geneva (law degree). Div. of Foreign Interests, Swiss Federal Political Dept, Berne, then served successively in London, Berne, Athens and (as Counsellor) Washington, 1942–60; Federal Office of Foreign Trade, Berne, 1960; Ambassador's Deputy, Swiss Embassy, Paris, 1962; Swiss Federal Council's Rep. at OECD, Paris, with rank of Ambassador, 1967; Swiss Ambassador to the Netherlands, 1969; Head of Swiss Mission to European Communities, Brussels, 1974. *Recreation:* golf. *Address:* 240 route de Lausanne, Chambésy, Geneva. *Clubs:* White's, Travellers'.

CAIN; see Nall-Cain, family name of Baron Brocket.

CAIN, Sir Edney; see Cain, Sir H. E. C.

CAIN, Sir Edward (Thomas), Kt 1972; CBE 1966; Commissioner of Taxation, Australia, 1964–76; retired; *b* Maryborough, Qld, Australia, 7 Dec. 1916; *s* of Edward Victor and Kathleen Teresa Cain; *m* 1942, Marcia Yvonne Cain (*née* Parbery); one *s* one *d. Educ:* Nudgee Coll., Queensland; Univ. of Queensland (BA, LLB). Commonwealth Taxation Office: in Brisbane, Sydney, Perth and Canberra, 1936–. Served War, 2/9th Bn, AIF, 1939–43. *Recreations:* golf, fishing. *Address:* 99 Buxton Street, Deakin, Canberra, ACT 2600, Australia. *T:* 811462. *Clubs:* Commonwealth, Royal Canberra Golf (Canberra); Royal Automobile (Melbourne).

CAIN, Maj.-Gen. George Robert T.; see Turner Cain.

CAIN, Sir (Henry) Edney (Conrad), Kt 1986; OBE 1976 (MBE 1965); FCCA; CA (Belize); Governor, Central Bank of Belize, 1982 and since 1991; *b* 2 Dec. 1924; *s* of Henry Edney Conrad I and Rhoda (*née* Stamp); *m* 1951, Leonie (*née* Locke). *Educ:* St George's Coll., Belize; St Michael's Coll., Belize; Balham and Tooting Coll. of Commerce, London. FCCA 1977 (ACCA 1961); CA Belize 1984. Belize Government Service, 1940–: Examr of Accts, Audit Dept, 1954; Auditor, Audit Dept, 1959; Asst Accountant Gen., 1961; Accountant Gen., 1963; Man. Dir, Monetary Authority of Belize, 1976; Ambassador to USA, 1983; High Comr to Canada (resident in Washington, DC), 1984; Financial Sec., Ministry of Finance, Belize, 1985–87; High Comr to UK, 1987–90. *Publication:* When the Angel says 'Write' (verse), 1948. *Recreations:* music, reading, current affairs. *Address:* PO Box 564, 18 Albert Street West, Belize City, Belize. *T:* 272325.

CAIN, Hon. John; MLA (Lab) for Bundoora, since 1976; Premier of Victoria, since 1982; *b* 26 April 1931; *s* of late Hon. John Cain; *m* 1955, Nancye Williams; two *s* one *d. Educ:* Melbourne Univ. (LLB). Practised as barrister and solicitor. Mem., Law Reform Commn, 1975–77. Pres., Law Inst. of Victoria, 1972–73 (Treasurer, 1969–70; Chm. of Council, 1971–72); Mem. Exec., Law Council of Australia, 1973–76. Vice-Chm., Vic. Br., Australian Labor Party, 1973–75; Mem., Parly Labor Exec., 1977–; Leader, State Labor Party, 1981–; Leader of Opposition, 1981–82; Minister for Fed. Affairs, 1982; Attorney-General of Vic, 1982–83. *Address:* 9 Magnolia Road, Ivanhoe, Vic 3079, Australia.

CAIN, John Clifford; research historian; Controller, Public Affairs, BBC, 1981–84; Hon. Vice-President, Broadcasting Support Services, since 1989 (Chairman, 1980–85; Trustee, 1985–89); *b* 2 April 1924; *s* of William John Cain and Florence Jessie (*née* Wood); *m* 1954, Shirley Jean Roberts; two *d. Educ:* Emanuel Sch.; Imperial Coll., Borough Road Coll., London Univ. (BSc); University Coll., London Univ. (MSc); BA (Hons) Open Univ., 1988. Served RAF (aircrew), 1944–47. Maths and science teacher in grammar, secondary modern and comprehensive schs and in polytechnic, 1950–59; Lectr, Science Museum, 1959–61; Asst Head of Sch. Broadcasting, Associated-Rediffusion, 1961–63; BBC Television: Producer; subseq. Sen. Producer, 1963–71; Asst Head of Further Educn Dept, 1971–72; Head, 1972–77; Asst Controller, Educn Br., BBC, 1977–80. Dir, Broadcasters' Audience Res. Bd, 1982–84. Mem., Health Educn Council, 1978–83. Member: RTS, 1984–; BAFTA, 1984–. FRSA 1990. *Publications:* Talking Machines, 1961; (jtly) Mathematics Miscellany, 1966; (contrib.) Culture, Education and the State, 1988; articles in EBU Review, Adult Educn, etc. *Recreations:* reading, gardening, music, theatre. *Address:* 63 Park Road, Chiswick, W4 3EY. *T:* 081–994 2712.

CAIN, Thomas William; QC 1989; HM Attorney General for Isle of Man, since 1980; *b* 1 June 1935; *s* of late James Arthur Cain and Mary Edith Cunningham (*née* Lamb); *m* 1961, Felicity Jane, *d* of late Rev. Arthur Stephen Gregory; two *s* one *d. Educ:* King's College Choir Sch., Cambridge; Marlborough Coll.; Worcester Coll., Oxford (BA 1958, MA 1961). National Service, 2nd Lieut RAC, 1953–55. Called to the Bar, Gray's Inn, 1959; Advocate, Manx Bar, 1961. Pres., I of M Law Soc., 1985–89. *Recreations:* sailing, Chairman, Manx Nature Conservation Trust. *Address:* Ivie Cottage, Kirk Michael, Isle of Man. *T:* Kirk Michael (0624878) 266.

CAINE, Emma Harriet; see Nicholson, E. H.

CAINE, Michael; actor; *b* Old Kent Road, London, 14 March 1933 (Maurice Joseph Micklewhite); *s* of late Maurice and of Ellen Frances Marie Micklewhite; *m* 1st, 1955, Patricia Haines (marr. diss.); one *d*; 2nd, 1973, Shakira Baksh; one *d. Educ:* Wilson's Grammar Sch., Peckham. Began acting in youth club drama gp. Served in Army, Berlin and Korea, 1951–53. Asst Stage Manager, Westminster Rep., Horsham, Sx, 1953; actor, Lowestoft Rep., 1953–55; Theatre Workshop, London, 1955; numerous TV appearances (over 100 plays), 1957–63; *play:* Next Time I'll Sing for You, Arts, 1963; *films:* A Hill in Korea, 1956; How to Murder a Rich Uncle, 1958; Zulu, 1964; The Ipcress File, 1965; Alfie, 1966; The Wrong Box, 1966; Gambit, 1966; Hurry Sundown, 1967; Woman Times Seven, 1967; Deadfall, 1967; The Magus, 1968; Battle of Britain, 1968; Play Dirty, 1968; The Italian Job, 1969; Too Late the Hero, 1970; The Last Valley, 1971; Get Carter, 1971; Zee & Co., 1972; Kidnapped, 1972; Pulp, 1972; Sleuth, 1973; The Black Windmill, Marseilles Contract, The Wilby Conspiracy, 1974; Fat Chance, The Romantic Englishwoman, The Man who would be King, Harry and Walter Go to New York, 1975; The Eagle has Landed, A Bridge Too Far, Silver Bears, 1976; The Swarm, 1977; California Suite, 1978; Ashanti, 1979; Beyond the Poseidon Adventure, 1979; The Island, 1979; Dressed to Kill, 1979; Escape to Victory, 1980; Death Trap, 1981; Jigsaw Man, 1982; Educating Rita, 1982; The Honorary Consul, 1982; Blame it on Rio, 1984; Water, 1985; The Holcroft Covenant, 1985; Hannah and Her Sisters (Academy Award), 1986; Half Moon Street, 1986; Mona Lisa, 1986; The Fourth Protocol, 1987; The Whistle Blower, 1987; Surrender, 1987; Jaws The Revenge, 1987; Without a Clue, 1989; Dirty Rotten Scoundrel, 1989; A Shock to the System, 1990; Bullseye, 1990; *films for TV:* Jack The Ripper, 1988; Jekyll and Hyde, 1989. *Recreations:* cinema, theatre, travel, gardening. *Address:* c/o Dennis Sellinger, International Creative Management, 388–396 Oxford Street, W1.

CAINE, Sir Michael (Harris), Kt 1988; Chairman, since 1979, Vice-Chairman, 1973–79, Chief Executive, 1975–84, Director, since 1964, Booker plc; *b* 17 June 1927; *s* of Sir Sydney Caine, KCMG and Muriel Anne (*née* Harris); *m* 1st, 1952, Janice Denise (*née* Mercer) (marr. diss. 1987); one *s* one *d*; 2nd, 1987, Emma Harriet Nicholson, *qv*. *Educ:* Bedales; Lincoln Coll., Oxford; George Washington Univ., USA. Joined Booker McConnell Ltd, 1952; Chm., Bookers Shopkeeping Holdings Ltd, 1963; Director: Arbor Acres Farm Inc., 1980–91; Commonwealth Equity Fund, 1990–. Chm., Council for Technical Educn and Training for Overseas Countries, 1973–75. Member: Council, Inst. of Race Relations, 1969–72; Council, Bedford Coll., London, 1966–85; IBA, 1984–89; Commonwealth Develt Corp., 1985– (Dep. Chm., 1989–); Governing Body: Inst. of Develt Studies, Sussex Univ., 1975–; NIESR, 1979–; Queen Elizabeth House, Oxford, 1983–; Chairman: UK Council for Overseas Student Affairs, 1980–; Council, Royal African Soc., 1984–; Commonwealth Scholarships Commn in the UK, 1987–; One World Broadcasting Trust, 1987–. *Address:* c/o Booker plc, Portland House, Stag Place, SW1E 5AY. *T:* 071–828 9850. *Club:* Reform.

CAINES, Eric; Director of Personnel, National Health Service, Department of Health, since 1990; *b* 27 Feb. 1936; *s* of Ernest and Doris Caines; *m* 1st, 1958 (marr. diss. 1984); three *s*; 2nd, 1984, Karen Higgs; two *s*. *Educ:* Rothwell Grammar School, Wakefield; Leeds Univ. (LLB Hons). Dip. Hist. Art, London Univ., 1984. Short Service Commission, RAEC, 1958–61. NCB, 1961–65; BBC, 1965–66; as Principal, Min. of Health, Management Side Sec., General Whitley Council, 1966–70; Sec., NHS Reorganisation Management Arrangements Study, 1970–73; Assistant Sec., DHSS, 1973–77; IMF/World Bank, Washington, 1977–79; Under Sec., DHSS, 1979, Dir, Regl Organisation, 1981–84; Dir, Personnel and Finance, Prison Dept, Home Office, 1984–87; Dir, Operational Strategy, DHSS, then DSS, 1987–90. Dir, Trebor Ltd, 1985–. *Recreation:* travelling on foot with a book. *Address:* Department of Health, Richmond House, 79 Whitehall, SW1A 2NS. *Club:* Athenæum.

CAINES, Sir John, KCB 1991 (CB 1983); Permanent Secretary, Department of Education and Science, since 1989; *b* 13 Jan. 1933; *s* of John Swinburne Caines and Ethel May Stenlake; *m* 1963, Mary Large; one *s* two *d*. *Educ:* Westminster Sch.; Christ Church, Oxford (MA). Asst Principal, Min. of Supply, 1957; Asst Private Sec., Min. of Aviation, 1960–61; Principal, Min. of Aviation, 1961–64; Civil Air Attaché in Middle East, 1964–66; Manchester Business Sch., 1967; Asst Sec., BoT, 1968; Sec., Commn on Third London Airport, 1968–71; Asst Sec., DTI, 1971–72; Principal Private Sec. to Sec. of State for Trade and Industry, 1972–74; Under-Sec., Dept of Trade, 1974–77; Sec., 1977–80, Mem. and Dep. Chief Exec., 1979–80, NEB; Dep. Sec., Dept of Trade, and Chief Exec., BOTB, 1980–82; Dep. Sec., Central Policy Review Staff, Cabinet Office, 1983; Dep. Sec., DTI, 1983–87; Permanent Sec., ODA, FCO, 1987–89. *Recreations:* travel, music, gardening, theatre. *Address:* Sanctuary Buildings, Great Smith Street, SW1.

CAIRD, Most Rev. Donald Arthur Richard; *see* Dublin, Archbishop of, and Primate of Ireland.

CAIRD, John Newport; Theatre director and writer; Hon. Associate Director, Royal Shakespeare Company; *b* 22 Sept. 1948; *s* of late Rev. George Bradford Caird, DPhil, DD, FBA and of Viola Mary Newport, MA; *m* 1st, 1972, Helen Frances Brammer (marr. diss. 1982); 2nd, 1982, Ann Dorzynski (marr. diss. 1990); two *s* one *d*; 3rd, 1990, Frances Ruffelle; one *s* one *d*. *Educ:* Selwyn House Sch., Montreal; Magdalen Coll. Sch., Oxford; Bristol Old Vic Theatre Sch. Fellow, Welsh Coll. of Music and Drama. Associate Dir, Contact Theatre, Manchester, 1974–76; directed, Contact: Look Back in Anger, Downright Hooligan, Twelfth Night; Resident Dir, 1977–82, Associate Dir, 1983–90, RSC; directed, RSC: Dance of Death, 1977; Savage Amusement, Look Out, Here Comes Trouble, 1978; Caucasian Chalk Circle, 1979; (co-dir, with Trevor Nunn) Nicholas Nickleby, London, New York and Los Angeles, 1980, 1982, 1986 (SWET Award, 1980, Tony Award, 1982, for Best Dir; televised, 1981); Naked Robots, Twin Rivals, 1981; Our Friends in the North, 1982; Peter Pan (co-dir with Trevor Nunn), 1982–84; Twelfth Night, Romeo and Juliet, 1983; The Merchant of Venice, Red Star, 1984; Philistines, 1985; Les Misérables (co-dir with Trevor Nunn), London, Washington, NY, Boston, Oslo, LA, Tokyo and Sydney, 1985–88 (Tony Award for Best Dir, 1986, 1987); Every Man in his Humour, Misalliance, 1986; A Question of Geography, The New Inn, 1987; As You Like It, A Midsummer Night's Dream, 1989. Directed: Song and Dance, London, 1982; As You Like It, Stockholm, 1984 (also for TV, 1985). Devised and dir., Intimate Letters (a series of concerts for actors and string quartet); wrote and directed: The Kingdom of the Spirit, London, 1986; Siegfried & Roy at the Mirage, Las Vegas, 1989; Children of Eden, a musical (with music and lyrics by Stephen Schwartz), London, 1991.

CAIRD, William Douglas Sime; Registrar, Family Division of High Court (formerly Probate, Divorce and Admiralty Division), 1964–82; *b* 21 Aug. 1917; *er s* of William Sime Caird and Elsie Amy Caird; *m* 1946, Josephine Mary, *d* of Peter and Elizabeth Seeney, Stratford on Avon; no *c*. *Educ:* Rutlish Sch., Merton. Entered Principal Probate Registry, 1937; Estabt Officer, 1954; Sec., 1959; Mem., Matrimonial Causes Rule Cttee, 1968–79. *Publications:* Consulting Editor, Rayden on Divorce, 10th edn 1967, 11th edn 1971, 12th edn 1974, 13th edn 1979. *Address:* 17 Pine Walk, Bookham, Surrey KT23 4AS. *T:* Bookham (0372) 456732.

CAIRNCROSS, Sir Alexander Kirkland, (Sir Alec Cairncross), KCMG 1967 (CMG 1950); FBA 1961; Chancellor, University of Glasgow, since 1972; Supernumerary Fellow, St Antony's College, Oxford, since 1978; *b* 11 Feb. 1911; 3rd *s* of Alexander Kirkland and Elizabeth Andrew Cairncross, Lesmahagow, Scotland; *m* 1943, Mary Frances Glynn, *d* of Maj. E. F. Glynn, TD, Ilkley; three *s* two *d*. *Educ:* Hamilton Academy; Glasgow and Cambridge Univs. Univ. Lectr, 1935–39; Civil Servant, 1940–45; Dir of Programmes, Min. of Aircraft Production, 1945; Economic Advisory Panel, Berlin, 1945–46; Mem. of Staff of The Economist, 1946. Mem. of Wool Working Party, 1946; Economic Adviser to: BoT, 1946–49; Organisation for European Economic Co-operation, 1949–50; Prof. of Applied Economics, Univ. of Glasgow, 1951–61; Dir, Economic Development Inst., Washington DC, 1955–56; Economic Adviser to HM Govt, 1961–64; Head of Govt Economic Service, 1964–69. Master of St Peter's Coll., Oxford, 1969–78, Hon. Fellow, 1978. Vis. Prof., Brookings Instn, Washington, DC, 1972; Leverhulme Vis. Prof., Inst. of Economic and Social Change, Bangalore, 1981; Leverhulme Emeritus Fellow, 1983–86. Chairman: independent advrs on reassessment of Channel Tunnel Project, 1974–75 (Adviser to Minister of Transport on Channel Tunnel Project, 1979–81); Commonwealth Secretariat Gp of Experts on Protectionism, 1982; Local Development Cttee, 1951–52; Member: Crofting Commn, 1951–54; Phillips Cttee, 1953–54; Anthrax Cttee, 1957–59; Radcliffe Cttee, 1957–59; Cttee on N Ireland, 1971; Cttee on Police Pay, 1978; Council of Management, Nat. Inst. of Economic and Social Research; Court of Governors, LSE, until 1989 (Hon. Fellow, 1980); Council, Royal Economic Soc. (Pres., 1968–70). President: Scottish Economic Soc., 1969–71; British Assoc. for Advancement of Science, 1970–71 (Pres. Section F, 1969); GPDST, 1972–. Houblon-Norman Trustee, 1982–86. Editor, Scottish Journal of Political Economy, 1954–61. For. Hon. Mem., Amer. Acad. of Arts and Scis, 1973. Hon. LLD: Mount Allison, 1962; Glasgow, 1966; Exeter, 1969; Hon. DLitt: Reading, 1968: Heriot-Watt, 1969; Hon. DSc(Econ.): Univ. of Wales, 1971; QUB, 1972; DUniv Stirling, 1973. *Publications:* Introduction to Economics, 1944, 6th edn 1982; Home and Foreign Investment, 1870–1913, 1953; Monetary Policy in a Mixed Economy, 1960; Economic Development and the Atlantic Provinces, 1961; Factors in Economic Development, 1962; Essays in Economic Management, 1971; Control of Long-term International Capital Movements, 1973; Inflation, Growth and International Finance, 1975; Science Studies (Nuffield Foundn report), 1980; Snatches (poems), 1981; (with Barry Eichengreen) Sterling in Decline, 1983; Years of Recovery, 1985; The Price of War, 1986; Economics and Economic Policy, 1986; A Country to Play With, 1987; (ed) The Diaries of Robert Hall, Vol. I 1989, Vol. II 1991; (with Nina Watts) The Economic Section 1939–61, 1989; Planning in Wartime, 1991. *Recreation:* writing. *Address:* 14 Staverton Road, Oxford OX2 6XJ. *T:* Oxford (0865) 52358.
See also F. A. Cairncross.

CAIRNCROSS, Frances Anne, (Mrs Hamish McRae); Environment Editor, The Economist, since 1989; *b* 30 Aug. 1944; *d* of Sir Alexander Kirkland Cairncross, *qv*; *m* 1971, Hamish McRae, *qv*; two *d*. *Educ:* Laurel Bank Sch., Glasgow; St Anne's Coll., Oxford (MA History); Brown Univ., Rhode Island (MAEcon). On Staff of: The Times, 1967–69; The Banker, 1969; The Observer, 1970–73; Economics Correspondent 1973–81, Women's Page Editor 1981–84, The Guardian; Britain Editor, The Economist, 1984–89. Member: SSRC Economics Cttee, 1972–76; Newspaper Panel, Monopolies Commn, 1973–80; Council, Royal Economic Soc., 1980–85; Council, PSI, 1987–90; Cttee of Inquiry into Proposals to Amend the Shops Act, 1983–84; Inquiry into British Housing, 1984–85. Director: Prolific Gp plc, 1988–89; Alliance & Leicester Building Soc., 1990–. Hon. Treas., Nat. Council for One Parent Families, 1980–83; Trustee, Kennedy Memorial Trust, 1974–90; *Publications:* Capital City (with Hamish McRae), 1971; The Second Great Crash (with Hamish McRae), 1973; The Guardian Guide to the Economy, 1981; Changing Perceptions of Economic Policy, 1981; The Second Guardian Guide to the Economy, 1983; Guide to the Economy, 1987; Costing the Earth, 1991. *Recreation:* child care. *Address:* 6 Canonbury Lane, N1 2AP. *T:* 071–359 4612.

CAIRNCROSS, Neil Francis, CB 1971; Deputy Under-Secretary of State, Home Office, 1972–80; *b* 29 July 1920; *s* of late James and Olive Hunter Cairncross; *m* 1947, Eleanor Elizabeth Leisten; two *s* one *d*. *Educ:* Charterhouse; Oriel Coll., Oxford. Royal Sussex Regt, 1940–45. Called to the Bar, 1948. Home Office, 1948; a Private Sec. to the Prime Minister, 1955–58; Sec., Royal Commn on the Press, 1961–62; Dep. Sec., Cabinet Office, 1970–72; Dep. Sec., NI Office, March-Nov. 1972. Member: Parole Bd, 1982–85; Home Grown Timber Adv. Cttee, 1981–90; (co-opted) Avon Probation Cttee, 1983–89. *Recreation:* painting. *Address:* Little Grange, The Green, Olveston, Bristol BS12 3EJ. *T:* Almondsbury (0454) 613060. *Club:* United Oxford & Cambridge University.

CAIRNS, family name of **Earl Cairns.**

CAIRNS, 6th Earl *cr* 1878; **Simon Dallas Cairns;** Baron Cairns 1867; Viscount Garmoyle 1878; Joint Chairman, S. G. Warburg & Co., since 1987 (Managing Director, 1979–85; a Vice-Chairman, 1985–87); Vice-Chairman, S. G. Warburg Group (formerly Mercury International Group), since 1987 (Director, since 1985); Chairman, Voluntary Service Overseas, since 1981 (Treasurer, 1974–81); Receiver-General of Duchy of Cornwall, since 1990; *b* 27 May 1939; *er s* of 5th Earl Cairns, GCVO, CB and of Barbara Jeanne Harrisson, *y d* of Sydney H. Burgess; *S* father, 1989; *m* 1964, Amanda Mary, *d* of late Major E. F. Heathcoat Amory, and of Mrs Roderick Heathcoat Amory, Oswaldkirk Hall, York; three *s*. *Educ:* Eton; Trinity Coll., Cambridge. Man. Dir, 1981–84, a Vice-Chm., 1984–86, Mercury Securities plc. Mem., City Capital Markets Cttee, 1989–. *Heir:* *s* Viscount Garmoyle, *qv*. *Address:* Bolehyde Manor, Allington, near Chippenham, Wilts SN14 6LW. *T:* Chippenham (0249) 652105; 2 Finsbury Avenue, EC2M 2PA. *Club:* Turf.

CAIRNS, Air Vice-Marshal Geoffrey Crerar, CBE 1970; AFC 1960; FRAeS 1979; FBIM; *b* 1926; *s* of late Dr J. W. Cairns, MD, MCh, DPH and Marion Cairns; *m* 1948, Carol (*d* 1985), *d* of H. I. F. Evernden, MBE; four *d*. *Educ:* Loretto School, Musselburgh; Cambridge Univ. Joined RAF, 1944; served: Sqdns 43 and 93, Italy; Sqdn 73, Malta, 1946–49; Sqdn 72, UK, 1949–51; Adjutant, Hong Kong Auxiliary Air Force; test pilot A&AEE, Boscombe Down, 1957–60; Jt Planning Staff, MoD, 1961; Chief Instructor, Helicopters, CFS, RAF Ternhill, 1963; JSSC 1966; Supt Flying A&AEE 1968; Dir, Defence Operational Requirements Staffs, MoD, 1970; Commandant, Boscombe Down, 1972–74; ACAS (Op. Requirements), MoD, 1974–76; Comdr, Southern Maritime Air Region, 1976–78; Chief of Staff No 18 Group, Strike Command, 1978–80. Consultant, Marconi Avionics, 1980–81. Dir, Trago Aircraft Ltd, 1982–87. *Recreations:* golf, railways. *Club:* Royal Air Force.

CAIRNS, Hugh John Forster; DM; FRS 1974; Professor of Microbiology, Harvard School of Public Health, since 1980; *b* 21 Nov. 1922. *Educ:* Oxford Univ. BA 1943; BM, BCh 1946; DM 1952. Surg. Registrar, Radcliffe Infirmary, Oxford, 1945; Med. Intern, Postgrad. Med. Sch., London, 1946; Paediatric Intern, Royal Victoria Infirmary, Newcastle, 1947; Chem. Pathologist, Radcliffe Infirmary, 1947–49; Virologist, Hall Inst., Melbourne, Aust., 1950–51; Virus Research Inst., Entebbe, Uganda, 1952–54; Research Fellow, then Reader, Aust. Nat. Univ., Canberra, 1955–63; Rockefeller Research Fellow, California Inst. of Technology, 1957; Nat. Insts of Health Fellow, Cold Spring Harbor, NY, 1960–61; Dir, Cold Spring Harbor Lab. of Quantitative Biology, 1963–68 (Staff Mem., 1968–); Prof of Biology (Hon.), State Univ. of New York, Stony Brook, 1968–73, Amer. Cancer Soc. Prof. 1968–73; Head of Imperial Cancer Research Fund Mill Hill Laboratories, 1973–80. *Address:* Department of Microbiology, Harvard School of Public Health, 677 Huntington Avenue, Boston, Massachusetts 02115, USA. *T:* (617) 732 1240.

CAIRNS, Dr James Ford; MHR (ALP) for Lalor, 1969–78 (for Yarra, 1955–69); *b* 4 Oct. 1914; *s* of James John Cairns and Letitia Cairns (*née* Ford); *m* 1939, Gwendolyn Olga

Robb; two *s*. *Educ*: Melton/Sunbury State Sch.; Northcote High Sch.; Melbourne Univ. MComm and PhD (Melb.). Australian Estates Co. Ltd, 1932; Victoria Police Force, 1935. Served War, AIF, 1945. Melbourne University: Sen. Tutor, Lectr, Sen. Lectr (Economic Hist.), 1946–55; Nuffield Dominion Fellow, Oxford Univ., 1951–52. Minister for Overseas Trade, 1972–74; Treasurer of Australia, 1974–75; Dep. Prime Minister, 1974–75; Minister for the Environment, Australia, 1975. *Publications*: Australia, 1951 (UK); Living with Asia, 1965; The Eagle and the Lotus, 1969; Tariffs or Planning, 1970; Silence Kills, 1970; The Quiet Revolution, 1972; Oil in Troubled Waters, 1976; Vietnam: Scorched Earth Reborn, 1976; Growth to Freedom, 1979; Survival Now, the Human Transformation, 1983; Human Growth: its source . . . and potential, 1985; Strength Within: towards an end to violence, 1988; The Untried Road, 1990; numerous articles in jls and press, incl. title Australia: History in Enc. Brit. *Recreations*: sleeping, reading.

CAIRNS, James George Hamilton Dickson; Chief Architect and Director of Works, Home Office, 1976–80; *b* 17 Sept. 1920; *s* of Percival Cairns and Christina Elliot Cairns; *m* 1944, G. Elizabeth Goodman; one *d*. *Educ*: Hillhead High Sch., Glasgow; London Polytechnic. ARIBA. Served War, Royal Corps of Signals (Intell.), 1941–46. Architects' Dept, GLC, 1946–75. Divisional Architect, Thamesmead New Town, awarded Sir Patrick Abercrombie Prize by Internat. Union of Architects, 1969. *Recreations*: golf, sailing. *Address*: Elmsleigh, 12 Elmstead Park Road, West Wittering, W Sussex PO20 8NQ. *T*: Birdham (0243) 513316. *Clubs*: Goodwood Golf; West Wittering Sailing.

CAITHNESS, 20th Earl of, *cr* 1455; **Malcolm Ian Sinclair**, PC 1990; FRICS; Lord Berriedale, 1455; Bt 1631; Minister of State, Foreign and Commonwealth Office, since 1990; *b* 3 Nov. 1948; *s* of 19th Earl of Caithness, CVO, CBE, DSO, DL, JP; *S* father, 1965; *m* 1975, Diana Caroline, *d* of Major Richard Coke, DSO, MC, DL; one *s* one *d*. *Educ*: Marlborough; Royal Agricl Coll., Cirencester. A Lord in Waiting (Govt Whip), 1984–85; parly spokesman on health and social security, 1984–85, on Scotland, 1984–86; Parly Under-Sec. of State, Dept of Transport, 1985–86; Minister of State: Home Office, 1986–88; DoE, 1988–89; Paymaster Gen., 1989–90. *Heir*: *s* Lord Berriedale, *qv*. *Address*: c/o House of Lords, SW1.

CAITHNESS, Archdeacon of; *see* Hadfield, Ven. J. C.

CALCUTT, Sir David (Charles), Kt 1991; QC 1972; Master of Magdalene College, Cambridge, since 1986 (Fellow Commoner, 1980–85); Chairman: Panel on Takeovers and Mergers, since 1989; Civil Service Arbitration Tribunal, since 1979; Institute of Actuaries' Appeal Board, since 1985; President, Lloyd's of London Appeal Tribunal, since 1987 (Deputy President, 1983–87); a Judge of the Courts of Appeal of Jersey and Guernsey, since 1978; Chancellor of the Dioceses of Exeter and of Bristol, since 1971 and of Gibraltar in Europe, since 1983; *b* 2 Nov. 1930; *s* of late Henry Calcutt; *m* 1969, Barbara, JP and Freeman, City of London, *d* of late Vivian Walker. *Educ*: Christ Church, Oxford (chorister); Cranleigh Sch. (music schol.); King's Coll., Cambridge (choral schol.; Stewart of Rannoch Schol.), 1952; prizeman; MA, LLB, MusB). Called to the Bar, Middle Temple, 1955 (Bencher, 1981); Harmsworth Law Schol., Garraway Rice Prize, 1956; Chm. of the Bar, 1984–85 (Vice-Chm., 1983–84). Dep. Chm., Somerset QS, 1970–71; a Recorder, 1972–89. Dept of Trade Inspector, Cornhill Consolidated Gp Ltd, 1974–77; Member: Criminal Injuries Compensation Bd, 1977–; Council on Tribunals, 1980–86; Chm., Falkland Is Commn of Enquiry, 1984; conducted: Cyprus Service Police Inquiry, 1985–86; Colin Wallace Inquiry, 1990; Member: Colliery Indep. Review Body, 1985–88; Interception of Communications Tribunal, 1986–; Conciliator, Internat. Centre for the Settlement of Investment Disputes, Washington DC, 1986–; Indep. Mem., Diplomatic Service Appeal Bd, 1986–; Home Office Assessor of Compensation for Miscarriages of Justice, 1989–; Chm., Cttee on Privacy and Related Matters, 1989–90. UK Deleg., Consultative Cttee, Bars and Law Socs, EEC, 1979–83. Fellow, Internat. Acad. of Trial Lawyers (NY), 1978–; Hon. Member: American Bar Assoc., 1985–; Canadian Bar Assoc., 1985–. Dir, Edington Music Fest., 1956–64. Dep. Chm., RCM, 1988–90 (FRCM 1988). Chairman: Council, Cranleigh and Bramley Schs, 1987– (Vice-Chm., 1983–87); Septemviri, Cambridge Univ., 1988–. Fellow, Winchester Coll., 1992. *Recreation*: living on Exmoor. *Address*: Magdalene College, Cambridge CB3 0AG; Lamb Building, Temple, EC4. *Clubs*: Athenæum, United Oxford & Cambridge University; New (Edinburgh).

CALCUTTA, Archbishop of, (RC), since 1986; **Most Rev. Henry Sebastian D'Souza**; *b* 20 Jan. 1926; *s* of George William and Aurelia Clotilde D'Souza. *Educ*: Papal Atheneum, Kandy (LPH, LD); Urban Univ., Rome (DCL). Nominated Archbishop of Cuttack-Bhubaneswar, 1974. Secretary General: Catholic Bishops' Conference of India, 1979–82; Federation of Asian Bishops' Confs, 1983–. Pres., Conf. of Catholic Bishops of India (Latin Rite), 1988–. *Address*: Archbishop's House, 32 Park Street, Calcutta 700016, India. *T*: 441960, 444666.

CALCUTTA, Bishop of, since 1982; **Rt. Rev. Dinesh Chandra Gorai**; *b* 15 Jan. 1934. *Educ*: Calcutta Univ. (BA 1956); Serampore Theological Coll. (BD 1959). Ordained, 1962; Methodist Minister in Calcutta/Barrackpore, 1968–70; first Bishop, Church of N India Diocese of Barrackpore, 1970–82; Dep. Moderator, 1980, Moderator, 1983–86, Church of N India. Hon. DD Bethel Coll., 1985. *Publication*: (ed) Transfer of Vision: a leadership development programme for the Church of North India 1983–1986, 1984. *Address*: Bishop's House, 51 Chowringhee Road, Calcutta 700 071, India. *T*: 44–5259.

CALDECOTE, 2nd Viscount *cr* 1939, of Bristol; **Robert Andrew Inskip**, KBE 1987; DSC 1941; DL; FEng 1977; Chairman: Delta Group plc (formerly Delta Metal Co.), 1972–82; Investors in Industry (formerly Finance for Industry), 1980–87; *b* 8 Oct. 1917; *o s* of Thomas Walker Hobart Inskip, 1st Viscount Caldecote, PC, CBE, and Lady Augusta Orr Ewing (*d* 1967), *widow* of Charles Orr Ewing, MP for Ayr Burghs and *e d* of 7th Earl of Glasgow; *S* father, 1947; *m* 1942, Jean Hamilla, *d* of late Rear-Adm. H. D. Hamilton; one *s* two *d*. *Educ*: Eton Coll.; King's Coll., Cambridge. BA Cantab 1939; MA 1944; Hon. LLD 1983. RNVR, 1939–45; RNC Greenwich, 1946–47; an Asst Manager, Vickers-Armstrong Naval Yard, Walker-on-Tyne, 1947–48; Fellow, King's Coll., and Lectr, Engineering Dept, Cambridge Univ., 1948–55; Man. Dir, English Electric Aviation, 1960–63; Dep. Man. Dir, British Aircraft Corp., 1961–67 (Dir, 1960–69); Dir, English Electric Co., 1953–69; Chm., Legal and General Gp, 1977–80. Chairman: EDC Movement of Exports, 1965–72; Export Council for Europe, 1970–71. Mem., H of L Select Cttee for Sci. and Technol., 1987–. President: Soc. of British Aerospace Cos, 1965–66; Internat. Assoc. of Aeronautical and Space Equipment Manufacturers, 1966–68; Parliamentary and Scientific Cttee, 1966–69; Fellowship of Engineering, 1981–86; RINA, 1987–90 (FRINA 1987). Director: Consolidated Gold Fields, 1969–78; Lloyds Bank, 1975–88; Lloyds Bank International, 1979–85; Equity Capital for Industry, 1980–85; W. S. Atkins Ltd, 1985–; Industry Ventures Ltd, 1989–. Member: Review Bd for Govt Contracts, 1969–76; Inflation Accounting Cttee, 1974–75; Engineering Industries Council, 1975–82; British Railways Bd, 1979–85; Adv. Council for Applied R & D, 1981–84; Engrg Council, 1981–85. Chairman: Design Council, 1972–80; BBC Gen. Adv. Council, 1982–85; Mary Rose Trust, 1983–; Crown Appts Commn, 1990. Pro-Chancellor, Cranfield Inst. of Technology, 1976–84. Mem., Church Assembly, 1950–55.

Mem. UK Delegn to UN, 1952. Fellow, Eton Coll., 1953–72; Pres., Dean Close Sch., 1960–90. DL Hants, 1991. Hon. FICE, 1981; Hon. FIMechE, 1982; Hon. FIEE, 1984; Hon. FIM 1984; Hon. FCSD (FSIAD 1976). Hon. DSc: Cranfield, 1976; Aston, 1979; City, 1982; Bristol, 1982; Hon. LLD: London, 1981; Cambridge, 1985. *Recreations*: sailing, shooting, golf. *Heir*: *s* Hon. Piers James Hampden Inskip [*b* 20 May 1947; *m* 1st, 1970, Susan Bridget, *d* of late W. P. Mellen; 2nd, 1984, Kristine Elizabeth, *d* of Harvey Holbrooke-Jackson; one *s*]. *Address*: Orchard Cottage, South Harting, Petersfield, Hants GU31 5NR. *T*: Harting (0730) 825529. *Clubs*: Pratt's, Athenæum, Royal Ocean Racing; Royal Yacht Squadron.

CALDER, Elisabeth Nicole; Publishing Director, Bloomsbury Publishing, since 1986; *b* 20 Jan. 1938; *d* of Florence Mary Baber and Ivor George Baber; *m* 1958, Richard Henry Calder (marr. diss. 1972); one *d* one *s*. *Educ*: Broadfields, Edgware; Palmerston North Girls' High Sch., NZ; Canterbury Univ., NZ (BA 1958). Reader, Metro-Goldwyn-Mayer story dept, 1969–70; Publicity Manager, Victor Gollancz, 1971–74; Editorial Director: Victor Gollancz, 1975–78; Jonathan Cape, 1979–86. *Recreations*: reading, thinking about gardening, junking. *Address*: Bloomsbury Publishing, 2 Soho Square, W1V 5DE. *T*: 071–494 2111. *Club*: Groucho.

CALDER, John Mackenzie; Managing Director: John Calder (Publishers) Ltd, 1950–91; Calder Publications Ltd, since 1991; President, Riverrun Press Inc., New York, since 1978; *b* 25 Jan. 1927; *e s* of James Calder, Ardargie, Forgandenny, Perthshire, and Lucianne Wilson, Montreal, Canada; *m* 1st, 1949, Mary Ann Simmonds; one *d*; 2nd, 1960, Bettina Jonic (marr. diss. 1975); one *d*. *Educ*: Gilling Castle, Yorks; Bishops College Sch., Canada; McGill Univ.; Sir George Williams Coll.; Zürich Univ. Studied political economy; subseq. worked in Calders Ltd (timber co.), Director; founded John Calder (Publishers) Ltd, 1949; Man. Dir, Calder & Boyars, 1964–75. Organiser of literary confs for Edinburgh Festival, 1962 and 1963, and Harrogate Festival, 1969. Founded Ledlanet Nights, 1963, in Kinross-shire (music and opera festival, closed 1974). Acquired book-selling business of Better Books, London, 1969, expanded Edinburgh, 1971. Dir of other cos associated with opera, publishing, etc, inc. Operabout Ltd, Canadian International Library Ltd, Canada. Active in fields related to the arts and on many cttees; Co-founder, Defence of Literature and the Arts Society; Chm., Fedn of Scottish Theatres, 1972–74. Contested (L): Kinross and W Perthshire, 1970; Hamilton, Oct. 1974; (European Parlt) Mid Scotland and Fife, 1979. FRSA 1974. Chevalier des Arts et des Lettres, 1975; Chevalier de l'Ordre nationale de mérite, 1983. *Publications*: (ed) A Samuel Beckett Reader, 1967; (ed) Beckett at 60, 1967; (ed) William Burroughs Reader, 1982; (ed) New Samuel Beckett Reader, 1983; (ed) Henry Miller Reader, 1985; (ed) The Nouveau Roman Reader, 1986; (ed) As No Other Dare Fail: for Samuel Beckett on his 80th birthday, 1986; The Defence of Literature (criticism), 1991; (ed) Gambit International Drama Review, etc; articles in many jls. *Recreations*: writing (several plays, stories; criticism, etc; translations); music, theatre, opera, reading, chess, lecturing, conversation; travelling, promoting good causes, fond of good food and wine. *Address*: Calder Educational Trust, 9–15 Neal Street, WC2H 9TU. *Clubs*: Caledonian; Scottish Arts (Edinburgh).

CALDER, Julian Richard; Director of Statistics, Board of Inland Revenue, since 1985; *b* 6 Dec. 1941; *s* of Donald Alexander and Ivy O'Nora Calder; *m* 1965, Avril Tucker; two *s*. *Educ*: Dulwich College; Brasenose College, Oxford; Birkbeck College, London. Statistician, 1973, Chief Statistician, 1978, Central Statistical Office; Chief Statistician, Board of Inland Revenue, 1981. *Recreations*: cycling, listening to music. *Address*: Statistics Division, Board of Inland Revenue, Somerset House, Strand, WC2R 1LB. *T*: 071–438 6609.

CALDER, Nigel David Ritchie, MA; science writer; *b* 2 Dec. 1931; *e s* of Baron Ritchie-Calder, CBE; *m* 1954, Elisabeth Palmer; two *s* three *d*. *Educ*: Merchant Taylors' Sch.; Sidney Sussex Coll., Cambridge. Physicist, Mullard Research Laboratories, 1954–56; Editorial staff, New Scientist, 1956–66; Science Editor, 1960–62; Editor, 1962–66. Science Correspondent, New Statesman, 1959–62 and 1966–71; Chairman, Assoc. of British Science Writers, 1962–64. Member: Initiative Group, Foundn Scientific Europe, 1987–90; RAS; RGS. (Jtly) UNESCO Kalinga Prize for popularisation of science, 1972. *Publications*: Electricity Grows Up, 1958; Robots, 1958; Radio Astronomy, 1958; (ed) The World in 1984, 1965; The Environment Game, 1967; (ed) Unless Peace Comes, 1968; Technopolis: Social Control of the Uses of Science, 1969; Living Tomorrow, 1970; (ed) Nature in the Round: a Guide to Environmental Science, 1973; Timescale, 1983; 1984 and After, 1983; The English Channel, 1986; The Green Machines, 1986; (ed) Future Earth, 1988; (ed) Scientific Europe, 1990; *books of own TV programmes*: The Violent Universe, 1969; The Mind of Man, 1970; The Restless Earth, 1972; The Life Game, 1973; The Weather Machine, 1974; The Human Conspiracy, 1975–76; The Key to the Universe, 1977; Spaceships of the Mind (TV series), 1978; Einstein's Universe, 1979; Nuclear Nightmares, 1979; The Comet is Coming!, 1980; Spaceship Earth, 1991. *Recreation*: sailing. *Address*: 8 The Chase, Furnace Green, Crawley, W Sussex RH10 6HW. *T*: Crawley (0293) 526693. *Clubs*: Athenæum; Cruising Association (Vice-Pres., 1981–84).

CALDER-MARSHALL, Arthur; author; *b* 19 Aug. 1908; *s* of late Arthur Grotjan Calder-Marshall and Alice Poole; *m* 1934, Violet Nancy Sales; two *d*. *Educ*: St Paul's Sch.; Hertford Coll., Oxford. *Publications*: *novels*: Two of a Kind, 1933; About Levy, 1933; At Sea, 1934; Dead Centre, 1935; Pie in the Sky, 1937; The Way to Santiago, 1940; A Man Reprieved, 1949; Occasion of Glory, 1955; The Scarlet Boy, 1961, rev. edn 1962; *short stories*: Crime against Cania, 1934; A Pink Doll, 1935; A Date with a Duchess, 1937; *for children*: The Man from Devil's Island, 1958; Fair to Middling, 1959; Lone Wolf: the story of Jack London, 1961; *travel*: Glory Dead, 1939; The Watershed, 1947; *biography*: No Earthly Command, 1957; Havelock Ellis, 1959; The Enthusiast, 1962; The Innocent Eye, 1963; Lewd, Blasphemous and Obscene, 1972; The Two Duchesses, 1978; *autobiography*: The Magic of My Youth, 1951, repr. 1990; *miscellaneous*: Challenge to Schools: public school education, 1935; The Changing Scene, 1937; The Book Front, ed J. Lindsay, 1947; Wish You Were Here: the art of Donald McGill, 1966; Prepare to Shed Them Now . . .: the biography and ballads of George R. Sims, 1968; The Grand Century of the Lady, 1976; *essays*: Sterne, in The English Novelists, ed D. Verschoyle, 1936; Films, in Mind in Chains, ed C. Day Lewis; *edited*: Tobias Smollett, Selected Writings, 1950; J. London, The Bodley Head Jack London, Vols 1–4, 1963–66; Charles Dickens, David Copperfield, 1967, Nicholas Nickleby, 1968, Oliver Twist, 1970; Bleak House, 1976; The Life of Benvenuto Cellini, 1968; Jack London, The Call of the Wild, and other stories, 1969; Jane Austen, Emma, 1970; Thomas Paine, Common Sense and the Rights of Man, 1970. *Address*: c/o Elaine Greene Ltd, 31 Newington Green, N16 9PW.

CALDERWOOD, Sir Robert, Kt 1990; Chief Executive, Strathclyde Regional Council, since 1980; *b* 1 March 1932; *s* of Robert Calderwood and Jessie Reid (*née* Marshall); *m* 1958, Meryl Anne (*née* Fleming); three *s* one *d*. *Educ*: William Hulme's Sch., Manchester; Manchester Univ. (LLB (Hons)). Admitted solicitor, 1956; Town Clerk: Salford, 1966–69; Bolton, 1969–73; Manchester, 1973–79. Dir, Glasgow Garden Fest. 1988 Ltd, 1985–88; Chm., Strathclyde Buses, 1989–. Member: Parole Bd for England and Wales, 1971–73; Soc. of Local Authority Chief Execs, 1974– (Pres., 1989–90); Scottish Consultative Cttee, Commn for Racial Equality, 1981–88. Dir, European Summer Special

Olympic Games 1990 (Strathclyde) Ltd, 1989–90. Mem. Council, Industrial Soc., 1983–; CBIM (Mem., Scottish Bd, 1982–); Companion, IWEM, 1983–89. *Recreations:* theatre, watching Rugby. *Address:* Strathclyde Regional Council, Strathclyde House, 20 India Street, Glasgow G2 4PF; 6 Mosspark Avenue, Milngavie, Glasgow G62 8NL.

CALDOW, William James, CMG 1977; Consultant, ICI plc, 1981–86; *b* 7 Dec. 1919; *s* of William Caldow and Mary Wilson Grier; *m* 1950, Monique Henriette Hervé, *d* of Gaétan Hervé, Chevalier de la Légion d'Honneur (member of French Resistance, executed 1944); one *s* (and one *s* decd). *Educ:* Marr College (Dux Medallist); Glasgow University (Scholar; MA Hons); Sorbonne. Captain, Intelligence Corps, 1940–45. Colonial Administrative Service, Gold Coast, later Ghana, 1947–59; War Office, later Ministry of Defence, 1959–80. *Recreations:* reading, music, bird watching. *Address:* 3 Pilgrims Way, Guildford, Surrey GU4 8AB. *T:* Guildford (0483) 62183.

CALDWELL, Surg. Vice-Adm. Sir Dick; *see* Caldwell, Surg. Vice-Adm. Sir E. D.

CALDWELL, Edward George, CB 1990; Parliamentary Counsel, since 1981; *b* 21 Aug. 1941; *s* of Arthur Francis Caldwell and Olive Caldwell (*née* Riddle); *m* 1965, Bronwen Anne, *d* of John Andrew Crockett and late Bronwen Crockett; two *d. Educ:* St Andrew's, Singapore; Clifton College; Worcester College, Oxford. Law Commission, 1967–69, 1975–77, 1986–88; joined Office of Parly Counsel, 1969. *Address:* Office of the Parliamentary Counsel, 36 Whitehall, SW1A 2AY. *T:* 071–210 6611.

CALDWELL, Surg. Vice-Adm. Sir (Eric) Dick, KBE 1969; CB 1965; Medical Director-General of the Royal Navy, 1966–69; Executive Director, Medical Council on Alcoholism, 1970–79; *b* 6 July 1909; *s* of late Dr John Colin Caldwell; *m* 1942, Margery Lee Abbott (*d* 1991). *Educ:* Edinburgh Acad.; Edinburgh Univ. MB, ChB Edinburgh 1933; LRCP, LRCSE, LRFPS(G) 1933; MD Edinburgh 1950; MRCP 1956; FRCP(Edin) 1962; FRCP(London) 1967. Joined Royal Navy, 1934. Served War of 1939–45 in Atlantic, Mediterranean and Pacific; survivor from torpedoeing of HMS Royal Oak and HMS Prince of Wales. Medical Specialist, RN Hosp., Hong Kong, 1947; Sen. Med. Specialist at RN Hosp., Haslar, 1956–58; Surg. Captain 1957; MO i/c of RN Hosp., Plymouth, 1963–66. RN Consultant in Medicine, 1962; Surg. Rear-Adm. 1963; Surg. Vice-Adm. 1966. QHP 1963–69. Gilbert Blane Gold Medal, 1962; FRSocMed. CStJ. *Recreations:* reading, travelling, trying to write. *Address:* Flat 10 Woodsford, 14 Melbury Road, Kensington, W14. *T:* 071–602 2225.

CALDWELL, Maj.-Gen. Frank Griffiths, OBE 1953 (MBE 1945); MC 1941 and Bar 1942; retired; *b* 26 Feb. 1921; *s* of William Charles Francis and Violet Marjorie Kathleen Caldwell; *m* 1945, Betty, *d* of Captain Charles Palmer Buesden; one *s* one *d. Educ:* Elizabeth Coll., Guernsey. Commnd Royal Engrs, 1940; served Western Desert RE, 1940–43 (MC and Bar); Special Air Service NW Europe, 1944–45 (MBE); Malaya, 1951–53 (OBE); Comdr RE, 2 Div. BAOR, 1961–63; Corps Comdr RE, 1 (BR) Corps, 1967–68; Dir Defence Operational Plans, MoD, 1970; Engineer in Chief (Army), 1970–72; Asst CGS (Operational Requirements), 1972–74. Col Comdt, RE, 1975–80. Belgian Croix de Guerre, 1940, and Croix Militaire, 1945. *Recreation:* ornithology. *Address:* Le Courtil Tomar, Rue des Pres, St Pierre du Bois, Guernsey.

CALDWELL, Prof. John Bernard, OBE 1979; PhD; FEng 1976; FRINA; Professor of Naval Architecture, University of Newcastle upon Tyne, since 1966 (Head of School of Marine Technology, 1975–80, 1986–88); *b* 26 Sept. 1926; *s* of John Revie Caldwell and Doris (*née* Bolland); *m* 1955, Jean Muriel Frances Duddridge; two *s. Educ:* Bootham Sch., York; Liverpool Univ. (BEng); Bristol Univ. (PhD). CEng, MIStructE; FRINA 1963. Res. Fellow, Civil Engrg, Bristol Univ., 1953; Sen. Scientific Officer 1955, Principal Sci. Off. 1958, Royal Naval Scientific Service; Asst Prof. of Applied Mechanics, RNC Greenwich, 1960–66; Newcastle upon Tyne University: Hd of Dept of Naval Architecture, 1966–83; Dean of Faculty of Engrg, 1983–86. Director: Nat. Maritime Inst. Ltd, 1983–85; Marine Design Consultants Ltd, 1985–89; Newcastle Technology Centre, 1985–90; Northern Engrg Centre, 1989–. Vis. Prof. of Naval Arch., MIT, 1962–63. President: N-E Coast Instn of Engrs and Shipbuilders, 1976–78; RINA, 1984–87 (Vice-Pres., 1977–84). Mem., Engineering Council, 1988– (Chm., Bd for Engrs' Registration, 1990–). Hon. DSc Gdansk Tech. Univ., 1985. Froude Medal, RINA, 1984; David W. Taylor Medal, SNAME, 1987. *Publications:* numerous papers on research and educn in naval arch. in Trans RINA. *Address:* The White House, Cadehill Road, Stocksfield, Northumberland NE43 7PT. *T:* Stocksfield (0661) 843445. *Club:* National Liberal.

CALDWELL, Philip; Senior Managing Director, Shearson Lehman Hutton Inc., since 1985; *b* Bourneville, Ohio, 27 Jan. 1920; *s* of Robert Clyde Caldwell and Wilhelmina (*née* Hemphill); *m* 1945, Betsey Chinn Clark; one *s* two *d. Educ:* Muskingum Coll. (BA Econs 1940); Harvard Univ. Graduate Sch. of Business (MBA Indust. Management, 1942). Served to Lieut, USNR, 1942–46. With Navy Dept, 1946–53 (Dep. Dir, Procurement Policy Div., 1948–53); joined Ford Motor Co., 1953: Vice Pres. and Gen. Man. Truck Ops, 1968–70; Pres. and Dir, Philco-Ford Corp. (subsid. of Ford Motor Co.), 1970–71; Vice Pres. Manufg Gp, N Amer. Automotive Ops, 1971–72; Chm. and Chief Exec. Officer, Ford of Europe, Inc., 1972–73; Dir, Ford Motor Co., 1973–; Exec. Vice Pres., Internat. Automotive Ops, 1973–77; Vice Chm. of Bd, 1977–79; Dep. Chief Exec. Officer, 1978–79; Pres., 1978–80; Chief Exec. Officer, 1979–85 and Chm. of Bd, 1980–85, retd; Director: Ford of Europe, 1972–85; Ford Latin America, 1973–85; Ford Mid-East and Africa, 1973–85; Ford Asia-Pacific, 1973–85; Ford Motor Credit Co., 1977–85; Ford of Canada, 1977–85; Mem., Eur. Adv. Council, 1976–88 (Chm., 1987–88). Director: Digital Equipment Corp., 1980–; Chase Manhattan Corp., and Chase Manhattan Bank, NA, 1982–85 (Mem., Chase Manhattan Bank Internat. Adv. Cttee, 1982–85); Federated Dept Stores, 1984–88; Russell Reynolds Associates, Inc., 1984–; Kellogg Co., 1985–; Shearson Lehman Brothers Hldgs Inc., 1985–87; Amer. Guarantee and Liability Insce Co., 1986–; Zurich Reinsurance Co. of New York, 1987–90; Zurich Hldg Co. of America Inc., 1989–; Detroit Symphony Orch., 1974–85; Harvard Business Sch. Associates, 1977–. Vice Chairperson, New Detroit, Inc., 1977–85; Vice Chm., Japan Soc., 1987–89 (Mem., 1983–89; Chm. Exec. Cttee, 1987–89); Member: US Chamber of Commerce Transportation Cttee, 1968–77; US Council, Internat. Chamber of Commerce, 1973–77; US Council for Internat. Business, 1977–85; Soc. of Automotive Engrs, 1969–85; Engrg Soc. of Detroit, 1970–85; Motor Vehicle Manufrs Assoc. of US, 1978–84 (Chm., 1978 and 1983; Mem., Motor Truck Cttee, 1964–70); Econ. Club of Detroit, 1977–86; Highway Users Fedn, 1977–85; INSEAD, 1978–81 (Chm., US Adv. Bd, 1979–84; Mem., Internat. Council, 1983–); Conf. Bd, 1979–; Cttee for Econ. Develt, 1979–; Business Higher Educn Forum, 1979–83; Business Council, 1980–; Policy Cttee, Business Roundtable, 1980–85; Trilateral Commn, 1980–86; Citizens Res. Council of Mich, 1980–85; Adv. Council on Japan–US Econ. Relations, 1981–85; US Trade Representative Adv. Cttee for Trade Negotiations, 1983–85; President's Export Council, 1985–89; Council on Foreign Relations, 1985–; Trustee: Muskingum Coll., 1967–; Winterthur Mus. and Gdns, 1986–. Hon. HHD Muskingum, 1974; Hon. DBA Upper Iowa Univ., 1978; Hon. LLD: Ohio Univ., 1974; Boston Univ. and Eastern Mich Univ., 1979; Miami Univ., 1980; Davidson Coll., 1982; Univ. of Mich, 1984. 1st William A. Jump Meml Award, 1950; Meritorious Civilian Service Award, US Navy, 1953;

Muskingum Coll. Alumni Dist. Service Award, 1978; Brigham Young Univ. Sch. of Management Internat. Exec. of the Year Award, 1983; Automotive Industry Leader of the Year, Automotive Hall of Fame, 1984; Harvard Business School: Club of Greater NY Business Statesman Award, 1984; Alumni Achievement Award, 1985. *Address:* Shearson Lehman Hutton Inc., 200 Vesey Street, New York, NY 10285-2000, USA. *Clubs:* Links, River (New York); Renaissance (Detroit).

CALDWELL-MOORE, Patrick; *see* Moore, P. C.

CALEDON, 7th Earl of, *cr* 1800; **Nicholas James Alexander;** Baron Caledon, 1790; Viscount Caledon, 1797; Lord Lieutenant of County Armagh, since 1989; *b* 6 May 1955; *s* of 6th Earl of Caledon, and Baroness Anne (*d* 1963), *d* of late Baron Nicolai de Graevenitz; *S* father, 1980; *m* 1st, 1979, Wendy (marr. diss.), *d* of Spiro Coumantaros and Mrs Suzanne Dayton; 2nd, 1989, Henrietta, *d* of John Newman, Compton Chamberlayne, Wilts; one *s. Educ:* Sandroyd School, Gordonstoun School (Round-Square House). *Recreations:* ski-ing, tennis, swimming, photography, travel. *Heir:* *s* Viscount Alexander, *qv. Address:* Caledon Castle, Caledon, Co. Tyrone, Northern Ireland. *T:* Caledon (0861) 232.

CALEDONIA, Bishop of, since 1981; **Rt. Rev. John Edward Hannen;** *b* 19 Nov. 1937; *s* of Charles Scott Hannen and Mary Bowman Hannen (*née* Lynds); *m* 1977, Alana Susan Long; two *d. Educ:* McGill Univ. (BA); College of the Resurrection (GOE). Asst Curate, St Alphege's, Solihull, Warwicks, 1961–64; Priest in Charge, Mission to the Hart Highway, Diocese of Caledonia, BC, 1965–67; Priest, St Andrew's, Greenville, BC, 1967–68; Priest in Charge, Church of Christ the King, Port Edward, BC, 1969–71; Rector, Christ Church, Kincolith, BC, 1971–81; Regional Dean of Metlakatla, 1972–78. *Recreations:* music, Irish wolfhounds. *Address:* Bishop's Lodge, 208 Fourth Avenue West, Prince Rupert, BC V8J 1P3, Canada. *T:* 624–6013.

CALGARY, Bishop of, since 1983; **Rt. Rev. John Barry Curtis;** *b* 19 June 1933; *s* of Harold Boyd Curtis and Eva B. Curtis (*née* Saunders); *m* 1959, Patricia Emily (*née* Simpson); two *s* two *d. Educ:* Trinity Coll., Univ. of Toronto (BA 1955, LTh 1958); Theological Coll., Chichester, Sussex. Deacon 1958, priest 1959; Asst Curate, Holy Trinity, Pembroke, Ont, 1958–61; Rector: Parish of March, Kanata, Ont, 1961–65; St Stephen's Church, Buckingham, Que, 1965–69; Church School Consultant, Diocese of Ottawa, 1969; Rector, All Saints (Westboro), Ottawa, 1969–78; Director of Programme, Diocese of Ottawa, 1978–80; Rector, Christ Church, Elbow Park, Calgary, Alta, 1980–83. Hon. DD Trinity Coll., Toronto, 1985. *Recreations:* reading, hiking, skiing, cycling. *Address:* 3015 Glencoe Road SW, Calgary, Alberta T2S 2L9, Canada. *T:* 403–243–3673; (home) 12 Varanger Place NW, Calgary, Alta T3A 0E9. *T:* 403–286–5127. *Club:* Ranchmen's (Calgary, Alta).

CALIGARI, Prof. Peter Douglas Savaria, PhD, DSc; Professor of Agricultural Botany, since 1986, and Head of Department of Agricultural Botany, since 1987, University of Reading; *b* 10 Nov. 1949; *s* of Kenneth Vane Savaria Caligari, DFM, RAF retd, and Mary Annetta (*née* Rock); *m* 1973, Patricia Ann (*née* Feeley); two *d. Educ:* Hereford Cathedral Sch.; Univ. of Birmingham (BSc Biol Sci., 1971; PhD Genetics, 1974; DSc Genetics, 1989). Res. Asst, 1971–74, Res. Fellow, 1974–81, Dept of Genetics, Univ. of Birmingham; SSO, 1981–84, PSO, 1984–86, Scottish Crop Res. Inst. FRSA 1990. Editor, Heredity, 1987–90 (Jun. Editor, 1985–87). *Publications:* (contrib.) The Potato Crop, 1991; scientific papers and reports on genetics and plant breeding (*c* 110 papers, *c* 20 reports). *Address:* Department of Agricultural Botany, School of Plant Sciences, University of Reading, Whiteknights, PO Box 221, Reading RG6 2AS. *T:* Reading (0734) 318091.

CALLADINE, Prof. Christopher Reuben, ScD; FRS 1984; Professor of Structural Mechanics, University of Cambridge, since 1986; Fellow of Peterhouse, since 1960; *b* 19 Jan. 1935; *s* of Reuben and Mabel Calladine (*née* Boam); *m* 1964, Mary R. H. Webb; two *s* one *d. Educ:* Nottingham High Sch.; Peterhouse, Cambridge; Massachusetts Inst. of Technology. Development engineer, English Electric Co., 1958; Demonstrator in Engrg, Univ. of Cambridge, 1960, Lectr, 1963; Reader, 1978. Vis. Research Associate, Brown Univ., 1963; Vis. Prof., Stanford Univ., 1969–70. *Publications:* Engineering Plasticity, 1969; Theory of Shell Structures, 1983; papers in engrg and biological jls. *Address:* 25 Almoners Avenue, Cambridge CB1 4NZ. *T:* Cambridge (0223) 246742.

CALLAGHAN, family name of **Baron Callaghan of Cardiff.**

CALLAGHAN OF CARDIFF, Baron *cr* 1987 (Life Peer), of the City of Cardiff in the County of South Glamorgan; **Leonard James Callaghan,** KG 1987; PC 1964; *b* 27 March 1912; *s* of James Callaghan, Chief Petty Officer, RN; *m* 1938, Audrey Elizabeth Moulton; one *s* two *d. Educ:* Elementary and Portsmouth Northern Secondary Schs. Entered Civil Service as a Tax Officer, 1929; Asst Sec., Inland Revenue Staff Fed., 1936–47 (with an interval during the War of 1939–45, when served in Royal Navy). Joined Labour Party, 1931. MP (Lab): S Cardiff, 1945–50; SE Cardiff, 1950–83; Cardiff S and Penarth, 1983–87. Parly Sec., Min. of Transport, 1947–50; Chm. Cttee on Road Safety, 1948–50; Parliamentary and Financial Sec., Admiralty, 1950–51; Opposition Spokesman: Transport, 1951–53; Fuel and Power, 1953–55; Colonial Affairs, 1956–61; Shadow Chancellor, 1961–64; Chancellor of the Exchequer, 1964–67; Home Secretary, 1967–70; Shadow Home Sec., 1970–71; Opposition Spokesman on Employment, 1971–72; Shadow Foreign Sec., 1972–74; Sec. of State for Foreign and Commonwealth Affairs, 1974–76; Minister of Overseas Develt, 1975–76; Prime Minister and First Lord of the Treasury, 1976–79; Leader, Labour Party, 1976–80; Leader of the Opposition, 1979–80. Father, House of Commons, 1983–87. Deleg. to Council of Europe, Strasburg, 1948–50 and 1954. Mem., Labour Party NEC, 1957–80; Treasurer, Labour Party, 1967–76, Vice-Chm. 1973, Chm. 1974. Consultant to Police Fedn of England and Wales and to Scottish Police Fedn, 1955–64. President: Adv. Cttee on Pollution of the Sea, 1963– (Chm., 1952–63); United Kingdom Pilots Assoc., 1963–76; Jt Pres., RIIA, 1983–. Hon. Pres., Internat. Maritime Pilots Assoc., 1971–76. Pres., UC Swansea, 1986–. Visiting Fellow, Nuffield Coll., Oxford, 1959–67, Hon. Life Fellow, 1967; Hon. Fellow: UC Cardiff, 1978; Portsmouth Polytechnic, 1981; Hon. LLD: Univ. of Wales, 1976; Sardar Patel Univ., India, 1978; Univ. of Birmingham, 1981; Univ. of Sussex, 1989. Hon. Bencher, Inner Temple, 1976. Hon. Freeman: City of Cardiff, 1974; City of Sheffield, 1979. Hubert H. Humphrey Internat. Award, 1978. Grand Cross, 1st class, Order of Merit of Federal Republic of Germany, 1979. *Publications:* A House Divided: the dilemma of Northern Ireland, 1973; Time and Chance (autobiog.), 1987. *Address:* House of Lords, SW1A 0PW. *See also* Hon. Peter Jay.

CALLAGHAN, Sir Allan (Robert), Kt 1972; CMG 1945; agricultural consultant, retired; *b* 24 Nov. 1903; *s* of late Phillip George Callaghan and late Jane Peacock; *m* 1928, Zillah May Sampson (*d* 1964); two *s* one *d* (and one *s* decd); *m* 1965, Doreen Rhys Draper. *Educ:* Bathurst High Sch., NSW; St Paul's Coll., Univ. of Sydney (BSc Agr. 1924); St John's Coll., Oxford (Rhodes Scholar, BSc 1926, DPhil 1928). Asst Plant Breeder, NSW, Dept of Agriculture, 1928–32; Principal, Roseworthy Agricultural Coll., South Australia, 1932–49; Asst Dir (Rural Industry) in Commonwealth Dept of War Organisation of Industry, 1943; Chm., Land Development Executive in South Australia, 1945–51; Dir of

Agriculture, South Australia, 1949–59; Commercial Counsellor, Australian Embassy, Washington, DC, 1959–65; Chm., Australian Wheat Bd, 1965–71. Farrer Medal (for distinguished service to Australian Agriculture), 1954; FAIAS 1959. *Publications:* (with A. J. Millington) The Wheat Industry in Australia, 1956; numerous articles in scientific and agricultural jls on agricultural and animal husbandry matters. *Recreations:* swimming, riding, gardening. *Address:* Tralee, 22 Murray Street, Clapham, SA 5062, Australia. *T:* 276–6524.

CALLAGHAN, Sir Bede (Bertrand), Kt 1976; CBE 1968; Managing Director, Commonwealth Banking Corporation, 1965–76; Chancellor of the University of Newcastle, NSW, 1977–88; *b* 16 March 1912; *s* of S. K. Callaghan and Amy M. Ryan; *m* 1940, Mary T. Brewer; three *d*. *Educ:* Newcastle High Sch. FAIB; FAIM. Commonwealth Bank, 1927. Mem. Board Executive Directors, IMF and World Bank, 1954–59; Gen. Man., Commonwealth Develt Bank of Australia, 1959–65; Chm., Aust. European Finance Corp. Ltd, 1971–76; Chm., Foreign Investment Review Bd, 1976–. Chm., Lewisham Hospital Adv. Bd, 1975–87. Chairman: Aust. Admin. Staff Coll., 1969–76; Inst. of Industrial Economics, 1976–88; Mem. Council, Univ. of Newcastle, NSW, 1966–88, Dep. Chancellor, 1973–77. Hon. DSc Newcastle, 1973. *Recreation:* lawn bowls. *Address:* 69 Darnley Street, Gordon, NSW 2072, Australia. *T:* (Sydney) 498–7583. *Club:* Union (Sydney).

CALLAGHAN, Rev. Brendan Alphonsus, SJ; Principal of Heythrop College, University of London, since 1985; *b* 29 July 1948; *s* of Dr Kathleen Callaghan (*née* Kavanagh) and Dr Alphonsus Callaghan. *Educ:* Stonyhurst; Heythrop, Oxon; Campion Hall, Oxford (MA 1977); Univ. of Glasgow (MPhil 1976); Heythrop Coll., Univ. of London (MTh 1979). FRSM; AFBPsS; CPsychol. Joined Society of Jesus, 1967; Clinical Psychologist, Glasgow, 1974–76; Middx Hosp., 1976–79; ordained priest, 1978; curate, St Aloysius, Glasgow, 1979–80; Lectr in Psychology, Heythrop, 1980–, Allen Hall, Chelsea, 1981–87. University of London: Chm., Bd of Examrs, Theol and Religious Studies, 1987–89; Schools Examn Bd, 1987–; Collegiate Council and Senate, 1989–; Institute of Medical Ethics: Hon. Asst/Associate Dir, 1976–89; Governing Body, 1989–. Vis. Lectr, Oblate Sch. of Theology, Natal, 1987; Vis. Prof., Fordham Univ., NY, 1990. Mem., Ethics Cttee, W Lambeth HA. Consultant Psychologist to Catholic Marriage Adv. Council, and to religious congregations and orders. *Publications:* Life Before Birth (with K. Boyd and E. Shotter), 1986; articles, reviews and verse in Br. JL Psych, Jl Med. Ethics, Heythrop Jl and magazines. *Recreations:* photography, long distance walking, poetry. *Address:* Heythrop College, 11–13 Cavendish Square, W1M 0AN. *T:* 071–580 6941, *Fax:* 071–580 5031.

CALLAGHAN, Rear-Adm. Desmond Noble, CB 1970; FRSA; Director-General, National Supervisory Council for Intruder Alarms, 1971–77; *b* 24 Nov. 1915; *s* of Edmund Ford Callaghan and Kathleen Louise Callaghan (*née* Noble): *m* 1948, Patricia Munro Geddes; one *s* two *d*. *Educ:* RNC Dartmouth. HMS Frobisher, 1933; RNEC Keyhan, 1934; HM Ships: Royal Oak, 1937; Iron Duke, 1938; Warspite, 1939; Hereward, 1941; Prisoner of War, 1941; HMS Argonaut, 1945; HMS Glory, 1946; RNC Dartmouth, 1947; Admiralty, 1949; C-in-C Med. Staff, 1950; HMS Excellent, 1953; HMS Eagle, 1956; RN Tactical Sch., 1958; Admiralty, 1960; HMS Caledonia, 1962; Admiralty, 1965; Vice-Pres. and Pres., Ordnance Board, 1968–71, retired 1971. *Recreations:* Rugby, tennis, swimming. *Address:* Bridge End, Abbotsbrook, Bourne End, Bucks SL8 5RE. *T:* Bourne End (06285) 20519.

CALLAGHAN, James; MP (Lab) Heywood and Middleton (Middleton and Prestwich, Feb. 1974–1983); *b* 28 Jan. 1927. Lectr, Manchester Coll., 1959–74. Metropolitan Borough Councillor, 1971–74. *Recreations:* sport and art. *Address:* 17 Towncroft Avenue, Middleton, Manchester.

CALLAN, Prof. Harold Garnet, FRS 1963; FRSE; MA, DSc; Professor of Natural History, St Salvator's College, St Andrews, 1950–82, now Emeritus; *b* 5 March 1917; *s* of Garnet George Callan and Winifred Edith Brazier; *m* 1944, Amarillis Maria Speranza, *d* of Dr R. Dohrn, Stazione Zoologica, Naples, Italy; one *s* two *d*. *Educ:* King's Coll. Sch., Wimbledon; St John's Coll., Oxford (Exhibitioner; Hon. Fellow, 1988). Casberd Scholar, St John's Coll., 1937; Naples Biological Scholar, 1938, 1939. Served War of 1939–45, Telecommunications Research Establishment, 1940–45, Hon. Commission, RAFVR. Senior Scientific Officer, ARC, Inst. of Animal Genetics, Edinburgh, 1946–50. Member: Advisory Council on Scientific Policy, 1963–64; SRC, 1972–76; Council, Royal Soc., 1974–76. Trustee, British Museum (Natural History), 1963–66. Vis. Prof., Univ. of Indiana, Bloomington, USA, 1964–65; Master of United Coll. of St Salvator and St Leonard's, 1967–68. Hon. Foreign Member: American Acad. of Arts and Scis, 1974; Accademia Nazionale dei Lincei, 1982. Hon. DSc St Andrews, 1984. *Publications:* Lampbrush Chromosomes, 1986; scientific papers, mostly on cytology and cell physiology. *Recreations:* shooting, carpentry. *Address:* 2 St Mary's Street, St Andrews, Fife KY16 8AY. *T:* St Andrews (0334) 72311.

CALLAN, Ivan Roy, CMG 1990; HM Diplomatic Service; Counsellor, Foreign and Commonwealth Office, since 1991; *b* 6 April 1942; *s* of Roy Ivan Callan and (Gladys) May Callan (*née* Coombe); *m* 1st, 1965, Hilary Flashman; one *d*; 2nd, 1987, Mary Catherine Helena Williams; two step *s* one step *d*. *Educ:* Reading Sch.; University Coll., Oxford. BA, Dip. Soc. Anthrop., BLitt, MA. Entered FCO, 1969; Middle East Centre for Arab Studies, 1970–71; Second, later First Sec., Beirut, 1971–75; FCO, 1975–80; First Sec. and Head of Chancery, Ottawa, 1980–83; Counsellor, Hd of Chancery and Consul-General, Baghdad, 1983–87; Consul-General, Jerusalem, 1987–90. *Address:* c/o Foreign and Commonwealth Office, King Charles Street, SW1A 2AH. *Club:* Commonwealth Trust.

CALLAN, Maj.-Gen. Michael, CB 1979; *b* 27 Nov. 1925; *s* of Major John Callan and Elsie Dorothy Callan (*née* Fordham); *m* 1948, Marie Evelyn Farthing; two *s*. *Educ:* Farnborough Grammar Sch., Hants. rcds, jssc, psc. Enlisted Hampshire Regt, 1943; commnd 1st (KGV's Own) Gurkha Rifles (The Malaun Regt), 1944; resigned commn, 1947; re-enlisted, 1948; re-commnd, RAOC, 1949; overseas service: India, Burma, French Indo China, Netherlands East Indies, 1944–47; Kenya, 1950–53; Malaya/Singapore, 1958–61; USA, 1966–68; Hong Kong, 1970–71; Comdr, Rhine Area, BAOR, 1975–76; Dir Gen., Ordnance Services, 1976–80. Col Comdt, RAOC, 1981–89; Hon. Col, SW London ACF, 1982–89. Registrar, Corporation of the Sons of the Clergy, 1982–83; consultant in defence logistics and admin, 1984–89. *Recreations:* sailing, DIY, gardening. *Address:* c/o Royal Bank of Scotland, Kirkland House, Whitehall, SW1A 2EB.

CALLARD, Sir Eric John, (Sir Jack Callard), Kt 1974; FEng; Chairman, British Home Stores Ltd, 1976–82 (Director 1975–82); *b* 15 March 1913; *s* of late F. Callard and Mrs A. Callard; *m* 1938, Pauline M. Pengelly; three *d*. *Educ:* Queen's Coll., Taunton; St John's Coll., Cambridge. 1st cl. Hons Mech. Sci. Tripos; BA 1935; MA 1973; Harvard Business Sch. (Adv. Management Programme, 1953). Joined ICI Ltd, 1935; seconded to Min. of Aircraft Prodn, 1942; ICI Paints Div., 1947 (Jt Man. Dir, 1955–59; Chm., 1959–64); Chairman: Deleg. Bd, ICI (Hyde) Ltd, 1959; ICI (Europa) Ltd, 1965–67; ICI Ltd, 1971–75 (Dir, 1964–75; Dep. Chm., 1967–71); Director: Pension Funds Securities Ltd, 1963–67; Imp. Metal Industries Ltd, 1964–67; Imp. Chemicals Insurance Ltd, 1966–70; Midland Bank Ltd, 1971–87; Ferguson Industrial Holdings, 1975–86; Commercial Union Assurance Co., 1976–83; Equity Capital for Industry, 1976–84. Member Council: BIM, 1964–69; Manchester Univ. Business Sch., 1964–71; Export Council for Europe, 1965–71; Member: CBI Steering Cttee on Europe, 1965–71; Cambridge Univ. Appointments Bd, 1968–71; CBI Overseas Cttee, 1969–71; Council of Industry for Management Educn, 1967–73; Royal Instn of GB, 1971–; Vice-Pres., Manchester Business Sch. Assoc., 1971– (Hon. Mem., 1966–; Pres., 1969–71); Pres., Industrial Participation Assoc., 1971–76 (Chm., 1967–71). Member: Hansard Soc. Commn on Electoral Reform, 1975–76; Cttee of Inquiry into Industrial Democracy, 1976–77. Trustee, Civic Trust, 1972–75; Governor, London Business Sch., 1972–75. Mem. Court, British Shippers' Council, 1972–75. FRSA 1970; CBIM (FBIM 1966); Hon. FIMechE. Hon. DSc Cranfield Inst. of Technology, 1974. *Recreations:* games, fishing. *Address:* Crookwath Cottage, High Row, Dockray, Penrith, Cumbria CA11 0LG. *Club:* Flyfishers'.

CALLAWAY, Betty; *see* Callaway-Fittall, B. D.

CALLAWAY, Sir Frank (Adams), Kt 1981; CMG 1975; OBE 1970; Professor and Head of Department of Music, University of Western Australia, 1959–84, Professor Emeritus, since 1985; *b* 16 May 1919; *s* of Archibald Charles Callaway and Mabel Callaway (*née* Adams); *m* 1942, Kathleen Jessie, *d* of R. Allan; two *s* two *d*. *Educ:* West Christchurch High Sch.; Dunedin Teachers' Coll., NZ; Univ. of Otago, NZ (MusB); Royal Academy of Music. FRAM, ARCM, FTCL; FACE. Head, Dept of Music, King Edward Tech. Coll., Dunedin, NZ, 1942–53; Reader in Music, Univ. of WA, 1953–59. Mem., RNZAF Band, 1940–42. Conductor: King Edward Tech. Coll. Symphony Orchestra, 1945–53; Univ. of WA Orchestral Soc., 1953–64; Univ. of WA Choral Soc., 1953–79; Guest Conductor: WA Symphony Orchestra; S Australia Symphony Orchestra; Adelaide Philharmonic Choir; Orpheus Choir, Wellington, NZ. Member: Australian Music Exams Bd, 1955–84 (Chm., 1964–66 and 1977–79); Adv. Bd, Commonwealth Assistance to Australian Composers, 1966–72; Australian Nat. Commn for UNESCO, 1968–82; Exec. Bd, Internat. Music Council of UNESCO, 1976–82 (Pres., 1980–81; Individual Mem., 1982–85, Life Mem. of Honour, 1986); Music Bd, Australia Council, 1969–74; Chairman: WA Arts Adv. Bd, 1970–73; WA Arts Council, 1973–79; Organizing Cttees, Aust. Nat. Eisteddfod 1979, Indian Ocean Fests, 1979, 1984; Indian Ocean Arts Assoc., 1980–85 (Pres., 1985–). Founding Pres. and Life Mem., Australian Soc. for Music Educn, 1966–71; Mem., Bd of Dirs, Internat. Soc. for Music Educn, 1958– (Pres., 1968–72, Treasurer, 1972–88, Hon. Pres., 1988–). Chm., Bd of Dirs, Internat. Acad. of Music, Nairobi, Kenya, 1985–; External Examiner (Music), Kenyatta Univ., Nairobi, 1985–87; Consultant, Frank Gallaway Internat. Resource Centre for Music Educn (Univ. of WA), 1988–. Foundn Mem., 1983, Pres., 1984–, WA Br., Lord's Taverners Australia. Founding Editor: Australian Jl of Music Educn, 1967–82; Studies in Music, 1967–84; Internat. Jl of Music Educn, 1983–85; also General Editor, Music Series and Music Monographs. W Australian Citizen of the Year, 1975. Hon. MusD: W Australia, 1975; Melbourne, 1982. Aust. Nat. Critics' Circle Award for Music, 1977; Sir Bernard Heinze Award for Service to Australian Music, 1988. *Publications:* (General Editor) Challenges in Music Education, 1975; (ed with D. E. Tunley) Australian Composition in the Twentieth Century, 1978. *Recreations:* reading, gardening, cricket. *Address:* 16 The Lane, Churchlands, WA 6018, Australia. *T:* 387.3345.

CALLAWAY-FITTALL, Betty Daphne, (Betty Callaway), MBE 1984; trainer of skaters; skating consultant to Ice Arena, Slough, since 1986; *b* 22 March 1928; *d* of William A. Roberts and Elizabeth T. Roberts; *m* 1st, 1949, E. Roy Callaway; 2nd, 1980, Captain W. Fittall (*d* 1990), British Airways, retd. *Educ:* Greycoat Sch., and St Paul's Convent, Westminster. Started teaching, Richmond Ice Rink, 1952; Nat. Trainer, W Germany, 1969–72; retired from full-time teaching, 1972. Commentator, ITV, 1984–. Pupils include: Angelika and Erich Buck (European Champions and 2nd in World Championship, 1972); Chrisztine Regoczy and Andras Sally (Hungarian and World Champions and Olympic silver medallists, 1980); Jayne Torvill and Christopher Dean (World Champions, 1981, 1982, 1983, 1984, European Champions, 1981, 1982, and Olympic gold medallists, 1984). Hon. Citizen, Ravensburg, Germany, 1972. Gold Medal, Nat. Skating Assoc., 1955; Hungarian Olympic Medal, 1980. *Recreations:* music, water ski-ing, gardening. *Address:* 35 Long Grove, Seer Green, Beaconsfield, Bucks HP9 2YN.

CALLENDER, Dr Maurice Henry; Ministry of Defence, 1977–80; retired, 1980; *b* 18 Dec. 1916; *s* of Harry and Lizbeth Callender; *m* 1941, Anne Kassel; two *s*. *Educ:* Univ. of Durham (MA, PhD). FSA. Commissioned: Royal Northumberland Fusiliers, 1939–41; RAF, 1941–45. Lectr, Huddersfield Technical Coll., 1945–47; Research, Univ. of Durham, 1947–49; Lectr, Bristol Univ. Extra-Mural Dept, 1949–53; MoD, 1953–62; Joint Services Staff Coll., 1959–60; Cabinet Office, 1962–64; MoD, 1964–70; Cabinet Office, 1970–73; Counsellor, Canberra, 1973–77. *Publications:* Roman Amphorae, 1965; various articles in archaeological jls. *Recreations:* oil painting, golf, bridge. *Address:* 24 Glanleam Road, Stanmore, Mddx. *T:* 081–954 1435. *Club:* Aldenham Golf and Country.

CALLER, Maxwell Marshall; Chief Executive, London Borough of Barnet, since 1989; *b* 9 Feb. 1951; *s* of Abraham Leon Caller and Cynthia Rachel Caller; *m* 1972, Linda Ann Wohlberg; three *s* one *d*. *Educ:* Newport High Sch.; University Coll. London (BSc Hons Engrg). CEng, MICE; MIWEM; CDipAF. GLC, 1972–74; Thames Water Authority, 1974–75; London Boroughs of: Hammersmith, 1975–78; Newham, 1978–81; Merton, 1981–85 (Asst Dir of Development); Barnet: Controller of Engrg Services, 1985–87; Dir of Technical Services, 1987–89. Adviser, Highways Cttee 1987–89, Public Works Cttee 1990–, AMA. *Recreations:* picking bluebells with Claire, work. *Address:* Town Hall, The Burroughs, Hendon, NW4 4BG. *T:* 081–202 8282.

CALLEY, Sir Henry (Algernon), Kt 1964; DSO 1945; DFC 1943; DL; Owner and Manager of a stud, since 1948; *b* 9 Feb. 1914; *s* of Rev. A. C. M. Langton and Mrs Langton (*née* Calley); changed surname to Calley, 1974; unmarried. *Educ:* St John's Sch., Leatherhead. Taught at Corchester. Corbridge-on-Tyne, 1933–35; Bombay Burmah Trading Corp., 1935–36; teaching, 1936–38; Metropolitan Police Coll., and Police Force, 1938–41; Royal Air Force, 1941–48; Pilot in Bombers, Actg Wing Comdr, 1944. Mem. Wiltshire CC, 1955; Chm. Finance Cttee, 1959–68; Chm. of Council, 1968–73; Chm. Wessex Area Conservative Assoc., 1963–66. DL Wilts, 1968.

CALLIL, Carmen Thérèse; Chairman, Virago Press, since 1972 (Managing Director, 1972–82); Managing Director, Chatto & Windus: The Hogarth Press, since 1983; *b* 15 July 1938; *d* of Frederick Alfred Louis Callil and Lorraine Clare Allen. *Educ:* Star of the Sea Convent, Gardenvale, Melbourne; Loreto Convent, Mandeville Hall, Melbourne; Melbourne Univ. (BA). Buyer's Asst, Marks & Spencer, 1963–65; Editorial Assistant: Hutchinson Publishing Co., 1965–66; B. T. Batsford, 1966–67; Publicity Manager, Panther Books, later also of Granada Publishing, 1967–70; André Deutsch, 1971–72; publicity for Ink newspaper, 1972; founded Carmen Callil Ltd, book publicity co., 1972; founded Virago Press, 1972, incorp. as co., 1973. Mem. Bd, Channel 4, 1985–. FRSA. *Recreations:* friends, reading, animals, films, gardening. *Address:* 20 Vauxhall Bridge Road, SW1V 2SA. *Club:* Groucho (Dir).

CALLINAN, Sir Bernard (James), AC 1986; Kt 1977; CBE 1971; DSO 1945; MC 1943; Consultant, Gutteridge, Haskins & Davey Pty Ltd, 1978–81 (Chairman and Managing Director, 1971–78); *b* 2 Feb. 1913; *s* of Michael Joseph Callinan and Mary Callinan (*née* Prendergast); *m* 1943, Naomi Marian Callinan (*née* Cullinan); five *s*. *Educ:* Univ. of Melbourne (BCE; Dip. Town and Regional Planning). Hon. FIE Aust (Pres., 1971–72; P. N. Russell Meml Medal, 1973); FICE; FTS. Lieut to Lt-Col, AIF, 1940–46. Asst Engr, A. Gordon Gutteridge, 1934; Associate, 1946, Sen. Partner, 1948–71, Gutteridge, Haskins & Davey. Chm., CCI Insurances Ltd, 1984–; Director: West Gate Bridge Authority, 1965– (Dep. Chm., 1971–81, Chm., 1981–82); British Petroleum Co. of Aust. Ltd, 1969–85; CSR Ltd, 1978–85. Commissioner: State Electricity Commn, 1963–83; Royal Commn of Inquiry, Aust. PO, 1973–74; Aust. Atomic Energy Commn, 1976–82; Australian Broadcasting Commn, 1977–82; Victorian Post Secondary Educn Commn, 1979–82. Chm., New Parlt House Authority (Canberra), 1979–85. Special Advr, Aust. Overseas Project Corp., 1978–82. Pres., Royal Humane Soc. of Australasia, 1986– (Dir, 1979–). Mem., Pontifical Commn on Justice and Peace, Rome, 1977–82. Councillor: La Trobe Univ., 1964–72; Melbourne Univ., 1976–81. Hon. Col, 4/19 Prince of Wales's Light Horse Regt, 1973–78. Hon. DEng Monash, 1984; Hon. LLD Melbourne, 1987. Kernot Meml Medal, Melbourne Univ., 1982. *Publications:* Independent Company, 1953, 3rd impression 1989; John Monash, 1981; contribs to Jl Instn of Engrs, Aust., Jl Royal Soc. of Vic. *Address:* 111 Sackville Street, Kew, Vic 3101, Australia. *T:* 817.1230. *Clubs:* Melbourne, Australian, Naval and Military (Melbourne); Melbourne Cricket (Pres., 1979–85).

CALLMAN, Clive Vernon; His Honour Judge Callman; a Circuit Judge, since 1973, assigned to South-Eastern Circuit; *b* 21 June 1927; *o s* of Felix Callman, DMD, LDS, RCS and Edith Callman, Walton-on-Thames, Surrey; *m* 1967, Judith Helen Hines, BA, DipSocStuds (Adelaide), *o d* of Gus Hines, OBE, JP, and Hilde Hines, St George's, Adelaide, S Aust.; one *s* one *d*. *Educ:* Ottershaw Coll.; St George's Coll., Weybridge; LSE, Univ. of London. BSc(Econ), Commercial Law. Called to the Bar, Middle Temple, 1951; Blackstone Pupillage Prizeman, 1951; practised as Barrister, London and Norwich, 1952–73 (Head of London chambers, 1963), South-Eastern Circuit; Hon. Mem., Central Criminal Court Bar Mess; Dep. Circuit Judge in Civil and Criminal Jurisdiction, 1971–73. Dir, Woburn Press, Publishers, 1971–73; dir of finance cos, 1961–73. University of London: Fac. Mem., Standing Cttee of Convocation, 1954–79; Senator, 1978–; Mem. Careers Adv. Bd, 1979–; Mem., Commerce Degree Bureau Cttee, 1980; Mem., Adv. Cttee for Magistrates' Courses, 1979–; Vice-Pres., Graduates' Soc.; Governor: Birkbeck Coll., 1982–; LSE, 1990–. Mem. Exec. Cttee, Soc. of Labour Lawyers, 1958; Chm., St Marylebone Constituency Labour Party, 1960–62. Mem. Council, Anglo-Jewish Assoc., 1956–. Editor, Clare Market Review, 1947; Member Editorial Board: Media Law and Practice, 1980–; Professional Negligence, 1985–; Jl of Child Law, 1989–. *Recreations:* reading, travelling, the arts. *Address:* 11 Constable Close, NW11 6UA. *T:* 081–458 3010. *Club:* Bar Yacht.

CALLOW, Henry William; His Honour Deemster Callow; HM Second Deemster, Isle of Man, since 1988; *b* 16 May 1926; 2nd *s* of Frederick Henry Callow and Elizabeth Callow (*née* Cowley); *m* 1952, Mary Elaine Corlett. *Educ:* Douglas High Sch.; King William's Coll., IOM. Served Army, 1945–48. Advocate, Manx Bar, 1950; High Bailiff and Coroner of Inquests, IOM, 1969–88; Chairman: IOM Criminal Injuries Compensation Tribunal, 1988–; IOM Licensing Appeal Court, 1988–. Chairman of Trustees: Noble's Hosp., IOM, 1987–; Ellan Vannin Home, 1988–. *Recreations:* music, walking. *Address:* 8 Marlborough Crescent, Clifton Park, Lezayre, Isle of Man. *T:* IOM (0624) 81–5929. *Clubs:* Manx Automobile (Douglas); Laxey Sailing (Laxey).

CALLOW, Simon Phillip Hugh; actor and director; *b* 15 June 1949; *s* of Neil Callow and Yvonne Mary Callow. *Educ:* London Oratory Grammar Sch.; Queen's Univ. Belfast; Drama Centre. London productions include: Schippel, 1975; A Mad World My Masters, 1977; Arturo Ui, Mary Barnes, 1978; As You Like It, Amadeus, NT, 1979; The Beastly Beatitudes of Balthazar B, Total Eclipse, Restoration, 1981; The Relapse, 1983; On the Spot, 1984; Kiss of the Spider Woman, 1985; Faust I and II, Lyric, Hammersmith, 1988; Single Spies (double bill: A Question of Attribution (also dir); An Englishman Abroad), NT, 1988, Queen's, 1989; *directed:* Loving Reno, Bush, 1984; The Passport, 1985, Nicolson Fights, Croydon, 1986, Offstage; Amadeus, Theatr Clwyd, 1986; The Infernal Machine, 1986; Così fan Tutte, Switzerland, 1987; Jacques and his Master, LA, 1987; Shirley Valentine, Vaudeville, 1988, NY, 1989; Die Fledermaus, Theatre Royal, Glasgow, 1988, 1989; Stevie Wants to Play the Blues, LA Theater Center, 1990; Carmen Jones, Old Vic, 1991; Ballad of the Sad Café, 1991. *Films:* Amadeus, 1983; A Room with a View, 1986; The Good Father, 1986; Maurice, 1987; Manifesto, 1988; Mr & Mrs Bridge, 1991; Postcards from the Edge, 1991; Crucifer of Blood, 1991. *Television series:* Chance in a Million, 1983, 1985–86; David Copperfield, 1986; *other television includes:* Cariani and the Courtesans, 1987; Charles Laughton (documentary), 1987; Old Flames, 1989; Revolutionary Witness, 1989. *Publications:* Being an Actor, 1984; A Difficult Actor: Charles Laughton, 1987; trans. Jacques et son Maître, by Kundera, 1986; trans. The Infernal Machine, by Jean Cocteau, 1987; Shooting the Actor, 1990. *Recreation:* planning the future of the British theatre. *Address:* c/o Marina Martin, 6a Danbury Street, N1 8JU. *T:* 071–359 3646.

CALMAN, Prof. Kenneth Charles; FRCP; FRCS; FRSE; Chief Medical Officer (at Department of Health and Social Security), Department of Education and Science, since 1991; *b* 25 Dec. 1941; *s* of Arthur McIntosh Calman and Grace Douglas Don; *m* 1967, Ann Wilkie; one *s* two *d*. *Educ:* Allan Glen's Sch., Glasgow; Univ. of Glasgow (BSc, MD, PhD). FRCSGlas 1971; FRCP 1985, FRCPE 1989; FRCGP 1989; MFCM 1989; FRCR 1990; FRCSE 1991; FRSE 1979. Hall Fellow in Surgery, Western Infirmary, Glasgow, 1968; Lectr in Surgery, Univ. of Glasgow, 1969; MRC Clinical Res. Fellow, Inst. of Cancer Res., London, 1972; University of Glasgow: Prof. of Clinical Oncology, 1974; Dean of Postgrad. Medicine and Prof. of Postgrad. Med. Educn, 1984–88; Chief Med. Officer, Scottish Office Home and Health Dept, 1989–91. *Publications:* Basic Skills for Clinical Housemen, 1971, 2nd edn 1983; Basic Principles of Cancer Chemotherapy, 1982; Invasion, 1984. *Publication:* Healthy Respect, 1987. *Recreations:* gardening, golf, collecting cartoons, Scottish literature. *Address:* 585 Anniesland Road, Glasgow G13 1UX. *T:* 041–954 9423.

CALMAN, Mel; artist, writer; cartoonist for The Times and others; *b* 19 May 1931; *s* of Clement and Anna Calman; *m* 1st, 1957, Pat McNeill (marr. diss.); two *d*; 2nd, Karen Usborne (marr. diss. 1982). *Educ:* Perse School, Cambridge; St Martin's School of Art, London (NDD); Goldsmiths' Coll., London (ATD). Cartoonist for Daily Express, 1957–63; BBC Tonight Programme, 1963–64; Sunday Telegraph, 1964–65; Observer, 1965–66; Sunday Times, 1969–84; The Times, 1979–. Free lance cartoonist for various magazines and newspapers, 1957–; also designer of book-jackets, advertising campaigns, and illustrator of books; started The Workshop-gallery, now The Cartoon Gall., devoted to original cartoons, illustrations etc., 1970; produced animated cartoon, The Arrow; syndicated feature, Men & Women, USA, 1976–82; original radio plays: Sweet Tooth, BBC Radio 3, 1987; Rabbit Man, BBC Radio 3, 1989. FRSA; FSIA; AGI. *Publications:* Through The Telephone Directory, 1962; Bed-Sit, 1963; Boxes, 1964; Calman & Women, 1967; The Penguin Calman, 1968; (contrib.) The Evacuees, ed B. S. Johnson, 1968; My God, 1970; Couples, 1972; This Pestered Isle, 1973; (contrib.) All Bull, ed B. S. Johnson, 1973; The New Penguin Calman, 1977; Dictionary of Psychoanalysis, 1979; "But It's My Turn to Leave You", 1980; "How About a Little Quarrel before Bed?", 1981; Help!, 1982; Calman Revisited, 1983; The Big Novel, 1983 (dramatised for radio, 1986); It's Only You That's Incompatible, 1984; "What Else Do You Do?" (autobiog.), 1986; Modern Times, 1988; Calman at the Movies, 1990; Merrie England plc, 1990; Calman at the Royal Opera House, 1990. *Recreations:* brooding and worrying. *Address:* 83 Lambs Conduit Street, WC1N 3NA. *T:* 071–242 5335. *Club:* Garrick.

CALNAN, Prof. Charles Dermod, MA, MB, BChir Cantab; FRCP; Director, Department of Occupational Dermatoses, St John's Hospital for Diseases of the Skin, 1974–82, retired; Honorary Consultant Dermatologist: Royal Free Hospital, 1958–82; St John's Hospital for Diseases of the Skin, London, 1958–82; *b* 14 Dec. 1917; *s* of James Calnan, Eastbourne, Sussex; *m* 1950, Josephine Gerard Keane, *d* of late Lt-Col Michael Keane, RAMC; three *s* one *d*. *Educ:* Stonyhurst Coll.; Corpus Christi Coll., Cambridge; London Hospital. 1st Cl. Hons Nat. Sci. Trip., Cambridge 1939. RAMC Specialist in Dermatology, Major, 1942–46; Marsden Prof., Royal Free Hosp., 1958; Visiting Research Associate, Univ. of Pennsylvania, 1959; Prof. of Dermatology, Inst. of Dermatology, 1960–74. WHO Cons. Adviser to Nat. Inst. of Dermatology of Thailand, 1971–. Editor: Transactions of the St John's Hosp. Dermatological Soc., 1958–75; Contact Dermatitis, 1975–. Mem. Brit. Assoc. of Dermatology. FRSocMed (Mem. Dermatological Section). Order of the White Elephant (Thailand), 1986. *Publications:* Atlas of Dermatology, 1974; various papers in med. and dermatological jls. *Recreations:* squash, books, theatre. *Address:* 109 Harley Street, W1.

CALNAN, Prof. James Stanislaus, FRCP; FRCS; Professor of Plastic and Reconstructive Surgery, University of London, at the Royal Postgraduate Medical School and Hammersmith Hospital, 1970–81, now Emeritus; *b* 12 March 1916; *e s* of James and Gertrude Calnan, Eastbourne, Sussex; *m* 1949, Joan (formerly County Councillor for Great Berkhamsted and Dacorum District Councillor, and Town Councillor, Berkhamsted), *e d* of George Frederick and Irene Maud Williams, Roath Park, Cardiff; one *d*. *Educ:* Stonyhurst Coll.; Univ. of London at London Hosp. Med. Sch. LDS RCS 1941; MRCS, LRCP 1943; DA 1944; DTM&H 1948; MRCP (London and Edinburgh) 1948; FRCS 1949. Served War of 1939–45, F/Lt RAF, UK, France, India. RMO, Hosp. for Tropical Diseases, 1948; Sen. Lectr, Nuffield Dept of Plastic Surgery, Oxford, 1954; Hammersmith Hospital and Royal Postgraduate Med. Sch.: Lectr in Surgery, 1960; Reader, 1965; Professor, 1970. Hunterian Prof. RCS, 1959. Vis. Prof. in Plastic Surgery, Univ. of Pennsylvania, 1959. Member: BMA, 1941–82; British Assoc. of Plastic Surgeons, 1949–71; Sen. Mem., Surgical Research Soc., 1962–. Fellow, Royal Soc. of Medicine, 1943; FCST 1966. Mem., Soc. of Authors, 1985–. Clemson Award for Bioengineering, 1980. *Publications:* Speaking at Medical Meetings, 1972, 2nd edn 1981; Writing Medical Papers, 1973; How to Speak and Write: a practical guide for nurses, 1975; One Way to do Research, 1976; Talking with Patients, 1983; Coping with Research: the complete guide for beginners, 1984; The Hammersmith 1935–1985: the first 50 years of the Royal Postgraduate Medical School, 1985; Principles of Surgical Research, 1989; contribs to medical and scientific jls and chapters in books, on cleft palate, wound healing, lymphatic diseases, venous thrombosis, research methods and organisation. *Recreations:* gardening, carpentry, reading and writing. *Address:* White Haven, 23 Kings Road, Berkhamsted, Herts HP4 3BH. *T:* Berkhamsted (0442) 862320; Royal Postgraduate Medical School, Ducane Road, W12 0HS. *T:* 081–743 2030.

See also Prof. C. D. Calnan.

CALNE, Sir Roy (Yorke), Kt 1986; MA, MS; FRCS; FRS 1974; Professor of Surgery, University of Cambridge, since 1965; Fellow of Trinity Hall, Cambridge, since 1965; Hon. Consulting Surgeon, Addenbrooke's Hospital, Cambridge, since 1965; *b* 30 Dec. 1930; *s* of Joseph Robert and Eileen Calne; *m* 1956, Patricia Doreen Whelan; two *s* four *d*. *Educ:* Lancing Coll.; Guy's Hosp. Med. Sch. MB, BS London with Hons (Distinction in Medicine), 1953. House Appts, Guy's Hosp., 1953–54; RAMC, 1954–56 (RMO to KEO 2nd Gurkhas); Deptl Anatomy Demonstrator, Oxford Univ., 1957–58; SHO Nuffield Orthopædic Centre, Oxford, 1958; Surg. Registrar, Royal Free Hosp., 1958–60; Harkness Fellow in Surgery, Peter Bent Brigham Hosp., Harvard Med. Sch., 1960–61; Lectr in Surgery, St Mary's Hosp., London, 1961–62; Sen. Lectr and Cons. Surg., Westminster Hosp., 1962–65. Royal Coll. of Surgeons: Hallet Prize, 1957; Jacksonian Prize, 1961; Hunterian Prof., 1962; Cecil Joll Prize, 1966; Mem. Ct of Examiners, 1970–76; Mem. Council, 1981–90; Vice-Pres., 1986–89; Hunterian Orator, 1989. Fellow Assoc. of Surgeons of Gt Brit.; Mem. Surgical Research Soc.; Pres., European Soc. for Organ Transplantation, 1983–84; Corresp. Fellow, Amer. Surgical Assoc., 1972, Hon. Fellow 1981; Hon. FRCP 1989. Hon. MD Oslo Univ., 1986. Prix de la Société Internationale de Chirurgie, 1969; Faltin Medal, Finnish Surgical Soc., 1977; Lister Medal, 1984; Fothergill Gold Medal, Med. Soc. of London, 1989; Cameron Prize, Edinburgh Univ., 1990; Ellison-Cliffe Medal, 1990. *Publications:* Renal Transplantations, 1963, 2nd edn 1967; (with H. Ellis) Lecture Notes in Surgery, 1965, 7th edn 1987; A Gift of Life, 1970; (ed and contrib.) Clinical Organ Transplantation, 1971; (ed and contrib.) Immunological Aspects of Transplantation Surgery, 1973; (ed and contrib.) Liver Transplantation, 1983; (ed and contrib.) Transplantation Immunology, 1984; Surgical Anatomy of the Abdomen in the Living Subject, 1988; papers on tissue transplantation and general surgery; sections in several surgical text-books. *Recreations:* tennis, squash, painting. *Address:* 22 Barrow Road, Cambridge. *T:* Cambridge (0223) 59831.

CALNE AND CALSTONE, Viscount; Simon Henry George Petty-Fitzmaurice; *b* 24 Nov. 1970; *s* and *heir* of Earl of Shelburne, *qv*.

CALOVSKI, Mitko; Yugoslav Ambassador to the Court of St James's and to the Republic of Ireland, 1985–89; *b* 3 April 1930; *m* Ilvana; one *s* one *d*. *Educ:* Higher School of Journalism and Diplomacy, Univ. of Belgrade. Posts with Federal Agencies, 1952–63; with Federal Board, later with Federal Conf. of Socialist Alliance of Working People of Yugoslavia, 1963–67; Consul-General in Toronto, Canada, 1967–71; Dir of Analysis and Policy Planning, Fed. Secretariat for Foreign Affairs, 1971–74; Dep. Sec.-Gen. of the Presidency, 1974–77; Ambassador to Canada, 1977–81; Mem., Federal Exec. Council and Federal Sec. for Information, 1982–85. Mem. of Yugoslavian Delegns to UN Gen. Assembly, non-aligned Summit and ministerial confs. *Address:* c/o Yugoslav Embassy, 5 Lexham Gardens, W8. *T:* 071–370 6105.

CALTHORPE; *see* Anstruther-Gough-Calthorpe, and Gough-Calthorpe.

CALTHORPE, 10th Baron *cr* 1796; **Peter Waldo Somerset Gough-Calthorpe;** Bt 1728; *b* 13 July 1927; *s* of late Hon. Frederick Somerset Gough-Calthorpe and Rose Mary Dorothy, *d* of late Leveson William Vernon-Harcourt; *S* brother, 1945; *m* 1st, 1956, Saranne (marr. diss. 1971; she *d* 1984), *o d* of James Harold Alexander, Ireland; 2nd, 1979, Elizabeth, *d* of James and Sibyl Young, Guildford, Surrey. *Heir:* none. *Address:* c/o Isle of Man Bank, 2 Athol Street, Douglas, Isle of Man.

CALVERLEY, 3rd Baron *cr* 1945; **Charles Rodney Muff;** Member of the West Yorkshire Metropolitan Police; *b* 2 Oct. 1946; *s* of 2nd Baron Calverley and of Mary, *d* of Arthur Farrar, Halifax; *S* father, 1971; *m* 1972, Barbara Ann, *d* of Jonathan Brown, Kelbrook, nr Colne; two *s*. *Educ:* Fulneck School for Boys. *Heir: s* Hon. Jonathan Edward Muff, *b* 16 April 1975. *Address:* 110 Buttershaw Lane, Wibsey, Bradford, W Yorks BD6 2DA.

CALVERT, Mrs Barbara Adamson, QC 1975; barrister-at-law; a Recorder of the Crown Court, since 1980; *b* 30 April 1926; *d* of late Albert Parker, CBE; *m* 1948, John Thornton Calvert, CBE (*d* 1987); one *s* one *d*. *Educ:* St Helen's, Northwood; London Sch. of Economics (BScEcon). Called to Bar, Middle Temple, 1959, Bencher 1982; admitted Sen. Bar of NI, 1978. Admin. Officer, City and Guilds of London Inst., 1961; practice at Bar, 1962–. Full-time Chm., Industrial Tribunals, London, 1986– (part-time Chm., 1974–86); Mem., Matrimonial Causes Rules Cttee, 1983–85. *Recreations:* gardening, swimming, poetry. *Address:* (home) 158 Ashley Gardens, SW1P 1HW; (chambers) 4 Brick Court, Temple, EC4Y 7AN. *Club:* Royal Fowey Yacht.

CALVERT, Denis; *see* Calvert, L. V. D.

CALVERT, Florence Irene, (Mrs W. A. Prowse); Principal, St Mary's College, University of Durham, 1975–77; *b* 1 March 1912; *d* of Ernest William Calvert and Florence Alice (*née* Walton); *m* 1977, William Arthur Prowse (*d* 1981). *Educ:* Univ. of Sheffield (BA, 1st Cl. Hons French and Latin, MA). Asst Language Teacher, Accrington Grammar Sch., 1936–39; Head, Modern Langs Dept, Accrington Girls' High Sch., 1939–48; Univ. of Durham: Lectr in Educn, 1948; Sen. Lectr, 1964–75. *Publications:* French Plays for the Classroom, 1951; L'Homme aux Mains Rouges, 1954; Contes, 1957; French by Modern Methods in Primary and Secondary Schools, 1965. *Address:* 7 St Mary's Close, Shincliffe, Durham DH1 2ND. *T:* Durham (091) 3865502.

CALVERT, Henry Reginald, Dr Phil; Keeper of Department of Astronomy and Geophysics in Science Museum, South Kensington, 1949–67; Keeper Emeritus, 1967–69; *b* 25 Jan. 1904; *e s* of late H. T. Calvert, MBE, DSc, of Min. of Health; *m* 1938, Eileen Mary Frow (*d* 1990); two *d*. *Educ:* Bridlington Sch., East Yorks; St John's Coll., Oxford (Scholar, MA); Univ. of Göttingen, Germany (Dr Phil). 1st Cl. Hons BSc (External) London, 1925; Goldsmiths' Company's Exhibitioner, 1925. Research Physicist, ICI, 1928–30; Research Physicist, Callender's Cable & Construction Co., 1932–34. Entered Science Museum, 1934; Dep. Keeper, 1946. Ballistics research for Min. of Supply, 1940–46. Hon. Treas., British Soc. for History of Science, 1952–63. Fellow Royal Astronomical Soc. *Publications:* Astronomy, Globes, Orreries and other Models, 1967; Scientific Trade Cards, 1971; papers in learned journals. *Recreations:* chess, bridge, croquet, gardening. *Address:* 17 Burnham Drive, Reigate, Surrey RH2 9HD. *T:* Reigate (0737) 246893.

CALVERT, (Louis Victor) Denis, CB 1985; Comptroller and Auditor General for Northern Ireland, 1980–89, retired; *b* 20 April 1924; *s* of Louis Victor Calvert, Belfast and Gertrude Cherry Hobson, Belfast; *m* 1949, Vivien Millicent Lawson; two *s* one *d*. *Educ:* Belfast Royal Academy; Queen's Univ., Belfast (BScEcon); Admin. Staff Coll., Henley-on-Thames. Served with RAF, 1943–47, navigator (F/O). Northern Ireland Civil Service, 1947–80: Min. of Agriculture, 1947–56; Dep. Principal 1951; Principal, Min. of Finance, 1956–63; Min. of Health and Local Govt, 1963–65; Asst Sec. 1964; Min. of Development, 1965–73; Sen. Asst Sec. 1970; Dep. Sec. 1971; Min. of Housing, Local Govt and Planning, 1973–76; DoE for NI, 1976–80. Mem. Bd, Internat. Fund for Ireland, 1989–. *Recreations:* gardening, golf, reading.

CALVERT, Norman Hilton; retired; Deputy Secretary, Departments of the Environment and of Transport, 1978–80; *b* 27 July 1925; *s* of Clifford and Doris Calvert; *m* 1st, 1949, May Yates (*d* 1968); one *s* one *d*; 2nd, 1971, Vera Baker. *Educ:* Leeds Modern Sch.; Leeds Univ.; King's Coll., Durham Univ. BA Hons 1st cl. Geography, 1950. Served Royal Signals, 1943–47: 81 (W African) Div., India, 1945–47. Min. of Housing and Local Govt: Asst Principal, 1950–55; Principal, 1956–64; Asst Sec., 1964–71; Sec., Water Resources Bd, 1964–68; Principal Regional Officer, Northern Region, 1969–71; Regional Dir, Northern Region, and Chm, Northern Econ. Planning Bd, 1971–73; Under Sec., DoE, 1971–78. *Recreations:* fell walking, listening to music, motoring. *Address:* 6 Monmouth Gardens, Beaminster, Dorset DT8 3BT. *T:* Beaminster (0308) 863366.

CALVERT, Phyllis; actress; *b* 18 Feb. 1915; *d* of Frederick and Annie Bickle; *m* 1941, Peter Murray Hill (*d* 1957); one *s* one *d*. *Educ:* Margaret Morris Sch.; Institut Français. Malvern Repertory Company, 1935; Coventry, 1937; York, 1938. First appeared in London in A Woman's Privilege, Kingsway Theatre, 1939; Punch Without Judy, Embassy, 1939; Flare Path, Apollo, 1942; Escapade, St James's, 1953; It's Never Too Late, Strand, 1954; River Breeze, Phoenix, 1956; The Complaisant Lover, Globe, 1959; The Rehearsal, Globe, 1961; Ménage à Trois, Lyric, 1963; Portrait of Murder, Savoy, Vaudeville, 1963; A Scent of Flowers, Duke of York's, 1964; Present Laughter, Queen's, 1965; A Woman of No Importance, Vaudeville, 1967; Blithe Spirit, Globe, 1970; Crown Matrimonial, Haymarket, 1973; Dear Daddy, Ambassadors, 1976; Mrs Warren's Profession, Worcester, 1977; She Stoops to Conquer, Old World, Exeter, 1978; Suite in Two Keys, tour, 1978; Before the Party, Queen's, 1980; Smithereens, Theatre Royal, Windsor, 1985; The Heiress, Chichester Fest., 1989. Started films, 1939. *Films include:* Kipps, The Young Mr Pitt, Man in Grey, Fanny by Gaslight, Madonna of the Seven Moons, They were Sisters, Time out of Mind, Broken Journey, My Own True Love, The Golden Madonna, A Woman with No Name, Mr Denning Drives North, Mandy, The Net, It's Never Too Late, Child in the House, Indiscreet, The Young and The Guilty, Oscar Wilde, Twisted Nerve, Oh! What a Lovely War, The Walking Stick. *Television* series and serials: Kate, 1970; Cover her Face, 1985; All Passion Spent, 1986; A Killing on the Exchange, 1987; Boon, 1987; Sophia and Constance, 1988; The Woman He Loved, 1988; Capsticks Law, 1989; plays: Death of a Heart, 1985; Across the Lake, 1988; Victoria Wood, 1989; After Henry, 1990. *Recreations:* swimming, gardening, collecting costume books. *Address:* Hill House, 118 High Street, Waddesdon, Bucks HP18 0JF.

CALVERT-SMITH, David; a Recorder of the Crown Court, since 1986; Senior Treasury Counsel, since 1991; *b* 6 April 1945; *s* of Arthur and Stella Calvert-Smith; *m* 1971, Marianthe Phoca. *Educ:* Eton; King's Coll., Cambridge (MA). Called to the Bar, Middle Temple, 1969; Jun. Treasury Counsel, 1986. *Recreations:* music, sports. *Address:* Queen Elizabeth Building, Temple, EC4. *T:* 071-583 5766.

CALVET, Jacques; President, Peugeot SA, since 1984; Referendary Councillor, Cour des Comptes (Audit Office), since 1963; *b* 19 Sept. 1931; *s* of Prof. Louis Calvet and Yvonne Calvet (*née* Olmières); *m* 1956, Françoise Rondot; two *s* one *d*. *Educ:* Lycée Janson-de-Sailly; Law Faculty, Paris (Licencié en droit; Dipl. Inst. d'Etudes Politiques; Dipl. d'Etudes Supérieures d'Economie Politique et des Sciences Economiques). Trainee, l'Ecole Nationale d'Administration, 1955–57; Audit Office, 1957–59; Office of Sec. of State for Finance, 1959–62, of Minister of Finance, 1962–66; Dep. Dir, 1964, Head of Dept, 1967, Central Finance Admin; Head of Finance Dept, Paris Préfecture, 1967–69; Asst Dir, later Dir, Office of Minister of Economy and Finance, 1969–74; Dir in Ministry of Finance, 1973; Asst Dir Gen., 1974, Dir Gen., 1976, Pres., 1979–82, Banque Nationale de Paris; Vice-Prés. du Conseil d'Administration, 1984, Prés, 1990, Automobile Peugeot; Prés. du Conseil d'Admin, Automobiles Citroën, 1983–. Administrator: Compagnie Générale des Eaux; Chaussures André; Galeries Lafayette; Société Générale; Pallas; Athéna; Consulting Advr, Banque de France; Member: Internat. Council, Morgan Bank; Internat. Adv. Council, Allianz. Officier de la Légion d'Honneur; Officier de l'ordre National du Mérite et du Mérite Agricole; Chevalier des Palmes académiques. *Address:* Peugeot SA, 75 avenue de la Grande Armée, 75116 Paris, France. *T:* 40.66.55.11.; Automobiles Citroën, 62 boulevard Victor Hugo, 92208 Neuilly-sur-Seine, France. *T:* 47.48.41.41.; 31 avenue Victor Hugo, 75116 Paris, France.

CALVIN, Prof. Melvin; University Professor of Chemistry, University of California, since 1971; Professor of Molecular Biology, 1963–80; *b* 8 April 1911; *s* of Rose and Elias Calvin; *m* 1942, Marie Genevieve Jemtegaard; one *s* two *d*. *Educ:* Univ. of Minnesota, Minneapolis (PhD). Fellow, Univ. of Manchester, 1935–37. Univ. of California, Berkeley: Instr., 1937; Asst Prof., 1941–45; Assoc. Prof., 1945–47; Prof., 1947–71; Dir, Laboratory of Chemical Biodynamics, 1960–80; Associate Dir, Lawrence Berkeley Lab., 1967–80. Foreign Mem., Royal Society, 1959. Member: Nat. Acad. of Sciences (US); Royal Netherlands Acad. of Sciences and Letters; Amer. Philos. Society. Nobel Prize in Chemistry, 1961; Davy Medal, Royal Society, 1964; Virtanen Medal, 1975; Gibbs Medal, 1977; Priestley Medal, 1978; Amer. Inst. Chemists Gold Medal, 1979; Nat. Medal of Science, 1989. Hon. Degrees: Michigan Coll. of Mining and Technology, 1955; Univ. of Nottingham, 1958; Oxford Univ., 1959; Northwestern Univ., 1961; Univ. of Notre Dame, 1965; Brooklyn Polytechnic Inst., 1969; Rijksuniversiteit-Gent, 1970; Columbia Univ., 1979. *Publications:* very numerous, including (7 books): Theory of Organic Chemistry (with Branch), 1941; Isotopic Carbon (with Heidelberger, Reid, Tolbert and Yankwich), 1949; Chemistry of Metal Chelate Compounds (with Martell), 1952; Path of Carbon in Photosynthesis (with Bassham), 1957; Chemical Evolution, 1961; Photosynthesis of Carbon Compounds (with Bassham), 1962; Chemical Evolution, 1969. *Address:* University of California, Berkeley, Calif 94720, USA; (home) 2683 Buena Vista Way, Berkeley, Calif 94708, USA. *T:* 848–4036.

CALVO, Roberto Q.; *see* Querejazu Calvo.

CALVOCORESSI, Peter (John Ambrose); author; *b* 17 Nov. 1912; *s* of Pandia Calvocoressi and Irene (Ralli); *m* 1938, Barbara Dorothy Eden, *d* of 6th Baron Henley; two *s*. *Educ:* Eton (King's Scholar); Balliol Coll., Oxford. Called to Bar, 1935. RAF Intelligence, 1940–45; Wing Comdr. Trial of Major War Criminals, Nuremberg, 1945–46. Contested (L) Nuneaton, 1945. Staff of Royal Institute of International Affairs, 1949–54 (Mem. Council, 1955–70); Dir of Chatto & Windus Ltd and The Hogarth Press Ltd, 1954–65; Editorial Dir, 1972–76, Publisher and Chief Exec., 1973–76, Penguin Books. Chm., Open Univ. Educnl Enterprises Ltd, 1979–88. Reader (part time) in International Relations, Univ. of Sussex, 1965–71; Member: Council, Inst. for Strategic Studies, 1961–71; Council, Inst. of Race Relations, 1970–71; UN Sub-Commn on the Prevention of Discrimination and Protection of Minorities, 1962–71; Chm., The Africa Bureau, 1963–71; Mem., Internat. Exec., Amnesty International, 1969–71; Chm., The London Library, 1970–73; Dep. Chm., N Metropolitan Conciliation Cttee, 1967–71. DUniv Open. *Publications:* Nuremberg: The Facts, the Law and the Consequences, 1947; Surveys of International Affairs, vol. 1, 1947–48, 1950; vol. 2, 1949–50, 1951; vol. 3, 1951, 1952; vol. 4, 1952, 1953; vol. 5, 1953, 1954; Middle East Crisis (with Guy Wint), 1957; South Africa and World Opinion, 1961; World Order and New States, 1962; World Politics since 1945, 1968, 6th edn 1991; (with Guy Wint) Total War, 1972, 2nd rev. edn 1989; The British Experience 1945–75, 1978; Top Secret Ultra, 1980; Independent Africa and the World, 1985; A Time for Peace, 1987; Who's Who in the Bible, 1987; Resilient Europe 1870–2000, 1991. *Recreation:* walking. *Address:* 1 Queen's Parade, Bath. *T:* Bath (0225) 333903. *Club:* Garrick.

CALVOCORESSI, Richard Edward Ion; Keeper, Scottish National Gallery of Modern Art, since 1987; *b* 5 May 1951; *s* of Ion Melville Calvocoressi and Katharine (*née* Kennedy); *m* 1976, Francesca Temple Roberts; one *s* two *d*. *Educ:* Eton; Brooke House, Market Harborough; Magdalen Coll., Oxford (Exhibnr; BA (Hons) English Lang. and Lit.); Courtauld Inst. of Art (MA Hist. of Art, 19th and 20th centuries). Research Assistant: Scottish Nat. Gall. of Modern Art, Edinburgh, 1977–79; Modern Collection, Tate Gall., 1979–82; Asst Keeper, Tate Gall., 1982–87. Art Advr, Chelmsford Mus., 1980–86. Governor, Glasgow Sch. of Art, 1988–. *Publications:* Alastair Morton and Edinburgh Weavers, 1978; James Cowie, 1979; Magritte, 1979, 3rd edn 1989; Miró Sculptures, 1981; Tinguely, 1982; Georg Baselitz Paintings, 1983; Reg Butler, 1983; Cross-Currents in Swiss Art, 1985; Marie Louise von Motesiczky, 1985; Oskar Kokoschka 1886–1980, 1986; (ed) Picabia 1879–1953, 1988; (ed) Scottish Art since 1900, 1989; Kokoschka and Scotland, 1990; contrib. British Sculpture in the 20th Century, 1981; contrib. Oskar Kokoschka Symposium, 1986; reviews and articles in TLS, Spectator, Burlington Magazine. *Address:* Scottish National Gallery of Modern Art, Belford Road, Edinburgh EH4 3DR.

CAMBELL, Rear-Adm. Dennis Royle Farquharson, CB 1960; DSC 1940; *b* 13 Nov. 1907; *s* of Dr Archibald Cambell and Edith Cambell, Southsea; *m* 1933, Dorothy Elinor Downes; two *d*. *Educ:* Westminster Sch. Joined RN, 1925, HMS Thunderer Cadet Training; trained as FAA pilot, 1931; 1st Capt. of HMS Ark Royal IV, 1955–56; retired, 1960. *Address:* c/o National Westminster Bank, High Street, Petersfield, Hants.

CAMBRIDGE, Alan John; HM Diplomatic Service, retired; *b* 1 July 1925; *s* of Thomas David Cambridge and Winifred Elizabeth (*née* Jarrett); *m* 1947, Thelma Elliot; three *s* one *d*. *Educ:* Beckenham Grammar Sch. Served War, FAA and RAFVR, 1943–47 (Air Gunner, Bomber Comd). War Pensions Office and MPNI, 1948–55; entered CRO, 1955; Chief Clerk: Madras, 1956–58; Kuala Lumpur, 1959–62; 2nd Sec., Salisbury, Fedn of Rhodesia and Nyasaland, 1962–65; 1st Sec. (Political), Freetown, 1965–66; UN Dept, FCO, 1966–68; 1st Sec., Prague, 1969; 1st Sec. (Consular/Aid), Suva, 1970–72; HM Consul, Milan, 1972–74; Asst Head of Inf. Dept, FCO, 1974–78; 1st Sec., Ankara, 1978–81; Asst Head, 1981–82, Head and Counsellor, 1983–85, Migration and Visa Dept, FCO; Assessor, FCO, 1985–90. *Recreations:* photography, swimming, tennis. *Address:* 9 The Ferns, Carlton Road, Tunbridge Wells TN1 2JT. *T:* Tunbridge Wells (0892) 31223. *Club:* Civil Service.

CAMBRIDGE, Sydney John Guy, CMG 1979; CVO 1979; HM Diplomatic Service, retired; *b* 5 Nov. 1928; *o s* of late Jack and Mona Cambridge; unmarried. *Educ:* Marlborough; King's Coll., Cambridge. Entered HM Diplomatic Service, Sept. 1952; Oriental Sec., British Embassy, Jedda, 1953–56; Foreign Office, 1956–60; First Sec., UK Delegn to United Nations, at New York, 1960–64; Head of Chancery, British Embassy, Djakarta, 1964–66; FO, 1966–70; Counsellor, British Embassy, Rome, 1970–73; Head of Financial Relations Dept, FCO, 1973–75; Counsellor, British High Commn, Nicosia, 1975–77; Ambassador: to Kuwait, 1977–82; to Morocco, 1982–84. *Address:* Saint Peter's House, Filkins, Lechlade, Glos GL7 3JQ.

CAMDEN, 6th Marquess *cr* 1812; **David George Edward Henry Pratt;** Baron Camden, 1765; Earl Camden, Viscount Bayham, 1786; Earl of Brecknock, 1812; *b* 13 Aug. 1930; *o s* of 5th Marquess Camden and Marjorie, Countess of Brecknock, DBE (*d* 1989); *S* father, 1983; *m* 1961, Virginia Ann (marr. diss. 1984), *o d* of late F. H. H. Finlaison, Arklow Cottage, Windsor, Berks; one *s* one *d* (and one *s* decd). Late Lieutenant, Scots Guards. *Educ:* Eton. Dir, Clive Discount Co. Ltd, 1958–69. *Heir: s* Earl of Brecknock, *qv*. *Address:* Cowdown Farm House, Andover, Hants SP11 6LE. *T:* Andover (0264) 352085.

CAMDEN, John; Chairman, RMC Group plc, since 1974 (Managing Director, 1966–85); *b* 18 Nov. 1925; *s* of late Joseph Reginald Richard John Camden and Lilian Kate McCann; *m* 1972, Diane Mae Friese; two *d* (and one *s* two *d* of former *m*). *Educ:* Worcester Royal Grammar Sch.; Birmingham Univ. (BSc). Royal Tank Corps and Intell. Corps, 1943–47. Joined RMC Group (formerly Ready Mixed Concrete Group), 1952; Dir responsible for Group's ops in Europe, 1962. Grand Decoration of Honour in Silver (Austria), 1978. *Recreations:* golf, gardening. *Address:* RMC Group plc, RMC House, Coldharbour Lane, Thorpe, Egham, Surrey TW20 8TD.

CAMDESSUS, Michel; Managing Director, International Monetary Fund, since 1987; *b* 1 May 1933; *s* of Alfred Camdessus and Madeleine Camdessus (*née* Cassembon); *m* 1957, Brigitte d'Arcy; two *s* four *d*. *Educ:* Inst. of Political Studies, Paris; Diploma, Nat. Sch. of Administration. Administrateur Civil, French Treasury, 1960; Financial Attaché, Permt French Delegn to European Communities, 1966–68; Asst Dir, Treasury, 1971, Dep. Dir, 1974, Dir, 1982; First Dep. Governor, Bank of France, Aug. 1984, Governor, Nov. 1984. Chm., Paris Club, 1978–84. Chevalier de la Légion d'Honneur; Chevalier de l'Ordre National du Mérite; Croix de la valeur militaire. *Address:* International Monetary Fund, 700 19th Street NW, Washington, DC 20431, USA. *T:* (202) 623–4600.

CAMERON, family name of **Baron Cameron of Lochbroom.**

CAMERON, Hon. Lord; John Cameron, KT 1978; Kt 1954; DSC; HRSA; FRSGS; a Senator of The College of Justice in Scotland and Lord of Session 1955–85; *b* 1900; *m* 1st, 1927, Eileen Dorothea (*d* 1943), *d* of late H. M. Burrell; one *s* two *d*; 2nd, 1944, Iris, *widow* of Lambert C. Shepherd. *Educ:* Edinburgh Acad.; Edinburgh Univ. Served European War, 1918–19, with RNVR. Advocate, 1924; Advocate-Depute, 1929–36; QC (Scotland), 1936. Served with RNVR, Sept. 1939–44 (despatches, DSC); released to reserve, Dec. 1944. Sheriff of Inverness, Elgin and Nairn, 1945; Sheriff of Inverness, Moray, Nairn and Ross and Cromarty, 1946–48; Dean of Faculty of Advocates, 1948–55. Member: Cttee on Law of Contempt of Court, 1972–; Royal Commn on Civil Liability and Compensation for Personal Injury, 1973–78. DL Edinburgh, 1953–84. Hon. FRSE 1983; Hon. FBA 1983. DUniv Edinburgh, 1983; Hon. LLD: Aberdeen; Glasgow; Edinburgh; Hon. DLitt Heriot-Watt. *Address:* 28 Moray Place, Edinburgh. *T:* 031–225 7585. *Clubs:* New, Scottish Arts (Edinburgh); Royal Forth Yacht.
See also Baron Cameron of Lochbroom, Hon. Lord Weir.

CAMERON OF LOCHBROOM, Baron *cr* 1984 (Life Peer), of Lochbroom in the District of Ross and Cromarty; **Kenneth John Cameron;** PC 1984; a Senator of the College of Justice in Scotland, since 1989; *b* 11 June 1931; *s* of Hon. Lord Cameron, *qv*; *m* 1964, Jean Pamela Murray; two *d*. *Educ:* The Edinburgh Academy; Corpus Christi Coll., Oxford (MA); Edinburgh Univ. (LLB). Served RN, 1950–52; commissioned RNVR, 1951 (Lt). Admitted Faculty of Advocates, 1958; QC (Scot.) 1972; Standing Junior to Dept of Transport, 1964–71; to DoE, 1971–72; Chairman of Industrial Tribunals in Scotland, 1966–81; Advocate Depute, 1981–84; Lord Advocate, 1984–89. Chm. of Pensions Appeal Tribunal (Scotland), 1975, Pres. 1976–84. Chairman: Cttee for Investigation in Scotland of Agricultural Marketing Schemes, 1980–84; Scottish Civic Trust; Edinburgh New Town Conservation Cttee. Pres., Scottish Council for Voluntary Orgns. FRSE 1990. *Recreations:* fishing, sailing, music. *Address:* 10 Belford Terrace, Edinburgh EH4 3DQ. *T:* 031–332 6636. *Clubs:* Scottish Arts, New (Edinburgh).

CAMERON, Prof. Alan Douglas Edward, FBA 1975; Anthon Professor of Latin Language and Literature, Columbia University, New York, since 1977; *b* 13 March 1938; *er s* of A. D. Cameron, Egham; *m* 1962, Averil Sutton (marr. diss. 1980; *see* Averil Cameron); one *s* one *d*. *Educ:* St Paul's Sch. (Schol.); New Coll., Oxford (Schol.). Craven Scholar 1958; 1st cl. Hon. Mods 1959; De Paravicini Scholar 1960; Chancellor's Prize for Latin Prose 1960; 1st cl. Lit. Hum. 1961; N. H. Baynes Prize 1967; John Conington Prize 1968. Asst Master, Brunswick Sch., Haywards Heath, 1956–57; Asst Lectr, then Lectr, in Humanity, Glasgow Univ., 1961–64; Lectr in Latin, 1964–71, Reader, 1971–72, Bedford Coll., London; Prof. of Latin, King's Coll., London, 1972–77. Vis. Prof., Columbia Univ., NY, 1967–68. Vis. Fellow, Humanities Research Centre, Australian National Univ., 1985. Fellow, Amer. Acad. of Arts and Sciences, 1979. *Publications:* Claudian: Poetry and Propaganda at the Court of Honorius, 1970; (contrib.) Prosopography of the Later Roman Empire, ed Jones, Morris and Martindale, i, 1971, ii, 1980; Porphyrius the Charioteer, 1973; Bread and Circuses, 1974; Circus Factions, 1976; Literature and Society in the Early Byzantine World, 1985; The Greek Anthology, 1986; articles and reviews in learned jls. *Recreation:* the cinema. *Address:* Columbia University, Morningside Heights, New York, NY 10027, USA.

CAMERON, Major Allan John, MBE 1988; JP; Vice Lord-Lieutenant, Highland Region (Ross and Cromarty), since 1977; *b* 25 March 1917; *s* of Col Sir Donald Cameron of Lochiel, KT, CMG (*d* 1951), and Lady Hermione Cameron (*d* 1978), *d* of 5th Duke of Montrose; *m* 1945, Mary Elizabeth Vaughan-Lee, Dillington, Somerset; two *s* two *d* (and one *s* decd.). *Educ:* Harrow; RMC Sandhurst. Served QO Cameron Highlanders, 1936–48; Major, Retd (POW Middle East, 1942). County Councillor, Ross-shire, 1955–75 (Chm. Educn Cttee, 1962–75); former Member: Red Deer Commn; Countryside Commn for Scotland; Broadcasting Council for Scotland. *Recreations:* curling (Past Pres. Royal Caledonian Curling Club), gardening, golf. *Address:* Allangrange, Munlochy, Ross-shire IV8 8NZ. *T:* Munlochy (046381) 249. *Club:* Naval and Military.
See also Col Sir Donald Cameron of Lochiel.

CAMERON, Prof. Averil Millicent, MA, PhD; FBA 1981; FSA 1982; Professor of Late Antique and Byzantine Studies, and Director, Centre for Hellenic Studies, King's College London, since 1988; *b* 8 Feb. 1940; *d* of T. R. Sutton, Leek, Staffs; *m* 1962, Alan Douglas Edward Cameron, *qv* (marr. diss. 1980); one *s* one *d*. *Educ:* Westwood Hall Girls' High Sch., Leek, Staffs; Somerville Coll., Oxford (Passmore Edwards Schol. 1960; Rosa Hovey Schol. 1962; MA); Univ. of Glasgow; University Coll. London (PhD; FKC 1987). King's College London: Asst Lectr, 1965; Lectr, 1968; Reader in Ancient History, 1970; Prof. of Ancient History, 1978–88; Head of Dept of Classics, 1984–89. Visiting Professor: Columbia Univ., 1967–68; Collège de France, 1987; Sather Prof., Univ. of Calif. at Berkeley, 1985–86; Vis. Member, Inst. of Advanced Study, Princeton, 1977–78; Summer Fellow, Dumbarton Oaks Center for Byzantine Studies, 1981; British Acad. Wolfson Res. Reader in Hist., 1990–92. Chm., British Nat. Byzantine Cttee, 1983–89; Vice-President: Roman Soc., 1983–; British Acad. Council, 1983–86. Editor, Jl of Roman Studies, 1985–90. *Publications:* Procopius, 1967; Agathias, 1970; Corippus: In laudem Iustini minoris, 1976; Change and Continuity in Sixth-Century Byzantium, 1981; (ed jtly) Images of Women in Antiquity, 1983; (ed jtly) Constantinople in the Eighth Century: the Parastaseis Syntomoi Chronikai, 1984; Procopius and the Sixth Century, 1985; (ed) History as Text: the writing of Ancient History, 1989; Christianity and the Rhetoric of Empire, 1991; numerous articles in learned jls.

CAMERON, Dr Clive Bremner; Dean, Institute of Cancer Research, London, 1978–82; *b* 28 Sept. 1921; *s* of Clive Rutherford and Aroha Margaret Cameron; *m* 1958, Rosalind Louise Paget; two *s* one *d*. *Educ:* King's Coll., Auckland, NZ; Otago Univ., NZ (MD). Consultant in Clinical Pathology, Royal Marsden Hospital, 1961–82; Chairman, SW Thames Regional Cancer Council, 1976–81. Mem. Bd of Governors, Royal Marsden Hosp., 1977–82. *Publications:* papers on steroid biochemistry, biochemical and other aspects of cancer. *Recreation:* country pursuits. *Address:* East Kennett Manor, Marlborough, Wilts SN8 5ET. *T:* Lockeridge (067286) 239.

CAMERON OF LOCHIEL, Colonel Sir Donald (Hamish), KT 1973; CVO 1970; TD 1944; JP; 26th Chief of the Clan Cameron; Lord-Lieutenant of County of Inverness, 1971–85 (Vice-Lieutenant, 1963–70); Chartered Accountant; *b* 12 Sept. 1910; *s* of Col Sir Donald Walter Cameron of Lochiel, KT, CMG, 25th Chief of the Clan Cameron, and Lady Hermione Emily Graham (*d* 1978), 2nd *d* of 5th Duke of Montrose; *S* father as 26th Chief, 1951; *m* 1939, Margaret, *o d* of Lieut-Col Hon. Nigel Gathorne-Hardy, DSO; two *s* two *d*. *Educ:* Harrow; Balliol Coll., Oxford. Joined Lovat Scouts, 1929; Major 1940; Lieut-Col 1945; Lieut-Col comdg 4/5th Bn (TA) QO Cameron Highlanders, 1955–57; Col 1957 (TARO). Hon. Colonel: 4/5th Bn QO Cameron Highlanders, 1958–67; 3rd (Territorial) Bn Queen's Own Highlanders (Seaforth and Camerons), 1967–69; 2nd Bn, 51st Highland Volunteers, 1970–75. Member (part-time): British Railways Bd, 1962–64; Scottish Railways Bd, 1964–72 (Chm. Scottish Area Bd, BTC, 1959–64); Transport Holding Co., 1962–65; Director: Royal Bank of Scotland, 1954–80 (Vice-Chm., 1969–80); Save & Prosper Gp, 1968–84; Culter Guard Bridge Holdings Ltd, 1970–77 (Chm., 1970–76); Scottish Widows Life Assurance Soc., 1955–81 (Chm., 1964–67). Crown Estate Comr, 1957–69. Chm., Scottish Cttee, Malcolm Sargent Cancer Fund for Children, 1975–91. President: Scottish Landowners Fedn, 1979–84; Royal Highland and Agricultural Soc. of Scotland, 1971, 1979 and 1987. Governor, Harrow Sch., 1967–77. *Heir: s* Donald Angus Cameron, younger of Lochiel [*b* 2 Aug. 1946; *m* 1974, Lady Cecil Kerr, *d* of Marquess of Lothian, *qv*; one *s* three *d*]. *Address:* Achnacarry, Spean Bridge, Inverness-shire. *T:* Spean Bridge (039781) 708. *Clubs:* Pratt's; New (Edinburgh).
See also A. J. Cameron.

CAMERON, Ellen; *see* Malcolm, E.

CAMERON, Sir (Eustace) John, Kt 1977; CBE 1970; MA Cantab; Tasmanian pastoralist, since 1946; *b* 8 Oct. 1913; *s* of Eustace Noel Cameron and Alexina Maria Cameron; *m* 1934, Nancie Ailsa Sutherland (OBE 1983) (*d* 1988); one *d*. *Educ:* Geelong Grammar Sch.; Trinity Coll., Cambridge. Served RANVR, 1942–46. ICI, 1938–41. State Pres., Liberal Party, 1948–52. Pres., Tasmanian Stockowners Assoc., 1965–68; Vice-Pres., Aust. Graziers, 1968–71. University of Tasmania: Mem. Council, 1956–82; Dep. Chancellor, 1964–72; Chancellor, 1973–81. Member: Selection Cttee, Winston Churchill Fellowship, 1965–74; CSIRO Adv. Cttee, 1959–77; Housing Loan Insurance Corp., 1970–73. Hon. LLD Tasmania, 1982. *Publications:* contrib. Australian Dictionary of Biography. *Recreations:* Australiana, gardening, pottering. *Address:* Lochiel, Ross, Tas 7209, Australia. *T:* Ross 815253. *Clubs:* Tasmanian (Hobart); Launceston (Launceston).

CAMERON, Rt. Rev. Ewen Donald; Assistant Bishop, Diocese of Sydney, since 1975; Registrar, Diocese of Sydney, since 1990; Member, Anglican-Roman Catholic International Commission, since 1983; *b* 7 Nov. 1926; *s* of Ewen Cameron, Balranald, NSW, and Dulce M. Cameron, Sydney, NSW; *m* 1952, Joan R., *d* of T. Wilkins, Mosman, NSW; one *s* two *d*. *Educ:* Sydney C of E Grammar Sch., N Sydney; Moore Theological Coll., Sydney. ACA (Aust.); BD (London); ThSchol (Aust. Coll. of Theol.). Public Accountancy, 1945–57. Lectr, Moore Theological Coll., 1960–63; Rector, St Stephen's, Bellevue Hill, 1963–65; Federal Secretary, CMS of Aust., 1965–72; Archdeacon of Cumberland with Sydney, 1972–75; Bishop of North Sydney, 1983–90. *Address:* 3 Mildura Street, Killara, NSW 2071, Australia. *T:* 02–498–5816. *Club:* Union (Sydney).

CAMERON, Francis (Ernest), MA, DipEth (Oxon); FRCO(CHM), ARAM; organist and ethnomusicologist; Choirmaster and Organist, City Church of St Michael at the North Gate, Oxford, since 1988; *b* London, 5 Dec. 1927; *er s* of Ernest and Doris Cameron; *m* 1952, Barbara Minns; three *d*. *Educ:* Mercers' Sch.; Caerphilly Boys' Secondary Sch.; Royal Acad. of Music; University Coll., Oxford. Henry Richards Prizewinner, RAM, 1946. Organist, St Peter's, Fulham, 1943; Pianist, Canadian Legion, 1944; Organist, St Luke's, Holloway, 1945; Sub-organist, St Peter's, Eaton Square, 1945; Organist, St James-the-Less, Westminster, 1946; commissioned RASC, 1948; Organ Scholar, University Coll., Oxford, 1950; Organist: St Anne's, Highgate, 1952; St Barnabas', Pimlico, 1953; St Mark's, Marylebone Road, 1957–58; Choirmaster, St Aloysius, Somers Town, 1959; Master of Music, Westminster Cathedral, 1959; Visiting Organist, Church of St Thomas of Canterbury, Rainham, Kent, 1961; Organist and Choirmaster, Church of Our Lady of the Assumption and St Gregory, Warwick Street, W1, 1962–68. Travel for UNESCO, 1952–55; Dep. Dir of Music, LCC (subsequently GLC), 1954–68; Asst-Dir of Music, Emanuel Sch., 1954; Music Master, Central Foundation Boys' Grammar Sch., 1956; Prof. of Organ and Composition, RAM, 1959–68; *locum tenens* Dir of Music, St Felix Sch., Southwold, 1963 and 1964; Asst Dir, 1968, Chm. of Musicology, 1974–79, NSW State Conservatorium of Music; Organist, Church of St Mary the Virgin, Iffley, 1980–88; Sen. Lectr, Musical Studies, Oxford Poly., 1982–86. Inaugural Conductor, Witan Operatic Soc., 1957–58; Conductor: "I Cantici", 1961–65; Francis Cameron Chorale, 1965–68; Singers of David, 1973–76; British Adjudicator, Fedn of Canadian Music Festivals, 1965; Examr Associated Bd of Royal Schools of Music, 1965–68; Dep. Chm., NSW Adv. Bd, Aust. Music Exams Bd, 1969–74. Field Officer, Deep Creek Aboriginal Monuments res. and recording prog., 1973; Mem., Lancefield Archaeol Expedn, 1975. President: "Open Score", 1946–68; Musicol Soc. of Aust., 1971–75 (jt leader, ethnomusicol expedn to New Hebrides, 1971–72); Sydney Univ. Anthropol Soc., 1974–75; Phoenix Photographic Circle, 1977–79; Conservatorium Professional Staff Assoc., 1978–79; Vice-Pres., Aust. Chapter, Internat. Soc. for Contemporary Music, 1970–77; Ed., INFO, European Seminar in Ethnomusicology, 1986–. Beethoven Commemorative Medal, Fed. Repub. of Germany, 1970. *Publications:* editor (with John Steele) Musica Britannica vol. xiv (The Keyboard Music of John Bull, part I), 1960; Old Palace Yard, 1963; Eight dances from Benjamin Cosyn's Second Virginal Book, 1964; I Sing of a Maiden, 1966; John Bull, ausgewählte Werke, 1967; I Believe, 1969; incidental music for film The Voyage of the New Endeavour, 1970; songs and incidental music for Congreve's Love for Love, 1972; Alleluia, 1990; contributor to: Church Music; Composer; The Conductor; Liturgy; Musical Times; Australian Jl of Music Education; Studies in Music; Music in Tertiary Educn; Con Brio; Musicology IV; Aust. Nat. Hist.; Nation Review; Quanta; ICTM (UK) Bulletin; Intercultural Music Studies. *Address:* 12 Norreys Avenue, Oxford OX1 4SS. *T:* Oxford (0865) 240058.

CAMERON, George Edmund, CBE 1970; retired; *b* 2 July 1911; *s* of William Cameron and Margaret Cameron (*née* Craig); *m* 1939, Winifred Audrey Brown; two *s*. *Educ:*

Ballymena Academy. Chartered Accountant, 1933; Partner, Wright Fitzsimons & Cameron, 1937–79. Pres., Inst. of Chartered Accountants in Ireland, 1960–61. *Recreations:* golf, gardening. *Address:* Ardavon, Glen Road, Craigavad, Co. Down. *T:* Holywood (02317) 2232. *Clubs:* Ulster (Belfast); Royal County Down Golf, Royal Belfast Golf.

CAMERON, Gordon Stewart, RSA 1971 (ARSA 1958); Senior Lecturer, School of Drawing and Painting, Duncan of Jordanstone College of Art, Dundee, 1952–81, retired; *b* Aberdeen, 27 April 1916; *s* of John Roderick Cameron; *m* 1962, Ellen Malcolm, *qv. Educ:* Robert Gordon's Coll., Aberdeen; Gray's Sch. of Art, Aberdeen. Part-time teaching, Gray's Sch. of Art, 1945–50; engaged on anatomical illustrations for Lockhart's Anatomy of the Human Body, 1945–48; apptd Lectr in Duncan of Jordanstone Coll. of Art, 1952. Awarded Davidson Gold Medal, 1939; Guthrie Award, 1944; Carnegie Travelling Schol., 1946. Work in Public Galleries: Aberdeen, Dundee, Perth, Edinburgh, Glasgow; also in private collections in Scotland, England, Ireland and America. *Recreation:* gardening. *Address:* 7 Auburn Terrace, Invergowrie, Dundee DD2 5AB. *T:* Dundee (0382) 562318.

CAMERON, Ian Alexander; Sheriff of Lothian and Borders at Edinburgh, since 1987; *b* 5 Nov. 1938; *s* of late James Cameron and of Isabella Cameron; *m* 1968, Dr Margaret Anne Innes; one *s. Educ:* Elgin Acad.; Edinburgh Univ. (MA); Aberdeen Univ. (LLB with dist.). Qualified as solicitor, 1961; Partner, Stewart & McIsaac, Solicitors, Elgin, 1962–87. *Recreations:* travel, railway history, hillwalking. *Address:* Achnacarry, Elgin IV30 1NU. *T:* Elgin 542731; 19/4 Damside, Dean Village, Edinburgh EH4 3BB. *T:* 031–220 1548. *Club:* Elgin.

CAMERON, Prof. Ian Rennell, FRCP; Professor of Medicine since 1979, and Principal since 1989, United Medical and Dental Schools of Guy's and St Thomas' Hospitals; Hon. Consultant Physician, St Thomas' Hospital, since 1970; *b* 20 May 1936; *s* of James and Frances Mary Cameron; *m* 1st, 1964, Jayne Bustard (marr. diss.); one *s* one *d;* 2nd, 1980, Jennifer, *d* of Stewart and Josephine Cowin. *Educ:* Westminster Sch.; Corpus Christi Coll., Oxford (BA 1958 1st Cl. Hons Animal Physiol; MA 1961; DM 1969); St Thomas's Hosp. Med. Sch. (BM BCh 1961). FRCP 1976. Jun. med. appts, St Thomas' Hosp., 1961–64; Lectr 1967, Sen. Lectr 1969, Reader 1975, St Thomas's Hosp. Med. Sch.; Res. Asst, Dept of Physiol, UCL, 1966–68; NIH Postdoctoral Fellowship at Cedars-Sinai Med. Center, LA, and Asst Prof., Dept of Physiol, UCLA, 1968–69; Medway HA, 1981–86. Examiner, Univ. of London Final MB, 1980–; Mem. Senate, Univ. of London, 1989–. Member: Assoc. of Physicians of GB and Ire., 1979–; Med. Res. Soc., 1966–; Physiol Soc., 1974–. FRSA 1990. *Publications:* Respiratory Disorders (with N. T. Bateman), 1983; papers in various med. and physiol jls. *Recreation:* collecting (books, paintings and ceramics). *Address:* 52 Beaconsfield Road, Blackheath, SE3 7LG. *T:* 081–853 1921. *Club:* Athenæum.

CAMERON, Sir James Clark, Kt 1979; CBE 1969; TD 1947; Visitor to Council, British Medical Association (past Chairman of Council, 1976–79); *b* 8 April 1905; *s* of Malcolm Clark Cameron, Rannoch, Perthshire; *m* 1933, Irene (*d* 1986), *d* of Arthur Ferguson, Perth; one *s* two *d. Educ:* Perth Academy; St Andrews Univ. (MB, ChB). FRCGP. Served War of 1939–45, as Captain RAMC attached to 1st Bn, The Rifle Bde (despatches), Calais; POW, 1940. Past Chm., Gen. Med. Services Cttee, BMA, 1964–74, and Hon. Life Member; Chm., Adv. Cttee for Gen. Practice Council for Post Grad. Med. Educn (England and Wales), 1971–79; Mem., Adv. Cttee on Med. Trng, Commn of the European Communities, 1976–82. Hon. Mem. Council, Cameron Fund Ltd, 1974. Gold Medal for distinguished merit, BMA, 1974. *Address:* 62 Haven Green Court, Haven Green, Ealing, W5 2UY. *T:* 081–997 8262.

See also S. M. C. Cameron, G. C. Ryan.

CAMERON, Prof. J(ames) Malcolm, MD, PhD; FRCSGlas, FRCPath, DMJ; Professor of Forensic Medicine, University of London, at The Royal London (formerly London) Hospital Medical College, since 1973, and Director, Department of Forensic Medicine; Ver Heyden De Lancey Readership in Forensic Medicine, Council of Legal Education, since 1978; Hon. Consultant: to The Royal London (formerly London) Hospital, since 1967; to the Army at Home, in Forensic Medicine, since 1971; to the Royal Navy, in Forensic Medicine, since 1972; to the Royal Air Force, since 1990; Hon. Medical Adviser to Amateur Swimming Association; Editor of Medicine, Science and Law, since 1970; *b* 29 April 1930; *s* of late James Cameron and Doris Mary Robertson; *m* 1956, Primrose Agnes Miller McKerrell, MCST; one *d. Educ:* The High Sch. of Glasgow; Univ. of Glasgow (MB, ChB, MD, PhD). Sen. Ho. Officer in Pathology, Southern Gen. Hosp., Glasgow, 1955–56; McIntyre Clin. Res. Schol., Depts of Path. and Surgery, Glasgow Roy. Infirm., 1956–57; Registrar in Orthop. Surg., Western Infirm., Glasgow, and The Royal Hosp. for Sick Children, Glasgow, 1957–59; Registrar in Lab. Med., 1959–60, and Sen. Registrar in Path., 1960–62, Southern Gen. Hosp., Glasgow; Lectr in Path., Univ. of Glasgow, 1962. The London Hosp. Med. Coll.: Lectr in Forensic Med., 1963–65; Sen. Lectr in Forensic Med., 1965–70; Reader in Forensic Med., 1970–72; Sen. Lectr in Forensic Med. at St Bartholomew's Hosp. Med. Coll., 1971–. Lectr to Metropolitan Police Detective Trng Sch., SW Detective Trng Sch., Bristol, and Special Investigation Br. of RMP, 1969; former Examiner in Forensic Med. to Univ. of Dublin; former Convenor for Exams of Dip. in Med. Jurisp. of Honourable Soc. of Apothecaries of London; former Mem. Council, Royal Coll. of Pathologists. Chm. and Hon. Sec., LEN Med. Cttee, 1990–. Member: BMA; Council, Brit. Assoc. in Forensic Med. (Pres., 1985–87); British Acad. of Forensic Sciences (Sec. Gen., 1970–85; Pres., 1978–79); Medico-Legal Soc. (past Vice-Pres.); FINA Med. Cttee, 1986–; Assoc. of Police Surgeons of GB (Hon. Fellow); Forensic Science Soc.; Assoc. of Clinical Pathologists; Pathological Soc. of GB and Ire.; Research Defence Soc.; Fellow, Amer. Acad. of Forensic Sciences; Mem., Academic Internationalis Medicinae Legalis et Medicinae Socialis. *Publications:* scientific papers in numerous learned jls, both med. and forensic. *Recreations:* sports medicine and legal medicine. *Address:* c/o Department of Forensic Medicine, The London Hospital Medical College, Turner Street, E1 2AD. *T:* 071–377 7622. *Clubs:* Savage, Royal Naval Medical.

CAMERON, Prof. James Munro; University Professor, St Michaels College, University of Toronto, 1971–78, now Emeritus; *b* 14 Nov. 1910; *o s* of Alan and Jane Helen Cameron; *m* 1933, Vera Shaw (*d* 1985); one *d* (one *s* decd). *Educ:* Central Secondary Sch., Sheffield; Keighley Grammar Sch.; Balliol Coll., Oxford (Scholar). Tutor, Workers' Educational Assoc., 1931–32; Staff Tutor, Univ. Coll., Southampton, 1932–35; Staff Tutor, Vaughan Coll., Leicester (Dept of Adult Education, Univ. Coll., Leicester), 1935–43. Univ. of Leeds: Staff Tutor for Tutorial Classes, 1943–47; Lectr in Philosophy, 1947–60 (Sen. Lectr from 1952); Acting Head of Dept of Philosophy, 1954–55 and 1959–60; Prof. of Philosophy, 1960–67; Master of Rutherford Coll., and Prof. of Philosophy, Univ. of Kent at Canterbury, 1967–71. Vis. Prof., Univ. of Notre Dame, Indiana, 1957–58, 1965; Terry Lectr, Yale Univ., 1964–65. Newman Fellow, Univ. of Melbourne, 1968; Christian Culture Award, Univ. of Windsor, Ont, 1972. Hon. DLittS St Michael's Coll., Univ. of Toronto, 1990. *Publications:* Scrutiny of Marxism, 1948; (trans. with Marianne Kuschnitzky) Max Picard, The Flight from God, 1951; John Henry Newman, 1956; The Night Battle, 1962; Images of Authority, 1966; (ed) Essay on Development (1845 edn), by J. H. Newman, 1974; On the Idea of a University, 1978; The Music is in the Sadness (poems), 1988; Nuclear Catholics and other Essays, 1990; articles and papers in many periodicals. *Address:* 360 Bloor Street E, Apt 409, Toronto, Ontario M4W 3M3, Canada.

CAMERON, Sir John; *see* Cameron, Hon. Lord.

CAMERON, Sir John; *see* Cameron, Sir E. J.

CAMERON, John Alastair, QC (Scot.) 1979; *b* 1 Feb. 1938; *s* of William Philip Legerwood Cameron and Kathleen Milthorpe (*née* Parker); *m* 1968, Elspeth Mary Dunlop Miller; three *s. Educ:* Trinity Coll., Glenalmond; Pembroke Coll., Oxford (MA). Called to the Bar, Inner Temple, 1963; admitted Mem., Faculty of Advocates, 1966, Vice-Dean, 1983–. Advocate-Depute, 1972–75; Standing Jun. Counsel: to Dept of Energy, 1976–79; to Scottish Develt Dept, 1978–79. Legal Chm., Pensions Appeal Tribunals for Scotland, 1979–85 (Pres., 1985–). *Publications:* Medical Negligence: an introduction, 1983; (contrib.) Reproductive Medicine and the Law, 1990. *Recreations:* travel, sport, Africana. *Address:* 4 Garscube Terrace, Edinburgh EH12 6BQ. *T:* 031–337 3460.

CAMERON, John Bell, CBE 1982; Chairman, British Rail (Scotland), and Scottish Member, British Rail Board, since 1988; Chairman, World Meats Group, International Federation of Agricultural Producers, since 1984; *b* 14 June 1939; *s* of John and Margaret Cameron; *m* 1964, Margaret (*née* Clapperton). *Educ:* Dollar Academy. AIAgrE; FRAgS. Studied agriculture in various countries, Scandinavia, S America and Europe, 1956–61; farmed in Scotland, 1961–64. National Farmers' Union of Scotland: Mem. National Council, 1964; Vice-Pres., 1976; Pres., 1979–84 (first long-term Pres.). Mem., Agricultural Praesidium of EEC, 1979–89; Chairman: EEC Adv. Cttee for Sheep Meat, 1982–89; UK Sheep Consultative Cttee, 1986–87. Chm. Governors, Dollar Acad., 1984–. Winner: George Headley Award to the UK Sheep Industry, 1986; Sir William Young Award to the Scottish Livestock Industry, 1986. *Recreations:* flying, shooting, travelling. *Address:* Balbuthie Farm, By Leven, Fife, Scotland. *T:* St Monans (03337) 210.

CAMERON, John Charles Finlay; Director, British Urban Regeneration Association, since 1989; Chairman, Highland Perthshire Development Company, since 1990; *b* 8 Feb. 1928; *s* of Robert John and Nancy Angela Cameron; *m* 1st, Ruth Thompson, Sydney, Australia; two *s* two *d*; 2nd, Nancy Foy, Redlands, Calif. *Educ:* privately; University Coll., Southampton. CEng, MICE, FCIT, CBIM. Royal Marines, 1946–48. British Railways, Southern Region, Civil Engineering, 1948; BR Transport Commn, 1957; BR Rlys Workshops, 1962; Rank Organisation, 1968–75. Mem., LTE, 1975–84. Dir-Gen. and Sec., CIT, 1983–88 (Hon. Vice Pres., 1988–91). Mem. Management Cttee, Abbotstone, Ag. Prop. Unit Trust. Vice-Pres., Westminster Br., BIM (Chm., 1985–88). Major, Engr and Transport Staff Corps, RE (TA). Liveryman, Carmen's Co. *Recreations:* book collecting and dealing, building, garden construction. *Address:* Clunemore Farm, Killiecrankie, Pitlochry, Perthshire PH16 5LS. *T:* Pitlochry (0796) 3470, *Fax:* Pitlochry (0796) 3030. *T:* 071–249 1177. *Club:* Oriental.

CAMERON, Prof. John Robinson; Regius Professor of Logic, University of Aberdeen, since 1979; *b* 24 June 1936; *s* of Rev. George Gordon Cameron and Mary Levering (*née* Robinson); *m* 1st, 1959, Mary Elizabeth Ranson (*d* 1984); one *s* two *d*; 2nd, 1987, Barbara Elizabeth Blair. *Educ:* Dundee High Sch.; Univ. of St Andrews (MA 1st Cl. Hons Maths, BPhil Philosophy); Univ. of Calif, Berkeley; Cornell Univ. Harkness Fellow, Berkeley and Cornell, USA, 1959–61; University of Dundee (formerly Queen's College): Asst in Phil., 1962–63; Lectr in Phil., 1963–73; Sen. Lectr in Phil., 1973–78. *Publications:* articles in phil jls. *Recreation:* bricolage. *Address:* 70 Cornhill Road, Aberdeen AB2 5DH. *T:* Aberdeen (0224) 486700.

CAMERON, John Taylor; *see* Coulsfield, Hon. Lord.

CAMERON, Sir John (Watson), Kt 1981; OBE 1960; President, J. W. Cameron & Co., since 1977; *b* 16 Nov. 1901; *s* of Captain Watson Cameron and Isabel Mann; *m* 1930, Lilian Florence Sanderson; one *s* two *d. Educ:* Lancing Coll. Commnd Durham RGA, 1920. Joined J. W. Cameron & Co., brewery co., 1922; Man. Dir, 1940; Chm., 1943–75. Mem., Northern Area, Economic League, 1950–80. Chm., 1964–69, Treasurer, 1967–72, Northern Area Cons. Party; Hartlepool Conservative Party: Chm., 1942–45; Pres., 1945–76; Patron, 1976–78; Pres. and Patron, 1978–. Chm., Hartlepools Hosp. Trust, 1973–80. *Recreations:* gardening, shooting, fishing. *Address:* Cowesby Hall, near Thirsk, N Yorks YO7 2JJ.

CAMERON, Prof. Kenneth, CBE 1987; FBA 1976; Professor of English Language, 1963–87, and Head of Department of English Studies, 1984–87, University of Nottingham; *b* Burnley, Lancs, 21 May 1922; *s* of late Angus W. Cameron and E. Alice Cameron, Habergham, Burnley; *m* 1947, Kathleen (*d* 1977), *d* of late F. E. Heap, Burnley; one *s* one *d. Educ:* Burnley Grammar Sch.; Univ. of Leeds (BA Hons, Sch. of English Language and Literature); PhD Sheffield. Served War, 1941–45, Pilot, RAF. Asst Lectr in English Language, Univ. of Sheffield, 1947–50; Nottingham University: Lectr in English Language, 1950–59; Sen. Lectr, 1959–62; Reader, 1962–63. External Prof., Loughborough Univ., 1990–; Leverhulme Emeritus Fellow, 1990–91. Sir Israel Gollancz Meml Lecture, British Academy, 1976; O'Donnell Lectr, 1979. Pres., Viking Soc., 1972–74; Hon. Dir, 1966–, Hon. Sec., 1972–, English Place-Name Soc. Gen. Editor, English Place-Name Survey, 1966–; Editor, Jl of the English Place-Name Soc., 1972–. FRHistS 1970; FSA 1984. Hon. FilDr Uppsala, 1977; Hon. LittD Sheffield, 1991. Sir Israel Gollancz Meml Prize, British Academy, 1969; Jöran Sahlgren prize, Royal Gustaf Adolfs Acad., Sweden, 1990. *Publications:* The Place-Names of Derbyshire, 1959; English Place-Names, 1961; Scandinavian Settlement in the Territory of the Five Boroughs: the place-name evidence, 1965; The Meaning and Significance of OE *walh* in English Place-Names, 1980; The Place-Names of the County of the City of Lincoln, 1985; *festschrift:* Studies in Honour of Kenneth Cameron, 1987; contribs to: Nottingham Medieval Studies; Medium Ævum; Mediaeval Scandinavia; Festschrifts, etc. *Recreations:* sports (supporting), home, "The Queens". *Address:* 16 The Cloisters, Beeston, Nottingham. *T:* Nottingham (0602) 254503.

CAMERON, Lewis; Sheriff of South Strathclyde, Dumfries and Galloway at Dumfries, since 1988; *b* 12 Aug. 1935; *s* of James Aloysius Cameron and Marie Isobel McKenzie; *m* 1962, Sheila Colette Gallacher; two *s* two *d. Educ:* Blairs Coll., Aberdeen; St Sulpice, Paris; Glasgow Univ. (MA, LLB). Admitted Solicitor, 1962. RAF (Nat. Service), 1954–56. Chm., Social Security Appeal Tribunals, 1983–88; Mem., Legal Aid Central Cttee, 1970–80; Legal Aid Sec., Airdrie, 1978–87; Dean, Airdrie Soc. of Solicitors, 1984–85; Tutor, Strathclyde Univ., 1981–88. Treas., Monklands Victim Support Scheme, 1983–88; Chairman: Dumfries and Galloway Family Conciliation Service, 1988–; Dumfries and Galloway Scottish Assoc. for Study of Delinquency, 1989–. Mem., Scotland Cttee, Nat. Children's Home, 1991–; Trustee, Oscar Marzaroli Trust, 1990–. *Publications:* articles in Law Society Jl. *Recreations:* cinema, theatre, tennis, travel. *Address:* Rose Cottage, Johnstonebridge, Dumfries and Galloway; Sheriff Court House, Dumfries DG1 2AN. *T:* Dumfries (0387) 62334. *Clubs:* New (St Andrews); Ross Priory (Gartocharn, Loch Lomond).

CAMERON, Roy James, CB 1982; PhD; Australian Statistician, 1977–85; *b* 11 March 1923; *s* of Kenneth Cameron and Amy Jean (*née* Davidson); *m* 1951, Dorothy Olive

Lober; two *s* one *d*. *Educ:* Univ. of Adelaide (BEc 1st Cl. Hons, MEc); PhD Harvard. Lecturer in Economics, Canberra University College, 1949–51; Economist, World Bank, 1954–56; Australian Treasury official, 1956–73; Australian Ambassador to OECD, Paris, 1973–77. Chairman: ACT Taxi Fares Adv. Cttee, 1987–89; Cttee of Inquiry into Distribution of Federal Roads Grants, 1985–86. Associate Comr, Industries Assistance Commn, 1989–90. Mem. Council, Canberra Coll. of Advanced Educn, 1986–89. *Recreation:* lawn bowls. *Address:* PO Box 305, Curtin, ACT 2605, Australia. *T:* 062 814522.

CAMERON, Sheila Morag Clark, (Mrs G. C. Ryan); QC 1983; a Recorder, since 1985; Vicar-General of the Province of Canterbury, since 1983; *b* 22 March 1934; *d* of Sir James Clark Cameron, *qv*, and Lady (Irene M.) Cameron; *m* 1960, Gerard Charles Ryan, *qv*; two *s*. *Educ:* Commonweal Lodge Sch., Purley; St Hugh's Coll., Oxford (MA). Called to the Bar, Middle Temple, 1957, Harmsworth Law Scholar, 1958, Bencher, 1988; Part-time Lectr in Law, Southampton Univ., 1960–64; part-time Tutor, Council of Legal Educn, 1966–71. Mem., Bar Council, 1967–70. Comr, Boundary Commn for England, 1989– (Asst Comr, 1981–89). Official Principal, Archdeaconry of Hampstead, 1968–86; Chancellor, Dio. of Chelmsford, 1969–; Chm., Archbishops' Group on the Episcopate, 1986–90; Member: Legal Adv. Commn, Gen. Synod of C of E, 1975–; Gen. Synod Marriage Commn, 1975–78; Council on Tribunals, 1986–90. Mem. Council, Wycombe Abbey Sch., 1972–86. *Address:* 2 Harcourt Buildings, Temple, EC4Y 9DB. *T:* 071–353 8415.

CAMERON, Stuart Gordon, MC 1943; Director, Royal Mint, since 1989; *b* 8 Jan. 1924; *s* of late James Cameron and Dora Sylvia (*née* Godsell); *m* 1946, Joyce Alice, *d* of Roland Ashley Wood; three *s* one *d*. *Educ:* Chigwell School, Essex. Served War, 2nd Gurkha Rifles, 1942–46 (MC). Managing Dir, 1976–78, Dep. Chm., 1978–80, Chm. and Chief Exec., 1980–89, Gallaher Ltd. Dir, American Brands Inc., 1980–89. *Address:* Otterholme, Holly Hill Lane, Sarisbury Green, near Southampton SO3 6AH. *Club:* Royal Thames Yacht.

CAMERON-RAMSAY-FAIRFAX-LUCY; *see* Fairfax-Lucy.

CAMERON WATT, Prof. Donald, FBA 1990; Stevenson Professor of International History in the University of London, since 1981; *b* 17 May 1928; *s* of late Robert Cameron Watt and Barbara, *d* of late Rt Rev. E. J. Bidwell, former Bishop of Ontario; *m* 1st, 1951, Marianne Ruth Grau (*d* 1962); one *s*; 2nd, 1962, Felicia Cobb Stanley; one step *d*. *Educ:* Rugby Sch.; Oriel Coll., Oxford. BA 1951, MA 1954; FRHistS. Asst Editor, Documents on German Foreign Policy, 1918–1945, in Foreign Office, 1951–54; Asst Lectr, Lectr, Sen. Lectr in Internat. History, LSE, 1954–66; Reader in Internat. History in Univ. of London, 1966; Titular Prof. of Internat. History, 1972–81. Editor, Survey of Internat. Affairs, Royal Inst. of Internat. Affairs, 1962–71; Rockefeller Research Fellow in Social Sciences, Inst of Advanced Internat. Studies, Washington, 1960–61; Official Historian, Cabinet Office Historical Section, 1978–. Sec., 1967, Chm., 1976–87, Assoc. of Contemporary Historians; Mem. Bd, Inst. of Contemporary British History, 1987–; Chm., Greenwich Forum, 1974–84; Sec.-Treasurer, Internat. Commn for the Hist. of Internat. Relations, 1982–. Member Editorial Board: Political Quarterly, 1969–; Marine Policy, 1978–; International History, 1984–; Intelligence and National Security, 1986–; Review of Internat. Studies, 1989–. FRSA 1990. *Publications:* Britain and the Suez Canal, 1956; (ed) Documents on the Suez Crisis, 1957; Britain looks to Germany, 1965; Personalities and Policies, 1965; (ed) Survey of International Affairs 1961, 1966; (ed) Documents on International Affairs 1961, 1966; (ed, with K. Bourne) Studies in International History, 1967; A History of the World in the Twentieth Century, Pt I, 1967; (ed) Contemporary History of Europe, 1969; (ed) Hitler's Mein Kampf, 1969; (ed) Survey of International Affairs 1962, 1969; (ed, with James Mayall): Current British Foreign Policy 1970, 1971; Current British Foreign Policy 1971, 1972; Current British Foreign Policy 1972, 1973; Too Serious a Business, 1975; (ed) Survey of International Affairs 1963, 1977; Succeeding John Bull: America in Britain's place 1900–1975, 1984; How War Came, 1989; (ed with Guido Di Tella): Argentina between the Great Powers, 1990. *Recreations:* exploring London, cats. *Address:* c/o London School of Economics and Political Science, Houghton Street, WC2A 2AE. *Club:* Players Theatre.

CAMILLERI, Victor; Ambassador and Permanent Representative for Malta to the United Nations, since 1991; *b* 8 Oct. 1942; *s* of John Camilleri and Esther (*née* Casingena); *m* 1967, Elizabeth Bernadette Heaney; two *s*. *Educ:* Lyceum, Malta; Birmingham Univ. (BA Hons English). Joined Min. of Foreign Affairs, Malta, 1968: 2nd Sec., 1968–74; 1st Sec., 1974–86; Counsellor, 1986–90; 1st Counsellor, 1990; postings in Rome, Brussels, NY and London; Ambassador; to UNIDO and UNESCO, 1981–85; to CSCE, 1985–86; Actg Sec., Min. of Foreign Affairs, 1986–87; Dep. High Comr, 1987–90, High Comr, 1991, London. *Recreations:* reading, swimming. *Address:* Permanent Mission of Malta to UN, 249 East 35th Street, New York, NY 10016, USA.

CAMM, Prof. A(lan) John, MD; FRCP, FACC, FESC; Prudential Professor of Clinical Cardiology, St George's Hospital Medical School, London University, since 1986; *b* 11 Jan. 1947; *s* of John Donald and Joan Camm; *m* 1987, Joy-Maria Frappell; one *s* one *d*. *Educ:* Guy's Hosp. Med. Sch., London Univ. (BSc 1968; MB BS 1971; MD 1981). LRCP, MRCS 1971; FACC 1981; FRCP 1984; FESC 1988. Guy's Hospital: House Surgeon, 1971; House Physician, 1971–72; Jun. Registrar, 1972; Jun. Lectr in Medicine, 1972–73; Registrar in Cardiology, 1973–74; Clin. Fellow in Cardiology, Univ. of Vermont, USA, 1974–75; St Bartholomew's Hospital: British Heart Foundn Res. Registrar, 1975–76, Sen. Registrar 1977–79; Wellcome Sen. Lectr and Hon. Consultant Cardiologist, 1979–83; Sir Ronald Bodley Scott Prof. of Cardiovascular Medicine, 1983–86. Freeman, City of London, 1984. CStJ 1990. *Publications:* First Aid, Step by Step, 1978; Pacing for Tachycardia Control, 1983; Heart Disease in the Elderly, 1984; Clinical Electrophysiology of the Heart, 1987; Heart Disease in Old Age, 1988; Clinical Aspects of Cardiac Arrhythmias, 1988; Diseases of the Heart, 1989; Heart Disease in Old Age, 1990; approx. 350 papers in major jls. *Recreations:* collector of prints, watercolours and other antiques, model railway enthusiast. *Address:* St George's Hospital Medical School, Cranmer Terrace, Tooting, SW17 0RE. *Club:* Athenæum.

CAMMELL, John Ernest; Head of Manufacturing Technology Division (formerly Mechanical Engineering and Manufacturing Technology Division), Department of Trade and Industry, since 1986; *b* 14 Nov. 1932; *s* of Ernest Alfred Cammell and Gladys Clara (*née* Burroughes); *m* 1976, Janis Linda Moody. *Educ:* Highfield Coll., Leigh-on-Sea, Essex. Mil. Service, Royal Signals. Joined Victualling Dept, Admiralty, 1952; DSIR, 1963; Min. of Technology, 1964; DTI, 1967; Dept of Industry, 1973; Dir, National Maritime Inst., 1981–84. Companion, IProdE, 1988. *Recreations:* amateur theatre, golf, cricket, eating. *Address:* 13 Vale Court, Acton, W3 7XW. *T:* 081–749 4747.

CAMOYS, 7th Baron *cr* 1264 (called out of abeyance, 1839); **Ralph Thomas Campion George Sherman Stonor;** Deputy Chairman, Barclays de Zoete Wedd (BZW), since 1987 (Chief Executive, 1986–88); Managing Director, 1978–84, Executive Vice-Chairman, 1984–86, Barclays Merchant Bank Ltd; Chairman, Jacksons of Piccadilly Ltd, 1968–85; *b* 16 April 1940; *s* of 6th Baron Camoys and Mary Jeanne (*d* 1987), *d* of late Captain Herbert Marmaduke Joseph Stourton, OBE; *S* father, 1976; *m* 1966, Elisabeth Mary Hyde, *d* of Sir William Stephen Hyde Parker, 11th Bt; one *s* three *d*. *Educ:* Eton Coll.; Balliol Coll., Oxford (MA). Gen. Manager and Director, National Provincial and Rothschild (London) Ltd, 1968; Man. Director, Rothschild Intercontinental Bank Ltd, 1969; Chief Exec. Officer and Man. Dir, 1975–77, Chm., 1977–78, Amex Bank Ltd; Director: Barclays Bank Internat. Ltd, 1980–84; Barclays Bank PLC, 1984–; Mercantile Credit Co. Ltd, 1980–84; National Provident Instn, 1982–. Pres., Mail Users' Assoc., 1977–84; Member: House of Lords EEC Select Cttee, 1979–81; Historic Bldgs and Monuments Commn for England, 1985–87; Royal Commn on Historical MSS, 1987–. Mem. Court of Assistants, Fishmongers' Co., 1980–. Order of Gorkha Dakshina Bahu, 1st class (Nepal), 1981. *Recreations:* the arts, shooting. *Heir:* *s* Hon. (Ralph) William (Robert Thomas) Stonor, *b* 10 Sept. 1974. *Address:* Stonor Park, Henley-on-Thames, Oxon RG9 6HF. *Clubs:* Boodle's, Pratt's; Leander (Henley-on-Thames).

CAMP, Jeffery Bruce, RA 1984 (ARA 1974); artist; Lecturer, Slade School of Fine Art. *Educ:* Edinburgh Coll. of Art. DA (Edin.). One-man exhibitions include: Galerie de Seine, 1958; Beaux Arts Gallery, 1959, 1961, 1963; New Art Centre, 1968; S London Art Gall., 1973 (retrospective); Serpentine Gall., 1978; Bradford City Art Gallery, 1979; Browse and Darby, 1984; Aldeburgh Fest., 1986; Nigel Greenwood Gall., 1986, 1990; Royal Acad., 1988 (retrospective); other exhibitions include: Hayward Annual, 1974, 1982, 1985; Serpentine Gall., 1974, 1987; Narrative Painting, ICA and Arts Council tour, 1979; British Council touring exhibns to China and Edinburgh, 1982, to India, 1985, to Kuala Lumpur, 1988; Chantrey Bicentenary, Tate Gall., 1981; The Hardwon Image, Tate Gall., 1984; group exhibn, Twinning Gall., NY, 1985; Peter Moores exhibn, Liverpool, 1986; Athena Art Awards, 1987. *Publication:* Draw, 1981. *Address:* c/o Nigel Greenwood Gallery, 4 New Burlington Street, W1X 1FE. *T:* 071–434 3795.

CAMP, William Newton Alexander; writer and political and corporate adviser; *b* 12 May 1926; *s* of I. N. Camp, OBE, Colonial Administrative Service, Palestine, and Freda Camp; *m* 1st, 1950, Patricia Cowan (marr. diss. 1973); two *s* one *d*; 2nd, 1975, Juliet Schubart, *d* of late Hans Schubart, CBE. *Educ:* Bradfield Coll.; Oriel Coll., Oxford (Classical Scholar, MA). Served in Army, 1944–47. Asst Res. Officer, British Travel and Holidays Assoc., 1950–54; Asst Sec., Consumer Adv. Council, BSI, 1954–59; Asst Sec., Gas Council, 1960–63; Public Relations Adviser, Gas Council (British Gas Corp.), 1963–67; Dir of Information Services, British Steel Corp., 1967–71; Mem., British Nat. Oil Corp., 1976–78. Special Adviser: milling and baking industries, 1972–90; British Leyland Motor Corp., 1975; railway trades unions, 1975–76; C. A. Parsons & Co. Ltd, 1976–77; Prudential Corp. (formerly Prudential Assurance Co.), 1978–88; Northern Engineering Industries plc, 1978–84; Corporate Advr, British Railways Bd, 1977–90. Director: Quartet Books, 1973–76; Westminster Communications Gp Ltd, 1989–90; Chm., Camden Consultants Ltd, 1975–91. Chm., Oxford Univ. Labour Club, 1949; contested (Lab) Solihull, 1950; Mem., Southwark Borough Council, 1953–56; Press Adviser (unpaid) to Prime Minister, Gen. Election, 1970. Founder Mem., Public Enterprise Group. *Publications:* *novels:* Prospects of Love, 1957; Idle on Parade, 1958 (filmed, 1959); The Ruling Passion, 1959; A Man's World, 1962; Two Schools of Thought, 1964; Flavour of Decay, 1967; The Father Figures, 1970; Stroke Counterstroke, 1986; *biography:* The Glittering Prizes (F. E. Smith), 1960. *Address:* 61 Gloucester Crescent, NW1 7EG. *T:* 071–482 5112; Keeper's Cottage, Marshfield, near Chippenham, Wilts SN14 8PD. *T:* Bath (0225) 891211. *Club:* Garrick.

CAMPBELL, family name of **Duke of Argyll,** of **Earl of Breadalbane,** of **Earl Cawdor,** and of **Barons Campbell of Alloway, Campbell of Croy, Campbell of Eskan, Colgrain** and **Stratheden.**

CAMPBELL OF ALLOWAY, Baron *cr* 1981 (Life Peer), of Ayr in the District of Kyle and Carrick; **Alan Robertson Campbell,** QC 1965; a Recorder of the Crown Court, 1976–89; *b* 24 May 1917; *s* of late J. K. Campbell; *m* 1957, Vivien, *y d* of late Comdr A. H. de Kantzow, DSO, RN. *Educ:* Aldenham; Ecole des Sciences Politiques, Paris; Trinity Hall, Cambridge. Called to Bar, Inner Temple, 1939, Bencher, 1972; Western Circuit. Commissioned RA (Suppl. Res.), 1939; served France and Belgium, 1939–40; POW, 1940–45. Consultant to sub-cttee of Legal Cttee of Council of Europe on Industrial Espionage, 1965–74; Chm., Legal Res. Cttee, Soc. of Conservative Lawyers, 1968–80. Member: Law Adv. Cttee, British Council, 1974–82; Management Cttee, UK Assoc. for European Law, 1975–90. *Publications:* (with Lord Wilberforce) Restrictive Trade Practices and Monopolies, 1956, 2nd edn, 1966, Supplements 1 and 2, 1973; Restrictive Trading Agreements in the Common Market, 1964, Supplement, 1965; Common Market Law, vols 1 and 2, 1969, vol. 3, 1973 and Supplement, 1975; Industrial Relations Act, 1971; EC Competition Law, 1980; Trade Unions and the Individual, 1980. *Address:* 2 King's Bench Walk, Temple, EC4. *T:* 071–353 9276. *Clubs:* Carlton (Mem., Political Cttee, 1967–79), Pratt's, Beefsteak.

CAMPBELL OF CROY, Baron *cr* 1974 (Life Peer), of Croy in the County of Nairn; **Gordon Thomas Calthrop Campbell,** PC 1970; MC 1944, and Bar, 1945; DL; Vice-Lord-Lieutenant, Highland Region (Nairn), since 1988; *b* 8 June 1921; *s* of late Maj.-Gen. J. A. Campbell, DSO; *m* 1949, Nicola Elizabeth Gina Madan; two *s* one *d*. *Educ:* Wellington and Hospital. War of 1939–45: commissioned in Regular Army, 1939; RA, Major, 1942; commanded 320 Field Battery in 15 Scottish Div.; wounded and disabled, 1945. Entered HM Foreign Service, 1946; served, until 1957, in FO, UK Delegn to the UN (New York), Cabinet Office (Private Sec. to Sec. of Cabinet) and Vienna. MP (C) Moray and Nairn, 1959–Feb. 1974; Asst Govt Whip, 1961–62; a Lord Comr of the Treasury and Scottish Whip, 1962–63; Joint Parly Under-Sec. of State, Scottish Office, 1963–64; Opposition Spokesman on Defence and Scottish Affairs, 1966–70; Sec. of State for Scotland, 1970–74. Vice-Pres., Parly Maritime Gp, 1986–. Oil industry consultant, 1975–; Partner in Holme Rose Farms and Estate, 1969–; Chm., Scottish Bd, 1976–, Dir, 1983–, Alliance and Leicester (formerly Alliance) Building Soc.; Chm., Stoic Financial Services (formerly Stoic Insurance Services), 1979–; Advisory Committee on Pollution of Sea: Vice-Pres., 1976–84; Acting Chm., 1980–82; Chm., 1987–89. Chm., Scottish Cttee, Internat. Year of Disabled, 1981; Mem., RA Council, Scotland, 1980–; Pres., Anglo-Austrian Soc., 1991–. Trustee, Thomson Foundn, 1980–; First Fellow, Nuffield Provincial Hospitals Trust Queen Elizabeth The Queen Mother Fellowship, 1980. DL Nairn, 1985. *Publication:* Disablement: Problems and Prospects in the UK, 1981. *Recreations:* music, birds. *Address:* Holme Rose, Cawdor, Nairnshire, Scotland. *T:* Croy (06678) 223.

CAMPBELL OF ESKAN, Baron *cr* 1966 (Life Peer), of Camis Eskan; **John (Jock) Middleton Campbell;** Kt 1957; Chairman, Commonwealth Sugar Exporters' Association, 1950–84; Trustee, Chequers Trust; *b* 8 Aug. 1912; *e s* of late Colin Algernon Campbell, Colgrain, Dunbartonshire and Underriver House, Sevenoaks, Kent and of Mary Charlotte Gladys (Barrington); *m* 1st, 1938, Barbara Noel (marr. diss. 1948), *d* of late Leslie Arden Roffey; two *s* two *d*; 2nd, 1949, Phyllis Jacqueline Gilmour Taylor (*d* 1983), *d* of late Henry Boyd, CBE. *Educ:* Eton; Exeter Coll., Oxford (Hon. Fellow, 1973). Chairman: Booker McConnell Ltd, 1952–66 (Pres., 1967–79); Statesman and Nation Publishing Co. Ltd, 1964–77; Statesman Publishing Co. Ltd, 1964–81. New Towns

Assoc., 1975–77; Director: London Weekend TV Ltd, 1967–74 (Dep. Chm., 1969–73); Commonwealth Develt Corp., 1968–81. Mem., Community Relations Commn, 1968–77 (a Dep. Chm., 1968–71). President: W India Cttee, 1957–77; Town & Country Planning Assoc., 1980–89. Chm., Governing Body, Imperial Coll. of Tropical Agriculture, 1945–55. First Freeman of Milton Keynes, 1982. DUniv Open, 1973. *Recreations:* reading, hitting balls, painting. *Address:* Lawers, Crocker End, Nettlebed, Oxfordshire. *T:* Nettlebed (0491) 641202. *Club:* All England Lawn Tennis.

CAMPBELL, Sir Alan (Hugh), GCMG 1979 (KCMG 1976; CMG 1964); HM Diplomatic Service, retired; Director, Agricole (UK) Ltd, since 1987; *b* 1 July 1919; *y s* of late Hugh Campbell and Ethel Campbell (*née* Warren); *m* 1947, Margaret Taylor; three *d*. *Educ:* Sherborne Sch.; Caius Coll., Cambridge. Served in Devonshire Regt, 1940–46. 3rd Sec., HM Foreign (now Diplomatic) Service, 1946; appointed to Lord Killearn's Special Mission to Singapore, 1946; served in Rome, 1952, Peking, 1955; UK Mission to UN, New York, 1961; Head of Western Dept, Foreign Office, 1965; Counsellor, Paris, 1967; Ambassador to Ethiopia, 1969–72; Asst Under-Sec. of State, FCO, 1972–74; Dep. Under-Sec. of State, FCO, 1974–76; Ambassador to Italy, 1976–79; Foreign Affairs adviser to Rolls Royce Ltd, 1979–81. Director: National Westminster Bank, 1979–89; Mercantile and General Reinsurance Co., 1979–89; H. Clarkson (Hldgs), 1979–89. Chairman: Soc. of Pension Consultants, 1982–87; British-Italian Soc., 1983–90; British Sch. at Rome, 1987–91 (Mem. Council, 1982–); Mem. Council, London Philharmonic Orchestra, 1982–90. Governor, Sherborne Sch., 1973–87 (Chm. of Governors, 1982–87). *Publications:* Colleagues and Friends (autobiog.), 1988; articles in Internat. Affairs. *Recreations:* lawn tennis, painting in watercolour. *Address:* 45 Carlisle Mansions, Carlisle Place, SW1P 1HY. *Clubs:* Brooks's, Beefsteak.

CAMPBELL, Hon. Alexander Bradshaw, PC (Canada) 1967; Judge, Supreme Court of Prince Edward Island, since 1978; *b* 1 Dec. 1933; *s* of Dr Thane A. Campbell and late Cecilia B. Campbell; *m* 1961, Marilyn Gilmour; two *s* one *d*. *Educ:* Dalhousie Univ. (BA, LLB). Called to Bar of Prince Edward Island, 1959; practised law with Campbell & Campbell, Summerside, PEI, 1959–66; QC (PEI) 1966. MLA, Prince Edward Island, 1965–78; Leader of Liberal Party, Dec. 1966–78; Premier, 1966–78; served (while Premier) as Attorney-Gen., 1966–69, Minister of Development, 1969–72, Minister of Agriculture, 1972–74, and Minister of Justice, 1974–78. Dir, Inst. of Man and Resources, 1976–80. Pres., Summerside YMCA, 1981–; Founder Pres., Summerside Area Historical Soc., 1983–; Founder Chm., PEI Council, Duke of Edinburgh Awards (Canada), 1984. Elder of Trinity United Church, Summerside. Hon. LLD: McGill 1967; PEI, 1978. *Recreations:* curling, skiing, golf, boating, gardening. *Address:* 330 Beaver Street, Summerside, PEI C1N 2A3, Canada. *T:* 436–2714. *Club:* Y's Men's (Summerside).

CAMPBELL, Alexander Buchanan, ARSA; FRIBA; architect; *b* 14 June 1914; *s* of Hugh Campbell and Elizabeth Flett; *m* 1939, Sheila Neville Smith; one *s* one *d*. *Educ:* Royal Technical Coll., Glasgow; Glasgow School of Art; Univ. of Strathclyde (BArch). ARSA 1973; PPRIAS. Assistant: Prof. T. Harold Hughes, 1937; G. Grey Wornum, 1938; City Architect, Glasgow, 1939; served War, Royal Engineers, 1940–46; Inspector, Inspectorate of Elect. and Mech. Equipment, 1947; Chief Technical Officer, Scottish Building Centre, 1948, Dep. Dir, 1949. Principal works include: Dollan Swimming Baths and Key Youth Centre, East Kilbride; Flats, Great Western Road, Glasgow; St Christopher's Church, Glasgow; Priesthill Church, Glasgow; St James Primary Sch., Renfrew; Callendar Park Coll. and Craigie College of Education at Falkirk and Ayr (Civic Trust Awards); High Rise Flats, Drumchapel. President: Glasgow Inst. of Architects, 1974–76; Royal Incorporation of Architects in Scotland, 1977–79. *Recreations:* music, art, golf, exhibiting show dogs. *Address:* 19 Lochan Avenue, Kirn, Dunoon, Argyll. *T:* Dunoon (0369) 3674. *Club:* Glasgow Art (President, 1972–74).

CAMPBELL, Prof. (Alexander) Colin (Patton), FRCPath, FRCPE; Procter Professor of Pathology and Pathological Anatomy, University of Manchester, 1950–73, now Professor Emeritus (formerly Dean, Faculty of Medicine and Pro-Vice Chancellor); formerly Director of Studies, Royal College of Pathologists; *b* 21 Feb. 1908; *s* of late A. C. Campbell, Londonderry; *m* 1943, Hon. Elisabeth Joan Adderley, 2nd *d* of 6th Baron Norton; one *s* one *d* (and one *s* decd). *Educ:* Foyle Coll., Londonderry; Edinburgh Univ. MB, ChB (Hons) Edinburgh 1930; FRCPE 1939. Rockefeller Fellow and Research Fellow in Neuropathology, Harvard Univ., 1935–36; Lectr in Neuropathology, Edinburgh Univ., 1937–39; Lectr in Pathology, Edinburgh Univ., and Pathologist, Royal Infirmary, Edinburgh, 1939–50. War service, 1940–46, RAFVR (Wing-Comdr). Hon. MSc Manchester, 1954. *Publications:* papers on pathological subjects in various medical and scientific jls. *Recreations:* carpentry and cabinet-making. *Address:* The Priory House, Ascott-under-Wychwood, Oxford OX7 6AW.

CAMPBELL, Prof. Alexander Elmslie, PhD; FRHistS; Professor of American History, University of Birmingham, 1972–87 (part-time, 1984–87; Director of American Studies, 1972–84); now Emeritus Professor; *b* 12 May 1929; *s* of Rev. John Young Campbell and Emma (*née* Wickert); *m* 1st, 1956, Sophia Anne Sonne (*d* 1972); one *s* one *d*; 2nd, 1983, Juliet Jeanne d'Auvergne Collings (*see* J. J. d'A. Campbell). *Educ:* Paisley Grammar Sch.; Perse Sch., Cambridge; St John's Coll., Cambridge (MA; PhD 1956). MA Oxon 1959. FRHistS 1970. Smith-Mundt Student, Harvard Univ., 1953–54; Fellow, King's Coll., Cambridge, 1955–59; Second Sec., HM Foreign Service, 1958–60; Fellow and Tutor in Mod. Hist., Keble Coll., Oxford, 1960–72, Emeritus Fellow 1981–. Vis. Professor: Hobart and William Smith Colls, NY, 1970; Columbia Univ., 1975; Univ. of Kansas, 1976; Stanford Univ., 1977. Mem., Inst. for Advanced Study, Princeton, 1975. *Publications:* Great Britain and the United States, 1895–1903, 1960; (ed) Expansion and Imperialism, 1970; America Comes of Age: the era of Theodore Roosevelt, 1971; (ed) The USA in World Affairs, 1974; articles and reviews in collections and jls. *Address:* 3 Belbroughton Road, Oxford OX2 6UZ. *T:* Oxford (0865) 58685. *Clubs:* Athenæum; Cosmos (Washington, DC).

CAMPBELL, Hon. Sir Anthony; *see* Campbell, Hon. Sir W. A.

CAMPBELL, Archibald, CMG 1966; Assistant Under-Secretary of State, Ministry of Defence, 1969–74, retired; *b* 10 Dec. 1914; *s* of late Archibald Campbell and Jessie Sanders Campbell (*née* Halsall); *m* 1939, Peggie Phyllis Hussey; two *s* one *d*. *Educ:* Berkhamsted Sch.; Hertford Coll., Oxford. BA Oxford 1935. Barrister at Law, Middle Temple. Administrative Service, Gold Coast, 1936–46; Colonial Office, 1946; Colonial Attaché, British Embassy, Washington, 1953–56; Asst Secretary, Colonial Office, 1956–59 and 1962–67; Chief Secretary, Malta, 1959–62; Asst Sec., MoD, 1967–69. Mem., British observer team, Rhodesian Elections, 1980. *Recreations:* cricket (capped for Bucks in Minor County Competition, 1951); fishing, gardening. *Address:* Bransbury, Long Park, Chesham Bois, Bucks HP6 5LF. *T:* Amersham (0494) 727727. *Club:* MCC.

CAMPBELL, Arthur McLure, CBE 1990; Principal Clerk of Session and Justiciary, Scotland, 1982–89, retired; Clerk of Committees, House of Lords (temporary), since 1991; *b* 15 Aug. 1932; *s* of late Hector Brownlie Campbell, MBE, AIPA and Catherine Smylie (*née* Renwick). *Educ:* Queen's Park Sch., Glasgow. Deptl Legal Qual., Scottish Court Service, 1956. National Service, FAA, 1950–52. Admiralty Supplies Directorate, 1953–54; entered Scottish Court Service (Sheriff Clerk Br.), 1954; Sheriff Clerk Depute, Kilmarnock, 1957–60; Sheriff Clerk of Orkney, 1961–65; seconded HM Treasury (O & M), 1965–69; Principal Sheriff Clerk Depute, Glasgow, 1969; Sheriff Clerk, Airdrie, 1969–72; Principal, Scottish Court Service Staff Trng Centre, 1973–74; Asst Sheriff Clerk of Glasgow, 1974–81. Secretary: Lord Chancellor's Cttee on Re-sealing of Probates and Confirmations, 1967–68; Scottish Office Cttee on Money Transfer Services, 1968–69; Chm., Simplified Divorce (Scotland) Implementation Gp, 1981–82 (Scottish Consumer Council Champion Award, 1983); Mem., Review Body on Use of Judicial Time in Superior Courts in Scotland, 1985–86. Chm., Sheriff Clerks' Assoc., 1971–72. *Address:* c/o Bank of Scotland, 56 Albert Street, Kirkwall, Orkney KW15 1HJ. *Clubs:* National Liberal, Civil Service.

CAMPBELL, Maj.-Gen. (Charles) Peter, CBE 1977; Director, Quicks (formerly H. & J. Quick) Group Plc, since 1982; *b* 25 Aug. 1926; *s* of late Charles Alfred Campbell and Blanche Campbell; *m* 1st, 1949, Lucy Kitching (*d* 1986); two *s*; 2nd, 1986, Elizabeth Tristram. *Educ:* Gillingham Grammar Sch.; Emmanuel Coll., Cambridge. FBIM. Commnd RE, 1945; psc 1957; DAA&QMG Trng Bde, RE, 1958–60; OC 11 Indep. Field Sqdn, RE, 1960–62; Jt Services Staff Coll., 1963; DAAG WO, 1963–65; Co. Comd, RMA Sandhurst, 1965–67; CO 21 Engr Regt, 1967–70; GSOI MoD, 1970–71; CRE 3 Div., 1971; Comd 12 Engr Bde, 1972–73; RCDS, 1974; COS HQ NI, 1975–77; Engineer-in-Chief (Army), 1977–80. Col Comdt, RE, 1981–86, Rep. Col Comdt, 1982; Hon. Colonel: RE (Vol.) (Explosive Ordnance Disposal), 1986–88; 101 (London) Engr Regt (Explosive Ordnance Disposal) (V), 1988–91. Chm., RE Assoc., 1983–89. *Recreations:* painting and collecting militaria. *Address:* c/o Lloyds Bank, Cox's and King's Branch, 7 Pall Mall, SW1Y 5NA. *Club:* Naval and Military.

CAMPBELL, Cheryl (Anne); actress; *b* 22 May 1949. *Educ:* Francis Bacon Grammar Sch., St Albans; London Acad. of Music and Dramatic Art (Rodney Millington Award). Formerly: student and acting Asst Stage Manager, Watford Palace Theatre; acted at Glasgow Citizens Theatre, Watford Rep., Birmingham Rep., King's Head and National Theatre; Nora in A Doll's House (SWET Award, 1983, for best actress of 1982 in a revival), and Diana in All's Well That Ends Well, RSC; title role in Miss Julie, Lyric, Hammersmith, and Duke of York's, 1983; Asta in Little Eyolf, Lyric, Hammersmith, 1985; title rôle in Daughter-in-Law, Hampstead, 1985; The Sneeze, Aldwych, 1988; Betrayal, Almeida, 1991. Television serials: Pennies from Heaven; Testament of Youth (Best Actress Award, BAFTA, and British Broadcasting Press Guild Award, 1979); Malice Aforethought; A Winter Harvest; Centrepoint. Films include Chariots of Fire, 1981; Greystoke, 1983; The Shooting Party, 1985. *Address:* c/o Michael Whitehall Ltd, 125 Gloucester Road, SW7 4TE. *T:* 071–244 8466.

CAMPBELL, Christopher James; Chairman, British Shipbuilders, since 1989; non-executive Member, National Bus Company, 1988–91 (Member, and chief negotiator, 1986–88); *b* 2 Jan. 1936; *s* of David Heggie Campbell and Nettie Phyllis (*née* Burgess). *Educ:* Epsom College. FCA. Served RAPC, 1959–61. Debenhams and subsidiaries, 1966–86, incl. Man. Dir, Hardy Amies, 1978–79; former Director: Debenhams dept store; Harvey Nichols; Lotus; Debenhams Finance; Debenhams (M & S). Finance Dir, Nat. Rivers Authy Adv. Cttee, 1988–89. Treas., Bow Gp, 1966. Captain Paymaster, HAC Inf. Bn, 1960–63. *Recreations:* reading, listening to music, entertaining, indifferent bridge, current affairs. *Address:* 19 Morpeth Mansions, Morpeth Terrace, SW1P 1ER. *T:* 071–630 7527. *Club:* Brooks's.

CAMPBELL, Sir Clifford (Clarence), GCMG 1962; GCVO 1966; Governor-General of Jamaica, 1962–73; *b* 28 June 1892; *s* of late James Campbell, civil servant, and Blanche, *d* of John Ruddock, agriculturist; *m* 1920, Alice Esthephene, *d* of late William Jolly, planter; two *s* two *d*. *Educ:* Petersfield Sch.; Mico Training Coll., Jamaica. Headmaster: Fullersfield Govt Sch., 1916–18; Friendship Elementary Sch., 1918–28; Grange Hill Govt Sch., 1928–44. Member Jamaica House of Representatives (Jamaica Labour Party) for Westmoreland Western, 1944–49; Chm., House Cttee on Education, 1945–49; 1st Vice-President, Elected Members Assoc., 1945; re-elected 1949; Speaker of the House of Representatives, 1950; Senator and President of the Senate, 1962. KStJ. *Recreations:* agricultural pursuits, reading. *Address:* 8 Cherry Gardens Avenue, Kingston 8, Jamaica. *Clubs:* (Hon. Member) Caymanas Golf and Country, Ex-Services, Kingston Cricket, Liguanea, Rotary, St Andrew's, Trelawny (all in Jamaica).

CAMPBELL, Colin; *see* Campbell, A. C. P.

CAMPBELL, Colin Malcolm; QC (Scot.) 1990; *b* 1 Oct. 1953; *s* of Malcolm Donald Campbell and Annabella Ferguson or Campbell; *m* 1977, Fiona Anderson; one *s* one *d* (and one *d* decd). *Educ:* Grove Acad., Broughty Ferry; Univ. of Dundee (LLB). Passed Advocate, 1977. Lectr, Dept of Scots Law, Univ. of Edinburgh, 1977–79; Standing Junior Counsel: to Scottish Develt Dept (all matters other than Planning), 1984–86; to Scottish Develt Dept (Planning), 1986–90. *Publications:* articles in Scots Law Times and Jl of Law Soc. of Scotland. *Recreation:* golf. *Address:* Advocates' Library, Parliament House, Edinburgh EH1 1RF. *T:* 031-226 5071. *Clubs:* New, Bruntsfield Links (Edinburgh).

CAMPBELL, Sir Colin Moffat, 8th Bt *cr* 1667, of Aberuchill and Kilbryde, Dunblane, Perthshire; MC 1945; Director, James Finlay plc, since 1971 (Chairman, 1975–90); *b* 4 Aug. 1925; *e s* of Sir John Campbell, 7th Bt and Janet Moffat (*d* 1975); *S* father, 1960; *m* 1952, Mary Anne Chichester Bain, *er d* of Brigadier G. A. Bain, Sandy Lodge, Chagford, Devon; two *s* (one *d* decd). *Educ:* Stowe. Scots Guards, 1943–47, Captain. Employed with James Finlay & Co. Ltd, Calcutta, 1948–58, Nairobi, 1958–71, Dep. Chm., 1973–75. President Federation of Kenya Employers, 1962–70; Chairman: Tea Board of Kenya, 1961–71; E African Tea Trade Assoc., 1960–61, 1962–63, 1966–67. Member: Scottish Council, CBI, 1979–85; Council, CBI, 1981–; Commonwealth Develt Corp., 1981–89 (Dep. Chm., 1983–89). CBIM 1980; FRSA 1982. *Recreations:* gardening, racing, cards, travel. *Heir:* *s* James Alexander Moffat Bain Campbell, *b* 23 Sept. 1956. *Address:* Kilbryde Castle, Dunblane, Perthshire. *T:* Dunblane (0786) 823104. *Clubs:* Boodle's; Western (Glasgow); Royal Calcutta Turf, Tollygunge (Calcutta); Nairobi (E Africa).

CAMPBELL, Prof. Colin Murray; Vice-Chancellor, University of Nottingham, since 1988; Professor Emeritus, Queen's University, Belfast; *b* 26 Dec. 1944; *s* of late Donald Campbell and of Isobel Campbell; *m* 1974, Elaine Carlisle; one *s* one *d*. *Educ:* Robert Gordon's Coll., Aberdeen; Univ. of Aberdeen (LLB 1st Cl. Hons). Lecturer: Faculty of Law, Univ. of Dundee, 1967–69; Dept of Public Law, Univ. of Edinburgh, 1969–73; Prof. of Jurisprudence, 1974–88, Dean of Faculty of Law, 1977–80, Pro-Vice-Chancellor, 1983–87, QUB. Member: Council, Soc. for Computers and Law, 1973–88; Standing Adv. Commn on Human Rights, 1977–80; Legal Aid Adv. Cttee, NI, 1978–82; Mental Health Legislation Rev. Cttee, NI, 1978–82; UGC, 1987–88; Nottingham Develt Enterprise, 1988–; UFC Scottish Cttee, 1989–. Chairman: QUBIS Ltd, 1983–88; Ind. Adv. Gp on Consumers Protection in NI, 1984; NI Economic Council, 1987– (Mem., 1985–); Lace Market Develt Co., 1989–; Human Fertilisation and Embryology Authy, 1990–. *Publications:* (ed jtly) Law and Society, 1979; (ed) Do We Need a Bill of Rights?, 1980; (ed) Data Processing and the Law, 1984; numerous articles in books and jls.

Recreations: sport, walking, music, reading. *Address:* University of Nottingham, Nottingham NG7 2RD.

CAMPBELL, David John G.; *see* Graham-Campbell.

CAMPBELL, Prof. Donald, CBE 1987; FCAnaes; FRCS; FFARCSI; FRCPGlas; Professor of Anaesthesia, University of Glasgow, since 1976 (Dean of Faculty of Medicine, 1987–91); President, Royal College of Physicians and Surgeons of Glasgow, from Nov. 1992; *b* 8 March 1930; *s* of Archibald Peter and Mary Campbell; *m* 1st, 1954, Nancy Rebecca McKintosh (decd); one *s* one *d*; 2nd, 1975, Catherine Conway Bradburn; two *d*. *Educ:* Hutchesons' Boys' Grammar Sch.; Univ. of Glasgow (MB, ChB). Lectr in Anaesthesia, 1959–60, Cons. Anaesthetist, 1960–76, Royal Inf., Glasgow. Vice-Dean, 1981–82, Dean, 1982–85, Faculty of Anaesthetists, RCS; Vice-Pres., RCS, 1985–87; Visitor, RCPSG, 1990–Nov. 1992. Chm., Scottish Council for Postgrad. Med. Educn, 1985–90. *Publications:* A Nurse's Guide to Anaesthetics, Resuscitation and Intensive Care, 1964, 7th edn 1983; Anaesthetics, Resuscitation and Intensive Care, 1965, 7th edn 1990; contribs to med. jls, mainly on anaesthesia and intensive therapy. *Recreations:* angling, curling. *Address:* Novar, 27 Tannoch Drive, Milngavie, Glasgow G62 8AR. *T:* 041–956 1736.

CAMPBELL, Donald le Strange, MC; Chairman, Harvest Hydroponics Ltd, since 1985; Director: Project Services Overseas Ltd, since 1974; Hovair International Ltd (formerly Hovair Systems Ltd), since 1974; Beechdean Farms, since 1966; *b* 16 June 1919; *s* of late Donald Fraser Campbell and of Caroline Campbell, Heacham, Norfolk; *m* 1952, Hon. Shona Catherine Greig Macpherson, *y d* of 1st Baron Macpherson of Drumochter; one *s* one *d*. *Educ:* Winchester Coll.; Clare Coll., Cambridge. Served War, 1939–45, Major RA (MC). EFCO Ltd, 1947–55; MEECO Ltd, 1955–61; Davy-Ashmore Ltd, 1961–67. Dep. Chm., BNEC Latin America, 1967. *Recreations:* farming, sailing, field sports. *Address:* Little Dartmouth House, Dartmouth, Devon TQ6 0JP. *Clubs:* Boodle's; Royal Yacht Squadron.

CAMPBELL, Duncan; Director, Countryside Commission for Scotland, since 1988; *b* 23 Sept. 1935; *s* of late Duncan Campbell, sometime Manager, Chartered Bank of India and Australasia, and Mary Beryl Campbell; *m* 1959, Morny Key; two *s*. *Educ:* Merchiston Castle Sch., Edinburgh; Edinburgh Univ.; Newcastle upon Tyne Univ. Nat. service, RHA, 1954–56. Forestry Commission: Forest Manager, 1960–73; Landscape Architect, 1973–80; Head of Design and Recreation Br., 1980–85; Head of Environment Br., 1985–88. *Publications:* articles in Landscape Design and Jl of RASE. *Recreations:* landscape appreciation, fishing. *Address:* Countryside Commission for Scotland, Battleby, Redgorton, Perth PH1 3EW. *T:* Perth (0738) 27921.

CAMPBELL, Prof. Fergus William, FRS 1978; Professor of Neurosensory Physiology, Physiological Laboratory, University of Cambridge, since 1983; Fellow of St John's College, Cambridge, since 1955; *b* 30 Jan. 1924; *s* of William Campbell and Anne Fleming; *m* 1948, Helen Margaret Cunningham; one *s* two *d* (and one *d* decd). *Educ:* Univ. of Glasgow (MA, MD, PhD, DOMS). Casualty and Eye Resident Surg., Western Infirmary, Glasgow, 1946–47; Asst, Inst. of Physiol., Glasgow, 1947–49, Lectr, 1949–52; Res. Graduate, Nuffield Lab. of Ophthalmology, Oxford, 1952–53; Univ. Lectr, 1953–72, Reader in Neurosensory Physiol., 1973–83, Physiol Lab., Cambridge. Hon. FBCO 1962. Hon. DSc: Glasgow, 1986; Aston, 1987. Tillyer Medal, Optical Soc. of America, 1980. *Publications:* papers on neurophysiology and psychophysics of vision in Jl Physiol., and Vision Res. *Recreations:* music, photography. *Address:* 96 Queen Ediths Way, Cambridge CB1 4PP. *T:* Cambridge (0223) 247578.

CAMPBELL, Graham Gordon, CB 1984; Under-Secretary, Department of Energy, 1974–84; *b* 12 Dec. 1924; *s* of late Lt-Col and Mrs P. H. Campbell; *m* 1955, Margaret Rosamond Busby; one *d*. *Educ:* Cheltenham Coll.; Caius Coll., Cambridge (BA Hist.). Served War, Royal Artillery, 1943–46. Asst Principal, Min. of Fuel and Power, 1949; Private Sec. to Parly Sec., Min. of Fuel and Power, 1953–54; Principal, 1954; Asst Sec., Min. of Power, 1965; Under-Sec., DTI, 1973. *Recreations:* watching birds, music, hill-walking, clearing scrub. *Address:* 3 Clovelly Avenue, Warlingham, Surrey CR6 9HZ. *T:* Upper Warlingham (0883) 624671.

CAMPBELL, Sir Guy (Theophilus Halswell), 5th Bt *cr* 1815; OBE 1954; MC 1941; Colonel, late 60th Rifles, El Kaimakam Bey, Camel Corps, Sudan Defence Force, and Kenya Regiment; *b* 18 Jan. 1910; *s* of Major Sir Guy Colin Campbell, 4th Bt, late 60th Rifles, and Mary Arabella Swinnerton Kemeys-Tynte, *sister* of 8th Lord Wharton; *S* father, 1960; *m* 1956, Lizbeth Webb, Bickenhall Mansions, W1; two *s*. *Educ:* St Aubyn's, Rottingdean; Eton Coll.; St Andrews Univ. War of 1939–45 (wounded); served in KOYLI, 1931–42; seconded to Camel Corps, Sudan Defence Force, 1939–47; Comd 2/7 and 7 Nuba Bns, 1943–47; Shifta Ops, Eritrea, 1946; Acting Brig., 1945, HQ SDF Group (N Africa); Palestine, 1948; Mil. Adviser to Count Folke Bernadotte and Dr Ralph Bunche of United Nations, 1948; attached British Embassy as Civil Affairs Officer, Cairo, 1948; British Mil. Mission to Ethiopia, in Ogaden Province, 1949–51; 2nd i/c 1/60th Rifles, BAOR, 1951; comd Kenya Regt (TF), 1952–56, Mau Mau ops; Head of British Mil. Mission to Libya, 1956–60; retired Aug. 1960. MoD, 1965–72. Col R of O, 60th Rifles. Provided historical research, costume, weapons etc for United Artists film Khartoum, 1964. C-in-C's (MELF) Commendation, 1945; Gold Medal of Emperor Haile Selassie (non-wearable). *Recreations:* painting, writing, watching cricket, Rugby football, golf. *Heir: s* Lachlan Philip Kemeys Campbell, The Royal Green Jackets [*b* 9 Oct. 1958; *m* 1986, Harriet Jane Sarah, *o d* of F. E. J. Girling, Malvern; one *s*]. *Address:* 18 Lansdown Terrace, Malvern Road, Cheltenham, Glos GL50 2JT. *Clubs:* Army and Navy, Special Forces; Puffins (Edinburgh); MCC, I Zingari; Royal and Ancient (St Andrews).

CAMPBELL, Maj.-Gen. Sir Hamish Manus, KBE 1963 (CBE 1958); CB 1961; Rev. Hamish Campbell, Order of Prémontré (White Canons), since 1984; ordained priest, 1988; *b* 6 Jan. 1905; *s* of late Major A. C. J. Campbell, Middlesex Regt and Army Pay Dept, and of Alice, *d* of late Comdr Yelverton O'Keeffe, RN; *m* 1929, Marcelle (*d* 1983), *d* of late Charles Ortlieb, Neuchâtel, Switzerland; one *s*. *Educ:* Downside School; New Coll., Oxford. Commissioned in Argyll and Sutherland Highlanders, 1927; transferred to Royal Army Pay Corps, 1937; Lieut-Colonel and Staff Paymaster (1st Class), temp. 1945, subs. 1951; Colonel and Chief Paymaster, temp. 1954, subs. 1955; Major-General, 1959. Command Paymaster: Sierra Leone, 1940–42; Burma, 1946–48; Malta, 1953. Deputy Chief, Budget and Finance Division, SHAPE, 1954–56; Commandant, RAPC Training Centre, 1956–59; Paymaster-in-Chief, War Office, 1959–63; retired, 1963. Col Comdt, RAPC, 1963–70. *Address:* Our Lady of England Priory, Storrington, Pulborough, West Sussex RH20 4LN. *T:* Storrington (0903) 742150.

CAMPBELL, Harold Edward; Director, Greater London Secondary Housing Association, 1978–83; Chairman, Sutton (Hastoe) Housing Association, 1975–85; *b* 28 Feb. 1915; *s* of Edward Inkerman Campbell and Florence Annie Campbell. *Educ:* Southbury Road Elementary Sch.; Enfield Central Sch. Asst Sec., 1946–64, Sec., 1964–67, Cooperative Party; Mem., 1967–73, Dep. Chm., 1969–73, Housing Corp. Gen. Manager, Newlon Housing Trust, 1970–76; Chairman: Cooperative Planning Ltd, 1964–74; Co-Ownership Develt Soc. Ltd, 1966–76; Sutton Housing Trust, 1973–80 (Trustee, 1967–86); Dir, Co-op. Housing Centre, and S British Housing Assoc., 1976–78; Dep. Chm., Stevenage Develt Corp., 1968–80; Mem., Cooperative Develt Agency, 1978–81; Pres., Enfield Highway Cooperative Soc. Ltd, 1976–85 (Dir, 1965–85); Dir, CWS Ltd, 1968–73. Chairman: DoE Working Party on Cooperative Housing, 1973–75; DoE Working Group on New Forms of Housing Tenure, 1976–77; Housing Assoc. Registration Adv. Cttee, 1974–79; Hearing Aid Council, 1970–71. Borough Councillor, Enfield, 1959–63. *Recreations:* music, theatre, cinema. *Address:* Apartado 606, 8200 Albufeira, Portugal.

CAMPBELL, Hugh, PhD; Industrial Adviser, Department of Trade and Industry, 1971–74, retired; *b* 24 Oct. 1916; *s* of Hugh Campbell and Annie C. Campbell (*née* Spence); *m* 1946, Sybil Marian Williams, MB, ChB (*d* 1988), *y d* of Benjamin and Sarah Williams; two *s*. *Educ:* University College Sch., London; St John's Coll., Cambridge (MA, PhD). Research, Dept of Colloid Science, Cambridge, 1938–45; Head of Physical Chem., Research Gp, May and Baker Ltd, 1945–61; Lectr, West Ham Techn. Coll., 1949–54; Research Manager, Chloride Electrical Storage Co. Ltd, 1961–65; Managing Dir: Alkaline Batteries Ltd, 1965–67; Electric Power Storage Ltd, 1968–71; Dir, Chloride Electrical Storage Co. Ltd, 1968–71. Career Consultant in Paris and London, 1974–78. *Publications:* papers on various subjects in scientific jls. *Recreations:* skiing, theatre, travelling. *Address:* 25 Kittiwake Drive, Kidderminster, Worcs DY10 4RS. *T:* Kidderminster (0562) 829626.

CAMPBELL, Hugh Hall, QC (Scot.) 1983; FCIArb; *b* 18 Feb. 1944; *s* of William Wright Campbell and Marianne Doris Stuart Hutchison or Campbell; *m* 1969, Eleanor Jane Hare; three *s*. *Educ:* Glasgow Acad.; Trinity Coll., Glenalmond (Alexander Cross Scholar); Exeter Coll., Oxford (Open Scholar in Classics; BA Hons, MA); Edinburgh Univ. (LLB Hons). FCIArb 1986. Called to the Scottish Bar, 1969; Standing Jun. Counsel to Admiralty, 1976. *Recreations:* music, hill-walking, golf. *Address:* 12 Ainslie Place, Edinburgh EH3 6AS. *T:* 031–225 2067. *Club:* Hon. Company of Edinburgh Golfers.

CAMPBELL, Ian, JP; CEng, MIMechE; national and local government consultant; Director, Dumbarton District Enterprise Trust, since 1987; *b* 26 April 1926; *s* of William Campbell and Helen Crockett; *m* 1950, Mary Millar; two *s* three *d*. *Educ:* Dumbarton Academy; Royal Technical Coll., Glasgow (now Strathclyde Univ.). Engineer with South of Scotland Electricity Board for 17 years. Councillor, Dumbarton, 1958–70; Provost of Dumbarton, 1962–70. MP (Lab): Dunbartonshire W, 1970–83; Dumbarton, 1983–87. PPS to Sec. of State for Scotland, 1976–79. Mem., Strathclyde Region Local Valuation Panel, 1988–. *Address:* The Shanacles, Gartocharn, Alexandria, Dunbartonshire G83 8NB. *T:* Alexandria (0389) 52286.

CAMPBELL, Ian Burns; His Honour Judge Ian Campbell; a Circuit Judge, since 1984; *b* 7 July 1938; *s* of late James Campbell and of Laura Woolnough Dransfield; *m* 1967, Mary Elisabeth Poole, BArch, MCD Liverpool; two *s* one *d*. *Educ:* Tiffin Boys' Sch.; Cambridge Univ. (MA, LLM, PhD). Called to the Bar, Middle Temple, 1966. French Govt Scholar, 1961–62; Asst Lectr in Law, Liverpool Univ., 1962–64, Lectr 1964–69; a Recorder, 1981–84. *Recreation:* cycling.

CAMPBELL, Ian Dugald, QHP 1977; FRCPE, FFCM; Treasurer, Royal College of Physicians of Edinburgh, 1981–85; *b* Dornie, Kintail, 22 Feb. 1916; *s* of John Campbell and Margaret Campbell; *m* 1943, Joan Carnegie Osborn; one *s* two *d*. *Educ:* Dingwall Acad.; Edinburgh Univ. (MB, ChB 1939). FRCPE 1973, FFCM 1974. Served War, 1941–46: UK, BAOR, MEF, RAMC; final appt OC Field Amb. (Lt-Col). Med. Supt, St Luke's Hosp., Bradford, 1946–49; Asst SMO, Leeds Reg. Hosp. Bd, 1949–57; Dep. Sen. Admin. MO, S-Eastern Reg. Hosp. Bd, Scotland, 1957–72, Sen. Admin. MO, 1972–73; Chief Admin. MO, Lothian Health Bd, 1973–80. WHO assignments, SE Asia, 1969, 1971, 1975. *Publications:* various medical. *Recreations:* fishing, shooting, golf. *Address:* 5 Succoth Park, Edinburgh EH12 6BX. *T:* 031–337 5965. *Clubs:* New (Edinburgh); Hon. Company of Edinburgh Golfers (Muirfield); Royal Burgess Golfing Society (Barnton, Edinburgh).

CAMPBELL, Ian James; defence and marine technology consultant; Director of Defence Science, Sema Scientific (formerly CAP Scientific), since 1987; Director of Defence Analysis, YARD Ltd, since 1989; *b* 9 June 1923; *s* of Allan and Elizabeth Campbell; *m* 1946, Stella Margaret Smith. *Educ:* George Heriot's Sch.; Edinburgh Univ. (MA). Op. Res. Sect., HQ Bomber Comd, 1943–46; Asst Lectr in Astronomy, St Andrews Univ., 1946–48; Royal Naval Scientific Service, 1948; Dept of Aeronaut. and Eng Res., Admiralty, 1948–49; Admiralty Res. Lab., 1949–59; Admiralty Underwater Weapons Estab., 1959–68; Chief Scientist, Naval Construction Res. Estab., 1969–73; Head of Weapons Dept, Admiralty Underwater Weapons Estab., 1973–76; Ministry of Defence: Dir of Res. (Ships), 1976–78; Scientific Advr to Ship Dept, 1976–81; Dir Gen. Res. Maritime, 1978–81; Technical Dir, CAP Scientific, 1983–87; Dir of Studies, Centre for Operational Res. and Defence Analysis, 1987–88. Chm., Res. Adv. Cttee, Electronic Engrg Assoc., 1989–. *Publications:* papers on fluid mechanics in scientific jls. *Address:* Claremont, North Street, Charminster, Dorchester, Dorset DT2 9QZ. *T:* Dorchester (0305) 264270.

CAMPBELL, Ian Macdonald, CVO 1977; BSc; FEng; FICE; Member, Economic and Social Committee, EEC, 1983–90; *b* 13 July 1922; *s* of late John Isdale Campbell; *m* 1946, Hilda Ann Williams; one *s* three *d*. *Educ:* University Coll., London (Fellow, 1984). BSc(Eng). British Rail: Chief Civil Engr, Scottish Region, 1965–68; Gen. Manager, E Region, 1970–73; Exec. Dir, BR, 1973–76; Bd Mem., 1977–87; Chm., Scottish Bd, 1983–88. Pres., ICE, 1981–82 (Vice-Pres., 1978–81). *Address:* Lochearnside, St Fillans, Perthshire.

CAMPBELL, Mrs Ian McIvor; *see* Corbet, Mrs Freda K.

CAMPBELL, Air Vice-Marshal Ian Robert, CB 1976; CBE 1964; AFC 1948; *b* 5 Oct. 1920; *s* of late Major and Hon. Mrs D. E. Campbell; *m* 1st, 1953, Beryl Evelyn Newbigging (*d* 1982); one *s*; 2nd, 1984, Elisabeth Guthrie. *Educ:* Eton; RAF Coll., Cranwell. Anti-Shipping Ops, 1940–42; POW, Italy and Germany, 1942–45; 540 Sqdn, Benson, 1946; psa 1949; PSO to C-in-C Far East, 1950; 124 (F) Wing Oldenburg, 1953; OC, RAF Sandwich, 1956; pfc 1957; OC 213 Sqdn, Bruggen, 1958; ACOS Plans HQ 2ATAF, 1959; OC, RAF Marham, 1961; MoD (Air) DASB, 1964; SASO, HQ No 1 Group, 1965; Air Attaché, Bonn, 1968; Dir of Management and Support Intell., MoD, 1970–73; C of S, No 18 (M) Group, Strike Command, 1973–75, retired. *Recreations:* shooting, travel. *Address:* Pike Farm, Fossebridge, Cheltenham, Glos GL54 3JR. *Clubs:* Boodle's, Royal Air Force.

CAMPBELL, Maj.-Gen. Ian Ross, CBE 1954; DSO and Bar, 1941; *b* 23 March 1900; *m* 1927, Patience Allison Russell (*d* 1961); one *d*; *m* 1967, Irene Cardamatis. *Educ:* Wesley Coll., Melbourne; Scots Coll., Sydney; Royal Military College, Duntroon, Canberra (Sword of Honour, 1922). psc Camberley, 1936–37. Served War of 1939–45, Middle East Campaigns, Libya, Greece and Crete (DSO and bar, Cross of Kt Comdr, Greek Order of Phœnix; pow 1941–45); comd Aust. forces in Korean War, 1951–53 (CBE); Comdt, Australian Staff Coll., 1953–54; Comdt, Royal Mil. Coll. Duntroon, 1954–57; retired,

1957, Mem. Federal Exec., RSL, 1955–56. Chm., NSW Div., Aust. Red Cross Soc., 1967–74. Pres., Great Public Schs Athletic Assoc., NSW, 1966–69. Hon. Col, NSW Scottish Regt, 1957–60. *Recreation:* reading. *Address:* 15/17 Wylde Street, Potts Point, Sydney, NSW 2011, Australia. *Clubs:* Australian, Royal Sydney Golf (Sydney).

CAMPBELL, Sir Ian (Tofts), Kt 1988; CBE 1984; VRD 1961; JP; Director, Conservative Board of Finance, 1978–90; Director of Finance and Administration, Scottish Conservative Party, 1988–90; *b* 3 Feb. 1923; *o s* of John Walter Campbell and Mary Hardie Campbell (*née* Scott); *m* 1961, Marion Kirkhope Paterson (*née* Shiel); one *d*. *Educ:* Daniel Stewart's College, Edinburgh. FInstD 1964. RN 1942–46, RNR 1946–65 (Comdr). Man. Dir, MacGregor Wallcoverings, 1966–78. Chm., Select Assured Properties, Glasgow, 1989–; Dep. Chm., Heath Collins Halden (Scotland), 1988– (Dir, 1987–); Director: Travel System, 1987–89; Hermiston Securities, 1990–. Mem., Transport Users' Cons. Cttee for Scotland, 1981–87. Councillor, City of Edinburgh District Council, 1984–88. JP Edinburgh, 1987. OStJ 1987. *Recreations:* golf, water colour painting, vintage cars. *Address:* Merleton, 10 Boswall Road, Edinburgh EH5 3RH. *T:* 031–552 4825. *Clubs:* Royal Over-Seas League; Caledonian (Edinburgh).

CAMPBELL of Succoth, Sir Ilay (Mark), 7th Bt *cr* 1808, of Succoth, Dunbartonshire; *b* 29 May 1927; *o s* of Sir George Ilay Campbell, 6th Bt; *S* father, 1967; *m* 1961, Margaret Minette Rohais, *o d* of J. Alasdair Anderson; two *d*. *Educ:* Eton; Christ Church, Oxford. BA 1952; MA 1970. Joint Scottish Agent for Messrs Christie, Manson & Woods; Chm., Christie's Scotland. Dir., High Craigton Farming Co. Mem., Historic Buildings Council for Scotland, 1989–. Pres., Assoc. for Protection of Rural Scotland, 1978–90. Mem., C of S Cttee for Artistic Matters (Covener, 1987–91). Hon. Vice Pres., Scotland's Gardens Scheme; Trustee, Crarae Gardens Charitable Trust. *Recreations:* heraldry, collecting heraldic bookplates, horticulture. *Heir:* none. *Address:* Crarae Lodge, Inveraray, Argyll PA32 8YA. *T:* Minard (0546) 86274. *Clubs:* Turf; Arts (Glasgow).
See also Sir Gregor MacGregor of MacGregor, Bt.

CAMPBELL, James, FBA 1984; FSA 1971; Fellow of Worcester College, since 1957 and Lecturer in Modern History, since 1958, Oxford University; *b* 26 Jan. 1935. *Educ:* Mill Road Mixed Infants, Clowne, Derbyshire and other primary schools; Lowestoft Grammar School; Magdalen College (Exhibitioner; BA 1955, MA). Junior Research Fellow, Merton College, 1956–57; Worcester College: Tutorial Fellow, 1957; Fellow Librarian, 1977–; Senior Proctor, Oxford Univ., 1973–74. Visiting Professor: Univ. of South Carolina, 1969; Univ. of Rochester, 1986–87. *Publications:* Norwich, 1975; (ed) The Anglo-Saxons, 1982; Essays in Anglo-Saxon History, 1986; articles in learned jls. *Recreation:* topography. *Address:* Worcester College, Oxford OX1 2HB. *T:* Oxford (0865) 278340. *Club:* United Oxford & Cambridge University.

CAMPBELL, James Hugh; Senior Partner, Bird Semple Fyfe Ireland, WS, Glasgow, Edinburgh and London, since 1987; President, Law Society of Scotland, May 1991–92 (Vice-President, 1990–91); *b* 13 Nov. 1926; *s* of William Campbell and Agnes Wightman Campbell; *m* 1953, Iris Burnside (*née* Hercus); two *s* one *d*. *Educ:* Univ. of Glasgow, 1944–45 and 1948–50 (BL). Service in RAF, Japan, 1946–48. Partner, Bird Son & Semple, 1952–73, Sen. Partner, 1965–73; Sen. Partner, Bird Semple & Crawford Herron, 1973–87. Mem. Council, Law Soc. of Scotland, 1986–. *Recreations:* music, reading, golf. *Address:* 24 Woodvale Avenue, Giffnock, Glasgow G46 6RQ. *T:* 041–638 2630. *Clubs:* Royal Scottish Automobile (Glasgow); East Renfrewshire Golf, Glasgow Golf.

CAMPBELL, John Davies, CVO 1980; CBE 1981 (MBE 1957); MC 1945, and bar 1945; company director; HM Diplomatic Service, retired; Consul-General, Naples, 1977–81; *b* 11 Nov. 1921; *s* of late William Hastings Campbell and of late The Hon. Mrs Campbell (Eugenie Anne Westenra, subsequently Harbord), *d* of 14th Baron Louth; *m* 1959, Shirley Bouch; one *s* two *d*. *Educ:* Cheltenham Coll.; St Andrews Univ. Served War, HM Forces, Argyll and Sutherland Highlanders and Popski's Private Army, 1940–46. HM Colonial Service (subseq. HMOCS), 1949–61 (despatches, 1957); HM Foreign (subseq. HM Diplomatic) Service, 1961; First Secretary, 1961; Counsellor, 1972; Counsellor (Information) Ottawa, 1972–77. Commendatore dell'ordine al merito della Repubblica Italiana, 1980. *Recreations:* golf, tennis. *Address:* Ridgeway, The Ludlow Road, Leominster, Herefordshire HR6 0DH. *T:* Leominster (0568) 2446. *Clubs:* Special Forces; Muthaiga Country (Nairobi) (Life Mem.); Mombasa.

CAMPBELL, John L., OBE 1990; owner of Heiskeir and Humla, of the Small Isles; formerly owner of Isle of Canna, which he presented to National Trust for Scotland, 1981; farmer (retired) and author; *b* 1 Oct. 1906; *e s* of late Col Duncan Campbell of Inverneill and Ethel Harriet, *e d* of late John I. Waterbury, Morristown, NJ; *m* 1935, Margaret Fay (author of Folksongs and Folklore of South Uist), *y d* of Henry Clay Shaw, Glenshaw, Pennsylvania (US); no *c*. *Educ:* Cargilfield; Rugby; St John's Coll., Oxford (Dipl. Rural Economy 1930; MA 1933, DLitt 1965). Sec., Barra Sea League, 1933–38. Curator of Woods on Isle of Canna for Nat. Trust for Scotland. FRSE 1989. Hon. LLD, St Francis Xavier Univ., Antigonish, NS, 1953; Hon. DLitt, Glasgow Univ., 1965. *Publications include:* Highland Songs of the Forty-Five, 1933, 2nd edn 1984; The Book of Barra (with Compton Mackenzie and Carl Hj. Borgstrom), 1936; Act Now for the Highlands and Islands (with Sir Alexander MacEwen, in which creation of Highland Develt Bd suggested for first time), 1939; Gaelic in Scottish Education and Life, 1945, 2nd edn 1950; Fr. Allan McDonald of Eriskay, Priest, Poet and Folklorist, 1954; Tales from Barra, told by the Coddy, 1960; Stories from South Uist, 1961; The Furrow Behind Me, 1962; Edward Lhuyd in the Scottish Highlands (with Prof. Derick Thomson), 1963; A School in South Uist (memoirs of Frederick Rea), 1964; Gaelic Poems of Fr. Allan McDonald, 1965; Strange Things (story of SPR enquiry into Highland second sight, with Trevor H. Hall), 1968; Hebridean Folksongs (waulking songs from South Uist and Barra) (with F. Collinson), vol. i, 1969, vol. ii, 1977, vol. iii, 1981; Canna, the Story of a Hebridean Island, 1984; Songs Remembered in Exile, traditional Gaelic songs from Nova Scotia, 1990; other pubns and articles on Highland history and Gaelic oral tradition, also on Hebridean entomology. *Recreations:* entomology, sea fishing, listening to old Gaelic stories. *Address:* Canna House, Isle of Canna, Scotland PH44 4RS.

CAMPBELL, (John) Quentin; Metropolitan Stipendiary Magistrate, since 1981; a Recorder, since 1989; *b* 5 March 1939; *s* of late John McKnight Campbell, OBE, MC, and late Katharine Margaret Campbell; *m* 1st, Penelope Jane Redman (marr. diss. 1976); three *s* one *d*; 2nd, 1977, Ann Rosemary Beeching; one *s* one *d*. *Educ:* Loretto Sch., Musselburgh, Scotland; Wadham Coll., Oxford (MA). Admitted as Solicitor, 1965; private practice, Linnell & Murphy, Oxford (Partner, 1968–80). Chm., Inner London Juvenile Courts, 1985–. Chairman, Bd of Governors, Bessels Leigh Sch., near Oxford, 1979–. *Recreations:* opera, gardening. *Address:* 12 Park Town, Oxford OX2 6SH. *T:* Oxford (0865) 56269. *Clubs:* Chelsea Arts; Frewen (Oxford).

CAMPBELL, Juliet Jeanne d'Auvergne, CMG 1988; HM Diplomatic Service, retired; Mistress of Girton College, Cambridge, since 1992; *b* 23 May 1935; *d* of Maj.-Gen. Wilfred d'Auvergne Collings, CB, CBE and of Nancy Draper Bishop; *m* 1983, Prof. Alexander Elmslie Campbell, *qv*. *Educ:* a variety of schools; Lady Margaret Hall, Oxford. BA. Joined Foreign Office 1957; Common Market Delegation, Brussels, 1961–63; FO, 1963–64; Second, later First Secretary, Bangkok, 1964–66; News Dept, FO, 1967–70; Head of Chancery, The Hague, 1970–74; European Integration Dept, FCO, 1974–77; Counsellor (Inf.), Paris, 1977–80; RCDS, 1981; Counsellor, Jakarta, 1982–83; Head of Training Dept, FCO, 1984–87; Ambassador to Luxembourg, 1988–91. *Address:* Girton College, Cambridge CB3 0JG. *Club:* United Oxford & Cambridge University.

CAMPBELL, Air Vice-Marshal Kenneth Archibald, CB 1989; consulting engineer; Air Officer Maintenance, RAF Support Command, 1987–89; *b* 3 May 1936; *s* of John McLean and Christina Campbell; *m* 1959, Isobel Love Millar; two *d*. *Educ:* George Heriot's Sch.; Glasgow Univ. (BSc); College of Aeronautics, Cranfield (MSc). Various engrg appts, RAF, 1959–90; Air Officer, Wales, 1977–79; Dir, Engrg Policy (RAF), 1981–83; AO, Engrg and Supply, RAF Germany, 1983–85; DG Personal Services (RAF), 1985–87. *Recreations:* golf, skiing. *Club:* Royal Air Force.

CAMPBELL, Rev. Laurence Jamieson; Methodist Minister, Trinity Church, Newport, Gwent Circuit, since 1989; *b* 10 June 1927; *er s* of George S. Campbell and Mary P. Paterson; *m* 1954, Sheena E. Macdonald; two *s* one *d*. *Educ:* Hillhead High Sch., Glasgow; Aberdeen Univ., Edinburgh Univ. (MA). Lieut RA, 1945–48. Housemaster, Alliance High Sch., Kenya, 1952–56; Presbyterian Church of E Africa, 1957–61; Educn Sec., Christian Council of Kenya, 1962; Headmaster: Alliance High Sch., Kenya, 1963–70; Kingswood Sch., Bath, 1970–87. Methodist minister, ordained 1988. Contested North Kenya Constituency, Kenya General Election, 1961. Mem. Council, Univ. of East Africa, 1963–69; Chm., Heads Assoc. of Kenya, 1965–69; Official of Kenya Commonwealth Games Team, 1970. Schoolmaster Fellow, Balliol Coll., Oxford, 1970. Chairman: Christians Abroad, 1977–81; Bloxham Project, 1981–84. *Recreations:* golf, athletics, church. *Address:* Trinity Manse, 46 Western Avenue, Newport, Gwent NP9 3SN. *Club:* Commonwealth Trust.

CAMPBELL, Leila; Chairman, Inner London Education Authority, 1977–78; *b* 10 Aug. 1911; *d* of Myer and Rebecca Jaffe; *m* 1940, Andrew Campbell (*d* 1968); one *d*. *Educ:* Belvedere Sch., Liverpool. Art Teacher's Dip. Dress designer, 1932–42; catering, 1942–46. Elected (Lab), Hampstead Bor. Council, 1961–65; elected new London Bor. of Camden, 1964–78 (later Alderman): Mem., Social Services Cttee; Chm., Libraries and Arts Cttee; elected LCC for Holborn and S St Pancras, 1958–65; elected GLC for Camden, 1964–67: Chm., Schools Sub-cttee; Rep. Camden on ILEA, 1970–78: Vice-Chm., Schs Cttee; Vice-Chm. of ILEA, 1967–77. *Recreations:* cooking, theatre, opera, jazz. *Address:* 56 Belsize Park, NW3 4EH. *T:* 071–722 7038.

CAMPBELL, Sir Matthew, KBE 1963; CB 1959; FRSE; Deputy Chairman, White Fish Authority, and Chairman, Authority's Committee for Scotland and Northern Ireland, 1968–78; *b* 23 May 1907; *s* of late Matthew Campbell, High Blantyre; *m* 1939, Isabella, *d* of late John Wilson, Rutherglen; two *s*. *Educ:* Hamilton Academy; Glasgow Univ. Entered CS, 1928, and after service in Inland Revenue Dept and Admiralty joined staff of Dept of Agriculture for Scotland, 1935; Principal, 1938; Assistant Sec., 1943; Under Sec., 1953; Sec., Dept of Agriculture and Fisheries for Scotland, 1958–68. *Address:* 10 Craigleith View, Edinburgh. *T:* 031–337 5168.

CAMPBELL, Menzies; *see* Campbell, W. M.

CAMPBELL, Sir Niall (Alexander Hamilton), 8th Bt *cr* 1831, of Barcaldine and Glenure; 15th Chieftain, Hereditary Keeper of Barcaldine Castle; Clerk to Justices of N Devon Divisions of Barnstaple, Bideford and Great Torrington and South Molton, since 1976; *b* 7 Jan. 1925; *o s* of Sir Ian Vincent Hamilton Campbell, 7th Bt, CB, and Madeline Lowe Reid (*d* 1929), *e d* of late Hugh Anglin Whitelocke, FRCS; *S* father, 1978; *m* 1st, 1949, Patricia Mary (marr. diss. on his petition, 1956), *d* of R. G. Turner; 2nd, 1957, Norma Joyce, *d* of W. N. Wiggin; two *s* two *d* (including twin *s* and *d*). *Educ:* Cheltenham College (Scholar); Corpus Christi Coll., Oxford. Called to the Bar, Inner Temple. Served War, 1943–46, Lieut Royal Marines; in Inf. bn, NW Europe campaign and on staff of Comdr RM training bde. Appts as Hosp. Administrator, 1953–70, inside and outside NHS, including St Mary's, Paddington, London Clinic, and Royal Hosp. and Home for Incurables, Putney (Chief Exec.); Dep. Chief Clerk, Inner London Magistrates' Courts, 1970–76, and Dep. Coroner, Inner London (South), Southwark. Mem. Exec. Cttee, N Devon Community Health Council; Governor, Grenville Coll., Bideford; Mem. Management Cttee, N Devon Cheshire Home. *Publication:* Making the Best Use of Bed Resources—monograph based on lecture sponsored by King Edward's Hospital Fund, 1965. *Recreations:* garden labour; writing letters to the Times, with little success; keeping a golden retriever; birds. *Heir: er s* Roderick Duncan Hamilton Campbell, of Barcaldine, Younger [*b* 24 Feb. 1961; *m* 1989, Jean Caroline, *d* of Laurie Bicknell, Braunton, Devon; one *d*]. *Address:* The Old Mill, Milltown, Muddiford, Barnstaple, Devon. *T:* Shirwell (027182) 341; The Law Courts, Civic Centre, Barnstaple. *T:* Barnstaple (0271) 22511; (seat) Barcaldine Castle, Benderloch via Connel, Argyllshire. *Club:* Marshalls (Barnstaple).

CAMPBELL, Niall Gordon; Under Secretary, Social Work Services Group, Scottish Office, since 1989; *b* 9 Nov. 1941; *s* of Ian M. Campbell and Jean G. Campbell; *m* 1975, Alison Margaret Rigg; three *s*. *Educ:* Edinburgh Academy; Merton College, Oxford (BA). Entered Scottish Office, 1964; Asst Sec., 1978; posts in Scottish Educn and Scottish Develt Depts. *Address:* 15 Warriston Crescent, Edinburgh EH3 5LA. *T:* 031–556 2895.

CAMPBELL, Maj.-Gen. Peter; *see* Campbell, Maj.-Gen. C. P.

CAMPBELL, Prof. Peter Nelson; Courtauld Professor of Biochemistry, and Director of the Courtauld Institute, Middlesex Hospital Medical School, London University, 1976–87, now Emeritus Professor; Editor in Chief, Biotechnology and Applied Biochemistry, since 1981; *b* 5 Nov. 1921; *s* of late Alan A. Campbell and Nora Nelson; *m* 1946, Mollie (*née* Manklow); one *s* one *d* (and one *s* decd). *Educ:* Eastbourne Coll.; Univ. Coll., London (Fellow, 1981). BSc, PhD, DSc, London; FIBiol. Research and Production Chemist with Standard Telephones and Cables, Ltd, 1942–46; PhD Student, UCL; 1946–47; Asst Lectr UCL, 1947–49; staff of Nat. Inst. for Med. Research, Hampstead and Mill Hill, 1949–54; Asst, Courtauld Inst. of Biochem., Middx Hosp. Med. Sch., 1954–57; Sen. Lectr, Middx Hosp. Med. Sch., 1957–64; Reader in Biochem., Univ. of London, 1964–67; Prof. and Head of Dept of Biochem., Leeds Univ., 1967–75. Hon. Consulting Chemical Pathologist to Middlesex Hosp., 1987–. Butland Vis. Prof., Univ. of Auckland, 1988. Chm., Assoc. of Researchers in Medicine and Sci., 1987–. Hon. Lectr, Dept of Biochem., UCL, 1954–67. Hon. Mem., Biochemical Soc., 1988. Diplôme d'Honneur, Fedn of European Biochemical Socs., 1981. *Publications:* Structure and Function of Animal Cell Components, 1966; (ed with B. A. Kilby) Basic Biochemistry for Medical Students, 1975; (ed) Biology in Profile, 1981; (with A. D. Smith) Biochemistry Illustrated, 1982, 2nd edn 1988; many scientific papers in Biochem. Jl. *Recreations:* theatre, travelling, conversation. *Address:* Department of Biochemistry and Molecular Biology, University College London, WC1E 6BT. *T:* 071–387 7050 ext. 2169.

CAMPBELL, Prof. Peter (Walter); Professor of Politics, Reading University, 1964–91; *b* 17 June 1926; *o s* of late W. C. H. and L. M. Campbell. *Educ:* Bournemouth Sch.; New Coll., Oxford. 2nd class PPE, 1947; MA 1951; Research Student, Nuffield Coll., Oxford, 1947–49. Asst Lecturer in Govt, Manchester Univ., 1949–52; Lectr, 1952–60; Vice-

Warden Needham Hall, 1959–60; Visiting Lectr in Political Science, Victoria Univ. Coll., NZ, 1954; Prof. of Political Economy, 1960–64, Dean, Faculty of Letters, 1966–69, Chm., Graduate Sch. of Contemporary European Studies, 1971–73, Reading University. Hon. Sec. Political Studies Assoc., 1955–58; Chm., Inst. of Electoral Research, 1959–65; Mem. Council, Hansard Soc. for Parly Govt, 1962–77; Editor of Political Studies, 1963–69; Hon. Treas., Joint Univ. Council for Social and Public Administration, 1965–69; Chm., Reading Romilly Assoc., 1965–69; Vice-Chm., Reading and District Council of Social Service, 1966–71; Vice-Pres., Electoral Reform Soc., 1972–; Mem., Nat. Cttee for Electoral Reform, 1976–; Hon. Treas., CAER, 1990–. Member: CNAA Bds and Panels, 1971–78; Social Studies Sub-Cttee, UGC, 1973–83. Co-Pres., Reading Univ. Cons. Assoc., 1961–91. Mem. Council, Campaign for Homosexual Equality, 1978–79; Convenor, Reading CHE, 1979–80; Vice-Pres., Conservative Gp for Homosexual Equality, 1988– (Chm., 1982–88); Mem. Exec. Cttee, Soc. for Individual Freedom, 1984–. Patron, Univ. of Buckingham, 1984–. *Publications:* (with W. Theimer) Encyclopædia of World Politics, 1950; French Electoral Systems and Elections, 1789–1957, 1958; (with B. Chapman) The Constitution of the Fifth Republic, 1958. Articles in British, French and New Zealand Jls of Political Science. *Recreations:* ambling, idling. *Address:* 6 Treyarnon Court, 37 Eastern Avenue, Reading RG1 5RX. *T:* Reading (0734) 661888. *Clubs:* Athenæum, United Oxford & Cambridge University.

CAMPBELL, Quentin; *see* Campbell, J. Q.

CAMPBELL, Robert, MSc; FICE; Management Consultant; Chairman and Chief Executive, Rem Campbell Management Ltd, since 1987; *b* 18 May 1929; *s* of Robert Stewart Campbell and Isobella Frances Campbell; *m* 1950, Edna Maud Evans. *Educ:* Emmanuel IGS; Loughborough Univ. (DLC (Hons), MSc). MIWES. Member of Gray's Inn, 1960. Contracts Engineer, Wyatts, Contractors, 1954–56; Chief Asst Engr, Stirlingshire and Falkirk Water Board, 1956–59; Water Engr, Camborne, 1959–60; Chief Asst City Water Engr, Plymouth, 1960–65; Civil Engr, Colne Valley Water Co., 1965–69; Engrg Inspector, Min. of Housing and Local Govt/DoE, 1969–74; Asst Dir, Resources, Planning, Anglian Water Authority, 1974–77; Chief Executive, Epping Forest Dist Council, 1977–79; Sec., ICE, 1979–81, and Man. Dir, Thomas Telford Ltd, Dir, Watt Cttee on Energy, and Hon. Sec., ICE Benevolent Fund, 1979–81; Chm., Rem Campbell Internat., 1981–87. Freeman of City of London, 1977; Liveryman of Horners' Co. 1977–. *Publication:* The Pricing of Water, 1973. *Recreations:* golf, music, caravanning, cricket. *Address:* 8 Tansy Close, Northampton NN4 9XW. *Club:* MCC.

CAMPBELL, Sir Robin Auchinbreck, 15th Bt *cr* 1628 (NS); *b* 7 June 1922; *s* of Sir Louis Hamilton Campbell, 14th Bt and Margaret Elizabeth Patricia (*d* 1985), *d* of late Patrick Campbell; *S* father, 1970; *m* 1st, 1948, Rosemary, (Sally) (*d* 1978), *d* of Ashley Dean, Christchurch, NZ; one *s* two *d*; 2nd, 1978, Mrs Elizabeth Gunston, *d* of Sir Arthur Colegate, Bembridge, IoW. Formerly Lieut (A) RNVR. *Heir: s* Louis Auchinbreck Campbell [*b* 17 Jan. 1953; *m* 1976, Fiona Mary St Clair, *d* of Gordon King; two *d*]. *Address:* Glen Dhu, Greta Valley, RMD, N Canterbury, New Zealand.

CAMPBELL, Ronald, (Ronnie); MP (Lab) Blyth Valley, since 1987; *b* 14 Aug. 1943; *m* Deirdre (*née* McHale); five *s* one *d*. *Educ:* Ridley High Sch., Blyth. Former miner. Member: Blyth Borough Council, 1969–74; Blyth Valley Council, 1974–88 (Chm., Environmental Health Cttee; Vice-Chm., Housing Cttee). Mem., NUM. *Address:* 68 Broadway, Blyth, Northumberland NE24 2PR; House of Commons, SW1A 0AA.

CAMPBELL, Ronald Francis Boyd, MA; *b* 28 Aug. 1912; *o s* of Major Roy Neil Boyd Campbell, DSO, OBE and Effie Muriel, *y d* of Major Charles Pierce, IMS; *m* 1939, Pamela Muriel Désirée, *o d* of H. L. Wright, OBE, late Indian Forest Service; one *s* two *d*. *Educ:* Berkhamsted Sch.; Peterhouse, Cambridge. Asst Master, Berkhamsted Sch., 1934–39. War of 1939–45: Supplementary Reserve, The Duke of Cornwall's Light Infantry, Sept. 1939; served in England and Italy; DAQMG, HQ 3rd Div., 1943; demobilized with hon. rank of Lt-Col, 1945. Housemaster and OC Combined Cadet Force, Berkhamsted Sch., 1945–51; Headmaster, John Lyon Sch., Harrow, 1951–68. Dir, Public Sch. Appointments Bureau, later Independent Schs Careers Orgn, 1968–78. Walter Hines Page Travelling Scholarship to USA, 1960. 1939–45 Star, Italy Star, Defence and Victory Medals; ERD (2 clasps). *Recreations:* sailing, fishing. *Address:* 30 Marine Drive, Torpoint, Cornwall PL11 2EH. *T:* Plymouth (0752) 813671. *Clubs:* East India, Devonshire, Sports and Public Schools, Royal Cruising.

CAMPBELL, Ross, DSC 1944; Partner, InterCon Consultants, Ottawa, since 1983; *b* 4 Nov. 1918; *s* of late William Marshall Campbell and of Helen Isabel Harris; *m* 1945, Penelope Grantham-Hill; two *s*. *Educ:* Univ. of Toronto Schs; Trin. Coll., Univ. of Toronto. BA, Faculty of Law, 1940. Served RCN, 1940–45. Joined Dept. of Ext. Affairs, Canada, 1945; Third Sec., Oslo, 1946–47; Second Sec., Copenhagen, 1947–50; European Div., Ottawa, 1950–52; First Sec., Ankara, 1952–56; Head of Middle East Div., Ottawa, 1957–59; Special Asst to Sec. of State for Ext. Aff., 1959–62; Asst Under-Sec. of State for Ext. Aff., 1962–64; Adviser to Canadian Delegns to: UN Gen. Assemblies, 1958–63; North Atlantic Coun., 1959–64; Ambassador to Yugoslavia, 1964–67, concurrently accredited Ambassador to Algeria, 1965–67; Ambassador and Perm. Rep. to NATO, 1967–73 (Paris May 1967, Brussels Oct. 1967); Ambassador to Japan, 1973–75, and concurrently to Republic of Korea, 1973. Chm., Atomic Energy of Canada Ltd, 1976–79; President: Atomic Energy of Canada International, 1979–80; Canus Technical Services Corp., Ottawa, 1981–83; Director: MBB Helicopter Canada Ltd, 1984–; UXB International (Canada) Inc., 1986–. *Recreation:* gardening. *Address:* Rivermead House, 890 Aylmer Road, Aylmer, Que J9H 5T8, Canada; (office) Suite 1003, 275 Slater Street, Ottawa K1P 5H9, Canada. *Clubs:* Rideau (Ottawa); Country (Lucerne).

CAMPBELL, Ross; Director, International Military Services Ltd, 1979–83, retired; *b* 4 May 1916; 2nd *s* of George Albert Campbell and Jean Glendinning Campbell (*née* Ross); *m* 1st, 1939, Emmy Zoph (marr. diss. 1948); one *s* one *d*; 2nd, 1952, Dr Diana Stewart (*d* 1977); one *d* (and one *d* decd); 3rd, 1979, Jean Margaret Turner (*née* Ballinger) (marr. diss. 1984). *Educ:* Farnborough Grammar Sch.; Reading Univ. CEng, FICE. Articled to Municipal Engr; Local Authority Engr, 1936–39; Air Min. (UK), 1939–44; Sqdn Ldr, RAF, Middle East, 1944–47; Air Min. (UK), 1947–52; Supt Engr, Gibraltar, 1952–55; Air Min. (UK), 1955–59; Chief Engr, Far East Air Force, 1959–62 and Bomber Comd, 1962–63; Personnel Management, MPBW, 1963–66; Chief Resident Engr, Persian Gulf, 1966–68; Dir Staff Management, MPBW, 1968–69; Dir of Works (Air), 1969–72; Under-Sec., and Dir of Defence Services II PSA, DoE, 1972–75. Dir, 1975–77, Dep. Chief Exec., 1977–79, Internat. Military Services Ltd. *Publications:* papers on professional civil engrg and trng in ICE Jl. *Recreations:* golf, music. *Address:* 41 Nightingale Road, Rickmansworth, Herts WD3 2DA. *T:* Rickmansworth (0923) 773744. *Clubs:* Royal Air Force; Denham Golf.

CAMPBELL, Sir Thomas C.; *see* Cockburn-Campbell.

CAMPBELL, Hon. Sir Walter (Benjamin), AC 1989; Kt 1979; Governor of Queensland, Australia, since 1985; *b* 4 March 1921; *s* of Archie Eric Gordon Campbell and Leila Mary Campbell; *m* 1942, Georgina Margaret Pearce; one *s* one *d* (and one *s* decd). *Educ:* Univ. of Queensland (MA, LLB; Hon. LLD 1980). Served War, RAAF, 1941–46 (pilot). Called to the Qld Bar, 1948; QC 1960; Judge, Supreme Court, Qld, 1967; Chief Justice, Qld, 1982–85. Chairman: Law Reform Commn of Qld, 1969–73; Remuneration Tribunal (Commonwealth), 1974–82; sole Mem., Academic Salaries Tribunal (Commonwealth), 1974–78. President: Qld Bar Assoc., 1965–67; Australian Bar Assoc., 1966–67; Mem. Exec., Law Council of Aust., 1965–67. Dir, Winston Churchill Meml Trust, 1969–80; Chm., Utah Foundn, 1977–85. Mem. Senate 1963–85, and Chancellor 1977–85, Univ. of Qld. Fellow Aust. Inst. Judicial Admin., 1986. KStJ 1986. Freeman, City of London, 1987; Liveryman, GAPAN, 1988. Hon. DLitt James Cook Univ., 1988. *Recreations:* golf, reading. *Address:* Government House, Brisbane, Qld 4001, Australia. *T:* 07 369 7744. *Clubs:* Queensland, Royal Queensland Golf (Brisbane); Australasian Pioneers (Sydney).

CAMPBELL, (Walter) Menzies, CBE 1987; QC (Scot.) 1982; MP Fife North East, since 1987 (L 1987–88, Lib Dem since 1988); *b* 22 May 1941; *s* of George Alexander Campbell and Elizabeth Jean Adam Phillips; *m* 1970, Elspeth Mary Urquhart or Grant-Suttie, *d* of Maj.-Gen. R. E. Urquhart, CB, DSO. *Educ:* Hillhead High School, Glasgow; Glasgow Univ. (MA 1962, LLB 1965; President of the Union, 1964–65); Stanford Univ., Calif. Advocate, Scottish Bar, 1968; Advocate Depute, 1977–80; Standing Jun. Counsel to the Army, 1980–82. Member: Clayson Cttee on licensing reform, 1971; Legal Aid Central Cttee, 1983–87; Scottish Legal Aid Bd, 1987; Broadcasting Council for Scotland, 1984–87. Part-time Chairman: VAT Tribunal, 1984–87; Medical Appeal Tribunal, 1985–87. Chm., Scottish Liberal Party, 1975–77; contested (L): Greenock and Port Glasgow, Feb. 1974 and Oct. 1974; E Fife, 1979; NE Fife, 1983; Lib. spokesman on arts, broadcasting and sport, 1987–88; Lib Dem spokesman on arts, broadcasting and sport, 1988, on defence, 1988–. Member: Select Cttee on Members Interests, 1987–90; Select Cttee on Trade and Industry, 1990–. Chm., Royal Lyceum Theatre Co., Edinburgh, 1984–87. Member: UK Sports Council, 1965–68; Scottish Sports Council, 1971–81. Governor, Scottish Sports Aid Foundn, 1981–; Trustee, Scottish Internat. Educn Trust, 1984–. AAA 220 Yards Champion, 1964 and 1967; UK 100 Metres Record Holder, 1967–74; competed at Olympic Games, 1964 and Commonwealth Games, 1966; Captain, UK Athletics Team, 1965 and 1966. *Recreations:* all sports, reading, music, theatre. *Address:* c/o House of Commons, SW1A 0AA. *T:* 071–219 4446. *Clubs:* National Liberal, Reform; Scottish Liberal (Edinburgh).

CAMPBELL, Hon. Sir (William) Anthony; Kt 1988; **Hon. Mr Justice Campbell;** a Judge of the High Court of Justice, Northern Ireland, since 1988; *b* 30 Oct. 1936; *s* of late H. E. Campbell and of Marion Wheeler; *m* 1960, Gail, *e d* of F. M. McKibbin; three *d*. *Educ:* Campbell Coll., Belfast; Queens' Coll., Cambridge. Called to the Bar, Gray's Inn, 1960; called to the Bar of NI, 1960 (Bencher, 1983; Chm., Exec. Council, 1985–87). Jun. Counsel to Attorney-Gen. for NI, 1971–74; QC (NI) 1974; Senior Crown Counsel in NI, 1984–88. Chm., NI Mountain Rescue Co-ordinating Cttee, 1985. Governor, Campbell Coll., 1976– (Chm., 1984–86); Mem. Council, St Leonards Sch., St Andrews, 1985–. *Recreations:* sailing, hill walking. *Address:* Royal Courts of Justice, Belfast BT1 3JY. *Club:* Royal Ulster Yacht.

See also J. E. P. Grigg.

CAMPBELL, Maj.-Gen. William Tait, CBE 1945 (OBE 1944); retired; *b* 8 Oct. 1912; *s* of late R. B. Campbell, MD, FRCPE, Edinburgh; *m* 1942, Rhoda Alice, *y d* of late Adm. Algernon Walker-Heneage-Vivian, CB, MVO, Swansea; two *d*. *Educ:* Cargilfield Sch.; Fettes Coll.; RMC Sandhurst. 2nd Lieut, The Royal Scots (The Royal Regt), 1933; served War of 1939–45: 1st Airborne Div. and 1st Allied Airborne Army (North Africa, Sicily, Italy and Europe). Lieut-Col Commanding 1st Bn The Royal Scots, in Egypt, Cyprus, UK and Suez Operation (despatches), 1954–57; Col, Royal Naval War Coll., Greenwich, 1958; Brig. i/c Admin. Malaya, 1962; Maj.-Gen., 1964; DQMG, MoD (Army Dept), 1964–67; Col, The Royal Scots (The Royal Regt), 1964–74. Dir, The Fairbridge Soc., 1969–78. US Bronze Star, 1945. *Recreations:* gardening, golf, shooting, fishing. *Address:* Ashwood, Boarhills, St Andrews, Fife KY16 8PR.

CAMPBELL-GRAY, family name of **Lord Gray.**

CAMPBELL-JOHNSON, Alan, CIE 1947; OBE 1946; Officer of US Legion of Merit, 1947; MA Oxon; FRSA, MRI; public relations consultant; *b* 16 July 1913; *o c* of late Lieut-Col James Alexander Campbell-Johnson and late Gladys Susanne Campbell-Johnson; *m* 1938, Imogen Fay de la Tour Dunlap; one *d* (one *s* decd). *Educ:* Westminster; Christ Church, Oxford (scholar). BA 2nd Cl. Hons Mod. Hist., 1935. Political Sec. to Rt Hon. Sir Archibald Sinclair, Leader of Parl. Lib. Party, 1937–40; served War of 1939–45, RAF; COHQ, 1942–43; HQ SACSEA (Wing Comdr i/c Inter-Allied Records Section), 1943–46. Contested (L) Salisbury and South Wilts. Div., Gen. Elections, 1945 and 1950. Press Attaché to Viceroy and Gov.-Gen. of India (Earl Mountbatten of Burma), 1947–48. Chm., Campbell-Johnson Ltd, Public Relations Consultants, 1953–78; Dir, Hill and Knowlton (UK) Ltd, 1976–85. Hon. Fellow Inst. of Public Relations, Pres. 1956–57. Hon. DLitt Southampton, 1990. *Publications:* Growing Opinions, 1935; Peace Offering, 1936; Anthony Eden: a biography, 1938, rev. edn 1955; Viscount Halifax: a biography, 1941; Mission with Mountbatten, 1951, repr. 1972. *Recreations:* watching cricket, listening to music. *Address:* 21 Ashley Gardens, Ambrosden Avenue, SW1P 1QD. *T:* 071–834 1532. *Clubs:* Brooks's, National Liberal, MCC.

CAMPBELL-JOHNSTON, Very Rev. Michael Alexander Ninian, SJ; Provincial, British Province of the Society of Jesus, since 1987; *b* 27 Sept. 1931; *s* of Ninian Campbell-Johnston and Marguerite Antoinette Shakespear. *Educ:* Beaumont College; Séminaire Les Fontaines, France (Lic Phil); LSE (BSc Econ, DipEd); Col. Max. Christi Regis, Mexico (STL). Dir, Guyana Inst. for Social Research and Action, 1967–75; Dir, Social Secretariat, Jesuit Generalate, Rome, 1975–84; Regional Co-ordinator, Jesuit Refugee Service for Mexico and Central America, El Salvador, 1984–87. Editor: Gisra; Promotio Justitiae. *Recreations:* reading, motorbike riding. *Address:* 114 Mount Street, W1Y 6AH. *T:* 071–499 0285.

CAMPBELL ORDE, Alan Colin, CBE 1943; AFC 1919; FRAeS; *b* Lochgilphead, Argyll, NB, 4 Oct. 1898; *s* of Colin Ridley Campbell Orde; *m* 1951, Mrs Beatrice McClure (*d* 1989), *e d* of late Rev. Eliott-Drake Briscoe. *Educ:* Sherborne. Served European War, 1916–18, Flight Sub-Lieut, Royal Navy, and Flying Officer, Royal Air Force; active service in Belgium, 1917; one of original commercial Pilots on London-Paris route with Aircraft Transport & Travel Ltd, 1919–20; Instructor and Adviser to Chinese Govt in Peking, 1921–23; Instructor and latterly Chief Test Pilot to Sir W. G. Armstrong-Whitworth Aircraft, Ltd, Coventry, 1924–36; Operational Manager, British Airways, Ltd, 1936–39; subseq. Operations Manager, Imperial Airways Ltd; was Ops Director BOAC, during first 4 years after its inception in 1939; thereafter responsible for technical development as Development Dir until resignation from BOAC Dec. 1957. *Recreation:* reading in bed. *Address:* Smugglers Mead, Stepleton, Blandford, Dorset. *T:* Child Okeford (0258) 860268. *Club:* Boodle's.

CAMPBELL-ORDE, Sir John A.; *see* Orde.

CAMPBELL-PRESTON, Dame Frances (Olivia), DCVO 1990 (CVO 1977); Woman of the Bedchamber to HM Queen Elizabeth the Queen Mother, since 1965; *b* 2 Sept. 1918; *d* of Lt-Col Arthur Grenfell and Hilda Margaret Grenfell (*née* Lyttelton); *m* 1938, Lt-Col George Patrick Campbell-Preston (*d* 1960), The Black Watch; two *s* two *d*. *Educ:* St Paul's Girls' Sch. WRNS, 1941–43. Mem., Argyll CC, 1960–64; Chm., Children's Panel, Argyle and Argyll and Bute, 1970–80. *Address:* The Turret Cottage, Inverawe, Taynuilt, Argyll PA35 1HU.

CAMPBELL-PRESTON of Ardchattan, Robert Modan Thorne, OBE 1955; MC 1943; TD; DL; Vice-Lieutenant, Argyll and Bute, 1976–90; *b* 7 Jan. 1909; *s* of Colonel R. W. P. Campbell-Preston, DL, JP, of Ardchattan and Valleyfield, Fife, and Mary Augusta Thorne, MBE; *m* 1950, Hon. Angela Murray (*d* 1981), 3rd *d* of 2nd Viscount Cowdray and *widow* of Lt-Col George Anthony Murray, OBE, TD (killed in action, Italy, 1945); one *d*. *Educ:* Eton; Christ Church, Oxford (MA). Lt Scottish Horse, 1927; Lt-Col 1945. Hon. Col, Fife-Forfar Yeo./Scottish Horse, 1962–67. Member Royal Company of Archers, Queen's Body Guard for Scotland. Joint Managing Director, Alginate Industries Ltd, 1949–74. DL 1951, JP 1950, Argyllshire. Silver Star (USA), 1945. *Recreations:* shooting, fishing, gardening. *Address:* Ardchattan Priory, by Oban, Argyll PA37 1RQ. *T:* Bonawe (063175) 274; 31 Marlborough Hill, NW8. *T:* 071–586 2291. *Club:* Puffin's (Edinburgh).
See also Duke of Atholl.

CAMPBELL-SAVOURS, Dale Norman; MP (Lab) Workington, Cumbria, since 1979; *b* 23 Aug. 1943; *s* of late John Lawrence and of Cynthia Lorraine Campbell-Savours; *m* 1970, Gudrun Kristin Runolfsdottir; three *s*. *Educ:* Keswick Sch.; Sorbonne, Paris. Dir, manufacturing co., 1969–77. Member, Ramsbottom UDC, 1972–73. Mem., TGWU and COHSE, 1970–. Contested (Lab): Darwen Division of Lancashire, gen. elections, Feb. 1974, Oct. 1974; Workington, by-election, 1976. *Address:* House of Commons, SW1.

CAMPDEN, Viscount; Anthony Baptist Noel; *b* 16 Jan. 1950; *s* and *heir* of 5th Earl of Gainsborough, *qv*; *m* 1972, Sarah Rose, *er d* of Col T. F. C. Winnington; one *s*. *Educ:* Ampleforth; Royal Agricultural Coll., Cirencester. *Heir:* *s* Hon. Henry Robert Anthony Noel, *b* 1 July 1977. *Address:* Top House, Exton, Rutland, Leics LE15 8AX. *T:* Oakham (0572) 812587; 105 Earls Court Road, W8. *T:* 071–370 5650. *Club:* Turf.
See also Sir F. S. W. Winnington, Bt.

CAMPION, Sir Harry, Kt 1957; CB 1949; CBE 1945; MA; retired as Director of Central Statistical Office, Cabinet Office, 1967; *b* 20 May 1905; *o s* of John Henry Campion, Worsley, Lancs. *Educ:* Farnworth Grammar Sch.; Univ. of Manchester. Rockefeller Foundation Fellow, United States, 1932; Robert Ottley Reader in Statistics, Univ. of Manchester, 1933–39. Dir. of Statistical Office, UN, 1946–47; Mem. of Statistical Commission, United Nations, 1947–67; Pres.: International Statistical Institute, 1963–67; Royal Statistical Society, 1957–59; Hon. LLD, Manchester, 1967. *Publications:* Distribution of National Capital; Public and Private Property in Great Britain; articles in economic and statistical journals. *Address:* Rima, Priory Close, Stanmore, Mddx HA7 3HW. *T:* 081–954 3267. *Club:* Reform.

CAMPION, Peter James, DPhil; FInstP; technical consultant; *b* 7 April 1926; *s* of Frank Wallace Campion and Gertrude Alice (*née* Lambert); *m* 1950, Beryl Grace Stanton, *e d* of John and Grace Stanton; one *s* one *d* (and one *s* decd). *Educ:* Westcliff High Sch., Essex; Exeter Coll., Oxford (MA, DPhil). FInstP 1964. RN, 1943. Nuffield Res. Fellow, Oxford, 1954; Chalk River Proj., Atomic Energy of Canada Ltd, 1955; National Physical Lab., Teddington, 1960–86: Supt, Div. of Radiation Science, 1964; Supt, Div. of Mech. and Optical Metrology, 1974; Dep. Dir, 1976. Mem., Comité Consultatif pour les Etalons de Mesure des Rayonnements Ionisante, 1963–79; Chm., Sect. II, reconstituted Comité Consultatif, Mesure des radionucléides, 1970–79; Mem., NACCB, 1984–86. Editor, Internat. Jl of Applied Radiation and Isotopes, 1968–71. *Publications:* A Code of Practice for the Detailed Statement of Accuracy (with A. Williams and J. E. Burns), 1973; technical and rev. papers in learned jls on neutron capture gamma rays, measurement of radioactivity, and on metrology generally. *Recreation:* winemaking and wine drinking.

CAMPLING, Very Rev. Christopher Russell; Dean of Ripon, since 1984; *b* 4 July 1925; *s* of Canon William Charles Campling; *m* 1953, Juliet Marian Hughes; one *s* two *d*. *Educ:* Lancing Coll.; St Edmund Hall, Oxford (MA; Hons Theol. cl. 2); Cuddesdon Theol. Coll. RNVR, 1943–47. Deacon 1951, priest 1952; Curate of Basingstoke, 1951–55; Minor Canon of Ely Cathedral and Chaplain of King's School, Ely, 1955–60; Chaplain of Lancing Coll., 1960–67; Vicar of Pershore with Pinvin and Wick and Birlingham, 1968–76; RD of Pershore, 1970–76; Archdeacon of Dudley and Director of Religious Education, Diocese of Worcester, 1976–84. Mem., General Synod of Church of England, 1970–; Chm., House of Clergy, Diocese of Worcester, 1981–84; Chm., Council for the Care of Churches, 1988–. Lectr, Leeds Parish Church, 1988–. *Publications:* The Way, The Truth and The Life: Vol. 1, The Love of God in Action, 1964; Vol. 2, The People of God in Action, 1964; Vol. 3, The Word of God in Action, 1965; Vol. 4, God's Plan in Acion, 1965; also two teachers' volumes; Words of Worship, 1969; The Fourth Lesson, Vol. 1 1973, Vol. 2 1974. *Recreations:* music, drama, golf. *Address:* The Minster House, Ripon, N Yorks HG4 1PE. *Club:* Naval.

CAMPORA, Dr Mario; Argentine Ambassador to the Court of St James's, since 1990; *b* 3 Aug. 1930; *m* 1972, Magdalena Teresa María Díaz Gavier; one *s* two *d*. *Educ:* Nat. Univ. of Rosario, Argentina (Dr in Diplomacy). Argentine Foreign Service, 1955–71 and 1973–75; Internat. Orgns Dept, Foreign Policy Bureau, and Legal Dept, Ministry for Foreign Affairs; has served in Geneva, Washington, The Hague, New Delhi, and as deleg. to UN and OAS; Mem., Justicialist Party, active in politics, 1971–73, 1975–; Ambassador Extraordinary, Argentine Special Mission for Disarmament, Geneva, 1985; Sec. of State, Ministry for Foreign Affairs, 1989–90. *Publications:* articles on foreign policy and international relations. *Address:* Argentine Embassy, 49 Belgrave Square, SW1X 8QZ. *T:* 071–235 3777.

CAMPOS, Prof. Christophe Lucien; Director, British Institute in Paris, since 1978; *b* 27 April 1938; *s* of Lucien Antoine Campos and Margaret Lilian (*née* Dunn); *m* 1977, Lucy Elizabeth Mitchell; one *s* four *d*. *Educ:* Lycée Lamoricière, Oran; Lycée Français de Londres; Lycée Henri IV, Paris; Gonville and Caius Coll., Cambridge. LèsL (Paris), PhD (Cantab). Lector in French, Gonville and Caius Coll., 1959; Lecturer in French: Univ. of Maryland, 1963; Univ. of Sussex, 1964; Lectr in English, Univ. i Oslo, 1969; Prof. of French, University Coll., Dublin, 1974. Gen. Editor, Franco-British Studies, 1988–. Chevalier de l'Ordre des Arts et des Lettres (France), 1988. *Publications:* The View of France, 1964; L'Enseignement de la civilisation française, 1988; contribs to Th. Qly, TLS, Univs Qly, Franco-British Studies. *Recreations:* bees, football, gastronomy, navigation. *Address:* 53 Houndean Rise, Lewes, Sussex.

CAMPOS, Roberto de Oliveira, Hon. GCVO 1976; Senator, House of Congress, Brazil, since 1982; *b* Cuiabá, Mato Grosso, 17 April 1917. *Educ:* Catholic Seminaries: Guaxupé and Belo Horizonte, Brazil (grad. Philosophy and Theol.); George Washington Univ., Washington (MA Econs); Columbia Univ., NYC (Hon. Dr). Entered Brazilian Foreign Service, 1939; Economic Counsellor, Brazil-US EDC, 1951–53; Dir 1952, Gen. Man. 1955, Pres. 1959, Nat. Economic Develt Bank; Sec. Gen., Nat. Develt Council, 1956–59; Delegate to internat. confs, incl. ECOSOC and GATT, 1959–61; Roving Ambassador for financial negotiations in W Europe, 1961; Ambassador of Brazil to US, 1961–63; Minister of State for Planning and Co-ord., 1964–67; Ambassador to UK, 1975–82. Prof., Sch. of Econs, Univ. of Brazil, 1956–61. Mem. or past Mem., Cttees and Bds on economic develt (particularly inter-Amer. econ. develt). *Publications:* Ensaios de História Econômica e Sociologia; Economia, Planejamento e Nacionalismo; A Moeda, o Govêrno e o Tempo; A Técnica e o Riso; Reflections on Latin American Development; Do outro lado da cerca; Temas e Sistemas; Ensaios contra a maré; Política Econômica e Mitos Políticos (jtly); Trends in International Trade (GATT report); Partners in Progress (report of Pearson Cttee of World Bank); A Nova Economia Brasileira; Formas Criativas do Desenvolvimento Brasileiro; Omundo que vejo e náo desejo; techn. articles and reports on develt and internat. econs, in jls. *Address:* House of Congress, Praça dos Tres Poderes, 70160 Brasilia DF, Brazil; 140 Francisco Otaviano, Ipanema, Rio de Janiero, Brazil.

CAMPS, William Anthony; Master of Pembroke College, Cambridge, 1970–81; *b* 28 Dec. 1910; *s* of P. W. L. Camps, FRCS, and Alice, *d* of Joseph Redfern, Matlock; *m* 1953, Miriam Camp, Washington, DC, *d* of Prof. Burton Camp, Wesleyan Univ., Connecticut. *Educ:* Marlborough Coll.; Pembroke Coll., Cambridge (Schol.). Fellow, Pembroke Coll., 1933; Univ. Lectr in Classics, 1939; Temp. Civil Servant, 1940–45; Asst Tutor, Pembroke Coll., 1945; Senior Tutor, 1947–62; Tutor for Advanced Students, 1963–70; Pres., 1964–70. Mem., Inst. for Advanced Study, Princeton, 1956–57; Vis. Assoc. Prof., UC Toronto, 1966; Vis. Prof., Univ. of North Carolina at Chapel Hill, 1969. *Publications:* edns of Propertius I, 1961, IV, 1965, III, 1966, II, 1967; An Introduction to Virgil's Aeneid, 1969; An Introduction to Homer, 1980; sundry notes and reviews in classical periodicals. *Recreations:* unremarkable. *Address:* c/o Pembroke College, Cambridge CB2 1RF. *T:* Cambridge (0223) 338100.

CAMROSE, 2nd Viscount, *cr* 1941, of Hackwood Park; **John Seymour Berry,** TD; Bt 1921; Baron 1929; Director, The Daily Telegraph plc; *b* 12 July 1909; *e s* of 1st Viscount Camrose and Mary Agnes (*d* 1962), *e d* of late Thomas Corns, 2 Bolton Street, W; *S* father, 1954; *m* 1986, Princess Joan Aly Khan. *Educ:* Eton; Christ Church, Oxford. Major, City of London Yeomanry, 1941–45. Served War of 1939–45, North African and Italian Campaigns, 1942–45 (despatches). MP (C) for Hitchin Division, Herts, 1941–45. Dep. Chm., The Daily Telegraph Ltd, 1939–87; Vice-Chm. Amalgamated Press Ltd, 1942–59. Younger Brother, Trinity House. *Heir:* *b* Baron Hartwell, *qv*. *Address:* 8a Hobart Place, SW1. *T:* 071–235 9900; Hackwood, Basingstoke, Hampshire. *T:* Basingstoke (0256) 464630. *Clubs:* Buck's, White's, Beefsteak, Marylebone Cricket (MCC); Royal Yacht Squadron (Trustee).

CANADA, Primate of All; *see* Peers, Most Rev. M. G.

CANADA, Primate of; *see* Quebec, Archbishop of, (RC).

CANADA, Metropolitan of the Ecclesiastical Province of; *see* Newfoundland, Western, Archbishop of.

CANAVAN, Dennis Andrew; MP (Lab) Falkirk West, since 1983 (West Stirlingshire, Oct. 1974–1983); *b* 8 Aug. 1942; *s* of Thomas and Agnes Canavan. *Educ:* St Columba's High Sch., Cowdenbeath; Edinburgh Univ. (BSc Hons, DipEd). Head of Maths Dept, St Modan's High Sch., Stirling, 1970–74; Asst Head, Holy Rood High Sch., Edinburgh, 1974. District Councillor, 1973–74; Leader of Labour Gp, Stirling District Council, 1974; Member: Stirling Dist Educn Sub-cttee, 1973–74; Stirlingshire Youth Employment Adv. Cttee, 1972–74. Sec., W Stirlingshire Constituency Labour Party, 1972–74; Labour Party Agent, Feb. 1974; Treasurer, Scottish Parly Lab. Gp, 1976–79, Vice-Chm., 1979–80, Chm., 1980–81. Sponsored by COHSE; Parly spokesman for Scottish Cttee on mobility for the disabled, 1977–; Mem., H of C Select Cttee on For. Affairs, 1982–; Vice-Chair: PLP NI Cttee, 1983–; PLP Foreign Affairs Cttee, 1983–; Chair, Parly Br, EIS, 1983–; Founder and Convener, All-Party Parly Scottish Sports Gp, 1987–. *Publications:* contribs to various jls on educn and politics. *Recreations:* hill walking, marathon running, swimming, reading, football (Scottish Univs football internationalist, 1966–67 and 1967–68; Hon. Pres., Milton Amateurs FC). *Address:* 15 Margaret Road, Bannockburn, Stirlingshire. *T:* Bannockburn (0786) 812581; House of Commons, SW1A 0AA. *T:* 071–219 3000. *Clubs:* Bannockburn Miners' Welfare (Bannockburn); Camelon Labour (Falkirk).

CANAVAN, Vincent Joseph; Sheriff of South Strathclyde, Dumfries and Galloway at Hamilton, since 1987; *b* 13 Dec. 1946; *s* of James Canavan and Catherine Ludivine Brogan; *m* 1973, Mary Allison; three *s* three *d*. *Educ:* St Aloysius Coll., Glasgow; Univ. of Glasgow (LLB Hons 1968). Qualified as Solicitor, 1970; passed Advocate, 1980. *Recreations:* reading history, Italian cuisine. *Address:* Sheriff Court, Almada Street, Hamilton, Lanarks ML3 0HF. *Club:* Edinburgh University Staff.

CANBERRA AND GOULBURN, Bishop of, since 1983; **Rt. Rev. Owen Douglas Dowling;** *b* 11 Oct. 1934; *s* of Cecil Gair Mackenzie Dowling and Winifred Hunter; *m* 1958, Beverly Anne Johnston (*d* 1985); two *s* one *d*. *Educ:* Melbourne High School; Trinity Coll., Melbourne Univ. (BA, DipEd, ThL). Victorian Education Dept, Secondary Teacher, 1956–60; ordained to ministry of Anglican Church, 1960; Asst Curate, Sunshine/Deer Park, Dio. Melbourne, 1960–62; Vicar of St. Philip's, W Heidelberg, 1962–65; Precentor and Organist, St Saviour's Cathedral, Goulburn, 1965–67; Rector of South Wagga Wagga, 1968–72; Rector of St. John's, Canberra, 1972–81; Archdeacon of Canberra, 1974–81; Asst Bishop, Dio. Canberra and Goulburn, 1981–83. *Recreations:* pipe organ and piano playing; squash. *Address:* (office) GPO Box 1981, Canberra, ACT 2601, Australia; (home) 51 Rosenthal Street, Campbell, ACT 2601. *T:* (06) 248 0716. *Clubs:* Canberra, Southern Cross (Canberra).

CANDELA OUTERINO, Felix; engineer and architect; Professor, Escuela Nacional de Arquitectura, University of Mexico, since 1953 (on leave of absence); *b* Madrid, 27 Jan. 1910; *s* of Felix and Julia Candela; *m* 1940, Eladia Martin Galan (*d* 1964); four *d*; *m* 1967, Dorothy H. Davies. *Educ:* Univ. of Madrid, Spain. Architect, Escuela Superior de Arquitectura de Madrid, 1935. Captain of Engineers, Republican Army, Spanish Civil War, 1936–39. Emigrated to Mexico, 1939; Mexican Citizen, 1941; USA citizen, 1978. General practice in Mexico as Architect and Contractor. Founded (with brother Antonio) Cubiertas ALA, SA, firm specializing in design and construction of reinforced concrete shell structures. Work includes Sports Palace for Mexico Olympics, 1968. Founding Mem., Internat. Acad. of Architecture, Sofia, 1986; Hon. Member: Sociedad de Arquitectos Colombianos, 1956; Sociedad Venezolana de Arquitectos, 1961; International Assoc. for Shell Structures, 1962; Acad. de Arquitectura de Mexico, 1983. Charles Elliot Norton Prof. of Poetry, Harvard Univ., for academic year, 1961–62; Jefferson Meml Prof., Univ. of Virginia, 1966; Andrew D. White Prof., Cornell Univ., 1969–74; Prof., Dept of Architecture, Univ. of Illinois at Chicago, 1971–78; Prof. Honorario: Escuela Tecnica Superior de Arquitectura de Madrid, 1969; Univ. Nacional Federico Villareal, Peru, 1977; William Hoffman Wood Prof., Leeds Univ., 1974–75. Gold Medal, Instn

Structural Engineers, England, 1961; Auguste Perret Prize of International Union of Architects, 1961; Alfred E. Lindau Award, Amer. Concrete Inst., 1965; Silver Medal, Acad. d'Architecture, Paris, 1980; Gold Medal, Consejo Superior de Arquitectos de España, 1981; Silver Medal, Union des Architects Bulgares, 1983; Gold Medal, Premio Antonio Camuñas, Madrid, 1985. Hon. Fellow American Inst. of Architects, 1963; Hon. Corr. Mem., RIBA, 1963; Plomada de Oro, Soc. de Arquitectos Mexicanos, 1963; Doctor in Fine Arts (*hc*): Univ. of New Mexico, 1964; Univ. of Illinois, 1979; Dr Ing *hc* Univ. de Santa Maria, Caracas, 1968; Dr *hc* Univ. of Sevilla, Spain, 1990. Order of Civil Merit, Spain, 1978. *Publications:* En Defensa del Formalismo, 1985; several articles in architectural and engineering magazines all around the world; *relevant publication:* Candela, the Shell Builder, by Colin Faber, 1963. *Address:* 6109 Bayberry Lane, Raleigh, NC 27612, USA. *T:* (919) 848–3303; Avenida America 14–7, Madrid 2, Spain. *T:* 356 0096.

CANDLIN, Prof. Christopher Noel; Professor of Linguistics, Macquarie University, Sydney, Australia, since 1987; Director, National Centre for English Language Teaching and Research, Macquarie University, since 1988; *b* 31 March 1940; *s* of Edwin Frank Candlin and Nora Candlin (*née* Letts); *m* 1964, Sally (*née* Carter); one *s* three *d*. *Educ:* Jesus Coll., Oxford (MA); Univ. of London (PGCE); Yale Univ. (MPhil). Research Associate, Univ. of Leeds, 1967–68; University of Lancaster: Lectr, 1968, later Sen. Lectr; Prof. of Linguistics and Modern English Language, 1981–87. Visiting Professor: Univ. of Giessen, 1975; Ontario Inst. for Studies in Educn, Toronto, 1983; East–West Centre, Honolulu, 1978; Univ. of Hawaii at Manoa, 1984; Univ. of Melbourne, 1985. FRSA. General Editor: Applied Linguistics and Language Study; Language in Social Life; Language Teacher Educn Scheme; Language Teaching Methodology Series. *Publications:* Challenges, 1978; The Communicative Teaching of English, 1981; Computers in English Language Teaching and Research, 1985; Language Learning Tasks, 1986; Language, Learning and Community, 1989; English at Work, 1991. *Recreations:* sailing, cooking. *Address:* School of English and Linguistics, Macquarie University, Sydney, NSW 2109, Australia.

CANDLISH, Thomas Tait, FEng 1980; Chairman, Historic Cars Ltd, since 1988; consultant, construction industry, since 1989; *b* 26 Nov. 1926; *s* of John Candlish and Elizabeth (*née* Tait); *m* 1964, Mary Trinkwon; two *s*. *Educ:* Perth Acad.; Glasgow Univ. (BSc Eng). FICE 1971. Served RE, 1946–49 (commnd). Student Engr, George Wimpey & Co. Ltd, 1944–46; rejoined Wimpey, 1951; served in: Borneo, 1951–54; Papua New Guinea, 1955–57; Arabian Gulf area, 1958–62; W Africa, 1962–65; Director: George Wimpey PLC, 1973–85 (Man. Dir, 1978–85); Wimpey Internat., 1973–85 (Chm., 1979–85); Wimpey ME & C, 1973–85; Wimpey Marine Ltd, 1975–85 (Chm., 1979–85); Brown & Root-Wimpey Highlands Fabricators, 1974–89 (Chm., 1981–86); British Smelter Constructions Ltd, 1977–83 (Chm., 1977–83); Hill Samuel Developments, 1978–85; A & P Appledore Holdings, 1979–85; Brown & Root (UK) Ltd, 1985–89; Chm., Howard Humphreys Gp Ltd, 1987–89. Chm., Export Gp for Constructional Industries, 1983–85; Member: EDC for Civil Engrg, 1979–82; British Overseas Trade Bd, 1984–87. *Recreations:* motor sport, ski-ing, golf. *Address:* Tithe Cottage, Dorney Wood Road, Burnham, Bucks SL1 8EQ. *Club:* Royal Automobile.

CANE, Prof. Violet Rosina; Professor of Mathematical Statistics, University of Manchester, 1971–81, now Emeritus; *b* 31 Jan. 1916; *d* of Tubal George Cane and Annie Louisa Lansdell. *Educ:* Newnham Coll., Cambridge (MA, Dipl. in Math. Stats). BoT, 1940; Univ. of Aberdeen, 1941; FO, 1942; Min. of Town and Country Planning, 1946; Statistician to MRC Applied Psychol. Unit, 1948; Queen Mary Coll., London, 1955; Fellow, Newnham Coll., Cambridge, 1957; Lectr, Univ. of Cambridge, 1960. Mem., UGC, 1974–79. Mem., Cambridge CC, 1965–72, 1982–90. Hon. MSc Manchester, 1974. *Publications:* (contrib.) Current Problems in Animal Behaviour, 1961; (contrib.) Perspectives in Probability and Statistics, 1975; papers in Jl of Royal Stat. Soc., Animal Behaviour, and psychol jls. *Recreation:* supporting old houses. *Address:* 13/14 Little St Mary's Lane, Cambridge CB2 1RR. *T:* Cambridge (0223) 357277; Statistical Laboratory, University of Cambridge, 16 Mill Lane, Cambridge CB2 1SB.

CANET, Maj.-Gen. Lawrence George, CB 1964; CBE 1956; BE; Master General of the Ordnance, Australia, 1964–67, retired; *b* 1 Dec. 1910; *s* of late Albert Canet, Melbourne, Victoria; *m* 1940, Mary Elizabeth Clift, *d* of Cecil Clift Jones, Geelong, Victoria; one *s*. *Educ:* RMC Duntroon; Sydney Univ. (BE). Served War of 1939–45 with 7th Australian Div. (Middle East and Pacific). GOC Southern Command, 1960–64. Brigadier 1953; Maj.-Gen. 1957. *Address:* 37 The Corso, Isle of Capri, Surfers Paradise, Qld 4217, Australia.

CANETTI, Elias; writer; *b* Ruschuk, Bulgaria, 25 July 1905; *e s* of late Jacques Canetti and Mathilde (*née* Arditi); *m* 1st, 1934, Venetia Taubner-Calderón (*d* 1963); 2nd; one *c*. *Educ:* schs in Manchester, Vienna and Zurich; Univ. of Vienna (DSc 1929). Settled in London, 1939. Prizes include: Prix Internat. de Paris, 1949; Austrian Prize for Literature, 1968; Kafka Prize, Austria, 1981; Nobel Prize for Literature, 1981. *Publications: plays:* Hochzeit, 1932; Komödie der Eitelkeit, 1934; Die Befristeten, 1952 (The Numbered, 1956); *novel:* Bie Blendung, 1935 (Auto da Fé, 1946); *non-fiction:* Fritz Wotruba, 1955; Masse und Macht, 1960 (Crowds and Power, 1962); Die Stimmen von Marrakesch, 1967 (The Voices of Marrakesh, 1978); Der andere Prozess, 1969 (Kafka's Other Trial, 1974); Die Provinz des Menschen: Aufzeichnungen 1942–1972, 1973 (The Human Province, 1979); Der Ohrenzeuge: 50 Charaktere, 1974 (Earwitness, 1979); *autobiography:* Die geretete Zunge, 1977 (The Tongue set Free, 1979); Die Fackel im Ohr, 1980 (The Torch in my Ear, 1989); Das Augenspiel, 1985 (The Play of the Eyes, 1990).

CANHAM, Bryan Frederick, (Peter), MC 1943; FCIS; Non-Executive Director, Eurofi (formerly Eurofi UK) plc (Chairman, 1981); *b* 11 April 1920; *s* of Frederick William Canham and Emma Louisa Martin; *m* 1944, Rita Gwendoline Huggett; one *s*. *Educ:* Trinity County Sch. FCIS 1968 (ACIS 1950). Served War, 1939–46: N Africa, Italy and NW Europe; Captain 1st Royal Tank Regt. Accounting and financial appts, Shell cos in Kenya, Tanzania and French W Africa, 1947–56; Controller, S Europe and N Africa, Shell Internat. Petroleum Co., 1956–60; Finance Dir, Shell Philippines and Ass. Cos, 1960–63; Finance Dir, Shell Malaysia and Ass. Cos, 1963–68; Personnel Adviser, finance and computer staff, Shell Internat. Pet. Co., 1968–73; Div. Hd, Loans, Directorate Gen. XVIII, Commn of European Communities, 1973–76, Dir, Investment and Loans, 1976–80. *Recreations:* reading, chess, pottering. *Address:* The Old Laundry, Penshurst, Kent TN11 8HY. *T:* Penshurst (0892) 870239; The Cottage, Stedham Hall, Stedham, W Sussex; (office) Guildgate House, Pelican Lane, Newbury, Berks RG13 1NX. *T:* Newbury (0635) 31900. *Club:* Muthaiga Country (Nairobi).

CANHAM, Paul George, LVO 1991; Official Secretary to Governor-General of New Zealand, 1985–90; *b* 25 Oct. 1933; *s* of George Ernest Canham and Ella Mary (*née* Mackenzie); *m* 1964, Diane Alderton; one *s* one *d*. *Educ:* Timaru Boys' High Sch.; Victoria Univ. of Wellington (BA, MA Hons History). Teacher: Pomfret Sch., Conn., 1957; Matamata Coll., NZ, 1960; Hauraki Plains Coll., 1967; Heretaunga Coll., 1969; Dep. Prin., Hutt Valley High Sch., 1973; Prin., Wanganui High Sch., 1979. *Recreations:* bridge, surfcasting. *Address:* 11B Tivoli Place, Christchurch 5, New Zealand. *T:* (03) 352–0323.

CANHAM, Peter; *see* Canham, B. F.

CANN, Charles Richard; Deputy Secretary, Ministry of Agriculture, Fisheries and Food, since 1991; *b* 3 Feb. 1937; *s* of Charles Alfred Cann and Grace Elizabeth Cann; *m* 1979, Denise Ann Margaret Love; two *s*. *Educ:* Merchant Taylors' Sch., Northwood, Mddx; St John's Coll., Cambridge (MA). Asst Principal, MAFF, 1960, Principal 1965; Cabinet Office, 1969–71; Asst Sec., MAFF, 1971; Under Sec., 1981; Fisheries Sec., MAFF, 1987–91. *Address:* c/o Ministry of Agriculture, Fisheries and Food, Whitehall Place East, SW1A 2HH.

CANN, Prof. Johnson Robin, ScD; Professor of Earth Sciences, University of Leeds, since 1989; *b* 18 Oct. 1937; *er s* of Johnson Ralph Cann and (Ethel) Mary (*née* Northmore); *m* 1963, Janet, *d* of late Prof. Charles John Hamson, QC; two *s*. *Educ:* St Alban's Sch.; St John's Coll., Cambridge (MA, PhD, ScD). Research fellow, St John's Coll., 1962–66; post-doctoral work in Depts of Mineralogy and Petrology, and Geodesy and Geophysics, Cambridge, 1962–66; Dept of Mineralogy, British Museum (Natural History), 1966–68; Lectr, then Reader, School of Environmental Sciences, Univ. of East Anglia, 1968–77; J. B. Simpson Prof. of Geology, Univ. of Newcastle upon Tyne, 1977–89; current research in hot springs of mid-ocean ridges, seafloor volcanoes, rocks of ocean floor, creation of oceanic crust, obsidian in archaeology. Member, then Chm., ocean crust panel, 1975–78, UK rep. on planning cttee, 1978–84, Jt Oceanographic Instns for Deep Earth Sampling; co-chief scientist on Glomar Challenger, 1976 and 1979; Adjunct Scientist, Woods Hole Oceanographic Instn, 1987–. Chm., UK Ocean Drilling Program Grants Cttee, 1987–. Mem., UGC physical sciences sub-cttee, 1982–88. Murchison Medal, Geol Soc. of London, 1990. *Publications:* papers in jls of earth science and archaeology. *Recreations:* gathering, music, local politics. *Address:* Department of Earth Sciences, University of Leeds, Leeds LS2 9JT. *T:* Leeds (0532) 335200.

CANNAN, Denis; dramatist and script writer; *b* 14 May 1919; *s* of late Captain H. J. Pullein-Thompson, MC, and late Joanna Pullein-Thompson (*née* Cannan); *m* 1st, 1946, Joan Ross (marr. diss.); two *s* one *d*; 2nd, 1965, Rose Evansky; he changed name to Denis Cannan, by deed poll, 1964. *Educ:* Eton. A Repertory factotum, 1937–39. Served War of 1939–45, Queen's Royal Regt, Captain (despatches). Actor at Citizens' Theatre, Glasgow, 1946–48. *Publications: plays:* Max (prod. Malvern Festival), 1949; Captain Carvallo (Bristol Old Vic and St James's Theatres), 1950; Colombe (trans. from Anouilh), New Theatre, 1951; Misery Me!, Duchess, 1955; You and Your Wife, Bristol Old Vic, 1955; The Power and The Glory (adaptation from Graham Greene), Phoenix Theatre, 1956, and Phœnix Theatre, New York, 1958; Who's Your Father?, Cambridge Theatre, 1958; US (original text), Aldwych, 1966; adapted Ibsen's Ghosts, Aldwych, 1966; One at Night, Royal Court, 1971; The Ik (adaptation and collaboration), 1975; Dear Daddy, Oxford Festival and Ambassadors, 1976 (Play of the Year award, 1976); the screenplays of several films; plays for TV and radio, adaptations for TV series. *Address:* 43 Osmond Road, Hove, Sussex BN3 1TF.

See also D. L. A. Farr.

CANNAN, Rt. Rev. Edward Alexander Capparis; Assistant Bishop, Diocese of Hereford, since 1986; *b* 25 Dec. 1920; *s* of Alexander and Mabel Capparis; *m* 1941, Eunice Mary Blandford; three *s*. *Educ:* St Marylebone Grammar School; King's College, London (BD, AKC). Served RAF, 1937–46 (despatches). Deacon 1950, priest 1951, dio. Salisbury; Curate, Blandford Forum, Dorset, 1950–53. Chaplain, RAF, 1953–74; RAF Cosford, 1953–54; Padgate, 1954–57; HQ 2 Gp, Germany, 1957–58; Lecturer, RAF Chaplains' Sch., 1958–60; RAF Gan, Maldive Islands, 1960–61; RAF Halton, 1961–62; Hereford, 1962–64; Khormaksar, Aden, 1964–66; Vice-Principal, RAF Chaplains' School, 1966–69; Asst Chaplain-in-Chief, 1969–74; Far East Air Force, Singapore, 1969–72; HQ Training Comd, 1972–73; Principal, RAF Chaplains' Sch., 1973–74; Hon. Chaplain to the Queen, 1972–74; Chaplain, St Margaret's Sch., Bushey, 1974–79; Bishop of St Helena, 1979–85. *Publication:* A History of the Diocese of St Helena and its Precursors 1502–1984, 1985. *Recreations:* gardening, house maintenance, photography. *Address:* Church Cottage, Allensmore, Hereford HR2 9AQ. *T:* Hereford (0432) 277357. *Club:* Royal Air Force.

CANNELL, Prof. Robert Quirk; Head of Crop and Soil Environmental Sciences Department, Virginia Polytechnic Institute and State University, since 1987; *b* 20 March 1937; *s* of William Watterson Cannell and Norah Isabel Corjeag; *m* 1962, Edwina Anne Thornborough; two *s*. *Educ:* King's Coll., Newcastle upon Tyne; Univ. of Durham (BSc, PhD). FIBiol 1986. Shell Chemical Co., London, 1959; School of Agriculture, Univ. of Newcastle upon Tyne, 1961; Dept of Agronomy and Plant Genetics, Univ. of Minnesota, 1968–69; Letcombe Lab., AFRC, Oxon, 1970; Dir, Welsh Plant Breeding Station, Aberystwyth, 1984–87. *Publications:* papers in agricultural science jls. *Address:* Department of Crop and Soil Environmental Sciences, Virginia Polytechnic Institute and State University, Blacksburg, Virginia 24061, USA. *T:* 703–231 6305. *Club:* Farmers.

CANNING, family name of **Baron Garvagh.**

CANNON, Prof. John Ashton, CBE 1985; PhD; Professor of Modern History, University of Newcastle upon Tyne, since 1976; Pro-Vice Chancellor, 1983–86; *b* 8 Oct. 1926; *s* of George and Gladys Cannon; *m* 1st, 1948, Audrey Elizabeth, *d* of G. R. Caple (marr. diss. 1953); one *s* one *d*; 2nd, 1953, Minna, *d* of Frederick Pedersen, Denmark; one *s* two *d*. *Educ:* Hertford Grammar Sch.; Peterhouse, Cambridge (MA 1955). PhD Bristol, 1958. Served RAF, 1947–49 and 1952–55. History of Parlt Trust, 1960–61; Univ. of Bristol: Lectr, 1961; Sen. Lectr, 1967; Reader, 1970; Dean, Faculty of Arts, Univ. of Newcastle upon Tyne, 1979–82. Member: UGC, 1983–89 (Vice-Chm., 1986–89; Chm., Arts Sub-Cttee, 1983–89); Open Univ. Vis. Cttee, 1988–. Lectures: Wiles, Queen's Univ. Belfast, 1982; Raleigh, British Acad., 1982; Prothero, RHistS, 1985; Stenton, Reading Univ., 1986. Chm., Radio Bristol, 1970–74. FRHistS; FRSA. *Publications:* The Fox-North Coalition: crisis of the constitution, 1970; Parliamentary Reform, 1640–1832, 1973; (ed with P. V. McGrath) Essays in Bristol and Gloucestershire History, 1976; (ed) The Letters of Junius, 1978; (ed) The Historian at Work, 1980; (ed) The Whig Ascendancy, 1981; Aristocratic Century, 1984; (ed jtly) The Blackwell Dictionary of Historians, 1988; (with R. Griffiths) The Oxford Illustrated History of the British Monarchy, 1988. *Recreations:* music, losing at tennis. *Address:* 17 Haldane Terrace, Jesmond, Newcastle upon Tyne NE2 3AN. *T:* Newcastle upon Tyne (091) 2815186.

CANNON, John Francis Michael; Keeper of Botany, Natural History Museum (formerly British Museum (Natural History)), 1977–90; *b* 22 April 1930; *s* of Francis Leslie Cannon and Aileen Flora Cannon; *m* 1954, Margaret Joy (*née* Herbert); two *s* one *d*. *Educ:* Whitgift Sch., South Croydon, Surrey; King's Coll., Newcastle upon Tyne, Univ. of Durham (BSc 1st Cl. Hons Botany). Dept of Botany, British Museum (Nat. History), 1952, Dep. Keeper 1972. President: Botanical Soc. of the British Isles, 1983–85; Ray Soc., 1986–. *Publications:* papers in scientific periodicals and similar pubns. *Recreations:* travel, music, gardening. *Address:* Barn Croft, Rodmell, near Lewes, E Sussex BN7 3HF.

CANNON, Richard Walter, CEng, FIEE; Joint Managing Director, 1977–83, Managing Director, 1983, Cable and Wireless plc; retired; *b* 7 Dec. 1923; *s* of Richard William Cannon and Lily Harriet Cannon (*née* Fewins); *m* 1949, Dorothy (formerly Jarvis); two *d. Educ:* Eltham Coll. Joined Cable and Wireless Ltd, 1941; Exec. Dir, 1973. Director: Batelco (Bahrain), 1981–90; Teletswana (Botswana), 1984–86. *Publications:* telecommunications papers for IEE and IERE.

CANNON, Thomas; Director, Manchester Business School, since 1989; *b* 20 Nov. 1945; *s* of Albert and Bridget Cannon; *m* 1971, Frances Cannon (*née* Constable); one *s* one *d*. *Educ:* St Francis Xavier's Grammar Sch., Liverpool; Borough Polytechnic. BSc (Hons) Sociology (London Univ. external degree). FIEx, FIPDM; FRSA. Res. Associate, Warwick Univ., 1969–71; Lectr, Middlesex Poly., 1971–72; Products Man., Imperial Gp, 1972–74; Lectr, Durham Univ., 1975–81; Prof., Univ. of Stirling, 1981–89. Member: ESRC; Industry, Environment and Economy RDG; Jt Cttee, ESRC/SERC; Chm., Jt Working Party, Scottish Examinations Bd. *Publications:* Advertising Research, 1972; Distribution Research, 1973; Advertising: the economic implications, 1974; How to Win Profitable Business, 1983; How to Win Business Overseas, 1984; Basic Marketing, 1991; Enterprise, 1991; papers in learned jls. *Recreations:* soccer, supporting Everton FC, walking, writing. *Address:* Manchester Business School, Booth Street West, Manchester M15 6PB. *T:* 061–275 6333.

CANNON-BROOKES, Peter, PhD; FMA, FIIC; international museum consultant; *b* 23 Aug. 1938; *s* of Victor Montgomery Cannon Brookes and Nancy Margaret (*née* Markham Carter); *m* 1966, Caroline Aylmer, *d* of John Aylmer Christie-Miller; one *s* one *d*. *Educ:* Bryanston; Trinity Hall, Cambridge (MA); Courtauld Inst. of Art, Univ. of London (PhD). FMA 1975. Gooden and Fox Ltd, London, 1963–64; Keeper, Dept of Art, City Museums and Art Gall., Birmingham, 1965–78; Sessional Teacher in History of Art, Courtauld Inst. of Art, London, 1966–68; Keeper of Dept of Art, Nat. Mus. of Wales, Cardiff, 1978–86; Mus. Services Dir, STIPPLE Database Services, 1986–90. Internat. Council of Museums: Mem. Exec. Bd, UK Cttee, 1973–81; Pres., Internat. Art Exhibns Cttee, 1977–79 (Dir, 1974–80; Sec., 1975–77); Dir, Conservation Cttee, 1975–81 (Vice Pres., 1978–81). Member: Town Twinning Cttee, Birmingham Internat. Council, 1968–78; Birm. Diocesan Synod, 1970–78; Birm. Diocesan Adv. Cttee for Care of Churches, 1972–78; Edgbaston Deanery Synod, 1970–78 (Lay Jt Chm., 1975–78); Society of Authors, 1972–; Art and Design Adv. Panel, Welsh Jt Educn Cttee, 1978–86; Welsh Arts Council, 1979–84 (Member: Art Cttee, 1978–84; Craft Cttee, 1983–87); Projects and Orgns Cttee, Crafts Council, 1985–87. President: Welsh Fedn of Museums and Art Galleries, 1980–82; S Wales Art Soc., 1980–87. Trustee, Welsh Sculpture Trust, 1981–; Consultant Curator, Tabley House Collection, 1988–. Editor, Museum Management and Curatorship, 1981–. Freeman 1969, Liveryman 1974, Worshipful Co. of Goldsmiths. FRSA. JP Birmingham, 1973–78, Cardiff, 1978–82. *Publications:* (with H. D. Molesworth) European Sculpture, 1964; (with C. A. Cannon-Brookes) Baroque Churches, 1969; Lombard Painting, 1974; After Gulbenkian, 1976; The Cornbury Park Bellini, 1977; Michael Ayrton, 1978; Emile Antoine Bourdelle, 1983; Ivor Roberts-Jones, 1983; Czech Sculpture 1800–1938, 1983; Paintings from Tabley, 1989; contrib. Apollo, Art Bull., Arte Veneta, Burlington Mag., Connoisseur, Internat. Jl of Museum Management and Curatorship, and Museums Jl. *Recreations:* photography, growing vegetables, cooking. *Address:* Thrupp House, Abingdon, Oxon OX14 3NE. *T:* Abingdon (0235) 520595, *Fax:* Abingdon (0235) 534817. *Clubs:* Athenæum; Birmingham (Birmingham).

CANSDALE, George Soper, BA, BSc, FLS; *b* 29 Nov. 1909; *y s* of G. W. Cansdale, Paignton, Devon; *m* 1940, Margaret Sheila, *o d* of R. M. Williamson, Indian Forest Service; two *s*. *Educ:* Brentwood Sch.; St Edmund Hall, Oxford. Colonial Forest Service, Gold Coast, 1934–48. Superintendent to Zoological Society of London, Regent's Park, 1948–53. Inventor, SWS Filtration Unit, 1975. IBM Award for Sustainable Development. *Publications:* The Black Poplars, 1938; Animals of West Africa, 1946; Animals and Man, 1952; George Cansdale's Zoo Book, 1953; Belinda the Bushbaby, 1953; Reptiles of West Africa, 1955; West African Snakes, 1961; Behind the Scenes at a Zoo, 1965; Animals of Bible Lands, 1970; articles in the Field, Geographical Magazine, Zoo Life, Nigerian Field, Natural History, etc. *Recreations:* natural history, photography, sailing. *Address:* Dove Cottage, Great Chesterford, Essex CB10 1PL. *T:* Saffron Walden (0799) 30274. *Club:* Commonwealth Trust.

CANT, Rev. Harry William Macphail; Minister of St Magnus Cathedral, Kirkwall, Orkney, 1968–90; Chaplain to the Queen in Scotland, 1972–91, and Extra Chaplain, since 1991; *b* 3 April 1921; *s* of late J. M. Cant and late Margaret Cant; *m* 1951, Margaret Elizabeth Loudon; one *s* two *d*. *Educ:* Edinburgh Acad.; Edinburgh Univ. (MA, BD); Union Theological Seminary, NY (STM). Lieut, KOSB, 1941–43; Captain, King's African Rifles, 1944–46; TA Chaplain, 7th Argyll and Sutherland Highlanders, 1962–70. Asst Minister, Old Parish Church, Aberdeen, 1950–51; Minister of Fallin Parish Church, Stirling, 1951–56; Scottish Sec., Student Christian Movt, 1956–59; Minister of St Thomas' Parish Church, 1960–68. *Publications:* Preaching in a Scottish Parish Church: St Magnus and Other Sermons, 1970; Springs of Renewal in Congregational Life, 1980; Light in the North, 1989. *Recreations:* angling, golf. *Address:* Quoylobs, Holm, Orkney KW17 2RY.

CANT, Robert (Bowen); *b* 24 July 1915; *s* of Robert and Catherine Cant; *m* 1940, Rebecca Harris Watt; one *s* two *d*. *Educ:* Middlesbrough High Sch. for Boys; London Sch. of Economics. BSc (Econ.) 1945. Lecturer in Economics, Univ. of Keele, 1962–66. Member: Stoke-on-Trent City Council, 1953–76; Staffs CC, 1973– (Chm., Educn Cttee, 1981–89). Contested (Lab) Shrewsbury, 1950, 1951; MP (Lab) Stoke-on-Trent Central, 1966–83. *Publication:* American Journey. *Recreation:* bookbinding. *Address:* (home) 119 Chell Green Avenue, Stoke-on-Trent, Staffordshire ST6 76A. *Club:* Chell Working Men's.

CANTACUZINO, Sherban, CBE 1988; FRIBA; Secretary, Royal Fine Art Commission, since 1979; *b* 6 Sept. 1928; *s* of Georges M. Cantacuzino and Sanda Stirbey; *m* 1954, Anne Mary Trafford; two *d* (one *s* decd). *Educ:* Winchester Coll.; Magdalene Coll., Cambridge (MA). Partner, Steane, Shipman & Cantacuzino, Chartered Architects, 1956–65; private practice, 1965–73; Asst Editor, Architectural Review, 1967–73, Exec. Editor, 1973–79. Sen. Lectr, Dept of Architecture, College of Art, Canterbury, 1967–70. Trustee: Thomas Cubitt Trust, 1978–; Conran Foundn, 1981–; Member: Arts Panel, Arts Council, 1977–80; Steering Cttee, Aga Khan Award for Architecture, 1980– (Mem., Master Jury, 1980); Council, RSA, 1980–85; Design Cttee, London Transport, 1981–82; Adv. Panel, Railway Heritage Trust, 1985–; Fabric Cttee, Canterbury Cathedral, 1987–; Chm., ICOMOS UK Cttee, 1987–. *Publications:* Modern Houses of the World, 1964, 3rd edn 1966; Great Modern Architecture, 1966, 2nd edn 1968; European Domestic Architecture, 1969; New Uses for Old Buildings, 1975; (ed) Architectural Conservation in Europe, 1975; Wells Coates, a monograph, 1978; (with Susan Brandt) Saving Old Buildings, 1980; The Architecture of Howell, Killick, Partridge and Amis, 1981; Charles Correa, 1984; (ed) Architecture in Continuity: building in the Islamic world today, 1985; Re/Architecture: old buildings/New uses, 1989; articles in Architectural Rev. *Recreations:* music, cooking. *Address:* 140 Iffley Road, W6 0PE. *T:* 081–748 0415. *Club:* Garrick.

CANTER, Prof. David Victor, PhD; FBPsS; Professor of Psychology and Head of Department of Psychology, University of Surrey, since 1987; *b* 5 Jan. 1944; *s* of late Hyman Victor Canter and Coralie Lilian Canter (*née* Hyam); *m* 1967, Sandra Lorraine Smith; one *s* two *d*. *Educ:* Liverpool Collegiate Grammar Sch.; Liverpool Univ. (BA Hons 1964; PhD 1969). Research Associate, Liverpool Univ., 1964–65; Strathclyde University: Res. Associate, 1966; Res. Fellow, Building Performance Res. Unit, 1967–70; Lectr, 1971–72; University of Surrey: Lectr, 1972–78; Reader, 1978–83; Personal Chair of Applied Psychology, 1983–87. CPsych 1988; FBIM; FAPA. Mem., Forensic Sci. Soc. Hon. Mem., Japanese Inst. of Architects, 1971. Man. Ed., Jl of Envmtl Psychology, 1981–. *Publications:* Architectural Psychology, 1970; Psychology for Architects, 1974; (ed jtly) Psychology and the Built Environment, 1974; Environmental Interaction, 1975; (with P. Stringer) Psychology of Place, 1977; (ed jtly) Designing for Therapeutic Environments, 1979; (ed) Fires and Human Behaviour, 1980, 2nd edn 1990; (ed jtly) Psychology in Practice, 1982; (ed) Facet Theory, 1985; (ed jtly) The Research Interview, 1985; (ed jtly) Environmental Perspectives, 1988; (ed jtly) Environmental Policy, Assessment and Communication, 1988; (ed jtly) New Directions in Environmental Participation, 1988; (ed jtly) Environmental Social Psychology, 1988; (with M. Comber and D. Uzzell) Football in its Place, 1989; contribs to learned jls, newspapers, radio, TV. *Recreations:* clarinet, collage, cantering, criminal profiling. *Address:* Department of Psychology, University of Surrey, Guildford GU2 5XH. *T:* Guildford (0483) 509176.

CANTERBURY, Archbishop of, since 1991; **Most Rev. and Rt. Hon. George Leonard Carey;** PC 1991; *b* 13 Nov. 1935; *s* of George and Ruby Carey; *m* 1960, Eileen Harmsworth Hood, Dagenham, Essex; two *s* two *d*. *Educ:* Bifrons Secondary Modern Sch., Barking; London College of Divinity; King's College, London. BD Hons, MTh; PhD London. National Service, RAF Wireless Operator, 1954–56. Deacon, 1962; Curate, St Mary's, Islington, 1962–66; Lecturer: Oak Hill Coll., Southgate, 1966–70; St John's Coll., Nottingham, 1970–75; Vicar, St Nicholas' Church, Durham, 1975–82; Principal, Trinity Coll., Stoke Hill, Bristol, 1982–87; Hon. Canon, Bristol Cathedral, 1983–87; Bishop of Bath and Wells, 1987–91. *Publications:* I Believe in Man, 1975; God Incarnate, 1976; (jtly) The Great Acquittal, 1980; The Meeting of the Waters, 1985; The Gate of Glory, 1986; The Message of the Bible, 1988; The Great God Robbery, 1989; I Believe, 1991; contributor to numerous jls. *Recreations:* reading, writing, walking. *Address:* Lambeth Palace, SE1 7JU. *T:* 071–928 8282.

CANTERBURY, Dean of; *see* Simpson, Very Rev. J. A.

CANTERBURY, Archdeacon of; *see* Till, Ven. M. S.

CANTLAY, George Thomson, CBE 1973; Partner, Murray & Co., 1979–83, subsequently Consultant; former Director: Parkfield Foundries (Tees-side) Ltd (Chairman, to 1984); A. B. Electronic Products Group PLC; Christie-Tyler Ltd; Welsh National Opera Ltd; *b* 2 Aug. 1907; *s* of G. and A. Cantlay; *m* 1934, Sibyl Gwendoline Alsop Stoker; one *s* one *d*. *Educ:* Glasgow High Sch. Member of Stock Exchange. Vice-Pres., Welsh Region, Inst. of Directors. KStJ 1985; FRSA. *Recreations:* music (opera), gardening. *Address:* 8 Park Road, Penarth CF6 2BD. *Clubs:* Carlton; Cardiff and County (Cardiff).

CANTLEY, Sir Joseph (Donaldson), Kt 1965; OBE 1945; Judge of the High Court of Justice, Queen's Bench Division, 1965–85; *b* 8 Aug. 1910; *er s* of Dr Joseph Cantley, Crumpsall, Manchester, and Georgina Cantley (*née* Kean); *m* 1966, Lady (Hilda Goodwin) Gerrard, *widow* of Sir Denis Gerrard. *Educ:* Manchester Grammar Sch.; Manchester Univ. Studentship and Certificate of Honour, Council of Legal Education, 1933; Barrister, Middle Temple, 1933 (Bencher 1963; Treasurer 1981); QC 1954. Served throughout War of 1939–45: Royal Artillery and on Staff; commnd 2nd Lieut RA, 1940; N Africa and Italy, 1942–45 (despatches twice); Lieut-Colonel and AAG, 1943–45. Recorder of Oldham, 1959–60; Judge of Salford Hundred Court of Record, 1960–65; Judge of Appeal, Isle of Man, 1962–65; Presiding Judge: Northern Circuit, 1970–74; South Eastern Circuit, 1980. Member, General Council of the Bar, 1957–61. Hon. Col, Manchester and Salford Univs OTC, 1971–77. Hon. LLD Manchester, 1968. *Club:* Travellers'.

CANTY, Brian George John, OBE 1988; HM Diplomatic Service; Governor of Anguilla, since 1989; *b* 23 Oct. 1931; *s* of George Robert Canty and Phœbe Charlotte Canty (*née* Cobb); *m* 1954, Maureen Kathleen Kenny; one *s* one *d*. *Educ:* South West Essex Technical College; external student, London University (Social Studies); RAF Staff College (psc 1970). RN 1950; Air Ministry, 1957; Financial Adviser's Office, Cyprus, 1960; MoD (Air), 1963; FCO, 1971; served Oslo, 1973, Kingston, 1977, Vienna, 1979; FCO, 1984; Dep. Governor, Bermuda, 1986. JP Bermuda, 1986. *Recreations:* sailing, skiing, DIY. *Address:* Government House, Old Ta, The Valley, Anguilla, British West Indies. *T:* Anguilla 2292. *Clubs:* Royal Automobile; Beefsteak (Vienna); Royal Bermuda Yacht.

CAPE, Donald Paul Montagu Stewart, CMG 1977; HM Diplomatic Service, retired; Ambassador and UK Permanent Representative to the Council of Europe, Strasbourg, 1978–83; *b* 6 Jan. 1923; *s* of late John Scarvell and Olivia Millicent Cape; *m* 1948, Cathune Johnston; four *s* one *d*. *Educ:* Ampleforth Coll.; Brasenose Coll., Oxford. Scots Guards, 1942–45. Entered Foreign Service, 1946. Served: Belgrade, 1946–49; FO, 1949–51; Lisbon, 1951–55; Singapore, 1955–57; FO, 1957–60; Bogota, 1960–61; Holy See, 1962–67; Head of Information Administration Dept, FCO, 1968–70; Counsellor, Washington, 1970–73; Counsellor, Brasilia, 1973–75; Ambassador to Laos, 1976–78. Administrator, Anglo-Irish Encounter, 1983–; Chm., Anglo-Portuguese Soc., 1988–. *Recreations:* tennis, walking, swimming, skiing. *Address:* Hilltop, Wonersh, Guildford, Surrey GU5 0QT.

CAPE, Maj.-Gen. Timothy Frederick, CB 1972; CBE 1966; DSO; idc, jssc, psc; FAIM; *b* Sydney, 5 Aug. 1915; *s* of C. S. Cape, DSO, Edgecliff, NSW; *m* 1961, Elizabeth (*d* 1985), *d* of Brig. R. L. R. Rabett; one *d*. *Educ:* Cranbrook Sch., Sydney; RMC Duntroon. Served with RAA, 1938–40; Bde Major Sparrow Force, Timor, 1942; GS01: (Air) New Guinea Force, 1942–43; (Ops) Melbourne, 1944; (Air) Morotai, 1945; (Ops) Japan, 1946–47; (Plans) Melbourne, 1948–49; Instructor, UK, 1950–52; Comdt, Portsea, 1954–56; Dep. Master-Gen. Ordnance, 1957–59; COS Northern Comd, Brisbane, 1961; Dir of Staff Duties, Army HQ, Canberra, 1962–63; Comdr, Adelaide, 1964; GOC Northern Comd, Brisbane, 1965–68; Master-General of the Ordnance, 1968–72; retd 1972. Nat. Chm., Royal United Services Inst. of Australia, 1980–83; Chm., Nat. Disaster Relief Cttee and Mem., Nat. Council, Australian Red Cross Soc., 1975–85. Bronze Star (US). *Address:* 20 Charlotte Street, Red Hill, ACT 2603, Australia. *Clubs:* Melbourne, Naval and Military (Melbourne); Commonwealth (Canberra); Union (Sydney); Royal Sydney Golf.

CAPE TOWN, Archbishop of, and Metropolitan of Southern Africa, since 1986; **Most Rev. Desmond Mpilo Tutu;** *b* 7 Oct. 1931; *s* of Zachariah and Aletta Tutu; *m* 1955, Leah Nomalizo Shenxane; one *s* three *d*. *Educ:* Western High, Johannesburg; Bantu Normal Coll., Pretoria (Higher Teachers' Dip.); Univ. of S Africa (BA); St Peter's Theol Coll., Johannesburg (LTh); King's Coll. London (BD, MTh; FKC 1978). Schoolmaster: Madibane High Sch., Johannesburg, 1954; Munsieville High Sch., Krugersdorp, 1955–57. Theological coll. student, 1958–60; deacon 1960, priest 1961, St Mary's Cathedral, Johannesburg. Curate: St Alban's Church, Benoni, 1960–61; St Philip's Church, Alberton, 1961–62; St Alban's, Golder's Green, London, 1962–65; St Mary's, Bletchingley, Surrey, 1965–66. Lecturer: Federal Theol Seminary, Alice, CP, 1967–69; Univ. of Botswana,

Lesotho and Swaziland, Roma, Lesotho, 1970–72; Associate Dir, Theol Education Fund (WCC) based in Bromley, Kent, and Curate, St Augustine's, Grove Park, 1972–75; Dean of Johannesburg, 1975–76; Bishop of Lesotho, 1976–78; Gen. Sec., South African Council of Churches, 1978–85; Asst Bishop of Johannesburg, 1978–85; Rector, St Augustine's Parish, Soweto, 1981–85; Bishop of Johannesburg, 1985–86. Chancellor, Univ. of Western Cape, Cape Town, 1988–. Pres., All Africa Conference of Churches, 1987–. Trustee, Phelps Stoke Fund, New York. Holds over thirty hon. degrees from academic institutions in UK, Europe and USA. Athena Prize, Onassis Foundation, 1980; Nobel Peace Prize, 1984; Albert Schweitzer Humanitarian Award, Emmanuel Coll., Boston, 1988. Order of Southern Cross (Brazil), 1987; Order of Merit of Brasilia (Brazil), 1987. *Publications:* Crying in the Wilderness, 1982; Hope and Suffering, 1983; The Words of Desmond Tutu, 1989; articles and reviews. *Recreations:* music, reading, jogging. *Address:* Bishopscourt, Claremont, CP, 7700, South Africa.

CAPE TOWN, Bishops Suffragan of; *see* Albertyn, Rt Rev. C. H.; Matolengwe, Rt Rev. P. M.; Quinlan, Rt. Rev. A. G.

CAPEL CURE, (George) Nigel, TD; JP; DL; *b* 28 Sept. 1908; *o s* of late Major George Edward Capel Cure, JP, Blake Hall, Ongar; *m* 1935, Nancy Elizabeth, *d* of late William James Barry, Great Witchingham Hall, Norwich; two *s* one *d*. *Educ:* Eton; Trinity Coll., Cambridge. DL and JP, 1947, High Sheriff, 1951, Essex; Vice-Lieutenant, later Vice Lord-Lieutenant, Essex, 1958–78; late of Blake Hall, Ongar. *Recreations:* shooting, cricket. *Address:* Ashlings, Moreton Road, Ongar, Essex. *T:* Ongar (0277) 362634. *Clubs:* MCC, City University.

CAPELL, family name of **Earl of Essex.**

CAPEY, Montague Martin; Director of Establishments and Organisation, Department of Education and Science, since 1988; *b* 16 July 1933; *s* of Ernest Paton Capey and Lettice Isabel Capey; *m* 1960, Diana Mary Barnes; one *s* one *d*. *Educ:* The Leys Sch., Cambridge; Clare Coll., Cambridge (MA); Didsbury Coll., Bristol; Univ. of Bristol (BA). Methodist Minister, 1958–71. Principal 1971–76, Asst Sec. 1976–88, DES. *Recreations:* gardening, music, planning to live in Cornwall. *Address:* Department of Education and Science, Sanctuary Buildings, Great Smith Street, SW1.

CAPLAN, Hon. Lord; Philip Isaac Caplan; a Senator of the College of Justice in Scotland, since 1989; *b* 24 Feb. 1929; *s* of Hyman and Rosalena Caplan; *m* 1st, 1953; two *s* one *d*; 2nd, 1974, Joyce Ethel Stone; one *d*. *Educ:* Eastwood Sch., Renfrewshire; Glasgow Univ. (MA, LLB). Solicitor, 1952–56; called to Bar, 1957; Standing Junior Counsel to Accountant of Court, 1964–70; QC (Scot.) 1970; Sheriff of Lothian and Borders, 1979–83; Sheriff-Principal of North Strathclyde, 1983–89. Member: Sheriff Court Rules Council, 1984–89; Adv. Council on Messengers-at-Arms and Sheriff Officers, 1987–89. Chairman: Plant Varieties and Seeds Tribunal, Scotland, 1977–79; Scottish Assoc. for Study of Delinquency, 1985–89 (Hon. Vice-Pres., 1990–); Scottish Assoc. of Family Conciliation Services, 1989–. Mem., Scottish Photographic Circle, 1986–. FRPS 1988; AFIAP 1985. *Recreations:* photography, reading, music. *Address:* Parliament House, Parliament Square, Edinburgh. *Club:* New (Edinburgh).

CAPLAN, Daniel; Under-Secretary, Department of the Environment, 1970–71; *b* 29 July 1915; *y s* of Daniel and Miriam Caplan; *m* 1945, Olive Beatrice Porter; no *c*. *Educ:* Elem. and Secondary Schools, Blackpool; St Catharine's Coll., Cambridge. Asst Principal, Import Duties Adv. Cttee, 1938; Private Secretary to three Permanent Secretaries, Ministry of Supply, 1940; Principal, 1942; Ministry of Supply Representative and Economic Secretary to British Political Representative in Finland, 1944–45; Asst Secretary, Board of Trade, 1948; Adviser to Chancellor of Duchy of Lancaster, 1957–60; Under-Secretary, Scottish Development Dept, 1963–65; Under-Secretary, National Economic Development Office, 1966; Asst Under-Sec. of State, DEA, 1966–69; Under-Sec., Min. of Housing and Local Govt, 1969–70; Consultant to Minister for Housing for Leasehold Charges Study, 1972–73. Indep. Review of Royal Commn on Historical Manuscripts, for HM Govt, 1980. *Publications:* People and Homes (indep. report on Landlord and Tenant Relations in England for British Property Fedn), 1975; Border Country Branch Lines, 1981; Report on the Work of the Royal Commission on Historical Manuscripts, 1981; The Waverley Route, 1985; The Royal Scot, 1987; The West Highland Line, 1988; numerous papers on religious and economic history in learned journals. *Recreations:* railways, historical research, gardening. *Address:* Knowle Wood, London Road, Cuckfield, West Sussex RH17 5ES. *T:* Haywards Heath (0444) 454301.

CAPLAN, Jonathan Michael; QC 1991; *b* 11 Jan. 1951; *s* of Dr Malcolm Denis Caplan and late Jean Hilary Caplan, JP. *Educ:* St Paul's Sch.; Downing Coll., Cambridge (MA). Called to Bar, Gray's Inn, 1973. Mem., General Council of Bar, 1986–90; Chairman: Bar Council Report on Televising the Courts, 1989; Public Affairs Cttee, Bar Council, 1991–. *Publications:* The Confait Confessions, 1977; (contrib.) Disabling Professions, 1978. *Recreations:* writing, tennis, collecting historical newspapers and manuscripts, Khmer and Thai sculpture, cinema, books. *Address:* 5 Paper Buildings, Temple, EC4Y 7HB. *T:* 071–583 6117; 2 Belsize Mews, Belsize Lane, NW3 5AT. *T:* 071–435 3354. *Club:* Queen's.

CAPLAN, Leonard, QC 1954; *b* 28 June 1909; *s* of late Henry Caplan, Liverpool; *m* 1st, 1942, Tania (*d* 1974); two *d*; 2nd, 1977, Mrs Korda Herskovits (marr. diss. 1989), NY. Served War of 1939–45, Royal Artillery (Anti-Tank): Staff Captain, 47th Div.; Staff Captain ("Q" Operations), Southern Command, engaged in D-Day Planning; passed Staff Coll., Camberley; Major, DAAG and Lt-Col, AAG, HQ Allied Land Forces, South East Asia. Called to the Bar, Gray's Inn, 1935; Master of the Bench, 1964; Vice-Treasurer, 1978; Treasurer, 1979; Master of the Library, 1980–86; joined South Eastern Circuit; Middle Temple, 1949; sometime Dep. High Ct Judge. Conservative candidate: Pontypool, 1935; N Hammersmith, 1945; N Kensington, 1950–51. Chm., Coll. Hall (Univ. of London), 1958–67. Chm., Mental Health Review Tribunal, SE Region, 1960–63; Vice-Chm., NI Detention Appeals Tribunal, 1973–75; Senate of Inns of Court and the Bar, 1975–81. Pres., Medico-Legal Soc., 1979–81. *Publication:* (with late Marcus Samuel, MP) The Great Experiment: a critical study of Soviet Five Year Plans, 1935. *Recreation:* yachting. *Address:* 1 Pump Court, Temple, EC4. *T:* 071–353 9332; Skol, Marbella, S Spain. *Clubs:* Savage, Authors', Royal Automobile.

CAPLAN, Philip Isaac; *see* Caplan, Hon. Lord.

CAPLAT, Moran Victor Hingston, CBE 1968; General Administrator, Glyndebourne Festival Opera, retired; *b* 1 Oct. 1916; *s* of Roger Armand Charles Caplat and Norah Hingston; *m* 1943, Diana Murray Downton; one *s* two *d* (and one *s* decd). *Educ:* privately; Royal Acad. of Dramatic Art. Actor, etc., 1934–39. Royal Navy, 1939–45. Glyndebourne: Asst to Gen. Man., 1945; Gen. Man., later known as Gen. Administrator, 1949–81. *Publication:* Dinghies to Divas (autobiog.), 1985. *Recreations:* gardening, sailing, wine. *Address:* Mermaid Cottage, 6 Church Road, Newick, Lewes, East Sussex BN8 4JU. *T:* Newick (082572) 2964. *Clubs:* Garrick, Royal Ocean Racing; Royal Yacht Squadron (Cowes).

See also D. N. O. Sekers.

CAPPER, Rt. Rev. Edmund Michael Hubert, OBE 1961; LTh (Dur.); Auxiliary Bishop in the Diocese of Gibraltar in Europe, since 1973; Assistant Bishop of Southwark, since 1981; *b* 12 March 1908; *e s* of Arthur Charles and Mabel Lavinia Capper; unmarried. *Educ:* St Joseph's Academy, Blackheath; St Augustine's College, Canterbury. Deacon, 1932, Priest, 1933. Royal Army Chaplains' Dept, 1942–46 (EA); Archdeacon of Lindi and Canon of Masasi Cathedral, 1947–54; Archdeacon of Dar es Salaam, 1954–58. Provost of the Collegiate Church of St Alban the Martyr, Dar es Salaam, Tanganyika, 1957–62; Canon of Zanzibar, 1954–62; Member, Universities' Mission to Central Africa, 1936–62; Chairman, Tanganyika British Legion Benevolent Fund, 1956–62; President, Tanganyika British Legion, 1960–62; Chaplain, Palma de Mallorca, 1962–67; Bishop of St Helena, 1967–73; Chaplain of St George's, Malaga, 1973–76. *Recreations:* swimming and walking. *Address:* Morden College, Blackheath, SE3 0PW. *T:* 081–858 9169. *Club:* Travellers'.

CAPRON, (George) Christopher; independent television producer; Director, Capron Productions, since 1987; *b* 17 Dec. 1935; *s* of late Lt-Col George Capron and Hon. Mrs (Edith) Christian Capron (*née* Hepburne-Scott); *m* 1958, Edna Naomi Goldrei; one *s* one *d*. *Educ:* Wellington Coll.; Trinity Hall, Cambridge (BA Hons Mod. Langs). Served Army, 12th Royal Lancers (Prince of Wales's), 1954–56. British Broadcasting Corporation: radio producer, 1963–67; television producer, 1967–76; Editor, Tonight, 1976–77; Editor, Panorama, 1977–79; Asst Head, 1979–81, Head, 1981–85, TV Current Affairs Programmes; Head of Parly Broadcasting, 1985–87. *Recreations:* village cricket, tennis. *Address:* 32 Amerland Road, SW18 1PZ; Southwick Hall, Oundle, Northants.

CAPSTICK, Brian Eric, QC 1973; **His Honour Judge Capstick;** a Circuit Judge, since 1985; *b* 12 Feb. 1927; *o s* of late Eric and Betty Capstick; *m* 1960, Margaret Harrison; one *s* one *d*. *Educ:* Sedbergh; Queen's Coll., Oxford (Scholar) (MA). Served HM Forces, 1945–48: 17/21st Lancers, Palestine, 1947–48. Tancred Student, and called to Bar, Lincoln's Inn, 1952; Bencher, 1980; a Recorder, 1980–85. Dep. Chm., Northern Agriculture Tribunal, 1976–; Asst Boundary Comr, 1978–85. Appeal Steward, British Board of Boxing Control, 1985–. *Recreations:* shooting, reading, cooking. *Address:* c/o Central Criminal Court, Old Bailey, EC4M 7EH. *Club:* Garrick.

CAPSTICK, Charles William, CMG 1972; Deputy Secretary, Food Safety Directorate, Ministry of Agriculture, Fisheries and Food, since 1989; *b* 18 Dec. 1934; *s* of William Capstick and Janet Frankland; *m* 1962, Joyce Alma Dodsworth; two *s*. *Educ:* King's Coll., Univ. of Durham (BSc (Hons)); Univ. of Kentucky, USA (MS). MAFF: Asst Agricl Economist, 1961; Principal Agricl Economist, 1966; Senior Principal Agricl Economist, 1968; Sen. Econ. Advr and Head, Milk and Milk Products Div., 1976; Under Sec., 1977, Dir of Econs and Statistics, 1977. Pres., Agricultural Economics Soc., 1983. *Recreations:* gardening, golf. *Address:* 7 Dellfield Close, Radlett, Herts. *T:* Radlett (09276) 7640.

CARBERY, 11th Baron *cr* 1715; **Peter Ralfe Harrington Evans-Freke;** Bt 1768; *b* 20 March 1920; *o s* of Major the Hon. Ralfe Evans-Freke, MBE (*yr s* of 9th Baron) (*d* 1969), and Vera (*d* 1984), *d* of late C. Harrington Moore; *S* uncle, 1970; *m* 1941, Joyzelle Mary, *o d* of late Herbert Binnie; three *s* two *d*. *Educ:* Downside School. MICE. Served War of 1939–45, Captain RE, India, Burmah. Member of London Stock Exchange, 1955–68. *Recreations:* hunting, tennis, winter sports. *Heir:* *e s* Hon. Michael Peter Evans-Freke [*b* 11 Oct. 1942; *m* 1967, Claudia Janet Elizabeth, *o d* of Captain P. L. C. Gurney; one *s* three *d*]. *Address:* 2 Hayes Court, Sunnyside, Wimbledon, SW19 4SH. *Clubs:* Kennel, Ski Club of Great Britain.

CARBERY, Prof. Thomas Francis, OBE 1983; Professor (part-time), Department of Marketing, University of Strathclyde, 1988–90, now Emeritus; Chairman, South of Scotland Electricity Consumers' Committee, since 1990; *b* 18 Jan. 1925; *o c* of Thomas Albert Carbery and Jane Morrison; *m* 1954, Ellen Donnelly; one *s* two *d*. *Educ:* St Aloysius Coll., Glasgow; Univ. of Glasgow and Scottish Coll. of Commerce. Cadet Navigator and Meteorologist, RAFVR, 1943–47; Min. of Labour, 1947–61; Sen. Lectr in Govt and Econs, Scottish College of Commerce, Glasgow, 1961–64; University of Strathclyde: Sen. Lectr in Govt-Business Relations, 1964–75; Head of Dept of Office Organisation, 1975–79, and Prof., 1979–85; Prof., Dept of Inf. Science, 1985–88, and Chm. of Dept, 1985–86. Member: IBA (formerly ITA), 1970–79 (Chm., Scottish Cttee, 1970–79); Royal Commn on Gambling, 1976–78; Central Transport Users' Consultative Cttee, 1976–80 (Chm., Scottish Transport Users' Consultative Cttee, 1976–80); European (later International) Adv. Council, Salzburg Seminar, 1980–91; Broadcasting Complaints Commn, 1981–86; Data Protection Tribunal, 1984–; Scottish Legal Aid Bd, 1986–; Press Council, 1987–90; Dep. Chm., Scottish Consumer Council, 1980–84 (Mem. 1977–80); Chm., Scottish Cttee, Information Technology, 1982–85; Ombudsman to Mirror Gp Newspapers Scottish titles, 1990–; Special Adviser, H of C Select Cttee on Scottish Affairs, 1982. Academic Governor, Richmond Coll., 1983–; Governor, St Aloysius' Coll., Glasgow, 1984–. Editor, Approaches to Information Technology (Plenum Press series), 1984–90. *Publication:* Consumers in Politics, 1969. *Recreations:* golf, conversation, spectating at Association football, listening to Radio 4, watching television. *Address:* 24 Fairfax Avenue, Glasgow G44 5AL. *T:* 041–637 0514. *Clubs:* University of Strathclyde, Glasgow Art, Ross Priory (Glasgow).

CARBONELL, William Leycester Rouse, CMG 1956; Commissioner of Police, Federation of Malaya, 1953–58, retired; *b* 14 Aug. 1912; *m* 1937; two *s*. *Educ:* Shrewsbury Sch.; St Catharine's Coll., Cambridge. Probationary Assistant Commissioner of Police, 1935; (title changed to) Asst Superintendent, 1938; Superintendent, 1949; Asst Commissioner, 1952; Senior, 1952; Commissioner, 1953. King's Police Medal, 1950. Perlawan Mangku Negara (PMN), Malaya, 1958. *Address:* Amery End, Tanhouse Lane, Alton, Hants.

CARDEN, Derrick Charles, CMG 1974; JP; HM Diplomatic Service, retired; HM Ambassador, Sudan, 1977–79; *b* 30 Oct. 1921; *s* of Canon Henry Craven Carden and Olive (*née* Gorton); *heir pres.* to Sir John Craven Carden, 7th Bt, *qv*; *m* 1952, Elizabeth Anne Russell; two *s* two *d*. *Educ:* Marlborough; Christ Church, Oxford. Sudan Political Service, 1942–54. Entered HM Diplomatic Service, 1954; Foreign Office, 1954–55; Political Agent, Doha, 1955–58; 1st Sec., Libya, 1958–62; Foreign Office, 1962–65; Head of Chancery, Cairo, 1965; Consul-General, Muscat, 1965–69; Dir, ME Centre of Arab Studies, 1969–73; Ambassador, Yemen Arab Republic, 1973–76. Governor, IDS, Sussex Univ., 1981–87. Mem. Bd, CARE Britain, 1988–90. JP Fareham, 1980. *Recreation:* pleasures of the countryside. *Address:* Wistaria Cottage, 174 Castle Street, Portchester, Hants PO16 9QH. *Club:* Vincent's (Oxford).

CARDEN, (Graham) Stephen (Paul), CBE 1986; TD 1968; DL; Partner, Cazenove & Co., since 1964; *b* 14 May 1935; *s* of late Paul Carden and Lilias Kathleen Carden. *Educ:* Harrow School. 9th Lancers, 1954–56. Cazenove & Co., 1956–; Dir, Greenfriar Investment Co., 1966–. City of London Yeomanry (Rough Riders) and on amalgamation, Inns of Court & City Yeomanry, 1956–74 (Jt Hon. Col 1989–); Col, TA, 1976–78; Chm., 1981–88, Vice Pres., 1988–, Greater London TAVRA; Vice-Chairman: Council, TAVRA, 1984–88; ACFA, 1989–; Hon. Col 71st (Yeomanry) Signal Regt, TA, 1989–. Comr, Royal Hosp., Chelsea, 1986–; Vice-Pres., Yeomanry Benevolent Fund, 1986–.

Chm., Fairbridge Soc., 1986–87 (Hon. Treas., 1964–87), Vice Chm. and Hon. Treas., Fairbridge Drake Soc., 1987–; Chm., London House for Overseas Graduates, 1990– (Gov., 1975–). DL Gtr London, 1983. *Recreations:* equestrian (mainly hunting), fishing, sailing, watching cricket. *Address:* 12 Warwick Square, SW1V 2AA. *T:* 071–834 8919. *Clubs:* Cavalry & Guards, White's, City of London, MCC, Royal Yacht Squadron.

CARDEN, Sir Henry (Christopher), 4th Bt *cr* 1887; OBE (mil.) 1945; Regular Army Officer (17th/21st Lancers), retired; *b* 16 Oct. 1908; *o s* of Sir Frederick H. W. Carden, 3rd Bt; *S* father, 1966; *m* 1st, 1943, Jane St C. Daniell (whom he divorced, 1960); one *s* one *d*; 2nd, 1962, Gwyneth S. Emerson (*née* Acland), *widow* of Flt-Lt R. Emerson, of Argentina (killed in action, RAF, 1944). *Educ:* Eton; RMC Sandhurst. 2/Lieut, 17/21 Lancers, 1928; served Egypt and India, 1930–39. Staff Coll., 1941; comd, 2 Armoured Delivery Regt, in France, 1944–45. CO 17/21 Lancers, in Greece and Palestine, 1947–48; War Office, 1948–51; Military Attaché in Stockholm, 1951–55; retired 1956. Comdr of the Order of the Sword (Sweden), 1954. *Recreations:* most field sports and games. *Heir:* *s* Christopher Robert Carden, *b* 24 Nov. 1946. *Address:* Moongrove, East Woodhay, near Newbury, Berks. *T:* Highclere (0635) 253661. *Club:* Cavalry and Guards.

CARDEN, Sir John Craven, 7th Bt, *cr* 1787; *b* 11 March 1926; *s* of Capt. Sir John V. Carden, 6th Bt and Dorothy Mary, *d* of Charles Luckrart McKinnon; *S* father, 1935; *m* 1947, Isabel Georgette, *y d* of late Robert de Hart; one *d*. *Educ:* Eton. *Heir:* *cousin* Derrick Charles Carden, *qv*. *Address:* PO Box N-3718, Nassau, Bahamas. *Club:* White's.

CARDEN, Richard John Derek; Fisheries Secretary, Ministry of Agriculture, Fisheries and Food, since 1991; *b* 12 June 1943; *s* of late John and Hilda Carden; *m* 1971, Pamela Haughton; one *s* one *d*. *Educ:* Merchant Taylors' Sch., Northwood; St John's Coll., Oxford (Craven Scholar, 1964; Derby Scholar, 1966; MA Lit. Hum. 1969; DPhil 1970); Freie Universität, Berlin. Research for Egypt Exploration Soc., 1969–70; entered Civil Service, MAFF, 1970; HM Treasury, 1977–79; MAFF, 1979–: Chief Regional Officer, Midlands and Western Region, 1983–86; Under Sec., Hd of European Community and Ext. Trade Policy, 1987–91. *Publications:* The Papyrus Fragments of Sophocles, 1974; articles on Greek literature. *Address:* c/o Ministry of Agriculture, Fisheries and Food, Nobel House, 17 Smith Square, SW1P 3JR.

CARDEN, Stephen; *see* Carden, G. S. P.

CARDIFF, Archbishop of, (RC), since 1983; **Most Rev. John Aloysius Ward,** OFM Cap; *b* 24 Jan. 1929; *s* of Eugene Ward and Hannah Ward (*née* Cheetham). *Educ:* Prior Park College, Bath. Received as Capuchin Franciscan Friar, 1945; solemn profession as Friar, 1950; ordained Priest, 1953; Diocesan Travelling Mission, Menevia, 1954–60; Guardian and Parish Priest, Peckham, London, 1960–66; Provincial Definitor (Councillor), 1963–69; Minister Provincial, 1969–70; General Definitor (Councillor), 1970–80; Bishop Coadjutor of Menevia, 1980–81; Bishop of Menevia, 1981–83. *Address:* Archbishop's House, 41–43 Cathedral Road, Cardiff, S Glamorgan CF1 9HD. *T:* Cardiff (0222) 220411.

CARDIFF, Jack; film director and cameraman; *b* 18 Sept. 1914; *s* of John Joseph and Florence Cardiff; *m* 1940, Julia Lily (*née* Mickleboro); three *s*. *Educ:* various schools, incl. Medburn Sch., Herts. Started as child actor, 1918; switched to cameras, 1928. World travelogues, 1937–39. Photographed, MOI Crown Film Unit: Western Approaches, 1942; best known films include: A Matter of Life and Death, Black Narcissus, The Red Shoes, Scott of the Antarctic, Under Capricorn, Pandora and the Flying Dutchman, African Queen, War and Peace. Started as Director, 1958. *Films include: directed:* Sons and Lovers, My Geisha, The Lion, The Long Ships, Young Cassidy, The Mercenaries, The Liquidator, Girl on a Motorcycle, The Mutation, Catseyes; *photographed:* Ride a Wild Pony, The Prince and the Pauper, Behind the Iron Mask, Death on the Nile, Avalanche Express, The Awakening, The Dogs of War, Ghost Story, The Wicked Lady, Scandalous, The Far Pavilions, The Last Days of Pompeii, Conan II, First Blood II. Awards: Academy Award (Oscar) Photography, Black Narcissus, 1947; Golden Globe Award, 1947; Coup Ce Soir (France), 1951; Film Achievement Award, Look Magazine; BSC Award, War and Peace; New York Critics Award for best film direction, Golden Globe Award, outstanding directorial award (all for Sons and Lovers); six Academy Award nominations. Hon. Dr of Art, Rome, 1953; Hon. Mem., Assoc. Française de Cameramen, 1971. *Publication:* Autobiography, 1975. *Recreations:* tennis, cricket, painting. *Address:* 32 Woodland Rise, N10. *Club:* MCC.

CARDIGAN, Earl of; David Michael James Brudenell-Bruce; Manager and owner, Savernake Forest, since 1974; *b* 12 Nov. 1952; *s* and *heir* of 8th Marquess of Ailesbury, *qv*; *m* 1980, Rosamond Jane, cookery author, *er d* of Captain W. R. M. Winkley, Wyke Champflower Manor, near Bruton, Somerset, and of Mrs Jane Winkley, Kepnal Cottage, Kepnal, Marlborough; one *s* one *d*. *Educ:* Eton; Rannoch; Royal Agricultural Coll., Cirencester. Sec., Marlborough Conservatives, 1985–; Mem. Exec., Devizes Constituency Cons. Assoc., 1988–. *Heir:* *s* Viscount Savernake, *qv*. *Address:* Savernake Lodge, Savernake Forest, Marlborough, Wilts.

CARDIN, Pierre; Chevalier de la Légion d'Honneur, 1983; couturier; *b* 2 July 1922. Designer: Paquin, Paris, 1945–46; Dior, Paris, 1946–50; founded own fashion house, 1950. Founder and Dir, Théâtre des Ambassadeurs, now Espace Pierre Cardin complex, 1970–; Chm., Maxim's Restaurant, 1981–. Designed costumes for films, including: Cocteau's La Belle et la Bête, 1946; The Yellow Rolls Royce, 1965. Retrospective exhibition, V & A, 1990. Dé d'Or, 1977, 1979, 1982; Fashion Oscar, 1985; prize of Foundn for Advancement of Garment and Apparel Res., Japan, 1988. Grand Officer, Order of Merit (Italy), 1988. *Address:* 59 rue du Faubourg Saint-Honoré, 75008 Paris, France.

CARDOSO E CUNHA, António José Baptista; Member of the European Commission, since 1986; Member of Portuguese Parliament, 1979–83 and since 1985; *b* 28 Jan. 1934; *s* of Arnaldo and Maria Beatriz Cardoso E Cunha; *m* 1958, Dea Cardoso E Cunha; four *s*. *Educ:* Instituto Superior Tecnico; Lisbon Univ. MSc Chem. Engrg. Professional engineer, Lisbon, 1957–65; Man. Dir/Chief Exec. Officer of private cos, Sa da Bandeira, Angola, 1965–77; in business, director of private cos, Lisbon, 1977–78 and 1982–85; Mem. Portuguese Government: Sec. of State for Foreign Trade, 1978, for Industry, 1979; Minister for Agriculture/Fisheries, 1980–82. Grand Croix, Leopold II, Belgium, 1980; Gran Cruz, Merito Agricola, Spain, 1981. *Address:* Campo Grande 30–7–F, 1700 Lisbon, Portugal. *T:* 772718.

CARDROSS, Lord; Henry Thomas Alexander Erskine; *b* 31 May 1960; *s* and *heir* of 17th Earl of Buchan, *qv*; *m* 1987, Charlotte, *d* of Hon. Matthew Beaumont and Mrs Alexander Maitland; one *s*.

CARDY, Prof. John Lawrence, PhD; FRS 1991; Professor of Physics, University of California, Santa Barbara, since 1977; *b* 19 March 1947; *s* of late George Laurence Cardy and Sarah Cardy; *m* 1985, Mary Ann Gilreath. *Educ:* Downing Coll., Cambridge (BA 1968; PhD 1971). Research Associate: European Orgn for Nuclear Res., Geneva, 1971–73; Daresbury Lab., 1973–74; Univ. of California, Santa Barbara, 1974–76; Fellow: European Orgn for Nuclear Res., 1976–77; Alfred P. Sloan Foundn, 1978; Guggenheim Foundn, 1986. *Publications:* Finite-Size Scaling, 1988; contrib. to learned jls. *Recreation:* mountaineering. *Address:* Department of Physics, University of California, Santa Barbara, Calif 93106, USA. *T:* (805) 893–2246.

CAREW, 6th Baron (UK) *cr* 1838; **William Francis Conolly-Carew,** CBE 1966; Baron Carew (Ireland), 1834; Bt Major retired, Duke of Cornwall's Light Infantry; *b* 23 April 1905; *e s* of 5th Baron and Catherine (*d* 1947), *o d* of late Thomas Conolly, MP, of Castletown, Co. Kildare; *S* father, 1927; *m* 1937, Lady Sylvia Maitland, CStJ (*d* 1991), *o d* of 15th Earl of Lauderdale; two *s* two *d*. *Educ:* Wellington; Sandhurst. Gazetted DCLI 1925; ADC to Governor and Comdr-in-Chief of Bermuda, 1931–36. Chm., British Legion, 1963–66; Pres., Irish Grassland Assn, 1949; Br. Govt Trustee, Irish Sailors' and Soldiers' Land Trust. CStJ. *Heir:* *s* Hon. Patrick Thomas Conolly-Carew, Captain Royal Horse Guards, retd [*b* 6 March 1938; *m* 1962, Celia, *d* of late Col Hon. (Charles) Guy Cubitt, CBE, DSO, TD; one *s* three *d*]. *Address:* The Dower House, Donadea House, Naas, Co. Kildare, Ireland. *T:* Naas (045) 68300.

CAREW, Sir Rivers (Verain), 11th Bt *cr* 1661; journalist; *b* 17 Oct. 1935; *s* of Sir Thomas Palk Carew, 10th Bt, and Phyllis Evelyn (*d* 1976), *o c* of Neville Mayman; *S* father, 1976; *m* 1968, Susan Babington (marr. diss. 1991), *yr d* of late H. B. Hill, London; one *s* three *d* (and one *s* decd). *Educ:* St Columba's Coll., Rathfarnham, Co. Dublin; Trinity Coll., Dublin. MA, BAgr (Hort.). Asst Editor, Ireland of the Welcomes (Irish Tourist Bd magazine), 1964–67; Joint Editor, The Dublin Magazine, 1964–69; Irish Television, 1967–; BBC World Service, 1987–. *Publication:* (with Timothy Brownlow) Figures out of Mist (verse). *Recreations:* reading; music; reflection. *Heir:* *s* Gerald de Redvers Carew, *b* 24 May 1975. *Address:* 148 Catharine Street, Cambridge CB1 3AR.

CAREW POLE, Col Sir John (Gawen), 12th Bt *cr* 1628; DSO 1944; TD; JP; Lord-Lieutenant of Cornwall, 1962–77; Member of the Prince of Wales's Council, 1952–68; Member, Jockey Club (incorporating National Hunt Committee), since 1969; Steward, National Hunt Committee, 1953–56; Member, Garden Society; *b* 4 March 1902; *e s* of late Lt-Gen. Sir Reginald Pole-Carew, KCB, of Antony, Cornwall, and Lady Beatrice Pole-Carew, *er d* of 3rd Marquess of Ormonde; *S* kinsman, 1926; *m* 1st, 1928, Cynthia Mary, OBE 1959 (*d* 1977), *o d* of Walter Burns, North Mymms Park, Hatfield; one *s* two *d*; 2nd, 1979, Joan, *widow* of Lt-Col Anthony Fulford, Dunsford, Devon. *Educ:* Eton; RMC, Sandhurst. Coldstream Guards, 1923–39; ADC to Commander-in-Chief in India, 1924–25; Comptroller to Governor-General, Union of S Africa, 1935–36; Palestine, 1936; commanded 5th Bn Duke of Cornwall's LI (TA), 1939–43; commanded 2nd Bn Devonshire Regt, 1944; Colonel, Second Army, 1944–45; Normandy, France, Belgium, Holland, Germany, 1944–45 (despatches, immediate DSO); raised and commanded post-war TA Bn, 4/5 Bn, DCLI, 1946–47; Hon. Col, 4/5 Bn DCLI (TA), 1958–60; Hon. Col DCLI (TA) 1960–67. Director: Lloyd's Bank, 1956–72 (Chm., Devon and Cornwall Cttee, 1956–72); English China Clays Ltd, 1969–73; Keith Prowse, 1969; Vice-Chm., Westward Television Ltd, 1960–72. Member: Central Transport Consultative Cttee for Great Britain, 1948–54; SW Electricity Consultative Council, 1949–52 (Vice-Chairman, 1951–52); Western Area Board, British Transport Commission, 1955–61. JP 1939, DL 1947, CA 1954–66, Cornwall; High Sheriff, Cornwall, 1947–48; Vice-Lt, Cornwall, 1950–62; Chairman Cornwall County Council, 1952–63. A Gentleman of HM Bodyguard of the Honourable Corps of Gentlemen-at-Arms, 1950–72, Standard Bearer, 1968–72. Prime Warden Worshipful Company of Fishmongers, 1969–70. KStJ 1972. Hon. LLD Exeter, 1979. *Recreations:* gardening, shooting, travel. *Heir:* *s* (John) Richard (Walter Reginald) Carew Pole, *qv*. *Address:* Horson House, Antony, Torpoint, Cornwall PL11 2PE. *T:* Plymouth (0752) 812406. *Clubs:* Army and Navy, Pratt's, MCC.
See also D. C. T. Quilter.

CAREW POLE, (John) Richard (Walter Reginald); DL; farmer and chartered surveyor; *b* 2 Dec. 1938; *s* and *heir* of Sir John Gawen Carew Pole, *qv*; *m* 1st, 1966, Hon. Victoria Marion Ann Lever (marr. diss. 1974), *d* of 3rd Viscount Leverhulme, *qv*; 2nd, 1974, Mary (MVO 1983), *d* of Lt-Col Ronald Dawnay; two *s*. *Educ:* Eton Coll.; Royal Agricultural Coll., Cirencester. ARICS 1967. Lieut, Coldstream Guards, 1958–63. Asst Surveyor, Laws & Fiennes, Chartered Surveyors, 1967–72. Dir, South West Venture Capital, 1985–87; Mem. Regional Bd, West of England, subseq. Portman, Bldg Soc., 1989–. Chm., Devon and Cornwall Police Authority, 1985–87 (Mem., 1973–89); Member: SW Area Electricity Bd, 1981–90; NT Cttee for Devon and Cornwall, 1979–83. President: Surf Life Saving Assoc. of GB, 1976–86; Royal Cornwall Agricultural Show, 1981; Governor: Seale Hayne Agric. Coll., 1979–89; Plymouth Coll., 1985–; Mem. Bd, Theatre Royal, Plymouth, 1985–. County Councillor, Cornwall, 1973– (Chairman: Planning Cttee, 1980–84; Finance Cttee, 1985–89; Property Cttee, 1989–); High Sheriff of Cornwall, 1979; DL Cornwall, 1988. Liveryman, Fishmongers' Co., 1960. *Recreations:* walking, gardening, daydreaming. *Address:* Antony House, Torpoint, Cornwall PL11 2QA. *T:* Plymouth (0752) 814914. *Clubs:* White's, Pratt's.

CAREY, Group Captain Alban M., CBE 1943; owner/farmer Church Farm, Great Witchingham, since 1973; *b* 18 April 1906; *m* 1934, Enid Morten Bond; one *s*. *Educ:* Bloxham. Commissioned RAF 1929; served in night bombers, flying boats and as flying boat and landplane instructor; Pilots Cert. no 5283 for Public Transport; Navigator's Licence no 175, 1936; Sen. Op. Trng Officer, Coastal Command, 1939–42; Station Commander: Pembroke Dock, 1942–43; Gibraltar, 1943–45; Haverfordwest, 1945; St Eval, 1945–46. Chairman: Shaw & Sons Ltd, 1946–79; Jordan & Sons Ltd, 1953–68; Hadden Best Ltd, 1957–72; Shaw & Blake Ltd, 1960–68; H. T. Woodrow & Co., 1961–68; Chirit Investment Co., 1970–; Leutromedia Computers Internat., 1971–; Maden Park Property Investment Co., 1975–; East Coast Plastics, 1984–; Viking Opticals, 1986–; Dep. Chm., Tridant Group Printers plc 1972–78; Sen. Partner, Park Farm Syndicate, Snettisham, 1988–. Pres., Nat. Assoc. of Engravers and Die Stampers, 1954; Pres., Central London Br., British Fedn of Printing Industries, 1963; Chm., Nat. Assoc. of Law Stationers, 1963–68; Pres., Egham and Thorpe, Royal Agr. Assoc., 1961, 1962; Chm., Egham and Dist Abbeyfield Assoc., 1970–82. Trustee: Pensthorpe Waterfowl Trust, 1986–; Thursford Collection of Steam Engines, 1990–. *Recreations:* shooting, fishing, yachting. *Address:* Church Farm, Great Witchingham, Norfolk NR9 5PQ. *T:* Norwich (0603) 872511. *Clubs:* Royal Air Force; Royal Air Force Yacht.

CAREY, Charles John; Member, European Communities' Court of Auditors, since 1983; *b* 11 Nov. 1933; *s* of Richard Mein Carey and Celia Herbert Amy (*née* Conway); *m* 1990, Elizabeth Dale (*née* Slade). *Educ:* Rugby; Balliol Coll., Oxford. HM Treasury: Asst Principal, 1957; Principal, 1962; Asst Sec., 1971; seconded to HM Diplomatic Service as Counsellor (Econs and Finance), Office of UK Perm. Rep. to EEC, Brussels, 1974–77; Under Sec., HM Treasury, 1978–83. Mem., CIPFA, 1988. *Recreations:* mountaineering, Bavarian baroque churches, Trollope novels. *Club:* United Oxford & Cambridge University.

CAREY, Brig. Conan Jerome; Director General, The Home Farm Trust Ltd, since 1988; *b* 8 Aug. 1936; *s* of Dr James J. Carey and Marion Carey; *m* 1966, Elizabeth Gay Docker, *d* of late Lt-Col L. R. Docker, OBE, MC, TD and Cynthia (*née* Washington); one *s* two *d*.

Educ: Belvedere College, Dublin; RMA Sandhurst; RMCS Shrivenham; Staff Coll., Camberley (psc). FIPM, FBIM. Enlisted Royal Hampshire Regt, 1954; Commissioned RASC, 1956; qualified aircraft pilot, 1960; seconded Army Air Corps, 1960–65; flying duties Malaya, Brunei, Borneo, Hong Kong, BAOR; transf. to RCT, 1965; Comdr 155 (Wessex) Regt RCT(V), 1976–78; Defence Staff, British Embassy, Washington DC, 1979–82; HQ BAOR, 1982; Dep. Dir-Gen., Transport and Movements, MoD, 1985; Comdr Training Gp, RCT, 1988. MInstD; FRSA. *Recreations:* amateur rugby, golf, tennis. *Address:* c/o Lloyds Bank, Corn Street, Bristol BS99 7LE. *Clubs:* Army & Navy; Tracy Park Golf and Country (Bath).

CAREY, D(avid) M(acbeth) M(oir), CBE 1983; MA, DCL Oxon; Joint Registrar to Faculty Office of Archbishop of Canterbury, since 1982; Legal Secretary to the Archbishop of Canterbury and Principal Registrar to the Province of Canterbury, 1958–82; Legal Secretary to the Bishops of Ely, 1953–82 and Gloucester, 1957–82; Registrar to the Diocese of Canterbury, 1959–82; *b* 21 Jan. 1917; *s* of Godfrey Mohun Carey, Sherborne, Dorset, and Agnes Charlotte Carey (*née* Milligan); *m* 1949, Margaret Ruth (*née* Mills), Highfield Sch., Liphook, Hants; three *s* one *d*. *Educ:* Westminster Sch. (King's Scholar); St Edmund Hall, Oxford. Articled Clerk, Messrs Lee, Bolton & Lee, 1938–40. Lt-Cdr (S) RNVR, 1940–46. Qualified Solicitor, 1947; Partnership with Lee, Bolton & Lee, 1948–82, Consultant, 1982–. Gov., Westminster Sch., 1960–. *Recreation:* fishing. *Address:* Two Trees, 30 Shepherds Way, Liphook, Hants GU30 7HF. *T:* Liphook (0428) 723452. *Club:* Army and Navy.

CAREY, de Vic Graham; QC (Guernsey) 1989; Attorney-General, since 1982, and Receiver-General, since 1985, Guernsey; *b* 15 June 1940; *s* of Victor Michael de Vic Carey and Jean Burnett (*née* Bullen); *m* 1968, Bridget Lindsay Smith; two *s* two *d*. *Educ:* Cheam Sch.; Bryanston Sch.; Trinity Hall, Cambridge (BA 1962; MA 1967). Admitted Solicitor, 1965; Advocate, Royal Court of Guernsey, 1966. People's Dep., States of Guernsey, 1976; Solicitor-Gen. for Guernsey, 1977–82. Mem., Gen. Synod of C of E, 1982–. *Address:* Les Padins, St Saviours, Guernsey. *T:* Guernsey (0481) 64587.

CAREY, Most Rev. and Rt. Hon. George Leonard; *see* Canterbury, Archbishop of.

CAREY, Godfrey Mohun Cecil; QC 1991; a Recorder of the Crown Court, since 1986; *b* 31 Oct. 1941; *s* of Dr Godfrey Fraser Carey, MVO and Prudence Loveday (*née* Webb); *m* 1st, 1965, Caroline Jane Riggall (marr. diss. 1975); one *s* one *d* (and one *s* decd); 2nd, 1978, Dorothy May Sturgeon (marr. diss. 1983); one *d*. *Educ:* Highfield, Liphook; Eton. Legal Advr, Small Engine Div., Rolls Royce Ltd, 1964–70. Called to the Bar, Inner Temple, 1969; in practice at the Bar, 1971–. *Recreations:* music, tennis, Woodruff. *Address:* 5 Paper Buildings, EC4Y 7HB. *T:* 071–583 6117. *Clubs:* Lansdowne, Annabels.

CAREY, Hugh Leo; Executive Vice-President, W. R. Grace and Co.; Director: American Blood Pressure, Inc.; Rooney, Pace, Inc.; *b* Brooklyn, NY, 11 April 1919; *s* of Denis Carey and Margaret (*née* Collins); *m* 1st, 1947, Helen Owen Twohy (*d* 1974); seven *s* four *d* one step *d* (and two *s* decd); 2nd, 1981, Evangeline Gouletas; one step *d*. *Educ:* St Augustine's Academy and High School, Brooklyn; St John's Coll.; St John's Law School. JD 1951. Served War of 1939–45 (Bronze Star, Croix de Guerre with Silver Star); with US Army in Europe, 1939–46, rank of Lt-Col. Joined family business (petrochemicals), 1947. Called to Bar, 1951. Member US House of Reps, rep. 12th District of Brooklyn, 1960–75 (Democrat); Deputy Whip; Governor of New York State, 1974–83. Chairman: NY City Sports Commn, 1983–; NY State World Trade Council, 1985–. *Address:* (office) 1114 Avenue of the Americas, New York, NY 10036, USA.

CAREY, Prof. John; FRSL 1982; Merton Professor of English Literature, Oxford University, since 1976; *b* 5 April 1934; *s* of Charles William Carey and Winifred Ethel Carey (*née* Cook); *m* 1960, Gillian Mary Florence Booth; two *s*. *Educ:* Richmond and East Sheen County Grammar Sch.; St John's Coll., Oxford (MA, DPhil). 2nd Lieut, East Surrey Regt, 1953–54; Harmsworth Sen. Scholar, Merton Coll., Oxford, 1957–58; Lectr, Christ Church, Oxford, 1958–59; Andrew Bradley Jun. Research Fellow, Balliol, Oxford, 1959–60; Tutorial Fellow: Keble Coll., Oxford, 1960–64; St John's Coll., Oxford, 1964–75. Principal book reviewer, Sunday Times, 1977–. Chm., Booker Prize Judges, 1982. *Publications:* The Poems of John Milton (ed with Alastair Fowler), 1968; Milton, 1969; (ed) Andrew Marvell, 1969; (ed) The Private Memoirs and Confessions of a Justified Sinner, by James Hogg, 1969, 2nd edn 1981; The Violent Effigy: a study of Dickens' imagination, 1973, 2nd edn 1991; (trans.) Milton, Christian Doctrine, 1973; Thackeray: Prodigal Genius, 1977; John Donne: Life, Mind and Art, 1981, 2nd edn 1990; (ed) William Golding—the Man and his Books: a tribute on his 75th birthday, 1986; Original Copy: selected journalism and reviews, 1987; (ed) The Faber Book of Reportage, 1987; (ed) Donne, 1990; articles in Rev. of English Studies, Mod. Lang. Rev., etc. *Recreations:* swimming, gardening, bee-keeping. *Address:* Brasenose Cottage, Lyneham, Oxon; 57 Stapleton Road, Headington, Oxford. *T:* Oxford (0865) 64304.

CAREY, Peter Philip, FRSL; writer; *b* 7 May 1943; *s* of Percival Stanley Carey and Helen Jean Carey; *m* 1st, 1964, Leigh Weetman; 2nd, Alison Margaret Summers; two *s*. *Educ:* Geelong Grammar Sch., Vic., Aust. FRSL 1988. Hon. DLitt Queensland, 1989. *Publications:* Fat Man in History, 1980; Bliss, 1981; Illywhacker, 1985; Oscar and Lucinda, 1988 (Booker Prize, 1988); The Tax Inspector, 1991. *Recreation:* sleeping. *Address:* c/o Rogers, Coleridge & White, Powis Mews, W11.

CAREY, Sir Peter (Willoughby), GCB 1982 (KCB 1976; CB 1972); Chairman, Dalgety PLC, since 1986 (Director, since 1983); Director: BPB Industries PLC, since 1983; Cable and Wireless PLC, since 1984; NV Philips Gloeilampenfabrieken, since 1984; *b* 26 July 1923; *s* of Jack Delves Carey and Sophie Carey; *m* 1946, Thelma Young; three *d*. *Educ:* Portsmouth Grammar Sch.; Oriel Coll., Oxford; Sch. of Slavonic Studies. Served War of 1939–45: Capt., Gen. List, 1943–45. Information Officer, British Embassy, Belgrade, 1945–46; FO (German Section), 1948–51; Bd of Trade, 1953; Prin. Private Sec. to successive Presidents, 1960–64; IDC, 1965; Asst Sec., 1963–67, Under-Sec., 1967–69, Bd of Trade; Under-Sec., Min. of Technology, 1969–71; Dep. Sec., Cabinet Office, 1971–72; Dep. Sec., 1972–73, Second Permanent Sec., 1973–74, DTI; Second Permanent Sec., 1974–76, Permanent Sec., 1976–83, DoI. Director: Morgan Grenfell Hldgs, then Morgan Grenfell Gp, 1983–90 (Chm., 1987–89); Westland Gp, 1986–88. Hon. LLD Birmingham, 1983; Hon. DSc Cranfield Inst. of Tech., 1984. *Recreations:* music, theatre, travel. *Address:* Rose Cottage, 67 Church Road, Wimbledon, SW19 5DQ. *T:* 081–947 5222. *Club:* United Oxford & Cambridge University.

CAREY EVANS, David Lloyd, OBE 1984; JP; DL; farmer; *b* 14 Aug. 1925; *s* of Sir Thomas Carey Evans, MC, FRCS and Lady Olwen Carey Evans, DBE; *m* 1959, Annwen Williams; three *s* one *d*. *Educ:* Rottingdean Sch.; Oundle Sch.; Univ. of Wales, Bangor. BSc (Agric) 1950. Sub-Lieut, RNVR, 1943–46; farming 1947–; Chm., Welsh Council, NFU, 1976–79; Welsh Representative and Chm., Welsh Panel, CCAHC, 1974–; Vice-Chm., WAOS, 1980–. JP Portmadoc, Gwynedd, 1969. DL Gwynedd 1988. *Address:* Eisteddfa, Criccieth, Gwynedd LL52 0PT. *T:* Criccieth (0766) 522104. *Club:* Sloane.

CAREY-FOSTER, George Arthur, CMG 1952; DFC 1944; AFC 1941; Counsellor, HM Diplomatic (formerly Foreign) Service, 1946–68; *b* 18 Nov. 1907; *s* of George Muir Foster, FRCS, MRCP, and Marie Thérèse Mutin; *m* 1936, Margaret Aloysius Barry Egan; one *d*. *Educ:* Clifton Coll., Bristol. Royal Air Force, 1929–35; Reserve of Air Force Officers, 1935–39; served War of 1939–45: Royal Air Force, 1939–46 (despatches, AFC, DFC), Group Capt. Served at Foreign Office, as Consul General at Hanover, as Counsellor and Chargé d'Affaires at Rio de Janeiro, Warsaw and The Hague, 1946–68; retired, 1968. *Recreations:* wine, gardening. *Address:* 25 Saffrons Court, Compton Place Road, Eastbourne, East Sussex BN21 1DX. *Clubs:* Royal Air Force; Haagsche (The Hague).

CAREY JONES, Norman Stewart, CMG 1965; Director, Development Administration, Leeds University, 1965–77; *b* 11 Dec. 1911; *s* of Samuel Carey Jones and Jessie Isabella Stewart; *m* 1946, Stella Myles (*d* 1990); two *s*. *Educ:* Monmouth Sch.; Merton Coll., Oxford. Colonial Audit Service: Gold Coast, 1935; Northern Rhodesia, 1939; British Honduras, 1946; Kenya, 1950; Asst Financial Sec., Treasury, Kenya, 1954; Dep. Sec., Min. of Agric., Kenya, 1956; Perm. Sec., Min. of Lands and Settlement, Kenya, 1962. *Publications:* The Pattern of a Dependent Economy, 1952; The Anatomy of Uhuru, 1966; Politics, Public Enterprise and The Industrial Development Agency, 1974; articles and reviews for: Journal of Rhodes-Livingstone Inst.; E African Economics Review; Africa Quarterly; Geog. Jl. *Address:* Mawingo, Welsh St Donats, near Cowbridge, S Glam CF7 7SS. *Club:* Commonwealth Trust.

CARINE, Rear-Adm. James; Chief of Staff to Commander-in-Chief Naval Home Command, 1989–91; *b* 14 Sept. 1934; *s* of Amos Carine and Kathleen Prudence Carine (*née* Kelly); *m* 1961, (Carolyn) Sally Taylor; three *s* one *d* (and two *s* decd). *Educ:* Victoria Road Sch., Castletown, IoM; King William's Coll., IoM. FCIS 1971. Joined Royal Navy 1951; Captain 1980; Sec., Second Sea Lord, 1979–82; SACLANT HQ, Norfolk, Va, 1982–85; Naval Home Staff, 1985–88; Commodore in Comd, HMS Drake, 1988–89. Liveryman, 1988, Mem., Court of Assistants, 1989, Chartered Secretaries' Co. KSG. *Recreations:* dinghy sailing, horse racing. *Club:* Royal Naval and Royal Albert Yacht (Portsmouth).

CARINGTON, family name of **Baron Carrington.**

CARLESS, Hugh Michael, CMG 1976; HM Diplomatic Service, retired; Executive Vice-President, Hinduja Foundation, since 1986; Vice Chairman, South Atlantic Council, since 1987; *b* 22 April 1925; *s* of late Henry Alfred Carless, CIE, and Gwendolen Pattullo; *m* 1956, Rosa Maria, *e d* of Martino and Ada Frontini, São Paulo; two *s*. *Educ:* Sherborne; Sch. of Oriental Studies, London; Trinity Hall, Cambridge. Served in Paiforce and BAOR, 1943–47; entered Foreign (subseq. Diplomatic) Service, 1950; 3rd Sec., Kabul, 1951; 2nd Sec., Rio de Janeiro, 1953; Tehran, 1956; 1st Sec., 1957; FO, 1958; Private Sec. to Minister of State, 1961; Budapest, 1963; Civil Service Fellow, Dept of Politics, Glasgow Univ., 1966; Counsellor and Consul-Gen., Luanda, 1967–70; Counsellor, Bonn, 1970–73; Head of Latin American Dept, FCO, 1973–77; Minister and Chargé d'Affaires, Buenos Aires, 1977–80; on secondment to Northern Engineering Industries International Ltd, 1980–82; Ambassador to Venezuela, 1982–85. *Recreations:* golf, history. *Address:* 15 Bryanston Square, W1H 7FF. *Clubs:* Travellers'; Royal Mid Surrey Golf.

CARLESS, Prof. John Edward, BPharm, MSc, PhD; Professor and Head of Department of Pharmaceutics, School of Pharmacy, London University, 1977–83, Emeritus Professor, since 1984; *b* 23 Nov. 1922; *s* of Alfred Edward Carless and Frances Mary (*née* Smith); *m* 1950, Dorothy Litherland; one *d* and two step *d*. *Educ:* Leominster Grammar Sch.; Leicester Coll. of Science and Technol. (BPharm); FPS 1947; Univ. of Manchester (MSc, PhD). MRPharmS. Asst Lectr in Pharmacy, Univ. of Manchester, 1947–54; Chelsea College: Sen. Lectr in Pharmaceutics, 1954–61; Reader, 1961–67; Prof. of Pharmaceutics, 1967–77. Member: Cttee on Safety of Medicines, 1976–78 (Mem., Sub-Cttee on Chemistry, Pharmacy and Standards, 1973–); Veterinary Products Cttee, 1978–85; Cttee on Review of Medicine, 1980–; UK Working Gp on iodine prophylaxis following nuclear accidents, 1989–90; Chm., Pharmacy Bd, CNAA, 1978–85. Chm., Reigate Photographic Soc., 1984–86; Governor, Reigate Sixth Form Coll., 1986–. Harrison Meml Medal, 1980. *Publications:* (ed jtly) Advances in Pharmaceutical Sciences: Vol. 1, 1964–vol. 5, 1982; (contrib.) Bentley's Text Book of Pharmaceutics, 1977. *Recreations:* photography, listening to records, bowls. *Address:* Manton, Colley Manor Drive, Reigate, Surrey RH2 9JS. *T:* Reigate (0737) 43670.

CARLETON, Mrs John; *see* Adam Smith, J. B.

CARLETON-SMITH, Maj.-Gen. Michael Edward, CBE 1980 (MBE 1966); Director-General, Marie Curie Memorial Foundation, since 1985; Chairman, Marie Curie Trading Co. Ltd, since 1990; *b* 5 May 1931; *s* of late Lt-Col D. L. G. Carleton-Smith; *m* 1963, Helga Katja Stoss; three *s*. *Educ:* Radley Coll.; RMA, Sandhurst. Graduate: Army Staff Coll.; JSSC; NDC; RCDS. Commissioned into The Rifle Brigade, 1951; Rifle Bde, Germany, 1951–53; active service: Kenya, 1954–55; Malaya, 1957; Exchange PPCLI, Canada, 1958–60; GSO2 General Staff, HQ1(BR) Corps, 1962–63; Rifle Brigade: Cyprus, Hong Kong, active service, Borneo, 1965–66; Sch. of Infantry Staff, 1967–68; Comd Rifle Depot, 1970–72; Directing Staff NDC, 1972–74; Col General Staff, HQ BAOR, 1974–77; Commander Gurkha Field Force, Hong Kong, 1977–79; Dep. Director Army Staff Duties, MoD, 1981; Defence Advr and Head of British Defence Liaison Staff, Canberra, Australia, also Mil. Advr, Canberra, and Wellington, NZ, and Defence Advr, PNG, 1982–85, retd. *Recreations:* riding, travel. *Address:* 28 Belgrave Square, SW1X 8QG.

CARLIER, Maj.-Gen. Anthony Neil, OBE 1982; Team Leader, Quartermaster General's Logistic Review, since 1991; *b* 11 Jan. 1937; *s* of Geoffrey Anthony George and Sylvia Maude Carlier; *m* 1974, Daphne Kathleen Humphreys; one *s* one *d*. *Educ:* Highgate Sch.; RMA Sandhurst; RMCS. BSc(Eng) London. Troop Comdr, Cyprus, 1962–64; GSO3, 19 Inf. Bde, Borneo, 1965–66; Instructor, RMA Sandhurst, 1967–70; Staff Course: RMCS Shrivenham, 1971; BRNC Greenwich, 1972; GSO2, Staff of Flag Officer, Carriers and Amphibious Ships, 1973–74; Sqn Comdr, 1975–76; Regtl Comdr, 1977–80; Mil. Asst to Army Bd Mem., 1980–83; Engr Gp Comdr, 1983–85; rcds, 1986; Comdr British Forces, Falkland Is, 1987–88; Chief, Jt Services Liaison Organisation, Bonn, 1989–90. *Recreations:* offshore sailing, fishing, gardening, DIY. *Clubs:* Victoria League; International Association of Cape Horners (St Malo).

CARLILE, Alexander Charles, QC 1984; MP Montgomery, since 1983 (L 1983–88, Lib Dem since 1988); a Recorder, since 1986; *b* 12 Feb. 1948; *s* of Erwin Falik, MD and Sabina Falik; *m* 1968, Frances, *d* of Michael and Elizabeth Soley; three *d*. *Educ:* Epsom Coll.; King's Coll., London (LLB; AKC). Called to the Bar, Gray's Inn, 1970. Chm., Welsh Liberal Party, 1980–82. Lib. spokesman, 1983–88, Soc & Lib Dem spokesman, 1988, on Home Office and Legal Affairs; Alliance spokesman on Legal Affairs, 1987; Lib Dem spokesman on Foreign Affairs, 1988–89, on Legal Affairs, 1989–90, on Trade and Industry, 1990–. Contested (L) Flint East, Feb. 1974, 1979. Member: Adv. Council on Public Records, 1989–; GMC, 1989–; Council, Howard League, 1989–. *Recreations:* reading, theatre. *Address:* Cil y Wennol, Berriew, Powys. *Clubs:* Reform, National Liberal; Bristol Channel Yacht, Swansea.

CARLILE, Rev. Edward Wilson; Liaison Officer, East Africa Church Army Appeal, 1981–84; *b* 11 June 1915; *s* of Victor Wilson and Elsie Carlile; *m* 1946, Elizabeth (*née* Bryant); two *s* one *d*. *Educ:* Epsom Coll.; King's Coll., London (BD). Chartered Accountant, 1939. Deacon, 1943; priest, 1944; Curate, All Saints, Queensbury, 1943–46; Hon. Asst Sec. of Church Army, 1946–49; Chief Sec. of Church Army, 1949–60; Vicar of St Peter's with St Hilda's, Leicester, 1960–73; Rector of Swithland, Leicester, 1973–76; Priest in Charge of St Michael and All Angels, Belgrave, Leicester, 1976–81. *Recreations:* race relations, evangelism, walking, travel, photography. *Address:* 120A Mount View Road, Sheffield S8 8PL. *T:* Sheffield (0742) 581098.

CARLILE, Thomas, CBE 1975; FEng; Chairman, Burnett and Hallamshire Holdings, 1985–88; *b* 9 Feb. 1924; *s* of late James Love Carlile and Isobel Scott Carlile; *m* 1955, Jessie Davidson Clarkson; three *d*. *Educ:* Minchenden County Sch.; City & Guilds Coll., London. Joined Babcock & Wilcox Ltd, 1944; Man. Dir, 1968–84, Dep. Chm., 1978–84, Babcock Internat. plc. Chm., Shipbuilding Industry Training Board, 1967–70; Dep. Chm., Police Negotiating Bd, 1987–. Mem., Energy Commn, 1977–79. Pres., Engineering Employers' Fedn, 1972–74, a Vice-Pres., 1979–84. Director: Chubb & Son plc, 1976–84; French Kier Hldgs Plc, 1985–86. FCGI 1978; FEng 1979. *Address:* 8 Aldenham Grove, Radlett, Herts WD7 7BW. *T:* Radlett (0923) 857033.

CARLILL, Rear Adm. John Hildred, OBE 1969; Royal Navy, retired 1982; *b* 24 Oct. 1925; *o s* of late Dr and Mrs H. B. Carlill; *m* 1955, (Elizabeth) Ann, *yr d* of late Lt Col and Mrs W. Southern; three *d*. *Educ:* RNC Dartmouth. psc 1961; jssc 1967. Served War 1939–45. Joined RN as Exec. Cadet 1939, transferred to Accountant Branch 1943; HMS Mauritius 1943–45. Comdr 1963, Captain 1972 (Sec. to FO Naval Air Comd, Dir Naval Manning and Training (S), Sec. to Second Sea Lord, Admty Interview Board, Cdre HMS Drake); Rear Admiral 1980; Adm. President, RNC Greenwich, 1980–82. Sec., Engineering Council, 1983–87. Chm., Guildford Sea Cadet Cttee, 1987; Pres., Guildford Br., RN Assoc., 1989–. Freeman: City of London, 1980; Drapers' Co., 1983. *Recreations:* walking, skiing, water colour painting. *Address:* Crownpits Barn, Crownpits Lane, Godalming, Surrey GU7 1NY. *T:* Godalming (0483) 415022.

CARLILL, Vice-Admiral Sir Stephen Hope, KBE 1957; CB 1954; DSO 1942; *b* Orpington, Kent, 23 Dec. 1902; *s* of late Harold Flamank Carlill; *m* 1928, Julie Fredrike Elisabeth Hildegard, *o d* of late Rev. W. Rahlenbeck, Westphalia; two *s*. *Educ:* Royal Naval Colleges, Osborne and Dartmouth. Lieut RN, 1925; qualified as Gunnery Officer, 1929; Commander 1937; Commanded HM Destroyers Hambledon, 1940, and Farndale, 1941–42; Captain 1942; Captain (D), 4th Destoyer Flotilla, HMS Quilliam, 1942–44 (despatches); Admiralty, 1944–46; Chief of Staff to C-in-C British Pacific Fleet, 1946–48; Captain, HMS Excellent, 1949–50; Commanded HMS Illustrious, 1950–51; Rear-Admiral, 1952; Senior Naval Member, Imperial Defence Coll., 1952–54; Vice-Admiral, 1954; Flag Officer, Training Squadron, 1954–55; Chief of Naval Staff, Indian Navy, 1955–58, retired. Representative in Ghana of West Africa Cttee 1960–66; Adviser to W Africa Cttee, 1966–67. *Recreations:* walking and gardening. *Address:* 22 Hamilton Court, Milford-on-Sea, Lymington, Hants SO41 0PR. *T:* Lymington (0590) 642958. *Club:* Naval and Military.

CARLISLE, family name of **Baron Carlisle of Bucklow.**

CARLISLE, 12th Earl of, *cr* 1661; **Charles James Ruthven Howard,** MC 1945; DL; Viscount Howard of Morpeth, Baron Dacre of Gillesland, 1661; Lord Ruthven of Freeland, 1651; *b* 21 Feb. 1923; *o s* of 11th Earl of Carlisle, and Lady Ruthven of Freeland (*d* 1982) (11th in line); *S* father, 1963; *m* 1945, Hon. Ela Beaumont, OStJ, *o d* of 2nd Viscount Allendale, KG, CB, CBE, MC; two *s* two *d*. *Educ:* Eton. Served War of 1939–45 (wounded twice, MC). Lieut late Rifle Brigade. Forestry Comr, 1967–70. DL Cumbria, 1984–. FRICS (FLAS 1953). *Heir: s* Viscount Morpeth, *qv*. *Address:* Naworth Castle, Brampton, Cumbria. *T:* Brampton (06977) 2621.

CARLISLE OF BUCKLOW, Baron *cr* 1987 (Life Peer), of Mobberley in the County of Cheshire; **Mark Carlisle,** PC 1979; QC 1971; DL; a Recorder of the Crown Court, 1976–79 and since 1981; a Judge of the Courts of Appeal, Jersey and Guernsey, since 1990; *b* 7 July 1929; 2nd *s* of late Philip Edmund and Mary Carlisle; *m* 1959, Sandra Joyce Des Voeux; one *d*. *Educ:* Radley Coll.; Manchester Univ. LLB (Hons) Manchester, 1952. Called to the Bar, Gray's Inn, 1953, Bencher 1980; Northern Circuit. Member Home Office Advisory Council on the Penal System, 1966–70. MP (C): Runcorn, 1964–83; Warrington S, 1983–87. Joint Hon. Secretary, Conservative Home Affairs Cttee, 1965–69; Conservative Front Bench Spokesman on Home Affairs, 1969–70; Parly Under-Sec. of State, Home Office, 1970–72; Minister of State, Home Office, 1972–74; Sec. of State for Educn and Science, 1979–81. Chairman: Cons. Home Affairs Cttee, 1983–87; Parole Review Cttee, 1987–88; Prime Minister's Adv. Cttee on Business Appts of Crown Servants, 1988–; Criminal Injuries Compensation Bd, 1989–. Treas., CPA, 1982–85, Dep. Chm., UK Br., 1985–87. Mem., Adv. Council, BBC, 1975–79. DL Cheshire, 1983. *Recreation:* golf. *Address:* Queen Elizabeth Building, Temple, EC4. *T:* 071-583 5766; 3 Holt Gardens, Mobberley, Cheshire. *T:* Mobberley (056587) 2275. *Club:* Garrick.

CARLISLE, Bishop of, since 1989; **Rt. Rev. Ian Harland;** *b* 19 Dec. 1932; *s* of late Canon Samuel James Harland and of Brenda Gwendolyn Harland; *m* 1967, Susan Hinman; one *s* three *d*. *Educ:* Dragon School, Oxford; Haileybury; Peterhouse, Cambridge (MA); Wycliffe Hall, Oxford. Teaching at Sunningdale School, 1956–58; Curate, Melton Mowbray, 1960–63; Vicar, Oughtibridge, Sheffield, 1963–72; Member, Wortley RDC, 1969–73; Vicar, St Cuthbert, Fir Vale, Sheffield, 1972–75; Priest-in-charge, All Saints, Brightside, 1973–75; RD of Ecclesfield, 1973–75; Vicar of Rotherham, 1975–79; RD of Rotherham, 1976–79; Archdeacon of Doncaster, 1979–85; Bishop Suffragan of Lancaster, 1985–89. Proctor in Convocation, 1975–85. *Recreations:* politics, sport. *Address:* Rose Castle, Dalston, Carlisle CA5 7BZ. *T:* Raughton Head (06996) 274.

CARLISLE, Dean of; *see* Stapleton, Very Rev. H. E. C.

CARLISLE, Archdeacon of; *see* Stannard, Ven. C. P.

CARLISLE, Brian Apcar, CBE 1974; DSC 1945; Chairman, Saxon Oil PLC, 1980–85; *b* 27 Dec. 1919; 2nd *s* of Captain F. M. M. Carlisle, MC; *m* 1953, Elizabeth Hazel Mary Binnie, 2nd *d* of Comdr J. A. Binnie, RN; one *s* three *d*. *Educ:* Harrow Sch.; Corpus Christi Coll., Cambridge. Royal Navy, 1940–46, served in N Atlantic, Channel and Mediterranean in HMS Hood and destroyers; Sudan Political Service, 1946–54, served in Kassala, Blue-Nile and Bahr-el-Ghazal Provinces; Royal Dutch/Shell Group, 1955–74: served in India with Burmah Shell, 1960–64; Regional Co-ordinator, Middle East, and Dir, Shell International Petroleum, 1970–74; participated in pricing negotiations with OPEC states, 1970–73; Dir, Home Oil Co. Ltd, 1977–80; Oil Consultant to Lloyds Bank International, 1975–81. Chm., Bd of Governors, Gordon's Sch. (formerly Gordon Boys' Sch.), 1985–. Chm., Sudan Church Assoc., 1982–. *Recreations:* gardening, crosswords, golf. *Address:* Heath Cottage, Hartley Wintney, Hants RG27 8RE. *T:* Hartley Wintney (025126) 2224.

CARLISLE, Hugh Bernard Harwood, QC 1978; a Recorder of the Crown Court, since 1983; *b* 14 March 1937; *s* of late W. H. Carlisle, FRCS (Ed), FRCOG, and Joyce Carlisle; *m* 1964, Veronica Marjorie, *d* of G. A. Worth, *qv*; one *s* one *d*. *Educ:* Oundle Sch.; Downing Coll., Cambridge. Nat. Service, 2nd Lt, RA. Called to the Bar, Middle Temple, 1961, Bencher, 1985. Jun. Treasury Counsel for Personal Injuries Cases, 1975–78. Dept of Trade Inspector: Bryanston Finance Ltd, 1978–87; Milbury plc, 1985–87. Member: Criminal Injuries Compensation Bd, 1982–; Bar Council, 1989–. *Recreations:* fishing, croquet. *Address:* 1 Temple Gardens, EC4Y 9BB. *T:* 071-583 1315. *Clubs:* Garrick, Hurlingham (Chm., 1982–85).

CARLISLE, Sir (John) Michael, Kt 1985; CEng, FIMechE, FIMarE; Director, Torday & Carlisle plc, since 1981; Chairman, Trent Regional Health Authority, since 1982; *b* 16 Dec. 1929; *s* of John Hugh Carlisle and Lilian Amy (*née* Smith); *m* 1957, Mary Scott Young; one *s* one *d*. *Educ:* King Edward VII Sch., Sheffield; Sheffield Univ. (BEng). Served Royal Navy (Lieut), 1952–54. Production Engr, Lockwood & Carlisle Ltd, 1954–57, Man. Dir, 1958–70, Chm. and Man. Dir, 1970–81; Dir of several overseas subsid. cos; Director: Eric Woodward (Electrical) Ltd, 1965–85; Diesel Marine Internat., 1981–89. Chairman: Sheffield AHA(T), 1974–82; N Sheffield Univ. HMC, 1971–74; Mem., Bd of Governors, United Sheffield Hosps, 1972–74; Mem. Council: Sheffield Chamber of Commerce, 1967–78; Production Engrg Res. Assoc., 1968–73; Chm., Sheffield Productivity Assoc., 1970; Pres., Sheffield Jun. Chamber of Commerce, 1967–68; non-exec. Director: Fenchurch Midlands Ltd, 1986–; Norhomes plc. Governor: Sheffield City Polytechnic, 1979–82 (Hon. Fellow, 1977); Sheffield High Sch., 1977–87; Member: Sheffield Univ. Court, 1968–; Sheffield Univ. Careers Adv. Bd, 1974–82; Nottingham Univ. Court, 1982–; Council, York Univ. Hon. LLD Sheffield, 1988. Freeman, Co. of Cutlers in Hallamshire. CBIM. *Recreations:* golf, country walking, horse riding, water colour painting, genealogy. *Address:* 7 Rushley Avenue, Dore, Sheffield S17 3EP. *T:* Sheffield (0742) 365988; St Ovin, Lastingham, N Yorks YO6 6TL. *Clubs:* Sickleholme Golf; Kirbymoorside Golf.

CARLISLE, John Russell; MP (C) Luton North, since 1983 (Luton West, 1979–83); *b* 28 Aug. 1942; *s* of Andrew and Edith Carlisle; *m* 1964, Anthea Jane Lindsay May; two *d*. *Educ:* Bedford Sch.; St Lawrence Coll.; Coll. of Estate Management, London. Sidney C. Banks Ltd, Sandy, 1964–78; Consultant: Louis Dreyfus plc, 1982–87; Barnet Devanney & Co. Ltd, 1987–; Barry Simmons PR, 1987–; non-exec. Dir, Bletchley Motor Gp, 1988–; Mem., London Corn Exchange, 1987–. Chm., Mid Beds Cons. Assoc., 1974–76. Chm., Cons Parly Cttee on Sport, 1981–82, 1983–84, 1985–; Vice Chm., All-Party Football Cttee, 1987–; Mem., Commons Select Cttee on Agriculture, 1985–88. Chm., British–S Africa Gp, 1987 (Sec., 1983–87); Treas., Anglo-Gibraltar Gp, 1981–82. Governor, Sports Aid Foundn (Eastern), 1985–. President: Luton 100 Club; Luton Band. *Recreations:* sport, music. *Address:* House of Commons, SW1A 0AA. *T:* 071-219 4571. *Clubs:* Farmers', MCC, Rugby.

CARLISLE, Kenneth Melville; MP (C) Lincoln, since 1979; Parliamentary Under-Secretary of State, Ministry of Defence, since 1990; *b* 25 March 1941; *s* of late Kenneth Ralph Malcolm Carlisle, TD and of Hon. Elizabeth Mary McLaren, *d* of 2nd Baron Aberconway; *m* 1986, Carla, *d* of A. W. Heffner, Md, USA; one *s*. *Educ:* Harrow; Magdalen Coll., Oxford (BA History). Called to Bar, Inner Temple, 1965. Brooke Bond Liebig, 1966–74; farming in Suffolk, 1974–. PPS to: Minister of State for Energy, 1981–83; Minister of State for Home Office, 1983–84; Sec. of State for NI, 1984–85; Home Secretary, 1985–87; an Asst Govt Whip, 1987–88; a Lord Comr of HM Treasury, 1988–90. *Recreations:* botany, gardening, walking, history. *Address:* House of Commons, SW1A 0AA.

CARLISLE, Sir Michael; *see* Carlisle, Sir J. M.

CARLOW, Viscount; Charles George Yuill Seymour Dawson-Damer; *b* 6 Oct. 1965; *s* and *heir* of 7th Earl of Portarlington, *qv*. *Educ:* Eton College; Univ. of Edinburgh (MA Hons 1988). A Page of Honour to the Queen, 1979–80. *Address:* 19 Coolong Road, Vaucluse, NSW 2030, Australia. *Club:* Royal Sydney Golf (Sydney).

CARLTON, Viscount; Reed Montagu Stuart Wortley; *b* 5 Feb. 1980; *s* and heir of Earl of Wharncliffe, *qv*.

CARLYLE, Joan Hildred; soprano; *b* 6 April 1931; *d* of late Edgar James and Margaret Mary Carlyle; *m*; two *d*. *Educ:* Howell's Sch., Denbigh, N Wales. Became Principal Lyric Soprano, Royal Opera House, Covent Garden, 1955; Oscar in Ballo in Maschera, 1957–58 season; Sophie in Rosenkavalier, 1958–59; Micaela in Carmen, 1958–59; Nedda in Pagliacci (new Zeffirelli production), Dec. 1959; Mimi in La Bohème, Dec. 1960; Titania in Gielgud production of Britten's Midsummer Night's Dream, London première, Dec. 1961; Pamina in Klemperer production of The Magic Flute, 1962; Countess in Figaro, 1963; Zdenko in Hartman production of Arabella, 1964; Sœur Angelica (new production), 1965; Desdemona in Otello, 1965, 1967; Sophie in Rosenkavalier (new production), 1966; Pamina in Magic Flute (new production), 1966; Arabella in Arabella, 1967; Marschallin in Rosenkavalier, 1968; Jenifer, Midsummer Marriage (new prod.), 1969; Donna Anna, 1970; Reiza, Oberon, 1970; Adrianna Lecouvreur, 1970; Russalka, for BBC, 1969; Elizabeth in Don Carlos, 1975. Roles sung abroad include: Oscar, Nedda, Mimi, Pamina, Zdenko, Micaela, Desdemona, Donna Anna, Arabella, Elizabeth. Has sung in Buenos Aires, Belgium, Holland, France, Monaco, Naples, Milan, Berlin, Capetown, Munich. Has made numerous recordings; appeared BBC, TV (in film). *Recreations:* gardening, cooking, interior decorating, countryside preservation. *Address:* The Griffin, Ruthin, Clwyd, N Wales. *T:* Ruthin (08242) 2792.

CARMAN, George Alfred, QC 1971; a Recorder of the Crown Court, 1972–84; *b* 6 Oct. 1929; *o s* of late Alfred George Carman and Evelyn Carman; *m* 1st, 1960, Cecilia Sparrow (marr. diss. 1976); one *s*; 2nd, 1976, Frances Elizabeth Venning (marr. diss. 1984). *Educ:* St Joseph's Coll., Blackpool; Balliol Coll., Oxford. First Class, Final Hons Sch. of Jurisprudence, 1952. Captain RAEC, 1948–49. Called to the Bar (King George V Coronation Schol.) Lincoln's Inn, 1953, Bencher 1978; practised on Northern Circuit. *Address:* New Court, Temple, EC4Y 9BE; 15 Evelyn Gardens, SW7. *Club:* Garrick.

CARMICHAEL, family name of **Baron Carmichael of Kelvingrove.**

CARMICHAEL OF KELVINGROVE, Baron *cr* 1983 (Life Peer), of Camlachie in the District of the City of Glasgow; **Neil George Carmichael;** *b* Oct. 1921; *m* 1948, Catherine McIntosh Rankin (*see* C. M. Carmichael) (marr. diss.); one *d*. *Educ:* Estbank Acad.; Royal Coll. of Science and Technology, Glasgow. Employed by Gas Board in Planning Dept. Past Member Glasgow Corporation. MP (Lab) Glasgow, Woodside, 1962–74, Glasgow, Kelvingrove, 1974–83; contested (Lab) Glasgow, Hillhead, 1983. PPS to Minister of Technology, 1966–67; Jt Parly Sec., Min. of Transport, 1967–69; Parly Sec., Min. of Technology, 1969–70; Parliamentary Under-Secretary of State: DoE, 1974–75; DoI, 1975–76; Mem., Select Cttee on Transport, 1980–83; Hon. Sec., Scottish Labour Gp of MPs, 1979–83. *Address:* House of Lords, SW1A 0PW; 53 Partick Hill Road, Glasgow G11 5AB.

CARMICHAEL, Catherine McIntosh, (Kay); social worker; *b* 22 Nov. 1925; *d* of John D. and Mary Rankin; *m* 1948, Neil George Carmichael (now Baron Carmichael of Kelvingrove, *qv*) (marr. diss.); one *d*; *m* 1987, David Vernon Donnison, *qv*. *Educ:* Glasgow and Edinburgh. Social worker, 1955–57; psychiatric social work, 1957–60; Dep. Dir, Scottish Probation Training Course, 1960–62; Lectr, 1962, Sen. Lectr, 1974–80, Dept of Social Administration and Social Work, Univ. of Glasgow. Mem., 1969–75, Dep. Chm., 1975–80, Supplementary Benefits Commn. *Recreation:* Alexander technique. *Address:* The Old Manse, Ardentinny, Argyll PA23 8TR. *T:* Ardentinny (036981) 298.

CARMICHAEL, Sir David William G. C.; *see* Gibson-Craig-Carmichael.

CARMICHAEL, Ian (Gillett); *b* 18 June 1920; *s* of Arthur Denholm Carmichael, Cottingham, E Yorks, and Kate Gillett, Hessle, E Yorks; *m* 1943, Jean Pyman Maclean (*d* 1983), Sleights, Yorks; two *d*. *Educ:* Scarborough Coll.; Bromsgrove Sch. Studied at RADA, 1938–39. Served War of 1939–45 (despatches). First professional appearance as a Robot in "RUR", by Karel and Josef Capek, The People's Palace, Stepney, 1939; *stage appearances* include: The Lyric Revue, Globe, 1951; The Globe Revue, Globe, 1952; High Spirits, Hippodrome, 1953; Going to Town, St Martin's, 1954; Simon and Laura, Apollo, 1954; The Tunnel of Love, Her Majesty's, 1958; The Gazebo, Savoy, 1960; Critic's Choice, Vaudeville, 1961; Devil May Care, Strand, 1963; Boeing-Boeing, Cort Theatre, New York, 1965; Say Who You Are, Her Majesty's, 1965; Getting Married, Strand, 1968; I Do! I Do!, Lyric, 1968; Birds on the Wing, O'Keefe Centre, Toronto, 1969; Darling I'm Home, S African tour, 1972; Out on a Limb, Vaudeville, 1976; Overheard, Theatre Royal, Haymarket, 1981; Pride and Prejudice, Theatre Royal, York and nat. tour, 1987; The Circle, nat. tour, 1990. *Films* include: (from 1955) Simon and Laura; Private's Progress; Brothers in Law; Lucky Jim; Happy is the Bride; The Big Money; Left, Right and Centre; I'm All Right Jack; School for Scoundrels; Light Up The Sky; Double Bunk; The Amorous Prawn; Hide and Seek; Heavens Above!; Smashing Time; The Magnificent Seven Deadly Sins; From Beyond the Grave; The Lady Vanishes; Diamond Skulls. *TV series* include: The World of Wooster; Bachelor Father; Lord Peter Wimsey; All For Love; Obituaries. Hon. DLitt Hull, 1987. *Publication:* Will the Real Ian Carmichael . . . (autobiog.), 1979. *Recreations:* cricket, gardening, photography and reading. *Address:* c/o London Management, 235/241 Regent Street, W1A 2JT. *Club:* MCC.

CARMICHAEL, Sir John, KBE 1955; Chairman, St Andrews Links Trust, 1984–88; *b* 22 April 1910; *s* of late Thomas Carmichael and Margaret Doig Coupar; *m* 1940, Cecilia Macdonald Edwards; one *s* three *d*. *Educ:* Madras Coll., St Andrews; Univ. of St Andrews; Univ. of Michigan (Commonwealth Fund Fellow). Guardian Assurance Co., Actuarial Dept, 1935–36; Sudan Govt Civil Service, 1936–59; Member, Sudan Resources Board and War Supply Dept, 1939–45; Secretary, Sudan Development Board, 1944–48; Asst Financial Secretary, 1946–48; Dep. Financial Secretary, 1948–53; Director, Sudan Gezira Board, 1950–54; Chm., Sudan Light and Power Co., 1952–54; Acting Financial Secretary, then Permanent Under Secretary to Ministry of Finance, 1953–55; Financial and Economic Adviser to Sudan Government, 1955–59. Member: UK delegation to General Assembly of UN, 1959; Scottish Gas Board, 1960–70; Scottish Industrial Develt Adv. Bd, 1973–80; Dep. Chm., ITA, 1960–64, Acting Chm., ITA, 1962–63; Chm., Herring Industry Bd, 1962–65; Director: Fisons Ltd, 1961–80 (Chief Executive, 1962–66, Dep. Chm., 1965–71); Grampian Television, 1965–72; Jute Industries Ltd, later Sidlaw Industries Ltd, 1966–80 (Dep. Chm., 1969; Chm., 1970–80); Royal Bank of Scotland, 1966–80; Adobe Oil and Gas Corp., Texas, 1973–85; Mem., Social and Economic Cttee, EEC, 1972–77. Pres., Senior Golfers' Soc., 1982–85. *Recreations:* golf, gardening. *Address:* Hayston Park, Balmullo, St Andrews, Fife KY16 0AN. *T:* Balmullo (0334) 870268. *Clubs:* Honourable Company of Edinburgh Golfers; Royal and Ancient Golf (St Andrews) (Captain, 1974–75); Augusta National Golf, Pine Valley Golf.

CARMICHAEL, Kay; *see* Carmichael, C. M.

CARMICHAEL, Keith Stanley, CBE 1981; FCA; Managing Partner, Longcrofts, 1981–90; *b* 5 Oct. 1929; *s* of Stanley and Ruby Dorothy Carmichael; *m* 1958, Cynthia Mary (née Jones); one *s*. *Educ:* Charlton House Sch.; Bristol Grammar Sch.; qualified as Chartered Accountant, 1951; FTII 1951, FCA 1961. Partner, Wilson Bigg & Co., 1957–69; Dir, H. Foulks Lynch & Co. Ltd, 1957–69; Dir, Radio Rentals Ltd, 1967–69; sole practitioner, 1969–81, 1990–. Mem., Monopolies and Mergers Commn, 1983–; Lloyd's Underwriter, 1976–90. Pres., Hertsmere Cons. Assoc. Chm. Bd of Governors, and Trustee, Rickmansworth Masonic Sch., 1984–. Freeman, City of London, 1960. FInstD. Mem., Editl Bd, Simon's Taxes, 1970–82. *Publications:* Spicer and Pegler's Income Tax (ed), 1965; Corporation Tax, 1966; Capital Gains Tax, 1968; Ranking Spicer and Pegler's Executorship Law and Accounts (ed), 1969, 1987; (with P. Wolstenholme) Taxation of Lloyd's Underwriters, 1980, 3rd edn 1988; contribs to Accountancy. *Recreations:* gardening, reading, golf. *Address:* 117 Newberries Avenue, Radlett, Herts WD7 7EN. *T:* Radlett (0923) 855098. *Clubs:* Carlton (Dep. Chm., 1989–), City of London, MCC, Lord's Taverners.

CARMICHAEL, Peter, CBE 1981; retired; self-employed consultant and horological specialist; *b* 26 March 1933; *s* of Robert and Elizabeth Carmichael; *m* 1st; two *s* four *d*; 2nd, 1980, June Carmichael (*née* Philip). *Educ:* Glasgow Univ. (BSc 1st Cl. Hons Physics). Design Engineer with Ferranti Ltd, Edinburgh, 1958–65; Hewlett-Packard: Project Leader, 1965–67 (Leader of Project Team which won Queen's Award to Industry for Technical Innovation, 1967); Production Engrg Manager, 1967–68; Quality Assurance Manager, 1968–73; Engrg Manager, 1973–75; Manufacturing Manager, 1975–76; Division Gen. Man., 1976–82, and Jt Managing Director, 1980–82. Scottish Development Agency: Dir, Small Business and Electronics, 1982–88; Gp Dir (East), 1988–89. Chairman: (non-exec.) Strathclyde Fabricators, 1989–; Wolfson Microelectronics, 1990–. Chm., Esmée Fairbairn Res. Centre, Heriot-Watt Univ., 1990–. Hon. DSc Heriot-Watt, 1984. *Recreations:* fishing, antique clock restoration. *Address:* 86 Craiglea Drive, Edinburgh EH10 5PH. *T:* (home) 031–447 6334; (office) 031–452 8568.

CARNAC; *see* Rivett-Carnac.

CARNARVON, 7th Earl of, *cr* 1793; **Henry George Reginald Molyneux Herbert,** KCVO 1982; KBE 1976; DL; Baron Porchester 1780; *b* 19 Jan. 1924; *o s* of 6th Earl of Carnarvon and of Catherine, *d* of late Jacob Wendell, New York; *S* father, 1987; *m* 1956, Jean Margaret, *e d* of Hon. Oliver Wallop, Big Horn, Sheridan Co., Wyoming, USA; two *s* one *d*. Late Lieut RHG; retired pay, 1947. Hon. Col, Hampshire Fortress Regt, RE (TA) 1963–67, retaining rank of Hon. Col. Racing Manager to the Queen, 1969–. Chairman: South East Economic Planning Council, 1971–79; Agricultural Research Council, 1978–82; Game Research Assoc., 1960–67 (Vice-Pres., 1967–); Stallion Adv. Cttee to Betting Levy Bd, 1974–86; Standing Conf. on Countryside Sports, 1978–; Newbury Racecourse plc, 1985–; Standing Conf. on London and SE Regl Planning Authys, 1989–; President: Thoroughbred Breeders' Assoc., 1969–74, 1986–91 (Chm. 1964–66); RASE, 1980–81. Member: Hampshire Agriculture Exec. Cttee, 1955–65; Nature Conservancy, 1963–66; Sports Council, 1965–70 (Chm., Planning Cttee, 1965–70); Forestry Commission, 1967–70; Pres., Hampshire and IoW Naturalist Trust, 1987–; President: Amateur Riders' Assoc., 1969–75; Hampshire County Cricket Club, 1966–68; Mem., Jockey Club, 1964– (Chm., Flat Pattern Cttee, 1967–85). CC Hants, 1954; County Alderman, 1965–74; Vice-Chm. County Council, 1971–74, Chm., New County Council, 1973–77; Vice-Chm., CC Assoc., 1972–74 (Chm. Planning Cttee, 1968–74); Member: Basingstoke Town Develt Jt Cttee, 1960–73; Andover Town Develt Jt Cttee, 1960–65. Verderer of the New Forest, 1961–65. DL Hants 1965. High Steward of Winchester, 1977. Hon. Fellow, Portsmouth Polytech., 1976. Hon. DSc Reading, 1980. *Heir:* *s* Lord Porchester, *qv*. *Address:* Milford Lake House, Burghclere, Newbury, Berks RG16 9EL. *T:* Highclere (0635) 253387. *Clubs:* White's, Portland.

CARNE, Dr Stuart John, CBE 1986 (OBE 1977); FRCGP; Senior Partner, Grove Health Centre, since 1967; Senior Tutor in General Practice, Royal Postgraduate Medical School, since 1970; *b* 19 June 1926; *s* of late Bernard Carne and Millicent Carne; *m* 1951, Yolande (*née* Cooper); two *s* two *d*. *Educ:* Willesden County Grammar Sch.; Middlesex Hosp. Med. Sch. MB BS; MRCS; LRCP; DCH. House Surgeon, Middlesex Hosp., 1950–51; House Physician, House Surgeon and Casualty Officer, Queen Elizabeth Hosp. for Children, 1951–52; Flight Lieut, Med. Branch, RAF, 1952–54; general practice in London, 1954–. DHSS appointments: Chm., Standing Med. Adv. Cttee, 1982–86 (Mem., 1974–86); Member: Central Health Services Council, 1976–79; Children's Cttee, 1978–81; Personal Social Services Council, 1976–80; Chm., Jt Cttee on Contraception, 1983–86 (Mem., 1975–86). Hon. Civil Consultant in Gen. Practice to RAF, 1974–. Royal College of General Practitioners: Mem. Council, 1961–; Hon.Treasurer, 1964–81; Pres., 1988–91; President: Section of General Practice, 1973–74, United Services Sect., 1985–87, RSocMed; Mem. Council, World Orgn of Nat. Colls and Acads of Gen. Practice and Family Medicine,1970–80 (Pres., 1976–78); Mem. Exec. Council, British Diabetic Assoc., 1981–87. Examnr in medicine, Soc. of Apothecaries, 1980–88. Chm., St Mary Abbots Court Ltd, 1981–. Hon. MO, 1959–89, Vice-Pres., 1989–, Queen's Park Rangers FC. Hon. Mem., BPA, 1982. *Publications:* Paediatric Care, 1976; (jtly) DHSS Handbook on Contraceptive Practice, 3rd edn 1984, 4th edn 1988; numerous articles in Lancet, BMJ and other jls. *Recreations:* music, theatre, photography, philately. *Address:* 5 St Mary Abbots Court, Warwick Gardens, W14 8RA. *T:* 071–602 1970. *Club:* Royal Air Force.

CARNEGIE, family name of **Duke of Fife** and of **Earls of Northesk** and **Southesk.**

CARNEGIE, Lt-Gen. Sir Robin (Macdonald), KCB 1979; OBE 1968; DL; Director General of Army Training, 1981–82, retired; *b* 22 June 1926; *yr s* of late Sir Francis Carnegie, CBE; *m* 1955, Iona, *yr d* of late Maj.-Gen. Sir John Sinclair, KCMG, CB, OBE; one *s* two *d*. *Educ:* Rugby. Commnd 7th Queen's Own Hussars, 1946; comd The Queen's Own Hussars, 1967–69; Comdr 11th Armd Bde, 1971–72; Student, Royal Coll. of Defence Studies, 1973; GOC 3rd Div., 1974–76; Chief of Staff, BAOR, 1976–78; Military Secretary, 1978–80. Col, The Queen's Own Hussars, 1981–87. DL Wilts, 1990. *Club:* Cavalry and Guards.

CARNEGIE, Sir Roderick (Howard), Kt 1978; FTS; Chairman, Hudson Conway Ltd, 1987; *b* 27 Nov. 1932; *s* of Douglas H. Carnegie and Margaret F. Carnegie; *m* 1959, Carmen, *d* of W. J. T. Clarke; three *s*. *Educ:* Geelong Church of England Grammar Sch.; Trinity Coll., Univ. of Melbourne; New Coll., Oxford Univ.; Harvard Business Sch., Boston. BSc; Dip. Agricl Economics, MA Oxon; MBA Harvard; FTS 1985. McKinsey & Co., New York, 1954–70: Principal, 1964–68, Director, 1968–70; Man. Dir, 1971–83, Chm. and Chief Exec., 1974–86, CRA Ltd. Director: Comalco Ltd, 1970–; Aust. Mining Industry Council, 1974– (a Sen. Vice-Pres., 1985–); Aust. and NZ Banking Gp Ltd; Mem., IBM Asia Pacific Gp. Member: General Motors Aust. Adv. Council, 1979–; Chm., Consultative Cttee on Relations with Japan, 1984–; Pres., Business Council of Aust., 1987–88; International Councillor: Morgan Guaranty Trust; The Brookings Instn. Mem., CSIRO Bd, 1987. Hon. DSc Newcastle, 1985. *Recreations:* surfing, tennis, reading. *Address:* Collins Street, Melbourne, Victoria 3000, Australia. *Clubs:* Melbourne (Victoria, Aust.); Links (New York).

CARNEGY OF LOUR, Baroness *cr* 1982 (Life Peer), of Lour in the District of Angus; **Elizabeth Patricia Carnegy of Lour;** DL; President for Scotland, Girl Guides Association, 1979–89; formerly a farmer; *b* 28 April 1925; *e d* of late Lt Col U. E. C. Carnegy, DSO, MC, DL, JP, 12th of Lour, and Violet Carnegy, MBE. *Educ:* Downham Sch., Essex. Served Cavendish Lab., Cambridge, 1943–46. With Girl Guides Assoc., 1947–: County Comr, Angus, 1956–63; Trng Adviser, Scotland, 1958–62; Trng Adviser, Commonwealth HQ, 1963–65; Pres. for Angus, 1971–79. Co-opted to Educn Cttee, Angus CC, 1967–75; Tayside Regional Council: Councillor, 1974–82; Convener: Recreation and Tourism Cttee, 1974–76; Educn Cttee, 1977–81. Chairman: Working Party on Prof. Trng for Community Education in Scotland, 1975–77; Tayside Cttee on Med. Res. Ethics, 1990–. Member: MSC, 1979–82 (Chm., Cttee for Scotland, 1981–83); Council for Tertiary Educn in Scotland, 1979–84; Scottish Economic Council, 1981–; Scottish Council for Community Educn, 1981–88 (Mem., 1978–88); H of L Select Cttee on European Communities, 1983–; Council, Open Univ., 1984–; Admin. Council, Royal Jubilee Trusts, 1985–88; Court, St Andrews Univ., 1991–; Trustee, Nat. Museums of Scotland, 1987–91. Hon. Pres., Scottish Library Assoc., 1989–. Hon. Sheriff, 1969–84; DL Angus, 1988. Hon. LLD Dundee, 1991. *Address:* Lour, by Forfar, Angus DD8 2LR. *T:* Inverarity (030782) 237; 33 Tufton Court, Tufton Street, SW1P 3QH. *T:* 071–222 4464. *Club:* Lansdowne.

CARNELL, Rev. Canon Geoffrey Gordon; Chaplain to The Queen, 1981–88; Non-Residentiary Canon of Peterborough Cathedral, 1965–85, Canon Emeritus since 1985; *b* 5 July 1918; *m* 1945, Mary Elizabeth Boucher Smith; two *s*. *Educ:* City of Norwich Sch.; St John's Coll., Cambridge (Scholar, 1937; BA 1940; Naden Divinity Student, 1940; Lightfoot Scholar, 1940; MA 1944); Cuddesdon Coll., Oxford. Ordained deacon, Peterborough Cathedral, 1942; priest, 1943. Asst Curate, Abington, Northampton, 1942–49; Chaplain and Lectr in Divinity, St Gabriel's Coll., Camberwell, 1949–53; Rector of Isham with Great and Little Harrowden, Northants, 1953–71; Rector of Boughton, Northampton, 1971–85. Examining Chaplain to Bishop of Peterborough, 1962–86; Dir, Post-Ordination Trng and Ordinands, 1962–86. Chaplain: to High Sheriff of Northants, 1972–73; to Mayor of Kettering, 1988–89. Mem., Ecclesiastical History Soc., 1979–; a Vice-Chm., Northants Record Soc., 1982–89. *Recreations:* walking, music, art history, local history. *Address:* 52 Walsingham Avenue, Barton Woods, Kettering, Northamptonshire NN15 5ER. *T:* Kettering (0536) 511415.

CARNELLEY, Ven. Desmond; Archdeacon of Doncaster, since 1985; Acting Director of Education, diocese of Sheffield, since 1991; *b* 28 Nov. 1929; *m* 1st, 1954, Dorothy Frith (*d* 1986); three *s* one *d*; 2nd, 1988, Marjorie Freeman. *Educ:* St John's Coll., York; St Luke's Coll., Exeter; William Temple Coll., Rugby; Ripon Hall, Oxford. BA (Open Univ.); Cert. Ed. (Leeds); Cert. Rel. Ed. (Exon). Curate of Aston, 1960–63; Priest-in-charge, St Paul, Ecclesfield, 1963–67; Vicar of Balby, Doncaster, 1967–72; Priest-in-charge, Mosborough, 1973; Vicar of Mosborough, 1974–85; RD of Attercliffe, 1979–84. *Recreations:* reading, theatre, walking in Derbyshire. *Address:* 1 Balmoral Road, Town Moor, Doncaster DN2 5BZ. *T:* Doncaster (0302) 325787.

CARNEY, Most Rev. James F.; *see* Vancouver, Archbishop of, (RC).

CARNEY, Michael; Secretary, Water Services Association (formerly Water Authorities Association), since 1987; *b* 19 Oct. 1937; *s* of Bernard Patrick Carney and Gwyneth (*née* Ellis); *m* 1963, Mary Patricia (*née* Davies); two *s* one *d*. *Educ:* University College of North Wales, Bangor (BA). Administrative Officer, NCB, 1962–65; Staff Officer to Dep. Chm., NCB, 1965–68; Electricity Council: Administrative Officer, 1968–71; Asst Sec. (Establishments), 1971–74; Sec., S Western Region, CEGB, 1974–80, Personnel Man., Midlands Region, 1980–82; Personnel Dir, Oxfam, 1982–87. *Recreations:* reading, book collecting, music, theatre. *Address:* 16 Brodrick Road, SW17 7DZ. *T:* 081–682 2830.

CARNLEY, Most Rev. Peter Frederick; *see* Perth (Australia), Archbishop of.

CARNOCK, 4th Baron *cr* 1916, of Carnock; **David Henry Arthur Nicolson;** Bt (NS) of that Ilk and Lasswade 1629, of Carnock 1637; Chief of Clan Nicolson; solicitor; *b* 10 July 1920; *s* of 3rd Baron Carnock, DSO, and Hon. Katharine (*d* 1968), *e d* of 1st Baron Roborough; *S* father, 1982. *Educ:* Winchester; Balliol Coll., Oxford (MA). Admitted Solicitor, 1949; Partner, Clifford-Turner, 1953–86. Served War of 1939–45, Royal Devon Yeomanry and on staff, Major. *Recreations:* shooting, fishing, gardening. *Heir: cousin* Nigel Nicolson, *qv*. *Address:* 90 Whitehall Court, SW1A 2EL; Ermewood House, Harford, Ivybridge, S Devon PL21 0JE. *Clubs:* Travellers', Beefsteak.

CARNWATH, Sir Andrew Hunter, KCVO 1975; DL; a Managing Director, Baring Brothers & Co. Ltd, 1955–74; Chairman, London Multinational Bank, 1971–74; *b* 26 Oct. 1909; *s* of late Dr Thomas Carnwath, DSO, Dep. CMO, Min. of Health, and Margaret Ethel (*née* McKee); *m* 1st, 1939, Kathleen Marianne Armstrong (*d* 1968); five *s* one *d*; 2nd, 1973, Joan Gertrude Wetherell-Pepper (Joan Alexander, author). *Educ:* Eton (King's Scholar; Hon. Fellow 1981). Served RAF (Coastal Comd Intelligence), 1939–45. Joined Baring Bros & Co. Ltd, 1928; rejoined as Head of New Issues Dept, 1945. Chm., Save and Prosper Group Ltd, 1961–80 (Dir, 1960–80); Director: Equity & Law Life Assurance Soc. Ltd, 1955–83; Scottish Agricultural Industries Ltd, 1969–75; Great Portland Estates Ltd, 1977–89. Member: London Cttee, Hongkong and Shanghai Banking Corp., 1967–74; Council, Inst. of Bankers, 1955– (Dep. Chm., 1969–70, Pres., 1970–72, Vice-Pres., 1972–); Cttee on Consumer Credit; Central Bd of Finance of Church of England (Chm., Investment Management Cttee), 1960–74; Chm., Chelmsford Diocesan Bd of Finance, 1969–75 (Vice-Chm., 1967–68). Member: Council, King Edward's Hosp. Fund for London, 1962–89 (Treasurer, 1965–74; Governor, 1976–85); Royal Commn for Exhibn of 1851, 1964–85; Council, Friends of Tate Gall., 1962–84 (Treasurer, 1966–82). Trustee: Imp. War Graves Endowment Fund, 1963–74, Chm., 1964–74; Thalidomide Children's Trust, 1980–85; Chairman: Manor Charitable Trustees, 1969–88; Baring Foundn, 1982–85. A Governor, Felsted Sch., 1965–81; Treasurer, Essex Univ., 1973–82 (DU Essex, 1983). Pres., Saffron Walden Conservative Assoc. until 1977. Musicians Company: Mem., Ct of Assts, 1973–; Master, 1981–82. Mem., Essex CC, 1973–77; High Sheriff, 1965, DL Essex, 1972–85. FCIB; FRSA. DU Essex, 1983. *Recreations:* crosswords, struggling with the piano, pictures. *Address:* Garden Flat, 39 Palace Gardens Terrace, W8 4SB. *T:* 071–727 9145. *Club:* Athenæum.
See also R. J. A. Carnwath.

CARNWATH, Robert John Anderson; QC 1985; Attorney General to the Prince of Wales, since 1988; *b* 15 March 1945; *s* of Sir Andrew Carnwath, *qv*; *m* 1974, Bambina D'Adda. *Educ:* Eton; Trinity Coll., Cambridge (MA, LLB). Called to the Bar, Middle Temple, 1968, Bencher 1991. Junior Counsel to Inland Revenue, 1980–85. Chm., Shepherds Bush Housing Assoc., 1988–. *Publications:* Knight's Guide to Homeless Persons Act, 1977; (with Rt Hon. Sir Frederick Corfield) Compulsory Acquisition and Compensation, 1978; various legal texts and reports on planning and local govt law. *Recreations:* violin, singing, tennis, etc. *Address:* 2 Chepstow Place, W2 4TA. *T:* 071-221 6226. *Club:* Garrick.

CARO, Sir Anthony (Alfred), Kt 1987; CBE 1969; sculptor; *b* 8 March 1924; *s* of Alfred and Mary Caro; *m* 1949, Sheila May Girling; two *s*. *Educ:* Charterhouse; Christ's Coll., Cambridge (Hon. Fellow, 1981); Regent Street Polytechnic; Royal Acad. Schs, London (Landseer Schol., 1st Landseer Award). Served FAA, 1944–46. Asst to Henry Moore, 1951–53; taught part-time, St Martin's Sch. of Art, 1953–79; taught sculpture at Bennington Coll., Vermont, 1963, 1965. Initiated and taught at Triangle Workshop, Pine Plains, NY, 1982–89. Visiting Artist, 1989: Univ. of Alberta; Red Deer Coll., Alberta. *One-man exhibitions include:* Galleria del Naviglio, Milan, 1956; Gimpel Fils, London, 1957; Whitechapel Art Gall., 1963; Andre Emmerich Gall., NY, 1964, 1966, 1968, 1970, 1972, 1973, 1974, 1977, 1978, 1979, 1982, 1984, 1986, 1988, 1989; Washington Gall. of Modern Art, Washington, DC, 1965; Kasmin Ltd, London, 1965, 1967, 1971, 1972; David Mirvish Gall., Toronto, 1966, 1971, 1974; Galerie Bischofberger, Zurich, 1966; Rijkmuseum, Kroller-Muller, Holland, 1967; Hayward Gall., 1969; British Section, X Bienal de São Paulo, 1969; Norfolk and Norwich Triennial Fest., 1973; Kenwood House, Hampstead, 1974, 1981; Galleria dell'Ariete, Milan, 1974; Galerie Andre Emmerich, Zurich, 1974, 1978, 1985; Mus. of Modern Art, NY, 1975 (toured to Walker Art Center, Minn, Mus. of Fine Arts, Houston, Mus. of Fine Arts, Boston); Richard Gray Gall., Chicago, 1976, 1978, 1986, 1989; Watson/de Nagy Gall., Houston, 1976; Lefevre Gall., London, 1976; Galerie Wentzel, Hamburg, 1976, 1978, Cologne, 1982, 1984, 1985, 1988; Galerie Piltzer-Rheims, Paris, 1977; Waddington & Tooth Galls, London, 1977; Waddington Galls, London, 1983, 1986; Harkus Krackow Gall., Boston, 1978, 1981, 1985; Knoedler Gall., London, 1978, 1982, 1983, 1984, 1986, 1989; Ace Gall., Venice, Calif, 1978, Vancouver, 1979; Kunsthalle Mannheim, 1979; Kunstverein Braunschweig, 1979; Kunstverein Frankfurt, 1979; Stadtische Galerie im Lenbachhaus, Munich, 1979; Gall. Kasahara, Osaka, Japan, 1979, 1990; York Sculptures, Christian Science Center, Boston, 1980; Acquavella Galls, NY, 1980, 1984, 1986; Galerie Andre, Berlin, 1980; Downstairs Gall., Edmonton, Alta, 1981; Storm King Art Center, Mountainville, NY, 1981; Stadtische Galerie im Stadel, Frankfurt, 1981; Saarland Mus., Saarbrucken, 1982; Gallery One, Toronto, 1982, 1985, 1987–88, 1990; Galerie de France, Paris, 1983; Martin Gerard Gall., Edmonton, 1984; Serpentine Gall., 1984; Whitworth Art Gall., Manchester, 1984; Leeds City Art Gall., 1984; Ordrupgaard Samlingen, Copenhagen, 1984; Kunstmuseum Düsseldorf, 1985; Joan Miró Foundn, Barcelona, 1985; C. Grimaldis Gall., Baltimore, 1985, 1987, 1989; Galerie Blanche, Stockholm , 1985; Galleri Lang, Malmö, 1985; Galerie Artek, Helsinki, 1985; Galleria Stendhal, Milan, 1985; Norrkipings Kunstmuseum, Sweden, 1985; Richard Galerie Joan Prats, Barcelona, 1986; Comune di Bogliasco, Genoa, 1986; Iglesia de San Esteban, Spain, 1986; La Lonja, Spain, 1987; Soledad Lorenzo Galerie, Madrid, 1987; Northern Centre for Contemp. Art, Sunderland, 1987; Sylvia Cordish Fine Art, Baltimore, 1988; Elisabeth Franck Gall., Belgium, 1988; Galerie Renée Ziegler, Zurich, 1988; Annely Juda Fine Art, 1989; Walker Hill Art Center, Seoul, 1989; Galeria Fluxis, Porto, 1989; Galerie Lelong, Paris, 1990; Baugre Palace, Antwerp, 1990. British Council touring exhibn, 1977–79: Tel Aviv, NZ and Australia. *Exhibited:* Venice Biennale, 1958, 1966; 1st Paris Biennale, 1959 (Sculpture Prize); Battersea Park Open Air Exhibns, 1960, 1963, 1966; Gulbenkian Exhibn, London, 1964; Documenta III, Kassel, 1965; Primary Structures, Jewish Mus., NY, 1966 (David Bright Prize); Pittsburgh Internat., 1967, 1968; Univ. of Pennsylvania, 1969; Everson Mus., Syracuse, 1976. Sculpture commnd by Nat. Gall. of Art, Washington, 1978. Member: Council, RCA, 1981–83 (Hon. Fellow 1986); Council, Slade Sch. of Art, 1982–; Trustee, Tate Gall., 1982–89. Hon. Mem., Amer. Acad. and Inst. of Arts and Letters, 1979; For. Hon. Mem., Amer. Acad. of Arts and Sciences, 1988. Lectures: William Townsend Meml, UCL, 1982; Delia Heron Meml, Falmouth Sch. of Art, 1985; Annual, Clore Gall., London, 1987. Hon. DLitt: East Anglia; York Univ., Toronto; Brandeis Univ., Mass; Hon. LittD Cambridge, 1985; DUniv Surrey, 1987; Hon. DFA Yale, 1989. Given key to City of New York, 1974. *Relevant publications:* Anthony Caro, by R. Whelan *et al*, 1974; Anthony Caro, by W. S. Rubin, 1975; Anthony Caro, by D. Waldman, 1982; Anthony Caro, by Terry Fenton, 1986. *Recreation:* listening to music. *Address:* 111 Frognal, Hampstead, NW3 6XR.

CARO, Prof. David Edmund, AO 1986; OBE 1977; MSc, PhD; FInstP, FAIP, FACE; Vice-Chancellor: University of Melbourne, 1982–87; (interim), Northern Territory University, 1988–89; *b* 29 June 1922; *s* of George Alfred Caro and Alice Lillian Caro; *m* 1954, Fiona Macleod; one *s* one *d*. *Educ:* Geelong Grammar Sch.; Univ. of Melbourne (MSc); Univ. of Birmingham (PhD). FInstP 1960, FAIP 1963, FACE 1982. Served War, RAAF, 1941–45. Demonstrator, Univ. of Melbourne, 1947–49; 1851 Overseas Res. Scholar, Birmingham, 1949–51; University of Melbourne: Lectr, 1952; Sen. Lectr, 1954; Reader, 1958; Foundn Prof. of Exper. Physics, 1961; Dean, Faculty of Science, 1970; Dep. Vice-Chancellor, 1972–77; Vice-Chancellor, Univ. of Tasmania, 1978–82. Chairman: Antarctic Res. Policy Adv. Cttee, 1979–85; Aust. Vice-Chancellors Cttee, 1982–83; Melbourne Theatre Co., 1982–87; SSAU Nominees Ltd, 1984–89; UniSuper Ltd, 1990–; Pres., Victorian Coll. of the Arts, 1989–. Member: Management Cttee, Royal Melbourne Hosp., 1982–. Hon. LLD: Melbourne, 1978; Tasmania, 1982; Hon. DSc Melbourne, 1987. *Publication:* (jtly) Modern Physics, 1961 (3rd edn 1978). *Recreations:* skiing, gardening, theatre. *Address:* 17 Fairbairn Road, Toorak, Vic 3142, Australia. *Clubs:* Melbourne (Melbourne); Peninsula Golf (Vic); Tasmanian (Hobart).

CAROL, Sister; *see* Griese, Sr Carol.

CAROLIN, Prof. Peter Burns, ARIBA; Professor of Architecture, University of Cambridge, and Fellow of Corpus Christi College, since 1989; *b* 11 Sept. 1936; *s* of late Joseph Sinclair Carolin and of Jean Bell Carolin (*née* Burns); *m* 1964, Anne-Birgit Warning; three *d*. *Educ:* Radley Coll.; Corpus Christi Coll., Cambridge (MA); University Coll. London (MA Architecture). Served RNR, Lieut, 1955–61. Asst to John Voelcker, 1960–63; Architect: with Colin St John Wilson, 1965–70; with Sir John Burnet, Tait and Partners, 1970–71; Associate, 1971–73, and Partner, 1973–80, Colin St John Wilson and Partners; Partner, Cambridge Design, 1980–81; Technical Ed., 1981–84, Editor, 1984–89, Architects' Jl; Co-founder, Facilities Newsletter, 1983. Magazine of Year Award (jtly), 1985; (jtly) numerous publishing awards, 1985–87. *Publications:* articles in professional jls in UK and Germany. *Recreation:* sailing. *Address:* 34 Selwyn Gardens, Cambridge CB3 9AY. *T:* Cambridge (0223) 352723; University of Cambridge Department of Architecture, 1 Scroope Terrace, Cambridge CB2 1PX. *T:* Cambridge (0223) 332958/9.

CARON, Leslie (Claire Margaret); film and stage actress; *b* 1 July 1931; *d* of Claude Caron and Margaret Caron (*née* Petit); *m* 1st, 1951, George Hormel (marr. diss.); 2nd, 1956, Peter Reginald Frederick Hall (marr. diss. 1965); one *s* one *d*; 3rd, 1969, Michael Laughlin (marr. diss.). *Educ:* Convent of the Assumption, Paris. With Ballet des Champs Elysées, 1947–50, Ballet de Paris, 1954. *Films include:* American in Paris, 1950; subsequently, Lili; The Glass Slipper; Daddy Long Legs; Gaby; Gigi; The Doctor's Dilemma; The Man Who Understood Women; The Subterraneans; Fanny; Guns of Darkness; The L-Shaped Room; Father Goose; A Very Special Favour; Promise Her Anything; Is Paris Burning?; Head of the Family; Madron; QB VII; Valentino; Sérail; L'homme qui aimait les femmes; The Contract; The Unapproachable; Master of the Game. *Plays:* Orvet, Paris, 1955; Gigi, London, 1956; Ondine, London, 1961; The Rehearsal, UK tour, 1983; On Your Toes, US tour, 1984. *Musical:* Grand Hotel, Berlin. *Television:* Tales of the Unexpected, 1982. *Publication:* Vengeance (short stories), 1982. *Recreation:* collecting antiques. *Address:* c/o James Fraser, Peters, Fraser & Dunlop, 5th Floor, The Chambers, Chelsea Harbour, Lots Road, SW10 0XF. *T:* 071–352 4446.

CARPENTARIA, Bishop of, since 1984; **Rt. Rev. Anthony Francis Hall-Matthews;** *b* 14 Nov. 1940; *s* of Rev. Cecil Berners Hall and Barbara (who *m* 1944, Rt Rev. Seering John Matthews); *m* 1966, Valerie Joan Cecil; two *s* three *d*. *Educ:* Sanctuary School, Walsingham, Norfolk; Southport School, Queensland; St Francis Theol Coll., Milton, Brisbane. ThL Aust. Coll. of Theology, 1962. Curate of Darwin, 1963–66; Chaplain, Aerial Mission, and Rector of Normanton with Croydon, 1966–76; Hon. Canon of Carpentaria, 1970–76; Archdeacon of Cape York Peninsula, 1976–84; Priest-in-charge of Cooktown, Dio. Carpentaria, 1976–84. *Recreations:* flying, reading, sailing. *Address:* Bishop's House, Thursday Island, Queensland 4875, Australia. *T:* (070) 691455.

CARPENTER; *see* Boyd-Carpenter.

CARPENTER, Very Rev. Edward Frederick, KCVO 1985; Dean of Westminster, 1974–85; Lector Theologiae of Westminster Abbey, 1958; *b* 27 Nov. 1910; *s* of Frederick James and Jessie Kate Carpenter; *m* Lilian Betsy Wright; three *s* one *d*. *Educ:* Strodes Sch., Egham; King's Coll., University of London. BA 1932, MA 1934, BD 1935, PhD 1943; AKC 1935; FKC 1951; Hon. DD London, 1976. Deacon, 1935; Priest, 1936; Curate, Holy Trinity, St Marylebone, 1935–41; St Mary, Harrow, 1941–45; Rector of Great Stanmore, 1945–51; Canon of Westminster, 1951; Treasurer, 1959–74; Archdeacon, 1963–74. Fellow of King's Coll., London University, 1954 (AKC 1935). Chairman Frances Mary Buss Foundation, 1956–; Chairman Governing Body of: North London Collegiate Sch.; Camden Sch. for Girls, 1956–; Chairman of St Anne's Soc., 1958–; Joint Chm., London Soc. of Jews and Christians, 1960–; Chm., CCJ, 1986–; Member, Central Religious Advisory Cttee serving BBC and ITA, 1962–67; Chairman: Recruitment Cttee, ACCM, 1967; Religious Adv. Cttee of UNA, 1969–; President: London Region of UNA, 1966–67; Modern Churchmen's Union, 1966–; World Congress of Faiths, 1966. *Publications:* Thomas Sherlock, 1936; Thomas Tenison, His Life and Times, 1948; That Man Paul, 1953; The Protestant Bishop, 1956; (joint author) of Nineteenth Century Country Parson, 1954, and of History of St Paul's Cathedral, 1957; Common Sense about Christian Ethics, 1961; (jtly) From Uniformity to Unity, 1962; (jtly) The Church's Use of the Bible, 1963; The Service of a Parson, 1965; (jtly) The English Church, 1966; (jtly) A House of Kings, 1966; Cantuar: the Archbishops in their office, 1971; contrib. Man of Christian Action, ed Ian Henderson, 1976; (with David Gentleman) Westminster Abbey, 1987. *Recreations:* walking, conversation, Association football. *Address:* 6 Selwyn Avenue, Richmond, Surrey.

CARPENTER, Ven. Frederick Charles; Archdeacon of the Isle of Wight, 1977–86, Archdeacon Emeritus since 1986; Priest-in-charge of the Holy Cross, Binstead, Isle of Wight, 1977–86; *b* 24 Feb. 1920; *s* of Frank and Florence Carpenter; *m* 1952, Rachel Nancy, *widow* of Douglas H. Curtis. *Educ:* Sir George Monoux Grammar Sch., Walthamstow; Sidney Sussex Coll., Cambridge (BA 1947, MA 1949); Wycliffe Hall, Oxford. Served with Royal Signals, 1940–46; Italy, 1944 (despatches). Curate of Woodford, 1949–51; Assistant Master and Chaplain, Sherborne School, Dorset, 1951–62;

Vicar of Moseley, Birmingham, 1962–68; Director of Religious Education, Diocese of Portsmouth, 1968–75; Canon Residentiary of Portsmouth, 1968–77. *Recreations:* music, gardening. *Address:* Gilston, Mount Pleasant, Stoford, Salisbury SP2 0PP. *T:* Salisbury (0722) 790335.

CARPENTER, George Frederick, ERD 1954; Assistant Under-Secretary of State, Ministry of Defence, 1971–77; *b* 18 May 1917; *s* of late Frederick and Ada Carpenter; *m* 1949, Alison Elizabeth (*d* 1978), *d* of late Colonel Sidney Smith, DSO, MC, TD and Elizabeth Smith, Longridge, Lancs; two step *d*. *Educ:* Bec Sch.; Trinity Coll., Cambridge (MA). Commnd Royal Artillery (Supplementary Reserve), July 1939; War Service, 1939–46, France, 1940 and AA Comd; joined War Office, 1946; Asst Sec., 1958; Comd Sec., Northern Comd, 1961–65; Inspector of Establishments (A), MoD, 1965–71. Silver Jubilee Medal, 1977. *Address:* 10 Park Meadow, Hatfield, Herts AL9 5HA. *T:* Hatfield (07072) 65581.

CARPENTER, Rt. Rev. Harry James, DD; *b* 20 Oct. 1901; *s* of William and Elizabeth Carpenter; *m* 1940, Urith Monica Trevelyan; one *s*. *Educ:* Churcher's Coll., Petersfield; Queen's Coll., Oxford. Tutor of Keble Coll., Oxford, 1927; Fellow, 1930; Warden of Keble Coll., 1939–55, Hon. Fellow, 1955; Hon. Fellow, Queen's Coll., Oxford, 1955; Canon Theologian of Leicester Cathedral, 1941–55; Bishop of Oxford, 1955–70. Hon. DD Oxon, 1955; Hon. DLitt Southampton, 1985. *Publications:* (ed) Bicknell, Thirty Nine Articles, 1955; contrib. to: Oxford Dictionary of the Christian Church, ed Cross, 1957; A Theological Word Book of the Bible, ed Richardson, 1963; The Interpretation of the Bible, ed Dugmore, 1944; Jl of Theological Studies. *Address:* St John's Home, St Mary's Road, Oxford OX4 1QE.

See also H. W. B. Carpenter.

CARPENTER, Harry Leonard, OBE 1991; sports commentator, BBC, since 1949; *b* 17 Oct. 1925; *s* of Harry and Adelaide May Carpenter; *m* 1950, Phyllis Barbara Matthews; one *s*. *Educ:* Ashburton School, Shirley; Selhurst Grammar School, Croydon. Greyhound Express, 1941; RN, 1943–46; Greyhound owner, 1946–48; Speedway Gazette, 1948–50; Sporting Record, 1950–54; Daily Mail, 1954–62; BBC TV, full-time 1962–. Sports Personality of the Year, TV and Radio Industries, 1989; Internat. Award, Amer. Sportscasters' Assoc., 1989. *Publications:* Masters of Boxing, 1964; Illustrated History of Boxing, 1975; The Hardest Game, 1981. *Recreations:* golf, chess, classical music. *Address:* BBC Television, Kensington House, W14. *T:* 081–743 1272.

CARPENTER, Humphrey William Bouverie, FRSL; author, broadcaster, musician; *b* 29 April 1946; *s* of Rt Rev. Harry James Carpenter, *qv*; *m* 1973, Mari Christina Prichard; two *d*. *Educ:* Dragon Sch., Oxford; Marlborough Coll.; Keble Coll., Oxford (MA, DipEd). FRSL 1983. BBC general trainee, 1968–70; staff producer, BBC Radio Oxford, 1970–74; freelance writer and broadcaster, 1975–. Founded, 1983, the band Vile Bodies, playing 1920s and 1930s dance music and jazz, resident at the Ritz Hotel, London, 1987–. *Publications:* A Thames Companion (with Mari Prichard), 1975; J. R. R. Tolkien: a biography, 1977; The Inklings (Somerset Maugham Award), 1978; Jesus (Past Masters series), 1980; (ed with Christopher Tolkien) The Letters of J. R. R. Tolkien, 1981; W. H. Auden: a biography, 1981 (E. M. Forster Award, Amer. Acad. of Arts and Letters, 1984); (with Mari Prichard) The Oxford Companion to Children's Literature, 1984; OUDS: a centenary history of the Oxford University Dramatic Society, 1985; Secret Gardens: the golden age of children's literature, 1985; Geniuses Together: American writers in Paris, 1987; A Serious Character: the life of Ezra Pound (Duff Cooper Meml Prize), 1988; The Brideshead Generation: Evelyn Waugh and his friends, 1989; *children's books:* The Joshers, 1977; The Captain Hook Affair, 1979; Mr Majeika, 1984; Mr Majeika and the Music Teacher, 1986; Mr Majeika and the Haunted Hotel, 1987; The Television Adventures of Mr Majeika, 1987; More Television Adventures of Mr Majeika, 1988; Mr Majeika and the Dinner Lady, 1989; Further Television Adventures of Mr Majeika, 1990; Mr Majeika and the School Play, 1991 (Mr Majeika books serialised on television, 1988–90). *Recreation:* sleep. *Address:* 6 Farndon Road, Oxford OX2 6RS. *T:* Oxford (0865) 56673.

CARPENTER, John; *see* Carpenter, V. H. J.

CARPENTER, Leslie Arthur; Director, Reed International PLC, since 1974 (Chief Executive, 1982–86; Chairman, 1985–87); *b* 26 June 1927; *s* of William and Rose Carpenter; *m* 1989, Louise Botting, *qv*. *Educ:* Hackney Techn. Coll. Director: Country Life, 1965; George Newnes, 1966; Odhams Press Ltd (Managing), 1968; International Publishing Corp., 1972; Reed International Ltd, 1974; IPC (America) Inc., 1975; Chairman: Reed Hldgs Inc. (formerly Reed Publishing Hldgs Inc.), 1977; Reed Publishing Hldgs Ltd, 1981; Chm. and Chief Exec., IPC Ltd, 1974; Chief Exec., Publishing and Printing, Reed International Ltd, 1979. Dir, Watmoughs (Hldgs) plc, 1988–. *Recreations:* racing, gardening. *Address:* 10 Park Square Mews, Upper Harley Street, NW1.

CARPENTER, Louise, (Mrs L. A. Carpenter); *see* Botting, Louise.

CARPENTER, Maj.-Gen. (Victor Harry) John, CB 1975; MBE 1945; FCIT; Senior Traffic Commissioner, Western Traffic Area and Licensing Authority, 1990–91; *b* 21 June 1921; *s* of Harry and Amelia Carpenter; *m* 1946, Theresa McCulloch; one *s* one *d*. *Educ:* Army schools; Apprentice Artificer RA; RMC Sandhurst. Joined the Army, Royal Artillery, 1936; commissioned into Royal Army Service Corps as 2nd Lieut, 1939. Served War of 1939–45 (Dunkirk evacuation, Western Desert, D-Day landings). Post-war appts included service in Palestine, Korea, Aden, and Singapore; also commanded a company at Sandhurst. Staff College, 1951; JSSC, 1960; served WO, BAOR, FARELF, 1962–71; Transport Officer-in-Chief (Army), MoD, 1971–73; Dir of Movements (Army), MoD, 1973–75; Chm., Traffic Comrs, NE Traffic Area (formerly Yorks Traffic Area), 1975–85; Traffic Comr, W Traffic Area, 1985–90. Col Comdt, 1975–87, Representative Col Comdt, 1976, 1978 and 1985, RCT; Nat. Chm., 1940 Dunkirk Veterans Assoc.; Pres., Artificers Royal Artillery Assoc.; Pres., RASC/RCT Assoc., 1977–87; Chm., Yorkshire Section, CIT, 1980–81. Hon. FIRTE 1987. *Recreation:* gardening. *Address:* c/o Lloyds Bank, 31 Fore Street, Taunton, Som TA1 1HN. *Club:* Royal Over-Seas League.

CARR, family name of **Baron Carr of Hadley.**

CARR OF HADLEY, Baron *cr* 1975 (Life Peer), of Monken Hadley; **(Leonard) Robert Carr,** PC 1963; FIC; *b* 11 Nov. 1916; *s* of late Ralph Edward and of Katie Elizabeth Carr; *m* 1943, Joan Kathleen, *d* of Dr E. W. Twining; two *d* (and one *s* decd). *Educ:* Westminster Sch. (Hon. Fellow, 1991); Gonville and Caius Coll., Cambridge, BA Nat. Sci. Hons, 1938; MA 1942. FIM 1957. Joined John Dale Ltd, 1938 (Dir, 1948–55; Chm., 1958–63); Director: Metal Closures Group Ltd, 1964–70 (Dep. Chm., 1960–63 and Jt Man. Dir, 1960–63); Carr, Day & Martin Ltd, 1947–55; Isotope Developments Ltd, 1950–55; Metal Closures Ltd, 1959–63; Scottish Union & National Insurance Co. (London Bd), 1958–63; S. Hoffnung & Co., 1963, 1965–70, 1974–80; Securicor Ltd and Security Services PLC, 1961–63, 1965–70, 1974–85; SGB Gp PLC, 1974–86; Prudential Assurance Co., 1976–85 (Dep. Chm., 1979–80, Chm., 1980–85); Prudential Corporation PLC, 1978–89 (Dep. Chm., 1979–80, Chm., 1980–85); Cadbury Schweppes PLC, 1979–87; Chm., Strategy Ventures, 1988–; Mem., London Adv. Bd, Norwich Union Insurance Gp, 1965–70, 1974–76; Member, Advisory Board: PA Strategy Partners, 1985–87; LEK Partnership, 1987–. Mem. Council, CBI, 1976–87 (Chm., Educn and Trng Cttee, 1977–82); Chm., Business in the Community, 1984–87. MP (C) Mitcham, 1950–74, Sutton, Carshalton, 1974–76; PPS to Sec. of State for Foreign Affairs, Nov. 1951–April 1955, to Prime Minister, April-Dec. 1955; Parly Sec., Min. of Labour and Nat. Service, Dec. 1955–April 1958; Sec. for Technical Co-operation, 1963–64; Sec. of State for Employment, 1970–72; Lord President of the Council and Leader of the House of Commons, April-Nov. 1972; Home Secretary, 1972–74. Governor: St Mary's Hosp., Paddington, 1958–63; Imperial Coll. of Science and Technology, 1959–63 and 1976–87 (Fellow 1985); St Mary's Medical Sch. Council, 1958–63; Hon. Treas., Wright Fleming Inst. of Microbiology, 1960–63. Pres., Consultative Council of Professional Management Orgns, 1976–. Duke of Edinburgh Lectr, Inst. of Building, 1976. Pres., Surrey CCC, 1985–86. *Publications:* (jt) One Nation, 1950; (jt) Change is our Ally, 1954; (jt) The Responsible Society, 1958; (jt) One Europe, 1965; articles in technical jls. *Recreations:* lawn tennis, music, gardening. *Address:* 14 North Court, Great Peter Street, SW1P 3LL. *Club:* Brooks's.

CARR, Sir (Albert) Raymond (Maillard), Kt 1987; DLitt (Oxon); FRHistS; FRSL; FBA 1978; Warden of St Antony's College, Oxford, 1968–87 (Sub-Warden, 1966–68); Fellow since 1964; *b* 11 April 1919; *s* of Reginald and Marion Maillard Carr; *m* 1950, Sara Strickland; three *s* one *d*. *Educ:* Brockenhurst Sch.; Christ Church, Oxford (Hon. Student 1986). Gladstone Research Exhnr, Christ Church, 1941; Lectr, UCL, 1945–46; Fellow of All Souls' Coll., 1946–53; Fellow of New Coll., 1953–64. Director, Latin American Centre, 1964–68. Chm. Soc. for Latin American Studies, 1966–68. Prof. of History of Latin America, Oxford, 1967–68. Distinguished Prof., Boston Univ., 1980. Mem., Nat. Theatre Bd, 1968–77. Hon. Fellow: Exeter Univ., 1987; St Antony's Coll., Oxford, 1988. Corresp. Mem., Royal Acad. of History, Madrid. Award of Merit, Soc. for Spanish Hist. Studies of the US, 1987; Leimer Award for Spanish Studies, Univ. of Augsburg, 1990. Grand Cross of the Order of Alfonso el Sabio (Spain), 1983; Order of Infante Dom Henrique (Portugal), 1989. *Publications:* Spain 1808–1939, 1966; Latin America (St Antony's Papers), 1969; (ed) The Republic and the Civil War in Spain, 1971; English Fox Hunting, 1976; The Spanish Tragedy: the Civil War in Perspective, 1977; (jtly) Spain: Dictatorship to Democracy, 1979; Modern Spain, 1980; (with Sara Carr) Fox-Hunting, 1982; Puerto Rico: a colonial experiment, 1984; (ed) The Spanish Civil War, 1986; articles on Swedish, Spanish and Latin American history. *Recreation:* fox hunting. *Address:* Burch, North Molton, South Molton EX36 3JU. *T:* Bishops Nympton (07697) 267. *Clubs:* Beefsteak, United Oxford & Cambridge University, Academy.

CARR, Very Rev. Arthur Wesley, PhD; Dean of Bristol, since 1987; *b* 26 July 1941; *s* of Arthur and Irene Carr; *m* 1968, Natalie Gill; one *d*. *Educ:* Dulwich College; Jesus Coll., Oxford (MA); Jesus Coll., Cambridge (MA); Ridley Hall, Cambridge; Univ. of Sheffield (PhD). Curate, Luton Parish Church, 1967–71; Tutor, Ridley Hall, Cambridge, 1970–71, Chaplain 1971–72; Sir Henry Stephenson Fellow, Dept of Biblical Studies, Univ. of Sheffield, 1972–74; Hon. Curate, Ranmoor, 1972–74; Chaplain, Chelmsford Cathedral, 1974–78; Dep. Director, Chelmsford Cathedral Centre for Research and Training, 1974–82; Dir of Training, Diocese of Chelmsford, 1976–82; Canon Residentiary, Chelmsford Cathedral, 1978–87. Mem., Gen. Synod of C of E, 1980–87, 1989–. Select Preacher, Univ. of Oxford, 1984–85; Hon. Fellow, New Coll., Edinburgh, 1986. *Publications:* Angels and Principalities, 1977; The Priestlike Task, 1985; Brief Encounters, 1985; The Pastor as Theologian, 1989; Ministry and the Media, 1990; articles in Theology, etc. *Recreations:* music, reading, writing, gardening. *Address:* The Deanery, 20 Charlotte Street, Bristol, Avon BS1 5PZ. *T:* Bristol (0272) 262443; (office) Bristol (0272) 264879, 250692, *Fax:* Bristol (0272) 253678.

CARR, Christopher; QC 1983; barrister; *b* 30 Nov. 1944; *s* of Edwin Wilfred Carr and Kathleen Carr; *m* 1989, Susan Ann Upjohn; two *d* one *s* of previous marriage. *Educ:* Skegness Grammar Sch.; London Sch. of Economics; Clare Coll., Cambridge. Called to the Bar, Lincoln's Inn, 1968. Lectr in Law, LSE, 1968–69 and 1972–73; Asst Prof. of Law, Univ. of British Columbia, 1969–72; Associate Prof. of Law, Univ. of Toronto, 1973–75; part-time Lectr, QMC, London, 1975–78; in practice at the Bar, 1975–. *Publications:* articles and notes in English and Canadian law jls. *Recreations:* mixed. *Address:* 1 Essex Court, Temple, EC4. *Club:* Athenæum.

CARR, Prof. Denis John; Professor, Research School of Biological Sciences, Australian National University, Canberra, 1968–80; *b* 15 Dec. 1915; *s* of James E. Carr and Elizabeth (*née* Brindley), Stoke-on-Trent, Staffs; *m* 1955, Stella G. M. Fawcett; no *c*. *Educ:* Hanley High Sch., Staffs; Manchester Univ. RAF, 1940–46. Manchester Univ.: undergraduate, 1946–49; Asst Lectr in Plant Ecology, 1949–53; Guest Research Worker at Max-Planck-Inst. (Melchers), Tübingen, 1952; Sen. Lectr in plant physiology, 1953, Reader, 1959, Melbourne; Prof. of Botany, Queen's Univ., Belfast, 1960–67. Hon. MSc Melbourne, 1958. *Publications:* Plant Growth Substances 1970, 1972; numerous papers in scientific jls. *Recreations:* research, music. *Address:* c/o Research School of Biological Sciences, ANU Canberra, PO Box 475, ACT 2601, Australia.

CARR, Donald Bryce, OBE 1985; Secretary, Cricket Council and Test and County Cricket Board, 1974–86, retired; *b* 28 Dec. 1926; *s* of John Lillingston Carr and Constance Ruth Carr; *m* 1953, Stella Alice Vaughan Simpkinson; one *s* one *d*. *Educ:* Repton Sch.; Worcester Coll., Oxford (MA). Served Army, 1945–48 (Lieut Royal Berks Regt). Asst Sec., 1953–59, Sec., 1959–62, Derbyshire CCC; Asst Sec., MCC, 1962–74. *Recreations:* golf, following most sports. *Address:* 28 Aldenham Avenue, Radlett, Herts WD7 8HX. *T:* Radlett 855602. *Clubs:* MCC, British Sportsman's, Lord's Taverners; Vincent's, Oxford University Cricket (Oxford).

CARR, Dr Eric Francis, FRCP, FRCPsych; Lord Chancellor's Medical Visitor, 1979–89; Member: Mental Health Act Commission, since 1983; Parole Board, since 1988; *b* 23 Sept. 1919; *s* of Edward Francis Carr and Maude Mary Almond; *m* 1954, Janet Gilfillan (marr. diss. 1980); two *s* one *d*. *Educ:* Mill Hill Sch.; Emmanuel Coll., Cambridge. MA, MB BChir; FRCP, 1971, FRCPsych, 1972; DPM. Captain, RAMC, 1944–46. Consultant Psychiatrist: St Ebba's Hosp., 1954–60; Netherne Hosp., 1960–67; Epsom and West Park Hosps, 1967–76; Hon. Consultant Psychiatrist, KCH, 1960–76; SPMO, DHSS, 1976–79. Fellow, RSocMed. *Recreations:* reading, listening to music, cooking. *Address:* 116 Holly Lane East, Banstead, Surrey. *T:* Burgh Heath (0737) 353675.

CARR, Glyn; *see* Styles, F. S.

CARR, Air Marshal Sir John Darcy B.; *see* Baker-Carr.

CARR, John Roger, CBE 1991; JP; Chairman, Countryside Commission for Scotland, since 1986 (Member, 1979–84; Vice-Chairman, 1984–85); *b* 18 Jan. 1927; *s* of James Stanley Carr and Edith Carr (*née* Robinson); *m* 1951, Catherine Elise Dickson-Smith; two *s*. *Educ:* Ackworth and Ayton (Quaker Schools). FRICS. Royal Marines, 1944–47; Gordon Highlanders (TA), 1950–54. Factor, Walker Scottish Estates Co., 1950–54; Factor, 1954–67, Dir and Gen. Man., 1967–88, Dir, 1988–, Moray Estates Devel Co. Dir, Strathearn Tourism Develt Co., 1959–. Mem., Wkg Party, Management Training for Leisure and Recreation in Scotland, 1986; Dir, Macaulay Land Use Res. Inst., 1987–.

Mem., Moray DC, 1974–80. JP Moray, 1975. FRSA. *Recreations:* most countryside pursuits. *Address:* Bradbush, Darnaway, Forres, Moray IV36 0SU. *T:* Brodie (03094) 249. *Club:* New (Edinburgh).

CARR, Rear-Adm. Lawrence George, CB 1971; DSC 1954; Chief of Naval Staff, New Zealand, and Member of the Defence Council, 1969–72; management consultant; *b* 31 Jan. 1920; *s* of late George Henry Carr and late Susan Elizabeth Carr; unmarried. *Educ:* Wellington Technical Coll., NZ; Victoria Coll., Univ. of New Zealand. Served War: entered RNZNVR, 1941; commissioned, 1942; on loan to RN, in HM Destroyers in N Atlantic, Medit., W Af. Coast, Eng. Channel, 1941–44; HMNZS Achilles in Pacific Theatre and NZ, 1945–46; permanent Commn, RNZN, 1946. Qual. as communications specialist, 1947; served in: British Medit. Fleet, 1948; RNZN, 1949–; various appts.; in command HMNZS Kaniere, in Korea, 1953–54 (DSC); Comdr Dec. 1953; Exec. Officer, HMNZS Philomel, 1954–55; jssc, 1956; Deputy Chief of Naval Personnel, 1957–59; Qual. Sen. Officers War Coll., Greenwich, 1959–60; Captain June 1960; in command HMNZS: Philomel, 1960–62, Taranaki, 1962–64; idc 1965; Commodore, Auckland, 1966–68. Chief of Naval Personnel, Second Naval Mem., NZ Naval Bd, 1968–69. Nat. Parly Cand., Nov. 1972; Chm., Nat. Party, Pakuranga Electorate, 1976–82. Exec. Dir, Laura Fergusson Trust for Disabled Persons (Auckland), 1982–85. Mem. Bd, Spirit of Adventure Trust, 1972–; Patron, Coastguard (NZ); Vice-Patron, Co. of Master Mariners, NZ. *Recreations:* golf, fishing, shooting, sailing, tennis, chess. *Address:* Unit 75 Remnera Gardens, 57 Richard Farrell Avenue, Remnera, Auckland, New Zealand. *Clubs:* Wellington, Royal New Zealand Yacht Squadron, Auckland Racing.

CARR, Maurice Chapman; His Honour Judge Carr; a Circuit Judge, since 1986; *b* 14 Aug. 1937; *s* of John and Elizabeth Carr; *m* 1959, Caryl Olson; one *s* one *d*. *Educ:* Hookergate Grammar Sch.; LSE (LLB); Harvard Univ. (LLM). Lectr in Law, 1960–62, Asst Prof. of Law, 1963–64, Univ. of British Columbia; Lecturer in Law: UCW, 1964–65; Univ. of Newcastle upon Tyne, 1965–69. Called to the Bar, Middle Temple, 1966. *Recreations:* walking, music. *Address:* 33 Broad Chare, Newcastle upon Tyne. *T:* Tyneside 091–232 0541.

CARR, Michael; MP (Lib Dem) Ribble Valley, since March 1991; *b* 31 Jan. 1946; *s* of James and Sheila Mary Carr; *m* 1st (wife *d* 1979); one *s*; 2nd, 1980, Georgina Clare; four *s* two *d*. *Educ:* St Joseph's Coll., Blackpool; Catholic Coll., Preston; Margaret McMillan Coll. of Educn, Bradford (CertEd); Bradford and Ilkley Community Coll. (DPSE). Engrg apprentice, 1962–63; Local Govt Officer, 1964–68; partner in family retail newsagency, 1968–70; Teacher of Geography: Brookside Sec. Sch., Middlesbrough, 1973–74; Stainsby Sch., Middlesbrough, 1974–75; Head of Geog., St Thomas Aquinas RC High Sch., Darwen, Lancs, 1975–82; Head of Gen. Studies, Blackthorn County Sec. Sch. and Blackthorn Wing of Fearns CS Sch., Bacup, 1982–87; Mem., Lancs Educn Cttee Sch. Support Team (Disruptive Behaviour), 1988–91. Mem., Sabden Parish Council, 1976–78, 1979–83; Mem. (C 1979–81, SDP 1981–83), Ribble Valley BC, 1979–83. Joined SDP, 1981; contested (SDP/Lib Alliance) Ribble Valley, 1983, 1987. Mem., NAS/UWT (Dist Sec., Rossendale Assoc., 1983–87; Press Officer, Lancs Fedn, 1983–87, 1988–90). *Recreations:* hill walking, cooking, music. *Address:* House of Commons, SW1A 0AA. *T:* 071–219 3450.

CARR, Peter Derek, CBE 1989; Chairman: Northern Regional Health Authority, since 1990; County Durham Development Co., since 1990; *b* 12 July 1930; *s* of George William Carr and Marjorie (*née* Tailby); *m* 1958, Geraldine Pamela (*née* Ward); one *s* one *d*. *Educ:* Fircroft Coll., Birmingham; Ruskin Coll., Oxford. National Service, RAF, 1951–53. Carpenter and joiner, construction industry, 1944–51 and 1953–56; college, 1956–60; Lectr, Percival Whitley Coll., Halifax, 1960–65; Sen. Lectr in Indust. Relations, Thurrock Coll., and part-time Adviser, NBPI, 1965–69; Director: Commn on Industrial Relations, 1969–74; ACAS, 1974–78; Diplomatic Service, Washington, 1978–83; Regl Dir, Northern Regl Office, Dept of Employment, and Leader, City Action Team, 1983–89. Vis. Fellow, Durham Univ., 1989–. *Publications:* directed study for CIR on worker participation and collective bargaining in Europe, and study for ACAS on industrial relations in national newspaper industry. *Recreations:* walking, cooking, furniture-making. *Address:* 4 Corchester Towers, Corbridge, Northumberland NE45 5NR. *T:* Hexham (0434) 632841.

CARR, Philippa; *see* Hibbert, Eleanor.

CARR, Sir Raymond; *see* Carr, Sir A. R. M.

CARR, Dr Thomas Ernest Ashdown, CB 1977; part-time medical referee, Department of Health and Social Security, 1979–87; retired; *b* 21 June 1915; *s* of late Laurence H. A. Carr, MScTech, MIEE, ARPS, Stockport, and late Norah E. V. Carr (*née* Taylor); *m* 1940, Mary Sybil (*née* Dunkey); one *s* two *d*. *Educ:* County High Sch. for Boys, Altrincham; Victoria Univ. of Manchester (BSc). MB, ChB 1939; FRCGP 1968; FFCM 1972; DObstRCOG. Jun. hosp. posts, Manchester and Ipswich, 1939–41; RAMC, UK and NW Europe, 1941–46 (Hon. Major, 1946). GP, Highcliffe, Hants, 1947; Mem. Hants Local Med. Cttee, 1952–55; Min. of Health: Regional Med. Officer, Southampton, 1956; Sen. Med. Officer, 1963; Principal Med. Officer, 1966; SPMO in charge of GP and Regional Med. Service, DHSS, 1967–79. Founder Mem., 1953, Provost of SE England Faculty 1962–64, Mem. Council 1964–66, RCGP; Chm., Guildford Div., BMA, 1988–89 (Mem. Exec. Cttee, Lambeth and Southwark Div., 1975–79). FRSocMed (Mem. Council, Gen. Practice Section, 1977–79). Member: Camping Club of GB and Ireland, 1976–83; Southampton Gramophone Soc., 1956–63 (Chm., 1957–58); Guildford Philharmonic Soc., 1964–89; Guildford Soc., 1968–89; Putney Music, 1989–; Putney Soc., 1989–; Consumers' Assoc., 1974–; Nat. Soc. of Non-Smokers (QUIT), 1981– (Chm., 1982–86, Vice-Pres., 1987–); British Humanist Assoc., 1965–; Fabian Soc., 1989–. *Publications:* papers on NHS practice organisation in Medical World, Practitioner, Update, Health Trends, faculty jls of RCGP, Proc. of RSM. *Recreations:* playing and listening to music, photography, country walks, foreign travel. *Address:* 17 Westpoint, Putney Hill, SW15 6RU. *T:* 081–788 9969. *Club:* Civil Service.

CARR, William Compton; *b* 10 July 1918; *m*; two *s* one *d*. *Educ:* The Leys Sch., Cambridge. MP (C) Barons Court, 1959–64; PPS to Min. of State, Board of Trade, 1963; PPS to Financial Sec. to the Treasury, 1963–64. *Recreations:* reading, theatre-going, skin diving, eating, dieting.

CARR-ELLISON, Sir Ralph (Harry), Kt 1973; TD; Chairman, Tyne Tees Television Ltd, since 1974 (Director since 1966); Chairman, Automobile Association, since 1986 (Vice Chairman, 1985–86); Lord-Lieutenant of Tyne and Wear, since 1984; *b* 8 Dec. 1925; *s* of late Major John Campbell Carr-Ellison; *m* 1951, Mary Clare, *d* of late Major Arthur McMorrough Kavanagh, MC; three *s* one *d*. *Educ:* Eton. Served Royal Glos Hussars and 1st Royal Dragoons, 1944–49; Northumberland Hussars (TA), (Lt-Col Comdg), 1949–69; TAVR Col, Northumbrian Dist, 1969–72; Col, Dep. Comdr (TAVR), NE Dist, 1973; Chm., N of England TA&VRA, 1976–80, Pres. 1987–90; ADC (TAVR) to HM the Queen, 1970–75; Hon. Colonel: Northumbrian Univs OTC, 1982–86; QOY, 1988–90 (Northumberland Hussars Sqn, 1986–88); Col Comdt, Yeomanry RAC TA, 1990–. Co. Comr, Northumberland Scouts, 1958–68; Mem. Cttee of Council, 1960–67, Mem. Council, 1982–, Scout Assoc. Chm., Berwick-on-Tweed Constituency Cons. Assoc., 1959–62, Pres., 1973–77; Northern Area Cons. Assocs: Treas., 1961–66, Chm., 1966–69; Pres., 1974–78; Vice Chm., Nat Union of Cons. and Unionist Assocs, 1969–71. Director: Newcastle & Gateshead Water Co., 1964–73; Trident Television, 1972–81 (Dep. Chm., 1976–81); Chm: Northumbrian Water Authority, 1973–82; North Tyne Area, Manpower Bd, MSC, 1983–84. Mem. Council, The Wildfowl Trust, 1981–88. Chm., Newcastle Univ. Develt Trust, 1978–81; Mem. Ct, Newcastle Univ., 1979–; Governor, Swinton Conservative College, 1967–81. FRSA 1983. High Sheriff, 1972, JP 1953–75, DL 1981–85, Vice Lord-Lieut, 1984, Northumberland. Hon. DCL Newcastle, 1989. KStJ 1984. *Recreation:* Jt Master, West Percy Foxhounds, 1950–90. *Address:* Hedgeley Hall, Powburn, Alnwick, Northumberland NE66 4HZ. *T:* Powburn (066578) 273; (office) Newcastle upon Tyne (091) 2610181. *Clubs:* Cavalry and Guards, White's, Pratt's; Northern Counties (Newcastle upon Tyne).

CARR-GOMM, Richard Culling, OBE 1985; Consultant to the Carr-Gomm Society and Morpeth Society (charity societies); *b* 2 Jan. 1922; *s* of Mark Culling Carr-Gomm and Amicia Dorothy (*née* Heming); *m* 1957, Susan, *d* of Ralph and Dorothy Gibbs; two *s* three *d*. *Educ:* Stowe School. Served War: commnd Coldstream Guards, 1941; served 6th Guards Tank Bde, NW Europe (twice wounded, mentioned in despatches); Palestine, 1945; ME; resigned commn, 1955. Founded: Abbeyfield Soc., 1956; Carr-Gomm Soc., 1965; Morpeth Soc., 1972. Templeton UK Project Award, 1984. Croix de Guerre (Silver Star), France, 1944. KStJ. *Publications:* Push on the Door (autobiog.), 1979; Loneliness—the wider scene, 1987. *Recreations:* golf, backgammon, painting. *Address:* 9 The Batch, Batheaston, Avon BA1 7DR. *T:* Bath (0225) 858434.

CARR LINFORD, Alan, RWS 1955 (ARWS 1949); ARE 1946; ARCA 1946; *b* 15 Jan. 1926; *m* 1948, Margaret Dorothea Parish; one *s* one *d*. *Educ:* Royal College of Art, and in Rome. Was awarded the Prix de Rome, 1947. *Recreation:* shooting.

CARREL, Philip, CMG 1960; OBE 1954; *b* 23 Sept. 1915; *s* of late Louis Raymond Carrel and Lucy Mabel (*née* Cooper); *m* 1948, Eileen Mary Bullock (*née* Hainworth); one *s* one *d*. *Educ:* Blundell's; Balliol. Colonial Admin. Service, 1938, Zanzibar Protectorate. EA Forces, 1940. Civil Affairs, 1941–47 (OETA); Civilian Employee Civil Affairs, GHQ MELF, 1947–49 (on secondment from Som. Prot.); Colonial Admin. Service (Somaliland Protectorate), 1947; Commissioner of Somali Affairs, 1953; Chief Sec. to the Government, Somaliland Protectorate, 1959–60. Cttee Sec., Overseas Relns, Inst. of Chartered Accountants in England and Wales, 1961–77; retired. *Address:* Lych Gates, 51 Chiltley Lane, Liphook, Hants GU30 7HJ. *T:* Liphook (0428) 722150.

CARRELL, Prof. Robin Wayne, FRSNZ 1980; FRCP; Professor of Haematology, University of Cambridge, since 1986; Fellow of Trinity College, Cambridge, since 1987; *b* 5 April 1936; *s* of Ruane George Carrell and Constance Gwendoline Carrell (*née* Rowe); *m* 1962, Susan Wyatt Rogers; two *s* two *d*. *Educ:* Christchurch Boys' High School, NZ; Univ. of Otago (MB ChB 1959); Univ. of Canterbury (BSc 1965); Univ. of Cambridge (MA, PhD 1968). FRACP 1973; FRCPath 1976; MRCP 1985, FRCP 1990. Mem., MRC Abnormal Haemoglobin Unit, Cambridge, 1965–68; Dir, Clinical Biochemistry, Christchurch Hosp., NZ, 1968–75; Lectr and Consultant in Clinical Biochem., Addenbrooke's Hosp. and Univ. of Cambridge, 1976–78; Prof. of Clinical Biochem., Christchurch Sch. of Clinical Medicine, Univ. of Otago, 1978–86. Mem., Gen. Bd, Univ. of Cambridge, 1989–. Commonwealth Fellow, St John's Coll. and Vis. Scientist, MRC Lab. of Molecular Biol., 1985. Pharmacia Prize for biochem. res., NZ, 1984; Hector Medal, Royal Soc., NZ, 1986. *Publications:* articles in sci. jls, esp. on genetic abnormalities of human proteins. *Recreations:* gardening, walking. *Address:* 19 Madingley Road, Cambridge CB3 0EG. *T:* Cambridge (0223) 312970.

CARRICK, 9th Earl of, *cr* 1748; **Brian Stuart Theobald Somerset Caher Butler;** Baron Butler (UK), 1912; Viscount Ikerrin, 1629; *b* 17 Aug. 1931; *o s* of 8th Earl of Carrick; *S* father, 1957; *m* 1st, 1951, (Mary) Belinda (marr. diss. 1976), *e d* of Major David Constable-Maxwell, TD, Bosworth Hall, near Rugby; one *s* one *d*; 2nd, 1986, Gillian, *er d* of Leonard Grimes. *Educ:* Downside. Chm., Balfour Maclaine Corp.; Director: Bowater Inc.; Bowater plc; Cargill plc; Cargill Financial Services Corp. Ltd; Chloride Eastern Industries Ltd. *Heir:* *s* Viscount Ikerrin, *qv*. *Address:* 10 Netherton Grove, SW10. *T:* 071–352 6328. *Clubs:* White's, Brooks's, Pratt's.

CARRICK, Edward; *see* Craig, E. A.

CARRICK, Hon. Sir John (Leslie), KCMG 1982; Senator, Commonwealth Parliament of Australia, 1971–87, retired; *b* 4 Sept. 1918; *s* of late A. J. Carrick and of E. E. Carrick; *m* 1951, Diana Margaret Hunter; three *d*. *Educ:* Univ. of Sydney (BEc; Hon. DLitt 1988). Res. Officer, Liberal Party of Aust., NSW Div., 1946–48, Gen. Sec., 1948–71; Minister: for Housing and Construction, 1975; for Urban and Regional Develt, 1975; for Educn, 1975–79; Minister Assisting Prime Minister in Fed. Affairs, 1975–78; Minister for Nat. Develt and Energy, 1979–83; Dep. Leader, 1978, Leader, 1978–83, Govt in the Senate. Vice-Pres., Exec. Council, 1978–82. Chairman: NSW Govt Cttee of Review of Schs, 1988–89; Gas Council of NSW, 1990–. Pres., Univ. of Sydney Dermatology Res. Foundn, 1989–. *Recreations:* swimming, reading. *Address:* 8 Montah Avenue, Killara, NSW 2071, Australia. *T:* 02 498 6326. *Clubs:* Australian (Sydney); Commonwealth (Canberra).

CARRICK, Roger John, CMG 1983; LVO 1972; HM Diplomatic Service; Ambassador to Republic of Indonesia, since 1990; *b* 13 Oct. 1937; *s* of John H. and Florence M. Carrick; *m* 1962, Hilary Elizabeth Blinman; two *s*. *Educ:* Isleworth Grammar Sch.; Sch. of Slavonic and East European Studies, London Univ. Served RN, 1956–58. Joined HM Foreign (subseq. Diplomatic) Service, 1956; SSEES, 1961; Sofia, 1962; FO, 1965; Paris, 1967; Singapore, 1971; FCO, 1973; Counsellor and Dep. Head, Personnel Ops Dept, FCO, 1976; Vis. Fellow, Inst. of Internat. Studies, Univ. of Calif, Berkeley, 1977–78; Counsellor, Washington, 1978; Hd, Overseas Estate Dept, FCO, 1982; Consul-Gen., Chicago, 1985–88; Asst Under-Sec. of State (Economic), FCO, 1988–90. Churchill Fellow (Life), Westminster Coll., Fulton, Missouri, 1987. *Publication:* East-West Technology Transfer in Perspective, 1978. *Recreations:* sailing, music, reading, avoiding gardening. *Address:* c/o Foreign and Commonwealth Office, SW1A 2AH. *Clubs:* Commonwealth Trust, Royal Over-Seas League; Mercantile (Jakarta).

CARRICK, Maj-Gen. Thomas Welsh, OBE 1959; retired; Specialist in Community Medicine, Camden and Islington Area Health Authority (Teaching), 1975–78; *b* 19 Dec. 1914; *s* of late George Carrick and late Mary Welsh; *m* 1948, Nan Middleton Allison; one *s*. *Educ:* Glasgow Academy; Glasgow Univ.; London Sch. of Hygiene and Tropical Med. MB, ChB 1937, FFPHM (FFCM 1972), DPH 1951, DIH 1961. House appts in medicine, surgery and urological surgery at Glasgow Royal Infirmary, 1937–38; Dep. Supt, Glasgow Royal Infirmary, 1939–40. Commissioned, RAMC, 1940. Later service appts include: Asst Dir, Army Health, 17 Gurkha Div., Malaya, 1961–63; Asst Dir, Army Health, HQ Scotland, 1964–65; Dir Army Personnel Research Estabt, 1965–68; Dep. Dir, Army Health, Strategic Command, 1968–70; Prof. of Army Health, Royal Army Med. Coll., 1970; Dir of Army Health and Research, MoD, 1971–72; Comdt and

Postgraduate Dean, Royal Army Medical Coll., Millbank, 1973–75, retd. Col Comdt, RAMC, 1975–79. Blackham Lectr, RIPH, 1977. QHS 1973. Pres., Blackmore Vale and Yeovil Centre, National Trust, 1979–85. OStJ 1946. *Publications:* articles in Jl of RAMC, Army Review, Community Health. *Recreations:* gardening, theatre.

CARRINGTON, 6th Baron (Ireland) *cr* 1796, (Great Britain) *cr* 1797; **Peter Alexander Rupert Carington,** KG 1985; GCMG 1988 (KCMG 1958); CH 1983; MC 1945; PC 1959; Chairman, Christies International plc, since 1988; Director, The Daily Telegraph plc, since 1990; Chancellor, Order of St Michael and St George, since 1984; *b* 6 June 1919; *s* of 5th Baron and Hon. Sibyl Marion (*d* 1946), *d* of 2nd Viscount Colville; *S* father, 1938; *m* 1942, Iona, *yr d* of late Sir Francis McClean; one *s* two *d. Educ:* Eton Coll.; RMC Sandhurst. Served NW Europe, Major Grenadier Guards. Parly Sec., Min. of Agriculture and Fisheries, 1951–54; Parly Sec., Min. of Defence, Oct. 1954–Nov. 1956; High Comr for the UK in Australia, Nov. 1956–Oct. 1959; First Lord of the Admiralty, 1959–63; Minister without Portfolio and Leader of the House of Lords, 1963–64; Leader of the Opposition, House of Lords, 1964–70 and 1974–79. Secretary of State: for Defence, 1970–74; for Energy, 1974; for For. and Commonwealth Affairs, 1979–82; Minister of Aviation Supply, 1971–74. Chm., Cons. Party Organisation, 1972–74. Chm., GEC, 1983–84; Sec.-Gen., NATO, 1984–88. Sec. for Foreign Correspondence and Hon. Mem., Royal Acad. of Arts, 1982–; Chm., Bd of Trustees, V & A Museum, 1983–88. Pres., The Pilgrims, 1983–. Hon Bencher, Middle Temple, 1983; Hon. Elder Brother of Trinity House, 1984. JP 1948, DL Bucks. Fellow of Eton Coll., 1966–81; Hon. Fellow, St Antony's Coll., Oxford, 1982. Hon. LLD: Cambridge, 1981; Leeds, 1981; Aberdeen, 1985; Hon. Dr Laws: Univ. of Philippines, 1982; Univ. of S Carolina, 1983; Harvard, 1986; Reading, 1989; Sussex, 1989; DUniv: Essex, 1983; Buckingham, 1989; Hon. DSc Cranfield, 1988. *Publication:* Reflect on Things Past (autobiog.), 1988. *Heir: s* Hon. Rupert Francis John Carington [*b* 2 Dec. 1948; *m* 1989, Daniela, *d* of Mr and Mrs Flavio Diotallevi; one *s*]. *Address:* 32a Ovington Square, SW3 1LR. *T:* 071–584 1476; The Manor House, Bledlow, near Aylesbury, Bucks. *T:* Princes Risborough (08444) 3499. *Clubs:* Pratt's, White's.

See also Baron Ashcombe.

CARRINGTON, Prof. Alan, FRS 1971; Royal Society Research Professor, Southampton University, 1979–84 and since 1987, Oxford University, 1984–87; *b* 6 Jan. 1934; *o s* of Albert Carrington and Constance (*née* Nelson); *m* 1959, Noreen Hilary Taylor; one *s* two *d. Educ:* Colfe's Grammar Sch.; Univ. of Southampton. BSc, PhD; MA Cantab., MA Oxon. Univ. of Cambridge: Asst in Research, 1960; Fellow of Downing Coll., 1960; Asst Dir of Res., 1963; Prof. of Chemistry, Univ. of Southampton, 1967; Fellow, Jesus Coll., Oxford, 1984–87. Tilden Lectr, Chem. Soc., 1972; Sen. Fellowship, SRC, 1976. Foreign Hon. Mem., Amer. Acad. of Arts and Scis, 1987. Hon. DSc Southampton, 1985. Harrison Mem. Prize, Chem. Soc., 1962; Meldola Medal, Royal Inst. of Chemistry, 1963; Marlow Medal, Faraday Soc., 1966; Corday Morgan Medal, Chem. Soc., 1967; Chem. Soc. Award in Structural Chemistry, 1970; Faraday Medal, RSC, 1985. *Publications:* (with A. D. McLachlan) Introduction to Magnetic Resonance, 1967; Microwave Spectroscopy of Free Radicals, 1974; numerous papers on topics in chemical physics in various learned jls. *Recreations:* family, music, fishing, golf, sailing. *Address:* 46 Lakewood Road, Chandler's Ford, Hants. *T:* Chandler's Ford (0703) 265092.

CARRINGTON, Maj.-Gen. Colin Edward George, CB 1991; CBE 1983; Director General Transport and Movements (Army), Ministry of Defence, 1988–91; *b* 19 Jan. 1936; *s* of Edgar John Carrington and Ruth Carrington (*née* West); *m* 1967, Joy Bracknell; one *s* one *d. Educ:* Royal Liberty Sch.; RMA Sandhurst. FCIT; FILDM. Troop Comdr, BAOR, 1956–59; Air Despatch duties, 1960–64; Instructor, RMA, 1964–68; Sqdn Comdr, BAOR, 1972–74; Directing Staff, Staff Coll., 1975–77; CO 1 Armd Div. Transport Regt, 1977–79; DCOS 1 Armd Div., 1979–82; RCDS 1983; Dir, Manning Policy (Army), 1984–86; Comd Transport 1 (BR) Corps, 1986–88. *Recreations:* gardening, reading. *Address:* c/o Lloyds Bank, Cox & King's Branch, 7 Pall Mall, SW1.

CARRINGTON, Matthew Hadrian Marshall; MP (C) Fulham, since 1987; *b* 19 Oct. 1947; *s* of Walter and Dilys Carrington; *m* 1975, Mary Lou Darrow; one *d. Educ:* London Lycée; Imperial Coll. of Science and Technol., London (BSc Physics); London Business Sch. (MSc). Prodn Foreman, GKN Ltd, 1969–72; banker: with The First National Bank of Chicago, 1974–78; with Saudi Internat. Bank, 1978–87. *Recreations:* cooking, political history. *Address:* House of Commons, SW1A 0AA.

CARROL, Charles Gordon; Director, Commonwealth Institute, Scotland, since 1971; *b* 21 March 1935; *s* of Charles Muir Carrol and Catherine Gray Napier; *m* 1970, Frances Anne, *o d* of John A. and Flora McL. Sinclair; three *s. Educ:* Melville Coll., Edinburgh; Edinburgh Univ. (MA); Moray House Coll. (DipEd). Education Officer: Govt of Nigeria, 1959–65; Commonwealth Inst., Scotland, 1965–71. Lay Member, Press Council, 1978–82. *Recreations:* walking, reading, cooking. *Address:* 11 Dukehaugh, Peebles, Scotland EH45 9DN. *T:* Peebles (0721) 21296.

CARROLL, Ven. Charles William Desmond; Archdeacon of Blackburn, 1973–86; Archdeacon Emeritus since 1986; Vicar of Balderstone, 1973–86; *b* 27 Jan. 1919; *s* of Rev. William and Mrs L. Mary Carroll; *m* 1945, Doreen Daisy Ruskell; three *s* one *d. Educ:* St Columba Coll.; Trinity Coll., Dublin. BA 1943; Dip. Ed. Hons 1945; MA 1946. Asst Master: Kingstown Grammar Sch., 1943–45; Rickerby House Sch., 1945–50; Vicar of Stanwix, Carlisle, 1950–59; Hon. Canon of Blackburn, 1959; Dir of Religious Education, 1959; Hon. Chaplain to Bishop of Blackburn, 1961; Canon Residentiary of Blackburn Cathedral, 1964. *Publication:* Management for Managers, 1968. *Address:* 11 Assheton Road, Blackburn BB2 6SF. *T:* Blackburn (0254) 51915. *Clubs:* Commonwealth Trust; Rotary (Blackburn).

CARROLL, Maj.-Gen. Derek Raymond, OBE 1958; retired; *b* 2 Jan. 1919; *er s* of late Raymond and Edith Lisle Carroll; *m* 1946, Bettina Mary, *d* of late Leslie Gould; one *s* two *d.* Enlisted TA, 1939; commnd into Royal Engineers, 1943; served Western Desert, 1941–43, Italy, 1943–44; psc 1945; various appts, 1946–66, in War Office (2), Germany (2), Sudan Defence Force, Libya, Malaya; CRE 4 Div., 1962–64; comd 12 Engr Bde, 1966–67; idc 1968; Dir, MoD, 1969–70; Chief Engr, BAOR, 1970–73; RARO, 1973.

CARROLL, Prof. John Edward, FEng 1985; Professor of Engineering, University of Cambridge, since 1983; Fellow of Queens' College, Cambridge, since 1967; *b* 15 Feb. 1934; *s* of Sydney Wentworth Carroll and May Doris Carroll; *m* 1958, Vera Mary Jordan; three *s. Educ:* Oundle Sch.; Queens' Coll., Cambridge (Wrangler; Foundn Schol., 1957). BA 1957; PhD 1961; FIEE; ScD 1982. Microwave Div., Services Electronic Res. Lab., 1961–67; Cambridge University: Lectr, 1967–76; Reader, 1976–83; Dep. Hd of Engrg Dept, 1986–90. Vis. Prof., Queensland Univ., 1982. Editor, IEE Jl of Solid State and Electron Devices, 1976–82. *Publications:* Hot Electron Microwave Generators, 1970; Physical Models of Semiconductor Devices, 1974; Solid State Devices (Inst. of Phys. vol. 57), 1980; Rate Equations in Semiconductor Electronics, 1986; contribs on microwaves, semiconductor devices and optical systems to learned jls. *Recreations:* swimming, piano, walking, reading thrillers, carpentry. *Address:* Engineering Department, Cambridge University, Trumpington Street, Cambridge CB2 1PZ. *T:* Cambridge (0223) 332799, *Fax:* Cambridge (0223) 332662.

CARROLL, Terence Patrick, (Terry); Treasury Director, National & Provincial Building Society, since 1990; Chairman, Bradford Breakthrough Ltd, since 1990; *b* 24 Nov. 1948; *s* of George Daniel Carroll and Betty Doreen Carroll (*née* Holmes); *m* 1st, 1971, Louise Mary (*née* Smith) (marr. diss. 1984); one *s*; 2nd, 1984, Penelope Julia, (Penny) (*née* Berry). *Educ:* Gillingham Grammar Sch.; Univ. of Bradford (BSc Business Studies). FCA 1980; MCT 1985; FCBSI 1986. Auditor and Computer Auditor, Armitage & Norton, 1970–76; Management Accountant, Bradford & Bingley Building Soc., 1976–80; Exec. and Mem. Stock Exchange, Sheppards & Chase, 1980–82; Treasurer, Halifax Building Soc., 1982–85; National & Provincial Building Society: Gen. Manager Finance, 1985–88 (acting Chief Exec., 1985–86); Finance Dir, 1987–90. MBIM. *Recreations:* golf, hockey, bridge. *Address:* National & Provincial Building Society, Provincial House, Bradford, West Yorks BD1 1NL. *T:* Bradford (0274) 842502, *Fax:* Bradford (0274) 304353. *Clubs:* Bradford; Ilkley Golf.

CARRUTHERS, Alwyn Guy; Director of Statistics, Department of Employment, 1981–83 (Deputy Director, 1972–80); *b* 6 May 1925; *yr s* of late John Sendall and of Lily Eden Carruthers, Grimsby; *m* 1950, Edith Eileen, *o d* of late William and Edith Addison Lumb; no *c. Educ:* Wintringham Grammar Sch., Grimsby; King's Coll., London Univ. BA First Cl. Hons in Mathematics, Drew Gold Medal and Prize, 1945. RAE, Farnborough, 1945–46; Instructor Lieut, RN, 1946–49; Rothamsted Experimental Station, 1949. Postgraduate Diploma in Mathematical Statistics, Christ's Coll., Cambridge, 1951. Bd of Trade and DTI Statistics Divisions, 1951–72. *Publications:* articles in official publications and learned jls. *Recreations:* gardening, music. *Address:* 24 Red House Lane, Bexleyheath, Kent DA6 8JD. *T:* 081–303 4898.

CARRUTHERS, Colin Malcolm, CMG 1980; HM Diplomatic Service, retired; Government and International Relations Consultant, World Vision International, since 1985; *b* 23 Feb. 1931; *s* of Colin Carruthers and late Dorothy Beatrice Carruthers; *m* 1954, Annette Audrey Buckton; three *s* one *d. Educ:* Monkton Combe School; Selwyn College, Cambridge (MA). Royal Signals, 1950–51; joined HMOCS Kenya, 1955; District Officer, Kenya, 1955–63; Dep. Civil Sec., Rift Valley Region, Kenya, 1963–65 (retired on Africanisation of post); Field Dir, Oxfam, Maseru, Lesotho, 1965–67; joined HM Diplomatic Service, 1968; First Sec. (Economic), Islamabad, 1969–73; First Sec., Ottawa, 1973–77; Counsellor and Hd of Chancery, Addis Ababa, 1977–80 (Chargé d'Affaires, 1978–79); Asst Election Comr, Zimbabwe-Rhodesia elecns, 1980; Head of South Pacific Dept, FCO, 1980–83, retired. UK Comr, British Phosphate Comrs, 1981–87. Governor, Monkton Combe Sch., 1984–. *Recreations:* tennis, golf, family. *Address:* Thornbury, Frant, near Tunbridge Wells, Kent TN3 9DH. *T:* Frant (089275) 238. *Clubs:* Commonwealth Trust; Hawks (Cambridge).

CARRUTHERS, George, OBE 1979; FCIT; Member of Board, 1979–82, Deputy Chief Executive, 1981–82, Consultant, 1983–84, National Bus Company; *b* 15 Nov. 1917; *s* of James and Dinah Carruthers; *m* 1941, Gabriel Joan Heath; one *s* one *d. Educ:* Nelson Sch., Wigton, Cumbria; St Edmund Hall, Oxford (BA). FBIM. Served War, Border Regt and Cameronians (Major), 1939–46 (despatches). Various management posts, Bus Industry (all at subsid. cos or Headquarters NBC): Eastern Counties, Norwich, 1946–59; Wilts and Dorset Omnibus Co., 1959–63; Dep. Gen. Manager, Hants and Dorset Omnibus Co., 1963–66; Gen. Manager, United Welsh-Swansea, 1967–69; Vice-Chm., South Wales (NBC), 1969–72; Regional Exec., Western Region (NBC), 1972–73; Gp Exec., NBC Headquarters, 1973–74; Director of Manpower, NBC HQ, 1974–79; Mem. for Personnel Services, 1979–81. Pres., Bus and Coach Council, 1983–84. *Publications:* papers for Jl and meetings of CIT (Road Passenger award for a paper, 1978). *Recreation:* the countryside. *Address:* 2 Mallard Close, Lower Street, Harnham, Salisbury, Wilts SP2 8JB. *T:* Salisbury (0722) 323084.

CARRUTHERS, James Edwin; Assistant Secretary, Royal Hospital Chelsea, since 1988; *b* 19 March 1928; *er s* of James and Dollie Carruthers; *m* 1955, Phyllis Williams; one *s. Educ:* George Heriot's Sch.; Edinburgh Univ. (MA; Medallist in Scottish Hist.). FSAScot. Lieut, The Queen's Own Cameron Highlanders, 1949–51, and TA, 1951–55. Air Ministry: Asst Principal, 1951; Private Sec. to DCAS, 1955; Asst Private Sec. to Sec. of State for Air, 1956; Principal, 1956; Min. of Aviation, 1960–62; Private Secretary: to Minister of Defence for RAF, 1965–67; to Parly Under Sec. of State for RAF, 1967; Asst Sec., 1967; Chief Officer, Sovereign Base Areas Admin, Cyprus, 1968–71; Dep. Chief of Public Relations, MoD, 1971–72; Private Sec. to Chancellor of Duchy of Lancaster, Cabinet Office, 1973–74; Sec., Organising Cttee for British Aerospace, DoI, 1975–77; Under-Sec., 1977; seconded as Asst to Chm., British Aerospace, 1977–79; Dir Gen., Royal Ordnance Factories (Finance and Procurement), 1980–83; Chm., C S Selection Bd, 1983–84; Asst Under Sec. of State, MoD, 1984–88. *Recreations:* painting, gardening, travel. *Address:* 6 Light Horse Court, Royal Hospital Chelsea, SW3 4SL.

CARRUTHERS, Hon. Norman Harry; Hon. Mr Justice Carruthers; Chief Justice of the Supreme Court of Prince Edward Island, since 1985; *b* 25 Oct. 1935; *s* of Lorne C. H. Carruthers and Jean R. Webster; *m* 1970, Diana C. Rodd; one *s* two *d. Educ:* Prince of Wales Coll.; Mount Allison Univ. (BSc, BEd); Dalhousie Law Sch. (LLB). Canadian Industries Ltd, 1956–59; schoolteacher, 1961–64; Lawyer, Foster, MacDonald and Carruthers, 1968–80; Chief Judge, Provincial Court, PEI, 1980–85. *Address:* 16 Trafalgar Street, Charlottetown, PEI C1A 3Z1, Canada. *T:* 902–566–3007; (office) 902–368–6023.

CARRUTHERS, William Buttrick; Regional Chairman, Industrial Tribunals, Bury St Edmunds, since 1990; *b* 1 Aug. 1929; *s* of Alexander Norman and Olive Carruthers; *m* 1961, Jennifer Stevens; one *s* two *d. Educ:* Middlesex School, Concord, Mass; Radley College; Clare College, Cambridge (BA Hons, LLB). Called to the Bar, Lincoln's Inn, 1954; practised in N Rhodesia (later Zambia), 1956–70; part time Chm., Industrial Tribunals, 1970; Chm., Industrial Tribunals, Bedford, 1975. *Recreations:* tennis, walking. *Address:* Worndith Hall, Kimbolton, Huntingdon, Cambs PE18 0JW. *T:* Huntingdon (0480) 860203.

CARSBERG, Sir Bryan (Victor), Kt 1989; Director General of Telecommunications, since 1984; *b* 3 Jan. 1939; *s* of Alfred Victor Carsberg and Maryllia (*née* Collins); *m* 1960, Margaret Linda Graham; two *d. Educ:* Berkhamsted Sch.; London Sch. of Econs and Polit. Science (MScEcon; Hon. Fellow, 1990). Chartered Accountant, 1960. Sole practice, chartered accountant, 1962–64; Lectr in Accounting, LSE, 1964–68; Vis. Lectr, Grad. Sch. of Business, Univ. of Chicago, 1968–69; Prof. of Accounting, Univ. of Manchester, 1969–81 (Dean, Faculty of Econ. and Social Studies, 1977–78); Arthur Andersen Prof. of Accounting, LSE, 1981–87; Dir of Res., ICA, 1981–87. Visiting Professor: of Business Admin, Univ. of Calif, Berkeley, 1974; of Accounting, LSE, 1988–89. Asst Dir of Res. and Technical Activities, Financial Accounting Standards Bd, USA, 1978–81; Vice-Chm., Accounting Standards Bd, 1990–. Mem. Council, ICA, 1975–79. Director: Economists Adv. Gp, 1976–84; Economist Bookshop, 1981–; Philip Allan (Publishers), 1981–; Mem., Bd, Radiocommunications Agency, 1990–. Mem., Council, Univ. of Surrey, 1990–. Hon. MAEcon Manchester, 1973. Chartered Accountants Founding Societies Centenary Award, 1988. *Publications:* An Introduction to Mathematical Programming for Accountants, 1969; (with H. C. Edey) Modern Financial Management, 1969; Analysis for Investment Decisions, 1974; (with E. V. Morgan and M. Parkin) Indexation and Inflation, 1975; Economics of Business Decisions, 1975; (with A. Hope) Investment Decisions under Inflation, 1976; (with A. Hope) Current Issues in Accountancy, 1977, 2nd edn 1984; (with J. Arnold and R. Scapens) Topics in Management Accounting, 1980; (with S. Lumby) The Evaluation of Financial Performance in the Water Industry, 1983; (with M. Page) Current Cost Accounting, 1984; (with M. Page *et al*) Small Company Financial Reporting, 1985. *Recreations:* road running, theatre, music, opera. *Address:* Oftel, Export House, Ludgate Hill, EC4M 7JJ. *T:* 071–822 1601.

CARSON, John, CBE 1981; Draper; Member (OUP) for Belfast North, Northern Ireland Assembly, 1982–86; *b* 1934. Member of the Orange Order; Member, Belfast District Council, (formerly Belfast Corporation), 1971–; Official Unionist Councillor for Duncairn; Lord Mayor of Belfast, 1980–81, 1985–86. MP (UU) Belfast North, Feb. 1974–1979. Dir, Laganside Corp., 1989; Vice-Chm., NI Youth Council, 1985. High Sheriff, Belfast, 1978. *Address:* 20 Cardy Road, Greyabbey, Co. Down, N Ireland.

CARSON, Robert Andrew Glendinning, FBA 1980; Keeper, Department of Coins and Medals, British Museum, 1978–83; *b* 7 April 1918; *s* of Andrew and Mary Dempster Carson; *m* 1949, Meta Fransisca De Vries; one *s* one *d. Educ:* Kirkcudbright Acad.; Univ. of Glasgow (MA (1st Cl. Hons Classics) 1940; Foulis Schol. 1940; Hon. DLitt 1983). FSA 1965. Served War, RA, 1940–46, NW Europe; 2nd Lieut 1941, Captain 1945. Asst Keeper, 1947, Dep. Keeper, 1965, Dept of Coins and Medals, British Museum. Pres., Internat. Numismatic Commn, 1979–86. Editor, Numismatic Chronicle, 1966–73; Mem., Adv. Cttee on Historic Wreck Sites, 1973–80; Pres., Royal Numismatic Soc., 1974–79 (Medallist, 1972; Hon. Fellow, 1980); Patron, Australian Numismatic Soc., 1984–. Hon. Vis. Fellow, Univ. of Tasmania, 1990. Hon. Assoc., Powerhouse Mus., Sydney, 1986. Hon. Member: Romanian Numismatic Soc., 1977; British Numismatic Soc., 1979; Corresponding Member: Amer. Numismatic Soc., 1967; Austrian Numismatic Soc., 1971; Foreign Mem., Finnish Soc. of Science and Letters, 1986. Medallist: Soc. française de Numismatique, 1970; Luxembourg Museum, 1971; Amer. Numismatic Soc., 1978. Silver Jubilee Medal, 1977. *Publications:* (with H. Mattingly and C. H. V. Sutherland) Roman Imperial Coinage, 1951–; ed, Essays in Roman Coinage presented to Harold Mattingly, 1956; (with P. V. Hill and J. P. C. Kent) Late Roman Bronze Coinage, 1960; Coins, ancient, mediæval and modern, 1962, 2nd edn 1972; Catalogue of Roman Imperial Coins in the British Museum, vol. VI, 1962; ed, Mints, Dies and Currency, 1971; Principal Coins of the Romans, vol. I, 1978, vol. II, 1980, vol. III, 1981; ed, Essays presented to Humphrey Sutherland, 1978; History of the Royal Numismatic Society, 1986; Coins of the Roman Empire, 1990; articles in Numismatic Chron., Rev. Numismatique, etc. *Address:* 2/2A Queen's Parade, Newport, NSW 2106, Australia.

CARSON, Air Cdre Robert John, CBE 1974; AFC 1964; Queen's Commendation (Air), 1962; Director, Leicestershire Medical Research Foundation, University of Leicester, since 1980; *b* 3 Aug. 1924; *e s* of Robert George and Margaret Etta Helena Carson; *m* 1945, Jane, *yr d* of James and Jane Bailie; three *d. Educ:* Regent House Sch., Newtownards, NI; RAF. MRAeS; MBIM; MIOM. India, Burma, Malaya, 1945–48; Rhodesia, 1949–50; Queens Univ. Air Sqdn, 1951–52; RAF HC Examining Unit, 1952–53; AHQ Iraq, 1953–54; RAF Staff Coll., 1955; Plans, Air Min., 1956–59; 16 Sqdn, Laarbruch, Germany, 1959–62; Wing Comdr Flying, RAF Swinderby, 1962–64; Air Warfare Coll., Manby, 1964; Chief Nuclear Ops, 2ATAF Germany, 1964–67; JSSC Latimer, 1967; Chief Air Planner, UK Delegn, Live Oak, SHAPE, 1968–71; Station Comdr, RAF Leeming, 1971–73; Overseas Coll. Defence Studies, Canada, 1973–74; Air Adviser, British High Commission, Ottawa, 1974–75; Defence Advr to British High Comr in Canada, 1975–78; Manager, Panavia Office, Ottawa, and Grumman Aerospace Corp., NY, 1978–80. County Chm., SSAFA, Leics, 1982–; Regional Rep., SSAFA, Midland (2), 1986–; Pres., Aircrew Assoc., Leics, 1984–. *Recreations:* Rugby, tennis, golf, gardening. *Address:* 20 Meadow Drive, Scruton, near Northallerton, North Yorks DL7 0QW. *T:* Northallerton (0609) 748656; c/o Lloyds Bank, 118 High Street, Northallerton, N Yorks DL7 8PW. *Clubs:* Royal Air Force; Royal Ottawa (Ottawa).

CARSON, William Hunter Fisher, OBE 1983; jockey; *b* 16 Nov. 1942; *s* of Thomas Whelan Carson and Mary Hay; *m* 1963, Carole Jane Sutton (marr. diss. 1979); three *s*; *m* 1982, Elaine Williams. *Educ:* Riverside, Stirling, Scotland. Apprenticed to Captain G. Armstrong, 1957; trans. to Fred Armstrong, 1963–66; First Jockey to Lord Derby, 1967; first classic win, High Top, 1972; Champion Jockey, 1972, 1973, 1978, 1980 and 1983; became First Jockey to W. R. Hern, 1977; also appointed Royal Jockey, riding Dunfermline to the Jubilee Oaks and St Leger wins in the colours of HM the Queen; won the 200th Derby on Troy, trained by W. R. Hern, 1979; the same combination won the 1980 Derby, with Henbit, and the 1980 Oaks, with Bireme; also won King George VI and Queen Elizabeth Stakes, on Troy, 1979, on Ela-Mana-Mou, 1980, on Petoski, 1985, on Nashwan, 1989; 1983 Oaks and St Leger, with Sun Princess; Ascot Gold Cup, on Little Wolf, 1983; St Leger, on Minster Son, 1988 (only jockey ever to breed and ride a Classic winner); Derby, on Nashwan, 1989; 1,000 Guineas, Oaks and Irish Derby, on Salsabil, 1990. During the 1989 season rode 50th Group One winner in England. *Recreation:* hunting. *Address:* Minster House, Barnsley, Cirencester, Glos GL7 5DZ.

CARSTAIRS, Charles Young, CB 1968; CMG 1950; *b* 30 Oct. 1910; *s* of late Rev. Dr G. Carstairs, DD and Elizabeth Huntly Carstairs (*née* Young); *m* 1939, Frances Mary (*d* 1981), *o d* of late Dr Claude Lionel Coode, Stroud, Glos; one *s* one *d. Educ:* George Watson's Boys' Coll., Edinburgh; Edinburgh Univ. Entered Home Civil Service, 1934, Dominions Office; transf. Colonial Office, 1935; Asst Private Sec. to Sec. of State for the Colonies, 1936; Private Sec. to Perm. Under-Sec. of State for the Colonies, 1937; Asst Sec., West India Royal Commn, 1938–39; West Indian, Prodn, Res. and Mediterranean Depts, 1939–47; Administrative Sec., Development and Welfare Organisation, British West Indies, 1947–50; Sec., British Caribbean Standing Closer Assoc. Cttee, 1948–49; Dir of Information Services, Colonial Office, 1951–53, Asst Under-Sec., 1953–62; Deputy Sec., Medical Research Council, 1962–65; Under-Secretary, MPBW: Directorate-Gen., R and D, 1965–67, Construction Economics, 1967–70; Special Advr, Expenditure Cttee, House of Commons, 1971–75; Clerk to Select Cttee on Commodity Prices, House of Lords, 1976–77. *Publications:* (contrib.) The New Select Committees, ed Gavin Drewry, 1985; (ed jtly) Parliament and International Relations, 1991. *Recreation:* bad watercolours. *Address:* 4 Church Court, 31 Monks Walk, Reigate, Surrey RH2 0ST. *T:* Reigate (0737) 244896. *Club:* Athenæum.

CARSTEN, Prof. Francis Ludwig, DPhil, DLitt Oxon; FBA 1971; Masaryk Professor of Central European History in the University of London, 1961–78; *b* 25 June 1911; *s* of Prof. Paul Carsten and Frida Carsten (*née* Born); *m* 1945, Ruth Carsten (*née* Moses); two *s* one *d. Educ:* Heidelberg, Berlin and Oxford Univs. Barnett scholar, Wadham Coll., Oxford, 1939; Senior Demy, Magdalen Coll., Oxford, 1942; Lectr in History, Westfield Coll., Univ. of London, 1947; Reader in Modern History, Univ. of London, 1960. Co-Editor, Slavonic and East European Review, 1966–84. *Publications:* The Origins of Prussia, 1954; Princes and Parliaments in Germany from the 15th to the 18th Century, 1959; The Reichswehr and Politics, 1918–1933, 1966; The Rise of Fascism, 1967, rev. edn, 1980; Revolution in Central Europe, 1918–1919, 1972; Fascist Movements in Austria, 1977; War against War: British and German Radical Movements in the First World War, 1982; Britain and the Weimar Republic, The British Documents, 1984; Essays in German History, 1985; The First Austrian Republic, 1986; A History of the Prussian Junkers, 1988; ed and contributor, The New Cambridge Modern History, vol. V: The Ascendancy of France, 1961; articles in English Historical Review, History, Survey, Historische Zeitschrift, etc. *Recreations:* gardening, climbing, swimming. *Address:* 11 Redington Road, NW3. *T:* 071–435 5522.

CARSTENS, Prof. Dr Karl; President of the Federal Republic of Germany, 1979–84; *b* 14 Dec. 1914; *s* of Dr Karl Carstens, teacher, and Gertrud (*née* Clausen); *m* 1944, Dr Veronica Carstens (*née* Prior). *Educ:* Univs of Frankfurt, Dijon, München, Königsberg, Hamburg, Yale. Dr Laws Hamburg 1936, LLM Yale 1949. Served with Army, 1939–45; lawyer, Bremen, 1945–49; rep. of Bremen in Bonn, 1949–54; rep. of Fed. Republic of Germany to Council of Europe, Strasbourg, 1954–55; teaching at Cologne Univ., 1950–73; Prof. of Constitutional and Internat. Law, 1960–73; FO, Bonn, 1955–60 (State Sec., 1960–66); Dep. Defence Minister, 1966–67; Head of Chancellor's Office, Bonn, 1968–69; Dir Research Inst., German Foreign Policy Assoc., 1969–72; Mem. German Bundestag (CDU), 1972–79; Leader of the Opposition, 1973–76; Pres. of Bundestag, 1976–79. Hon. Citizen: Berlin, Bonn. Charlemagne Prize, 1984; Bremische Senatsmedaille in Gold, 1985; Robert Schuman Prize, 1985; Stresemann Medaille, 1985. Sonderstufe Grosskreuz Bundesverdienstkreuz, 1979; Dr *hc* Univs. of Tokyo, Coimbra, St Louis, Dijon and Speyer. Ehrenkreuz Bundeswehr in Gold, 1987; Schleyer Prize, 1987. *Publications:* Grundgedanken der amerikanischen Verfassung und ihre Verwirklichung, 1954; Das Recht des Europarats, 1956; Politische Führung—Erfahrungen im Dienst der Bundesregierung, 1971; Bundestagsreden und Zeitdokumente, 1977; Reden und Interviews, 5 vols, 1980–84; Anthologie Deutsche Gedichte, 1983; Wanderungen in Deutschland, 1985; Vom Geist der Freiheit, 1989. *Address:* 5300 Bonn 1, Bundeshaus, Germany.

CARSWELL, John Patrick, CB 1977; FRSL; Secretary, British Academy, 1978–83, now emeritus; Honorary Research Fellow, Department of History, University College London, since 1983; *b* 30 May 1918; *s* of Donald Carswell, barrister and author, and Catherine Carswell, author; *m* 1944, Ianthe Elstob; two *d. Educ:* Merchant Taylors' Sch.; St John's Coll., Oxford (MA). Served in Army, 1940–46. Entered Civil Service, 1946. Joint Sec., Cttee on Economic and Financial Problems of Provision for Old Age (Phillips Cttee), 1953–54; Asst Sec., 1955; Principal Private Sec. to Minister of Pensions and Nat. Insurance, 1955–56; Treasury, 1961–64; Under-Sec., Office of Lord Pres. of the Council and Minister for Science, 1964, Under-Sec., DES and Ministry of Health, 1964–74; Sec., UGC, 1974–77. Life Mem., Inst. of Historical Research, Univ. of London, 1984; FRSL 1984. *Publications:* The Prospector, 1950; The Old Cause, 1954; The South Sea Bubble, 1960; (ed with L. A. Dralle) The Diary and Political Papers of George Bubb Dodington, 1965; The Civil Servant and his World, 1966; The Descent on England, 1969; From Revolution to Revolution: English Society 1688–1776, 1973; Lives and Letters, 1978; The Exile: a memoir of Ivy Litvinov, 1983; Government and the Universities in Britain, 1986; The Porcupine: a life of Algernon Sidney, 1989; The Northern Heights: how Kenwood was saved, 1992; contribs to Times Literary Supplement and other periodicals. *Address:* 5 Prince Arthur Road, NW3 6AX. *T:* 071–794 6527. *Club:* Garrick.

CARSWELL, Hon. Sir Robert (Douglas), Kt 1988; **Hon. Mr Justice Carswell;** a Judge of the High Court of Northern Ireland, since 1984; *b* 28 June 1934; *er s* of late Alan E. Carswell and of Nance E. Carswell; *m* 1961, Romayne Winifred Ferris, OBE, *o d* of late James Ferris, JP, Greyabbey, Co. Down, and of Eileen Ferris, JP; two *d. Educ:* Royal Belfast Academical Instn; Pembroke Coll., Oxford (Schol.; 1st Cl. Honour Mods, 1st Cl. Jurisprudence, MA; Hon. Fellow, 1984); Univ. of Chicago Law Sch. (JD). Called to Bar of N Ireland, 1957, and to English Bar, Gray's Inn, 1972; Counsel to Attorney-General for N Ireland, 1970–71; QC (NI), 1971; Sen. Crown Counsel in NI, 1979–84; Bencher, Inn of Court of N Ireland, 1979. Chancellor, Dios of Armagh and of Down and Dromore, 1990–. Chairman: Council of Law Reporting for NI, 1987–; Law Reform Adv. Cttee for NI, 1989–. Governor, Royal Belfast Academical Instn, 1967–, Chm. Bd of Governors, 1986–; Pro-Chancellor and Chm. Council, Univ. of Ulster, 1984–. *Publications:* Trustee Acts (Northern Ireland), 1964; articles in legal periodicals. *Recreation:* golf. *Address:* Royal Courts of Justice, Belfast BT1 3JF. *Club:* Ulster Reform (Belfast).

CARTER; *see* Bonham-Carter and Bonham Carter.

CARTER, family name of **Baron Carter.**

CARTER, Baron *cr* 1987 (Life Peer), of Devizes in the County of Wiltshire; **Denis Victor Carter;** agricultural consultant and farmer, since 1957; *b* 17 Jan. 1932; *s* of Albert William and Annie Julia Carter; *m* 1957, Teresa Mary Greengoe; one *d* (one *s* decd). *Educ:* Xaverian Coll., Brighton; East Sussex Inst. of Agriculture; Essex Inst. of Agriculture (NDA, Queen's Prize); Oxford Univ. (BLitt). Nat. Service, Canal Zone, GHQ MELF, 1950–52. Audit clerk, 1949–50 and 1952–53; farmworker, 1953–54; student of agriculture, 1954–57. Founded AKC Ltd, Agricultural Accounting and Management, 1957; commenced farming, Oxfordshire, Hants and Wilts, 1975. Sen. Research Fellowship in Agricultural Marketing, MAFF, 1970–72. Dep. Chief Opposition Whip, H of L, 1990–. Opposition frontbench spokesman on agric. and rural affairs, 1987–, also on social security, 1988–, and health, 1989–. Contested (Lab) Basingstoke, 1970. *Recreations:* walking, reading, supporting Southampton Football Club. *Clubs:* Farmers'; Turners (Stockbridge); Grasshoppers (Amesbury).

CARTER, Andrew; HM Diplomatic Service; Deputy Governor, Gibraltar, since 1990; *b* 4 Dec. 1943; *s* of Eric and Margaret Carter; *m* 1st, 1973, Anne Caroline Morgan (marr. diss. 1986); one *d*; 2nd, 1988, Catherine Mary Tyler; one *d. Educ:* Latymer Upper Sch., Hammersmith; Royal Coll. of Music; Jesus Coll., Cambridge (Scholar 1962; MA). FRCO; LRAM; ARCM. Asst Master, Marlborough Coll., 1965–70. Joined HM Diplomatic Service, 1971; Warsaw, 1972; Geneva, 1975; Bonn, 1975; FCO, 1978; Brussels, 1986. *Recreation:* music. *Address:* c/o Foreign and Commonwealth Office, SW1.

CARTER, Angela; author and reviewer; *b* 1940; *m*; one *s. Educ:* Bristol Univ. Fellow in Creative Writing, Sheffield Univ., 1976–78. Judge, Booker McConnell Prize, 1983. Screenplay (jtly), The Company of Wolves, 1984. *Publications: fiction: novels:* Shadow Dance, 1966; The Magic Toyshop (John Llewellyn Rhys Prize), 1967 (screenplay, 1986); Several Perceptions (Somerset Maugham Award), 1968; Heroes and Villains, 1969; Miss Z, the Dark Young Lady, 1970; Love, 1971; The Infernal Desire Machines of Doctor Hoffman, 1972; The Passion of New Eve, 1977; Nights at the Circus (jtly, James Tait Black Meml Prize), 1984; Wise Children, 1991; *short stories:* Fireworks, 1974; The Bloody Chamber and other stories (Cheltenham Fest. of Lit. Award), 1979; Black Venus, 1985; (ed) Wayward Girls and Wicked Women, 1986; (contrib.) The Virago Book of Ghost Stories, 1987; (ed) The Virago Book of Fairy Stories, 1990; Come unto these Yellow Sands: four radio plays, 1984; *for children:* (jtly) Martin Leman's Comic and Curious Cats, 1979; (jtly) Moonshadow, 1982; (jtly) Sleeping Beauty and other favourite fairy tales (Kate Greenaway Medal), 1983; *non-fiction:* The Sadeian Woman: an exercise in cultural history, 1979; Nothing Sacred: selected writings, 1982; contrib. New Society,

Guardian, etc. *Address:* c/o Virago Press Ltd, Centro House, 20–23 Mandela Street, Camden Town, NW1 0HQ.

CARTER, Bernard Thomas; Hon. RE 1975; full-time artist (painter and etcher), since 1977; *b* 6 April 1920; *s* of Cecil Carter and Ethel Carter (*née* Darby); *m* Eugenie Alexander, artist and writer; one *s*. *Educ:* Haberdashers' Aske's; Goldsmith's College of Art, London Univ. NDD, ATD. RAF, 1939–46. Art lectr, critic and book reviewer, 1952–68; National Maritime Museum: Asst Keeper (prints and drawings), 1968; Dep. Keeper (Head of Picture Dept), 1970; Keeper (Head of Dept of Pictures and Conservation), 1972–77. One-man exhibns in London: Arthur Jeffress Gall., 1955; Portal Gall., 1963, 1965, 1967, 1969, 1974, 1978, 1979, 1981, 1984, 1987 and 1990; mixed exhibns: Royal Academy, Arts Council, British Council and galleries in Europe and USA; works in public collections, galleries abroad and British educn authorities, etc. TV and radio include: Thames at Six, Pebble Mill at One, Kaleidoscope, London Radio, etc. *Publication:* Art for Young People (with Eugenie Alexander), 1958. *Recreations:* reading, listening to music, gardening, theatre. *Address:* 56 King George Street, Greenwich, SE10 8QD. *T:* 081–858 4281.

CARTER, Dr Brandon, FRS 1981; Directeur de Recherche (Centre National de la Recherche Scientifique), Observatoire de Paris-Meudon, since 1986; *b* Sydney, Australia, 26 May 1942; *s* of Harold Burnell Carter and Mary (*née* Brandon Jones); *m* 1969, Lucette Defrise; three *d*. *Educ:* George Watson's Coll., Edinburgh; Univ. of St Andrews; Pembroke Coll., Cambridge (MA, PhD 1968, DSc 1976). Res. Student, Dept of Applied Maths and Theoretical Physics, Cambridge, 1964–67; Res. Fellow, Pembroke Coll., Cambridge, 1967–68; Staff Mem., Inst. of Astronomy, Cambridge, 1968–73; Univ. Asst Lectr, 1973–74, Univ. Lectr, 1974–75, Dept of Applied Maths and Theoretical Physics, Cambridge; Maître de Recherche, co-responsable Groupe d'Astrophysique Relativiste (CNRS), Paris-Meudon, 1975–86. *Recreation:* wilderness. *Address:* 19 rue de la Borne au Diable, 92310 Sèvres, France. *T:* (Paris) 4534—46–77.

CARTER, Bruce; *see* Hough, R. A.

CARTER, Sir Charles (Frederick), Kt 1978; FBA 1970; President, Policy Studies Institute, since 1989; Vice-Chancellor, University of Lancaster, 1963–79; *b* Rugby, 15 Aug. 1919; *y s* of late Frederick William Carter, FRS; *m* 1944, Janet Shea; one *s* two *d*. *Educ:* Rugby Sch.; St John's Coll., Cambridge. Friends' Relief Service, 1941–45; Lectr in Statistics, Univ. of Cambridge, 1945–51; Fellow of Emmanuel Coll., 1947–51 (Hon. Fellow, 1965–); Prof. of Applied Economics, The Queen's Univ., Belfast, 1952–59; Stanley Jevons Prof. of Political Economy and Cobden Lectr, Univ. of Manchester, 1959–63. Chairman: Science and Industry Cttee, RSA, British Assoc. and Nuffield Foundn, 1954–59; Schools' Broadcasting Council, 1964–71; Joint Cttee of the Univs and the Accountancy Profession, 1964–70; Adv. Bd of Accountancy Educn, 1970–76; North-West Economic Planning Council, 1965–68; Centre for Studies in Social Policy, 1972–78; PO Rev. Cttee, 1976–77; NI Economic Council, 1977–87; Sec.-Gen., Royal Econ. Soc., 1971–75; Member: UN Expert Cttee on Commodity Trade, 1953; Capital Investment Advisory Cttee, Republic of Ireland, 1956; British Assoc. Cttee on Metric System, 1958; Council for Scientific and Industrial Research, 1959–63; Commn on Higher Education, Republic of Ireland, 1960–67; Heyworth Cttee on Social Studies, 1963; Advisory Council on Technology, 1964–66; North Western Postal Bd, 1970–73; President: Manchester Statistical Soc., 1967–69; BAAS, 1981–82. Joint Editor: Journal of Industrial Economics, 1955–61; Economic Journal, 1961–70; Editor, Policy Studies, 1980–88. Chm. Council, Goldsmiths' Coll., Univ. of London, 1988–. Fellow, Internat. Acad. of Management; Hon. Member, Royal Irish Academy; Trustee: Joseph Rowntree Meml Trust, 1966– (Vice-Chm., 1981–); Sir Halley Stewart Trust, 1969– (Chm., 1986–); Chairman: West Cumbria Arts Trust (formerly Rosehill Theatre Trust), 1984–; Learning from Experience Trust, 1986–. Hon. DEconSc, NUI, 1968; Hon. DSc: NUU, 1979; Lancaster, 1979; QUB, 1980; Hon. LLD: TCD, 1980; Liverpool, 1982. *Publications:* The Science of Wealth, 1960, 3rd edn 1973; (with W. B. Reddaway and J. R. N. Stone) The Measurement of Production Movements, 1948; (with G. L. S. Shackle and others) Uncertainty and Business Decisions, 1954; (with A. D. Roy) British Economic Statistics, 1954; (with B. R. Williams) Industry and Technical Progress, 1957; Investment in Innovation, 1958; Science in Industry, 1959; (with D. P. Barritt) The Northern Ireland Problem, 1962, 2nd edn 1972; Wealth, 1968; (with G. Brosan and others) Patterns and Policies in Higher Education, 1971; On Having a Sense of all Conditions, 1971; (with J. L. Ford and others) Uncertainty and Expectation in Economics, 1972; Higher Education for the Future, 1980; (with J. H. M. Pinder) Policies for a Constrained Economy, 1982; articles in Economic Journal, etc. *Recreation:* gardening. *Address:* 1 Gosforth Road, Seascale, Cumbria CA20 1PU. *T:* Seascale (09467) 28359. *Club:* National Liberal.

CARTER, David; *see* Carter, R. D.

CARTER, Prof. David Craig, FRCSE; FRCSGlas; Regius Professor of Clinical Surgery, Edinburgh University, since 1988; *b* 1 Sept. 1940; *s* of Horace Ramsay Carter and Mary Florence Carter (*née* Lister); *m* 1967, Ilske Ursula Luth; two *s*. *Educ:* Cockermouth Grammar Sch.; St Andrews Univ. (MB ChB, MD). British Empire Cancer Campaign Fellow, 1967; Lecturer in Surgery: Edinburgh Univ., 1969; Makerere Univ., Uganda, 1972; Wellcome Trust Sen. Lectr, Edinburgh Univ., 1974, seconded for 12 months to Center for Ulcer Res. and Educn, LA, 1976; Sen. Lectr in Surgery, Edinburgh Univ., 1974–79; St Mungo Prof. of Surgery, Glasgow Univ., 1979–88. Chairman: Scottish Foundn for Surgery in Nepal, 1988–; Scottish Council for Postgrad. Med. Educn, 1990–. Member: Council, RCSE, 1980–90; James IV Assoc. of Surgeons, 1981–; Internat. Surgical Gp, 1984–. Mem., Broadcasting Council, BBC Scotland, 1989–. Co-Editor, British Journal of Surgery, 1986–91; General Editor, Operative Surgery, 1983–. *Publications:* Peptic Ulcer, 1983; Principles and Practice of Surgery, 1985; Pancreatitis, 1988; numerous contribs to surgical and gastroenterological jls. *Recreations:* music, golf. *Address:* 19 Buckingham Terrace, Edinburgh EH4 3AD. *T:* 031–332 5554. *Clubs:* New (Edinburgh); Royal & Ancient Golf (St Andrews); Luffness Golf.

CARTER, Sir Derrick (Hunton), Kt 1975; TD 1952; Vice-Chairman, Remploy Ltd, 1976–78 (Chairman, 1972–76; Director, 1967–79); *b* 7 April 1906; *s* of Arthur Hunton Carter, MD and Winifred Carter, Sedbergh; *m* 1st, 1933, Phyllis, *d* of Denis Best, Worcester; one *s* one *d*; 2nd, 1948, Madeline, *d* of Col D. M. O'Callaghan, CMG, DSO; one *d*. *Educ:* Haileybury Coll.; St John's Coll., Cambridge (MA). 2nd Lieut, 27th (LEE) Bn RE, TA, 1936, mobilised Aug. 1939; in AA until Dec. 1941; 1st War Advanced Class; Major RA, Dept Tank Design; comd Armament Wing of DTD, Lulworth, 1942–45 (Lt-Col). Civil Engr, Dominion Bridge Co., Montreal, 1927–28; Res. Engr, Billingham Div., ICI, 1928–33; Asst Sales Controller, ICI, London, 1933–38; Asst Sales Man., ICI, 1938–39 and 1945–47; Gen. Chemicals Div., ICI: Sales Control Man., 1947; Commercial Dir, 1951; Man. Dir, 1953; Chm., 1961; also Chm. Alkali Div., 1963; Chm. (of merged Divs as) Mond Div., 1964; retd from ICI, 1967. Chm., United Sulphuric Acid Corp. Ltd, 1967–71; Chm., Torrance & Sons Ltd, 1971–79; Director: Avon Rubber Co. Ltd, 1970–81; Stothert & Pitt Ltd, 1971–79; BICERI Ltd, 1967–90. Mem. Exec. Cttee, Gloucestershire Council for Small Industries in Rural Areas, 1970–86. Mem. Council of Management, Nat. Star Centre for Disabled Youth, 1977–82; Vice-Pres., Glos Assoc. of Boys' Clubs. Freeman of City of London, 1973; Liveryman, Worshipful Co. of Coachmakers and Coach Harness Makers, 1973. *Recreations:* shooting, gardening. *Address:* Withington House, Withington, Cheltenham, Glos GL54 4BB. *T:* Withington (024289) 286. *Club:* Army and Navy.

CARTER, Dorothy Ethel Fleming, (Jane); energy adviser; World Bank consultant; Partner, International Energy Efficiency Consultants; Vice President, British Institute of Energy Economics; *b* 29 Aug. 1928; *d* of late Charles Edward Starkey and Doris Alma Starkey (*nee* Fleming); *m* 1952, Frank Arthur (Nick) Carter; two *d*. *Educ:* Dame Allen's Girls' Sch.; Swansea High Sch.; LSE (BSc (Econ) 1951). Joined CS as Exec. Officer, BoT, 1947; Principal, 1966; Min. of Technology, 1969–70; DTI, 1970–73; Asst Sec., Pay Bd, 1973–74; Dept of Energy, 1974–82, Under Sec., 1979–82. Ecole Nat. d'Admin, Paris, 1976. Vis. Prof., Institut d'Economie et de Politique de l'Energie, Grenoble, 1987–88. Pres., Internat. Assoc. of Energy Economists, 1986–. *Recreations:* travelling, reading. *Address:* 27 Gilkes Crescent, Dulwich Village, SE21 7BP. *T:* 081–693 1889. *Club:* Reform.

CARTER, Douglas, CB 1969; Under-Secretary, Department of Trade and Industry, 1970–71; *b* 4 Dec. 1911; 3rd *s* of Albert and Mabel Carter, Bradford, Yorks; *m* 1935, Alice, *d* of Captain C. E. Le Mesurier, CB, RN; three *s* one *d*. *Educ:* Bradford Grammar Sch.; St John's Coll., Cambridge (Scholar). First Cl. Hons, Historical Tripos Part I and Economics Tripos Part II. Wrenbury Research Scholarship in Economics, Cambridge, 1933. Asst Principal, Board of Trade, 1934; Sec., Imperial Shipping Cttee, 1935–38; Princ. BoT, 1939; Asst Sec., BoT, 1943; Chm., Cttee of Experts in Enemy Property Custodianship, Inter-Allied Reparations Agency, Brussels, 1946; Controller, Import Licensing Dept, 1949; Distribution of Industry Div., BoT, 1954; Industries and Manufactures Div., 1957; Commercial Relations and Exports Div., 1960; Under-Sec., 1963; Tariff Div., 1965. *Publications:* articles in bridge magazines. *Recreations:* reading, golf, bridge, travel. *Address:* 12 Garbrand Walk, Ewell Village, Epsom, Surrey. *T:* 081–394 1316. *Club:* Walton Heath Golf.

CARTER, Elliott (Cook), DrMus; composer; *b* New York City, 11 Dec. 1908; *m* 1939, Helen Frost-Jones; one *s*. *Educ:* Harvard Univ. (MA); Ecole Normale, Paris (DrMus). Professor of Greek and Maths, St John's Coll., Annapolis, 1940–42; Professor of Music: Columbia Univ., 1948–50; Yale Univ., 1960–61. *Compositions include:* First Symphony, 1942–43; Quartet for Four Saxophones, 1943; Holiday Overture, 1944; Ballet, The Minotaur, 1946–47; Woodwind Quintet, 1947; Sonata for Cello and Piano, 1948; First String Quartet, 1950–51; Sonata for Flute, Oboe, Cello and Harpsichord, 1952; Variations for Orchestra, 1953; Second String Quartet, 1960 (New York Critics' Circle Award; Pulitzer Prize; Unesco 1st Prize); Double Concerto for Harpsichord and Piano, 1961 (New York Critics' Circle Award); Piano Concerto, 1967; Concerto for Orchestra, 1970; Third String Quartet, 1971 (Pulitzer Prize); Duo for Violin and Piano, 1973–74; Brass Quintet, 1974; A Mirror on which to Dwell (song cycle), 1976; A Symphony of Three Orchestras, 1977; Syringa, 1979; Night Fantasies (for piano), 1980; In Sleep in Thunder, 1982; Triple Duo, 1983; Penthode, 1985; Fourth String Quartet, 1986; Oboe Concerto, 1988; Three Occasions for Orchestra, 1989. Member: Nat. Inst. of Arts and Letters, 1956 (Gold Medal for Music, 1971); Amer. Acad. of Arts and Sciences (Boston), 1962; Amer. Acad. of Arts and Letters, 1971; Akad. der Kunste, Berlin, 1971. Hon. degrees incl. MusD Cantab, 1983. Sibelius Medal (Harriet Cohen Foundation), London, 1961; Premio delle Muse, City of Florence, 1969; Handel Medallion, New York City, 1978; Mayor of Los Angeles declared Elliott Carter Day, 27 April 1979; Ernst Von Siemens Prize, Munich, 1981; Gold Medal, MacDowell Colony, 1983; National Medal of Arts, USA, 1985. *Publication:* The Writings of Elliott Carter, 1977; *relevant publication:* The Music of Elliott Carter, by David Schiff, 1983.

CARTER, Eric Bairstow, BSc(Eng); CEng, FIMechE, FRAeS, FIProdE; Consultant Engineer, 1972–78; *b* 26 Aug. 1912; *s* of John Bolton Carter and Edith Carter (*née* Bairstow); *m* 1st, 1934, Lily (*d* 1981), *d* of John Charles and Ethel May Roome (*née* Bates); one *d*; 2nd, 1981, Olive Hicks Wright, *d* of Major William George and Olive Theresa Groombridge (*née* Hicks). *Educ:* Halifax Technical Coll. Staff appt, Halifax Tech. Coll., 1932; Supt and Lectr, Constantine Technical Coll., Middlesbrough, 1936; apptd to Air Min. (Engine Directorate), Sept. 1939; subseq. Air Min. appts to engine firms and at HQ. Asst Dir (Research and Develt, Ramjets and Liquid Propellant Rockets), Dec. 1955; Dir (Engine Prod.), 1960; Dir (Engine R&D), 1963; Dir-Gen. (Engine R&D), Min. of Technology, later MoD (Aviation Supply), 1969–72. Chm., Gas Turbine Collaborative Cttee, 1969–70. *Address:* 15 Colyford Road, Seaton, Devon EX12 2DP.

CARTER, Eric Stephen, CBE 1986; Convener, Standing Conference on Countryside Sports, since 1988; *b* 23 June 1923; *s* of Albert Harry Carter, MBE and Doris Margaret (*née* Mann); *m* 1948, Audrey Windsor; one *s*. *Educ:* Grammar Sch., Lydney; Reading Univ. BSc (Agric) 1945. Techn. Officer, Gloucester AEC, 1945–46; Asst District Officer, Gloucester NAAS, 1946–49, Dist Off. 1949–57; Sen. Dist Off., Lindsey (Lincs) NAAS, 1957–63, County Agric. Off. 1963–69; Yorks and Lancs Region: Dep. Regional Dir, NAAS, 1969–71; Regional Agric. Off., ADAS, 1971–73; Regional Off. (ADAS), 1973–74; Chief Regional Off., MAFF, 1974–75; Dep. Dir-Gen., Agricl Develt and Advisory Service, 1975–81; Adviser, Farming and Wildlife Trust, 1981–88. Member: Nuffield Farming Scholarships Trust Selection Cttee, 1981–; Adv. Cttee, Welsh Plant Breeding Station, 1987–; Governing Body, AFRC Inst. for Grassland and Envmtl Res., 1989–. FIBiol 1974, CBiol 1974; FRAgS 1985; Hon. FRASE 1988. Editor, Jl of Royal Agricl Soc. of England, 1985–. *Publications:* (with M. H. R. Soper) Modern Farming and the Countryside, 1985; (with M. H. R. Soper) Farming the Countryside, 1991; contrib. agric. and techn. jls. *Recreations:* gardening, reading, music, countryside. *Address:* 15 Farrs Lane, East Hyde, Luton, Beds LU2 9PY. *T:* Harpenden (0582) 760504. *Club:* Farmers'.

CARTER, Francis Jackson, CMG 1954; CVO 1963; CBE 1946; Under-Secretary of State of Tasmania and Clerk of Executive Council, 1953–64; also permanent head of Premier's and Chief Secretary's Department; *b* Fremantle, W Australia, 9 Sept. 1899; *s* of late Francis Henry Carter, formerly of Bendigo, Victoria; *m* 1926, Margaret Flora, *d* of late William Thomas Walker, Launceston; two *s* one *d*. *Educ:* Hobart High Sch.; Univ. of Tasmania. Entered Tasmanian Public Service, 1916; transferred to Hydro-Electric Dept, 1925; Asst Secretary, Hydro-Electric Commn, 1934; Secretary to Premier, 1935–39; Dep. Under-Secretary of State, 1939–53; served War of 1939–45 as State Liaison Officer to Commonwealth Dept of Home Security; Official Secretary for Tasmania in London, 1949–50; State Director for Royal Visits, 1954, 1958, 1963, and Thai Royal Visit, 1962. Executive Member, State Economic Planning Authority, 1944–55; Chairman, Fire Brigades Commn of Tasmania, 1945–70. Grand Master GL of Tasmania, 1956–59. FCIS, FCIM. JP 1939. *Recreations:* music, golf and lawn bowls. *Address:* 568 Churchill Avenue, Sandy Bay, Hobart, Tasmania 7005. *T:* Hobart 252 382. *Clubs:* Royal Automobile of Tasmania, Masonic (Hobart).

CARTER, Frank Ernest Lovell, CBE 1956 (OBE 1949); FSA; Director General of the Overseas Audit Service, 1963–71; *b* 6 Oct. 1909; *s* of Ernest and Florence Carter; *m* 1966,

Gerda (*née* Gruen) (*d* 1981). *Educ:* Chigwell Sch.; Hertford Coll., Oxford. Served in Overseas Audit Service in: Nigeria, 1933–42; Sierra Leone, 1943; Palestine, 1944–45; Aden and Somaliland, 1946–49; Tanganyika, 1950–54; Hong Kong, 1955–59; Deputy Director in London, 1960–62. Part-time Adviser: FCO, 1972–76; ODM, 1977–81. FSA 1983. *Address:* 8 The Leys, N2 0HE. *T:* 081–458 4684. *Club:* East India.

CARTER, Frederick Brian; QC 1980; **His Honour Judge Carter;** a Circuit Judge, since 1985; *b* 11 May 1933; *s* of late Arthur and Minnie Carter; *m* 1960, Elizabeth Hughes, JP, *d* of late W. B. Hughes and of Mrs B. M. Hughes; one *s* three *d* (and one *s* decd). *Educ:* Stretford Grammar Sch.; King's Coll., London (LLB). Called to Bar, Gray's Inn, 1955, practised Northern Circuit, 1957–85; Prosecuting Counsel for Inland Revenue, Northern Circuit, 1973–80; a Recorder, 1978–85. *Recreations:* golf, travel. *Address:* 23 Lynton Park Road, Cheadle Hulme, Cheadle, Cheshire SK8 6JA. *Clubs:* Big Four (Manchester); Chorlton-cum-Hardy Golf.

CARTER, His Eminence G(erald) Emmett, Cardinal; CC 1983; Archbishop Emeritus of Toronto (Archbishop, 1978–90); *b* Montreal, Quebec, 1 March 1912; *s* of Thomas Carter and Mary Kelty. *Educ:* Univ. of Montreal (BA, MA, PhD); Grand Seminary of Montreal (STL). Founder, Director and Teacher at St Joseph's Teachers' Coll., Montreal, 1939–61; Auxiliary Bishop of London, Ont., 1961; Bishop of London, 1964. Cardinal, 1979. Chairman, Internat. Cttee for English in the Liturgy, 1971; President, Canadian Catholic Conf. of Bishops, 1975–77. Elected Member, Permanent Council of the Synod of Bishops in Rome, 1977. Hon. LLD: Univ. of W Ontario, 1964; Concordia Univ., 1976; Univ. of Windsor, 1977; McGill Univ., Montreal, 1980; Notre Dame Univ., 1981; Hon. DD, Huron Coll., Univ. of W Ont., 1978; Hon. DHL, Duquesne Univ., Pittsburg, 1965; Hon. DLitt, St Mary's Univ., Halifax, 1980. *Publications:* The Catholic Public Schools of Quebec, 1957; Psychology and the Cross, 1959; The Modern Challenge, 1961. *Recreations:* tennis, skiing. *Address:* Chancery Office, 355 Church Street, Toronto, Ontario M5B 1Z8, Canada. *T:* 416/977–1500.

CARTER, Godfrey James, CBE 1984; Parliamentary Counsel, 1972–79; *b* 1 June 1919; *s* of Captain James Shuckburgh Carter, Grenadier Guards (killed in action, 1918), and Diana Violet Gladys Carter (*née* Cavendish); *m* 1946, Cynthia, *e d* of Eric Strickland Mason; three *s*. *Educ:* Eton (KS); Magdalene Coll., Cambridge. BA 1945, LLM 1946. War Service (Rifle Bde), Middle East, 1940–43 (twice wounded). Called to Bar, Inner Temple, 1946; Asst Parly Counsel, 1949–56; commercial dept, Bristol Aeroplane Co. Ltd, and Bristol Siddeley Engines Ltd, 1956–64; re-joined Parly Counsel Office, 1964; Dep. Counsel, 1970. *Address:* Old Bournstream House, Wotton-under-Edge, Glos. *T:* Dursley (0453) 843246. *Clubs:* Travellers'; Wotton-under-Edge Probus.

CARTER, James Earl, Jr, (Jimmy); President of the United States of America, 1977–81; *b* Plains, Georgia, USA, 1 Oct. 1924; *s* of late James Earl Carter and Lillian (*née* Gordy); *m* 1946, Rosalynn Smith; three *s* one *d*. *Educ:* Plains High Sch.; Georgia Southwestern Coll.; Georgia Inst. of Technology; US Naval Acad. (BS); Union Coll., Schenectady, NY (post grad.). Served in US Navy submarines and battleships, 1946–53; Ensign (commissioned, 1947); Lieut (JG) 1950, (SG) 1952; retd from US Navy, 1953. Became farmer and warehouseman, 1953, farming peanuts at Plains, Georgia, until 1977. Member: Sumter Co. (Ga) School Bd, 1955–62 (Chm. 1960–62); Americus and Sumter Co. Hosp. Authority, 1956–70; Sumter Co. (Ga) Library Bd, 1961; President: Plains Develt Corp., 1963; Georgia Planning Assoc., 1968; Chm., W Central Georgia Area Planning and Develt Commn, 1964; Dir, Georgia Crop Improvement Assoc., 1957–63 (Pres., 1961). State Chm., March of Dimes, 1968–70; Dist Governor, Lions Club, 1968–69. State Senator (Democrat), Georgia, 1963–67; Governor of Georgia, 1971–75. Chm., Congressional Campaign Cttee, Democratic Nat. Cttee, 1974; Democratic Candidate for the Presidency of the USA, 1976. Founder, Carter Center, Emory Univ, 1982. Mem., Bd of Dirs, Habitat for Humanity, 1984–87; Chairman, Board of Trustees: Carter Center, Inc., 1986–; Carter-Menil Human Rights Foundn, 1986–; Global 2000 Inc., 1986–; Chairman: Council of Freely-Elected Heads of Government, 1986–; Council of Internat. Negotiation Network, 1991–. Distinguished Prof., Emory Univ., 1982–. Baptist. Hon. LLD: Morehouse Coll., and Morris Brown Coll., 1972; Notre Dame, 1977; Emory Univ., 1979; Kwansei Gakuim Univ., Japan, and Georgia Southwestern Coll., 1981; New York Law Sch., and Bates Coll., 1985; Centre Coll., and Creighton Univ., 1987; Hon. DE Georgia Inst. Tech., 1979; Hon. PhD: Weizmann Inst. of Science, 1980; Tel Aviv Univ., 1983; Haifa Univ., 1987; Hon. DHL Central; Connecticut State Univ., 1985. Awards include: Gold Medal, Internat. Inst. for Human Rights, 1979; Internat. Mediation Medal, American Arbitration Assoc., 1979; Harry S. Truman Public Service Award, 1981; Ansel Adams Conservation Award, Wilderness Soc., 1982; Distinguished Service Award, Southern Baptist Convention, 1982; Human Rights Award, Internat. League for Human Rights, 1983; Albert Schweitzer Prize for Humanitarianism, 1987; Jefferson Award, Amer. Inst. of Public Service, 1990. *Publications:* Why Not the Best?, 1975; A Government as Good as its People, 1977; Keeping Faith: memoirs of a President, 1982; The Blood of Abraham, 1985; (with Rosalynn Carter) Everything to Gain: making the most of the rest of your life, 1987; An Outdoor Journal, 1988. *Address:* (office) The Carter Center, One Copenhill, Atlanta, Georgia 30307, USA.

CARTER, Maj.-Gen. James Norman, CB 1958; CBE 1955 (OBE 1946). *Educ:* Charterhouse; RMC Sandhurst. Commissioned The Dorset Regt, 1926; Captain, The Royal Warwickshire Regt, 1936; Lieut-Colonel, 1948; Colonel, 1950; Brigadier, 1954; Maj.-General, 1957. Asst Chief of Staff, Organisation and Training Div., SHAPE, 1955–57; Commander British Army Staff, British Joint Services Mission, Washington, 1958–60; Military Attaché, Washington, Jan.-July 1960; General Secretary, The Officers' Assoc., 1961–63.

CARTER, Jane; *see* Carter, D. E. F.

CARTER, Sir John, Kt 1966; QC (Guyana) 1962; Guyana Diplomatic Service, retired; *b* 27 Jan. 1919; *s* of Kemp R. Carter; *m* 1959, Sara Lou (formerly Harris); two *s* three *d*. *Educ:* University of London and Middle Temple, England. Called to English Bar, 1942; admitted to Guyana (late British Guiana) Bar, 1945; Member of Legislature of Guyana, 1948–53 and 1961–64; Pro-Chancellor, Univ. of Guyana, 1962–66; Ambassador of Guyana to US, 1966–70; High Comr for Guyana in UK, 1970–76; Ambassador to China and Korea, 1976–81 and to Japan, 1979–81; High Comr to Jamaica, 1981–83. *Recreations:* cricket, swimming. *Address:* 3603 East West Highway, Chevy Chase, Maryland 20815, USA. *Clubs:* MCC; Georgetown (Guyana).

CARTER, Sir John (Alexander), Kt 1989; Chairman, Stock Land & Estates Ltd, since 1987; *b* 2 Nov. 1921; *s* of Allan Randolph Carter and Beatrice Alice Carter; *m* 1954; two *d*. *Educ:* Duke of York's Royal Military Sch., Dover, Kent. Served Territorial Army, 1939–45: Warwicks Yeo., RA and Loyal N Lancs Regt. Founder Chm., Carter Holdings PLC, 1964–89. Co-opted Mem., Conservative Central Bd of Finance, 1983–87; Conservative Party, East of England: Chm., Industrial Council, 1983–87; Chm., Property Adv. Bd, 1986–87. CStJ 1990; Chm. Council, Order of St John for Essex, 1988–. *Recreations:* golf, swimming, reading. *Address:* Cobblers, Mill Road, Stock, near Ingatestone, Essex CM4 9RG. *T:* Stock (0277) 840580. *Clubs:* Carlton, St Stephen's Constitutional, Institute of Directors.

CARTER, Dr (John) Timothy, FRCP, FFOM; Director of Medical Services, since 1983 and of Health Policy, since 1989, Health and Safety Executive; *b* 12 Feb. 1944; *s* of Reginald John Carter and Linda Mary (*née* Briggs); *m* 1967, Judith Ann Lintott; one *s* two *d*. *Educ:* Dulwich Coll.; Corpus Christi Coll., Cambridge (MB, MA); University Coll. Hosp., London. FFOM 1984; FRCP 1987. London Sch. of Hygiene, 1972–74 (MSc). MO, British Petroleum, 1974–78; SMO, BP Chemicals, 1978–83. Member: MRC, 1983–; Bd, Faculty of Occupnl Medicine, 1982–88; Hon. Sec., Occupnl Medicine Section, RSM, 1979–83; Pres., British Occupnl Hygiene Soc., 1987–88. *Publications:* articles on investigation and control of occupnl health hazards and med. history. *Recreation:* history—natural, medical and local. *Address:* 41 Clarence Road, St Albans, Herts AL1 4NP.

CARTER, Peers Lee, CMG 1965; HM Diplomatic Service, retired; Member since 1984, Chairman since 1989, and Trustee, Afghanaid; *b* 5 Dec. 1916; *s* of Peers Owen Carter; *m* 1940, Joan Eleanor Lovegrove; one *s*. *Educ:* Radley; Christ Church, Oxford. Entered HM Foreign Service, 1939. Joined the Army in 1940; served in Africa (with Gen. Leclerc) and Europe (SOE). HM Embassy, Baghdad, 1945; First Secretary, Commissioner-General's Office, Singapore, 1951; Counsellor HM Embassy, Washington, 1958; (Temp. duty) UK Delegation to UN, New York, 1961; Head of UK Permanent Mission, Geneva, 1961; Inspector of Foreign Service Establishments, 1963–66; Chief Inspector of HM Diplomatic Service, 1966–68; Ambassador to Afghanistan, 1968–72; Ministerial Interpreter and Asst Under-Sec. of State, FCO, 1973–76. Dir, Afghanistan Support Cttee, 1981–84; Member: Bureau Internat. Afghanistan, Paris, 1985–; Internat. Assoc. of Conference Interpreters, 1976–87. Sardar-e A'ala, Afghanistan, 1971. *Recreations:* mountain walking, photography. *Address:* Dean Land Shaw, by Jobes, Balcombe, Sussex RH17 6HZ. *T:* Balcombe (0444) 811205. *Clubs:* Special Forces, Travellers'.

CARTER, Peter Basil; QC 1990; Emeritus Fellow, Wadham College, Oxford, since 1988 (Fellow, 1949–88); *b* 10 April 1921; *s* of Albert George Carter and Amy Kathleen FitzGerald (*née* Arthur); *m* 1st, 1960, Elizabeth Maxwell (*née* Ely) (decd); 2nd, 1982, Lorna Jean (*née* Sinclair). *Educ:* Loughborough GS; Oriel Coll., Oxford (BA 1st Cl. Hons Jurisprudence; BCL 1st Cl. Hons; Vinerian Scholar, 1949; MA). War Service, RAC, 1941–46 (Croix de Guerre, 1944). Called to the Bar, Middle Temple, 1947; Hon. Bencher, 1981. Curator, Bodleian Library, Oxford, 1963–88; Sen. Bursar, Wadham Coll., Oxford, 1965–77. Inns of Court School of Law: Lectr in Conflict of Laws, 1960–89; Lectr in Evidence, 1971–; Hon. Reader, 1985–. Visiting Professor of Law: Univ. of Melbourne, 1953; Univ. of Florida, 1955; New York Univ., 1961 and 1969; Osgoode Hall Law Sch., Ont, 1971, 1973, 1978 and 1982; Walter S. Owen Prof., Univ. of British Columbia, 1986; Canada Commonwealth Vis. Fellow, Faculty of Law, Univ. of Toronto, 1970; delivered Gen. Course of Lectures on Private Internat. Law, The Hague Acad. of Internat. Law, 1981. Rapporteur, Cttee on Transnational Recognition and Enforcement of Foreign Public Laws, Internat. Law Assoc., 1984–88. Gen. Comr for Income Tax Appeals, E Oxfordshire, 1965– (Chm., 1991–). Dir (non-exec.), University Life Assurance Soc., 1969– (Chm., 1980–). FInstD 1984. JP Oxon, 1959–88. Jt Editor, International and Comparative Law Qly, 1961–. *Publications:* Essays on the Law of Evidence (with Sir Zelman Cowen), 1956; Cases and Statutes on Evidence, 1981, 2nd edn 1990; articles, mostly on private internat. law or law of evidence, in British Yearbook of Internat. Law, Internat. and Comparative Law Qly, Law Qly Rev., Cambridge Law Jl, Modern Law Rev., etc. *Recreation:* appreciating architecture. *Address:* Wadham College, Oxford OX1 3PN. *T:* Oxford (0865) 277900; Fountain Court, Temple, EC4Y 9DH. *T:* 071–583 3335. *Club:* United Oxford & Cambridge University.

CARTER, Sir Philip David, Kt 1991; CBE 1982; Managing Director, Littlewoods Organisation, 1976–83; Chairman, Merseyside Tourism Board, since 1986; *b* 8 May 1927; *s* of Percival Carter and Isobell (*née* Stirrup); *m* 1946, Harriet Rita (*née* Evans); one *s* two *d*. *Educ:* Waterloo Grammar Sch., Liverpool. Volunteered for Fleet Air Arm, 1945. Professional career in Littlewoods Organisation, 1948–83. Chm., Mail Order Traders Assoc. of GB, 1979–83; Pres., European Mail Order Traders Assoc., 1983; Chm., Man Made Fibres Sector Wkg Party, 1980–; Member: Jt Textile Cttee, NEDO, 1979–; Distributive Trades EDC, 1980–; Merseyside Develt Corp., 1981–91 (Chm., 1987–91); Merseyside Residuary Body, 1986–. Vice-Chm., 1980–86, Chm., 1986–, Empire Theatre Trust, Liverpool. Chm., Liverpool Conservative Assoc., 1985–. Chm., Everton FC, 1978–91; Pres., Football League, 1986–88. *Recreations:* football, squash, music, theatre. *Address:* Oak Cottage, Noctorum Road, Noctorum, Wirral, Merseyside L43 9UQ. *T:* 051–652 4053.

CARTER, Raymond John, CBE 1991; Executive, since 1980, Director, since 1983, Marathon Oil Co.; *b* 17 Sept. 1935; *s* of John Carter; *m* 1959, Jeanette Hills; one *s* two *d*. *Educ:* Mortlake Co. Secondary Sch.; Reading Technical Coll.; Staffordshire Coll. of Technology. National Service, Army, 1953–55. Sperry Gyroscope Co.: Technical Asst, Research and Development Computer Studies, 1956–65. Electrical Engineer, Central Electricity Generating Bd, 1965–70, Mem., CEGB Management, 1979–80. Mem., Gen. Adv. Council, BBC, 1974–76. Mem. Easthampstead RDC, 1963–68. Contested: Wokingham, Gen. Elec., 1966; Warwick and Leamington, By-elec., March 1968; MP (Lab) Birmingham, Northfield, 1970–79; Parly Under-Sec. of State, Northern Ireland Office, 1976–79. Member: Public Accounts Cttee, 1973–74; Parly Science and Technology Cttee, 1974–76; Interim Adv. Cttee (Teachers' Pay and Conditions), DES, 1987–; author of Congenital Disabilities (Civil Liability) Act, 1976. Delegate: Council of Europe, 1974–76; WEU, 1974–76. Trustee, BM (Nat. Hist.), 1986–. Co-cataloguer and exhibitor, works of Sir John Betjeman, 1983. *Recreations:* running, reading, book collecting. *Address:* 1 Lynwood Chase, Warfield Road, Bracknell, Berkshire RG12 2JT. *T:* Bracknell (0344) 420237.

CARTER, Air Commodore Robert Alfred Copsey, CB 1956; DSO 1942; DFC 1943; Royal Air Force, retired; *b* 15 Sept. 1910; *s* of S. H. Carter and S. Copsey; *m* 1947, Sally Ann Peters, Va, USA; two *s* one *d*. *Educ:* Portsmouth Grammar Sch.; RAF Coll., Cranwell. Cranwell Cadet, 1930–32; commissioned in RAF, 1932; served in India, 1933–36; grad. RAF School of Aeronautical Engineering, 1938; served in Bomber Command, 1940–45; commanded 103 and 150 Sqdns; Station Comdr, RAF, Grimsby; grad. RAF Staff Coll., 1945; attended US Armed Forces Staff Coll., Norfolk, Va, USA, 1947; attached to RNZAF, 1950–53; comd. RAF Station, Upwood, 1953–55; SASO, RAF Transport Command, 1956–58; Director of Personal Services, Air Ministry, 1958–61; AO i/c Admin, HQ, RAF Germany, 1961–64; retired 1964. MRAeS 1960; CEng, 1966. *Club:* Royal Air Force.

CARTER, Robert William Bernard, CMG 1964; HM Diplomatic Service, retired; *b* 1913; 3rd *s* of late William Joseph Carter and late Lucy (*née* How); *m* 1945, Joan Violet, *o d* of Theodore and Violet Magnus; one *s* two *d* (and one *d* decd). *Educ:* St Bees Sch., Cumberland; Trinity Coll., Oxford (Scholar). Asst Master, Glenalmond, Perthshire, 1936. Served with the Royal Navy, 1940–46; Lieut, RNVR. Administrative Assistant, Newcastle upon Tyne Education Cttee, 1946; Principal, Board of Trade, 1949; Trade Commissioner:

Calcutta, 1952; Delhi, 1955; Accra, 1956; Principal Trade Commissioner, Colombo (Assistant Secretary), 1959; Senior British Trade Commissioner in Pakistan, 1961; Minister (Commercial), Pakistan, and Dep. High Comr, Karachi, 1967–68; Dep. High Comr, 1969–73 and Consul-Gen., 1973, Melbourne. *Recreations:* reading, travelling, collecting beer-mugs. *Address:* The Old Parsonage, Heywood, Westbury, Wilts BA13 4NB. *T:* Westbury (0373) 822194. *Club:* Oriental.

CARTER, Roland; retired; Visiting Fellow, Institute for Research in the Social Sciences, York University, since 1990; *b* 29 Aug. 1924; *s* of Ralph Carter; *m* 1950, Elisabeth Mary Green; one *s* two *d.* *Educ:* Cockburn High Sch., Leeds; Leeds Univ. Served War of 1939–45: Queen's Royal Regt, 1944; 6th Gurkha Rifles, 1945; Frontier Corps (South Waziristan and Gilgit Scouts), 1946. Seconded to Indian Political Service, as Asst Political Agent, Chilas, Gilgit Agency, 1946–47; Lectr, Zurich Univ. and Finnish Sch. of Economics, 1950–53. Joined Foreign Service, 1953: FO, 1953–54; Third Sec., Moscow, 1955; Germany, 1956–58; Second Sec., Helsinki, 1959 (First Sec., 1962); FO, 1962–67; Kuala Lumpur, 1967–69; Ambassador to People's Republic of Mongolia, 1969–71; seconded to Cabinet Office, 1971–74; Counsellor: Pretoria, 1974–77; FCO, 1977–80, retired. Area Appeals Manager, N and NE England, Nat. Soc. for Cancer Relief, 1981–89. *Publication:* Näin Puhutaan Englantia (in Finnish; with Erik Erämetsä), 1952. *Recreations:* music, linguistics, Indian studies. *Address:* Post Cottage, Langton, Malton, N Yorks YO17 9QP.

CARTER, (Ronald) David, CBE 1980; RDI 1975; Chairman, DCA Design International Ltd; *b* 30 Dec. 1927; *s* of H. Miles Carter and Margaret Carter; *m* 1953, Theo (Marjorie Elizabeth), *d* of Rev. L. T. Towers; two *s* two *d.* *Educ:* Wyggeston Sch., Leicester; Central Sch. of Art and Design, London. Served RN, 1946–48. Appts in industry, 1951–60; Principal, David Carter Associates, 1960–75. Visiting Lectr, Birmingham Coll. of Industrial Design, 1960–65. Examnr, RCA, 1976–79 and 1987–90. Mem., Design Council, 1972–84 (Dep. Chm., 1975–84; Chm., Report on Industrial Design Educn in UK, 1977). Pres., Soc. of Industrial Artists and Designers, 1974–75; Mem., Art and Design Cttee, CNAA, 1975–77; Chm., DATEC, 1977–82; Mem., Nat. Adv. Body, Higher Educn Art and Design Working Party, 1982–84; Royal Fine Arts Comr, 1986–. Chm., Design Mus. (formerly Conran Foundn), 1986– (Trustee, 1981–); Moderator, Hong Kong Polytechnic, 1981–86; Mem., Prince of Wales Award for Indust. Innovation, 1981–85. Governor, London Inst., 1988–. Design Awards, 1961, 1969, 1983; Duke of Edinburgh Prize for Elegant Design, 1967. FSIA 1967; FRSA 1975. *Recreations:* making coarse soup, galloping, County Cork. *Address:* 43 Beauchamp Avenue, Leamington Spa, Warwickshire. *T:* Leamington Spa (0926) 424864. *Club:* Reform.

CARTER, Ronald Louis, DesRCA; RDI 1971; FCSD (FSIAD 1961); private consultancy design practice, since 1974; *b* 3 June 1926; *s* of Harry Victor Carter and Ruth Allensen; *m* 1st (marr. diss.); three *d*; 2nd, 1985, Ann McNab; one step *s* two step *d.* *Educ:* Birmingham Central College of Art: studied Industrial and Interior Design (NDD; Louisa Anne Ryland Schol. for Silver Design), 1946–49; Royal College of Art: studied Furniture Design (1st Cl. Dip.; Silver Medal for work of special distinction; Travelling Schol. to USA), 1949–52; DesRCA; Fellow, RCA, 1966; Hon. Fellow, 1974. Staff Designer with Corning Glass, 5th Avenue, NY City, 1952–53; freelance design practice, Birmingham and London, 1954; Tutor, School of Furniture, RCA, 1956–74; Partner: Design Partners, 1960–68; Carter Freeman Associates, 1968–74; Dir, Miles-Carter, 1980–. *Recreations:* fishing, fly designing. *Address:* 35 Great Queen Street, WC2B 5AA. *T:* 071–242 2291.

CARTER, Timothy; *see* Carter, J. T.

CARTER, Air Vice-Marshal Wilfred, CB 1963; DFC 1943; international disaster consultant; *b* 5 Nov. 1912; *s* of late Samuel Carter; *m* 1950, Margaret Enid Bray; one *d* (one *s* decd). Educ: Witney Grammar Sch. RAF, 1929. Served War of 1939–45 with Bomber Command in UK and Middle East. Graduate, Middle East Centre for Arab Studies, 1945–46. Air Adviser to Lebanon, 1950–53; with Cabinet Secretariat, 1954–55; OC, RAF, Ternhill, 1956–58; Sen. RAF Dir, and later Commandant, Jt Services Staff Coll.; Asst Chief of Staff, Cento, 1960–63; Asst Commandant, RAF Staff Coll., 1963–65; AOA, HQ Bomber Command, 1965–67; Dir, Austr. Counter Disaster Coll., 1969–78. Gordon Shephard Memorial Prize (for Strategic Studies), 1955, 1956, 1957, 1961, 1965, 1967. Officer, Order of Cedar of Lebanon, 1953. *Publications:* Disaster Preparedness and Response, 1985; Disaster Management, 1991. *Recreations:* walking, swimming. *Address:* Blue Range, Macedon, Vic 3440, Australia.

CARTER, William Nicholas, (Will Carter), OBE 1984; Senior Partner, Rampant Lions Press, since 1967; *b* 24 Sept. 1912; *s* of Thomas Buchanan Carter and Margaret Theresa Stone; *m* 1939, Barbara Ruth Digby; one *s* three *d.* *Educ:* Sunningdale Sch.; Radley. Served War, RN, 1941–46: S Atlantic, Coastal Forces Eastern Med.; commnd 1943. Gen. career in printing, advertising, typography and inscriptional letter-carving; founded Rampant Lions Press, 1949. Artist-in-Residence, Dartmouth Coll., NH, USA, 1969. Member: Royal Mint Adv. Cttee, 1971–; Arch. Adv. Panel, Westminster Abbey, 1979–. Hon. Fellow, Magdalene Coll., Cambridge, 1977. Frederick W. Goudy Award, Rochester Inst. of Technol., New York State, 1975; Silver Jubilee Medal, 1977. *Publication:* (with Wilfrid Blunt) Italic Handwriting, 1954. *Address:* 12 Chesterton Road, Cambridge CB4 3AB. *T:* Cambridge (0223) 357553. *Club:* Double Crown (Pres., 1961).

CARTER, Sir William (Oscar), Kt 1972; Consultant, Daynes, Hill and Perks, Solicitors, Norwich; *b* 12 Jan. 1905; *s* of late Oscar Carter and Alice Carter; *m* 1934, Winifred Thompson. *Educ:* Swaffham Grammar Sch.; City of Norwich Sch. Admitted Solicitor of Supreme Court of Judicature, 1931. Served War, 1940–45, RAF (Wing Comdr), UK and Middle East. Mem. Council, The Law Society, 1954–75, Vice-Pres. 1970, Pres. 1971–72; President: East Anglian Law Soc., 1952–80; Norfolk and Norwich Incorporated Law Soc., 1959; Internat. Legal Aid Assoc., 1974–80; Life Mem. Council, Internat. Bar Assoc. (first Vice-Pres., 1976–78). Member: County Court Rules Cttee, 1956–60; Supreme Court Rules Cttee, 1960–75; Criminal Injuries Compensation Board, 1967–82 (Dep. Chm., 1977–82). Former Chm., Mental Health Review Tribunals for E Anglian and NE Thames RHA Areas. Upper Warden, 1984, Master, 1985–86, Worshipful Co. of Glaziers; Hon. Mem., The Fellows of American Bar Foundn. *Recreations:* swimming, walking, foreign travel. *Address:* 83 Newmarket Road, Norwich NR2 2HP. *T:* Norwich (0603) 53772. *Clubs:* Army and Navy; Norfolk (Norwich).

CARTER-JONES, Lewis; *b* Gilfach Goch, S Wales, 17 Nov. 1920; *s* of Tom Jones, Kenfig Hill, Bridgend, Glam.; *m* 1945, Patricia Hylda, *d* of late Alfred Bastiman, Scarborough, Yorks; two *d.* *Educ:* Bridgend County Sch.; University Coll. of Wales, Aberystwyth (BA; Chm. Student Finance Cttee; Capt, Coll., Univ. and County Hockey XI). Served War of 1939–45 (Flight Sergeant Navigator, RAF). Head of Business Studies, Yale Grammar Technical Sch., Wrexham, 1950–64. Contested (Lab) Chester, by-election, 1956, and general election, 1959. MP (Lab) Eccles, 1964–87. Chairman: Cttee for Research for Apparatus for Disabled, 1973–80; Anglo-Columbian Gp, 1975–87; PLP Disablement Gp, 1975–81; PLP Aviation Gp, 1978–87. Exec. Mem., UK Br., CPA, 1983–87; Secretary: Indo-British Parly Gp, 1966–87; All-Party BLESMA Gp, 1973–87; All Party Aviation Gp, 1980–87. Hon. Parliamentary Adviser: RNIB, 1973–87; British Assoc. of Occupational Therapists; Soc. of Physiotherapists, until 1987. Mem., Gen. Adv. Council, IBA, 1982–87. Chm., British Cttee, Rehabilitation International, 1978–; Vice-President: Wales Council for the Disabled, 1981–; RADAR, 1987–; Member: Disablement Services Authority, 1987–; Disabled Persons Transport Adv. Cttee, Dept of Transport, 1988–; Trustee, Granada Telethon, 1987–. Dir, Possum Controls Ltd, 1974–. *Address:* Cader Idris, 5 Cefn Road, Rhosnesni, Wrexham, Clwyd LL13 9NF.

CARTER-RUCK, Peter Frederick; Senior Partner, Peter Carter-Ruck and Partners, Solicitors, since 1981 (Senior Partner, Oswald Hickson, Collier & Co., 1945–81); *b* 26 Feb. 1914; *s* of Frederick Henry Carter-Ruck and Nell Mabel Carter-Ruck; *m* 1940, Pamela Ann, *o d* of late Gp Capt. Reginald Stuart Maxwell, MC, DFC, AFC, RAF; one *d* (one *s* decd). *Educ:* St Edward's, Oxford; Law Society; Solicitor of the Supreme Court (Hons). Admitted Solicitor, 1937; served RA, 1939–44, Captain Instr in gunnery. Specialist Member, Council of Law Soc., 1971–84; Chairman: Law Soc. Law Reform Cttee, 1980–83; Media Cttee, Internat. Bar Assoc., 1983–85; Mem., Council of Justice (Internat. Commn of Jurists), 1968–; President: City of Westminster Law Soc., 1975–76 (Hon. Life Pres., 1988); Media Soc., 1981–82 and 1984–86. Governor, St Edward's Sch., Oxford, 1950–78; past Chm. and Founder Governor, Shiplake Coll., Henley; Mem. Livery, City of London Solicitors' Co., 1949–; Underwriting Mem. of Lloyd's. *Publications:* Libel and Slander, 1953, 3rd edn 1985; (with Ian Mackrill) The Cyclist and the Law, 1953; (with Edmund Skone James) Copyright: modern law and practice, 1965; Memoirs of a Libel Lawyer, 1990. *Address:* 75 Shoe Lane, EC4A 3BQ. *T:* 071–379 3456; Latchmore Cottage, Great Hallingbury, Bishop's Stortford, Herts. *T:* Bishop's Stortford (0279) 654357; Eilagadale, N Ardnamurchan, Argyll. *T:* Kilchoan (09723) 267. *Clubs:* Carlton, Garrick, Press; Royal Yacht Squadron, Lloyd's Yacht, Law Society Yacht (past Commodore), Royal Ocean Racing, Ocean Cruising (past Commodore).

CARTIER, Rudolph; Drama Producer, Television, since 1953; also Producer Television Operas, since 1956; *b* Vienna, Austria, 17 April 1908; *s* of Joseph Cartier; *m* 1949, Margaret Pepper; two *d.* *Educ:* Vienna Academy of Music and Dramatic Art (Max Reinhardt's Master-class). Film director and Scenario writer in pre-war Berlin; came to Britain, 1935; joined BBC Television. Productions include: Arrow to the Heart, Dybbuk, Portrait of Peter Perowne, 1952; It is Midnight, Doctor Schweitzer, L'Aiglon, The Quatermass Experiment, Wuthering Heights, 1953; Such Men are Dangerous, That Lady, Captain Banner, Nineteen-Eightyfour, 1954; Moment of Truth, The Creature, Vale of Shadows, Quatermass II, The Devil's General, 1955; The White Falcon, The Mayerling Affair, The Public Prosecutor, The Fugitive, The Cold Light, The Saint of Bleecker Street, Dark Victory, Clive of India, The Queen and the Rebels, 1956; Salome, Ordeal by Fire, Counsellor-at-Law, 1957; Captain of Koepenick, The Winslow Boy, A Tale of Two Cities, Midsummer Night's Dream, 1958; Quatermass and the Pit, Philadelphia Story, Mother Courage and her Children, (Verdi's) Othello, 1959; The White Guard, Glorious Morning, Tobias and the Angel (Opera), 1960; Rashomon, Adventure Story, Anna Karenina, Cross of Iron, 1961; Doctor Korczuk and the Children, Sword of Vengeance, Carmen, 1962; Anna Christie, Night Express, Stalingrad, 1963; Lady of the Camelias, The Midnight Men, The July Plot, 1964; Wings of the Dove, Ironhand, The Joel Brand Story, 1965; Gordon of Khartoum, Lee Oswald, Assassin, 1966; Firebrand, The Burning Bush, 1967; The Fanatics, Triumph of Death, The Naked Sun, The Rebel, 1968; Conversation at Night, An Ideal Husband, 1969; Rembrandt, The Bear (Opera), The Year of the Crow, 1970; The Proposal, 1971; Lady Windermere's Fan, 1972; The Deep Blue Sea, 1973; Fall of Eagles (episodes Dress Rehearsal, End Game), 1974; Loyalties, 1976; Gaslight, 1977. Prod. Film, Corridor of Mirrors. Directed Film, Passionate Summer. Guild of Television Producers and Directors "Oscar" as best drama producer of 1957. *Recreations:* motoring, serious music, going to films or watching television, stamp-collecting. *Address:* 26 Lowther Road, Barnes, SW13 9ND.

CARTIER-BRESSON, Henri; photographer; *b* France, 22 Aug. 1908. Studied painting with André Lhote, 1927–28. Asst Dir to Jean Renoir, 1936–39; Co-founder, Magnum Photos, 1947. Photographs exhibited: Mexico; Japan; Mus. of Modern Art, NY, 1947, 1968, 1987; Villa Medicis, Rome; Louvre, 1955, 1967, Grand Palais, 1970, Paris; V&A, 1969; Manege, Moscow, 1972; Edinburgh Festival, 1978; Hayward Gall., London, 1978; drawings exhibited: Carlton Gall., NY, 1975; Bischofberger Gall., Zürich, 1976; Forcalquier Gall., France, 1976; Mus. of Modern Art, Paris, 1981; Mus. of Modern Art, Mexico, 1982; French Inst., Stockholm, 1983; Pavilion of Contemporary Art, Milan, 1983; Mus. of Modern Art, Oxford, 1984; Palace Liechtenstein, Vienna, Salzburg, 1985; Herstand Gall., NY, 1987; drawings exhibited: Ecole des Beaux Arts, Paris, 1989; le Printemps Tokio, 1989; Fondation Gianadda, Switzerland, 1990; Villa Medici, Rome, 1990. Collection of 390 photographs at DeMenil Foundn, Houston, USA, V&A, Univ. of Fine Arts, Osaka, Japan, Bibliothèque Nationale, Paris. Documentary films: on hosps, Spanish Republic, 1937; (with J. Lemare) Le Retour, 1945; (with J. Boffety) Impressions of California, 1969; (with W. Dombrow) Southern Exposures, 1970. Mem., Amer. Acad. of Arts and Scis, 1974. Hon. DLitt Oxon, 1975. Awards: US Camera, 1948; Overseas Press Club of America, 1949; Amer. Soc. of Magazine Photography, 1953; Photography Soc. of America, 1958; Overseas Press Club, 1954 (for Russia), 1960 (for China), 1964 (for Cuba); German Photographic Soc.; Hasselblad, 1983; Novecento, Palermo, 1986; Japanese Photographic Soc., 1989. *Publications:* (ed) Images à la Sauvette (The Decisive Moment), 1952; Verve, 1952; The Europeans; Moscow, 1955; From One China to the Other, 1956; Photographs by Cartier-Bresson; Flagrants Délits (The World of Henri Cartier-Bresson, 1968); (with F. Nourrissier) Vive la France, 1970; Cartier-Bresson's France, 1971; (jtly) L'Homme et la Machine, 1972 (Man and Machine, 1969) for IBM; Faces of Asia, 1972; A Propos de l'URSS, 1973 (About Russia, 1974); Henri Cartier-Bresson Pocket Book, 1985; Henri Cartier-Bresson in India, 1988; Traits pour Traits (Line by Line, 1989) (drawings); L'Amérique Furtivement, 1991; *relevant publications:* Yves Bonnefoy, Henri Cartier-Bresson, Photographer, 1979; André P. de Mandiargues, Photoportrait, 1985. *Address:* c/o Magnum Photos, 5 impasse Piver, 75011 Paris, France, and Moreland Building, 25 Old Street, EC1V 9HL; c/o Helen Wright, 135 East 74th Street, New York, NY 10021, USA; c/o John Hillelson, Room 198 Temple Chambers, Temple Avenue, EC4Y 0DT.

CARTLAND, Dame Barbara (Hamilton), DBE 1991; authoress and playwright; *d* of late Major Bertram Cartland, Worcestershire Regiment; *m* 1st, 1927, Alexander George McCorquodale (whom she divorced, 1933; he *d* 1964), of Cound Hall, Cressage, Salop; one *d*; 2nd, 1936, Hugh (*d* 1963), 2nd *s* of late Harold McCorquodale, Forest Hall, Ongar, Essex; two *s*. Published first novel at the age of twenty-one, which ran into five editions; designed and organised many pageants in aid of charity, including Britain and her Industries at British Legion Ball, Albert Hall, 1930; carried the first aeroplane-towed glider-mail in her glider, the Barbara Cartland, from Manston Aerodrome to Reading, June 1931; 2 lecture tours in Canada, 1940; Hon. Junior Commander, ATS and Lady Welfare Officer and Librarian to all Services in Bedfordshire, 1941–49; Certificate of Merit, Eastern Command, 1946; County Cadet Officer for St John Ambulance Brigade in Beds, 1943–47, County Vice-Pres. Cadets, Beds, 1948–50; organised and produced the St John Ambulance Bde Exhibn, 1945–50; Chm., St John Ambulance Bde Exhibn Cttee, 1944–51; County Vice-Pres.: Nursing Cadets, Herts, 1951 (instigated a govt enquiry into the housing conditions of old people, 1955); Nursing Div., Herts, 1966; CC Herts (Hatfield Div.), 1955–64; Chm., St John Council, Herts, 1972–; Dep. Pres., St John Amb. Bde, Herts, 1978–; Pres., Herts Br. of Royal Coll. of Midwives, 1961. Had Law of England changed with regard to sites for gypsies so that their children can go to school; founded Cartland Onslow Romany Trust, with private site in Hatfield for family of Romany Gypsies. Founder and Pres., Nat. Assoc. for Health, 1964–. DStJ 1972 (Mem. Chapter Gen.). FRSA. Bishop Wright Air Industry Award for contrib. to aviation in 1931, Kennedy Airport, 1984; Médaille de Vermeil de la Ville de Paris (Gold Medal of City of Paris) for Achievement, for sales of 25 million books in France, 1988. Bestselling author in the world (Guinness Book of Records); broke world record for last 12 years, by writing an average of 23 books a year. *Publications: novels:* Jigsaw, 1923; Sawdust; If the Tree is Saved; For What?; Sweet Punishment; A Virgin in Mayfair; Just off Piccadilly; Not Love Alone; A Beggar Wished; Passionate Attainment; First Class, Lady?; Dangerous Experiment; Desperate Defiance; The Forgotten City; Saga at Forty; But Never Free; Bitter Winds of Love; Broken Barriers; The Gods Forget; The Black Panther; Stolen Halo; Now Rough-Now Smooth; Open Wings; The Leaping Flame; A Heart is Broken; Escape from Passion; The Dark Stream; Towards the Stars; Armour against Love; Out of Reach; The Hidden Heart; Against the Stream; Again this Rapture; The Dream Within; Where is Love?; No Heart is Free; Sleeping Swords; Love is Mine; The Passionate Pilgrim; Blue Heather; Wings on My Heart; The Kiss of Paris; Love Forbidden; Lights of Love; The Thief of Love; Theft of a Heart; The Sweet Enchantress; The Kiss of Silk; The Price is Love; The Runaway Heart; A Light to the Heart; Love is Dangerous; Danger by the Nile; Love on the Run; A Hazard of Hearts; A Duel of Hearts; A Knave of Hearts; The Enchanted Moment; The Little Pretender; A Ghost in Monte Carlo; Love is an Eagle; Love is the Enemy; Cupid Rides Pillion; Love Me Forever; Elizabethan Lover; Desire of the Heart; The Enchanted Waltz; The Kiss of the Devil; The Captive Heart; The Coin of Love; Stars in My Heart; Sweet Adventure; The Golden Gondola; Love in Hiding; The Smuggled Heart; Love under Fire; The Messenger of Love; The Wings of Love; The Hidden Evil; The Fire of Love; The Unpredictable Bride; Love Holds the Cards; A Virgin in Paris; Love to the Rescue; Love is Contraband; The Enchanting Evil; The Unknown Heart; The Secret Fear; The Reluctant Bride; The Pretty Horse-Breakers; The Audacious Adventuress; Halo for the Devil; The Irresistible Buck; Lost Enchantment; The Odious Duke; The Wicked Marquis; The Complacent Wife; The Little Adventure; The Daring Deception; No Darkness for Love; Lessons in Love; The Ruthless Rake; Journey to Paradise; Love is Innocent; The Mask of Love; A Sword to the Heart; The Karma of Love; The Magnificent Marriage; Bewitched; The Impetuous Duchess; The Shadow of Sin; The Tears of Love; The Devil in Love; The Frightened Bride; The Flame is Love; A Very Naughty Angel; Call of the Heart; As Eagles Fly; Say Yes, Samantha; An Arrow of Love; A Gamble with Hearts; A Kiss for the King; A Frame of Dreams; Fragrant Flowers; The Dangerous Dandy; The Bored Bridegroom; The Penniless Peer; The Cruel Count; The Castle of Fear; The Glittering Lights; Fire on the Snow; The Elusive Earl; Moon over Eden; The Golden Illusion; No Time for Love; The Husband Hunters; The Slaves of Love; Passions in the Sand; An Angel in Hell; The Wild Cry of Love; The Blue-Eyed Witch; The Incredible Honeymoon; A Dream from the Night; Conquered by Love; Never Laugh at Love; The Secret of the Glen; The Dream and the Glory; The Proud Princess; Hungry for Love; The Heart Triumphant; The Disgraceful Duke; The Taming of Lady Lorinda; Vote for Love; The Mysterious Maid-Servant; The Magic of Love; Kiss the Moonlight; Love Locked In; The Marquis who Hated Women; Rhapsody of Love; Look Listen and Love; Duel with Destiny; The Wild Unwilling Wife; Punishment of a Vixen; The Curse of the Clan; The Outrageous Lady; A Touch of Love; The Love Pirate; The Dragon and the Pearl; The Temptation of Torilla; The Passion and the Flower; Love, Lords and Ladybirds; Love and the Loathsome Leopard; The Naked Battle; The Hell-Cat and the King; No Escape From Love; A Sign of Love; The Castle Made for Love; The Saint and the Sinner; A Fugitive from Love; Love Leaves at Midnight; The Problems of Love; The Twists and Turns of Love; Magic or Mirage; The Ghost who Fell in Love; The Chieftain without a Heart; Lord Ravenscar's Revenge; A Runaway Star; A Princess in Distress; The Judgement of Love; Lovers in Paradise; The Race for Love; Flowers for the God of Love; The Irresistible Force; The Duke and the Preacher's Daughter; The Drums of Love; Alone in Paris; The Prince and the Pekinese; A Serpent of Satan, 1978; Love in the Clouds, 1978; The Treasure is Love, 1978; Imperial Splendour, 1978; Light of the Moon, 1978; The Prisoner of Love, 1978; Love in the Dark, 1978; The Duchess Disappeared, 1978; Love Climbs In, 1978; A Nightingale Sang, 1978; Terror in the Sun, 1978; Who can Deny Love?, 1978; Bride to the King, 1978; Only Love, 1979; The Dawn of Love, 1979; Love Has His Way, 1979; The Explosion of Love, 1979; Women Have Hearts, 1979; A Gentleman in Love, 1979; A Heart is Stolen, 1979; The Power and the Prince, 1979; Free From Fear, 1979; A Song of Love, 1979; Love for Sale, 1979; Little White Doves of Love, 1979; The Perfection of Love, 1979; Lost Laughter, 1979; Punished with Love, 1979; Lucifer and the Angel, 1979; Ola and the Sea Wolf, 1979; The Prude and the Prodigal, 1979; The Goddess and the Gaiety Girl, 1979; Signpost to Love, 1979; Money, Magic and Marriage, 1979; From Hell to Heaven, 1980; Pride and The Poor Princess, 1980; The Lioness and The Lily, 1980; A Kiss of Life, 1980; Love At The Helm, 1980; The Waltz of Hearts, 1980; Afraid, 1980; The Horizons of Love, 1980; Love in the Moon, 1980; Dollars for the Duke, 1981; Dreams Do Come True, 1981; Night of Gaiety, 1981; Count the Stars, 1981; Winged Magic, 1981; A Portrait of Love, 1981; River of Love, 1981; Gift of the Gods, 1981; The Heart of the Clan, 1981; An Innocent in Russia, 1981; A Shaft of Sunlight, 1981; Love Wins, 1981; Enchanted, 1981; Wings of Ecstasy, 1981; Pure and Untouched, 1981; In the Arms of Love, 1981; Touch a Star, 1981; For All Eternity, 1981; Secret Harbour, 1981; Looking for Love, 1981; The Vibration of Love, 1981; Lies for Love, 1981; Love Rules, 1981; Moments of Love, 1981; Lucky in Love, 1981; Poor Governess, 1981; Music from the Heart, 1981; Caught by Love, 1981; A King in Love, 1981; Winged Victory, 1981; The Call of the Highlands, 1981; Love and the Marquis, 1981; Kneel for Mercy, 1981; Riding to the Moon, 1981; Wish for Love, 1981; Mission to Monte Carlo, 1981; A Miracle in Music, 1981; A Marriage Made in Heaven, 1981; From Hate to Love, 1982; Light of the Gods, 1982; Love on the Wind, 1982; The Duke Comes Home, 1982; Journey to a Star, 1983; Love and Lucia, 1983; The Unwanted Wedding, 1983; Gypsy Magic, 1983; Help from the Heart, 1983; A Duke in Danger, 1983; Tempted to Love, 1983; Lights, Laughter and a Lady, 1983; The Unbreakable Spell, 1983; Diona and a Dalmatian, 1983; Fire in the Blood, 1983; The Scots Never Forget, 1983; A Rebel Princess, 1983; A Witch's Spell, 1983; Secrets, 1983; The Storms of Love, 1983; Moonlight on the Sphinx, 1983; White Lilac, 1983; Revenge of the Heart, 1983; Bride of a Brigand, 1983; Love Comes West, 1983; Theresa and a Tiger, 1983; An Island of Love, 1983; Love is Heaven, 1983; Miracle for a Madonna, 1984; A Very Unusual Wife, 1984; The Peril and the Prince, 1984; Alone and Afraid, 1984; Terror for a Teacher, 1984; Royal Punishment, 1984; The Devilish Deception, 1984; Paradise Found, 1984; Love is a Gamble, 1984; A Victory for Love, 1984; Look with Love, 1984; Never Forget Love, 1984; Helga in Hiding, 1984; Safe at Last, 1984; Haunted, 1984; Crowned with Love, 1984; Escape, 1984; The Devil Defeated, 1985; The Secret of the Mosque, 1985; A Dream in Spain, 1985; The Love Trap, 1985; Listen to Love, 1985; The Golden Cage, 1985; Love Casts Out Fear, 1985; A World of Love, 1985; Dancing on a Rainbow, 1985; Love Joins the Clans, 1985; An Angel Runs Away, 1985; Forced into Marriage, 1985; Bewildered in Berlin, 1985; Wanted—a Wedding Ring, 1985; Starlight Over Tunis, 1985; The Earl Escapes, 1985; The Love Puzzle, 1985; Love and Kisses, 1985; Sapphires in Siam, 1985; A Caretaker of Love, 1985; Secrets of the Heart, 1985; Riding to the Sky, 1986; Lovers in Lisbon, 1986; Love is Invincible, 1986; The Goddess of Love, 1986; An Adventure of Love, 1986; A Herb for Happiness, 1986; Only a Dream, 1986; Saved by Love, 1986; Little Tongues of Fire, 1986; A Chieftain Finds Love, 1986; The Lovely Liar, 1986; The Perfume of the Gods, 1986; A Knight in Paris, 1987; Revenge is Sweet, 1987; The Passionate Princess, 1987; Solita and the Spies, 1987; The Perfect Pearl, 1987; Love is a Maze, 1987; A Circus for Love, 1987; The Temple of Love, 1987; The Bargain Bride, 1987; The Haunted Heart, 1987; Real Love or Fake, 1987; A Kiss from a Stranger, 1987; A Very Special Love, 1987; A Necklace of Love, 1987; No Disguise for Love, 1987; A Revolution of Love, 1988; The Marquis Wins, 1988; Love is the Key, 1988; Free as the Wind, 1988; Desire in the Desert, 1988; A Heart in the Highlands, 1988; The Music of Love, 1988; The Wrong Duchess, 1988; The Taming of a Tigress, 1988; Love Comes to the Castle, 1988; The Magic of Paris, 1988; Stand and Deliver Your Heart, 1988; The Scent of Roses, 1988; Love at First Sight, 1988; The Secret Princess, 1988; Heaven in Hong Kong, 1988; Paradise in Penang, 1988; A Game of Love, 1988; The Sleeping Princess, 1988; A Wish Comes True, 1988; Loved for Himself, 1988; Two Hearts in Hungary, 1988; A Theatre of Love, 1988; A Dynasty of Love, 1988; Magic from the Heart, 1988; Windmill of Love, 1988; Love Strikes Satan, 1988; The Earl Rings a Belle, 1988; The Queen Saves the King, 1988; Love Lifts the Curse, 1988; Beauty or Brains, 1988; Too Precious to Lose, 1988; Hiding, 1988; A Tangled Web, 1988; Just Fate, 1988; A Miracle in Mexico, 1988; Warned by a Ghost, 1988; Terror from the Throne, 1988; The Cave of Love, 1988; The Peaks of Ecstasy, 1988; A Kiss in Rome, 1988; Hidden by Love, 1988; Walking to Wonderland, 1988; Lucky Logan Finds Love, 1988; Born of Love, 1988; The Angel and the Rake, 1988; The Queen of Hearts, 1988; The Wicked Widow, 1988; To Scotland and Love, 1988; Love and War, 1988; Love at the Ritz, 1989; The Dangerous Marriage, 1989; Good or Bad, 1989; This is Love, 1989; Seek the Stars, 1989; Escape to Love, 1989; Look with the Heart, 1989; Safe in Paradise, 1989; Love in the Ruins, 1989; A Coronation of Love, 1989; A Duel of Jewels, 1989; The Duke is Trapped, 1989; Just a Wonderful Dream, 1989; Love and The Cheetah, 1989; Drena and the Duke, 1989; A Dog, a Horse and a Heart, 1989; Never Lose Love, 1989; The Eyes of Love, 1989; The Duke's Dilemma, 1989; Saved by a Saint, 1989; Beyond the Stars, 1990; The Spirit of Love, 1991; *philosophy:* Touch the Stars; *sociology:* You in the Home; The Fascinating Forties; Marriage for Moderns; Be Vivid, Be Vital; Love, Life and Sex; Look Lovely, Be Lovely; Vitamins for Vitality; Husbands and Wives; Etiquette; The Many Facets of Love; Sex and the Teenager; Charm; Living Together; Woman the Enigma; The Youth Secret; The Magic of Honey; Health Food Cookery Book; Book of Beauty and Health; Men are Wonderful; The Magic of Honey Cookbook; Food for Love; Recipes for Lovers; The Romance of Food; Getting Older, Growing Younger; The Etiquette of Romance, 1985; *biography:* Ronald Cartland, 1942; Bewitching Women; The Outrageous Queen; Polly, My Wonderful Mother, 1956; The Scandalous Life of King Carol; The Private Life of Charles II; The Private Life of Elizabeth, Empress of Austria; Josephine, Empress of France; Diane de Poitiers; Metternich, the Passionate Diplomat; *historical:* A Year of Royal Days, 1988; Royal Jewels, 1989; Royal Lovers, 1989; Royal Eccentrics, 1989; *autobiography:* The Isthmus Years, 1943; The Years of Opportunity, 1947; I Search for Rainbows, 1967; We Danced All Night, 1919–1929, 1971; I Seek the Miraculous, 1978; *general:* Useless Information (foreword by Earl Mountbatten of Burma); Light of Love (prayers), 1978; Love and Lovers (pictures), 1978; Barbara Cartland's Book of Celebrities, 1982; Barbara Cartland's Scrapbook, 1980; Romantic Royal Marriages, 1981; Written with Love, 1981; *verse:* Lines on Love and Life; *plays:* Blood Money, 1925; French Dressing (with Bruce Woodhouse), 1943; *revue:* The Mayfair Revue; *radio play:* The Caged Bird; *television:* Portrait of Successful Woman, 1957; This is Your Life, 1958 and 1989; Success Story, 1959; Midland Profile, 1961; No Looking Back-a Portrait of Barbara Cartland, 1967; The Frost Programme, 1968; The Time of Your Life (programme about the first glider air mail, 1931), BBC1, 1985; *radio:* The World of Barbara Cartland, 1970, and many other radio and television appearances. Editor of the Common Problem, by Ronald Cartland, 1943. *Address:* Camfield Place, Hatfield, Herts. *T:* Potters Bar (0707) 42612, 42657.

See also Countess Spencer.

CARTLAND, Sir George (Barrington), Kt 1963; CMG 1956; BA; Vice-Chancellor of the University of Tasmania, 1968–77; Chairman, Australian National Accreditation Authority for Translators and Interpreters, 1977–83; *b* 22 Sept. 1912; *s* of William Arthur and Margaret Cartland, West Didsbury; *m* 1937, Dorothy Rayton; two *s*. *Educ:* Manchester Central High Sch.; Manchester Univ.; Hertford Coll., Oxford. Entered Colonial Service, Gold Coast, 1935; served Colonial Office, 1944–49; Head of African Studies Br. and Ed. Jl of Afr. Adminis., 1945–49; Sec. London Afr. Conf., 1948; Admin. Sec., Uganda, 1949; Sec. for Social Services and Local Govt, Uganda, 1952; Min. for Social Services, Uganda, 1955; Min. of Education and Labour, Uganda, 1958; Chief Sec., Uganda, 1960; Deputy Gov. of Uganda, 1961–62 (Acting Gov., various occasions, 1952–62); Registrar of Univ. of Birmingham, 1963–67. Part-time Mem., West Midlands Gas Bd, 1964–67. Member: Exec. Cttee, Inter Univ. Council for Higher Educn Overseas (UK), 1963–67; Commonwealth Scholarship Commn (UK), 1964–67. Dep. Chm., Australian Vice-Chancellors' Cttee, 1975 and 1977. Chairman: Adv. Cttee on National Park in SW Tasmania, 1976–78; Tasmanian Council of Australian Trade Union Trng Authority, 1979. Appointed to review: Library and Archives Legislation of Tasmania, 1978; Tasmanian Govt Admin, 1979. Mem., Australian Nat. Cttee of Hoover Awards for Marketing, 1968–82. Chm., St John Council, Uganda, 1958–59; Pres., St John Council, Tasmania, 1969–78. Member Council: Makerere Coll., 1952–60; Royal Tech. Coll., Nairobi, 1952–60; UC of Rhodesia, 1963–67; Univ. of S Pacific, 1972–76. FACE 1970. Hon. LLD Univ. of Tasmania, 1978. KStJ 1972; awarded Belgian Congo medal, 1960. *Publication:* (jtly) The Irish Cartlands and Cartland Genealogy, 1978. *Recreation:* fly fishing. *Address:* 5 Aotea Road, Sandy Bay, Hobart, Tasmania 7005. *Clubs:* Athenæum; Tasmanian, Royal Tasmanian Yacht (Hobart).

CARTLEDGE, Sir Bryan (George), KCMG 1985 (CMG 1980); Principal of Linacre College, Oxford, since 1988; *b* 10 June 1931; *s* of Eric Montague George Cartledge and Phyllis (*née* Shaw); *m* 1960, Ruth Hylton Gass, *d* of John Gass; one *s* one *d*. *Educ:* Hurstpierpoint; St John's Coll., Cambridge (Hon. Fellow, 1985). Queen's Royal Regt, 1950–51. Commonwealth Fund Fellow, Stanford Univ., 1956–57; Research Fellow, St Antony's Coll., Oxford, 1958–59 (Hon. Fellow, 1987). Entered HM Foreign (subseq. Diplomatic) Service, 1960; served in FO, 1960–61; Stockholm, 1961–63; Moscow, 1963–66; DSAO, 1966–68; Tehran, 1968–70; Harvard Univ., 1971–72; Counsellor, Moscow, 1972–75; Head of E European and Soviet Dept, FCO, 1975–77; Private Sec. (Overseas Affairs) to Prime Minister, 1977–79; Ambassador to Hungary, 1980–83; Asst Under-Sec. of State, FCO, 1983–84; Dep. Sec. of the Cabinet, 1984–85; Ambassador to the Soviet Union, 1985–88. *Address:* Linacre College, Oxford OX1 3JA. *Club:* United Oxford & Cambridge University.

CARTTISS, Michael Reginald Harry; MP (C) Great Yarmouth, since 1983; *b* Norwich, 11 March 1938; *s* of Reginald Carttiss and Doris Culling. *Educ:* Filby County Primary

Sch.; Great Yarmouth Tech. High Sch.; Goldsmiths' Coll., London Univ. (DipEd); LSE (part time, 1961–64). Nat. Service, RAF, 1956–58. Teacher: Orpington, Kent, and Waltham Cross, Herts, 1961–64; Oriel Grammar Sch., 1964–69; Cons. Party Agent, Gt Yarmouth, 1969–82. Member: Norfolk CC, 1966–85 (Vice-Chm., 1972, Chm., 1980–85, Educn Cttee); Gt Yarmouth BC, 1973–82 (Leader, 1980–82). Chm., Norfolk Museums Service, 1981–85; Mem., E Anglian RHA, 1981–85; Comr, Gt Yarmouth Port and Haven Commn, 1982–86. *Recreations:* reading, writing, talking, walking, theatre. *Address:* c/o House of Commons, SW1A 0AA; Main Road, Filby, Great Yarmouth, Norfolk NR29 3HN; (office) The Precinct, Market Gates, Great Yarmouth, Norfolk.

CARTWRIGHT, David Edgar, DSc; FRS 1984; Assistant Director, Institute of Oceanographic Sciences, Bidston Observatory, Birkenhead, 1973–86, retired; *b* 21 Oct. 1926; *s of* Edgar A. Cartwright and Lucienne Cartwright (*née* Tartanson); *m* 1952, Anne-Marie Guerin; two *s* two *d. Educ:* St John's Coll., Cambridge (BA); King's Coll., London (BSc, DSc). Dept of Naval Construction, Admiralty, Bath, 1951–54; Nat. Inst. of Oceanography (later Inst. of Oceanographic Sciences), Wormley, Surrey: Sci. Officer, rising to Individual Merit SPSO, 1954–73; Research Associate, Univ. of California, La Jolla, 1964–65; Sen. Res. Associate, NASA–Goddard Space Flight Center, Greenbelt, Md, 1987–89; Consultant, NASA, 1990–91. Mem., Royal Astronomical Soc., 1976–; Fellow, Amer. Geophysical Union, 1991–. *Publications:* over 90 papers on marine sci. research; reviews, etc, in various learned jls. *Recreations:* music, walking, travel. *Address:* 3 Borough House, Borough Road, Petersfield, Hants GU32 3LF. *T:* Petersfield (0730) 67195.

CARTWRIGHT, Rt. Rev. (Edward) David; *b* 15 July 1920; *o c of* John Edward Cartwright and Gertrude Cartwright (*née* Lusby), North Somercotes and Grimsby, Lincs; *m* 1946, Elsie Irene, *o c of* Walter and Jane Elizabeth Rogers, Grimsby; one *s* two *d. Educ:* Grimsby Parish Church Choir Sch.; Lincoln Sch.; Selwyn Coll. and Westcott House, Cambridge. 2nd Cl. Hons Hist. Tripos Pt 1, 1940; 2nd Cl.Hons Theol Tripos Pt 1, 1942; Steel Univ. Student in Divinity, 1941; BA 1941, MA 1945; Pres., SCM in Cambridge, 1941–42. Deacon, 1943; Priest, 1944; Curate of Boston, 1943–48; Vicar: St Leonard's, Redfield, Bristol, 1948–52; Olveston with Aust, 1952–60; Bishopston, 1960–73; Secretary, Bristol Diocesan Synod, 1967–73; Hon. Canon of Bristol Cathedral, 1970–73; Archdeacon of Winchester and Vicar of Sparsholt with Lainston, 1973–84; Hon. Canon of Winchester Cathedral, 1973–88; Bishop Suffragan of Southampton, 1984–88. Dir of Studies, Bristol Lay Readers, 1956–72; Proctor in Convocation, Mem. of Church Assembly and General Synod, 1956–73, 1975–83. Member: Central Bd of Finance of C of E, 1970–73; C of E Pensions Bd, 1980–84. Church Commissioner, 1973–83 (Mem. Board of Governors, 1978–83); Member: Dilapidations Legislation Commn, 1958–64; Working Party on Housing of Retired Clergy, 1972–73; Differential Payment of Clergy, 1976–77. Secretary, Bristol Council of Christian Churches, 1950–61; Chm., Winchester Christian Council, 1976–77; Pres., Southampton Council of Churches, 1984–88. Chm., Christian Aid Cttee: Bristol, 1956–73; Winchester, 1974–81. Anglican-Presbyterian Conversations, 1962–66; Convocations Jt Cttees on Anglican-Methodist Union Scheme, 1965. *Recreations:* book-hunting and rose-growing. *Address:* Bargate House, 25 Newport, Warminster, Wilts BA12 8RH. *T:* Warminster (0985) 216298.

CARTWRIGHT, Frederick; see Cartwright, W. F.

CARTWRIGHT, Harry, CBE 1979 (MBE 1946); MA, CEng, MIMechE, MIEE; Director, Atomic Energy Establishment, Winfrith, 1973–83; *b* 16 Sept. 1919; *s of* Edwin Harry Cartwright and Agnes Alice Cartwright (*née* Gillibrand); *m* 1950, Catharine Margaret Carson Bradbury; two *s. Educ:* William Hulme's Grammar Sch., Manchester; St John's Coll., Cambridge (Schol.). 1st cl. Mechanical Sciences Tripos, 1940. Served War, RAF, 1940–46: Flt Lt, service on ground radar in Europe, India and Burma. Decca Navigator Co., 1946–47; English Electric Co., 1947–49; joined Dept of Atomic Energy, Risley, as a Design and Project Engr, 1949; Chief Engr, 1955; Dir in charge of UKAEA consultancy services on nuclear reactors, 1960–64; Dir, Water Reactors, 1964–70, and as such responsible for design and construction of Winfrith 100 MW(e) SGHWR prototype power station; Dir, Fast Reactor Systems, 1970–73. Pres., British Nuclear Energy Soc., 1979–82; Pres., European Nuclear Soc., 1983–85 (Vice-Pres., 1980–83). Chm. of Trustees, Corfe Castle Charities, 1991–. Chm. of Govs, Purbeck Sch., 1985–88. *Publications:* various techn. papers. *Recreations:* walking, gardening, golf. *Address:* Tabbit's Hill House, Corfe Castle, Wareham, Dorset BH20 5HZ. *T:* Corfe Castle (0929) 480582. *Club:* United Oxford & Cambridge University.

CARTWRIGHT, John Cameron; JP; MP Woolwich, since 1983 (SDP, 1983–90; Social Democrat, since 1990) (Greenwich, Woolwich East, Oct. 1974–1983: Lab, 1974–81; SDP, 1981–83); *b* 29 Nov. 1933; *s of* Aubrey John Randolph Cartwright and Ivy Adeline Billie Cartwright; *m* 1959, Iris June Tant; one *s* one *d. Educ:* Woking County Grammar School. Exec. Officer, Home Civil Service, 1952–55; Labour Party Agent, 1955–67; Political Sec., RACS Ltd, 1967–72; Director, RACS Ltd, 1972–74. Leader, Greenwich Borough Council, 1971–74. Mem., Labour Party Nat. Exec. Cttee, 1971–75 and 1976–78. PPS to Sec. of State for Education and Science, 1976–77; Chm., Parly Labour Party Defence Group, 1979–81; Mem., Select Cttee on Defence, 1979–82 and 1986–; SDP party spokesman on environment, 1981–87, on defence and foreign affairs, 1983–87; SDP/Liberal Alliance spokesman on defence, 1987; SDP Parly Whip, 1983–; Vice Pres., SDP, 1987–88, Pres., 1988–. Jt Chm., Council for Advancement of Arab British Understanding, 1983–87; Vice-Chm., GB-USSR Assoc., 1983–; Mem., Calcutt Cttee on Privacy and Related Matters, 1989–90. Vice-Pres., Assoc. of Metropolitan Authorities, 1974–. Trustee, Nat. Maritime Museum, 1976–83. JP Inner London, 1970–. *Publication:* (jtly) Cruise, Pershing and SS20, 1985. *Recreations:* do-it-yourself, reading, watching television. *Address:* 17 Commonwealth Way, SE2 0JZ. *T:* 081–311 4394.

CARTWRIGHT, Dame Mary Lucy, DBE 1969; FRS 1947; ScD Cambridge 1949; MA Oxford and Cambridge; DPhil Oxford; Hon. LLD (Edin.) 1953; Hon. DSc: Leeds, 1958; Hull, 1959; Wales, 1962; Oxford, 1966; Brown (Providence, RI), 1969; Fellow of Girton College, Cambridge, 1930–49, and since 1968; *b* 1900; *d of late* W. D. Cartwright, Rector of Aynhoe. *Educ:* Godolphin Sch., Salisbury, and St Hugh's Coll., Oxford. Asst Mistress, Alice Ottley Sch., Worcester, 1923–24, Wycombe Abbey Sch., Bucks, 1924–27; read for DPhil, 1928–30; Yarrow Research Fellow of Girton Coll., 1930–34; Univ. Lectr in Mathematics, Cambridge, 1935–59; Mistress of Girton Coll., Cambridge, 1949–68; Reader in the Theory of Functions, Univ. of Cambridge, 1959–68, Emeritus Reader, 1968–; Visiting Professor: Brown Univ., Providence, RI, 1968–69; Claremont Graduate Sch., California, 1969–70; Case Western Reserve, 1970; Polish Acad. of Sciences, 1970; Univ. of Wales, 1971; Case Western Reserve, 1971. Consultant on US Navy Mathematical Research Projects at Stanford and Princeton Universities, Jan.-May 1949. Comdt, British Red Cross Detachment, Cambs 112, 1940–44. Fellow of Cambridge Philosophical Soc.; President: London Math. Soc., 1961–63; Mathematical Assoc., 1951–52 (now Hon. Mem.). Hon. FIMA, 1972; Hon. FRSE. Sylvester Medal, Royal Soc., 1964; De Morgan Medal, London Mathematical Soc., 1968; Medal of Univ. of Jyväskylä, Finland, 1973. Commander, Order of the Dannebrog, 1961. *Publications:* Integral Functions (Cambridge Tracts in Mathematics and Mathematical Physics), 1956; math. papers in various journals.

Address: 38 Sherlock Close, Cambridge CB3 0HP. *T:* Cambridge (0223) 352574.
See also W. F. Cartwright.

CARTWRIGHT, Rt. Rev. Richard Fox; Assistant Bishop, Diocese of Truro, since 1982, and Diocese of Exeter, since 1988; *b* 10 Nov. 1913; *s of late* Rev. George Frederick Cartwright, Vicar of Plumstead, and Constance Margaret Cartwright (*née* Clark); *m* 1947, Rosemary Magdalen, *d of* Francis Evelyn Bray, Woodham Grange, Surrey; one *s* three *d. Educ:* The King's School, Canterbury; Pembroke Coll., Cambridge (BA 1935, MA 1939); Cuddesdon Theological Coll. Deacon, 1936; Priest, 1937; Curate, St Anselm, Kennington Cross, 1936–40; Priest-in-Charge, Lower Kingswood, 1940–45; Vicar, St Andrew, Surbiton, 1945–52; Proctor in Convocation, 1950–52; Vicar of St Mary Redcliffe, Bristol (with Temple from 1956 and St John Bedminster from 1965), 1952–72; Hon. Canon of Bristol, 1960–72; Suffragan Bishop of Plymouth, 1972–81. Sub-Chaplain, Order of St John, 1957–; Director: Ecclesiastical Insurance Office Ltd, 1964–85; Allchurches Trust Ltd, 1985–. Chm. Governors, Kelly Coll., 1973–88. Hon. DD Univ. of the South, Tennessee, 1969. *Recreations:* fly-fishing, gardening, water-colour painting. *Address:* 5 Old Vicarage Close, Ide, near Exeter, Devon EX2 9RT. *T:* Exeter (0392) 211270. *Club:* Army and Navy.

CARTWRIGHT, Dame Silvia (Rose), DBE 1989; **Chief Judge Dame Silvia Cartwright;** Chief District Court Judge, New Zealand, since 1989; *b* 7 Nov. 1943; *d of* Monteith Poulter and Eileen Jane Poulter, both of Dunedin, NZ; *m* 1969, Peter John Cartwright. *Educ:* Univ. of Otago, NZ (LLB). Partner, Harkness Henry & Co., Barristers and Solicitors, Hamilton, NZ, 1971–81; Dist Court and Family Court Judge, 1981–89. Mem., Commn for the Future, 1975–80; conducted Inquiry into: Soc. Sci. Funding in NZ, 1986–87; Treatment of Cervical Cancer at Nat. Women's Hosp., Auckland, NZ, 1987–88. *Publications:* UNESCO Monograph, 1985; Report of the Cervical Cancer Inquiry, 1988; contrib. Jl of Assoc. of Family and Conciliation Courts (US). *Recreations:* reading, gardening, boating. *Address:* Chief Judge's Chambers, Box 10167, The Terrace, Wellington, New Zealand. *T:* (04) 4985002, *Fax:* (04) 737917.

CARTWRIGHT, (William) Frederick, CBE 1977; DL; MIMechE; Director, BSC (International) Ltd; a Deputy Chairman, British Steel Corporation, 1970–72; Group Managing Director, S Wales Group, British Steel Corporation, 1967–70; Chairman, The Steel Co. of Wales Ltd, 1967 (Managing Director, 1962–67); *b* 13 Nov. 1906; *s of* William Digby Cartwright, Rector of Aynhoe; *m* 1937, Sally Chrystobel Ware; two *s* one *d. Educ:* Rugby Sch. Joined Guest, Keen and Nettlefold, Dowlais, 1929; gained experience at steelworks in Germany, Luxembourg and France, 1930; Asst Works Manager, 1931, Tech. Asst to Managing Director, 1935, Dir and Chief Engineer, 1940, Dir and General Manager, 1943, Guest, Keen and Baldwin, Port Talbot Works; Dir and General Manager, Steel Co. of Wales, 1947; Asst Man. Dir and General Manager of the Steel Div., The Steel Co. of Wales Ltd, 1954. Pres., Iron and Steel Inst., 1960. Dir, Lloyds Bank, 1968–77 (Chm., S Wales Regional Bd, 1968–77). Dir, Develt Corp for Wales. Freeman of Port Talbot, 1970. DL, County of Glamorgan; High Sheriff, Glamorgan, 1961. OStJ. Hon. LLD Wales, 1968. Bessemer Gold Medal, 1958; Frederico Giolitti Steel Medal, 1960. *Recreations:* riding and yachting. *Address:* Castle-upon-Alun, St Brides Major, near Bridgend, Mid Glam CF32 0TN. *T:* Southern-down (0656) 298. *Clubs:* Royal Ocean Racing, Royal Cruising; Royal Yacht Squadron.
See also Dame Mary Cartwright.

CARTWRIGHT SHARP, Michael; see Sharp, J. M. C.

CARUS, Louis Revell, Hon. RAM, FRSAMD, FRCM, FBSM; Artistic Director, International String Quartet Week, since 1985; Principal, Birmingham School of Music, 1975–87; *b* Kasauli, India, 22 Oct. 1927; *s of* Lt-Col Martin and Enid Carus-Wilson; *m* 1951, Nancy Reade Noell; two *s* one *d. Educ:* Rugby Sch.; Brussels Conservatoire (Premier Prix); Peabody Conservatory, USA. LRAM. Scottish National Orchestra, 1950; solo violinist and chamber music specialist, 1951–; Head of Strings, Royal Scottish Academy of Music, 1956; Scottish Trio and Piano Quartet, New Music Group of Scotland, 1956–75; Northern Sinfonia, Monteverdi Orchestras, 1963–73; Orchestra Da Camera, 1975; Adjudicator, 1960–; Examr, Associated Bd of Royal Schs of Music, 1976–. Pres., ISM, 1986–87; FRSAMD 1976; Hon. RAM 1977; FRCM 1983; FBSM 1988. Fellow, Birmingham Polytechnic, 1988. *Publications:* various musical journalism, eg, daily press, Strad Magazine, ISM Jl, Gulbenkian Report. *Recreations:* painting, gardening, travel. *Address:* 15 Kings End Road, Powick, Worcester WR2 4RA. *T:* Worcester (0905) 831715. *Clubs:* Royal Society of Musicians, Incorporated Society of Musicians, European String Teachers Association; Rotary (Worcester).

CARUS, Roderick; QC 1990; a Recorder since 1990; *b* 4 June 1944; *s of* Anthony and Kathleen Carus; *m* 1972, Hilary Mary (*née* Jones); two *s* two *d. Educ:* Wirral GS, Merseyside; University Coll., Oxford (BA Law); Manchester Business Sch. (Postgrad. Diploma in Advanced Business Studies). Called to the Bar, Gray's Inn, 1971. Merchant bank, investments, 1966–70. Asst Recorder, 1987–90. *Recreations:* chess, crosswords, fishing, gardening. *Address:* Yealand House, Park Road, Hale, Cheshire WA15 9LQ. *Club:* Hale Conservative.

CARVER, family name of **Baron Carver.**

CARVER, Baron *cr* 1977 (Life Peer); **Field-Marshal (Richard) Michael (Power) Carver,** GCB 1970 (KCB 1966; CB 1957); CBE 1945; DSO 1943 and Bar 1943; MC 1941; designated British Resident Commissioner in Rhodesia, 1977–78; Chief of the Defence Staff, 1973–76; *b* 24 April 1915; *2nd s of late* Harold Power Carver and late Winifred Anne Gabrielle Carver (*née* Wellesley); *m* 1947, Edith, *d of* Lt-Col Sir Henry Lowry-Corry, MC; two *s* two *d. Educ:* Winchester Coll.; Sandhurst. 2nd Lieut Royal Tank Corps, 1935; War of 1939–45 (despatches twice); GSO1, 7th Armoured Div., 1942; OC 1st Royal Tank Regt, 1943; Comdr 4th Armoured Brigade, 1944; Tech. Staff Officer (1), Min. of Supply, 1947; Joint Services Staff Coll., 1950; AQMG, Allied Land Forces, Central Europe, 1951; Col GS, SHAPE 1952; Dep. Chief of Staff, East Africa, 1954 (despatches); Chief of Staff, East Africa, 1955; idc 1957; Dir of Plans, War Office, 1958–59; Comdr 6th Infty Brigade, 1960–62; Maj.-Gen. 1962; GOC, 3 Div., 1962–64, also Comdr Joint Truce Force, Cyprus, and Dep. Comdr United Nations' Force in Cyprus, 1964; Dir, Army Staff Duties, Min. of Defence, 1964–66; Lt-Gen. 1966; comd FE Land Forces, 1966–67; Gen., 1967; C-in-C, Far East, 1967–69; GOC-in-C, Southern Command, 1969–71; Chief of the General Staff, 1971–73; Field-Marshal 1973. Col Commandant: REME 1966–76; Royal Tank Regt, 1968–72; RAC, 1974–77; ADC (Gen.) 1969–72. *Publications:* Second to None (History of Royal Scots Greys, 1919–45), 1954; El Alamein, 1962; Tobruk, 1964; (ed) The War Lords, 1976; Harding of Petherton, 1978; The Apostles of Mobility, 1979; War Since 1945, 1980; A Policy for Peace, 1982; The Seven Ages of the British Army, 1984; Dilemmas of the Desert War, 1986; Twentieth Century Warriors, 1987; Out of Step: memoirs of Field-Marshal Lord Carver, 1989. *Address:* Wood End House, Wickham, Fareham, Hants PO17 6JZ. *T:* Wickham (0329) 832143. *Club:* Anglo-Belgian.

CARVER, James, CB 1978; CEng, FIMinE; consulting mining engineer; *b* 29 Feb. 1916; *s* of late William and Ellen Carver; *m* 1944, Elsie Sharrock; one *s* two *d* (of whom one *s* one *d* are twins). *Educ:* Wigan Mining and Technical Coll. Certificated Mine Manager. Asst Mine Manager, Nos 5, 6 and 7 mines, Garswood Hall, Lancs, 1941–43; HM Jun. Inspector Mines and Quarries, W Midlands Coalfields, 1943; Dist Inspector, Mines and Quarries, N Staffordshire, 1951; Senior District Inspector: M&Q, London Headquarters, 1957; M&Q, Doncaster Dist (in charge), 1962; Principal Inspector, M&Q, London Headquarters, 1967; Dep. Chief, M&Q, 1973; Chief Inspector, M&Q, 1975–77; Member, Health and Safety Exec., 1976–77. *Publications:* author or co-author, papers in Trans IMinE; several papers to internat. mining confs. *Recreation:* golf. *Address:* 196 Forest Road, Tunbridge Wells, Kent TN2 5JB. *T:* Tunbridge Wells (0892) 26748. *Club:* Nevill Golf (Tunbridge Wells).

CARVILL, Patrick; Permanent Secretary, Department of Education for Northern Ireland, since 1990; *b* 13 Oct. 1943; *s* of Bernard and Susan Carvill; *m* 1965, Vera Abbott; two *s*. *Educ:* St Mary's Christian Brothers Grammar School, Belfast; Queen's Univ., Belfast (BA Hons). Min. of Fuel and Power, Westminster, 1965; Min. of Development, Stormont, 1967; Min. of Community Relations, 1969; Asst Sec., Dept. of Educn, 1975–83; Under-Secretary: Dept of Finance and Personnel, 1983–88; Dept. of Econ. Develt, 1988–89; Dept. of Finance and Personnel, 1989–90. *Recreations:* reading, hill-walking, diving. *Address:* c/o Department of Education for Northern Ireland, Rathgael House, Balloo Road, Bangor, Co. Down BT19 2PR.

CARY, family name of **Viscount Falkland.**

CARY, Sir Roger Hugh, 2nd Bt *cr* 1955; a consultant to BBC's Director-General, since 1986; *b* 8 Jan. 1926; *o s* of Sir Robert (Archibald) Cary, 1st Bt, and Hon. Rosamond Mary Curzon (*d* 1985), *d* of late Col Hon. Alfred Nathaniel Curzon; *S* father, 1979; *m* 1st, 1948, Marilda (marr. diss. 1951), *d* of Major Pearson-Gregory, MC; one *d*; 2nd, 1953, Ann Helen Katharine, *e d* of Hugh Blair Brenan, OBE (formerly Asst Sec., Royal Hosp., Chelsea); two *s* one *d*. *Educ:* Ludgrove; Eton; New Coll., Oxford (BA Mod. Hist. 1949). Enlisted Grenadier Guards, 1943; Lieut 1945; Staff Captain and Instr, Sch. of Signals, Catterick, 1946; Signals Officer, Guards Trng Bn, 1946–47; R of O 1947. Sub-editor and Leader-writer, The Times, 1949–50; Archivist, St Paul's Cathedral, 1950; joined BBC, 1950: attached Home Talks, 1951; Producer, Overseas Talks, 1951–56; Asst, European Talks, 1956–58; Dep. Editor, The Listener, 1958–61; Man. Trng Organiser, 1961–66; Asst, Secretariat, 1966–72, Sen. Asst, 1972–74; Sec., Central Music Adv. Cttee, 1966–77, 1982–83; Special Asst (Public Affairs), 1974–77; Special Asst to Alasdair Milne, when Man. Dir, BBC TV, 1977–82; Chief Asst to Sec., BBC, 1982–83; Chief Asst to Dir of Progs, BBC TV, 1983–86; Research, Richard Cawston's documentary film, Royal Family, 1969; Secretary: Sims Cttee on portrayal of violence on TV, 1979, Wyatt Cttee revision 1983; Wenham Cttee on Subscription Television, 1980–81; Cotton Cttee on Sponsorship and BBC TV, 1981; British Deleg., Internat. Art-Historical Conf., Amsterdam, 1952; Salzburg Scholar in Amer. Studies, 1956. Associate, RHistS. Trustee, Kedleston, 1988–. *Recreations:* looking at pictures, collecting books. *Heir:* *s* Nicolas Robert Hugh Cary [*b* 17 April 1955; *m* 1979, Pauline Jean, *d* of Dr Thomas Ian Boyd; three *s*]. *Address:* 23 Bath Road, W4 1LJ. *Clubs:* Pratt's, First Guards; The Bushmen.

CASALONE, Carlo D.; *see* Dionisotti-Casalone.

CASE, Anthea Fiendley, (Mrs D. C. Case); Under Secretary, HM Treasury, since 1988; *b* 7 Feb. 1945; *d* of Thomas Fiendley Stones and of late Bess Stones (*née* Mackie); *m* 1967, David Charles Case; two *d*. *Educ:* Christ's Hospital, Hertford; St Anne's Coll., Oxford (BA). HM Treasury: Asst Principal, 1966–70; Private Sec. to Financial Sec., 1970–71; Principal, 1971–79; Asst Sec., 1980–88. *Address:* HM Treasury, Parliament Street, SW1. *T:* 071–270 4400.

CASE, Humphrey John; Keeper, Department of Antiquities, Ashmolean Museum, 1973–82; *b* 26 May 1918; *s* of George Reginald Case and Margaret Helen (*née* Duckett); *m* 1st, 1942, Margaret Adelia (*née* Eaton); 2nd, 1949, Jean Alison (*née* Orr); two *s*; 3rd, 1979, Jocelyn (*née* Herickx). *Educ:* Charterhouse; St John's Coll., Cambridge (MA); Inst. of Archaeology, London Univ. Served War, 1939–46. Ashmolean Museum: Asst Keeper, 1949–57; Sen. Asst Keeper, 1957–69; Dep. Keeper, Dept of Antiquities, 1969–73. Vice-Pres., Prehistoric Soc., 1969–73; has directed excavations in England, Ireland and France. FSA 1954. *Publications:* in learned jls (British and foreign): principally on neolithic in Western Europe, prehistoric metallurgy and regional archaeology. *Recreations:* reading, music, gardening. *Address:* Pitt's Cottage, 187 Thame Road, Warborough, Wallingford, Oxon OX10 7DH.

CASE, Captain Richard Vere Essex, DSO 1942; DSC 1940; RD; RNR retired; Royal Naval Reserve ADC to the Queen, 1958; Chief Marine Superintendent, Coast Lines Ltd and Associated Companies, 1953–69; *b* 13 April 1904; *s* of late Prof. R. H. Case; *m* 1940, Olive May, *d* of H. W. Griggs, Preston, near Canterbury, Kent; one *s* one *d*. *Educ:* Thames Nautical Training Coll., HMS Worcester. Joined RNR 1920; commenced service in Merchant Service, 1920; Master's Certificate of Competency, 1928; Captain RNR, 1953; served War of 1939–45 (DSO, DSC and Bar, RD and Clasp). *Recreation:* bowls. *Address:* 14 Aigburth Hall Road, Liverpool L19 9DQ. *T:* 051–427 1016. *Clubs:* Athenæum (Liverpool); Liverpool Cricket.

CASEY, Most Rev. Eamonn; *see* Galway and Kilmacduagh, Bishop of, (RC).

CASEY, Rt. Hon. Sir Maurice Eugene, Kt 1991; PC 1986; **Rt. Hon. Mr Justice Casey;** Judge of Court of Appeal of New Zealand, since 1986; *b* 28 Aug. 1923; *s* of Eugene Casey and Beatrice Casey; *m* 1948, Stella Katherine Wright (*see* Dame Stella Casey); three *s* six *d*. *Educ:* St Patrick's Coll., Wellington; Victoria Univ. (LLM Hons). Served War, Naval Officer, 1943–45. Barrister and Solicitor, 1946; Vice Pres., Auckland Dist Law Soc., 1974; Judge, Supreme (now High) Court, 1974. Chm., Penal Policy Review Cttee, 1981. *Publication:* Hire Purchase Law in New Zealand, 1961. *Address:* 5/144 Oriental Parade, Wellington, New Zealand. *T:* (04) 843–258. *Clubs:* Wellington; Northern (Auckland).

CASEY, Michael Bernard; Chairman, Sallingbury Casey Ltd (formerly Michael Casey & Associates Ltd) Management Consultants; Director, Marlar International Ltd; *b* 1 Sept. 1928; *s* of late Joseph Bernard Casey, OBE, and Dorothy (*née* Love); *m* 1963, Sally Louise, *e d* of James Stuart Smith; two *s* two *d*. *Educ:* Colwyn Bay Grammar Sch.; LSE (Scholar in Laws, 1952; LLB 1954). RAF, 1947–49. Principal, MAFF, 1961; Office of the Minister for Science, 1963–64; Asst Sec., DEA, 1967; DTI (later Dept of Prices and Consumer Protection), 1970; Under Sec., DTI, 1975–77; a Dep. Chm. and Chief Exec., British Shipbuilders, 1977–80; Chm. and Man. Dir, Mather & Platt, 1980–81. *Recreations:* golf, chess, bridge. *Address:* 3 Barkston Gardens, SW5 0ER. *T:* 071–244 6124. *Club:* Reform.

CASEY, Michael Vince, OBE 1990; BSc(Eng), FEng 1985; FIMechE; retired, 1990; *b* 25 May 1927; *s* of Charles John Casey and May Louise Casey; *m* 1954, Elinor Jane (*née* Harris) (*d* 1987); two *s* two *d*. *Educ:* Glossop Grammar Sch.; The College, Swindon. BSc(Eng) Hons London. Premium Apprentice, GWR Locomotive Works, Swindon, 1944–49; Univ. of London External Degree Course, 1949–52; British Rail Western Region: Locomotive Testing and Experimental Office, Swindon, 1952–58; Supplies and Contracts Dept, Swindon, 1958–61; Chief Mechanical and Electrical Engr's Dept, Paddington, 1961–63; Area Maintenance Engr, Old Oak Common, 1963–66; Chief Mech. and Elec. Engr's Dept, Paddington, 1966–71; Chief Mech. and Elec. Engineer: Scottish Region, Glasgow, 1971–76; Eastern Region, York, 1976–78; Engrg Dir, British Rail Engrg Ltd, 1978–82; Dir, Mechanical and Electrical Engrg, BRB, 1982–87; Project Dir (BR Engrg), 1987–89; Chief Engr, Channel Tunnel Rail Link, BR, 1989–90. *Recreations:* gardening, philately. *Address:* Hunters Ride, Stoke Row Road, Peppard, Henley-on-Thames RG9 5EJ. *T:* Kidmore End (0734) 722653.

CASEY, Rt. Rev. Patrick Joseph; Former Bishop of Brentwood; *b* 20 Nov. 1913; *s* of Patrick Casey and Bridget Casey (*née* Norris). *Educ:* St Joseph's Parochial Sch., Kingsland; St Edmund's Coll., Ware. Ordained priest, 1939; Asst, St James's, Spanish Place, 1939–61; Parish Priest of Hendon, 1961–63; Vicar Gen. of Westminster, 1963; Domestic Prelate, and Canon of Westminster Cathedral, 1964; Provost of Westminster Cathedral Chapter, 1967; Auxiliary Bishop of Westminster and Titular Bishop of Sufar, 1966–69; Bishop of Brentwood, 1969–79, then Apostolic Administrator; Parish Priest, Our Most Holy Redeemer and St Thomas More, Chelsea, 1980–89. *Address:* 7 Cliffsea Grove, Leigh-on-Sea, Essex SS9 1NG.

CASEY, Dr Raymond, FRS 1970; retired; Senior Principal Scientific Officer (Special Merit), Institute of Geological Sciences, London, 1964–79; *b* 10 Oct. 1917; *s* of Samuel Gardiner Casey and Gladys Violet Helen Casey (*née* Garrett); *m* 1943, Norah Kathleen Pakeman (*d* 1974); two *s*. *Educ:* St Mary's, Folkestone; Univ. of Reading. PhD 1958; DSc 1963. Geological Survey and Museum: Asst 1939; Asst Exper. Officer 1946; Exper. Officer 1949; Sen. Geologist 1957; Principal Geologist 1960. *Publications:* A Monograph of the Ammonoidea of the Lower Greensand, 1960–80; (ed, with P. F. Rawson) The Boreal Lower Cretaceous, 1973; numerous articles on Mesozoic palaeontology and stratigraphy in scientific press. *Recreation:* research into early Russian postal and military history (Pres., British Soc. of Russian Philately). *Address:* 38 Reed Avenue, Orpington, Kent. *T:* Farnborough (Kent) (0689) 51728.

CASEY, Dame Stella (Katherine), DBE 1990; *b* 22 May 1924; *d* of William Wright and Stella Hickey; *m* 1948, Maurice Eugene Casey (*see* Rt Hon. Sir M. E. Casey); three *s* six *d*. *Educ.* Rahotu Sch.; Opunake Dist High Sch.; Victoria Univ. (BA). Voluntary service: Catholic Women's League of NZ, 1967–; Nat. Council of Women of NZ, 1976–; NZ Fedn of Univ. Women, 1969–; World Union of Catholic Women's Organisations, 1975–79; Hato Petra Coll. Assoc., 1968–73; Girl Guides Assoc., 1968–75; Bd of Governors, Sacred Heart Coll., 1976–82. Member: Cttee on Secondary Educn, 1975–76; Working Party, Teacher Training Review, 1977–78; Christchurch Polytechnic Council, 1979–82; Nat. Adv. Cttee on Women and Educn, 1982–83; Dep. Chm., Adv. Cttee on Women's Affairs, 1981–84. *Publications:* Drugs and the Young New Zealander, 1968. *Address:* 5 Dorchester, 144 Oriental Parade, Wellington, New Zealand. *T:* 04–843–258.

CASH, Sir Gerald (Christopher), GCMG 1980; GCVO 1985 (KCVO 1977); OBE 1964; JP; Governor-General, Commonwealth of the Bahamas, 1979–88 (Acting Governor-General, 1976–79); Consultant Counsel, Cash, Fountain & Co., Nassau, since 1989; *b* Nassau, Bahamas, 28 May 1917; *s* of late Wilfred Gladstone Cash and of Lillian Cash; *m* Dorothy Eileen (*née* Long); two *s* one *d*. *Educ:* Govt High Sch., Nassau. Called to the Bar, Middle Temple, 1948. Counsel and Attorney, Supreme Court of Bahamas, 1940. Member: House of Assembly, Bahamas, 1949–62; Exec. Council, 1958–62; Senate, 1969–73 (Vice-Pres., 1970–72; Pres., 1972–73). Chm., Labour Bd, 1950–52. Member: Bd of Educn, 1950–62; Police Service Commn, 1964–69; Immigration Cttee, 1958–62; Road Traffic Cttee, 1958–62. Rep. Bahamas, Independence Celebrations of Jamaica, Trinidad and Tobago, 1962. Chairman: Vis. Cttee, Boys Indust. Sch., 1952–62; Bd of Governors, Govt High Sch., 1949–63 and 1965–76; Bahamas National Cttee, United World Colls, 1977–. Formerly: Hon. Vice-Consul for Republic of Haiti; Vice-Chancellor, Anglican Dio.; Admin. Adviser, Rotary Clubs in Bahamas to Pres. of Rotary Internat.; Treasurer and Dir, YMCA; Treas., Bahamas Cricket Assoc.; Chm., Boy Scouts Exec. Council; Mem. Board: Dirs of Central Bank of Bahamas; Dirs of Bahamas Assoc. for Mentally Retarded. Formerly: President: Rotary Club of E Nassau; Gym Tennis Club; Florida Tennis Assoc.; Bahamas Lawn Tennis Assoc.; Bahamas Table Tennis Assoc.; Vice-President: Boy Scouts Assoc.; Olympic Assoc., Amateur Athletic Assoc., Swimming Assoc., Football Assoc., Bahamas. JP Bahamas, 1940. Coronation Medal, 1953; Silver Jubilee Medal, 1977; Silver Medal, Olympic Order, 1983. *Recreations:* golf, tennis, table tennis, swimming. *Address:* 4 Bristol Street, PO Box N-476, Nassau, Bahamas. *T:* 809–393–4767, 809–393–2062. *Clubs:* Commonwealth Trust; Kingston Cricket (Jamaica); Lyford Cay, Paradise Island Golf, South Ocean Golf, Ambassador Golf, Gym Tennis (Nassau).

CASH, William Nigel Paul; MP (C) Stafford, since 1984; *b* 10 May 1940; *s* of Paul Trevor Cash, MC (killed in action Normandy, July 13, 1944) and Moyra Roberts (*née* Morrison); *m* 1965, Bridget Mary Lee; two *s* one *d*. *Educ:* Stonyhurst Coll.; Lincoln Coll., Oxford (MA History). Qualified as Solicitor, 1967; Partner, Dyson Bell & Co., 1971–79; William Cash & Co. (constitutional and administrative lawyer), 1979–. Chairman: Cons. Backbench Cttee on European Affairs, 1989–; All Party Cttee on E Africa, 1988– (Sec., 1984–88); Vice-Chairman: Cons. Small Business Bureau, 1984–89; Cons. Constitutional Cttee, 1985–87; Member: Select Cttee on European Legislation, 1985–; Select Cttee on Employment, 1989–; Standing Cttee: on Financial Services, 1985–86; on Banking, 1986–87; on Broadcasting, 1989. Dir, Ironbridge Gorge Museum Trust, 1980–. *Recreations:* history, cricket, the heritage. *Address:* Upton Cressett Hall, near Bridgnorth, Shropshire. *T:* Morville 307. *Clubs:* Carlton; Vincent's (Oxford); Free Foresters CC; Lords and Commons Cricket (Sec., 1988–).

CASHEL AND EMLY, Archbishop of, (RC), since 1988; **Most Rev. Dermot Clifford.** *Address:* Archbishop's House, Thurles, Co. Tipperary, Ireland.

CASHEL AND OSSORY, Bishop of, since 1980; **Rt. Rev. Noel Vincent Willoughby;** *b* 15 Dec. 1926; *s* of George and Mary Jane Willoughby; *m* 1959, Valerie Moore, Dungannon, Tyrone; two *s* one *d*. *Educ:* Tate School, Wexford; Trinity Coll., Dublin (Scholar, Moderator and Gold Medallist in Philosophy). Deacon 1950, priest 1951, Armagh Cathedral; Curate: Drumglass Parish, 1950–53; St Catherine's, Dublin, 1953–55; Bray Parish, 1955–59; Rector: Delgany Parish, 1959–69; Glenageary Parish, 1969–80; Hon. Sec., General Synod, 1976–80; Treasurer, St Patrick's Cathedral, Dublin, 1976–80; Archdeacon of Dublin, 1979–80. *Recreations:* gardening, golf, tennis, fishing. *Address:* The Palace, Kilkenny, Ireland. *T:* Kilkenny 21560.

CASHMAN, John Prescott; Under-Secretary, Department of Health (formerly of Health and Social Security), 1973–88; *b* 19 May 1930; *s* of late John Patrick Cashman and late Mary Cashman (*née* Prescott). *Educ:* Balliol Coll., Oxford. MA (English Lang. and Lit.). Army (Intell. Corps), 1948–49. Entered Min. of Health, 1951; Principal 1957; Private Sec. to Minister, 1962–65; Asst Sec. 1965; Nuffield Foundn Trav. Fellow, 1968–69; Private Sec. to Sec. of State, 1969. Trustee, Macfarlane Trust, 1989–; Mem. Exec. Council,

Hospital Saving Assoc., 1989–. *Address:* 3 Paul Gardens, Croydon, Surrey CR0 5QL. *T:* 081–681 6578.

CASHMORE, Prof. Roger John, DPhil; FInstP; Professor of Experimental Physics, since 1991, and Fellow of Balliol College, since 1979, Oxford University; *b* 22 Aug. 1944; *e s* of C. J. C. and E. M. Cashmore; *m* 1971, Elizabeth Ann, *d* of Rev. S. J. C. Lindsay; one *s*. *Educ:* Dudley Grammar Sch.; St John's Coll., Cambridge (schol.; BA 1965; MA); Balliol Coll., Oxford (DPhil 1969). FInstP 1985. Weir Jun. Res. Fellow, University Coll., Oxford, 1967–69; 1851 Res. Fellow, 1968; Res. Associate, Stanford Linear Accelerator Centre, Calif, 1969–74; Oxford University: Res. Officer, 1974–79; Lectr, Christ Church, 1976–78; Sen. Res. Fellow, Merton Coll., 1977–79; Tutor, Balliol Coll., and Univ. Lectr in Physics, 1979–90; Reader in Experimental Physics, 1990–91. SERC Sen. Res. Fellow, 1982–87; Vis. Prof., Vrije Univ., Brussels, 1982; Guest Scientist, Fermilab, Chicago, 1986. Mem., policy and prog. cttees, CERN, Deutsches Electronen–Synchrotron, Hamburg, and SERC. C.V. Boys Prize, Inst. of Physics, 1983. *Publications:* contrib. Nuclear Physics, Physics Letters, Phys. Rev., Phys. Rev. Letters. *Recreations:* sports, wine. *Address:* Balliol College, Oxford OX1 3BJ.

CASS, Edward Geoffrey, CB 1974; OBE 1951; Alternate Governor, Reserve Bank of Rhodesia, 1978–79; *b* 10 Sept. 1916; *s* of Edward Charles and Florence Mary Cass; *m* 1941, Ruth Mary Powley; four *d*. *Educ:* St Olave's; Univ. Coll., London (Scholar); BSc (Econ.) London (1st Cl.) 1937; The Queen's Coll., Oxford (Scholar); George Webb Medley Scholarship, 1938; BA Oxon (1st Cl. PPE) 1939, MA 1987. Lecturer in Economics, New Coll., Oxford, 1939. From 1940 served in Min. of Supply, Treasury, Air Ministry, MoD; Private Sec. to the Prime Minister, 1949–52; Chief Statistician, Min. of Supply, 1952; Private Sec. to Min. of Supply, 1954; Imperial Defence Coll., 1958; Asst Under-Sec. of State (Programmes and Budget), MoD, 1965–72; Dep. Under-Sec. of State (Finance and Budget), MoD, 1972–76. Mem., Review Bd for Govt Contracts, 1977–84; Chm., Verbatim Reporting Study Gp, 1977–79. *Address:* 60 Rotherwick Road, NW11 7DB. *T:* 081–455 1664.

CASS, Geoffrey Arthur, MA; CBIM, FIIM; Chief Executive, Cambridge University Press, since 1972; Fellow of Clare Hall, Cambridge, since 1979; Chairman: Council of Governors, Royal Shakespeare Company, since 1985 (Governor, since 1975); National Training and International Matches, Lawn Tennis Association, since 1985; *b* 11 Aug. 1932; *o c* of late Arthur Cass and Jessie Cass (*née* Simpson), Darlington and Oxford; *m* 1957, Olwen Mary, *o c* of late William Leslie Richards and of Edith Louisa Richards, Llanelli and Brecon; four *d*. *Educ:* Queen Elizabeth Grammar Sch., Darlington (Head of Sch.); Jesus Coll., Nuffield Coll., and Dept of Social and Admin. Studies, Oxford Univ. (BA 1954; MA 1958); MA Cantab, 1972. FInstD 1968; FIWM, FIIM 1979; CBIM 1980. Commnd RAFVR, fighter control, 1954; served RAF, 1958–60: Air Min. Directorate of Work Study; Pilot Officer, 1958; Flying Officer, 1960. Consultant: PA Management Consultants Ltd, 1960–65; British Communications Corp., and Controls and Communications Ltd, 1965; Dir, Controls and Communications Ltd, 1966–69; Managing Director, George Allen and Unwin Ltd, 1967–71; Director: Weidenfeld (Publishers) Ltd, 1972–74; Chicago Univ. Press (UK), 1971–86; Mem., Jesus Coll., Cambridge, 1972–; Univ. Printer, 1982–83. Member: Univ. of Cambridge Cttee of Management of Fenner's (and Exec. Cttee), 1976–; Univ. of Cambridge Careers Service Syndicate (formerly Appts Bd), 1977– (Exec. Cttee, 1982–); Governing Syndicate, Fitzwilliam Mus., Cambridge, 1977–78; Chm. Governors, Perse Sch. for Girls, Cambridge, 1978–88. Chm., Royal Shakespeare Theatre Trust, 1983– (Founder Mem. Council, 1967–); Mem. Council, RSC, 1975– (Mem. 1976–, Chm. 1982–, F and GP Cttee); Trustee and Guardian, Shakespeare Birthplace Trust, 1982–. Director: Newcastle Theatre Royal Trust, 1984–89; Cambridge Theatre Co., 1986–. Cambs County LTA: Mem. Exec., 1974–84; Chm., F and GP Cttee, 1982–84; Captain 1974–78; Pres., 1980–82; Hon. Life Vice-Pres., 1982–; Lawn Tennis Assoc. of GB: Member: Management Cttee, 1985–; Council, 1976–; Nat. Trng and Internat. Match Cttee (Davis Cup, Fedn Cup, Wightman Cup, etc), 1982–; Wimbledon Championships: Member: Cttee of Management, 1990–; Jt Finance Bd, 1989–; British Jun. Championships Cttee of Management, 1983– (Chm., 1985–); Nat. Championships Cttee of Management, 1988–89; Rules and Internat. Cttee, 1980–81; Re-orgn Wkg Party, 1984–85. Tennis singles champion: Durham County, 1951; Cambridgeshire, 1975; Oxford University: tennis Blue, 1953, 1954, 1955 (Sec., 1955); badminton, 1951, 1952 (Captain, 1952); Chm., Cambridge Univ. Lawn Tennis Club, 1977– (Hon. Cambridge tennis Blue, 1980); played in Wimbledon Championships, 1954, 1955, 1956, 1959; played in inter-county lawn tennis championships for Durham County, then for Cambridgeshire, 1952–82; Brit. Veterans (over 45) singles champion, Wimbledon, 1978; Mem., Brit. Veterans' Internat. Dubler Cup Team, Barcelona, 1978, Milano Marittima, 1979 (Captain). Chevalier, Ordre des Arts et des Lettres (France), 1982. *Publications:* contrib. scientific and technical jls and periodicals (Britain, France, Italy) on econ. and social effects of automation; articles on publishing. *Recreations:* lawn tennis, theatre, running. *Address:* Middlefield, Huntingdon Road, Cambridge CB3 0LH. *Clubs:* Hurlingham, Queen's, Institute of Directors, International Lawn Tennis of GB, The 45, Veterans' Lawn Tennis of GB; Cambridge University Lawn Tennis.

CASS, John, QPM 1979; National Co-ordinator of Regional Crime Squads, 1981–84; Security Consultant; *b* 24 June 1925; *m* 1948, Dilys Margaret Hughes, SRN; three *d*. *Educ:* Nelson Sch., Wigton, Cumbria. Served no 40 RM Commando, 1944–45. Joined Metropolitan Police, 1946; Comdt, Detective Training Sch., Hendon, 1974; Commander: CID, New Scotland Yard, 1975; Complaints Bureau, 1978; Serious Crime Squads, New Scotland Yard, 1980. UK Rep., Interpol Conf. on crime prediction, Paris, 1976. Student in Criminology, Cambridge Univ., 1966. Adviser, Police Staff Coll., on multi-Force major investigations, 1982–83; Chief Investigator, War Crimes Inquiry, Home Office, 1988–89. Mem., British Acad. of Forensic Scis, 1965. Member: Association of Chief Police Officers; Metropolitan Police Commanders' Assoc.; Internat. Police Assoc. Freeman, City of London, 1979. *Recreations:* Lakeland, walking, wild life; and Janet (BA), Anne (BDS), Sarah (LLB), James, Gwilym and Bryn. *Address:* 30 Latchingdon Court, Forest Road, E17 6JT. *T:* 081–521 1580; Carmarthen (0267) 236948. *Club:* Special Forces.

CASS, Sir John (Patrick), Kt 1978; OBE 1960; Director: Farmers and Graziers Co-operative Co., since 1962; The Land Newspaper Ltd, since 1964; Queensland Country Life Newspaper, since 1977; *b* 7 May 1909; *s* of Phillip and Florence Cass; *m* 1932, Velma Mostyn; two *s*. *Educ:* Christian Brothers College, Young, NSW. Gen. Pres., Farmers and Settlers Assoc. of NSW, 1954–59; Senior Vice-Pres., Aust. NFU, 1960–70; Chm., NSW Wheat Research Cttee, 1954–72; Mem., Aust. Wheat Board, 1952–77, Chm., 1972–77. Agricultural Man of the Year in Australia, 1977. *Address:* Stoney Ridge, Crowther, NSW 2692, Australia. *Clubs:* Royal Automobile of Australia, Royal Automobile of Victoria.

CASSAR, Francis Felix Anthony; Chargé d'affaires, Maltese Embassy, Baghdad, 1988; *b* 10 May 1934; *s* of Carmelo and Filomena Cassar; *m* 1969, Doreen Marjorie; two *s*. *Educ:* Primary Sch., Malta; Lyceum, Malta. Emigrated to UK, 1953. Studied mech. engrg, 1953–58; Man. Dir of own motor engrg co.; Co. Sec., Malta Drydocks (UK) Ltd, 1975. Sec., Maltese Labour Movt (UK), 1960–71; active in the Movt for Colonial Freedom; represented Malta Labour Party in the UK, 1971–81, also at meetings of the Bureau of the Socialist International. High Comr for Malta in London, 1985–87. Mem., Inst of Management, 1977. JP Brentford and Ealing, Tottenham, 1972–80. *Recreations:* music, football, DIY. *Address:* c/o Ministry of Foreign Affairs, Valletta, Malta.

CASSEL, family name of **Baroness Mallalieu.**

CASSEL, His Honour Sir Harold (Felix), 3rd Bt *cr* 1920; TD 1975; QC 1970; a Circuit Judge, 1976–88; *b* 8 Nov. 1916; 3rd *s* of Rt Hon. Sir Felix Cassel, 1st Bt, PC, QC (*d* 1953), and Lady Helen Cassel (*d* 1947); *S* brother, 1969; *m* 1st, 1940, Ione Jean Barclay (marr. diss. 1963); three *s* one *d*; 2nd, 1963, Mrs Eileen Elfrida Smedley. *Educ:* Stowe; Corpus Christi Coll., Oxford. Served War of 1939–45, Captain, 1941, Royal Artillery. Called to Bar, Lincoln's Inn, 1946. Recorder of Great Yarmouth, 1968–71, Hon. Recorder, 1972–. JP Herts, 1959–62; Dep. Chm., Herts QS, 1959–62. Mem. Council, BCEL, 1988–. *Recreations:* shooting, swimming, travelling. *Heir:* *s* Timothy Felix Harold Cassel, *qv*. *Address:* 49 Lennox Gardens, SW1. *T:* 071–584 2721.

CASSEL, Timothy Felix Harold; QC 1988; *b* 30 April 1942; *s* of Sir Harold Cassel, Bt, *qv*; *m* 1st, 1971, Jenifer Puckle (marr. diss. 1976); one *s* one *d*; 2nd, 1979, Ann Mallalieu (*see* Baroness Mallalieu); two *d*. *Educ:* Eton College. Called to the Bar, Lincoln's Inn, 1965; Jun. Prosecuting Counsel at Central Criminal Court, 1978, Sen. Prosecuting Counsel, 1986–88; Asst Boundaries Comr, 1979–85. *Address:* Studdridge Farm, Stokenchurch, Bucks. *T:* Radnage (024026) 2303. *Club:* Garrick.

CASSELL, Frank, CB 1987; Economic Minister, Washington, and UK Executive Director, International Monetary Fund and World Bank, 1988–90; *b* 21 August 1930; *s* of Francis Joseph Cassell and Ellen Blanche Cassell (*née* Adams); *m* 1957, Jean Seabrook; two *s* one *d*. *Educ:* Borden Grammar School; LSE (BSc Econ). Asst City Editor, News Chronicle, 1953–58; Dep. Editor, The Banker, 1958–65; HM Treasury: Economic Adviser, 1965; Senior Economic Adviser, 1968; Under Sec., 1974; Deputy Sec., 1983–88. Vis. Scholar, Federal Reserve Bank of Minneapolis, 1970. *Publications:* Gold or Credit?, 1965; articles on economic policy, 1953–65. *Recreations:* walking, watching cricket, reading history. *Address:* c/o National Westminster Bank, Addiscombe, Surrey CR0 6RB.

CASSELS, Field-Marshal Sir (Archibald) James (Halkett), GCB 1961 (CB 1950); KBE 1952 (CBE 1944); DSO 1944; Chief of the General Staff, Ministry of Defence, 1965–68; *b* 28 Feb. 1907; *s* of late General Sir Robert A. Cassels, GCB, GCSI, DSO; *m* 1st, 1935, Joyce (*d* 1978), *d* of late Brig.-Gen. Henry Kirk and Mrs G. A. McL. Sceales; one *s*; 2nd, 1978, Joy (Mrs Kenneth Dickson). *Educ:* Rugby Sch.; RMC, Sandhurst. 2nd Lieut Seaforth Highlanders, 1926; Lieut 1929; Capt. 1938; Major 1943; Col 1946; temp. Maj.-Gen. 1945; Maj.-Gen. 1948; Lieut-Gen. 1954; Gen. 1958. Served War of 1939–45 (despatches twice): BGS 1944; Bde Comd 1944; GOC 51st Highland Div., 1945; GOC 6th Airborne Div., Palestine, 1946 (despatches); idc, 1947; Dir Land/Air Warfare, War Office, 1948–49; Chief Liaison Officer, United Kingdom Services Liaison Staff, Australia, 1950–51; GOC 1st British Commonwealth Div. in Korea (US Legion of Merit), 1951–52; Comdr, 1st Corps, 1953–54; Dir-Gen. of Military Training, War Office, 1954–57; Dir of Emergency Operations Federation of Malaya, 1957–59; PMN (Panglima Mangku Negara), 1958; GOC-in-C, Eastern Command, 1959; C-in-C, British Army of the Rhine and Comdr NATO Northern Army Group, 1960–63; Adjutant-Gen. to the Forces, 1963–64; Field-Marshal, 1968. ADC Gen. to the Queen, 1960–63. Col Seaforth Highlanders, 1957–61; Col Queen's Own Highlanders, 1961–66; Colonel Commandant: Corps of Royal Military Police, 1957–68; Army Physical Training Corps, 1961–65. Pres., Company of Veteran Motorists, 1970–73. *Recreations:* follower of all forms of sport. *Address:* Hamble End, Barrow, Bury St Edmunds, Suffolk IP29 5BE. *Club:* Cavalry and Guards (Hon. Mem.).

CASSELS, Prof. James Macdonald, FRS 1959; Lyon Jones Professor of Physics, University of Liverpool, 1960–82, Emeritus Professor, since 1982; Chairman, Igitur Ltd, since 1986; *b* 9 Sept. 1924; *s* of Alastair Macdonald Cassels and Ada White Cassels (*née* Scott); *m* 1st, 1947, Jane Helen Thera Lawrence (*d* 1977); one *s* one *d*; 2nd, 1986, Analesia Theresa Bestman (marr. diss. 1989). *Educ:* Rochester House Sch., Edinburgh; St Lawrence Coll., Ramsgate; Trinity College, Cambridge (Coutts Trotter Student, 1948–49). BA, MA, PhD (Cantab.). Harwell Fellow and Principal Scientific Officer, Atomic Energy Research Establishment, Harwell, 1949–53. Lecturer, 1953, subseq. Senior Lecturer, University of Liverpool; Prof. of Experimental Physics, University of Liverpool, 1956–59; Extraordinary Fellow, Churchill Coll., Cambridge, 1959–60; Visiting Prof., Cornell Univ., 1959–60. Mem., Combined Heat and Power Cttee, Dept of Energy, 1974–79. Mem. Council, Royal Soc., 1968–69. Hon. Mem., Combined Heat and Power Assoc., 1979–. Hon. Fellow, Univ. of Liverpool, 1982–83. Rutherford Medal, Inst. of Physics, 1973. *Publications:* Basic Quantum Mechanics, 1970; contributions to: scientific journals on atomic, nuclear and elementary particle physics; govt reports on district heating and combined heat and power. *Recreations:* fishing, classic cars, talking. *Address:* 18 St Michael at Pleas, Norwich NR3 1EP. *T:* Norwich (0603) 660999; Igitur Ltd, 29 Sandy Way, Skelmersdale, Lancs WN8 8LF. *T:* Skelmersdale (0695) 22251.

CASSELS, Sir John (Seton), Kt 1988; CB 1978; Director General, National Economic Development Office, 1983–88; Director, National Commission on Education, since 1991; *b* 10 Oct. 1928; *s* of Alastair Macdonald Cassels and Ada White Cassels (*née* Scott); *m* 1956, Mary Whittington; two *s* two *d*. *Educ:* Sedbergh Sch., Yorkshire; Trinity Coll., Cambridge (1st cl. Hons, Classics, 1951). Rome Scholar, Classical Archaeology, 1952–54. Entered Ministry of Labour, 1954; Secretary of the Royal Commission on Trade Unions and Employers' Associations, 1965–68; Under-Sec., NBPI, 1968–71; Managing Directors' Office, Dunlop Holdings Ltd, 1971–72; Chief Exec., Training Services Agency, 1972–75; Dir, Manpower Services Commn, 1975–81; Second Permanent Sec., MPO, 1981–83. Member Council: Inst. of Manpower Studies, 1982– (Pres., 1989–); Policy Studies Inst., 1983–88; Industrial Soc., 1984–; CRAC, 1988–; Assoc. for Consumer Res., 1989–; Dir, Volunteers (PTP) Trust (Chm., 1990–91); Chairman: UK Skills, 1990–; Consumer Assoc. Ltd, 1990–91. Non-exec. Dir, Ealing HA, 1990–91. Associate Fellow, Templeton Coll., Oxford, 1988–; Dist. Vis. Fellow, 1989, Sen. Fellow, 1990, PSI. CBIM; FIPM; Hon. CGIA 1989. *Publication:* Britain's Real Skill Shortage—and what to do about it, 1990. *Address:* 10 Beverley Road, Barnes, SW13 0LX. *T:* 081–876 6270. *Club:* Reform.

CASSELS, Prof. John William Scott, FRS 1963; FRSE 1981; MA, PhD; Sadleirian Professor of Pure Mathematics, Cambridge University, 1967–84; Head of Department of Pure Mathematics and Mathematical Statistics, 1969–84; *b* 11 July 1922; *s* of late J. W. Cassels (latterly Dir of Agriculture in Co. Durham) and late Mrs M. S. Cassels (*née* Lobjoit); *m* 1949, Constance Mabel Merritt (*née* Senior); one *s* one *d*. *Educ:* Neville's Cross Council Sch., Durham; George Heriot's Sch., Edinburgh; Edinburgh and Cambridge Univs. MA Edinburgh, 1943; PhD Cantab, 1949. Fellow, Trinity, 1949–; Lecturer, Manchester Univ., 1949; Lecturer, Cambridge Univ., 1950; Reader in Arithmetic, 1963–67. Mem. Council, Royal Society, 1970, 1971 (Sylvester Medal, 1973); Vice Pres., 1974–78, Mem. Exec., 1978–82, Internat. Mathematical Union; Pres., London Mathematical Soc., 1976–78. Dr (*hc*) Lille Univ., 1965; Hon. ScD Edinburgh, 1977. De Morgan Medal, London Mathematical Soc., 1986. *Publications:* An Introduction to Diophantine Approximation, 1957; An Introduction to the Geometry of Numbers, 1959;

Rational Quadratic Forms, 1978; Economics for Mathematicians, 1981; Local Fields, 1986; papers in diverse mathematical journals on arithmetical topics. *Recreations:* arithmetic (higher only), gardening (especially common vegetables). *Address:* 3 Luard Close, Cambridge CB2 2PL. *T:* Cambridge (0223) 246108; (office) Cambridge (0223) 337975.

CASSELS, Adm. Sir Simon (Alastair Cassillis), KCB 1982; CBE 1976; *b* 5 March 1928; *o s* of late Comdr A. G. Cassels, RN, and Clarissa Cassels (*née* Motion); *m* 1962, Jillian Francies Kannreuther; one *s* one *d*. *Educ:* RNC, Dartmouth. Midshipman 1945; Commanding Officer: HM Ships Vigilant, Roebuck, and Tenby, 1962–63; HMS Eskimo, 1966–67; HMS Fearless, 1972–73; Principal Staff Officer to CDS, 1973–76; CO HMS Tiger, 1976–78; Asst Chief of Naval Staff (Op. Requirements), 1978–80; Flag Officer, Plymouth, Port Adm. Devonport, Comdr Central Sub Area Eastern Atlantic and Comdr Plymouth Sub Area Channel, 1981–82; Second Sea Lord, Chief of Naval Personnel and Adm. Pres., RNC, Greenwich, 1982–86. Dir Gen., TSB Foundn for Eng. and Wales, 1986–90. Younger Brother of Trinity House, 1963. Pres., Regular Forces Employment Assoc., 1990– (Chm., 1989). Freeman, City of London, 1983; Liveryman, Shipwrights' Co., 1984. FRGS. *Publication:* Peninsular Portrait 1811–1814, 1963. *Recreations:* family, water colours, historical research. *Address:* c/o Lloyds Bank, Broadway, Worcs. *Club:* Army and Navy.

CASSEN, Prof. Robert Harvey; Director, Queen Elizabeth House, International Development Centre, University of Oxford, and Professorial Fellow, St Antony's College, since 1986; *b* 24 March 1935; *s* of John and Liliane Cassen; *m* 1989, Sun Shuyun. *Educ:* Bedford School; New Coll., Oxford (BA LitHum, MA); Univ. of California, Berkeley; Harvard (PhD Econ). Dept of Economics, LSE, 1961–69; Sen. Economist, ODM, 1966–67; First Sec. (Econ.), New Delhi, 1967–68; Sen. Economist, World Bank, Washington, 1969–72 and 1980–81; Fellow, Inst. of Develt Studies, Sussex Univ., 1972–86; Sen. Res. Fellow, Centre for Population Studies, LSHTM, 1976–77. Special Adviser, H of C Select Cttee on Overseas Develt, 1973–74; Secretariat, Brandt Commn, 1978–79 and 1981–82; Mem., Bd of Trustees, Population Council, NY, 1978–87; UK Mem., UN Cttee for Develt Planning, 1982–84. *Publications:* India: Population, Economy, Society, 1978; (ed and contrib.) Planning for Growing Populations, 1979; (ed and contrib.) World Development Report, 1981; (ed and contrib.) Rich Country Interests and Third World Development, 1982; (ed) Soviet Interests in the Third World, 1985; Does Aid Work? (report), 1986; contribs to learned jls. *Recreations:* music and other pursuits. *Address:* Queen Elizabeth House, 21 St Giles, Oxford OX1 3LA. *T:* Oxford (0865) 273600.

CASSIDI, Adm. Sir (Arthur) Desmond, GCB 1983 (KCB 1978); President, Royal Naval Association, since 1987; Deputy Grand President, British Commonwealth Ex-Services League, since 1986; defence consultant; *b* 26 Jan. 1925; *s* of late Comdr Robert A. Cassidi, RN and late Clare F. (*née* Alexander); *m* 1st, 1950, Dorothy Sheelagh Marie (*née* Scott) (*d* 1974); one *s* two *d*; 2nd, 1982, Dr Deborah Marion Pollock (*née* Bliss), FRCS. *Educ:* RNC Dartmouth. Qual. Pilot, 1946; CO, 820 Sqdn (Gannet aircraft), 1955; 1st Lieut HMS Protector, 1955–56; psc 1957; CO, HMS Whitby, 1959–61; Fleet Ops Officer Home Fleet, 1962–64; Asst Dir Naval Plans, 1964–67; Captain (D) Portland and CO HMS Undaunted, 1967–68; idc 1969; Dir of Naval Plans, 1970–72; CO, HMS Ark Royal, 1972–73; Flag Officer Carriers and Amphibious Ships, 1974–75; Dir-Gen., Naval Manpower and Training, 1975–77; Flag Officer, Naval Air Command, 1978–79; Chief of Naval Personnel and Second Sea Lord, 1979–82; C-in-C Naval Home Comd, 1982–85; Flag ADC to the Queen, 1982–85. Mem. Adv. Council, Science Museum, 1979–84, Trustee, 1984–; Pres., FAA Museum, 1985–. FRSA 1986. *Recreation:* country pursuits. *Address:* c/o Barclays Bank, 16 Whitehall, SW1A 2EA.

CASSIDY, Bryan Michael Deece; Member (C) Dorset East and Hampshire West, European Parliament, since 1984; *b* 17 Feb. 1934; *s* of late William Francis Deece Cassidy and Kathleen Selina Patricia Cassidy (*née* Geraghty); *m* 1960, Gillian Mary Isobel Bohane; one *s* two *d*. *Educ:* Ratcliffe College; Sidney Sussex College, Cambridge. MA (Law). Commissioned RA, 1955–57 (Malta and Libya); HAC, 1957–62. With Ever Ready, Beecham's and Reed International (Dir, European associates). Mem. Council, CBI, 1981–84. Dir Gen., of a trade assoc., 1981–84. Contested (C) Wandsworth Central, 1966; Mem. GLC (Hendon North), 1977–86 (opposition spokesman on industry and employment, 1983–84). *Recreations:* history, country sports, theatre. *Address:* 11 Esmond Court, Thackeray Street, W8 5HB. *T:* 071–937 3558; (office) The Stables, White Cliff Gardens, Blandford DT11 7BU. *T:* Blandford (0258) 452420.

CASSIDY, Most Rev. Edward; *see* Cassidy, Most Rev. I. E.

CASSIDY, Ven. George Henry; Archdeacon of London and Canon Residentiary of St Paul's Cathedral, since 1987; *b* 17 Oct. 1942; *s* of Joseph Abram Cassidy and Ethel McDonald; *m* 1966, Jane Barling Stevens; two *d*. *Educ:* Belfast High School; Queen's Univ., Belfast (BSc 1965; Cert. Bib. Studies 1968); University Coll., London (MPhil 1967); Oak Hill Theological College. MRTPI 1969. Civil Servant: N Ireland, 1967–68; Govt of Kenya, 1968–70. Curate, Christ Church, Clifton, Bristol, 1972–75; Vicar: St Edyth, Sea Mills, Bristol, 1975–82; St Paul's, Portman Square, W1, 1982–87. Trustee, City Parochial Foundn, 1987–. Freeman, Tylers' & Bricklayers' Co., 1988; Hon. Chaplain, Chartered Accountants' Co., 1990. *Recreations:* Rugby football, art, chamber music, walking in the Quantocks. *Address:* 2 Amen Court, EC4M 7BU. *T:* 071–248 3312. *Club:* National.

CASSIDY, Very Rev. Herbert; Dean of Armagh and Keeper of the Library, since 1989; *b* 25 July 1935; *s* of Herbert Cassidy and Fredericka Jane Summerville; *m* 1961, Elizabeth Ann Egerton; one *s* two *d*. *Educ:* Cork Grammar Sch.; Trinity Coll., Dublin (BA 1957; MA 1965). Curate Assistant: Holy Trinity, Belfast, 1958–60; Christ Church, Londonderry, 1960–62; Rector: Aghavilly and Derrynoose, 1962–65; St Columba's, Portadown, 1965–85; Dean of Kilmore, 1985–89. *Publications:* various pamphlets. *Recreations:* music, travel. *Address:* The Library, Abbey Street, Armagh BT61 7DY. *T:* Armagh (0861) 523142.

CASSIDY, His Eminence Cardinal (Idris) Edward, AC 1990; Titular Archbishop of Amantia, since 1970; President, Pontifical Council for Promoting Christian Unity, since 1989; *b* 5 July 1924; *s* of Harold George Cassidy and Dorothy May Philipps. *Educ:* Parramatta High Sch.; St Patrick's Coll., Manly; Lateran Univ., Rome. Dr in Canon Law and Diploma of Pontifical Eccl. Acad., Rome. Ordained priest, 1949; India, 1955–62; Ireland, 1962–67; El Salvador, 1967–69; Counsellor, Apostolic Nunciature, Argentina, 1969–70; ordained bishop, Rome, 1970; Apostolic Pro-Nuncio: to Republic of China, 1970–79; to Bangladesh, 1973–79; to Lesotho, 1979–84, and Apostolic Delegate to Southern Africa; to the Netherlands, 1984–88; Substitute of Vatican Secretariat of State, 1988–89. Cardinal, 1991. Orders from China, Netherlands and Italy. *Recreations:* tennis, golf. *Address:* Pontifical Council for Christian Unity, 00120 Vatican City, Rome, Italy. *T:* 6698 4181.

CASSIDY, Most Rev. Joseph; *see* Tuam, Archbishop of, (RC).

CASSIDY, Dr Sheila Anne; Medical Director, St Luke's Hospice, Plymouth, since 1982; *b* 18 Aug. 1937; *d* of late Air Vice-Marshal John Reginald Cassidy and Barbara Margaret Cassidy. *Educ:* Univ. of Sydney; Somerville Coll., Oxford (BM BCh 1963; MA). Worked in Oxford and Leicester to 1971; went to Chile to work, 1971; arrested for treating wounded revolutionary, 1975; tortured and imprisoned 2 months, released Dec. 1975; lectured on human rights; in monastic religious order, 1978–80; returned to medicine, 1980; lecturer in UK and overseas, preacher, writer, broadcaster. Hon. DSc Exeter, 1991. Valiant for Truth Media Award, 1977. *Publications:* Audacity to Believe, 1977; Prayer for Pilgrims, 1979; Sharing the Darkness, 1988; Good Friday People, 1991. *Recreations:* writing, sewing, creative pursuits, reading, TV. *Address:* St Luke's Hospice, Stamford Road, Turnchapel, Plymouth. *T:* Plymouth (0752) 401172.

CASSILLIS, Earl of; Archibald Angus Charles Kennedy; *b* 13 Sept. 1956; *s* and *heir* of 7th Marquess of Ailsa, *qv*; *m* 1979, Dawn Leslie Anne Keen (marr. diss. 1989); two *d*. *Recreations:* shooting, ski-ing, cadets and youth-work. *Address:* Cassillis House, Maybole, Ayrshire. *T:* Dalrymple (029256) 310. *Club:* New (Edinburgh).

CASSILLY, Prof. Richard; operatic tenor; Professor, School of Fine Arts, Boston University, since 1986; *b* Washington, DC, 14 Dec. 1927; *s* of Robert Rogers Cassilly and Vera F. Swart; *m* 1st, 1951, Helen Koliopoulos; four *s* three *d*; 2nd, 1985, Patricia Craig. *Educ:* Peabody Conservatory of Music, Baltimore, Md. New York City Opera, 1955–66; Chicago Lyric, 1959–; Deutsche Oper, Berlin, 1965–; Hamburgische Staatsoper, 1966–; San Francisco Opera, 1966–; Covent Garden, 1968–; Staatsoper, Vienna, 1969–; La Scala, Milan, 1970–; Staatsoper, Munich, 1970–; Paris Opera, 1972–; Metropolitan Opera, NY, 1973–; *Television:* Otello, Peter Grimes, Fidelio, Wozzeck, Die Meistersinger; numerous recordings. Kammersänger, Hamburg, 1973; Distinguished Alumni Award, Peabody, 1977; Gold Medal, Acad. of Vocal Arts, Philadelphia, 1984. *Address:* c/o Boston University School of Fine Arts, 855 Commonwealth Avenue, Boston, Mass 02215, USA.

CASSIRER, Mrs Reinhold; *see* Gordimer, Nadine.

CASSON, (Frederick) Michael, OBE 1983; self-employed potter, since 1945 (first workshop, 1952); *b* 2 April 1925; *s* of William and Dorothy Casson; *m* 1955, Sheila Wilmot; one *s* two *d*. *Educ:* Tollington Grammar Sch.; Hornsey Coll. of Art (Art Teachers Dip.). First pots made 1945; has continued to make functional pots from opening of first workshop, 1952; at present making stoneware and porcelain pots fired with wood. Teaches part-time, all ages, 1946–; at present teaching history of ceramics and lecturing in USA. Founder member: Craftsmen Potters Assoc., 1958 (Chm., 1963–67); Harrow Studio Pottery Course, 1963; Vice-Chm., Crafts Council of GB, 1986–88. Presenter, The Craft of the Potter, BBC TV series, 1975. Gold Medal, Prague Internat. Acad. of Ceramic Art, 1964. *Publications:* Pottery in Britain Today, 1967; The Craft of the Potter, 1976, 2nd edn, 1980; many articles in Crafts, Ceramic Review, Ceramics Monthly (USA). *Recreation:* history - particularly the history of crafts. *Address:* Wobage Farm, Upton Bishop, near Ross-on-Wye, Herefordshire HR9 7QP. *T:* Upton Bishop (098985) 233.

CASSON, Sir Hugh (Maxwell), CH 1985; KCVO 1978; Kt 1952; RA 1970; RDI 1951; MA Cantab; RIBA, FCSD; President of the Royal Academy, 1976–84; Professor of Environmental Design, 1953–75, Provost, 1980–86, Royal College of Art; Member, Royal Mint Advisory Committee, since 1972; *b* 23 May 1910; *s* of late Randal Casson, ICS; *m* 1938, Margaret Macdonald Troup (*see* Margaret MacDonald Casson); three *d*. *Educ:* Eastbourne Coll.; St John's Coll., Cambridge. Craven Scholar, British Sch. at Athens, 1933; in private practice as architect since 1937 with late Christopher Nicholson; served War of 1939–45, Camouflage Officer in Air Ministry, 1940–44; Technical Officer Ministry of Town and Country Planning, 1944–46; private practice, Sen. Partner, Casson Conder & Partners, 1946–48; Dir. of Architecture, Festival of Britain, 1948–51. Master of Faculty, RDI, 1969–71. Mem., Royal Fine Art Commn, 1960–83; Trustee: British Museum (Nat. Hist.), 1976–86; Nat. Portrait Gall., 1976–84; Mem. Bd, British Council, 1977–81. Mem., Royal Danish Acad., 1954; Hon. Associate, Amer. Inst of Architects, 1968; Hon. Mem., Royal Canadian Acad. of Arts, 1980. Hon. Dr: RCA 1975; Southampton, 1977; Hon. LLD, Birmingham, 1977; Hon. DLitt Sheffield, 1986. Hon. Fellow University Coll. London, 1983. Albert Medal, RSA, 1984. Italian Order of Merit, 1980. Regular contributor as author and illustrator to technical and lay Press. *Publications:* New Sights of London (London Transport), 1937; Bombed Churches, 1946; Homes by the Million (Penguin), 1947; (with Anthony Chitty) Houses-Permanence and Prefabrication, 1947; Victorian Architecture, 1948; Inscape: the design of interiors, 1968; (with Joyce Grenfell) Nanny Says, 1972; Diary, 1981; Hugh Casson's London, 1983; Hugh Casson's Oxford, 1988. *Recreation:* drawing. *Address:* 6 Hereford Mansions, Hereford Road, W2 5BA. *T:* (office) 071–221 7774.

CASSON, Margaret MacDonald, (Lady Casson); architect, designer; Senior Tutor, School of Environmental Design, Royal College of Art, retired 1974; *b* 26 Sept. 1913; 2nd *d* of James MacDonald Troup, MD, and Alberta Davis; *m* 1938, Hugh Maxwell Casson, *qv*, three *d*. *Educ:* Wychwood Sch., Oxford; Bartlett Sch. of Architecture, University Coll. London; Royal Inst. of British Architecture. Office of late Christopher Nicholson, 1937–38; private practice, S Africa, 1938–39; Designer for Cockade Ltd, 1946–51; Tutor, Royal Coll. of Art, 1952–72; private practice as Architect and Designer for private and public buildings and interiors, also of china, glass, carpets, furniture, etc. Design consultant to various cos; Member: Council for Design Council, 1967–73 (Chm. Panel for Design Council Awards for Consumer Goods, 1972); Three-Dimensional Design Panel of NCDAD, 1962–72 (Ext. Assessor for NCDAD, 1962–65); Council of RCA, 1970; Arts Council, 1972–75; Adv. Council of V&A Museum, 1975–80; Craft Adv. Cttee, 1976–82; Royal Soc. of Arts, 1977–82; Stamp Adv. Cttee, PO, 1980–; Design Cttee, London Transport, 1980–88; Council, Zoological Soc. of London, 1983–86. Mem. Bd of Governors: Wolverhampton Coll. of Art, 1964–66; West of England Coll. of Art, 1965–67; BFI, 1973–79. FSIAD; Sen. Fellow RCA; Hon. Fellow, Royal Acad., 1985. Art photographer (as Margaret MacDonald): exhibited: London 1984, 1985 and 1986; USA, 1988; RPS, Bath, 1989; Tokyo, 1989; NY, 1990. *Address:* 6 Hereford Mansions, Hereford Road, W2 5BA. *T:* 071–727 2999.

CASSON, Prof. Mark Christopher; Professor of Economics, since 1981, and Head of Department of Economics, since 1987, University of Reading; *b* 17 Dec. 1945; *s* of Stanley Christopher Casson and Dorothy Nowell Barlow; *m* 1975, Janet Penelope Close; one *d*. *Educ:* Manchester Grammar Sch.; Univ. of Bristol (BA 1st cl. hons 1966); Churchill Coll., Cambridge (graduate student). Lecturer in Economics, 1969, Reader, 1977, Univ. of Reading. Mem. Council, REconS, 1985–90. *Publications:* Introduction to Mathematical Economics, 1973; (jtly) The Future of the Multinational Enterprise, 1976; Alternatives to the Multinational Enterprise, 1979; Youth Unemployment, 1979; Unemployment: a disequilibrium approach, 1981; The Entrepreneur: an economic theory, 1982; Economics of Unemployment: an historical perspective, 1983; (ed) The Growth of International Business, 1983; (jtly) The Economic Theory of the Multinational Enterprise: selected papers, 1985; (jtly) Multinationals and World Trade: vertical integration and the division of labour in world industries, 1986; The Firm and the Market: studies in multinational enterprise and the scope of the firm, 1987; Enterprise and Competitiveness: a systems view of international business, 1990; (ed) Entrepreneurship, 1990; (ed) Multinational Corporations, 1990; Economics of Business Culture: game theory, transaction costs and economic performance, 1991; (ed) Global Research Strategy and International Competitiveness, 1991; (ed) International Business and Global Integration, 1991. *Recreations:* collecting old books, studying old railways, visiting old churches. *Address:* 6 Wayside Green, Woodcote, Reading RG8 0QJ. *T:* (home) Checkendon (0491) 681483; (office) Reading (0734) 318227.

CASSON, Michael; *see* Casson, F. M.

CASTILLO, Rudolph Innocent, MBE 1976; first resident High Commissioner for Belize in Canada, since 1990; Representative to International Civil Aviation Organisation, since 1991; business consultant; *b* 28 Dec. 1927; *s* of late Justo S. and Marcelina Castillo; *m* 1947, Gwen Frances Powery; three *s* four *d. Educ:* St John's Coll., Belize. Training Assignments with BBC and COI, London. Lectr in Maths, Spanish and Hist., St John's Coll., 1946–52; Radio Belize: Announcer, 1952–53; Sen. Announcer, 1953–55; Asst Prog. Organizer, 1955–59; Govt Information Services: Information Officer, 1959–62; Chief Information Officer, 1962–74; Permanent Secretary: Agriculture, 1974–76; Education, 1976–79; Sec. to Cabinet, 1980–83; Chief of Protocol, 1981–83; first High Comr for Belize in London, and first Belize Ambassador to France, Fed. Republic of Germany, Holy See, EEC and Unesco, 1983–85; retired from public service, 1985. TV Commercial Productions (script writing, shooting supervision, voicing commentary). *Recreations:* photography, theatre, watercolour painting. *Address:* 112 Kent Street, Suite 2005, Ottawa, Ont K1P 5P2, Canada.

CASTLE, family name of **Baroness Castle of Blackburn.**

CASTLE OF BLACKBURN, Baroness *cr* 1990 (Life Peer), of Ibstone in the County of Buckinghamshire; **Barbara Anne Castle;** PC 1964; BA; Member (Lab) Greater Manchester West, European Parliament, 1984–89 (Greater Manchester North, 1979–84); Leader, British Labour Group, 1979–85, Vice-Chairman of Socialist Group, 1979–86, European Parliament; *b* 6 Oct. 1910; *d* of Frank and Annie Rebecca Betts; *m* 1944, Edward Cyril Castle (later Baron Castle (*d* 1979); no *c. Educ:* Bradford Girls' Grammar Sch.; St Hugh's Coll., Oxford. Elected to St Pancras Borough Council, 1937; Member Metropolitan Water Board, 1940–45; Asst Editor, Town and County Councillor, 1936–40; Administrative Officer, Ministry of Food, 1941–44; Housing Correspondent and Forces Adviser, Daily Mirror, 1944–45. MP (Lab) Blackburn, 1945–50, Blackburn East, 1950–55, Blackburn, 1955–79. Member of National Executive Cttee of Labour Party, 1950–85; Chairman Labour Party, 1958–59 (Vice-Chm. 1957–58). Minister of: Overseas Development, 1964–65; Transport, 1965–68; First Secretary of State and Sec. of State for Employment and Productivity, 1968–70; Sec. of State for Social Services, 1974–76. Co-Chm., Women's Nat. Commn, 1975–76. Hon. Fellow, St Hugh's Coll., Oxford, 1966. Hon. DTech: Bradford, 1968; Loughborough, 1969. *Publications:* part author of Social Security, edited by Dr Robson, 1943; The Castle Diaries 1974–76, 1980, vol. II, 1964–70, 1984; Sylvia and Christabel Pankhurst, 1987. *Recreations:* poetry and walking. *Address:* House of Lords, SW1A 0PW.

CASTLE, Enid; JP; Principal, The Cheltenham Ladies' College, since 1987; *b* 28 Jan. 1936; *d* of Bertram and Alice Castle. *Educ:* Hulme Grammar Sch. for Girls, Oldham; Royal Holloway Coll., Univ. of London. BA Hons History. Colne Valley High Sch., Yorks, 1958–62; Kenya High Sch., Nairobi, 1962–65; Queen's Coll., Nassau, Bahamas, 1965–68; Dep. Head, Roundhill High Sch., Leicester, 1968–72; Headmistress: High Sch. for Girls, Gloucester, 1973–81; Red Maids' Sch., Bristol, 1982–87. JP Glos, 1989. *Recreations:* tennis, squash, bridge, choral music. *Address:* The Cheltenham Ladies' College, Cheltenham, Glos GL50 3EP.

CASTLE STEWART, 8th Earl, *cr* 1800 (Ireland); **Arthur Patrick Avondale Stuart;** Viscount Stuart, 1793; Baron, 1619; Bt 1628; *b* 18 Aug. 1928; 3rd but *e* surv. *s* of 7th Earl Castle Stewart, MC, and Eleanor May, *er d* of late S. R. Guggenheim, New York; *S* father, 1961; *m* 1952, Edna Fowler; one *s* one *d. Educ:* Brambletye; Eton; Trinity Coll., Cambridge (BA). Lieut Scots Guards, 1949. FBIM. *Heir: s* Viscount Stuart, *qv. Address:* Stone House Farm, East Pennard, Shepton Mallet, Somerset BA4 6RZ. *T:* Ditcheat (074986) 240; Stuart Hall, Stewartstown, Co. Tyrone. *T:* Stewartstown (086873) 208. *Club:* Carlton.

CASTLEMAINE, 8th Baron *cr* 1812; **Roland Thomas John Handcock,** MBE (mil.) 1981; Lieutenant Colonel, Army Air Corps; *b* 22 April 1943; *s* of 7th Baron Castlemaine and Rebecca Ellen (*d* 1978), *o d* of William T. Soady, RN; *S* father, 1973; *m* 1st, 1969, Pauline Anne (marr. diss.), *e d* of John Taylor Bainbridge; 2nd, 1989, Lynne Christine, *e d* of Maj. Justin Michael Gurney, RAEC; one *s. Educ:* Campbell Coll., Belfast. psc, ph (cfs). *Heir: s* Hon. Ronan Michael Edward Handcock, *b* 27 March 1989. *Address:* c/o Lloyds Bank, Aldershot, Hants.

CASTLEMAN, Christopher Norman Anthony; corporate adviser; Chief Executive, LIT Holdings, since 1989; *b* 23 June 1941; *s* of late S. Phillips and of Mrs Joan S. R. Pyper; *m* 1st, 1965, Sarah Victoria (*née* Stockdale) (*d* 1979); one *s* one *d*; 2nd, 1980, Caroline Clare (*née* Westcott) (marr. diss. 1990); two *d*; 3rd, 1990, Suzy M. Diamond (*née* Twycross). *Educ:* Harrow; Clare Coll., Cambridge (MA Law). Joined M. Samuel & Co. Ltd, 1963; General Manager, Hill Samuel Australia Ltd, 1970–72; Director, Hill Samuel & Co. Ltd, 1972; Man. Dir, Hill Samuel Group (SA) Ltd and Hill Samuel (SA) Ltd, 1978–80; Chief Executive: Hill Samuel Gp Plc, 1980–87; Blue Arrow PLC, 1987–88; Dir, Macquarie Bank Ltd, 1985; Chm., Nat. Investment Hldgs, 1988–90. *Recreations:* sport, travel. *Address:* 20 Regent Street, SW1Y 4PZ. *T:* 071–839 8411.

CASTLEREAGH, Viscount; Frederick Aubrey Vane-Tempest-Stewart; *b* 6 Sept. 1972; *s* and *heir* of 9th Marquess of Londonderry, *qv.*

CASTON, Geoffrey Kemp, CBE 1990; Vice-Chancellor, University of the South Pacific, since 1983; *b* 17 May 1926; *s* of late Reginald and Lilian Caston, West Wickham, Kent; *m*; two *s* one *d. Educ:* St Dunstans Coll.; (Major Open Scholar) Peterhouse, Cambridge (MA). First Cl. Pt 1 History; First Cl. Pt II Law (with distinction) and Geo. Long Prize for Jurisprudence, 1950; Harvard Univ. (Master of Public Admin. 1951; Frank Knox Fellow, 1950–51). Sub-Lt, RNVR, 1945–47. Colonial Office, 1951–58; UK Mission to UN, New York, 1958–61; Dept of Techn. Co-op., 1961–64; Asst Sec., Dept of Educn and Sci. (Univs and Sci. Branches), 1964–66; Jt Sec., Schools Council, 1966–70; Under-Secretary, UGC, 1970–72; Registrar of Oxford Univ. and Fellow of Merton Coll., Oxford, 1972–79; Sec.-Gen., Cttee of Vice-Chancellors and Principals, 1979–83. Sec., Assoc. of First Div. Civil Servants, 1956–58; Adv. to UK Delegn to seven sessions of UN Gen. Assembly, 1953–63; UK Rep. on UN Cttee on Non-Self-Governing Territories, 1958–60; UN Techn. Assistance Cttee, 1962–64; Mem., UN Visiting Mission to Trust Territory of Pacific Islands, 1961. Chm., SE Surrey Assoc. for Advancement of State Educn, 1962–64; UK Delegn to Commonwealth Educn Conf., Ottawa, 1964. Ford Foundn travel grants for visits to schools and univs in USA, 1964, 1967, 1970. Vis. Associate, Center for Studies in Higher Educn, Univ. of Calif, Berkeley, 1978–. Chairman: Planning Cttee, 3rd and 4th Internat. Curriculum Confs, Oxford, 1967, New York, 1968; Ford Foundn Anglo-American Primary Educn Project, 1968–70; Library Adv. Council (England), 1973–78; Nat. Inst. for Careers Educn and Counselling, 1975–83; DES/DHSS Working Gp on Under 5s Res., 1980–82; Vice-Chm., Educnl Res. Bd, SSRC, 1973–77; Member: Steering Gp, OECD Workshops on Educnl Innovation, Cambridge 1969, W Germany, 1970, Illinois 1971; Exec. Cttee, Inter-Univ. Council for Higher Educn Overseas, 1977–83; Council, Univ. of Papua New Guinea, 1984–; Council, ACU, 1987–88; Governor, Centre for Educnl Development Overseas, 1969–70; Dep., Admin. Bd, Internat. Assoc. of Univs, 1990–. Hon. LLD Dundee, 1982; Hon. DLitt Deakin, 1991. *Publications:* contribs to educnl jls. *Address:* University of the South Pacific, Suva, Fiji.

CASTRO, Rev. Emilio Enrique; General Secretary, World Council of Churches, since 1985; *b* Uruguay, 2 May 1927; *s* of Ignacio Castro and Maria Pombo; *m* 1951, Gladys Nieves; one *s* one *d. Educ:* Union Theol. Seminary, Buenos Aires (ThL); University of Basel (post graduate work, 1953–54); University of Lausanne (doctoral candidate, 1983–84). Ordained, 1948; Pastor: Durazno and Trinidad (Uruguay), 1951–53; Central Methodist Church, La Paz, 1954–56; Central Methodist Church, Montevideo, 1957–65; concurrently Prof. of Contemp. Theol. Thought, Mennonite Seminary, Montevideo; Coordinator, Commn for Evangelical Unity in Latin America, 1965–72; Exec. Sec., S American Assoc. of Theol. Schools, 1966–69; Pres., Methodist Church in Uruguay, 1970–72; Dir, WCC Commn on World Mission and Evangelism, 1973–83. Chm., Fellowship of Christians and Jews in Uruguay, 1962–66; Moderator, Conf. on future of CCIA, Netherlands, 1967; Chm., WCC's Agency for Christian Literature Develt, 1970–72. Hon. DHL Westmar Coll., USA, 1984. *Publications:* Jesus the Conqueror, 1956; When Conscience Disturbs, 1959; Mission, Presence and Dialogue, 1963; A Pilgrim People, 1965; Reality and Faith, 1966; Amidst Evolution, 1975; Towards a Latin American Pastoral Perspective, 1973; Sent Free: Mission and Unity in the Perspective of the Kingdom, 1985; When we pray together, 1989; (ed and contrib.) Christian Century, 1971–75; (ed and contrib.) International Review of Mission, 1973–83; (ed) To the Wind of God's Spirit: Reflections on the Canberra Theme, 1991; numerous articles in several languages. *Recreation:* basket ball. *Address:* World Council of Churches, PO Box 2100, 150 route de Ferney, 1211 Geneva 2, Switzerland.

CATCHESIDE, David Guthrie, DSc London; FRS 1951; Hon. Research Associate, Waite Agricultural Research Institute, South Australia, since 1975; *b* 31 May 1907; *s* of late David Guthrie Catcheside and Florence Susanna (*née* Boxwell); *m* 1931, Kathleen Mary Whiteman; one *s* one *d. Educ:* Strand Sch.; King's Coll., University of London. Asst to Professor of Botany, Glasgow Univ., 1928–30; Asst Lecturer, 1931–33, and Lecturer in Botany, University of London (King's Coll.), 1933–36; International Fellow of Rockefeller Foundation, 1936–37; Lecturer in Botany, University of Cambridge, 1937–50; Lecturer and Fellow, Trinity Coll., Cambridge, 1944–51; Reader in Plant Cytogenetics, Cambridge Univ., 1950–51; Prof. of Genetics, Adelaide Univ., S. Australia, 1952–55; Prof. of Microbiology, Univ. of Birmingham, 1956–64; Prof. of Genetics, 1964–72, Dir, 1967–72, Vis. Fellow, 1973–75, Res. Sch. of Biol Scis, ANU. Research Associate, Carnegie Instn of Washington, 1958. Visiting Professor, California Inst. of Technology, 1961. Foreign Associate, Nat. Acad. of Sciences of USA, 1974. Foundation FAA, 1954; FKC 1959. *Publications:* Botanical Technique in Bolles Lee's Microtomists' Vade-Mecum, 1937–50; Genetics of Micro-organisms, 1951; Genetics of Recombination, 1977; Mosses of South Australia, 1980; papers on genetics and cytology. *Address:* 16 Rodger Avenue, Leabrook, SA 5068, Australia.

CATCHPOLE, Nancy Mona, OBE 1987; Consultant to Royal Society of Arts for the Women's Training Roadshow Programme, since 1989; *b* 6 Aug. 1929; *d* of George William Page and Mona Dorothy Page (*née* Cowin), New Eltham; *m* 1959, Geoffrey David Arthur Catchpole; one *s* one *d. Educ:* Haberdashers' Aske's Hatcham Girls' Sch.; Bedford Coll., Univ. of London. BA Hons (History). Asst mistress, Gravesend Grammar Sch. for Girls, 1952–56; i/c History, Ipswich High Sch. GPDST, 1956–62; part time lectr in History and General Studies, Bath Tech. Coll., 1977–. Sec., Bath Assoc. of University Women, 1970–75; Regional Rep. on Exec., BFUW, 1975–77, Vice-Pres., 1977–80, Pres., 1981–84. Women's National Commission: Co-Chairman, 1983–85; Immediate Past Co-Chairman, 1985–86; part-time Sec. with special responsibility for Women's Trng Roadshow prog., 1985–88; Actg Sec., March–Dec. 1988; Consultant to Industry Matters, for Women's Trng Roadshow prog., 1989. Vice-Chm., Women's Working Group for Industry Year 1986, 1985–. Sec., Bath Branch, Historical Assoc., 1975–79; a Governor, Weston Infants' Sch., Bath, 1975–85 (Chm., 1981–83; Vice-Chm., 1983–86). Member: Managers, Eagle House Community Sch., Somerset CC, 1979–82; Case Cttee, Western Nat. Adoption Soc., 1975–77; Wessex RHA, 1986–90; Avon FHSA Service Cttee, 1990–. FRSA 1986. *Recreations:* listening, viewing, talking, writing. *Address:* 66 Leighton Road, Weston, Bath, Avon BA1 4NG. *T:* Bath (0225) 423338. *Club:* Crosby Hall.

CATER, Antony John E., *see* Essex-Cater.

CATER, Douglass; writer and educator in USA, since 1968; President, Washington College, Chestertown, Maryland, 1982–90; Founding Fellow, and Trustee since 1982, Aspen Institute (Director, Programme on Communications and Society, 1970–76); *b* Montgomery, Ala, 24 Aug. 1923; *s* of Silas D. Cater and Nancy Chesnutt; *m* 1950, Libby Anderson; two *s* two *d. Educ:* Philip Exeter Acad. (grad.); Harvard Univ. (AB, MA). Served War, 1943–45, with OSS. Washington Editor, The Reporter (Magazine), 1950–63; Nat. Affairs Editor, 1963–64; Special Assistant: to Sec. of Army, 1951; to the President of the United States, 1964–68. Vice-Chm., The Observer, 1976–81. Consultant to Dir, Mutual Security Agency, 1952. Visiting Professor, 1959–: Princeton Univ.; Weslyan Univ., Middletown, Conn; Stanford Univ., etc. Guggenheim Fellow, 1955; Eisenhower Exchange Fellow, 1957; George Polk Meml Award, 1961; NY Newspaper Guild, Page One Award, 1961. Mem., Delta Sigma Chi. *Publications:* (with Marquis Childs) Ethics in a Business Society, 1953; The Fourth Branch of Government, 1959; Power in Washington, 1963; The Irrelevant Man, 1970. *Address:* c/o Washington College, Chestertown, Md 21620, USA.

CATER, Sir Jack, KBE 1979 (CBE 1973; MBE 1956); JP; Consultant, Hong Kong Nuclear Investment Co., since 1990 (Managing Director, 1987–89); Director, Guangdong Nuclear Power Joint Venture Co. Ltd, 1986–89 (First Deputy General Manager, 1985–86); *b* 21 Feb. 1922; *yr s* of Alfred Francis Cater and Pamela Elizabeth Dukes; *m* 1950, Peggy Gwenda Richards; one *s* two *d. Educ:* Sir George Monoux Grammar Sch., Walthamstow. Served War of 1939–45, Sqdn Ldr, RAFVR; British Military Administration, Hong Kong, 1945; joined Colonial Administrative Service, 1946, appointed Hong Kong; attended 2nd Devonshire Course, Oxford (The Queen's Coll.), 1949–50; various appts, incl. Registrar of Co-operative Societies and Director of Marketing, Dir of Agriculture and Fisheries, Dep. Economic Sec.; IDC 1966; Defence Sec./Special Asst to Governor/Dep. Colonial Sec. (Special Duties), 1967; Executive Dir, HK Trade Development Council, 1968–70; Director, Commerce and Industry, 1970–72; Secretary for Information, 1972; for Home Affairs and Information, 1973; Commissioner, Independent Commn Against Corruption, 1974–78; Chief Secretary, Hong Kong, 1978–81; actg Governor and Dep. Governor on several occasions; MEC and MLC, variously 1970–81; Hong Kong Comr in London, 1982–84; Adviser to Consultative

Cttee for the Basic Law, Hong Kong, 1986–90. Director: Hong Kong Cable Communications Ltd, 1990–; Hoare Govett (Asia) Ltd (also Consultant), 1990–; The Scottish Asian Development Co. Ltd, 1990–; Consultant: Philips & Co., China and Hong Kong, 1990–; Internat. Bechtel Inc., 1990–. Pres., Agency for Volunteer Service, Hong Kong, 1982–; Member: Internat. Bd of Dirs, United World Colls, UK, 1981–; Court, Univ. of Hong Kong, 1982–. Hon. DSSc Univ. of Hong Kong, 1982. *Recreations:* work, walking, bridge, reading, watching television. *Address:* (office) Hong Kong Nuclear Investment Co. Ltd, 147 Argyle Street, Kowloon, Hong Kong. *T:* Hong Kong 7608058; (home) 97 Kadoorie Avenue, Kowloon, Hong Kong. *T:* Hong Kong 7154004. *Clubs:* Hong Kong, Royal Hong Kong Jockey (Hong Kong).

CATER, Sir John Robert, (Sir Robin), Kt 1984; Chairman, Distillers Co. Ltd, 1976–83; *b* 25 April 1919; *s* of Sir John Cater; *m* 1945, Isobel Calder Ritchie; one *d. Educ:* George Watson's Coll., Edinburgh; Cambridge Univ. (MA). Trainee, W. P. Lowrie & Co. Ltd, 1946; James Buchanan & Co. Ltd, 1949: Dir 1950; Prodn Dir 1959; Prodn Asst, Distillers Co. Ltd, Edinburgh: Prodn Asst, 1959; Dir, 1967–83 (Mem., Management Cttee); Dep. Chm., 1975–76; Man. Dir, John Haig & Co. Ltd, 1965–70; Non-Exec. Dir, United Glass, 1969, Chm. 1972. *Recreations:* music, theatre, fishing, golf (Walker Cup team, 1955; played for Scotland, 1952–56). *Address:* Avernish, Elie, Fife, Scotland KY9 1DA. *Clubs:* New (Edinburgh); Royal and Ancient (St Andrews); The Golf House (Elie).

CATFORD, (John) Robin, CBE 1990; Secretary for Appointments to the Prime Minister and Ecclesiastical Secretary to the Lord Chancellor, since 1982; *b* 11 Jan. 1923; *er s* of late Adrian Leslie Catford and Ethel Augusta (*née* Rolfe); *m* 1948, Daphne Georgina, *o d* of late Col J. F. Darby, CBE, TD; three *s* one *d. Educ:* Hampton Grammar Sch.; Univ. of St Andrews (BSc); St John's Coll., Cambridge (DipAgric). Sudan Civil Service: Dept of Agriculture and Forests: Kordofan Province, 1946; Equatoria Province, 1948; Blue Nile Province (secondment to White Nile Schemes Bd), 1952–55; various posts in industry and commerce, mainly in UK, 1955–66; Home Civil Service: Principal, MAFF, 1966; sec. to Cttee of Inquiry on Contract Farming, 1971; Asst Sec., 1972; Under-Sec. (Agricultural Resources Policy and Horticulture), 1979; transferred to PM's Office, 1982. Member: Economic Development Cttee for Hotels and Catering, 1972–76; EDC for Agriculture, 1979–82. Mem. Chichester Dio. Synod, 1979–84 and 1988–90. *Recreations:* sailing, theatre, avoiding gardening. *Address:* 10 Downing Street, SW1A 2AA. *Club:* United Oxford & Cambridge University.

CATHCART, family name of **Earl Cathcart.**

CATHCART, 6th Earl *cr* 1814; **Alan Cathcart,** CB 1973; DSO 1945; MC 1944; Viscount Cathcart, 1807; Baron Greenock (United Kingdom) and 15th Baron Cathcart (Scotland), 1447; Major-General; *b* 22 Aug. 1919; *o s* of 5th Earl and Vera, *d* of late John Fraser, of Cape Town; *S* father, 1927; *m* 1st, 1946, Rosemary (*d* 1980), *yr d* of late Air Commodore Sir Percy Smyth-Osbourne, CMG, CBE; one *s* two *d*; 2nd, 1984, Marie Isobel Lady Weldon. *Educ:* Eton; Magdalene Coll., Cambridge. Served War of 1939–45 (despatches, MC, DSO). Adjt RMA Sandhurst, 1946–47; Regimental Adjt Scots Guards, 1951–53; Brigade Major, 4th Guards Brigade, 1954–56; Commanding Officer, 1st Battalion Scots Guards, 1957; Lt-Col comd Scots Guards, 1960; Colonel AQ Scottish Command, 1962–63; Imperial Defence Coll., 1964; Brigade Comdr, 152 Highland Brigade, 1965–66; Chief, SHAPEX and Exercise Branch SHAPE, 1967–68; GOC Yorkshire District, 1969–70; GOC and British Comdt, Berlin, 1970–73; retd. A Dep-Chm. of Cttees and Dep. Speaker, House of Lords. Ensign, Queen's Body Guard for Scotland, Royal Company of Archers. Pres., ACFA, 1975–82; Dep. Grand Pres., British Commonwealth Ex-Services League, 1976–86. Pres., RoSPA, 1982–86. Cdre, RYS, 1974–80. GCStJ 1986 (KStJ 1985); Lord Prior, Order of St John of Jerusalem, 1986–88 (Vice Chancellor, 1984–86). *Heir: s* Lord Greenock, *qv. Address:* Moor Hatches, West Amesbury, Salisbury, Wilts. *Clubs:* Brooks's; Royal Yacht Squadron (Cowes).

CATHERWOOD, Sir (Henry) Frederick (Ross), Kt 1971; Member (C) Cambridge and North Bedfordshire, European Parliament, since 1984 (Cambridgeshire, 1979–84); a Vice-President of the European Parliament, since 1989; Director, Goodyear Great Britain Ltd; *b* 30 Jan. 1925; *s* of late Stuart and of Jean Catherwood, Co. Londonderry; *m* 1954, Elizabeth, *er d* of late Rev. Dr D. M. Lloyd Jones, Westminster Chapel, London; two *s* one *d. Educ:* Shrewsbury; Clare Coll., Cambridge. Articled Price, Waterhouse & Co.; qualified as Chartered Accountant, 1951; Secretary, Laws Stores Ltd, Gateshead, 1952–54; Secretary and Controller, Richard Costain Ltd, 1954–55; Chief Executive, 1955–60; Asst Managing Director, British Aluminium Co. Ltd, 1960–62; Managing Director, 1962–64; Chief Industrial Adviser, DEA, 1964–66; Dir-Gen., NEDC, 1966–71; Managing Dir and Chief Executive, John Laing & Son Ltd, 1972–74. Chm., Cttee for External Economic Relations, European Parlt, 1979–84; Dep. Chm., EDG, Eur. Parlt, 1983–87. British Institute of Management: Mem. Council, 1961–66, 1969–79; Vice-Chm., 1972; Chm., 1974–76; Vice-Pres., 1976–. Member of Council: NI Development Council, 1963–64; RIIA, 1964–77; BNEC, 1965–71; NEDC, 1964–71; Chm., BOTB, 1975–79. Vice-Pres., 1976, Pres., 1977, Fellowship of Independent Evangelical Churches; Chm. of Council, 1971–77, Pres., 1983–84, Univs and Colls Christian Fellowship (formerly Inter-Varsity Fellowship); Mem., Central Religious Adv. Cttee to BBC and IBA, 1975–79. Hon. DSc Aston, 1972; Hon. DSc (Econ.) QUB, 1973; Hon. DUniv Surrey, 1979. *Publications:* The Christian in Industrial Society, 1964, rev. edn 1980 (Nine to Five, USA, 1983); The Christian Citizen, 1969; A Better Way, 1976; First Things First, 1979; God's Time God's Money, 1987; David: Poet, Soldier, King, 1991. *Recreations:* music, gardening, reading. *Address:* Sutton Hall, Balsham, Cambridgeshire; (office) Shire Hall, Castle Hill, Cambridge CB3 0AW. *T:* Cambridge (0223) 317672. *Club:* United Oxford & Cambridge University.

CATHERWOOD, Herbert Sidney Elliott, CBE 1979; former Chairman of Ulsterbus and Citybus; *b* 1929. *Educ:* Belfast Royal Academy, N Ireland. Chairman, Ulsterbus Ltd, from inception, 1967; Member, NI Transport Holding Co., 1968; became Director of Merger of Belfast Corporation Transport with Ulsterbus, 1972. Director: RMC Catherwood; Sea Ferry Parcels. Member: NE Area Board, Ulster Bank, 1976. *Address:* Boulderstone House, 917 Antrim Road, Templepatrick, Co. Antrim, N Ireland.

CATLIN, John Anthony; Deputy Solicitor, Department of the Environment, since 1989 (Assistant Solicitor, 1984–89); *b* 25 Nov. 1947; *s* of John Vincent Catlin and Kathleen Glover Catlin (*née* Brand); *m* 1974, Caroline Jane Goodman; one *s* two *d. Educ:* Ampleforth Coll., York; Birmingham Univ. (LLB 1969). Solicitor of the Supreme Court, 1972. Articled Clerk, 1970–72, Asst Solicitor, 1972–75, Gregory Rowcliffe & Co.; Legal Asst, 1975–78, Sen. Legal Asst, 1978–84, Treasury Solicitor's Dept. *Recreations:* music, travel. *Address:* Department of the Environment, 2 Marsham Street, SW1P 3EB. *T:* 071–276 4702.

CATLING, Hector William, CBE 1989 (OBE 1980); MA, DPhil, FSA; Director of the British School at Athens, 1971–89, retired; *b* 26 June 1924; *s* of late Arthur William Catling and Phyllis Norah Catling (*née* Vyvyan); *m* 1948, Elizabeth Anne (*née* Salter); two *s* one *d. Educ:* The Grammar Sch., Bristol; St John's Coll., Oxford (Hon. Fellow 1986). Casberd Exhbr, 1948, BA 1950, MA 1954, DPhil 1957. Served War, RNVR, 1942–46. At Univ.: undergrad. 1946–50, postgrad. 1950–54. Goldsmiths' Travelling Schol., 1951–53. Archaeological Survey Officer, Dept of Antiquities, Cyprus, 1955–59; Asst Keeper, Dept of Antiquities, Ashmolean Museum, Univ. of Oxford, 1959–64, Sen. Asst Keeper, 1964–71. Fellow, 1967–71, Supernumerary Fellow, 1991–, Linacre Coll., Oxford. Sanders Meml Lectr, Sheffield, 1979; Myres Meml Lectr, Oxford, 1987; Mitford Meml Lectr, St Andrews, 1989. Corresp. Mem., German Archaeological Inst., 1961; Hon. Mem., Greek Archaeological Soc., 1975 (Counsellor, 1987–). Hon. Dr Athens, 1987. *Publications:* Cypriot Bronzework in the Mycenaean World, 1964; contribs to jls concerned with prehistoric and classical antiquity in Greek lands. *Recreation:* ornithology. *Address:* Dunford House, Langford, Lechlade, Glos GL7 3LN. *Club:* Athenæum.

CATLING, Sir Richard (Charles), Kt 1964; CMG 1956; OBE 1951; QPM; CPM 1942; *b* 22 Aug. 1912; *y s* of late William Catling, Leiston, Suffolk; *m* 1951, Mary Joan Feyer (*née* Lewis) (*d* 1974). *Educ:* The Grammar School, Bungay, Suffolk. Palestine Police, 1935–48; Federation of Malaya Police, 1948–54; Commissioner of Police, Kenya, 1954–63; Inspector General of Police, Kenya, 1963–64; Police Advr to Jordan Govt, 1971–75. Security/Safety Consultant to Guthrie Corp., London, 1965–88. KPM 1945. Officer Brother, OStJ, 1956. Freeman, City of London, 1979. *Recreations:* fishing, sailing. *Address:* Hall Fen House, Irstead, Norfolk NR12 8XT. *Club:* East India.

CATLOW, Prof. Charles Richard Arthur; Wolfson Professor of Natural Philosophy at Royal Institution of Great Britain, since 1989; *b* 24 April 1947; *s* of Rolf M. Catlow and Constance Catlow (*née* Aldred); *m* 1978, Carey Anne Chapman; one *s. Educ:* Clitheroe Royal Grammar School; St John's College, Oxford (MA, DPhil). Research Fellow, Oxford Univ., 1973–76; Lectr, Dept of Chemistry, UCL, 1976–85; Prof. of Physical Chemistry, Univ. of Keele, 1985–89. *Publications:* (jtly) Point Defects in Materials, 1988; ed jtly and contrib. to works on computational and materials sciences; papers in learned jls. *Recreations:* reading, music, walking. *Address:* Royal Institution of Great Britain, 21 Albemarle Street, W1X 4BS. *T:* 071–409 2992.

CATO, Sir Arnott Samuel, KCMG 1983; Kt 1977; PC (Barbados) 1976; President of the Senate of Barbados, 1976–86; *b* St Vincent, 24 Sept. 1912. *Educ:* St Vincent Grammar Sch. (St Vincent Scholar, 1930); Edinburgh Univ. (MB, ChB). Returned to St Vincent; Asst Resident Surgeon, Colonial Hosp., 1936–37; Ho. Surg., Barbados Gen. Hosp., 1937–41; private practice from 1941; Vis. Surgeon, Barbados Gen. Hosp., later Queen Elizabeth Hosp., and Chm. Med. Staff Cttee 1965–70. Past Pres., Barbados Br. BMA. Chm., Barbados Public Service Commn, 1972–76; (Prime Minister's Nominee) Senate of Barbados, following Gen. Election of Sept. 1976; Actg Governor Gen. for periods in 1976, 1980, 1981, 1983, 1984, 1985 and 1986. Hon. LLD, Univ. of West Indies, 1978. *Address:* Little Kent, Kent, Christ Church, Barbados.

CATO, Brian Hudson; Full-time Chairman of Industrial Tribunals, since 1975, Regional Chairman, Newcastle upon Tyne, since 1989; *b* 6 June 1928; *s* of Thomas and Edith Willis Cato; *m* 1963, Barbara Edith Myles; one *s. Educ:* LEA elem. and grammar schs; Trinity Coll., Oxford; RAF Padgate. MA Oxon, LLB London. RAF, 1952–54. Called to Bar, Gray's Inn, 1952; in practice NE Circuit, 1954–75; a Recorder of the Crown Court, 1974–75. Special Lectr (part-time) in Law of Town and Country Planning, King's Coll., now Univ. of Newcastle, 1956–75; Hon. Examnr, Inst. of Landscape Architects, 1960–75. Pres., N of England Medico-legal Soc., 1973–75. Freeman of City of Newcastle upon Tyne by patrimony; Mem. Plumbers', Hostmen's, Goldsmiths' and Colliers' Companies; Founder Mem. Scriveners' Co. Freeman, City of London, 1985. Hon. ALI. *Recreations:* bibliomania, antiquarian studies, family life. *Address:* 46 Bemersyde Drive, Newcastle upon Tyne NE2 2HJ. *T:* Newcastle (091) 2814226; 2 Croft Place, Newton-by-the-Sea, Alnwick, Northumberland NE66 1UF. *T:* Embleton (066576) 334.

CATO, Rt. Hon. (Robert) Milton, PC 1981; Barrister; Leader of the Opposition, St Vincent and the Grenadines, since 1984 (Prime Minister, 1979–84); *b* 3 June 1915; *m* Lucy Claxton. *Educ:* St Vincent Grammar Sch. Called to the Bar, Middle Temple, 1948; in private practice. Served War of 1939–45, Canadian Army. Leader, St Vincent Labour Party; Premier of St Vincent, 1967–72, 1974–79; former Minister of Finance. Mem., Kingstown Town Bd, 1952–59 (Chm., 1952–53); former Mem., Public Service Commn. A Governor, Caribbean Reg. Develt Bank for St Vincent. Former Pres., St Vincent Cricket Assoc. *Address:* PO Box 138, Kingstown, St Vincent and the Grenadines. *Club:* Kingstown.

CATOVSKY, Julia Margaret, (Mrs Daniel Catovsky); *see* Polak, J. M.

CATTANACH, Bruce Macintosh, PhD, DSc; FRS 1987; Head of Genetics Division, MRC Radiobiology Unit, Chilton, since 1987; *b* 5 Nov. 1932; *s* of James and Margaretta Cattanach; *m* 1966, Margaret Bouchier Crewe; two *d. Educ:* King's Coll., Univ. of Durham (BSc, 1st Cl. Hons); Inst. of Animal Genetics, Univ. of Edinburgh (PhD, DSc). Scientific Staff, MRC Induced Mutagenesis Unit, Edinburgh, 1959–62, 1964–66; NIH Post Doctoral Res. Fellow, Biology Div., Oak Ridge Nat. Lab., Tenn, USA, 1962–64; Sen. Scientist, City of Hope Med. Centre, Duarte, Calif, 1966–69; Scientific Staff, MRC Radiobiology Unit, Chilton, Oxon, 1969–86. *Publications:* contribs to several learned jls on X-chromosome inactivation, sex determination, mammalian chromosome imprinting, and genetics generally. *Recreations:* squash; breeding, showing and judging pedigree dogs. *Address:* Down's Edge, Reading Road, Harwell, Oxon OX11 0JJ. *T:* Abingdon (0235) 835410.

CATTANACH, Brig. Helen, CB 1976; RRC 1963; Matron-in-Chief (Army) and Director of Army Nursing Services, Queen Alexandra's Royal Army Nursing Corps, 1973–76; *b* 21 June 1920; *d* of late Francis Cattanach and Marjory Cattanach (*née* Grant). *Educ:* Elgin Academy; trained Woodend Hospital, Aberdeen. Joined QAIMNS (R) 1945; service in India, Java, United Kingdom, Singapore, Hong Kong and Germany, 1945–52; MELF, Gibraltar and UK, 1953–57; Staff Officer, MoD, 1958–61; Inspector of Recruiting, QARANC, 1961–62; Hong Kong, 1963–64; Matron: BMH Munster, 1968; Cambridge Military Hosp., Aldershot, 1969–71; Dir of Studies, QARANC, 1971–72. QHNS 1973–76. Col Comdt QARANC, 1978–81. Governor, Royal Scottish Corp., 1976–. CStJ 1976 (OStJ 1971). *Address:* 22 Southview Court, Hill View Road, Woking, Surrey GU22 7RP.

CATTELL, George Harold Bernard; Group Managing Director, FMC, 1978–84; Chief Executive, NFU Holdings Ltd, since 1978; Director, Agricultural Credit Corporation, since 1980; *b* 23 March 1920; *s* of H. W. K. Cattell; *m* 1951, Agnes Jean Hardy; three *s* one *d. Educ:* Royal Grammar Sch., Colchester. Served Regular Army, 1939–58; psc 1954; despatches, Malaya, 1957; retired as Major, RA. Asst Director, London Engineering Employers' Assoc., 1958–60; Group Industrial Relations Officer, H. Stevenson & Sons, 1960–61; Director, Personnel and Manufacturing, Rootes Motors Ltd, 1961–68; Managing Director, Humber Ltd, Chm., Hills Precision Diecasting Ltd, Chm., Thrupp & Maberly Ltd, 1965–68; Dir, Manpower and Productivity Services, Dept of Employment and Productivity, 1968–70; Dir-Gen., NFU, 1970–78. Member Council: Industrial Soc. 1965–84; CBI, 1970–84. FRSA; FBIM. AMN Federation of Malaya, 1958. *Recreations:* tennis, fishing. *Address:* Little Cheveney, Yalding, Kent ME18 6DY. *T:* Hunton (06272) 365. *Club:* Institute of Directors.

CATTERALL, Dr John Ashley, FIM, FInstP; Secretary, The Institute of Metals, since 1988; *b* 26 May 1928; *s* of John William Catterall and Gladys Violet Catterall; *m* 1960, Jennifer Margaret Bradfield; two *s*. *Educ:* Imperial Coll. of Science and Technol., London (BSc, PhD, DIC). ARSM; FIM 1964; FInstP 1968; CEng 1978. National Physical Lab., 1952–74; Dept of Industry, 1974–81; Head, Energy Technology Div., and Dep. Chief Scientist, Dept of Energy, 1981–83; Sec., SERC, 1983–88. Inst. of Metals Rosenhain Medal for Physical Metallurgy, 1970. *Publications:* (with O. Kubaschewski) Thermochemical Data of Alloys, 1956; contrib. Philos. Mag., Jl Inst. of Physics, Jl Inst. of Metals. *Recreation:* sailing. *Address:* 65 Hamilton Avenue, Pyrford, Woking, Surrey GU22 8RU. *T:* Byfleet (09323) 46707.

CATTERALL, John Stewart; Managing Director, CIPFA Consultancy for Health, since 1989; Deputy Director, Finance, National Health Service Management Board, since 1985; *b* 13 Jan. 1939; *s* of John Bernard and Eliza Catterall; *m* 1965, Ann Beryl Hughes; two *s*. *Educ:* Blackpool Tech. Coll. and Sch. of Art. Mem. CIPFA. Posts in local authorities, 1961–70; Management Accountant, Cambridgeshire and Isle of Ely CC, 1970–72, Chief Accountant, 1972–73; Asst County Treasurer, Financial Planning and Accounting, Cambs CC, 1973–76; Dist. Treasurer, Southampton and SW Hants DHA, 1976–78, Area Treasurer, 1978–82; Regional Treasurer, NE Thames RHA, 1982–85; Head of Health Services, 1985–89, Head of Health Adv. Services, 1989, CIPFA. *Publications:* contribs to professional jls. *Recreations:* golf, swimming, reading. *Address:* Birkdale, Green Lane, Chilworth, Southampton. *T:* Southampton (0703) 769402.

CATTERMOLE, Joan Eileen, (Mrs J. Cattermole); *see* Mitchell, Prof. J. E.

CATTERMOLE, Lancelot Harry Mosse, ROI 1938; painter and illustrator; *b* 19 July 1898; *s* of Sidney and Josephine Cattermole; *g s* of George Cattermole (1800–1868), painter in water-colours and oils and illustrator of works by Charles Dickens and Sir Walter Scott; *m* 1937, Lydia Alice Winifred Coles, BA; no *c*. *Educ:* Holmsdale House Sch., Worthing, Sussex; The Robert May Grammar Sch., Odiham, Hants. Senior Art Scholarship to Slade Faculty of Fine Art, University of London, and Central School of Arts and Crafts, London, 1923–26. Exhibitor RA, ROI, RBA, RP, etc, and Provincial Art Galleries; works acquired by National Army Mus., London, and Royal Naval Mus., Portsmouth. Signs work Lance Cattermole. *Recreations:* reading, bridge. *Address:* Horizon, 17 Palmers Way, High Salvington, Worthing, W Sussex BN13 3DP. *T:* Worthing (0903) 60436.

CATTO, family name of **Baron Catto.**

CATTO, 2nd Baron, *cr* 1936, of Cairncatto; Bt *cr* 1921; **Stephen Gordon Catto;** President, Morgan Grenfell Group plc, since 1987 (Chairman, Morgan Grenfell Group plc, 1980–87); Chairman, Yule Catto & Co. plc, since 1971; Director: The General Electric Co. plc, since 1959; News International plc, since 1969; Times Newspapers Holdings Ltd, since 1981, and other companies; *b* 14 Jan. 1923; *o s* of 1st Baron Catto and Gladys Forbes (*d* 1980), *d* of Stephen Gordon; *S* father 1959; *m* 1st, 1948, Josephine Innes (marr. diss. 1965), *er d* of G. H. Packer, Alexandria, Egypt; two *s* two *d*; 2nd, 1966, Margaret, *d* of J. S. Forrest, Dilston, Tasmania; one *s* one *d*. *Educ:* Eton; Cambridge Univ. Served with RAFVR, 1943–47. Dir, 1957, Chief Exec., 1973–74, and Chm., 1973–79, Morgan Grenfell & Co. Ltd; Chairman: Australian Mutual Provident Soc. (UK branch) 1972–91; Pearl Gp, 1989–91. Member, Advisory Council, ECGD, 1959–65; part-time Mem., London Transport Bd, 1962–68; Mem., London Adv. Cttee, Hong Kong & Shanghai Banking Corp., 1966–80. Chm. Council, RAF Benevolent Fund, 1978–91; Trustee and Chm., Exec. Cttee, Westminster Abbey Trust, 1973–. *Heir:* *s* Hon. Innes Gordon Catto, *b* 7 Aug. 1950. *Address:* Morgan Grenfell Group plc, 23 Great Winchester Street, EC2P 2AX; 41 William Mews, Lowndes Square, SW1X 9HQ. *Clubs:* Oriental; Melbourne (Australia).

CATTO, Henry Edward; Director, United States Information Agency, since 1991; *b* 6 Dec. 1930; *s* of Henry E. Catto and Maurine H. Catto; *m* 1958, Jessica Hobby; two *s* two *d*. *Educ:* Williams Coll. (BA). Businessman, San Antonio, Texas, 1952–69; Dep. US Rep., Orgn of American States, 1969–71; US Ambassador to El Salvador, 1971–73; US Chief of Protocol, 1974–76; Consultant, Washington DC, 1977–81; Asst Sec. of Defense, 1981–83; Vice-Chm., H & C Communications, 1983–89; US Ambassador to UK, 1989–91. *Recreations:* tennis, hiking, running, ski-ing, golf. *Address:* 7718 Georgetown Pike, McLean, Va 22102, USA; United States Information Agency, 301 4th Street SW, Washington, DC 20547.

CAUGHEY, Sir Thomas Harcourt Clarke, KBE 1972 (OBE 1966); JP; Executive Chairman, Smith & Caughey Ltd, since 1975 (Managing Director, 1962–85); *b* Auckland, 4 July 1911; *s* of James Marsden Caughey; *m* 1939, Patricia Mary, *d* of Hon. Sir George Panton Finlay; one *s* two *d*. *Educ:* King's Coll., Auckland; Auckland Univ. Major, Fiji Military Forces (Pacific), 1942–44. Director: New Zealand Insurance Corp., 1981–86 (Dep. Chm., 1981–86); South British Insurance Co., 1963–81; New Zealand Guardian Trust Co., 1963–86. Member: Caughey Preston Trust Bd, 1950–79 (Chm., 1954–79); Eden Park Trustees; Auckland Hosps Bd, 1953–74 (Chm., 1959–74); Hosps Adv. Council, 1960–74; Vice-Pres., NZ Exec. Hosps Bds Assoc., 1960–74; Chairman: NZ MRC, 1966–71; Social Council of NZ, 1971–73; Pres., Auckland Med. Res. Foundn, 1978–84. CStJ. Hon. LLD Auckland, 1986. Mem., All Black Rugby Team, 1932–37. *Recreations:* gardening, swimming. *Address:* 7 Judges Bay Road, Auckland, NZ. *Club:* Northern (Auckland, NZ).

CAULCOTT, Thomas Holt; management consultant; Vice Chairman, Committee of Management, Hanover Housing Association, since 1990 (Member, since 1988); Councillor, South Shropshire District Council, since 1991; *b* 7 June 1927; *s* of late L. W. Caulcott and Doris Caulcott; *m* 1st, 1954, C. Evelyn Lowden (marr. diss. 1987); one *d* (and one *s* decd); 2nd, 1988, Jane Marguerite Allsopp. *Educ:* Solihull Sch.; Emmanuel Coll., Cambridge. Asst Principal, Central Land Bd and War Damage Commn, 1950–53; transferred to HM Treasury, 1953; Private Sec. to Economic Sec. to the Treasury, 1955; Principal, Treasury supply divs, 1956–60; Private Sec. to successive Chancellors of the Exchequer, Sept. 1961–Oct. 1964; Principal Private Sec. to First Sec. of State (DEA), 1964–65; Asst Sec., HM Treasury, 1965–66; Min. of Housing and Local Govt, 1967–69; Civil Service Dept, 1969–70; Under-Sec., Machinery of Govt Gp, 1970–73; Principal Finance Officer, Local Govt Finance Policy, DoE, 1973–76; Sec., AMA, 1976–82; Chief Exec., Birmingham City Council, 1982–88. Harkness Fellowship, Harvard and Brookings Instn, 1960–61; Vis. Fellow, Dept of Land Economy, Univ. of Cambridge, 1984–85; Hon. Fellow: Inst. of Local Govt Studies, Univ. of Birmingham, 1979–; Birmingham Polytechnic, 1990. *Address:* 37 Lower Broad Street, Ludlow, Shropshire SY8 1PH. *T:* Ludlow (0584) 875154.

CAULFEILD, family name of **Viscount Charlemont.**

CAULFIELD, Sir Bernard, Kt 1968; Judge of the High Court of Justice, Queen's Bench Division, 1968–89; Presiding Judge, Northern Circuit, 1976–80; *b* 24 April 1914; *y s* of late John Caulfield and late Catherine Quinn; *m* 1953, Sheila Mary, *o d* of Dr J. F. J. Herbert; three *s* one *d*. *Educ:* St Francis Xavier's Coll.; University of Liverpool. LLB 1938, LLM 1940, Hon. LLD 1980. Solicitor, 1940. Army Service, 1940–46; Home and MEF; Commnd, Dec. 1942, RAOC; released with Hon. rank of Major. Barrister-at-Law, Lincoln's Inn, 1947 (Bencher, 1968); joined Midland Circuit, 1949; QC 1961; Recorder of Coventry, 1963–68; Dep. Chairman QS, County of Lincoln (Parts of Lindsey), 1963–71; Leader, Midland Circuit, 1965–68; Comr of Assize, 1967. Mem., General Council of Bar, 1965–68; Mem. Senate, 1984, Treasurer and Dean of Chapel, Lincoln's Inn, 1987; Mem. Inns of Court Council, 1987. Hon. Mem., Northern Circuit Bar Mess, 1979. *Address:* Ingleby, near Lincoln, LN1 2PQ.

CAULFIELD, Ian George; Clerk of the Council and Chief Executive, Warwickshire County Council, and Clerk to the Warwickshire Lieutenancy, since 1986; *b* 14 Dec. 1942; *s* of William and Elizabeth Caulfield; *m* 1967, Geraldine Mary Hind; three *s*. *Educ:* Liverpool Inst. High Schs for Boys; Univ. of Manchester (BA Hons Geography); Liverpool Poly. (DipTP). Jun. Planning Assistant, Liverpool City, 1964–65; Planning Assistant, Lancs CC, 1965–69; Sen. Planning Officer, Hants CC, 1969–74; Asst Hd, Res. and Intelligence Unit, 1974–76, Prin. Assistant to Chief Exec., 1976–78, Oxford CC; Asst Exec., 1978–83, Dep. Clerk and Asst Chief Exec., 1983–86, Warwicks CC. *Publication:* (jtly) Planning for Change: strategic planning and local government, 1989. *Recreation:* sport, particularly soccer. *Address:* 52 Northumberland Road, Leamington Spa, Warwicks CV32 6HB. *T:* Leamington Spa (0926) 423625.

CAULFIELD, Patrick; artist; *b* London, 29 Jan. 1936; *s* of Patrick and Annie Caulfield; *m* 1968, Pauline Jacobs; three *s*. *Educ:* Acton Central Secondary Modern Sch.; Chelsea Sch. of Art; RCA. Served RAF, 1953–56. Taught at Chelsea Sch. of Art, 1963–71. First exhibited, FBA Galls, 1961; group exhibitions include: Whitechapel, Tate, Hayward, Waddington and Tooth Galls, and ICA, in London; Walker Art Gall., Liverpool; and exhibns in Paris, Brussels, Milan, NY, São Paulo, Berlin, Lugano, Dortmund, Bielefeld and Helsinki. One-man exhibitions include: Robert Fraser Gall., London, 1965, 1967; Robert Elkon Gall., NY, 1966, 1968; Waddington Galls, 1969, 1971, 1973, 1975, 1979, 1981, and 1985; Tate Gall. (retrospective), 1981; also in Italy, France, Australia, Belgium, USA and Japan. Design for Party Game (ballet), Covent Garden, 1984. Work in public collections incl. Tate Gall.; V&A; Walker Art Gall., Liverpool; Whitworth Art Gall., and Manchester City Art Gall.; and museums and galls in GB, Australia, USA, W Germany and Japan. *Address:* c/o Waddington Galleries, 2 Cork Street, W1X 1PA; 6 Primrose Hill Studios, Fitzroy Road, NW1.

CAUSEY, Prof. Gilbert, FRCS; retired; Sir William Collins Professor of Anatomy, Royal College of Surgeons, Professor of Anatomy, University of London, and Conservator of Hunterian Museum, 1952–70; *b* 8 Oct. 1907; 2nd *s* of George and Ada Causey; *m* 1935, Elizabeth, *d* of late F. J. L. Hickinbotham, JP, and of Mrs Hickinbotham; two *s* three *d*. *Educ:* Wigan Grammar Sch.; University of Liverpool. MB, ChB (1st Hons.), 1930; MRCS, LRCP, 1930; FRCS 1933; DSc 1964; FDSRCS 1971. Gold Medallist in Anatomy, Surgery, Medicine, and Obstetrics and Gynæcology; Lyon Jones Scholar and various prizes. Member of Anatomical and Physiological Societies. Asst Surgeon, Walton Hospital, Liverpool, 1935; Lecturer in Anatomy, University College, London, 1948; Rockefeller Foundation Travelling Fellow, 1950. John Hunter Medal, 1964; Keith Medal, 1970. *Publications:* The Cell of Schwann, 1960; Electron Microscopy, 1962; contributions to various scientific texts and journals. *Recreation:* music. *Address:* Orchard Cottage, Bodinnick-by-Fowey, Cornwall PL23 1LX. *T:* Polruan (072687) 433.

CAUSLEY, Charles Stanley, CBE 1986; poet; broadcaster; *b* Launceston, Cornwall, 24 Aug. 1917; *o s* of Charles Causley and Laura Bartlett. *Educ:* Launceston National Sch.; Horwell Grammar Sch.; Launceston Coll.; Peterborough Training Coll. Served on lower-deck in Royal Navy (Communications Branch), 1940–46. Literary Editor, 1953–56, of BBC's West Region radio magazines Apollo in the West and Signature. Awarded Travelling Scholarships by Society of Authors, 1954 and 1966. Mem., Arts Council Poetry Panel, 1962–66. Hon. Vis. Fellow in Poetry, Univ. of Exeter, 1973. FRSL 1958. Hon. DLitt Exeter, 1977; Hon. MA Open, 1982. Awarded Queen's Gold Medal for Poetry, 1967; Cholmondeley Award, 1971; Kurt Maschler Award, 1987; Ingersoll Prize, 1990. *Publications:* Hands to Dance (short stories), 1951, rev. edn as Hands to Dance and Skylark, 1979; *poetry:* Farewell, Aggie Weston, 1951; Survivor's Leave, 1953; Union Street, 1957; Peninsula (ed), 1957; Johnny Alleluia, 1961; Dawn and Dusk (ed), 1962; Penguin Modern Poets 3 (with George Barker and Martin Bell), 1962; Rising Early (ed), 1964; Modern Folk Ballads (ed), 1966; Underneath the Water, 1968; Figure of 8, 1969; Figgie Hobbin, 1971; The Tail of the Trinosaur, 1973; (ed) The Puffin Book of Magic Verse, 1974; Collected Poems 1951–1975, 1975; The Hill of the Fairy Calf, 1976; (ed) The Puffin Book of Salt-Sea Verse, 1978; The Animals' Carol, 1978; (ed) Batsford Book of Stories in Verse for Children, 1979; (trans.) 25 Poems by Hamdija Demirović, 1980; (ed) The Sun, Dancing, 1982; Secret Destinations, 1984; 21 Poems, 1986; (trans.) Kings' Children, 1986; Early in the Morning, 1986; Jack the Treacle Eater, 1987; A Field of Vision, 1988; The Young Man of Cury, 1991; Bring in the Holly, 1991; *children's stories:* Three Heads made of Gold, 1978; The Last King of Cornwall, 1978; *verse plays:* The Gift of a Lamb, 1978; The Ballad of Aucassin and Nicolette, 1981; *libretto:* Jonah (music by William Mathias), 1990; contrib. to many anthologies of verse in Great Britain and America. *Recreations:* the theatre; European travel; the re-discovery of his native town; playing the piano with expression. *Address:* 2 Cyprus Well, Launceston, Cornwall PL15 8BT. *T:* Launceston (0566) 772731.

CAUTE, (John) David, MA, DPhil; writer; *b* 16 Dec. 1936; *m* 1st, 1961, Catherine Shuckburgh (marr. diss. 1970); two *s*; 2nd, 1973, Martha Bates; two *d*. *Educ:* Edinburgh Academy; Wellington; Wadham Coll., Oxford. Scholar of St Antony's Coll., 1959. Spent a year in the Army in the Gold Coast, 1955–56, and a year at Harvard Univ. on a Henry Fellowship, 1960–61. Fellow of All Souls Coll., Oxford, 1959–65; Visiting Professor, New York Univ. and Columbia Univ., 1966–67; Reader in Social and Political Theory, Brunel Univ., 1967–70. Regents' Lectr, Univ. of Calif., 1974; Vis. Prof., Bristol Univ., 1985. Literary Editor, New Statesman, 1979–80. Co-Chm., Writers' Guild, 1981–82; Chm., Sinclair Fiction Prize, 1984. *Plays:* Songs for an Autumn Rifle, staged by Oxford Theatre Group at Edinburgh, 1961; The Demonstration, Nottingham Playhouse, 1969; The Fourth World, Royal Court, 1973; Brecht and Company, BBC TV, 1979; BBC Radio: Fallout, 1972; The Zimbabwe Tapes, 1983; Henry and the Dogs, 1986; Sanctions, 1988. *Publications:* At Fever Pitch (novel), 1959 (Authors' Club Award and John Llewelyn Rhys Prize, 1960); Comrade Jacob (novel), 1961; Communism and the French Intellectuals, 1914–1960, 1964; The Left in Europe Since 1789, 1966; The Decline of the West (novel), 1966; Essential Writings of Karl Marx (ed), 1967; Fanon, 1970; The Confrontation: a trilogy, 1971 (consisting of The Demonstration (play), 1970; The Occupation (novel), 1971; The Illusion, 1971); The Fellow-Travellers, 1973, rev. edn 1988; Collisions, 1974; Cuba, Yes?, 1974; The Great Fear: the anti-communist campaign under Truman and Eisenhower, 1978; Under the Skin: the Death of White Rhodesia, 1983; The K-Factor (novel), 1983; The Espionage of the Saints, 1986; News from Nowhere (novel), 1986; Sixty Eight: the year of the barricades, 1988; Veronica—Or the Two Nations (novel), 1989; *as John Salisbury: novels:* The Baby-Sitters, 1978; Moscow Gold, 1980. *Address:* 41 Westcroft Square, W6 0TA.

CAVALIERO, Roderick; Deputy Director General, British Council, 1981–88 (Assistant Director General, 1977–81); *b* 21 March 1928; *s* of Eric Cavaliero and Valerie (*née* Logan); *m* 1957, Mary McDonnell; one *s* four *d. Educ:* Tonbridge School; Hertford Coll., Oxford. Teaching in Britain, 1950–52; teaching in Malta, 1952–58; British Council Officer, 1958–88 (service in India, Brazil, Italy). Chm., Educnl and Trng Export Cttee, 1979–88; Dir, Open Univ. Educnl Enterprises, 1980–88; Pres., British Educnl Equipment Assoc., 1987–. Mem., British Section, Franco-British Council, 1981–88. Exec. Trustee, Charles Wallace India Trust, 1981–. Mem. Council, British Sch. at Rome; Trustee, St George's English Sch., Rome. *Publications:* Olympia and the Angel, 1958; The Last of the Crusaders, 1960. *Address:* 10 Lansdowne Road, Tunbridge Wells, Kent TN1 2NJ. *T:* Tunbridge Wells (0892) 33452.

CAVALLERA, Rt. Rev. Charles; *b* Centallo, Cuneo, Italy, 1909. *Educ:* International Missionary College of the Consolata of Turin; Pontifical Univ. of Propaganda Fide of Rome (degree in Missionology). Sec. to Delegate Apostolic of British Africa, 1936–40; Vice-Rector, then Rector, of Urban Coll. of Propaganda Fide of Rome, 1941–47; formerly Titular Bishop of Sufes; Vicar-Apostolic of Nyeri (Kenya), 1947–53; Bishop of Nyeri, 1953–64; Bishop of Marsabit, 1964–81. *Address:* Missioni Consolata, Viale Mura Aurelie 12, 00165 Rome, Italy.

CAVAN, 13th Earl of, *cr* 1647 (Ire.); **Roger Cavan Lambart;** Baron Cavan 1618; Baron Lambart 1618; Viscount Kilcoursie 1647; *b* 1 Sept. 1944; *s* of Frederick Cavan Lambart (*d* 1963) and Audrey May, *d* of Albert Charles Dunham. *Educ:* Wilson's School, Wallington, Surrey. *Address:* 34 Woodleigh Gardens, SW16.
Has not yet established his right to the peerage.

CAVANAGH, John Bryan; Dress Designer; Chairman and Managing Director, John Cavanagh Ltd, retired 1974; *b* 28 Sept. 1914; *s* of Cyril Cavanagh and Anne (*née* Murphy). *Educ:* St Paul's School. Trained with Captain Edward Molyneux in London and Paris, 1932–40. Joined Intelligence Corps, 1940, Captain (GS, Camouflage), 1944. On demobilisation, 1946, travelled throughout USA studying fashion promotion. Personal Assistant to Pierre Balmain, Paris, 1947–51; opened own business, 1952; opened John Cavanagh Boutique, 1959. Elected to Incorporated Society of London Fashion Designers, 1952 (Vice-Chm., 1956–59). Took own complete Collection to Paris, 1953; designed clothes for late Princess Marina and wedding dresses for the Duchess of Kent and Princess Alexandra. Gold Medal, Munich, 1954. *Recreations:* the theatre, swimming, travelling. *Address:* 10 Birchlands Avenue, SW12.

CAVE, Alexander James Edward, MD, DSc, FRCS, FLS; Emeritus Professor of Anatomy, University of London; *b* Manchester, 13 Sept. 1900; *e s* of late John Cave and Teresa Anne d'Hooghe; *m* 1st, 1926, Dorothy M. Dimbleby (*d* 1961); one *d*; 2nd, 1970, Catherine Elizabeth FitzGerald. *Educ:* Manchester High Sch.; Victoria University of Manchester. MB, ChB (distinction Preventive Medicine) 1923; MD (commendation) 1937; DSc, 1944; FRCS, 1959; DSc London, 1967. Senior Demonstrator (later Lecturer) in Anatomy, University of Leeds, 1924–34; Senior Demonstrator of Anatomy and Curator of Anatomical Museum, University College, London, 1934–35; Asst Conservator of Museum (1935–46), Arnott Demonstrator (1936–46), Arris and Gale Lectr, 1932, 1941, Professor of Human and Comparative Anatomy (1941–46), and Wood Jones Medalist 1978, Royal College of Surgeons of England; Prof. of Anatomy, St Bartholomew's Hospital Medical Coll., University of London, 1946–67, now Member Board Governors. Hunterian Trustee; Stopford Lecturer, 1967; Morrison Watson Research Fellow, 1961–72. Late Examiner in Anatomy, University of London, Royal University of Malta, Universities of Cambridge and Ireland, Primary FRCS and English Conjoint Board; Fellow (formerly Council Mem. and Pres.), Linnean Society; Fellow and Hon. Res. Associate (late Vice-Pres. and Council Mem.) and Silver Medallist Zoological Society; Life-Member (late Council Mem., Hon. Secretary and Recorder, Vice-Pres.) Anatomical Soc.; Hon. Associate BM (Nat. Hist.); Mem., American Assoc. of Physical Anthropologists. Liveryman, Soc. of Apothecaries. *Publications:* various papers on human and comparative anatomy, physical anthropology and medical history. *Address:* 18 Orchard Avenue, Church End, Finchley, N3. *T:* 081–346 3340. *Club:* Athenæum.

CAVE, Sir Charles (Edward Coleridge), 4th Bt, *cr* 1896; JP; DL; *b* 28 Feb. 1927; *o s* of Sir Edward Charles Cave, 3rd Bt, and Betty (*d* 1979), *o d* of late Rennell Coleridge, Salston, Ottery St Mary; *S* father 1946; *m* 1957, Mary Elizabeth, *yr d* of late John Francis Gore, CVO, TD; four *s. Educ:* Eton. Lieut The Devonshire Regt, 1946–48. CC Devon, 1955–64; High Sheriff of Devonshire, 1969. JP Devon 1972, DL Devon 1977. FRICS. *Heir: s* John Charles Cave [*b* 8 Sept. 1958; *m* 1984, Carey D., *er d* of John Lloyd, Langport, Somerset; one *s* one *d*]. *Address:* Sidbury Manor, Sidmouth, Devon EX10 0QE. *T:* Sidbury (03957) 207.

CAVE, Sir (Charles) Philip H.; *see* Haddon-Cave.

CAVE, John Arthur, FCIB; Chairman: Midland Bank Finance Corporation Ltd, 1975–79; Midland Montagu Leasing Ltd, 1975–79; Forward Trust Ltd, 1975–79; Director, Midland Bank Ltd, 1974–79; *b* 30 Jan. 1915; *s* of Ernest Cave and Eva Mary Cave; *m* 1937, Peggy Pauline, *y d* of Frederick Charles Matthews Browne; two *s* two *d. Educ:* Loughborough Grammar Sch. FCIB (FIB 1962). Served War, Royal Tank Regt, 1940–46. Entered Midland Bank, Eye, Suffolk, 1933; Manager, Threadneedle Street Office, 1962–64; Jt Gen. Man., 1965–72; Asst Chief Gen. Man., 1972–74; Dep. Chief Gen. Man., 1974–75. Dir, Midland Bank Trust Co. Ltd, 1972–76. Mem. Council, Inst. of Bankers, 1967–75 (Dep. Chm., 1973–75). Hon. Captain and Founder, Midland Bank Sailing Club (Cdre, 1967–75). *Recreation:* sailing. *Address:* Dolphin House, Centre Cliff, Southwold, Suffolk. *T:* Southwold (0502) 722232. *Club:* Royal Norfolk and Suffolk Yacht (Lowestoft).

CAVE, Prof. Terence Christopher, FBA 1991; Professor of French Literature, Oxford University, since 1989; Fellow and Tutor in French, St John's College, Oxford, since 1972; *b* 1 Dec. 1938; *s* of Alfred Cyril Cave and Sylvia Norah (*née* Norman); *m* 1965, Helen Elizabeth Robb (marr. diss. 1990); one *s* one *d. Educ:* Winchester Coll.; Gonville and Caius Coll., Cambridge (MA; PhD). University of St Andrews: Assistant, 1962–63; Lectr, 1963–65; University of Warwick: Lectr, 1965–70; Sen. Lectr, 1970–72. Visiting Professor: Cornell Univ., 1967–68; Univ. of California, Santa Barbara, 1976; Univ. of Virginia, Charlottesville, 1979; Univ. of Toronto, 1991; Royal Norwegian Soc. of Scis and Letters, Trondheim, 1991; Visiting Fellow: All Souls Coll., Oxford, 1971; Princeton Univ., 1984; Hon. Sen. Res. Fellow, Inst. of Romance Studies, Univ. of London. Mem., Academia Europaea. *Publications:* Devotional Poetry in France, 1969; Ronsard the Poet, 1973; The Cornucopian Text: problems of writing in the French Renaissance, 1979; Recognitions: a study in poetics, 1988; articles and essays in learned jls, collective vols, etc. *Recreation:* music. *Address:* St John's College, Oxford OX1 3JP. *T:* Oxford (0865) 277345.

CAVE-BROWNE-CAVE, Sir Robert, 16th Bt, *cr* 1641; President of Seaboard Chemicals Ltd; *b* 8 June 1929; *s* of 15th Bt, and Dorothea Plewman, *d* of Robert Greene Dwen, Chicago, Ill; *S* father 1945; *m* 1st, 1954, Lois Shirley, (marr. diss. 1975), *d* of John Chalmers Huggard, Winnipeg, Manitoba; one *s* one *d*; 2nd, 1977, Joan Shirley, d of Dr Kenneth Ashe Peacock, West Vancouver, BC. *Educ:* University of BC (BA 1951). KSJ 1986. *Heir: s* John Robert Charles Cave-Browne-Cave, *b* 22 June 1957. *Address:* 20901–83 Avenue, RR11, Langley, BC V3A 6Y3, Canada.

CAVELL, Rt. Rev. John Kingsmill; Assistant Bishop, Diocese of Salisbury, since 1988; Hon. Canon, Salisbury Cathedral, since 1988; *b* 4 Nov. 1916; *o s* of late William H. G. Cavell and Edith May (*née* Warner), Deal, Kent; *m* 1942, Mary Grossett (*née* Penman) (*d* 1988), Devizes, Wilts; one *d. Educ:* Sir Roger Manwood's Sch., Sandwich; Queens' Coll., Cambridge (MA; Ryle Reading Prize); Wycliffe Hall, Oxford. Ordained May 1940; Curate: Christ Church, Folkestone, 1940; Addington Parish Church, Croydon, 1940–44; CMS Area Secretary, dio. Oxford and Peterborough, and CMS Training Officer, 1944–52; Vicar: Christ Church, Cheltenham, 1952–62; St Andrew's, Plymouth, 1962–72; Rural Dean of Plymouth, 1967–72; Prebendary of Exeter Cathedral, 1967–72; Bishop Suffragan of Southampton, 1972–84; Bishop to HM Prisons and Borstals, 1975–85. Hon. Canon, Winchester Cathedral, 1972–84. Proctor in Convocation; Member of General Synod (Mem., Bd for Social Responsibility, 1982–84); Surrogate. Chm., Home Cttee, CMS London; Chm., Sarum Dio. Readers' Bd, 1984–88. Chaplain, Greenbank and Freedom Fields Hosps, Plymouth; Member: Plymouth City Educn Cttee, 1967–72; City Youth Cttee; Plymouth Exec. Council NHS, 1968–72; Chairman: Hants Assoc. for the Deaf, 1972–84; Salisbury Diocesan Assoc. for the Deaf, 1988–91; Pres., Hants Genealogical Soc., 1979–84; Vice-Pres., Soc. of Genealogists. Fellow, Pilgrim Soc., Massachusetts, 1974–84. Patron, Southampton RNLI Bd, 1976–84. Governor: Cheltenham Colls of Educn; King Alfred's College of Educn, 1973–84; Croft House Sch., Shillingstone, 1986–88; Chairman: St Mary's Coll. Building Cttee, 1957–62; Talbot Heath Sch., Bournemouth, 1975–84; Queensmount Sch., Bournemouth, 1980–84. *Recreations:* historical research, genealogy, philately, cricket. *Address:* Strathmore, 5 Constable Way, West Harnham, Salisbury, Wilts SP2 8LN. *T:* Salisbury (0722) 334782.

CAVENAGH, Prof. Winifred Elizabeth, OBE 1977; JP; PhD, BScEcon; Professor of Social Administration and Criminology, University of Birmingham, 1972–76, now Emeritus; Barrister-at-Law; *d* of Arthur Speakman and Ethel Speakman (*née* Butterworth); *m* 1938, Hugh Cavenagh; one step *s. Educ:* London Sch. of Economics, Univ. of London. BSc Econ (London); PhD (Birm.). Called to the Bar, Gray's Inn, 1964. With Lewis's Ltd, 1931–38; Min. of Labour, 1941–45. Univ. of Birmingham, 1946–. Birmingham: City Educn Cttee (co-opted expert), 1946–66; City Magistrate, 1949– (Dep. Chm., 1970–78); Police Authority, 1970–78. Governor, Birmingham United Teaching Hosps (Ministerial appt, 1958–64); W Midlands Economic Planning Council, 1967–71; Indep. Mem. of Wages Councils; Home Office Standing Advisory Cttee on Probation, 1958–67; Lord Chancellor's Standing Adv. Cttee: on Legal Aid, 1960–71; on Training of Magistrates, 1965–73. Nat. Chm., Assoc. of Social Workers, 1955–57; Council, Magistrates Assoc. (co-opted expert), 1965–78; BBC Gen. Adv. Council, 1977–80; Chm., Industrial Tribunal, 1974–77; Hon. Mem., Internat. Assoc. of Juvenile and Family Courts. Visiting Prof., Univ of Ghana, 1971; Eleanor Rathbone Meml Lectr, 1976; Moir Cullis Lectr Fellowship, USA, 1977, Canada, 1980. *Publications:* Four Decades of Students in Social Work, 1953; The Child and the Court, 1959; Juvenile Courts, the Child and the Law, 1967; contrib. articles to: Public Administration, Brit. Jl Criminology, Justice of the Peace, Social Work To-day, etc. *Recreations:* theatre, music, films. *Address:* 25 High Point, Richmond Hill Road, Edgbaston, Birmingham B15 3RU. *T:* 021–454 0109. *Club:* University Women's.

CAVENAGH-MAINWARING, Captain Maurice Kildare, DSO 1940; Royal Navy; joined Simpson (Piccadilly) Ltd, 1961; *b* 13 April 1908; *yr s* of Major James Gordon Cavenagh-Mainwaring, Whitmore Hall, Whitmore, Staffordshire; *m* Iris Mary, *d* of late Colonel Charles Denaro, OBE; one *s. Educ:* RN College, Dartmouth. Joint Services Staff College, 1951–52; HMS St Angelo and Flag Captain to Flag Officer, Malta, 1952–54; President, Second Admiralty Interview Board, 1955–56; Naval Attaché, Paris, 1957–60. ADC to the Queen, 1960. Retired from RN, 1960. Cross of Merit Sovereign Order, Knights of Malta, 1955; Comdr Légion d'Honneur, 1960. *Address:* 47 Cadogan Gardens, SW3 2TH. *T:* 071–584 7870. *Club:* Naval and Military.

CAVENDISH, family name of **Barons Cavendish of Furness, Chesham,** of **Duke of Devonshire,** and of **Baron Waterpark.**

CAVENDISH OF FURNESS, Baron *cr* 1990 (Life Peer), of Cartmel in the County of Cumbria; **Richard Hugh Cavendish;** Chairman, Holker Estate Group of Companies (interests including agricultural and urban property, leisure, mineral extraction, export, construction and forestry), since 1971; a Lord in Waiting (Government Whip), since 1990; *b* 2 Nov. 1941; *s* of late Richard Edward Osborne Cavendish and of Pamela J. Lloyd Thomas; *m* 1970, Grania Mary Caulfeild; one *s* two *d. Educ:* Eton. International banking, 1961–71. Chm., Morecambe and Lonsdale Conservative Assoc., 1975–78. Chm. Governors, St Anne's Sch., Windermere, 1983–89. Mem., Cumbria CC, 1985–90. High Sheriff 1978, DL 1988, Cumbria. FRSA. *Recreations:* gardening, National Hunt racing, collecting drawings, reading, travel. *Address:* Holker Hall, Cark-in-Cartmel, Cumbria LA11 7PL. *T:* Flookburgh (05395) 58220. *Clubs:* Brooks's, Pratt's, White's.

CAVENDISH, Lady Elizabeth (Georgiana Alice), LVO 1976; JP; Extra Lady-in-Waiting to Princess Margaret, since 1951; Chairman, Cancer Research Campaign, since 1981; Member, Press Complaints Commission, since 1991; *b* 24 April 1926; *d* of 10th Duke of Devonshire, KG, and Lady Mary Cecil, GCVO, CBE (*d* 1988), *d* of 4th Marquess of Salisbury, KG, GCVO. *Educ:* private. Member: Advertising Standards Authority, 1981–91; Marre Cttee on Future of Legal Profession, 1986–89; Lay Mem., Senate of Inns of Court's Professional Conduct Cttee of Bar Council and Disciplinary Cttee Tribunal, 1983–. Chm., Bd of Visitors, Wandsworth Prison, 1970–73; Mem. Council, St Christopher's Hospice, Sydenham, 1991–. JP London, 1961; Chairman: N Westminster Magistrates' Court PSD, 1980–83; Inner London Juvenile Courts, 1983–86. *Address:* 19 Radnor Walk, SW3 4BP. *T:* 071–352 0774; Moor View, Edensor, Bakewell, Derbyshire DE4 1PH. *T:* Baslow (0246) 2204.
See also Duke of Devonshire.

CAVENDISH, Maj.-Gen. Peter Boucher, CB 1981; OBE 1969; DL; retired; Chairman, Military Agency for Standardisation and Director, Armaments Standardisation and Interoperability Division, International Military Staff, HQ NATO, 1978–81; *b* 26 Aug. 1925; *s* of late Brig. R. V. C. Cavendish, OBE, MC (killed in action, 1943) and Helen Cavendish (*née* Boucher); *m* 1952, Marion Loudon (*née* Constantine); three *s. Educ:* Abberley Hall, Worcester; Winchester Coll.; New Coll., Oxford. Enlisted 1943; commnd The Royal Dragoons, 1945; transf. 3rd The King's Own Hussars, 1946; Staff Coll., Camberley, 1955; served Palestine, BAOR, Canada and N Africa to 1966; CO 14th/20th King's Hussars, 1966–69; HQ 1st British Corps, 1969–71; Comdt RAC Centre, 1971–74; Canadian Defence Coll., 1975; Sec. to Mil. Cttee and Internat. Mil. Staff, HQ NATO, 1975–78. Colonel, 14th/20th King's Hussars, 1976–81; Hon. Col, The Queen's Own Mercian Yeomanry, TAVR, 1982–87; Col Comdt, Yeomanry RAC TA, 1986–90. Mem., Peak Park Jt Planning Bd, 1982–91 (Vice-Chm., 1987–91). FBIM 1979. High Sheriff, 1986–87, DL 1989, Derbys. *Recreations:* shooting, country pursuits, DIY. *Address:*

The Rock Cottage, Middleton-by-Youlgrave, Bakewell, Derbys DE4 1LS. *T:* Matlock (0629) 636225.

CAWDOR, 6th Earl *cr* 1827; **Hugh John Vaughan Campbell,** FSA; FRICS; Baron Cawdor, 1796; Viscount Emlyn, 1827; *b* 6 Sept. 1932; *er s* of 5th Earl Cawdor, TD, FSA, and Wilma Mairi (*d* 1982), *e d* of late Vincent C. Vickers; *S* father, 1970; *m* 1st, 1957, Cathryn (marr. diss. 1979), 2nd *d* of Maj.-Gen. Sir Robert Hinde, KBE, CB, DSO; two *s* three *d*; 2nd, 1979, Countess Angelika Ilona Lazansky von Bukowa. *Educ:* Eton; Magdalen Coll., Oxford; Royal Agricultural Coll., Cirencester. High Sheriff of Carmarthenshire, 1964. *Heir: s* Viscount Emlyn, *qv. Address:* Cawdor Castle, Nairn. *Clubs:* Pratt's, White's.

CAWLEY, family name of **Baron Cawley.**

CAWLEY, 3rd Baron, *cr* 1918; **Frederick Lee Cawley,** 3rd Bt, *cr* 1906; *b* 27 July 1913; *s* of 2nd Baron and Vivienne (*d* 1978), *d* of Harold Lee, Broughton Park, Manchester; *S* father 1954; *m* 1944, Rosemary Joan, *y d* of late R. E. Marsden; six *s* one *d. Educ:* Eton; New Coll., Oxford. BA Nat. Science (Zoology), 1935, MA 1942. Called to the Bar, Lincoln's Inn, 1938; practised at the Patent Bar, 1946–73. Served War of 1939–45 in Europe; Capt. RA Leicestershire Yeomanry (wounded). Mem. Woking UDC, 1949–57. Dep.-Chm. of Cttees, House of Lords, 1958–67; Mem., Jt Parly Cttees: Consolidation Bills, 1956–73; Delegated Legislation, 1972–73; Ecclesiastical, 1974; Chm. of many Private Bill Select Cttees. *Recreations:* gardening, shooting. *Heir: s* Hon. John Francis Cawley [*b* 28 Sept. 1946; *m* 1979, Regina Sarabia, *e d* of late Marqués de Hazas, Madrid; three *s* one *d*]. *Address:* Bircher Hall, Leominster, Herefordshire HR6 0AX. *T:* Yarpole (056885) 218. *Club:* Farmers'.

CAWLEY, Sir Charles (Mills), Kt 1965; CBE; Chief Scientist, Ministry of Power, 1959–67; a Civil Service Commissioner, 1967–69; *b* 17 May 1907; *s* of John and Emily Cawley, Gillingham, Kent; *m* 1934, Florence Mary Ellaline, *d* of James Shepherd, York; one *d. Educ:* Sir Joseph Williamson's Mathematical Sch., Rochester; Imperial Coll. of Science and Technology (Royal College of Sci.). ARCS, BSc (First Cl. Hons in Chem.), DIC; MSc; PhD; FRSC; DSc(London); SFInstF; FRSA; Fellow, Imperial Coll. of Science and Technology. Fuel Research Station, DSIR, 1929–53. Imperial Defence Coll., 1949. A Dir, Headquarters, DSIR, 1953–59. Chm., Admiralty Fuels and Lubricants Advisory Cttee, 1957–64. Melchett Medal, Inst. of Fuel, 1968. *Publications:* Papers in various scientific and technical journals. *Address:* 8 Glen Gardens, Ferring-by-Sea, Worthing, West Sussex BN12 5HG.

CAWLEY, Prof. Robert Hugh, PhD; FRCP, FRCPsych; Professor of Psychological Medicine, University of London, at King's College School of Medicine and Dentistry (formerly King's College Hospital Medical School), and Institute of Psychiatry, and Consultant Psychiatrist, King's College Hospital, 1975–89; now Emeritus Professor; *b* 16 Aug. 1924; *yr s* of Robert Ernest Cawley and Alice Maud (*née* Taylor); *m* 1985, Elizabeth Ann, *d* of Eugene Malachy Doris and Mary Doris (*née* Crummie). *Educ:* Solihull Sch.; Univ. of Birmingham (BSc Hons Zool., PhD, MB, ChB); Univ. of London (DPM). FRCP 1975; FRCPsych 1971, Hon. FRCPsych 1990. Univ. of Birmingham: Res. Scholar, 1947; Res. Fellow, 1949; Halley Stewart Res. Fellow, 1954; House Phys. and Surg., Queen Elizabeth Hosp., Birmingham, 1956–57; Registrar, then Sen. Registrar, Bethlem Royal and Maudsley Hosps, 1957–60; Clin. Lectr, Inst. of Psych., 1960–62; Sen. Lectr and First Asst in Psych., Univ. of Birmingham, and Hon. Consultant, United Birm. Hosps and Birm. RHB, 1962–67; Phys., 1967–75, and Consultant Psychiatrist, 1967–89, Bethlem Royal and Maudsley Hosps. Consultant Advr (Psychiatry) to DHSS, 1984–89; Civilian Advr in Psychiatry to RAF, 1986–89. Mem., MRC, 1979–83 (Chm., Neurosciences Bd, 1979–81). Chief Examr, Royal Coll. of Psychiatrists, 1981–88. *Publications:* papers on biological, medical and psychiatric subjects in scientific books and jls. *Address:* Flat 2, 24 Earl's Court Square, SW5 9DN. *Club:* Athenæum.

CAWS, Richard Byron, CBE 1984; Chairman, Caws Morris Associates Ltd, Chartered Surveyors, London, since 1987; Senior Consultant (Real Estate), Goldman Sachs International Corp. (London), since 1987; *b* 9 March 1927; *s* of Maxwell and Edith S. Caws; *m* 1948, Fiona Muriel Ruth Elton Darling; one *s* two *d* (and one *s* decd). Partner: Nightingale Page & Bennett, Chartered Surveyors, Kingston upon Thames, 1944–60; Debenham Tewson & Chinnocks, 1961–87. Crown Estate Comr, 1971–. Member: Commn for the New Towns, 1976– (Chm., Property Cttee, 1978–); Dobry Cttee on Review of the Dev. Control System, 1973–75; DoE Adv. Gp on Commercial Property Dev., 1973–77; DoE Property Adv. Gp, 1978–88. Gov., Royal Agricl Coll., 1985–88. Master, Worshipful Co. of Chartered Surveyors, 1982–83. FRICS (Chm., Jun. Orgn, RICS, 1959–60). *Recreations:* sailing, travel. *Address:* 36 Mount Park Road, Ealing, W5 2RS. *Clubs:* Boodle's, Royal Thames Yacht, Little Ship.

CAWSON, Prof. Roderick Anthony, MD; FDS, RCS and RCPS Glasgow; FRCPath; Professor (Hon. Consultant) and Head of Department of Oral Medicine and Pathology, United Medical and Dental Schools, Guy's Hospital, 1966–86, now Emeritus; *b* 23 April 1921; *s* of Capt. Leopold Donald Cawson and Ivy Clunies-Ross; *m* 1949, Diana Hall, SRN; no *c. Educ:* King's College Sch. Wimbledon; King's College Hosp. Med. Sch. MD (London); MB, BS, BDS (Hons) (London); FDS, RCS; FDS, RCPS Glasgow; MRCPath; LMSSA. Served RAF, 1944–48; Nuffield Foundn Fellow, 1953–55; Dept of Pathology, King's Coll. Hosp., Sen. Lectr in Oral Pathology, King's Coll. Hosp. Med. Sch., 1955–62; Sen. Lectr in Oral Pathology, Guy's Hosp. Med. Sch., 1962–66. Examinerships: Pathology (BDS) London, 1965–69; Univ. of Wales, 1969–71; Dental Surgery (BDS), Glasgow, 1966–70; BChD Leeds, 1966–70; Newcastle, 1967–71; FDS, RCPS Glasgow, 1967–86; BDS Lagos, 1975–; RCPath, 1984–87. Chairman: Dental Formulary Sub-cttee (BMA); Dental and Surgical Materials Cttee, Medicines Division, 1976–80; recently First Chm, Univ. Teachers' Gp (BDA). *Publications:* Essentials of Dental Surgery and Pathology 1962, 4th edn, 1984; Medicine for Dental Students (with R. H. Cutforth), 1960; (with R. G. Spector) Clinical Pharmacology in Dentistry, 1975, 5th edn 1989; Aids to Oral Pathology and Diagnosis, 1981; (with C. Scully) Medical Problems in Dentistry, 1982, 2nd edn 1987; (with A. W. McCracken and P. B. Marcus) Pathology: the mechanisms of disease, 1982, 2nd edn 1989; (with A. W. McCracken) Clinical and Oral Microbiology, 1982; (with J. W. Eveson) Oral Pathology and Diagnosis, 1987; numerous papers, etc, in med. and dental jls. *Recreations:* reading, music, gardening (reluctantly). *Address:* 40 Court Lane, Dulwich, SE21 7DR. *T:* 081–693 5781.

CAWTHRA, Rear-Adm. Arthur James, CB 1966; Admiral Superintendent, HM Dockyard, Devonport, 1964–66; *b* 30 Sept. 1911; *s* of James Herbert Cawthra, MIEE, and Margaret Anne Cawthra; *m* 1959, Adrien Eleanor Lakeman Tivy, *d* of Cecil B. Tivy, MCh, Plymouth; one *s* (and one *s* decd). *Educ:* abroad. Joined Royal Navy, 1930; Imperial Defence Course, 1956; HMS Fisgard, 1958–59; Dir Underwater Weapons, Admiralty, 1960–63. Capt. 1955; Rear-Adm. 1964.

CAWTHRA, David Wilkinson, FEng, FICE; Chief Executive, Balfour Beatty, since 1990; *b* 5 March 1943; *s* of Jack and Dorothy Cawthra; *m* 1967, Maureen Williamson; one *s* one *d. Educ:* Heath Grammar Sch., Halifax; Univ. of Birmingham (BSc Hons). FIHT. Mitchell Construction Co., 1963–73; Tarmac Construction, 1973–78; Balfour Beatty Construction, 1979–87; Managing Dir, Balfour Beatty, 1988. Dir, BICC, 1988. CBIM. *Recreations:* golf, hill walking. *Address:* 7 Mayday Road, Thornton Heath, Surrey CR7 7XA. *T:* 081–684 6922. *Club:* Royal Automobile.

CAYFORD, Dame Florence Evelyn, DBE 1965; JP; Mayor, London Borough of Camden, 1969; *b* 14 June 1897; *d* of George William and Mary S. A. Bunch; *m* 1923, John Cayford; two *s. Educ:* Carlton Road Sch.; St Pancras County Secondary Sch., Paddington Technical Institute. Alderman, LCC, 1946–52; Member: LCC for Shoreditch and Finsbury, 1952–64; GLC (for Islington) and ILEA, 1964–67. Chairman: Hospital and Medical Services Cttee LCC, 1948; (Health Cttee). Division 7, 1948–49, Division 2 in 1949; Health Cttee, 1953–60; Welfare Cttee, 1965, of LCC; Metropolitan Water Bd, 1966–67 (Vice-Chm., 1965–66). Mem. Hampstead Borough Council, 1937–65 (Leader of Labour Group, 1945–58), Councillor for Kilburn until 1945, Alderman, 1945–65; Chm., LCC, 1960–61; Chairman: (Hampstead), Maternity and Child Welfare Cttee, 1941–45, Juvenile Court Panel, 1950–62; Dep. Mayoress, Camden Borough Council, 1967–68. Probation Cttee, 1959–; Leavesden Hosp. Management Cttee, 1948–63; Harben Secondary Sch., 1946–61. Member: Co-operative Political Party (ex-Chm. and Sec.); Co-operative Soc.; Labour Party; National Institute for Social Work Training, 1962–65; Min. of Health Council for Training of Health Visitors, 1962–65; Min. of Health Council for Training in Social Work, 1962–65. Chm., YWCA Helen Graham Hse, 1972–. JP, Inner London, 1941–. Freeman, London Borough of Camden (formerly Borough of Hampstead), 1961. Noble Order, Crown of Thailand, 3rd Class, 1964. *Address:* 26 Hemstal Road, Hampstead, NW6. *T:* 071–624 6181.

CAYGILL, Hon. David Francis; MP (Lab) St Albans, New Zealand, since 1978; *b* 15 Nov. 1948; *s* of Bruce Allott Caygill and Gwyneth Mary Caygill; *m* 1974, Eileen Ellen Boyd; one *s* three *d. Educ:* St Albans Primary Sch.; Christchurch Boys' High Sch.; Univ. of Canterbury (BA, LLB). Pres., Univ. of Canterbury Students' Assoc., 1971. Barrister and Solicitor, 1974–78; Christchurch City Councillor, 1971–80; Minister of Trade and Industry, Minister of Nat. Develt, Associate Minister of Finance, 1984–87; Minister of Health, Dep. Minister of Finance, 1987–88; Minister of Finance, 1988–90. *Recreations:* collecting and listening to classical records, following American politics. *Address:* Parliament House, Wellington, New Zealand. *T:* 719.991. *Club:* St Albans Shirley.

CAYLEY, Sir Digby (William David), 11th Bt *cr* 1661; MA Cantab; sometime dealer in antiques; currently employed at Denzil Grant Antiques, Long Melford, Suffolk; *b* 3 June 1944; *s* of Lieut-Comdr W. A. S. Cayley, RN (*d* 1964) (*g g s* of 7th Bt), and of Natalie M. Cayley, BA; *S* kinsman, 1967; *m* 1969 (marr. diss. 1987); two *d. Educ:* Malvern Coll.; Downing Coll., Cambridge. Asst Classics Master, Portsmouth Grammar Sch., 1968–73; Stonyhurst Coll., 1973–81; Manager, C. P. Stockbridge Ltd, Cambs, 1982–83. *Recreation:* solitude. *Heir: cousin* George Paul Cayley [*b* 23 May 1940; *m* 1967, Shirley Southwell, *d* of Frank Woodward Petford; two *s*]. *Address:* Drake House, 1 Water Lane, Little Whelnetham, Bury St Edmunds, W Suffolk IP30 0DU. *T:* Bury St Edmunds (0284) 868245.

CAYZER, family name of **Barons Cayzer** and **Rotherwick.**

CAYZER, Baron *cr* 1982 (Life Peer), of St Mary Axe in the City of London; **William Nicholas Cayzer;** Bt 1921; Chairman: British and Commonwealth Shipping Co. Ltd, 1958–87; Caledonia Investments PLC, since 1958; *b* 21 Jan. 1910; *s* of Sir August Cayzer, 1st Bt, and Ina Frances (*d* 1935), 2nd *d* of William Stancombe, Blounts Ct, Wilts; *S* to father's baronetcy, 1943; *m* 1935, Elizabeth Catherine, *d* of late Owain Williams and *g d* of Morgan Stuart Williams, Aberpergwm, Glamorgan; two *d. Educ:* Eton; Corpus Christi Coll., Cambridge. Director: Clan Line Steamers Ltd, 1938–87 (Chm.); Cayzer, Irvine & Co. Ltd, 1939–87 (Chm.); Union-Castle Mail Steamship Co. Ltd and associated cos, 1956–87 (Chm.); Air Hldgs Ltd, 1962–87 (Chm.); Meldrum Investment Trust, 1971–(Chm.). Chm. Liverpool Steamship Owners Association, 1944–45; Pres. Chamber of Shipping of the UK, 1959; Pres. Inst. of Marine Engineers, 1963. Chairman: Gen. Council of Brit. Shipping, 1959; Chamber of Shipping's British Liner Cttee, 1960–63; Mem., MoT Shipping Adv. Panel, 1962–64; sometime Mem. Mersey Dock and Harbour Board; sometime Mem. National Dock Labour Board. Prime Warden, Shipwrights Company, 1969. *Heir* (to baronetcy): none. *Address:* The Grove, Walsham-le-Willows, Suffolk. *T:* Walsham-le-Willows (03598) 263; 95j Eaton Square, SW1. *T:* 071–235 5551. *Club:* Brooks's.

See also M. K. B. Colvin.

CAYZER, Sir James Arthur, 5th Bt, *cr* 1904; *b* 15 Nov. 1931; *s* of Sir Charles William Cayzer, 3rd Bt, MP (*d* 1940), and Beatrice Eileen (*d* 1981), *d* of late James Meakin and Emma Beatrice (later wife of 3rd Earl Sondes); *S* brother, 1943. *Educ:* Eton. *Heir: cousin*, Baron Cayzer, *qv. Address:* Kinpurnie Castle, Newtyle, Angus PH12 8TW. *T:* Newtyle (08285) 207. *Club:* Carlton.

CAZALET, Hon. Sir Edward (Stephen), Kt 1988; DL; **Hon. Mr Justice Cazalet;** a Judge of the High Court of Justice, Family Division, since 1988; *b* 26 April 1936; *s* of late Peter Victor Ferdinand Cazalet and Leonora Cazalet (*née* Rowley); *m* 1965, Camilla Jane (*née* Gage); two *s* one *d. Educ:* Eton Coll. (Fellow, 1989); Christ Church, Oxford (MA Jurisprudence). Called to the Bar, Inner Temple, 1960, Bencher, 1985. QC 1980; a Recorder, 1985–88; Family Division Liaison Judge for SE Circuit, 1990–. Chairman, Horserace Betting Levy Appeal Tribunal, 1977–88. Chm. Trustees, Charles Douglas-Home Award, 1986–. DL E Sussex, 1989. *Recreations:* riding, ball games, chess. *Address:* Royal Courts of Justice, Strand, WC2. *Clubs:* White's, Garrick, Wig and Pen.

CAZALET, Sir Peter (Grenville), Kt 1989; Chairman, APV plc, since 1989; Deputy Chairman, GKN, since 1989; *b* 26 Feb. 1929; *e s* of Vice-Adm. Sir Peter (Grenville Lyon) Cazalet, KBE, CB, DSO, DSC, and of Lady (Elise) Cazalet (*née* Winterbotham); *m* 1957, Jane Jennifer, *yr d* of Charles and Nancy Rew, Guernsey, CI; three *s. Educ:* Uppingham Sch., Uppingham, Rutland; Magdalene Coll., Cambridge (Schol.; MA Hons). General Manager, BP Tanker Co. Ltd, 1968; Regional Co-ordinator, Australasia and Far East, 1970; Pres., BP North America Inc., 1972–75; Director: Standard Oil Co. of Ohio, 1973–75; BP Trading Ltd, 1975; Peninsular & Oriental Steam Navigation Co., 1980–; Man. Dir, 1981–89, Dep. Chm., 1986–89, BP; Chm., BP Oil International, 1981–89. Dir, De La Rue Co., 1983–. Chm., Armed Forces Pay Review Body, 1989–; Mem., Top Salaries Review Body, 1989–. A Vice-Pres., ME Assoc.; Hon. Sec., King George's Fund for Sailors; Trustee: Uppingham Sch., 1976–; Wellcome Trust, 1989–; Mem., Gen. Cttee, Lloyd's Register of Shipping, 1981– (Mem. Bd, 1981–86). CBIM 1982. Liveryman: Tallow Chandlers' Co. (Master, 1991–92); Shipwrights' Co. *Recreations:* theatre, fishing. *Address:* APV plc, 1 Lygon Place, SW1W 0JR. *T:* 071–730 7244. *Clubs:* Brooks's, Royal Wimbledon Golf, MCC.

CECIL, family name of **Baron Amherst of Hackney, Marquess of Exeter, Baron Rockley,** and **Marquess of Salisbury.**

CECIL, Henry Richard Amherst; Trainer of Racehorses; *b* 11 Jan. 1943; *s* of late Hon. Henry Kerr Auchmuty Cecil and of Elizabeth Rohays Mary (who *m* 2nd, Sir Cecil Boyd-Rochfort, KCVO), *d* of Sir James Burnett, 13th Bt, CB, CMG, DSO; *m* 1966, Julia (marr.

diss. 1990), *d* of Sir Noel Murless; one *s* one *d*. *Educ:* Canford School. Commenced training under flat race rules, 1969; previously Assistant to Sir Cecil Boyd-Rochfort. Leading Trainer, 1976, 1978, 1979, 1982, 1984, 1985, 1987, 1988, 1990. *Publication:* On the Level (autobiog.), 1983. *Recreation:* gardening. *Address:* Warren Place, Newmarket, Suffolk CB8 8QQ. *T:* Newmarket (0638) 662387.

CECIL, Rear-Adm. Sir (Oswald) Nigel Amherst, KBE 1979; CB 1978; *b* 11 Nov. 1925; *s* of Comdr the Hon. Henry M. A. Cecil, OBE, RN, and the Hon. Mrs Henry Cecil; *m* 1961, Annette (CStJ 1980), *d* of Maj. Robert Barclay, TD, Bury Hill, near Dorking, Surrey; one *s*. *Educ:* Royal Naval Coll., Dartmouth. Joined Navy, 1939; served during War, 1939–45. In comd, HM MTB 521, 1946–48; Flag Lieut to Admiral, BJSM, Washington, 1950–52; Comdr, 1959; Chief Staff Officer, London Div. RNR, 1959–61; in comd: HMS Corunna, 1961–63; HMS Royal Arthur, 1963–66; Captain 1966; Staff of Dep. Chief of Defence Staff (Operational Requirements), 1966–69; Captain (D) Dartmouth Trng Sqdn and in comd HMS Tenby and HMS Scarborough, 1969–71; Senior British Naval Officer, S Africa, and Naval Attaché, Capetown, as Cdre, 1971–73; Dir, Naval Operational Requirements, 1973–75; Naval ADC to the Queen, 1975; Rear-Adm., 1975; NATO Comdr SE Mediterranean, 1975–77; Comdr British Forces Malta, and Flag Officer Malta, 1975–79; Lieut Gov., Isle of Man, 1980–85. FBIM 1980. KStJ 1980 (OStJ 1971). *Recreations:* racing, cricket, tennis. *Address:* c/o C. Hoare & Co., 37 Fleet Street, EC4P 4DQ. *Clubs:* White's, MCC.

CECIL, Robert, CMG 1959; author; HM Diplomatic Service, retired; Chairman, Institute for Cultural Research, since 1968; *b* 25 March 1913; *s* of late Charles Cecil; *m* 1938, Kathleen, *d* of late Col C. C. Marindin, CBE, DSO; one *s* two *d*. *Educ:* Wellington Coll.; Caius Coll., Cambridge. BA Cantab. 1935, MA 1961. Entered HM Foreign Service, 1936; served in Foreign Office, 1939–45; First Sec., HM Embassy, Washington, 1945–48; assigned to Foreign Office, 1948; Counsellor and Head of American Dept, 1951; Counsellor, HM Embassy, Copenhagen, 1953–55; HM Consul-Gen., Hanover, 1955–57; Counsellor, HM Embassy, Bonn, 1957–59; Dir-Gen., British Information Services, New York, 1959–61; Head of Cultural Relations Dept, FO, 1962–67. Reader in Contemp. German Hist., Reading Univ., 1968–78; Chm., Grad. Sch. of Contemp. European Studies, 1976–78. *Publications:* Levant and other Poems, 1940; Time and other Poems, 1955; Life in Edwardian England, 1969; The Myth of the Master Race: Alfred Rosenberg and Nazi ideology, 1972; Hitler's Decision to Invade Russia, 1941, 1976; (ed) The King's Son (anthology), 1980; (contrib.) The Missing Dimension, 1984; A Divided Life: a biography of Donald Maclean, 1988. *Recreations:* gardening, chess, etc. *Address:* Hambledon, Hants PO7 6RU. *T:* Hambledon (070132) 669. *Club:* Royal Automobile.

CELAC, Sergiu; Ambassador of Romania to the Court of St James's, since 1990; *b* Bucharest, 26 May 1939; *s* of Nicolae and Elena Celac; *m* 1964, Rea-Silvia Casu. *Educ:* Bucharest Univ. Joined Foreign Service, 1961; Private Sec. to Dep. Foreign Minister, 1963–69; Dep. Dir, then Dir, Policy Planning, Min. of Foreign Affairs, 1969–74; interpreter at Presidency, 1974–78; reader, Scientific and Encyclopaedic Publishing House, 1978–89; Minister of Foreign Affairs, Dec. 1989–June 1990. Mem., Nat. Council, Romanian Writers' Union, 1990–. Hon. Nat. Pres., Romanian Shooting and Fishing Sports Union, 1990; Mem., Journalists' Soc. of Romania, 1991. *Publications:* studies and essays on political sci.; trans. novels and poetry from and into Russian and English. *Recreation:* shooting. *Address:* Romanian Embassy, 4 Palace Green, W8 4QD. *T:* 071–937 9666; 1 Belgrave Square, SW1.

CELIBIDACHE, Sergiu; Chief Conductor, Munich Philharmonic Orchestra, since 1979; Composer and Guest Conductor to leading orchestras all over the world; *b* Rumania, 28 June 1912; *s* of Demosthene Celibidache; *m* Maria Celibidache. *Educ:* Jassy; Berlin. Doctorate in mathematics, musicology, philosophy and Buddhist religion. Conductor and Artistic Dir, Berlin Philharmonic Orchestra, 1946–51. Member: Royal Acad. of Music, Sweden; Acad. of Music, Bologna. German Critics' Prize, 1953; Berlin City Art Prize, 1955; Grand Cross of Merit, Federal Republic of Germany, 1954. *Recreations:* skiing, water-skiing. *Address:* Munich Philharmonic Orchestra, 8000 Munich 2, Rindermarkt 3–4/III, Germany.

CENTRAL AFRICA, Archbishop of, since 1980; **Most Rev. Walter Paul Khotso Makhulu;** Bishop of Botswana, since 1979; *b* Johannesburg, 1935; *m* 1966, Rosemary Sansom; one *s* one *d*. *Educ:* St Peter's Theological Coll., Rosettenville; Selly Oak Colls, Birmingham. Deacon 1957, priest 1958, Johannesburg; Curate: Johannesburg, 1957–60; Botswana, 1961–63; St Carantoc's Mission, Francistown, Botswana, 1961–63; St Andrew's Coll., Selly Oak, Birmingham, 1963–64; Curate: All Saints, Poplar, 1964–66; St Silas, Pentonville, with St Clement's, Barnsbury, 1966–68; Vicar of St Philip's, Battersea, 1968–75; Secretary for E Africa, WCC, 1975–79; a President: WCC, 1983–91; All Africa Conf. of Churches, 1981–86. Hon. DD: Kent, 1988; Gen. Theol Seminary, NY, 1990. Officier, Ordre des Palmes Académiques (France), 1981. *Address:* PO Box 769, Gaborone, Botswana.

CHABAN-DELMAS, Jacques Pierre Michel; Commander Légion d'Honneur; Compagnon de la Libération; Deputy, Department of Gironde, since 1946; Mayor of Bordeaux, since 1947; *b* Paris, 7 March 1915; *s* of Pierre Delmas and Georgette Delmas (*née* Barrouin); *m* 1947 (2nd marr.), Mme Geoffray (*née* Marie Antoinette Iôn) (*d* 1970); two *s* two *d*; *m* 1971, Mme Micheline Chavelet. *Educ:* Lycée Lakanal, Sceaux; Faculté de Droit, Paris; Ecole Libre des Sciences Politiques (Dip.). Licencié en droit. Journalist with l'Information, 1933. Served War of 1939–45: Army, 1939–40 (an Alpine Regt); joined the Resistance; *nom de guerre* of Chaban added (Compagnon de la Libération, Croix de Guerre); attached to Min. of Industrial Production, 1941; Inspector of Finance, 1943; Brig.-Gen., 1944; Nat. Mil. Deleg. (co-ord. mil. planning) Resistance, 1944; Inspector Gen. of Army, 1944; Sec.-Gen., Min. of Inf., 1945. Deputy for Gironde (Radical), 1946. Leader of Gaullist group (Républicans Sociaux) in Nat. Assembly, 1953–56; also Mem. Consultative Assembly of Council of Europe; Minister of State, 1956–57; Minister of Nat. Defence, 1957–58; Pres., Nat. Assembly, France, 1958–69, 1978–81 and 1986–88; Prime Minister, June 1969–July 1972. Président: Communauté urbain de Bordeaux, 1983–; Conseil régional d'Aquitaine, 1985–. *Publication:* L'ardeur, 1976. *Address:* 36 rue Emile Fourcand, 33000 Bordeaux, France; Mairie de Bordeaux, 33000 Bordeaux, France.

CHACKSFIELD, Air Vice-Marshal Sir Bernard, KBE 1968 (OBE 1945); CB 1961; CEng, FRAeS 1968; *b* 13 April 1913; *s* of Edgar Chacksfield, Ilford, Essex; *m* 1st, 1937, Myrtle, (*d* 1984), *d* of Walter Matthews, Rickmansworth, Herts; two *s* two *d* (and one *s* decd); 2nd, 1985, Mrs Elizabeth Beatrice Ody. *Educ:* Co. High Sch., Ilford; RAF, Halton; RAF Coll., Cranwell. Service: NW Frontier, 1934–37; UK, India, Burma, Singapore, 1939–45 (OBE); Air Min., 1945–48; Western Union (NATO), Fontainebleau, 1949–51; RAF Staff Coll., 1951–53; Fighter Command, 1954–55; Director, Guided Weapons (trials), Min. of Supply, 1956–58; IDC, 1959; SASO, Tech. Trg Comd, RAF, 1960; AOC No. 22 Group RAF Technical Training Command, 1960–62; Comdt-Gen., RAF Regiment and Inspector of Ground Defence, 1963–68; retired 1968. Chm., Burma Star Council, 1977– (Vice-Chm., 1974–76). Chm., Bd of Management, Royal Masonic Hosp., 1988– (Mem., 1987–88); Chairman of Governors: Bedstone College, 1978–90 (Governor, 1970); Wye Valley Sch. (formerly Deyncourt Sch.), 1978–89 (Governor, 1977). Order of Cloud and Banner with special rosette (Chinese), 1941. *Recreations:* scouting (HQ Comr, Air Activities, 1959–72; Chief Comr for England, 1968–77), sailing, fencing (Pres. RAF Fencing Union, 1963–68), gliding, travel, model aircraft (Pres. British Model Flying Assoc. (formerly Soc. Model Aircraft Engrs, GB), 1965–), modern Pentathlon (Pres., RAF Pentathlon Assoc., 1963–68), shooting (Chm. RAF Small Arms Assoc., 1963–68); swimming; youth work, amateur dramatics. *Address:* 8 Rowan House, Bourne End, Bucks. *T:* Bourne End (06285) 20829. *Club:* Royal Air Force.

CHADDOCK, Prof. Dennis Hilliar, CBE 1962; Professor of Engineering Design, University of Technology, Loughborough, 1966–73, retired; Professor Emeritus, 1974; Consultant Proprietor, Quorn Engineering, since 1974; *b* 28 July 1908; *m* 1937, Stella Edith Dorrington; one *s* one *d* (and one *s* decd). *Educ:* University Coll. Sch. Engineering Apprentice, Sa Adolph Saurer, Switzerland, 1927–30; Research Engineer, Morris Commercial Cars Ltd, Birmingham, 1930–32; Asst Road Motor Engineer, LMS Railway Co., Euston, 1932–41. BSc (Eng) Hons, London, 1933; MSc (Eng) London, 1938. HM Forces, 1941–46; Inspecting Officer, Chief Inspector of Armaments, 1941–43; Dep. Chief Inspecting Officer, 1943–45; Chief Design Officer, Armament Design Estabt, 1945–46; relinquished commission with rank of Lieut-Col, 1946. Superintendent, Carriage Design Branch of Armament Design Estabt, 1947–50; Imperial Defence Coll., 1951; Dep. Chief Engineer, 1952–55; Principal Superintendent, Weapons and Ammunition Div., Armament Research and Development Estabt, 1955–62; Dir of Artillery Research and Development, Ministry of Defence (Army) 1962–66. *Recreation:* model engineering. *Address:* 29 Paddock Close, Quorndon, Leics LE12 8BJ. *T:* Quorn (0509) 412607.

CHADWICK, Charles McKenzie, OBE 1984; British Council Director (formerly Representative), Poland, 1989–92; *b* 31 July 1932; *s* of late Trevor McKenzie Chadwick and of Marjorie Baron; *m* 1965, Evelyn Ingeborg Ihlenfeldt; one *s*. *Educ:* Charterhouse School; Trinity Coll., Toronto (BA). Army service, 1950–52; HMOCS Provincial Administration, Northern Rhodesia, 1958–64; Lectr, 1964–66, and Head, Administrative Training, 1966–67, Staff Trng Coll., Lusaka; British Council Officer, 1967–92; service in Kenya, Nigeria, Brazil, London; British Election Supervisor, Zimbabwe, 1980; British Council Rep., Canada, 1981–88. *Address:* 25A Denning Road, NW3 1ST.

CHADWICK, Derek James, DPhil; CChem, FRSC; Director, Ciba Foundation, since 1988; *b* 9 Feb. 1948; *s* of Dennis Edmund and Ida Chadwick; *m* 1980, Susan Reid; two *s*. *Educ:* St Joseph's Coll., Blackpool; Keble Coll., Oxford (BA, BSc, MA, DPhil). FRSC 1982; MACS 1989. ICI Fellow, Cambridge Univ., 1972–73; Prize Fellow, Magdalen Coll., Oxford, 1973–77; Lectr and Sen. Lectr, Liverpool Univ., 1977–88. Member: Sci. Cttee, Louis Jeantet Foundn, Geneva, 1989–; Hague Club of European Foundn Dirs, 1989–; Sci. Adv. Cttee, Assoc. of Med. Res. Charities, 1990–. *Publications:* chapters in: Aromatic and Heteroaromatic Chemistry, 1979; Comprehensive Heterocyclic Chemistry, 1984; The Research and Academic Users' Guide to the IBM PC, 1988; many papers in chemistry jls, eg, Jl Chem. Soc., Tetrahedron, Tet. Letters, etc. *Recreations:* music, ski-ing. *Address:* 4 Bromley Avenue, Bromley, Kent BR1 4BQ. *T:* 081–460 3332; The Ciba Foundation, 41 Portland Place, W1N 4BN. *T:* 071–636 9456.

CHADWICK, Gerald William St John, (John Chadwick), CMG 1961; HM Diplomatic Service, retired; Director, London Science Centre, 1981; *b* 28 May 1915; *s* of late John F. Chadwick, Solicitor; *m* 1938, Madeleine Renée Boucheron; two *s*. *Educ:* Lancing; St Catharine's Coll., Cambridge (open Exhibitioner). Asst Principal, Colonial Office, 1938; transf. Dominions Office, following demobilisation, 1940; Sec., Parl. Mission to Newfoundland, 1943; further missions to Newfoundland and Bermuda, 1946 and 1947; attended United Nations, 1949; Office of UK High Commission, Ottawa, 1949–52; Counsellor, British Embassy, Dublin, 1952–53; UK Delegn to NATO, Paris, 1954–56; Asst Sec., CRO, 1956; Asst Under-Sec. of State, CRO, 1960–66; first Dir, Commonwealth Foundn, 1966–80. Governor, Commonwealth Inst., 1967–80. Certificate of Merit, Canadian Historical Soc., 1968. *Publications:* The Shining Plain, 1937; Newfoundland: Island into Province, 1967; International Organisations, 1969; (ed jtly) Professional Organisations in the Commonwealth, 1976; The Unofficial Commonwealth, 1982; contrib. to A Decade of the Commonwealth 1955–64, 1966; numerous reviews and articles. *Recreation:* travel.

CHADWICK, Rt. Rev. Graham Charles; Assistant Bishop of Liverpool, since 1990; *b* 3 Jan. 1923; *s* of William Henry and Sarah Ann Chadwick; *m* 1955, Jeanne Suzanne Tyrell; one *s*. *Educ:* Swansea Grammar School; Keble Coll., Oxford (MA); St Michael's Coll., Llandaff. RNVR, 1942–46. Deacon 1950, priest 1951; Curate, Oystermouth, Dio. Swansea and Brecon, 1950–53; Diocese of Lesotho, 1953–63; Chaplain, University Coll., Swansea, 1963–68; Senior Bursar, Queen's Coll., Birmingham, 1968–69; Diocesan Missioner, Lesotho, and Warden of Diocesan Training Centre, 1970–76; Bishop of Kimberley and Kuruman, 1976–82; Chaplain, St Asaph Cathedral, and Advr on Spirituality, Dio. of St Asaph, 1983–90. *Address:* 423 Eaton Road, West Derby, Liverpool L12 2AJ. *T:* 051–228 2891.

CHADWICK, Professor Henry, KBE 1989; DD; FBA 1960; MRIA; Master of Peterhouse, Cambridge, since 1987; Regius Professor Emeritus of Divinity, University of Cambridge, 1983 (Regius Professor, 1979–83); Hon. Canon Emeritus of Ely; *b* 23 June 1920; 3rd *s* of late John Chadwick, Barrister, Bromley, Kent, and Edith (*née* Horrocks); *m* 1945, Margaret Elizabeth, *d* of late W. Pemell Brownrigg; three *d*. *Educ:* Eton (King's Scholar); Magdalene Coll., Cambridge (Music Schol.). John Stewart of Rannoch Scholar, 1939. MusB. Asst Master, Wellington Coll., 1945; University of Cambridge: Fellow of Queens' Coll., 1946–58; Hon. Fellow, 1958; Junior Proctor, 1948–49. Regius Professor of Divinity and Canon of Christ Church, Oxford, 1959–69; Dean of Christ Church, Oxford, 1969–79 (Hon. Student, 1979); Pro-Vice-Chancellor, Oxford Univ., 1974–75; Delegate, OUP, 1960–79; Fellow, Magdalene Coll., Cambridge, 1979–87 (Hon. Fellow 1962). Fellow, Eton, 1976–79; Hon. Fellow: St Anne's Coll., Oxford, 1979; Trinity Coll., Cambridge, 1987. Gifford Lectr, St Andrews Univ., 1962–64; Birkbeck Lectr, Cambridge, 1965; Burns Lectr, Otago, 1971; Sarum Lectr, Oxford, 1982–83. Editor, Journal of Theological Studies, 1954–85. Member, Anglican-Roman Catholic International Commn, 1969–81 and 1983–90. Mem., Amer. Philosophical Soc.; For. Hon. Mem., Amer. Acad. Arts and Sciences; Correspondant de l'Académie des Inscriptions et des Belles Lettres, Institut de France; Mem., Société des Bollandistes, Brussels; Corresponding Member: Göttingen Acad. of Scis; Rhineland Acad. of Scis. Hon. DD, Glasgow, Yale, Leeds and Manchester; Hon. Teol Dr, Uppsala; D Humane Letters, Chicago. Humboldt Prize, 1983; Lucas Prize, Tübingen, 1991. *Publications:* Origen, Contra Celsum, 1953, 3rd edn 1980; Alexandrian Christianity (with J. E. L. Oulton), 1954; Lessing's Theological Writings, 1956; The Sentences of Sextus, 1959; Early Christian Thought and the Classical Tradition, 1966; The Early Church (Pelican), 1967; The Treatise on the Apostolic Tradition of St Hippolytus of Rome, ed G. Dix (rev. edn), 1968; Priscillian of Avila, 1976; Boethius, 1981; History and Thought of the Early Church, 1982; Augustine, 1986; (ed) Atlas of the Christian Church, 1987; Augustine's Confessions, 1991; Heresy and Orthodoxy in the Early Church, 1991; (contrib.) Oxford History of the Classical World, 1986.

Recreation: music. *Address:* Peterhouse, Cambridge, CB2 1RD. *T:* Cambridge (0223) 338211.
See also W. O. Chadwick.

CHADWICK, John; *see* Chadwick, G. W. St J.

CHADWICK, John, FBA 1967; MA; LittD; Perceval Maitland Laurence Reader in Classics, University of Cambridge, 1969–84; Hon. Fellow, Downing College, Cambridge, since 1984 (Collins Fellow, 1960–84); *b* 21 May 1920; *yr s* of late Fred Chadwick; *m* 1947, Joan Isobel Hill; one *s*. *Educ:* St Paul's Sch.; Corpus Christi Coll., Cambridge. Editorial Asst, Oxford Latin Dictionary, Clarendon Press, 1946–52; Asst Lectr in Classics, 1952–54, Lectr in Classics, 1954–66, Reader in Greek Language, 1966–69, Univ. of Cambridge. Corresponding Member: Deutsches Archäologisches Inst., 1957; Austrian Acad. of Scis, 1974; Associé étranger, Acad. des Inscriptions et Belles-Lettres, Institut de France, 1985; Pres., Swedenborg Soc., 1987–88. Hon. Councillor, Athens Archaeol Soc., 1988 (Hon. Fellow, 1974). Hon. Dr of Philosophical Sch., University of Athens, 1958; Hon. DLitt, Trinity Coll., Dublin, 1971; Hon. Dr: Université Libre de Bruxelles, 1969; Euskal Herriko Unibertsitatea, Vitoria, Spain, 1985; Univ. of Salzburg, 1990. Medal of J. E. Purkyně Univ., Brno, 1966. Comdr, Order of the Phoenix, Greece, 1984. *Publications:* (jtly) The Medical Works of Hippocrates, 1950; (jtly) Documents in Mycenaean Greek, 1956, rev. edn 1973; The Decipherment of Linear B, 1958, 2nd edn 1967 (trans. into 12 languages); The Pre-history of the Greek Language (in Camb. Ancient History), 1963; The Mycenaean World, 1976 (trans. into 6 languages); (ed jtly) Corpus of Mycenaean Inscriptions from Knossos, Vol. I, 1986; Linear B and Related Scripts, 1987; (trans.) E. Swedenborg, The True Christian Religion, 1988; articles in learned jls on Mycenaean Greek. *Recreation:* travel. *Address:* 75 Gough Way, Cambridge CB3 9LN. *T:* Cambridge (0223) 356864.

CHADWICK, Hon. Sir John Murray, Kt 1991; ED; **Hon. Mr Justice Chadwick;** a Judge of the High Court of Justice, Chancery Division, since 1991; *b* 20 Jan. 1941; *s* of Hector George Chadwick and Margaret Corry Laing; *m* 1975, Diana Mary Blunt; two *d*. *Educ:* Rugby School; Magdalene Coll., Cambridge (MA). Called to the Bar, Inner Temple, 1966, Bencher, 1986; QC 1980; Judge of Courts of Appeal of Jersey and Guernsey, 1986–91; a Recorder, 1989–91. *Recreation:* sailing. *Address:* Royal Courts of Justice, Strand, WC2A 2LL. *Clubs:* Cavalry and Guards; Royal Yacht Squadron (Cowes).

CHADWICK, Sir Joshua Kenneth B.; *see* Burton-Chadwick.

CHADWICK, Lynn Russell, CBE 1964; sculptor since 1948; *b* 24 Nov. 1914; *s* of late Verner Russell Chadwick and Margery Brown Lynn; *m* 1942, Charlotte Ann Secord; one *s*; *m* 1959, Frances Mary Jamieson (*d* 1964); two *d*; *m* 1965, Eva Reiner; one *s*. *Educ:* Merchant Taylors' Sch. Architectural Draughtsman, 1933–39; Pilot, FAA, 1941–44. Exhibitions have been held in London, in various galleries, by the Arts Council and British Council; his works have also been shown in numerous international exhibitions abroad, including Venice Biennale, 1956 (Internat. Sculpture Prize). *Works in public collections:* Great Britain: Tate Gallery, London; British Council, London; Arts Council of Great Britain; Victoria and Albert Museum; Pembroke Coll., Oxford; City Art Gallery, Bristol; Art Gallery, Brighton; Whitworth Art Gallery, University of Manchester; France: Musée National D'Art Moderne, Paris; Holland: Boymans van Beuningen Museum, Rotterdam; Germany: Municipality of Recklinghausen; Staatliche Graphische Sammlung, Munich; Staatische Kunstmuseum, Duisburg; Sweden: Art Gallery, Gothenburg; Belgium: Musées Royaux des Beaux-Arts de Belgique, Brussels; Italy: Galleria D'Arte Moderna, Rome; Museo Civico, Turin; Australia: National Gallery of SA, Adelaide; Canada: National Gallery of Canada, Ottawa; Museum of Fine Arts, Montreal; USA: Museum of Modern Art, New York; Carnegie Institute, Pittsburgh; University of Michigan; Albright Art Gallery, Buffalo; Art Institute, Chicago; Chile: Inst. de Artes Contemporáneas, Lima. Officier des Arts et des Lettres (France), 1986. *Address:* Lypiatt Park, Stroud, Glos GL6 7LL.

CHADWICK, Owen; *see* Chadwick, W. O.

CHADWICK, Peter, PhD, ScD; FRS 1977; Professor of Mathematics, University of East Anglia, 1965–91; Dean of School of Mathematics and Physics, 1979–82; *b* 23 March 1931; *s* of Jack Chadwick and late Marjorie Chadwick (*née* Castle); *m* 1956, Sheila Gladys Salter, *d* of late Clarence F. and Gladys I. Salter; two *d*. *Educ:* Huddersfield Coll.; Univ. of Manchester (BSc 1952); Pembroke Coll., Cambridge (PhD 1957, ScD 1973). Scientific Officer, then Sen. Scientific Officer, Atomic Weapons Res. Estabt, Aldermaston, 1955–59; Lectr, then Sen. Lectr, in Applied Maths, Univ. of Sheffield, 1959–65. Vis. Prof., Univ. of Queensland, 1972. Member: Exec. Cttee, Internat. Soc. for Interaction of Mechanics and Maths, 1983–88; British Nat. Cttee for Theoretical and Applied Mechanics, 1969–75, 1985–89. Jt Exec. Editor, Qly Jl of Mechanics and Applied Maths, 1965–72, Trustee, 1977–91. Hon. DSc Glasgow, 1991. *Publications:* Continuum Mechanics, 1976; numerous papers on theoretical solid mechanics and the mechanics of continua in various learned journals and books. *Address:* 8 Stratford Crescent, Cringleford, Norwich NR4 7SF. *T:* Norwich (0603) 51655.

CHADWICK, Robert Everard; Director, Leeds Permanent Building Society, 1974–86 (President, 1983–85); *b* 20 Oct. 1916; *s* of Robert Agar Chadwick and Aline Chadwick; *m* 1948, Audrey Monica Procter; two *s* one *d*. *Educ:* Oundle; Leeds Univ. (LLB). Served RA, 1939–46. Solicitor, 1938–82; Director: J. Hepworth & Son, 1946–81 (Chm., 1956–81); John Waddington, 1954–77 (Chm., 1969–77); Magnet Joinery, 1969–77; Robert Glew & Co., 1969–77; W Riding Reg. Bd, Barclays Bank, 1972–82. *Recreations:* hill walking, fishing. *Address:* Baxters Fold, Cracoe, Skipton, N Yorks BD23 6LB. *T:* Cracoe (075673) 233. *Club:* Leeds (Leeds).

CHADWICK, (William) Owen, OM 1983; KBE 1982; FBA 1962; Fellow of Selwyn College, Cambridge, since 1983; Chancellor, University of East Anglia, since 1985; *b* 20 May 1916; 2nd *s* of John Chadwick and Edith (*née* Horrocks); *m* 1949, Ruth, *e d* of B. L. Hallward, *qv*; two *s* two *d*. *Educ:* Tonbridge; St John's Coll., Cambridge, and took holy orders. Fellow of Trinity Hall, Cambridge, 1947–56, Hon. Fellow, 1959; Master of Selwyn Coll., Cambridge, 1956–83; Dixie Professor of Ecclesiastical History, 1958–68; Regius Prof. of Modern History, 1968–83; Vice-Chancellor, Cambridge Univ., 1969–71. Chm. Trustees, University Coll., later Wolfson Coll., Cambridge, 1965–77, Hon. Fellow 1977. Pres., British Academy, 1981–85. Chm., Archbishops' Commn on Church and State, 1966–70; Mem., Royal Commn on Historical MSS, 1984–. Chm. of Trustees, Nat. Portrait Gall., 1988– (Trustee, 1978–). Hon. Mem., American Acad. of Arts and Scis, 1977. Hon. Fellow, St John's Coll., Cambridge, 1964; Hon. FRSE. Hon. DD: St Andrews; Oxford; Hon. DLitt: Kent; Bristol; London; Leeds; Hon. LittD: UEA; Cambridge; Hon. Dr of Letters, Columbia; Hon. LLD Aberdeen. Wolfson Literary Prize, 1980. *Publications include:* John Cassian, 1950; From Bossuet to Newman, 1957; Victorian Miniature, 1960; The Reformation, 1964; The Victorian Church, 1966, 1971; The Secularization of the European Mind in the 19th Century, 1976; Acton and Gladstone, 1976; Catholicism and History, 1978; The Popes and European Revolution, 1981; Britain and the Vatican during the Second World War, 1986; Michael Ramsey: a life, 1990; The Spirit of the Oxford Movement, 1990; contrib. to Studies in Early British History, 1954. *Recreations:* opera; Cambridge XV versus Oxford, 1936–38. *Address:* 67 Grantchester Street, Cambridge CB3 9HZ.
See also Henry Chadwick.

CHADWICK-JONES, Prof. John Knighton, PhD, DSc(Econ); Professor of Psychology, Saint Mary's University, Halifax, Canada, since 1974; *b* 26 July 1928; *s* of Thomas Chadwick-Jones and Cecilia Rachel (*née* Thomas); *m* 1965, Araceli Carceller y Bergillos, PhD; two *s* one *d*. *Educ:* Bromsgrove Sch.; St Edmund Hall, Oxford (MA). PhD Wales, 1960; DSc(Econ) Wales, 1981. FBPsS. Scientific Staff, Nat. Inst. of Industrial Psychol., London, 1957–60; Lectr, then Sen. Lectr, in Industrial Psychol., UC, Cardiff, 1960–66; Reader in Social Psychol., Flinders Univ. of South Australia, 1967–68; Dir, Occupational Psychol. Res. Unit, UC, Cardiff, 1968–74; Mem., Exec. Cttee, Bd of Governors, Saint Mary's Univ., 1975–78. Canada Soc. Scis and Humanities Res. Council Leave Fellow: Darwin Coll., Cambridge, 1980–81; MRC Unit on Develt and Integration of Behaviour, Cambridge, 1984–85; Visiting Fellow: Clare Hall, Cambridge, 1982; Wolfson Coll., Cambridge, 1984–85; Wolfson Coll., Oxford, 1988–89; St Edmund's Coll., Cambridge, 1990. Dir, Cambridge Canadian Trust (Toronto), 1988–. Fellow: Amer. Psychol Assoc.; Canadian Psychol Assoc. *Publications:* Automation and Behavior: a social psychological study, 1969; Social Exchange Theory: its strueture and influence in social psychology, 1976; (jtly) Brain, Environment and Social Psychology, 1979; Absenteeism in the Canadian Context, 1979; (jtly) Social Psychology of Absenteeism, 1982; articles in academic jls. *Address:* 1105 Belmont-on-the-Arm, Halifax, Nova Scotia B3H 1J2, Canada.

CHADWYCK-HEALEY, Sir Charles (Edward), 5th Bt *cr* 1919, of Wyphurst, Cranleigh, Co. Surrey and New Place, Luccombe, Somerset; Chairman: Chadwyck-Healey Ltd, since 1973; Chadwyck-Healey Inc., since 1981; Chadwyck-Healey France SA, since 1985; *b* 13 May 1940; *s* of Sir Charles Arthur Chadwyck-Healey, 4th Bt, OBE, TD, and of Viola, *d* of late Cecil Lubbock; *S* father, 1986; *m* 1967, Angela Mary, *e d* of late John Metson; one *s* two *d*. *Educ:* Eton; Trinity Coll., Oxford (MA). Hon. Pres., European Information Assoc. *Heir:* *s* Edward Alexander Chadwyck-Healey, *b* 2 June 1972. *Address:* Manor Farm, Bassingbourn, Cambs SG8 5NX. *T:* Royston (0763) 242447. *Club:* Brooks's.

CHAIR, Somerset de; *see* de Chair.

CHAKAIPA, Most Rev. Patrick; *see* Harare, Archbishop of, (RC).

CHALDECOTT, John Anthony; Keeper, Science Museum Library, South Kensington, 1961–76; *b* 16 Feb. 1916; *o s* of Wilfrid James and Mary Eleanor Chaldecott; *m* 1940, Kathleen Elizabeth Jones; one *d*. *Educ:* Latymer Upper Sch., Hammersmith; Brentwood Sch.; Borough Road Coll., Isleworth; University College, London. BSc 1938, MSc 1949, PhD 1972. FInstP; CPhys. Meteorological Branch, RAFVR, 1939–45 (despatches). Lecturer, Acton Technical Coll., 1945–48; entered Science Museum as Asst Keeper, Dept of Physics, 1949; Deputy Keeper and Secretary to Advisory Council, 1957. Pres., British Society for the History of Science, 1972–74. *Publications:* Josiah Wedgwood: the arts and sciences united (with J. des Fontaines and J. Tindall), 1978; Science Museum handbooks; papers on the history of science. *Address:* 7 Ravens Court, St John's Road, Eastbourne, E Sussex BN20 7HY.

CHALFONT, Baron, *cr* 1964 (Life Peer); **Alun Arthur Gwynne Jones,** PC 1964; OBE 1961; MC 1957; Chairman, VSEL Consortium plc, since 1987; Chairman, All Party Defence Group, House of Lords, since 1980; Chairman, Radio Authority, since 1991; *b* 5 Dec. 1919; *s* of Arthur Gwynne Jones and Eliza Alice Hardman; *m* 1948, Dr Mona Mitchell; one *d* decd. *Educ:* West Monmouth Sch. Commissioned into South Wales Borderers (24th Foot), 1940; served in: Burma 1941–44; Malayan campaign 1955–57; Cyprus campaign 1958–59; various staff and intelligence appointments; Staff Coll., Camberley, 1950; Jt Services Staff Coll., 1958; Russian interpreter, 1951; resigned commission, 1961, on appt as Defence Correspondent, The Times; frequent television and sound broadcasts and consultant on foreign affairs to BBC Television, 1961–64; Minister of State, Foreign and Commonwealth Office, 1964–70; UK Permanent Rep. to WEU, 1969–70; Foreign Editor, New Statesman, 1970–71. Dep. Chm., IBA, 1989–90. Director: W. S. Atkins International, 1979–83; IBM UK Ltd, 1973–90 (Mem. IBM Europe Adv. Council, 1973–90); Lazard Bros & Co. Ltd, 1983–90; Shandwick plc, 1985–; Triangle Holdings, 1986–; Chairman: Industrial Cleaning Papers, 1979–86; Peter Hamilton Security Consultants Ltd, 1984–86; President: Abington Corp. (Consultants) Ltd, 1981–; Nottingham Bldg Soc., 1983–90. President: Hispanic and Luso Brazilian Council, 1975–80; RNID, 1980–; Llangollen Internat. Music Festival, 1979–; Freedom in Sport, 1982–; Chairman: UK Cttee for Free World, 1981–; Eur. Atlantic Gp, 1983–; Member: IISS; Bd of Governors, Sandle Manor Sch. MRI; MInstD. FRSA. Hon. Fellow UCW Aberystwyth, 1974. Liveryman, Worshipful Co. of Paviors. Freeman, City of London. *Publications:* The Sword and The Spirit, 1963; The Great Commanders, 1973; Montgomery of Alamein, 1976; (ed) Waterloo: battle of three armies, 1979; Star Wars: suicide or survival, 1985; Defence of the Realm, 1987; By God's Will: a portrait of the Sultan of Brunei, 1989; contribs to The Times, and other national and professional journals. *Recreations:* formerly Rugby football, cricket, lawn tennis; now music and theatre. *Address:* House of Lords, SW1A 0PW. *Clubs:* Garrick, MCC, Lord's Taverners, City Livery.

CHALK, Hon. Sir Gordon (William Wesley), KBE 1971; Hon. LLD; company director and business consultant; MP (Queensland), 1947–76; Minister for Transport, Govt of Queensland, 1957–65, Deputy Premier and Treasurer, 1965–76; Leader, Liberal Party of Australia (Queensland Div.), 1965–76; voluntarily retired, 1976; *b* 1913; of British parentage; *m* 1937, Ellen Clare Grant; one *s* one *d*. *Educ:* Gatton Senior High Sch., Qld. Formerly: Queensland Sales Manager, Toowoomba Foundry Pty Ltd; Registered Taxation Agent. Mem. Senate, Griffith Univ., 1976–84. Hon. LLD Queensland Univ., 1974. *Address:* 277 Indooroopilly Road, Indooroopilly, Qld. 4068, Australia. *T:* Brisbane 3711598. *Clubs:* Tattersall's (Brisbane, Qld); Rotary International (Gatton, Qld); Southport Yacht.

CHALKER, Rt. Hon. Lynda, PC 1987; MP (C) Wallasey since Feb. 1974; Minister of State, since 1986 and Minister for Overseas Development, since 1989, Foreign and Commonwealth Office (Deputy to Secretary of State, 1987–89); *b* 29 April 1942; *d* of late Sidney Henry James Bates and Marjorie Kathleen Randell; *m* 1st, 1967, Eric Robert Chalker (marr. diss. 1973); no *c*; 2nd, 1981, Clive Landa. *Educ:* Heidelberg Univ.; London Univ.; Central London Polytechnic. Statistician with Research Bureau Ltd (Unilever), 1963–69; Dep. Market Research Man. with Shell Mex & BP Ltd, 1969–72; Chief Exec. of Internat. Div. of Louis Harris International, 1972–74. Opposition Spokesman on Social Services, 1976–79; Parly Under-Sec. of State, DHSS, 1979–82, Dept of Transport, 1982–83; Minister of State, Dept of Transport, 1983–86. Jt Sec., Cons. Health and Social Services Cttee, 1975–76; Chm., Greater London Young Conservatives, 1969–70; Nat. Vice-Chm., Young Conservatives, 1970–71. Member: BBC Gen. Adv. Cttee, 1975–79; RIIA, 1977–. *Publications:* (jtly) Police in Retreat (pamphlet), 1967; (jtly) Unhappy Families (pamphlet), 1971; (jtly) We are Richer than We Think, 1978; Africa: turning the tide, 1989. *Recreations:* music, cooking, theatre, driving. *Address:* House of Commons, SW1A 0AA. *T:* 071–219 5098.

CHALKLEY, David Walter; Chairman, Inner London Education Authority, 1979–80; *b* 11 May 1915; *m* 1941, Hilda Davis; one *s* one *d*. *Educ:* Sellincourt Sch.; Battersea Polytechnic. Parliamentary Labour Candidate: NW Croydon, 1959; Brentford-Chiswick, 1964; Mayor of Mitcham, 1961; Mem., GLC, 1964–67 and 1970–81 (for Deptford). *Publication:* article on Labour organisation and class voting in constituencies. *Recreation:* travel. *Club:* Progressive (Tooting).

CHALLEN, Rt. Rev. Michael Boyd, AM 1988; Executive Director, Brotherhood of St Laurence, since 1991; *b* 27 May 1932; *s* of late B. Challen; *m* 1961, Judith, *d* of A. Kelly; two *d*. *Educ:* Mordialloc High School; Frankston High School; Univ. of Melbourne (BSc 1955); Ridley College, Melbourne (ThL 1956). Deacon 1957, priest 1958; Curate of Christ Church, Essendon, 1957–59; Member, Melbourne Dio. Centre 1959–63; Director, 1963–69; Priest-in-charge, St Luke, Fitzroy, 1959–61; St Alban's, N Melbourne, 1961–65; Flemington, 1965–69; Dir, Anglican Inner-City Ministry, 1969; Dir, Home Mission Dept, Perth, 1971–78; Priest-in-charge, Lockridge with Eden Hill, 1973; Archdeacon, Home Missions, Perth, 1975–78; Asst Bp, dio. of Perth, WA, 1978–91; Exec. Dir, Anglican Health and Welfare Service, Perth, 1977–78. *Address:* 67 Brunswick Street, Fitzroy, Vic 3065, Australia. *T:* 03 4197055, *Fax:* 03 4172691.

CHALLENS, Wallace John, CBE 1967 (OBE 1958); Director, Atomic Weapons Research Establishment, Aldermaston, 1976–78; *b* 14 May 1915; *s* of late Walter Lincoln Challens and Harriet Sybil Challens (*née* Collins); *m* 1st, 1938, Winifred Joan Stephenson (*d* 1971); two *s*; 2nd, 1973, Norma Lane. *Educ:* Deacons Sch., Peterborough; University Coll., Nottingham; BSc (Hons) London. Research Dept, Woolwich, 1936; Projectile Develt Estabt, Aberporth, 1939. British Commonwealth Scientific Office, Washington, 1946; Armament Research Estabt, Fort Halstead, 1947; Atomic Weapons Research Estabt: Fort Halstead, 1954; Aldermaston, 1955–78. Scientific Dir of trials at Christmas Island, 1957. Appointed: Chief of Warhead Develt, 1959; Asst Dir, 1965; Dep. Dir, 1972. FInstP 1944. US Medal of Freedom (Bronze) 1946. *Recreation:* golf. *Address:* Far End, Crossborough Hill, Basingstoke, Hampshire RG21 2AG. *T:* Basingstoke (0256) 464986.

CHALLIS, Dr Anthony Arthur Leonard, CBE 1980; Chief Scientist, Department of Energy, 1980–83; *b* 24 Dec. 1921; *s* of Leonard Hough Challis and Dorothy (*née* Busby); *m* 1947, L. Beryl Hedley; two *d*. *Educ:* Newcastle upon Tyne Royal Grammar Sch.; King's Coll., Univ. of Durham. 1st cl. hons BSc Chemistry; PhD. Imperial Chemical Industries: joined Billingham Div., 1946; Research Man., HOC Div., 1962; Research Dir, Mond Div., 1966; Head of Corporate Lab., 1967; Gen. Man. Planning, 1970; Sen. Vice-Pres., ICI Americas Inc., 1975–76; Dir, Polymer Engrg, SRC, 1976–80. Mem., SERC (formerly SRC), 1973–83; Pres., PRI, 1985–87 (Chm. Council, 1983–85). Associate Prof., Wolfson Unit on Processing Materials, Stirling Univ., 1968. Mem. Court, Univ. of Stirling, 1968–74. Mem., Horners' Co. *Publications:* contrib. chem, energy and managerial jls. *Recreations:* music, walking, narrow boat. *Address:* Classeys, Low Ham, Langport, Somerset TA10 9DP.

CHALLIS, Margaret Joan, MA; Headmistress of Queen Anne's School, Caversham, 1958–77; *b* 14 April 1917; *d* of R. S. Challis and L. Challis (*née* Fairbairn). *Educ:* Girton Coll., Cambridge. BA Hons., English Tripos, 1939, MA, 1943, Cambridge. English Mistress: Christ's Hospital, Hertford, 1940–44; Dartford Grammar School for Girls, 1944–45; Cheltenham Ladies' Coll., 1945–57. Housemistress at Cheltenham Ladies' Coll., 1949–57. *Recreations:* local history, music, old churches. *Address:* 30 Eldorado Crescent, Cheltenham, Glos GL50 2PY. *T:* Cheltenham (0242) 245605.

CHALMERS, Ian Pender, OBE 1980; HM Diplomatic Service; Counsellor, Foreign and Commonwealth Office, since 1987; *b* 30 Jan. 1939; *s* of John William Pender Chalmers and Beatrice Miriam Emery; *m* 1962, Lisa Christine Hay; two *s* two *d* (and one *d* decd). *Educ:* Hordle House, Harrow; Trinity College Dublin. Joined HM Diplomatic Service, 1963; Second Sec., Beirut, 1966–68; FCO, 1968–70; First Sec., Warsaw, 1970–72; FCO, 1972–76; First Sec., Paris, 1976–80; FCO, 1980–84; Counsellor, UK Mission to UN, Geneva, 1984–87. *Recreations:* reading, ski-ing, travel, watching sport. *Address:* c/o Foreign and Commonwealth Office, SW1A 2AH.

CHALMERS, Neil Robert, PhD; Director, The Natural History Museum (formerly British Museum (Natural History)), since 1988; *b* 19 June 1942; *s* of William King and Irene Margaret Chalmers (*née* Pemberton); *m* 1970, Monica Elizabeth Byanjeru (*née* Rusoke); two *d*. *Educ:* King's College Sch., Wimbledon; Magdalen Coll., Oxford (BA); St John's Coll., Cambridge (PhD). Lectr in Zoology, Makerere University Coll., Kampala, 1966–69; Scientific Dir, Nat. Primate Res. Centre, Nairobi, 1969–70; Open University: Lectr, subseq. Sen. Lectr, then Reader in Biology, 1970–85; Dean of Science, 1985–88. *Publications:* Social Behaviour in Primates, 1979; numerous papers on animal behaviour in Animal Behaviour and other learned jls. *Recreations:* music, squash. *Address:* The Natural History Museum, Cromwell Road, SW7 5BD.

CHALMERS, Patrick Edward Bruce; Controller, BBC Scotland, since 1983; *b* Chapel of Garioch, Aberdeenshire, 26 Oct. 1939; *s* of L. E. F. Chalmers, farmer, Lethenty, Inverurie, and Helen Morris Campbell; *m* 1963, Ailza Catherine Reid, *d* of late William McGibbon, Advocate in Aberdeen; three *d*. *Educ:* Fettes Coll., Edinburgh; N of Scotland Coll. of Agriculture (NDA); Univ. of Durham (BScA). Joined BBC as radio talks producer, BBC Scotland, 1963; television producer, 1965; sen. producer, Aberdeen, 1970; Head of Television, Scotland, 1979–82; Gen. Man., Co-Productions, London, 1982. President: Edinburgh Television Fest., 1984–; BAFTA, Scotland, 1990. Mem., Grampian Region Children's Panel, 1974–79. FRSA 1990. Bailie of Bennachie, 1975. *Recreations:* skiing, gardening. *Address:* c/o BBC, Queen Margaret Drive, Glasgow G12 8DG. *Clubs:* New (Edinburgh); Royal Northern (Aberdeen); Kandahar Ski.

CHALMERS, Thomas Wightman, CBE 1957; *b* 29 April 1913; *s* of Thomas Wightman Chalmers and Susan Florence Colman. *Educ:* Bradfield Coll.; King's Coll., London. Organ Scholar, King's Coll., London, 1934–36; BSc (Engineering), 1936. Joined BBC programme staff, 1936; successively announcer, Belfast and London; Overseas Presentation Director; Chief Assistant, Light Programme, 1945, Controller, 1948–50; Director, Nigerian Broadcasting Service, 1950–56, on secondment from BBC; Controller, North Region, BBC, 1956–58; Director of the Tanganyika Broadcasting Corporation, 1958–62; Deputy Regional Representative, UN Technical Assistance Board, East and Central Africa, 1962–64; Special Asst, Overseas and Foreign Relations, BBC, 1964–71; Chief Exec., Radio Services, United Newspapers Ltd, and Dir, Radio Fleet Productions Ltd, 1971–75. *Recreations:* travel, literature, music.

CHALMERS, William Gordon, CB 1980; MC 1944; Crown Agent for Scotland, 1974–84; *b* 4 June 1922; *s* of Robert Wilson Chalmers and Mary Robertson Chalmers (*née* Clark); *m* 1948, Margaret Helen McLeod; one *s* one *d*. *Educ:* Robert Gordon's Coll., Aberdeen; Aberdeen Univ. (BL). University, 1940–42 and 1947–48; served with Queen's Own Cameron Highlanders, 1942–47; Solicitor in Aberdeen, 1948–50; Procurator Fiscal Depute at Dunfermline, 1950–59; Senior Procurator Fiscal Depute at Edinburgh, 1959–63; Asst in Crown Office, 1963–67; Deputy Crown Agent, 1967–74. Jt Hd, War Crimes Enquiry in UK, 1988–89. *Recreations:* golf, bridge. *Address:* 3/4 Rocheid Park, East Fettes Avenue, Edinburgh EH4 1RP. *T:* 031–332 7937.

CHALONER, family name of Baron Gisborough.

CHALONER, Prof. William Gilbert, FRS 1976; Hildred Carlile Professor of Botany and Head of School of Life Sciences, Royal Holloway and Bedford New College, University of London, since 1985 (at Bedford College, 1979–85); *b* London, 22 Nov. 1928; *s* of late Ernest J. and L. Chaloner; *m* 1955, Judith Carroll; one *s* two *d*. *Educ:* Kingston Grammar Sch.; Reading Univ. (BSc, PhD). 2nd Lt RA, 1955–56. Lectr and Reader, University Coll., London, 1956–72. Visiting Prof., Pennsylvania State Univ., USA, 1961–62; Prof. of Botany, Univ. of Nigeria, 1965–66; Prof. of Botany, Birkbeck Coll., Univ. of London, 1972–79. Wilmer D. Barrett Prof. of Botany, Univ. of Mass, 1988–91. Member: Senate, Univ. of London, 1983–; Bd of Trustees, Royal Botanic Gardens, Kew, 1983–. President: Palaeontological Assoc., 1976–78; Internat. Orgn of Palaeobotany, 1981–87; Linnean Soc., 1985–88; Vice-Pres., Geol Soc. London, 1985–86. Corresponding Mem., Botanical Soc. of Amer., 1987–. Associé Etranger de l'Acad. des Scis, Inst. de France, 1989. Linnean Medal (Botany), Linnean Soc., 1991. *Publications:* papers in Palaeontology and other scientific jls, dealing with fossil plants. *Recreations:* swimming, tennis, visiting USA. *Address:* 20 Parke Road, SW13 9NG. *T:* 081–748 3863.

CHAMBERLAIN, Prof. Geoffrey Victor Price, RD 1974; MD; FRCS, FRCOG; Professor and Chairman, Obstetrics and Gynaecology, St George's Hospital Medical School, since 1982; *b* 21 April 1930; *s* of late Albert Chamberlain and Irene Chamberlain (*née* Price); *m* 1956, Jocelyn Olivia Kerley, *d* of late Sir Peter Kerley, KCVO, CBE; three *s* two *d*. *Educ:* Llandaff Cathedral Sch.; Cowbridge; University Coll. and UCH, London (Goldsmith Schol. 1948; MB 1954; Fellow, UCL, 1987); MD 1968; FRCS 1960; FRCOG 1978. Residencies at RPMS, Gt Ormond St, Queen Charlotte's and Chelsea Hosps, KCH, 1955–69; Tutor, George Washington Med. Sch., Washington DC, 1965–66; Consultant Obstetrician and Gynaecologist, Queen Charlotte's and Chelsea Hosps, 1970–82. RNR, 1955–74, Surgeon Comdr. Member: Council, RSocMed, 1977–84 (Council, Obst. Sect., 1970–87; Council, Open Sect., 1987–); Council, RCOG, 1971–77, 1982–87 (Vice-Pres., 1984–87); Chairman: Med. Cttee, Nat. Birthday Trust, 1982–; Blair Bell Res. Soc., 1977–80; Assoc. of Profs of Obstetrics and Gynaecology, 1989–; Fulbright Fellow, RCOG, 1966; Thomas Eden Fellow, RCOG, 1966; Vis. Professor: Beckman, USA, 1984; Daphne Chung, Hong Kong, 1985; Edwin Tooth, Brisbane, 1987; S African Representative Cttee, 1988. Hon. FACOG. Freeman, City of London, 1982. Foundn Prize, Amer. Assoc. of Obstetricians, 1967. Editor, Contemporary Reviews in Obstetrics and Gynaecology, 1987–. *Publications:* Safety of the Unborn Child, 1969; Lecture Notes in Obstetrics, 1975, 5th edn 1985; British Births, 1970; Placental Transfer, 1979; Clinical Physiology in Obstetrics, 1980; Tubal Infertility, 1982; Pregnant Women at Work, 1984; Prepregnancy Care, 1985; Birthplace, 1987; Lecture Notes in Gynaecology, 1988; Manual of Obstetrics, 1988; (ed) Obstetrics by Ten Teachers, 15th edn, 1990 (contrib. 13th edn 1980, 14th edn 1985); (ed) Gynaecology by Ten Teachers, 15th edn, 1990 (contrib. 13th edn 1980, 14th edn 1985); contribs to BMJ, Lancet, UK and overseas Jls of Obst. and Gyn. *Recreations:* travel, labouring in wife's garden. *Address:* 10 Burghley Road, Wimbledon, SW19 5BH. *T:* 081–947 7558; Groose Cottage, Cwm Ivy, Llanmadoc, Gower, Glamorgan.

CHAMBERLAIN, George Digby, CMG 1950; Chief Secretary, Western Pacific High Commission, 1947–52; *b* 13 Feb. 1898; *s* of Digby Chamberlain, late Knockfin, Knaresborough; *m* 1931, Kirsteen Miller Holmes; one *d* (one *s* decd). *Educ:* St Catharine's Coll., Cambridge. War Service, 1917–19, with Rifle Brigade, Lieut RARO. Asst District Commissioner, Gold Coast, 1925; Asst Principal, Colonial Office, 1930–32; Asst Colonial Secretary, Gold Coast, 1932; Asst Chief Secretary, Northern Rhodesia, 1939; Colonial Secretary, Gambia, 1943–47; Acting Governor, Gambia, July-Nov. 1943, and June-Aug. 1944; Acting High Commissioner, Western Pacific, Jan.-April, and Sept. 1951–July 1952; retired 1952. *Recreations:* shooting, fishing. *Address:* 18 Douglas Crescent, Edinburgh EH12 5BA. *Club:* New (Edinburgh).

CHAMBERLAIN, Air Vice-Marshal George Philip, CB 1946; OBE 1941; RAF, retired; *b* 18 Aug. 1905; *s* of G. A. R. Chamberlain, MA, FLAS, FRICS, Enville, Staffordshire; *m* 1930, Alfreda Rosamond Kedward; one *s* one *d*. *Educ:* Denstone Coll.; Royal Air Force Coll., Cranwell. Commissioned RAF, 1925. On loan to Min. of Civil Aviation, 1947–48; Imperial Defence Coll., 1949; AOA 205 Group, MEAF, 1950; AOC Transport Wing, MEAF, 1951–52; Commandant, RAF Staff Coll., Andover, 1953–54; AO i/c A, HQ Fighter Command, 1954–57; Dep. Controller of Electronics, Min. of Supply, 1957–59, Min. of Aviation, 1959–60; Managing Director, Collins Radio Co. of England, 1961–66, non-executive director, 1967–75. *Recreations:* gardening, walking. *Address:* Little Orchard, 12 Adelaide Close, Stanmore, Middlesex HA7 3EL. *T:* 081–954 0710. *Club:* Royal Air Force.

CHAMBERLAIN, Kevin John; Deputy Legal Adviser, Foreign and Commonwealth Office, since 1990; *b* 31 Jan. 1942; *s* of Arthur James Chamberlain and Gladys Mary (*née* Harris); *m* 1967, Pia Rosita Frauenlob; one *d*. *Educ:* Wimbledon Coll.; King's Coll., London (LLB). Called to the Bar, Inner Temple, 1965. Asst Legal Adviser, FCO, 1965–74; Legal Adviser: British Mil. Govt, Berlin, 1974–76; British Embassy, Bonn, 1976–77; Asst Legal Adviser, FCO, 1977–79; Legal Counsellor, FCO, 1979–83; Counsellor (Legal Advr), Office of UK Perm. Rep. to EC, Brussels, 1983–87; Legal Counsellor, FCO, 1987–90. *Recreations:* opera, riding, tennis, skiing. *Address:* c/o Foreign and Commonwealth Office, SW1A 2AH.

CHAMBERLAIN, (Leslie) Neville, CBE 1990; Chief Executive, British Nuclear Fuels plc, since 1986; *b* 3 Oct. 1939; *s* of Leslie Chamberlain and Doris Anne Chamberlain (*née* Thompson); *m* 1971, Joy Rachel Wellings; one *s* three *d*. *Educ:* King James Grammar School, Bishop Auckland; King's College, Univ. of Durham. UKAEA, 1962–71; Urenco Ltd, 1971–77; British Nuclear Fuels: Fuel Production, 1977–81; Enrichment Business Manager, 1981–84; Dir, Enrichment Div., 1984–86. *Recreations:* horse racing, swimming, music. *Address:* British Nuclear Fuels plc, Risley, Warrington, Cheshire WA3 6AS. *T:* Warrington (0925) 835006.

CHAMBERLAIN, Michael Aubrey, FCA; Senior Partner, KPMG Peat Marwick McLintock, Leicester, since 1974; *b* 16 April 1939; *s* of George Thomas Everard Chamberlain and Doris (*née* Arden). *Educ:* Repton Sch., Derbys. FCA 1963. Vice-Pres., Inst. of Chartered Accountants in England and Wales, 1991–June 1992. Chm., Leicester Diocesan Bd of Finance, 1983–. *Address:* Peat House, 1 Waterloo Way, Leicester LE1 6LP. *T:* Leicester (0533) 471122. *Club:* Savile.

CHAMBERLAIN, Neville; *see* Chamberlain, L. N.

CHAMBERLAIN, Prof. Owen, AB, PhD; Professor of Physics, University of California, 1958–89, now Emeritus; *b* San Francisco, 10 July 1920; *s* of W. Edward Chamberlain and Genevieve Lucinda Owen; *m* 1943, Babette Copper (marr. diss. 1978); one *s* three *d*; *m* 1980, June Greenfield Steingart. *Educ:* Philadelphia; Dartmouth Coll., Hanover, NH

(AB). Atomic research for Manhattan District, 1942, transferred to Los Alamos, 1943; worked in Argonne National Laboratory, Chicago, 1947–48, and studied at University of Chicago (PhD); Instructor in Physics, University of California, 1948; Asst Professor, 1950; Associate Professor, 1954. Guggenheim Fellowship, 1957; Loeb Lecturer in Physics, Harvard Univ., 1959. Nobel Prize (joint) for Physics, 1959. Fellow: American Phys. Soc.; Amer. Acad. of Arts and Scis; Mem., Nat. Acad. of Sciences, 1960. *Publications:* papers in Physical Review, Physical Review Letters, Nature, Nuovo Cimento. *Address:* Department of Physics, University of California, Berkeley, California 94720, USA.

CHAMBERLAIN, Peter Edwin, FEng; FRINA; Assistant Under Secretary of State, Defence Research Agency Implementation Team, Ministry of Defence, since 1989; *b* 25 July 1939; *s* of Dr Eric Alfred Charles Chamberlain, OBE, FRSE, and Winifred Louise (Susan) (*née* Bone); *m* 1963, Irene May Frew; two *s* one *d*. *Educ:* Royal High Sch.; Edinburgh Univ. (Keasby Schol., BSc); RN Colls Manadon and Greenwich. RCNC. Asst Constructor, ship and submarine design, ME and Bath, 1963–68; Constructor: submarine design, Bath, 1968–69; submarine construction, Birkenhead, 1969–72; ship structures R&D, Dunfermline, 1972–74; postgrad. programmes in Naval Architecture, UCL, 1974–77; ship design, Bath, 1977–78; Chief Constructor: Hd of Secretariat, Bath, 1978–80; Surface Ship Forward Design, Bath, 1980–82; RCDS 1983; Asst Sec., Hd of Secretariat to Master Gen. of Ordnance, London, 1984–85; Under Sec., Dir Gen. Future Material Programmes (Naval), London, 1985–87; Dep. Controller Warship Equipments, MoD, 1987–88; Chief Underwater Systems Exec., MoD, 1988–89. FEng 1988. *Recreations:* jogging, music, visual arts, poetry, computing. *Address:* Ministry of Defence, St George's Court, 14 New Oxford Street, WC1A 1EJ.

CHAMBERLAIN, Hon. Sir (Reginald) Roderic (St Clair), Kt 1970; Judge of the Supreme Court of South Australia, 1959–71; *b* 17 June 1901; *s* of late Henry Chamberlain; *m* 1929, Leila Macdonald Haining; one *d*. *Educ:* St Peter's Coll.; Adelaide Univ. Crown Prosecutor, 1928; KC 1945; Crown Solicitor, 1952–59; Chm., SA Parole Board, 1970–75. Chm., Anti-Cancer Foundn. *Publication:* The Stuart Affair, 1973. *Recreations:* golf, bridge. *Address:* 72 Moseley Street, Glenelg South, SA 5045, Australia. *T:* 95.2036. *Clubs:* Adelaide, Royal Adelaide Golf (Adelaide).

CHAMBERLAIN, Richard, TD 1949; Chief Master of the Supreme Court, Chancery Division, 1985–86 (Master, 1964–84); *b* 29 Jan. 1914; *o s* of late John Chamberlain and Hilda (*née* Poynting); *m* 1938, Joan, *d* of late George and Eileen Kay; two *s* one *d*. *Educ:* Radley Coll.; Trinity Coll., Cambridge (MA). Admitted Solicitor, 1938. Served War, 1939–45: Devon Regt, TJFF, Staff Coll., Haifa. Partner, Kingsford Dorman & Co., 1948–64. Asst, Worshipful Co. of Solicitors of the City of London, 1966, Warden, 1973–74, Master, 1975. *Publication:* Asst Editor, Supreme Court Practice, 1967. *Recreations:* gardening, photography, travel, grandparental duties. *Address:* 23 Drax Avenue, Wimbledon, SW20 0EG. *T:* 081–946 4219. *Club:* Garrick.

CHAMBERLAIN, Hon. Sir Roderick; *see* Chamberlain, Hon Sir (Reginald) R.

CHAMBERLAIN, William Richard Frank, DL; Chairman, Test and County Cricket Board, since 1990; *b* 13 April 1925; *s* of Lt-Comdr Richard Chamberlain and Elizabeth Chamberlain (*née* Robson); *m* 1960, Gillian Diarmid Castle; one *s* one *d*. *Educ:* Uppingham School. Served Fleet Air Arm 1943–46. Chairman: Chamberlain Phipps, 1975–87; Stead & Simpson, 1984–89; Regional Dir, Nat. Westminster Bank, 1983–90; Dir, Kingsgrange, 1989–. Chm., Northants CCC, 1985–90; Chm., Cricket Council, 1990. Freeman, City of London; Master, Patternmaker's Co., 1987. High Sheriff, 1990, DL 1991, Northants. *Recreations:* cricket, shooting. *Address:* Manor House, Swineshead, Bedford MK44 2AF. *T:* Bedford (0234) 708283. *Clubs:* Naval & Military, MCC.

CHAMBERLEN, Nicholas Hugh; Chairman, Clive Discount Company, since 1977; *b* 18 April 1939; *s* of Rev. Leonard Saunders Chamberlen, MC, and Lillian Margaret (*née* Webley); *m* 1962, Jane Mary Lindo; three *s* one *d*. *Educ:* Sherborne Sch.; Lincoln Coll., Oxford (BA Hons). Nat. Cash Register Co., 1962–67; Clive Discount Co. Ltd, 1967–. *Recreations:* shooting, golf, cricket. *Address:* Ryders Wells House, Ringmer, East Sussex BN8 5RN. *Clubs:* Portland, Turf.

CHAMBERS, Prof. Andrew David; Professor of Internal Auditing, City University Business School, since 1983; *b* 7 April 1943; *s* of Lewis Harold and Florence Lilian Chambers; *m* 1st, 1969, Mary Elizabeth Ann Kilbey (marr. diss. 1984); two *s*; 2nd, 1987, Celia Barrington (*née* Pruen); one *s* one *d*, and one step *s*. *Educ:* St Albans Sch.; Hatfield Coll., Univ. of Durham (BA Hons). FCA, FBCS, FCCA, FIIA. Arthur Andersen & Co., 1965–69; Barker & Dobson, 1969–70; United Biscuits, 1970–71; City University Business School: Lectr in Computer Applications in Accountancy, 1971–74; Leverhulme Sen. Res. Fellow in Internal Auditing, 1974–78; Sen. Lectr in Audit and Management Control, 1978–83; Administrative Sub-Dean, 1983–86; Acting Dean, 1985–86; Dean, 1986–91; Head of Dept of Business Studies, 1986–89. Warden, Northampton Hall, City Univ., 1983–86 (Dep. Warden, 1972–76). Vis. Prof. in Computer Auditing, Univ. of Leuven, Belgium, 1980–81, 1992–. Consultant: MacIntyre Hudson, Chartered Accountants, 1987–89; BBHW, Chartered Accountants, 1990–; Director: Nat. Home Loans Hldgs; Nat. Mortgage Bank; Management Audit. Member Council: BCS, 1979–82 (Mem., Tech. Bd; Chm., Meetings Cttee); IIA, 1985–86 (Chm., Res. Cttee); Member: IT Cttee, ICA, 1986–; Educn, Training and Technol. Transfer Cttee, British Malaysian Soc., 1987–90; MBA Adv. Bd, Ashridge Management Coll., 1986–; British Acad. of Management, 1990–. Hon. Auditor, RSAA, 1986–91. FRSA. Gov., Islington Green Comprehensive Sch., 1989–. Member, Editorial Board: Computer Fraud and Security, 1981–87; Managerial Auditing Jl, 1986–. *Publications:* (with O. J. Hanson) Keeping Computers Under Control, 1975; (ed) Internal Auditing: developments and horizons, 1979; Internal Auditing: theory and practice, 1981, 2nd edn (with G. M. Selim and G. Vinten) 1987; Computer Auditing, 1981, 3rd edn (with J. M. Court) 1991; papers in learned jls. *Recreations:* family, conservation. *Address:* City University Business School, Frobisher Crescent, Barbican Centre, EC2Y 8HB. *T:* 071–920 0111. *Clubs:* Reform, Travellers', Institute of Directors.

CHAMBERS, Dr Douglas Robert; HM Coroner, Inner North London, since 1970; *b* 2 Nov. 1929; *s* of Douglas Henry Chambers and Elizabeth Paterson; *m* 1955, Barbara June Rowe; one *s* two *d*. *Educ:* Shene Grammar Sch.; King's College, London. MB BS; AKC 1953; LLB 1960; MA Univ. of Wales, 1989. Called to the Bar, Lincoln's Inn, 1965. RAF Med. Br., 1955–58; Med. Advr, Parke Davis, 1959–61, Nicholas Laboratories, 1961–63, Pharmacia, 1964–65; Med. Dir, Hoechst Pharmaceuticals, 1965–70; Dep. Coroner, West London, 1969–70. Vis. Lectr, City Univ., 1976–; Hon. Sen. Clin. Lectr in med. law, UCL, 1978–; Hon. Sen. Lectr, medical law, Royal Free Hosp., 1978–. Chairman: Richmond Div., BMA, 1969–70; Animal Research and Welfare Panel, Biological Council, 1986–; Pres., Library (sci. research) section, RSocMed, 1979–80; Pres., British sect., Anglo-German Med. Soc., 1980–84; Pres., Coroners' Soc., 1985–86. Hon. Mem., British Micro-circulation Soc., 1986 (Hon. Treas., 1968–86). Dist Comr, Richmond & Barnes Dist Scouts, 1976–85 (Silver Acorn 1984). Pres., Kensington Rowing Club, 1973–78. Baron C. ver Heyden de Lancey Prize for services to law and medicine, RSocMed, 1990. *Publications:* (jtly) Coroners' Inquiries, 1985; papers on medico-legal subjects. *Recreation:* local history of coroners and of scouting. *Address:* 4 Ormond Avenue, Richmond, Surrey TW10 6TN. *T:* (home) 081–940 7745, (court) 071–387 4882. *Clubs:* Wig and Pen; Auriol-Kensington Rowing.

CHAMBERS, Hon. George Michael; MP (People's National Movement), St Ann's, 1966–86; Prime Minister and Minister of Finance and Planning, Trinidad and Tobago, 1981–86; *b* 4 Oct. 1928; *m* 1956, Juliana; one *d*. *Educ:* Nelson Street Boys' RC Sch.; Burke's Coll.; Osmond High Sch.; Wolsey Hall, Oxford. Parly Sec., Min. of Finance, 1966; Minister of Public Utilities and Housing, 1969; Minister of State in Min. of National Security and Minister of State in Min. of Finance, Planning and Develt, 1970; Minister of National Security, Nov. 1970; Minister of Finance, Planning and Development, 1971–73; Minister of Finance, 1973–75; Minister of Educn and Culture, 1975–76; Minister of Industry and Commerce and Minister of Agriculture, Lands and Fisheries, 1976–81. Formerly, Asst Gen. Sec. and Mem. Central Exec., Gen. Council, and Res. and Disciplinary Cttees, People's National Movement. Chm. Bd of Governors, World Bank and IMF, 1973; Governor, Caribbean Develt Bank, 1981.

CHAMBERS, Harry Heyworth; Assistant Secretary, Ministry of Defence, since 1988; *b* 7 Nov. 1926; *s* of Francis Charles Chambers and Margaret Chambers; *m* 1st, 1955, Stella Howard (decd); 2nd, 1965, Elizabeth Mary Sansom; one *d*. *Educ:* Liverpool Collegiate Sch.; Liverpool Univ. (BComm). RAF 1945–48. Joined Automotive Products Co. Ltd, 1951, Manager, Service Div., 1956; Principal, 1971, Asst Sec., 1976, MoD; Counsellor (Defence Supply), British Embassy, Bonn, 1984–88. *Recreations:* mountaineering, translating.

CHAMBERS, Nicholas Mordaunt; QC 1985; a Recorder, since 1987; *b* 25 Feb. 1944; *s* of Marcus Mordaunt Bertrand Chambers and Lona Margit Chambers (*née* Gross); *m* 1966, Sarah Elizabeth, *er d* of Thomas Herbert Fothergill Banks; two *s* one *d*. *Educ:* King's School, Worcester; Hertford College, Oxford (BA 1965). Called to the Bar, Gray's Inn, 1966. *Recreation:* sketching. *Address:* 1 Brick Court, Temple, EC4. *T:* 01–583 0777. *Clubs:* Garrick, Lansdowne.

CHAMBERS, Robert Alexander H.; *see* Hammond-Chambers.

CHAMBERS, Prof. Robert Guy; Professor of Physics, University of Bristol, 1964–90, Emeritus 1990; *b* 8 Sept. 1924; *s* of A. G. P. Chambers; *m* 1st, 1950, Joan Brislee (marr. diss. 1981); one *d*; 2nd, 1988, Susan Eden. *Educ:* King Edward VI Sch., Southampton; Peterhouse, Cambridge. Work on tank armament (Ministry of Supply), 1944–46; Electrical Research Association, 1946–47; Royal Society Mond Laboratory, Cambridge, 1947–57; Stokes Student, Pembroke Coll., 1950–53; PhD 1952; ICI Fellow, 1953–54; NRC Post-doctoral Fellow, Ottawa, 1954–55; University Demonstrator, Cambridge, 1955–57; Bristol University: Sen. Lectr, 1958–61; Reader in Physics, 1961–64; Dean of Science, 1973–76, 1985–88; Pro-Vice-Chancellor, 1978–81. Member: Physics Cttee, 1967–71, Nuclear Physics Bd, 1971–74, Sci. Bd, 1975–78, SRC; Physical Sci. Sub-Cttee, UGC, 1974–81. Institute of Physics: Mem., Publications Cttee, 1969–81 (Chm., 1977–81); Vice-Pres., 1977–81. Chairman: SLS (Information Systems) Ltd, 1986–89; Track Analysis Systems Ltd, 1986–. *Publications:* various papers in learned journals on the behaviour of metals at low temperatures. *Recreation:* hill-walking. *Address:* 9 Apsley Road, Clifton, Bristol BS8 2SH. *T:* Bristol (0272) 739833.

CHAMBERS, Dr Timothy Lachlan, FRCP; Consultant Physician, Royal Hospital for Sick Children, Bristol and Paediatric Department, Southmead Hospital, since 1979; *b* 11 Feb. 1946; adopted *s* of late Victor Lachlan Chambers, Purley and Elsie Ruth Chambers (*née* Reynolds); *m* 1971, (Elizabeth) Joanna, *d* of late John Carrington Ward, Barnstone and Joan La Fontaine Ward; one *s* two *d*. *Educ:* Wallington County Grammar Sch.; King's College London; King's Coll. Hosp. Med. Sch. (MB BS 1969). MRCP 1972; FRCPE 1985; MFPaed RCPI 1989. Jun. med. posts, London and SE England; Tutor in paed. and child health, Univ. of Leeds, 1973–76 (Sen. Registrar in medicine, 1974–75); Physician, Derbyshire Children's Hosp., City Hosp. and Nottingham Hosp., 1976–79; University of Bristol: Clinical Lectr in Child Health, 1979–; Clinical Dean, Southmead Hosp., 1983–90. Mem. Council, RCP, 1979–80, 1981–82, 1990–; Mem., BPA, 1976 (Hon. Sec., 1984–89); Mem., BMA, 1979 (Chm., Paed. Sub-Cttee, Central Consultants and Specialists, 1989–); Pres., Union of Nat. Eur. Paed. Socs and Assocs, 1990–. Examnr to med. bodies and univs. Chm., Regional Cttee on Specialist Training, SW RHA, 1987–. Member: Medico-Legal Soc.; Philosophical Soc., Oxford; British Assoc. for Paed. Nephrology. FRSocMed 1977. Liveryman, Apothecaries' Soc., 1985. *Publications:* Fluid Therapy in Childhood, 1987; contribs to med. and lay jls and collective works. *Recreation:* attacking fast bowling. *Address:* 4 Clyde Park, Bristol BS6 6RR. *T:* Bristol (0272) 742814; 2 Clifton Park, Bristol BS8 3BS. *T:* Bristol (0272) 730622. *Clubs:* Athenæum, Army and Navy.

CHAMIER, Anthony Edward Deschamps; Head of Schools 3 Branch, Department of Education and Science, since 1989; *b* 16 Aug. 1935; *s* of late Brig. George Chamier, OBE and of Marion (*née* Gascoigne), Achandounie, Alness, Ross-shire; *m* 1962, Anne-Carole Tweeddale Dalling, *d* of William and Kathleen Dalling, Transvaal, S Africa; one *s* one *d*. *Educ:* Stowe, Buckingham; Trinity Hall, Cambridge; Yale Univ. (Henry Fellow). Military service, 1st Bn Seaforth Highlanders, 1953–55. HM Foreign (later Diplomatic) Service, 1960; Third Secretary, Foreign Office, 1960–62; Second Sec., Rome, 1962–64; Asst Political Adviser, HQ Middle East Comd, Aden, 1964–66; First Sec., FCO, 1966–71; Head of Chancery, Helsinki, 1971–72; seconded, later transf. to Dept of Educn and Science; Principal, 1972–73; Principal Private Sec. to Sec. of State for Educn and Science, 1973–74; Asst Sec., 1974–79; Under Sec., 1980–; Dir of Estabts and Orgn, 1980–84; Head, Further and Higher Educn Br. 1, 1985–89. *Recreations:* walking, shooting, gardening. *Address:* Department of Education and Science, Sanctuary Buildings, Great Smith Street, SW1. *Club:* Army and Navy.

CHAMPERNOWNE, David Gawen, MA; FBA 1970; Professor of Economics and Statistics, Cambridge University, 1970–78, now Emeritus; Fellow of Trinity College at Cambridge, since 1959; *b* Oxford, 9 July 1912; *s* of late F. G. Champernowne, MA, Bursar of Keble Coll., Oxford; *m* 1948, Wilhelmina Dullaert; two *s*. *Educ:* The College, Winchester; King's Coll., Cambridge. Asst Lecturer at London Sch. of Economics, 1936–38; Fellow of King's Coll., Cambridge, 1937–48; University Lecturer in Statistics at Cambridge, 1938–40; temp. Civil Servant, 1940–45; Dir of Oxford Univ. Institute of Statistics, 1945–48; Fellow of Nuffield Coll., Oxford, 1945–59; Prof. of Statistics, Oxford Univ., 1948–59; Reader in Economics, Cambridge Univ., 1959–70. Editor, Economic Jl, 1971–76. *Publications:* Uncertainty and Estimation in Economics (3 vols), 1969; The Distribution of Income between Persons, 1973; sundry articles on mathematics, statistics and economics in learned jls, 1933–. *Address:* 20 Manor Court, Grange Road, Cambridge CB3 9BE. *T:* Cambridge (0223) 328477; Trinity College, Cambridge.

CHAMPION, John Stuart, CMG 1977; OBE 1963; HM Diplomatic Service, retired; *b* 17 May 1921; *er s* of Rev. Sir Reginald Champion, KCMG, OBE and Margaret, *d* of late Very Rev. W. M. Macgregor, DD, LLD; *m* 1944, Olive Lawrencina, *o d* of late Lawrence Durning Holt, Liverpool; five *s* two *d*. *Educ:* Shrewsbury Sch.; Balliol Coll., Oxford (Schol., BA). Commnd 11 Hussars PAO, 1941–46. Colonial Service (later HMOCS),

Uganda, 1946–63: District Officer; Secretariat, 1949–52; Private Sec. to Governor, 1952; Asst Financial Sec., 1956; Actg Perm. Sec., Min. of Health, 1959; Perm. Sec., Min. of Internal Affairs, 1960; retd 1963; Principal, CRO, 1963; 1st Sec., FCO, 1965; Head of Chancery, Tehran, 1968; Counsellor, Amman, 1971; FCO 1973; British Resident Comr, Anglo/French Condominium of the New Hebrides, 1975–78. Mem., West Midlands RHA, 1980–81; Chm., Herefordshire HA, 1982–86. Governor, Royal National Coll. for the Blind, 1980– (Vice-Chm., 1985–); Chairman: St John Council for Hereford and Worcester, 1987–; Friends of Hereford Cathedral, 1988–. OStJ 1987. *Recreations:* hill walking, golf, music. *Address:* Farmore, Callow, Hereford HR2 8DB. *T:* Hereford (0432) 274875. *Club:* Commonwealth Trust.

CHAN, Cho-chak John, LVO 1986; OBE 1985; Secretary for Trade and Industry, Hong Kong Government, since 1989; *b* 8 April 1943; *s* of late Kai Kit Chan and of Yuk Ying Wong; *m* 1965, Wai-chun Agnes Wong; one *s* one *d*. *Educ:* St Rose of Lima's Sch.,; Wah Yan Coll., Kowloon; La Salle Coll., Univ. of Hong Kong (BA (Hons), DMS). Commerce and Industry Dept, 1964; Economic Br., Govt Secretariat, 1970; Private Sec. to Gov., 1973; City Dist Comr (Hong Kong), 1975; Asst Dir of Home Affairs, 1976; Dep. Dir of Trade, 1977; Exec. Dir and Gen. Man., Sun Hung Kai Finance Co. Ltd, 1978; Principal Assistant Secretary: for Security, Govt Secretariat, 1980; for CS, 1982; Dep. Dir of Trade, 1983; Dep. Sec. (Gen. Duties), 1984; Dir of Inf. Services, 1986; Dep. Chief Sec., 1987. *Recreations:* swimming, ten-pin bowling, music, reading. *Address:* Government Secretariat, Lower Albert Road, Central, Hong Kong. *T:* 8102885. *Clubs:* Royal Hong Kong Jockey; Hong Kong.

CHAN, Rt. Hon. Sir Julius, KBE 1980 (CBE 1975); PC 1981; MP 1968; Parliamentary Leader, People's Progress Party, Papua New Guinea, since 1970; *b* 29 Aug. 1939; *s* of Chin Pak and Tingoris Chan; *m* 1966, Stella Ahmat. *Educ:* Marist Brothers Coll., Ashgrove, Qld; Univ. of Queensland, Australia (Agricl Science). Co-operative Officer, Papua New Guinea Admin, 1960–62; private business, coastal shipping and merchandise, 1963–70. Minister for Finance, 1972–77; Dep. Prime Minister and Minister for Primary Industry, 1977–78; Prime Minister of PNG, 1980–82; Minister for Finance and Planning, 1985–86; Dep. Prime Minister, 1985–88; Minister for Trade and Industry, 1986–88. Governor: World Bank/IMF, 1976; Asian Development Bank, 1977. Fellow, Internat. Bankers Assoc., USA, 1976. Attended meetings and conferences worldwide as rep. of PNG, latterly as leader of PNG delegn, 1970–; made State and official visits to Australia, Rep. of Korea, China, Vanuatu, Indonesia, UK, France, Italy, NZ. Hon. DEc Dankook (Republic of Korea) 1978; Hon. Dr Technol., Univ. of Technol., PNG, 1983. *Recreations:* swimming, walking, boating. *Address:* PO Box 717, Rabaul, Papua New Guinea.

CHAN, Nai Keong, CBE 1985; JP; FEng 1986; Group Managing Director, Cavendish International Holdings Limited, since 1987; *b* 17 Nov. 1931; two *s* one *d*. FICE. FIStructE, FHKIE. Public Works Dept, Hong Kong: pupil engineer, Roads Office, 1952; Civil Engineering Office, 1960; Senior Engineer, 1964; Chief Engineer, Highways Office, 1969; Principal Govt Engineer, 1973, i/c Tuen Mun New Town develt; Principal Govt Engineer, Highways Office, 1978; Dir, Engineering Dept, 1980; Dep. Dir, Public Works, 1981; Dep. Sec. for Lands and Works, 1982; Sec. for Lands and Works, 1983–86. JP Hong Kong, 1972. Hon. DTech Loughborough, 1984. *Recreations:* bridge, swimming, yoga, music. *Address:* c/o Cavendish International Holdings Ltd, Room 1108, Hutchison House, 10 Harcourt Road, Hong Kong. *T:* 5–246123. *Clubs:* Hongkong; Royal Golf, Royal HK Jockey, Pacific, Chinese, HK Country, Chinese Recreation.

CHANCE, Sqdn Ldr Dudley Raymond, FRGS; a Recorder of the Crown Court, 1980–86; *b* 9 July 1916; *s* of Captain Arthur Chance, Sherwood Foresters, and Byzie Chance; *m* 1958, Jessie Maidstone, widow, *d* of John and Alice Dewing. *Educ:* Nottingham High Sch.; London Univ. (BA Oriental Religions and Philosophies, LLB 1969); BA Hons Internat. Politics and For. Policy, Open Univ., 1980. Called to Bar, Middle Temple, 1955. Commissioned in Royal Air Force, 1936; served Egypt, Transjordan, 1936–37; Bomber Comd (4 Gp), 1938; served in Bomber Comd Nos 97 and 77 Sqdns; took part in first raids on Norway; crashed off Trondheim; picked up later from sea by HMS Basilisk, later sunk at Dunkirk; Air Ministry, Whitehall, 1941–42, later in 2 Group, Norfolk, 21 Sqdn; also served in SEAC, Bengal/Burma. Sqdn Ldr, RAFO, until March 1961; gazetted to retain rank of Sqdn Ldr from that date. Member: panel of Chairmen of Medical Appeal Tribunals (DHSS), 1978–88; panel of Independent Inspectors for motorway and trunk road inquiries for DoE, 1978–83. Contested (C) Norwich North, 1959. FRGS 1979. *Recreations:* violin, painting. *Address:* Lamb Buildings, Temple, EC4; Fenners Chambers, 4 Madingley Road, Cambridge. *Club:* Goldfish (RAF aircrew rescued from sea).

CHANCE, Sir (George) Jeremy (ffolliott), 4th Bt *cr* 1900, of Grand Avenue, Hove; retired; *b* 24 Feb. 1926; *s* of Sir Roger James Ferguson Chance, 3rd Bt, MC and Mary Georgina (*d* 1984), *d* of Col William Rowney; *S* father, 1987; *m* 1950, (cousin) Cecilia Mary Elizabeth, *d* of Sir William Hugh Stobart Chance, CBE; two *s* two *d*. *Educ:* Gordonstoun School; Christ Church, Oxford (MA). Sub-Lieut RNVR, 1944–47. Harry Ferguson Ltd, 1950–53; Massey-Ferguson, 1953–78; Director, Massey-Ferguson (UK) Ltd, 1973–78; farmer, 1978–87. *Recreations:* making lakes, planting trees, choral singing, painting. *Heir:* *s* (John) Sebastian Chance [*b* 2 Oct. 1954; *m* 1977, Victoria Mary, *d* of Denis McClean; two *s* one *d*]. *Address:* Rhosgyll Fawr, Chwilog, Pwllheli, Gwynedd LL53 6TQ. *T:* Chwilog (0766) 810584.

CHANCE, Michael Spencer; Deputy Director, Serious Fraud Office, 1987–90; Consultant, Cameron Markby Hewitt, since 1991; *b* 14 May 1938; *s* of Florence and Ernest Horace Chance; *m* 1962, Enid Mabel Carter; three *d*. *Educ:* Rossall School. Solicitor. With Challinor & Roberts, Warley, 1962–70; Senior Asst Prosecuting Solicitor, Sussex Police Authy, 1970–72; Office of Director of Public Prosecutions, 1972–86: Asst Dir, 1981–86; Chief Crown Prosecutor, North London, 1986–87; Asst Head of Legal Services, Crown Prosecution Service, 1987. *Address:* 16 Frithsden, Hemel Hempstead HP1 3DD.

CHANCELLOR, Alexander Surtees; Editor, The Independent Magazine, since 1988; *b* 4 Jan. 1940; *s* of Sir Christopher Chancellor, CMG and of Sylvia Mary, OBE, *e d* of Sir Richard Paget, 2nd Bt and Lady Muriel Finch-Hatton, *d* of 12th Earl of Winchilsea and Nottingham; *m* 1964, Susanna Elisabeth Debenham; two *d*. *Educ:* Eton College; Trinity Hall, Cambridge. Reuters News Agency, 1964–74; ITN, 1974–75; Editor: The Spectator, 1975–84; Time and Tide, 1984–86; Dep. Editor, Sunday Telegraph, 1986; US Editor, The Independent, 1986–88. *Address:* c/o The Independent, 40 City Road, EC1Y 2DB. *Club:* Garrick.

CHANDLER, Sir Colin (Michael), Kt 1988; Managing Director, since 1990, Chief Executive, since 1991, Vickers PLC; *b* 7 Oct. 1939; *s* of Henry John Chandler and Mary Martha (*née* Bowles); *m* 1964, Jennifer Mary Crawford; one *s* one *d*. *Educ:* St Joseph's Acad.; Hatfield Polytechnic. FCMA. Commercial Apprentice, De Havilland Aircraft Co., 1956–61; Contracts Officer, Hawker Siddeley Aviation, Hatfield, 1962–66; Hawker Siddeley Aviation, Kingston: Commercial Manager, 1967–72; Exec. Dir, Commercial, 1973–76; Exec. Dir and Gen. Manager, 1977; British Aerospace, Kingston: Divl Man. Dir., 1978–82; Gp Marketing Dir, 1983–85; Hd of Defence Export Services, MoD, 1985–89. Non-Exec. Dir, Siemens Plessey Electronic Systems, 1990–. Mem., Engrg Council, 1991–. Commander, Order of the Lion of Finland, 1982. *Recreations:* jogging, playing tennis, reading, listening to music. *Address:* c/o Vickers PLC, Millbank Tower, Millbank, SW1P 4RA. *T:* 071–828 7777. *Clubs:* Reform, Mark's.

CHANDLER, Edwin George, CBE 1979; FRIBA, FRTPI; City Architect, City of London, 1961–79; *b* 28 Aug. 1914; *e s* of Edwin and Honor Chandler; *m* 1938, Iris Dorothy, *o d* of Herbert William Grubb; one *d*. *Educ:* Selhurst Grammar Sch., Croydon. Asst Architect, Hants County Council and City of Portsmouth, 1936–39. Served in HMS Vernon, Mine Design Dept, 1940–45. Gained distinction in thesis, ARIBA, 1942, FRIBA 1961. Dep. Architect and Planning Officer, West Ham, 1945–47; City Architect and Planning Officer, City of Oxford, 1947–61. Member: RIBA Council, 1950–52; Univ. Social Survey Cttee, Oxford; City of London Archaeological Trust; Trustee, Silver Jubilee Walkway Trust; Chm., Bd of Alleyn's Estate, Dulwich; Gov., James Allen's Sch., Dulwich. Liveryman, Gardeners' Co. (Master, 1988–89); Mem., Court of Common Council, Corp. of London (Cornhill Ward), 1982–, Deputy, 1986–. *Publications:* Housing for Old Age, 1939; City of Oxford Development Plan, 1950; articles contrib. to press and professional jls. *Recreations:* landscaping, travel, swimming. *Clubs:* Guildhall, Dulwich.

CHANDLER, Sir Geoffrey, Kt 1983; CBE 1976; Chairman, National Council for Voluntary Organisations, since 1989; Industry Adviser, Royal Society of Arts, since 1987; *b* 15 Nov. 1922; *s* of Frederick George Chandler, MD, FRCP, and Marjorie Chandler; *m* 1955, Lucy Bertha Buxton; four *d*. *Educ:* Sherborne; Trinity Coll., Cambridge (MA History). Military Service, 1942–46: Captain 60th Rifles; Political Warfare Exec., Cairo; Special Ops Exec. (Force 133), Greece; Anglo-Greek Information Service, W Macedonia, 1945; Press Officer, Volos and Salonika, 1946. Cambridge Univ., 1947–49; Captain, Univ. Lawn Tennis, 1949. BBC Foreign News Service, 1949–51; Leader Writer and Features Editor, Financial Times, 1951–56; Commonwealth Fund Fellow, Columbia Univ., New York, 1953–54; Shell Internat. Petroleum Co.: Manager, Econs Div., 1957–61; Area Co-ordinator, W Africa, 1961–64; Chm. and Man. Dir, Shell Trinidad Ltd, 1964–69; Shell Internat. Petroleum Co.: Public Affairs Co-ordinator, 1969–78; Dir, 1971–78; Dir, Shell Petroleum Co.; and Shell Petroleum NV, 1976–78; Dir Gen., NEDO, and Mem., NEDC, 1978–83; Dir, Industry Year 1986, 1984–86; Leader, RSA Industry Matters team, 1987–89. Pres., Inst. of Petroleum, 1972–74. Member: Council and Exec. Cttee, Overseas Develt Inst., 1969–78; British Overseas Trade Adv. Council, 1978–82; Council and Exec. Cttee, VSO. Chm., BBC Consultative Group on Industrial and Business Affairs, and Mem. BBC Gen. Adv. Council, 1983–88; Chm., Consultative Council, Soc. of Educn Officers Schools Curriculum Award, 1984–; Member: Wilton Park Academic Council, 1983–87; Council for Charitable Support, 1990–; Associate, Ashridge Management Coll., 1983–89; Pres., Assoc. for Management & Business Educn, 1986–90; Trustee, Charities Aid Foundn, 1990–; Dir, Blackheath Preservation Trust. FRSA. Hon. Mem., CGLI, 1988. Hon. Fellow: Sheffield City Polytechnic, 1981; Girton Coll., Cambridge, 1986; Hon. FInstPet 1982. Hon. DBA Internat. Management Centre from Buckingham, 1986; Hon. DSc: CNAA, 1986; Bradford, 1987; Aston, 1987; Hon. CGIA 1987. *Publications:* The Divided Land: an Anglo-Greek Tragedy, 1959; (jtly) The State of the Nation: Trinidad & Tobago in the later 1960s, 1969; articles on oil, energy, transnational corporations, and development; numerous speeches, urging employee participation, coherent British indust. policy and the need for clearly articulated business principles. *Recreations:* working in woodland, gardening, playing the oboe. *Address:* (office) 8 John Adam Street, WC2N 6EZ. *T:* 071-930 5115; (home) 46 Hyde Vale, Greenwich, SE10 8HP. *T:* 081–692 5304. *Clubs:* Athenæum; Hawks (Cambridge).

CHANDLER, George, MA, PhD, FLA, FRHistS; FRSA; International Adviser and Editor in Library and Information Science; *b* England, 2 July 1915; *s* of W. and F. W. Chandler; *m* 1937, Dorothy Lowe; one *s*. *Educ:* Central Grammar Sch., Birmingham; Leeds Coll. of Commerce; University of London. ALAA 1974. Birmingham Public Libraries, 1931–37; Leeds Public Libraries, 1937–46; WEA Tutor Organiser, 1946–47; Borough Librarian, Dudley, 1947–50; Dep. City Librarian, Liverpool, 1950–52, City Librarian, 1952–74; Dir-Gen., Nat. Library of Australia, 1974–80. Sec. Dudley Arts Club, 1948–50; Pres., Internat. Assoc. of Met. City Libraries, 1968–71; Pres. 1962–71 (Hon. Sec. 1957–62), Soc. of Municipal and County Chief Librarians; Dir, 1962–74 (Hon. Sec. 1955–62), Liverpool and District Scientific, Industrial and Research Library Advisory Council; Hon. Librarian, 1957–74 (Hon. Sec. 1950–57), Historic Soc. of Lancs and Ches; Chm., Exec. Cttee, 1965–70, President, 1971, Library Assoc.; Member: DES Library Adv. Council for England and Wales, 1965–72; British Library Organising Cttee, 1972–73; British Library Bd, 1973–74. Hon. Editor, Internat. Library Review, 1969–. Unesco expert in Tunisia, 1964. *Publications:* Dudley, 1949; William Roscoe, 1953; Liverpool 1207–1957; Liverpool Shipping, 1960; Liverpool under James I, 1960; How to Find Out, 1963 (5th edn 1982); Four Centuries of Banking: Martins Bank, Vol. I, 1964, Vol. II, 1968; Liverpool under Charles I, 1965; Libraries in the Modern World, 1965; How to Find Out About Literature, 1968; Libraries in the East, 1971; Libraries, Bibliography and Documentation in the USSR, 1972; Victorian and Edwardian Liverpool and the North West, 1972; An Illustrated History of Liverpool, 1972; (ed) International Librarianship, 1972; Merchant Venturers, 1973; Victorian and Edwardian Manchester, 1974; Liverpool and Literature, 1974; Recent Developments in International and National Library and Information Services, 1982; (ed) International Series of Monographs on Library and Information Science; (ed) series, Recent Advances in Library and Information Services, 1981–; contributions to educl and library press. *Recreations:* writing, research; walking; foreign travel. *Address:* 43 Saxon Close, Stratford-upon-Avon, Warwickshire CV37 7DX.

CHANDLER, Tony John; *b* 7 Nov. 1928; *s* of Harold William and Florence Ellen Chandler; *m* 1954, Margaret Joyce Weston; one *s* one *d*. *Educ:* King's Coll., London. MSc. PhD, AKC, MA. Lectr, Birkbeck Coll., Univ. of London, 1952–56; University Coll. London: Lectr, 1956–65; Reader in Geography, 1965–69; Prof. of Geography, 1969–73; Prof. of Geography, Manchester Univ., 1973–77; Master of Birkbeck Coll., Univ. of London, 1977–79. Sec., Royal Meteorological Soc., 1969–73, Vice-Pres., 1973–75. Member: Council, NERC; Health and Safety Commn; Cttee of Experts on Major Hazards; Royal Soc. Study Gp on Pollution in the Atmosphere, 1974–77; Clean Air Council; Royal Commn on Environmental Pollution, 1973–77; Standing Commn on Energy and the Environment 1978. *Publications:* The Climate of London, 1965; Modern Meteorology and Climatology, 1972, 2nd edn 1981; contribs to: Geographical Jl, Geography, Weather, Meteorological Magazine, Bulletin of Amer. Meteorological Soc., etc. *Recreations:* horology, music, reading, travel. *Address:* 44 Knoll Rise, Orpington, Kent BR6 0EL. *T:* Orpington (0689) 832880.

CHANDLEY, Peter Warren, MVO 1981; HM Diplomatic Service; Ambassador to People's Republic of the Congo, 1990–91; *b* 24 Nov. 1934; *s* of Samuel and Freda Chandley; *m* 1961, Jane Williams. *Educ:* Manchester Warehousemen and Clerks Orphan School, Cheadle Hulme. Clerk, Min. of Fuel and Power, 1953; Nat. Service, RAF, 1953–55; FO, 1955; served Tripoli, 1955; Kabul, 1958; Havana, 1960; Phnom Penh, 1962; Madagascar, 1966; FCO, 1969; Nairobi, 1972; Kampala, 1976; Oslo, 1977; FCO, 1981; Abidjan, 1986. Ridder 1st Class, Order of St Olav (Norway), 1981. *Recreations:* bird-watching, reading, conservation activities. *Address:* Foreign and Commonwealth Office, King Charles Street, SW1A 2AH.

CHANDOS, 3rd Viscount *cr* 1954, of Aldershot; **Thomas Orlando Lyttelton;** Banker, since 1974, Director, since 1985, Kleinwort, Benson Ltd; *b* 12 Feb. 1953; *s* of 2nd Viscount Chandos and of Caroline Mary (who *m* 1985, Hon. David Hervey Erskine), *d* of Rt Hon. Sir Alan Lascelles, GCB, GCVO, CMG, MC; *S* father, 1980; *m* 1985, Arabella Sarah, *d* of Adrian Bailey and Lady Mary Russell; two *s* one *d*. *Educ:* Eton; Worcester College, Oxford (BA). *Heir:* *s* Hon. Oliver Antony Lyttelton, *b* 21 Feb. 1986. *Address:* 149 Gloucester Avenue, NW1. *T:* 071–722 8329.

CHANDOS-POLE, Lt-Col John, CVO 1979; OBE 1951; JP; Lord-Lieutenant for Northamptonshire, 1967–84; *b* 20 July 1909; *s* of late Brig.-Gen. Harry Anthony Chandos-Pole, CBE, DL, JP and late Ada Ismay, Heverswood, Brasted, Kent; *m* 1952, Josephine Sylvia (*d* 1990), *d* of late Brig.-Gen. Cyril Randell Crofton, CBE, Limerick House, Milborne Port, near Sherborne; two step-*d*. *Educ:* Eton; Magdalene Coll., Cambridge (MA). 2nd Lieut Coldstream Guards, 1933; ADC: to Governor of Bombay, May-Nov., 1937; to Governor of Bengal, Nov. 1937–June 1938, Oct. 1938–Feb. 1939, also to Viceroy of India, June-Oct., 1938. Served War of 1939–45: France and Belgium (wounded); Palestine, 1948 (wounded, despatches); commanded 1st Bn, Coldstream Guards, 1947–48; Guards Depot, 1948–50; 2nd Bn, Coldstream Guards, 1950–52. Lieut-Col 1949; retired, 1953. A Member of the Hon. Corps of Gentlemen-at-Arms, 1956–79 (Harbinger, 1966–79). DL 1965, JP 1957, Northants. KStJ 1975. *Recreations:* racing and travel. *Address:* Newnham Hall, Daventry, Northants NN11 6HQ. *T:* Daventry (0327) 702711. *Clubs:* Boodle's, Pratt's.

CHANDOS-POLE, Major John Walkelyne, DL, JP; *b* 4 Nov. 1913; *o s* of late Col Reginald Walkelyne Chandos-Pole, TD, JP, Radburne Hall; *m* 1947, Ilsa Jill, *er d* of Emil Ernst Barstz, Zürich; one *d* (one *s* decd). *Educ:* Eton; RMC, Sandhurst. Commissioned Grenadier Guards, 1933; ADC to Viceroy of India, 1938–39; retired, 1947. JP 1951, DL 1961, Derbys; High Sheriff of Derbys, 1959. *Recreation:* shooting. *Address:* Radburne Hall, Kirk Langley, Derby DE6 4LZ. *T:* Kirk Langley (033124) 246. *Clubs:* Army and Navy, Lansdowne; MCC; County (Derby).

See also Sir E. J. Chichester, Bt.

CHANDRACHUD, Hon. Yeshwant Vishnu; Chief Justice of India, 1978–85; *b* Poona (Maharashtra), 12 July 1920; *s* of Vishnu Balkrishna Chandrachud and Indira; *m* Prabha; one *s* one *d*. *Educ:* Bombay Univ. (BA, LLB). Advocate of Bombay High Court, 1943, civil and criminal work; part-time Prof. of Law, Government Law Coll., Bombay, 1949–52; Asst Govt Pleader, 1952; Govt Pleader, 1958; Judge, Bombay High Court, 1961–72; one-man Pay Commn for Bombay Municipal Corporation officers, later Arbitrator in dispute between Electricity Supply and Transport Undertaking and its employees' union; one-man Commn to inquire into circumstances leading to death of Deen Dayal Upadhyaya; Judge, Supreme Court of India, 1972–78. President: Internat. Law Assoc. (India Branch), 1978–; Indian Law Inst., 1978–. *Address:* (official) c/o Supreme Court of India, New Delhi, India. *T:* 387165.

CHANDRASEKHAR, Prof. Sivaramakrishna, FRS 1983; Professor, Raman Research Institute, Bangalore, 1971–90, Bhatnagar Fellow, since 1990; *b* 6 Aug. 1930; *s* of S. Sivaramakrishnan and Sitalaxmi; *m* 1954, Ila Pinglay; one *s* one *d*. *Educ:* Nagpur Univ. (MSc, DSc); Pembroke Coll., Cambridge (PhD 1958; ScD 1987). Res. Schol., Raman Res. Inst., Bangalore, 1950–54; 1851 Exhibn Schol., Cavendish Lab., Cambridge, 1954–57; DSIR Fellow, Dept of Crystallography, UCL, 1957–59; Res. Fellow, Davy Faraday Res. Lab., Royal Instn, 1959–61; Prof. and Hd of Dept of Physics, Univ. of Mysore, 1961–71; Nehru Vis. Prof., and Fellow Pembroke Coll., Cambridge, 1986–87; India Corresp., Royal Soc., 1987–. *Publications:* Liquid Crystals, 1977; editor of several books; contrib. scientific papers to learned jls. *Address:* Raman Research Institute, Bangalore 560080, India. *T:* (office) 340124 ext. 225, 345267; (home) 342356.

CHANDRASEKHAR, Subrahmanyan, FRS 1944; Morton D. Hull Distinguished Service Professor of Theoretical Astrophysics, University of Chicago, USA, 1937–85, now Emeritus; *b* 19 Oct. 1910; *m* 1936, Lalitha Doraiswamy. *Educ:* Presidency Coll., Madras; Trinity Coll., Cambridge (Government of Madras Research Scholar, PhD 1933, ScD 1942). Fellow of Trinity Coll., Cambridge, 1933–37, Hon. Fellow 1981. Managing Editor Astrophysical Journal, 1952–71. Nehru Memorial Lecture, India, 1968. Member: Nat. Acad. of Sciences (Henry Draper Medal, 1971); Amer. Philosophical Soc.; Amer. Acad. of Arts and Sciences (Rumford Medal, 1957). Hon. DSc Oxon 1972. Bruce Gold Medal, Astr. Soc. Pacific, 1952; Gold Medal, Royal Astronomical Soc. London, 1953; Royal Medal, Royal Society, 1962; Nat. Medal of Science (USA), 1966; Heineman Prize, Amer. Phys. Soc., 1974; (jtly) Nobel Prize for Physics, 1983; Copley Medal, Royal Soc., 1984; Dr Tomalla Prize, Eidgenössische Technische Hochschule, Zürich, 1984. *Publications:* An Introduction to the Study of Stellar Structure, 1939; Principles of Stellar Dynamics, 1942; Radiative Transfer, 1950; Hydrodynamic and Hydromagnetic Stability, 1961; Ellipsoidal Figures of Equilibrium, 1969; The Mathematical Theory of Black Holes, 1983; Eddington: the most distinguished astro-physicist of his time, 1983; Truth and Beauty: aesthetics and motivations in science, 1987; Selected Papers, 6 vols, 1989–90; various papers in current scientific periodicals. *Address:* Laboratory for Astrophysics and Space Research, University of Chicago, 933 East 56th Street, Chicago, Illinois 60637, USA. *T:* (312) 702–7860. *Club:* Quadrangle (Chicago).

CHANEY, Hon. Sir Frederick (Charles), KBE 1982 (CBE 1969); AFC 1945; Chairman, Home Building Society, 1974–87; *b* 12 Oct. 1914; *s* of Frederick Charles Chaney and Rose Templar Chaney; *m* 1938; four *s* three *d*. *Educ:* Aquinas Coll.; Claremont Coll. Served War, RAAF, 1940–45. Teacher, 1936–40 and 1946–55. MHR (L) Perth, 1955–69; Govt Whip, 1961–63; Minister for the Navy, 1963–66; Administrator, Northern Territory, 1970–73. Lord Mayor of Perth, WA, 1978–82. Dep. Pres., King's Park Bd, 1981–84. *Recreation:* golf. *Address:* 9A Melville Street, Claremont, WA 6010, Australia. *T:* 384.0596. *Clubs:* West Australian Cricket Assoc., East Perth Football (Perth); Mount Lawley Golf (WA).

CHANG-HIM, Most Rev. French Kitchener; *see* Indian Ocean, Archbishop of the.

CHANNON, Prof. Derek French, DBA; Professor of Management, Imperial College of Science, Technology and Medicine, since 1990; *b* 4 March 1939; *s* of John French and Betty Blanche Channon; *m* 1963, Ann Lesley (marr. diss. 1986); one *s* one *d*. *Educ:* University Coll. London (BSc); Manchester Business Sch. (MBA); Harvard Graduate Sch. of Business (DBA). Marketing management, Royal Dutch Shell Gp, 1960–68; Lectr in Marketing, Manchester Business Sch., 1968–70; Ford Foundn European Doctoral Fellow, Harvard Bus. Sch., 1968–71; Manchester Business School: Sen. Res. Fellow, 1971–76; Prof. of Strategic Management and Marketing, 1977–89; Associate Dir, 1985–87. Jt Man. Dir, Evode Holdings PLC, 1976–77. Director: Strategic Management Soc., 1982– (Pres. 1985–88); Bray Technologies, 1983–; Royal Bank of Scotland, 1988–. *Publications:* Strategy and Structure of British Enterprise, 1973; (with J. Stopford and B. Norburn) Business Policy, 1975; British Banking Strategy and the International Challenge, 1977; The Service Industries, 1978; (with R. M. Jalland) Multi-national Strategic Planning, 1979; British Transnational Bank Strategy, 1979; (with J. Stopford and J. Constable) Cases in Strategic Management, 1980; (with P. Rushton) Retail Electronic Banking and Point of Sale, 1982; Bank Strategic Management and Marketing, 1986; Global Banking Strategy, 1988. *Recreations:* golf, tennis. *Address:* Imperial College, 53 Prince's Gate, Exhibition Road, SW7.

CHANNON, Rt. Hon. (Henry) Paul (Guinness); PC 1980; MP (C) for Southend West, since Jan. 1959; *b* 9 Oct. 1935; *o s* of late Sir Henry Channon, MP, and of late Lady Honor Svejdar (*née* Guinness), *e d* of 2nd Earl of Iveagh, KG; *m* 1963, Ingrid Olivia Georgia Guinness (*née* Wyndham); one *s* one *d* (and one *d* decd). *Educ:* Lockers Park, Hemel Hempstead; Eton Coll., Christ Church, Oxford. 2nd Lieut Royal Horse Guards (The Blues), 1955–56. Pres. of Oxford Univ. Conservative Association, 1958. Parly Private Sec. to: Minister of Power, 1959–60; Home Sec., 1960–62; First Sec. of State, 1962–63; PPS to the Foreign Sec., 1963–64; Opposition Spokesman on Arts and Amenities, 1967–70; Parly Sec., Min. of Housing and Local Govt, June-Oct. 1970; Parly Under-Sec. of State, DoE, 1970–72; Minister of State, Northern Ireland Office, March-Nov. 1972; Minister for Housing and Construction, DoE, 1972–74; Opposition Spokesman on: Prices and Consumer Protection, March-Sept. 1974; environmental affairs, Oct. 1974–Feb. 1975; Minister of State, CSD, 1979–81; Minister for the Arts, 1981–83; Minister for Trade, 1983–86; Sec. of State for Trade and Industry, 1986–87; Sec. of State for Transport, 1987–89. Dep. Leader, Cons. Delegn to WEU and Council of Europe, 1976–79. Mem., Gen. Adv. Council to ITA, 1964–66. *Address:* House of Commons, SW1.

CHANTRY, Dr George William, CEng, FIEE; CPhys; FInstP; Director European Operations, Carnahan & Associates; Consultant to Ministry of Defence on Strategic Defence Initiative Technology Transfer, since 1990; *b* 13 April 1933; *s* of George William Chantry and Sophia Veronica (*née* Johnston); *m* 1956, Diana Margaret Rhodes (*née* Martin); two *s* one *d*. *Educ:* Christ Church, Oxford (DPhil 1959, MA 1960). CEng, FIEE 1976; FInstP 1974. Res. Associate, Cornell Univ., 1958; National Physical Lab., Dept of Industry: Sen. Res. Fellow, 1960; Sen. Scientific Officer, 1962; Principal Sci. Officer, 1967; Sen. Principal Sci. Officer, 1973; Dep. Chief Sci. Officer, DoI HQ, 1982, seconded to FCO; Counsellor (Sci. and Tech.), Bonn and Berne, 1982; Res. and Technol. Policy Div., DTI, 1985; seconded to MoD as Asst Dir for Industry in SDI Participation Office, 1985. Past Chm., European Molecular Liquids Gp; Mem., Science Educn and Technol. Bd, IEE, 1980–82. Editor, Proc. IEE, Part A, 1981–. *Publications:* Submillimetre Spectroscopy, 1971; High-Frequency Dielectric Measurement, 1972; Submillimetre Waves and their Applications, 1978; Modern Aspects of Microwave Spectroscopy, 1980; Long-Wave Optics, 1983; papers in learned literature. *Recreations:* philately, bridge, gardening, music. *Address:* 42 Cranwell Grove, Shepperton, Mddx TW17 0JR. *T:* Chertsey (0932) 560524.

CHAPLAIS, Pierre Théophile Victorien Marie; Médaille de la Résistance, 1946; FBA 1973; Reader in Diplomatic in the University of Oxford, 1957–87, now Reader Emeritus; Professorial Fellow, Wadham College, Oxford, 1964–87, now Emeritus Fellow; *b* Châteaubriant, Loire-Atlantique, France, 8 July 1920; *s* of late Théophile Chaplais and Victorine Chaplais (*née* Roussel); *m* 1948, Mary Doreen Middlemast; two *s*. *Educ:* Collège St-Sauveur, Redon, Ille-et-Vilaine; Univ. of Rennes, Ille-et-Vilaine (Licence en Droit, Licence ès-Lettres); Univ. of London (PhD). Editor, Public Record Office, London, 1948–55; Lectr in Diplomatic, Univ. of Oxford, 1955–57; Literary Dir, Royal Hist. Soc., 1958–64. Corresp. Fellow, Mediaeval Acad. of America, 1979. *Publications:* Some Documents regarding . . . The Treaty of Brétigny, 1952; The War of St Sardos, 1954; Treaty Rolls, vol. I, 1955; (with T. A. M. Bishop) Facsimiles of English Royal Writs to AD 1100 presented to V. H. Galbraith, 1957; Diplomatic Documents, vol. I, 1964; English Royal Documents, King John-Henry VI, 1971; English Medieval Diplomatic Practice, Part II, 1975, Part I, 1983; Essays in Medieval Diplomacy and Administration, 1981; articles in Bulletin of Inst. of Historical Research, English Hist. Review, Jl of Soc. of Archivists, etc. *Recreations:* gardening, fishing. *Address:* Lew Lodge, Lew, Oxford OX8 2BE. *T:* Bampton Castle (0993) 850613.

CHAPLIN, Arthur Hugh, CB 1970; Principal Keeper of Printed Books, British Museum, 1966–70; *b* 17 April 1905; *er s* of late Rev. Herbert F. Chaplin and Florence B. Lusher; *m* 1938, Irene Marcousé (*d* 1990). *Educ:* King's Lynn Grammar Sch.; Bedford Modern Sch.; University Coll., London. Asst Librarian: Reading Univ. 1927–28; Queen's Univ., Belfast, 1928–29; Asst Keeper, Dept of Printed Books, British Museum, 1930–52; Dep. Keeper, 1952–59; Keeper, 1959–66. Exec. Sec., Organizing Cttee of Internat. Conf. on Cataloguing Principles, Paris, 1961; Mem. Council, Library Assoc. 1964–70; Pres., Microfilm Assoc. of GB, 1967–71; Mem. Senate, Univ. of London, 1973–79. Fellow UCL, 1969. *Publications:* contributions to Jl Documentation, Library Assoc. Record, Library Quarterly, and to Cataloguing Principles and Practice (ed M. Piggott), 1954; Tradition and Principle in Library Cataloguing, 1966; GK: 150 Years of the General Catalogue of Printed Books, 1987. *Address:* 44 Russell Square, WC1B 4JP. *T:* 071–636 7217.

CHAPLIN, John Cyril, CBE 1988; FEng 1987; FRAeS; Member, Civil Aviation Authority and Group Director, Safety Regulation (formerly Safety Services), 1983–88; *b* 13 Aug. 1926; *s* of late Ernest Stanley Chaplin and Isabel Chaplin; *m* 1949, Ruth Marianne Livingstone; two *s* two *d*. *Educ:* Keswick School. Miles Aircraft, 1946; Vickers-Supermarine, 1948; Handley Page, 1950; Somers-Kendall Aircraft, 1952; Heston Aircraft, 1956; Air Registration Board, 1958; Civil Aviation Authority, 1972, Dir-Gen. Airworthiness, 1979. *Publications:* papers to RAeS. *Recreations:* sailing, photography. *Address:* Norman Croft, Mattingley, Basingstoke, Hants RG27 8LF. *T:* Reading (0734) 326207. *Club:* Cruising Association.

CHAPLIN, Sir Malcolm Hilbery, Kt 1991; CBE 1984; Senior Partner, Hilbery Chaplin. *Educ:* Rugby Sch.; Trinity Hall, Cambridge (MA 1961). FRICS. Freeman, City of London. *Address:* Hilbery Chaplin, 4 Eastern Road, Romford RM1 3PL.

CHAPLIN , (Sybil) Judith; Head of Prime Minister's Political Office, since 1990; *b* 19 Aug. 1939; *d* of Theodore and Sybil Schofield; *m* 1st, 1962, Hon. Robin Walpole (*see* Lord Walpole) (marr. diss. 1979); two *s* two *d*; 2nd, 1984, Michael Chaplin, CBE, JP, RIBA. *Educ:* Wycombe Abbey; Girton Coll., Cambridge (MA Econs); Univ. of E Anglia (DipEcon). Headmistress, nursery and preparatory sch., 1967–74; Martin & Acock, Accountants, 1977–81; partner in family farm; Conservative Res. Dept, 1983–86; Hd, Policy Unit, Inst. of Dirs, 1986–88; Special Advr to Chancellor of Exchequer, 1988–90 (Rt Hon. Nigel Lawson, 1988–89, Rt Hon. John Major, 1989–90). Norfolk County Councillor, 1974–85 (Chm., Educn Cttee); Member: ACC, 1977–84 (Vice-Chm., Educn Cttee; Mem., Burnham Cttee); Secondary Examn Council, 1983–86; Interim Adv. Body on Teachers' Pay, 1987–88. Prospective Parly Cand. (C) Newbury, 1990. *Recreations:* walking, riding, opera.

CHAPMAN, family name of **Baron Northfield.**

CHAPMAN, Angela Mary, (Mrs I. M. Chapman); Headmistress, Central Newcastle High School (GPDST), since 1985; *b* 2 Jan. 1940; *d* of Frank Dyson and Mary Rowe; *m* 1959, Ian Michael Chapman; two *s*. *Educ:* Queen Victoria High Sch., Stockton; Univ. of Bristol (BA Hons French); Sorbonne (Dip. de Civilisation Française). Teacher of French, Bede Sch., Sunderland, 1970–80; Dep. Headmistress, Newcastle-upon-Tyne Church High

Sch., 1980–84. *Recreations:* Western Front 1914–18, walking, tennis. *Address:* 14 Alpine Way, Sunderland, Tyne and Wear SR3 1TN.

CHAPMAN, Ben; *see* Chapman, J. K.

CHAPMAN, Charles Cyril Staplee; consultant; Member for Corporate Development and Finance, UK Atomic Energy Authority, 1988–90; *b* 9 Aug. 1936; *s* of Thomas John Chapman and Gertrude Gosden Chapman; *m* 1963, Lorraine Dorothy Wenborn; two *s*. *Educ:* St Peter's Sch., York; Univ. of Sheffield (BSc Hons). British Petroleum Co., 1958, Manager, Chemicals, Corporate Planning, Minerals, 1962–85; Senior Strategy Advisor, British Telecom, 1986–88. *Recreation:* growing rhododendrons.

CHAPMAN, Prof. Christopher Hugh; Scientific Advisor, Schlumberger Cambridge Research, since 1991; *b* 5 May 1945; *s* of John Harold Chapman and Margaret Joan Weeks; *m* 1974, Lillian Tarapaski; one *s* one *d*. *Educ:* Latymer Upper School; Christ's College, Cambridge (MA); Dept of Geodesy and Geophysics, Cambridge (PhD). Asst Prof., Univ. of Alberta, 1969–72, Associate Prof., 1973–74; Asst Prof., Univ. of California, Berkeley, 1972–73; University of Toronto: Associate Prof., 1974–80; Prof., 1980–84; Killam Research Fellow, 1981–83; Adjunct Prof., 1984–88; Prof. of Physics, 1988–90; Prof. of Geophysics, Dept of Earth Scis, and Fellow, Christ's Coll., Cambridge, 1984–88. Green Scholar, Univ. of California, San Diego, 1978–79, 1986. *Publications:* research papers in sci. jls. *Recreations:* sailing, photography, woodwork. *Address:* Schlumberger Cambridge Research, High Cross, Madingley Road, Cambridge CB3 0EL. *T:* Cambridge (0223) 315576.

CHAPMAN, His Honour Cyril Donald, QC 1965; a Circuit Judge, 1972–86; *b* 17 Sept. 1920; *s* of Cyril Henry Chapman and Frances Elizabeth Chapman (*née* Braithwaite); *m* 1st, 1950, Audrey Margaret Fraser (*née* Gough) (marr. diss., 1959); one *s*; 2nd, 1960, Muriel Falconer Bristow; one *s*. *Educ:* Roundhay Sch., Leeds; Brasenose Coll., Oxford (MA). Served RNVR, 1939–45. Called to Bar, 1947; Harmsworth Scholar, 1947; North Eastern Circuit, 1947; Recorder of Huddersfield, 1965–69, of Bradford, 1969–71. Contested (C) East Leeds 1955, Goole 1964, Brighouse and Spenborough, 1966. *Recreation:* walking. *Address:* Hill Top, Collingham, Wetherby, W Yorks. *T:* Collingham Bridge (0937) 72813. *Club:* Leeds (Leeds).

CHAPMAN, Daniel Ahmling; *see* Chapman Nyaho.

CHAPMAN, Sir David (Robert Macgowan), 3rd Bt *cr* 1958, of Cleadon, Co. Durham; Director, Wise Speke Ltd, Stock and Share Brokers, Newcastle upon Tyne; *b* 16 Dec. 1941; *s* of Sir Robert Macgowan Chapman, 2nd Bt, CBE, TD and of Barbara May, *d* of Hubert Tonks; *S* father, 1987; *m* 1965, Maria Elizabeth de Gosztonyi-Zsolnay, *o d* of Dr N. de Mattyasovsky-Zsolnay; one *s* one *d*. *Educ:* Marlborough; McGill Univ., Montreal (BCom). Director: North of England Building Soc., 1974–; Breathe North Ltd, 1988–; British Lung Foundation Ltd, 1989–. Chm., Northern Unit, Stock Exchange, 1988–; Mem., Stock Exchange Council, 1979–88. Gov., St Aidan's Coll., Durham, 1987–. *Heir: s* Michael Nicholas Chapman, *b* 21 May 1969. *Address:* Westmount, 14 West Park Road, Cleadon, Sunderland, Tyne and Wear SR6 7RR; Wise Speke Ltd, Commercial Union House, 39 Pilgrim Street, Newcastle upon Tyne NE1 6RQ.

CHAPMAN, Prof. Dennis, FRS 1986; Professor of Biophysical Chemistry, since 1977, and Head of Department of Protein and Molecular Biology, since 1988, and Vice Dean, since 1990, Royal Free Hospital School of Medicine, University of London; *b* 6 May 1927; *s* of George Henry Chapman and Katherine Magnus; *m* 1949, Elsie Margaret (*d* 1989); two *s* one *d*. *Educ:* London Univ. (BSc; DSc); Liverpool Univ. (PhD); Cambridge Univ. Comyns Berkeley Fellow, Gonville and Caius Coll., Cambridge, 1960–63; Head of Gen. Research Div., Unilever Ltd, Welwyn, 1963–69; Professor Associate, Biophysical Chem., Sheffield Univ., 1968–76; Sen. Wellcome Trust Research Fellow, Dept of Chemistry, Chelsea Coll., Univ. of London, 1976–77; Head of Div. of Basic Med. Scis, Royal Free Hosp. Sch. of Medicine, London Univ., 1988–89. Hon. MRCP 1988. Hon. DSc: Utrecht, 1976; Meml, Canada, 1980. *Publications:* Biological Membranes, vol. I–vol. V, 1968–84; 400 scientific publications in biochemical jls. *Recreations:* tennis, golf, walking. *Address:* Department of Protein and Molecular Biology, Royal Free Hospital School of Medicine, Rowland Hill Street, NW3 2PF. *T:* 071–794 0500, ext. 3246.

CHAPMAN, (Francis) Ian, CBE 1988; Chairman and Managing Director, Chapmans Publishers, since 1989; Chairman: Radio Clyde Holdings (formerly Radio Clyde) PLC, since 1972; The Listener Publications PLC, since 1988; *b* 26 Oct. 1925; *s* of late Rev. Peter Chapman and Frances Burdett; *m* 1953, Marjory Stewart Swinton; one *s* one *d*. *Educ:* Shawlands Academy, Glasgow. Served RAF, 1943–44; worked in coal mines as part of national service, 1945–47. Joined Wm Collins Sons & Co. Ltd, 1947 as management trainee; Sales Manager, 1955; Gp Sales Dir, 1960; Jt Man. Dir, 1968–76; Dep. Chm., William Collins Hldgs, 1976–81; Chm., William Collins Publishers Ltd, 1979–81; Chm. and Gp Chief Exec., William Collins plc, 1981–89. Chairman: Harvill Press Ltd, 1976–89; Hatchards Ltd, 1976–89; Ancient House Bookshop (Ipswich) Ltd, 1976–89; Co-Chm. and Actg Chief Exec., Harper & Row, NY, 1987–89. Director: Independent Radio News, 1984–85; Pan Books Ltd, 1962–84 (Chm., 1974–76); Book Tokens Ltd, 1981–; Stanley Botes Ltd, 1985–89; (non-exec.) Guinness PLC, 1986–91; (non-exec.) United Distillers PLC, 1987–91. Mem. Council, Publishers' Assoc., 1963–76, 1977– (Vice Pres., 1978–79 and 1981–82; Pres., 1979–81; Vice-Chm., 1981); Member: Bd, Book Develt Council, 1967–73; Governing Council, Scottish Business in the Community, 1983–; Dir, Scottish Opera, Theatre Royal Ltd, 1974–79; Trustee, Book Trade Benevolent Soc., 1982–. Chm. Council, Strathclyde Univ. Business School, 1985–88. FRSA 1985; CBIM 1982. Hon. DLitt Strathclyde, 1990. Scottish Free Enterprise Award, 1985. *Publications:* various articles on publishing in trade jls. *Recreations:* music, golf, reading, skiing. *Address:* (business) Chapmans Publishers Ltd, 141–143 Drury Lane, Covent Garden, WC2B 5TB. *T:* 071–379 9799; Kenmore, 46 The Avenue, Cheam, Surrey SM2 7QE. *T:* 081–642 1820. *Clubs:* Garrick, Groucho, MCC; Royal Wimbledon Golf; Prestwick Golf; Walton Heath Golf.

CHAPMAN, Frederick John; Treasurer, since 1989, and Vice-President, since 1990, Varity Corporation (Treasurer (Europe), 1988–89), (on secondment); Principal Establishment and Finance Officer (Under Secretary), Export Credits Guarantee Department, since 1985; *b* 24 June 1939; *s* of late Reginald John Chapman and Elizabeth Chapman; *m* 1964, Paula Brenda Waller; one *s* two *d*. *Educ:* Sutton County Grammar Sch. Joined ECGD, 1958; Principal, 1969; Asst Sec., 1977; Under Sec., 1982. *Recreations:* reading, music. *Address:* Clinton House, 2 Ludlow Road, Maidenhead, Berks SL6 2RH. *T:* Maidenhead (0628) 31908.

CHAPMAN, Prof. Garth; Professor of Zoology, Queen Elizabeth College, University of London, 1958–82, now Emeritus (Vice Principal, 1974–80; Acting Principal, Sept. 1977–March 1978; Fellow, 1984); *b* 8 Oct. 1917; *o s* of E. J. Chapman and Edith Chapman (*née* Attwood); *m* 1941, Margaret Hilda Wigley; two *s* one *d*. *Educ:* Royal Grammar Sch., Worcester; Trinity Hall, Cambridge (Major Scholar); ScD Cantab 1977. FIBiol 1963; FKC 1985. Telecommunications Research Establishment, Ministry of Aircraft Production, 1941–45; Asst Lectr in Zoology, 1945–46, Lectr in Zoology, 1946–58, QMC, Univ. of London; Dean, Faculty of Science, Univ. of London, 1974–78. Vis. Prof., Univ. of California, Berkeley, 1967, Los Angeles, 1970–71. Member: Cttee for Commonwealth Univ. Interchange, British Council, 1978–80; Inter-Univ. Council for Higher Educn Overseas, 1973–83; Council, Westfield Coll., Univ. of London, 1978–84; Central Research Fund Cttee B, 1978–82; Management Cttee of Univ. Marine Biological Station, Millport, 1975–82. *Publications:* Zoology for Intermediate Students (with W. B. Barker), 1964; Body Fluids and their Functions, 1967; various on structure and physiology of marine invertebrates. *Recreations:* gardening; wood-engraving. *Address:* The Grove, Callis Street, Clare, Suffolk CO10 8PX. *T:* Clare (0787) 277235. *Club:* Athenæum.

CHAPMAN, Geoffrey Lloyd; Vice Judge Advocate General, since 1984; *b* 20 Oct. 1928; *o s* of Sydney Leslie Chapman and Dora Chapman (*née* Lloyd); *m* 1958, Jean, *er d* of Valentine Harry Coleman and Marjorie Coleman (*née* Poston); one *s* two *d*. *Educ:* Latymer Upper School; Christ Church, Oxford (MA, BCL). National Service, 1947–49 (commissioned RASC). Called to the Bar, Inner Temple, 1953; practised London and Western Circuit; Legal Asst, Min. of Labour and Nat. Service, 1957; Legal Asst, JAG's Office, 1958; Dep. Judge Advocate, 1961 (Germany, 1963–66, Cyprus, 1969–72); Asst JAG, 1971 (Germany, 1972–76); Dep. JAG, British Forces in Germany, 1979–82. *Recreations:* beagling, reading. *Address:* Thurston Lodge, Doods Road, Reigate, Surrey RH2 0NT. *T:* Reigate (0737) 247860.

CHAPMAN, Sir George (Alan), Kt 1982; FCA; FCIS; Senior Partner, Chapman Ross & Co., Chartered Accountants; *b* 13 April 1927; *s* of late Thomas George Chapman and of Winifred Jordan Chapman; *m* 1950, Jacqueline Sidney (*née* Irvine); two *s* five *d*. *Educ:* Trentham Sch.; Hutt Valley High Sch.; Victoria University. Fellow, Chartered Inst. of Secretaries, 1969 (Mem., 1948–); Fellow, NZ Soc. of Accountants, 1969 (Mem., 1948–). Joined Chapman Ross & Co., 1948. Chairman: Norwich Union General Insurance (formerly Norwich Winterthur) (NZ), 1985– (Dir, 1982–); BNZ Finance, 1979–88 (Dir, 1977–88); Mitel Telecommunications, 1984–; Pilkington (formerly Pilkington Brothers) (NZ), 1989– (Dir, 1982–); Director: Bank of New Zealand, 1968–86 (Dep. Chm., 1976–86); Maui Developments Ltd, 1979–85; Offshore Mining Co. Ltd, 1979–85; Liquigas Ltd, 1981–85 (Chm., 1982–84); NZ Bd, Norwich Union Life Insurance Soc., 1982–; Skellerup Industries Ltd, 1982–90 (Dep. Chm., 1984–87); Skellerup Industries, Malaysia, 1986–90; State Insurance, 1990–. NZ National Party: Member, 1948–; Vice-Pres., 1966–73; Pres., 1973–82. Councillor, Upper Hutt Bor. Council, 1952–53, Deputy Mayor, Upper Hutt, 1953–55; Member: Hutt Valley Drainage Bd, 1953–55; Heretaunga Bd of Governors, 1953–55; Pres., Upper Hutt Chamber of Commerce, 1956–57. *Publication:* The Years of Lightning, 1980. *Recreations:* golf, reading, tennis. *Address:* 53 Barton Avenue, Heretaunga, Wellington, New Zealand. *T:* 283–512. *Clubs:* Wellington Golf, Wellington Racing.

CHAPMAN, Ian; *see* Chapman, F. I.

CHAPMAN, James Keith, (Ben); Deputy Regional Director, Northwest, and Director, Merseyside, Department of Trade and Industry, since 1991; *b* 8 July 1940; *s* of John Hartley and Elsie Vera Chapman; *m* (marr. diss); three *d*. *Educ:* Appleby Grammar Sch., Appleby in Westmorland. Pilot Officer, RAFVR, 1959–61. Min. of Pensions and Nat. Insce, 1958–62; Min. of Aviation/BAA, 1962–67; Rochdale Cttee of Inquiry into Shipping, 1967–70; BoT, 1970–74; First Sec. (Commercial), Dar es Salaam, 1974–78; First Sec. (Econ.), Accra, 1978–81; Asst Sec., DTI, 1981–87; Commercial Counsellor, Peking, 1987–90. FBIM. *Recreations:* opera, theatre, music, walking. *Address:* 18 The Keep, Pond Road, Blackheath, SE3 0AF; 14 Murton View, Appleby in Westmorland, Cumbria CA16 6RF; (office) Graeme House, Derby Square, Liverpool L2 7UP.

CHAPMAN, John Henry Benjamin, CB 1957; CEng; FRINA; RCNC; *b* 28 Dec. 1899; *s* of Robert Henry Chapman and Edith Yeo Chapman (*née* Lillicrap); *m* 1929, Dorothy Rowlerson (*d* 1991); one *s* one *d*. *Educ:* HM Dockyard Sch., Devonport; RNC Greenwich. Dir of Naval Construction, Admiralty, 1958–61. Dir, Fairfield S & E Co. Ltd, 1962–66; Consultant, Upper Clyde Shipbuilders, 1966–68. Mem. of Royal Corps of Naval Constructors, 1922–61; Hon. Vice-Pres., RINA. *Address:* The Small House, Delling Lane, Bosham, W Sussex PO18 8NR. *T:* Bosham (0243) 573331. *Club:* Bosham Sailing.

CHAPMAN, Kathleen Violet, CBE 1956; RRC 1953 (ARRC 1945); QHNS 1953–56; Matron-in-Chief, Queen Alexandra's Royal Naval Nursing Service, 1953–56, retired; *b* 30 May 1903; *d* of late Major H. E. Chapman, CBE, DL Kent, Chief Constable of Kent, and Mrs C. H. J. Chapman. *Educ:* Queen Anne's, Caversham. Trained St Thomas's Hospital, 1928–32.

CHAPMAN, Leslie Charles; Founder and Chairman, Campaign to Stop Waste in Public Expenditure, since 1981; *b* 14 Sept. 1919; *e s* of Charles Richard Chapman and Lilian Elizabeth Chapman; *m* 1947, Beryl Edith England; one *s*. *Educ:* Bishopshalt Sch. Served War, Army, 1939–45. Civil Service, 1939 and 1945–74; Regional Dir, Southern Region, MPBW and PSA, 1967–74. Chm. and mem., various cttees; Mem. (pt-time), LTE, 1979–80. *Publications:* Your Disobedient Servant, 1978, 2nd revised edn 1979; Waste Away, 1982. *Recreations:* reading, music, gardening. *Address:* Cae Caradog, Ffarmers, Llanwrda, Dyfed SA19 8NQ. *T:* Pumpsaint (05585) 504.

CHAPMAN, Mark Fenger, CVO 1979; HM Diplomatic Service, retired; Member, Police Complaints Authority, since 1991; *b* 12 Sept. 1934; *er s* of late Geoffrey Walter Chapman and of Esther Maria Fenger; *m* 1959, Patricia Mary Long; three *s* (and one *s* decd). *Educ:* Cranbrook Sch.; St Catharine's Coll., Cambridge. Entered HM Foreign Service, 1958; served in: Bangkok, 1959–63; FO, 1963–67; Head of Chancery, Maseru, 1967–71; Asst Head of Dept, FCO, 1971–74; Head of Chancery, Vienna, 1975–76; Dep. High Comr and Counsellor (Econ. and Comm.), Lusaka, 1976–79; Diplomatic Service Inspector, 1979–82; Counsellor, The Hague, 1982–86; Ambassador to Iceland, 1986–89. *Address:* c/o Barclays Bank, Holt, Norfolk NR25 6BQ. *Club:* Commonwealth Trust.

CHAPMAN, Ven. Michael Robin; Archdeacon of Northampton, since 1991; *b* 29 Sept. 1939; *s* of Frankland and Kathleen Chapman; *m* 1973, Bernadette Taylor; one *s* one *d*. *Educ:* Lichfield Cathedral Sch.; Ellesmere Coll.; Leeds Univ. (BA 1961); Coll. of the Resurrection, Mirfield. Ordained, dio. of Durham, deacon, 1963, priest, 1964; curate, St Columba, Sunderland, 1963–68; Chaplain, RN, 1968–84; Vicar, St John the Evangelist, Farnham, 1984–91; Rural Dean of Farnham, 1988–91. *Recreations:* flying light aircraft, music, hill walking. *Address:* 11 The Drive, Northampton NN1 4RZ. *T:* Northampton (0604) 714015.

CHAPMAN, Prof. Norman Bellamy, MA, PhD; CChem, FRSC; G. F. Grant Professor of Chemistry, Hull University, 1956–82, now Emeritus; Pro-Vice-Chancellor, 1973–76; *b* 19 April 1916; *s* of Frederick Taylor Chapman and Bertha Chapman; *m* 1949, Fonda Maureen Bungey; one *s* one *d*. *Educ:* Barnsley Holgate Grammar Sch.; Magdalene Coll., Cambridge (Entrance Scholar). 1st Cl. Parts I and II Nat. Sciences Tripos, 1937 and 1938; BA 1938, MA 1942, PhD 1941. Bye-Fellow, Magdalene Coll., 1939–42; Univ. Demonstrator in Chemistry, Cambridge, 1945; Southampton Univ.: Lectr, 1947; Senior Lectr, 1949; Reader in Chemistry, 1955. R. T. French Visiting Prof., Univ. of Rochester, NY, 1962–63; R. J. Reynolds Vis. Prof., Duke Univ., N Carolina, 1971; Cooch Behar

Prof., Calcutta, 1982. Universities Central Council on Admissions: Dep. Chm., 1979–83; Chm., Technical Cttee, 1974–79; Chm., Statistics Cttee, 1983–89. Hon. DSc Hull, 1984. *Publications:* (ed with J. Shorter) Advances in Free Energy Relationships, 1972; (ed) Organic Chemistry, Series One, vol. 2: Aliphatic Compounds (MTP Internat. Review of Science), 1973, Series Two, vol 2, 1976; Correlation Analysis in Chemistry: recent advances, 1978; contribs to Jl Chem. Soc., Analyst, Jl Medicinal Chem., Tetrahedron, Jl Organic Chemistry, Chemistry and Industry. *Recreations:* music, gardening, cricket, Rugby football. *Address:* 5 The Lawns, Molescroft, Beverley HU17 7LS. *T:* Hull (0482) 860553.

CHAPMAN, Roy de Courcy; Headmaster of Malvern College, since 1983; *b* 1 Oct. 1936; *s* of Edward Frederic Gilbert Chapman and Aline de Courcy Ireland; *m* 1959, Valerie Rosemary Small; two *s* one *d*. *Educ:* Dollar Academy; St Andrews Univ. (Harkness Schol.: MA 1959); Moray House Coll. of Educn, Edinburgh. Asst Master, Trinity Coll., Glenalmond, 1960–64; Marlborough College: Asst Master, 1964–68; Head of Mod. Langs, 1968–75; OC CCF, 1969–75; Rector of Glasgow Acad., 1975–82. Chm., Common Entrance Bd, 1988–. *Publications:* Le Français Contemporain, 1971; (with D. Whiting) Le Français Contemporain: Passages for translation and comprehension, 1975. *Recreations:* France, brewing, wine-making. *Address:* Headmaster's House, Malvern College, Worcs WR14 3HW. *T:* Malvern (0684) 574472.

CHAPMAN, Roy John, FCA; Senior Partner, Arthur Andersen, since 1989; *b* 30 Nov. 1936; *s* of William George Chapman and Frances Harriet Chapman; *m* 1961, Janet Gibbeson Taylor; two *s* one *d*. *Educ:* Kettering Grammar Sch.; St Catharine's Coll., Cambridge (Athletics Blue; MA). FIMC, FBIM, FBPICS. Joined Arthur Andersen & Co., Chartered Accountants, 1958; consulting, UK and abroad, incl. France, USA, Algeria, Greece, Turkey, Thailand and Switzerland, 1964–84; admitted to Partnership, 1970; Hd of Financial Services Practice, 1970–84; Man. Partner, London, 1984–89; Mem., Internat. Bd, 1988–. Mem., Adv. Council, London Enterprise Agency, 1985–88. Mem. Governing Body, SOAS, London, 1990–. London Marathon, 1983 (Save the Children). Mem., various professional cttees, 1971–. *Publications:* contribs to professional jls. *Recreations:* cricket, walking, opera, literature, idling. *Address:* 9 Chislehurst Road, Bickley, Kent BR1 2NN. *T:* 081–467 3749. *Clubs:* United Oxford & Cambridge University, MCC; Hawks (Cambridge).

CHAPMAN, Sydney Brookes, RIBA; FRTPI; MP (C) Chipping Barnet, since 1979; a Lord Commissioner of HM Treasury (Government Whip), since 1990; Chartered Architect and Chartered Town and Country Planner; private planning consultant (non-practising); freelance writer; *b* 17 Oct. 1935; *m* 1976, Claire Lesley McNab (*née* Davies); two *s* one *d*. *Educ:* Rugby Sch.; Manchester University. DipArch 1958; ARIBA 1960; DipTP 1961; AMTPI 1962; FFB 1980. Nat. Chm., Young Conservatives, 1964–66 (has been Chm. and Vice-Chm. at every level of Movt); Sen. Elected Vice-Chm., NW Area of Nat. Union of C and U Assocs, 1966–70. Contested (C) Stalybridge and Hyde, 1964; MP (C) Birmingham, Handsworth, 1970–Feb. 1974; PPS to Sec. of State for Transport, 1979–81, to Sec. of State for Social Services, 1981–83; an Asst Govt Whip, 1988–90. Member: Select Cttee on Environment, 1983–87; House of Commons Services Cttee, 1983–87; Jt Cttee on Private Bill Procedure, 1987–88. Chm., Parly Consultants Gp, British Consultants Bureau, 1980–88. Lectr in Arch. and Planning at techn. coll., 1964–70; Dir (Information), British Property Fedn, 1976–79; Dir (non-exec.), Capital and Counties plc, 1980–88; consultant to YJ Lovell (Holdings) plc, 1982–88. Originator of nat. tree planting year, 1973; President: Arboricultural Assoc., 1983–89; London Green Belt Council, 1985–89; Chm., Queen's Silver Jubilee London Tree Group, 1977; Vice-Chm., Wildlife Link, 1985–89; Patron, Tree Council. RIBA: Vice-Pres., 1974–75; Chm., Public Affairs Bd, 1974–75; Mem. Council, 1972–77. President: Friends of Barnet Hosps, 1981–; Friends of Peter Pan Homes, 1981–; Barnet Soc., 1990–. Hon. Assoc. Mem., BVA, 1983–; Hon. ALI; FRSA; Hon. FIAAS 1987; Hon. FFB 1989. *Publications:* Town and Countryside: future planning policies for Britain, 1978; regular contributor to bldg and property jls and to political booklets. *Recreation:* tree spotting. *Address:* House of Commons, SW1A 0AA.

CHAPMAN NYAHO, Daniel Ahmling, CBE 1961; Director: Pioneer Tobacco Co. Ltd, Ghana (Member of British-American Tobacco Group), since 1967; Standard Bank Ghana Ltd, 1970–75; *b* 5 July 1909; *s* of William Henry Chapman and Jane Atsiamesi (*née* Atriki); *m* 1941, Jane Abam (*née* Quashie); two *s* four *d* (and two *d* decd). *Educ:* Bremen Mission Schs, Gold Coast and Togoland; Achimota Coll., Ghana; St Peter's Hall, Oxford. Postgraduate courses at Columbia Univ. and New York Univ.; Teacher, Government Senior Boys' School, Accra, 1930; Master, Achimota Coll., 1930–33, 1937–46. Area Specialist, UN Secretariat, Lake Success and New York, 1946–54; Sec. to Prime Minister and Sec. of Cabinet, Gold Coast/Ghana, 1954–57; Ghana's Ambassador to USA and Permanent Representative at UN, 1957–59; Headmaster, Achimota Sch., Ghana, 1959–63; Dir, UN Div. of Narcotic Drugs, Geneva, 1963–66; Ambassador (Special Duties), Min. of External Affairs, Ghana, 1967. Gen. Sec., All-Ewe Conf., 1944–46; Commonwealth Prime Ministers' Conf., 1957; Mem., Ghana delegn to the conf. of indep. African States, Accra, 1958. First Vice-Chm., Governing Council of UN Special Fund, 1959; Chairman: Mission of Indep. African States to Cuba, Dominican Republic, Haiti, Venezuela, Bolivia, Paraguay, Uruguay, Brazil, Argentina, Chile, 1958; Volta Union, 1968–69. Vice-Chairman: Commn on Univ. Educn in Ghana, 1960–61; Ghana Constituent Assembly, 1978–79. Member: Board of Management, UN Internat. Sch., New York, 1950–54, 1958–59; UN Middle East and N. Africa Technical Assistance Mission on Narcotics Control, 1963; Dir, UN Consultative Gp on Narcotics Control in Asia and Far East, Tokyo, 1964; Member: Political Cttee of Nat. Liberation Council, 1967; Board of Trustees of General Kotoka Trust Fund, 1967–83; Chairman: Arts Council of Ghana, 1968–69; Council of Univ. of Science and Technology, Kumasi, 1972; Bd. of Directors, Ghana Film Industry Corporation, 1979–80; Ghana National Honours and Awards Cttee, 1979–80. Darnforth Vis. Lectr, Assoc. Amer. Colls, 1969, 1970. Hon. LLD Greenboro Agric. and Techn. Coll., USA, 1958. Fellow, Ghana Acad. of Arts and Sciences. *Publications:* Human Geography of Eweland, 1946; Our Homeland—Book I: South-East Gold Coast, 1945; (Ed.) The Ewe News-Letter, 1945–46. *Recreations:* music, gardening, walking. *Address:* (office) Tobacco House, Kwame Nkrumah Avenue, PO Box 5211, Accra, Ghana. *T:* 221111; (home) 9 Ninth Avenue, Tesano, Accra, Ghana. *T:* 227180.

CHAPPELL, (Edwin) Philip, CBE 1976; Adviser, Association of Investment Trust Companies, since 1986; non-executive Director, Fisons, and other companies; Chairman, Thames Customer Service Committee, since 1990; *b* 12 June 1929; *s* of late Rev. C. R. Chappell; *m* 1962, Julia Clavering House, *d* of late H. W. House, DSO, MC; one *s* three *d*. *Educ:* Marlborough Coll.; Christ Church, Oxford (MA). Joined Morgan Grenfell, 1954; Dir, Morgan Grenfell & Co. Ltd, 1964–85; a Vice-Chm., Morgan Grenfell Hldgs, 1975–85; Chm., ICL, 1980–81. Chairman: Nat. Ports Council, 1971–77; EDC for Food and Drink Manufacturing Industry, 1976–80. Member: Council, Institute of Bankers, 1971–85; Business Educn Council, 1974–80; SITPRO Board, 1974–77; (non exec.) British Rail Property Bd, 1986–. Governor of BBC, 1976–81. Treasurer: RSA, 1982–87; City Univ., 1987–. *Publication:* Pensions and Privilege, 1988. *Address:* 22 Frognal Lane, NW3 7DT. *T:* 071–435 8627. *Clubs:* Athenæum, Garrick.

CHAPPELL, William; dancer, designer, producer; *b* Wolverhampton, 27 Sept. 1908; *s* of Archibald Chappell and Edith Eva Clara Blair-Staples. *Educ:* Chelsea School of Art. Studied dancing under Marie Rambert. First appearance on stage, 1929; toured Europe with Ida Rubinstein's company, working under Massine and Nijinska; danced in many ballets, London, 1929–34; joined Sadler's Wells Co., 1934, and appeared there every season; Army service, 1940–45; designed scenery and costumes at Sadler's Wells, 1934–, and Covent Garden, 1947–, including Les Rendezvous, Les Patineurs, Coppelia, Giselle, Handel's Samson, Frederick Ashton's Walk to the Paradise Garden, and Ashton's Rhapsody (costumes); for many revues and London plays. Produced Lyric Revue, 1951, Globe Revue, 1952, High Spirits, Hippodrome, 1953, At the Lyric, 1953, Going to Town, St Martin's, 1954 (also arranging dances for many of these); An Evening with Beatrice Lillie, Globe, 1954 (asst prod.); Time Remembered, New, 1955; Moby Dick, Duke of York's, 1955 (with Orson Welles); The Buccaneer, Lyric, Hammersmith, 1955; The Rivals, Saville; Beaux' Stratagem, Chichester; Violins of St Jacques (also wrote libretto), Sadler's Wells; English Eccentrics; Love and a Bottle; Passion Flower Hotel, Prince of Wales Theatre; Travelling Light; Espresso Bongo; Living for Pleasure, Saville and Garrick Theatres; Where's Charley?; appeared in and assisted Orson Welles with film The Trial; The Chalk Garden, Haymarket, 1971; Offenbach's Robinson Crusoe (1st English perf.), Camden Festival, 1973; Cockie, Vaudeville, 1973; Oh, Kay!, Westminster, 1974; National Tour, In Praise of Love, 1974; Fallen Angels, Gate Theatre, Dublin, 1975; Marriage of Figaro (designed and directed), Sadler's Wells, 1977; The Master's Voice, Dublin, 1977; Memoir, Ambassadors, 1978; Gianni Schicci, Sadler's Wells, 1978; Nijinsky (film), 1979; Same Time Next Year, Dublin, 1980; A Little Bit on the Side (revue, with Beryl Reid), 1983; For Dublin Theatre Festival: A Moon for the Misbegotten, 1976; The Rivals, 1976; Speak of the Devil (musical), designs for Giselle, inc. 2 prodns for Anton Dolin, 1980; dir. Arsenic and Old Lace, 1985; design for Merle Park's costume as Fanny Ellsler, Vienna Opera House, 1985; Choreographed: Travesties, RSC Aldwych, 1974, NY, 1975; Bloomsbury, Phoenix, 1974; Directed, designed costumes and choreographed: Purcell's Fairy Queen, London Opera Centre, 1974; Donizetti's Torquato Tasso, Camden Festival, 1975; Lully's Alceste, London Opera Centre, 1975; restaged original designs for Ashton's Capriole Suite and Valses Nobles et Sentimentales, Sadler's Wells Royal Ballet, 1987; teacher and adviser for: Nureyev season, 1979; Joffrey Ballet, NY, 1979. TV shows. Illustrator of several books. *Publications:* Studies in Ballet; Fonteyn; (ed and jt author) Edward Burra: a painter remembered by his friends, 1982; (ed) Well, Dearie: the letters of Edward Burra, 1985. *Recreations:* reading, cinema, painting. *Address:* 25 Rosenau Road, Battersea, SW11 4QN.

CHAPPLE, family name of **Baron Chapple.**

CHAPPLE, Baron *cr* 1985 (Life Peer), of Hoxton in Greater London; **Francis Joseph Chapple;** General Secretary, Electrical, Electronic, Telecommunication and Plumbing Union, 1966–84; *b* Shoreditch, 1921; *m*; two *s*. *Educ:* elementary school. Started as Apprentice Electrician; Member ETU, 1937–83; Shop Steward and Branch Official; Member Exec. Council, 1958; Asst General Secretary, 1963–66. Mem., Gen. Council of TUC, 1971–83, Chm. 1982–83; Gold Badge of Congress, 1983. Member: National Exec. Cttee of Labour Party, 1965–71; Cttee of Inquiry into Shipping, 1967; Royal Commn on Environmental Pollution, 1973–77; Horserace Totalisator Bd, 1976–90; Energy Commn, 1977–79; NEDC, 1979–83; Nat. Nuclear Corp., 1980–86; Southern Water Authority, 1983–89; Director: Inner City Enterprises, 1983–88; N. G. Bailey Orgn, 1989–. *Publication:* (autobiog.) Sparks Fly, 1984. *Recreation:* racing pigeons. *Address:* c/o Electrical, Electronic, Telecommunication and Plumbing Union, Hayes Court, West Common Road, Bromley BR2 7AU.

CHAPPLE, Gen. Sir John, GCB 1988 (KCB 1985); CBE 1980 (MBE 1969); Chief of the General Staff, 1988–Feb. 1992; Aide-de-Camp General to the Queen, 1987–Feb. 1992; *b* 27 May 1931; *s* of C. H. Chapple; *m* 1959, Annabel Hill; one *s* three *d*. *Educ:* Haileybury; Trinity Coll., Cambridge (MA). Joined 2nd KEO Goorkhas, 1954; served Malaya, Hong Kong, Borneo; Staff Coll., 1962; jssc 1969; Commanded 1st Bn 2nd Goorkhas, 1970–72; Directing Staff, Staff Coll., 1972–73; Commanded 48 Gurkha Infantry Bde, 1976; Gurkha Field Force, 1977; Principal Staff Officer to Chief of Defence Staff, 1978–79; Comdr, British Forces Hong Kong, and Maj.-Gen., Brigade of Gurkhas, 1980–82; Dir of Military Operations, 1982–84; Dep. Chief of Defence Staff (Progs and Personnel), 1985–87; C-in-C, UKLF, 1987–88. Col, 2nd Goorkhas, 1986–. Hon. Col, Oxford Univ. OTC, 1988–. Services Fellow, Fitzwilliam Coll., Cambridge, 1973. Member: Council, Nat. Army Museum; Soc. for Army Historical Res.; Trustee, WWF, UK. FZS (Mem. Council), FLS, FRGS (Mem. Council). OStJ. *Club:* Beefsteak.

CHARD, Prof. Timothy, MD; FRCOG; Professor of Reproductive Physiology, St Bartholomew's Hospital Medical College, since 1973; *b* 4 June 1937; *s* of Henry Francis and Dorothea Elaine Chard; *m* 1977, Linda Kay Elmore; two *s*. *Educ:* Merchant Taylors' School; St Thomas's Hosp. Med. Sch. Junior med. posts, 1960–65; MRC Clinical Research Fellow, 1965–68; Sen. Lectr, St Bartholomew's Hosp., 1968–73. *Publications* (jointly): Radioimmunoassay, 1978, 3rd edn 1987; Placental Function Tests, 1982; Basic Sciences for Obstetrics, 1984, 2nd edn 1987; Computing for Clinicians, 1988. *Recreations:* fine arts, venture capital. *Address:* 509 Mountjoy House, Barbican, EC2Y 8BP. *T:* 071–628 4570.

CHARING CROSS, Archdeacon of; *see* Fulham, Bishop of.

CHARKHAM, Jonathan Philip; Adviser to the Governors, Bank of England, since 1988 (Chief Advr, 1985–88); *b* 17 Oct. 1930; *s* of late Louis Charkham and Phoebe Beatrice Barquet (*née* Miller); *m* Moira Elizabeth Frances, *d* of late Barnett A. Salmon and of Molly Salmon; twin *s* one *d*. *Educ:* St Paul's Sch. (scholar); Jesus Coll., Cambridge (Exhibitioner). BA 1952. Called to Bar, Inner Temple, 1953. Morris Charkham Ltd, 1953–63 (Man. Dir, 1957–63); Div. Dir, Rest Assured Ltd, 1963–68. Civil Service Department: Principal, Management Services, later Pay, 1969–73; Asst Sec., 1973–78, Personnel Management, 1973–75; Dir, Public Appts Unit, 1975–82; Under Sec., 1978, Management and Organisation, 1980–82; on secondment from Bank of England as Dir, PRO NED, 1982–85. Member: Council, Royal Inst. of Public Admin., 1981–82; Industry and Finance Cttee, NEDC, 1988–90; Steering Cttee, Corporate Takeovers Inquiry, 1990–; Instnl Investors Project Adv. Bd, Columbia Univ. of NY Center for Law and Econ. Studies, 1989–; City Transportation Task Force, 1990–. Duke of Edinburgh's 7th Commonwealth Study Conf., 1990–. Cttee, Knightsbridge Assoc., 1989–. Chm., CU Labour Club, 1952. Master, Worshipful Co. of Upholders, 1979–80, 1980–81. FRSA; CBIM. *Publications:* booklets and pamphlets on non-executive directors, boards and shareholders. *Recreations:* music, playing golf, antique furniture, wine. *Address:* 22 Montpelier Place, SW7 1HL. *T:* 071–589 9879. *Clubs:* Athenæum, MCC, City Livery.

CHARKIN, Richard Denis Paul; Executive Director, Reed International Books, since 1988; *b* 17 June 1949; *s* of Frank Charkin and Mabel Doreen Charkin (*née* Rosen); *m* 1972, Susan Mary Poole; one *s* two *d*. *Educ:* Haileybury and ISC; Trinity College, Cambridge (MA). Science Editor, Harrap & Co., 1972; Sen. Publishing Manager,

Pergamon Press, 1973; Oxford University Press: Medical Editor, 1974; Head of Science and Medicine, 1976; Head of Reference, 1980; Managing Dir, Academic, 1984; Octopus Publishing Group (Reed International Books), 1988. Vis. Fellow, Green College, Oxford, 1987. *Recreations:* music, cricket. *Address:* 52 Southmoor Road, Oxford OX2 6RD.

CHARLEMONT, 14th Viscount *cr* 1665 (Ire.); **John Day Caulfeild;** Baron Caulfeild of Charlemont 1620 (Ire.); *b* 19 March 1934; *s* of Eric St George Caulfeild (*d* 1975) and of Edith Evelyn, *d* of Frederick William Day, Ottawa; *S* uncle, 1985; *m* 1st, 1964, Judith Ann (*d* 1971), *d* of James E. Dodd; one *s* one *d*; 2nd, 1972, Janet Evelyn, *d* of Orville R. Nancekivell. *Heir: s* Hon. John Dodd Caulfeild, *b* 15 May 1966. *Address:* 39 Rossburn Drive, Etobicoke, Ontario M9C 2P9, Canada.

CHARLES, Rt. Rev. Adrian Owen, RFD 1983; ED 1976; Bishop of Western Region (Assistant Bishop of Diocese of Brisbane), since 1984; Bishop to Australian Defence Force, since 1989; *b* 31 July 1926; *s* of Robert Charles and Alice (*née* Donovan); *m* 1955, Leonie Olive (*née* Robinson); one *s* one *d*. *Educ:* Slade Sch., Warwick, Qld; St Francis Coll., Univ. of Qld; Anglican Central Coll., Canterbury (ThL, Diploma in Divinity). Ordained priest, 1952; Royal Australian Army Chaplains Dept, 1955–83; Rector: Christ Church, St Lucia, Brisbane, 1958–66; St Paul's, Ipswich, 1966–71; Dir, Religious Studies, Christ Church Grammar Sch., Perth, 1971–72; Dean, St James' Cathedral, Townsville, 1972–77; Rector, St David's, Chelmer, Brisbane, 1977–83; Sen. Chaplain, 1st Mil. Dist, 1981–83; Archdeacon and Chaplain to Archbishop of Brisbane, 1981–83; Bishop of Southern Region, 1983–84. *Recreations:* reading, cricket, golf, theatre. *Address:* Lethbridge, 19 East Street, Toowoomba, Qld 4350, Australia. *T:* (076) 327240. *Clubs:* United Service (Brisbane); Middle Ridge Golf (Toowoomba); Officers Mess, Aviation Regiment (Oakey).

CHARLES, Arthur William Hessin; First Junior Counsel to HM Treasury on Chancery Matters, since 1989; *b* 25 March 1948; *s* of Arthur Attwood Sinclair Charles and May Davies Charles (*née* Westerman); *m* 1974, Lydia Margaret Ainscow; one *s* one *d*. *Educ:* Malvern College; Christ's College, Cambridge (MA Hons). Called to the Bar, Lincoln's Inn, 1971; Junior Counsel to the Crown (Chancery), 1986. *Recreations:* golf, tennis. *Address:* 13 Old Square, Lincoln's Inn, WC2 3UA. *T:* 071–404 4800. *Clubs:* Hawks (Cambridge); Denham Golf.

CHARLES, Bernard Leopold, QC 1980; **His Honour Judge Charles;** a Circuit Judge, since 1990; *b* 16 May 1929; *s* of Chaskiel Charles and Mary Harris; *m* 1958, Margaret Daphne Abel; one *s* two *d*. *Educ:* King's Coll., Taunton. Called to the Bar, Gray's Inn, 1955. Practised in London and on South Eastern Circuit, 1956–90; a Recorder, 1985–90. *Recreations:* music, politics. *Address:* Lamb Building, Temple, EC4. *T:* 01–353 6701; 12 East 41st Street, New York, NY 10017, USA.

CHARLES, Hon. Eugenia; *see* Charles, Hon. M. E.

CHARLES, Jack; Director of Establishments, Greater London Council, 1972–77, retired; *b* 18 Jan. 1923; *o s* of late Frederick Walter Charles and of Alice Mary Charles; *m* 1959, Jean, *d* of late F. H. Braund, London; one *s* one *d*. *Educ:* County High Sch., Ilford. Air Min., 1939–42; RAF, 1942–46; Min. of Supply, 1947–59 (Private Sec. to Minister of Supply, 1952–54); War Office, 1959–60; UKAEA, 1960–68 (Authority Personnel Officer, 1965–68); Dep. Dir of Estabs, GLC, 1968–72. *Recreations:* gardening, walking. *Address:* Kings Warren, Enborne Row, Wash Water, Newbury, Berks RG15 0LY. *T:* Newbury (0635) 30161.

CHARLES, James Anthony, ScD; FEng 1983; Reader in Process Metallurgy, University of Cambridge, 1978–90, now Emeritus; Fellow, St John's College, Cambridge, since 1963; *b* 23 Aug. 1926; *s* of John and Winifred Charles; *m* 1951, Valerie E. King; two *s*. *Educ:* Imperial College of Science and Technology, Royal School of Mines (BScEng, ARSM); MA, ScD Cantab; FIM, MIMM; FRSA. J. Stone & Co. Ltd, 1947–50; British Oxygen Ltd, 1950–60; Dept of Metallurgy and Materials Science, Univ. of Cambridge, 1960–90. Syndic, Fitzwilliam Museum, 1986–. Sir George Beilby Medal and Prize, RIC, Soc. Chem. Ind. and Inst. of Metals, 1965; Sir Robert Hadfield Medal, Metals Soc., 1977; Kroll Medal, Inst. of Metals, 1989. *Publications:* Oxygen in Iron and Steel Making, 1956; Selection and Use of Engineering Materials, 1984, 2nd edn 1989; numerous papers on the science and technology of metals and archaeometallurgy. *Recreations:* gardening, walking, listening to music, archaeology. *Address:* New Lodge, 22 Mingle Lane, Stapleford, Cambridge CB2 5BG. *T:* Cambridge (0223) 843812.

CHARLES, Sir Joseph (Quentin), Kt 1984; Managing Director, J. Q. Charles Ltd; *b* 25 Nov. 1908; *s* of Martineau Charles; *m* 1934, Albertha L. Yorke; three *s* two *d*. *Educ:* St Mary's Coll., St Lucia. Commission Agent's Clerk, 1927–33. Started J. Q. Charles as a small provision wholesale and retail business, 1933, incorporated 1944; business has grown to become classified retailer of cars, foods, building materials and hardware, dry goods and wearing apparel; also started several light manufacturing industries; St Lucia Co-operative Bank, 1937 (Founding Director for 43 years, Pres., 1974–79); Past Chairman: St Lucia Agricl & Industrial Bank; St Lucia Banana Growers Assoc., 1963–67; Dir, Copra Manufacturers Ltd. Mem., Castries City Council. *Address:* c/o J. Q. Charles Ltd, PO Box 279, Castries, St Lucia, West Indies. *T:* (home) 20656.

CHARLES, Leslie Stanley Francis; Director, Birmid Qualcast plc, 1981–88, retired; *b* 28 July 1917; *s* of Samuel Francis Charles and Lena Gwendolyn (*née* Reed); *m* 1941, Henrietta Elizabeth Calvin Thomas; one *s*. *Educ:* Cardiff High Sch.; University Coll. of S Wales and Mon, Univ. of Wales (BScEng London, 1st Cl. Hons). Grad. Engr, Metropolitan Vickers Ltd, 1936–39; Regular Officer, REME, 1939–54; Consultant, Urwick Orr & Partners Ltd, 1954–60; Chief Engr Ops, UKAEA, 1960–63; Dir of Factories, Raleigh Industries Ltd, 1963–66; Man. Dir, Aluminium Wire & Cable Co. Ltd, 1966–68; British Aluminium Co. Ltd: Dep. Man. Dir, 1968–79; Man. Dir, 1979–82. Chm., European Aluminium Assoc., 1981–84. *Recreations:* golf, bridge, music. *Address:* Crana, Claydon Lane, Chalfont St Peter, Bucks SL9 8JU. *T:* Gerrards Cross (0753) 884290.

CHARLES, Hon. (Mary) Eugenia; Prime Minister and Minister of Finance, Commonwealth of Dominica, since 1980; MP (Dominica Freedom Party) Roseau, since 1970; *b* 15 May 1919; *d* of John Baptiste Charles and Josephine (*née* Delauney). *Educ:* Convent High Sch., Roseau, Dominica; St Joseph's Convent, St George's, Grenada; University Coll., Univ. of Toronto (BA); London Sch. of Econs and Pol. Science. Called to the Bar, Inner Temple, 1947; admitted to practice, Dominica, 1949. Entered Parlt, 1970; Leader of the Opposition, 1975–79. *Recreations:* reading, gardening, travelling. *Address:* Office of the Prime Minister, Roseau, Commonwealth of Dominica. *T:* 82401, ext. 300.

CHARLES, Michael Geoffrey A.; *see* Audley-Charles.

CHARLESTON, Robert Jesse, FSA; FSGT. Keeper of the Department of Ceramics, Victoria and Albert Museum, 1963–76; *b* 3 April 1916; *s* of late Sidney James Charleston, Lektor, Stockholms Högskola; *m* 1941, Joan Randle; one *s* one *d*. *Educ:* Berkhamsted Sch., Herts; New College, Oxford. Army (Major, RAPC), 1940–46; Asst, Bristol Museum, 1947; Asst Keeper, Victoria and Albert Museum, 1948; Deputy Keeper, 1959. W. E. S.

Turner Meml Lectr, Sheffield Univ., 1979. Mem., Reviewing Cttee on Export of Works of Art, 1979–84. President: The Glass Circle, 1957–; Fellows of the Corning Mus. of Glass, 1980–. Award winner, Glass Sellers' Co., 1986. *Publications:* Roman Pottery, 1955; (ed) English Porcelain, 1745–1850, 1965; (ed) World Ceramics, 1968; (with Donald Towner) English Ceramics, 1580–1830, 1977; Islamic Pottery, 1979; Masterpieces of Glass, 1980; The James A. de Rothschild Collection: (with J. G. Ayers) Meissen and Oriental Porcelain, 1971; (with Michael Archer and M. Marcheix) Glass and Enamels, 1977; Maioliche e Porcellane: Inghilterra, Paisi Scandinavi, Russia, 1982; English Glass, 1984; numerous articles and reviews in The Connoisseur, Jl of Glass Studies, Burlington Magazine, etc. *Recreations:* foreign travel, music. *Address:* Whittington Court, Whittington, near Cheltenham, Glos GL54 4HF.

CHARLESWORTH, Arthur Leonard, FCIOB; Joint Managing Director, John Mowlem Co., 1978–89; Non-Executive Director, John Mowlem Group, since 1989; *b* 11 June 1927; *s* of William Henry and Florence Alice Charlesworth; *m* 1948, June Edith (*née* Sims); one *s* two *d*. *Educ:* Wandsworth Grammar Sch. Joined John Mowlem Co., 1941; Dir, Mowlem (Building), 1965, John Mowlem & Co., 1969; Man. Dir, John Mowlem & Co., 1978; Jt Man. Dir, Mowlem Group, 1986. CBIM; FRSA. *Recreation:* golf. *Address:* 61 Vicarage Road, SW14 8RY. *T:* 081–876 6724. *Club:* Richmond Golf.

CHARLESWORTH, Prof. Brian, PhD; FRS 1991; Professor, Department of Ecology and Evolution, University of Chicago, since 1985; *b* 29 April 1945; *s* of Francis Gustave Charlesworth and Mary (*née* Ryan); *m* 1967, Deborah Maltby; one *d*. *Educ:* Queen's Coll., Cambridge (BA Natural Scis; PhD Genetics). Post-Doctoral Fellow, Univ. of Chicago, 1969–71; Lectr in Genetics, Univ. of Liverpool, 1971–74; Lectr, 1974–82, Reader, 1982–84, in Biology, Univ. of Sussex; Chm., Dept of Ecology and Evolution, Univ. of Chicago, 1986–91. *Publications:* Evolution in Age-Structured Populations, 1980; papers in Nature, Science, Genetics, Genetical Res., Evolution, Amer. Naturalist, Procs Roy. Soc. *Recreations:* reading, listening to classical music, walking. *Address:* Department of Ecology and Evolution, University of Chicago, 1101 E 57th Street, Chicago, Ill 60637, USA. *T:* 312–702–8942.

CHARLESWORTH, Peter James; His Honour Judge Charlesworth; a Circuit Judge, since 1989; *b* 24 Aug. 1944; *s* of late Joseph William Charlesworth and of Florence Mary Charlesworth; *m* 1967, Elizabeth Mary Postill; one *s* one *d*. *Educ:* Hull Grammar Sch.; Leeds Univ. (LLB 1965, LLM 1966). Called to the Bar, Inner Temple, 1966. In practice on North-Eastern Circuit, 1966–89; a Recorder, 1982–89. *Recreations:* tennis, ski-ing, Rugby football (spectating), walking. *Address:* Daleswood, Creskeld Gardens, Bramhope, Leeds LS16 9EN. *T:* Leeds (0532) 674377. *Clubs:* Hull Rugby League Football (Vice-Pres.); Leeds YMCA Tennis.

CHARLESWORTH, Stanley, OBE 1980; National Secretary, National Council of YMCAs, 1975–80; *b* 20 March 1920; *s* of Ernest and Amy Charlesworth; *m* 1942, Vera Bridge; three *d*. *Educ:* Ashton under Lyne Grammar Sch.; Manchester Coll. of Commerce. YMCA: Area Sec., Community Services, 1943–52, Dep. Sec., 1952–57; Asst Regional Sec., NW Region, 1957–67, Regional Sec., 1967–75. *Recreations:* sailing, golf, walking, gardening. *Address:* Inchcape, Maes Y Cnwce, Newport, Dyfed SA42 0RS. *Clubs:* Rotary (Fishguard and Goodwick); YMCA (Manchester).

CHARLISH, Dennis Norman; Panel Chairman, Civil Service Selection Board, 1978–88 (Resident Chairman, 1975–78); *b* 24 May 1918; *s* of Norman Charlish and Edith (*née* Cherriman); *m* 1941, Margaret Trevor, *o d* of William Trevor and Margaret Ann Williams, Manchester; one *d*. *Educ:* Brighton Grammar Sch.; London Sch. of Economics. Rosebery Schol., 1947; BSc (Econ) 1st class hons., 1951. Joined Civil Service as Tax Officer, Inland Revenue, 1936; Exec. Officer, Dept of Overseas Trade, 1937; Dep. Armament Supply Officer, Admty, 1941; Principal, BoT, 1949; Asst Secretary, 1959; Imperial Defence Coll., 1963; Under-Sec., BoT, 1967–69; Min. of Technology, 1969–70; Head of Personnel, DTI, 1971–74, Dept of Industry, 1974–75. *Address:* 28 Multon Road, SW18 3LH.

CHARLTON, Bobby; *see* Charlton, Robert.

CHARLTON, (Foster) Ferrier (Harvey), CBE 1986; DFC 1945; Partner, 1953–88, Senior Partner, 1985–88, Linklaters & Paines, Solicitors; *b* 26 March 1923; *s* of Foster Ferrier Charlton and Esther Naomi French Charlton (*née* Brown); *m* 1950, Doris Winnifred (Lola) Marson; one *s* three *d*. *Educ:* Rugby Sch.; Wadham Coll., Oxford (MA, PPE 1st Cl. 1947). RAFVR (Pilot), 1941–53; served W Africa, India, Ceylon, 8 Sqdn and 200 Sqdn, RAF, 1944–45. Articles with Linklaters & Paines, 1948; qualified as solicitor, 1950; Partner, 1953–88. Director: Short Bros, 1958–89; Law Debenture Corp., 1988–. Mem., City/Industry Task Force, CBI, 1987. *Publications:* legal articles. *Recreation:* gardening (Pres., Alpine Garden Soc., to 1991). *Address:* 19 Kippington Road, Sevenoaks, Kent TN13 2LJ. *T:* Sevenoaks (0732) 453370.

CHARLTON, (Frederick) Noel, CB 1961; CBE 1946; *b* 4 Dec. 1906; *s* of late Frederick William Charlton and Marian Charlton; *m* 1932, Maud Helen Rudgard; no *c*. *Educ:* Rugby School; Hertford Coll., Oxford Univ. (MA). Admitted a Solicitor, 1932; in private practice as Solicitor in London, 1932–39. War Service, 1939–46 (attained rank of Colonel, Gen. List). Joined Treasury Solicitor's Dept, 1946; Principal Asst Solicitor (Litigation), Treasury Solicitor's Dept, 1956–71; Sec., Lord Chancellor's Cttee on Defamation, 1971–74; with Dept of Energy (Treasury Solicitor's Branch), 1975–81, retired. Chairman, Coulsdon and Purley UDC, 1953–54 and 1964–65; Hon. Alderman, London Borough of Croydon. Bronze Star (USA), 1945. *Recreations:* golf, travel. *Address:* 4 Newton Road, Purley, Surrey CR8 3DN. *T:* 081–660 2802. *Club:* Army and Navy.
See also T. A. G. Charlton.

CHARLTON, Graham; *see* Charlton, T. A. G.

CHARLTON, Prof. Graham, MDS; FDSRCSE; Professor of Conservative Dentistry, University of Edinburgh, since 1978 (Dean of Dental Studies, 1978–83); *b* 15 Oct. 1928; *s* of Simpson R. Charlton and Georgina (*née* Graham); *m* 1956, Stella Dobson; two *s* one *d*. *Educ:* Bedlington Grammar Sch., Northumberland; St John's Coll., York (Teaching Cert.); King's Coll., Univ. of Durham (BDS); Univ. of Bristol (MDS). Teacher, Northumberland, 1948–52; National Service, 1948–50; Dental School, 1952–58; General Dental Practice, Torquay, 1958–64; University of Bristol: Lecturer, 1964–72; Cons. Sen. Lectr, 1972–78; Dental Clinical Dean, 1975–78. *Address:* Carnethy, Bog Road, Penicuik, Midlothian EH26 9BT. *T:* Penicuik (0968) 73639.

CHARLTON, John, (Jack Charlton), OBE 1974; Manager, Republic of Ireland Football Team, since 1986; broadcaster; *b* 8 May 1935; *s* of Robert and Elizabeth Charlton; *m* 1958, Patricia; two *s* one *d*. *Educ:* Hirst Park Sch., Ashington. Professional footballer, Leeds United, 1952–73; Manager: Middlesbrough, 1973–77; Sheffield Wednesday FC, 1977–83; Newcastle United FC, 1984–85. Mem., Sports Council, 1977–82. *Recreations:* shooting, fishing, gardening. *Address:* c/o Football Association of the Republic of Ireland, 8 Merrion Square, Dublin 2, Ireland.
See also Robert Charlton.

CHARLTON, Prof. Kenneth; Emeritus Professor of History of Education, King's College, University of London, since 1983; *b* 11 July 1925; 2nd *s* of late George and Lottie Charlton; *m* 1953, Maud Tulloch Brown, *d* of late P. R. Brown, MBE and M. B. Brown; one *s* one *d*. *Educ:* City Grammar Sch., Chester; Univ. of Glasgow. MA 1949, MEd 1953, Glasgow. RNVR, 1943–46. History Master, Dalziel High Sch., Motherwell, and Uddingston Grammar Sch., 1950–54; Lectr in Educn, UC N Staffs, 1954–64; Sen. Lectr in Educn, Keele Univ., 1964–66; Prof. of History and Philosophy of Educn, Birmingham Univ., 1966–72; Prof. of History of Educn and Head of Dept of Educn, King's Coll., Univ. of London, 1972–83. *Publications:* Recent Historical Fiction for Children, 1960, 2nd edn 1969; Education in Renaissance England, 1965; contrib. Educnl Rev., Brit. Jl Educnl Psych., Year Bk of Educn, Jl Hist. of Ideas, Brit. Jl Educnl Studies, Internat. Rev. of Educn, Trans Hist. Soc. Lancs and Cheshire, Irish Hist. Studies, Northern Hist., Hist. of Educn, Hist. of Educn Quarterly. *Recreations:* gardening, listening to music. *Address:* 128 Ridge Langley, Sanderstead, Croydon CR2 0AS.
See also P. Charlton.

CHARLTON, Philip, OBE 1987; FCIB; CBIM; Group Managing Director, 1986–88, Chief Executive, 1988–89, Deputy Chairman, 1990–91, TSB Group plc; *b* 31 July 1930; *s* of George and Lottie Charlton; *m* 1953, Jessie Boulton; one *s* one *d*. *Educ:* Chester Grammar School. Entered service of Chester Savings Bank, 1947; Gen. Manager, Chester, Wrexham and N Wales Savings Bank, 1966–75; Gen. Manager, TSB Wales & Border Counties, 1975–81; TSB Group Central Executive: Dep. Chief Gen. Manager, 1981–82; Chief Gen. Manager, 1982–85; Mem., TSB Central Bd, 1976–77, 1981–90; Director: TSB Computer Services (Wythenshawe) Ltd, 1976–81; TSB Trust Co. Ltd, 1979–82; TSB Gp Computer Services Ltd, 1981–; Central Trustee Savings Bank, later TSB Bank, 1982–89; TSB (Holdings) Ltd, 1982–; Hill Samuel Gp, 1987–89. Council Mem., 1968–71, Hon. Treasurer, 1975–77, Savings Bank Inst.; Vice Pres., Internat. Savings Banks Inst. (Geneva), 1988–; Mem., Bd of Admin, European Savings Banks Gp, Brussels, 1989–. Chm., TSB Nat. Sports Council, 1979–82. FCIB (FIB 1977; Mem. Council, 1982–; Dep. Chm., 1989; Pres., 1990–); CBIM 1983. *Recreations:* music, swimming, sport. *Address:* 62 Quinta Drive, Arkley, near Barnet, Herts EN5 3BE. *T:* 081–440 4477. *Clubs:* Royal Automobile; City (Chester).
See also Prof. K. Charlton.

CHARLTON, Robert, (Bobby Charlton), CBE 1974 (OBE 1969); Director, Manchester United Football Club, since 1984; *b* 11 Oct. 1937; *s* of Robert and Elizabeth Charlton; *m* 1961, Norma; two *d*. *Educ:* Bedlington Grammar Sch., Northumberland. Professional Footballer with Manchester United, 1954–73, for whom he played 751 games and scored 245 goals; FA Cup Winners Medal, 1963; FA Championship Medals, 1956–57, 1964–65 and 1966–67; World Cup Winners Medal (International), 1966; European Cup Winners medal, 1968. 100th England cap, 21 April 1970; 106 appearances for England, 1957–73. Manager, Preston North End, 1973–75. Mem., Adv. Council, BBC NW. Hon. Fellow, Manchester Polytechnic, 1979. Hon. MA Manchester Univ. *Publications:* My Soccer Life, 1965; Forward for England, 1967; This Game of Soccer, 1967; Book of European Football, Books 1–4, 1969–72. *Recreation:* golf. *Address:* Garthollerton, Chelford Road, Ollerton, near Knutsford, Cheshire.
See also John Charlton.

CHARLTON, (Thomas Alfred) Graham, CB 1970; Secretary, Trade Marks, Patents and Designs Federation, 1973–84; *b* 29 Aug. 1913; 3rd *s* of late Frederick William and Marian Charlton; *m* 1940, Margaret Ethel, *yr d* of A. E. Furst; three *d*. *Educ:* Rugby School; Corpus Christi Coll., Cambridge. Asst Principal, War Office, 1936; Asst Private Secretary to Secretary of State for War, 1937–39; Principal, 1939; Cabinet Office, 1947–49; Asst Secretary, 1949; International Staff, NATO, 1950–52; War Office, later MoD, 1952–73; Asst Under-Sec. of State, 1960–73. Coronation Medal, 1953. *Recreations:* golf, gardening. *Address:* Victoria House, Elm Road, Penn, Bucks HP10 8LQ. *T:* Penn (049481) 3195.
See also Frederick Noel Charlton.

CHARLTON, Prof. Thomas Malcolm, FRSE 1973; historian of engineering science; Jackson Professor of Engineering, University of Aberdeen, 1970–79, now Emeritus; *b* 1 Sept. 1923; *s* of William Charlton and Emily May Charlton (née Wallbank); *m* 1950, Valerie, *d* of late Dr C. McCulloch, Hexham; two *s* (and one *s* decd). *Educ:* Doncaster Grammar Sch. BSc (Eng) London, MA Cantab. Junior Scientific Officer, Min. of Aircraft Prodn, TRE, Malvern, 1943–46; Asst Engr, Merz & McLellan, Newcastle upon Tyne, 1946–54; Univ. Lectr in Engrg, Cambridge, 1954–63; Fellow and Tutor, Sidney Sussex Coll., 1959–63; Prof. of Civil Engrg, Queen's Univ., Belfast, 1963–70; Dean, Faculty of Applied Science, QUB, 1967–70. Vis. Prof. of Civil Engineering, Univ. of Newcastle upon Tyne, 1982–89. Council, Instn of Civil Engrs of Ireland, 1965–69. For. Mem., Finnish Acad. of Technical Sciences, 1967. Personal Symposium, Turin Politecnico, 1989. Bd of Finance, Hereford Dio., 1980. *Publications:* Model Analysis of Structures, 1954, new edn 1966; (contrib.) Hydro-electric Engineering Practice, 1958; Energy Principles in Applied Statics, 1959; Analysis of Statically-indeterminate Frameworks, 1961; Principles of Structural Analysis, 1969, new edn 1977; Energy Principles in Theory of Structures, 1973; (contrib.) The Works of I. K. Brunel, 1976; A History of Theory of Structures in the Nineteenth Century, 1982; (contrib.) Encyclopaedia of Building Technology, 1986; Professor Emeritus (autobiog.), 1991; papers on energy principles, hist. of structures. *Recreations:* ecclesiastical history, golf. *Address:* The Old School House, Burwell, Cambridge CB5 0BB. *T:* Newmarket (0638) 741351.

CHARNLEY, Sir (William) John, Kt 1981; CB 1973; MEng, FEng, FRAeS, FRInstNav; consultant in advanced technology; *b* 4 Sept. 1922; *s* of George and Catherine Charnley; *m* 1945, Mary Paden; one *s* one *d*. *Educ:* Oulton High Sch., Liverpool; Liverpool Univ. MEng 1945. Aerodynamics Dept, RAE Farnborough, 1943–55; Supt. Blind Landing Experimental Unit, 1955–61; Imperial Defence Coll., 1962; Head of Instruments and Electrical Engineering Dept, 1963–65, Head of Weapons Dept, 1965–68, RAE Farnborough; Head of Research Planning, 1968–69, Dep. Controller, Guided Weapons, Min. of Technology, later MoD, 1969–72; Controller, Guided Weapons and Electronics, MoD (PE), 1972–73; Chief Scientist (RAF), 1973–77, and Dep. Controller, R&D Establishments and Res. C, MoD, 1975–77; Controller, R&D Establishments and Res., MoD, 1977–82. Director: Fairey Holdings Ltd, 1983–86; Winsdale Investments Ltd, 1985–88. Technical Advr, Monopolies and Mergers Commn, 1982; Specialist Advr to House of Lords Select Cttee on Science and Technology, 1986. Chm., Civil Aviation Res. and Develt Programme Bd, 1984–; Mem., Air Traffic Control Bd, 1985–. Pres., Royal Inst. of Navigation, 1987–90. Trustee, Richard Ormonde Shuttleworth Remembrance Trust, 1987–. Hon. DEng Liverpool, 1988. Gold Medal, RAeS, 1980. *Publications:* papers on subjects in aerodynamics, aircraft all weather operation, aircraft navigation, defence R&D. *Address:* Kirkstones, 29 Brackendale Close, Camberley, Surrey GU15 1HP. *T:* Camberley (0276) 22547. *Club:* Royal Air Force.

CHARNOCK, Henry, FRS 1976; Professor of Physical Oceanography, 1966–71 and 1978–86, now Emeritus, Deputy Vice-Chancellor, 1982–84, Southampton University; *b* 25 Dec. 1920; *s* of Henry Charnock and Mary Gray McLeod; *m* 1946, Eva Mary Dickinson; one *s* two *d*. *Educ:* Queen Elizabeth's Grammar Sch., Municipal Techn. Coll., Blackburn; Imperial Coll., London. Staff, Nat. Inst. of Oceanography, 1949–58 and 1959–66; Reader in Physical Oceanography, Imperial Coll., 1958–59; Dir, Inst. of Oceanographic Scis (formerly Nat. Inst. of Oceanography), 1971–78. President: Internat. Union of Geodesy and Geophysics, 1971–75; RMetS, 1982–84; Vice-Pres., Scientific Cttee on Oceanic Res., 1980–82 (Sec., 1978–80); Mem., Royal Commn on Environmental Pollution, 1985–. *Publications:* papers in meteorological and oceanographic jls. *Address:* 5 Links View Way, Southampton SO1 7GR. *T:* Southampton (0703) 769629.

CHARTERIS, family name of **Baron Charteris of Amisfield** and of **Earl of Wemyss.**

CHARTERIS OF AMISFIELD, Baron *cr* 1978 (Life Peer), of Amisfield, E Lothian; **Martin Michael Charles Charteris,** GCB 1977 (KCB 1972; CB 1958); GCVO 1976 (KCVO 1962; MVO 1953); QSO 1978; OBE 1946; PC 1972; Hon. RA 1981; Provost of Eton, 1978–91; Chairman of Trustees, National Heritage Memorial Fund, since 1980; *b* 7 Sept. 1913; 2nd *s* of Hugo Francis, Lord Elcho (killed in action, 1916); *g s* of 11th Earl of Wemyss; *m* 1944, Hon. Mary Gay Hobart Margesson, *yr d* of 1st Viscount Margesson, PC, MC; two *s* one *d*. *Educ:* Eton; RMC Sandhurst. Lieut KRRC, 1936; served War of 1939–45; Lieut-Colonel, 1944. Private Secretary to Princess Elizabeth, 1950–52; Asst Private Secretary to the Queen, 1952–72; Private Secretary to the Queen and Keeper of HM's Archives, 1972–77. A Permanent Lord in Waiting to the Queen, 1978–. Director: Claridge's Hotel, 1978–; Connaught Hotel, 1978–; De La Rue Co., 1978–85; Rio Tinto Zinc Corp., 1978–84. Trustee, BM, 1979–89. Hon. DCL Oxon, 1978; Hon. LLD London, 1981. *Recreation:* sculpting. *Address:* Wood Stanway House, Wood Stanway, Glos GL54 5PE. *T:* Stanton (038673) 480. *Club:* White's.
See also Baron Pearson of Rannoch.

CHARTERIS, Leslie; FRSA; author; *b* 12 May 1907; *m* 1st, Pauline Schishkin (divorced, 1937); one *d*; 2nd, Barbara Meyer (divorced, 1941); 3rd, Elizabeth Bryant Borst (divorced, 1951); 4th, Audrey Long. *Educ:* Rossall; Cambridge Univ. Many years of entertaining, but usually unprofitable, travel and adventure; after one or two false starts created character of "The Saint" (trans. into 15 languages besides those of films, radio, television, and the comic strip). *Publications:* Meet the Tiger, 1928; Enter the Saint; The Last Hero; Knight Templar; Featuring the Saint; Alias the Saint; She was a Lady (filmed 1938 as The Saint Strikes Back); The Holy Terror (filmed 1939 as The Saint in London); Getaway; Once More the Saint; The Brighter Buccaneer; The Misfortunes of Mr Teal; Boodle; The Saint Goes On; The Saint in New York (filmed 1938); Saint Overboard, 1936; The Ace of Knaves, 1937; Thieves Picnic, 1937; (trans., with introd.) Juan Belmonte, Killer of Bulls: The Autobiography of a Matador, 1937; Prelude for War, 1938; Follow the Saint, 1938; The Happy Highwayman, 1939; The First Saint Omnibus, 1939; The Saint in Miami, 1941; The Saint Goes West, 1942; The Saint Steps In, 1944; The Saint on Guard, 1945; The Saint Sees it Through, 1946; Call for the Saint, 1948; Saint Errant, 1948; The Second Saint Omnibus, 1952; The Saint on the Spanish Main, 1955; The Saint around the World, 1957; Thanks to the Saint, 1958; Señor Saint, 1959; The Saint to the Rescue, 1961; Trust the Saint, 1962; The Saint in the Sun, 1964; Vendetta for the Saint, 1965 (filmed 1968); The Saint on TV, 1968; The Saint Returns, 1969; The Saint and the Fiction Makers, 1969; The Saint Abroad, 1970; The Saint in Pursuit, 1971; The Saint and the People Importers, 1971; Paleneo, 1972; Saints Alive, 1974; Catch the Saint, 1975; The Saint and the Hapsburg Necklace, 1976; Send for the Saint, 1977; The Saint in Trouble, 1978; The Saint and the Templar Treasure, 1979; Count on the Saint, 1980; The Fantastic Saint, 1982; Salvage for the Saint, 1983; Supervising Editor of the Saint Magazine, 1953–67; Editorial Consultant of the (new) Saint Magazine, 1984–85; columnist, Gourmet Magazine, 1966–68; concurrently has worked as special correspondent and Hollywood scenarist; contributor to leading English and American magazines and newspapers. *Recreations:* eating, drinking, horseracing, loafing. *Address:* 3/4 Great Marlborough Street, W1V 2AR. *Clubs:* Mensa, Yacht Club de Cannes.

CHARVET, Richard Christopher Larkins, RD 1972; JP; Associate Director, Anglo Soviet Shipping Co. Ltd, since 1988; *b* 12 Dec. 1936; *s* of Patrice and late Eleanor Charvet; *m* 1990; two *s* one *d* by a previous marriage. *Educ:* Rugby. MITT, ACIArb; FCIS; FBIM; MIFF. FRSA 1985. National Service, Royal Navy, 1955–57; Mem., London Div., RNR, 1955–. Union Castle Line, 1957–58; Killick Martin & Co. Ltd, Shipbrokers, 1958–81; Vogt and Maguire Ltd, Shipbrokers, 1981–88. Chairman: City Br., St John Ambulance Appeal, 1985–; City Br., RNLI, 1986–. Mem., Court of Common Council for Aldgate Ward, City of London, 1970–76; Alderman, Aldgate Ward, 1976–85; Sheriff, 1983–84. Prime Warden, Worshipful Co. of Shipwrights, 1985–86 (Renter Warden, 1984–85); Master, Guild of World Traders, 1991. JP 1976. CStJ 1989. Hon. JSM, Malaysia, 1974. *Publication:* Peter and Tom in the Lord Mayor's Show, 1982. *Recreations:* gardening, travel, sailing. *Clubs:* United Wards, Aldgate Ward, Lime Street Ward.

CHASE, Robert John; HM Diplomatic Service; Head of Resource Management Department, Foreign and Commonwealth Office, since 1990; *b* 13 March 1943; *s* of late Herbert Chase and of Evelyn Chase; *m* 1966, Gillian Ann Chase (née Shelton); one *s* two *d*. *Educ:* Sevenoaks Sch.; St John's Coll., Oxford. MA (Mod. Hist.). Entered HM Diplomatic Service, 1965; Third, later Second Sec., Rangoon, 1966–69; UN Dept, FCO, 1970–72; First Sec. (Press Attaché), Brasilia, 1972–76; Hd Caribbean Section, Mexico and Caribbean Dept, FCO, 1976–80; on secondment as a manager to Imperial Chemical Industries PLC, 1980–82; Asst Hd S American Dept, FCO, 1982–83; Asst Hd, Maritime, Aviation and Environment Dept, FCO, 1983–84; Counsellor (Commercial), Moscow, 1985–88; Overseas Inspector, FCO, 1988–89. *Recreations:* military history, visiting historic sites, tennis. *Address:* c/o Foreign and Commonwealth Office, King Charles Street, SW1A 2AH. *T:* 071–210 4722; Forest House, Bishops Down Park Road, Tunbridge Wells, Kent. *T:* Tunbridge Wells (0892) 21623.

CHASE, Roger Robert, FIPM; Director of Personnel, BBC, 1989–91; *b* 19 Sept. 1928; *s* of Robert Joseph Chase and Lillian Ada (née Meredith); *m* 1958, Geraldine Joan Whitlamsmith; three *d*. *Educ:* Gosport Grammar Sch. Served RN, 1947–49. Joined BBC, 1944; Engrg Div., 1944–47 and 1949–67; Television Personnel Dept, 1967–74; Head, Central Services Dept, 1974–76; Controller, Personnel, Television, 1976–82; Dep. Dir of Personnel, 1982–89. *Recreation:* sailing. *Address:* Vernons, Vernons Road, Chappel, Colchester, Essex CO6 2AQ. *T:* Colchester (0206) 240143. *Club:* Royal Naval Sailing Association.

CHATAWAY, Rt. Hon. Christopher John, PC 1970; Chairman, Crown Communications Group PLC, since 1987; Chairman, Civil Aviation Authority, since 1991; *b* 31 Jan. 1931; *m* 1st, 1959, Anna Lett (marr. diss. 1975); two *s* one *d*; 2nd, 1976, Carola Walker; two *s*. *Educ:* Sherborne Sch.; Magdalen Coll., Oxford. Hons. Degree, PPE. President OUAC, 1952; rep. Great Britain, Olympic Games, 1952 and 1956; briefly held world 5,000 metres record in 1954. Junior Exec. Arthur Guinness Son & Co., 1953–55; Staff Reporter, Independent Television News, 1955–56; Current Affairs Commentator for BBC Television, 1956–59. Elected for N Lewisham to LCC, 1958–61. MP (C): Lewisham North, 1959–66; Chichester, May 1969–Sept. 1974; PPS to Minister of Power, 1961–62; Joint Parly Under-Secretary of State, Dept of Education and Science,

1962–64; Minister of Posts and Telecommunications, 1970–72; Minister for Industrial Develt, DTI, 1972–74. Chm., London Broadcasting Co., 1981–; Director: British Electric Traction Co., 1974–; RBC Dominion Securities International Ltd (formerly Orion Royal Bank), 1988– (Man. Dir, 1974–80, Vice Chm., 1980–88). Treasurer, Nat. Cttee for Electoral Reform, 1976–84; Chairman: Action Aid (formerly Action in Distress), 1986– (Treas., 1976–86); Groundwork Foundn, 1985–. Alderman, GLC, 1967–70; Leader Educn Cttee, ILEA, 1967–69. Hon. DLitt Loughborough, 1985. Nansen Medal, 1960. *Publication:* (with Philip Goodhart) War Without Weapons, 1968. *Address:* 27 Randolph Crescent, W9.

CHATER, Dr Anthony Philip John; Editor, Morning Star, since 1974; parents both shoe factory workers; *m* 1954, Janice (*née* Smith); three *s. Educ:* Northampton Grammar Sch. for Boys; Queen Mary Coll., London. BSc (1st cl. hons Chem.) 1951, PhD (Phys.Chem.) 1954. Fellow in Biochem., Ottawa Exper. Farm, 1954–56; studied biochem. at Brussels Univ., 1956–57; Teacher, Northampton Techn. High Sch., 1957–59; Teacher, Blyth Grammar Sch., Norwich, 1959–60; Lectr, subseq. Sen. Lectr in Phys. Chem., Luton Coll. of Technology, 1960–69; Head of Press and Publicity of Communist Party, 1969–74; Nat. Chm. of Communist Party, 1967–69. Contested (Com) Luton, Nov. 1963, 1964, 1966, 1970. Mem. Presidential Cttee, World Peace Council, 1969–. *Publications:* Race Relations in Britain, 1966; numerous articles. *Recreations:* walking, swimming, music, camping.

CHATER, Nancy, CBE 1974; Headmistress, Stanley Park Comprehensive School, Liverpool, 1964–75, retired; *b* 18 July 1915; *d* of William John and Ellen Chater. *Educ:* Northampton Sch. for Girls; Girton Coll., Cambridge (Math. Schol., Bell Exhibr, MA); Cambridge Trng Coll. for Women (CertifEd). Asst Mistress, Huddersfield College Grammar Sch. for Boys, 1940–42; Asst Mistress, Fairfield High Sch. for Girls, Manchester, 1942–45; Sen. Maths Mistress, Thistley Hough High Sch., Stoke-on-Trent, 1945–49; Sen. Lectr, Newland Park Trng Coll. for Teachers, 1949–55; Dep. Head, Whitley Abbey Comprehensive Sch., Coventry, 1955–63. *Publications:* contrib. Math. Gazette. *Address:* c/o Priory Comprehensive School, Priory Road, Liverpool L4 2SL. *T:* 051–263 5665. *Clubs:* Soroptimist International, Business and Professional Women's.

CHATFIELD, family name of **Baron Chatfield.**

CHATFIELD, 2nd Baron *cr* 1937, of Ditchling; **Ernle David Lewis Chatfield;** *b* 2 Jan. 1917; *s* of 1st Baron Chatfield, PC, GCB, OM, KCMG, CVO (Admiral of the Fleet Lord Chatfield), and Lillian Emma St John Matthews (*d* 1977); *S* father, 1967; *m* 1969, (Felicia Mary) Elizabeth, *d* of late Dr John Roderick Bulman, Hereford. *Educ:* RNC Dartmouth; Trinity Coll., Cambridge. ADC to Governor-General of Canada, 1940–44. *Heir:* none. *Address:* 535 Island Road, Victoria, BC V8S 2T7, Canada.

CHATFIELD, John Freeman, CBE 1982; DL; Chairman, Association of County Councils, since 1989; Consultant Solicitor in private practice, since 1989; *b* 28 Oct. 1929; *s* of Cecil Freeman Chatfield and Florence Dorothy Chatfield; *m* 1954, Barbara Elizabeth Trickett. *Educ:* Southdown Coll., Eastbourne; Roborough Sch., Eastbourne; Lawrence Sheriff Sch., Rugby; Lewes Grammar Sch.; Law Soc. Sch. (Final, 1951). Solicitor, 1952; Sen. Partner, Hart Reade & Co., Eastbourne, 1976–89. Mem., E Sussex CC (Leader, 1981–85; Chm., 1985–87); Chairman: Sussex Police Authy, 1982–85; Police Cttee, ACC, 1982–85; Official Side, Police Negotiating Bd, 1982–85; Mem., Police Adv. Bd, England and Wales, 1980–85; Vice-Chm., ACC, 1986–89; Chm., UK Local Authorities Internat. Bureau, 1989–; first Chm., Internat. Council for Local Envmt Initiatives, 1990–; Pres., Consultative Council of Local and Regional Authorities in Europe, 1990–; a Vice-Pres., CEMR, 1989–; Leader, UK Delegn, 1989–, Mem., Standing Cttee, CLRAE. DL E Sussex, 1986. *Recreations:* music, theatre. *Address:* Underhill House, East Dean, Eastbourne, E Sussex BN20 0DB. *T:* Eastbourne (0323) 423397.

CHATT, Prof. Joseph, CBE 1978; ScD; FRS 1961; Professor of Chemistry, University of Sussex, 1964–80; now Emeritus; Director, Research Unit of Nitrogen Fixation, ARC, 1963–80 (in Sussex, 1964–80); *b* 6 Nov. 1914; *e s* of Joseph and M. Elsie Chatt; *m* 1947, Ethel, *y d* of Hugh Williams, St Helens, Lancs; one *s* one *d. Educ:* Nelson Sch., Wigton, Cumberland; Emmanuel Coll., Cambridge (PhD 1940; ScD 1956; Hon. Fellow, 1978). Research Chemist, Woolwich Arsenal, 1941–42; Dep. Chief Chemist, later Chief Chemist, Peter Spence & Sons Ltd, Widnes, 1942–46; ICI Research Fellow, Imperial Coll., London, 1946–47; Head of Inorganic Chemistry Dept, Butterwick, later Akers, Research Laboratories, ICI Ltd, 1947–60; Group Manager, Research Dept, Heavy Organic Chemicals Div., ICI Ltd, 1961–62; Prof. of Inorganic Chem., QMC, Univ. of London, 1964. Visiting Professor: Pennsylvania State Univ., 1960; Yale Univ., 1963; Royal Society Leverhulme, Univ. of Rajasthan, India, 1966–67; Univ. of S Carolina, 1968. Royal Society of Chemistry (formerly Chemical Society): Mem. Council, 1952–65, 1972–76; Hon. Sec., 1956–62; Vice-Pres., 1962–65, 1972–74; Pres. Dalton Div., 1972–74; Organometallic Chem. Award, 1970; Pres., Section B, BAAS, 1974–75; Member: Chemical Council, 1958–60; Commn on Nomenclature of Inorganic Chemistry, Internat. Union of Pure and Applied Chemistry, 1959–81, Hon-Sec., 1959–63, Chm., 1976–81; ARC Adv. Cttee on Plants and Soils, 1964–67; Comité de Direction du Laboratoire de Chimie de Coordination, Toulouse, 1974–77; Council, Royal Soc., 1975–77; national and internat. cttees concerned with chemistry, incl. Parly and Scientific Cttee. Founder, Internat. Confs on Coordination Chemistry, 1950. Lectures: Tilden, 1961–62; Liversidge, 1971–72; Debye, Cornell, 1975; Nyholm, 1976–77; Arthur D. Little, MIT, 1977; Julius Steiglitz, Chicago, 1978; Columbia, 1978 (and Chandler Medal); Univ. of Western Ontario, 1978; John Stauffer, S California, 1979; Dwyer Meml Lectr and Medallist, Univ. of NSW, 1980; Sunner Meml Lectr, Univ. of Lund, 1982. Gordon Wigan Prize for Res. in Chem., Cambridge, 1939; Amer. Chem. Soc. Award for dist. service to Inorganic Chemistry, 1971; Chugaev Commem. Dipl. and Medal, Kurnakov Inst. of Gen. and Inorganic Chemistry, Soviet Acad. of Sciences, 1976; Davy Medal of Royal Soc., 1979; Wolf Foundn Prize for Chemistry, 1981; G.W. Wheland Award (lecture, medal and prize), Univ. of Chicago, 1983. Hon. DSc: East Anglia, 1974; Sussex, 1982; Hon. Dr Pierre et Marie Curie, Paris, 1981; Filosofie Doctor *hc* Lund, Sweden, 1986. Sócio corresp., Academia das Ciências de Lisboa, 1978; Hon. Life Mem., NY Acad. of Sciences, 1978; For. Fellow, Indian Nat. Science Acad., 1980; Hon. Fellow, Indian Chem. Soc., 1983; Hon. Mem., Royal Physiographical Soc., Lund, 1984; Hon. For. Mem., Amer. Acad. of Arts and Scis, 1985. *Publications:* scientific papers, mainly in Jl Chem. Soc. *Recreations:* numismatics, art, history, travel. *Address:* 16 Tongdean Road, Hove, East Sussex BN3 6QE. *T:* Brighton (0273) 554377. *Club:* Civil Service.

CHATTEN, Harold Raymond Percy, CB 1975; RCNC; Chief Executive, Royal Dockyards, 1975–79, and Head of Royal Corps of Naval Constructors, Apr.-Sept. 1979, Ministry of Defence. Production Manager, HM Dockyard, Chatham, 1967–70; General Manager, HM Dockyard, Rosyth, Fife, 1970–75. MA Cambridge 1946. *Address:* c/o National Westminster Bank, 39 Milsom Street, Bath.

CHATTERJEE, Dr Satya Saran, OBE 1971; JP; FRCP, FRCPE; Consultant Chest Physician and Physician in Charge, Department of Respiratory Physiology, Wythenshawe Hospital, Manchester, 1959–88; *b* 16 July 1922; *m* 1948, Enid May (*née* Adlington); one *s* two *d. Educ:* India, UK, Sweden and USA. MB, BS; FCCP (USA). Asst Lectr, Dept of Medicine, Albany Med. Coll. Hosp., NY, 1953–54; Med. Registrar, Sen. Registrar, Dept of Thoracic Medicine, Wythenshawe Hosp., Manchester, 1954–59. Mem., NW RHA, 1976–. Chairman: NW Conciliation Cttee, Race Relations Board, 1972–77; Overseas Doctors Assoc., 1975–81 (Pres., 1981–87); Member: Standing Adv. Council on Race Relations, 1977–86; GMC, 1979–; NW Adv. Council, BBC, 1987–; Vice-Pres., Manchester Council for Community Relations, 1974–. President: Rotary Club, Wythenshawe, 1975–76; Indian Assoc., Manchester, 1962–71. *Publications:* research papers in various projects related to cardio/pulmonary disorders. *Address:* March, 20 Macclesfield Road, Wilmslow, Cheshire SK9 2AF. *T:* Wilmslow (0625) 522559.

CHATTO, Beth, VMH 1988; Creator and Managing Director of The Beth Chatto Gardens; *b* 27 June 1923; *d* of William George and Bessie Beatrice Little; *m* 1943, Andrew Edward Chatto; two *d. Educ:* Colchester County High Sch.; Hockerill Training Coll. for Teachers. No formal horticultural educn; parents enthusiastic gardeners; husband's lifelong study of natural associations of plants was original inspiration in use of species plants in more natural groupings; Sir Cedric Morris' knowledge and generosity with many rare plants from his rich collection at Benton End, Suffolk, became basis for gdns at Elmstead Market; began career demonstrating flower arranging; Beth Chatto Gardens, 1960–, Nursery, 1967–; a keen advocate of organic gardening and diet for over 40 yrs. Founder Mem., Colchester Flower Club (2nd Flower Club in England). Lectures throughout UK; lecture tours and talks: USA, 1983, 1984 and 1986; Holland and Germany, 1987; Australia and Toronto, 1989. DUniv Essex, 1988. Lawrence Meml Medal, RHS, 1988. *Publications:* The Dry Garden, 1978; The Damp Garden, 1982; Plant Portraits, 1985; The Beth Chatto Garden Notebook, 1988; The Green Tapestry, 1989 (also USA); articles in Popular Gardening, Englishwoman's Garden, Horticulture, Amer. Jl of Hort., Sunday Telegraph, and Hortus. *Recreations:* family, cooking, entertaining, music, reading—and always creating the garden. *Address:* The Beth Chatto Gardens, Elmstead Market, Colchester, Essex CO7 7DB. *T:* Wivenhoe (020622) 2007.

CHAUDHURI, Prof. Kirti Narayan, PhD; FBA 1990; Vasco da Gama Professor of the History of European Expansion, European University Institute, Florence, since 1991; *b* 8 Sept. 1934; *s* of Nirad C. Chaudhuri, *qv*; *m* 1961, Surang Chaudhuri; one *s. Educ:* privately in India; London Univ. (BA Hons Hist., 1959; PhD 1961). Derby Postgrad. Schol., London Univ., 1959–61; School of Oriental and African Studies, London University: Res. Fellow in Econ. Hist., 1961–63; Lectr in Econ. Hist. of Asia, 1963–74; Reader, 1974–81; Prof. of Econ. Hist. of Asia, 1981–91; Chairman: S Asia Area Studies Centre, 1982–85; History Exam. Bd, 1982–87. *Publications:* The English East India Company: the study of an early joint-stock company 1600–1640, 1965; The Economic Development of India under the East India Company 1814–58: a selection of contemporary writings, 1971; The Trading World of Asia and the English East India Company 1660–1760, 1978; Trade and Civilisation in the Indian Ocean: an economic history from the rise of Islam to 1750, 1985; Asia before Europe: the economy and civilisation in the Indian Ocean from the rise of Islam to 1750, 1990; contribs to Econ. Hist. Rev., Eng. Histl Rev., Jl of European Econ. Hist., Jl of RAS, Modern Asian Studies, TLS. *Recreations:* mountain walking, sailing, exploration, collecting modern prints and vintage watches, photography, wine tasting. *Address:* Istituto Universitario Europeo, CP No 2330, 1–50100 Firenze, Italy. *Club:* Athenæum.

CHAUDHURI, Nirad Chandra, FRSL; FRAS; author and broadcaster; *b* Bengal, 23 Nov. 1897; *s* of Upendra Narayan Chaudhuri and Sushila, of Banagram, Bengal; *m* 1932, Amiya Dhar; three *s. Educ:* Calcutta University. BA (Hons) 1918. Resident in UK, 1970–. University Lectures include: Chicago; Texas Univ. at Austin; Pennsylvania; Potsdam; Boston; Oxford; Canadian Univs. DUniv Stirling 1978. Broadcasting on radio and TV; television appearances include: A Brown Man in Search of Civilization (feature on life), 1972; Everyman, 1983; Springing Tiger, 1984. *Publications:* The Autobiography of an unknown Indian, 1951; A Passage to England, 1959; The Continent of Circe, 1965 (Duff Cooper Meml Prize, 1966); The Intellectual in India, 1967; Woman in Bengali Life, 1967 (in Bengali language); To Live or not to Live, 1970; Scholar Extraordinary: life of F. Max Muller, 1974; Clive of India, 1975; Culture in the Vanity Bag, 1976; Hinduism, 1979, Italian trans. 1980, Japanese trans. 1985; Thy Hand, Great Anarch!, 1987; contribs to The Times, TLS, The Daily Telegraph, Guardian, London Magazine, Encounter, The New English Review, Spectator, The Atlantic Monthly (USA), Pacific Affairs (USA), major Indian newspapers and magazines. *Recreations:* music, gardening, walks. *Address:* 20 Lathbury Road, Oxford OX2 7AU. *T:* Oxford (0865) 57683.
See also K. N. Chaudhuri.

CHAUVIRÉ, Yvette, Commandeur de la Légion d'Honneur, 1988 (Officier, 1974); Commandeur des Arts et des Lettres, 1975; Commandeur, Ordre National du Mérite, 1981 (Officier, 1972); ballerina assoluta, since 1950; *b* Paris, 22 April 1917. *Educ:* Ecole de la Danse de l'Opéra, Paris. Paris Opera Ballet, 1931; first major rôles in David Triomphant and Les Créatures de Prométhée; Danseuse étoile 1942; danced Istar, 1941; Monte Carlo Opera Ballet, 1946–47; returned to Paris Opera Ballet, 1947–49. Has appeared at Covent Garden, London; also danced in the USA, and in cities of Rome, Moscow, Leningrad, Berlin, Buenos Aires, Johannesburg, Milan, etc; official tours: USA 1948; USSR 1958, 1966, 1969; Canada 1967; Australia. Leading rôles in following ballets: Les Mirages, Lac des Cygnes, Sleeping Beauty, Giselle, Roméo et Juliette, Suite en Blanc, Le Cygne (St Saens), La Dame aux Camélias, etc; acting rôle, Reine Léda, Amphitryon 38, Paris, 1976–77; La Comtessa de Doris in Raymonda, Paris, 1983. Choreographer: La Péri, Roméo et Juliette, Le Cygne; farewell performances: Paris Opera, Giselle, Nov. 1972, Petrouchka and The Swan, Dec. 1972; Berlin Opera, Giselle, 1973; Director, Giselle (150th anniv. celebration), Marseille Opera Ballet, 1991. Artistic and Tech. Adviser, Paris Opera, 1963–72, teacher of dance for style and perfection, 1970–; Artistic Director: Acad. Internat. de la Danse, Paris, 1972–76; Acad. ARIMA, Kyoto, Japan, 1981. *Films:* La Mort du Cygne, 1937 (Paris); Carrousel Napolitain, 1953 (Rome); Dominique Delouche présente un grand portrait sur Yvette Chauviré, une Etoile pour l'exemple, 1988. *Publication:* Je suis Ballerine. *Recreations:* painting and drawing, collections of swans. *Address:* 21 Place du Commerce, Paris 75015, France.

CHAVASSE, Christopher Patrick Grant, MA; Clerk to the Worshipful Company of Grocers, 1981–88; *b* 14 March 1928; *s* of late Grant Chavasse and of Maureen Shingler (*née* Whalley); *m* 1955, Audrey Mary Leonard; two *s* one *d. Educ:* Bedford Sch.; Clare Coll., Cambridge (Exhibitioner). Commissioned The Rifle Brigade, 1947; served in Palestine (despatches), 1948; RAFVR 1949. Admitted Solicitor, 1955; Partner: Jacobs & Greenwood, 1960; Woodham Smith, 1970; President, Holborn Law Soc., 1977–78. Trustee, NADFAS, 1983–90; Chm., NADFAS Tours Ltd, 1986–. Vice-Pres. Chiltern Decorative and Fine Art Soc., 1986–. Hon. Steward of Westminster Abbey, 1950–; Treasurer, St Mary-le-Bow Church, 1981–88. Secretary: Governing Body of Oundle and Laxton Schs, 1981–88; The Grocers' Charity, 1981–88. Mem. Ct, Corp. of Sons of the Clergy, 1985–. *Publications:* Conveyancing Costs, 1971; Non-Contentious Costs, 1975; The Discretionary Items in Contentious Costs, 1980; various articles in Law Society's Gazette, New Law Jl, Solicitors Jl, and others. *Address:* Duncannon House, Stoke Gabriel,

Totnes, S Devon TQ9 6QY. *T:* Stoke Gabriel (080428) 291. *Clubs:* Royal Air Force; Leander.

CHAYTOR, Sir George Reginald, 8th Bt *cr* 1831; *b* 28 Oct. 1912; *s* of William Richard Carter Chaytor (*d* 1973) (*g s* of 2nd Bt) and Anna Laura (*d* 1947), *d* of George Fawcett; *S* cousin, Sir William Henry Clervaux Chaytor, 7th Bt, 1976. *Heir: cousin* (Herbert) Gordon Chaytor [*b* 15 June 1922; *m* 1947, Mary Alice, *d* of Thomas Craven; three *s*]. *Address:* 46044 Bonny Avenue, Chilliwack, BC V2P 3H6, Canada.

CHEADLE, Sir Eric (Wallers), Kt 1978; CBE 1973; DL; Deputy Managing Director, International Thomson Organisation Ltd, 1959–74; retired 1974 after 50 years service with the same company (Hultons/Allied Newspapers/Kemsleys/The Thomson Organisation); Director, Thomson International Press Consultancy Ltd; *b* 14 May 1908; *s* of Edgar and Nellie Cheadle; *m* 1938, Pamela, *d* of Alfred and Charlotte Hulme; two *s*. *Educ:* Farnworth Grammar Sch. Editorial Staff, Evening Chronicle and Daily Dispatch, Manchester, 1924–30; Publicity Manager, Allied Newspapers Ltd, 1931–37; Publicity Manager-in-Chief, Allied Newspapers Group, 1938; Organiser, War Fund for the Services, 1939. Served War, RAFVR, Sqdn Ldr, 1941–46. Dir and Gen. Manager, Kemsley Newspapers Ltd, 1947–53. Member: Council, Newspaper Publishers Assoc., 1947–74; Council, Newspaper Soc., 1959–78 (Pres., 1970–71; Chm., Editorial Cttee, 1971–78; Mem., Appeal Cttee, 1979–); Council, NEDC for Printing and Publishing Industry; Jt Bd for Nat. Newspaper Industry, 1965–67; Bd, FIEJ/INCA (Fédération Internationale des Editeurs de Journaux et Publications), 1972–76; Caxton Quincentenary Commem. Cttee, 1976; UK Newsprint Users' Cttee (Founder Mem.); Science Mus. Adv. Cttee (Printing); Chm., Jt Cttee, Newspaper and Periodicals Publishers and Distributors, 1979–85; Pres., Manchester Publicity Assoc., 1972–74 (former Hon. Sec.; Gold Medal, 1973). Member: London Adv. Bd, Nat. and Provincial Building Soc.; Council, Imperial Soc. of Kts Bachelor, 1979–. Pres., Printers' Charitable Corp., 1973–74 (Life Vice-Pres., 1975, Chm. of Council, 1975–81, Trustee, 1981–); Member: Council, Chest, Heart and Stroke Assoc., 1981– (Chm., Appeal Adv. Cttee); Appeal Council, Coll. of Arms Quincentenary Appeal, 1982; Special Cttee, Herts Isotope Cancer Scanner Appeal, 1982–84; Children's Assessment Clinic Appeal, 1984–86; St Albans City Hosp. Rehabilitation Unit Appeal, 1986–88; Cttee, St Bride's Appeal for Restoration and Develt, 1987–90; Chairman: Nat. Stroke Campaign, 1986–88; St Albans Women Against Cancer Appeal, 1988–89; Trustees and Management Group, St Albans Cathedral Trust; Soc. of St Michaels; Vice Chm., Shrine of St Alban Restoration Appeal, 1990–; Vice-Pres., NW Herts Macmillan Cancer Centre Appeal; Trustee, Herts Groundwork Trust, 1986–; Dir, Herts Building Preservation Trust Ltd, 1981–84; Mem., Ver Valley Soc. Hon. Life Member: Friends of St Albans City Hosp., 1984; Independent Adoption Soc., 1978; Hon. Chm., PS Tattershall Castle (Victoria Embankment) Trust. President: Assoc. of Lancastrians in London, 1959 and 1973–74; Herts Br., E-SU, 1989–. Hon. Lay Canon, Cathedral and Abbey Church of St Alban, 1989. DL Hertford, 1985. Editor, Chivalry Newspaper, 1986–. *Publication:* (ed) The Roll of Knights Bachelor, 1981. *Recreations:* watching cricket, talking newspapers. *Address:* The Old Church House, 172 Fishpool Street, St Albans, Herts AL3 4SB. *T:* St Albans (0727) 59639. *Clubs:* Wig and Pen, Press, Variety, MCC, Porters Park Golf (Captain, 1974–75).

CHECKETTS, Sir David (John), KCVO 1979 (CVO 1969; MVO 1966); Squadron Leader, retired; an Extra Equerry to the Prince of Wales, since 1979; *b* 23 Aug. 1930; 3rd *s* of late Reginald Ernest George Checketts and late Frances Mary Checketts; *m* 1958, Rachel Leila Warren Herrick; one *s* three *d*. Flying Training, Bulawayo, Rhodesia, 1948–50; 14 Sqdn, Germany, 1950–54; Instructor, Fighter Weapons Sch., 1954–57; Air ADC to C-in-C Malta, 1958–59; 3 Sqdn, Germany, 1960–61; Equerry to Duke of Edinburgh, 1961–66, to the Prince of Wales, 1967–70; Private Sec. to the Prince of Wales, 1970–79. Director: Brieftag Ltd; Global Print Air Ltd; Global Airline Printing Ltd; Samson Press Ltd; Seeatic Marine Ltd; Global Money Placement. Chairman: Rainbow Boats Trust; Wilderness Foundn. *Recreation:* ornithology. *Address:* Church Cottage, Winkfield, Windsor, Berks. *T:* Winkfield Row (0344) 882289. *Club:* Whitefriars.

CHECKETTS, Guy Tresham, CBE 1982; Deputy Chairman and Managing Director, Hawker Siddeley International, 1975–90, retired; *b* 11 May 1927; *s* of John Albert and Norah Maud Checketts; *m* 1957, Valerie Cynthia Stanley; four *s*. *Educ:* Warwick Sch.; Birmingham Univ. BScEng Hons; CEng, MIEE. British Thompson Houston Co., Rugby, 1948–51; Brush Group, 1951–57; Hawker Siddeley International, 1957–90. Chm., SE Asia Trade Adv. Gp, 1979–83; Mem., BOTB, 1981–84. *Recreation:* sailing. *Club:* Royal Over-Seas League.

CHECKLAND, Michael; Director-General, BBC, since 1987; *b* 13 March 1936; *s* of Leslie and Ivy Florence Checkland; *m* 1st, 1960–83; two *s* one *d*; 2nd, 1987, Sue Zetter. *Educ:* King Edward's Grammar Sch., Fiveways, Birmingham; Wadham Coll., Oxford (BA Modern History; Hon. Fellow, 1989). FCMA. Accountant: Parkinson Cowan Ltd, 1959–62; Thorn Electronics Ltd, 1962–64; BBC: Senior Cost Accountant, 1964; Head of Central Finance Unit, 1967; Chief Accountant, Central Finance Services, 1969; Chief Accountant, Television, 1971; Controller, Finance, 1976; Controller, Planning and Resource Management, Television, 1977; Director of Resources, Television, 1982; Dep. Dir-Gen., 1985; Director: BBC Enterprises, 1979– (Chm., 1986–87); Visnews, 1980–85. Vice-Pres., 1985–, Fellow 1987–, RTS; Pres., Commonwealth Broadcasting Assoc., 1987–88; Vice-Pres., EBU, 1991–. *Recreations:* sport, music, travel. *Address:* BBC, Broadcasting House, W1A 1AA. *T:* 071–580 4486.

CHEDLOW, Barry William, QC 1969; a Recorder of the Crown Court, since 1974; Member, Criminal Injuries Compensation Board, since 1976; *b* Macclesfield, 8 Oct. 1921; *m* Anne Sheldon, BA; one *s* one *d*. *Educ:* Burnage High Sch.; Manchester Univ. Served RAF, 1941–46: USAAF, Flying Instructor, 1942; Flt-Lt 1943. Called to Bar, Middle Temple, 1947, Bencher, 1976; Prizeman in Law of Evidence. Practises in London, Midland and Oxford Circuit. *Publications:* author and editor of various legal text-books. *Recreations:* flying (private pilot's licence, singles, twins, helicopters), languages, sailing. *Address:* 12 King's Bench Walk, Temple, EC4. *T:* 071–583 0811; Little Kimblewick Farm, Finch Lane, Amersham, Bucks. *T:* Little Chalfont (0494) 762156.

CHEESEMAN, Prof. Ian Clifford, PhD; ARCS; CEng, FRAeS; Professor of Helicopter Engineering, University of Southampton, 1970–82, now Emeritus and part time; consultant in aeronautical, acoustic and general engineering matters; *b* 12 June 1926; *s* of Richard Charles Cheeseman and Emily Ethel Clifford; *m* 1957, Margaret Edith Pither; one *s* two *d*. *Educ:* Andover Grammar Sch.; Imperial Coll. of Science and Technology. Vickers Supermarine Ltd, 1951–53; Aeroplane and Armament Estab., 1953–56; Atomic Weapons Res. Estab., 1956–58; Nat. Gas Turbine Estab., 1958–70. Res. Dir, 1983–87, Dir and Consultant, 1987–88, Stewart Hughes Ltd, Southampton. Pres., Airship Assoc., 1986–. *Publications:* contribs to Jl RAeS, Jl CIT, Jl Sound and Vibration, Procs Phys. Soc. 'A', Vertica. *Recreations:* dog breeding, gardening, photography, historical research. *Address:* Abbey View, Tarrant Keynston, Blandford Forum, Dorset DT11 9JE. *T:* Blandford (0258) 56877.

CHEETHAM, Anthony John Valerian; Chairman and Chief Executive, Random Century Group, since 1989; *b* 12 April 1943; *s* of Sir Nicolas Cheetham, *qv*; *m* 1st, 1969, Julia Rollason (marr. diss.); two *s* one *d*; 2nd, 1979, Rosemary de Courcy; two *d*. *Educ:* Eton Coll.; Balliol Coll., Oxford (BA Hons Modern History). Editorial Dir, Sphere Books, 1968; Managing Director: Futura Publications, 1973; Macdonald Futura, 1979; Chm., Century Publishing, 1982–85; Man. Dir, Century Hutchinson, 1985. *Publication:* Richard III, 1972. *Recreations:* walking, tennis, gardening. *Address:* 20 Grove Park, SE5 8LH. *T:* 071–733 8204.

CHEETHAM, Prof. Anthony Kevin, FRSC; Professor of Materials, University of California, Santa Barbara, since 1991; Professor of Solid State Chemistry, Royal Institution, since 1986; Emeritus Student, Christ Church, Oxford, since 1991; *b* 16 Nov. 1946; *s* of Norman James Cheetham and Lilian Cheetham; *m* 1984, Janet Clare (*née* Stockwell); one *s* one *d*, and one *s* one *d* from a previous marriage. *Educ:* Stockport Grammar Sch.; St Catherine's Coll., Oxford (Hon. Scholar); Wadham Coll., Oxford (Sen. Scholar). BA (Chem.) 1968; DPhil 1971. University of Oxford: Cephalosporin Fellow, Lincoln Coll., 1971–74; Lectr in Inorganic Chem., St Hilda's Coll., 1971–85; Lectr in Chemical Crystallography, 1974–90; Tutor in Inorganic Chem., Christ Church, 1974–91; Reader in Inorganic Materials, 1990–91. Visiting Professor: Arizona State Univ., 1977; Univ. of California, Berkeley, 1979; Vis. Foreign Scientist, Amer. Chem. Soc., 1981. Mem. Scientific Council, Institut Laue-Langevin, Grenoble, 1988–90. Dir, Gen. Funds Investment Trust plc, 1984–87. Corday-Morgan Medal and Prize, RSC, 1982; Solid State Chemistry Award, RSC, 1988. *Publications:* Inorganic Solids: techniques (with P. Day), 1986; contribs to sci. jls. *Recreations:* cricket, stock market. *Address:* 1695 East Valley Road, Montecito, Calif 93108, USA.

CHEETHAM, Francis William, OBE 1979; FMA; Director, Norfolk Museums Service, 1974–90; *b* 5 Feb. 1928; *s* of Francis Cheetham and Doris Elizabeth Jones; *m* 1954, Monica Fairhurst; three *s* one *d*. *Educ:* King Edward VII Sch., Sheffield; Univ. of Sheffield (MA). Dep. Art Dir and Curator, Castle Museum, Nottingham, 1960–63; Dir, City of Norwich Museums, 1963–74. Winston Churchill Fellow, 1967. Member: Management Cttee, Norfolk and Norwich Triennial Fest., 1966–89; Crafts Council, 1978–81; Management Cttee, Eastern Arts Assoc., 1978–79, 1987–89; Bd, Norwich Puppet Theatre, 1981–87; Founder Mem., National Heritage, 1970; Chairman: Norfolk and Norwich Film Theatre, 1968–70; Norfolk Contemporary Crafts Soc., 1972–85 (Life Pres., 1985). Museums Association: AMA 1959; FMA 1966; Hon. Treasurer, 1970–73; Vice-Pres., 1977–78, 1979–80; Pres., 1978–79; Chm., Soc. of County Museum Dirs, 1974–77; Museum Advr to ACC, 1976–84. Member: Exec. Bd, ICOM (UK), 1981–84; Bd, Radio Broadland (ILR Station), 1983–. FRSA 1986. *Publications:* Medieval English Alabaster Carvings in the Castle Museum, Nottingham, 1962, revd edn 1973; English Medieval Alabasters, 1984; contrib. Jl of Museums Assoc. *Recreations:* hill-walking, listening to music, especially early and baroque. *Address:* 25 St Andrew's Avenue, Thorpe St Andrew, Norwich NR7 0RG. *T:* Norwich (0603) 34091.

CHEETHAM, John Frederick Thomas, CB 1978; Secretary, Exchequer and Audit Department, 1975–79; *b* 27 March 1919; *s* of late James Oldham Cheetham, MA, BCom; *m* 1943, Yvonne Marie Smith; one *s* one *d*. *Educ:* Penarth Grammar Sch.; Univ. of Wales. Entered Exchequer and Audit Dept, 1938; War Service, Royal Artillery, 1939–46; Office of Parly Comr for Administration, 1966–69; Dep. Sec., Exchequer and Audit Dept, 1973–74. *Recreations:* tennis, food and wine. *Address:* 70 Chatsworth Road, Croydon, Surrey CR0 1HB. *T:* 081–688 3740. *Club:* MCC.

CHEETHAM, Juliet; Professor and Director, Social Work Research Centre, Stirling University, since 1986; *b* 12 Oct. 1939; *d* of Harold Neville Blair and Isabel (*née* Sanders); *m* 1965, Christopher Paul Cheetham; one *s* two *d*. *Educ:* St Andrews Univ. (MA); Oxford Univ. (Dip. in Social and Admin. Studies). Qual. social worker. Probation Officer, Inner London, 1960–65; Lectr in Applied Social Studies, and Fellow of Green Coll., Oxford Univ., 1965–85. Member: Cttee of Enquiry into Immigration and Youth Service, 1966–68; Cttee of Enquiry into Working of Abortion Act, 1971–74; NI Standing Adv. Commn on Human Rights, 1974–77; Central Council for Educn and Trng in Social Work, 1973–89; Commn for Racial Equality, 1977–84; Social Security Adv. Cttee, 1983–; CNAA Social Scis Cttee, 1989–. *Publications:* Social Work with Immigrants, 1972; Unwanted Pregnancy and Counselling, 1977; Social Work and Ethnicity, 1982; Social Work with Black Children and their Families, 1986; contrib. collected papers and prof. jls. *Recreation:* canal boats. *Address:* 34 Danube Street, Edinburgh EH4 1NT. *T:* 031–343 1108; Social Work Research Centre, Department of Sociology, University of Stirling, Stirling FK9 4LA. *T:* Stirling (0786) 67724.

CHEETHAM, Sir Nicolas (John Alexander), KCMG 1964 (CMG 1953); *b* 8 Oct. 1910; *s* of late Sir Milne Cheetham, KCMG, and late Mrs Nigel Law, CBE, DStJ; *m* 1st, 1937, Jean Evison Corfe (marr. diss. 1960); two *s*; 2nd, 1960, Lady Mabel Brooke (*née* Jocelyn). *Educ:* Eton College; Christ Church, Oxford. Entered HM Diplomatic Service, 1934; served in Foreign Office and at Athens, Buenos Aires, Mexico City and Vienna; UK Deputy Permanent Representative on North Atlantic Council, 1954–59; HM Minister to Hungary, 1959–61; Assistant Under-Secretary, Foreign Office, 1961–64; Ambassador to Mexico, 1964–68. *Publications:* A History of Mexico, 1970; New Spain, 1974; Mediaeval Greece, 1981; Keepers of the Keys: the Pope in history, 1982. *Address:* 50 Cadogan Square, SW1X 0JW. *T:* 071–589 5624. *Club:* Travellers'.

See also A. J. V. Cheetham.

CHEEVERS, William Harold; Director of Engineering, Granada Television, 1970–73, retired; *b* 20 June 1918; *m* 1964, Shirley Cheevers; one *s*. *Educ:* Christ's Coll., London. Engineer, BBC Television, 1938–39. War Service, Army, PoW, 1941–45. Sen. Engr, BBC Television, 1946–54; Planning Engr, Radio-Corp. of America, in USA and Canada, 1954–55; Head of Engineering, Associated Rediffusion, 1955–60; Gen. Manager, Westward Television, Jt Man. Dir, 1963–67, Man. Dir, 1967–70; Dir, ITN News, 1967–70, and of IT Publications; also Director: Keith Prowse, 1963–70; Direct Line Services, 1964–87; Prowest, 1967–70; Penwell Ltd, 1971–88. Chm., British Regional Television Assoc., 1968–69. Fellow British Kinematograph Soc.; MInstD; MBIM; AssIEE. *Publications:* articles for most TV Jls, and Symposiums, at home and abroad. *Recreations:* boating, golf, reading. *Address:* 52 Preston Down Road, Paignton, Devon TQ3 1DU. *T:* Paignton (0803) 524455. *Club:* Royal Western Yacht Club of England (Plymouth).

CHEKE, Dudley John, CMG 1961; MA Cantab; HM Diplomatic Service, retired; *b* 14 June 1912; *s* of late Thomas William Cheke, FRIC; *m* 1944, Yvonne de Méric (*d* 1991), *d* of late Rear-Adm. M. J. C. de Méric, MVO; two *s*. *Educ:* St Christopher's, Letchworth; Emmanuel Coll., Cambridge. Entered HM Consular Service, 1934; served in Japan, Manchuria, Korea, 1935–41; served 1942–44, in East Africa and Ceylon; Foreign Office, 1945–49 and 1958–61; UK delegation to OEEC, Paris, 1949–50; Commissioner-Gen.'s Office, Singapore, 1950–51; idc 1952; HM Consul-Gen., Frankfurt-am-Main, 1953–55, Osaka-Kobe, 1956–58; Mem. of Foreign Service Corps of Inspectors, 1961–63; Minister, Tokyo, 1963–67; Ambassador to the Ivory Coast, Niger and Upper Volta, 1967–70.

Chm., Japan Soc., 1979–82. *Recreations:* theatre, birdwatching, gardening. *Address:* Honey Farm, Bramley, Basingstoke, Hants RG26 5DE. *Clubs:* United Oxford & Cambridge University; Union Society (Cambridge).

CHELMER, Baron *cr* 1963 (Life Peer), of Margaretting; **Eric Cyril Boyd Edwards,** Kt 1954; MC 1944; TD; JP; DL; *b* 9 Oct. 1914; *s* of Col C. E. Edwards, DSO, MC, TD, DL, JP, and Mrs J. Edwards; *m* 1939, Enid, *d* of F. W. Harvey; one *s*. *Educ:* Felsted Sch. Solicitor, 1937; LLB (London) 1937. Served Essex Yeomanry, 1940–54 (MC), Lieut-Col Commanding, 1945–46. Chm., Provident Financial Gp, 1976–83 (Dir, 1970–83); Chm. and Dir, Greycoat Group, 1977–85; Director: NEM Group, 1970–86; NEL Assurance, 1970–86. National Union of Conservative Associations: Chm., 1956; Pres., 1967; Chm., Review Cttee, 1970–73; Chm., Nat. Exec. Cttee of Conservative and Unionist Assoc., 1957–65; Conservative Party: Jt Treas., 1965–77; Mem. Adv. Cttee on Policy, 1956–85. Member: Political Cttee, Carlton Club, 1961; Cttee of Musicians' Benevolent Fund; Ralph Vaughan Williams Trust. JP Essex, 1950; DL Essex 1971. *Recreation:* "improving". *Address:* Peacocks, Margaretting, Essex CM4 9HY. *Clubs:* Carlton, Buck's, Royal Ocean Racing.

See also D. Edwards, J. T. Edwards.

CHELMSFORD, 3rd Viscount *cr* 1921, of Chelmsford; **Frederic Jan Thesiger;** Baron Chelmsford, 1858; Lloyd's Insurance Broker; Director, Willis Corroon (formerly Willis Faber) plc; *b* 7 March 1931; *s* of 2nd Viscount Chelmsford and of Gilian (*d* 1978), *d* of late Arthur Nevile Lubbock; *S* father, 1970; *m* 1958, Clare Rendle, *d* of Dr G. R. Rolston, Haslemere; one *s* one *d*. Formerly Lieut, Inns of Court Regt. *Heir:* *s* Hon. Frederic Corin Piers Thesiger, *b* 6 March 1962. *Address:* 26 Ormonde Gate, SW3; Hazelbridge Court, Chiddingfold, Surrey.

CHELMSFORD, Bishop of, since 1986; **Rt. Rev. John Waine;** Clerk of the Closet to the Queen, since 1989; *b* 20 June 1930; *s* of late William and Ellen Waine; *m* 1957, Patricia Zena Haikney; three *s*. *Educ:* Prescot Grammar Sch.; Manchester Univ. (BA); Ridley Hall, Cambridge. Deacon 1955, Priest 1956; Curate of St Mary, West Derby, 1955–58; Curate in Charge of All Saints, Sutton, 1958–60; Vicar of Ditton, 1960–64; Vicar of Holy Trinity, Southport, 1964–69; Rector of Kirkby, 1969–75; Bishop Suffragan of Stafford, 1975–78; Bishop of St Edmundsbury and Ipswich, 1978–86. ChStJ 1983. *Recreations:* music, gardening. *Address:* Bishopscourt, Margaretting, Ingatestone, Essex CM4 0HD. *Club:* Royal Air Force.

CHELMSFORD, Provost of; *see* Moses, Very Rev. J. H.

CHELSEA, Viscount; Charles Gerald John Cadogan; *b* 24 March 1937; *o s* of 7th Earl Cadogan, *qv*; *m* 1st, 1963, Lady Philippa Wallop (*d* 1984), *d* of 9th Earl of Portsmouth; two *s* one *d*; 2nd, 1989, Jennifer Jane Greig Rae, *d* of J. E. K. Rae and Mrs S. Z. de Ferranti. *Educ:* Eton. Chm., Leukaemia Research Fund, 1985–. Freeman, City of London, 1979; Liveryman, GAPAN. *Heir:* *s* Hon. Edward Charles Cadogan, *b* 10 May 1966. *Address:* 7 Smith Street, SW3 4EE. *T:* 071–730 2465; Marndhill, Ardington, near Wantage, Oxon OX12 8PN. *T:* Abingdon (0235) 833273. *Clubs:* White's, Royal Automobile.

CHELTENHAM, Archdeacon of; *see* Lewis, Ven. J. A.

CHELTON, Captain Lewis William Leonard, RN; Secretary, Engineering Council, since 1987; *b* 19 Dec. 1934; *s* of Lewis Walter Chelton and Doris May Chelton (*née* Gamblin); *m* 1957, Daphne Joan Landon; three *s*. *Educ:* Royal Naval College, Dartmouth. Called to the Bar, Inner Temple, 1966. Entered RN as Cadet, 1951; served in ships and shore estabts, home and abroad; Fleet Supply Officer, 1979–81; Captain, 1981; Chief Naval Judge Advocate, 1982–84; retired (voluntarily), 1987. *Recreations:* shooting, gardening, country life. *Address:* Palmers Green House, Hatch Beauchamp, near Taunton, Som TA3 6AE. *T:* Hatch Beauchamp (0823) 480221. *Club:* Farmers'.

CHEN Zhaoyuan; Ambassador Extraordinary and Plenipotentiary of the People's Republic of China to the Court of St James's, 1983–85; *b* 14 Nov. 1918; *m* 1946, Ma Lansen; two *s* one *d*. *Educ:* university. Counsellor, Sweden, 1952–58; Dep. Head, Internat. Orgns and Confs Dept, Foreign Ministry, 1958–61; Counsellor, India, 1961–70; Ambassador to: Burma, 1971–73; Spain, 1973–76; India, 1976–79; Head, Second Dept of Asian Affairs, 1980–82. *Recreations:* reading, football, tennis. *Address:* c/o Foreign Ministry, Beijing, People's Republic of China.

CHENERY, Peter James; Secretary, British Council, since 1990; *b* 24 Oct. 1946; *s* of Dudley James Chenery and Brenda Dorothy (*née* Redford); *m* 1979, Alice Blanche Faulder; three *d*. *Educ:* Forest Sch.; Christ Church, Oxford (MA). Teacher, Ghana Teaching Service, 1967–70; joined British Council, 1970: Amman, 1971–73; Middle East Dept, 1973–76; Riyadh, 1977; Freetown, 1978–80; Jedda, 1981–84; Sana'a, 1984–88; Munich, 1988–90. *Recreations:* amusing conversation, beers of the world, early English coins. *Address:* The British Council, 10 Spring Gardens, SW1A 2BN. *T:* 071–930 8466. *Club:* Leander.

CHENEY, Richard Bruce; Secretary of Defense, USA, since 1989; *b* 30 Jan. 1941; *s* of Richard H. Cheney and Marjorie Dickey Cheney; *m* 1964, Lynne Ann Vincent; two *d*. *Educ:* Casper Elementary Sch.; National County High Sch.; Univ. of Wyoming (BA 1965; MA 1966); Univ. of Wisconsin. Public service, Wyoming, 1965–69; Federal service, 1969–73; Vice-Pres., Bradley Woods, 1973–74; Dep. Asst to Pres. Ford, 1974–75; Asst to Pres. Ford and White House Chief of Staff, 1975–77; Mem. (Republican) for Wyoming House of Representatives, 1978–89; Chm., Repub. Policy Cttee, 1981, Repub. House Conf., 1987; Repub. House Whip, 1988; Mem., Cttees on Interior and Insular Affairs, Intelligence, Iran Arms Deals. *Publication:* (with Lynne V. Cheney) Kings of the Hill, 1983. *Recreation:* tennis. *Address:* The Pentagon, Washington, DC 20301, USA. *T:* 202/695–5261.

CHERENKOV, Prof. Pavel Alexeevich; Soviet physicist; Member of the Institute of Physics, Academy of Sciences of the USSR; *b* 27 July 1904. *Educ:* Voronezh State Univ., Voronezh, USSR. Discovered the Cherenkov Effect, 1934. Corresp. Mem., 1964–70, Academician, 1970–, USSR Acad. of Scis. Awarded Stalin Prize, 1946; Nobel Prize for Physics (joint), 1958. *Address:* Academy of Sciences of the USSR, Leninsky Prospekt 14, Moscow V-71, USSR.

CHERKASSKY, Shura; pianist; *b* 7 Oct. 1911; *s* of late Isaac and Lydia Cherkassky; *m* 1946, Genia Ganz (marr. diss. 1948). *Educ:* Curtis Institute of Music, Pa, USA (diploma). Plays with the principal orchestras and conductors of the world and in all the major series and festivals in Asia, America, Australia and Europe. Has made numerous recordings. *Address:* c/o Artist Management International, 12/13 Richmond Buildings, W1V 5AF.

CHERMAYEFF, Serge, FRIBA, FRSA; architect; author; abstract painter; *b* 8 Oct. 1900; *s* of Ivan and Rosalie Issakovitch; changed surname by deed poll to Chermayeff and adopted British nationality, 1927; *m* 1928, Barbara Maitland May; two *s*. *Educ:* Harrow Sch. Journalist, 1918–22; studied architecture, 1922–25; principal work in England, studios for BBC; Modern Exhibitions; Gilbey's Offices; ICI Laboratories; in Partnership: Bexhill Pavilion. Professor, Brooklyn Coll., 1942–46; Pres. and Dir, Inst. of Design, Chicago, 1946–51; Prof., Harvard Univ., 1953–62; Prof., Yale Univ., 1962–71, now Emeritus. Hon. Fellow, Assoc. of Columbian Architects. Hon. Dr of Fine Art, Washington Univ., 1964; Hon. Dr of Humanities, Ohio State Univ., 1980. Gold Medal, Royal Architectural Inst., Canada, 1974; AIA and Assoc. of Collegiate Schs 1980 Award for excellence in educn; Misha Black Meml Medal for significant contribn to design educn, SIAD, 1980; Gold Medal, NY State Univ. at Buffalo, 1982. *Publications:* Art and Architectural Criticism; ARP, 1939; Community and Privacy, 1963; Shape of Community, 1970; Design and the Public Good (Collected Works), 1982. *Address:* Box 1472, Wellfleet, Mass 02667, USA.

CHERMONT, Jayme Sloan, KCVO (Hon.) 1968; Brazilian Ambassador to the Court of St James's, 1966–68, retired; *b* 5 April 1903; *s* of Ambassador E. L. Chermont and Mrs Helen Mary Chermont; *m* 1928, Zaïde Alvim de Mello Franco Chermont (decd); no *c*. *Educ:* Law Sch., Rio de Janeiro Univ. Entered Brazilian Foreign Office, 1928; served in Washington, 1930–32; Rio de Janeiro, 1932–37; London, 1937; transf. to Brazil, 1938; 1st Sec., 1941; Buenos Aires, 1943–45; transf. to Brazil, 1945; Counsellor, Brussels, 1948–50; Minister Counsellor, London (periodically Chargé d'Affaires), 1950–53; various appts, Brazilian FO, 1953–57; Consul-Gen., New York, 1957–60; Ambassador to Haiti, 1960–61; Head of Political and Cultural Depts, Brazil, 1961; Sec.-Gen., FO, 1962–63; Ambassador to Netherlands, 1963–66. Headed Brazilian Delegn to UN Gen. Assembly, 1962. Holds Orders from many foreign countries. *Recreations:* golf, chess, bridge, stamps, coins, books. *Address:* Rua Siqueira Campos no 7–7, Copacabana, Rio de Janeiro, Brasil. *Clubs:* Jockey, Country, Itanhangá Golf (Rio).

CHERRY, Bridget Katherine, FSA; Editor, Buildings of England, since 1983; *b* 17 May 1941; *d* of Norman Stayner Marsh, *qv*; *m* 1966, John Cherry, *qv*; one *s* one *d*. *Educ:* Oxford High Sch. for Girls; Lady Margaret Hall, Oxford (BA Modern Hist.); Courtauld Inst. of Art, Univ. of London (Dip. Hist. of Art). FSA 1980. Asst Librarian, Conway Library, Courtauld Inst., 1964–68; Res. Asst to Sir Nikolaus Pevsner, Buildings of England, 1968–83. Mem., Royal Commn on Historical Monuments of England, 1987–; English Heritage: Mem., London Adv. Cttee, 1985–; Mem., Historic Buildings Adv. Cttee, 1986–. *Publications:* reviser or part author, 2nd edns, Buildings of England series, incl. London I, 3rd edn 1973, Wiltshire, 1975, Hertfordshire, 1977, London 2: South, 1983, Devon, 1989; London 3: North West, 1991; articles and reviews on arch. subjects in learned jls. *Recreation:* walking. *Address:* Buildings of England, Penguin Books, 27 Wrights Lane, W8 5TZ. *T:* 071–928 2200.

CHERRY, Colin; Director of Operations, Inland Revenue, 1985–90; *b* 20 Nov. 1931; *s* of late Reginald Cherry and Dorothy (*née* Brooks); *m* 1958, Marjorie Rose Harman; two *d*. *Educ:* Hymers Coll., Hull. Joined Inland Revenue, 1950; HM Inspector of Taxes, 1960; Under Sec., 1985. *Recreations:* music, chrysanthemums, photography. *Address:* 13 Wathen Road, Dorking, Surrey RH4 1JZ. *Club:* Reform.

CHERRY, Prof. Gordon Emanuel; Professor of Urban and Regional Planning, University of Birmingham, since 1976; *b* 6 Feb. 1931; *s* of Emanuel and Nora Cherry; *m* 1957, Margaret Mary Loudon Cox; one *s* two *d*. *Educ:* Holgate and District Grammar Sch., Barnsley; QMC, Univ. of London (BA(Hons) Geog. 1953). Variously employed in local authority planning depts, 1956–68; Research Officer, Newcastle upon Tyne City Planning Dept, 1963–68; University of Birmingham: Sen. Lectr and Dep. Dir, Centre for Urban and Regional Studies, 1968–76; Dean, Fac. of Commerce and Social Science, 1981–86; Head, Sch. of Geography, 1987–91. Chm., Planning History Gp, 1974–. Member: Local Govt Boundary Commn for England, 1979–89; Adv. Cttee on Landscape Treatment of Trunk Roads, 1984–; Trustee, Bournville Village Trust, 1979–. FRICS; Pres., RTPI, 1978–79; FRSA 1991. Hon. DSc Heriot-Watt, 1984. *Publications:* Town Planning in its Social Context, 1970, 2nd edn 1973; (with T. L. Burton) Social Research Techniques for Planners, 1970; Urban Change and Planning, 1972; The Evolution of British Town Planning, 1974; Environmental Planning, Vol. II: National Parks and Recreation in the Countryside, 1975; The Politics of Town Planning, 1982; (with J. L. Penny) Holford: a study in planning, architecture and civic design, 1986; Cities and Plans, 1988; Editor: Urban Planning Problems, 1974; Rural Planning Problems, 1976; Shaping an Urban World, 1980; Pioneers in British Planning, 1981; (with A. R. Sutcliffe) Planning Perspectives, 1986–. *Recreations:* work, professional activities, church ecumenism, sport, reading, music, enjoyment of family life. *Address:* Quaker Ridge, 66 Meriden Road, Hampton in Arden, West Midlands B92 0BT. *T:* Hampton in Arden (06755) 3200.

CHERRY, John, FSA, FRHistS; Deputy Keeper, Department of Medieval and Later Antiquities, British Museum, since 1981 (Acting Keeper, 1991); *b* 5 Aug. 1942; *s* of Edwin Lewis Cherry and Vera Edith Blanche (*née* Bunn); *m* 1966, Bridget Katherine Marsh (*see* B. K. Cherry); one *s* one *d*. *Educ:* Portsmouth Grammar Sch.; Christ Church, Oxford (Open Scholar 1960, MA). British Museum: Asst Keeper, Dept of British and Medieval Antiquities, 1964–69; Asst Keeper, Dept of Medieval and Later Antiquities, 1969–81. Dir, British Archaeological Assoc., 1977–82; Sec., Soc. of Antiquaries of London, 1986–. *Publications:* (jtly) The Ring from Antiquity to the 20th Century, 1981; (ed with I. H. Longworth) Archaeology in Britain since 1945, 1986; Medieval Decorative Art, 1991; articles in learned jls on topics of medieval archaeology. *Address:* 58 Lancaster Road, N4 4PT. *T:* 071–272 0578.

CHERRY, John Mitchell; QC 1988; a Recorder, since 1987; *b* 10 Sept. 1937; *s* of John William and Dorothy Mary Cherry; *m* 1972, Eunice Ann Westmoreland; two *s* two *d*. *Educ:* Cheshunt Grammar Sch.; Council of Legal Education. Called to the Bar, Gray's Inn, 1961. *Recreations:* cricket, Rugby, food, wine. *Address:* Winterton, Turkey Street, Enfield, Middx EN1 4RJ. *T:* Lea Valley (0992) 719018.

CHERRYMAN, John Richard, QC 1982; *b* 7 Dec. 1932; *s* of Albert James and Mabel Cherryman; *m* 1963, Anna Greenleaf Collis; three *s* one *d*. *Educ:* Farnham Grammar Sch.; London School of Economics (LLB Hons); Harvard Law Sch. Called to Bar, Gray's Inn, 1955. *Recreation:* splitting hairs. *Address:* 4 Stone Buildings, Lincoln's Inn, WC2.

CHESHAM, 6th Baron, *cr* 1858; **Nicholas Charles Cavendish;** *b* 7 Nov. 1941; *s* of 5th Baron Chesham, TD, PC and of Mary Edmunds, *d* of late David G. Marshall; *S* father, 1989; *m* 1st, 1965, Susan Donne Beauchamp (marr. diss. 1969); 2nd, 1973, Suzanne Adrienne, *d* of late Alan Gray Byrne; two *s*. *Educ:* Eton. Chartered Accountant. *Recreations:* tennis, ski-ing, shooting. *Heir:* *s* Hon. Charles Gray Compton Cavendish, *b* 11 Nov. 1974. *Address:* Latimer, 54B Wentworth Road, Vaucluse, NSW 2030, Australia. *T:* (02) 3375023. *Clubs:* Pratt's; Australian (Sydney); Royal Sydney Golf.

CHESHIRE, family name of **Baron Cheshire**.

CHESHIRE, Baron *cr* 1991 (Life Peer), of Woodhall in the county of Lincolnshire; **Geoffrey Leonard Cheshire,** VC 1944; OM 1981; DSO 1940 and two Bars 1941, 1943; DFC 1941; RAF retired; *b* 7 Sept. 1917; *s* of late Geoffrey Chevalier Cheshire, FBA, DCL, and late Primrose Barstow; *m* 2nd, 1959, Susan Ryder (*see* Baroness Ryder of Warsaw); one *s* one *d*. *Educ:* Stowe Sch.; Merton Coll., Oxford. 2nd Class Hon. Sch. of Jurisprudence, 1939; OU Air Sqdn, 1936; RAFVR, 1937; Perm. Commn RAF, 1939; trained Hullavington; served Bomber Comd, 1940–45: 102 Sqdn, 1940; 35 Sqdn, 1941;

CO 76 Sqdn, 1942; RAF Station, Marston Moor, 1943; CO 617 Sqdn (Dambusters), 1943; attached Eastern Air Command, South-East Asia, 1944; British Joint Staff Mission, Washington, 1945; official British observer at dropping of Atomic Bomb on Nagasaki, 1945; retd Dec. 1945. Founder of Cheshire Foundation Homes (270 Homes in 50 countries); Co-founder of Ryder Cheshire Mission for the Relief of Suffering; Founder Chm., World War Meml Fund for Disaster Relief, 1989–. Member: Pathfinders Assoc.; Air Crew Assoc. Pres., British Soc. of the Turin Shroud. Hon. LLD: Liverpool, 1973; Manchester Polytechnic, 1979; Nottingham, 1981; Birmingham, 1986; Hon. DCL: Oxon, 1984; Kent, 1986. Variety Club Humanitarian Award (jtly with wife), 1975. *Publications:* Bomber Pilot, 1943; Pilgrimage to the Shroud, 1956; The Face of Victory, 1961; The Hidden World, 1981; The Light of Many Suns, 1985. *Relevant publications:* Cheshire, VC, by Russell Braddon, 1954; No Passing Glory, by Andrew Boyle, 1955; New Lives for Old, by W. W. Russell, 1963. *Recreation:* tennis. *Address:* 26 Maunsel Street, SW1P 2QN. *T:* 071–828 1822. *Clubs:* Royal Air Force, Queen's (Hon. Life Mem.), All England Lawn Tennis.

CHESSELLS, Arthur David, (Tim); Chairman, North East Thames Regional Health Authority, since1990; *b* 15 June 1941; *s* of late Brig. Arthur Chessells and Carmel (*née* McGinnis); *m* 1966, Katharine, *d* of Dick and Rachel Goodwin; two *s* two *d*. *Educ:* Stonyhurst Coll. CA 1965. Partner, Arthur Young, 1972–89; Mem., Kent AHA, 1979–82; Vice-Chm., Tunbridge Wells HA, 1982–88; Mem., SE Thames RHA, 1988–90. Dir, Odgers and Co. Ltd, 1989–, and other cos; Chm., James Chandler (Lewes) Ltd, 1991–. Mem. Council, St Christopher's Hospice, 1989–. Trustee: Kent Community Housing Trust, 1990–; Stonyhurst Charitable Fund, 1980–. *Recreations:* reading, shooting, gardening. *Address:* North East Thames Regional Health Authority, 40 Eastbourne Terrace, W2 3QR. *T:* 071–262 8011. *Club:* Carlton.

CHESSHYRE, (David) Hubert (Boothby), LVO 1988; FSA; Chester Herald of Arms, since 1978; *b* 22 June 1940; *e s* of late Col Hubert Layard Chesshyre and of Katharine Anne (*née* Boothby), Canterbury, Kent. *Educ:* King's Sch., Canterbury; Trinity Coll., Cambridge (MA); Christ Church, Oxford (DipEd 1967). FSA 1977. Taught French in England and English in France, at intervals 1962–67; wine merchant (Moët et Chandon and Harvey's of Bristol), 1962–65; Hon. Artillery Co., 1964–65 (fired salute at funeral of Sir Winston Churchill, 1965); Green Staff Officer at Investiture of the Prince of Wales, 1969; Rouge Croix Pursuivant, 1970–78, and on staff of Sir Anthony Wagner, Garter King of Arms, 1971–78. Member: Council, Heraldry Soc., 1973–85; Bach Choir, 1979–; Madrigal Soc., 1980–. Hon. Genealogist to Royal Victorian Order, 1987–; Sec., Most Noble Order of the Garter, 1988–. Lectr, NADFAS, 1982–. Lay Clerk, Southwark Cathedral, 1971–. Freeman, City of London, 1975. *Publications:* (Eng. lang. editor) C. A. von Volborth, Heraldry of the World, 1973; The Identification of Coats of Arms on British Silver, 1978; (with A. J. Robinson) The Green: a history of the heart of Bethnal Green, 1978; (with Adrian Ailes) Heralds of Today, 1986; Dictionary of British Arms, vol. I, 1992; genealogical and heraldic articles in British Heritage and elsewhere. *Recreations:* singing, gardening, mountain walking, motorcycling, squash. *Address:* Hawthorn Cottage, 1 Flamborough Walk, E14 7LS. *T:* 071-790 7923; College of Arms, Queen Victoria Street, EC4V 4BT. *T:* 071–248 1137.

CHESTER, Bishop of, since 1982; **Rt. Rev. Michael Alfred Baughen;** *b* 7 June 1930; *s* of Alfred Henry and Clarice Adelaide Baughen; *m* 1956, Myrtle Newcomb Phillips; two *s* one *d*. *Educ:* Bromley County Grammar Sch; Univ. of London; Oak Hill Theol Coll. BD (London). With Martins Bank, 1946–48, 1950–51. Army, Royal Signals, 1948–50. Degree Course and Ordination Trng, 1951–56; Curate: St Paul's, Hyson Green, Nottingham, 1956–59; Reigate Parish Ch., 1959–61; Candidates Sec., Church Pastoral Aid Soc., 1961–64; Rector of Holy Trinity (Platt), Rusholme, Manchester, 1964–70; Vicar of All Souls, Langham Place, W1, 1970–75; Rector, 1975–82; Area Dean of St Marylebone, 1978–82; a Prebendary of St Paul's Cathedral, 1979–82. *Publications:* Moses and the Venture of Faith, 1979; The Prayer Principle, 1981; II Corinthians: a spiritual health-warning to the Church, 1982; Chained to the Gospel, 1986; Evidence for Christ, 1986; Editor: Youth Praise, 1966; Youth Praise II, 1969; Psalm Praise, 1973; consultant editor, Hymns for Today's Church, 1982. *Recreations:* music, railways, touring. *Address:* Bishop's House, Chester CH1 2JD. *T:* Chester (0244) 350864.

CHESTER, Dean of; *see* Smalley, Very Rev. S. S.

CHESTER, Archdeacon of; *see* Gear, Ven. M. F.

CHESTER, Dr Peter Francis, FInstP; FIEE; Executive Director, Technology and Environment, National Power Company, since 1990; *b* 8 Feb. 1929; *s* of late Herbert and of Edith Maud Chester (*née* Pullen); *m* 1953, Barbara Ann Collin; one *s* four *d*. *Educ:* Gunnersbury Grammar Sch.; Queen Mary College, London. BSc 1st Physics 1950; PhD London 1953. Post-doctoral Fellow, Nat. Research Council, Ottawa, 1953–54; Adv. Physicist, Westinghouse Res. Labs, Pittsburgh, 1954–60; Head of Solid State Physics Section, CERL, 1960–65; Head of Fundamental Studies Section, CERL, 1965–66; Res. Man., Electricity Council Res. Centre, 1966–70; Controller of Scientific Services, CEGB NW Region, 1970–73; Dir, Central Electricity Res. Labs, 1973–82; a Dir, Technol. Planning and Res., Div., CEGB, 1982–86; Dir, Environment, CEGB, 1986–89. Science Research Council: Mem., 1976–80; Mem., Science Bd, 1972–75; Chm., Energy Round Table and Energy Cttee, 1975–80. Vice-Pres., Inst. of Physics, 1972–76. A Dir, Fulmer Res. Inst., 1976–83. Faraday Lectr, IEE, 1984–85. Robens Coal Science Medal, 1985. *Publications:* original papers in solid state and low temperature physics, reports on energy and the environment, and acid rain. *Address:* National Power Company, 15 Newgate Street, EC1A 7AU.

CHESTER JONES, Prof. Ian, DSc; Professor of Zoology, University of Sheffield, 1958–81, now Emeritus Professor; Independent Research Worker, Pathology, Sheffield Medical School, since 1987; *b* 3 Jan. 1916; *s* of late H. C. Jones; *m* 1942, Nansi Ellis Williams; two *s* one *d*. *Educ:* Liverpool Institute High Sch. for Boys; Liverpool Univ. BSc 1938; PhD 1941; DSc 1958. Served in Army, 1941–46 (despatches). Commonwealth Fund Fellow, Harvard Univ., 1947–49; Senior Lecturer in Zoology, Univ. of Liverpool, 1955. Milton Fellow, Harvard Univ., 1960; Vis. Prof., Coll. of William and Mary, Virginia, 1968–69. Ian Chester Jones Internat. Lectureship for Distinction in Comparative Endocrinology, triennium. Chm., Soc. for Endocrinology, 1966 (Sir Henry Dale medal, 1976, Hon. Fellow): Hon. FZS; Hon. FIBiol; Hon. Fellow: Amer. Soc. of Zoologists; NY Acad. of Scis. Dr de l'Université de Clermont (*hc*), 1967. *Publications:* The Adrenal Cortex, 1957; Integrated Biology, 1971; General, Comparative and Clinical Endocrinology of the Adrenal Cortex, vol. 1, 1976, vol. 2, 1978, vol. 3, 1980; Fundamentals of Comparative Vertebrate Endocrinology, 1987. *Address:* 36 Sale Hill, Sheffield S10 5BX.

CHESTERFIELD, Archdeacon of; *see* Phizackerley, Ven. G. R.

CHESTERMAN, Sir Ross, Kt 1970; MSc, PhD; DIC; Warden of Goldsmiths' College (University of London), 1953–74; Hon. Fellow, 1980; Master of the College of Design, Craft and Technology (formerly College of Craft Education), since 1982 (Vice-Master, 1960–82; Dean, 1958–60); *b* 27 April 1909; *s* of late Dudley and Ettie Chesterman; *m* 1st, 1938, Audrey Mary Horlick (*d* 1982); one *s* one *d*; 2nd, 1985, Patricia Burns Bell. *Educ:* Hastings Grammar Sch.; Imperial College of Science, London (scholar). Acland English Essay Prizeman, 1930; 1st class hons BSc (Chem.), 1930; MSc 1932; Lecturer in Chemistry, Woolwich Polytechnic; PhD 1937; Science master in various grammar schools; Headmaster, Meols Cop Secondary Sch., Southport, 1946–48. Chief County Inspector of Schools, Worcestershire, 1948–53. Educnl Consultant to numerous overseas countries, 1966–73. Ford Foundation Travel Award to American Univs, 1966. Chairman: Standing Cttee on Teacher Trng; Nat. Council for Supply and Trng of Teachers Overseas, 1971; Adv. Cttee for Teacher Trng Overseas, FCO (ODA), 1972–74. Fellow *hc* of Coll. of Handicraft, 1958. Liveryman and Freeman of Goldsmiths' Co., 1968. *Publications:* The Birds of Southport, 1947; chapter in The Forge, 1955; chapter in Science in Schools, 1958; Teacher Training in some American Universities, 1967; scientific papers in chemical journals and journals of natural history; articles in educational periodicals. *Recreations:* music, painting, travel. *Address:* The Garden House, 6 High Street, Lancaster LA1 1LA. *T:* Lancaster (0524) 65687.

CHESTERS, Rt. Rev. Alan David; *see* Blackburn, Bishop of.

CHESTERS, Prof. Charles Geddes Coull, OBE 1977; BSc, MSc, PhD; FRSE; FLS; FInstBiol; Professor of Botany, University of Nottingham, 1944–69, now Emeritus Professor; *b* 9 March 1904; *s* of Charles and Margaret Geddes Chesters; *m* 1928, Margarita Mercedes Cathie Maclean; one *s* one *d*. *Educ:* Hyndland Sch.; Univ. of Glasgow. Lecturer in Botany, 1930, Reader in Mycology, 1942, Univ. of Birmingham. *Publications:* scientific papers on mycology and microbiology, mainly in Trans. British Myc. Soc., Ann. Ap. Biol., Jl Gen. Microb. *Recreations:* photography and collecting fungi. *Address:* Grandage Cottages, Quenington, near Cirencester, Glos GL7 5DB.

CHESTERS, Dr John Hugh, OBE 1970; FRS 1969; FEng; Consultant, since 1971; *b* 16 Oct. 1906; 2nd *s* of Rev. George M. Chesters; *m* 1936, Nell Knight, Minnesota, USA; three *s* one *d*. *Educ:* High Pavement Sch., Nottingham; King Edward VII Sch., Sheffield; Univ. of Sheffield. BSc Hons Physics, 1928; PhD 1931; DSc Tech 1945; Hon. DSc 1975. Metropolitan-Vickers Research Schol., Univ. Sheff., 1928–31. Robert Blair Fellowship, Kaiser-Wilhelm Inst. für Silikatforschung, Berlin, 1931–32; Commonwealth Fund Fellowship, Univ. of Illinois, 1932–34; United Steel Cos Ltd: in charge of Refractories Section, 1934–45; Asst Dir of Research, 1945–62; Dep. Dir of Research, United Steel Cos Ltd, 1962–67, Midland Group, British Steel Corporation, 1967–70; Dir, Corporate Labs, BISRA, 1970–71. Chm., Watt Cttee on Energy, 1976–86. President: Brit. Ceramic Soc., 1951–52; Inst. of Ceramics, 1961–63; Iron and Steel Inst., 1968–69; Inst. of Fuel, 1972–73. Foreign Associate, Nat. Acad. of Engineering, USA, 1977. Fellow, Fellowship of Engineering, 1978; SFInstF, FIM, FICeram; Fellow, Amer. Ceramic Soc. Hon. FInstE 1986. Iron and Steel Inst., Bessemer Gold Medal, 1966; John Wilkinson Gold Medal, Staffs Iron and Steel Inst., 1971; American Inst. Met. Eng: Robert Hunt Award, 1952; Benjamin Fairless Award, 1973. *Publications:* Steelplant Refractories, 1945, 2nd edn 1957; Iron and Steel, 1948; Refractories: production and properties, 1973; Refractories for Iron- and Steelmaking, 1974; numerous articles in Jl of Iron and Steel Inst., Trans Brit. Cer. Soc., Jl Amer. Cer. Soc., Jl Inst. of Fuel, etc. *Recreations:* foreign travel, fishing. *Address:* 21 Slayleigh Lane, Sheffield S10 3RF. *T:* Sheffield (0742) 301257.

CHESTERTON, David; Under Secretary, Northern Ireland Office, since 1985; *b* 30 Nov. 1939; *s* of Raymond and Joyce Chesterton; *m* 1st, 1965, Ursula Morgan; one *s* three *d*; 2nd, 1977, Lindsay Fellows; three step *d*. *Educ:* Reading Sch.; St Catherine's Coll., Oxford (BA). Editorial Assistant: Financial World, 1961–62; Fleet Street Letter, 1962–65; Producer, BBC External Services, 1965–68, Exec. Producer, 1968–74; Northern Ireland Office: Principal, 1974–80; Asst Sec., 1980–85. *Recreation:* walking. *Address:* Northern Ireland Office, Whitehall, SW1.

CHESTERTON, Dame Elizabeth (Ursula), DBE 1987 (OBE 1977); architect and town planner; *b* 12 Oct. 1915; *d* of late Maurice Chesterton, architect, and Dorothy (*née* Deck). *Educ:* King Alfred Sch.; Queen's Coll., London; Architectural Assoc. Sch. of Architecture, London. AA Dipl. (Hons) 1939; ARIBA 1940; DistTP 1968; FRTPI 1967 (AMTPI 1943). Asst County Planning Officer, E Suffolk CC, 1940–47; Develt Control Officer, Cambs CC Planning Dept, 1947–51; Mem. Staff: Social Res. Unit, Dept of Town Planning, UCL, 1951–53; Architectural Assoc. Sch. of Architecture, 1954–61. Member: Council, Architectural Assoc., 1964–67; Royal Fine Art Commn, 1970–; Historic Buildings Council, 1973–84; Historic Bldgs Adv. Cttee, 1984–88, Historic Areas Adv. Cttee, 1984–, English Heritage; BR Environment Panel, 1983–88; BR Architecture Panel, 1988–; Architecture Panel, 1978–90, Council, 1984–90, National Trust. FRSA 1982. Reports prepared: Report on Local Land Use for the Dartington Hall Trustees, 1957; (jtly) The Historic Core of King's Lynn: study and plan, 1964; Plan for the Beaulieu Estate, 1966; North West Solent Shore Estates Report, 1969; Snowdon Summit Report for Countryside Commission, 1974; Plans for Quarries and Rail Distribution Depots, Foster Yeoman and Yeoman (Morvern), 1974–81; Central Area Study, Chippenham, for North Wiltshire District Council, 1975–80; The Crumbles, Eastbourne, for Chatsworth Settlement, 1976; Aldeburgh, Suffolk, for Aldeburgh Soc., 1976; Old Market Conservation and Redevelopment Study, for City of Bristol and Bristol Municipal Charities, 1978; Uplands Landscape Study, for Countryside Commission, 1980. *Recreations:* gardening, travel. *Address:* 12 The Mount, NW3 6SZ. *T:* 071–435 0666 and 071–580 6396.

CHESTERTON, Sir Oliver (Sidney), Kt 1969; MC 1943; Consultant, Chestertons, Chartered Surveyors, London, since 1980 (Partner, 1936, Senior Partner, 1945–80); President, Woolwich Equitable Building Society, since 1986; *b* 28 Jan. 1913; *s* of Frank and Nora Chesterton; *m* 1944, Violet Ethel Jameson; two *s* one *d*. *Educ:* Rugby Sch. Served War of 1939–45, Irish Guards. Director: Woolwich Equitable Building Soc., 1962–86 (Chm., 1976–83); Property Growth Assurance, 1972–85; London Life Assoc., 1975–84; Estates Property Investment Co., 1979–88. Vice-Chm., Council of Royal Free Med. Sch., 1964–77; Crown Estate Comr, 1969–82. Past Pres., Royal Instn of Chartered Surveyors, Hon. Sec., 1972–79; Pres., Commonwealth Assoc. Surveying and Land Economy, 1969–77; first Master, Chartered Surveyors' Co., 1977–78. Governor, Rugby Sch., 1972–88. *Recreations:* golf, fishing, National Hunt racing. *Address:* Hookfield House, Abinger Common, Dorking, Surrey RH5 6JF. *Clubs:* White's; Rye Golf; New Zealand Golf.

CHESWORTH, Air Vice-Marshal George Arthur, CB 1982; OBE 1972; DFC 1954; Deputy Chairman: SEC Ltd, since 1989; Moray, Badenoch and Strathspey Enterprise Co., since 1991; *b* 4 June 1930; *s* of Alfred Matthew Chesworth and Grace Edith Chesworth; *m* 1951, Betty Joan Hopkins; two *d* (one *s* decd). *Educ:* Carshalton and Wimbledon. Joined RAF, 1948; commissioned, 1950; 205 Flying boat Sqdn, FEAF, 1951–53 (DFC 1954); RAF Germany, RAF Kinloss, RAF St Mawgan, 1956–61; RN Staff Coll., 1963; MoD, 1964–67; OC 201 Nimrod Sqdn, 1968–71 (OBE); OC RAF Kinloss, 1972–75; Air Officer in Charge, Central Tactics & Trials Orgn, 1975–77; Director, RAF Quartering, 1977–80; C of S to Air Comdr CTF 317 during Falkland Campaign, Apr.–June 1982 (CB); C of S, HQ 18 Gp, RAF, 1980–84. Chief Exec., Glasgow Garden Fest. (1988),

1985–89. Chm., ATC Council for Scotland and NI, 1989–; Vice Chm. (Air), Highland TAVR, 1990–. Develt Dir, Military and Aerospace Mus. (Aldershot) Trust, 1990–; Mem. Management Bd, RAF Benevolent Fund Home, Alastrean House, Tarland, Aberdeenshire, 1990–. *Address:* Pindlers Croft, Lower Califer, Forres, Moray IV36 0RN. *T:* Forres (0309) 74136.

CHETWODE, family name of **Baron Chetwode.**

CHETWODE, 2nd Baron *cr* 1945, of Chetwode; **Philip Chetwode;** Bt, 1700; *b* 26 March 1937; *s* of Capt. Roger Charles George Chetwode (*d* 1940; *o s* of Field Marshal Lord Chetwode, GCB, OM, GCSI, KCMG, DSO) and Hon. Molly Patricia Berry, *d* of 1st Viscount Camrose (she *m* 2nd, 1942, 1st Baron Sherwood, from whom she obtained a divorce, 1948, and *m* 3rd, 1958, late Sir Richard Cotterell, 5th Bt, CBE); *S* grandfather, 1950; *m* 1st, 1967, Mrs Susan Dudley Smith (marr. diss. 1979); two *s* one *d*; 2nd, 1990, Mrs Fiona Holt. Educ: Eton. Commissioned Royal Horse Guards, 1956–66. *Heir: s* Hon. Roger Chetwode, *b* 29 May 1968. *Address:* The Mill House, Chilton Foliat, Hungerford, Berks. *Club:* White's.

CHETWOOD, Sir Clifford (Jack), Kt 1987; FCIOB, FRSH; Chairman, George Wimpey PLC, since 1984 (a Group Managing Director, 1979–90; Chief Executive, 1982–90); *b* 2 Nov. 1928; *s* of Stanley Jack Chetwood and Doris May Palmer; *m* 1953, Pamela Phyllis Sherlock; one *s* three *d*. George Wimpey & Co. Ltd, later George Wimpey PLC: Director, 1969; Chm., Bd of Management, 1975–79; Chairman: Wimpey Construction UK, 1979–83; Wimpey Homes Holdings, 1981–83. Pres., Building Employers' Confedn, 1989–; Chm., Construction ITB, 1990. Mem. Council, Imperial Soc. of Knights Bachelor, 1988–; Trustee: V & A Museum, 1985–; London Zoological Soc. Develt Trust, 1986–90; Chm. of Trustees, Develt Trust, ICE, 1988–. FRSA; Hon. FICE, 1990. Prince Philip Medal, CGLI, 1987. Man of the Year, Architects and Surveyors Inst., 1989. *Recreations:* Real tennis, lawn tennis. *Address:* Wineberry House, The Drive, Eaton Park, Cobham, Surrey. *T:* Cobham (09328) 62389.

CHETWYN, Robert; *b* 7 Sept. 1933; *s* of Frederick Reuben Suckling and Eleanor Lavinia (*née* Boffee). *Educ:* Rutlish, Merton, SW; Central Sch. of Speech and Drama. First appeared as actor with Dundee Repertory Co., 1952; subseq. in repertory at Hull, Alexandra Theatre, Birmingham, 1954; Birmingham Repertory Theatre, 1954–56; various TV plays, 1956–59; 1st prodn, Five Finger Exercise, Salisbury Playhouse, 1960; Dir of Prodns, Opera Hse, Harrogate, 1961–62; Artistic Dir, Ipswich Arts, 1962–64; Midsummer Night's Dream, transf. Comedy (London), 1964; Resident Dir, Belgrade (Coventry), 1964–66; Assoc. Dir, Mermaid, 1966, The Beaver Coat, three one-act plays by Shaw; There's a Girl in My Soup, Globe, 1966 and Music Box (NY), 1967; A Present for the Past, Edinburgh Fest., 1966; The Flip Side, Apollo, 1967; The Importance of Being Earnest, Haymarket, 1968; The Real Inspector Hound, Criterion, 1968; What the Butler Saw, Queens, 1968; The Country Wife, Chichester Fest., 1968; The Bandwaggon, Mermaid, 1968 and Sydney, 1970; Cannibal Crackers, Hampstead, 1969; When We are Married, Strand, 1970; Hamlet, in Rome, Zurich, Vienna, Antwerp, Cologne, then Cambridge (London), 1971; Parents Day, Globe, 1972; Restez Donc Jusq'au Petit Dejeuner, Belgium, 1973; Who's Who, Fortune, 1973; At the End of the Day, Savoy, 1973; Chez Nous, Globe, 1974; Qui est Qui, Belgium, 1974; The Doctor's Dilemma, Mermaid, 1975; Getting Away with Murder, Comedy, 1976; Private Lives, Melbourne, 1976; It's All Right If I Do It, Mermaid, 1977; A Murder is Announced, Vaudeville, 1977; Arms and The Man, Greenwich, 1978; LUV, Amsterdam, 1978; Brimstone and Treacle, Open Space, 1979; Bent, Royal Court and Criterion, 1979; Pygmalion, National Theatre of Belgium, 1979; Moving, Queen's, 1980; Eastward Ho!, Mermaid, 1981; Beethoven's 10th, Vaudeville, 1983 (also Broadway, New York); Number One, Queen's, 1984; Why Me?, Strand, 1985; Selling The Sizzle, Hampstead, 1988. Has produced and directed for BBC (incl. series Private Shulz, by Jack Pullman, film, That Uncertain Feeling, Born In the Gardens) and ITV (Irish RM first series, Small World, Case of the Late Pig). Trustee, Dirs' Guild of GB, 1984–. *Publication:* (jtly) Theatre on Merseyside (Arts Council report), 1973. *Recreations:* tennis, films, gardening. *Address:* 1 Wilton Court, Eccleston Square, SW1V 1PH.

CHETWYND, family name of **Viscount Chetwynd.**

CHETWYND, 10th Viscount *cr* 1717 (Ireland); **Adam Richard John Casson Chetwynd;** Baron Rathdowne, 1717 (Ireland); Life Assurance Agent, Prudential Assurance Co. of South Africa Ltd, Sandton Branch, Johannesburg; *b* 2 Feb. 1935; *o s* of 9th Viscount and Joan Gilbert (*d* 1979), *o c* of late Herbert Alexander Casson, CSI, Ty'n-y-coed, Arthog, Merioneth; *S* father, 1965; *m* 1st, 1966, Celia Grace (marr. diss. 1974), *er d* of Comdr Alexander Robert Ramsay, DSC, RNVR, Fasque, Borrowdale, Salisbury, Rhodesia; twin *s* one *d*; 2nd, 1975, Angela May, *o d* of Jack Payne McCarthy, 21 Llanberis Grove, Nottingham. *Educ:* Eton. Fellow, Inst. of Life and Pension Advrs, 1982. 2nd Lieut Cameron Highlanders, 1954–56. With Colonial Mutual Life Assurance Soc. Ltd, Salisbury, Rhodesia, then Johannesburg, 1968–78; Prudential Assurance and London Life Assoc. of Africa, 1978–. Freeman, Guild of Air Pilots and Air Navigators. Life and Qualifying Mem., Million Dollar Round Table, 1979–91; qualified Top of the Table, 1984–91; Holder, Internat. Quality Award, 1978–91. *Recreations:* travel. *Heir: s* Hon. Adam Douglas Chetwynd, *b* 26 Feb. 1969. *Address:* c/o J. G. Ouvry Esq., Lee Bolton & Lee, 1 The Sanctuary, Westminster, SW1P 3JT. *Clubs:* Rand (Johannesburg); Rotary (Morningside).

CHETWYND, Sir Arthur (Ralph Talbot), 8th Bt *cr* 1795; President: Brocton Hall Communications Ltd, Toronto, since 1978; Post Productions Inc.; Chairman, Board of Directors, Chetwynd Films Ltd, Toronto, since 1977 (Founder, President and General Manager, 1950–76); *b* Walhachin, BC, 28 Oct. 1913; *o s* of Hon. William Ralph Talbot Chetwynd, MC, MLA (*d* 1957) (*b* of 7th Bt), and Frances Mary (*d* 1986), *d* of late James Jupe; *S* uncle, 1972; *m* 1940, Marjory May McDonald, *er d* of late Robert Bruce Lang, Vancouver, BC, and Glasgow, Scotland; two *s*. *Educ:* Vernon Preparatory School, BC; University of British Columbia (Physical Education and Recreation). Prior to 1933, a rancher in interior BC; Games Master, Vernon Prep. School, BC, 1933–36, also Instructor, Provincial Physical Education and Recreation; Chief Instructor, McDonald's Remedial Institute, Vancouver, 1937–41; Director of Remedial Gymnastics, British Columbia Workmen's Compensation Board, 1942; RCAF, 1943–45; Associate in Physical and Health Education, Univ. of Toronto, also Publicity Officer, Univ. of Toronto Athletic Assoc., 1946–52. Former Dir, NZ Lamb Co. Ltd. Former Chairman: Canterbury Cathedral Appeal in Canada; Codrington Coll. (Barbados) Appeal in Canada; Toronto Branch, Royal Commonwealth Soc.; Pres., Empire Club of Canada, 1974–75; Member: Monarchist League of Canada; Military and Hospitaller Order of St Lazarus of Jerusalem, Canada. KCLJ. Hon. Mem., Order of Barbados (SCM), 1984. *Recreations:* photography, travelling, swimming. *Heir: er s* Robin John Talbot Chetwynd [*b* 21 Aug. 1941; *m* 1st, 1967, Heather Helen (marr. diss. 1986), *d* of George Bayliss Lothian; one *s* one *d*; 2nd, 1986, Donna Preece]. *Address:* #3–117 King Street East, Cobourg, Ont K9A 1L2, Canada. *Clubs:* Albany, Toronto Hunt (Toronto).

CHETWYND-TALBOT, family name of **Earl of Shrewsbury and Waterford.**

CHETWYND-TALBOT, Richard Michael Arthur; *see* Talbot.

CHEUNG, Sir Oswald (Victor), Kt 1987; CBE 1976 (OBE 1972); QC (Hong Kong) 1965; Member, Executive Council, Hong Kong, 1974–86; *b* 22 Jan. 1922; *s* of Cheung U Pui and Elizabeth Ellis; *m* 1963, Pauline Cheng; one *s*. *Educ:* Diocesan Boys' Sch.; Hong Kong Univ.; University Coll., Oxford (BA 1949, MA 1963). Called to the Bar, Lincoln's Inn, 1951; Bencher, 1987. Magistrate, 1951–52; Hong Kong Bar, 1952–; Mem., Legislative Council, Hong Kong, 1970–81 (Senior Unofficial Mem., 1978–81); Chairman: Criminal Injuries Compensation Bd; Law Enforcement Injuries Compensation Bd. Director: Mass Transit Railway Corp., 1975–89; Hong Kong Electric (Holdings) Ltd; Cavendish International Holding Ltd; Ciba-Geigy (HK) Ltd. Member: Criminal Injuries Compensation Bd; Law Enforcement Injuries Compensation Bd; Univ. and Polytechnic Grants Cttee, 1970–78; Court, Hong Kong Univ. Trustee, Croucher Foundn; Chm., Children's Meals Soc., 1966–81; Steward, Royal Hong Kong Jockey Club, 1977– (Chm. of Stewards, 1986–89). Captain, Royal Hong Kong Regt, 1956–62, Hon. Col, 1977–82. Fellow, Internat. Acad. of Trial Lawyers. Hon. LLD Hong Kong, 1979. *Recreations:* photography, racing, travel. *Address:* New Henry House, 10th Floor, 10 Ice House Street, Hong Kong. *T:* 524–2156. *Clubs:* Turf, Oriental; Royal Hong Kong Jockey, Hong Kong, Royal Hong Kong Golf, Country, Chinese.

CHEW, (Victor) Kenneth, TD 1958; Fellow of the Science Museum, London; *b* 19 Jan. 1915; *yr s* of Frederick and Edith Chew. *Educ:* Christ's Hospital; Christ Church, Oxford (Scholar). 1st class, Final Honours School of Natural Science (Physics), 1936; BA (Oxon) 1936, MA 1964. Asst Master, King's Sch., Rochester, 1936–38; Winchester Coll., 1938–40. Served War: Royal Signals, 1940–46. Asst Master, Shrewsbury Sch., 1946–48 and 1949–58; Lecturer in Education, Bristol Univ., 1948–49. Entered Science Museum as Asst Keeper, 1958; Deputy Keeper and Sec. to Advisory Council, 1967; Keeper, Dept of Physics, 1970–78. *Publications:* official publications of Science Museum. *Recreations:* hill walking, photography. *Address:* 701 Gilbert House, Barbican, EC2.

CHEWTON, Viscount; James Sherbrooke Waldegrave; *b* 8 Dec. 1940; *e s* of 12th Earl Waldegrave, *qv*; *m* 1986, Mary Alison Anthea, *d* of late Sir Robert Furness, KBE, CMG, and of Lady Furness, 13 Emmanuel Road, Cambridge; two *s*. *Educ:* Eton Coll.; Trinity Coll., Cambridge. *Heir: s* Hon. Edward Robert Waldegrave, *b* 10 Oct. 1986. *Address:* West End Farm, Chewton Mendip, Bath. *Club:* Beefsteak.

CHEYNE, Major Sir Joseph (Lister Watson), 3rd Bt *cr* 1908; OBE 1976; Curator, Keats Shelley Memorial House, Rome, 1976–90; *b* 10 Oct. 1914; *e s* of Sir Joseph Lister Cheyne, 2nd Bt, MC, and Nelita Manfield (*d* 1977), *d* of Andrew Pringle, Borgue; *S* father, 1957; *m* 1st, 1938, Mary Mort (marr. diss. 1955; she *d* 1959), *d* of late Vice-Adm. J. D. Allen, CB; one *s* one *d*; 2nd, 1955, Cicely, *d* of late T. Metcalfe, Padiham, Lancs; two *s* one *d*. *Educ:* Stowe Sch.; Corpus Christi Coll., Cambridge. Major, The Queen's Westminsters (KRRC), 1943; Italian Campaign. 2nd Sec. (Inf.), British Embassy, Rome, 1968, 1st Sec., 1971, 1st Sec. (Inf.), 1973–76. *Heir: s* Patrick John Lister Cheyne [*b* 2 July 1941; *m* 1968, Helen Louise Trevor, *yr d* of Louis Smith, Southsea; one *s* three *d*]. *Address:* Leagarth, Fetlar, Shetland; Po' di Serse, Via Po' del Vento, Paciano (PG) 06060, Italy. *T:* 075–830129. *Clubs:* Boodle's; Circolo della Caccia (Rome).

CHEYSSON, Claude, Commander Legion of Honour; Croix de Guerre (5 times); Member, European Parliament, since 1989; Board Member, Le Monde, since 1978; President: Institut Pierre Mendes-France, since 1988; Arche de la Fraternité, since 1989; *b* 13 April 1920; *s* of Pierre Cheysson and Sophie Funck-Brentano; *m* 1969, Danièle Schwarz; one *s* two *d* (and two *s* one *d* by former marrs). *Educ:* Coll. Stanislas, Paris; Ecole Polytechnique; Ecole Nationale d'Administration. Escaped from occupied France, 1943; Tank Officer, Free French Forces, France and Germany, 1944–45. Liaison Officer with German authorities, Bonn, 1948–52; Political Adviser to Viet Nam Govt, Saigon, 1952–53; Personal Adviser: to Prime Minister of France, Paris, 1954–55; to French Minister of Moroccan and Tunisian Affairs, 1956; Sec.-Gen., Commn for Techn. Cooperation in Africa, Lagos, Nairobi, 1957–62; Dir-Gen., Sahara Authority, Algiers, 1962–66; French Ambassador in Indonesia, 1966–69; Pres., Entreprise Minière et Chimique, 1970–73; European Comr (relations with Third World), 1973–81, 1985–89; Minister for External Relations, 1981–84. Town Councillor, Bargemon, 1983–89. Grand Cross, Grand Officer and Comdr of many national orders; US Presidential Citation. Dr *hc* Univ. of Louvain; Joseph Bech Prize, 1978; Luderitz Prize, 1983. *Publications:* articles on Europe, and develt policies. *Recreation:* ski-ing. *Address:* 52 rue de Vaugirard, 75006 Paris, France. *T:* 40 63 61 76.

CHIANG KAI-SHEK, Madame (Mayling Soong Chiang); Chinese sociologist; *y d* of C. J. Soong; *m* 1927, Generalissimo Chiang Kai-Shek (*d* 1975). *Educ:* Wellesley Coll., USA. LHD, John B. Stetson Univ., Deland, Fla, Bryant Coll., Providence, RI, Hobart and William Smith Colls, Geneva, NY; LLD, Rutgers Univ., New Brunswick, NJ, Goucher Coll., Baltimore, MD, Wellesley Coll., Wellesley, Mass, Loyola Univ., Los Angeles, Cal., Russell Sage Coll., Troy, NY, Hahnemann Medical Coll., Philadelphia, Pa, Wesleyan Coll., Macon, Ga, Univ. of Michigan, Univ. of Hawaii; Hon. FRCS. First Chinese woman appointed Mem. Child Labor Commn; Inaugurated Moral Endeavor Assoc.; established schools in Nanking for orphans of Revolutionary Soldiers; former Mem. Legislative Yuan; served as Sec.-General of Chinese Commission on Aeronautical Affairs; Member Chinese Commission on Aeronautical Affairs; Director-General of the New Life Movement and Chairman of its Women's Advisory Council; Founder and Director: National Chinese Women's Assoc. for War Relief; National Assoc. for Refugee Children; Chinese Women's Anti-Aggression League; Huashing Children's Home; Cheng Hsin Medical Rehabilitation Center for Post Polio Crippled Children. Chm., Fu Jen Catholic University. Governor, Nat. Palace Museum. Frequently makes inspection tours to all sections of Free China where personally trained girl workers carry on war area and rural service work; accompanies husband on military campaigns; first Chinese woman to be decorated by National Govt of China. Recipient of highest military and Civil decorations; Hon. Chm., British United Aid to China Fund, China; Hon. Chm., Soc. for the Friends of the Wounded; Hon. President, American Bureau for Medical Aid to China; Patroness, International Red Cross Commn; Hon. President, Chinese Women's Relief Assoc. of New York; Hon. Chairman, Canadian Red Cross China Cttee; Hon. Chairman, Board of Directors, India Famine Relief Cttee; Hon. Mem., New York Zoological Soc.; Hon. Pres., Cttee for the Promotion of the Welfare of the Blind; Life Mem., San Francisco Press Club and Associated Countrywomen of the World; Mem., Phi Beta Kappa, Eta Chapter; first Hon. Member, Bill of Rights Commemorative Society; Hon. Member: Filipino Guerrillas of Bataan Assoc.; Catherine Lorillard Wolf Club. Medal of Honour, New York City Federation of Women's Clubs; YWCA Emblem; Gold Medal, New York Southern Soc.; Chi Omega Nat. Achievement Award for 1943; Gold Medal for distinguished services, National Institute for Social Sciences; Distinguished Service Award, Altrusa Internat. Assoc.; Churchman Fifth Annual Award, 1943; Distinguished Service Citation, All-American Conf. to Combat Communism, 1958; Hon. Lieut-Gen. US Marine Corps. *Publications:* China in Peace and War, 1939; China Shall Rise Again, 1939; This is Our China, 1940; We Chinese Women, 1941; Little Sister Su, 1943; Ten Eventful Years, for Encyclopædia Britannica, 1946; Album of Reproduction of Paintings, vol. I, 1952, vol. II,

1962; The Sure Victory, 1955; Madame Chiang Kai-Shek Selected Speeches, 1958–59; Madame Chiang Kai-shek Selected Speeches, 1965–66; Album of Chinese Orchid Paintings, 1971; Album of Chinese Bamboo Paintings, 1972; Album of Chinese Landscape Paintings, 1973; Album of Chinese Floral Paintings, 1974; Conversations with Mikhail Borodin, 1977; Religious Writings 1934–63, 1964.

CHIASSON, Most Rev. Donat; *see* Moncton, Archbishop of, (RC).

CHIBA, Kazuo; Counselor, Mitsui & Co. Ltd; *b* 19 April 1925; *s* of Shin-ichi and Miyoko Chiba; *m* 1954, Keiko Okamoto; one *s* one *d. Educ:* Univ. of Tokyo (LLB 1949); Fletcher Sch. of Law and Diplomacy, Medford, Mass, USA (MA 1951). Joined Min. of Foreign Affairs, Tokyo, 1948; Geneva, 1956; Iran, 1958; Min. of For. Affairs, 1962; Washington, DC, 1964; Dir, N America Div., N American Affairs Bureau, Min. of For. Affairs, 1967; Minister, Moscow, 1972; Consul-Gen., Atlanta, Ga, 1974; Consul-Gen., West Berlin, 1976; Dir Gen., Middle Eastern and African Affairs Bureau, Min. of For. Affairs, 1978; Ambassador: to Sri Lanka, 1980; in Geneva (Perm. Mission of Japan to internat. orgns), 1982–87; to UK, 1988–91. Chairman: GATT Council, 1984–85; GATT Contracting Parties, 1985–86. *Recreations:* reading (history), travel, music, art. *Address:* Mitsui & Co. Ltd, 2-1 Ohtemachi 1-Chome, Chiyoda-ku, Tokyo 100, Japan.

CHIBNALL, Marjorie McCallum, MA, DPhil; FSA; FBA 1978; Fellow of Clare Hall, Cambridge, since 1975; *b* 27 Sept. 1915; *d* of J. C. Morgan, MBE; *m* 1947, Prof. Albert Charles Chibnall, FRS (*d* 1988); one *s* one *d* and two step *d. Educ:* Shrewsbury Priory County Girls' Sch.; Lady Margaret Hall, Oxford; Sorbonne, Paris. BLitt, MA, DPhil (Oxon); PhD (Cantab). Amy Mary Preston Read Scholar, Oxford, 1937–38; Goldsmiths' Sen. Student, 1937–39; Nursing Auxiliary, 1939; Susette Taylor Research Fellow, Lady Margaret Hall, Oxford, 1940–41; Asst Lectr, University Coll., Southampton, 1941–43; Asst Lectr, 1943–45, Lectr, 1945–47, in Medieval History, Univ. of Aberdeen; Lectr in History, later Fellow of Girton Coll., Cambridge, 1947–65; Research Fellow, Clare Hall, Cambridge, 1969–75; Leverhulme Emeritus Fellowship, 1982. Prothero Lectr, RHistS, 1987. Vice-Pres., Selden Soc., 1987–90. Corresp. Fellow, Medieval Acad. of America, 1983. Hon. Fellow, Girton Coll., Cambridge, 1988. Hon. DLitt Birmingham, 1979. *Publications:* The English Lands of the Abbey of Bec, 1946; Select Documents of the English Lands of the Abbey of Bec, 1951; The *Historia Pontificalis* of John of Salisbury, 1956; The Ecclesiastical History of Orderic Vitalis, 6 vols, 1969–80; Charters and Custumals of the Abbey of Holy Trinity Caen, 1982; The World of Orderic Vitalis, 1984; Anglo-Norman England 1066–1166, 1986; (ed) Anglo-Norman Studies, XII, 1990, XIII, 1991; numerous articles and reviews, principally in English and French historical jls. *Address:* Clare Hall, Cambridge CB3 9AL. *T:* Cambridge (0223) 353923. *Club:* University Women's.

CHICHESTER, family name of **Marquess of Donegall.**

CHICHESTER, 9th Earl of, *cr* 1801; **John Nicholas Pelham;** Bt 1611; Baron Pelham of Stanmer, 1762; *b* (posthumous) 14 April 1944; *s* of 8th Earl of Chichester (killed on active service, 1944) and Ursula (*d* 1989) (she *m* 2nd, 1957, Ralph Gunning Henderson; marr. diss. 1971), *o d* of late Walter de Pannwitz, de Hartekamp, Bennebroek, Holland; *S* father, 1944; *m* 1975, Mrs June Marijke Hall; one *d. Recreations:* music, flying. *Heir: kinsman* Richard Anthony Henry Pelham [*b* 1 Aug. 1952; *m* 1987, Georgina, *d* of David Gilmour; two *s*]. *Address:* Little Durnford Manor, Salisbury, Wilts.

CHICHESTER, Viscount; James Chichester; *b* 19 Nov. 1990; *s* and *heir* of Earl of Belfast, *qv.*

CHICHESTER, Bishop of, since 1974; **Rt. Rev. Eric Waldram Kemp,** MA Oxon, DD; *b* 27 April 1915; *o c* of Tom Kemp and Florence Lilian Kemp (*née* Waldram), Grove House, Waltham, Grimsby, Lincs; *m* 1953, Leslie Patricia, 3rd *d* of late Rt Rev. K. E. Kirk, sometime Bishop of Oxford; one *s* four *d. Educ:* Brigg Grammar Sch., Lincs; Exeter Coll., Oxford; St Stephen's House, Oxford. Deacon 1939; Priest 1940; Curate of St Luke, Southampton, 1939–41; Librarian of Pusey House, Oxford, 1941–46; Chaplain of Christ Church Oxford, 1943–46; Actg Chap., St John's Coll., Oxford, 1943–45; Fellow, Chaplain, Tutor, and Lectr in Theology and Medieval History, Exeter Coll., Oxford, 1946–69; Dean of Worcester, 1969–74. Exam. Chaplain: to Bp of Mon, 1942–45; to Bp of Southwark, 1946–50; to Bp of St Albans, 1946–69; to Bp of Exeter, 1949–69; to Bp of Lincoln, 1950–69. Proctor in Convocation for University of Oxford, 1949–69. Bp of Oxford's Commissary for Religious Communities, 1952–69; Chaplain to the Queen, 1967–69. Canon and Prebendary of Caistor in Lincoln Cathedral, 1952; Hon. Provincial Canon of Cape Town, 1960–; Bampton Lecturer, 1959–60. FRHistS 1951. Hon. DLitt Sussex, 1986; Hon. DD Berne, 1987. *Publications:* (contributions to) Thy Household the Church, 1943; Canonization and Authority in the Western Church, 1948; Norman Powell Williams, 1954; Twenty-five Papal Decretals relating to the Diocese of Lincoln (with W. Holtzmann), 1954; An Introduction to Canon Law in the Church of England, 1957; Life and Letters of Kenneth Escott Kirk, 1959; Counsel and Consent, 1961; The Anglican-Methodist conversations: A Comment from within, 1964; (ed) Man: Fallen and Free, 1969; Square Words in a Round World, 1980; contrib. to English Historical Review, Jl of Ecclesiastical History. *Recreations:* music, travel. *Address:* The Palace, Chichester, W Sussex PO19 1PY. *T:* Chichester (0243) 782161. *Club:* National Liberal.

CHICHESTER, Dean of; *see* Treadgold, Very Rev. J. D.

CHICHESTER, Archdeacon of; *see* Brotherton, Ven. J. M.

CHICHESTER, Sir (Edward) John, 11th Bt *cr* 1641; *b* 14 April 1916; *s* of Comdr Sir Edward George Chichester, 10th Bt, RN, and late Phyllis Dorothy, *d* of late Henry F. Compton, Minstead Manor, Hants; *S* father, 1940; *m* 1950, Hon. Mrs Anne Rachel Pearl Moore-Gwyn, *widow* of Capt. Howel Moore-Gwyn, Welsh Guards, and *d* of 2nd Baron Montagu of Beaulieu and of Hon. Mrs Edward Pleydell-Bouverie; two *s* two *d* (and one *d* decd). *Educ:* Radley; RMC Sandhurst. Commissioned RSF, 1936. Patron of one living. Served throughout War of 1939–45. Was employed by ICI Ltd, 1950–60. A King's Foreign Service Messenger, 1947–50. Formerly Capt., Royal Scots Fusiliers and Lieut RNVR. *Heir: s* James Henry Edward Chichester [*b* 15 Oct. 1951; *m* 1990, Anne, *d* of Major J. W. Chandos-Pole, *qv*; one *s*]. *Address:* Battramsley Lodge, Boldre, Lymington, Hants. *Club:* Naval.

CHICHESTER-CLARK, family name of **Baron Moyola.**

CHICHESTER-CLARK, Sir Robert, (Sir Robin Chichester-Clark), Kt 1974; Director, Welbeck Group Ltd; management consultant; *b* 10 Jan. 1928; *s* of late Capt. J. L. C. Chichester-Clark, DSO and Bar, DL, MP, and Mrs C. E. Brackenbury; *m* 1st, 1953, Jane Helen Goddard (marr. diss. 1972); one *s* two *d*; 2nd, 1974, Caroline, *d* of Anthony Bull, *qv*; two *s. Educ:* Royal Naval Coll.; Magdalene Coll., Cambridge (BA Hons Hist. and Law). Journalist, 1950; Public Relations Officer, Glyndebourne Opera, 1952; Asst to Sales Manager, Oxford Univ. Press, 1953–55. MP (UU) Londonderry City and Co., 1955–Feb. 1974; PPS to Financial Secretary to the Treasury, 1958; Asst Government Whip (unpaid), 1958–60; a Lord Comr of the Treasury, 1960–61; Comptroller of HM Household, 1961–64; Chief Opposition Spokesman on N Ireland, 1964–70, on Public Building and Works and the Arts, 1965–70; Minister of State, Dept of Employment, 1972–74. Hon. FIWM 1972. *Recreations:* fishing, reading. *Club:* Brooks's.

See also P. Hobhouse, Baron Moyola.

CHICK, John Stephen; HM Diplomatic Service; Consul-General, Geneva, 1985–89; *b* 5 Aug. 1935; *m* 1966, Margarita Alvarez de Sotomayor; one *s* three *d. Educ:* St John's Coll., Cambridge (BA 1959). Entered FO, 1961; Madrid, 1963–66; First Sec., Mexico City, 1966–69; FCO, 1969–73; First Sec. and Head of Chancery, Rangoon, 1973–76; Consul, Luxembourg, 1976–78; Consul-Gen., Buenos Aires, 1978–81; Head of Arms Control Dept, FCO, 1981–83; Head of S Pacific Dept, FCO, 1983–85. *Address:* c/o Foreign and Commonwealth Office, SW1.

CHIENE, John; Deputy Chairman, County NatWest Ltd, 1989–90; *b* 27 Jan. 1937; *s* of John and Muriel Chiene; *m* 1st, 1965, Anne; one *s* one *d*; 2nd, 1987, Carol; one *d. Educ:* Rugby; Queen's Coll., Cambridge (BA). Wood Mackenzie: joined, 1962; Man. Partner, 1969; Sen. Partner, 1974; Jt Chief Exec., Hill Samuel & Co. Ltd (who had merged with Wood Mackenzie), 1987; Chm., County NatWest Securities, on their merger with Wood Mackenzie, 1988–89. *Recreations:* golf, opera, ski-ing. *Address:* 7 St Leonard's Terrace, SW3 4QB. *Clubs:* Cavalry and Guards, City of London; New (Edinburgh).

CHIEPE, Hon. Gaositwe Keagakwa Tibe, PMS 1975; MBE 1962; FRSA; Minister for External Affairs, since 1984; *b* 20 Oct. 1922; *d* of late T. Chiepe. *Educ:* Fort Hare, South Africa (BSc, EdDip); Bristol Univ., UK (MA (Ed)). Asst Educn Officer, 1948–53; Educn Officer and Schools Inspector, 1953–62; Sen. Educn Officer, 1962–65; Dep. Dir of Educn, 1965–67; Dir of Educn, 1968–70; Diplomat, 1970–; High Comr to UK and Nigeria, 1970–74; Ambassador: Denmark, Norway, Sweden, France and Germany, 1970–74; Belgium and EEC, 1973–74; Minister of Commerce and Industry, 1974–77; Minister for Mineral Resources and Water Affairs, 1977–84. Chairman: Africa Region, CPA, 1981–83; Botswana Branch, CPA, 1981–. Member: Botswana Society; Botswana Girl Guide Assoc.; Internat. Fedn of University Women. Hon. Pres., Kalahari Conservation Soc.; Patron, Botswana Forestry Assoc. Hon. LLD Bristol, 1972. FRSA 1973. *Recreations:* gardening, a bit of swimming (in Botswana), reading. *Address:* Department of External Affairs, Private Bag 001, Gabarone, Botswana.

CHIKETA, Stephen Cletus; High Commissioner for Zimbabwe in London, since 1990; *b* 16 Sept. 1942; *s* of Mangwiro S. Chiketa and Mary Magdalene (*née* Chivero); *m* 1981, Juliet Joalane; one *s* two *d. Educ:* Univ. of South Africa (BA Hons); Univ. of Basutoland, Botswana and Swaziland (BA, PGCE). Asst Teacher, Swaziland schs, 1967–73; part-time Lectr, Univ. of Botswana, Lesotho and Swaziland, 1972–73; Principal, High School in Lesotho, 1974–80; Under Sec., Min. of Foreign Affairs, 1982; Dep. Perm. Rep., UN, 1982–86; Dep. Sec., Min. of Foreign Affairs, 1986–87; Ambassador to Romania and Bulgaria, 1987–90. *Publications:* history articles in Swaziland weekly newspapers. *Recreations:* photography, tennis, reading, table tennis, cards. *Address:* Zimbabwe High Commission, 429 Strand, WC2R 0SA. *T:* 071–836 7755.

CHILCOT, John Anthony, CB 1990; Permanent Under Secretary of State, Northern Ireland Office, since 1990; *b* 22 April 1939; *s* of Henry William Chilcot and Catherine Chilcot (*née* Ashall); *m* 1964, Rosalind Mary Forster. *Educ:* Brighton Coll. (Lyon Scholar); Pembroke Coll., Cambridge (Open Scholar; MA). Joined Home Office, 1963; Asst Private Sec. to Home Secretary (Rt Hon. Roy Jenkins), 1966; Private Sec. to Head of Civil Service (late Baron Armstrong of Sanderstead), 1971–73; Principal Private Secretary to Home Secretary (Rt Hon. Merlyn Rees; Rt Hon. William Whitelaw), 1978–80; Asst Under-Sec. of State, Dir of Personnel and Finance, Prison Dept, 1980–84; Under-Sec., Cabinet Office (MPO), 1984–86; Asst Under Sec. of State, 1986 (seconded to Schroders, 1986–87), Dep. Under Sec. of State, 1987–90, Home Office. Dir, RTZ Pillar, 1986–90. *Recreations:* reading, music and opera, travel. *Address:* c/o Northern Ireland Office, Whitehall, SW1. *Club:* Travellers'.

CHILD, Christopher Thomas; National President, Bakers' Union, 1968–77; former Consultant to Baking Industry, Industrial Relations Officer and Training Officer, Baking Industry and Health Food Products, 1970–85; *b* 8 Jan. 1920; *s* of late Thomas William and Penelope Child; *m* 1943, Lilian Delaney; two *s* one *d. Educ:* Robert Ferguson Sch., Carlisle; Birmingham Coll. of Food and Domestic Science. Apprenticed baker, 1936; gained London City and Guilds final certificates in Breadmaking, Flour Confectionery and Bakery Science, 1951, and became Examiner in these subjects for CGLI. Full-time trade union official in Birmingham, 1958. Member: Birmingham Trades Council Exec., 1958–68; Adv. Council, Midland Regional TUC, 1959–68; Disablement Adv. Cttee, Birmingham, 1959–68. Former Chairman: Nat. Council Baking Education; Nat. Joint Apprenticeship Council for Baking. Mem., Industrial Training Bd, Food, Drink and Tobacco, 1968–78; former Vice-Pres., EEC Food Group and Mem., EEC Cttees on Food Products, Vocational Training, and Food Legislation; former Sec., Jt Bakers' Unions of England, Scotland and Ireland. Mem., TEC C4 programme Cttee, Hotel, Food, Catering and Institutional Management. *Recreations:* fishing, gardening, climbing in English Lake District. *Address:* 200 Bedford Road, Letchworth, Herts SG6 4EA. *T:* Letchworth (0462) 672170.

CHILD, Clifton James, OBE 1949; MA, PhM, FRHistS; Administrative Officer, Cabinet Office Historical Section, 1969–76, retired; *b* Birmingham, 20 June 1912; *s* of late Joseph and Georgina Child; *m* 1938, Hilde Hurwitz; two *s. Educ:* Moseley Grammar Sch.; Universities of Birmingham, Berlin and Wisconsin. Univ. of Birmingham: Entrance Schol., 1929; Kenrick Prizeman, 1930; BA 1st class hons, 1932; Francis Corder Clayton Research Schol., 1932–34; MA 1934. Univ. of Wisconsin: Commonwealth Fund Fellow, 1936–38; PhM 1938. Educn Officer, Lancs Community Council, 1939–40. Joined Foreign Office, 1941; Head of American Section, FO Research Dept, 1946–58; African Section, 1958–62; Dep. Librarian and Departmental Record Officer, 1962; Librarian and Keeper of the Papers, FO, 1965–69; Cabinet Office, 1969–76. FRHistS 1965. *Publications:* The German-Americans in Politics, 1939; (with Arnold Toynbee and others) Hitler's Europe, 1954; contribs to learned periodicals in Britain and US. *Recreations:* gardening, foreign travel. *Address:* Westcroft, Westhall Road, Warlingham, Surrey CR6 9HB. *T:* Upper Warlingham (0883) 622540.

CHILD, Sir (Coles John) Jeremy, 3rd Bt *cr* 1919; actor; *b* 20 Sept. 1944; *s* of Sir Coles John Child, 2nd Bt, and Sheila (*d* 1964), *e d* of Hugh Mathewson; *S* father, 1971; *m* 1971, Deborah Jane (*née* Snelling) (marr. diss. 1976); one *d*; *m* 1978, Jan (marr. diss. 1986), *y d* of B. Todd, Kingston upon Thames; one *s* one *d*; *m* 1987, Libby Morgan; one *s* one *d. Educ:* Eton; Univ. of Poitiers (Dip. in Fr.). Trained at Bristol Old Vic Theatre Sch., 1963–65; Bristol Old Vic, 1965–66; repertory at Windsor, Canterbury and Colchester; Conduct Unbecoming, Queen's, 1970; appeared at Royal Court, Mermaid and Bankside Globe, 1973; Oh Kay, Westminster, 1974; Donkey's Years, Globe, 1977; Hay Fever, Lyric, Hammersmith, 1980; *films include:* Privilege, 1967; Oh What a Lovely War!, 1967; The Breaking of Bumbo, 1970; Young Winston, 1971; The Stud, 1976; Quadrophenia, 1978; Sir Henry at Rawlinson's End, 1979; Chanel Solitaire, 1980; High Road to China, 1982; Give my Regards to Broad Street, 1983; *TV series:* Father, Dear

Father, Glittering Prizes, Wings, Edward and Mrs Simpson, When the Boat Comes In, Bird of Prey, The Jewel in the Crown, Fairly Secret Army, Hart to Hart, First Among Equals. *Recreations:* travel, squash, flying, photography. *Heir:* s Coles John Alexander Child, *b* 10 May 1982. *Clubs:* Garrick, Roehampton.

CHILD, Denis Marsden, CBE 1987; Chairman: International Commodities Clearing House, since 1990 (a Director, 1982–86); Lombard North Central PLC, since 1991; *b* 1 Nov. 1926; *s* of late Percival Snowden Child and Alice Child (*née* Jackson); *m* 1973, Patricia Charlton; two *s* one *d* by previous marr. *Educ:* Woodhouse Grove Sch., Bradford. Joined Westminster Bank, Leeds, 1942; RN, 1944–48; rejoined Westminster Bank; National Westminster Bank: Asst Area Manager, Leeds, 1970; Area Manager, Wembley, 1972; Chief Manager, Planning and Marketing, 1975; Head, Management Inf. and Control, 1977; Gen. Manager, Financial Control Div., 1979; Director, 1982–, NatWest Bank and subsids; Dep. Gp Chief Exec., 1982–87. Chairman: Exec. Cttee, BBA, 1986–87; Council, Assoc. for Payment Clearing Services, 1985–86; Financial Markets Cttee, Fedn Bancaire, EC, 1985–87; Director: Eurotunnel Gp, 1985–; Investors Compensation Scheme Ltd, 1988–. Bd Mem., CAA, 1986–90. Member: Accounting Standards Cttee, 1985–90; Securities and Investments Bd, 1986–; IBM UK Pensions Trust, 1984–. FCIB; FCT; FBIM. *Recreations:* golf, gardening. *Address:* Hill House, Ascott, Shipston on Stour, Warwicks CV36 5PP. *T:* Long Compton (060884) 268. *Club:* Stoke Poges Golf.

CHILD, Sir Jeremy; *see* Child, Sir C. J. J.

CHILD, Mark Sheard, PhD; FRS 1989; Aldrichian Praelector in Chemistry, University of Oxford, since 1989, and Fellow of St Edmund Hall, Oxford, since 1966; *b* 17 Aug. 1937; *s* of George Child and Kathleen (*née* Stevenson); *m* 1964, Daphne Hall; one *s* two *d*. *Educ:* Pocklington Sch., Yorks; Clare Coll., Cambridge (BA, PhD). Vis. Scientist, Berkeley, California, 1962–63; Lecturer in Theoretical Chemistry: Glasgow Univ., 1963–66; Oxford Univ., 1966–89. *Publication:* Molecular Collision Theory, 1974. *Recreations:* gardening, walking. *Address:* St Edmund Hall, Oxford. *T:* Oxford (0865) 279000.

CHILD VILLIERS, family name of **Earl of Jersey.**

CHILE, Bishop of, since 1977; **Most Rev. Colin Frederick Bazley;** Presiding Bishop (Primate) of the Province of the Southern Cone of America, since 1989; *b* 27 June 1935; *s* of Reginald Samuel Bazley and Isabella Davies; *m* 1960, Barbara Helen Griffiths; three *d*. *Educ:* Birkenhead School; St Peter's Hall, Oxford (MA); Tyndale Hall, Bristol. Deacon 1959, priest 1960; Assistant Curate, St Leonard's, Bootle, 1959–62; Missionary of S American Missionary Society in Chile, 1962–69; Rural Dean of Chol-Chol, 1962–66; Archdeacon of Temuco, 1966–69; Assistant Bishop for Cautin and Malleco, Dio. Chile, Bolivia and Peru, 1969–75; Assistant Bishop for Santiago, 1975–77; Bishop of Chile, Bolivia and Peru, 1977; diocese divided, Oct. 1977; Bishop of Chile and Bolivia until Oct. 1981, when diocese again divided; Presiding Bishop of the Anglican Council for South America, 1977–83. *Recreations:* football (Liverpool supporter) and fishing on camping holidays. *Address:* Iglesia Anglicana, Casilla 50675, Correo Central, Santiago, Chile. *T:* 8212478.

CHILSTON, 4th Viscount *cr* 1911, of Boughton Malherbe; **Alastair George Akers-Douglas;** Baron Douglas of Baads, 1911; film producer; *b* 5 Sept. 1946; *s* of Ian Stanley Akers-Douglas (*d* 1952) (*g s* of 1st Viscount) and of Phyllis Rosemary (who *m* 2nd, John Anthony Cobham Shaw, MC), *d* of late Arthur David Clere Parsons; *S* cousin, 1982; *m* 1971, Juliet Anne, *d* of Lt-Col Nigel Lovett, Glos Regt; three *s*. *Educ:* Eton College; Madrid Univ. *Recreation:* sailing. *Heir:* *s* Hon. Oliver Ian Akers-Douglas, *b* 13 Oct. 1973. *Address:* The Old Rectory, Twyford, near Winchester, Hants. *T:* Twyford (0962) 712300.

CHILTON, Air Marshal Sir (Charles) Edward, KBE 1959 (CBE 1945); CB 1951; RAF (retired); *o s* of J. C. Chilton; *m* 1st, 1929, Betty Ursula (*d* 1963), 2nd *d* of late Bernard Temple Wrinch; one *s*; 2nd, 1964, Joyce Cornforth. Royal Air Force general duties branch; Air Commodore, 1950; Air Vice-Marshal, 1954; Air Marshal, 1959. Dep. Air Officer i/c Administration, Air Command, SE Asia, 1944; AOC Ceylon, 1946; Imperial Defence Coll., 1951; AOC Gibraltar, 1952; Asst Chief of the Air Staff (Policy), 1953–54; SASO, HQ Coastal Command, 1955; AOC Royal Air Force, Malta, Fortress Comdr, Malta, and Dep. Comdr-in-Chief (Air), Allied Forces Mediterranean, 1957–59; AOC-in-C, Coastal Command and Maritime Air Commander Eastern Atlantic Area, and Commander Maritime Air, Channel and Southern North Sea, 1959–62. Consultant and Dir, IBM (Rentals) UK, 1963–78. Specialist navigator (Air Master navigator certificate) and Founder Fellow (Vice-Pres. 1949–51, 1959–61, 1963–65), Royal Institute of Navigation. Pres. RAF Rowing Club, 1956; Vice-Adm. and Hon. Life Mem. RAF Sailing Assoc.; Hon. Vice-Pres. RAF Swimming Assoc. FInstD. Freeman, City of London. Grand Cross of Prince Henry the Navigator (Portugal), 1960; Order of Polonia Restituta, Poland, 1980. *Publications:* numerous contributions to Service and other journals, on maritime-air operations and air navigation, and biographical papers on Rear-Adm. Sir Murray Sueter, CB, Wing Comdr J. C. Porte, CMG, Air Chief Marshal Sir Philip Joubert, and Air Chief Marshal The Hon. Sir Ralph Cochrane. *Recreations:* sailing, sea fishing and country walking. *Address:* 11 Charles House, Phyllis Court Drive, Henley-on-Thames, Oxon. *Clubs:* Royal Air Force; (Vice-Patron) Royal Gibraltar Yacht; Phyllis Court (Henley).

CHILTON, Brig. Sir Frederick Oliver, Kt 1969; CBE 1963 (OBE 1957); DSO 1941 and bar 1944; Chairman, Repatriation Commission, Australia, 1958–70; *b* 23 July 1905. *Educ:* Univ. of Sydney (BA, LLB). Solicitor, NSW, 1929. Late AIF; served War of 1939–45, Libya, Greece, New Guinea and Borneo (despatches, DSO and bar); Controller of Joint Intelligence, 1946–48; Asst Sec., Dept of Defence, Australia, 1948–50; Dep. Sec., 1950–58. *Address:* 30 Hudson Parade, Clareville Beach, NSW 2107, Australia. *Clubs:* Melbourne, Union, Naval and Military (Melbourne).

CHILVER, family name of **Baron Chilver.**

CHILVER, Baron *cr* 1987 (Life Peer), of Cranfield in the County of Bedfordshire; **Henry Chilver;** Kt 1978; FRS 1982; FEng 1977; CBIM; Chairman, ECC Group (formerly English China Clays), since 1989 (Director, since 1973); Chairman: Universities Funding Council, since 1988; Milton Keynes Development Corporation, since 1983; *b* 30 Oct. 1926; *e s* of A. H. Chilver and A. E. Mack; *m* 1959, Claudia M. B. Grigson, MA, MB, BCh, *o d* of Sir Wilfrid Grigson; three *s* two *d*. *Educ:* Southend High Sch.; Bristol Univ. (Albert Fry Prize 1947). Structural Engineering Asst, British Railways, 1947; Asst Lecturer, 1950, Lecturer, 1952, in Civil Engineering, Bristol Univ.; Demonstrator, 1954, Lectr, 1956, in Engineering, Cambridge Univ.; Fellow of Corpus Christi Coll., Cambridge, 1958–61 (Hon. Fellow, 1981); Chadwick Prof. of Civil Engineering, UCL, 1961–69; Vice-Chancellor, Cranfield Inst. of Technology, 1970–89; Director: Centre for Environmental Studies, 1967–69; Node Course (for civil service and industry), 1974–75. Chm., BASE Internat. Hldgs, 1988–; Director: SKF (UK), 1972–80; De La Rue Co., 1973–81; SE Reg., Nat. Westminster Bank, 1975–83; Delta Gp, 1977–84; Powell Duffryn, 1979–89; TR Technology Investment Trust, 1982–88; Hill Samuel Gp, 1983–87; Britoil, 1986–88; Porton Internat., 1989–; Ling Dynamic Systems, 1989–; ICI, 1990–. Chairman: PO, 1980–81; Higher Educn Review Body, NI, 1978–81; Univs' Computer Bd, 1975–78; RAF Trng and Educn Adv. Cttee, 1976–80; Adv. Council, RMCS, Shrivenham, 1978–83; Working Gp on Advanced Ground Transport, 1978–81; Electronics EDC, 1980–85; ACARD, 1982–85; Interim Adv. Cttee on Teachers' Pay, 1987–91; Innovation Adv. Bd, DTI, 1989–. Member: Ferrybridge Enquiry Cttee, 1965; Management Cttee, Inst. of Child Health, 1965–69; ARC, 1967–70 and 1972–75; SRC, 1970–74; Beds Educn Cttee, 1970–74; Planning and Transport Res. Adv. Council, 1972–79; Cttee for Ind. Technologies, 1972–76; ICE Special Cttee on Educn and Trng, 1973 (Chm.); CNAA, 1973–76; Royal Commn on Environmental Pollution, 1976–81; Standing Commn on Energy and the Environment, 1978–81; Adv. Bd for Res. Councils, 1982–85; Bd, Nat. Adv. Body for Local Authority Higher Educn, 1983–85. Dep. Pres., Standing Conf. on Schools Sci. and Technol.; Assessor, Inquiry on Lorries, People and the Envt, 1979–80. President: Inst. of Management Services, 1982–; Inst. Materials Management, 1986–; Vice-Pres., ICE, 1981–83; Mem., Smeatonian Soc. of Civil Engrs. Member Council: Birkbeck Coll., 1980–82; Cheltenham Coll., 1980–88. Lectures: STC Communications, 1981; O'Sullivan, Imperial Coll., 1984; Lady Margaret Beaufort, Bedford, 1985; Fawley, Southampton Univ., 1985; Lubbock, Oxford, 1990. Telford Gold Medal, ICE, 1962; Coopers Hill War Meml Prize, ICE, 1977. Hon. DSc: Leeds, 1982; Bristol, 1983; Salford, 1983; Strathclyde, 1986; Bath, 1986; Cranfield, 1989; Buckingham, 1990; Compiègne, 1990. *Publications:* Problems in Engineering Structures (with R. J. Ashby), 1958; Strength of Materials (with J. Case), 1959; Thin-walled Structures (ed), 1967; papers on structural theory in engineering journals. *Address:* ECC Group plc, 125 Wood Street, EC2V 7AQ. *T:* 071-696 9229. *Clubs:* Athenæum, United Oxford & Cambridge University.

CHILVER, Brian Outram; Chairman, Seafield, since 1990; *b* 17 June 1933; *s* of late Bertram Montagu Chilver and of Edith Gwendoline Chilver; *m* 1956, Erica Mary; two *s* two *d*. *Educ:* University College Sch. FCA 1965; ACMA 1966. Temple Gothard & Co., 1949–55 (articled clerk); National Service, RAF, 1955–57; Barton Mayhew & Co., 1957–59; Temple Gothard & Co., 1959–85 (Partner, 1960, Senior Partner, 1975); Chm., Laing Properties, 1987–90. *Recreations:* walking, swimming, reading, music. *Address:* Bretaye, Limbourne Lane, Fittleworth, West Sussex RH20 1HR; (office) 9 Chesterfield Street, W1X 7HF.

CHILVER, Elizabeth Millicent, (Mrs R. C. Chilver); Principal of Lady Margaret Hall, Oxford, 1971–79, Honorary Fellow, 1979; *b* 3 Aug. 1914; *o d* of late Philip Perceval Graves and late Millicent Graves (*née* Gilchrist); *m* 1937, Richard Clementson Chilver, CB (*d* 1985). *Educ:* Benenden Sch., Cranbrook; Somerville Coll., Oxford (Hon. Fellow, 1977). Journalist, 1937–39; temp. Civil Servant, 1939–45; Daily News Ltd, 1945–47; temp. Principal and Secretary, Colonial Social Science Research Council and Colonial Economic Research Cttee, Colonial Office, 1948–57; Director, Univ. of Oxford Inst. of Commonwealth Studies, 1957–61; Senior Research Fellow, Univ. of London Inst. of Commonwealth Studies, 1961–64; Principal, Bedford Coll., Univ. of London, 1964–71, Fellow, 1974. Mem. Royal Commn on Medical Education, 1965–68. Trustee, British Museum, 1970–75; Mem. Governing Body, SOAS, Univ. of London, 1975–80. Médaille de la Reconnaissance française, 1945. *Publications:* articles on African historical subjects. *Address:* 47 Kingston Road, Oxford OX2 6RH. *T:* Oxford (0865) 53082.

CHILWELL, Hon. Sir Muir Fitzherbert, Kt 1989; **Hon. Mr Justice Chilwell;** Judge of the High Court (formerly Supreme Court) of New Zealand, since 1973; *b* 12 April 1924; *s* of Benjamin Charles Chilwell and Loris Madeleine Chilwell; *m* 1947, Lynette Erica Frances Cox; two *d* (one *s* decd). *Educ:* Auckland University Coll., Univ. of New Zealand (LLB 1949; LLM Hons 1950). Law Clerk, 1941–49; admitted Barrister and Solicitor, 1949; Partner, Haddow, Haddow & Chilwell, later Haddow Chilwell Pain & Palmer, 1949–65; QC 1965; admitted Victorian Bar (Aust.) and QC Vict. 1970; Admin. Div., High Court, 1982; Lectr, Univ. of Auckland, 1950 and 1953–60. Member: Contracts and Commercial Law Reform Cttee, 1966–68 (Chm., 1968–73); Law Revision Commn, 1968–73; Disciplinary Cttee, NZ Law Soc., 1971–73; Council, Legal Educn, NZ, 1985– (Assessor in Law of Contract, 1964–67); Chm., Legal Res. Foundn, 1977–81; Mem. Council, Auckland Dist Law Soc., 1960–67, Pres., 1967–68; Pres., Auckland Medico-Legal Soc., 1969–70, Life Mem., 1989. Silver Jubilee Medal, 1977; Commemoration Medal, NZ, 1990. *Recreation:* boating. *Address:* 87 St Heliers Bay Road, Auckland 5, New Zealand. *T:* 557 999. *Club:* Royal New Zealand Yacht Squadron.

CHING, Henry, CBE 1982; Secretary General, Caritas–Hong Kong, since 1990; *b* 2 Nov. 1933; *s* of Henry Ching, OBE and Ruby Irene Ching; *m* 1963, Eileen Frances Peters; two *d*. *Educ:* Diocesan Boys' School, Hong Kong; Hong Kong Univ. (BA Hons); Wadham Coll., Oxford (MA, DipEd). Schoolmaster, 1958–61; Hong Kong Civil Service: various appts, 1961–73; Principal Asst Financial Sec., 1973–76; Dep. Financial Sec., 1976–83; Sec. for Health and Welfare and MLC, Hong Kong, 1983–85, retired. Chief Administrator, Hong Kong Foundn, 1989. *Recreations:* cricket, rowing. *Address:* 39 Saiala Road, East Killara, NSW 2071, Australia.

CHINN, Sir Trevor (Edwin), Kt 1990; CVO 1989; Chairman, since 1973 and Chief Executive, since 1987, Lex Service PLC (Managing Director, 1968–86); *b* 24 July 1935; *s* of Rosser and Susie Chinn; *m* 1965, Susan Speelman; two *s*. *Educ:* Clifton Coll.; King's Coll., Cambridge. Dir, Lex Service, 1959–. Chm., Robins Cinemas Ltd, 1990. Member: Governing Council, Business in the Community, 1983–; Council, Royal Shakespeare Theatre, 1982–; Bd of Govs, Jewish Agency. Pres. and Chm. Bd, Joint Israel Appeal; Chm., Britain/Israel Public Affairs Centre. Vice Chm., Wishing Well Appeal, Gt Ormond St Hosp. for Sick Children, 1985–89. Trustee: Duke of Edinburgh's Award Scheme, 1979–88; Royal Acad. Trust, 1989–; Hampstead Theatre Trust, 1990. Freeman of the City of London. Chief Barker, Variety Club of GB, 1977, 1978. *Address:* Lex House, 17 Connaught Place, W2 2EL. *T:* 071–723 1212.

CHINNERY, (Charles) Derek; Controller, Radio 1, BBC, 1978–85; *b* 27 April 1925; *s* of Percy Herbert and Frances Dorothy Chinnery; *m* 1953, Doreen Grace Clarke. *Educ:* Gosforth Grammar School. Youth in training, BBC, 1941; RAF Cadet Pilot, 1943. BBC: Technical Asst, 1947; Programme Engineer, 1948; Studio Manager, 1950; Producer, 1952; Executive Producer, 1967; Head of Radio 1, 1972. *Recreations:* DIY, sailing. *Address:* 2 Meads Brow, Eastbourne BN20 7UP.

CHIONA, Most Rev. James; *see* Blantyre, Archbishop of, (RC).

CHIPIMO, Elias Marko; Chairman, Standard Bank Zambia Ltd, 1976–80 (Deputy Chairman, 1975); *b* 23 Feb. 1931; *s* of Marko Chipimo, Zambia (then Northern Rhodesia); *m* 1959, Anna Joyce Nkole Konie; four *s* three *d*. *Educ:* St Canisius, Chikuni, Zambia; Munali; Fort Hare Univ. Coll., SA; University Coll. of Rhodesia and Nyasaland; Univ. of Zambia (LLB 1985). Schoolmaster, 1959–63; Sen. Govt Administrator, 1964–67; High Comr for Zambia in London, and Zambian Ambassador to the Holy See, 1968–69; Perm. Sec., Min. of Foreign Affairs, 1969. Chairman: Zambia Stock Exchange Council, 1970–72; Zambia Nat. Bldg Soc., 1970–71; Dep. Chm., Development Bank of Zambia Ltd, 1973–75; Director: Zambia Airways Corp., 1975–81; Zambia Bata Shoe Co. Ltd, 1977–. Mem., Nat Council for Sci. Res., 1977–80. President: Lusaka Branch, Zambia Red Cross, 1970–75; Zambia Red Cross Soc., 1990– (Vice-Pres., 1976–90); Mem., Zambia

Univ. Council, 1970–76; Dir, Internat. Sch. of Lusaka, 1970–76. Cllr, Lusaka City Council, 1974–80. Representative: Knights of Malta, 1978–; Commonwealth Soc., 1979–88. *Publications:* Our Land and People, 1966; Tied Loans and the Role of Banks (vol. 2 of International Financing of Economic Development), 1978; articles in Univ. of Zambia Jl. *Recreations:* rose gardening, reading, general literature, linguistics, philosophy, politics, economics, discussions, chess, growing roses. *Address:* PO Box 32115, 10101 Lusaka, Zambia.

CHIPP, David Allan; Director, Reuter Foundation, 1986–90; *b* 6 June 1927; *s* of late Thomas Ford Chipp and late Isabel Mary Ballinger; unmarried. *Educ:* Geelong Grammar Sch., Australia; King's Coll., Cambridge (MA). Served with Middlesex Regt, 1944–47; Cambridge, 1947–50. Joined Reuters as Sports Reporter, 1950; Correspondent for Reuters: in SE Asia, 1953–55; in Peking, 1956–58; various managerial positions in Reuters, 1960–68; Editor of Reuters, 1968; Editor in Chief, Press Assoc., 1969–86. An Indep. Dir, The Observer, 1985–; Director: TV-am News Co., 1986–; Lloyds of London Press, 1990–. Mem., Press Complaints Commn, 1991–. *Recreations:* reading, opera. *Address:* 2 Wilton Court, 59/60 Eccleston Square, SW1V 1PH. *T:* 071–834 5579. *Clubs:* Garrick; Leander (Henley-on-Thames).

CHIPPERFIELD, Geoffrey Howes; Second Permanent Secretary, Department of the Environment, and Chief Executive, Property Services Agency, since 1991; *b* 20 April 1933; *s* of Nelson Chipperfield and Eleanor Chipperfield; *m* 1959, Gillian James; two *s*. *Educ:* Cranleigh; New Coll., Oxford. Called to the Bar, Gray's Inn, 1955. Joined Min. of Housing and Local Govt, 1956; Harkness Fellow, Inst. of Govtl Studies, Univ. of Calif, Berkeley, 1962–63; Principal Private Sec., Minister of Housing, 1968–70; Sec., Greater London Develt Plan Inquiry, 1970–73; Under Sec., 1976, Dep. Sec., 1982–87, DoE; Dep. Sec., Dept of Energy, 1987–89; Perm. Under-Sec. of State, DoE, 1989–91. *Recreations:* reading, gardening. *Address:* Department of the Environment, 2 Marsham Street, SW1P 3EB. *Club:* United Oxford & Cambridge University.

CHIPPINDALE, Christopher Ralph, PhD; FSA; Editor, Antiquity, since 1987; Assistant Curator, Cambridge University Museum of Archaeology, and Bye-Fellow, Girton College, Cambridge, since 1988; *b* 13 Oct. 1951; *s* of Keith and Ruth Chippindale; *m* 1976, Anne Lowe; two *s* two *d*. *Educ:* Sedbergh School; St John's College, Cambridge (BA Hons); Girton Coll., Cambridge (PhD). FSA; MIFA. Editor, freelance, Penguin Books, Hutchinson Publishing Group, 1974–82; Res. Fellow in Archaeology, Girton Coll., Cambridge, 1985–88. *Publications:* Stonehenge Complete, 1983; (ed jtly) The Pastmasters, 1989; (jtly) Who owns Stonehenge?; articles in jls. *Recreations:* archaeology, worrying. *Address:* 85 Hills Road, Cambridge.

CHIRAC, Jacques René; Prime Minister of France, 1974–76 and 1986–88; President, Rassemblement pour la République, 1976–81 and since 1982; Mayor of Paris, since 1977; *b* Paris, 29 Nov. 1932; *s* of François Chirac, company manager and Marie-Louise (*née* Valette); *m* 1956, Bernadette Chodron de Courcel; two *s*. *Educ:* Lycée Carnot and Lycee Louis-le-Grand, Paris; Diploma of Inst. of Polit. Studies, Paris, and of Summer Sch., Harvard Univ., USA. Served Army in Algeria. Ecole Nat. d'Admin, 1957–59; Auditor, Cour des Comptes, 1959; Head Dept: Sec.-Gen. of Govt, 1962; Private Office of Georges Pompidou, 1962–67; Counsellor, Cour des Comptes, 1965–; State Secretary: Employment Problems, 1967–68; Economy and Finance, 1968–71; Minister for Parly Relations, 1971–72; Minister for Agriculture and Rural Development, 1972–74; Home Minister, March-May 1974; Sec.-Gen., UDR, Dec. 1974–June 1975. Deputy from Corrèze, elected 1967, 1968, 1973, 1976 (UDR), 1978 (RFR), and 1981; Member from Meymac, Conseil Général of Corrèze, 1968–, Pres. 1970–. Mem., European Parlt, 1979–80. Treasurer, Claude Pompidou Foundn (charity for elderly and for handicapped children), 1969–. Grand-Croix, Ordre national du Mérite; Croix de la valeur militaire; Chevalier du Mérite agricole, des Arts et des Lettres, de l'Etoile noire, du Mérite sportif, du Mérite touristique; Médaille de l'Aéronautique. *Publications:* a thesis on development of Port of New Orleans, 1954; Discours pour la France à l'heure du choix, la lueur d'espérance: réflexion du soir pour le matin, 1978. *Address:* Hôtel de Ville de Paris, 75196 Paris RP, France.

CHISHOLM, Prof. Alexander William John; Professorial Fellow, University of Salford, since 1987; *b* 18 April 1922; *s* of Thomas Alexander Chisholm and Maude Mary Chisholm (*née* Robinson); *m* 1945, Aline Mary (*née* Eastwood); one *s* one *d*. *Educ:* Brentwood Sch., Essex; Northampton Polytechnic; Manchester Coll. of Science and Technology; Royal Technical Coll., Salford (BSc(Eng) London). CEng, FIMechE, FIProdE. Section Leader, Res. Dept, Metropolitan Vickers Electrical Co. Ltd, 1944–49; Sen. Scientific Officer, then Principal Scientific Officer, Nat. Engrg Lab., 1949–57; UK Scientific Mission, British Embassy, USA, 1952–54; Head of Dept of Mechanical Engrg, then Prof. of Mechanical Engrg, Royal Coll. of Advanced Technology, Salford, 1957–67; University of Salford: Prof. of Mech. Engineering, 1967–82; Research Prof. in Engrg., 1982–87; Chm., Salford Univ. Industrial Centre Ltd, 1976–82. Visitor, Cambridge Univ. Engrg Dept and Vis. Fellow, Wolfson Coll., 1973–74. Chm., Industrial Admin and Engrg Prodn Gp, IMechE, 1960–62. Nat. Council for Technological Awards: Chm., Mechanical/Prodn Engrg Cttee, 1960–63; Vice-Chm., Bd of Studies in Engrg and Governor, 1963–65. Chm., Engrg Profs Conf., 1976–80; Member: Technology Cttee, UGC, 1969–74; Engrg Processes Cttee, SERC, 1980–83. Pres., CIRP, 1983–84 (Chm., UK Bd, 1977–88; Hon. Life Mem. 1987). Mem., Court, Cranfield Inst. of Technology, 1974–91. Whitworth Prize, IMechE, 1965. *Publications:* numerous on production process technology, manufacturing systems, industrial research, educn and training of engineers, human factors in manufacturing. *Recreations:* hill walking, sailing. *Address:* 12 Legh Road, Prestbury, Macclesfield, Cheshire SK10 4HX. *T:* Prestbury (0625) 829412. *Club:* Athenæum.

CHISHOLM, Archibald Hugh Tennent, CBE (mil.) 1946; MA; *b* 17 Aug. 1902; 2nd *s* of late Hugh Chisholm and Mrs Chisholm (*née* Harrison), Rush Park, Co. Antrim; *m* 1939, Josephine (*d* 1983), *e d* of J. E. Goudge, OBE, ICS; one *s* one *d* (and one *d* decd). *Educ:* Westminster (Exhibnr and Mure Schol.); Christ Church, Oxford (schol.). Wall Street Journal of NY, 1925–27; The British Petroleum Co. (then Anglo-Persian/Anglo-Iranian Oil Co.), Iran and Kuwait, 1928–36 and London, 1945–72. Editor of The Financial Times, 1937–40; Army, 1940–45 (despatches twice, CBE). FZS; FInstPet. Chevalier, Légion d'Honneur. *Publication:* The First Kuwait Oil Concession Agreement: a Record of the Negotiations, 1911–1934, 1975. *Address:* 107 Hamilton Terrace, NW8 9QY. *T:* 071–289 0713; The Coach House, Charlton House, Tetbury, Glos. *T:* Tetbury (0666) 54339. *Clubs:* Athenæum, Naval and Military, Beefsteak, MCC.

CHISHOLM, Prof. Geoffrey Duncan, FRCSE, FRCPE, FRCS; Professor of Surgery, University of Edinburgh, since 1977; Director, Nuffield Transplant Unit, Edinburgh, since 1977; *b* 30 Sept. 1931; *s* of Sedman Arthur Chisholm and Ellen Marion Chisholm (*née* Friston); *m* 1962, Angela Jane Holden; two *s*. *Educ:* Scots Coll., Wellington, NZ; Malvern Coll.; St Andrews Univ. (MB ChB 1955, ChM 1965). FRCSE 1959, FRCS 1960, FRCPE 1990. BPMF Travelling Fellow, 1961–62; Res. Fellow, Johns Hopkins Hosp., Baltimore, 1961–62; Consultant Urol Surgeon, Hammersmith Hosp., 1967–77; Hon. Consultant Urol Surgeon, Western Gen. Hosp., Edinburgh, 1977–. Hon. Sen. Lecturer: RPMS, 1967–77; Inst. of Urology, Univ. of London, 1972–. Chairman: British Prostate Gp, 1975–80; Conf. Roy. Colls and Faculties (Scotland), 1989–; Vice-Pres., British Assoc. of Surgical Oncologists, 1980–81; Chm., European Soc. of Urol Oncology and Endocrinology, 1984–85; President: British Assoc. of Urol Surgeons, 1986–88; RCSE 1988– (Mem. Council, 1984–); FRSocMed (Mem. Council, 1974–76); Fellow, Assoc. Surg. GB and Ireland, 1967; Founder Mem., British Transplant Soc., 1972; Corresp. Mem., Amer. Assoc. Genito-urinary Surg., 1980; Hon. Mem., Dutch, Australasian, Greek and S African Urol Assocs; Member: Internat. Soc. of Urology; Internat. Continence Soc. Hon. FRACS 1990; Hon. FCSSA 1990. Vis. Professorships include Rotterdam, Strasbourg, Aachen, Cairo, San Diego, Dallas; lectures in UK, USA and Australia. Managing Editor, Urological Research, 1977–81; Editor, British Jl of Urology, 1977–; Series Editor, Clinical Practice in Urology, 1981– (9 vols). Francisco Diaz Medal, Spanish Assoc. of Urology, 1985; Pybus Medal, N of England Surgical Soc., 1986; St Peter's Medal, British Assoc. of Urol Surgeons, 1989. *Publications:* Tutorials in Postgraduate Medicine, 1980; (jtly) Scientific Foundations of Urology, 1982, 2nd edn 1990; (jtly) Surgical Management, 1984, 2nd edn 1991; contribs to learned jls. *Recreations:* medical journalism, wine tasting. *Address:* University Department of Surgery/Urology, Western General Hospital, Edinburgh EH4 2XU. *T:* 031–315 2522; 8 Ettrick Road, Edinburgh EH10 5BJ. *T:* 031–229 7173. *Club:* New (Edinburgh).

CHISHOLM, John Alexander Raymond, CEng; Chief Executive, Defence Research Agency, since 1991; *b* 27 Aug. 1946; *s* of Ruari Ian Lambert Chisholm and Pamela Harland Chisholm; *m* 1969, Catherine Alexandra (*née* Pana); one *s* one *d*. *Educ:* Univ. of Cambridge (MA). MIEE. Vauxhall Motors, 1964–69; Scicon Ltd, 1969–79; Cap Scientific Ltd, 1979–88; Man. Dir, 1981–88; Chm., 1986–88; Chm., Yard Ltd, 1986–88; UK Man. Dir, Sema Group plc, 1988–91. Pres., Electronic and Business Equipment Assoc., 1989–90. *Recreations:* ski-ing, water-ski-ing, wind-surfing, golf. *Address:* 13 The Green, Woughton-on-the-Green, Milton Keynes, Bucks MK6 3BE. *T:* Milton Keynes (0908) 670714.

CHISHOLM, Prof. Malcolm Harold, PhD; FRS 1990; Distinguished Professor of Chemistry, Indiana University, since 1985; *b* 15 Oct. 1945; *s* of Angus and Gweneth Chisholm; *m* 1st, 1969, Susan (marr. diss.); one *s*; 2nd, 1982, Cynthia; two *s*. *Educ:* London Univ. (BSc 1966; PhD 1969). Sessional Lectr, Univ. of W Ontario, 1970–72; Asst Prof. of Chemistry, Princeton Univ., 1972–78; Associate Prof., 1978–80, Prof., 1980–85, Indiana Univ. Guggenheim Fellow, 1985–86. FAAAS 1987. Hon. DSc London, 1980. RSC Award for Chem. and Electrochem. of Transition Elements, 1987; Alexander von Humboldt Sen. Scientist Award, 1988; (jtly) ACS Nobel Laureate Signature Award, 1988; ACS Award in Inorganic Chm., 1989. *Publications:* author or co-author of numerous publications, mostly in chem. jls. *Recreations:* squash, gardening. *Address:* 515 Hawthorne, Bloomington, Ind 47405, USA. *T:* (812) 855–6606; 38 Norwich Street, Cambridge CB2 1EW. *T:* Cambridge (0223) 312392.

CHISHOLM, Prof. Michael Donald Inglis; Professor of Geography, University of Cambridge, since 1976; Professorial Fellow, St Catharine's College, Cambridge, since 1976; *b* 10 June 1931; *s* of M. S. and A. W. Chisholm; *m* 1st, 1959, Edith Gretchen Emma (*née* Hoof) (marr. diss. 1981); one *s* two *d*; 2nd, 1986, Judith Carola Shackleton (*née* Murray). *Educ:* St Christopher Sch., Letchworth; St Catharine's Coll., Cambridge (MA). MA Oxon. Nat. Service Commn, RE, 1950–51. Deptl Demonstrator, Inst. for Agric. Econs, Oxford, 1954–59; Asst Lectr, then Lectr in Geog., Bedford Coll., London, 1960–64; Vis. Sen. Lectr in Geog., Univ. of Ibadan, 1964–65; Lectr, then Reader in Geog., Univ. of Bristol, 1965–72; Prof. of Economic and Social Geography, Univ. of Bristol, 1972–76. Associate, Economic Associates Ltd, consultants, 1965–77; Mem. SSRC, and Chm. of Cttees for Human Geography and Planning, 1967–72; Member: Local Govt Boundary Commn for England, 1971–78; Rural Develt Commn, 1981–90; English Adv. Cttee on Telecommunications, 1990–. Mem. Council, Inst. of British Geographers, 1961 and 1962, Junior Vice-Pres., 1977, Sen. Vice-Pres., 1978, Pres. 1979. Conservator of River Cam, 1979–, Chm., 1991–. Gill Memorial Prize, RGS, 1969. Geography Editor for Hutchinson Univ. Lib., 1973–82. *Publications:* Rural Settlement and Land Use: an essay in location, 1962; Geography and Economics, 1966; (ed jtly) Regional Forecasting, 1971; (ed jtly) Spatial Policy Problems of the British Economy, 1971; Research in Human Geography, 1971; (ed) Resources for Britain's Future, 1972; (jtly) Freight Flows and Spatial Aspects of the British Economy, 1973; (jtly) The Changing Pattern of Employment, 1973; (ed jtly) Studies in Human Geography, 1973; (ed jtly) Processes in Physical and Human Geography: Bristol Essays, 1975; Human Geography: Evolution or Revolution?, 1975; Modern World Development, 1982; Regions in Recession and Resurgence, 1990; (ed jtly) Shared Space: Divided Space, 1990; papers in Farm Economist, Oxford Econ. Papers, Trans Inst. British Geographers, Geography, Geographical Jl, Applied Statistics, Area, etc. *Recreations:* gardening, theatre, opera, interior design. *Address:* Department of Geography, Downing Place, Cambridge CB2 3EN.

CHISHOLM, Roderick Æneas, CBE 1946; DSO 1944; DFC and bar; AE; ARCS; BSc; *b* 23 Nov. 1911; *s* of Edward Consitt Chisholm and Edith Maud Mary Cary Elwes; *m* 1945, Phillis Mary Sanchia, *d* of late Geoffrey A. Whitworth, CBE; one *s* two *d*. *Educ:* Ampleforth Coll.; Imperial Coll. of Science and Technology, London. AAF, 1932–40; Royal Air Force, 1940–46 (Air Cdre). *Publication:* Cover of Darkness, 1953. *Address:* Ladywell House, Alresford, Hants.

CHISLETT, Derek Victor; Warden, Sackville College, since 1988; *b* 18 April 1929; *s* of Archibald Lynn Chislett and Eva Jessie Collins; *m* 1954, Joan Robson; two *d*. *Educ:* Christ's Hospital. Admiralty, 1946–53; HM Forces, 1947–49; Nat. Assistance Board, 1953–66; Min. of Social Security, 1966–68; Department of Health and Social Security, 1968–88: Under Sec., 1983; Controller, Newcastle Central Office, 1983–86; Dir of Finance (Social Security), 1986–88. Dir, Pennington Robson, 1989–. Mem. Exec. Cttee, Nat. Assoc. of Almshouses, 1989–. Trustee: Down's Syndrome Assoc., 1989–; Motability Tenth Anniversary Trust, 1989–; Independent Living Fund, 1990–. *Recreations:* opera, walking, bee-keeping. *Address:* Sackville College, East Grinstead, W Sussex. *T:* East Grinstead (0342) 326561.

CHISWELL, Rt. Rev. Peter; *see* Armidale, Bishop of.

CHISWELL, Maj.-Gen. Peter Irvine, CB 1985; CBE 1976 (OBE 1972; MBE 1965); Director, Buckland Leadership Development Centre, since 1989; *b* 19 April 1930; *s* of late Col Henry Thomas Chiswell, OBE (late RAMC) and of Gladys Beatrice Chiswell; *m* 1958, Felicity Philippa, *d* of R. F. Martin; two *s*. *Educ:* Allhallows School; RMA Sandhurst. Commissioned Devonshire Regt, 1951; transf. Parachute Regt, 1958; DAAG HQ Berlin Inf. Bde, 1963–65; Brigade Major, 16 Para Bde, 1967–68; GSO1 (DS), Staff Coll., 1968–69; CO 3 PARA, 1969–71; Col GS (Army Training), 1971–74; Comd British Contingent DCOS UN Force Cyprus, 1974–76; Comd, 44 Para Bde, 1976–78; ACOS (Operations), HQ Northern Army Gp, 1978–81; Comd, Land Forces NI, 1982–83; GOC Wales, 1983–85. Vice-Chm., ACFA, 1988–; Mem., Welsh Adv. Bd, Welsh Wildlife Appeal, 1988–. Gov., Christ Coll., Brecon, 1987–. *Recreations:* travel, sailing.

CHITNIS, family name of **Baron Chitnis.**

CHITNIS, Baron *cr* 1977 (Life Peer), of Ryedale, N Yorks; **Pratap Chidamber Chitnis;** Chairman, British Refugee Council, 1986–89; *b* 1 May 1936; *s* of late Chidamber N. Chitnis and Lucia Mallik; *m* 1964, Anne Brand; one *s* decd. *Educ:* Penryn Sch.; Stonyhurst Coll.; Univs of Birmingham (BA) and Kansas (MA). Admin. Asst, Nat. Coal Board, 1958–59; Liberal Party Organisation: Local Govt Officer, 1960–62; Agent, Orpington Liberal Campaign, 1962; Trng Officer, 1962–64; Press Officer, 1964–66; Head of Liberal Party Organisation, 1966–69. Sec., 1969–75, Chief Exec. and Dir, 1975–88, Joseph Rowntree Social Service Trust. Mem., Community Relations Commn, 1970–77; Chm., BBC Immigrants Programme Adv. Cttee, 1979–83 (Mem., 1972–77). Chm., Refugee Action, 1981–86. Reported on elections in: Zimbabwe, 1979; (jtly) Guyana, 1980; El Salvador, 1982, 1984, 1988 and 1989; Nicaragua, 1984. *Address:* Quartier des Trois Fontaines, 84490 Vaucluse, France.

CHITTY, Alison Jill; theatre designer; *b* 16 Oct. 1948; *d* of Ernest Hedley Chitty and Irene Joan Waldron. *Educ:* King Alfred School, London; St Martin's School of Art; Central School of Art and Design (Degree in Theatre Design); Arts Council Scholarship. Victoria Theatre, Stoke-on-Trent, 1970–79 (designed over 40 productions; Head of Design 4 years); designer, 1970–, for *stage:* Hampstead Theatre, Riverside studios, Sheffield, RSC, NT, Haymarket, Stratford East, Playhouse (Rose Tattoo, 1991); for *opera:* Opera North, Houston Grand Opera, Glyndebourne, Royal Opera House (Gawain, 1991); for *films:* Blue Jean, Aria, Life is Sweet. *Address:* c/o Curtis Brown Associates, 162–168 Regent Street, W1R 5TB.

CHITTY, Dr Anthony; Director of Corporate Engineering, Northern Engineering Industries, since 1989 (Deputy Director, 1988–89); *b* 29 May 1931; *s* of Ashley George Chitty and Doris Ellen Mary Buck; *m* 1956, Audrey Munro; two *s* one *d*. *Educ:* Glynn Grammar Sch., Epsom; Imperial Coll., London. BSc, PhD, DIC; CEng. GEC Res. Labs, 1955; Hd, Creep of Steels Lab., ERA, 1959; GEC Power Gp, 1963; Chief Metallurgist (Applications), C. A. Parsons, 1966; Dir, Advanced Technol. Div., Clarke Chapman-John Thompson, 1973; Internat. Res. and Develt, 1978; Gen. Manager, Engrg Products, N.E.I. Parsons, 1979; Regional Industrial Adviser, NE Region, DTI, 1984–88. Vis. Prof., Univ. of Aston in Birmingham, 1977–84. Chairman: Bd of Newcastle Technol. Centre, 1988–90 (Dep. Chm., 1985–88); Centre for Adhesive Technol, 1990–; Member, Board: Newcastle Univ. New Ventures Ltd, 1989–; Newcastle Polytechnic Products Ltd, 1989–. *Publications:* research publications in the fields of materials and welding for power generation. *Recreations:* hill walking, gardening. *Address:* 1 Willow Way, Darras Hall, Ponteland, Northumberland NE20 9RJ. *T:* Ponteland (0661) 23899.

CHITTY, (Margaret) Beryl, (Mrs Henry Fowler), CMG 1977; HM Diplomatic Service, retired; *b* 2 Dec. 1917; *d* of Wilfrid and Eleanor Holdgate; *m* 1st, 1949, Keith Chitty, FRCS (*d* 1958); 2nd, 1989, Henry Fowler, CD, Kingston, Jamaica. *Educ:* Belvedere Sch. (GPDST), Liverpool; St Hugh's Coll., Oxford (BA, MA; Hon. Fellow, 1982). Dominions Office, 1940; Private Sec. to Parly Under-Sec. of State, 1943–45; Principal, 1945; CRO, 1947–52; First Sec., Commonwealth Office, 1958; UK Mission to UN, New York, 1968–70; FCO, 1970–71; Dep. (and Acting) British High Comr in Jamaica, 1971–75; Head of Commonwealth Co-ord. Dept, FCO, 1975–77. Appeal Sec., St Hugh's Coll., Oxford, 1978–81; Appeal Dir, St Peter's Coll., Oxford, 1982–88. Non-Press Mem., Press Council, 1978–80. Mem., Governing Body, Queen Elizabeth House, Oxford, 1977–80. *Address:* 79 Bainton Road, Oxford OX2 7AG. *T:* Oxford (0865) 53384.

CHITTY, Susan Elspeth, (Lady Chitty); author; *b* 18 Aug. 1929; *d* of Rudolph Glossop and Mrs E. A. Hopkinson; *m* 1951, Sir Thomas Willes Chitty, Bt, *qv*; one *s* three *d*. *Educ:* Godolphin Sch., Salisbury; Somerville Coll., Oxford. Mem. editorial staff, Vogue, 1952–53; subseq. journalist, reviewer, broadcaster and lecturer. *Publications: novels:* Diary of a Fashion Model, 1958; White Huntress, 1963; My Life and Horses, 1966; *biographies:* The Woman who wrote Black Beauty, 1972; The Beast and the Monk, 1975; Charles Kingsley and North Devon, 1976; Gwen John 1876–1939, 1981; Now to My Mother, 1985; That Singular Person Called Lear, 1988; *non-fiction:* (with Thomas Hinde) On Next to Nothing, 1976; (with Thomas Hinde) The Great Donkey Walk, 1977; The Young Rider, 1979; *edited:* The Intelligent Woman's Guide to Good Taste, 1958; The Puffin Book of Horses, 1975; As Once in May, by Antonia White, 1983. *Recreations:* riding, travel. *Address:* Bow Cottage, West Hoathly, Sussex RH19 4QF. *T:* Sharpthorne (0342) 810269.

CHITTY, Sir Thomas Willes, 3rd Bt *cr* 1924; author (as Thomas Hinde); *b* 2 March 1926; *e s* of Sir (Thomas) Henry Willes Chitty, 2nd Bt, and Ethel Constance (*d* 1971), *d* of S. H. Gladstone, Darley Ash, Bovingdon, Herts; *S* father, 1955; *m* 1951, Susan Elspeth (*see* S. E. Chitty); one *s* three *d*. *Educ:* Winchester; University Coll., Oxford. Royal Navy, 1944–47. Shell Petroleum Co., 1953–60. Granada Arts Fellow, Univ. of York, 1964–65; Visiting Lectr, Univ. of Illinois, 1965–67; Vis. Prof., Boston Univ., 1969–70. *Publications: novels:* Mr Nicholas, 1952; Happy as Larry, 1957; For the Good of the Company, 1961; A Place Like Home, 1962; The Cage, 1962; Ninety Double Martinis, 1963; The Day the Call Came, 1964; Games of Chance, 1965; The Village, 1966; High, 1968; Bird, 1970; Generally a Virgin, 1972; Agent, 1974; Our Father, 1975; Daymare, 1980; *non-fiction:* (with wife, as Susan Hinde) On Next to Nothing, 1976; (with Susan Chitty) The Great Donkey Walk, 1977; The Cottage Book, 1979; Stately Gardens of Britain, 1983; Forests of Britain, 1985; (ed) The Domesday Book: England's heritage, then and now, 1986; Courtiers: 900 years of court life, 1986; Tales from the Pumproom: an informal history of Bath, 1988; Roads and Ways of Britain, 1990; *autobiography:* Sir Henry and Sons, 1980; *biography:* A Field Guide to the English Country Parson, 1983; Capability Brown, 1986; *anthology:* Spain, 1963. *Heir: s* Andrew Edward Willes Chitty, *b* 20 Nov. 1953. *Address:* Bow Cottage, West Hoathly, Sussex RH19 4QF. *T:* Sharpthorne (0342) 810269.

CHOLERTON, Frederick Arthur, CBE 1978; *b* 15 April 1917; *s* of Frederick Arthur Cholerton and Charlotte (*née* Wagstaffe); *m* 1939, Ethel (*née* Jackson); one *s* decd. *Educ:* Penkhull Secondary Sch., Stoke-on-Trent. Locomotive driver, British Rail, 1934–77; Trade Union work with ASLEF, 1934–71. City of Stoke-on-Trent: Councillor, 1951–87; Leader of Council, 1976–81; Lord Mayor, 1971–72; Staffordshire County Council: Councillor, 1973–89; Vice-Chm., 1973–76; Chm., 1977 and 1981–89; Opposition Leader, 1977–81. Director: North Staffordshire South Cheshire Broadcasting (Signal Radio), Ltd, 1982–88; Longton Enterprise Ltd, 1980–; 1986 Nat. Garden Festival, Stoke-on-Trent, Staffordshire Ltd, 1983–88; W Midlands Industrial Develt Bd, 1983–89; Staffordshire Cable, 1988–. Trustee, Central Telephon, 1990–. JP Stoke-on-Trent, 1956–74. MUniv Keele, 1988. *Recreations:* sports, gardening, politics, voluntary work for charities. *Address:* 12 Werburgh Drive, Trentham, Stoke-on-Trent ST4 8JP. *T:* Stoke-on-Trent (0782) 657457.

CHOLMELEY, John Adye, FRCS; Surgeon, Royal National Orthopædic Hospital, 1948–70, Hon. Consulting Surgeon, since 1970; Chairman of Joint Examining Board for Orthopædic Nursing, 1959–83; *b* 31 Oct. 1902; *s* of Montague Adye Cholmeley and Mary Bertha Gordon-Cumming; unmarried. *Educ:* St Paul's Sch.; St Bartholomew's Hosp. MRCS, LRCP 1926; MB, BS London 1927; FRCS 1935; Resident appts St Bart's Hosp., 1928–30; Asst MO: Lord Mayor Treloar Cripples' Hosp., Alton, 1930–32; Alexandra Orth. Hosp., Swanley, 1933–34; Resident Surg. and Med. Supt, Country Br., Royal Nat. Orth. Hosp., Stanmore, 1940–48 (Asst Res. Surg., 1936–39); former Orthopædic Surg., Clare Hall Hosp., Neasden Hosp. Mem. Internat. Soc. of Orthopædic Surgery and Trauma (Société Internationale de Chirurgie Orthopédique et de Traumatologie, SICOT); FRSocMed (Pres. Orthopædic Sect., 1957–58); Fellow Brit. Orth. Assoc. *Publications:* History of the Royal National Orthopaedic Hospital, 1985; articles on orthopædic subjects, particularly tuberculosis and poliomyelitis in med. jls. *Address:* 14 Warren Fields, Valencia Road, Stanmore, Mddx HA7 4JQ. *T:* 081–954 6920.

CHOLMELEY, Sir Montague (John), 6th Bt *cr* 1806; *b* 27 March 1935; *s* of 5th Bt and Cecilia, *er d* of W. H. Ellice; *S* father, 1964; *m* 1960, Juliet Auriol Sally Nelson; one *s* two *d*. *Educ:* Eton. Grenadier Guards, 1954–64. *Heir: s* Hugh John Frederick Sebastian Cholmeley, *b* 3 Jan. 1968. *Address:* Church Farm, Burton le Coggles, Grantham, Lincs. *T:* Corby Glen (047684) 329. *Clubs:* White's, Cavalry and Guards.

CHOLMONDELEY, family name of **Marquess of Cholmondeley,** and of **Baron Delamere.**

CHOLMONDELEY, 7th Marquess of, *cr* 1815; **David George Philip Cholmondeley;** Bt 1611; Viscount Cholmondeley (Ire.), 1661; Baron Cholmondeley of Namptwich (Eng.), 1689; Earl of Cholmondeley, Viscount Malpas, 1706; Baron Newborough (Ire.), 1715; Baron Newburgh (Gt Brit.), 1716; Earl of Rocksavage, 1815; Joint Hereditary Lord Great Chamberlain of England (acting for the reign of Queen Elizabeth II); *b* 27 June 1960; *s* of 6th Marquess of Cholmondeley, GCVO, MC and of Lavinia Margaret, *d* of late Col John Leslie, DSO, MC; *S* father, 1990. *Heir: cousin* Charles George Cholmondeley, *b* 18 March 1959. *Address:* Cholmondeley Castle, Malpas, Cheshire.

CHOLMONDELEY CLARKE, Marshal Butler; Master of the Supreme Court of Judicature (Chancery Division), since 1973; *b* 14 July 1919; *s* of Major Cecil Cholmondeley Clarke and Fanny Ethel Carter; *m* 1947, Joan Roberta Stephens; two *s*. *Educ:* Aldenham. Admitted a solicitor, 1943; Partner, Burton Yeates & Hart, Solicitors, London, WC2, 1946–72. Pres., City of Westminster Law Soc., 1971–72; Mem. Council, Law Soc., 1966–72; Chm., Family Law Cttee, 1970–72; Chm., Legal Aid Cttee, 1972; Chancery Procedure Cttee, 1968–72; Ecclesiastical Examiner, Dio. London; Trustee, United Law Clerks' Soc. *Publication:* The Supreme Court Practice (Chancery ed.), 1985, 1991. *Recreation:* reading. *Address:* 16 Cheyne Court, SW3 5TP. *Club:* Turf.

CHOMSKY, Prof. (Avram) Noam, PhD; Institute Professor, Massachusetts Institute of Technology, since 1976 (Ferrari P. Ward Professor of Modern Languages and Linguistics, 1966–76); *b* Philadelphia, 7 Dec. 1928; *s* of late William Chomsky and of Elsie Simonofsky; *m* 1949, Carol Doris Schatz; one *s* two *d*. *Educ:* Central High Sch., Philadelphia; Univ. of Pennsylvania (PhD); Society of Fellows, Harvard, 1951–55. Massachusetts Institute of Technology: Asst Prof., 1955–58; Associate Prof., 1958–61; Prof. of Modern Langs, 1961–66. Res. Fellow, Harvard Cognitive Studies Center, 1964–65. Vis. Prof., Columbia Univ., 1957–58; Nat. Sci. Foundn Fellow, Inst. for Advanced Study, Princeton, 1958–59; Linguistics Soc. of America Prof., Univ. of Calif, LA, 1966; Beckman Prof., Univ. of Calif, Berkeley, 1966–67; Vis. Watson Prof., Syracuse Univ., 1982; Lectures: Shearman, UCL, 1969; John Locke, Oxford, 1969; Bertrand Russell Meml, Cambridge 1971; Nehru Meml, New Delhi, 1972; Whidden, McMaster Univ., 1975; Huizinga Meml, Leiden, 1977; Woodbridge, Columbia, 1978; Kant, Stanford, 1979. Member: Nat. Acad. of Scis; Amer. Acad. of Arts and Scis; Linguistic Soc. of America; Amer. Philosophical Assoc.; Bertrand Russell Peace Foundn; Utrecht Soc. of Arts and Scis; Deutsche Akademie der Naturforscher Leopoldina; Aristotelian Soc., GB; Corresp. Mem., British Acad., 1974; Hon. Mem., Ges. für Sprachwissenschaft, Germany, 1990. Fellow, Amer. Assoc. for Advancement of Science; William James Fellow, Amer. Psychological Assoc., 1990. Mem., Council, Internat. Confedn for Disarmament and Peace, 1967. Hon. FBPsS; Hon. FRAI 1990. Hon. DLitt: London, 1967; Visva-Bharati, West Bengal, 1980; Hon. DHL: Chicago, 1967; Loyola Univ., Chicago, 1970; Swarthmore Coll., 1970; Bard Coll., 1971; Delhi, 1972; Massachusetts, 1973; Pennsylvania, 1985. Distinguished Scientific Contribution Award, Amer. Psychological Assoc., 1984; Kyoto Prize in Basic Science, Inamori Foundn, 1988; Orwell Award, Nat. Council of Teachers of English, 1987, 1989. *Publications:* Syntactic Structures, 1957; Current Issues in Linguistic Theory, 1964; Aspects of the Theory of Syntax, 1965; Cartesian Linguistics, 1966; Topics in the Theory of Generative Grammar, 1966; Language and Mind, 1968; (with Morris Halle) Sound Pattern of English, 1968; American Power and the New Mandarins, 1969; At War with Asia, 1970; Problems of Knowledge and Freedom, 1971; Studies on Semantics in Generative Grammar, 1972; For Reasons of State, 1973; The Backroom Boys, 1973; Peace in the Middle East?, 1974; (with Edward Herman) Bains de Sang, 1974; Reflections on Language, 1975; The Logical Structure of Linguistic Theory, 1975; Essays on Form and Interpretation, 1977; Human Rights and American Foreign Policy, 1978; Language and Responsibility, 1979; (with Edward Herman) Political Economy of Human Rights, 1979; Rules and Representations, 1980; Radical Priorities, 1981; Lectures on Government and Binding, 1981; Towards a New Cold War, 1982; Some Concepts and Consequences of the Theory of Government and Binding, 1982; Fateful Triangle: the United States, Israel and the Palestinians, 1983; Modular Approaches to the Study of the Mind, 1984; Turning the Tide, 1985; Barriers, 1986; Pirates and Emperors, 1986; Knowledge of Language: its nature, origin and use, 1986; Generative Grammar: its basis, development and prospects, 1987; On Power and Ideology, 1987; Language in a Psychological Setting, 1987; Language and Problems of Knowledge, 1987; The Chomsky Reader, 1987; The Culture of Terrorism, 1988; (with Edward Herman) Manufacturing Consent, 1988; Necessary Illusions, 1989; Deterring Democracy, 1991. *Recreation:* gardening. *Address:* Department of Linguistics and Philosophy, Massachusetts Institute of Technology, 20D-219, 77 Massachusetts Avenue, Cambridge, Mass 02139, USA. *T:* 617–253–7819.

CHOPE, Christopher Robert, OBE 1982; barrister; MP (C) Southampton Itchen, since 1983; Parliamentary Under-Secretary of State, (Minister for Roads and Traffic), Department of Transport, since 1990; *b* 19 May 1947; *s* of late His Honour Robert Charles Chope and of Pamela Durell; *m* 1987, Christo Hutchinson; one *d*. *Educ:* St Andrew's Sch., Eastbourne; Marlborough Coll.; St Andrews Univ. (LLB Hons). Called to the Bar, Inner Temple, 1972. Mem., Wandsworth Borough Council, 1974–83; Chm., Housing Cttee, 1978–79; Leader of Council, 1979–83. PPS to Minister of State, HM Treasury, 1986; Parly Under-Sec. of State, DoE, 1986–90. Jt Sec., Cons. Backbench Environment Cttee, 1983–86; Mem., Select Cttee on Procedure, 1984–86. Mem. Exec. Cttee, Soc. of Cons. Lawyers, 1983–86. *Address:* 12 King's Bench Walk, Temple, EC4. *T:* 071–353 5892. *Clubs:* Royal Southampton Yacht; Bitterne Conservative.

CHORLEY, family name of **Baron Chorley.**

CHORLEY, 2nd Baron *cr* 1945, of Kendal; **Roger Richard Edward Chorley,** FCA; Chairman, National Trust, since 1991; *b* 14 Aug. 1930; *er s* of 1st Baron Chorley, QC, and Katharine Campbell (*d* 1986), *d* of late Edward Hopkinson, DSc; *S* father, 1978; *m* 1964, Ann, *d* of late A. S. Debenham; two *s*. *Educ:* Stowe Sch.; Gonville and Caius Coll., Cambridge (BA). Pres., CU Mountaineering Club. Expedns to Himalayas, 1954

(Rakaposhi), 1957 (Nepal); joined Cooper Brothers & Co. (later Coopers & Lybrand), 1955; New York office, 1959–60; Pakistan (Indus Basin Project), 1961; Partner, 1967–89; Hon. Sec., Climbers Club, 1963–67; seconded to Nat. Bd for Prices and Incomes as accounting adviser, 1965–68; Mem. Management Cttee, Mount Everest Foundn, 1968–70; Visiting Prof., Dept of Management Sciences, Imperial Coll. of Science and Technology, Univ. of London, 1979–82. Dep. Chm., British Council, 1990– (Mem. Bd, 1981–). National Trust: Member: Finance Cttee, 1970–; Exec. Cttee, 1989–; Council, 1989–. Member: Royal Commn on the Press, 1974–77; Finance Act 1960 Tribunal, 1974–79; Ordnance Survey Rev. Cttee, 1978–79; British Council Rev. Cttee, 1979–80; Nat. Theatre Bd, 1980–; Top Salaries Review Body, 1981–; Ordnance Survey Adv. Bd, 1983–85; H of L Select Cttee on Sci. and Technology, 1983, 1987, 1988, 1989; NERC, 1988–; Council, City and Guilds of London Inst., 1977–90; Council, RGS, 1984– (Pres., 1987–90); Council, RSA, 1987–89; Chm., Cttee into Handling of Geographic Information, 1985–87. Pres., Alpine Club, 1983–85. Hon. DSc Reading, 1990. *Recreation:* mountains. *Heir:* s Hon. Nicholas Rupert Debenham Chorley, b 15 July 1966. *Address:* House of Lords, SW1. *Club:* Alpine.

CHORLEY, Francis Kenneth, CBE 1982; FEng, FIEE; Board Member (part-time), Civil Aviation Authority, since 1987; Chairman: 3 NET Ltd, since 1987; Waycom Holdings Ltd, since 1989; *b* 29 July 1926; *s* of late Francis Henry Chorley and Eva Ellen Chorley; *m* 1954, Lorna Stella Brooks; two *s*. *Educ:* Rutlish Sch., Merton. With Plessey Co., 1951–60; Tech. Dir, Epsylon Industries, 1960–63; Divl Manager, GEC Electronics Ltd, 1963–64; Dir and Gen. Manager, then Man. Dir, GEC-AEI Electronics Ltd, 1964–67; Dir and Gen. Manager, GEC-AEI Telecommunications Ltd, 1967–74; Man. Dir, Plessey Avionics and Communications Div., 1974–78; Man. Dir and Dep. Chm., Plessey Electronic Systems Ltd, 1979–83; Exec. Chm., Plessey Telecommunications & Office Systems Ltd, 1983–86; Bd Mem., 1978–86, Dep. Chief Exec., 1983–86, The Plessey Co. plc; Dir, Pirelli Focom, 1987–. Member: Engineering Council, 1986–; Council, CGLI, 1983–. Pres., IERE, 1987–88; Vice-Pres., TEMA, 1986–87. FInstD; FRSA; CBIM. Prince Philip Medal, CGLI, 1983. *Recreations:* photography, music, sailing. *Address:* 15 Crown Reach, Grosvenor Road, SW1V 3JY. *T:* 071–828 5824. *Clubs:* East India; Royal Air Force Yacht.

CHORLEY, Prof. Richard John; Professor of Geography, University of Cambridge, since 1974; Fellow of Sidney Sussex College, Cambridge, since 1962 (Vice-Master, 1990); *b* 4 Sept. 1927; *s* of Walter Joseph Chorley and Ellen Mary Chorley; *m* 1965, Rosemary Joan Macdonald More; one *s* one *d*. *Educ:* Minehead Grammar Sch.; Exeter Coll., Oxford. MA (Oxon), ScD (Cantab). Lieut, RE, 1946–48. Fulbright Schol., Columbia Univ., 1951–52; Instructor: in Geography, Columbia Univ., 1952–54; in Geology, Brown Univ., 1954–57; Cambridge University: Demonstrator in Geography, 1958–62; Lectr in Geography, 1962–70, Reader, 1970–74. British rep. on Commn on Quantitative Techniques of Internat. Geographical Union, 1964–68; Dir, Madingley Geog. Courses, 1963–. First Hon. Life Mem., British Geomorphological Res. Gp, 1974; Corresponding Mem., Italian Geographical Soc. Gill Meml Medal, 1967, Patron's Medal, 1987, RGS; Hons Award, Assoc. of Amer. Geographers, 1981; David Linton Award, 1984. *Publications:* co-author of: The History of the Study of Landforms, Vols I, II and III, 1964, 1973, 1991; Atmosphere, Weather and Climate, 1968; Network Analysis in Geography, 1969; Physical Geography, 1971; Environmental Systems, 1978; Geomorphology, 1984; co-editor of: Frontiers in Geographical Teaching, 1965; Models in Geography, 1967; editor of: Water, Earth and Man, 1969; Spatial Analysis in Geomorphology, 1972; Directions in Geography, 1973; contribs to: Jl of Geology, Amer. Jl of Science, Bulletin of Geolog. Soc. of Amer., Geog. Jl, Geol. Magazine, Inst. of Brit. Geographers, etc. *Recreations:* gardening, theatre. *Address:* 76 Grantchester Meadows, Newnham, Cambridge CB3 9JL.

CHOUFFOT, Geoffrey Charles, CBE 1983 (MBE 1965); Director and Treasurer, St Wilfrid's Hospice (South Coast) Ltd, since 1987; Deputy Chairman, Civil Aviation Authority, 1980–83, retired; *m* 1941, June Catherine, *d* of Rev. W. Peebles Fleming; one *s* two *d*. Group Director, Safety Services, Civil Aviation Authority, 1978–80. *Club:* Royal Air Force.

CHRÉTIEN, Hon. Jean, PC (Canada); QC; MP (L) Beauséjour, New Brunswick, since 1990; Leader of the Opposition, since 1990; *b* 11 Jan. 1934; *s* of Wellie Chrétien and Marie Boisvert Chrétien; *m* 1957, Aline Chaine; two *s* one *d*. *Educ:* Trois-Rivières; Joliette; Shawinigan; Laval Univ. (BA, LLL). Called to the Bar, and entered Shawinigan law firm of Chrétien, Landry, Deschênes, Trudel and Normand, 1958; Counsel, Lang Michener Lawrence and Shaw, 1986–90; Director: Shawinigan Sen. Chamber of Commerce, 1962; Bar of Trois-Rivières, 1962–63. Govt of Canada: MP (L) St Maurice, 1963–86; Parly Sec. to Prime Minister, 1965, and to Minister of Finance, 1966; Minister of State, 1967; Minister of National Revenue, Jan. 1968; Minister of Indian and Northern Affairs, July 1968; Pres., Treasury Bd, 1974; Minister of Industry, Trade and Commerce, 1976; Minister of Finance, 1977–79; Minister of Justice, responsible for constitutional negotiations, Attorney General, Minister of State for Social Develt, 1980–82; Minister of Energy, 1982–84; Deputy Prime Minister and External Affairs Minister, 1984; External Affairs Critic for official Opposition, 1984–86. Elected Leader, Liberal Party of Canada, June 1990. Hon LLD: Wilfred Laurier Univ., 1981; Laurentian Univ., 1982; Univ. of W Ontario, 1982; York Univ., Ont., 1986; Univ. of Alberta, 1987; Lakehead Univ., 1988. *Recreations:* skiing, fishing, golf, reading, classical music. *Address:* Room 409 S, House of Commons, Ottawa, Ont K1A 0A6, Canada.

CHRIMES, Henry Bertram, DL; Chairman, Liverpool Daily Post and Echo Ltd, 1976–85; *b* 11 March 1915; *s* of Sir Bertram Chrimes, CBE, and Mary (*née* Holder); *m* 1946, Suzanne, *d* of W. S. Corbett-Lowe, Sodylt Hall, Ellesmere; one *s* three *d*. *Educ:* Oundle; Clare Coll., Cambridge. Served War of 1939–45: RA, India and Burma, Bde Major (despatches). Cooper & Co.'s Stores Ltd, 1945–60 (Man. Dir, 1954–60); Ocean Transport & Trading Ltd, 1960–85 (Dep. Chm., 1971–75); Liverpool Daily Post & Echo Ltd, 1963–85; Member, Liverpool Bd, Barclays Bank Ltd, 1972–83. Member: Council, Univ. of Liverpool, 1951–87 (Pres., 1975–81; Pro-Chancellor, 1981–Nov. 1987); Univ. Authorities Panel, 1976–87; Dir, Univs Superannuation Scheme Ltd, 1980–85; Vice-Pres., Liverpool Sch. of Tropical Medicine, 1981–87; Mem., 1951–, Vice-Pres., 1973–, Liverpool Council of Social Service (Chm., 1964–70); President: Merseyside Pre-Retirement Assoc., 1977–87; Royal Liverpool Seamen's Orphan Instn, 1980–86. DL 1974, High Sheriff 1978–79, Merseyside. Hon. LLD Liverpool, 1987. *Recreations:* books, gardening. *Address:* Bracken Bank, Heswall, Merseyside L60 4RP. *T:* 051–342 2397. *Clubs:* Reform; Racquet (Liverpool).
See also R. G. Toulson.

CHRIST CHURCH, Dublin, Dean of; *see* Salmon, Very Rev. T. N. D. C.

CHRIST CHURCH, Oxford, Dean of; *see* Heaton, Very Rev. E. W.

CHRISTCHURCH, Bishop of, since 1990; **Rt. Rev. David John Coles;** *b* 23 March 1943; *s* of Samuel Arthur and Evelyn Ann Coles; *m* 1970, Ceridwyn Mary Parr; one *s* one *d*. *Educ:* Auckland Grammar Sch.; Univ. of Auckland (MA Hons 1967); Univ. of Otago (BD 1969; MTh 1971); Univ. of Manchester (PhD 1974); Melbourne Coll. of Divinity (Dip. Religious Educn). Deacon 1968, priest 1969; Curate, St Mark, Remuera, Auckland, 1968–70; Asst Chaplain, Selwyn Coll., Dunedin, 1970–71; Curate, Fallowfield, 1972–73; Chaplain, Hulme Hall, Univ. of Manchester, 1973–74; Vicar of: Glenfield, 1974–76; Takapuna, 1976–80; Examining Chaplain to Bp of Auckland, 1974–80; Dean and Vicar of St John's Cathedral, Napier, dio. Waiapu, 1980–84; Dean of Christchurch and Vicar-General, dio. Christchurch, 1984–90. *Recreations:* music, ski-ing, tramping. *Address:* Bishop's House, 80 Bealey Avenue, Christchurch 8001, New Zealand. *T:* (09) 662653.

CHRISTENSEN, Eric Herbert, CMG 1968; Chairman, Victrose Holdings (Channel Islands) Ltd, since 1985; Director: Seagull Cold Stores, since 1980; Gambia Oil Company Ltd, since 1985; *b* 29 Oct. 1923; *s* of George Vilhelm Christensen and Rose Fleury; *m* 1951, Diana, *d* of Rev. J. Dixon-Baker; four *s* three *d*. Teacher, St Augustine's Sec. Sch., Bathurst, 1941–43; Military Service, W African Air Corps (RAF), Bathurst, 1944–45; Clerk, The Secretariat, Bathurst, 1946–47; Head of Chancery, then Vice-Consul, French Consulate, Bathurst, 1947–60; acted as Consul on several occasions; Attaché, Senegalese Consulate-Gen., Bathurst, 1961–65, acted as Consul-Gen. on several occasions; Asst Sec. (Ext. Affairs), Gambia Govt, 1965; Principal Asst Sec., Prime Minister's Office, Bathurst, 1966–67; Sec.-Gen., President's Office, Perm. Sec., Min. of External Affairs, and Sec. to the Cabinet, The Gambia, 1967–78; also Hd, Public Service, 1967–78. Foreign decorations include: Grand Officer, Order of the Brilliant Star of China (Taiwan), 1966; Officer, Order of Merit of Islamic Republic of Mauritania, 1967; Knight Commander's Cross, Badge and Star, Order of Merit of Federal Republic of Germany, 1968; Order of Republic of Nigeria, 1970; Grand Officer, National Order of Republic of The Gambia, 1970; Order of Diplomatic Merit, Republic of Korea, 1970, and also those from Egypt, Republic of Guinea and Republic of Liberia; Comdr, Nat. Order of the Lion, Senegal, 1972; Chevalier de la Légion d'Honneur, 1975. *Recreations:* reading, photography, philately, chess. *Address:* Sir Dawda Kairaba Jawara Avenue, Kombo St Mary, The Gambia. *T:* Serekunda 2222.

CHRISTENSEN, Jens; Commander First Class, Order of the Dannebrog; Hon. GCVO; Ambassador of Denmark to Organization for Economic Co-operation and Development, since 1989; *b* 30 July 1921; *s* of Christian Christensen and Sophie Dorthea Christensen; *m* 1st, 1950, Tove (*née* Jessen) (*d* 1982); one *s* two *d*; 2nd, 1983, Vibeke Pagh. *Educ:* Copenhagen Univ. (MPolSc 1945). Joined Danish Foreign Service, 1945; Head of Section, Econ. Secretariat of Govt, 1947; Sec. to OECD Delegn in Paris, 1949 and to NATO Delegn, 1952; Hd of Sect., Min. of Foreign Affairs, 1952, Actg Hd of Div., 1954; Chargé d'Affaires *a.i.* and Counsellor of Legation, Vienna, 1957; Asst Hd of Econ.-Polit. Dept, Min. of For. Affairs, 1960; Dep. Under-Sec., 1961; Under-Sec. and Hd of Econ.-Polit. Dept, 1964–71; Hd of Secretariat for Europ. Integration, 1966; Ambassador Extraord. and Plenipotentiary, 1967; State Sec. for Foreign Econ. Affairs, 1971; Ambassador to the Court of St James's, 1977–81; Pres., Danish Oil and Natural Gas Co., 1980–84; Ambassador to Austria, 1984–89. Governor for Denmark, The Asian Development Bank, 1967–73. Knight Grand Cross: Order of Icelandic Falcon; Order of Northern Star, Sweden; Order of St Olav, Norway; Royal Victorian Order; Austrian Order of Honour. *Address:* Délégation Danoise auprès de l'OCDE, 6 rue Jean Richepin, 75116 Paris, France.

CHRISTIAN, Clifford Stuart, CMG 1971; consultant in environmental matters; *b* 19 Dec. 1907; *s* of Thomas William and Lily Elizabeth Christian; *m* 1933, Agnes Robinson; four *d*. *Educ:* Univ. of Queensland (BScAgr); Univ. of Minnesota (MS). Officer-in-charge: Northern Australia Regional Survey Section, 1946–50; Land Research and Regional Survey Section, CSIRO, 1950–57; Chief, Div. of Land Research, CSIRO, 1957–60; Mem. Executive, CSIRO, 1960–72. Adviser, Ranger Uranium Environmental Inquiry, 1975–76. Farrer Memorial Medal, 1969. FAIAS; FWA; Fellow, Aust. Acad. of Technological Sciences and Engrg. Hon. DScAgr Queensland, 1978. *Publications:* A Review Report, Alligator Rivers Study (with J. Aldrick), 1977; chapter contribs to books; articles in various pubns mainly concerning natural resources. *Recreation:* photography. *Address:* 6 Baudin Street, Forrest, ACT 2603, Australia. *T:* 062 952495.

CHRISTIAN, Prof. John Wyrill, FRS 1975; Professor of Physical Metallurgy, Oxford University, 1967–88, now Emeritus; Fellow of St Edmund Hall, Oxford, 1963–88, now Senior Research Fellow; *b* 9 April 1926; *e s* of John Christian and Louisa Christian (*née* Crawford); *m* 1949, Maureen Lena Smith; two *s* one *d*. *Educ:* Scarborough Boys' High Sch.; The Queen's Coll., Oxford. BA 1946, DPhil 1949, MA 1950. Pressed Steel Co. Ltd Research Fellow, Oxford University, 1951–55; Lectr in Metallurgy, 1955–58; George Kelley Reader in Metallurgy, 1958–67. Visiting Prof.: Univ. of Illinois, 1959; Case Inst. of Technology, USA, 1962–63; MIT and Stanford Univ., 1971–72. Lectures: Williams, MIT, 1971; Hume-Rothery Meml, 1976; Inst. of Metals, AIME, 1981; Campbell Meml, ASM, 1982. Rosenhain medallist of Inst. of Metals, 1969; Mehl Medallist of AIME, 1981; Platinum Medallist of Metals Soc., 1984; Gold Medallist Acta Metallurgica, 1984. Editor: Progress in Materials Science, 1970–; Jl Less Common Metals, 1976–85. *Publications:* Metallurgical Equilibrium Diagrams (with others), 1952; The Theory of Transformations in Metals and Alloys, 1965, 2nd rev. edn, 1975; contribs to scientific jls. *Address:* 11 Charlbury Road, Oxford OX2 6UT. *T:* Oxford (0865) 58569.

CHRISTIAN, Prof. Reginald Frank; Professor of Russian, St Andrews University, since 1966; *b* Liverpool, 9 Aug. 1924; *s* of late H. A. Christian and late Jessie Gower (*née* Scott); *m* 1952, Rosalind Iris Napier; one *s* one *d*. *Educ:* Liverpool Inst.; Queen's Coll., Oxford (Open Scholar; MA). Hon. Mods Class. (Oxon), 1943; 1st cl. hons Russian (Oxon), 1949. Commnd RAF, 1944; flying with Atlantic Ferry Unit and 231 Sqdn, 1943–46. FO, British Embassy, Moscow, 1949–50; Lectr and Head of Russian Dept, Liverpool Univ., 1950–55; Sen. Lectr and Head of Russian Dept, Birmingham Univ., 1956–63; Vis. Prof. of Russian, McGill Univ., Canada, 1961–62; Prof. of Russian, Birmingham Univ., 1963–66; Exchange Lectr, Moscow, 1964–65. Mem. Univ. Ct, 1971–73 and 1981–85, Associate Dean, Fac. of Arts, 1972–73, Dean, Fac. of Arts, 1975–78, St Andrews Univ. Pres., British Univs Assoc. of Slavists, 1967–70; Member: Internat. Cttee of Slavists, 1970–75; UGC Atkinson Cttee, 1978–81. *Publications:* Korolenko's Siberia, 1954; (with F. M. Borras) Russian Syntax, 1959, 2nd rev. edn, 1971; Tolstoy's War and Peace: a study, 1962; (with F. M. Borras) Russian Prose Composition, 1964, 2nd rev. edn, 1974; Tolstoy: a critical introduction, 1969; Tolstoy's Letters, 2 vols, 1978; Tolstoy's Diaries, 2 vols, 1985; numerous articles and reviews in Slavonic and E European Review, Slavonic and E European Jl, Mod. Languages Review, Survey, Forum, Birmingham Post, Times Lit. Supp., Oxford Slavonic Papers, etc. *Recreations:* fell-walking, violin. *Address:* 20 Shoregate, Crail, Fife. *T:* Crail (0333) 50101; Scioncroft, Knockard Road, Pitlochry, Perthshire. *T:* Pitlochry (0796) 2993.

CHRISTIANSON, Alan, CBE 1971; MC 1945; Deputy Chairman, South of Scotland Electricity Board, 1967–72; retired; *b* 14 March 1909; *s* of Carl Robert Christianson; *m* 1936, Gladys Muriel Lewin, *d* of William Barker; two *d*. *Educ:* Royal Grammar Sch., Newcastle upon Tyne; FCA, CompIEE. Served as Major, RA, 1939–45: comd Field Battery, 1943–45. Central Electricity Bd, 1934–48; Divisional Sec., British Electricity Authority, SW Scotland Div., 1948–55; Dep. Sec., S of Scotland Electricity Bd, 1955–62;

Chief Financial Officer, 1962–65; Gen. Man., Finance and Administration, 1965–67. *Recreation:* golf. *Address:* Tynedale, Lennox Drive East, Helensburgh, Dunbartonshire G84 9JD. *T:* Helensburgh (0436) 74503.

CHRISTIE, Ann Philippa; *see* Pearce, A. P.

CHRISTIE, Campbell; General Secretary, Scottish Trades Union Congress, since 1986; *b* 23 Aug. 1937; *s* of Thomas Christie and Johnina Rolling; *m* 1962, Elizabeth Brown Cameron; two *s*. *Educ:* Albert Sen. Secondary Sch., Glasgow. Civil Service, 1954–72: Admiralty, 1954–59; DHSS, 1959–72; Society of Civil and Public Servants, 1972–85: Asst Sec., 1972–73; Asst Gen. Sec., 1973–75; Dep. Gen. Sec., 1975–85. *Address:* 31 Dumyat Drive, Falkirk, Stirlingshire FK1 5PA. *T:* Falkirk (0324) 24555.

CHRISTIE, Charles Henry; Director of Studies, Britannia Royal Naval College, Dartmouth, 1978–86; *b* 1 Sept. 1924; *s* of late Lieut-Comdr C. P. Christie and Mrs C. S. Christie; *m* 1950, Naida Joan Bentley; one *s* three *d*. *Educ:* Westminster Sch. (King's Scholar); Trinity Coll., Cambridge (Exhibitioner). Served 1943–46, RNVR (despatches, 1945). Trinity Coll., Cambridge, 1946–49; Asst Master, Eton Coll., 1949–57; Under Master and Master of Queen's Scholars, Westminster Sch., 1957–63; Headmaster, Brighton Coll., 1963–71; Warden, St Edward's Sch., Oxford, 1971–78. Vis. Prof., US Naval Acad., Annapolis, 1986–88. Prime Warden, Dyers' Co., 1983–84. *Address:* 8 Paddox Close, Squitchey Lane, Oxford OX2 7LR.

CHRISTIE, Sir George (William Langham), Kt 1984; DL; Chairman, Glyndebourne Productions Ltd; *b* 31 Dec. 1934; *o s* of John Christie, CH, MC, and Audrey Mildmay Christie; *m* 1958, Patricia Mary Nicholson; three *s* one *d*. *Educ:* Eton. Asst to Sec. of Calouste Gulbenkian Foundation, 1957–62. Chm. of Glyndebourne Productions, 1956–, and of other family companies. Mem., Arts Council of GB, 1988– (Chm., Adv. Panel on Music, 1988–). Founder Chm., The London Sinfonietta, 1968–88. DL E Sussex, 1983. Hon. FRCM 1986; Hon. FRNCM 1986. Cavaliere al Merito della Repubblica Italiana, 1977. *Address:* Glyndebourne, Lewes, E Sussex BN8 5UU. *T:* Ringmer (0273) 812250.

CHRISTIE, Herbert; Director, Research Department, European Investment Bank, since 1983; *b* 26 Sept. 1933; *s* of Brig.-Gen. H. W. A. Christie, CB, CMG, and Mary Ann Christie; *m* 1982, Gilberte F. M. V. Desbois; one *s*. *Educ:* Methodist Coll., Belfast; Univ. of St Andrews (MA). Asst Lectr, Univ. of Leeds, 1958–60; Econ. Asst, HM Treasury, 1960–63; First Sec., Washington, DC, 1963–66; Econ. Adviser, J. Henry Schroder Wagg and Co. Ltd, 1966–71, with secondment as Econ. Adviser, NBPI, 1967–71; Sen. Econ. Adviser, Min. of Posts and Telecommunications, 1971–74, and Dept of Prices and Consumer Protection, 1974–76; Econ. Adviser, EEC Commn, Brussels, 1976–78; Under Sec., HM Treasury, 1978–83. *Publications:* contrib. to books and learned jls. *Recreations:* languages, foreign travel. *Address:* c/o European Investment Bank, 100 boulevard Konrad Adenauer, L2950 Luxembourg. *T:* Luxembourg 4379.

CHRISTIE, Prof. Ian Ralph, FBA 1977; Astor Professor of British History, University of London at University College, 1979–84, now Professor Emeritus; Hon. Research Fellow, University College London, since 1984; *b* 11 May 1919; *s* of John Reid Christie and Gladys Lilian (*née* Whatley). *Educ:* privately; Worcester Royal Grammar Sch.; Magdalen Coll., Oxford, 1938–40 and 1946–48 (MA). Served War, RAF, 1940–46. University Coll. London: Asst Lectr in Hist., 1948; Lectr, 1951; Reader, 1960; Prof. of Modern British History, 1966; Dean of Arts, 1971–73; Chm. History Dept, 1975–79. Ford Lectr, Oxford Univ., 1983–84. Jt Literary Dir, Royal Hist. Soc., 1964–70, Mem. Council, 1970–74. Mem. Editorial Bd, History of Parliament Trust, 1973–. *Publications:* The End of North's Ministry, 1780–1782, 1958; Wilkes, Wyvill and Reform, 1962; Crisis of Empire: Great Britain and the American Colonies, 1754–1783, 1966; (ed) Essays in Modern History selected from the Transactions of the Royal Historical Society, 1968; Myth and Reality in late Eighteenth-century British Politics, 1970; (ed) The Correspondence of Jeremy Bentham, vol. 3, 1971; (with B. W. Labaree) Empire or Independence, 1760–1776, 1976; (with Lucy M. Brown) Bibliography of British History, 1789–1851, 1977; Wars and Revolutions: Britain, 1760–1815, 1982; Stress and Stability in Late Eighteenth Century Britain: reflections on the British avoidance of revolution, 1984; contrib. to jls. *Recreation:* walking. *Address:* 10 Green Lane, Croxley Green, Herts WD3 3HR. *T:* Rickmansworth (0923) 773008. *Club:* Commonwealth Trust.

CHRISTIE, John Arthur Kingsley; Under-Secretary, Ministry of Agriculture, Fisheries and Food, 1970–75; *b* 8 Feb. 1915; *s* of Harold Douglas Christie and Enid Marian (*née* Hall); *m* 1951, Enid Margaret (*née* Owen); one *s* two *d*. *Educ:* Rugby Sch.; Magdalen Coll., Oxford. BA (1st cl. Hon. Mods, 1st cl. Litt. Hum.). Asst Principal, Min. of Agriculture, 1937–41; Sub-Lt, RNVR, 1941–45; Asst Private Sec. to Lord President of the Council, 1945–47; Min. of Agriculture: Principal, 1947–52; Asst Sec., 1952–70. *Recreation:* music. *Address:* Westfield, 16 Knole Road, Sevenoaks, Kent TN13 3XH. *T:* Sevenoaks (0732) 451423.

CHRISTIE, John Belford Wilson, CBE 1981; Sheriff of Tayside, Central and Fife (formerly Perth and Angus) at Dundee, 1955–83; *b* 4 May 1914; *o s* of late J. A. Christie, Advocate, Edinburgh; *m* 1939, Christine Isobel Syme, *o d* of late Rev. J. T. Arnott; four *d*. *Educ:* Merchiston Castle Sch.; St John's Coll., Cambridge; Edinburgh Univ. Admitted to Faculty of Advocates, 1939. Served War of 1939–45, in RNVR, 1939–46. Sheriff-Substitute of Western Div. of Dumfries and Galloway, 1948–55. Mem., Parole Bd for Scotland, 1967–73; Mem., Queen's Coll. Council, Univ. of St Andrews, 1960–67; Mem. Univ. Court, 1967–75, and Hon. Lectr, Dept of Private Law, Univ. of Dundee. Hon.LLD Dundee, 1977. KHS 1988. *Recreations:* curling, golf. *Address:* Annsmuir Farm, Ladybank, Fife KY7 7RE. *T:* Ladybank (0337) 30480. *Clubs:* New (Edinburgh); Royal and Ancient (St Andrews).

CHRISTIE, John Rankin, CB 1978; Deputy Master and Comptroller of the Royal Mint, 1974–77; *b* 5 Jan. 1918; *s* of Robert Christie and Georgina (*née* Rankin); *m* 1941, Constance May, *d* of Henry Gracie; one *s* two *d*. *Educ:* Ormskirk Gram. Sch.; London Sch. of Economics. War Office, 1936–39; Min. of Supply, 1939; Royal Artillery, 1943–47; Min. of Supply, 1947; Admin. Staff Coll., 1949; Air Ministry, 1954; Private Sec. to Ministers of Supply, 1955–57; Asst Sec., 1957; British Defence Staffs, Washington, 1962–65; Under-Sec., Min. of Aviation, 1965–67, Min. of Technology, 1967–70, Min. of Aviation Supply, 1970–71; Asst Under-Sec. of State, MoD, 1971–74. *Recreations:* travel, bird-watching. *Address:* Twitten Cottage, East Hill, Oxted, Surrey RH8 9AA. *T:* Oxted (0883) 713047.

CHRISTIE, Julie (Frances); actress; *b* 14 April 1940; *d* of Frank St John Christie and Rosemary Christie (*née* Ramsden). *Educ:* Convent; Brighton Coll. of Technology; Central Sch. of Speech and Drama. *Films:* Crooks Anonymous, 1962; The Fast Lady, 1962; Billy Liar, 1963; Darling, 1964 (Oscar, NY Film Critics Award, Br. Film Academy Award, etc); Young Cassidy, 1964; Dr Zhivago, 1965 (Donatello Award); Fahrenheit 451, 1966; Far from the Madding Crowd, 1966; Petulia, 1967; In Search of Gregory, 1969; The Go-Between, 1971; McCabe and Mrs Miller, 1972; Don't Look Now, 1973; Shampoo, 1974; Heaven Can Wait, 1978; Memoirs of a Survivor, 1981; The Animals Film, 1982; Return of the Soldier, 1982; Heat and Dust, 1983; The Gold Diggers, 1984; Power, 1987; Miss

Mary, 1987; McCabe and Mrs Miller, 1990. Motion Picture Laurel Award, Best Dramatic Actress, 1967; Motion Picture Herald Award, Best Dramatic Actress, 1967. *Address:* c/o ICM Ltd, 388–396 Oxford Street, W1.

CHRISTIE, Hon. Sir Vernon (Howard Colville), Kt 1972; Speaker of the Legislative Assembly, Victoria, 1967–73; MLA (L) for Ivanhoe, Victoria, 1955–73; *b* Manly, NSW, 17 Dec. 1909; *s* of C. Christie, Sydney; *m* 1936, Joyce, *d* of F. H. Hamlin; one *s* one *d*. Chm. Cttees, Legislative Assembly, 1956–61, 1965–68; Director: Australian Elizabethan Theatre Trust, 1969–78; Australian Ballet Foundn, 1969–84; Qld Ballet. Hon. Life Mem., Victoria Br., CPA. AASA; FCIS; AFAIM. *Recreations:* bowls, sailing, music, ballet and the arts, conservation, fly fishing. *Address:* Rothes, 51 Colburn Avenue, Victoria Point, Qld 4163, Australia. *Club:* Queensland (Brisbane).

CHRISTIE, Sir William, Kt 1975; MBE 1970; JP; Lord Mayor of Belfast, 1972–75; a Company Director; *b* 1 June 1913; *s* of Richard and Ellen Christie, Belfast; *m* 1935, Selina (*née* Pattison); one *s* two *d* (and one *s* decd). *Educ:* Ward Sch., Bangor, Northern Ireland. Belfast City Councillor, 1961; High Sheriff of Belfast, 1964–65; Deputy Lord Mayor, 1969; Alderman, 1973–77. JP Belfast, 1951; DL Belfast, 1977. Freeman, City of London, 1975. Salvation Army Order of Distinguished Auxiliary Service, 1973. *Recreations:* travel, walking, boating, gardening.

CHRISTIE, William James; Sheriff of Tayside, Central and Fife at Kirkaldy, since 1979; *b* 1 Nov. 1932; *s* of William David Christie and Mrs Anne Christie; *m* 1957, Maeve Patricia Gallacher; three *s*. *Educ:* Holy Cross Acad., Edinburgh; Edinburgh Univ. LLB. Nat. Service, 1954–56; commnd Royal Scots. Private Practice, 1956–79. Mem. Council, Law Soc. of Scotland, 1975–79; President: Soc. of Procurators of Midlothian, 1977–79; Soc. of Solicitors in the Supreme Court, 1979. *Recreations:* music, reading, shooting. *Address:* Sheriff Court House, Whytescauseway, Kirkcaldy, Fife KY1 1XQ. *Club:* New (Edinburgh).

CHRISTISON, Gen. Sir (Alexander Frank) Philip, 4th Bt *cr* 1871; GBE 1948 (KBE 1944); CB 1943; DSO 1945; MC (and Bar); DL; *b* 17 Nov. 1893; 2nd *s* of Sir Alexander Christison, 2nd Bt, and Florence (*d* 1949), *d* of F. T. Elworthy; *S* half-brother, 1945; *m* 1st, 1916, Betty (*d* 1974), *d* of late Rt Rev. A. Mitchell, Bishop of Aberdeen and Orkney; (one *s* killed in action in Burma, 7 March 1942) two *d* (and one *d* decd); 2nd, 1974, Vida Wallace Smith, MBE. *Educ:* Edinburgh Academy; Oxford Univ. (BA); Hon. Fellow, University Coll., Oxford, 1973. 2nd Lieut Cameron Highlanders, 1914; Capt. 1915; Bt Major, 1930; Bt Lt-Col 1933; Lt-Col Duke of Wellington's Regt, 1937; Col 1938; comd Quetta Bde, 1938–40; Comdt Staff Coll., Quetta, 1940–41; Brig. Gen. Staff, 1941; Maj.-Gen. 1941; Lt-Gen. 1942; Gen. 1947; comd XXXIII and XV Indian Corps, 1942–45; Temp. Comdr 14th Army, 1945; C-in-C, ALFSEA, 1945; Allied Comdr Netherland East Indies, 1945–46; GOC-in-C Northern Command, 1946; GOC-in-C Scottish Command and Governor of Edinburgh Castle, 1947–49; ADC Gen. to the King, 1947–49; retired pay, 1949. Col, The Duke of Wellington's Regt, 1947–57; Col, 10th Princess Mary's Own Gurkha Rifles, 1947–57; Hon. Col, 414 Coast Regt Royal Artillery, 1950–57. Dir, Cochran and Co. Ltd, 1951–66; Chm., Alban Timber Ltd, 1953–78. Fruit farmer, 1949–. President: Scottish Unionist Party, 1957–58; Army Cadet Force, Scotland; Earl Haig Fund; Vice-President: Burma Star Assoc.; Officers' Assoc.; Scottish Salmon Angling Fedn, 1969; Chm., Lodge Trust for Ornithology, 1969; Chm. and Pres., Clarsach Soc., 1947–. DL Roxburghshire, 1956. FSA Scot, 1957. Chinese Order of Cloud and Banner with Grand Cordon, 1949. Hon. Fellow, Mark Twain Soc., USA, 1977. *Publications:* Birds of Northern Baluchistan, 1940; Birds of Arakan (with Aubrey Buxton), 1946. *Heir:* none. *Recreations:* ornithology, Celtic languages, field sports. *Address:* The Croft, Melrose, Roxburghshire TD6 9QS. *T:* Melrose (089682) 2456. *Club:* New (Edinburgh).

CHRISTMAS, Arthur Napier, BSc(Eng), CEng, FIEE, FRAeS; Chief Scientific Officer and Director of Materials Quality Assurance, Ministry of Defence, 1971–74, retired; *b* 16 May 1913; *s* of Ernest Napier and Florence Elizabeth Christmas; *m* 1940, Betty Margaret Christmas (*née* Bradbrook); one *s* one *d*. *Educ:* Holloway Sch.; Northampton Technical Coll., London (BSc (Hons)). BEAIRA, 1934–37; Post Office Research Station, 1937–46; Prin. Scientific Officer, Min. of Supply, 1946–51; Sec., British Washington Guided Missile Cttee, 1951–54; Sen. Prin. Scientific Officer, Armament Research and Develt Estabt, 1954–59; DCSO, 1959; Dir, Guided Weapons Research and Techniques, Min. of Aviation, 1959–62; Dir for Engrg Develt, European Launcher Develt Org., 1962–67; Prin. Supt, Royal Armament Research and Develt Estabt, 1967–71. *Recreations:* sailing, mountain walking, music. *Address:* Old Farm Cottage, Itchenor, Sussex. *T:* Birdham (0243) 512224. *Clubs:* Itchenor Sailing, Island Sailing.

CHRISTODOULOU, Anastasios, CBE 1978; Secretary-General, Association of Commonwealth Universities, since 1980; Joint Secretary, UK Commonwealth Scholarship Commission, since 1980; Executive Secretary, Marshall Scholarships Commemoration Commission, since 1980; *b* Cyprus, 1 May 1932; *s* of Christodoulos and Maria Haji Yianni; *m* 1955, Joan P. Edmunds; two *s* two *d*. *Educ:* St Marylebone Grammar Sch.; The Queen's Coll., Oxford (MA). Colonial Administrative Service, Tanganyika (Tanzania), 1956–62; served as District Commissioner and Magistrate. Univ. of Leeds Administration, 1963–68: Asst Registrar, 1963–65; Dep. Sec., 1965–68; Secretary, Open Univ., 1969–80. Chm., Surrey Univ. Centre for Commonwealth and European Educnl Develt, 1990–; Vice-Chm., Commonwealth Inst., 1981–89; Member: Bd of Trustees, Harlow Campus, Meml Univ. of Newfoundland, 1980–; Exec. Cttee, Council for Educn in Commonwealth, 1980–; Fulbright Commn, 1980–; Bd of Trustees, Richmond Coll., London, 1988–; Bd of Govs, Commonwealth of Learning, 1988–. Member, Court: Exeter Univ., 1980–; Hull Univ., 1980–; RCA, 1980–. FRSA. Hon. Prof., Univ. of Mauritius, 1986. Hon. DUniv: Open, 1981; Athabasca, 1981. *Recreations:* sport, music, bridge; international and Commonwealth relations. *Address:* 22 Kensington Court Gardens, W8 5QP. *T:* 071–937 4626. *Club:* Commonwealth Trust.

CHRISTOFAS, Sir Kenneth (Cavendish), KCMG 1983 (CMG 1969); MBE 1944; HM Diplomatic Service, retired; *b* 18 Aug. 1917; *o s* of late Edward Julius Goodwin and of Lillian Christofas (*step-s* of late Alexander Christofas); *m* 1948, Jessica Laura (*née* Sparshott); two *d*. *Educ:* Merchant Taylors' Sch.; University Coll., London (Fellow, 1976). Served War of 1939–45 (MBE): commissioned in The Queen's Own Royal West Kent Regt, 1939; Adjt 1940; Staff Capt. 1941; DAAG 1942; Staff Coll., Quetta, 1944; AAG 1944; GSO1, War Office, 1946. Resigned from Army with Hon. rank of Lieut-Col and joined Sen. Br. of HM Foreign Service, 1948 (HM Diplomatic Service after 1965); served in Foreign Office, 1948–49 and 1951–55; Rio de Janeiro, 1949–51; Rome, 1955–59 and as Dep. Head of UK Delegn to European Communities, Brussels, 1959–61; seconded to CRO for service as Counsellor in the British High Commn, Lagos, 1961–64 and to Colonial Office as Head of Economic Dept, 1965–66; on sabbatical year at Univ. of London, 1964–65; Counsellor in Commonwealth Office, then in FCO, 1966–69; Minister and Dep. Head of UK Delegn to EEC, 1969–72 (acting Head, March-Oct. 1971); Cabinet Office, on secondment, 1972–73; Director General, Secretariat, Council of Ministers of the European Communities, 1973–82, Hon. Dir Gen. 1982–. Pres., Crabtree Foundn, 1985; Hon. Pres. UK Branch, Assoc. of Former Officials of European Communities,

1986–. Gold Medal, Eur. Parlt, 1982. Order of Polonia Restituta (Poland), 1944. *Recreations:* railways, music. *Address:* 3 The Ridge, Bolsover Road, Eastbourne, Sussex BN20 7JE. *T:* Eastbourne (0323) 22384. *Club:* East India, Devonshire, Sports and Public Schools.

CHRISTOFF, Boris; opera singer (bass); *b* Plovdiv, near Sofia, Bulgaria, 18 May 1919; *s* of Kyryl and Rayna Teodorova; *m* Franca, *d* of Raffaello de Rensis. *Educ:* Univ. of Sofia (Doctor of Law). Joined Gussla Choir and Sofia Cathedral Choir as soloist. Obtained scholarship, through King Boris III of Bulgaria, to study singing in Rome under Riccardo Stracciari; made concert début at St Cecilia Academy in Rome, 1946 and operatic début, 1946; Covent Garden début, 1950, as Boris Godunov and Philip II; subsequently has appeared at all leading European and American opera houses; American début, Metropolitan Opera House, 1950; as Boris Godunov, San Francisco, 1956. Principal rôles include: Boris Godunov, King Philip, Galitzky, Konchak, Don Quixote, Dositheus, Ivan the Terrible, Ivan Susanin, Mephistopheles, Moses, Don Basilio, Pizarro, Simon Boccanegra. Has made numerous recordings, including opera and songs, winning many prix du disque; these include particularly the complete lyric works of the five great Russian composers. Now making concert appearances. Hon. Mem. Théâtre de l'Opéra, Paris, Mem. La Scala, Milan. Holds foreign decorations. Commendatore della Repubblica Italiana. *Address:* Villa Leccio, Buggiano (PT), Italy.

CHRISTOPHER, Ann, RA 1989(1); ARA 1980; RWA 1983; sculptor; *b* 4 Dec. 1947; *d* of William and Phyllis Christopher; *m* 1969, Kenneth Cook. *Educ:* Harrow School of Art (pre-Diploma); West of England College of Art (DipAD Sculpture). Prizewinner, Daily Telegraph Young Sculptors Competition, 1971; Arts Council grants, 1973–76. *Exhibitions include:* Oxford Gallery, Oxford, 1973, 1974, 1978; Festival Gall., Bath, 1973; London Group exhibns, 1975, 1977; Park Street Gall., Bristol, 1978, 1980; Dorset County Mus. and Art Gall. (retrospective), 1989; Royal Academy, Summer Exhibns, 1971–. *Work in Collections:* Bristol City Art Gallery; Contemporary Arts Soc.; Chantrey, London; Glynn Vivian Art Gall., Swansea; Royal West of England Academy. *Recreation:* cinema. *Address:* The Stable Block, Hay Street, Marshfield, near Chippenham, Wilts SN14 8PF.

CHRISTOPHER, Anthony Martin Grosvenor, CBE 1984; General Secretary, Inland Revenue Staff Federation, 1976–88; *b* 25 April 1925; *s* of George Russell Christopher and Helen Kathleen Milford Christopher (*née* Rowley); *m* 1962, Adela Joy Thompson. *Educ:* Cheltenham Grammar Sch.; Westminster Coll. of Commerce. Articled Pupil, Agric. Valuers, Gloucester, 1941–44; RAF, 1944–48; Inland Revenue, 1948–57; Asst Sec. 1957–60, Asst Gen. Sec. 1960–74, Jt Gen. Sec. 1975, Inland Revenue Staff Fedn; Member: TUC General Council, 1976–89 (Chm., 1988–89); TUC Economic Cttee, 1977–89; TUC Education Cttee, 1977–85; TUC Educn and Training Cttee, 1985–86; TUC Employment Policy and Orgn Cttees, 1985–89; TUC International Cttee, 1982–89; TUC Finance and General Purposes Cttee, 1983–89; TUC Media Working Group, 1979–89 (Chm., 1985–89); TUC Employment Policy and Orgn Cttee, 1979–85; TUC Social Insurance Cttee, 1986–89; Mems Auditor, ICFTU, 1984–. Member: Tax Reform Cttee, 1974–80; Tax Consultative Cttee, 1980–88; Royal Commn on Distribution of Income and Wealth, 1978–79; IBA, 1978–83; Council, Inst. of Manpower Studies, 1984–89; ESRC, 1985–88; GMC, 1989–. Chm., Tyre Industry EDC, 1983–86; Vice Pres., Building Socs Assoc., 1985–90; Director: Civil Service Building Soc., 1958–87 (Chm., 1978–87); Trades Union Unit Trust, 1981– (Chm., 1983–); Birmingham Midshires Building Soc., 1987–88; Policy Studies Inst. Council, 1983–; Member: Bd, Civil Service Housing Assoc., 1958– (Vice-Chm., 1988); Council, Nat. Assoc. for Care and Resettlement of Offenders, 1956– (Chm., 1973–); Home Sec.'s Adv. Council for Probation and After-care, 1967–77; Inner London Probation and After-care Cttee, 1966–79; Audit Commn, 1989–; Broadcasting Complaints Commn, 1989–; Council, 1985–90, Assembly, 1990–, SCF; Chm., Alcoholics Recovery Project, 1970–76; Member: Home Sec.'s Working Party on Treatment of Habitual Drunken Offenders, 1969–71; Inquiry into Rover Cowley Works Closure, 1990. Trustee: Commonwealth Trades Union Council Charitable Trust, 1985–; Inst. for Public Policy Res., 1989– (Treas., 1990). Vis. Fellow, Univ. of Bath, 1981–; Mem. Council, Royal Holloway and Bedford New Coll., 1985–89. FRSA 1989. *Publications:* (jtly) Policy for Poverty, 1970; (jtly) The Wealth Report, 1979; (jtly) The Wealth Report 2, 1982. *Recreations:* gardening, reading, music. *Address:* c/o Lloyds Bank, 130 High Street, Cheltenham, Glos GL50 1EW. *Club:* Wig and Pen.

CHRISTOPHER, Colin Alfred; General Secretary, Furniture, Timber and Allied Trades Union, since 1986; *b* 6 Nov. 1932; *s* of Alfred and Ivy Christopher; *m* 1952, Mary (*née* Wells); one *s* one *d*. *Educ:* Woodland Secondary Modern Sch., Gillingham, Kent. Apprentice upholsterer, furniture industry, 1947–52. Nat. Service, RAOC, 1952–54. Dist Organiser of FTAT for Kent/Sussex/Hampshire area, 1968; Nat. Trade Organiser for Soft Furnishing and Bedding Sect., 1978. Mem. Bd, FIRA, 1986–; Member: Furniture EDC, 1986–; Exec. Cttee, IFBWW, 1990. Active Mem, British Labour Party, at Constituency and Nat. Level, 1960–. *Recreations:* gardening, reading, classical music, ballet. *Address:* Furniture, Timber and Allied Trades Union, Fairfields, Roe Green, Kingsbury, NW9 0PT. *T:* 081–204 0273.

CHRISTOPHER, John Anthony, CB 1983; BSc; FRICS; Chief Valuer, Valuation Office, Inland Revenue, 1981–84, retired; *b* 19 June 1924; *s* of John William and Dorothy Christopher; *m* 1947, Pamela Evelyn Hardy; one *s* one *d* (and one *s* decd). *Educ:* Sir George Monoux Grammar Sch., Walthamstow; BSc Estate Management (London). Chartered Surveyor; LCC Valuation Dept, 1941. Served War, RAF, 1943–47. Joined Valuation Office, 1952; District Valuer and Valuation Officer, Lincoln, 1965; Superintending Valuer, Darlington, 1972; Asst Chief Valuer, 1974; Dep. Chief Valuer, Valuation Office, Inland Revenue, 1978. *Recreation:* golf. *Address:* 40 Svenskaby, Orton Wistow, Peterborough, Cambs PE2 0YZ. *T:* Peterborough (0733) 238199.

CHRISTOPHERSEN, Henning; a Vice-President, Commission of the European Communities, since 1985; *b* Copenhagen, 8 Nov. 1939; *m* Jytte Christophersen; three *c*. *Educ:* Copenhagen University (Graduated in economics, 1965). Head, Economic Div., Danish Fedn of Crafts and Smaller Industries, 1965–70; economics reporter for periodical NB, 1970–71, for weekly Weekendavisen, 1971–78. MP (Liberal) for Hillerød, 1971–85; Nat. Auditor, 1976–78; Minister for Foreign Affairs, 1978–79; Pres., Liberal Party Parly Gp, 1979–82; Dep. Prime Minister and Minister for Finance, 1982–84. Mem., parly finance and budget cttee, 1972–76 (Vice-Chm., 1975); Chm., parly foreign affairs cttee, 1979–81; Mem., Nordic Council, 1981–82. Dep. Leader, Danish Liberal Party, Venstre, 1972–77; Political spokesman of Liberal MPs, 1973–78; Acting Leader, Liberal Party, 1977, Party Leader, 1978–84. Vice-Pres., Fedn of European Liberals and Democrats, 1980–84. *Address:* Commission of the European Communities, 200 Rue de la Loi, 1049 Brussels, Belgium.

CHRISTOPHERSON, Sir Derman (Guy), Kt 1969; OBE 1946; FRS 1960; FEng 1976; DPhil (Oxon) 1941; MICE, FIMechE; Master, Magdalene College, Cambridge, 1979–85; *b* 6 Sept. 1915; *s* of late Derman Christopherson, Clerk in Holy Orders, formerly of Blackheath, and Edith Frances Christopherson; *m* 1940, Frances Edith (*d* 1988), *d* of late James and Martha Tearle; three *s* one *d*. *Educ:* Sherborne Sch.; University Coll., Oxford (Hon. Fellow, 1977). Henry Fellow at Harvard Univ., 1938; Scientific Officer, Research and Experiments Dept, Ministry of Home Security, 1941–45; Fellow, Magdalene Coll., Cambridge, 1945 (Hon. Fellow 1969), Bursar, 1947; University Demonstrator, Cambridge Univ. Engineering Dept, 1945, Lecturer, 1946; Professor of Mechanical Engineering, Leeds Univ., 1949–55; Prof. of Applied Science, Imperial Coll. of Science and Technology, 1955–60; Vice-Chancellor and Warden, Durham Univ., 1960–78. Mem. Council of Institution of Mechanical Engineers, 1950–53; Clayton Prize, Instn of Mechanical Engineers, 1963. Chairman: Cttee of Vice-Chancellors and Principals, 1967–70; Central Council for Educn and Training in Social Work, 1971–79; CNAA (Chm., Educn Cttee), 1966–74; Board of Washington New Town Develt Corp., 1964–78; SRC, 1965–70; Jt Standing Cttee on Structural Safety, Instns of Civil and Structural Engrs, 1983–88. Member: Council, Royal Soc., 1975; British Library Adv. Council, 1984–; Chm., Royal Fine Art Commn, 1980–85 (Mem., 1978). Fellow, Imperial Coll. of Science and Technology, 1966. Hon. DCL: Kent, 1966; Newcastle, 1971; Durham, 1986; Hon DSc: Aston, 1967; Sierra Leone, 1970; Cranfield Inst. of Technology, 1985; Hon. LLD: Leeds, 1969; Royal Univ. of Malta, 1969; DTech Brunel, 1979. *Publications:* The Engineer in The University, 1967; The University at Work, 1973; various papers in Proc. Royal Soc., Proc. IMechE, Jl of Applied Mechanics, etc. *Address:* 43 Lensfield Road, Cambridge CB2 1EN. *Club:* United Oxford & Cambridge University.

CHRISTOPHERSON, Harald Fairbairn, CMG 1978; Commissioner of Customs and Excise, 1970–80, retired; *b* 12 Jan. 1920; *s* of late Captain H. and Mrs L. G. L. Christopherson; *m* 1947, Joyce Winifred Emmett (*d* 1979); one *s* two *d*. *Educ:* Heaton Grammar Sch., Newcastle upon Tyne; King's Coll., Univ. of Durham (BSc and DipEd). Served in RA, 1941–46, Captain 1945. Teacher and lecturer in mathematics, 1947–48. Entered administrative class, Home CS, Customs and Excise, 1948; seconded to Trade and Tariffs Commn, W Indies, 1956–58; Asst Sec., 1959; seconded to Treasury, 1965–66; Under Sec., 1969. Senior Clerk, Committee Office: House of Commons, 1980–85; House of Lords, 1985–86. Mem. Cttee for Southern Region, Nat. Trust, 1986–. *Recreations:* music, travel. *Address:* 57a York Road, Sutton, Surrey SM2 6HN. *T:* 081–642 2444. *Club:* Reform.

CHRISTOPHERSON, Romola Carol Andrea; Director of Information, Department of Health (formerly of Health and Social Security), since 1986; *b* 10 Jan. 1939; *d* of Albert Edward Christopherson and Kathleen Christopherson (*née* Marfitt). *Educ:* Collegiate School for Girls, Leicester; St Hugh's College, Oxford (BA Hons English). DSIR, Min. of Technology, 1962; DoE, 1970; Min. of Agriculture, Fisheries and Food, 1978; N Ireland Office, 1981; Dep. Press Sec. to Prime Minister, 1983; Head of Inf., Dept of Energy, 1984. *Recreations:* amateur dramatics, antiques. *Address:* Department of Health, Richmond House, Whitehall, SW1.

CHUA, Nam-Hai, FRS 1988; Andrew W. Mellon Professor and Head of Laboratory of Plant Molecular Biology, Rockefeller University, since 1981; *b* 8 April 1944; *m* 1970, Suat Choo Pearl; two *d*. *Educ:* Univ. of Singapore (BSc Botany and Biochem.); Harvard Univ. (AM, PhD Biol.). Lectr, Biochem. Dept, Univ. of Singapore, 1969–71; Rockefeller University, Cell Biology Department: Res. Associate, 1971–73; Asst Prof., 1973–77; Associate Prof., 1977–81. Fellow, Acad. Sinica, Taipei, 1988; Associate Fellow, Third World Acad. of Scis, 1988. *Publications:* Methods in Chloroplast Molecular Biology, 1982; Plant Molecular Biology, 1987; numerous papers in professional jls. *Recreations:* squash, ski-ing. *Address:* 32 Walworth Avenue, Scarsdale, NY 10583, USA. *T:* (914) 723-0335.

CHUBB, family name of **Baron Hayter.**

CHUBB, Anthony Gerald Trelawny, FCA; Chairman, Foseco (formerly Foseco Minsep) PLC, 1986–90; *b* 6 April 1928; *s* of Ernest Gerald Trelawny Chubb and Eunice Chubb; *m* 1951, Beryl Joyce (*née* Cross); two *s*. *Educ:* Wylde Green Coll., Sutton Coldfield. FCA 1962 (ACA 1951); ACMA 1956. CBIM 1981. Joined Foundry Services Ltd, 1951; Man. Dir, Foseco UK, 1964–69; Dir, Foseco Ltd, 1966; Man. Dir, Foseco International, 1969–78; Dep. Gp Man. Dir, 1974–79, Gp Man. Dir, 1979–86, Foseco Minsep PLC; Chm., Electrocomponents PLC, 1986–90 (Dep. Chm., 1983–86; Dir, 1980–90). *Recreations:* golf, gardening, reading. *Address:* Heathcroft, Hartopp Road, Sutton Coldfield, West Midlands B74 2RQ.

CHUBB, Prof. Frederick Basil, MA, DPhil, LittD; Professor of Political Science, Dublin University, Trinity College, since 1960; *b* 8 Dec. 1921; *s* of late Frederick John Bailey Chubb and Gertrude May Chubb, Ludgershall, Wilts; *m* 1st, 1946, Margaret Gertrude Rafther (*d* 1984); no *c*; 2nd, 1985, Orla, *d* of Seán and Veronica Sheehan; one *d*. *Educ:* Bishop Wordsworth's Sch., Salisbury; Merton Coll., Oxford. BA 1946; MA Oxon; MA Dublin; DPhil Oxon 1950; LittD Dublin 1976. Lecturer in Political Science, Trinity Coll., Dublin, 1948; Fellow in Polit. Sci., 1952; Reader in Polit. Sci., 1955; Bursar, 1957–62. Chm., Comhairle na n-Ospidéal, 1972–78; Chm., Employer-Labour Conf., 1970; MRIA 1969. *Publications:* The Control of Public Expenditure, 1952; (with D. E. Butler (ed) and others) Elections Abroad, 1959; A Source Book of Irish Government, 1964, 2nd edn 1983; (ed with P. Lynch) Economic Development and Planning, 1969; The Government and Politics of Ireland, 1970, 2nd edn 1982; Cabinet Government in Ireland, 1974; The Constitution and Constitutional Change in Ireland, 1978; The Politics of the Irish Constitution, 1991; articles in learned jls. *Recreation:* fishing. *Address:* 19 Clyde Lane, Ballsbridge, Dublin 4. *T:* 684625.

CHUBB, John Oliver, CMG 1976; HM Diplomatic Service, retired; Counsellor, Foreign and Commonwealth Office, 1973–80; *b* 21 April 1920; *s* of Clifford Chubb and Margaret Chubb (*née* Hunt); *m* 1945, Mary Griselda Robertson (marr. diss. 1980); one *s* two *d*. *Educ:* Rugby; Oxford (MA). Served War, Scots Guards, 1940–46. Joined Diplomatic Service, 1946; Beirut, 1947; Bagdad, 1948–49; Canal Zone, 1950–52; Cyprus, 1953; FO, 1954–56; Tokyo, 1957–61; FO, 1961–63; Hong Kong, 1964–66; FO, 1967. Chm., St John's Wood Soc., 1978–83. *Recreations:* reading, spectator sports, golf, gardening, sailing. *Address:* Clayhill House, Clayhill, Beckley, near Rye, East Sussex TN31 6SQ. *T:* Northiam (0797) 252268. *Clubs:* Athenæum, MCC; Royal & Ancient Golf (St Andrews); Rye Golf, Senior Golfers' Society.

CHUMAS, Henry John, CMG 1991; TD 1969; Director General, Directorate General for Customs Union and Indirect Taxation, Commission of the European Communities, 1989–90 (Director, 1986–89); retired; *b* 21 Dec. 1933; *s* of Charles Savel Chumas and Bertha Emily Pratley; *m* 1956, Maureen Audry Collin; one *s* two *d* (and one *d* decd). *Educ:* Ealing Grammar Sch. for Boys; Sch. of Slavonic Studies, Cambridge Univ. Intelligence Corps, TA, 1957–71, Major and Co. Comdr, Intelligence and Security Gp, 1969–71. Immigration Officer, Home Office, 1955–61; HM Customs and Excise: Asst Principal, 1962–64; Principal, 1964–69; Sloan Fellow, London Grad. Sch. of Business Studies, 1969–70; Asst Sec., 1970–73; Dir, Customs Union service, Commn of EC, 1973–86. *Recreation:* ski-ing, sailing. *Address:* Les Peupliers, Chemin Perrey, 27680 Trouville la Haule, France. *T:* 32 42 88 31.

CHUNG, Kyung-Wha, Korean Order of Merit; concert violinist; *b* 26 March 1948; *d* of Chun-Chai Chung and Won-Sook (Lee) Chung; *m*; two *s*. *Educ:* Juilliard Sch. of Music, New York. Moved from Korea to New York, 1960; 7 years' study with Ivan Galamian, 1960–67; New York début with New York Philharmonic Orch., 1967; European début with André Previn and London Symphony Orch., Royal Festival Hall, London, 1970. First prize, Leventritt Internat. Violin Competition, NY, 1967. *Address:* c/o 86 Hatton Garden, EC1.

CHUNG, Sir Sze-yuen, GBE 1989 (CBE 1975; OBE 1968); Kt 1978; PhD; FEng, JP; Founding Chairman, Hong Kong University of Science and Technology, since 1987; Chairman, Hong Kong Hospital Authority, since 1990; *b* 3 Nov. 1917; *m* 1942, Nancy Cheung (*d* 1977); one *s* two *d*. *Educ:* Hong Kong Univ. (BScEng 1st Cl. Hons, 1941); Sheffield Univ. (PhD 1951). FEng 1983; FIMechE 1957, Hon. FIMechE 1983; Hon. FHKIE 1976; FIMfgE (FIProdE 1958); CBIM (FBIM 1978). Consulting engr, 1952–56; Gen. Man., Sonca Industries (now Sonca Products), 1956–60, Man. Dir 1960–77, Chm. 1977–88. Director: China Light & Power Co., 1968–; World Internat. Hldgs, 1983–; Hong Kong Telecommunications, 1988–. Mem., Hong Kong Legislative Council, 1965–74, Sen. Mem., 1974–78; Mem., Hong Kong Exec. Council, 1972–80, Sen. Mem., 1980–88. Chairman: Standing Commn on CS Salaries and Conditions of Service, 1980–88; Hong Kong Provisional Hosp. Authy, 1988–90; Hong Kong Productivity Council, 1974–76; Asian Product. Orgn, 1969–70; Hong Kong Industrial Design Council, 1969–75; Fedn of Hong Kong Industries, 1966–70 (Hon. Life Pres. 1974); Hong Kong Metrication Cttee, 1969–73; Hong Kong–Japan Business Co-operation Cttee, 1983–88; Hong Kong–US Econ. Co-operation Cttee, 1984–88. Founding Chairman: Hong Kong Polytechnic, 1972–86; City Polytechnic of Hong Kong, 1984 (Founding Fellow, 1986). Pres., Engrg Soc. of Hong Kong, 1960–61. LLD (*hc*): Chinese Univ. of Hong Kong, 1983; Sheffield, 1985; DSc (*hc*) Hong Kong Univ., 1976; DEng (*hc*) Hong Kong Polytechnic, 1989; DBA (*hc*) City Polytechnic of Hong Kong, 1989. JP Hong Kong, 1964. Man of the Year, Hong Kong Business Today magazine, 1985. Defence Medal, 1948; Silver Jubilee Medal, 1977; Gold Medal, Asian Productivity Orgn, 1980. Japanese Order of Sacred Treasure (3rd cl.), 1983. *Publications:* contrib. Proc. IMechE, Jl Iron and Steel Inst., and Jl Engrg Soc. of Hong Kong. *Recreations:* swimming, hiking, badminton, windsurfing. *Address:* House 25, Bella Vista, Silver Terrace Road, Clear Water Bay, Kowloon, Hong Kong. *T:* Hong Kong 7610281, 7192857. *Clubs:* Hong Kong, Royal Hong Kong Jockey, Kowloon Cricket (Hong Kong); Pacific (Kowloon).

CHURCH, Ian David; Editor, Official Report (Hansard), House of Commons, since 1989; *b* 18 Oct. 1941; *s* of John Jasper and Violet Kathleen Church; *m* 1964, Christine Stevenson; one *d*. *Educ:* Roan School. Journalist with Press Association, 1964; The Scotsman, 1966; The Times, 1968; joined Hansard, 1972; Dep. Editor, 1988. Pres., Commonwealth Hansard Editors' Assoc., 1989–. *Recreations:* photography, writing fiction. *Address:* Department of the Official Report, House of Commons, SW1A 0AA.

CHURCH, James Anthony; *see* Church, Tony.

CHURCH, John Carver, CMG 1986; CVO 1988; MBE 1970; HM Diplomatic Service, retired; Chairman, ECU Internacional SA (business management services), Barcelona, since 1990; *b* 8 Dec. 1929; *s* of Richard Church, CBE, FRSL, and Catherina Church; *m* 1953, Marie-Geneviève Vallette; two *s* two *d*. *Educ:* Cranbrook Sch., Kent; Ecole Alsacienne, Paris; Christ's Coll., Cambridge (MA 1953). Reuters News Agency, 1953–59; Central Office of Information, 1959–61; Commonwealth Relations Office: Information Officer, Calcutta, 1961–65; Foreign and Commonwealth Office: Second Secretary (Commercial) Rio de Janeiro, 1966–69; First Sec. (Information) Tel Aviv, 1969–74; First Sec., News Dept, FCO, 1974–77; Consul (Commercial) Milan, 1977–78; Consul-General: São Paulo, 1978–81; Naples, 1981–86; Barcelona, 1986–89. *Recreations:* reading, swimming, skiing. *Address:* 124 Chesterton Road, W10 6EP. *T:* 081–969 8251.

CHURCH, Prof. Ronald James H.; *see* Harrison-Church.

CHURCH, Tony, (James Anthony Church); Dean of the National Theatre Conservatory, Denver, USA, since 1989; *b* 11 May 1930; *s* of Ronald Frederic and Margaret Fanny Church; *m* 1958, Margaret Ann Blakeney; one *s* two *d*. *Educ:* Hurstpierpoint Coll.; Clare Coll., Cambridge. MA 1954. First perf. as professional, Arts Theatre, London, 1953; frequent television, radio, regional theatre perfs; founder mem., RSC, 1960, and Associate Artist, 1960–; roles there include: Henry IV; Polonius (twice); King Lear; John of Gaunt; Friar Laurence; Ulysses; Pandarus; York in Richard II; Trelawney in Maydays; Horsham in Waste; Director of Nuclear Plant in Sarcophagus; Wizard in Wizard of Oz, 1987; Cymbeline, Gonzalo and Antigonus in the late Shakespeares, NT, 1988. Toured USA extensively, 1974–: King Lear, 1982; Falstaff (Santa Cruz), 1984; Prospero, Shylock (Colorado), 1987; recorded 26 Shakespeare roles, 1956–66. Founder dir, Northcott Theatre, Exeter, 1967–71; Dir of Drama, GSMD, 1982–88; Drama Advr, Hong Kong Govt, 1982–85. Member: Arts Council 1982–85 (Chm., Drama Panel, 1982–85); British Council Drama Cttee, 1985–88. Hon. MA Exeter, 1971. *Recreations:* listening to music, narrowboats, travel. *Address:* 1050 13th Street, Denver, Colorado 80204, USA. *T:* 303 8934200; 38 Rosebery Road, N10 2LJ.

CHURCHER, Maj.-Gen. John Bryan, CB 1952; DSO 1944, Bar 1946; retired; Director and General Secretary, Independent Stores Association, 1959–71; *b* 2 Sept. 1905; *s* of late Lieut-Col B. T. Churcher, Wargrave, Berks, and Beatrice Theresa Churcher; *m* 1937, Rosamond Hildegarde Mary, *y d* of late Frederick Parkin, Truro Vean, Truro, Cornwall; one *s* two *d*. *Educ:* Wellington Coll., Berks; RMC Sandhurst. Commissioned DCLI, 1925; Lieut, 1927; Capt. KSLI, 1936; Staff Coll., 1939; served War of 1939–45 (despatches, DSO and Bar); commanded: 1 Bn Hereford Regt, 1942–44; 159 Inf. Bde, 1944–46; 43 Div., 1946; Northumbrian Dist., 1946; 2 Div., 1946; 3 Div., 1946–47; 5 Div., 1947–48; Brig., Imperial Defence Coll., 1948; BGS, Western Command, 1949–51; Chief of Staff, Southern Comd, 1951–54; GOC, 3rd Inf. Div., 1954–57; Dir of Military Training at the War Office, 1957–59; retired, 1959. ADC to King George VI, 1949–52; ADC to the Queen to 1952. *Address:* 34 Oaks Drive, Colchester, Essex CO3 3PS. *T:* Colchester (0206) 574525.

CHURCHHOUSE, Prof. Robert Francis, CBE 1982; PhD; Professor of Computing Mathematics, University College, Cardiff, since 1971; *b* 30 Dec. 1927; *s* of Robert Francis Churchhouse and Agnes Howard; *m* 1954, Julia McCarthy; three *s*. *Educ:* St Bede's Coll., Manchester; Manchester Univ. (BSc 1949); Trinity Hall, Cambridge (PhD 1952). Royal Naval Scientific Service, 1952–63; Head of Programming Gp, Atlas Computer Lab., SRC, 1963–71. Vis. Fellow, St Cross Coll., Oxford, 1972–90. Chm., Computer Bd for Univs and Res. Councils, 1979–82; Mem., Welsh Cttee, UFC, 1989–. Pres., IMA, 1986–87. KSG 1988. *Publications:* (ed jtly) Computers in Mathematical Research, 1968; (ed jtly) The Computer in Literary and Linguistic Studies, 1976; Numerical Analysis, 1978; papers in math. and other jls. *Recreations:* cricket, astronomy. *Address:* 15 Holly Grove, Lisvane, Cardiff CF4 5UJ. *T:* Cardiff (0222) 750250. *Club:* Challenor.

CHURCHILL; *see* Spencer-Churchill.

CHURCHILL, 3rd Viscount *cr* 1902; **Victor George Spencer;** Baron 1815; Investment Manager, Central Board of Finance of the Church of England and Charities Official Investment Fund; Director: Local Authorities' Mutual Investment Trust; Church, Charity and Local Authority Fund Managers Ltd; *b* 31 July 1934; *s* of 1st Viscount Churchill, GCVO, and late Christine Sinclair (who *m* 3rd, Sir Lancelot Oliphant, KCMG, CB); *S* half-brother, 1973. *Educ:* Eton; New Coll., Oxford (MA). Lieut, Scots Guards, 1953–55. Morgan Grenfell & Co. Ltd, 1958–74. *Heir* (to Barony only): Richard Harry Ramsay Spencer [*b* 11 Oct. 1926; *m* 1958, Antoinette Rose-Marie de Charrière; two *s*]. *Address:* 6 Cumberland Mansions, George Street, W1H 5TE.

CHURCHILL, Diana (Josephine); actress, stage and screen; *b* Wembley, 21 Aug. 1913; *d* of Joseph H. Churchill, MRCS, LRCP and Ethel Mary Nunn; *m* Barry K. Barnes (*d* 1965); *m* 1976, Mervyn Johns. *Educ:* St Mary's Sch., Wantage; Guildhall Sch. of Music (scholarship). First professional appearance in Champion North, Royalty, 1931; subsequently in West End and in Repertory. Old Vic Season, 1949–50, New Theatre, as Rosaline in Love's Labour's Lost, Miss Kate Hardcastle in She Stoops to Conquer, Lizaveta Bogdanovna in A Month in the Country and Elise in The Miser; High Spirits, London Hippodrome, 1953; The Desperate Hours, London Hippodrome, 1955; Hamlet, Stratford-on-Avon Festival, 1956; Lady Fidget in The Country Wife, Royal Court Theatre, 1956; The Rehearsal, Globe Theatre, 1961; The Winter's Tale, Cambridge, 1966; The Farmer's Wife, Chichester, 1967; Heartbreak House, Chichester, later Lyric, 1967. Has also appeared in several films. *Address:* c/o Stella Richards Management, 42 Hazlebury Road, SW6.

CHURCHILL, John George Spencer; mural and portrait, townscape, landscape painter; sculptor, lecturer and author since 1932; *b* 31 May 1909; *s* of John Strange Spencer Churchill and Lady Gwendoline Bertie; *m* 1st, 1934, Angela Culme Seymour; one *d*; 2nd, 1941, Mary Cookson; 3rd, 1953, Kathlyn Tandy (*d* 1957); 4th, 1958, Lullan Boston (marr. diss. 1972). *Educ:* Harrow School; Pembroke Coll., Oxford; Royal Coll. of Art; Central Sch. of Art; Westminster Sch. of Art; Ruskin Sch. of Art, Oxford; private pupil of Meninsky, Hubbard, Nicholson and Lutyens. Stock Exchange, 1930–32. Served War, Major GSO, RE, 1939–45. Mural and portrait, townscape and landscape paintings in England, France, Spain, Portugal, Italy, Switzerland, Belgium and America, 1932–80. Lectr in America, 1961–69. *Work includes:* incised relief carving on slate and cement cast busts, in Marlborough Pavilion at Chartwell, Westerham, Kent (National Trust), 1949; reportage illustrations and paintings of Spanish Revolution, 1936, and Evacuation of BEF from Dunkirk, 1940 (in Illustrated London News); London from the South Bank, in Simpsons, Piccadilly, 1957; painting of forest destruction for WWF, 1985. Mem., Soc. of Mural Painters. *Publications:* Crowded Canvas, 1960; A Churchill Canvas, 1961 (USA), serialised in Sunday Dispatch and Atlantic Monthly, USA; Varnishing Day, 1986; contrib. illustr.: Country Life, Connoisseur, etc. *Recreations:* music, travel. *Address:* (professional) 40 Elsham Road, W14. *T:* 071–602 4666; (domicile) Appartement Churchill, 83360 Grimaud, France. *T:* 94.43.21.31. *Clubs:* Press, Chelsea Arts; Cincinatti (Washington, DC, USA).

See also Baron Ashburton.

CHURCHILL, Winston Spencer; MP (C) Davyhulme, Manchester, since 1983 (Stretford, Lancs, 1970–83); author; journalist; *b* 10 Oct. 1940; *s* of late Randolph Frederick Edward Spencer Churchill, MBE and of Hon. Mrs Averell Harriman, *e d* of 11th Baron Digby, KG, DSO, MC, TD; *m* 1964, Mary Caroline, (Minnie), d'Erlanger, *d* of late Sir Gerard d'Erlanger, CBE, Chairman of BOAC; two *s* two *d*. *Educ:* Eton; Christ Church, Oxford (MA). Correspondent in Yemen, Congo and Angola, 1963; Presenter, This Time of Day, BBC Radio, 1964–65; Correspondent: Borneo and Vietnam, 1966; Middle East, 1967; Chicago, Czechoslovakia, 1968; Nigeria, Biafra and Middle East, for The Times, 1969–70; Special Correspondent, China, 1972, Portugal, 1975. Lecture tours of the US and Canada, 1965, 1969, 1971, 1973, 1975, 1978, 1980, 1981, 1984, 1985, 1989, 1990. Contested Gorton Div. of Manchester in Bye-election, Nov. 1967. PPS to Minister of Housing and Construction, 1970–72, to Minister of State, FCO, 1972–73; Sec., Cons. Foreign and Commonwealth Affairs Cttee, 1973–76; Conservative Party front-bench spokesman on Defence, 1976–78. Member: Select Cttee on Defence, 1983–; Select Cttee on H of C (Services), 1985–86. Vice-Chm., Cons. Defence Cttee, 1979–83; Cons. Party Co-ordinator for Defence and Multilateral Disarmament, 1982–84; Mem. Exec., 1922 Cttee, 1979–85, Treas., 1987–88. Pres., Bristol Univ. Cons. Assoc., 1977–. Sponsored Motor Vehicles (Passenger Insce) Act 1972, Crown Proceedings (Armed Forces) Act 1987. Pres., Trafford Park Indust. Council, 1971–. Member, Council: Consumers' Assoc., 1990–; British Kidney Patients Assoc., 1990–. Trustee: Winston Churchill Meml Trust, 1968–; Nat. Benevolent Fund for the Aged, 1974–; Governor, English-Speaking Union, 1975–80; Vice-Pres., British Technion Soc., 1976–. Hon. Fellow, Churchill Coll., Cambridge, 1969. Hon. LLD, Westminster Coll., Fulton, Mo, USA, 1972. *Publications:* First Journey, 1964; Six Day War, 1967; Defending the West, 1981; Memories and Adventures, 1989. *Recreations:* tennis, sailing, ski-ing. *Address:* House of Commons, SW1A 0AA. *Clubs:* White's, Buck's, Press.

CHURSTON, 5th Baron *cr* 1858; **John Francis Yarde-Buller;** Bt 1790; *b* 29 Dec. 1934; *s* of 4th Baron Churston, VRD and Elizabeth Mary (*d* 1951), *d* of late W. B. du Pre; *S* father, 1991; *m* 1973, Alexander Joanna, *d* of A. G. Contomichalos; one *s* two *d*. *Educ:* Eton Coll. 2nd Lt RHG, 1954. *Heir:* *s* Hon. Benjamin Anthony Francis Yarde-Buller, *b* 13 Sept. 1974. *Address:* Yowlestone House, Puddington, Tiverton, Devon EX16 8LN. *T:* Tiverton (0884) 860328. *Clubs:* Buck's, White's.

CHUTE, Marchette; author; *b* 16 Aug. 1909; *d* of William Young Chute and Edith Mary Pickburn; unmarried. *Educ:* Univ. of Minnesota (BA). Doctor of Letters: Western Coll., 1952; Carleton Coll., 1957; Dickinson Coll., 1964. Mem., American Acad. of Arts and Letters. Outstanding Achievement Award, Univ. of Minnesota, 1958; co-winner of Constance Lindsay Skinner Award, 1959. *Publications:* Rhymes about Ourselves, 1932; The Search for God, 1941; Rhymes about the Country, 1941; The Innocent Wayfaring, 1943; Geoffrey Chaucer of England, 1946; Rhymes about the City, 1946; The End of the Search, 1947; Shakespeare of London, 1950; An Introduction to Shakespeare, 1951 (English title: Shakespeare and his Stage); Ben Jonson of Westminster, 1953; The Wonderful Winter, 1954; Stories from Shakespeare, 1956; Around and About, 1957; Two Gentle Men: the Lives of George Herbert and Robert Herrick, 1959; Jesus of Israel, 1961; The Worlds of Shakespeare (with Ernestine Perrie), 1963; The First Liberty: a history of the right to vote in America, 1619–1850, 1969; The Green Tree of Democracy, 1971; PEN American Center: a history of the first fifty years, 1972; Rhymes About Us, 1974; various articles in Saturday Review, Virginia Quarterly Review, etc. *Recreations:* walking, reading, talking. *Address:* 66 Glenbrook Road, Morris Plains, NJ 07950, USA. *T:* 201–540–1069. *Clubs:* Royal Society of Arts; PEN, Renaissance Society of America (New York).

CHYNOWETH, David Boyd; Director of Finance, Lothian Regional Council, since 1985; *b* 26 Dec. 1940; *s* of Ernest and Blodwen Chynoweth; *m* 1968, Margaret Slater; one *s* two *d*. *Educ:* Simon Langton Sch., Canterbury; Univ. of Nottingham (BA). IPFA 1966; FCCA 1983. Public Finance posts with Derbs CC, 1962 and London Borough of

Ealing, 1965; Asst County Treas., Flints CC, 1968; Dep. County Treas., West Suffolk CC, 1970; County Treasurer, S Yorks CC, 1973. Mem. Council, CIPFA, 1983–; Mem. Investment Protection Cttee, Nat. Assoc. of Pension Funds; Pres., Assoc. of Public Service Finance Officers, 1981–82. *Recreations:* sailing, photography. *Address:* Regional Headquarters, George IV Bridge, Edinburgh EH1 1UQ. *T:* 031-229 9292. *Club:* Royal Over-Seas League.

CHYNOWETH, Rt. Rev. Neville James, ED 1966; *b* 3 Oct. 1922; *s* of Percy James and Lilian Chynoweth; *m* 1951, Joan Laurice Wilson; two *s* two *d. Educ:* Manly High School; Sydney Univ. (MA); Melbourne Coll. of Divinity (BD); Moore Theological Coll. (ThL). Assistant, St Michael's, Sydney, 1950; Rector, Kangaroo Valley, 1951–52; Chaplain, Royal Prince Alfred Hospital, 1952–54; Rector: St John's, Deewhy, 1954–63; St Anne's, Strathfield, 1963–66; All Saints, Canberra, 1966–71; St Paul's, Canberra, 1971–74; Archdeacon of Canberra, 1973–74; Assistant Bishop of Canberra and Goulburn, 1974–80; Bishop of Gippsland, 1980–87. *Recreations:* music, biography. *Address:* 79 Carruthers Street, Curtin, Canberra, ACT 2605, Australia. *T:* (06) 2810518.

CITRINE, family name of **Baron Citrine.**

CITRINE, 2nd Baron *cr* 1946, of Wembley; **Norman Arthur Citrine,** LLB; solicitor in general practice, retired 1984; author, editor, lecturer, advocate; *b* 27 Sept. 1914; *er s* of 1st Baron Citrine, GBE, PC, and Doris Helen (*d* 1973), *d* of Edgar Slade; *S* father, 1983; *m* 1939, Kathleen Alice, *d* of George Thomas Chilvers; one *d. Educ:* University Coll. Sch., Hampstead; Law Society's Sch., London. Admitted solicitor of Supreme Court (Hons), 1937; LLB (London), 1938. Served War of 1939–45, Lieut RNVR, 1940–46. Legal Adviser to Trades Union Congress, 1946–51; re-entered general legal practice, 1951. Pres., Devon and Exeter Law Soc., 1971. *Publications:* War Pensions Appeal Cases, 1946; Guide to Industrial Injuries Acts, 1948; Citrine's Trade Union Law, 1950, 3rd edn, 1967; Citrine's ABC of Chairmanship, 1952–82. *Recreations:* yachting, camping, hiking, music, literature, art and numerous creative pursuits. *Heir: b* Dr the Hon. Ronald Eric Citrine [*b* 19 May 1919; *m* 1945, Mary, *d* of Reginald Williams]. *Address:* Casa Katrina, The Mount, Opua, Bay of Islands, New Zealand.

CLAGUE, Joan; Director of Nursing Services, Marie Curie Memorial Foundation, 1986–90; *b* 17 April 1931; *d* of James Henry Clague and Violet May Clague (*née* Johnson). *Educ:* Malvern Girls' Coll.; Guy's Hosp.; Hampstead Gen. Hosp.; Simpson Meml Maternity Pavilion. Asst Regional Nursing Officer, Oxford Regional Hosp. Bd, 1965–67; Principal, then Chief Nursing Officer, St George's Hosp. Bd of Governors, 1967–73; Area Nursing Officer, Merton, Sutton and Wandsworth AHA, 1973–81; Regl Nursing Officer, NE Thames RHA, 1981–86. Pres., Assoc. of Nurse Administrators, 1983–85. WHO Fellow, 1969; Smith and Nephew EEC Scholar, 1981. *Recreations:* walking, domestic pursuits. *Address:* 7 Tylney Avenue, SE19 1LN. *T:* 081–670 5171.

CLAMAGERAN, Alice Germaine Suzanne; Director, School of Social Workers, Centre Hospitalier Universitaire de Rouen, 1942–73; President, International Council of Nurses, 1961–65; *b* 5 March 1906; *d* of William Clamageran, shipowner at Rouen and of Lucie Harlé. *Educ:* Rouen. Nursing studies: Red Cross School of Nurses, Rouen; Ecole Professionnelle d'Assistance aux Malades, Paris. Tutor, Red Cross Sch. for Nurses, Rouen, 1931–42 (leave, for course in Public Health at Florence Nightingale Internat. Foundn, London, 1934–35). War service (6 months), 1939–40. President: Bd of Dirs, Fondation Edith Seltzer (Sanatorium Chantoiseau, Briançon) for Nurses, Social Workers and Medical Auxiliaries; Assoc. Médico-Sociale Protestante de Langue Française; Hon. Pres. Nat. Assoc. of Trained Nurses in France. Hon. Fellow, Royal Coll. of Nursing of UK, 1977. Médaille de Bronze de l'Enseignement Technique, 1960; Officier dans l'Ordre de la Santé Publique, 1961; Chevalier, Légion d'Honneur, 1962. *Address:* Hautonne, 27310 Bourg-Achard, France.

CLANCARTY, 8th Earl of, *cr* 1803; **William Francis Brinsley Le Poer Trench;** Baron Kilconnel, 1797; Viscount Dunlo, 1801; Baron Trench (UK), 1815; Viscount Clancarty (UK), 1823; Marquess of Heusden (Kingdom of the Netherlands), 1818; author; *b* 18 Sept. 1911; 5th *s* of 5th Earl of Clancarty and of Mary Gwatkin, *d* of late W. F. Rosslewin Ellis; *S* half-brother, 1975; *m* 1st, 1940, Diana Joan (marr. diss. 1947), *yr d* of Sir William Younger, 2nd Bt; 2nd, 1961, Mrs Wilma Dorothy Millen Belknap (marr. diss. 1969), *d* of S. R. Vermilyea, USA; 3rd, 1974, Mrs Mildred Alleyn Spong (*d* 1975); 4th, 1976, May, *widow* of Commander Frank M. Beasley, RN and *o d* of late E. Radonicich. *Educ:* Nautical Coll., Pangbourne. Founder Pres., Contact International; Chm., House of Lords UFO Study Gp. *Publications:* (as Brinsley Le Poer Trench): The Sky People, 1960; Men Among Mankind, 1962; Forgotten Heritage, 1964; The Flying Saucer Story, 1966; Operation Earth, 1969; The Eternal Subject, 1973; Secret of the Ages, 1974. *Recreations:* Ufology, travel, walking. *Heir: nephew* Nicholas Power Richard Le Poer Trench, *b* 1 May 1952. *Address:* 51 Eaton Place, Belgravia, SW1. *Club:* Buck's.

CLANCHY, Joan Lesley, (Mrs Michael Clanchy); Headmistress, North London Collegiate School, since 1986; *b* 26 Aug. 1939; *d* of Leslie and Mary Milne; *m* 1962, Dr Michael Clanchy; one *s* one *d. Educ:* St Leonard's Sch., St Andrews; St Hilda's Coll., Oxford. MA; DipEd. Schoolteacher: Woodberry Down Sch., London, 1962–63; The Park Sch., Glasgow, 1967–76. Headmistress, St George's Sch., Edinburgh, 1976–85. *Address:* 28 Hillfield Road, NW6 1PZ.

CLANCY, His Eminence Cardinal Edward Bede; *see* Sydney, Archbishop of, (RC).

CLANFIELD, Viscount; Ashton Robert Gerard Peel; *b* 16 Sept. 1976; *s* and *heir* of 3rd Earl Peel, *qv.*

CLANMORRIS, 8th Baron *cr* 1800 (Ire.); **Simon John Ward Bingham;** FCA; *b* 25 Oct. 1937; *s* of 7th Baron Clanmorris and of Madeleine Mary, *d* of late Clement Ebel; *S* father, 1988; *m* 1971, Gizella Maria, *d* of Sandor Zverkó; one *d. Educ:* Downside; Queens' College, Cambridge (MA). ACA 1965, FCA 1975. *Heir: cousin* John Temple Bingham [*b* 22 Feb. 1923; *m* 1949, Joan Muriel Bowen (*d* 1955)]. *Address:* Falkland House, Marloes Road, W8 5LF.

See also Hon. Charlotte Bingham.

CLANWILLIAM, 7th Earl of, *cr* 1776 (Ire.); **John Herbert Meade;** Bt 1703; Viscount Clanwilliam, Baron Gillford 1766; Baron Clanwilliam (UK) 1828; *b* 27 Sept. 1919; 2nd *s* of Adm. Hon. Sir Herbert Meade-Fetherstonhaugh, GCVO, CB, DSO (*d* 1964) (3rd *s* of 4th Earl) and Margaret Ishbel Frances (*d* 1977), *d* of Rt. Rev. Hon. Edward Carr Glyn, DD; *S* cousin, 1989; *m* 1956, Maxine, *o d* of late J. A. Hayden-Scott; one *s* two *d. Educ:* RNC Dartmouth. *Heir: s* Lord Gillford, *qv. Address:* House of Lords, SW1A 0PW. *Club:* Turf.

CLAPHAM, His Honour Brian Ralph; a Circuit Judge, South East Circuit, 1974–85; *b* 1 July 1913; *s* of Isaac Clapham and Laura Alice Clapham (*née* Meech); *m* 1961, Margaret Warburg; two *s. Educ:* Tonbridge Sch.; Wadham Coll., Oxford; University Coll. London (LLB; LLM 1976). Called to Bar, Middle Temple, 1936. Contested (Lab): Tonbridge, 1950; Billericay, 1951, 1955; Chelmsford, 1959. Councillor, Tonbridge and Southborough UDCs, 1947–74; Chm., Tonbridge UDC, 1959–60. Governor, West Kent Coll. Freeman of City of London. BA Open, 1981. FCIArb 1988. *Recreations:* walking and talking.

CLAPHAM, Sir Michael (John Sinclair), KBE 1973; Chairman: IMI Ltd, 1974–81; BPM Holdings Ltd, 1974–81; *b* 17 Jan. 1912; *s* of late Sir John Clapham, CBE and Lady Clapham, Cambridge; *m* 1935, Hon. Elisabeth Russell Rea, *d* of 1st Baron Rea of Eskdale; two *s* one *d* (and one *s* decd). *Educ:* Marlborough Coll.; King's Coll., Cambridge (MA). Apprenticed as printer with University Press, Cambridge, 1933–35; Overseer and later Works Man., Percy Lund Humphries & Co. Ltd, Bradford, 1935–38; joined ICI Ltd as Man., Kynoch Press, 1938; seconded, in conseq. of developing a diffusion barrier, to Tube Alloys Project (atomic energy), 1941–45; Personnel Dir, ICI Metals Div., 1946; Midland Regional Man., ICI, 1951; Jt Man. Dir, ICI Metals Div., 1952; Chm. 1959; Dir, ICI, 1961–74, Dep. Chm. 1968–74; served as Overseas Dir; Dir, ICI of Austr. & NZ Ltd, 1961–74; Director: Imp. Metal Industries Ltd, 1962–70; Lloyds Bank Ltd, 1971–82 (Dep. Chm., 1974–80); Grindlay's Bank Ltd, 1975–84; Associated Communications Corp., 1982–88; Heytesbury (UK) Ltd, 1988–90. Mem., General Motors European Adv. Council, 1975–82. Dep. Pres., 1971–72, Pres., 1972–74, CBI. Member: IRC, 1969–71; Standing Adv. Cttee on Pay of Higher Civil Service, 1968–71; Review Body on Doctors' and Dentists' Remuneration, 1968–70; Birmingham Educn Cttee, 1949–56; W Mids Adv. Coun. for Techn., Commercial and Art Educn, and Regional Academic Bd, 1952; Life Governor, Birmingham Univ., 1955 (Mem. Coun., 1956–61); Member: Court, Univ. of London, 1969–85; Govt Youth Service Cttee (Albemarle Cttee), 1958; CNAA, 1964–77 (Chm., 1971–77); NEDC, 1971–76; Pres., Inst. of Printing, 1980–82. Hon. DSc Aston, 1973; Hon. LLD: CNAA, 1978; London, 1984. *Publications:* Printing, 1500–1730, in The History of Technology, Vol. III, 1957; Multinational Enterprises and Nation States, 1975; various articles on printing, personnel management and education. *Recreations:* sailing, canal boating, cooking. *Address:* 26 Hill Street, W1X 7FU. *T:* 071–499 1240. *Club:* Royal Yacht Squadron.

See also B. D. Till.

CLAPHAM, Peter Brian, PhD; CEng, FInstP; Director, National Physical Laboratory, since 1990; *b* 3 Nov. 1940; *s* of Wilfred Clapham and Una Frances (*née* Murray); *m* 1965, Jean Margaret (*née* Vigil); two *s. Educ:* Ashville Coll., Harrogate; University Coll. London (BSc, PhD). Research in optics and metrology, NPL, 1960–70; Sec., Adv. Cttee on Res. on Measurements and Standards, 1970–71; res. management and head of marketing, NPL, 1972–81; Res. and Technology Policy, DoI, 1981–82; Supt of Div. of Mech. and Optical Metrology, NPL, 1982–84; Dir 1985, Chief Exec. 1989, Nat. Weights and Measures Lab. Member: Presidential Council of Internat. Orgn of Legal Metrology, 1985–90; Chm., W European Legal Metrology Cooperation, 1989–90. Internat. Cttee of Weights and Measures, 1991–; *Publications:* numerous sci. contribs to learned jls. *Recreations:* peregrination, crafts. *Address:* c/o National Physical Laboratory, Teddington, Mddx.

CLAPP, Captain Michael Cecil, CB 1982; FBIM, MNI; RN retired; *b* 22 Feb. 1932; *s* of Brig. Cecil Douglas Clapp, CBE and Mary Elizabeth Emmeline Palmer Clapp; *m* 1975, Sarah Jane Alexander; one *s* two *d. Educ:* Chafyn Grove Sch., Salisbury; Marlborough College. Joined Royal Navy, 1950; HMS Norfolk, 1972; Directorate of Naval Plans, MoD, 1974; in Command, HMS Leander, 1977; Jt Maritime Op. Trng Staff, 1979; Commodore, Amphibious Warfare, Staff of Third Flotilla, 1980–83 (South Atlantic Campaign, 1982). Mem., Stock Exchange, 1987–. Governor: Kelly Coll., 1985–; St Michael Sch., Tavistock, 1985–. *Recreations:* sailing, shooting, fishing, skiing, genealogy, country life. *Address:* c/o Lloyds Bank, 234 High Street, Exeter, Devon EX4 3NL.

CLARE; *see* Sabben-Clare.

CLARE, Prof. Anthony Ward, MD; FRCPsych; FRCPI; Clinical Professor of Psychiatry, Trinity College, Dublin, and Medical Director, St Patrick's Hospital, Dublin, since 1989; *b* 24 Dec. 1942; *s* of Bernard Joseph Clare and Mary Agnes (*née* Dunne); *m* 1966, Jane Carmel Hogan; three *s* four *d. Educ:* Gonzaga Coll., Dublin; University Coll., Dublin. MB, BCh, BAO 1966, MD 1982; MPhil 1972; FRCPsych 1985 (MRCPsych 1973), FRCPI 1983 (MRCPI 1971). Auditor, Literary and Historical Soc., 1963–64. Internship, St Joseph's Hosp., Syracuse, New York, 1967; psychiatric training, St Patrick's Hosp., Dublin, 1967–69; Psychiatric Registrar, Maudsley Hosp., London, 1970–72, Sen. Registrar, 1973–75; research worker, General Practice Research Unit, Inst. of Psychiatry, 1976–79, Sen. Lectr, 1980–82; Prof. and Head of Dept of Psychol Medicine, St Bartholomew's Hosp. Med. Coll., 1983–88. Radio series: In the Psychiatrist's Chair, 1982–; All in the Mind, 1988–; TV series: Motives, 1983. *Publications:* Psychiatry in Dissent, 1976, 2nd edn 1980; (ed with P. Williams) Psychosocial Disorders in General Practice, 1979; (with S. Thompson) Let's Talk About Me, 1981; (ed with R. Corney) Social Work and Primary Health Care, 1982; (ed with M. Lader) Psychiatry and General Practice, 1982; In the Psychiatrist's Chair, 1984; Lovelaw, 1986. *Recreations:* tennis, broadcasting, theatre, family life. *Address:* 87 Coper's Cope Road, Beckenham, Kent BR3 1NR. *T:* 081–650 1784; Delville, Lucan, Co. Dublin. *T:* Dublin 6798055.

CLARE, Herbert Mitchell N.; *see* Newton-Clare.

CLARENDON, 7th Earl of, 2nd *cr* 1776; **George Frederick Laurence Hyde Villiers;** Chairman, since 1985, and Managing Director, since 1962, Seccombe Marshall and Campion plc; *b* 2 Feb. 1933; *o s* of Lord Hyde (*d* 1935) and Hon. Marion Féodorovna Louise Glyn, Lady Hyde (*d* 1970), *er d* of 4th Baron Wolverton; *S* grandfather, 1955; *m* 1974, Jane Diana, *d* of late E. W. Dawson; one *s* one *d*. Page of Honour to King George VI, 1948–49; Lieut RHG, 1951–53. *Heir: s* Lord Hyde, *qv. Address:* 5 Astell Street, SW3 3RT. *T:* 071–352 9131; Soberton Mill, Swanmore, Hants SO3 2QF. *T:* Wickham (0329) 833118.

CLARFELT, Jack Gerald; Chairman: Linhay Meats Ltd, since 1982; Linhay Frizzell Insurance Brokers Ltd, since 1984; *b* 7 Feb. 1914; *s* of Barnett Clarfelt and Rene (*née* Frankel); *m* 1948, Baba Fredman; one *s* one *d. Educ:* Grocers' Co. Sch.; Sorbonne. Qualified as Solicitor, 1937; Man. Dir, Home Killed Meat Assoc., 1940–43 and 1945–54; Queen's Royal Surreys, 1943–45; Man. Dir, Fatstock Marketing Corp., 1954–60; Chm., Smithfield & Zwanenberg Gp Ltd, 1960–75; Exec. Dep. Chm., 1975–79, Dir, 1979–83, FMC Ltd. Dir, S. and W. Berisford Ltd, 1973–75. Farming, Hampshire. Master, Worshipful Co. of Butchers, 1978. *Recreations:* golf, swimming. *Address:* Linhay Meads, Timsbury, Romsey, Hants SO51 0LA. *T:* Braishfield (0794) 68243. *Clubs:* City Livery, Farmers'.

See also R. E. Rhodes.

CLARIDGE, Prof. Michael Frederick; Professor of Entomology and Head of School of Biology, University of Wales College of Cardiff, since 1989; *b* 2 June 1934; *s* of Frederick William Claridge and Eva Alice (*née* Jeffrey); *m* 1967, Lindsey Clare Hellings; two *s* one *d. Educ:* Lawrence Sheriff Sch., Rugby; Keble Coll., Oxford (MA, DPhil). Lectr in Zoology 1959–74, Sen. Lectr in Zoology 1974–77, Univ. Coll., Cardiff; Reader in Entomology 1977–83, Prof. of Entomology, 1983–88, Univ. of Wales, Cardiff. Pres., Linnean Soc. of London, 1988–91. *Publications:* chapters in: The Leafhoppers and

Planthoppers, 1985; Organization of Communities – Past and Present, 1987; Prospects in Systematics, 1988; papers in Biol Jl of Linnean Soc., Ecological Entomology, Amer. Naturalist. *Recreations:* classical music, cricket, natural history. *Address:* School of Pure and Applied Biology, University of Wales College of Cardiff, Cardiff CF1 3TL. *T:* Cardiff (0222) 874147.

CLARK; *see* Chichester-Clark.

CLARK; *see* Stafford-Clark.

CLARK, Rt. Rev. Alan Charles; *see* East Anglia, Bishop of, (RC).

CLARK, Rt. Hon. Alan (Kenneth McKenzie), PC 1991; MP (C) Plymouth Sutton, since Feb. 1974; Minister of State, Ministry of Defence, since 1989; historian; *b* 13 April 1928; *s* of Baron Clark (Life Peer), OM, CH, KCB, CLit, FBA and late Elizabeth Martin; *m* 1958, (Caroline) Jane Beuttler; two *s*. *Educ:* Eton; Christ Church, Oxford (MA). Household Cavalry (Training Regt), 1946; RAuxAF, 1952–54. Barrister, Inner Temple, 1955. Mem., Inst. for Strategic Studies, 1963. Parly Under Sec. of State, Dept of Employment, 1983–86; Minister for Trade, 1986–89. Vice-Chm., Parly Defence Cttee, 1980–. Chm., Internal Market Council of the BEF in EEC Ministers, 1986–87. Mem., RUSI. *Publications:* The Donkeys, A History of the BEF in 1915, 1961; The Fall of Crete, 1963; Barbarossa, The Russo-German Conflict, 1941–45, 1965; Aces High: the war in the air over the Western Front 1914–18, 1973; (ed) A Good Innings: the private papers of Viscount Lee of Fareham, 1974. *Address:* Saltwood Castle, Kent CT21 4QU. *T:* Hythe (0303) 267190. *Clubs:* Brooks's, Pratt's.

CLARK, Alan Richard; HM Diplomatic Service; Consul-General, Montreal, since 1990; *b* 4 Sept. 1939; *s* of George Edward Clark and Norah Ivy Maria Clark (*née* Hope); *m* 1961, Ann Rosemary (*née* Hosford); one *s*. *Educ:* Chatham House Grammar Sch., Ramsgate. Foreign Office, 1958; HM Forces, 1960–62; FO 1962; served Tehran, 1964–66; Jedda, 1966–68; Second Sec. (Economic), later First Sec., Paris, 1969–71; FCO, 1972–76; Freetown, 1976–80; FCO, 1980–84; secondment (with rank of Counsellor) to Vickers Shipbuilding and Engineering Ltd, 1984–86; Counsellor and Head of Chancery, Bucharest, 1986–89. *Recreations:* swimming, walking, reading. *Address:* c/o Foreign and Commonwealth Office, SW1A 2AH. *Club:* Commonwealth Trust.

CLARK, Albert William; His Honour Judge Clark; a Circuit Judge, since 1981; *b* 23 Sept. 1922; *s* of William Charles Clark and Cissy Dorothy Elizabeth Clark; *m* 1951, Frances Philippa, *d* of Dr Samuel Lavington Hart, Tientsin; one *s* one *d*. *Educ:* Christ's Coll., Finchley. War service, 1941–46, Royal Navy. Called to Bar, Middle Temple, 1949; Clerk of Arraigns, Central Criminal Court, 1951–56; Clerk to the Justices, E Devon, 1956–70; Metropolitan Magistrate, 1970–80; Acting Dep. Chm., Inner London QS, 1971; Dep. Circuit Judge, 1972–80. Mem., Central Council of Probation and After-Care Cttees, 1975–81. *Recreations:* fly-fishing, seafishing, walking, travel to remote places. *Address:* 31 Hill Court, Wimbledon Hill Road, Wimbledon, SW19 7PD. *T:* 081–947 8041.

CLARK, Alistair Campbell; WS; Partner, Blackadder Reid Johnston (formerly Reid Johnston Bell & Henderson), Solicitors, Dundee, since 1961; *b* 4 March 1933; *s* of Peter Campbell Clark and Janet Mitchell Scott or Clark; *m* 1960, Evelyn M. Johnston; three *s*. *Educ:* St Andrews Univ. Admitted solicitor, 1957. WS 1991. Hon. Sheriff, Tayside Central and Fife, 1986–. Mem. Council, Law Soc. of Scotland, 1982– (Pres., 1989–90); Dean, Faculty of Procurators and Solicitors, Dundee, 1979–81. Sec., Royal Dundee Blindcraft Products; Founder Chm., Broughty Ferry Round Table; Founder Pres., Claverhouse Rotary Club, Dundee. *Recreations:* family, travel, erratic golf. *Address:* (office) 34 Reform Street, Dundee DD1 1RJ. *T:* Dundee (0382) 29222. *Club:* New (Edinburgh).

CLARK, Brian Robert, FRSL 1985; playwright; *b* 3 June 1932; *s* of Leonard and Selina Clark; *m* (marr. diss.); two *s*; *m* 1990, Cherry Potter. *Educ:* Merrywood Grammar Sch., Bristol; Redland Coll. of Educn, Bristol; Central Sch. of Speech and Drama, London; Nottingham Univ. BA Hons English. Teacher, 1955–61, and 1964–66; Staff Tutor in Drama, Univ. of Hull, 1966–70. Since 1971 has written some thirty television plays, incl. Whose Life Is It Anyway? and The Saturday Party; also series: Telford's Change; Late Starter. Stage plays: Whose Life Is It Anyway? (SWET award for Best Play, 1977; filmed, 1982); Can You Hear Me At the Back?, 1978; Campions Interview; Post Mortem; Kipling, London and NY, 1985; The Petition, NY and Nat. Theatre, 1986; (with Kathy Levin) Hopping to Byzantium, Germany 1989, Sydney, Aust., 1990. Founded Amber Lane Press, publishing plays and books on the theatre, 1978. *Publications:* Group Theatre, 1971; Whose Life Is It Anyway?, 1978; Can You Hear Me At the Back?, 1979; Post Mortem, 1979; The Petition, 1986. *Address:* c/o Judy Daish Associates, 83 Eastbourne Mews, W2 6LQ. *T:* 071–262 1101. *Club:* Garrick.

CLARK, Charles Anthony, (Tony); Under Secretary, Higher Education, Department of Education and Science, since 1989; *b* 13 June 1940; *s* of late Stephen and Winifred Clark; *m* 1968, Penelope Margaret (*née* Brett); one *s* two *d*. *Educ:* King's Coll. Sch., Wimbledon; Pembroke Coll., Oxford (MA Nat. Sci.). Pressed Steel Co., 1961; Hilger & Watts Ltd, 1962–65; DES, 1965–; seconded to UGC, 1971–73; Under Sec., 1982–; Hd of Finance Br. and Prin. Finance Officer, 1987–89. *Recreations:* running, gardening, sailing. *Address:* Department of Education and Science, Sanctuary Buildings, Great Smith Street, SW1.

CLARK, Charles David Lawson; Legal Adviser: Publishers' Association, since 1984; Copyright Licensing Agency, since 1988 (Chairman, 1985–88); General Counsel, International Publishers Copyright Council, since 1990; *b* 12 June 1933; *s* of Alec Fulton Charles Clark, CB, and of Mary Clark; *m* 1960, Fiona McKenzie Mill; one *s* three *d*. *Educ:* Edinburgh Acad.; Jesus Coll., Oxford (Exhibnr; MA). Called to the Bar, Inner Temple, 1960. Second Lieut 4th Regt RHA. Editor: Sweet and Maxwell, 1957–60; Penguin Books, 1960–66; Managing Director: Penguin Educn, 1966–72; Allen Lane the Penguin Press, 1967–69; Dir, LWT (Holdings) Ltd, 1982–84. Chairman: Bookrest, 1975–78; Book Marketing Council, 1979–81; Hutchinson Publishing Group, 1972–80 (Man. Dir, 1972); Chief Exec., Hutchinson Ltd, 1980–84. A Mem. of Bd, CICI, 1989–. Member: Book Trade Working Party, 1970–72; Brit. Copyright Council, 1976–79 and 1984– (Treas. 1987–); Council of Management, CLIP, 1990–; Council of Management, MIND, the Nat. Assoc. of Mental Health, 1970–79 (Chm. MIND, 1976–79, Vice-Pres., 1980–). *Publications:* (ed) Publishing Agreements, 1980, 3rd edn 1988; articles on publishing topics. *Recreations:* singing lieder, golf. *Address:* 19 Offley Road, SW9 0LR. *T:* 071–735 1422. *Clubs:* Groucho, Le Beaujolais.

CLARK, Rt. Hon. Charles Joseph, (Joe); PC (Canada); MP (Progressive C) Rocky Mountain, later Yellowhead, Constituency, since 1972; Minister for Constitutional Affairs, since 1991; *b* 5 June 1939; *s* of Charles and Grace Clark; *m* 1973, Maureen McTeer (she retained her maiden name); one *d*. *Educ:* High River High Sch.; Univ. of Alta (BA History); Univ. of Alberta (MA Polit. Sci.). Journalist, Canadian Press, Calgary Herald, Edmonton Jl, High River Times, 1964–66; Prof. of Political Science, Univ. of Alberta, Edmonton, 1966–67; Exec. Asst to Hon. Robert L. Stanfield, Leader of HM's Loyal Opposition, 1967–70. Leader of HM's Loyal Opposition, Canada, 1976–79; Prime Minister of Canada, 1979–80; Leader of HM's Loyal Opposition, 1980–83; Sec. of State for External Affairs, 1984–91. Pres., Queen's Privy Council for Canada, 1991–. Hon. LLD: New Brunswick, 1976; Calgary, 1984; Alberta, 1985. Alberta Award of Excellence, Alberta Univ., 1983. *Recreations:* riding, reading, walking, film going. *Address:* House of Commons, Ottawa, Ont K1A 0A6, Canada.

CLARK, Christopher Harvey; QC 1989; a Recorder, since 1986; *b* 20 Dec. 1946; *s* of Harvey Frederick Beckford Clark and Winifred Julia Clark; *m* 1972, Gillian Elizabeth Ann Mullen; one *s* two *d*. *Educ:* Taunton's Grammar Sch., Southampton; The Queen's Coll., Oxford (BA 1968; MA 1987). Called to the Bar, Gray's Inn, 1969; Mem., Western Circuit, 1969–; Mem., Chambers of Mr J. Hampden Inskip, QC, 1974–; Asst Recorder, 1982. *Recreations:* amateur dramatics, golf, cricket, gardening, youth club work, local community affairs, ski-ing, writing and producing pantomimes. *Address:* 3 Pump Court, Temple, EC4Y 7AJ. *T:* 071–353 0711; 31 Southgate Street, Winchester, Hants SO23 9EE. *Club:* Hampshire (Winchester).

CLARK, Sir Colin (Douglas), 4th Bt *cr* 1917, of Dunlambert, City of Belfast; MC 1945; *b* 20 July 1918; *s* of Sir George Ernest Clark, 2nd Bt and Norah Anne (*d* 1966), *d* of W. G. Wilson; *S* brother, 1991; *m* 1946, Margaret Coleman, *d* of Maj.-Gen. Sir Charlton Watson Spinks, KBE, DSO and *widow* of Maj. G. W. Threlfall, MC; one *s* two *d*. *Educ:* Eton; Cambridge Univ. (BA 1939; MA 1944). Served War 1939–45; Major RE; despatches, 1944. *Heir:* *s* Jonathan George Clark [*b* 9 Oct. 1947; *m* 1971, Susan Joy, *d* of Brig. T. I. G. Gray; one *s* two *d*]. *Address:* Flaxpool House, Crowcombe, Taunton, Somerset TA4 4AW.

CLARK, David Beatson, CBE 1986; TD 1966; DL; Executive Chairman, Beatson Clark plc, 1984–88; *b* 5 May 1933; *s* of late Alec Wilson Clark, OBE, JP, DSc(Tech) and Phyllis Mary Clark; *m* 1959, Ann Morgan Mudford; two *s* one *d*. *Educ:* Wrekin College; Keele Univ. (BA Hons Physics and Econs). Beatson Clark: joined 1958; Managing Dir, 1971; Chm. and Managing Dir, 1979. Non-Executive Director: Royal Bank of Scotland, 1988–91; Yorkshire Electricity Gp, 1990– (Mem., Yorkshire Electricity Bd, 1980–90); Rotherham TEC, 1990–. President: Rotherham Chamber of Commerce, 1975–76; Sheffield Br., BIM, 1983–86; Glass Manufacturers' Fedn, 1982–83; Member: Council, Univ. of Sheffield, 1984–; Rotherham HA, 1985–. Liveryman, Glass Sellers' Co., 1967; Freeman, Cutlers' Co. in Hallamshire, 1980. DL S Yorks, 1990. Hon. Fellow, Sheffield City Polytechnic, 1988. *Address:* Sorrelstan, 142 Moorgate Road, Rotherham, South Yorks S60 3AZ. *T:* Rotherham (0709) 365539. *Clubs:* Army and Navy, City Livery.

CLARK, David (George); MP (Lab) South Shields, since 1979; *b* 19 Oct. 1939; *s* of George and Janet Clark; *m* 1970, Christine Kirkby; one *d*. *Educ:* Manchester Univ. (BA(Econ), MSc); Sheffield Univ. (PhD 1978). Forester, 1956–57; Laboratory Asst in Textile Mill, 1957–59; Student Teacher, 1959–60; Student, 1960–63; Pres., Univ. of Manchester Union, 1963–64; Trainee Manager in USA, 1964; University Lecturer, 1965–70. Contested Manchester (Withington), Gen. Elec. 1966; MP (Lab) Colne Valley, 1970–Feb. 1974; contested Colne Valley, Oct. 1974; Opposition spokesman on Agriculture and Food, 1973–74, on Defence, 1980–81, on the Environment, 1981–86; opposition front bench spokesman on: environmental protection and develt, 1986–87; food, agriculture and rural affairs, 1987–. Pres., Open Spaces Soc., 1979–88. *Publications:* The Industrial Manager, 1966; Colne Valley: Radicalism to Socialism, 1981; Victor Grayson, Labour's Lost Leader, 1985; various articles on Management and Labour History. *Recreations:* fell-walking, ornithology, gardening. *Address:* House of Commons, SW1A 0AA.

CLARK, David John; Head of Social Security Division C, Department of Social Security, since 1990; *b* 20 Sept. 1947; *m* 1970, Caroline Russell; two *s* two *d*, one foster *d*. *Educ:* Univ. of Kent at Canterbury (MA). Department of Health and Social Security, later Department of Social Security: Asst Principal, 1969; Principal, 1973; Asst Sec., 1983; Under Sec., 1990. *Address:* Department of Social Security, 1–11 John Adam Street, WC2N 6HT. *T:* 071–962 8451.

CLARK, Denis; His Honour Judge Denis Clark; a Circuit Judge, since 1988; *b* 2 Aug. 1943; twin *s* of John and Mary Clark; *m* 1967, Frances Mary (*née* Corcoran); four *d*. *Educ:* St Anne's RC Primary, Rock Ferry, Birkenhead; St Anselm's Coll., Birkenhead; Sheffield Univ. LLB. Called to the Bar, Inner Temple, 1966; practised Northern Circuit, 1966–88; a Recorder, 1984–88. *Recreations:* medieval history, cricket, theatre. *Address:* c/o The Queen Elizabeth II Law Courts, Derby Square, Liverpool L2 1XA.

CLARK, Derek John, FCIS; Secretary, Institution of Structural Engineers, since 1982; *b* 17 June 1929; *s* of Robert Clark and Florence Mary (*née* Wise); *m* 1949, Edna Doris Coome; one *s* one *d*. *Educ:* Selhurst Grammar Sch., Croydon; SE London Technical Coll. FCIS 1982 (ACIS 1961). National Service, RAF, 1948–49. Corp. of Trinity House, 1949–66; RICS, 1966–71; ICMA, 1971–82. *Recreations:* athletics (until 1961), squash. *Address:* 7 Elvington Green, Hayesford Park, Bromley, Kent BR2 9DE. *T:* 081–460 9055. *Club:* Anglo-Belgian.

CLARK, Desmond; *see* Clark, John Desmond.

CLARK, Douglas Henderson, MD, FRCSEd, FRCSGlas, FRCPEd; Consultant Surgeon, Western Infirmary, Glasgow, since 1950; *b* 20 Jan. 1917; *s* of William and Jean Clark; *m* 1950, Morag Clark (decd); three *s*. *Educ:* Ayr Acad.; Glasgow Univ. (ChM 1950, MD Hons 1956). FRCSEd, FRCSGlas 1947, FRCPEd 1982. Captain RAMC, 1941–47. Miners Welfare Scholar, 1936; Fulbright Scholar, 1952; William Stewart Halsted Fellow, Johns Hopkins Hosp., 1952–53. Vis. Lectr in America, S Africa, Australia and NZ. Pres., RCPGlas, 1980–82; Dir, James IV Assoc. of Surgeons, 1979–. Hon. FRCS 1982, Hon. FRCSI 1982. Hon. DSc Glasgow, 1983. *Publications:* papers on gastro-enterology and thyroid disease; chapters in text-books. *Address:* 36 Southbrae Drive, Glasgow G13 1PZ. *T:* 041–959 3556.

CLARK, Lt-Gen. Findlay; *see* Clark, Lt-Gen. S. F.

CLARK, Sir Francis (Drake), 5th Bt *cr* 1886, of Melville Crescent, Edinburgh; *b* 16 July 1924; *s* of Sir Thomas Clark, 3rd Bt and Ellen Mercy (*d* 1987), *d* of late Francis Drake; *S* brother, 1991; *m* 1958, Mary, *d* of late John Alban Andrews, MC, FRCS; one *s*. *Educ:* Edinburgh Acad. RN 1943–46. Dir, Clark Travel Service Ltd, London, 1948–80. *Recreations:* tennis, cricket, music, gardening. *Heir:* *s* Edward Drake Clark, *b* 27 April 1966. *Address:* Woodend Cottages, Burgh-next-Aylsham, Norfolk NR11 6TS.

CLARK, (Francis) Leo, QC 1972; **His Honour Judge Leo Clark;** a Circuit Judge, since 1976; Designated Judge and Liaison Judge, Oxford Combined Court Centre, since 1983; *b* 15 Dec. 1920; *s* of Sydney John Clark and Florence Lilian Clark; *m* 1st, 1957, Denise Jacqueline Rambaud; one *s*; 2nd, 1967, Dr Daphne Margaret Humphreys. *Educ:* Bablake Sch.; St Peter's Coll., Oxford (MA). Called to Bar, Lincoln's Inn, 1947. Dep. Chm., Oxford County QS, 1970; a Recorder of the Crown Court, 1972–76. Hon. Recorder, City of Oxford, 1989–. *Recreations:* tennis, travel. *Address:* The Ivy House, Charlbury, Oxon. *Clubs:* Hurlingham; Union (Oxford).

CLARK WHO'S WHO 1992 350

CLARK, Gerald, CBE 1990; Inspector of Companies, Companies Investigation Branch, Department of Trade and Industry, 1984–90; *b* 18 Sept. 1933; *s* of John George and Elizabeth Clark (*née* Shaw); *m* 1958, Elizabeth McDermott; one *s*. *Educ:* St Cuthbert's Grammar School, Newcastle upon Tyne. Chartered Secretary. National Health Service, Northumberland Exec. Council, 1949–55; National Coal Board 1955–60; Board of Trade, Official Receiver's Service, 1960–71; Companies Investigation Branch, 1971–79; Official Receiver, High Court of Justice, 1981–83; Principal Examiner, Companies Investigation Branch, 1983–84. *Recreations:* music, photography.

CLARK, Gerald Edmondson, CMG 1989; HM Diplomatic Service; UK Permanent Representative to International Atomic Energy Agency, United Nations Development Organisation, and to United Nations in Vienna, since 1987, with personal rank of Ambassador; *b* 26 Dec. 1935; *s* of Edward John Clark and Irene Elizabeth Ada Clark (*née* Edmondson); *m* 1967, Mary Rose Organ; two *d*. *Educ:* Johnston Grammar School, Durham; New College, Oxford. MA. Foreign Office, 1960; Hong Kong, 1961; Peking, 1962–63; FO, 1964–68; Moscow, 1968–70; FCO, 1970–73; Head of Chancery, Lisbon, 1973–77; Asst Sec., Cabinet Office, 1977–79; seconded to Barclays Bank International, 1979–81; Commercial Counsellor, Peking, 1981–83; FCO, 1984–87. *Recreations:* architecture, economics and politics. *Address:* c/o Foreign and Commonwealth Office, SW1A 2AH. *Clubs:* Athenæum, Commonwealth Trust; Jockety (Austria).

CLARK, Grahame; *see* Clark, J. G. D.

CLARK, Gregor Munro; Assistant Legal Secretary to the Lord Advocate and Scottish Parliamentary Counsel, since 1979; *b* 18 April 1946; *s* of Ian Munro Clark and Norah Isobel Joss; *m* 1974, Jane Maralyn Palmer; one *s* two *d*. *Educ:* Queen's Park Senior Secondary Sch., Glasgow; St Andrews Univ. (LLB Hons). Admitted Faculty of Advocates, 1972; entered Lord Advocate's Dept, 1974; Asst Parly Draftsman, then Dep. Parly Draftsman, 1974–79. *Recreations:* music, opera, Scandinavian languages and literature. *Address;* 1 Old Pound Yard, High Street, Great Shelford, Cambridge CB2 5EH. *T:* Cambridge (0223) 841990.

CLARK, Rt. Hon. Helen Elizabeth; PC 1990; MP (Lab) Mount Albert, New Zealand, since 1981; Deputy Leader of the Opposition, New Zealand, since 1990; *b* 26 Feb. 1950; *d* of George and Margaret Clark; *m* 1981, Dr Peter Byard Davis. *Educ:* Epsom Girls' Grammar School; Auckland Univ. (BA 1971; MA Hons 1974). Junior Lectr in Political Studies, Auckland Univ., 1973–75; UGC Post Graduate Scholar, 1976; Lectr, Political Studies Dept, Auckland Univ., 1977–81. Minister: of Housing, of Conservation, 1987–89; of Health, of Labour, 1989–90; Dep. Prime Minister, 1989–90. *Recreations:* theatre, music, tennis, reading. *Address:* Parliament House, Wellington, New Zealand. *T:* 04–719–999.

CLARK, Henry Maitland; Head of Information, Council for Small Industries in Rural Areas, 1977–89; feature writer, Avon Advertiser, since 1989; *b* 11 April 1929; *s* of Major H. F. Clark, Rockwood, Upperlands, Co. Londonderry; *m* 1972, Penelope Winifred Tindal; one *s* two *d*. *Educ:* Shrewsbury Sch.; Trinity Coll., Dublin; Trinity Hall, Cambridge. Entered Colonial Service and appointed District Officer, Tanganyika, 1951; served in various Districts of Tanganyika, 1951–59; resigned from Colonial Service, 1959. MP (UU) Antrim North (UK Parliament), Oct. 1959–1970; Chm. Conservative Trade and Overseas Develt Sub-Cttee; Member: British Delegation to Council of Europe and WEU, 1962–65; Advisory Council Food Law Res. Centre, Univ. of Brussels; Exec. Cttee, Lepra (British Leprosy Relief Assoc.); Select Cttee on Overseas Aid and Develt, 1969–70; Grand Jury, Co. Londonderry, 1970. A Commonwealth Observer, Mauritius General Election, 1967. Wine merchant, IDV Ltd and Cock Russell Vintners, 1972–76. Vice-Pres., Dublin Univ. Boat Club. *Recreations:* rowing coach, sailing, shooting, golf, collecting old furniture. *Address:* Rockwood, Upperlands, Co. Derry, Northern Ireland. *T:* Maghera (0648) 42237; Staddles, Hindon Lane, Tisbury, Wilts. *T:* Tisbury (0747) 870330. *Clubs:* Kildare Street and University (Dublin); Royal Portrush Golf.

See also H. W. S. Clark.

CLARK, (Henry) Wallace (Stuart), MBE 1970; DL; Director, Wm Clark & Sons, Linen Manufacturers, since 1972, non-executive Director, since 1987; *b* 20 Nov. 1926; *s* of Major H. F. Clark, MBE, JP, RA, Rockwood, Upperlands, and Sybil Emily (*née* Stuart); *m* 1957, June Elisabeth Lester Deane; two *s*. *Educ:* Shrewsbury School. Lieut, RNVR, 1945–47 (bomb and mine disposal); Cattleman, Merchant Navy, 1947–48. District Comdt, Ulster Special Constabulary, 1955–70; Major, Ulster Defence Regt, 1970–81. Foyle's Lectr, USA tour, 1964. Led Church of Ireland St Columba commemorative curragh voyage, Derry to Iona, 1963. Mem., Cttee of Management, RNLI. DL 1962, High Sheriff 1969, Co. Londonderry. *Publications:* (jtly) North and East Coasts of Ireland, 1957; (jtly) South and West Coasts of Ireland, 1962, 2nd edn 1970; Guns in Ulster, 1967; Rathlin Disputed Island, 1972; Sailing Round Ireland, 1976; Linen on the Green, 1982. *Recreations:* sailing, writing. *Address:* Gorteade Cottage, Upperlands, Co. Londonderry, N Ireland BT46 5SB. *T:* Maghera (0648) 42737. *Clubs:* Royal Cruising, Irish Cruising (Cdre 1962).

See also H. M. Clark.

CLARK, Ian Robertson, CBE 1979; Chairman, Ventures Division, Richard Costain Ltd, since 1987; *b* 18 Jan. 1939; *s* of Alexander Clark and Annie Dundas Watson; *m* 1961, Jean Scott Waddell Lang; one *s* one *d*. *Educ:* Dalziel High Sch., Motherwell. FCCA, IPFA. Trained with Glasgow Chartered Accountant; served in local govt, 1962–76, this service culminating in the post of Chief Executive, Shetland Islands Council; full-time Mem., BNOC, from 1976 until privatisation in 1982; Jt Man. Dir, Britoil plc, 1982–85. Member: Scottish Economic Council, 1978–87; Glasgow Univ. Court, 1980–87. Hon. LLD Glasgow, 1979. *Publications:* Reservoir of Power, 1980; contribs to professional and religious periodicals. *Recreations:* theology, general reading, walking. *Address:* 16 Pan's Gardens, Camberley, Surrey GU15 1HY. *T:* Camberley (0276) 685728.

CLARK, James Leonard; Under Secretary, Establishment Personnel Division, Departments of Industry and Trade Common Services, 1980–83 (Under Secretary, Department of Trade, 1978–80); *b* 8 Jan. 1923; *s* of James Alfred and Grace Clark; *m* 1954, Joan Pauline Richards. *Educ:* Mercers' School. Lieut (A), Fleet Air Arm, 1942–46. Clerical Officer, HM Treasury, 1939; Private Sec. to successive First Secs of State, 1964–67; Cabinet Office, 1969–71; Asst Sec., Price Commn, 1973–75; Dept of Industry, 1975–78. CBI, 1983–85; Hd of Administration, SIB, 1985–89. *Address:* 4 Westcott Way, Cheam, Surrey SM2 7JY. *T:* 081–393 2622.

CLARK, James McAdam, CVO 1972; MC 1944; HM Diplomatic Service, retired; *b* 13 Sept. 1916; *er s* of late James Heriot Clark of Wester Coltfield, and late Ella Catherine McAdam; *m* 1946, Denise Thérèse, *d* of late Dr Léon Dufournier, Paris; two *d*. *Educ:* Edinburgh Univ. BSc (Hons) Tech. Chemistry, 1938. Asst Lectr, Edinburgh Univ., 1938–39. Served Royal Artillery, 1939–46 (MC), rank of Capt.; Royal Mil. Coll. of Science, 1945–46 (pac). Min. of Fuel and Power, 1947–48. Entered Foreign (now Diplomatic) Service, 1948; FO, 1948–50; Head of Chancery, Quito, 1950–53; FO, 1953–56; Head of Chancery, Lisbon, 1956–60; Counsellor, UK Rep. to and Alternate Gov. of Internat. Atomic Energy Agency, Vienna, 1960–64; Head of Scientific Relations Dept, FO, 1964–66; Counsellor on secondment to Min. of Technology, 1966–70; Consul-Gen., Paris, 1970–77. Officer Order of Christ of Portugal, 1957. *Publications:* a number of poems and articles. *Recreations:* golf, sailing, music, disputation. *Address:* Hill Lodge, Aldeburgh, Suffolk IP15 5DU. *Clubs:* Aldeburgh Yacht, Aldeburgh Golf.

CLARK, Rt. Hon. Joe; *see* Clark, Rt Hon. C. J.

CLARK, Sir John (Allen), Kt 1971; Chief Executive Officer, The Plessey Company plc, 1962–89; Chairman, GEC-Plessey Telecommunications Holdings, 1988–89; *b* 14 Feb. 1926; *e s* of late Sir Allen Clark and Lady (Jocelyn) Clark, *d* of late Percy and Madeline Culverhouse; *m* 1952, Deirdre Kathleen (marr. diss. 1962), *d* of Samuel Herbert Waterhouse and Maeve Murphy Waterhouse; one *s* one *d*; *m* 1970, Olivia, *d* of H. Pratt and of late Mrs R. S. H. Shepard; twin *s* one *d*. *Educ:* Harrow; Cambridge. Served War of 1939–45; commnd RNVR (2nd Lieut). Received early industrial training with Metropolitan Vickers and Ford Motor Co.; spent over a year in USA, studying the electronics industry. Asst to Gen. Manager, Plessey International Ltd, 1949; Dir and Gen. Man., Plessey (Ireland) Ltd, and Wireless Telephone Co. Ltd, 1950; appointed to main board, The Plessey Co. Ltd, 1953; Gen. Man., Plessey Components Group, 1957; Dep. Chm., The Plessey Co. Ltd, 1967–70, Chm., 1970–89. Director: International Computers Ltd, 1968–79; Banque Nationale de Paris Ltd, 1976–89. Pres., Telecommunication Engineering and Manufacturing Assoc., 1964–66, 1971–73; Vice-President: Inst. of Works Managers; Engineering Employers' Fedn. Member: Nat. Defence Industries Council; Engineering Industries Council, 1975–89. CompIEE; FIM. Order of Henry the Navigator, Portugal, 1973. *Recreations:* horseriding, shooting. *Address:* Redenham Park, Redenham, near Andover, Hants SP11 9AH. *Club:* Boodle's.

See also Michael W. Clark.

CLARK, Prof. J(ohn) Desmond, CBE 1960; PhD, ScD; FBA 1961; FSA 1952; FRSSAf 1959; Professor of Anthropology, University of California, Berkeley, USA, 1961–86, now Emeritus Professor; *b* London, 10 April 1916; *s* of late Thomas John Chown Clark and Catharine (*née* Wynne); *m* 1938, Betty Cable, *d* of late Henry Lea Baume and late Frances M. S. (*née* Brown); one *s* one *d*. *Educ:* Monkton Combe Sch.; Christ's Coll., Cambridge. PhD in Archaeology (Cambridge), 1950; ScD Cantab 1975. Dir, Rhodes-Livingstone Museum, Livingstone, N Rhodesia, 1938–61. Has conducted excavations in Southern, East and Equatorial Africa, the Sahara, Ethiopia, Syria, 1938–, India, 1980–82, China, 1990, 1991. Military Service in East Africa, Abyssinia, The Somalilands and Madagascar, 1941–46. Founder Mem. and Sec., N Rhodesia Nat. Monuments Commn, 1948–61. Corr. Mem. Scientific Coun. for Africa South of the Sahara, 1956–64, etc. Lectures: Faculty Res. Berkeley, 1979; Raymond Dart, Johannesburg, 1979; Mortimer Wheeler, British Acad., 1981; John Mulvaney, ANU, 1991; Distinguished, Amer. Anthropol Assoc., 1992. Fellow, Amer. Acad. of Arts and Sciences, 1965; Foreign Associate, Nat. Acad. of Science, USA, 1986. Hon. DSc: Univ. of the Witwatersrand, 1985; Univ. of Cape Town, 1985. Huxley Medal, RAI, 1974; Gold Medal, Soc. of Antiquaries of London, 1985; Fellows Medal, Calif. Acad. of Scis, 1987; Gold Medal, Archaeological Inst. of America, 1989. Comdr, Nat. Order of Senegal, 1968. *Publications:* The Prehistoric Cultures of the Horn of Africa, 1954; The Prehistory of Southern Africa, 1959; The Stone Age Cultures of Northern Rhodesia, 1960; Prehistoric Cultures of Northeast Angola and their Significance in Tropical Africa, 1963; (ed) Proc. 3rd Pan-African Congress on Pre-history, 1957; (comp.) Atlas of African Pre-history, 1967; (ed, with W. W. Bishop) Background to Evolution in Africa, 1967; Kalambo Falls Prehistoric Site, vol. I, 1969, vol. II, 1973; The Prehistory of Africa, 1970; (ed) Cambridge History of Africa, vol I, 1982; (ed with G. R. Sharma) Palaeoenvironment and Prehistory in the Middle Son Valley, India, 1983; (ed with Steven A. Brandt) From Hunters to Farmers: the causes and consequences of food production in Africa, 1984; contribs to learned journals on prehistoric archaeology. *Recreations:* gardening, walking, photography. *Address:* 1941 Yosemite Road, Berkeley, Calif 94707, USA. *T:* 525/4519 Area Code 415. *Clubs:* Commonwealth Trust, United Oxford & Cambridge University.

CLARK, John Edward; Secretary, National Association of Local Councils, since 1978; *b* 18 Oct. 1932; *s* of Albert Edward Clark and Edith (*née* Brown); *m* 1969, Judith Rosemary Lester; one *s* one *d* (and one *d* decd). *Educ:* Royal Grammar Sch., Clitheroe; Keble Coll., Oxford (MA, BCL). Called to the Bar, Gray's Inn, 1957; practised at the Bar, 1957–61. Dep. Sec., National Assoc. of Local (formerly Parish) Councils, (part-time) 1959–61, (full-time) 1961–78. *Publications:* chapters on local govt, public health, and theatres, in Encyclopaedia of Court Forms, 2nd edn 1964 to 1975. *Recreations:* gardening, walking; indoor games, collecting detective fiction. *Address:* 113 Turney Road, SE21 7JB. *T:* 071–274 1381.

CLARK, Prof. (John) Grahame (Douglas), CBE 1971; FBA 1951; MA, PhD, ScD (Cantab); Master of Peterhouse, 1973–80 (Fellow, 1950–73, Honorary Fellow, 1980); *b* 28 July 1907; *s* of Lt-Col Charles Douglas Clark and Maude Ethel Grahame Clark (*née* Shaw); *m* 1936, Gwladys Maude (*née* White); two *s* one *d*. *Educ:* Marlborough Coll.; Peterhouse, Cambridge. Served War of 1939–45, RAFVR, in Photographic Interpretation, 1941–43, and Air Historical Br., 1943–45. Research Student, 1930–32, and Bye-Fellow, 1933–35, of Peterhouse; Faculty Asst Lectr in Archæology, Cambridge, 1935–46, and Univ. Lectr, 1946–52; Disney Prof. of Archæology, Cambridge, 1952–74; Head of Dept of Archæology and Anthropology, Cambridge, 1956–61 and 1968–71. Lectures: Munro, in Archæology, Edinburgh Univ., 1949; Reckitt, British Acad. 1954; Dalrymple in Archæology, Glasgow Univ., 1955; G. Grant MacCurdy, Harvard, 1957; Mortimer Wheeler Meml, New Delhi, 1978; William Evans Vis. Prof., Univ. of Otago, NZ, 1964; Commonwealth Vis. Fellow, Australia, 1964; Hitchcock Prof., Univ. of California, Berkeley, 1969; Leverhulme Vis. Prof., Uppsala, 1972. Member: Ancient Monuments Board, 1954–77; Royal Commn on Historical Monuments, 1957–69; a Trustee, BM, 1975–80; Pres., Prehistoric Soc., 1958–62; Vice-Pres., Soc. of Antiquaries, 1959–62. Hon. Editor, Proceedings Prehistoric Soc., 1935–70. Hon. Corr. Mem., Royal Soc. Northern Antiquaries, Copenhagen, 1946, and of Swiss Prehistoric Soc., 1951; Fellow, German Archæological Inst., 1954; Hon. Member: RIA, 1955; Archaeol. Inst. of America, 1977; Foreign Member: Finnish Archæological Soc., 1958; Amer. Acad. of Arts and Sciences (Hon.) 1961; Royal Danish Acad. of Sciences and Letters, 1964; Royal Netherlands Acad. of Sciences, 1964; For. Fellow, Royal Society of Sciences, Uppsala, 1964; For. Associate, Nat. Acad. of Sciences, USA, 1974; Royal Soc. of Humane Letters, Lund, 1976. Hon. DLitt: Sheffield, 1971; National Univ. of Ireland, 1976; Fil dr, Uppsala, 1977. Hodgkins Medal, Smithsonian Institution, 1967; Viking Medal, Wenner-Gren Foundn, 1971; Lucy Wharton Drexel Gold Medal, Museum, Univ. of Pennsylvania, 1974; Gold Medal, Soc. of Antiquaries, 1978; Chanda Medal, Asiatic Soc., Calcutta, 1979; Erasmus Prize, Netherlands Foundn, 1991. Comdr, Order of the Danebrog, 1961. *Publications:* The Mesolithic Settlement of Northern Europe, 1936; Archæology and Society 1939, 1947 and 1957; Prehistoric England, 1940, 1941, 1945, 1948, 1962; From Savagery to Civilization, 1946; Prehistoric Europe, The Economic Basis, 1952; Excavations at Star Carr, 1954; The Study of Prehistory, 1954; World Prehistory, An Outline, 1961; (with Stuart Piggott) Prehistoric Societies, 1965; The Stone Age Hunters, 1967; World Prehistory, a new outline, 1969; Aspects of Prehistory, 1970; The Earlier Stone Age

Settlement of Scandinavia, 1975; World Prehistory in New Perspective, 1977; Sir Mortimer and Indian Archaeology (Wheeler Memorial Lectures, 1978), 1979; Mesolithic Prelude, 1980; The Identity of Man (as seen by an archaeologist), 1982; Symbols of Excellence, 1986; Economic Prehistory, 1989; Prehistoric Archaeology at Cambridge and Beyond, 1989; Time and Space in History, 1991; numerous papers in archæological journals. *Recreations:* gardening, travel, contemporary art. *Address:* 36 Millington Road, Cambridge CB3 9HP. *Club:* United Oxford & Cambridge University.

CLARK, Sir John S.; *see* Stewart-Clark.

CLARK, June; *see* Clark, M. J.

CLARK, Ven. Kenneth James, DSC 1944; Archdeacon of Swindon, 1982–May 1992; *b* 31 May 1922; *er s* of Francis James Clark and Winifred Adelaide Clark (*née* Martin); *m* 1948, Elisabeth Mary Monica Helen Huggett; three *s* three *d. Educ:* Watford Grammar School; St Catherine's Coll., Oxford (MA); Cuddesdon Theological Coll. Midshipman RN, 1940; Lieutenant RN, 1942; served in submarines, 1942–46. Baptist Minister, Forest Row, Sussex, 1950–52; Curate of Brinkworth, 1952–53; Curate of Cricklade with Latton, 1953–56; Priest-in-Charge, then Vicar (1959), of Holy Cross, Inns Court, Bristol, 1956–61; Vicar: Westbury-on-Trym, 1961–72; St Mary Redcliffe, Bristol, 1972–82; Hon. Canon of Bristol Cathedral, 1974. Member, Gen. Synod of C of E, 1980–92. *Recreations:* music, travel, gardening. *Address:* (until May 1992) 70 Bath Road, Swindon, Wilts SN1 4AY. *T:* Swindon (0793) 695059; (from May 1992) 6 Saxon Road, Harnham, Salisbury, Wilts SP2 8JZ. *T:* Salisbury (0722) 523952.

CLARK, Leo; *see* Clark, F. L.

CLARK, Leslie Joseph, CBE 1977; BEM 1942; FEng; Chairman, Victor Products (Wallsend) Ltd, 1977–79; Special Adviser on the international gas industry to the Chairman of British Gas, since 1975; Chairman, Northern Gas Region (formerly Northern Gas Board), 1967–75; *b* 21 May 1914; *s* of Joseph George Clark and Elizabeth (*née* Winslow); *m* 1940, Mary M. Peacock; one *s* one *d. Educ:* Stationers' Company's Sch.; King's Coll., London, BSc(Eng), 1st Cl. Hons, 1934; MSc 1948. Engineer, Gas Light & Coke Co., then North Thames Gas Board. Chief Engineer, North Thames Gas Board, 1962–65 (pioneered work for development of sea transp. of liquefied natural gas, 1954–63), Dep. Chm., 1965–67. Pres., Instn of Gas Engineers, 1965–66; Pres., IGU, 1973–76 (Vice.-Pres., 1970–73). Member: Court, Univ. of Newcastle upon Tyne, 1972–; Council, Univ. of Durham, 1975–78. CEng, FICE, FIMechE, FIGasE, FInstE, MIEE, AMIChemE. Founder Fellow, Fellowship of Engineering, 1976. Elmer Sperry Award, USA, 1979. *Publications:* technical papers to Instns of Gas Engineers and Mech. Engrs, Inst. of Fuel, World Energy Conf., Internat. Gas Union, etc. *Recreations:* model engineering, walking, photography, music. *Address:* Hillway, New Ridley Road, Stocksfield, Northumberland NE43 7QB. *T:* Stocksfield (0661) 842339.

CLARK, Luther Johnson, (John); Chief Executive and Managing Director, BET, since 1991; *b* 27 Aug. 1941; *s* of E. T. Clark and Mary Opal Clark; *m* 1965, Judith Dooley; one *s* one *d. Educ:* Wharton Sch. of Finance & Commerce, Univ. of Pennsylavania (BS Econs/ Finance 1963); Wharton Graduate Sch. of Finance & Commerce (MBA Marketing/ Finance 1968). Captain, US Marine Corps, 1963–66. Singer Co.: joined 1968; Corp. Vice-Pres., 1978–81; Pres. and Chief Exec., Europe, Africa and Middle East, 1982–85; Exec. Vice-Pres., V. F. Corp., 1986–87; Chm. and Chief Exec., Core-Mark Internat. Inc., 1988–90. *Address:* BET, Stratton House, Piccadilly, W1X 6AS. *T:* 071–629 8886.

CLARK, Lynda Margaret; QC (Scot.) 1989. *Educ:* St Andrews Univ. (LLB Hons); Edinburgh Univ. (PhD). Lectr, Univ. of Dundee, 1973–76; admitted Advocate, Scots Bar, 1977; called to the English Bar, Inner Temple, 1988. *Address:* Advocates' Library, Parliament Square, Edinburgh. *T:* 031–226 2881.

CLARK, Malcolm, CB 1990; Inspector General, Insolvency Service, Department of Trade and Industry, 1984–89, retired; *b* 13 Feb. 1931; *s* of late Percy Clark and Gladys Helena Clark; *m* 1956, Beryl Patricia Dale; two *s. Educ:* Wheelwright Grammar Sch., Dewsbury, Yorks. FCCA 1980. Department of Trade and Industry Insolvency Service: Examiner, 1953–62; Sen. Examiner, 1962–66; Asst Official Receiver, Rochester, 1966–70; Official Receiver, Lytham St Annes, 1970–79; Principal Inspector of Official Receivers, 1979–81; Dep. Inspector Gen., 1981–84. *Recreations:* theatre, gardening, reading. *Address:* c/o Room 622, Bridge Place, 88/89 Eccleston Square, SW1V 1PT.

CLARK, Rev. Canon Malcolm Aiken; Dean, Collegiate Church of St Vincent since 1982, Dean of Edinburgh, 1983–85, Hon. Canon, since 1985; *b* 3 Oct. 1905; *s* of Hugh Aiken Clark, MB, CM, and Agnes Roberta Douglas Baxter; *m* 1936, Margherita Felicinna Columba Gannaway (*d* 1973); two *s* one *d. Educ:* Drax, Yorks; High School of Glasgow; Lichfield Theological College. Deacon 1934, priest 1935, Glasgow; Curate, St John's, Greenock; Rector, All Saints, Lockerbie, 1938–49, with All Saints, Langholm, 1939–42. Chaplain, RAFVR, 1942–46. Priest-in-charge, St Mary's, Dalkeith, 1949–56; Rector, Good Shepherd, Murrayfield, 1956–77; retired; warrant to officiate, dio. Edinburgh. Chaplain of St Vincent, Edinburgh, Order of St Lazarus of Jerusalem, 1977; Canon 1980, Dean 1982; also Canon of Cathedral Church of St Mary, Edinburgh and Dean, 1983. FSA (Scot.) 1979. *Address:* 12 St Vincent Street, Edinburgh EH3 6SH. *T:* 031–557 3662.

CLARK, Prof. (Margaret) June, FRCN; Professor of Nursing and Head of School of Health Care Studies, Middlesex Polytechnic, since 1990; *b* 31 May 1941; *d* of Ernest Harold Hickery and Marion Louise Hickery (*née* Walters); *m* 1966, Roger Michael Geoffrey Clark; one *s* one *d. Educ:* Pontywaun Grammar Sch.; University College London (BA Hons Classics 1962); University College Hosp. (SRN 1965); Royal college of Nursing (RHV 1967); Univ. of Reading (MPhil 1972); PhD South Bank Polytechnic 1985. FRCN 1982. Nurse, 1965; health visitor, 1967; clinical nursing appts, combined with teaching and research while bringing up a family; resumed as health visitor, Berks, 1981; Senior Nurse (Research), 1983; Health Authority posts: Special Projects Co-ordinator, Lewisham and N Southwark, 1985–86; Dir, Community Nursing Services, W Lambeth, 1986–88; Chief Nursing Adviser, Harrow, 1988–90. Pres., RCN, 1991–. Council of Europe Fellow, 1981. *Publications:* A Family Visitor, 1973; (with R. Hiller) Community Care, 1975; What Do Health Visitors Do?, 1981; (with S. Parsonage) Infant Feeding and Family Nutrition, 1981; (with J. Henderson) Community Health, 1983; (with M. Baly) District Nursing, 1981; contribs to nursing and med. jls. *Recreations:* travel, family caravan on South Wales coast. *Address:* 39 Ramsbury Drive, Earley, Reading RG6 2RT. *T:* Reading (0734) 663489.

CLARK, Dr Michael; MP (C) Rochford, since 1983; *b* 8 Aug. 1935; *s* of late Mervyn Clark and of Sybilla Norma Clark (*née* Winscott); *m* 1958, Valerie Ethel, *d* of C. S. Harbord; one *s* one *d. Educ:* King Edward VI Grammar School, East Retford; King's College London (BSc (1st cl. Hons) Chemistry, 1956; FKC 1987); Univ. of Minnesota (Fulbright Scholar, 1956–57); St John's College, Cambridge (PhD 1960). FRSC 1988. Research Scientist, later Factory Manager, ICI, 1960–66; Smith's Industries Ltd, 1966–69; PA International Management Consultants, 1969–73; Marketing Manager, St Regis Paper Co., 1973–78; Dir, Courtenay Stewart International, 1978–81; PA International Management Consultants, 1981–. Treasurer, 1975–78, Chm., 1980–83, Cambs Cons. Assoc.; Cons. Eastern Area Exec., 1980–83; contested (C) Ilkeston, 1979. Member: Parly Select Cttee for Energy, 1983– (Chm., 1989–); Council, Parly IT Cttee, 1984–90; Vice-Chm., All Party Gp for the Chemical Industry, 1990– (Hon. Sec. 1985–90); Hon. Secretary: Parly and Scientific Cttee, 1985–88; Parly Anglo-Nepalese Soc., 1985–; Parly Anglo-Malaŵi Gp, 1987–; Parly Space Cttee, 1989–91; Cons. Backbench Energy Cttee, 1986–87 (Vice-Chm., 1987–90); Chm., IPU, 1990– (Mem. Exec., 1987–90). Governor, Melbourn Village Coll., 1974–83 (Chm., 1977–80). *Publication:* The History of Rochford Hall, 1990. *Recreations:* history, DIY, gardening. *Address:* 82 Marsham Court, Marsham Street, SW1. *T:* 071–828 0620; Rochford Hall, Rochford, Essex SS4 1NW. *T:* Southend-on-Sea (0702) 542042. *Clubs:* Carlton; Rochford Conservative.

CLARK, Michael William, CBE 1977; DL; landowner; Deputy Chairman and Deputy Chief Executive, Plessey Co. plc, 1970–87; *b* 7 May 1927; *yr s* of late Sir Allen Clark and late Jocelyn Anina Maria Louise Clark (*née* Emerson Culverhouse); *m* 1st, 1955, Shirley (*née* MacPhadyen) (*d* 1974); two *s* one *d* (and one *d* decd); 2nd, 1985, Virginia, Marchioness Camden. *Educ:* Harrow. 1st Foot Guards, Subaltern, 1945–48. Ford Motor Co.; Bendix Aviation (USA); Plessey Co. plc, 1950–87 (formed Electronics Div., 1951; Main Bd Dir, 1953); Dir, Corporate Planning, 1965, Man. Dir, Telecommunications Gp, 1967; Chm., Plessey Electronic Systems Ltd, 1976–87. Member: Electronics EDC, 1975–80; Council, Inst. of Dirs; Nat. Electronics Council; Ct of Univ. of Essex. President: Essex Br., SSAFA, 1988–; Essex Br., Grenadier Guards Assoc., 1988–. Comp. IEE, 1964; Comp. IERE, 1965. FBIM 1974. DL Essex, 1988. *Recreations:* fishing, shooting, forestry. *Address:* Braxted Park, Witham, Essex CM8 3EN. *Clubs:* Boodle's, Pratt's.

See also Sir J. A. Clark.

CLARK, Oswald William Hugh, CBE 1978; Assistant Director-General, Greater London Council, 1973–79; *b* 26 Nov. 1917; *s* of late Rev. Hugh M. A. Clark and Mabel Bessie Clark (*née* Dance); *m* 1966, Diana Mary (*née* Hine); one *d. Educ:* Rutlish Sch., Merton; Univ. of London (BA; BD Hons). Local Govt Official, LCC (later GLC), 1937–79. Served War, HM Forces, 1940–46: Major, 2nd Derbyshire Yeo., Eighth Army, Middle East, NW Europe. Member: Church Assembly (later General Synod), 1948–90; Standing and Legislative Cttees, 1950–90; Standing Orders Cttee (Chm.), 1950–90; Crown Appts Commn, 1987–90; Chm., House of Laity, 1979–85 (Vice-Chm., 1970–79); a Church Commissioner, 1958–88, Mem. Bd of Governors, 1966–68, 1969–73, 1977–88; Vice-Pres., Corp. of Church House, 1981–. Principal, Soc. of the Faith, 1987–. Parish Clerk, St Laurence Pountney, 1986–. Life Fellow, Guild of Guide Lectrs, 1982. *Recreations:* London's history and development, commemorative and Goss china, heraldry. *Address:* 8 Courtlands Avenue, Hampton, Middlesex TW12 3NT. *T:* 081–979 1081. *Clubs:* Cavalry and Guards, Pratt's.

CLARK, Air Vice-Marshal Paul Derek, CEng; FRAeS; Air Officer, Engineering and Supply, Headquarters Strike Command, since 1991; *b* 19 March 1939; *s* of John Hayes Clark and Kathleen Clark; *m* 1963, Mary Elizabeth Morgan; two *d. Educ:* Orange Hill Grammar Sch.; RAF Henlow Technical Coll. BA Open Univ., 1985. CEng 1970; FRAeS 1987. Commnd Engr Br., RAF, 1961; RAF Wittering, 1961–63, Topcliffe, 1963, Wittering, 1964–69, Cranwell, 1969–70; RAF Staff Coll., Bracknell, 1971; HQ Logistics Comd, USAF, 1972–74; HQ Strike Comd, 1974–76; Nat. Defence Coll., 1977; OC Engrg Wing, RAF Leuchars, 1977–79; HQ No 1 Gp, RAF Bawtry, 1980–81; Stn Comdr No 30 Maintenance Unit, RAF Sealand, 1981–83; RCDS, 1984; MoD, 1985–86; Directorate Electronics Radar Air, MoD (PE), 1986–87; Dir, European Helicopter 101 Project, MoD (PE), 1987–89; Comdt RAF Signals Engrg Estabt, 1990–91. *Recreations:* theatre, art, high handicap golfing. *Club:* Royal Air Force.

See also Prof. T. J. H. Clark.

CLARK, Paul Nicholas Rowntree; His Honour Judge Paul Clark; a Circuit Judge, since 1985; *b* 17 Aug. 1940; *s* of late Henry Rowntree Clark and of Gwendoline Victoria Clark; *m* 1967, Diana Barbara Bishop; two *s* one *d. Educ:* Bristol Grammar Sch.; New Coll., Oxford (Open Schol.; MA (Lit. Hum.)). Called to the Bar, Middle Temple, 1966 (Harmsworth Schol.), Bencher 1982; in practice on Midland and Oxford (formerly Oxford) Circuit, 1966–85; a Recorder, 1981–85. *Address:* 2 Harcourt Buildings, Temple, EC4Y 9DB. *T:* 071–353 6961. *Club:* Garrick.

CLARK, Petula, (Sally Olwen); singer, actress; *b* 15 Nov. 1934; *d* of Leslie Clark; *m* 1961, Claude Wolff; one *s* two *d.* Own BBC radio series, Pet's Parlour, 1943; early British films include: Medal for the General, 1944; I Know Where I'm Going, 1945; Here Come the Huggetts, 1948; Dance Hall, 1950; White Corridors, 1951; The Card, 1951; Made in Heaven, 1952; The Runaway Bus, 1953; That Woman Opposite, 1957. Began career as singer in France, 1959. Top female vocalist, France, 1962; Bravos du Music Hall award for outstanding woman in show business, France, 1965; Grammy awards for records Downtown and I Know A Place. Numerous concert and television appearances in Europe and USA including her own BBC TV series. *Films:* Finian's Rainbow, 1968; Goodbye Mr Chips, 1969; Second to the Right and Straight on till Morning, 1982; *musicals:* The Sound of Music, Apollo Victoria, 1981; (also composer and creator) Someone Like You, Strand, 1990. *Address:* c/o John Ashby, Hindworth Management Ltd, 235 Regent Street, W1.

CLARK, Ramsey; lawyer in private practice, New York City, since 1969; *b* Dallas, Texas, 18 Dec. 1927; *s* of late Thomas Clark, and of Mary Ramsey; *m* 1949, Georgia Welch, Corpus Christi, Texas; one *s* one *d. Educ:* Public Schs, Dallas, Los Angeles, Washington; Univ. of Texas (BA); Univ. of Chicago (MA, JD). US Marine Corps, 1945–46. Engaged private practice of law, Dallas, 1951–61; Asst Attorney Gen., Dept of Justice, 1961–65; Dep. Attorney Gen., 1965–67, Attorney Gen., 1967–69. *Address:* 37 West 12th Street, New York, NY 10011, USA.

CLARK, Richard David; Chief Executive, and Clerk to the Lieutenancy, Devon County Council, since 1989; *b* 2 Sept. 1934; *s* of David and Enid Clark; *m* 1958, Pamela Mary (*née* Burgess); two *d. Educ:* Keele Univ. (BA, DipEd); Univ. de Paris, Sorbonne. Teaching, Woodberry Down Comprehensive School, 1957–61; Education Admin., Herts CC, 1961–69; Asst Educn Officer, Lancs CC, 1969–71; Second Dep. County Educn Officer, Hants CC, 1972–76; Chief Educn Officer, Glos CC, 1976–83; County Educn Officer, Hants CC, 1983–88; Associate Clerk to Devon and Cornwall Police Authority, 1989–; Dir, Devon and Cornwall TEC, 1989–. Mem., Adv. Cttee on Supply and Educn of Teachers. Adviser to: Burnham Cttee, 1982–87; Educn Cttee, ACC, 1982–89, 1990–; Council of Local Educn Authorities, 1983–89. Fellow Commoner, Churchill Coll., Cambridge, 1983; Vis. Fellow, Southampton Univ., 1986–88. FRSA 1977. *Recreations:* books, gardening. *Address:* Bickwell Brook, Bickwell Valley, Sidmouth, Devon EX10 8SQ. *T:* Sidmouth (0395) 514937. *Club:* Sidmouth Gentlemans.

CLARK, Sir Robert (Anthony), Kt 1976; DSC 1944; Deputy Chairman, TSB Group plc, 1989–91 (Director, 1987–91); *b* 6 Jan. 1924; *yr s* of John Clark and Gladys Clark (*née* Dyer); *m* 1949, Andolyn Marjorie Lewis; two *s* one *d. Educ:* Highgate Sch.; King's Coll., Cambridge. Served War, Royal Navy, 1942–46 (DSC). Partner with Slaughter and May, Solicitors, 1953–61; Director: Alfred McAlpine plc (formerly Marchwiel plc), 1957–;

Hill Samuel Bank Ltd, merchant bankers (formerly Philip Hill, Higginson, Erlangers Ltd, then Hill Samuel & Co. Ltd), 1961– (Chm., 1974–87); Bank of England, 1976–85; Eagle Star Holdings Ltd, 1976–87; Rover Gp plc (formerly BL plc), 1977–88; Shell Transport and Trading Co., plc, 1982–; SmithKline Beecham plc, 1987– (Vice-Chm.); Racal Telecom PLC, 1988–; Chairman: Hill Samuel Gp plc, 1980–88 (Chief Exec., 1976–80); IMI plc, 1981–89; Marley plc, 1985–89. Chairman: Industrial Development Adv. Bd, 1973–80; Review Body on Doctors' and Dentists' Remuneration, 1979–86; Council, Charing Cross and Westminster Med. Sch., 1982–; Dir, ENO, 1983–87. Hon. DSc Cranfield Inst. of Technol., 1982. *Recreations*: reading, music, collecting books. *Address*: Munstead Wood, Godalming, Surrey GU7 1UN. *T*: Godalming (04868) 7867; Hill Samuel Bank Ltd, 100 Wood Street, EC2P 2AJ. *T*: 071–628 8011. *Club*: Pratt's.

CLARK, Prof. Robert Bernard, DSc, PhD; FIBiol, FRSE; Professor of Zoology, University of Newcastle upon Tyne, since 1966; *b* 13 Oct. 1923; *s* of Joseph Lawrence Clark and Dorothy (*née* Halden); *m* 1st, 1956, Mary Eleanor (*née* Laurence) (marr. diss.); 2nd, 1970, Susan Diana (*née* Smith); one *s* one *d. Educ*: St Marylebone Grammar Sch.; Chelsea Polytechnic (BSc London 1944); University Coll., Exeter (BSc 1950); Univ. of Glasgow (PhD 1956); DSc London 1965. FIBiol 1966, FLS 1969, FRSE 1970. Asst Experimental Officer, DSIR Road Research Laboratory, 1944; Asst to Prof. of Zoology, Univ. of Glasgow, 1950; Asst Prof., Univ. of California (Berkeley), 1953; Lectr in Zoology, Univ. of Bristol, 1956; Head of Dept of Zoology and Dir of Dove Marine Laboratory, Univ. of Newcastle upon Tyne, 1966–77, Dir of Research Unit on Rehabilitation of Oiled Seabirds, 1967–76; Dir of NERC Research Unit on Rocky Shore Biology, 1981–87. Member: NERC, 1971–77 and 1983–86; Royal Commn on Environmental Pollution, 1979–83; Adv. Cttee on Pesticides, 1986–; Mem. Council, Nature Conservancy, 1975. *Publications*: Neurosecretion (ed, jtly), 1962; Dynamics in Metazoan Evolution, 1964, corrected repr. 1967; Practical Course in Experimental Zoology, 1966; (jtly) Invertebrate Panorama, 1971; (jtly) Synopsis of Animal Classification, 1971; (ed, jtly) Essays in Hydrobiology, 1972; (ed) The Long-Term Effects of Oil Pollution on Marine Populations, Communities and Ecosystems, 1982; Marine Pollution, 1986, 2nd edn 1989; The Waters Around the British Isles: their conflicting uses, 1987; (ed jtly) Environmental Effects of North Sea Oil and Gas Development, 1987; Founder, 1968, and ed, Marine Pollution Bulletin; numerous papers in learned jls. *Recreations*: architecture, music, unambitious gardening, reading undemanding novels. *Address*: Department of Biology, The University, Newcastle upon Tyne NE1 7RU. *T*: Newcastle upon Tyne 091–222 6656; Highbury House, Highbury, Newcastle upon Tyne NE2 3LN. *T*: Newcastle upon Tyne 091–281 4672.

CLARK, Rev. Canon Robert James Vodden; *b* 12 April 1907; *s* of Albert Arthur Clark and Bessie Vodden; *m* 1934, Ethel Dolina McGregor Alexander; one *d. Educ*: Dalry Normal Practising Episcopal Church Sch., Edinburgh; Church Army Coll.; Coates Hall Theol. Coll. Ordained, 1941. Men's Social Dept, Church Army, 1926; varied work in homes for men; special work in probation trng home under Home Office, 1934–39; St Paul and St George, Edinburgh, 1941–44; Rector, St Andrew's, Fort William, 1944–47; seconded to Scottish Educn Dept as Warden-Leader of Scottish Centre of Outdoor Trng, Glenmore Lodge, 1947–49; Curate i/c St David's, Edinburgh, 1949–54; Rector of Christ Church, Falkirk, 1954–69; Rector of St Leonards, Lasswade, 1969–79; Canon, Edinburgh, 1962; Dean of Edinburgh, 1967–76; Hon. Canon, Edinburgh, 1976; retd 1979. Mem., Royal Highland and Agric. Soc. *Recreations*: mountaineering, photography. *Address*: 15 North Street, St Andrews, Fife, Scotland KY16 9PW.

CLARK, Prof. Robin Jon Hawes, FRS 1990; Sir William Ramsay Professor and Head of Department of Chemistry, University College London, since 1989; *b* 16 Feb. 1935; *s* of Reginald Hawes Clark, JP and Marjorie Alice Clark (*née* Thomas); *m* 1964, Beatrice Rawdin Brown, JP; one *s* one *d. Educ*: Christ's Coll., NZ; Canterbury University Coll., Univ. of NZ (BSc 1956; MSc (1st cl. hons) 1958); University Coll. London (British Titan Products Scholar and Fellow; PhD 1961); DSc London 1969. FRSC 1969. University College London: Asst Lectr in Chemistry, 1962; Lectr 1963–71; Reader 1972–81; Prof., 1982–89; Dean of Faculty of Science, 1988–89. Mem., Senate and Academic Council, Univ. of London, 1988–. Visiting Professor: Columbia, 1965; Padua, 1967; Western Ontario, 1968; Texas A&M, 1978; Bern, 1979; Fribourg, 1979; Auckland, 1981; Odense, 1983; Sydney, 1985; Bordeaux, 1988. Royal Society of Chemistry: Tilden Lectr, 1983–84; Nyholm Lectr, 1989–90; Thomas Graham Lectr, 1991; Mem., Dalton Divl Council, 1985–88, Vice-Pres., 1988–90. Member: SRC Inorganic Chem. Panel, 1977–80; SERC Post-doctoral Fellowships Cttee, 1983; Chm., Steering Cttee, Internat. Confs on Raman Spectroscopy, 1990–. Chm., Adv. Council, Ramsay Meml Fellowships Trust, 1989–. Mem., Academia Europaea, 1990. Hon. FRSNZ, 1989. *Publications*: The Chemistry of Titanium and Vanadium, 1968; (jtly) The Chemistry of Titanium, Zirconium and Hafnium, 1973; (jtly) The Chemistry of Vanadium, Niobium and Tantalum, 1973; (ed jtly) Advances in Spectroscopy, vols 1–19, 1975–91; (ed jtly) Raman Spectroscopy, 1988; (ed) monographs on Inorganic Chemistry, 1978–; over 300 contribs to learned jls, in fields of transition metal chem. and spectroscopy. *Recreations*: golf, tennis, swimming, skiing, long distance walking, travel, bridge, music, theatre, wine. *Address*: Christopher Ingold Laboratories, University College London, 20 Gordon Street, WC1H 0AJ; 3a Loom Lane, Radlett, Herts WD7 8AA. *T*: Radlett (0923) 857899. *Clubs*: Athenæum; Porters Park Golf (Radlett).

CLARK, Prof. Ronald George, FRCSE, FRCS; Professor of Surgery, since 1972, Pro-Vice-Chancellor, since 1988, University of Sheffield; Consultant Surgeon; Northern General Hospital, since 1966; Royal Hallamshire Hospital, since 1966; *b* 9 Aug. 1928; *s* of late George Clark and of Gladys Clark; *m* 1960, Tamar Welsh Harvie; two *d. Educ*: Aberdeen Acad.; Univ. of Aberdeen. MB, ChB; FRCSE 1960; FRCS 1980. House appts, Aberdeen Royal Infirmary, 1956–57; Registrar, Western Infirmary, Glasgow, 1958–60; Surgical Res. Fellow, Harvard, USA, 1960–61; Lectr in Surgery, Univ. of Glasgow, 1961–65; Sheffield University: Sen. Lectr in Surgery, 1966–72; Dean, Faculty of Medicine and Dentistry, 1982–85. Examiner, Universities of: Aberdeen, Glasgow, Edinburgh, Liverpool, Newcastle, Leicester, London, Southampton, Malta, Ibadan, Jos. Chm., European Soc. for Parenteral and Enteral Nutrition, 1982–; Council Mem., Nutrition Soc., 1982–85; Scientific Governor, British Nutrition Foundn, 1982–; Member: GMC, 1983–; GDC, 1990–; Assoc. of Surgeons of GB and Ireland, 1968–; Surgical Res. Soc., 1969–. Mem., Editorial Bd, Scottish Medical Jl, 1962–65; Editor-in-Chief, Clinical Nutrition, 1980–82. *Publications*: contribs to books and jls on surgical topics and metabolic aspects of acute disease. *Recreation*: golf. *Address*: Brookline, 2 Chesterwood Drive, Sheffield S10 5DU. *T*: Sheffield (0742) 663601. *Club*: Commonwealth Trust.

CLARK, Lt-Gen. (Samuel) Findlay, CBE 1945; CD 1950; MEIC; MCSEE; PEng; *b* 17 March 1909; *m* 1937, Leona Blanche Seagram. *Educ*: Univ. of Manitoba (BScEE); Univ. of Saskatchewan (BScME). Lieut, Royal Canadian Signals, 1933. Associate Prof. of Elec. and Mechan. Engrg (Capt.) at RMC Kingston, 1938. Overseas to UK, Aug. 1940 (Major); Comd 5th Canadian Armd Div. Sigs Regt (Lt-Col), 1941. GSO1 Can. Mil. HQ, London, 1942; Staff Course, Camberley, England (Col), 1942–43; CSO, HQ 2nd Canadian Corps until end of War (Brig. 1943). Dep. Chief of Gen. Staff, 1945; Imperial Defence Coll.,

1948; Canadian Mil. Observer on Western Union Mil. Cttee; Maj.-Gen. 1949; Canadian Mil. Rep. NATO, London, 1949; Chm., Joint Staff, CALE, London, 1951; QMG of Canadian Army, 1951; GOC Central Comd, 1955; CGS, Sept. 1958–61. Chm., Nat. Capital Commission, 1961–67. Past Col Comdt, Royal Canadian Corps of Signals. FRCGS. Legion of Merit (USA), 1945; Comdr Order of Orange Nassau (Netherlands), 1945. OStJ 1975. *Address*: 301–1375 Newport Avenue, Victoria, BC V8S 5E8, Canada. *T*: 592 4338. *Club*: Union (Victoria).

CLARK, Sir Terence (Joseph), KBE 1990; CMG 1985; CVO 1978; HM Diplomatic Service; Ambassador to Oman, since 1990; *b* 19 June 1934; *s* of Joseph Clark and Mary Clark; *m* 1960, Lieselotte Rosa Marie Müller; two *s* one *d. Educ*: Thomas Parmiter's, London. RAF (attached to Sch. of Slavonic Studies, Cambridge), 1953–55; Pilot Officer, RAFVR, 1955. HM Foreign Service, 1955; ME Centre for Arab Studies, 1956–57; Bahrain, 1957–58; Amman, 1958–60; Casablanca, 1961–62; FO, 1962–65; Asst Polit. Agent, Dubai, 1965–68; Belgrade, 1969–71; Hd of Chancery, Muscat, 1972–73; Asst Hd of ME Dept, FCO, 1974–76; Counsellor (Press and Information), Bonn, 1976–79; Chargé d'Affaires, Tripoli, Feb.-March 1981; Counsellor, Belgrade, 1979–82. Dep. Leader, UK Delegn, Conf. on Security and Co-operation in Europe, Madrid, 1982–83; Hd of Information Dept, FCO, 1983–85; Ambassador to Iraq, 1985–89. Commander's Cross, Order of Merit of Fed. Republic of Germany, 1978. *Recreations*: Salukis, tennis. *Address*: c/o Foreign and Commonwealth Office, SW1A 2AH. *Clubs*: Commonwealth Trust, Hurlingham.

CLARK, Sir Thomas (Edwin), Kt 1986; retired director; non-executive Deputy Chairman, Ceramco, since 1984; farming since 1986; *b* 6 Aug. 1916; *s* of Thomas Edwin and Margaret Clark; *m* 1st, 1938, Joan Mary Hodgson (marr. diss. 1954); one *s* two *d* (and one *d* decd); 2nd, 1954, Josephine Mary Buckley (*d* 1962); one *s* two *d*; 3rd, 1963, Patricia Mary France; two *s* one *d. Educ*: King's College, Auckland. General labourer, Amalgamated Brick and Pipe Co., 1932; Asst Factory Manager, 1937; Associate Director, 1939; Manager, R & D, 1938; Gen. Manager, 1942; Director and Jt Gen. Manager, 1946 (with brother M. M. Clark); Jt Man. Dir, 1954; company name changed to Ceramco, 1964; Man. Dir, 1972, retired 1984. Director: Geothermal Energy NZ (Dep. Chm.); Rinnai NZ; Morlynn, Australia; Southern Pacific Boatyard. Chm., West Auckland Hospice Trust. *Recreations*: motor racing, yachting, gardening. *Address*: Aotea Farms, South Kaipara Heads, RDI Helensville, New Zealand. *T*: 854 SKH. *Clubs*: Auckland; Royal NZ Yacht Squadron, Titirangi Golf, Helensville Golf.

CLARK, Prof. Timothy John Hayes, FRCP; Consultant Physician to Royal Brompton National Heart and Lung Hospital (formerly Brompton Hospital), since 1970; Dean, and Professor of Pulmonary Medicine, National Heart and Lung Institute, since 1990; *b* 18 Oct. 1935; *s* of John and Kathleen Clark; *m* 1961, Elizabeth Ann Day; two *s* two *d. Educ*: Christ's Hospital; Guy's Hospital Medical Sch. BSc 1958; MB BS (Hons) 1961, MD 1967 London. FRCP 1973 (LRCP 1960, MRCP 1962); MRCS 1960. Fellow, Johns Hopkins Hosp., Baltimore USA, 1963; Registrar, Hammersmith Hosp., 1964; Lecturer and Sen. Lectr, Guy's Hospital Med. Sch., 1966; Consultant Physician, Guy's Hosp., 1968–90; Prof. of Thoracic Med., Guy's Hosp. Med. Sch., later UMDS, 1977–89; Dean: Guy's Hosp., 1984–89; UMDS, 1986–89; Pro-Vice-Chancellor for Medicine and Dentistry, Univ. of London, 1987–89. Mem., Council of Governors, UMDS, 1982–89, 1990–. Specialist Adviser to Social Services Cttee, 1981 and 1985. Special Trustee, Guy's Hosp., 1982–86. Pres., British Thoracic Soc., 1990–91. *Publications*: (jtly) Asthma, 1977, 2nd edn, 1983; (ed) Small Airways in Health and Disease, 1979; (jtly) Topical Steroid Treatment of Asthma and Rhinitis, 1980; (ed) Clinical Investigation of Respiratory Disease, 1981; (jtly) Practical Management of Asthma, 1985; articles in British Medical Jl, Lancet, and other specialist scientific jls. *Recreation*: cricket. *Address*: 8 Lawrence Court, NW7 3QP. *T*: 081–959 4411. *Club*: MCC.

CLARK, Tony; *see* Clark, C. A.

CLARK, Wallace; *see* Clark, H. W. S.

CLARK, Rt. Hon. Sir William (Gibson), Kt 1980; PC 1990; MP (C) Croydon South, since 1974 (E Surrey, 1970–74); *b* 18 Oct. 1917; *m* 1944, Irene Dorothy Dawson Rands; three *s* one *d. Educ*: London. Mem. Association of Certified Accountants, 1941. Served in Army, 1941–46 (UK and India), Major. Mem. Wandsworth Borough Council, 1949–53 (Vice-Chm. Finance Cttee). Contested (C) Northampton, 1955; MP (C) Nottingham South, 1959–66. Opposition Front Bench Spokesman on Economics, 1964–66; Chairman: Select Cttee on Tax Credits, 1973; Cons. Back-bench Finance Cttee, 1979–. Jt Deputy Chm., Conservative Party Organisation, 1975–77 (Jt Treasurer, 1974–75). Chm., Anglo-Austrian Soc., 1983–. Hon. Nat. Dir, Carrington £2 million Appeal, 1967–68. Freeman, City of London, 1987. Grand Gold Cross (Austria), 1989. *Recreation*: gardening. *Address*: The Clock House, Box End, Bedford. *T*: Bedford (0234) 852361; 3 Barton Street, SW1. *T*: 071–222 5759. *Clubs*: Carlton, Buck's.

CLARK, William P.; Counsel, Rogers & Wells, lawyers, since 1985; Chief Executive Officer, Clark Co.; *b* 23 Oct. 1931; *s* of William and Bernice Clark; *m* 1955, Joan Brauner; three *s* two *d. Educ*: Stanford Univ., California; Loyola Law Sch., Los Angeles, California. Admitted to practice of law, California, 1958; Sen. Member, law firm, Clark, Cole & Fairfield, Oxnard, Calif, 1958–67. Served on Cabinet of California, Governor Ronald Reagan, first as Cabinet Secretary, later as Executive Secretary, 1967–69; Judge, Superior Court, State of California, County of San Luis Obispo, 1969–71; Associate Justice: California Court of Appeal, Second District, Los Angeles, 1971–73; California Supreme Court, San Francisco, 1973–81; Dep. Secretary, Dept of State, Washington, DC, 1981–82; Assistant to Pres. of USA for Nat. Security Affairs, 1982–83; Sec. of the Interior, 1983–85. Chm., Presidential Task Force on Nuclear Weapons Program Management, 1985; Member: Commn on Defense Management, 1985–86; Commn on Integrated Long-Term Strategy, 1987. Trustee, Ronald Reagan Presidential Foundn, 1988. *Publications*: judicial opinions in California Reports, 9 Cal. 3d through 29 Cal. 3d. *Recreations*: ranching, horseback riding, outdoor sports. *Address*: (office) 1737 H Street NW, Washington, DC 20006, USA; Clark Company, 1031 Pine Street, Paso Robles, Calif 93446, USA. *Clubs*: Bohemian (San Francisco); California Cattleman's Association; Rancheros Visitadores (California).

CLARK-EDDINGTON, Paul; *see* Eddington.

CLARK HUTCHISON; *see* Hutchison.

CLARKE, Prof. Alan Douglas Benson, CBE 1974; Professor of Psychology, University of Hull, 1962–84, now Emeritus; *b* 21 March 1922; *s* of late Robert Benson Clarke and late Mary Lizars Clarke; *m* 1950, Prof. Ann Margaret (*née* Gravely); two *s. Educ*: Lancing Coll.; Univs of Reading and London. 1st cl. hons BA Reading 1948; PhD London 1950; FBPsS. Reading Univ., 1940–41 and 1946–48. Sen. Psychol., 1951–57 and Cons. Psychol., 1957–62, Manor Hosp., Epsom. Dean of Faculty of Science, 1966–68, and Pro-Vice-Chancellor 1968–71, Univ. of Hull. Rapporteur, WHO Expert Cttee on Organization of Services for Mentally Retarded, 1967; Mem. WHO Expert Adv. Panel on Mental Health, 1968–85; Chm., Trng Council for Teachers of Mentally Handicapped, 1969–74; Hon.

Vice-Pres., Nat. Assoc. for Mental Health, 1970–; President: Internat. Assoc. for Sci. Study of Mental Deficiency, 1973–76 (Hon. Past-Pres., 1976–88; Hon. Life Pres., 1988–); BPsS, 1977–78. Member: Personal Social Services Council, 1973–77; DHSS/SSRC Organizing Gp Transmitted Deprivation, 1974–83 (Chm. 1978–83); Cons., OECD/NZ Conf. on Early Childhood Care and Educn, 1978; Chairman: Sec. of State's Adv. Cttee on Top Grade Clinical Psychologist Posts and Appts, NHS, 1981–82; Adv. Cttee, Thomas Coram Res. Unit, Univ. of London Inst. of Educn, 1981–. Lectures: Maudsley, RMPA, 1967; Stolz, Guy's Hosp., 1972; Tizard Meml, Assoc. for Child Psychol. and Psychiatry, 1983. Hon. Life Mem., Amer. Assoc. on Mental Deficiency, 1975 (Research award, 1977, with Ann M. Clarke). Hon. FRCPsych 1989. Hon. DSc Hull, 1986. (With Ann M. Clarke) Distinguished Achievement Award for Scientific Lit., Internat. Assoc. for Scientific Study of Mental Deficiency, 1982. Editor, Brit. Jl Psychol., 1973–79; Mem., Editorial Bds of other jls. *Publications* (with Ann M. Clarke): Mental Deficiency: the Changing Outlook, 1958, 4th edn 1985; Mental Retardation and Behavioural Research, 1973; Early Experience: myth and evidence, 1976; (with B. Tizard) Child Development and Social Policy: the life and work of Jack Tizard, 1983; (with P. Evans) Combating Mental Handicap, 1991; numerous in psychol and med. jls. *Address:* 55 Newland Park, Hull HU5 2DR. *T:* Hull (0482) 444141.

CLARKE, Allen; *see* Clarke, C. A. A.

CLARKE, Anthony Peter; QC 1979; a Recorder, since 1985; *b* 13 May 1943; *s* of Harry Alston Clarke and Isobel Clarke; *m* 1968, Rosemary (*née* Adam); two *s* one *d*. *Educ:* Oakham Sch.; King's Coll., Cambridge (Econs Pt I, Law Pt II; MA). Called to the Bar, Middle Temple, 1965; Bencher, 1987. *Recreations:* golf, tennis, holidays. *Address:* 2 Essex Court, Temple, EC4Y 9AP. *T:* 071–583 8381.

CLARKE, Arthur Charles, CBE 1989; *b* 16 Dec. 1917; *s* of Charles Wright Clarke and Nora Mary Willis; *m* 1953, Marilyn Mayfield (marr. diss. 1964). *Educ:* Huish's Grammar Sch., Taunton; King's Coll., London (BSc); FKC 1977. HM Exchequer and Audit Dept, 1936–41. Served RAF, 1941–46. Instn of Electrical Engineers, 1949–50. Techn. Officer on first GCA radar, 1943; originated communications satellites, 1945. Chm., British Interplanetary Soc., 1946–47, 1950–53. Asst Ed., Science Abstracts, 1949–50. Since 1954 engaged on underwater exploration on Gt Barrier Reef of Australia and coast of Ceylon. Extensive lecturing, radio and TV in UK and US. Chancellor, Moratuwa Univ., Sri Lanka, 1979–; Vikram Sarabhai Prof., Physical Research Lab., Ahmedabad, 1980; Marconi Fellowship, 1982; FRAS. Unesco, Kalinga Prize, 1961; Acad. of Astronautics, 1961; World Acad. of Art and Science, 1962; Stuart Ballantine Medal, Franklin Inst., 1963; Westinghouse-AAAS Science Writing Award, 1969; Amer. Inst. of Aeronautics and Astronautics: Aerospace Communications Award, 1974; Hon. Fellow, 1976; Nebula Award, Science Fiction Writers of America, 1972, 1974, 1979; John Campbell Award, 1974; Hugo Award, World Science Fiction Convention, 1974, 1980; Marconi Internat. Fellowship, 1982; Vidya Jyothi Medal (Presidential Science Award), 1986; Grand Master, SF Writers of America, 1986; Charles Lindbergh Award, 1987. *Publications: non-fiction:* Interplanetary Flight, 1950; The Exploration of Space, 1951; The Young Traveller in Space, 1954 (publ. in USA as Going into Space); The Coast of Coral, 1956; The Making of a Moon, 1957; The Reefs of Taprobane, 1957; Voice Across the Sea, 1958; The Challenge of the Spaceship, 1960; The Challenge of the Sea, 1960; Profiles of the Future, 1962; Voices from the Sky, 1965; (with Mike Wilson): Boy Beneath the Sea, 1958; The First Five Fathoms, 1960; Indian Ocean Adventure, 1961; The Treasure of the Great Reef, 1964; Indian Ocean Treasure, 1964; (with R. A. Smith) The Exploration of the Moon, 1954; (with Editors of Life) Man and Space, 1964; (ed) The Coming of the Space Age, 1967; The Promise of Space, 1968; (with the astronauts) First on the Moon, 1970; Report on Planet Three, 1972; (with Chesley Bonestell) Beyond Jupiter, 1973; The View from Serendip, 1977; (with Simon Welfare and John Fairley) Arthur C. Clarke's Mysterious World, 1980 (also TV series); (with Simon Welfare and John Fairley) Arthur C. Clarke's World of Strange Powers, 1984 (also TV series); Ascent to Orbit, 1984; 1984: Spring, 1984; (with Peter Hyams) The Odyssey File, 1985; (with editors of OMNI) Arthur C. Clarke's July 20, 2019, 1986; (with Simon Welfare and John Fairley) Arthur C. Clarke's Chronicles of the Strange and Mysterious, 1987; Astounding Days, 1988; *fiction:* Prelude to Space, 1951; The Sands of Mars, 1951; Islands in the Sky, 1952; Against the Fall of Night, 1953; Childhood's End, 1953; Expedition to Earth, 1953; Earthlight, 1955; Reach for Tomorrow, 1956; The City and the Stars, 1956; Tales from the White Hart, 1957; The Deep Range, 1957; The Other Side of the Sky, 1958; Across the Sea of Stars, 1959; A Fall of Moondust, 1961; From the Ocean, From the Stars, 1962; Tales of Ten Worlds, 1962; Dolphin Island, 1963; Glide Path, 1963; Prelude to Mars, 1965; The Nine Billion Names of God, 1967; (with Stanley Kubrick) novel and screenplay, 2001: A Space Odyssey, 1968; The Lost Worlds of 2001, 1972; Of Time and Stars, 1972; The Wind from the Sun, 1972; Rendezvous with Rama, 1973; The Best of Arthur C. Clarke, 1973; Imperial Earth, 1975; The Fountains of Paradise, 1979; 2010: Space Odyssey II, 1982 (filmed 1984); The Songs of Distant Earth, 1986; 2061: Odyssey III, 1988; (with Gentry Lee) Cradle, 1988; Rama II, 1989; Tales from Planet Earth, 1990; The Ghost from the Grand Banks, 1990; The Garden of Rama, 1991; papers in Electronic Engineering, Wireless World, Wireless Engineer, Aeroplane, Jl of British Interplanetary Soc., Astronautics, etc. *Recreations:* diving, table-tennis. *Address:* 25 Barnes Place, Colombo 7, Sri Lanka. *T:* Colombo 699757, 694255, *Fax:* Colombo 698730; c/o David Higham Associates, 5 Lower John Street, Golden Square, W1R 3PE. *Club:* British Sub-Aqua.

CLARKE, Arthur Grenfell, CMG 1953; *b* 17 Aug. 1906; *m* 1st, 1934, Rhoda McLean Arnott (*d* 1980); 2nd, 1980, Violet Louise Riley. *Educ:* Mountjoy Sch., Dublin; Dublin Univ. Appointed Cadet Officer, Hong Kong, 1929; entered service of Hong Kong Government, 1929; interned in Stanley Camp during Japanese occupation; Financial Sec., 1952–62; retired, 1962. *Address:* Foxdene, Brighton Road, Foxrock, Dublin 18. *T:* 894368.

CLARKE, Dr Arthur S.; Keeper, Department of Natural History, Royal Scottish Museum, 1980–83, retired; *b* 11 Feb. 1923; *yr s* of late Albert Clarke and Doris Clarke (*née* Elliott); *m* 1951, Joan, *er d* of Walter Andrassy; one *s* one *d*. *Educ:* Leeds Boys' Modern School; Aireborough Grammar School; Leeds Univ. (BSc 1948, PhD 1951). Pilot, RAF, 1943–46. Assistant Lecturer, Glasgow Univ., 1951; Asst Keeper, Royal Scottish Museum, 1954; Deputy Keeper, 1973. *Address:* Rose Cottage, Yarrow, Selkirk TD7 5LB.

CLARKE, Sir Ashley; *see* Clarke, Sir H. A.

CLARKE, Bernard; *see* Clarke, J. B.

CLARKE, Prof. Bryan Campbell, DPhil; FRS 1982; Foundation Professor of Genetics, University of Nottingham, since 1971; *b* 24 June 1932; *s* of Robert Campbell Clarke and Gladys Mary (*née* Carter); *m* 1960, Ann Gillian, *d* of late Prof. John Jewkes, CBE; one *s* one *d*. *Educ:* Fay Sch., Southborough, Mass, USA; Magdalen Coll. Sch., Oxford; Magdalen Coll., Oxford (MA, DPhil). FLS 1980. National Service, 1950–52 (Pilot Officer, RAF). Nature Conservancy Res. Student, Oxford Univ., 1956; Asst 1959, Lectr 1963, Reader 1969, Dept of Zoology, Univ. of Edinburgh. Res. Fellow, Stanford Univ., 1973; SRC Sen. Res. Fellow, 1976–81. Joint Founder, Population Genetics Gp, 1967; Pres., Section D (Biology), BAAS, 1989; Vice-President: Genetical Soc., 1981; Linnean Soc., 1985–87; Soc. for Study of Evolution, USA, 1990–; Chm., Terrestrial Life Sciences Cttee, NERC, 1984–87. Scientific expeditions to: Morocco, 1955; Polynesia, 1962, 1967, 1968, 1980 and 1982. Lectures: Special, London Univ., 1973; Official Visitor, Australian Genetics Soc., 1979; Nelson, Rutgers Univ., 1980; R. A. Fisher, La Trobe Univ., 1986; Walton, Virginia Univ., 1988. Editor: Heredity, 1978–85; Proceedings of the Royal Society, Series B, 1989–. *Publications:* Berber Village, 1959; contrib. scientific jls, mostly on ecological genetics and evolution. *Recreations:* sporadic painting and gardening; archaeology, computing. *Address:* Linden Cottage, School Lane, Colston Bassett, Nottingham NG12 3FD. *T:* Kinoulton (0949) 81243. *Club:* Royal Air Force.

CLARKE, Sir (Charles Mansfield) Tobias, 6th Bt *cr* 1831; *b* Santa Barbara, California, 8 Sept. 1939; *e s* of Sir Humphrey Orme Clarke, 5th Bt, and Elisabeth (*d* 1967), *d* of Dr William Albert Cook; *S* father, 1973; *m* 1971, Charlotte (marr. diss. 1979), *e d* of Roderick Walter; *m* 1984, Teresa L. A. de Chair, *d* of Somerset de Chair, *qv*; one *s* two *d*. *Educ:* Eton; Christ Church, Oxford (MA); Univ. of Paris; New York Univ. Graduate Business Sch. Bankers Trust Co., NY, 1963–80 (Vice-Pres., 1974–80). Hon. Treas., 1980–, Vice-Chm., 1990–, Standing Council of the Baronetage; Editor and originator, The Baronets Journal, 1987–; Trustee, Baronets Trust, 1989–. *Recreations:* fox hunting, gardening, photography, stimulating conversation; Pres., Bibury Cricket Club. *Heir: s* (Charles Somerset) Lawrence Clarke, *b* 12 March 1990. *Address:* South Lodge, 80 Campden Hill Road, W8 7AA. *T:* 071–937 3932, *Fax:* 071–938 2955; The Church House, Bibury, Cirencester, Glos GL7 5NR. *T:* Bibury (0285) 740225. *Clubs:* Boodle's, Pratt's; Pilgrims; Jockey (Paris); The Brook, Racquet & Tennis (New York).

CLARKE, Christopher Michael; Keeper, National Gallery of Scotland, since 1987; *b* 29 Aug. 1952; *s* of Patrick Reginald Clarke and Margaret Catherine Clarke (*née* Waugh); *m* 1978, Deborah Clare Cowling; two *s*. *Educ:* Felsted; Manchester Univ. (BA (Hons) History of Art). Art Asst, York City Art Gall., 1973–76; Res. Asst, British Mus., 1976–78; Asst Keeper in Charge of Prints, Whitworth Art Gall., Manchester Univ., 1978–84; Asst Keeper, Nat. Gall. of Scotland, 1984–87. Vis. Fellow, Yale Center for British Art, 1985. *Publications:* Pollaiuolo to Picasso: Old Master prints in the Whitworth Art Gallery, 1980; The Tempting Prospect: a social history of English watercolours, 1981; (co-ed with N. Penny) The Arrogant Connoisseur: Richard Payne Knight, 1982; The Draughtsman's Art: Master Drawings in the Whitworth Art Gallery, 1983; Lighting up the Landscape: French Impressionism and its origins, 1986; Corot and the Art of Landscape, 1991; articles, reviews, etc, in Apollo, Art Internat., Burlington Magazine, Museums Jl. *Recreations:* golf, travel. *Address:* 9A Summerside Street, Trinity, Edinburgh EH6 4NT.

CLARKE, Christopher Simon Courtenay Stephenson; QC 1984; a Recorder, since 1990; *b* 14 March 1947; *s* of late Rev. John Stephenson Clarke and of Enid Courtenay Clarke; *m* 1974, Caroline Anne Fletcher; one *s* two *d*. *Educ:* Marlborough College; Gonville and Caius College, Cambridge (MA). Called to the Bar, Middle Temple, 1969; Attorney of Supreme Court of Turks and Caicos Islands, 1975–. Councillor, Internat. Bar Assoc., 1988–. *Address:* 42 The Chase, SW4. *T:* 071–622 0765; Brick Court Chambers, 15/19 Devereux Court, WC2R 3JJ. *T:* 071–583 0777. *Clubs:* Brooks's, Hurlingham.

CLARKE, (Cyril Alfred) Allen, MA; Headmaster, Holland Park Secondary School, 1957–71; *b* 21 Aug. 1910; *s* of late Frederick John Clarke; *m* 1934, Edna Gertrude Francis (decd); three *s*. *Educ:* Langley Sch., Norwich; Culham Coll. of Educn, Oxon; Birkbeck Coll., Univ. of London; King's Coll., Univ. of London. Entered London Teaching Service, 1933; Royal Artillery, 1940–46; Staff Officer (Major) in Educn Br. of Mil. Govt of Germany, 1945–46; Asst Master, Haberdashers' Aske's Hatcham Boys' Sch., 1946–51; Headmaster: Isledon Sec. Sch., 1951–55; Battersea Co. Sec. Sch., 1955–57. *Recreations:* photography, writing, reading, archaeology. *Address:* 16 Plasset Drive, Attleborough, Norfolk NR17 2NU. *T:* Attleborough (0953) 454518.

CLARKE, Prof. Sir Cyril (Astley), KBE 1974 (CBE 1969); FRS 1970; MD, ScD, FRCP, FRCOG; FIBiol; Emeritus Professor and Hon. Nuffield Research Fellow, Department of Genetics, and Hon. Research Fellow, Department of Geriatric Medicine, University of Liverpool (Professor of Medicine, 1965–72, Director, Nuffield Unit of Medical Genetics, 1963–72, and Nuffield Research Fellow, 1972–76); Consultant Physician, United Liverpool Hospitals (David Lewis Northern, 1946–58, Royal Infirmary since 1958) and to Broadgreen Hospital since 1946; *b* 22 Aug. 1907; *s* of Astley Vavasour Clarke, MD, JP, and Ethel Mary Clarke, *d* of H. Simpson Gee; *m* 1935, Frieda (Féo) Margaret Mary, *d* of Alexander John Campbell Hart and Isabella Margaret Hart; three *s*. *Educ:* Wyggeston Grammar Sch., Leicester; Oundle Sch.; Gonville and Caius Coll., Cambridge; Guy's Hosp. (Schol.). 2nd Class Hons, Natural Science Tripos Pt I; MD Cantab 1937; ScD Cantab 1963. FRCP 1949; FRCOG 1970; FRACP 1973; FRCPI 1973; FRSA 1973; FFCM 1974; FACP 1976; Fellow Ceylon Coll. of Physicians 1974; FRCPE 1975; FRCP(C) 1977; FLS 1981. House Phys., Demonstr in Physiology and Clin. Asst in Dermatology, Guy's Hosp., 1932–36. Life Insurance practice, Grocers' Hall, EC2, 1936–39. Served, 1939–46, as Med Specialist, RNVR: HM Hosp. Ship Amarapoora (Scapa Flow and N Africa), RNH Seaforth and RNH Sydney. After War, Med. Registrar, Queen Elizabeth Hosp., Birmingham. Visiting Prof. of Genetics, Seton Hall Sch. of Med., Jersey City, USA, 1963; Lectures: Lumleian, RCP, 1967; Ingleby, Univ. of Birmingham, 1968; Foundn, RCPath, 1971; Inaugural Faculty, Univ. of Leeds, 1972; P. B. Fernando Meml, Colombo, 1974; Marsden, Royal Free Hosp., 1976; Linacre, 1978; New Ireland, UCD, 1979; William Meredith Fletcher Shaw, RCOG, 1979; Harveian Oration, RCP, 1979; Sir Arthur Hall Meml, Sheffield, 1981; Ransom, Univ. of Nottingham, 1990. Examr in Med., Dundee Univ., 1965–69. Pres., RCP, 1972–77 (Censor, 1967–69, Sen. Censor, 1971–72, Dir, Med. Services Study Group, 1977–83, Dir, Med. Res. Unit, 1983–88); Pres. Liverpool Med. Instn, 1970–71; Chairman: British Heart Foundn Council, 1982–87; British Soc. for Res. on Ageing, 1987–; Member: MRC Working Party, 1966; Sub-Cttee of Dept of Health and Social Security on prevention of Rhesus hæmolytic disease, 1967–82 (Chm., 1973–82); Bd of Governors, United Liverpool Hosps, 1969; Assoc. of Hungarian Medical Socs, 1973; Res. Adv. Cttee Royal Hosp. and Home, Putney, 1988–; President: Harveian Soc.; Royal Entomological Soc. of London, 1991–; Governor and Councillor, Bedford Coll., 1974, Chm. of Council, 1975–85. Chm., Cockayne Trust Fund, Natural History Museum, 1974–. Hon. Fellow, Caius Coll., Cambridge, 1974; Leverhulme Emeritus Fellow, 1980. Hon. FRCPE 1981; Hon. FRCPath 1981; Hon. FRSM 1982; Hon. Mem., Liverpool Med. Inst., 1981. Hon. DSc: Edinburgh, 1971; Leicester, 1971; East Anglia, 1973; Birmingham, Liverpool and Sussex, 1974; Hull, 1977; Wales, 1978; London, 1980. Gold Medal in Therapeutics, Worshipful Soc. of Apothecaries, 1970; James Spence Medal, Brit. Paediatric Assoc., 1973; Addingham Medal, Leeds, 1973; John Scott Medal and Award, Philadelphia, 1976; Fothergillian Medal, Med. Soc., 1977; Gairdner Award, 1977; Ballantyne Prize, RCPEd, 1979; (jtly) Albert and Mary Lasker Foundn Award, 1980; Linnean Medal for Zoology, 1981; Artois-Baillet Latour Health Prize, 1981; Gold Medal, RSM, 1986; Buchanan Medal, Royal Soc., 1990. *Publications:* Genetics for the Clinician, 1962; (ed) Selected Topics in Medical Genetics, 1969; Human Genetics and Medicine, 1970, 3rd edn 1987; (with R. B. McConnell) Prevention of Rhesus

Hæmolytic Disease, 1972; (ed) Rhesus Hæmolytic Disease: selected papers and extracts, 1975; many contribs med. and scientific jls, particularly on prevention of Rhesus hæmolytic disease and on evolution of mimicry in swallowtail butterflies. *Recreations:* small boat sailing, breeding swallowtail butterflies. *Address:* 43 Caldy Road, West Kirby, Wirral, Merseyside L48 2HF. *T:* 051–625 8811. *Clubs:* Athenæum; Explorers' (New York); Oxford and Cambridge Sailing Society (Pres., 1975–77); West Kirby Sailing, Royal Mersey Yacht; United Hospitals Sailing (Pres.).

CLARKE, David Clive; QC 1983; a Recorder, since 1981; *b* 16 July 1942; *s* of Philip George Clarke and José Margaret Clarke; *m* 1969, Alison Claire, *d* of Rt Rev. Percy James Brazier; three *s*. *Educ:* Winchester Coll.; Magdalene Coll., Cambridge. BA 1964, MA 1968. Called to the Bar, Inner Temple, 1965. In practice, Northern Circuit, 1965–. *Recreations:* exploring canals, sailing, swimming. *Address:* 5 Essex Court, Temple, EC4Y 9AH. *T:* 071–353 4363; 25 Byrom Street, Manchester M3 4PF. *T:* 061–834 5238. *Clubs:* Trearddur Bay Sailing (Anglesey); Oxton Cricket (Birkenhead).

CLARKE, David Stuart; Executive Chairman, Macquarie Bank Ltd, since 1985; Chairman, Barlile Corporation Ltd, since 1986; Chairman, Australian Opera, since 1986 (Deputy Chairman, 1982–86); *b* 3 Jan. 1942; *s* of Stuart Richardson Clarke and Ailsie Jean Talbot Clarke; *m* 1964, Margaret Maclean Partridge; two *s*. *Educ:* Knox Grammar Sch.; Sydney Univ. (BEcon Hons); Harvard Univ. (MBA). Director: Darling & Co. Ltd (now Schroder Australia Ltd), 1968–71; Babcock Aust. Holdings Ltd, 1972–81; Chairman: Accepting Houses Assoc. of Aust. (now Aust. Merchant Bankers Assoc.), 1974–76; Sceggs Darlinghurst Ltd, 1976–79; Jt Man. Dir 1971–77, Man. Dir 1977–84, Hill Samuel Aust. Ltd; Director: Hill Samuel & Co. Ltd (London), 1978–84; Hooker Corp. Ltd, 1984–86; Reil Corp. Ltd, 1986–87. Member: Lloyds of London, 1983–; Aust. Stock Exch. (Sydney) Ltd, 1987–; Fed. Govt Cttee under Financial Corporations Act, 1975–85; Exec. Cttee, Cttee for Econ. Devel t of Australia, 1982–. Member: Council, Royal Agricl Soc. of NSW, 1986–; Harvard Bus. Sch. Alumni Council, 1986–89. Hon. Fed. Treas., Liberal Party of Aust., 1987–89. Chm., Salvation Army Red Shield Appeal, 1990– (Cttee Mem., 1985–88; Dep. Chm., 1989–90). Treas., NSW Rugby Union, 1989–. *Recreations:* opera, ski-ing, tennis, golf, bridge, philately, personal computers, ballet, wine. *Address:* 57 Bulkara Road, Bellevue Hill, NSW 2023, Australia. *T:* 61 2 327 5724. *Clubs:* Australian, Harvard of Australia (Pres. 1977–79), Royal Sydney Golf, Elanora Country, Cabbage Tree (Sydney).

CLARKE, Donald Roberts; Finance Director, 3i (formerly Investors in Industry) Group plc, 1988–91; *b* 14 May 1933; *s* of Harold Leslie Clarke and Mary Clarke; *m* 1959, Susan Charlotte Cotton; one *s* three *d*. *Educ:* Ealing Grammar Sch.; The Queen's Coll., Oxford (MA). FCA 1970 (ACA 1960); FCT 1981. Articled Peat Marwick Mitchell & Co., 1957–62; Accountant, The Collingwood Group, 1962–64; Industrial and Commercial Finance Corporation: Investigating Accountant, 1964; Controller, 1964–67; Br. Manager, 1967–68; Co. Sec., 1968–73; Investors in Industry Gp (formerly Finance for Industry): Sec./Treasurer, 1973–76; Asst Gen. Man., 1976–79; Gen. Man., Finance, 1979–88. Dir, Consumers' Assoc. Ltd, 1990–. Member: UGC, 1982–85; Industrial, Commercial and Prof. Liaison Gp, National Adv. Body for Local Authority Higher Educn, 1983–85; Continuing Educn Standing Cttee, Nat. Adv. Body for Local Authority Higher Educn and UGC, 1985–89; Council, RHBNC, 1987–. *Recreations:* music, gardening, photography.

CLARKE, Most Rev. Edwin Kent, DD. *Educ:* Bishop's Univ., Lennoxville (BA 1954, LST 1956); Union Seminary, NY (MRE 1960); Huron Coll., Ontario (DD). Deacon 1956, priest 1957, Ottawa. Curate of All Saints, Westboro, 1956–59; Director of Christian Education, Diocese of Ottawa, 1960–66; Rector of St Lambert, Montreal, 1966–73; Diocesan Sec., Diocese of Niagara, 1973–76; Archdeacon of Niagara, 1973–76; Bishop Suffragan of Niagara, 1976–79; Bishop of Edmonton, 1980; Archbishop of Edmonton and Metropolitan of Rupert's Land, 1986–87. *Address:* RR#3, Pembroke, Ontario K8A 6W4, Canada.

CLARKE, Edwin (Sisterson), MD, FRCP; Hon. Curator, Sherrington Room, University Laboratory of Physiology, Oxford University, since 1985; Director, Wellcome Institute for the History of Medicine, 1973–79, retired; *b* Felling-on-Tyne, 18 June 1919; *s* of Joseph and Nellie Clarke; *m* 1st, 1949, Margaret Elsie Morrison (marr. diss.); two *s*; 2nd, 1958, Beryl Eileen Brock (marr. diss.); one *d*; 3rd, 1982, Gaynor Crawford. *Educ:* Jarrow Central Sch.; Univ. of Durham Med. Sch. (MD); Univ. of Chicago Med. Sch. (MD). Neurological Specialist, RAMC, 1946–48; Nat. Hosp., Queen Square, 1950–51; Postgrad. Med. Sch. of London, 1951–58; Lectr in Neurology and Consultant Neurologist to Hammersmith Hosp., 1955–58; Asst Sec. to Wellcome Trust, 1958–60; Asst Prof., History of Medicine, Johns Hopkins Hosp. Med. Sch., 1960–62; Vis. Assoc. Prof., History of Medicine, Yale Univ. Med. Sch., 1962–63; Med. Historian to Wellcome Historical Med. Library and Museum, 1963–66; Sen. Lectr and Head of Sub-Dept of History of Medicine, University Coll. London, 1966–72, Reader, 1972–73. *Publications:* (jtly) The Human Brain and Spinal Cord, 1968; (ed) Modern Methods in the History of Medicine, 1971; (jtly) An Illustrated History of Brain Function, 1972; (trans.) Die historische Entwicklung der experimentellen Gehirn- und Rückenmarksphysiologie vor Flourens, by M. Neuburger, 1981; (jtly) Nineteenth Century Origins of Neuroscientific Concepts, 1987; articles in jls dealing with neurology and with history of medicine.

CLARKE, Elizabeth Bleckly, CVO 1969; MA; JP; Headmistress, Benenden School, Kent, 1954–Dec. 1975; *b* 26 May 1915; *d* of Kenneth Bleckly Clarke, JP, MRCS, LRCP, Cranborne, Dorset, and Dorothy Milborough (*née* Hasluck). *Educ:* Grovely Manor Sch., Boscombe, Hants; St Hilda's Coll., Oxford, 1933–37. BA 1936, BLitt and MA 1940. Asst Mistress, The Grove Sch., Hindhead, 1937–39; Benenden Sch., 1940–47; called to the Bar, Middle Temple, 1949; Vice-Principal, Cheltenham Ladies' Coll., 1950–54. JP, County of Kent, 1956. *Recreations:* walking, gardening, local history. *Address:* Minden, 1 Waterloo Place, Cranbrook, Kent TN17 3JH. *T:* Cranbook (0580) 712139. *Club:* English-Speaking Union.

CLARKE, Sir Ellis (Emmanuel Innocent), TC 1969; GCMG 1972 (CMG 1960); Kt 1963 (but does not use the title within Republic of Trinidad and Tobago); President of Trinidad and Tobago, 1976–86 (Governor General and C-in-C, 1973–76); *b* 28 Dec. 1917; *o c* of late Cecil Clarke and of Mrs Elma Clarke; *m* 1952, Eyrmyntrude (*née* Hagley); one *s* one *d*. *Educ:* St Mary's Coll., Trinidad (Jerningham Gold Medal, 1936, and other prizes). London Univ. (LLB 1940); called to the Bar, Gray's Inn, 1940. Private practice at Bar of Trinidad and Tobago, 1941–54; Solicitor-Gen., Oct. 1954; Dep. Colonial Sec., Dec. 1956; Attorney-Gen., 1957–62; Actg Governor, 1960; Chief Justice designate, 1961; Trinidad and Tobago Perm. Rep. to UN, 1962–66; Ambassador: to United States, 1962–73; to Mexico, 1966–73; Rep. on Council of OAS, 1967–73. Chm. of Bd, British West Indian Airways, 1968–72. KStJ 1973. *Address:* Port of Spain, Trinidad. *Clubs:* Queen's Park Cricket (Port of Spain); Trinidad Turf, Arima Race (Trinidad); Tobago Golf (President, 1969–75).

CLARKE, Frederick, BSc; FBCS; Director, DS Information Systems, since 1991; *b* 8 Dec. 1928; *s* of George and Edna Clarke; *m* 1955, Doris Thompson (marr. diss. 1987); two *d*; *m* 1988, Dorothy Sugrue. *Educ:* King James I Grammar Sch., Bishop Auckland; King's Coll., Durham Univ. (BSc 1951). FBCS 1972. Served RAF, 1951–54. Schoolmaster, 1954–57; IBM, 1957–82 (final appts, Gen. Man. and Dir); Chm., Royal Ordnance plc (formerly Royal Ordnance Factories), 1982–85. Chm., Lingfield Park Racecourse, 1988–90; Dir, Leisure Investments, 1985–90. Mem., Reading Univ. Council, 1980–88. Freeman, City of London, 1987. *Recreations:* golf, cricket, racing, reading. *Address:* Arran, Bute Avenue, Petersham, Richmond, Surrey TW10 7AX.

CLARKE, Geoffrey, RA 1976 (ARA 1970); ARCA; artist and sculptor; *b* 28 Nov. 1924; *s* of John Moulding Clarke and Janet Petts; two *s*. *Educ:* Royal College of Art (Hons). Exhibitions: Gimpel Fils Gallery, 1952, 1955; Redfern Gallery, 1965; Tranman Gallery, 1975, 1976, 1982. Works in public collections: Victoria and Albert Museum; Tate Gallery; Arts Council; Museum of Modern Art, NY; etc. Prizes for engraving: Triennial, 1951; London, 1953, Tokyo, 1957. Commissioned work includes: iron sculpture, Time Life Building, New Bond Street; cast aluminium relief sculpture, Castrol House, Marylebone Road; mosaics, Liverpool Univ. Physics Block and Basildon New Town; stained glass windows for Treasury, Lincoln Cathedral; bronze sculpture, Thorn Electric Building, Upper St Martin's Lane; relief sculpture on Canberra and Oriana; 3 stained glass windows, high altar, cross and candlesticks, the flying cross and crown of thorns, all in Coventry Cathedral; sculpture, Nottingham Civic Theatre; UKAEA Culham; Westminster Bank, Bond Street; Univs of Liverpool, Exeter, Cambridge, Oxford, Manchester, Lancaster and Loughborough; screens in Royal Military Chapel, Birdcage Walk. Further work at Chichester, Newcastle, Manchester, Plymouth, Ipswich, Canterbury, Taunton, Winchester, St Paul, Minnesota, Lincoln, Nebraska, Newcastle Civic Centre, Wolverhampton, Leicester, Churchill Coll., Aldershot, Suffolk Police HQ, All Souls, W1, The Majlis, Abu Dhabi, York House, N1.

CLARKE, Graham Neil; Editor, Amateur Gardening, since 1986; *b* 23 July 1956; *s* of Henry Charles Owen Clarke, RVM and Doris May Clarke; *m* 1980, Denise Carole (*née* Anderson); one *d*. *Educ:* Rutherford Sch., N London; Wisley School of Horticulture (WisCertHort). Staff gardener, Buckingham Palace, 1975–76; Nurseryman, Hyde Park, 1976; Amateur Gardening: Sub-Editor, 1976–79; Chief Sub-Editor, 1979–81; Dep. Editor, 1981–86; Editor, Home Plus Magazine, 1984–85. FLS. *Publications:* Step by Step Pruning, 1985; Autumn and Winter Colour in the Garden, 1986; Complete Book of Plant Propagation, 1990. *Recreations:* hospital broadcasting, philately, gardening. *Address:* c/o Amateur Gardening, Westover House, West Quay Road, Poole, Dorset BH15 1JG. *T:* Poole (0202) 680586. *Club:* Royal Horticultural Society Garden (Surrey).

CLARKE, Guy Hamilton, CMG 1959; HM Ambassador to Nepal, 1962–63, retired; *b* 23 July 1910; 3rd *s* of late Dr and Mrs Charles H. Clarke, Leicester. *Educ:* Wyggeston Grammar Sch., Leicester; Trinity Hall, Cambridge. Probationer Vice-Consul, Levant Consular Service, Beirut, 1933; transf. to Ankara, 1936; Corfu, 1940; Adana, 1941; Baltimore, 1944; has since served at: Washington, Los Angeles (Consul 1945), Bangkok, Jedda, Kirkuk (Consul 1949), Bagdad, Kirkuk (Consul-Gen. 1951); Ambassador to the Republic of Liberia, 1957–60, and to the Republic of Guinea, 1959–60; Mem. United Kingdom Delegation to United Nations Gen. Assembly, New York, 1960; HM Consul-General, Damascus, Feb. 1961, and Chargé d'Affaires there, Oct. 1961–Jan. 1962. *Address:* 10 Fairlawn House, Christchurch Road, Winchester, Hants SO23 9SR.

CLARKE, Dr Helen, FRA, FRHistS; Director, Society of Antiquaries, since 1990; *b* 25 Aug. 1939; *d* of George Parker and Helen (*née* Teare); *m* 1967, Giles Colin Scott Clarke; one *s*. *Educ:* Univ. of Birmingham (BA; PhD); Univ. of Lund, Sweden. FSA 1972; FRHistS 1990. Dir of Excavations, King's Lynn, 1963–67; Res. Fellow, Sch. of History, Birmingham Univ., 1965–67; Lecturer in Medieval Archaeology: Glasgow Univ., 1967–69; UCL, 1976–90. Editor and Translator: Royal Swedish Acad. of History and Antiquaries, 1975–; Bd of National Antiquaries, Sweden (also Consultant), 1990–; Consultant, English Heritage, 1987–. Member: Svenska Arkeologiska Samfundet, 1988; Vetenskapssocieten i Lund, 1988. Hon. Fil Dr Lund, 1991. *Publications:* Regional Archaeologies: East Anglia, 1971; Excavations in King's Lynn, 1963–1970, 1977; The Archaeology of Medieval England, 1984, 2nd edn 1986; Towns in the Viking Age, 1991. *Recreations:* attending opera, watching cricket, food, wine. *Address:* Kynance, Clarence Road, Tunbridge Wells, Kent TN1 1HE. *T:* Tunbridge Wells (0892) 525484.

CLARKE, Sir (Henry) Ashley, GCMG 1962 (KCMG 1952; CMG 1946); GCVO 1961; FSA; President, Venice in Peril Fund, since 1983 (Vice-Chairman, 1970–83); *b* 26 June 1903; *e s* of H. H. R. Clarke, MD; *m* 1st, 1937, Virginia (marr. diss. 1960), *d* of Edward Bell, New York; 2nd, 1962, Frances (OBE 1984), *d* of John Molyneux, Stourbridge, Worcs. *Educ:* Repton; Pembroke Coll., Cambridge. Entered Diplomatic Service, 1925; 3rd Sec., Budapest and Warsaw; 2nd Sec., Constantinople, FO and Gen. Disarmament Conf, Geneva; 1st Sec., Tokyo; Counsellor, FO; Minister, Lisbon and Paris; Deputy Under-Sec., FO; Ambassador to Italy, 1953–62, retd. London Adviser, Banca Commerciale Italiana, 1962–71; Sec.-Gen., Europa Nostra, 1969–70. Governor: BBC, 1962–67; Brit. Inst. of Recorded Sound, 1964–67; Member: Council, British Sch. at Rome, 1962–78; Exec. Cttee, Keats-Shelley Assoc., 1962–71; D'Oyly Carte Trust, 1964–71; Adv. Council, V&A Mus., 1969–73; Nat. Theatre Bd, 1962–66; Governing Body, RAM, 1967–73; Chairman: British-Italian Soc., 1962–67; Italian Art and Archives Rescue Fund, 1966–70; Royal Acad. of Dancing, 1964–69. Mem. Gen. Bd, Assicurazioni Generali of Trieste, 1964–84. Hon. Dr of Political Science, Genoa, 1956; Hon. Academician, Accademia Filarmonica Romana, 1962; FSA 1985; Hon. Fellow: Pembroke Coll., Cambridge, 1962; Ancient Monuments Soc., 1969– (Vice-Pres., 1982–); Royal Acad. of Music, 1971; Ateneo Veneto, 1973. Freeman, City of Venice, 1985. Pietro Torta Prize, 1974 and Bolla Award, 1976 (for conservation in Venice). Knight Grand Cross of the Order of Merit of the Republic of Italy, 1957; Knight Grand Cross, Order of St Gregory the Great, 1976; Knight of St Mark, 1979. *Publication:* Restoring Venice: The Madonna dell'Orto (with P. Rylands), 1977. *Recreation:* music. *Address:* Bushy Cottage, The Green, Hampton Court, Surrey KT8 9BS. *T:* 081–943 2709; Fondamenta Bonlini 1113, Dorsoduro, 30123 Venice, Italy. *T:* 041–5206530. *Clubs:* Athenæum, Garrick.

CLARKE, Henry Benwell; Deputy Chief Executive, Crown Estate Commission, since 1988; *b* 30 Jan. 1950; *yr s* of late Stephen Lampard Clarke and Elinor Wade Clarke (*née* Benwell); *m* 1973, Verena Angela Lodge; three *s* one *d*. *Educ:* St John's Sch., Leatherhead; South Bank Polytechnic (BSc Estate Management 1972); Imperial College London (MSc Management Science 1977; DIC 1977). ARICS 1973, FRICS 1986; ACIArb 1979. British Rail Property Board: S Region, 1972–78; NW Region, 1978–82; E Region, 1982–85; Regional Estate Surveyor and Manager, Midland Region, 1985–86; Chief Estate Surveyor, HQ, 1986–87; Nat. Develt Manager, 1987–88; Crown Estate: Acting Chief Exec. and Accounting Officer, 1989. Mem., Gen. Council, British Property Fedn, 1989–. Mem. Council, Christian Union for Estate Profession, 1983–88; Mem. Bd, Youth with a Mission (England), 1990–; advisor to various Christian trusts. MBIM. *Recreations:* reading, walking, architecture, Church. *Address:* 42 Wordsworth Road, Harpenden, Herts AL5 4AF. *Club:* National.

CLARKE, Hilton Swift, CBE 1984; President, Atlantic International Bank Ltd, since 1987 (Director, 1969–86, Chairman, 1973–86); *b* 1 April 1909; *yr s* of Frederick Job

Clarke; *m* 1st, 1934, Sibyl Muriel (*d* 1975), *d* of late C. J. C. Salter; one *s*; 2nd, 1984, Ann Elizabeth, *d* of late Leonard James Marchant. *Educ*: Highgate School. FCIB. Bank of England, 1927–67; former Director: Charterhouse Group Ltd, 1967–82 (Chm. Charterhouse Japhet Ltd, 1971–73); United Dominions Trust Ltd, 1967–81; Guthrie Corp., 1967–79; Bank of Scotland Ltd (London Bd), 1967–79; Chairman: Astley & Pearce, 1981–86 (Dir, 1975–86); Exco International plc, 1981–84 (Dir, 1981–86). Freeman, City of London, 1973. Hon. FRCGP 1975. *Recreation*: gardening. *Address*: 4 Coverdale Avenue, Cooden, Bexhill, E Sussex TN39 4TY. *T*: Cooden (04243) 5030. *Clubs*: Overseas Bankers', City of London, Sloane; Cooden Beach Golf.

CLARKE, James Samuel, MC 1943 and Bar 1944; Under-Secretary and Principal Assistant Solicitor, Inland Revenue, 1970–81, retired; Managing Director, Bishop and Clarke Ltd, since 1981; *b* 19 Jan. 1921; *s* of James Henry and Deborah Florence Clarke; *m* 1949, Ilse Cohen; two *d*. *Educ*: Reigate Grammar Sch.; St Catharine's Coll., Cambridge (MA). Army Service, 1941–45: Royal Irish Fusiliers; served 1st Bn N Africa and Italy; Major 1943. Called to Bar, Middle Temple, 1946. Entered Legal Service (Inland Rev.), 1953; Sen. Legal Asst, 1958; Asst Solicitor, 1965. *Recreations*: gardening, sailing. *Address*: Dormers, The Downs, Givons Grove, Leatherhead, Surrey KT22 8LH. *T*: Leatherhead (0372) 378254. *Clubs*: National Liberal, Royal Automobile.

CLARKE, Prof. John, FRS 1986; Professor of Physics, University of California, Berkeley, since 1973; *b* 10 Feb. 1942; *s* of Victor Patrick and Ethel May Clarke; *m* 1979, Grethe F. Pedersen; one *d*. *Educ*: Christ's Coll., Cambridge (BA, MA 1968); Darwin Coll., Cambridge (PhD 1968). Postdoctoral Scholar, 1968, Asst Prof., 1969, Associate Prof., 1971–73, Univ. of California, Berkeley. Alfred P. Sloan Foundn Fellow, 1970; Adolph C. and Mary Sprague Miller Inst. for Basic Research into Science Prof., 1975; John Simon Guggenheim Fellow, 1977; Vis. Fellow, Clare Hall, Cambridge, 1989. FAAAS 1982; Fellow, Amer. Phys. Soc., 1985. Charles Vernon Boys Prize, Inst. of Physics, 1977; Calif. Scientist of the Year, 1987; Fritz Loudon Meml Award for Low Temperature Physics, 1987. *Publications*: numerous contribs to learned jls. *Address*: Department of Physics, University of California, Berkeley, Calif 94720, USA. *T*: (415) 642–3069.

CLARKE, (John) Bernard; Manager, YMCA Training For Life; Director: Manchester Travel Services; Greater Manchester Museum of Science and Industry; *b* 10 March 1934; *s* of John Clarke and Alice (*née* Hewitt); *m* 1955, Patricia Powell; four *s* two *d*. *Educ*: St Mary's RC Sch., Stockport. Employed by BRB and National Carriers Ltd, 1948–85. Mem., Stockport Metrop. Bor. Council, 1963–74 (Leader, 1972–74); Leader, Greater Manchester CC, 1981–86 (Mem., 1973–86, Leader of Labour Gp, 1978–86). *Recreations*: angling, gardening. *Address*: 22 Fallowfield Road, North Reddish, Stockport SK5 6XT.

CLARKE, Prof. John Frederick, FRS 1987; Professor of Theoretical Gas Dynamics, Cranfield Institute of Technology, since 1972; *b* 1 May 1927; *s* of Frederick William Clarke and Clara Auguste Antonie (*née* Nauen); *m* 1953, Jean Ruth Gentle; two *d*. *Educ*: Warwick School; Queen Mary Coll., Univ. of London. BSc Eng 1st Cl. Hons, David Allan Low Prize, PhD; FRAeS, FIMA. Qualified Service Pilot, RN, 1946–48; Aerodynamicist, English Electric Co., 1956–57; Lectr, Coll. of Aeronautics, 1958–65 (Vis. Associate Prof. and Fulbright Scholar, Stanford Univ., 1961–62); Reader, Cranfield Inst. of Technology, 1965–72. Vis. Prof. at univs in USA, Australia and Europe; Vis. Res. Fellow, Centre for Non-linear Studies, Univ. of Leeds, 1987–; Benjamin Meaker Vis. Prof., Univ. of Bristol, 1988–89. Member: NATO Collaborative Research Grants Panel, 1987–90; Esso Energy Award Cttee, 1988–; Maths Cttee, SERC, 1990–. Mem., Editl Bd, Qly Jl Mech. Appl. Math., 1982–. FRSA 1985. *Publications*: (with M. McChesney) The Dynamics of Real Gases, 1964; (with M. McChesney) Dynamics of Relaxing Gases, 1976; contribs to professional jls on gas dynamics and combustion theory. *Recreation*: Sunday painter. *Address*: Aerodynamics, Cranfield Institute of Technology, Bedford MK43 0AL. *T*: Bedford (0234) 750111; Field House, Green Lane, Aspley Guise MK17 8EN. *T*: Milton Keynes (0908) 582234.

CLARKE, Prof. John Innes, DL; Professor of Geography, 1968–90, Pro-Vice-Chancellor and Sub-Warden, 1984–90, University of Durham; *b* 7 Jan. 1929; *s* of Bernard Griffith Clarke and Edith Louie (*née* Mott); *m* 1955, Dorothy Anne Watkinson; three *d*. *Educ*: Bournemouth Sch.; Univ. of Aberdeen (MA 1st cl., PhD); Univ. of Paris (French Govt scholar). FRGS 1963. RAF 1952–54 (Sword of Merit, 1953). Asst Lectr in Geog., Univ. of Aberdeen, 1954–55; Prof. of Geog., Univ. Coll. of Sierra Leone, 1963–65; University of Durham: Lectr in Geog., 1955–63; Reader in Geog., 1965–68; Acting Principal, Trevelyan Coll., 1979–80. Visiting Professor: Univ. of Wisconsin, 1967–68; Cameroon, 1965, 1966, 1967; Clermont-Ferrand, 1974; Cairo, 1982; Shanghai, 1986. Acting Chm., Human Geog. Cttee, SSRC, 1975; RGS rep. on British Nat. Cttee for Geography, 1976–81, 1988–89; Chairman: IGU Commn on Population Geography, 1980–88; Higher Educn Support for Industry in the North, 1987–89. Chm., Durham DHA, 1990–. Vice-Pres., Eugenics Soc., 1981–84. DL Durham, 1990. FRSA 1990. Silver Medal, RSGS, 1947. *Publications*: Iranian City of Shiraz, 1963; (jtly) Africa and the Islands, 1964, 4th edn 1977; Population Geography, 1965, 2nd edn 1972; (with B. D. Clark) Kermanshah: an Iranian Provincial City, 1969; Population Geography and the Developing Countries, 1971; (jtly) People in Britain: a census atlas, 1980; *edited*: Sierra Leone in Maps, 1966, 2nd edn 1969; An Advanced Geography of Africa, 1975; Geography and Population: approaches and applications, 1984; *co-edited*: Field Studies in Libya, 1960; Populations of the Middle East and North Africa: a geographical approach, 1972; Human Geography in France and Britain, 1976; Régions Géographiques et Régions d'Aménagements, 1978; Change and Development in the Middle East, 1981; Redistribution of Population in Africa, 1982; Population and Development Projects in Africa, 1985; Population and Disaster, 1989; Mountain Population Pressure, 1990; author of many learned articles. *Recreations*: travel, sports (now vicariously), countryside, family history. *Address*: Tower Cottage, The Avenue, Durham DH1 4EB. *T*: Durham (091) 3848350.

CLARKE, (John) Neil; Chairman, British Coal, since 1991; *b* 7 Aug. 1934; *s* of late George Philip Clarke and Norah Marie Clarke (*née* Bailey); *m* 1958, Sonia Heather Beckett; three *s*. *Educ*: Rugby School; King's College London (LLB). FICA 1959. Partner, Rowley, Pemberton, Roberts & Co., 1960–69; Charter Consolidated, 1969–88: Dir, 1973; Exec. Dir, 1974; Man. Dir, 1979; Chief Exec., 1980; Dep. Chm. and Chief Exec., 1982–88; Chairman: Johnson Matthey, 1984–89; Molins, 1989–91 (Dir, 1987–91); Genchem Holdings, 1989–; Director: Anglo American Corp. of SA, 1976–90; Consolidated Gold Fields, 1982–89; Travis Perkins, 1990–. *Recreations*: music, tennis, golf. *Address*: High Willows, 18 Park Avenue, Farnborough Park, Orpington, Kent BR6 8LL. *T*: Farnborough, Kent (0689) 851651; (office) 071–235 2020. *Clubs*: MCC; Royal West Norfolk Golf, Addington Golf.

CLARKE, Sir Jonathan (Dennis), Kt 1981; **His Honour Judge Sir Jonathan Clarke**; a Circuit Judge, since 1982; *b* 19 Jan. 1930; *e s* of late Dennis Robert Clarke, Master of Supreme Court, and of Caroline Alice (*née* Hill); *m* 1956, Susan Margaret Elizabeth (*née* Ashworth); one *s* three *d*. *Educ*: Kidstones Sch.; University Coll. London. Admitted Solicitor, 1956; partner in Townsends, solicitors, 1959–82; a Recorder of the Crown Court, 1972–82. Mem. Council, Law Soc., 1964–82, Pres., 1980–81; Sec., Nat. Cttee of

Young Solicitors, 1962–64; Member: Matrimonial Causes Rule Cttee, 1967–78; Legal Studies Bd, CNAA, 1968–75; Judicial Studies Bd, 1979–82; Governor, College of Law, 1970–90, Chm. of Governors, 1982. *Recreations*: sailing, skiing. *Address*: c/o Midland Bank, The Forum, Marlborough Road, Swindon, Wilts. *Clubs*: Farmers'; Royal Western Yacht, Law Society Yacht.

CLARKE, Rt. Hon. Kenneth (Harry); PC 1984; QC 1980; MP (C) Rushcliffe Division of Nottinghamshire since 1970; Secretary of State for Education and Science, since 1990; *b* 2 July 1940; *e c* of Kenneth Clarke, Nottingham; *m* 1964, Gillian Mary Edwards; one *s* one *d*. *Educ*: Nottingham High Sch.; Gonville and Caius Coll., Cambridge (BA, LLB). Chm., Cambridge Univ. Conservative Assoc., 1961; Pres., Cambridge Union, 1963; Chm., Fedn Conservative Students, 1963. Called to Bar, Gray's Inn 1963, Hon. Bencher, 1989; Mem., Midland Circuit. Research Sec., Birmingham Bow Group, 1965–66; contested Mansfield (Notts) in General Elections of 1964 and 1966. PPS to Solicitor General, 1971–72; an Asst Govt Whip, 1972–74 (Govt Whip for Europe, 1973–74); a Lord Comr, HM Treasury, 1974; Parly Sec., DoT, later Parly Under Sec. of State for Transport, 1979–82; Minister of State (Minister for Health), DHSS, 1982–85; entered Cabinet as Paymaster General and Minister for Employment, 1985–87; Chancellor of Duchy of Lancaster and Minister for Trade and Industry (with additl responsibility to co-ordinate Govt policy on Inner Cities), 1987–88; Sec. of State for Health, 1988–90. Mem., Parly delegn to Council of Europe and WEU, 1973–74; Sec., Cons. Parly Health and Social Security Cttee, 1974; Opposition Spokesman on: Social Services, 1974–76; Industry, 1976–79. Hon. LLD Nottingham, 1989. *Publications*: New Hope for the Regions, 1969; pamphlets published by Bow Group, 1964–. *Recreations*: modern jazz music; watching Association Football and cricket, bird-watching. *Address*: House of Commons, SW1A 0AA.

CLARKE, Prof. Malcolm Roy, FRS 1981; Senior Principal Scientific Officer, Marine Biological Association of the UK, 1978–87; *b* 24 Oct. 1930; *s* of Cecil Dutfield Clarke and Edith Ellen Woodward; *m* 1958, Dorothy Clara Knight; three *s* one *d*. *Educ*: eleven schools and finally Wallingford County Grammar Sch.; Hull Univ. BSc 1955, PhD 1958, DSc 1978. National Service, Private, RAMC, 1949–50. Teacher, 1951; Hull Univ., 1951–58; Whaling Inspector in Antarctic, 1955–56; Scientific Officer, later PSO, Nat. Inst. of Oceanography, 1958–71; led Oceanographic Expedns on RRS Discovery, RRS Challenger, RRS Frederick Russell and RV Sarsia; PSO, Marine Biol Assoc. of UK, 1972–78. Vis. Prof. in Zoology, Liverpool Univ., 1987–90. *Publications*: (ed jtly) Deep Oceans, 1971; Identification of Cephalopod Beaks, 1986; (ed jtly) Evolution, vol. 10, The Mollusca, 1986, vol. 11, Form and Function, 1987, vol. 12, Palaeontology and Neontology of the Cephalopoda, 1987; (ed jtly) Identification of "Larval" Cephalopods, 1987; papers on squids and whales in Jl of Marine Biol Assoc. etc, and a Discovery Report, 1980. *Recreations*: boating, painting. *Address*: Ridge Court, Court Road, Newton Ferrers, S Devon PL8 1DD. *T*: Plymouth (0752) 872738.

CLARKE, Marshal Butler C.; see Cholmondeley Clarke.

CLARKE, Prof. Martin Lowther; *b* 2 Oct. 1909; *s* of late Rev. William Kemp Lowther Clarke; *m* 1942, Emilie de Rontenay Moon (*d* 1991), *d* of late Dr R. O. Moon; two *s*. *Educ*: Haileybury Coll.; King's Coll., Cambridge. Asst, Dept of Humanity, Edinburgh Univ., 1933–34; Fellow of King's Coll., Cambridge, 1934–40; Asst Lecturer in Greek and Latin, University Coll., London, 1935–37. Foreign Office, 1940–45. Lecturer, 1946–47, and Reader, 1947–48, in Greek and Latin, University Coll., London; Prof. of Latin, University Coll. of North Wales, 1948–74, Vice-Principal, 1963–65, 1967–74. *Publications*: Richard Porson, 1937; Greek Studies in England, 1700 to 1830, 1945; Rhetoric at Rome, 1953; The Roman Mind, 1956; Classical Education in Britain, 1500–1900, 1959; George Grote, 1962; Bangor Cathedral, 1969; Higher Education in the Ancient World, 1971; Paley, 1974; The Noblest Roman, 1981. *Address*: 61 Ilges Lane, Cholsey, Wallingford OX10 9PA. *T*: Cholsey (0491) 651389.

CLARKE, Mary; Editor, Dancing Times, since 1963; *b* 23 Aug. 1923; *d* of Frederick Clarke and Ethel Kate (*née* Reynolds); unmarried. *Educ*: Mary Datchelor Girls' School. London Corresp., Dance Magazine, NY, 1943–55; London Editor, Dance News, NY, 1955–70; Asst Editor and Contributor, Ballet Annual, 1952–63; joined Dancing Times as Asst Editor, 1954. Dance critic, The Guardian, 1977–. Queen Elizabeth II Coronation Award, Royal Acad. of Dancing, 1990. *Publications*: The Sadler's Wells Ballet: a history and an appreciation, 1955; Six Great Dancers, 1957; Dancers of Mercury: the story of Ballet Rambert, 1962; ed (with David Vaughan) Encyclopedia of Dance and Ballet, 1977; (with Clement Crisp): Ballet, an Illustrated History, 1973; Making a Ballet, 1974; Introducing Ballet, 1976; Design for Ballet, 1978; Ballet in Art, 1978; The History of Dance, 1981; Dancer, Men in Dance, 1984; Ballerina, 1987; contrib. Encycl. Britannica. *Address*: 54 Ripplevale Grove, N1 1HT. *T*: 071–607 3422. *Club*: Gautier.

CLARKE, Matthew Gerard; QC (Scot) 1989; *s* of Thomas Clarke and Ann (*née* Duddy). *Educ*: Holy Cross High Sch., Hamilton; Univ. of Glasgow (MA; LLB). Solicitor, 1972. Lectr, Dept of Scots Law, Edinburgh Univ., 1972–78; admitted to Faculty of Advocates, 1978; Standing Junior Counsel to Scottish Home and Health Dept, 1983–89. Member: Consumer Credit Licensing Appeal Tribunal, 1976–; Estate Agents Tribunals, 1980–; Chm. (part-time), Industrial Tribunals, 1987–. Mem., UK Delegn, Council of the Bars and Laws Socs of EC, 1989–. Publication: (Scottish Editor) Sweet & Maxwell's Encyclopaedia of Consumer Law, 1980–. *Recreations*: opera, chamber music, the music of Schubert, travel. *Address*: 12 Strathearn Place, Edinburgh EH9 2AL. *T*: 031–447 6074. *Club*: Scottish Arts (Edinburgh).

CLARKE, Michael Gilbert; Chief Executive, Local Government Management Board, since 1990; *b* 21 May 1944; *s* of Rev. Canon Reginald Gilbert Clarke and Marjorie Kathleen Clarke; *m* 1967, Angela Mary Cook; one *s* two *d*. *Educ*: Queen Elizabeth Grammar Sch., Wakefield; Sussex Univ. (BA 1966; MA 1967). Teaching Assistant, Essex Univ., 1967–69; Lectr and Dir of Studies in Politics, Edinburgh Univ., 1969–75; Asst Dir and Depute Dir, Policy Planning, Lothian Regl Council, 1975–81; Dir, LGTB, 1981–90. Chm., RIPA, 1990–. Mem., Gen. Synod of C of E, 1990–. Vice-Chm. of Govs, St George's Sch., Harpenden. Hon. Fellow, Birmingham Univ., 1983. *Publications*: (ed) C. F. Strong, Modern Political Constitutions, 1975; Getting the Balance Right, 1990; Choices for Local Government: the 1990s and beyond, 1991; contribs on local govt matters to various books and jls. *Recreations*: church, family, gardening. *Address*: Bramble Corner, Devonshire Road, Harpenden, Herts AL5 4TJ. *T*: Harpenden (0582) 762051. *Club*: Reform.

CLARKE, Neil; see Clarke, J. N.

CLARKE, Norman, OBE 1982; Secretary and Registrar, Institute of Mathematics and its Applications, from its foundation, 1964–87, now Emeritus; *b* 21 Oct. 1916; *o s* of late Joseph Clarke and of Ellen Clarke, Oldham; *m* 1940, Hilda May Watts; two *d*. *Educ*: Hulme Grammar Sch., Oldham; Univ. of Manchester (BSc). FInstP; FIMA, Hon. FIMA 1990. Pres., Manchester Univ. Union, 1938–39. External Ballistics Dept, Ordnance Bd, 1939–42; Armament Res. Estabt, Br. for Theoretical Res., 1942–45; Dep. Sec., Inst.

Physics, 1945–65; Hon. Sec., Internat. Commn on Physics Educn, 1960–66. Southend-on-Sea County Borough Council: Mem., 1961–74; Alderman, 1964–74; Chm. of Watch Cttee, 1962–69 and of Public Protection Cttee, 1969–78; Vice-Chm., Essex Police Authority, 1969–85; Member: Essex CC, 1973–85; Southend-on-Sea Borough Council, 1974– (Mayor, 1975–76; Chm., Highways Cttee, 1980–84; Leader, 1984–87, 1990–; Leader, Cons. Gp, 1984–). *Publications:* papers on educn; editor and contributor: A Physics Anthology: (with S. C. Brown) International Education in Physics; Why Teach Physics; The Education of a Physicist; contributor: A Survey of the Teaching of Physics in Universities (Unesco); Metrication. *Recreations:* cricket, gastronomy, photography. *Address:* 106 Olive Avenue, Leigh-on-Sea, Essex SS9 3QE. *T:* Southend-on-Sea (0702) 558056; Institute of Mathematics and its Applications, 16 Nelson Street, Southend-on-Sea, Essex SS1 1EF. *T:* Southend-on-Sea (0702) 354020. *Club:* MCC.

CLARKE, Norman Eley, CB 1985; Deputy Secretary, Department of Health and Social Security, later Department of Social Security, 1982–88; *b* 11 Feb. 1930; *s* of Thomas John Laurence Clarke and May (*née* Eley); *m* 1953, Pamela Muriel Colwill; three *s* one *d*. *Educ:* Hampton Grammar Sch. Grade 5 Officer, Min. of Labour and National Service, 1948–56; Asst Principal, Principal, Asst Sec., Under Sec., 1956–82, with Nat. Assistance Bd, Cabinet Office, Min. of Social Security, DHSS and DSS. *Recreations:* reading, bridge, watching Queens Park Rangers, talking. *Address:* Northwood, Dartnell Avenue, West Byfleet, Surrey. *T:* Byfleet (0932) 346043.

CLARKE, Prof. Patricia Hannah, DSc; FRS 1976; Emeritus Professor, University of London, since 1984; Hon. Research Fellow, Chemical and Biochemical Engineering Department, University College London, since 1984; *b* 29 July 1919; *d* of David Samuel Green and Daisy Lilian Amy Willoughby; *m* 1940, Michael Clarke; two *s*. *Educ:* Howells Sch., Llandaff; Girton Coll., Cambridge (BA). DSc London. Armament Res. Dept, 1940–44; Wellcome Res. Labs, 1944–47; National Collection of Type Cultures, 1951–53; Lectr, Dept of Biochemistry, UCL, 1953; Reader in Microbial Biochemistry, 1966, Prof. of Microbial Biochemistry 1974–84. Leverhulme Emer. Fellow, 1984–87; Hon. Professorial Fellow, UWIST, Univ. of Wales, 1984–90; Kan Tong-Po Prof., Chinese Univ. of Hong Kong, 1986. Chm., Inst. for Biotechnological Studies, 1986–87. Hon. Gen. Sec., Soc. for General Microbiology, 1965–70; Mem., CNAA, 1973–79. Lectures: Royal Soc. Leeuwenhoek, 1979; Marjory Stephenson, Soc. for Gen. Microbiology, 1981; A. J. Kluyver, Netherlands Soc. for Microbiology, 1981. A Vice-Pres., Royal Soc., 1981–82. Hon. DSc: Kent, 1984; CNAA, 1990. *Publications:* Genetics and Biochemistry of Pseudomonas (ed with M. H. Richmond), 1975; papers on genetics, biochemistry and enzyme evolution in Jl of Gen. Microbiol. and other jls. *Recreations:* walking, gardening, dress-making. *Address:* 7 Corinium Gate, Cirencester, Glos GL7 2PX.

CLARKE, Peter, CBE 1983; PhD, CChem, FRSC, FInstPet; Principal, Robert Gordon's Institute of Technology, Aberdeen, 1970–85, retired; Chairman, Scottish Vocational Education Council, since 1985; *b* 18 March 1922; *er s* of Frederick John and Gladys May Clarke; *m* 1947, Ethel Jones; two *s*. *Educ:* Queen Elizabeth's Grammar Sch., Mansfield; University Coll., Nottingham (BSc). Industrial Chemist, 1942; Sen. Chemistry Master, Buxton Coll., 1947; Lectr, Huddersfield Technl Coll., 1949; British Enka Ltd, Liverpool, 1956; Sen. Lectr, Royal Coll. of Advanced Tech., Salford, 1962; Head of Dept of Chemistry and Biology, Nottingham Regional Coll. of Technology, 1963; Vice-Principal, Huddersfield Coll. of Technology, 1965–70. Member: SERC (formerly SRC), 1978–82; Council for Professions Supplementary to Medicine, 1977–85; Scottish Technical Educn Council, 1982–85; CNAA, 1982–87 (Chm., Cttee for Scotland, 1983). Chm., Assoc. of Principals of Colleges (Scotland), 1976–78; Pres., Assoc. of Principals of Colleges, 1980–81. Chairman: Aberdeen Enterprise Trust, 1984–; Industrial Trng Centre Aberdeen Ltd, 1989–. FRSA 1986. Burgess of Guild, City of Aberdeen, 1973. Hon. LLD Aberdeen, 1985. *Publications:* contribs to Jl of Chem. Soc., Chemistry and Industry. *Recreations:* gardening, swimming. *Address:* Dunaber, 12 Woodburn Place, Aberdeen AB1 8JR.

CLARKE, Major Peter Cecil, CVO 1969 (LVO 1964); Chief Clerk, Duchy of Lancaster, and Extra Equerry to HRH Princess Alexandra, the Hon. Mrs Angus Ogilvy; *b* 9 Aug. 1927; *s* of late Captain E. D. Clarke, CBE, MC, Binstead, Isle of Wight; *m* 1950, Rosemary Virginia Margaret Harmsworth, *d* of late T. C. Durham, Appomattox, Virginia, USA; one *s* two *d*. *Educ:* Eton; RMA, Sandhurst. 3rd The King's Own Hussars and 14th/20th King's Hussars, 1945–64; Adjt 3rd The King's Own Hussars, GSO2 2 Inf. Div., psc 1959. Seconded as Asst Private Secretary to HRH Princess Marina, Duchess of Kent, 1961–64; Comptroller, 1964–68; Comptroller to HRH Princess Alexandra, 1964–69. JP Hants, 1971–81. *Recreations:* golf, fishing. *Address:* 6 Gordon Place, W8. *T:* 071–937 0356. *Club:* Cavalry and Guards.

CLARKE, Prof. Peter Frederick, LittD; FBA 1989; Professor of Modern British History, Cambridge University, since 1991; Fellow of St John's College, Cambridge, since 1980; *b* 21 July 1942; *s* of late John William Clarke and of Winifred Clarke (*née* Hadfield); *m* 1st, 1969, Dillon Cheetham (marr. diss. 1990); two *d*; 2nd, 1991, Maria Tippett, Vancouver. *Educ:* Eastbourne Grammar Sch.; St John's Coll., Cambridge (BA 1963; MA 1967; PhD 1967; LittD 1989). FRHistS 1972. Asst Lectr and Lectr in History, 1966–78, Reader in Modern Hist., 1978–80, UCL; Cambridge University: Tutor, St John's Coll., 1982–87; Sec., Faculty Bd of Hist., 1985–86; Reader in Modern History, 1987–91. Vis. Prof. of Modern British Hist., Harvard Univ., 1974; Vis. Fellow, Res. Sch. of Social Scis, ANU, 1983. Mem. Council, RHistS, 1979–83. Chm., S Cambs Area Party, SDP, 1981–82. Jt Review Ed., History, 1967–73; Chm., Editl Bd, Twentieth Century British History, 1988–. *Publications:* Lancashire and the New Liberalism, 1971; Liberals and Social Democrats, 1978, 2nd edn 1981; The Keynesian Revolution in the Making, 1988, 2nd edn 1990; A Question of Leadership: from Gladstone to Thatcher, 1991; articles in learned jls; contribs to TLS, London Rev. of Books, etc. *Recreations:* walking, cooking. *Address:* St John's College, Cambridge CB2 1TP. *T:* Cambridge (0223) 338726.

CLARKE, Peter James; Secretary of the Forestry Commission, since 1976; *b* 16 Jan. 1934; *s* of Stanley Ernest Clarke and Elsie May (*née* Scales); *m* 1966, Roberta Anne, *y d* of Robert and Ada Browne; one *s* one *d*. *Educ:* Enfield Grammar Sch.; St John's Coll., Cambridge (MA). Exec. Officer, WO, 1952–62 (univ., 1957–60), Higher Exec. Officer, 1962; Sen. Exec. Officer, Forestry Commn, 1967, Principal 1972; Principal, Dept of Energy, 1975. *Recreations:* gardening, walking, sailing. *Address:* 5 Murrayfield Gardens, Edinburgh EH12 6DG. *T:* 031–337 3145. *Club:* Commonwealth Trust.

CLARKE, Robert Cyril; Chairman, United Biscuits (Holdings) plc, since 1990 (Group Chief Executive, 1986–90); *b* 28 March 1929; *s* of Robert Henry Clarke and Rose Clarke (*née* Bratton); *m* 1952, Evelyn (Lynne) Mary, *d* of Cyrus Harper and Ann Ellen Harper (*née* Jones); three *s* one *d*. *Educ:* Dulwich Coll.; Pembroke Coll., Oxford (MA Hist.). Served Royal West Kent Regt, 1947–49. Joined Cadbury Bros, as trainee, 1952; Gen. Manager, John Forrest, 1954; Marketing Dir, Cadbury Confectionery, 1957; Man. Dir, 1962–69, Chm., 1969–71, Cadbury Cakes; Dir, Cadbury Schweppes Foods, 1969–71; Man. Dir, McVitie & Cadbury Cakes, 1971–74; Dir, 1974–, Chm. and Man. Dir, 1984–, United Biscuits UK; Man. Dir, UB Biscuits, 1977–84; Dir, United Biscuits (Holdings), 1984–. Non-Exec. Mem., Thames Water, 1988–. Member: Council, Cake and Biscuit Alliance, 1965–83; Council, ISBA, 1977–84; Resources Cttee, Food and Drink Fedn, 1984–86; EDC, Food and Drink Industry, 1984–86. FIGD, CBIM. *Recreations:* reading, walking, renovating old buildings, planting trees. *Address:* United Biscuits (Holdings) plc, Syon Lane, Isleworth, Middx TW7 5NN.

CLARKE, Rev. Robert Sydney; whole-time Chaplain, Winchester Health Authority, since 1985; Chaplain to HM the Queen, since 1987; *b* 31 Oct. 1935; *s* of George Sydney and Elizabeth Clarke. *Educ:* St Dunstan's College; King's Coll., Univ. of London (AKC 1964). Chaplain: New Cross Hospital, Wolverhampton, 1970–74; Herrison and West Dorset County Hosp., Dorchester, 1974–79; Westminster Hosp. and Westminster Medical School, Univ. of London, 1979–85. *Recreations:* breeding and showing dogs, music, travel, DIY. *Address:* 22 The Harrage, Romsey, Hants SO51 8HE. *T:* Romsey (0794) 524215. *Club:* Kennel.

CLARKE, Robin Mitchell, MC 1944; JP; DL; Chairman, Gatwick Airport Consultative Committee, 1982–90; *b* 8 Jan. 1917; *e s* of Joseph and Mary Clarke; *m* 1946, Betty Mumford; twin *s* and *d*. *Educ:* Ruckholt Central Sch., Leyton. Middleton and St Bride's Wharf, Wapping, 1932–34; Town Clerk's Office, City of Westminster, 1935–40. War of 1939–45: 12th Regt, RHA (HAC) and 142 (Royal Devon Yeomanry) Fd Regt, RA; Major, 1944; served Sicily and Italy (wounded, despatches, MC). Town Clerk's Office, Westminster, 1946–48; Crawley Development Corporation, 1948–62; Manager, Crawley, Commn for the New Towns, 1962–78; Chief Exec., New Towns Commn, 1978–82. Vice-Pres., St Catherine's Hospice, Crawley, 1989– (Chm., 1983–89). Master, Worshipful Co. of Chartered Secs and Administrators, 1984–85. ACIS 1949; FCIS 1959 (Mem. Nat. Council, 1968–87; Pres., 1978). JP Crawley, 1971; DL West Sussex, 1982. FRSA 1980. *Address:* Mayford Cottage, 89 Golden Avenue, East Preston, W Sussex BN16 1QT. *T:* Rustington (0903) 771739. *Club:* Army and Navy.

CLARKE, Roger Eric; Under Secretary, Public Transport Directorate, Department of Transport, since 1989; *b* 13 June 1939; *s* of Frederick Cuérel Clarke and late Hilda Josephine Clarke; *m* 1983, Elizabeth Jane, *d* of Gordon W. Pingstone and Anne Ellen Pingstone; one *d*. *Educ:* UCS, Hampstead; Corpus Christi Coll., Cambridge (MA). Various posts in civil aviation divs of Min. of Aviation, BoT and Depts of Trade and Transport, 1961–72 and 1980–; Air Traffic Rights Advr to Govt of Fiji, 1972–74; Asst Sec., Insce and Overseas Trade Divs, Dept of Trade, 1975–80; Under Sec., 1985–. Non-Exec. Dir, Earls Court and Olympia Ltd, 1989–. *Recreations:* family, friends, church, garden, walking, theatre, music, languages, travel. *Address:* PTR Directorate, Department of Transport, 2 Marsham Street, SW1P 3EB. *T:* 071–276 5020. *Club:* Reform.

CLARKE, Roger Howard, PhD; Director, National Radiological Protection Board, since 1987; *b* 22 Aug. 1943; *s* of late Harold Pardoe and Laurie Gwyneth Clarke; *m* 1966, Sandra Ann (*née* Buckley); one *s* one *d*. *Educ:* King Edward VI Sch., Stourbridge; Univ. of Birmingham (BSc, MSc); Polytechnic of Central London (PhD). Res. Officer, Berkeley Nuclear Laboratories, CEGB, 1965–77; Hd of Nuclear Power Assessments, NRPB, 1978–83; Bd Sec., 1983–87. Deleg. to UN Sci. Cttee on the Effects of Atomic Radiation, 1979–; Chm., OECD Nuclear Energy Agency Cttee on Radiation Protection and Public Health, 1987–; Member: Gp of Experts, Article 31, Euratom, 1988–; Internat. Commn on Radiol Protection, 1989– (Chm., Cttee on Application of Commn's Recommendations, 1989–; Sec., Cttee on Secondary Standards, 1985–89). *Publications:* Carcinogenesis and Radiation Risk (with W. V. Mayneord), 1975; numerous papers in sci. and technical literature. *Recreations:* gardening, theatre, travel. *Address:* Corner Cottage, Woolton Hill, Newbury, Berks RG15 9XJ. *T:* Highclere (0635) 253957.

CLARKE, Major Sir Rupert William John, 3rd Bt *cr* 1882; MBE 1943; late Irish Guards; Chairman: United Distillers Co., 1960–88; National Australia Bank Ltd (formerly National Bank of Australasia), since 1986 (Director, since 1955); Bank of South Pacific, since 1986; First National Ltd; International Ranch Management Services Pty Ltd; P & O Australia Ltd, since 1983 (Director, since 1980); *b* 5 Nov. 1919; *s* of 2nd Bt and Elsie Florence (who *m* 2nd, 1928, 5th Marquess of Headfort), *d* of James Partridge Tucker, Devonshire; *S* father, 1926; *m* 1947, Kathleen, *d* of P. Grant Hay, Toorak, Victoria, Australia; two *s* one *d* (and one *s* decd). *Educ:* Eton; Magdalen Coll., Oxford (MA). Hon. Fellow, Trinity Coll., Melbourne, 1981. Served War of 1939–45 (despatches, MBE). Chm., Cadbury Schweppes Australia Ltd (formerly Schweppes (Australia)), 1955–89; Dir, Cadbury Schweppes, 1977–85. Director: Conzinc Riotinto of Australia, 1962–87; Custom Credit Corp.; Morganite Australia Pty (Chm., 1976–84); National Australia Gp (UK), 1990–. Dir, Royal Humane Soc. of Australasia. Mem. Cttee, Vict. Amateur Turf Club (Chm., 1972–88). Hon. Consul General for Monaco, 1975– (Hon. Consul, 1961). Chevalier de la Légion d'Honneur, 1979; Ordre des Grimaldis (Monaco); Officer, Order of Leopold (Belgium), 1989. *Heir: s* Rupert Grant Alexander Clarke, LLB (Hons) [*b* 12 Dec. 1947; *m* 1978, Susannah, *d* of Sir Robert Law-Smith, *qv*; one *s* two *d*]. *Address:* Bolinda Vale, Clarkefield, Vic 3430, Australia; Richmond House, 56 Avoca Street, South Yarra, Vic 3141. *Clubs:* Cavalry and Guards, Lansdowne; Melbourne, Athenæum, Australian (Melbourne); Union (Sydney); Queensland (Brisbane).

CLARKE, Samuel Harrison, CBE 1956; MSc; Hon. MIFireE; *b* 5 Sept. 1903; *s* of Samuel Clarke and Mary Clarke (*née* Clarke); *m* 1st, 1928, Frances Mary Blowers (*d* 1972); one *s* two *d*; 2nd, 1977, Mrs Beryl N. Wood; two step *d*. *Educ:* The Brunts Sch., Mansfield; University Coll., Nottingham (MSc London). Forest Products Res. Laboratory of DSIR, 1927; Fire Research Div., Research and Experiments Dept, Ministry of Home Security, 1940; Dir of Fire Research, DSIR, and Fire Offices Cttee, 1946–58; Dir of Fuel Research Station, DSIR, 1958; Dir, Warren Spring Laboratory, DSIR, 1958–63; Careers Officer, Min. of Technology, 1963–67 (DSIR, 1964–65). Mem. Stevenage Development Corporation, 1962–71; Vice-Pres., Herts Assoc. for Care and Resettlement of Offenders. *Publications:* papers in scientific and technical jls. *Recreations:* exchanging ideas, painting. *Address:* 14 Silam Road, Stevenage, Herts SG1 1JH.

See also S. L. H. Clarke.

CLARKE, Samuel Laurence Harrison, CBE 1988; CEng, FIEE; Assistant Technical Director, GEC plc, since 1981; Chairman, Image Store Holdings plc, since 1989; *b* 16 Dec. 1929; *s* of Samuel Harrison Clarke, *qv*; *m* 1952, Ruth Joan Godwin, *yr d* of Oscar and Muriel Godwin; one *s* three *d*. *Educ:* Westminster Sch.; Trinity Coll., Cambridge (BA). Technical Dir, GEC-Elliott Automation Ltd, 1970–74; Technical Dir (Automation), GEC-Marconi Electronics Ltd, 1974–81; Director, GEC Computers Ltd, 1971–83. Dep. Dir, 1983–87, Dir, 1987, Alvey Programme, DTI. *Publications:* various papers in learned and technical jls. *Recreations:* ski-ing, Scottish dancing, sailing. *Address:* Laureldown, 31 Craigweil Avenue, Radlett, Herts WD7 7ET. *T:* Radlett (0923) 852418.

CLARKE, Stanley George, CBE 1975; Chief Inspector of the Prison Service, 1971–74; Member: Prisons Board, 1971–74; Parole Board, 1975–78; *b* Dunfermline, 5 May 1914; *s* of Stanley and Catherine Clarke; *m* 1940, Mary Preston Lewin; one *s* one *d*. *Educ:* Sutton High Sch., Plymouth (school colours: cricket, Rugby, soccer). Civil Service Clerk: Dartmoor Prison, 1931; Lowdham Grange Borstal, 1933; North Sea Camp, 1935; Borstal Housemaster: Portland, 1937; North Sea Camp, 1939. Served War, 1941–45 (despatches): Sqdn Ldr, RAF. Borstal Housemaster: Hollesley Bay Colony, 1945; Gaynes Hall, 1946.

Dep. Governor, Manchester Prison, 1947; Governor: Norwich Prison, 1949; Nottingham Prison, 1952; Eastchurch Prison, 1955; Liverpool Prison, 1959. Asst Dir of Prisons, in charge of North Region, 1964; Asst Controller, Prison Dept, 1970. *Address:* 17 Grundy's Lane, Malvern Wells, Worcs WR14 4HS.

CLARKE, Mrs Stella Rosemary, JP; DL; Chairman of Council, Bristol University, since 1987 (Member, since 1982); Director, Fosters Rooms Ltd, since 1975; *b* 16 Feb. 1932; *d* of John Herbert and Molly Isabel Bruce King; *m* 1952, Charles Nigel Clarke; four *s* one *d. Educ:* Cheltenham Ladies' Coll.; Trinity Coll. Dublin. Long Ashton RDC: Councillor, Chm. Council, Housing and Public Health Cttees, 1955–73; Mem., Woodspring Dist Council, 1973–76; co-opted Mem., Somerset CC, Social Services and Children's Cttee, 1957–73. A Governor, BBC, 1974–81. Purchased and restored Theatre Royal, Bath, with husband, 1974–76. Chm., new initiatives in training and housing of the young and unemployed, 1982–. Member: Housing Corp., 1988–; Bristol Develt Corp., 1989–. JP Bristol, 1968 (Chm., Bench, 1991–); DL Avon, 1986. *Recreations:* family and the variety of life. *Address:* Gatcombe Court, Flax Bourton, near Bristol BS19 1PX. *T:* Bristol (0272) 393141.

CLARKE, Brig. Terence Hugh, CBE 1943; *b* 17 Feb. 1904; *e s* of late Col Hugh Clarke, AM, Royal Artillery, and Mrs Hugh Clarke, Bunces, Kennel Ride, Ascot; *m* 1928, Eileen Armistead (*d* 1982), Hopelands, Woodville, NZ; two *d. Educ:* Temple Grove; Haileybury Coll.; RMA Sandhurst. 2nd Lieut Glos Regt, 1924; served India, 1924–27; China, 1928; India, 1928–31, in IA Ordnance Corps; England, 1931–33, Glos Regt; transferred to RAOC, 1933; Norway, 1940 (despatches); DDOS 1st Army, 1942, as Brig. (despatches, CBE); DDOS 2nd Army, 1944; Normandy to Luneberg, Germany (despatches); comd RAOC Training Centre, 1946; DDOS Southern Command, 1948–50; retired from Army, 1950, to enter industry as a Dir of public and private companies, retired. MP (C) Portsmouth West, 1950–66; contested (C) Portsmouth West, 1966, 1970. *Recreations:* capped six times for the Army at Rugby and boxed heavyweight for Army; sailing, ski-ing and horse racing.

CLARKE, Thomas, CBE 1980; JP; MP (Lab) Monklands West, since 1983 (Coatbridge and Airdrie, June 1982–1983); *b* 10 Jan. 1941; *s* of James Clarke and Mary (*née* Gordon). *Educ:* All Saints Primary Sch., Airdrie; Columba High Sch., Coatbridge; Scottish College of Commerce. Started working life as office boy with Glasgow Accountants' firm; Asst Director, Scottish Council for Educational Technology, before going to Parliament. Councillor: (former) Coatbridge Council, 1964; (reorganised) Monklands District Council, 1974; Provost of Monklands, 1975–77, 1977–80, 1980–82. Vice-President, Convention of Scottish Local Authorities, 1976–78, President, 1978–80. Opposition front-bench spokesman on: Scottish Affairs, 1987; health and social security (personal social services), 1987–90. Chm., PLP Foreign Affairs Cttee, 1983–86. Author and main sponsor, Disabled Persons (Consultation, Representation and Services) Act, 1986. Director, award winning amateur film, Give Us a Goal, 1972; former President, British Amateur Cinematographers' Central Council. JP County of Lanark, 1972. *Recreations:* films, reading, walking. *Address:* 37 Blairhill Street, Coatbridge, Lanarkshire ML5 1PG. *T:* Coatbridge (0236) 22550. *Clubs:* Coatbridge Municipal Golf, Easter Moffat Golf.

CLARKE, Sir Tobias; *see* Clarke, Sir C. M. T.

CLARKE, Tom; freelance screenwriter, playwright; *b* 7 Nov. 1918; *s* of Herman C. Clarke and May Dora Carter; *m* 1st, 1945, B. D. Gordon; one *s* three *d*; 2nd, 1953, J. I. Hampton; two *s*; 3rd, 1960, Ann Wiltshire; one *d. Educ:* Tonbridge School. Served War, Royal Artillery, 1939–46 (Captain). Called to Bar, Gray's Inn, 1951. Freelance writer, 1958–. TV plays and films include: Mad Jack, 1971; Stocker's Copper, 1972; Billion Dollar Bubble, 1975; Muck and Brass, 1982; Past Caring, 1986; stage play, Come Again, 1983. Grand Prize, Monte Carlo TV Festival, 1972; UNRRA Silver Dove, 1972; Mention d'Honneur, Prague TV Festival, 1973; Writer's Guild Award, 1973; BAFTA Award, 1973; Mention d'Honneur, Venice Film Festival, 1985; Best Screenplay, Prague TV Fest., 1987. *Recreations:* nursing hypochondria and awaiting fulfilment of optimistic astrological predictions. *Address:* c/o Judy Daish Associates, 83 Eastbourne Mews, W2 6LQ. *T:* 071–262 1101.

CLARKE, William Malpas, CBE 1976; Chairman: Grindlays Bank (Jersey), since 1981; ANZ Merchant Bank, since 1987 (Director, since 1985); Transatlantic Capital (Biosciences) Ltd, since 1989; Central Banking Publications Ltd, since 1990; *b* 5 June 1922; *o s* of late Ernest and Florence Clarke; *m* 1st, 1946, Margaret Braithwaite; two *d*; 2nd, 1973, Faith Elizabeth Dawson. *Educ:* Audenshaw Grammar Sch.; Univ. of Manchester. Served Royal Air Force, 1941–46; Flying Instructor, 1942–44; Flight-Lieut, 1945. Editorial Staff, Manchester Guardian, 1948–55; The Times, 1955–66: City Editor, 1957–62; Financial and Industrial Editor, 1962–66; Editor, The Banker, March-Sept. 1966, Consultant 1966–76. Dir, 1968–76, Dep. Chm. and Dir Gen., 1976–87, British Invisible Exports Council (formerly Cttee on Invisible Exports); Deputy Chairman: City Communications Centre, 1976–87; Trade Indemnity Co. Ltd, 1980–86; Director: ANZ Grindlays Bank (formerly Grindlays Bank), 1966–85, 1987–; Euromoney Ltd, 1969–84; Trade Indemnity plc, 1971–87; Swiss Reinsurance Co. (UK) plc, 1977–; ANZ Holdings, 1985–87. Chm., Harold Wincott Financial Journalist Press Award Panel, 1971–. Governor, The Hospitals for Sick Children, 1984–90; Chm., Wishing Well Redevelt Appeal Trust, 1985–. *Publications:* The City's Invisible Earnings, 1958; The City in the World Economy, 1965; Private Enterprise in Developing Countries, 1966; (ed, as Director of Studies) Britain's Invisible Earnings, 1967; (with George Pulay) The World's Money, 1970; Inside the City, 1979, rev. edn 1983; How the City of London Works, 1986, rev. edn 1988; The Secret Life of Wilkie Collins, 1988; Planning for Europe: 1992, 1989. *Recreations:* books, theatre. *Address:* 37 Park Vista, Greenwich, SE10. *T:* 081–858 0979. *Club:* Reform.

CLARKE HALL, Denis; architect; President, Architectural Association, 1958–59; Chairman, Architects Registration Council of the UK, 1963–64; *b* 4 July 1910; *m* 1936, Mary Garfitt; one *s* two *d. Educ:* Bedales. Holds AA Dip. *Address:* Moorhouse, Iping, Midhurst, W Sussex.

CLARKSON, Ven. Alan Geoffrey; Archdeacon of Winchester since 1984; Vicar of Burley, Ringwood, since 1984; *b* 14 Feb. 1934; *s* of Instructor Captain Geoffrey Archibald Clarkson, OBE, RN and Essie Isabel Bruce Clarkson; *m* 1959, Monica Ruth (*née* Lightburne); two *s* one *d. Educ:* Sherborne School; Christ's Coll., Cambridge (BA 1957, MA 1961); Wycliffe Hall, Oxford. Nat. Service Commn, RA, 1952–54. Curate: Penn, Wolverhampton, 1959–60; St Oswald's, Oswestry, 1960–63; Wrington with Redhill, 1963–65; Vicar, Chewton Mendip with Emborough, 1965–74; Vicar of St John Baptist, Glastonbury with Godney, 1974–84; Priest in Charge: West Pennard, 1981–84; Meare, 1981–84; St Benedict, Glastonbury, 1982–84. Proctor in Convocation, 1970–75, 1990–. Hon. Canon, Winchester Cathedral, 1984. *Recreations:* music, gardening, carpentry, wood-turning. *Address:* The Vicarage, Church Corner, Burley, Ringwood BH24 4AP. *T:* Burley (04253) 2303.

CLARKSON, Prof. Brian Leonard, DSc; FEng 1986; Principal, University College of Swansea, since 1982; Vice-Chancellor, University of Wales, 1987–89; *b* 28 July 1930; *s* of L. C. Clarkson; *m* 1953, Margaret Elaine Wilby; three *s* one *d. Educ:* Univ. of Leeds (BSc, PhD; Hon. DSc 1984). FRAeS; Fellow, Soc. of Environmental Engineers; FInst Acoustics. George Taylor Gold Medal, RAeS, 1963. Dynamics Engineer, de Havilland Aircraft Co., Hatfield, Herts, 1953–57; Southampton University: Sir Alan Cobham Research Fellow, Dept of Aeronautics, 1957–58; Lectr, Dept of Aeronautics and Astronautics, 1958–66; Prof. of Vibration Studies, 1966–82; Dir, Inst. of Sound and Vibration Res., 1967–78; Dean, Faculty of Engrg and Applied Science, 1978–80; Deputy Vice-Chancellor, 1980–82. Sen. Post Doctoral Research Fellow, Nat. Academy of Sciences, USA, 1970–71 (one year's leave of absence from Southampton). Vice-Chm., ACU, 1990–. Sec., Internat. Commn on Acoustics, 1975–81. Pres., Fedn of Acoustical Socs of Europe, 1982–84. Member: SERC, 1984–88; CNAA, 1988–. Hon. DSc: Southampton, 1987; Universiti Sains Malaysia, 1990. *Publications:* author of sections of three books: Technical Acoustics, vol. 3 (ed Richardson) 1959; Noise and Acoustic Fatigue in Aeronautics (ed Mead and Richards), 1967; Noise and Vibration (ed White and Walker), 1982; (ed) Stochastic Problems in Dynamics, 1977; technical papers on Jet Noise and its effect on Aircraft Structures, Jl of Royal Aeronautical Soc., etc. *Recreations:* walking, gardening, travelling, golf. *Address:* University College of Swansea, Singleton Park, Swansea SA2 8PP. *T:* Swansea (0792) 295154.

CLARKSON, Derek Joshua; QC 1969; **His Honour Judge Clarkson;** a Circuit Judge, since 1977; Middlesex Liaison Judge, since 1985; *b* 10 Dec. 1929; *o s* of Albert and Winifred Charlotte Clarkson (*née* James); *m* 1960, Peternella Marie-Luise Ilse Canenbley; one *s* one *d. Educ:* Pudsey Grammar Sch.; King's Coll., Univ. of London. LLB (1st cl. Hons) 1950. Called to Bar, Inner Temple, 1951; Nat. Service, RAF, 1952–54 (Flt Lt). In practice as Barrister, 1954–77; Prosecuting Counsel to Post Office on North-Eastern Circuit, 1961–65; Prosecuting Counsel to Inland Revenue on North-Eastern Circuit, 1965–69; Recorder of Rotherham, 1967–71; Recorder of Huddersfield, 1971; a Recorder of the Crown Court, 1972–77. Mem., Gen. Council of the Bar, 1971–73. Inspector of companies for the Department of Trade, 1972–73, 1975–76. *Recreations:* theatre-going, walking, book collecting. *Address:* Millbank Court, 24 John Islip Street, Westminster, SW1; 72A Cornwall Road, Harrogate, N Yorks.

CLARKSON, Prof. Geoffrey Peniston Elliott, PhD; Professor of Business Administration, since 1980, and Dean, College of Business Administration, since 1977, Northeastern University, Boston; Visiting Professor, Sloan School of Management, Massachusetts Institute of Technology, since 1975; *b* 30 May 1934; *s* of George Elliott Clarkson and Alice Helene (*née* Manneberg); *m* 1960, Eleanor M. (*née* Micenko); two *d. Educ:* Carnegie-Mellon Univ., Pittsburgh, Pa (BSc, MSc, PhD). Asst Prof., Sloan Sch. of Management, MIT, 1961–65, Associate Prof., 1965–67. Vis. Ford Foundn Fellow, Carnegie-Mellon Univ., 1965–66; Vis. Prof., LSE, 1966–67; Nat. Westminster Bank Prof. of Business Finance, Manchester Business Sch., Univ. of Manchester, 1967–77. Dir of and consultant to public and private manufng and financial services cos, 1969–. *Publications:* Portfolio Selection: a simulation of trust investment, USA 1962 (Ford Dissertation Prize, 1961); The Theory of Consumer Demand: a critical appraisal, USA 1963; Managerial Economics, 1968; (with B. J. Elliott) Managing Money and Finance, 1969 (3rd edn 1982); Jihad, 1981. *Recreations:* fishing, sailing, reading. *Address:* PO Box 1600, Waltham, Mass 02254, USA. *Club:* Royal Automobile.

CLARKSON, Gerald Dawson, CBE 1990; QFSM 1983; Chief Fire Officer and Chief Executive, London Fire and Civil Defence Authority, 1987–91, retired; *b* 4 June 1939; *s* of Alexander Dickie Clarkson and Agnes Tierney Price; *m* 1959, Rose Lilian Hodgson; one *s* one *d. Educ:* Westminster Technical Coll.; Polytechnic of Central London (BA Hons). FIMS, FBIM, FRSH. Served Royal Engineers, 1960–61. Joined London Fire Bde, 1961; Dep. Chief Officer, 1983; Reg. Fire Comdr No 5, Greater London Region, 1987–91. Member: Central Fire Bdes Adv. Council, 1987–91; Fire Service Central Examinations Bd, 1987–; Adviser: Nat. Jt Council for Local Authorities Fire Bdes, 1987–; Assoc. of Metropolitan Authorities, 1987–91; Chm., Fedn of British Fire Orgns, 1990–91; Dir, Nat. Fire Protection Assoc., USA, 1990–; President: London Fire Brigade Widows' and Orphans' Friendly Soc., 1987–91; Commonwealth and Overseas Fire Service Assoc., 1990–. Ext. Examr for Govt, Singapore Fire Service, 1990–. Freeman, City of London, 1985; Founder Master, Guild of Firefighters, 1988. OStJ 1989 (Mem., London Dist Council, 1987–). Hon. FIFireE, 1989. *Recreations:* reading, golf, sailing, fishing. *Address:* Oldfield Lodge, Oldfield Road, Bickley, Bromley, Kent BR1 2LE. *Club:* East India.

CLARKSON, Patrick Robert James; QC 1991; *b* 1 Aug. 1949; *s* of Commander Robert Anthony Clarkson, LVO, RN and Sheelagh Clarissa Neale; *m* 1975, Bridget Cecilia Doyne; two *s* one *d. Educ:* Winchester. Called to the Bar, Lincoln's Inn, 1972. *Recreations:* cricket, motor racing, literature, country. *Address:* 1 Serjeants Inn, EC4Y 1NH. *T:* 071–583 1355.

CLARKSON, Dr Peter David; Executive Secretary, Scientific Committee on Antarctic Research, since 1989; *b* 19 June 1945; *s* of Maurice Roland Clarkson and Jessie Yoxall (*née* Baker); *m* 1974, Rita Margaret Skinner; one *d. Educ:* Epsom Coll.; Univ. of Durham (BSc 1967); Univ. of Birmingham (PhD 1977). FGS 1980. Geologist with British Antarctic Survey, 1967–89: wintered in Antarctica, Halley Bay, 1968 and 1969; Base Comdr, 1969; Antarctic field seasons in Shackleton Range (leader 3 times), 1968–78; in S Shetland Is, 1974–75; in Antarctic Peninsula, 1985–86 (leader). UK adviser to PROANTAR, Brazil, 1982. Hon. Sec., Trans-Antarctic Assoc., 1980–. Polar Medal, 1976. *Publications:* articles on Antarctic geology. *Recreations:* walking, woodwork, photography, music, all matters Antarctic. *Address:* Scott Polar Research Institute, Lensfield Road, Cambridge CB2 1ER. *T:* Cambridge (0223) 62061; 35 King's Grove, Barton, Cambridge CB3 7AZ. *T:* Cambridge (0223) 263417. *Club:* Antarctic.

CLARRICOATS, Prof. Peter John Bell, FRS 1990; FEng; Professor of Electronic Engineering, Queen Mary and Westfield (formerly Queen Mary) College, University of London, since 1968, and Head of Department, since 1979; *b* 6 April 1932; *s* of John Clarricoats and Cecilia (*née* Bell); *m* 1st, 1955, Gillian (*née* Hall) (marr. diss. 1962); one *s* one *d*; 2nd, 1968, Phyllis Joan (*née* Lloyd); two *d* one step *s* one step *d. Educ:* Minchenden Grammar Sch.; Imperial College. BSc (Eng), PhD, DSc (Eng) 1968; FInstP 1964, FIEE 1967, FIEEE 1967, FCGI 1980, FEng 1983. Scientific Staff, GEC, 1953–58; Lectr, Queen's Univ. Belfast, 1959–62; Sheffield Univ., 1962–63; Prof. of Electronic Engineering, Univ. of Leeds, 1963–67. Mem., Governing Body, QMC, 1976–79, Dean of Engineering, 1977–80. Chm., British Nat. Cttee for Radio Sci., 1985. Chairman: 1st Internat. Conf. on Antennas and Propagation, IEE, 1978; European Microwave Conf., 1979; Mil. Microwaves Conf., 1988. Distinguished Lectr, IEEE, 1987–88. Institution of Electrical Engineers: Mem. Council, 1964–67, 1977–80; Chm., Electronics Div., 1978–79; awards: Premia, Electronics Section, 1960, 1961; Marconi, 1974; Coopers Hill Meml Prize, 1964; IEEE Cert. of Appreciation, EUREL European Microwave Prize, IEE Measurement Prize, J. J. Thomson Medal, IEE, 1989. Co-Editor, Electronics Letters (IEE Jl), 1964–. *Publications:* Microwave Ferrites, 1960; (with A.D. Olver) Corrugated Horns for Microwave Antennas, 1984; papers on antennas and waveguides. *Recreations:* music, photography, formerly squash and mountaineering. *Address:* 7 Falcon Close, Sawbridgeworth, Herts CM21 0AX. *T:* Bishop's Stortford (0279) 723561.

CLATWORTHY, Robert, RA 1973 (ARA 1968); sculptor; *b* 31 Jan. 1928; *s* of E. W. and G. Clatworthy; *m* 1954, Pamela Gordon (marr. diss.); two *s* one *d*. *Educ:* Dr Morgan's Grammar Sch., Bridgwater. Studied West of England Coll. of Art, Chelsea Sch. of Art, The Slade. Teacher, West of England Coll. of Art, 1967–71. Visiting Tutor, RCA, 1960–72; Mem., Fine Art Panel of Nat. Council for Diplomas in Art and Design, 1961–72; Governor, St Martin's Sch. of Art, 1970–71; Head of Dept of Fine Art, Central Sch. of Art and Design, 1971–75. Exhibited: Hanover Gall., 1954, 1956; Waddington Galls, 1965; Holland Park Open Air Sculpture, 1957; Battersea Park Open Air Sculpture, 1960, 1963; Tate Gallery, British Sculpture in the Sixties, 1965; British Sculptors 1972, Burlington House; Basil Jacobs Fine Art Ltd, 1972; Diploma Galls, Burlington Ho., 1977; Photographers Gall., 1980; Quinton Green Fine Art, London, 1986; British Sculpture 1950–65, New Art Centre, 1986; Chapman Gall., (now Keith Chapman), 1988, 1989, 1990; Austin Desmond Fine Art, 1991. Work in Collections: Arts Council, Contemporary Art Soc., Tate Gallery, Victoria and Albert Museum, Greater London Council, Nat. Portrait Gall. (portrait of Dame Elisabeth Frink, 1985). Monumental Horse and Rider, Finsbury Avenue, London, 1984. *Address:* Moelfre, Cynghordy, Llandovery, Dyfed SA20 0UW. *T:* Llandovery (0550) 20201. *Club:* Chelsea Arts.

CLAUSEN, Alden Winship, (Tom); Chairman and Chief Executive, BankAmerica Corporation, 1986–90; Director, Wellcome plc, since 1986; *b* 17 Feb. 1923; *s* of Morton and Elsie Clausen; *m* 1950, Mary Margaret Crassweller; two *s*. *Educ:* Carthage Coll. (BA 1944); Univ. of Minnesota (LLB 1949); Grad. Harvard Advanced Management Program, 1966. Admitted to Minnesota Bar, 1949. Joined Bank of America, 1949: Vice-Pres., 1961–65; Sen. Vice-Pres., 1965–68; Exec. Vice-Pres., 1968–69; Vice-Chm. of Bd, 1969; Pres. and Chief Exec. Officer, 1970–81; Pres., The World Bank, 1981–86. President: Fed. Adv. Council, 1972; Internat. Monetary Conf., Amer. Bankers' Assoc., 1977. Former Director: US-USSR Trade and Econ. Council, 1974–81; Nat. Council for US-China Trade, 1974–81; Co-Chm., Japan-California Assoc., 1973–80. Hon. LLD: Carthage, 1970; Lewis and Clark, 1978; Gonzaga Univ., 1978; Univ. of Notre Dame, 1981; Hon. DPS Univ. Santa Clara, 1981. *Address:* c/o BankAmerica Corporation, PO Box 37000, San Francisco, Calif 94137, USA.

CLAVELL, James; author, screenwriter, film director and producer; *s* of late Comdr R. C. Clavell, OBE, RN and Eileen Ross Clavell; *m* 1953, April, *d* of late Comdr W. S. Stride, DSO, RN; two *d*. *Educ:* Portsmouth Grammar Sch. Served World War II, Captain, RA; POW Far East, 1941–45. Emigrated to USA, 1953. Screenwriter: The Fly, 1958; Watussi, 1958; The Great Escape, 1960; Satan Bug, 1962; 633 Squadron, 1963; director, Where's Jack?, 1968; writer/producer/director: Five Gates to Hell, 1959; Walk Like a Dragon, 1960; To Sir with Love, 1966; Last Valley, 1969; Children's Story . . . But Not for Children, 1982; exec. producer, Shōgun (TV series), 1980 (Emmy, Peabody, Critics, Golden Globe Awards, 1981) (musical, 1990); Noble House, 1986. Pilot: Multi-engine, Instrument Rating, Helicopter. Hon. DLitt: Maryland, 1980; Bradford, 1986. Goldener Eiger (Austria), 1972. *Publications:* King Rat, 1962; Tai-Pan, 1966; Shōgun, 1976; Noble House, 1980; The Children's Story but not for Children (novella), 1982; (forward to) Sun Tsu; The Art of War, 1983; Thrump-O-moto (fantasy), 1985; Whirlwind, 1986. *Address:* c/o Foreign Rights, Inc., 136 E 57th Street, New York, NY 10022, USA.

CLAXTON, Rt. Rev. Charles Robert, MA, DD; *b* 16 Nov. 1903; *s* of Herbert Bailey and Frances Ann Claxton; *m* 1930, Agnes Jane Stevenson; two *s* two *d*. *Educ:* Monkton Combe Sch.; Weymouth Coll.; Queen's Coll., Cambridge. Deacon, 1927; Priest, 1928; Curate, St John's, Stratford, E15, 1927–29; St John, Redhill, 1929–33; St Martin-in-the-Fields, 1944–46; Vicar Holy Trinity, Bristol, 1933–38; Hon. Canon of Bristol Cathedral, 1942–46; Hon. Chaplain to Bishop of Bristol, 1938–46; Hon. Chaplain to Bishop of Rochester, 1943–46; Rector of Halsall, near Ormskirk, Lancs, 1948–59; Suffragan Bishop of Warrington, 1946–60; Bishop of Blackburn, 1960–71; Asst Bishop, dio. of Exeter, 1972–89. Hon. Officiating Chaplain, RN, 1978. *Recreation:* golf. *Address:* St Martins, 18 Prestbury Park, Collar House Drive, Prestbury, Cheshire SK10 4AP. *T:* Prestbury (0625) 829864.

CLAXTON, Maj.-Gen. Patrick Fisher, CB 1972; OBE 1946; General Manager, Regular Forces Employment Association, 1971–81; *b* 13 March 1915; *s* of late Rear-Adm. Ernest William Claxton and Kathleen O'Callaghan Claxton, formerly Fisher; *m* 1941, Jóna Gudrún Gunnarsdóttir (*d* 1980); two *d*. *Educ:* Sutton Valence Sch.; St John's Coll., Cambridge (BA). Served GHQ, India, 1943–45; Singapore, 1945–46; WO, 1946–48; British Element Trieste Force, 1949–51; HQ, BAOR, 1952–54; RASC Officers' Sch., 1955–56; Amphibious Warfare HQ and Persian Gulf, 1957–58; Col, WO, 1959–60; Brig., WO, 1961–62; DST, BAOR, 1963–65; CTO, BAOR, 1965–66; Comdt, Sch. of Transport, and ADC to the Queen, 1966–68; Transport Officer-in-Chief (Army), 1969–71, retired; Col. Comdt, RCT, 1972–80. Governor and Mem. Administrative Bd, Corps of Commissionaires, 1977–90. FCIT. *Publication:* The Regular Forces Employment Association 1885–1985, 1985. *Address:* The Lodge, Beacon Hill Park, Hindhead, Surrey GU26 6HU. *T:* Hindhead (0428) 604437. *Club:* MCC.

CLAY, His Honour John Lionel, TD 1961; a Circuit Judge, 1977–88; *b* 31 Jan. 1918; *s* of Lionel Pilleau Clay and Mary Winifred Muriel Clay; *m* 1952, Elizabeth, *d* of Rev. Canon Maurice and Lady Phyllis Ponsonby; one *s* three *d*. *Educ:* Harrow Sch.; Corpus Christi Coll., Oxford (MA). Served War of 1939–45 (despatches): in 1st Bn Rifle Bde, N Africa (8th Army), Italy, 1941–44; Instr, Infantry Heavy Weapons Sch., 1944–45; 1st Bn Rifle Bde, Germany, 1945–46. London Rifle Bde Rangers (TA); Major, 2nd i/c Bn and 23 SAS (TA), 1948–60. Called to the Bar, Middle Temple, 1947; a Recorder of the Crown Court, 1975–76. Chm., Horserace Betting Levy Appeal Tribunal for England and Wales, 1974–77. Freeman of City of London, 1980; Liveryman, Gardeners' Co., 1980. *Recreations:* gardening, fishing. *Address:* Newtimber Place, Hassocks, Sussex BN6 9BU.

CLAY, John Martin; Deputy Chairman: Hambros plc, 1986–90 (Director, since 1970); Hambros Bank Ltd, 1972–84 (Director, 1961–84); *b* 20 Aug. 1927; *s* of late Sir Henry Clay and Gladys Priestman Clay; *m* 1952, Susan Jennifer, *d* of Lt-Gen. Sir Euan Miller, KCB, KBE, DSO, MC; four *s*. *Educ:* Eton; Magdalen Coll., Oxford. Chairman: Johnson & Firth Brown Ltd, 1973–; Hambro Life Assurance Ltd, 1978–84. Dir, Bank of England, 1973–83. Mem., Commonwealth Develt Corp., 1970–88. FBIM 1971. *Recreation:* sailing. *Club:* Royal Thames Yacht.

CLAY, Prof. Dame Marie (Mildred), DBE 1987; Professor of Education, University of Auckland, New Zealand, 1975–91, now Emeritus, and Head of Department of Education, 1975–78 and 1986–88; *b* 3 Jan. 1926; *d* of Donald Leolin Irwin and Mildred Blanche Irwin (*née* Godier); *m* 1951, Warwick Victor Clay; one *s* one *d*. *Educ:* Wellington East Girls' College; Wellington Teachers' College; Univ. of New Zealand (MA Hons, DipEd); Univ. of Minnesota; Univ of Auckland (PhD). Teacher Training, 1943–45; Teacher of Retarded Children, 1945; Asst Psychologist, 1948–50; Fulbright Scholar, Univ. of Minnesota, 1950–51; Teacher, 1953–54; Psychologist, 1955–59; University of Auckland: Univ. Lectr, 1960–67; Sen. Lectr, 1968–72; Associate Prof., 1973–74. Distinguished Vis. Prof., Ohio State Univ., 1984–85; Vis. Fellow, Wolfson Coll., Oxford, 1987–88; George A. Miller Vice-Prof., Univ. of Illinois, 1991. Pres.-elect, Internat. Reading Assoc., 1991–92. FNZPsS 1978; Hon. FNZEI 1976. Mackie Medal, ANZAAS, 1983. *Publications:* What Did I Write, 1975; Reading: the patterning of complex behaviour, 1972, 2nd edn 1979; The Early Detection of Reading Difficulties, 1972, 3rd edn 1985; Children of Parents Who Separate, 1978; Reading Begins at Home, 1979; Observing Young Readers, 1982; Round About Twelve, 1983; Writing Begins at Home, 1987; Quadruplets and Higher Multiple Births, 1989; Becoming Literate: the Construction of Inner Control, 1991. *Address:* Flat 4, 153 Bassett Road, Auckland 5, New Zealand. *T:* (064) (09) 547–047.

CLAY, Sir Richard (Henry), 7th Bt *cr* 1841, of Fulwell Lodge, Middlesex; *b* 2 June 1940; *s* of Sir Henry Felix Clay, 6th Bt, and of Phyllis Mary, *yr d* of late R. H. Paramore, MD, FRCS; *S* father, 1985; *m* 1963, Alison Mary, *d* of Dr James Gordon Fife; three *s* two *d*. *Educ:* Eton. FCA 1966. *Recreation:* sailing. *Heir:* *s* Charles Richard Clay, *b* 18 Dec. 1965. *Address:* The Copse, Shiplate Road, Bleadon, Avon BS24 0NX. *Club:* Aldeburgh Yacht.

CLAY, Robert Alan; MP (Lab) Sunderland North, since 1983; *b* 2 Oct. 1946; *m* 1980, Uta Christa. *Educ:* Bedford Sch.; Gonville and Caius Coll., Cambridge. Busdriver, Tyne and Wear PTE, 1975–83. Branch Chm., GMBATU, 1977–83. Treas., 1983–86, Sec., 1986–87, Campaign Gp of Labour MPs. *Recreations:* walking, reading. *Address:* (constituency office) 7 Bridge House, Bridge Street, Sunderland SR1 1TE. *T:* 091–567 8878; 12 Park Parade, Roker, Sunderland, Tyne and Wear; House of Commons, SW1A 0AA. *T:* 071–219 6230.

CLAY, Trevor, CBE 1990; MPhil; SRN, RMN; FRCN; General Secretary of the Royal College of Nursing of the United Kingdom, 1982–89 (Deputy General Secretary, 1979–82); *b* 10 May 1936; *s* of Joseph Reginald George and Florence Emma Clay. *Educ:* Nuneaton and Bethlem Royal and Maudsley Hosps. (SRN 1957; RMN 1960); MPhil Brunel Univ. 1976. FRCN 1985. Staff Nurse and Charge Nurse, Guy's Hosp., London, 1960–65; Asst Matron in charge of Psychiatric Unit, Queen Elizabeth II Hosp., Welwyn Garden City, 1965–67; Asst Regional Nursing Officer, NW Metropolitan Regional Hosp. Board, 1967–69; Director of Nursing, Whittington Hosp., London, 1969–70; Chief Nursing Officer, N London Group HMC, 1970–74; Area Nursing Officer, Camden and Islington Area Health Authority, 1974–79. Lay Mem., Employment Appeal Tribunal, 1991–. Advr, IHSM Consultants, 1989–. First Vice-Pres., Internat. Council of Nurses, 1989– (Mem. Bd, 1985–89); Chm., Bd of Management, Portsmouth and RN Sch. of Nursing, 1991–; Member: Council, Royal Nat. Pension Fund for Nurses, 1989–; Council, British Lung Foundn, 1989–; Council of Management, London Lighthouse, 1989–; Council of Management, Inst. of Nursing, Oxford, 1989–. Pres., Breath Easy, 1991–. Hon. DArt Bristol Polytechnic, 1990. *Publications:* Nurses: power and politics, 1987; thesis on The Workings of the Nursing and Midwifery Advisory Committees in the NHS since 1974; various articles on nursing and health care. *Recreations:* breathing, good friends, Mozart and Sondheim. *Address:* c/o The Royal College of Nursing, 20 Cavendish Square, W1M 0AB.

CLAYDON, Geoffrey Bernard, CB 1990; Assistant Treasury Solicitor, Department of Transport, since 1990; *b* 14 Sept. 1930; *s* of Bernard Claydon and Edith Mary (*née* Lucas); unmarried. *Educ:* Leeds Modern; King Edward's, Birmingham; Birmingham Univ. (LLB). Articled at Pinsent & Co., Birmingham, 1950; admitted Solicitor, 1954. Legal Asst, 1959, Sen. Legal Asst, 1965, Treasury Solicitor's Dept; Asst Solicitor, DTI, 1973; Asst Treasury Solicitor, 1974; Principal Asst Treasury Solicitor and Legal Advr, Dept of Energy, 1980. Mem., Editorial Bd, Jl of Energy and Natural Resources Law, 1983–90. Sec., National Tramway Museum, 1958–84 (Vice-Chm., 1969–); Vice-Pres., Light Rail Transit Assoc. (formerly Light Railway Transport League), 1968– (Chm. of League, 1963–68); Chairman: Tramway and Light Railway Soc., 1967–; Consultative Panel for Preservation of British Transport Relics, 1982–; Mem., Inst. of Transport Admin, 1972–. *Recreations:* rail transport, travel. *Address:* 23 Baron's Keep, W14 9AT. *T:* 071–603 6400. *Club:* Royal Automobile.

CLAYMAN, David; Managing Director, Esso UK plc, since 1986; *b* 28 May 1934; *s* of Maurice and Nancy Clayman; *m* 1956, Patricia Moore; two *s*. *Educ:* Purley Grammar Sch.; University College London (BSc Chem. Engrg). Joined Esso Petroleum Co., 1956; Supply Manager, London, 1966–67, Esso Europe Inc., 1970–71; Marketing Div. Dir, 1971–79; Exec. Asst to Chm., Exxon Corp., 1979–80; Dir, Esso Petroleum Co., 1982, 1986–; Pres., Esso Africa Inc., 1983–85; Director: Esso Europe Inc., 1985; Esso Exploration and Production UK, 1986–; Esso Pension Trust, 1986–; Mainline Pipeline, 1986–. Vice-Pres., 1987–88, Pres., 1988–, UKPIA; Director: GCBS, 1986–87; Foundn for Management Educn, 1986–. *Recreation:* golf. *Address:* Esso House, Victoria Street, SW1E 5JW. *T:* 071–245 3788. *Club:* Burhill Golf.

CLAYSON, Christopher William, CBE 1974 (OBE 1966); retired; *b* 11 Sept. 1903; *s* of Christopher Clayson and Agnes Lilias Montgomerie Hunter; *m* 1st, 1933, Elsie Webster Breingan; 2nd, 1988, Anne Dorothy Miller or Middlemiss. *Educ:* George Heriot's Sch.; Edinburgh University. MB, ChB 1926; DPH 1929; MD (Gold Medal) Edinburgh 1936; FRCPE 1951; FRCP 1967. Physician: Southfield Hosp., Edinburgh, 1931–44; Edinburgh City Hosp., 1939–44; Lectr in Tuberculosis Dept, Univ. of Edinburgh, 1939–44; Med. Supt, Lochmaben Hosp., 1944–48; Consultant Phys. in Chest Medicine, Dumfries and Galloway, 1948–68; retd from clinical practice, 1968. Served on numerous Govt and Nat. Health Service cttees, 1948–; Chairman: Scottish Licensing Law Cttee, 1971–73; Scottish Council for Postgrad. Med. Educn, 1970–74. Pres., RCPE, 1966–70; Mem., Scottish Soc. of Physicians; Mem., Thoracic Soc.; Hon. FACP 1968; Hon. FRACP 1969; Hon. FRCPGlas 1970; Hon. FRCGP 1971; Hon. FRCPE 1990. William Cullen Prize, RCPE, 1978. *Publications:* various papers on tuberculosis problem and on alcoholism in leading medical jls. *Recreations:* gardening, fishing. *Address:* Cockiesknowe, Lochmaben, Lockerbie, Dumfriesshire. *T:* Lochmaben (0387) 810231. *Clubs:* Caledonian; New (Edinburgh).

CLAYTON, Prof. Dame Barbara (Evelyn), (Dame Barbara Klyne), DBE 1988 (CBE 1983); MD, PhD; FRCP, FRCPath; Hon. Research Professor in Metabolism, Faculty of Medicine, University of Southampton, since 1987 (Professor of Chemical Pathology and Human Metabolism, 1979–87, and Dean of the Faculty of Medicine 1983–86); *b* 2 Sept. 1922; *m* 1949, William Klyne; one *s* one *d*. *Educ:* Univ. of Edinburgh (MD, PhD). FRCP 1972; FRCPath 1971; FRCPE 1985. Consultant in Chem. Pathology, Hosp. for Sick Children, London, 1959–70; Prof. of Chem. Pathology, Inst. of Child Health, Univ. of London, 1970–78. Hon Consultant, 1979–, Mem., 1983–87, Southampton and SW Hants HA. Member: Commonwealth Scholarship Commn, 1977–; Royal Commn on Environmental Pollution, 1981–; Standing Med. Adv. Cttee (DHSS), 1981–87; Cttee on Toxicity of Chemicals in Food, Consumer Products and the Environment, DoH (formerly DHSS), 1977–; Systems Bd, MRC, 1974–77; British Nat. Cttee on Problems of the Environment, 1988–89; Council, British Nutrition Foundn, 1987–; WHO Expert Adv. Panel on Nutrition, 1988–; Chairman: Adv. Cttee on Borderline Substances, 1971–83; MRC Adv. Gp on Lead and Neuropsychol Effects in Children, 1983–; Cttee on Med. Aspects of Contaminants in Air, Soil and Water, 1984–; Standing Cttee on Postgrad. Med. Educn, 1988–; Med. and Scientific Panel, Leukaemia Res. Fund, 1989–; MRC Cttee on Toxic Hazards in the Workplace and the Environment, 1989–. Council, RCPath, 1982–(Pres., 1984–87); GMC, 1983–87. President: Assoc. of

Clinical Biochemists, 1977, 1978; Soc. for Study of Inborn Errors of Metabolism, 1981–82; Biomedical Scis Sect., BAAS, 1989–90; British Dietetic Assoc., 1989–. Member: Bd of Govs, Hosps for Sick Children, London, 1968–78; Scientific Adv. Cttee, Assoc. of Med. Res. Charities, 1990–. Hon. Member: BPA, 1987; Soc. for Study of Inborn Errors of Metabolism, 1988; Assoc. of Clinical Biochemists, 1990; Corresponding Mem., Gesellschaft für Laboratoriumsmedizin, 1990. Hon. Fellow: British Dietetic Assoc., 1976; Faculty of Pathology, RCPI, 1986; Amer. Soc. of Clin. Pathologists, 1987. Hon. DSc Edinburgh, 1985. Jessie MacGregor Prize for Med. Sci., RCPE, 1985; Wellcome Prize, Assoc. of Clin. Biochemists, 1988. *Publications:* contrib. learned jls, incl. Jl Endocrinol., Arch. Dis. Childhood, and BMJ. *Recreations:* natural history, walking. *Address:* 16 Chetwynd Drive, Bassett, Southampton SO2 3HZ. *T:* Southampton (0703) 769937.

CLAYTON, Captain Sir David (Robert), 12th Bt *cr* 1732, of Marden; Shipmaster since 1970; *b* 12 Dec. 1936; *s* of Sir Arthur Harold Clayton, 11th Bt, DSC, and of Alexandra, Lady Clayton, *d* of late Sergei Andreevsky; *S* father, 1985; *m* 1971, Julia Louise, *d* of late Charles Henry Redfearn; two *s. Educ:* HMS Conway. Joined Merchant Service, 1953; promoted to first command as Captain, 1970. *Recreations:* shooting, sailing. *Heir:* *s* Robert Philip Clayton, *b* 8 July 1975. *Address:* Rock House, Kingswear, Dartmouth, Devon TQ6 0BX. *T:* Kingswear (080425) 433. *Club:* Royal Dart Yacht (Kingswear).

CLAYTON, Prof. Frederick William; Professor of Classics, 1948–75, and Public Orator, 1965–73, University of Exeter; *b* 13 Dec. 1913; *s* of late William and Gertrude Clayton, Liverpool; *m* 1948, Friederike Luise Büttner-Wobst; two *s* two *d. Educ:* Liverpool Collegiate Sch.; King's Coll., Cambridge. Members' Essay Prizes (Latin and English), Porson Prize, Browne Medal, 1933; Craven Scholar in Classics, 1934; Chancellor's Medal for Classics, 1935; Fellow of King's Coll., 1937. Served War, Nov. 1940–Oct. 1946, Signals, Field Security, RAF Intelligence, India. *Publications:* The Cloven Pine, 1942; various articles. *Address:* Halwill, Clydesdale Road, Exeter, Devon. *T:* Exeter (0392) 71810.

  See also G. Clayton.

CLAYTON, Air Marshal Sir Gareth (Thomas Butler), KCB 1970 (CB 1962); DFC 1940, and Bar, 1944; Air Secretary, Ministry of Defence, 1970–72, retired; *b* 13 Nov. 1914; *s* of Thomas and Katherine Clayton; *m* 1938, Elisabeth Marian Keates; three *d. Educ:* Rossall Sch. Entered RAF, 1936; served in various Bomber and Fighter Squadrons, 1936–44; RAF Staff Coll., 1944; Air Attaché, Lisbon, 1946–48; various command and staff appts, 1948–58; idc 1959; Air Ministry, 1960–61; Air Officer Commanding No. 11 Group, RAF, 1962–63; Chief of Staff, Second Allied Tactical Air Force, Germany, 1963–66; Dir-Gen., RAF Personal Services, 1966–69; Chief of Staff, HQ RAF Strike Command, 1969–70. Life Vice-Pres., RAFA (Chm., 1978–80). *Address:* Polstead, near Colchester CO6 5AD. *Club:* Royal Air Force.

CLAYTON, Prof. George; Newton Chambers Professor of Applied Economics, University of Sheffield, 1967–83, Pro-Vice-Chancellor, 1978–82, now Emeritus Professor; Partner, Clayton and Law, economic and financial consultants, since 1988; *b* 15 July 1922; *s* of late William Clayton and late Gertrude Alison Clarke Clayton; *m* 1948, Rhiannon Jones, JP; two *s* two *d. Educ:* Liverpool Collegiate Sch.; King's Coll., Cambridge. Served War of 1939–45: Pilot, RAF, 1941–45; Pilot, Fleet Air Arm, 1945, Acting Sqdn Ldr. Univ. of Liverpool: Asst Lectr, 1947–50; Lectr, 1950–57; Sen. Lectr, 1957–60 and 1961–63; Sen. Simon Res. Fellow, Univ. of Manchester, 1960–61; Prof. and Head of Dept of Econs, UCW Aberystwyth, 1963–67; Luis Olariaga Lectr, Madrid Univ., 1959; Special Univ. Lectr, London, 1970; Page Fund Lectr, UC Cardiff, 1970. Member: Council, Royal Econ. Soc., 1965–68; (part-time) East Midland Gas Bd, 1967–70; Crowther Cttee on Consumer Credit, 1968–70; Scott Cttee on Property Bonds and Equity-linked Insce, 1970–72; Econs Cttee, SSRC, 1978–82 (Vice-Chm., 1979–82). Non-exec. Dir, Pioneer Mutual Assurance Co., 1976–90; Consultant, Eastern Caribbean Central Bank, 1987–. Chm., British, Canadian and Amer. Mission to British Honduras, 1966; Econ. Adviser: Govt of Tanzania, 1965–66; Govt of Gibraltar, 1973–. Chm., Assoc. of Univ. Teachers of Economics, 1973–78. *Publications:* (contrib.) A New Prospect of Economics, ed G. L. S. Shackle, 1956; (contrib.) Banking in Western Europe, ed R. S. Sayers, 1959; Insurance Company Investment, 1965; Problems of Rail Transport in Rural Wales: Two Case Studies, 1967; Monetary Theory and Monetary Policy in the 1970s, 1971; British Insurance, 1971; articles in Econ. Jl, etc. *Recreations:* tennis, sailing, theatre, fell walking. *Address:* 108 Westbourne Road, Sheffield S10 2QT. *T:* Sheffield (0742) 681833. *Clubs:* Hawks (Cambridge); Sheffield (Sheffield).

  See also Prof. F. W. Clayton.

CLAYTON, Jack; film director; *b* 1921; *m* Christine Norden (marr. diss.); *m* Katherine Kath (marr. diss.). Entered film industry, 1935. Served War of 1939–45, RAF Film Unit. Production Manager: An Ideal Husband; Associate Producer: Queen of Spades; Flesh and Blood; Moulin Rouge; Beat the Devil; The Good Die Young; I am a Camera; Producer and Director: The Bespoke Overcoat, 1955; The Innocents, 1961; Our Mother's House, 1967; Director: Room at the Top, 1958; The Pumpkin Eater, 1964; The Great Gatsby, 1974; Something Wicked This Way Comes, 1983; The Lonely Passion of Judith Hearne, 1989. *Address:* c/o Batya Films, Heron's Flight, Highfield, Marlow, Bucks SL7 2LE.

CLAYTON, John Pilkington, CVO 1986 (LVO 1975); MA, MB, BChir; Apothecary to HM Household at Windsor, 1965–86; Surgeon Apothecary to HM Queen Elizabeth the Queen Mother's Household at the Royal Lodge, Windsor, 1965–86; Senior Medical Officer, Eton College, 1965–86 (MO, 1962–65); *b* 13 Feb. 1921; *s* of late Brig.-Gen. Sir Gilbert Clayton, KCMG, KBE, CB, and Enid, *d* of late F. N. Thorowgood. *Educ:* Wellington Coll.; Gonville and Caius Coll., Cambridge; King's Coll. Hospital. RAFVR, 1947–49; Sqdn Ldr 1949. Senior Resident, Nottingham Children's Hosp., 1950. MO, Black and Decker Ltd, 1955–70; MO, 1953–62, SMO 1962–81, Royal Holloway Coll. *Address:* Knapp House, Market Lavington, near Devizes, Wilts SN10 4DP.

CLAYTON, Prof. Keith Martin, CBE 1984; Professor of Environmental Sciences, since 1967 and Dean, School of Environmental Sciences, University of East Anglia; *b* 25 Sept. 1928; *s* of Edgar Francis Clayton and Constance Annie (*née* Clark); *m* 1st, 1950 (marr. diss. 1976); three *s* one *d*; 2nd, 1976. *Educ:* Bedales Sch.; Univ. of Sheffield (MSc). PhD London. Demonstrator, Univ. of Nottingham, 1949–51. Served RE, 1951–53. Lectr, London Sch. of Economics, 1953–63; Reader in Geography, LSE, 1963–67; Univ. of E Anglia: Founding Dean, Sch. of Environmental Scis, 1967–71; Pro-Vice-Chancellor, 1971–73; Dir, Centre of E Anglian Studies, 1974–81; Vis. Professor, State Univ. of New York at Binghamton, 1960–62. Member: Natural Environment Res. Council, 1970–73; UGC, 1973–84; Nat. Radiological Protection Bd, 1980–85; Nat. Adv. Bd for Local Authority Higher Educn, 1982–84; Cttee on Med. Aspects of Radiation in Environment, DHSS, 1985–; Envmt Cttee, MoD, 1990–. Pres., IBG, 1984. Patron's Medal, RGS, 1989. *Publications:* Editor and publisher, Geo Abstracts, 1960–85. *Recreations:* gardening, work. *Address:* Well Close, Pound Lane, Thorpe, Norwich NR7 0UA. *T:* Norwich (0603) 33780.

CLAYTON, Lucie; see Kark, Evelyn F.

CLAYTON, Margaret Ann; Under Secretary, Police Department, Home Office, since 1990; *b* 7 May 1941; *d* of late Percy Thomas Clayton and of Kathleen Clayton (*née* Payne). *Educ:* Christ's Hospital, Hertford; Birkbeck Coll., London (BA, MSc). Entered Home Office, 1960; Executive Officer/Asst Principal, 1960–67; Asst Private Secretary to Home Secretary, 1967–68; Principal, 1968–75 (seconded to Cabinet Office, 1972–73); Asst Sec., 1975–82; Asst Under Sec. of State, 1983; Dir of Services, Prison Service, 1986–90. Resident Chairman, Civil Service Selection Board, 1983. *Recreations:* equitation, gardening, theatre. *Club:* Reform.

CLAYTON, Michael Aylwin; Editor of Horse and Hound, since 1973; *b* 20 Nov. 1934; *s* of Aylwin Goff Clayton and late Norah (*née* Banfield); *m* 1st, 1959, Mary L. B. Watson (marr. diss.); one *s* one *d*; 2nd, 1979, Barbara Jane Ryman (*née* Whitfield) (marr. diss. 1988); 3rd, 1988, Marilyn Crowhurst (*née* Orrin). *Educ:* Bournemouth Grammar School. National Service, RAF, 1954–56. Reporter: Lymington Times and New Milton Advertiser, 1951–54; Portsmouth Evening News, 1956–57; London Evening News, 1957–61; reporter/feature writer, New Zealand Herald, 1961; reporter, London Evening Standard, 1961, Dep. News Editor, 1962–64; News Editor, Southern Ind. Television, 1964–65; staff correspondent, BBC TV and radio (incl. Vietnam, Cambodia, India, Pakistan and Middle East), 1965–73; Presenter, Today, BBC Radio 4, 1973–75. Chm., British Soc. of Magazine Editors, 1986. Mem., Press Complaints Commn, 1991–. *Publications:* A Hunting We Will Go, 1967; (with Dick Tracey) Hickstead—the First Twelve Years, 1972; (ed) The Complete Book of Showjumping, 1975; (ed) Cross-Country Riding, 1977; The Hunter, 1980; The Golden Thread, 1984; Prince Charles: horseman, 1987; The Chase: a modern guide to foxhunting, 1987. *Recreations:* foxhunting, music. *Address:* King's Reach Tower, Stamford Street, SE1 9LS.

CLAYTON, Michael Thomas Emilius, CB 1976; OBE 1958; *b* 15 Sept. 1917; *s* of Lt-Col Emilius Clayton, OBE, RA and Irene Dorothy Constance (*née* Strong); *m* 1942, Mary Margery Pate; one *d. Educ:* Bradfield College, Berks. Attached War Office, 1939 and Ministry of Defence, 1964–76. *Recreations:* philately, country pursuits generally. *Address:* Hillside Cottage, Marshwood, Bridport, Dorset DT6 5QF. *T:* Hawkchurch (02977) 452.

CLAYTON, Richard Henry Michael, (William Haggard); writer; *b* 11 Aug. 1907; *o s* of late Rev. Henry James Clayton and late Mabel Sarah Clayton (*née* Haggard); *m* 1936, Barbara, *e d* of late Edward Sant, Downton, Wilts; one *s* one *d. Educ:* Lancing; Christ Church, Oxford. Indian Civil Service, 1931–39; Indian Army, 1939–46 (GSO1 1943); BoT, 1947–69 (Controller of Enemy Property, 1965–69). *Publications:* Slow Burner, The Telemann Touch, 1958; Venetian Blind, 1959; Closed Circuit, 1960; The Arena, 1961; The Unquiet Sleep, 1962; The High Wire, 1963; The Antagonists, 1964; The Hard Sell, The Powder Barrel, 1965; The Power House, 1966; The Conspirators, The Haggard Omnibus, 1967; A Cool Day For Killing, 1968; The Doubtful Disciple, Haggard For Your Holiday, 1969; The Hardliners, 1970; The Bitter Harvest, 1971; The Protectors, 1972; The Little Rug Book (non-fiction), 1972; The Old Masters, 1973; The Kinsmen, 1974; The Scorpion's Tail, 1975; Yesterday's Enemy, 1976; The Poison People, 1977; Visa to Limbo, 1978; The Median Line, 1979; The Money Men, 1981; The Mischief Makers, 1982; The Heirloom, 1983; The Need to Know, 1984; The Meritocrats, 1985; The Martello Tower, 1986; The Diplomatist, 1987; The Expatriates, 1989; The Vendettists, 1990. *Address:* 3 Linkside, Frinton-on-Sea, Essex CO13 9EN. *Club:* Travellers'.

CLAYTON, Sir Robert (James), Kt 1980; CBE 1970 (OBE 1960); FEng, FInstP, FRAeS, FIEE, FIEEE; Technical Director, The General Electric Co. plc, 1968–83; GEC Director, 1978–83; *b* 30 Oct. 1915; *m* 1949, Joy Kathleen King; no *c. Educ:* Cambridge Univ. (Scholar, Christ's Coll.; MA; Hon. Fellow, 1983). GEC Research Labs, 1937; Manager, GEC Applied Electronics Labs, 1955; Dep. Dir, Hirst Research Centre, 1960; Man. Dir, GEC (Electronics), 1963; Man. Dir, GEC (Research), 1966. Member: Adv. Council for Applied R&D, 1976–80 (Chm. of Groups producing reports on Applications of Semiconductors, Computer Aided Design and Manufacture, and Inf. Technology); Adv. Council on R&D for Fuel and Power, 1976–83; NEB, 1978–80; Adv. Council, Science Mus., 1980–83, Trustee, 1984–90; British Library Bd, 1983–87; UGC, 1982–89; Monopolies and Mergers Commn, 1983–89; Chairman: Computer Systems and Electronics Requirements Bd, DoI, 1978–81; Open Technology Steering Gp, MSC, 1983–84; Policy Cttee, IT Skills Agency, 1985–88. Chm., Electronics Engrg Assoc., 1965; President: IEE, 1975–76 (Chm., Electronics Div., 1968–69); Inst. of Physics, 1982–84; Assoc. for Science Educn, 1983; IInfSc, 1985–86; Vice-President: Fellowship of Engineering, 1980–82; IERE, 1983–84. Vis. Prof., Electrical Engrg Dept, Imperial Coll. of Science and Technology, 1971–77; Lectures: IEE Faraday; CEI Graham Clarke; Christopher Hinton, Fellowship of Engineering. Hon. FIEE 1982. Hon. DSc: Aston, 1979; Salford, 1979; City, 1981; Oxon, 1988; Hon. DEng Bradford, 1985. *Publications:* The GEC Research Laboratories 1919–1984, 1989; (ed) A Scientist's War—the Diary of Sir Clifford Paterson, 1991; papers in Proc. IEE (premium awards). *Address:* c/o GEC Hirst Research Centre, East Lane, Wembley, Mddx. *T:* 081–908 9004. *Club:* United Oxford & Cambridge University.

CLAYTON, Prof. Robert Norman, FRS 1981; Professor, Departments of Chemistry and of the Geophysical Sciences, University of Chicago, since 1966; *b* 20 March 1930; *s* of Norman and Gwenda Clayton; *m* 1971, Cathleen Shelburne Clayton; one *d. Educ:* Queen's Univ., Canada (BSc, MSc); California Inst. of Technol. (PhD). Res. Fellow, Calif. Inst. of Technol., 1955–56; Asst Prof., Pennsylvania State Univ., 1956–58; University of Chicago: Asst Prof., 1958–62; Associate Prof., 1962–66. *Publications:* over 100 papers in geochemical journals. *Address:* 5201 South Cornell, Chicago, Ill 60615, USA. *T:* 312–643–2450.

CLAYTON, Stanley James; Town Clerk of the City of London 1974–82; *b* 10 Dec. 1919; *s* of late James John Clayton and late Florence Clayton; *m* 1955, Jean Winifred, *d* of late Frederick Etheridge; one *s* one *d. Educ:* Ensham Sch.; King's Coll., London (LLB). Served War of 1939–45, commnd RAF. Admitted Solicitor 1958. City of Westminster, 1938–52; Camberwell, 1952–60; Asst Solicitor, Holborn, 1960–63; Deputy Town Clerk: Greenwich, 1963–65; Islington, 1964–69; City of London, 1969–74. Comdr, Order of Dannebrog (Denmark); holds other foreign orders. *Address:* 27 Lakeside, Beckenham, Kent BR3 2LX. *Club:* Royal Air Force.

CLEALL, Charles; author; *b* 1 June 1927; *s* of Sydney Cleal and Dorothy Bound; *m* 1953, Mary, *yr d* of G. L. Turner, Archery Lodge, Ashford, Mddx; two *d. Educ:* Hampton Sch.; Univ. of London (BMus); Univ of Wales (MA); Jordanhill Coll. of Educn, Glasgow. ADCM, GTCL, FRCO(CHM), LRAM, HonTSC. Command Music Adviser, RN, 1946–48; Prof. of Singing and Voice Production, TCL, 1949–52; Conductor, Morley Coll. Orch., 1949–51; Choral Scholar, Westminster Abbey, 1949–52; Organist and Choirmaster, Wesley's Chapel, City Road, EC4, 1950–52; Conductor, Glasgow Choral Union, 1952–54; BBC Music Asst, Midland Region, 1954–55; Music Master, Glyn County Sch., Ewell, 1955–66; Conductor, Aldeburgh Festival Choir, 1957–60; Organist and Choirmaster: St Paul's, Portman Sq., W1, 1957–61; Holy Trinity, Guildford, 1961–65; Lectr in Music, Froebel Inst., 1967–68; Adviser in Music, London Borough of Harrow, 1968–72; Warden, Education Section, ISM, 1971–72; music specialist, N Div.,

HM Inspectorate of Schs in Scotland, 1972–87. Regd Teacher, Sch. of Sinus Tone, 1985–. Editor, Jl of Ernest George White Soc., 1983–88. Presented papers at: study-conf. of teachers of singing, The Maltings, Snape, 1976; Nat. Course on Develt of Young Children's Musical Skills, Univ. of Reading Sch. of Educn, 1979; annual conf., Scottish Fedn of Organists, 1980; Nat. Conf., Assoc. of Music Advisers in Scotland, 1987. Internat. Composition Prizeman of Cathedral of St John the Divine, NY; Limpus Fellowship Prizeman of RCO. *Publications:* Voice Production in Choral Technique, 1955, rev. edn 1970; The Selection and Training of Mixed Choirs in Churches, 1960; Sixty Songs from Sankey, 1960; (ed) John Merbecke's Music for the Congregation at Holy Communion, 1963; Music and Holiness, 1964; Plainsong for Pleasure, 1969; Authentic Chanting, 1969; Guide to Vanity Fair, 1982. *Recreations:* watching sea-birds, reading, writing, walking. *Address:* 10 Carronhall, Stonehaven, Aberdeen AB3 2HF.

CLEARY, Denis Mackrow, CMG 1967; HM Diplomatic Service, retired; *b* 20 Dec. 1907; *s* of late Francis Esmonde Cleary and late Emmeline Marie Cleary (*née* Mackrow); *m* 1st, 1941, Barbara Wykeham-George (*d* 1960); 2nd, 1962, Mary Kent (*née* Dunlop), *widow* of Harold Kent; one step-*d*. *Educ:* St Ignatius Coll. and St Olave's Sch.; St John's Coll., Cambridge (Major Schol.). 1st Class Hons Pts I and II, Math. Tripos; BA 1930; MA 1934. Asst Principal, India Office, 1931; Principal, 1937; seconded to Min. of Home Security, 1940–44; Dep. Principal Officer to Regional Commissioner, Cambridge, March 1943–Sept. 1944; seconded to Foreign Office (German Section) as Asst Sec., 1946–49; transferred to CRO and posted to Delhi as Counsellor, 1949–51; Dep. High Commissioner, Wellington, 1955–58; Mem. of British Delegn to Law of the Sea Conf., Geneva, 1960; Dep. High Comr, Nicosia, 1962–64; Head of Atlantic Dept, Commonwealth Office, 1964–68 (Mem., Cttee for Exports to the Caribbean, 1965–67); retd 1968; re-employed in Internat. Div., DHSS, 1968–72; UK Delegate to Public Health Cttees, Council of Europe, 1968–72; Chm., Council of Europe Med. Fellowships Selection Cttee, 1972–74. *Recreations:* gardening, walking. *Address:* High Gate, Burwash, East Sussex TN19 7LA. *T:* Burwash (0435) 882712.

CLEARY, Jon Stephen; novelist; *b* 22 Nov. 1917; *s* of Matthew Cleary and Ida (*née* Brown); *m* 1946, Constantine Lucas; one *d* (and one *d* decd). *Educ:* Marist Brothers' Sch., Randwick, NSW. Variety of jobs, 1932–40; served with AIF, 1940–45; freelance writer, 1945–48; journalist with Australian News and Information Bureau: London, 1948–49; New York, 1949–51; subseq. full-time writer. Jt winner, Nat. Radio Play Contest, ABC, 1945; regional winner, NY Herald Tribune World Short Story Contest, 1950. *Publications:* These Small Glories (short stories), 1946; You Can't See Round Corners, 1947 (2nd Prize, Novel Contest, Sydney Morning Herald); The Long Shadow, 1949; Just Let Me Be, 1950 (Crouch Gold Medal for best Australian novel); The Sundowners, 1952; The Climate of Courage, 1953; Justin Bayard, 1955; The Green Helmet, 1957; Back of Sunset, 1959; North from Thursday, 1960; The Country of Marriage, 1962; Forests of the Night, 1963; A Flight of Chariots, 1964; The Fall of an Eagle, 1964; The Pulse of Danger, 1966; The High Commissioner, 1967; The Long Pursuit, 1967; Season of Doubt, 1968; Remember Jack Hoxie, 1969; Helga's Web, 1970; Mask of the Andes, 1971; Man's Estate, 1972; Ransom, 1973; Peter's Pence, 1974 (Edgar Award for best crime novel); The Safe House, 1975; A Sound of Lightning, 1976; High Road to China, 1977; Vortex, 1977; The Beaufort Sisters, 1979; A Very Private War, 1980; The Golden Sabre, 1981; The Faraway Drums, 1981; Spearfield's Daughter, 1982; The Phoenix Tree, 1984; The City of Fading Light, 1985; Dragons at the Party, 1987; Now and Then, Amen, 1988; Babylon South, 1989; Murder Song, 1990; Pride's Harvest, 1991. *Recreations:* tennis, reading. *Address:* c/o Harper/Collins, 77–85 Fulham Palace Road, W6 8JB.

CLEARY, Sir Joseph Jackson, Kt 1965; *b* 26 Oct. 1902; *s* of Joseph Cleary, JP; *m* 1945, Ethel McColl. *Educ:* Holy Trinity C of E Sch., Anfield, Liverpool; Skerry's Coll., Liverpool. Alderman, 1941, JP, 1927 for Liverpool; Lord Mayor of Liverpool, 1949–50. Contested East Toxteth Div., Liverpool, March 1929 and May 1929; West Derby, Oct. 1931; MP (Lab) Wavertree Div. of Liverpool, Feb.-Oct. 1935. Lecture tour to Forces in Middle East, 1945. Freeman, City of Liverpool, 1970. *Recreations:* football (Association), tennis. *Address:* 115 Riverview Heights, Liverpool L19 0LQ. *T:* 051–427 2133.

CLEASBY, Very Rev. Thomas Wood Ingram; Dean of Chester, 1978–86, Dean Emeritus, since 1986; *b* 27 March 1920; *s* of T. W. Cleasby, Oakdene, Sedbergh, Yorks, and Jessie Brown Cleasby; *m* 1st, 1956, Olga Elizabeth Vibert Douglas (*d* 1967); one *s* one *d* (and one *d* decd); 2nd, 1970, Monica, *e d* of Rt Rev. O. S. Tomkins, *qv*; one *d*. *Educ:* Sedbergh Sch., Yorks; Magdalen Coll., Oxford; Cuddesdon Coll., Oxford. BA, MA (Hons Mod. History) 1947. Commissioned, 1st Bn Border Regt, 1940; served 1st Airborne Div., 1941–45, Actg Major. Ordained, Dio. Wakefield, 1949 (Huddersfield Parish Church). Domestic Chaplain to Archbishop of York, 1952–56; Anglican Chaplain to Univ. of Nottingham, 1956–63; Archdeacon of Chesterfield, 1963–78; Vicar of St Mary and All Saints, Chesterfield, 1963–70; Rector of Morton, Derby, 1970–78. *Recreations:* fell-walking, bird-watching, gardening, fishing. *Address:* Low Barth, Dent, Cumbria LA10 5SZ. *T:* Dent (05875) 476.

CLEAVER, Anthony Brian; Chief Executive, since 1986, and Chairman, since 1990, IBM United Kingdom Holdings Ltd; *b* 10 April 1938; *s* of late William Brian Cleaver and Dorothea Early Cleaver (*née* Peeks); *m* 1962, Mary Teresa Cotter; one *s*. *Educ:* Berkhamsted Sch.; Trinity Coll., Oxford (Schol.; MA; Hon. Fellow 1989). Joined IBM United Kingdom, 1962; IBM World Trade Corp., USA, 1973–74; Dir, DP Div., IBM UK, 1977; Vice-Pres. of Marketing, IBM Europe, Paris, 1981–82; Gen. Man., IBM UK, 1984. Dir and Mem. Audit Cttee, General Accident, 1988–. Dir, Nat. Computing Centre, 1976–80. Dir, ENO, 1988–; Member Board: UK Centre for Econ. and Environmental Develt, 1985–; Business in the Community, 1985– (Chm., Business in the Envmt Target Team, 1988–; Mem., President's Cttee, 1988–); RIPA, 1985–89; Assoc. for Business Sponsorship of the Arts, 1985–. Member: Electronics EDC, NEDO, 1986–; CBI, 1986– (Mem., President's Cttee, 1988–); BOTB, 1988–91; Nat. Trng Task Force, 1989–; Council, Foundn for Educn Business Partnerships, 1989–; HRH Duke of Edinburgh's Seventh Commonwealth Study Conf. Council, 1990–. Mem., President's Cttee, Oxford Univ. Appeal, 1988–; Appeal Chm., Trinity Coll., Oxford, 1989–. Mem. Council, WWF, 1988–. Member Council: Templeton Coll., Oxford, 1982–; PSI, 1985–88; Chm. Govs, Birkbeck Coll., 1989–. *Recreations:* music, especially opera; sport, especially cricket. *Address:* PO Box 41, North Harbour, Portsmouth, Hants PO6 3AU. *T:* Portsmouth (0705) 321212. *Clubs:* Reform, MCC.

CLEAVER, Leonard Harry, FCA; JP; *b* 27 Oct. 1909; *s* of late Harry Cleaver, OBE, JP; *m* 1938, Mary Richards Matthews; one *s*. *Educ:* Bilton Grange and Rugby. Chartered Accountant: articled Agar, Bates, Neal & Co., Birmingham; Sec. and Chief Accountant, Chance Bros Ltd, 1935–51; Partner, Heathcote & Coleman, 1951–59. MP (C) Yardley Div. of Birmingham, 1959–64; PPS to Parly Sec. to Min. of Housing and Local Govt, 1963–64; contested Yardley Div. of Birmingham, 1964, 1966. Member: Smethwick Nat. Savings Cttee, 1939–45; Birmingham Probation Cttee, 1955–73; Central Council, Probation and After-Care Cttees for England and Wales, 1966–73. Treasurer: Deritend Unionist Assoc., 1945–48; Yardley Div. Unionist Assoc., 1971–73 (Chm., 1973–74). Governor, Yardley Educnl Foundn, 1966–70. JP Birmingham, 1954; City Councillor, Birmingham, 1966–70. *Recreations:* Rugby football, fishing, philately. *Address:* 6 The Retreat, Leamington Road, Broadway, Worcs WR12 7DZ. *T:* Broadway (0386) 852090.

CLEAVER, Air Vice-Marshal Peter (Charles), CB 1971; OBE 1945; *b* 6 July 1919; *s* of William Henry Cleaver, Warwick; *m* 1948, Jean, *d* of J. E. B. Fairclough, Ledbury; two *s*. *Educ:* Warwick Sch.; Coll. of Aeronautics (MSc). Staff Coll., Haifa, 1945; idc 1966. HM Asst Air Attaché, Bucharest, 1947–49; Coll. of Aeronautics, Cranfield, 1950–52; Structural Research, RAE Farnborough, 1952–55; Min. of Supply, 1955–57; HQ FEAF, 1957–60; Maintenance Comd, 1960–63; OC, Central Servicing Develt Estabt, 1963–64; Air Officer Engineering: HQ Flying Trg Comd, 1964–66; HQ FEAF, 1967–69; Air Support Command, 1969–72; retired 1972. Sec., Cranfield Inst. of Technology, 1973–78. Governor, Warwick Schs Foundn, 1978–85; Chm. Governors, Warwick Sch., 1980–85. CEng, FRAeS. *Recreation:* gardening. *Address:* Willow House, Watling Street, Little Brickhill, Milton Keynes MK17 9LS. *Club:* Royal Air Force.

CLEAVER, William Benjamin, CEng, FIMinE; JP; Deputy Director, South Wales Area, National Coal Board, 1969–85; *b* 15 Sept. 1921; *s* of David John Cleaver and Blodwen (*née* Miles); *m* 1943, Mary Watkin (*née* James); one *s* two *d*. *Educ:* Pentre (Rhondda) Grammar Sch.; University Coll. Cardiff (BSc Hons). National Coal Board: Manager: N Celynen Collieries, Gwent, 1947; Oakdale Colliery, Gwent, 1950; Production Manager (Group), S Wales, 1953; Area General Manager, No 2 S Wales Area, 1958. Sec., Contemporary Art Soc. for Wales, 1972–; Member: Welsh Arts Council, 1977–83 (Vice-Chm., 1980–83); Arts Council of GB, 1980–83; Council, Nat. Museum of Wales, 1982–; Exec. Cttee, Council of Museums in Wales, 1983– (Chm., 1986–). Founder Pres., Cardiff Jun. Ch. of Commerce, 1953. Rugby Union Football: Cardiff RFC, 1940–50; Welsh Rugby International, 1947–50 (14 caps); British Lion to NZ and Aust., 1950; Barbarian Rugby Club, 1946; Founder Chm., Welsh Youth Rugby Union, 1949–57. JP Cardiff 1973. OStJ 1961. *Recreations:* theatre, fine arts. *Address:* 29 Lon-y-deri, Rhiwbina, Cardiff CF4 6JN. *T:* Cardiff (0222) 693242. *Clubs:* Savile; Cardiff and County (Cardiff).

CLEDWYN OF PENRHOS, Baron *cr* 1979 (Life Peer), of Holyhead in the Isle of Anglesey; **Cledwyn Hughes,** CH 1977; PC 1966; Leader of the Opposition, House of Lords, since 1982 (Deputy Leader of the Opposition, 1981–82); *b* 14 Sept. 1916; *er s* of Rev. Henry David and Emily Hughes; *m* 1949, Jean Beatrice Hughes; one *s* one *d*. *Educ:* Holyhead Grammar Sch.; University Coll. of Wales, Aberystwyth (LLB). Solicitor, 1940. Served RAFVR, 1940–45. Mem. Anglesey County Council, 1946–52. Contested (Lab) Anglesey, 1945 and 1950; MP (Lab) Anglesey, 1951–79; Opposition spokesman for Housing and Local Govt, 1959–64; Minister of State for Commonwealth Relations, 1964–66; Sec. of State for Wales, 1966–68; Min. of Agriculture, Fisheries and Food, 1968–70; Opposition spokesman on Agriculture, Fisheries and Food, 1970–72; Commissioner of the House of Commons, 1979; Chm., House of Lords Select Cttee on Agriculture and Food, 1980–83. Chairman: Welsh Parliamentary Party, 1953–54; Welsh Labour Group, 1955–56; Parly Labour Party, Oct. 1974–1979 (Vice-Chm., March-Oct. 1974); Welsh Cttee on Economic and Industrial Affairs, 1982–84. Member: Cttee of Public Accounts, 1957–64; Cttee of Privileges, 1974–79. Jt Chm. TUC/Labour Party Liaison Cttee, 1974–79. Vice-Pres., Britain in Europe, 1975. Mem. Parly Delegn to Lebanon, 1957; represented British Govt at Kenya Republic Celebrations, 1964; led UK Delegn to The Gambia Independence celebrations, 1965; Mission to Rhodesia, July 1965; led UK Mission on Contingency Planning to Zambia, 1966; led Parliamentary Delegn to USSR, 1977; Prime Minister's Envoy to Southern Africa, Nov.-Dec. 1978. Director: Shell UK Ltd, 1980–84; Anglesey Aluminium Ltd, 1980–; Holyhead Towing Ltd, 1980–; a Regional Advr in Midland Bank, with special responsibilities for Wales, 1979–. Member, County Councils' Assoc., 1980–; Chm., Welsh Theatre Co., 1981–85; President: Housing and Town Planning Council, 1980–; Age Concern, Wales, 1980–85; Soc. of Welsh People Overseas, 1979–91; UCW, Aberystwyth, 1976–85; Assembly of Welsh Counties, 1990–. Pro-Chancellor, Univ. of Wales, 1985–. Hon. Freedom of Beaumaris, 1972; Freeman, Borough of Anglesey, 1976. Hon. LLD Wales, 1970. Alderman, Anglesey CC, 1973. *Publication:* Report on Conditions in St Helena, 1958. *Address:* Penmorfa, Trearddur, Holyhead, Gwynedd. *T:* Trearddur Bay (0407) 860544. *Club:* Travellers'.

CLEERE, Henry Forester, FSA; Director, Council for British Archaeology, 1974–91; *b* 2 Dec. 1926; *s* of late Christopher Henry John Cleere and Frances Eleanor (*née* King); *m* 1st, 1950, Dorothy Percy (marr. diss.); one *s* one *d*; 2nd, 1975, Pamela Joan Vertue; two *d*. *Educ:* Beckenham County Sch.; University Coll. London (BA Hons 1951); Univ. of London Inst. of Archaeology (PhD 1981). FSA 1967. Commissioned Royal Artillery, 1944–48. Successively, Production Editor, Asst Sec., Man. Editor, Dep. Sec., Iron and Steel Inst., 1952–71; Industrial Development Officer, UN Industrial Develt Org., Vienna, 1972–73. Member: Exec. Cttee, ICOMOS, 1981–90; Scientific Cttee, Centro Universitario Europeo per i Beni Culturali, 1985–. Pres., Sussex Archaeol Soc., 1987–91. MIFA 1982; FBIM; FRSA 1991. Winston Churchill Fellow, 1979; Hon. Vis. Fellow, Univ. of York, 1988–; Vis. Res. Fellow, Univ. de Paris I (Sorbonne), 1989; UK Trust Sen. Fellow, Indian Nat. Trust for Art and Cultural Heritage, 1990. Editor, Antiquity, 1992. *Publications:* Approaches to the Archaeological Heritage, 1984; (with D. W. Crossley) The Iron Industry of the Weald, 1985; Archaeological Heritage Management in the Modern World, 1988; papers in British and foreign jls on aspects of early ironmaking, Roman fleets, etc. *Recreations:* gardening, beekeeping, cookery. *Address:* Acres Rise, Lower Platts, Ticehurst, Wadhurst, East Sussex TN5 7DD. *T:* Ticehurst (0580) 200752. *Club:* Athenæum.

CLEESE, John Marwood; writer and actor; Founder and Director, Video Arts Ltd; *b* 27 Oct. 1939; *s* of Reginald and Muriel Cleese; *m* 1st, 1968, Connie Booth (marr. diss. 1978); one *d*; 2nd, 1981, Barbara Trentham (marr. diss. 1990); one *d*. *Educ:* Clifton Sports Acad.; Downing College, Cambridge (MA). Started making jokes professionally, 1963; started on British television, 1966; TV series have included: The Frost Report, At Last the 1948 Show, Monty Python's Flying Circus, Fawlty Towers. Films include: Interlude, The Magic Christian, And Now For Something Completely Different, Monty Python and the Holy Grail, Romance with a Double Bass, Life of Brian, Privates on Parade, The Meaning of Life, Yellowbeard, Silverado, Clockwise, A Fish Called Wanda, Erik the Viking. Hon. LLD St Andrews. *Publications:* (with Robin Skynner) Families and How to Survive Them, 1983; The Golden Skits of Wing Commander Muriel Volestrangler FRHS and Bar, 1984; (with Connie Booth) The Complete Fawlty Towers, 1989. *Recreations:* gluttony, sloth. *Address:* c/o David Wilkinson, 115 Hazlebury Road, SW6 2LX.

CLEGG, Brian George Herbert; management consultant and company director; *b* 10 Dec. 1921; *s* of Frederic Bradbury Clegg and Gladys Butterworth; *m* 1st, 1949, Iris May Ludlow; one *s* one *d*; 2nd, 1976, Anne Elizabeth Robertson; one *s*. *Educ:* Manchester Grammar Sch.; Trinity Coll., Cambridge (Open Math. Schol., MA). FIS, FIM, CEng, FIGasE, MBIM. Sci. Officer, Min. of Supply, 1942; Hon. Flt-Lt, RAFVR. Statistician, Liverpool Gas Co., 1946; Market and Operational Res. Man., Southern Gas Bd, 1957; Commercial Man., Southern Gas Bd, 1961; Dep. Dir of Marketing, Gas Council, 1968; Dir of Marketing, British Gas Corp., 1972; Chairman, Northern Region of British Gas Corp., 1975–82, retired. Director: Pershke Price Service Organisation Ltd, 1984–;

Priceacre Ltd, 1990–. *Publications:* numerous articles and papers on marketing and fuel matters. *Recreations:* swimming, ice-skating, electronic organ. *Address:* 30 The Pines, 40 The Avenue, Poole, Dorset BH13 6HJ.

CLEGG, Professor Edward John, MD, PhD; FIBiol; Regius Professor of Anatomy, University of Aberdeen, 1976–89; Professor of Biological Anthropology, University of Aberdeen, 1990–91; *b* 29 Oct. 1925; *s* of Edward Clegg and Emily Armistead; *m* 1958, Sheila Douglas Walls; two *d* (and one *d* decd). *Educ:* High Storrs Grammar Sch., Sheffield; Univ. of Sheffield (MB, ChB Hons 1948, MD 1964). PhD Liverpool, 1957; FIBiol 1974. RAMC, 1948–50 and RAMC (TA), 1950–61; late Major, RAMC (RARO). Demonstr, Asst Lectr and Lectr in Anatomy, Univ. of Liverpool, 1952–63; Lectr, Sen. Lectr and Reader in Human Biology and Anatomy, Univ. of Sheffield, 1963–77. MO, British Kangchenjunga Expedn, 1955; Sci. Mem., Chogolungma Glacier Expedn, 1959; Leader, WHO/IBP Expedn, Simien Mountains, Ethiopia, 1967. Pres., Anat. Soc. of GB and Ire, 1988–89; Chm., Soc. for the Study of Human Biology, 1988–91. *Publications:* The Study of Man: an introduction to human biology, 1968 (2nd edn 1978); papers on anatomy, endocrinology and human biology. *Recreations:* mountaineering, fishing, sailing, music. *Address:* 22 Woodburn Avenue, Aberdeen AB1 8JQ; c/o School of Biomedical Sciences, Marischal College, Aberdeen AB9 1AS. *T:* Aberdeen (0224) 273081. *Clubs:* Alpine; Wayfarers (Liverpool).

CLEGG, Prof. Hugh Armstrong; Emeritus Professor of Industrial Relations, University of Warwick, since 1983; *b* 22 May 1920; *s* of late Rev. Herbert Hobson Clegg and of Mabel (*née* Duckering); *m* 1941, Mary Matilda (*née* Shaw); two *s* two *d*. *Educ:* Kingswood Sch., Bath; Magdalen Coll., Oxford. Served War, 1940–45; Official Fellow, Nuffield Coll., Oxford, 1949–66, Emeritus Fellow, 1966–; Prof. of Industrial Relns, Univ. of Warwick, 1967–79, Titular Prof. and Leverhulme Res. Fellow, 1979–83. Chm., Civil Service Arbitration Tribunal, 1968–71; Dir, Industrial Relations Res. Unit, SSRC, 1970–74; Member: Royal Commn on Trade Unions and Employers' Assocs, 1965–68; Cttee of Inquiry into Port Transport Industry, 1964–65; Ct of Inquiry into Seamen's Dispute, 1966–67; Nat. Board for Prices and Incomes, 1966–67; Ct of Inquiry into Local Authorities' Manual Workers' Pay Dispute, 1970; Council, ACAS, 1974–79; Chm., Standing Commn on Pay Comparability, 1979–80. Hon. DLitt Warwick, 1987. *Publications:* Labour Relations in London Transport, 1950; Industrial Democracy and Nationalisation, 1951; The Future of Nationalisation (with T. E. Chester), 1953; General Union, 1954; Wage Policy in the Health Service (with T. E. Chester), 1957; The Employers' Challenge (with R. Adams), 1957; A New Approach to Industrial Democracy, 1960; Trade Union Officers (with A. J. Killick and R. Adams), 1961; General Union in a Changing Society, 1964; A History of British Trade Unions: Vol. I (with A. Fox and A. F. Thompson), 1964, Vol. II, 1985; The System of Industrial Relations in Great Britain, 1970; How to run an Incomes Policy and Why we made such a Mess of the Last One, 1971; Workplace and Union (with I. Boraston and M. Rimmer), 1975; Trade Unionism under Collective Bargaining, 1976; The Changing System of Industrial Relations in Great Britain, 1979. *Recreations:* walking, beer. *Address:* 7 John Nash Square, Regency Drive, Kenilworth, Warwicks. *T:* Kenilworth (0926) 50794.

CLEGG, Philip Charles; His Honour Judge Clegg; a Circuit Judge, since 1987; *b* 17 Oct. 1942; *s* of Charles and Patricia Clegg; *m* 1965, Caroline Frances Peall; one *s* two *d*. *Educ:* Rossall; Bristol Univ. (LLB Hons). Called to the Bar, Middle Temple, 1966; in practice on Northern Circuit; Asst Recorder, 1980–83; a Recorder, 1983–87. *Recreations:* sailing, model engineering. *Address:* Hillside Cottage, The Hill, Polstead, near Colchester, Essex CO6 5AL.

CLEGG, Richard Ninian Barwick, QC 1979; a Recorder of the Crown Court, since 1978; *b* 28 June 1938; *o s* of Sir Cuthbert Clegg, TD; *m* 1963, Katherine Veronica, *d* of A. A. H. Douglas; two *s* one *d*. *Educ:* Aysgarth; Charterhouse; Trinity Coll., Oxford (MA). Captain of Oxford Pentathlon Team, 1959. Called to Bar, Inner Temple, 1960, Bencher, 1985. Chm., NW section of Bow Group, 1964–66; Vice-Chm., Bow Group, 1965–66; Chm., Winston Circle, 1965–66; Pres., Heywood and Royton Conservative Assoc., 1965–68. *Publication:* (jtly) Bow Group pamphlet, Towards a New North West, 1964. *Recreations:* sport, music, travel. *Address:* The Old Rectory, Brereton, via Sandbach, Cheshire CW11 9RY. *T:* Holmes Chapel (0477) 32358; 5 Essex Court, Temple, EC4. *T:* 071–353 4365. *Club:* Lansdowne.

CLEGG, (Ronald) Anthony, (Tony); Chairman, E & F Securities Ltd; Chairman and Chief Executive, Mountleigh Group plc, 1983–89; *b* 8 April 1937; *s* of Stanley and Cicely Clegg; *m* 1963, Dorothy Eve Glaze; three *d*. *Educ:* Bickerton House, Southport, Lancs. Joined Mountain Mills Co. Ltd as manager, 1961; Dir, 1963; Dir, Leigh Mills Co. Ltd (a publicly quoted co.), when Mountain Gp merged with it, 1966; Jt Man. Dir, Leigh Mills Co. Ltd, 1972; responsible for the transformation of the Gp from textile manufg to a property investment and develt co., 1976–82; the co. changed its name to Mountleigh Gp. Dir, Wembley plc, 1987–90. Chairman: British Soc. for Clinical Cytology Appeal; Leeds General Infirmary NHS Trust; Leeds Special Appeal Cancer Res. Macmillan Fund; Trustee, and Dep. Chm. F and GP Cttee, Prince's Youth Business Trust; Council Member: Yorkshire Agricl Soc.; Home Farm Trust, Yorks. Patron, Leeds Riding for the Disabled. FInstD; CBIM. Liveryman, Co. of Turners. *Recreations:* riding, racehorses, Highland cattle breeding, music. *Address:* The Old Hall, Bramham, Wetherby, West Yorkshire LS23 6QR.

CLEGG, Sir Walter, Kt 1980; *b* 18 April 1920; *s* of Edwin Clegg; *m* 1951, Elise Margaret Hargreaves. *Educ:* Bury Grammar Sch.; Arnold Sch., Blackpool; Manchester Univ. Law Sch. Articled to Town Clerk, Barrow-in-Furness, 1937. Served in Royal Artillery, 1939–46 (commnd 1940). Qualified as Solicitor, 1947; subsequently in practice. Lancashire CC, 1955–61. MP (C): N Fylde, 1966–83; Wyre, 1983–87. Opposition Whip, 1967–69; a Lord Comr, HM Treasury, 1970–72; Vice-Chamberlain, HM Household, 1972–73, Comptroller, 1973–74; an Opposition Whip, March-Oct. 1974. Hon. Sec., Cons. Housing and Local Govt Cttee, 1968–69; Mem. Exec., 1922 Cttee, 1975–76, Hon. Treasurer 1976–87; Chm., Cons. NW Members Group, 1977–87; Mem. Exec., IPU, 1980–85, CPA, 1980–85; Chm., Parly All-Party Solicitors Gp, 1979–87. Vice-Chm., Assoc. of Conservative Clubs, 1969–71, Pres. 1977–78, Vice-Pres. 1982; Pres., Cons. NW Provincial Area, 1982–. Pres., Central and W Lancs Chamber of Commerce, 1981. *Recreation:* reading. *Address:* Beech House, Raikes Road, Little Thornton, near Blackpool, Lancs. *T:* Cleveleys (0253) 826131. *Club:* Garrick.

CLEGG, William; QC 1991; *b* 5 Sept. 1949; *s* of Peter Hepworth Clegg and Sheila Clegg; *m* 1974, Wendy Doreen Chard; one *s* one *d*. *Educ:* St Thomas More High School; Bristol Univ. (LLB). Called to the Bar, Gray's Inn, 1972; in practice, SE Circuit. *Recreations:* squash, cricket. *Address:* 3 Hare court, Temple, EC4Y 7BJ. *T:* 071–353 7561. *Club:* Sudbury Racquet Centre.

CLEGG-HILL, family name of **Viscount Hill.**

CLELAND, Dame Rachel, DBE 1980 (CBE 1966; MBE 1959); *b* Peppermint Grove, Jan. 1906; *d* of W. H. Evans, Perth, WA; *m* 1928, Sir Donald Cleland, *s* of E. D. Cleland; two *s*. *Educ:* Methodist Ladies' Coll., Perth, WA; Kindergarten Training Coll. Pres., Girl Guide Assoc., Papua and New Guinea, 1952–66; President: Red Cross, Papua and New Guinea, 1952–66; Branch of Aust. Pre-Sch. Assoc. (TPNG), 1952–66; Patron WA Branch, Soc. of Women Writers (Aust.). *Publication:* Pathways to Independence: official and family life in Papua New Guinea 1951–1976, 1984, 2nd edn 1985. *Recreations:* music, theatre, reading. *Address:* 2/24 Richardson Avenue, Claremont, WA 6010, Australia. *Club:* Queen's (Sydney).

CLELAND, William Paton, FRCP, FRCS, FACS; Consulting Surgeon, National Heart and Chest Hospital; Consulting Thoracic Surgeon, King's College Hospital; Emeritus Consultant to the RN; late Adviser in Thoracic Surgery to the Department of Health and Social Security; *b* 30 May 1912; *o s* of late Sir John Cleland, CBE; *m* 1940, Norah, *d* of George E. Goodhart; two *s* one *d*. *Educ:* Scotch Coll., Adelaide; Univ. of Adelaide, S Australia. MB, BS (Adelaide). Resident appts, Royal Adelaide and Adelaide Children's Hosps, 1935–36; MRCP 1939; House Physician and Resident Surgical Officer, Brompton Chest Hosp., 1939–41. Served in EMS as Registrar and Surgeon, 1939–45. FRCS 1946. Consultant Thoracic Surg., King's Coll. Hosp., 1948; Surgeon, Brompton Chest Hospital, 1948; Sen. Lectr in Thoracic Surgery, Royal Postgrad. Med. Sch., 1949; Dir, Dept of Surgery, Cardio-Thoracic Inst., Brompton Hosp. Member: Assoc. Thoracic Surgeons of Gt Brit. and Ire.; Thoracic Soc.; British Cardiac Soc.; Amer. Coll. of Surgeons. Editor, Jl of Cardiovascular Surgery, 1978–83. Comdr, Order of Lion of Finland; Comdr, Order of Icelandic Falcon. *Publications:* (jt author) Medical and Surgical Cardiology, 1969; chapters on thoracic surgery in British Surgical Practice, Diseases of the Chest (Marshall and Perry), Short Practice of Surgery (Bailey and Love), and Operative Surgery (Rob and Rodney Smith); articles on pulmonary and cardiac surgery in medical literature. *Recreations:* fishing, gardening. *Address:* Green Meadows, Goodworth Clatford, Andover, Hants SP11 7HH. *T:* Andover (0264) 324327.

CLELLAND, David Gordon; MP (Lab) Tyne Bridge, since Dec. 1985; *b* 27 June 1943; *s* of Archibald and Ellen Clelland; *m* 1965, Maureen; two *d*. *Educ:* Kelvin Grove Boys' School, Gateshead; Gateshead and Hebburn Technical Colleges. Apprentice electrical fitter, 1959–64; electrical tester, 1964–81. Gateshead Borough Council: Councillor, 1972–86; Recreation Chm., 1976–84; Leader of Council, 1984–85. Nat. Sec., Assoc. of Councillors, 1981–85. Member: Home Affairs Select Cttee, 1986–88; Energy Select Cttee, 1989–. Chm., Backbench Envmt Cttee; Sec., Northern Gp of Lab MPs. *Recreation:* golf. *Address:* Ground Floor, Old Bank, Swinburne Street, Gateshead NE8 1AN. *T:* 091–477 2559.

CLEMENS, Clive Carruthers, CMG 1983; MC 1946; HM Diplomatic Service, retired; High Commissioner in Lesotho, 1981–84; *b* 22 Jan. 1924; British; *s* of late M. B. Clemens, Imperial Bank of India, and late Margaret Jane (*née* Carruthers); *m* 1947, Philippa Jane Bailey; three *s*. *Educ:* Blundell's Sch.; St Catharine's Coll., Cambridge. War Service 1943–46: commissioned in Duke of Cornwall's Light Infantry; served in India and Burma, 1944–45. Entered HM Foreign Service and apptd to FO, 1947; Third Sec., Rangoon, 1948; Third (later Second) Sec., Lisbon, 1950; FO, 1953; First Sec., Budapest, 1954; Brussels, 1956; Seoul, 1959; FO, 1961; Strasbourg (UK Delegn to Council of Europe), 1964; Counsellor, Paris, 1967; Principal British Trade Comr, Vancouver, 1970–74; Dep. Consul-Gen., Johannesburg, 1974–78; Consul-Gen., Istanbul, 1978–81. *Recreations:* birdwatching, photography. *Address:* 9 Saxonhurst, Downton, Salisbury, Wilts.

CLEMENT, David James; financial consultant, since 1985; *b* 29 Sept. 1930; *s* of James and Constance Clement; *m* 1958, Margaret Stone; two *s* one *d*. *Educ:* Chipping Sodbury Grammar Sch.; Univ. of Bristol (BA). IPFA. Internal Audit Asst, City of Bristol, 1953–56; Accountancy/Audit Asst, 1956–60, Chief Accountancy Asst, 1960–65, City of Worcester; Dep. Chief Finance Officer, Runcorn Develt Corp., 1965–68; Chief Finance Officer, Antrim and Ballymena Develt Commn, 1968–72; Asst Sec., Dept of Finance, NI, 1972–75, Dep. Sec., 1975–80; Under Sec., DoE, NI, 1980–84. *Recreations:* lawn tennis, Association football, contract bridge, philately.

CLEMENT, David Morris, CBE 1971; FCA, IPFA; Hon. FCGI; Chairman, Joint Mission Hospital Equipment Board Ltd, 1978–85; *b* 6 Feb. 1911; 2nd *s* of Charles William and Rosina Wannell Clement, Swansea; *m* 1938, Kathleen Mary (*d* 1991), *o d* of Ernest George Davies, ACA, Swansea; one *d*. *Educ:* Bishop Gore's Grammar Sch., Swansea. Mem. Inst. Chartered Accountants, 1933. A. Owen John & Co., Swansea, and Sissons Bersey Gain Vincent & Co., London, Chartered Accts, 1928–35; ICI Ltd, Lime Gp, 1935–40; Chloride Electrical Storage Co. Ltd, 1941–46; National Coal Board: Sec., North Western Div., 1946–49; Chief Acct, Northern and Durham Divs, 1950–55; Dep. Dir-Gen. of Finance, 1955–61; Dir-Gen. of Finance, 1961–69; Bd Mem., 1969–76; Chairman: NCB (Ancillaries) Ltd, 1973–79; Redwood-Corex Services Ltd, 1978–82. Chm., Public Corporations Finance Gp, 1975–76. Dep. Chm., Horizon Exploration Ltd, 1978–80. Underwriting Member of Lloyd's, 1978–. Member: Aircraft and Shipbuilding Industries Arbitration Tribunals, 1980–83; Council, CIPFA, 1975–76; Council, CGLI (Hon. Treas.), 1978–82. *Recreations:* golf, photography. *Address:* 19 The Highway, Sutton, Surrey. *T:* 081–642 3626. *Clubs:* Royal Automobile, Directors'.

See also D. J. Mellor.

CLEMENT, John; Chairman, Unigate Group, 1977–91; non-executive Chairman, The Littlewoods Organisation, 1982–90; *b* 18 May 1932; *s* of Frederick and Alice Eleanor Clement; *m* 1956, Elisabeth Anne (*née* Emery); two *s* one *d*. *Educ:* Bishop's Stortford College. Howards Dairies, Westcliff on Sea, 1949–64; United Dairies London Ltd, 1964–69; Asst Managing Director, Rank Leisure Services Ltd, 1969–73; Chairman, Unigate Foods Div., 1973; Chief Executive, Unigate Group, 1976–90. Dir, Eagle Star Holdings plc, 1981–86. Mem., Securities and Investments Bd, 1986–89. CBIM (FBIM 1977). *Recreations:* shooting, sailing, bridge, Rugby, tennis. *Address:* Tuddenham Hall, Tuddenham, Ipswich, Suffolk IP6 9DD. *T:* Witnesham (047385) 217. *Clubs:* Farmers', London Welsh Rugby Football; Cumberland Lawn Tennis; Royal Harwich Yacht.

See also R. Clement.

CLEMENT, John Handel, CB 1980; Member, Midland Bank plc Advisory Council for Wales, since 1985; Adviser to Gooding Group, since 1985; *b* 24 Nov. 1920; *s* of late William and Mary Hannah Clement; *m* 1946, Anita Jones; one *d* (and one *d* decd). *Educ:* Pontardawe Grammar Sch. RAF, 1940–46, Flt Lt (despatches). Welsh Board of Health: Clerical Officer, 1938; Exec. Officer, 1946; Higher Exec. Officer, 1948; Sen. Exec. Officer, 1956; Principal, Welsh Office, Min. of Housing and Local Govt, 1960, Asst Sec., 1966; Private Sec. to Sec. of State for Wales, 1966; Under-Sec., 1971–81, Dir of Industry Dept, 1976–81, Welsh Office. Sec., Council for Wales, 1955–59; Chm., Welsh Planning Bd, 1971–76. Mem., Wales Tourist Bd, 1982–88. Hon. MA Wales, 1982. *Recreations:* Welsh Rugby, fishing. *Address:* 6 St Brioc Road, Heath, Cardiff CF4 4HJ. *T:* Cardiff (0222) 624192.

CLÉMENT, René; Officier de la Légion d'Honneur; Commandeur, Ordre National du Mérite; Commandeur des Arts et des Lettres; film director; *b* Bordeaux, 18 March 1913; *s* of Jean Maurice Clément and Marguérite Clément (*née* Bayle); *m* 1st, 1940, Bella

Gurwich (decd); 2nd, 1987, Johanna Harwood. *Educ:* Ecole nationale supérieure des beaux-arts. *Films:* Soigne ton Gauche (short), 1936; *documentaries:* L'Arabie Interdite, 1937; La Grande Chartreuse, 1938; La Bièvre, 1939; Le Triage, 1940; Ceux du Rail, 1942; La Grande Pastorale, 1943; Chefs de Demain, 1944; *feature films:* La Bataille du Rail, 1946 (Cannes Fest. Prize); Le Père Tranquille, 1946; Les Maudits, 1947 (Cannes Fest. Prize); Au-delà des Grilles, 1948 (US Academy Award, British award); Le Chateau de Verre, 1950; Jeux Interdits, 1952 (US Academy Award, British award and Grand Internat. Prize Venice Biennale); Monsieur Ripois, 1954 (Cannes Fest. Prize); Gervaise, 1955 (Venice Internat. Prize); Barrage contre le Pacifique, 1958; Plein Soleil, 1959; Quelle Joie de Vivre, 1961; Le Jour et l'Heure, 1962; Les Félins, 1964; Paris, Brûle-t-il?, 1966 (Prix Europa); Le Passager de la Pluie, 1969; La Maison sous les Arbres, 1971; La Course du lièvre à travers les champs, 1971; The Baby Sitter, 1975. Founder Mem., Institut des hautes études cinématographiques; Mem., Institut de France. *Publication:* (with C. Audry) Bataille du rail, 1947. *Recreations:* antiques, painting, yachting. *Address:* 5 Avenue de St Roman, 98000 Monte Carlo, Monaco.

CLEMENT, Richard, (Dick); freelance writer, director and producer; *b* 5 Sept. 1937; *s* of Frederick and Alice Eleanor Clement; *m* 1st, Jennifer F. Sheppard (marr. diss. 1981); three *s* one *d*; 2nd, 1982, Nancy S. Campbell; one *d*. *Educ:* Bishop's Stortford Coll.; Westminster Sch., Conn, USA. Co-writer (with Ian La Frenais): *television:* The Likely Lads, 1964–66; Whatever Happened to the Likely Lads, 1972–73; Porridge, 1974–76; Thick as Thieves, 1974; Going Straight, 1978; Auf Wiedersehen, Pet, 1984; Freddie and Max, 1990; *films:* The Jokers, 1967; Otley, 1968; Hannibal Brooks, 1968; Villain, 1971; Porridge, 1979; Water, 1984; Vice Versa, 1987; The Commitments, 1991; Director: *films:* Otley, 1968; A Severed Head, 1969; Porridge, 1979; Bullshot, 1983; Water, 1984; Co-Producer (with Ian La Frenais) Vice Versa, 1987; *stage:* Billy, 1974; Anyone for Denis?, 1981. *Recreations:* work, tennis, dinner; supporting Essex at cricket and Los Angeles Dodgers at baseball. *Address:* 9700 Yoakum Drive, Beverly Hills, Calif 90210, USA. *T:* 213–276–4916.

See also John Clement.

CLEMENTS, Alan William, CBE 1990; Chairman, David S. Smith (Holdings), since 1991; *b* 12 Dec. 1928; *s* of William and Kathleen Clements; *m* 1953, Pearl Dorling; two *s* one *d*. *Educ:* Culford School, Bury St Edmunds; Magdalen College, Oxford (BA Hons). HM Inspector of Taxes, Inland Revenue, 1952–56; ICI: Asst Treasurer, 1966; Dep. Treasurer, 1971; Treasurer, 1976; Finance Director, 1979–90. Non-Exec. Director: Trafalgar House PLC, 1980–; Cable & Wireless PLC, 1985–; Guinness Mahon Hldgs, 1988–. Lay Mem., Internat. Stock Exchange, 1984–88. *Publications:* articles on finance in jls. *Recreations:* golf, music, reading.

CLEMENTS, Andrew Joseph; Music Critic, Financial Times, since 1979; *b* 15 Sept. 1950; *s* of Joseph George Clements and Linda Helen Clements; *m* 1977, Kathryn Denise Coltman; two *d*. *Educ:* Crypt Sch., Gloucester; Emmanuel Coll., Cambridge (BA). Music Critic, New Statesman, 1977–88; Editor, Musical Times, 1987–88. *Recreation:* gardening. *Address:* c/o Financial Times, One Southwark Bridge, SE1 9HL.

CLEMENTS, Julia; *see* Seton, Lady, (Julia).

CLEMENTS, Rt. Rev. Kenneth John; *b* 21 Dec. 1905; *s* of John Edwin Clements and Ethel Evelyn Clark; *m* 1935, Rosalind Elizabeth Cakebread; one *s* two *d*. *Educ:* Highgate Sch., London; St Paul's Coll., University of Sydney. BA (Hons) 1933; ThD 1949. Registrar, Diocese of Riverina, 1933–37; Rector of: Narrandera, NSW, 1937–39; Tumbarumba, NSW, 1939–43; Gunning, NSW, 1943–44; Director of Studies, Canberra Grammar Sch., Canberra, ACT, 1945; Registrar Diocese of Canberra and Goulburn, 1946–56; Archdeacon of Goulburn, 1946–56; Asst Bishop of Canberra and Goulburn, 1949–56; Bishop of Grafton, NSW, 1956–61; Bishop of Canberra and Goulburn, 1961–71; retired, 1971. *Address:* 5 Quorn Close, Buderim, Qld 4556, Australia.

CLEMENTS, Richard Harry; author and journalist; Consultant, Project Development International Inc. (New York), since 1989; *b* 11 Oct. 1928; *s* of Harry and Sonia Clements; *m* 1952, Bridget Mary MacDonald; two *s*. *Educ:* King Alfred Sch., Hampstead; Western High Sch., Washington, DC; Regent Street Polytechnic. Middlesex Independent, 1949; Leicester Mercury, 1951; Editor, Socialist Advance (Labour Party Youth paper), 1953; industrial staff, Daily Herald, 1954; joined Tribune, 1956, Editor, 1961–82; Political Adviser to the Leader of the Opposition, Rt Hon. Michael Foot, 1982–83; Exec. Officer to Leader of the Opposition, Rt Hon. Neil Kinnock, 1983–87. *Publication:* Glory without Power: a study of trade unions, 1959. *Recreation:* woodwork. *Address:* 53B Hendon Lane, N3 1SG.

CLEMENTS, Prof. Ronald Ernest; Samuel Davidson Professor of Old Testament Studies, King's College, University of London, since 1983; *b* 27 May 1929; *m* 1955, Valerie Winifred (*née* Suffield); two *d*. *Educ:* Buckhurst Hill County High Sch.; Spurgeon's Coll.; Christ's Coll., Cambridge; Univ. of Sheffield. MA, DD Cantab. Asst Lectr 1960–64, Lectr 1960–67, Univ. of Edinburgh; Lectr, Univ. of Cambridge, 1967–83. Hon. For. Sec., SOTS, 1973–83 (Pres., 1985–); Hon. Mem., OTWSA, 1979–. Hon. DLitt Acadia, Nova Scotia, 1982. *Publications:* God and Temple, 1965; Prophecy and Covenant, 1965; Old Testament Theology, 1978; Isaiah 1–39, 1979; A Century of Old Testament Study, 1976, 2nd edn 1983; Prayers of the Bible, 1986; Jeremiah, 1988; (ed) The World of Ancient Israel, 1989; contrib. Vetus Testamentum, Jl of Semitic Studies. *Recreations:* reading, travel, photography. *Address:* 8 Brookfield Road, Coton, Cambridge CB3 7PT.

CLEMINSON, Sir James (Arnold Stacey), KBE 1990; Kt 1982; MC 1945; DL; Vice-Chairman, Norwich Union, since 1981 (Director, since 1979); Director: Eastern Counties Newspaper Group, since 1987; J. H. Fenner plc, since 1989; Riggs National Bank of Washington, since 1991; *b* 31 Aug. 1921; *s* of Arnold Russel Cleminson and Florence Stacey; *m* 1950, Helen Juliet Measor; one *s* two *d*. *Educ:* Rugby Sch. Served War, 1940–46, mainly in Parachute Regt. Reckitt & Colman, 1946–86: Chief Exec., 1973–80; Chm., 1977–86; Chairman: Jeyes Hygiene, 1986–89; Riggs A P Bank, 1987–91 (Dir, 1985–); Director: United Biscuits, 1982–89; Member: Council, CBI, 1978– (Dep. Pres., 1983; Pres., 1984–86); London Cttee, Toronto Dominion Bank, 1982–90; NEDC, 1984–86. Jt Chm., Netherlands British Chamber of Commerce Council, 1978–84; Chairman: Food and Drink Industries Council, 1983–84; Nurses' Independent Pay Review Body, 1986–90; BOTB, 1986–90. Pres., Endeavour Trng, 1984–; Trustee: Airborne Forces Security Fund; Army Benevolent Fund. Pro-Chancellor, Hull Univ., 1985; Hon. LLD Hull, 1985. DL Norfolk, 1983. *Recreations:* field sports, golf. *Address:* Loddon Hall, Hales, Norfolk NR14 6TB. *Clubs:* Boodle's; Norfolk (Norwich).

CLEMITS, John Henry, RIBA; FRSA; Managing Director, PSA Projects Cardiff, since 1990; *b* 16 Feb. 1934; *s* of late Cyril Thomas Clemits and Minnie Alberta Clemits; *m* 1958, Elizabeth Angela Moon; one *s* one *d*. *Educ:* Sutton High Sch.; Plymouth College of Art. ARIBA (Dist. in Thesis). National Service, RAF, 1959–61; Captain, RE (TA), 43 Wessex Div. and Royal Monmouthshire RE (Militia), 1964–69. Plymouth City Architects Dept, 1954–59; Watkins Gray & Partners, Architects, Bristol, 1961–63; SW RHB, 1963–65; Architect, MPBW, Bristol, 1965–69; Sen. Architect, MPBW, Regional HQ, Rheindahlen, Germany, 1969–71; Naval Base Planning Officer, MPBW, Portsmouth, 1971–73; Suptg Architect, PSA, Directorate of Bldg Develt, 1973–75; Suptg Planning Officer, PSA, Rheindahlen, 1975–79; Dir of Works (Army), PSA, Chessington, 1979–85; Dir for Wales, PSA, Central Office for Wales, DoE, 1985–90. Chm., Cowbridge Choral Soc., 1988–90. *Recreations:* golf, music, DIY. *Address:* The Lodge, Hendrescythan, Creigiau, Cardiff CF4 8NN. *T:* Pentyrch (0222) 891786. *Clubs:* Civil Service, Naval.

CLEMITSON, Ivor Malcolm; *b* 8 Dec. 1931; *s* of Daniel Malcolm Clemitson and Annie Ellen Clemitson; *m* 1960, Janet Alicia Meeke; one *s* one *d*. *Educ:* Harlington Primary Sch.; Luton Grammar Sch.; London Sch. of Economics (BScEcon); Bishops Theol College. Deacon 1958, Priest 1959. Curate: St Mary's (Bramall Lane), Sheffield, 1958–61; Christ Church, Luton, 1962–64; Industrial Chaplain, Dio. St Albans, 1964–69; Dir of Industrial Mission, Dio. Singapore, 1969–70; Research Officer, National Graphical Assoc., 1971–74. MP (Lab) Luton East, Feb. 1974–1979; contested (Lab) Luton South, 1983. *Publication:* (with George Rodgers) A Life to Live, 1981. *Recreations:* watching football, theatre, travel.

CLEMOES, Prof. Peter Alan Martin, PhD (Cantab); FRHistS; FSA; Elrington and Bosworth Professor of Anglo-Saxon, Cambridge University, 1969–82, Emeritus Professor since 1982; Official Fellow of Emmanuel College, Cambridge, 1962–69, Professorial Fellow 1969–82, Life Fellow since 1982; Fellow, Queen Mary College, London University, since 1975; *b* 20 Jan. 1920; *o s* of Victor Clemoes and Mary (*née* Paton); *m* 1956, Jean Elizabeth, *yr d* of Sidney Grew; two *s*. *Educ:* Brentwood Sch.; Queen Mary Coll., London; King's Coll., Cambridge. BA London (1st Cl. Hons English) 1950; Soley Student, King's Coll., Cambridge, 1951–53; Research Fellow, Reading Univ., 1954–55; PhD Cambridge 1956. Lectr in English, Reading Univ., 1955–61; Lectr in Anglo-Saxon, Cambridge Univ., 1961–69; Emmanuel College, Cambridge: Coll. Lectr in English, 1963–69 and Dir of Studies in English, 1963–65; Tutor, 1966–68; Asst Librarian, 1963–69. Hon. Sen. Res. Fellow, KCL, 1987–89. Mem., Council of Early English Text Soc., 1971–. Pres., Internat. Soc. of Anglo-Saxonists, 1983–85; Dir, Fontes Anglo-Saxonici (a register of written sources used by authors in Anglo-Saxon England), 1985–. Founder and Chief Editor, Anglo-Saxon England, 1972–89. *Publications:* The Anglo-Saxons, Studies . . . presented to Bruce Dickins (ed and contrib.), 1959; General Editor of Early English Manuscripts in Facsimile (Copenhagen), 1963–74, and co-editor of vol. XIII, 1966, vol. XVIII, 1974; Rhythm and Cosmic Order in Old English Christian Literature (inaug. lecture), 1970; England before the Conquest: Studies . . . presented to Dorothy Whitelock (co-ed and contrib.), 1971; textual and critical writings, especially on the works of Ælfric and Old English poetry. *Festschrift:* Learning and Literature in Anglo-Saxon England: studies presented to Peter Clemoes on the occasion of his sixty-fifth birthday, ed Michael Lapidge and Helmut Gneuss, 1985. *Address:* 14 Church Street, Chesterton, Cambridge CB4 1DT. *T:* Cambridge (0223) 358655.

CLEOBURY, Nicholas Randall, MA; FRCO; conductor; *b* 23 June 1950; *s* of John and Brenda Cleobury; *m* 1978, Heather Kay; one *s* one *d*. *Educ:* King's Sch., Worcester; Worcester Coll., Oxford (MA Hons). Assistant Organist: Chichester Cathedral, 1971–72; Christ Church, Oxford, 1972–76; Chorus Master, Glyndebourne Opera, 1977–79; Asst Director, BBC Singers, 1977–79; Conductor: main BBC, provincial and London orchestras and opera houses, also in Austria, Belgium, Denmark, France, Germany, Holland, Italy, Norway, Spain, Sweden; regular BBC, TV appearances. Principal Opera Conductor, Royal Academy of Music, 1981–88; Artistic Dir, Aquarius, 1983–; Principal Conductor: Cambridge Symphony Orch., 1990–; Eastern Sinfonia, 1990–; Principal Guest Conductor, Gävle, Sweden, 1989–91. Music Dir, Broomhill Arts, 1990–; Artistic Dir, Cambridge Fest., 1992–. Hon. RAM 1985 (Hon. ARAM 1983). *Recreations:* reading, food, wine, theatre, walking, cricket. *Address:* China Cottage, Church Lane, Petham, Canterbury CT4 5RD. *T:* Petham (0227) 70584. *Club:* Savage.

See also S. J. Cleobury.

CLEOBURY, Stephen John, FRCO; Fellow, Director of Music and Organist, King's College, Cambridge, since 1982; Organist, Cambridge University, since 1991; *b* 31 Dec. 1948; *s* of John Frank Cleobury and Brenda Julie (*née* Randall); *m* 1971, Penelope Jane (*née* Holloway); two *d*. *Educ:* King's Sch., Worcester; St John's Coll., Cambridge (MA, MusB). FRCO 1968. Organist, St Matthew's, Northampton, 1971–74; Sub-Organist, Westminster Abbey, 1974–78; Master of Music, Westminster Cathedral, 1979–82. President: IAO, 1985–87; Cathedral Organists' Assoc., 1988–90; RCO, 1990–Oct. 1992 (Hon. Sec., 1981–90); Mem. Council, RSCM, 1982–. Conductor, CUMS, 1983–. *Recreations:* playing chess, watching cricket, reading railway timetables. *Address:* 85 Gough Way, Newnham, Cambridge CB3 9LN. *T:* (college) Cambridge (0223) 350411, ext. 224.

See also N. R. Cleobury.

CLERK of Penicuik, Sir John Dutton, 10th Bt *cr* 1679; CBE 1966; VRD; FRSE 1977; JP; Lord-Lieutenant of Midlothian since 1972 (Vice-Lieutenant, 1965–72); Cdre RNR; retd; *b* 30 Jan. 1917; *s* of Sir George James Robert Clerk of Penicuik, 9th Bt, and Hon. Mabel Honor (*d* 1974), *y d* of late Col Hon. Charles Dutton and *sister* of 6th Baron Sherborne, DSO; *S* father, 1943; *m* 1944, Evelyn Elizabeth Robertson; two *s* two *d*. *Educ:* Stowe. Brig., 1973–89, Ensign, 1989–, Queen's Body Guard for Scotland, Royal Company of Archers. JP 1955, DL 1956, Midlothian. *Heir:* *s* Robert Maxwell Clerk, Younger of Penicuik [*b* 3 April 1945; *m* 1970, Felicity Faye, *yr d* of George Collins, Bampton, Oxford; two *s* one *d*. *Educ:* Winchester Coll.; London Univ. (BSc (Agric)). FRICS]. *Address:* Penicuik House, Penicuik, Midlothian EH26 9LA. *T:* Penicuik (0968) 74318. *Clubs:* Royal Over-Seas League; New (Edinburgh).

CLERKE, Sir John Edward Longueville, 12th Bt *cr* 1660; Captain Royal Wilts Yeomanry, RAC, TA; *b* 29 Oct. 1913; *er s* of Francis William Talbot Clerke (killed in action, 1916), *e s* of 11th Bt, and late Albinia Mary, *er d* of Edward Henry Evans-Lombe (who *m* 3rd, 1923, Air Chief Marshal Sir Edgar Rainey Ludlow-Hewitt, GCB, GBE, CMG, DSO, MC); *S* grandfather, 1930; *m* 1948, Mary (marr. diss. 1987), *d* of late Lt-Col I. R. Beviss Bond, OBE, MC; one *s* two *d*. *Heir:* *s* Francis Ludlow Longueville Clerke [*b* 25 Jan. 1953; *m* 1982, Vanessa Anne, *o d* of late Charles Cosman Citron and of Mrs Olga May Citron, Mouille Point, Cape Town; one *s* one *d*]. *Address:* 48 Savernake Avenue, Melksham, Wilts SN12 7HD. *T:* Melksham (0225) 703994.

CLEVELAND, Archdeacon of; *see* Hawthorn, Ven. C. J.

CLEVELAND, Harlan; Professor, 1980–88 and Dean, 1980–87, Hubert H. Humphrey Institute of Public Affairs, University of Minnesota, now Professor Emeritus; *b* 19 Jan. 1918; *s* of Stanley Matthews Cleveland and Marian Phelps (*née* Van Buren); *m* 1941, Lois W. Burton; one *s* two *d*. *Educ:* Phillips Acad., Andover, Mass; Princeton Univ.; Oxford Univ. Farm Security Admin., Dept of Agric., 1940–42; Bd of Econ. Warfare (subseq. Foreign Econ. Admin.), 1942–44; Exec. Dir Econ. Sect., 1944–45, Actg Vice-Pres., 1945–46, Allied Control Commn, Rome; Mem. US Delegn, UNRRA Council, London, 1945; Dept Chief of Mission, UNRRA Italian Mission, Rome, 1946–47; Dir, UNRRA China Office, Shanghai, 1947–48; Dir, China Program, Econ. Coop. Admin., Washington, 1948–49; Dept Asst Adminstr, 1949–51; Asst Dir for Europe, Mutual Security Agency,

1952–53; Exec. Editor, The Reporter, NYC, 1953–56, Publisher, 1955–56; Dean, Maxwell Sch. of Citizenship and Pub. Affairs, Syracuse Univ., 1956–61; Asst Sec. for Internat. Orgn Affairs, State Dept, 1961–65; US Ambassador to NATO, 1965–69; Pres., Univ. of Hawaii, 1969–74; Dir, Program in Internat. Affairs, Aspen Inst. for Humanistic Studies, 1974–80. Distinguished Vis. Tom Slick Prof. of World Peace, Univ. of Texas at Austin, 1979. Delegate, Democratic National Convention, 1960. Chm., Weather Modification Adv. Bd, US Dept of Commerce, 1977–78; Chm., Nat. Retiree Volunteer Center, 1989–. Pres., World Acad. of Art and Sci., 1991–. Holds hon. degrees and foreign orders; US Medal of Freedom, 1946. Woodrow Wilson Award, Princeton Univ., 1968; Prix de Talloires, Groupe de Talloires, 1981. *Publications:* Next Step in Asia (jtly), 1949; (ed jtly) The Art of Overseasmanship, 1957; (jtly) The Overseas Americans, 1960; (ed) The Promise of World Tensions, 1961; (ed jtly) The Ethic of Power, 1962; (ed jtly) Ethics and Bigness, 1962; The Obligations of Power, 1966; NATO: the Transatlantic Bargain, 1970; The Future Executive, 1972; China Diary, 1976; The Third Try at World Order, 1977; (jtly) Humangrowth: an essay on growth, values and the quality of life, 1978; (ed) Energy Futures of Developing Countries, 1980; (ed jtly) Bioresources for Development, 1980; (ed) The Management of Sustainable Growth, 1981; The Knowledge Executive, 1985; The Global Commons, 1990. *Address:* Hubert H. Humphrey Institute of Public Affairs, HHH Center, 301 19th Avenue South, Minneapolis, Minn 55455, USA. *T:* (612) 625–6062, *Fax:* (612) 625–6351. *Clubs:* Century (NY); International (Washington); Waikiki Yacht (Honolulu).

CLEVERLEY FORD, Rev. Preb. Douglas William; Chaplain to The Queen, 1973–84; *b* 4 March 1914; *yr s* of late Arthur James and Mildred Ford; *m* 1939, Olga Mary, *er d* of late Dr Thomas Bewley and Elizabeth Gilbart-Smith; no *c*. *Educ:* Great Yarmouth Grammar Sch.; Univ. of London. BD, MTh, ALCD (1st cl.). Deacon 1937, Priest 1938. London Coll. of Divinity: Tutor, 1937–39; Lectr, 1942–43 and 1952–58; Lectr, Church Army Trng Coll., 1953–60. Curate of Bridlington, Yorks, 1939–42; Vicar of Holy Trinity, Hampstead, 1942–55; Vicar of Holy Trinity with All Saints Church, South Kensington, 1955–74; Senior Chaplain to Archbishop of Canterbury, 1975–80; Hon. Dir, Coll. of Preachers, 1960–73; Rural Dean of Westminster, 1965–74; Prebendary of St Paul's Cathedral, 1968, now Prebendary Emeritus; Provincial Canon of York, 1969–; Lectr, Wey Inst. of Religious Studies, 1980–84; Tutor, Southwark Ordination Course, 1980–86. Six Preacher, Canterbury Cathedral, 1982–. Chm., Queen Alexandra's House, Kensington Gore, 1966–74; Mem. Governing Body, Westminster City Sch. and United Westminster Schs, 1965–74; Hon. Life Governor: British and Foreign Bible Soc., 1948; Church's Ministry among the Jews, 1955. Queen's Jubilee Medal, 1977. *Publications:* An Expository Preacher's Notebook, 1960; The Christian Faith Explained, 1962; A Theological Preacher's Notebook, 1962; A Pastoral Preacher's Notebook, 1965; A Reading of St Luke's Gospel, 1967; Preaching at the Parish Communion, Vol. 1 1967, Vol. 2 1968, Vol. 3 1969; Preaching Today, 1969; Preaching through the Christian Year, 1971; Praying through the Christian Year, 1973; Have You Anything to Declare?, 1973; Preaching on the Special Occasions, 1974, Vol. 2 1981; Preaching at the Parish Communion (Series III), 1975; New Preaching from the Old Testament, 1976; New Preaching from the New Testament, 1977; The Ministry of the Word, 1979; Preaching through the Acts of the Apostles, 1979; More Preaching from the New Testament, 1982; More Preaching from the Old Testament, 1983; Preaching through the Psalms, 1984; Preaching through the Life of Christ, 1985; Preaching on Devotional Occasions, 1986; From Strength to Strength, 1987; Preaching the Risen Christ, 1988; Preaching on Great Themes, 1989; Preaching on the Holy Spirit, 1990; God's Masterpieces, 1991; contrib. Churchman's Companion 1967, Expository Times. *Recreations:* gardening, music, languages. *Address:* Rostrevor, Lingfield, Surrey RH7 6BZ. *Club:* Athenæum.

CLEWS, Michael Arthur; Master of the Supreme Court Taxing Office, 1970–87; *b* Caudebec, France, 16 Sept. 1919; *s* of late Roland Trevor Clews and late Marjorie (*née* Baily); *m* 1947, Kathleen Edith, *d* of late Adam Hollingworth, OBE, JP, and Gertrude (*née* Bardsley); three *c*. *Educ:* Epworth Coll., Rhyl; Clare Coll., Cambridge (MA). Served in Indian Army (Major, RA and V Force), 1940–46. Solicitor, 1953; Partner, W. H. House & Son, and Knocker & Foskett, Sevenoaks, 1957–70. Mem., Lord Chancellor's Adv. Cttee on Legal Aid, 1977–84. *Address:* Hameau de Coriolan 9, 83120 Plan de la Tour, Var, France.

CLIBBORN, Donovan Harold, CMG 1966; HM Diplomatic Service, retired; *b* 2 July 1917; *s* of Henry Joseph Fairley Clibborn and Isabel Sarah Jago; *m* 1st, 1940, Margaret Mercedes Edwige Nelson (*d* 1966); one *s* two *d*; 2nd, 1973, Victoria Ondiviela Garvi; one step *s* two step *d*. *Educ:* Ilford High Sch.; St Edmund Hall, Oxford (MA). Laming Travelling Fellow, Queen's Coll., Oxford, 1938–40. Entered Consular Service, 1939; Vice-Consul, Genoa, 1939–40. Army Service, 1940–45: Intelligence Corps and Royal Signals, Western Desert, Sicily, Italy, NW Europe (despatches); Major, 1944. Foreign Office, 1945–46; Consul, Los Angeles, 1946–48; Foreign Office, 1948–50; 1st Sec. (UK High Commn, India), Madras, 1950–52; 1st Sec. (Information), Rio de Janeiro, 1952–56; 1st Sec. (Commercial), Madrid, 1956–60; Consul (Commercial), Milan, 1960–62; Counsellor (Economic), Tehran, 1962–64; Counsellor, Rio de Janeiro, 1964–66; Consul-General, Barcelona, 1966–70; Ambassador, El Salvador, 1971–75. *Recreations:* reading, music, perpetrating light verse. *Address:* Paseo del Dr Moragas 188, Atico 1A, Barberá del Vallés, Prov. Barcelona 08210, Spain. *T:* Barcelona 7185377.

See also J. D. N. dalla R. Clibborn.

CLIBBORN, John Donovan Nelson dalla Rosa; HM Diplomatic Service; Counsellor, Washington, since 1988; *b* 24 Nov. 1941; *s* of Donovan Harold Clibborn, *qv*; *m* 1968, Juliet Elizabeth Pagden; one *s* two *d*. *Educ:* Downside Sch., Stratton-on-the-Fosse, Bath; Oriel Coll., Oxford (1st Cl. Hon. Mods and Lit.Hum. BA, MA). Joined HM Diplomatic Service, 1965; FCO, 1965–67; 3rd, subseq. 2nd Sec., Nicosia, 1967–69; FCO, 1970–72; 1st Secretary: Bonn, 1972–75; UK Mission to EC, Brussels, 1975–78; Jt Res. Centre, EEC, 1978–81; FCO, 1981–88. Member: Soc. for the Promotion of Roman Studies, 1963–; Soc. for the Promotion of Hellenic Studies, 1964–; Palestine Exploration Fund, 1965–. *Recreations:* classical literature, ancient history. *Address:* c/o Foreign and Commonwealth Office, SW1. *Club:* Athenæum.

CLIBBORN, Rt. Rev. Stanley Eric Francis B.; *see* Manchester, Bishop of.

CLIBURN, Van, (Harvey Lavan Cliburn Jr); pianist; *b* Shreveport, La, 12 July 1934; *o c* of Harvey Lavan Cliburn and Rildia Bee (*née* O'Bryan). *Educ:* Kilgore High Sch., Texas; Juilliard Sch. of Music, New York. Made début in Houston, Texas, 1947; subsequently has toured extensively in United States and Europe. Awards include first International Tchaikovsky Piano Competition, Moscow, 1958, and every US prize, for pianistic ability. *Recreation:* swimming. *Address:* 455 Wilder Place, Shreveport, La 71104, USA.

CLIFFORD, family name of **Baron Clifford of Chudleigh.**

CLIFFORD OF CHUDLEIGH, 14th Baron *cr* 1672; **Thomas Hugh Clifford;** Count of The Holy Roman Empire; *b* 17 March 1948; *s* of 13th Baron Clifford of Chudleigh, OBE and of Hon. Katharine Vavasseur Fisher, 2nd *d* of 2nd Baron Fisher; *S* father, 1988; *m* 1980, (Muriel) Suzanne, *d* of Major Campbell Austin and Mrs Campbell Austin; two *s* one *d*. *Educ:* Downside Abbey. Commnd Coldstream Guards, 1967; stationed British Honduras, 1967–68; Instructor, Guards Depot, 1968–69; Northern Ireland (three 6-month periods), 1969–70 and 1971–72; ADC to Chief of Defence Staff, 1972–73; served with Ace Mobile Force, 1973; Adjutant, Guards Depot, 1973–75. Royal Agricultural College, Cirencester, 1976–78. *Recreations:* shooting, fishing, tennis, croquet. *Heir: s* Hon. Alexander Thomas Hugh Clifford, *b* 24 Sept. 1985. *Address:* Ugbrooke Park, Chudleigh, South Devon TQ13 0AD. *T:* (office) Chudleigh (0626) 852179.

CLIFFORD, Clark McAdams; Senior Partner, Clifford & Warnke, since 1969; Special Counsel and Special Envoy of the President of the United States; *b* 25 Dec. 1906; *s* of Frank Andrew Clifford and Georgia (*née* McAdams); *m* 1931, Margery Pepperell Kimball; three *d*. *Educ:* Washington Univ., St Louis (LLB). Served US Naval Reserve, 1944–46 (Naval Commendation Ribbon). Practised law in St Louis, 1928–43; specialised in trial cases, corporation and labour law; Special Counsel to President of US, 1946–50; Senior Partner, Clifford & Miller, 1950–68; Secretary of Defense, USA, 1968–69. Dir, Knight-Ridder Newspapers; Chm. Bd, First American Bankshares, Inc. (formerly Financial General Bankshares). Medal of Freedom with Distinction, USA, 1969. *Recreation:* golf. *Address:* 815 Connecticut Avenue, Washington, DC 20006, USA.

CLIFFORD, Most Rev. Dermot; *see* Cashel and Emly, Archbishop of, (RC).

CLIFFORD, Rev. Paul Rowntree, MA; President, Selly Oak Colleges, Birmingham, 1965–79; *b* 21 Feb. 1913; *s* of Robert and Harriet Rowntree Clifford; *m* 1st, 1947, Marjory Jean Tait (*d* 1988); one *s* one *d*; 2nd, 1989, Dorothy Marion White, OBE. *Educ:* Mill Hill Sch.; Balliol Coll., Oxford; Mansfield and Regents Park Colls, Oxford. MA (Oxon) 1939. West Ham Central Mission, London: Asst Minister, 1938–43; Supt Minister, 1943–53; McMaster Univ., Hamilton, Canada: Asst Prof. of Homiletics and Pastoral Theology, 1953–59; Dean of Men and Chm. of Dept of Religion, 1959–64; Prof. of Religion, 1964–65. Hon. Treas., Internat. Assoc. for Mission Studies, 1974–88; Sec., Foundn for Study of Christianity and Society, 1980–90. *Publications:* The Mission of the Local Church, 1953; The Pastoral Calling, 1959; Now is the Time, 1970; Interpreting Human Experience, 1971; The Death of the Dinosaur, 1977; Politics and the Christian Vision, 1984; Government by the People?, 1986; articles in Jl of Religion, Metaphysical Review, Dialogue, Canadian Jl of Theology, Scottish Jl of Theology, Foundations, Religious Studies. *Recreations:* golf, gardening. *Address:* 12 Ravens Court, St John's Road, Eastbourne, Sussex BN20 7HY. *Club:* Reform (Chm., 1987–89).

CLIFFORD, Sir Roger (Joseph), 7th Bt *cr* 1887; *b* 5 June 1936; *s* of Sir Roger Charles Joseph Gerard Clifford, 6th Bt and Henrietta Millicent Kiver (*d* 1971); *S* father 1982; *m* 1968, Joanna Theresa, *d* of C. J. Ward, Christchurch, NZ; two *d*. *Educ:* Beaumont College, England. *Recreations:* golf, Rugby football. *Heir: b* Charles Joseph Clifford [*b* 5 June 1936; *m* 1983, Sally Green]. *Address:* 135 Totara Street, Christchurch, New Zealand. *T:* 485958. *Clubs:* Blenheim (Bleinheim, NZ); Christchurch Golf.

CLIFFORD, Timothy Peter Plint, BA, AMA; Director, National Galleries of Scotland, since 1984; *b* 26 Jan. 1946; *s* of Derek Plint Clifford and late Anne (*née* Pierson); *m* 1968, Jane Olivia, *yr d* of Sir George Paterson, *qv*; one *d*. *Educ:* Sherborne, Dorset; Perugia Univ. (Dip. Italian); Courtauld Inst., Univ. of London (BA Hons, History of Art). Dip. Fine Art, Museums Assoc., 1972. Asst Keeper, Dept of Paintings, Manchester City Art Galleries, 1968–72, Acting Keeper, 1972; Asst Keeper, Dept of Ceramics, Victoria and Albert Mus., London, 1972–76; Asst Keeper, Dept of Prints and Drawings, British Mus., London, 1976–78; Dir, Manchester City Art Galls, 1978–84. Member: Manchester Diocesan Adv. Cttee for Care of Churches, 1978–84; NACF Cttee (Cheshire and Gtr Manchester Br.), 1978–84; North Western Museum and Art Gall. Service Jt Adv. Panel, 1978–84; Cttee, ICOM (UK), 1980–82; Chm., Internat. Cttee for Museums of Fine Art, ICOM, 1980–83 (Mem., Exec. Cttee, 1983–88); Member: Museums and Galleries Commn, 1983–88; British Council, 1987– (Fine Arts Adv. Cttee, 1988–); Founder and Committee Member: Friends of Manchester City Art Galls, 1978–84; Patrons and Associates, Manchester City Art Galls, 1979–; Mem. Exec. Cttee, Scottish Museums Council, 1984–. Cttee Mem., Derby Internat. Porcelain Soc., 1983–86; Vice Pres., Turner Soc., 1984–86, and 1989–; Mem., Adv. Cttee, Come and See Scotland's Churches, 1989–90. Vice-Pres., Frigate Unicorn Preservation Soc., 1987–. Trustee, Lake Dist Art Gall. and Mus. Trust, 1989–. Mem., Accadèmia Italiana delle Arti Applicate, 1988–. FRSA; FSA(Scot) 1986. Freeman: Goldsmiths' Co., 1989; City of London, 1989. Cavaliere al Ordine della Repubblica Italiana, 1988. *Publications:* (with Derek Clifford) John Crome, 1968; (with Dr Ivan Hall) Heaton Hall, 1972; (with Dr T. Friedmann) The Man at Hyde Park Corner: sculpture by John Cheere, 1974; Vues Pittoresques de Luxembourg ... par J. M. W. Turner, (Luxembourg) 1977; Ceramics of Derbyshire 1750–1975 (ed, H. G. Bradley), 1978; J. M. W. Turner, Acquerelli e incisioni, (Rome) 1980; Turner at Manchester, 1982; contrib. Burlington Magazine, etc. *Recreations:* shooting, bird watching, entomology. *Address:* National Galleries of Scotland, The Mound, Edinburgh EH2 2EL. *Clubs:* Turf, Beefsteak; New (Edinburgh).

CLIFFORD, William Henry Morton, CB 1972; CBE 1966; Legal Consultant, Civil Service College, 1974–79, retired; *b* 30 July 1909; *s* of Henry Edward Clifford, FRIBA, Glasgow, and Margaret Alice, *d* of Dr William Gibson, Campbeltown, Argyll; *m* 1936, Katharine Winifred, *d* of Rev. H. W. Waterfield, Temple Grove, Eastbourne; one *s* two *d*. *Educ:* Tonbridge Sch.; Corpus Christi Coll., Cambridge. Admitted a solicitor, 1936. Entered Solicitor's Department, GPO, 1937. Served in Army, 1939–45: Major GS, Army Council Secretariat, WO, 1944–45. Transferred to Solicitor's Office, Min. of National Insurance, 1945; Assistant Solicitor, Min. of Pensions and Nat. Insurance (later Min. of Social Security), 1953; Solicitor, DHSS (formerly Min. of Social Security), 1968–74. *Recreations:* reading, listening to music (especially opera), genealogy, walking, sailing. *Address:* Woodbrook, 9 Lake Road, Tunbridge Wells, Kent TN4 8XT. *T:* Tunbridge Wells (0892) 21612.

CLIFFORD-TURNER, Raymond; solicitor; Senior Partner, Clifford-Turner, 1941–81; *b* 7 Feb. 1906; *s* of Harry Clifford-Turner, solicitor; *m* 1st, 1933, Zoë Vachell (*d* 1984); one *s* two *d*; 2nd, 1988, Diana Dumergue Edwards. *Educ:* Rugby Sch.; Trinity Coll., Cambridge. Solicitor, 1930; Partner, Clifford-Turner & Co., 1931. Dir, Transport Holding Co., 1962–73. Wing Commander, RAFVR. *Recreations:* golf, racing. *Address:* Garden Flat, 86 Eaton Place, SW1. *T:* 071–235 2443; Childown, Longcross, near Chertsey, Surrey KT16 0EH. *T:* Ottershaw (093287) 2608. *Clubs:* Portland; Berkshire; Swinley.

CLIFT, Richard Dennis, CMG 1984; HM Diplomatic Service, retired; furniture restorer; *b* 18 May 1933; *s* of late Dennis Victor Clift and Helen Wilmot Clift (*née* Evans); *m* 1st, 1957, Barbara Mary Travis (marr. diss. 1982); three *d*; 2nd, 1982, Jane Rosamund Barker (*née* Homfray). *Educ:* St Edward's Sch., Oxford; Pembroke Coll., Cambridge. BA 1956. FO, 1956–57; Office of British Chargé d'Affaires, Peking, 1958–60; British Embassy, Berne, 1961–62; UK Delegn to NATO, Paris, 1962–64; FO, 1964–68; Head of Chancery, British High Commn, Kuala Lumpur, 1969–71; FCO, 1971–73; Counsellor (Commercial), Peking, 1974–76; Canadian Nat. Defence Coll., 1976–77; seconded to NI

Office, 1977–79; Hd of Hong Kong Dept, FCO, 1979–84; High Comr in Freetown, 1984–86; Political Advr, Hong Kong Govt, 1987–89. Student, London Coll. of Furniture, 1989–91. *Recreations:* sailing, walking. *Address:* 18 Langwood Chase, Teddington, Middx.

CLIFT, Prof. Roland, FEng 1986; Professor of Chemical Engineering, University of Surrey, since 1981; *b* 19 Nov. 1942; *s* of Leslie William Clift and Ivy Florence Gertrude Clift (*née* Wheeler); *m* 1st, 1968, Rosena Valory (*née* Davison); one *d*; 2nd, 1979, Diana Helen (*née* Manning); two *s. Educ:* Trinity Coll., Cambridge (BA 1963; MA 1967); PhD McGill 1970. CEng, FIChem E. Technical Officer (Chem. Engr), ICI, 1964–67; Lectr, Asst Prof. and Associate Prof., McGill Univ., 1967–75; Lectr, Imperial Coll., London, 1975–76; Lectr, Univ. of Cambridge, 1976–81; Fellow, Trinity Coll., Cambridge, 1976–81 (Praelector, 1980–81). Vis. Prof., Univ. di Napoli, 1973–74; Dir, Clift Mar Associates, 1986–. Chm., Clean Technology Management Cttee, SERC, 1990–. Mem., Governing Body, Charterhouse Sch., 1982–91. Hon. Citizen of Augusta, Georgia, 1987. Editor in Chief, Powder Technology, 1987–. *Publications:* (jtly) Bubbles, Drops and Particles, 1978; (ed jtly) Fluidization, 1985. *Recreation:* music. *Address:* Department of Chemical and Process Engineering, University of Surrey, Guildford, Surrey GU2 5XH. *T:* Guildford (0483) 509239.

CLIFTON, Lord; Ivo Donald Stuart Bligh; *b* 17 April 1968; *s* and *heir* of 11th Earl of Darnley, *qv*.

CLIFTON, Bishop of (RC), since 1974; **Rt. Rev. Mervyn Alban Newman Alexander,** DD; *b* London, 29 June 1925; *s* of William Paul Alexander and Grace Evelyn Alexander (*née* Newman). *Educ:* Bishop Wordsworth School, Salisbury; Prior Park College, Bath; Gregorian University, Rome (DD 1951). Curate at Pro-Cathedral, Clifton, Bristol, 1951–63; RC Chaplain, Bristol University, 1953–67; Parish Priest, Our Lady of Lourdes, Weston-super-Mare, 1967–72; Auxiliary Bishop of Clifton and Titular Bishop of Pinhel, 1972–74; Vicar Capitular of Clifton, 1974. *Address:* St Ambrose, Leigh Woods, Bristol BS8 3PW. *T:* Bristol (0272) 733072.

CLIFTON, Lt-Col Peter Thomas, CVO 1980; DSO 1945; DL; JP; Standard Bearer, HM Body Guard of Honourable Corps of Gentlemen at Arms, 1979–81; *b* 24 Jan. 1911; *s* of Lt-Col Percy Robert Clifton, CMG, DSO, TD, Clifton Hall, Nottingham; *m* 1st, 1934, Ursula (marr. diss. 1936), *d* of Sir Edward Hussey Packe; 2nd, 1948, Patricia Mary Adela, DStJ (who *m* 1935, Robert Cobbold, killed in action 1944), *d* of Major J. M. Gibson-Watt, Doldowlod, Radnorshire; two *d. Educ:* Eton; RMC Sandhurst. 2nd Lieut Grenadier Guards, 1931; served War of 1939–45: France, 1939–40; Italy, 1944–45; Lt-Col 1944; Palestine, 1945–47. Mem. HM Body Guard of Hon. Corps of Gentlemen at Arms, 1960–81 (Clerk of the Cheque and Adjutant, 1973–79). DL Notts 1954; JP Notts 1952–59, Hants 1964. *Address:* Dummer House, Basingstoke, Hants RG25 2AG. *T:* Dummer (0256) 397306. *Clubs:* Cavalry and Guards, White's; Royal Yacht Squadron.
See also Baron Gibson-Watt, Baron Wrottesley.

CLINCH, David John; Secretary, Open University, since 1981; *b* 14 Feb. 1937; *s* of Thomas Charles Clinch and Madge Isabel Clinch (*née* Saker); *m* 1963, Hilary Jacques; one *s* one *d. Educ:* Nautical Coll., Pangbourne; St Cuthbert's Soc., Univ. of Durham (BA); Indiana Univ. (MBA). National Service, Royal Navy (Sub-Lieut), Supply and Secretariat, 1955–57. Administrator, Univ. of Sussex, 1963–69; Deputy Secretary and Registrar, Open University, 1969–81; Registrar Counterpart, Allama Iqbal Open Univ., Pakistan, 1976–77. Member: Conf. of Univ. Administrators, 1973–; Conf. of Registrars and Secs, 1981– (Chm., 1990–91); British Fulbright Scholars Assoc., 1978–. Dir, Nat. Educnl Resources Information Service Trust, 1989–; Trustee, Open Univ. Superannuation Scheme, 1989–. *Recreations:* gardening, music, natural history, reading, walking. *Address:* 39 Tudor Gardens, Stony Stratford, Milton Keynes MK11 1HX. *T:* Milton Keynes (0908) 562475.

CLINTON; *see* Fiennes-Clinton, family name of Earl of Lincoln.

CLINTON, 22nd Baron *cr* 1299 (title abeyant 1957–65); **Gerard Nevile Mark Fane Trefusis;** DL; landowner; *b* 7 Oct. 1934; *s* of Capt. Charles Fane (killed in action, 1940); assumed by deed poll, 1958, surname of Trefusis in addition to patronymic; *m* 1959, Nicola Harriette Purdon Coote; one *s* two *d. Educ:* Gordonstoun. Took seat in House of Lords, 1965. Mem., Prince of Wales's Councils, 1968–79. JP Bideford, 1963–83; DL Devon, 1977. *Recreations:* shooting, fishing, forestry. *Heir: s* Hon. Charles Patrick Rolle Fane Trefusis, *b* 21 March 1962. *Address:* Heanton Satchville, near Okehampton, North Devon EX20 3QE. *T:* Dolton (08054) 224. *Club:* Boodle's.

CLINTON, (Robert) Alan; Director, since 1986, Managing Director, since 1987, Picton House Group of Companies, property development cos; *b* 12 July 1931; *s* of John and Leah Clinton; *m* 1956, Valerie Joy Falconer. *Educ:* George Dixon Grammar Sch., Edgbaston, Birmingham. On leaving school, joined the Post Office, 1948; Member, North Western Postal Board, 1970; Asst Director (Personnel), London, 1975; Asst Director (Operations), London, 1976; Director of Eastern Postal Region, Colchester, 1978; Director of Postal Operations, London, 1979; Member Post Office Board, 1981–85: for Mails Network and Develt, 1981; for Mails Ops and Estates, 1982; for Corporate Services, 1984–85; Man. Dir, Counter Services, 1984–85. FCIT 1982. Mem., Worshipful Company of Carmen, 1981; Freeman of City of London, 1979. *Recreations:* music, walking, sailing. *Address:* Summer Cottage, The Quay, St Osyth, Clacton-on-Sea, Essex CO16 8EW. *T:* St Osyth (0255) 820368; Flat 19, 4 Crane Court, Fleet Street, EC4A 2EJ. *T:* 071–353 7509. *Clubs:* City of London, City Livery; Colne Yacht (Brightlingsea).

CLINTON-DAVIS, family name of **Baron Clinton-Davis**.

CLINTON-DAVIS, Baron *cr* 1990 (Life Peer), of Hackney in the London Borough of Hackney; **Stanley Clinton Clinton-Davis;** consultant on European affairs and law, S. J. Berwin & Co., solicitors, since 1989; Senior Adviser on European Affairs, Hill and Knowlton, since 1989; *b* 6 Dec. 1928; *s* of Sidney Davis; name changed to Clinton-Davis by deed poll, 1990; *m* 1954, Frances Jane Lucas; one *s* three *d. Educ:* Hackney Downs Sch.; Mercers' Sch.; King's Coll., London University. LLB 1950; admitted Solicitor 1953. Mem. Exec. Council, Nat. Assoc. of Labour Student Organisations, 1949–50. Councillor, London Borough of Hackney, 1959; Mayor of Hackney, 1968. Contested (Lab): Langstone Div. of Portsmouth, 1955; Yarmouth, 1959 and 1964. MP (Lab) Hackney Central, 1970–83; Parly Under-Sec. of State, Dept of Trade, 1974–79; Opposition spokesman on trade, prices and consumer protection, 1979–81, on foreign affairs, 1981–83; Opposition frontbench spokesman on transport, H of L, 1990–. Mem., Commn of EC, 1985–89. Chm., Adv. Cttee on Pollution of the Sea, 1984–85, 1989–; Chair, Refugee Council, 1989–. Member: Council and Exec. Cttee, Justice; Exec. Cttee, Lab. Finance and Industry Gp; APEX; UN Selection Cttee for Sasakawa, Envmt Project; Bd, Jewish Chronicle; formerly Mem., Bd of Deputies of British Jews; Parly Relations Sub-Cttee of the Law Soc. Mem. Council, British Maritime League, 1989–. Pres., Hackney Br., Multiple Sclerosis Soc.; Vice-Pres., Hackney Assoc. for Disabled; Mem. Rotary Club, Hackney; Trustee, Bernt Carlsson Trust (One World), 1989–. Hon. Mem., 1979, and former Trustee, NUMAST (formerly Merchant Navy and Airline Officers' Assoc.). First Medal for Outstanding Services to Animal Welfare in Europe, Eurogroup for Animal Welfare, 1988. Grand Cross, Order of Leopold II, Belgium (for services to EC), 1990. *Recreations:* golf, Association football, reading biographical histories. *Address:* c/o S. J. Berwin & Co., 236 Gray's Inn Road, WC1X 8HB.

CLITHEROE, 2nd Baron *cr* 1955, of Downham; **Ralph John Assheton;** Bt 1945; Lord of the Honor of Clitheroe and Hundred of Blackburn; DL; Chairman, Yorkshire Bank, since 1990; *b* 3 Nov. 1929; *s* of 1st Baron Clitheroe, KCVO, PC, FSA, and Sylvia Benita Frances, Lady Clitheroe, FRICS, FLAS, (*d* 1991), *d* of 6th Baron Hotham; *S* father, 1984; *m* 1961, Juliet, *d* of Lt-Col Christopher Lionel Hanbury, MBE, TD; two *s* one *d. Educ:* Eton; Christ Church, Oxford (Scholar, MA). Served as 2nd Lieut Life Guards, 1948–49. Chairman: RTZ Chemicals Ltd, 1973–87; RTZ Borax Ltd, 1979–89; US Borax and Chemical Corp., 1979–89; RTZ Oil & Gas Ltd, 1983–88; Director: Borax Consolidated, 1960–89; RTZ Corp., 1968–89; First Interstate Bank of California, 1981–89; TR Natural Resources Investment Trust, 1982–87; American Mining Congress, 1982–89; Halliburton Co., Texas, 1987–. Mem., Council, Chemical Industries Assoc., 1984–88. Liveryman, Skinners' Co. DL Lancs, 1986. *Heir: s* Hon. Ralph Christopher Assheton, *b* 19 March 1962. *Address:* Downham Hall, Clitheroe, Lancs. *Clubs:* Boodle's, Pratt's, Royal Automobile.

CLIVE, Viscount; John George Herbert; Assistant Professor, Redeemer College, Ontario, Canada, since 1990; *b* 19 May 1952; *s* and *heir* of Earl of Powis, *qv*; *m* 1977, Marijke, *d* of Martin Guther, Hamilton, Canada; one *s* two *d. Educ:* Wellington; McMaster Univ., Ontario, Canada (MA). Formerly Lectr, McMaster Univ. *Heir: s* Hon. Jonathan Nicholas William Herbert, *b* 5 Dec. 1979. *Address:* c/o Marrington Hall, Chirbury, Montgomery, Powys SY15 6DR.

CLIVE, Eric McCredie; a Scottish Law Commissioner, since 1981; *b* 24 July 1938; *s* of Robert M. Clive and Mary L. D. Clive; *m* 1962, Kay M. McLeman; one *s* three *d. Educ:* Univs of Edinburgh (MA, LLB with dist.); Michigan (LLM); Virginia (SJD). Solicitor. Lecturer 1962–69, Sen. Lectr 1969–75, Reader 1975–77, Professor of Scots Law 1977–81, Univ. of Edinburgh. *Publications:* Law of Husband and Wife in Scotland, 1974, 2nd edn 1982; (jtly) Scots Law for Journalists, 1965, 5th edn 1988; articles and notes in legal jls. *Recreations:* beekeeping, hill-walking, chess. *Address:* 14 York Road, Edinburgh EH5 3EH. *T:* 031–552 2875.

CLIVE, Nigel David, CMG 1967; OBE 1959; MC 1944; TD; HM Diplomatic Service, retired; *b* 13 July 1917; *s* of late Horace David and Hilda Mary Clive; *m* 1949, Maria Jeanne Tambakopoulou. *Educ:* Stowe; Christ Church, Oxford (Scholar). Commissioned 2nd Mddx Yeomanry, 1939; served in Middle East and Greece. Joined Foreign Office, 1946; served Athens, 1946–48; Jerusalem, 1948; FO, 1948–50; Baghdad, 1950–53; FO, 1953–58; Tunis, 1958–62; Algiers, 1962–63; FO, 1964–65; Head of Information Research Dept, FCO (formerly FO), 1966–69; Adviser to Secretary-General of OECD, 1970–80. FRSA 1989. *Publication:* A Greek Experience 1943–1948, 1985. *Recreations:* reading, travel. *Address:* Flat 2, 41 Lowndes Square, SW1X 9JL. *T:* 071–235 1186. *Clubs:* Brooks's, Special Forces, MCC.

CLOAKE, John Cecil, CMG 1977; HM Diplomatic Service, retired; *b* 2 Dec. 1924; *s* of late Dr Cecil Stedman Cloake, Wimbledon, and Maude Osborne Newling; *m* 1956, Margaret Thomure Morris, Washington, DC, USA; one *s. Educ:* King's Coll. Sch., Wimbledon; Peterhouse, Cambridge. Served in Army, 1943–46 (Lieut RE). Foreign Office, 1948; 3rd Sec., Baghdad, 1949, and Saigon, 1951; 2nd Sec., 1952; FO, 1954; Private Sec. to Permanent Under-Sec., 1956, and to Parly Under-Sec., 1957; 1st Sec., 1957; Consul (Commercial), New York, 1958; 1st Sec., Moscow, 1962; FO, 1963; DSAO, 1965; Counsellor, 1966; Head of Accommodation Dept, 1967; Counsellor (Commercial), Tehran, 1968–72; Fellow, Centre for International Studies, LSE, 1972–73; Head of Trade Relations and Exports Dept, FCO, 1973–76; Ambassador to Bulgaria, 1976–80. Member: Council, British Inst. of Persian Studies, 1981– (Hon. Treas. 1982–90); Cttee of Honour for Bulgarian 1300th Anniv., 1981. Chairman: Richmond Museum Project, 1983–86; Richmond Soc. History Section, 1975–76, 1984–85; Richmond Local Hist. Soc., 1985–90 (Pres., 1990–); Mus. of Richmond, 1986–. *Publications:* Templer: Tiger of Malaya, 1985; Richmond Past, 1991; articles on local history. *Recreations:* gardening, painting, architecture, local history, genealogy. *Address:* 4 The Terrace, Richmond Hill, Richmond, Surrey TW10 6RN.

CLODE, Dame (Emma) Frances (Heather), DBE 1974 (CBE 1969; OBE 1955; MBE 1951); Chairman, Women's Royal Voluntary Service, 1971–74; *b* 12 Aug. 1903; *d* of Alexander and Florence Marc; *m* 1927, Colonel Charles Clode (then Captain in Royal Norfolk Regt); one *s. Educ:* privately. Joined WRVS, 1939; served in Cambridge, 1940–45; WRVS Headquarters, 1945; Vice-Chm. 1967. CStJ 1973. *Address:* 19 Rusher's Close, Pershore, Worcs WR10 1HF.

CLOGHER, Bishop of, since 1986; **Rt. Rev. Brian Desmond Anthony Hannon;** *b* 5 Oct. 1936; *s* of late Ven. Arthur Gordon Hannon and of Hilda Catherine Stewart-Moore Hannon (*née* Denny); *m* 1964, Maeve Geraldine Audley (*née* Butler); three *s. Educ:* Mourne Grange Prep. School, Co. Down; St Columba's Coll., Co. Dublin; Trinity Coll., Dublin (BA Hons 1959, 1st Class Divinity Testimonium 1961). Deacon 1961, priest 1962; Diocese of Derry: Curate-Assistant, All Saints, Clooney, Londonderry, 1961–64; Rector of Desertmartin, 1964–69; Rector of Christchurch, Londonderry, 1969–82; RD of Londonderry, 1977–82; Diocese of Clogher: Rector of St Macartin's Cathedral, Enniskillen, 1982–86; Canon of Cathedral Chapter, 1983; Dean of Clogher, 1985. Chm. of Western (NI) Education and Library Bd, 1989–91; Mem., WCC Central Cttee, 1983–. Hon. MA TCD, 1962. *Publication:* (editor/author) Christ Church, Londonderry—1830 to 1980—Milestones, Ministers, Memories, 1980. *Recreations:* walking, music, travel, sport. *Address:* The See House, Fivemiletown, Co. Tyrone, Northern Ireland BT75 0QP. *T:* Fivemiletown (03655) 21265.

CLOGHER, Bishop of, (RC), since 1979; **Most Rev. Joseph Duffy,** DD; *b* 3 Feb. 1934; *s* of Edward Duffy and Brigid MacEntee. *Educ:* St Macartan's College, Monaghan; Maynooth College. MA, BD, HDipEd. Ordained priest, 1958; Teacher, 1960–72; Curate, 1972–79. *Publications:* Patrick in his own words, 1972; Lough Derg Guide, 1980. *Recreations:* local history, travel. *Address:* Bishop's House, Monaghan, Ireland. *T:* 047–81019.

CLOSE, Richard Charles, FCA; Board Member for Corporate Finance and Planning, Post Office, since 1989; *b* 3 Sept. 1949; *s* of Richard Alwen Close and Marjorie Ann Close; *m* 1973, Elizabeth Janet Beatrice Brown; one *s* one *d. Educ:* Canford Sch., Wimborne, Dorset; Sidney Sussex Coll., Cambridge Univ. (MA). Qualified Inst. of Chartered Accountants, 1974; FCA 1979; FCT 1990. Arthur Young & Co., Chartered Accountants, 1971–74; Arthur Young, Milan, Italy, 1974–81; Regional Dir Internal Audit, Europe, ME and Africa, Sperry Corp., 1981–84; European Treasurer, Sperry Corp., 1984–86; Finance Dir, Unisys Ltd, 1986–87; Corporate Finance Dir, Post Office, 1987–89. *Publications:* contribs to financial jls. *Recreations:* tennis, fishing, walking. *Address:* 9 Birnam Close, Send Marsh, Ripley, Surrey GU23 6JH. *T:* Guildford (0483) 224755.

CLOSE, Roy Edwin, CBE 1973; *b* 11 March 1920; *s* of Bruce Edwin and Minnie Louise Close; *m* 1947, Olive Joan Forty; two *s*. *Educ:* Trinity County Sch., N London. Served Army, 1939–46; SAS, 1943–46 (Captain). Editorial Staff, The Times; Asst Editor, The Times Review of Industry, 1949–56; Executive, Booker McConnell GP; Dir, Bookers Sugar Estates, 1957–65; Directing Staff, Admin. Staff Coll., Henley, 1965; Industrial Adviser, NEDO, 1966–69; Industrial Dir, NEDO, 1969–73; MSc Univ. of Aston in Birmingham, 1973; Chm., Univ. of Aston Management Centre; Dean of Faculty of Management, 1973–76; Dir. Gen., BIM, 1976–85; Proprietor, Management Adv. Services. Director: Davies and Perfect, 1985–87; Flextech plc, 1985–87; Kepner Tregoe Ltd, 1986–89; Broad Street Group, 1986–91 (Chm., 1986–88). Chairman: Open Univ. Management Educn Sector Bd, 1984–87; Open Business Sch., 1984–87; Open Business Sch. Industrial and Professional Adv. Cttee, 1988–. Chm., Conservation Foundn, 1987– (Dir, 1986–). Mem. Council, Farm–Africa, 1987–. CBIM (FBIM 1979); FIIM (FIWM 1979); FRSA 1980. DUniv Open, 1987. *Publications:* various articles on industrial, economic subjects. *Recreations:* swimming, walking, reading, listening to music. *Address:* Cathedral Cottage, North Elmham, Dereham, Norfolk NR20 5JU. *Clubs:* Reform, Special Forces.

CLOTHIER, Sir Cecil (Montacute), KCB 1982; QC 1965; Chairman, Council on Tribunals, since 1989; *b* 28 Aug. 1919; *s* of Hugh Montacute Clothier, Liverpool; *m* 1943, Mary Elizabeth (*d* 1984), *o d* of late Ernest Glover Bush; one *s* two *d*. *Educ:* Stonyhurst Coll.; Lincoln Coll., Oxford (BCL, MA; Hon. Fellow 1984). Served 1939–46, 51 (Highland) Div.; British Army Staff, Washington, DC; Hon. Lt-Col Royal Signals. Called to Bar, Inner Temple, 1950, Bencher, 1973. Recorder of Blackpool, later of the Crown Court, 1965–78; Judge of Appeal, IoM, 1972–78. A Legal Assessor to Gen. Medical and Gen. Dental Councils, 1972–78; Mem., Royal Commn on NHS, 1976–78; Parly Comr for Admin, and Health Service Comr for England, Wales and Scotland, 1979–84; Chm., Police Complaints Authority, 1985–89; Mem., Top Salaries Rev. Body, 1989–; Vice-Pres., Interception of Communications Tribunal, 1986–. John Snow Meml lectr (Assoc. of Anaesthetists of GB and Ireland/Amer. Assoc. of Anaesthesiologists), 1981. Hon. Mem., Assoc. of Anaesthetists of GB and Ireland, 1987; Hon. FRPharmS 1990. Rock Carling Fellow, Nuffield Provincial Hosps Trust, 1987. Hon. LLD Hull, 1982. *Address:* 2 King's Bench Walk, Temple, EC4Y 7DE.

CLOUDSLEY-THOMPSON, Prof. John Leonard, MA, PhD (Cantab), DSc (London); FRES, FLS, FZS, FIBiol, FWAAS; Professor of Zoology, Birkbeck College, University of London, 1972–86, now Emeritus (Reader 1971–72); *b* Murree, India, 23 May 1921; *s* of Dr Ashley George Gyton Thompson, MA, MD (Cantab), DPH, and Muriel Elaine (*née* Griffiths); *m* 1944, Jessie Anne Cloudsley, MCSP, DipBS, LCAD; three *s*. *Educ:* Marlborough Coll.; Pembroke Coll., Univ. of Cambridge. War of 1939–45: commissioned into 4th Queen's Own Hussars, 1941; transf. 4th Co. of Lond. Yeo. (Sharpshooters); N Africa, 1941–42 (severely wounded); Instructor (Capt.), Sandhurst, 1943; rejoined regt for D Day (escaped from Villers Bocage), Caen Offensive, etc, 1944 (Hon. rank of Capt. on resignation). Lectr in Zoology, King's Coll., Univ. of London, 1950–60; Prof. of Zoology, Univ. of Khartoum, and Keeper, Sudan Nat. Hist. Museum, 1960–71. Nat. Science Foundn Sen. Res. Fellow, Univ. of New Mexico, Albuquerque, USA, 1969; Visiting Professor: Univ. of Kuwait, 1978 and 1983; Univ. of Nigeria, Nsukka, 1981; Univ. of Qatar, 1986; Sultan Qaboos Univ., Muscat, 1988; Leverhulme Emeritus Fellow, 1987–89; Visiting Research Fellow: ANU, 1987; Namib Desert Ecol. Res. Unit, Namibia, 1989. Hon. Consultant: Univ. of Malaya, 1969; Arabian Gulf Univ., Bahrain, 1986; Univ. of Kuwait, 1990. Took part in: Cambridge Iceland Expedn, 1947; Expedn to Southern Tunisia, 1954; univ. expedns with his wife to various parts of Africa, 1960–73, incl. Trans-Sahara crossing, 1967. Chairman: British Naturalists' Assoc., 1974–83 (Vice-Pres., 1985–); Biological Council, 1977–82 (Medal, 1985). President: British Arachnological Soc., 1982–85 (Vice-Pres., 1985–86); British Soc. for Chronobiology, 1985–87; Vice-President: Linnean Soc., 1975–76 and 1977–78; 1st World Congress of Herpetology, 1989. Hon. Member: Royal African Soc., 1969 (Medal, 1969); British Herpetological Soc., 1983 (Pres., 1991–). Liveryman, Worshipful Co. of Skinners, 1952–. Silver Jubilee Gold Medal and Hon. DSc, Khartoum, 1981. Inst. of Biology K. S. S. Charter Award, 1981; J. H. Grundy Medal, Royal Army Med. Coll., 1987; Foundn for Envmtl Conservation Prize, Geneva, 1989. Editor: Jl of Arid Environments (assisted by wife), Vol. 1, 1978–; (with wife) Natural History of the Arabian Gulf (book series), 1981–82; Adaptations of Desert Organisms (book series), 1989–. *Publications:* Biology of Deserts (ed), 1954; Spiders, Scorpions, Centipedes and Mites, 1958 (2nd edn 1968); Animal Behaviour, 1960; Rhythmic Activity in Animal Physiology and Behaviour, 1961; Land Invertebrates (with John Sankey), 1961; Life in Deserts (with M. J. Chadwick), 1964; Desert Life, 1965; Animal Conflict and Adaptation, 1965; Animal Twilight: man and game in eastern Africa, 1967; Microecology, 1967; Zoology of Tropical Africa, 1969; The Temperature and Water Relations of Reptiles, 1971; Desert Life, 1974; Terrestrial Environments, 1975; Insects and History, 1976; Evolutionary Trends in the Mating of Arthropoda, 1976; (ed jtly) Environmental Physiology of Animals, 1976; Man and the Biology of Arid Zones, 1977; The Water and Temperature Relations of Woodlice, 1977; The Desert, 1977; Animal Migration, 1978; Why the Dinosaurs Became Extinct, 1978; Wildlife of the Desert, 1979; Biological Clocks: their functions in nature, 1980; Tooth and Claw: defensive strategies in the animal world, 1980; (ed) Sahara Desert, 1984; Guide to Woodlands, 1985; Evolution and Adaptation of Terrestrial Arthropods, 1988; Ecophysiology of Desert Arthropods and Reptiles, 1991; (novel) Nile Quest, 1991; contribs to Encyclopædia Britannica, Encyclopedia Americana; shorter monographs and eleven children's books; many scientific articles in learned jls, etc. *Recreations:* music (especially opera), photography, travel. *Address:* Department of Biology (Medawar Building), University College, Gower Street, WC1E 6BT; 10 Battishill Street, N1 1TE.

CLOUGH, Alan; *see* Clough, J. A.

CLOUGH, (Arthur) Gordon; broadcaster and writer, freelance since 1973; *b* 26 Aug. 1934; *s* of late James Stanley Gordon Clough and Annie Clough; *m* 1959, Carolyn Stafford (marr. diss. 1991); one *s* three *d*. *Educ:* Bolton Sch., Bolton, Lancs; Magdalen Coll., Oxford (William Doncaster Schol.; BA Mod Langs, French and Russian). National Service, RN, 1953–55. BBC: Studio Man., 1958–60; Russian Service, 1960–68 (Prog. Organiser, 1963–68); Radio News Features, Sen. Duty Ed., 1968–73; 1973–: freelance presenter, World at One, PM, World this Weekend; co-chm. and question setter, Round Britain Quiz, Round Europe Quiz and Transatlantic Quiz; presenter, Twentyfour Hours, BBC World Service. Writer/Reporter for many documentary progs for BBC Radio Four and World Service, notably: Let there be No More War, 1985; Revolution Without Shots, 1987; The Indissoluble Union, 1989 (Sony Award, Best Documentary Feature, Current Affairs, 1990); Whose shall be the Land?, 1990; Death of a Superpower, 1991. Sony Award, Best Current Affairs Prog., World this Weekend,1984. *Publications:* translations from Russian: Years off my Life, General A. V. Gorbatov, (with Tony Cash), 1964; The Ordeal, V. Bykov, 1972; Hostages, G. Svirsky, 1976; The Yawning Heights, A. Zinoviev, 1979; The Radiant Future, A. Zinoviev, 1981; translations from French: The Elusive Revolution, Raymond Aron, 1971; The Art of the Surrealists, A. Alexandrian, 1972; (with Peter Sadecky) Octobriana, Progressive Political Pornography, 1972; occasional articles in The Listener, etc. *Recreations:* cooking, crossword puzzles, coarse chess. *Address:* c/o BBC, Broadcasting House, W1A 1AA.

CLOUGH, (John) Alan, CBE 1972; MC 1945; Chairman, Textile Research Council, 1984–89; Chairman, British Mohair Holdings plc (formerly British Mohair Spinners Ltd), 1980–84 (Deputy Chairman, 1970–80, Chief Executive, 1977–80, Joint Managing Director, 1980–83); *b* 20 March 1924; *s* of late John Clough and Yvonne (*née* Dollfus); *m* 1st, 1949, Margaret Joy Catton (marr. diss.); one *s* two *d*; 2nd, 1961, Mary Cowan Catherwood; one *s* one *d*. *Educ:* Marlborough Coll.; Leeds Univ. HM Forces, Queen's Bays, 1942–47, N Africa and Italy (Captain); TA Major, Yorkshire Hussars, 1947–55. Mayor, Co. of Merchants of Staple of England, 1969–70. Chairman: Wool Industries Res. Assoc., 1967–69; Wool Textile Delegn, 1969–72; Member: Wool Textile EDC, 1967–72; Jt Textile Cttee, NEDO, 1972–74; President: Comitextil (Co-ordinating Cttee for Textile Industries in EEC), Brussels, 1975–77; British Textile Confedn, 1974–77; Textile Inst., 1979–81; Confedn of British Wool Textiles, 1982–84. CompTI 1975. Hon. DSc Bradford, 1987. *Recreations:* fishing, gardening, travel. *Address:* The Hays, Monks Eleigh, Suffolk IP7 7AE. *T:* Bildeston (0449) 740364. *Club:* Boodle's.

CLOUGH, Philip Gerard; Hon. Mr Justice Clough; Justice of Appeal, Hong Kong, since 1986; *b* 11 March 1924; *s* of Gerard Duncombe Clough and Grace Margaret (*née* Phillips); *m* 1st, Mary Elizabeth Carter (marr. diss.); one *s*; 2nd, Margaret Joy Davies; one *s* one *d*. *Educ:* Dauntsey's Sch.; King's Coll., Cambridge (Exhibnr; MA). War service, Sub Lieut (A) RNVR, 1942–46. Called to the Bar, Inner Temple, 1949; Colonial Legal Service: Federal Counsel, Malaya, 1951–58; Chancery Bar, Lincoln's Inn, 1958–78; Legal Affairs Advr, Brunei, 1978–81; Dist Judge, Hong Kong, 1981–83; High Court Judge, Hong Kong, 1983–86. *Address:* Supreme Court, Queensway, Hong Kong. *T:* 5–8254603. *Clubs:* Garrick; Hong Kong.

CLOUGH, Prunella; painter; *b* 1919; *d* of Eric Clough Taylor, poet and civil servant, and Thora Clough Taylor. *Educ:* privately; Chelsea Sch. of Art. Exhibited at Leger Gallery, 1947; Roland Browse & Delbanco, 1949; Leicester Galleries, 1953; Whitechapel Gallery, 1960; Grosvenor Gallery, 1964, 1968; Graves Art Gallery, Sheffield, 1972; New Art Centre, 1975, 1979; Serpentine Gallery, 1976; Warwick Arts Trust, 1982; Annely Juda Fine Art, 1989. City of London Midsummer Prize, 1977. *Address:* 19 Sherbrooke Road, SW6 7HX.

CLOUTMAN, Air Vice-Marshal Geoffrey William, CB 1980; FDSRCS; Director of Dental Services, Royal Air Force, 1977–80; *b* 1 April 1920; *s* of Rev. Walter Evans Cloutman and Dora Cloutman; *m* 1949, Sylvia Brown; three *d*. *Educ:* Cheltenham Grammar Sch.; Queen Mary Coll., and The London Hosp., Univ. of London. LDSRCS 1942, FDSRCS 1954. House Surg., London Hosp., 1942; joined RAFVR, 1942; War Service, UK and India; specialisation in preventive dentistry, 1948–55; dental hygiene trng; oral surgery appts, 1955–73: RAF Hosps, Fayid, Akrotiri, Aden, Wegberg, Wroughton, Uxbridge; Principal Dental Off., Strike Comd, 1973; QHDS, 1976–80. *Publications:* papers in Brit. Dental Jl and Dental Practitioner. *Recreations:* English church music, cricket, Rugby, Wells Cathedral (Sub-Deacon, 1984–), history of Wells Cathedral and Bishop's Palace. *Address:* Ivy Cottage, 27 Millers Gardens, Wells, Somerset BA5 2TN.

CLOVER, His Honour Robert Gordon, TD 1951; QC 1958; JP; a Circuit Judge (formerly Judge of County Courts), 1965–82; *b* 14 Nov. 1911; *m* 1947, Elizabeth Suzanne (*née* McCorquodale); two *s*. *Educ:* Lancing Coll.; Exeter Coll., Oxford. MA, BCL Oxford. Called to Bar, Lincoln's Inn, 1935. Served in RA, 1939–45 (despatches, 1944). Practised on Northern Circuit, 1935–61; Recorder of Blackpool, 1960–61; Dep. Comr for purposes of Nat. Insurance Acts, 1961–65; Dep. Chm., Bucks QS, 1969–71; Chm., Marlow Magistrates Court, 1972–79. JP Bucks, 1969. *Address:* 10 Westcliff, Sheringham, Norfolk NR26 8JT.

CLOWES, A. W.; General Secretary, Ceramic and Allied Trades Union, since 1980; *b* 17 Dec. 1931. Has been in the Industry since leaving school. Asst Gen. Sec., Ceramic and Allied Trades Union, 1975–80. *Address:* Ceramic and Allied Trades Union, Hillcrest House, Garth Street, Hanley, Stoke-on-Trent, Staffordshire ST1 2AB. *T:* Stoke-on-Trent (0782) 272755.

CLOWES, Col Sir Henry (Nelson), KCVO 1981 (CVO 1977); DSO 1945; OBE 1953; *b* 21 Oct. 1911; *yr s* of late Major E. W. Clowes, DSO, Bradley Hall, Ashbourne, Derbs; *m* 1941, Diana Katharine, MBE, *er d* of late Major Basil Kerr, DSC; one *s*. *Educ:* Eton; Sandhurst. Served in Scots Guards, 1931–57: Adjt RMA Sandhurst, 1940–41; psc 1941; Bde Major 4th Inf. Bde, 1942–44; comd 2nd Bn Scots Guards, 1944–46; jssc 1947; cmd 1st Bn Scots Guards, 1947–50; War Office (AG4), 1950–52; AAG Scottish Comd, 1952–54; Lt-Col comdg Scots Guards, 1954–57; retired 1957. Mem. Her Majesty's Body Guard, 1961; Clerk of the Cheque and Adjt, 1966; Standard Bearer, 1973–76; Lieut, 1976–81. *Recreations:* shooting, fishing. *Address:* 57 Perrymead Street, SW6 3SN. *T:* 071–736 7901. *Clubs:* Cavalry and Guards, Pratt's, Shikar.

CLUCAS, Sir Kenneth (Henry), KCB 1976 (CB 1969); Permanent Secretary, Department of Trade, 1979–82; Chairman, Nuffield Foundation Committee of Inquiry into Pharmacy, 1983–86; *b* 18 Nov. 1921; *o s* of late Rev. J. H. Clucas and Ethel Clucas (*née* Sim); *m* 1960, Barbara, *e d* of Rear-Adm. R. P. Hunter, USN (Retd), Washington, DC; two *d*. *Educ:* Kingswood Sch.; Emmanuel Coll., Cambridge. Royal Signals, 1941–46 (despatches). Joined Min. of Labour as Asst Principal, 1948; 2nd Sec. (Labour), British Embassy, Cairo, 1950; Principal, HM Treasury, 1952; Min. of Labour, 1954; Private Sec. to Minister, 1960–62; Asst Sec., 1962; Under-Sec., 1966–68; Sec., Nat. Bd for Prices and Incomes, 1968–71; First Civil Service Comr, and Dep. Sec., CSD, 1971–73; Dep. Sec., DTI, 1974; Permanent Sec., Dept of Prices and Consumer Protection, 1974–79. Member: Council on Tribunals, 1983–89; Adv. Panel, Freedom of Information Campaign, 1984–; RIPA Wkg Gp on Politics and the Civil Service, 1985–86; Council, FIMBRA, 1986–; Chairman: Cttee of Inquiry into Advertising Controls, 1986–87; Monitoring Cttee, ABI Code of Practice, 1989–; Dep. Chm., CIBA Foundn Media Resource Steering Cttee, 1984–; Chm., Lloyd's Wkg Pty on Consumer Guarantees, 1985; Lloyd's Members Ombudsman, 1988–. Chm., Nat. Assoc. of Citizens' Advice Bureaux, 1984–89 (Vice Chm., 1983–84; Chm. Surrey and W Sussex Area Cttee, 1982–84); Mem. Management Cttee, Godalming CAB, 1982–85. Hon. FRPharmS, 1989. *Address:* Cariad, Knoll Road, Godalming, Surrey. *T:* Godalming (0483) 416430.

CLUFF, John Gordon, (Algy); Chairman, since 1979, and Chief Executive, since 1971, Cluff Resources (formerly Cluff Oil); Chairman, The Spectator, since 1985 (Proprietor, 1981–85); *b* 19 April 1940; *s* of late Harold Cluff and of Freda Cluff, Waldeshare House, Waldeshare, Kent. *Educ:* Stowe Sch. 2/Lieut, Grenadier Guards, 1959; Captain, Guards Independent Parachute Co., 1963; served W Africa, Cyprus, Malaysia, retd 1964. Director: Henry Sotheran & Sons; Apollo Magazine. Trustee, Anglo–Hong Kong Trust. *Address:* 58 St James's Street, SW1A 1LD; Clova House, Lumsden, West Aberdeenshire AB5 4YJ. *T:* Rhynie (04646) 336. *Clubs:* White's, Boodle's, Beefsteak, Turf; Royal Northern (Aberdeen); Royal St George's (Sandwich); Travellers' (Paris).

CLUSKEY, Frank; TD (Lab) for Dublin South, since 1987; *b* April 1930; *m* Eileen Gillespie (decd); one *s* two *d*. *Educ:* St Vincent's Sch., Glasnevin; Harvard Univ., USA. A Branch Sec., Workers' Union of Ireland, 1954–68; Member, Dublin City Council, 1960–63; Lord Mayor of Dublin, 1968–69. TD (Lab) Dublin S Central, 1965–81 and 1982–83; Member: Cttee of Public Accounts and Cttee of Procedure, 1965–69 and 1970–73; Parly Sec. to Min. of Social Welfare, 1973–77; former Labour Opposition Front Bench Spokesman on Justice, Social Welfare, and Labour; Leader of the Labour Party, Ireland, 1977–81; Minister for Trade and Commerce, 1982–83. Mem., European Parlt, 1981–82. *Address:* 1 Glasnevin Park, Dublin 11, Ireland.

CLUTTERBUCK, Vice-Adm. Sir David Granville, KBE 1968; CB 1965; *b* Gloucester, 25 Jan. 1913; *m* 1937, Rose Mere Vaile, Auckland, NZ; two *d*. Joined RN, 1929. Served War of 1939–45 (despatches twice): navigating officer of cruisers HMS Ajax, 1940–42, HMS Newfoundland, 1942–46 (present Japanese surrender at Tokyo). Subsequently commanded destroyers Sluys and Cadiz, 1952–53; Naval Attaché at British Embassy, Bonn; Capt. (D) of Third Training Squadron in HMS Zest, Londonderry, 1956–58; commanded cruiser HMS Blake, 1960–62; Chief of Staff to C-in-C Home Fleet and C-in-C Allied Forces Eastern Atlantic, 1963–66; Rear-Adm., 1963; Vice-Adm. 1966; Dep. Supreme Allied Comdr, Atlantic, 1966–68. *Address:* Burrard Cottage, Walhampton, Lymington, Hampshire. *Clubs:* Army and Navy; Royal Lymington Yacht.

CLUTTERBUCK, Maj.-Gen. Richard Lewis, CB 1971; OBE 1958; writer, lecturer and broadcaster; *b* London, 22 Nov. 1917; *s* of late Col L. St J. R. Clutterbuck, OBE, late RA, and late Mrs I. J. Clutterbuck; *m* 1948, Angela Muriel Barford; three *s*. *Educ:* Radley Coll.; Pembroke Coll., Cambridge. MA Cantab (Mech. Scis); PhD (Econ. and Pol.), London Univ., 1971. Commd in RE, 1937; War Service: France, 1940; Sudan and Ethiopia, 1941; Western Desert, 1941–43; Italy, 1944; subseq. service in: Germany, 1946 and 1951–53; Italy, 1946; Palestine, 1947; Malaya, 1956–58; Christmas Island (Nuclear Trials), 1958; USA, 1961–63; Singapore, 1966–68. Instructor, British Army Staff Coll., 1953–56; Instructor, US Army Staff Coll., 1961–63; idc 1965; Chief Engr, Far East Land Forces, 1966–68; Engr-in-Chief (Army), 1968–70; Chief Army Instructor, Royal Coll. of Defence Studies, 1971–72, retired. Col Comdt, RE, 1972–77. Sen. Lectr and Reader, Dept of Politics, Univ. of Exeter, 1972–83. FICE. *Publications:* Across the River (as Richard Jocelyn), 1957; The Long Long War, 1966; Protest and the Urban Guerrilla, 1973; Riot and Revolution in Singapore and Malaya, 1973; Living with Terrorism, 1975; Guerrillas and Terrorists, 1977; Britain in Agony, 1978, rev. edn 1980; Kidnap and Ransom, 1978; The Media and Political Violence, 1981, rev. edn 1983; Industrial Conflict and Democracy, 1984; Conflict and Violence in Singapore and Malaysia, 1985; The Future of Political Violence, 1986; Kidnap, Hijack and Extortion, 1987; Terrorism and Guerrilla Warfare, 1990; Terrorism, Drugs and Crime in Europe after 1992, 1990; contribs to British and US jls. *Address:* Department of Politics, University of Exeter, Exeter EX4 4RJ. *Clubs:* Commonwealth Trust, Army and Navy.

CLUTTON, Rafe Henry, FRICS; Partner in Cluttons, Chartered Surveyors, London, since 1955 (Senior Partner, since 1982); *b* 13 June 1929; *s* of late Robin John Clutton and Rosalie Muriel (*née* Birch); *m* 1954, Jill Olwyn Evans; four *s* one *d*. *Educ:* Tonbridge Sch., Kent. FRICS 1959. Director: Legal & General Group PLC (formerly Legal & General Assurance Soc. Ltd), 1972–; Haslemere Estates plc, 1990–. Member: Royal National Theatre Bd, 1976–; Salvation Army London Adv. Bd, 1971–; Royal Commn for Exhibn of 1851, 1988–. Governor, Royal Foundn of Grey Coat Hosp., 1967– (Chm., 1981–). FRSA 1990. *Recreations:* family, books, conservation. *Address:* Fairfield, North Chailey, Sussex BN8 4DH. *T:* Newick (082572) 2431. *Clubs:* Royal Thames Yacht, City of London.

CLUTTON-BROCK, Arthur Guy; independent social worker, 1965–72, retired; *b* 5 April 1906; *s* of late Henry Alan Clutton-Brock and late Rosa Clutton-Brock; *m* 1934, Francys Mary Allen; one *d*. *Educ:* Rugby Sch.; Magdalene Coll., Cambridge (Hon. Fellow, 1973). Cambridge House, 1927; Rugby House, 1929; Borstal Service, 1933; Principal Probation Officer for the Metropolitan Police Court District, 1936; Head of Oxford House, 1940; Christian Reconstruction in Europe, 1946; Agricultural Labourer, 1947; Agriculturalist at St Faith's Mission, 1949; Field Worker of African Development Trust, 1959–65; deported from Rhodesia by rebel regime, 1971. Treasurer, Cold Comfort Farm Soc., 1966. *Publications:* Dawn in Nyasaland, 1959; Cold Comfort Confronted, 1973. *Address:* Gelli Uchaf, Llandyrnog, Clwyd LL16 4HR.

CLUTTON-BROCK, Timothy Hugh, PhD; ScD; Lecturer in Zoology, University of Cambridge, since 1987; *b* 13 Aug. 1946; *s* of Hugh Alan Clutton-Brock and Eileen Mary Stableforth; *m* 1980, Dafila Kathleen Scott; one *s* one *d*. *Educ:* Rugby Sch.; Magdalene Coll., Cambridge (BA, MA, PhD, ScD). NERC res. fellowship, Animal Behaviour Res. Gp, Oxford, 1972; Lectr in Ethology, Univ. of Sussex, 1973; Sen. Res. Fellow in Behavioural Ecology, King's Coll., Cambridge, 1976; SERC Advanced Fellow, Dept of Zoology, Cambridge, 1981; Royal Soc. Res. Fellow in Biology, 1983. Chm., IUCN Deer Specialist Gp, 1980–. Jt Editor, Princeton Monographs in Behavioral Ecology, 1982–. Scientific Medal, Zoological Soc. of London, 1984. *Publications:* (ed) Primate Ecology, 1977; (ed) Readings in Sociobiology, 1978; Red Deer: the behaviour and ecology of two sexes, 1982; (ed) Rhum, Natural History of an Island, 1987; (ed) Reproductive Success, 1988; Red Deer in the Highlands, 1989; The Evolution of Parental Care, 1991; approx. 100 sci. papers on animal behaviour, ecology and evolution in Nature, Jl Animal Ecol., Evolution, Amer. Naturalist, Jl of Zoology, Animal Behaviour, Behaviour, Behavioral Ecol. and Sociobiol., Folia Primatologica and other jls. *Recreations:* bird watching, fish watching, fishing. *Address:* White Roses, Reach, Cambridgeshire CB5 0JQ; Department of Zoology, Downing Street, Cambridge CB2 3EJ. *T:* Cambridge (0223) 336600.

CLWYD, 3rd Baron *cr* 1919; **John Anthony Roberts;** Bt 1908; *b* 2 Jan. 1935; *s* of 2nd Baron Clwyd and Joan de Bois (*d* 1985); *d* of late Charles R. Murray; *S* father, 1987; *m* 1969, Geraldine, *yr d* of Charles Eugene Cannons, Sanderstead; three *s*. *Educ:* Harrow; Trinity College, Cambridge. Called to the Bar, Gray's Inn, 1970. *Heir: s* Hon. John Murray Roberts, *b* 27 Aug. 1971. *Address:* 24 Salisbury Avenue, Cheam, Sutton, Surrey SM1 2DJ.

CLWYD, Ann; journalist and broadcaster; MP (Lab) Cynon Valley, since May 1984; *b* 21 March 1937; *d* of Gwilym Henri Lewis and Elizabeth Ann Lewis; *m* 1963, Owen Dryhurst Roberts, TV director and producer. *Educ:* Halkyn Primary Sch.; Holywell Grammar Sch.; The Queen's Sch., Chester; University Coll., Bangor. Former: Student-teacher, Hope Sch., Flintshire; BBC Studio Manager; freelance reporter, producer; Welsh corresp., The Guardian and The Observer, 1964–79; Vice-Chm., Welsh Arts Council, 1975–79. Member: Welsh Hospital Board, 1970–74; Cardiff Community Health Council, 1975–79; Royal Commn on NHS, 1976–79; Working Party, report, Organisation of Out-Patient Care, for Welsh Hosp. Bd; Working Party, Bilingualism in the Hospital Service; Labour Party Study Gp., People and the Media; Arts Council of Gt Britain, 1975–80; Chm., Cardiff Anti-Racialism Cttee, 1978–80; Labour Party NEC, 1983–84. Chm., Labour back-bench cttee on Health and Social Security, 1985–87; Vice-Chm., Labour back-bench cttee on Defence, 1985–87; Opposition front-bench spokesperson on women, 1987–88, on educn, 1987–88, on overseas develt and co-operation, 1989–. Member: NUJ; TGWU. Contested (Lab): Denbigh, 1970; Gloucester, Oct. 1974; Mem. (Lab) Mid and West Wales, European Parlt, 1979–84. *Address:* 6 Deans Court, Dean Street, Aberdare, Mid Glam. *T:* Aberdare (0685) 871394.

CLYDE, Hon. Lord; James John Clyde; a Senator of the College of Justice in Scotland, since 1985; *b* 29 Jan. 1932; *s* of Rt Hon. Lord Clyde; *m* 1963, Ann Clunie Hoblyn; two *s*. *Educ:* Edinburgh Academy; Corpus Christi Coll., Oxford (BA); Edinburgh Univ. (LLB). Called to Scottish Bar, 1959; QC (Scot.) 1971; Advocate-Depute, 1973–74. Chancellor to Bishop of Argyll and the Isles, 1972–85; a Judge of the Courts of Appeal of Jersey and Guernsey, 1979–85. Chairman: Med. Appeal Tribunal, 1974–85; Cttee of Investigation for Scotland on Agricl Mktg, 1984–85; Scottish Valuation Adv. Council, 1987– (Mem., 1972–). Mem., UK Delegn to CCBE, 1978–84 (Leader, 1981–84). Hon. Pres., Scottish Young Lawyers' Assoc., 1988–; Vice-Pres., Royal Blind Asylum and Sch., 1987–; Assessor to Chancellor, Court of Edinburgh Univ., 1989–; Dir, Edinburgh Acad., 1979–88; Trustee: St Mary's Music Sch., 1976–; Nat. Library of Scotland, 1977–; Chm. of Govs, St George's Sch. for Girls, 1989–; Gov., Napier Polytechnic, 1989–. *Publication:* (ed jtly) Armour on Valuation, 3rd edn, 1961, 5th edn, 1985. *Recreations:* music, gardening. *Address:* 9 Heriot Row, Edinburgh EH3 6HU. *T:* 031–556 7114. *Club:* New (Edinburgh).

CLYDESMUIR, 2nd Baron *cr* 1948, of Braidwood; **Ronald John Bilsland Colville,** KT 1972; CB 1965; MBE 1944; TD; Lord High Commissioner to the General Assembly, Church of Scotland, 1971 and 1972; Lord-Lieutenant, Lanarkshire, since 1963; a Captain, Royal Company of Archers, Queen's Body Guard for Scotland, 1985–88, Captain General since 1988; *b* 21 May 1917; *s* of 1st Baron Clydesmuir, PC, GCIE, TD, and Agnes Anne (*d* 1970), CI 1947, Kaisar-i-Hind Gold Medal; *S* father, 1954; *m* 1946, Joan Marguerita, *d* of Lt-Col E. B. Booth, DSO, Darver Castle, Co. Louth; two *s* two *d*. *Educ:* Charterhouse; Trinity Coll., Cambridge. Served in The Cameronians (Scottish Rifles), 1939–45 (MBE, despatches). Commanded 6/7th Bn The Cameronians, TA, 1953–56. Director: Colvilles Ltd, 1958–70; British Linen Bank (Governor, 1966–71); Bank of Scotland (Dep. Governor, 1971–72, Governor, 1972–81); Scottish Provident Instn, 1954–88; Scotbits Securities Ltd, 1960–78; The Scottish Western Investment Co., 1965–78; BSC Strip Mills Div., 1970–73; Caledonian Offshore Co. Ltd, 1971–87; Barclays Bank, 1972–82; Chm., North Sea Assets Ltd, 1972–87. President: Scottish Council (Development and Industry), 1978–86 (Chm., Exec. Cttee, 1966–78); Scottish Council of Physical Recreation, 1964–72; Scottish Br., National Playing Fields Assoc.; Chm., Council, Territorial, Auxiliary and Volunteer Reserve Assocs, 1969–73, Pres., 1974–81; Chm., Lanarkshire T&AFA, 1957–63, Pres. 1963–68; Pres., Lowland TA&VRA. Hon. Colonel: 6th/7th (Territorial) Bn, The Cameronians (Scottish Rifles), 1967–71; 52 Lowland Volunteers, T&AVR, 1970–75. Chm., Scottish Outward Bound Assoc. Trustee, MacRobert Trusts. DL Lanarkshire, 1955, Vice-Lieut, 1959–63. Hon. LLD Strathclyde, 1968; Hon. DSc Heriot-Watt, 1971. *Recreations:* shooting, fishing. *Heir: s* Hon. David Ronald Colville [*b* 8 April 1949; *m* 1978, Aline Frances, *er d* of Peter Merriam, Holton Lodge, Holton St Mary, Suffolk; one *s* two *d*]. *Address:* Langlees House, Biggar, Lanarkshire ML12 6NP. *T:* Biggar (0899) 20057. *Club:* New (Edinburgh).

See also Captain N. E. F. Dalrymple Hamilton.

COADY, Aubrey William Burleton, CMG 1959; Chairman, Electricity Commission of NSW, 1959–75 (Member since 1950); *b* Singleton, NSW, 15 June 1915; *s* of W. A. Coady, Belmont; *m* 1964, Phyllis K., *d* of late G. W. Mathews. *Educ:* Newcastle High Sch.; Sydney Univ. (BA, BEc). Under-Sec. and Comptroller of Accounts, NSW Treasury, 1955–59. *Address:* 42 Rickard Avenue, Mosman, NSW 2088, Australia.

COALES, Prof. John Flavell, CBE 1974 (OBE 1945); FRS 1970; FEng; Professor of Engineering, Cambridge University, 1965–74, now Emeritus; Fellow of Clare Hall, 1964–74, now Emeritus; *b* 14 Sept. 1907; *s* of John Dennis Coales and Marion Beatrice Coales (*née* Flavell); *m* 1936, Mary Dorothea Violet, *d* of Rev. Guthrie Henry Lewis Alison; two *s* two *d*. *Educ:* Berkhamsted Sch.; Sidney Sussex Coll., Cambridge (MA; ScD 1985). Admty Dept of Scientific Res., 1929–46; Res. Dir, Elliott Bros (London) Ltd, 1946; Engrg Dept, Cambridge Univ.: Asst Dir of Res., 1953; Lectr, 1956; Reader in Engrg, 1958; Prof., 1965. Part-time Mem., E Electricity Bd, 1967–73. Director: Tube Investments Technological Centre, 1955–60; TI R&D Bd, 1960–65; BSA Metal Components, 1967–73; BSA Gp Res. Bd (Dep. Chm.), 1967–73; Delta Materials Research Ltd, 1974–77. Mackay Vis. Prof. of Electrical Engrg, Univ. of Calif., Berkeley, 1963. Internat. Fedn of Automatic Control: MEC, 1957; Vice-Pres., 1961; Pres., 1963. Brit. Conf. on Automation and Computation: Gp B Vice-Chm., 1958; Chm., 1960. UK Automation Council: Chm. Res. and Develt Panel, 1960–63; Chm. For. Relations Panel, 1960–64; Vice-Chm., 1961–63; Chm., 1963–66. Instn of Electrical Engrs: Mem. Council, 1953–55, 1964–77; Chm., Measurement Section, 1953; Chm., Control and Automation Div., 1965, etc; Vice-Pres., 1966–71; Pres., 1971–72. Council of Engineering Institutions: Vice-Chm., 1974; Chm., 1975 (Mem. Council for Envtl Sci. and Engrg, 1973–76); Chm., Commonwealth Bd for Engrg Educn and Training, 1976–80; Pres., World Environment and Resources Council, 1973–74. Pres., Soc. of Instrument Technology, 1958. Past Member, Gen. Bd and Exec. Cttee of Nat. Physical Laboratory; Member: Adv. Council, RMCS, 1963–73; Educn Adv. Cttee for RAF, 1967–76; Trng and Educn Adv. Cttee of RAF, 1976–79; Court of Cranfield Inst. of Technology, 1970–82; Governing Body, Nat. Inst. of Agric. Engrg, 1970–75; Envtl Design and Engrg Res. Cttee, DoE Bldg Res. Estab., 1973–76; British Council Sci. Adv. Cttee, 1973–75; Engrg and Bldgs Bd, ARC, 1973–77; British Library Adv. Council, 1975–81; Chm., IFAC Pubns Managing Bd, 1976–87. Governor: Hatfield Coll. of Technology, 1951–68; Hatfield Polytechnic, 1969–70 (Hon. Fellow, 1971–). FICE, FIEE (Pres., IEE, 1971–72; Hon. FIEE 1985), FIEEE, FIAgrE, FInstP; Founder Fellow, Fellowship of Engineering, 1976 (Mem., Exec. Cttee and Chm., Activities Cttee, 1976–80); Hon. Mem., Inst. of Measurement and Control, 1971. For. Mem., Serbian Acad. of Scis, 1981. Hon. DSc City Univ., 1970; Hon. DTech Loughborough, 1977; Hon. DEng Sheffield, 1978. Harold Hartley Medal, 1971; Giorgio Quazza Medal, IFAC, 1981 (first recipient); Honda Prize, 1982. *Publications:* (ed) Automatic and Remote Control (Proc. First Congr. of Internat. Fedn of Automatic Control), 1961; original papers on radio direction finding, radar, information theory, magnetic amplifiers, automatic control, automation and technical education. *Recreations:* mountaineering, gardening. *Address:* 14 Chesterford House, Southacre Drive, Cambridge CB2 2TZ. *Clubs:* Athenæum, Alpine.

COATES, Sir Anthony Robert M.; *see* Milnes Coates.

COATES, David Randall; Chief Economic Adviser, Department of Trade and Industry, since 1990; *b* 22 March 1942. *Educ:* Leeds Grammar Sch.; Queen's Coll., Oxford; LSE. Res. Assistant, Univ. of Manchester and Manchester Business Sch., 1966–68; Economic Advr, Min. of Technology and DTI, 1968–74; Sen. Economic Advr, Dept of Trade and DTI, 1974–82; Asst Sec., DTI, 1982–89; Grade 3, DTI, 1989. *Recreations:* family, gardening, travel, music. *Address:* Department of Trade and Industry, 1 Victoria Street, SW1H 0ET. *T:* 071–215 5073.

COATES, Dudley James; Director of Regional Management, Ministry of Agriculture, Fisheries and Food, since 1989; *b* 15 Sept. 1946; *o s* of Edward and Margot Coates; *m*

1969, Dr Jean Walsingham; two *d*. *Educ:* Westcliff High School for Boys; Univ. of Sussex (BA (Hons)). Joined MAFF as Asst Principal, 1968; Second Sec., UK Delegn to the EC, Brussels, 1970–72; Principal, MAFF, 1973; Lectr, Civil Service Coll., 1978–81; Head of Animal Health Div. II, 1981–83, Head of Financial Management Team, 1983–87, MAFF; Dir Gen. of Corporate Services, Intervention Bd for Agricultural Produce, 1987–89. Mem., Methodist Conference, 1988–89. *Publication:* (contrib.) Policies into Practice (ed David Lewis and Helen Wallace), 1984. *Recreations:* Christian activities, cycling. *Address:* Ministry of Agriculture, Fisheries and Food, Nobel House, 17 Smith Square, SW1P 3JR. *T:* 071–238 6717.

COATES, Sir Ernest (William), Kt 1973; CMG 1970; State Director of Finance and Permanent Head of Victoria Treasury, Australia, 1959–77; *b* 30 Nov. 1916; *s* of Thomas Atlee Coates; *m* 1st, 1943, Phylis E. Morris (*d* 1971); one *s* three *d*; 2nd, 1974, Patricia Ann (*d* 1986), *d* of late C. A. Fisher, Herts. *Educ:* Ballarat High Sch.; Univ. of Melbourne. BCom. Member: Bd of State Savings Bank of Victoria, 1960–77; Nat. Debt Commn, Australia, 1963–78; Australian Universities Commn, 1968–77; Aust. Administrative Appeals Tribunal, 1978–86. Dir, Equity Trustees Executors and Agency Co. Ltd, 1978–89. Chairman: Australian Selection Cttee, Harkness Fellowships, 1975–83; Rhodes Scholarship Selection Cttee (Victoria), 1981 (Mem., 1977–81). Hon. LLD Melbourne, 1979. *Recreations:* golf, music. *Address:* 64 Molesworth Street, Kew, Victoria 3101, Australia. *T:* 8618226. *Clubs:* Melbourne (Melbourne); Green Acres Golf, Lorne Golf.

COATES, Brig. Sir Frederick (Gregory Lindsay), 2nd Bt *cr* 1921; *b* 19 May 1916; *o s* of Sir William Frederick Coates, 1st Bt, Belfast, N Ireland; *S* father, 1932; *m* 1940, Joan Nugent, *d* of late Maj.-Gen. Sir Charlton Spinks, KBE, DSO; one *s* two *d*. *Educ:* Eton; Sandhurst. Commissioned Royal Tank Regt, 1936; served War of 1939–45, North Africa and NW Europe (wounded twice); Min. of Supply, 1947–53; Asst Military Attaché, Stockholm, 1953–56; British Joint Services Mission, Washington, 1956–58; Comdt, RAC School of Tank Technology, 1958–61; Asst Dir of Fighting Vehicles, and Col GS, War Office and MoD, 1961–66; Brig., British Defence Staff, Washington, DC, 1966–69; Mil. Dep. to Head of Defence Sales, 1969–71; retired 1971. *Heir:* *s* David Charlton Frederick Coates [*b* 16 Feb. 1948; *m* 1973, Christine Helen, *d* of Lewis F. Marshall; two *s*]. *Address:* Launchfield, Briantspuddle, Dorchester, Dorset DT2 7HN. *Clubs:* Royal Ocean Racing; Royal Yacht Squadron; RMYC; RLymYC; Island Sailing; RAC Yacht.

COATES, Prof. Geoffrey Edward, MA, DSc; Professor of Chemistry, University of Wyoming, 1968–79, now Emeritus; *b* 14 May 1917; *er s* of Prof. Joseph Edward Coates, OBE; *m* 1951, Winifred Jean Hobbs; one *s* one *d*. *Educ:* Clifton Coll.; Queen's Coll., Oxford. Research Chemist, Magnesium Metal Corp., 1940–45; Univ. of Bristol: Lecturer in Chemistry, 1945–53; Sub-Warden of Wills Hall, 1946–51; Prof. of Chemistry, Univ. of Durham, 1953–68. *Publications:* Organo-metallic Compounds (monograph), 1956, 3rd edn (2 vols), 1967–68; Principles of Organometallic Chemistry, 1968; papers in scientific journals. *Address:* 1801 Rainbow Avenue, Laramie, Wyoming 82070, USA. *Club:* Commonwealth Trust.

See also J. F. Coates.

COATES, James Richard; Under Secretary, Railways Directorate, Department of Transport, since 1985; *b* 18 Oct. 1935; *s* of William Richard Coates and Doris Coral (*née* Richmond); *m* 1969, Helen Rosamund Rimington; one *s* one *d*. *Educ:* Nottingham High Sch.; Clare Coll., Cambridge (MA). Joined Ministry of Transport, 1959; Private Sec. to Permanent Sec., 1962–63; Principal, 1963; Private Sec. to Secretary of State for Local Govt and Regional Planning, 1969, and to Minister of Transport, 1970–71; Asst Sec., DoE, 1971; Under Secretary, 1977; Dir, London Reg., PSA, 1979–83; Under Sec., Dept of Transport, 1983–. *Recreations:* listening to music, gardening. *Address:* Department of Transport, 2 Marsham Street, SW1.

COATES, John Francis, OBE 1955; Deputy Director, Ship Design, Ministry of Defence, 1977–79, retired; *b* 30 March 1922; *s* of Joseph Edward Coates and Ada Maria Coates; *m* 1954, Jane Waymouth; two *s*. *Educ:* Clifton Coll.; Queen's Coll., Oxford (MA 1946). Entered RCNC, 1943; RCDS, 1971; Supt, Naval Construction Res. Estabt, Dunfermline, 1974. Dir, The Trireme Trust, 1985–. Hon. DSc Bath, 1989. *Publications:* (with J. S. Morrison) The Athenian Trireme, 1986; papers on naval architecture of ancient ships. *Recreation:* nautical research. *Address:* Sabinal, Lucklands Road, Bath BA1 4AU. *T:* Bath (0225) 423696.

See also Prof. G. E. Coates.

COATES, Prof. John Henry, FRS 1985; Sadleirian Professor of Pure Mathematics, and Professorial Fellow of Emmanuel College, Cambridge University, since 1986; *b* 26 Jan. 1945; *s* of J. R. Coates and Beryl (*née* Lee); *m* 1966, Julie Turner; three *s*. *Educ:* Australian National Univ. (BSc); Trinity Coll., Cambridge (PhD). Assistant Prof., Harvard Univ., 1969–72; Associate Prof., Stanford Univ., 1972–74; Univ. Lectr, Cambridge, and Fellow, Emmanuel Coll., 1974–77; Prof., ANU, 1977–78; Prof. of Maths, Univ. de Paris, Orsay, 1978–86, Ecole Normale Supérieure, Paris, 1985–86. Pres., London Math. Soc., 1988–90; Vice-Pres., Internat. Mathematical Union, 1991–. *Address:* Emmanuel College, Cambridge CB2 3AP; 104 Mawson Road, Cambridge CB2 3AP. *T:* Cambridge (0223) 60884.

COATES, Kenneth Sidney; Member (Lab) Nottingham, European Parliament, since 1989; Special Professor in Adult Education, University of Nottingham, since 1990 (Reader, 1980–89); *b* 16 Sept. 1930; *s* of Eric Arthur Coates and Mary Coates; *m* 1969, Tamara Tura; three *s* three *d* (and one *d* decd). *Educ:* Nottingham Univ. (Mature State Scholar, 1956; BA 1st Cl. Hons Sociology, 1959). Coal miner, Notts Coalfield, 1948–56; student, 1956–60; Asst Tutor, Tutor, and Sen. Tutor in Adult Educn, Univ. of Nottingham, 1960–89. Chm., Human Rights Subcttee, Eur. Parlt, 1989–. Member: Bertrand Russell Peace Foundn, 1965–; Inst. of Workers' Control, 1968–; Jt Sec., European Nuclear Disarmament Liaison Cttee, 1981–89. *Publications:* (with A. J. Topham) Industrial Democracy in Great Britain, 1967, 3rd edn 1976; (with R. L. Silburn) Poverty, the Forgotten Englishmen, 1970, 4th edn 1983; (with A. J. Topham) The New Unionism, 1972, 2nd edn 1974; (with A. J. Topham) Trade Unions in Britain, 1980, 3rd edn 1988; Heresies, 1982; The Most Dangerous Decade, 1984; (with A. J. Topham) Trade Unions and Politics, 1986; Think Globally, Act Locally, 1988. *Recreations:* walking, reading. *Address:* Bertrand Russell House, Gamble Street, Nottingham NG7 4ET. *T:* Nottingham (0602) 784504.

COATES, Michael Arthur, FCA; Chairman, Price Waterhouse, World Firm, 1982–88; *b* 12 May 1924; *yr s* of late Joseph Michael Smith Coates, OBE, Elmfield, Wylam, Northumberland, and late Lillian Warren Coates (*née* Murray); *m* 1st, 1952, Audrey Hampton Thorne (marr. diss. 1970); one *s* two *d*; 2nd, 1971, Sally Rogers (marr. diss. 1980). *Educ:* Uppingham Sch. Admitted Mem., Inst. of Chartered Accountants, 1951. Served RA, mainly in ME and Italy, 1942–47. Articled with Price Waterhouse & Co., Newcastle, 1942; returned to Price Waterhouse, 1947; transf. to London, 1954; Partner, Price Waterhouse & Co., 1959–82, Dep. Sen. Partner, 1974–75, Sen. Partner, 1975–82; Chm., Price Waterhouse Internat. Manpower Cttee, 1971–74; Mem., Policy Cttee, 1974–88. *Recreations:* diverse, including music, modern painting, antiques, gardens, reading, railways, photography. *Address:* 20 Wilton Crescent, SW1. *T:* 071–235 4423; Cantray House, Croy, Inverness-shire IV1 2PW. *T:* Croy (06678) 204.

COATES, Reginald Charles, FEng 1978; Emeritus Professor of Civil Engineering, University of Nottingham, since 1983; *b* 28 June 1920; *s* of Wilfrid and Margaret Anne Coates; *m* 1942, Doris Sheila (*née* Sharrad) (*d* 1988); two *s* one *d*. *Educ:* New Mills Grammar Sch.; The Herbert Strutt Sch., Belper, Derbyshire; University Coll., Nottingham. Served War of 1939–45, Corps of Royal Engineers. Univ. of Nottingham: Lectr in Civil Engineering, 1946; Sen. Lectr, 1953; Prof. and Head of Dept of Civil Engrg, 1958–82; Dep. Vice-Chancellor, 1966–69; Prof. and Hd, Dept of Civil Engrg, Papua New Guinea Univ. of Technol., 1982–85. Member: Council, Instn of Civil Engineers, 1967–72 (Vice-Pres., 1975–78, Pres., 1978–79); Sheffield Regional Hosp. Bd, 1971–74; Notts AHA, 1974–75; Council, Construction Industry Research and Information Assoc., 1978–82; Adv. Cttee, Books for Overseas, British Council, 1974–82; Construction and Housing Res. Adv. Council, DoE, 1976–79. *Publications:* (with M. G. Coutie and F. K. Kong) Structural Analysis, 1972, 3rd edn 1987; occasional articles in technical press. *Recreations:* cooking and idling. *Address:* 13 Metcalfe Close, Southwell, Notts NG25 0JE.

COATS, Sir Alastair Francis Stuart, 4th Bt, *cr* 1905; *b* 18 Nov. 1921; *s* of Lieut-Col Sir James Stuart Coats, MC, 3rd Bt and Lady Amy Coats (*d* 1975), *er d* of 8th Duke of Richmond and Gordon; *S* father, 1966; *m* 1947, Lukyn, *d* of Capt. Charles Gordon; one *s* one *d*. *Educ:* Eton. Served War of 1939–45, Coldstream Guards (Capt.). *Heir:* *s* Alexander James Coats, *b* 6 July 1951. *Address:* Birchwood House, Durford Wood, Petersfield, Hants. *T:* Liss (0730) 892254.

COATS, Sir William David, Kt 1985; DL; Chairman, Coats Patons PLC, 1981–86 (Deputy Chairman, 1979–81); Deputy Chairman, Clydesdale Bank, since 1985 (Director, since 1962); *b* 25 July 1924; *s* of Thomas Heywood Coats and Olivia Violet Pitman; *m* 1950, Hon. Elizabeth Lilian Graham MacAndrew; two *s* one *d*. *Educ:* Eton Coll. Entered service of Coats Patons PLC, 1948: Director: The Central Agency Ltd (subsid. co.), 1953–55; Coats Patons PLC, 1960–86; Murray Caledonian Trust Co. Ltd, 1961–81; Weir Group Ltd, 1970–83; Murray Investment Trusts, 1986–. Mem., S of Scotland Electricity Bd, 1972–81. Hon. LLD Strathclyde, 1977. DL Ayr and Arran, 1986. *Recreations:* shooting and golf. *Address:* The Cottage, Symington, Ayrshire KA1 5QG. *T:* Symington (0563) 830287. *Club:* Western (Glasgow).

COBB, Henry Nichols; Partner, Pei Cobb Freed and Partners, Architects, since 1960; *b* 8 April 1926; *s* of Charles Kane Cobb and Elsie Quincy Cobb; *m* 1953, Joan Stewart Spaulding; three *d*. *Educ:* Harvard College (AB 1947); Harvard Graduate Sch. of Design (MArch 1949). Architectural Div., Webb & Knapp, 1950–60; Pei Cobb Freed & Partners (formerly I. M. Pei & Partners), 1960–. Sch. of Architecture, Yale University: William Henry Bishop Vis. Prof., 1973, 1978; Charlotte Sheperd Davenport Vis. Prof., 1975; Graduate School of Design, Harvard: Studio Prof. and Chm., Dept of Architecture, 1980–85; Adjunct Prof. of Architecture and Urban Design, 1985–88; Vis. Lectr, 1988–. Hon. DFA Bowdoin Coll., 1985; Dr Technical Scis *hc*, Swiss Fed. Inst. of Technol., 1990. *Publications:* Where I Stand, 1980; Architecture and the University, 1985. *Address:* Pei Cobb Freed & Partners, 600 Madison Avenue, New York, NY 10022, USA. *T:* 212–751–3122. *Clubs:* Century, Knickerbocker (NY).

COBB, Henry Stephen, CBE 1991; FSA; FRHistS; Clerk of the Records, House of Lords, 1981–91; *b* 17 Nov. 1926; *y s* of Ernest Cobb and Violet Kate Cobb (*née* Sleath), Wallasey; *m* 1969, Eileen Margaret Downer. *Educ:* Birkenhead Sch.; London School of Economics (BA, MA); Liverpool Univ. (Dip. Archive Admin). Archivist, Church Missionary Soc., 1951–53; Asst Archivist, House of Lords, 1953–59, Asst Clerk of the Records, 1959–73, Dep. Clerk, 1973–81. Lecturer in Palaeography, School of Librarianship, North London Polytechnic, 1973–77. Mem. Council: British Records Assoc., 1978–81; Society of Archivists, 1970–82 (Chm., 1982–84); Chm., London Record Soc., 1984–. Mem. Cttee of Management, Inst. of Historical Research, 1986–90. FSA 1967; FRHistS 1970. *Publications:* (ed) The Local Port Book of Southampton 1439–40, 1961; (ed with D. J. Johnson) Guide to the Parliament and the Glorious Revolution Exhibition, 1988; (ed) The Overseas Trade of London: Exchequer Customs Accounts 1480–1, 1990; contribs to Economic History Rev., Jl of Soc. of Archivists, Archives, etc. *Recreations:* music, historical research. *Address:* 1 Child's Way, Hampstead Garden Suburb, NW11 6XU. *T:* 081–458 3688.

COBB, Richard Charles, CBE 1978; FBA 1967; Professor of Modern History, University of Oxford, 1973–84; Senior Research Fellow of Worcester College, Oxford, 1984–87; *b* 20 May 1917; *s* of Francis Hills Cobb, Sudan Civil Service, and Dora Cobb (*née* Swindale); *m* 1963, Margaret Tennant; three *s* one *d*. *Educ:* Shrewsbury Sch.; Merton Coll., Oxford (Hon. Fellow 1980). Postmastership in History, Merton, 1934. HM Forces, 1942–46. Research in Paris, 1946–55; Lectr in History, UCW Aberystwyth, 1955–61; Sen. Simon Res. Fellow, Manchester, 1960; Lectr, University of Leeds, 1962; Fellow and Tutor in Modern History, Balliol Coll., 1962–72, Hon. Fellow, 1977; Reader in French Revolutionary History, Oxford, 1969–72. Vis. Prof. in the History of Paris, Collège de France, 1971. Lectures: Ralegh, British Academy, 1974; Zaharoff, Oxford, 1976; Helmsley, Brandeis, 1981. DUniv Essex, 1981; Hon. LittD Leeds, 1988; Hon. DLitt Cambridge, 1989. Chevalier des Palmes Académiques, 1956; Officier de l'Ordre National du Mérite, 1977; Chevalier de la Légion d'Honneur, 1985. *Publications:* L'armée révolutionnaire à Lyon, 1952; Les armées révolutionnaires du Midi, 1955; Les armées révolutionnaires, vol. 1, 1961, vol. 2, 1963 (English trans., by Marianne Elliott, as The People's Armies: instrument of the Terror in the Departments, April 1793 to Floréal Year II, 1987); Terreur et Subsistances, 1965; A Second Identity: essays on France and French history, 1969; The Police and the People: French Popular Protest 1789–1820, 1970; Reactions to the French Revolution, 1972; Paris and its Provinces 1792–1802, 1975; A Sense of Place, 1975; Tour de France, 1976; Death in Paris 1795–1801, 1978 (Wolfson Prize, 1979); Streets of Paris, 1980; Promenades, 1980; French and Germans, Germans and French, 1983; People and Places, 1985; *autobiography:* Still Life: sketches from a Tunbridge Wells childhood, 1983 (J. R. Ackerley Prize); A Classical Education, 1985; Something to Hold Onto: autobiographical sketches, 1988. *Address:* Worcester College, Oxford OX1 2HB.

COBB, Timothy Humphry, MA; *b* 4 July 1909; *s* of Humphry Henry Cobb and Edith Muriel (*née* Stogdon); *m* 1952, Cecilia Mary Josephine, *d* of W. G. Chapman; two *s* one *d*. *Educ:* Harrow; Magdalene Coll., Cambridge. Asst Master, Middlesex Sch., Concord, Mass, USA, 1931–32; Bryanston Sch., Blandford, Dorset, 1932–47, Housemaster, Head of Classics, Estate Bursar; Headmaster of King's Coll., Budo, Kampala, Uganda, 1947–58; formerly Sec., Uganda Headmasters' Association; Headmaster, Dover College, 1958–73. *Publication:* Certificate English Language Practice, 1958. *Recreations:* music, railways, producing vegetables. *Address:* Parkgate Farm, Framlingham, Woodbridge, Suffolk IP13 9JH. *T:* Badingham (072875) 672. *Clubs:* MCC, Commonwealth Trust; Bluemantles Cricket (Tunbridge Wells and W Kent).

COBBAN, Sir James (Macdonald), Kt 1982; CBE 1971; TD; MA; DL; JP; Headmaster of Abingdon School, 1947–70; b 14 Sept. 1910; s of late A. M. Cobban, MIStructE, Scunthorpe, Lincs; m 1942, Lorna Mary (d 1961), er d of late G. S. W. Marlow, BSc, FRIC, barrister-at-law, Sydenham; four d (one s decd). Educ: Pocklington Sch.; Jesus Coll., Cambridge (Scholar); Univ. of Vienna. Classical Tripos, Part I, 1931, Part II, 1932; Sandys Student, 1932: Thirlwall Medallist and Gladstone Prizeman, 1935; MA, Cambridge; MA, Oxford (Pembroke Coll.). Asst Master, King Edward VI Sch., Southampton, 1933–36; Class. Sixth Form Master, Dulwich Coll., 1936–40, 1946–47. Intelligence Corps (TA), 1941; GSO3, Directorate of Mil. Intelligence, 1941; Intermediate War Course, Staff Coll., 1943; DAQMG, Combined Ops HQ, 1943; Staff Officer, CCG, 1944 (Lt-Col 1945). Rep. Diocese of Oxford on Gen. Synod, 1970–85 (Panel of Chairmen 1979–81); Vice-Pres., Dio. Synod, 1975–82; Chm., Abingdon Co. Bench, 1964–74; Member: Cttee GBA, 1972– (Dep. Chm., 1976–82; Hon. Life Mem., 1981); Direct Grant Schs Jt Cttee, 1966–80 (Chm., 1975–80); Cttee, GBGSA, 1976–81; Council, Ind. Schs Careers Orgn, 1972–80; Cttee, United Soc. Christian Lit., 1974–83; Thames Valley Police Authority, 1973–80; Vale of White Horse DC, 1973–76; Governor: Stowe Sch., 1970–83; Wellington Coll., 1970–81; Campion Sch., Athens, 1980–83; Sch. of St Helen and St Katharine, 1954–80, 1983–87 (Chm., 1958–67); Abingdon Coll. of Further Education, 1974–80; St Stephen's House, Oxford, 1982–85; Gloucester School of Ministry, 1984–86. JP Berks, 1950, Oxon, 1974; DL Berks, 1966, Oxon, 1974. Publications: Senate and Provinces, 78–49 BC, 1935; (in collaboration) Civis Romanus, 1936; Pax et Imperium, 1938; Church and School, 1963. Address: 10 Coverdale Court, Preston Road, Yeovil BA21 3AQ. T: Yeovil (0935) 77835.

COBBETT, David John, TD 1973; ERD 1962; railway and transportation management consultant; b 9 Dec. 1928; m 1952, Beatrix Jane Ogilvie Cockburn; three s. Educ: Royal Masonic Sch. FCIT. Gen. Railway admin. and managerial positions, 1949–67; Divl Movements Manager, Liverpool Street, 1967; Divl Manager, Norwich (British Railways Bd), 1968–70; Asst Managing Dir, Freightliners Ltd, 1970–73; Dep. Gen. Manager, British Railways Bd Scottish Region, 1973; Gen. Manager, British Railways Scottish Region, 1974–76; Chm., British Transport Ship Management, Scotland, 1974–76; Gen. Manager, BR Eastern Region, 1976–77; British Railways Board: Export Dir (Special Projects), 1977–78; Dir, Strategic Studies, 1978–83; Dir, Information Systems and Technology, 1983–85. Dir, Transmark, 1978. Chm., Railway Benevolent Instn, 1984– (Dep. Chm., 1981–84). Bt Col, Royal Corps of Transport (RARO), 1974. Recreations: military matters, historical reading, games. Address: Ballytruim, Newtonmore, Inverness-shire PH20 1DS. T: Newtonmore (05403) 269. Clubs: Army and Navy; MCC.

COBBOLD; see Lytton Cobbold, family name of Baron Cobbold.

COBBOLD, 2nd Baron cr 1960, of Knebworth; **David Antony Fromanteel Lytton Cobbold**; Managing Director, Gaiacorp Currency Managers, since 1991 (Director, since 1989); b 14 July 1937; s of 1st Baron Cobbold, KG, GCVO, PC, and of Lady Hermione Bulwer-Lytton, er d of 2nd Earl of Lytton, KG, GCSI, GCIE, PC; assumed by deed poll, 1960, additional surname of Lytton; S father, 1987; m 1961, Christine Elizabeth, 3rd d of Major Sir Dennis Frederic Bankes Stucley, 5th Bt; three s one d. Educ: Eton College; Trinity Coll., Cambridge (BA Hons Moral Sciences). Fellow, Assoc. of Corporate Treasurers. PO, RAF, 1955–57. NATO Flying Training Scheme, Canada 1956–57. Morgan Guaranty Trust Co., New York, 1961–62; Bank of London and South America Ltd, London, Zürich, Barcelona, 1962–72; Treasurer, Finance for Industry Ltd, 1974–79; Manager Treasury Div., BP Finance International, The British Petroleum Co. plc, 1979–87; Gen. Manager Financial Markets, TSB England & Wales plc, 1987–88; Dir, Hill Samuel Bank Ltd, and Head of TSB-Hill Samuel Treasury Div., 1988–89. Chm. and Man. Dir, Lytton Enterprises Ltd, Knebworth House, 1971–; Dir, 39 Production Co., 1988–. Mem., Finance and Policy Cttee, Historic Houses Assoc., 1973– (Hon. Treas., 1988–); Chm., Stevenage Community Trust, 1990–. Contested (L): Bishop Auckland, Oct. 1974; Hertfordshire, European Parly Election, 1979. Recreation: travel. Heir: s Hon. Henry Fromanteel Lytton Cobbold, b 12 May 1962. Address: Knebworth House, Knebworth, Herts. T: Stevenage (0438) 812261.

COBBOLD, (Michael) David (Nevill), CBE 1983; MA; DL; Consultant, Beachcroft Stanleys (formerly Beachcrofts), Solicitors, since 1983; Senior Partner, Stileman Neate & Topping, 1959–83; b 21 Oct. 1919; s of late Geoffrey Wyndham Nevill Cobbold and Cicely Helen Cobbold; m 1949, Ann Rosemary Trevor; two s one d (and one s decd). Educ: Charterhouse; New Coll., Oxford (MA); RMA, Sandhurst. War of 1939–45: commissioned and served with 2nd Bn, The Buffs, 1940–45. Admitted Solicitor, 1949. Westminster City Council: Member, 1949–86; Leader, 1964–65, 1976–83; Alderman, 1962–78; Mayor of Westminster, 1958–59; Lord Mayor and Dep. High Steward of Westminster, 1973–74. London Boroughs Association: Hon. Treas., 1977–84; Chm., Gen. Purposes Cttee, 1978–86; Dep. Chm., 1984–86. Chairman: London Boroughs Grants Cttee, 1985–86; London Area Social Responsibility Cttee, 1988–; Member: DoE Housing Act Gp, 1970–76; Adv. Cttee on Local Govt Audit, 1979–82; Royal Parks Constabulary Cttee, 1985–89. Pres., Beckenham Conservative Assoc., 1974–. DL Greater London, 1967–. Recreations: watching grandchildren and weeds grow: encouraging the former, discouraging the latter. Address: Tudor House, Childrey, Wantage OX12 9XQ.

COBBOLD, Patrick Mark; b 20 June 1934; s of late Captain J. M. Cobbold and Lady Blanche Cobbold. Educ: Eton. Served Scots Guards, 1953–57; ADC to the Governor of the Bahamas, 1957–60; Tolly Cobbold Breweries, 1961–89. Chm., Ipswich Town FC, 1976–. Recreations: fishing, shooting, football. Address: Glemham Hall, Woodbridge, Suffolk. T: Wickham Market (0728) 746219. Clubs: White's, Pratt's.

COBBOLD, Rear-Adm. Richard Francis; Assistant Chief of Defence Staff, Operational Requirements (Sea), since 1991; b 25 June 1942; s of Geoffrey Francis and Elizabeth Mary Cobbold; m 1975, Anne Marika Hjörne; one s one d. Educ: Bryanston Sch.; BRNC Dartmouth. Early service, RN: HMS Kent; Staff of FO Naval Flying Training; HMS Juno; HMS Hermes; loan to RAN; RN Staff College 1973; Arctic Flight in comd, 1973–74; 814 Sqdn, Sen. Observer, 1974–75; MoD, 1975–77; HMS Mohawk in comd, 1977–79; MoD, 1979–83; RCDS 1984; HMS Brazen in comd, 1985–86; Dir of Defence Concepts, MoD, 1987–88; Captain 2nd Frigate Sqdn, 1989–90. Recreations: ski-ing, most sports, gardening, naval history. Address: c/o Ministry of Defence, SW1A 2HB. Club: Naval and Military.

COBHAM, 11th Viscount cr 1718; **John William Leonard Lyttelton**; Bt 1618; Baron Cobham 1718; Lord Lyttelton, Baron of Frankley 1756 (renewed 1794); Baron Westcote (Ire.) 1776; b 5 June 1943; e s of 10th Viscount Cobham, KG, PC, GCMG, GCVO, TD, and Elizabeth Alison Viscountess Cobham (d 1986), d of J. R. Makeig-Jones, CBE; S father, 1977; m 1974, Penelope Ann, e d of late Roy Cooper, Moss Farm, Ollerton, near Knutsford, Cheshire. Educ: Eton; Christ's College, New Zealand; Royal Agricultural College, Cirencester. Recreations: cricket, shooting. Heir: b Hon. Christopher Charles Lyttelton [b 23 Oct. 1947; m 1973, Tessa Mary, d of late Col A. G. J. Readman, DSO; one s one d]. Address: Hagley Hall, near Stourbridge, West Midlands DY9 9LG. T: Hagley

(0562) 885823; 20 Kylestrome House, Cundy Street, Ebury Street, SW1. T: 071–730 5756. Club: MCC.

COBHAM, Michael John, CBE 1981; FRAeS; CBIM; Chairman, FR Group plc (formerly Flight Refuelling (Holdings) Ltd), since 1969 (Chief Executive, 1969–Feb. 1992); b 22 Feb. 1927; s of Sir Alan John Cobham, KBE, AFC, and Lady (Gladys) Cobham; m 1st, 1954, June Oakes (marr. diss. 1972); 2nd, 1973, Nadine Felicity, e d of William Abbott, Wimborne, Dorset; one d. Educ: Malvern; Trinity Coll., Cambridge (BA 1949, MA 1965). Served RN, 1945–47. Called to the Bar, Inner Temple, 1952; practised, 1954–55. Flight Refuelling Ltd: Dir, 1952; Man. Dir, 1964–77. Pres., 1976–77, Treasurer, 1980–84, SBAC; Mem. Council, Inst. of Dirs, 1976–. Chm., Air League, 1990–; Trustee, Fleet Air Arm Museum. Recreations: ski-ing, sailing. Address: FR Group plc, Brook Road, Wimborne, Dorset BH21 2BJ. Clubs: Naval and Military; Royal Thames Yacht; Royal Southern Yacht (Hamble).

COBURN, Prof. Kathleen, OC 1974; Professor of English, Victoria College, University of Toronto, 1953–71, now Emeritus; author; b 1905; d of Rev. John Coburn and Susannah Coburn. Educ: University of Toronto (MA); Oxford University (BLitt). Imperial Order of the Daughters of the Empire (IODE) Travelling Scholarship, 1930–31. Formerly Lectr, Asst Prof., and Assoc. Prof. of English, Victoria College, University of Toronto. University Women's Internat. Senior Fellowship, 1948–49; John Simon Guggenheim Memorial Fellowship, 1953–54, renewed, 1957–58; Commonwealth Visiting Fellowship (Univ. of London), 1962–63. FRSC 1958. Hon. Fellow, St Hugh's Coll., Oxford, 1970; Hon. Fellow, Champlain Coll., Trent Univ., Ont., 1972; Corresp. FBA, 1973. DHL: Haverford, 1972; Princeton, 1983; Hon. LLD, Queen's Univ., Kingston, Ontario, 1964; Hon. DLitt: Trent Univ., 1972; Cambridge, 1975; Toronto, 1978; Hon. DSL Toronto, 1986. Rose Mary Crawshay Prize for English Literature (Brit. Acad.), 1958, 1990; Chauveau Medal, RSC. Publications: (ed) The Philosophical Lectures of S. T. Coleridge, 1949; Inquiring Spirit, 1951, revd edn 1979; (ed) The Letters of Sara Hutchinson, 1954; (ed) The Notebooks of S. T. Coleridge, vol. i, 1957, vol. ii, 1961, vol. iii, 1973, vol. iv, 1990; Coleridge: A Collection of Critical Essays, 1967; The Self-Conscious Imagination (Riddell Meml Lectures), 1972; Coleridge, a Bridge Between Science and Poetry: reflections on the bicentenary of his birth, Discourse, Royal Institution, 1972; In Pursuit of Coleridge, 1977; Experience into Thought: perspectives in the Coleridge notebooks, Alexander Lectures, 1979; general editor, The Collected Coleridge, 1968–. Address: Victoria College, 73 Queen's Park Crescent, Toronto, Ontario M5S 1K7, Canada.

COCHRAN, William; PhD, MA; FRS 1962; Professor of Natural Philosophy, University of Edinburgh, 1975–87, retired; b 30 July 1922; s of James Cochran and Margaret Watson Cochran (née Baird); m 1953, Ingegerd Wall; one s two d. Educ: Boroughmuir Sch., Edinburgh; Edinburgh Univ. Asst Lectr, Edinburgh Univ., 1943–46; Demonstrator and Lectr, Univ. of Cambridge, 1948–62; Reader in Physics, Univ. of Cambridge, 1962–64. Fellow of Trinity Hall, Cambridge, 1951–64; University of Edinburgh: Prof. of Physics, 1964–75; Dean, Faculty of Science, 1978–81; Vice-Principal, 1984–87. Research fellowships abroad, 1950–51, 1958–59, 1970. Hon. Fellow, Trinity Hall, Cambridge, 1982. Guthrie medallist, Inst. Physics and Phys. Soc., 1966; Hughes medallist, Royal Soc., 1978; Potts medallist, Franklin Inst., 1985. Publications: Vol. III of The Crystalline State (with Prof. H. Lipson), 1954, new edn 1966; Dynamics of Atoms in Crystals, 1973. Recreations: Scots verse, family history. Address: Department of Physics, The University, The King's Buildings, Edinburgh EH9 3JZ; 71 Clermiston Road, Edinburgh.

COCHRANE, family name of **Earl of Dundonald** and **Baron Cochrane of Cults**.

COCHRANE, Lord; **Archie Iain Thomas Blair Cochrane**; b 14 March 1991; s and heir of Earl of Dundonald, qv.

COCHRANE OF CULTS, 4th Baron cr 1919; **Ralph Henry Vere Cochrane**; DL; Chairman, Craigtoun Meadows Ltd; b 20 Sept. 1926; 2nd s of 2nd Baron Cochrane of Cults, DSO and Hon. Elin Douglas-Pennant (d 1934), y d of 2nd Baron Penrhyn; S brother, 1990; m 1956, Janet Mary Watson, d of late William Hunter Watson Cheyne, MB, MRCS, LRCP; two s. Educ: Eton; King's Coll., Cambridge (MA). Served RE, 1945–47 (Lt). Formerly: Vice-Chm., Cupar-Fife Savings Bank; Dir for Fife, Tayside Savings Bank. Underwriting Mem. of Lloyds, 1965–. Gen. Comr for Income Tax. Mem., Queen's Body Guard for Scotland (Royal Co. of Archers). DL Fife. Heir: s Hon. Thomas Hunter Vere Cochrane, LLB, ACII, b 7 Sept. 1957. Address: Cults House, Cupar, Fife KY15 5RD. Club: New (Edinburgh).

COCHRANE, (Alexander John) Cameron, MBE 1987; MA; first Headmaster, Prince Willem-Alexander College, Holland, since 1988; b 19 July 1933; s of late Dr Alexander Younger Cochrane and of Jenny Johnstone Cochrane; m 1958, Rosemary Aline, d of late Robert Alexander Ogg and of Aline Mary Ogg; one s two d. Educ: The Edinburgh Academy; University Coll., Oxford. National Service in RA, 1952–54. Asst Master, St Edward's Sch., Oxford, 1957–66; Warden, Brathay Hall, Ambleside, Cumbria, 1966–70; Asst Dir of Educn, City of Edinburgh, 1970–74; Headmaster, Arnold Sch., Blackpool, 1974–79; Headmaster, Fettes Coll., Edinburgh, 1979–88. Member: Lancashire CC Educn Cttee, 1976–79; Council, Outward Bound Trust, 1979–88; Scottish Cttee, Duke of Edinburgh's Award, 1981–86; Chairman: Outward Bound Ullswater, 1979–84; Outward Bound Loch Eil, 1984–88; Lothian Fedn of Boys' Clubs, 1981–84 (Vice-Pres., 1986–). Commandant, XIII Commonwealth Games Village, Edinburgh, 1986. Governor: Aiglon Coll.; Pocklington Sch. Hon. Fellow, Dept of Educnl Studies, Univ. of Edinburgh, 1973–74. Recreations: games, the countryside, music. Address: Prince Willem-Alexander College, Gravenallee 22, 7591 PE Denekamp, Holland. Clubs: Public Schools, MCC; Vincent's (Oxford); New (Edinburgh).

COCHRANE, Christopher Duncan; QC 1988; b 29 Aug. 1938; s of Harold Hubert and Joan Cochrane; m 1st, 1960, Caroline Beatrice Carey; two d; 2nd, 1970, Patricia Joan Godley; 3rd, 1984, Doreen Ann Suffolk; one step d. Educ: Ampleforth Coll.; Magdalen Coll., Oxford (Schol.; MA). Called to the Bar, Middle Temple, 1965; a Recorder, 1985. Recreations: travel, theatre, spectator sport, dining out. Address: 8 New Square, Lincoln's Inn, WC2A 3QP. T: 071–242 4986.

COCHRANE, Sir (Henry) Marc (Sursock), 4th Bt cr 1903; b 23 Oct. 1946; s of Sir Desmond Oriel Alastair George Weston Cochrane, 3rd Bt, and of Yvonne Lady Cochrane (née Sursock); S father, 1979; m 1969, Hala (née Es-Said); two s one d. Educ: Eton; Trinity Coll., Dublin (BBS, MA). Director: Hambros Bank Ltd, 1979–85; GT Management PLC, 1986–. Hon. Consul General of Ireland in Beirut, 1979–84. Trustee, Chester Beatty Library and Gall. of Oriental Art, Dublin. Recreations: skiing, target shooting, electronics. Heir: s Alexander Desmond Cochrane, b 7 May 1973. Address: Woodbrook, Bray, Co. Wicklow, Ireland. T: 821421; Palais Sursock, PO Box 154, Beirut, Lebanon. T: 331607.

COCKBURN, Prof. Forrester, MD; FRCPGlas; FRCPEd; Samson Gemmell Professor of Child Health, University of Glasgow, since 1977; b 13 Oct. 1934; s of Forrester Cockburn and Violet E. Bunce; m 1960, Alison Fisher Grieve; two s. Educ: Leith Acad.; Univ. of Edinburgh (MD). DCH Glasgow. FRCPE 1971; FRCPGlas 1978. Med. trng, Royal Infirmary of Edinburgh, Royal Hosp. for Sick Children, and Simpson Memorial

Maternity Pavilion, Edinburgh, 1959–63; Huntingdon Hertford Foundn Res. Fellow, Boston Univ., Mass, 1963–65; Nuffield Sen. Res. Fellow, Univ. of Oxford, 1965–66; Wellcome Trust Sen. Med. Res. Fellow, Univ. of Edin. and Simpson Meml Maternity Pavilion, 1966–71; Sen. Lectr, Dept of Child Life and Health, Univ. of Edin., 1971–77. *Publications:* Neonatal Medicine, 1974; The Cultured Cell in Inherited Metabolic Disease, 1977; Inborn Errors of Metabolism in Humans, 1980; (with O. P. Gray) Children—A Handbook for Children's Doctors, 1984; (with J. H. Hutchison) Practical Paediatric Problems, 6th edn 1986; (with T. L. Turner and J. Douglas) Craig's Care of the Newly Born Infant, 8th edn 1988; Fetal and Neonatal Growth, 1988; contrib. Fetal and Neonatal Nutrition. *Recreation:* sailing. *Address:* University Department of Child Health, Royal Hospital for Sick Children, Yorkhill, Glasgow G3 8SJ. *T:* 041–339 8888.

COCKBURN, Sir John (Elliot), 12th Bt of that Ilk, *cr* 1671; *b* 7 Dec. 1925; *s* of Lieut-Col Sir John Cockburn, 11th Bt of that Ilk, DSO and Isabel Hunter (*d* 1978), *y d* of late James McQueen, Crofts, Kirkcudbrightshire; *S* father, 1949; *m* 1949, Glory Patricia, *er d* of Nigel Tudway Mullings; three *s* two *d*. *Educ:* RNC Dartmouth; Royal Agricultural Coll., Cirencester. Served War of 1939–45, joined RAFVR, July 1944. *Recreation:* reading. *Heir: s* Charles Christopher Cockburn [*b* 19 Nov. 1950; *m* 1985, Ruth, *d* of Samuel Bell; one *s* one *d* (twins)]. *Address:* 48 Frewin Road, SW18. *Club:* Naval and Military.

COCKBURN, Sir Robert, KBE 1960 (OBE 1946); CB 1953; PhD, MSc, MA; FEng 1977; FInstP; Senior Research Fellow, Churchill College, Cambridge, 1970–77; Chairman, National Computing Centre, 1970–77; *b* 31 March 1909; 2nd *s* of late Rev. R. T. Cockburn, Columba Manse, Belford, Northumberland; *m* 1935, Phyllis Hoyland; two *d*. *Educ:* Southern Secondary Sch. and Municipal Coll., Portsmouth; London Univ. BSc 1928, MSc 1935, PhD 1939, London; MA Cantab 1973. Taught Science at West Ham Municipal Coll., 1930–37; research in communications at RAE Farnborough, 1937–39; in radar at TRE Malvern, Worcs, 1939–45; in atomic energy at AERE Harwell, 1945–48; Scientific Adviser to Air Min., 1948–53; Princ. Dir of Scientific Research (Guided Weapons and Electronics), Ministry of Supply, 1954–55; Deputy Controller of Electronics, Ministry of Supply, 1955–56; Controller of Guided Weapons and Electronics, Ministry of Supply, 1956–59; Chief Scientist of Ministry of Aviation, 1959–64; Dir, RAE, Farnborough, 1964–69. Chairman: Television Adv. Cttee for Posts and Telecommunications, 1971–73; BBC Engineering Adv. Cttee, 1973–81. Hon. FRAeS, 1970. Congressional Medal for Merit, 1947. *Publications:* scientific papers. *Recreations:* sailing, modelling. *Address:* 1 Firethorn Close, Longmead, Fleet, Hants GU13 9TR. *T:* Fleet (0252) 615518. *Clubs:* Athenæum; Offshore Cruising.

COCKBURN, William, CBE 1989; TD 1980; Managing Director, Royal Mail, The Post Office, since 1986; *b* 28 Feb. 1943. Entered Post Office, 1961; held various junior and middle management positions; Personal Assistant to Chm. of PO, 1971–73; Asst Dir of Finance and Planning, 1973–77; Dir, Central Finance Planning, 1977–78; Dir, Postal Finance, 1978–79; Dir, London Postal Region, 1979–82; apptd Mem., PO Board, 1981, Mem. for Finance, Counter Services and Planning, 1982–84; Mem. for Royal Mail Operations, 1984–86. Non-exec. Dir, V. A. T. Watkins Holdings Ltd, 1985–; Dir, Business in the Community, 1990–. Col, RE Postal and Courier Service (V), 1986–. *Address:* Royal Mail Headquarters, 148–166 Old Street, EC1V 9HQ.

COCKBURN-CAMPBELL, Sir Thomas; 6th Bt, *cr* 1821; *b* 8 Dec. 1918; *e s* of Sir Alexander Thomas Cockburn-Campbell, 5th Bt, and Maude Frances Lorenzo (*d* 1926), *o d* of Alfred Giles, Kent Town, Adelaide, SA; *S* father, 1935; *m* 1st, 1944, Josephine Zoi (marr. diss. 1981), *e d* of Harold Douglas Forward, Curjardine, WA; one *s*; 2nd, 1982, Janice Laraine, *y d* of William John Pascoe, Bundoora, Vic. *Educ:* Melbourne C of E Grammar Sch. *Heir: s* Alexander Thomas Cockburn-Campbell [*b* 16 March 1945; *m* 1969, Kerry Ann, *e d* of Sgt K. Johnson; one *s* one *d*]. *Address:* 14 Lincoln Street, York, WA 6302, Australia.

COCKCROFT, Dr Janet Rosemary, OBE 1975; Chairman, Bottoms Mill Co. Ltd, Todmorden, since 1980 (Director, since 1961, Deputy Chairman, 1974–80); *b* 26 July 1916; *er d* of late Major W. G. Mowat, MC, TD, JP, of Bucholllie, Lybster, Caithness, Scotland, and late Mary Mowat; *m* 1942, Major Peter Worby Cockcroft (*d* 1980); two *s* one *d*. *Educ:* Glasgow Univ. MB, ChB 1938. Ho. Surg. and Ho. Phys., Glasgow Royal Infirmary, 1938–39; GP, 1939–43; Asst MOH, Co. of Caithness, 1943–46; MO, Maternity and Child Welfare, Halifax, 1950–53; Part-time MOH, WRCC, 1953–67; MO, Family Planning Assoc., 1947–75 (Halifax and Sowerby Bridge Clinics); MO, British Red Cross, Halifax, 1960–66; Chairman: N Midlands FPA Doctors' Gp, 1966–68; Halifax FPA Clinic, 1963–75. Mem., Food Additives and Contaminants Cttee, MAFF, 1972–81; Chm., Consumers' Cttees for England and Wales and for GB, MAFF, 1975–82; Vice-Pres., 1969–70, Pres., 1970–72, Nat. Council of Women of GB; Vice-Pres., Internat. Council of Women, 1973–76; UK Rep., UN Status of Women Commn, 1973–79 (Vice Chm., 1976; Chm., 1978–80); Member: BBC Northern Adv. Council, 1975–79; Gen. Adv. Council, BBC, 1980–87. Elder, United Reformed Church, 1973–. *Publication:* Not a Proper Doctor (autobiog.), 1986. *Recreations:* travel, reading. *Address:* Dalemore, Savile Park, Halifax, W Yorks HX1 3EA. *T:* Halifax (0422) 352621. *Club:* Naval and Military.

COCKCROFT, John Hoyle; Chairman, Commed Publishing Ltd, telecommunications co., since 1989 (Director, since 1983); various electronics consultancies, since 1977; *b* 6 July 1934; *s* of late Lionel Fielden Cockcroft and of Jenny Hoyle; *m* 1971, Tessa Fay Shepley; three *d*. *Educ:* Primary, Trearddur House; Oundle; St John's Coll., Cambridge (Sen. Maj. Scholar (History), 1953). MA Hons History and Econs 1958; Pres., Cambridge Union, 1958. Royal Artillery, 2nd Lieut, 1953–55. Feature Writer and Investment Analyst, Financial Times, 1959–61; Economist, GKN, 1962–67 (re-acquisitions, 1962–65); seconded to Treasury, Public Enterprises Div., 1965–66; Econ. Leader-writer, Daily Telegraph, 1967–74. MP (C) Nantwich, Feb. 1974–1979; Mem. Select Cttee on Nationalised Industries, 1975–79; Company Secretaries Bill (Private Member's), 1978. Dir, BR (Eastern Region), 1984–89; Laurence Prust, stockbrokers, 1986–90; Consultant: and historian, GKN, 1971–76; British Field Sports Soc., 1975–76; Financial Public Relations Internat., 1975–76; Edman Gp, 1976–77; Mail Users' Assoc., 1976–79; Inst. of Chartered Secretaries, 1977–79; Datsun (Nissan) UK, 1980–81; Cray Electronics, 1982–84; Dowty Gp, 1983–86; Wedgwood, 1983–84; Crystalate, 1983–86; Camden Associates (political PR), 1984–88; Cambridge Corp. Consultants, 1989–; Gen. Aviation Manufacturers and Traders Assoc. (GAMTA) Ltd, 1991–; Premier Administration (American Express), 1991–. Advr and consultant, NEI History Archives, 1980–85. Member Council: European Movement, 1973–74, 1983–84; Conservative Gp for Europe, 1980–87; Member: Cttee, Assoc. of Youth Clubs, 1970–74; PITCOM, 1985–90; Cons. Computer Forum, 1983–; Epping Cons. Supper Club Cttee, 1984–90. Treasurer, Cambridge Univ. Cons. Assoc., 1958. Author, Belgium Quarterly Economic Review, EIU, 1969–71; columnist: and contributor, Microscope, 1982–85; electronic money transmission, Banking World, 1984–86; Westminster Watch, Electronics Times, 1985–90. *Publications:* (jtly) Reforming the Constitution, 1968; (jtly) Self-Help Reborn, 1969; Why England Sleeps, 1971; (jtly) An Internal History of Guest Keen and Nettlefolds, 1976; Microtechnology in Banking, 1984; Microelectronics (booklet), 1979 and 1982; leaders and leader page articles, Daily and Sunday Telegraphs, 1979–87. *Recreations:* walking, reading, swimming, entertaining. *Address:* Mitchell's Farmhouse, Stapleford Tawney, Essex RM4 1SS. *T:* Stapleford (04028) 254; 137 Dulwich Road, SE24 0NG. *T: 071–733 3456*. *Club:* Cambridge Union Soc.

COCKCROFT, Sir Wilfred (Halliday), Kt 1983; Chairman, Educational Project Resources, since 1989; *b* 7 June 1923; *s* of Wilfred Cockcroft and Bessie Halliday; *m* 1st, 1949, Barbara Rhona Huggan; two *s*; 2nd, 1982, Vivien, *o d* of Mr and Mrs David Lloyd. *Educ:* Keighley Boys' Grammar Sch.; Balliol Coll., Oxford (Williams Exhibnr, 1941, Hon. Scholar, 1946). MA, DPhil Oxon; FIMA 1973; FRSA 1983. Technical Signals/Radar Officer, RAF, 1942–46. Asst Lectr, Univ. of Aberdeen, 1949, Lectr 1950; Lectr, Univ. of Southampton, 1957, Reader 1960; G. F. Grant Prof. of Pure Mathematics, Univ. of Hull, 1961; Vice-Chancellor, NUU, 1976–82; Chm. and Chief Exec., Secondary Exams Council, 1983–88. Vis. Lectr and Prof., Univs of Chicago, Stanford, State Univ. of NY, 1954, 1959, 1967. University Grants Committee: Mem., 1973–76; Mem., Math. Sciences Subcttee, 1967–72, Chm. 1973–76; Chm., Educn Subcttee, 1973–76; Mem., Management and Business Studies Subcttee, and Educnl Technology Subcttee, 1973–76. Science and Engineering Research Council (formerly Science Research Council): Mem., 1978–82; Mem., Maths Sub-Cttee, 1964–68 (Chm., 1969–73); Mem., Science Bd, 1969–73; Chm., Postgraduate Trng Cttee, 1979–82. Chairman: Nuffield Maths Project Consultative Cttee, 1963–71; Specialist Conf. on Maths in Commonwealth Schs, Trinidad, 1968. Cttee to review Rural Planning Policy, DoE, NI, 1977–78; Cttee to consider teaching of maths in schs in England and Wales, 1978–82; Standing Conference on Univ. Entrance, 1979–82; Nat. Foundn for Educnl Res., 1988–90; Royal Soc. Maths Curriculum Subcttee, 1991–; Member: Computer Bd for Univs and Res. Councils, 1975–76; US/UK Educnl Commn, 1977–80; Educn Cttee, Royal Soc., 1990–. Member, Council: London Mathematical Soc., 1973–76; IMA, 1974–77, 1982–85. Hon. Fellow, Humberside Higher Educn Coll., 1987; Hon. Mem., CGLI, 1987. Hon. DSc: Kent, 1983; Southampton, 1986; DUniv Open, 1984. *Publications:* Your Child and Mathematics, 1968; Complex Numbers, 1972. *Recreations:* mathematics textbook writing and editing, golf, swimming, sketching, bad piano playing. *Address:* The Old Rectory, Warmington, OX17 1BU. *T:* Farnborough (029589) 531; (office) 126–128 Cromwell Road, SW7 4ET. *T:* 071–373 7716. *Club:* Athenæum.

COCKELL, Michael Henry; a Deputy Chairman of Lloyd's, 1986; *b* 30 Aug. 1933; *s* of Charles and Elise Seaton; *m* 1961, Elizabeth Janet Meikle; one *s* three *d*. *Educ:* Harrow School. Underwriter for G. N. Rouse Syndicate 570, 1968–90; Chm., M. H. Cockell & Co., 1978; Senior Partner, M. H. Cockell & Partners, 1986. Dep. Chm., Lloyd's Non-Marine Assoc., 1982, Chm., 1983–; Mem. Council, Lloyd's, 1984–87, 1990–. *Recreations:* all sport (especially cricket), ornithology, music (not loud pop), gardening, countryside. *Address:* Hill Harbour House, Hellingly, Hailsham, East Sussex. *T:* Hailsham (0323) 845081. *Clubs:* City of London, MCC.

COCKERAM, Eric (Paul); JP; *b* 4 July 1924; *er s* of Mr and Mrs J. W. Cockeram; *m* 1949, Frances Irving; two *s* two *d*. *Educ:* The Leys Sch., Cambridge. Served War, 1942–46: Captain The Gloucestershire Regt; "D Day" landings (wounded and later discharged). MP (C): Bebington, 1970–Feb. 1974; Ludlow, 1979–87. PPS: to Minister for Industry, 1970–72; to Minister for Posts and Telecommunications, 1972; to Chancellor of Exchequer, 1972–74. Mem., Select Cttee on Corporation Tax, 1971, on Industry and Trade, 1979–87; Mem., Public Accounts Cttee, 1983–87. Pres., Menswear Assoc. of Britain, 1964–65. Mem., Bd of Governors, United Liverpool Hosps, 1965–74; Chm., Liverpool NHS Exec. Council, 1970. Chairman: Watson Prickard Ltd, 1966–; Johnson Fry (Northern) Ltd, 1988–; Director: TSB (NW), 1968–83; TSB (Wales & Border Counties), 1983–; Liverpool Building Soc., 1975–82 (Vice-Chm., 1981–82); Midshires Building Soc., 1982–; Muller Group (UK) Ltd, 1983–; Member of Lloyd's. Liveryman, Worshipful Co. of Glovers, 1969–, Mem. Court, 1979–. Freeman: City of London; City of Springfield, Ill. JP, City of Liverpool, 1960. *Recreations:* bridge, golf, shooting, country walking. *Address:* Fairway Lodge, Caldy, Wirral, Cheshire L48 1NB. *T:* 051–625 1100. *Club:* Carlton.

COCKERELL, Sir Christopher (Sydney), Kt 1969; CBE 1966; RDI 1987; FRS 1967; designer and inventor; *b* 4 June 1910; *s* of late Sir Sydney Cockerell; *m* 1937, Margaret Elinor Belsham; two *d*. *Educ:* Gresham's; Peterhouse, Cambridge (Hon. Fellow, 1974). Pupil, W. H. Allen & Sons, Bedford, 1931–33; Radio Research, Cambridge, 1933–35; airborne and navigational equipment research and development (36 patents), Marconi Wireless Telegraph Co. Ltd, 1935–51; inventor of and engaged on hovercraft since 1953 (56 patents); Consultant (hovercraft), Ministry of Supply, 1957–58; Consultant: Hovercraft Development Ltd, 1958–70 (Dir, 1959–66); British Hovercraft Corp., 1973–79; Chm., Ripplecraft Co. Ltd, 1950–79; Founder and Chm., Wavepower Ltd, 1974–82 (3 patents), Consultant, 1982–88. Foundn Pres., Internat. Air Cushion Engrg Soc., 1969–71 (Vice-Pres., 1971–); Pres., UK Hovercraft Soc., 1972–; Member, Min. of Technology's Adv. Cttee for Hovercraft, 1968–70. A Trustee of National Portrait Gallery, 1967–79. Hon. Fellow: Swedish Soc. of Aeronautics, 1963; Soc. of Engineers, 1966; Manchester Inst. of Sci. and Tech., 1967; Downing Coll., Cambridge, 1969. Hon. Mem., Southampton Chamber of Commerce, 1967. Hon. DSc: Leicester, 1967; Heriot-Watt, 1971; London, 1975; Hon. Dr RCA, 1968. Hon. Freeman, Borough of Ramsgate, 1971. Viva Shield, Worshipful Co. of Carmen, 1961; RAC Diamond Jubilee Trophy, 1962. Thulin Medal, Swedish Soc. of Aeronautics, 1963; Howard N. Potts Medal, Franklin Inst., 1965; Albert Medal, RSA, 1966; Churchill Medal, Soc. of Engineers, 1966; Royal Medal, Royal Soc., 1966; Mitchell Memorial Medal, Stoke-on-Trent Assoc. of Engineers, 1967; Columbus Prize, Genoa, 1968; John Scott Award, City of Philadelphia, 1968; Elmer A. Sperry Award, 1968; Gold Medal, Calais Chamber of Commerce, 1969; Bluebird Trophy, 1969; James Alfred Ewing Medal, ICE, 1977; James Watt Internat. Gold Medal, IMechE, 1983. *Recreations:* the visual arts, gardening, fishing. *Address:* 16 Prospect Place, Hythe, Hants SO4 6AU.

COCKERILL, Geoffrey Fairfax, CB 1980; Secretary, University Grants Committee, 1978–82; *b* 14 May 1922; *e s* of late Walter B. Cockerill and Mary W. Cockerill (*née* Buffery); *m* 1959, Janet Agnes Walters, JP, MA, *d* of late Archibald J. Walters, MBE, and Elsie Walters; two *s*. *Educ:* Humberstone Foundation Sch.; UC Nottingham. BA London 1947. Royal Artillery, 1941–45 (Captain). Min. of Labour, 1947; Min. of Educn, 1952; Private Sec. to last Minister of Educn and Secs of State for Educn and Science, 1963–65; Asst Sec., 1964; Sec., Public Schools Commn, 1966–68; Jt Sec., Schools Council for Curriculum and Examinations, 1970–72; Under-Sec., DES, 1972–77; Dep. Sec., 1978. Chairman: Anglo-Amer. Primary Educ. Project, 1970–72; Working Party on Nutritional Aspects of School Meals, 1973–75; Kingston-upon-Thames CAB, 1985–88; Member: Adv. Gp on London Health Services, 1980–81; RCN Commn on Nursing Educn, 1984–85; RCN Strategy Gp, 1985–; UGC, Univ. of S Pacific, 1984–87; Vice-Pres., Experiment in Internat. Living, 1989–. Reviewed for Government: Central Bureau for Educational Visits and Exchanges, 1982; Youth Exchanges, 1983; Nat. Youth Bureau, 1983; Consultant to Cttee of Vice-Chancellors and Principals, 1984–85. Hon. Senior Research Fellow, KCL, 1982–86. *Recreations:* gardening, photography. *Address:* 29 Lovelace Road, Surbiton, Surrey KT6 6NS. *T:* 081–399 0125. *Clubs:* Athenæum, National Liberal, Commonwealth Trust.

COCKERTON, Rev. Canon John Clifford Penn; Rector of Wheldrake with Thorganby, since 1985 (Rector of Wheldrake, 1978–85); Canon of York (Prebend of Dunnington), since 1987; b 27 June 1927; s of late William Penn Cockerton and Eleanor Cockerton; m 1974, Diana Margaret Smith (d 1987), d of Mr and Mrs W. Smith, Upper Poppleton, York. Educ: Wirral Grammar Sch.; Univ. of Liverpool; St Catherine's Society, Oxford; Wycliffe Hall, Oxford. Asst Master, Prenton Secondary Sch., 1949–51; Deacon 1954; Priest 1955; Asst Curate, St Helens Parish Church, 1954–58; Tutor 1958–60, Chaplain 1960–63, Cranmer Hall, Durham; Vice-Principal, St John's Coll., Durham, 1963–70; Principal, St John's College and Cranmer Hall, Durham, 1970–78. Examining Chaplain to Bishop of Durham, 1971–73; Proctor in Convocation, 1980–85. Recreation: music. Address: The Rectory, 3 Church Lane, Wheldrake, York YO4 6AW. T: Wheldrake (0904) 448230.

COCKETT, Frank Bernard, MS, FRCS; Consulting Surgeon to: St Thomas' Hospital; King Edward VII Hospital for Officers, London; b Rockhampton, Australia, 22 April 1916; s of late Rev. Charles Bernard Cockett, MA, DD; m 1945, Felicity Ann (d 1958), d of Col James Thackeray Fisher, DSO, Frieston, near Grantham, Lincs; one s two d; m 1960, Dorothea Anne Newman; twin s. Educ: Bedford Sch.; St Thomas's Hosp. Med. Sch. BSc (1st Cl. Hons), 1936; MRCS, LRCP 1939; MB, BS (London) 1940; FRCS Eng 1947; MS (London) 1953. Sqdn Ldr (Surgical Specialist) RAFVR, 1942–46; Surgical Registrar, St Thomas' Hosp., 1947–48; Resident Asst Surg., St Thomas' Hosp., 1948–50, Consultant, 1954–81; Senior Lecturer in Surgery, St Thomas's Hosp. Med. Sch., 1950–54; Consultant, King Edward VII Hosp. for Officers, 1974–81. Fellow Assoc. of Surgs of Gt Brit.; Mem. European Soc. of Cardiovascular Surgery; Pres., Vascular Surgical Soc. of GB and Ireland, 1980; Chm., Venous Forum, RSM, 1986–87. Publications: The Pathology and Surgery of the Veins of the Lower Limb, 1956, 2nd edn 1976; several contribs to Operative Surgery (ed. C. G. Rob and Rodney Smith), 1956; various papers in medical and surgical journals. Recreations: sailing, tennis, squash, gardening, collecting marine paintings. Address: 14 Essex Villas, Kensington, W8 7BN. T: 071-937 9883. Clubs: Lansdowne, Little Ship; Island Sailing.

COCKETT, Geoffrey Howard; consultant; Chief Scientific Officer, Ministry of Defence, and Deputy Director, Royal Armament Research and Development Establishment, 1983–86; b 18 March 1926; s of late William Cockett and Edith (née Dinham); m 1951, Elizabeth Bagshaw; two d. Educ: King Edward VI Sch., Southampton; Univ. of Southampton (BSc, Hons Maths, and Hons Physics). FInstP; CPhys. Royal Aircraft Establishment, 1948–52; Armament Research Estabt, Woolwich, 1952–62; RARDE, 1962–68; Supt of Physics Div., Chemical Defence Estabt, 1968–71; RARDE: Supt, Optics and Surveillance Systems Div., 1971–76; Head, Applied Physics Group, 1976–83. (Jtly) Gold Medal, Congrès des Materiaux Résistant à Chaud, Paris, 1951. Publications: official reports; scientific and technical papers in various learned jls. Recreations: opera, photography, under gardening. Address: Royal Armament Research and Development Establishment, Fort Halstead, Sevenoaks, Kent TN14 7BP. T: Knockholt (0959) 32222.

COCKFIELD, family name of **Baron Cockfield.**

COCKFIELD, Baron cr 1978 (Life Peer), of Dover in the County of Kent; **Francis Arthur Cockfield,** Kt 1973; PC 1982; a Vice-President, Commission of the European Communities, 1985–88; b 28 Sept. 1916; 2nd s of late Lieut C. F. Cockfield (killed on the Somme in Aug. 1916) and Louisa (née James); m Aileen Monica Mudie, choreographer. Educ: Dover Grammar Sch.; London Sch. of Economics (LLB, BSc (Econ.)). Called to Bar, Inner Temple, 1942. Home Civil Service, Inland Revenue, 1938; Asst Sec. to Board of Inland Revenue, 1945; Commissioner of Inland Revenue, 1951–52; Dir of Statistics and Intelligence to Board of Inland Revenue, 1945–52; Boots Pure Drug Co. Ltd: Finance Dir, 1953–61; Man. Dir. and Chm. Exec. Management Cttee, 1961–67. Chm., Price Commn, 1973–77. Minister of State, HM Treasury, 1979–82; Sec. of State for Trade, 1982–83; Chancellor of the Duchy of Lancaster, 1983–84. Mem., NEDC, 1962–64, 1982–83; Advr on Taxation Policy to Chancellor of Exchequer, 1970–73. Mem., Court of Governors, Univ. of Nottingham, 1963–67. Pres., Royal Statistical Soc., 1968–69. Hon. Fellow, LSE, 1972. Hon. LLD Fordham Univ., NY, 1989; Sheffield, 1990; DUniv Surrey, 1989. Grand Cross, Order of Leopold II, Belgium, 1990. Address: House of Lords, SW1.

COCKIN, Rt. Rev. George Eyles Irwin; Assistant Bishop, Diocese of York, since 1969; b 15 Aug. 1908; s of late Charles Irwin Cockin, Solicitor, and Judith Cockin. Educ: Repton; Leeds University (BA); Lincoln Theological College. Tutor, St Paul's College, Awka, Nigeria, 1933–40; Supervisor, Anglican Schools, E Nigeria, 1940–52. Deacon, 1953, Priest, 1954; Curate, Kimberworth, Rotherham, 1953–55; Sen. Supervisor, Anglican Schools, E Nigeria, 1955–58; Canon, All Saints Cathedral, Onitsha, 1957; first Bishop of Owerri, 1959–69. Rector of Bainton, dio. York, 1969–78; Rural Dean of Harthill, 1973–78.

COCKING, Prof. Edward Charles Daniel, FRS 1983; Professor of Botany and Head of Department of Botany, University of Nottingham, since 1969; b 26 Sept. 1931; y s of late Charles Cocking and of Mary (née Murray); m 1960, Bernadette Keane; one s one d. Educ: Buckhurst Hill County High Sch., Essex; Univ. of Bristol (BSc, PhD, DSc). FIBiol. Civil Service Commission Research Fellow, 1956–59; Lecturer in Plant Physiology, Univ. of Nottingham, 1959–66, Reader, 1966–69. S. Yoshida Meml Lecture, Hangzhou Univ., China, 1987. Member: Lawes Agricl Trust Cttee, Rothamsted Experimental Stn, 1987–; Adv. Cttee on Forest Res., Forestry Commn, 1987–; Council, Royal Soc., 1986–88; AFRC, 1990– (Royal Soc. Assessor, 1988–90). Mem., Bd of Trustees, Royal Botanic Gardens, Kew, 1983–; Member, Governing Body: Glasshouse Crops Res. Inst., 1983–87; British Soc. Horticultural Res., 1987–89. Pres., Sect. K, BAAS, 1983. Publications: Introduction to the Principles of Plant Physiology (with W. Stiles, FRS), 3rd edn 1969; numerous scientific papers in botanical/genetics jls on plant genetic manipulations. Recreations: walking, travelling, especially by train, occasional chess. Address: Department of Botany, University of Nottingham, University Park, Nottingham NG7 2RD. T: Nottingham (0602) 484848, ext. 2201; 30 Patterdale Road, Woodthorpe, Nottingham NG5 4LQ. T: Nottingham (0602) 262452.

COCKRAM, Sir John, Kt 1964; Director, 1952–79, General Manager, 1941–73, The Colne Valley Water Company; Director, 1970–86, Chairman, 1971–86, Rickmansworth Water Co. (formerly Rickmansworth and Uxbridge Valley Water Co.); b 10 July 1908; s of Alfred John and Beatrice Elizabeth Cockram; m 1937, Phyllis Eleanor, d of Albert Henning; one s two d. Educ: St Aloysius Coll., Highgate. Chartered Accountant. Member: Herts CC, 1949–74 (Chm. 1961–65); Thames Conservancy, 1954–74; Exec. Cttee, British Waterworks Assoc., 1948–74 (Pres., 1957–58); Central Advisory Water Cttee, 1955–73; Thames Water Authy, 1973–76. Life Mem., Water Cos Assoc., 1985 (Mem., 1950–85; Chm., 1950–79; Dep. Pres., 1979–85). Life Governor, Haileybury. Recreations: fishing, gardening. Address: Rebels' Corner, The Common, Chorleywood, Hertfordshire WD3 5LT.

COCKS, family name of **Barons Cocks of Hartcliffe** and **Somers.**

COCKS OF HARTCLIFFE, Baron cr 1987 (Life Peer), of Chinnor in the County of Oxfordshire; **Michael Francis Lovell Cocks,** PC 1976; b 19 Aug. 1929; s of late Dr H. F. Lovell Cocks; m 1st, 1954, Janet Macfarlane; two s two d; 2nd, 1979, Valerie Davis. Educ: Bristol University. Various posts in education from 1954; Lectr, Bristol Polytechnic, 1968. Contested (Lab): Bristol West, 1959; South Gloucestershire, 1964, 1966. MP (Lab) Bristol S, 1970–87. An Asst Govt Whip, 1974–76; Parly Sec. to the Treasury and Govt Chief Whip, 1976–79; Opposition Chief Whip, 1979–85. Publication: Labour and the Benn Factor, 1989. Recreations: swimming, listening to music, reading.

COCKS, Anna Gwenllian S.; see Somers Cocks.

COCKS, Rt. Rev. Francis William, CB 1959; b 5 Nov. 1913; o s of late Canon W. Cocks, OBE, St John's Vicarage, Felixstowe; m 1940, Irene May, (Barbara) (d 1989), 2nd d of H. Thompson, Bridlington; one s one d. Educ: Haileybury; St Catharine's Coll., Cambridge; Westcott House. Played Rugby Football for Cambridge Univ., Hampshire and Eastern Counties, 1935–38. Ordained, 1937. Chaplain RAFVR, 1939; Chaplain RAF, 1945; Asst Chaplain-in-Chief, 1950; Chaplain-in-Chief, and Archdeacon, Royal Air Force, 1959–65; Rector and Rural Dean of Wolverhampton, 1965–70; Bishop Suffragan of Shrewsbury, 1970–80. Hon. Chaplain to HM the Queen, 1959–65. Prebendary of S Botolph in Lincoln Cathedral, 1959; Canon Emeritus, 1965–70; Prebendary of Lichfield Cathedral, 1968–70; Select Preacher, Univ. of Cambridge, 1960; Hon. Canon of Lichfield Cathedral, 1970–. Dir, Mercia Television, 1980–81. Mem. of Council, Haileybury and Imperial Service Coll., 1949–87; Pres., Haileybury Soc., 1976–77. Fellow, Woodard Schools, 1970–83; Mem. Council: Denstone Sch., 1970–72; Shrewsbury Sch., 1971–80; Ellesmere Coll., 1971–80. Archbishops' Advr to HMC, 1975–80. President: Shropshire Horticultural Soc., 1979; Shropshire and W Midlands Agric. Soc., 1980; Buccaneers CC, 1965–89. Recreations: playing golf, watching TV, reading. Address: 41 Beatrice Avenue, Felixstowe, Suffolk IP11 9HB. T: Felixstowe (0394) 283574. Clubs: MCC, Royal Air Force; Hawks (Cambridge).

COCKS, Freda Mary, OBE 1972; JP; Deputy Leader, Birmingham City Council, 1982–86; b 30 July 1915; d of Frank and Mary Wood; m 1942, Donald Francis Melvin, s of Melvin J. Cocks; one d (and one d decd). Educ: St Peter's Sch., Harborne; Queen's Coll., Birmingham. Birmingham Council, 1957–78: Alderman, 1965–74; Lord Mayor of Birmingham, 1977–78; Dep. Chm., Housing Cttee, 1968–70, Chm. 1970–72. Founder Sec., Birmingham Sanatoria League of Friends, 1950–68; Founder, Birm. Hosps Broadcasting Assoc., 1952–78; Member: Little Bromwich Hosp. Management Cttee, 1953–68; West Birmingham Health Authority, 1981–; Vice-Pres. and Mem., Nat. Careers Assoc., 1985–. Conservative Women's Central Council: Chm., 1968–71; Chm., Gen. Purposes Cttee, 1978; service on housing, finance, policies, and land cttees; President: Edgbaston Conservative Assoc., 1980–; Mission to Seamen, Birmingham, 1981–. JP Birmingham, 1968. Hon. Freeman: City of Birmingham, 1986; Du-Panne, Belgium, 1978. Recreations: hospitals and housing. Address: 332–4 Hagley Road, Edgbaston, Birmingham B17 8BH. T: 021–420 1140.

COCKS, Dr Leonard Robert Morrison, (Dr Robin Cocks), TD 1979; Keeper of Palaeontology, Natural History Museum (formerly British Museum (Natural History)), since 1986; b 17 June 1938; s of late Ralph Morrison Cocks and of Lucille Mary Cocks (née Blackler); m 1963, Elaine Margaret Sturdy; one s two d. Educ: Felsted School; Hertford College, Oxford (BA, MA, DPhil, DSc). FGS. Commissioned Royal Artillery 1958; active service Malaya, 1958–59; DSIR Research Student, Oxford Univ., 1962–65; British Museum (Nat. Hist.), 1965–; Dep. Keeper of Palaeontology, 1980–86. Geologist, Royal Engineers, 1970–83; Member: Council, Palaeontological Assoc., 1969–82, 1986–88 (Editor, 1971–82, Pres., 1986–88); Council, Geological Soc., 1982–89 (Sec., 1985–89); NERC Geological Res. Grants Cttee, 1978–81, 1984. Comr, Internat. Commn on Zoological Nomenclature, 1982–. Vis. Fellow, Southampton Univ., 1988–91. Publications: The Evolving Earth, 1979; papers in sci. jls on Ordovician-Silurian biostratigraphy and brachiopods, esp. from Britain, Canada, Norway, Sweden, China. Recreations: country pursuits. Address: Department of Palaeontology, Natural History Museum, Cromwell Road, SW7 5BD. T: 071–938 8845.

COCKS, Robin; see Cocks, L. R. M.

COCKSHAW, Alan, FEng 1986; FICE; FIHT; Chairman, Amec plc, since 1988 (Group Chief Executive, 1984–88); b 14 July 1937; s of John and Maud Cockshaw; m 1960, Brenda Payne; one s three d. Educ: Farnworth Grammar Sch.; Leeds Univ. (BSc). FIHT 1968; FICE 1985. Chief Executive: Fairclough Civil Engrg, 1978–85; Fairclough Parkinson–Mining, 1982–85; Fairclough Engrg, 1983–84. Recreations: Rugby (both codes), cricket, walking, gardening. Address: Red Hill House, 4 Waterbridge, The Green, Worsley, Manchester M28 4NL. T: 061–794 5972.

COCKSHUT, Gillian Elise, (Mrs A. O. J. Cockshut); see Avery, G. E.

CODD, Ronald Geoffrey, CEng; Managing Partner, Inter-Change Associates; b 20 Aug. 1932; s of Thomas Reuben Codd and Betty Leyster Codd (née Sturt); m 1960, Christine Ellen Léone Robertson; one s two d. Educ: Cathedral Sch., Llandaff; The College, Llandovery. FBCS; FBIM; CEng 1990. Dip. in Company Direction, 1989. Served RAF, Transport Comd, 1952–57. Rolls Royce, Aero-Engine Div., 1957–58; International Computers, 1958–61; Marconi Co., 1961–70; J. Bibby & Sons, Liverpool, 1970–74; Weir Gp, Glasgow, 1974–80; Brooke Bond Gp, 1981–86; ECGD: Dir responsible for management of wide ranging change, introduction of new inf. management techniques and services and development of new risk management techniques in relation to country underwriting policy, 1986–90; Under Sec., Information and Risks Management, 1986–90. MInstD. Freeman, City of London, 1990; Liveryman, Co. of Inf. Technologists, 1990. Publications: contributor to business magazines. Recreations: competitive and leisure sailing, theatre, practical pastimes. Address: Chesterton House, Three Gates Lane, Haslemere, Surrey GU27 2LD. Club: Royal Northern and Clyde Yacht.

CODRINGTON, John Ernest Fleetwood, CMG 1968; b 1919; s of late Stewart Codrington; m 1951, Margaret, d of late Sir Herbert Hall Hall, KCMG; three d. Educ: Haileybury; Trinity Coll., Cambridge. Served RNVR, 1940–42: HMS Enchantress, HMS Vanity; Royal Marines, 1942–46: 42 (RM) Commando; Colonial Administrative Service, 1946: Gold Coast (later Ghana), 1947–58; Nyasaland, 1958–64; Financial Sec., Bahamas, 1964–70; Bahamas Comr in London, 1970–73, acting High Comr, 1973–74; Financial Sec., Bermuda, 1974–77. Recreation: sailing. Address: Chequers Close, Lymington, Hants SO41 8AH. Clubs: Army and Navy; Royal Lymington Yacht.

CODRINGTON, Sir Simon (Francis Bethell), 3rd Bt cr 1876; b 14 Aug. 1923; s of Sir Christopher William Gerald Henry Codrington, 2nd Bt, and Joan Mary Hague-Cook (d 1961); S father, 1979; m 1st, 1947, Joanne (marr. diss. 1959), d of J. W. Molineaux and widow of William Humphrey Austin Thompson; 2nd, 1959, Pamela Joy Halliday Wise (marr. diss. 1979); three s; 3rd, 1980, Sarah Gwynne Gaze (née Pennell) (marr. diss.). Educ: Eton. Late Coldstream Guards. Heir: s Christopher George Wayne Codrington, b 20 Feb. 1960. Address: Dodington, Chipping Sodbury, Bristol. T: Chipping Sodbury (0454) 312354.

CODRINGTON, Sir William (Alexander), 8th Bt *cr* 1721; FNI; in command with Worldwide Shipping; Port Captain, Hong Kong, for Worldwide Shipping Agency, since 1979; *b* 5 July 1934; *e s* of Sir William Richard Codrington, 7th Bt, and Joan Kathleen Birellu, *e d* of Percy E. Nicholas, London, NW; *S* father, 1961. *Educ:* St Andrew Coll., S Africa; S African Naval Coll., General Botha. FNI 1976. Joined Merchant Navy, 1952; joined Union Castle Mail Steamship Co., 1960; Master Mariner's Certificate of Competency, 1961. Joined Worldwide Shipping 1976. Mem., Hon. Co. of Master Mariners. Pres., Tooting and Balham Sea Cadet Unit. *Recreations:* model engineering, sailing. *Heir: b* Giles Peter Codrington, *b* 28 Oct. 1943. *Address:* Flat A, 1st Floor, Seaview Gardens, 31 Cloudview Road, Hong Kong; 99 St James Drive, Wandsworth Common, SW17 7RP. *Club:* Foreign Correspondents (Hong Kong).

CODRON, Michael Victor, CBE 1989; theatrical producer; *b* 8 June 1930; *s* of I. A. Codron and Lily (*née* Morgenstern). *Educ:* St Paul's Sch.; Worcester Coll., Oxford (BA). Director: Aldwych Theatre; Adelphi Theatre; Hampstead Theatre; Theatres Mutual Insurance Co.; Bd mem., Royal Nat. Theatre; Co-owner, Vaudeville Theatre. Productions include: Share My Lettuce, Breath of Spring, 1957; Dock Brief and What Shall We Tell Caroline?, The Birthday Party, Valmouth, 1958; Pieces of Eight, 1959; The Wrong Side of the Park, The Caretaker, 1960; Three, Stop It Whoever You Are, One Over the Eight, The Tenth Man, Big Soft Nellie, 1961; Two Stars for Comfort, Everything in the Garden, Rattle of a Simple Man, 1962; Next Time I'll sing to You, Private Lives (revival), The Lovers and the Dwarfs, Cockade, 1963; Poor Bitos, The Formation Dancers, Entertaining Mr Sloane, 1964; Loot, The Killing of Sister George, Ride a Cock Horse, 1965; Little Malcolm and his Struggle against the Eunuchs, The Anniversary, There's a Girl in my Soup, Big Bad Mouse, 1966; The Judge, The Flip Side, Wise Child, The Boy Friend (revival), 1967; Not Now Darling, The Real Inspector Hound, 1968; The Contractor, Slag, The Two of Us, The Philanthropist, 1970; The Foursome, Butley, A Voyage Round my Father, The Changing Room, 1971; Veterans, Time and Time Again, Crown Matrimonial, My Fat Friend, 1972; Collaborators, Savages, Habeas Corpus, Absurd Person Singular, 1973; Knuckle, Flowers, Golden Pathway Annual, The Norman Conquests, John Paul George Ringo . . . and Bert, 1974; A Family and A Fortune, Alphabetical Order, A Far Better Husband, Ashes, Absent Friends, Otherwise Engaged, Stripwell, 1975; Funny Peculiar, Treats, Donkey's Years, Confusions, Teeth 'n' Smiles, Yahoo, 1976; Dusa, Stas, Fish & Vi, Just Between Ourselves, Oh, Mr Porter, Breezeblock Park, The Bells of Hell, The Old Country, 1977; The Rear Column, Ten Times Table, The Unvarnished Truth, The Homecoming (revival), Alice's Boys, Night and Day, 1978; Joking Apart, Tishoo, Stage Struck, 1979; Dr Faustus, Make and Break, The Dresser, Taking Steps, Enjoy, 1980; Hinge and Bracket at the Globe, Rowan Atkinson in Revue, House Guest, Quartermaine's Terms, 1981; Season's Greetings, Noises Off, Funny Turns, The Real Thing, 1982; The Hard Shoulder, 1983; Benefactors, 1984; Why Me?, Jumpers, Who Plays Wins, Look, No Hans!, 1985; Made in Bangkok, Woman in Mind, 1986; Three Sisters, A View from the Bridge, 1987; Hapgood, Uncle Vanya, Re: Joyce, The Sneeze, Henceforward, 1988; The Cherry Orchard, 1989; Man of the Moment, Look Look, Hidden Laughter, Private Lives, 1990; *film:* Clockwise, 1986. *Recreation:* collecting Caroline memorabilia. *Address:* Aldwych Theatre Offices, Aldwych, WC2B 4DF. *Club:* Garrick.

COE, Denis Walter; Joint Founder and Hon. Executive Chairman, British Youth Opera, since 1987; *b* 5 June 1929; *s* of James and Lily Coe, Whitley Bay, Northumberland; *m* 1953, Margaret Rae (marr. diss. 1979), *d* of William and Ida Chambers; three *s* one *d*; *m* 1979, Diana Rosemary, *d* of Maxwell and Flora Barr. *Educ:* Bede Trng Coll., Durham; London Sch. of Economics. Teacher's Certificate, 1952; BSc (Econ.) 1960; MSc (Econ.) 1966. National Service in RAF, 1947–50; Junior and Secondary Schoolmaster, 1952–59; Dep. Headmaster, Secondary Sch., 1959–61; Lectr in Govt, Manchester Coll. of Commerce, 1961–66. Contested (Lab) Macclesfield, 1964; MP (Lab) Middleton, Prestwich and Whitefield, 1966–70; Parly deleg. to Council of Europe and WEU, 1968–70. Dean of Students, NE London Polytechnic, 1970–74; Asst Dir, Middx Polytechnic, 1974–82; Dir of Cleveland Arts, 1986–89; Founder/Dir., Cleveland Music Fest., 1985–89. Member: Governing Council, Nat. Youth Theatre, 1968–; Planning Cttee, Arts Council, 1987–90. Vice-Pres., SKILL (formerly Nat. Bureau for Handicapped Students), 1983– (Chm., 1975–83). *Recreations:* music, drama, walking.

COE, Sebastian Newbold, OBE 1990 (MBE 1982); Member: Health Education Authority, since 1987; Olympic Committee, Medical Commission, since 1987; *b* 29 Sept. 1956; *s* of Peter and Angela Coe; *m* 1990, Nicola McIrvine. *Educ:* Loughborough University (BSc Hons Economics and Social History). Won gold medal for running 1500m and silver medal for 800m at Moscow Olympics, 1980; gold medal for 1500m and silver medal for 800m at Los Angeles Olympics, 1984; European Champion for 800m, Stuttgart, 1986; set world records at 800m, 1000m and mile, 1981. Research Assistant, Loughborough Univ., 1981–84. Sports Council: Mem., 1983–89; Vice-Chm., 1986–89, Chm., Olympic Review Gp, 1984–85. Associate Mem., Académie des Sports, France; Mem., Athletes Commn, Internat. Olympic Cttee, Lausanne. Chm., Diadora (UK), 1987–. Prospective Parly Candidate (C) Falmouth-Camborne, 1989–. Hon. DTech Loughborough, 1985; Hon. DSc Hull, 1988. Principe de Asturias award (Spain), 1987. *Publications:* (with David Miller) Running Free, 1981; (with Peter Coe) Running for Fitness, 1983; The Olympians, 1984. *Recreations:* listening to recorded or preferably live jazz, theatre, reading, avoiding all strenuous activity away from the track. *Clubs:* East India, Sportsman's.

COEN, Massimo (Aldo), Cavaliere al Merito del Lavoro 1982; Grande Ufficiale nell'Ordine al Merito della Repubblica Italiana 1979; Chairman and Managing Director: Granosa Trading Co. Ltd, since 1946; Florence (Arts & Crafts) Ltd, since 1946; Thames Rugs & Tweed Fabrics Ltd, since 1959; President: Italian Chamber of Commerce for Great Britain, since 1978; Etrufin Reserco Ltd, since 1985; *b* Bologna, 29 July 1918; *s* of Cavaliere Ragioniere Terzo Coen and Delia Coen Guetta; *m* 1946, Thelma Doreen Kelley; one *s* three *d*. *Educ:* Liceo Marco Foscarini, Venice (dipl. 1937); Padua University; London School of Economics. Came to London from Venice because of racial laws, 1939; interned in Isle of Man, June-Dec. 1940; Netherland Shipping & Trading Cttee Ltd, Jan.-April 1941; Italian Section, BBC External Services, 1941–46 (Shift Leader and Senior Announcer Translator); Granosa Trading Co. Ltd and subsidiaries (dealing in textiles), 1946–. Councillor, Italian Chamber of Commerce for GB, 1951–72, Vice-Pres., 1972–78; Chm., Club di Londra, 1985–. Many radio plays, talks and commentaries during the war years. Acted in Snowbound, 1947, Hotel Sahara, 1951. Cavaliere 1956, Ufficiale 1968, Commendatore 1972, nell'Ordine al Merito della Repubblica Italiana. *Recreations:* shooting, fishing, golf; formerly competition skiing and fencing. *Address:* 14 Acacia Road, St John's Wood, NW8 6AN. *T:* 071–722 2459; (office) 071–323 5551, *Fax:* 071–323 5653.

COETZEE, Prof. John M.; writer; Professor of General Literature, University of Cape Town, since 1983; *b* 9 Feb. 1940; one *d* (one *s* decd). Educ: Univ. of Cape Town (MA); Univ. of Texas (PhD). FRSL 1988. Assistant Professor of English, State University of New York at Buffalo, 1968–71; Lectr in English, Univ. of Cape Town, 1972–82; Butler Prof. of English, State Univ. of New York at Buffalo, 1984; Hinkley Prof. of English, Johns Hopkins Univ., 1986, 1989. Hon. Fellow, MLA, 1989. Hon. DLitt: Strathclyde, 1985; State Univ. of New York, 1989. *Publications:* Dusklands, 1974; In the Heart of the Country, 1977 (CNA Literary Award, 1977; filmed as Dust, 1986); Waiting for the Barbarians, 1980 (CNA Literary Award, 1980; James Tait Black Prize, 1980; Geoffrey Faber Award, 1980); Life and Times of Michael K, 1983 (CNA Literary Award, 1983; Booker-McConnell Prize, 1983; Prix Femina Etranger, 1985); Foe, 1986 (Jerusalem Prize, 1987); (ed with André Brink) A Land Apart, 1986; White Writing, 1988; Age of Iron, 1990 (Sunday Express Award, 1990); essays in Comp. Lit., Jl of Mod. Lit., Linguistics, Mod. Lang. Notes, Pubns of MLA, etc. *Address:* PO Box 92, Rondebosch, Cape Province, 7700, South Africa.

COFFER, David Edwin, CBE 1973 (OBE 1963); General Secretary, The Royal British Legion, 1959–78; *b* 18 Sept. 1913; *s* of David Gilbertson Coffer and Florence Ellen Gard; *m* 1947, Edith Mary Moulton; three *d*. *Educ:* Colfe Grammar Sch. Member: Supplementary Benefits Appeal Tribunals, 1978–85; Central Advisory Cttee on War Pensions, 1976–87; Bromley, Croydon and Sutton War Pensions Cttee, 1953–87, Chm., 1976–87; Patron, SE County, Royal British Legion, 1978–. *Address:* 47 Malvern Road, Orpington, Kent BR6 9HA. *T:* Orpington (0689) 829007.

COFFEY, Rev. David Roy; General Secretary, Baptist Union of Great Britain, since 1991; *b* 13 Nov. 1941; *s* of Arthur Coffey and Elsie Maud Willis; *m* 1966, Janet Anne Dunbar; one *s* one *d*. *Educ:* Spurgeon's Coll. (BA London). Ordained, 1967; Minister: Whetstone Baptist Church, Leicester, 1967–72; North Cheam Baptist Ch., London, 1972–80; Sen. Minister, Upton Vale Baptist Ch., Torquay, 1980–88; Sec. for Evangelism, BUGB, 1988–91. Pres., BUGB, 1986–87. *Publication:* Build that Bridge – a Study in Conflict and Reconciliation, 1986. *Recreations:* music, walking. *Address:* Baptist House, PO Box 44, 129 Broadway, Didcot, Oxon OX11 8RT. *T:* Didcot (0235) 512077.

COFFIN, Cyril Edwin, CBE 1984; Director General, Food Manufacturers' Federation, 1977–84; *b* 29 June 1919; *m* 1947, Joyce Mary Tobitt; one *s* one *d* (and one *d* decd). *Educ:* King's Coll. Sch., Wimbledon; King's Coll., Cambridge. War service, 1939–45, Captain RIASC; jssc 1950. Civil servant, 1946–77; Alternate UK Governor, Internat. Atomic Energy Agency, 1964; Under-Secretary: Min. of Technology, 1966, later DTI; Dept of Prices and Consumer Protection, 1974–77. FRSA 1979. *Publications:* Working with Whitehall, 1987; articles in various jls. *Recreations:* music, learning languages. *Address:* 54 Cambridge Avenue, New Malden, Surrey KT3 4LE. *T:* 081–942 0763. *Clubs:* Athenæum; Union (Cambridge).

COGGAN, Baron *cr* 1980 (Life Peer), of Canterbury and of Sissinghurst in the County of Kent; **Rt. Rev. and Rt. Hon. (Frederick) Donald Coggan;** PC 1961; Royal Victorian Chain, 1980; MA; DD; *b* 9 Oct. 1909; *s* of late Cornish Arthur Coggan and late Fannie Sarah Coggan; *m* 1935, Jean Braithwaite Strain; two *d*. *Educ:* Merchant Taylors' School; St John's College, Cambridge; Wycliffe Hall, Oxford. Late Schol. of St John's Coll., Cambridge, 1st cl. Or. Lang. Trip. pt i, 1930; BA (1st cl. Or. Lang. Trip. pt ii) and Jeremie Sep. Prize, 1931, Naden Div. Student, 1931; Tyrwhitt Hebrew Schol. and Mason Prize, 1932; MA 1935. Asst Lectr in Semitic Languages and Literature, University of Manchester, 1931–34; Curate of St Mary Islington, 1934–37; Professor of New Testament, Wycliffe College, Toronto, 1937–44; Principal of the London College of Divinity, 1944–56; Bishop of Bradford, 1956–61; Archbishop of York, 1961–74; Archbishop of Canterbury, 1974–80. Chairman of the Liturgical Commission, 1960–64. President, Society for Old Testament Studies, 1967–68; first Life President, Church Army, 1981. Pro-Chancellor, York Univ., 1962–74, Hull Univ., 1968–74. Prelate, Order of St John of Jerusalem, 1967–90. Wycliffe Coll., Toronto: BD 1941, DD (*hc*) 1944; DD (Lambeth) 1957; Hon. DD: Cambridge, 1962; Leeds, 1958; Aberdeen, 1963; Tokyo, 1963; Saskatoon, 1963; Huron, 1963; Hull, 1963; Manchester, 1972; Moravian Theol Seminary, 1976; Virginia Theol Seminary, 1979. Hon. LLD Liverpool, 1972; HHD Westminster Choir Coll., Princeton, 1966; Hon. DLitt Lancaster, 1967; STD (*hc*) Gen. Theol Seminary, NY, 1967; Hon. DCL Kent, 1975; DUniv York, 1975; FKC, 1975. Hon. Freeman, City of Canterbury, 1976. *Publications:* A People's Heritage, 1944; The Ministry of the Word, 1945; The Glory of God, 1950; Stewards of Grace, 1958; Five Makers of the New Testament, 1962; Christian Priorities, 1963; The Prayers of the New Testament, 1967; Sinews of Faith, 1969; Word and World, 1971; Convictions, 1975; On Preaching, 1978; The Heart of the Christian Faith, 1978; The Name above All Names, 1981; Sure Foundation, 1981; Mission to the World, 1982; Paul—Portrait of a Revolutionary, 1984; The Sacrament of the Word, 1987; Cuthbert Bardsley: bishop, evangelist, pastor, 1989; God of Hope, 1991; contributions to Theology, etc. *Recreations:* gardening, motoring, music. *Address:* 28 Lions Hall, St Swithun Street, Winchester SO23 9HW. *T:* Winchester (0962) 864289. *Club:* Athenæum.

COGHILL, Sir Egerton James Nevill Tobias, (Sir Toby Coghill), 8th Bt *cr* 1778; investment counsellor, Valn-Trac Research; *b* 26 March 1930; *s* of Sir Joscelyn Ambrose Cramer Coghill, 7th Bt and Elizabeth Gwendoline (*d* 1980), *d* of John B. Atkins; *S* father, 1983; *m* 1958, Gabriel Nancy, *d* of Major Dudley Claud Douglas Ryder; one *s* one *d*. *Educ:* Gordonstoun; Pembroke College, Cambridge. E-SU Walter Hines Page Scholar to USA. Architectural Asst with Sir Frederick Gibberd & Ptnrs, 1952–55; Industrial Developer, 1955–58; Admin. Manager, McKinsey and Co. Inc., 1959–61; Supply teacher, LCC, 1961–62; Housemaster, Aiglon Coll., Switzerland (Chm. Govs, 1991–), 1962–64; Headmaster, Aberlour House, 1964–89. Director: Aiglon Coll., Switzerland (Chm. Govs, 1991–); Rannoch Sch., Perthshire; Rosebrae Sch., Moray. *Recreation:* country sports. *Heir: s* Patrick Kendal Farley Coghill, *b* 3 Nov. 1960. *Address:* Sourden, Rothes, Aberlour, Banffshire AB38 7AE. *Club:* Royal Ocean Racing.

COGMAN, Very Rev. Frederick Walter; Dean of Guernsey, 1967–78; Rector of St Peter Port, Guernsey, 1976–78; *b* 4 March 1913; *s* of William Frederick Cogman and Mabel Cozens; *m* 1940, Rose Hélène Mauger; one *s* one *d*. *Educ:* Rutlish Sch., Merton; King's Coll., London. Asst Priest, Upton-cum-Chalvey, Slough, 1938–42; Chaplain and Housemaster, St George's Sch., Harpenden, 1942–48; Rector of St Martin, Guernsey, 1948–76. *Recreations:* music, painting. *Address:* Oriana Lodge, Rue des Fontenelles, Forest, Guernsey, CI.

COHAN, Robert Paul, CBE 1989; Founder Artistic Director, Contemporary Dance Trust; *b* 27 March 1925; *s* of Walter and Billie Cohan; British citizen, 1989. *Educ:* Martha Graham Sch., NYC. Joined Martha Graham Co., 1946; Partner, 1950; Co-Dir, Martha Graham Co., 1966; Artistic Dir, Contemporary Dance Trust Ltd, 1967; Artistic Dir and Principal Choreographer, 1969–87, Dir, 1987–89, London Contemporary Dance Theatre; Artistic Advr, Batsheva Co., Israel, 1980; Director: York Univ., Toronto Choreographic Summer Sch., 1977; Gulbenkian Choreographic Summer Sch., Univ. of Surrey, 1978, 1979, 1982; Banff Sch. of Fine Arts Choreographic Seminar, Canada, 1980; New Zealand Choreographic Seminar, 1982; Choreographic Seminar, Simon Frazer Univ., Vancouver, 1985; Internat. Dance Course for Professional Choreographers and Composers, Surrey Univ., 1985, 1989. With London Contemporary Dance Theatre has toured Britain, E and W Europe, S America, N Africa and USA; major works created: Cell, 1969 (recorded for

BBC TV, 1982); Stages, 1971; Waterless Method of Swimming Instruction, 1974 (recorded for BBC TV); Class, 1975; Stabat Mater, 1975 (recorded for BBC TV); Masque of Separation, 1975; Khamsin, 1976; Nympheas, 1976 (recorded for BBC TV, 1983); Forest, 1977 (recorded by BBC TV); Eos, 1978; Songs, Lamentations and Praises, 1979; Dances of Love and Death, 1981; Agora, 1984; A Mass for Man, 1985 (recorded for BBC TV); Ceremony, 1986; Interrogations, 1986; Video Life, 1986; Phantasmagoria, 1987. Hon. Fellow, York Univ., Toronto. Evening Standard Award for most outstanding achievement in ballet, 1975; Soc. of West End Theatres Award for most outstanding achievement in ballet, 1978. *Publication:* The Dance Workshop, 1986. *Recreation:* dancing. *Address:* The Place, 17 Dukes Road, WC1. *T:* 071–387 0161.

COHEN; *see* Waley-Cohen.

COHEN, His Honour Arthur; *see* Cohen, His Honour N. A. J.

COHEN, Prof. Bernard Woolf; Slade Professor, and Chair of Fine Art, University of London, since 1988; *b* 28 July 1933; *s* of Victor and Leah Cohen; *m* 1959, Jean Cohen; one *s* one *d. Educ:* Slade School of Fine Art, University Coll. London (Dip. Fine Art). Head of Painting, Wimbledon Sch. of Art, 1980–87. Vis. Prof., Univ. of New Mexico, USA, 1969–70. First one man exhibn, Gimpel Fils Gall., 1958, again in 1960; other exhibitions: Molton Gall., 1962; Kazmin Gall., Bond Street, 1963, 1964, 1967; Waddington Gall., 1974, 1977, 1979, 1990; First New York exhibn, Betty Parsons Gall., 1967; major retrospective, Hayward Gall., 1972; print retrospective, Tate Gall., 1976; represented GB at Venice Biennale, 1966. Work in collections of Tate Gall., Mus. of Modern Art, New York; Fogg Mus., Mass; Minneapolis Walker Art Centre; Carnegie Inst., Pittsburgh, and others. *Recreations:* painting, travel, food, wine, music. *Address:* Slade School of Fine Art, University College London, Gower Street, WC1E 6BT. *T:* 071–387 7050.

COHEN, Betty; *see* Jackson, B.

COHEN, Sir Edward, Kt 1970; company director; Solicitor; Consultant, Corrs, solicitors, Melbourne, Australia; *b* 9 Nov. 1912; *s* of Brig. Hon. H. E. Cohen; *m* 1939, Meryl D., *d* of D. G. Fink; one *s. Educ:* Scotch Coll., Melbourne (Exhibnr in Greek and Roman History); Ormond Coll., Univ. of Melbourne (LLB; Aust. Blue Athletics, Hockey). Served, 1940–45: AIF, 2/12 Fd Regt, 9th Div. Artillery, Captain 1942. Partner, Pavey, Wilson, Cohen & Carter, 1945–76; Director: Carlton and United Breweries, 1947–84 (Chm., 1967–84); Swan Brewery, 1947–57; Associated Pulp & Paper Mills Ltd, 1951–83 (Dep. Chm. 1981–83); Electrolytic Zinc Co., A'asia, 1951–84 (Chm., 1960–84); Glazebrooks Paints and Chemicals Ltd, 1951–61; Standard Mutual Bldg Soc., 1951–64; E. Z. Industries, 1956–84 (Chm., 1960–84, Pres., 1984–); Pelaco Ltd, 1959–68; Commercial Union Assurance, 1960–82 (Chm., 1964–82); Union Assce Soc. of Aust., 1960–75 (Local Advisor, 1951–60); Michaelis Bayley Ltd, 1964–80; Qld Brewery (later CUB Qld), 1968–84; Herald and Weekly Times Ltd, 1974–77 (Vice-Chm., 1976–77); Chairman: Derwent Metals, 1957–84; CUB Fibre Containers, 1963–84; Emu Bay Railway Co., 1967–84; Manufrs Bottle Co., Vic, 1967–84; Northern Aust. Breweries (CUB (N Qld)), 1967–84; Nat. Commercial Union, 1982–84. Past Member: Faculty of Law of Melbourne Univ.; Internat. Hse Council, Melbourne Univ.; Council of Legal Education and Bd of Examiners. Mem. Council Law Inst. of Victoria, 1959–68, Pres. 1965–66. Chairman: Pensions Cttee, Melbourne Legacy, 1961–84 (Mem., 1955–84); Royal Women's Hosp. 1968 Million Dollar Bldg Appeal; Eileen Patricia Goulding Meml Fund Appeal, 1983; Life Governor: Austin, Prince Henry's, Royal Children's, Royal Melbourne, Royal Women's Hosps; Corps of Commissionaires; Adult Deaf and Dumb Soc. of Victoria. Hon. Solicitor, Queens Fund, 1951–. *Address:* 722 Orrong Road, Toorak, Victoria 3142, Australia; (office) 600 Bourke Street, Melbourne, Victoria 3000, Australia. *Clubs:* Naval and Military, Victoria Racing, Royal Automobile (all in Melbourne).

COHEN, George Cormack; Sheriff-Substitute of the Lothians and Peebles at Edinburgh, 1955–66; *b* 16 Dec. 1909; *s* of J. Cohen and Mary J. Cormack, Melfort House, Bearsden, Dunbartonshire; *m* 1939, Elizabeth, *d* of James H. Wallace, Malvern; one *s* one *d. Educ:* Kelvinside Academy, Glasgow; Glasgow Univ. MA 1930, LLB 1934. Admitted to Scottish Bar, 1935; Sheriff-Substitute of Caithness at Wick, 1944–51; of Ayr and Bute at Kilmarnock, 1951–55. *Recreations:* travel, gastronomy, philately, gardening. *Address:* 37B Lauder Road, Edinburgh EH9 1UE. *T:* 031–668 1689.

COHEN, Prof. Gerald Allan, FBA 1985; Chichele Professor of Social and Political Theory and Fellow of All Souls, Oxford, since Jan. 1985; *b* 14 April 1941; *s* of Morrie Cohen and Bella Lipkin; *m* 1965, Margaret Florence Pearce; one *s* two *d. Educ:* Morris Winchevsky Jewish School, Montreal; Strathcona Academy, Montreal; Outremont High School, Montreal; McGill University (BA 1961); New College, Oxford (BPhil 1963). Lectr in Philosophy, University College London, 1963, Reader, 1978–84. Vis. Asst Prof. of Political Science, McGill Univ., 1965; Vis. Associate Prof. of Philosophy, Princeton Univ., 1975. *Publications:* Karl Marx's Theory of History: a defence, 1978; History, Labour and Freedom: themes from Marx, 1988; articles in anthologies, philosophical and social-scientific jls. *Recreations:* Guardian crosswords, the visual arts. *Address:* All Souls College, Oxford OX1 4AL. *T:* Oxford (0865) 279339.

COHEN, Harry; MP (Lab) Leyton, since 1983; accountant; *b* 10 Dec. 1949. Mem., Waltham Forest Borough Council, 1972–83 (formerly Chm., Planning Cttee and Sec., Labour Group). Member: CIPFA; NALGO. *Address:* House of Commons, SW1A 0AA.

COHEN, Ivor Harold, CBE 1985; TD 1968; Chairman, Remploy Ltd, since 1987; *b* 28 April 1931; *s* of Jack Cohen and Anne (*née* Victor); *m* 1963, Betty Edith, *yr d* of Reginald George and Mabel Appleby; one *d. Educ:* Central Foundation Sch., EC2; University Coll. London (BA (Hons) Mod. Hist.; Fellow, 1987). Nat. Service, Royal Signals, 1952–54 (2nd Lieut); TA, Royal Signals, 1954–69 (Major 1964). Engrg industry, 1954–57; range of managerial posts, Mullard Ltd (subsid. of Philips (UK)), 1957–77; Dir, Philips Lighting, 1977–79; Man. Dir, Mullard Ltd, 1979–87; Dir, Philips Electronics (UK) Ltd, 1984–87. Non-Executive Director: AB Electronic Products Gp plc, 1987–; Océ (UK) Ltd, 1988–; PA Holdings Ltd, 1989–; Redifon Holdings Ltd, 1989–; Redifon Ltd, 1989–; Cons., Comet Gp plc, 1987–90; Advr, Alan Patricof Associates, 1987–. Member: IT Adv. Panel, 1981–86; Teletext and Viewdata Steering Gp, DTI, 1981–86; Electronic Components EDC, NEDO, 1980–88; Electronics Ind. EDC, NEDO, 1982–86; Steering Cttee, Telecom. Infrastructure, DTI, 1987–88; Computing Software and Communications Requirements Bd, DTI, 1984–88; Steering Bd, Radiocommunications Agency, DTI, 1990–; Electronics Ind. Sector Gp, NEDO, 1988– (Chm., 1990–); Chm., Electronic Applications Sector Gp, NEDO, 1988–90; Member Council: Electronic Components Ind. Fedn, 1980–87; European Electronic Components Assoc., 1985–87; Dir, Radio Industries Council, 1980–87. Mem., Schs Examinations and Assessment Council, 1988–90; British Schools Technology: Mem. Council of Management, 1984–87, Trustee Dir, 1987–89; Mem., Management Adv. Gp IT Res. Inst., Brighton Poly., 1987–. CompIEE 1988; Hon. Mem. CGLI, 1989; FInstD 1988; FRSA 1984. Freeman, City of London, 1982; Liveryman, Sci. Instrument Makers' Co., 1982. Mem., Editl Bd, Nat. Electronics Review, 1987–90. *Publications:* articles on electronics policy and marketing and use of inf. technology in the technical press. *Recreations:* opera, reading, occasional sculpting, walking in towns. *Address:* 24 Selborne Road, Croydon, Surrey CR0 5JQ. *Clubs:* Army and Navy, East India.

COHEN, Laurence Jonathan, FBA 1973; Fellow and Praelector in Philosophy, 1957–90, Senior Tutor, 1985–90, Queen's College, Oxford, now Emeritus Fellow; British Academy Reader in Humanities, Oxford University, 1982–84; *b* 7 May 1923; *s* of Israel and Theresa Cohen; *m* 1953, Gillian Mary Slee; three *s* one *d. Educ:* St Paul's Sch., London; Balliol Coll., Oxford (MA 1947, DLitt 1982). Served War: Naval Intell. in UK and SEAC, 1942–45, and Lieut (Sp.) RNVR. Asst in Logic and Metaphysics, Edinburgh Univ., 1947; Lectr in Philosophy, St Andrews Univ. at Dundee, 1950; Commonwealth Fund Fellow in Logic at Princeton and Harvard Univs, 1952–53. Vis. Lectr, Hebrew Univ. of Jerusalem, 1952; Visiting Professor: Columbia Univ., 1967; Yale Univ., 1972; Northwestern Univ. Law Sch., 1988; Hon. Prof., Northwest Univ., Xian, China, 1987. Vis. Fellow, ANU, 1980. British Acad. Philosophical Lectr, 1975; Fry Lectr, Bristol Univ., 1976; Austin Lectr, UK Assoc. for Legal and Social Philos., 1982. Sec., Internat. Union of History and Philosophy of Science (Div. of Logic Methodology and Philosophy of Science), 1975–83, Pres., 1987–91; Pres., British Soc. for Philosophy of Science, 1977–79; Chm., British Nat. Cttee for Logic, Methodology and Philosophy of Science, 1987–91; Mem., Comité Directeur, Fédn Internat. des Socs de Philosophie, 1983–. General Editor, Clarendon Library of Logic and Philosophy, 1973–. *Publications:* The Principles of World Citizenship, 1954; The Diversity of Meaning, 1962; The Implications of Induction, 1970; The Probable and the Provable, 1977; (ed jtly) Applications of Inductive Logic, 1980; (ed jtly) Logic, Methodology and Philosophy of Science, 1982; The Dialogue of Reason, 1986; An Introduction to the Philosophy of Induction and Probability, 1989. *Recreations:* gardening; work for Council for Protection of Rural England. *Address:* Queen's College, Oxford OX1 4AW.

COHEN, Hon. Leonard Harold Lionel; barrister-at-law; *b* 1 Jan. 1922; *s* of Rt Hon. Lord Cohen, PC (Life Peer), and Adelaide, Lady Cohen (*née* Spielmann); *m* 1949, Eleanor Lucy Quixano Henriques; two *s* one *d. Educ:* Eton Coll.; New Coll., Oxford (MA). War Service, Rifle Bde (wounded), Captain, 1941–45. Called to Bar, Lincoln's Inn, 1948, Bencher, 1989; practised at Chancery Bar, 1949–61. Chm., Secure Retirement PLC, 1987–; Dir, M. Samuel & Co. Ltd (subseq. Hill Samuel & Co. Ltd), 1961–76. Dir-Gen., Accepting Houses Cttee, 1976–82; Chairman: United Services Trustee, 1976–82; Council, Royal Free Hosp. Med. Sch., 1982–; Community Trust for Berkshire, 1988–; Pres., Jewish Colonization Assoc., 1976–. Master of the Skinners' Co., 1971–72. Hon. Col, 39th (City of London) Signal Regt (V), 1973–78. High Sheriff of Berks, 1987–88. *Recreations:* shooting, golf, reading, opera. *Address:* Dovecote House, Swallowfield Park, Reading RG7 1TG. *T:* Reading (0734) 884775. *Club:* White's.

COHEN, Dr Louis; Executive Secretary, Institute of Physics, 1966–90, retired; *b* 14 Oct. 1925; *s* of late Harry Cohen and Fanny Cohen (*née* Abrahams); *m* 1948, Eve G. Marsh; one *s* two *d. Educ:* Manchester Central High Sch.; Manchester Univ.; Imperial Coll., London. BSc, PhD, FInstP. Research Physicist, Simon-Carves Ltd, 1953–63; Research Manager, Pyrotenax Ltd, 1963–66. Hon. Sec., Council of Science and Technology Insts, 1969–87; Treasurer, European Physical Soc., 1968–73; Corresp. Mem., Manchester Literary and Philosophical Soc., 1963. FRSA. *Publications:* papers and articles on physics and related subjects. *Recreations:* cooking, books, music, the theatre. *Address:* Flat 1, 21 Hamilton Road, W5 2EE. *T:* 081–579 2227.

COHEN, Michael Antony; Chief Executive, The Guinness Trust, since 1987; *b* 18 April 1940; *s* of Gerald and Beatrice Cohen; *m* 1967, Jennifer Audrey Price; one *s* two *d. Educ:* Quarry Bank Grammar School, Liverpool; Univ. of Liverpool (BA Hons Econ.). FCA; MIH. Articled clerk, 1962–65; Accountant and Planning Manager, Bank of London & S America, 1965–72; posts in European and US banking, Lloyds Bank, 1972–78; Internat. Project Finance Manager, Lloyds Bank, 1978–82; Regional Dir, London and SE, Housing Corp., 1982–87. Mem. Council, London Borough of Barnet, 1972–78; Chairman: Barnet Arts Workshop, 1984–; St Mungo Community Housing Assoc.; Barnet Housing Aid Centre, 1990–. Dir, Phoenix Cinema Trust Ltd, 1989–. *Recreations:* walking, eating, France, theatre, finding time. *Address:* 6 Talbot Avenue, East Finchley, N2 0LS. *T:* 081–883 9433.

COHEN, Lt-Col Mordaunt, TD 1954; DL; Regional Chairman of Industrial Tribunals, 1976–89 (Chairman, 1974–76); *b* 6 Aug. 1916; *s* of Israel Ellis Cohen and Sophie Cohen; *m* 1953, Her Honour Judge Myrella Cohen, *qv*; one *s* one *d. Educ:* Bede Collegiate Sch. for Boys, Sunderland. Admitted solicitor, 1938. Served War, RA, 1940–46: seconded RWAFF; despatches, Burma campaign; served TA, 1947–55: CO 463(M) HAA Regt, RA(TA), 1954–55. Alderman, Sunderland Co. Bor. Council, 1967–74; Chm., Sunderland Educn Cttee, 1970–72; Chm., NE Council of Educn Cttees, 1971; Councillor, Tyne and Wear CC, 1973–74; Dep. Chm., Northern Traffic Comrs, 1973–74. Chm., Mental Health Review Tribunal, 1967–76. Chm. of Governors, Sunderland Polytechnic, 1969–72; Mem. Court, Univ. of Newcastle upon Tyne, 1968–72. Pres., Sunderland Law Soc., 1970; Hon. Life Pres., Sunderland Hebrew Congregation; Mem., Bd of Deputies of British Jews (Chm., Provincial Cttee; Dir, Central Enquiry Desk); former Mem., Chief Rabbinate Council; Mem., NEC, Ajex; Life Pres., Sunderland Br., Ajex; Trustee: Ajex Charitable Trust; Colwyn Bay Synagogue Trust. DL Tyne and Wear, 1986. *Recreations:* watching sport, playing bowls; communal service, promoting inter-faith understanding. *Address:* Flat 1, Peters Lodge, 2 Stonegrove, Edgware, Middlesex HA8 7TY.

COHEN, Myrella, QC 1970; **Her Honour Judge Myrella Cohen;** a Circuit Judge, since 1972; *b* 16 Dec. 1927; *d* of late Samuel and Sarah Cohen, Manchester; *m* 1953, Lt-Col Mordaunt Cohen, *qv*; one *s* one *d. Educ:* Manchester High Sch. for Girls; Colwyn Bay Grammar Sch.; Manchester Univ. (LLB 1948). Called to the Bar, Gray's Inn, 1950. Recorder of Hull, 1971. Mem., Parole Bd, 1983–86. *Address:* c/o The Crown Court, Wood Green, N22 5LF. *Club:* Soroptimist Club of Great Britain.

COHEN, Lt-Col Nathan Leslie, OBE 1990; TD 1949; JP; *b* 13 Jan. 1908; *s* of Reuben and Maud Cohen; unmarried. *Educ:* Stockton-on-Tees Grammar Sch.; Clifton Coll. In private practice as a Solicitor until 1939; called to the Bar, Lincoln's Inn, 1954. War Service, Aug. 1939–May 1945. Senior Legal Officer (Lt-Col), Military Govt, Carinthia, Austria, 1945–49; Pres. of Sessions Courts, Malaya, 1949–57; Justice of the Special Courts, Cyprus, 1958–59; Judge of HM Court of Sovereign Base Areas of Akrotiri and Dhekalia, Cyprus, 1960–61; Adjudicator under Immigration Appeals Act, 1970–71. Mem., Cleveland Co. Social Services Cttee 1978–80. Dist Hd, Forces Relief Soc., Stockton, 1975–; Vice-President: Northern Area, Royal British Legion; Cleveland British Red Cross Soc.; Patron, Durham and Cleveland Royal British Legion, 1985–; President: Stockton Physically Handicapped Club, 1990–; St John Ambulance Assoc., Stockton and Thornaby. SBStJ 1980. JP Stockton-on-Tees, 1967. Diamond Jubilee Medal (Johore), 1955; Colonial Police Medal, 1956; Royal Brit. Legion Gold Badge, 1979; British Red Cross Badge of Honour, 1981, Voluntary Medical Service Medal, 1982. *Recreations:* travelling, reading. *Address:* 35 Richmond Road, Stockton-on-Tees, Cleveland TS18 4DS. *T:* Stockton (0642) 674831. *Club:* Royal Over-Seas League.

COHEN, His Honour (Nathaniel) Arthur (Jim), JP; County Court Judge, Circuit No 38, 1955–56, Circuit No 43, 1956–60, Circuit No 56, 1960–70, retired; *b* 19 Jan. 1898; 2nd *s* of late Sir Benjamin Arthur Cohen, KC, and Lady Cohen; *m* 1st, 1927, Judith Luard (marr. diss.); two *s*; 2nd, 1936, Joyce Collingridge. *Educ:* Rugby; CCC, Oxford (BA). Served European War, 1916–19, Royal Navy. Called to Bar, Inner Temple, 1923. War of 1939–45: recalled to RN and placed on Emergency List with rank of Commander. Legal Adviser to UNRRA, 1946–49; Dep. Chm., Foreign Compensation Commn, 1950–55. JP Surrey, 1958. *Recreations:* golf, music. *Address:* Bay Tree Cottage, Crockham Hill, Edenbridge, Kent. *Club:* United Oxford & Cambridge University.

COHEN, Prof. Philip, PhD; FRS 1984; FRSE 1984; Royal Society Research Professor, University of Dundee, since 1984; *b* 22 July 1945; *s* of Jacob Davis Cohen and Fanny (*née* Bragman); *m* 1969, Patricia Townsend Wade; one *s* one *d. Educ:* Hendon County Grammar Sch.; University Coll. London (BSc 1st Cl. Hons (Biochemistry Special), 1966; PhD Biochem., 1969). SRC/NATO Postdoctoral Res. Fellow, Dept of Biochem., Univ. of Washington, Seattle, USA, 1969–71; Univ. of Dundee: Lectr in Biochem., 1971–78; Reader in Biochem., 1978–81; Prof. of Enzymology, 1981–84. Mem., Eur. Molecular Biology Orgn, 1982–. Anniversary Prize, Fedn of Eur. Biochemical Socs, 1977; Colworth Medal, British Biochemical Soc., 1978. *Publications:* Control of Enzyme Activity, 1976, 2nd edn 1983; (ed series) Molecular Aspects of Cellular Regulation: vol. 1, 1980; vol. 2, 1982; vol. 3, 1984; vol. 4, 1985; vol. 5, 1988; vol. 6, 1991; over 250 original papers and revs in scientific jls. *Recreations:* chess, golf, natural history. *Address:* Inverbay II, Invergowrie, Dundee DD2 5DQ. *T:* Dundee (0382) 562328.

COHEN, Dr Richard Henry Lionel, CB 1969; Chief Scientist, Department of Health and Social Security, 1972–73, retired; *b* 1 Feb. 1907; *y s* of Frank Lionel and Bertha Hendelah Cohen; *m* 1934, Margaret Clarkson Deas; one *s. Educ:* Clifton Coll.; King's Coll., Cambridge; St Bartholomew's Hospital. Miscellaneous hosp. appts, 1940–46; MRC, 1948–62; Dep. Chief Med. Off., MRC, 1957–62; Dept of Health and Social Security (formerly Min. of Health), 1962–73. *Address:* The End House South, Lady Margaret Road, Cambridge CB3 0BJ. *Club:* Reform.

COHEN, Prof. Robert Donald, MD, FRCP; Professor of Medicine and Director, Academic Medical Unit, London Hospital Medical College, University of London, since 1981 (Professor of Metabolic Medicine, 1974–81); *b* 11 Oct. 1933; *s* of Dr Harry H. and Ruby Cohen; *m* 1961, Dr Barbara Joan Boucher; one *s* one *d. Educ:* Clifton Coll.; Trinity Coll., Cambridge. MA, MD (Cantab). Hon. Cons. Physician, London Hosp., 1967; Chm., Editorial Bd, Clinical Science and Molecular Medicine, 1973–74; Dir, Academic Unit of Metabolism and Endocrinology, London Hosp. Med. Coll., 1974; Chairman: Adv. Cttee on the Application of Computing Science to Medicine and the Nat. Health Service, 1976–77; DHSS Computer R&D Cttee, 1977–80; Jt Cttee on Higher Med. Trng, 1983–90 (Chm., Special Adv. Cttee on Gen. Internal Medicine, 1983–90); DHSS/MRC Monitoring Cttee on Magnetic Resonance Imaging, 1986–89; Review Body, British Diabetic Assoc., 1990–; Member: GMC, 1988–; Council, Imperial Cancer Res. Fund, 1989–. *Publications:* Clinical and Biochemical Aspects of Lactic Acidosis (with H. F. Woods), 1976; (jtly) The Metabolic and Molecular Basis of Acquired Disease, 1990; papers in Clin. Sci. and Molecular Med., BMJ, Lancet, Biochemical Journal. *Address:* Medical Unit, The Royal London Hospital, Whitechapel Road, E1 1BB. *T:* 071–377 7110.

COHEN, Stanley; *b* 31 July 1927; *s* of Thomas and Teresa Cohen; *m* 1954, Brenda P. Rafferty; three *s* one *d. Educ:* St Patrick's and St Charles' Schools, Leeds. Served in Royal Navy, 1947–49. Employed in Clothing Industry, 1943–47 and 1949–51; Clerical Officer with British Railways, 1951–70. Mem. Leeds City Council, 1952–71; elected Alderman, 1968. Parly Candidate (Lab) Barkston Ash County Constituency, 1966; MP (Lab) Leeds South East, 1970–83. PPS to Minister of State, DES, 1976–79. Mem., Duke of Edinburgh's Commonwealth Study Conf. to Australia, 1968. *Recreations:* walking, camping, driving. *Address:* 9 Pendil Close, Whitkirk, Leeds LS15 0NE. *T:* Leeds (0532) 649568. *Clubs:* Crossgates Recreational; Irish Centre (Leeds).

COHEN, Prof. Stanley, PhD; Professor of Criminology, Hebrew University, Jerusalem, since 1981; *b* 23 Feb. 1942; *s* of Ray and Sie Cohen; *m* 1963, Ruth Kretzmer; two *d. Educ:* Univ. of Witwatersrand, Johannesburg (BA); LSE, Univ. of London (PhD). Psychiatric social worker, 1963–64; Lectr in Sociology: Enfield Coll., 1965–67; Univ. of Durham, 1967–72; Sen. Lectr in Sociol., Univ. of Essex, 1972–74, Prof. of Sociol., 1974–81. Sellin-Glueck Award, Amer. Soc. of Criminology, 1985. *Publications:* Images of Deviance, 1971; Folk Devils and Moral Panics, 1972; Psychological Survival, 1972; The Manufacture of News, 1973; Escape Attempts, 1976; Prison Secrets, 1978; Social Control and the State, 1984; Visions of Social Control: crime, punishment and classification, 1985; Against Criminology, 1988. *Address:* Institute of Criminology, Hebrew University, Mount Scopus, Jerusalem 91905, Israel.

COHEN, Prof. Stanley; Distinguished Professor, Department of Biochemistry, Vanderbilt University School of Medicine, since 1986; *b* 17 Nov. 1922; *s* of Louis Cohen and Fruma Feitel; *m* 1st, 1951, Olivia Larson; three *s*; 2nd, 1981, Jan Elizabeth Jordan. *Educ:* Brooklyn Coll., NY; Oberlin Coll., Ohio; Univ. of Michigan (BA, PhD). Teaching Fellow, Dept of Biochem., Univ. of Michigan, 1946–48; Instructor, Depts of Biochem. and Pediatrics, Univ. of Colorado Sch. of Medicine, 1948–52; Fellow, Amer. Cancer Soc., Dept of Radiology, Washington Univ., St Louis, 1952–53; Vanderbilt University School of Medicine, Nashville: Asst Prof. of Biochem., 1959–62; Associate Prof., 1962; Prof. 1967–86. Mem., Editl Bds of learned jls. Mem., Nat. Acad. of Science, and other sci. bodies. Hon. DSc Chicago, 1985. Nobel Prize for Physiology or Medicine, 1986 (jtly); other prizes and awards. *Publications:* papers in learned jls on cell biology, human developmental biology, embryology. *Address:* Department of Biochemistry, Vanderbilt University School of Medicine, 507 Light Hall, Nashville, Tenn 37232–0146, USA.

COHEN, Prof. Sydney, CBE 1978; FRS 1978; Professor of Chemical Pathology, Guy's Hospital Medical School, 1965–86, now Emeritus Professor, University of London; *b* Johannesburg, SA, 18 Sept. 1921; *s* of Morris and Pauline Cohen; *m* 1950, June Bernice Adler, JP, *d* of Dr and Mrs L. D. Adler; one *s* one *d. Educ:* King Edward VIIth Sch., Johannesburg; Witwatersrand and London Univs. MD, PhD. Lectr, Dept of Physiology, Witwatersrand Univ., 1947–53; Scientific Staff, Nat. Inst. for Med. Research, London, 1954–60; Reader, Dept of Immunology, St Mary's Hosp. Med. Sch., 1960–65. Mem., MRC, 1974–76; Chm., Tropical Med. Research Bd, MRC, 1974–76; Chm., WHO Scientific Gp on Immunity to Malaria, 1976–81; Mem., WHO expert adv. panel on malaria, 1977–89; Mem. Council, Royal Soc., 1981–83; Royal Soc. Assessor, MRC, 1982–84; Consultant, Amer. Inst. of Biol Scis, 1987–. Nuffield Dominion Fellow in Medicine, 1954; Founder Fellow, RCPath, 1964; William Julius Mickle Fellow, Univ. of London, 1986. Hon. DSc Witwatersrand, 1987. *Publications:* papers on immunology and parasitic diseases in sci. jls. *Recreations:* golf, gardening, forestry. *Address:* 4 Frognal Rise, NW3 6RD. *T:* 071–435 6507; Hafodfraith, Llangurig, Powys SY18 6QG. *Club:* Royal and Ancient (St Andrews).

COHN, Prof. Norman, MA; DLitt; FBA 1978; FRHistS; historian; Astor-Wolfson Professor, University of Sussex, 1973–80, now Professor Emeritus; *b* London, 12 Jan. 1915; *yr s* of late August Cohn, barrister-at-law, Middle Temple, and Daisy (*née* Reimer); *m* 1941, Vera, *d* of late Mark and Eva Broido, St Petersburg; one *s. Educ:* Gresham's Sch., Holt (Scholar); Christ Church, Oxford (Scholar). 1st Class Hons, Sch. of Medieval and Mod. Languages, 1936; DLitt Glasgow, 1957. Served War of 1939–45, Queen's Royal Regt and Intell. Corps. Lectr in French, Glasgow Univ., 1946–51; Professor of French: Magee Univ. Coll. (then associated with TCD), 1951–60; King's Coll., Durham Univ., 1960–63; changed career to become Dir, Columbus Centre, Sussex Univ. and Gen. Editor, Columbus Centre's Studies in the Dynamics of Persecution and Extermination, 1966–80; Professorial Fellow, Sussex Univ., 1966–73; advr on comparative study of genocide, Concordia Univ., Montreal, 1982–85; advr, Montreal Inst. for Genocide Studies, 1985–; Vis. Prof., KCL, 1986–89. Hugh Le May Fellow, Rhodes Univ., 1950; Fellow, Center for Advanced Study in the Behavioral Sciences, Stanford, Calif, 1966; Vis. Fellow, Center for Humanities, Wesleyan Univ., Conn, 1971; Fellow, Netherlands Inst. for Advanced Study, 1975–76; Canadian SSHRC Vis. Fellow, 1982, Canadian Commonwealth Vis. Fellow, 1983. Hon. LLD Concordia Univ., 1985. *Publications:* Gold Khan and other Siberian legends, 1946; The Pursuit of the Millennium: revolutionary millenarians and mystical anarchists of the middle ages, 1957, rev. edns 1961, 1970; Warrant for Genocide: the myth of the Jewish world-conspiracy and the Protocols of the Elders of Zion, 1967, rev. edn 1981 (Anisfield-Wolf Award in Race Relations, 1967); Europe's Inner Demons: an enquiry inspired by the great witch-hunt, 1975, rev. edn 1976; contributor to various symposia, learned jls, and reviews. *Recreations:* walking, travel, looking at pictures, butterfly-watching. *Address:* Orchard Cottage, Wood End, Ardeley, Herts SG2 7AZ. *T:* Stevenage (0438) 85247. *Club:* Athenæum.

COHN, Prof. Paul Moritz, FRS 1980; Emeritus Professor of Mathematics, University of London, and Hon. Research Fellow in Mathematics, University College London, since 1989; *b* Hamburg, 8 Jan. 1924; *o c* of late James Cohn and late Julia Cohn (*née* Cohen); *m* 1958, Deirdre Sonia Sharon; two *d. Educ:* Trinity Coll., Cambridge. BA 1948, MA, PhD 1951. Chargé de Recherches, Univ. de Nancy, 1951–52; Lectr, Manchester Univ., 1952–62; Reader, London Univ., at Queen Mary Coll., 1962–67; Prof. of Maths, London Univ. at Bedford Coll., 1967–84, at UCL, 1984–86; Astor Prof. of Maths, UCL, 1986–89. Visiting Professor: Yale Univ., 1961–62; Univ. of California (Berkeley), 1962; Univ. of Chicago, 1964; State Univ. of New York (Stony Brook), 1967; Rutgers Univ., 1967–68; Univ. of Paris, 1969; Tulane Univ., 1971; Indian Inst. of Technology, Delhi, 1971; Univ. of Alberta, 1972, 1986; Carleton Univ., Ottawa, 1973; Technion, Haifa, 1975; Iowa State Univ., 1978; Univ. of Bielefeld, 1979; Bar Ilan Univ., Ramat Gan, 1987. Member: Mathematics Cttee, SRC, 1977–80; Council, Royal Soc., 1985–87; London Mathematical Society: Sec., 1965–67; Mem. Council, 1968–71, 1972–75, 1979–84; Pres., 1982–84; Editor, London Math. Soc. Monographs, 1968–77, 1980–. Lester R. Ford Award (Mathematical Assoc. of America), 1972; Senior Berwick Prize, London Mathematical Soc., 1974. *Publications:* Lie Groups, 1957; Linear Equations, 1958; Solid Geometry, 1961; Universal Algebra, 1965, 2nd edn 1981 (trans foreign langs); Free Rings and their Relations, 1971, 2nd edn 1985; Algebra, vol. I, 1974, 2nd edn 1982, vol. II, 1977, 2nd edn 1989, vol. III, 1990; Skewfield Constructions, 1977; papers on algebra in various mathematical periodicals. *Recreations:* linguistics, etymology. *Address:* Department of Mathematics, University College London, Gower Street, WC1E 6BT. *T:* 071–387 7050.

COILEY, John Arthur, PhD; Keeper, National Railway Museum, York, since 1974; *b* 29 March 1932; *o s* of Arthur George Coiley and Stella Coiley (*née* Chinnock); *m* 1956, Patricia Anne Coiley, BA, (*née* Dixon); two *s* one *d. Educ:* Beckenham and Penge Grammar Sch.; Selwyn Coll., Cambridge (BA, PhD Metallurgy). Scientific Officer, UKAEA, Harwell, 1957–60; Aeon Laboratories, Egham, 1960–65; Development Manager, Fulmer Research Laboratories, 1965–73; Asst Keeper, Science Museum, 1973–74. Vice-President, Internat. Assoc. of Transport Museums, 1977–. *Publication:* (jtly) Images of Steam, 1968, 2nd edn 1974. *Recreations:* photography, motoring. *Address:* 4 Beech Close, Farnham, Knaresborough, N Yorkshire HG5 9JJ. *T:* Boroughbridge (0423) 340497.

COKAYNE, family name of **Baron Cullen of Ashbourne.**

COKE, family name of **Earl of Leicester.**

COKE, Viscount; Edward Douglas Coke; *b* 6 May 1936; *s* and *heir* of 6th Earl of Leicester, *qv*; *m* 1st, 1962, Valeria Phyllis (marr. diss. 1985), *e d* of late L. A. Potter; two *s* one *d*; 2nd, 1986, Mrs Sarah de Chair. *Educ:* St Andrew's, Grahamstown, CP, S Africa. *Recreations:* skiing, shooting. *Heir: s* Hon. Thomas Edward Coke, *b* 6 July 1965. *Address:* Holkham, Wells-next-the-Sea, Norfolk. *Clubs:* Brooks's, White's, Farmers'.

COKER, Peter Godfrey, RA 1972 (ARA 1965); ARCA 1953; *b* 27 July 1926; *m* 1951, Vera Joyce Crook; one *s* decd. *Educ:* St Martin's Sch. of Art; Royal Coll. of Art (Royal Schol.). Brit. Inst. Schol., 1954. Arts Council Award to Artists, 1976. One-man Exhibitions: Zwemmer Gall., 1956, 1957, 1959, 1964, 1967; Magdalene Street Gall., Cambridge, 1968; Stone Gall., Newcastle, 1969; Thackeray Gall., London, 1970, 1972, 1974, 1975, 1976, 1978; Gallery 10, London, 1980, 1982, 1984, 1986, 1988; Flying Colours Gall., Edinburgh, 1990. Retrospective Exhibitions: Minories, Colchester, 1972; Victoria Gall., Bath, 1972; Morley Gall., London, 1973; Mappin Art Gall., Sheffield, 1973; Chelmsford and Essex Museum, 1978; Royal Acad., 1979; Fitzwilliam Mus., Cambridge, 1989 (working drawings and sketchbooks, 1955–88). Represented in Group Exhibitions: Tate Gall., 1958; Jordan Gall., Toronto, 1958; John Moores, Liverpool, 1959, 1961; Northampton, 1960; Europaisches Forum, Alpbach, Austria, 1960; Neue Galerie, Linz, 1960; RCA, 1952–62; Painters in E Anglia, Arts Council, 1966; Bicentenary Exhibn, Royal Acad., 1768–1968, 1968; British Painting 1900–1960, Sheffield and Aberdeen, 1975–76; British Painting 1952–77, RA; Recent Chartrey Purchases, Tate Gall., 1981; Acquisitions since 1980, Tate Gall., 1982; The Forgotten Fifties, Sheffield and UK tour, 1984; Exhibition Road, RCA, 1988. Works in permanent collections: Tate Gall.; British Museum; Scottish Nat. Gall. of Modern Art; Arts Council; Contemp. Art Soc., GB; Contemp. Art Soc., Wales; Chantrey Bequest; Nat. Portrait Gall.; V&A; Nat. Maritime Museum; Stedelijk Museum Ostend; Eastern Arts Assoc.; Rugby Library and Museum; Chelmsford and Essex Museum; Castle Museum, Norwich; Fitzwilliam Mus., Cambridge; Art Galls and Museums of Carlisle, Ipswich, Leicester, Rochdale, Doncaster; Art Galls of Bath (Victoria), Batley, Birmingham, Coventry (Herbert), Kendal (Abbot Hall), Kettering, Leeds City, Manchester City, Sheffield City, Southport (Atkinson), Salford; RCA; RA; Minories, Colchester; Beecroft Art Gall., Southend-on-Sea; Educn Cttees of Nottingham, Essex, Derbyshire, Lancs, ILEA; Liverpool Univ. *Publication:* Etching Techniques, 1976. *Address:* The Red House, Mistley, Manningtree, Essex. *T:* Colchester (0206) 392179.

COLBECK-WELCH, Air Vice-Marshal Edward Lawrence, CB 1961; OBE 1948; DFC 1941; Royal Air Force, retired; *b* 29 Jan. 1914; *s* of Major G. S. M. Colbeck-Welch, MC, Collingham, Yorks; *m* 1938, Doreen (*d* 1988), *d* of T. G. Jenkin, Sliema, Malta; one *s* two *d. Educ:* Leeds Grammar Sch. Commnd RAF, 1933; No. 22 Sqdn, RAF, 1934–37;

CFS Instructor Course, 1937; Flying Instr RAuxAF Sqdns, 1937–39; Staff duties, 1940; OC No. 29 Night Fighter Sqdn, 1941–42; Staff Coll., 1942; Staff duties, 1943–44; Staff duties in 2nd TAF and OC No. 139 (Bomber) Wing, 1944–45; Air Min. Dep. Dir Air Defence, 1945–47; Staff duties in USA, 1947–50; OC Fighter Stations (2), 1950–53; Air Min. Personnel Staff duties, 1954–55; student, idc 1956; Comdt Central Fighter Estab., 1957–58; SASO, HQ No 13 (F) Group, 1959; SASO, HQ Fighter Comd RAF, 1960–63. *Recreation:* sailing. *Address:* La Cote au Palier, St Martin, Jersey, CI. *Clubs:* Royal Channel Islands Yacht, St Helier Yacht.

COLBERT, Claudette; Chevalier, Légion d'Honneur, 1988; stage and film actress; *b* Paris, 13 Sept. 1903; *d* of Georges Chauchoin and Jeanne Loew; *m* 1st, Norman Foster (marr. diss.); 2nd, Dr Joel J. Pressman (*d* 1968). Went to America, 1908. First appearances: New York Stage, 1923; London stage, 1928. Returned to Broadway stage, 1958–60. After success on Broadway, entered films, 1929. *Plays include:* Wild Westcotts, The Marionette Man, We've Got to Have Money, The Cat Came Back, Leah Kleschna, High Stakes, A Kiss in the Taxi, The Ghost Train, The Pearl of Great Price, The Barker, The Mulberry Bush, La Gringa, Within the Law, Fast Life, Tin Pan Alley, Dynamo, See Naples and Die, The Marriage-Go-Round, The Kingfisher, Talent for Murder, Aren't We All?. *Films include:* For the Love of Mike, The Lady Lies, Manslaughter, The Smiling Lieutenant, Sign of the Cross, Cleopatra, Private Worlds, Maid of Salem, It Happened One Night (Academy Award, 1934), The Gilded Lily, I Met Him in Paris, Bluebeard's Eighth Wife, Zaza, Midnight, Drums Along the Mohawk, Skylark, Remember the Day, Palm Beach Story, No Time for Love, So Proudly We Hail, Without Reservations, The Secret Heart, The Egg and I, Sleep My Love, Three Came Home, The Secret Fury, The Planter's Wife, Destiny, Versailles, Parrish, Since You Went Away (Academy Award nomination). *Film for television:* The Two Mrs Grenvilles, 1988 (Golden Globe award). Kennedy Center Honors Award, 1989. *Address:* Bellerive, St Peter, Barbados, West Indies.

COLCHESTER, Area Bishop of, since 1988; **Rt. Rev. Michael Edwin Vickers;** *b* 13 Jan. 1929; *s* of William Edwin and Florence Alice Vickers; *m* 1960, Janet Cynthia Croasdale; three *d*. *Educ:* St Lawrence Coll., Ramsgate; Worcester Coll., Oxford (BA Mod. History, 1952, MA 1956); Cranmer Hall, Durham (DipTheol with distinction, 1959). Company Secretary, Hoares (Ceylon) Ltd, 1952–56; Refugee Administrator for British Council for Aid to Refugees, 1956–57; Lay Worker, Diocese of Oklahoma, 1959; Curate of Christ Church, Bexleyheath, 1959–62; Sen. Chaplain, Lee Abbey Community, 1962–67; Vicar of St John's, Newland, Hull, 1967–81; Area Dean, Central and North Hull, 1972–81; Archdeacon of E Riding, 1981–88. Chm., York Diocesan House of Clergy, 1975–85; Canon and Prebendary of York, 1981–88. Mem., Gen. Synod, 1975–88 (Proctor in Convocation, 1975–85). *Recreations:* gardening, fell-walking, travel, drama. *Address:* 1 Fitzwalter Road, Lexden, Colchester, Essex CO3 3SS. *T:* Colchester (0206) 576648.

COLCHESTER, Archdeacon of; *see* Stroud, Ven. E. C. F.

COLCHESTER, Rev. Halsey Sparrowe, CMG 1968; OBE 1960; MA Oxon; Priest in Charge, Great Tew, Oxfordshire, 1981–87 and since 1990; *b* 5 March 1918; *s* of late Ernest Charles Colchester; *m* 1946, Rozanne Felicity Hastings Medhurst, *d* of late Air Chief Marshal Sir Charles Medhurst, KCB, OBE, MC; four *s* one *d*. *Educ:* Uppingham Sch.; Magdalen Coll., Oxford. Served Oxf. and Bucks Lt Inf., 1940–43; 2nd SAS Regt, 1944–46 (despatches); Captain. Joined Diplomatic Service, 1947; FO 1948–50; 2nd Sec., Istanbul, 1950–54; FO 1954–56; Consul, Zürich, 1956–60; 1st Sec., Athens, 1960–64; FO 1964–68; Counsellor, Paris, 1968–72; retired from Diplomatic Service, 1972; Ordinand at Cuddesdon Theological Coll., 1972–73; Deacon, 1973; Priest, 1974; Curate, Minchinhampton, Glos, 1973–76; Vicar of Bollington, Cheshire, 1976–81. *Recreations:* theatre-going, wild flowers. *Address:* The Vicarage, Great Tew, Oxford OX7 4AG. *T:* Great Tew (060883) 293. *Club:* Travellers'.

See also N. B. S. Colchester.

COLCHESTER, Nicholas Benedick Sparrowe; Deputy Editor, The Economist, since 1989; *b* 30 Dec. 1946; *s* of Rev. Halsey Sparrowe Colchester, *qv*; *m* 1976, Laurence Lucie Antoinette Schloesing; two *s*. *Educ:* Radley Coll.; Magdalen Coll., Oxford (BA). Joined Financial Times, 1968: New York Corresp., 1970–73; Bonn Corresp., 1974–77; For. Editor, 1981–86; joined The Economist, 1986. Chevalier de l'Ordre National du Mérite (France), 1988. *Publication:* Europe Relaunched (jtly), 1990. *Recreations:* music, theatre. *Address:* 37 Arundel Gardens, W11 2LW. *T:* 071–221 2829. *Club:* Garrick.

COLCHESTER, Trevor Charles, CMG 1958; *b* London, 18 April 1909; *s* of Charles Colchester; *m* 1937, Nancy Joan Russell; one *d*. *Educ:* Corpus Christi Coll., Cambridge (MA). Colonial Service, 1931–64; in Kenya, Zanzibar, and Northern Rhodesia. Sec. to Cabinet, Kenya, 1954–57; Permanent Sec., Kenya, 1957–61. Sec., Commonwealth Assoc. of Architects, 1964–74; Consultant, Commonwealth Legal Education Assoc., 1974–84. Hon. FRIBA 1975. *Recreations:* conservation, gardening, fly-fishing, music. *Address:* Plomesgate, Aldeburgh, Suffolk IP15 5QB. *T:* Aldeburgh (0728) 452871.

COLDRICK, Albert Percival, OBE 1974; FCIT 1972; Chairman: National Health Service SE Thames Appeals Tribunal, 1974–89; Executive Committee, Industrial Participation Association, since 1974; *b* 6 June 1913; *s* of Albert Percival and Florence Coldrick; *m* 1938, Esther Muriel Blades; three *s*. *Educ:* Britannia Bridge Elementary Sch.; Wigan Mining and Technical College. Railway Controller, 1933–47; Transport Salaried Staffs' Assoc.: full-time Officer, 1948–62; Sen. Asst Sec., 1962–66; Asst Gen. Sec., 1967; Gen. Sec., 1968–73. Member: General Council, TUC, 1968–73; Industrial Tribunal, 1975–84. Mem., Midlands and West Region Rlys Bd, 1975–77. Chm., Foundn for Industrial Understanding, 1979–; Vice Chm., Nat. Exam. Bd for Supervisory Management, 1979. Jt Editor, International Directory of the Trade Union Movement, 1977–. *Recreations:* reading, golf, walking, photography. *Address:* 10 Murray Avenue, Bromley, Kent BR1 3DQ. *T:* 081–464 4089. *Club:* Royal Over-Seas League.

COLDSTREAM, Sir George (Phillips), KCB 1955 (CB 1949); KCVO 1968; QC 1960; *b* 20 Dec. 1907; *s* of late Francis Menzies Coldstream; *m* 1st, 1934, Mary Morna (marr. diss. 1948), *o d* of Major and Mrs A. D. Carmichael, Meigle, Perthshire; one *d* (and one *d* decd); 2nd, Sheila Hope, *widow* of Lt-Col J. H. H. Whitty, DSO, MC. *Educ:* Rugby; Oriel Coll., Oxford. Called to the Bar, Lincoln's Inn, 1930. Bencher, 1954; Asst to Parly Counsel to Treasury, 1934–39; Legal Asst, Lord Chancellor's Office, 1939–44; Dep. Clerk of the Crown, 1944–54; Clerk of the Crown in Chancery and Permanent Sec. to the Lord Chancellor, 1954–68. Member: British War Crimes Executive, 1944–46; Evershed Cttee on Supreme Court Practice and Procedure, 1947–53; British team, Anglo-Amer. Legal Exchanges, 1961–69; Royal Commn on Assizes and Quarter Sessions, 1967–70; Top Salaries Review Body, 1971–82. Sec., Party Leaders Conf. on Reform of House of Lords, Feb.–May 1948. Special Consultant, Amer. Inst. of Judicial Admin, NY, 1968–71. Part-time Chm., Industrial Tribunals, 1975–80. Chm., Council of Legal Educn, 1970–73. Pres., Old Rugbeian Soc., 1978–80. Hon. Mem., American Bar Assoc., 1969; Hon. Fellow, Amer. Coll. of Trial Lawyers, 1969. Hon. LLD Columbia Univ., 1966. *Address:* The Gate House, Seaford, East Sussex BN25 2AH. *T:* Seaford (0323) 892801. *Clubs:* Athenæum; Royal Cruising.

COLDSTREAM, Prof. John Nicolas, FSA; FBA 1977; Yates Professor of Classical Art and Archaeology, University College London, since 1983; *b* 30 March 1927; *s* of Sir John Coldstream and Phyllis Mary Hambly; *m* 1970, Imogen Nicola Carr. *Educ:* Eton; King's College, Cambridge (Class. Tripos, BA 1951, MA 1956). FSA 1964. Nat. Service, Buffs and HLI (Egypt and Palestine), 1945–48. Asst Master, Shrewsbury Sch., 1952–56; Temp. Asst Keeper, Dept of Greek and Roman Antiquities, BM, 1956–57; Macmillan Student, British Sch. at Athens, 1957–60; Bedford College, London: Lectr, 1960–66; Reader, 1966–75; Prof. of Aegean Archaeology, 1975–83. Geddes-Harrower Vis. Prof. of Classical Archaeology, Univ. of Aberdeen, 1983. Mem., 1966–, Chm., 1987–, Managing Cttee, British Sch. at Athens. Chm., Nat. Organizing Cttee, XI Internat. Congress of Classical Archaeol., London, 1978. Mem., Deutsches Archäologisches Inst., 1978; Corr. Mem., Rheinisch-Westfälische Akademie der Wissenschaften, 1984. Hon. Fellow, Archaiologikē Hetaireia Athenōn, 1987. Editor, Annual of the British School at Athens, 1968–73. *Publications:* Greek Geometric Pottery, 1968; (with G. L. Huxley) Kythera: Excavations and Studies, 1972; Knossos: The Sanctuary of Demeter, 1973; Geometric Greece, 1977; articles in British and foreign classical and archaeological journals. *Recreations:* music, travel. *Address:* 180 Ebury Street, SW1.

COLDWELLS, Rev. Canon Alan Alfred; Canon of St George's Chapel, Windsor, since 1987; *b* 15 Jan. 1930; *yr s* of late Alfred Carpenter Coldwells and of Leila Philis Eugenie Coldwells (*née* Livings); *m* 1963, Mary Patricia, *d* of A. L. Hemsley; one *s* two *d*. *Educ:* Haileybury and ISC; University Coll., Oxford (MA); Wells Theological Coll. Deacon 1955, priest 1956; Curate, St Andrew's Parish, Rugby, 1955–62; Curate in charge, St George's, Rugby, 1956–62; Vicar of Sprowston and Rector of Beeston St Andrew, Norfolk, 1962–73; RD, Norwich North, 1970–72; Director, Samaritans, Norwich, 1970–72; Rector of Rugby, 1973–87; RD of Rugby, 1973–78; Hon. Canon, Coventry Cathedral, 1983. *Publication:* The Story of St Andrew's, Rugby, 1979. *Recreations:* art, painting, local history. *Address:* 6 The Cloisters, Windsor Castle, Berks SL4 1NJ. *T:* Windsor (0753) 866313.

COLE, family name of **Earl of Enniskillen.**

COLE, Sir (Alexander) Colin, KCVO 1983 (CVO 1979; MVO 1977); TD 1972; FSA; Garter Principal King of Arms, since 1978; *b* 16 May 1922; *er s* of Capt. Edward Harold Cole, and Blanche Ruby Lavinia (*née* Wallis) (both decd); *m* 1944, Valerie, *o d* of late Capt. Stanley Walter Card; four *s* three *d*. *Educ:* Dulwich; Pembroke Coll. Cambridge; Brasenose Coll., Oxford. BCL Oxon; MA Oxon. Served War of 1939–45, Capt. Coldstream Guards. Barrister-at-law (Inner Temple), 1949, Hon. Bencher, 1988. Fitzalan Pursuivant of Arms Extraordinary, 1953; Portcullis Pursuivant of Arms, 1957; Windsor Herald of Arms, 1966. Major, 6th (Volunteer) Bn, Queen's Regt, 1971–73, Col RARO (Brevet, 1973); Hon. Col, 6/7 Bn, Queen's Regt, 1981–86. Mem. Court of Common Council of City of London (Castle Baynard Ward), 1964–; Sheriff, City of London, 1976–77. Freeman of City of London, Freeman and Liveryman, Scriveners', Basketmakers and Painter Stainers Companies of London. Fellow Heraldry Soc.; Hon. Heraldic Adviser, Monumental Brass Soc.; Registrar and Librarian, College of Arms, 1967–74. Knight Principal, Imperial Soc. of Knights Bachelor, 1983–; Pres., Royal Soc. of St George, 1982–. FRSA 1979. OStJ. *Publications:* articles on heraldry and kindred subjects in their appropriate journals; illus. Visitations of London (1568) and Wiltshire (1623) (Harleian Soc.). *Recreations:* art, archæology, architecture, wine-bibbing. *Address:* College of Arms, Queen Victoria Street, EC4. *T:* 071–248 1188; Holly House, Burstow, Surrey. *Clubs:* Cavalry and Guards, City Livery.

COLE, Prof. Boris Norman, BSc(Eng) (London), PhD (Birmingham), WhSch, CEng, FIMechE, FInstP; Professor of Mechanical Engineering, 1962–88, Head of Department of Mechanical Engineering, 1962–87, University of Leeds, now Professor Emeritus; *b* 8 Jan. 1924; *s* of James Edward Cole and Gertrude Cole; *m* 1945, Sibylle Duijts; two *s* one *d*. *Educ:* King Edward's Sch., Birmingham. Apprenticed to Messrs Belliss and Morcom Ltd, Engineers, Birmingham. Dept of Mech. Engrg, Univ. of Birmingham: Lectr, 1949–55; Sen. Lectr, 1955–58; Reader, 1958–62; Chm. of Faculty Bd of Applied Sciences, Birmingham Univ., 1955–57 and 1959–62. Dir, Univ. of Leeds Industrial Services Ltd. Member: Smethwick Co. Borough Educn Cttee, 1957–60; Engrg Materials Res. Requirements Bd, 1974–78, and various other govt cttees; Governor, Engrg Industries Training Bd, Leeds Training Centre, 1967–82. Prizewinner, IMechE, 1953 and 1962. *Publications:* numerous in fields of solid and fluid mechanics and in engineering education. *Recreations:* walking, music, social history of engineering. *Address:* 6 Wedgewood Grove, Leeds LS8 1EG. *T:* Leeds (0532) 664756.

COLE, (Claude Neville) David, CBE 1977; JP; Deputy Managing Director, International Thomson Organisation plc, 1985–86 (Joint Deputy Managing Director, 1980–84); Chairman, Thomson Foundation, since 1986; *b* 4 June 1928; 2nd *s* of late W. J. Cole and of Mrs M. J. Cole; *m* 1951, Alma Gwlithyn Williams (*d* 1990); one *s* one *d* (one *s* decd). *Educ:* Royal Masonic School; Harvard Business Sch. Journalist: Merthyr Express; South Wales Echo; Daily Graphic (Manchester); Daily Sketch (London); Daily Recorder; Empire News (Cardiff); Editor, Western Mail, Cardiff, 1956–59; Managing Director: Western Mail and Echo Ltd, 1959–67 (now Chm.); Newcastle Chronicle and Journal Ltd, 1967–69; Thomson Regional Newspapers Ltd: Asst Man. Dir and Editorial Dir, 1969–72; Man. Dir and Chief Exec., 1972–82; Chm., 1980–82; Chm. and Chief Exec., Thomson Information Services, 1982–84. Chairman: Rainbird Publishing Gp, 1980–85; Hamish Hamilton, 1982–85; Thomson Books, 1980–85; Janes Publishing Co., 1981–86; Director: Thomson Organisation (Exec. Bd), 1973–80; Reuters Ltd, 1976–81; Press Assoc. (Chm. 1976–77, 1977–78); Welsh Nat. Opera Co. Ltd, 1960–71; Chairman: Celtic Press Ltd; Cole Cttee on Recruitment of Nurses in Wales, 1961–63; Working Party on Welsh Tourism, 1963–64; Barry Development Partnership, 1986–88; Civic Trust for Wales, 1986–; Director: Welsh Develt Agency, 1987–90; Celtic Trees plc. Member: Council, Newspaper Soc., 1974– (Pres., 1982); Press Council, 1976–80; PIRA Council, 1984–86; Trustee, Reuters Ltd, 1983–. Member: Court of Governors of Univ. of Wales, 1962–; Council of Univ. of Wales, 1962–; Council of Welsh National Sch. of Medicine, 1964–67; Council, Univ. of Wales Coll., Cardiff, 1988–; Governing Body of Cardiff Coll. of Music and Drama, 1963–67; Council of Cardiff New Theatre Trust, 1964–67; Welsh Nat. Theatre Cttee; Aberfan Disaster Fund, 1966–67; Welsh Hospitals Bd, 1962–67. Vice-Patron, Coun. for Wales, Brit. Empire and Commonwealth Games. Pres., Tenovus, 1963–. FBIM. Hon. LLD Wales, 1989. OStJ. *Publications:* This and Other Worlds (poems), 1975; Meeting Places and other poems, 1977; Mount of Angels (poems), 1978. *Recreations:* two of the three R's. *Address:* Longacre, 14 The Paddocks, Penarth, S Glam CF6 2BW. *T:* Penarth (0222) 703487. *Clubs:* East India, Devonshire, Sports and Public Schools; Cardiff and County (Cardiff).

COLE, Sir Colin; *see* Cole, Sir A. C.

COLE, David; *see* Cole, C. N. D.

COLE, Sir David (Lee), KCMG 1975 (CMG 1965); MC 1944; HM Diplomatic Service, retired; *b* 31 Aug. 1920; *s* of late Brig. D. H. Cole, CBE, LittD, and Charlotte Cole (*née* Wedgwood); *m* 1945, Dorothy (*née* Patton); one *s*. *Educ:* Cheltenham Coll.; Sidney

Sussex Coll., Cambridge. MA (1st Cl. Hons History). Served Royal Inniskilling Fusiliers, 1940–45. Dominions Office, 1947; seconded to Foreign Office for service with UK Delegn to UN, New York, 1948–51; First Sec., Brit. High Commn, New Delhi, 1953–56; Private Sec. to Rt Hon. the Earl of Home (Sec. of State for Commonwealth Relations and Lord President of the Council), 1957–60; Head of Personnel Dept, CRO, 1961–63; British Dep. High Comr in Ghana, 1963–64; British High Comr in Malawi, 1964–67; Minister (Political), New Delhi, 1967–70; Asst Under-Sec. of State, FCO, 1970–73; Ambassador to Thailand, 1973–78. *Publications:* Thailand: Water Colour Impressions, 1977; Rough Road to Rome, 1983. *Recreation:* watercolour painting (exhibited RI, RBA). *Address:* 19 Burghley House, Somerset Road, Wimbledon, SW19 5JB.

COLE, Eileen Marie Lucy, CBE 1987; Chief Executive, Research International (Unilever Ltd), 1973–85 (in Rotterdam, 1973–77), retired 1985; Director (non-executive), Post Office, since 1980; Director (part-time), London Regional Transport, 1984–88; *b* 22 April 1924; *d* of Arthur Walter Cole and Mary Agnes Boyd. *Educ:* grammar schs; Girton Coll., Cambridge (BA Hons Econ.). Joined Unilever as trainee, 1948; with associated cos and market res. div. of Unilever, 1948–60; Market Research Controller, Lever Bros Ltd, 1960–64; Research Bureau Ltd: Dir, 1964–67; Chm. and Man. Dir, 1967–72. Vice-Pres., 1979–, and Full Mem., UK Market Res. Soc. (Chm., 1977–79; Hon. Life Mem., 1985); Council Mem., Women in Management, 1971–; Mem., Careers Advisory Services: Cambridge Univ., 1968–75, 1979–83; Reading Univ., 1970–76, 1979–. FBIM; Mem., Inst. of Dirs. *Publications:* various in learned jls connected with market research. *Recreations:* gardening, cooking, reading, theatre. *Address:* Nicholas Farm, Lower Wield, Alresford, Hants SO24 9RX.

COLE, Maj.-Gen. Eric Stuart, CB 1960; CBE 1945; retired; Director of Telecommunications, War Office, 1958–61; *b* 1906; *s* of John William Cole; *m* 1941, Doris Cole. Served Palestine, 1936–39; War of 1939–45 in Italy, France, Greece (despatches, CBE); Maj.-Gen., 1958. Col Comdt Royal Corps of Signals, 1962–67. Pres., Radio Soc. of GB, 1961. Pres., Army Golf Soc., 1971–73. *Address:* 28 Royal Avenue, Chelsea, SW3. *Clubs:* Army and Navy, MCC, Roehampton.

COLE, Frank; *see* Cole, (George) Francis.

COLE, George; actor on stage, screen, radio and television; *b* 22 April 1925; *m* 1st, 1954, Eileen Moore (marr. diss. 1966); one *s* one *d*; 2nd, 1967, Penelope Morrell; one *s* one *d*. *Educ:* Surrey County Council Secondary Sch., Morden. Made first stage appearance in White Horse Inn, tour and London Coliseum, 1939; Cottage to Let, Birmingham, 1940; West End and on tour, 1940–41; subseq. West End plays included Goodnight Children, New, 1942; Mr Bolfry, Playhouse, 1943. Served in RAF, 1943–47. Returned to stage in Dr Angelus, Phoenix, 1947; The Anatomist, Westminster, 1948; Mr Gillie, Garrick, 1950; A Phoenix too Frequent and Thor with Angels, Lyric, Hammersmith, 1951; Misery Me, Duchess, 1955; Mr Bolfry, Aldwych, 1956; Brass Butterfly, Strand, 1958; The Bargain, St Martin's, 1961; The Sponge Room and Squat Betty, Royal Court, 1962; Meet Me on the Fence (tour), 1963; Hedda Gabler, St Martin's, 1964; A Public Mischief, St Martin's, 1965; Too True To Be Good, Strand, 1965; The Waiting Game, Arts, 1966; The Three Sisters, Royal Court, 1967; Doubtful Haunts, Hampstead, 1968; The Passionate Husband, 1969; The Philanthropist, Mayfair, 1971; Country Life, Hampstead, 1973; Déjà Revue, New London, 1974; Motive (tour), 1976; Banana Ridge, Savoy, 1976; The Case of the Oily Levantine, Guildford, 1977; Something Afoot, Hong Kong, 1978; Brimstone and Treacle, Open Space, 1979; Liberty Hall, Greenwich, 1980; The Pirates of Penzance, Drury Lane, 1982; A Month of Sundays, Duchess, 1986; A Piece of My Mind, Apollo, 1987; Peter Pan, Cambridge, 1987; The Breadwinner (tour). *Films include:* Cottage to Let, 1941; Morning Departure, Laughter in Paradise, Scrooge, Top Secret, 1949–51; Will Any Gentleman?, The Intruder, 1952; Happy Ever After, Our Girl Friday, 1953; Belles of St Trinian's, 1954; Quentin Durward, 1955; The Weapon, It's a Wonderful World, The Green Man, 1956; Blue Murder at St Trinian's, Too Many Crooks, Don't Panic Chaps, The Bridal Path, 1957–59; The Pure Hell of St Trinian's, Cleopatra, Dr Syn, 1961–62; One Way Pendulum, Legend of Dick Turpin, 1964; Great St Trinian's Train Robbery, 1965; The Green Shoes, 1969; Vampire Lovers, 1970; Girl in the Dark, 1971; The Blue Bird, 1975; Minder on the Orient Express (TV film), 1985. TV Series include Life of Bliss (also radio), A Man of our Times, Don't Forget to Write, Minder (7 series), The Bounder (2 series), Blott on the Landscape, Comrade Dad, Life after Life, Single Voices. *Address:* Donnelly, Newnham Hill Bottom, Nettlebed, Oxon.

COLE, George Francis, (Frank); Founder Director, Frank Cole (Consultancy) Ltd, since 1979; Director: Alexander Stenhouse UK Ltd (formerly Reed Stenhouse UK Ltd), since 1981; William Mitchell (Sinkers) Ltd (Chairman, 1982–89); Mitchell-Grieve Ltd, since 1989; *b* 3 Nov. 1918; *m*; Gwendoline Mary Laver (decd); two *s* one *d*; Barbara Mary Booth (*née* Gornall). *Educ:* Manchester Grammar Sch. Dir and Gen. Manager, Clarkson Engineers Ltd, 1944–53; Gen. Man., Ariel Motors Ltd (BSA Group), 1953–55; Dir, then Man. Dir, Vono Ltd, 1955–67. Past Chairman: Grovewood Products Ltd; Portways Ltd; R. & W. H. Symington Holdings Ltd; National Exhibition Centre Ltd; Crane's Screw (Hldgs); Stokes Bomford (Holdings) Ltd; Debenholt Ltd; Stokes Bomford (Foods) Ltd; James Cooke (Birmingham) Ltd; Franklin Medical Ltd; Aero Needles Gp plc; Needle Industries Gp Ltd; F. J. Neve & Co. Ltd; Wild Barnsley Engrg Gp Ltd; Past Director: Duport Ltd; Shipping Industrial Holdings Ltd; G. Clancey Ltd; Armstrong Equipment PLC (retd as Dep. Chm., 1989). Pres., Birmingham Chamber of Commerce and Industry, 1968–69. Leader of Trade Missions to West Germany, Yugoslavia, Romania and Hungary. CBIM; Life Governor, Birmingham Univ.; Liveryman of City of London. Radio and Television appearances. *Publications:* press articles on economics, exports, etc. *Recreations:* tennis (doubles second round, singles quarter-finalist, Nat. Veterans Championships of GB, Wimbledon, 1990), oil painting, snooker, gardening. *Address:* Northcot, 128 Station Road, Balsall Common, Coventry, West Midlands CV7 7FF. *T:* Berkswell (0676) 32105.

COLE, Humphrey John Douglas; retired; Deputy Secretary and Chief Economic Adviser, Department of Transport, and Chief Economic Adviser, Department of the Environment, 1983–87; *b* 30 Jan. 1928; *s* of late G. D. H. Cole and Dame Margaret I. Cole, DBE; *m* 1955, Hilda Annette Robinson; two *s* one *d*. *Educ:* Winchester Coll.; Trinity Coll., Cambridge. Research, Oxford Inst. of Statistics, 1950–61; Head, Economic Indicators and Foreign Trade, OECD Statistics Div., 1961–66; Dept of Economic Affairs: Senior Economic Adviser (Regional), 1966–67; Asst Dir of Economics, 1967–69; Dir of Economics, Min. of Technology, 1969–70; Dir of Econs (Urban and Highways), DoE, 1970–72; Dir Gen., Econs and Resources, DoE, 1972–76; Chief Economic Advr, DoE and Dept of Transport, 1976–82. *Publications:* articles in Bulletin of Inst. of Statistics, 1950–61. *Recreation:* walking. *Address:* 3 The Mead, W13. *T:* 081–997 8285.

COLE, James S.; *see* Stuart-Cole.

COLE, John Morrison; Political Editor, BBC, since 1981; *b* 23 Nov. 1927; *s* of George Cole and Alice Jane Cole; *m* 1956, Margaret Isobel, *d* of Mr and Mrs John S. Williamson, Belfast; four *s*. *Educ:* Fortwilliam and Skegoneill Primary Schs, Belfast; Belfast Royal Acad.; London Univ. (BA External). Belfast Telegraph, 1945–56: successively reporter, industrial, municipal and political correspondent; The Guardian: Reporter, 1956–57; Labour Correspondent, 1957–63; News Editor, 1963–69; Dep. Editor, 1969–75; The Observer: Asst Editor, 1975; Dep. Editor, 1976–81. *Publications:* The Poor of the Earth, 1976; The Thatcher Years: a decade of revolution in British politics, 1987; contrib. to books on British and Irish politics. *Recreations:* reading, travel. *Address:* BBC Office, House of Commons, Westminster, SW1A 0AA. *T:* 071–219 4765. *Club:* Athenæum.

COLE, Prof. John Peter; Professor of Human and Regional Geography (formerly of Regional Geography), University of Nottingham, since 1975; *b* Sydney, Australia, 9 Dec. 1928; *s* of Philip and Marjorie Cecelia Cole; *m* 1952, Isabel Jesús Cole (*née* Urrunaga); two *s*. *Educ:* Bromley Grammar Sch.; Univ. of Nottingham (State Schol., BA, MA, PhD, DLitt); Collegio Borromeo, Pavia Univ., Italy (British Council Schol.). Demonstrator, Univ. of Nottingham, 1951–52; Nat. Service with RN, Jt Services Sch. for Linguists, Russian Language Interpreter, 1952–54 (Lt Comdr RNR, retired); Oficina Nacional de Planeamiento y Urbanismo, Lima, Peru, 1954–55; Lectr in Geography, Univ. of Reading, 1955–56; Lectr in Geography, Univ. of Nottingham, 1956–69. Reader, 1969–75; Vis. Lectr or Prof., Univs of Washington, Columbia, Mexico, Valparaíso, Nanjing, Beijing. *Publications:* Geography of World Affairs, 1959, 6th edn 1983; (with F. C. German) Geography of the USSR, 1961, 2nd edn 1970; Italy, 1964; Latin America, 1965, 2nd edn 1975; (with C. A. M. King) Quantitative Geography, 1968; (with N. J. Beynon) New Ways in Geography, 1968, 2nd edn 1982; Situations in Human Geography, 1975; The Development Gap, 1981; Geography of the Soviet Union, 1984; China 1950–2000 Performance and Prospects, 1985; The Poverty of Marxism in Contemporary Geographical Applications and Research, 1986; Development and Underdevelopment, 1987; (with T. Buck) Modern Soviet Economic Performance, 1987; contribs to learned jls, UK and overseas. *Recreations:* travel, languages, pen drawing and painting, gardening. *Address:* 10 Ranmore Close, Beeston, Nottingham NG9 3FR. *T:* Nottingham (0602) 250409.

COLE, Prof. Monica M.; Professor of Geography, 1964–87, and Director of Research in Geobotany, Terrain Analysis and related Resource Use, 1975–87, Royal Holloway and Bedford New College (formerly at Bedford College), University of London, now Professor Emeritus; Leverhulme Emeritus Professorial Research Fellow, since 1988; *b* 5 May 1922; *d* of William Henry Parnall Cole and Dorothy Mary Cole (*née* Thomas). *Educ:* Wimbledon County Grammar Sch.; Bedford Coll., Univ. of London. Research Asst, Min. of Town and Country Planning, Cambridge, 1944–45; Postgrad. study, Univ. of London, 1945–46; Lectr in Geography: Univ. of Capetown, 1947; Univ. of Witwatersrand, 1948–51, Univ. of Keele, 1951–64. Assoc. Prof., Univ. of Idaho summer sch., 1952; Vis. Lectr, Univs of Queensland, Melbourne, and Adelaide, 1960. Mem. British delegn Internat. Geographical Congress in: Washington, 1952; Rio de Janeiro, 1956; London, 1964; New Delhi, 1968; Montreal, 1972; Tokyo, 1980; Paris, 1984; Participant, Internat. Savannas Symposia, Venezuela, 1964, S Africa, 1979, Australia, 1984. Research: savannas, vegetation, soils and geomorphology: S Africa, 1948–51; Brazil, 1956, 1965; Central and E Africa, 1959; Australia, 1960, 1962, 1963, 1965, 1966, 1967, 1968, 1971, 1972, 1975, 1976, 1980, 1984; Venezuela, 1964; Southern Africa, 1967, 1968, 1978, 1979, 1980, 1983; plant indicators of mineralization: Australia, Africa, Brazil, UK, Finland, Japan, 1964–73, 1977, 1978, 1980, 1984, 1985; remote sensing for terrain analysis: Australia, UK, 1970–76, 1983–85, China, 1981. Principal Investigator, SPOT IMAGE, 1986–. *Publications:* The Transvaal Lowveld, 1956; South Africa, 1961, 1966; The Savannas: biogeography and geobotany, 1986; contribs to Geograph. Jl, Geography, Trans Inst. Brit. Geographers, S African Geograph. Jl, Trans Instn Mining and Metallurgy, Proc. Royal Soc., Jl Applied Ecology, ESRO, Procs Symposium Frascati, Jl Biogeography, S Africa Geol Soc., CIMM and COSPAR Conf. Procs, Advances in Space Res., Ecological Studies, Environmental Pollution, and many papers in conf. procs. *Recreations:* painting, photography, tennis, walking, climbing. *Address:* Royal Holloway and Bedford New College, Egham Hill, Egham, Surrey TW20 0EX.

COLE, Peter Geoffrey; journalist; Editor, News Review, The Sunday Times, since 1990; *b* 16 Dec. 1945; *s* of Arthur and Elizabeth Cole; *m* 1982, Jane Ellison; one *s* one *d*. *Educ:* Tonbridge Sch.; Queens' Coll., Cambridge. Reporter, Evening News, 1968–72; Diary Editor, Evening Standard, 1976–78; News Editor, Deputy Editor, The Guardian, 1978–88; Editor, Sunday Correspondent, 1988–90. *Publication:* Can You Positively Identify This Man? (with Peter Pringle), 1975. *Recreations:* music, reading, armchair sport. *Address:* 15 Fairlawn Avenue, W4 5EF. *Club:* Plymouth Argyle Supporters' (London Branch).

COLE, Richard Raymond Buxton; His Honour Judge Richard Cole; a Circuit Judge, since 1984; *b* 11 June 1937; *s* of Raymond Buxton Cole, DSO, TD, DL, and Edith Mary Cole; *m* 1962, Sheila Joy Rumbold; one *s* one *d*. *Educ:* Dragon School, St Edward's, Oxford. Admitted as Solicitor 1960; Partner in Cole & Cole Solicitors, Oxford, 1962–84; Recorder, 1976–84. Mem., Parole Bd, 1981–83. Pres., Berks, Bucks and Oxon Law Soc., 1981–82. Mem. Governing Body, Dragon Sch., 1975–, Chm., 1986–. Chm., Burford Parish Council, 1976–79, first Town Mayor, 1979. *Recreations:* sport, gardening. *Clubs:* MCC; Frewen (Oxford).

COLE, Robert Templeman, CBE 1981; FEng 1982; DL; Chairman, Conder Group plc, 1979–87; *b* 14 Dec. 1918; *s* of Percival P. Cole and Amy Gladys Cole (*née* Templeman); *m* 1947, Elspeth Lawson; one *s* one *d*. *Educ:* Harrow; Cambridge Univ. (MA). FIStructE. Served RAF, 1940–46. Hampshire County Council, 1946–47; Founder Partner, Conder Engineering, 1947; Chairman: Conder Engineering Co. Ltd, 1950; Conder International Ltd, 1964. DL Hants 1988. Hon. DSc Southampton, 1980. *Recreations:* gliding, jogging, travel. *Address:* Dragons, 69 Chilbolton Avenue, Winchester, Hampshire SO22 5HJ. *T:* Winchester (0962) 854565.

COLE, Sir (Robert) William, Kt 1981; Director, Legal and General, Australia, since 1987; *b* 16 Sept. 1926; *s* of James Henry and Rita Sarah Cole; *m* 1956, Margaret Noleen Martin; one *s* one *d*. *Educ:* Univ. of Melbourne (BCom). Joined Australian Public Service, 1952; Res. Officer, Treasury, 1952–57; Technical Asst, IMF, Washington, 1957–59; various positions, Treasury, 1959–70; Dir, Bureau of Transport Econs, Dept of Shipping and Transport, 1970–72; First Asst Sec., Gen. Financial and Economic Policy Div., Treasury, 1972–76; Australian Statistician, 1976; Sec., Dept of Finance, 1977–78; Chm., Public Service Bd, 1978–83; Sec., Defence Dept, 1983–86. Hon. Treas., Winston Churchill Meml Trust. *Recreations:* reading, fishing, wine. *Address:* 1/106 Mugga Way, Red Hill, ACT 2603, Australia. *T:* Canberra 957089. *Club:* Commonwealth (Canberra).

COLE, Ven. Ronald Berkeley; Archdeacon Emeritus of Leicester; *b* 20 Oct. 1913; *s* of James William and Florence Caroline Cole; *m* 1943, Mabel Grace Chapman; one *s* one *d*. *Educ:* Bishop's Coll., Cheshunt. Registrar, London County Freehold and Leasehold Properties Ltd, 1934–40. Deacon, 1942; Priest, 1943; Curate, Braunstone, Leicester, 1942–48; Succentor, Leicester Cathedral, 1948–50; Vicar of St Philip, Leicester, 1950–73; Archdeacon of Loughborough, 1953–63, of Leicester, 1963–80; Residentiary Canon of Leicester Cathedral, 1977–80. Hon. Chaplain, 1949–53, Examining Chaplain, 1956–80, to Bishop of Leicester. RD of Repps, dio. Norwich, 1983–86. Hon. DLitt Geneva Theol.

Coll., 1972. *Recreations:* gardening, motoring. *Address:* Harland Rise, 70 Cromer Road, Sheringham, Norfolk NR26 8RT.

COLE, Sir William; see Cole, Sir R. W.

COLE, William Charles, LVO 1966; DMus; FSA, FRAM, FRCM; FRCO; The Master of the Music at the Queen's Chapel of the Savoy since 1954; Member Council, Royal College of Organists, since 1960 (Hon. Treasurer, 1964–85; President, 1970–72); Member, Central Music Library Council (formerly Committee), since 1964, Chairman, since 1973; b 9 Oct. 1909; s of Frederick George Cole and Maria (*née* Fry), Camberwell, London; m 1st, Elizabeth Brown Caw (d 1942); three d; 2nd, Winifred Grace Mitchell (d 1991); one s. *Educ:* St Olave's Grammar Sch.; RAM. Organist and Choirmaster, Dorking Parish Church, 1930; Music Master, Dorking County Sch., 1931; served War of 1939–45, in Air Ministry; Hon. Musical Dir, Toynbee Hall, 1947–58; Prof. of Harmony and Composition, and Lectr in History of Music, Royal Academy of Music, 1945–62; Royal Academy of Dancing: Lectr, 1948–62; Chm., Music Cttee, 1961–68; Mem., Exec. Council, 1965–68; Mem., Grand Council, 1976–88; Conductor: People's Palace Choral Soc., 1947–63; Leith Hill Musical Festival, 1954–77; Sec., Associated Bd of Royal Schools of Music, 1962–74; Hon. Sec., Royal Philharmonic Soc., 1969–80. President: Surrey County Music Assoc., 1958–76; The London Assoc. of Organists, 1963–66. Member: Governing Cttee, Royal Choral Soc., 1972– (Chm., Music Cttee, 1975–78); Exec. Cttee, Musicians' Benevolent Fund, 1972–. Mem. Education Cttee, Surrey CC, 1951–62. *Publications:* Rudiments of Music, 1951; chapter on Development of British Ballet Music, in The Ballet in Britain, 1962; The Form of Music, 1969; articles in various musical jls and in various learned jls on stained glass. *Recreation:* stained glass. *Address:* Barnacre, Wood Road, Hindhead, Surrey GU26 6PX. *T:* Hindhead (042873) 4917. *Club:* Garrick.

COLE, Maj.-Gen. William Scott, CB 1949; CBE 1946; b 29 March 1902; s of late William Scott Cole; m 1st, 1948, Kathleen Winifred Coleing (marr. diss. 1970); one d; 2nd, 1971, Alice Rose Pitts, *widow* of Dr G. T. Pitts. *Educ:* Victoria Coll., Jersey; RMA Woolwich. Commissioned into the Corps of Royal Engineers, 1921. Served War of 1939–45; Temp. Brig., 1943; Substantive Col, 1945; Subs. Brig., 1951; temp. Maj.-Gen., 1955; Subs. Maj.-Gen., 1956; retd 1958. *Club:* Army and Navy.

COLE-HAMILTON, Arthur Richard, BA; CA; FIB (Scot); Chief Executive, Clydesdale Bank PLC, since 1987; b 8 May 1935; s of John Cole-Hamilton, *qv*; m 1963, Prudence Ann; one s two d. *Educ:* Ardrossan Academy; Loretto School; Cambridge Univ. (BA). Commissioned Argyll and Sutherland Highlanders, 1960–62. Brechin Cole-Hamilton & Co. (Chartered Accountants), 1962–67; Clydesdale Bank, 1967–: Manager, Finance Corp. and Money Market, 1971; Asst Manager, Chief London Office, 1971; Supt of Branches, 1974; Head Office Manager, 1976; Asst Gen. Manager, 1978; Gen. Manager, 1979; Dep. Chief Gen. Manager, Feb. 1982; Chief Gen. Manager, July 1982; Dir, 1984–; Deputy Chairman: Cttee of Scottish Clearing Bankers, 1989–91 (Chm., 1985–87); Scottish Council for Develt and Industry, 1989–; Dir, Glasgow Chamber of Commerce, 1985–. Pres., Inst. of Bankers in Scotland, 1988–90. Mem. Council, Inst. of Chartered Accts of Scotland, 1981–85. Mem., Highland Brigade. Trustee, Nat. Galls of Scotland, 1986–; Mem. Exec. Cttee, Erskine Hosp., 1976–. *Recreation:* golf. *Address:* Clydesdale Bank PLC, 30 St Vincent Place, Glasgow G1 2HL. *T:* 041–248 7070. *Clubs:* Western (Glasgow); Royal and Ancient Golf, Prestwick Golf.

COLE-HAMILTON, John, CBE 1954; DL; b 15 Oct. 1899; s of late Col A. R. Cole-Hamilton; m 1930, Gladys Cowie; one s two d. *Educ:* Royal Academy, Irvine. Served European War, 1914–19, with RFC and RAF. Major, Home Guard, 1942. DL for County of Ayr, 1951. *Address:* Beltrim House, Kilwinning, Ayrshire.
See also A. R. Cole-Hamilton.

COLEBROOK, Philip Victor Charles, CEng, MIChemE; retired 1984; Managing Director, Imperial Continental Gas Association, 1973–84 (Director, 1971; Director, CompAir Ltd, 1980–84); Director: Calor Group Ltd, 1969–84; Century Power & Light Ltd, 1980–84; Contibel SA (Belgium), 1978–84; b 8 March 1924; s of Frederick Charles Colebrook and Florence Margaret (*née* Cooper); m 1946, Dorothy Ursula Kemp; one s three d. *Educ:* Andover Grammar Sch.; Guildford Technical Coll.; Battersea Polytechnic, London. Served War of 1939–45, RNVR. Joined Pfizer as Works and Production Manager, 1952; Dir, 1956, Man. Dir, 1958–69, Pfizer Ltd; Chm. and Man. Dir, Pfizer Gp, 1961–69; Vice-Pres., Pfizer Internat., 1967–69; Man. Dir, Calor Gas Holding Co., 1969–80. Member: NHS Affairs Cttee, Assoc. of the British Pharmaceutical Industry, 1963–67; CBI Cttee on State Intervention in Private Business, 1975–78. Trustee and Mem. of Steering Cttee, Univ. of Kent at Canterbury, 1964–65. *Publication:* Going International, 1972. *Recreations:* sailing, ski-ing, golf. *Club:* Royal Cornwall Yacht.

COLEBY, Anthony Laurie; Executive Director, Bank of England, since 1990; b 27 April 1935; s of Dr Leslie James Moger Coleby and Laurie Coleby (*née* Shuttleworth); m 1966, Rosemary Melian Elisabeth, d of Sir Peter Garran, KCMG; one s two d. *Educ:* Winchester; Corpus Christi, Cambridge (BAEcon, MA). Bank of England: joined, 1961; Assistant Chief, Overseas Dept, 1969; Adviser, Overseas Dept, 1972; Dep. Chief Cashier, 1973; Asst Dir, 1980–86; Chief Monetary Advr to the Governor, 1986–90. Personal Asst to Managing Director, International Monetary Fund, 1964–67. *Recreations:* choral singing, railways and transport. *Address:* Bank of England, EC2R 8AH. *T:* 071–601 4444. *Club:* Overseas Bankers'.

COLECLOUGH, Peter Cecil; Chairman, Howard Machinery Ltd, 1969–82 (Director, 1950–82); Director: National Westminster Bank (Chairman SE Region), 1976–86; NCR Ltd, 1971–87; b 5 March 1917; s of late Thomas James Coleclough and of Hilda Emma (*née* Ingram); m 1944, Pamela Beresford (*née* Rhodes); one s (and one s decd). *Educ:* Bradfield. Served War, Cheshire Yeomanry, 1939; commnd into Roy. Warwickshire Regt, 1940; served until 1946. Mem., FBI/CBI Council, 1962–72; Chm., E Region, CBI, 1971–72; Leader, OECD/BIAC Investment Gp to Ceylon, 1968 and 1969; Chm., Meat and Livestock Commn, 1971–74; Pres., Agricl Engrs Assoc., 1971–72; Pres., Royal Warrant Holders Assoc., 1971–72. Chm., Appeals and Management Cttee, S Essex Medical Educn and Research Trust, 1969–75. CBIM 1976; FRSA 1977. *Recreation:* fishing. *Address:* Longlands Hall, Stonham Aspal, Stowmarket, Suffolk IP14 6AR. *T:* Stowmarket (0449) 711242. *Club:* Naval and Military.

COLEGATE, Isabel Diana, (Mrs Michael Briggs); novelist; b 10 Sept. 1931; d of Sir Arthur Colegate, sometime MP, and Winifred Mary, d of Sir William Worsley, 3rd Bt; m 1953, Michael Briggs; two s one d. *Educ:* Runton Hill Sch., Norfolk. Worked as literary agent at Anthony Blond (London) Ltd, 1952–57. FRSL 1981. Hon. MA Bath, 1988. *Publications:* The Blackmailer, 1958; A Man of Power, 1960; The Great Occasion, 1962 (re-issued as Three Novels, 1983); Statues in a Garden, 1964; Orlando King, 1968; Orlando at the Brazen Threshold, 1971; Agatha, 1973 (re-issued as The Orlando Trilogy, 1984); News from the City of the Sun, 1979; The Shooting Party, 1980 (W. H. Smith Literary Award, 1980; filmed, 1985); A Glimpse of Sion's Glory, 1985; Deceits of Time, 1988; The Summer of the Royal Visit, 1991. *Recreation:* walking the dog. *Address:* Midford Castle, Bath BA2 7BU.

COLEGATE, Raymond, CBE 1982; FCIT 1983; air transport consultant; Member, Civil Aviation Authority, 1974–90, retired (Group Director, Economic Services, later Economic Regulation, 1977–89); b 31 Aug. 1927; s of Ernest William and Violet Colegate; m 1961, Sally Healy; one s one d. *Educ:* County Sch. for Boys, Gravesend; LSE. BA London (Hons History). Joined BoT, 1949; seconded to Central Statistical Office, 1952–53; Asst Private Sec. to President, 1955–56; seconded to Treasury, 1957–59; seconded to EFTA Secretariat, Geneva and Brussels, 1960–64; CRE Dept, BoT, 1964–67; Aviation Dept, BoT/DTI, 1967–72; Head, Economic Policy and Licensing Div., CAA, 1972–75; Head, Economic Dept, CAA, 1975–77. Vice-Pres., CIT, 1988–91. *Publications:* articles. *Recreations:* music, travel, thinking. *Address:* 40 Lebanon Park, Twickenham TW1 3DG. *T:* 081–892 0084.

COLEMAN, Prof. Alice Mary; Professor of Geography, King's College, London, since 1987; b 8 June 1923; d of Bertie Coleman and Elizabeth Mary (*née* White). *Educ:* Clarendon House Sch.; Furzedown Training Coll. (Cert. of Educn); Birkbeck Coll., Univ. of London (BA Hons 1st Cl.); King's Coll., Univ. of London (MA with Mark of Distinction). FKC 1980. Geography Teacher, Northfleet Central Sch. for Girls, 1943–48; Geography Dept, King's Coll., London: Asst Lectr, 1948; Lectr, 1951; Sen. Lectr, 1963; Reader, 1965. Vis. Prof. for Distinguished Women Social Scientists, Univ. of Western Ontario, 1976; BC/Mombusho Prof. of Geog., Hokkaido Univ. of Educn at Asahikawa, 1985. Initiated and directed Second Land Utilisation Survey of Britain, 1960–; Dir, Design Improvement Controlled Experiment, 1988–. Gill Meml Award, RGS, 1963; The Times-Veuve Clicquot Award, 1974; Busk Award, RGS, 1987. *Publications:* The Planning Challenge of the Ottawa Area, 1969; Utopia on Trial, 1985; 120 land-use maps in eleven colours at the scale of 1:25,000; over 200 academic papers. *Recreations:* reading, graphology. *Address:* King's College, Strand, WC2R 2LS. *T:* 071–836 5454, ext. 2610.

COLEMAN, Arthur Percy; Deputy Director and Secretary to the Board of Trustees, British Museum (Natural History), 1976–82 (Museum Secretary, 1965–76); b 8 Feb. 1922; s of late Percy Coleman and Gladys May Coleman (*née* Fisher); m 1948, Peggy (*née* Coombs); two d. *Educ:* Wanstead Co. High Sch.; Bristol Univ. War Service in 1st King George V Own Gurkha Rifles, 1943–47; Min. of Public Building and Works, 1948–61; HM Treasury, 1961–64. *Recreations:* wild life, music. *Address:* Candleford, Hurst, Beaminster, Dorset DT8 3ES. *T:* Beaminster (0308) 862155.

COLEMAN, Bernard, CMG 1986; HM Diplomatic Service, retired; Ambassador to Paraguay, 1984–86; b 3 Sept. 1928; s of William Coleman and Ettie Coleman; m 1950, Sonia Dinah (*née* Walters); two d. *Educ:* Alsop High Sch., Liverpool. HM Forces (RAEC), 1946–48. Entered Foreign (later Diplomatic) Service, 1950; FO, 1950–53; Lima, 1953–56; Detroit, 1956–59; Second Secretary (Information): Montevideo, 1959–62; Caracas, 1962–64; First Sec. (Inf.), Caracas, 1964–66; FCO, 1967–69; First Sec. (Inf.), Ottawa, 1969–73; FCO, 1973–74; seconded to DTI, 1974–75; Consul-Gen., Bilbao, 1976–78; First Sec. (Commercial), Dublin, 1979–80; High Commissioner, Tonga, 1980–83. *Recreations:* golf, bowls, bridge, reading, walking, travel.

COLEMAN, Prof. Donald Cuthbert, LittD; FBA 1972; Professor of Economic History, Cambridge University, 1971–81, now Emeritus; Fellow of Pembroke College, Cambridge; b 21 Jan. 1920; s of Hugh Augustus Coleman and Marian Stella Agnes Cuthbert; m 1954, Jessie Ann Matilda Child (*née* Stevens). *Educ:* Haberdashers' Aske's, Hampstead (now Elstree); London Sch. of Economics, Univ. of London. Worked in London, in insurance, 1937–39; admitted LSE, 1939. Served War, in Army, 1940–46: commissioned Royal Warwickshire Regt, 1941; transf. RA, 1942; active service in N Africa, Italy and Greece. Returned to LSE, 1946; BSc(Econ), 1st Cl. Hons. 1949; Leverhulme Research Studentship, 1949–51; PhD 1951. Lectr in Industrial History, LSE, 1951–58; Reader in Economic History, 1958–69; Prof. of Economic History, 1969–71; Hon. Fellow, LSE, 1984. Visiting Associate Prof. of Economics, Yale Univ., 1957–58. Lectures: Neale, UCL, 1979; Creighton, Univ. of London, 1989. Governor, Pasold Research Fund, 1977–, Chm. of Governors, 1986–. English Editor, Scandinavian Economic History Review, 1952–61; Editor, Economic History Review, 1967–72. FRHistS. *Publications:* The British Paper Industry, 1495–1860, 1958; Sir John Banks: Baronet and Businessman, 1963; Courtaulds: an economic and social history, vols 1 & 2, 1969, vol. 3, 1980; What Has Happened to Economic History? (Inaug. Lect.), 1972; Industry in Tudor and Stuart England, 1975; The Economy of England 1450–1750, 1977; (ed with A. H. John) Trade, Government and Economy in Pre-Industrial England, 1977; (ed with P. Mathias) Enterprise and History, 1984; History and the Economic Past, 1987; numerous articles in: Economic History Review, Economica, Historical Jl, etc. *Recreations:* music, gardening, reading. *Address:* Over Hall, Cavendish, Sudbury, Suffolk CO10 8BP. *T:* Glemsford (0787) 280325.

COLEMAN, Isobel Mary; see Plumpstead, I. M.

COLEMAN, John Ennis, CB 1990; Legal Adviser, Department of Education and Science, 1983–90, retired; b 12 Nov. 1930; o s of late Donald Stafford Coleman and Dorothy Jean Balieff (*née* Ennis); m 1958, Doreen Gwendoline Hellinger; one s one d. *Educ:* Dean Close Sch., Cheltenham; Dulwich Coll.; Worcester Coll., Oxford (MA). Solicitor (Hons), 1957. Legal Asst, Treasury Solicitor's Dept, 1958; Senior Legal Asst, 1964; Asst Solicitor, 1971; Under Sec. (Legal), Depts of Industry and Trade, 1980–83.

COLEMAN, Rt. Rev. Peter Everard; see Crediton, Bishop Suffragan of.

COLEMAN, Prof. Robert George Gilbert; Professor of Comparative Philology, University of Cambridge, since 1985; Fellow of Emmanuel College, Cambridge, since 1960; b 2 Oct. 1929; s of George Gilbert Coleman and Rosina Emily (*née* Warner); m 1958, Dorothy Gabe (separated 1990); one s. *Educ:* Rongotai and Wellington Colls, NZ; Victoria Univ. of Wellington (MA 1951); Emmanuel Coll., Cambridge (BA 1954; Burney Prize (shared), 1955; MA 1980). Lecturer: Dept of Humanity, Aberdeen Univ., 1955–60; Faculty of Classics, Cambridge Univ., 1960–85; Tutor, 1963–71, Librarian, 1980–85, Emmanuel Coll., Cambridge. *Publications:* (ed, with commentary) Vergil's Eclogues, 1977; essays and papers in classical and philological jls. *Recreations:* music, conversation, exploring strange towns. *Address:* 7 Linton Road, Balsham, Cambridge CB1 6HA. *T:* Cambridge (0223) 893086.

COLEMAN, Robert John; Director, Approximation of Laws, Freedom of Establishment, and Freedom to Provide Services, European Commission, since 1990; b 8 Sept. 1943; s of Frederick and Kathleen Coleman; m 1966, Malinda Tigay Cutler; two d. *Educ:* Univ. of Oxford (MA); Univ. of Chicago (JD). Called to the Bar, Inner Temple, 1969. Lectr in Law, Univ. of Birmingham, 1967–70; Barrister at Law, 1970–73; European Commission: Administrator, subseq. principal administrator, 1974–82; Dep. Head of Div., safeguard measures and removal of non-tariff barriers, 1983; Head of Div., Intellectual Property and Unfair Competition, 1984–87; Dir, Public Procurement, 1987–90. *Publications:* contribs and articles on legal and policy issues, concerning corporate accounting, employee participation and intellectual property. *Recreations:* cycling, music. *Address:* 114 rue des Deux Tours, 1030 Brussels, Belgium. *T:* Brussels 218 38 65.

COLEMAN, Ronald Frederick, CB 1991; DSc; CChem, FRSC; Chief Engineer and Scientist, Department of Trade and Industry, 1987–March 1992; *b* 10 Nov. 1931; *s* of late Frederick George Coleman and of Dorothy Alice Coleman (*née* Smith); *m* 1954, Maureen Mary Salt; one *s* one *d*. *Educ:* King Edward VI Sch., Birmingham; College of Technology, Birmingham (BSc, DSc). Chance Brothers Glassworks, Smethwick, 1949–54; UKAEA: Aldermaston, 1954–71; Harwell, 1972; Laboratory of the Government Chemist, 1973–77; National Physical Laboratory, 1977–81; Government Chemist, 1981–87. Visiting Professor: Kingston Polytechnic, 1981–; Royal Holloway and Bedford New Coll., 1985–. Pres., British Acad. of Forensic Sciences, 1982–83. Member: SERC, 1987–March 1992; AFRC, 1987–March 1992. Chm., Bd of Govs, Kingston Polytechnic, 1991–. DUniv Surrey, 1987; Hon. DSc Poly. of Central London, 1989. *Publications:* various papers on analytical chemistry, nuclear chemistry and forensic science. *Recreations:* music, golf, gardening. *Address:* 6 Hurstwood, Ascot, Berks SL5 9SP. *T:* Ascot (0344) 22336.

COLEMAN, Terry, (Terence Francis Frank); reporter and author; Associate Editor, The Independent, since 1989; *b* 13 Feb. 1931; *s* of J. and D. I. B. Coleman; *m* 1st, 1954, Lesley Fox-Strangeways Vane (marr. diss.); two *d*; 2nd, 1981, Vivien Rosemary Lumsdaine Wallace; one *s* one *d*. *Educ:* 14 schs. LLB London. Formerly: Reporter, Poole Herald; Editor, Savoir Faire; Sub-editor, Sunday Mercury, and Birmingham Post; Reporter and then Arts Corresp., The Guardian, 1961–70, Chief Feature Writer, 1970–74; Special Writer with Daily Mail, 1974–76; The Guardian: Chief Feature Writer, 1976–79, writing mainly political interviews, inc. last seven British Prime Ministers; NY Correspondent, 1981; special corresp., 1982–89. Feature Writer of the Year, British Press Awards, 1982; Journalist of the Year, Granada Awards, 1987. *Publications:* The Railway Navvies, 1965 (Yorkshire Post prize for best first book of year); A Girl for the Afternoons, 1965; (with Lois Deacon) Providence and Mr Hardy, 1966; The Only True History: collected journalism, 1969; Passage to America, 1972; (ed) An Indiscretion in the Life of an Heiress (Hardy's first novel), 1976; The Liners, 1976; The Scented Brawl: collected journalism, 1978; Southern Cross, 1979; Thanksgiving, 1981; Movers and Shakers: collected interviews, 1987; Thatcher's Britain, 1987. *Recreations:* cricket, opera, circumnavigation. *Address:* c/o A. D. Peters, The Chambers, Chelsea Harbour, SW10 0XF. *Club:* MCC.

COLEMAN, Rt. Rev. Prof. William Robert, DD; former Professor of Humanities, York University, Toronto; *b* Ulverton, Quebec, 16 Aug. 1917; *s* of Rev. Stanley Harold Coleman and Mary Ann Coleman (*née* Armstrong); *m* 1947, Mary Elizabeth Charmes, *er d* of Thomas Summers and Marion Wilson; one *s* two *d*. *Educ:* St Mary's Collegiate Inst.; Brantford Collegiate Inst.; University Coll. and Wycliffe Coll. (BD); Univ. of Toronto (MA); Union Theological Seminary, New York (STM); Univs of Cambridge and Edinburgh. Deacon, 1942; Priest, 1943; Curate, Church of the Epiphany, Sudbury, Ont., 1942–43; Priest-in-charge, 1943–45; post-graduate study, 1945–47; Prof. of Religious Philosophy and Ethics, Wycliffe Coll., 1947–50; Dean of Divinity and Harold Prof., Bishop's Coll., Lennoxville, Quebec, 1950–52; Principal, Huron Coll., London, Ont., 1952–61; Bishop of Kootenay, 1961–65. FRSA, London. DD Wycliffe Coll., 1951. DD (Hon.) Huron Coll., 1961; DD (Hon.) Trinity Coll., Toronto, 1962. *Publications:* contributed to: In Such an Age (ed W. C. Lockhart), 1951; The Church in the Sixties (ed. P. Jefferson), 1962.

COLERAINE, 2nd Baron *cr* 1954, of Haltemprice; **James Martin Bonar Law;** *b* 8 Aug. 1931; *s* of 1st Baron Coleraine, PC, *y s* of Rt Hon. Andrew Bonar Law, and Mary Virginia (*d* 1978), *d* of A. F. Nellis, Rochester, NY; *S* father, 1980; *m* 1st, 1958, Emma Elizabeth Richards (marr. diss.); two *d*; 2nd, 1966, (Anne) Patricia, *yr d* of Major-Gen. R. H. Farrant, CB; one *s* two *d*. *Educ:* Eton; Trinity College, Oxford. *Heir: s* Hon. James Peter Bonar Law, *b* 23 Feb. 1975. *Address:* 5 Kensington Park Gardens, W11 3HB.

See also Baron Ironside.

COLERIDGE, family name of **Baron Coleridge.**

COLERIDGE, 5th Baron *cr* 1873, of Ottery St Mary; **William Duke Coleridge;** *b* 18 June 1937; *s* of 4th Baron Coleridge, KBE, and Cecilia Rosamund (*d* 1991), *d* of Adm. Sir William Wordsworth Fisher, GCB, GCVO; *S* father, 1984; *m* 1st, 1962, Everild Tania (marr. diss. 1977), *d* of Lt-Col Beauchamp Hambrough, OBE; one *s* two *d*; 2nd, 1977, Pamela, *d* of G. W. Baker, *qv*; two *d*. *Educ:* Eton; RMA Sandhurst. Commissioned into Coldstream Guards, 1958; served King's African Rifles, 1962–64; commanded Guards Parachute Company, 1970–72. *Heir:* Hon. James Duke Coleridge, *b* 5 June 1967. *Address:* The Chanters House, Ottery St Mary, Devon EX11 1DQ. *T:* Ottery St Mary (0404) 812417.

COLERIDGE, David Ean; Chairman, Sturge Holdings PLC, since 1978; Chairman of Lloyd's, 1991 (Deputy Chairman, 1985, 1988, 1989); *b* 7 June 1932; *s* of Guy Cecil Richard Coleridge, MC and Katherine Cicely Stewart Smith; *m* 1955, Susan Senior; three *s*. *Educ:* Eton. Glanvill Enthoven, 1950–57; R. W. Sturge & Co., 1957–: Dir, 1966–; Chm., A. L. Sturge (Holdings) Ltd (now Sturge Holdings PLC), 1978–. Chm., Oxford Agency Hldgs Ltd, 1987–90; Director: R. A. Edwards (Holdings) Ltd, 1985–90; Wise Speke Hldgs Ltd, 1987–. Member: Cttee of Lloyd's Underwriting Agents Assoc., 1974–82 (Chm., 1981–82); Council and Cttee of Lloyd's, 1983–86, 1988–. *Recreations:* golf, racing, gardening, family. *Address:* Spring Pond, Wispers, near Midhurst, W Sussex. *T:* Midhurst (073081) 3277; 37 Egerton Terrace, SW3. *T:* 071–581 1756. *Clubs:* City of London, Mark's.

See also N. D. Coleridge.

COLERIDGE, Geraldine Margaret, (Gill), (Mrs D. R. Leeming); Partner, Rogers Coleridge and White, Literary Agency, since 1988; *b* 26 May 1948; *d* of Antony Duke Coleridge and June Marion Caswell; *m* 1974, David Roger Leeming; two *s*. *Educ:* Queen Anne's School, Caversham; Marlborough Secretarial College, Oxford. BPC Partworks, Sidgwick & Jackson, Bedford Square Book Bang, to 1971; Publicity Manager, Chatto & Windus, 1971–72; Dir and Literary Agent, Anthony Sheil Associates, 1973–88. Pres., Assoc. of Authors' Agents, 1988–91. *Recreations:* reading, music. *Address:* 113 Calabria Road, N5 1HS. *T:* 071–226 5875.

COLERIDGE, Lady (Marguerite) Georgina; *b* 19 March 1916; *d* of 11th Marquess of Tweeddale; *m* 1941, Arthur Coleridge (*d* 1988), *yr s* of John Duke Coleridge; one *d*. *Educ:* home, abroad as a child. Freelance writer, Harpers Bazaar, etc., 1936–; joined National Magazine Co.: Circulation Dept, 1937; Advertisement Dept., 1938; joined Country Life, 1945; Editor of Homes and Gardens, 1949–63; Chm., Inst. of Journalists (London District), 1954, Fellow 1970; Chm., Women's Press Club, 1959 (Pres., 1965–67). Dir, Country Life Ltd, 1962–74; Dir, George Newnes Ltd, 1963–69; Publisher: Homes and Gardens; Woman's Journal, 1969–71; Ideal Home, 1970–71; Dir, Special Projects, IPC Women's Magazines, 1971–74; Consultant: IPC Women's Magazines, 1974–82; Public Relations Counsel Ltd, 1974–85 (Dir, 1978–85). Mem., Internat. Assoc. of Women and Home Page Journalists, 1968–74; Associate, Women in Public Relations, 1972–; Associate Mem., Ladies Jockeys Assoc. of GB, 1973–; Founder Mem., Media Soc. Ltd (Inst. of Journalists Foundn), 1973–76; Member: Information Cttee, Brit. Nutrition Foundn, 1975–79; Information Cttee, RCP, 1977–81; Vice-Pres., Greater London Fund for the Blind, 1981–; Pres., Friends of Moorfields, 1981–. Freeman, Worshipful Co. of Stationers and Newspapermakers, 1973. *Publications:* Grand Smashional Pointers (book of cartoons), 1934; I Know What I Like (clichés), 1959; That's Racing, 1978; many features for various jls. *Recreations:* racing, writing, cooking; nothing highbrow. *Address:* 33 Peel Street, W8 7PA. *T:* 071–727 7732.

COLERIDGE, Nicholas David; Editorial Director, Condé Nast Publications, since 1989; *b* 4 March 1957; *s* of David Ean Coleridge, *qv*; *m* 1989, Georgia Metcalfe; one *s*. *Educ:* Eton; Trinity Coll., Cambridge. Associate Editor, Tatler, 1979–81; Columnist, Evening Standard, 1981–84; Features Editor, Harpers and Queen, 1985–86, Editor, 1986–89. Young Journalist of the Year, British Press Awards, 1983. *Publications:* Tunnel Vision, collected journalism, 1982; Around the World in 78 Days, 1984; Shooting Stars, 1984; The Fashion Conspiracy, 1988; How I Met My Wife and other stories, 1991. *Address:* 24 Chepstow Crescent, W11. *T:* 071–221 4293. *Club:* Harry's Bar.

COLES, Sir (Arthur) John, KCMG 1989 (CMG 1984); HM Diplomatic Service; Deputy Under Secretary of State, Foreign and Commonwealth Office, since 1991; *b* 13 Nov. 1937; *s* of Arthur Strixton Coles and Doris Gwendoline Coles; *m* 1965, Anne Mary Sutherland Graham; two *s* one *d*. *Educ:* Magdalen Coll. Sch., Brackley; Magdalen Coll., Oxford (BA 1960). Served HM Forces, 1955–57. Joined HM Diplomatic Service, 1960; Middle Eastern Centre for Arabic Studies, Lebanon, 1960–62; Third Sec., Khartoum, 1962–64; FO (later FCO), 1964–68; Asst Political Agent, Trucial States (Dubai), 1968–71; FCO, 1971–75; Head of Chancery, Cairo, 1975–77; Counsellor (Developing Countries), UK Perm. Mission to EEC, 1977–80; Head of S Asian Dept, FCO, 1980–81; Private Sec. to Prime Minister, 1981–84; Ambassador to Jordan, 1984–88; High Commissioner to Australia, 1988–91. *Recreations:* walking, cricket, bird-watching, reading, music. *Address:* c/o Foreign and Commonwealth Office, King Charles Street, SW1. *Club:* United Oxford & Cambridge University.

COLES, Bruce; *see* Coles, N. B. C.

COLES, Prof. Bryan Randell, DPhil; FRS 1991; FInstP; Pro-Rector, since 1986 and Professor of Solid State Physics, since 1966, Imperial College, University of London; Dean of the Royal College of Science, 1984–86; *b* 9 June 1926; *s* of Charles Frederick Coles and Olive Irene Coles; *m* 1955, Merivan Robinson; two *s*. *Educ:* Canton High Sch., Cardiff; Univ. of Wales, Cardiff (BSc); Jesus Coll., Univ. of Oxford (DPhil). FInstP 1972. Lectr in Metal Physics, Imperial Coll., London, 1950; Res. Fellow, Carnegie Inst. of Technol., Pittsburgh, 1954–56. Vis. Prof., Univ. of Calif, San Diego, 1962 and 1969; Hill Vis. Prof., Univ. of Minnesota, 1983. Vice-Pres., Inst. of Physics, 1968–72; Mem. Physics Cttee, SRC, 1972–76 (Chm. 1973–76); Chm., Neutron Beam Cttee, SERC, 1985–88. Chm. Bd of Dirs, Taylor & Francis Ltd (Scientific Publishers), 1976–. *Publications:* Electronic Structures of Solids (with A. D. Caplin), 1976; papers on structure, electrical properties, superconductivity and magnetic properties of metals and alloys in Philosoph. Magazine, Advances in Physics, Jl of Physics. *Recreations:* music, natural history, theatre. *Address:* 61 Courtfield Gardens, SW5 0NQ. *T:* 071–373 3539.

COLES, Rt. Rev. David John; *see* Christchurch, Bishop of.

COLES, Gerald James Kay; QC 1976; **His Honour Judge Gerald Coles;** a Circuit Judge, since 1985; *b* 6 May 1933; *o s* of James William Coles and Jane Elizabeth Coles; *m* 1958, Kathleen Yolande, *e d* of Alfred John Hobson, FRCS, and Kathleen Elizabeth Hobson; three *s*. *Educ:* Coatham Sch., Redcar; Brasenose Coll., Oxford; Harvard Law Sch., Harvard Univ. Meritorious Award, Hastings Schol., Queen's Coll., Oxford, 1949; Akroyd Open Schol. 1950; BA 1954, BCL 1955, Oxon; Westengard Schol., Harvard Law Sch., 1955; LLM 1956. Called to Bar, Middle Temple, 1957; practised at Bar, London and NE Circuit, 1957–85; Prosecuting Counsel to Inland Revenue, 1971–76; a Recorder, 1972–85. *Recreations:* music, theatre, photography. *Address:* Redwood, Dean Lane, Hawksworth, Guiseley, Leeds, Yorks LS20 8NY. *Club:* Yorkshire (York).

COLES, Sir John; *see* Coles, Sir A. J.

COLES, John Morton, ScD, PhD; FBA 1978; Professor of European Prehistory, University of Cambridge, 1980–86; Fellow of Fitzwilliam College, since 1963, Honorary Fellow, 1987; *b* 25 March 1930; *s* of Edward John Langdon Coles and Alice Margaret (*née* Brown); *m* 1985, Bryony Jean Orme; two *s* two *d* of previous marr. *Educ:* Woodstock, Ontario; Univ. of Toronto (BA); Univ. of Cambridge (MA, ScD); Univ. of Edinburgh (PhD). Research Fellow, Univ. of Edinburgh, 1959–60; Asst Lectr, 1960–65, Lectr, 1965–76, Reader, 1976–80, Univ. of Cambridge. President, Prehistoric Soc., 1978–82. FSA 1963, Vice-Pres., 1982–86. *Publications:* The Archaeology of Early Man (with E. Higgs), 1969; Field Archaeology in Britain, 1972; Archaeology by Experiment, 1973; (with A. Harding) The Bronze Age in Europe, 1979; Experimental Archaeology, 1979; (with B. Orme) Prehistory of the Somerset Levels, 1980; The Archaeology of Wetlands, 1984; (with B. J. Coles) Sweet Track to Glastonbury: the Somerset Levels in prehistory, 1986; (ed with A. Lawson) European Wetlands in Prehistory, 1987; Meare Village East, 1987; (with B. J. Coles) People of the Wetlands, 1989; Images of the Past, 1990; contrib. Proc. Prehist. Soc., Antiquaries Jl, Antiquity, Somerset Levels Papers, etc. *Recreations:* music, wetlands, woodlands. *Address:* Fursdon Mill Cottage, Thorverton, Devon EX5 5JS. *T:* Exeter (0392) 860125.

COLES, Kenneth George, BE; FIE(Aust); CEng, FIMechE, FAIM; Chairman, Conveyor Co. of Australia Pty Ltd, 1957–91; *b* Melbourne, 30 June 1926; *s* of Sir Kenneth Coles; *m* 1st, 1950, Thalia Helen (marr. diss. 1980); one *s* two *d*; 2nd, 1985, Rowena Danziger. *Educ:* The King's Sch., Parramatta, NSW; Sydney Univ. (BE 1948). FIE(Aust) 1986; FIMechE 1969; FAIM 1959. Gained engrg experience in appliance manufacturing and automotive industries Nuffield Aust. Pty Ltd, Gen. Motors Holdens Pty Ltd and Frigidaire, before commencing own business manufacturing conveyors, 1955; Chm & Man. Dir, K. G. Coles & Co. Pty Ltd, 1955–76, Chm. 1976–; Chm. & Man. Dir, K. G. C. Magnetic Tape Pty Ltd, 1973–80. Director: Australian Oil & Gas Corp. Ltd, 1969–89 (Dep. Chm., 1984–89); A. O. G. Minerals Ltd, 1969–87 (Dep. Chm., 1984–87); Coles Myer Ltd (formerly G. J. Coles & Coy Ltd), 1976–; Electrical Equipment Ltd, 1976–84; Permanent Trustee Co. Ltd, 1978– (Vice Chm., 1990–); Centre for Industrial Technol. Ltd, 1985–87; Chatham Investment Co. Ltd, 1987–; NRMA Insurance Ltd, 1989–90; Stockland Trust Group, 1990–; Chairman: Innovation Council of NSW Ltd, 1984–89 (Dir, 1982–89); Australian Corporate Training Centre Pty Ltd, 1991–. Gen. Councillor, NSW Br., Metal Trades Industries Assoc. of Australia, 1976–; Member: Internat. Solar Energy Soc., 1957–; Science & Industry Forum, Australian Academy of Science, 1983–; Mem. and Employers' Rep., NSW Bd of Secondary Educn, 1987–90. Mem. Council, Nat. Roads and Motorists Assoc., NSW, 1986–90. Councillor and Mem. Bd of Governors, Ascham Sch., 1972–82; Employers' Rep., NSW Secondary Schs Bd, 1979–83. Fellow, Senate, Sydney Univ., 1983–. *Address:* 2/24 Rosemont Avenue, Woollahra, NSW 2025, Australia. *T:* 328.6084. *Clubs:* Union (Sydney), Sydney Rotary; Royal Sydney Golf; RACV (Melbourne).

COLES, Dame Mabel Irene, DBE 1971 (CBE 1965); President: Royal Women's Hospital, Melbourne, 1968–72; Australian Women's Liberal Club, since 1965; Director, Asthma

Foundation of Victoria, 1965; *d* of late E. Johnston; *m* 1927, Sir Edgar Coles (*d* 1981); one *s* two *d*. Associated with Royal Women's Hosp. for 30 years; Chairman: Ladies Cttee for (two) $1,000,000 appeals; (two) Door Knock Appeals; Asthma Ladies' Appeal Cttee; Patroness: Family Planning Assoc. of Vic.; Rheumatism and Arthritis Assoc. of Vic.; Frankston Musical Soc. Life Mem., Australian Nat. Meml Theatre Ltd. Trustee, Mayfield Centre. *Recreations:* dogs, horses, walking. *Address:* Hendra, Williams Road, Mount Eliza, Vic. 3930, Australia. *Clubs:* Alexandra, Peninsula Country (Melbourne).

COLES, Norman, CB 1971; *b* 29 Dec. 1914; *s* of Fred and Emily Coles; *m* 1947, Una Valerie Tarrant; five *s*. *Educ:* Hanson High Sch., Bradford; Royal College of Science; City and Guilds Coll. Head, Armament Dept, RAE, 1959; Dir Gen. Equipment Research and Development, Min. of Aviation, 1962; Dep. Controller: of Aircraft (RAF), Min. of Technology, 1966–68; of Guided Weapons, Min. of Technology, 1968–69; Dep. Chief Adviser (Research and Studies), MoD, 1969–71; Dep. Controller, Establishments and Research, MoD, 1971–75. *Recreations:* carpentry, crossword puzzles. *Address:* Castle Gate, 27 Castle Hill, Banwell, Weston-super-Mare, Avon. *T:* Banwell (0934) 822019.

COLES, (Norman) Bruce (Cameron); QC 1984; a Recorder, since 1986; *b* 28 Feb. 1937; *s* of Sir Norman Coles and of Dorothy Verna (*née* Deague); *m* 1961, Sally Fenella Freeman; one *s* three *d*. *Educ:* Melbourne Grammar Sch.; Univ. of Melbourne (LLB); Magdalen Coll., Oxford Univ. (BCL). 2nd Lieut, 6th Bn Royal Melbourne Regt, 1956–59. Associate to Sir Owen Dixon, Chief Justice of High Court of Australia, 1959–60; called to English Bar, Middle Temple, 1963, Bencher, 1991; admitted to Bar of Supreme Court of Victoria, 1964. Assistant Recorder, 1982. Mem. Council, Oxfam, 1985–. *Recreations:* mountaineering, cycling, theatre, music. *Address:* Fountain Court, Temple, EC4Y 9DH. *T:* 071–583 3335. *Clubs:* Gentian Mountaineering (Glos); Cyclist Touring (Surrey).

COLESHILL, Archdeacon of; *see* Cooper, Ven. J. L.

COLFOX, Sir (William) John, 2nd Bt *cr* 1939; JP; DL; *b* 25 April 1924; *yr* and *o* surv. *s* of Sir (William) Philip Colfox, 1st Bt, MC, and Mary (Frances) Lady Colfox (*d* 1973); *S* father, 1966; *m* 1962, Frederica Loveday, *d* of Adm. Sir Victor Crutchley, VC, KCB, DSC; two *s* three *d*. *Educ:* Eton. Served in RNVR, 1942–46, leaving as Lieut. Qualified Land Agent, 1950. Chm., Land Settlement Assoc., 1980–81. Vice-Chm., TSW, 1981–. JP Dorset, 1962, High Sheriff of Dorset, 1969, DL Dorset, 1977. *Heir: s* Philip John Colfox, *b* 27 Dec. 1962. *Address:* Symondsbury House, Bridport, Dorset. *T:* Bridport (0308) 22956.

COLGAN, Samuel Hezlett; His Honour Judge Colgan; a Circuit Judge, since 1990; *b* 10 June 1945; *s* of late Henry George Colgan and of Jane Swan Hezlett. *Educ:* Foyle College, Londonderry; Trinity College Dublin (MA, LLB). Called to the Bar, Middle Temple, 1969; a Recorder, SE Circuit, 1987. *Recreations:* travelling, the arts, reading, tennis. *Address:* Lord Chancellor's Department, SE Circuit, New Cavendish House, 18 Maltravers Street, WC2R 3EU.

COLGRAIN, 3rd Baron *cr* 1946, of Everlands; **David Colin Campbell;** *b* 24 April 1920; *s* of 2nd Baron Colgrain, MC, and of Margaret Emily (*d* 1989), *d* of late P. W. Carver; *S* father, 1973; *m* 1st, 1945, Veronica Margaret (marr. diss. 1964), *d* of late Lt-Col William Leckie Webster, RAMC; one *s* one *d*; 2nd, 1973, Mrs Sheila M. Hudson. *Educ:* Eton; Trinity Coll., Cambridge. Served War of 1939–45, 9th Lancers. Manager, Grindlays Bank Ltd, India and Pakistan, 1945–49; joined Antony Gibbs and Sons Ltd, 1949, Director, 1954–83, retired; Chm., Alexander and Berendt Ltd, 1967–. Jt Treasurer, Royal Assoc. for Disability and Rehabilitation. *Heir: s* Hon. Alastair Colin Leckie Campbell [*b* 16 Sept. 1951; *m* 1979, Annabel Rose, *yr d* of Hon. Robin Warrender, *qv*; two *s*]. *Address:* Bushes Farm, Weald, Sevenoaks, Kent.

COLHOUN, Prof. John; Barker Professor of Cryptogamic Botany, University of Manchester, 1960–80, now Emeritus; Dean, Faculty of Science, 1974 and 1975; Pro-Vice-Chancellor, 1977–80; *b* 15 May 1913; *yr s* of late James and Rebecca Colhoun, Castlederg, Co. Tyrone; *m* 1949, Margaret, *e d* of late Prof. Gilbert Waterhouse, LittD, and Mary Elizabeth, *e d* of Sir Robert Woods; three *d*. *Educ:* Edwards Sch., Castlederg, Co. Tyrone; The Queen's Univ. of Belfast; Imperial Coll. of Science, London Univ. BSc, MAgr (Belfast), PhD, DSc (London), MSc (Manchester), DIC. Min. of Agriculture for Northern Ireland: Research Asst, 1939–46; Senior Scientific Officer, 1946–50; Principal Scientific Officer, 1951–60. The Queen's Univ., Belfast: Asst Lecturer in Agricultural Botany, 1940–42; Asst Lectr 1942–45, Jun. Lectr 1945–46, Lectr 1946–54, Reader 1954–60, in Mycology and Plant Pathology. Warden of Queen's Chambers, 1942–49. FLS 1955. FIBiol 1963. President: British Mycological Soc., 1963; The Queen's Univ. Assoc., 1960–61; The Queen's Univ. Club, London, 1983–85. Chm., Fedn of British Plant Pathologists, 1968; Hon. Mem., British Soc. for Plant Pathology, 1989. Jt Editor, Jl of Phytopathology (Phytopath. Zeitschrift), 1973–91. *Publications:* Diseases of the Flax Plant, 1947; Club Root Disease of Crucifers caused by *Plasmodiophora brassicae* Woron, 1958; numerous papers in Annals of Applied Biology, Annals of Botany, Trans Brit. Mycological Soc., Nature, Phytopath. Z. *Address:* 12 Southdown Crescent, Cheadle Hulme, Cheshire SK8 6EQ. *T:* 061–485 2084. *Club:* Athenæum.

COLIN, Rt. Rev. Gerald Fitzmaurice, MA; an Assistant Bishop, Diocese of Lincoln, since 1979; *b* 19 July 1913; *s* of Frederick Constant Colin and Jemima Fitzmaurice; *m* 1941, Iris Susan Stuart Weir; three *s* two *d*. *Educ:* Mountjoy Sch.; Trinity Coll., Dublin. MA (TCD) 1946. Deacon, 1936; Priest, 1937. St George's, Dublin, 1938; Chancellor's Vicar, St Patrick's Cathedral, Dublin, 1938; RAFVR, 1939–47; Vicar of Frodingham, Dio. of Lincoln, 1947–66; Bishop Suffragan of Grimsby, 1966–78. Canon of Lincoln Cathedral, 1960; Rural Dean of Manlake, 1960; Proctor in Convocation, 1960–65, 1966–70. *Recreation:* fishing. *Address:* Orchard Close, St Mary's Lane, Louth, Lincs LN11 0DT. *T:* Louth (0507) 602600.

COLL, Elizabeth Anne Loosemore E.; *See* Esteve-Coll.

COLL BLASINI, Néstor; Grand Cross, Libertador Simón Bolivar; Venezuelan Ambassador, retired 1991; *b* 10 June 1931; *s* of Guillermo Coll Nuñez and María de Lourdes Blasini de Coll; *m* 1952, Maritza Barrios de Coll; five *s* one *d*. *Educ:* Colegio La Salle, Caracas; Univ. Católica Andres Bello, Caracas. Entered Foreign Service, 1958, as Third Secretary, later Second Sec.; Head of Office that revised Reciprocal Commercial Treaty between Venezuela and USA; Economic Counsellor, Colombia; Minister Counsellor, Head of Cabinet of Min. of Foreign Affairs; Director of Frontiers, 1969; Ambassador of Venezuela in Panama, 1969–71; Asst Director General, Min. of For. Affairs, actg as Dir Gen. on several occasions, 1971–74; Ambassador of Venezuela: in Sweden and Finland, 1974–76; in Turkey, 1976–78; in Finland, 1978–79; in Italy, 1979–82; in UK, 1982–84; in Israel, 1984–91. Member: Sociedades Bolivarianas, Venezuela, Italy and Honduras; Academia Tiberina, Rome; Sociedad de Estudios Históricos Mirandinos, Venezuela. Grand Cross: Cavalieri di Gran Croce (Italy), Condor de los Andres (Bolivia), Libertador San Martin (Argentina), Yugoslav Flag (Yugoslavia), Polar Star (Sweden), and other decorations. *Publications:* La Opinion Publica en America Latina (Colombia), 1963; various articles in Latin American newspapers. *Recreations:* reading, music, golf, ULM pilot, IP shooting. *Club:* Lagunita Country, Los Canales Country (Caracas).

COLLARD, Douglas Reginald, OBE 1976; HM Diplomatic Service, retired; Member Council, Anglo-Arab Association, since 1990 (Director, 1976–90); Director, Arab British Centre, 1981–90; Secretary, Saudi British Society, 1986–90; *b* 7 April 1916; *s* of late Hebert Carthew Collard and late Mary Ann (*née* Pugh); *m* 1947, Eleni Alkmini Kiortsi (marr. diss. 1969), Greece; two *s* three *d*. *Educ:* Wallasey Grammar Sch.; privately. Army Service, 1940–46 (despatches); UNRRA, Greece, 1946–47; Asst Commercial Adviser, British Econ. Mission to Greece, 1947; Consul, Patras, Greece, 1947–52; Beirut, 1952–54; 2nd Sec. (Commercial); Khartoum, 1954–56; Copenhagen, 1958–61; FCO, 1956–58 and 1967–69; 1st Sec. (Commercial): Tripoli, 1961–65; Lahore, 1965–67; Montevideo, 1969–71; 1st Sec., later Counsellor (Commercial), Algiers, 1971–73; Consul-Gen., Bilbao, 1973–76. *Recreations:* reading, walking. *Address:* Flat 23, Westminster Court, 23 Cambridge Park, Wanstead, E11 2PU. *T:* 081–530 8308.

COLLEE, Prof. John Gerald, CBE 1991; MD; FRCPath; FRCPE; Robert Irvine Professor of Bacteriology and Head of Department of Medical Microbiology (formerly Department of Bacteriology), University of Edinburgh, 1979–91; Chief Bacteriologist to Edinburgh Royal Infirmary and Consultant Bacteriologist, Lothian Health Board, 1979–91; Consultant Adviser in Microbiology to Scottish Home and Health Department, 1986–91; *b* 10 May 1929; *s* of John Gerald Collee and Mary Hay Wilson Kirsopp Cassels; *m* 1952, Isobel McNay Galbraith; two *s* one *d*. *Educ:* Bo'ness Acad.; Edinburgh Acad.; Edinburgh Univ. MB ChB, MD (Gold Medal). Ho. Phys., 1951–52. AMS (Captain RAMC), 1952–54. Lectr in Bacteriology, Edinburgh, 1955–63; WHO Vis. Prof. of Bacteriol., Baroda, 1963–64; Sen. Lectr, Edinburgh, and Hon. Cons. Bacteriologist, 1964–70; Reader in Bacteriol. 1970–74, Personal Prof. of Bacteriol. 1974–79, Edinburgh. Member: Scottish Health Service Planning Council Adv. Gp on Infection, 1981–90; Jt Cttee on Vaccination and Immunisation, 1982–; Cttee on Safety of Medicines, 1987–89; Cttee on Vaccination and Immunisation Procedures, MRC, 1988–. *Publications:* Applied Medical Microbiology, 1976, 2nd edn 1981; contrib. and ed several textbooks, incl. Mackie and McCartney's Practical Medical Microbiology, 1989; many sci. papers on aspects of infection, anaerobes of clin. importance, antimicrobial drugs and immunization. *Recreations:* woodwork, mechanics, fishing, music, painting. *Address:* 204 Newhaven Road, Edinburgh EH6 4QE. *T:* 031–552 8810. *Club:* Scottish Arts (Edinburgh).

COLLENDER, Andrew Robert; QC 1991; *b* 11 Aug. 1946; *s* of John Collender and Kathleen (*née* Lemon); *m* 1974, Titia Tybout; two *s*. *Educ:* Mt Pleasant Boys High Sch., Rhodesia; Univ. of Bristol (LLB Hons). Called to the Bar, Lincoln's Inn, 1969; an Asst Recorder, 1989–. *Recreations:* playing the violin, sailing, riding. *Address:* 2 Temple Gardens, Temple, EC4Y 9AY. *T:* 071–583 6041.

COLLETT, Sir Christopher, GBE 1988; JP; Partner in Ernst & Young, Chartered Accountants, London; Lord Mayor of London, 1988–89; *b* 10 June 1931; 2nd *s* of Sir Henry Seymour Collett, 2nd Bt, and Lady (Ruth Mildred) Collett (*née* Hatch); *m* 1959, Christine Anne, *d* of Oswald Hardy Griffiths, Nunthorpe, Yorks; two *s* one *d*. *Educ:* Harrow; Emmanuel Coll., Cambridge. MA; FCA. Nat. Service, RA and Surrey Yeomanry; Captain TA (RA). Articled with Cassleton Elliott & Co., Chartered Accountants, 1954; qualified, 1958; Partner, Ghana 1960, London 1963; firm merged to become Josolyne Miles and Cassleton Elliott, Josolyne Layton Bennett & Co., Arthur Young, and now Ernst & Young. Mem., Court of Common Council (Broad Street Ward), City of London, 1973–79; Alderman, 1979–; Sheriff, City of London, 1985–86. Master, Worshipful Co. of Glovers, 1981; Hon. Liveryman, Haberdashers' Co., 1990; Member: Guild of Freemen, 1983–; Worshipful Co. of Chartered Accts in Eng. and Wales, 1984– (Liveryman, 1984; Asst, 1986); City of London TAVR Cttee, 1980–; Council Mem., Action Research for the Crippled Child, 1984–. Governor: Haberdashers' Aske's Schs, Elstree, 1982–; Music Therapy Gp Ltd, 1986–; Bridewell Royal Hosp., 1987–; Hon. Treas., Lee House, Wimbledon. Pres., Broad Street Ward Club, 1979–. JP City of London, 1979. Hon. DSc City, 1988. KStJ 1988. Order of Merit (cl. II), State of Qatar, 1985; Orden del Merito Civil (cl. II), Spain, 1986; Commander, Order of Merit, Federal Republic of Germany, 1986; CON, 1st cl. (Nigeria), 1989. *Recreations:* gardening, fishing. *Address:* 121 Home Park Road, Wimbledon, SW19. *Clubs:* City of London, City Livery.

COLLETT, Sir Ian (Seymour), 3rd Bt *cr* 1934; *b* 5 Oct. 1953; *s* of David Seymour Collett (*d* 1962), and of Sheila Joan Collett (who *m* 1980, Sir James William Miskin, *qv*), *o d* of late Harold Scott; *S* grandfather, 1971; *m* 1982, Philippa, *o d* of James R. I. Hawkins, Preston St Mary, Suffolk; one *s* one *d*. *Educ:* Lancing College, Sussex. Notary Public, 1985. Mem., Law Society, 1979. Governor, Felixstowe College, 1986–. *Recreations:* golf, fishing, cricket, shooting. *Heir: s* Anthony Seymour Collett, *b* 27 Feb. 1984. *Address:* Pound Farm, Great Glemham, Saxmundham, Suffolk. *Clubs:* MCC; Aldeburgh Golf.

COLLEY, Maj.-Gen. (David) Bryan (Hall), CB 1988; CBE 1982 (OBE 1977; MBE 1968); FCIT; Director-General, Road Haulage Association, since 1988; *b* 5 June 1934; *s* of Lawson and Alice Colley; *m* 1957, Marie Thérèse (*née* Préfontaine); one *s* one *d*. *Educ:* King Edward's Sch., Birmingham; RMA, Sandhurst. Commissioned: RASC, 1954; RCT, 1965; regimental appts in Germany, Belgium, UK, Hong Kong and Singapore; Student, Staff Coll., Camberley, 1964; JSSC Latimer, 1970; CO Gurkha Transport Regt and 31 Regt, RCT, 1971–74; Staff HQ 1st (British) Corps, 1974–77; Comd Logistic Support Gp, 1977–80; Col AQ (Ops and Plans) and Dir Admin. Planning, MoD (Army), 1980–82; Comd Transport 1st (British) Corps, 1983–86; Dir Gen., Transport and Movts (Army), 1986–88, retired. Col Comdt, RCT, 1988–. Freeman, City of London, 1986; Hon. Liveryman, Worshipful Co. of Carmen, 1986. *Recreations:* travel, walking. *Address:* c/o Midland Bank, Redditch, Worcs B97 4EA. *Club:* Army and Navy.

COLLEY, Surg. Rear-Adm. Ian Harris, OBE 1963; Member, Committee of Management, Royal National Lifeboat Institution, since 1982; *b* 14 Oct. 1922; *s* of Aubrey James Colley and Violet Fulford Colley; *m* 1952, Joy Kathleen (*née* Goodacre). *Educ:* Hanley Castle Grammar Sch.; King's Coll., London and King's Coll. Hosp. MB, BS 1948; DPH; MFOM; FFCM. Royal Naval Medical Service, 1948–80: MO HMS Cardigan Bay and HMS Consort, 1949–52; service with Fleet Air Arm, 1955–78: as PMO HMS Centaur; MO i/c Air Med. Sch.; Pres., Central Air Med. Bd; Comd MO to Flag Officer, Naval Air Comd; Surg. Rear Adm. (Ships and Estabs), 1978–80, retired. QHP 1978–80. Consultant in Aviation Medicine; former Examr to Conjoint Bd, Royal College of Surgeons and Royal College of Physicians for DipAvMed. Vice-Pres., RNLI, 1989– (Chm., Med. and Survival Cttee, 1984–88). CStJ 1980. *Publications:* papers in field of aviation medicine. *Address:* c/o Royal Bank of Scotland, Inveraray, Argyll PA32 8TY.

COLLIE, Alexander Conn, MBE 1979; JP; Chairman, Aberdeen Tourist Board, since 1984; Lord Provost of the City of Aberdeen, 1980–84; Member: Aberdeen District Council, since 1975; Aberdeen Licensing Board, since 1984; *b* 1 July 1913; *s* of late Donald and Jane Collie; *m* 1942, Elizabeth Keith Macleod (*d* 1985); two *s*. *Educ:* Ferryhill Sch., Aberdeen; Ruthrieston Sch., Aberdeen. Member: Aberdeen Town Council, 1947–75; Aberdeen Harbour Board, 1947–74; North of Scotland Hydro-Electric

Consultative Council, until Oct. 1980; Past Member: Scottish Sports Council; Scottish Bakers' Union Exec. Council. JP Aberdeen, 1956. OStJ 1981. *Address:* (home) 43 Brimmond Place, Aberdeen AB1 3EN. *T:* Aberdeen (0224) 874972.

COLLIER, family name of **Baron Monkswell.**

COLLIER, Andrew James, CB 1976; Deputy Secretary, Department of Health and Social Security, 1973–82; *b* 12 July 1923; *s* of Joseph Veasy Collier and Dorothy Murray; *m* 1950, Bridget, *d* of George and Edith Eberstadt, London; two *d. Educ:* Harrow; Christ Church, Oxford. Served Army, RHA, 1943–46. Entered HM Treasury, 1948; Private Sec. to: Sir Henry Wilson Smith, 1950; Sir Leslie Rowan, 1951; Chancellors of the Exchequer, 1956–59 (Rt Hon. Harold Macmillan, Rt Hon. Peter Thorneycroft, Rt Hon. Heathcoat Amory); Asst Sec., 1961; Under-Sec., 1967; Under-Secretary: Civil Service Dept, 1968–71; DHSS, 1971–73. Consultant, 1983–. *Address:* 10 Lambourne Avenue, SW19 7DW. *T:* 081–879 3560. *Club:* Athenæum.

COLLIER, Andrew John; Chief Education Officer, Lancashire County Council, since 1980; *b* 29 Oct. 1939; *s* of Francis George Collier and Margaret Nancy (*née* Nockles); *m* 1964, Gillian Ann (*née* Churchill); two *d. Educ:* University College Sch.; St John's Coll., Cambridge (MA). Assistant Master, Winchester Coll., 1962–68; Hampshire County Educn Dept, 1968–71; Buckinghamshire County Educn Dept, 1971–77; Dep. Chief Educn Officer, Lancashire, 1977–80. Member: Open Univ. Vis. Cttee, 1982–88; Council for Accreditation of Teacher Educn, 1984–89; Nat. Training Task Force, 1989–; Chm., County Educn Officers' Soc., 1987–88; Treas., Soc. of Educn Officers, 1987– (Pres., 1990). Liveryman, Worshipful Company of Wheelwrights, 1972. Mem. Council, Univ. of Lancaster, 1981–86, 1988–. *Publications:* (contrib.) New Directions for County Government, 1989; articles in jls. *Recreations:* music, walking, gardening. *Address:* County Hall, Preston, Lancs PR1 8RJ. *T:* Preston (0772) 263646. *Clubs:* Athenæum; Leander (Henley-on-Thames).

COLLIER, John Gordon, FRS 1990; FEng; Chairman, Nuclear Electric plc, since 1990; *b* London, 22 Jan. 1935; *s* of John Collier and Edith Georgina (*née* de Ville); *m* 1956, Ellen Alice Mary Mitchell; one *s* one *d. Educ:* St Paul's Sch., Hammersmith; University Coll. London (BScEng). FIMechE, FIChemE, FINucE. AERE, Harwell: apprenticeship in mech. and chem. engrg, 1951–56; SO, then SSO, Chem. Engrg Div., 1957–62; Sect. Hd, then Br. Hd, Exptl Engrg Br., Adv. Reactor Engrg Div., Atomic Energy of Canada Ltd (on leave of absence from UKAEA), 1962–64; SSO, then PSO, Chem. Engrg Div., AERE, Harwell, 1964–66; Hd, Engrg Div., Atomic Power Constructions Ltd, R&D Lab., Heston, 1966–70; UKAEA, Harwell: Hd of Engrg Scis Gp, later Engrg Scis Br., 1970–75; Hd of Chem. Engrg Div., 1975–77; Mem., Atomic Energy Technical Unit responsible to Dep. Chm., UKAEA, 1977–79; Hd, Atomic Energy Technical Unit, 1979–81; Dir of Technical Studies, UKAEA, Harwell, 1981–82; Dir, Safety and Reliability Directorate, UKAEA, Culcheth, 1982–83; Dir Gen., Generation Develt and Construction Div. of CEGB, Barnwood, Glos, 1983–86; Dep. Chm., 1986, Chm., 1987–90, UKAEA. Chm., Nationalised Industries Chairmen's Gp, 1990–. Hon. DSc Cranfield, 1988. *Publications:* Convective Boiling and Condensation, 1972, 2nd edn 1981; (jtly) Introduction to Nuclear Power, 1987. *Recreations:* cricket, music. *Address:* Nuclear Electric plc, Barnett Way, Barnwood, Glos GL4 7RS.

COLLIER, Kenneth Gerald; Principal, College of the Venerable Bede, Durham, 1959–75; *b* 1910; *m* 1938, Gwendoline Halford; two *s. Educ:* Aldenham Sch.; St John's Coll., Cambridge. MA 1935; Diploma in Education (Oxon) 1945. Technical translation, Stockholm, 1931–32; Schoolmaster, 1933–41; Royal Ordnance Factories, 1941–44; Physics Master, Lancing Coll., 1944–49; Lectr, St Luke's Coll., Exeter, 1949–59. Editor, Education for Teaching, 1953–58. Chm., Assoc. Teachers in Colls and Depts of Education, 1964–65. Vis. Prof. of Education, Temple Univ., Philadelphia, 1965, 1968. Consultant to Council for Educational Technology, 1971–80. British Council tours, 1976–79: India (consultations in Delhi, Patna and Calcutta); Brazil (consultant to British Sch. in São Paulo; lectures at univs); Portugal (consultant to Eng. lang. schs). Hon. Research Fellow, Univ. of East Anglia, 1978–81. *Publications:* The Science of Humanity, 1950; The Social Purposes of Education, 1959; New Dimensions in Higher Education, 1968; (ed) Innovation in Higher Education, 1974; (ed) Values and Moral Development in Higher Education, 1974; (ed) Evaluating the New BEd, 1978; (ed) The Management of Peer-Group Learning, 1983; A New Teaching, A New Learning: a guide to theological education, 1989; contribs to: Sixth Form Citizens, 1950; Religious Faith and World Culture (New York), 1951; Internat. Encyclopedia of Educn, 1985; articles in educational and other jls. *Recreations:* local history, music, the film. *Address:* 4 Robson Terrace, Shincliffe, Durham DH1 2NL. *T:* Durham (091) 3841647.

COLLIER, Lesley Faye; Principal Dancer with the Royal Ballet, since 1972; *b* 13 March 1947; *d* of Roy and Mavis Collier; twin *s. Educ:* The Royal Ballet School, White Lodge, Richmond. Joined Royal Ballet, 1965; has danced most principal roles in the Royal repertory. Evening Standard Ballet Award, 1987. *Address:* c/o Royal Ballet Company, 155 Talgarth Road, W14.

COLLIER, Prof. Leslie Harold, MD, DSc; FRCP, FRCPath; Professor of Virology, University of London, 1966–86, now Emeritus; Consulting Pathologist, Royal London Hospital (formerly London Hospital), since 1987; *b* 9 Feb. 1921; *s* of late Maurice Leonard Collier and Ruth (*née* Phillips); *m* 1942, Adeline Barnett; one *s. Educ:* Brighton Coll.; UCH Med. Sch. MD London 1953; DSc London 1968; MRCP 1969; FRCPath 1975; FRCP 1980. House Phys., UCH, 1943; served RAMC, 1944–47; Asst Pathologist, St Helier Hosp., Carshalton, 1947; Lister Inst. of Preventive Medicine, 1948–78: Head, Dept of Virology, 1955–74; Dep. Dir, 1968–74; Dir, Vaccines and Sera Laboratories, 1974–78; Hon. Dir, MRC Trachoma Unit, 1957–73; Prof. of Virology and Sen. Lectr, Jt Dept of Virology, London Hosp. Med. Coll. and St Bartholomew's Hosp. Med. Coll., 1978–86; Hd, Dept of Virology, London Hosp. Med. Coll., 1982–86. Hon. Consultant in Virology, Tower Hamlets HA, 1978–86. Pres., Sect. of Pathology, RSM, 1986–88. Chibret Gold Medal, Ligue contre le Trachome, 1959; Luys Prize, Soc. de Médecine de Paris, 1963. *Publications:* (ed jtly) Topley and Wilson's Principles of Bacteriology, Virology and Immunology, 8th edn, 1990; papers in med. and scientific jls. *Recreations:* various. *Address:* 8 Peto Place, Regent's Park, NW1 4DT. *T:* 071–487 4848.

COLLIER-WRIGHT, John Hurrell, CBE 1966; Member, British Transport Docks Board, 1974–77; *b* 1 April 1915; *s* of John Robert Collier Collier-Wright and Phyllis Hurrell Walters; *m* 1940, Pauline Beatrice Platts; three *s* (and one *s* decd). *Educ:* Bradfield Coll.; Queen's Coll., Oxford (MA). FCIT. Traffic Apprentice, LNER, 1936–39. Served War of 1939–45, RE, France, Iraq and Iran (Lt-Col; US Legion of Merit). East African Railways and Harbours, 1946–64; Chief Commercial Supt; joined British Transport Docks Bd, 1964; Chief Commercial Man., 1964–70; Asst Man. Dir, 1970–72; Dep. Man. Dir, 1972–77; Dir, British Transport Advertising, 1966–81. *Address:* 62 Marygate, York YO3 7BH. *Club:* Nairobi (Kenya).

COLLIGAN, John Clifford, CBE 1963 (OBE 1957); Director-General, Royal National Institute for the Blind, 1950–72; Secretary, British Wireless for the Blind Fund, 1950–84; Hon. Treasurer and Life Member, World Council for the Blind, since 1969 (British Representative, 1954–69); *b* 27 Oct. 1906; *s* of John and Florence Colligan, Wallasey, Cheshire; *m* 1st, 1934, Ethel May Allton (*d* 1948); one *s* one *d*; 2nd, 1949, Frances Bird (*d* 1988); 3rd, 1989, Beryl May Johns. *Educ:* Liscard High Sch., Wallasey. Dep. Sec., National Institute for the Blind, 1945–49. *Publications:* The Longest Journey, 1969; various articles on blind welfare. *Recreations:* watching cricket, walking, gardening. *Address:* 11 Townfield Lane, Chalfont St Giles, Bucks HP8 4QW. *T:* Chalfont St Giles (02407) 4264.

COLLIN, Maj.-Gen. Geoffrey de Egglesfield, CB 1975; MC 1944; DL; *b* 18 July 1921; *s* of late Charles de Egglesfield Collin and Catherine Mary Collin; *m* 1949, Angela Stella (*née* Young); one *s* three *d. Educ:* Wellington Coll., Berks. Served War of 1939–45: commissioned as 2nd Lt, RA, 1941; in India and Burma, 1942–45. Qualified as Army Pilot, 1946; attended Staff Coll., Camberley, 1951; Instructor at RMA, Sandhurst, 1954–56; served Kenya, 1956–58; JSSC, 1958; Instructor at Staff Coll., Camberley, 1960–62; comd 50 Missile Regt, RA, 1962–64; GSO 1 Sch. of Artillery, 1965; CRA, 4th Div., 1966–67; attended Imperial Defence College, London, 1968; Comdt, Royal School of Artillery, 1969–71; Maj.-Gen. RA, HQ BAOR, 1971–73; GOC North East District, York, 1973–76; retired 1976. Col Comdt, RA, 1976–83 (Rep. Col Comdt, 1982). Chairman: CS Selection Bd, 1981– (Mem., 1978); Retired Officer Selection Bd, 1979–. Hon. Dir, Great Yorks Show, 1976–87; Pres., Yorks Agricl Soc., 1988–89. DL N Yorks, 1977. *Recreations:* fishing, ornithology, music, keeping gun dog and garden under control. *Address:* c/o Lloyds Bank, 8 Cambridge Crescent, Harrogate HG1 1PQ. *Club:* Army and Navy.

COLLIN, Jack, MA, MD; FRCS; Clinical Reader in Surgery, University of Oxford, Consultant Surgeon, John Radcliffe Hospital, Oxford and Fellow of Trinity College, Oxford, since 1980; Chairman, Faculty of Clinical Medicine, University of Oxford, since 1990; *b* 23 April 1945; *s* of John Collin and Amy Maud Collin; *m* 1971, Christine Frances Proud; three *s* one *d. Educ:* Univ. of Newcastle (MB BS, MD); Mayo Clinic, Minn. University of Newcastle: Demonstrator in Anatomy, 1969–70; Sen. Res. Associate, 1973–75; Registrar in Surgery, Royal Victoria Infirmary, Newcastle, 1971–80; Mayo Foundn Fellow, Mayo Clinic, Minn, 1977. Moynihan Fellow, Assoc. of Surgeons of GB and Ire., 1980. Royal College of Surgeons: Arris and Gale Lectr, 1976; Jacksonian Prize, 1977; Hunterian Prof., 1988–89. Non-exec. Dir, Nuffield Orthopaedic Centre NHS Trust, 1990. *Publications:* papers on vascular surgery, intestinal myoelectrical activity and absorption, parenteral nutrition and pancreatic and intestinal transplantation. *Recreations:* gardening, walking. *Address:* Nuffield Department of Surgery, John Radcliffe Hospital, Oxford. *T:* Oxford (0865) 221284, 221286.

COLLING, Rev. Canon James Oliver; Rector of Warrington, since 1973; Canon Diocesan of Liverpool Cathedral, since 1976; Chaplain to the Queen, since 1990; *b* 3 Jan. 1930; *e s* of late Leonard Colling and Dorothy Colling (*née* Atherton); *m* 1957, Jean Wright; one *s* one *d* (one twin *s* decd). *Educ:* Leigh Grammar Sch.; Univ. of Manchester (BA 1950); Cuddesdon Coll., Oxford. Commissioned RAF, 1950–52 (Nat. Service). Deacon 1954; priest 1955; Asst Curate, Wigan Parish Church, 1954–59; Vicar of Padgate, 1959–71, Rector, 1971–73; Rural Dean of Warrington, 1970–82 and 1987–89, Area Dean, 1989–. Chairman: Warrington CHC, 1974–82; Warrington Community Council, 1974–87; Vice-Chm., Warrington HA, 1982–89. Chairman: Warrington C of E Educnl Trust, 1973–; Warrington and Dist Soc. for the Deaf, 1974–; Warrington Charities Trust, 1989–; Mem., Cheshire Family Health Services Authority, 1990–. Chm. Governors, Sir Thomas Boteler High Sch., Warrington, 1988–. *Recreations:* gardening, looking at buildings and places, local history. *Address:* The Rectory, Warrington, Cheshire WA1 2TL. *T:* Warrington (0925) 35020.

COLLINGRIDGE, Jean Mary, (Mrs A. R. Collingridge); Chief Executive, Employment Division of the Manpower Services Commission, 1979–82, retired; Member, Civil Service Appeal Board, since 1984; *b* 9 March 1923; *d* of Edgar and Elsie Bishop; *m* 1951, Albert Robert Collingridge; one *d. Educ:* County High School, Loughton, Essex; University College London (BSc Econ); LSE (Social Science Course). Asst Personnel Officer, C. and J. Clark, 1945–49; Personnel Manager, Pet Foods Ltd, 1949–50; Ministry of Labour/Department of Employment: Personnel Management Adviser and Industrial Relations Officer, 1950–65; Regl Industrial Relations Officer/Sen. Manpower Adviser, 1965–71; Assistant Secretary, Office of Manpower Economics 1971–73, Pay Board 1973–74, Dept of Employment HQ 1974–76; Dep. Chief Exec., Employment Service Div. of Manpower Services Commn, 1976–79. Chm., Kent Area Manpower Bd, 1983–88. Personnel Advr, St James's Church, Piccadilly, 1989–. *Publication:* (jtly) Personnel Management in the Small Firm, 1953. *Recreations:* home and garden. *Address:* 21 Burnham Wood, Fareham, Hants PO16 7UD. *T:* Fareham (0329) 284589.

COLLINGS, Juliet Jeanne d'Auvergne; *see* Campbell, J. J. d'A.

COLLINGWOOD, John Gildas, FEng, FIChemE; Director: Unilever Ltd, 1965–77; Unilever NV, 1965–77; Head of Research Division of Unilever Ltd, 1961–77; *b* 15 June 1917; *s* of Stanley Ernest Collingwood and Kathleen Muriel (*née* Smalley); *m* 1942, Pauline Winifred (*née* Jones); one *s* one *d. Educ:* Wycliffe Coll., Stonehouse, Glos; University Coll. London (BSc). English Charcoal, 1940–41; British Ropeway Engrg Co, 1941–44; De Havilland Engines, 1944–46; Olympia Oil and Cake Mills Ltd, 1946–49; British Oil and Cake Mills Ltd, 1949–51; Mem., UK Milling Group of Unilever Ltd, 1951–60; Dir, Advita Ltd, 1951–60; Dir, British Oil & Cake Mills Ltd, 1955–60. Instn of Chemical Engrs: Mem. Research Cttee, 1963–68; Mem. Council, 1964–67. Mem. Council of Univ. of Aston, 1971–83 (Chm., Academic Advisory Cttee, 1964–71); Mem., Research Cttee, CBI, 1970–71; Member: Council for Scientific Policy, 1971–72; Exec. Cttee, British Nutrition Foundn, 1978–82 (Council, 1970–85); Food Standards Cttee, 1972–80; Royal Commn on Environmental Pollution, 1973–79; Standing Commn on Energy and the Environment, 1978–81. A Gen. Sec., BAAS, 1978–83, 1986–88. Vice President: Nat. Children's Home, 1989– (Chm., F and GP Cttee, 1983–89); Council of Governors, Wycliffe Coll., Stonehouse, Glos, 1989– (Mem. Council, 1967–; Chm. Council, 1985–89). Hon. DSc Aston, 1966; Fellow, University Coll. London, 1970. *Recreations:* sailing, music. *Address:* 54 Downs Road, Coulsdon, Surrey CR5 1AA. *T:* Downland (0737) 554817. *Club:* Athenæum.

COLLINS, Andrew David; QC 1985; a Recorder, since 1986; *b* 19 July 1942; *s* of Rev. Canon Lewis John Collins, MA, and Diana (*née* Elliot); *m* 1970, Nicolette Anne Sandford-Saville; one *s* one *d. Educ:* Eton; King's Coll., Cambridge (BA, MA). Called to the Bar, Middle Temple, 1965. *Address:* 4/5 Gray's Inn Square, Gray's Inn, WC1R 5AY. *T:* 071–404 5252.

COLLINS, Sir Arthur (James Robert), KCVO 1980; *b* 10 July 1911; *s* of Col William Fellowes Collins, DSO, and Lady Evelyn Collins (*née* Innes Ker), OBE; *m* 1965, Elizabeth, *d* of Rear-Adm. Sir Arthur Bromley, Bt, and *widow* of 6th Baron Sudeley (*died* on war service, 1941). *Educ:* Eton; Christ Church, Oxford (MA). Admitted a Solicitor, 1935; Partner, Withers, 1937, Sen. Partner, 1962–81, now Consultant. Served with Royal Horse Guards, 1938–46; Adjt, 2nd Household Cavalry Regt, 1940–44 (despatches), Major 1943.

Address: Kirkman Bank, Knaresborough, N Yorks HG5 9BT. *T:* Harrogate (0423) 863136; 38 Clarence Terrace, NW1. *T:* 071–723 4198. *Clubs:* Turf, White's.

COLLINS, Arthur John, OBE 1973; HM Diplomatic Service, retired; *b* 17 May 1931; *s* of Reginald and Margery Collins; *m* 1952, Enid Maureen, *d* of Charles and Sarah Stableford; one *s* one *d.* *Educ:* Purley Grammar Sch. Served RAF, 1949–51. Min. of Health, 1951–68 (Private Sec. to Perm. Sec., 1960–61, and to Parly Sec., 1962–63); transf. to HM Diplomatic Service, 1968; FCO, 1968–69; First Secretary and Head of Chancery: Dhaka, 1970–71; Brasilia, 1972–74; Asst Head of Latin America and Caribbean Depts, FCO, 1974–77; Counsellor, UK Del. to OECD, Paris, 1978–81; High Comr, Papua New Guinea, 1982–85; adviser on management, FCO, 1986–88; FCO rep. (protocol), 1988–. *Recreations:* beekeeping, downland walking. *Address:* 60 Dean Court Road, Rottingdean, Sussex BN2 7DJ. *Club:* Commonwealth Trust.

COLLINS, Basil Eugene Sinclair, CBE 1983; Chairman, Nabisco Group, 1984–89; *b* 21 Dec. 1923; *s* of Albert Collins and Pauline Alicia (*née* Wright); *m* 1942, Doris Slott; two *d.* *Educ:* Great Yarmouth Grammar School. Sales Manager, L. Rose & Co. Ltd, 1945; Export Dir, Schweppes (Overseas) Ltd, 1958; Group Admin Dir, Schweppes Ltd, 1964, Chm. of Overseas Gp 1968; Chm. of Overseas Gp, Cadbury Schweppes Ltd, 1969, Dep. Man. Dir 1972, Man. Dir 1974, Dep. Chm. and Group Chief Exec., Cadbury Schweppes plc, 1980–83; Director: Thomas Cook Gp, 1980–85; British Airways Bd, 1982–88; Royal Mint, 1984–88. Royal College of Nursing: Chm., Finance and General Purposes Cttee, 1970–86; Hon. Treasurer, 1970–86; Vice-Pres., 1972, Life Vice-Pres., 1986. Fellow Inst. of Dirs, 1974, Council Mem., 1982–89; Managing Trustee, Inst. of Economic Affairs, 1987–; Mem. Council, UEA, 1987–. FZS 1975; CBIM (FBIM 1976); Fellow, Amer. Chamber of Commerce, 1979, Dir 1984–89. FRSA 1984. *Recreations:* music, languages, travel, English countryside. *Address:* Wyddial Parva, Buntingford, Herts SG9 0EL. *Club:* Carlton.

COLLINS, Gerard; *see* Collins, James G.

COLLINS, Henry Edward, CBE 1948; FEng 1976; Consulting Mining Engineer; *b* 4 Oct. 1903; *s* of James Collins; *m* 1934, Cecilia Harris (*d* 1975); no *c.* *Educ:* Rotherham Grammar Sch.; Univ. of Sheffield (MEng). Sen. Lectr in Mining, Univ. of Sheffield, 1935–38; Manager, Rossington Main Colliery, Doncaster, 1939–42; Agent, Markham Colliery, Doncaster, 1942–44; Chief Mining Agent, Doncaster Amalgamated Collieries Ltd, 1944–45; Dir Coal Production, CCG, 1945–47; British Chm., UK/US Coal Control Gp, Germany (later Combined Coal Control Gp), 1947–50; Production Dir, Durham Div., NCB, 1950–56; Dir-Gen. of Reconstruction, NCB, 1956–57; Board Mem. for Production, NCB, 1957–67; Consultant to NCB, 1967–69. Mem., Govtl Cttee on Coal Derivatives, 1959–60; Chairman: NCB Opencast Executive, 1961–67; NCB Brickworks Executive, 1962–67; Whittlesea Central Brick Co. Ltd, 1966–67; Field Research Steering Cttee, Min. of Power, 1964–67; Past Director: Omnia Concrete Sales Ltd; Bradley's (Concrete) Ltd; Powell Duffryn Technical Services Ltd; Inter-Continental Fuels Ltd. Member: Minister of Power's Adv. Council on Research and Develt, 1963–67; Min. of Power Nat. Jt Pneumoconiosis Cttee, 1964–67; Safety in Mines (Adv.) Bd; Mining Qualifications Bd, 1962–69. Pres., Inst. of Mining Engineers, 1962, Hon. Fellow, 1988. *Publications:* Mining Memories and Musings: the autobiography of a mining engineer, 1985; numerous papers on mining engineering subjects. *Address:* Rising Sun, 22a West Side, Wimbledon Common, SW19 4UF. *T:* 081–946 3949. *Club:* Athenæum.

COLLINS, (James) Gerard; TD (FF) Limerick West, since 1967; Minister for Foreign Affairs, Republic of Ireland, since 1989; *b* Abbeyfeale, Co. Limerick, 16 Oct. 1938; *s* of late James J. Collins, TD and Margaret Collins; *m* 1969, Hilary Tattan. *Educ:* University Coll., Dublin (BA). Teacher. Asst Gen. Sec., Fianna Fáil, 1965–67. Parly Sec. to Ministers for Industry and Commerce and for the Gaeltacht, 1969–70; Minister for Posts and Telegraphs, 1970–73; opposition front-bench spokesman on agriculture, 1973–75; spokesman on justice, 1975–77; Minister for Justice, 1977–81 and 1987–89; Minister for Foreign Affairs, March-Dec. 1982; opposition front-bench spokesman on foreign affairs, 1983–87. Mem., Consultative Assembly, Council of Europe, 1973–77; Chm., Parly Cttee on Secondary Legislation of European Communities, 1983–. Mem., Limerick CC, 1974–77. *Address:* The Hill, Abbeyfeale, Co. Limerick.

COLLINS, Prof. Jeffrey Hamilton, FRSE; FEng 1981; Chairman, Parallel Computing Centre, Edinburgh University, since 1991; Senior Technical Specialist, Lothian Regional Council, since 1991; *b* 22 April 1930; *s* of Ernest Frederick and Dora Gladys Collins; *m* 1956, Sally Parfitt; two *s.* *Educ:* London Univ. (BSc, MSc, DSc). FIEE, FInstP, FIEEE; CEng, CPhys. GEC Research Laboratories, London, 1951–56; Ferranti Ltd, Edinburgh, 1956–57; Univ. of Glasgow, 1957–66; Research Engr, Stanford Univ., Calif, 1966–68; Dir of Physical Electronics, Rockwell International, Calif, 1968–70; University of Edinburgh: Research Prof., 1970–73; Prof. of Industrial Electronics, 1973–77; Prof. of Electrical Engrg and Hd of Dept, 1977–84; Emeritus Prof., 1984; Head of Computing Centre, 1990. Dir, Automation and Robotics Res. Inst., and Prof. of Electrical Engrg, Univ. of Texas at Arlington, 1987–90. Member: Electronics Res. Council, 1979; Computer Bd for Univs and Res. Councils, 1985–86. Director: MESL, 1970–79; Racal-MESL, 1979–81; Advent Technology, 1981–86; Filtronics Components, 1981–85; Burr-Brown Ltd, 1985; River Bend Bank, Fort Worth, 1987–90. Member Honour Societies: Eta Kappa Nu; Tau Beta Pi; Upsilon Pi Epsilon; Phi Beta Delta. *Publications:* Computer-Aided Design of Surface Acoustic Wave Devices, 1976; over 190 articles in learned soc. electrical engrg jls. *Recreations:* music, DIY, tennis. *Address:* 3/4 St Teresa Place, Edinburgh EH10 5UB.

COLLINS, John Alexander; Chairman and Chief Executive, Shell UK, since 1990; *b* 10 Dec. 1941; *s* of John Constantine Collins and Nancy Isobel Mitchell; *m* 1965, Susan Mary Hooper. *Educ:* Campbell Coll., Belfast; Reading Univ. Joined Shell International Chemicals, 1964; various appointments in Shell in Kenya, Nigeria, Columbia and UK, until 1989; Supply and Marketing Co-ordinator, and Dir, Shell Internat. Petroleum Co. Ltd, 1989–90. *Recreations:* opera, theatre, sailing, riding, golf, tennis, a love of the New Forest. *Address:* Shell UK Ltd, Shell-Mex House, Strand, WC2R 0DX.

COLLINS, John Ernest Harley, MBE 1944; DSC 1945 and Bar 1945; DL; Chairman: Morgan Grenfell Holdings Ltd, 1974–79; Guardian Royal Exchange Assurance, 1974–88; *b* 24 April 1923; *o s* of late G. W. Collins, Taynton, Glos; *m* 1st, 1946, Gillian (*d* 1981), *e d* of 2nd Baron Bicester; one *s* one *d*; 2nd, 1986, Jennifer Faith, *widow* of Capt. A. J. A. Cubitt. *Educ:* King Edward's Sch., Birmingham; Birmingham Univ. Royal Navy, 1941–46. Morgan Grenfell & Co. Ltd, 1946, Dir 1957. Director: Royal Exchange Assce, 1957; Rank Hovis McDougall Ltd, 1965–91; Charter Consolidated Ltd, 1966–83; Hudson's Bay Co., 1957–74. Chm. United Services Trustee, 1968–76. DL Oxon, 1975; High Sheriff, Oxon, 1975. KStJ 1983. *Recreations:* shooting, stalking, fishing. *Address:* Chetwode Manor, Buckingham MK18 4BB. *T:* Finmere (0280) 848333. *Club:* White's.

COLLINS, (John) Martin, QC 1972; a Judge of the Courts of Appeal of Jersey and Guernsey, since 1984; *b* 24 Jan. 1929; *s* of John Lissant Collins and Marjorie Mary Collins; *m* 1957, Daphne Mary, *d* of George Martyn Swindells, Prestbury; two *s* one *d.* *Educ:* Uppingham Sch.; Manchester Univ. (LLB). Called to Bar, Gray's Inn, 1952, Bencher, 1981; called to the Bar of Gibraltar, 1990. Dep. Chm., Cumberland QS, 1969–72; a Recorder, 1972–88. Member: Senate of Inns of Court and Bar, 1981–84; Gen. Council of the Bar, 1991. Chm., Management Cttee, Gray's Inn, 1990. *Address:* 10 Essex Street, Outer Temple, WC2R 3AA; 19 avenue Messine, 75008 Paris, France; 15 Ranelagh Grove, SW1. *Clubs:* Athenæum, Carlton.

COLLINS, John Morris; a Recorder of the Crown Court, since 1980; *b* 25 June 1931; *s* of late Emmanuel Cohen, MBE, and Ruby Cohen; *m* 1968, Sheila Brummer; one *d.* *Educ:* Leeds Grammar Sch.; The Queen's Coll., Oxford (MA LitHum). Called to Bar, Middle Temple, 1956, Member of North Eastern Circuit; a Deputy Circuit Judge, 1970. Pres., Leeds Jewish Representative Council, 1986–89. *Publications:* Summary Justice, 1963; various articles in legal periodicals, etc. *Recreation:* walking. *Address:* (home) 14 Sandhill Oval, Leeds LS17 8EA. *T:* Leeds (0532) 686008; (professional) Pearl Chambers, East Parade, Leeds LS1 5BZ. *T:* Leeds (0532) 451986.

COLLINS, Kenneth Darlingston; Member (Lab) East Strathclyde, European Parliament, since 1979; *b* 12 Aug. 1939; *s* of Nicholas Collins and Ellen Williamson; *m* 1966, Georgina Frances Pollard; one *s* one *d.* *Educ:* St John's Grammar Sch.; Hamilton Acad.; Glasgow Univ. (BSc Hons); Strathclyde Univ. (MSc). Left school, 1956; steelworks apprentice, 1956–59; univ., 1960–65; planning officer, 1965–66; WEA Tutor-Organiser, 1966–67; Lecturer: Glasgow Coll. of Bldg, 1967–69; Paisley Coll. of Technol., 1969–79. European Parliament: Dep. Leader, Labour Gp, 1979–84; Socialist spokesman on envmt, public health and consumer protection, 1984–89; Chm., Cttee on Envmt, Public Health and Consumer Protection, 1979–84 and 1989– (Vice Chm., 1984–87). Dir, Inst. for Eur. Envmt Policy, London; Eur. Advr, ACTT, EETPU and NALGO. Member: East Kilbride Town and Dist Council, 1973–79; Lanark CC, 1973–75; East Kilbride Develt Corp., 1976–79; Chm., NE Glasgow Children's Panel, 1974–76. Member: Socialist Internat. Envmt Cttee; Fabian Soc.; Amnesty Internat.; Labour Movement in Europe; World Disarmament Movement; Scottish Educn and Action for Develt; Friends of the Earth (Scotland); Hon. Vice-President: Royal Envmtl Health Inst. of Scotland, 1983–; Internat Fedn on Envmtl Health, 1987–; Inst. of Trading Standards Admin; Socialist Envmt and Resources Assoc. Fellow, Industry and Parlt Trust, 1984–. *Publications:* contributed to European Parliament reports. *Recreations:* Labour Party, music, boxer dogs, cycling. *Address:* 11 Stuarton Park, East Kilbride, Lanarkshire G74 4LA. *T:* East Kilbride (03552) 37282.

COLLINS, Lesley Elizabeth; *see* Appleby, L. E.

COLLINS, Margaret Elizabeth, CBE 1983; RRC; Matron-in-Chief, Queen Alexandra's Royal Naval Nursing Service, 1980–83; *b* 13 Feb. 1927; *d* of James Henry Collins and Amy Collins. *Educ:* St Anne's Convent Grammar Sch., Southampton. RRC 1978 (ARRC 1965). Royal Victoria Hosp., Bournemouth, SRN 1949; West Middlesex Hosp., CMB Part 1; entered QARNNS as Nursing Sister, 1953; accepted for permanent service, 1958; Matron, 1972; Principal Matron, 1976. SSStJ 1978. QHNS, 1980–83. *Recreations:* gardening, theatre-going. *Address:* Lancastria, First Marine Avenue, Barton-on-Sea, Hants BH25 6DP. *T:* New Milton (0425) 612374.

COLLINS, Martin; *see* Collins, J. M.

COLLINS, Michael; aerospace consultant; Vice President, LTV Aerospace and Defense Company (formerly Vought Corporation), 1980–85; former NASA Astronaut; Command Module Pilot, Apollo 11 rocket flight to the Moon, July 1969; *b* Rome, Italy, 31 Oct. 1930; *s* of Maj.-Gen. and Mrs James L. Collins, Washington, DC, USA; *m* 1957, Patricia M. Finnegan, Boston, Mass; one *s* two *d.* *Educ:* St Albans Sch., Washington, DC (grad.). US Mil. Academy, West Point, NY (BSc); advanced through grades to Colonel; Harvard Business Sch. (AMP), 1974. Served as an experimental flight test officer, Air Force Flight Test Center, Edwards Air Force Base, Calif; he was one of the third group of astronauts named by NASA in Oct. 1963; served as backup pilot for Gemini 7 mission; as pilot with John Young on the 3–day 44–revolution Gemini 10 mission, launched 18 July 1966, he shared record-setting flight (successful rendezvous and docking with a separately launched Agena target vehicle; completed two periods of extravehicular activity); Command Module Pilot for Apollo flight, first lunar landing, in orbit 20 July 1969, when Neil Armstrong and Edwin Aldrin landed on the Moon. Asst Sec. of State for Public Affairs, US, 1970–71; Dir, Nat. Air and Space Museum, Smithsonian Institution, 1971–78; Under Sec., Smithsonian Inst., 1978–80. Maj. Gen. Air Force Reserve, retired. Dir, AF Historical Foundn; Member: Bd of Trustees, Rand Corp.; Bd of Trustees, Nat. Geographic Soc.; Washington Historical Monument Soc.; Soc. of Experimental Test Pilots; Internat. Acad. of Astronautics of Internat. Astronautical Fedn; Washington Inst. of Foreign Affairs. FAIAA; Fellow, Amer. Astronautical Soc. Member, Order of Daedalians. Hon. degrees from: Stonehill Coll.; St Michael's Coll.; Northeastern Univ.; Southeastern Univ. Presidential Medal of Freedom, NASA; FAI Gold Space Medal; DSM (NASA); DSM (AF); Exceptional Service Medal (NASA); Astronaut Wings; DFC. *Publications:* Carrying the Fire (autobiog.), 1974; Flying to the Moon and Other Strange Places (for children), 1976; Liftoff, 1988. *Recreations:* fishing, handball. *Address:* LTV Corporation, 1025 Thomas Jefferson Street NW, Washington, DC 20007, USA. *Clubs:* Alfalfa, Alibi (Washington, DC).

COLLINS, Michael Brendan, OBE 1983 (MBE 1969); HM Diplomatic Service; HM Consul-General, Istanbul, since 1988; *b* 9 Sept. 1932; *s* of Daniel James Collins, GM and Mary Bridget Collins (*née* Kennedy); *m* 1959, Maria Elena Lozar. *Educ:* St Illtyd's College, Cardiff; University College London. HM Forces, 1953–55. FO 1956; Santiago, Chile, 1959; Consul, Santiago, Cuba, 1962; FO, 1964; Second, later First, Sec. (Admin.) and Consul, Prague, 1967; Dep. High Comr, Bathurst, The Gambia, 1970; Head of Chancery, Algiers, 1972; First Sec., FCO, 1975; Consul Commercial, Montreal, 1978; Consul for Atlantic Provinces of Canada, Halifax, 1981; Counsellor (Economic and Commercial), Brussels, 1983. *Recreations:* fishing, shooting, golf, walking, reading, music. *Address:* c/o Foreign and Commonwealth Office, SW1A 2AH; British Consulate General, Beyoglu, Istanbul, Turkey. *T:* 144 7540. *Club:* Army and Navy.

COLLINS, Michael Geoffrey; QC 1988; *b* 4 March 1948; *s* of Francis Geoffrey Collins and Margaret Isabelle Collins; *m* 1985, Bonnie Gayle Bird. *Educ:* Peterhouse, Rhodesia (now Zimbabwe); Exeter Univ. (LLB). Called to the Bar, Gray's Inn, 1971. *Publication:* contributor, Private International Litigation, 1988. *Recreations:* golf, tennis, watercolours, amateur dramatics. *Address:* 4 Essex Court, Temple, EC4Y 9AJ. *T:* 071–583 9191.

COLLINS, Michael John; clarinettist; Professor, Royal College of Music, since 1983; *b* 27 Jan. 1962; *s* of Gwendoline Violet and Fred Allenby Collins. *Educ:* Royal Coll. of Music (ARCM, Clarinet and Piano with Hons). BBC Young Musician of the Year, 1978. Principal clarinet: London Sinfonietta, 1982–; Nash Ensemble, 1982–88; Philharmonia Orchestra, 1988–. Musicians' Co. Medal, 1980; competition winner: Leeds, 1980; Concert Artists' Guild, NY, 1982 (Amcon Award); Internat Rostrum of Young Performers, Unesco, 1985; Tagore Gold Medal, 1982. *Recreations:* walking, driving, wildlife. *Address:* 59 Harlington Road West, Feltham, Middx TW14 0JG. *T:* 081–890 9326.

COLLINS, Neil Adam; City Editor, Daily Telegraph, since 1986; *b* 20 Jan. 1947; *s* of Clive and Joan Collins; *m* 1981, Vivien Goldsmith; one *d. Educ:* Uppingham School; Selwyn College, Cambridge (MA). Editor, Investors Guardian, 1973–74; Daily Mail, 1974–79; City Editor: Evening Standard, 1979–84; Sunday Times, 1984–86. *Recreations:* walking, wine. *Address:* 26 Lloyd Square, WC1X 9AD. *T:* 071–833 0497.

COLLINS, Miss Nina; *see* Lowry, Mrs N. M.

COLLINS, Pauline; actress (stage and television); *b* Exmouth, Devon, 3 Sept. 1940; *d* of William Henry Collins and Mary Honora Callanan; *m* John Alderton, *qv;* two *s* one *d. Educ:* Convent of the Sacred Heart, Hammersmith, London; Central Sch. of Speech and Drama. *Stage:* 1st appearance in A Gazelle in Park Lane, Theatre Royal, Windsor, 1962; 1st London appearance in Passion Flower Hotel, Prince of Wales, 1965; The Erpingham Camp, Royal Court, 1967; The Happy Apple, Hampstead, 1967, and Apollo, 1970; Importance of Being Earnest, Haymarket, 1968; The Night I chased the Women with an Eel, 1969; Come As You Are (3 parts), New, 1970; Judies, Comedy, 1974; Engaged, National Theatre, Old Vic, 1975; Confusions, Apollo, 1976; Rattle of a Simple Man, Savoy, 1980; Romantic Comedy, Apollo, 1983; Shirley Valentine, Vaudeville, 1988, NY, 1989 (Tony Award, Best Actress, 1989); *television,* 1962–: series: Upstairs Downstairs; No Honestly; P. G. Wodehouse; Thomas and Sarah; The Black Tower; Forever Green; plays: Long Distance Information, 1979; Knockback, 1984; *film:* Shirley Valentine, 1989 (Evening Standard Film Actress of the Year, 1989; BAFTA Best Actress Award, 1990). *Address:* c/o James Sharkey Associates, 15 Golden Square, W1R 3AG.

COLLINS, Peter G., RSA 1974 (ARSA 1966); painter in oil; lecturer, Duncan of Jordanstone College of Art, Dundee; *b* Inverness, 21 June 1935; *s* of E. G. Collins, FRCSE; *m* 1959, Myra Mackintosh (marr. diss. 1978); one *s* one *d. Educ:* Fettes Coll., Edinburgh; Edinburgh Coll. of Art. Studied in Italy, on Andrew Grant Major Travelling Scholarship, 1957–58. Work in permanent collections: Aberdeen Civic; Glasgow Civic; Scottish Arts Council. *Recreations:* music, art-historical research. *Address:* Royal Scottish Academy, The Mound, Edinburgh; The Cottage, Hilltown of Ballindean, Inchture, Perthshire.

COLLINS, Air Vice-Marshal Peter Spencer, CB 1985; AFC 1961; Consultant Director, Marconi Radar Systems, since 1988; Consultant, GEC-Marconi Research Centre, since 1989; *b* 19 March 1930; *s* of Frederick Wilbore Collins and Mary (*née* Spencer); *m* 1953, Sheila Mary (*née* Perks); three *s* one *d. Educ:* Royal Grammar Sch., High Wycombe; Univ. of Birmingham (BA (Hons) History). FBIM 1979. Joined RAF, 1951; flying tours incl. service on squadron nos: 63, 141, 41, AWDS, AFDS; RAF Handling Sqdn, nos 23 and 11; commanded: 111 Sqdn, 1970–72; RAF Gütersloh, 1974–76; staff tours include: Air Ministry, 1962–64; Strike Comd HQ, 1968–70 and 1972–74; Dir of Forward Policy (RAF), 1978–81; SASO, HQ 11 Gp, 1981–83; DG, Communications, Inf. Systems and Orgn (RAF), 1983–85; psc 1965, rcds 1977; retired 1985. Dir, Business Develt, Marconi Radar Systems, 1986–88. *Publications:* contribs to service jls and to Seaford House Papers, 1978. *Recreations:* golf, music, stock market. *Address:* Babylon, Boreham, Essex CM3 3EJ. *Club:* Royal Air Force.

COLLINS, Philip; singer, drummer, songwriter, actor and record producer; Trustee, Prince's Trust, since 1983; patron of numerous charities; *b* 30 Jan. 1951; *s* of Greville and June Collins; *m* 1st, 1976 (marr. diss.); one *s* one *d;* 2nd, 1984, Jill Tavelman; one *d. Educ:* primary and secondary schs; Barbara Speake Stage Sch. Played parts in various television, film and stage productions, 1965–67; mem. of various rock groups, 1967–70; drummer, 1970–, lead singer, 1975–, Genesis; started writing songs, 1976; toured Japan, USA and Europe, 1978, 1987; first solo album, 1981; solo world tours, 1985, 1990; started producing records for other artists, 1981. *Albums* include: *with Genesis:* Nursury Crime, 1971; Foxtrot, 1972; Genesis Live, 1973; Selling England by the Pound, 1973; The Lamb Lies Down on Broadway, 1974; A Trick of the Tail, 1976; Genesis Rock Roots, 1976; Wind and Wuthering, 1977; Genesis Seconds Out, 1977; And Then There Were Three, 1978; Duke, 1980; Abacab, 1981; Three Sides Live, 1982; Genesis, 1983; Invisible Touch, 1986; *solo:* Face Value, 1981; Hello . . . I must be Going, 1982; No Jacket Required, 1985; But Seriously, 1989. Lead role, film, Buster, 1988. Numerous awards, incl. Grammy (seven), Ivor Novello (six), Brit (four), Variety Club of GB (two), Silver Clef (two), and Elvis awards. *Address:* c/o Hit & Run Music, 25 Ives Street, SW3 2ND.

COLLINS, Prof. Philip Arthur William; Emeritus Professor of English, University of Leicester, since 1982; *b* 28 May 1923; *er s* of Arthur Henry and Winifred Nellie Collins; *m* 1st, 1952, Mildred Lowe (marr. diss. 1963); 2nd, 1965, Joyce Dickins; two *s* one *d. Educ:* Brentwood Sch.; Emmanuel Coll., Cambridge (Sen. Schol.). MA 1948. Served War (RAOC and Royal Norfolk Regt), 1942–45. Leicester: Staff Tutor in Adult Educn, 1947; Warden, Vaughan Coll., 1954; Sen. Lectr in English, 1962–64; Prof., 1964–82; Head, English Dept, 1971–76, 1981–82; Public Orator, 1975–78, 1980–82. Visiting Prof.: Univ. of California, Berkeley, 1967; Columbia, 1969; Victoria Univ., NZ, 1974. Sec., Leicester Theatre Trust Ltd, 1963–87; Member: Drama Panel, Arts Council of Gt Britain, 1970–75; National Theatre Bd, 1976–82; British American Drama Acad. Bd, 1983–; Pres., Dickens Fellowship, 1983–85; Chm. Trustees, Dickens House Museum, 1984–; Chm., Tennyson Soc., 1984–. Many overseas lecture-tours; performances, talks and scripts for radio and television. *Publications:* James Boswell, 1956; (ed) English Christmas, 1956; Dickens and Crime, 1962; Dickens and Education, 1963; The Canker and the Rose (Shakespeare Quater-centenary celebration) perf. Mermaid Theatre, London, 1964; The Impress of the Moving Age, 1965; Thomas Cooper the Chartist, 1969; A Dickens Bibliography, 1970; Dickens's Bleak House, 1971; (ed) Dickens, the Critical Heritage, 1971; (ed) A Christmas Carol: the public reading version, 1971; Reading Aloud: a Victorian Métier, 1972; (ed) Dickens's Public Readings, 1975; Dickens's David Copperfield, 1977; (ed) Dickens: Interviews and Recollections, 1981; (ed) Thackeray: Interviews and Recollections, 1983; Trollope's London, 1983; (ed) Dickens: Sikes and Nancy and other Readings, 1983; Tennyson, Poet of Lincolnshire, 1984; (co-ed) The Annotated Dickens, 1986; contrib. to: Encyclopaedia Britannica, Listener, TLS, sundry learned journals. *Recreations:* theatre, music. *Address:* 26 Knighton Drive, Leicester LE2 3HB. *T:* Leicester (0533) 706026.

COLLINS, Stuart Verdun, CB 1970; retired; Chief Inspector of Audit, Department of the Environment (formerly Ministry of Housing and Local Government), 1968–76; *b* 24 Feb. 1916; *m* 1st, 1942, Helen Simpson (*d* 1968); two *d;* 2nd, 1970, Joan Mary Walmsley (widow); one *step s* two *step d. Educ:* Plymouth Coll. Entered Civil Service as Audit Assistant in the District Audit Service of the Ministry of Health, 1934; appointed District Auditor for the London Audit District, 1958. IPFA, FBCS. *Recreations:* golf, do-it-yourself, sailing. *Address:* Kemendine, Court Wood, Newton Ferrers, Devon PL8 1BW.

COLLINS, Terence Bernard; Chairman, 1984–87, Group Managing Director, 1975–86, Berger Jenson Nicholson; *b* 3 March 1927; *s* of George Bernard Collins and Helen Teresa Collins; *m* 1956, Barbara (*née* Lowday); two *s* two *d. Educ:* Marist Coll., Hull; Univ. of St Andrews (MA Hons). Trainee, Ideal Standard, 1951–52; Blundell Spence: Area Manager, 1953–55; Regl Manager, 1955–57; Nat. Sales Manager, 1957–59; Berger Jenson Nicholson: Sales Manager, 1959–62; Man. Dir, Caribbean, 1962–69; Overseas Regl Exec., 1969–70; Gp Dir UK, 1971–74. Chairman: Cranfield Conf. Services Ltd, 1987–; Cranfield Ventures Ltd, 1990–; Director: A. G. Stanley Hldgs, 1977–87; Hoechst UK, 1979–87; Hoechst Australia Investments, 1980–87; Mayborn Gp PLC, 1986–; Phoenix Develts Ltd, 1987–; Aldehurst Consultants Ltd, 1987–; C.I.T. Holdings Ltd, 1989–; Cranfield Precision Engineering Ltd, 1990–; Member: Management Bd, Kingline Consultants Ltd, 1989–90; Bd, Atlas Economic Foundn UK, 1986–. Mem., Duke of Edinburgh's Award Internat. Panel, 1978–86. Mem., Ct and Council, Cranfield Inst. of Technology, 1977–; Vice-Chm. Council, 1987–, Chm., F and GP Cttee, 1987–, Univ. of Buckingham. *Recreations:* golf, music, gardening. *Address:* Aldehurst, Church Walk, Aldeburgh, Suffolk IP15 5DX. *Clubs:* Directors; Aldeburgh Golf.

COLLINS, Brig. Thomas Frederick James, CBE 1945 (OBE 1944); JP; DL; *b* 9 April 1905; *s* of Capt. J. A. Collins and Emily (*née* Truscott); *m* 1942, Marjorie Morwenna, *d* of Lt-Col T. Donnelly, DSO; one *d. Educ:* Haileybury; RMC, Sandhurst. Gazetted to Green Howards, 1924; Staff College, 1938. Served War of 1939–45 (despatches twice, OBE, CBE): France, 1940, NW Europe, 1944–45. Retired, with rank of Brig., 1948. Essex County Council: CC, 1960; Vice-Chm., 1967; Chm., 1968–71. JP 1968, DL 1969, Essex. Comdr, Order of Leopold II (Belgium), 1945. *Recreation:* shooting. *Address:* Ashdon Hall, Saffron Walden, Essex CB10 2HF. *T:* Ashdon (079984) 232. *Club:* Army and Navy.

COLLINS, William Janson; Chairman, William Collins Sons & Co. (Holdings) Ltd, 1976–81; *b* 10 June 1929; *s* of late Sir William Alexander Roy Collins, CBE, and Lady Collins (Priscilla Marian, *d* of late S. J. Lloyd); *m* 1951, Lady Sara Elena Hely-Hutchinson, *d* of 7th Earl of Donoughmore; one *s* three *d. Educ:* Magdalen Coll., Oxford (BA). Joined William Collins Sons & Co. Ltd, 1952; Dir, then Man. Dir, 1967; Vice-Chm., 1971; Chm., 1976. *Recreations:* Royal tennis, shooting, fishing, tennis, golf. *Address:* House of Craigie, by Kilmarnock, Ayrshire KA1 5NA. *T:* Craigie (056386) 246. *Clubs:* Boodle's; All England Lawn Tennis and Croquet.

COLLINSON, Prof. Patrick, PhD; FBA 1982; FRHistS, FAHA; Regius Professor of Modern History, University of Cambridge, since 1988; Fellow of Trinity College, Cambridge, since 1988; *b* 10 Aug. 1929; *s* of William Cecil Collinson and Belle Hay (*née* Patrick); *m* 1960, Elizabeth Albinia Susan Selwyn; two *s* two *d. Educ:* King's Sch., Ely; Pembroke Coll., Cambridge (Exhibnr 1949, Foundn Scholar 1952; BA 1952, 1st Cl. Hons Hist. Tripos Pt II; Hadley Prize for Hist., 1952). PhD London, 1957; FRHistS 1967 (Mem. Council, 1977–81, Vice-Pres., 1983–87); FAHA 1974. University of London: Postgrad. Student, Royal Holloway Coll., 1952–54; Res. Fellow, Inst. of Hist. Res., 1954–55; Res. Asst, UCL, 1955–56; Lectr in Hist., Univ. of Khartoum, 1956–61; Asst Lectr in Eccles. Hist., King's Coll., Univ. of London, 1961–62, Lectr, 1962–69 (Fellow 1976); Professor of History: Univ. of Sydney, 1969–75; Univ. of Kent at Canterbury, 1976–84; Prof. of Modern Hist., Sheffield Univ., 1984–88. Vis. Fellow, All Souls Coll., Oxford, 1981; Andrew W. Mellon Fellow, Huntington Library, California, 1984. Lectures: Ford's, in Eng. Hist., Univ. of Oxford, 1978–79; Birkbeck, Univ. of Cambridge, 1981; Stenton Meml, Univ. of Reading, 1985; Neale Meml, Univ. of Manchester, 1986; Anstey Meml, Univ. of Kent, 1986; Neale Meml, UCL, 1987; F. D. Maurice, KCL, 1990. Pres., Ecclesiastical Hist. Soc., 1985–86. Mem. Council, British Acad., 1986–89. Mem., Academia Europaea, 1989; Corresp. Mem., Massachusetts Historical Soc., 1990. DUniv York, 1988; Hon. DLitt Kent at Canterbury, 1989. Chm., Adv. Editorial Bd, Jl of Ecclesiastical History, 1982–. *Publications:* The Elizabethan Puritan Movement, 1967 (USA 1967; repr. 1982); Archbishop Grindal 1519–1583: the struggle for a Reformed Church, 1979 (USA 1979); The Religion of Protestants: the Church in English Society 1559–1625 (Ford Lectures, 1979), 1982; Godly People: essays on English Protestantism and Puritanism, 1983; English Puritanism, 1983; The Birthpangs of Protestant England: religious and cultural change in the 16th and 17th centuries, 1988; articles and revs in Bull. Inst. Hist. Res., Eng. Hist. Rev., Jl of Eccles. Hist., Studies in Church Hist., TLS. *Recreations:* mountains, fishing, music, gardening. *Address:* 23 Hinton Avenue, Cambridge; The Winnats, Cannonfields, Hathersage, Sheffield S30 1AG; Trinity College, Cambridge CB2 1TQ; Faculty of History, West Road, Cambridge.

COLLISON, family name of **Baron Collison.**

COLLISON, Baron (Life Peer) *cr* 1964, of Cheshunt; **Harold Francis Collison,** CBE 1961; Chairman, Supplementary Benefits Commission, 1969–75; *b* 10 May 1909; *m* 1946, Ivy Kate Hanks. *Educ:* The Hay Currie LCC Sch.; Crypt Sch., Gloucester. Firstly, worked in a commercial office in London; farm worker in Glos, 1934–53. National Union of Agricultural Workers (later Nat. Union of Agricultural and Allied Workers): District Organiser in Gloucester and Worcs, 1944; Nat. Officer, 1946; General Secretary, 1953–69. Mem., TUC Gen. Coun., 1953–69, Chm., 1964–65; Chm., Social Insce and Industrial Welfare Cttee of TUC, 1957–69. President: Internat. Fedn of Plantation, Agricultural and Allied Workers, 1960–76; Assoc. of Agriculture, 1976–84; Member: Coun. on Tribunals, 1959–69; Nat. Insce Adv. Cttee, 1959–69; Governing Body of ILO, 1960–69; Pilkington Cttee on Broadcasting, 1960–62; Central Transport Consultative Cttee, 1962–70; Agric. Adv. Council, 1962–80; Adv. Cttee on Agricultural Educn, 1963; Royal Commn on Trades Unions and Employers' Assocs, 1965–68; Home-Grown Cereals Authority, 1965–78; former Member: Industrial Health Adv. Cttee; Economic Develt for Agriculture; Industrial Consultative Cttee, Approach to Europe; Overseas Labour Consultative Cttee; Agric. Productivity Cttee, British Productivity Council; Chairman: Land Settlement Assoc., 1977–79 (Vice-Chm., 1964–77); Agric. Apprenticeship Council, 1968–74; Mem., N Thames Gas Board (part-time), 1961–72. Mem., Governing Body, Brooklands Technical Coll., Weybridge, 1970–85 (Chm., 1977–85). *Recreations:* gardening, chess. *Address:* Honeywood, 163 Old Nazeing Road, Broxbourne, Herts EN10 6QT. *T:* Hoddesdon (0992) 463597.

COLLYEAR, Sir John (Gowen), Kt 1986; FEng 1979; Chairman, United Machinery Group Ltd, since 1987; *b* 19 Feb. 1927; *s* of John Robert Collyear and Amy Elizabeth Collyear (*née* Gowen); *m* 1953, Catherine Barbara Newman; one *s* two *d. Educ:* Leeds Univ. (BSc). FIMechE, FIProdE; CBIM. Graduate apprentice and Production Engr, Joseph Lucas Industries, 1951; Glacier Metal Company Ltd: Production Engr, 1953; Production Manager, 1956; Chief Production Engr, 1956; Factory Gen. Manager, 1959; Managing Director, 1969; Bearings Div. Man. Dir, Associated Engineering Ltd, 1972; Group Man. Dir, AE plc, 1975, Chm., 1981–86. Chairman: MK Electric Gp PLC, 1987–88; Fulmer Ltd, 1987–91; Dir, Hollis plc, 1987–88. Chm., Technology Requirements Bd, DTI, 1985–88. Pres., MIRA, 1987–. FRSA 1987. *Publications:* Management Precepts, 1975; The Practice of First Level Management, 1976. *Recreations:* golf, bridge, piano music. *Address:* Walnut Tree House, Nether Westcote, Oxon OX7 6SD. *T:* Shipton-under-Wychwood (0993) 831247. *Club:* Athenæum.

COLMAN, Anthony David, QC 1977; barrister-at-law; a Recorder, since 1986; *b* 27 May 1938; *s* of Solomon Colman and late Helen Colman; *m* 1964, Angela Glynn; two *d. Educ:* Harrogate Grammar Sch.; Trinity Hall, Cambridge (Aldis Schol.; Double First in Law Tripos; MA). FCIArb 1978. Called to the Bar, Gray's Inn, 1962, Master of the Bench, 1986. Mem., Bar Council, 1990– (Chm., Trust Funds Cttee, 1988–); Treasurer, Commercial Bar Assoc., 1989–; Chm., Lloyd's Disciplinary Cttee for PCW and Minet, 1984; Mem., Cttee of Enquiry into Fidentia at Lloyd's, 1982–83. *Publications:* Mathew's

Practice of the Commercial Court (1902), 2nd edn, 1967; The Practice and Procedure of the Commercial Court, 1983, 3rd edn, 1990. *Recreations:* cricket, tennis, music, gardening, the 17th Century, Sifnos, the River Chess. *Address:* 4 Essex Court, Temple, EC4Y 9AJ. *T:* 071–583 9191.

COLMAN, Anthony John; Chairman, Retail Solutions Ltd, since 1991; Leader of Council, London Borough of Merton, since 1991 (Councillor, since 1990); *b* 24 July 1943; *s* of late William Benjamin Colman and Beatrice (*née* Hudson); *m* Juliet Annabelle, *d* of Alec and June Owen; four *s* two *d* by prev. *ms. Educ:* Paston Grammar Sch.; Magdalene Coll., Cambridge (MA); Univ. of E Africa, 1964–66; LSE, 1966. Unilever (United Africa Co.), 1964–69; Burton Group, 1969–90: Merchandise Manager, Buying and Merchandising Dir, Top Shop, 1969–76; Asst Man. Dir, Womenswear Sector, 1976–81; Director: Burton Menswear, Top Man, 1976–81; Dorothy Perkins, 1979–81; Dir, 1981–90. Chairman: Prime Retail, 1990–92; Urban Culture, 1991–; New Order, 1991–; East Ocean Trading, 1991–; Director: GLE, 1990– (Chm., GLE Development Capital, 1990–); Aztec, 1990–. Chm., Low Pay Unit, 1990–; Vice-Chm., ALA, 1991–; Member: Price Commn, 1977–79; Exec., Labour Finance & Industry Gp; Labour Party Enquiry into Educn & Trng in Europe, 1991–. Contested (Lab), SW Herts, 1979. Industrial Fellow, Kingston Polytechnic, 1983–. FRSA 1983. *Address:* 14 Lambourne Avenue, Wimbledon Village, SW19 7DW. *T:* 081–879 0045. *Club:* Reform.

COLMAN, David Stacy, MA; retired; *b* Broughty Ferry, Angus, 1 May 1906; *yr s* of Dr H. C. Colman; *m* 1934, Sallie Edwards (*d* 1970). *Educ:* Shrewsbury Sch.; Balliol Coll., Oxford (Scholar). 1st Class Hon. Mods, 1926; 1st Class Lit. Hum., 1928. Asst Master at Shrewsbury Sch., 1928–31 and 1935–36; Fellow of Queen's Coll., Oxford and Praelector in Classics and Ancient History, 1931–34; Headmaster, C of E Grammar Sch., Melbourne, 1937–38; Shrewsbury School: Asst Master, 1938–66; Master of Day Boys, 1949–61; Librarian, 1961–66. Mem Council, Soc. for Promotion of Roman Studies, 1958–61, Classical Assoc., 1961–64. *Publication:* Sabrinae Corolla: The Classics at Shrewsbury School under Dr Butler and Dr Kennedy, 1950. *Address:* 19 Woodfield Road, Shrewsbury SY3 8HZ. *T:* Shrewsbury (0743) 353749. *Clubs:* National Liberal; Leander; Salop (Shrewsbury).

COLMAN, Sir Michael (Jeremiah), 3rd Bt *cr* 1907; Chairman, Reckitt and Colman plc, since 1986; *b* 7 July 1928; *s* of Sir Jeremiah Colman, 2nd Bt, and Edith Gwendolyn Tritton; *S* father, 1961; *m* 1955, Judith Jean Wallop, *d* of Vice-Adm. Sir Peveril William-Powlett, KCB, KCMG, CBE, DSO; two *s* three *d. Educ:* Eton. Director: Reckitt & Colman plc; Foreign and Colonial Ventures Advisors Ltd, 1988–. Member: Council of Royal Warrant Holders, 1977–, Pres., 1984–85; Trinity House Lighthouse Bd, 1985–. Member: Council, Chemical Industries Assoc., 1982–84; Bd, UK Centre for Econ. and Environmental Develt, 1985–. Mem., Council, Scout Assoc., 1985–. Mem. Gen. Council and Mem. Finance Cttee, King Edward's Hosp. Fund for London, 1978–; Associate Trustee, St Mary's Hosp., 1988–; Trustee, Royal Foundn of Grey Coat Hosp., 1989–. Capt., Yorks Yeomanry, RARO, 1967. Mem. Ct, Skinners' Co., 1985– (Master, 1991–May 1992). FRSA. *Recreations:* farming, shooting. *Heir: s* Jeremiah Michael Powlett Colman [*b* 23 Jan. 1958; *m* 1981, Susan Elizabeth, *yr d* of John Henry Britland, York; two *s* one *d*]. *Address:* Malshanger, Basingstoke, Hants. *T:* Basingstoke (0256) 780241; 40 Chester Square, SW1; Tarvie, Bridge of Cally, Blairgowrie, Perthshire. *T:* Strathardle (025081) 264. *Club:* Cavalry and Guards.

COLMAN, Timothy James Alan; Lord-Lieutenant of Norfolk, since 1978; *b* 19 Sept. 1929; 2nd but *o* surv. *s* of late Captain Geoffrey Russell Rees Colman and Lettice Elizabeth Evelyn Colman, Norwich; *m* 1951, Lady Mary Cecelia (Extra Lady in Waiting to Princess Alexandra), twin *d* of late Lt-Col Hon. Michael Claude Hamilton Bowes Lyon and Elizabeth Margaret, Glamis; two *s* three *d. Educ:* RNC, Dartmouth and Greenwich. Lieut RN, 1950, retd 1953. Chm., Eastern Counties Newspapers Group Ltd; Director: Reckitt & Colman plc, 1978–89; Anglia Television Ltd; Whitbread & Co. PLC, 1980–86; Trustee, Carnegie UK Trust (Chm., 1983–87). Pro-Chancellor, Univ. of E Anglia (Chm. Council, 1973–86); Chairman: Trustees, Norfolk and Norwich Triennial Festival, 1974–; Royal Norfolk Agricl Assoc., 1985– (Pres., 1982). Member: Countryside Commn, 1971–76; Water Space Amenity Commn, 1973–76; Adv. Cttee for England, Nature Conservancy Council, 1974–80; Eastern Regional Cttee, National Trust, 1967–71; Pres., Norfolk Naturalists Trust, 1962–78. JP 1958, DL 1968, High Sheriff 1970, Norfolk. Hon. DCL E Anglia, 1973. KStJ 1979. *Address:* Bixley Manor, Norwich, Norfolk NR14 8SJ. *T:* Norwich (0603) 625298. *Clubs:* Turf, Pratt's; Royal Yacht Squadron.

COLNBROOK, Baron *cr* 1987 (Life Peer), of Waltham St Lawrence in the Royal County of Berkshire; **Humphrey Edward Gregory Atkins,** KCMG 1983; PC 1973; *b* 12 Aug. 1922; *s* of late Capt. E. D. Atkins, Nyeri, Kenya Colony; *m* 1944, Margaret, *d* of Sir Robert Spencer-Nairn, 1st Bt; one *s* three *d. Educ:* Wellington Coll. Special entry cadetship, RN, 1940; Lieut RN, 1943; resigned, 1948. MP (C): Merton and Morden, Surrey, 1955–70; Spelthorne, 1970–87. PPS to Civil Lord of the Admiralty, 1959–62; Hon. Sec. Conservative Parly Defence Cttee, 1965–67; Opposition Whip, 1967–70; Treasurer of HM Household and Dep. Chief Whip, 1970–73; Parly Sec. to the Treasury and Govt Chief Whip, 1973–74; Opposition Chief Whip, 1974–79; Secretary of State for N Ireland, 1979–81; Lord Privy Seal, 1981–82. Chm., Select Cttee on Defence, 1984–87. Pres., Nat. Union of Conservative and Unionist Assocs, 1985–86. Underwriting Mem. of Lloyd's. Mem., Press Complaints Commn, 1991–. Vice-Chm., Management Cttee, Outward Bound Trust, 1966–70; Chm., Airey Neave Trust, 1984–90. *Address:* Tuckenhams, Waltham St Lawrence, Reading, Berks RG10 0JH. *Club:* Brooks's.

COLOMBO, Metropolitan Archbishop of, (RC), since 1977; **Most Rev. Nicholas Marcus Fernando,** STD; *b* 6 Dec. 1932. *Educ:* St Aloysius' Seminary, Colombo; Universitas Propaganda Fide, Rome. BA (London); PhL (Rome); STD (Rome). Mem., Sacred Congregation for Evangelization of Peoples; Pres., Catholic Bishops' Conf. of Sri Lanka, 1989–April 1992. *Address:* Archbishop's House, Borella, Colombo 8, Sri Lanka. *T:* 695471/2/3.

COLOMBO, Emilio; Deputy (Christian Democrat), Italian Parliament, since 1948; Minister of Foreign Affairs, Italy, 1980–83; *b* Potenza, Italy, 11 April 1920. *Educ:* Rome Univ. Deputy, Constituent Assembly, 1946–48; Under-Secretary: of Agriculture, 1948–51; of Public Works, 1953–55; Minister: of Agriculture, 1955–58; of Foreign Trade, 1958–59; of Industry and Commerce, 1959–60, March-April 1960, July 1960–63; of the Treasury, 1963–70, Feb.-May 1972, 1974–76; Prime Minister, 1970–72; Minister of State for UN Affairs, 1972–73; Minister of Finance, 1973–74. European Parliament: Mem., 1976–80; Chm., Political Affairs Cttee, 1976–77; Pres., 1977–79. Formerly Vice-Pres., Italian Catholic Youth Assoc. Charlemagne Prize, 1979. *Address:* Camera dei Deputati, Rome, Italy; Via Aurelia 239, Rome, Italy.

COLQUHOUN, Andrew John, PhD; Secretary and Chief Executive, Institute of Chartered Accountants in England and Wales, since 1990; *b* 21 Sept. 1949; *s* of late Kenneth James Colquhoun, MC, and of Christine Mary Colquhoun (*née* Morris); *m* 1975, Patricia Beardall; one *s* one *d. Educ:* Tiffin Sch.; Nottingham Univ. (BSc 1st Cl. Hons 1971); Glasgow Univ. (PhD 1974); City Univ. Business Sch. (MBA Dist. 1987). Joined HM Diplomatic Service, 1974; Third Sec., FCO, 1974–75; Second Sec., MECAS, 1975–77; Second, later First, Sec., Damascus, 1977–79; First Sec., Tel Aviv, 1979–81; Principal, Cabinet Office, 1981–83; Planning Staff, FCO, 1983–84; Shandwick Consultants (on secondment to ICA), 1984–86; Dir of Educn and Trng, ICA, 1987–90. Sec., Consultative Cttee of Accountancy Bodies, 1990–. *Publications:* various articles on accountancy, educn and recruitment in nat., educnl and professional press. *Recreations:* boating, bird watching, country life, reading. *Address:* PO Box 433, Chartered Accountants' Hall, Moorgate Place, EC2P 2BJ; 17 By Sunte, Lindfield, West Sussex. *T:* Haywards Heath (0444) 414705.

COLQUHOUN, Maj.-Gen. Sir Cyril (Harry), KCVO 1968 (CVO 1965); CB 1955; OBE 1945; late Royal Artillery; Secretary of the Central Chancery of the Orders of Knighthood, 1960–68; Extra Gentleman Usher to the Queen since 1968; *b* 1903; *s* of late Capt. Harry Colquhoun; *m* 1930, Stella Irene, *d* of late W. C. Rose, Kotagiri, India, and Cheam, Surrey; one *s. Educ:* RMA, Woolwich. Commnd RA, 1923; served War of 1939–45 (despatches, OBE); Palestine, 1946–48 (despatches); Comdr, 6th, 76th and 1st Field Regiments; CRA 61st Div., 1945; CRA 6th Airborne Div., 1947–48; CRA 1st Infantry Div., 1949–50; Comdt, Sch. of Artillery, 1951–53; GOC 50th (Northumbrian) Infantry Div. (TA), and Northumbrian District, 1954–56; GOC Troops, Malta, 1956–59; retired 1960. Col Commandant: Royal Artillery, 1962–69; Royal Malta Artillery, 1962–70. *Recreations:* gardening, shooting. *Address:* Longwalls, Shenington, Banbury, Oxon OX15 6NQ. *T:* Edge Hill (029587) 246. *Club:* Army and Navy.

COLQUHOUN, Prof. David, FRS 1985; Professor of Pharmacology, University College London, since 1983; *b* 19 July 1936; *s* of Gilbert Colquhoun and Kathleen Mary (*née* Chambers); *m* 1976, Margaret Ann Boultwood; one *s. Educ:* Birkenhead Sch.; Liverpool Technical Coll.; Leeds Univ. (BSc); Edinburgh Univ. (PhD). Lectr, Dept of Pharmacol., UCL, 1964–70; Vis. Asst, then Associate Prof., Dept of Pharmacol., Yale Univ. Med. Sch., 1970–72; Sen. Lectr, Dept of Pharmacol., Univ. of Southampton Med. Sch., 1972–75; Sen. Lectr, Dept of Pharmacol., St George's Hosp. Med. Sch., 1975–79; Reader, Dept of Pharmacol., UCL, 1979–83. Guest Prof., Max-Planck-Institut für Medizinische Forschung, Heidelberg, 1990–91. Krantz Lectr, Univ. of Maryland, 1987. Trustee, Sir Ronald Fisher Meml Cttee, 1975–. Alexander von Humboldt Prize, 1990. Member Editorial Board: Jl of Physiology, 1974–81; Series B, Proceedings of Royal Soc. *Publications:* Lectures on Biostatistics, 1971; articles in Jl of Physiology, British Jl of Pharmacology, Proc. of Royal Soc., etc. *Recreations:* walking, running, sailing, linear algebra. *Address:* 7 Beech Close, Walton-on-Thames, Surrey KT12 5RG. *T:* Walton-on-Thames (0932) 244021.

COLQUHOUN, Rev. Canon Frank, MA; Canon Residentiary of Norwich Cathedral, 1973–78, Canon Emeritus, since 1978; Vice-Dean, 1974–78; *b* 28 Oct. 1909; *s* of Rev. R. W. Colquhoun; *m* 1st, 1934, Dora Gertrude Hearne Slater; one *s* one *d*; 2nd, 1973, Judy Kenney. *Educ:* Warwick Sch.; Durham Univ. LTh 1932, BA 1933, MA 1937, Durham. Deacon, 1933; Priest, 1934; Curate, St Faith, Maidstone, 1933–35; Curate, New Malden, Surrey, 1935–39; Vicar, St Michael and All Angels, Blackheath Park, SE3, 1939–46; Editorial Sec., Nat. Church League, 1946–52; Priest-in-Charge, Christ Church, Woburn Square, WC1, 1952–54; Vicar of Wallington, Surrey, 1954–61; Canon Residentiary of Southwark Cathedral, 1961–73; Principal, Southwark Ordination Course, 1966–72. Editor, The Churchman, 1946–53. *Publications:* The Living Church in the Parish (ed), 1952; Harringay Story, 1954; Your Child's Baptism, 1958; The Gospels, 1961; Total Christianity, 1962; The Catechism, 1963; Lent with Pilgrim's Progress, 1965; Christ's Ambassadors, 1965; (ed) Parish Prayers, 1967; (ed) Hard Questions, 1967; Preaching through the Christian Year, 1972; Strong Son of God, 1973; Preaching at the Parish Communion, 1974; Contemporary Parish Prayers, 1975; (ed) Moral Questions, 1977; Hymns that Live, 1980; Prayers that Live, 1981; New Parish Prayers, 1982; Family Prayers, 1984; Fourfold Portrait of Jesus, 1984; A Hymn Companion, 1985; Preaching on Favourite Hymns, 1986; (ed) Your Favourite Songs of Praise, 1987; Sing to the Lord, 1988; Prayers for Today, 1989; More Preaching on Favourite Hymns, 1990; God of our Fathers, 1990. *Recreations:* writing, listening to music. *Address:* 21 Buckholt Avenue, Bexhill-on-Sea, East Sussex TN40 2RS. *T:* Bexhill (0424) 221138.

COLQUHOUN OF LUSS, Captain Sir Ivar (Iain), 8th Bt *cr* 1786; JP; DL; Hon. Sheriff (formerly Hon. Sheriff Substitute); Chief of the Clan; Grenadier Guards; *b* 4 Jan. 1916; *s* of Sir Iain Colquhoun, 7th Bt, and Geraldine Bryde (Dinah) (*d* 1974), *d* of late F. J. Tennant; *S* father, 1948; *m* 1943, Kathleen, 2nd *d* of late W. A. Duncan and of Mrs Duncan, 53 Cadogan Square, SW1; one *s* one *d* (and one *s* decd). *Educ:* Eton. JP 1951, DL 1952, Dunbartonshire. *Heir: s* Malcolm Rory Colquhoun, Younger of Luss [*b* 20 Dec. 1947; *m* 1st, 1978, Susan Timmerman (marr. diss.); one *s*; 2nd, 1989, Katharine, *e d* of A. C. Mears; one *s*]. *Address:* Camstraddan, Luss, Dunbartonshire; Eilean da Mheinn, Crinan, Argyllshire; 26A Thorney Crescent, SW11. *Clubs:* White's, Royal Ocean Racing.

See also Duke of Argyll.

COLQUHOUN, Ms Maureen Morfydd; political researcher and writer; Director, Westminster Democratic Studies Ltd, since 1989; *b* 12 Aug. 1928; *m* 1949, Keith Colquhoun (marr. diss. 1980); two *s* one *d*. Partner, 1975–, Ms Barbara Todd; extended family, two *d*. Mem. Labour Party, 1945–; Councillor: Shoreham UDC, 1965–74; Adur District Council, 1973–74; County Councillor, West Sussex CC, 1971–74; Mem., Hackney BC, 1982–90. MP (Lab) Northampton North, Feb. 1974–1979. Information Officer, Gingerbread, 1980–82. Hon. Sec., All-Party Parly Gp on AIDS, 1987–88. Trustee and Hon. Treas., Albany Soc., 1980–90. *Publication:* A Woman In the House, 1980. *Recreations:* walking, jazz, opera, theatre. *Address:* 19 Vicars Close, E9 7HT.

COLSTON, Colin Charles; QC 1980; **His Honour Judge Colston;** a Circuit Judge, since 1983; Resident Judge, St Albans, since 1989; *b* 2 Oct. 1937; *yr s* of late Eric Colston, JP, and Catherine Colston; *m* 1963, Edith Helga, JP, *d* of Med. Rat Dr Wilhelm and Frau Gisela Hille, St Oswald/Freistadt, Austria; two *s* one *d. Educ:* Rugby Sch.; The Gunnery, Washington, Conn, USA; Trinity Hall, Cambridge (MA). National Service, RN, 1956–58; commissioned, RNR, 1958–64. Called to the Bar, Gray's Inn, 1962; Midland and Oxford Circuit (formerly Midland Circuit); Recorder of Midland Circuit, 1968–69; Member, Senate of Inns of Court and Bar, 1977–80; Recorder of the Crown Court, 1978–83. Mem., Criminal Cttee, Judicial Studies Bd, 1989–. Chm., St Albans Diocesan Bd of Patronage, 1987–. *Address:* The Crown Court, St Albans, Herts.

COLSTON, Michael; Chairman: Colston Consultants Ltd, since 1989; Quit Ltd, since 1989; *b* 24 July 1932; *s* of Sir Charles Blampied Colston, CBE, MC, DCM, FCGI and Lady (Eliza Foster) Colston, MBE; *m* 1st, 1956, Jane Olivia Kilham Roberts (marr. diss.); three *d*; 2nd, 1977, Judith Angela Briggs. *Educ:* Ridley Coll., Canada; Stowe; Gonville and Caius Coll., Cambridge. Joined 17th/21st Lancers, 1952; later seconded to 1st Royal Tank Regt for service in Korea. Founder Dir, Charles Colston Group Ltd (formerly Colston Appliances Ltd) together with late Sir Charles Colston, 1955, Chm. and Man. Dir, 1969–89; Chm. and Man. Dir, Colston Domestic Appliances Ltd, 1969–79. Chairman: Tallent Engineering Ltd, 1969–89; Tallent Holdings plc, 1989–90; ITS Rubber Ltd, 1969–85; Dishwasher Council, 1970–75. Chm., Assoc. Manufrs of Domestic

Electrical Appliances, 1976–79. Member Council: Inst. of Directors, 1977– (Pres., Thames Valley Br., 1983–); CBI, 1984–90 (Chm., S Regl Council, 1986–88); British Electrotechnical Approvals Bd, 1976–79; SMMT, 1987–90. *Recreations:* fishing, shooting, tennis; founder Cambridge Univ. Water Ski Club. *Address:* C6 Albany, Piccadilly, W1V 9RF. *T:* 071–734 2452.

COLT, Sir Edward (William Dutton), 10th Bt *cr* 1694; MB, MRCP, FACP; Assistant Attending Physician, St Luke's-Roosevelt Hospital, New York; Assistant Professor of Clinical Medicine (part-time), Columbia University, New York; *b* 22 Sept. 1936; *s* of Major John Rochfort Colt, North Staffs Regt (*d* 1944), and of Angela Miriam Phyllis (*née* Kyan; she *m* 1946, Capt. Robert Leslie Cock); *S* uncle, 1951; *m* 1st, 1966, Jane Caroline (marr. diss. 1972), *d* of James Histed Lewis, Geneva and Washington, DC; 2nd, 1979, Suzanne Nelson (*née* Knickerbocker); one *s* one *d*. *Educ:* Stoke House, Seaford; Douai Sch.; University Coll., London. Lately: Medical Registrar, UCH; House Physician, Brompton Hosp. *Publications:* contribs, especially on sports medicine, particularly running, to British and American med. jls. *Recreations:* cycling, jogging, skiing, squash. *Heir: s* Tristan Charles Edward Colt, *b* 27 June 1983. *Address:* 12 E 88 Street, New York, NY 10128, USA.

COLTHURST, Sir Richard La Touche, 9th Bt *cr* 1744; *b* 14 Aug. 1928; *er s* of Sir Richard St John Jefferyes Colthurst, 8th Bt, and Denys Maida Hanmer West (*d* 1966), *e d* of Augustus William West; *S* father, 1955; *m* 1953, Janet Georgina, *d* of L. A. Wilson-Wright, Coolcarrigan, Co. Kildare; three *s* one *d*. *Educ:* Harrow; Peterhouse, Cambridge (MA). Liveryman of Worshipful Company of Grocers. Mem., Internat. Dendrology Soc. *Recreations:* forestry, cricket, tennis, swimming. *Heir: s* Charles St John Colthurst [*b* 21 May 1955; *m* 1987, Nora Mary, *d* of Mortimer Kelleher, Dooniskey, Lissarda, Co. Cork; one *s* one *d*. *Educ:* Eton; Magdalene Coll., Cambridge (MA); University Coll., Dublin]. *Clubs:* City University, MCC.

COLTMAN, (Arthur) Leycester (Scott); HM Diplomatic Service; Ambassador to Cuba, since 1991; *b* 24 May 1938; *s* of late Arthur Cranfield Coltman and Vera Vaid; *m* 1969, Maria Piedad Josefina Cantos Aberasturi; two *s* one *d*. *Educ:* Rugby School; Magdalene Coll., Cambridge. Foreign Office, 1961–62; Third Secretary, British Embassy, Copenhagen, 1963–64; Second Secretary, Cairo 1964–65, Madrid 1966–69; Manchester Business School, 1969–70; Foreign Office, 1970–74; Commercial Secretary, Brasilia, 1974–77; Foreign Office, 1977–79; Counsellor, Mexico City, 1979–83; Counsellor and Hd of Chancery, Brussels, 1983–87; Head: Mexico and Central America Dept, 1987–90; Latin America Dept, 1990. *Recreations:* squash, chess, bridge, music. *Address:* c/o Foreign and Commonwealth Office, King Charles Street, SW1A 2AH.

COLVILLE, family name of **Viscount Colville of Culross** and of **Baron Clydesmuir.**

COLVILLE OF CULROSS, 4th Viscount *cr* 1902; **John Mark Alexander Colville;** QC; 14th Baron (Scot.) *cr* 1604; 4th Baron (UK) *cr* 1885; Chairman, Parole Board, since 1988; a Recorder, since 1990; *b* 19 July 1933; *e s* of 3rd Viscount and Kathleen Myrtle (*d* 1986), OBE 1961, *e d* of late Brig.-Gen. H. R. Gale, CMG, RE, Bardsey, Saanichton, Vancouver Island; *S* father, 1945; *m* 1st, 1958, Mary Elizabeth Webb-Bowen (marr. diss. 1973); four *s*; 2nd, 1974, Margaret Birgitta, Viscountess Davidson, LLB, JP, Barrister, *o d* of Maj.-Gen. C. H. Norton, CB, CBE, DSO; one *s*. *Educ:* Rugby (Scholar); New Coll., Oxford (Scholar) (MA). Lieut Grenadier Guards Reserve. Barrister-at-law, Lincoln's Inn, 1960 (Buchanan prizeman), Bencher, 1986; QC 1978. Minister of State, Home Office, 1972–74. Dir, Securities Assoc., 1987–91. Chm., Norwich Information and Technology Centre, 1983–85; Director: Rediffusion Television Ltd, 1961–68; British Electric Traction Co. Ltd, 1968–72, 1974–84 (Dep. Chm., 1980–81); Mem., CBI Council, 1982–84. Chairman: Mental Health Act Commn, 1983–88; Alcohol Res. and Educn Council, 1984–90; UK rep., UN Human Rights Commn, 1980–83; Mem., UN Working Gp on Disappeared Persons, 1980–84 (Chm., 1981–84); Special Rapporteur on Human Rights in Guatemala, 1983–86. Reports on Prevention of Terrorism Act and NI Emergency Powers Act, for HM Govt, 1986–. Mem. Council, Univ. of E Anglia, 1968–72. Mem., Royal Company of Archers (Queen's Body Guard for Scotland). Hon. Mem., Rating and Valuation Assoc. Governor, BUPA, 1990–. *Heir: s* Master of Colville, *qv*. *Address:* House of Lords, SW1A 0PW.
See also Baron Carrington.

COLVILLE, Master of; Hon. Charles Mark Townshend Colville; *b* 5 Sept. 1959; *s* and *heir* of 4th Viscount Colville of Culross, *qv*. *Educ:* Rugby; Univ. of Durham. *Address:* Rookyards, Spexhall, near Halesworth, Suffolk. *T:* Ilketshall (098681) 318.

COLVILLE, Lady Margaret; an Extra Woman of the Bedchamber to HM Queen Elizabeth the Queen Mother, since 1990; *b* 20 July 1918; *d* of 4th Earl of Ellesmere; *m* 1948, Sir John Rupert Colville, CB, CVO (*d* 1987); two *s* one *d*. Served War of 1939–45 in ATS (Junior Subaltern). Lady in Waiting to the Princess Elizabeth, Duchess of Edinburgh, 1946–49. *Address:* The Close, Broughton, near Stockbridge, Hants SO20 8AA. *T:* Romsey (0794) 301331.
See also Duke of Sutherland.

COLVIN, Andrew James; Comptroller and City Solicitor, City of London, since 1989; *b* 28 April 1947; *s* of Gilbert Russell Colvin, OBE, MA, and Dr Beatrice Colvin, MRCS, LRCP, DPH; *m* 1971, Helen Mary Ryan; one *s* three *d*. *Educ:* qualified Solicitor, 1975. Articled to Borough Solicitor, subseq. Asst Town Clerk, London Borough of Ealing, 1971–82; Dep. Town Clerk and Borough Solicitor, Royal Borough of Kensington and Chelsea, 1982–89. Freeman, City of London, 1989. *Recreations:* sailing, music, cycling. *Address:* Guildhall, EC2P 2EJ.

COLVIN, David, CBE 1991; Chief Adviser in Social Work, The Scottish Office, 1980–91; Interim Director of Social Work, Shetland Islands Council, 1991; *b* 31 Jan. 1931; *s* of James Colvin and Mrs Crawford Colvin; *m* 1957, Elma Findlay, artist; two *s* three *d*. *Educ:* Whitehill Sch., Glasgow; Glasgow and Edinburgh Univs. Probation Officer, Glasgow City, 1955–60; Psychiatric Social Worker, Scottish Prison and Borstal Service, Scottish Home and Health Dept, 1960–61; Sen. Psychiatric Social Worker, Crichton Royal Hosp., Child Psychiatric Unit, 1961–65; Director, Family Casework Unit, Paisley, 1965–66; Welfare Officer, SHHD, 1966–68; Social Work Adviser, Social Work Services Gp, Scottish Educn Dept, 1968, and subseq. At various times held office in Howard League for Penal Reform, Assoc. of Social Workers and Inst. for Study and Treatment of Delinquency. Sen. Associate Research Fellow, Brunel Univ., 1978. Chm., Scotland Cttee, Nat. Children's Homes, 1991. Gov., Nat. Inst. for Social Work, 1986–89. Hon. Adviser, British Red Cross, 1982–. *Recreations:* collector; swimming, climbing, golf, gardens, social affairs. *Address:* The Studio, 53 Windsor Place, Edinburgh EH15 2AF. *Clubs:* Commonwealth Trust; Scottish Arts (Edinburgh).

COLVIN, David Hugh; HM Diplomatic Service; Head of South East Asian Department, Foreign and Commonwealth Office, since 1988; *b* 23 Jan. 1941; 3rd *s* of Major Leslie Hubert Boyd Colvin, MC, and Edna Mary (*née* Parrott); *m* 1971, (Diana) Caroline Carew, *y d* of Gordon MacPherson Lang Smith and Mildred (*née* Carew-Gibson); one *s* one *d*. *Educ:* Lincoln Sch.; Trinity Coll., Oxford (MA). Assistant Principal, Board of

Trade, 1966. Joined HM Foreign (later Diplomatic) Service, 1967; Central Dept, FO, 1967; Second Secretary, Bangkok, 1968–71; European Integration Dept, FCO, 1971–75; First Sec., Paris, 1975–77; First Sec. (Press and Inf.), UK Permanent Representation to the European Community, 1977–82; Asst Sec., Cabinet Office, 1982–85; Counsellor and Hd of Chancery, Budapest, 1985–88. *Recreations:* military history, squash, tennis, shooting. *Address:* c/o Foreign and Commonwealth Office, SW1; 15 Westmoreland Terrace, SW1V 4AG. *T:* 071–834 2900. *Club:* Travellers'.

COLVIN, Howard Montagu, CVO 1983; CBE 1964; MA; FBA 1963; FRHistS; FSA, 1980; Fellow of St John's College, Oxford, 1948–87, now Emeritus (Tutor in History, 1948–78; Librarian, 1950–84); Reader in Architectural History, Oxford University, 1965–87; Member: Historic Buildings Council for England, 1970–84; Historic Buildings and Monuments Commission, 1984–85; Historic Buildings Advisory Committee, since 1984; Royal Commission on Ancient and Historical Monuments of Scotland, 1977–89; Royal Commission on Historical Manuscripts, 1981–88; Reviewing Committee on the Export of Works of Art, 1982–83; Royal Fine Art Commission, 1962–72; Royal Commission on Historical Monuments, England, 1963–76; President, Society of Architectural Historians of Great Britain, 1979–81; *b* 15 Oct. 1919; *s* of late Montagu Colvin; *m* 1943, Christina Edgeworth, *d* of late H. E. Butler, Prof. of Latin at University Coll., London; two *s*. *Educ:* Trent Coll.; University Coll., London (Fellow, 1974). Served in RAF, 1940–46 (despatches). Asst Lecturer, Dept of History, University Coll., London, 1946–48. Hon. FRIBA; Hon. FSA (Scot.) 1986. DUniv York, 1978. Wolfson Literary Award, 1978. *Publications:* The White Canons in England, 1951; A Biographical Dictionary of English Architects 1660–1840, 1954; (General Editor and part author) The History of the King's Works, 6 Vols, 1963–82; A History of Deddington, 1963; Catalogue of Architectural Drawings in Worcester College Library, 1964; Architectural Drawings in the Library of Elton Hall (with Maurice Craig), 1964; (ed with John Harris) The Country Seat, 1970; Building Accounts of King Henry III, 1971; A Biographical Dictionary of British Architects 1600–1840, 1978; (introduction) The Queen Anne Churches, 1980; (ed with John Newman) Roger North, Of Architecture, 1981; Unbuilt Oxford, 1983; Calke Abbey, Derbyshire, 1985; The Canterbury Quadrangle, St John's College, Oxford, 1988; (with J. S. G. Simmons) All Souls: an Oxford college and its buildings, 1989; Architecture and the After-Life, 1991; articles on mediæval and architectural history in Archaeological Journal, Architectural Review, etc. *Recreation:* gardening. *Address:* 50 Plantation Road, Oxford OX2 6JE. *T:* Oxford (0865) 57460.

COLVIN, John Horace Ragnar, CMG 1968; HM Diplomatic Service, retired; Director, Robert Fraser and Partners; *b* Tokyo, 18 June 1922; *s* of late Adm. Sir Ragnar Colvin, KBE, CB and Lady Colvin; *m* 1st, 1948, Elizabeth Anne Manifold (marr. diss., 1963); one *s* one *d*; 2nd, 1967, Moranna Sibyl de Lerisson Cazenove; one *s* one *d*. *Educ:* RNC Dartmouth; University of London. Royal Navy, 1935–51. Joined HM Diplomatic Service, 1951; HM Embassies, Oslo, 1951–53 and Vienna, 1953–55; British High Commn, Kuala Lumpur, 1958–61; HM Consul-General, Hanoi, 1965–67; Ambassador to People's Republic of Mongolia, 1971–74; HM Embassy, Washington, 1977–80. Dir for Internat. Relations, Chase Manhattan Bank, 1980–86. Member: Research Council, Pacific Forum; Political Council, Asiaweek. *Address:* 12A Evelyn Mansions, Carlisle Place, SW1. *Clubs:* Brooks's, Beefsteak.

COLVIN, Michael Keith Beale; MP (C) Romsey and Waterside, since 1983 (Bristol North West, 1979–83); *b* 27 Sept. 1932; *s* of late Captain Ivan Beale Colvin, RN, and Mrs Joy Colvin, OBE; *m* Hon. Nichola, *e d* of Baron Cayzer, *qv*; one *s* two *d*. *Educ:* Eton; RMA, Sandhurst; Royal Agricultural Coll., Cirencester. Served Grenadier Guards, 1950–57; Temp. Captain; served BAOR, Berlin, Suez campaign, Cyprus. J. Walter Thompson & Co. Ltd, 1958–63. Councillor: Andover RDC, 1965–72; Test Valley Bor. Council, 1972–74 (first Vice Chm.); Dep. Chm., Winchester Constituency Conservative Assoc., 1973–76; Mem. (part-time), Cons. Res. Dept, 1975–79. Chairman: Conservative Aviation Cttee, 1982–83, 1987–; Cttee of W Country Cons. MPs, 1982–83; Vice-Chm., Conservative Smaller Businesses Cttee, 1980–83; Member: Select Cttee on Employment, 1981–83; Select Cttee on Energy, 1990–; Sec., Conservative Shipping and Shipbuilding Cttee, 1981–83; Parly Adviser to Play Board, 1983–86; PPS to Baroness Young, Dep. Foreign Sec., FCO, 1983–85, and to Richard Luce, Minister for Arts, 1983–87. President: Hampshire Young Farmers Clubs, 1973–74; Test Valley Br., CPRE, 1974–; Mem., Southern Sports Council, 1970–74; Vice-Chm., British Field Sports Soc., 1987–; Chm., Council for Country Sports, 1988–. Governor, Enham Village Centre. *Address:* Tangley House, near Andover, Hants SP11 0SH. *T:* Chute Standen (026470) 215. *Clubs:* Turf, Pratt's.

COLWYN, 3rd Baron, *cr* 1917; **Ian Anthony Hamilton-Smith,** CBE 1989; Bt 1912; Dental Surgeon since 1966; *b* 1 Jan. 1942; *s* of 2nd Baron Colwyn and Miriam Gwendoline, *d* of Victor Ferguson; *S* father 1966; *m* 1st, 1964, Sonia Jane (marr. diss. 1977), *d* of P. H. G. Morgan, The Eades, Upton-on-Severn; one *s* one *d*; 2nd, 1977, Nicola Jeanne, *d* of Arthur Tyers, The Avenue, Sunbury-on-Thames; two *d*. *Educ:* Cheltenham Coll.; Univ. of London. BDS London 1966; LDS, RCS 1966. *Recreations:* music, dance band and orchestra, golf. *Heir: s* Hon. Craig Peter Hamilton-Smith, *b* 13 Oct. 1968. *Address:* (practice) 53 Wimpole Street, W1.

COLYER, John Stuart, QC 1976; a Recorder, since 1986; *b* 25 April 1935; *s* of late Stanley Herbert Colyer, MBE, and Louisa (*née* Randle); *m* 1961, Emily Warner, *o d* of late Stanley Leland Dutrow and Mrs Dutrow, Blue Ridge Summit, Pa, USA; two *d*. *Educ:* Dudley Grammar Sch.; Shrewsbury; Worcester Coll., Oxford (Open History Scholarship; BA 1955, MA 1961). 2nd Lieut RA, 1954–55. Called to the Bar, Middle Temple, 1959 (Bencher, 1983); Instructor, Univ. of Pennsylvania, Philadelphia, 1959–60, Asst Prof., 1960–61; practised English bar, Midland and Oxford Circuit (formerly Oxford Circuit), 1961–; Hon. Reader, 1985– and Mem. Council, 1985–, Council of Legal Educn (Lectr (Law of Landlord and Tenant), 1970–89); Chm., Lawyers' Christian Fellowship, 1981–89; Mem., Anglo-American Real Property Inst., 1980– (Treasurer, 1984). Blundell Meml Lectr, 1977, 1982, 1986. *Publications:* (ed jtly) Encyclopaedia of Forms and Precedents (Landlord and Tenant), vol. XI, 1965, vol. XII, 1966; A Modern View of the Law of Torts, 1966; Landlord and Tenant, in Halsbury's Laws of England, 4th edn, 1981; Gen. Ed., Megarry's The Rent Acts, 11th edn, 1988; articles in Conveyancer and other professional jls. *Recreations:* entertaining my family; opera; cultivation of cacti and of succulents (esp. Lithops); gardening generally; travel. *Address:* Falcon Chambers, Falcon Court, EC4Y 1AA. *T:* 071–353 2484, *Fax:* 071–353 1261.

COLYER-FERGUSSON, Sir James Herbert Hamilton, 4th Bt, *cr* 1866; *b* 10 Jan. 1917; *s* of Max Christian Hamilton Colyer-Fergusson (*d* on active service, 1940) and Edith Jane (*d* 1936), singer, *d* of late William White Miller, Portage la Prairie, Manitoba; *S* grandfather, 1951. *Educ:* Harrow; Balliol Coll., Oxford. BA 1939; MA 1945. Formerly Capt., The Buffs; served War of 1939–45 (prisoner-of-war, 1940). Entered service of former Great Western Railway Traffic Dept, 1947, later Operating Dept of the Western Region of British Rlys. Personal Asst to Chm. of British Transport Commission, 1957; Passenger Officer in SE Division of Southern Region, BR, 1961; Parly and Public Correspondent, BRB, 1967; Deputy to Curator of Historical Relics, BRB, 1968. Retired.

Heir: none. *Address:* 61 Onslow Square, SW7. *Club:* Naval and Military.
See also Sir Lingard Goulding, Bt, Viscount Monckton of Brenchley.

COLYTON, 1st Baron, *cr* 1956; **Henry Lennox d'Aubigné Hopkinson,** PC 1952; CMG 1944; *b* 3 Jan. 1902; *e s* of late Sir Henry Lennox Hopkinson, KCVO; *m* 1st, 1927, Alice Labouisse (*d* 1953), *d* of Henry Lane Eno, Bar Harbor, Maine, USA; one *s*; 2nd, 1956, Mrs Barbara Addams, *d* of late Stephen Barb, New York. *Educ:* Eton Coll.; Trinity Coll., Cambridge (BA History and Modern Languages Tripos). Entered Diplomatic Service, 1924; 3rd Sec., Washington, 1924; 2nd Sec., Foreign Office, 1929; Stockholm, 1931; Asst Private Sec. to Sec. of State for Foreign Affairs, 1932; Cairo, 1934; 1st Sec., 1936; Athens, 1938; War Cabinet Secretariat, 1939; Private Sec. to Permanent Under-Sec. for Foreign Affairs, 1940; Counsellor and Political Advr to Minister of State in the Middle East, 1941; Minister Plenipotentiary, Lisbon, 1943; Dep. Brit. High Comr in Italy, and Vice-Pres., Allied Control Commn, 1944–46. Resigned from Foreign Service to enter politics, 1946; Head of Conservative Parly Secretariat and Jt Dir, Conservative Research Dept, 1946–50; MP (C) Taunton Div. of Somerset, 1950–56; Sec. for Overseas Trade, 1951–52; Minister of State for Colonial Affairs, 1952–Dec. 1955; Mem., Consultative Assembly, Council of Europe, 1950–52; Delegate, General Assembly, United Nations, 1952–55; Chairman: Anglo-Egyptian Resettlement Board, 1957–60; Joint East and Central African Board, 1960–65; Tanganyika Concessions Ltd, 1965–72. Royal Humane Society's Award for saving life from drowning, 1919. OStJ 1959. Grand Cross, Order of Prince Henry the Navigator (Portugal), 1972; Dato, Order of the Stia Negara (Brunei), 1972; Grand Star, Order Paduka Stia Negara (Brunei), 1978; Commander, Order of the Zaire (Congo) 1971. *Heir: g s* Alisdair John Munro Hopkinson [*b* 7 May 1958; *m* 1980, Philippa J., *yr d* of Peter J. Bell; two *s*]. *Address:* Le Formentor, avenue Princesse Grace, Monte Carlo, Monaco. *T:* (93) 30 92 96. *Clubs:* Buck's, White's, Beefsteak.

COMBER, Ven. Anthony James; Archdeacon of Leeds, since 1982; *b* 20 April 1927; *s* of late Norman Mederson Comber and Nellie Comber. *Educ:* Leeds Grammar School; Leeds Univ. (MSc Mining); St Chad's Coll., Durham (DipTh); Munich Univ. Colliery underground official, 1951–53. Vicar: Oulton, 1960–69; Hunslet, 1969–77; Rector of Farnley, 1977–82. *Publication:* (contrib.) Today's Church and Today's World, 1977. *Recreations:* politics; walking in Bavaria. *Address:* 712 Foundry Lane, Leeds LS14 6BL. *T:* Leeds (0532) 602069.

COMBERMERE, 5th Viscount, *cr* 1826; **Michael Wellington Stapleton-Cotton;** Bt 1677; Baron Combermere, 1814; Lecturer in Biblical and Religious Studies, University of London, Department of Extra-Mural Studies, since 1972; Senior Lecturer, Centre for Extra-Mural Studies, Birkbeck College, since 1988; *b* 8 Aug. 1929; *s* of 4th Viscount Combermere and Constance Marie Katherine (*d* 1968), *d* of Lt-Col Sir Francis Dudley W. Drummond, KBE; *S* father, 1969; *m* 1961, Pamela Elizabeth, *d* of Rev. R. G. Coulson; one *s* two *d*. *Educ:* Eton; King's Coll., Univ. of London. Palestine Police, 1947–48; Royal Canadian Mounted Police, 1948–50; Short-service commn as gen. duties Pilot, RAF, 1950–58, retd as Flt-Lt; Sales Rep., Teleflex Products Ltd, 1959–62; read Theology, KCL, 1962–67 (BD, MTh). Chm., World Congress of Faiths, 1983–88. *Heir: s* Hon. Thomas Robert Wellington Stapleton-Cotton, *b* 30 Aug. 1969. *Address:* 46 Smith Street, SW3. *T:* 071–352 1319. *Club:* Royal Automobile.

COMBS, Sir Willis (Ide), KCVO 1974; CMG 1962; HM Diplomatic Service, retired; *b* Melbourne, 6 May 1916; *s* of Willis Ide Combs, Napier, New Zealand; *m* 1942, Grace Willis; two *d*. *Educ:* Dannevirke High Sch.; Victoria Coll., NZ; St John's Coll., Cambridge. Served in HM Forces, 1940–46. Apptd Mem. Foreign Service, 1947; transf. to Paris as 2nd Sec. (Commercial), Dec. 1947; 1st Sec., Nov. 1948; transf. to Rio de Janeiro, as 1st Sec., 1951; to Peking as 1st Sec. and Consul, 1953 (Chargé d'Affaires, 1954); Foreign Office, 1956; to Baghdad as Counsellor (Commercial), 1959; Diplomatic Service Inspector, 1963; Counsellor, British Embassy, Rangoon, 1965; Asst Under-Sec. of State, FCO, 1968; Ambassador to Indonesia, 1970–75. *Address:* Sunset, Wadhurst Park, Wadhurst, East Sussex. *Club:* United Oxford & Cambridge University.
See also Viscount Raynham.

COMFORT, Alexander, PhD, DSc; physician; poet and novelist; Adjunct Professor, Neuropsychiatric Institute, University of California at Los Angeles, since 1980; Consultant, Ventura County Hospital (Medical Education), since 1981; *b* 10 Feb. 1920; *s* of late Alexander Charles and Daisy Elizabeth Comfort; *m* 1st, 1943, Ruth Muriel Harris (marr. diss. 1973); one *s*; 2nd, 1973, Jane Tristram Henderson. *Educ:* Highgate Sch.; Trinity Coll., Cambridge (Robert Styring Scholar Classics, and Senior Scholar, Nat. Sciences); London Hospital (Scholar). 1st Cl. Nat. Sc. Tripos, Part I, 1940; 2nd Cl. Nat. Sc. Tripos, 1st Div. (Pathology), 1941; MRCS, LRCP 1944; MB, BCh Cantab 1944; MA Cantab 1945; DCH London 1945; PhD London 1949 (Biochemistry); DSc London 1963 (Gerontology). Refused military service in war of 1939–45. Lectr in Physiology, London Hospital Medical Coll., 1948–51; Hon. Research Associate, Dept of Zoology, 1951–73, and Dir of Research, Gerontology, 1966–73, UCL; Clin. Lectr, Dept Psychiatry, Stanford Univ., 1974–83; Prof., Dept of Pathol., Univ. of Calif Sch. of Med., Irvine, 1976–78; Consultant psychiatrist, Brentwood VA Hospital, LA, 1978–81. Pres., Brit. Soc. for Research on Ageing, 1967; Member: RSocMed.; Amer. Psychiatric Assoc. *Publications: fiction:* No Such Liberty, 1941; The Almond Tree, 1943; The Powerhouse, 1944; Letters from an Outpost (stories), 1947; On this side Nothing, 1948; A Giant's Strength, 1952; Come Out to Play, 1961; Tetrarch (trilogy), 1980; Imperial Patient, 1987; The Philosophers, 1989; *poetry:* France and Other Poems, 1942; A Wreath for the Living, 1943; Elegies, 1944; The Song of Lazarus (USA), 1945; The Signal to Engage, 1947; And All but He Departed, 1951; Haste to the Wedding, 1961; Poems, 1979; *plays:* Into Egypt, 1942; Cities of the Plain (melodrama), 1943; Gengulphus, 1948; *songs:* Are You Sitting Comfortably?, 1962; *translation:* The Koka Shastra, 1964; *non-fiction:* The Silver River (travel), 1937; Art and Social Responsibility (essays), 1947; First Year Physiological Technique (textbook), 1948; The Novel and Our Time (criticism), 1948; Barbarism and Sexual Freedom (essays), 1948; Sexual Behaviour in Society (social psychology), 1950; The Pattern of the Future (broadcast lectures), 1950; Authority and Delinquency in the Modern State (social psychology), 1950; The Biology of Senescence (textbook), 1956, 2nd edn 1964, 3rd edn 1978; Darwin and the Naked Lady (essays), 1961; Sex and Society (social psychology), 1963; Ageing, the Biology of Senescence (textbook), 1964; The Process of Ageing (science), 1965; Nature and Human Nature (science), 1966; The Anxiety Makers (medical history), 1967; The Joy of Sex (counselling), 1973; More Joy (counselling), 1974; A Good Age, 1976; (ed) Sexual Consequences of Disability, 1978; I and That: notes on the Biology of Religion, 1979; (with Jane T. Comfort) The Facts of Love, 1979; A practice of Geriatric Psychiatry, 1979; What is a Doctor? (essays), 1980; Reality and Empathy, 1983; (with Jane T. Comfort) What about Alcohol? (textbook), 1983. *Address:* The Windmill House, Cranbrook, Kent TN17 3AH.

COMFORT, Anthony Francis; HM Diplomatic Service, retired; *b* Plymouth, 12 Oct. 1920; *s* of Francis Harold Comfort and Elsie Grace (*née* Martin); *m* 1948, Joy Margaret Midson; two *s* one *d*. *Educ:* Bristol Grammar Sch.; Oriel Coll., Oxford. Entered Foreign Service, 1947; 2nd Sec. (Commercial), Athens, 1948–51; Consul, Alexandria, 1951–53; 1st Sec. (Commercial), Amman, 1953–54; Foreign Office, 1954–57; seconded to Colonial Office, 1957–59; 1st Sec. (Commercial), Belgrade, 1959–60; 1st Sec. and Consul, Reykjavik, 1961–65; Inspector of Diplomatic Establishments, 1965–68, retired 1969. *Recreations:* walking, gardening, looking at churches. *Address:* Nymet Cottage, Trowbridge Road, Bradford on Avon, Wilts BA15 1EE. *T:* Bradford-on-Avon (02216) 6046.

COMFORT, Dr Charles Fraser, OC; CD; RCA; artist and author; Emeritus Director, National Gallery of Canada, 1965; *b* Edinburgh, 22 July 1900; *m* 1924, Louise Chase, Winnipeg; two *d*. *Educ:* Winnipeg Sch. of Art and Art Students' League, New York. Cadet Officer, Univ. of Toronto Contingent of Canadian OTC, 1939; Commnd Instr in Infantry Weapons, 1940; Sen. Canadian War Artist (Army) Major, 1942–46 (UK, Italy and NW Europe). Head of Dept of Mural Painting, Ontario Coll. of Art, 1935–38; Associate Prof., Dept of Art and Archaeology, Univ. of Toronto, 1946–60 (Mem. staff, 1938); Dir, Nat. Gall. of Canada, 1959. Gold Medal and cash award, Great Lakes Exhibn, Albright Gall., Buffalo, NY, 1938; has travelled widely in Europe; Royal Society Fellowship to continue research into problems of Netherlandish painting, 1955–56; studied under Dr William Heckscher of Kunsthistorisch Inst., Utrecht. *Works include:* landscape painting and portraiture (oils and water colour); mural paintings and stone carvings in many public buildings. Pres., Royal Canadian Academy of Arts, 1957–60; Past Pres., Canadian Soc. of Painters in Water Colour; Past Pres. and Charter Mem., Canadian Group of Painters; Mem., Ontario Soc. of Artists. Dr of Laws *hc:* Mount Allison Univ., 1958; Royal Military Coll., Canada, 1980. Medaglia Benemerito della culturale (Italy), 1963; Univ. of Alberta National Award in painting and related arts, 1963. Centennial Decoration, 1967; OC 1972; Queen's Jubilee Medal, 1978. *Publications:* Artist at War, 1956 (Toronto); contrib. to Royal Commission Studies Report on National Development in the Arts, Letters and Sciences, Vol. II, 1951; contrib. various art and literary publications.

COMMAGER, Henry Steele, MA Oxon; MA Cantab; Professor of American History, 1956–72, Simpson Lecturer, since 1972, Amherst College; Professor of History, Columbia University, 1938–56; Hon. Professor, University of Santiago de Chile; *b* 25 Oct. 1902; *s* of James W. Commager and Anna Elizabeth Dan; *m* 1st, 1928, Evan Carroll; one *s* two *d*; 2nd, 1979, Mary Powlesland. *Educ:* Univ. of Chicago; Univ. of Copenhagen. AB, Univ. of Chicago, 1923; MA, 1924; PhD, 1928; Scholar Amer-Scand. Foundation, 1924–25; taught History, New York Univ., 1926–29; Prof. of History, 1929–38. Lectr on American History, Cambridge Univ., 1942–43; Hon. Fellow, Peterhouse; Pitt Prof. of Amer. Hist., Cambridge Univ., 1947–48; Lectr, Salzburg Seminar in Amer. Studies, 1951; Harold Vyvyan Harmsworth Prof. of American History, Oxford Univ., 1952; Gotesman Lectr, Upsala Univ., 1953; Special State Dept lectr to German Univs, 1954; Zuskind Prof., Brandeis Univ., 1954–55; Prof., Univ. of Copenhagen, 1956; Visiting Prof., Univ. of Aix-Provence, summer 1957; Lectr, Univ. of Jerusalem, summer 1958; Commonwealth Lectr, Univ. of London, 1964; Harris Lectr, Northwestern Univ., 1964; Visiting Prof., Harvard, Chicago, Calif, City Univ. NY, Nebraska, etc. Editor-in-Chief, The Rise of the American Nation, 50 vols; Consultant, Office War Information in Britain and USA; Mem. US Army War Hist. Commn; Mem. Historians Commn on Air Power; special citation US Army; Consultant US Army attached to SHAEF, 1945. Trustee; American Scandinavian Foundation; American Friends of Cambridge Univ. Member: Mass Historical Soc.; American Antiquarian Soc.; Colonial Soc. of Mass; Amer. Acad. of Arts and Letters (Gold Medal for History, 1972). Hon degrees: EdD Rhode I; LittD: Washington, Ohio Wesleyan, Pittsburgh, Marietta, Hampshire Coll., 1970; Adelphi Coll., 1974; NY State, 1985; Rutgers, 1988; DLitt: Cambridge, Franklin-Marshall, W Virginia, Michigan State; LHD: Brandeis, Puget Sound, Hartford, Alfred; LLD: Merrimack, Carleton; Dickinson Coll., 1967; Franklin Pierce Coll., 1968; Columbia Univ., 1969; Ohio State, 1970; Wilson Coll., 1970; W. C. Post Coll., 1974; Alassa Univ., 1974; DHL: Maryville Coll., 1970; Univ. of Mass, 1972. Pepper Medal for contrib. to social democracy, 1984; Jefferson Medal, Council for Advancement and Support of Educn, 1987; Gold Medal for Arts, Brandeis Univ., 1988. Knight of Order of Dannebrog (Denmark), 1957 (1st cl.). *Publications:* Theodore Parker, 1936; Growth of the American Republic, 1930, 2 vols 1939; sub-ed (with S. E. Morison) Documents of American History, 1934, 9th edn 1974; Heritage of America (with A. Nevins), 1939; America: Story of a Free People (with A. Nevins), 1943, new edn 1966; Majority Rule and Minority Rights, 1944; Story of the Second World War, 1945; ed Tocqueville, Democracy in America, 1947; ed America in Perspective, 1947; ed The St Nicholas Anthology, 1947; The American Mind, 1950; The Blue and the Gray, 2 vols 1950; Living Ideas in America, 1951; Robert E. Lee, 1951; Freedom, Loyalty, Dissent, 1954 (special award, Hillman Foundation); Europe and America since 1942 (with G. Bruun), 1954; Joseph Story, 1956; The Spirit of Seventy-Six, 2 vols (with R. B. Morris); Crusaders for Freedom; History: Nature and Purpose, 1965; Freedom and Order, 1966; Search for a Usable Past, 1967; Was America a Mistake?, 1968; The Commonwealth of Learning, 1968; The American Character, 1970; The Use and Abuse of History, 1972; Britain Through American Eyes, 1974; The Defeat of America, 1974; Essays on the Enlightenment, 1974; The Empire of Reason, 1978; edited: Atlas of American Civil War; Winston Churchill, History of the English Speaking Peoples; Why the Confederacy Lost the Civil War; Major Documents of the Civil War; Theodore Parker, an Anthology; Immigration in American History; Lester Ward and the Welfare State; The Struggle for Racial Equality; Joseph Story, Selected Writings and Judicial Opinions; Winston Churchill, Marlborough, 1968; American Destiny, 12 vols. *Recreation:* music. *Address:* Amherst College, Mass 01002, USA. *Clubs:* Lansdowne (London); Century (New York); St Botolph (Boston); (former Pres.) PEN (American Centre).

COMPSTON, Alastair; *see* Compston, D. A. S.

COMPSTON, Christopher Dean, MA; **His Honour Judge Compston;** a Circuit Judge, since 1986; *b* 5 May 1940; *s* of Vice Adm. Sir Peter Maxwell Compston, *qv*; *m* 1st, 1968, Bronwen Henniker Gotley (marr. diss. 1982); one *s* one *d* (and one *s* decd); 2nd, 1983, Caroline Philippa, *d* of Paul Odgers, *qv*; one *s* one *d*. *Educ:* Epsom Coll. (Prae Sum.); Magdalen Coll., Oxford (MA). Called to the Bar, Middle Temple, 1965; a Recorder, 1982–86. Mem. Senate, Inns of Court, 1983–86. *Recreation:* the arts. *Address:* 6 King's Bench Walk, Temple, EC4.

COMPSTON, Prof. (David) Alastair (Standish), FRCP; Professor of Neurology, University of Cambridge, since 1989; Fellow of Jesus College, Cambridge, since 1990; *b* 23 Jan. 1948; *s* of late Nigel Dean Compston and of Diana Mary Compston (*née* Standish); *m* 1973, Juliet Elizabeth, *d* of Sir Denys Lionel Page, FBA; one *d*. *Educ:* Rugby Sch.; Middlesex Hospital Med. Sch., London Univ. (MB BS (Hons); PhD). Jun. Hosp. appts, Nat. Hosp. for Nervous Diseases, 1972–82; Cons. Neurologist, University Hosp. of Wales, 1982–87; Prof. of Neurology, Univ. of Wales Coll. of Medicine, 1987–88. *Publications:* contribs to human and experimental demyelinating diseases, in learned jls. *Recreations:* walking, reading. *Address:* Pembroke House, Mill Lane, Linton, Cambridge CB1 6JY. *T:* Cambridge (0223) 893414.

COMPSTON, Vice-Adm. Sir Peter (Maxwell), KCB 1970 (CB 1967); *b* 12 Sept. 1915; *s* of Dr G. D. Compston; *m* 1st, 1939, Valerie Bocquet (marr. diss.); one *s* one *d*; 2nd,

1953, Angela Brickwood. *Educ:* Epsom Coll. Royal Navy, 1937; specialised in flying duties. Served 1939–45, HMS Ark Royal, Anson, Vengeance; HMCS Warrior, 1946; HMS Theseus, 1948–50 (despatches); Directorate of RN Staff Coll., 1951–53; Capt. 1955; in comd HMS Orwell and Capt. 'D' Plymouth, 1955–57; Imperial Defence Coll., 1958; Naval Attaché, Paris, 1960–62; in comd HMS Victorious, 1962–64; Rear-Adm., Jan. 1965; Chief of British Naval Staff and Naval Attaché, Washington, 1965–67; Flag Officer Flotillas, Western Fleet, 1967–68; Dep. Supreme Allied Comdr, Atlantic, 1968–70, retired. Life Vice Pres., RNLI; Mem., Cttee, Royal Humane Soc. *Recreations:* theatre, country life. *Address:* Holmwood, Stroud, near Petersfield, Hants GU32 3PJ. *Club:* Army and Navy.

See also C. D. Compston.

COMPSTON, Prof. William, PhD; FRS 1987; FAA; Professor in Isotope Geochemistry, Research School of Earth Sciences, Australian National University, since 1987; *b* 19 Feb. 1931; *s* of late J. A. Compston; *m* 1952, Elizabeth Blair; three *s* one *d*. *Educ:* Christian Brothers' Coll., Fremantle; Univ. of WA (BSc (Hons); PhD). Res. Fellow, CIT, 1956–58; Res. Fellow, Dept of Terrestrial Magnetism, Carnegie Inst. of Washington, 1958; Lectr, Univ. of WA, 1959–60; Fellow, then Sen. Fellow, 1961–74, Professorial Fellow, 1974–87, ANU. *Address:* Research School of Earth Sciences, Australian National University, GPO 4, Canberra, ACT 2601, Australia.

COMPTON, family name of **Marquess of Northampton.**

COMPTON, Earl; Daniel Bingham Compton; *b* 16 Jan. 1973; *s* and *heir* of Marquess of Northampton, *qv*.

COMPTON, Denis Charles Scott, CBE 1958; professional cricketer, retired 1957; Sunday Express Cricket Correspondent, since 1950; BBC Television Cricket Commentator, since 1958; *b* 23 May 1918; *m* 1st; one *s*; 2nd; two *s*; 3rd, 1975, Christine Franklin Tobias; two *d*. *Educ:* Bell Lane Sch., Hendon. First played for Middlesex, 1936. First played for England *v* New Zealand, 1937; *v* Australia, 1938; *v* West Indies, 1939; *v* India, 1946; *v* S Africa, 1947. Played in 78 Test matches; made 123 centuries in first-class cricket. Association football: mem. of Arsenal XI; England XI, 1943; Editor, Denis Compton's Annual, 1950–57. *Publications:* Playing for England, 1948; Testing Time for England, 1948; In Sun and Shadow, 1952; End of an Innings, 1958, repr. 1988; Denis Compton's Test Diary, 1964; (jtly) Cricket and All That, 1978. *Recreation:* golf. *Address:* c/o Sunday Express, Fleet Street, EC4P 4JT. *Clubs:* MCC, Middlesex CC (Pres., 1990–91); Wanderers (Johannesburg).

COMPTON, Sir Edmund (Gerald), GCB 1971 (KCB 1965, CB 1948); KBE 1955; MA; Hon. FRAM; FRCM; *b* 30 July 1906; *er s* of late Edmund Spencer Compton, MC, Pailton House, Rugby; *m* 1934, Betty Tresyllian, CBE (*d* 1987), 2nd *d* of late Hakewill Tresyllian Williams, DL, JP, Churchill Court, Kidderminster; one *s* four *d*. *Educ:* Rugby (Scholar); New Coll., Oxford (Scholar); 1st Class Lit. Hum., 1929; Hon. Fellow 1972. Entered Home Civil Service, 1929; Colonial Office, 1930; transf. to HM Treasury, 1931; Private Sec. to Financial Sec. to Treasury, 1934–36; seconded to Min. of Aircraft Production as Private Sec. to Minister, 1940; Min. of Supply, 1941; Asst Sec., HM Treasury, 1942, Under-Sec., 1947, Third Sec., 1949–58; Comptroller and Auditor General, Exchequer and Audit Dept, 1958–66; Parly Comr for Administration, 1967–71, and in NI, 1969–71. Chm., English Local Govt Boundary Commn, 1971–78. Chairman: Irish Sailors and Soldiers Land Trust, 1946–86; Milibern Trust, 1968–88; BBC Programmes Complaints Commn, 1972–81; Governing Body, Royal Acad. of Music, 1975–81. *Recreations:* music, water-colour sketching. *Address:* 1/80 Elm Park Gardens, SW10 9PD. *T:* 071–351 3790. *Clubs:* Athenæum, Boodle's.

See also Viscount De L'Isle.

COMPTON, Rt. Hon. John George Melvin, PC 1983; Prime Minister of St Lucia, since 1982, and Minister for Finance, Planning and Development; *b* 1926; *m*; five *c*. *Educ:* London School of Economics. Called to the Bar, Gray's Inn; practice in St Lucia, 1951. Indep. Mem., Legislative Council, 1954; joined Labour Party, 1954; Dep. Leader, 1957–61; resigned, and formed Nat. Labour Movement, 1961 (later United Workers' Party; Leader, 1964); Chief Minister of St Lucia, 1964–67, Premier, 1967–79, Prime Minister, Feb.-July 1979, 1982–. *Address:* Office of the Prime Minister, Castries, St Lucia.

COMPTON, Michael Graeme, CBE 1987; Keeper of Museum Services, Tate Gallery, 1970–87, retired; *b* 29 Sept. 1927; *s* of Joseph Nield Compton, OBE, and Dorothy Margaret Townsend Compton; *m* 1952, Susan Paschal Benn; two *d*. *Educ:* Courtauld Institute, London (BA Hons History of Art). Asst to Director, Leeds City Art Gallery and Templenewsam, 1954–57; Keeper of Foreign Schools, Walker Art Gallery, Liverpool, 1957–59; Dir, Ferens Art Gall., Hull, 1960–65; Asst Keeper, Modern Collection, Tate Gall., 1965–70. Frederick R. Weisman Art Foundn Award, 1991. *Publications:* Optical and Kinetic Art, 1967; Pop Art, 1970; (jtly) Catalogue of Foreign Schools, Walker Art Gallery, 1963; Marcel Broodthaers, 1989; articles in art jls, exhibn catalogues. *Address:* Michaelmas Lodge, Rockfield Road, Oxted, Surrey RH8 0HB.

COMPTON, Robert Edward John; DL; Chairman: Time-Life International Ltd, 1979–90 (Chief Executive Officer, 1985–88); Time SARL, 1985–90; *b* 11 July 1922; *yr s* of late Major Edward Robert Francis Compton, JP, DL, and Sylvia Farquharson of Invercauld; *m* 1951, Ursula Jane Kenyon-Slaney; two *s*. *Educ:* Eton; Magdalen Coll., Oxford, 1940–41. Served War, Coldstream Guards, 1941–46 (4 medals, wounded); Mil. Asst to British Ambassador, Vienna (temp. Major), 1946. Studied fruit growing and horticulture (Diploma), 1946–48; with W. S. Crawford Ltd, Advertising Agency, 1951–54; Sen. Acct Exec., Crawfords Internat., 1954; joined Time International, 1954; advertising sales, 1954–58, UK Advtsg Dir, 1958–62; also Dir, Time-Life Internat. Ltd, 1958–79; New Projects Dir, Time-Life Internat. Europe, 1962–65; Public Affairs Dir, Europe, Time-Life Internat. Ltd, 1965. Chairman: Newby Hall Estate Co., 1964–69; CXL UK Ltd, 1971–73; Pres., Highline Finances Services, SA, and Dir, Highline Leasing Ltd, 1985–; Bd Dir, Extel Corp., Chicago, 1973–80; Dir, Transtel Communications Ltd, Slough, 1974–. FInstD 1958. National Trust: Vice-Chm., Yorks, 1970–85; Mem. Properties Cttee, 1970–85; Mem., Gardens Panel, 1970–85 and 1988–; Chm., Nat. Council for the Conservation of Plants and Gardens, 1988–; Pres., Dales Centre, 1979–85; President: Ripon Tourist Assoc., 1977–; N of England Horticultural Soc., 1984–86; Pres., Northern Horticultural Soc., 1986–. High Sheriff, 1978–79, DL 1981, N Yorks. *Recreations:* gardening, shooting, golf, music. *Address:* Newby Hall, Ripon, Yorkshire HG4 5AE. *T:* Boroughbridge (0423) 322583; Flat 2, 17 Brompton Square, SW3. *Clubs:* White's, Buck's; Swinley Forest (Ascot).

See also Captain A. A. C. Farquharson of Invercauld.

COMPTON MILLER, Sir John (Francis), Kt 1969; MBE (mil.) 1945; TD; MA Oxon; Barrister-at-Law; Senior Registrar, The Family Division (formerly Probate, Divorce and Admiralty Division), 1964–72 (Registrar, 1946–64), retired 1972; *b* 11 May 1900; 3rd *s* of Frederic Richard Miller, MD and Effie Anne, *d* of Samson Rickard Stuttaford; *m* 1st, 1925, Alice Irene Mary (*d* 1931), *er d* of John Scales Bakewell; one *s*; 2nd, 1936, Mary, *e d* of Rev. Alexander MacEwen Baird-Smith; one *s* one *d*. *Educ:* Colet Court; St Paul's Sch.; New Coll., Oxford. Called to Bar, Inner Temple, 1923; went the Western Circuit, practised Criminal, Common Law, Probate and Divorce Courts. Major, Inns of Court Regt, TA, 1936; OC No 21 Recep. Unit; Asst Comdt, Army Tech. Sch. (Boys), Chepstow. A Deputy Judge Advocate, United Kingdom and North West Europe, 1969. Examiner, Council of Legal Education, 1951–64. UK Rep., Council of Europe Sub-Cttee on Registration of Wills, 1970. *Publications:* I Tried My Hand at Verse, 1968; Further Verse, 1970; The Miraculous Cornfield, 1978; The Chinese Saucer, 1980; Poems '81, 1981; Selected Poems, 1982; Miscellany, 1983; And So It Went, 1985; An Ambit Small, 1986. *Recreations:* painting (Dip., City of London Art Exhibn, 1979), versing, heraldic art. *Address:* 2 Crown Office Row, Temple, EC4. *T:* 071–583 1352. *Club:* Garrick (Life Mem.).

COMRIE, Rear-Adm. (Alexander) Peter, CB 1982; defence equipment consultant; Director, A. Comrie & Sons Ltd, since 1983; *b* 27 March 1924; *s* of Robert Duncan Comrie and Phyllis Dorothy Comrie; *m* 1945, Madeleine Irene (*née* Bullock) (*d* 1983); one *s* one *d*. *Educ:* Sutton Valence Sch., Kent; County Technical Coll., Wednesbury, Staffs, and in the Royal Navy. Joined Royal Navy, 1945; served in cruisers, frigates, minesweepers and RN air stations; RCDS 1973; Captain HMS Daedalus, 1974; Director of Weapons Coordination and Acceptance (Naval), 1975; Deputy Controller Aircraft, MoD, 1978–81; Dir-Gen. Aircraft (Navy), 1981–83, retired. Vice Pres., IEE, 1988–91 (Mem. Council, 1981–84); Member: IEE Electronics Divisional Bd, 1976–77; IEE Qualifications Bd, 1981–88; Chairman: IEE International (formerly Overseas) Bd, 1988–91; Executive Gp Cttee 3, Engrg Council, 1986–. FIEE 1975; FRAeS 1978; Eur Ing 1987. *Recreations:* sailing, swimming, DIY. *Address:* c/o National Westminster Bank, 23 West Street, Havant, Hants PO9 1EU. *Clubs:* Commonwealth Trust; Hayling Island Sailing.

COMYN, Hon. Sir James, Kt 1978; Judge of the High Court of Justice, Queen's Bench Division, 1979–85 (Family Division, 1978–79), resigned due to ill-health, Sept. 1985; *b* Co. Dublin, 8 March 1921; *o s* of late James Comyn, QC, Dublin and late Mary Comyn; *m* 1967, Anne (solicitor), *d* of late Philip Chaundler, MC, solicitor, Biggleswade, and late Mrs Chaundler; one *s* one *d*. *Educ:* Oratory Sch.; New Coll., Oxford (MA). Ex-Pres. of Oxford Union. With Irish Times (briefly), BBC and various war-time orgns, 1938–44. Inner Temple, 1942; called to Irish Bar, 1947, Hong Kong Bar, 1969; QC 1961. Recorder of Andover, 1964–71; Hon. (life) Recorder of Andover, 1972; a Recorder of the Crown Court, 1972–77. Master of the Bench, Inner Temple, 1968; Mem. and Chm., Bar Council, 1973–74. Chairman: Court Line Enquiry, 1972–73; Solihull Hosp. Enquiry, 1974. Mem., Parole Bd, 1982–84, Vice-Chm. 1983–84. A Governor of the Oratory Sch., 1964–90; President: Oratory Sch. Assoc. (Sch. and Prep. Sch.), 1983–90; Oratory Sch. Soc. (old boys), 1984–. Owner of the "Clareville" herd of pedigree Aberdeen-Angus. *Publications:* Their Friends at Court, 1973; Irish at Law: a selection of famous and unusual cases, 1981; Lost Causes, 1982; Summing It Up (memoirs), 1991; various vols of light verse and books and articles on legal subjects. *Recreations:* cattle-breeding, farming, golf, planting trees. *Address:* Belvin, Tara, Co. Meath, Ireland. *Club:* Royal Dublin Society.

COMYNS, Jacqueline Roberta; a Metropolitan Stipendiary Magistrate, since 1982; *b* 27 April 1943; *d* of late Jack and of Belle Fisher; *m* 1963, Malcolm John Comyns, medical practitioner; one *s*. *Educ:* Hendon County Grammar Sch.; London Sch. of Econs and Pol. Science (LLB Hons 1964). Called to the Bar, Inner Temple, 1969. Practised on South Eastern Circuit. *Recreations:* theatre, bridge, travel. *Address:* Tower Bridge Magistrates' Court, Tooley Street, SE1 2JY. *T:* 071–407 4232.

CONAN DOYLE, Air Comdt Dame Jean (Lena Annette), (Lady Bromet), DBE 1963 (OBE 1948); AE; Director of the Women's Royal Air Force, 1963–66, retired; *b* 21 Dec. 1912; *d* of late Sir Arthur Conan Doyle and Lady Conan Doyle (*née* Jean Leckie); *m* 1965, Air Vice-Marshal Sir Geoffrey Bromet, KBE, CB, DSO, DL (*d* 1983). *Educ:* Granville House, Eastbourne. Joined No 46 (Co. of Sussex) ATS, RAF Company, Sept. 1938; commnd in WAAF, 1940; served in UK, 1939–45; commnd in RAF, 1949; Comd WRAF Admin Officer: BAFO, Germany, 1947–50; HQ Tech. Trng Comd, 1950–52 and 1962–63; Dep. Dir, 1952–54 and 1960–62; OC, RAF Hawkinge, 1956–59; Inspector of the WRAF, 1954–56 and 1959–60. Hon. ADC to the Queen, 1963–66. A Governor, Royal Star and Garter Home, 1968–82; Mem. Council, Officers' Pensions Soc., 1970–75, a Vice-Pres. 1981–88; Mem. Cttee, Not Forgotten Assoc., 1975–91, a Pres. 1981–91. Holder of USA copyright on her father's published works. *Recreation:* attempting to paint. *Address:* Flat 6, 72 Cadogan Square, SW1X 0EA. *Clubs:* Naval and Military, Royal Air Force.

CONANT, Sir John (Ernest Michael), 2nd Bt *cr* 1954; farmer and landowner, since 1949; *b* 24 April 1923; *s* of Sir Roger Conant, 1st Bt, CVO, and Daphne, Lady Conant, *d* of A. E. Learoyd; *S* father, 1973; *m* 1950, Periwinkle Elizabeth (*d* 1985), *d* of late Dudley Thorp, Kimbolton, Hunts; two *s* two *d* (and one *s* decd). *Educ:* Eton; Corpus Christi Coll., Cambridge (BA Agric). Served in Grenadier Guards, 1942–45; at CCC Cambridge, 1946–49. Farming in Rutland, 1950–; High Sheriff of Rutland, 1960. *Recreations:* fishing, shooting, tennis. *Heir:* *s* Simon Edward Christopher Conant, *b* 13 Oct. 1958. *Address:* Lyndon Hall, Oakham, Rutland LE15 8TU. *T:* Manton (057285) 275.

CONCANNON, Rt. Hon. John Dennis, (Rt. Hon. Don Concannon), PC 1978; *b* 16 May 1930; *m* 1953, Iris May Wilson; two *s* two *d*. *Educ:* Rossington Sec. Sch. Coldstream Guards, 1947–53; Mem. Nat. Union of Mineworkers, 1953–66; Branch Official, 1960–65. Mem., Mansfield Town Council, 1962–66. MP (Lab) Mansfield, 1966–87. Asst Govt Whip, 1968–70; Opposition Whip, 1970–74; Vice-Chamberlain, HM Household, 1974; Parly Under-Sec. of State, NI Office, 1974–76; Minister of State, NI Office, 1976–79; Opposition Spokesman for Defence, 1979–80, for NI, 1980–83. Mem., Commonwealth War Graves Commn, 1986–. *Recreations:* cricket, basket-ball. *Address:* 69 Skegby Lane, Mansfield, Notts NG19 6QS. *T:* Mansfield (0623) 27235.

CONDON, Denis David, OBE 1964; retired; Senior Representative at Lloyd's of London for Neilson McCarthy, Consultants, 1968–75; *b* 23 Oct. 1910; *s* of Capt. D. Condon and Mrs A. E. Condon; *m* 1933, Mary Marson; one *d*. *Educ:* Paston Grammar Sch., North Walsham, Norfolk. Journalist until 1939. War Service with Royal Artillery, UK and Burma (Major). Joined India Office, 1946; CRO, 1947; served India, Ceylon, Australia, Nigeria; Head of News Dept, CO, 1967–68. *Recreations:* fishing, bird-watching, gardening. *Address:* Rose Cottage, Weir, Dulverton, Somerset TA22 9NB. *T:* Dulverton (0398) 23309. *Clubs:* Gymkhana (Delhi); Australasian Pioneers (Sydney).

CONGLETON, 8th Baron *cr* 1841; **Christopher Patrick Parnell;** Bt 1766; *b* 11 March 1930; 3rd *s* of 6th Baron Congleton (*d* 1932) and Hon. Edith Mary Palmer Howard (MBE 1941) (she *m* 2nd, 1946, Flight Lieut A. E. R. Aldridge, who died 1950), *d* of late R. J. B. Howard and late Lady Strathcona and Mount Royal; *S* brother, 1967; *m* 1955, Anna Hedvig, *d* of G. A. Sommerfelt, Oslo, Norway; two *s* three *d*. *Educ:* Eton; New Coll., Oxford (BA 2nd cl. Hons, 1954; MA 1988). Mem., Salisbury and Wilton RDC, 1964–74; Vice-President: RDCA, 1973–74; Assoc. of District Councils, 1974–79; Chm., Salisbury and S Wilts Museum, 1972–77; Pres., Nat. Ski Federation of GB, 1976–81; Mem., Adv. Bd for Redundant Churches, 1981–87. Trustee: Sandroyd Sch. Trust, 1975– (Chm., 1980–84); Wessex Med. Trust, 1984–90; Southampton Univ. Develt Trust,

1986–. Hon. LLD Southampton, 1990. *Heir:* *s* Hon. John Patrick Christian Parnell [*b* 17 March 1959; *m* 1985, Marjorie-Anne, *o d* of John Hobdell, Cobham, Surrey; two *s*]. *Address:* Ebbesbourne Wake, Salisbury, Wilts SP5 5JW.

CONGO, Sonia, (Mrs C. W. Congo); *see* Lawson, S.

CONGREVE, Ambrose, CBE 1965; responsible for Humphreys & Glasgow Ltd, 1939–83; *b* London, 4 April 1907; *s* of Major John Congreve, DL, JP, and Helena Blanche Irene Ponsonby, *d* of 8th Earl of Bessborough; *m* 1935, Marjorie, *d* of Dr Arthur Graham Glasgow, London, and Richmond, Virginia, and Margaret, *d* of John P. Branch, President of Virginia's Merchants National Bank. *Educ:* Eton; Trinity Coll., Cambridge. Employed by Unilever Ltd, in England and China, 1927–36; joined Humphreys & Glasgow Ltd, as Director, 1936; responsible for the company, 1939–83, in succession to Dr Glasgow who founded the firm in 1892. Served War of 1939–45: Air Intelligence for Plans and Bomber Command, then Min. of Supply. Hon. Fellow IChemE 1967. Veitch Meml Medal, RHS, 1987. *Recreation:* collection and large-scale outdoor cultivation in Ireland of plant species and hybrids from all over the world. *Address:* Mount Congreve, Waterford, Ireland. *T:* Waterford 84103; Warwick House, Stable Yard, St James's, SW1. *T:* 071–839 3301. *Club:* Beefsteak.

CONI, Peter Richard Carstairs, OBE 1987; QC 1980; a Recorder, since 1985; *b* 20 Nov. 1935; *s* of late Eric Charles Coni and Leslie Sybil Carstairs (*née* Pearson). *Educ:* Uppingham; St Catharine's Coll., Cambridge (MA). Called to the Bar, Inner Temple, 1960, Bencher, 1986. Steward, Henley Royal Regatta, 1974 (Chm. Cttee of Management, 1977–); Pres., London Rowing Club, 1988–; Chm., 1986 World Rowing Championships Cttee (FISA Medal of Honour, 1986); Member: Exec. Cttee, Amateur Rowing Assoc., 1968– (Chm., 1970–77); Exec. Cttee, Central Council of Physical Recreation, 1978–80; Nat. Olympic Cttee, 1990–. Mem., Thames Water Authority, 1978–83. Treas., FISA, 1990–. Mem., Ct of Assts, Needlemakers' Co., 1983–. *Recreations:* rowing, sports administration, good food, modern art. *Address:* 3 Churton Place, SW1V 2LN. *T:* 071–828 2135. *Clubs:* Athenæum, Garrick, London Rowing; Leander (Henley-on-Thames).

CONINGSBY, Thomas Arthur Charles; QC 1986; Chancellor of the Diocese of York, since 1977, of the Diocese of Peterborough since 1989; Vicar General of the Province of York, since 1980; a Recorder, since 1986; *b* 21 April 1933; *s* of Francis Charles and Eilleen Rowena Coningsby; *m* 1959, Elaine Mary Coningsby; two *s* three *d.* *Educ:* Epsom; Queens' Coll., Cambridge (MA). Called to the Bar, Gray's Inn, 1957. Member: Lord Chancellor's Matrimonial Causes Rule Cttee, 1986–89; Gen. Council of the Bar, 1988–90; Supreme Court Procedure Cttee, 1988–; Chm., Family Law Bar Assoc., 1988–90 (Sec., 1986–88). Member, General Synod, 1970– (Member: Legal Adv. Commn, 1975–; Fees Adv. Commn, 1979–). *Recreation:* lawn tennis. *Address:* Leyfields, Chipstead, Surrey CR3 3SG. *T:* Downland (07375) 53304. *Club:* Athenæum.

CONLAN, Bernard; engineer; *b* 24 Oct. 1923; *m*; one *d.* *Educ:* Manchester Primary and Secondary Schs. Mem., AEU, 1940–, Officer, 1943–87. City Councillor, Manchester, 1954–66. Joined Labour Party, 1942; contested (Lab) High Peak, 1959. MP (Lab) Gateshead East, 1964–87. A Vice-Chm., Parly Lab. Party Trade Union Gp, 1974–. Member: House of Commons Expenditure Cttee (since inception), 1971–79; Trade and Industry Select Cttee, 1983–86; Select Cttee on Defence, 1979–83. *Address:* 33 Beccles Road, Sale, Cheshire M33 3RP. *T:* 061–973 3991.

CONN, Edward, CBE 1979; FRCVS; Technical Consultant, Norbrook Laboratories Ltd, Newry, Northern Ireland, 1983–90, retired; *b* 25 March 1918; *s* of late Edward and Elizabeth Conn; *m* 1st, 1943, Kathleen Victoria Sandford (*d* 1974); three *d*; 2nd, 1975, Lilian Frances Miley. *Educ:* Coleraine Academical Instn; Royal (Dick) Veterinary Sch., Edinburgh Univ. Qual. Vet. Surgeon, 1940; Diploma; MRCVS 1940; FRCVS 1984. Gen. practice, Coleraine, 1940–43; Chief Vet. Officer, Hampshire Cattle Breeders, 1943–47; Dept of Agriculture, NI, 1947–83, Chief Vet. Officer, 1958–83. Governor, Coleraine Academical Instn, 1972–. *Recreations:* golf, walking; watching all sports, particularly Rugby and athletics. *Address:* Ardeena, 23 The Brae, Groomsport, Co. Down, BT19 2JQ. *Clubs:* Clandeboye Golf; Bangor Rugby and Athletic.

CONN, Prof. John Farquhar Christie, DSc; CEng; FRINA; John Elder Professor of Naval Architecture, University of Glasgow, 1957–73; *b* 5 July 1903; *s* of Alexander Aberdein Conn and Margaret Rhind Wilson; *m* 1935, Doris Maude Yeatman; one *s* one *d.* *Educ:* Robert Gordon's Coll., Aberdeen; Glasgow Univ. Apprenticeship at Alexander Hall and Co. Ltd, Aberdeen, 1920–25; employed in several shipyards; Scientific staff, Ship Div., National Physical Laboratory, 1929–44; Chief Naval Architect, British Shipbuilding Research Association, 1945–57. Hon. Vice-Pres., RINA. *Publications:* various papers in Trans. of Royal Instn of Naval Architects and other learned societies. *Recreations:* music, reading. *Address:* 14 Elm Walk, Bearsden, Glasgow G61 3BQ. *T:* 041–942 4640.

CONNALLY, John Bowden; lawyer; *b* 27 Feb. 1917; *s* of John Bowden Connally and Lela (*née* Wright); *m* 1940, Idanell Brill; two *s* one *d.* *Educ:* Univ. of Texas (LLB). Served US Navy, 1941–46. Pres. and Gen. Manager, KVET radio stn, 1946–49; Admin. Asst to Lyndon Johnson, 1949; employed with Powell, Wirtz & Rauhut, 1950–52; Attorney to Richardson & Bass, oil merchants, 1952–61; Sec. US Navy, 1961; Governor of Texas, 1962–68; Secretary of the Treasury, USA, 1971–72. Member: President's Adv. Cttee on Exec. Organisation, 1969–70; President's Foreign Intelligence Adv. Bd, 1972–74 and 1976–77; US Adv. Cttee on reform of Internat. Monetary System, 1973–74; Partner, Vinson Elkins, 1969–71, 1972–85; Director: The Methodist Hospital, 1977–; Ford Motor Co., 1981–87; Coastal Corp., 1988–; Maxxam Inc., 1988–; Kaiser Tech, 1988–; Kaiser Aluminum and Chemical, 1988. *Address:* 5847 San Felipe, Suite 2600, Houston, Texas 77057, USA.

CONNELL, Charles Percy; Puisne Judge, Kenya Colony, 1951–64, retired; *b* 1 Oct. 1902; *s* of late C. R. Connell, Barrister-at-Law and late K. Adlard; *m* 1946, Mary O'Rourke. *Educ:* Charterhouse; New Coll., Oxford (Hons, Jurisprudence). Called to Bar, Lincoln's Inn, 1927. Joined Kenya Judicial Service, 1938 (Resident Magistrate). Served War of 1939–45 (8th Army Clasp and war medals); commissioned King's African Rifles, 1941; British Military Administration (Legal and Judicial), Eritrea and Tripolitania, 1942–46. Acting Puisne Judge, Kenya, 1950, retired 1964. *Recreations:* tennis, cricket and trout fishing. *Address:* c/o Isle of Man Bank, Bowring Road, Ramsey, Isle of Man.

CONNELL, Most Rev. Desmond; *see* Dublin, Archbishop of, and Primate of Ireland, (RC).

CONNELL, George Edward, OC 1987; PhD; FCIC; FRSC; President, University of Toronto, 1984–90; *b* 20 June 1930; *m* 1955, Sheila Horan; two *s* two *d.* *Educ:* Univ. of Toronto (BA, PhD Biochemistry). FCIC 1971; FRSC 1975. Post-doctoral Fellow, Div. of Applied Biol., National Res. Council, Ottawa, Ont, 1955–56; Fellow, National Science Foundn (US), Dept of Biochem., New York University Coll. of Medicine, 1956–57; University of Toronto: Asst Prof. of Biochem., 1957–62; Associate Prof. of Biochem., 1962–65; Prof. and Chm. Dept of Biochem., 1965–70; Associate Dean, Faculty of Med., 1972–74; Vice-Pres., Res. and Planning, 1974–77; Pres. and Vice-Chancellor, Univ. of Western Ontario, 1977–84. Chairman: Exec. Cttee, Internat. Congress of Biochem., 1979; Nat. Round Table on Envmt and Economy, 1991–; Vice-Chm., Envmtl Assessment Bd, Ontario, 1990–; Member: MRC of Canada, 1966–70; Ont Council of Health, 1978–84; Bd of Dirs and Nat. Exec. Cttee, Canadian Arthritis and Rheumatism Soc., 1965–75; Bd of Dirs, Nat. Inst. of Nutrition, 1984–91; Bd of Dirs, Southam Inc., 1985–; Council, Ont Univs, 1977–90 (Chm., 1981–83); Bd of Governors, Upper Canada Coll., 1982–90; Bd of Trustees, Royal Ont Mus., 1984–90. Hon. LLD: Trent, 1984; Univ. of Western Ont, 1985; McGill, 1987. *Publications:* scientific papers in jls incl. Canadian Jl of Biochem., Biochemical Jl (UK), and Jl of Immunol. *Recreations:* skiing, tennis, wilderness canoe trips. *Address:* 240 Walmer Road, Toronto, Ont M5R 3R7, Canada. *Clubs:* University, Queen's (Toronto).

CONNELL, Prof. John Jeffrey, CBE 1985; PhD; FRSE; FIFST; Director, Torry Research Station, Aberdeen (Ministry of Agriculture, Fisheries and Food), 1979–87 (Assistant Director, 1969–79); Emeritus Professor, Aberdeen University, 1987; *b* 2 July 1927; *s* of John Edward Connell and Margaret Connell; *m* 1950, Margaret Parsons; one *s* two *d* (and one *d* decd). *Educ:* Burnage High Sch.; Univ. of Manchester (BSc 1947); Univ. of Edinburgh (PhD 1950). FIFST 1970; FRSE 1984. Torry Research Station: Scientific Officer, 1950; Sen. Sci. Officer, 1955; Principal Sci. Officer, 1961; Dep. Chief Sci. Officer, 1979; Officer i/c Humber Lab., Hull (Sen. Principal Sci. Officer), 1968–69. Res. Associate, 1969–79 and Hon. Res. Lectr, 1979–83, Aberdeen Univ. Mem., Fisheries Res. and Develt Bd, 1979–84. *Publications:* Control of Fish Quality, 1975, 3rd edn 1990 (Spanish edn 1978); Trends in Fish Utilisation, 1982; scientific and technical papers related to use of fish as food. *Recreations:* music, hill walking. *Address:* 61 Burnieboozle Crescent, Aberdeen AB1 8NR. *T:* Aberdeen (0224) 315852.

CONNELL, John MacFarlane; Chairman, The Distillers Company plc, 1983–86; *b* 29 Dec. 1924; *s* of late John Maclean Connell and Mollie Isobel MacFarlane; *m* 1949, Jean Matheson Sutherland Mackay, *d* of late Major George Sutherland Mackay and late Christine Bourne; two *s.* *Educ:* Stowe; Christ Church, Oxford. Joined Tanqueray, Gordon & Co. Ltd, 1946, Export Dir 1954, Man. Dir 1962–70; Dir, Distillers Co. Ltd, 1965, Mem., Management Cttee, 1971–86; Chm., United Glass Holdings plc, 1979–83. Chm., Gin Rectifiers and Distillers Assoc., 1968–71. Pres., Royal Warrant Holders Assoc., 1975. *Recreations:* golf, shooting, fishing. *Clubs:* East India; Royal and Ancient (St Andrews).

CONNELL, John Morris, OBE 1991; Chairman, Noise Abatement Society, since 1964; *b* 13 Sept. 1911; *s* of late James and Florence Connell; *m* 1939, Gertrude, *d* of late Judge Johann Adler, Vienna; three *d.* *Educ:* BeckenhamTechnical Sch.; Goldsmiths' Coll. MInstM 1935; MIPR 1965. Wholesale meat salesman, Smithfield Market, 1930–39; dir, own meat business, 1939–56; RN, 1941–46; company directorships, 1956–. Founded Noise Abatement Soc., 1959, Hon. Sec., 1959–64; Co-Founder, and Hon. Treasurer, Instn of Environmental Scis, 1970–; Co-Founder, Internat. Assoc. Against Noise, Zürich, 1960. *Publications:* articles and letters in the press. *Recreations:* gardening, reading newspapers. *Address:* 12 Hengist Way, Bromley, Kent BR2 0NS. *T:* 081–460 3146.

CONNELL, Michael Bryan; QC 1981; barrister-at-law; a Recorder of the Crown Court, since 1980; *b* 6 Aug. 1939; *s* of Lorraine Connell and of late Joan Connell; *m* 1965, Anne Joan Pulham; three *s* one *d.* *Educ:* Harrow; Brasenose Coll., Oxford (MA Jurisprudence). Called to the Bar, Inner Temple, 1962, Bencher, 1988. Governor, Harrow Sch., 1983–. Mem., Jockey Club, 1988–. *Recreations:* steeplechasing, cricket, foxhunting. *Address:* Queen Elizabeth Buildings, Temple, EC4. *T:* 071–583 7837. *Club:* Buck's.

CONNELL, Dame Ninette; *see* de Valois, Dame Ninette.

CONNELL, Dr Philip Henry, CBE 1986; Emeritus Physician, The Bethlem Royal Hospital and The Maudsley Hospital, 1986 (Physician, 1963–86); *b* 6 July 1921; *s* of George Henry Connell and Evelyn Hilda Sykes; *m* 1st, 1948, Marjorie Helen Gilham; two *s*; 2nd, 1973, Cecily Mary Harper. *Educ:* St Paul's Sch.; St Bartholomew's Hosp., London. MD, BS, MRCS, FRCP, FRCPsych, DPM (academic). St Stephen's Hosp., Fulham Road, 1951–53; Registrar and Sen. Registrar, The Bethlem Royal Hosp. and the Maudsley Hosp., 1953–57; Cons. Psychiatrist, Newcastle Gen. Hosp. and Physician i/c Child Psychiatry Unit, Newcastle Gen. Hosp. in assoc. with King's Coll., Durham Univ., and Assoc. Phys., Royal Victoria Infirm., 1957–63. Extensive nat. and internat. work on drug addiction and dependence (incl. work for WHO, Council of Europe and CENTO), and on maladjusted and psychiatrically ill children and adolescents. Mem. numerous adv. cttees and working parties, including: Standing Mental Health Adv. Cttee, DHSS (formerly Min. of Health), 1966–72 (Vice Chm., 1967–72); Standing Adv. Cttee on Drug Dependence (Wayne Cttee), 1966–71 (Mem., Hallucinogens Sub-Cttees on Cannabis, 1967–68, and on LSD and Amphetamines, 1968–70); Consultant Adviser (Addiction) to DHSS, 1965–71 and 1981–86; Pres., Soc. for Study of Addiction, 1973–78; Vice Pres., Internat. Council on Alcohol and Addictions, 1982– (Chm., Scientific and Prof. Adv. Bd, 1971–79, Mem., Bd of Management, 1984–88); Chairman: Inst. for Study of Drug Dependence, 1975–90; Adv. Council on Misuse of Drugs, 1982–88; Sec. of State for Transport's Adv. Panel on Driving and Alcohol and Substance Misuse, 1988–; Member: Council, RMPA, 1962–67; Cttee of Management, Inst. of Psychiatry, 1968–74; Trethowan Cttee on Role of Psychologists in Health Service, 1968–72; Standing Mental Health Adv. Cttee, DHSS, 1966–71; GMC, 1979–81 (Preliminary Screener for Health, 1982–84, 1989–91; Dep. Screener, 1984–89); Vice-Pres., RCPsych, 1979–81 (Mem. Council, 1971–81; Chm., Child and Adolescent Specialist Section, 1971–74; observer on Council as Coll. appointee to GMC, 1981–). Dent Meml Lectr, KCL and Soc. for Study of Addiction, 1985. Member of Bd of Governors: Bethlem Royal and Maudsley Hosps, 1966–73; Mowden Hall Sch., 1976–82. Mem., editorial bds, various jls. *Publications:* Amphetamine Psychosis (monograph), 1958; (ed jtly) Cannabis and Man, 1975; numerous chapters in books, papers in sci. jls and proc. sci. confs. *Recreations:* theatre, bridge. *Address:* 25 Oxford Road, Putney, SW15 2LG. *T:* 081–788 1416; 21 Wimpole Street, W1M 7AD. *T:* 071–636 2220. *Club:* Athenæum.

CONNELL-SMITH, Prof. Gordon Edward, PhD; FRHistS; Professor of Contemporary History, University of Hull, 1973–85; *b* 23 Nov. 1917; 2nd *s* of George Frederick Smith and Margaret Smith (*née* Woolerton); surname changed to Connell-Smith by deed-poll, 1942; *m* 1954, Wendy Ann (*d* 1987), *o d* of John Bertram and Kathleen Tomlinson; one *s* one *d.* *Educ:* Richmond County Sch., Surrey; University Coll. of SW of England, Exeter (BA); Birkbeck Coll., London (PhD). FRHistS 1959. Served War, RA and Staff, 1940–46 (Staff Major). Julian Corbett Prize, Inst. of Historical Res., 1949; University of Hull: Staff Tutor/Lectr in Adult Educn and History Depts, 1952–63; Sen. Lectr, 1963–69; Reader in Contemp. Internat. History, 1969–73. Mem., Cttee of Management, Univ. of London Inst. of Latin Amer. Studies, 1973–85. Chm., Latin American Newsletters, Ltd, London, 1969–72. *Publications:* Forerunners of Drake, 1954; Pattern of the Post-War World, 1957; The Inter-American System, 1966 (Spanish edn 1971); (co-author) The Relevance of History, 1972; The United States and Latin America, 1974 (Spanish edn 1977); The Future of History, 1975; Latin American Relations with the World 1826–1976, 1976; contrib. to Bull. Inst. of Historical Res., Contemp. Rev., Econ. History Rev., Eng. Historical

Rev., History, Internat. Affairs, Jl of Latin Amer. Studies, World Today, etc. *Recreations:* travel, sport. *Address:* 7 Braids Walk, Kirk Ella, Hull HU10 7PA. *T:* Hull (0482) 652624.

CONNELLY, Thomas John; Director of Services, General and Municipal Workers' Union, 1978–85, retired; *b* 24 Dec. 1925; *s* of William and Jane Connelly; *m* 1952, Naomi Shakow; one *s* one *d. Educ:* Priory St Elementary Sch., Colchester; Ruskin Coll.; Lincoln Coll., Oxford. BA 1955. Research Officer: Amalgamated Soc. of Woodworkers, 1955–63; G&MWU, 1963–66; Adviser, Industrial Relations Prices and Incomes Bd, 1966–68; various posts, finally as Chief Officer, Race Relations Bd, 1968–77; apptd Chief Executive, Commn for Racial Equality, 1977, but withdrew from appt. *Publication:* The Woodworkers 1860–1960, 1960. *Recreations:* reading, music. *Address:* 2 Caroline Court, 25 Lovelace Road, Surbiton, Surrey. *T:* 081–399 9223.

CONNER, Rev. David John; Vicar, St Mary the Great with St Michael, Cambridge, since 1987; Rural Dean of Cambridge, since 1989; *b* 6 April 1947; *s* of William Ernest Conner and Joan Millington Conner; *m* 1969, Jayne Maria Evans; two *s. Educ:* Erith Grammar School; Exeter College, Oxford (Symes Exhibnr; MA); St Stephen's House, Oxford. Asst Chaplain, St Edward's School, Oxford, 1971–73; Chaplain, 1973–80; Team Vicar, Wolvercote with Summertown, Oxford, 1976–80; Senior Chaplain, Winchester College, 1980–86. *Address:* Great St Mary's Vicarage, 39 Madingley Road, Cambridge CB3 0EL. *T:* Cambridge (0223) 355285.

CONNERY, Sean, (Thomas Connery); actor; *b* 25 Aug. 1930; *s* of Joseph and Euphamia Connery; *m* 1st, 1962, Diane (marr. diss. 1974), *d* of Sir Raphael West Cilento, MD and of Lady Cilento; one *s* (and one step *d*); 2nd, 1975, Micheline Roquebrune. Served Royal Navy. Dir, Tantallon Films Ltd, 1972–. Has appeared in films: No Road Back, 1956; Action of the Tiger, 1957; Another Time, Another Place, 1957; Hell Drivers, 1958; Tarzan's Greatest Adventure, 1959; Darby O'Gill and the Little People, 1959; On the Fiddle, 1961; The Longest Day, 1962; The Frightened City, 1962; Woman of Straw, 1964; The Hill, 1965; A Fine Madness, 1966; Shalako, 1968; The Molly Maguires, 1968; The Red Tent (1st Russian co-production), 1969; The Anderson Tapes, 1970; The Offence, 1973; Zardoz, 1973; Ransom, 1974; Murder on the Orient Express, 1974; The Wind and the Lion, 1975; The Man Who Would Be King, 1975; Robin and Marian, 1976; The First Great Train Robbery, 1978; Cuba, 1978; Meteor, 1979; Outland, 1981; The Man with the Deadly Lens, 1982; Wrong is Right, 1982; Five Days One Summer, 1982; Highlander, 1986; The Name of the Rose, 1987; The Untouchables, 1987 (Best Supporting Actor, Academy Awards, 1988); The Presidio, 1989; Indiana Jones and the Last Crusade, 1989; Family Business, 1990; The Hunt for Red October, 1990; The Russia House, 1991; Highlander II—The Quickening, 1991; *as James Bond:* Dr No, 1963; From Russia With Love, 1964; Goldfinger, 1965; Thunderball, 1965; You Only Live Twice, 1967; Diamonds are Forever, 1971; Never Say Never Again, 1983. FRSAMD 1984. Hon. DLitt Heriot-Watt, 1981. Commander, Order of Arts and Literature (France), 1987. *Recreations:* oil painting, golf, reading, cooking.

CONNOLLY, Edward Thomas; Regional Chairman of Industrial Tribunals, since 1988; *b* 5 Sept. 1935; *s* of Edward Connolly and Alice Joyce; *m* 1962, Dr Pamela Marie Hagan; one *s* one *d. Educ:* St Mary's Coll., Crosby; Prior Park Coll.; Liverpool Univ. (LLB). Qualified as solicitor, 1960. Asst Solicitor, Lancs CC, 1960–63; Asst Prosecuting Solicitor, Liverpool City Council, 1963–65; Dep. Chief Legal Officer, Skelmersdale Develt Corp., 1965–68; Asst Clerk of the Peace, Lancs CC, 1968–71; Dep. Circuit Administrator, Northern Circuit, 1971–76; Chm. of Industrial Tribunals, 1976–88. *Address:* (office) Alexander House, 14–22 The Parsonage, Manchester M3 2JA. *T:* 061–833 0581. *Club:* Royal Automobile.

CONNOR, Bishop of, since 1987; **Rt. Rev. Samuel Greenfield Poyntz;** *b* 4 March 1926; *s* of James and Katharine Jane Poyntz; *m* 1952, Noreen Henrietta Armstrong; one *s* two *d. Educ:* Portora Royal School, Enniskillen; Univ. of Dublin. Mod., Mental and Moral Sci. and Oriental Langs, 1948; 1st cl. Div. Test., 1950; MA 1951; BD 1953; PhD 1960. Deacon 1950, priest 1951; Curate Assistant: St George's, Dublin, 1950–52; Bray, 1952–55; St Michan and St Paul, Dublin, 1955–59; Rector of St Stephen's, Dublin, 1959–67; Vicar of St Ann's, Dublin, 1967–78; Archdeacon of Dublin, 1974–78; Exam. Chaplain to Archbishop of Dublin, 1974–78; Bishop of Cork, Cloyne and Ross, 1978–87. Chairman: Youth Dept, British Council of Churches, 1965–69; Irish Council of Churches, 1986–88; Vice-Pres., BCC, 1987–90. *Publications:* The Exaltation of the Blessed Virgin Mary, 1953; St Stephen's—One Hundred and Fifty Years of Worship and Witness, 1974; Journey towards Unity, 1975; St Ann's—the Church in the heart of the City, 1976; (ed) Church the Way, the Truth, and Your Life, 1955; Our Church—Praying with our Church Family, 1983. *Recreations:* interest in Rugby football, stamp collecting. *Address:* Bishop's House, 22 Deramore Park, Belfast BT9 5JU.

CONNOR, Prof. James Michael, FRCPGlas, FRCPE; Burton Professor of Medical Genetics, Glasgow University, since 1987; *b* 18 June 1951; *s* of James Connor and Mona Connor (*née* Hall); *m* 1979, Dr Rachel Alyson Clare Brooks; two *d. Educ:* Liverpool Univ. (BSc (Hons); MB ChB (Hons); MD). MRCP 1977; FRCPGlas 1988; FRCPE 1990. Gen. med. professional trng in various Liverpool hosps, 1975–77; Resident in Internal Medicine, Johns Hopkins Hosp., Baltimore, 1977–78; Univ. Res. Fellow, Dept of Medicine, Liverpool Univ., 1978–81; Instr in Med. Genetics, John Hopkins Hosp., 1981–82; Cons. in Med. Genetics, 1982–84, Wellcome Trust Sen. Lectr in Med. Genetics, 1984–87, Duncan Guthrie Inst. of Med. Genetics, Glasgow. *Publications:* Essential Medical Genetics, 1984, 3rd edn 1990; Prenatal Diagnosis in Obstetric Practice, 1989; articles on various aspects of human gene mapping, molecular pathology and clin. applications of DNA probes. *Recreations:* windsurfing, fly-fishing. *Address:* Westbank Cottage, 84 Montgomery Street, Eaglesham, Strathclyde G76 0AU. *T:* Eaglesham (03553) 2626.

CONNOR, Jeremy George; Metropolitan Stipendiary Magistrate, since 1979; a Recorder, since 1986; *b* 14 Dec. 1938; *s* of Joseph Connor and Mabel Emmeline (*née* Adams), ARCA. *Educ:* Beaumont; University Coll., London (LLB; DRS). Called to the Bar, Middle Temple, 1961; S Eastern Circuit. Apptd to Treasury List, Central Criminal Court, 1973; a Chm., Inner London Juvenile Cts, 1980–. Chm., Inner London and City Probation Cttee, 1989–; Mem. Exec. Cttee, Central Council of Probation for England and Wales, 1982–89. Mem., Judicial Studies Bd, 1990–. Pres., British Acad. of Forensic Scis, 1989–90 (Chm., Exec. Council, 1983–86; Mem. Council, 1982–). Underwriting Mem. of Lloyd's. Freeman, City of London, 1980; Liveryman, Fanmakers' Co., 1981 (Mem., Livery Cttee, 1987–). *Publications:* chapter in Archbold, Criminal Pleading, Evidence and Practice, 38th and 39th edns. *Recreations:* travel, theatre, occasional broadcasting. *Address:* Bow Street Magistrates' Court, WC2. *Clubs:* Garrick, Royal Society of Medicine.

CONNOR, Roger David; His Honour Judge Connor; a Circuit Judge, since 1991; *b* 8 June 1939; *s* of Thomas Bernard Connor and Susie Violet Connor (*née* Spittlehouse); *m* 1967, Sandra Home Holmes; two *s. Educ:* Merchant Taylors' School; Brunel College of Advanced Science and Technology; The College of Law. Solicitor; articled to J. R. Hodder, 1963–68; Asst Solicitor, 1968–70; Partner, Hodders, 1970–83; Metropolitan Stipendiary Magistrate, 1983–91; a Recorder, 1987–91. *Recreations:* music, golf, gardening, bee keeping. *Address:* c/o Crown Court, Aylesbury, Bucks. *Club:* Beaconsfield Golf.

CONOLLY, Mrs Yvonne Cecile; Senior Inspector for Primary Education, London Borough of Islington, since 1989; *b* 12 June 1939; *d* of Hugh Augustus and Blanche Foster; *m* 1965, Michael Patrick Conolly; one *d. Educ:* Westwood High Sch., Jamaica; Shortwood Coll., Jamaica (Teachers' CertEd); Polytechnic, N London (BEd Hons Primary Educn). Primary school teacher: Jamaica, 1960–63; London, 1963–68; Head Teacher, London, 1969–78; ILEA Inspector, Multi-ethnic Education, 1978–81; Inspector of Primary Schools, 1981–90, Dist Primary Inspector, 1988–90, ILEA. Member: Home Secretary's Adv. Council on Race Relations, 1977–86; IBA, 1982–86; Consumer Protection Adv. Cttee, 1974–75. Governor, former Centre for Information and Advice on Educnl Disadvantage, 1975–80; (first) Chm., Caribbean Teachers' Assoc., 1974–76. *Publications:* (contrib.) Mango Spice, book of 44 Caribbean songs for schools, 1981; (contrib.) Against the Tide, 1990. *Recreations:* special interest in the activities of ethnic minority groups; travelling, conversing.

CONOLLY-CAREW, family name of **Baron Carew.**

CONQUEST, (George) Robert (Acworth), OBE 1955; writer; *b* 15 July 1917; *s* of late Robert Folger Westcott Conquest and Rosamund, *d* of H. A. Acworth, CIE; *m* 1st, 1942, Joan Watkins (marr. diss. 1948); two *s*; 2nd, 1948, Tatiana Mihailova (marr. diss. 1962); 3rd, 1964, Caroleen Macfarlane (marr. diss. 1978); 4th, 1979, Elizabeth, *d* of late Col Richard D. Neece, USAF. *Educ:* Winchester; Magdalen Coll., Oxford. MA Oxon 1972; DLitt 1975. Oxf. and Bucks LI, 1939–46; Foreign Service, 1946–56; Fellow, LSE, 1956–58; Vis. Poet, Univ. of Buffalo, 1959–60; Literary Editor, The Spectator, 1962–63; Fellow: Columbia Univ., 1964–65; Woodrow Wilson International Center, 1976–77; Hoover Instn, 1977–79 and 1981–; Distinguished Vis. Scholar, Heritage Foundn, 1980–81; Research Associate, Harvard Univ., 1982–83; Adjunct Fellow, Center for Strategic and Internat. Studies, 1983–. FRSL 1972. *Publications:* Poems, 1955; A World of Difference, 1955; (ed) New Lines, 1956; Common Sense About Russia, 1960; Power and Policy in the USSR, 1961; Courage of Genius, 1962; Between Mars and Venus, 1962; (ed) New Lines II, 1963; (with Kingsley Amis) The Egyptologists, 1965; Russia after Khrushchev, 1965; The Great Terror, 1968; Arias from a Love Opera, 1969; The Nation Killers, 1970; Lenin, 1972; Kolyma, 1978; The Abomination of Moab, 1979; Present Danger, 1979; Forays, 1979; We and They, 1980; (with Jon Manchip White) What to do when the Russians Come, 1984; Inside Stalin's Secret Police, 1985; The Harvest of Sorrow, 1986; New and Collected Poems, 1988; Tyrants and Typewriters, 1989; Stalin and the Kirov Murder, 1989; The Great Terror Reassessed, 1990; Stalin Then and Now, 1991. *Address:* c/o Brown Shipley & Co., Founder's Court, Lothbury, EC2; 52 Peter Coutts Circle, Stanford, Calif 94305, USA. *Club:* Travellers'.

CONRAN, Elizabeth Margaret, MA, FMA; Curator, The Bowes Museum, Barnard Castle, since 1979; *b* 5 May 1939; *d* of James Johnston and Elizabeth Russell Wilson; *m* 1970, George Loraine Conran (*d* 1986); one *d. Educ:* Falkirk High Sch.; Glasgow Univ. (MA). FMA 1969. Res. Asst, Dept of History of Fine Art, Glasgow Univ., 1959–60; Asst Curator, The Iveagh Bequest, Kenwood, 1960–63; Keeper of Paintings, City Art Galls, Manchester, 1963–74; Arts Adviser, Greater Manchester Council, 1974–79. FRSA 1987. *Publications:* exhibn catalogues; articles in art and museum jls. *Recreations:* gardens, ballet. *Address:* 31 Thorngate, Barnard Castle, Co. Durham DL12 8QB. *T:* Teesdale (0833) 31055.

CONRAN, Jasper Alexander Thirlby; Designer (mens and womens wear) and Managing Director, Jasper Conran Ltd, since 1978; *b* 12 Dec. 1959; *s* of Sir Terence Conran, *qv* and Shirley Conran, *qv. Educ:* Bryanston School, Dorset; Parsons School of Art and Design, New York. Costumes for Anouilh's The Rehearsal, 1990 (Laurence Olivier Award, 1991). Fil d'Or (Internat. Linen Award), 1982 and 1983; British Fashion Council Designer of the Year Award, 1986–87; Fashion Group of America Award, 1987. *Address:* 49/50 Great Marlborough Street, W1V 1DB. *T:* 071–437 0386.

CONRAN, Shirley Ida; writer; *b* 21 Sept. 1932; *d* of W. Thirlby Pearce and Ida Pearce; *m* 1955, Sir Terence Conran (marr. diss. 1962); two *s. Educ:* St Paul's Girls' Sch.; Southern College of Art, Portsmouth. Fabric Designer and Director of Conran Fabrics, 1956–62; Member, Selection Cttee, Design Centre, 1961–69. Journalist; (first) Woman's Editor, Observer Colour Magazine, 1964; Woman's Editor, Daily Mail, 1969; Life and Style Editor, Over 21, 1972–74. *Publications:* Superwoman, 1975, revd edn as Down with Superwoman, 1990; Superwoman Year Book, 1976; Superwoman in Action, 1977; (with E. Sidney) Futurewoman, 1979; Lace (novel), 1982; The Magic Garden, 1983; Lace 2 (novel), 1985; Savages (novel), 1987. *Recreations:* reading, swimming, Yoga. *Address:* 39 avenue Princesse Grace, Monaco.
See also J. A. T. Conran.

CONRAN, Sir Terence (Orby), Kt 1983; Chairman: RSCG Conran Design (formerly Conran Design Group/Conran Associates), since 1971; The Conran Shop Ltd, since 1976; Conran Roche, since 1980; Jasper Conran Ltd, since 1982; Bibendum Restaurant Ltd, since 1986; Benchmark Ltd, since 1989; Blueprint Café Ltd, since 1989; Terence Conran Ltd, since 1990; Conran Shop Holdings Ltd, since 1990; *b* 4 Oct. 1931; *m*; two *s*; *m* 1963, Caroline Herbert; two *s* one *d. Educ:* Bryanston, Dorset. Chm., Conran Holdings Ltd, 1965–68; Jt Chm., Ryman Conran Ltd, 1968–71; Chairman: Habitat Group Ltd, 1971–88; Habitat France SA, 1973–88; Conran Stores Inc., 1977–88; J. Hepworth & Son Ltd, 1981–83 (Dir, 1979–); Habitat Mothercare Ltd, 1982–88; Heal & Sons Ltd, 1983–87; Richard Shops, 1983–87; Storehouse plc, 1986–90 (Chief Exec., 1986–88; non-exec. Dir, 1990); Butlers Wharf Ltd, 1984–90; Le Pont de la Tour Ltd, 1991–; Director: Conran Ink Ltd, 1969–; The Neal Street Restaurant, 1972–89; Conran Octopus, 1983–; BhS plc, 1986–88; Savacentre Ltd, 1986–88; Michelin House Investment Co. Ltd, 1989–; Vice-Pres., FNAC, 1985–89. Estabd Conran Foundn for Design Educn and Research, 1981–. Mem., Royal Commn on Environmental Pollution, 1973–76. Member: Council, RCA, 1978–81, 1986–; Adv. Council, V&A Mus., 1979–83; Trustee: V&A Museum, 1984–90; Design Museum, 1989–. RSA Presidential Medal for Design Management to Conran Group; RSA Presidential Award for Design Management to Habitat Designs Ltd, 1975; SIAD Medal, 1981; Assoc. for Business Sponsorship of the Arts and Daily Telegraph Award to Habitat Mothercare, 1982; RSA Bicentenary Medal, 1982; President's Award, D&AD, 1989. Hon. FRIBA 1984. *Publications:* The House Book, 1974; The Kitchen Book, 1977; The Bedroom & Bathroom Book, 1978; (with Caroline Conran) The Cook Book, 1980; The New House Book, 1985; Conran Directory of Design, 1985; Plants at Home, 1986; The Soft Furnishings Book, 1986; Terence Conran's France, 1987; Terence Conran's DIY by Design, 1989; Terence Conran's Garden DIY by Design, 1990. *Recreations:* gardening, cooking. *Address:* 512 The Butler Wharf Building, 36 Shad Thames, SE1 2YE. *T:* 071–378 1161.
See also J. A. T. Conran.

CONROY, Harry; Campaigns Director, Scottish Constitutional Convention, since 1990; General Secretary, National Union of Journalists, 1985–90; *b* Scotland, 6 April 1943; *s* of Michael Conroy and Sarah (*née* Mullan); *m* 1965, Margaret Craig (*née* Campbell); twin *s* one *d.* Trainee Lab. Technician, Southern Gen. Hosp., 1961–62; Night Messenger (copy boy), 1962–63, Jun. Features Sub-Editor, 1963–64, Scottish Daily Express; Daily Record:

Reporter, 1964–66 and 1967–69; Financial Correspondent, 1969–85; Reporter, Scottish Daily Mail, 1966–67. Mem., ASTMS, 1961–62. National Union of Journalists: Mem., 1963–; Mem., Nat. Exec. Council, 1976–85; Vice-Pres., 1980–81; Pres., 1981–82. Associate Mem., GMBATU, 1984–85. *Recreations:* stamp and post-card collecting, supporting Glasgow Celtic FC. *Address:* 15 Swallow Rise, Walderslade, Chatham, Kent ME5 7QB.

CONS, Hon. Sir Derek, Kt 1990; **Hon. Mr Justice Cons;** Vice President, Court of Appeal, Supreme Court of Hong Kong, since 1986; *b* 15 July 1928; *s* of Alfred Henry Cons and Elsie Margaret (*née* Neville); *m* 1952, Mary Roberta Upton Wilkes. *Educ:* Rutlish; Birmingham Univ. (LLB (Hons)). Called to Bar, Gray's Inn, 1953. RASC (2nd Lieut), 1946–48. Magistrate, Hong Kong, 1955–62, Principal Magistrate, 1962–66; District Judge, 1966–72; Judge of Supreme Court of Hong Kong, 1972–80, Justice of Appeal, 1980–86. *Recreations:* golf, skiing. *Address:* The Supreme Court, Hong Kong; Mulberry Mews, Church Street, Fordingbridge, Hants SP6 1BE. *Clubs:* Bramshaw Golf (Hants); Hong Kong, Royal Hong Kong Yacht, Shek O Country (Hong Kong).

CONSTABLE, (Charles) John, DBA; CBIM; management educator and consultant; Chairman, Bright Tech Ltd, since 1989; Director-General, British Institute of Management, 1985–86; *b* 20 Jan. 1936; *s* of Charles and Gladys Constable; *m* 1960, Elisabeth Mary Light; three *s* one *d*. *Educ:* Durham Sch.; St John's Coll., Cambridge (MA); Royal Sch. of Mines, Imperial Coll. London (BSc); Harvard Grad. Sch. of Bus. Admin. (DBA). NCB, 1959–60; Wallis & Linnel Ltd, 1960–63; Arthur Young & Co., 1963–64; Lectr and Sen. Lectr, Durham Univ. Business Sch., 1964–71; Prof. of Operations Management, Business Policy, 1971–82, Dir 1982–85, Cranfield Sch. of Management. Non-executive Director: IMS Ltd, 1984–; Lloyds Abbey Life (formerly Abbey Life), 1987–. Member: Heavy Electrical EDC, NEDO, 1977–87; N Beds HA, 1987–90; Res. Grants Bd, ESRC, 1989–90. Dep. Chm. of Govs, Harpur Trust, 1988– (Governor, 1979–). *Publications:* (jtly) Group Assessment Programmes, 1966; (jtly) Operations Management Text and Cases, 1976; (jtly) Cases in Strategic Management, 1980; The Making of British Managers (BIM/CBI report), 1987. *Recreations:* golf, family. *Address:* 20 Kimbolton Road, Bedford MK40 2NR. *T:* Bedford (0234) 212576.

CONSTABLE, Sir Robert Frederick S.; *see* Strickland-Constable.

CONSTANT, Antony; Group Management Development Executive, the Delta Group plc (formerly Delta Metal Co. Ltd), retired 1980 (Group Archivist, 1980–83); *b* 1916; *s* of Frederick Charles and Mary Theresa Constant; *m* 1947, Pamela Mary Pemberton (*d* 1989); one *s*. *Educ:* Dover Coll.; King's Coll., Cambridge. Asst master, Oundle Sch., 1939–45; Staff of Dir of Naval Intelligence, Admiralty, 1940–44; Educational Adviser to the Control Commission, Germany, 1945. Asst Master, and Asst House Master of School House, Rugby Sch., 1945–49; Rector of Royal Coll., Mauritius, 1949–53; Dir of Studies, RAF Coll., Cranwell, 1953–59; Educational Adviser: RAF Benevolent Fund, 1953–78; to MoD and Chm. of Joint-Services Working Party, 1959–62; joined Delta Group of Companies, 1963, as Head of Group Training Dept. Mem. Bd for Postgraduate Studies, and Mem. Faculty Bd, Management Centre, Univ. of Aston, 1973–77. *Publications:* The Percy Lane Group 1932–82, 1982; various articles on historical geography, ships and shipping. *Recreations:* genealogy, ornithology, ships. *Address:* Old Bonham's, Wardington, near Banbury, Oxon OX17 1SA.

CONSTANTINE, family name of **Baron Constantine of Stanmore.**

CONSTANTINE OF STANMORE, Baron *cr* 1981 (Life Peer), of Stanmore in Greater London; **Theodore Constantine;** Kt 1964; CBE 1956; AE 1945; DL; *er s* of Leonard and Fanny Louise Constantine; *m* 1935, Sylvia Mary (*d* 1990), *y d* of Wallace Henry Legge-Pointing; one *s* one *d*. *Educ:* Acton Coll. Personal Asst to Chm. of public company, 1926–28; Executive in industry, 1928–38; Managing Dir of public company subsidiary, 1938–39. Served War of 1939–45, AAF (AEA 1945). Dir of Industrial Holding Company, 1956–59; Chm. of Public Companies, 1959–86. Organisational work for Conservative Party as Constituency Chm., Area Chm., Mem. Nat. Exec. Cttee, Policy Cttee, Nat. Advisory Cttee on Publicity. Chm., Nat. Union Cons. and Unionist Assocs, 1967–68, Pres. 1980. Trustee, Sir John Wolstenholme Charity; Master, Worshipful Co. of Coachmakers, 1975; Freeman of City of London, 1949. High Sheriff of Greater London, 1967; DL Greater London, 1967–85. *Recreations:* watching motor racing, reading, walking. *Address:* House of Lords, SW1A 0PW. *Club:* Carlton.

CONSTANTINE, Air Chief Marshal Sir Hugh (Alex), KBE 1958 (CBE 1944); CB 1946; DSO 1942; Co-ordinator, Anglo-American Community Relations, Ministry of Defence (Air), 1964–77; *b* 23 May 1908; *s* of Fleet Paymaster Henry Constantine, RN, and Alice Louise Squire; *m* 1937, Helen, *d* of J. W. Bourke, Sydney, Australia; one *d*. *Educ:* Christ's Hosp.; Royal Air Force Coll., Cranwell. Pilot Officer in RAF, 1927; 56 (F) Sqdn, 1928–29; Flying Instructor, RAF Coll., 1930–31; CFS Instructor, 1932–33 and 1937; No 1 Armoured Car Co. (Iraq), 1934–36 (Palestine, despatches); Sqdn Ldr, 1936; 214 Bomber Sqdn, 1937–38; Sqdn Ldr Examining Wing, CFS, 1939; graduated Staff Coll., Andover, 1940; served in Bomber Comd, 1940–45 (Gp Capt. 1941; despatches four times); Wing Comdr (Ops) No 3 Gp, 1940, (Flying) No 11 OTU, 1941; comd RAF Elsham Wolds, 1941–42; SASO No 1 (B) Gp, 1943; Dep. SASO Bomber Comd, 1944; Air Vice-Marshal, Jan. 1945, and commanded No 5 (B) Group Bomber Command; Chief Intelligence Officer, BAFO and Control Commission, Germany, 1946; idc, 1947; SASO, 205 Gp (Egypt), 1948–49; Dir of Intelligence, Air Min., 1950–51; AO i/c A, Fighter Comd, 1952–53; AOC No 25 Group, Flying Training Command, 1954–56; Deputy Chief of Staff (Plans and Operations), SHAPE, NATO, 1956–59; Comdt, ATC, 1959–60; AOC-in-C, Flg Trng Comd, 1959–61; Commandant, Imperial Defence Coll., 1962–64; retired 1964. Air Marshal, 1957; Air Chief Marshal, 1961. Patron, Central Flying Sch. Assoc., 1979–84. Governor, Christ's Hospital, 1963 – (Almoner, 1969–85). Hon. LLD Warwick, 1978. Order of Polonia Restituta (2nd Class), 1945. *Recreations:* Rugby (English Trial, 1934), Eastern Counties, RAF and Leicester; golf. *Address:* 14 Cadogan Court, Draycott Avenue, SW3 3BX. *T:* 071–581 8821. *Club:* Royal Air Force.

CONTI, Rt. Rev. Mario Joseph; *see* Aberdeen, Bishop of, (RC).

CONTI, Tom; actor, since 1960; director; *b* Scotland, 1942; *m* Kara Wilson; one *d*. London appearances include: Savages, Royal Court and Comedy, 1973; Other People, The Black and White Minstrels, Hampstead; The Devil's Disciple, RSC Aldwych, 1976; Whose Life is it Anyway?, Mermaid and Savoy, 1978, NY 1979 (SWET Award for Best Actor in a new play, Variety Club of GB Award for Best Stage Actor, 1978, Tony Award for Best Actor, 1979); They're Playing Our Song, Shaftesbury, 1980; Romantic Comedy, Apollo, 1983; An Italian Straw Hat, Shaftesbury, 1986; *directed:* Last Licks, Broadway, 1979; Before the Party, Oxford Playhouse and Queen's, 1980; The Housekeeper, Apollo, 1982; Treats, Hampstead, 1989; *films include:* Galileo, Flame, 1974; Eclipse, 1975; Full Circle, The Duellists, 1977; The Wall, 1980; Merry Christmas, Mr Lawrence, 1983; Reuben, Reuben, 1983; American Dreamer, 1985; Miracles, 1985; Saving Grace, 1986; Heavenly Pursuits, 1987; Beyond Therapy, 1987; The Dumb Waiter (USA); White Roses; Shirley Valentine, 1989; Two Brothers Running; *television appearances include:*

Madame Bovary, The Norman Conquests, Glittering Prizes, The Beate Klarsfeld Story, Fatal Dosage, The Quick and the Dead, Blade on the Feather. *Address:* c/o Chatto & Linnit, Prince of Wales Theatre, Coventry Street, W1.

CONTOGEORGIS, George; Member, Commission of the European Communities, 1981–85; *b* 21 Nov. 1912; *s* of Leonidas and Angeliki Contogeorgis; *m* 1949, Mary Lazopoulou. *Educ:* Athens Sch. (now University) of Economic and Commercial Sciences. Ministry of Trade, Greece: Administrator, 1937; Chief of Section, 1945; Dir, 1952; Dir Gen., 1964–67, resigned. Gen. Sec., Tourism, Govt of Nea Dimokratia, 1974; Dep. Minister of Co-ordination (Econs), 1974–77; Minister for EEC Affairs, 1977–81; Minister of Nat. Economy, 1989–90. MP, 1977–81. Grand Comdr, Order of the Phoenix (Greece), 1966; Grand Croix de l'Ordre de Leopold II (Belgium), 1984. *Publication:* Greece in Europe, 1985. *Address:* Rue Anagnostopoulon 26, Athens 10673, Greece. *T:* 361.68.44.

CONWAY, (David) Martin; President, Selly Oak Colleges, Birmingham, since 1986; *b* 22 Aug. 1935; *s* of Geoffrey S. and Dr Elsie Conway; *m* 1962, Ruth, *d* of Rev. Richard Daniel; one *s* two *d*. *Educ:* Sedbergh Sch.; Gonville and Caius Coll., Cambridge (BA, MA); and by friends and fellow Christians in many different cultures. Internat. Sec., SCM of GB and Ire., 1958–61; Study Sec., World Student Christian Fedn, Geneva, 1961–67; Sec. for Chaplaincies in Higher Educn, Gen. Synod of C of E, 1967–70; Publications Sec., WCC, 1970–74; Asst Gen. Sec. for Ecumenical Affairs, BCC, 1974–83; Dir, Oxford Inst. for Church and Society, and Tutor, Ripon Coll., Cuddesdon, Oxford, 1983–86. Simultaneous interpreter at assemblies and major world confs of WCC, 1961–; Consultant, Faith and Order Commn, WCC, 1971–82; Consultant, 1974–83, and Mem., 1986–, C of E Bd for Mission and Unity. Editor: The Ecumenical Review, 1972–74; Christians Together, 1983–; Oxford Papers on Contemporary Society, 1984–86. *Publications:* The Undivided Vision, 1966; (ed) University Chaplain?, 1969; The Christian Enterprise in Higher Education, 1971; Seeing Education Whole, 1971; Look Listen Care, 1983; contribs to Student World, New Christian, Audenshaw Papers, Internat. Rev. of Mission, etc. *Recreations:* other people—family, friends, colleagues; travel, music. *Address:* President's House, Selly Oak Colleges, Birmingham B29 6LQ. *T:* 021–472 4231.

CONWAY, Derek Leslie; MP (C) Shrewsbury and Atcham, since 1983; *b* 15 Feb. 1953; *s* of Leslie and Florence Conway; *m* 1980, Colette Elizabeth Mary (*née* Lamb); two *s* one *d*. *Educ:* Beacon Hill Boys' School. Borough Councillor and Dep. Leader of the Opposition, Gateshead Metropolitan Borough Council, 1974–78; Mem., Tyne and Wear Metropolitan County Council, 1977–83 (Leader, 1979–82); Member Board: Washington Develt Corp., 1979–83; North of England Develt Council, 1979–83; Newcastle Airport, 1980–83; Northern Arts, 1980–83. Principal Organiser, Action Research for the Crippled Child, 1974–83. PPS to Minister of State, Welsh Office, 1988–. Member: Select Cttee on Agric., 1987; Select Cttee on Transport, 1987–88; Chm., British–Morocco Parly Gp, 1988–. Member, Conservative Party Committees: Nat. Exec. Cttee, 1971–81; Nat. Gen. Purposes Cttee, 1972–74; Nat. Local Govt Cttee, 1979–83; Nat. Vice-Chm., Young Conservatives, 1972–74. Commnd RMA Sandhurst into Royal Regt of Fusiliers; Major, 5th Bn (TA) Light Infantry. *Recreation:* gardening. *Address:* House of Commons, SW1. *T:* 071–219 3000. *Clubs:* Farmers'; Beaconsfield (Shrewsbury).

CONWAY, Most Rev. Dominic J.; *see* Elphin, Bishop of, (RC).

CONWAY, Prof. Gordon Richard, FIBiol; Representative for India, Nepal and Sri Lanka, The Ford Foundation, since 1989; *b* 6 July 1938; *s* of Cyril Gordon Conway and Thelma (*née* Goodwin); *m* 1965, Susan Mary, *d* of Harold Edward Mumford and Ellen Martha (*née* Bingham); one *s* two *d*. *Educ:* Kingston Grammar Sch.; Kingston Polytechnic; University Coll. of North Wales, Bangor (BSc 1959). DipAgricSci, Cambridge, 1960; DTA University Coll. of West Indies, Trinidad, 1961; PhD Univ. of California, Davis, 1969; FIBiol 1978. Research Officer (Entomology), Agric. Res. Centre, State of Sabah, Malaysia, 1961–66; Statistician, Inst. Ecology, Univ. of California, Davis, 1966–69; Imperial College, London: Res. Fellow and Lectr, Dept of Zoology and Applied Entomology, 1970–76; Dir, 1977–80, Chm., 1980–86, Centre for Envtl Technol.; Reader in Environmental Management, Univ. of London, 1976–80; Prof. of Environmental Technol., 1980–88. Dir, Sustainable Agric. Prog., Internat. Inst. for Envt and Develt, 1986–88. Vis Prof., Imperial Coll., 1989–. Mem., Royal Commn on Environmental Pollution, 1984–88. *Publications:* Pest and Pathogen Control, 1984; (jtly) After the Green Revolution, 1990; (jtly) Unwelcome Harvest: agriculture and pollution, 1991; papers and reports on agricl ecology. *Recreations:* travel, music. *Address:* Ford Foundation, 55 Lodi Estate, New Delhi 110003, India.

CONWAY, Prof. John Horton, FRS 1981; John von Neumann Professor of Mathematics, Princeton University, USA. *Educ:* Gonville and Caius Coll., Cambridge. BA 1959; MA 1963; PhD 1964. Univ. Lectr in Pure Maths, Cambridge, to 1973; Reader in Pure Mathematics and Mathematical Statistics, 1973–83; Prof. of Maths, 1983; Fellow: Sidney Sussex Coll., Cambridge; Gonville and Caius Coll., Cambridge, 1968. Polya Prize, London Mathematical Soc., 1987. *Publications:* Regular Algebra and Finite Machines, 1971; On Numbers and Games, 1976; Atlas of Finite Groups, 1985. *Address:* Department of Mathematics, Princeton University, Fine Hall, Washington Road, Princeton, NJ 08544, USA.

CONWAY, Martin; *see* Conway, D. M.

CONWAY, Sari Elizabeth; Director of Education, City of Bradford Metropolitan Council, since 1991; *b* 3 March 1951; *d* of Gordon and Gladys Mary Wright; *m* 1973, Vincent Conway; three *s*. *Educ:* Leeds Polytechnic (Teaching Cert.); Leeds Univ. (Advanced Diploma in Guidance and Counselling; Postgrad. Cert. in Educn of Maladjusted Children); Nottingham Univ. (MPhil). Teacher of Home Econs, Leeds LEA, 1973–75; Head of Girls' Studies, Nat. Children's Home, Leeds, 1975–77; Sen. Mistress, Disruptive Unit, and Head of Girls' Studies, Calderdale, 1977–79; part-time Adult Educn Tutor/Organiser, Youth Worker, and Lectr in Further Educn, Derbys, 1979–82; Educn Advr, Leics CC, 1982–88; Asst Dir of Community and Continuing Educn, South Tyneside MBC, 1988–91. *Publication:* Educational Perceptions of Unemployed Adolescents in an LEA, 1984. *Recreations:* travel, dressmaking, theatre, voluntary youth work. *Address:* Byers Green House, Byers Green, near Spennymoor, Co. Durham DL16 7NL. *T:* Spennymoor (0388) 60952.

CONWAY MORRIS, Dr Simon, FRS 1990; University Lecturer in Palaeontology, since 1983, and Fellow of St John's College, since 1987, Cambridge; *b* 6 Nov. 1951; *s* of Richard Conway Morris and Barbara Louise Maxwell; *m* 1975, Zoë Helen James; two *s*. *Educ:* Univ. of Bristol (BSc Hons); Univ. of Cambridge (PhD). Research Fellow, St John's Coll., Cambridge, 1975–79; Lectr, Open Univ., 1979–83. Gallagher Vis. Scientist, Univ. of Calgary, 1981; Nuffield Sci. Res. Fellowship, 1987–88; Merrill W. Haas Vis. Dist. Prof., Univ. of Kansas, 1988. Mem. Council, Systematics Assoc., 1981–85. Walcott Medal, Nat. Acad. of Scis, 1987; Charles Schuchert Award, Paleontol. Soc., 1989. *Publications:* contribs to professional jls. *Recreations:* travel, wine, punting. *Address:* Department of Earth Sciences, Downing Street, Cambridge CB2 3EQ. *T:* Cambridge (0223) 333414.

CONYNGHAM, family name of **Marquess Conyngham.**

CONYNGHAM, 7th Marquess *cr* 1816; **Frederick William Henry Francis Conyngham;** Baron Conyngham, 1781; Viscount Conyngham, 1789; Earl Conyngham, Viscount Mount Charles, 1797; Earl of Mount Charles, Viscount Slane, 1816; Baron Minster (UK), 1821; late Captain Irish Guards; *b* 13 March 1924; *e s* of 6th Marquess Conyngham and Antoinette Winifred (*d* 1966), *er d* of late J. W. H. Thompson; *S* father, 1974; *m* 1st, 1950, Eileen Wren (marr. diss. 1970), *o d* of Capt. C. W. Newsam, Ashfield, Beauparc, Co. Meath; three *s*; 2nd, 1971, Mrs Elizabeth Anne Rudd; 3rd, 1980, Mrs D. G. A. Walker (*d* 1986); 4th, 1987, Annabelle Agnew. *Educ:* Eton. *Heir: s* Earl of Mount Charles, *qv*. *Address:* Bifrons, near Canterbury; Cronk Ghennie House, Ramsey, Isle of Man. *Club:* Royal St George Yacht.

COOGAN, Ven. Robert Arthur William; Archdeacon of Hampstead, since 1985; *b* 11 July 1929; *s* of Ronald Dudley Coogan and Joyce Elizabeth Coogan (*née* Roberts). *Educ:* Univ. of Tasmania (BA); Univ. of Durham (DipTheol). Asst Curate, St Andrew, Plaistow, 1953–56; Rector of Bothwell, Tasmania, 1956–62; Vicar: North Woolwich, 1962–73; St Stephen, Hampstead, 1973–77; Priest in Charge, All Hallows, Gospel Oak, 1974–77; Vicar of St Stephen with All Hallows, Hampstead, 1977–85; Priest in Charge: Old St Pancras with St Matthew, 1976–80; St Martin with St Andrew, Gospel Oak, 1978–81; Area Dean, South Camden 1975–81, North Camden 1978–83; Prebendary of St Paul's Cathedral, 1982–85. Commissary for Bishop of Tasmania, 1968–88; Exam. Chaplain to Bishop of Edmonton, 1985–. *Recreations:* reading, gardening, travel. *Address:* 27 Thurlow Road, Hampstead, NW3 5PP. *T:* 071-435 5890. *Club:* Oriental.

COOK, Sir Alan (Hugh), Kt 1988; FRS 1969; Master of Selwyn College, Cambridge University, since 1983; *b* 2 Dec. 1922; *s* of late Reginald Thomas Cook, OBE, and of Ethel Cook; *m* 1948, Isabell Weir Adamson; one *s* one *d*. *Educ:* Westcliff High Sch. for Boys; Corpus Christi Coll. Cambridge. MA, PhD, ScD. Admty Signal Estabt, 1943–46; Research Student, then Res. Asst, Dept of Geodesy and Geophysics, Cambridge, 1946–51; Metrology Div., Nat. Physical Laboratory, Teddington, 1952; Vis. Fellow, Jt Inst. for Laboratory Astrophysics, Boulder, Colorado, 1965–66; Supt, Standards (subseq. Quantum Metrology) Div., Nat. Physical Laboratory, 1966–69; Prof. of Geophysics, Univ. of Edinburgh, 1969–72; Cambridge University: Jacksonian Prof. of Natural Philosophy, 1972–90; Fellow, King's Coll., 1972–83; Head of Dept of Physics, 1979–84. Vis. Prof. and Green Schol., Univ. of Calif. at Los Angeles, Berkeley and San Diego, 1981–82. Mem. SERC, 1984–88. FInstP; FRSE 1970; Foreign Fellow, Acad. Naz. dei Lincei, 1971. Pres., RAS, 1977–79. Fellow, Explorers' Club, NY, 1980. C. V. Boys Prize, Inst. of Physics, 1967. *Publications:* Gravity and the Earth, 1969; Global Geophysics, 1970; Interference of Electromagnetic Waves, 1971; Physics of the Earth and Planets, 1973; Celestial Masers, 1977; Interiors of the Planets, 1980; The Motion of the Moon, 1988; many contribs learned jls on gravity, artificial satellites, precise measurement, fundamental constants of physics and astronomy, history of science. *Recreations:* amateur theatre, travel, painting. *Address:* Master's Lodge, Selwyn College, Cambridge CB3 9DQ. *T:* Cambridge (0223) 335889; Cavendish Laboratory, Madingley Road, Cambridge CB3 0HE. *T:* Cambridge (0223) 337200.

COOK, (Alfred) Melville, MusDoc, FRCO; Hon. FRCCO; Organist and Choirmaster of the Metropolitan United, Toronto, 1967–86; *b* 18 June 1912; *s* of Harry Melville and Vera Louis Cook; *m* 1944, Marion Weir Moncrieff (*d* 1985); no *c*. *Educ:* King's Sch., Gloucester. Chorister, 1923–28, Asst Organist, 1932–37, Gloucester Cathedral. Organist and Choirmaster: All Saints, Cheltenham, 1935–37; Leeds Parish Church, 1937–56. MusDoc Durham, 1940. Served War in RA, 1941–46. Organist and Master of the Choristers, Hereford Cathedral, 1956–66. Conductor, Three Choirs Festival, Hereford, 1958, 1961, 1964; Conductor, Hereford Choral Soc., 1957–66. Organist and Choirmaster, All Saints', Winnipeg; Conductor of the Winnipeg Philharmonic Choir, Canada, 1966. *Recreations:* walking, swimming. *Address:* Flat 6, The Gate House, East Approach Drive, Pittville, Cheltenham GL52 3JE.

COOK, Ann; *see* Christopher, A.

COOK, Maj.-Gen. Arthur Thompson, FRCP, FRCPE; Director of Army Medicine, 1977–81; *b* 21 Oct. 1923; *s* of Thomas and Mabel Elizabeth Cook; *m* 1960, Kathleen Lane; two *s* one *d*. *Educ:* China Inland Mission Sch., Chefoo, N China; City of London Sch.; St Thomas' Hosp., London (MB). FRCP 1955, FRCPE 1954. Joined RAMC, 1948. QHP, 1977–81. *Address:* The Old Cricketers, Cricket Hill, Yateley, Camberley, Surrey GU17 7BA. *T:* Yateley (0252) 879452.

COOK, Mrs Beryl Frances; painter; *b* 10 Sept. 1926; *d* of Adrian Lansley and Ella Farmer-Francis; *m* 1948, John Victor Cook; one *s*. *Educ:* Kendrick Girls' Sch., Reading, Berks. *Exhibitions:* Plymouth Arts Centre, 1975; Whitechapel Art Gallery, London, 1976; The Craft of Art, Walker Art Gallery, 1979; Musée de Cahors, 1981; Chelmsford Museum, 1982; Portal Gall., 1985; travelling, Plymouth, Stoke-on-Trent, Preston, Nottingham and Edinburgh, 1988–89. *Publications:* The Works, 1978; Private View, 1980; Seven Years and a Day (illustrations), 1980; One Man Show, 1981; Bertie and the Big Red Ball (illustrations), 1982; My Granny (illustrations), 1983; Beryl Cook's New York, 1985; Beryl Cook's London, 1988; Mr Norris Changes Trains (illustrations), 1990. *Recreation:* reading. *Address:* Glanville House, 3 Athenæum Street, The Hoe, Plymouth PL1 2RQ.

COOK, Brian Francis, FSA; Keeper of Greek and Roman Antiquities, British Museum, since 1976; *b* 13 Feb. 1933; *yr s* of late Harry Cook and Renia Cook; *m* 1962, Veronica Dewhirst. *Educ:* St Bede's Grammar Sch., Bradford; Univ. of Manchester (BA); Downing Coll. and St Edmund's House, Cambridge (MA); British Sch. at Athens. FSA 1971. NCO 16/5 Lancers, 1956–58. Dept of Greek and Roman Art, Metropolitan Museum of Art, New York: Curatorial Asst, 1960; Asst Curator, 1961; Associate Curator, 1965–69; Asst Keeper, Dept of Greek and Roman Antiquities, BM, 1969–76. Corr. Mem., German Archaeol. Inst., 1977. *Publications:* Inscribed Hadra Vases in the Metropolitan Museum of Art, 1966; Greek and Roman Art in the British Museum, 1976; The Elgin Marbles, 1984; The Townley Marbles, 1985; Greek Inscriptions, 1987; (ed) The Rogozen Treasure, 1989; articles and revs on Greek, Etruscan and Roman antiquities in Brit. and foreign periodicals. *Recreations:* reading, gardening. *Address:* 4 Belmont Avenue, Barnet, Herts. *T:* 081–440 6590. *Club:* Challoner.

COOK, Brian Hartley K.; *see* Kemball-Cook.

COOK, Charles Alfred George, MC 1945; GM 1945; FRCS; Consultant Ophthalmic Surgeon: Guy's Hospital, 1954–73; Moorfields Eye Hospital, 1956–73; Teacher of Ophthalmology, University of London (Guy's Hospital and Institute of Ophthalmology), 1955–73; *b* 20 Aug. 1913; *s* of late Charles F. Cook and Beatrice Grist; *m* 1939, Edna Constance Dobson; one *s* one *d*. *Educ:* St Edward's Sch., Oxford; Guy's Hospital. MRCS, LRCP 1939; DOMS (Eng.), 1946; FRCS 1950. Capt. and Major RAMC, 1939–45. Moorfields Eye Hospital: Clinical Asst, 1946–47; Ho. Surg., 1948–49; Sen. Resident Officer, 1950; Chief Clin. Asst, 1951–55. Sen. Registrar, Eye Dept, Guy's Hospital, 1951–55; Moorfields Research Fellow, Inst. of Ophthalmology, 1951–58; Ophthalmic Surg., West Middlesex Hospital, 1954–56. Mem., Court of Examrs, RCS; Examr for DOMS, RCP and RCS; Examr Brit. Orthoptic Board; Sec., Ophthalmological Soc. of UK, 1956–57. Member: Cttee of Management, Inst. of Ophthalmology, 1960–63 (Vice-Dean of Inst., 1959–62); Cttee of Management, London Refraction Hosp., 1983–; Council, Coll. of Opth. Opticians, 1979–83 (Hon. Fellow 1982); Bd of Governors, Faculty of Dispensing Opticians, 1980–84. Governor: Royal Nat. Coll. for Blind, 1967–; Moorfields Eye Hosp., 1962–65. Hon. DSc Aston, 1983. Renter Warden, Upper Warden, then Master, Worshipful Co. of Spectacle Makers, 1975–81. Freeman, City of London. *Publications:* (ed) S. Duke Elder, Embryology, vol. 3, 1963; (contrib.) Payling, Wright and Symers, Systematic Pathology, 1966; (jt) May and Worth, Diseases of the Eye, 1968; articles in Brit. Jl of Ophthalmology, Trans Ophthalmological Soc., Jl of Pathology and other Med. Jls. *Recreations:* swimming, reading; an interest in all outdoor recreations. *Address:* 13 Clarence Terrace, Regent's Park, NW1 4RD. *T:* 071–723 5111. *Clubs:* Athenæum, Garrick.

COOK, Sir Christopher Wymondham Rayner Herbert, 5th Bt *cr* 1886; company director since 1979; Director, Diamond Guarantees Ltd, since 1980; *b* 24 March 1938; *s* of Sir Francis Ferdinand Maurice Cook, 4th Bt and Joan Loraine, *d* of John Aloysius Ashton-Case; *S* father, 1978; *m* 1st, 1958, Mrs Malina Gunasekera (from whom he obtained a divorce, 1975); one *s* one *d*; 2nd, 1975, Mrs Margaret Miller, *d* of late John Murray; one *s* one *d*. *Educ:* King's School, Canterbury. *Recreation:* golf. *Heir: s* Richard Herbert Aster Maurice Cook, *b* 30 June 1959. *Address:* La Fontenelle, Ville au Roi, St Peter Port, Guernsey, CI.

COOK, David Somerville; solicitor; Senior Partner, Messrs Sheldon & Stewart, Solicitors, Belfast; Lord Mayor of Belfast, 1978–79; *b* 25 Jan. 1944; *s* of Francis John Granville Cook, *qv*; *m* 1972, Mary Fionnuala Ann Deeny; four *s* one *d*. *Educ:* Campbell Coll., Belfast; Pembroke Coll., Cambridge (MA). Alliance Party of Northern Ireland: Founder Member, 1970; Hon. Treasurer, 1972–75; Central Executive Cttee, 1970–78, 1980–85; Dep. Leader, 1980–84. Chm., NI Voluntary Trust, 1979–. Mem., Belfast City Council, 1973–85; Mem. (Alliance) for Belfast S, NI Assembly, 1982–86; contested (Alliance): Belfast South, Feb. 1974, by-elections March 1982 and Jan. 1986, gen. election, 1987; N Ireland, European Parly elecn, 1984. Trustee, Ulster Museum, 1974–85; Vice Pres., NI Council on Alcohol, 1978–83; Mem. NI Council, European Movement, 1980–84. Dir, Ulster Actors' Co. Ltd, 1981–85. Mem., Royal Naval Assoc. Obtained Orders of Mandamus and fines for contempt of court against Belfast City Council, following its unlawful protest against the Anglo-Irish Agreement, 1986, 1987. *Recreations:* clearing undergrowth, wine, marmalade making, observing politicians from a distance. *Address:* Banford House, Tullylish, Gilford, Co. Down BT63 6DL. *Clubs:* Ulster Reform, Ulster Arts (Belfast).

COOK, Derek Edward, TD 1967; Deputy Chairman and Group Managing Director, Pilkington, since 1987; *b* 7 Dec. 1931; 2nd *s* of late Mr and Mrs H. E. Cook; *m* 1968, Prudence Carolyn Wilson; one *s* one *d*. *Educ:* Fyling Hall; Denstone Coll.; Corpus Christi Coll., Oxford (MA); Salford Univ.; Huddersfield Tech. Coll. FSS; FTI, CText. Commissioned Z Battery, BAOR, 1951; W Riding Artillery, 1952–68. Tootal, 1955–61; John Emsley, 1961–63; Man. Dir, A. & S. Henry & Co. (Bradford), 1963–70; Man. Dir, 1971–75, Chm., 1975–79, Fibreglass Pilkington, India; Director: R. H. Windsor, India, 1976–79; Killick Halco, India, 1977–79; Chm., Pilkington Cos, S Africa and Zimbabwe, 1979–84; Chm., Pilkington Glass Ltd, 1982–85; former Dir, Pilkington Holdings Inc., Triplex Safety Glass Co., Pilkington Floatglas AB, Flachglas AG, Rowntree plc. Director: Libby-Owens-Ford Co., USA, 1987–; Charter Consolidated, 1988–; Powell Duffryn, 1989–; Leeds Permanent Building Soc., 1991–. Member: Council of Industry and Parlt Trust, 1987–; Council, CBI, 1988–; Mem. Court, 1988–; Dir, 1989–, Leeds Univ. Foundn. Dir, Publications Bd, Textile Inst., 1989–. Mem., Cook Soc., 1985–. CBIM. Liveryman, Glass Sellers' Co., 1991–. *Recreations:* sailing, general sporting and country life interests. *Address:* Windmill Farm, Wrigley Lane, Over Alderley, Macclesfield, Cheshire SK10 4SA. *T:* Macclesfield (0625) 827985. *Clubs:* Oriental, Army and Navy, Cavalry and Guards, Royal Thames, Royal Ocean Racing; Leander (Henley); St James's, Racquets (Manchester); Rand, Country (Johannesburg); Royal Yorkshire Yacht, Royal Bombay Yacht.

COOK, Francis; MP (Lab) Stockton North, since 1983; *b* 3 Nov. 1935; *s* of James Cook and Elizabeth May Cook; *m* 1959, Patricia, *d* of Thomas and Evelyn Lundrigan; one *s* three *d*. *Educ:* Corby School, Sunderland; De La Salle College, Manchester; Institute of Education, Leeds. Schoolmaster, 9½ years; Construction Project Manager with Capper-Neill International. *Recreations:* climbing, fell walking, singing, swimming. *Address:* 37 Windlestone Road, Billingham, Cleveland TS23 3JW. *T:* Stockton (0642) 370641.

COOK, Francis John Granville, MA Cantab; Headmaster of Campbell College, Belfast, 1954–71; *b* 28 Jan. 1913; *o s* of late W. G. Cook and Nora Braley; *m* 1942, Jocelyn McKay, *d* of late John Stewart, Westholm, Dunblane, Perthshire; one *s* two *d*. *Educ:* Wyggeston Sch.; Downing Coll., Cambridge. Historical Tripos, Law Tripos; Squire Scholar; Tancred Studentship, Lincoln's Inn. Asst Master, Rossall Sch., 1937; served War, 1940–46, with Royal Navy; Headmaster of Junior Sch., Rossall Sch., 1949–54. *Recreations:* gardening, books, people. *Address:* 49 Bryansford Village, Newcastle, Co. Down BT33 0PT. *T:* Newcastle (Co. Down) (03967) 25165.
See also D. S. Cook.

COOK, Frank Patrick, (Pat); Member, Commission for Local Administration in England and first Local Ombudsman for the North and North Midlands, 1974–85; *b* 28 March 1920; *o c* of Frank Cook, FRCS, FRCOG and Edith Harriet (*née* Reid); *m* 1st, 1945, Rosemary Eason (marr. diss. 1975); two *s* one *d*; 2nd, 1975, Margaret Rodgers, 2nd *d* of Dr J. W. Rodgers, PhD; one *s*. *Educ:* Rugby; Trinity Hall, Cambridge (Open Schol.); LSE (Personnel Management). Royal Marines, 1939–46; Courtaulds Ltd, 1946–56; Nat. Coal Board, 1956–61; Venesta Ltd, 1961–64; Principal, British Transport Staff Coll., 1964–69; First Chief Exec., English Tourist Board, 1970–74. Chm., Microtest Research Ltd, 1982–87. Indep. Mem., Council, FIMBRA, 1988–90; a Vice President: IPM, 1965–67; RCN, 1973–; Member: Nat. Nursing Staff Cttee, 1967–72; Brighton and Lewes HMC, 1972–74; Ombudsman Adv. Bd, Internat. Bar Assoc., 1975–85; Exec. Cttee, Fawcett Soc., 1975–77; Council, Univ. of York, 1979–85; Merchant Taylors' Co. of York, 1981–; N Yorks FPC, 1985–87. Inquiry into provision for health care in St Helens and Knowsley, 1990. Governor: Martin House Hospice for Children, 1984–86; Bootham and The Mount Quaker Schs, 1987–89. Chm., Cleeve Abbey Action Council of Management, 1988–91. Hon. LLD Hull, 1986. *Publications:* Shift Work, 1954; Ombudsman (autobiog.), 1981; articles on personnel management. *Address:* Mellory, Old Cleeve, near Minehead, Somerset TA24 6HS. *T:* Washford (0984) 40176. *Club:* Naval and Military.

COOK, George David, CEng, FIEE; Consultant, Quantel Ltd, since 1985; *b* 23 Sept. 1925; *s* of late John and Jean C. Cook; *m* 1954, Sylvia Ann Sampson; two *d*. *Educ:* Hendon College of Technology. BBC Planning and Installation Dept, 1947; Asst to Supt Engineer, Television Outside Broadcasts, 1955; Head of Engineering, Wales, 1963; Asst Chief Engr, Television, 1967; Chief Engr Transmitters, 1974; Asst Dir of Engrg, 1978; Dep. Dir of Engrg, 1984–85. *Recreations:* golf, theatre. *Address:* 26 Ridge Lane, Watford, Herts WD1 3TA. *T:* Watford (0923) 29638.

COOK, George Steveni L.; *see* Littlejohn Cook.

COOK, Harold James; a Metropolitan Stipendiary Magistrate, since 1975; *b* 25 Jan. 1926; *s* of Harold Cook and Gwendoline Lydia (*née* List); *m* 1952, Mary Elizabeth (*née* Edwards); one *s*. *Educ:* The John Lyon Sch., Harrow; Edinburgh Univ. RN, 1943–47. Civil Service, 1947–52. Called to the Bar, Gray's Inn, 1952; Dep. Chief Clerk, Bow Street, and later Thames, Magistrates' Courts, 1952–54; Inner London QS, 1955; Dep. Clerk to Justices, Gore Div., Mddx, 1956–60; Clerk to Justices, Highgate Div., 1961, and also Barnet and South Mymms Divs, 1968. *Publications:* contrib. legal jls. *Address:* West London Magistrates' Court, Southcombe Street, W14.

COOK, Rt. Rev. Henry George; retired; *b* Walthamstow, London, England, 12 Oct. 1906; *s* of Henry G. Cook and Ada Mary Evans; *m* 1935, Opal May Thompson, Sarnia, Ont, *d* of Wesley Thompson and Charity Ellen Britney; two *s* one *d*. *Educ:* Ingersoll Collegiate Inst., Ont; Huron Coll. (LTh); Univ. of Western Ont, London, Canada (BA). Deacon, 1935, Priest, 1936; Missionary at Fort Simpson, 1935–43; Canon of Athabasca, 1940–43; Incumbent S Porcupine, Ont., 1943–44; Archdeacon of James Bay, 1945–48; Principal, Bp Horden Sch., Moose Factory, 1945–48; Mem., Gen Synod Exec., 1943–47; Supt of Indian Sch. Admin., 1948–62; Bishop Suffragan of the Arctic, 1963–66, of Athabasca, 1966–70 (the area of Mackenzie having been part first of one diocese and then of the other, constituted an Episcopal District, 1970); Bishop of Mackenzie, 1970–74. RCN(R) Chaplain, 1949–56. Hon. DD Huron Coll. and Univ. of Western Ont. 1946. *Recreations:* fishing, coin collecting, model carving. *Address:* 15 Plainfield Court, Stittsville, Ont K2S 1B9, Canada.

COOK, Cdre Henry Home; Chairman, Chiltern Society, since 1988; Director of Public Relations, Scientific Exploration Society, 1984–88; *b* 24 Jan. 1918; *o s* of George Home Cook, Edinburgh; *m* 1943, Theffania, *yr d* of A. P. Saunders, Gerrards Cross; two *s* two *d*. *Educ:* St Lawrence Coll., Ramsgate; Pangbourne College. Entered RN as Paymaster Cadet, 1936; Comdr 1955; Captain 1963; Cdre 1970. Naval Sec. to Vice-Adm. Sir Guy Sayer, 1953–59; Sqdn Supply Officer, 1st S/m Sqdn, 1959; Comdr, RNC Greenwich, 1961; Naval Attaché, Ankara, 1964; Dir of Public Relations (RN), 1966; Defence Adviser to British High Comr, and Head of British Defence Liaison Staff, Ottawa, 1970–72; retired, 1973. ADC to HM the Queen, 1971–72. A Gen. Comr of Income Tax, 1983–. Dir, Ellerman City Liners Ltd, 1973–80. Pres., Anchorites, 1978; Vice-Pres., Inst. of Admin. Management, 1983–. FInstAM 1973 (Chm., 1982). DipCAM 1975. *Recreations:* fencing, swimming, sailing. *Address:* Ramblers Cottage, Layters Green, Chalfont St Peter, Bucks. *T:* Gerrards Cross (0753) 883724. *Club:* Army and Navy.

COOK, Rear-Adm. James William Dunbar, CB 1975; DL; Chairman, Surrey Branch of Soldiers', Sailors', and Airmen's Families Association; *b* 12 Dec. 1921; *s* of James Alexander Cook, Pluscarden, Morayshire; *m* 1949, Edith May Williams; one *s* two *d*. *Educ:* Bedford Sch.; HMS Worcester. CO, HM Ships Venus, Dido and Norfolk; Sen. British Naval Officer, S Africa, 1967–69 (as Cdre); Dir RN War College, 1969–71; Asst Chief of Naval Staff (Ops), 1973–75; retired from RN, 1975. Comdr 1957; Captain 1963; Rear-Adm. 1973; jssc 1958; sowc 1970. Mem. Council, King George's Fund for Sailors. Gov., Royal Naval Sch., Haslemere, 1989–. Pres., Age Concern (Haslemere), 1990. DL Surrey, 1989. *Recreations:* golf, gardening. *Address:* Springways Cottage, Farnham Lane, Haslemere, Surrey. *T:* Haslemere (0428) 643615. *Club:* Army and Navy.

COOK, John, FRCSEd; FRSE 1970; Consultant Surgeon, Eastern General Hospital, Edinburgh, 1964–87; *b* 9 May 1926; *s* of George Cook and Katherine Ferncroft (*née* Gauss); *m* 1953, Patricia Mary Bligh; one *s* four *d*. *Educ:* Fettes Coll., Edinburgh; Edinburgh Univ. (MB 1949, ChM 1963). FRCSEd 1954. Served Med. Br., RAF, 1950–52 (Flt Lieut). House Surgeon, Royal Infirmary, Edinburgh, 1949; Res. Asst, Radcliffe Infirm., Oxford, 1954–55; First Asst, Dept of Surg., Makerere University Coll., Uganda, 1955–64 (Reader in Surg., 1962–64). Royal Coll. of Surgeons of Edinburgh: Hon. Sec., 1969–72; Mem. Council, 1974–84. Representative Mem., GMC, 1982–86; Hon. Sec., Internat. Fedn of Surgical Colls, 1974–84. Hon. Fellow, Polish Assoc. of Surgeons, 1981. *Publications:* contrib. surgical jls. *Recreations:* music, fishing. *Address:* Medwel, Pleasant Row, Clehonger, Hereford HR2 9RE.

COOK, Dr John Barry; Headmaster of Epsom College, since 1982; *b* 9 May 1940; *er s* of Albert Edward and late Beatrice Irene Cook, Gloucester; *m* 1964, Vivien Margaret Roxana Lamb, *o d* of Victor and late Marjorie Lamb, St Albans; two *s* one *d*. *Educ:* Sir Thomas Rich's Sch., Gloucester; King's Coll., Univ. of London (BSc 1961, AKC 1961); Guy's Hosp. Med. Sch. (PhD 1965). Guy's Hospital Medical School: Biophysics research, 1961–64; Lectr in Physics, 1964–65; Haileybury College: Asst Master, 1965–72; Senior Science Master and Head of Physics Dept, 1967–72; Headmaster of Christ Coll., Brecon, 1973–82. Church in Wales: Mem. Governing Body, 1976–83; Coll. of Episcopal Electors, 1980–83. Chairman: S Wales ISIS, 1978–82; Academic Policy Cttee, HMC, 1985–88. *Publications:* (jtly) Solid State Biophysics, 1969; Multiple Choice Questions in A-level Physics, 1969; Multiple Choice Questions in O-level Physics, 1970; papers in Nature, Molecular Physics, Internat. Jl of Radiation Biology, Jl of Scientific Instruments, Educn in Science, Conference and Trends in Education. *Recreations:* sports, philately. *Address:* Headmaster's House, Epsom College, Epsom, Surrey KT17 4JQ. *T:* Epsom (0372) 722118.

COOK, John Edward E.; *see* Evan-Cook.

COOK, Prof. John Manuel, FSA; FBA 1974; Professor of Ancient History and Classical Archæology, Bristol University, 1958–76 (formerly Reader); *b* 11 Dec. 1910; *s* of late Rev. C. R. Cook; *m* 1st, 1939, Enid May (*d* 1976), *d* of Dr W. A. Robertson; two *s*; 2nd, 1977, Nancy Easton Law, MA, *widow* of Ralph Hamilton Law. *Educ:* Marlborough; King's Coll., Cambridge. Sir William Browne's Medal for Greek Ode, 1933; Members' Latin Essay Prize, 1933; Augustus Austen Leigh Student in King's Coll., 1934; Asst in Humanity and Lectr in Classical Archæology, Edinburgh Univ., 1936–46; Dir of British Sch. of Archæology at Athens, 1946–54; Dean, Faculty of Arts, 1966–68, Pro-Vice-Chancellor, 1972–75, Bristol Univ. C. E. Norton Lectr of the Archaeological Inst. of America, 1961–62; Visiting Prof., Yale Univ., 1965; Gray Memorial Lectr, Cambridge, 1969; Geddes-Harrower Prof., Univ. of Aberdeen, 1977. Served in Royal Scots, Force 133 (despatches), and HQ Land Forces, Greece (Lt-Col). *Publications:* The Greeks in Ionia and the East, 1962; (with W. H. Plommer) The Sanctuary of Hemithea at Kastabos, 1966; The Troad, an archaeological and historical study, 1973; The Persian Empire, 1983; chapters in: Cambridge Ancient History; Cambridge History of Iran. *Address:* 8 Dalrymple Crescent, Edinburgh EH9 2NU.

COOK, Joseph, CChem, FRSC; management consultant; *b* 7 April 1917; *y s* of Joseph Cook, MBE, JP, and Jane Cook (*née* Adams), Cumberland; *m* 1950, Betty, *d* of James and Elizabeth Barlow, Standish, Lancs; two *d*. *Educ:* Whitehaven Grammar Sch.; Univ. of Liverpool (BSc, DipEd). RAF, 1939–40. Posts in Ministries of Supply, Aviation, Technology and Defence 1941–59; Dir, ROF Burghfield, 1959–65; Gp Dir, Ammunition Factories, 1966; Dir Gen. (Prodn), ROF, 1966–74; Man. Dir, Millbank Tech. Services Ordnance Ltd, 1974–77 (on secondment from MoD). *Recreations:* gardening, golf. *Address:* Abbots-wood, Bramley Road, Pamber End, near Basingstoke, Hants RG26 5QP. *T:* Basingstoke (0256) 850304.

COOK, Melville; *see* Cook, Alfred Melville.

COOK, Michael John; His Honour Judge Michael Cook; a Circuit Judge, since 1986; *b* 20 June 1930; *s* of George Henry Cook and Nora Wilson Cook (*née* Mackman); *m* 1st, 1958, Anne Margaret Vaughan; three *s* one *d*; 2nd, 1974, Patricia Anne Sturdy; one *d*. *Educ:* Leeds Grammar Sch.; Worksop Coll.; Univ. of Leeds (LLB 2(1) Cl. Hons). Admitted Solicitor, 1953. National Service, commnd Royal Artillery, 1954. Willey Hargrave & Co., Solicitors, to 1957; Ward Bowie, Solicitors, 1957–86 (Senior Partner, 1965–86); a Recorder, 1980–86. Past Hon. Sec. and Pres., London Solicitors' Litigation Assoc.; Member: Solicitors Disciplinary Tribunal, 1975–86; Law Society sub-cttees and working parties. Mem. Council, Royal Med. Foundn, 1990. Freeman, City of London, 1990. *Publications:* The Courts and You, 1976; The Taxation of Contentious Costs, 1979; The Taxation of Solicitors Costs, 1986; (contrib.) Butterworth's Costs and County Court Precendents and Pleadings, 1989. *Recreations:* tennis, gardening, theatre, sitting on moving horses.

COOK, Norman Charles, BA; FSA, FMA; *b* 24 Jan. 1906; *s* of George and Emily Cook; *m* 1934, Dorothy Ida Waters; one *s* one *d*. *Educ:* Maidstone Grammar Sch. Maidstone Museum, 1924–37; Morven Institute of Archaeological Research, Avebury, 1937–39; Curator, Southampton Museum, 1947–50; Director: Guildhall Museum, 1950–71; Museum of London, 1970–72. Hon. Sec., 1954–59, Pres., 1964–65, Museums Assoc. Vice-Pres., Soc. of Antiquaries, 1967–72. Hon. Curator, Wells Mus., Som, 1972–82. *Recreation:* archæology. *Address:* 6 St Thomas Terrace, Wells, Somerset BA5 2XG.

COOK, Norman Edgar, CBE 1980; writer; *b* 4 March 1920; *s* of Edgar James and Kate Cook; *m* 1942, Mildred Warburton; three *s*. *Educ:* Cowley Grammar Sch., St Helens. TA (Royal Corps of Signals), 1939; served war, UK, Sierra Leone, Gold Coast. Min. of Information, 1943–45; Editor, Northwich Guardian, 1945–47; Liverpool Daily Post, 1947–49; Information Officer, Air Ministry, 1949–53; Liverpool Daily Post and Echo: Night News Editor, 1953–55; Dep. News Editor, 1955–59; London Editor, 1959–72; Exec. News Editor, 1972–77; Editor, 1978–79, retired 1979, then chief book critic, 1980–90, Liverpool Daily Post. *Publications:* numerous articles and reviews. *Recreations:* walking, reading, playing the piano. *Address:* 7 Trinity Gardens, Southport, Lancashire PR8 1AU. *T:* Southport (0704) 531268. *Club:* Athenæum (Liverpool).

COOK, Pat; *see* Cook, F. P.

COOK, Prof. Paul Derek, MBE 1985; PhD; CEng; Chairman and Managing Director, Scientifica-Cook Ltd, since 1962; Professor of Laser Technology, Brunel University, since 1986; *b* 12 March 1934; *s* of James Walter Cook and Florence Jefferay; *m* 1954, Frances Ann James; four *d*. *Educ:* Queen Mary Coll., London (BSc Hons; PhD 1963; Sir John Johnson Scholar, 1959). CEng, MIEE 1963. Res. Scientist: MRC, 1960–62; Middlesex Hosp. Med. Sch., 1962–65. Scientific Adviser to: Minister for the Envmt and Countryside, DoE, 1990–; British Gas, 1990–; Laser Consultant, BAe, 1986–; Consultant, W Midlands Police. Responsible for design and develt of numerous laser systems used in med. and mil. estabts throughout world, incl. ophthalmic LaserSpec; major contrib. to Europe's first laser gyroscope in 1970's; invention of laser instrument that improves safety of motorists by detecting and correcting night myopia. Dep. Chm., Conserve, 1990–; Founder/Pres., British Science and Technol. Trust, 1985– (Chm., Cttee selecting Sci-Tech Careers Award winners, 1988–); UK Pres., Japanese Zen Nippon Airinkai, 1978–81. *Recreations:* breeding and rearing exotic Japanese carp, cultivating Japanese bonzai. *Address:* Carlton House, 78 Bollo Bridge Road, W3 8AU; Physics Department, Brunel University, Uxbridge, Mddx UB8 3PH.

COOK, Peter Edward; writer; entertainer; *b* 17 Nov. 1937; *s* of Alexander and Margaret Cook; *m* 1st, 1964, Wendy Snowden; two *d*; 2nd, 1973, Judy Huxtable. *Educ:* Radley Coll.; Pembroke Coll., Cambridge (BA). Part-author and appeared in: *revues:* Pieces of Eight, 1958; One Over the Eight, 1959; Beyond the Fringe, 1959–64 (London and New York); Behind the Fridge, 1971–72 (Australia and London); Good Evening, 1973–75 (US); *television:* Not Only but Also (four series, BBC), 1965–71; Revolver (ITV series), 1978. *Films:* The Wrong Box, 1965; Bedazzled, 1967; A Dandy in Aspic, 1968; Monte Carlo or Bust, 1969; The Bed-Sitting Room, 1970; The Rise and Rise of Michael Rimmer, 1971; The Hound of the Baskervilles, 1978; Derek and Clive, 1981; Yellowbeard, 1983; Whoops Apocalypse, 1987; Mr Jolly Lives Next Door, 1987. *Publication:* Dud and Pete: The Dagenham Dialogues, 1971. *Recreations:* gambling, gossip, golf. *Address:* c/o Wright & Webb, Syrett and Sons, 10 Soho Square, W1. *T:* 071–734 9641.

COOK, Dr Peter John; Director, British Geological Survey, since 1990; *b* 15 Oct. 1938; *s* of John and Rose Cook; *m* 1961, Norma Irene Walker; two *s*. *Educ:* Durham Univ. (BSc Hons, DSc); ANU (MSc); Univ. of Colorado (PhD). Geologist to Sen. Geologist, BMR, Canberra, 1961–76; Sen. Res. Fellow, ANU Res. Sch. of Earth Sci., 1976–82 (Vis. Fellow, 1982–90); Chief of Div./Chief Res. Scientist, BMR, 1982–90 (Prof., Univ. Louis Pasteur, Strasbourg, 1989); Chairman: Consortium for Ocean Geosci., 1980–82; Commonwealth/State Hydrogeol. Cttee, 1983–88; Member: Adv. Cttee, Aust. Nuclear Sci. and Tech. Orgn, 1984–90; Geolog. Adv. Panel, BM (Nat. Hist.), 1990–; Council, MIRO, 1991–; Vice-Chm., Ocean Sci. Resources Programme, IOC, 1984–. *Publications:* contribs to several books, and to learned jls. *Recreations:* ski-ing, hiking, travel. *Address:* British Geological Survey, Keyworth, Nottingham NG12 5GG. *T:* Plumtree (06077) 6111.

COOK, Reginald, FCA; Chairman, South Wales Electricity Board, 1977–81; Member, Electricity Council, 1977–81; *b* 29 Dec. 1918; *s* of Harold Cook and Gwendolyn Cook, Birmingham; *m* 1945, Constance Irene Holt, Norden, Lancs; one *s* one *d*. *Educ:* Rochdale High Sch.; Manchester Univ. (BA). Admin. Staff Coll. Served War, 1939–46; Staff Captain, RA. Local Govt Service with Corporations of Manchester, West Bromwich and York, 1946–52; Midlands Electricity Board: accountancy posts, 1952–59; Chief Accountant, 1959–69; Exec. Mem., 1964–69; Dep. Chm., S Wales Electricity Bd, 1969–77. FBIM; CompIEE. Gold Medal, IMTA, 1949. *Recreations:* countryside activities, gardening, golf, bridge. *Address:* Heppleshaw, Itton, Chepstow, Gwent. *T:* Shirenewton (02917) 265.

COOK, Brig. Richard Arthur, CBE 1961; *b* 26 May 1908; *m* 1940, Sheila Mary Ostell Prosser; two *s*. *Educ:* St Paul's; RMA, Woolwich. Commissioned, Royal Artillery, 1928. Posted to India, 1933. Served War of 1939–45 in India and Burma: Staff Coll., 1941; Regimental Comd, 1943; Joint Services Staff Coll., 1947; Col, 1948; Col Administrative Plans, GHQ, MELF, 1948–51; CRA (Brig.) 16th Airborne Div., 1954–56; NATO Defence Coll., 1957; BGS, Southern Command, 1958–61; retired from Army, 1961. *Address:* 3 Meadow Court, Whiteparish, Wilts. *T:* Whiteparish (0794) 884409. *Club:* Army and Navy.

COOK, Robert Finlayson, (Robin F. Cook); MP (Lab) Livingston, since 1983 (Edinburgh Central, Feb. 1974–1983); *b* 28 Feb. 1946; *s* of Peter Cook, headmaster and Christina Cook (*née* Lynch); *m* 1969, Margaret K. Whitmore, medical consultant; two *s*.

Educ: Aberdeen Grammar Sch.; Univ. of Edinburgh. MA Hons English Lit. Tutor-Organiser with WEA, 1970–74. Chm., Scottish Assoc. of Labour Student Organisations, 1966–67; Sec., Edinburgh City Labour Party, 1970–72; Mem., Edinburgh Corporation, 1971–74, Chm. Housing Cttee, 1973–74. An Opposition Treasury spokesman, 1980–83; opposition front bench spokesman on: European and community affairs, 1983–84; trade, 1986–87; health, 1987–; Labour's Campaigns Co-ordinator, 1984–86. Mem., Tribune Group. *Recreations:* eating, reading, talking. *Address:* c/o House of Commons, SW1A 0AA. *T:* 071–219 5120.

COOK, Maj.-Gen. Robert Francis Leonard, MSc, MPhil; CEng, FIEE; CPhys; Signal Officer-in-Chief (Army), since 1989, and Director General Command, Control, Communications and Information Systems (Army), since 1990; *b* 18 June 1939; *s* of Lt-Col Frank Leonard Cook and Louise Alicia (*née* Davis); *m* 1961, Gillian Margaret Lowry; one *s* two *d. Educ:* Karachi Grammar Sch., Pakistan; St John's Coll., Southsea; University Coll. of Wales; Welbeck Coll.; RMA Sandhurst; RMCS; Staff Coll., Camberley; NATO Defence Coll., Rome. BSc 1962, MSc 1964, London; MPhil (Strategic Studies) Wales, 1989. Commnd Royal Signals, 1959; served Germany, Malaysia, UK, 1959–70; Directorate of Manning (Army), MoD, 1972; OC 7 Armd Bde, Signal Sqn, 1973; Project Management Staff, MoD (PE), 1975; Lt-Col DS, RMCS, 1976; CO 4 Armd Div. HQ and Signal Regt, 1978; Logistics Staff, HQ BAOR, 1981; Colonel, MoD Operational Requirements Staff, 1982; Brig., Comd 1 Signal Bde, 1 (BR) Corps, 1983; Sec., NATO Mil. Cttee, NATO HQ, Brussels, 1986. Freeman, City of London, 1989; Liveryman, Engineers' Co., 1990. *Recreations:* mountain walking, winter and water sports, music, travel, wine. *Address:* c/o Lloyds Bank, 8 Market Place, Faringdon, Oxon SN7 7HN. *Club:* Army and Navy.

COOK, Prof. Robert Manuel, FBA 1976; Laurence Professor of Classical Archaeology, University of Cambridge, 1962–76; *b* 4 July 1909; *s* of Rev. Charles Robert and Mary Manuel Cook; *m* 1938, Kathleen (*d* 1979), *d* of James Frank and Ellen Hardman Porter. *Educ:* Marlborough Coll.; Cambridge Univ. Walston Student, Cambridge Univ., 1932; Asst Lectr in Classics, Manchester Univ., 1934; Lectr, 1938; Sub-warden, St Anselm's Hall, Manchester, 1936–38; Laurence Reader in Classical Archaeology, Cambridge Univ., 1945, Ord. Mem., German Archaeological Inst., 1953. Chm., Managing Cttee, British School at Athens, 1983–87. *Publications:* Corpus Vasorum Antiquorum, British Museum 8, 1954; Greek Painted Pottery, 1960, 2nd edn 1972; The Greeks till Alexander, 1962; (with Kathleen Cook) Southern Greece: an archaeological guide, 1968; Greek Art, 1972; Clazomenian Sarcophagi, 1981. *Address:* 15 Wilberforce Road, Cambridge CB3 0EQ. *T:* Cambridge (0223) 352863.

See also Prof. J. M. Cook.

COOK, Robin; *see* Cook, Robert F.

COOK, William Birkett, MA; Master of Magdalen College School, Oxford, 1972–91; *b* 30 Aug. 1931; *e s* of late William James and Mildred Elizabeth Cook, Headington, Oxford; *m* 1958, Marianne Ruth, *yr d* of late A. E. Taylor, The Schools, Shrewsbury; one *s* one *d* (and one *d* decd). *Educ:* Dragon Sch.; Eton (King's Schol.); Trinity Coll., Cambridge (Schol.). National Service, 1950–51 (commnd in RA). Porson Prizeman, 1953; 1st cl. Classical Tripos Pt I, 1953, Pt II, 1954; Henry Arthur Thomas Student, 1954; MA Oxon by incorporation, 1972. Asst Master, Shrewsbury Sch., 1955–67, and Head of Classical Faculty, 1960–67; Headmaster of Durham Sch., 1967–72. Governor, Oxford High Sch., 1979–. *Recreations:* music, gardening, Scottish country dancing. *Address:* 27 St Andrew's Road, Headington, Oxford OX3 9DL. *T:* Oxford (0865) 63190.

COOKE, Alexander Macdougall, DM; FRCP; Hon. Consulting Physician, United Oxford Hospitals, 1966; *b* 17 Oct. 1899; *s* of Arthur Clement Cooke, OBE and Isobel Gilles Macdougall; *m* Vera (*d* 1984), *d* of Charles Hermann Lea; one *s* three *d. Educ:* Merchant Taylors' School; Jesus College, Oxford; St Thomas's Hosp. (Mead Medal, 1923). 1st Cl. Hons Nat. Sci. 1920; BM 1923; DM 1933; MRCP 1926, FRCP 1935. War Service, Royal Fusiliers, RFC and RAF, 1917–18. Resident Asst Physician, 1927–28, 1st Asst, Professorial Med. Unit, 1928–30 and Dep. Dir, 1930–32, St Thomas's Hosp.; Physician, Radcliffe Infirmary, 1932–66; May Reader in Medicine, 1933–47; Clinical Sub-Dean, Oxford Medical Sch., 1939–49; Fellow of Merton Coll., Oxford, 1942–66, Emeritus Fellow, 1966–. Lectures: Lumleian, RCP, 1955; Langdon-Brown, RCP, 1968; Litchfield, Oxford, 1964; Stopford Meml, Manchester, 1973. Royal College of Physicians: Examr, 1943–47 and 1952–62; Councillor, 1953–55; Censor, 1956–58; Sen. Censor, 1959–60; Oxford Univ. Rep., GMC, 1963–73. FRSocMed 1924, Hon. Fellow 1972 (Pres., Section of Medicine, 1960–62); Mem., Assoc. of Physicians, 1936 (Exec. Cttee, 1950–53), Hon. Mem., 1966; Hon. Mem., Royal Coll. of Radiologists. Sec. to Editors, 1937–50 and Editor, 1951–65, Quarterly Jl of Medicine. *Publications:* A History of the Royal College of Physicians of London, Vol. III, 1972; Sir E. Farquhar Buzzard, Bt, KCVO, 1975; The Cookes Tale, 1991; articles and papers on medicine and med. hist. *Recreation:* inertia. Address: Grove Cottage, St Cross Road, Oxford OX1 3TX. *T:* Oxford (0865) 242419. *Club:* Athenæum.

COOKE, (Alfred) Alistair, KBE (Hon.) 1973; journalist and broadcaster; *b* 20 Nov. 1908; *s* of Samuel Cooke and Mary Elizabeth Byrne; *m* 1st, 1934, Ruth Emerson; one *s*; 2nd, 1946, Jane White Hawkes; one *d. Educ:* Blackpool Grammar Sch.; Jesus Coll., Cambridge (Scholar; Hon. Fellow, 1986); Yale Univ.; Harvard. Founded Cambridge University Mummers, 1928; First Class, English Tripos, 1929; Second Class, 1930. Editor, The Granta, 1931; Commonwealth Fund Fellow, 1932–34. BBC Film Critic, 1934–37; London Correspondent for NBC, 1936–37; Commentator on American Affairs for BBC, 1938–; Special Correspondent on American Affairs, The London Times, 1938–40; American Feature Writer, The Daily Herald, 1941–43; UN Correspondent of the Manchester Guardian (which changed name to Guardian, 1959), 1945–48; Chief Correspondent in US of The Guardian, 1948–72. Master of ceremonies: Ford Foundation's television programme, Omnibus, 1952–61; UN television programme, International Zone, 1961–67; Masterpiece Theatre, 1971–. Wrote and narrated, America: a personal history of the United States, BBC TV, 1972–73 (Peabody Award for meritorious services to broadcasting, 1972; Writers' Guild of GB award for best documentary of 1972; Dimbleby Award, Soc. of Film and TV Arts, 1973; four Emmy awards of (US) Nat. Acad. of TV Arts and Sciences, 1973). Hon. LLD: Edinburgh, 1969; Manchester, 1973; Hon. LittD: St Andrews, 1975; Cantab, 1988. Peabody Award for internat. reporting, 1952 and 1983; Benjamin Franklin Medal, RSA, 1973; Howland Medal, Yale Univ., 1977. *Publications:* (ed) Garbo and the Night Watchmen, 1937, repr. 1972; Douglas Fairbanks: The Making of a Screen Character, 1940; A Generation on Trial: USA v Alger Hiss, 1950; Letters from America, 1951; Christmas Eve, 1952; A Commencement Address, 1954; (ed) The Vintage Mencken, 1955; Around the World in Fifty Years, 1966; Talk about America, 1968; Alistair Cooke's America, 1973; Six Men, 1977; The Americans: fifty letters from America on our life and times, 1979; (with Robert Cameron) Above London, 1980; Masterpieces, 1982; The Patient has the Floor, 1986; America Observed, 1988. *Recreations:* playing golf, watching tennis, music. *Address:* 1150 Fifth Avenue, New York City; Nassau Point, Cutchogue, Long Island, NY, USA. *Clubs:* Athenæum; Lotos, National Arts (New York); National Press (Washington); San Francisco Golf.

COOKE, Rear-Adm. Anthony John, CB 1980; Private Secretary to Lord Mayor of London, since 1981; *b* 21 Sept. 1927; *s* of Rear-Adm. John Ernest Cooke, CB; *m* 1951, Margaret Anne, *d* of Frederick Charles Hynard; two *s* three *d. Educ:* St Edward's Sch., Oxford. Entered RN 1945; specialised in navigation, 1953; Army Staff Coll., 1958; Sqdn Navigating Officer, HMS Daring, Second Destroyer Sqdn, 1959–61; Staff Navigating Officer to Flag Officer, Sea Trng, 1961; Comdr 1961; Directorate of Naval Ops and Trade, 1961–63; i/c HMS Brighton, 1964–66; Directorate of Navigation and Tactical Control, 1966; Captain 1966; Captain of Dockyard and Queen's Harbourmaster, Singapore, 1967–69; Captain 1st Destroyer Sqdn, Far East, later Divnl Comdr 3rd Div. Western Fleet, i/c HMS Galatea, 1969–71; Dir, Royal Naval Staff Coll., 1971–73; Cdre Clyde i/c Clyde Submarine Base, 1973–75; Rear-Adm. 1976; Senior Naval Mem., Directing Staff, RCDS, 1975–78; Adm. Pres., RNC Greenwich, 1978–80, retd. Police Foundn, 1980–81. A Younger Brother, Trinity House, 1974. Freeman, City of London, 1979; Mem.,, Court of Assts, Shipwrights' Co., 1990–. OStJ 1990. *Recreation:* philately. *Address:* Chalkhurst, Eynsford, Kent DA4 0HT. *T:* Farningham (0322) 862789. *Club:* City Livery.

COOKE, Brian, JP; Circuit Administrator, South Eastern Circuit, since 1989; *b* 16 Jan. 1935; *s* of Norman and Edith Cooke; *m* 1958, Edith Mary Palmer; two *s* one *d. Educ:* Manchester Grammar Sch.; University Coll. London (LLB). Served Royal Air Force, 1956–59. Called to Bar, Lincoln's Inn, 1959; Dept of Director of Public Prosecutions, 1960–68; Deputy Clerk of the Peace, Inner London Quarter Sessions, 1968–71; Dep. Circuit Administrator, North Eastern Circuit, 1971–81, Circuit Administrator 1981–82; Sec. of Commissions, 1982–88, Hd of Judicial Appointments Gp, 1987–88, Lord Chancellor's Dept. JP Mddx, 1985. *Recreations:* tennis, walking, theatre, music. *Address:* Circuit Office, New Cavendish House, 18 Maltravers Street, WC2R 3EU.

COOKE, Prof. Brian Ernest Dudley; Professor Emeritus, University of Wales, 1983; Professor of Oral Medicine and Oral Pathology, University of Wales, Dean of Welsh National School of Medicine Dental School and Consultant Dental Surgeon to University Hospital of Wales, 1962–82; *b* 12 Jan. 1920; *e s* of Charles Ernest Cooke and Margaret Beatrice Wood; *m* 1948, Marion Neill Orkney Hope; one *s* one *d. Educ:* Merchant Taylors' Sch.; London Univ. LDSRCS 1942; LRCP, MRCS 1949; FDSRCS 1952; MDSU London 1959; MRCPath 1965, FRCPath 1974. Served RNVR (Dental Br.), 1943–46. Nuffield Dental Fellow, 1950–52; Trav. Nuffield Fellow, Australia, 1964. Lectr 1952–57, Reader in Dental Med. 1958–62, Guy's Hosp. Dental School. Rep. Univ. of Wales on Gen. Dental Council, 1964–82; Mem. Bd of Faculty of Dental Surgery, RCS England, 1964–72 (Vice-Dean 1971–72); Chm., Dental Educn Adv. Council, GB, 1975–78 (Mem. 1962–82); Sec.-Gen., Assoc. for Dental Educn in Europe, 1982–84. Adviser in Dental Surgery to Welsh Hosp. Bd, 1962–74; Civilian Consultant in Dental Surgery to RN, 1967–. Hon. Adviser, Editorial Bd, British Jl of Dermatology, 1967–76. Mem., S Glamorgan AHA, 1974–76. Mem. Bd of Governors: United Cardiff Hosps, 1965–71; HMC (Cardiff) Univ. Hosp. of Wales, 1971–74. Vice-Provost, Welsh Nat. Sch. of Medicine, 1974–76. Examr in Dental Surgery and Oral Pathology, Liverpool, Manchester and London Univs; Examr for Primary Fellowship in Dental Surgery, RCS, 1967–73. Hon. Mem., Pierre Fauchard Acad., 1967. Charles Tomes Lectr, RCS, 1963; Guest Lectr, Students' Vis. Lectrs Trust Fund, Witwatersrand Univ., 1967; Vis. Prof., Univ. of Sydney Dental Sch., 1986–87. Pres., Section of Odontology, RSocMed, 1975 (Hon. Mem., 1990); Founder Pres., British Soc. for Oral Medicine, 1981. Hon. Coll. Fellow, Univ. of Wales Coll. of Medicine, 1990. Cartwright Prize and Medal, RCS, 1955; Chesterfield Prize and Medal, St John's Hosp. for Diseases of Skin, 1955. *Publications:* (jtly) Oral Histopathology, 1959, 2nd edn 1970; scientific contribs to medical and dental jls. *Recreations:* various. *Address:* 38 St Aidan Crescent, Heath, Cardiff CF4 4AU. *T:* Cardiff (0222) 693503.

COOKE, Sir Charles Fletcher F.; *see* Fletcher-Cooke.

COOKE, Cynthia Felicity Joan, CBE 1975; RRC 1969; Matron-in-Chief, Queen Alexandra's Royal Naval Nursing Service, 1973–76; *b* 11 June 1919; *d* of late Frank Alexander Cooke, MBE, DCM, and of Ethel May (*née* Buckle). *Educ:* Rosa Bassett Sch. for Girls; Victoria Hosp. for Children, Tite Street, Chelsea; RSCN, 1940; University Coll. Hosp., London, SRN, 1942; Univ. of London, Sister Tutor Diploma, 1949. Joined QARNNS, 1943; served in: Australia, 1944–45; Hong Kong, 1956–58; Malta, 1964–66. HMS: Collingwood, Gosling, Goldcrest; RN Hospitals: Chatham, Plymouth, Haslar. Principal Tutor, Royal Naval School of Nursing, 1967–70; Principal Matron, RN Hosp., Haslar, 1970–73. QHNS 1973–76. CStJ 1975. *Address:* The Banquet House, Kings Head Mews, The Pightle, Needham Market, Suffolk IP6 8AQ.

COOKE, Col Sir David (William Perceval), 12th Bt *cr* 1661; Director of Finance and Resources, Bradford City Technology College; *b* 28 April 1935; *s* of Sir Charles Arthur John Cooke, 11th Bt, and Diana (*d* 1989), *o d* of late Maj.-Gen. Sir Edward Maxwell Perceval, KCB, DSO; *S* father, 1978; *m* 1959, Margaret Frances, *o d* of Herbert Skinner, Knutsford, Cheshire; three *d. Educ:* Wellington College; RMA Sandhurst; Open Univ. (BA). FCIT, FBIM, AMInstTA. Commissioned 4/7 Royal Dragoon Guards, 1955; served BAOR, 1955–58; transferred to RASC, 1958; served: BAOR, 1958–60; France, 1960–62; Far East, 1962–65; UK. Transferred to RCT on formation, 1965, and served UK, 1965–76, and BAOR, 1976–80; AQMG, MoD, 1980–82; Comdr, Transport and Movements, HQ British Forces, Hong Kong, 1982–84; Comdr, Transport and Movts, NW Dist, Western Dist and Wales, 1984–87; Col, Movements 1 (Army), MoD, 1987–90. Operational service: Brunei, 1962; Malay Peninsula, 1964–65; N Ireland, 1971–72. Attended Staff Coll., Camberley, 1968 and Advanced Transport Course, 1973–74. Col 1984. Queen's Jubilee Medal, 1977. *Recreations:* fishing, ornithology, military history. *Heir: cousin* Edmund Harry Cooke-Yarborough [*b* 25 Dec. 1918; *m* 1952, Anthea Katharine, *er d* of J. A. Dixon; one *s* one *d*]. *Address:* c/o Midland Bank, Knutsford, Cheshire. *Clubs:* Royal Aeronautical Society, Royal Over-Seas League.

COOKE, George Venables, CBE 1978; *b* 8 Sept. 1918; *s* of William Geoffrey Cooke and Constance Eva (*née* Venables); *m* 1941, Doreen (*née* Cooke); one *s* two *d. Educ:* Sandbach Sch., Cheshire; Lincoln Coll., Oxford, 1936–39 and 1946. MA, DipEd (Oxon). Served Army, 1939–46 (Major). Teacher, Manchester Grammar Sch., 1947–51; Professional Asst (Educn), W Riding of Yorkshire CC, 1951–53; Asst Dir of Educn, Liverpool, 1953–58; Dep. Dir of Educn, Sheffield, 1958–64; Dir of Educn, Lindsey (Lincs) CC, 1965–74; County Educn Officer, Lincolnshire CC, 1974–78; Gen. Sec., Soc. of Education Officers, 1978–84. Chm., Secretary of State's Adv. Cttee on Handicapped Children, 1973–74; Vice-Chm., Nat. Cttee of Enquiry into Special Educn (Warnock Cttee), 1974–78; Member: Jt Adv. Cttee on Agricultural Educn (Hudson Cttee), 1971–74; Parole Bd, 1984–87. Pres., Soc. of Educn Officers, 1975–76; Chm., County Educn Officers' Soc., 1976–77. Chm., Lincs and Humberside Arts, 1987–. *Recreations:* golf, gardening. *Address:* White House, Grange Lane, Riseholme, Lincoln LN2 2LQ. *T:* Lincoln (0522) 522667. *Club:* Royal Over-Seas League.

COOKE, George William, CBE 1975; FRS 1969; Chief Scientific Officer, Agricultural Research Council, 1975–81, retired; *b* 6 Jan. 1916; *s* of late William Harry Cooke and late Sarah Jane Cooke (*née* Whittaker); *m* 1944, Elizabeth Hannah Hill; one *s* one *d*. *Educ:* Loughborough Grammar Sch.; University Coll., Nottingham. BSc (Chem.) London Univ., 1937, PhD London, 1940. Awarded Min. of Agric. Research Schol., tenable at Rothamsted Experimental Station, 1938; apptd Scientific Officer there, 1941, and Prin. Sc. Officer, 1951; Head of Chemistry Dept, 1956–75; Deputy Dir, 1962–75 (acting Dir, 1972–73). Chm., Agriculture Group of Soc. of Chem. Industry, 1956–58; President: Fertiliser Soc., London, 1961–62; British Soc. of Soil Science, 1976–78. Lectures: Amos Meml, East Malling Res. Station, 1967; Francis New Meml, Fertiliser Soc., 1971; Clive Behrens, Univ. of Leeds, 1972–73; Scott Robertson Meml, QUB, 1973; Macaulay, Macaulay Inst. for Soil Res., 1979; Blackman, Oxford Univ., 1980; Boyd Orr Meml, Nutrition Soc., 1981. Hon. MRIA, 1980; Hon. FRAgS 1981; For. Mem., Lenin All-Union Acad. of Agric. Scis, USSR, 1972. Research Medal of Royal Agricultural Soc., 1967; Soc. of Chem. Industry Medal, 1983. *Publications:* Fertilizers and Profitable Farming, 1960; The Control of Soil Fertility, 1967; Fertilizing for Maximum Yield, 1972, 3rd edn 1982 (trans. Japanese, 1986); many papers in scientific jls on soil science, crop nutrition and fertilizers. *Recreation:* boats. *Address:* 33 Topstreet Way, Harpenden, Herts AL5 5TU. *T:* Harpenden (0582) 712899. *Club:* Farmers'.

COOKE, Gilbert Andrew, FCA; Chairman and Chief Executive, C. T. Bowring & Co. Ltd, 1982–88; Director, Marsh & McLennan Companies Inc., 1980–88; *b* 7 March 1923; *s* of Gilbert N. Cooke and Laurie Cooke; *m* 1949, Katherine Margaret Mary McGovern; one *s* one *d*. *Educ:* Bournemouth Sch. FCA 1950. Sen. Clerk, chartered accountants, 1950–54; Bowmaker Ltd: Chief Accountant, 1955; Dir, 1968; Man. Dir, 1968; Dep. Chm. and Chief Exec., 1972; C. T. Bowring & Co. Ltd: Dir, 1969; Gp Man. Dir, 1976–82. Chm., Bowring UK, 1984–88. Chm., Finance Houses Assoc., 1972–74. *Recreations:* music, reading. *Address:* Kilmarth, Onslow Road, Burwood Park, Walton-on-Thames, Surrey. *T:* Walton-on-Thames (0932) 240451.

COOKE, Jean Esme Oregon, RA 1972 (ARA 1965); (professional name Jean E. Cooke); Lecturer in Painting, Royal College of Art, 1964–74; *b* 18 Feb. 1927; *d* of Arthur Oregon Cooke, Grocer, and of Dorothy Emily Cooke (*née* Cranefield); *m* 1953, John Randall Bratby (marr. diss.), *qv*; three *s* one *d*. *Educ:* Blackheath High Sch.; Central Sch. of Arts and Crafts, Camberwell; City and Guilds; Goldsmiths' Coll. Sch. of Art; Royal Coll. of Art. NDD in Sculpture, 1949. Pottery Workshop, 1950–53. Member: Council, Royal Acad., 1983–85; Academic Bd, Blackheath Sch. of Art, 1986–; Governor: Central Sch. of Art and Design, 1984–; Tertiary Educn Bd, Greenwich, 1984–. Life Pres., Friends of Woodlands Art Gall., Blackheath, 1990. Purchase of self-portrait, 1969, and portrait of John Bratby (called Lilly, Lilly on the Brow), 1972, by Chantry Bequest; portraits: Dr Egon Wellesz and Dr Walter Oakshott for Lincoln Coll., Oxford; Mrs Bennett, Principal, for St Hilda's Coll., Oxford, 1976; Peter Carlisle, 1985–86; Clare Chalmers and Jane Lee, 1987–88; John Petty, 1989. Started Homage to Birling Gap (large painting), 1985. Television film: Portrait of John Bratby, BBC, 1978. *One-man shows:* Establishment Club, 1963; Leicester Gall., 1964; Bear Lane Gall., Oxford, 1965; Arun Art Centre, Arundel; Ashgate Gall., Farnham; Moyan Gall., Manchester; Bladon Gall., Hampshire, 1966; Lane Gall., Bradford, 1967; Gallery 66, Blackheath, 1967; Motley Gall., Lewisham, 1968; Phoenix, Suffolk, 1970; New Grafton Gall., 1971; Ansdell Gall., 1974; Woodlands Gall., Blackheath, 1976; J. K. Taylor Gall., Cambridge, 1976; Garden Gall., Greenwich, 1983; Alpine Gall., 1986; Friends Room, RA, 1990; Bardolf Hall, Sussex, 1990, in aid of Birling Gap Safety Boat; Blackheath Concert Halls, 1990; Linton Court Gall., Settle, 1991; open studio for: Greenwich Festival, 1977–89; Blackheath High Sch. Art Fund, 1979; Bakehouse Gall., Blackheath, 1980; open studio in aid of: Royal Acad. Trust, 1982; Birling Gap Safety Boat, 1989. *Works exhibited:* annually, RA, 1956–; Furneaux Gall., 1968; Upper Grosvenor Gall., 1968; Ashgate Gall., 1973; Agnews, 1974; Gall. 10, Richmond Hill, 1974; Leonie Jonleigh Gall., 1976; Dulwich Coll. Picture Gall., 1976; British Painting 1952–77, Royal Acad., 1977; Business Art Galleries, 1978; New Ashgate Gall., 1979; Tate Gall., 1979; Grosvenor Street Gall., 1979, 1980; Norwich Gall., 1979, 1980; Imp. Coll. Gall., 1980; Patrick Seale Gall., Belgravia, 1981; WEA, 1987; Foss Gall. Gp, 1987, 1988, 1990; RCA, 1988; Hurlingham Gall., 1990; Patterson Gall., 1990. *Publications:* Contemporary British Artists; The Artist, 1980; The Artist's Garden, 1989. *Recreations:* ungardening, talking, shouting, walking along the beach. *Address:* 7 Hardy Road, Blackheath, SE3 7NS. *T:* 081–858 6288.

COOKE, Jeremy Lionel; QC 1990; *b* 28 April 1949; *s* of Eric Edwin Cooke and Margaret Lilian Cooke; *m* 1972, Barbara Helen Willey; one *s* two *d*. *Educ:* Whitgift Sch., Croydon; St Edmund Hall, Oxford (MA Jurisprudence, 1st cl. Hons 1970; Rugby blue, 1968, 1969). Admitted Solicitor, 1973; with Coward Chance, 1973–76; called to the Bar, Lincoln's Inn, 1976. *Address:* 7 King's Bench Walk, Temple, EC4Y 7AS. *T:* 071–583 0404.

COOKE, John Arthur; Head of Central Unit, since 1989, and Director, Deregulation Unit, since 1990, Department of Trade and Industry; *b* 13 April 1943; *er s* of late Dr Arthur Hafford Cooke, MBE and Ilse Cooke (*née* Sachs); *m* 1970, Tania Frances, 2nd *d* of A. C. Crichton; one *s* two *d*. *Educ:* Dragon Sch.; Magdalen Coll. Sch., Oxford; Univ. of Heidelberg; King's Coll., Cambridge (Exhibnr, Sen. Scholar, BA History 1964, MA 1968); LSE. Mem., Cambridge Univ. expedition to Seistan, 1966. Asst Principal, Board of Trade, 1966; Second, later First, Sec., UK Delegn to European Communities, 1969–73; DTI, 1973–76; Office of UK Perm. Rep. to European Communities, 1976–77; Dept of Trade, 1977–80 (at Inst. Internat. d'Administration Publique, Paris, 1979); Asst Sec., Dept of Trade, 1980–84; seconded to Morgan Grenfell & Co. as Asst Dir, 1984–85; DTI, 1985–; Under Sec., Overseas Trade Div. 2, 1987–89. Dir (non-exec.), RTZ Pillar Ltd, 1990–. Mem. Bd, St Luke's Community Trust, 1985–. *Recreations:* reading, travelling, looking at buildings. *Address:* c/o Department of Trade and Industry, Ashdown House, 123 Victoria Street, SW1E 6RB. *Clubs:* United Oxford & Cambridge University; Cambridge Union.

COOKE, Air Vice-Marshal John Nigel Carlyle, CB 1984; OBE 1954; Consultant Physician, King Edward VII Hospital, Midhurst, since 1988; *b* 16 Jan. 1922; *s* of Air Marshal Sir Cyril Bertram Cooke, KCB, CBE and Phyllis Amelia Elizabeth Cooke; *m* 1958, Elizabeth Helena Murray Johnstone; two *s* one *d*. *Educ:* Felsted Sch.; St Mary's Hosp., Paddington (MD, BS(London)). FRCP, FRCPEd, MRCS, MFOM. House Physician, St Mary's, Paddington, 1945; RAF medical Br., 1945–85; Sen. Registrar, St George's, London, 1956–58; Consultant Physician, RAF, 1958–85; overseas service in Germany, Singapore, Aden; Prof. of Aviation Medicine, 1974–79; Dean of Air Force Medicine, 1979–83; Senior Consultant, RAF, 1983–85. UK Mem., Medical Adv. Bd, European Space Agency, 1978–84; Consultant to CAA, UK, 1972–; Consultant Advr to Sultan of Oman's Air Force, 1985–. Chairman: Defence Med. Services Postgrad. Council, 1980–82; Ethics Cttee, RAF Inst. of Aviation Medicine, 1987–89; Pres., Assoc. of Aviation Med. Examiners, 1986–. QHP 1979–85. *Publications:* articles on metabolic and aviation medicine subjects in numerous medical jls. *Recreations:* gliding, fly fishing. *Club:* Royal Air Force.

COOKE, Joseph; *see* Cooke, P. J. D.

COOKE, Kenneth; *see* Cooke, R. K.

COOKE, (Patrick) Joseph (Dominic), FIMC; Managing Director, Daily Telegraph, since 1987; *s* of Patrick Cooke and Mary (*née* Naughton); *m* 1960, Margaret Mary Brown; two *s* four *d*. *Educ:* St Joseph's Coll.; University Coll., Galway (BE). CEng, MICE, MIMechE; FIMC 1968; MBIM; AIIRA. United Steel Cos, 1952–54; Workington Iron & Steel Co., 1954–61; Urwick, Orr and Partners Ltd, 1961–73: Sen. Partner, 1967; Principal Partner, 1970; founded Cooke Management Consultants Ltd, 1973; Non-Exec. Dir, EMAP plc, 1984–; Consultant, Daily Telegraph, 1985–87; Non-Exec. Dir, IFRA, 1990–. Sandford Smith Award, Inst. Management Consultants, 1967. *Recreations:* golf, gardening. *Address:* Daily Telegraph plc, 181 Marsh Wall, E14 9SR. *T:* 071–538 5000.

COOKE, Peter; *see* Cooke, W. P.

COOKE, Peter Maurice; Regional Administrator, Oxford Regional Health Authority, 1980–85; *b* Feb. 1927; *s* of late Reginald and Grace Cooke; *m* 1956, Daphne Joyce (*née* Annoot); two *s*. *Educ:* Bristol Grammar Sch.; Corpus Christi Coll., Oxford (MA). 3rd Royal Tank Regt, 1946–48. FHSM. Admin. Assistant, Central Middlesex and Taunton HMCs, 1951–59; Asst Sec., NW Met Regional Hosp. Bd, 1959–63; Group Secretary: W Suffolk and Ipswich and District HMCs, 1963–73; Area Administrator, Suffolk AHA, 1973–80. *Recreations:* golf, choral singing. *Address:* Haremire House, Buckland, near Faringdon, Oxon SN7 8QS. *T:* Buckland (036787) 603.

COOKE, Randle Henry, LVO 1971; Managing Director, Randle Cooke and Associates, Recruitment Consultants, since 1987; *b* 26 April 1930; *o s* of late Col H. R. V. Cooke, Dalicote Hall, Bridgnorth, Salop and Mrs E. F. K. Cooke, Brodawel, Tremeirchion, N Wales; *m* 1961, Clare, *d* of C. J. M. Bennett, *qv*; one *s* one *d*. *Educ:* Heatherdown, Ascot; Eton College. 2nd Lieut, 8th King's Royal Irish Hussars, 1949; served Korea, 1950–53 with Regt and USAF (POW); ADC to GOC 7th Armoured Div., 1955; Regimental Adjt, 1957; Instructor, RMA Sandhurst, 1960; Sqdn Comdr, The Queen's Royal Irish Hussars, Malaya, Borneo and Germany, 1963; GSO3 (SD), HQ 1st Div., 1965. Equerry to the Duke of Edinburgh, 1968–71; Private Sec. to Lord Mayor of London, 1972–74. Dir, Personnel and Administration, Alginate Industries plc, 1974–78; Managing Director: ARA International Ltd, 1984–86; Mervyn Hughes International Ltd, 1986–87. Freeman of City of London, 1971. *Recreations:* most things to do with water. *Address:* Coney Hill House, Great Missenden, Bucks. *T:* Great Missenden (02406) 2147. *Club:* Cavalry and Guards.

COOKE, (Richard) Kenneth, OBE 1945; **His Honour Judge Cooke;** a Circuit Judge, since 1980; *b* 17 March 1917; *s* of Richard and Beatrice Mary Cooke; *m* 1st, 1945, Gwendoline Mary Black (*d* 1985); no *c*; 2nd, 1986, E. A. Rowlands (*née* Bachmann). *Educ:* Sebright Sch., Wolverley; Birmingham Univ. Admitted Solicitor (Hons), 1939; Birmingham Law Soc. Prizeman. Sqdn Leader, RAFVR, 1939–45. Solicitor in private practice specialising in Magistrates' Courts, 1945–52; Clerk: to Prescot and St Helens Justices, 1952–57; to Rotherham County Borough and WR Justices, 1957–64; to Bradford City Justices, 1964–70; Metropolitan Stipendiary Magistrate, 1970–80; a Recorder of the Crown Court, 1972–80. Mem. Council, Magistrates' Assoc., 1973–89 (Chm. Legal Cttee; Hon. Sec. Inner London Branch, 1972–89; a Dep. Chm., 1981–82; Pres., SE London Br., 1985–89); Member: Lord Chancellor's Adv. Cttee on the Training of Magistrates, 1978–85; Adv. Bd, Crime Concern Trust, 1988–. Reader, Rochester Dio., 1970–. Hon. Mem., Justices' Clerks Soc., 1988. *Publications:* contribs to Criminal Law Review, Justice of the Peace and Local Govt Review, etc. *Recreations:* fishing, choral singing, sampling bin ends. *Address:* The Bridewell, 6 Liskeard Close, Chislehurst, Kent BR7 6RT. *T:* 081–467 3908.

COOKE, Rt. Hon. Sir Robin (Brunskill), KBE 1986; Kt 1977; PC 1977; PhD; **Rt. Hon. Mr Justice Cooke;** President, Court of Appeal of New Zealand, since 1986 (Judge, 1976–86); *b* 9 May 1926; *s* of Hon. Philip Brunskill Cooke, MC (Judge of Supreme Court), and Valmai Digby Gore; *m* 1952, Phyllis Annette Miller; three *s*. *Educ:* Wanganui Collegiate Sch.; Victoria University Coll., Wellington (LLM); Clare Coll., Cambridge; Gonville and Caius Coll., Cambridge (MA, PhD). Trav. Scholarship in Law, NZ, 1950; Fellow, Gonville and Caius Coll., Cambridge, 1952 (Yorke Prize, 1954), Hon. Fellow, 1982. Called to the Bar, Inner Temple, 1954, Hon. Bencher 1985; practised at NZ Bar, 1955–72; QC 1964; Judge of Supreme Court, 1972; Pres., Court of Appeal of Western Samoa, 1982. Chm., Commn of Inquiry into Housing, 1970–71. Vis. Fellow, All Souls Coll., Oxford, 1990. Sultan Azlan Shah Law Lectr, Malaysia, 1990. Hon. LLD: Victoria Univ. of Wellington, 1989; Cambridge Univ., 1990; Hon. DCL Oxford, 1991. *Publications:* (ed) Portrait of a Profession (Centennial Book of NZ Law Society), 1969; articles in law reviews. *Recreations:* running, theatre, The Times crossword. *Address:* 4 Homewood Crescent, Karori, Wellington, New Zealand. *T:* 768–059. *Clubs:* United Oxford & Cambridge University; Wellington, Wellington Golf (NZ).

COOKE, Roger Arnold; His Honour Judge Roger Cooke; a Circuit Judge, since 1989; *b* 30 Nov. 1939; *s* of Stanley Gordon and Frances Mabel Cooke; *m* 1970, Hilary Robertson; two *s* two *d*. *Educ:* Repton; Magdalen Coll., Oxford (BA 1961; MA 1966). Astbury Scholar, Middle Temple, 1962; called to the Bar, Middle Temple, 1962 (*ad eund* Lincoln's Inn, 1967); in practice, Chancery Bar, 1963–89; Asst Recorder, 1982–87; Recorder, 1987–89. Sec., Chancery Bar Assoc., 1979–89; Mem., Bar Disciplinary Tribunal, 1988–89. MRI. *Recreations:* gardening, photography, history, amateur dramatics, old buildings, food. *Address:* The Law Courts, Woodall House, Lordship Lane, N22.

COOKE, Roger Malcolm; Deputy Managing Partner, UK, Arthur Andersen, and Area Co-Ordindator, Tax Europe, since 1989; *b* 12 March 1945; *s* of Sidney and Elsie Cooke; *m* 1968, Antoinette; one *s* one *d*. FCA, FTII. Qualified Chartered Accountant, 1968; Arthur Andersen & Co.: joined 1968, Tax Div.; Partner, 1976; Head, London Tax Div., 1979; area co-ordinator, tax practice, Europe, Middle East, Africa and India, 1989–. *Publication:* Establishing a Business in the United Kingdom, 1978. *Recreations:* playing squash and tennis, travel, ski-ing, cricket, football, good food. *Address:* (office) 1 Surrey Street, WC2R 2PS. *T:* 071–438 3207. *Club:* Royal Berkshire Racquets and Health.

COOKE, Prof. Ronald Urwick, MSc, PhD, DSc; Professor and Head of Department of Geography, since 1981, Dean of Arts, since 1991, and Vice-Provost, since 1991, University College London; *b* 1 Sept. 1941; *y s* of Ernest Cooke and Lillian (*née* Mount), Maidstone, Kent; *m* 1968, Barbara Anne, *d* of A. Baldwin; one *s* one *d*. *Educ:* Ashford Grammar Sch.; University College London, Univ. of London (BSc 1st Cl. Hons, MSc, PhD, DSc); FGS. Lectr, UCL, 1961–75; Prof. of Geography, 1975–81, Dean of Science, 1978–80, and Vice-Principal, 1979–80, Bedford Coll., Univ. of London. Amer. Council of Learned Societies Fellow, UCLA, 1964–65 and 1973; Vis. Professor: UCLA, 1968; Univ. of Arizona, Tucson, 1970; Arizona State Univ., Tempe, 1988. Desert research in N and S America, N Africa and ME. Chm., Geomorphological Services Ltd, 1986–90. Chm., British Geomorphological Res. Group, 1979; Mem. Council: RGS, 1980–83 (Back Grant, 1977); Inst. of British Geographers, 1973–75 (Pres., 1991–). *Publications:* (ed with J. H. Johnson) Trends in Geography, 1969; (with A. Warren) Geomorphology in Deserts, 1973; (with

J. C. Doornkamp) Geomorphology in Environmental Management, 1974, 2nd edn 1990; (with R. W. Reeves) Arroyos and Environmental Change in the American Southwest, 1976; (contrib.) Geology, Geomorphology and Pedology of Bahrain, 1980; (contrib.) Urban Geomorphology in Drylands, 1982; Geomorphological Hazards in Los Angeles, 1984; contribs mainly on desert and applied geomorphology in prof. jls. *Address:* Department of Geography, University College London, 26 Bedford Way, WC1H 0AP. *T:* 071–387 7050. *Club:* Athenæum.

COOKE, Roy, MA; JP; Director of Coventry School Foundation, since 1977; *b* Manchester, 6 May 1930; *s* of Reginald Herbert Cooke and Alice Cooke; *m* 1957, Claire Marion Medlicott Woodward, *d* of Lt-Col C. S. Woodward, CBE, JP, DL and Irene Anne Woodward, Glamorgan; three *s.* *Educ:* Manchester Grammar Sch. (schol.); Trinity Coll., Oxford (schol.; BA 1951; MA 1955; DipEd). Army service, 1951–54; commnd RAEC; Staff Officer in Germany (Captain, actg Major). Assistant Master: Gillingham Grammar Sch., Kent, 1955–56; Woking Grammar Sch., Surrey, 1956–58; Manchester Grammar Sch., 1958–64; Head of For. Langs, Stockport Sch., 1964–68; Headmaster: Gravesend Sch. for Boys, 1968–74; King Henry VIII Sch., Coventry, 1974–77. JP Kent, 1972, W Midlands, 1976. *Recreations:* photography, gardening, fell-walking, music. *Address:* 10 Stivichall Croft, Coventry CV3 6GN. *Club:* East India.

COOKE, Thomas Fitzpatrick, TD 1946; Lord Lieutenant, City of Londonderry, 1975–86; *b* 10 July 1911; *s* of Thomas Fitzpatrick Cooke and Aileen Frances Cooke; *m* 1946, Ruth, *d* of Rt Hon. Sir Anthony Brutus Babington, QC; one *s* one *d.* *Educ:* Stowe; Trinity Coll., Dublin (Dip. in Commerce). Served War, 1939–46, Captain, RA. Chm., Londonderry Port and Harbour Commissioners, 1967–73. Alderman, Londonderry Corp., 1946–52; High Sheriff, County of Londerry, 1949; DL 1950, High Sheriff, 1971–72, City of Londonderry. *Recreations:* gardening, shooting, fishing. *Address:* The Lodge, 5 Edenreagh Road, Eglinton, Londonderry BT47 3AR. *T:* Eglinton (0504) 810256. *Club* Northern Counties (Londonderry).

COOKE, Victor Alexander, OBE 1981; DL; CEng, FIMechE; Chairman: Henry R. Ayton Ltd, Belfast, 1970–89; Springvale EPS (formerly Polyproducts) Ltd, since 1964; *b* 18 Oct. 1920; *s* of Norman Victor Cooke and Alice Harman Cooke (*née* Peavey); *m* 1951, Alison Sheila Casement; two *s* one *d.* *Educ:* Marlborough Coll., Wilts; Trinity Coll., Cambridge (MA). Engineer Officer, Royal Navy, 1940–46 (Lieut (E) RN). Henry R. Ayton Ltd, Belfast, 1946–89; Chairman: Belfast Savings Bank, 1963; Harland & Wolff Ltd, 1980–May 1981 (Dir, 1970–87); Dir, NI Airports, 1970–85. Member: Senate, Parliament of N Ireland, 1960–68; N Ireland Economic Council, 1974–78; Commissioner, Belfast Harbour, 1968–79; Commissioner of Irish Lights, 1983– (Chm. of Comrs, 1990–). DL Co. Antrim, 1970. *Recreations:* sailing, shooting. *Club:* Naval.

COOKE, (William) Peter; Chairman, Price Waterhouse Regulatory Advisory Service, since 1989; *b* 1 Feb. 1932; *s* of late Douglas Edgar Cooke, MC and Florence May (*née* Mills); *m* 1957, Maureen Elizabeth, *er d* of late Dr E. A. Haslam-Fox; two *s* two *d.* *Educ:* Royal Grammar Sch., High Wycombe; Kingswood Sch., Bath; Merton Coll., Oxford (MA). Entered Bank of England, 1955; Bank for Internat. Settlements, Basle, 1958–59; Personal Asst to Man. Dir, IMF, Washington, DC, 1961–65; Sec., City Panel on Takeovers and Mergers, 1968–69; First Dep. Chief Cashier, Bank of England, 1970–73; Adviser to Governors, 1973–76; Hd of Banking Supervision, 1976–85; Associate Dir, 1982–88. Chairman: City EEC Cttee, 1973–80; Group of Ten Cttee on Banking Regulations and Supervisory Practices at BIS, Basle, 1977–88. Dir., Safra Republic Holdings SA, 1989–. Member: Bd, The Housing Corp., 1988–; Nat. Cttee, Church Housing Assoc., 1977–. Governor, Pangbourne Coll., 1982–. *Recreations:* music, golf, travel. *Address:* (office) Southwark Towers, 32 London Bridge Street, SE1 9SY; (home) Fourways, Oxford Road, Gerrards Cross, Bucks SL9 7DJ. *Clubs:* Reform, Overseas Bankers; Denham Golf.

COOKE-PRIEST, Rear Adm. Colin Herbert Dickinson; Flag Officer, Naval Aviation, since 1990; *b* 17 March 1939; *s* of Dr William Hereward Dickinson Priest and Harriet Lesley Josephine Priest (*née* Cooke); *m* 1965, Susan Mary Diana Hobler; two *s* two *d.* *Educ:* St Pirans, Maidenhead; Marlborough Coll.; BRNC, Dartmouth. Entered RN, 1957; Lieut, 1960; exchange service with RAN, 1968–70; commanded: HMS Plymouth, 1975–76; HMS Berwick, 1976; Airwarfare Directorate, Naval Staff, MoD, 1977–79; Naval Asst to Adm. Sir James Eberle, 1979–81; Asst Dir, Naval Air Warfare, 1981–82; CO, HMS Boxer, 1983–85; Dir, Maritime Tactical Sch., 1985–87; CO, HMS Brilliant and Capt. Second Frigate Sqn, 1987–89; Dep. Asst Chief of Staff (Ops) to Supreme Allied Comdr Europe, 1989–90. Freeman, City of London, 1985; Hon. Liveryman, Coachmakers' and Coachharness Makers' Co., 1985. *Recreations:* hockey, cricket, golf. *Address:* FONA Headquarters, RNAS Yeovilton, Ilchester, Somerset BA22 8HL. *Club:* Royal Navy of 1765 and 1785.

COOKSEY, David James Scott; Chairman, Advent Ltd, since 1987 (Managing Director, 1981–87); Chairman, Audit Commission for Local Government in England and Wales, since 1986; *b* 14 May 1940; *s* of Dr Frank S. Cooksey, CBE, and Muriel M. Cooksey; *m* 1973, Janet Clouston Bewley Wardell-Yerburgh (*née* Cathie, *widowed* 1970); one *s* one *d*, and one step *d.* *Educ:* Westminster Sch.; St Edmund Hall, Oxford Univ. (MA). Dir of Manufacturing, Formica International, 1969–71; Man. Dir, Intercobra Ltd, 1971–80; Director: Advent International Corp., 1985–90; Advent International plc, 1989–90; Electra Risk Capital, 1981–90; Macro 4, 1982–88; Agricultural Genetics Co., 1983–; European Silicon Structures, 1985–. Member: Council, CBI, 1976–88; Scottish Economic Council, 1980–87; Vice Chancellors and Principals Adv. Cttee on Industry, 1984–87; Council, British Venture Capital Assoc., 1983–89 (Chm., 1983–84); Innovation Adv. Bd, DTI, 1988–; Sci. and Industry Cttee, BAAS, 1988–. Mem., Pres's Cttee, Campaign for Oxford, 1988–. Trustee: Zool Soc. of London Develt Trust, 1987–; Inter Action, 1990–. *Publications:* papers in Philosophical Mag., Jl of Physics and Chemistry of Solids, Jl of Inst. of Metals. *Recreations:* sailing, property restoration, music, theatre. *Address:* 25 Buckingham Gate, SW1E 6LD. *T:* 071–630 9811. *Clubs:* Royal Thames Yacht; New (Edinburgh).

COOKSON, Catherine Ann, OBE 1985; author, since 1950; *b* 20 June 1906; *d* of Catherine Fawcett; *m* 1940, Thomas Cookson. Member: Society of Authors; Writers' and Authors' Guild. Paul Harris Fellow, Rotary International, Hexham, 1985. Catherine Cookson Foundation, Newcastle Univ., established 1985. Hon. MA Newcastle upon Tyne, 1983. Freeman of South Shields, 1978. *Publications:* Kate Hannigan, 1950; The Fifteen Streets, 1951 (staged 1987, London 1988); Colour Blind, 1953; Maggie Rowan, 1954; A Grand Man, 1954 (filmed as Jacqueline, 1956); The Lord and Mary Ann, 1956; Rooney, 1957 (filmed 1958); The Menagerie, 1958; The Devil and Mary Ann, 1958; Slinky Jane, 1959; Fanny McBride, 1959; Fenwick Houses, 1960; Love and Mary Ann, 1961; The Garment, 1962; Life and Mary Ann, 1962; The Blind Miller, 1963; Hannah Massey, 1964; Marriage and Mary Ann, 1964; The Long Corridor, 1965; Mary Ann's Angels, 1965; Matty Doolin, 1965; The Unbaited Trap, 1966; Katie Mulholland, 1967; Mary Ann and Bill, 1967; The Round Tower, 1968 (RSL Winifred Holtby Award for Best Regional Novel); Joe and the Gladiator, 1968; Our Kate (autobiog.), 1969; The Nice Bloke, 1969; The Glass Virgin, 1970; The Invitation, 1970; The Nipper, 1970; The Dwelling Place, 1971; Feathers in the Fire, 1971; Pure as the Lily, 1972; Blue Baccy, 1972; The Mallen Streak, 1973; The Mallen Girl, 1974; The Mallen Litter, 1974; Our John Willie, 1974; The Invisible Cord, 1975; The Gambling Man, 1975 (staged 1985); The Tide of Life, 1976; Mrs Flannagan's Trumpet, 1976; The Girl, 1977; Go Tell It To Mrs Golightly, 1977; The Cinder Path, 1978; The Man Who Cried, 1979; Tilly Trotter, 1980; Lanky Jones, 1980; Tilly Trotter Wed, 1981; Tilly Trotter Widowed, 1982; The Whip, 1983; Hamilton, 1983; The Black Velvet Gown, 1984; Goodbye Hamilton, 1984; A Dinner of Herbs, 1985; Harold, 1985; The Moth, 1986; Catherine Cookson Country (memoirs), 1986; Bill Bailey, 1986; The Parson's Daughter, 1987; Bill Bailey's Lot, 1987; The Cultured Handmaiden, 1988; Bill Bailey's Daughter, 1988; Let Me Make Myself Plain, 1988; The Harrogate Secret, 1989; The Black Candle, 1989; The Wingless Bird, 1990; The Gillyvors, 1990; My Beloved Son, 1991; *as Catherine Marchant:* Heritage of Folly, 1962; Fen Tiger, 1963; House of Men, 1964; Martha Mary Crawford, 1975; The Slow Awakening, 1976; The Iron Façade, 1977. *Recreations:* painting, gardening. *Address:* c/o Anthony Sheil Associates, 43 Doughty Street, WC1N 2LF. *Club:* PEN (English Centre).

COOKSON, Lt-Col Michael John Blencowe, OBE 1986; TD 1969; Vice Lord Lieutenant of Northumberland, since 1987; land owner, agriculturist; *b* 13 Oct. 1927; *s* of late Col John Charles Blencowe Cookson, DSO, TD, DL; *m* 1957, Rosemary Elizabeth, *d* of David Aubrey Haggie; one *s* three *d.* *Educ:* Eton; Cirencester Agricl Coll., 1951–52. Served with: E African Forces, Kenya, 1947–48; Northumberland Hussars (TA), 1952–69; Queen's Own Yeomanry, 1969–72; Chm., Northumberland Hussars (TA) Regtl Assoc., 1977–87. Hon. Col, Northumberland Hussars Sqn QOY, 1988–. Chm., Co. Cttee, Northumberland Assoc. Boys' Clubs, 1974–86 (Mem., 1964–73). Chm., Northumberland Queen's Silver Jubilee Appeal, 1978. High Sheriff, 1976, DL 1983, Northumberland. *Recreations:* hunting (Joint Master: Haydon Foxhounds, 1955–57; Morpeth Foxhounds, 1960–64, 1971–), gardening. *Address:* Meldon Park, Morpeth, Northumberland NE61 3SW. *T:* Hartburn (067072) 661. *Club:* Northern Counties (Newcastle upon Tyne).

COOKSON, Prof. Richard Clive, MA, PhD; FRS 1968, FRSC; Research Professor of Chemistry in the University of Southampton, 1983–85, Emeritus Professor, since 1985 (Professor of Chemistry, 1957–83); *b* 27 Aug. 1922; *s* of late Clive Cookson; *m* 1948, Ellen Fawaz; two *s.* *Educ:* Harrow Sch.; Trinity Coll., Cambridge. BA 1944; MA, PhD Cantab 1947. Research Fellow, Harvard Univ., 1948; Research Div. of Glaxo Laboratories Ltd, 1949–51; Lectr, Birkbeck Coll., London Univ., 1951–57. *Publications:* papers, mainly in Jl Chem. Soc. *Address:* Manor House, Stratford Tony, Salisbury, Wilts SP5 4AT.

COOKSON, Roland Antony, CBE 1974 (OBE 1946); Chairman, Lead Industries Group Ltd (until 1967 known as Goodlass Wall & Lead Industries Ltd), 1962–73 (Director, 1948–80, a Managing Director, 1952–62); Chairman, Consett Iron Co. Ltd, 1966–67 (Director 1955; Acting Chairman 1964); Director of Lloyds Bank Ltd, 1964–79 (Chairman, Northern Regional Board, 1965–79); *b* 12 Dec. 1908; *s* of late Bryan Cookson; *m* 1st, 1931, Rosamond Gwladys (*d* 1973), *er d* of late Sir John S. Barwick, 2nd Bt; one *d*; 2nd, 1974, Dr Anne Aitchison, *widow* of Sir Stephen Charles de Lancey Aitchison, 3rd Bt. *Educ:* Harrow; Magdalen Coll., Oxford. Vice-Chm., Northern Regional Board for Industry, 1949–65; Mem., Northern Economic Planning Council, 1965–68; Pres., Tyneside Chamber of Commerce, 1955–57; Chm., Northern Regional Council, CBI, 1970–72 (Vice-Chm., 1968–70); Mem., Port of Tyne Authority, 1968–74. Mem., Court and Council, Univ. of Newcastle upon Tyne (Vice-Chm. of Council, 1985–); Chm., Careers Adv. Board, Univs of Newcastle upon Tyne and Durham, 1962–73. Hon. DCL Newcastle, 1974. *Recreations:* music, fishing. *Address:* The Brow, Wylam, Northumberland NE41 8DQ. *T:* Wylam (0661) 853888. *Clubs:* Brooks's; Northern Counties (Newcastle upon Tyne).

COOLEY, Sir Alan (Sydenham), Kt 1976; CBE 1972; FIE; Secretary, Department of Productivity, 1977–80, retired 1981; *b* 17 Sept. 1920; *s* of Hector William Cooley and Ruby Ann Cooley; *m* 1949, Nancie Chisholm Young; four *d.* *Educ:* Geelong Grammar Sch.; Melbourne Univ. (BEngSc). Cadet Engr, Dept of Supply, 1940–43; Engrg Rep., London, 1951–52; Manager, Echuca Ball Bearing Factory, 1953–55; Supply Rep., Washington, 1956–57; Manager, Small Arms Factory, Lithgow, 1958–60; Dept of Supply: First Asst Sec. (Management Services and Planning), 1961–62; Controller-Gen. (Munitions Supply), 1962–66; Sec., 1966–71; Chm., Australian Public Service Bd, 1971–77. *Recreations:* golf, fishing. *Address:* PO Box 105, Milton, NSW 2538, Australia.

COOLS-LARTIGUE, Sir Louis, Kt 1968; OBE 1955; KStJ 1975; Governor of Dominica, 1967–78; *b* 18 Jan. 1905; *s* of Theodore Cools-Lartigue and Emily (*née* Giraud); *m* 1932, Eugene (*née* Royer); two *s* four *d.* *Educ:* Convents, St Lucia and Dominica; Dominica Grammar Sch. Clerk, Dominica Civil Service, 1924; Chief Clerk to Administrator and Clerk of Councils, 1932; Colonial Treas., Dominica, 1940, St Vincent, 1945; Asst Administrator, St Lucia, 1949; Chief Sec., Windward Is, 1951, retd 1960 on abolition of office; performed duties of Governor's Dep., Windward Is, over fifty times; Speaker of Legislative Council, Dominica, 1961–67; Speaker of House of Assembly, Dominica, March-Oct. 1967. *Recreations:* tennis, swimming. *Address:* 7 Virgin Lane, Roseau, Commonwealth of Dominica, West Indies.

COOMBE, Gerald Hugh; His Honour Judge Gerald Coombe; a Circuit Judge, since 1986; *b* 16 Dec. 1925; *s* of William Stafford Coombe and Mabel Florence Coombe; *m* 1957, Zoë Margaret Richards; one *s* one *d.* *Educ:* Alleyne's School, Dulwich; Hele's School, Exeter; Exeter College, Oxford. MA 1950. RAF (Navigator), 1944–48; Solicitor, 1953; Partner, Whitehead Monckton & Co., Maidstone, 1956–86; HM Coroner, Maidstone, 1962–86; a Recorder, 1983–86. *Club:* Royal Air Force.

COOMBE, Michael Rew; His Honour Judge Coombe; a Circuit Judge, since 1985; *b* 17 June 1930; *s* of late John Rew Coombe and Phyllis Mary Coombe; *m* 1961, Elizabeth Anne Hull; two *s* one *d* (and one *s* decd). *Educ:* Berkhamsted; New Coll., Oxford. MA (Eng. Lang. and Lit.). Called to Bar, Middle Temple, 1957 (Harmsworth Scholar), Bencher 1984. 2nd Prosecuting Counsel to the Inland Revenue at Central Criminal Court and 5 Courts of London Sessions, 1971; 2nd Counsel to the Crown at Inner London Sessions, Sept. 1971; 1st Counsel to the Crown at Inner London Crown Court, 1974; 4th Junior Treasury Counsel at Central Criminal Court, 1974, 2nd Jun. Treasury Counsel, 1975, 1st Jun. Treasury Counsel, 1977; Recorder of the Crown Court, 1976–85; Sen. Prosecuting Counsel to the Crown, CCC, 1978–85. *Recreations:* theatre, antiquity, art and architecture, printing. *Address:* Central Criminal Court, EC4M 7EH.

COOMBES, Keva Christopher; Member (Lab) Liverpool City Council, since 1986 (Leader, 1987–90); Consultant, David Phillips Harris & Whalley, solicitors, since 1986; *b* 23 Dec. 1949; *s* of Arthur Edward Coombes and Beatrice Claire Coombes; *m* 1970, Kathy Gannon; two *s* one *d.* *Educ:* Chatham House Grammar Sch.; Univ. of East Anglia (BA). Admitted Solicitor, 1977. Member: Liverpool CC, 1976–80; Merseyside CC, 1981–86 (Leader, 1982–86). Contested (Lab) Hyndburn, 1987. *Address:* c/o David Phillips Harris & Whalley, 23 Moorfields, Liverpool L2 2BQ. *T:* 051–236 3340.

COOMBS, Anthony Michael Vincent; MP (C) Wyre Forest, since 1987; *b* 18 Nov. 1952; *s* of Clifford Keith Coombs and Celia Mary Gostling (*née* Vincent); *m* 1984, Andrea Caroline (*née* Pritchard); one *s*. *Educ:* Bilton Grange Sch.; Charterhouse; Worcester Coll., Oxford (MA). Birmingham City Council: Mem., 1978–; Deputy Chairman: Educn Cttee, 1982–84; Social Services Cttee, 1982–84; Cons. spokesman on educn, Birmingham MDC, 1984–86. PPS to Minister of State, Home Office, 1989–91. Sec., Cons. Back-Bench Educn Cttee, 1987–90. Dir of several cos in Midlands, and Man. Dir, Grevayne Properties Ltd, 1972–. Pres., Wyre Forest "Solidarity" Campaign, 1987–. Chm. of Governors, Perry Common Sch., Birmingham, 1978–; Governor: King Edward Foundn, 1982–88; Birmingham Coll. of Tourism, 1982–88. *Publications:* Reviving our Inner Cities, Bow Group Paper, 1986; numerous articles in newspapers and jls. *Recreations:* golf, tennis, occasional football, music, theatre. *Address:* Morningside, 35 Tilehouse Green Lane, Knowle, Solihull, W Midlands. *T:* Knowle (0564) 77544; 47 Clarence Street, Kidderminster. *T:* Kidderminster (0562) 752439.

COOMBS, Derek Michael; Chairman, Hardanger Properties plc, since 1976; *b* 12 Aug. 1937; *m* 1986, Jennifer Lonsdale; two *s*, and one *s* one *d* by previous marriage. *Educ:* Rydal Prep. Sch.; Bromsgrove. Chm. and Man. Dir, S & U Stores plc, 1976–; Dir, Metalrax Group plc, 1975–. Political journalist. MP (C) Yardley, 1970–Feb. 1974. Successfully introduced unsupported Private Member's Bill for relaxation of Earnings Rule, 1972, establishing parly record for a measure of its kind; author of Cons. rate scheme for Oct. 1974 Gen. Election; specialist on economic affairs. Lectured on foreign affairs at Cons. weekend confs. Active pro-European. Governor, Royal Hosp. and Home for Incurables. Named as one of top 100 in report, The British Entrepreneur 1988. *Publications:* numerous articles on home, economic and foreign affairs. *Recreations:* friends, reading, tennis, skiing. *Address:* Cheyne Row, SW3. *T:* 071–352 6709.

COOMBS, Douglas Stafford, PhD; Controller, Books Division, British Council, 1980–83, retired; *b* 23 Aug. 1924; *s* of Alexander John Coombs and Rosina May (*née* Stafford); *m* 1950, Valerie Nyman; one *s* three *d*. *Educ:* Royal Liberty Sch., Romford; University College of Southampton; University College London (BA Hons, PhD). Served Royal Air Force, 1943–47. Lecturer in History, University College of the Gold Coast (subseq. Univ. of Ghana), 1952–60; British Council, 1960–: Nigeria, 1960–62; Overseas Student Centre, London, 1962–67; Bombay, 1967–73; Representative: Zambia, 1973–76; Yugoslavia, 1976–79; Visiting Fellow, Postgrad. School of Librarianship and Information Science, Univ. of Sheffield, 1979–80. Chm. Editorial Cttee and Mem. Exec. Cttee, Byways and Bridleways Trust, 1984–; Chm., Wootton Rivers Village Soc., 1985–88. *Publications:* The Conduct of the Dutch, 1958; The Gold Coast, Britain and The Netherlands, 1963; Spreading the Word: the library work of the British Council, 1988; articles in historical jls. *Recreations:* travel, slow jogging, watching cricket. *Address:* The Long House, Primrose Hill, Wootton Rivers, Marlborough, Wilts SN8 4NJ. *T:* Marlborough (0672) 810201.

COOMBS, Herbert Cole, MA, PhD; FAA; FAHA; FASSA; Visiting Fellow, Centre for Resource and Environmental Studies, Australian National University, since 1976; *b* 24 Feb. 1906; *s* of Francis Robert Henry and Rebecca Mary Coombs; *m* 1931, Mary Alice Ross; three *s* one *d*. *Educ:* Univ. of Western Australia, Perth, WA (MA); LSE (PhD). School teacher, Education Dept, WA, 1929; Asst Economist, Commonwealth Bank of Australia, 1935; Economist to Commonwealth Treasury, 1939; Mem., Commonwealth Bank Board, 1942; Dir of Rationing, 1942; Dir-Gen. of Post-War Reconstruction, 1943; Governor, Commonwealth Bank of Australia, 1949–60; Chm., Commonwealth Bank Board, 1951–60; Governor and Chm. of Board, Reserve Bank of Australia, 1960–68; Chancellor, ANU, 1968–76. Chairman: Australian Elizabethan Theatre Trust, 1954–68; Australian Council for Arts, 1968–74; Australian Council for Aboriginal Affairs, 1968–76; Royal Commn on Australian Govt Admin, 1974–76. Hon. LLD: Melbourne; ANU; Sydney; Hon. DLitt WA; Hon. DSc NSW; Hon. Fellow LSE, 1961. *Publications:* The Fragile Pattern, 1970; Other People's Money, 1971; Kulinma: Listening to Aboriginal Australians, 1978; Trial Balance—issues in my working life, 1981; (jtly) A Certain Heritage: programs by and for Aborigines, 1983; Towards a National Aboriginal Conference, 1985; The Waitangi Treaty and Aborigines (Boyer Lect.), 1988; (jtly) Land of Promises—economic development and aborigines of the East Kimberly, 1989; The Return of Scarcity—Essays Economic and Ecological, 1989. *Recreations:* walking, cooking, listening to music. *Address:* 119 Milson Road, Cremorne, NSW 2090, Australia.

COOMBS, Ven. Peter Bertram; Archdeacon of Reigate, since 1988; *b* 30 Nov. 1928; *s* of Bertram Robert and Margaret Ann Coombs; *m* 1953, Catherine Ann (*née* Buckwell); one *s* one *d*. *Educ:* Reading Sch.; Bristol Univ. (MA 1960); Clifton Theological Coll. Curate, Christ Church, Beckenham, 1960–64; Rector, St Nicholas, Nottingham, 1964–68; Vicar, Christ Church, New Malden, 1968–75; Rural Dean of Kingston upon Thames, 1970–75; Archdeacon of Wandsworth, 1975–88. *Recreations:* walking, sketching. *Address:* 89 Nutfield Road, South Merstham, Redhill, Surrey RH1 3HD. *T:* Merstham (0737) 642375.

COOMBS, Prof. Robert Royston Amos, ScD; FRS 1965; FRCPath 1969; Quick Professor in Immunology, University of Cambridge, 1966–88, now Emeritus; Fellow of Corpus Christi College, since 1962; *b* 9 Jan. 1921; *s* of Charles Royston Amos and Edris Owen Amos (formerly Coombs); *m* 1952, Anne Marion Blomfield; one *s* one *d*. *Educ:* Diocesan Coll., Cape Town; Edinburgh and Cambridge Univs. BSc, MRCVS Edinburgh 1943; PhD Cambridge 1947. Stringer Fellow, King's Coll., Cambridge, 1947–56; Asst Director of Research, Dept of Pathology, University of Cambridge, 1948; Reader in Immunology, University of Cambridge, 1963–66. Foreign Corres., Royal Belgium Acad. of Medicine, 1979. Hon. FRCP 1973; Hon. Fellow, Amer. Coll. of Allergists, 1979; Hon. Member: Amer. Assoc. of Immunologists, 1973–; British Blood Transfusion Soc., 1984–; British Soc. of Immunology, 1988–; British Soc. Allergy and Clin. Immunology, 1988–; Pathol. Soc. of GB and Ire. Hon. MD Linköping Univ. 1973; Hon. dr med. vet. Copenhagen, 1979; Hon. DSc: Guelph, 1981; Edinburgh, 1984. Landsteiner Award, Amer. Assoc. of Blood Banks, 1961; Gairdner Foundn Award, 1965; Henry Steele Gold Medal, RCVS, 1966; James Calvert Spence Medal, British Paediatric Assoc., 1967; Philip Levine Medal, Amer. Soc. Clin. Pathol, 1969; Clemens von Pirquet Medal, Austrian Soc. of Allergy and Immunology, 1988. *Publications:* (with Anne M. Coombs and D. G. Ingram) Serology of Conglutination and its relation to disease, 1960; (ed with P. G. H. Gell) Clinical Aspects of Immunology, 1963, 3rd edn (also with P. J. Lachmann), 1975; numerous scientific papers on immunology. *Recreation:* retreat to the country. *Address:* 6 Selwyn Gardens, Cambridge. *T:* Cambridge (0223) 352681.

COOMBS, Simon Christopher; MP (C) Swindon, since 1983; *b* 21 Feb. 1947; *s* of late Ian Peter Coombs and of Rachel Robins Coombs; *m* 1983, Kathryn Lee Coe Royce. *Educ:* Reading University (BA, MPhil); Wycliffe College. Marketing Executive, British Telecom and Post Office, Data and Telex, 1970–82; Marketing Manager, Telex Networks, British Telecom, 1982–83. Mem., Southern Electricity Consultative Council, 1981–84. Reading Borough Council: Mem., 1969–84; Chm., Transportation Cttee, 1976–83; Vice-Chm., Policy Cttee, 1976–83; Dep. Leader, 1976–81; Chief Whip, 1983. PPS to Rt Hon. Kenneth Baker, MP, Minister of State for Industry and IT, 1984–85, to Hon. William Waldegrave, MP, Parly Under-Sec. of State DoE, and Rt Hon. Lord Elton, Minister of State for the Environment, 1985. Member: Select Cttee on Employment, 1987–; British-American Parly Gp, 1983–; CPA, 1983–; Chairman: Cable TV Gp, 1987– (Sec, 1986–87); British Malaŵi Parly Gp, 1989– (Sec., 1985–89); Parly Food and Health Forum, 1989– (Sec., 1985–89); Treasurer, Parly IT Cttee, 1987–. Vice-Chm., Cons. Tourism Cttee, 1988–; Chm., Cons. Party, Wessex Area, 1980–83; Chm., Wessex Area Young Conservatives, 1973–76; Pres., Wilts Young Conservatives, 1984–; Vice Pres., N Wilts Disabled Drivers, 1985–. Member University Court: Univ. of Reading; Univ of Bath. *Recreations:* music, cricket, philately, reading, writing. *Address:* House of Commons, SW1A 0AA. *T:* 071–219 5049. *Clubs:* Swindon Conservative; Hampshire Cricket.

COONEY, Raymond George Alfred, (Ray Cooney); actor, author, director, theatrical producer; created Theatre of Comedy at Shaftesbury Theatre, and Little Theatre of Comedy at Ambassadors Theatre, 1983; *b* 30 May 1932; *s* of Gerard Cooney and Olive (*née* Clarke); *m* 1962, Linda Dixon; two *s*. *Educ:* Alleyn's Sch., Dulwich. First appeared in Song of Norway, Palace, 1946; toured in Wales, 1954–56; subseq. played in: Dry Rot and Simple Spymen, Whitehall; Mousetrap, Ambassador; Charlie Girl, Adelphi; Not Now Darling, Savoy (also film); Not Now Comrade (film); Run for your Wife, Guildford; Two into One, Leicester and Guildford. Productions (some jointly) include: Thark (revival); Doctor at Sea; The Queen's Highland Servant; My Giddy Aunt; Move Over Mrs Markham; The Mating Game; Lloyd George Knew My Father; That's No Lady-That's My Husband; Say Goodnight to Grandma; Two and Two Make Sex; At the End of the Day; Why Not Stay for Breakfast?; A Ghost on Tiptoe; My Son's Father; The Sacking of Norman Banks; The Bedwinner; The Little Hut; Springtime for Henry; Saint Joan; The Trials of Oscar Wilde; The Dame of Sark; Jack the Ripper; There Goes the Bride (and played leading role, Ambassadors, 1974); Ipi Tombi; What's a Nice Country Like US Doing In a State Like This?; Some of My Best Friends Are Husbands; Banana Ridge; Fire Angel; Elvis; Whose Life is it Anyway? (London and NY); Clouds; Chicago; Bodies; Beatlemania; Not Now Darling (revival); Hello Dolly (revival); Duet for One (London and NY); They're Playing Our Song; Children of a Lesser God; Run for your Wife; Aladdin; See How They Run; Pygmalion; Two Into One; Passion Play; Loot (revival); Intimate Exchanges; Wife Begins at Forty; An Italian Straw Hat (revival); It Runs in the Family; Out of Order. *Publications:* (with H. and M. Williams) Charlie Girl, 1965; *plays:* (with Tony Hilton) One for the Pot, 1961; Chase Me Comrade, 1964; (with Tony Hilton) Stand by your Bedouin, 1966; (with John Chapman) Not Now Darling, 1967; (with John Chapman) My Giddy Aunt, 1968; (with John Chapman) Move Over Mrs Markham, 1969; (with Gene Stone) Why Not Stay for Breakfast?, 1970; (with John Chapman) There Goes the Bride, 1973; Run for Your Wife, 1981; Two into One, 1983; Wife Begins at Forty, 1986; It Runs in the Family, 1989; Out of Order, 1990. *Recreations:* tennis, swimming, golf. *Address:* Duchess Theatre, Catherine Street, WC2B 5LA. *Club:* Dramatists'.

COOP, Sir Maurice (Fletcher); Kt 1973; Solicitor; *b* 11 Sept. 1907; *s* of George Harry and Ada Coop; *m* 1948, Elsie Hilda Brazier. *Educ:* Epworth Coll., Rhyl; Emmanuel Coll., Cambridge (BA). Admitted Solicitor of Supreme Court, 1932. Sec., Dunlop Rubber Co. Ltd, 1948–68; Dir, Dunlop Rubber Co. Ltd, 1966–70. Chm., Standing Adv. Cttee to Govt on Patents, 1972–74. *Recreations:* Association football, cricket. *Address:* 39 Hill Street, Berkeley Square, W1X 7FG. *T:* 071-491 4549. *Club:* United Oxford & Cambridge University.

COOPER, family name of **Viscount Norwich.**

COOPER; *see* Ashley-Cooper, family name of Earl of Shaftesbury.

COOPER, Very Rev. Alan; *see* Cooper, Very Rev. W. H. A.

COOPER, Rev. Albert Samuel; Moderator, Free Church Federal Council, 1973–74; *b* 6 Nov. 1905; *s* of Samuel and Edith Cooper; *m* 1936, Emily (*d* 1983), *d* of Hugh and Emily Williams; one *s* one *d*. *Educ:* Birkenhead Inst.; London Univ. (external student; BA Hons Philosophy); Westminster Coll., Cambridge (DipTheol); Fitzwilliam House, Cambridge (BA Theol Tripos, MA). Ordained 1936. Pastoral charges: St Columba's Presbyterian Church, Grimsby, 1936–41; Blundellsands Presbyt. Ch., Liverpool, 1941–44; St Columba's Presbyt. Ch., Cambridge, 1944–60; St Columba's Presbyt. (later United Reformed) Ch., Leeds, 1960–72, retd 1972. Free Church Chaplain. Fulbourn Mental Hosp., Cambridgeshire, 1950–60. Moderator, Presbyt. Ch. of England, 1968–69. *Address:* 6 Abbeyfield House, 596 Old Chester Road, Rock Ferry, Birkenhead, Merseyside L42 4NW. *T:* 051-645 0418.

COOPER, Andrew Ramsden, CBE 1965; FEng 1977; FIEE; Industrial Consultant, since 1966; Member for Operations and Personnel, Central Electricity Generating Board, 1957–66; *b* 1 Oct. 1902; *s* of Mary and William Cooper, Rotherham, Yorks; *m* 1922, Alice Robinson (marr. diss. 1982); one *s* two *d*; *m* 1982, Helen Louise Gordon. *Educ:* Rotherham Grammar Sch.; Sheffield Univ. Colliery Engineer, Yorks and Kent, 1918–28; Chief Electrical Engineer, Pearson & Dorman Long, 1928; Personal Asst to G. A. Mower, London, 1934; joined Central Electricity Board Operation Dept, NW England and N Wales, 1935; transf. to HQ, 1937; Operation Engineeer, SE and E England, 1942; Chief Operation Engineer to Central Electricity Board, 1944; Controller, Merseyside and N Wales Div. (Central Electricity Authority), 1948–52; NW Div., 1952–54; N West, Merseyside and N Wales Reg., 1954–57; Mem. Ops and Personnel, CEGB, 1957–66. Inventor, ARCAID Deaf/Blind Conversation Machine; Pres. Electricity Industries Benevolent Assoc., 1964–65; Mem, GB-USSR Cttee, 1967–. Faraday Lectr, 1952–53. CEng, FIEE; SFInstE; Hon. Life FIEEE. Pres., CIGRE, 1966–72. Bernard Price Meml Lectr, S African Inst. of Electr. Engrg, 1970; Meritorious Service Award, Power Engrg Soc. of America, 1972; Willans Medal, IEE, 1952; Thornton Medal, AMEME, 1961; Donor, Power/Life Award, Power Engrg Soc., IEEE, 1970. Hon. Mem., Batti-Wallahs Assoc. Hon. MEng Liverpool Univ., 1954. *Publications include:* Load Dispatching, with Special Reference to the British Grid System (a paper receiving John Hopkinson Award, 1948, and Willans Medal, 1952, IEE); The Human Approach to Management, 1989. *Recreations:* golf, art, music, writing, broadcasting, lecturing. *Address:* 32 Vanbrugh Court, 9 Eaton Gardens, Hove, E Sussex BN3 3TN. *T:* Brighton (0273) 724572. *Clubs:* Savile, Commonwealth Trust, Energy Industries, 25, Dynamcables; West Hove Golf.

COOPER, Beryl Phyllis, QC 1977; a Recorder of the Crown Court, since 1977; *b* 24 Nov. 1927; *o c* of late Charles Augustus Cooper and Phyllis Lillie (*née* Burrows). *Educ:* Surbiton High Sch. (Head Girl, 1945–46); Univ. of Birmingham (BCom 1950; Hon. Sec., Guild of Undergrads, 1949–50). Called to the Bar, Gray's Inn, 1960, Bencher, 1988; Dep. Circuit Judge, 1972–77; Dep. High Court Judge, 1980–. Hosp. Adminstr, Royal Free Hosp., 1951–57. Formerly: Councillor, St Pancras Metrop. Bor. Council; Mem., Homeopathic Hosp. Cttee; Mem., Bd of Visitors, Wandsworth Prison. Conservative Parly Candidate, Stepney, 1966; Founder Mem., Bow Gp (former Sec. and Council Mem.); Mem. Exec. Cttee, Soc. of Cons. Lawyers, 1981–87. Chm., Justice Report on Fraud Trials, 1985–86. Member: Cripps Cttee, Women and the Law; Home Office Cttee on Criminal Statistics (Perks Cttee); Housing Corp., 1976–79; Lambeth, Southwark and Lewisham AHA (Teaching), 1980–82; Criminal Injuries Compensation Bd, 1978–; Review Body for Nursing Staff, Midwives, Health Visitors, and Professions Allied to

Medicine, 1983–90; Council of Justice, 1986–; Family Law Bar Assoc. Cttee, 1986–88. *Publications:* pamphlets for CPC, Justice, etc.; articles on social, legal, criminal and local govt matters. *Recreations:* travel, swimming, golf, gardening. *Address:* 31 Alleyn Park, Dulwich, SE21 8AT. *T:* 081–670 7012; 2 Dr Johnson's Buildings, Temple, EC4Y 7AY. *T:* 071–353 5371; 8d South Cliff Tower, Eastbourne, Sussex. *T:* Eastbourne (0323) 32884. *Clubs:* English-Speaking Union; Caledonian (Edinburgh); Royal Eastbourne Golf, Dulwich and Sydenham Hill Golf.

COOPER, Prof. Cary Lynn; Professor of Organisational Psychology, University of Manchester, since 1975; *b* 28 April 1940; *s* of Harry and Caroline Cooper; *m* 1984, Rachel Faith Cooper; two *d*; one *s* one *d* from previous marr. *Educ:* Univ. of California (BS, MBA); Univ. of Leeds (PhD). FBPsS 1982. Lectr in Psychology, Univ. of Southampton, 1967–73. Advr to WHO and ILO, 1982–84. Mem., Bd of Trustees, Amer. Inst. of Stress, 1984–; Pres., British Acad. of Management, 1987–90. Myers Lectr, BPsS, 1986. FRSA 1990. Hon. MSc Manchester, 1979. Editor, Jl of Organizational Behavior, 1980–; Associate Ed., Stress Medicine, 1987–. *Publications:* T-Groups, 1971; Group Training for Individual and Organizational Development, 1973; Theories of Group Processes, 1975; Developing Social Skills in Managers, 1976; OD in the US and UK, 1977; Understanding Executive Stress, 1978; Advances in Experiential Social Processes, vol. 1, 1978, vol. 2, 1980; Stress at Work, 1978; Executives under Pressure, 1978; Behavioural Problems in Organizations, 1979; The Quality of Working Life in Western and Eastern Europe, 1979; Learning from Others in Groups, 1979; The Executive Gypsy, 1979; Current Concerns in Occupational Stress, 1980; Developing Managers for the 1980's, 1980; Combating Managerial Obsolescence, 1980; The Stress Check, 1980; White Collar and Professional Stress, 1981; Improving Interpersonal Relations, 1981; (jtly) Groups at Work, 1981; Executive Families Under Stress, 1981; (jtly) After Forty, 1981; Coping with Stress at Work, 1982; Psychology and Management, 1982; (jtly) Management Education, 1982; (jtly) Introducing Organization Behaviour, 1982; (jtly) High Pressure, 1982; Stress Research, 1983; (jtly) Human Behaviour in Organizations, 1983; (jtly) Stress and the Woman Manager, 1983; Public Faces, Private Lives, 1984; (jtly) Working Women, 1984; (jtly) Psychology for Managers, 1984; Psychosocial Stress and Cancer, 1984; (jtly) Women in Management, 1984; (jtly) The Change Makers, 1985; (jtly) Job Stress and Blue Collar Work, 1985; (jtly) International Review of Industrial and Organizational Psychology: 1986, 1986, 1987, 1988, 1989, 1990; (jtly) Man and Accidents Offshore, 1986; (jtly) Stress and the Nurse Manager, 1986; (jtly) Pilots under Stress, 1986; (jtly) Psycho-social Factors at Work, 1987; (jtly) Retirement in Industrialized Societies, 1987; Living with Stress, 1988; Stress and Breast Cancer, 1988; (jtly) High Fliers, 1988; (jtly) Early Retirement, 1989; (jtly) Career Couples: contemporary lifestyles and how to manage them, 1989; (jtly) Understanding Stress: health care professionals, 1990; (jtly) Managing People at Work, 1990; articles on social science and medicine, stress medicine. *Recreations:* reading 19th century Russian fiction, writing children's stories, squash. *Address:* 25 Lostock Hall Road, Poynton, Cheshire SK12 1DP. *T:* Poynton (0625) 871450. *Club:* St James's.

COOPER, Derek Macdonald; author, broadcaster and journalist; *b* 25 May 1925; *s* of George Stephen Cooper and Jessie Margaret Macdonald; *m* 1953, Janet Marian Feaster; one *s* one *d*. *Educ:* Raynes Park Grammar Sch.; Portree High Sch.; University Coll., Cardiff; Wadham Coll., Oxford (MA Hons). Served RN, 1943–47. Joined Radio Malaya as producer, 1950, retired as Controller of Progs, 1960; Producer, Roving Report, ITN, 1960–61; has worked widely as presenter, interviewer and writer in both television and radio. *Radio* programmes include: Today; Ten O'clock; Newstime; PM; Town and Country; A La Carte; Home This Afternoon; Frankly Speaking; Two of a Kind; You and Yours; Northbeat; New Worlds; Asian Club; Speaking For Myself; Conversations with Cooper; Friday Call; It's Your Line; Offshore Britons; Person to Person; The Food Programme; Meridien book programme; *television* programmes include: World in Action; Tomorrow's World; Breathing Space; A Taste of Britain; The Caterers; World About Us; I Am An Engineer; Men and Materials; Apart from Oil; Money Wise; One in a Hundred; The Living Body; From the Face of the Earth; This Food Business. Columnist: The Listener; Guardian; Observer magazine; Sunday Standard (House of Fraser Press Award, 1984); Homes & Gardens; Saga magazine; Woman's Journal; Scotland on Sunday; regular contributor to: In Britain; Taste; A La Carte; The West Highland Free Press; Signature. Founder Mem. and first Chm., 1985–88, Pres., 1988–, Guild of Food Writers. Glenfiddich Trophy as Wine and Food Writer, 1973, 1980; Broadcaster of the Year, 1984. *Publications:* The Bad Food Guide, 1967; Skye, 1970, 2nd edn 1977; The Beverage Report, 1970; The Gullibility Gap, 1974; Hebridean Connection, 1977; Guide to the Whiskies of Scotland, 1978; Road to the Isles, 1979 (Scottish Arts Council Award, 1980); (with Dione Pattullo) Enjoying Scotch, 1980; Wine With Food, 1982, 2nd edn 1986; (with Fay Godwin) The Whisky Roads of Scotland, 1982; The Century Companion to Whiskies, 1983; Skye Remembered, 1983; The World Of Cooking, 1983; The Road to Mingulay, 1985; The Gunge File, 1986; A Taste of Scotch, 1989. *Address:* 4 St Helena Terrace, Richmond, Surrey TW9 1NR. *T:* 081–940 7051; Seafield House, Portree, Isle of Skye. *T:* Portree (0478) 2380.

COOPER, Wing Comdr Donald Arthur, CBE 1990; AFC 1961; Chief Inspector, Air Accidents Investigation Branch, Department of Transport, 1986–90; *b* 27 Sept. 1930; *s* of A. A. Cooper and E. B. Cooper (*née* Edmonds); *m* 1958, Belinda, 3rd *d* of Adm. Sir Charles Woodhouse, KCB and of Lady Woodhouse; three *s*. *Educ:* Queen's Coll., British Guiana; RAF Coll., Cranwell. BA Open. ATPL (H) 1961, ATPL (A) 1972. FRAeS. Served on fighter and trng sqdns, 1952–56; Empire Test Pilot's Sch., 1957; RAE Farnborough, 1958–60; RAF sc 1961; Sqdn Comdr CFS Helicopter Wing, 1962–64; HQ FTC, 1964–66; Defence Operational Requirements Staff, MoD, 1966–70; joined Accidents Investigation, BoT, on retirement, 1970. *Recreations:* walking, ballroom dancing, amateur dramatics. *Address:* 7 Lynch Road, Farnham, Surrey GU9 8BZ.

COOPER, Rt Hon. Sir Frank, GCB 1979 (KCB 1974; CB 1970); CMG 1961; PC 1983; Chairman, High Integrity Systems Ltd, since 1986; Director: Babcock International Group, 1983–90; Morgan Crucible, since 1983; N. M. Rothschild & Sons, since 1983; *b* 2 Dec. 1922; *s* of late V. H. Cooper, Fairfield, Manchester; *m* 1948, Peggie, *d* of F. J. Claxton; two *s* one *d*. *Educ:* Manchester Grammar Sch.; Pembroke Coll., Oxford (Hon. Fellow, 1976). War of 1939–45: Pilot, Royal Air Force, 1941–46. Asst Principal, Air Ministry, 1948; Private Secretary: to Parly Under-Sec. of State for Air, 1949–51; to Permanent Under-Sec. of State for Air, 1951–53; to Chief of Air Staff, 1953–55; Asst Sec., Head of the Air Staff, Secretariat, 1955–60; Dir of Accounts, Air Ministry, 1961–62; Asst Under-Sec. of State, Air Min., 1962–64, Min. of Defence, 1964–68; Dep. Under-Sec. of State, Min. of Defence, 1968–70; Dep. Sec., CSD, 1970–73; Permanent Under-Secretary of State: NI Office, 1973–76; MoD, 1976–82. Hon. Consultant, RUSI, 1982–. Chm., United Scientific Hldgs, 1985–89. Mem., Adv. Council on Public Records, 1989–. Chm., Inst. of Contemp. British Hist., 1986–. Member Council: KCL, 1981–89; Imperial Coll., 1983– (Chm., 1988–); Chm. Delegacy, King's Coll. Med. and Dental Sch., 1983–89; Chm., Liddell Hart Trustees, 1987–; Gov., Cranbrook Sch., 1982– (Chm., 1984–). FKC 1987; FIC 1988. *Recreation:* walking. *Address:* 34 Camden Park Road, Chislehurst, Kent BR7 5HG. *Clubs:* Athenæum, Royal Air Force.

COOPER, Sir (Frederick Howard) Michael C.; *see* Craig-Cooper.

COOPER, Wing Comdr Geoffrey; free-lance writer; architect; Secretary, Friends of Gideons, since 1988 (Member, Gideons, since 1988); fundraising on Mary Whitehouse Trust; *b* 18 Feb. 1907; *s* of Albert Cooper, Leicester, and Evelyn J. Bradnam, Hastings. *Educ:* Wyggeston Gram. Sch., Leicester; Royal Grammar School, Worcester. Accountancy, business management. Auxiliary Air Force, 1933; BOAC, 1939. Royal Air Force 1939–45, Pilot (mentioned in despatches). MP (Lab) for Middlesbrough West Div., 1945–51. Farming in Jersey, CI, 1951–61; founder and one of first directors, Jersey Farmers' Co-operative; Chm. Jersey Branch, RAFA. Architecture and land develt, Bahama Is, 1962–77; Pres., Estate Developers Ltd. Writing and social welfare voluntary work in S London, 1977–84; Captain, 56th London Boys' Brigade. *Publications:* Cæsar's Mistress (exposé of BBC and nationalisation); articles in England, Bahamas and USA on civil aviation, business management and government methods. *Recreations:* portrait and landscape painting, swimming. *Address:* PO Box N7117, Nassau, Bahamas; 91 Connor Court, Battersea Park, SW11 5HG. *Club:* Royal Air Force.

COOPER, George A.; marketing and business consultant; Chairman, Independent Television Publications Ltd, 1971–89; *b* 9 Oct. 1915; *s* of late Joseph Cooper; *m* 1944, Irene Burns; one *d*. Exec. with internat. publishing gp; served War of 1939–45, Royal Artillery (Captain); Exec., Hulton Press, 1949–55; Director: ABC Television Ltd, 1955–77; Thames Television Ltd, 1968 (Man. Dir, 1974–77); Independent Television News, 1976–77; Chm., Network Programme Cttee of Independent Television, 1975–77. FRTS 1987. *Recreations:* golf, walking. *Address:* 43 Rivermill, 151 Grosvenor Road, SW1V 3JN. *T:* 071-821 9305. *Clubs:* Royal Automobile, Thirty.

COOPER, George Edward; Chairman, North Thames Gas Region (formerly North Thames Gas Board), 1970–78; Part-time Member, British Gas Corporation, 1973–78; *b* 25 Jan. 1915; *s* of H. E. Cooper and R. A. Jones, Wolverhampton; *m* 1941, Dorothy Anne Robinson; one *s*. *Educ:* Wolverhampton Municipal Grammar Sch. Wolverhampton and Walsall Corp., 1933–40. Served War, 1940–45, with RA in Middle East (Bimbashi Sudan Defence Force), Captain. Qualified as Accountant, Inst. of Municipal Treasurers and Accountants (now Chartered Inst. of Public Accountants), 1947; Hemel Hempstead Development Corp., 1948–50; W Midlands Gas Bd (finally Dep. Chm.), 1950–70. IPFA (FIMTA 1965); CIGasE 1968. Officer OStJ 1976. *Recreations:* photography, geology, golf. *Club:* City Livery.

COOPER, Gen. Sir George (Leslie Conroy), GCB 1984 (KCB 1979); MC 1953; DL; Chief Royal Engineer, since 1987; *b* 10 Aug. 1925; *s* of late Lt-Col G. C. Cooper and Mrs Y. V. Cooper, Bulmer Tye House, Sudbury; *m* 1957, Cynthia Mary Hume; one *s* one *d*. *Educ:* Downside Sch.; Trinity Coll., Cambridge. Commnd 1945; served with Bengal Sappers and Miners, 1945–48; Korea, 1952–53; psc 1956; jssc 1959; Instructor, RMA Sandhurst, 1959–62 and Staff Coll., Camberley, 1964; GSO1, 1st Div., 1964–66; CRE, 4th Div., 1966–68; MoD, 1968–69; Comdr, 19th Airportable Bde, 1969–71; Royal Coll. of Defence Studies, 1972; Dep. Dir Army Trng, 1973–74; GOC SW District, 1974–75; Dir, Army Staff Duties, 1976–79; GOC SE District, 1979–81; Adjt-Gen., 1981–84, retd. ADC General to the Queen, 1982–84. Mem., UK Bd of Management, and Dir of Management Develt, GEC, 1985–86. Colonel Commandant: RE, 1980–; RPC, 1981–85; Col, Queen's Gurkha Engineers, 1981–91. Chm., Knightstone Syndicate Management (formerly HGP Managing Agency), 1991– (Dir, 1990–91). Lay Rep., Senate and Bar Council Disciplinary Bodies, 1984–90. Chm., Infantile Hypercalcæmia Foundn, 1980–; Mem. Council, Action Research (formerly Nat. Fund for Res. into Crippling Diseases), 1982–. DL Essex, 1990. *Recreations:* shooting, gardening. *Address:* c/o Barclays Bank, 3–5 King Street, Reading, Berks RG1 2HD. *Clubs:* Army and Navy, MCC.

COOPER, Henry, OBE 1969; company director since 1972; *b* 3 May 1934; *s* of late Henry William Cooper and Lily Nutkins; *m* 1960, Albina Genepri; two *s*. *Educ:* Athelney Street Sch., Bellingham. Professional boxer, 1954–71. Presenter, Be Your Own Boss (series), Channel 4, 1983. KSG 1978. *Film:* Royal Flash, 1975. *Publications:* Henry Cooper: an autobiography, 1972; The Great Heavyweights, 1978; Henry Cooper's Book of Boxing, 1982; Henry Cooper's 100 Greatest Boxers, 1990. *Recreation:* golf. *Address:* 36 Brampton Grove, NW4.

COOPER, Imogen; concert pianist; *b* 28 Aug. 1949; *d* of late Martin Du Pré Cooper, CBE; *m* 1982, John Alexander Batten. *Educ:* Paris Conservatoire, with Jacques Février and Yvonne Lefébure, 1961–67 (Premier Prix, 1967); privately in Vienna, with Alfred Brendel. Plays regularly with all major British orchestras; regular appearances at Proms, 1975–; first British pianist, and woman, to have appeared in South Bank Piano Series, 1975; British festivals include Bath, Cheltenham, Harrogate, Brighton and Edinburgh. Overseas engagements in Germany, Austria, Holland, France, Scandinavia, Spain, USA, Italy, NZ and Japan. Recordings include: Mozart's Concerti for Two and Three Pianos, with Alfred Brendel and Acad. of St Martin-in-the-Fields; Schubert's late works. Mozart Meml Prize, 1969. *Recreations:* Romanesque architecture, reading, hill-walking. *Address:* c/o Joy Nebus, Artists Management, PO Box 355, 3860 AJ Nijkerk, The Netherlands. *T:* (31) 3494–53444, *Fax:* 60411.

COOPER, Jilly, (Mrs Leo Cooper); author; *b* 21 Feb. 1937; *d* of Brig. W. B. Sallitt, OBE, and Mary Elaine Whincup; *m* 1961, Leo Cooper; one *s* one *d*. *Educ:* Godolphin Sch., Salisbury. Reporter, Middlesex Independent, Brentford, 1957–59; followed by numerous short-lived jobs as account executive, copy writer, publisher's reader, receptionist, puppy fat model, switchboard wrecker, and very temporary typist. Columnist: Sunday Times, 1969–82; Mail on Sunday, 1982–87. *Publications:* How to Stay Married, 1969; How to Survive from Nine to Five, 1970 (new edn as Work and Wedlock, 1978); Jolly Super, 1971; Men and Super Men, 1972; Jolly Super Too, 1973; Women and Super Women, 1974 (new edn as Super Men and Super Women, 1977); Jolly Superlative, 1975; Super Jilly, 1977; Class, 1979; The British in Love, 1980; (with Tom Hartman) Violets and Vinegar, 1980; Supercooper, 1980; Intelligent and Loyal, 1981; Jolly Marsupial, 1982; (with Imperial War Museum) Animals in War, 1983; The Common Years, 1984; Leo and Jilly Cooper on Cricket, 1985; (with Patrick Lichfield) Hot Foot to Zabrieskie Point, the Unipart Calendar Book, 1985; How to Survive Christmas, 1986; Leo and Jilly Cooper on Horse Mania, 1986; Turn Right at the Spotted Dog, 1987; Angels Rush In, 1990; *novels:* Emily, 1975; Bella, 1976; Harriet, 1976; Octavia, 1977; Prudence, 1978; Imogen, 1978; Riders, 1985; Rivals, 1988; Polo, 1991; *short stories:* Love and Other Heartaches, 1981; *for children:* Little Mabel, 1980; Little Mabel's Great Escape, 1981; Little Mabel Wins, 1982; Little Mabel Saves the Day, 1985. *Recreations:* merry-making, wild flowers, music, mongrels. *Address:* c/o Desmond Elliott, 15–17 King Street, St James's, SW1.

COOPER, Joan Davies, CB 1972; Hon. Research Fellow, University of Sussex, since 1979; *b* 12 Aug. 1914; *d* of late Valentine Holland Cooper and of Wynnefred Louisa Cooper; unmarried. *Educ:* Fairfield High Sch., Manchester; University of Manchester (BA). Asst Dir of Educn, Derbyshire CC, 1941; Children's Officer, E Sussex CC, 1948; Chief Inspector, Children's Dept, Home Office, 1965–71; Dir, Social Work Service, DHSS, 1971–76; Nat. Inst. for Social Work, 1976–77. Mem., SSRC, 1973–76. Vice Pres.,

Nat. Children's Bureau, 1964–; Chairman: Parents for Children, 1979–87; NACRO Adv. Council on Juvenile Crime, 1982–87; Central Council for Educn and Trng in Social Work, 1984–86; E Sussex Care for the Carers, 1985–. Chm., Internat. Conf. on Data Protection, 1987. Trustee, Homestart, 1981–89. FRAI 1972. *Publications:* Patterns of Family Placement, 1978; Social Groupwork with Elderly Patients, 1981; Creation of the British Personal Social Services, 1962–74, 1983. *Recreation:* walking. *Address:* 44 Greyfriars Court, Court Road, Lewes, East Sussex BN7 2RF. *T:* Lewes (0273) 472604. *Club:* University Women's.

COOPER, Ven. John Leslie; Archdeacon of Coleshill, since 1990; *b* 16 Dec. 1933; *s* of Iris and Leslie Cooper; *m* 1959, Gillian Mary Dodds; two *s* one *d. Educ:* Tiffin School, Kingston, Surrey; Chichester Theological Coll. BD 1965, MPhil 1978, London Univ. (External Student). National Service, RA; commissioned, 1952–54. General Electric Co. management trainee, 1954–59; Chichester Theolog. Coll., 1959–62; Asst Curate, All Saints, Kings Heath, Birmingham, 1962–65; Asst Chaplain, HM Prison, Wandsworth, 1965–66; Chaplain: HM Borstal, Portland, Dorset, 1966–68; HM Prison, Bristol, 1968–72; Research Fellow, Queen's Coll., Birmingham, 1972–73; Priest-in-Charge 1973–81, Vicar 1981–82, St Paul's, Balsall Heath, Birmingham. Examining Chaplain to Bishop of Birmingham, 1981–82; Archdeacon of Aston, and Canon Residentiary, St Philip's Cathedral, Birmingham, 1982–90. *Recreations:* music, reading, squash, walking, travel, carpentry, gardening, photography. *Address:* 93 Coleshill Road, Marston Green, Birmingham B37 7HT. *T:* 021–779 4959, *Fax:* 021–779 6555.

COOPER, Prof. John Philip, CBE 1983; DSc; FRS 1977; FIBiol; Emeritus Professor of Agricultural Botany, University of Wales, 1984; *b* Buxton, Derbyshire, 16 Dec. 1923; *o s* of Frank Edward and Nora Goodwin Cooper; *m* 1951, Christine Mary Palmer; one *s* three *d. Educ:* Stockport Grammar Sch.; Univ. of Reading (BSc 1945, PhD 1953, DSc 1964); FitzWilliam House, Cambridge (DipAgrSc 1946). Scientific Officer, Welsh Plant Breeding Station, 1946–50; Lectr, Univ. of Reading, 1950–54; Welsh Plant Breeding Station, University College of Wales, Aberystwyth: Plant Geneticist, 1950–59; Head, Dept of Develtl Genetics, 1959–75; Dir, and Prof. of Agricl Botany, 1975–83. Consultant, FAO Headquarters, Rome, 1956; Nuffield Royal Society Bursary, CSIRO, Canberra, 1962; Visiting Professor: Univ. of Kentucky, 1965; Univ. of Khartoum, 1975; Univ. of Reading, 1984–89. Member: UK Seeds Exec., 1979–86; Internat. Bd for Plant Genetics Resources, 1981–86. *Publications:* (ed, with P. F. Wareing) Potential Crop Production, 1971; (ed) Photosynthesis and Productivity in Different Environments, 1975; various papers on crop physiology and genetics in sc. jls. *Recreations:* walking, field archaeology. *Address:* 31 West End, Minchinhampton, Glos. *T:* Brimscombe (0453) 882533. *Club:* Farmers'.

COOPER, Rear-Adm. John Spencer, OBE 1974; RN retired, 1988; an operations manager, Ferranti International, since 1988; *b* 5 April 1933; *s* of Harold Spencer Cooper and Barbara (*née* Highet); *m* 1966, Jacqueline Street (*née* Taylor); two *d. Educ:* St Edward's Sch., Oxford; Clare Coll., Cambridge (MA 1959). Electrical cadet, 1951; Lieut 1957; joined Submarines for Polaris programme, 1966; Comdr 1969, Captain 1976; Director, Trials (Polaris), 1976–78; Cdre 1981; Dir, Weapons (Stragetic Systems), 1981–83; Dir Gen., Strategic Weapon Systems, 1983–85; Chief Strategic Systems Exec., MoD, 1985–88. *Recreation:* sailing. *Address:* 3 Burlington Avenue, Kew Gardens, Richmond, Surrey TW9 4DF. *T:* 081-876 3675.

COOPER, Joseph, OBE 1982; pianist and broadcaster; *b* 7 Oct. 1912; *s* of Wilfrid Needham and Elsie Goodacre Cooper; *m* 1st, 1947, Jean (*d* 1973), *d* of late Sir Louis Greig, KBE, CVO; no *c*; 2nd, 1975, Carol, *d* of Charles and Olive Borg. *Educ:* Clifton Coll. (music schol.); Keble Coll., Oxford (organ schol.). MA (Oxon), ARCM (solo piano). Studied piano under Egon Petri, 1937–39. Served War, in RA, 1939–46. Solo pianist debut, Wigmore Hall, 1947 (postponed, Oct. 1939, owing to War); concerto debut, Philharmonia Orchestra, 1950; BBC debut Promenade Concerts Royal Albert Hall, 1953. Since then has toured in: British Isles, Europe, Africa, India, Canada. Many solo piano records. Chm., BBC TV prog., Face The Music, 1966–84. Hon. Chm., Barclaycard Composer of the Year Competition, 1983. Liveryman, Worshipful Co. of Musicians, 1963–; Member: Music Panel of Arts Council (and Chm. piano sub-cttee), 1966–71; Council, Musicians Benevolent Fund, 1987–; Trustee, Countess of Munster Musical Trust, 1975–80. Governor, Clifton College. Ambrose Fleming award, Royal Television Soc., 1961; Music Trades Assoc. Record Award, 1976. *Publications:* Hidden Melodies, 1975; More Hidden Melodies, 1976; Still More Hidden Melodies, 1978; Facing the Music (autobiog.), 1979; Arrangement of Vaughan Williams Piano Concerto for 2 pianos (in collab. with composer). *Recreations:* jigsaws, church architecture. *Address:* Octagon Lodge, Ranmore, near Dorking, Surrey RH5 6SX. *T:* East Horsley (04865) 2658. *Club:* Garrick.

COOPER, Prof. Kenneth Ernest; Emeritus Professor of Bacteriology, Bristol University, 1968; *b* 8 July 1903; *s* of E. Cooper; *m* 1930, Jessie Griffiths; no *c. Educ:* Tadcaster Grammar Sch.; Leeds Univ. BSc 1925, PhD 1927 Leeds; LRCP MRCS 1936; FIBiol. Leeds University: Research Asst in Chemotherapy, 1928–31; Research Asst in Bacteriology, 1931–36; Lectr in Bacteriology, 1936–38; Bristol University: Lectr in Bacteriology, 1938–46; Reader in Bacteriology, 1946–50; Prof. of Bacteriology, 1951–68; Dep. Dean of the Faculty of Science, 1955–58. Hon. Gen. Sec. of Soc. for Gen. Microbiology, 1954–60, Hon. Treas., 1961–68, Hon. Mem., 1969. *Publications:* numerous papers in medical, chemical and bacteriological journals. *Recreations:* golf, chess. *Address:* Flat 22, Oaklands, Elton Road, Clevedon, Avon BS21 7QZ. *T:* Clevedon (0272) 343310.

COOPER, Kenneth Reginald, CB 1991; Chief Executive, The British Library, 1984–91; *b* 28 June 1931; *s* of Reginald and Louisa May Cooper; *m* 1955, Olga Ruth (*née* Harvey); two *s* two *d. Educ:* Queen Elizabeth's Grammar Sch., Barnet; New Coll., Oxford (MA). FIPM; FITD (Pres., 1981–83); FIInfSc (Pres., 1988–89). Various appointments, Min. of Labour, 1954–62; Principal, HM Treasury, 1962–65; Principal Private Secretary to Minister of Labour, 1966–67; Asst Sec. for Industrial Training, Min. of Labour, 1967–70; Chief Executive: Employment Services Agency, 1971–75; Training Services Agency, 1975–79; Dir Gen., Nat. Fedn of Building Trades Employers, 1979–84. Vis. Prof., Strathclyde Univ., 1987–. Dep. Chm., CICI, 1988–. CBIM 1989. *Recreations:* music, Rugby football.

COOPER, Prof. Leon N., PhD ; Thomas J. Watson, Sr, Professor of Science, Brown University, Providence, RI, since 1974; Co-Director, Center for Neural Science; *b* NYC, 28 Feb. 1930; *s* of Irving Cooper and Anna Cooper (*née* Zola); *m* 1969, Kay Anne Allard; two *d. Educ:* Columbia Univ. (AB 1951, AM 1953, PhD 1954). Nat. Sci. Foundn post-doctoral Fellow, and Mem., Inst. for Advanced Study, 1954–55; Res. Associate, Univ. of Illinois, 1955–57; Asst Prof., Ohio State Univ., 1957–58; Associate Prof., Brown Univ., 1958–62, Prof., 1962–66, Henry Ledyard Goddard Prof., 1966–74. Consultant, various governmental agencies, industrial and educational organizations. Lectr, Summer Sch., Varenna, Italy, 1955; Visiting Professor: Brandeis Summer Inst., 1959; Bergen Internat. Sch. Physics, Norway, 1961; Scuola Internazionale di Fisica, Erice, Italy, 1965; Ecole Normale Supérieure, Centre Universitaire Internat., Paris, 1966; Cargèse Summer Sch., 1966; Radiation Lab., Univ. of Calif at Berkeley, 1969; Faculty of Scis, Quai St Bernard, Paris, 1970, 1971; Brookhaven Nat. Lab., 1972; Chair of Math. Models of Nervous System, Fondation de France, 1977–83; Mem., Conseil Supérieur de la Recherche, l'Université René Descartes, Paris, 1981–87. Alfred P. Sloan Foundn Res. Fellow, 1959–66; John Simon Guggenheim Meml Foundn Fellow, 1965–66. Co-Chm., Bd of Dirs, Nestor Inc. Fellow: Amer. Physical Soc.; Amer. Acad. of Arts and Sciences. Member: Amer. Philosoph. Soc.; National Acad. of Sciences; Sponsor Fedn of Amer. Scientists; Soc. for Neuroscience, Amer. Assoc. for Advancement of Science; Defense Science Bd. Mem. Bd of Govs, Internat. Neural Network Soc. (Jtly) Comstock Prize, Nat. Acad. of Scis, 1968; (jtly) Nobel Prize for Physics, 1972; Award of Excellence, Grad. Fac. Alumni, Columbia Univ., 1974; Déscartes Medal, Acad. de Paris, Univ. René Déscartes, 1977. Yrjö Reenpää Medal, Finnish Cultural Foundn, 1982; John Jay Award, Columbia Univ, 1985. Hon. DSc: Columbia, 1973; Sussex, 1973; Illinois, 1974; Brown, 1974; Gustavus Adolphus Coll., 1975; Ohio State Univ., 1976; Univ. Pierre et Marie Curie, Paris, 1977. Public lectures, internat. confs, symposia. *Publications:* Introduction to the Meaning and Structure of Physics, 1968; (contrib.) The Physicist's Conception of Nature, 1973; contrib. The Many Body Problem, 1963; contrib. to numerous jls incl. Physics Rev., Amer. Jl Physics, Biological Cybernetics, Procs of the US Nat. Acad. of Scis. *Recreations:* music, theatre, skiing. *Address:* 49 Intervale Road, Providence, RI 02906, USA. *T:* (401)-421-1181; Physics Department, Brown University, Providence, RI 02912, USA. *T:* (401)-863-2172. *Clubs:* University, Faculty (Providence, RI).

COOPER, Louis Jacques B.; *see* Blom-Cooper.

COOPER, Margaret Jean Drummond, OBE 1980; Chief Education Officer, General Nursing Council for England and Wales, 1974–82; *b* 24 March 1922; *d* of Canon Bernard R. Cooper and A. Jean Cooper (*née* Drackley). *Educ:* School of St Mary and St Anne, Abbots Bromley; Royal College of Nursing; Open Univ. (BA 1987). SRN, SCM, RNT. Nursing trng and early posts, Leicester Royal Infirmary, 1941–47; Midwifery trng, General Lying-in Hosp., SW1 and Coventry and Warwicks Hosp.; Nurse Tutor, Middlesex Hosp., 1953–55; Principal Tutor: General Hosp., Northampton, 1956–63; Addenbrooke's Hosp., Cambridge, 1963–68; Principal, Queen Elizabeth Sch. of Nursing, Birmingham, 1968–74. Chm., General Nursing Council for England and Wales, 1971–74 (Mem., 1965 and 1970). *Recreations:* birds, books, buildings. *Address:* 28 Lambert Cross, Saffron Walden, Essex CB10 2DP.

COOPER, Nigel Cookson; General Secretary, British Amateur Athletic Board, 1982–87; *b* 7 May 1929; *s* of Richard and Violet Sarah Cooper; *m* 1972, Elizabeth Gillian Smith; two *s* one *d. Educ:* Leeds Training Coll., Leeds Univ. (LLB); State Univ. of Iowa, USA (MA). Teacher, primary and secondary schools, 1950–59; Lecturer: Trent Park Training Coll., 1959–61; Loughborough Training Coll., 1961–64; Provincial Supervisor (Schools and Community) for Nova Scotia, Canada, 1964–65; County Organiser of Schools for Norfolk, 1965–68; Asst Education Officer for Oldham, 1970–72; Asst Director of Educn for British Families Educn Service in Europe, 1972–78; Registrar, Kelvin Grove College of Advanced Education, Brisbane, Australia, 1978–82. *Recreations:* playing the trumpet, squash, jogging. *Address:* 24 Southfields, East Molesey, Surrey KT8 0BP. *T:* 081–398 6076.

COOPER, Sir Patrick Graham Astley, 6th Bt *cr* 1821; Director, Crendon Concrete Co. Ltd, Long Crendon, 1973–83; *b* 4 Aug. 1918; *s* of late Col C. G. A. Cooper, DSO, RA and I. M. M. A. Cooper, Abergeldie, Camberley, Surrey; *S* cousin, Sir Henry Lovick Cooper, 5th Bt, 1959; *m* 1942, Audrey Ann Jervoise, *d* of late Major D. P. J. Collas, Military Knight of Windsor; one *s* two *d. Educ:* Marlborough Coll. Qualified RICS, 1949; Sen. Asst Land Comr, Min. of Agric., Fisheries and Food, 1950–59. Joined Crendon Concrete Co. Ltd, 1959. Served 1939–40, Gunner, RA, 52 AA Bde TA (invalided out). *Recreations:* golf, tennis. *Heir: s* Alexander Paston Astley Cooper [*b* 1 Feb. 1943; *m* 1974, Minnie Margaret, *d* of Charles Harrison]. *Address:* Monkton Cottage, Burton Lane, Monks Risborough, Aylesbury, Bucks. *T:* Princes Risborough (08444) 4210.

COOPER, Philip John, CB 1989; Comptroller-General of Patents, Designs and Trade Marks, Department of Trade and Industry, 1986–89; *b* 15 Sept. 1929; *s* of Charles Cooper and Mildred Annie Marlow; *m* 1st, 1953, Dorothy Joan Chapman (*d* 1982); two *d*; 2nd, 1986, Pamela Mary Pysden (*d* 1988). *Educ:* Deacon's Sch., Peterborough; University Coll., Leicester. BSc (Chem. 1st Cl. Hons). CChem, FRSC. Joined Dept (later Laboratory) of Govt Chemist, 1952; Nat. Service, 2nd Lt, R Signals, 1953–55; Dept of Scientific and Ind. Res., 1956–67; Principal, Min. of Technology, 1967; Prin. Private Sec. to Minister for Industrial Develt, 1972–73; Asst Sec., 1973–79, Under Sec., 1979–89, DoI and DTI; Dir, Warren Spring Lab., DTI, 1984–85. *Publications:* various papers on analytical and chemical matters. *Address:* Abbottsmead, 27 Sandy Lane, Kingswood, Surrey KT20 6ND.

COOPER, Sir Richard (Powell), 5th Bt *cr* 1905, of Shenstone Court, Co. Stafford; *b* 13 April 1934; *s* of Sir Francis Ashmole Cooper, 4th Bt and of Dorothy Frances Hendrika, *d* of late Emile Deen; *S* father, 1987; *m* 1957, Angela Marjorie, *e d* of Eric Wilson, Norton-on-Tees; one *s* two *d. Educ:* Marlborough. *Recreation:* foxhunting. *Heir: s* Richard Adrian Cooper, *b* 21 Aug. 1960. *Address:* Lower Farm, Chedington, Beaminster, Dorset DT8 3HY. *T:* Corscombe (093589) 463. *Clubs:* Buck's, Carlton.

COOPER, Robert Francis, MVO 1975; HM Diplomatic Service; Head of Policy Planning Staff, Foreign and Commonwealth Office, since 1989; *b* 28 Aug. 1947; *s* of Norman and Frances Cooper. *Educ:* Delamere Sch., Nairobi; Worcester Coll., Oxford (BA); Univ. of Pennsylvania (MA). Joined FCO 1970; Tokyo 1972; London 1977; seconded to Bank of England, 1982; UK Rep. to EC, 1984; Head of Management Review Staff, FCO, 1987; Head of Far Eastern Dept, FCO, 1987. *Recreations:* Shakespeare, bridge, bicycling. *Address:* Foreign and Commonwealth Office, SW1.

COOPER, Robert George, CBE 1987; Chairman, Northern Ireland Fair Employment Commission (formerly Agency), since 1976; Member, Northern Ireland Standing Advisory Commission on Human Rights, since 1976; *b* 24 June 1936; *er s* of William Hugh Cooper and Annie (*née* Pollock); *m* 1974, Patricia, *yr d* of Gerald and Sheila Nichol, Belfast; one *s* one *d. Educ:* Foyle Coll., Londonderry; Queen's Univ., Belfast (LLB). Industrial Relations, International Computers Ltd, Belfast, 1958–63; Asst Sec., Engineering Employers' Fedn, NI, 1963–67, Sec. 1967–72; Gen. Sec., Alliance Party of Northern Ireland, 1972–73. Member (Alliance): West Belfast, NI Assembly, 1973–75; West Belfast, NI Constitutional Convention, 1975–76; Minister, Manpower Services, NI, 1974. *Address:* Lynwood, 104 Bangor Road, Holywood, Co. Down, N Ireland. *T:* Holywood (02317) 2071.

COOPER, Ronald Cecil Macleod, CB 1981; Deputy Secretary, Department of Transport, 1986–90; *b* 8 May 1931; *s* of Cecil Redvers Cooper and Norah Agnes Louise Cooper (*née* Macleod); *m* 1st, 1953, June Bicknell (marr. diss. 1967); 2nd, 1967, Christine Savage; one *s* two *d. Educ:* Royal Grammar Sch., Newcastle upon Tyne; St Edmund Hall, Oxford (MA). Asst Principal, Min. of Supply, 1954–59; Principal, Min. of Aviation, 1959–62; on loan to European Launcher Develt Org., Paris, 1962–67; Asst Sec., Min. of Technology, 1968–70, DTI, 1970–73; Under Sec., Dept of Trade, 1973–78; Sec., Price Commn, 1979;

Dep. Sec. and Principal Estabt and Finance Officer, DTI, 1979–85. *Recreations:* music, reading.

COOPER, Hon. Russell; *see* Cooper, Hon. T. R.

COOPER, Sidney G.; *see* Grattan-Cooper.

COOPER, Sidney Pool; Head of Public Services, British Museum, 1973–76; *b* 29 March 1919; *s* of late Sidney Charles Henry Cooper and Emily Lilian Baptie; *m* 1940, Denise Marjorie Peverett; two *s* one *d*. *Educ:* Finchley County Sch.; Northern Polytechnic (BSc); University Coll. London (MSc). Laboratory of the Government Chemist, 1947; Asst Keeper, National Reference Library of Science and Invention, British Museum, 1963; Dep. Keeper, NRLSI, 1969. *Recreations:* gardening, golf. *Address:* 98 Kings Road, Berkhamsted, Herts HP4 3BP. *T:* Berkhamsted (0442) 864145.

COOPER, Maj.-Gen. Sir Simon Christie, KCVO 1991; General Officer Commanding London District and Major General Commanding Household Division, 1989–91, retired; *b* 5 Feb. 1936; *s* of Maj.-Gen. Kenneth Christie Cooper, CB, DSO, OBE and Barbara Harding-Newman; *m* 1967, Juliet Elizabeth Palmer; one *s* one *d*. *Educ:* Winchester College; rcds, psc. Commissioned Life Guards, 1956; served Aden, London, BAOR, 1957–63; Captain-Adjt, Household Cavalry Regt, 1963–65; ADC to CDS Earl Mountbatten of Burma, 1965–66; Borneo, Malaya, 1966–67; Staff Coll., 1968; BAOR, 1969–75; CO Life Guards, 1974–76; GSO1, Staff Coll., 1976–78; OC Household Cavalry and Silver Stick in Waiting, 1978–81; Commander, RAC Centre, 1981–82; RCDS, 1983; Dir, RAC, 1984–87; Comdt, RMA, Sandhurst, 1987–89. Hon. Colonel: Westminster Dragoons, 1987–; Royal Yeomanry, 1987–. *Recreations:* cricket, skiing, sailing, shooting. *Club:* MCC.

COOPER, Susie, (Mrs Susan Vera Barker), OBE 1979; RDI 1940; FRSA; Senior Designer for Josiah Wedgwood & Sons Ltd, since 1966; *b* 29 Oct. 1902; *d* of John Cooper and Mary-Ann (*née* Adams); *m* 1938, Cecil Barker (*d* 1972); one *s*. *Educ:* Mollart House, Hanley; Burslem School of Art. Resident designer, Gray's Pottery, 1924; founded Susie Cooper Pottery, 1929; designed and produced tableware for Royal Pavilion, Festival of Britain, on South Bank, 1951. Dr RCA 1987. *Recreations:* gardening, seed painting.

COOPER, (Theo) Russell; MLA (National Party) for Roma, Queensland, since 1983; Leader of the Opposition, Queensland, since 1989; *b* 4 Feb. 1941; *s* of Theo Beverley Cooper and Muriel Frances Cooper; *m* 1965, Penelope Anne Parkinson; one *s* three *d*. *Educ:* Surfers Paradise State Sch.; Correspondence Sch.; Toowoomba Prep. Sch.; King's Sch., Parramatta. Councillor, 1976–88, Dep. Chm., 1983–88, Bendemere Shire Council; Vice-Pres., Roma Electorate NP Council, 1982–84; Chm., Wallumbilla-Yuleba Branch, NP, 1974–84. Minister for: Corrective Services and Admin. Services, 1987–89; Police and Emergency Services, 1989; Premier of Qld, Sept.–Dec. 1989. Vice-Pres., Maranoa Graziers Assoc., 1979–80 (Chm., Wallumbilla Br.); Pres., Roma and Dist Amateur Race Club, 1981–83. *Recreations:* golf, tennis (active), Rugby League, Rugby Union, cricket. *Address:* Donnabar, Wallumbilla, Qld 4428, Australia. *T:* (076) 234341. *Clubs:* Brisbane, Polo (Brisbane); Maranoa (Roma).

COOPER, Hon. Warren Ernest; MP (National Party) Otago, since 1975; Minister of Defence and of Local Government; Minister responsible for War Pensions, Radio and Television, New Zealand; *b* Dunedin, 21 Feb. 1933; *s* of William Cooper; *m* 1959, Lorraine Margaret, *d* of Angus T. Rees; three *s* two *d*. *Educ:* Musselburgh Sch.; King's High Sch., Dunedin. Formerly Minister of Tourism, Minister of Regional Develt, Minister in charge of Publicity and in charge of Govt Printing Office; Postmaster Gen., 1980; Minister of Broadcasting and Assoc. Minister of Finance, 1981; Minister of Foreign Affairs and Overseas Trade, 1981–84. Mem., Cabinet Cttees on Expenditure Control, State Sector, Environment and External Relns. Member Executive: S Island Publicity Assoc., 1971; NZ Municipal Assoc. Life Mem. and former Pres., Queenstown Jaycees. Mayor of Queenstown, 1968–71. JP Queenstown. *Address:* Parliament House, Wellington, New Zealand; 12 Cluny Avenue, Kelburn, Wellington, New Zealand.

COOPER, Dame Whina, ONZ 1991; DBE 1981 (CBE 1974; MBE 1953); JP; New Zealand President, Maori Land Rights, since 1975; *b* 9 Dec. 1895; *d* of Heremia Te Wake, JP (a Chief of Ngati-Manawa hapu of Te Rarawa tribe) and Kare Pouro; *m* 1st, 1916, Richard Gilbert (decd); one *d* (one *s* decd); 2nd, 1935, William Cooper (decd); two *s* two *d*. *Educ:* St Joseph's Coll., Greenmeadows, Napier, NZ. Proficiency Cert.; qualified as school teacher. Teacher, Pawarenga Sch., Northland, 1917; postmistress and storekeeper, Panguru, 1940 (Pres., Panguru Federated Farmers, 1940). Active in Maori land devel schemes, 1930; President: (first), Maori Women's Welfare League, 1952; Te Unga Waka Marae Soc., 1960; Maori Progressive Cultural Org., 1966; Pres. and Maori Land Rights Leader who led the Great Maori Land March to Parliament, 1975. Had the honour of being the first woman to cross the threshold of Waitangi House, 1949. Pres., Hokianga Rugby Union, 1947; Mem., Whangarei Gun Club, 1930–38. JP Auckland, 1952. *Publication:* Notable New Zealanders, 1979; *relevant publication:* Whina, by Michael King, 1983. *Recreations:* hockey, netball, table tennis. *Address:* 4 McCulloch Road, Panmure, Auckland, New Zealand. *T:* Auckland 578–534.

COOPER, William, (Harry Summerfield Hoff), FRSL; novelist; *b* 4 Aug. 1910; *m* 1951, Joyce Barbara Harris (*d* 1988); two *d*. *Educ:* Christ's Coll., Cambridge. Assistant Commissioner, Civil Service Commission, 1945–58; Personnel Consultant to: UKAEA, 1958–72; CEGB, 1958–72; Commn of European Communities, 1972–73; Asst Dir, Civil Service Selection Bd, 1973–75; Mem. Bd of Crown Agents, 1975–77; Personnel Advr, Millbank Technical Services, 1975–77. Adjunct Prof. of English Lit., Syracuse Univ., 1977–90. *Publications:* (as H. S. Hoff) Trina, 1934; Rhéa, 1935; Lisa, 1937; Three Marriages, 1946; (as William Cooper) Scenes from Provincial Life, 1950; The Struggles of Albert Woods, 1952; The Ever-Interesting Topic, 1953; Disquiet and Peace, 1956; Young People, 1958; C. P. Snow (British Council Bibliographical Series, Writers and Their Work, No 115) 1959; Prince Genji (a play), 1960; Scenes from Married Life, 1961; Memoirs of a New Man, 1966; You Want The Right Frame of Reference, 1971; Shall We Ever Know?, 1971; Love on the Coast, 1973; You're Not Alone, 1976; Scenes from Metropolitan Life, 1982; Scenes from Later Life, 1983; From Early Life (autobiog.), 1990; Immortality at any Price, 1991. *Address:* 22 Kenilworth Court, Lower Richmond Road, SW15 1EW. *T:* 081 788–8326. *Club:* Savile.

COOPER, Sir William (Daniel Charles), 6th Bt *cr* 1863, of Woollahra; Company Director of The Garden Maintenance Service and G.M.S. Vehicles; *b* 5 March 1955; *s* of Sir Charles Eric Daniel Cooper, 5th Bt, and of Mary Elisabeth, *e d* of Captain J. Graham Clarke; *S* father, 1984; *m* 1988, Julia Nicholson. *Educ:* Northease Manor, Lewes, Sussex. *Heir: b* George John Cooper, *b* 28 June 1956. *Address:* 1 Victoria Cottages, Andover Road, Micheldever Station, near Winchester, Hants SO21 3AX.

COOPER, Maj.-Gen. William Frank, CBE 1971; MC 1945; consultant; *b* 30 May 1921; *s* of Allan Cooper, Officer of Indian State Railways, and Margaret Cooper; *m* 1945, Elisabeth Mary Finch; one *s* one *d*. *Educ:* Sherborne Sch.; RMA Woolwich. Commnd in RE, 1940; served N Africa and Italy (MC; despatches 1944); Malaya, 1956–58 (despatches); S Arabia, 1963–65 (OBE); Chief Engr FARELF, 1968–70; Dep. Dir Army Staff Duties, MoD, 1970–72; Dir, Mil. Assistance Office, 1972–73; DQMG, 1973–76, retd. Col Comdt, RE, 1978–83. Dir, Gin Rectifiers and Distillers Assoc. and Vodka Trade Assoc., 1976–90. *Recreations:* fishing, birdwatching, theatre, gardening. *Address:* c/o Lloyds Bank, High Street, Guildford, Surrey. *Club:* Army and Navy.

COOPER, Very Rev. (William Hugh) Alan; Priest-in-charge of Chrishall, 1981–88; *b* 2 June 1909; *s* of William and Ethel Cooper; *m* 1st, 1940, Barbara (*née* Bentall); one *s* two *d*; 2nd, 1980, Muriel Barnes. *Educ:* King's Coll. Sch., Wimbledon; Christ's Coll., Cambridge (MA); St John's Hall, London. ALCD. Curate of Lee, 1932–36; Holy Trinity, Cambridge, 1936–38; CMS Missionary and Diocesan Missioner of Dio. Lagos, 1938–41; Curate of Farnham, 1941–42; Rector of Ashtead, 1942–51; Vicar of St Andrew, Plymouth, 1951–62; Preb. of Exeter Cathedral, 1958–62; Provost of Bradford, 1962–77; Hon. Assistant to Bishop of Karachi, 1977–80. Hon. MA Bradford, 1978. *Address:* 4 Eastgate Gardens, Guildford, Surrey GU1 4AZ.

COOPER, Prof. Sir William M.; *see* Mansfield Cooper.

COORAY, (Bulathsinhalage) Anura (Siri); His Honour Judge Cooray; a Circuit Judge, since 1991; *b* 20 Jan. 1936; *s* of (Bulathsinhalage) Vincent Cooray, accountant, and Dolly Perera Manchanayake, Etul Kotte, Sri Lanka; *m* 1957, Manel Therese, *d* of late George Perera, planter, and late Myrtle Perera, Kandy, Sri Lanka; two *s* three *d*. *Educ:* Christian Coll., Kotte, Sri Lanka; London Univ. Called to the Bar, Lincoln's Inn, 1968. Served RAF, Cranwell and Locking, 1952–55 (RAF Boxing Assoc. Sigrist Trophy, 1953–54); served Royal Ceylon Air Force, 1955–60. Practised in Common Law Chambers at Middle Temple; later, Dep. Head of Chambers at No 1 Gray's Inn Sq.; Mem., South Eastern Circuit; Prosecuting Counsel for DPP and Met. Police Solicitors, 1969–82; a Metropolitan Stipendiary Magistrate, 1982–91; a Recorder, 1989–91. Mem., Cttee of Magistrates, 1989. *Recreations:* wine making (and tasting too!), gardening. *Address:* 1 Gray's Inn Square, WC1R 5AA; Kingsland, Etul Kotte, Kotte, Sri Lanka.

COOTE, Sir Christopher (John), 15th Bt *cr* 1621; Senior Baronetcy of Ireland in use; *b* 22 Sept. 1928; *s* of Rear-Adm. Sir John Ralph Coote, 14th Bt, CB, CBE, DSC, and of Noreen Una, *o d* of late Wilfred Tighe; *S* father, 1978; *m* 1952, Anne Georgiana, *d* of Lt-Col Donald Handford; one *s* one *d*. *Educ:* Winchester; Christ Church, Oxford (MA 1957). Coffee and tea merchant. *Heir: s* Nicholas Patrick Coote [*b* 28 July 1953; *m* 1980, Mona, *d* of late Moushegh Bedelian; one *s* one *d*].

COOTE, Prof. John Haven; Bowman Professor, since 1987, Head of Department of Physiology, since 1984, and Head of School of Basic Medical Sciences, since 1988, Birmingham University; *b* 5 Jan. 1937; *m* 1976, Susan Hylton; one *s* two *d*. *Educ:* Royal Free Hosp. Sch. of Medicine (BSc (Hons) Physiol.; PhD London); DSc Birmingham 1980. CBiol, FIBiol 1988. Prof. of Physiology, Birmingham Univ., 1984–. Vis. Scientist, Inst. de Medicina Experimental, Univ. of Caracas, Venezuela, 1971; Visiting Professor, Department of Physiology: Inst. of Gerontology, Tokyo, 1974–75; Inst. of Physiological Scis, Warsaw, 1977–78. *Publications:* contribs to Jl of Physiol., Jl of the Autonomic Nervous System, Brain Res. *Recreation:* mountaineering. *Address:* Physiology Department, University of Birmingham, Birmingham B15 2TT.

COOTE, John Oldham; Captain, RN; *b* 13 Aug. 1921; *o s* of F. Stanley Coote, OBE, KStJ and Edith F. Coote; *m* 1944, Sylvia Mary (*née* Syson); three *d*. *Educ:* China Inland Mission Sch., Chefoo; Felsted. Royal Navy, as submarine specialist, 1940–60 (despatches 1944). Joined Beaverbrook Newspapers, 1960 (Vice-Chm. and Man. Dir, 1968–74; Dep. Chm. and Gp Man. Dir, 1974–75). Mem., Newspaper Publishers Assoc., 1968–75; Chm., Newsvendors Benevolent Inst. Festival Appeal, 1974. Dir Gen., British Film Prodn Assoc., 1976–77. Consultant, Boeing Marine Systems, 1980–87. Mem. Council, King George's Fund for Sailors, 1968–90 (Chm. Appeal Cttee, 1983–88); Trustee: Submarine Meml Museum, 1968–90; Devas Boys' Club, 1967–85; Chm., Petworth House Tennis Court, 1986–. *Publications:* Shell Pilot to the English Channel: Part 1 (South Coast), 1982; Part 2 (N France and Channel Islands), 1985; Shell Guide to Yacht Navigation, 1987; (ed and contrib.) The Faber Book of the Sea, 1989; Submariner, 1991; contrib. defence and yachting pubns. *Recreations:* performing arts, offshore sailing, Real tennis. *Address:* Titty Hill, Iping, Midhurst, W Sussex GU29 0PL. *Clubs:* Garrick, Royal Ocean Racing; Royal Yacht Squadron; Cruising of America.

COOTE, Rt. Rev. Roderic Norman, DD; *b* 13 April 1915; *s* of late Comdr B. T. Coote and late Grace Harriet (*née* Robinson); *m* 1964, Erica Lynette, *d* of late Rev. E. G. Shrubbs, MBE; one *s* two *d*. *Educ:* Woking County Sch.; Trinity Coll., Dublin. Curate Asst, St Bartholomew's, Dublin, 1938–41; Missionary Priest in the Diocese of Gambia and the Rio Pongas, 1942; Bishop of Gambia and the Rio Pongas, 1951–57; Suffragan Bishop of Fulham, 1957–66; Suffragan Bishop of Colchester, 1966–87; Archdeacon of Colchester, 1969–72. Member, General Synod of Church of England, 1969–72. *Recreations:* walking, piano (composer and broadcaster); Irish Champion 120 yds Hurdles. *Address:* 58 Broom Park, Teddington TW11 9RS.

COPAS, Most Rev. Virgil, KBE 1982; DD; Archbishop Emeritus (RC) of Port Moresby and of Kerema; Member of Religious Order of Missionaries of Sacred Heart (MSC); *b* 19 March 1915; *s* of Cornelius Copas and Kathleen (*née* Daly). *Educ:* St Mary's Coll. and Downlands Coll., Toowoomba, Queensland. Sec. to Bp L. Scharmach, Rabaul, New Britain, New Guinea, 1945–51; Religious Superior, Dio. of Darwin, Australia, 1954–60; Bishop of Port Moresby, 1960–66; Archbishop of Port Moresby, 1966–76, resigned in favour of a national archbishop; Archbishop of Kerema, 1976–88. Initiated into 3 tribal gps of people in Papua New Guinea. *Address:* 12/64 Esplanade, Surfers Paradise, Qld 4217, Australia.

COPE, David Robert, MA; Master of Marlborough College, since April 1986; *b* 24 Oct. 1944; *yr s* of Dr C. L. Cope; *m* 1966, Gillian Margaret Peck; one *s* two *d*. *Educ:* Winchester Coll. (Scholar); Clare Coll., Cambridge (Scholar). 1st Cl. Hons Hist. Tripos Part II, 1965; BA 1965; MA 1972. Asst Master, Eton Coll., 1965–67; Asst British Council Rep. (Cultural Attaché), Mexico City, 1968–70; Asst Master, Bryanston Sch., 1970–73; Headmaster: Dover College, 1973–81; British Sch. of Paris, 1981–86. FRSA. *Recreations:* music, tennis, travel. *Address:* The Master's Lodge, Marlborough College, Wilts SN8 1PA. *T:* Marlborough (0672) 512140. *Club:* Athenæum.

COPE, David Robert; Director, UK Centre for Economic and Environmental Development, since 1986; *b* 7 July 1946; *s* of Lawrence William and Ethel Anne Cope; *m* (separated). *Educ:* Fitzwilliam Coll., Cambridge Univ. (MA); London School of Economics (MScEcon, with dist.). Res. Officer, University Coll. London, 1969–70; Lectr, Nottingham Univ., 1970–81; Environment Team Leader, Internat. Energy Agency Coal Unit, 1981–86; Special Lectr in Energy and Environment Studies, Nottingham Univ., 1985–; Vis. Lectr, Cambridge Univ., 1988. *Publications:* Energy Policy and Land Use Planning (with P. Hills and P. James), 1984; numerous papers on energy and environment topics. *Recreations:* hill walking, woodworking. *Address:* UK Centre for Economic and Environmental Development, Suite E, 3 King's Parade, Cambridge CB2 1SJ. *T:* Cambridge (0223) 67799, *Fax:* (0223) 67794.

COPE, Prof. F(rederick) Wolverson, DSc, CEng, FIMinE, FGS; Consultant Geologist; Professor of Geology and Head of Geology Department, University of Keele, 1950–76, now Professor Emeritus; *b* 30 July 1909; *e s* of late Fred and Ida Mary Cope (*née* Chappells), Macclesfield; *m* 1st, 1935, Ethel May Hitchens, BSc (*d* 1961); one *s* two *d*; 2nd, 1962, Evelyn Mary Swales, BA, AKC, *d* of late John Frederick and Ada Mary Swales, Kingston-upon-Hull; one *d. Educ:* The King's Sch., Macclesfield; Univs of Manchester (DSc 1946) and London. Brocklehurst Scholar, 1928; John Dalton Prize, 1930; BSc with First Class Honours in Geology, 1931; MSc, Mark Stirrup Res. Scholar, Manchester, 1932. Demonstrator in Geology, Bedford Coll., Univ. of London, 1933–34; Daniel Pidgeon Fund, Geol. Soc. of London, 1937; Prin. Geologist in Geological Survey of GB, 1934–50 (discoverer of Formby oilfield, 1937); Murchison Award of Geol. Soc. of London, 1948; Vis. Prof. of Geology, Univ. of Pisa, 1964. Sometime Examr, Univs of Bristol, Exeter, London, Manchester, Nottingham, Sheffield and Wales. FGS 1934 (Senior Fellow 1984); FIMinE 1968; CEng 1969. Chm., Essex Gp of Geologists' Assoc., 1980–; Hon. Mem., Geologists' Assoc., 1982. *Publications:* The North Staffordshire Coalfields, in Coalfields of Great Britain (ed by late Sir Arthur Trueman), 1954; Geology Explained in the Peak District, 1976; various research publications mainly in the fields of stratigraphy and palaeontology. *Recreations:* hill walking, landscape sketching, servicing own cars, travel, geology, ornithology, Italy, reading and speaking Italian. *Address:* 6 Boley Drive, Clacton-on-Sea, Essex CO15 6LA. *T:* Clacton-on-Sea (0255) 421829.

COPE, Hon. James Francis, CMG 1978; Speaker of the Australian House of Representatives, 1973–75; *b* 26 Nov. 1907; *s* of G. E. Cope; *m* 1931, Myrtle Irene, *d* of S. J. Hurst; one *d. Educ:* Crown Street Public Sch., NSW. Hon. Treaurer, NSW Br., Aust. Glass Workers' Union; Delegate to Federal Council, 1953–55. MHR (Lab) for divs of: Cook, 1955; Watson, 1955–69; Sydney, 1969–75. *Recreations:* billiards, horse racing, cricket, football. *Address:* 1/38–40 Fontainebleau Street, Sans Souci, NSW 2219, Australia.

COPE, Rt. Hon. Sir John (Ambrose), Kt 1991; PC 1988; MP (C) Northavon, since 1983 (South Gloucestershire, Feb. 1974–1983); Deputy Chariman, Conservative Party, since 1990; *b* 13 May 1937; *s* of George Cope, MC, FRIBA, Leicester; *m* 1969, Djemila Lovell Payne, *d* of Col P. V. L. Payne, Martinstown, Dorset and Mrs Tanetta Blackden; two *d. Educ:* Oakham Sch., Rutland. Chartered Accountant; Company Director. Commnd RA and RE, Nat Service and TA. Conservative Research Dept, 1965–67; Personal Asst to Chm. of Conservative Party, 1967–70; contested (C) Woolwich East, 1970; Special Asst to Sec. of State for Trade and Industry, 1972–74; a Govt Whip, 1979–87, and Lord Comr of HM Treasury, 1981–83; Treas. of HM Household and Dep. Chief Whip, 1983–87; Minister of State: Dept of Employment and Minister for Small Businesses, 1987–89; NI Office, 1989–90; Formerly Secretary: Cons. Parly Finance Cttee; Parly Gp for Concorde; Vice Chm., Cons. Parly Smaller Business Cttee, 1977–79 (Sec., 1975–77). Pres., Inst. of Business Counsellors, 1988–90; Hon. Vice-Pres., National Chamber of Trade. Patron, Avon Riding for the Disabled. *Publication:* (with Bernard Weatherill) Acorns to Oaks (Policy for Small Business), 1967. *Recreation:* woodwork. *Address:* House of Commons, SW1A 0AA. *Clubs:* Carlton, Beefsteak; Tudor House (Chipping Sodbury), Chipping Sodbury Yacht.

COPE, Maclachlan Alan Carl S.; *see* Silverwood-Cope.

COPE, Wendy Mary; writer, freelance since 1986; *b* 21 July 1945; *d* of Fred Stanley Cope and Alice Mary (*née* Hand). *Educ:* Farringtons Sch.; St Hilda's Coll., Oxford (MA); Westminster College of Education, Oxford (DipEd). Teacher in London primary schs, 1967–81 and 1984–86; Arts editor, ILEA Contact, 1982–84; Television columnist, The Spectator, 1986–90. Cholmondeley Award for Poetry, 1987. *Publications:* Making Cocoa for Kingsley Amis (poems), 1986; Twiddling Your Thumbs (rhymes for children), 1988; (ed) Is That The New Moon?, 1989; The River Girl, 1991. *Recreations:* music, swimming. *Address:* c/o Faber and Faber, 3 Queen Square, WC1N 3AU.

COPELAND, Hon. Dame Joyanne Winifred; *see* Bracewell, Hon. Dame J. W.

COPEMAN, Harold Arthur; Under-Secretary, HM Treasury, 1972–76; *b* 27 Jan. 1918; *s* of H. W. M. and G. E. Copeman; *m* 1948, Kathleen (Kay) Gadd; one *s. Educ:* Manchester Grammar Sch.; The Queen's Coll., Oxford. BA, 1st Cl. Hons in PPE, 1939; MA. Served War, Army: Cheshire Regt, RA (Instructor in Gunnery) and Ordnance Board (Applied Ballistics Dept), 1940–45. HM Treasury, 1946–76. Consultant, Fiscal Affairs Dept, IMF, 1982. Vis. Fellow, Warwick Univ., 1976–84. *Publications:* (jtly) Health Care: priorities and management, 1980; The National Accounts: a short guide, 1981; Singing in Latin, 1990; A Pocket Singing in Latin, 1990. *Recreations:* music, Latin pronunciation, photography. *Address:* 22 Tawney Street, Oxford. *T:* Oxford (0865) 243830.

COPISAROW, Sir Alcon (Charles), Kt 1988; DSc, FInstP; CEng; FIEE; FZS; company chairman; a Chairman, General Commissioners for Income Tax, since 1975; *b* 25 June 1920; *o s* of late Dr Maurice Copisarow, Manchester; *m* 1953, Diana, *y d* of Ellis James Castello, MC, Bucklebury, Berks; two *s* two *d. Educ:* Manchester Central Grammar Sch.; University of Manchester; Imperial Coll. of Science and Technology; Sorbonne, Paris. Council of Europe Research Fellow. Served War, 1942–47; Lieut RN, 1943–47; British Admiralty Delegn, Washington, 1945. Home Civil Service, 1946–66; Office of Minister of Defence, 1947–54. Scientific Counsellor, British Embassy, Paris, 1954–60. Dir, Forest Products Research Laboratory, Dept of Scientific and Industrial Research, 1960–62; Chief Technical Officer, Nat. Economic Development Council, 1962–64; Chief Scientific Officer, Min. of Technology, 1964–66. Dir, McKinsey & Co. Inc., 1966–76; non-exec. Dir, British Leyland, 1976–77; Mem., BNOC, 1980–83; Dir, Touche Remnant Holdings, 1985–89. Chairman: Commonwealth Forest Products Conf., Nairobi, 1962; CENTO Conf. on Investment in Science, Teheran, 1963; Member: Scientific Manpower Cttee, Advisory Council on Scientific Policy, 1963–64; Econ. Develt Cttees for Electronics Industry and for Heavy Electrical Industry; Trop. Prod. Adv. Cttee, 1965–66; Press Council, 1975–81; External Mem., Council of Lloyd's, 1982–90. Dep. Chm., Bd of Governors, English-Speaking Union, 1976–83; Chm., Youth Business Initiative, subseq. The Prince's Youth Business Trust, 1982–87. Dir, Windsor Fest., 1983–; Trustee, Duke of Edinburgh's Award, 1978–84; Member Council: Royal Jubilee Trusts, 1981–87; Zoological Soc., 1990–91. Governor, Benenden Sch., 1976–86. Freeman, City of London, 1981. Hon. FTCL. *Address:* 25 Launceston Place, W8 5RN. *Clubs:* Athenæum, Beefsteak, MCC.

COPLAND, Rev. Canon Charles McAlester; *b* 5 April 1910; *s* of Canon Alexander Copland and of Violet Williamina Somerville McAlester; *m* 1946, Gwendoline Lorimer Williamson; two *d. Educ:* Forfar Academy; Denstone Coll.; Corpus Christi Coll., Cambridge (MA); Cuddesdon College. Reserve of Officers, 1933–38. Curate, Peterborough Parish Church, 1934–38; Mission Priest, Chanda, CP, India, 1938–53 (Head of Mission, 1942–53); Canon of Nagpur, 1952; Rector, St Mary's, Arbroath, 1953–59; Canon of Dundee, 1953; Provost of St John's Cathedral, Oban, 1959–79, also Dean of Diocese of Argyll and The Isles, 1977–79; Hon. Canon of Oban, 1979. *Publication:* Chanda: history of a mission, 1988. *Recreations:* formerly Rugby football, athletics; rifle shooting (shot for Cambridge, for Scotland 1932–84). *Address:* Fir Cottage, South Crieff Road, Comrie, Perthshire PH6 2HF. *T:* Comrie (0764) 70185.

COPLESTON, Ernest Reginald, CB 1954; Secretary, Committee of Enquiry into the Governance of the University of London, 1970–72; *b* 16 Nov. 1909; *s* of F. S. Copleston, former Chief Judge of Lower Burma; *m* Olivia Green. *Educ:* Marlborough Coll.; Balliol Coll., Oxford. Inland Revenue Dept, 1932; Treasury, 1942; Under-Sec., 1950; Dep. Sec., 1957–63, Sec., 1963–69, UGC; retired. *Address:* Arden, Bears Lane, Lavenham, Suffolk CO10 9RT. *T:* Lavenham (0787) 247470.

COPLESTON, Rev. Frederick Charles, SJ; MA Oxon, DPhil Rome, Gregorian Univ.; FBA 1970; Principal of Heythrop College, University of London, 1970–74; Emeritus Professor of University of London, 1974; Dean, Faculty of Theology, 1972–74; *b* 10 April 1907; *s* of F. S. Copleston, former Chief Judge of Lower Burma, and N. M. Little. *Educ:* Marlborough Coll.; St John's Coll., Oxford (Hon. Fellow, 1975). Entered Catholic Church, 1925; Soc. of Jesus, 1930; ordained 1937. Prof. of History of Philosophy: Heythrop Coll., Oxford, 1939–70, and Univ. of London, 1972–74; Gregorian Univ., Rome, 1952–68; Dean of Faculty of Theology, Univ. of London, 1972–74; Visiting Professor: Univ. of Santa Clara, Calif., 1974–75 and 1977–82; Univ. of Hawaii, 1976; Gifford Lectr, Univ. of Aberdeen, 1979–80. Hon. Dr (Theology), Uppsala, Sweden, 1983; Hon. DLitt St Andrews, 1990. *Publications:* Friedrich Nietzsche, Philosopher of Culture, 1942, new edn 1975; St Thomas and Nietzsche, 1944; Arthur Schopenhauer, Philosopher of Pessimism, 1946; A History of Philosophy: vol. 1, Greece and Rome, 1946; revised 1947; vol. 2, Augustine to Scotus, 1950; vol. 3, Ockham to Suárez, 1953; vol. 4, Descartes to Leibniz, 1958; vol. 5, Hobbes to Hume, 1959; vol. 6, Wolff to Kant, 1960; vol. 7, Fichte to Nietzsche, 1963; vol. 8, Bentham to Russell, 1966; vol. 9, Maine de Biran to Sartre, 1975); Medieval Philosophy, 1952; Existentialism and Modern Man, 1948; Aquinas (Pelican), 1955; Contemporary Philosophy, 1956, rev. edn 1972; A History of Medieval Philosophy, 1972; Religion and Philosophy, 1974; Philosophers and Philosophies, 1976; On the History of Philosophy, 1979; Philosophies and Cultures, 1980; Religion and the One, 1982; Philosophy in Russia, 1986; Russian Religious Philosophy, 1988; articles in learned journals. *Address:* 114 Mount Street, W1Y 6AH. *T:* 071-493 7811.

COPLESTONE-BOUGHEY, His Honour John Fenton; a Circuit Judge (formerly Judge of the County Courts), 1969–85; *b* 5 Feb. 1912; *o s* of late Comdr A. F. Coplestone-Boughey, RN; *m* 1944, Gilian Beatrice, *e d* of late H. A. Counsell, Appleby; one *s* one *d. Educ:* Shrewsbury School; Brasenose Coll., Oxford (Open Exhibitioner, Matthew Arnold Prizeman). Inner Temple, Entrance Scholar 1934, Barrister 1935. Legal Assistant, Min. of Health, 1937–40. Royal Artillery, 1940–46; Advanced Class, Military Coll. of Science, 1945. Chester Chronicle & Associated Newspapers, Ltd: Dir, 1947–56; Dep. Chm., 1956–65. Chairman, Nat. Insurance Tribunals (SW London), 1951–69; Referee, Nat. Service and Family Allowances Acts, 1957–69. Battersea etc Hospital Management Cttee: Member 1960–69, Chairman 1969–74; Mem., Wandsworth etc AHA, 1973–82. Chm., Chelsea Housing Improvement Soc., 1981–84. Governor, St Thomas' Hosp., 1971–74; Special Trustee, St George's Hospital, 1974–, Chm. of Trustees 1980–84. Mem. Council, Queen's Coll., London, 1976–, Vice-Chm. 1979–84, Chm. 1984–. *Publications:* contrib. to Halsbury's Laws of England. *Recreations:* walking, travel. *Address:* 82 Oakley Street, SW3 5NP. *T:* 071-352 6287. *Club:* Athenæum.

COPLEY, John (Michael Harold); opera director; *b* 12 June, 1933; *s* of Ernest Harold Copley and Lilian Forbes. *Educ:* King Edward's, Five Ways, Birmingham; Sadler's Wells Ballet Sch.; Central Sch. of Arts and Crafts, London (Dip. with Hons in Theatre Design). Appeared as the apprentice in Britten's Peter Grimes for Covent Garden Opera Co, 1950; stage managed: both opera and ballet companies at Sadler's Wells, in Rosebery Avenue, 1953–57; also various musicals, plays, etc, in London's West End, incl. The World of Paul Slickey and My Fair Lady. Joined Covent Garden Opera Co.: Dep. Stage Manager, 1960; Asst Resident Producer, 1963; Associate Resident Producer, 1966; Resident Producer, 1972; Prin. Resident Producer, 1975–88. *Productions include:* at Covent Garden: Suor Angelica, 1965; Cosi fan Tutte, 1968, 1981; Orpheo ed Euridice, 1969; Le Nozze di Figaro, 1971, 1985; Don Giovanni, 1973; La Bohème, 1974, 1985; Faust, 1974; L'elisir d'amore, 1975, 1981, 1985; Benvenuto Cellini, 1976; Ariadne auf Naxos, 1976; Maria Stuarda; Royal Silver Jubilee Gala, 1977; Werther, 1979; La Traviata, Lucrezia Borgia, 1980; Alceste, 1981; Semele, 1982, 1988; Norma, 1987; *at London Coliseum (for Sadler's Wells, subseq. ENO):* Carmen, Il Seraglio, Il Trovatore, La Traviata, Mary Stuart; Rosenkavalier, La Belle Hélène, 1975; Werther, 1977; Manon, Aida, Julius Caesar, Les Mamelles de Tirésias, 1979; *Athens Festival:* Macbeth; *Netherlands Opera:* Lucia; *Opera National de Belge:* Lucia; Hansel and Gretel, 1991; *Wexford Festival:* La Clemenza di Tito; L'Infedelta delusa; *Dallas Civic Opera, Texas:* Lucia; *Chicago Lyric Opera:* Lucia; La Bohème, 1983; Orlando, 1986; Tancredi, 1989; The Barber of Seville, 1989; *Canadian Opera, Toronto:* Lucia; Falstaff; La Bohème, 1984; Adriana Lecouvreur, La Forza del Destino, 1987; *Greek Nat. Opera:* Madame Butterfly; Otello; *Australian Opera:* Fidelio, Nozze di Figaro, Rigoletto, Magic Flute, Jenufa, Ariadne auf Naxos, Madame Butterfly, Fra Diavolo, Macbeth, La Traviata, Manon Lescaut, Lucia di Lammermoor, Tosca, Manon; Adriana Lecouvreur, 1984; Peter Grimes, 1986; Carmen, 1987; La Forza del Destino, 1988; *Victoria State Opera:* Don Carlos, 1984; La Bohème, 1985; *WNO:* La Traviata, Falstaff, Peter Grimes, Tosca; Peter Grimes, 1983; *Opera North:* Les Mamelles de Tirésias, Madama Butterfly; *Scottish Opera:* Lucia, Ballo in Maschera, Dido and Aeneas; Acis and Galatea for English Opera Group in Stockholm, Paris, Aldeburgh Fest.; *New York City Opera:* Le Nozze di Figaro; Der Freischutz; Don Quichotte; *Santa Fé Opera:* Ariodanie, 1987; Così fan tutte, 1988; Der Rosenkavalier, La Traviata, 1989; La Bohème, 1990; *Ottawa Festival:* Midsummer Night's Dream; Eugene Onegin, 1983; *Vancouver Opera:* Carmen; *San Francisco Opera:* Julius Caesar; The Midsummer Marriage, 1983; Don Giovanni, 1984; Orlando, 1985; Le Nozze di Figaro, Eugene Onegin, 1986; La Traviata, 1987; Idomeneo, 1989; *San Diego Opera:* Eugene Onegin, 1985; Le Nozze di Figaro, 1986; Così fan tutte, 1991; *Staatsoper Munich:* Adriana Lecouvreur, 1984; *Deutsche Opera, Berlin:* L'Elisir d'amore, 1988; *Metropolitan Opera, NY:* Julius Caesar, 1988, Semiramide, 1990. Sang as soloist in Bach's St John Passion, Bremen, Germany, 1965; appeared as Ferdy in John Osborne's play, A Patriot for Me, at Royal Court Theatre, 1965. Co-directed (with Patrick Garland): Fanfare for Europe Gala, Covent Garden, 3 Jan. 1973; Fanfare for Elizabeth gala, Covent Garden, 21 April 1986. *Recreation:* cooking. *Address:* 9D Thistle Grove, SW10 9RR.

COPP, Darrell John Barkwell, OBE 1981; General Secretary, Institute of Biology, 1951–82; *b* 25 April 1922; *s* of J. J. H. Copp and L. A. Hoad; *m* 1944, Margaret Henderson; two *s* one *d. Educ:* Taunton's Sch., Southampton; Southampton Univ. (BSc). Scientific Officer, Admty Signals Estabt, 1942–45; Asst Sec., British Assoc. for Advancement of Science, 1947–51. Sec., Council for Nature, 1958–63; originator and co-ordinator of first National Nature Week, 1963. Hon. Treas., Parly and Scientific Cttee, 1980–83; Sec., European Community Biologists' Assoc., 1975–85. Trustee, Rye Art Gall., 1985–90. Hon. MTech Bradford, 1975; Hon. FIBiol 1984. *Publications:* reports and reviews in scientific jls. *Recreations:* mountain walking, renovating country cottages. *Address:* Underhill Farmhouse, Wittersham, Tenterden, Kent TN30 7EU. *T:* Wittersham (0797) 270633.

COPP, Prof. (Douglas) Harold, CC 1980 (OC 1971); MD, PhD; FRS 1971; FRSC; FRCP(C); Professor of Physiology, University of British Columbia, Canada, since 1950;

b 16 Jan. 1915; *s* of Charles J. Copp and Edith M. O'Hara; *m* 1939, Winnifred A. Thompson; three *d*. *Educ:* Univ. of Toronto, Canada (BA, MD); Univ. of California, Berkeley, Calif (PhD); British Columbia College of Physicians and Surgeons (Lic.). Asst Prof. of Physiology, Calif, 1945–50. Co-ordinator, Health Scis, Univ. of British Columbia, 1976–77; Head of Dept of Physiology, Univ. of British Columbia, 1950–80. FRSC 1959 (Mem. Council, 1973–75, 1977–; Vice-Pres., and Pres. Academy of Science, 1978–81); FRCP(C) 1974. Hon. LLD: Queen's Univ., Kingston, Ont, 1970; Univ. of Toronto, 1970; Hon. DSc: Univ. of Ottawa, 1973; Acadia Univ., 1975; Univ. of British Columbia, 1980. Discovered calcitonin (ultimobranchial hormone) and stanniocalcin (corpuscles of Stannius). *Recreation:* gardening. *Address:* 4755 Belmont Avenue, Vancouver, British Columbia V6T 1A8, Canada. *T:* 604–224–3793.

COPPEN, Dr Alec James, MD, DSc; FRCP, FRCPsych; Director, Medical Research Council Neuropsychiatry Laboratory, and Emeritus Consultant Psychiatrist, West Park Hospital, Epsom, Surrey, since 1974; *b* 29 Jan. 1923; *y s* of late Herbert John Wardle Coppen and Marguerite Mary Annie Coppen; *m* 1952, Gunhild Margareta, *y d* of late Albert and Sigrid Andersson, Båstad, Sweden; one *s*. *Educ:* Dulwich Coll.; Univ. of Bristol (MB, ChB 1953; MD 1958; DSc 1978); Maudsley Hosp.; Univ. of London (DPM 1957); MRCP 1975, FRCP 1980, FRCPsych 1971. Registrar, then Sen. Registrar, Maudsley Hosp., 1954–59; MRC Neuropsychiatry Research Unit, 1959–74, MRC External Staff, 1974–; Consultant Psychiatrist: St Ebba's Hosp., 1959–64; West Park Hosp., 1964–; Hon. Cons. Psychiatrist, St George's Hosp., 1965–70. Head of WHO designated Centre for Biological Psychiatry in UK, 1974–; Consultant, WHO, 1977–; Examiner, Royal Coll. of Psychiatry, 1973–77; Andrew Woods Vis. Prof., Univ. of Iowa, 1981; Lectr to learned socs and univs in Europe, N and S America, Asia and Africa. Mem. Council, RMPA (Chm., Research and Clinical Section), 1965–70; Chairman, Biolog. Psychiatry Section, World Psychiatric Assoc., 1972; President, British Assoc. of Psychopharmacology, 1975; Member: Internat. Coll. Neuropsychopharm., 1960– (Mem. Council, 1979; Pres., 1988–90); RSM, 1960–; British Pharmacol. Soc., 1977–; Special Health Auth., Bethlem Royal and Maudsley Hosp., 1982–; Hon. Member: Mexican Soc. for Biolog. Psychiatry, 1973–; Mexican Inst. of Culture, 1974–; Swedish Psychiatric Assoc., 1977–; European Collegium Neuro-Psychipharmacolgicum, 1987–; Corresponding Member: Amer. Coll. of Neuropsychopharm., 1977–; Deutsche Gesellschaft für Psychiatrie und Nervenheilkunde; Distinguished Fellow, APA, 1981. Freeman, City of London, 1980; Soc. of Apothecaries: Yeoman, 1980; Liveryman 1985. Anna Monika Prize, 1969. *Publications:* (jtly) Recent Developments in Schizophrenia, 1967; (jtly) Recent Developments in Affective Disorders, 1968; (jtly) Psychopharmacology of Affective Disorders, 1979; contribs to text books; papers in Nature, Lancet, BMJ, etc (Current Contents Citation Classic, 1978, Biochemistry of the Affective Disorders). *Recreations:* golf, opera. *Address:* 5 Walnut Close, Epsom, Surrey KT18 5JL. *T:* Epsom (03727) 20800. *Clubs:* Athenæum, Royal Automobile.

COPPLESTONE, Frank Henry; Managing Director, Southern Television Ltd, 1976–88; Director, Westcountry Television Ltd; *b* 26 Feb. 1925; 2nd *s* of late Rev. Frank T. Copplestone; *m* 1st, 1950, Margaret Mary (*d* 1973), *d* of late Edward Walker; three *s*; 2nd, 1977, Penny Perrick (marr. diss. 1988); one step *s* one step *d*; 3rd, 1989, Fenella, *widow* of Prof. Gamini Salgado; one step *s* one step *d*. *Educ:* Truro Sch.; Nottingham Univ. (BA). Royal Horse Artillery, 1943–47. Pres., Univ. of Nottingham Union, 1952–53; Pres., Nat. Union of Students, 1954–56; Internat. Research Fellow, 1956–58; Regional Officer, Independent Television Authority, 1958–62; Head of Regional Services, ITA, 1962–63; Head of Programme Services, ITA, 1963–67; Controller, ITV Network Programme Secretariat, 1967–73; Dir, ITV Programme Planning Secretariat, 1973–75; Director: Independent Television News Ltd, 1977–81; Independent Television Publications Ltd, 1976–81. Mem., Broadcasters' Audience Res. Bd, 1981. *Recreations:* sailing, reading, music. *Address:* Pen an Mor, 39 Esplanade, Fowey, Cornwall PL23 1HY. *T:* Fowey (0726) 832818; Flat 1A, Fraser House, 190 Cromwell Road, SW5 0SL. *T:* 071–373 8631. *Clubs:* Reform; Royal Fowey Yacht, Fowey Gallants Sailing.

COPPOCK, Surgeon Rear-Adm. (D) David Arthur, CB 1990; Director, Defence Dental Services, 1988–90; *b* 19 April 1931; *s* of Oswald John Coppock and Ada Katherine Beaven; *m* 1956, Maria Averil Ferreira (*d* 1985); two *d*; *m* 1990, Sally Annette Arnold. *Educ:* Bishop Wordsworth School; Guy's Hosp. (BDS); George Washington Univ. (MSc). Entered RN 1955; HM Ships Eagle, 1956, Tamar, Hong Kong, 1959, Hermes, 1963, Rooke, Gibraltar, 1965; US Navy exchange, 1972; Dep. Dir, Naval Dental Services, 1980; Comd Dental Surgeon to C-in-C Naval Home Command, 1983. QHDS. OStJ. *Recreations:* fishing, tennis, golf. *Address:* Breamore Lodge, West Street, Hambledon, Hants PO7 4RW. *T:* Hambledon (070132) 566. *Club:* Royal Society of Medicine.

COPPOCK, Prof. John Terence, (Terry), CBE 1987; FBA 1975; FRSE 1976; Secretary and Treasurer, Carnegie Trust for the Universities of Scotland, since 1986; *b* 2 June 1921; *s* of late Arthur Coppock and late Valerie Margaret Coppock (*née* Phillips); *m* 1953, Sheila Mary Burnett (*d* 1990); one *s* one *d*. *Educ:* Penarth County Sch.; Queens' Coll., Cambridge. MA (Cantab); PhD (London). Civil Servant: Lord Chancellor's Dept, Min. of Works, Board of Customs and Excise, 1938–47. Served War, Army (commissioned Welch Regt, 1941), 1939–46. Cambridge Univ., 1947–50. University Coll. London (Dept of Geography): successively, Asst Lecturer, Lecturer, Reader, 1950–65, Fellow, 1987; Ogilvie Prof. of Geography, Univ. of Edinburgh, 1965–86, Professor Emeritus, 1987–. Visiting Professor: Loughborough Univ., 1986–89; Birkbeck Coll., London, 1986–. Chm., British Acad./British Lity review panel on information needs in the humanities, 1990. Member: Scottish Sports Council, 1976–87; Ordnance Survey Rev. Cttee, 1978–79. FRSA 1980; FRSGS 1988. Ed., Internat. Jl of Geographical Information Systems, 1986–. *Publications:* The Changing Use of Land in Britain (with R. H. Best), 1962; An Agricultural Atlas of England and Wales, 1964, 2nd edn 1976; Greater London (ed, with H. C. Prince), 1964; An Agricultural Geography of Great Britain, 1971; Recreation in the Countryside: a Spatial Analysis (with B. S. Duffield), 1975; Spatial Dimensions of Public Policy (ed, with W. R. D. Sewell), 1976; An Agricultural Atlas of Scotland, 1976; Second Homes: Curse or Blessing? (ed), 1977; Public Participation in Planning (ed, with W. R. D. Sewell), 1977; Land Use and Town and Country Planning (with L. F. Gebbett), 1978; Land Assessment in Scotland (ed, with M. F. Thomas), 1980; Agriculture in Developed Countries, 1984; Innovation in Water Management (with W. R. D. Sewell and A. Pitkethly), 1986; Geography, Planning and Policy Making (ed, with P. T. Kivell), 1986; numerous papers: mainly in geographical, but also historical, planning and agricultural periodicals, mainly on theme of rural land use in Great Britain. *Recreations:* listening to music, natural history. *Address:* 57 Braid Avenue, Edinburgh EH10 6EB. *T:* 031–447 3443.

COPPOLA, Francis Ford; Artistic Director, Zoetrope Studios, since 1969; *b* 7 April 1939; *s* of late Carmine Coppola and of Italia Pennino; *m* 1963, Eleanor Neil; one *s* one *d* (and one *s* decd). *Educ:* Hofstra Univ. (BA); Univ. of Calif, LA (MFA). Films directed: Dementia 13, 1963; You're a Big Boy Now, 1967; Finian's Rainbow, 1968; The Rain People, 1969; The Godfather, 1972; The Conversation, 1974; The Godfather Part II, 1974; Apocalypse Now, 1979; One From the Heart, 1981; The Outsiders, 1983; Rumble Fish, 1983; The Cotton Club, 1984; Peggy Sue Got Married, 1987; Gardens of Stone, 1988; Tucker: The Man and his Dream, 1988; New York Stories (Life Without Zoe), 1989; The Godfather Part III, 1991. Commandeur, Ordre des Arts et des Lettres, 1983. *Recreations:* reading, writing, scientific discovery. *Address:* Zoetrope Studios, 916 Kearny Street, San Francisco, Calif 94133, USA. *T:* (415) 788-7500.

CORBEN, Albert Edward; Assistant Under Secretary of State, Radio Regulatory Department, Home Office (and subsequently with Department of Trade and Industry), 1980–83, retired; *b* 25 Nov. 1923; *s* of Ebenezer Joseph James Corben and Frances Flora (*née* Orchard); *m* 1953, Doris Dodd; two *s*. *Educ:* Portsmouth Grammar Sch.; Sir John Cass Technical Inst. Served Royal Artillery, 1943–47. Entered Home Office, as Executive Officer, 1947; Higher Executive Officer, 1955–62; Sen. Executive Officer, 1962–66; Principal, 1966–72; Secretary to Advisory Council on Penal System, 1966–68; Sen. Principal, 1972–73; Asst Sec., 1973–80. *Recreations:* swimming, golf, walking. *Address:* The Gables, 30 Kingswood Road, Bromley, Kent BR2 0NF. *T:* 081–460 4106.

CORBET, Mrs Freda (Kunzlen), (Mrs Ian McIvor Campbell), BA; JP; *b* 1900; *d* of James Mansell; *m* 1925, William Corbet (*d* 1957); *m* 1962, Ian McIvor Campbell (*d* 1976). *Educ:* Wimbledon County Sch.; University Coll., London. Called to Bar, Inner Temple, 1932. MP (Lab) NW Camberwell, later Peckham Div. of Camberwell, 1945–Feb. 1974. Awarded Freedom of Southwark, 1974. JP, Co. London, 1940. *Address:* 39 Gravel Road, Bromley, Kent.

CORBET, Dr Gordon Barclay; zoologist; *b* 4 March 1933; *s* of George and Mary Corbet; *m* 1959, Elizabeth Urquhart; one *s* one *d*. *Educ:* Morgan Acad., Dundee; Univ. of St Andrews. BSc, PhD. Asst Lectr in Biology, Sir John Cass Coll., London, 1958–59; British Museum (Natural History): Sen., later Principal, Scientific Officer, Dept of Zoology, 1960–71; Dep. Keeper of Zoology, 1971–76; Hd, Dept of Central Services, 1976–88. *Publications:* The Terrestrial Mammals of Western Europe, 1966; Finding and Identifying Mammals in Britain, 1975; The Handbook of British Mammals (with H. N. Southern), 1977, 3rd edn 1991; The Mammals of the Palaearctic Region, 1978; The Mammals of Britain and Europe, 1980; A World List of Mammalian Species (with J. E. Hill), 1980, 3rd edn 1991. *Recreations:* bird-watching, walking. *Address:* 27 Farnaby Road, Bromley, Kent BR1 4BL. *T:* 081–460 2439.

CORBET, Lieut-Col Sir John (Vincent), 7th Bt, *cr* 1808; MBE 1946; DL; JP; RE (retired); *b* 27 Feb. 1911; *s* of Archer Henry Corbet (*d* 1950) and Anne Maria (*d* 1951), *d* of late German Buxton; *S* kinsman, Sir Gerald Vincent Corbet, 6th Bt, 1955; *m* 1st, 1937, Elfrida Isobel Francis; 2nd, 1948, Doreen Elizabeth Stewart (*d* 1964), *d* of Arthur William Gibbon Ritchie; 3rd, 1965, Annie Elizabeth Lorimer, MBE, MSc, Dunedin, NZ. *Educ:* Shrewsbury Sch.; RMA; Magdalene Coll., Cambridge. BA 1933, MA 1972. 2nd Lieut, RE, 1931; served North-West Frontier, India, 1935, and War of 1939–45 in India, Burma and Malaya (despatches, MBE); Lieut-Col, 1953; retd 1955. DL County of Salop, 1961; JP 1957; High Sheriff of Salop, 1966; CC Salop, 1963–81. OStJ; Mem., Church Assembly, later General Synod, 1960–75; former Chm., Board of Visitors, Stoke Heath Borstal. *Address:* Acton Reynald, near Shrewsbury, Salop SY4 4DS. *T:* Clive (093928) 259. *Club:* Royal Thames Yacht.

CORBETT, family name of **Baron Rowallan.**

CORBETT, Rev. Canon Charles Eric. *Educ:* Jesus College, Oxford (BA 1939, MA 1943); Wycliffe Hall, Oxford. Deacon 1940, priest 1941, St Asaph; Curate of Gresford, 1940–44; CF, 1944–47; Curate of Eglwys-Rhos, 1947–49; Rector of Harpurhey, 1949–54; Vicar of St Catherine's, Wigan, 1954–61; Vicar of St Luke, Farnworth, 1961–71; Rural Dean of Farnworth, 1964–71; Archdeacon of Liverpool, 1971–79; Canon-Treasurer of Liverpool Cathedral, 1979–83. *Address:* 80 Latham Avenue, Helsby, Cheshire WA6 0EB. *T:* Helsby (09282) 724184.

CORBETT, Captain Hugh Askew, CBE 1968; DSO 1945; DSC 1943; RN; (Retired); *b* 25 June 1916; *s* of late Rev. F. St John Corbett, MA, FRSL, FRHistS and late Elsie L. V. Askew; *m* 1945, Patricia Nancy, *d* of late Thomas Patrick Spens, OBE, MC, LLD; three *s*. *Educ:* St Edmund's Sch., Canterbury. Joined Royal Navy, 1933; HMS Cæsar as Capt. (D), 8th Destroyer Sqdn, 1961–63; HMS Fearless, 1965–67 (Capt.). *Address:* Holly Cottage, 3 Clare Road, Cambridge. *T:* Cambridge (0223) 357735.

CORBETT, Prof. John Patrick, MA; Professor of Philosophy, University of Bradford, 1972–76; *b* 5 March 1916; *s* of E. S. H. and K. F. Corbett; *m* 1st, 1940, Nina Angeloni; two *s*; 2nd, 1968, Jan Adams; two *d*. *Educ:* RNC, Dartmouth; Magdalen Coll., Oxford. Lieut, RA, 1940; POW in Germany, 1940–45. Fellow of Balliol, 1945–61; Prof. of Philosophy, Univ. of Sussex, 1961–72; Jowett Lectr in Philosophy. Council of Europe Fellow, 1957; Visiting Lectr, Yale Univ., 1958; NATO Fellow, 1960; Vis. Prof., Univ. of Toronto, 1968. *Publications:* Europe and the Social Order, 1959; Ideologies, 1965. *Address:* Kalokhorio, Limassol, Cyprus.

CORBETT, Michael McGregor; Hon. Mr Justice Corbett; Chief Justice of South Africa, since 1989; *b* 14 Sept. 1923; *s* of Alan Frederick Corbett and Johanna Sibella McGregor; *m* 1949, Margaret Murray Corbett (*née* Luscombe); two *s* two *d*. *Educ:* Rondebosch Boys' High Sch.; Univ. of Cape Town (BA, LLB); Trinity Hall, Cambridge (Elsie Ballot Scholarship, 1946; Law Tripos 1st cl. 1947; LLB 1st cl. 1948). Enlisted S African Tank Corps, 1942, commissioned 1943; active service, Egypt and Italy with Royal Natal Carbineers, 1943–44. Admitted Advocate, Cape Bar, 1948; QC 1961; Judge, Cape Provincial Div., Supreme Court, 1963; Judge of Appeal, 1974. Hon. Bencher, Lincoln's Inn, 1991. Hon. LLD: Cape Town, 1982; Orange Free State, 1990; Rhodes, 1990. *Publications:* (jtly) The Quantum of Damages in Bodily and Fatal Injury Cases, 1960, 3rd edn 1985; (jtly) The Law of Succession in South Africa, 1980. *Recreations:* tennis, walking. *Address:* 18 Ladies Mile Extension, Constantia, Cape 7800, South Africa. *Clubs:* City and Civil Service (Cape Town); Kelvin Grove (Newlands, Cape).

CORBETT, Prof. Peter Edgar; Yates Professor of Classical Art and Archaeology in the University of London (University College), 1961–82, now Professor Emeritus; *b* 19 June 1920; 2nd *s* of Ernest Oliver Corbett and Margaret Edgar. *Educ:* Bedford Sch.; St John's Coll., Oxford. Royal Artillery, 1940–41, RAFVR, 1942–45. Thomas Whitcombe Greene Scholar, and Macmillan Student of British School at Athens, 1947–49; Asst Keeper in Dept of Greek and Roman Antiquities, British Museum, 1949–61. Lectr in Classics, Univ. of Calif, Los Angeles, 1956. Pres., Soc. for Promotion of Hellenic Studies, 1980–83. *Publications:* The Sculpture of the Parthenon, 1959; (with A. Birchall) Greek Gods and Heroes, 1974; articles in Jl of Hellenic Studies, Hesperia, Annual of Brit. School at Athens, BM Quarterly, Bulletin of the Inst. of Classical Studies. *Address:* 30 The Terrace, Barnes, SW13 0NR.

CORBETT, Maj.-Gen. Robert John Swan, CB 1991; General Officer Commanding London District and Major-General Commanding Household Division, since 1991; *b* 16 May 1940; *s* of Robert Hugh Swan Corbett and Pearl Patricia Elizabeth Corbett (*née* Cavan-Lambart); *m* 1966, Susan Margaret Anne O'Cock; three *s*. *Educ:* Woodcote House; Shrewsbury School; Army Staff Coll., 1973; US Armed Forces Staff Coll., 1980.

Commissioned Irish Guards, 1959; served UK, Cyprus, Hong Kong, BAOR; Brigade Major, HQ Household Div., 1980–81; CO, 1st Bn Irish Guards (4 Armoured Brigade, BAOR), 1981–84; Chief of Staff, British Forces Falkland Is, 1984–85; Comdr, 5th Airborne Brigade, 1985–87; Mem., RCDS, 1987; Dir, Defence Programme, MoD, 1987–89; GOC Berlin (British Sector) and British Comdt, Berlin, 1989–90; attached HQ BAOR, 1990–91. Regtl Lt-Col, Irish Guards, 1988. *Recreations:* travel, reading, tennis, ski-ing, English church architecture. *Clubs:* Pratt's, Army and Navy.

CORBETT, Robin; MP (Lab) Birmingham, Erdington, since 1983; communication and public affairs consultant; *b* 22 Dec. 1933; *s* of Thomas Corbett and Marguerite Adele Mainwaring; *m* 1970, Val Hudson; one *d*. *Educ:* Holly Lodge Grammar Sch., Smethwick. Newspaper and magazine journalist, 1950–69; Editorial Staff Develt Exec., IPC Magazines, 1969–72; Sen. Lab. Adviser, IPC Magazines, 1972–74. Mem. Nat. Union of Journalists Nat. Exec. Council, 1965–69. MP (Lab) Hemel Hempstead, Oct. 1974–1979; opposition front bench spokesman on home affairs, 1985–. Chairman: PLP Agric. Gp, 1977–78; PLP Home Affairs Cttee, 1984–86; Sec., PLP Civil Liberties Gp, 1974–79; Member: Expenditure Cttee, 1976–79; Commons Home Affairs Cttee, 1984–86; PLP Campaign Unit, 1985–86; Vice Chm., All Party Animal Welfare Gp, 1976–79; Jt Sec., All Party Anzac Gp, 1985–; Jt Vice-Chm., All Party Motor Industry Gp, 1987–. Vice-Chm., Friends of Cyprus, 1987–. Mem., Food and Agriculture Sub-Cttee, Labour Party Nat. Exec. Cttee, 1974–79; Chm., farm animal welfare co-ordinating exec., 1977–. Member, Council: RCVS, 1989–; SCF, 1987–90; sponsor, Terrence Higgins Trust, 1987–. Fellow, Industry and Parlt Trust, 1979. *Publications:* (jtly) Can I Count on your Support?, 1986; On the Campaign Trail, 1987. *Recreations:* visiting North Wales; pottering. *Address:* House of Commons, SW1A 0AA. *Clubs:* Castle Vale Residents Association; Forget-Me-Not (Erdington).

CORBETT, Ronald Balfour, OBE 1978; comedian/character actor; *b* 4 Dec. 1930; *s* of William Balfour Corbett and Anne Elizabeth Corbett; *m* 1965, Anne Hart; two *d*. *Educ:* James Gillespie Sch., Edinburgh; Royal High Sch., Edinburgh. *Films:* Top of the Form; You're Only Young Once; Casino Royale, 1966; No Sex Please, We're British, 1974; *television:* Frost Report, 1966–67; Frost on Sunday, 1968–69; The Two Ronnies (12 in series), 1971–85; The Two Ronnies Christmas Special, 1982, 1987; Variety Specials, 1977; Sorry! (8 in series), 1981–; *theatre:* Twang (Lionel Bart musical), 1965; Cinderella, London Palladium, Christmas 1971–72; two seasons at London Palladium, 1978, 1983. *Publications:* Small Man's Guide to Life; Armchair Golf, 1986. *Recreations:* golf, racing, soccer, cooking. *Address:* Fairways, Shirley Church Road, Addington Park, Surrey. *Clubs:* Turf, Annabel's; Addington Golf (Surrey); Gullane Golf (East Lothian).

CORBETT, Lt-Col Uvedale, CBE 1984; DSO 1944; DL; *b* 12 Sept. 1909; *s* of Major C. U. Corbett, Stableford, Bridgnorth, Shropshire; *m* 1st, 1935, Veronica Marian Whitehead (marr. diss., 1952); two *s* one *d*; 2nd, 1953, Mrs Patricia Jane Walker (*d* 1985); 3rd, 1987, Mrs Peggy Roberts. *Educ:* Wellington (Berks); RMA, Woolwich. Commissioned Royal Artillery, 1929; relinquished command 3rd Regt RHA 1945; retired. MP (C) Ludlow Div. of Shropshire, 1945–51. Chm., Sun Valley Poultry Ltd, 1961–83. DL Hereford and Worcester, 1983. *Address:* Shobdon Court, Leominster, Herefordshire HR6 9LZ. *T:* Kingsland (056881) 260. *Club:* Army and Navy.

CORBIN, Maurice Haig Alleyne; Justice of Appeal, Supreme Court, Trinidad and Tobago, 1972–81; *b* 26 May 1916; *s* of L. A. Corbin; *m* 1943, Helen Jocelyn Child; one *s* two *d*; *m* 1968, Jean Barcant. *Educ:* Harrison Coll., Barbados; Queen's Royal Coll., Trinidad. Solicitor, 1941; appointed Magistrate, Trinidad, 1945; called to the Bar, Middle Temple, 1949; Crown Counsel, 1953; Registrar, Supreme Court, 1954; Puisne Judge, Supreme Court, 1957–72. *Recreation:* tennis. *Address:* 77 Brook Road, Goodwood Park, Trinidad. *Club:* Queen's Park Cricket (Port of Spain, Trinidad).

CORBY, Sir (Frederick) Brian, Kt 1989; FIA; Chairman, Prudential Corporation plc, since 1990; a Director, Bank of England, since 1985; *b* 10 May 1929; *s* of Charles Walter and Millicent Corby; *m* 1952, Elizabeth Mairi McInnes; one *s* two *d*. *Educ:* Kimbolton Sch.; St John's Coll., Cambridge (MA). Joined Prudential Assce Co. Ltd, 1952; Dep. Gen. Manager, 1974; Gen. Manager, 1976–79; Gp Gen. Manager, Prudential Corp. Ltd, 1979–82; Dir, 1981–89, Chief Gen. Manager, 1982–85, Chm., 1985–89, Prudential Assce Co. Ltd; Chief Exec., Prudential Corp., 1982–90. Dir, 1982–90, Chm., 1985–90, Mercantile & General Reinsce Co. Chm., South Bank Bd, 1990–. Vice-President, Inst. of Actuaries, 1979–82; Chm., Assoc. of British Insurers, 1985–87; Pres., CBI, 1990–May 1992. Hon. DSc City, 1989. *Publications:* contribs to Jl of Inst. of Actuaries. *Recreations:* reading, golf. *Address:* Prudential Corporation plc, 1 Stephen Street, W1P 2AP.

CORBY, George Arthur; international meteorological consultant; *b* 14 Aug. 1917; *s* of Bertie John Corby and Agnes May (*née* Dale); *m* 1951, Gertrude Anne Nicoll; one *s* one *d*. *Educ:* St Marylebone Grammar Sch.; Univ. of London (BSc Special Maths 1st Cl.). Architect's Dept. LCC, 1936–42; entered Met. Office, 1942; Flt Lt, RAFVR, 1943; Sqdn Leader, Dep. Chief Met. Officer, ACSEA, 1945–46; Sen. Met. Off., Northolt Airport, 1947–53; research, 1953–73; Dep. Dir for Communications and Computing, 1973–76; Dir of Services and Dep. Dir Gen., 1976–78. Vice-Pres., Royal Meteorol Soc., 1975–77. *Publications:* official scientific pubns and res. papers on mountain airflow, dynamical meteorol., and numerical forecasting. *Recreations:* music, photography, cross-country skiing. *Address:* Kings Barn, High Street, Harwell, Oxon OX11 0EY. *T:* Abingdon (0235) 832883.

CORBYN, Jeremy Bernard; MP (Lab) Islington North, since 1983; *b* 26 May 1949; *s* of David Benjamin Corbyn. *Educ:* Adams Grammar Sch., Newport, Shropshire. NUPE Official, 1975–83; sponsored NUPE MP. Mem., Haringey Borough Council, 1974– (Chm., Community Develt Cttee 1975–78, Public Works 1978–79, Planning Cttee 1980–81, 1982–83). Sec., PLP Latin America, Central America and Caribbean Group, 1984–; Vice-Chm., PLP Health Cttee, 1984–. Vice-Chair, London Gp of Lab MPs, 1985; Secretary: Campaign for Non-alignment, 1986; Campaign Gp of Lab MPs, 1987. Vice-Chm., London Labour Party. *Address:* (office) 129 Seven Sisters Road, N7 7QG. *T:* 071–263 9450; House of Commons, SW1A 0AA. *T:* 071–219 3545.

CORCORAN, Hon. James Desmond, AO 1982; MP (Labor) Hartley, South Australia, 1977–82; *b* 8 Nov. 1928; *s* of James and Catherine Corcoran; *m* 1957, Carmel Mary Campbell; four *s* four *d*. *Educ:* Tantanoola Public School. Enlisted Australian Regular Army, 1950; served Korea, Japan, Malaya and New Guinea (despatches twice); discharged, rank of Captain, 1962. Entered politics, contested and won House of Assembly seat of Millicent, S Aust. Parliament, 1962, Member for Coles, 1975; held portfolios of Minister of Lands, Irrigation, Repatriation, Immigration and Tourism, in Labor Govt, 1965–68; Dep. Leader of Opposition, 1968–70; Dep. Premier, Minister of Works and Minister of Marine, 1970–77, additionally Minister of Environment, 1977–79; Premier, Treasurer, and Minister of Ethnic Affairs, of S Australia, Feb.-Sept. 1979. *Address:* 1 Aringa Court, Rostrevor, SA 5073, Australia.

CORDEIRO, His Eminence Cardinal Joseph; *see* Karachi, Archbishop of, (RC).

CORDEROY, Rev. Graham Thomas; Minister, Hutton and Shenfield Union Church, since 1987; *b* 15 April 1931; *s* of Thomas and Gladys Corderoy; *m* 1957, Edna Marian Barnes; six *d*. *Educ:* Emanuel Sch., London; Manchester Univ. (BA Theology 1957). Ordained 1957; King's Lynn, 1957–62; commissioned RAF Chaplain, 1962; Principal Chaplain, Church of Scotland and Free Churches, and Hon. Chaplain to the Queen, 1984–87. Inst. of Alcohol Studies Bd, 1986–. *Recreations:* Rugby referee 1964–87; Gilbert and Sullivan buff. *Address:* San Michele, Friars Close, Shenfield, Essex CM15 8HX. *T:* Brentwood (0277) 211322. *Club:* Royal Air Force.

CORDINER, William Lawson; HM Diplomatic Service; High Commissioner, Kingdom of Tonga, and Consul for Pacific Islands under American sovereignty South of the Equator, since 1990; *b* 9 March 1935; *s* of late Alexander Lamb Cordiner and Jessie Cordiner; *m* 1958, Anne Milton; one *s*. *Educ:* Peterhead Acad.; Boroughmuir, Edinburgh. Inland Revenue, 1952–60; E African Common Services Orgn, 1960–67; HM Diplomatic Service: London, 1967–68; Saigon, 1968–70; Addis Ababa, 1971–74; Kuwait, 1974–75; Baghdad, 1975–77; on secondment to Export Div., DHSS, 1977–79; Rhodesia Dept, FCO, 1979–80; Govt Rep., Antigua and Barbuda, and St Kitts Nevis, 1980–83; Consul for Pacific NW of USA, Seattle, 1983–87; Asst, Commonwealth Co-ordination Dept, FCO, 1988–90. British Delegn Sec., Commonwealth Heads of Govt Meeting, Kuala Lumpur, 1989. Hon. Citizen of Washington State, 1987; Hon. Ambassador of Goodwill, Washington State, 1987. *Recreations:* golf, gardening, oil painting, travel, music. *Address:* c/o Foreign and Commonwealth Office, King Charles Street, SW1. *Club:* Commonwealth Trust.

CORDINGLEY, Maj-Gen. John Edward, OBE 1959; *b* 1 Sept. 1916; *s* of Air Vice-Marshal Sir John Cordingley, KCB, KCVO, CBE, and late Elizabeth Ruth Carpenter; *m* 1st, 1940, Ruth Pamela (marr. diss. 1961), *d* of late Major S. A. Boddam-Whetham; two *s*; 2nd, 1961, Audrey Helen Anne, *d* of late Maj-Gen. F. G. Beaumont-Nesbitt, CVO, CBE, MC; two step *d*. *Educ:* Sherborne; RMA, Woolwich. 2nd Lieut RA, 1936; served War of 1939–45, Europe and India. Brigade Comdr, 1961–62; Imperial Defence Coll., 1963; Dir of Work Study, Min. of Defence (Army), 1964–66; Dep. Dir, RA, 1967–68; Maj-Gen., RA, BAOR, 1968–71, retired. Controller, Royal Artillery Instn, 1975–82; Chm. Bd of Management, RA Charitable Fund, 1977–82. Col Comdt, RA, 1973–82. Bursar, Sherborne Sch., 1971–74; Chm., J. W. Carpenter Ltd, 1984–87. Fellow, Inst. of Work Study Practitioners, 1965; MBIM 1966; FInstD 1985. *Recreations:* golf and gardening. *Address:* Church Farm House, Rotherwick, Basingstoke, Hants RG27 9BG. *T:* Hook (025676) 2734. *Clubs:* Army and Navy; Senior Golfers.

CORDINGLY, David Michael Bradley, DPhil; Head of Exhibitions, National Maritime Museum, since 1988; *b* 5 Dec. 1938; *s* of late Rt Rev. Eric Cordingly, MBE, sometime Bishop of Thetford, and of Mary Mathews; *m* 1971, Shirley Elizabeth Robin; one *s* one *d*. *Educ:* Christ's Hosp., Horsham; Oriel Coll., Oxford; (MA); Univ. of Sussex (DPhil). Graphic designer, 1960–68; Exhibn designer at BM, 1968–71; Keeper of Art Gall., Royal Pavilion and Museums, Brighton, 1971–78; Asst Dir, Mus. of London, 1978–80; Asst Keeper, 1980–82, Dep. Keeper, 1982–86, Keeper of Pictures, 1986–88, Nat. Maritime Mus. FRSA 1974. Order of the White Rose of Finland, 1986. *Publications:* Marine Painting in England, 1974; Painters of the Sea, 1979; (with W. Percival Prescott) The Art of the Van de Veldes, 1982; Nicholas Pocock, 1986; Captain James Cook, Navigator, 1988; articles in Apollo, Connoisseur and Burlington Magazine. *Recreations:* sailing, carpentry. *Address:* National Maritime Museum, Greenwich, SE10 9NF. *T:* 081–858 4422.

CORDLE, John Howard; *b* 11 Oct. 1912; *s* of late Ernest William Cordle; *m* 1st, 1938 (marr. diss., 1956); three *s* (and one *s* one *d* decd); 2nd, 1957 (marr. diss. 1971), *e d* of Col A. Maynard, OBE; one *s* three *d*; 3rd, 1976, Terttu, *y d* of Mikko Heikura, Finland; two *s*. *Educ:* City of London Sch. Served RAF (commissioned), 1940–45. Man. Dir 1946–68, Chm. 1968–81, E. W. Cordle & Son Ltd. Proprietor, Church of England Newspaper, 1959–60, Dir, 1960–71. Member: Archbishops of Canterbury and York Commission on Evangelism, 1945–46; Church Assembly, 1946–53; Oxford Churches Patronage Trust, 1947– (Chm., 1955–); Ecclesiastical Cttee of H of C, 1975–77; Hon. Treas., The World's Evangelical Alliance, 1949–53. Lay-Reader, Rochester, 1940–. Mem. of Lloyd's, 1952. Freeman of City of London, 1956, and Mem., Founders' Livery Co. (Master, 1990–91). Prospective Parly Cand. (C) NE Wolverhampton, 1949; contested (C) Wrekin Div., 1951; MP (C) Bournemouth E and Christchurch, Oct. 1959–1974, Bournemouth E, 1974–77; Chairman: West Africa Cttee, Conservative Commonwealth Council, 1962–77; Church and Parliament All-Party Gp, 1975–77; Sec., All Party Anglo-Libyan Gp, H of C, 1964–67. Member UK Delegation to: Council of Europe, Strasbourg, 1974–77 (Vice-Chm., Parly and Public Relations Cttee, 1976–77); WEU, Paris, 1974–77; Rapporteur, 1976–77, to Cttee on Social and Health Questions, on the institution of Internat. Medical Card. Primrose League: Chm., Finance Cttee, 1964–67; Hon. Treas., 1964–67; Chm., Gen. Purposes Cttee, 1967–68. Chm., Wessex Aid to Addicts Gp, 1985–; Pres. Salisbury District Speech-impaired Children Trust, 1988–; Governor, London Coll. of Divinity, 1947–52; Life Governor: St Mary's and St Paul's Coll., Cheltenham; Epsom Coll.; Mem. Court of University of Southampton, 1960–77. Gold Staff Officer, Coronation, 1953. Grand Band, Order of the Star of Africa (Liberia), 1964. *Recreations:* shooting, golf, gardening. *Address:* Malmesbury House, The Close, Salisbury, Wilts. *Clubs:* Carlton, National (Trustee, 1946–), English-Speaking Union, Commonwealth Trust.

See also Viscount Cowdray.

CORDY, Timothy Soames; Chief Executive, Royal Society for Nature Conservation, since 1987; *b* 17 May 1949; *s* of John Knutt Cordy and Margaret Winifred Cordy (*née* Sheward); *m* 1974, Dr Jill Margaret Tattersall; one *s* one *d*. *Educ:* Dragon Sch., Oxford; Sherborne Sch.; Durham Univ. (BA); Glasgow Univ. (MPhil). MRTPI 1976. Leicester City Council, 1974–85 (Asst City Planning Officer, 1980–85); Communauté Urbaine de Strasbourg, 1978–79; Asst Chief Exec., Bolton MBC, 1985–87. Director: UK 2000, 1987–; Volunteer Centre UK, 1989–; Age Resource, 1991–. *Publications:* articles on housing renewal, local economic develt, Asian retailing. *Recreations:* music, France, food. *Address:* RSNC, The Green, Witham Park, Lincoln LN5 7JR. *T:* Lincoln (0522) 544400.

COREN, Alan; writer and broadcaster; *b* 27 June 1938; *s* of Samuel and Martha Coren; *m* 1963, Anne Kasriel; one *s* one *d*. *Educ:* East Barnet Grammar Sch.; Wadham Coll., Oxford (Open scholar; MA); Yale; Univ. of California, Berkeley. Asst Editor, Punch, 1963–66, Literary Editor 1966–69, Dep. Editor 1969–77, Editor, 1978–87; Editor, The Listener, 1988–89. TV Critic, The Times, 1971–78; Columnist: Daily Mail, 1972–76; Mail on Sunday, 1984–; The Times, 1988–; contributor to: Sunday Times, Atlantic Monthly, TLS, Observer, Tatler, London Review of Books. Commonwealth Fellowship, 1961–63. Rector, St Andrews Univ., 1973–76. *Publications:* The Dog It Was That Died, 1965; All Except the Bastard, 1969; The Sanity Inspector, 1974; The Bulletins of Idi Amin, 1974; Golfing For Cats, 1975; The Further Bulletins of Idi Amin, 1975; The Lady From Stalingrad Mansions, 1977; The Peanut Papers, 1977; The Rhinestone as Big as the Ritz, 1979; Tissues for Men, 1980; The Best of Alan Coren, 1980; The Cricklewood Diet, 1982; Present Laughter, 1982; (ed) The Penguin Book of Modern Humour, 1983; Bumf, 1984; Something For The Weekend, 1986; Bin Ends, 1987; Seems Like Old Times, 1989;

More Like Old Times, 1990; (ed) The Pick of Punch (annual), 1979–87; (ed) The Punch Book of Short Stories, Bk 1, 1979, Bk 2, 1980, Bk 3, 1981; The Arthur Books (for children), 1976–83. *TV series:* The Losers, 1978. *Recreations:* bridge, riding, broadcasting. *Address:* Robson Books, Bolsover House, Clipstone Street, W1P 7EB.

CORFIELD, Rt. Hon. Sir Frederick (Vernon), PC 1970; Kt 1972; QC 1972; a Recorder of the Crown Court, 1979–87; *b* 1 June 1915; *s* of late Brig. F. A. Corfield, DSO, OBE, IA, and M. G. Corfield (*née* Vernon); *m* 1945, Elizabeth Mary Ruth Taylor; no *c*. *Educ:* Cheltenham Coll. (Scholar); RMA, Woolwich. Royal Artillery, 1935; 8th Field Regt, RA, India, 1935–39; served War of 1939–45; Actg Captain and Adjutant, 23rd Field Regt, BEF, 3rd Div., 1939; 51st (Highland) Div., 1940 (despatches); prisoner of war, Germany, 1940–45. Called to Bar, Middle Temple, 1945; Bencher, 1980; JAG's Branch, WO, 1945–46; retired, 1946; farming, 1946–56. MP (C) South Gloucester, 1955–Feb. 1974; Jt Parly Sec., Min. of Housing and Local Govt, 1962–64; Minister of State, Board of Trade, June-Oct. 1970; Minister of Aviation Supply, 1970–71; Minister for Aerospace, DTI, 1971–72. Mem., British Waterways Bd, 1974–83 (Vice-Chm., 1980–83); Dir, Mid-Kent Water Co. Chm., London and Provincial Antique Dealers' Assoc., 1975–89. Pres., Council, Cheltenham Coll., 1985–88. *Publications:* Corfield on Compensation, 1959; A Guide to the Community Land Act, 1976; (with R. J. A. Carnworth) Compulsory Acquisition and Compensation, 1978. *Recreation:* gardening. *Address:* Wordings Orchard, Sheepscombe, near Stroud, Glos GL6 7RE. *Club:* Army and Navy.

CORFIELD, Sir Kenneth (George), Kt 1980; FEng; Chairman, 1979–85, and Managing Director, 1969–85, STC PLC (formerly Standard Telephones & Cables plc); Chairman: Standard Telephones and Cables (Northern Ireland), 1974–85; Distributed Information Processing Ltd, since 1987; Tanks Consolidated Investments, 1990–; Vice-President, ITT Europe Inc., 1967–85; *b* 27 Jan. 1924; *s* of Stanley Corfield and Dorothy Elizabeth (*née* Mason); *m* 1960; one *d*. *Educ:* South Staffs Coll. of Advanced Technology. FEng 1979, FIMechE, CBIM. Management Develt, ICI Metals Div., 1946–50; Man. Dir, K. G. Corfield Ltd, 1950–60; Exec. Dir, Parkinson Cowan, 1960–66; Dep. Chm., STC Ltd, 1969–79; Sen. Officer, ITT Corp. (UK), 1974–84. Director: Midland Bank Ltd, 1979–91; Britoil PLC, 1982–88; Octagon Investment Management, 1987–. Chairman: EDC for Ferrous Foundries Industry, 1975–78; British Engrg Council, 1981–85; Defence Spectrum Review, 1985–88; Radio Spectrum Review, 1990–; Mem., ACARD, 1981–84. President: TEMA, 1974–80; BAIE, 1975–79; Vice-Pres., Engineering Employers' Fedn, 1979–85; Member Council: CBI, 1971–85; Inst. of Dirs, 1981– (Pres. 1984–85); BIM, 1978– (Vice-Pres. 1978–83). Trustee, Science Museum, 1984– (Mem. Adv. Council, 1975–83). CompIEE 1974, Hon. FIEE 1985. Hon. Fellow: Sheffield Polytechnic, 1983; Wolverhampton Polytechnic, 1986. DUniv: Surrey, 1976; Open, 1985; Hon. DSc: City, 1981; Bath, 1982; Aston in Birmingham, 1985; Hon. DScEng London, 1982; Hon. DSc (Engrg) QUB, 1982; Hon. LLD Strathclyde, 1982; Hon. DTech Loughborough, 1983; Hon. DEngrg Bradford, 1984. Bicentennial Medal for design, RSA, 1985. *Publications:* Product Design, Report for NEDO, 1979; No Man An Island, 1982 (SIAD Award). *Recreations:* shooting, photography, music. *Address:* 6 John Street, WC1N 2ES. *Club:* Carlton.

CORK AND ORRERY, 13th Earl of, *cr* 1620; **Patrick Reginald Boyle;** Baron Boyle of Youghall, 1616; Viscount Dungarvan, 1620; Viscount Kinalmeaky, Baron Boyle of Bandon Bridge and Baron Boyle of Broghill (Ireland), 1628; Earl of Orrery, 1660; Baron Boyle of Marston, 1711; writer, artist and broadcaster; *b* 7 Feb. 1910; *s* of Major Hon. Reginald Courtenay Boyle, MBE, MC (*d* 1946), and Violet (*d* 1974), *d* of late Arthur Flower; *S* uncle, 12th Earl of Cork and Orrery, 1967; *m* 1952, Dorothy Kate (*d* 1978), *o d* of late Robert Ramsden, Meltham, Yorks; *m* 1978, Mary Gabrielle Walker, *widow* of Kenneth Macfarlane Walker and *o d* of late Louis Ginnett. *Educ:* Harrow Sch.; Royal Military College, Sandhurst. Royal Ulster Rifles, 1930–33; Capt. London Irish Rifles, Royal Ulster Rifles (TA), 1935–38. Served War of 1939–45 with Royal Ulster Rifles and Parachute Regt. Dep. Speaker and Dep. Chm. of Cttees, House of Lords, 1973–78; Mem., British Delegn to Inter-Parly Conf., Tokyo, 1974, Madrid, 1976. Past Pres. and Exec. Chm., British Cancer Council; Dir, Cancer Research Campaign; Mem., Council of Management, St Christopher's Hospice, Sydenham (Vice Pres., 1988–). Hereditary Life Governor and Exec. Chm., Christian Faith Soc. (Vice-Pres., 1988). FRSA 1947. *Publications:* (author and illustrator) Sailing in a Nutshell, 1935; (jointly) Jungle, Jungle, Little Chindit, 1946. Contribs to the Hibbert Jl. *Recreations:* oil-painting, gardening. *Heir:* *b* Hon. John William Boyle, DSC [*b* 12 May 1916; *m* 1943, Mary Leslie, *d* of late Gen. Sir Robert Gordon Finlayson, KCB, CMG, DSO; three *s*]. *Address:* Flint House, Heyshott, Midhurst, W Sussex. *Club:* Cork and County (Cork).

CORK, CLOYNE, AND ROSS, Bishop of, since 1988; **Rt. Rev. Robert Alexander Warke;** *b* 10 July 1930; *s* of Alexander and Annie Warke; *m* 1964, Eileen Charlotte Janet Minna Skillen; two *d*. *Educ:* Mountmellick National School; The King's Hospital; Trinity Coll., Dublin (BA 1952, BD 1960); Union Theol Seminary, New York (Dip. in Ecumenical Studies). Ordained, 1953; Curate: St Mark's, Newtownards, 1953–55; St Catherine's, Dublin, 1956–59; Rathfarnham, Dublin, 1959–64; Rector: Dunlavin, Hollywood and Ballymore-Eustace, 1964–67; Drumcondra, North Strand and St Barnabas, 1967–71; Zion, Dublin, 1971–88; Archdeacon of Dublin, 1980–88. *Publications:* St Nicholas Church and Parish, 1967; Light at Evening Time, 1986; The Passion according to St Matthew, 1990. *Recreations:* following sport, theatre, reading. *Address:* The Palace, Bishop Street, Cork, Ireland. *T:* Cork (021) 271214.

CORK, Sir Kenneth (Russell), GBE 1978; FCA; Chairman: Advent Eurofund, since 1982; Advent Capital, since 1985; Advent Management Ltd, since 1988; Richmount Enterprize Zone Managers Ltd, since 1988; Laser Richmount Ltd, since 1990; Vice-Chairman, Ladbroke Group, since 1986; Senior Partner, Cork Gully, Chartered Accountants, 1980–83 (Senior Partner, W. H. Cork, Gully & Co., 1946–80); Lord Mayor of London for 1978–79; *b* 21 Aug. 1913; *s* of William Henry Cork and Maud Alice (*née* Nunn); *m* 1937, Nina Lippold; one *s* one *d*. *Educ:* Berkhamsted. ACA 1937, FCA 1946 (Founding Socs' Centenary Award, 1981). Enlisted HAC, 1938; called up, 1939; served in North Africa and Italy, 1939–45 (rank Lt-Col). Common Councilman, City of London, 1951–70; Alderman, City of London (Ward of Tower), 1970; Sheriff, City of London, 1975–76; Liveryman, Worshipful Co. of Horners (Mem. Court, 1970, Renter Warden, 1978, Master, 1980); Master, Worshipful Co. of Chartered Accountants in England and Wales, 1984–85 (Sen. Warden, 1983–84). One of HM Lieutenants, City of London, 1979–. Chairman: EEC Bankruptcy Convention Adv. Cttee to Dept Trade, 1973; Insolvency Law Review Cttee, 1977–82. Chairman: NI Finance Corp., 1974–76; NI Develt Agency, 1976–77, Hon. Consultant, 1977–. Mem., Cttee to Review the Functioning of Financial Institutions, 1977–. President: Inst. of Credit Management Ltd; City Branch, Inst. of Dirs, 1981–. Director: Aitken Hume International; Brent Walker Hldgs, 1986–89. Vice-Chm., Arts Council of GB, 1986–87 (Mem., 1985–87); Chm., Arts Council Enquiry into Professional Theatre in England, 1986–87; Governor, Royal Shakespeare Theatre, 1967–89 (Chm., 1975–85; Pres., 1986–89); Dir, Shakespeare Theatre Trust (Chm. 1967–75). Treas., Royal Concert, 1970. Chm. of Governors, Berkhamsted Sch. FRSA 1970; FICM; CBIM 1979 (President: S Bucks Br.; City Br., 1986–); FCIS 1979; FInstD. KStJ 1979. Hon. DLitt City Univ., 1978. Hon. GSM. Insol Scroll of Honour, 1989. Commandeur de l'Ordre du Merite (France); Order of Rio Branco, cl. III (Brazil); Grande Oficiàl da Ordem Militaire de Cristo (Portugal); Order of Diplomatic Service Merit Gwanghwa Medal (Korea). *Publication:* Cork on Cork (autobiog.), 1988. *Recreations:* sailing, photography, painting. *Address:* Cherry Trees, Grimms Hill, Great Missenden, Bucks HP16 9BG. *T:* Great Missenden (02406) 2628. *Clubs:* Athenæum, Royal Thames Yacht, City Livery, Cornhill (Pres. 1984), Little Ship; Itchenor Sailing, Royal Southern Yacht (Southampton).

See also R. W. Cork.

CORK, Roger William; Partner: Cork Gully; Coopers & Lybrand Deloitte; *b* 31 March 1947; *s* of Sir Kenneth Cork, *qv*; *m* 1970, Barbara Anita Pauline, *d* of Reginald Harper; one *s* two *d*. *Educ:* St Martin's School, Northwood; Uppingham School. FCA, FICM, FIPA. Partner, W. H. Cork Gully, 1970, changed to Cork Gully, 1980; associated with Coopers & Lybrand, 1980, changed to Coopers and Lybrand Deloitte, 1990. Chm. of Governors, St Dunstan's Coll. Educnl Foundn. Freeman, City of London; Alderman, Tower Ward, City of London, 1983–. Master, Bowyers' Co. *Recreations:* sailing, photography, DIY. *Address:* Rabbs, The Lee, Great Missenden, Bucks HP16 9NX. *T:* The Lee (024020) 296. *Clubs:* City Livery, Royal Yachting Association.

CORKERY, Michael; QC 1981; *b* 20 May 1926; *o s* of late Charles Timothy Corkery and of Nellie Marie Corkery; *m* 1967, Juliet Shore Foulkes, *o d* of late Harold Glyn Foulkes; one *s* one *d*. *Educ:* The King's Sch., Canterbury. Commissioned in Welsh Guards, 1945; served until 1948. Called to Bar, Lincoln's Inn, 1949, Bencher 1973, Master of the Library, 1991. Mem., South Eastern Circuit; 3rd Junior Prosecuting Counsel to the Crown at the Central Criminal Court, 1959; 1st Junior Prosecuting Counsel to the Crown, 1964; 5th Senior Prosecuting Counsel to the Crown, 1970; 3rd Sen. Prosecuting Counsel, 1971; 2nd Sen. Prosecuting Counsel, 1974; 1st Sen. Prosecuting Counsel, 1977–81. Mem., Hong Kong Bar Assoc., 1981–. *Recreations:* shooting, sailing, gardening, music. *Address:* 5 Paper Buildings, Temple, EC4.

CORLETT, Clive William; Under Secretary, Board of Inland Revenue, since 1985; *b* 14 June 1938; *s* of F. William and Hanna Corlett; *m* 1964, Margaret Catherine Jones; one *s*. *Educ:* Birkenhead Sch.; Brasenose Coll., Oxford (BA PPE). Merchant Navy, 1957. Joined Inland Revenue, 1960; seconded to: Civil Service Selection Bd, 1970; HM Treasury, 1972–74 (as Private Sec. to Chancellor of Exchequer) and 1979–81. *Address:* Board of Inland Revenue, Somerset House, Strand, WC2.

CORLETT, Ewan Christian Brew, OBE 1985; MA, PhD; FEng 1978; Chairman, Burness, Corlett Group (formerly Burness, Corlett & Partners Ltd), since 1954; *b* 11 Feb. 1923; *s* of Malcolm James John and Catherine Ann Corlett; *m* 1946, Edna Lilian Büggs; three *s*. *Educ:* King William's Coll., IOM; Oxford Univ. (MA Engrg Sci.); Durham Univ. (PhD Naval Architecture). Dept of Director of Naval Construction, Admiralty, Bath, 1944–46; Tipton Engrg Co., Tipton, 1946–47; Aluminium Develt Assoc. Research Scholar, Durham Univ., 1947–50; Naval Architect, British Aluminium Co., 1950–53; Design Dir, Burness, Corlett & Partners Ltd, 1953–54, Man. Dir, 1954–88. Chm. Council, RINA, 1977–79, Vice-Pres., 1971–82, Hon. Vice-Pres., 1982. Home Office Assessor (Technical Inquiries), 1959–80. Hon. Naval Architect and Vice-Pres., SS Great Britain Project. Mem. Board, Nat. Maritime Inst., 1978–82; Trustee, Nat. Maritime Museum, 1974–. Mem. Court, Shipwrights' Co., 1976–, Prime Warden 1990. *Publications:* The Iron Ship, 1976, revised edn 1990; The Revolution in Merchant Shipping 1950–1980, 1980. numerous papers to learned instns. *Recreations:* sailing, painting, astronomy. *Address:* Cottimans, Port-e-Vullen, Isle of Man. *T:* Ramsey, IOM, (0624) 814009. *Club:* Manx Sailing and Cruising.

CORLETT, Gerald Lingham; Chairman, Higsons Brewery plc, 1980–88; *b* 8 May 1925; *s* of Alfred Lingham Corlett and Nancy Eileen Bremner; *m* 1957, Helen Bromfield Williamson; three *s* one *d*. *Educ:* Rossall School; Aberdeen University (short war-time course). RA, 1943–47 (Lieut, Royal Indian Artillery). Higsons Brewery, 1947–88. Director: Westminster (Liverpool) Trust Co., 1960–; Midshires Building Soc. (Northern Bd), 1977–87; Radio City (Sound of Merseyside), 1982–88 (Chm., 1985–88); Boddington Gp, 1985–88. Member, Council: Brewers' Soc., 1964–88; Rossall Sch., 1956–. Mem., Brewers' Co., 1983–. *Recreation:* family. *Address:* Kirk House, 4 Abbey Road, West Kirby, Merseyside L48 7EW. *T:* 051–625 5425. *Clubs:* Liverpool Racquet; West Kirby Sailing.

CORLEY, Sir Kenneth (Sholl Ferrand), Kt 1972; Chairman and Chief Executive, Joseph Lucas (Industries) Ltd, 1969–73; *b* 3 Nov. 1908; *s* of late S. W. Corley and late Mrs A. L. Corley; *m* 1937, Olwen Mary Yeoman; one *s* one *d*. *Educ:* St Bees, Cumberland. Joined Joseph Lucas Ltd, 1927; Director, 1948. Pres., Birmingham Chamber of Commerce, 1964. Governor, Royal Shakespeare Theatre; Life Governor, Birmingham Univ.; Pres., Soc. of Motor Mfrs and Traders, 1971. Chm. Governors, St Bees Sch., 1978–84. Chevalier, Légion d'Honneur, 1975. *Recreations:* fell-walking, bee-keeping, theatre. *Address:* 34 Dingle Lane, Solihull, West Midlands B91 3NG. *T:* 021–705 1597; Yewtree, Wasdale, Cumbria CA20 1EU. *T:* Wasdale (09467) 26285. *Club:* Royal Automobile.

CORLEY, His Honour Michael Early Ferrand; a Circuit Judge (formerly County Court Judge), 1967–82; *b* 11 Oct. 1909; *s* of late Ferrand Edward Corley, Christian College, Madras, and Elsie Maria Corley. *Educ:* Marlborough; Oriel Coll., Oxford. Called to Bar, 1934. War Service, RNVR, 1940–46. *Publication:* At The Gates—Tomorrow, 1983. *Address:* The Old Rectory, Rectory Road, Broome, Norfolk NR35 2HU.

CORLEY, Peter Maurice Sinclair; Under Secretary, Department of Trade and Industry, since 1981; *b* 15 June 1933; *s* of Rev. James Maurice Corley, MLitt and Mrs Barbara Shearer Corley; *m* 1961, Dr Marjorie Constance Doddridge; two *d*. *Educ:* Marlborough Coll.; King's Coll., Cambridge (MA). Min. of Power, 1957–61; Min. of Transport, 1961–65; BoT, 1965–69; Commercial Sec., Brussels, 1969–71; Asst Sec., DTI, 1972–75; Dir Gen., Econ. Co-operation Office, Riyadh, 1976–78; Dept of Industry, 1978–81. *Recreation:* bookbinding. *Address:* c/o Department of Trade and Industry, 1 Victoria Street, SW1H 0ET. *Club:* United Oxford & Cambridge University.

CORLEY, Roger David; Managing Director, Clerical, Medical and General Life Assurance Society, since 1982; *b* 13 April 1933; *s* of Thomas Arthur and Erica Trent Corley; *m* 1964, Brigitte Roeder; three *s*. *Educ:* Hymers College, Hull; Univ. of Manchester (BSc). FIA 1960. Joined Clerical Medical, 1956: Investment Manager, 1961–72; Actuary, 1972–80; Dir, 1975–; Dep. Gen. Manager and Actuary, 1980–82. Pres., Inst. of Actuaries, 1988–90 (Mem. Council, 1976–; Hon. Sec., 1980–82; Vice-Pres., 1985–88); Vice Pres., Internat. Actuarial Assoc., 1990– (Mem. Council, 1983–; Nat. Correspondent for England, 1984–90); Mem., Deutsche Gesellschaft für Versicherungsmathematik, 1975–. Sen. Warden, Actuaries' Co., 1991– (Mem. Court, 1985–). FRSA 1990. *Recreations:* theatre, travel, music. *Address:* (office) The Little Adelphi, 10 John Adam Street, WC2N 6HA. *Club:* Army and Navy.

CORLEY SMITH, Gerard Thomas, CMG 1952; HM Diplomatic Service, retired; *b* 30 July 1909; *s* of late Thomas and Nina Smith; *m* 1937, Joan Haggard (*d* 1984); one *s* three *d* *Educ:* Bolton Sch.; Emmanuel Coll., Cambridge. Gen. Consular Service, 1931; has served in Paris, Oran, Detroit, La Paz, Milan, St Louis, New York, Brussels, and at various times in the Foreign Office. Became 1st Sec. and Consul, on appt as Labour Attaché to Embassy in Brussels 1945; Counsellor UK Deleg. to UNO at New York and UK Alternate Rep. on UN Economic and Social Council, 1949–52; Press Counsellor, Brit. Embassy, Paris, 1952–54; Labour Counsellor, Brit. Embassy, Madrid, 1954–59; British Ambassador: to Haiti, 1960–62; to Ecuador, 1962–67. Sec. Gen., Charles Darwin Foundn for the Galapagos Islands, 1972–82. Grand Officer, Order of Merit (Ecuador), 1980. *Recreations:* music, mountains, birds. *Address:* Greensted Hall, Chipping Ongar, Essex CM5 9LD. *T:* Ongar (0277) 362031. *Club:* Travellers'.

CORMACK, Prof. Allan MacLeod; University Professor, Tufts University, since 1980; *b* 23 Feb. 1924; *s* of George Cormack and Amelia MacLeod; *m* 1950, Barbara Jeanne Seavey; one *s* two *d*. *Educ:* Univ. of Cape Town (BSc, MSc). Research Student, St John's Coll., Cambridge. Lecturer, Univ. of Cape Town, 1950–56; Research Fellow, Harvard Univ., 1956–57; Tufts University: Asst Prof., 1957–60; Associate Prof., 1960–64; Prof. of Physics, 1964–80; Chairman, Physics Dept, 1968–76. Nelson Medical Lectr, Univ. of Calif. Davis, 1985; Watkins Vis. Prof., Wichita State Univ., 1986. Fellow, Amer. Physical Soc., 1964; Fellow, Amer. Acad. of Arts and Sciences, 1980; Mem., Nat. Acad. of Sciences, 1983; Hon. Member: Swedish Neuroradiological Soc., 1979; S African Inst. of Physics, 1985; Amer. Assoc. of Physicists in Medicine, 1988; Foreign Fellow, Royal Soc. of S Africa, 1983. Hon. DSc Tufts Univ., 1980. Ballou Medallist, Tufts Univ., 1978; (jtly) Nobel Prize for Physiology or Medicine, 1979; Medal of Merit, Univ. of Cape Town, 1980; Mike Hogg Medallist, Univ. of Texas, 1981; Nat. Medal of Sci., 1990. *Publications:* articles on nuclear and particle physics, computed tomography, and related mathematics. *Address:* 18 Harrison Street, Winchester, Mass 01890, USA. *T:* 617–729–0735.

CORMACK, John, CB 1982; Director, Parliamentary and Law, Institute of Chartered Accountants of Scotland, 1987–88 (Assistant Director, 1984–87); Fisheries Secretary, Department of Agriculture and Fisheries for Scotland, 1976–82; *b* 27 Aug. 1922; *yr s* of late Donald Cormack and Anne Hunter Cormack (*née* Gair); *m* 1947, Jessie Margaret Bain; one *s* one *d* (and one *d* decd). *Educ:* Royal High Sch., Edinburgh. Served RAPC, 1941–46; Captain and Command Cashier, CMF, 1946. Entered Department of Agriculture for Scotland, 1939: Principal, 1959; Private Sec. to Sec. of State for Scotland, 1967–69; Asst Sec., 1969; Under Sec., 1976. *Recreations:* golf, music. *Address:* 57 Craigmount Avenue North, Edinburgh EH12 8DN.

CORMACK, Sir Magnus (Cameron), KBE 1970; *b* Caithness, Scotland, 12 Feb. 1906; *s* of William Petrie Cormack and Violet McDonald Cameron; *m* 1935, Mary Gordon Macmeiken; one *s* three *d*. *Educ:* St Peter's Sch., Adelaide, S Aust. Farmer and Grazier. Served War, 1940–44; Aust. Imperial Forces, SW Pacific Area, Major. Pres., Liberal Party Organisation, 1947–49; Senator for Victoria, 1951–53 and 1962–78; President of the Senate, 1971–74. *Recreation:* deep sea sailing. *Club:* Australian (Melbourne).

CORMACK, Patrick Thomas; MP (C) Staffordshire South, since 1983 (Cannock, 1970–74; Staffordshire South West, 1974–83); *b* 18 May 1939; *s* of Thomas Charles and Kathleen Mary Cormack, Grimsby; *m* 1967, Kathleen Mary McDonald; two *s*. *Educ:* St James' Choir School and Havelock School, Grimsby; Univ. of Hull. Second Master, St James' Choir School, Grimsby, 1961–66; Company Education and Training Officer, Ross Group Ltd, Grimsby, 1966–67; Assistant Housemaster, Wrekin College, Shropshire, 1967–69; Head of History, Brewood Grammar School, Stafford, 1969–70. Vis. Lectr, Univ. of Texas, 1984. Dir, Historic House Hotels Ltd, 1981–89; Chm., Aitken Dott Ltd (The Scottish Gallery), 1983–89. Trustee, Historic Churches Preservation Trust, 1972–; Pres., Staffs Historic Buildings Trust, 1983–; Member: Historic Buildings Council, 1979–84; Faculty Jurisdiction Commn, 1979–84; Heritage in Danger (Vice-Chm., 1974–); Council for British Archaeology, 1979–; Royal Commn on Historical Manuscripts, 1981–; Council for Independent Educn (Chm., 1979–); Lord Chancellor's Adv. Cttee on Public Records, 1979–84; Council, Georgian Gp, 1985–; Council, Winston Churchill Meml Trust, 1983–. Member: Select Cttee on Educn, Science and Arts, 1979–84; Chairman's Panel, H of C, 1983–; Chm., H of C Works of Art Cttee, 1987–; Member: All Party Heritage Cttee (Chm. 1979–); Cons. Party Arts and Heritage Cttee, 1979–84 (Chm.); Chm., Cons. Party Adv. Cttee on Arts and Heritage, 1988–. Chm. Editorial Bd, Parliamentary Publications, 1983–. FSA 1978. Rector's Warden, 1978–90, Parly Warden, 1990–, St Margaret's Church, Westminster. Mem., Worshipful Co. of Glaziers, 1979–; Freeman, City of London, 1979. Hon. Citizen of Texas, 1985. *Publications:* Heritage in Danger, 1976; Right Turn, 1978; Westminster: Palace and Parliament, 1981; Castles of Britain, 1982; Wilberforce—the Nation's Conscience, 1983; Cathedrals of England, 1984. *Recreations:* fighting philistines, walking, visiting old churches, avoiding sitting on fences. *Address:* House of Commons, SW1A 0AA. *Clubs:* Athenæum, Brooks's.

CORMACK, Robert Linklater Burke, CMG 1988; HM Diplomatic Service; Ambassador to Sweden, since 1991; *b* 29 Aug. 1935; *s* of late Frederick Eunson Cormack, CIE, and Elspeth Mary (*née* Linklater), Dounby, Orkney; *m* 1962, Eivor Dorotea Kumlin; one *s* two *d*. *Educ:* Trinity Coll., Glenalmond; Trinity Hall, Cambridge (BA Agric.). National Service, The Black Watch, 1954–56. Dist Officer, Kenya (HMOCS), 1960–64; entered CRO (subseq. Diplomatic Service), 1964: Private Sec. to Minister of State, 1964–66; 1st Secretary: Saigon, 1966–68; Bombay, 1969–70; Delhi, 1970–72; FCO, 1972–77; Counsellor and Consul-Gen., Kinshasa, 1977–79; RCDS, 1980; Counsellor (Economic and Commercial), Stockholm, 1981–85; Hd of Information Technology Dept, FCO, 1985–87; Ambassador, Zaire, 1987–91. *Address:* Westness, Rousay, Orkney KW17 2PT.

CORNBERG, Mrs Sol; *see* Gaskin, Catherine.

CORNELIUS, David Frederick, CPhys, FInstP; FIHT; Director, Transport and Road Research Laboratory, Crowthorne, since 1989 (Acting Director, 1988–89); *b* 7 May 1932; *s* of Frederick M. N. and Florence K. Cornelius; *m* 1956, Susan (*née* Austin); two *s* two *d*. *Educ:* Teignmouth Grammar Sch.; Exeter University Coll. (BSc (Hons) Physics). Royal Naval Scientific Service, 1953–58; UKAEA, 1958–64; Research Manager, Road Research Laboratory, 1964–72; Asst Director, Building Research Estabt, 1973–78; Head, Research, Transport and Special Programmes, 1978–80, Transport Science Policy Unit, 1980–82, Dept of Transport; Asst Dir, 1982–84, Dep. Dir, 1984–88, Transport and Road Res. Lab. FRSA. *Publications:* scientific papers to nat. and internat. confs and in jls of various professional instns on range of topics in tribology and highway transportation. *Recreations:* swimming, cycling, youth work, antiques. *Address:* Transport and Road Research Laboratory, Old Wokingham Road, Crowthorne, Berkshire RG11 6AU. *T:* Crowthorne (0344) 770001. *Club:* Civil Service.

CORNELL, Ward MacLaurin; retired; Deputy Minister, Ministry of Housing (formerly Ministry of Municipal Affairs and Housing), Province of Ontario, 1980–88; *b* London, Ont, 4 May 1924; *m* Georgina Saxon; three *s* two *d*. *Educ:* Pickering Coll.; Univ. of Western Ontario. Lectr in English and History, Pickering Coll., Ont, 1949–54; Vis. Lectr, Conestoga Coll.; Gen. Manager, Broadcast Div. (Radio), Free Press Printing Co., 1954–67; Pres., Creative Projects in Communications, 1967–72; Agent-Gen. for Ont. in UK, 1972–78; Gen. Manager, European Ops, Lenroc Internat. Ltd, 1978–80; Dep. Minister, Min. of Citizenship and Culture, Province of Ontario, 1980–82. *Recreations:* reading, tennis, travelling. *Address:* RR1, Uxbridge, Ontario L0C 1K0, Canada.

CORNER, Edred John Henry, CBE 1972; FRS 1955; FLS; Professor of Tropical Botany, University of Cambridge, 1966–73, now Emeritus; *b* 12 Jan. 1906; *s* of late Edred Moss Corner and Henrietta Corner (*née* Henderson); *m* 1953, Helga Dinesen Sondergoord; one *s* two *d* (by 1st *m*). *Educ:* Rugby Sch. Asst Dir, Gardens Dept, Straits Settlements, 1929–45; Principal Field Scientific Officer, Latin America, Unesco, 1947–48; Lecturer in Botany, Cambridge, 1949–59; Reader in Plant Taxonomy, 1959–65; Fellow, Sidney Sussex Coll., Cambridge, 1959–73. Member: American Mycological Soc.; Brit. Mycological Soc.; French Mycological Soc.; Fellow, American Assoc. for the Advancement of Science; Corr. Member: Botanical Soc. of America; Royal Netherlands Botanical Soc.; Hon. Member: Japanese Mycological Soc; Czechoslovak Scientific Soc. for Mycology. Mem., Governing Body of Rugby Sch., 1959–75. Darwin Medal, Royal Soc., 1960; Patron's Medal, RGS, 1966; Gold Medal, Linnean Soc. of London, 1970; Victoria Medal of Honour, RHS, 1974; Allerton Award, Pacific Tropical Botanical Garden, Hawaii, 1981; Internat. Prize for Biology, Japan Acad., 1985. *Publications:* Wayside Trees of Malaya (2 vols), 1940, 3rd edn 1988; A Monograph of Clavaria and allied genera, 1950; Life of Plants, 1964; Natural History of Palms, 1966; Monograph of Cantharelloid Fungi, 1966; Boletus in Malaysia, 1972; Seeds of Dicotyledons, 2 vols, 1976; The Marquis: a tale of Syonan-to, 1981; Biographical Memoir of HM Hirohito, Emperor of Japan, 1990. *Address:* 91 Hinton Way, Great Shelford, Cambs CB2 5AH. *T:* Cambridge (0223) 842167.

CORNER, Frank Henry, CMG 1980; retired New Zealand Civil Servant and Diplomat; *b* 17 May 1920; *y s* of Charles William Corner, Napier, NZ, and Sybil Corner (*née* Smith); *m* 1943, Lynette Robinson; two *d*. *Educ:* Napier Boys' High Sch.; Victoria Univ. of Wellington. MA, 1st cl. History; James Macintosh and Post-graduate Scholar. External Affairs Dept, NZ, and War Cabinet Secretariat, 1943; 1st Sec., NZ Embassy, Washington, 1948–51; Sen. Counsellor, NZ High Commn, London, 1952–58; Dep. Sec. NZ Dept of External Affairs, 1958–62; Perm. Rep. (Ambassador) to UN, 1962–67; Ambassador of NZ to USA, 1967–72; Permanent Head of Prime Minister's Dept, 1973–75; Secretary of Foreign Affairs, 1973–80; Administrator of Tokelau, 1976–85. Chm., NZ Defence Cttee of Enquiry, 1985–86. Mem., NZ Delegn to Commonwealth Prime Ministers' Meetings, 1944, 1946, 1951–57, 1973, 1975, 1977, 1979; Deleg. to UN Gen. Assembly, 1949–52, 1955, 1960–68, 1973, 1974; NZ Rep. to UN Trusteeship Council, 1962–66 (Pres., 1965–66; Chm., UN Vis. Mission to Micronesia, 1964); NZ Rep. on UN Security Coun., 1966; Adviser, NZ Delegn: Paris Peace Conf., 1946; Geneva Conf. on Korea, 1954; numerous other internat. confs as adviser or delegate. Mem., Bd of NZ-US Educnl Foundn, 1980–88; Patron, Assoc. of NZ Art Socs, 1973–88; Mem. Council, Victoria Univ. of Wellington, 1981–87. FRSA. *Recreations:* the arts, gardening, wine. *Address:* 26 Burnell Avenue, Wellington 1, NZ. *T:* 737–022; 29 Kakariki Grove, Waikanae. *T:* 36235.

CORNER, Philip; Director General of Quality Assurance, Ministry of Defence Procurement Executive, 1975–84, retired; Chairman, Institute of Quality Assurance's Management Board (for qualification and registration scheme for lead assessors of quality assurance management system), since 1984; *b* 7 Aug. 1924; *s* of late William Henry Corner and Dora (*née* Smailes); *m* 1948, Nora Pipes (*d* 1984); no *c*; *m* 1985, Paula Mason. *Educ:* Dame Allan's Boys' Sch., Newcastle upon Tyne; Bradford Technical Coll.; RNEC Manadon; Battersea Polytechnic. BScEng (London); CEng 1966; MIMechE 1952; MIEE 1957; Hon. FIQA 1985. Short Bros (Aeronautical Engrs), 1942–43; Air Br., RN, Sub-Lieut RNVR, 1944–46; LNER Co., 1946–47; Min. of Works, 1947–50; Min. of Supply, 1950; Ministry of Defence: Dir of Guided Weapons Prodn, 1968–72; Dir of Quality Assurance (Technical), 1972–75. Member: Metrology and Standards Requirements Bd, DoI, 1974–84; Adv. Council for Calibration and Measurement, DoI, 1975–84; BSI Quality Assurance Council, 1979–84; BSI Bd, 1980–84. *Recreations:* gardening, listening to music, building and flying radio controlled model aircraft. *Address:* 3 The Green, Dyke Road, Hove, E Sussex BN3 6TH.

CORNESS, Sir Colin Ross, Kt 1986; Chairman: Redland PLC, since 1977 (Managing Director, 1967–82; Chief Executive, 1977–91); Nationwide Building Society, since 1991; a Director, Bank of England, since 1987; *b* 9 Oct. 1931; *s* of Thomas Corness and Mary Evlyne Corness. *Educ:* Uppingham Sch.; Magdalene Coll., Cambridge (BA 1954, MA 1958); Graduate Sch. of Business Admin, Harvard, USA (Advanced Management Program Dip. 1970). Called to the Bar, Inner Temple, 1956. Dir, Taylor Woodrow Construction Ltd, 1961–64; Man. Dir, Redland Tiles Ltd, 1965–70. Director: Chubb & Son PLC, 1974–84 (Dep. Chm., 1984); W. H. Smith & Son (Holdings) PLC, 1980–87; Gordon Russell PLC, 1985–89; Courtaulds PLC, 1986–; S. G. Warburg Gp, 1987–; Unitech, 1987–; Union Camp Corp., 1991–. Chm., Building Centre, 1974–77; Pres., Nat. Council of Building Material Producers, 1985–87; Member: EDC for Building, 1980–84; Industrial Develt Adv. Bd, 1982–84. Mem., UK Adv. Bd, British-American Chamber of Commerce, 1987–. *Recreations:* tennis, travel, music. *Address:* Redland House, Reigate, Surrey RH2 0SJ. *T:* Reigate (0737) 242488. *Clubs:* Cavalry and Guards, White's; Australian (Sydney).

CORNFORD, Sir (Edward) Clifford, KCB 1977 (CB 1966); FEng 1980; Chief of Defence Procurement, Ministry of Defence, 1977–80; *b* 6 Feb. 1918; *s* of John Herbert Cornford; *m* 1945, Catherine Muir; three *s* three *d*. *Educ:* Kimbolton Sch.; Jesus Coll., Cambridge (BA). Joined RAE, 1938. Operational Research with RAF, 1939–45. Guided Weapons Res. at RAE, 1945–60; jssc 1951; Head of Guided Weapons Dept, RAE, 1956–61; Min. of Defence: Chm., Def. Res. Policy Staff, 1961–63; Asst Chief Scientific Adviser, 1963–64; Chief Scientist (Army), Mem. Army Board, Ministry of Defence, 1965–67; Chm. Programme Evaluation Group, MoD, 1967–Jan. 1968; Dep. Chief Adviser (Research and Studies), MoD, 1968–69; Controller of Guided Weapons and Electronics, Min. of Technology, later Min. of Aviation Supply and MoD (Procurement Executive), 1969–72; Ministry of Defence (PE): Controller (Policy), 1972–74; Dep. Chief Exec., 1974–75; Chief Exec. and Permanent Under Sec. of State, 1975–77. Mem., PO Board, 1981–87. FRAeS. *Publications:* on aeronautical subjects in jls of learned socs and technical publications. *Recreation:* travelling. *Address:* The Spinney, 7 Ash Grove, Liphook, Hants GU30 7HZ. *T:* Liphook (0428) 722780. *Club:* Athenæum.

CORNFORD, James Peters; Director, Institute for Public Policy Research, since 1989; *b* 1935; *s* of John Cornford and Rachel Peters; *m* 1960, Avery Amanda Goodfellow; one *s* three *d*. *Educ:* Winchester Coll.; Trinity Coll., Cambridge (MA). Fellow, Trinity Coll., Cambridge, 1960–64; Harkness Fellow, 1961–62; Univ. of Edinburgh: Lectr in Politics, 1964–68; Prof. of Politics, 1968–76; Dir, Outer Circle Policy Unit, 1976–80; Dir, Nuffield Foundn, 1980–88. Vis. Fellow, All Souls Coll., Oxford, 1975–76; Vis. Prof., Birkbeck Coll., Univ. of London, 1977–80. Mem., Cttee of Inquiry into Educn of Children from Ethnic Minority Gps (DES), 1981–85. Dir, Job Ownership Ltd, 1979–. Mem. Bd, Co-op. Develt Agency, 1987–90. Chairman of Council: RIPA, 1984–85; Campaign for Freedom of Information, 1984–. Literary Editor, The Political Quarterly,

1976–. *Publications:* contrib.: Cleavages, Ideologies and Party Systems, ed Allardt and Littunen, 1965; Ideas and Institutions of Victorian Britain, ed Robson, 1967; International Guide to Election Statistics, ed Meyriat and Rokkan, 1969; Government and Nationalism in Scotland, ed Wolfe, 1969; Mass Politics, ed Rokkan and Allardt, 1970; Philosophy, Politics and Society IV, ed Laslett, Runciman and Skinner, 1972; (ed) The Failure of the State, 1975; (ed) William Stubbs, The Constitutional History of England, 1979; contrib. to jls. *Address:* 9 Wallingford Avenue, W10 6QA. *T:* 081–968 6109.

CORNFORTH, Sir John (Warcup), AC 1991; Kt 1977; CBE 1972; FRS 1953; DPhil; Royal Society Research Professor, University of Sussex, 1975–82, now Emeritus; *b* 7 Sept. 1917; *er s* of J. W. Cornforth, Sydney, Aust.; *m* 1941, Rita, *d* of W. C. Harradence; one *s* two *d*. *Educ:* Sydney High Sch.; Universities of Sydney and Oxford. BSc Sydney 1937; MSc Sydney, 1938; 1851 Exhibition Overseas Scholarship, 1939–42; DPhil Oxford, 1941; scientific staff of Med. Research Coun., 1946–62; Dir, Shell Research, Milstead Lab. of Chem. Enzymology, 1962–75. Assoc. Prof. in Molecular Sciences, Univ. of Warwick, 1965–71; Vis. Prof., Univ. of Sussex, 1971–75; Hon. Prof., Beijing Med. Univ., 1986–. Lectures: Pedler, Chem. Soc., 1968–69; Max Tishler, Harvard Univ., 1970; Robert Robinson, Chem. Soc., 1971–72; Sandin, Univ. of Alberta, 1977. For. Hon. Mem., Amer. Acad., 1973; Corresp. Mem., Aust. Acad., 1977; For. Associate, US Nat. Acad. of Scis, 1978; For. Mem., Royal Netherlands Acad. of Scis, 1978. Hon. Fellow, St Catherine's Coll., Oxford, 1976; Hon. DSc: ETH Zürich, 1975; Oxford, Warwick, Dublin, Liverpool, 1976; Aberdeen, Hull, Sussex, Sydney, 1977. Corday-Morgan Medal and Prize, Chem. Soc., 1953; (with G. J. Popjak) CIBA Medal, Biochem. Soc., 1965; Flintoff Medal, Chem. Soc., 1966; Stouffer Prize, 1967; Ernest Guenther Award, Amer. Chem. Soc., 1969; (with G. J. Popjak) Davy Medal, Royal Soc., 1968; Prix Roussel, 1972; (jtly) Nobel Prize for Chemistry, 1975; Royal Medal, Royal Soc., 1976; Copley Medal, Royal Soc., 1982. Has been deaf since boyhood. *Publications:* numerous papers on organic chemical and biochemical subjects. *Recreations:* lawn tennis, chess, gardening. *Address:* Saxon Down, Cuilfail, Lewes, East Sussex BN7 2BE.

CORNISH, Francis; *see* Cornish, R. F.

CORNISH, Jack Bertram; HM Civil Service; Under-Secretary, Department of Health and Social Security, 1976–78; *b* 26 June 1918; *s* of Bertram George John Cornish and Nora Jarmy; *m* 1946, Mary Milton; three *d*. *Educ:* Price's Grammar Sch., Fareham; Cotham Grammar Sch., Bristol. Admiralty, 1937–61: London, Bath, Plymouth, Singapore; DHSS, 1961–78. Supply Ships in Singapore and Newfoundland, 1941 and 1942. *Recreations:* music, painting, gardening. *Address:* 13 Kingsley Road, Kingsbridge, South Devon TQ7 1EY. *T:* Kingsbridge (0548) 2585.

CORNISH, James Easton; European Market Strategist, County NatWest Securities Ltd, since 1990; *b* 5 Aug. 1939; *s* of Eric Easton Cornish and Ivie Hedworth (*née* McCulloch); *m* 1968, Ursula Pink; one *s*. *Educ:* Eton Coll.; Wadham Coll., Oxford (BA); Harvard. Joined FO, 1961; Bonn, 1963; British Mil. Govt, Berlin, 1965; FCO, 1968; Washington, 1973; Dep. Head of Planning Staff, FCO, 1977; Central Policy Rev. Staff, 1980; seconded to Phillips & Drew, 1982; resigned HM Diplomatic Service, 1985; Manager, Internat. Dept, Phillips & Drew, 1982–87; Asst Dir, subseq. Associate Dir, County Securities Ltd, 1987–. *Address:* c/o County NatWest Securities Ltd, 135 Bishopsgate, EC2.

CORNISH, (Robert) Francis, LVO 1978; HM Diplomatic Service; Counsellor, Foreign and Commonwealth Office, since 1990; *b* 18 May 1942; *s* of Mr and Mrs C. D. Cornish; *m* 1964, Alison Jane Dundas; three *d*. *Educ:* Charterhouse; RMA Sandhurst. Commissioned 14th/20th King's Hussars, 1962–68; HM Diplomatic Service 1968; served Kuala Lumpur, Jakarta and FCO, 1969–76; First Sec., Bonn, 1976–80; Asst Private Sec. to HRH the Prince of Wales, 1980–83; High Comr, Brunei, 1983–86; Counsellor (Inf.), Washington, and Dir, British Inf. Service, NY, 1986–90. *Address:* c/o Foreign and Commonwealth Office, SW1A 2AH; 28 Embercourt Road, Thames Ditton, Surrey. *T:* 081–398 8054. *Club:* Cavalry and Guards.

CORNISH, William Herbert, CB 1955; Receiver for the Metropolitan Police District, 1961–67; *b* 2 Jan. 1906; *s* of late Rev. Herbert H. Cornish and Susan Emerson; *m* 1938, Eileen May Elizabeth Cooney; two *d*. *Educ:* Wesley Coll., Dublin; Trinity Coll., Dublin. Scholar, 1st Cl. Moderator with Large Gold Medal in Modern History and Political Science. Entered Home Office, 1930; Asst Sec., 1942; Asst Under-Sec. of State, 1952–60. *Recreations:* gardening and music. *Address:* 2 Tormead, Dene Road, Northwood, Mddx HA6 2BX. *T:* Northwood (09274) 21933.

CORNISH, Prof. William Rodolph, FBA 1984; Professor of Law and Fellow of Magdalene College, Cambridge University, since 1990; *b* 9 Aug. 1937; *s* of Jack R. and Elizabeth E. Cornish, Adelaide, S Australia; *m* 1964, Lovedy E. Moule; one *s* two *d*. *Educ:* Univs of Adelaide (LLB) and Oxford (BCL). Lectr in Law, LSE, 1962–68; Reader in Law, Queen Mary Coll., London, 1969–70; Prof. of English Law, LSE, 1970–90. *Publications:* The Jury, 1968; (Jt Editor) Sutton and Shannon on Contracts, 1970; (jtly) Encyclopedia of United Kingdom and European Patent Law, 1977; Intellectual Property, 1981, 2nd edn 1989; Law and Society in England 1750–1950, 1989; articles etc in legal periodicals. *Address:* Magdalene College, Cambridge.

CORNOCK, Maj.-Gen. Archibald Rae, CB 1975; OBE 1968; FBIM; Chairman, London Electricity Consultative Council, 1980; *b* 4 May 1920; *s* of Matthew Cornock and Mrs Mary Munro MacRae; *m* 1951, Dorothy Margaret Cecilia; two *d*. *Educ:* Coatbridge. MBIM 1965. NW Frontier, 1940–42; Burma, 1942–43; transf. Royal Indian Navy, 1943; Burma (Arakan), 1944–46; Gordon Highlanders, 1947–50; transf. RAOC, 1950; psc 1954; GSO2 Intelligence, 1955–57; DAQMG Northern Army Gp, 1959–61; comd 16 Bn RAOC, 1961–64; SEATO Planning Staff, Bangkok, 1964; Defence Attaché, Budapest, 1965–67; Comdt 15 Base Ordnance Depot, 1967; DDOS Strategic Comd, 1968–70; Brig. Q (Maint.), MoD, 1970–72; Dir of Clothing Procurement, 1972; Dir of Army Quartering, 1973–75. Col Comdt, RAOC, 1976–80. Chm., Army Athletic Assoc., 1968–75; Mem. Council, Back Pain Assoc., 1979–. *Recreations:* sailing, opera, golf. *Address:* 20 Claremont, St Johns Avenue, Putney Hill, SW15 2AB. *Clubs:* Royal Thames Yacht, Roehampton; Highland Brigade.

CORNOCK, Maj-Gen. Charles Gordon, CB 1988; MBE 1974; Bursar, Cranleigh School, since 1990; *b* 25 April 1935; *s* of Gordon Wallace Cornock and Edith Mary (née Keeley); *m* 1963, Kay Smith; two *s*. *Educ:* King Alfred Sch., Plön, Germany; RMA, Sandhurst. Commnd RA, 1956; served, 1957–71: 33 Para Lt Regt; 1 RHA; RMA, Sandhurst; Staff Coll., Camberley; BMRA; Armed Forces Staff Coll., Norfolk, Va; Second in Comd, 1972–74 and CO 1974–76, 7 Para RHA; GSO1 DS Staff Coll., Camberley, 1977–78; Col GS HQ UKLF, 1979; CRA 3rd Armoured Div., 1980–81; RCDS, 1982; Dep. Comdt, Staff Coll., Camberley, 1983; Dir, RA, 1984–86; C of S and Head of UK Delegn, Live Oak, SHAPE, 1986–89. Col Comdt RA, 1986–; Rep. Col Comdt, RA, 1991–92. Pres., RA Golfing Soc., 1989–; Vice-Pres., Army Hockey Assoc. FBIM. *Recreations:* hockey, tennis, golf, skiing, water skiing. *Address:* Oranmore. Horseshoe Lane, Cranleigh, Surrey. *Clubs:* Special Forces; West Hill Golf; La Moye Golf (Jersey).

CORNWALL, Archdeacon of; *see* Ravenscroft, Ven. R. L.

CORNWALL, Ian Wolfran, PhD London; Reader in Human Environment, University of London, 1965–74; *b* 28 Nov. 1909; *s* of Lt-Col J. W. Cornwall, CIE, IMS, and Effie E. C. (*née* Sinclair), *d* of Surg.-Gen. D. Sinclair, IMS; *m* 1st, 1937, Anna Margareta (*née* Callear) (*d* 1967); two *s*; 2nd, 1974, Mary L. Reynolds (*née* Miller). *Educ:* private sch.; Wellington Coll., Berks; St John's Coll., Cambridge (BA). Teaching, clerking, pharmaceutical manufacturing, selling, 1931–39; Postal and Telegraph Censorship, Press Censorship, MOI, 1939–45. London Univ. Inst. of Archaeology: Student, 1945–47 (Diploma, 1947); Secretary, 1948–51. University teacher and researcher, 1951–74, retd. (PhD London, 1952). Life Mem., Geologists' Assoc. Henry Stopes Memorial Medal, Geologists' Assoc., 1970. *Publications:* Bones for the Archaeologist, 1956, rev. edn 1975; Soils for the Archaeologist, 1958; The Making of Man, 1960 (Carnegie Medal of Library Assoc.); The World of Ancient Man, 1964; Hunter's Half Moon (fiction), 1967; Prehistoric Animals and their Hunters, 1968; Ice Ages, 1970. Contribs to specialist jls. *Recreations:* geology, gardening, photography. *Address:* 5 Westmead Road, Fishbourne, Chichester, W Sussex PO19 3JD.

CORNWALL-LEGH, family name of **Baron Grey of Codnor.**

CORNWALLIS, family name of **Baron Cornwallis.**

CORNWALLIS, 3rd Baron *cr* 1927, of Linton, Kent; **Fiennes Neil Wykeham Cornwallis,** OBE 1963; DL; *b* 29 June 1921; *s* of 2nd Baron Cornwallis, KCVO, KBE, MC, and Cecily Etha Mary (*d* 1943), *d* of Sir James Walker, 3rd Bt; *S* father, 1982; *m* 1st, 1942, Judith Lacy Scott (marr. diss. 1948); one *s* (one *d* decd); 2nd, 1951, Agnes Jean Russell Landale; one *s* three *d*. *Educ:* Eton. Served War, Coldstream Guards, 1940–44. Pres., British Agricultural Contractors Assoc., 1952–54; Pres., Nat. Assoc. of Agricultural Contractors, 1957–63 and 1986–; Vice-Pres., Fedn of Agricl Co-operatives, 1984–86; Chm., Smaller Firms Council, CBI, 1978–81. Representative, Horticultural Co-operatives in the EEC, 1974–87. Director: Checkers Ltd; Town & Country Building Soc.(formerly Planet, then Magnet & Planet, Bld Soc.) 1967– (Chm., 1973–75; Dep. Chm., 1975–77; Chm., 1978–81 and 1991–). Mem., Bd of Trustees, Chevening Estate, 1979–. Fellow, Inst. of Horticulture, 1986. Pro Grand Master, United Grand Lodge of England, 1982–. DL Kent, 1976. *Recreation:* fishing. *Heir: s* Hon. (Fiennes Wykeham) Jeremy Cornwallis [*b* 25 May 1946; *m* 1969, Sara Gray de Neufville, *d* of Lt-Col Nigel Stockwell, Benenden, Kent; one *s* two *d*]. *Address:* Ruck Farm, Horsmonden, Tonbridge, Kent TN12 8DT. *T:* Brenchley (089272) 2267; 25B Queen's Gate Mews, SW7 5QL. *T:* 071–589 1167. *Clubs:* Brooks's, Pratt's, Farmers'.

CORNWELL, David John Moore, (John le Carré); writer; *b* 19 Oct. 1931; *s* of Ronald Thomas Archibald Cornwell and Olive (*née* Glassy); *m* 1954, Alison Ann Veronica Sharp (marr. diss. 1971); three *s*; *m* 1972, Valerie Jane Eustace; one *s*. *Educ:* Sherborne; Berne Univ.; Lincoln Coll., Oxford (1st cl. Modern Languages; Hon. Fellow 1984). Taught at Eton, 1956–58. Mem. of HM Foreign Service, 1960–64. Hon. Dr, Exeter, 1990. Cartier Diamond Dagger, CWA, 1988. *Publications:* Call for the Dead, 1961 (filmed as The Deadly Affair, 1967); A Murder of Quality, 1962; The Spy Who Came in from the Cold, 1963 (Somerset Maugham Award; Crime Writers' Assoc. Gold Dagger) (filmed); The Looking-Glass War, 1965 (filmed); A Small Town in Germany, 1968; The Naïve and Sentimental Lover, 1971; Tinker, Tailor, Soldier, Spy, 1974 (televised 1979); The Honourable Schoolboy, 1977 (James Tait Black Meml Prize; Crime Writers' Assoc. Gold Dagger); Smiley's People, 1980 (televised 1982); The Little Drummer Girl, 1983 (filmed 1985); A Perfect Spy, 1986 (televised 1987); The Russia House, 1989 (filmed 1991); The Secret Pilgrim, 1991. *Address:* David Higham Associates, 5–8 Lower John Street, Golden Square, W1R 4HA.

CORNWELL, Roger Eliot, FCA; Chairman, Louis Dreyfus & Co. Ltd, since 1982 (Director since 1978); *b* 5 Feb. 1922; *s* of Harold and Kathleen Cornwell. *Educ:* St Albans Sch.; Jesus Coll., Oxford (MA). FCA 1976. *Address:* 42 Brompton Square, SW3 2AF.

CORREA, Charles Mark; Padma Shri, 1972; architect; *b* 1 Sept. 1930; *s* of Carlos M. Correa and Ana Florinda de Heredia; *m* 1961, Monika Sequeira; one *s* one *d*. *Educ:* Univ. of Michigan (BArch); MIT (MArch). Private practice, Bombay, 1958–; work includes: Mahatma Gandhi Memorial, Sabarmati Ashram; State Assembly for Madhya Pradesh; low cost housing projects in Delhi, Bombay, Ahmedabad and other cities in India; Chief Architect for planning of New Bombay; Founder Mem., Steering Cttee, Aga Khan Award for Architecture, 1977–86. Jawaharlal Nehru Vis. Prof. and Fellow of Churchill Coll., Cambridge, 1985–86. Hon. FAIA 1979. Hon. Dr Univ. of Michigan, 1980. Royal Gold Medal for Architecture, RIBA, 1984; Gold Medal, Indian Inst. of Architects, 1987; Gold Medal, IUA, 1990. *Publication:* The New Landscape, 1984; *relevant publication:* S. Cantacuzino, Charles Correa, 1984. *Recreations:* tennis, model trains, chess. *Address:* 9 Mathew Road, Bombay 400004, India. *T:* 811.1976/811.1858. *Clubs:* Bombay Gymkhana, United Services, Willingdon Sports, Bombay Sailing Association (Bombay); Bangalore (Bangalore).

CORRIE, John Alexander; *b* 29 July 1935; *s* of John Corrie and Helen Brown; *m* 1965, Jean Sandra Hardie; one *s* two *d*. *Educ:* Kirkcudbright Acad.; George Watson's Coll.; Lincoln Agric. Coll., NZ. Farmed in NZ, 1955–59, in Selkirk, 1959–65 and in Kirkcudbright, 1965–. Lectr for British Wool Marketing Bd and Agric. Trng Bd, 1966–74; Mem. Cttee, National Farmers Union, 1964–74 (Vice-Chm. Apprenticeship Council, 1971–74); Nuffield Scholar in Agriculture, 1972. District Officer, Rotary International, 1973–74 (Community service). Nat. Chm., Scottish Young Conservatives, 1964. Contested (C): North Lanark, 1964; Central Ayr, 1966; Cunninghame N, 1987. MP (C): Bute and N Ayr, Feb. 1974–1983; Cunninghame N, 1983–87. Opposition spokesman on educn in Scotland, Oct. 1974–75; an Opposition Scottish Whip, 1975–76 (resigned over Devolution); PPS to Sec. of State for Scotland, 1979–81; Mem., Council of Europe and WEU, 1982–87. Treas., Scottish Cons. Back Bench Cttee, 1980, Chm. 1981–82; Leader, Cons. Gp on Scottish Affairs, 1982–84; Sec., Cons. Backbench Fish-farming Cttee, 1982–86. Mem. European Parlt, 1975–76 and 1977–79 (Mem. Cttees of Agriculture, Reg. Develt and Transport). Vice-President: EEC-Turkey Cttee, 1975–76; EEC Fisheries Cttee, 1977–79; EEC Mediterranean Agricl Cttee, 1977–79; Rapporteur for EEC Fisheries Policy, 1977–78. Chm., Transport Users' Consultative Cttee for Scotland, 1989–; Mem., Central Transport Consultative Cttee, 1989–. Mem. Council, Scottish Landowners Fedn, 1990; Dir, Ayr Agricl Soc., 1990. Industry and Parlt Trust Fellowship with Conoco (UK) Ltd, 1986–87. *Publications:* (jtly) Towards a European Rural Policy, 1978; Towards a Community Forestry Policy, 1979; Fish Farming in Europe, 1979; The Importance of Forestry in the World Economy, 1980. *Recreations:* shooting, fishing, riding, tennis, golf, curling, bridge. *Address:* Park of Tongland, Kirkcudbright, Scotland DG6 4NE. *Clubs:* Annabel's; Royal Automobile (Glasgow).

CORRIE, W(allace) Rodney, CB 1977; *b* 25 Nov. 1919; *o c* of late Edward and Mary Ellen Corrie; *m* 1952, Helen Margaret (*née* Morice), *widow* of Flt-Lt A. H. E. Kahn; one *s* one *d*. *Educ:* Leigh Grammar School; Christ's Coll., Cambridge (BA 1941, MA 1944). Served Royal Signals, 1940–46 (despatches). Entered Civil Service, Min. of Town and

Country Planning, 1947; Min. of Housing and Local Govt, 1951; Asst Secretary, 1961; Assistant Under-Secretary of State, DEA, 1969; Under-Secretary: Min. of Housing and Local Govt, 1969; Dept of the Environment, 1970; Chm., NW Econ. Planning Bd, 1969–80, and Regl Dir (NW), DoE, 1971–80, Dept of Transport, 1976–80. *Recreations:* exploring byways, catching up on things. *Address:* Brambledown, Chapel Lane, Hale Barns, Cheshire WA15 0AJ.

CORRIGAN, Margaret Mary; Member, Radio Authority, since 1991; *d* of Joseph Hamilton and Mary Anna (*née* Monaghan); *m* 1979, Gerard Michael Corrigan; one *s* one *d. Educ:* Univ. of Strathclyde (BA Hons English). Trainee journalist with newspaper/magazine publishers D. C. Thomson, Dundee, 1977–78; Advertising Copywriter and Acct Exec., Austin Knight Advertising, Glasgow, 1978–81; Depute Dir of Public Relns, Cumbernauld Develt Corp., 1981–83. *Recreations:* swimming, music, theatre; member of Linlithgow Amateur Musical Productions.

CORRIGAN, Thomas Stephen; Chairman, Post Office Users' National Council, since 1984; Director, McNicholas Construction Holdings, since 1988; Director of other companies; *b* 2 July 1932; *s* of Thomas Corrigan and Renée Victorine Chaborel; *m* 1963, Sally Margaret Everitt; two *d. Educ:* Beulah Hill; Chartered Accountant (Scottish Inst.). Nat. Service, Army, 1955–57. Chief Accountant, Lobitos Oilfields, 1957–62; Exec., Keyser Ullmann, 1962–64; Inveresk Group: Finance Controller, 1964; Finance Dir, 1966; Man. Dir, 1971–74; Chm., 1974–83. Chairman: Havelock Europa, 1983–89; Rex Stewart Gp Ltd, 1987–90. Pres., British Paper and Board Industry Fedn, 1975–77; Vice-Pres., European Confedn of Pulp, Paper and Board Industries, 1982–83; Mem., NEDC (Tripartite Sector Working Party on paper industry), 1976–77. Master: Makers of Playing Cards Co., 1978–79; Stationers and Newspaper Makers' Co., 1990–91. FRSA. *Recreations:* golf, bridge, tennis, travel. *Address:* Woodend, The Chase, Kingswood, Surrey KT20 6HZ. *T:* Mogador (0737) 832709. *Clubs:* MCC, Royal Automobile, City Livery.

CORRIGAN-MAGUIRE, Mairead; Co-Founder, Community of the Peace People; *b* 27 Jan. 1944; *d* of Andrew and Margaret Corrigan; *m* 1981, Jackie Maguire; one *s* and three step *c. Educ:* St Vincent's Primary Sch., Falls Road, Belfast; Miss Gordon's Commercial Coll., Belfast. Secretarial qualification. Confidential Sec. to Managing Director, A. Guinness Son & Co. (Belfast) Ltd, Brewers, Belfast. Initiator of Peace Movement in Northern Ireland, Aug. 1976; Chm., Peace People Organisation, 1980–81. Hon. Dr of Law, Yale Univ., 1976; Nobel Prize for Peace (jtly), 1976; Carl-Von-Ossietzky Medaille for Courage, Berlin, 1976. *Recreations:* voluntary community and youth work. *Address:* 224 Lisburn Road, Belfast 9, N Ireland. *T:* (business) (0232) 663465.

CORRIN, John Bowes, OBE 1983; *b* 26 Oct. 1922; *s* of Harold R. Corrin and Mabel F. Corrin; *m* 1948, José M. Sharman; one *s* one *d. Educ:* Berkhamsted. FCA 1945 (Auditing Prize). Partner, Thornton Baker, later Grant Thornton, 1949–87; Dir, Anglia, later Nationwide Anglia Building Soc., 1964–89 (Chm., 1981–85). Pres., Leics and Northants Soc. of Chartered Accountants, 1959; past Pres., Northampton Conservative Assoc. Mayor, Northampton, 1964–65; Hon. Freeman, Borough of Northampton, 1972. *Recreation:* golf. *Address:* Tynwald, Sandy Lane, Church Brampton, Northampton NN6 8AX. *T:* Northampton (0604) 845301. *Clubs:* Northampton County; Northamptonshire County Golf.

CORRIN, John William; His Honour Deemster Corrin; HM's First Deemster, Clerk of the Rolls and Deputy Governor of the Isle of Man, since 1988; *b* 6 Jan. 1932; *s* of Evan Cain Corrin and Dorothy Mildred Corrin; *m* 1961, Dorothy Patricia, *d* of late J. S. Lace; one *d. Educ:* Murrays Road Primary Sch., Douglas; King William's Coll., IOM. Admitted to Manx Bar, 1954. Attorney Gen., IOM, 1974–80; Second Deemster, 1980–88. Chairman (all IOM): Criminal Injuries Compensation Tribunal, 1980–88; Licensing Appeal Court, 1980–88; Prevention of Fraud (Unit Trust) Tribunal, 1980–88; Income Tax Appeal Comrs, 1988–; Tynwald Ceremony Arrangements Cttee, 1988–. Chairman: Manx Blind Welfare Soc.; Manx Workshop for the Disabled; Council, Postgrad. Med. Centre; Hon. Mem., IOM Med. Soc.; President: IOM Br., Crossroads Care; Island Bridge Club; Lon Dhoo Male Voice Choir; IOM Br., SSAFA; Manx Asthma Assoc.; Chm., Douglas Buxton Music Trust; Trustee: Manx Foundn for Physically Disabled; Manx Methodist Church. *Recreations:* music, gardening, bridge, *Address:* Carla Beck, 28 Devonshire Road, Douglas, Isle of Man. *T:* Douglas (0624) 621806. *Club:* Ellan Vannin (Douglas) (Past Pres.).

CORRY; *see* Lowry-Corry, family name of Earl of Belmore.

CORRY, Viscount; John Armar Galbraith Lowry-Corry; *b* 2 Nov. 1985; *s* and *heir* of Earl of Belmore, *qv.*

CORRY, Lt-Comdr Sir William (James), 4th Bt *cr* 1885, of Dunraven, Co. Antrim; RN retired; *b* 1 Aug. 1924; *s* of Sir James Perowne Ivo Myles Corry, 3rd Bt and Molly Irene, *d* of Major O. J. Bell; *S* father, 1987; *m* 1945, Pamela Diana Mary, *d* of late Lt-Col J. B. Lapsley, MC; four *s* two *d. Educ:* RNC Dartmouth. Joined RN, 1938; Lt-Comdr 1953; retired, 1977. *Recreation:* beagling. *Heir:* s James Michael Corry [*b* 3 Oct. 1946; *m* 1973, Sheridan Lorraine, *d* of A. P. Ashbourne; three *s*]. *Address:* East Hillerton House, Bow, Crediton, Devon EX17 5AD. *T:* Bow (03633) 82407.

CORSAR, Hon. Mary Drummond; Chairman, Women's Royal Voluntary Service, since 1988; *b* 8 July 1927; *o d* of Lord Balerno, CBE, TD, DL and Mary Kathleen Smith; *m* 1953, Col Charles Herbert Kenneth Corsar, LVO, OBE, TD, DL; two *s* two *d* (and one *d* decd). *Educ:* Westbourne, Glasgow; St Denis, Edinburgh; Edinburgh Univ. (MA Hons). Dep. Chief Comr, Girl Guides, Scotland, 1972–77; Chm., Scotland WRVS, 1981–88. Member: Vis. Cttee, Glenochil Young Offenders Instn, 1976–; Parole Bd for Scotland, 1982–89. Hon. Pres., Scottish Women's AAA, 1973–. Member: Exec. Cttee, Trefoil Centre for Handicapped, 1975–; Convocation, Heriot Watt Univ., 1986–; Royal Anniversary Trust, 1990–. Gov., Fettes Coll., 1984–. *Recreation:* hill walking. *Address:* Burg, Torloisk, Isle of Mull, Argyll PA74 6NH. *T:* Ulva Ferry (06885) 289; 234 Stockwell Road, SW9 9SP. *T:* 071–416 0146. *Clubs:* Lansdowne; New (Edinburgh) (Associate Mem.).

CORTAZZI, Sir (Henry Arthur) Hugh, GCMG 1984 (KCMG 1980; CMG 1969); HM Diplomatic Service, retired; Director: Hill Samuel Bank Ltd, since 1984; Foreign and Colonial Pacific Trust, since 1984; GT Japan Investment Trust plc, since 1984; Thornton Pacific (formerly Pacific) Investment Trust, since 1986; *b* 2 May 1924; *m* 1956, Elizabeth Esther Montagu; one *s* two *d. Educ:* Sedbergh Sch.; St Andrews and London Univs. Served in RAF, 1943–47; joined Foreign Office, 1949; Third Sec., Singapore, 1950–51; Third/Second Sec., Tokyo, 1951–54; FO, 1954–58; First Sec., Bonn, 1958–60; First Sec., later Head of Chancery, Tokyo, 1961–65; FO, 1965–66; Counsellor (Commercial), Tokyo, 1966–70; Royal Coll. of Defence Studies, 1971–72; Minister (Commercial), Washington, 1972–75; Dep. Under-Sec. of State, FCO, 1975–80; Ambassador to Japan, 1980–84. Mem., ESRC, 1984–. Pres., Asiatic Soc. of Japan, 1982–83; Chm., Japan Soc. of London, 1985–. Mem., Council and Court, Sussex Univ., 1985–. Hon. Fellow, Robinson Coll., Cambridge, 1988. Hon. Dr Stirling, 1988. *Publications:* trans. from Japanese, Genji Keita: The Ogre and other stories of the Japanese Salarymen,

1972; The Guardian God of Golf and other humorous stories, 1972, reprinted as The Lucky One, 1980; (ed) Mary Crawford Fraser, A Diplomat's Wife in Japan: sketches at the turn of the century, 1982; Isles of Gold: antique maps of Japan, 1983; Higashi No Shimaguni, Nishi No Shimaguni (collection of articles and speeches in Japanese), 1984; Dr Willis in Japan, 1985; (ed) Mitford's Japan, 1985; Victorians in Japan: in and around the Treaty Ports, 1987; for Japanese students of English: Thoughts from a Sussex Garden (essays), 1984; Second Thoughts (essays), 1986; Japanese Encounter, 1987; Zoku, Higashi no Shimaguni, Nishi no Shimaguni, 1987; (ed with George Webb) Kipling's Japan, 1988; The Japanese Achievement: a short history of Japan and Japanese culture, 1990; articles on Japanese themes in English and Japanese pubns. *Recreations:* Japanese studies, the arts including antiques. *Address:* c/o Hill Samuel Bank Ltd, 100 Wood Street, EC2P 2AJ. *Club:* Royal Air Force.

CORVEDALE, Viscount; Benedict Alexander Stanley Baldwin; *b* 28 Dec. 1973; *s* and *heir* of 4th Earl Baldwin of Bewdley, *qv.*

CORY, (Charles) Raymond, CBE 1982; Chairman: John Cory & Sons Ltd, since 1965 (Director since 1948); Milford Haven Port Authority (formerly Conservancy Board), since 1982; *b* 20 Oct. 1922; *s* of Charles and Ethel Cory; *m* 1st, 1946, Vivienne Mary Roberts (*d* 1988), Kelowna, BC, Canada; three *d*; 2nd, 1989, Betty Horley. *Educ:* Harrow; Christ Church, Oxford. Served RNVR, Ord. Seaman to Lieut, 1942–46; Russian and N Atlantic convoys and Normandy landings (C-in-C's Commendation June 1944). Vice-Chm., A. B. Electronics Products Group PLC, 1979–. Dir and Mem. Executive, Baltic and Internat. Maritime Conf., Copenhagen, 1957–67; Mem., Lloyd's Register of Shipping, 1963–67. Chairman: Barry Pilotage Authority, 1963–74 (Mem. 1953); Port Talbot Pilotage Authority, 1970–74; SE Wales Pilotage Authority, 1974–80; Welsh Council Mission to Seamen, 1984–; Vice-Chm., BTDB, 1969–79 (Mem., 1966–79; Chm., S Wales Local Bd, 1966); Pres., Cardiff Chamber of Commerce, 1959–60. Chm., S Glamorgan HA, 1974–84. Church in Wales: Member: Governing Body, 1957–60; Rep. Body, 1960– (Dep. Chm., 1985–; Treasurer, 1988–); Finance Cttee, 1960–88 (Vice-Chm. 1971, Chm. 1975–88); Dep. Chm., Finance and Resources Cttee, 1988–. RNLI: Chm. Cardiff Br., 1950–73; Mem. Cttee of Management, 1954–; Vice-Pres. 1969–; Dep. Chm., 1985–; Mem., Exec. Cttee, 1970–. Chm., Council, Univ. of Wales Coll. of Medicine, 1988– (Mem., 1984–). *Publication:* A Century of Family Shipowning, 1954. *Recreations:* skiing, sailing, gardening. *Address:* The Coach House, Llanblethian, Cowbridge, South Glamorgan. *T:* Cowbridge (04463) 2251. *Club:* Cardiff and County.

CORY, Sir (Clinton Charles) Donald, 5th Bt *cr* 1919, of Coryton, Whitchurch, Glamorgan; *b* 13 Sept. 1937; *s* of Sir Clinton James Donald Cory, 4th Bt and of Mary, *o d* of Dr Arthur Douglas Hunt; *S* father, 1991.

CORY, John; Vice Lord-Lieutenant of South Glamorgan, since 1990; Director, John Cory & Sons Ltd, since 1949; *b* 30 June 1928; *s* of John and Cecil Cory; *m* 1965, Sarah Christine, *d* of John Meade, JP, DL; two *d. Educ:* Eton; Trinity College, Cambridge. Chm., Cardiff RDC, 1971–72. Member, Governing Body, 1957–74, Representative Body, 1960–, Church in Wales. Pres., Nat. Light Horse Breeding Soc., 1977–78. Joint Master, Glamorgan Hounds, 1962–67. High Sheriff, 1959, JP 1961, DL 1968, Glamorgan. KStJ. *Address:* The Grange, St Brides-super-Ely, Cardiff CF5 6XA. *T:* Peterston-super-Ely (0446) 760211. *Club:* Cardiff and County (Cardiff).

CORY, Raymond; *see* Cory, C. R.

CORY-WRIGHT, Sir Richard (Michael), 4th Bt *cr* 1903; *b* 17 Jan. 1944; *s* of Capt. A. J. J. Cory-Wright (killed in action, 1944), and of Susan Esterel (who *m* 2nd, 1949, late Lt-Col J. E. Gurney, DSO, MC), *d* of Robert Elwes; *S* grandfather, 1969; *m* 1976, Veronica, *o d* of James Bolton; three *s. Educ:* Eton; Birmingham Univ. *Heir:* s Roland Anthony Cory-Wright, *b* 11 March 1979. *Address:* Cox's Farm, Winterbrook Lane, Wallingford, Oxon OX10 9RE.

COSGRAVE, Liam, SC; *b* April 1920; *s* of late William T. Cosgrave; *m* 1952, Vera Osborne; two *s* one *d. Educ:* Synge Street Christian Brothers; Castlenock College, Dublin; King's Inns. Served in Army during Emergency. Barrister-at-Law, 1943; Senior Counsel, 1958. Member, Dail Eireann, 1943–81; Chairman Public Accounts Committee, 1945; Parliamentary Secretary to Taoiseach and Minister for Industry and Commerce, 1948–51; Minister for External Affairs, 1954–57; Leader, Fine Gael Party, 1965–77; Taoiseach (Head of Govt of Ireland), 1973–77; Minister for Defence, 1976. Leader first delegation from Ireland to the UN Assembly. Hon. LLD: Duquesne Univ., Pittsburg, Pa, and St John's Univ., Brooklyn, 1956; de Paul Univ., Chicago, 1958; NUI, 1974; Dublin Univ., 1974. Knight Grand Cross of Pius IX, 1956. *Address:* Beechpark, Templeogue, Co. Dublin.

COSGRAVE, Patrick John, PhD; writer; *b* 28 Sept. 1941; *s* of Patrick John Cosgrave and Margaret FitzGerald; *m* 1st, 1965, Ruth Dudley Edwards (marr. diss.); 2nd, 1974, Norma Alicia Green (marr. diss.); one *d*; 3rd, 1981, Shirley Ward. *Educ:* St Vincent's Sch., Dublin; University Coll., NUI, Dublin (BA, MA); Univ. of Cambridge (PhD). London Editor, Radio Telefis Eireann, 1968–69; Conservative Research Dept, 1969–71; Political Editor, The Spectator, 1971–75; Features Editor, Telegraph Magazine, 1974–76. Special Adviser to Rt Hon. Mrs Margaret Thatcher, 1975–79. Managing Editor, Quartet Crime (Quartet Books), 1979–81. *Publications:* The Public Poetry of Robert Lowell, 1970; Churchill at War: Alone, 1974; Cheyney's Law (novel), 1977; Margaret Thatcher: a Tory and her party, 1978, 2nd edn as Margaret Thatcher: Prime Minister, 1979; The Three Colonels (novel), 1979; R. A. Butler: an English Life, 1981; Adventure of State (novel), 1984; Thatcher: the First Term, 1985; Carrington: a life and a policy, 1985; The Lives of Enoch Powell, 1989; contribs to Proc. of Royal Irish Academy, Irish Historical Studies, Encounter, Policy Rev., New Law Jl. *Recreations:* thriller fiction, cooking, roses, cricket. *Address:* 21 Thornton Road, SW12 0JX. *T:* 081–671 0637.

COSGROVE, Hazel Josephine, (Mrs J. A. Cosgrove); *see* Aronson, H. J.

COSSERAT, Kay, RDI 1986; Director, Cosserat Design Ltd, since 1976; Part-time Lecturer, Royal College of Art, since 1990, and Chelsea School of Art, since 1985; *b* 24 Oct. 1947; *d* of Robert and Elizabeth Macklam; *m* 1972, Christopher Graham Peloquin Cosserat; two *s. Educ:* Cleveland Sch., Eaglescliffe; Goldsmiths' Sch. of Art (Dip AD 1st cl. Hons); Royal Coll. of Art (MA Textiles 1972); Sanderson Travel Scholarship, 1972. Formed Cosserat Design Partnership, 1974; Founder Mem., London Designer Collections, 1974; currently producing textile and garment designs on a consultancy basis. Mem., Fashion and Textile Bd, CNAA, 1978. Part-time Lecturer: St Martins Sch. of Art, 1972–80; RCA, 1976–79; External Assessor: Central Sch. of Art, 1982–85; Trent Poly., 1983–85; Liverpool Poly., 1985–87; Huddersfield Poly., 1985–88; QUB, 1990–; Winchester Sch. of Art, 1991–. *Recreations:* gardening, ski-ing, collecting '30s pottery. *Address:* Cosserat Design Ltd, 1 Second Avenue, Milton Keynes MK1 1ED.

COSSHAM, Christopher Hugh, CB 1989; Senior Assistant Director of Public Prosecutions (Northern Ireland), 1973–89; *b* 12 April 1929; *s* of Lorimer and Gwendolin Cossham; *m* 1958, Joanna Howard Smith; one *s* one *d. Educ:* Monkton Combe Sch.; Bristol Univ. Called to Bar, Gray's Inn, 1958. Board of Trade, 1958–62; Director of

Public Prosecutions Dept, 1962–73. Dep. Metropolitan Stipendiary Magistrate, 1938–86. Mem., Wkg Party on handling of complaints against police, 1974. *Recreations:* cycling, listening to music, writing humorous verse. *Address:* Valhalla, 1 The Grange, High Street, Portishead, Avon BS20 9QL. *T:* Portishead (0272) 845237. *Clubs:* Civil Service, Northern Law.

COSSONS, Neil, OBE 1982; Director, Science Museum, since 1986; *b* 15 Jan. 1939; *s* of Arthur Cossons and Evelyn (*née* Bettle); *m* 1965, Veronica Edwards; two *s* one *d*. *Educ:* Henry Mellish Sch., Nottingham; Univ. of Liverpool (MA). FSA 1968; FMA 1970; FRSA 1988. Curator of Technology, Bristol City Museum, 1964; Dep. Dir, City of Liverpool Museums, 1969; Dir, Ironbridge Gorge Museum Trust, 1971; Dir, Nat. Maritime Museum, 1983–86. Comr, Historic Buildings and Monuments Commn for England, 1989– (Mem., Ancient Monuments Adv. Cttee, 1984–); Member: Curatorium Internat. Committee for the Conservation of the Industrial Heritage, 1973–78; BBC General Adv. Council, 1987–90; NEDO Tourism and Leisure Industries Sector Gp (formerly Leisure Industries EDC), 1987–90; Council, RCA, 1989–; Design Council, 1990–. President: Assoc. for Industrial Archaeology, 1977–80; Assoc. of Independent Museums, 1983– (Chm., 1978–83); Museums Assoc., 1981–82. Trustee, Civic Trust, 1987–. Gov., Imperial Coll. of Sci., Technology and Medicine, 1989–. Hon. Fellow, RCA, 1987. Hon. DSocSc Birmingham, 1979; DUniv Open, 1984; Hon. DLitt: Liverpool, 1989; Bradford, 1991. Norton Medlicott Medal, Historical Assoc., 1991. *Publications:* Contractors' Locomotives GCR, 1963; (with R. A. Buchanan) Industrial Archaeology of the Bristol Region, 1968; (with K. Hudson) Industrial Archaeologists' Guide, 1969, 2nd edn 1971; Industrial Archaeology, 1975, 2nd edn 1987; (ed) Transactions of the First International Congress on the Conservation of Industrial Monuments, 1975; (ed) Rees's Manufacturing Industry, 1975; (with H. Sowden) Ironbridge—Landscape of Industry, 1977; (with B. S. Trinder) The Iron Bridge—Symbol of the Industrial Revolution, 1979, 2nd edn (Japanese) 1989; (ed) Management of Change in Museums, 1985; numerous papers in Museums Jl and elsewhere. *Recreations:* travel, design. *Address:* Science Museum, SW7 2DD; Church Hill, Ironbridge, Shropshire TF8 7PW. *T:* Ironbridge (095243) 2701. *Club:* Athenæum.

COSTAIN, Noel Leslie, OBE 1964; Director of Works, University of Sheffield, 1964–78; *b* 11 Jan. 1914; *s* of George Wesley Costain and Minnie Grace Pinson; *m* 1945, Marie José Elizabeth (*née* Bishton); two *d*. *Educ:* King Edward's Sch., Five Ways, Birmingham; Univ. of Birmingham (BSc). CEng, MICE, FINucE. Engineer with Sir R. MacAlpine & Sons, 1937–38; Epsom and Ewell BC, 1939; Air Min., Directorate-Gen. of Works; Section Officer, Orkneys and Shetlands, 1940–43; Prin. Works Officer, Sierra Leone, 1944–46; Superintending Engr, Air Ministry, 1946–51; RAF Airfield Construction Br.: Cmdg 5352 Wing, Germany, and OC, RAF Church Lawford, 1951–54; Superintending Engr, Works Area, Bristol, 1954–58; Chief Engr, MEAF, 1958–60; Chief Resident Engr, BMEWS, Fylingdales, 1960–63. Vice-Chm., Yorkshire Univs Air Squadron Cttee. Mem. Council, Instn of Nuclear Engineers, 1965; Vice-Pres., 1969; President, 1972–76. *Recreations:* travel, gardening. *Address:* Villa Marie José, Avenida 3 no 59, Urbanisation Hacienda Las Chapas, Marbella, Málaga, Spain.

COSTAIN, Peter John, FCA; Group Chief Executive, Costain Group Plc, since 1980; Director, Pearl Group, since 1990; *b* 2 April 1938; *s* of Sir Albert Costain; *m* 1963, Victoria M. Pope; three *s*. *Educ:* Charterhouse. Peat Marwick Mitchell & Co., 1956–63; Richard Costain Ltd, 1963–65; Costain Australia Ltd, 1965–: Board Member, 1967; Managing Director, 1971; Chief Executive, 1973. Mem., London Adv. Bd, Westpac Banking Corp., 1981–86. FAIB. *Recreations:* sailing, skiing, golf. *Address:* 21 Caroline Terrace, SW1. *Clubs:* Royal Thames Yacht; Athenæum (Melbourne); Rye Golf, Royal St George's Golf.

COSTANZI, Edwin J. B.; *see* Borg-Costanzi.

COSTAR, Sir Norman (Edgar), KCMG 1963 (CMG 1953); *b* 18 May 1909. *Educ:* Battersea Grammar School; Jesus Coll., Cambridge. Asst Principal, Colonial Office, 1932; Private Sec. to Permanent Under Sec., Dominions Office, 1935; served in UK High Commissioner's Offices, Australia, 1937–39, New Zealand, 1945–47. Principal, 1938; Asst Sec., 1946. Dep. High Commissioner, Ceylon, 1953–57; Asst Under-Sec., Commonwealth Relations Office, 1958–60; Dep. High Commissioner in Australia, 1960–62; High Commissioner: Trinidad and Tobago, 1962–66; Cyprus, 1967–69. Adjudicator, Immigration Appeals, 1970–81. *Club:* United Oxford & Cambridge University.

COSTELLO, Gordon John; Chief Accountant of the Bank of England, 1975–78; *b* 29 March 1921; *s* of late Ernest James Costello and Hilda May Costello; *m* 1946, Joan Lilian Moore; two *s* one *d*. *Educ:* Varndean Sch. Served War, 1939–45 (RA). Bank of England, 1946; worked in various Departments; Asst Chief Accountant, 1964; Asst Sec., 1965; Dep. Sec., 1968; Dep. Chief Cashier, 1970. *Recreations:* music, travel, walking, tennis. *Address:* 26 Peacock Lane, Brighton, Sussex BN1 6WA. *T:* Brighton (0273) 552344.

COT, Pierre Donatien Alphonse, Commander Legion of Honour; Croix de Guerre; Ingénieur général des ponts et chaussées; *b* 10 Sept. 1911; *s* of late Donatien Cot, Engr-Gen. and Naval Hydrographer, Membre de l'Institut, and Yvonne (*née* Bunout); *m* 1939, Claude Bouguen; two *s* two *d*. *Educ:* Lycée Louis-le-Grand, Paris; Ecole Polytechnique, Paris. Licencié ès Sciences. Govt Civil Engr, Paris, 1936; Chief Engineer of Port of Le Havre, 1945; Techn. Manager, 1951, Dir-Gen., 1955–67, and Administrator, 1967–75, Paris Airport Authority; Pres., Air France, 1967–74; Pres.-Dir-Gen., Soc. Gén. d'Entreprises, 1974–79, now Président d'Honneur. Pres., Institut géographique national, 1967–75. Médaille de l'Aéronautique; Officer du Mérite Touristique. Hon. MVO. Médaille de vermeil de la Ville de Paris, 1972. *Address:* 69 rue de l'Assomption, 75016 Paris, France.

COTES, Peter, (Sydney Arthur Boulting); author, lecturer, play producer, stage, film and television director; *e s* of Arthur Boulting and Rose Bennett; *m* 1st, 1938, Myfanwy Jones (marr. diss.); 2nd, 1948, Joan Miller (*d* 1988). *Educ:* Taplow; Italia Conti and privately. Was for some years an actor; made theatrical debut, Portsmouth Hippodrome, in the arms of Vesta Tilley. Formed own independent play-producing co. with Hon. James Smith, 1949, presented Rocket to the Moon, St Martin's Theatre, and subsequently produced, in association with Arts Council of Great Britain, notable seasons in Manchester and at Embassy and Lyric Theatres, Hammersmith. Founded: New Lindsey, 1946; New Boltons, 1951. West-End Productions include: Pick Up Girl, 1946; The Animal Kingdom, 1947; The Master Builder, 1948; Miss Julie, 1949; Come Back, Little Sheba, 1951; The Father, 1951; The Biggest Thief in Town, 1951; The Mousetrap, 1952; The Man, 1952; A Pin to see the Peepshow, Broadway, 1953; Happy Holiday, 1954; Hot Summer Night, 1958; Epitaph for George Dillon (Holland), 1959; The Rope Dancers, 1959; Girl on the Highway, 1960; A Loss of Roses, 1962; The Odd Ones, 1963; Hidden Stranger, Broadway, 1963; What Goes Up. . .!, 1963; So Wise, So Young, 1964; Paint Myself Black, 1965; The Impossible Years, 1966; Staring at the Sun, 1968; Janie Jackson, 1968; The Old Ladies, 1969; Look, No Hands!, 1971. Films: The Right Person; Two Letters; Jane Clegg; Waterfront; The Young and the Guilty; has prod. and adapted numerous plays for BBC Television and ITV; was Sen. Drama Dir, AR-TV, 1955–58; producing stage plays and films, 1959–60; Supervising Producer of Drama Channel 7, Melbourne, 1961; produced and adapted plays for Anglia TV, 1964; produced first TV series of P. G. Wodehouse short stories, on BBC; wrote George Robey centenary TV Tribute, BBC Omnibus series, 1969; wrote and dir. in One Pair of Eyes series, BBC TV, 1970; has written, adapted and narrated many productions for radio incl. Back into the Light, The Prime Minister of Mirth, Mervyn Peake, Portrait of an Actor; collaborated 1980–81 on: The Song is Ended, Who Were You With Last Night, Whose Your Lady Friend, The Black Sheep of the Family (BBC); scripted: Old Stagers, 1979–87; This Fabulous Genius (BBC), 1980; Wee Georgie Wood (BBC), 1980. FRSA; Member: Theatrical Managers' Assoc.; Medico-Legal Soc.; Our Society; Guild of Drama Adjudicators. Kt of Mark Twain, 1980. *Publications:* No Star Nonsense, 1949; The Little Fellow, 1951; A Handbook of Amateur Theatre, 1957; George Robey, 1972; The Trial of Elvira Barney, 1976; Circus, 1976; Origin of a Thriller, 1977; JP (The Man Called Mitch), 1978; Misfit Midget, 1979; Portrait of an Actor, 1980; (jtly) The Barbirollis: a musical marriage, 1983; Dickie: the story of Dickie Henderson, 1988; contrib. to The Field, Spectator, Queen, Guardian, etc. *Address:* 7 Hill Lawn Court, Chipping Norton, Oxon OX7 5NF. *Recreations:* book collecting, writing letters, criminology. *Clubs:* Savage, Our Society.

COTILL, John Atrill T.; *see* Templeton-Cotill.

COTRUBAS, Ileana, (Mme Manfred Ramin); opera singer, retired 1990; *b* Rumania; *d* of Vasile and Maria Cotrubas; *m* 1972, Manfred Ramin. *Educ:* Conservatorul Ciprian Porumbescu, Bucharest. Opera and concert engagements all over Europe, N America and Japan. Formerly permanent guest at Royal Opera House, Covent Garden; Member, Vienna State Opera; also frequently sang in Scala, Milan, Munich, Berlin, Paris, Chicago, NY Metropolitan Opera. Main operatic roles: Susanna, Pamina, Gilda, Traviata, Manon, Tatyana, Mimi, Melisande, Amina, Elisabetta, Nedda, Marguerite. Has made numerous recordings. Kammersängerin, Austria, 1981; Grand Officer, Sant Iago da Espada (Portugal), 1990.

COTTAM, Harold; UK Managing Partner, Ernst & Young, since 1987; *b* 12 Oct. 1938; *s* of Frank and Elizabeth Cottam; *m* 1962, Lyn Minton; two *d*. *Educ:* Bedford School. FCA. Smith Kline UK, 1964–66; Simon Engineering Group, 1966–68; Ernst & Whinney, subseq. Ernst & Young, 1968–. *Recreations:* music, tennis. *Address:* Ernst & Young, Becket House, 1 Lambeth Palace Road, SE1 7EU. *T:* 071–931 3002.

COTTENHAM, 8th Earl of, *cr* 1850; **Kenelm Charles Everard Digby Pepys;** Bt 1784 and 1801; Baron Cottenham, 1836; Viscount Crowhurst, 1850; *b* 27 Nov. 1948; *s* of 7th Earl of Cottenham and Lady Angela Isabel Nellie Nevill, *d* of 4th Marquess of Abergavenny; *S* father, 1968; *m* 1975, Sarah, *d* of Captain S. Lombard-Hobson, CVO, OBE, RN; two *s* one *d*. *Educ:* Eton. *Heir: s* Viscount Crowhurst, *qv*.

See also Baron McGowan.

COTTER, Lt-Col Sir Delaval James Alfred, 6th Bt, *cr* 1763; DSO 1944; late 13th/18th Royal Hussars; *b* 29 April 1911; *s* of 5th Bt and Ethel Lucy (*d* 1956), *d* of Alfred Wheeler; *S* father, 1924; *m* 1st, 1943, Roma (marr. diss., 1949), *widow* of Sqdn Ldr K. A. K. MacEwen and *o d* of late Adrian Rome, Dalswinton Lodge, Salisbury, SR; two *d*; 2nd, 1952, Mrs Eveline Mary Paterson (*d* 1991), *widow* of Lieut-Col J. F. Paterson, OBE, and *d* of late E. J. Mardon, ICS (retired). *Educ:* Malvern Coll; RMC, Sandhurst. Served War of 1939–45 (DSO); retired, 1959. JP Wilts, 1962–63. *Heir: n* Patrick Laurence Delaval Cotter [*b* 21 Nov. 1941; *m* 1967, Janet, *d* of George Potter, Barnstaple; one *s* two *d*]. *Address:* Green Lines, Iwerne Courtney, Blandford Forum, Dorset DT11 8QR.

COTTERELL, Geoffrey; author; *b* 24 Nov. 1919; *yr s* of late Graham Cotterell and Millicent (*née* Crews). *Educ:* Bishops Stortford College. Served War of 1939–45, Royal Artillery, 1940–46. *Publications:* Then a Soldier, 1944; This is the Way, 1947; Randle in Springtime, 1949; Strait and Narrow, 1950; Westward the Sun, 1952 (repr. 1973); The Strange Enchantment, 1956 (repr. 1973); Tea at Shadow Creek, 1958; Tiara Tahiti, 1960 (filmed 1962, screenplay with Ivan Foxwell); Go, said the bird, 1966; Bowers of Innocence, 1970; Amsterdam, the life of a city, 1972. *Recreation:* golf. *Address:* 2 Fulbourne House, Blackwater Road, Eastbourne, Sussex BN20 7DN. *Clubs:* Royal Automobile; Cooden Beach Golf.

COTTERELL, Sir John (Henry Geers), 6th Bt *cr* 1805; Chairman, Radio Wyvern, since 1981; *b* 8 May 1935; *s* of Sir Richard Charles Geers Cotterell, 5th Bt, CBE, and Lady Lettice Cotterell (*d* 1973), *d* of 7th Earl Beauchamp; *S* father, 1978; *m* 1959, Vanda Alexandra Clare, *d* of Major Philip Alexander Clement Bridgewater; three *s* one *d*. *Educ:* Eton; RMA Sandhurst. Officer, Royal Horse Guards, 1955–61. Vice-Chm. Hereford and Worcs CC, 1973–77, Chm., 1977–81. Pres., Nat. Fedn of Young Farmers Clubs, 1986– (Dep. Pres., 1979–86); Mem., Jockey Club, 1990–. Chairman: Hereford Mappa Mundi Trust, 1990; Rural Voice, 1991. *Recreations:* cricket, shooting. *Heir: s* Henry Richard Geers Cotterell [*b* 22 Aug. 1961; *m* 1986, Carolyn, *er d* of John Beckwith-Smith, Maybanks Manor, Rudgwick, Sussex; one *d*]. *Address:* Garnons, near Hereford. *T:* Bridge Sollars (098122) 232. *Club:* White's.

COTTERILL, Kenneth William, CMG 1976; Chairman, Commercial and Political Risk Consultants Ltd, since 1986 (Deputy Chairman, 1981–86); *b* 5 June 1921; *s* of William and Ada May Cotterill; *m* 1948, Janet Hilda Cox; one *d*. *Educ:* Sutton County Sch.; London School of Economics, BSc (Econ). Served War in Royal Navy, 1941–46. After the war, joined ECGD; Principal, 1956; Asst Sec., 1966; Under Sec., 1970; Dep. Head of Dept, 1976–81. Dir, Tarmac Internat., 1981–86; Consultant: NEI International, 1981–87; Barclays Bank, 1981–87. *Recreations:* reading, walking, gardening. *Address:* 15 Minster Drive, Croydon CR0 5UP. *T:* 081–681 6700.

COTTESLOE, 4th Baron (UK) *cr* 1874; **John Walgrave Halford Fremantle,** GBE 1960; TD; Bt 1821; Baron of Austrian Empire, *cr* 1816; *b* 2 March 1900; *s* of 3rd Baron Cottesloe, CB and Florence (*d* 1956), *d* of Thomas Tapling; *S* father 1956; *m* 1st, 1926, Lady Elizabeth Harris (marr. diss., 1945; she *d* 1983), *o d* of 5th Earl of Malmesbury; one *s* one *d*; 2nd, 1959, Gloria Jean Irene Dunn; one *s* two *d*. *Educ:* Eton; Trinity Coll., Cambridge. BA (Hons) Mechanical Sciences 1921; MA 1924. Served as OC 251 (Bucks) AA Battery RA (TA), 1938–39; GSO 1 att. 2nd Armoured Division, 1940; Senior Military Liaison Officer to Regional Commissioner, NE Region, 1940–41; GSO 1 (Technical) AA Command, 1941–42; Commanding Officer, 20 LAA Regt RA, 1942–44; GSO 1 (Radar) War Office, 1944–45. Mem. LCC, 1945–55. Chm., Thomas Tapling & Co. Ltd; Vice-Chm., PLA, 1956–67. Chairman: Tate Gallery, 1959–60; Arts Council of Gt Britain, 1960–65; South Bank Theatre Bd (from inception), 1962–77 (Cottesloe theatre part of Nat. Theatre complex, opened 1976); Adv. Council and Reviewing Cttee on Export of Works of Art, 1954–72; Heritage in Danger, 1973–; Royal Postgrad. Med. Sch., 1949–58 (Fellow); NW Met. Reg. Hosp. Bd, 1953–60; Hammersmith and St Mark's Hospital, 1968–74; Northwick Park Hosp. Adv. Cttee, 1970–74; a Governor, King Edward's Hosp. Fund for London, 1973–83. Chairman: British Postgraduate Medical Fedn, 1958–72; Nat. Rifle Assoc., 1960–72; Vice-Chm., City Parochial Foundn, 1972–77; Pres., Hospital Saving Assoc., 1973–; Hon. Sec. Amateur Rowing Assoc., 1932–46; a

Steward of Henley Royal Regatta; Pres., Leander, 1957–62. Chm., The Dogs' Home, Battersea, 1970–83. Former DL County of London (later Greater London). *Recreations:* rowed in winning crews in Oxford and Cambridge Boat Race, 1921 and 1922 and in Grand Challenge Cup, Henley, 1922; Captain of English VIII at Bisley on 25 occasions and has shot in English VIII on 37 occasions and won Match Rifle Championship six times, with many other first prizes for long-range shooting. *Heir: s* Comdr Hon. John Tapling Fremantle, *qv. Address:* 33 Edna Street, SW11 3DP. *T:* 071–585 0208. *Clubs:* Travellers'; Leander.

See also T. G. M. Brooks.

COTTHAM, George William; Chairman and Managing Director: Yorkshire Rider Ltd, since 1986; Rider Holdings Ltd, since 1988; Rider York Ltd, since 1990; *b* 11 July 1944; *s* of George William and Elizabeth Cottham; *m* 1967, Joan Thomas; two *d. Educ:* Univ. of London; Polytechnic of Liverpool; Liverpool Coll. of Commerce. BSc 1st Cl. Hons, LLB 2nd Cl. Hons. FCIT. Various posts, Liverpool City Transport, 1960–74; District Transport Manager, St Helens, 1974–77; Transport General Manager, Newport, 1977–80; Gen. Manager, Cleveland Transit, 1980–83; Dir Gen., W Yorks PTE, 1983–86. *Recreations:* family, home, garden, music, photography. *Address:* Brow Lee, 118 Huddersfield Road, Brighouse, West Yorkshire. *T:* Brighouse (0484) 713019.

COTTON; *see* Stapleton-Cotton, family name of Viscount Combermere.

COTTON, Bernard Edward, CBE 1976; Chairman, South Yorkshire Residuary Body, 1985–89; *b* 8 Oct. 1920; *s* of Hugh Harry Cotton and Alice Cotton; *m* 1944, Stephanie Anne, *d* of Rev. A. E. and Mrs Furnival; three *s. Educ:* Sheffield City Grammar Sch.; Sheffield Univ. Served Army, 1939–45, latterly as Lieut, Worcs Yeomanry (53rd Airlanding Light Regt RA). Joined Round Oak Steelworks, Brierley Hill, 1949, Sales Man., 1954–57; Gen. Man., Samuel Osborn (Canada) Ltd, Montreal, 1957–63; Samuel Osborn & Co. Ltd: Sales Dir, 1963–69; Man. Dir, 1969; Chm. and Chief Exec., 1969–78; Pres., 1978–80. Dir, Renold Ltd, 1979–84; Dep. Chm., Baker Perkins plc, 1983–86. Chairman: Yorks and Humberside Reg. Econ. Planning Council, 1970–79; Health Service Supply Council, 1980–85; Mem., BR Eastern Bd, 1977–85; Pres., Yorks and Humberside Develt Assoc., 1973–84. Chm., BIM Working Party on Employee Participation, 1975. Pro Chancellor, Sheffield Univ., 1982–87. Master, Cutlers' Co. in Hallamshire, 1979–80. Hon. Fellow, Sheffield City Poly., 1980. Hon. LLD Sheffield, 1988. CBIM. *Recreations:* gardening and other quiet pursuits. *Address:* Stubbin House, Carsick Hill Road, Sheffield S10 3LU. *T:* Sheffield (0742) 303082. *Club:* Sheffield (Sheffield).

COTTON, Christopher P.; *see* Powell-Cotton.

COTTON, Diana Rosemary, (Mrs R. B. Allan); QC 1983; *b* 30 Nov. 1941; *d* of Arthur Frank Edward and Muriel Cotton; *m* 1966, Richard Bellerby Allan; two *s* one *d. Educ:* Berkhamsted School for Girls; Lady Margaret Hall, Oxford (MA). Joined Middle Temple, 1961; called to Bar, 1964; Bencher, 1990; Member, Midland and Oxford Circuit; a Recorder of the Crown Court, 1982. Mem., Criminal Injuries Compensation Bd, 1989–. *Recreation:* her family and other animals. *Address:* Devereux Chambers, Devereux Court, Temple, WC2R 3JJ. *T:* 071–353 7534. *Club:* Western (Glasgow).

COTTON, Henry Egerton, JP; Lord-Lieutenant and Custos Rotulorum, Metropolitan County of Merseyside, since 1989; *b* 21 July 1929; *s* of Vere Egerton Cotton, CBE, TD, LLD, and Elfreda Helen Cotton (*née* Moore); *m* 1955, (Elizabeth Margaret) Susan Peard; one *s* one *d. Educ:* Durnford and Brockhurst Prep. Schs; Rugby Sch.; Magdalene Coll., Cambridge (MA). National Service, RA, 1947–49; Territorials, 59th Med. Regt RA (Lieut), 1949–55. Owen Owen Ltd, 1952–89; Development Dir, T. J. Hughes & Co., 1986–89. Liverpool Playhouse: Dir, 1967–73; Chm., 1973–82; Pres., 1989–; Dir, Northern Ballet Th., 1977–; Governor: Liverpool Polytechnic, 1988–; Blue Coat Sch., Liverpool, 1970–; Vice-Pres. and Life Gov., Liverpool Coll., 1989–. Trustee: Childwall Open Spaces Trust, 1970–; Skelton Bounty, 1988–; Nat. Museums and Galls on Merseyside, 1991–; Chairman: Local Radio Council (Radio Merseyside), 1976–79; Drama Panel, Merseyside Arts Assoc., 1980–82. Vice Chm., Liverpool Dio. Bd of Finance, 1968–75; Chm., Liverpool Cathedral Exec. Cttee, 1979–; Dir, Liverpool Cathedral Estates, 1991–. Patron, St Mary's Ch., Grassendale, Liverpool, 1969–. High Sheriff of Merseyside, 1986–87. KStJ 1989. *Recreations:* travel, theatre, canals, gardening. *Address:* Norwood, Grassendale Park, Liverpool L19 0LP. *T:* 051–427 3122.

COTTON, John Anthony; His Honour Judge Cotton; a Circuit Judge, since 1973; *b* 6 March 1926; *s* of Frederick Thomas Hooley Cotton and Catherine Mary Cotton; *m* 1960, Johanna Aritia van Lookeren Campagne; three *s* two *d. Educ:* Stonyhurst Coll.; Lincoln Coll., Oxford. Called to the Bar, Middle Temple, 1949; Dep. Chm., W Riding of Yorks QS, 1967–71; Recorder of Halifax, 1971; a Recorder and Hon. Recorder of Halifax, 1972–73. Pres., S Yorks Br., Magistrates' Assoc., 1982–. *Recreation:* golf. *Address:* 81 Lyndhurst Road, Sheffield S11 9BJ. *T:* Sheffield (0742) 585569.

COTTON, Sir John Richard, KCMG 1969 (CMG 1959); OBE 1947 (MBE 1944); retired from HM Diplomatic Service, 1969; Adjudicator, Immigration Appeals, 1970–81; *b* 22 Jan. 1909; *s* of late J. J. Cotton, ICS, and late Gigia Ricciardi Arlotta; *m* 1937, Mary Bridget Connors, Stradbally, County Waterford, Ireland; three *s. Educ:* Wellington Coll.; RMC, Sandhurst. Commissioned 1929; 8th King George's Own Light Cavalry (IA), 1930–34; transferred to Indian Political Service, 1934; served in: Aden, Abyssinia (Attaché HM Legation, 1935), Persian Gulf, Rajputana, Hyderabad, Kathiawar, Baroda, New Delhi (Dep. Sec. Political Dept). Transferred to HM Foreign Service, 1947; served in Karachi (First Sec.), 1947–48, Foreign Office, 1949–51, Madrid (Commercial Counsellor, HM Embassy), 1951–54; Consul-Gen., Brazzaville, 1954–55, Leopoldville, 1955–57; Counsellor (Commercial), HM Embassy, Brussels, 1957–62. Consul-Gen., São Paulo, Brazil, 1962–65; Ambassador to Kinshasa, Congo Republic (now Zaire), and to Burundi, 1965–69. *Recreation:* golf. *Address:* Lansing House, Hartley Wintney, Hants RG27 8RY. *T:* Hartley Wintney (0252) 842681. *Club:* Army and Navy.

COTTON, Leonard Thomas, MCh; FRCS; Surgeon, King's College Hospital, since 1957; Surgeon, Queen Victoria Hospital, East Grinstead, and St Luke's Nursing Home for the Clergy; Dean, King's College Hospital Medical School, 1978–87 (Vice-Dean, 1976–77); *b* 5 Dec. 1922; *s* of Edward Cotton and Elizabeth (*née* Webb); *m* 1946, Frances Joanna Bryan; one *s* two *d. Educ:* King's College Sch., Wimbledon; Oriel Coll., Oxford; King's Coll. Hospital. MRCS, LRCP 1946; BM, BCh Oxon 1946; FRCS 1950; MCh Oxon 1957. House Surgeon, King's College Hospital, 1946; Resident Surgical Officer, Royal Waterloo Hospital, 1947; Resident Surgical Officer, Weymouth and District Hospital, 1948; National Service, Surgical Specialist RAMC, 1949–51; Senior Registrar and Registrar, King's College Hospital, 1951–57; Surgical Tutor, King's Coll. Hospital Medical Sch., 1957–65. FRSM; Member: Surgical Research Soc., Assoc. of Surgeons; Vascular Surgical Soc.; Ct of Examiners, RCS. Hunterian Prof., RCS. FKC 1983. *Publications:* (ed) Hey Groves' Synopsis of Surgery; co-author, short text-book of Surgery; contributions to medical journals. *Recreations:* gardening, reading. *Address:* 3 Dome Hill Park, Sydenham Hill, SE26 6SP. *T:* 081–778 8047; Private Wing, King's College Hospital, Denmark Hill, SE5 8RX. *T:* 071–274 8670.

COTTON, Hon. Sir Robert Carrington, KCMG 1978; Chairman of Directors: Cottons Pty, since 1965; Kleinwort Benson Australian Income Fund Inc., since 1986; Senior Advisor, Hill & Knowlton Inc., since 1988; *b* 29 Nov. 1915; *s* of H. L. Carrington Cotton; *m* 1937, Eve Elizabeth Macdougall; one *s* two *d. Educ:* St Peter's Coll., Adelaide, SA. FASA. State President of Liberal Party (NSW), 1956–59; Federal Vice-Pres., 1960–61; elected to Senate, 1965; Minister for Civil Aviation, 1969–72; Shadow Minister for Manufacturing Industry (in Opposition), 1972–75; Minister for Industry and Commerce, 1975–77; Australian Consul-Gen. in NY, 1978–81; Ambassador to USA, 1982–85. Chm., Australian Political Exchange Cttee, 1981–. *Recreations:* swimming, writing, photography. *Address:* 75 Pacific Road, Palm Beach, NSW 2108, Australia. *T:* 919.5456. *Clubs:* Oriental; The Brook (NY); Australian (Sydney); Commonwealth (Canberra, ACT).

COTTON, William Frederick, (Bill Cotton), CBE 1989 (OBE 1976); Managing Director, Television, BBC, 1984–88; Chairman, Noel Gay Television, since 1988; Director, Noel Gay Organisation, since 1988; *b* 23 April 1928; *s* of late William Edward (Billy) Cotton and Mabel Hope; *m* 1st, 1950, Bernadine Maud (*née* Sinclair); three *d*; 2nd, 1965, Ann Corfield (*née* Bucknall); one step *d*; *m* 1990, Kathryn Mary (*née* Ralphes). *Educ:* Ardingly College. Jt Man. Dir, Michael Reine Music Co., 1952–56; BBC-TV: Producer, Light Entertainment Dept, 1956–62; Asst Head of Light Entertainment, 1962–67; Head of Variety, 1967–70; Head of Light Entertainment Gp, 1970–77; Controller, BBC 1, 1977–81; Dep. Man. Dir, 1981–82; Dir of Programmes, Television, and Dir of Develt, BBC, 1982; Chm., BBC Enterprises, 1982–86 and 1987–88 (Vice Chm., 1986–87). Non-exec. Dir, Alba plc, 1988–. FRTS 1983. *Recreation:* golf. *Address:* c/o Noel Gay Organisation, 24 Denmark Street, WC2. *Club:* Royal & Ancient Golf (St Andrews).

COTTRELL, Sir Alan (Howard), Kt 1971; FRS 1955; FEng; Master of Jesus College, Cambridge, 1974–86 (Hon. Fellow 1986); Vice-Chancellor, University of Cambridge, 1977–79; *b* 17 July 1919; *s* of Albert and Elizabeth Cottrell; *m* 1944, Jean Elizabeth Harber; one *s. Educ:* Moseley Grammar Sch.; University of Birmingham. BSc 1939; PhD 1942; ScD(Cantab) 1976. Lectr in Metallurgy, University of Birmingham, 1943–49; Prof. of Physical Metallurgy, University of Birmingham, 1949–55; Deputy Head of Metallurgy Division, Atomic Energy Research Establishment, Harwell, Berks, 1955–58; Goldsmiths' Prof. of Metallurgy, Cambridge Univ., 1958–65; Fellow of Christ's Coll., Cambridge, 1958–70, Hon. Fellow, 1970; Dep. Chief Scientific Adviser (Studies), Min. of Defence, 1965–67, Chief Adviser, 1967; Dep. Chief Scientific Advr to HM Govt, 1968–71, Chief Scientific Advr, 1971–74. Part-time Mem., UKAEA, 1962–65, 1983–87; Member: Adv. Council on Scientific Policy, 1963–64; Central Adv. Council for Science and Technology, 1967–; Exec. Cttee, British Council, 1974–87; Adv. Council, Science Policy Foundn, 1976–; Security Commn, 1981–. Dir, Fisons plc, 1979–90. A Vice-Pres., Royal Society, 1964, 1976, 1977. Foreign Hon. Mem., American Academy of Arts and Sciences, 1960; Foreign Associate, Nat. Acad. of Sciences, USA, 1972; Hon. Mem., Amer. Soc. for Metals, 1972 (Fellow 1974); Foreign Associate, Nat. Acad. of Engrg, USA, 1976; Hon. Member: Metals Soc., 1977 (Hon. FIM, 1989); Japan Inst. of Metals, 1981. FIC 1991; FEng 1979; Fellow, Royal Swedish Acad. of Scis; Hon. Fellow, Internat. Congress on Fracture, 1985–. Hon. DSc: Columbia Univ., 1965; Newcastle Univ., 1967; Liverpool Univ., 1969; Manchester, 1970; Warwick, 1971; Sussex, 1972; Bath, 1973; Strathclyde, 1975; Cranfield, 1975; Aston, 1975; Oxford, 1979; Birmingham, 1983; DUniv Essex, 1982; Hon. DEng Tech. Univ. of Nova Scotia, 1984. Rosenhain Medallist of the Inst. of Metals; Hughes Medal, 1961, Rumford Medal, 1974, Royal Society; Inst. of Metals (Platinum) Medal, 1965; Réaumur Medal, Société Française de Métallurgie, 1964; James Alfred Ewing Medal, ICE, 1967; Holweck Medal, Société Française de Physique, 1969; Albert Sauveur Achievement Award, Amer. Soc. for Metals, 1969; James Douglas Gold Medal, Amer. Inst. of Mining, Metallurgy and Petroleum Engrs, 1974; Harvey Science Prize, Technion Israel Inst., 1974; Acta Metallurgica Gold Medal, 1976; Guthrie Medal and Prize, Inst. of Physics, 1977; Gold Medal, Amer. Soc. for Metals, 1980; Brinell Medal, Royal Swedish Acad. of Engrg Sciences, 1980; Kelvin Medal, ICE, 1986; Hollomon Award, Acta Metallurgica, 1991. *Publications:* Theoretical Structural Metallurgy, 1948, 2nd edn 1955; Dislocations and Plastic Flow in Crystals, 1953; The Mechanical Properties of Matter, 1964; Theory of Crystal Dislocations, 1964; An Introduction to Metallurgy, 1967; Portrait of Nature, 1975; Environmental Economics, 1978; How Safe is Nuclear Energy?, 1981; Introduction to the Modern Theory of Metals, 1988; scientific papers to various learned journals. *Recreation:* music. *Address:* 40 Maids Causeway, Cambridge CB5 8DD. *T:* Cambridge (0223) 63806.

COTTRELL, Bryce Arthur Murray; Fellow and Funding Director, Corpus Christi College, Oxford, since 1990; *b* 16 Sept. 1931; *s* of late Brig. A. F. B. Cottrell, DSO, OBE and Mrs M. B. Cottrell (*née* Nicoll); *m* 1955, Jeane Dolores Monk; two *s* two *d. Educ:* Charterhouse; Corpus Christi Coll., Oxford (MA). Joined Phillips-Drew, 1955; Partner, 1963; Sen. Partner, 1983; Chm., 1985–88. *Recreations:* sport, railways. *Address:* Portreeves House, East Street, Tonbridge TN9 1HP. *T:* Tonbridge (0732) 773277. *Club:* City of London.

COTTRELL, Richard John; Director, Advanced Transport for Avon Ltd; Managing Partner, RCA International; Director, Advanced Transport Projects Ltd; *b* 11 July 1943; *s* of John Cottrell and Winifred (*née* Barter); *m* 1st, 1965, Dinah Louise (*née* David) (marr. diss. 1986); two *d*; 2nd, 1987, Tracy Katherine (née Wade); one *d. Educ:* Court Fields Sch., Wellington, Somerset. Journalist: Wellington Weekly News, 1958; South Devon Jl, 1960; Topic (internat. news weekly), 1962; Evening Argus, Brighton, 1963; Lincolnshire Standard, 1964; Evening Post, Bristol, 1965; TWW, subseq. HTV, 1967–79. Contested (C) Bristol, European Parly elecn, 1989. MEP (C) Bristol, 1979–89; Sec., backbench cttee, European Dem. Gp, 1979; Member: Transport Cttee, 1979–83; External Econ. Relns Cttee, 1979–82; Information Cttee, 1981–84; ACP-EEC Convention, 1981–84; Agriculture Cttee, 1982–86; Rules Cttee, 1982–89; Environment Cttee, 1983–89; Budget Cttee, 1983–86; Energy Cttee, 1986–88; deleg. to China, 1987. European Vice-Pres., Assoc. of District Councils; Vice-President: Nat. Council on Inland Transport; Railway Develt Soc. *Publications:* Energy, the Burning Question for Europe (jtly), 1981; (ed and contrib.) Transport for Europe, 1982; Blood on their Hands: the killing of Ann Chapman, 1987; The Sacred Cow, 1987; contribs to Encounter, Contemporary Review. *Recreations:* travel, reading, transport studies, appreciation of real ale. *Address:* Dean House, Bower Ashton, Bristol. *T:* Bristol (0272) 663404, Brussels 646.2593, Washington 202 639 4082, Warsaw 275155.

COTTS, Sir (Robert) Crichton Mitchell, 3rd Bt, *cr* 1921; *b* 20 Oct. 1903; *yr s* of Sir William Dingwall Mitchell Cotts, 1st Bt, KBE, MP (*d* 1932), and Agnes Nivison (*d* 1966), 2nd *d* of late Robert Sloane; *S* brother, 1964; *m* 1942, Barbara (*d* 1982), *o d* of late Capt. Herbert J. A. Throckmorton, Royal Navy; two *s* two *d* (and one *d* decd). Late Temp. Major, Irish Guards; USSR, White Sea, 1941–42. *Heir: s* Richard Crichton Mitchell Cotts, *b* 26 July 1946. *Address:* 16 High Street, Needham Market, Suffolk.

COUCHMAN, James Randall; MP (C) Gillingham, since 1983; *b* 11 Feb. 1942; *s* of Stanley Randall Couchman and Alison Margaret Couchman; *m* 1967, Barbara Jean (*née*

Heilbrun); one *s* one *d. Educ:* Cranleigh School; King's College, Newcastle upon Tyne; Univ. of Durham. Oil industry, 1964–70; Public House Manager, family company, 1970–74; Gen. Manager, family licensed trade co., 1974–80, Director, 1980–. Councillor, London Borough of Bexley, 1974–82 (Chm., Social Services, 1975–78, 1980–82). Chm., Bexley HA, 1981–83. Member: Assoc. of Metropolitan Authorities Social Services Cttee, 1975–80; Central Council for Educn and Training of Social Workers, 1976–80; Governor, Nat. Inst. for Social Workers, 1976–80. PPS to Minister of State for Social Security, 1984–86, to Minister of Health, 1986–88, to Chancellor of Duchy of Lancaster, 1988–89, to Sec. of State for Social Security, 1989–90. Member: Social Services Select Cttee, 1983–85; Select Cttee on Health, 1990–. Fellow, Industry and Parlt Trust, 1987. Mem., Vintners' Co. *Recreations:* travel, reading, listening to music, politics. *Address:* c/o House of Commons, SW1A 0AA.

COUCHMAN, Martin; Secretary, National Economic Development Council, since 1988; *b* 28 Sept. 1947; *s* of late Frederick Alfred James Couchman and of Pamela Mary Couchman (*née* Argent); *m* 1983, Carolyn Mary Constance Roberts; two *s* one *d. Educ:* Sutton Valence Sch.; Exeter Coll., Oxford (BA Jurisprudence). Building Industry, 1970–77; National Economic Development Office, 1977–: Industrial Advr, 1977–84; Hd of Administration, 1984–87; on secondment as UK Dir of European Year of the Environment, 1987–88. FRSA 1988. *Recreations:* Anglo-Saxon history, armchair archaeology, amateur dramatics. *Address:* The Old Rectory, Halstead, Kent TN14 7HG. *T:* Knockholt (0959) 32253.

COULL, Prof. Alexander, PhD; DSc; FRSE; FICE, FIStructE; Regius Professor of Civil Engineering, University of Glasgow, since 1977; *b* 20 June 1931; *s* of William Coull and Jane Ritchie (*née* Reid); *m* 1962, Frances Bruce Moir; one *s* two *d. Educ:* Peterhead Acad.; Univ. of Aberdeen (BScEng, PhD; DSc 1983). FRSE 1971; FICE 1972, FIStructE 1973; Res. Asst, MIT, USA, 1955; Struct. Engr, English Electric Co. Ltd, 1955–57; Lectr in Engrg, Univ. of Aberdeen, 1957–62; Lectr in Civil Engrg, Univ. of Southampton, 1962–66; Prof. of Struct. Engrg, Univ. of Strathclyde, 1966–76. Chm., Clyde Estuary Amenity Council, 1981–86. *Publications:* Tall Buildings, 1967; Fundamentals of Structural Theory, 1972; (with B. Stafford Smith) Tall Building Structures: Planning Analysis and Design, 1991; author or co-author of 130 res. papers in scientific jls. *Recreations:* golf, hill walking, ski-ing. *Address:* 11 Blackwood Road, Milngavie, Glasgow G62 7LB. *T:* 041–956 1655. *Club:* Buchanan Castle Golf (Drymen).

COULL, Maj.-Gen. John Taylor, FRCS; FRCSE; QHS 1988; Director of Army Surgery, since 1988; *b* 4 March 1934; *s* of late John Sandeman Coull and Ethel Marjory (*née* Taylor); *m* 1958, Mildred Macfarlane; three *s. Educ:* Robert Gordon's College; Aberdeen Univ. Med. Sch. MB ChB. House appts, Aberdeen Royal Infirmary, 1958–60; Commissioned RAMC, 1960; Surgeon: Colchester Mil. Hosp., 1960–63; Queen Alexander Mil. Hosp., 1963; Sen. Registrar, Edinburgh East Gen. Hosp., 1963–65; Royal Herbert Hosp., 1965–67; Sen. Registrar, Birmingham Accident Hosp., 1967; Consultant Surgeon, BMH Singapore, 1967–70; Lectr, Dept of Orthopaedics, Univ. of Edinburgh, 1970–71; Consultant Orthopaedic Surgeon, BAOR, 1971–77; Consultant Adviser in Orthop. Surgery and Sen. Consultant, Queen Elizabeth Mil. Hosp., 1977–86; Consulting Surgeon, HQ BAOR, 1986–88. GSM N Ireland, 1976; Mitchiner Medal, RCS, 1980. OStJ. *Publications:* chapters in: Field Pocket Surgery, 1981; R. Smith's The Hand, 1985; Trauma, 1989; articles in learned jls. *Recreations:* home maintenance, carpentry, gardening, travel. *Address:* c/o Royal Bank of Scotland, Farnborough, Hants. *Club:* Royal Society of Medicine.

COULSFIELD, Hon. Lord; John Taylor Cameron; a Senator of the College of Justice in Scotland, since 1987; *b* 24 April 1934; *s* of late John Reid Cameron, MA, formerly Director of Education, Dundee; *m* 1964, Bridget Deirdre Sloan; no *c. Educ:* Fettes Coll.; Corpus Christi Coll., Oxford; Edinburgh Univ. BA (Oxon), LLB (Edinburgh). Admitted to Faculty of Advocates, 1960. Lecturer in Public Law, Edinburgh Univ., 1960–64. QC (Scot.) 1973; Keeper of the Advocates' Library, 1977–87; an Advocate-Depute, 1977–79. Judge, Courts of Appeal of Jersey and Guernsey, 1986–87. Chm., Medical Appeal Tribunals, 1985–87. *Publications:* articles in legal jls.

COULSHED, Dame (Mary) Frances, DBE 1953 (CBE 1949); TD 1951; Brigadier, Women's Royal Army Corps, retired; *b* 10 Nov. 1904; *d* of Wilfred and Maud Coulshed. *Educ:* Parkfields Cedars, Derby; Convent of the Sacred Heart, Kensington. Served War of 1939–45 (despatches); North-West Europe, 1944–45, with General Headquarters Anti-Aircraft Troops and at Headquarters Lines of Communications; Deputy Dir, Anti-Aircraft Command, 1946–50; Dep. Dir, War Office, July-Dec. 1950; Director, WRAC, 1951–54. ADC to the King, 1951, to the Queen, 1952–54. Order of Leopold I of Belgium with palm, Croix de Guerre with palm, 1946. *Address:* 815 Endsleigh Court, Upper Woburn Place, WC1.

COULSON, Mrs Ann Margaret; General Manager, Age Concern, Solihull, since 1991; *b* 11 March 1935; *d* of Sidney Herbert Wood and Ada (*née* Mills); *m* 1958, Peter James Coulson; two *s* one *d. Educ:* The Grammar Sch., Chippenham, Wilts; UCL (BScEcon); Univ. of Manchester (DSA); Wolverhampton Technical Teachers' Coll. (CertEd). Hosp. Admin, 1956–62; Lectr in Econs and Management, Bromsgrove Coll. of Further Educn, 1968–76; Asst Dir, North Worcestershire Coll., 1976–80; Service Planning and Develt Co-ordinator, 1980–83, Regl Planning Administrator, 1983–88, Dir of Planning, 1988–91, W Midlands RHA. City of Birmingham Dist Council, 1973–79; special interest in Social Services. Mem., IBA, 1976–81. FBIM. *Recreations:* cooking, music, theatre. *Address:* Rowans, Leamington Hastings, near Rugby, Warwicks CV23 8DY. *T:* Marton (0926) 633264.

COULSON, His Honour (James) Michael; a Circuit Judge, Midland and Oxford Circuit, 1983–90; *b* 23 Nov. 1927; *s* of William Coulson, Wold Newton Hall, Driffield, E Yorks; *m* 1st, 1955, Dilys Adair Jones (marr. diss.); one *s*; 2nd, 1977, Barbara Elizabeth Islay, *d* of Dr Roland Moncrieff Chambers; one *s* one *d. Educ:* Fulneck Sch., Yorks; Merton Coll., Oxford; Royal Agricultural Coll., Cirencester. Served E Riding Yeomanry (Wenlocks Horse); Queen's Own Yorks Yeomanry (Major). Called to Bar, Middle Temple, 1951; Mem. North Eastern Circuit; Asst Recorder of Sheffield, 1965–71; Dep. Chm., NR of Yorks QS, 1968–71; a Chm. of Industrial Tribunals, 1968–83; a Recorder of the Crown Court, 1981–83. Dep. Chm., Northern Agricl Land Tribunal, 1967–73. Former Mem., Tadcaster RDC. MP (C) Kingston-upon-Hull North, 1959–64; PPS to Solicitor Gen., 1962–64; Mem., Executive Cttee, Conservative Commonwealth Council. Sometime Sec., Bramham Moor and York and Ainsty Point to Point Race Meetings. *Recreations:* hunting, reading, travel. *Address:* The Tithe Barn, Wymondham, Melton Mowbray, Leics. *Club:* Cavalry and Guards.

COULSON, Sir John Eltringham, KCMG 1957 (CMG 1946); President, Hampshire Branch, British Red Cross Society, 1972–79; Secretary-General of EFTA, 1965–72, retired; *b* 13 Sept. 1909; *er s* of H. J. Coulson, Bickley, Kent; *m* 1944, Mavis Ninette Beazley; two *s. Educ:* Rugby; Corpus Christi Coll., Cambridge (Hon. Fellow 1975). Entered Diplomatic Service in 1932. Served in Bucharest, Min. of Econ. Warfare, War Cabinet Office, Foreign Office and Paris. Sometime Dep. UK representative to UN, New York; Asst Under-Sec., Foreign Office, 1952–55; Minister British Embassy, Washington, 1955–57; Asst to Paymaster-Gen., 1957–60; Ambassador to Sweden, 1960–63; Dep. Under-Sec. of State, Foreign Office, 1963–65; Chief of Administration of HM Diplomatic Service, Jan.-Sept. 1965. Director: Atlas Copco (GB), 1972–80; Sheerness Steel Co., 1972–84. Knight Grand Cross, Order of the North Star, Sweden, 1982. *Recreations:* fishing, golf. *Address:* The Old Mill, Selborne, Hants. *Club:* Brooks's.

COULSON, Michael; *see* Coulson, J. M.

COULTASS, (George Thomas) Clive; historian; Senior Keeper, Department of Film, Imperial War Museum, London, 1979–91; Keeper of Audio-Visual Records, 1983–91; *b* 5 July 1931; *m* 1962, Norma Morris. *Educ:* Tadcaster Grammar Sch.; Univ. of Sheffield (BA Hons). Teacher in various London schools, 1955–62; Lectr/Sen. Lectr in History, James Graham Coll., Leeds, 1962–69; Keeper of Film Programming, Imperial War Museum, 1969–70; Keeper, Dept of Film, 1970–83. Vice-Pres., Internat. Assoc. for Audio-Visual Media in Hist. Res. and Educn, 1978–85. Organiser: various film historical confs, 1973–90; exhibn on British film and World War II, 1982. *Publications:* Images for Battle, 1989; sections in: The Historian and Film, 1976; Britain and the Cinema in the Second World War, 1988; articles in various historical jls. *Recreations:* travel, music, including opera, reading. *Address:* 39 Fairfield Grove, SE7 8UA.

COULTHARD, Air Vice-Marshal Colin Weal, CB 1975; AFC 1953 (Bar 1958); retired; *b* 27 Feb. 1921; *s* of late George Robert Coulthard and Cicely Eva Coulthard (*née* Minns); *m* 1st, 1941, Norah Ellen Creighton (marr. diss.); one *s* two *d*; 2nd, 1957, Eileen Pamela (*née* Barber); one *s. Educ:* Watford Grammar Sch.; De Havilland Aeronautical Tech. Sch. Commissioned RAF, 1941; Fighter Pilot, 1942–45 (despatches, 1945); HQ Fighter Comd, 1948–49; RAF Staff Coll., 1950; OC 266 Sqn, Wunstorf, 1952–54, DFLS, CFE, 1955; OC Flying, 233(F) OCU, 1956–57; OC AFDS, CFE, 1957–59; HQ Fighter Comd, 1959–60; Stn Cdr, Gutersloh, 1961–64; MoD, 1964–66; SOA, AHQ Malta, 1966–67; DOR 1(RAF), MoD, 1967–69; Air Attaché, Washington, DC, 1970–72; Mil. Dep. to Head of Defence Sales, MoD, 1973–75. Governor, Truro Sch., 1981–91. Hon. FRAeS 1975. *Recreations:* walking, shooting, motor sport. *Address:* Fiddlers, Old Truro Road, Goonhavern, Truro TR4 9NN. *T:* Zelah (087254) 312. *Club:* Royal Air Force.

COULTHARD, William Henderson, CBE 1968; MSc, CEng, FIMechE, FRPS; Deputy Director, Royal Armament Research and Development Establishment, 1962–74; *b* 24 Nov. 1913; *s* of William and Louise Coulthard, Flimby, Cumberland; *m* 1942, Peggie Frances Platts Taylor, Chiselhurst; one *d* (one *s* decd). *Educ:* Flimby, Workington Schs; Armstrong Coll., University of Durham. Mather Schol., University of Durham, 1932. Linen Industry Research Assoc., 1934; Instrument Dept, Royal Aircraft Estabt, 1935; Air Ministry HQ, 1939; Sqdn Ldr RAFVR, 1944; Official German Translator, 1945; Air Photography Div., RAE, 1946; Supt, later Dep. Dir, Fighting Vehicles Research and Development Estabt, 1951. *Publications:* Aircraft Instrument Design, 1951; Aircraft Engineer's Handbook, 1953; (trans.) Mathematical Instruments (Capellen), 1948; (trans.) Gyroscopes (Grammel), 1950; articles in technical journals. *Recreations:* art history (Diploma in History of Art, London Univ., 1964); languages. *Address:* Argyll, Francis Close, Ewell, Surrey. *T:* 081–337 4909.

COULTON, Very Rev. Nicholas Guy; Provost of St Nicholas' Cathedral, Newcastle-upon-Tyne, since 1990; *b* 14 June 1940; *s* of Nicholas Guy Coulton and Audrey Florence Furneaux Coulton (*née* Luscombe); *m* 1978, Edith Mary Gainford; one *s* two *d. Educ:* Blundell's School, Tiverton; Cuddesdon Coll., Oxford. BD London 1972. Admitted Solicitor, 1962; Asst Solicitor, Burges, Salmon & Co., Bristol, 1962–65. Ordination training, 1965–67; Curate of Pershore Abbey with Birlingham, Wick and Pinvin, 1967–71; Domestic Chaplain to Bishop of St Albans, 1971–75; Vicar of St Paul's, Bedford, 1975–90. Proctor in Convocation, 1985–90; Hon. Canon of St Alban's Cathedral, 1989–90. *Publication:* Twelve Years of Prayer, 1989. *Recreations:* gardening, reading, listening to music, historical exploration, rearing children, horse-riding, sailing, ski-ing. *Address:* The Cathedral Vicarage, 26 Mitchell Avenue, West Jesmond, Newcastle-upon-Tyne NE2 3LA. *T:* 091–232 1939.

COUNSELL, Hazel Rosemary; Her Honour Judge Hazel Counsell; a Circuit Judge, since 1978; *b* 7 Jan. 1931; *d* of late Arthur Henry Counsell and Elsie Winifred Counsell; *m* 1980, Peter Fallon, *qv. Educ:* Clifton High Sch.; Switzerland; Univ. of Bristol (LLB). Called to the Bar, Gray's Inn, 1956; Western Circuit, 1956–; a Recorder of the Crown Court, 1976–77. Legal Dept, Min. of Labour, 1959–62. Governor, Colston Girls Sch. *Recreations:* reading, swimming, travel. *Address:* The Crown Court, The Guildhall, Broad Street, Bristol.

COUNSELL, His Honour Paul Hayward; a Circuit Judge, 1973–90; *b* 13 Nov. 1926; twin *s* of Frederick Charles Counsell and Edna Counsell; *m* 1959, Joan Agnes Strachan; one *s* two *d. Educ:* Colston Sch., Bristol; Queen's Coll., Oxford (MA). Served RAF, 1944–48. Admitted Solicitor, 1951; called to Bar, Inner Temple, 1962. Northern Rhodesia: Crown Solicitor, 1955–56; Crown Counsel, 1956–61; Resident Magistrate, 1958; Dir of Public Prosecutions, 1962–63; Solicitor General, 1963–64; QC 1963; Acting Attorney General, 1964; Solicitor-General, Zambia, 1964, MLC 1963–64. In chambers of Lord Hailsham, Temple, 1965–73; Dep. Circuit Judge, 1971–73. Chm., Industrial Tribunal, 1970–73. *Recreation:* model engineering.

COUPER, Prof. Alastair Dougal, FNI; FRICS; FCIT; Professor of Maritime Studies, University of Wales College of Cardiff (formerly University of Wales Institute of Science and Technology), since 1970; *b* 4 June 1931; *s* of Daniel Alexander Couper and Davina Couper (*née* Rilley); *m* 1958, Norma Milton; two *s* two *d. Educ:* Robert Gordon's School of Navigation (Master Mariner); Univ. of Aberdeen (MA, DipEd); Australian National Univ. (PhD). FCIT 1974; FNI 1979; FRICS 1986. Cadet and Navigating Officer, Merchant Navy, 1947–57; student, Univ. of Aberdeen, 1958–62, postgraduate teaching course, 1962–63; Research Schol., Sch. of Pacific Studies, ANU, Canberra, 1963–66; Lectr, Univ. of Durham, 1967–70. Prof., World Maritime Univ. (UN), Malmö, Sweden, 1987–89 (on secondment). UN Consultant, 1972–; Chm., Maritime Bd, CNAA, 1978–85; Assessor, Chartered Inst. of Transport, 1976–85; Founder Mem., Council, British Maritime League, 1982–85; Mem. Exec. Bd, Law of the Sea Inst., USA, 1989–. Editor (and Founder), Journal of Maritime Policy and Management, 1973–84. *Publications:* Geography of Sea Transport, 1971; The Law of the Sea, 1978; (ed) Times Atlas of the Oceans, 1983; contrib. Pacific, in World Atlas of Agriculture, 1969; Pacific in Transition (ed Brookfield), 1973; New Cargo Handling Techniques: implications for port employment and skills, 1986; (ed) Development and Social Change in the Pacific, 1988; several UN Reports, UNCTAD, ILO, IMO; articles in jls; conf. papers. *Recreations:* hill walking, sailing, archaeology, Pacific history. *Address:* University of Wales College of Cardiff, Cardiff CF1 3YP. *T:* Cardiff (0222) 874000.

COUPER, Heather Anita, FRAS; science broadcaster and author, since 1983; *b* 2 June 1949; *o d* of George Couper Elder Couper and late Anita Couper (*née* Taylor). *Educ:* St Mary's Grammar Sch., Northwood, Mddx; Univ. of Leicester (BSc Hons Astronomy and Physics); Univ. of Oxford. FRAS 1970. Management trainee, Peter Robinson Ltd,

1967–69; Res. Asst, Cambridge Observatories, 1969–70; Lectr, Greenwich Planetarium, Old Royal Observ., 1977–83. President: Brit. Astron. Assoc., 1984–86; Jun. Astron. Soc., 1987–89. Presenter on television: Heavens Above, 1981; Spacewatch, 1983; The Planets, 1985; The Stars, 1988; The Neptune Encounter, 1989; Presenter on radio: Science Now, 1983; Cosmic Pursuits, 1985; The John Dunn Programme, 1990; Seeing Stars, 1991; also appearances and interviews on wide variety of television and radio progs. Astronomy columnist: The Independent; The Sunday Post. Dir, Pioneer Productions, 1988–. Hon. DLitt Loughborough, 1991. *Publications:* (jtly) Space Frontiers, 1978; Exploring Space, 1980; (jtly) Heavens Above, 1981; (jtly) The Restless Universe, 1982; (jtly) Physics, 1983; (jtly) Astronomy, 1983; Journey into Space, 1984; (jtly) Starfinder, 1984; (jtly) The Halley's Comet Pop-Up Book, 1985; (jtly) The Universe: a 3-dimensional study, 1985; (jtly) The Planets, 1985; (jtly) The Stars, 1988; Space Scientist series, 1985–87: Comets and Meteors; The Planets; The Stars; jointly: The Sun; The Moon; Galaxies and Quasars; Satellites and Spaceprobes; Telescopes and Observatories; numerous articles in nat. newspapers and magazines. *Recreations:* travel, the English countryside, chamber music; wine, food and winemaking. *Address:* c/o David Higham Associates, 5–8 Lower John Street, Golden Square, W1R 4HA.

COUPER, Sir (Robert) Nicholas (Oliver), 6th Bt *cr* 1841; *b* 9 Oct. 1945; *s* of Sir George Robert Cecil Couper, 5th Bt, and Margaret Grace (*d* 1984), *d* of late Robert George Dashwood Thomas; *S* father, 1975; *m* 1972, Curzon Henrietta (marr. diss. 1986), *d* of late Major George Burrell MacKean, DL, JP; one *s* one *d. Educ:* Eton; RMA, Sandhurst. Major, Blues and Royals; retired, 1975. Now working with Lane Fox as an estate agent. *Heir: s* James George Couper, *b* 27 Oct. 1977. *Address:* 38 Bampton Street, Tiverton, Devon EX16 6AH.

COUPLAND, Prof. Rex Ernest; Professor of Human Morphology, 1967–89, and Dean of Medicine, 1981–87, University of Nottingham; Hon. Consultant, Trent Regional Hospital Board, 1970–89; *b* 30 Jan. 1924; *s* of late Ernest Coupland, company dir and Doris Coupland; *m* 1947, Lucy Eileen Sargent; one *s* one *d. Educ:* Mirfield Grammar Sch.; University of Leeds. MB, ChB with honours, 1947; MD with distinction, 1952; PhD 1954; DSc 1970. House appointments, Leeds General Infirmary, 1947; Demonstrator and Lecturer in Anatomy, University of Leeds, 1948, 1950–58; Asst Prof. of Anatomy, University of Minnesota, USA, 1955–56; Prof. of Anatomy, Queen's Coll., Dundee, University of St Andrews, 1958–67. Medical Officer, RAF, 1948–50. FRSE 1960. Member: Biological Research Board of MRC, 1964–70; Med. Adv. Bd, Crippling Diseases Foundn, 1971–75; CMO's Academic Forum, 1984–89; Chm., MRC Non-Ionizing Radiations Cttee, 1970–89; Derbyshire AHA, 1978–81; Trent RHA, 1981–88; Chm., Nottingham Div., BMA, 1978–79; GMC, 1982–88; Med. sub-cttee, UGC, 1984–89. President: Anat. Soc. GB and Ireland, 1976–78; British Assoc. of Clinical Anat., 1977–82. Wood Jones Medal for contrib. to clinical anatomy, RCS, 1984. *Publications:* The Natural History of the Chromaffin Cell, 1965; (ed jtly) Chromaffin, Enterochromaffin and Related Cells, 1976; (ed jtly) Peripheral Neuroendocrine Interaction, 1978; papers in jls of anatomy, physiology, endocrinology, pathology and pharmacology on endocrine and nervous systems and in jls of radiology on NMR imaging; *chapters on:* Anatomy of the Human Kidney, in Renal Disease (ed Black), 1962, 1968, 1973; The Chromaffin System, in Catecholamines (ed Blaschko and Muscholl), 1973; The Blood Supply of the Adrenal Gland, in Handbook of Physiology, 1974; The Adrenal Medulla, in The Cell in Medical Science (ed Beck and Lloyd), 1976; Endocrine System, in Textbook of Human Anatomy (ed W. J. Hamilton), 1976; *contribs to:* Hormones and Evolution, Vol. I, ed Barrington, 1979; Biogenic Amines in Development, ed Parvez and Parvez, 1980; Hormones in Human Tissues, Vol. I, ed Fotherby and Pal, 1981; Asst Editor, Gray's Anatomy (ed Davies), 1967. *Recreations:* shooting, gardening. *Address:* Foxhollow, Quaker Lane, Farnsfield, Newark, Notts NG22 8EE. *T:* Mansfield (0623) 882028.

COURAGE, Richard Hubert, DL; *b* 23 Jan. 1915; *s* of Raymond Courage and Mildred Frances Courage (formerly Fisher); *m* 1st, 1941, Jean Elizabeth Agnes Watson (*d* 1977), *d* of late Sir Charles Cuningham Watson, KCIE, CSI, ICS; two *s* (and one *s* decd); 2nd, 1978, Phyllida Anne, *widow* of J. D. Derouet. *Educ:* Eton. Served War of 1939–45: Northants Yeomanry, 1939–46, Major (despatches). Director: Courage Ltd, 1948–75 (Chm., 1959–75); Imperial Group Ltd, 1972–75; Norwich Union Insce Group, 1975–80; Chm., London Adv. Bd, Norwich Union Insce Gp, 1975–80 (Dir, 1964–80). Governor, Brentwood Sch., Essex, 1959– (Chm., 1976–89). JP Essex, 1955–85; DL Essex, 1977. *Recreations:* yachting and shooting. *Address:* Chainbridge, Mountnessing, near Brentwood, Essex CM15 8SG. *T:* Brentwood (0277) 222206.

COURAGE, Maj.-Gen. Walter James, MBE 1979; Chief Joint Services Liaison Officer, BAOR, Bonn, since 1990; *b* 25 Sept. 1940; *s* of late Walter Henry Phipps and of Nancy Mary Courage (*née* Reeves, now Gardner), and step *s* of late Lt-Col Nigel Anthony Courage, MC; *m* 1964, Lavinia Patricia, *d* of late John Emerson Crawhall Wood; one *s* one *d. Educ:* Abingdon Sch.; RMA, Sandhurst. Commnd 5th Royal Inniskilling Dragoon Guards, 1961; served BAOR, Libya and Canada, 1961–81; commanded Regt, 1982–84; Div. Col Staff Coll., 1985; Comdr 4th Armoured Bde, 1985–88; Chief of Staff, UN Force in Cyprus, 1988–90. *Recreations:* shooting, cricket, ski-ing, polo, fine art. *Address:* c/o Lloyds Bank, Cox's and King's Branch, 7 Pall Mall, SW1Y 5NH. *Clubs:* Cavalry and Guards, MCC; I Zingari.

COURCEL, Baron de; (Geoffroy Chodron de Courcel), Hon. GCVO 1950; MC 1943; Grand' Croix de la Légion d'Honneur, 1980; Compagnon de la Libération, 1943; Croix de Guerre, 1939–45; President, Institute Charles de Gaulle, since 1985; *b* Tours, Indre-et-Loire, 11 Sept. 1912; *s* of Louis Chodron de Courcel, Officer, and Alice Lambert-Champy; *m* 1954, Martine Hallade; two *s. Educ:* Stanislas Coll.; University of Paris. DenDr, LèsL, Dip. Ecole des Sciences Politiques. Attaché, Warsaw, 1937; Sec., Athens, 1938–39; Armée du Levant, 1939; joined Free French Forces, June 1940; Chef de Cabinet, Gén. de Gaulle, London, 1940–41; Captain 1st Spahis marocains Regt, Egypt, Libya and Tunisia, 1941–43; Dep.-Dir of Cabinet, Gén de Gaulle, Algiers, 1943–44; Mem. Conseil de l'Ordre de la Libération, 1944; Regional Comr for Liberated Territories, 1944; in charge of Alsace-Lorraine Dept, Min. of Interior, 1944–45; Counsellor, 1945; in Min. of Foreign Affairs: Dep. Dir Central and N European Sections, 1945–47; First Counsellor, Rome, 1947–50; Minister Plen., 1951; Dir Bilateral Trade Agreements Section, 1951; Dir African and ME Section, 1953; Dir Gen., Polit. and Econ. Affairs, Min. of Moroccan and Tunisian Affairs, 1954; Perm. Sec., Nat. Defence, 1955–58; Ambassador, Perm. Rep. to NATO, 1958; Sec.-Gen. Présidence de la République, 1959–62; Ambassador to London, 1962–72; Sec.-Gen., Min. of For. Affairs, 1973–76. Pres., France–GB Assoc., 1978–87. Ambassadeur de France, 1965; Hon. DCL Oxon, 1970; Hon. LLD Birmingham, 1972. *Publication:* L'influence de la Conférence de Berlin de 1885 sur le droit Colonial International, 1936. *Recreations:* shooting, swimming. *Address:* 7 rue de Médicis, 75006 Paris, France; La Ravinière, Fontaines en Sologne, 41250 Bracieux, France.

COURCY; *see* de Courcy.

COURT, Hon. Sir Charles (Walter Michael), AK 1982; KCMG 1979; Kt 1972; OBE 1946; MLA (Liberal Party) for Nedlands, 1953–82; Premier of Western Australia,

1974–82; also Treasurer, and Minister co-ordinating Economic and Regional Development, 1974–82; *b* Crawley, Sussex, 29 Sept. 1911; *s* of late W. J. Court, Perth; *m* 1936, Rita M., *d* of L. R. Steffanoni; five *s. Educ:* Leederville and Rosalie State Schs; Perth Boys' Sch. Chartered Accountant, 1933; Partner, Hendry, Rae & Court, 1938–70. Served AIF, 1940–46; Lt-Col. State Registrar, Inst. Chartered Accountants in Aust. (WA Br.), 1946–52, Mem. State Council, 1952–55. Dep. Leader, 1957–59, 1971–72, and Leader, 1972–74, of Opposition, WA; Minister, Western Australia: for Industrial Development and the NW, 1959–71; for Railways, 1959–67; for Transport, 1965–66. Chm., Adv. Cttee under WA Prices Control Act, 1948–52; President: WA Band Assoc., 1954–59; Order of Australia Assoc., 1987–89. Hon. Colonel: WA Univ. Regt, 1969–75; SAS Regt, 1976–80. Paul Harris Fellow, Rotary, 1982. FCA; FCIS; FASA. Hon. FAIM 1980. Freeman: City of Nedlands, 1982; Shire of West Kimberley, WA, 1983. Hon. LLD Univ. of WA, 1969; Hon. DTech WA Inst. of Technol., 1982. Manufacturers' Export Council Award, 1969; James Kirby Award, Inst. of Production Engrs, 1971; Australian Chartered Accountant of the Year, 1983. Life Member: Musicians Union, 1953; ASA, 1979; Returned Services League, 1981; Inst. of Chartered Accountants in Australia, 1982. Order of the Sacred Treasure, 1st cl. (Japan), 1983. *Publications:* many professional papers on accountancy, and papers on economic and resource development. *Recreations:* music, yachting. *Address:* 46 Waratah Avenue, Nedlands, WA 6009, Australia. *Clubs:* Weld, Western Australia, Commercial Travellers Association (Perth); Nedlands and Perth Rotary, Lions.

COURT, Emeritus Prof. (Seymour) Donald (Mayneord), CBE 1969; MD; FRCP; *b* 4 Jan. 1912; *s* of David Henry and Ethel Court; *m* 1939, Dr Frances Edith Radcliffe; two *s* one *d. Educ:* Adams Grammar Sch., Wem; Birmingham Univ (MB, ChB, 1936; MD 1947); FRCP 1956. Resident Hosp. appts Birmingham Gen. Hosps, and Hosp. for Sick Children, London, 1936–38; Paediatric Registrar, Wander Scholar, Westminster Hosp., 1938–39; Physician, EMS, 1939–46; Nuffield Fellow in Child Health, 1946–47; Reader in Child Health, University of Durham, 1947–55; James Spence Prof. of Child Health, Univ. of Newcastle upon Tyne, 1955–72, Emeritus Professor, 1972. Chm., Child Health Services Cttee for Eng. and Wales, 1973–76. Pres., British Paediatric Assoc., 1973–76. FRCGP *ad eundem* 1982; Hon. FRSM 1986. James Spence Medal, British Paed. Assoc., 1978; Nils Rosén von Rosenstein Medal, Swedish Paed. Assoc., 1979. *Publications:* (jointly) Growing Up in Newcastle upon Tyne, 1960; (ed) The Medical Care of Children, 1963; (ed jointly) Paediatrics in the Seventies, 1972; (jointly) The School Years in Newcastle upon Tyne, 1974; (ed jtly) Fit for the Future, 1976; contributions to special jls and text books on respiratory infection in childhood. *Recreations:* walking, natural history, poetry. *Address:* 8 Towers Avenue, Jesmond, Newcastle upon Tyne NE2 3QE. *T:* Newcastle upon Tyne (091) 2814884.

COURTAULD, Rev. (Augustine) Christopher (Caradoc); Vicar of St Paul's, Knightsbridge, since 1978; *b* 12 Sept. 1934; *s* of late Augustine Courtauld and of Lady Butler of Saffron Walden; *m* 1978, Dr Elizabeth Ann Molland, MD, FRCPath, *d* of late Rev. Preb. John W. G. Molland; two *d. Educ:* Trinity College, Cambridge (BA 1958, MA 1961); Westcott House, Cambridge. Deacon 1960, priest 1961, Manchester; Curate of Oldham, 1960–63; Chaplain: Trinity College, Cambridge, 1963–68; The London Hospital, 1968–78. *Recreation:* sailing. *Address:* St Paul's Vicarage, 32 Wilton Place, SW1X 8SH.

COURTENAY, family name of **Earl of Devon.**

COURTENAY, Lord; Hugh Rupert Courtenay; DL; landowner, farmer; *b* 5 May 1942; *o s* of 17th Earl of Devon, *qv; m* 1967, Dianna Frances, *er d* of J. G. Watherston, Jedburgh, Roxburghshire; one *s* three *d. Educ:* Winchester; Magdalene Coll., Cambridge (BA). ARICS. Captain, Wessex Yeomanry, retd. Chm., Devon Br., CLA, 1987–89. DL Devon, 1991. *Recreations:* riding, hunting, shooting. *Heir: s* Hon. Charles Peregrine Courtenay, *b* 14 Aug. 1975. *Address:* Powderham Castle, near Exeter, Devon EX6 8JQ. *T:* Starcross 890370.

COURTENAY, Thomas Daniel, (Tom Courtenay); actor; *b* 25 Feb. 1937; *s* of late Thomas Henry Courtenay and Annie Eliza Quest; *m* 1st, 1973, Cheryl Kennedy (marr. diss. 1982); 2nd, 1988, Isabel Crossley. *Educ:* Kingston High Sch., Hull; University Coll., London. RADA, 1958–60; started acting professionally, 1960; Old Vic, 1960–61: Konstantin Treplieff, Poins, Feste and Puck; Billy Liar, Cambridge Theatre, June 1961–Feb. 1962 and on tour; Andorra, National Theatre (guest), 1964; The Cherry Orchard, and Macbeth, Chichester, 1966; joined 69 Theatre Co., Manchester, 1966: Charley's Aunt, 1966; Romeo, Playboy of the Western World, 1967; Hamlet (Edinburgh Festival), 1968; She Stoops to Conquer, (transferred to Garrick), 1969; Peer Gynt, 1970; Charley's Aunt, Apollo, 1971; Time and Time Again, Comedy, 1972 (Variety Club of GB Stage Actor Award, 1972); The Norman Conquests, Globe, 1974; The Fool, Royal Court, 1975; Prince of Homburg, The Rivals, Manchester (opening prods of The Royal Exchange), 1976; Otherwise Engaged, NY, 1977; Clouds, Duke of York's, 1978; Crime and Punishment, Manchester, 1978; The Dresser, Manchester and Queen's, 1980 (Drama Critics Award and New Standard Award for best actor, 1980), NY 1981; The Misanthrope, Manchester and Round House, 1981; Andy Capp, Manchester and Aldwych, 1982; Jumpers, Manchester, 1984; Rookery Nook, Shaftesbury, 1986; The Hypochondriac, Lyric, Hammersmith, 1987; Dealing with Clair, Richmond, 1988. Began acting in films, 1962. *Films:* The Loneliness of the Long Distance Runner; Private Potter; Billy Liar; King and Country (Volpi Cup, 1964); Operation Crossbow; King Rat; Dr Zhivago; The Night of the Generals; The Day the Fish Came Out; A Dandy in Aspic; Otley; One Day in the Life of Ivan Denisovitch; Catch Me a Spy; The Dresser (Golden Globe); The Last Butterfly; Let Him Have It; Redemption. Has appeared on Television. Best Actor Award, Prague Festival, 1968; TV Drama Award (for Oswald in Ghosts), 1968. *Recreations:* listening to music (mainly classical, romantic and jazz); watching sport (and occasionally taking part in it, in a light-hearted manner), bird watching, astronomy. *Address:* Putney. *Club:* Garrick.

COURTNEY, Prof. Edward, MA; Professor of Classics, since 1982, Leonard Ely Professor of Humanistic Studies, since 1986, Stanford University; *b* 22 March 1932; *s* of George and Kathleen Courtney; *m* 1962, Brenda Virginia Meek; two *s. Educ:* Royal Belfast Academical Instn; Trinity Coll., Dublin (BA). BA (by incorporation) 1955, MA 1957, Oxford. University studentship, Dublin, 1954–55; Research Lectr, Christ Church, Oxford, 1955–59; Lectr in Classics, 1959, Reader in Classics, 1970, Prof. of Latin, 1977, King's Coll., London. *Publications:* (ed) Valerius Flaccus, Argonautica (Leipzig), 1970; (ed jtly) Juvenal, Satires 1, 3, 10, 1977; (ed jtly) Ovid, Fasti (Leipzig), 1978, 3rd edn 1988; A Commentary on the Satires of Juvenal, 1980; (ed) Juvenal, The Satires, a text, 1984; (ed) Statius, Silvae, 1990; The Poems of Petronius, 1991; many articles and reviews. *Recreation:* chess (schoolboy champion of Ireland, 1950). *Address:* 1011 Cathcart Way, Stanford, Calif 94305, USA. *T:* (415) 856–3010.

COURTNEY, Roger Graham; Chief Executive, Building Research Establishment, Department of the Environment, since 1990; *b* 11 July 1946; *s* of late Ronald Samuel Courtney and of Marjorie Dixon Courtney; *m* 1973, Rosemary Madeleine Westlake;

four d. *Educ:* Roan School for Boys, SE3; Trinity Coll., Cambridge (MA); Univ. of Bristol (MSc); Brunel Univ. (MTech(OR)). Building Research Station (later, Building Research Establishment), 1969–77: res. on bldg and urban services and energy conservation; Sci. Officer, 1969–72; Sen. Sci. Officer, 1972–75; PSO, 1975–81; Inner Cities Directorate, DoE, 1977–78; Sci. and Technology Secretariat, Cabinet Office, 1978–84 (Sec. to ACARD and IT Adv. Panel); SPSO, 1981–83; DCSO, 1983–86; Technical Dir, Energy Efficiency Office, Dept of Energy, 1984–86; Dep. Dir, 1986–88, Dir, 1988–90, BRE. *Publications:* papers in sci. and professional jls. *Address:* Building Research Establishment, Garston, Watford WD2 7JR. *T:* Watford (0923) 894040.

COURTOWN, 9th Earl of, *cr* 1762; **James Patrick Montagu Burgoyne Winthrop Stopford;** Baron Courtown (Ire.), 1758; Viscount Stopford, 1762; Baron Saltersford (GB), 1796; *b* 19 March 1954; *s* of 8th Earl of Courtown, OBE, TD, DL, and of Patricia, 3rd *d* of Harry S. Winthrop, Auckland, NZ; *S* father, 1975; *m* 1985, Elisabeth, *yr d* of I. R. Dunnett, Broad Campden, Glos; one *s* one *d*. *Educ:* Eton College; Berkshire Coll. of Agriculture; RAC, Cirencester. ARICS. *Heir: s* Viscount Stopford, *qv.*

COUSE, Philip Edward, FCA; Partner, Coopers & Lybrand Deloitte (formerly Coopers & Lybrand), 1966–91; *b* 24 March 1936; *s* of Oliver and Marion Couse; *m* 1st, Jane Nicholson (marr. diss. 1973); two *s* one *d*; 2nd, Carol Ann Johannessen Pruitt; one step-*d*. *Educ:* Uppingham Sch.; Hackley Sch., USA. Qualified as Chartered Accountant, 1961. Birmingham Chartered Accountants' Students Society: Sec., 1958–59; Chm., 1967–69; Pres., 1977–78; Birmingham and West Midlands Soc. of Chartered Accountants: Mem. Cttee, 1974–, Pres., 1982–83; Institute of Chartered Accountants: Mem. Council, 1978–; Chm. of various cttees; Vice-Pres., 1987–88; Dep. Pres., 1988–89; Pres., 1989–90; Chartered Accountants' Dining Club: Mem. Cttee, 1981–; Treas., 1985–89; Pres., 1989–91. Dir, Hillstone Sch. Trust, Malvern, 1971–86; Chairman: Edgbaston C of E Coll. for Girls, 1982–88; Birmingham Rep. Theatre Foundn, 1991–; Member: Birmingham Dio. Bd of Finance, 1991–; Council of Management, Ironbridge Heritage Foundn, 1991–; Trustee and Treas., Birmingham Eye Foundn, 1981–91. Liveryman, Co. of Chartered Accountants in England and Wales, 1977– (Mem., Court, 1987–90). *Recreations:* music, horse racing, woodwork. *Address:* 15 Chad Road, Edgbaston, Birmingham B15 3ER. *Clubs:* Royal Automobile; Birmingham (Birmingham).

COUSINS, Brian Harry, CBE 1981; Principal Establishment and Finance Officer, Lord Chancellor's Department, since 1989; *b* 18 July 1933; *s* of late William and Ethel Margaret Cousins; *m* 1957, Margaret (*née* Spark); two *s*. *Educ:* Devonport High School. Served RAF, pilot, 1952–54. Joined Ministry of Defence, 1954; Private Sec. to Permanent Secretary, 1962–65; Private Sec. Parliamentary Secretary, 1971–72; ndc 1972; Civil Sec., British Forces Germany, 1973–76; Asst Under Sec. of State, MoD, 1981–85, 1986–89; Chm., CSSB, 1985–86. *Recreations:* tennis, music, gardening.

COUSINS, Air Vice-Marshal David, CB 1991; AFC 1980; Director General Aircraft 2, Ministry of Defence Procurement Executive, since 1989; *b* 20 Jan. 1942; *s* of late Peter and Irene Cousins; *m* 1966, Mary Edith McMurray, *e d* of Rev. A. W. S. Holmes; two *s* one *d*. *Educ:* St Edward's Sch., Malta; Prince Rupert's Sch., Wilhelmshaven; RAF College. 92 Sqn (Lightnings), 1965–68; ADC to CAS, 1968–70; 15 Sqn (Buccaneers), 1970–73; Air Plans, HQ RAF Germany, 1973; RAF Staff Coll., 1974; Staff Officer to ACAS (OR), 1975–77; OC 16 Sqn (Buccaneers), 1977–80; Central Trials and Tactics Orgn, 1980; PSO to CAS, 1981–83; OC RAF Laarbruch, 1983–85; RCDS 1986; Dir, Air Offensive, MoD, 1987–89. ADC to the Queen, 1984–85. *Recreations:* squash, dinghy sailing, horology. *Address:* Ministry of Defence (PE), St Giles Court, WC2H 8LD. *Clubs:* Royal Air Force, London Corinthian Sailing.

COUSINS, James Mackay; MP (Lab) Newcastle upon Tyne Central, since 1987; *b* 21 Feb. 1944; *m*; two *s* (one step *s* two step *d*). *Educ:* New Coll., Oxford (Schol.); London School of Economics. Contract Researcher, and Lectr in steel, shipbuilding and inner city job markets for trade unions, Commn on Industrial Relns and Depts of Employment and the Environment. Member: Wallsend Borough Council, 1969–73; Tyne and Wear County Council, 1973–86 (Dep. Leader, 1981–86). Founder, North Low Pay Unit. Member: CND; ASTMS. *Address:* (office) Burt Hall, Northumberland Road, Newcastle upon Tyne NE1 8LD; House of Commons, SW1A 0AA.

COUSINS, John Peter; Managing Director, Cousins Financial Services Ltd (Gibraltar), since 1990; *b* 31 Oct. 1931; *s* of Rt Hon. Frank Cousins, PC; *m* 1976, Pauline Cousins (*née* Hubbard); three *d*. *Educ:* Doncaster Central Sch. Motor engineering apprentice, 1947–52; RAF Engineering, 1952–55; BOAC cabin crew and clerical work, 1955–63; Full Time Official, TGWU, 1963–75, Nat. Sec., 1966–75; Dir of Manpower and Industrial Relations, NEDO, 1975–79; Dir of Personnel, Plessey Telecommunications and Office Systems Ltd, 1979–81; Dir of Personnel and Industrial Relns, John Brown PLC, 1981–83; Gen. Sec., Clearing Bank Union, 1983–86; Head of Personnel, Scottish Daily Record & Sunday Mail (1986) Ltd, 1987; Personnel Dir, Maxwell Pergamon Publishing Corp., 1988–89; Sen. Consultant, Contract 2000, 1989–90. Mem., Transport and Local Govt Cttees, TUC; UK Deleg., ILO; International Transport Workers Federation: Member: Aviation Sect.; Local Govt Cttee; Chemical Cttee; Civil Aviation Cttee; Mem. Industrial Training Bds. Member: Countryside Commn, 1972–84; New Towns Commn, 1975–79; Sandford Cttee to review National Parks in England and Wales, 1972–73; Council, RSPB, 1982; Bd of Trustees, Royal Botanic Gardens, Kew, 1983–88. Chm., British Council of Productivity Assocs, 1977–82. Travelling Fellow, Kingston Reg. Management Centre, 1977. FBIM. *Recreation:* music. *Address:* 1 White House, Vicarage Crescent, Battersea, SW11 3LJ.

COUSINS, Philip, CB 1982; Deputy Comptroller and Auditor General, National Audit Office (formerly Secretary, Exchequer and Audit Department), 1979–84; *b* 28 Feb. 1923; *s* of Herbert and Ella Cousins; *m* 1948, Ruby Laura Morris; two *d*. *Educ:* Royal Liberty School, Romford. Served in Royal Air Force, 1943–47. Joined Treasury, 1949; Under Secretary, 1974–79. *Address:* 102 Philbeach Gardens, SW5 9ET. *T:* 071–373 6164.

COUSTEAU, Jacques-Yves; Commandeur, Légion d'Honneur; Croix de Guerre with Palm; Officier du Mérite Maritime; Chevalier du Mérite Agricole; Officier des Arts et des Lettres; Member of Académie Française, 1989; marine explorer; *b* 11 June 1910; *s* of Daniel and Elizabeth Cousteau; *m* 1937, Simone Melchior (*d* 1990); one *s* (and one *s* decd). *Educ:* Stanislas, Paris; Navy Academy, Brest. Lt de vaisseau, War of 1939–45. Inventor with Emile Gagnan, 1943, of the Aqualung, a portable breathing device for divers; development with Lucien Malavard and Bertrand Charrier of Turbosail system, 1985. Established Undersea Research Group, 1946; Founder and President: Campagnes Océanographiques Françaises, 1950; Centre d'Etudes Marines Avancées, 1952; since 1951 has made annual oceanographic expdns on his ship Calypso, and has made film records of his undersea expdns since 1951; took part in making of the Bathyscaphe; promoted Conshelf saturation dive programme, 1962–65; Founder, Cousteau Soc., 1973. Dir, Musée Océanographique, Monaco, 1957–88; Gen. Sec., Internat. Commn for Scientific Exploration of the Mediterranean Sea, 1966. For. Assoc. Mem., Nat. Acad. Scis, USA, 1968; Corresp. Mem., Hellenic Inst. of Marine Archaeology, 1975; Hon. Mem., Indian Acad. of Scis, 1978. Hon. DSc: California 1970; Brandeis 1970; Rensselaer Polytechnic

Inst., 1979; Harvard, 1979; Ghent, 1983; Dr *hc* Univ. Autónoma de Guadalajara, 1989. Gold Medal, RGS, 1963; Pott's Medal, Franklin Inst., 1970; Gold Medal, Nat. Geographic Soc., and Gold Medal Grand Prix d'Océanographie Albert Ier, 1971; Grande Médaille d'Or, Soc. d'encouragement au Progrès, 1973; Award of New England Aquarium, 1973; Prix de la couronne d'or, 1973; Polena della Bravura, 1974; Gold Medal "Sciences" (Arts, Sciences, Lettres), 1974; Fellow, BAFTA, 1975; Manley Bendall Prize, Marine Acad., 1976; Special Cervia prize, 1976; Internat. Pahlavi Environment Prize, 1977; Jean Sainteny Prize, 1980; Kiwanis Internat. Europe Prize, 1980; Lindbergh Award, 1982; Neptune Award, Amer. Oceanic Orgn, 1982; Bruno H. Schubert Foundn Award, 1983; US Presidential Medal of Freedom, 1985; Founder's Award, Internat. Council of Nat. Acad. of Arts and Scis, 1987; inducted into Diving Equipment Manufrs Assoc. Hall of Fame, 1989 (Reaching Out Award, 1989). *Publications:* Par 18 mètres de fond, 1946; La Plongée en Scaphandre, 1950; (with Frederic Dumas) The Silent World, 1953 (New York and London), first published in English, then in 21 other languages; (ed with James Dugan) Captain Cousteau's Underwater Treasury, 1959 (London); The Living Sea, 1963 (London); World Without Sun, 1965 (film awarded Oscar, 1966); (with P. Cousteau) The Shark, 1970; with P. Diolé: Life and Death in a Coral Sea, 1971; Diving for Sunken Treasure, 1971; The Whale: mighty monarch of the sea, 1972; Octopus and Squid, 1973; Galapagos, Titicaca, the Blue Holes: three adventures, 1973; The Ocean World of Jacques Cousteau (21 vol. encyclopedia), 1973; Diving Companions, 1974; Dolphins, 1975; Jacques Cousteau: the ocean world, 1979; The Cousteau Almanac, 1981; Jacques Cousteau's Calypso, 1983; (with Mose Richards) Jacques Cousteau's Amazon Journey, 1984; Jacques Cousteau: Whales, 1988; articles in National Geographical Magazine, 1952–66. *Films:* The Silent World (Grand Prix, Gold Palm, Cannes 1956; Oscar, 1957); The Golden Fish (Oscar, best short film, 1959); World without Sun (Oscar, 1965); Voyage to the Edge of the World, 1975; Cries from the Deep, 1982; St Lawrence: stairway to the sea, 1982; Jacques Cousteau: the first seventy-five years, 1985; Riders of the Wind, 1986; Island of Peace, 1988; Outrage at Valdez, 1990; Lilliput in Antarctica, 1990; *TV film series:* The Undersea World of Jacques Cousteau, 1968–76 (numerous Emmy awards); Oasis in Space, 1977; The Cousteau Odyssey, 1977–82; Cousteau/Amazon, 1982–85; Cousteau/Mississippi, 1985; Cousteau/Rediscovery of the World, 1985–. *Address:* The Cousteau Society Inc., 930 West 21st Street, Norfolk, Va 23517, USA.

COUTTS; see Money-Coutts.

COUTTS, Gordon; see Coutts, T. G.

COUTTS, Herbert, FSAScot; FMA; City Curator, City of Edinburgh Museums and Art Galleries, since 1973; *b* 9 March 1944; *s* of late Herbert and Agnes Coutts, Dundee; *m* 1970, Angela Elizabeth Mason Smith; one *s* three *d*. *Educ:* Morgan Acad., Dundee. FSAScot 1965; AMA 1970, FMA 1976. Asst Keeper of Antiquities and Bygones, Dundee City Museums, 1965–68, Keeper, 1968–71; Supt, Edinburgh City Museums, 1971–73. Vice-Pres., Museums Assts Gp, 1967–70; Member: Govt Cttee on Future of Scotland's National Museums and Galleries, 1979–80 (report publd 1981); Council, Museums Assoc., 1977–78, 1987–; Council, Soc. of Antiquaries of Scotland, 1981–82; Bd, Scottish Museums Council, 1985–88, 1990–; Museums Advr, COSLA Arts and Recreation Cttee, 1985–90. Member: Paxton House Trust, 1988–; E Lothian Community Develt Trust, 1989–. Building Projects: City of Edinburgh Art Centre (opened 1980); Museum of Childhood Extension (opened 1986); People's Story Museum (opened 1989). Exhibitions at City of Edinburgh Art Centre: The Emperor's Warriors, 1985; Gold of the Pharaohs, 1988; Gold of Peru, 1990. Contested (Lab) Angus South, 1970. SBStJ 1977. *Publications:* Ancient Monuments of Tayside, 1970; Tayside Before History, 1971; Edinburgh: an illustrated history, 1975; (ed) Gold of the Pharaohs, 1988; (ed) Gold of Peru, 1990; guide books, exhibn catalogues; contrib. Museums Jl and archaeol jls. *Recreations:* relaxing with family, gardening, going to the opera, writing, reading, walking. *Address:* Kirkhill House, Queen's Road, Dunbar, East Lothian EH42 1LN. *T:* Dunbar (0368) 63113.

COUTTS, Ian Dewar, CBE 1982; in practice as chartered accountant, since 1950; Member, Forestry Commission, since 1984; Director, Eastern Electricity plc, since 1990 (Member, Eastern Electricity Board, 1982–90); *b* 15 May 1927; *s* of David Dewar Coutts and Dorothy Helen Coutts; *m* 1st, 1950, Sheila Margaret Cargill (marr. diss. 1983); one *s* two *d*; 2nd 1983, Hilary Ballard; one *s* one *d*. *Educ:* Ipswich Sch.; Culford Sch. Chartered Accountant, 1949. Served 1st Essex Regt, 1946–48. Norfolk County Councillor, 1970–89; Leader, Norfolk CC, 1973–79. Chm., ACC Finance Cttee, 1977–83; Mem., Consultative Council on Local Govt Finance, 1977–83. Mem., Local Govt Audit Commn, 1983–90. Chm., S Norfolk Conservative Assoc., 1970–73; Parly Cand., Norwich S, 1979. Mem., Council, Univ. of East Anglia, 1974–86. *Recreation:* sailing. *Address:* 2 The Close, Norwich NR1 4DJ. *T:* Norwich (0603) 612311. *Club:* Royal Automobile.

COUTTS, Prof. John Archibald; Professor of Jurisprudence in the University of Bristol, 1950–75, now Emeritus; Pro-Vice Chancellor, 1971–74; *b* 29 Dec. 1909; *e s* of Archibald and Katherine Jane Coutts; *m* 1940, Katherine Margaret Alldis; two *s*. *Educ:* Merchant Taylors', Crosby; Downing Coll., Cambridge (MA, LLB). Barrister Gray's Inn, 1933; lectured in Law: University Coll., Hull, 1934–35; King's Coll., London, 1935–36; Queen's Univ., Belfast, 1936–37; Trinity Coll., Dublin, 1937–50; Prof. of Laws, University of Dublin, 1944–50. Fellow, Trinity College, Dublin, 1944–50. Visiting Professor: Osgoode Hall Law Sch., Toronto, 1962–63; Univ. of Toronto, 1970–71, 1975–76. *Publications:* The Accused (ed); contributions to legal journals. *Address:* 22 Hurle Crescent, Clifton, Bristol BS8 2SZ. *T:* Bristol (0272) 736984.

COUTTS, T(homas) Gordon, QC (Scotland) 1973; *b* 5 July 1933; *s* of Thomas Coutts and Evelyn Gordon Coutts; *m* 1959, Winifred Katherine Scott, MLitt; one *s* one *d*. *Educ:* Aberdeen Grammar Sch.; Aberdeen Univ. (MA, LLB). Admitted Faculty of Advocates, 1959; Standing Junior Counsel to Dept Agric. (Scot.), 1965–73. Temporary Judge, Court of Session, Scotland, 1991–. Part-time Chairman: Industrial Tribunals, 1972–; Medical Appeal Tribunal, 1984–; VAT Tribunal, 1990–. *Recreations:* golf, stamp collecting. *Address:* 6 Heriot Row, Edinburgh EH3 6HU. *Club:* New (Edinburgh).

COUVE DE MURVILLE, Maurice; Commandeur de la Légion d'Honneur; Ambassadeur de France; Member of Senate, for Paris, since 1986; *b* 24 Jan. 1907; *m* 1932, Jacqueline Schweisguth; three *d*. *Educ:* Paris Univ. Inspecteur des finances, 1930; directeur des finances extérieures, 1940; membre du Comité français de la libération nationale (Alger), 1943; représentant de la France, Conseil consultatif pour l'Italie, 1944; Ambassador in Rome, 1945; directeur général des affaires politiques, Ministère des Affaires Etrangères, 1945–50; Ambassador in Egypt, 1950–54; French Permanent Rep., NATO, Sept. 1954–Jan. 1955; Ambassador in the US, 1955–56; Ambassador of France to the Federal Republic of Germany, 1956–58; Ministre des Affaires Etrangères, 1958–68, de l'Economie et des Finances, June–July 1968; Prime Minister of France, 1968–69; Deputy, French Nat. Assembly, Paris 8ème Arrondissement, 1973–86. *Publications:* Une Politique étrangère 1958–69, 1973; Le Monde en face, 1989. *Address:* 44 rue du Bac, 75007 Paris, France.

COUVE DE MURVILLE, Most Rev. Maurice Noël Léon; see Birmingham, Archbishop of, (RC).

COUZENS, Sir Kenneth (Edward), KCB 1979 (CB 1976); Chairman, Coal Products, since 1988; Director, Crédit Lyonnais Capital Markets, since 1989; *b* 29 May 1925; *s* of Albert Couzens and May Couzens (*née* Biddlecombe); *m* 1947, Muriel Eileen Fey; one *s* one *d. Educ:* Portsmouth Grammar Sch.; Caius Coll., Cambridge. Inland Revenue, 1949–51; Treasury, 1951–68, and 1970–82; Civil Service Dept, 1968–70. Private Sec. to Financial Sec., Treasury, 1952–55, and to Chief Sec., 1962–63; Asst Sec., 1963–69; Under-Secretary: CSD, 1969–70; Treasury, 1970–73; Dep. Sec., Incomes Policy and Public Finance, 1973–77; Second Perm. Sec. (Overseas Finance), 1977–82; Perm. Under-Sec. of State, Dept of Energy, 1983–85. Dep. Chm., NCB, subseq. British Coal, 1985–88. Chm., Monetary Cttee, European Community, 1982; Mem., UK Adv. Bd, Nat. Econ. Res. Assocs, 1986–. *Address:* Coverts Edge, Woodsway, Oxshott, Surrey. *T:* Oxshott (0372) 843207. *Club:* Reform.

COVACEVICH, Sir (Anthony) Thomas, Kt 1978; DFC 1943; Senior Partner, MacDonnells, Solicitors and Notaries Public, Cairns, Queensland, Australia, since 1963 (Partner, 1939); *b* 1 March 1915; *s* of Prosper and Ellen Covacevich; *m* 1944, Gladys Rose (*née* Bryant); one *s* one *d. Educ:* Townsville and Brisbane Grammar Schools. Admitted Solicitor, Supreme Court of Queensland, 1938. Formerly Director of five publicly listed Australian companies, including Foxwood Ltd, a timber company (Chm.). *Recreation:* fishing. *Address:* 17 Temora Close, Edge Hill, Cairns, Queensland, Australia. *T:* 51 4000; Box 5046, Cairns Mail Centre, Queensland 4870, Australia. *Clubs:* North Queensland (Townsville, Qld); Cairns Game Fishing (Cairns, Qld).

COVEN, Major Edwina Olwyn, CBE 1988; JP; DL; HM Lieutenant, City of London, since 1981; Director, since 1985 and Deputy Chairman, since 1990, TV-am; *b* 23 Oct. 1921; *d* of Sir Samuel Instone, DL, and Lady (Alice) Instone; *m* 1951, Frank Coven, *qv. Educ:* Queen's Coll., London; St Winifred's, Ramsgate; Lycée Victor Duruy, Paris; Marlborough Gate Secretarial Coll., London (1st Cl. Business Diploma). Volunteered for Mil. Service, Private ATS; commnd ATS (subseq. WRAC); Army Interpreter (French); served UK and overseas, incl. staff appts, Plans and Policy Div., Western Union Defence Org. and NATO, Directorate Manpower Planning, WO, 1942–56. 1959–: Children's Writer, Fleetway Publications; Gen. Features Writer, National Magazine Co.; Reporter, BBC Woman's Hour; performer and adviser, children's and teenage progs, ITV. Mem. Adv. Council, Radio London (BBC), 1978–81. Chm., Davbro Chemists, 1967–71; stores consultant on promotion and fashion, 1960–77; Mem., Women's Adv. Cttee (Clothing and Footwear Sub-Cttee), BSI, 1971–73. JP Inner London, North Westminster, 1965–72 (Dep. Chm., 1971–72); JP City of London Commn, 1969–88 (Dep. Chm., 1971–88); Greater London: DL 1987, Rep. DL Hammersmith and Fulham, 1989–; Mem., Central Council Probation and After-Care Cttee, 1971; Chm., City of London Probation and After-Care Cttee, 1971–77; Chm, City of London Police Cttee, 1984–87 (Dep. Chm., 1983–84); Mem., Police Cttee, AMA, 1985–. Mem., Jt Cttee of Management, London Court of Internat. Arbitration 1983–89. Dowgate Ward, City of London: Court of Common Council, 1972–; elected Alderman, 1973 and 1974; Deputy, 1975–. Chief Commoner, City of London, 1987–88. Freedom, City of London, 1967; Mem., Guild of Freemen, City of London, 1971; Freeman, Loriners' Co., 1967; Liveryman, Spectacle Makers' Co., 1972; Hon. Liveryman, Lightmongers' Co., 1990. Member: Council, WRAC Assoc., 1973–90 (Vice Pres., 1984–88; Vice-Chm., 1985–89; Chm., 1989–90); TAVRA, City of London, 1979–86; Associated Speakers, 1975–; London Home Safety Council, 1980–84; Vice Chm., Cities of London and Westminster Home Safety Council, 1984–89; Vice President: Nat. Org. for Women's Management Educn, 1983–90; FANY, 1989–; Operation Raleigh, 1989–; Chm., Cttee for Celebration of 800th Year of Mayoralty, Corp. of London, 1988–90. Mem., Bd of Governors, City of London Sch., 1972–77; Chm., Bd of Governors, City of London Sch. for Girls, 1978–81; Mem., Royal Soc. of St George, 1972–; Chm., Vintry and Dowgate Wards Club, 1977. FRSA 1988. Hon. Captain of Police, Salt Lake City, 1986; Order of Wissam Alouite, Cl. III (Morocco), 1987. OStJ 1987. *Publication:* Tales of Oaktree Kitchen, 1959 (2nd edn 1960; adapted for ITV children's educnl series). *Recreations:* looking after much-loved husband and homemaking generally; lawn tennis; watching a variety of spectator sports. *Address:* 22 Cadogan Court, Draycott Avenue, SW3 3BX. *T:* 071–589 8286. *Clubs:* Queen's, Hurlingham; Devonshire (Eastbourne).

COVEN, Frank; London and European Director, The Nine Television Network of Australia, since 1974; *b* 26 April 1910; *s* of Isaac L. Coven and Raie Coven; *m* 1951, Edwina Coven (*née* Instone), *qv. Educ:* The Perse, Cambridge; France and Germany. Studied film prodn, UFA and EFA Studios, Berlin. TA (Ranks), 1938; War Service, 1939–45 (commnd 1941). Film admin and prodn, Gaumont British Studies, 1932; Studio Manager, Gainsborough Pictures, 1935; TV prodn, BBC/Daily Mail, 1937–38; Jt Dep. Organiser, Daily Mail Ideal Home Exhibition (radio, television, special features), 1945; Manager, Public Relations, Associated Newspapers, 1949; interviews, Wimbledon tennis commentaries, children's series "Write it Yourself" BBC TV, 1949–54 (subseq. ITV); TV Adviser, Bd of Associated Newspapers, 1953, Associated Rediffusion, 1954; London Rep., Television Corporation Ltd, Sydney, and Herald-Sun Pty, Melbourne, 1954; Dir, Compagnie Belge Transmarine SA and Imperial Stevedoring Co. SA, 1959; Head of Publicity and Promotions, Associated Newspapers, 1961; 1962: Dir, Associated Newspapers Gp; Dir, Bouverie Investments Ltd; Managing Director: Northcliffe Developments Ltd; Frank Coven Enterprises Ltd, presenting (with John Roberts) plays in London, incl. The Professor, How's the World Treating You? and, with London Traverse Theatre Co., works by Saul Bellow and others, 1964–69; Gen. Man., United Racecourses Ltd (Epsom, Sandown Park, Kempton Park), 1970, Man. Dir 1970, Vice-Chm. 1972. Mem., Variety Club of GB. Mem., Royal Soc. of St George, 1972. *Publications:* various Daily Mail Guides to Television Development in UK. *Recreations:* lawn tennis, swimming, study of varied media (current affairs). *Address:* 22 Cadogan Court, Draycott Avenue, SW3 3BX. *T:* 071–589 8286. *Clubs:* Savage, Saints and Sinners; Hurlingham, Queen's; Devonshire (Eastbourne).

COVENEY, Prof. James; Professor of French, University of Bath, 1969–85, now Professor Emeritus; *b* 4 April 1920; *s* of James and Mary Coveney; *m* 1955, Patricia Yvonne Townsend; two *s. Educ:* elementary schools; St Ignatius Coll., Stamford Hill, London; Univ. of Reading (BA, 1st Cl. hons French, 1950); Univ. of Strasbourg (Dr Univ. 1953). Clerical Officer, LCC, 1936–40. Served War of 1939–45: enlisted in ranks of The Welch Regt, 1940; commnd in Queen's Own Royal West Kent Regt, 1941; served subsequently as Pilot in RAF; Flt-Lt, 1945. Univ. of Strasbourg: French Govt Research Scholar, 1950–51; Lecteur d'anglais, 1951–53. Lectr in French, Univ. of Hull, 1953–58; Asst Dir of Exams (Mod. Langs), Civil Service Commn, 1958–59; UN Secretariat, New York, 1959–61; NATO Secretariat, 1961–64; University of Bath: Sen. Lectr and Head of Mod. Langs, 1964–68; Head of Sch. of Mod. Langs, 1969–77 and 1980–83; Jt Dir, Centre for European Ind. Studies, 1969–75. Visiting Professor: Ecole Nat. d'Administration, Paris, 1974–85; Univ. of Buckingham, 1974–86; Bethlehem Univ., 1985; Univ. of Limerick, 1987–. Language Trng Adviser, McKinsey & Co. Inc., 1967–73. Governor, Bell Educnl Trust, 1972–88. Consultant, Gulf Centre for Strategic Studies, 1986–. Member: Nat. Council for Modern Languages, 1972–75 (Sec. 1972–74); Jt Sec., Assoc. of Univ. Profs of French, 1973–79. Member: British-French Mixed Cultural Commn, 1973–79; Cttee of Management, British Inst. in Paris, 1975–79; Council, Fédération Britannique de l'Alliance Française, 1976–81; Exec. Cttee, Council for the Advancement of Arab-British Understanding, 1987–; RIIA, 1987–. FRSA 1974. Corresp. Mem., Académie des Sciences, Agriculture, Arts et Belles Lettres, Aix-en-Provence, 1975. Chevalier de l'Ordre des Palmes Académiques, 1978; Officier de l'Ordre National du Mérite, 1986. *Publications:* La Légende de l'Empereur Constant, 1955; (jtly) Glossary of French and English Management Terms, 1972; (jtly) Le français pour l'ingénieur, 1974; (jtly) Glossary of German and English Management Terms, 1977; (jtly) Glossary of Spanish and English Management Terms, 1978; (jtly) Guide to French Institutions, 1978; (jtly) English-Portuguese Business Dictionary, 1982; (jtly) Dictionary of Management Terms in English-French-Arabic, 1990; (jtly) Glossary of French and English Business Management Terms, 1991; articles in British, French and American periodicals. *Address:* 40 Westfield Close, Bath BA2 2EB. *T:* Bath (0225) 316670. *Club:* Travellers'.

COVENEY, Michael William; theatre critic, The Observer, since 1990; *b* 24 July 1948; *s* of William Coveney and Violet Amy Coveney (*née* Perry); *m* 1977, Susan Monica Hyman; one *s. Educ:* St Ignatius College, London; Worcester College, Oxford. Editor, Plays and Players, 1975–78; theatre critic, Financial Times, 1981–89. *Publication:* The Citz, 1990. *Recreations:* music, tennis, travel. *Address:* c/o The Observer, Chelsea Bridge House, Queenstown Road, SW8 4NN.

COVENTRY, family name of **Earl of Coventry.**

COVENTRY, 11th Earl of, *cr* 1697; **George William Coventry;** Viscount Deerhurst, 1697; *b* 25 Jan. 1934; *o s* of 10th Earl and Hon. Nesta Donne Philipps, *e d* of 1st Baron Kylsant; *S* father, 1940; *m* 1st, 1955, Marie Farquhar-Medart (marr. diss. 1963); one *s*; 2nd, 1969, Ann (marr. diss. 1975), *d* of F. W. J. Cripps, Bickley, Kent; 3rd, 1980, Valerie Anne Birch, Southport. *Educ:* Eton; RMA, Sandhurst. *Heir: s* Viscount Deerhurst, *qv. Address:* Earls Croome Court, Earls Croome, Worcester.

See also Earl of Harrowby.

COVENTRY, Bishop of, since 1985; **Rt. Rev. Simon Barrington-Ward;** Prelate of the Most Distinguished Order of St Michael and St George, since 1989; *b* 27 May 1930; *s* of Robert McGowan Barrington-Ward and Margaret Adele Barrington-Ward; *m* 1963, Jean Caverhill Taylor; two *d. Educ:* Eton; Magdalene Coll., Cambridge (MA; Hon. Fellow, 1987). Lektor, Free Univ., Berlin, 1953–54; Westcott House, Cambridge, 1954–56; Chaplain, Magdalene Coll., Cambridge, 1956–60; Assist Lectr in Religious Studies, Univ. of Ibadan, 1960–63; Fellow and Dean of Chapel, Magdalene Coll., Cambridge, 1963–69; Principal, Crowther Hall, Selly Oak Colls, Birmingham, 1969–74; Gen. Sec., CMS, 1975–85; Hon. Canon of Derby Cathedral, 1975–85; a Chaplain to the Queen, 1984–85. Chairman: Partnership for World Mission, 1986–; Internat. Affairs Cttee, Bd for Social Responsibility of Gen. Synod, 1987–. Pres., St John's Coll., Nottingham, 1987. FRAI. Hon. DD Wycliffe Coll., Toronto, 1984. *Publications:* contributor to: Christianity in Independent Africa (ed Fasholé Luke and others), 1978; Today's Anglican Worship (ed C. Buchanan), 1980; Renewal—An Emerging Pattern, by Graham Pulkingham and others, 1980; A New Dictionary of Christian Theology (ed Alan Richardson and John Bowden), 1983; Love Will Out (anthology of news letters), 1988; Christianity Today, 1988; (contrib.) The World's Religions, 1988; CMS Newsletter, 1975–85. *Address:* Bishop's House, Davenport Road, Coventry, W Midlands CV5 6PW.

COVENTRY, Archdeacon of; *see* Russell, Ven. H. I. L.

COVENTRY, Provost of; *see* Petty, Very Rev. J. F.

COVENTRY, Rev. John Seton, SJ; Master, St Edmund's House, Cambridge, 1976–85; *b* 21 Jan. 1915; *yr s* of late Seton and Annie Coventry, Barton-on-Sea, Hants. *Educ:* Stonyhurst; Campion Hall, Oxford. MA Oxon 1945. Entered Society of Jesus, 1932; ordained, 1947; Prefect of Studies, Beaumont, 1950; Rector, Beaumont, 1956–58; Provincial, English Province of Soc. of Jesus, 1958–64; Lectr in Theology, Heythrop Coll., 1965–76. *Publications:* Morals and Independence, 1946; The Breaking of Bread, 1950; Faith Seeks Understanding, 1951; The Life Story of the Mass, 1959; The Theology of Faith, 1968; Christian Truth, 1975; Faith in Jesus Christ, 1980; Reconciling, 1985. *Address:* 10 Albert Road, Birmingham B17 0AN. *T:* 021–427 2628.

COVINGTON, Nicholas; Director, Office of Manpower Economics, 1986–89; *b* 9 June 1929; *s* of late Cyril Tim Covington and Margaret Joan (*née* Bray); *m* 1st, 1953, Patricia Sillitoe (marr. diss.); one *s* two *d*; 2nd, 1983, Kathleen Hegarty. *Educ:* Cranleigh Sch.; Oriel Coll., Oxford (BA). RAF, 1947–49. Metal Box Co. Ltd, 1952–57; Gen. Manager and Dir, Garnier & Co. Ltd, 1957–66; entered Min. of Labour, 1966; Asst Sec., 1971; Industrial Relns Div., Dept of Employment, 1976–86. *Recreations:* history, walking. *Address:* Dovecote House, Lower Slaughter, near Cheltenham, Glos GL54 2HY.

COWAN, Brig. Alan; *see* Cowan, Brig. J. A. C.

COWAN, Prof. Charles Donald, (Jeremy), CBE 1988; MA Cantab, PhD London; FRAS; Chairman of Convocation, University of London, since 1990; *b* London, 18 Nov. 1923; *s* of W. C. Cowan and Minnie Ethel (*née* Farrow); *m* 1st, 1945, Mary Evelyn (marr. diss. 1960), *d* of Otto Vetter, Perth, WA; two *d*; 2nd, 1962, Daphne Eleanor, *d* of Walter Rishworth Whittam, Rangoon. *Educ:* Kilburn Grammar Sch.; Peterhouse, Cambridge. Served Royal Navy, 1941–45. Lecturer in History, Raffles Coll., Singapore, 1947–48, and University of Malaya, 1948–50; School of Oriental and African Studies, University of London: Lectr in the History of South-East Asia, 1950–60; Prof., 1961–80, Prof. of Oriental History, 1980–89; Dir, 1976–89; Pro-Vice-Chancellor, 1985–86, Dep. Vice-Chancellor, 1988–90, London Univ. Visiting Prof. of Southeast Asian Hist., Cornell Univ., 1960–61. Governor: James Allen's Girls School, 1977–89; Alleyn's Coll. of God's Gift, Dulwich, 1980–; Richmond Coll., 1988–. *Publications:* Nineteenth Century Malaya, 1961; (ed) The Economic Development of South-East Asia, 1964; (ed) The Economic Development of China and Japan, 1964; (with P. L. Burns) Sir Frank Swettenham's Malayan Journals, 1975; (with O. L. Wolters) Southeast Asian History and Historiography, 1976. *Address:* University of London, Senate House, WC1E 7HU. *T:* 071–636 8000.

COWAN, Brig. Colin Hunter, CBE 1984; Chief Executive, Cumbernauld Development Corporation, 1970–85; *b* 16 Oct. 1920; *s* of late Lt-Col S. Hunter Cowan, DSO and Mrs Jean Hunter Cowan; *m* 1st, 1949, Elizabeth Williamson, MD (*d* 1985); two *s* one *d*; 2nd, 1988, Mrs Jen Burnett, *widow* of A. H. Burnett. *Educ:* Wellington Coll.; RMA Woolwich; Trinity Coll., Cambridge (MA). MICE. Comd Engineer Regt, 1960–63; Defence Adviser, UK Mission to the UN, 1964–66; Brigadier Engineer Plans, MoD (Army), 1968–70. DL Dunbartonshire, 1973–88. *Recreations:* music, photography. *Address:* 12B Greenhill Gardens, Edinburgh EH10 4BW. *T:* 031–447 9768. *Club:* New (Edinburgh).

COWAN, Brig. (James) Alan (Comrie), MBE 1956; Secretary, Government Hospitality Fund, since 1980; *b* 20 Sept. 1923; *s* of late Alexander Comrie Cowan and Helen May Isobel (*née* Finlayson); *m* 1948, Jennifer Evelyn Bland; two *s* one *d. Educ:* Rugby Sch., Warwicks. Commnd Rifle Bde, 1942; served War, Italy and Egypt, 1942–46; served Army, 1947–60: OU Trng Corps, BAOR, Army Staff Coll., WO, Kenya and Malaya;

DS, Army Staff Coll., 1961–63; CO 1 Royal Leicesters, later 4 Royal Anglian, UK, Aden and Malta, 1964–66; GSO1 17 Div., Malaysia, 1966–67; Col GS MoD, 1967–69; Comd 8 Inf. Bde, NI, 1970–71; DAG HQ UKLF, 1972–75; entered Civil Service and joined NI Office, with responsibility for industrial, economic and social affairs, 1975; Principal, 1975–78; Asst Sec., 1978–80. *Recreations:* current affairs, music, theatre, the countryside. *Address:* c/o C. Hoare & Co., 37 Fleet Street, EC4P 4DQ. *Clubs:* Army and Navy, MCC.

COWAN, James Robertson, CBE 1983 (OBE 1974); CEng, FIMinE; Chairman, NCB Coal Products, 1985–88; *b* 12 Sept. 1919; *s* of John and Jean Cowan; *m* 1945, Harriet Good Forrest; two *d. Educ:* Dalziel High Sch., Motherwell; Glasgow Univ. (BSc 1st Cl. Hons). CEng, FIMinE 1971. National Coal Board: Dir, Scottish Area, 1970–80; Bd Mem., 1977–85; Mem. for Industrial Relns, 1980–85; Dep. Chm., 1982–85. Chm., Scottish Brick Corp., 1980– (Dir. 1974–); Dir, British Investment Trust, 1978–. Vis. Prof., Strathclyde Univ., 1978. CBIM. *Recreation:* golf. *Address:* 31 Muirfield Park, Gullane, Scotland EH31 2DY. *T:* Gullane (0620) 843398. *Club:* Caledonian.

COWAN, Jeremy; *see* Cowan, C. D.

COWAN, Lionel David, (Nick Cowan); personnel management consultant; *b* 18 Dec. 1929; *m* 1953, Pamela Ida, *e d* of Hubert and Winifred Williams, Totton, Hants; one *s* two *d. Educ:* Surbiton County Grammar Sch. FBIM 1972; CIPM 1979 (AMIPM 1965). Served Royal Navy, 1945–61: Fleet Air Arm Aircrew (Lieut), 1953; Sen. Instr, RAN, 1958–60. Training Officer, Shoe and Allied Trades Res. Assoc., 1961–62; Perkins Engines Gp, 1962–72 (Dir of Personnel and Industrial Relns 1970–72); Dir of Personnel, Philips Electronic and Associated Industries, 1972–78; Gp Personnel Dir, Unigate Ltd, 1978–79; Dir and Sec., Fedn of London Clearing Bank Employers, 1980–87; Personnel Dir, TSB England & Wales, 1987–89. Chm., W Lambeth HA, 1982–86; Member: Editorial Panel, Personnel Management, 1967–91; BIM Adv. Bd on Industrial Relations, 1970–75; Employment Relns Cttee, IPM, 1971–81; Council, Independent Res. and Assessment Centre, 1975–89; Engrg Industry Trng Bd, 1976–79; Employment Appeal Tribunal, 1976–; Editorial Panel, Industrial Relns Law Reports, 1977–; Employment Policy Cttee, CBI, 1978–89; Civil Service Arbitration Tribunal, 1979–; CBI Council, 1980–87; Central Arbitration Cttee, 1984–; Youth Training Bd, 1984–85; Equal Opportunities Commn, 1988–91; NEDO Enquiry, Industrial Relns Trng for Managers, 1976, Supply and Demand for Skilled Manpower, 1977. Vice-Pres. (Employee Relations), IPM, 1977–79. Director, Oxford Univ. Business Summer Sch., 1980. Lecturer and writer on personnel management and industrial relations. *Publications:* Personnel Management and Banking, 1984; The Clearing Banks and the Trade Unions, 1984; numerous articles, papers and other pubns on various aspects of personnel management and industrial relations. *Recreations:* things Spanish, music and opera, bridge. *Address:* 15 Somerville Road, Cobham, Surrey KT11 2QT. *T:* Oxshott (0372) 843441. *Club:* Naval and Military.

COWAN, Sir Robert, Kt 1989; Chairman, Highlands and Islands Enterprise (formerly Highlands and Islands Development Board), Inverness, since 1982; *b* 27 July 1932; *s* of Dr John McQueen Cowan and May Cowan; *m* 1959, Margaret Morton (*née* Dewar); two *d. Educ:* Edinburgh Academy; Edinburgh Univ. (MA). Fisons Ltd, 1958–62; Wolsey Ltd, 1962–64; PA Management Consultants Ltd, 1965–82. Member: Bd, Scottish Develt Agency, 1982–91; BBC Broadcasting Council for Scotland, 1984–89; BBC Gen. Adv. Council, 1989–; Scottish PO Bd, 1990–. Mem., Court, Aberdeen Univ., 1989–; Gov., Napier Coll., Edinburgh, 1989–. Hon. LLD Aberdeen, 1987. *Recreation:* sailing. *Address:* The Old Manse, Farr, Inverness-shire IV1 2XA. *Clubs:* New (Edinburgh); Highland (Inverness); Hong Kong (Hong Kong).

COWAN, William Graham, MBE 1943; Chairman, J. H. Carruthers & Co. Ltd, since 1981 (Managing Director, 1981–84); *b* 29 April 1919; *s* of William Cowan, WS, Edinburgh, and Dorothy Isobel Horsbrugh; *m* 1960, Karen Wendell Hansen, Crestwood, NY; two *s* one *d. Educ:* Edinburgh Academy; Cambridge Univ. (MA). CEng, FIMechE, FCSD, FSA(Scot), FRSA. Served 1940–46, Royal Engrs and Gen. Staff, Africa, Italy (Lt-Col). Asst Man. Dir, North British Locomotive Co. Ltd, 1947–50; Man. Dir, J. H. Carruthers and Co. Ltd, 1950–79. Dir, Glasgow Sch. of Art, 1979–82. Mem. Exec. Cttee, Scottish Council (Develt and Industry), 1972–74; Pres., Scottish Engrg Employers' Assoc., 1972. Member: Design Council, 1974–78 (Chm., Scottish Cttee, 1976–78); Council, Nat. Trust for Scotland, 1984–89; Dir, Scottish Transport Group, 1977–80. *Address:* The Old Inn, Fowlis Wester, Perthshire. *T:* Madderty (076483) 319. *Club:* New (Edinburgh).

COWAN, Dr William Maxwell, FRS 1982; Vice President and Chief Scientific Officer, Howard Hughes Medical Insitute, since 1988; *b* 27 Sept. 1931; *s* of Adam Cowan and Jessie Sloan Cowan (*née* Maxwell); *m* 1956, Margaret Sherlock; two *s* one *d. Educ:* Univ. of the Witwatersrand, S Africa (BSc Hons); Hertford Coll., Oxford Univ. (MA, DPhil, BM, BCh). University Lecturer in Anatomy, Oxford, 1958–66; Fellow of Pembroke Coll., Oxford, 1958–66 (Hon. Fellow, 1986); Associate Prof., Univ. of Wisconsin, 1966–68; Washington University, St Louis: Professor and Head of Dept of Anatomy, Sch. of Medicine, 1968–80; Director, Div. of Biological Sciences, 1975–80; Salk Institute for Biological Studies: non-resident Fellow, 1977–80; Professor, 1980–86; Vice Pres. and Dir, Develt Neurobiol., 1980–86; Provost and Exec. Vice-Chancellor, Washington Univ., St Louis, 1986–87. Mem., Amer. Philosophical Soc., 1987. Fellow, Amer. Acad. of Arts and Scis, 1975; For. Mem., Norwegian Acad. of Scis, 1980; Foreign Associate: US National Academy of Sciences, 1981; Royal Soc. of S Africa, 1986. Hon. Fellow, Pembroke Coll., Oxford, 1986. *Publications:* The Use of Axonal Transport for Studies of Neuronal Connectivity, 1975; Aspects of Cellular Neurobiology, 1978; Studies in Developmental Neurobiology, 1981; Annual Reviews of Neuroscience, Vol. 1 1978, Vols 2–13, 1979–90. *Recreations:* photography, reading, travel. *Address:* Howard Hughes Medical Institute, 6701 Rockledge Drive, Bethesda, Md 20817, USA. *T:* (301) 571–0320.

COWARD, David John, CMG 1965; OBE 1962; Registrar General, Kenya, 1955–82; *b* 21 March 1917; *s* of late Robert J. Coward, Exmouth, Devon; *m* 1954, Joan, *d* of late Reginald Frank, Doncaster; three *d. Educ:* Exmouth Grammar Sch. and Law Society's Sch. of Law. FCIS 1961; ACIArb 1984. Admitted a solicitor, 1938. Joined RN as a rating at outbreak of war, 1939; commissioned, 1941; demobilized as Lieut-Comdr (S) RNVR, 1947. ADC to Governor of Trinidad, 1947. Joined Colonial Legal Service, 1948, Asst Registrar Gen., Kenya; Dep. Registrar Gen., 1952; Registrar Gen., Official Receiver and Public Trustee, 1955–82. Acted as Permanent Sec. for Justice and Constitutional Affairs, 1963–64. Served in Kenya Police Reserve, 1949–63, latterly as Senior Superintendent i/c Nairobi Area. Chm., Working Party on future of Company Secretarial Profession in Kenya; Mem. Accountants' Registration Bd, 1978–82; Trustee, Nat. Museums of Kenya, 1979–82. Silver Medal, Internat. Olympic Cttee, 1981. *Recreation:* golf. *Address:* North Perretts, Spinney Lane, West Chiltington, W Sussex RH20 2NX. *T:* Storrington (0903) 742521. *Clubs:* Naval; Nairobi and Limuru Country (Kenya).

COWARD, Vice Adm. Sir John (Francis), KCB 1990; DSO 1982; Commandant, Royal College of Defence Studies, since 1992; *b* 11 Oct. 1937; *s* of Reginald John Coward and Isabelle (*née* Foreman); *m* 1963, Diana (*née* Taylor); two *s. Educ:* Downside; RNC, Dartmouth. Served submarines, 1959–76, i/c HMS Oracle and HMS Valiant; Naval Asst to First Sea Lord, 1978–80; i/c HMS Brilliant, 1980–82; S Atlantic, 1982; Dir, Naval Operational Requirements, 1984; Rear Adm. 1987; Flag Officer: Sea Trng, 1987–88; Flotilla One, 1988–89; Submarines, and Comdr Submarine Forces Eastern Atlantic, 1989–91; Vice Adm. 1989. Younger Brother, Trinity Hse. *Recreations:* sailing, gardening, golf. *Clubs:* Royal Naval Sailing Association; Royal Yacht Squadron.

COWARD, John Stephen, QC 1984; barrister-at-law; a Recorder of the Crown Court, since 1980; *b* 15 Nov. 1937; *s* of Frank and Kathleen Coward; *m* 1967, Ann Lesley Pye; four *d. Educ:* King James Grammar Sch., Almondbury, Huddersfield; University Coll. London (LLB). Lecturer in Law and Constitutional History, University Coll. London and Police Staff Coll., 1962–64; called to the Bar, Inner Temple, 1964; in practice on Midland and Oxford Circuit, 1964–. *Recreation:* trying to grow calceolarias and a decent row of peas. *Address:* The Grange, Scaldwell, Northampton NN6 9JP. *T:* Northampton (0604) 880255. *Clubs:* Northampton and County (Northampton); Scaldwell (Scaldwell, Northants).

COWARD, Richard Edgar; retired; Director for Library Planning, OCLC Inc., 1980–81; *b* 1927; *s* of Edgar Frank Coward and Jean (*née* McIntyre); *m* 1949, Audrey Scott Lintern; one *s* two *d. Educ:* Richmond Grammar Sch., Surrey. FLA. Dir Gen., Bibliographic Servs Div., British Library, 1975–79. Member: Adv. Cttee on BBC Archives, 1976–79; Library Adv. Council (England), 1976–. *Address:* Gaios, Paxos, Greece; 12 Marylebone Mews, W1M 7LF. *T:* 071–486 7316.

COWBURN, Norman; Chairman, Britannia Building Society, 1987–90 (Managing Director, 1970–84; Deputy Chairman, 1986–87); *b* 5 Jan. 1920; *s* of Harold and Edith Cowburn; *m* 1945, Edna Margaret Heatley; two *s* one *d. Educ:* Queen Elizabeth's Grammar Sch., Blackburn. FCIS, FBS. Burnley Building Soc., 1936. Served War, 1940–46. Burnley Building Soc., 1946; Leek and Westbourne Building Soc., 1954 (re-named Britannia Building Soc., Dec. 1975). *Recreations:* golf, gardening. *Address:* Greywoods, Birchall, Leek, Staffs. *T:* Leek (0538) 383214.

COWDEROY, Brenda; General Secretary, Girls' Friendly Society, 1978–85; *b* 27 June 1925; *o c* of late Frederick Cowderoy and of Evelyn Cowderoy (*née* Land). *Educ:* Surbiton High Sch.; St Hugh's Coll., Oxford (MA). Called to Bar, Gray's Inn, 1949. John Lewis Partnership: Asst Legal Adviser, 1954–56; Head of Legal Dept, 1956–70; Nat. Gen. Sec., YWCA, 1971–77. FBIM. *Recreations:* gardens, golf. *Address:* 26 Rossetti Road, Birchington, Kent CT7 9ER. *Club:* Commonwealth Trust.

COWDRAY, 3rd Viscount, *cr* 1917; **Weetman John Churchill Pearson,** TD; Bt, *cr* 1894; Baron, *cr* 1910; Captain, Sussex Yeomanry; Chairman, S. Pearson & Son Ltd, 1954–77; President, Pearson Plc, since 1983; *b* 27 Feb. 1910 (twin); *s* of 2nd Viscount and Agnes Beryl (*d* 1948), *d* of Lord Edward Spencer Churchill; *S* father, 1933; *m* 1st, 1939, Lady Anne Bridgeman (from whom he obtained a divorce, 1950), *d* of 5th Earl of Bradford; one *s* two *d*; 2nd, 1953, Elizabeth Georgiana Mather, 2nd *d* of Sir Anthony Mather-Jackson, 6th Bt; one *s* two *d. Educ:* Eton; Christ Church, Oxford. Parliamentary Private Sec. to Under-Sec. of State for Air, 1941–42. *Recreations:* polo, shooting, fishing. *Heir: s* Hon. Michael Orlando Weetman Pearson [*b* 17 June 1944; *m* 1977, Ellen (marr. diss.), *yr d* of late Hermann Erhardt; *m* 1987, Marina, *d* of John H. Cordle, *qv* and Mrs H. J. Ross Skinner; two *d*]. *Address:* Cowdray Park, Midhurst, West Sussex. *T:* Midhurst (0730) 812461; Dunecht, Skene, Aberdeenshire. *T:* Dunecht (03306) 244. *Clubs:* Cavalry and Guards, White's.

See also Duke of Atholl, Baron Cranworth.

COWDREY, Colin; *see* Cowdrey, M. C.

COWDREY, Rev. Herbert Edward John, FBA 1991; Senior Research Fellow in Modern History, St Edmund Hall, Oxford, since 1987; *b* 29 Nov. 1926; *s* of Herbert and Winifred Cowdrey; *m* 1959, Judith Watson Davis; one *s* two *d. Educ:* Queen Mary's Sch., Basingstoke; Trinity Coll., Oxford (BA Modern Hist. and Theology, 1951; MA); St Stephen's House, Oxford. Nat. service, RN, 1945–47. Deacon, 1952; priest, 1953; Tutor and Chaplain, St Stephen's House, Oxford, 1952–56; Fellow and Tutor in Modern History, St Edmund Hall, Oxford, 1956–87. *Publications:* The Cluniacs and the Gregorian Reform, 1970; The Epistolae vagantes of Pope Gregory VII, 1972; Two Studies in Cluniac History, 1978; The Age of Abbot Desiderius, 1983; Popes, Monks and Crusaders, 1984; articles and reviews in learned jls. *Recreations:* travel, listening to music, gardening. *Address:* 30 Oxford Road, Old Marston, Oxford OX3 0PQ. *T:* Oxford (0865) 243360; St Edmund Hall, Oxford OX1 4AR. *T:* Oxford (0865) 279015.

COWDREY, (Michael) Colin, CBE 1972; Chairman, International Cricket Council, since 1989; Consultant, Barclays Bank PLC; *b* 24 Dec. 1932; *s* of Ernest Arthur Cowdrey and Kathleen Mary Cowdrey (*née* Taylor), BEM; *m* 1956, Penelope Susan Cowdrey (*née* Chiesman) (marr. diss. 1985); three *s* one *d*; *m* 1985, Lady Herries of Terregles, *qv. Educ:* Homefield, Sutton, Surrey; Tonbridge; Brasenose Coll., Oxford. Cricket: 5 years Tonbridge Sch. XI (Capt., 1949–50); Public Schs (Lord's) (Capt. 1950); (3 years) Oxford XI (Capt. 1954); Kent Cap, 1951 (Captain, 1957–71); 117 appearances for England, 1954–75; Capt. 23 times; 11 Overseas Tours; 107 centuries in first class cricket, of which 22 were Test centuries; on retirement in 1975, held record for most runs and most catches in Test Matches. Runner-up Amateur Rackets Title, Queen's Club, 1953 and Doubles, 1965. Chm., Internat. Cricket Conf., 1986–87. Mem. Council, Winston Churchill Meml Trust, 1969–88. Mem. Council, Britain Australia Soc. Master, Skinners' Co., 1985; Freeman, City of London, 1962. *Publications:* Cricket Today, 1961; Time for Reflection, 1962; Tackle Cricket This Way, 1969; The Incomparable Game, 1970; MCC: the Autobiography of a Cricketer, 1976. *Recreation:* golf. *Address:* Angmering Park, Littlehampton, W Sussex BN16 4EX. *T:* Patching (090674) 423. *Clubs:* MCC (Mem. Cttee; Pres., 1986–87), Boodle's.

COWE, (Robert George) Collin; Fellow and Senior Bursar, Magdalen College, Oxford, 1970–80; *b* 24 Sept. 1917; *s* of Peter and Annie Cowe, Berwick-upon-Tweed; *m* 1943, Gladys May, *d* of William Greenwood Wright and Jessie Wright, Bingley, Yorks; one *d. Educ:* The Duke's Sch., Alnwick; The Grammar Sch., Berwick-upon-Tweed; Edinburgh Univ. MA (Hons Classics) 1939; MA Oxon, 1970. Served Royal Regiment of Artillery, Field Branch, 1939–46; Major, RA, 1944–46; Instructor in Gunnery, Sch. of Artillery, UK, and CMF, 1943–46. National Coal Board, 1947–70; Private Sec. to Chm., 1947–49; Principal Private Sec. to Chm., 1949–52; Sec., East Midlands Div., 1952–55; Staff Dir, North-Eastern Div., 1955–58; Dep.-Sec. to NCB, 1958–59; Sec., 1960–67; Man. Dir, Associated Heat Services Ltd (associate co. of NCB), 1967–69. Mem., Advisory Council, BBC Radio Oxford, 1985–88. *Recreation:* listening to overseas broadcasts, especially BBC World Service. *Address:* Brookside Cottage, Brook End, Chadlington, Oxford OX7 3NF. *T:* Chadlington (060876) 373.

COWELL, John Richard; Secretary, Royal Horticultural Society, 1975–88; *b* 30 April 1933; *er s* of late Frank Richard Cowell, CMG, PhD, and Lilian Margaret (*née* Palin); *m* 1972, Josephine Suzanne Elizabeth, *d* of I.A.F. Craig, Nun Monkton, Yorks; two *s* one *d. Educ:* Westminster Sch.; Trinity Coll., Cambridge (MA). Secretariat: London Chamber of Commerce, 1957–58; Royal Horticultural Soc., 1958–88. Mem. Council, London Children's Flower Soc., 1988–. *Recreations:* gardening, fishing. *Address:* The Old House,

Boreham Street, near Hailsham, E Sussex BN27 4SF. *T:* Herstmonceux (0323) 832128. *Club:* Athenæum.

COWELL, Prof. Raymond; Director and Chief Executive, Nottingham Polytechnic (formerly Trent Polytechnic Nottingham), since 1988; *b* 3 Sept. 1937; *s* of Cecil Cowell and Susan Cowell (*née* Green); *m* 1963, Sheila (*née* Bolton); one *s* one *d*. *Educ:* St Aidan's Grammar Sch., Sunderland; Bristol Univ. (BA, PhD); Cambridge Univ. (PGCE). Head of English, Nottingham Coll. of Educn, 1970–73; Dean of Humanities 1974–81, Dep. Rector 1981–87, Sunderland Polytechnic. Member: CNAA, 1974–77 and 1981–85; Unit for Develt of Adult and Continuing Educn, 1986–90; Management Cttee, Cttee of Dirs of Polys, 1989–; British Council Cttee for Internat. Co-op. in Higher Educn, 1990; Bd, Greater Nottingham TEC, 1990. *Publications:* Twelve Modern Dramatists, 1967; W. B. Yeats, 1969; (ed) Richard II, 1969; Critics on Yeats, 1971; Critics on Wordsworth, 1973; The Critical Enterprise, 1975; articles and reviews on higher education. *Recreations:* literature, music, travelling. *Address:* Edwalton, Nottingham NG12 4AA. *T:* Nottingham (0602) 418418. *Club:* National Liberal.

COWEN, Rt. Hon. Sir Zelman, AK 1977; GCMG 1977 (CMG 1968); GCVO 1980; Kt 1976; PC 1981; QC; Provost of Oriel College, Oxford, 1982–90; Pro-Vice-Chancellor, University of Oxford, 1988–90; *b* 7 Oct. 1919; *s* of late Bernard and of Sara Cowen; *m* 1945, Anna Wittner; three *s* one *d*. *Educ:* Scotch Coll., Melbourne; Univ. of Melbourne; New and Oriel Colls, Oxford. BA 1939, LLB 1941, LLM 1942, Melbourne; BCL, MA 1947, DCL 1968, Oxford. Lieut, RANVR, 1941–45. Called to Bar, Gray's Inn, 1947; Hon. Bencher, 1978; called to Vic (Aust.) Bar, 1951, Queensland Bar, 1971; QC 1972. Victorian Rhodes Schol., 1941; Vinerian Schol., Oxford Univ., 1947. Fellow and Tutor, Oriel Coll., Oxford, 1947–50, Hon. Fellow 1977; Prof. of Public Law and Dean of Faculty of Law, Univ. of Melbourne, 1951–66; Dominion Liaison Officer to Colonial Office (UK), 1951–66; Prof. Emer., Univ. of Melbourne, 1967; Vice-Chancellor and Professor, Univ. of New England, Armidale, NSW, 1967–70; Vice-Chancellor, Qld Univ., 1970–77; Governor-General of Australia, 1977–82. Vis. Professor: Univ. of Chicago, 1949; Harvard Law Sch. and Fletcher Sch. of Law and Diplomacy, 1953–54 and 1963–64; Univ. of Utah, 1954; Univ. of Illinois, 1957–58; Washington Univ., St Louis, 1959; Tagore Law Prof., Univ. of Calcutta, 1975; Menzies Schol. in Res., Univ. of Va, 1983. For. Hon. Mem., Amer. Acad. of Arts and Sciences, 1965. Broadcaster on radio and TV on nat. and internat. affairs; Mem. and Chm., Victorian State Adv. Cttee of Australian Broadcasting Commn (at various times during 1950's and 1960's); Mem., Chief Justice's Law Reform Cttee, 1951–66; President: Asthma Foundn of Victoria, 1963–66; Adult Educn Assoc. of Australia, 1968–70; Aust. Inst. of Urban Studies, 1973–77; Mem., Law Reform Commn, Australia, 1976–77; Chairman: Aust. Vice-Chancellors' Cttee, 1977; Aust. Studies Centre Cttee, London, 1982–90; Nat Council, Australian Opera, 1983–; Press Council, 1983–88; Trustees, Visnews Ltd, 1986–; Victoria League for Commonwealth Friendship, 1987–89. Mem., Club of Rome, 1974–77. Academic Governor, Bd of Governors, Hebrew Univ. of Jerusalem, 1969–77, 1982–; Mem., Academic Bd of Govrs, Tel Aviv Univ., 1983–. Trustee: Van Leer Inst. of Jerusalem, 1985– (Chm. Trustees, 1988–); Winston Churchill Meml Trust, 1987–; Sir Robert Menzies Meml Trust, 1987–. Hon. LLD: Hong Kong, 1967; Queensland, 1972; Melbourne, 1973; Western Australia, 1981; Turin, 1981; ANU, 1985; Tasmania, 1990; Hon. DLitt: New England, 1979; Sydney, 1980; James Cook Univ. of N Qld, 1982; Oxford, 1983; Hon. DHL: Hebrew Union Coll., Cincinnati, 1980; Redlands Univ., Calif., 1986; DUniv.: Newcastle, 1980; Griffith, 1981; Hon. DPhil: Hebrew Univ. of Jerusalem, 1982; Tel Aviv, 1985. FRSA 1971; Hon. FASSA 1977; Hon. FACE 1978; Hon. FRAIA 1978; Hon. FTS 1979; Hon. FRACP 1979; Hon. FAHA 1980; Hon. FASA 1980; Hon. FRACMA 1981; Hon. FRACOG 1981; Hon. FCA 1981; Hon. FACRM 1982; Hon. Fellow: New Coll. Oxford 1978; University House, ANU, 1978; ANZAAS 1983; TCD, 1985. KStJ (A) 1977. Kt Grand Cross, Order of Merit (Italy), 1990. *Publications:* (ed jtly) Dicey's Conflict of Laws, 1949; Australia and the United States: Some Legal Comparisons, 1954; (with P. B. Carter) Essays on the Law of Evidence, 1956; American-Australian Private International Law, 1957; Federal Jurisdiction in Australia, 1959; (with D. M. da Costa) Matrimonial Causes Jurisdiction, 1961; Sir John Latham and other papers, 1965; British Commonwealth of Nations in a Changing World, 1964; Isaac Isaacs, 1967; The Private Man, 1969; Individual Liberty and the Law, 1977; The Virginia Lectures, 1984; Reflections on Medicine, Biotechnology, and the Law, 1986; A Touch of Healing, 1987; articles and chapters in legal works in UK, US, Canada, Germany, Australia. *Recreations:* swimming, music, performing and visual arts. *Address:* Commonwealth Offices, 4 Treasury Place, Melbourne, Vic 3002, Australia. *Clubs:* United Oxford & Cambridge University; Queensland (Brisbane); Pioneer (Sydney).

COWEY, Prof. Alan, PhD; FRS 1988; Professor of Physiological Psychology, and Professorial Fellow of Lincoln College, University of Oxford, since 1981; Director, Oxford Research Centre in Brain and Behaviour, since 1991; *b* 28 April 1935; *s* of Harry and Mary Cowey; *m* 1959, Patricia Leckonby; three *d*. *Educ:* Bede Grammar Sch., Sunderland; Emmanuel Coll., Cambridge (MA, PhD). Rockefeller Foundn Fellow, Center for Brain Research, Univ. of Rochester, New York, 1961–62; Univ. Demonstrator in Experimental Psychology, Cambridge, 1962–67; Fellow and Coll. Tutor, Emmanuel Coll., Cambridge, 1964–67; Vis. Sen. Fulbright Fellow, Psychology Dept, Harvard Univ., 1967; Sen. Res. Officer, Inst. of Experimental Psychology, Univ. of Oxford, 1967–68; Nuffield Sen. Res. Fellow, Lincoln Coll., Oxford, 1968–81; Henry Head Res. Fellow of Royal Society, 1968–73; Reader in Physiolog. Psychology, Oxford Univ., 1973–81. Member: MRC Neurosciences Grants Cttee, 1974–77 (Chm., 1979–81); MRC Neurosciences Board, 1979–83 (Chm., 1981–83); Mem. Council, MRC, 1981–85. Pres., European Brain and Behaviour Soc., 1986–88. Spearman Medal, British Psychological Soc., 1967. *Publications:* numerous articles in psychological and physiological jls. *Recreations:* squash, swimming, reading. *Address:* Department of Experimental Psychology, South Parks Road, Oxford OX1 3UD. *T:* Oxford (0865) 271351.

COWEY, Brig. Bernard Turing Vionnée, DSO 1945; OBE 1976; DL; *b* 20 Nov. 1911; *s* of late Lt-Col R. V. Cowey, DSO, RAMC and late Mrs B. A. Cowey (*née* Blancke); *m* 1947, Margaret Heath Dean (*née* Godwin). *Educ:* Wellington; RMC Sandhurst. Commnd The Welch Regt, 1931; served War of 1939–45: N Africa, 1939–41 (despatches 1941); psc 1941; India, 1942–43; Burma, 1944–45; CO 2 York and Lancs, 1944; CO 2 Welch, 1945–47; Co. Comdr RMA Sandhurst, 1947–49; Chief Instructor, Staff Coll., Quetta, 1952–53; CO 1 Welch, 1953–56; Comd (Brig.) 9 Indep. Armd Bde Gp TA, 1956 and 148 Inf. Bde Gp TA, 1956–58; Inspector of Intelligence, 1961–63; retd 1963. Sec., Notts T&AFA, 1965–67; TAVR Council (formerly TA Council): Dep. Sec., 1967–72; Sec., 1973–75. Regional Organiser, Army Benevolent Fund, 1975–; Regional Sec., British Field Sports Soc., 1976–83. DL Notts, 1973. *Recreations:* Rugby football (played for Wales, Barbarians and Army, 1934–35; Chm., Army Rugby Union Referees Soc., 1963–73); Arab horses (Hon. Show Dir, Arab Horse Show, 1968–81). *Address:* Trent Hills Farm, Flintham, Newark, Notts NG23 5LL. *T:* Newark (0636) 525274. *Clubs:* Army and Navy, British Sportsman's.

COWGILL, Bryan; television producer; *b* 27 May 1927; *m* 1966, Jennifer E. Baker; two *s*. *Educ:* Clitheroe Grammar School. Marine, subseq. Lieut, 3rd Royal Marine Commando Bde, SE Asia, 1943–47. Copy boy, then reporter, then feature writer with Lancashire Evening Post and Preston Guardian Group, 1942–50; edited local newspaper, Clitheroe, 1950–55; joined BBC TV as Outside Broadcasts prodn asst, 1955; produced Sportsview and Grandstand, 1957–63; Head of BBC Sport, 1963; Head of TV Outside Broadcasts Group, 1972; Controller, BBC1, 1974–77; Dir, News and Current Affairs, BBC, 1977; Man. Dir, Thames Television, 1977–85; Dep. Chm., Mirror Gp Newspapers, 1986–87; Man. Dir, Championship Television, 1989–90. Chairman: Euston Films, 1977–85; Cosgrove Hall Productions, 1977–85; Thames Television Internat., 1982–85; WTN (formerly UPITN), 1983–85; Thames Cable and Satellite Services, 1984–85. FRTS 1984. *Recreation:* golf. *Address:* 68 Chiswick Staithe, Hartington Road, W4 3TP.

COWIE, Hon. Lord; William Lorn Kerr Cowie; a Senator of the College of Justice in Scotland, since 1977; *b* 1 June 1926; *s* of late Charles Rennie Cowie, MBE and Norah Slimmon Kerr; *m* 1958, Camilla Henrietta Grizel Hoyle; two *s* two *d*. *Educ:* Fettes Coll.; Clare Coll., Cambridge; Glasgow Univ. Sub-Lieut RNVR, 1944–47; Cambridge, 1947–49; Glasgow Univ., 1949–51; Mem., Faculty of Advocates, 1952; QC (Scotland) 1967. *Address:* 20 Blacket Place, Edinburgh EH9 1RL. *T:* 031–667 8238. *Clubs:* New (Edinburgh); Royal Scottish Automobile (Glasgow).

COWIE, Mervyn Hugh, CBE 1960; ED 1954; FCA; *b* 13 April 1909; *s* of Capt. Herbert Hugh Cowie, JP; *m* 1st, 1934, Erica Mary Beaty (*d* 1956); two *s* one *d*; 2nd, 1957, Valori Hare Duke; one *s* one *d*. *Educ:* Brighton; Brasenose Coll., Oxford. Hon. Game Warden, 1932–; Mem. Nairobi District Council, 1932–36; KAR, Reserve of Officers, 1932–38 (3rd and 5th Battalions); Kenya Regt, 1939; served War of 1939–45; Abyssinia, Middle East, Madagascar (retd Lieut-Col). MLC Kenya, 1951–60; Dir of Manpower, Mau-Mau Emergency, 1953–56. Founder and Dir, Royal National Parks of Kenya, 1946–66. Vice-Pres. E African Tourist Travel Assoc., 1950–65; Mem. Nat. Parks Commn, Internat. Union for Conservation of Nature, 1959–66; Hon. Trustee, Uganda Nat. Parks, 1950–; Vice-Pres., Fauna Preservation Soc., London; Trustee, East African Wild Life Soc.; Financial Dir, African Med. and Res. Foundn (Flying Doctor Services), 1972–79. TV and Radio (BBC Natural History Section). Editor, Royal Nat. Parks of Kenya Annual Reports, 1946–65. Lectures (tours USA and Britain). Gold Medal, San Diego Zool Soc., 1972. Order of the Golden Ark, Netherlands, 1975. *Publications:* Fly Vulture, 1961; I Walk with Lions (USA), 1964; African Lion, 1965. Contributor to International Journals and Conferences. *Recreations:* flying and wild life conservation. *Address:* Kikenni, Walnut Tree Farm, Benhall, Saxmundham, Suffolk IP17 1JB. *T:* Saxmundham (0728) 603397. *Clubs:* Shikar; Explorer's (New York); Muthaiga Country (Nairobi).

COWIE, William Lorn Kerr; *see* Cowie, Hon. Lord.

COWLEY, 7th Earl *cr* 1857; **Garret Graham Wellesley;** Baron Cowley, 1828; Viscount Dangan, 1857; Investment Partner, Thos R. Miller & Son (Bermuda), Isle of Man, since 1990; *b* 30 July 1934; 3rd *s* of 4th Earl Cowley (*d* 1962) and of Mary (Elsie May), Countess Cowley; *S* nephew, 1975; *m* Paige Deming, Reno, Nevada; one *s* five *d*, and one *s* one *d* of former marriage. *Educ:* Univ. of S California (BSc Finance 1957); Harvard Univ. (MBA 1962). Investment Research Analyst: Wells Fargo Bank, San Francisco, 1962–64; Dodge & Cox, San Francisco, 1964–66; Asst Head, Investment Research Dept, Wells Fargo Bank, 1966–67; Vice-Pres., Investment Counsel, Thorndike, Doran, Paine & Lewis, Los Angeles, 1967–69; Sen. Vice-Pres., Exec. Cttee Mem., Securities, Real Estate and Company Acquisition Advisor, Shareholders Capital Corp., Los Angeles, 1969–74; Vice-Pres., and Sen. Investment Manager, Trust Dept, Bank of America, San Francisco, 1974–78; Gp Vice-Pres. and Dir, Internat Investment Management Service, Bank of America NT & SA, 1980–85; Director: Bank of America Internat., London, 1978–85; BankAmerica Trust Co. (Hong Kong), 1980–85; Bank of America Banking & Trust Co. (Gibraltar), 1981–85; Bank of America Trust Co. (Jersey), 1982–85; Bank of America Banking & Trust Co. (Nassau), 1982–85; Bank of America Banking & Trust Co. (Cayman), 1982–85; indep. financial advr and co. dir, 1985–90. Served US Army Counter Intelligence Corps, primarily in France, 1957–60. Member: Assoc. of Conservative Peers, 1981–; Parly Arts and Heritage Gp, 1981–, Defence Gp, 1982–, and Anglo-Amer. Gp, 1987–, H of L. *Heir:* *s* Viscount Dangan, *qv*. *Address:* PO Box 221, Douglas, Isle of Man; Château du Tignet, 06530 Peymeinade, France. *Clubs:* Brooks's; Harvard (San Francisco).

COWLEY, Prof. Alan Herbert, FRS 1988; Richard J. V. Johnson Regents Professor of Chemistry, University of Texas at Austin, since 1989; *b* 29 Jan. 1934; *s* of late Herbert Cowley and of Dora Cowley; *m* 1975, Deborah Elaine Cole; two *s* three *d*. *Educ:* Univ. of Manchester (BSc, MSc; Dalton Chem. Schol., 1956–58; PhD 1958). Technical Officer, ICI, 1960–61; University of Texas at Austin: Asst Prof. of Chemistry, 1962–67; Associate Prof., 1967–70; Prof., 1970–84; George W. Watt Centennial Prof., 1984–88; Sir Edward Frankland Prof. of Inorganic Chem., Imperial Coll., London, 1988–89. Deutsche Akademische Austausdienst Fellow, 1973; Guggenheim Fellow, 1976–77; Lectures: Jeremy I. Musher Meml, Hebrew Univ., Jerusalem, 1979; Mobay, Univ. of New Hampshire, 1985; Karcher, Univ. of Oklahoma, 1985; Reilly, Univ. of Notre Dame, 1987; Vis. Prof., Univ. of Western Ont., 1987. Member: Chem. Soc., subseq. RSC, 1961 (Award for Main-Gp Element Chem., 1980; Centenary Medal and Lectureship, 1986); Amer. Chem. Soc., 1962 (Southwest Regl Award, 1986). Stiefvater Meml Award and Lectureship, Univ. of Nebraska, 1987. Member, Editorial Board: Inorganic Chemistry, 1979–83; Chemical Reviews, 1984–88; Polyhedron, 1984–; Jl of Amer. Chem. Soc., 1986–; Jl of Organometallic Chemistry, 1987–; Mem. Bd, Inorganic Syntheses, 1983–. *Publications:* approximately 300 pubns in learned jls. *Recreations:* squash, sailing, music. *Address:* Department of Chemistry, University of Texas at Austin, Austin, Tex 78712, USA.

COWLEY, Rev. Canon Colin Patrick; Rector of Wonston, Winchester, 1955–71; Canon of Winchester, 1950–55, Hon. Canon, 1955; Canon Emeritus, 1971; *b* 3 Aug. 1902; *er s* of Rev. H. G. B. Cowley; *m* 1930, Dorothea Minna Pott (*d* 1980); three *d*. *Educ:* Winchester; Hertford Coll., Oxford. Curate at St Mary's, Bridport, 1926–28; Curate at St Mary Abbots, Kensington, 1928–35; Rector of Shenfield, Essex, 1935–50. Chaplain to the Forces, 1940–45. *Recreation:* coping with old age. *Address:* Brendon House, Park Road, Winchester, Hants.

COWLEY, Maj.-Gen. John Cain, CB 1971; DL; Paymaster-in-Chief and Inspector of Army Pay Services, Ministry of Defence, 1967–72, retired; with de Zoete and Bevan, Stockbrokers, 1972–79; *b* 17 July 1918; *er s* of late Philip Richard and Eleanor Cowley, Ballaquane, Peel, Isle of Man; *m* 1948, Eileen Rosemary, CBE 1982, *d* of late George Percival Stewart, Aigburth, Liverpool; three *s*. *Educ:* Douglas School, Isle of Man. War of 1939–45: commissioned, RAPC, 1940; served: Palestine, Western Desert, Italy, France, Belgium, Holland, Germany. Dep. Asst Adj.-Gen., Middle East, 1949–51; GSOI, with Permanent Under Sec., War Office, 1952–54; West African Frontier Force, 1956–59; Dep. Paymaster-in-Chief: War Office, 1960–63; BAOR, 1963–65; Chief Paymaster, Eastern Command, 1965–67. Capt. 1946, Maj. 1953, Lt-Col 1955, Col. 1960, Brig. 1963, Maj.-Gen. 1967; psc, 1948; jssc, 1955; Administrative Staff Coll., 1960. Col Comdt, RAPC, 1974–79. Chm., W Sussex, Duke of Edinburgh's Award Scheme, 1986–. Vice-Pres., St Catherine's Hospice, 1981–; Governor, St Michaels, Burton Park, 1982–88 (Chm.

of Govs, 1986–88). High Sheriff, W Sussex, 1984–85; DL W Sussex, 1986. *Recreations:* shooting, fishing, ornithology. *Address:* The Old Post Office, Nuthurst, Horsham, West Sussex RH13 6LH. *T:* Lower Beeding (0403) 891266. *Club:* Army and Navy.

COWLEY, Lt-Gen. Sir John Guise, GC (AM 1935); KBE 1958 (CBE 1946; OBE 1943); CB 1954; late RE; Chairman, Polamco Ltd, since 1976; *b* 20 Aug. 1905; *s* of Rev. Henry Guise Beatson Cowley, Fourgates, Dorchester, Dorset; *m* 1941, Irene Sybil, *d* of Percy Dreuille Millen, Berkhamsted, Herts; one *s* three *d. Educ:* Wellington Coll.; RMA Woolwich. 2nd Lieut RE 1925; Capt. 1936; Major 1940; Lieut-Col 1941; Brig. 1943; Maj.-Gen. 1953; Lieut-Gen. 1957. Served War of 1939–45, Middle East, Italy, and North-West Europe (despatches four times, OBE). Chief of Staff, HQ, Eastern Command, 1953–56; Vice-QMG, 1956–57; Controller of Munitions, Ministry of Supply, 1957–60; Master-Gen. of the Ordnance, War Office, 1960–62; retd, 1962. Col Commandant: Royal Pioneer Corps, 1961–67; Royal Engineers, 1961–70. Chairman: Bowmaker Ltd, 1962–71; Wilverley Securities Ltd, 1970–73; Keith and Henderson Ltd, 1973–76; Director: British Oxygen Ltd, 1962–76; Alastair Watson Ltd, 1962–70; C. T. Bowring and Co. Ltd, 1969–71. Pres., New Forest Preservation Soc., 1982–. Governor, Wellington Coll., 1960–76, Vice-Pres. and Chm. of Governors, 1969–76, Pres. OW Soc. 1979–; Chairman of Governors: Eagle House Sch., 1968–76; Bigshotte Sch., 1968–76; Brockenhurst Sixth Form Coll., 1977–84. Knight Comdr Order of Orange Nassau (Netherlands). FRSA. *Recreations:* bridge, croquet. *Address:* Whitemoor, Sandy Down, Boldre, Lymington, Hants SO41 8PN. *T:* Lymington (0590) 23369.

COWLEY, Dr John Maxwell, FRS 1979; FAA; Galvin Professor of Physics, since 1970, and Regents' Professor, since 1988, Arizona State University, USA; *b* 18 Feb. 1923; *s* of Alfred E. and Doris R. Cowley; *m* 1951, Roberta J. (*née* Beckett); two *d. Educ:* Univ. of Adelaide (BSc 1942, MSc 1945, DSc 1957); MIT (PhD 1949). FAA 1961. Res. Officer, CSIRO, Australia, 1945–62; Prof. of Physics, Univ. of Melbourne, 1962–70. International Union of Crystallography: Mem. Exec. Cttee, 1963–69; Chm., Commn on Electron Diffraction, 1987–; Ewald Prize, 1987. *Publications:* Diffraction Physics, 1975; approx. 300 articles in learned jls. *Recreations:* painting, music. *Address:* 2625 E Southern Avenue C-90, Tempe, Ariz 85282, USA. *T:* (602) 831–3123.

COWLEY, Kenneth Martin, CMG 1963; OBE 1956; *b* 15 May 1912; *s* of late Robert Martin Cowley, OBE, and late Mabel Priscilla Cowley (*née* Lee); *m* 1948, Barbara (*née* Tannahill); one *s* (and one step *s*). *Educ:* Merchant Taylors' Sch., Crosby; Exeter Coll., Oxford. District Officer, Kenya, 1935–44; Asst Sec., 1944–46; District Comr, 1946–49; Actg Native Courts Officer, 1949–53; Sec. for African Affairs, 1953–56; Provincial Commissioner, Southern Province, Kenya, 1956–63 (despatches, 1957); Sec., Kenya Regional Boundaries and Constituencies Commns, 1962; Sen. Administrative Manager, Express Transport Co. Ltd, Kenya, 1963–70. Sec., Overseas Service Pensioners' Assoc., 1971–79. *Recreation:* natural history. *Address:* Oakview Cottage, Cricket Green, Hartley Wintney, Hants RG27 8PZ. *T:* Hartley Wintney (025126) 4210. *Club:* Nairobi (Kenya).

COWLEY, Prof. Roger Arthur, FRS 1978; FRSE 1972; Dr Lee's Professor of Experimental Philosophy, and Fellow of Wadham College, University of Oxford, since 1988; *b* 24 Feb. 1939; *s* of Cecil A. Cowley and Mildred S. Cowley; *m* 1964, Sheila J. Wells; one *s* one *d. Educ:* Brentwood Sch., Essex; Cambridge Univ. (MA, PhD). Fellow, Trinity Hall, Cambridge, 1962–64; Research Officer, Atomic Energy of Canada Ltd, 1964–70; Prof. of Physics, Edinburgh Univ., 1970–88. Max Born Medal, 1973; Holweck Medal and Prize, 1990. *Publication:* Structural Phase Transitions, 1981. *Address:* Clarendon Laboratory, Parks Road, Oxford OX1 3PU. *T:* Oxford (0865) 272224; Tredinnock, Harcourt Hill, Oxford OX2 9AS. *T:* Oxford (0865) 247570.

COWLING, Gareth; *see* Cowling, T. G.

COWLING, Maurice John; Fellow of Peterhouse, Cambridge, since 1963; *b* 6 Sept. 1926; *s* of Reginald Frederick Cowling and May (*née* Roberts). *Educ:* Battersea Grammar Sch.; Jesus Coll., Cambridge (Historical Tripos, Pt I 1948, Pt II 1949). Served British and Indian Armies (Captain Queen's Royal Regt), 1944–48. Fellow, Jesus Coll., Cambridge, 1950–53; Res. Fellow, Univ. of Reading, 1953–54; FO, 1954; Mem. Editorial Staff: The Times, 1955–56; Daily Express, 1957–58; Fellow, Jesus Coll., Cambridge, 1961–63; Lectr in History, then Reader in Modern English History, Univ. of Cambridge, 1961–88. Olin Vis. Prof. of Religion, Columbia Univ., 1989. Literary Editor, The Spectator, 1970–71. Founder Mem. and Mem. Exec. Cttee, Salisbury Gp, 1978–. Contested (C) Bassetlaw, 1959; Mem., Cambs and Isle of Ely CC, 1966–70. *Publications:* The Nature and Limits of Political Science, 1963; Mill and Liberalism, 1963, 2nd edn 1989; Disraeli, Gladstone and Revolution, 1967; The Impact of Labour, 1971; The Impact of Hitler, 1975; (ed) Conservative Essays, 1978; Religion and Public Doctrine in Modern England, Vol. i 1980, Vol. ii 1985. *Address:* Peterhouse, Cambridge CB2 1RD. *T:* Cambridge (0223) 338251.

COWLING, (Thomas) Gareth; Stipendiary Magistrate for Hampshire, since 1989; *b* 12 Nov. 1944; *s* of late Clifford Cowling and of Beryl Elizabeth Cowling (*née* Thomas); *m* 1970, Jill Ann Stephens; one *s* one *d. Educ:* Eastbourne Coll.; College of Law. Articled to Clifford Cowling, of Clifford Cowling & Co., Hampshire, 1964; admitted Solicitor of Supreme Court, 1969; Solicitor, Solicitor's Dept, New Scotland Yard, 1969–72; called to Bar, Middle Temple, 1972; private practice at Bar, London and Winchester, Western Circuit, 1972–88; Metropolitan Stipendiary Magistrate, 1988–89. *Recreations:* family life, eating and drinking with friends, trying to play tennis and badminton, opera. *Address:* c/o The Law Courts, Winston Churchill Avenue, Portsmouth, Hants PO1 2DQ. *Clubs:* Hampshire (Winchester); Bourne (Farnham).

COWPERTHWAITE, David Jarvis; Under-Secretary, Scottish Home and Health Department, 1974–81, retired; *b* 14 Sept. 1921; *s* of J. J. Cowperthwaite and Mrs J. W. B. Cowperthwaite (*née* Jarvis); *m* 1944, Patricia Stockdale; two *d. Educ:* Edinburgh Academy; Exeter Coll., Oxford (MA). Nigerian Admin. Service, 1942–48; joined Home Civil Service (Scottish Home Dept), 1948. *Recreations:* cricket, golf. *Address:* 69 Northumberland Street, Edinburgh EH3 6JG. *T:* 031–557 0215.

See also Sir J. J. Cowperthwaite.

COWPERTHWAITE, Sir John James, KBE 1968 (OBE 1960); CMG 1964; International Adviser to Jardine Fleming & Co. Ltd, Hong Kong, 1972–81; Financial Secretary, Hong Kong, 1961–71; *b* 25 April 1915; *s* of late John James Cowperthwaite and Jessie Wemyss Barron Jarvis Cowperthwaite; *m* 1941, Sheila Mary, *d* of Alexander Thomson, Aberdeen; one *s. Educ:* Merchiston Castle Sch.; St Andrews Univ; Christ's Coll., Cambridge. Entered Colonial Administrative Service, Hong Kong, 1941; seconded to Sierra Leone, 1942–45. *Address:* 25 South Street, St Andrews, Fife. *T:* St Andrews (0334) 74759. *Clubs:* Royal Hong Kong Jockey, Royal Hong Kong Golf; Royal and Ancient.

COWTAN, Maj.-Gen. Frank Willoughby John, CBE 1970 (MBE 1947); MC 1942 and Bar, 1945; *b* 10 Feb. 1920; *s* of late Air Vice-Marshal F. C. Cowtan, CB, CBE, KHS and late Mrs N. A. Cowtan (*née* Kennedy); *m* 1949, Rose Isabel Cope; one *s* one *d. Educ:* Wellington Coll.; RMA Woolwich. 2nd Lieut Royal Engineers, 1939; served War of 1939–45, BEF, N Africa, Italy, NW Europe (Captain); Palestine, Kenya, Middle East, 1945–50 (Major); psc 1951; Middle East, UK, BAOR, 1952–58; Liaison Officer to US Corps of Engrs, USA, 1958–60 (Bt Lt-Col); CO 131 Parachute Engr Regt, 1960–62; CO Victory Coll., RMA Sandhurst, 1962–65 (Lt-Col); Comd 11 Engr Bde, BAOR, 1965–67 (Brig.); ndc (Canada) 1967–68; Dir of Quartering (Army), 1968–70; Dep. QMG, MoD(AD), 1970–71; Comdt, RMCS, 1971–75, retired. Hon. Col, 131 Indep. Commando Sqn, RE, 1975–80; Col Comdt RE, 1977–82. Dep. Dir, CLA Game Fair, 1978–86. *Recreations:* golf, shooting, wildfowling, sailing, travel, languages. *Address:* Rectory Cottage, Coleshill, Swindon, Wilts. *Club:* Army and Navy.

COX; *see* Roxbee Cox, family name of Baron Kings Norton.

COX, family name of **Baroness Cox.**

COX, Baroness *cr* 1982 (Life Peer), of Queensbury in Greater London; **Caroline Anne Cox;** a Deputy Speaker, House of Lords, since 1986; Director, Nursing Education Research Unit, Chelsea College, University of London, 1977–84; *b* 6 July 1937; *d* of Robert John McNeill Love, MS, FRCS and Dorothy Ida Borland; *m* 1959, Dr Murray Cox, FRCPsych; two *s* one *d. Educ:* Channing School. BSc (Sociology, 1st Cl. Hons) 1967, MSc (Economics) 1969, London Univ.; FRCN 1985. SRN, London Hosp., 1958; Staff Nurse, Edgware Gen. Hosp., 1960; Research Associate, Univ. of Newcastle upon Tyne, 1967–68. Department of Sociology, Polytechnic of North London: Lecturer, Senior Lectr, Principal Lectr, 1969–74; Head of Department, 1974–77. Vis. Prof., Faculty of Health and Social Work, Anglia Coll., 1990–. Dir, Centre for Policy Studies, 1983–85. A Baroness in Waiting, April–Aug. 1985. Chairman: Academic Council for Peace and Freedom, 1984–; Jagiellonian Trust, 1984–; Parental Alliance for Choice in Education, 1985–; Health Studies Cttee, CNAA, 1987–; Mem., Council and Management Cttee, Freedom Assoc., 1985–; Mem. Council, Lindley Educnl Trust, 1988–. Gov., Dorset Inst., 1988–. Mem. Council of Management, St Christopher's Hospice, 1986–; Vice Pres., RCN, 1990–. Patron: Medical Aid for Poland Fund; Assoc. for a Free Russia. Co-editor, Internat. Jl of Nursing Studies. Hon. PhD Polish Univ. in London. Commander's Cross, Order of Merit (Poland), 1990. *Publications:* (ed jtly) A Sociology of Medical Practice, 1975; (jtly) Rape of Reason: The Corruption of the Polytechnic of North London, 1975; (jtly) The Right to Learn, 1982; Sociology: A Guide for Nurses, Midwives and Health Visitors, 1983; (jtly) The Insolence of Office, 1989; (jtly) Choosing a State School: how to find the best education for your child, 1989. *Recreations:* campanology, squash, hill walking. *Address:* The White House, Wyke Hall, Gillingham, Dorset SP8 5NS. *T:* Gillingham (07476) 3436; 1 Arnellan House, 144–146 Slough Lane, Kingsbury, NW9 8XJ. *T:* 081–204 2321. *Clubs:* Commonwealth Trust, Royal Over-Seas League.

COX, Alan George, CBE 1988; FCA; Chief Executive, ASW Holdings PLC, since 1987; *b* 23 Aug. 1936; *s* of late George Henry Cox and of Florence Ivy Cox. *Educ:* Oldbury Grammar Sch. FCA 1959; ACMA 1961. Chm. and Chief Exec., GKN Rolled and Bright Steel Ltd, 1978–80; Corporate Management Dir, GKN, PLC, 1980–81; Chm. and Chief Exec., Allied Steel and Wire Ltd, 1981–87. *Recreations:* cookery, opera, walking. *Address:* PO Box 207, St Mellons, Cardiff CF3 0YJ. *Club:* Cardiff and County.

COX, Alan Seaforth; Clerk to the Grocers' Company, 1965–81; Secretary, Grocers' Trust Company Ltd, 1968–81; *b* 15 Oct. 1915; *m* 1st, 1944, Jean Heriot-Maitland (marr. diss. 1952); one *s*; 2nd, 1954, Mary Thornton (*d* 1990); three *s* one *d.* Served War: London Scottish and Gold Coast Regt, 1939–45; Staff Officer, WO, 1945–46. Farming and banking, Argentine (Patagonia), 1947–52; joined Grocers' Co., 1954. Sec., Governing Body of Oundle Sch., 1965–81. Hon. Mem. Ct, Grocers' Co., 1981–. *Recreations:* bridge, cribbage, dining and wining. *Address:* The Mount, Winchelsea, East Sussex TN36 4EG. *T:* Rye (0797) 226543.

COX, His Honour Albert Edward; a Circuit Judge, 1977–89; *b* 26 Sept. 1916; *s* of Frederick Stringer Cox; *m* 1962, Alwyn Winifred Cox, JP. Admitted Solicitor, 1938; Principal Partner, Claude Hornby & Cox, 1946–76. A Recorder of the Crown Court, 1972–77. President: London Criminal Courts Solicitors' Assoc., 1967–68; British Acad. of Forensic Science, 1977–78; Mem., Parole Board, 1971–75; Chm., London (Metropolis) Licensing Planning Cttee, 1979–84. *Address:* 38 Carlton Hill, NW8 0JY; Petit Bois, Teilhet, Arriège, France.

COX, Alister Stransom, MA; Headmaster, Royal Grammar School, Newcastle upon Tyne, since 1972; *b* 21 May 1934; *s* of Rev. Roland L. Cox and F. Ruth Cox; *m* 1960, Janet (*née* Williams); one *s* two *d. Educ:* Kingswood School, Bath; New College, Oxford (Scholar). Hon. Mods (1st Class); Lit. Hum. BA 1957, MA 1961. Sixth Form Master, Clifton Coll., 1957–63; Head of Classics, Wellington Coll., 1963–69; Dep. Head, Arnold Sch., Blackpool, 1969–72. Vis. Lectr in Greek, Bristol Univ., 1968. Founder Mem., Sinfonia Chorus, Northern Sinfonia of England, 1973– (Mem., Management Cttee, 1980–85). FRSA 1982. *Publications:* Lucretius on Matter and Man, 1967; Didactic Poetry, in Greek and Latin Literature (ed Higginbotham), 1969; articles in Greece and Rome, Times Educnl Supp. and educnl jls. *Recreations:* music, especially singing; Lake District fell walking. *Address:* 39 The Grove, Gosforth, Newcastle upon Tyne NE3 1NH. *T:* 091–285 7735.

COX, Anthony; *see* Cox, J. A.

COX, Anthony Robert, PhD, CEng; Superintendent, Radiation Science and Acoustics, National Physical Laboratory, since 1988; *b* 30 Nov. 1938; *s* of Robert George Cox and Gladys Cox; *m* 1963, Constance Jean Hammond; one *s* two *d. Educ:* Brockley County School; Imperial College, London. BScEng (Metallurgy). ARSM, MIM. RARDE, 1960–69; Exchange Scientist, US Naval Research Lab., Washington DC, 1969–71; Dep. Materials Supt, RARDE, 1971–75; Asst Dir, Armour and Materials, Military Vehicle Engineering Estab., 1975–80; MoD Central Staffs Defence Science, 1980–83; Counsellor, Science and Technol., Washington DC, 1983–87. *Publications:* papers on refractory metals, structure and strengthening mechanism on high strength steel, fractography, explosive effects, archaeological artefacts corrosion, composites, space, robotics, science policy, metrology. *Recreations:* sailing, squash, skiing, foreign travel. *Address:* 4 Ridgelands, Fetcham, Surrey KT22 9DB.

COX, Sir Anthony (Wakefield), Kt 1983; CBE 1972; FRIBA, AADip; Consultant, Architects' Co-Partnership, since 1980; *b* 18 July 1915; *s* of late William Edward Cox, CBE, and of Elsie Gertrude Wakefield; *m* 1943, Susan Babington Smith, ARIBA, AADip; two *d. Educ:* Mill Hill Sch.; Architectural Association Sch. of Architecture, London. RIBA Journal, 1938–39; Jt Editor of Focus, 1938–39; founder partner, Architects' Co-Partnership, 1939; Sir Alexander Gibb & Partners, ordnance factories and hostels, 1940–42. Served War: Royal Engineers, Western Europe and India, 1943–46; Hertfordshire CC Schools, 1946–47; reabsorbed in Architects' Co-Partnership, 1947; part-time teaching AA Sch. of Architecture, 1948–54; Mem. Council: Architectural Assoc., 1956–64 (Pres. 1962–63); RIBA, 1967–72; Member: Bd of Educn, RIBA, 1967–73; Royal Fine Art Commn, 1970–85; Bd, Property Services Agency, 1979–81, Adv. Bd, 1981–84. *Works include* Depts of: Chemistry at Univ. of Leicester and University Coll., London; Chemistry and Biochemistry at Imperial Coll. of Science and Technology; buildings for: Inst. of Psychiatry, London; the Maudsley Hosp., London. *Publications:*

(jtly) Design for Health Care, 1981; Hospitals and Health Care Facilities, 1990. *Recreations:* reading, listening, looking, making. *Address:* 5 Bacon's Lane, Highgate, N6 6BL. *T:* 081–340 2543.
See also O. J. Cox.

COX, Prof. Archibald; Carl M. Loeb University Professor, Harvard University, 1976–84, now Emeritus; Visiting Professor of Law, Boston University, since 1984; Chairman, Governing Board, Common Cause, since 1980; *b* 17 May 1912; *s* of Archibald Cox and Frances Bruen (*née* Perkins); *m* 1937, Phyllis Ames; one *s* two *d.* *Educ:* St Paul's Sch., Concord; Harvard Univ. AB 1934, LLB 1937. Admitted to Mass Bar, 1937. Gen. practice with Ropes, Gray, Best, Coolidge & Rugg, 1938–41; Office of Solicitor-Gen., US Dept of Justice, 1941–43; Assoc. Solicitor, Dept of Labor, 1943–45; Lectr on Law, Harvard, 1945–46, Prof. of Law, 1946–61; Solicitor-Gen., US Dept of Justice, 1961–65; Williston Prof. of Law, Harvard Law Sch., 1965–76. Pitt Prof., Univ. of Cambridge, 1974–75. Co-Chm., Constrn Industry Stablizn Commn, 1951–52; Chm., Wage Stablzn Bd, 1952; Mem. Bd Overseers, Harvard, 1962–65. Special Watergate Prosecutor, 1973. Hon. LLD: Loyola, 1964; Cincinnati, 1967; Rutgers, Amherst, Denver, 1974; Harvard, 1975; Michigan, 1976; Wheaton, 1977; Northeastern, 1978; Clark, 1980; Notre Dame, 1983; Hon. LHD: Hahnemann Med. Coll., 1980; Univ. of Mass, 1981; Illinois, 1985. *Publications:* Cases on Labor Law, 9th edn 1981; (jtly) Law and National Labor Policy, 1960; Civil Rights, the Constitution and the Courts, 1967; The Warren Court, 1968; The Role of the Supreme Court in American Government, 1976; Freedom of Expression, 1981; The Court and the Constitution, 1987; miscellaneous articles. *Address:* PO Box 393, Wayland, Mass 01778, USA; (office) Harvard Law School, Cambridge, Mass 02138, USA. *T:* 1–617–495–3133. *Clubs:* Somerset (Boston, Mass); Century Association (New York).
See also A. Cox, Jr.

COX, Archibald, Jr; President and Chief Executive Officer, The First Boston Corporation; *b* 13 July 1940; *s* of Archibald Cox, *qv*; *m* 1977, Jean Inge; two *s* one *d.* *Educ:* Harvard Coll. (ABEcon 1962); Harvard Business Sch. (MBA 1964). Associate 1964–70, Vice Pres. 1971–72, Man. Dir, 1973–88, Morgan Stanley & Co. Incorp.; Man. Dir and Head of London Office, Morgan Stanley Internat., 1977–88. Mem., Securities and Investments Board, 1986–88. *Recreations:* cycling, hiking, sailing, ski-ing. *Address:* 969 Fifth Avenue, New York, NY 10021, USA. *T:* 212–734–7169. *Clubs:* Royal Automobile; New York Yacht.

COX, Arthur George Ernest S.; *see* Stewart Cox.

COX, Brian; *see* Cox, Charles B.

COX, Brian Dennis; actor, director, teacher and writer; *b* 1 June 1946; *s* of Charles Mcardle Campbell Cox and Mary Ann Gillerline (*née* Mccann); *m* 1968, Caroline Burt (marr. diss. 1987); one *s* one *d.* *Educ:* LAMDA. *Stage appearances:* début, Dundee Rep., 1961; Royal Lyceum, Edinburgh, 1965–66; Birmingham Rep., 1966–68; As You Like It, Birmingham and Vaudeville (London début), 1967; title role, Peer Gynt, Birmingham, 1967; When We Dead Awaken, Edinburgh Fest., 1968; In Celebration, Royal Court, 1969; The Wild Duck, Edinburgh Festival, 1969; The Big Romance, Royal Court, 1970; Don't Start Without Me, Garrick, 1971; Mirandolina, Brighton, 1971; Getting On, Queen's, 1971; The Creditors, Open Space, 1972; Hedda Gabler, Royal Court, 1972; Playhouse, Nottingham: Love's Labour's Lost, title role, Brand, What The Butler Saw, The Three Musketeers, 1972; Cromwell, Royal Court, 1973; Royal Exchange, Manchester: Arms and the Man, 1974; The Cocktail Party, 1975; Pilgrims Progress, Prospect Th., 1975; Emigres, Nat. Theatre Co., Young Vic, 1976; Olivier Theatre: Tamburlaine The Great, 1976; Julius Caesar, 1977; The Changeling, Riverside Studios, 1978; National Theatre: title role, Herod, The Putney Debates, 1978; On Top, Royal Court, 1979; Macbeth, Cambridge Th. and tour of India, 1980; Summer Party, Crucible, 1980; Have You Anything to Declare?, Manchester then Round House, 1981; title role, Danton's Death, Nat. Theatre Co., Olivier, 1982; Strange Interlude, Duke of York, 1984 (Drama Mag. Best Actor Award, 1985), Nederlander, NY, 1985; Rat in the Skull, Royal Court, 1984 (Drama Mag. and Olivier Best Actor Awards, 1985) and NY, 1985; Fashion, The Danton Affair, Misalliance, Penny for a Song, 1986, The Taming of the Shrew, Titus Andronicus (title rôle), 1987, The Three Sisters, 1989, RSC, and Titus Andronicus on tour, Madrid, Paris, Copenhagen, 1988 (Olivier Award, Best Actor in a Revival, and Drama Mag. Best Actor Award for RSC 1988 season); Frankie and Johnny in the Clare-de-Lune, Comedy, 1989; Richard III, and title rôle, King Lear, National and world tour, 1990–91; *films:* Nicholas and Alexandra, 1971; In Celebration, 1975; Manhunter, 1986; Shoot for the Sun, 1986; Hidden Agenda, 1990; *TV appearances:* Churchill's People: The Wallace, 1972; The Master of Ballantrae, 1975; Henry II, in The Devil's Crown, 1978; Thérèse Raquin, 1979; Dalhousie's Luck, Bothwell, 1980; Bach, 1981; Pope John Paul II, 1984; Florence Nightingale, 1985; Beryl Markham: a shadow in the sun, 1988; Secret Weapon, 1990; Acting in Tragedy (BBC Masterclass), 1990; Lost Language of the Cranes, The Cloning of Joanna May, 1991; *directed:* Edinburgh Festival: The Man with a Flower in his Mouth, The Stronger, 1973; Orange Tree, Richmond: I Love My Love, 1982; Mrs Warren's Profession, 1989; The Crucible, Moscow Art Theatre, London and Edinburgh, 1988–89. Internat. Theatre Inst. Award, 1990. *Publications:* Salem to Moscow: an actor's Odyssey, 1991; The Lear Diaries, 1992. *Recreation:* keeping fit. *Address:* c/o Jeremy Conway Ltd, 18–21 Jermyn Street, SW1Y 6HP. *T:* 071–287 0077. *Club:* Savile.

COX, Brian (Robert) Escott, QC 1974; a Recorder of the Crown Court, since 1972; *b* 30 Sept. 1932; *yr s* of late George Robert Escott Cox; *m* 1st, 1956; one *s* two *d*; 2nd, 1969, Noelle Gilormini; one *s* one *d.* *Educ:* Rugby Sch.; Oriel Coll., Oxford (BA, MA). Called to Bar, Lincoln's Inn, 1954, Bencher, 1985. Midland and Oxford Circuit. *Address:* 1 King's Bench Walk, Temple, EC4. *T:* 071–353 8436.

COX, Prof. (Charles) Brian, CBE 1990; John Edward Taylor Professor of English Literature, since 1976, Pro-Vice-Chancellor, since 1987, University of Manchester; *b* 5 Sept. 1928; *s* of late Hedley E. Cox and Rose Thompson; *m* 1954, Jean Willmer; one *s* two *d.* *Educ:* Wintringham Sec. Sch.; Pembroke Coll., Cambridge (MA, MLitt). Lectr, Univ. of Hull, 1954–66; Manchester University: Prof. of English Lit., 1966–76; Dean, Faculty of Arts, 1984–86. Vis. Associate Prof., Univ. of Calif, Berkeley, 1964–65; Brown Fellow, Univ. of the South, Sewanee, Tennessee, 1980; Lord Northcliffe Lectr, UCL, 1991. Pres., Nat. Council for Educnl Standards, 1984–89 (Chm., 1979–84); Mem., Kingman Cttee, 1987–88; Chm., Nat. Curriculum English Working Gp, 1988–89. Co-editor: Critical Qly, 1959–; Black Papers on Education, 1969–77. *Publications:* The Free Spirit, 1963; (ed with A. E. Dyson) Modern Poetry, 1963; (ed with A. E. Dyson) Practical Criticism of Poetry, 1965; Joseph Conrad: the modern imagination, 1974; Every Common Sight (poems), 1981; Two-Headed Monster (poems), 1985. *Recreations:* Manchester United, walking. *Address:* 20 Park Gates Drive, Cheadle Hulme, Stockport SK8 7DF. *T:* 061–485 2162. *Club:* Lansdowne.

COX, Prof. Christopher Barry, PhD, DSc; Professor, Division of Biosphere Sciences, since 1988, and Assistant Principal, since 1989, King's College London; *b* 29 July 1931; *s* of Herbert Ernest Cox and May Cox; *m* 1961, Sheila (*née* Morgan); two *s* one *d.* *Educ:* St Paul's Sch., Kensington; Balliol Coll., Oxford (MA); St John's Coll., Cambridge (PhD); DSc London. Asst Lectr in Zoology, King's Coll. London, 1956–59; Harkness Fellow of Commonwealth Fund, at Mus. of Comparative Zoology, Harvard, 1959–60; King's College London: Lectr in Zoology, 1959–66; Sen. Lectr, 1966–69; Reader, 1970–76; Prof., 1976–82; Head: Dept of Zoology, 1982–85; Dept of Biology, 1985–88. Mem. Council, Palaeontological Assoc., 1967–69, 1974; Vice-Pres., 1969–81. Editor, Palaeontology, 1975–79. Palaeontological collecting expedns to Central Africa, 1963; Argentina, 1967; N Brasil, 1972; Qld, Aust., 1978. *Publications:* Prehistoric Animals, 1969; Biogeography—an ecological and evolutionary approach, 1973, 4th edn 1985; Prehistoric World, 1975; Illustrated Encyclopedia of Prehistoric Animals, 1988; Atlas of The Living World, 1989; History of Planet Earth, 1991; research papers on vertebrate palaeontology and historical biogeography, in Phil. Trans. Royal Soc., Proc. Zool. Soc., Nature, Bull. Brit. Mus. (Nat. Hist.), Jl Biogeog., etc. *Recreations:* gardening, theatre. *Address:* Conifers, Grange Road, Leatherhead, Surrey KT22 7JS. *T:* Ashtead (0372) 273167.

COX, Prof. Sir David (Roxbee), Kt 1985; PhD; FRS 1973; Warden of Nuffield College, Oxford, since 1988; *b* 15 July 1924; *s* of S. R. Cox, Handsworth, Birmingham; *m* 1948, Joyce (*née* Drummond), Keighley, Yorks; three *s* one *d.* *Educ:* Handsworth Grammar Sch., Birmingham; St John's Coll., Cambridge (MA). PhD Leeds, 1949. Posts at Royal Aircraft Establishment, 1944–46; Wool Industries Research Assoc., 1946–50; Statistical Laboratory, Cambridge, 1950–55; Visiting Prof., University of N Carolina, 1955–56; Reader in Statistics, Birkbeck College, 1956–60, Professor of Statistics, 1961–66; Prof. of Statistics, 1966–88 and Head of Dept of Maths, 1970–74, Imperial Coll. of Sci. and Technology. SERC Sen. Res. Fellow, 1983–88. President: Bernoulli Soc., 1979–81; Royal Statistical Soc., 1980–82. For. Mem., Royal Danish Acad. of Scis and Letters, 1983; For. Hon. Mem., Amer. Acad. of Arts and Sciences, 1974; For. Associate, Nat. Acad. of Scis, USA, 1988. Hon. FIA 1991. Hon. DSc: Reading, 1982; Bradford, 1982; Helsinki, 1986; Heriot-Watt, 1987; Limburg's Univ. Centrum, 1988; Queen's Univ., Kingston, Ont, 1989; Waterloo Univ., 1991. Weldon Meml Prize, Univ. of Oxford, 1984; Kettering Medal, General Motors Cancer Foundn, 1990. Editor of Biometrika, 1966–. *Publications:* Statistical Methods in the Textile Industry, 1949 (jt author); Planning of Experiments, 1958; (jtly) Queues, 1961; Renewal Theory, 1962; (jtly) Theory of Stochastic Processes, 1965; (jtly) Statistical Analysis of Series of Events, 1966; Analysis of Binary Data, 1970, 2nd edn 1989; (jtly) Theoretical Statistics, 1974; (jtly) Problems and Solutions in Theoretical Statistics, 1978; (jtly) Point Processes, 1980; (jtly) Applied Statistics, 1981; (jtly) Analysis of Survival Data, 1984; (jtly) Asymptotic Methods, 1989; papers in Jl of Royal Statistical Society, Biometrika, etc. *Address:* Nuffield College, Oxford OX1 1NF.

COX, Dennis George; Under-Secretary (Industrial Relations), Department of Employment, 1971–74; a Deputy Chairman, Central Arbitration Committee, 1977–84; *b* 23 Feb. 1914; *s* of George and Amelia Cox; *m* 1938, Victoria Barraclough; two *s.* *Educ:* University College Sch.; Queens' Coll., Cambridge. Royal Navy, 1942–45; served with Netherlands and Norwegian navies, Lieut RNVR. Entered Min. of Labour, 1936; Asst Sec. 1966; Regional Controller, SW Region. *Recreations:* gardening, fishing. *Address:* 22 Ashley Court, Morpeth Terrace, SW1; Church Cottage, Laughton, Lewes, East Sussex. *T:* Ripe (032183) 382. *Club:* Army and Navy.

COX, Edward; *see* Cox, A. E.

COX, Sir (Ernest) Gordon, KBE 1964; TD; DSc; FRS 1954; FRSC; FInstP; FIBiol; Secretary of the Agricultural Research Council, 1960–71; *b* 24 April 1906; *s* of Ernest Henry Cox (*d* 1987) and Rosina Ring; *m* 1st, 1929, Lucie Grace Baker (*d* 1962); one *s* one *d*; 2nd, 1968, Prof. Mary Rosaleen Truter, DSc, *d* of Dr D. N. Jackman. *Educ:* City of Bath Boys' Sch.; University of Bristol. Research Asst, Davy-Faraday Laboratory, Royal Institution, 1927; Chemistry Dept, Univ. of Birmingham, 1929–41 (Reader in Chemical Crystallography, 1940); Prof. of Inorganic and Structural Chemistry, University of Leeds, 1945–60; commissioned in Territorial Army, 1936; special scientific duties, War Office, 1942–44; attached to HQ staff of 21 Army Group, France and Germany, as Technical Staff Officer, Grade I, 1944–45. Vice-Pres., Institute of Physics, 1950–53; Mem. Agric. Research Council, 1957–60. Hon. DSc: Newcastle, 1964; Birmingham, 1964; Bath, 1973; East Anglia, 1973; Hon. LLD Bristol, 1969; Hon. ARCVS, 1972. *Publications:* numerous scientific papers in jls of various learned societies, chiefly on the crystal structures of chemical compounds. *Recreations:* music, gardening, natural history. *Address:* 117 Hampstead Way, NW11 7JN. *T:* 081–455 2618. *Clubs:* Athenæum, English-Speaking Union, Lansdowne.
See also K. G. Cox, P. A. Cox.

COX, Sir Geoffrey (Sandford), Kt 1966; CBE 1959 (MBE 1945); *b* 7 April 1910; *s* of Sandford Cox, Wellington, NZ, and Mary Cox (*née* MacGregor); *m* 1935, Cecily Barbara Talbot Turner; two *s* two *d.* *Educ:* Southland High Sch., New Zealand; Otago Univ., New Zealand (MA); Rhodes Scholar, 1932–35; Oriel Coll., Oxford (BA). Reporter, Foreign and War Corresp. News Chronicle, 1935–37, Daily Express, 1937–40. Enlisted New Zealand Army, 1940; commissioned, Dec. 1940; served in 2 New Zealand Div., Greece, Crete, Libya, Italy; Major, Chief Intelligence Officer, Gen. Freyberg's staff (despatches twice). First Sec. and Chargé d'Affaires, NZ Legation, Washington, 1943; NZ Rep., first UNRRA Conf., 1943; Political Corresp., News Chronicle, 1945; Asst Editor, News Chronicle 1954. Regular Contributor, BBC radio and TV, 1945–56; Editor and Chief Exec., Independent Television News, 1956–68; founded News at Ten, 1967; Dep. Chm., Yorkshire Television, 1968–71; Chm., Tyne Tees Television, 1971–74; Chm., LBC Radio, 1978–81; independent Dir, The Observer, 1981–89. TV Producers' Guild Award Winner, 1962; Fellow, Royal TV Soc. (Silver Medal, 1963; Gold Medal, 1978); Fellow, British Kinematograph and TV Soc. *Publications:* Defence of Madrid, 1937; The Red Army Moves, 1941; The Road to Trieste, 1946; The Race for Trieste, 1977; See It Happen, 1983; A Tale of Two Battles, 1987; Countdown to War, 1988. *Recreations:* fishing, tracing Roman roads. *Club:* Garrick.

COX, Sir (George) Trenchard; *see* Cox, Sir Trenchard.

COX, Sir Gordon; *see* Cox, Sir E. G.

COX, Major Horace B. T.; *see* Trevor Cox.

COX, Surgeon Rear-Adm. James, OBE 1964; QHS 1982; FFARCS; Surgeon Rear Admiral, Support Medical Services, 1983–84, retired; *b* 4 Feb. 1928; *s* of James Wolseley Cox and Gladys May Cox (*née* Watkinson); *m* 1952, Elizabeth Jennings; one *s* one *d.* *Educ:* Durham Sch.; Durham Univ. (MB BS 1951). FFARCS 1960. HMS Birmingham, 1952–54; Consultant Anaesthetist, RN Hospitals: Plymouth, 1955–59; Chatham, 1959–61; Plymouth, 1962–65; Gibraltar, 1965–69; Plymouth, 1969–71; Principal Medical Officer, HMS Bulwark, 1971–72; Consultant Anaesthetist, RN Hospitals: Plymouth, 1972–75; Haslar, 1975–77; Staff Medical Officer to MGRM Commando Forces, 1977–80; Medical Officer in Charge, RN Hospital Stonehouse, 1980–82; Surgeon Rear-Adm. (Naval Medicine and Trng), 1982–83. *Recreations:* fishing, gardening. *Address:* c/o National Westminster Bank PLC, 87 Grey Street, Newcastle upon Tyne NE1 6ER.

COX, (James) Anthony; His Honour Judge Anthony Cox; a Circuit Judge, since 1976; *b* 21 April 1924; *s* of Herbert Sidney Cox and Gwendoline Margaret Cox; *m* 1950, Doris Margaret Fretwell; three *s* one *d*. *Educ:* Cotham Sch., Bristol; Bristol Univ. LLB Hons 1948. War Service, Royal Marines, 1943–46. Called to Bar, Gray's Inn, 1949; a Recorder of the Crown Court, 1972–76. Pres., Anchor Soc., 1985–86. *Recreations:* cricket, sailing, golf, the arts. *Address:* c/o Courts Administrator, The Castle, Exeter, Devon. *Clubs:* MCC; Royal Western Yacht (Plymouth); Yealm Yacht; Bigbury Golf.

COX, John; Production Director, Royal Opera House, Covent Garden, since 1988; *b* 12 March 1935; *s* of Leonard John Cox and Ethel M. (*née* McGill). *Educ:* Queen Elizabeth's Hosp., Bristol; St Edmund Hall, Oxford (BA). Freelance director of plays, opera, revue and musicals in Britain and abroad, incl. La Scala, Milan, and Metropolitan Opera, New York, Vienna, Stockholm, Brussels, Amsterdam, Florence, Sydney, Cologne, Frankfurt, Munich, Salzburg, Spoleto, Wexford, Santa Fe, Houston, San Francisco, Washington, 1959–; Dir of Prodn, Glyndebourne Festival Opera, 1971–81; Gen. Adminr, 1981–85, Artistic Dir, 1985–86, Scottish Opera. A Board Mem., Greenwich Theatre. Productions include: *opera:* Glyndebourne: Richard Strauss cycle, Rake's Progress, The Magic Flute, La Cenerentola; ENO: Così Fan Tutte, Patience; Scottish Opera: L'Egisto, Manon Lescaut, Marriage of Figaro, Lulu; Royal Opera: Manon Lescaut, Die Fledermaus, Guillaume Tell, Capriccio, Die Meistersinger. *Address:* 7 West Grove, SE10 8QT. *T:* 081–692 2450. *Club:* Garrick.

COX, John Colin Leslie; Director General, Chemical Industries Association, since 1987; *b* 23 Oct. 1933; *s* of late Dr Leslie Reginald Cox, OBE, FRS, and Hilda Cecilia Cox; *m* 1983, Avril Joyce Butt; one *s* one *d*. *Educ:* University College Sch., London; Queens' Coll., Cambridge (BA). National Service, 2nd Lieut, 2nd 10th Princess Mary's Own Gurkha Rifles, 1956–58 (GSM Malaya 1958). Joined Shell Group, 1958–: Executive positions in Shell Ghana, 1962–65, and in Shell Gp in London, 1966–77; Shell Chemicals UK: Personnel Dir, 1978–81; Dir, Business Develt, and chm. of subsid. cos, 1981–86. FRSA 1989. *Recreations:* sailing, antiques, country pursuits, photography. *Address:* Chemical Industries Association, Kings Buildings, Smith Square, SW1P 3JJ. *T:* 071–931 7859. *Clubs:* Army and Navy, Hurlingham; Leander (Henley on Thames); Royal Solent Yacht (IoW).

COX, Vice-Adm. Sir John (Michael Holland), KCB 1982; Director, Sound Alive, since 1988; Flag Officer Naval Air Command, 1982–83; *b* Peking, China, 27 Oct. 1928; *s* of late Thomas Cox, MBE, and of Daisy Anne Cox; *m* 1962, Anne Garden Farquharson Seth-Smith; one *s* one *d*. *Educ:* Hilton Coll., Natal, SA. Joined BRNC, 1946; ADC to C-in-C Allied Forces, N Europe, 1952–53; ADC to Governor of Victoria, 1955; commanded HM Ships: Dilston, 1957 (despatches); Stubbington, 1958; sc Camberley, 1960; Cadet Trng Officer, BRNC Dartmouth, 1962; CSO, London Div., RNR, 1963; commanded HMS: Surprise, 1964; Naiad, 1965; Comdr, Sea Trng, Staff of Flag Officer Sea Trng, 1967; Naval Attaché, Bonn, 1969; comd HMS Norfolk, 1972; Dir, Naval Ops and Trade, 1973–75; Comdr, Standing Naval Force Atlantic, 1976–77; COS to C-in-C, Naval Home Command, 1977–79; Flag Officer Third Flotilla and Comdr Anti-Submarine Group Two, 1979–82. Dir, Spastics Soc., 1983–88. *Recreations:* tennis, skiing. *Club:* Lansdowne.

COX, Dr Keith Gordon, FRS 1988; Reader in Petrology, Department of Earth Sciences, Oxford University, since 1990; Fellow of Jesus College, Oxford, since 1973; *b* 25 April 1933; *s* of Sir (Ernest) Gordon Cox, *qv*; *m* 1960, Gillian Mary Palmer; two *s* one *d*. *Educ:* Leeds Grammar Sch.; Queen's Coll., Oxford (MA); Leeds Univ. (PhD). Lectr in Geology, Univ. of Edinburgh, 1962–71; Lectr, Dept of Earth Scis, Oxford Univ., 1972–90. Editor: Earth & Planetary Science Letters, 1981–85; Jl of Petrology, 1981–83. *Publications:* (with J. D. Bell and R. J. Pankhurst) The Interpretation of Igneous Rocks, 1979; scientific papers, mainly in field of basalt petrology. *Recreation:* water colours. *Address:* 59 Bagley Wood Road, Kennington, Oxford OX1 5LY. *T:* Oxford (0865) 735590.

See also P. A. Cox.

COX, Sir Mencea Ethereal, Kt 1980; Member of the Senate, Barbados; *b* 28 Nov. 1906; *s* of James William Cox and Charlotte Matilda Cox, Plymouth Brethren. *Educ:* elementary and private (languages: English, Latin, French, Spanish). Formerly worked in carpentry, engineering and hired car driving, and as garage owner; also in wholesale and retail business. Elected to Parliament, 1944; Member of the then Governor's Exec. Council, 1948; following the introduction of ministerial system of Govt in 1954, apptd Minister of Communications, Works and Housing, 1954, then Minister of Trade, Industry, Tourism and Labour, 1956–61; concurrently, 1958–61, Dep. Premier and Leader of House of Assembly. *Recreations:* horse racing, cricket. *Address:* Ambury, Clapham St Michael, Barbados, WI. *T:* 77766.

COX, Norman Ernest, CMG 1973; MA; HM Diplomatic Service, retired; *b* 28 Aug. 1921; *s* of late Ernest William Cox and late Daisy Beatrice (*née* Edmonds); *m* 1945, Maruja Margarita (*née* Cruz); one *s* one *d*. *Educ:* Lycée Français de Madrid; King's Coll., London. Tax Officer, Inland Revenue, 1938–41; Army, Intell. Corps, 1941–45: Gibraltar, 1942–45; Attaché, Madrid, 1945–47; FO, 1947–50; 2nd Sec., Sofia, 1950–52; 2nd Sec., Montevideo, 1952–54; FO, 1954–57; Dep. Regional Information Officer for SE Asia, Singapore, 1957–60; FO, 1960–62: Laos Conf., Geneva, 1961; Sec. to UK Conf. Delegn to ECSC, Luxemburg, 1962–63; 1st Sec. (Commercial), Madrid, 1963–66; Counsellor (Information), Mexico, Regional Information Officer for Central American Republics, PRO to Duke of Edinburgh for 1968 Olympics, 1966–68; Counsellor (Commercial), Moscow, 1969–72; Inst. of Latin American Studies, London Univ., 1972–73; Diplomatic Service Inspector, 1973–74; Ambassador to: Ecuador, 1974–77; Mexico, 1977–81. Vice-Pres., British Mexican Soc., 1985– (Chm., 1982–84). *Publication:* (jtly) Politics in Mexico, 1985. *Recreations:* swimming, walking, travelling, archaeology, history, linguistics, comparative religion. *Club:* Royal Automobile.

COX, Oliver Jasper, CBE 1982; RIBA; retired 1985; Partner, Shankland/Cox Partnership, 1965–85; *b* 20 April 1920; *s* of William Edward and Elsie Gertrude Cox; *m* 1953, Jean; one *s* two *d*. *Educ:* Mill Hill Sch.; Architectural Association School of Architecture (AADip Hons). DistTP. Architects Dept, Herts CC, New Schools Division, 1948–49; Architects Dept, LCC Housing Division, 1950–59; Dep. Chief Architect, and Leader, Research and Development Gp, Min. of Housing and Local Govt, 1960–64. *Recreations:* painting, drawing and screen printing. *Address:* 22 Grove Terrace, NW5 1PL. *T:* 071–485 6929.

See also Sir A. W. Cox, P. W. Cox.

COX, Patricia Ann, CB 1989; Under Secretary, Scottish Home and Health Department, 1985–88, retired; *b* 25 May 1931; *d* of Sir (Ernest) Gordon Cox, *qv*. *Educ:* Leeds Girls' High Sch.; Newnham Coll., Cambridge (MA). Asst Principal, Dept of Health for Scotland, 1953; Principal: SHHD, 1959–62; HM Treasury, 1962–65; SHHD, 1965–67; Asst Sec., 1967–76, Under Sec., 1976–85, Scottish Educn Dept. *Publication:* Sandal Ash (novel for children), 1950. *Recreations:* opera, archaeology, needlework, walking. *Address:* 2 Gloucester Place, Edinburgh EH3 6EF. *T:* 031–225 6370.

See also K. G. Cox.

COX, Patricia Anne, (Mrs Roger Cox); *see* Edwards, P. A.

COX, Paul William; freelance artist and illustrator, since 1982; *b* 31 July 1957; *s* of Oliver Jasper Cox, *qv*; *m* 1987, Julia Claire Nichol. *Educ:* Port Regis and Stanbridge Earls School; Camberwell Sch. of Art and Crafts (BA Hons); Royal Coll. of Art (MA). Contributor to: The Times, Daily Telegraph, Independent, Spectator, Punch, Sunday Times, Observer; founder contributor to Blueprint, 1984; designed PO stamps for 600th Lord Mayor's Show, 1989; exhibns of watercolour drawings, Workshop Gallery, Illustrators' Gallery, Chris Beetles Gallery. Vis Lectr in Illustration, Camberwell Sch. of Art and Crafts, 1982–90. *Publications:* illustrated books: Experiences of an Irish RM, 1984; The Common Years, 1984; A Varied Life, 1984; The Outing, 1985; The Character of Cricket, 1986; Romantic Gardens, 1988; Evacuee, 1988; Rebuilding the Globe, 1989; Dear Boy, 1989; Leave it to Psmith, 1989; Three Men in a Boat, 1989. *Address:* The Old Rectory, Tilney All Saints, King's Lynn, Norfolk PE34 4SJ. *Club:* Chelsea Arts.

COX, Peter Arthur, BSc Eng; FEng, FICE; FCGI; consulting engineer; *b* 30 Oct. 1922; *m* 1944, Rosemary; one *s* two *d*. *Educ:* Westcliff High Sch., Essex; City and Guilds Coll., Imperial Coll., London (FIC 1991). Commissioned, Royal Engineers, 1942 (despatches). Lewis & Duvivier, 1947; Rendel Palmer & Tritton, 1952; Peter Lind & Co. Ltd, 1954; Sir Bruce White Wolfe Barry & Partners, 1955; Rendel Palmer & Tritton Ltd, Consulting Engineers, 1956, Partner, 1966, Sen. Partner, 1978–85, Chm., 1985–88. Chm., Ceemaid Ltd, 1984–85. Member: Dover Harbour Bd, 1983–89; Nat. Maritime Inst. Ltd, 1983–85; British Maritime Technology Ltd, 1986–. Institution of Civil Engineers: Pres., 1980–81; Mem., Infrastructure Policy (formerly Planning) Gp, 1981– (Chm. 1981–84); Chm., Legal Affairs Cttee, 1988–; Mem., Smeatonian Soc. of Civil Engrs, 1980–. Mem., Commonwealth Scholarship Commn, 1982–88. Pres., Old Centralians, 1989–90. Governor, Westminster Coll., 1990–. *Publications:* papers to Instn of Civil Engrs on Leith Harbour and Belfast Dry Dock; many papers to conferences. *Recreations:* walking, gardening. *Address:* 18 Ranmore Avenue, Croydon, Surrey CR0 5QA. *Club:* East India.

COX, Peter Denzil John H.; *see* Hippisley-Cox, P. D. J.

COX, Peter Richmond, CB 1971; Deputy Government Actuary, 1963–74; *b* 3 Sept. 1914; *s* of Richard R. Cox, Civil Servant, and Nellie (*née* Richmond); *m* 1971, Faith Blake Schenk. *Educ:* King's Coll. Sch., Wimbledon. Entered Government Actuary's Dept, 1933. Qualified as Fellow, Institute of Actuaries, 1939. Joint Hon. Sec., Institute of Actuaries, 1962–64 (Vice-Pres., 1966–68). Pres., Eugenics Soc., 1970–72. Chm., CS Insurance Soc., 1973–78. Silver Medal, Inst. of Actuaries, 1975. *Publications:* Demography, 1950 (5 edns); (with R. H. Storr-Best) Surplus in British Life Assurance, 1962; (ed jtly) Population and Pollution, 1972; Resources and Population, 1973; Population and the New Biology, 1974; Equalities and Inequalities in Education, 1975; various papers on actuarial and demographic subjects. *Recreations:* music, painting, gardening. *Address:* The Level House, Mayfield, East Sussex TN20 6BW. *T:* Mayfield (0435) 872217. *Club:* Actuaries.

COX, Philip (Joseph), DSC 1943; QC 1967; a Recorder, and Honorary Recorder of Northampton, since 1972; *b* 28 Sept. 1922; *s* of Joseph Parriss Cox, Rugby; *m* 1951, Margaret Jocelyn Cox, *d* of R. C. H. Cox, Purley, Surrey; one *s* one *d*. *Educ:* Rugby Sch; Queens' Coll., Cambridge. RNVR, 1942–46 (Lieut). Called to Bar, Gray's Inn, 1949; Bencher, 1972 (Vice-Treas., 1990; Treas., 1991); practised at Bar, Birmingham, 1949–67. Mem. County Court Rules Cttee, 1962–68; Dep. Chm., Northants QS, 1963–71; Dep. Chm., Warwicks QS, 1966–71; Leader, Midland and Oxford Circuit, 1975–79; Mem. Senate, Inns of Court and Bar, 1974–80. Legal Assessor to Disciplinary Cttee, RCVS, 1969–; Chm., Cttee of Enquiry into London Smallpox Outbreak, 1973; Chairman: Code of Practice Cttee, Assoc. of British Pharmaceut. Industry, 1978–; Code of Practice Cttee, Internat. Fedn of Pharmaceut. Manufacturers Assocs, 1985–; Gen. Optical Council, 1985–88; Code of Practice Cttee, Nat. Office of Animal Health, 1987–. Pres., Mental Health Review Tribunals, 1984–. Pres., Edgbaston Liberal Assoc., 1974–86. *Recreations:* sailing, golf, gardening, reading. *Address:* (home) 9 Sir Harry's Road, Edgbaston, Birmingham B15 2UY. *T:* 021–440 0278; (chambers) 1 King's Bench Walk, Temple, EC4Y 7DB. *Clubs:* Naval; Birmingham; Royal Cruising, Bar Yacht.

COX, Richard Charles, MBE 1961; HM Diplomatic Service, retired; *b* 27 May 1920; *s* of Charles Victor Cox and Marjorie Eleanor Cox (*née* Fox); *m* 1941, Constance (*née* Goddard); one *s*. *Educ:* Gravesend Grammar Sch.; BA Open Univ., 1985. Served War of 1939–45, RAF; released with rank of Sqdn Leader, 1946. Entered Colonial Office, 1937; Dominions Office, 1946; High Commn, Colombo, 1949–52; Second Sec., Calcutta, 1953–54; CRO, 1954–56; First Sec., Bombay, 1956–59; CRO, 1960–63; First Sec., Valletta, 1964–68; FCO, 1968–72; NI Office, 1972–74; Dep. Sec. Gen., Cento, 1975–77. *Recreations:* swimming, gardening, watching Rugby football. *Address:* 31 Lotfield Street, Orwell, near Royston, Herts SG8 5QT. *T:* Cambridge (0223) 207969.

COX, Roger Charles; His Honour Judge Roger Cox; a Circuit Judge, since 1988; *b* 18 April 1941; *s* of late Reginald William Cox and of Hilda Cox; *m* 1970, Patricia Anne Edwards, *qv*. *Educ:* Cheltenham Grammar Sch.; Birmingham Univ. (LLB, LLM). Called to the Bar, Gray's Inn, 1965. Asst Lectr, Faculty of Law, Bristol Univ., 1964–66; Lord Justice Holker Sen. Schol., Gray's Inn, 1966; a Recorder, 1986. *Recreations:* travel, music, theatre, reading. *Address:* Southwark Crown Court, 1 English Grounds, Battlebridge Lane, SE1. *T:* 071–403 4141.

COX, Roy Arthur, CBE 1987; JDipMA; FCA, FCMA, FCBSI, CBIM; Chief General Manager, 1970–85, Director, 1976–89, Alliance and Leicester (formerly Alliance) Building Society; *b* 30 Nov. 1925; *s* of J. W. Arthur Cox; *m* 1st, 1951, Joy (*née* Dunsford); one *s* one *d*; 2nd, 1980, Audrey (*née* Brayham). *Educ:* Isleworth Grammar Sch. FCA 1953; FCMA 1957; FCBSI (FBS 1971); CBIM 1980. War Service, 1944–47. Wells & Partners, Chartered Accountants, 1942–49; Colombo Commercial Co. Ltd, 1950–61; Urwick, Orr & Partners, Management Consultants, 1961–65; Alliance Building Society: Sec., 1965; Gen. Man., 1967. Dir, Southern Bd, Legal & General Assce Soc. Ltd, 1972–86. Building Societies Association: Chm., S Eastern Assoc., 1972–74; Mem. Council, 1973–87; Chm., Gen. Purposes and Public Relations Cttee, 1975–77; Dep. Chm., Council, 1983–85; Chm., Council, 1985–87. Member: Royal Commn on Distribution of Income and Wealth, 1974–78; SE Electricity Bd, 1983–90; Dep. Chm., Seeboard plc, 1990–; Chairman: PO Staff Superannuation Scheme, 1986–; PO Pension Scheme, 1987–. Underwriting Mem., Lloyd's. *Recreations:* golf, bridge. *Address:* The Yett, 281 Dyke Road, Hove, E Sussex BN3 6PD.

COX, Stephen James; Director General, Commonwealth Institute, since 1991; *b* 5 Dec. 1946; *s* of late Harold James West Cox and of Norah Cox (*née* Wilkinson); *m* 1969, Pauline Victoria Greenwood; one *s* one *d*. *Educ:* Queen Elizabeth Grammar Sch., Blackburn; Atlantic Coll.; Birmingham Univ. (BA Hons Geography 1969); Leeds Univ. (Postgrad. Dip. ESL 1970); Sussex Univ. (MA Educn 1977). VSO, Bolivia, 1965–66. British Council: Warsaw, 1970; Western Europe Dept, London, 1973; Accra, 1977; Staff Training Dept, 1981; Chm., British Council Whitley Council, Trade Union Side, 1981–84; Educn Attaché, Washington DC, 1984–85; Asst Sec., Royal Society, 1985–91. FRGS. *Recreations:* cricket, travel, visiting galleries. *Address:* Commonwealth Institute,

Kensington High Street, W8 6NQ. *T:* 071–603 4535, *Fax:* 071–602 7374. *Club:* Middlesex County Cricket.

COX, Thomas Michael; MP (Lab) Tooting, since 1974 (Wandsworth Central, 1970–74); *b* London, 1930. *Educ:* state schools; London Sch. of Economics. Electrical worker. Former Mem., Fulham Borough Council; contested (Lab) GLC elections, 1967; contested (Lab) Stroud, 1966. An Asst Govt Whip, 1974–77; a Lord Comr of the Treasury, 1977–79. Member: ETU; Co-operative Party. *Address:* House of Commons, SW1A 0AA.

COX, Sir Trenchard, Kt 1961; CBE 1954; MA; FRSA (Vice-President 1964–68); FMA; FSA; Director and Secretary, Victoria and Albert Museum, 1956–66; *b* 31 July 1905; *s* of late William Pallett Cox and Marion Beverley; *m* 1935, Mary Désirée (*d* 1973), *d* of late Sir Hugh Anderson, Master of Gonville and Caius Coll., Cambridge. *Educ:* Eton; King's Coll., Cambridge. Worked as volunteer at the National Gallery and Brit. Museum (Dept of Prints and Drawings), 1929–32; spent a semester at the University of Berlin in the Dept of Arts, 1930; Asst to the Keeper, Wallace Collection, 1932–39; seconded for war-time duties, to Home Office, 1940–44; Dir of Birmingham Museum and Art Gallery, 1944–55. Member: Ancient Monuments Board for England, 1959–69; Standing Commn on Museums and Galleries, 1967–77. People's Warden, St Martin-in-the Fields, 1968–79. Hon. DLitt Birmingham, 1956. Hon. Fellow, Royal Acad., 1981. Chevalier, Légion d'Honneur, 1967. *Publications:* The National Gallery, a Room-to-Room Guide, 1930; Jehan Foucquet, Native of Tours, 1931; part editor of the Catalogue to the Exhibition of French Art at Burlington House, Jan.-March 1932; The Renaissance in Europe, 1933; A General Guide to the Wallace Collection, 1933; A Short Illustrated History of the Wallace Collection and its Founders, 1936; David Cox, 1947; Peter Bruegel, 1951; Pictures: a Handbook for Curators, 1956. *Recreations:* reading, travelling. *Address:* 33 Queen's Gate Gardens, SW7. *T:* 071–584 0231. *Club:* Athenæum.

COX, William Trevor; *see* Trevor, William.

COXETER, Harold Scott Macdonald, FRS 1950; PhD Cambridge, 1931; Professor of Mathematics, University of Toronto, 1948–80, now Emeritus Professor; *b* 9 Feb. 1907; *s* of Harold Samuel Coxeter and Lucy (*née* Gee); *m* 1936, Hendrina Johanna Brouwer, The Hague; one *s* one *d*. *Educ:* King Alfred Sch., London; St George's Sch., Harpenden; Trinity Coll., Cambridge. Entrance Scholar, Trinity Coll., 1926; Smith's Prize, 1931. Fellow Trinity Coll., Cambridge, 1931–36; Rockefeller Foundation Fellow, Princeton, 1932–33; Procter Fellow, Princeton, 1934–35; Asst Prof., 1936–43, Associate Prof., 1943–48, University of Toronto. Visiting Professor: Notre Dame, 1947; Columbia Univ., 1949; Dartmouth Coll., 1964; Univ. of Amsterdam, 1966; Univ. of Edinburgh, 1967; Univ. of E Anglia, 1968; ANU, 1970; Univ. of Sussex, 1972; Univ. of Warwick and Univ. of Utrecht, 1976; Calif. Inst. of Technology, 1977; Univ. of Bologna, 1978. Editor Canadian Jl of Mathematics, 1948–57. President: Canadian Mathematical Congress, 1965–67; Internat. Mathematical Congress, 1974. Foreign Mem., Koninklijke Nederlandse Akademie van Wetenschappen, 1975; Hon. Member: Mathematische Gesellschaft, Hamburg, 1977; Wiskundig Genootschap, Amsterdam, 1978; London Mathematical Soc., 1978. Hon. LLD: Alberta, 1957; Trent, 1973; Toronto, 1979; Hon. DMath Waterloo, 1969; Hon. DSc: Acadia, 1971; Carleton, 1984; McMaster, 1988; Hon. Dr rer. nat. Giessen, 1984. *Publications:* Non-Euclidean Geometry, 1942 and 1965; Regular Polytopes, 1948, 1963 and 1973; The Real Projective Plane, 1949, 1955 and 1959; (with W. O. J. Moser) Generators and Relations, 1st edn, 1957, 4th edn, 1980; Introduction to Geometry, 1961 and 1969; Projective Geometry, 1964, 2nd edn, revd 1987; (with S. L. Greitzer) Geometry Revisited, 1967; Twelve Geometric Essays, 1968; Regular Complex Polytopes, 1974, 2nd edn 1990; (with W. W. Rouse Ball) Mathematical Recreations and Essays, 11th edn 1939, 13th edn 1987; (with R. W. Frucht and D. L. Powers) Zero-symmetric Graphs, 1981; various mathematical papers. *Recreations:* music, travel. *Address:* 67 Roxborough Drive, Toronto M4W 1X2, Canada.

COYLE, Eurfron Gwynne, (Mrs Michael Coyle); *see* Jones, E. G.

COYNE, James Elliott; Canadian banker and financial consultant; *b* Winnipeg, 17 July 1910; *s* of James Bowes Coyne and Edna Margaret Coyne (*née* Elliott); *m* 1957, Meribeth Stobie; one *s* one *d*. *Educ:* University of Manitoba (BA); University of Oxford (BCL). RCAF (Flying Officer), 1942–44. Admitted to the Bar, Manitoba, 1934; solicitor and barrister in Manitoba, 1934–38; Financial Attaché, Canadian Embassy, Washington, DC, 1941; Mem. War-time Prices and Trade Board, Ottawa, 1942 (Dep.-Chm.). Bank of Canada, Ottawa: Asst to the Governors, 1944–49; Deputy-Governor, 1950–54; Governor, 1955–61. *Address:* 16 Ruskin Row, Winnipeg, Manitoba R3M 2R9, Canada.

COZENS, Brig. Dame (Florence) Barbara, DBE 1963; RRC 1958; *b* 24 Dec. 1906; *d* of late Capt. A. Cozens, S Staffs. *Educ:* Seabury Sch., Worthing. Nurse Training: The Nightingale Sch., St Thomas' Hosp., London, 1928–32. Joined QAIMNS, 1933. Served War of 1939–45, England and Continent. Lieut-Col 1954; Col 1958; Brig. 1960; Matron-in-Chief and Dir of Army Nursing Services, 1960–64, retd; Chief Nursing Officer to St John Ambulance Brigade, 1965–72. Col Commandant, QARANC, 1966–69. DStJ 1972.

COZENS, Air Cdre Henry Iliffe, CB 1946; AFC 1939; RAF retired; *b* 13 March 1904; *m* 1956, Gillian Mary, *o d* of Wing Comdr O. R. Pigott, Wokingham, Berks; one *s* two *d*. *Educ:* St Dunstan's Coll.; Downing Coll., Cambridge. MA 1934. Commissioned in RAF, 1923; Mem. of British Arctic Air Route Expedition, 1930–31. Served War of 1939–45 (AFC, CB). idc 1947. Vice-Pres., British Schs Exploring Soc., 1969–90. *Address:* Horley Manor, Banbury, Oxon. *Club:* Royal Air Force.

COZENS, Robert William, CBE 1989; QPM 1981; police management consultant; Director, Police Requirements for Science and Technology, Home Office, 1985–88, retired; *b* 10 Nov. 1927; *s* of Sydney Robert and Rose Elizabeth Cozens; *m* 1952, Jean Dorothy Banfield; one *s* one *d*. *Educ:* Stoke C of E Sch., Guildford. Constable to Chief Superintendent, Surrey Constabulary, 1954–72; Asst Dir, Command Courses, Police Staff Coll., Bramshill, 1972–74; Asst Chief Constable, S Yorks Police, 1974–78; seconded to Federal Judicial Police in Mexico for advisory duties, 1975; Dep. Chief Constable, Lincs Police, 1978–81; Chief Constable, W Mercia Constabulary (Hereford, Worcester and Shropshire), 1981–85. *Recreations:* tennis, squash, badminton. *Address:* Woodstock, 10 Ridgemoor Close, Hindhead, Surrey GU26 6QX.

CRABB, Most Rev. Frederick Hugh Wright, BD, DD; Interim Rector, St Peter's, Calgary; *b* Luppitt, Devon, 24 April 1915; *s* of William Samuel and Florence Mary Crabb; *m* 1946, Alice Margery Coombs; two *s* two *d*. *Educ:* Luppitt Parochial Sch.; Univ. of London (St John's Hall, Highbury, London). BD Lond. (1st Cl. Hons); ALCD (1st Cl. Hons). Asst Curate, St James', West Teignmouth, Devon, 1939–41; Asst Priest, St Andrew's, Plymouth, 1941–42; Missionary at Akot, S Sudan, 1942–44; Principal, Bishop Gwynne Divinity Sch., S Sudan, 1944–51; Vice Principal, London Coll. of Divinity, 1951–57; Principal, Coll. of Emmanuel and St Chad, Saskatoon, Sask., 1957–67; Assoc. Priest, Christ Church, Calgary, Alberta, 1967–69; Rector, St Stephen's Church, Calgary, 1969–75; Bishop of Athabasca, 1975–83; Metropolitan of Rupert's Land, 1977–82. Mem. Governing Council, Athabasca Univ., 1982–85. Hon. DD: Wycliffe Coll., Toronto, 1960; St Andrew's Coll., Saskatoon, 1967; Coll. of Emmanuel and St Chad, Saskatoon, 1979. *Publication:* (jtly) Rupert's Land: A Cultural Tapestry, 1988. *Recreations:* gardening, mountain hiking. *Address:* 3483 Chippendale Drive NW, Calgary, Alberta T2L 0W7, Canada.

CRABB, Tony William; Deputy Director of Broadcasting, Radio Television Hong Kong, since 1988; *b* 27 June 1933; *s* of William Harold Crabb and Ellen Emily Crabb; *m* 1957, Brenda Margaret (*née* Sullman); one *s* one *d*. *Educ:* Chiswick Grammar School; London School of Economics (BScEcon); Intelligence Corps Russian Interpreters Course, 1952–54. BBC, 1957–88; seconded as news adviser to Govt of Libya, 1968–69; Managing Editor: BBC TV News, 1979–82; BBC Breakfast Time, 1982–84; Controller, Corporate News Services, BBC, 1984–87; Special Asst, News and Current Affairs, BBC, 1987–88. *Address:* B2, 17th Floor, 1 Ventris Road, Happy Valley, Hong Kong. *Club:* Foreign Correspondents' (Hong Kong).

CRABBE, Kenneth Herbert Martineau, TD; *b* 4 Nov. 1916; *m* 1st, 1940, Rowena Leete (*d* 1981); one *s*; 2nd, 1982, Belinda V. Fitzherbert (*née* Batt); three step *s* one step *d*. *Educ:* Stowe Sch. Commnd TA, 1937; psc; Major. Member, Stock Exchange, London, 1937–; Mem. Council, The Stock Exchange, 1963–78 (Dep. Chm., 1970–73). *Recreations:* golf, fishing, shooting, painting. *Address:* Spandrels, Walliswood, Dorking, Surrey RH5 5RJ. *T:* Oakwood Hill (030679) 275. *Clubs:* Boodle's; West Sussex Golf.

CRABBE, Mrs Pauline, (Mrs Joseph Benjamin), OBE 1969; JP; National Vice-Chairman, Brook Advisory Centres, 1980–86; *b* 1 April 1914; *y d* of Cyril and Edith Henriques, Kingston, Jamaica; *m* 1st, 1936, Geoffrey Henebery (marr. diss. 1948); one *d*; 2nd, 1949, Neville Crabbe (marr. diss. 1960); one *s*; 3rd, 1969, Joseph Benjamin; three step *s*. *Educ:* Highgate Convent; London Academy of Music and Drama; London Univ. (extra-mural course in Psychology). Actress and broadcaster, 1945–53; secretarial work with British Actors' Equity and WEA, 1953–56; then with Old People's Welfare and London Council of Social Service, 1956–57; Welfare Sec. and Dep. Gen. Sec. to Nat. Council for Unmarried Mother and her Child, 1957–69; Conciliation Officer for Race Relations Bd, 1969–71; Sec., 1971–76, Sen. Counsellor, 1976–80, London Brook Adv. Centres. Founder Mem., Haverstock Housing Trust for Fatherless Families, 1966; Mem. Bd, Housing Corp., 1968–75; Member: Community Relations Commn, 1972–77; Standing Adv. Council on Race Relations, 1977–; Parole Bd, 1978–82. Hon. Fellow, Manchester Polytechnic, 1979. Radio and TV broadcaster and panellist. JP London, 1967. FRSA 1972. *Publications:* articles and book reviews in social work jls. *Recreations:* entertaining, walking, indoor gardening, the theatre and the arts. *Address:* 88 Osprey House, Sillwood Place, Brighton, Sussex. *Club:* Magistrates' Association.

CRABBE, Reginald James Williams, FIA, FSS; President for Life, Provident Life Association Ltd (Chairman, 1967–82, and President, 1982–86, Provident Life Association of London Ltd); Chairman: United Standard Insurance Co. Ltd, 1967–79; Vigilant Assurance Co. Ltd, 1970–79; *b* 22 June 1909; *e s* of late Harry James and Annie Martha Crabbe; *m* 1948, Phyllis Maud Smith; two *d*. *Educ:* Chigwell Sch., Essex. Entered National Mutual Life Assurance Soc., 1926; FIA 1933; joined Provident Life as Asst Actuary, 1935; Man. Dir, 1956–74; Dir, 1956–86; Dep. Chm., 1971–85, Chm., 1975–77, Cope & Timmins Holdings. Chm., Life Offices' Assoc., 1965, 1966. *Publication:* (with C. A. Poyser, MA, FIA) Pension and Widows' and Orphans' Funds, 1953. *Recreations:* reading, gardening, music, art. *Address:* Fairways, 166 Lower Green Road, Esher, Surrey KT10 8HA. *T:* Esher (0372) 462219.

CRABBIE, Christopher Donald; HM Diplomatic Service; Counsellor, British Embassy, Paris, since 1990; *b* 17 Jan. 1946; *s* of William George Crabbie and Jane (*née* Coe). *Educ:* Rugby Sch.; Newcastle Univ.; Liverpool Univ.; Corpus Christi Coll., Oxford. Second Sec., FCO, 1973; First Secretary: Nairobi, 1975; Washington, 1979; FCO, 1983; Counsellor and Hd of European Communities Div., HM Treasury, 1985; Counsellor, FCO, 1987; Dep. UK Perm. Rep., OECD, Paris, 1990. *Recreations:* ski-ing, flying, sailing, gardening. *Address:* c/o Foreign and Commonwealth Office, SW1. *Club:* New (Edinburgh).

CRABBIE, Mrs (Margaret) Veronica, CBE 1977; *b* 26 Nov. 1910; *d* of late Sir Christopher Nicholson Johnston (Lord Sands, Senator of the College of Justice, Scotland), and Lady Sands; *m* 1938, John Patrick Crabbie; two *s* one *d*. *Educ:* St Denis Sch., Edinburgh; Queen Margaret's Sch., Escrick, York. Chairman: Edinburgh Home for Mothers and Infants, 1951–66; Walpole Housing Assoc., 1969–72; Scottish Council for the Unmarried Mother and her Child, 1966–72; WRVS, Scotland, 1972–77. *Recreation:* curling. *Club:* New (Edinburgh).

CRABTREE, Maj.-Gen. Derek Thomas, CB 1983; General Manager, Regular Forces Employment Association, since 1987; *b* 21 Jan. 1930; *s* of late William Edward Crabtree and of Winifred Hilda Burton; *m* 1960, Daphne Christine Mason; one *s* one *d*. *Educ:* St Brendan's Coll., Bristol. Commissioned, 1953; Regimental Service: 13th/18th Royal Hussars (QMO), 1953–56; Royal Berkshire Regt, 1956–59; Technical Staff Course, RMCS, 1960–62; sc Camberley, 1964; BM 11 Inf. Bde, BAOR, 1965–67; CO 1st Bn Duke of Edinburgh's Royal Regt, UK and Berlin, 1970–72; Col GS, MGO Secretariat, MoD, 1974–76; Dep. Comdr and Chief of Staff Headquarters British Forces Hong Kong, 1976–79; Dep. Comdt RMCS, 1979–80; Dir Gen. of Weapons (Army), MoD, 1980–84. Sen. Mil. Advr, Short Bros, 1984–86. Col, Duke of Edinburgh's Royal Regt, 1982–87, 1988–89. *Recreations:* most outdoor sports, pottering in the house and garden. *Club:* Army and Navy.

CRABTREE, Jonathan; His Honour Judge Crabtree; a Circuit Judge, since 1986; *b* 17 April 1934; *s* of Charles H. Crabtree and Elsie M. Crabtree; *m* 1st, 1957, Caroline Ruth Keigwin (*née* Oliver) (marr. diss. 1976); one *s* three *d* (and one *s* decd); 2nd, 1980, Wendy Elizabeth Hudson (*née* Ward). *Educ:* Bootham; St John's Coll., Cambridge (MA, LLM). Called to Bar, Gray's Inn, 1958. A Recorder, 1974–86. *Recreations:* cricket, cooking, history, archaeology. *Address:* c/o Crown Court, Sheffield. *T:* Sheffield (0742) 755866.

CRABTREE, Prof. Lewis Frederick, PhD, FRAeS; FAIAA; Sir George White Professor of Aeronautical Engineering, University of Bristol, 1973–85, now Emeritus; *b* 16 Nov. 1924; *m* 1955, Averil Joan Escott; one *s* one *d*. *Educ:* Univ. of Leeds; Imperial Coll. of Science and Technology; Cornell Univ., USA. BSc (Mech. Eng) Leeds, 1945; DIC (Aeronautics), 1947; PhD (Aero Eng), Cornell, 1952. Air Engr Officer, RNVR, 1945–46. Grad. apprentice, Saunders-Roe Ltd, E Cowes, IoW, 1947–50; ECA Fellowship, Grad. Sch. of Aero. Engrg, Cornell Univ., 1950–52; Aerodynamics Dept, RAE, Farnborough, 1953–73; Head of: Hypersonics and High temperature Gasdynamics Div., 1961–66; Low Speed Aerodynamics Div., 1966–70; Propulsion Aerodynamics and Noise Div., 1970–73. Visiting Prof., Cornell Univ., 1957. Chm., Brecknock Wildlife Trust, 1988–. Lectures to RAeS: Lanchester Meml, 1977; Handley Page, 1979; Barnwell, 1981. Pres., RAeS, 1978–79 (Usborne Meml Prize, 1955). *Publications:* Elements of Hypersonic Aerodynamics, 1965; contributor to: Incompressible Aerodynamics, 1960; Laminar Boundary Layers, 1963; Engineering Structures, 1983; articles chiefly in Jl RAeS, Aeron. Quart., Jl Aeron. Sci., Jahrbuch der WGLR, and Reports and Memos of ARC. *Address:* Dan-y-Coity, Talybont-on-Usk, Brecon LD3 7YN. *T:* Talybont-on-Usk (087487) 216.

CRABTREE, Simon; *see* Wharton, Michael B.

CRACKNELL, Malcolm Thomas; His Honour Judge Cracknell; a Circuit Judge, since 1989; *b* 12 Dec. 1943; *s* of late Percy Thomas Cracknell and of Doris Louise Cracknell; *m* 1st, 1968, Ann Carrington (*née* Gooding) (marr. diss. 1980); one *s* one *d*; 2nd, 1988, Felicity Anne Davies; one *d*. *Educ:* Royal Liberty Sch., Romford; Hull Univ. (LLB); King's Coll., London (LLM). Called to Bar, Middle Temple, 1969. Lectr in Law, Univ. of Hull, 1968–74; Barrister, NE Circuit, 1970–89; a Recorder, 1988. *Recreations:* golf, gardening, walking, cricket, reading. *Address:* Garden House, High Street, Boston Spa, West Yorkshire LS23 6DR. *T:* Boston Spa (0937) 842085.

CRACKNELL, (William) Martin; Chief Executive, Glenrothes Development Corporation, since 1976; *b* 24 June 1929; *s* of John Sidney Cracknell and Sybil Marian (*née* Wood); *m* 1962, Gillian Goatcher; two *s* two *d*. *Educ:* St Edward's School, Oxford; RMA Sandhurst. Regular Army Officer, Royal Green Jackets, 1949–69; British Printing Industries Fedn, 1969–76. Mem. Exec., Scottish Council (Develt and Industry), 1984–90; Chm., Scottish Cttee, German Chamber of Commerce and Industry in UK, 1987–. Director: Glenrothes Enterprise Trust, 1983–89; New Enterprise Develt, 1987–90. *Address:* Alburne Knowe, Orchard Drive, Glenrothes, Fife. *T:* Glenrothes (0592) 752413. *Club:* Guid (Glenrothes) (Chm.).

CRACROFT, Air Vice-Marshal Peter Dicken, CB 1954; AFC 1932; *b* 29 Nov. 1907; *s* of Lt-Col H. Cracroft, Bath; *m* 1932, Margaret Eliza Sugden Patchett; two *s*. *Educ:* Monkton Combe Sch., Bath. Commissioned RAF 1927; Fleet Air Arm, 1928–31; Central Flying Sch. Instructors' Course, 1931; Flying Instructor, Leuchars, 1931–35; Adjt HMS Courageous, 1936–37; Chief Flying Instructor, Oxford Univ. Air Sqdn, 1937–39; RAF Stn Mount Batten, 1939–40; Air Staff, Coastal Command, 1940–41; OC RAF Station, Chivenor, 1941–43; SASO 19 Gp (later 17 Gp), 1933–44; OC 111 Op. Trg Unit, Bahamas, 1944–45; SASO HQ Air Comd, SE Asia, Mil. Gov. Penang, 1945; AOC Bombay, 1945–46; SASO, HQ 19 Gp, 1946–48; RAF Dir and CO, Jt Anti-Submarine Sch., Londonderry, 1948–50; Sen. Air Liaison Officer, S Africa, 1950–52; AOC 66 Gp, Edinburgh, 1952–53; Senior Air Staff Officer, Headquarters Coastal Command, 1953–55; AOC Scotland and 18 Group, 1955–58; retired from RAF, Dec. 1958. *Recreations:* tennis, fishing, shooting. *Address:* Alderney House, Burton Bradstock, Bridport, Dorset DT6 4NQ. *T:* Burton Bradstock (0308) 897270. *Club:* Royal Air Force.

CRADDOCK, (William) Aleck, LVO 1981; Director, Harrods Ltd, 1964–88 (Managing Director, 1980–84, Chairman, 1981–86, Deputy Chairman, 1987–88); Director, Cartier Ltd, since 1986; *b* Nov. 1924; *m* 1947, Olive May Brown; one *s* one *d*. *Educ:* City of London School. Joined Druce and Craddock, Craddock and Tomkins Ltd (family firm), Meat and Provision Merchants, Marylebone, London, 1946; joined Harrods Ltd as Asst to Food Manager, 1954; Member of the Board, 1964; Director and General Manager, 1970; Asst Managing Director, 1975; a Director of House of Fraser, 1980–91. Vice Chm., Drapers Cottage Homes, 1987– (Pres., Appeal, 1985–86); Pres., Twenty Club, 1988. Liveryman, Worshipful Company of Cooks, 1972. Cavaliere Ufficiale (Fourth Cl.), Order Al Merito Della Repubblica Italiana, 1980. *Recreations:* fell walking, golf, watercolour painting. *Address:* 17 Tretawn Park, Mill Hill, NW7 4PS. *Club:* Guards' Polo (Life Mem.).

CRADOCK, John Anthony, CB 1980; MBE 1952; Deputy Secretary, Ministry of Defence, 1981–82; *b* 19 Oct. 1921; *o s* of John Cradock and Nan Cradock (*née* Kelly); *m* 1948, Eileen (*née* Bell); one *s* one *d*. *Educ:* St Brendan's College, Bristol; Bristol Univ. (BA 1946). Military service, 1941–46 (Captain Royal Signals); Malayan Civil Service, 1946–57; War Office, 1957–67; MoD, 1967–75; Under Sec., N Ireland Office, 1975–77; MoD, 1977–82. *Recreations:* gardening, walking. *Address:* c/o Lloyds Bank, Morpeth, Northumberland NE61 1AN.

CRADOCK, Sir Percy, GCMG 1983 (KCMG 1980; CMG 1968); the Prime Minister's foreign policy adviser, since 1984; *b* 26 Oct. 1923; *m* 1953, Birthe Marie Dyrlund. *Educ:* St John's Coll., Cambridge (Hon. Fellow, 1982). Served Foreign Office, 1954–57; First Sec., Kuala Lumpur, 1957–61, Hong Kong, 1961, Peking, 1962; Foreign Office, 1963–66; Counsellor and Head of Chancery, Peking, 1966–68; Chargé d'Affaires, Peking, 1968–69; Head of Planning Staff, FCO, 1969–71; Under-Sec., Cabinet Office, 1971–75; Ambassador to German Democratic Republic, 1976–78; Leader, UK Delegn to Comprehensive Test Ban Discussions at Geneva, 1977–78; Ambassador to People's Republic of China, 1978–83; Leader of UK team in negotiations over Hong Kong, 1983; Dep. Under Sec. of State, FCO, supervising Hong Kong negotiations, 1984. *Address:* c/o 10 Downing Street, SW1. *Club:* Reform.

CRADOCK-HARTOPP, Sir J. E.; *see* Hartopp.

CRAFT, Prof. Ian Logan, FRCS; FRCOG; Director, London Fertility Centre, since 1990; *b* 11 July 1937; *s* of Reginald Thomas Craft and Lois Mary (*née* Logan); *m* 1959, Jacqueline Rivers Symmons; two *s*. *Educ:* Owens Sch., London; Westminster Med. Sch., Univ. of London (MB, BS). FRCS 1966; MRCOG 1970, FRCOG 1986. Sen. Registrar, Westminster Hosp. Teaching Gp (Westminster Hosp. and Kingston Hosp.), 1970–72; Sen. Lectr and Consultant, Inst. of Obstetrics and Gynaecology, Queen Charlotte's Hosp., London, 1972–76; Prof. of Obstetrics and Gynaecology, Royal Free Hosp., London, 1976–82; Dir of Gynaecology, Cromwell Hosp., 1982–85; Dir of Fertility and Obstetric Studies, Humana Hosp. Wellington, 1985–90. FRSocMed. *Publications:* contrib. BMJ, Lancet and other medical jls. *Recreations:* art, music, ornithology, sports of most types. *Address:* 17 Park St James, Prince Albert Road, NW8 7LE. *T:* 071–586 6001; Medicraft Services Ltd, Cozens House, 112A Harley Street, W1N 1AF. *T:* 071–224 0707.

CRAFT, Prof. Maurice, PhD, DLitt; Foundation Dean of Humanities and Social Science, Hong Kong University of Science and Technology, since 1989; *b* 4 May 1932; *er s* of Jack and Polly Craft, London; *m* 1957, Alma, *y d* of Elio and Dinah Sampson, Dublin; two *d*. *Educ:* LCC Elem. Sch. and Colfe's Grammar Sch., SE13; LSE, Univ. of London (BSc Econ); Sch. of Education, Trinity Coll., Univ. of Dublin (HDipEd); Inst. of Education, Univ. of London (AcadDipEd); Dept of Sociology, Univ. of Liverpool (PhD 1972); Univ. of Nottingham (DLitt 1990). 2/Lt RAOC (Nat. Service), 1953–55. Asst Master, Catford Secondary Sch., SE6, 1956–60; Princ. Lectr and Head of Dept of Sociology, Edge Hill Coll. of Education, Ormskirk, Lancs, 1960–67; Sen. Lectr in Education, i/c Advanced Courses, Univ. of Exeter, 1967–73; Sub-Dean, Faculty of Educn, 1969–73; Prof. of Education, and Chairman, Centre for the Study of Urban Education, La Trobe Univ., Melbourne, 1973–75; Goldsmiths' Prof. of Education, Inst. of Educn, Univ. of London, and Head of Dept of Advanced Studies in Education, Goldsmiths' Coll., 1976–80; Univ. of Nottingham: Prof. of Educn, and Hd, Div. of Advanced Studies, 1980–89; Dean, Faculty of Educn, 1981–83; Chm., Sch. of Educn, 1983–85, 1988–89; Pro-Vice-Chancellor, 1983–87. Adviser: Devon CC, 1970–72; Aust. Federal Poverty Commn, 1974–75; State Coll., Vict., Aust., 1974–75; SSRC, 1974–; Assoc. of Commonwealth Univs, 1976, 1979; CNAA, 1978–; Centre for Advice and Inf. on Educn Disadvantage (Chm., Teacher Educn Working Gp, 1979–80); Schools Council, 1979; CRE (Chm., Teacher Educn Adv. Gp, 1980–84); H of C Home Affairs Cttee, 1981; Swann Cttee, 1982–84; Council for Educn and Trng in Youth and Community Work (Chm., In-service Wkg Gp, 1983); UNESCO, 1985. Mem., UK Delegn to EEC Colloquium on Ethnic Min. Educn, Brussels, 1979, 1982; UK delegate to: Council of Europe Seminars on Intercultural Trng of Teachers, Lisbon, 1981, Rome, 1982, Strasbourg, 1983; UNESCO Colloquium on Educnl Disadvantage, Thessalonika, 1984. Member: Management Cttee, Sociology of Educn Abstracts 1965–; Editl Bd, Jl of Multilingual and Multicultural Develt, 1979–; Editl Bd, Multicultural Educn Abstracts, 1981–; Council of Validating Univs, 1982–89 (Vice-Chm., 1987–89); E Midlands Reg. Consultative Gp on Teacher Educn, 1980–84 (Chm., 1980–84); Exec. Cttee, Univs Council for Educn of Teachers, 1984–88 (Chm., Standing Cttee on Validation, 1984–87); Cttee of Vice-Chancellors and Principals, 1986–88 (Cttee on Validation, 1986–88). FRSA 1989. *Publications:* (ed jtly) Linking Home and School, 1967 (3rd edn, 1980); (ed jtly) Guidance and Counselling in British Schools, 1969 (2nd edn, 1974); (ed) Family, Class and Education: a Reader, 1970; Urban Education—a Dublin case study, 1974; School Welfare Provision in Australia, 1977; (ed) Teaching in a Multicultural Society: the Task for Teacher Education, 1981; (jtly) Training Teachers of Ethnic Minority Community Languages, 1983; (ed jtly) Change in Teacher Education, 1984; (ed) Education and Cultural Pluralism, 1984; The Democratisation of Education, 1985; Teacher Education in a Multicultural Society, 1986; contrib. to numerous books and to the following jls: Educnl Research, Internat. Review of Educn, Educnl Review, Social and Econ. Admin., Cambridge Jl of Educn, Educn for Teaching, British Jl of In-Service Educn, Internat. Social Work, Aust. Jl of Social Work, Aust. Educnl Researcher, THES, Higher Educn Jl, New Society, Education, Administration, New Era, Studies. *Recreations:* music, walking. *Address:* Hong Kong University of Science and Technology, 13/F World Shipping Centre, Harbour City, Hong Kong. *T:* 3021448. *Club:* Royal Over-Seas League.

CRAGG, Rt. Rev. (Albert) Kenneth, DPhil; *b* 8 March 1913; *yr s* of Albert and Emily Cragg; *m* 1940, Theodora Melita (*d* 1989), *yr d* of John Wesley Arnold; three *s* (one *d* decd). *Educ:* Blackpool Grammar Sch.; Jesus Coll., Oxford; Tyndale Hall, Bristol. BA Oxon 2nd Cl. Hons Mod. Hist., 1934; MA Oxon 1938; DPhil 1950. Ellerton Theol. Essay Prize, Oxford, 1937; Green Moral Philos. Prize, Oxford, 1947. Deacon, 1936; Priest, 1937; Curate, Higher Tranmere Parish Church, Birkenhead, 1936–39; Chaplain, All Saints', Beirut, Lebanon, 1939–47; Warden, St Justin's House, Beirut, 1942–47; Asst Prof. of Philos., Amer. University of Beirut, 1942–47; Rector of Longworth, Berks, 1947–51; Sheriff's Chap., Berks, 1948; Prof. of Arabic and Islamics, Hartford Seminary, Conn, USA, 1951–56; Rockefeller Travelling Schol., 1954; Res. Canon, St George's Collegiate Church, Jerusalem, 1956–61; Fellow, St Augustine's Coll., Canterbury, 1959–60, Sub-Warden, 1960–61, Warden, 1961–67; Examng Chaplain to Archbishop of Canterbury, 1961–67; Hon. Canon of Canterbury, 1961–80; Asst Bishop to Archbishop in Jerusalem, 1970–74; Reader in Religious Studies, Sussex Univ., and Asst Bishop, dio. of Chichester, 1973–78; Vicar of Helme, W Yorks, and Asst Bishop, dio. Wakefield, 1978–81; Asst Bishop, dio. Oxford, 1982–. Select Preacher: Cambridge, 1961; Dublin, 1962; Oxford, 1974. Proctor in Convocation, Canterbury, 1965–68; Visiting Prof., Union Theological Seminary, New York, 1965–66; Lectr, Faculty of Divinity, Cambridge, 1966; Jordan Lectr, Sch. of Oriental and African Studies, University of London, 1967; Vis. Prof., University of Ibadan, Nigeria, 1968; Bye-Fellow, Gonville and Caius Coll., Cambridge, 1968–74; Vis. Prof., Virginia Theol Seminary, 1984, 1985. Editor, The Muslim World Quarterly, 1952–60. *Publications:* The Call of the Minaret, 1956, 2nd edn 1986; Sandals at the Mosque, 1959; The Dome and the Rock, 1964; Counsels in Contemporary Islam, 1965; Christianity in World Perspective, 1968; The Privilege of Man, 1968; The House of Islam, 1969; Alive to God, 1970; The Event of the Qur'ān, 1971; The Mind of the Qur'ān, 1973; The Wisdom of the Sufis, 1976; The Christian and Other Religion, 1977; Islam from Within, 1979; This Year in Jerusalem, 1982; Muhammad and the Christian, 1983; The Pen and the Faith, 1985; Jesus and the Muslim, 1985; The Christ and the Faiths, 1986; Readings in the Qur'ān, 1988; What Decided Christianity, 1989; The Arab Christian, 1991; translated: City of Wrong, 1959; The Theology of Unity, 1965; A Passage to France, 1976; The Hallowed Valley, 1977; Contributor: Journal of World History, 1957; Religion in the Middle East, 1969. *Address:* Appletree Cottage, Ascott-under-Wychwood, Oxford OX7 6AG.

CRAGG, Anthony John; Director General of Management Audit, Ministry of Defence, since 1991; *b* 16 May 1943; *s* of Leslie Cragg and late Gwendolen Cragg (*née* Pevler); *m* 1971, Jeanette Ann Rix; two *d*. *Educ:* Hastings Grammar School; Lincoln College, Oxford (BA). Ministry of Defence, 1966–: Asst Private Sec. to Sec. of State for Defence, 1974; UK Delegn to NATO, 1977; Asst Sec., 1979; Chief Officer, Sovereign Base Area, Cyprus, 1983–85; RCDS 1988; Asst Under Sec. of State, 1990. *Recreations:* swimming, the performing arts. *Address:* Ministry of Defence, Whitehall, SW1. *T:* 071–218 9000.

CRAGG, James Birkett; Emeritus Professor of Environmental Science, University of Calgary, Alberta; *b* 8 Nov. 1910; *s* of late A. W. Cragg, N Shields; *m* 1937, Mary Catherine Macnaughtan (marr. diss. 1968); four *s* (and one *s* one *d* decd); *m* Jean Moore. *Educ:* private sch.; Tynemouth High Sch.; Durham Univ. BSc King's Coll., University of Durham, 1933; DThPT, 1934; MSc, 1937; DSc Newcastle, 1965. Demonstrator, Physiology Dept, Manchester Univ., 1935; Asst Lecturer, and later Lecturer, in Zoology, University Coll. of North Wales, 1937; seconded to Agricultural Research Council, 1942; Scientific Officer, ARC Unit of Insect Physiology, 1944; Reader in Zoology, Durham Colls, in University of Durham, 1946; Prof. of Zoology, University of Durham, 1950–61; Dir, Merlewood Research Station (Nature Conservancy, NERC), Grange-over-Sands, Lancs, 1961–66; Dir, Environmental Sciences Centre, and Prof. of Biology, 1966–72, Killam Meml Prof., 1966–76, Vice-Pres. (Academic), 1970–72, Univ. of Calgary, Alberta. Pres., British Ecol. Soc., 1960–61; Former Chairman: Commn for Ecology; Internat. Union for Conservation of Nature; Convenor, Internat. Biological Programme PT Cttee; Mem., Internat. Biological Programme Cttees; Consultant, Ford Foundation, 1965. Commonwealth Prestige Fellow (New Zealand), 1964. Jubilee medal, 1977. Hon. FIBiol 1981. *Publications:* papers in scientific periodicals; formerly Editor, Advances in Ecological Research. *Recreation:* books. *Address:* 2112 Uralta Road, Calgary, Alberta T2N 4B4, Canada. *Club:* Athenæum.

CRAGG, Rt. Rev. Kenneth; *see* Cragg, Rt. Rev. A. K.

CRAGGS, Prof. James Wilkinson, BSc, PhD; Professor of Engineering Mathematics, University of Southampton, 1967–81; *b* 3 Feb. 1920; *s* of Thomas Gibson Craggs and Margaret (*née* Wilkinson); *m* 1946, Mary Baker; two *s* one *d*. *Educ:* Bede Collegiate Sch., Sunderland; University of Manchester. BSc 1941, PhD 1948, Manchester; PhD Cambridge, 1953. Junior Lectr, Royal Military Coll. of Science, 1941–45; Asst Lectr, University of Manchester, 1947–49; Lecturer, Queen's Coll., Dundee, 1951–52; King's Coll., Newcastle upon Tyne: Lectr, 1952–56; Senior Lecturer, 1956–60; Reader in Mathematics, 1960–61; Prof. of Mathematics, University of Leeds, 1961–63; Prof. of Applied Mathematics, Melbourne Univ., 1963–67. *Publications:* contrib. learned journals regarding the mechanics of solids and fluids. *Recreation:* Methodist lay preacher. *Address:* 23 Redhill, Bassett, Southampton SO1 7BR.

CRAGGS, Prof. John Drummond, MSc, PhD, FInstP; retired; Professor of Electronic Engineering, University of Liverpool, 1955–82; *b* 17 May 1915; *s* of Thomas Lawson

Craggs and Elsie Aidrienne Roberts; *m* 1941, Dorothy Ellen Margaret Garfitt; two *d.* *Educ:* Huddersfield Coll.; University of London. Research Student, King's Coll., London Univ., 1937–38; Metropolitan-Vickers High Voltage Research Laboratory, Manchester, 1938–48; University of California, Radiation Laboratory, 1944–45; apptd Sen. Lectr, 1948, and, later, Reader, Dept of Electrical Engineering, University of Liverpool. A Pro-Vice-Chancellor, Liverpool Univ., 1969–72. Hon. DSc NUI, 1986. *Publications:* Counting Tubes, 1950 (with S. C. Curran); Electrical Breakdown of Gases, 1953; High Voltage Laboratory Technique, 1954 (with J. M. Meek); Electrical Breakdown of Gases (with J. M. Meek), 1978; papers in various professional jls. *Address:* Stone Cottage, Newton-cum-Larton, West Kirby, Wirral, Merseyside L48 1PG. *T:* 051–625 5055.

CRAIB, Douglas Duncan Simpson, CBE 1974; DL; FRAgS 1971; farmer, 1937–83; Member, Potato Marketing Board of Great Britain, 1968–83; *b* 5 April 1914; *s* of Peter Barton Salsbury Simpson and Helen Duncan; changed name by deed poll, 1930; *m* 1939, Moyra Louise Booth; one *s* one *d.* *Educ:* Aberdeen Grammar Sch.; Dundee High School. Commerce, 1934. Captain, 7th Bn Seaforth Highlanders, 1939–42. Dir, NALCO Ltd, Aberdeen, 1956–68. Chm., Elec. Cons. Council, N Scotland Area, 1971–79; Mem., N of Scotland Hydro-Elec. Bd, 1971–79. Dir, Royal Highland and Agric. Soc. of Scotland, 1961–74 (Chm., 1967–69; Hon. Sec. and Hon. Treas., 1970–74; Hon. Vice-Pres., 1978–79, 1987–88); Member: Highland Agric. Exec. Cttee, 1958–72 (Chm., 1970–72); Scottish Agric. Consultative Panel, 1963–87; Scottish Council of Technical Educn, 1973–85 (Assessor, 1981–85); President: Moray Area, NFU, 1945; Moray Farmers' Club, 1950; Governor: N of Scotland Coll. of Agriculture, 1970–84; Rowett Res. Inst., Aberdeen, 1973–86; Trustee, The MacRobert Trusts, Scotland, 1970–84. DL Moray 1974. *Address:* The Old School, Mosstodloch, Fochabers, Morayshire IV32 7LE. *T:* Fochabers (0343) 820733. *Clubs:* Farmers'; Elgin (Elgin, Morayshire).

CRAIG, family name of **Viscount Craigavon** and of **Baron Craig of Radley.**

CRAIG OF RADLEY, Baron *cr* 1991 (Life Peer), of Helhoughton in the County of Norfolk; **Marshal of the Royal Air Force David Brownrigg Craig,** GCB 1984 (KCB 1981; CB 1978); OBE 1967; Chief of the Defence Staff, 1988–91; *b* 17 Sept. 1929; *s* of Major Francis Brownrigg Craig and Mrs Olive Craig; *m* 1955, Elisabeth June Derenburg; one *s* one *d.* *Educ:* Radley Coll.; Lincoln Coll., Oxford (MA; Hon. Fellow 1984). Commnd in RAF, 1951; OC RAF Cranwell, 1968–70; ADC to the Queen, 1969–71; Dir, Plans and Ops, HQ Far East Comd, 1970–71; OC RAF Akrotiri, 1972–73; ACAS (Ops), MoD, 1975–78; AOC No 1 Group, RAF Strike Command, 1978–80; Vice-Chief of Air Staff, 1980–82; AOC-in-C, RAF Strike Command and C-in-C, UK Air Forces, 1982–85; CAS, 1985–88. Air ADC to the Queen, 1985–88. *Recreations:* fishing, shooting, golf. *Address:* c/o Royal Bank of Scotland, 9 Pall Mall, SW1Y 5LX. *Club:* Royal Air Force.

CRAIG, Sir (Albert) James (Macqueen), GCMG 1984 (KCMG 1981; CMG 1975); HM Diplomatic Service, retired; Director General, Middle East Association, since 1985; Visiting Professor in Arabic, and Lecturer at Pembroke College, University of Oxford, 1985–91; *b* 13 July 1924; *s* of James Craig and Florence Morris; *m* 1952, Margaret Hutchinson; three *s* one *d.* *Educ:* Liverpool Institute High Sch.; Univ. of Oxford. Queen's Coll., Oxford (Exhibr), 1942; 1st cl. Hon. Mods Classics, 1943 (Hon. Schol.); Army, 1943–44; 1st cl. Oriental Studies (Arabic and Persian), 1947; Sen. Demy, Magdalen Coll., 1947–48; Lectr in Arabic, Durham Univ., 1948–55; seconded to FO, 1955 as Principal Instructor at Middle East Centre for Arab Studies, Lebanon; joined Foreign Service substantively, 1956; served: FO, 1958–61; HM Political Agent, Trucial States, 1961–64; 1st Sec., Beirut, 1964–67; Counsellor and Head of Chancery, Jedda, 1967–70; Supernumerary Fellow, St Antony's Coll., Oxford, 1970–71; Head of Near East and N Africa Dept, FCO, 1971–75; Dep. High Comr, Kuala Lumpur, 1975–76; Ambassador to: Syria, 1976–79; Saudi Arabia, 1979–84. Director: Saudi-British Bank, 1985–; Hong Kong Egyptian Bank, 1987–; Special Adviser, Hong Kong Bank Gp, 1985–; Chm., Roxby Engineering Internat., 1988–. Pres., British Soc. for ME Studies, 1987–; Vice-Chm., Middle East Internat., 1990–. Sen. Associate Mem., St Antony's Coll., Oxford, 1989. Hon. Fellow, Middle East Centre, Durham Univ., 1987–. OStJ 1985; Mem. Council, Order of St John, 1985–90. *Address:* c/o 33 Bury Street, SW1Y 6AX. *T:* 071–839 2137. *Club:* Travellers'.

CRAIG, Mrs Barbara Denise, MA Oxon; Principal of Somerville College, Oxford, 1967–80, Honorary Fellow, 1980; *b* 22 Oct. 1915; *o d* of John Alexander Chapman and Janie Denize (*née* Callaway); *m* 1942, Wilson James Craig, CBE (*d* 1989); no *c.* *Educ:* Haberdashers' Aske's Girls' Sch., Acton; Somerville Coll., Oxford. Craven Fellow, 1938; Goldsmiths' Sen. Student, 1938; Woolley Fellow in Archæology of Somerville Coll., 1954–56. Temp. Asst Principal, Mins of Supply and Labour, 1939–40; Asst to Prof. of Greek, Aberdeen Univ., 1940–42; Temp. Asst Principal, Min. of Home Security, 1942; Temp. Principal, Min. of Production, 1943–45. Unofficial work as wife of British Council officer in Brazil, Iraq, Spain, Pakistan, 1946–65; from 1956, archæological work on finds from British excavations at Mycenae. *Recreations:* bird-watching (Mem. Brit. Ornithologists' Union); walking. *Address:* The Wynd, Gayle, Hawes, North Yorkshire DL8 3SD. *T:* Wensleydale (0969) 667289.

CRAIG, Charles (James); opera singer (tenor); *b* 3 Dec. 1920; *s* of James and Rosina Craig; *m* 1946, Dorothy Wilson; one *s* one *d.* *Educ:* in London. Protégé of Sir Thomas Beecham; Principal Tenor with Carl Rosa Opera Co., 1953–56; joined Sadler's Wells Opera Co., 1956. Appears regularly at Internat. Opera Houses, incl. Covent Garden, Milan, Rome, Vienna, Paris, Berlin, Buenos Aires, etc; repertoire of 48 operas, incl. Otello, Aida, Turandot, Norma, Andrea Chenier, Die Walküre, Götterdämmerung, Lohengrin, etc. Concerts, TV and radio, and records. International Opera Medal Award, 1962. *Recreations:* motoring, cooking. *Address:* Whitfield Cottage, Whitfield, Northants.

CRAIG, Cdre Christopher John Sinclair, CB 1991; DSC 1982; RN; Chief of Staff to Flag Officer, Naval Aviation, since 1991; *b* 18 May 1941; *s* of Richard Michael Craig and Barbara Mary Craig; *m* 1973, Daphne Joan Underwood; two *s.* *Educ:* Portchester Sch., Bournemouth. Joined RN as officer cadet, 1959; qualified as Naval helicopter pilot, 1963; operational flying and sea service (Far East), 1963–70; in comd HMS Monkton, 1970–72, naval air sqdns 705 and 826, 1973–76; Asst Sec. to Chiefs of Staff, 1978–80; in command: HMS Alacrity, 1980–82 (incl. Falklands War); HMS Avenger and Fourth Frigate Sqdn, 1986–87; RNAS Portland/HMS Osprey, 1987–89; HMS Drake, 1989–90; RN Forces Afloat, Gulf War, 1991. United States Bronze Star, 1991. *Recreations:* walking, reading, golf, horse-racing. *Address:* National Westminster Bank, 5 Old Christchurch Road, Bournemouth, Hants BH1 1DU.

CRAIG, Prof. David Parker, AO 1985; FRS 1968; FAA 1969; FRSC; University Fellow and Emeritus Professor, Australian National University, since 1985; *b* 23 Dec. 1919; *s* of Andrew Hunter Craig, Manchester and Sydney, and Mary Jane (*née* Parker); *m* 1948, Veronica, *d* of Cyril Bryden-Brown, Market Harborough and Sydney; three *s* one *d.* *Educ:* Sydney Church of England Grammar Sch.; University of Sydney; University Coll., London. MSc (Sydney) 1941, PhD (London) 1950, DSc (London) 1956. Commonwealth Science Scholar, 1940. War Service: Capt., Australian Imperial Force, 1941–44. Lectr in Chemistry, University of Sydney, 1944–46; Turner and Newall Research Fellow, 1946–49, and Lectr in Chemistry, University Coll., London, 1949–52; Prof. of Physical Chemistry, Univ. of Sydney, 1952–56; Prof. of Chemistry, University Coll., London, 1956–67; Prof. of Chemistry, 1967–85, Dean, Research Sch. of Chemistry, 1970–73 and 1977–81, ANU. Vis. Prof., UCL, 1968–; Firth Vis. Prof., Univ. of Sheffield, 1973; Vis. Prof., University Coll., Cardiff, 1975–89. Part-time Mem., CSIRO Exec., 1980–85. Chm., Adv. Cttee, Aust. Nat. Botanic Gdns, 1986–89. Pres., Australian Acad. of Sci., 1990–. Fellow of University Coll., London, 1964–. Hon. FRSC 1987. Hon. Dr Chem Bologna, 1985; Hon. DSc Sydney, 1985. *Publications:* books and original papers on chemistry in scientific periodicals. *Address:* 199 Dryandra Street, O'Connor, ACT 2601, Australia. *Club:* Athenæum.

CRAIG, Douglas, OBE 1965; freelance opera producer, adjudicator and lecturer; *b* 26 May 1916; *m* 1955, Dorothy Dixon; two *d.* *Educ:* Latymer Upper Sch.; St Catharine's Coll., Cambridge (MA). FRCM, FRSA. Winchester Prize, Cambridge, 1938. Intell. Corps, 1940–46, Major 1944. Baritone, Sadler's Wells Opera and elsewhere, 1946–; Artistic Dir, Opera for All, 1949–65; Stage Dir, Glyndebourne, 1952–55; Asst Gen. Man., Glyndebourne, 1955–59; Producer, Royal Coll. of Music, 1958–; Freelance Opera Producer, 1959–; Dep. Dir, London Opera Centre, 1965–66; Administrator, Welsh Nat. Opera, 1966–70; Dir, Sadler's Wells Theatre, 1970–78; Dir, Opera and Drama Sch., RCM, 1976–80. Master Teacher in Residence, Adelaide Coll. of the Arts, 1981; taught in Adelaide, Canberra, Melbourne, Sydney and Hong Kong, 1984 (specialist tour award from British Council); prodns for S Australia Coll. of Advanced Educn and for NSW State Conservatorium of Music, master classes and lectures, Australia, 1985; Nat. Adjudicator, Australian Singing Competition, 1985. Pres., Council of Friends of Sadler's Wells, 1987–; Vice Pres., Sussex Opera and Ballet Soc., 1974–. Mem. Exec. and Editor, Music Jl of ISM, 1979–84. *Publication:* (ed) Delius: Koanga (opera), 1975. *Recreation:* travel. *Address:* 43 Park Road, Radlett, Herts WD7 8EG. *T:* Radlett (0923) 857240. *Club:* Garrick.

CRAIG, Edward Anthony, (works also under name of Edward Carrick), FRSA; writer and lecturer, designer for film and theatre; independent film art director; *b* 3 Jan. 1905; *s* of late Edward Gordon Craig, CH; *m* 1960, Mary, *d* of late Lieut-Col H. A. Timewell, OBE. Studied art, the theatre and photography in Italy, 1917–26; has discovered numerous documents of great value to the history of the theatre; Art Dir to the Welsh Pearson Film Co., 1928–29; Art Dir for Associated Talking Pictures, 1932–36; Supervising Art Dir, Criterion Film, 1937–39; established AAT Film Sch., 1937; Art Dir to the Crown Film Unit (Ministry of Information), 1939–46; Executive Art Dir, Independent Producers (Rank), 1947–49; wood-engravings, oil paintings, and scene designs exhibited at: the St George's Gallery, 1927 and 1928; at the Redfern Gallery, 1929, 1931, 1938; The Grubb Group, 1928–38; also in the principal Galleries of Canada and North America; designer of scenes and costumes for numerous London productions and at Stratford-upon-Avon, 1949. *Official Purchasers:* the British Museum; Victoria and Albert Museum; Metropolitan Museum, New York; Yale Univ., USA; The University, Austin, Texas. *Publications:* Designing for Moving Pictures, 1941; Meet the Common People, 1942; Art and Design in British Films, 1948; Designing for Films, 1949; Gordon Craig, The Story of his Life, 1968, Polish trans., 1977, Amer. edn 1985; (in Italian) Fabrizio Carini Motta, 1972; William Nicolson's An Alphabet, 1978; Robinson Crusoe and Gordon Craig, 1979; William Nicolson's An Almanac, 1980; (ed) Gordon Craig: the last eight years, by Ellen Gordon Craig, 1983; Baroque Theatre Construction, 1982. *Illustrations:* The Georgics of Virgil, 1931, etc; books of verse by John Keats, Edith Sitwell, Edmund Blunden, W. H. Davies, etc. *Recreations:* books and music. *Address:* Southcourt Cottage, Long Crendon, Aylesbury, Bucks HP18 9AQ.

CRAIG, George Charles Graham; Principal Establishment Officer, Welsh Office, since 1986; *b* 8 May 1946; *s* of late George Craig and of E. S. Craig (*née* Milne); *m* 1968, (Ethne) Marian, *er d* of late H. H. A. Gallagher and of E. F. Gallagher; two *s* one *d.* *Educ:* Brockley County Grammar Sch.; Nottingham Univ. (BA). Asst Principal, Min. of Transport, 1967; Welsh Office: Private Sec. to Minister of State, 1970–72; Principal, 1972; PPS to Sec. of State for Wales, 1978–80; Asst Sec., 1980; Under Sec., 1986. Methodist Local Preacher. *Address:* Welsh Office, Cathays Park, Cardiff CF1 3NQ. *T:* Cardiff (0222) 825111.

CRAIG, Sir James; *see* Craig, Sir A. J. M.

CRAIG, Dr (James) Oscar (Max Clark), FRCS, FRCSI, FRCR; Consultant Radiologist since 1963, and Hon. Senior Clinical Lecturer, since 1987, St Mary's Hospital, London; President, Royal College of Radiologists, 1989–Sept. 1992; *b* 7 May 1927; *s* of James Oscar Max Clark Craig and Olivia Craig; *m* 1950, Louise Burleigh; four *d.* *Educ:* Royal College of Surgeons in Ireland. LRCP&SI 1950; FRCSI 1956; DMRD 1959; FRCR (FFR 1962); FRCS 1982; MRCP 1989. Asst GP, 1950–51; Ho. Surg., St Helier Hosp., Carshalton, 1951–52; Gen. practice, Sutton, 1952–54. Surg., RAF, 1954–56. Sen. Ho. Officer, Surgery, Hammersmith Hosp., 1956–57; Registrar and Sen. Registrar, Dept of Radiology, St Mary's Hosp., London, 1957–63; Lectr in Radiology, London Univ., 1963–87; Dir of Clinical Studies, 1969–75, Dir of Post Grad. Studies, 1979–81, St Mary's Hosp. Med. Sch. Hon. FFR RCSI 1985. *Publications:* numerous papers and chapters in books on clinical radiology, phlebography, lymangiography, gastro-intestinal radiology, medico-lectal medicine and the develt of digital radiology. *Recreation:* country-walking. *Address:* The White House, 18 Sandy Lane, Cheam, Surrey SM2 7NR. *T:* 081–642 2696. *Clubs:* Garrick, MCC.

CRAIG, John Egwin, OBE 1990; FCA 1961; Director, Standard Chartered PLC, since 1989; Chairman: Greyfriars Investment Co. PLC, since 1989; Jupiter European Investment Trust PLC, since 1990; *b* 16 Aug. 1932; *s* of late Thomas Joseph Alexander Craig, CIE, and Mabel Frances (*née* Quinnell); *m* 1959, Patricia Costa Lopes; three *s.* *Educ:* Charterhouse. Cooper Bros (later Coopers & Lybrands), 1958–61; Council of Stock Exchange, 1961–64; N. M. Rothschild & Sons, 1964–91, Dir, 1970–91; Man. Dir, N. M. Rothschild, 1981–89; Govt Dir, Internat. Fund for Ireland, 1989–. Mem. Exec. Council, BBA, 1981–89 (Chm., 1987–89). Mem. Council, LPO, 1983–87. FRSA 1988. *Address:* Saxonbury House, Frant, near Tunbridge Wells, Kent TN3 9HJ. *Club:* Brooks's.

CRAIG, John Frazer; Deputy Secretary (Head of Economic and Industrial Affairs), Welsh Office, since 1990; *b* 8 Nov. 1943; *s* of late John Frazer Craig and Margaret Jane Gibson Craig; *m* 1973, Janet Elizabeth. *Educ:* Robert Richardson Grammar Sch., Sunderland. Customs and Excise, 1961–69; Nat. Bd for Prices and Incomes, 1969–70; Welsh Office, 1970–: Private Sec. to Perm. Sec., 1972–74; Private Sec. to Sec. of State for Wales, 1980–82; Asst Sec., 1982–85, Under Sec. (Dir), 1985–87, Industry Dept; Under Sec. (Principal Finance Officer), Welsh Office, 1987–90. *Address:* c/o Welsh Office, Cathays Park, Cardiff CF1 3NQ. *T:* Cardiff (0222) 825111.

CRAIG, Rev. Maxwell Davidson; General Secretary, Action of Churches Together in Scotland, since 1990; Chaplain to The Queen in Scotland, since 1986; *b* 25 Dec. 1931; *s* of Dr William Craig and Alice M. Craig (*née* Semple); *m* 1957, Janet Margaret Macgregor; one *s* three *d.* *Educ:* Oriel Coll., Oxford (MA (Hons) Lit.Hum.); Edinburgh Univ. (BD);

Princeton Theol Seminary, NJ (ThM). 2nd Lieut, 1st Bn Argyll and Sutherland Highlanders, 1954–56. Ministry of Labour: Asst Principal, 1957–61; Pvte Sec. to Parly Sec., 1959–61. Fulbright Schol., Princeton, 1964; ordained minister, Grahamston Parish Church, Falkirk, 1966; Minister, Wellington Church, Glasgow, 1973–89; Minister, St Columba's Parish Church, Aberdeen, 1989–90. Convener of the Church and Nation Cttee, Church of Scotland, 1984–88. Chairman: Falkirk Children's Panel, 1970; Hillhead Housing Assoc., 1977–89. *Publication*: Stella: the story of Stella J. Reekie, 1984. *Recreations*: hill-walking, sailing, reading. *Address*: Scottish Churches' House, Dunblane, Perthshire FK15 0AJ. *T*: Dunblane (0786) 823588.

CRAIG, Norman; Assistant Under-Secretary of State, Ministry of Defence, 1972–79; *b* 15 May 1920; *s* of George Craig, OBE; *m* 1st, 1946, Judith Margaret Newling (marr. diss. 1957); one *s*; 2nd, 1960, Jane Hudson; two *s* one *d*. *Educ*: Penarth County Sch.; Cardiff Univ. Army Service, Royal Sussex Regt, 1940–47. Board of Trade, 1948; Min. of Supply (later Aviation), 1953; Private Sec. to Minister, 1959–60; Min. of Technology, 1964; Sec. to Cttee of Inquiry into Aircraft Industry, 1964–65; course at IDC, 1968; MoD, 1971. Lord Chancellor's Department: official, 1979–85; consultant, 1986–87; lay observer, 1990. *Publication*: The Broken Plume, 1982. *Address*: 51 Hayes Lane, Beckenham, Kent BR3 2RE. *T*: 081–650 7916.

CRAIG, Oscar; *see* Craig, J. O. M. C.

CRAIG, Very Rev. Prof. Robert, CBE 1981; Moderator of the General Assembly of the Church of Scotland, 1986–87; Minister, St Andrew's Scots Memorial Church, Jerusalem, 1980–85; Principal and Vice-Chancellor, 1969–80, Professor of Theology, 1963–80, University of Zimbabwe (formerly University of Rhodesia), now Emeritus; *b* 22 March 1917; *s* of late John Craig, stone-mason, and late Anne Peggie, linen-weaver; *m* 1950, Olga Wanda, *d* of late Michael and of Helena Strzelec; one *s* one *d*. *Educ*: Fife CC schs; St Andrews Univ.; Union Theol Seminary, NY. MA (Ordinary) 1938, BD with distinction in Systematic Theology 1941, PhD 1950, St Andrews; STM *magna cum laude* Union Theol Seminary 1948. Pres., Students' Rep. Council, Chm. Union Debating Soc., Berry Schol. in Theology, St Andrews Univ., 1941; Asst Minister, St John's Kirk, Perth, 1941–42, ordained 1942; Chaplain (4th class), Army, 1942–47: infantry bns, NW Europe, 1944–45 (despatches, Normandy,1944); Palestine, Egypt, 1945–47; HCF 1947. Hugh Black Fellow and Instructor in Systematic Theology, Union Theol Seminary, 1947–48; Dep. Leader, Iona Community, Scotland, 1948–50; Natal Univ.: Prof. of Divinity, 1950–57; College Dean, Adviser of Students and personal rep. of Principal and Vice-Chancellor, 1953–54; Prof. of Religion, Smith Coll., Mass, 1958–63; UC Rhodesia and Nyasaland: Prof. of Theology, 1963; Dean, Faculty of Arts, 1965; Vice-Principal, 1966; Actg Principal, 1967 and 1969. External Examiner: Boston, Cape Town, London, McGill, Natal, Rhodes, Surrey, Witwatersrand Univs, various times, 1950–90. Vis. Lectr, Ecumenical Inst., Bossey, Switz., 1955; John Dewey Mem. Lectr, Vermont Univ., 1961; Ainslie Meml Lectr, Rhodes Univ., 1965. Jerusalem appointments: Pres., Ecumenical Theol Res. Fraternity, 1983–85 (Mem. 1980–85); Member: Ecumenical Friends Gp, 1980–85; Council, Interfaith Cttee, 1981–85; Bd of Dirs, Internat. YMCA, 1982–85 (Vice-Chm., 1984, Chm., 1984–85); Exec. Cttee, Spafford Community Centre, 1982–85; Chm., Church of Scotland Israel Council, 1981–85; Jt Pres., Soc. of Friends of St Andrew's Church, Jerusalem, 1985–; Moderator, Presbytery of Jerusalem, 1982–84; Mem., Jerusalem Cttee, Jerusalem Foundn, 1989–. Brit. Council Commonwealth Interchange Fellow, Cambridge Univ., 1966. Hon. Chaplain: Kingdom and Angus Br., Normandy Veterans' Assoc., 1987–; Scottish Br., Palestine Police Assoc., 1988–. Hon. DD St Andrews, 1967; Hon. LLD: Witwatersrand 1979; Birmingham, 1980; Natal, 1981; Hon. DLitt Zimbabwe, 1981. Hon. Fellow, Zimbabwe Inst. of Engineers, 1976. Golden Jubilee Medal, Witwatersrand Univ., 1977; City of Jerusalem Medal, 1985. *Publications*: The Reasonableness of True Religion, 1954; Social Concern in the Thought of William Temple, 1963; Religion: Its Reality and Its Relevance, 1965; The Church: Unity in Integrity, 1966; Religion and Politics: a Christian view, 1972; On Belonging to a University, 1974; The Task of the Church in Today's World, 1989. *Recreations*: the cinema, theatre, contemporary and recent history, light classical music, listening and talking to people. *Address*: West Port, Falkland, Fife KY7 7BL. *T*: Falkland (0337) 57238. *Clubs*: Kate Kennedy, University Staff, Students' Union (St Andrews); YMCA, Rainbow (Jerusalem).

CRAIG, Thomas Rae, CBE 1969 (OBE 1945); TD; DL; retired; Deputy Governor, The Bank of Scotland, 1972–77; *b* 11 July 1906; *s* of Sir John Craig, CBE, and Jessie Craig (*née* Sommerville); *m* 1931, Christina Gay (*née* Moodie); three *s* one *d*. *Educ*: Glasgow Academy; Lycée Malherbe, Caen, Normandy. Served War of 1939–45: Lt-Col 6th Cameronians; AA and QMG 52nd (Lowland) Div. Dir of Colvilles Ltd, 1935; Man. Dir, 1958; Dep. Chm., 1961; Chm. and Man. Dir, 1965–68. Mem. Bd, BSC, 1967–72. Formerly Dir of companies. Mem., Convocation of Strathclyde Univ. DL Dunbartonshire, 1973. Hon. LLD: Strathclyde, 1968; Glasgow, 1970. OStJ. *Recreation*: farming. *Address*: Invergare, Rhu, Dunbartonshire. *T*: Rhu (0436) 820427. *Club*: Royal Scottish Automobile (Glasgow).

CRAIG, Rt. Hon. William, PC (N Ire.) 1963; solicitor and company director; *b* 2 Dec. 1924; *s* of late John Craig and Mary Kathleen Craig (*née* Lamont); *m* 1960, Doris Hilgendorff; two *s*. *Educ*: Dungannon Royal Sch.; Larne Grammar Sch.; Queen's Univ., Belfast. Served War of 1939–45, Royal Air Force, 1943–46. Qualified as solicitor, 1952. MP (U) Larne Div. of Antrim, NI Parliament, 1960–73; Mem. (Vanguard Unionist Progressive), N Antrim, NI Assembly, 1973–75; Mem. (UUC), E Belfast, NI Constitutional Convention, 1975–76; MP (UU) Belfast East, Feb. 1974–79. Chief Whip, Parliament of Northern Ireland, 1962–63; Minister of Home Affairs, 1963–64, and 1966–68; Minister of Health and Local Government, 1964; Minister of Development, 1965–66. Founder: Ulster Vanguard, 1972 (Leader, 1972–77); Vanguard Unionist Party, 1973 (Leader, 1973–77). Member: Council of Europe, 1976–79; WEU, 1976–79. *Recreations*: travel, motoring, shooting.

CRAIG-COOPER, Sir (Frederick Howard) Michael, Kt 1991; CBE 1982; TD 1968 (3 bars); DL; Director: Craig-Lloyd, since 1968; Carre Orban Partners, since 1989; management consultant, since 1984; *b* 28 Jan. 1936; *s* of late Frederick William Valentine Craig-Cooper and of Elizabeth Oliver-Thompson (*née* Macdonald) (she *m* 1978, Col J. H. Carroll-Leahy, MC); *m* 1968, Elizabeth Snagge, MVO; one *s*. *Educ*: Horris Hill; Stowe; College of Law. Solicitor, 1961. National Service, RA, 1954–56; TA, 1956–88; Comdr, Naval Gunfire Liaison Officer, 29 Commando Regt, RA, 1972–75; Mem., Greater London TAVRA (Chm., Employers Support Cttee, 1987–90). Jaques & Co., 1956–61; Allen & Overy, 1962–64; Inco, 1964–85; Dir, Paul Ray Internat., 1984 (merged with Carre Orban & Partners, 1989). Royal Borough of Kensington & Chelsea: Councillor, 1968–74; Chief Whip, 1971–74; Chm. Finance Cttee, 1972–74; Alderman, 1974–78; Mem. Investment Panel, 1973–. Contested (C) Houghton-le-Spring, 1966, 1970; Chairman: Chelsea Cons. Assoc., 1974–77 (Pres., 1983–); Cons. Nat. Property Adv. Cttee, 1986–. Trustee, Copper Develt Trust Fund, 1974–85; Mem. Council, Mining Assoc., 1977–82. Freeman, City of London, 1964; Liveryman, Drapers' Co., 1970– (Mem. Court of Assistants, 1987–). DL Greater London, 1986–; Rep. DL Kensington & Chelsea, 1987–. KStJ 1990 (Chm., Council for London, 1990–). Officer, SMO Malta, 1986. *Recreation*: admiring wife's gardening. *Address*: Carre Orban and Paul Ray International, 44 St James's Place, SW1A 1NS. *Clubs*: Pratt's, White's.

CRAIG-McFEELY, Comdt Elizabeth Sarah Ann, CB 1982; Director, Women's Royal Naval Service, 1979–82; *b* 28 April 1927; *d* of late Lt-Col Cecil Michael Craig McFeely, DSO, OBE, MC, and late Nancy Sarah (*née* Mann, later Roberts). *Educ*: St Rose's Convent, Stroud, Glos; Anstey College of Physical Educn, Birmingham. DipPhysEducn London. Taught PE at St Angela's Ursuline Convent Sch., 1948–52; joined WRNS, 1952; Third Officer, 1953; served in various Royal Naval, Royal Marines and Royal Naval Reserve Estabts, 1952–67; in charge, WRNS, Far Eastern Fleet, 1967–69; various appts, MoD (Navy), 1969–74; HMS Centurion, 1974–76; Supt WRNS, 1977. Naval member, NAAFI Bd of Management, 1977–79; Hon. ADC to the Queen, 1979–82; retired 1982. *Recreations*: gardening and country pursuits. *Address*: Moonrakers, Mockbeggar Lane, Biddenden, Kent TN27 8ES. *T*: Biddenden (0580) 291325.

CRAIGAVON, 3rd Viscount *cr* 1927, of Stormont, Co. Down; **Janric Fraser Craig;** Bt 1918; *b* 9 June 1944; *s* of 2nd Viscount Craigavon; *S* father, 1974. *Educ*: Eton; London Univ. (BA, BSc). FCA. *Heir*: none. *Address*: 17 Launceston Place, W8 5RL. *T*: 071–937 3898.

CRAIGEN, Desmond Seaward; Director: Prudential Corporation plc, 1982–89; Pioneer Concrete (Holdings) Ltd, 1982–89; *b* 31 July 1916; *s* of late John Craigen and Ann Amelia Craigen (*née* Brebner); *m* 1961, Elena Ines (*née* Oldham Florez); one *s* one *d*. *Educ*: Holloway Sch.; King's Coll., London (BA Hons). Prudential Assurance Co. Ltd, 1934–81; India, 1950–57; attached O&M Div., Treasury, 1957–58; Dep. General Manager, 1968–69; General Manager, 1969–78; Chief General Manager, 1979–81; Chm., Vanbrugh Life Assurance Co. Ltd, 1982–87. Served War of 1939–45: 53rd Reconnaisance Regt RAC (Major; despatches). *Recreations*: music, reading. *Address*: 44 Crondace Road, SW6 4BT.

CRAIGEN, James Mark, JP; Director and Secretary, Scottish Federation of Housing Associations, since 1988; freelance writer; *b* 2 Aug. 1938; *e s* of James Craigen, MA and Isabel Craigen; *m* 1971, Sheena Millar. *Educ*: Shawlands Academy, Glasgow; Strathclyde University. MLitt, Heriot-Watt, 1974. CBIM. Compositor, 1954–61. Industrial Relations Asst, Scottish Gas Bd, 1963–64; Head of Organisation and Social Services at Scottish TUC, 1964–68; Asst Sec., and Industrial Liaison Officer, Scottish Business Educn Council, 1968–74. Glasgow City Councillor, 1965–68, Magistrate, 1966–68. Member: Scottish Ambulance Service Bd, 1966–71; Race Relations Bd, Scottish Conciliation Cttee, 1967–70; Police Adv. Bd for Scotland, 1970–74. Contested Ayr constituency, 1970. MP (Lab and Co-op) Glasgow Maryhill, Feb. 1974–1987 (retired on grounds of experience, not age). PPS to Rt Hon. William Ross, MBE, MP, Sec. of State for Scotland, 1974–76; Opposition Spokesman on Scottish Affairs, 1983–85. Member: Select Cttee on Employment, 1979–83 (Chm., 1982–83); Select Cttee on Scottish Affairs, 1987; Chairman: Co-op. Party Parly Group, 1978–79; Scottish Group, Labour MPs, 1978–79; PLP Employment Gp, 1981–83. Mem., UK Delegn to Council of Europe Assembly, 1976–80. Mem., NUJ. Trustee, Industry and Parliament Trust, 1983–88 (Fellow, 1978–79). Mem., Bd of Trustees, Nat. Museums of Scotland, 1985–. Hon. Vice-Pres., Building Societies Assoc., 1985–88. Hon. Lectr, Strathclyde Univ., 1980–85. JP: Glasgow, 1966; Edinburgh, 1975. *Publications*: (contrib.) Forward! Labour Politics in Scotland 1888–1988, 1989; contribs to Co-operative News, The Scotsman, Glasgow Herald. *Address*: 38 Downie Grove, Edinburgh EH12 7AX.

CRAIGIE, Dr Hugh Brechin, CBE 1965; Principal Medical Officer, Mental Health Division, Scottish Home and Health Department, retired; *b* 19 May 1908; *s* of late Hugh Craigie; *m* 1st, 1933, Lillia Campbell (*d* 1958), *d* of Dr George Campbell Murray; two *s* (and one *s* decd); 2nd, 1962, Eileen (MBE 1950), *d* of F. S. Lyons. *Educ*: Manchester Grammar Sch.; Manchester Univ. House Physician, Manchester Royal Infirmary, 1931–32; Asst Medical Officer, Monsall Fever Hosp., Manchester, 1932–33; Senior Medical Officer, County Mental Hosp., Lancaster, 1933–46; Dep. Med. Supt, County Mental Hosp., Whittingham, 1946; HM Senior Medical Commissioner, General Board of Control for Scotland, 1947. Served War of 1939–45 (despatches), RAMC (Hon. Lieut-Col). *Publications*: various papers on psychiatry. *Address*: Saviskaill, Westerdunes Park, North Berwick EH39 5HJ.

CRAIGIE, John Hubert, OC 1967; FRS 1952; *b* 8 Dec. 1887; *s* of John Yorston Craigie and Elizabeth Mary Pollock; *m* 1926, Miriam Louise, *d* of Allen R. Morash and Clara Louise (*née* Smith). *Educ*: Harvard Univ. (AB); University of Minnesota (MSc); University of Manitoba (PhD). Dalhousie Univ., 1914. Served European War, 1914–18, Canadian Expeditionary Force, 1915–18; Indian Army, 1918–20. Canada Dept of Agriculture: Plant Pathologist, 1925–27; Senior Plant Pathologist, 1927–28; Officer-in-Charge (of Laboratory), Dominion Laboratory of Plant Pathology, Winnipeg, 1928–45; Associate Dir, Science Service, Canada Dept of Agriculture, Ottawa, 1945–52; retired 1952. Hon. DSc: University of British Columbia, 1946; University of Manitoba, 1959; Hon. LLD: University of Saskatchewan, 1948; Dalhousie Univ., 1951. *Publications*: papers in scientific journals. *Address*: 950 Bank Street, Ottawa, Ontario K1S 5G6, Canada.

CRAIGMYLE, 3rd Baron, *cr* 1929, of Craigmyle; **Thomas Donald Mackay Shaw;** Chairman: Craigmyle & Co. Ltd; Claridge Mills Ltd; *b* 17 Nov. 1923; *s* of 2nd Baron and Lady Margaret Cargill Mackay (*d* 1958), *e d* of 1st Earl of Inchcape; *S* father, 1944; *m* 1955, Anthea Esther Christine, *y d* of late E. C. Rich; three *s* three *d*. *Educ*: Eton; Trinity Coll., Oxford (MA). Served RNVR, 1943–46. FRSA. Kt Grand Cross of Obedience, SMO Malta, and Pres., British Assoc., 1989– (Hospitaller, 1962–73; Sec.-Gen., 1979–83; Vice-Pres., 1983–89). KStJ 1989. *Publication*: (ed with J. Gould) Your Death Warrant?, 1971. *Recreation*: home baking. *Heir*: *s* Hon. Thomas Columba Shaw [*b* 19 Oct. 1960; *m* 1987, Alice, second *d* of David Floyd; two *s*]. *Address*: 18 The Boltons, SW10 9SY; Scottas, Knoydart, Inverness-shire PH41 4PL. *Clubs*: Caledonian; Royal Thames Yacht; Bengal (Calcutta).

See also W. B. Dean.

CRAIGTON, Baron, *cr* 1959 (Life Peer); **Jack Nixon Browne,** PC 1961; CBE 1944; *b* 3 Sept. 1904; *m* 1950, Eileen Nolan, *d* of late Henry Whitford Nolan, London. *Educ*: Cheltenham Coll. Served War of 1939–45, RAF (Balloon Command), Actg Group Capt. Contested (C) Govan Div., Glasgow, in 1945; MP (C) Govan Div., 1950–55; MP (C) Craigton Div. of Glasgow, 1955–Sept. 1959; Parly Private Sec. to Sec. of State for Scotland, 1952–April 1955; Parly Under-Sec., Scottish Office, April 1955–Oct. 1959; Minister of State, Scottish Office, Nov. 1959–Oct. 1964. Westminster Chamber of Commerce: Mem., General Purposes Cttee, 1948; Mem., Exec. Cttee, 1950; Chm., 1954; Pres., 1966–83. Chm., United Biscuits (Holdings) Ltd, 1967–72. Pres., Commercial Travellers Benevolent Instn, 1976–. Vice-Pres., World Wildlife Fund (British Nat. Appeal), 1979; Chm., Fauna Preservation Soc., 1981–83 (Vice-Chm., 1970–80); Chairman: Council for Environmental Conservation, 1972–83; All-Party Conservation Group of both Houses of Parliament, 1972–; Fedn of Zoological Gardens, 1975–81; Mem., Jersey Wildlife Preservation Trust Council, 1970– (Internat. Trustee, 1972–).

RSA: Mem. Council, 1975–81; Mem., Environment Cttee, 1975–83. *Recreation:* gardening. *Address:* Friary House, Friary Island, Wraysbury, near Staines, Middlesex TW19 5JR. *T:* Wraysbury (0784) 482213. *Club:* Buck's.

CRAIK, Duncan Robert Steele, CB 1979; OBE 1971; Auditor-General for Australia, 1973–81; *b* 17 Feb. 1916; *s* of Henry Steele Craik and Lilian Kate Ellis; *m* 1943, Audrey Mavis Ion; four *d. Educ:* Univ. of Sydney (BEc). FASA 1973–87; FAIM 1975–86; FRAIPA 1983. Commonwealth Bank, 1933–40; Taxation Br., 1940–60; Treasury: Asst Sec., 1960–66; First Asst Sec., 1966–69; Dep. Sec., 1969–73. Part-time Mem., Admin. Appeals Tribunal, 1981–86. Mem. Council, ANU, 1981–83. *Recreations:* bowls, gardening. *Address:* 78 Grayson Street, Hackett, ACT 2602, Australia.

CRAIK, Roger George, QC (Scot.) 1981; Sheriff of Lothian and Borders, since 1984; *b* 22 Nov. 1940; *s* of George and Frances Craik; *m* 1964, Helen Sinclair Sutherland; one *s* one *d. Educ:* Lockerbie Academy; Breadalbane Academy, Aberfeldy; George Watson's Boys' Coll.; Edinburgh Univ. (MA 1960, LLB 1962). Qualified as solicitor, 1962; worked for Orr Dignam & Co., Solicitors, Pakistan, 1963–65; called to Scottish Bar, 1966. Standing junior counsel to Min. of Defence (Army), 1974–80; Advocate Depute, 1980–83. Mem., Sheriff Court Rules Council, 1990–. *Recreations:* Scottish antiquities, modern jazz. *Address:* Sheriff Court House, Lawnmarket, Edinburgh.

CRAM, Alastair Lorimer, MC 1945; Appellate Judge, Supreme Court of Appeal, Malawi, 1964–68, retired; in private practice at Scots Bar, Edinburgh; *b* 25 Aug. 1909; *m* 1951, Isobel Nicholson; no *c. Educ:* Perth Academy; Edinburgh University (LLB). Solicitor, 1933; private practice, 1935–39; admitted Scots Bar, 1946. Served in HM Army, 1939–48: POW, successful escapes; RA, SAS, Intelligence Corps, Counsel War Crimes Group NW Europe, Major; GSO 2. Resident Magistrate, Kenya, 1948; Actg Puisne Judge, 1953–56; Sen. Resident Magistrate, Kenya, 1956; Temp. Puisne Judge, 1958–60; Puisne Judge, High Court of Nyasaland, 1960; acting Chief Justice and (briefly) Governor-General, Malawi, 1965; Legal Dept, Scottish Office, 1971–74. Athlete, climber, and traveller: in Alps, 1930–60, and Himalayas, 1960 and 1963; in African, Asian and South American deserts, 1940–66; in Amazon basin and Peruvian Andes, 1966; in Atlas Mts, 1971; in Great Dividing Range, Australia, N-S traverse, 1981–84. *Publications:* Editor, Kenya Law Reports, 1952–56; contribs law reports, legal and mountaineering jls. *Recreations:* shooting, sound-recordings, photography (still and cine), orchid-collecting, languages. *Address:* 5 Upper Dean Terrace, Edinburgh. *T:* 031–332 5441. *Clubs:* Alpine; Scottish Mountaineering (Edinburgh).

CRAM, Prof. Donald James; University Professor Emeritus, University of California, Los Angeles, since 1990; *b* 22 April 1919; *s* of William Moffet and Joanna Shelley Cram; *m* 1969, Jane L. Maxwell. *Educ:* Rollins Coll., Fla (BS); Univ. of Nebraska (MS); Harvard Univ. (PhD). Chemist, Merck & Co., 1942–45; University of California, LA, 1947–90: Instr, ACS Fellow, 1947–48; Asst Prof., 1948–51; Associate Prof., 1951–56; Prof. of Chemistry, 1956; S. Winstein Prof. of Chemistry, 1985; Univ. Prof., 1988. Guggenheim Fellow, 1955. Centenary Lectr, London, 1976. Chemical Consultant: Upjohn Co., 1952–88; Union Carbide Corp., 1961–82; Eastman Kodak, 1982–; Technicon Co., 1984–; Istituto Guido Donegani, Milan, 1988–. MACS 1949; MRSC 1955; MNAS 1961; Mem., Amer. Acad. of Arts and Scis, 1967; Sigma Xi, Phi Beta Kappa (Hon.). Hon. Dr: Uppsala, 1977; Rollins, 1988; Hon. DSc, S California, 1983. Nobel Laureate, Chemistry, 1987. ACS Awards: Creative Work in Org. Chem., 1965; Arthur C. Cope, for Dist Achievement, 1974; Roger Adams, in Org. Chem., 1985; Willard Gibbs Medal 1985; Richard Tolman Medal 1985; Calif. Scientist of the Year, 1974. Fields of interest in org. chem.: molecular complexation, stereochemistry, carbanions, carbonium ions, organosulfur chemistry, paracyclophanes, mold metabolites. *Publications:* Organic Chemistry (jtly), 1959, 4th edn (jtly), 1980 (trans. into 12 langs); Carbanions, 1965; Elements of Organic Chemistry (jtly), 1967; Essence of Organic Chemistry (jtly), 1978; From Design to Discovery, 1990; numerous articles in ACS Jl, Jl Org. Chem., Chemical Communications, Angewandte Chemie, Tetrahedron. *Recreations:* surfing, ski-ing, tennis, guitar, reading. *Address:* 1250 Roscomare Road, Los Angeles, California 90077, USA. *Club:* San Onofre Surfing (California).

CRAMER, Hon. Sir John (Oscar), Kt 1964; FREI; QRV; MHR (L) for Bennelong, New South Wales, 1949–74; Managing Director, Cramer Brothers, real estate auctioneers; *b* Quirindi, NSW, 18 Feb. 1896; *s* of J. N. Cramer, Quirindi; *m* 1922, Mary, (Dame Mary Cramer, DBE) (*d* 1984), *d* of William M. Earls; two *s* two *d. Educ:* state public schs; business coll. Mayor of North Sydney, 1940–41; Member: Sydney County Council, 1935– (Chm., 1946–49); Statutory Cttee on Public Works, 1949–56 (Chm., 1955–56); Executive Building Industry Congress of New South Wales; Executive of Liberal Party of Australia, NSW Division (a founder of Provisional Exec.). Minister for the Army, 1956–63. Patron: Anzac Meml Club, N Sydney; RSL, N Ryde, NSW. *Recreation:* bowls. *Address:* Unit 2, 5 Morton Street, Wollstonecraft, NSW 2065, Australia. *T:* 957 2774. *Club:* Rotary.

CRAMOND, Ronald Duncan, CBE 1987; Chairman, Scottish Museums Council, since 1990; Member, Countryside Commission for Scotland, since 1988; *b* 22 March 1927; *s* of Adam and Margaret Cramond; *m* 1954, Constance MacGregor (*d* 1985); one *s* one *d. Educ:* George Heriot's Sch.; Edinburgh Univ. (MA). Sen. Medallist History 1949. FBIM; FSAScot 1978. Commnd Royal Scots, 1950. Entered War Office, 1951; Private Sec. to Parly Under-Sec. of State, Scottish Office, 1956; Principal, Dept of Health for Scotland, 1957; Mactaggart Fellow (Applied Econs), Glasgow Univ., 1962; Haldane Medallist in Public Admin, 1964; Asst Sec., Scottish Develt Dept, 1966, Under Sec., 1973; Under Sec., Dept of Agric. and Fisheries for Scotland, 1977; Dep. Chm., Highlands and Islands Develt Bd, 1983–88. Dir, Cairngorm Chairlift Co., 1988–90. Member: Scottish Museums Adv. Bd, 1984–85; Scottish Tourist Board, 1985–88; Trustee: Nat. Museums of Scotland, 1985–; Scottish Civic Trust, 1988–; Vice-Pres., Architectural Heritage Soc. of Scotland, 1988–. *Publication:* Housing Policy in Scotland, 1966. *Recreations:* golf, hill walking, testing a plastic hip. *Address:* Scottish Museums Council, 20–22 Torphichen Street, Edinburgh EH3 8JB. *Club:* Scottish Arts (Edinburgh).

CRAMOND, Dr William Alexander, OBE 1960; FRSE; Professor of Clinical Psychiatry, Flinders University, South Australia, 1983–91; *b* 2 Oct. 1920; *er s* of William James Cramond, MBE and of May Battisby, Aberdeen; *m* 1949, Bertine J. C. Mackintosh, MB, ChB, FRANZCP, Dornoch; one *s* one *d. Educ:* Robert Gordon's Coll., Aberdeen; Aberdeen Univ. MB, ChB, MD, FRCPsych, FRANZCP, FRACP, DPM. Physician Supt, Woodilee Mental Hosp., Glasgow, 1955–61; Dir of Mental Health, S Australia, 1961–65; Prof. of Mental Health, Univ. of Adelaide, 1963–71; Principal Medical Officer in Mental Health, Scottish Home and Health Dept, 1971–72; Dean of Faculty of Medicine and Prof. of Mental Health, Univ. of Leicester, 1972–75; Principal and Vice-Chancellor, Stirling Univ., 1975–80; Dir of Mental Health Services, NSW, 1980–83; Clinical Dir, Cleland House, Glenside Hosp., SA, 1983–85. Hon. Prof., Clinical Psychiatry, Sydney, 1980–83. DUniv Stirling, 1984. *Publications:* papers on psychosomatic medicine and on care of dying in Brit. Jl Psychiat., Lancet, BMJ. *Recreations:* walking, reading, theatre. *Address:* 28 Tynte Street, North Adelaide, SA 5006, Australia. *Club:* Adelaide (Adelaide).

CRAMP, Prof. Rosemary Jean, CBE 1987; Visiting Fellow, All Souls College, Oxford, 1992; Professor of Archaeology, University of Durham, 1971–90, now Emeritus; *b* 6 May 1929; *er d* of Robert Kingston and Vera Cramp, Cranoe Grange, Leics. *Educ:* Market Harborough Grammar Sch.; St Anne's Coll., Oxford (MA, BLitt). Lectr, St Anne's Coll., Oxford, 1950–55; Lectr, Durham Univ., 1955, Sen. Lectr, 1966. Commissioner: Royal Commn on Ancient and Historical Monuments of Scotland, 1975–; Historic Bldgs and Monuments Commn, 1984–89 (Mem., Adv. Cttee (Archaeology), 1984–89). Mem., Adv. Bd for Redundant Churches. Trustee, British Museum, 1978–. Pres., Council for British Archaeology, 1989–. Pres., Cumberland and Westmorland Antiquarian and Archaeol Soc., 1984–87. Gen. Editor, Corpus of Anglo-Saxon Stone Sculpture, 1974–. *Publications:* Corpus of Anglo-Saxon Stone Sculpture, vol. I, Durham and Northumberland, 1984, vol. 2, (with R. N. Bailey) Cumberland and Westmorland, 1986; contribs in the field of Early Monasticism, Early Medieval Sculpture and Northern Archaeology. *Address:* 5 Leazes Place, Durham DH1 1RE.

CRAMPTON, (Arthur Edward) Seán, MC 1943; GM(mil.) 1944; TD 1946; FRBS 1965 (ARBS 1952); sculptor; *b* 15 March 1918; *e s* of late Joshua Crampton, architect, and Ethel Mary (*née* Dyas); *m* 3rd, 1959, Patricia, *e d* of L. J. Cardew Wood; one *s* one *d*; three *d* by former marriages. *Educ:* St Joseph de Cluny, Stafford; Vittoria Jun. Sch. of Art, Birmingham; Birmingham Central Coll. of Art; London; Paris. Served TA, London Irish Rifles, Western Desert, Sicily, Italy, 1938–46. Prof. de Sculpture, Anglo-French Art Centre, 1946–50; served on juries for Thomas More and Winston Churchill meml statues. Member, Art Workers Guild, 1971 (Master, 1978); Pres., RBS, 1966–71. Mem., Accademia Italia, 1981. Governor: Camberwell Sch. of Arts and Crafts, 1970–88 (Chm., 1983–88); London Inst., 1986–88. FRSA 1973. *Exhibitions: general:* RA and RI Galls, 1950–; *one-man:* fourteen exhibns in London, 1948–82. *Major heroic size works:* Persephone, Crowmallie, Aberdeen; Horseman (RBS Silver Medal, 1965); Simon de Montfort, County Hall, Leics; Three Judges, Churchill Coll., Cambridge; Three Kings, Knochallachie, Aberdeen; Stability, Burgess Hill; Cascade, Duke of Westminster, Eaton, Chester; Two Geese, Goose Green, Altrincham (Civic Trust Award, 1984); Bird Flight, St John's Coll., Cambridge; *works in churches:* St Mary and Child, Midhurst; Our Lady, St Michael and Crucifix, Wolverhampton; Crucifix, Church of Child Jesus, Birmingham; Risen Christ and sanctuary furniture, St Vincent's Convent, Mill Hill; Our Lady and Child, Convent of Sisters of Mercy, Brentwood; Crucifix, St Cedd's, Goodmayes; Our Lady, St Mary's Coll., Wallasey; Cross Motif, St Thomas More, Manor House; Risen Christ, St Albans, Derby; Stations of the Cross, St Edmunds, Calne (RBS Medal, 1986), etc. *Publication:* Humans, Beasts, Birds (with Hicks and Anderson), 1981. *Recreations:* gardening, painting, cooking. *Address:* Rookery Farmhouse, Calne, Wilts SN11 0LH. *T:* Calne (0249) 814068. *Clubs:* Athenæum, Chelsea Arts.

CRAMPTON, Peter Duncan; Member (Lab) Humberside, European Parliament, since 1989; *b* 10 June 1932; *s* of Edmund Crampton and Louisa Crampton (*née* Thurman); *m* 1955, Councillor Margaret Eva McMillan; two *s. Educ:* Blackpool Grammar School; Nottingham Univ. (BA Hons Geography); Birmingham Univ. (MA African Studies); Hull Univ. (Dip. W European Studies); London Univ. (PGCE). Casual work, mainly as farm worker, 1954–55; Statistician, Plessey Co., 1955–56; Geography Teacher, Coventry, 1957–61; Educn Officer, Uganda, 1961–64; Lectr i/c Geography, Technical Coll., Birmingham, 1964–70; Lectr in Geography, Hull Coll. of Educn, then Humberside Coll. of HE, 1970–85; part-time work as lectr, writer, parly assistant, 1985–89. Chairman: European Nuclear Disarmament Campaign, 1984–86; Internat. Cttee, CND, 1988–. First Vice-Pres., Political Affairs Cttee, European Parlt, 1989–. *Publications:* (contrib.) Voices for One World, 1988; articles in jls on population geography in Africa, electoral behaviour and nuclear disarmament. *Recreations:* travel, hill walking, music. *Address:* 135 Westbourne Avenue, Hull. *T:* Hull (0482) 449337.

CRAMPTON SMITH, Alex; *see* Smith, Alexander C.

CRAN, James Douglas; MP (C) Beverley, since 1987; *b* 28 Jan. 1944; *s* of James Cran and Jane McDonald Cran, Aberdeenshire; *m* 1973, Penelope Barbara Wilson; one *d. Educ:* King's Coll., Univ. of Aberdeen (MA Hons). Researcher, Cons. Res. Dept, 1970–71; Sec., 1971–73, Chief Exec., 1973–79, Nat. Assoc. of Pension Funds; Northern Dir, 1979–84, West Midlands Dir, 1984–87, CBI. Mem., Select Cttee on Trade and Industry, 1987–. Mem. Court, Univ. of Hull, 1987–. *Recreations:* travelling; reading biographies, autobiographies and history. *Address:* House of Commons, SW1A 0AA. *T:* 071–219 3000.

CRAN, Mark Dyson Gordon; QC 1988; *b* 18 May 1948; *s* of William Broadbent Gordon Cran and Diana Rosemary Cran (*née* Mallinson); *m* 1983, Prudence Elizabeth Binning (marr. diss.). *Educ:* Gordonstoun; Millfield; Bristol Univ. (LLB). Called to the Bar, Gray's Inn, 1973. *Recreations:* country sports, convivial disputation, natural history, travel, English language and theatre. *Address:* Brick Court Chambers, 15/19 Devereux Court, WC2R 3JJ. *T:* 071–583 0777.

CRANBORNE, Viscount; Robert Michael James Cecil; DL; *b* 30 Sept. 1946; *s* and *heir* of 6th Marquess of Salisbury, *qv*; *m* 1970, Hannah Ann, *er d* of Lt-Col William Joseph Stirling of Keir; two *s* three *d. Educ:* Eton; Oxford. MP (C) Dorset South, 1979–87. DL Dorset, 1987. *Heir: s* Hon. Robert Edward William Cecil, *b* 18 Dec. 1970. *Address:* Manor House, Cranborne, Dorset.

CRANBROOK, 5th Earl of, *cr* 1892; **Gathorne Gathorne-Hardy;** Viscount Cranbrook, 1878; Baron Medway, 1892; DL; Chairman, English Nature, since 1990; *b* 20 June 1933; *er s* of 4th Earl of Cranbrook, CBE, and of the Dowager Countess of Cranbrook (Fidelity, OBE 1972, *o d* of late Hugh E. Seebohm); *S* father, 1978; *m* 1967, Caroline, *o d* of Col Ralph G. E. Jarvis, Doddington Hall, Lincoln; two *s* one *d. Educ:* Eton; Corpus Christi Coll., Cambridge (MA); University of Birmingham (PhD). Asst, Sarawak Museum, 1956–58; Fellow, Yayasan Siswa Lokantara (Indonesia), 1960–61; Sen. Lectr in Zoology, Univ. of Malaya, 1961–70. Editor of Ibis, 1973–80. Non-exec. Dir, Anglian Water, 1987–. Member: Royal Commn on Environmental Pollution, 1981–; NERC, 1982–88; Broads Authy, 1988–; Harwich Haven Authy, 1989–; Environment Sub-cttee, H of L Select Cttee on European Communities, 1979–85, 1987–90 (Chm., 1980–83 and 1987–90); Suffolk Coastal DC, 1974–83; Pres., Suffolk Trust for Nature Conservation, 1979–. Skinner and Freeman of the City of London. DL Suffolk, 1984. FLS; FZS; FRGS; FIBiol; MBOU. DSc Aberdeen. OStJ. *Publications:* Mammals of Borneo, 1965, 2nd edn 1977; Mammals of Malaya, 1969, 2nd edn 1978; (with D. R. Wells) Birds of the Malay Peninsula, 1976; Riches of the Wild: mammals of South East Asia, 1987; (ed) Key Environments: Malaysia, 1988. *Heir: s* Lord Medway, *qv. Address:* c/o National Westminster Bank, St James's Square, SW1Y 4JX.

CRANE, Prof. (Francis) Roger; Professor of Law, Queen Mary College, University of London, 1965–78, now Emeritus; *b* 19 Dec. 1910; *m* 1938, Jean Berenice Hadfield (*d* 1986); two *s* one *d. Educ:* Highgate Sch.; University Coll., London. LLB 1933; Solicitor, 1934, Clifford's Inn Prize. Lecturer in Law; King's Coll. and private practice, 1935–38; Lecturer in Law, University of Manchester, 1938–46; Prof. of Law, University of Nottingham, 1946–52; Prof. of English Law, King's Coll., London, 1952–65; Dean of the

Faculty of Law, QMC, London, 1965–76. University of London: Mem. Senate, 1969–71, 1973–78; Chm. Academic Council, 1975–78; Mem. Court, 1975–78. Visiting Professor: Tulane Univ., 1960; University of Khartoum, 1963; Dean of the Faculty of Law and Visiting Prof., University of Canterbury (New Zealand), 1964; Vis. Professor: Univ. of Melbourne, 1972; Monash Univ., 1972; Univ. of Sydney, 1980. Served War of 1939–45: Royal Corps of Signals, Major, 1944. Pres., Soc. of Public Teachers of Law, 1975–76. FKC 1976; Fellow QMC 1980. *Publications:* (jointly) A Century of Family Law, 1957; articles and notes in legal periodicals. *Address:* 25 Winston Drive, Isham, Kettering, Northants NN14 1HS. *T:* Burton Latimer (0536) 723938.

See also P. F. Crane.

CRANE, Geoffrey David; Head of Freight Directorate, Department of Transport, 1989–90; *b* 13 Oct. 1934; *s* of late Frederick David Crane and Marion Doris Crane; *m* 1962, Gillian Margaret, *d* of late Harry Thomas Austin; one *d*. *Educ:* City of London Sch. (John Carpenter Schol.); Trinity Hall, Cambridge (Schol., MA). Served RAF, 1956–58, Flying Officer. Assistant Principal, Min. of Works, 1958; Asst Private Sec. to Minister of Works, 1961–62; Principal, 1962; Secretary, Historic Buildings Council for Scotland and Ancient Monuments Bd for Scotland, 1962–66; Private Sec. to Minister of Public Building and Works, 1968–69; Asst Sec., Machinery of Govt Div., CSD, 1970–72; Dep. Dir, Central Unit on Environmental Pollution, DoE, 1972–76; Personnel Management and Trng, 1976–78, Under Sec. and Dir of Res. Ops, 1978–80, Dir, Personnel Management and Trng, 1981–85, Regl Dir, Eastern Region, 1985–89, DoE and Dept of Transport. *Recreations:* music, industrial archaeology, mathematics. *Address:* 6 The Paddock, Datchet, Berks SL3 9DL. *Clubs:* Royal Air Force, Civil Service.

CRANE, Sir James (William Donald), Kt 1980; CBE 1977; HM Chief Inspector of Constabulary, 1979–82; *b* 1 Jan. 1921; *s* of late William James Crane and Ivy Winifred Crane; *m* 1942, Patricia Elizabeth Hodge; one *s* one *d*. *Educ:* Hampshire schs. Served RE, RA, Royal Hampshire Regt, 1939–46. Joined Metrop. Police, 1946; Comdr and Dep. Asst Comr, Fraud Squad and Commercial Br., 1970–76; Inspector of Constabulary, 1976–79. Member: Parole Bd, 1983–85; Fraud Trials Cttee, 1984–85. Mem. Council, Univ. of Wales Coll. of Cardiff, 1988–. *Recreations:* gardening, walking, reading. *Address:* Home Office, 50 Queen Anne's Gate, SW1H 9AT. *Club:* Commonwealth Trust.

CRANE, Peter Francis; His Honour Judge Crane; a Circuit Judge, since 1987; *b* 14 Jan. 1940; *s* of Prof. Francis Roger Crane, *qv*, and late Jean Berenice Crane (*née* Hadfield); *m* 1967, Elizabeth Mary Pittman; four *d*. *Educ:* Nottingham High Sch.; Highgate Sch.; Gonville and Caius Coll., Cambridge (MA, LLM); Tulane Univ., New Orleans (LLM). Called to the Bar, Gray's Inn, 1964 (Barstow Scholar, 1963); in practice on Midland and Oxford Circuit, 1965–87; Recorder, 1982–87. Mem., Senate of Inns of Court and the Bar, 1983–86 (Member: Professional Conduct Cttee, 1984–86; Bar Cttee, 1985–86). Chairman: Kettering Constituency Liberal Assoc., 1981–84; Pytchley Parish Council, 1985–86. *Publication:* (co-ed) Phipson on Evidence, 14th edn, 1990. *Recreations:* walking, gardening, reading, wine. *Address:* The Glebe House, Pytchley, Northants NN14 1EW. *T:* Kettering (0536) 790322. *Club:* Northampton and County (Northampton).

CRANE, Roger; *see* Crane, F. R.

CRANFIELD, Rev. Prof. Charles Ernest Burland, FBA 1982; Emeritus Professor of Theology, University of Durham, since 1980; *b* 13 Sept. 1915; *s* of Charles Ernest Cranfield and Beatrice Mary Cranfield (*née* Tubbs); *m* 1953, Ruth Elizabeth Gertrude, *d* of Rev. T. Bole; two *d*. *Educ:* Mill Hill Sch.; Jesus Coll., Cambridge; Wesley House, Cambridge. MA Cantab. Research in Basel, cut short before it properly began by outbreak of war. Probationer in Methodist Church, 1939; ordained 1941; Minister, Shoeburyness; Chaplain to the Forces, 1942–46; from end of hostilities worked with German prisoners-of-war and was first staff chaplain to POW Directorate, War Office; Minister, Cleethorpes, 1946–50; admitted to Presbyterian Church of England (now United Reformed Church) as a minister, 1954. Lecturer in Theology, Durham Univ., 1950–62; Sen. Lectr, 1962–66; Reader, 1966–78; Prof. of Theology (personal), 1978–80. Joint general editor, new series of International Critical Commentary, 1966–. Hon. DD Aberdeen, 1980. Burkitt Medal for Biblical Studies, 1989. *Publications:* The First Epistle of Peter, 1950, 4th imp. 1958; The Gospel according to Saint Mark, 1959, supplemented and somewhat revised over the years, 10th imp. 1989; I and II Peter and Jude, 1960; A Ransom for Many, 1963; The Service of God, 1965; A Commentary on Romans 12–13, 1965; A Critical and Exegetical Commentary on the Epistle to the Romans, vol. 1 1975, 6th (corrected) imp. 1987, vol. 2 1979, 5th (corrected) imp. 1989; Romans: a shorter commentary, 1985, 3rd imp. 1987; If God Be For Us: a collection of sermons, 1985; The Bible and Christian Life: a collection of essays, 1985; contribs to composite works and to various theological periodicals. *Address:* 30 Western Hill, Durham City DH1 4RL. *T:* Durham (091) 3843096.

CRANLEY, Viscount; Rupert Charles William Bullard Onslow; *b* 16 June 1967; *s* and *heir* of 7th Earl of Onslow, *qv*. *Educ:* Eton; Western Kentucky Univ., USA. *Recreations:* photography, riding, shooting.

CRANMER, Philip; Secretary, Associated Board of the Royal Schools of Music, 1974–83; *b* 1 April 1918; *s* of Arthur Cranmer and Lilian Phillips; *m* 1939, Ruth Loasby; one *s* three *d*. *Educ:* Wellington; Christ Church, Oxford (BMus, MA). Asst Music Master, Wellington Coll. 1938–40; served RA, 1940–46; Major, Education Officer, Guards Div., 1946; Dir of Music, King Edward's Sch., Birmingham, 1946; Staff Accompanist, Midland Region, BBC, 1948; Lectr in Music, Birmingham Univ., 1950; Hamilton Harty Prof. of Music, Queen's Univ., Belfast, 1954–70; Prof. of Music, Univ. of Manchester, 1970–74. Pres., Incorporated Soc. of Musicians, 1971; Chm., Musicians' Benevolent Fund, 1980–87. FRCO 1947; Hon. RAM 1967; FRNCM 1974; FRCM 1976. Hon. DMus QUB, 1985. Chevalier de l'Ordre de Léopold II, 1947; Croix de Guerre Belge, 1947. *Publications:* The Technique of Accompaniment, 1970; Sight-reading for Young Pianists, 1979; How to Follow a Score, 1982; Two Sonatinas for piano duet, 1981 and 1985. *Address:* Quince Cottage, Underhill Lane, Clayton, Hassocks, W Sussex BN6 9PJ.

CRANSTON, Prof. Maurice (William); Professor of Political Science at the London School of Economics, 1969–85 (seconded as Professor of Political Science, European University Institute, 1978–81); *b* 8 May 1920; *o c* of William Cranston and Catherine Harris; *m* 1958, Baroness Maximiliana von und zu Fraunberg; two *s*. *Educ:* London Univ.; St Catherine's, Oxford (MA, BLitt; Hon. Fellow, 1984). London Civil Defence during war, 1939–45. Lecturer (part-time) in Social Philosophy, London Univ., 1950–59; Reader (previously Lecturer) in Political Science at London Sch. of Economics, 1959–69. Visiting Prof. of Government: Harvard Univ., 1965–66; Dartmouth Coll., USA, 1970–71; Univ. of British Columbia, 1973–74; Univ. of California, 1976; Ecole des Hautes Etudes, Paris, 1977; Woodrow Wilson Center, Washington, 1982; Fondation Thiers, Paris, 1983; Univ. of California, 1986–91; Carlyle Lectr, Oxford Univ., 1984. Pres., Institut International de Philosophie Politique, 1976–79; Vice-Pres. de l'Alliance Française en Angleterre, 1964–. Literary Adviser to Methuen Ltd, 1959–69. FRSL. Foreign Hon. Mem., Amer. Acad. of Arts and Sciences, 1970–. Commandeur de l'Ordre des Palmes Académiques (France), 1986. *Publications:* Freedom, 1953; Human Rights Today, 1954 (revised edn 1962); John Locke: a biography, 1957 (James Tait Black Memorial Prize); Jean-Paul Sartre, 1962; What Are Human Rights? (New York), 1963, 2nd rev. edn (London), 1973; Western Political Philosophers (ed), 1964; A Glossary of Political Terms, 1966; Rousseau's Social Contract, 1967; Political Dialogues, 1968; La Quintessence de Sartre (Montreal), 1969; Language and Philosophy (Toronto), 1969; The New Left (ed), 1970; (ed with R. S. Peters) Hobbes and Rousseau, 1972; The Mask of Politics, 1973; (ed with P. Mair) Idéologie et Politique, 1980; Langage et Politique, 1981; (ed with Lea Boralevi) Culture et Politique, 1982; Jean-Jacques: the early life and work of Jean-Jacques Rousseau 1712–1754, 1983; Rousseau's Discourse on Inequality, 1984; Philosophers and Pamphleteers, 1986; The Noble Savage: Jean-Jacques Rousseau 1754–1762, 1991. *Recreation:* walking. *Address:* 1A Kent Terrace, Regent's Park, NW1 4RP. *T:* 071–262 2698. *Club:* Garrick.

CRANSTON, Prof. William Ian; Professor of Medicine, United Medical and Dental Schools of Guy's and St Thomas' Hospitals (formerly St Thomas's Hospital Medical School), since 1964; *b* 11 Sept. 1928; *s* of Thomas and Margaret Cranston; *m* Pamela Isabel Pearson; four *s*. *Educ:* High Sch. for Boys, Glasgow; Aberdeen Grammar Sch.; Boys' High Sch., Oswestry; University of Aberdeen, FRCP London 1965 (MRCP 1952); MB, ChB (Hons), 1949; MD Aberdeen 1957; MA Oxon. 1962. Royal Infirmary, Aberdeen: House Physician, 1949–50; Medical Registrar, 1952–53; Asst in Medical Unit, St Mary's Hospital, Paddington, 1953–56; 1st Asst in Dept of Regius Prof. of Med., Radcliffe Inf., Oxford, 1961–64. Mem., Med. Res. Soc. *Recreations:* reading, gardening, painting. *Address:* United Medical and Dental Schools, St Thomas' Hospital, Albert Embankment, SE1 7EH.

CRANWORTH, 3rd Baron, *cr* 1899; **Philip Bertram Gurdon;** Lieutenant, Royal Wiltshire Yeomanry; *b* 24 May 1940; *s* of Hon. Robin Gurdon (killed in action, 1942) and Hon. Yoskyl Pearson (she *m* 2nd, 1944, as his 2nd wife, Lieut-Col. Alistair Gibb, and 3rd, 1962, as his 2nd wife, 1st Baron McCorquodale of Newton, PC, KCVO; she *d* 1979), *d* of 2nd Viscount Cowdray; *S* grandfather, 1964; *m* 1968, Frances Henrietta Montagu Douglas Scott, *d* of late Lord William Scott and of Lady William Scott, Beechwood, Melrose; two *s* one *d*. *Educ:* Eton; Magdalene Coll., Cambridge. *Heir:* *s* Hon. Sacha William Robin Gurdon, *b* 12 Aug. 1970. *Address:* Grundisburgh Hall, Woodbridge, Suffolk IP13 6TW.

See also Marquess of Huntly.

CRASTON, Rev. Canon (Richard) Colin; Rector of St Paul with Emmanuel, Bolton, since 1986 (Vicar, 1954); Hon. Canon, Manchester Cathedral, since 1968; Area Dean of Bolton, since 1972; Chaplain to the Queen, since 1985; *b* 31 Dec. 1922; *s* of Albert Edward Craston and Ethel Craston; *m* 1948, Ruth Taggart; one *s* one *d*. *Educ:* Preston Grammar Sch.; Univ. of Bristol (BA Hons); Univ. of London (BD Hons); Tyndale Hall, Bristol. Served War, RN, 1941–46. Ordained 1951; Curate, St Nicholas, Durham, 1951–54. Chm., House of Clergy, Dio. of Manchester, 1982–; Member: Gen. Synod, 1970– (Mem., Standing Cttee, 1975–); Anglican Consultative Council, 1981– (Mem., Standing Cttee, 1981–, Vice-Chm., 1986–90; Chm., 1990–); Crown Appts Commn, 1982–. *Publications:* Biblical Headship and the Ordination of Women, 1986; (ed) Open to the Spirit—Essays on Renewal, 1987; (contrib.) Authority in the Anglican Communion, 1987; (jtly) Anglicanism and the Universal Church, 1990; contrib. Anvil, and Modern Churchman. *Recreation:* football and cricket spectating. *Address:* St Paul's Vicarage, 174 Chorley New Road, Bolton BL1 4PF. *T:* Bolton (0204) 42303. *Club:* Union Jack.

CRATHORNE, 2nd Baron *cr* 1959; **Charles James Dugdale;** Bt 1945; DL; consultant and lecturer in Fine Art; Marketing Director, Blakeney Hotels Ltd, since 1981; *b* 12 Sept. 1939; *s* of 1st Baron Crathorne, PC, TD, and Nancy, OBE (*d* 1969), *d* of Sir Charles Tennant, 1st Bt; *S* father, 1977; *m* 1970, Sylvia Mary, *yr d* of Brig. Arthur Herbert Montgomery, OBE, TD; one *s* two *d*. *Educ:* Eton College; Trinity Coll., Cambridge. MA Cantab (Fine Arts). Impressionist and Modern Painting Dept, Sotheby & Co., 1963–66; Assistant to the President, Parke-Bernet, New York, 1966–69; James Dugdale & Associates, London, Independent Fine Art Consultancy Service, 1969–77; James Crathorne & Associates, 1977–; Dir, Woodhouse Securities, 1989–. Member: Yorks Regl Cttee, NT, 1978–84 and 1988–; Council, RSA, 1982–88; Exec. Cttee, Georgian Gp, 1985– (Chm., 1990–); Cons. Adv. Gp on Arts and Heritage, 1988–; Design Panel, Sheffield Develt Corp., 1989–; President: Cleveland Assoc., NT, 1982–; Yarm Civic Soc., 1987–; Hambledon Dist, CPRE, 1988–; Cleveland Family History Soc., 1988–; Cleveland Sea Cadets, 1988–; Vice Pres., Cleveland Wildlife Trust, 1990–; Patron, Cleveland Community Foundn, 1990–. Member: Works of Art Sub-Cttee, H of L, 1983–; Editorial Bd, House Magazine, 1983–; Hon. Sec., All-Party Parly Arts and Heritage Gp, 1981–. Trustee: Captain Cook Trust, 1978–; Georgian Theatre Royal, Richmond, Yorks, 1970–; Christian Inheritance, 1989–; Patron, Attingham Trust for Study of the British Country House. Church Warden, All Saints, Crathorne, 1977–. Annual lecture tours to America, 1970–; lecture series, Metropolitan Mus., NY, 1981; Australian Bicentennial Lecture Tour, 1988. Mem. Ct, Univ. of Leeds, 1985–; Gov., Queen Margaret's Sch. York Ltd, 1986–. FRSA 1972. DL Cleveland, 1983. *Exhibition:* Photographs, Middlesbrough Art Gall., 1980. *Publications:* Edouard Vuillard, 1967; (co-author) Tennant's Stalk, 1973; (co-author) A Present from Crathorne, 1989; contribs to Apollo and The Connoisseur. *Recreations:* photography, travel, collecting, shooting, fishing, music. *Heir:* *s* Hon. Thomas Arthur John Dugdale, *b* 30 Sept. 1977. *Address:* Crathorne House, Yarm, Cleveland TS15 0AT. *T:* Stokesley (0642) 700431; 52 Lower Sloane Street, SW1W 8BS. *T:* 071–730 9131, (office) 071–730 5420; House of Lords, SW1.

CRAUFURD, Sir Robert (James), 9th Bt *cr* 1781; Member of the London Stock Exchange; *b* 18 March 1937; *s* of Sir James Gregan Craufurd, 8th Bt and of Ruth Marjorie, *d* of Frederic Corder; *S* father, 1970; *m* 1st, 1964, Catherine Penelope (marr. diss.), *yr d* of late Captain Horatio Westmacott, Torquay; three *d*; 2nd, 1987, Georgina Anne, *d* of late John D. Russell, Lymington. *Educ:* Harrow; University College, Oxford. Elected Member of the London Stock Exchange, 1969. Associated with Greig, Middleton & Co. *Address:* 7 Waldemar Avenue, SW6 5LB.

CRAVEN, family name of **Earl of Craven.**

CRAVEN, 9th Earl of, *cr* 1801; **Benjamin Robert Joseph Craven;** Baron Craven, 1665; Viscount Uffington, 1801; *b* 13 June 1989; *s* of 8th Earl and of Teresa Maria Bernadette Craven; *S* father, 1990. *Heir:* *cousin* Rupert José Evelyn Craven, Lt-Comdr RN [*b* 22 March 1926; *m* 1955, Margaret Campbell (*d* 1985), *d* of Alexander Smith, MBE].

CRAVEN, Archdeacon of; *see* Smith, Ven. B. A.

CRAVEN, John Anthony; Chairman, Morgan Grenfell Group PLC, since 1989 (Chief Executive, 1987–89); Member, Board of Managing Directors, Deutsche Bank AG, Frankfurt, since 1990; *b* 23 Oct. 1940; *s* of William Herbert Craven and Hilda Lucy Craven; *m* 1st, 1961, Gillian Margaret (*née* Murray); one *s* one *d*; 2nd, 1970, Jane Frances (*née* Stiles-Allen); three *s*. *Educ:* Michaelhouse, S Africa; Jesus Coll., Cambridge (BA Hons Law); Queen's Univ., Kingston, Ont. Clarkson Gordon & Co., Toronto, Chartered Accountants, 1961–64; Wood Gundy, Investment Bankers, 1964–67; S. G. Warburg & Co., 1967–73, Dir 1969–73; Gp Chief Exec., White Weld & Co. Ltd, 1973–78; Vice

Chm., S. G. Warburg & Co., 1979; Founder and Chm., Phoenix Securities Ltd, 1981–; Dir, Mercury Securities Ltd, 1979; non-exec. Chm., Tootal Group PLC, 1985–91. Mem., Conseil d'Administration, Société Générale de Surveillance, Switzerland, 1989–; Dir, SIB, 1990–. Member: Ontario Inst. of Chartered Accts; Canadian Inst. of Chartered Accountants. *Recreations:* hunting, shooting, skiing. *Address:* Morgan Grenfell Group, 23 Great Winchester Street, EC2P 2AX. *Clubs:* City; Links (New York).

CRAVEN, Air Marshal Sir Robert Edward, KBE 1970 (OBE 1954); CB 1966; DFC 1940; *b* 16 Jan. 1916; *s* of Gerald Craven, Port Elizabeth, S Africa, and Edith Craven, York; *m* 1940, Joan Peters (*d* 1991); one *s* one *d. Educ:* Scarborough Coll. MN, 1932–37; Pilot Officer, RAF, 1937; 201, 210, 228 Sqdns, 1937–41; RAF Staff Coll., 1942; Staff Appts: Coastal Command, 1942 (despatches thrice); Directing Staff, RAF Staff Coll., 1944; HQ, Mediterranean and Middle East, Cairo, 1945; CO Eastleigh, Kenya, 1946; RN Staff Coll., 1948; Directing Staff, Joint Services Staff Coll., 1949; Standing Group, NATO Washington, 1951; RAF St Eval, 1954; Directing Staff, RAF Staff Coll., 1957; Group Capt. 1957; CO RAF Lyneham, 1959; Director, Personal Services, RAF, 1961; Air Cdre 1961; Air Officer Admin., Transport Comd, 1964; Air Vice-Marshal, 1965; SASO, Flying Training Comd, 1967–68, Training Comd, 1968–69; Commander, Maritime Air Forces, 1969–72, retired. Order of Menelik (Ethiopia), 1955. *Recreations:* water fowl breeding, antique furniture restoration and reproduction. *Address:* Letcombe House, Letcombe Regis, Oxon OX12 9LD. *Club:* Royal Air Force.

CRAWFORD, 29th Earl of, *cr* 1398, **AND BALCARRES,** 12th Earl of, *cr* 1651; **Robert Alexander Lindsay,** PC 1972; Lord Lindsay of Crawford, before 1143; Lord Lindsay of Balcarres, 1633; Lord Balniel, 1651; Baron Wigan (UK), 1826; Baron Balniel (Life Peer), 1974; Premier Earl of Scotland; Head of House of Lindsay; DL; *b* 5 March 1927; *er s* of 28th Earl of Crawford and 11th of Balcarres, KT, GBE, and of Mary, 3rd *d* of late Lord Richard Cavendish, PC, CB, CMG; *S* father, 1975; *m* 1949, Ruth Beatrice, *d* of Leo Meyer-Bechtler, Zürich; two *s* two *d. Educ:* Eton; Trinity College, Cambridge. Served with Grenadier Guards, 1945–49. MP (C) Hertford, 1955–74, Welwyn and Hatfield, Feb.-Sept. 1974; Parliamentary Private Secretary: to Financial Secretary of Treasury, 1955–57; to Minister of Housing and Local Government, 1957–60; Opposition front-bench spokesman on health and social security, 1967–70; Minister of State for Defence, 1970–72; Minister of State for Foreign and Commonwealth Affairs, 1972–74. First Crown Estate Comr, 1980–85. Chm., Lombard North Central Bank, 1976–80; Director: Nat. Westminster Bank, 1975–88; Scottish American Investment Co., 1978–88; a Vice-Chm., Sun Alliance & London Insurance Gp, 1975–91. President, Rural District Councils Assoc., 1959–65; Chairman: National Association for Mental Health, 1963–70; Historic Buildings Council for Scotland, 1976–83; Royal Commn on Ancient and Historical Monuments of Scotland, 1985–; Bd of Trustees, Nat. Library of Scotland, 1990–. DL Fife. *Heir: s* Lord Balniel, *qv. Address:* Balcarres, Colinsburgh, Fife KY9 1HL.

CRAWFORD, Andrew Charles, PhD; FRS 1990; Reader in Sensory Physiology, Cambridge University, since 1987; Fellow of Trinity College, Cambridge, since 1974; *b* 12 Jan. 1949; *s* of Charles and Vera Crawford; *m* 1974, Catherine Jones; one *s* one *d. Educ:* King Edward VI Camp Hill Sch., Birmingham; Downing Coll., Cambridge (BA 1970); Emmanuel Coll., Cambridge (MA, PhD 1974). Cambridge University: Research Fellow, Emmanuel Coll., 1972; Univ. Demonstrator, 1974; Lectr, 1977. *Publications:* contribs on physiology of hearing, in learned jls. *Address:* Physiological Laboratory, Downing Street, Cambridge CB2 3EG. *T:* Cambridge (0223) 333879.

CRAWFORD, Douglas; *see* Crawford, G. D.

CRAWFORD, Prof. Sir Frederick (William), Kt 1986; FEng 1985; Vice-Chancellor, Aston University, since 1980; *b* 28 July 1931; *s* of William and Victoria Maud Crawford; *m* 1963, Béatrice Madeleine Jacqueline Hutter, LèsL, MA, PhD, Paris; one *s* one *d. Educ:* George Dixon Grammar Sch., Birmingham; Univ. of London (BSc Eng (1st cl. hons), MSc, DSc); Univ. of Liverpool (DipEd, PhD, DEng). Pres., Guild of Undergraduates, 1955–56; Mem. Court, 1955–62 and 1981–; Treas., NUS, 1957–59; Winner, NUS-Observer Fifth Nat. Student Debating Tourn., 1958. ACT Birmingham 1952; FIEE 1965; FIEEE 1972; FInstP 1964; FAPS 1965; FIMA 1978; CBIM 1986. Research Trainee, J. Lucas Ltd, 1948–52; Scientist, NCB Mining Res. Estabt, 1956–57; Sen. Lectr in Elec. Engrg, CAT Birmingham, 1958–59; Stanford University, California, 1959–82: Res. Associate, W. W. Hansen Labs of Physics, 1959–64; Institute for Plasma Research: Prof. (Research), 1964–67; Associate Prof., 1967–69; Prof., 1969–82; Consulting Prof., 1983–84; Chm., 1974–80; Dir, Centre for Interdisciplinary Res. and Associate Dean of Graduate Studies, 1973–77. Vis. Scientist, French Atomic Energy Commn, and Cons. to Comp. Française Thomson-Houston, 1961–62; Vis. Professor: Japan, 1969; Univ. of Paris, 1971; Australia, 1972; Mathematical Inst., Oxford Univ., also Vis. Fellow, St Catherine's Coll., Oxford, 1977–78. Union Radio-Scientifique Internationale: Member: US Nat. Cttee, 1975–81; UK Nat. Cttee, 1980–84; Commn H (Waves in Plasmas); US Chm., 1975–78; Internat. Chm., 1978–81; UK Rep., 1982–84; Chm. Internat. Sci. Cttee, Internat. Conf. on Phenomena in Ionised Gases, 1979–81; Dir, Sigma Xi, 1976–78; Mem. Council, Amer. Assoc. of Univ. Profs, 1980–82; Univ. Space Research Association: Member: Council, 1973–81 (Chm. 1977–78); Bd of Trustees, 1975–81 (Chm. 1976–77); Mem. numerous cttees on Space Shuttle, NASA, 1972–80. Vice-Chm., Parly and Scientific Cttee, 1989–. Mem., Council, IEE, 1985–88 and 1989–. Director: Aston Technical Management and Planning Services, 1980–; Birmingham Technology Ltd, 1982–; West Midlands Technology Transfer Centre, 1985–; Legal & General Gp plc, 1988–; Bowater plc, 1989–; PowerGen plc, 1990–. Member: US-UK Educnl Commn, 1981–84; Ct, Birmingham Univ., 1980–85; British-North American Cttee, 1987–; Franco-British Council, 1987–; Vice-Pres., Birmingham Civic Soc., 1990– (Chm., 1983–88). Vice-Pres., Birmingham Br. E-SU, 1980–. Patron, Midlands Centre, Royal TV Soc., 1980–. Freeman, City of London, 1986; Mem. Court of Assistants, Worshipful Co. of Engineers, 1989–. Hon. FIL, 1987. Mem. Editorial Board: Jl of Applied Phys. and Appl. Phys. Letters, 1976–78; Oxford Univ. Press Engrg Science Series, 1979–. *Publications:* numerous papers on plasma physics in sci. books and jls. *Address:* Vice-Chancellor's Office, Aston University, Birmingham B4 7ET. *T:* 021–359 3611. *Club:* Athenæum.

CRAWFORD, (George) Douglas; journalist, Glasgow Herald, since 1989; *b* 1 Nov. 1939; *s* of Robert and Helen Crawford; *m* 1964, Joan Burnie; one *s* one *d. Educ:* Glasgow Academy; St Catharine's Coll., Cambridge (MA). Features Editor, Business, 1961–63; Industrial Corresp., Glasgow Herald, 1963–66; Editor, Scotland Magazine, 1966–70; Dir, Polecon Gp of Cos, 1970–89. MP (SNP) Perth and East Perthshire, Oct. 1974–1979; contested (SNP) Perth and Kinross, 1983. *Recreations:* hill-walking, swimming, playing piano and clavichord, watching cricket. *Address:* 43b 1 William Street, Edinburgh EH3 7LW. *Clubs:* Savile; Scottish Arts (Edinburgh).

CRAWFORD, Hon. Sir George (Hunter), Kt 1972; Judge of the Supreme Court of Tasmania 1958–81; *b* 12 Dec. 1911; *s* of Frederick Charles Crawford and Ruby Priscilla (*née* Simpson); *m* 1st, 1936, Helen Zoë (*d* 1976), *d* of Dr Bruce Arnold Anderson; two *s* one *d*; 2nd, 1979, Nancy Jean Garrott (*née* Findlay). *Educ:* East Launceston State Sch.; Launceston Church Grammar Sch.; Univ. of Tasmania (LLB). Barrister and Solicitor, 1934–58; Mem. Cttee, Northern Law Society, 1946–58 (Vice-Pres. 1957–58). Served (including War): AMF, 1929–40; AIF, 1940–44, Lt-Col. Councillor, Northern Br., Royal Soc. of Tasmania, 1954–72 (Chm., 1957–58 and 1966–68); Mem. Cttee, Tasmanian Historical Res. Assoc., 1960–62 (Chm., 1961–62); Mem. Bd, Launceston Church Grammar Sch., 1946–71 (Chm., 1958–65); Mem. Bd, Cradle Mountain-Lake St Clair Nat. Park; Mem. Adv. Cttee, Cradle Mountain, 1956–71; Pres., N Tasmania Branch, Roy. Commonwealth Soc., 1974–76. Col Comdt, Royal Regt of Australian Artillery, in Tasmania Command, 1972–78. *Recreations:* music, historical research. *Address:* 1/39 David Street, Launceston, Tasmania 7250, Australia. *T:* Launceston 312271. *Club:* Launceston (Launceston).

CRAWFORD, Maj.-Gen. George Oswald, CB 1956; CBE 1944; Director of Ordnance Services, War Office, 1958–61; *b* 12 Nov. 1902; *s* of late Col Arthur Gosset Crawford, Nailsworth, Glos; *m* Sophie Cecilia (*d* 1974), *d* of J. C. Yorke, JP, Langton, Dwrbach, Pembs; two *s* one *d*; *m* 1974, Ella Brown. *Educ:* Bradfield; RMC. 2nd Lieut Glos Regt, 1922; transf. RAOC 1928. Served CMF, 1942–45; Lieut-Col 1942; Brig. 1943; Dep. Dir of Ordnance Services, Western Command, 1947–51; DDOS, Southern Command, 1951–55; ADC to the Queen, 1954–55; Maj.-Gen. 1955; Inspector, Royal Army Ordnance Corps, 1955–57; Commandant Mechanical Transport Organisation, Chilwell, 1957–58; Col Comdt RAOC, 1960–66. *Address:* Gwyers, Dinton, Wilts.

See also Wilson Stephens.

CRAWFORD, Iain; Director, Veterinary Field Service, Ministry of Agriculture, Fisheries and Food, since 1988; *b* 8 April 1938; *s* of James and Agnes Crawford, Baillieston,, Glasgow; *m* 1962, Janette Mary Allan; two *s* one *d. Educ:* Coatbridge High Sch., Lanarks; Glasgow Univ. (BVMS). MRCVS 1961. Entered private vet. practice, 1961; joined MAFF as a Vet. Officer, 1968; Dep. Regl Vet. Officer, Bristol, 1981; Vet. Head of Sect. (Regl Vet. Officer), 1983; Asst Chief Vet. Officer, 1986. *Recreations:* sailing, walking. *Address:* 14 Camilla Close, Great Bookham, Leatherhead, Surrey KT23 4BU.

CRAWFORD, Prof. James Richard, DPhil; Challis Professor of International Law, 1986–March 1992, and Dean, Faculty of Law, 1990–March 1992, University of Sydney; Whewell Professor of International Law, University of Cambridge, from April 1992; *b* 14 Nov. 1948; *s* of James Allen and Josephine Margaret Crawford; *m* 1971, Marisa Lurgina (marr. diss. 1991); two *d. Educ:* Adelaide Univ. (LLB Hons; BA 1971); Oxford Univ. (DPhil 1977). Called to the Bar, High Court of Australia, 1979. University of Adelaide: Lectr, 1974; Sen. Lectr, 1977; Reader, 1982; Prof. of Law, 1983. Comr, Australian Law Reform Commn, 1982–90. *Publications:* The Creation of States in International Law, 1979; Australian Courts of Law, 1982, 2nd edn 1988; (ed) The Rights of Peoples, 1988. *Recreations:* cricket, reading. *Address:* (until March 1992) c/o Law School, University of Sydney, 173 Phillip Street, NSW 2006, Australia; (from April 1992) c/o Faculty of Law, University of Cambridge, Cambridge CB2 1TU.

CRAWFORD, John Michael; Director of Education (formerly Chief Education Officer), Birmingham, 1977–88; *b* 6 Dec. 1938; *s* of James and Emily Crawford; *m* 1962, Geraldine Kay Weaver; two *d. Educ:* Ipswich Sch.; University Coll., London (BA); Fitzwilliam House, Cambridge. Asst Master, Merchant Taylor's, Crosby, 1961–63; Admin. Asst, E Suffolk CC, 1963–66; Sen. Admin. Asst, Lancs CC, 1966–68; Asst Educn Officer, W Riding CC, 1968–73; Dep. Educn Officer, Birmingham, 1973–77. *Address:* July Green, Snuff Mill Walk, Bewdley, Worcs. *T:* Bewdley (0299) 400174.

CRAWFORD, Lionel Vivian, FRS 1988; Principal Scientist, Imperial Cancer Research Fund; Tumour Virus Group, Department of Pathology, Cambridge University, since 1988; *b* 30 April 1932; *s* of John Mitchell Crawford and Fanny May Crawford (*née* Barnett); *m* 1957, Elizabeth Minnie (*née* Green); one *d. Educ:* Rendcomb College, Cirencester; Emmanuel College, Cambridge (BA, MA, PhD). Virus Lab., Berkeley, Calif., 1958–59; Calif. Inst. of Technology, 1959–60; Inst. of Virology, Glasgow, 1960–68; Molecular Virology Lab., Imperial Cancer Res. Fund, 1968–88. Member: Soc. for Gen. Microbiology; EMBO. FRSE 1970. *Publications:* numerous scientific articles. *Recreation:* restoring old houses.

CRAWFORD, Michael, OBE 1987; actor since 1955; *b* 19 Jan. 1942. *Educ:* St Michael's Coll., Bexley; Oakfield Sch., Dulwich. In orig. prodn of Britten's Noyes Fludde and of Let's Make an Opera; *stage appearances include:* Come Blow Your Horn, Prince of Wales, 1961; Travelling Light, 1965; The Anniversary, 1966; No Sex Please, We're British, Strand, 1971; Billy, Drury Lane, 1974; Same Time, Next Year, Prince of Wales, 1976; Flowers for Algernon, Queen's, 1979; Barnum, Palladium, 1981, 1983, Victoria Palace, 1985–86; The Phantom of the Opera, Her Majesty's, 1986, NY, 1988 (Tony Award, Best Actor in a Musical), Los Angeles, 1989. *Films include:* Soap Box Derby; Blow Your Own Trumpet; Two Left Feet; The War Lover; Two Living, One Dead; The Knack, 1964; A Funny Thing Happened on the Way to the Forum, 1965; The Jokers, How I Won the War, 1966; Hello Dolly, 1968; The Games, 1969; Hello and Goodbye, 1970; Alice in Wonderland, 1972; The Condorman, 1980. Numerous radio broadcasts and TV appearances; *TV series include:* Some Mothers Do 'Ave 'Em; Chalk and Cheese. *Address:* c/o Duncan Heath Associates Ltd, Paramount House, 162/170 Wardour Street, W1. *T:* 071–439 1471.

CRAWFORD, Prof. Michael Hewson, FBA 1980; Professor of Ancient History, University College London, since 1986; *b* 7 Dec. 1939; *s* of late Brian Hewson Crawford and Margarethe Bettina (*née* Nagel). *Educ:* St Paul's School; Oriel College, Oxford (BA, MA). Scholar, British School at Rome, 1962–64; Jane Eliza Procter Visiting Fellow, Princeton Univ., 1964–65; Cambridge University: Research Fellow, 1964–69, Fellow, 1969–86, Christ's Coll.; Lectr, 1969–86. Visiting Professor: Univ. of Pavia, 1983; Ecole Normale Supérieure, Paris, 1984; Univ. of Padua, 1986; Sorbonne, Paris, 1989; San Marino, 1989; Milan, 1990; L'Aquila, 1990; Paris, 1991. Joint Director: Excavations of Fregellae, 1980–86; Valpolcevera Project, 1987–. Chm., JACT Ancient History Cttee, 1978–84; Vice-Pres., Roman Soc., 1981–. Membro Straniero, Istituto Lombardo, 1990. Editor: Papers of the British Sch. at Rome, 1975–79; Jl of Roman Studies, 1980–84. *Publications:* Roman Republican Coin Hoards, 1969; Roman Republican Coinage, 1974; The Roman Republic, 1978; La Moneta in Grecia e a Roma, 1981; (with D. Whitehead) Archaic and Classical Greece, 1982; Sources for Ancient History, 1983; Coinage and Money under the Roman Republic, 1985; (with M. Beard) Rome in the Late Republic, 1985; L'impero romano e la struttura economica e sociale delle province, 1986; (with A. M. Burnett) The Coinage of the Roman World in the Late Republic, 1987; (with C. Ligota and B. B. Trapp) Medals and Coins from Bude to Mommsen, 1990; contribs to Annales, Economic History Rev., Jl of Roman Studies, etc. *Address:* University College, Gower Street, WC1E 6BT.

CRAWFORD, Peter John, QC 1976; **His Honour Judge Peter Crawford;** a Circuit Judge, since 1988; *b* 23 June 1930; *s* of William Gordon Robertson and Doris Victoria Robertson (*née* Mann, subseq. Crawford); *m* 1st, 1955, Jocelyn Lavender; two *s* two *d*; 2nd, 1979, Ann Allen Travis. *Educ:* Berkhamsted Sch.; Brasenose Coll., Oxford (MA). Called to Bar, Lincoln's Inn, 1953; Bencher, 1984; a Recorder, 1974–88. Pres., Trent Region, Mental Health Review Tribunal, 1986–; Vice Chm., Appeal Cttee, ICA,

1987–88; Mem., Council of Justice, 1986–88. Mem., Paddington Borough Council, 1962–65; Chm., W London Family Service Unit, 1972–79; Mem., Family Service Units Nat. Council, 1975–81. *Recreation:* sailing. *Address:* The Law Courts, St Aldates, Oxford OX1 1TL. *Club:* Garrick.

CRAWFORD, Robert Gammie, CBE 1990; Chairman, Highlands and Islands Airports Ltd, since 1986; *b* 20 March 1924; *s* of William and Janet Beveridge Crawford; *m* 1947, Rita Veiss; one *d*. *Educ:* Robert Gordon's Coll., Aberdeen. Solicitor of the Supreme Court, England. Navigator, RAF, 1942–47. Practised as Solicitor, 1950–73, Partner, Ince and Co. (Internat. Shipping Lawyers); Chm., Silver Line Ltd, 1974–; Director: UK Freight Demurrage and Defence Assoc. Ltd, 1976– (Chm., 1987–90); UK Mutual Steamship Assurance Assoc. Ltd, 1980– (Chm., 1983–90); Avdel (formerly Newman Industries PLC), 1983–; Chm., UK Mutual War Risk Assoc. Ltd, 1982– (Dir, 1980–). Mem., Lloyd's, 1975. Member: Bd, CAA, 1984–; Bd, Lloyd's Register of Shipping, 1982–; Bd, PLA, 1985– (Vice Chm., 1986–). Freeman, City of London, 1988. *Recreations:* shooting, golf, reading, conversation. *Address:* 9 London House, Avenue Road, NW8 7PX. *T:* 071–483 2754; West Mains of Auchenhove, Lumphanan, Aberdeenshire. *T:* Lumphanan (03398) 83667. *Club:* Carlton.

CRAWFORD, (Robert) Norman, CBE 1973; Chairman, R. N. Crawford & Co., Business Advisors, since 1968; Director, William Clark & Sons, 1983–88 (Chief Executive, 1983–87); *b* 14 June 1923; *s* of Wm Crawford and Annie Catherine (*née* Rexter); *m* 1948, Jean Marie Patricia (*née* Carson); one *s* five *d*. *Educ:* Foyle Coll., Londonderry; Queen's Univ., Belfast (BComSc). FCA. Sec./Accountant, John McNeill Ltd, 1948–60; Dep. Man. Dir, McNeill Group Ltd, 1960–66, Man. Dir 1966–68; Chm., N Ireland Transport Holding Co., 1968–75; Divisional Hd, NI Develt Agency, 1976–82. Pres., N Ireland Chamber of Commerce and Industry, 1966–67; Chairman: N Ireland Regional Bd, BIM, 1966–69; Nature Reserves Cttee, 1967–85; NI Outward Bound Assoc., 1969–76 (Pres., 1983–); Open Door Housing Assoc., 1979–84; Retirement Assoc. of NI, 1982–83; Mem., CEED, 1985–. Member Senate, Queen's University, Belfast (Pres., Queen's Univ. Assoc., 1982–83); Pres., Foyle Coll. Old Boys' Assoc., 1981–82. Chm., NI Wildlife Campaign, 1986–88. FRSA. *Address:* 4 Fort Road, Helens Bay, Bangor, Co. Down BT19 1LD. *T:* Helens Bay (0247) 853661. *Club:* Ulster Reform (Belfast).

CRAWFORD, Sir (Robert) Stewart, GCMG 1973 (KCMG 1966; CMG 1951); CVO 1955; HM Diplomatic Service, retired; *b* 27 Aug. 1913; *s* of late Sir William Crawford, KBE, head of W. S. Crawford Ltd, advertising agents; *m* 1938, Mary Katharine, *d* of late Eric Corbett, Gorse Hill, Witley, Surrey; three *s* one *d* (and one *s* decd). *Educ:* Gresham's Sch., Holt; Oriel Coll., Oxford. Home Civil Service (Air Ministry), 1936; Private Sec. to Chief of Air Staff, 1940–46; Asst Sec., Control Office for Germany and Austria, 1946; Foreign Office, 1947; Counsellor, British Embassy, Oslo, 1954–56; Counsellor, later Minister, British Embassy, Baghdad, 1957–59; Dep. UK Delegate to OEEC Paris, 1959–60; Asst Under Sec., Foreign Office, 1961–65; Political Resident, Persian Gulf, 1966–70; Dep. Under-Sec. of State, FCO, 1970–73. Chm., Cttee on Broadcasting Coverage, 1973–74; Mem., BBC Gen. Adv. Council, 1976–84; Chm., Broadcasters' Audience Res. Bd, 1980–88. *Recreations:* opera, bookbinding. *Address:* 19 Adam Court, Bell Street, Henley-on-Thames, Oxon RG9 2BJ. *T:* Henley (0491) 574702. *Clubs:* United Oxford & Cambridge University; Phyllis Court (Henley-on-Thames).

CRAWFORD, Robert William Kenneth; Deputy Director-General, Imperial War Museum, since 1982; *b* 3 July 1945; *s* of late Hugh Merrall Crawford, FCA, and Mary Crawford (*née* Percival); *m* 1975, Vivienne Sylvia Polakowski; one *d* one *s*. *Educ:* Culford Sch.; Pembroke Coll., Oxford (Cleobury Schol.; BA). Joined Imperial War Museum as Research Asst, 1968: Head of Research and Information Office, 1971–89; Keeper, Dept of Photographs, 1975–83; Asst Director, 1979–82. *Address:* c/o Imperial War Museum, Lambeth Road, SE1 6HZ. *T:* 071–416 5206.

CRAWFORD, Prof. Sir Theodore, (Sir Theo), Kt 1973; Professor of Pathology in the University of London, 1948–77, Professor Emeritus, 1977; Director of Pathological Services, St George's Hospital and Medical School, 1946–77; *b* 23 Dec. 1911; *s* of late Theodore Crawford and late Sarah Mansfield; *m* 1st, 1938, Margaret Donald Green, MD (*d* 1973); two *s* three *d*; 2nd, 1974, Priscilla Leathley Chater. *Educ:* St Peter's Sch., York; Glasgow Academy; Glasgow Univ. BSc, 1932; MB, ChB, 1935; Hon. LLD, 1979. FRFPS, 1938; MD 1941; Bellahouston Gold Medal (Glasgow Univ.), 1941; MRCP 1960; FRCPGlas 1962; FRCPath 1963, FRCP 1964; FRCPA 1972; Hall Tutorial and Research Fellow, 1936–38. Asst Physician, Glasgow, Royal Hosp. for Sick Children, 1936–38; Lecturer in Pathology (Glasgow Univ.), 1939–46. Served War of 1939–45, Major RAMC, 1941–45. Mem. of the Medical Research Council, 1960–64 (and Mem. Cell Board, 1974–78); Registrar, Coll. of Pathologists, 1963–68; Consultant Adviser in Pathology to Dept of Health and Social Security and Chm. of its Central Pathology Cttee, 1969–78. Royal Society of Medicine (Pres. Section of Pathology, 1961–62); Royal Coll. of Pathologists: Vice-Pres., 1968–69; Pres., 1969–72; Hon. Fellow, 1983; Mem., Pathological Soc. of Great Britain, etc.; Chm., Scientific Cttee, British Empire Cancer Campaign, 1969–78 (Hon. Sec., 1955–67; Hon. Sec. of the Campaign, 1967–70); Vice-Pres., Cancer Res. Campaign, 1979–. Member: Council Epsom Coll., 1949–71; Standing Medical Advisory Cttee, Health Services Council, 1964–69; Cttee on Safety of Medicines, 1969–77 (Vice-Chm., 1976–77); Army Pathology Adv. Cttee, 1970–75; DHSS Cttee on Smoking and Health, 1973–79; Chm., Medical Adv. Gp to The Brewers' Soc., 1982–87 (Mem., 1972–87). *Publications:* (ed) Modern Trends in Pathology, 1967; Pathology of Ischaemic Heart Disease, 1977; scientific papers in Lancet, British Medical Journal, British Journal of Surgery, Archives of Disease in Childhood, British Journal of Opthalmology, Journal of Pathology and Bacteriology, etc. *Recreations:* horticulture, growing trees, walking, music. *Address:* 9 Asher Reeds, Langton Green, Tunbridge Wells, Kent TN3 0AL. *T:* Langton (0892) 863341. *Club:* Sloane.

CRAWFORD, Vice-Adm. Sir William (Godfrey), KBE 1961; CB 1958; DSC 1941; *b* 14 Sept. 1907; *s* of late H. E. V. Crawford, Wyld Court, Axminster, and late Mrs M. E. Crawford; *m* 1939, Mary Felicity Rosa, *d* of late Sir Philip Williams, 2nd Bt; three *s* one *d*. *Educ:* RN Coll., Dartmouth. Lieut RN, 1929; specialised in gunnery, 1932; Lieut-Comdr, 1937; Gunnery Officer, HMS Rodney, 1940–42; Comdr Dec. 1941; Exec. Officer, HMS Venerable, 1944–46; Capt. 1947; in comd HMS Pelican and 2nd Frigate Flotilla, Med., 1948–49; Dep.-Dir RN Staff Coll., 1950–52; in comd HMS Devonshire, 1952–53; in comd RN Coll., Dartmouth, 1953–56; Rear-Adm. 1956; Imperial Defence Coll., 1956–58; Flag Officer, Sea Training, 1958–60; Vice-Adm. 1959; Comdr British Navy Staff and Naval Attaché Washington, 1960–62; retired list, 1963. Dir, Overseas Offices, BTA, 1964–72. *Recreations:* sailing, fishing. *Address:* Broadlands, Whitchurch Canonicorum, Bridport, Dorset DT6 6RJ. *T:* Chideock (0297) 89591. *Clubs:* Naval and Military; Cruising.

CRAWFORD, William Hamilton Raymund, QC 1980; **His Honour Judge Crawford;** a Circuit Judge, since 1986; *b* 10 Nov. 1936; *s* of Col Mervyn Crawford, DSO, DL, JP, and Martha Hamilton Crawford; *m* 1965, Marilyn Jean Colville; one *s* two *d*. *Educ:* West Downs, Winchester; Winchester Coll.; Emmanuel Coll., Cambridge (BA). Called to the Bar, Inner Temple, 1964; Dep. Chm., Agricultural Land Tribunal, 1978; a Recorder, 1979–86. *Recreations:* hill farming, fishing, shooting (shot for GB in Kolapore Match, and for Scotland in Elcho and Twenty Matches on several occasions; mem., Scottish Rifle Team, Commonwealth Games, Jamaica, 1966). *Address:* c/o The Crown Court, Newcastle-upon-Tyne. *Clubs:* Naval and Military; Northern Counties (Newcastle).

CRAWLEY, Aidan Merivale, MBE; Chairman, London Weekend Television, 1967–71, President 1971–73; *b* 10 April 1908; *s* of late Canon A. S. Crawley; *m* 1945, Virginia Cowles, OBE (*d* 1983); one *d* (two *s* decd). *Educ:* Harrow; Oxford. Journalist, 1930–36; Educational Film Producer, 1936–39. AAF, 601 Sqdn, 1936–40; Asst Air Attaché, Ankara, Belgrade (resident Sofia), May 1940–March 1941; joined 73 (F) Sqdn, Egypt; shot down July 1941; prisoner until May 1945. MP (Lab) Buckingham Div. of N Bucks, 1945–51; Parliamentary Private Sec. to successive Secs of State for the Colonies, 1945 and 1946–47; Parliamentary Under-Sec. of State for Air, 1950–51; resigned from the Labour Party, 1957; MP (C) West Derbyshire, 1962–68; Editor-in-Chief, Independent Television News Ltd, 1955–56; making television documentaries for BBC, 1956–60; Mem. Monckton Commission on Federation of Rhodesia and Nyasaland, 1960. Pres., MCC, 1973. *Publications:* Escape from Germany, 1956; De Gaulle: A Biography, 1969; The Rise of Western Germany 1945–72, 1973; Dial 200-200, 1980; Leap Before You Look (autobiog.) 1988. *Recreation:* cricket; Co-Founder, Haig Nat. Village Cricket Championship, 1971. *Address:* Oak Cottage, Queen Street, Farthinghoe, Northants NN13 5NY. *T:* Banbury (0295) 710419. *Clubs:* Clermont; MCC, Queen's.

CRAWLEY, Charles William; Hon. Fellow of Trinity Hall, 1971; University Lecturer in History, 1931–66; Vice-Master of Trinity Hall, Cambridge, 1950–66, Emeritus Fellow, 1966; *b* 1 April 1899; *s* of Charles Crawley, barrister of Lincoln's Inn, and Augusta, *d* of Rt Rev. Samuel Butcher, Bishop of Meath; *m* 1930, Kathleen Elizabeth (*d* 1982), *d* of Lieut-Col H. G. Leahy, OBE, RA; four *s* one *d*. *Educ:* Winchester (Scholar); Trinity Coll., Cambridge (Scholar). Fellow of Trinity Hall, 1924–66. Asst Tutor, 1927, Acting Senior Tutor, 1940, Senior Tutor, 1946–58. *Publications:* The Question of Greek Independence, 1821–1833, 1930, repr. 1973; (ed) New Cambridge Modern History, Vol. IX, 1965; John Capodistrias: unpublished documents, 1970; Trinity Hall: the history of a Cambridge College, 1350–1975, 1976. *Address:* 93 Castelnau, SW13 9EL.

See also J. M. Crawley.

CRAWLEY, Mrs Christine Mary; Member (Lab) Birmingham East, European Parliament, since 1984; Chair, Women's Rights Committee; *b* 1 Jan. 1950; *m*; three *c* (incl. twins). *Educ:* Notre Dame Catholic Secondary Girls' School, Plymouth; Digby Stuart Training College, Roehampton. Formerly teacher; S Oxfordshire District Council; contested (Lab) Staffordshire SE, gen. election, 1983. *Address:* c/o Birmingham District Labour Party, 16 Bristol Street, Birmingham B5 7AA.

CRAWLEY, Rt. Rev. David; *see* Kootenay, Bishop of.

CRAWLEY, Desmond John Chetwode, CMG 1964; CVO 1961; HM Diplomatic Service, retired; *b* 2 June 1917; *s* of late Lieutenant-Colonel C. G. C. Crawley, OBE and late Agnes Luke; *m* 1945, Daphne Lesley (*d* 1989), *y d* of late Sir Vere Mockett, MBE, and late Ethel Norah Gaddum Tomkinson; two *s* one *d*. *Educ:* King's Sch., Ely; Queen's Coll., Oxford. Entered Indian Civil Service, serving in Madras Presidency, 1939; entered Indian Political Service, serving in Baluchistan, 1946; entered Commonwealth Relations Office, 1947, and served in London, Calcutta, and on loan to the Foreign Office in Washington; Principal Private Secretary to Sec. of State for Commonwealth Relations, 1952–53; British Dep. High Commissioner in Lahore, Pakistan, 1958–61; Imperial Defence Coll., 1962; British High Commissioner in Sierra Leone, 1963–66; Ambassador to Bulgaria, 1966–70; Minister to Holy See, 1970–75. Coronation Medal, 1953. Knight Grand Cross, Order of St Gregory the Great, 1973. *Address:* 35 Chartfield Avenue, SW15. *T:* 081–788 9529. *Club:* United Oxford & Cambridge University.

CRAWLEY, Frederick William, FCIB; Chairman: Betta Stores PLC, since 1990; Alliance & Leicester Building Society, since 1991 (Director, since 1988; Deputy Chairman, 1990–91); Deputy Chairman, Girobank PLC, since 1990; Director: Barratt Developments PLC, since 1988; Lloyds Development Capital, since 1988; *b* 10 June 1926; *s* of William Clement Crawley and Elsie Florence Crawley; *m* 1951, Ruth Eva Jungman; two *d*. Joined Lloyds Bank, 1942; Chief Accountant, 1969–72; Asst Chief Gen. Man., 1977–78; Dep. Chief Gen. Man., 1978–82; Chief Exec., Lloyds Bank, Calif, 1982–83; Dep. Chief Gen. Man., 1983–84, Chief Gen. Man., 1984–85, Dep. Chief Exec., 1985–87, Lloyds Bank plc. Chm., Black Horse Agencies Ltd, 1985–88; Director: Black Horse Life Assce Co., 1977–82; Lloyds Bank Unit Trust Managers, 1977–82; Lloyds Leasing, 1977–82; Lloyds Development Capital, 1981–82; Lloyds Bank International, 1982–83; Internat. Commodies Clearing House Hldgs, 1984–87; Lloyds Bank, 1984–88; Lloyds Bank Export Finance, 1985–87; Lloyds Bowmaker Finance, 1985–87; FS Assurance, 1988–90. RAF Benevolent Fund: Hon. Treas., 1988–, and Dir, 1988–, Internat. Air Tattoo; Dir, Battle of Britain Appeal, 1988–. FCIB (FIB 1971); CBIM. *Recreations:* aviation, shooting, photography. *Address:* 4 The Hexagon, Fitzroy Park, N6 6HR. *T:* 081–341 2279. *Club:* Overseas Bankers.

CRAWLEY, John Cecil, CBE 1972 (MBE 1944); Chairman of Trustees of Visnews, 1976–86; *b* 1909; *s* of John and Kathleen Crawley; *m* 1933, Constance Mary Griffiths; two *d*. *Educ:* William Ellis Sch. War Service, Army, 1939–45. Journalism: Reynolds, 1927; Central News Agency, 1928; National Press Agency, 1929; Press Secretaries, 1933; BBC: Sub-Editor, 1945; Foreign Correspondent, New York, 1959–63; Foreign News Editor, 1963–67; Editor of News and Current Affairs, 1967–71; Chief Asst to Dir-Gen., BBC, 1971–75. *Recreations:* walking, bird-watching. *Address:* 157 Clarence Gate Gardens, NW1 6AP. *T:* 071–723 6876.

CRAWLEY, John Maurice; Under Secretary (Principal Finance Officer and Director of Manpower and Support Services), Inland Revenue; *b* 27 Sept. 1933; *s* of Charles William Crawley, *qv*; *m* 1978, Jane Meadows Rendel; three *s*. *Educ:* Rugby Sch.; New Coll., Oxford (MA). Assistant Principal, Inland Revenue, 1959; Principal, 1963; Asst Secretary, 1969; Under Sec., 1979; seconded to Cabinet Office (Central Policy Review Staff), 1973–76 and 1979–81. *Recreations:* music, walking. *Address:* Somerset House, Strand, WC2.

CRAWLEY-BOEVEY, Sir Thomas (Michael Blake), 8th Bt *cr* 1784; *b* 29 Sept. 1928; *er s* of Sir Launcelot Valentine Hyde Crawley-Boevey, 7th Bt, and Elizabeth Goodeth (*d* 1976), *d* of Herbert d'Auvergne Innes, late Indian Police; *S* father, 1968; *m* 1957, Laura Coelingh (*d* 1979); two *s*. *Educ:* Wellington Coll.; St John's Coll., Cambridge (BA 1952, MA 1956). 2nd Lieut, Durham Light Infantry, 1948. With Shipping Agents, 1952–61; with Consumers' Association, 1961–82; Editor: Money Which?, 1968–76; Which?, 1976–82; Editor-in-Chief, Which? magazines, 1980–82. Mem. Council, Insce Ombudsman Bureau, 1985–. *Publications:* Buying, Selling and Owning Shares, 1987; Finance Your Future, 1989. *Heir: er s* Thomas Hyde Crawley-Boevey, *b* 26 June 1958. *Address:* Trebanau, Cilycwm, Llandovery, Dyfed SA20 0HP. *T:* Llandovery (0550) 20496. *Clubs:* Gower and Swansea Bay Windsurfing, Grafham Water Sailing.

CRAWSHAW, 4th Baron, *cr* 1892; **William Michael Clifton Brooks;** Bt *cr* 1891; *b* 25 March 1933; *s* of 3rd Baron and Sheila (*d* 1964), *o d* of late Lieut-Col P. R. Clifton, CMG, DSO; *S* father, 1946. *Educ:* Eton; Christ Church, Oxford. Jt Master, Oxford Univ. Drag Hounds, 1952–53. Treasurer, Loughborough Div. Conservative Assoc., 1954–58; County Commissioner, Leics Boy Scouts, 1958–. Pres., Leics Assoc. of the Disabled; Chm., Quorn Hunt Cttee, 1971–. Lord of the Manor of Long Whatton. Patron of the Living of Shepshed. *Heir:* *b* Hon. David Gerald Brooks [*b* 14 Sept. 1934; *m* 1970, Belinda Mary, *d* of George Burgess, Melbourne, and of Mrs J. P. Allen, Coleman's Hatch, Sussex; four *d*. *Educ:* Eton; Royal Agricultural College, Cirencester]. *Address:* Whatton, Loughborough, Leics. *TA:* Kegworth. *Clubs:* Boodle's, MCC.

CRAWSHAY, Elisabeth Mary Boyd, (Lady Crawshay), CBE 1986; JP, DL; Chairman, Local Government Boundary Commission, Wales, since 1979; Deputy Chief Commissioner, St John's Ambulance Brigade, Wales, 1979–84; *b* 2 July 1927; *d* of Lt-Col Guy Franklin Reynolds, late 9th Lancers, and Katherine Isobel (*née* Macdonell); *m* 1950, Col Sir William (Robert) Crawshay, *qv*. *Educ:* Convent of Sacred Heart, Roehampton; St Anne's Coll., Oxford (MA). Mem., Mental Health Act Commn, 1983–88. DL Gwent 1978; JP Abergavenny, 1972, Chm., Juvenile Bench, 1980–, Mem., Borstal Board of Visitors, 1975–84. DJStJ 1970. *Address:* Llanfair Court, Abergavenny, Gwent NP7 9BB.

CRAWSHAY, Col Sir William (Robert), Kt 1972; DSO 1945; ERD; TD; Vice Lord-Lieutenant of Gwent, since 1979; *b* 27 May 1920; *o s* of late Captain J. W. L. Crawshay, MC, Caversham Park, Oxon, and late Hon. Mrs. George Egerton, Brussels; *m* 1950, Elisabeth Mary Boyd Reynolds (*see* Lady Crawshay). *Educ:* Eton. Served Royal Welch Fus.(SR), 1939–46; SOE 1944 (DSO, despatches twice); TA, 1947–62, Parachute Regt, Welch Regt, SW Brigade. ADC to HM the Queen, 1966–71. Hon. Colonel: 3rd RRW (V) Bn, 1970–82; Cardiff Univ. OTC, 1977–85. Mem., Arts Council of GB, 1962–74; Chairman: Welsh Arts Council, 1968–74; Council, University Coll. of Cardiff, 1966–87; Member: Council and Court, Univ. of Wales, 1967; Welsh Council, 1966–69, 1970–; Council and Court, Nat. Museum of Wales, 1966– (Pres., 1977–82). Pres., Royal British Legion, Wales Area, 1974–88. Mem., Crafts Adv. Council, 1974–78. Hon. LLD, Univ. of Wales, 1975. DL Glamorgan, 1964, Monmouthshire, 1970, Gwent, 1974. Chevalier, Légion d'honneur, 1956; Croix de Guerre (France) with Palms twice, 1944, 1945. KStJ (formerly KJStJ) 1969. *Address:* Llanfair Court, Abergavenny, Gwent NP7 9BB. *Clubs:* White's; Cardiff and County (Cardiff).

CRAXTON, Antony, CVO 1977 (MVO 1968); freelance television consultant; *b* 23 April 1918; 2nd *s* of late Harold Craxton, OBE, and Essie Craxton; *m* 1944, Anne Sybil Cropper (marr. diss. 1978); one *s* one *d*. *Educ:* St George's Chapel Choir Sch., Windsor; Royal Acad. of Music; Gordonstoun Sch., Scotland. Joined BBC Radio, 1941; Home and Overseas Announcer, 1942–45; joined TV Service as Outside Broadcast Producer, 1951; resp. for coverage of all major Royal occasions, 1953–77, Jubilee Day being 200th broadcast involving the Queen and Royal Family; retd, 1979. Helped pioneer presentation of internat. cricket, rugby and golf in early 50s; covered over 100 orchestral concert relays from many parts of country, 1953–71. Chief Royal Occasions: Queen's 1st Christmas Television Broadcast and Prince Philip's 1st major TV appearance, Round the World in 40 Minutes, 1957; Princess Margaret's Wedding, 1960; Duke of Kent's Wedding, 1961; Princess Alexandra's Wedding, 1963; State Funeral of Sir Winston Churchill, 1965; Investiture of Prince Charles as Prince of Wales, 1969; Lying in State of Duke of Windsor, 1972; Queen's Silver Wedding Celebrations, 1972; Princess Anne's Wedding, 1973; Funeral of Duke of Gloucester, 1974; Funeral of Field-Marshal Montgomery, 1976; Queen's Silver Jubilee Day Celebrations, 1977; 10 State visits abroad and 19 visits by Foreign Heads of State to Britain, 1954–76. News Chronicle Readers' Award for Prince Philip's Round the World Documentary, 1957; Guild of TV Producers' Award for Princess Alexandra's Wedding, 1963; French TV Internat. Award for Investiture of Prince Charles, 1970; BAFTA Award for Jubilee Day (1977), 1978. Silver Jubilee Medal, 1977. *Recreations:* golf, cricket, classical music. *Address:* 14 Kidderpore Avenue, NW3. *Clubs:* MCC, Lord's Taverners, Eccentric.

CREAGH, Maj.-Gen. Sir Kilner Rupert B.; *see* Brazier-Creagh.

CREAMER, Brian; Consulting Physician, St Thomas' Hospital, London, 1991 (Physician, 1959–91); Senior Lecturer in Medicine, United Medical and Dental Schools (St Thomas's), 1959–91; Hon. Consultant in Gastroenterology to the Army, 1970–90; *b* 12 April 1926; *s* of late L. G. Creamer and Mrs Creamer, Epsom; *m* 1953, Margaret Holden Rees; two *s* one *d*. *Educ:* Christ's Hosp.; St Thomas' Hosp. MB, BS Hons London, 1948; MD London, 1952; FRCP 1966 (MRCP 1950); Research Asst, Mayo Clinic, Rochester, USA, 1955–56; Dean: St Thomas's Hosp. Med. Sch., 1979–84; UMDS of Guy's and St Thomas's Hosps, 1984–86. Vis. Prof., Shiraz Univ., Iran, 1977–78. Sir Arthur Hurst Memorial Lectr, 1968; Watson Smith Lectr, RCP, 1971. Member: SE Thames RHA, 1982–85; Medway DHA, 1987–89; W Lambeth DHA, 1989–90. Member: British Soc. of Gastroenterology; Assoc. of Physicians of GB and NI; Exec. Subcttee, Univ. Hosps Assoc., 1981–86. Chm. Council, Trinity Hospice, 1987–. Member: Collegiate Council, Univ. of London, 1980–86; Senate, Univ. of London, 1981–86; Council of Almoners, Christ's Hosp., 1986–. *Publications:* (ed) Modern Trends in Gastroenterology, vol. 4, 1970; (ed) The Small Intestine, 1974; contributions to med. jls. *Recreations:* drawing and painting, gardening, and listening to music. *Address:* Vine House, Highfields, East Horsley KT24 5AA. *T:* East Horsley (04865) 3320.

CREAN, Hon. Frank; *b* Hamilton, Vic, 28 Feb. 1916; *s* of J. Crean; *m* 1946, Mary, *d* of late A. E. Findlay; three *s*. *Educ:* Hamilton High Sch.; Melbourne High Sch.; Melbourne Univ. BA Hons; BCom. DPA; FASA. Income Tax Assessor, 1934–45. MLA: for Albert Park, Vic, 1945–47; for Prahran, 1949–51; MHR for Melbourne Ports, 1951–77; Mem. Exec., Federal Parly Labour Party, 1956–72, Dep. Leader, 1975–76; Mem., Jt Parly Cttee on Public Accounts, 1952–55; Treasurer, Commonwealth of Australia, 1972–74; Minister for Overseas Trade, 1974–75, also Deputy Prime Minister, 1975. Chm., Council of Adult Educn, 1947–74. Pres., Vict. Br., Aust. Inst. Internat. Affairs, 1983–86; Chm., Vict. Br., Freedom from Hunger Campaign, 1979. *Publication:* (with W. J. Byrt) Government and Politics in Australia, 1972, 2nd edn 1982. *Address:* 31/27 Queens Road, Melbourne, Vic 3004, Australia.

CREASY, Leonard Richard, CB 1972; OBE 1961; CEng, FICE, FIStructE; civil engineer in private practice with son, since 1974; *b* 20 Dec. 1912; *s* of William and Ellen Creasy; *m* 1937, Irene Howard; one *s* one *d*. *Educ:* Wimbledon Technical Coll. BSc(Eng) London. Served War, RE, E Africa, 1944–46. Service in Industry, 1928–34; HM Office of Works, Asst Engr, 1935; Min. of Works, Suptg Engr, 1959; MPBW: Dir, Civil Engrg, 1966; Dir, Central Services, 1968; Dir of Civil Engrg Develt, Dept of the Environment, 1970–73. Concerned with Inquiries into disasters at Aberfan, Ronan Point and Brent, and with design of Radio and Radar Towers, London Heathrow and Birmingham; Plant House, Royal Botanical Gardens, Edinburgh; Wind Tunnels, Bedford RAE; and other structures. Bronze Medal, Reinforced Concrete Assoc.; Manby and Telford Premiums, Instn Civil Engrs; Pres., Instn Struct. Engrs, 1973 (Bronze Medal and Certif. of Merit of the Instn). *Publications:* Pre-stressed Concrete Cylindrical Tanks, 1961; James Forrest Lecture, 1968; many other papers on civil and structural engrg projects and engrg economics. *Recreations:* music, opera, languages. *Address:* 5 The Oaks, Epsom, Surrey KT18 5HH. *T:* Epsom (0372) 722361.

CREDITON, Bishop Suffragan of, since 1984; **Rt. Rev. Peter Everard Coleman;** *b* 28 Aug. 1928; *s* of Geoffrey Everard Coleman and Lilian Coleman; *m* 1960, HSH Princess Elisabeth-Donata Reuss; two *s* two *d*. *Educ:* Haileybury; King's Coll., London Univ. (LLB, AKC); Bristol Univ. (MLitt). Mil. Service, RHG and RA, 1947–49. Called to the bar, Middle Temple, 1965. Ordained, Bristol, 1955; Chaplain and Lectr, King's Coll., London, 1960–66; Vicar of St Paul's, Clifton, and Chaplain, Bristol Univ., 1966–71; Canon Residentiary and Dir of Training, Bristol, 1971–81; Archdeacon of Worcester, 1981–84. Clerical Member, Court of Arches, 1980–91; Mem. General Synod, 1974–81, 1990–. Fellow, Woodard Corp., 1985–. Jt Editor, Theology, 1982–. *Publications:* Experiments with Prayer, 1961; A Christian Approach to Television, 1968; Christian Attitudes to Homosexuality, 1980; Gay Christians—a moral dilemma, 1989; Contrib. Digest. *Recreations:* film making, fishing. *Address:* 10 The Close, Exeter EX1 1EZ. *Club:* Commonwealth Trust.

CREE, Brig. Gerald Hilary, CBE 1946; DSO 1945; Colonel, The Prince of Wales's Own Regiment of Yorkshire, 1960–70; *b* 23 June 1905; *s* of late Maj.-Gen. Gerald Cree; *m* 1945, Joan Agnes, *d* of late Lt-Col W. R. Eden, RA; one *d*. *Educ:* Kelly Coll.; RMC Sandhurst. Commissioned, The West Yorks Regt, 1924; King's African Rifles, 1931–36; comd 2nd Bn West Yorks Regt, 1942–44; 1st Bn 1946–48; Comdr 25 (East African) Infantry Bde, 1944–45 and Brig. 1953. Served Palestine, East Africa, Abyssinia, Western Desert, Iraq, Burma, 1938–45. Commander 127 (East Lancs) Infantry Brigade (TA), 1953–56; Col, The West Yorks Regt, 1956–57, Col, PWO Regt of Yorkshire, 1960–70, retd. *Address:* Laurels, Sharpham Drive, Totnes, Devon.

CREEGGAN, Rt. Rev. Jack Burnett; *b* 10 Nov. 1902; *s* of Alfred Henry Creeggan and Mary Laura (*née* Sheffield); *m* 1931, Dorothy Jarman (*née* Embury); one *s* one *d*. *Educ:* Deseronto (Ont) Public and High Schs; Queen's Univ. (BA); Bishop's Univ. (LST). Priest, 1928; served in many parishes in Dio. Ontario; Canon, St George's Cathedral, Kingston, Ont, 1952; Archdeacon of: Ontario, 1953; Frontenac, 1962; Kingston, 1969; Bishop of Ontario, 1970–74. Prolocutor, Lower House, Provincial Synod of Ont., 1963. Hon. DCL, Bishop's Univ., Lennoxville, PQ, 1971. *Recreations:* curling, golf. *Address:* Apt 112, 32 Ontario Street, Kingston, Ontario K7L 2Y1, Canada. *T:* 542–5319.

CREEK, Malcolm Lars, LVO 1980; OBE 1985; HM Diplomatic Service, retired; Consul-General, Auckland, 1988–90; *b* 2 April 1931; *s* of Edgar Creek and Lily Creek (*née* Robertshaw); *m* 1st, 1953, Moira Pattison (marr. diss. 1970); one *s* one *d*; 2nd, 1970, Gillian Bell; one *s* two *d*. *Educ:* Belle Vue School, Bradford. BA Hons London. National Service, 1950–52. Foreign Office, 1953; served Mogadishu, Harar, Mexico City, Abidjan, Chile; First Sec., San José, 1968; Havana, 1971; FCO, 1974; Head of Chancery, Tunis, 1978; Lima, 1981; High Comr, Vanuatu, 1985. *Recreations:* reading, family history, cricket. *Address:* 17 Bertram Drive North, Meols, Wirral, Merseyside L47 0LN. *T:* 051–632 5520. *Club:* Yorkshire County Cricket.

CREESE, Nigel Arthur Holloway, AM 1988; Executive Officer, Association of Heads of Independent Schools of Australia, since 1989 (Chairman, 1985–87); *b* 4 June 1927; *s* of late H. R. Creese; *m* 1951, Valdai (*née* Walters); two *s* two *d*. *Educ:* Blundell's Sch.; Brasenose Coll., Oxford. Assistant Master: Bromsgrove Sch., 1952–55; Rugby Sch., 1955–63; Headmaster: Christ's Coll., Christchurch, NZ, 1963–70; Melbourne Grammar Sch., 1970–87. *Recreations:* Nordic ski-ing, tennis. *Address:* 75 Charles Street, Kew, Vic 3101, Australia. *Club:* Melbourne (Melbourne).

CREIGHTMORE, Peter Beauchamp; Master of Supreme Court, Queen's Bench Division, since 1975; *b* 15 Jan. 1928; *s* of late Maximilian Louis Creightmore, MRCS, LRCP and Mary Arnell Beauchamp; *m* 1957, June Patricia, *d* of Harold William Hedley, Captain Suez Canal Co. (Pilote Majeur), and Gwendoline Pugh; one *s* one *d*. *Educ:* Geelong Grammar Sch. (H. H. Whittingham Student, 1945); Worcester Coll., Oxford (MA). O/Sig, RNVR, 1952, commnd 1955. Called to Bar, Inner Temple, 1954; Oxford, later Oxford and Midland, Circuit. *Recreation:* music. *Address:* Royal Courts of Justice, Strand, WC2.

CREIGHTON, Alan Joseph, CEng, FRINA; RCNC; Chief Underwater Systems Executive, Ministry of Defence, since 1989; *b* 21 Nov. 1936; *s* of Joseph Kenneth and Iris Mary Creighton; *m* 1959, Judith Bayford; two *d*. *Educ:* Gillingham County Grammar School; Royal Naval College, Greenwich. Joined Admiralty, 1953; Cadetship to Royal Corps of Naval Constructors, 1957; pass out, RNC Greenwich, 1961; RCDS 1980; secondment to industry, 1981; resumed MoD (PE) career, 1984; Dir Gen., Surface Ships, 1986–89. *Recreations:* music, dinghy sailing, cabinet making. *Address:* Home Farm Cottage, West Littleton, Marshfield SN14 8JE. *T:* Bath (0225) 891021.

CREIGHTON, Harold Digby Fitzgerald; Chairman, since 1987, and Chief Executive, since 1982, Farmer Stedall plc (Deputy Chairman, 1982–87); *b* 11 Sept. 1927; *s* of late Rev. Digby Robert Creighton and Amy Frances Rohde; *m* 1964, Harriett Mary Falconer Wallace, *d* of late A. L. P. F. Wallace of Candacraig (Mem., Queen's Body Guard for Scotland); four *d*. *Educ:* Haileybury. National Service, Army (Lieut), India and ME, 1945–48. Consolidated Tin Smelters, Penang, 1950–52; Dir, machine tool companies, London, 1952–63; Chm., Scottish Machine Tool Corp. Ltd, Glasgow, 1963–68. Chm., 1967–75, Editor, 1973–75, The Spectator. *Address:* 5 Upper Brook Street, W1. *Clubs:* Beefsteak, Brooks's, Oriental.
See also Baron Fairhaven.

CREMONA, Hon. John Joseph; Judge, since 1965, Vice-President, since 1986, European Court of Human Rights; Judge, since 1985, Vice-President, since 1987, European Tribunal in matters of State immunity; Emeritus Professor, University of Malta, since 1965; Chief Justice of Malta and President of the Constitutional Court, Court of Appeal and Court of Criminal Appeal, 1971–81; *b* 6 Jan. 1918; *s* of late Dr Antonio Cremona, KM, MD and Anne (*née* Camilleri); *m* 1949, Marchioness Beatrice Barbaro of St George; one *s* two *d*. *Educ:* Malta Univ. (BA 1936, LLD *cum laude* 1942); Rome Univ. (DLitt 1939); London Univ. (BA 1st Cl. Hons 1946, PhD in Laws 1951). DrJur Trieste, 1972. Crown Counsel, 1947; Lectr in Constitutional Law, Malta Univ., 1947–65, Prof. of Criminal Law, 1959–65; Attorney-Gen., 1957–64; Vice-Pres., Constitutional Court and Court of Appeal, 1965–71; sometime Actg Governor General and Actg Pres., Republic of Malta. Chm., UN Cttee on Elimination of Racial Discrimination (CERD), 1986–88 (Mem., 1984–88). Chairman: Human Rights Section, World Assoc. of Lawyers; Planning Council, Foundn for Internat. Studies, Malta Univ.; Vice-Pres., Internat. Inst. of Studies, Documentation and Info. for the Protection of Envt, Italy; Member: Cttee of Experts of Human Rights and Cttee on State Immunity, Council of Europe, Strasbourg; Scientific Council, Revue des Droits de l'Homme, Paris; Patronage Cttee, Europäische Grundrechte Zeitschrift, Strasbourg; Scientific Council Centro Internazionale per Protezione dei Diritti dell' Uomo, Pesaro, Italy; Editorial Adv. Board: Checklist of Human Rights Documents, NY; Human Rights Law Jl, Arlington, Va; delegate and rapporteur, internat. confs. FRHistS;

Fellow *ex titulo*, Internat. Acad. of Legal Medicine and Social Medicine; Hon. Fellow, LSE; Hon. Mem., Real Acad. de Jurisprudencia y Legislacion, Madrid. Kt Comdr, 1968, Grand Officier, 1989, Order of Merit, Italy, 1968; Kt, Sovereign Military Order of Malta, 1966; KSG, 1972; Kt Comdr, 1971, Grand Cross of Merit, 1981, Constantinian Order of St George; KStJ 1984 (Chm., St John Council, Malta, 1983–); Chevalier de la Légion d'Honneur, France, 1990. *Publications:* The Treatment of Young Offenders in Malta, 1956; The Malta Constitution of 1835, 1959; The Doctrine of Entrapment in Theft, 1959; The Legal Consequences of a Conviction, 1962; The Constitutional Development of Malta, 1963; From the Declaration of Rights to Independence, 1965; Human Rights Documentation in Malta, 1966; Selected Papers 1946–1989, 1990; articles in French, German, Italian and American law jls. *Recreation:* gardening. *Address:* Villa Barbaro, Main Street, Attard, Malta. *T:* 440818.

CRESPI, (Caesar) James, QC 1984; a Recorder of the Crown Court, since 1973. *Educ:* Trinity Hall, Cambridge (BA). Called to the Bar, Middle Temple, 1951, South Eastern Circuit. *Address:* 5 Paper Buildings, Temple, EC4Y 7HB. *T:* 071–583 6117. *Club:* Garrick.

CRESPIN, Régine; Officier de la Légion d'Honneur, 1981 (Chevalier, 1969); Commandeur de l'Ordre National du Mérite, 1987 (Chevalier, 1965); Commandeur des Arts et des Lettres, 1974; soprano singer; Professor of Singing, Conservatoire National Supérieur de Musique de Paris, since 1976; *b* Marseille, 23 Feb.; *d* of Henri Crespin and Marguerite (*née* Meirone); *m* 1962, Lou Bruder, French novelist, critic, poet, translator. *Educ:* Nîmes; Conservatoire National, Paris (Baccalauréat). Worked at the Opera, Paris, 1951–, in all the famous opera houses of Europe and all over the world, giving concerts, recitals, etc.; *Operas include:* Otello, Tosca, Il Trovatore, Le Nozze di Figaro, Ballo in Maschera, Der Rosenkavalier, Tannhäuser, Lohengrin, Die Walküre, Parsifal, Les Troyens, Dialogues of the Carmelites, Tales of Hoffmann, Iphigenie auf Tauris, Carmen, Le Medium. *Publication:* La vie et l'amour d'une femme (autobiog.), 1982. *Recreations:* sea, sun, sleep, books, theatre; and my dog! *Address:* 3 Avenue Frochot, 75009 Paris, France.

CRESSON, Edith; Commandeur du Mérite Agricole, 1983; Prime Minister of France, since 1991; Mayor of Chatellerault, Vienne, since 1983; *b* 27 Jan. 1934; *née* Campion; *m* Jacques Cresson; two *d*. *Educ:* Diplômée de l'Ecole des Hautes Etudes Commerciales; Dr en démographie (doctoral thesis: the life of women in a rural district of Guémené-Penfao, Loire-Atlantique). Mem., Convention des Institutions Républicaines (responsible for agricl problems), 1966; Dir of Studies, Bureau des Etudes Economiques privés (dealing especially with industrial investment, particularly in Canada); National Secretary, Parti Socialiste (in charge of youth organisation), 1974; Mem. Directing Cttee, Parti Socialiste; contested (for Parti Socialiste) Châtellerault, 1975; elected to European Assembly, 1979 (Mem., Cttee on Agriculture); Minister: of Agriculture, France, 1981–83; of For. Trade and Tourism, 1983–84; for Industrial Redeployment and Foreign Trade, 1984–86; for European Affairs, 1988–90; Pres.-Dir Gen., Schneider Industries Services Internat., 1990–91. Pres., Assoc. Démocratique des Français à l'Etranger, 1986–. Mayor of Thure, Vienne, 1977; Member, Conseil Général of Vienne, 1982–. *Publication:* Avec le soleil, 1976. *Address:* Hôtel Matignon, 57 rue de Varenne, 75007 Paris, France; La Mairie, 86108 Chatellerault cedex, France.

CRESSWELL, Rev. Amos Samuel; Chairman, Plymouth and Exeter District of the Methodist Church, 1976–91; President of the Methodist Conference, 1983–84; *b* Walsall Wood, 21 April 1926; *s* of Amos and Jane Cresswell; *m* 1956, Evelyn Rosemary Marchbanks; two *s* one *d*. *Educ:* Queen Mary's Grammar School, Walsall; University College, Durham Univ.; Wesley House, and Fitzwilliam Coll., Cambridge; Theological Seminary, Bethel bei Bielefeld, Westphalia. BA (Dunelm), Classics, 1947; BA (Cantab), Theology, 1952, MA (Cantab) 1956. Teacher of English and Latin, High School for Boys, Colchester, 1947–49; Methodist Minister, Clitheroe Circuit, 1949–50; Asst Tutor in New Testament, Richmond Coll., London, 1953–56; Minister in Darlaston (Slater St), 1956–61; Tutor in New Testament, Cliff Coll., Derbyshire, 1961–66; Minister in Bramhall Circuit (Cheadle Hulme), 1966–73; Superintendent Minister, Welwyn Garden City, 1973–76. Pres., Devonshire Assoc., 1985–86. Editor, Advance (religious weekly, formerly Joyful News), 1961–63. *Publications:* The Story of Cliff (a history of Cliff College), 1965, 2nd edn 1983; The Story They Told (a short study of the Passion Narratives in the Gospels), 1966; Life Power and Hope—a study of the Holy Spirit, 1972; Lord! I've had enough! (a collection of sermons), 1991. *Recreations:* compulsive watching of sport (especially West Bromwich Albion); collecting Roman Imperial coins; reading about American Civil War; listening to music and to Shakespeare. *Address:* 85 Sandringham Drive, Paignton, Devon TQ3 1HH.

CRESSWELL, Helen, (Mrs Brian Rowe); freelance author and television scriptwriter; *b* July 1934; *d* of Annie Edna Clarke and Joseph Edward Cresswell; *m* 1962, Brian Rowe; two *d*. *Educ:* Nottingham Girls' High Sch.; King's College London (BA English Hons). *Television series:* Lizzie Dripping, 1973–75; Jumbo Spencer, 1976; The Bagthorpe Saga, 1980; numerous TV plays. *Publications:* Sonya-by-the-Shire, 1961; Jumbo Spencer, 1963; The White Sea Horse, 1964; Pietro and the Mule, 1965; Jumbo Back to Nature, 1965; Where the Wind Blows, 1966; Jumbo Afloat, 1966; The Piemakers, 1967; A Tide for the Captain, 1967; The Signposters, 1968; The Sea Piper, 1968; The Barge Children, 1968; The Night-watchman, 1969; A Game of Catch, 1969; A Gift from Winklesea, 1969; The Outlanders, 1970; The Wilkses, 1970; The Bird Fancier, 1971; At the Stroke of Midnight, 1971; The Beachcombers, 1972; Lizzie Dripping, 1972; The Bongleweed, 1972; Lizzie Dripping Again, 1974; Butterfly Chase, 1975; The Winter of the Birds, 1975; My Aunt Polly, 1979; My Aunt Polly By the Sea, 1980; Dear Shrink, 1982; The Secret World of Polly Flint, 1982; Ellie and the Hagwitch, 1984; The Bagthorpe Saga: Pt 1, Ordinary Jack, 1977; Pt 2, Absolute Zero, 1978; Pt 3, Bagthorpes Unlimited, 1978; Pt 4, Bagthorpes v The World, 1979; Pt 5, Bagthorpes Abroad, 1984; Pt 6, Bagthorpes Haunted, 1985; Moondial, 1987; Time Out, 1987; Bagthorpes Liberated, 1988; Rosie and the Boredom Eater, 1989; Whatever Happened in Winklesea?, 1989; Bagthorpes and the Black Hole, 1990; Meet Posy Bates, 1990; Posy Bates Again, 1991; Lizzie Dripping and the Witch, 1991. *Recreations:* watercolour painting, collecting books, antiques and coincidences, sundial watching. *Address:* Old Church Farm, Eakring, Newark, Notts NG22 0DA. *T:* Mansfield (0623) 870401.

CRESSWELL, Hon. Sir Peter (John), Kt 1991; **Hon. Mr Justice Cresswell;** a Judge of the High Court of Justice, Queen's Bench Division, since 1991; *b* 24 April 1944; *s* of Jack Joseph and Madeleine Cresswell; *m* 1972, Caroline Ward; one *s* (and one *s* decd). *Educ:* St John's Sch., Leatherhead; Queens' Coll., Cambridge (MA, LLM). Called to the Bar, Gray's Inn, 1966 (Malcolm Hilbery Award), Bencher, 1989; QC 1983; a Recorder, 1986–91. Mem., Senate of Inns of Court and Bar, 1981–84, 1985–86; Chm., Common Law and Commercial Bar Assoc., 1985–87; Mem., 1987–88, Vice Chm., 1989, Chm., 1990, Gen. Council of the Bar. Mem., Council and Exec. Cttee, Cystic Fibrosis Res. Trust, 1983–. Hon. Mem., Canadian Bar Assoc., 1990. *Publication:* Encyclopaedia of Banking Law, 1982, and 15 subseq. service issues. *Recreations:* fly-fishing, river management, the Outer Hebrides. *Address:* Royal Courts of Justice, Strand, WC2A 2LL. *Club:* Flyfishers'.

CRESWELL, Jack Norman; Deputy Chairman of Lloyd's, 1972, 1974; *b* 20 April 1913; *s* of late Sydney and Dora Creswell; *m* 1938, Jean (Lilian Jane) Maxwell; two *s*. *Educ:* Highgate School. Served War, 1942–46, 2nd Household Cavalry Regt; Captain and Adjt, The Life Guards, 1945–46. Member of Lloyd's, 1946: Mem. Cttee, 1969–72, 1974; Mem. Cttee Lloyd's Underwriters Non-Marine Assoc., 1968–74, Chm. 1973. *Recreations:* photography, family croquet. *Address:* Lullington Court, near Polegate, E Sussex BN26 5QY. *T:* Alfriston (0323) 870548. *Club:* Devonshire (Eastbourne).

CRETNEY, Prof. Stephen Michael, DCL; FBA 1985; Professor of Law, University of Bristol, since 1984 (Dean of the Faculty of Law, 1984–88); *b* 25 Feb. 1936; *yr s* of late Fred and Winifred M. V. Cretney; *m* 1973, Antonia Lois Vanrenen, *o d* of Lt-Comdr A. G. G. Vanrenen, RN; two *s*. *Educ:* Queen's Road Primary Sch., Cheadle Hulme; Manchester Warehousemen and Clerks' Orphan Schs, Cheadle Hulme; Magdalen Coll., Oxford (Demy in Mod. Hist.; 1st Cl. Hons Jurisprudence, 1959; DCL, 1985). Nat. Service, Intell. Corps, 1954–56. Solicitor. Partner, Macfarlanes, London, 1964; Lecturer: Kenya Sch. of Law, Nairobi, 1966; Southampton Univ., 1968; Fellow and Tutor, Exeter Coll., Oxford, 1969–78; a Law Comr, 1978–83. Pt-time Chm. of Social Security Appeal Tribunals, 1985–, of Med. Appeal Tribunals, 1989–. Member: Departmental Cttee on Prison Disciplinary System, 1984–85; Family and Civil Cttee, Judicial Studies Bd, 1985–90; Lord Chancellor's Adv. Cttee on Legal Educn, 1987–88; Cttee for Social Scis, CNAA, 1987–90; Committee of Management: Centre for Socio-Legal Studies, Oxford Univ., 1985–; Inst. for Advanced Legal Studies, 1985–. Chm., Cttee of Heads of Univ. Law Schs, 1986–88. Trustee, Bristol Courts Family Conciliation Service, 1984–87. A Gen. Comr of Income Tax, 1970–78. *Publications:* Theobald on Wills, (ed jtly) 13th edn 1970; Principles of Family Law, 1974, 5th edn (ed jtly) 1990; Family Law (Teach Yourself series), 1982; The Enduring Power of Attorney, 1986, 3rd edn 1991; Elements of Family Law, 1987, 2nd edn 1991; articles and notes in legal jls. *Recreations:* cooking, taking snapshots. *Address:* Faculty of Law, Wills Memorial Building, Queen's Road, Bristol BS8 1RJ. *T:* Bristol (0272) 303371; 15 Canynge Square, Clifton, Bristol BS8 3LA. *T:* Bristol (0272) 732983. *Club:* United Oxford & Cambridge University.

CREW, Air Vice-Marshal Edward Dixon, CB 1973; DSO 1944 and Bar 1950; DFC 1941 and Bar 1942; FRAeS 1972; Planning Inspectorate, Department of the Environment, 1973–87; *b* 24 Dec. 1917; *er s* of F. D. Crew, MB, MRCS, LRCP; *m* 1945, Virginia Martin; one *s*. *Educ:* Felsted Sch.; Downing Coll., Cambridge (MA). Commissioned RAFVR, 1939; served War of 1939–45: night fighter sqdns; 604 sqdn, 85 Sqdn; Comd 96 Sqdn; permanent commission, 1945. Malayan Emergency, Comd No 45 Sqdn, 1948–50; on exchange, RCAF, 1952–54; CFE, 1954–56; Comd RAF Brüggen, Germany, 1959–62; Comdr, Air Forces Borneo, 1965–66; AOC Central Reconnaissance Estabt, 1968; Dep. Controller, Nat. Air Traffic Services, 1969–72; various Air Staff jobs at Air Min. and MoD; retd 1973. *Recreation:* golf. *Address:* National Westminster Bank, 10 Benet Street, Cambridge. *Club:* Royal Air Force.

CREWE, Albert V., PhD; Professor, Department of Physics and the Enrico Fermi Institute, since 1963 (Assistant Professor, 1956–59; Associate Professor, 1959–63; William E. Wrather Distinguished Service Professor, 1977), Dean of Physical Sciences Division, 1971–81, University of Chicago; *b* 18 Feb. 1927; *m* 1949, Doreen Patricia Blunsdon; one *s* three *d*. *Educ:* Univ. of Liverpool (BS, PhD). Asst Lectr, 1950–52, Lectr, 1952–55, Univ. of Liverpool; Div. Dir, Particle Accelerator Division, Argonne National Laboratory, 1958–61; Dir, Argonne National Laboratory, 1961–67. Pres., Orchid One Corp., 1987–. Member: Nat. Acad. of Sciences; Amer. Acad. of Arts and Sciences. Hon. FRMS 1984. Named Outstanding New Citizen by Citizenship Council of Chicago, 1962; received Immigrant's Service League's Annual Award for Outstanding Achievement in the Field of Science, 1962; Illinois Sesquicentennial Award, 1968; Industrial Research Award, 1970; Distinguished Service Award, Electron Microscope Soc. of America, 1976; Albert A. Michelson Award, Franklin Inst., 1977; Ernst Abbe Award, NY Microscope Soc., 1979; Duddell Medal, Inst. of Physics, 1980. *Publications:* Research USA (with J. J. Katz), 1964; contribs to: Proc. Royal Soc.; Proc. Phys. Soc.; Physical Review; Science; Physics Today; Jl of Applied Physics; Reviews of Scientific Instruments; Optik; Ultramicroscopy, etc. *Address:* 63 Old Creek Road, Palos Park, Illinois, USA. *T:* 708–448–8738. *Clubs:* Quadrangle, Wayfarers' (Chicago).

CREWE, Prof. Ivor Martin; Professor of Government, University of Essex, since 1982; *b* 15 Dec. 1945; *s* of Francis and Lilly Crewe; *m* 1968, Jill Barbara (*née* Gadian); two *s* one *d*. *Educ:* Manchester Grammar Sch.; Exeter Coll., Oxford (MA); London School of Economics (MScEcon). Assistant Lecturer, Univ. of Lancaster, 1967–69; Junior Research Fellow, Nuffield Coll., Oxford, 1969–71; Lectr, Dept of Govt, Univ. of Essex, 1971–74; Dir SSRC Data Archive, 1974–82. Co-Dir, Feb. 1974, Oct. 1974, 1979 British Election Studies; elections analyst for: BBC TV, 1982–; The Times, 1990–. Editor, 1977–82, Co-editor, 1984–, British Journal of Political Science. *Publications:* (with A. H. Halsey) Social Survey of the Civil Service (HMSO), 1969; ed, British Political Sociology Yearbook, vol. 1 1974, vol. 2 1975; (with Bo Sarlvik) Decade of Dealignment, 1983; (with Anthony Fox) British Parliamentary Constituencies, 1984; (ed jtly) Electoral Change in Western Democracies, 1985; (ed jtly) Political Communications: the general election campaign of 1983, 1987; (with Anthony Fox) The British Electorate 1963–87; articles in various academic jls on public opinion and elections in Britain. *Recreation:* opera. *Address:* 141 Maldon Road, Colchester, Essex CO3 3BJ. *T:* Colchester (0206) 760745.

CREWE, Quentin Hugh; writer and journalist; *b* 14 Nov. 1926; *s* of Major Hugh Crewe and Lady Annabel Crewe; *m* 1st, 1956, Martha Sharp; one *s* one *d*; 2nd, 1961, Angela Huth; one *d* (one *s* decd); 3rd, 1970, Susan Cavendish (marr. diss.); one *s* one *d*. *Educ:* Eton; Trinity Coll., Cambridge. Joined Evening Standard, 1953; subseq. worked for Queen, Vogue, Daily Mail, Sunday Mirror; freelance, 1970–, contrib. to Times, Sunday Times, Sunday Telegraph, and Spectator. *Publications:* A Curse of Blossom, 1960; Frontiers of Privilege, 1961; Great Chefs of France, 1978; Pocket Book of Food, 1980; In Search of the Sahara, 1983; The Last Maharaja, 1985; Touch the Happy Isles, 1987; In the Realms of Gold, 1989; Well, I forget the rest, 1991. *Recreation:* travel. *Address:* Le Grand Banc, 04110 Oppedette, France. *T:* 92 759554, *Fax:* 92 759647.

CRIBB, Air Cdre Peter Henry, CBE 1957; DSO 1942, and Bar, 1944; DFC 1941; JP; retired 1983; *b* 28 Sept. 1918; *s* of late Charles B. Cribb and Mrs Ethel Cribb; *m* 1949, Vivienne Janet, *yr d* of late Col S. T. J. Perry, MC, TD, DL, Oxton, Birkenhead, Ches; three *s*. *Educ:* Bradford Grammar Sch.; Prince Henry's Sch., Otley. Flt Cadet, RAF Coll., 1936–38; Flying duties in Bomber Comd, 1938–45 (Comd No. 582 Sqdn, RAF Little Staughton); Comdg RAF Salbani, RAF Peshawar, India and Staff No. 1 Indian Gp, 1945–47; OC 203 Sqdn, 1947, and HQ Staff, 1950, Coastal Comd; RAF Staff Coll., Bracknell, 1951; Asst Dir Tech. Intell., Air Min., 1951–53; Gp Capt. Plans and Policy, HQ Bomber Comd, 1953–57; 2nd TAF, Germany (OC Oldenburg, Ahlhorn and Gutersloh), 1957–60; Air Min., Dep. Dir Air Staff Briefing, 1959–61, Dir, 1961–62; SASO, Air Forces, Middle East, 1962–63; IDC, 1964; Deputy to Asst Chief of Defence Staff (Joint Warfare), MoD 1965–66; retired, 1966. Administrative Manager, Goldsworthy Mining Ltd, 1966–68. Associate Fellow, Australian Inst. of Management, 1969; Past State Pres., Ryder-Cheshire Foundn of WA, Inc.; Pres., Pathfinder Assoc. of

WA; Mem., West Perth (WA) Rotary. Mem., Australian Faceters Guild. JP Western Australia, 1968. *Recreations:* fishing, facetting gem stones. *Address:* Peniston, 66 Sherington Road, Greenwood, WA 6024, Australia.

CRICHTON, family name of **Earl of Erne.**

CRICHTON, Viscount; John Henry Michael Ninian Crichton; *b* 19 June 1971; *s* and *heir* of Earl of Erne, *qv*.

CRICHTON, Sir Andrew Maitland-Makgill-, Kt 1963; Director, P&OSN Co., 1957–81; Vice-Chairman, Port of London Authority, 1967–76 (Member, 1964–67); *b* 28 Dec. 1910; *s* of late Lt-Col D. M.-M.-Crichton, Queen's Own Cameron Highldrs, and Phyllis (*née* Cuthbert); *m* 1948, Isabel, *d* of Andrew McGill, Sydney, NSW. *Educ:* Wellington Coll. Joined Gray, Dawes & Co., 1929; transf. India to Mackinnon Mackenzie & Co. (Agents of BI Co. and for P & O on Indian Continent and in parts of Far East), 1931. Joined IA, 1940; DDM (Shipping), Col, at GHQ India, 1944. Mackinnon Mackenzie, Calcutta, 1945–48; P&O Co., UK (Gen. Manager, 1951); Chm., Overseas Containers Ltd, 1965–73; former Director: Standard Chartered Group; Inchcape Insurance Hldgs Ltd; London Tin Corp.; Dir, Butler's Warehousing & Distrib. Ltd. Chairman: Nat. Assoc. Port Employers, 1958–65; EDC for GPO, 1965–70; Vice-Chm., British Transport Docks Bd, 1963–68; Member: Baltic Exchange; Nat. Freight Corp., 1969–73; Court of The Chartered Bank; Police Council for GB (Arbitrator), 1969–79; Industrial Arbitration Bd. FRSA; FCIT (a past Vice-Pres.). *Recreations:* golf, music. Freeman, Co. of Watermen and Lightermen. *Address:* 55 Hans Place, Knightsbridge, SW1. *T:* 071–584 1209. *Clubs:* City of London, Caledonian.
See also Maj.-Gen. Edward Maitland-Makgill-Crichton.

CRICHTON, Charles Ainslie; film director; *b* 6 Aug. 1910; *s* of John Douglas Crichton and Hester Wingate Ainslie; *m* 1st, 1936, Vera Pearl Harman-Mills; two *s*; 2nd, 1962, Nadine Haze. *Educ:* Oundle; Univ. of Oxford (BA History). Pictures, 1944–88, include: Painted Boats, Hue and Cry, Against the Wind, Dance Hall, Lavender Hill Mob (Dirs' Guild Awards Nomination, 1953), Hunted, Titfield Thunderbolt, The Love Lottery, Divided Heart, Man in the Sky, Battle of the Sexes, The Third Secret, He Who Rides a Tiger, A Fish Called Wanda (Directors' Guild Awards Nomination, 1989; Oscar Nomination, 1989; BAFTA Award, 1989; Evening Standard Award, 1989). Television: Danger Man, The Avengers, Strange Report, Black Beauty, Space 1999, Dick Turpin, Smuggler; Video Arts shorts. *Recreations:* fishing, photography. *Address:* 1 Southwell Gardens, SW7 4SB.

CRICHTON, David George, LVO 1968; British Consul-General, Nice, 1970–74; *b* 31 July 1914; *e s* of late Col Hon. Sir George Crichton, GCVO; *m* 1941, Joan Fenella, *d* of late Col D. W. Cleaver, DSO; one *s* one *d*. *Educ:* Eton. Worked as journalist, Reading and Manchester, and on Daily Telegraph, Paris and London, 1933–39; served War of 1939–45 in Derbyshire Yeomanry (despatches); Major 1944; entered Foreign Service, 1946; served in Belgrade, Singapore, Alexandria, Miami, La Paz and Santiago. *Address:* Church House, Medstead, Alton, Hampshire GU34 5LT. *T:* Alton (0420) 62632. *Club:* Boodle's.
See also R. J. V. Crichton.

CRICHTON, Maj.-Gen. Edward Maitland-Makgill-, OBE 1948 (MBE 1945); GOC 51st Highland Division, 1966–68, retired; *b* 23 Nov. 1916; *s* of late Lt-Col D. E. Maitland-Makgill-Crichton, Queen's Own Cameron Highlanders and Phyllis (*née* Cuthbert); *m* 1951, Sheila Margaret Hibbins, Bexhill-on-Sea; three *s*. *Educ:* Bedford Sch.; RMC Sandhurst. 2nd Lieut Queen's Own Cameron Highlanders, 1937; Adjt 5th Bn Cameron Highlanders, 1939; served with 5th Cameron Highlanders and 51 (Highland) Div., N Africa, Sicily, Normandy, NW Europe, 1940–45; GSO 1, HQ British Commonwealth Occupation Force, Japan, 1946–47; Mobilisation Br., WO 1948–50; 1st Bn Cameron Highlanders, Tripoli and Canal Zone, 1950–52; Jt Services Staff Coll., 1953; GSO 1, 3rd Inf. Div. (UK Strategic Reserve), Canal Zone, Egypt, UK and Suez, 1953–57; with 1st Bn Cameron Highlanders, Aden, 1957; comd 1st Liverpool Scottish, 1958–61; Comdr 152 (Highland) Inf. Bde, 1962–64; Dep. Dir Army Staff Duties, MoD, 1965–66. *Recreations:* shooting, golf, gardening, fishing. *Address:* 211 Braid Road, Edinburgh EH10 6HT. *T:* 031–447 5662.
See also Sir Andrew Maitland-Makgill-Crichton.

CRICHTON, Nicholas; Metropolitan Stipendiary Magistrate, since 1987; an Assistant Recorder, since 1991; *b* 23 Oct. 1943; s of Charles Ainslie Crichton and Vera Pearl McCallum; *m* 1973, Ann Valerie (*née* Jackson); two *s*. *Educ:* Haileybury & ISC; Queen's Univ., Belfast (LLB, 2nd Cl. Hons). Schoolmaster, Pembroke House Sch., Gilgil, Kenya, 1963; cowhand, Montana, USA, 1966; articled to late T. J. Burrows, Currey & Co., SW1, 1968–70; Assistant Solicitor: Currey & Co., 1970–71; Nicholls Christie & Crocker, 1972–74; Partner, Nicholls Christie & Crocker, 1974–86. *Recreations:* cricket (playing, coaching and watching), golf, watching rugby, gardening, walking, reading. *Address:* c/o Magistrates' Court, 58 Bow Road, E3 4DJ. *Clubs:* Middlesex CC; Old Haileyburian RFC; Flackwell Heath Golf.

CRICHTON, Col Richard John Vesey, CVO 1986; MC 1940; *b* 2 Nov. 1916; *s* of late Col Hon. Sir George Crichton, GCVO, and Lady Mary Crichton; *m* 1948, Yvonne Avril Catherine, *d* of late Dr and Mrs H. E. Worthington; three *s*. *Educ:* Eton; RMC, Sandhurst. Commissioned 2/Lieut Coldstream Guards, 1936; served World War II: Belgium, 1940, Italy, 1943–44 (twice wounded, MC, despatches); Commanded: 1st Bn Coldstream Guards, 1954–57; Coldstream Guards, 1958–61, retired 1961. Comptroller, Union Jack Services Clubs, 1964–66; Member, HM Body Guard, Hon. Corps of Gentlemen at Arms, 1966–86; Clerk of the Cheque and Adjutant, 1979–81; Lieutenant, 1981–86. Mem., Hants CC and Police Authority, 1964–67. *Publication:* The Coldstream Guards 1946–1970, 1972. *Address:* Eglinton Lodge, Hartley Wintney, Hampshire RG27 8JW. *Club:* Cavalry and Guards.
See also D. G. Crichton.

CRICHTON-BROWN, Sir Robert, KCMG 1980; Kt 1972; CBE 1970; TD; Executive Chairman, Rothmans International plc, 1985–88; *b* Melbourne, 23 Aug. 1919; *s* of late L. Crichton-Brown, Sydney; *m* 1941, Norah Isabelle, *d* of late A. E. Turnbull; one *s* one *d*. *Educ:* Sydney Grammar Sch. Served War, 1939–45, BEF; Major, Royal Artillery and Gen. Staff, France, Iceland, India, Burma (despatches twice). Chairman: Lumley Corp. Ltd (formerly Edward Lumley Ltd), 1974–89 (Man. Dir, 1952–82); Lumley Life Ltd, 1961–87 (Dir, 1961–89); Lumley Gen. Insce Ltd, 1974–88 (Dir, 1952–88); NEI Pacific Ltd, 1961–85; Rothmans of Pall Mall (Australia) Ltd, 1981–85 (Dir, 1971–85 and 1987–88); Commercial Banking Co. of Sydney Ltd, 1976–82 (Dir, 1970–82); Commercial & General Acceptance Ltd, 1977–82; Westham Dredging Co. Pty Ltd, 1975–85; Vice Chairman: Nat. Australia Bank Ltd, 1982–85; Custom Credit Corp., 1982–85; Director: Daily Mail and General Trust Ltd (UK), 1979–; Edward Lumley Hldgs, 1989–. Fed. Pres., Inst. of Dirs in Aust., 1967–80 (Chm., NSW Branch, 1965–80; Councillor, 1980–89; Hon. Life Mem.). Mem. Federal Exec. and Federal Hon. Treas., Liberal Party of Australia, 1973–85. Pres., Med. Foundn, Sydney Univ., 1962–87; Dir, Royal Prince Alfred Hosp., 1970–84; Hon. Life Governor, Aust. Postgraduate Fedn in Medicine; Member: Cttee, RACP, 1973–85; Adv. Bd, Girl Guides Assoc. of Australia, 1973–85; Adv. Bd, Salvation Army, 1973–85; Internat. Forum and Panel, Duke of Edinburgh's Award, 1979–84 (Nat. Co-ordinator, Duke of Edinburgh's Award Scheme in Aust., 1979–84); Council, Imperial Soc. of Knights Bachelor (Vice-Chm., Pacific Reg.); Nat. Councillor, Scout Assoc. of Aust., 1980–85; Council, Cutty Sark Maritime Trust, 1989– (Mem. Council, Maritime Trust, 1987–89; Gov., Cutty Sark Soc., 1987–89). Underwriting Mem. of Lloyd's, 1946–. Hon. Fellow, Sydney Univ., 1987. Mem., Australia's winning Admiral's Cup Team (Balandra), UK, 1967; winner, Sydney-Hobart Yacht Race (Pacha), 1970. *Clubs:* White's, Royal Cruising; Royal Yacht Squadron; Australian, Union (Sydney); Cruising Yacht Club of Australia, Royal Sydney Yacht Squadron, Royal Prince Alfred Yacht.

CRICHTON-MILLER, Donald, TD; MA; *b* 1906; *s* of late Hugh Crichton-Miller, MA, MD, FRCP; *m* 1931, Monica, *d* of late B. A. Glanvill, JP, Bromley, Kent; two *s* one *d*. *Educ:* Fettes Coll., Edinburgh; Pembroke Coll., Cambridge (Exhibitioner). Played Rugby Football for Cambridge and Scotland; Asst Master: Monmouth Sch., 1929–31; Bryanston Sch., 1931–34; Stowe Sch., 1934–36; Head Master: Taunton Sch., Somerset, 1936–45; Fettes Coll., 1945–58; Stowe Sch., 1958–63. Carried out education surveys in Pakistan, 1951, and Malta, 1956. *Recreations:* governing schools and managing properties. *Address:* Glencorse, Compton, Newbury, Berks RG16 0RE. *T:* Compton (0635) 578384.

CRICHTON-STUART, family name of **Marquess of Bute.**

CRICK, Alan John Pitts, OBE 1956; *b* 14 May 1913; *er s* of Owen John Pitts Crick and Margaret Crick (*née* Daw), late of Minehead, Somerset; *m* 1941, Norah (*née* Atkins) (*d* 1984); two *d*. *Educ:* Latymer Upper Sch.; King's Coll., London Univ. (MA); Heidelberg Univ. (Dr.phil). Vice-Consul, British Consulate-Gen., Free City of Danzig, 1938–39. Served War, Army, 1939–46: Egypt and Libya, 1941–43, HQ Eighth Army; NW Europe, 1944–46 (despatches); Major, GSO2, Intell., SHAEF; HQ 21 Army Group and HQ BAOR. Min. of Defence Jt Intell. Bureau, 1946–63; jssc, 1948; British Jt Services Mission, Washington, 1953–56; Asst Dir, Jt Intell. Bureau, 1957–63; idc, 1960; Counsellor, British Embassy, Washington, 1963–65; Asst Sec., Cabinet Office, 1965–68; Def. Intell. Staff, MoD, 1968–73; Director of Economic Intelligence, MoD, 1970–73. Adviser to Commercial Union Assurance Co., 1973–78. *Recreations:* travel, antiquarian interests, books. *Address:* 16 Church Square, Rye, East Sussex TN31 7HE. *T:* Rye (0797) 222050. *Clubs:* Naval and Military; Dormy House (Rye).
See also R. P. Crick.

CRICK, Prof. Bernard, BSc (Econ.), PhD (London); writer; Emeritus Professor, University of London; *b* 16 Dec. 1929; *s* of Harry Edgar and Florence Clara Crick. *Educ:* Whitgift Sch.; University Coll., London. Research student, LSE, 1950–52; Teaching Fellow, Harvard, 1952–54; Asst Prof., McGill, 1954–55; Vis. Fellow, Berkeley, 1955–56; Asst Lectr, later Lectr, later Sen. Lectr, LSE, 1957–65; Prof. of Political Theory and Institutions, Sheffield Univ., 1965–71; Prof. of Politics, Birkbeck Coll., Univ of London, 1971–84. Jt Editor, Political Quarterly, 1966–80; Chm., Political Qly Publishing Co., 1980–. Joint Sec., Study of Parlt Gp, 1964–68. Hon. Pres., Politics Assoc., 1970–76; Mem., Council of the Hansard Soc., 1962–. Hon. Fellow, Univ. of Edinburgh, 1986. Hon. DSc Belfast, 1986; Hon. DLitt: Sheffield, 1990; E London Poly., 1990. *Publications:* The American Science of Politics, 1958; In Defence of Politics, 1962, 3rd edn 1982 (trans. German, Japanese, Spanish, Italian); The Reform of Parliament, 1964, 2nd edn 1968; (ed) Essays on Reform, 1967; (ed with W. A. Robson) Protest and Discontent, 1970; (ed) Machiavelli: The Discourses, 1971; Political Theory and Practice, 1972; (ed with W. A. Robson) Taxation Policy, 1973; Basic Forms of Government, 1973; Crime, Rape and Gin, 1975; (ed with Alex Porter) Political Education and Political Literacy, 1978; George Orwell: a Life, 1980, 2nd edn 1982; (ed) Unemployment, 1981; (ed) Clarendon edn, Orwell's Nineteen Eighty-Four, 1984; (ed with Audrey Coppard) Orwell Observed, 1984; Socialism, 1987; Essays on Politics and Literature, 1989; Political Thoughts and Polemics, 1990; (ed) National Identities, 1991. *Recreations:* polemicising, book- and theatre-reviewing, hill-walking, bee-keeping. *Address:* 8A Bellevue Terrace, Edinburgh EH7 4DT. *T:* 031–557 2517. *Clubs:* Savile; Scottish Arts (Edinburgh).

CRICK, Francis Harry Compton, FRS 1959; BSc London, PhD Cantab; J. W. Kieckhefer Distinguished Professor, The Salk Institute, since 1977; Adjunct Professor of Chemistry and Psychology, University of California, San Diego; *b* 8 June 1916; *e s* of late Harry Crick and late Annie Elizabeth (*née* Wilkins); *m* 1st, 1940, Ruth Doreen Dodd (divorced, 1947); one *s*; 2nd, 1949, Odile Speed; two *d*. *Educ:* Mill Hill Sch.; University Coll., London; Caius Coll., Cambridge (Hon. Fellow, 1976). Scientist in Admiralty, 1940–47; Strangeways Laboratory, Cambridge, 1947–49; MRC Lab. of Molecular Biology, Cambridge, 1949–77; Brooklyn Polytechnic, NY, USA, 1953–54. Vis. Lectr Rockefeller Inst., NY, USA, 1959; Vis. Prof., Chemistry Dept, Harvard, 1959; Fellow, Churchill Coll., Cambridge, 1960–61; Vis. Biophysics Prof., Harvard, 1962; Non-resident Fellow, Salk Inst. for Biological Studies, San Diego, 1962–73; Ferkauf Foundn Visiting Prof., Salk Inst., 1976–77; Fellow, UCL, 1962; For. Hon. Mem., Amer. Acad. of Arts and Sciences, 1962; Hon. Mem., Amer. Soc. Biological Chem., 1963; Hon. MRIA, 1964; Hon. Fellow: Churchill Coll., Cambridge, 1965; Caius Coll., Cambridge, 1976; FAAAS 1966; Hon. FRSE, 1966; Fellow, INSA, 1982; Hon. Fellow, Indian Acad. of Scis, 1985; For. Associate, US Nat. Acad. of Sciences, 1969; Mem., German Acad. of Science, Leopoldina, 1969; For. Mem., American Philos. Soc., Philadelphia, 1972; Hon. Mem., Hellenic Biochem. and Biophys. Soc., 1974. Associate For. Mem., French Acad. of Scis, 1978. Lectures: Bloor, Rochester, USA, 1959; Korkes Meml, Duke Univ., 1960; Herter, Johns Hopkins Sch. of Medicine, USA, 1960; Franklin Harris, Mount Zion Hosp., 1962; Holme, London, 1962; Henry Sidgewick Meml, Cambridge, 1963; Harveian, London, 1963; Graham Young, Glasgow, 1963; Robert Boyle, Oxford, 1963; James W. Sherrill, Scripps Clinic, 1964; Elisha Mitchel Meml, N Carolina, 1964; Vanuxem, Princeton, 1964; Charles West, London, 1964; William T. Sedgwick Meml, MIT, 1965; A. J. Carlson Meml, Chicago, 1965; Failing, Univ. of Oregon, 1965; Robbins, Pomona Coll., 1965; Telford Meml, Manchester, 1965; Kinnaird, Regent St Polytechnic, 1965; John Danz, Univ. of Washington, 1966; Sumner, Cornell, 1966; Royal Society Croonian, 1966; Cherwell-Simon Meml, Oxford, 1966; Genetical Soc. Mendel, 1966; Rickman Godlee, UCL, 1968; Shell, Stanford Univ., 1969; Evarts A. Graham Meml, Washington Univ., St Louis Missouri; Gehrmann, Illinois Univ., 1973; Cori, Buffalo, NY, 1973; Jean Weigle Meml, Calif Inst. of Technology, 1976; John Stauffer Distinguished, Univ. of Southern Calif, 1976; Smith Kline and French, Univ. of Calif, SF, 1977; Henry Failing Distinguished, Oregon, 1977; Paul Lund, Northwestern, 1977; Steenbock, Wisconsin, 1977; 8th Sir Hans Krebs, and medal, FEBS, Copenhagen, 1977; Lynen, Miami, 1978; Briody Meml, New Jersey, 1979; Dupont, Harvard, 1979; Ferguson, Mo, 1980; George W. Gardiner Meml, New Mexico, 1981; Jean Weigle Meml, Geneva, 1981; Rand Meml, Los Angeles, 1983; Daniel Coir Gilman, Baltimore, 1983; Beatty Memls, McGill Univ., 1985; Ojemann, Univ. of Iowa, 1988. Warren Triennial Prize, Boston, USA (with J. D. Watson), 1959; Lasker Award (jointly), 1960; Prix Charles Léopold Mayer, French Académies des Sciences, 1961; Research Corp. Award (with J. D. Watson), 1961; Gairdner Foundation Award, Toronto, 1962; Nobel Prize for Medicine (jointly), 1962; Royal Medal, Royal Soc., 1972; Copley Medal, Royal Soc., 1976; Michelson-Morley Award, Cleveland, 1981;

Benjamin P. Cheney Medal, Spokane, Washington, 1986; Golden Plate Award, Phoenix, 1987; Albert Medal, RSA, 1987; Wright Prize VIII, Harvey Mudd Coll., Calif., 1988; Joseph Priestly Award, Dickinson Coll., Pennsylvania, 1988. *Publications:* Of Molecules and Men, 1966; Life Itself, 1981; What Mad Pursuit - a personal view of scientific discovery, 1988; papers and articles on molecular and cell biology and on neurobiology in scientific journals. *Address:* The Salk Institute for Biological Studies, PO Box 85800, San Diego, Calif 92136–8500, USA; 1792 Colgate Circle, La Jolla, Calif 92037, USA.

CRICK, R(onald) Pitts, FRCS, DOMS; Honorary Ophthalmic Surgeon, King's College Hospital, since 1982 (Ophthalmic Surgeon, 1950–82); Recognised Teacher in the Faculty of Medicine, University of London, 1960–82, Emeritus Lecturer, King's College Hospital Medical School, 1982; Visiting Research Fellow, University of Sussex, since 1976; *b* 5 Feb. 1917; *yr s* of Owen J. Pitts Crick and Margaret Daw, Minehead, Som; *m* 1941, Jocelyn Mary Grenfell Robins, *yr d* of Leonard A. C. Robins and Geraldine Grenfell, Hendon; four *s* one *d. Educ:* Latymer Upper Sch., London; King's Coll. and (Science Schol.) King's Coll. Hosp. Med. Sch., Univ. of London. MRCS, LRCP 1939. Surgeon, MN, 1939–40; Surg. Lieut, RNVR, 1940–46. Ophthalmic Registrar, King's Coll. Hosp., 1946–48; DOMS 1946. Surgical First Asst, Royal Eye Hosp., 1947–50; Ophth. Surg., Epsom County Hosp., 1948–49; Ophth. Registrar, Belgrave Hosp. for Children, 1948–50; Ophth. Surg., Sevenoaks Hosp., 1948–50; Sen. Ophthalmic Surg., Royal Eye Hosp., 1950–69; Ophthalmic Surg., Belgrave Hosp. for Children, 1950–66. Chm., Ophthalmic Post-Grad. Trng, SE Thames RHA, 1972–82. Examr to RCS for Diploma in Ophthalmology, 1961–68. FRCS 1950; FCOphth 1988. Hon. Ophth. Surg., Royal London Soc. for the Blind, 1954–57. FRSocMed, Vice-Pres. Ophthalmological Section, 1964, and Mem. Council Ophthalmolog. Section, 1953–54 and 1956–58. Member: Oxford Ophthalmolog. Congress; Southern Ophthalmolog. Soc. (Vice-Pres., 1969; Pres., 1970). Chm., Internat. Glaucoma Assoc., 1975; Charter Member: Internat. Glaucoma Congress, USA, 1977–; Internat. Assoc. of Ocular Surgeons, 1981. Sir Stewart Duke-Elder Glaucoma Award, Internat. Glaucoma Congress, 1985; Lederle Medal for Ophthalmology, Amer. Soc. of Contemp. Ophthalmol., 1985. *Publications:* All About Glaucoma, 1981; A Textbook of Clinical Ophthalmology, 1986; Cardiovascular Affections, Arteriosclerosis and Hypertension (Section in Systemic Ophthalmology, ed A. Sorsby), 1950 and 1958; Computerised Monitoring of Glaucoma (Section in Glaucoma, ed J. G. Bellows), 1979; Diagnosis of Primary Open Angle Glaucoma (in Glaucoma, ed J. E. Cairns), 1986; medical and ophthalmic contribs to Brit. Jl Ophthalmology, BMJ, Lancet, Jl RN Med. Service, Trans Ophthalmolog. Soc. of the UK, etc. *Recreations:* walking, motoring, sailing. *Address:* Ophthalmic Department, King's College Hospital, Denmark Hill, SE5 9RS. *T:* 071–274 6222 ext. 3534; Sandbanks House, 2 Panorama Road, Sandbanks, Poole, Dorset BH13 7RD. *T:* Canford Cliffs (0202) 707560. *Clubs:* Royal Automobile; Royal Motor Yacht.
See also A. J. P. Crick.

CRICKHOWELL, Baron *cr* 1987 (Life Peer), of Pont Esgob in the Black Mountains and County of Powys; **Roger Nicholas Edwards**, PC 1979; Chairman, National Rivers Authority, since 1989 (Chairman, Advisory Committee, 1988–89); Director: HTV Group, since 1987; Associated British Ports Holdings, since 1988; Anglesey Mining, since 1988 (Vice-Chairman); Harlech Fine Art Holdings and subsidiaries, since 1989; *b* 25 Feb. 1934; *s* of late (H. C.) Ralph Edwards, CBE, FSA, and Marjorie Ingham Brooke; *m* 1963, Ankaret Healing; one *s* two *d. Educ:* Westminster Sch.; Trinity Coll., Cambridge, 1954–57; read History: BA 1957, MA, 1968. Member of Lloyds, 1965–. MP (C) Pembroke, 1970–87. Sec. of State for Wales, 1979–87. Opposition spokesman on Welsh affairs, 1975–79. Pres., Univ. of Wales Coll. of Cardiff, 1988– (Hon. Fellow, UC, Cardiff, 1985–88). President: Contemporary Art Society for Wales, 1988–; SE Arts Assoc., 1988–; Mem. Council, Welsh Nat. Opera, 1988–; Mem., Cttee, AA, 1988–. *Publications:* articles and reviews in The Connoisseur and other jls. *Recreations:* fishing, gardening, collecting watercolours and drawings. *Address:* Pont Esgob Mill, Fforest Coal Pit, near Abergavenny, Gwent NP7 7LS; 4 Henning Street, SW11 3DR. *Club:* Cardiff and County.

CRICKMAY, John Rackstrow, FRICS; Chairman, Percy Bilton PLC, 1984–89 (Director, 1980–89); *b* 16 May 1914; *s* of Edward John Crickmay and Constance May Bowyer; *m* 1939, Margaret Hilda Rainer; one *s. Educ:* Brighton Coll. Legal & General Assurance Society: Surveyor, 1936–46; Chief Estates Surveyor, 1946–74. Artist Rifles, 1936; Royal Regt of Artillery, 1939–46: served in Far East, 1940–45 (POW, 1942–45); TEM 1946. Cons. to property interests, 1974–; Dir, Ecclesiastical Insce Office, 1980–84. President: British Chapter Real Property Fedn, 1966; Chartered Auctioneers & Estate Agents Inst., 1968; Mem. Council, RICS, 1972–85, Hon. Treas., 1980–85. Gov., Royal Star & Garter, Richmond, 1975–90; Dep. Chm., Christ's Hosp., 1984–89, Almoner, 1977–89. Master, Ironmongers' Co., 1976–77. Hon. Fellow, Coll. of Estate Management, Reading, 1988. Medal of Internat. Real Estate Fedn, 1974; Silver Jubilee Medal, 1977. *Recreations:* cricket, golf. *Address:* Old Walls, Rectory Lane, Pulborough, West Sussex RH20 2AF. *T:* Pulborough (07982) 2336. *Clubs:* Oriental, MCC; West Sussex Golf.

CRIGHTON, Prof. David George; Professor of Applied Mathematics, University of Cambridge and Fellow of St John's College, Cambridge, since 1986; *b* 15 Nov. 1942; *s* of George Wolfe Johnston Crighton and Violet Grace Crighton (*née* Garrison); *m* 1st, 1969, Mary Christine West (marr. diss. 1985); one *s* one *d*; 2nd, 1986, Johanna Veronica Hol. *Educ:* St John's College, Cambridge (BA 1964, MA 1980); Imperial College London (PhD 1969). Research Asst, Imperial College London, 1967–74; Prof. of Applied Mathematics, Univ. of Leeds, 1974–85. *Publications:* papers on fluid mechanics and wave theory in jls, conf. procs. *Recreations:* music, opera. *Address:* The Laurels, 58 Girton Road, Girton, Cambridge CB3 0LN. *T:* Cambridge (0223) 277100.

CRIGMAN, David Ian; QC 1989; *b* 16 Aug. 1945; *s* of late Jack Crigman and of Sylvia Crigman; *m* 1980, Judith Ann Penny; one *s. Educ:* King Edward's Sch., Birmingham; Univ. of Leeds (LLB Hons). Called to the Bar, Gray's Inn, 1969; a Recorder, 1985. *Recreations:* tennis, ski-ing, writing, travel. *Address:* 1 Fountain Court, Steelhouse Lane, Birmingham B4 6DR. *T:* 021–236 5721.

CRILL, Sir Peter (Leslie), Kt 1987; CBE 1980; FCIArb; Bailiff of Jersey, and President of the Court of Appeal of Jersey, since 1986; Judge, Court of Appeal of Guernsey, since 1986; *b* 1 Feb. 1925; *s* of S. G. Crill, Connetable of St Clement, 1916–58, and Olive Le Gros; *m* 1953, A. F. R. Dodd, MB, *d* of E. A. Dodd, JP, Dromara, NI; three *d. Educ:* Victoria Coll., Jersey; Exeter Coll., Oxford (King Charles I Scholar; MA; Hon. Fellow, 1991). Called to the Bar, Middle Temple, 1949; called to the Jersey Bar, 1949. In private practice in Jersey, 1949–62. States of Jersey Deputy for St Clement, 1951–58; States of Jersey Senator, 1960–62; Solicitor General, Jersey, 1962–69; Attorney General, Jersey, 1969–75. Dep. Bailiff, 1975–86. Mem. Council, University of Buckingham. Pres., La Société Jersiaise, 1980–85. *Recreations:* music, books, horses, boats, pottering about. *Address:* Beechfield House, Trinity, Jersey, Channel Islands. *T:* Jersey (0534) 20270. *Clubs:* United Oxford & Cambridge University; United, Victoria (Jersey); Royal Yacht Squadron, Royal CI Yacht, St Helier Yacht.

CRIPPIN, Harry Trevor, FCIS; Chief Executive and Town Clerk, Cardiff City Council, 1979–88; *b* 14 May 1929; *s* of Harry and Mary Elizabeth Crippin; *m* 1959, Hilda Green,

JP; one *s* one *d. Educ:* Leigh Grammar Sch., Lancs. DMA; FBIM; FCIS 1975. Asst Town Clerk, Manchester, 1970–74; City Sec., Cardiff CC, 1974–79. OStJ 1986. *Address:* 37 Ely Road, Llandaff, Cardiff CF5 2JF. *T:* Cardiff (0222) 564103.

CRIPPS, family name of **Baron Parmoor.**

CRIPPS, Anthony L.; *see* Cripps, M. A. L.

CRIPPS, Sir (Cyril) Humphrey, Kt 1989; DL; MA; CChem, FRSC; Managing Director, Pianoforte Supplies Ltd, Roade, Northampton, since 1960, Chairman since 1979; Founder Member, Cripps Foundation, Chairman since 1979; Chairman: Velcro Industries NV, since 1973; Air BVI, 1971–86; *b* 2 Oct. 1915; *o s* of Sir Cyril Thomas Cripps, MBE, and Lady (Amy) Cripps; *m* 1942, Dorothea Casson, *o d* of Reginald Percy Cook, architect; two *s* one *d* (and one *s* decd). *Educ:* Northampton Grammar Sch. (schol.); St John's Coll., Cambridge (Nat. Sci. Prelim. Cl. 1, Tripos Pts I and II, Cl. 2; BA, MA). FCS 1935; FRIC 1977; FRSC 1979. Founder of private businesses in UK, Australia, Canada and Brit. Virgin Islands. Member, Northamptonshire CC, 1963–74 (Leader of Independents, to 1974; formerly Vice-Chm., Educn and Planning Cttees); Mem., (new) Northants CC, 1973–81; Board Mem., Northampton Develt Corp., 1968–85. Life Mem., Ct, Univ. of Nottingham, 1953; Governor: Northampton Grammar Sch., 1963–74; Northampton Sch. for Boys, 1977–81; (Vice-Chm., 1970–81, 1986–88, Chm., 1988–, Foundn Trust); Northampton High Sch. for Girls, 1966– (Chm., 1972–84); Foundn Governor, Bilton Grange Prep. Sch., 1957–80. Trustee, Cripps Postgrad. Med. Centre, Northampton Gen. Hosp., 1969–; Member of Trusts: Peterborough Cath., 1975–; All Saints Church, Northampton, 1975–; Trustee, Univ. of Nottingham Develt Trust, 1990–. Hon. Fellow: Cambridge Univ.: St John's, 1966; Magdalene, 1971; Selwyn, 1971; Queens', 1979; Cripps Hall, Nottingham Univ., 1959; Hon. DSc Nottingham, 1975; Hon. LLD Cantab 1976; Pres., Johnian Soc., 1966. Liveryman, Worshipful Co. of Wheelwrights, 1957, Mem. Court 1970, Master 1982; Liveryman, Worshipful Co. of Tallow Chandlers, 1983; Freeman, City of London (by redemption), 1957. High Sheriff, Northants, 1985–86; DL Northants, 1986. *Recreations:* travel, photography, natural history—entomology (espec. Rhopalocera), philately. *Address:* Bull's Head Farm, Stoke Goldington, Newport Pagnell, Bucks MK16 8LP. *T:* Stoke Goldington (090855) 223.

CRIPPS, Sir John Stafford, Kt 1978; CBE 1968; Chairman, Countryside Commission, 1970–77; *b* 10 May 1912; *s* of late Rt Hon. Sir Stafford Cripps, PC, CH, FRS, QC, and Isobel (Dame Isobel Cripps, GBE); *m* 1st, 1936, Ursula (marr. diss. 1971), *d* of late Arthur C. Davy; four *s* two *d*; 2nd, 1971, Ann Elizabeth Farwell. *Educ:* Winchester; Balliol Coll., Oxford. 1st Class Hons Politics, Philosophy and Economics (Modern Greats). Editor, The Countryman, 1947–71. Filkins Parish Councillor, 1946–87; Witney Rural District Councillor, 1946–74; Chairman: Rural District Councils' Association, 1967–70; Rural Cttee of Nat. Council of Social Service; Member: Oxfordshire Planning Cttee, 1948–69; W Oxfordshire Technical Coll. Governors, 1951–70; South East Economic Planning Council, 1966–73; Nature Conservancy, 1970–73; Exec. Cttee, CPRE, 1963–69; Inland Waterways Amenity Advisory Council, 1968–73; Defence Lands Cttee, 1971–73; Water Space Amenities Commn, 1977–80; Development Commn, 1978–82. President: Oxfordshire Rural Community Council, 1982–; Camping and Caravanning Club of GB and Ireland, 1981–91. Prepared report on Accommodation for Gypsies, 1976. *Address:* Fox House, Filkins, Lechlade, Glos GL7 3JQ. *TA:* Filkins. *T:* Filkins (036786) 209. *Club:* Farmers'.
See also A. T. Ricketts.

CRIPPS, (Matthew) Anthony Leonard, CBE 1971; DSO 1943; TD 1947; QC 1958; a Recorder, 1972–85 (Recorder of Nottingham, 1961–71); Deputy Senior Judge, British Sovereign Base Areas, Cyprus, 1978–90; *b* 30 Dec. 1913; *s* of late Major Hon. L. H. Cripps; *heir-pres.* to 4th Baron Parmoor, *qv; m* 1941, Dorothea Margaret (Surrey CC 1965–67), *d* of G. Johnson Scott, Ashby-de-la-Zouch; three *s. Educ:* Eton; Christ Church, Oxford; Combined Army and RAF Staff Coll., 1944–45. Royal Leicestershire Regt, TA, 1933. Served War of 1939–45: Norway, Sweden, Finland, Iceland, N Africa, Italy, Egypt, 1939–44 (Capt. to Lt-Col); Staff Officer, Palestine and Syria, 1944–46. Barrister-at-law, Middle Temple, 1938 (Bencher 1965; Treasurer, 1983), Inner Temple, 1961, Hong Kong, 1974 and Singapore, 1987. Hon. Judge of Court of Arches, 1969–80. Comr for Local Govt Petitions, 1978–84. Chairman: Disciplinary Cttees, Milk Marketing Bd, 1956–90, Potato and Egg Marketing Bds, 1956–67; Isle of Man Govt Commn on Agricultural Marketing, 1961–62; Home Sec.'s Adv. Cttee on Service Candidates, 1966– (Dep. Chm., 1965); Nat. Panel, Approved Coal Merchants Scheme, 1972–89; Legal Adv. Cttee, RSPCA, 1978–90; Univ. of London Appeals Cttee, 1980–90. Member: Agricultural Wages Bd, 1964–67; Northumberland Cttee of Inquiry into Foot and Mouth Disease, 1968–69; Cttee of Inquiry, Export of Live Animals for Slaughter, 1973–74. Pres., Coal Trade Benevolent Assoc., 1983. Mem., Ct of Assts, Fuellers' Co., 1985– (Master, 1990). *Publications:* Agriculture Act 1947, 1947; Agriculture Holdings Act, 1948, 1948; (ed) 9th edn, Cripps on Compulsory Purchase: Powers, Procedure and Compensation, 1950; legal articles, especially on agricultural matters, for Law Jl and Encyclopaedia Britannica. *Recreations:* family life, writing. *Address:* 1 Harcourt Buildings, Temple EC4Y 9DA. *T:* 071–353 9421; Woodhurst, McCrae's Walk, Wargrave, Berks RG10 8LN. *T:* Wargrave (073522) 3449. *Clubs:* Brooks's, Lansdowne; Phyllis Court (Henley-on-Thames).

CRISP, Prof. Arthur Hamilton, MD, DSc; FRCP, FRCPE, FRCPsych; Professor of Psychiatry, University of London at St George's Hospital Medical School, since 1967, and Dean, Faculty of Medicine, University of London, 1976–80; *b* 17 June 1930; *s* of John and Elizabeth Crisp; *m* 1958, Irene Clare (*née* Reid); three *s. Educ:* Watford Grammar Sch.; Univ. of London (MD; DSc). FRCP 1973, FRCPE 1972, FRCPsych 1971. Previously Lectr, then Sen. Lectr in Psych., Middlesex Hosp. Med. Sch., London. Chairman: Educn Cttee, GMC, 1982–88; Adv. Cttee on Med. Educn, EEC, 1983–85. *Publications:* (jtly) Sleep, Nutrition and Mood, 1976; Anorexia Nervosa: Let Me Be, 1980; (jtly) Anorexia Nervosa and the Wish to Change, 1990; approx. 300 articles in learned jls. *Recreations:* golf, study of the River Wandle. *Address:* 113 Copse Hill, Wimbledon, SW20 0NT. *T:* 081–946 0976. *Clubs:* Athenæum; Royal Wimbledon Golf, Aldeburgh Golf.

CRISP, Sir (John) Peter, 4th Bt *cr* 1913; *b* 19 May 1925; *o s* of Sir John Wilson Crisp, 3rd Bt, and Marjorie (*d* 1977), *d* of F. R. Shriver; *S* father, 1950; *m* 1954, Judith Mary, *d* of late H. E. Gillett; three *s* one *d. Educ:* Westminster. *Heir: s* John Charles Crisp, *b* 10 Dec. 1955. *Address:* Crabtree Cottage, Drungewick Lane, Loxwood, Billingshurst, West Sussex RH14 0RP. *T:* Loxwood (0403) 752374.

CRITCHETT, Sir Ian (George Lorraine), 3rd Bt *cr* 1908; BA Cantab; HM Diplomatic Service, retired; Counsellor, Foreign and Commonwealth Office, 1977–80; *b* 9 Dec. 1920; *s* of Sir Montague Critchett, 2nd Bt, and Innes (*d* 1982), 3rd *d* of late Col F. G. A. Wiehe, The Durham Light Infantry; *S* father, 1941; *m* 1st, 1948, Paulette Mary Lorraine (*d* 1962), *e d* of late Col H. B. Humfrey; 2nd, 1964, Jocelyn Daphne Margret, *e d* of Comdr C. M. Hall, Higher Boswarva, Penzance, Cornwall; one *s* one *d. Educ:* Harrow; Clare Coll., Cambridge. RAFVR, 1942–46. Joined Foreign Office, 1948; 3rd Sec. (Commercial), at Vienna, 1950–51; 2nd Sec. (Commercial) at Bucharest, 1951–53; 2nd Sec. at Cairo, 1956; First Sec., FO, 1962. *Heir: s* Charles George Montague Critchett, *b* 2 April 1965.

Address: Uplands Lodge, Pains Hill, Limpsfield, Oxted, Surrey RH8 0RF. *Clubs:* Travellers', MCC.

CRITCHLEY, Julian Michael Gordon; MP (C) Aldershot, since 1974 (Aldershot and North Hants, 1970–74); writer, broadcaster and journalist; *b* 8 Dec. 1930; *s* of Dr Macdonald Critchley, *qv*; *m* 1955, Paula Joan Baron (divorced 1965); two *d*; *m* 1965, Mrs Heather Goodrick; one *s* one *d*. *Educ:* Shrewsbury; Sorbonne; Pembroke Coll., Oxford (MA). MP (C) Rochester and Chatham, 1959–64; contested Rochester and Chatham, 1966. Mem., Armed Forces Select Cttee. Vice-Chairman: Cons. Party Broadcasting Cttee, 1975; Cons. Party Defence Cttee, 1979–87; Chm., Cons. Party Media Cttee, 1976–81; Mem., One Nation Gp of Cons. MPs. Delegate to WEU and Council of Europe; Chm., WEU Defence Cttee; Deleg. to N Atlantic Assembly. Chm., Bow Gp, 1966–67; Pres., Atlantic Assoc. of Young Political Leaders, 1968–70. Steward, British Boxing Bd of Control, 1987–. *Publications:* (with O. Pick) Collective Security, 1974; Warning and Response, 1978; The North Atlantic Alliance and the Soviet Union in the 1980s, 1982; (jtly) Nuclear Weapons in Europe, 1984; Westminster Blues, 1985; (ed) Britain: a view from Westminster, 1986; Heseltine: the unauthorised biography, 1987; Palace of Varieties: an insider's view of Westminster, 1989; Hung Parliament, 1991; various Bow Group and CPC pamphlets. *Recreations:* watching boxing, the country, reading military history, looking at churches, collecting early Staffordshire. *Address:* The Brewer's House, 18 Bridge Square, Farnham, Surrey. *T:* Farnham (0252) 722075.

CRITCHLEY, Macdonald, CBE 1962; MB, ChB 1st Class Hons (Bristol), MD; FRCP; Consulting Neurologist; *b* 2 Feb. 1900; *s* of Arthur Frank and Rosina Matilda Critchley; *m* 1st, Edna Auldeth Morris (decd); two *s*; 2nd, Eileen Hargreaves. *Educ:* Christian Brothers Coll.; Univ. of Bristol (Lady Haberfield Scholarship in Medicine, Markham Skerritt Prize for Original Research). MD 1925. Goulstonian Lectr, RCP, 1930; Hunterian Prof., RCS, 1935; Royal Coll. of Physicians: Bradshaw Lectr, 1942; Croonian Lectr, 1945; Harveian Orator, 1966; Pres., World Fedn of Neurology, 1965–73; Hon. Consulting Neurologist, King's Coll. Hosp.; Hon. Consulting Physician, National Hosp., Queen Square; formerly Dean, Inst. of Neurology; Neurological Physician, Royal Masonic Hosp.; formerly Neurologist to Royal Hosp. and Home for Incurables, Putney. Consulting Neurologist to Royal Navy, 1939–77; Long Fox Lectr, Univ. of Bristol, 1935; William Withering Lectr, Univ. of Birmingham, 1946; Tisdall Lectr, Univ. of Manitoba, 1951; Semon Lectr, Univ. of London, 1951; Sherrington Lectr, Univ. of Wisconsin; Orator, Medical Soc. of London, 1955. Pres. Harveian Soc., 1947. Hunterian Orator, 1957; Doyne Memorial Lectr, 1961; Wartenberg Lectr, 1961; Victor Horsley Memorial Lectr, 1963; Honyman Gillespie Lectr, 1963; Schorstein Lectr, 1964; Hughlings Jackson Lectr and Medallist, RSM, 1964; Gowers Lectr and Medallist, 1965; Veraguth Gold Medallist, Bern, 1968; Sam T. Orton Award for work on Dyslexia, 1974; Arthur Hall Memorial Lectr, 1969; Rickman Godlee Lectr, 1970; Cavendish Lectr, 1976; Vis. Prof., Winston-Salem, NC, 1983. Pres. Assoc. of British Neurologists, 1962–64; Second Vice-Pres., RCP, 1964; Mem., GMC, 1957–73; Founder-Pres., Migraine Trust. Hon. FACP; MD Zürich *hc*; DenM (Aix-Marseille) *hc*; MD Madrid *hc*; Hon. Fellow: Faculty of History and Philosophy of Medicine and Pharmacy; Pan-African Assoc. of Neurological Scis; Hon. Mem., RSM; Hon. Corresp. Mem. Académie de Médecine de France, Norwegian Academy of Science and Letters, Royal Academy of Medicine, Barcelona, and Neurological Socs of France, Switzerland, Holland, Turkey, Uruguay, US, Canada, Australia, Brazil, Argentine, Germany, Chile, Spain, Roumania, Norway, Czechoslovakia, Greece, Italy, Bulgaria, Hungary, Peru, Poland and Sweden. Visiting Prof., Univs of: Istanbul, 1949; California, 1950 and 1964; Hawaii, 1966. Master, Worshipful Soc. of Apothecaries, 1956–57. Served European War, 1917–18; Surgeon Captain RNVR, 1939–46. *Publications:* Mirror Writing; Neurology of Old Age; Observations on Pain; Language of Gesture; Shipwreck-survivors; Sir William Gowers; The Parietal Lobes; The Black Hole; Developmental Dyslexia; Aphasiology; The Dyslexic Child; Silent Language; (ed jtly) Music and the Brain, 1976; (jtly) Dyslexia defined, 1978; The Divine Banquet of the Brain, 1979; The Citadel of the Senses, 1986; The Ventricle of Memory, 1990; various articles on nervous diseases. *Address:* Hughlings House, Mill Lane, Nether Stowey, Bridgwater, Somerset TA5 1NL.
    See also J. M. G. Critchley.

CRITCHLEY, Philip, CB 1990; Director of Contracts, Highways Administration and Maintenance, 1985–90, Director of Network Management and Maintenance, 1990–91, Department of Transport; *b* 31 Jan. 1931; *s* of Henry Stephen and Edith Adela Critchley; *m* 1962, Stella Ann Barnes; two *s* one *d*. *Educ:* Manchester Grammar Sch.; Balliol Coll., Oxford (MA, 2nd Classical Mods and Greats). National Service, Intelligence Corps, 1953–55. Joined Min. of Housing and Local Govt (now Dept of Environment), 1955: Principal, 1960; Asst Sec., 1969; Under Sec., 1980; Dir of Waste Disposal, 1983. FRSA. *Recreations:* philosophy, writing poetry. *Address:* Redstone House, Maidstone Road, Ashford, Kent TN25 4NP. *T:* Ashford (0233) 621037. *Clubs:* Blackheath Harriers; Oxford Union Society.

CRITCHLEY, Tom; international business adviser, since 1990; UK Chairman, Anglo-Soviet Health-care Group, since 1989; Senior Partner, Tom Critchley Associates, since 1990; *b* 17 Aug. 1928; *s* of late Leonard and Jessie Critchley; *m* 1951, Margaret Bland; one *s*. *Educ:* Sheffield College of Technology. Davy-Ashmore Group, 1951–66; Cammell Laird and Upper Clyde Groups, 1966–69; J. C. B. Group, 1969–70; EMI Group, 1970–80; Head, Investment Casting Mission to Canada; UN Adviser to Tanzanian Govt; Adviser to UN High Commn for Refugees; Chm., MATC Ltd; Senior Partner, internat. consultancy practice, 1980–85; Under Sec., Dept of Health (formerly DHSS), and NHS Management Bd Mem., 1986–90; Head, healthcare missions to Japan, Philippines, Indonesia, USSR and Poland, 1989–90. Chm., UK Trade Assoc., 1990–; Mem. Board, Nat. Inst. of Govt Purchasing, USA, 1977–78; Sen. UK Deleg., Internat. Fedn of Purchasing & Materials Management, 1980–85; Dir, Internat. Management Inst., Paris, 1980–88; Faculty Mem., Management Centre Europe, Brussels, 1980–85; Mem., Business in the Community, 1989–. Inst. of Purchasing & Supply: Fellow, 1967; Chm. Council, 1974–75; Pres., 1977–78; Chm., Ext. Affairs, 1978–82; Mem., Internat. Council, 1979–82. *Recreations:* competitive sports, live theatre, North American history. *Address:* 3 Lincoln Close, Stoke Mandeville, Bucks HP22 5YS.

CROAN, Thomas Malcolm; Sheriff of North Strathclyde, since 1983; *b* 7 Aug. 1932; *s* of John Croan and Amelia Sydney; *m* 1959, Joan Kilpatrick Law; one *s* three *d*. *Educ:* St Joseph's Coll., Dumfries; Edinburgh University. MA 1953; LLB 1955. Admitted to Faculty of Advocates, 1956; Standing Junior Counsel, to Scottish Develt Dept, 1964–65 and (for highways work) 1967–69; Advocate Depute, 1965–66; Sheriff of Grampian, Highland and Islands (formerly Aberdeen, Kincardine and Banff), 1969–83. *Recreations:* sailing, reading. *Address:* Overdale, 113 Bentinck Drive, Troon KA10 6JB.

CROCKATT, Lieut Comdr (Douglas) Allan, OBE 1981 (MBE 1971); RD 1978; RNR retd; Vice Lord-Lieutenant of West Yorkshire, since 1985; *b* 31 Jan. 1923; *s* of late Douglas Crockatt, JP, LLD and Ella Crockatt (*née* Lethem); *m* 1946, Helen Townley Tatton (*d* 1985), *d* of late Capt. T. A. Tatton, MC; one *d*. *Educ:* Bootham School, York; Trinity Hall, Cambridge; Dept of Navigation, Southampton Univ. RNVR 1942–46,

Western Approaches and N Russia; RNVSR 1946–64; RNR active list, 1964–82. Director: Johnson Group Cleaners, 1961–84 (Dep. Chm., 1976–84); Johnson Group Inc. (USA) (formerly Apparelmaster Inc.), 1975–84 (Dep. Chm., 1981–84); local Dir, Martins and Barclays Banks W Yorks Bd, 1964–84. Mem., Multiple Shops' Fedn Council, 1972–77. Life Vice-Pres., W Yorks Branch Magistrates' Assoc., 1980 (Hon. Sec., 1958–72; Chm., 1975–77; Pres., 1977–79); Mem. Council, Magistrates' Assoc., 1959–80 (Chm., Training Cttee, 1974–80); Member: Lord Chancellor's Adv. Cttee for training of Magistrates, 1964–79; Lord Chancellor's Magistrates' Courts Rule Cttee, 1979–81. CC, W Riding of Yorks, 1953–58; JP 1956, DL 1971, West (formerly WR) Yorks. Freeman, City of London, 1958; Liveryman, Dyers' Co., 1958. Hon. LLD Leeds, 1990. *Recreations:* cricket, sailing, fishing. *Address:* Paddock House, Sicklinghall, Wetherby, W Yorks LS22 4BJ. *T:* Wetherby (0937) 62844. *Clubs:* Army and Navy; RN Sailing Association, Driffield Anglers'.

CROCKER, His Honour Peter Vernon; a Circuit Judge, 1974–91; *b* 29 June 1926; *s* of Walter Angus Crocker and Fanny Victoria Crocker (*née* Dempster); *m* 1950, Nancy Kathleen Sargent. *Educ:* Oundle; Corpus Christi Coll., Cambridge (BA). Called to Bar, Inner Temple, 1949. *Recreations:* gardening, tennis, swimming.

CROCKER, Sir Walter (Russell), KBE 1978 (CBE 1955); Australian diplomat, retired 1970; Lieutenant-Governor of South Australia, 1973–82; *b* 25 March 1902; *e s* of late Robert Crocker and Alma Bray, Parnaroo, SA; *m* 1951, Claire (marr. diss. 1968), *y d* of F. J. Ward, Headmaster of Prince Alfred Coll., Adelaide, and *widow* of Dr John Gooden, Physicist; two *s*. *Educ:* University of Adelaide; Balliol Coll., Oxford; Stanford University, USA. Entered Colonial Administrative Service (Nigeria), 1930; transf. to League of Nations, 1934, and to ILO (Asst to Dir-Gen); Served War, 1940–45 (Lt-Col, Croix de Guerre avec palme, Ordre royal du Lion, Belgium); Farming at Parnaroo, 1946; UN Secretariat (Chief of Africa Sect.), 1946–49; Prof. of Internat. Relations, Aust. Nat. Univ., 1949–52; Actg Vice-Chancellor, 1951; High Commissioner for Australia to India, 1952–55; Ambassador of Australia to Indonesia, 1955–57; High Comr to Canada, 1957–58; High Comr for Australia to India and Ambassador to Nepal, 1958–62; Amb. of Australia to the Netherlands and Belgium, 1962–65; Ambassador to Ethiopia and High Commissioner to Kenya and Uganda, 1965–67; Ambassador to Italy, 1967–70. Hon. Colonel, Royal South Australia Regt, 1977–. L'Ordre royal du Lion (Belgium), 1945; Cavaliere di Gr. Croce dell'Ordine al Merito (Italy), 1970; Order of Malta (Grand' Uffiziale del Merito Melitense), 1975. *Publications:* The Japanese Population Problem, 1931; Nigeria, 1936; On Governing Colonies, 1946; Self-Government for the Colonies, 1949; Can the United Nations Succeed?, 1951; The Race Question as a factor in International Relations, 1955; Nehru, 1965; Australian Ambassador, 1971; Memoirs, 1981; Sir Thomas Playford, 1983. *Recreations:* gardening, walking, music; previously skiing, tennis. *Address:* 256 East Terrace, Adelaide, SA 5000, Australia. *Club:* Adelaide.

CROCKETT, Andrew Duncan; Executive Director, Bank of England, since 1989; *b* 23 March 1943; *s* of Dr Andrew Stuart Crockett and Sheilah Crockett (*née* Stewart); *m* 1966, Marjorie Frances Hlavacek; two *s* one *d*. *Educ:* Queens' College, Cambridge (MA Econ.); Yale Univ. (MA). Bank of England, 1966–72; International Monetary Fund, 1972–89. *Publications:* Money: theory, policy, institutions, 1973; International Money: issues and analysis, 1977; contribs to professional jls. *Recreations:* reading, golf, tennis. *Address:* Bank of England, Threadneedle Street, EC2R 8AH. *T:* 071–601 4212.

CROCKFORD, Brig. Allen Lepard, CBE 1955 (OBE 1945); DSO 1943; MC 1916; TD 1942; late Hon. Colonel RAMC 54 and 56 Division (TA); *b* 11 Sept. 1897; *s* of late J. A. V. Crockford, West Worthing, Sussex; *m* 1924, Doris Ellen Brookes-Smith; one *s* two *d*. *Educ:* Gresham's Sch.; King's Coll., Cambridge; St Thomas's Hosp. Glos Regt, BEF (Capt.; wounded), 1915–19. BA Cantab, 1920; MA 1926; MB, BCh Cantab, 1922; Gen. Practice, 1924–39; RAMC (TA): served with 43rd, Guards Armoured, 46th and 56th Divs, BNAF and CMF (Col), 1939–45; Gen. Practice, 1945–46; Medical Sec., St Thomas's Hosp. Medical Sch., London, SE1, 1946–64. Col (TA), ADMS, 56 Armoured Div., 1947; Brig. (TA); DDMS AA Comd, 1949; KHS 1952; QHS 1952–57; OStJ 1954. *Recreation:* cassette playing. *Address:* Overstone, Elvaston Road, Hexham, Northumberland NE46 2HH.

CROFT, family name of **Baron Croft.**

CROFT, 2nd Baron *cr* 1940, of Bournemouth; **Michael Henry Glendower Page Croft;** Bt 1924; *b* 20 Aug. 1916; *s* of 1st Baron Croft, PC, CMG, and Hon. Nancy Beatrice Borwick (*d* 1949), *y d* of 1st Baron Borwick; *S* father, 1947; *m* 1948, Lady Antoinette Fredericka Conyngham (*d* 1959), *o d* of 6th Marquess Conyngham; one *s* one *d*. *Educ:* Eton; Trinity Hall, Cambridge (BA). Served War of 1939–45, Capt. RASC. Called to the Bar, Inner Temple, 1952. Director: Henry Page & Co. Ltd, 1946–57; Ware Properties Ltd, 1958–65; Hereford and Worcester, Building Preservation Trust Ltd, 1986–. Underwriting Mem., Lloyd's, 1971–. Member Executive Cttee: Contemporary Arts Soc., 1960–68 and 1970–81 (Hon. Sec., 1971–76, Hon. Treasurer, 1976–80, Vice-Chm., 1980–81); British Museum Soc., 1969–76. Hon. Keeper of Contemporary Art, Fitzwilliam Museum, Cambridge, 1984. FRSA. OStJ. *Heir: s* Hon. Bernard William Henry Page Croft [*b* 28 Aug 1949. *Educ:* Stowe; Univ. of Wales, Cardiff. BScEcon]. *Address:* Croft Castle, near Leominster, Herefordshire; 19 Queen's Gate Gardens, SW7 5LZ. *Club:* Athenæum.

CROFT, David Legh, QC 1982; **His Honour Judge Croft;** a Circuit Judge, since 1987; *b* 14 Aug. 1937; *s* of late Alan Croft and of Doreen Mary Berry (*née* Mitchell); *m* 1963, Susan Mary (*née* Bagnall); two *s*. *Educ:* Haileybury and ISC; Nottingham Univ. (LLB). Called to the Bar, Middle Temple, 1960; called to the Hong Kong Bar, 1984; a Recorder, 1985–87. *Recreations:* patience and reflection at leisure.

CROFT, (Ivor) John, CBE 1982; painter; Head of Home Office Research and Planning Unit, 1981–83 (Head, Home Office Research Unit, 1972–81); *b* 6 Jan. 1923; *s* of Oswald Croft and Doris (*née* Phillips). *Educ:* Westminster Sch.; Christ Church, Oxford (MA); Inst. of Education, Univ. of London (MA); LSE. Temp. jun. admin. officer, FO, 1942–45; asst teacher, LCC, 1949–51; Inspector, Home Office Children's Dept, 1952–66; Sen. Research Officer, Home Office Research Unit, 1966–72. Member: Criminological Scientific Council, Council of Europe, 1978–83, Chm., 1981–83; Conservative Study Gp on Crime, 1983–87; Kensington Crime Prevention Panel, 1984–87; Cttee, Peel Heritage Trust, 1989–; Tribunal under I of M Interception of Communications Act, 1989–. Governor, ILEA Secondary Schs, 1959–68. Mem. Exec. Cttee, English Assoc., 1966–77 (Hon. Treas. 1972–75); Chm., Pembridge Assoc., 1985–87. Group shows, 1958, 1963, 1967, 1968, 1969, 1973; one-man shows, 1970, 1971. *Publications:* booklets and pamphlets, and various studies of crime, criminological research and the administration of justice. *Address:* 30 Stanley Road, Peel, Isle of Man. *Club:* Reform.

CROFT, Col Noel Andrew Cotton, DSO 1945; OBE 1970; MA Oxon; Essex Regiment; retired; *b* 30 Nov. 1906; *s* of late Rev. Canon R. W. Croft, MA; *m* 1952, Rosalind, 2nd *d* of late Comdr A. H. de Kantzow, DSO, RN; three *d*. *Educ:* Lancing Coll.; Stowe Sch.; Christ Church, Oxford; Sch. of Technology, Manchester. Cotton Trade, 1929–32; Mem.

British Trans-Greenland Expedition, 1933–34; ADC to Maharajah of Cooch Behar, India, 1934–35; Second-in-Command, Oxford Univ. Arctic Expedition to North-East Land, 1935–36; Ethnological Exped. to Swedish Lapland, 1938; Sec. to Dir of Fitzwilliam Museum, Cambridge, 1937–39. Served War of 1939–45, Capt. 1939; WO Mission to Finno-Russian War, 1939–40; Bde Intelligence Officer Independent Companies, Norwegian Campaign, 1940; Combined Ops, 1940–41; Major, 1941; Asst Mil. Attaché, Stockholm, 1941–42; sea or parachute ops in Tunisia, Corsica, Italy, France, and Denmark, 1943–45; Lieut-Col 1945; Asst Dir Scientific Research, War Office, 1945–49; WO Observer on Canadian Arctic "Exercise Musk-Ox", 1945–46, and on NW Frontier Trials, India, 1946–47; attached Canadian Army, 1947–48; GSO1, War Office, 1949–51; Liaison Officer HQ Continental Army, USA, 1952–54; comd The Infantry Junior Leaders Bn, 1954–57; Col 1957; Comdt Army Apprentices Sch., Harrogate, 1957–60; Comdt, Metropolitan Police Cadet Corps, 1960–71. Vice-Pres., Women's Transport Service (FANY), 1987– (Chm., 1972–87). Corresp. Fellow, Arctic Inst. of North America; Mem., Reindeer Council of UK, 1949–89 (Chm., 1962–82). Polar Medal (clasp Arctic, 1935–36), 1942; Back Award, RGS, 1946 and 1947. *Publications:* (with A. R. Glen) Under the Pole Star, 1937; Polar Exploration, 1939, 2nd edn 1947. *Recreations:* mountaineering, ski-ing, sailing, photography. *Address:* River House, Strand-on-the-Green, W4. *T:* 081–994 6359. *Clubs:* Alpine, Special Forces, Geographical.

CROFT, Sir Owen (Glendower), 14th Bt *cr* 1671; grazier; *b* 26 April 1932; *s* of Sir Bernard Hugh Denman Croft, 13th Bt, and of Helen Margaret (*née* Weaver); *S* father, 1984; *m* 1959, Sally Patricia, *d* of Dr T. M. Mansfield, Brisbane; one *s* two *d*. *Educ:* Armidale School, NSW. Dep. Chm., Council of Advice to Rural Lands Protection Bds of NSW; Member: Vertebrate Pest Control Adv. Cttee of NSW; NSW Footrot Strategic Plan Steering Cttee; NSW Non-Indigenous Species Adv. Cttee; Chm., Armidale Dist Adv. Cttee to NSW Nat. Parks and Wildlife Service. *Recreations:* tennis; National Trust activities. *Heir: s* Thomas Jasper Croft, *b* 3 Nov. 1962. *Address:* Salisbury Court, Uralla, NSW 2358, Australia. *T:* 067/784624.

CROFT, Roy Henry Francis, CB 1983; Executive Director and Chief Operating Officer, Securities and Investments Board, since 1985; *b* 4 March 1936; *s* of late William Henry Croft and Dorothy Croft; *m* 1961, Patricia Ainley; one *s* two *d*. *Educ:* Isleworth Grammar Sch.; Christ's Coll., Cambridge (MA). BoT, 1959; Treasury, 1961–62; DEA, 1964–67; Private Sec. to Pres. Bd of Trade, 1968–70; Cabinet Office, 1970–72; Civil Aviation Div., Dept of Trade, 1973–76; Finance and Economic Appraisal Div., DoI, 1976–79; Posts and Telecommunications Div., DoI, 1979–80; Dep. Sec. DTI, 1980–85. *Address:* Gavrelle House, 2–14 Bunhill Row, EC1Y 8RA.

CROFT, Stanley Edward, TD 1951; life insurance consultant; formerly HM Diplomatic Service; *b* 18 Oct. 1917; *s* of Edward John and Alice Lucy Croft; *m* 1950, Joan Mary Kaye; four *s* two *d*. *Educ:* Portsmouth Grammar School. TA, 1939; served War of 1939–45, RA, Middle East, Aden, Italy, Germany. Min. of Labour, 1935; Admty, 1937–39 and 1946–47; transf. to Diplomatic Service, 1947; Vice-Consul, Barcelona, 1950; 2nd Sec., Lahore, 1951; Washington, 1955; Madrid, 1956; 1st Sec., FO, 1960; Consul, Geneva, 1961; FO and CRO, 1965–70; Consul-Gen., Madrid, 1970; Counsellor and Consul-Gen., Luanda, 1974–77. Abbey Life Assurance Co., 1977–90. *Recreations:* swimming, tennis, camping, fishing, carpentry.

CROFT, Sir Thomas (Stephen Hutton), 6th Bt *cr* 1918, of Cowling Hall, Yorkshire; Principal, Thomas Croft, Architect, since 1988; *b* 12 June 1959; *o s* of Major Sir John Croft, 5th Bt and of Lucy Elizabeth, *d* of late Major William Dallas Loney Jupp, OBE; *S* father, 1990. *Educ:* King's Sch., Canterbury; University Coll., London (BSc); Royal Coll. of Art, London (MA). Architect, Richard Meier & Partners, Architects, New York, 1985–86; Project Architect, Rick Mather, Architects, London, 1986–88. *Heir: uncle* Cyril Bernard Croft, *b* 6 June 1918. *Address:* 53 Leinster Square, W2 4PU.

CROFTON, family name of **Baron Crofton.**

CROFTON, 7th Baron *cr* 1797 (Ire.); **Guy Patrick Gilbert Crofton;** Bt 1758; Major, 9/12 Royal Lancers (Prince of Wales's); *b* 17 June 1951; *s* of 5th Baron Crofton and of Ann Pamela, *d* of Gp Capt. Charles Herbert Tighe, OBE, DFC; *S* brother, 1989; *m* 1985, Gillian, *o d* of Harry Godfrey Mitchell Bass, *qv*; twin *s*. *Educ:* Theresianistische Akademie, Vienna; Midhurst GS. Commissioned 9/12 Royal Lancers, 1971. *Recreations:* shooting, ski-ing. *Heir: er* twin *s* Hon. Edward Harry Piers Crofton, *b* 23 Jan. 1988. *Address:* c/o Royal Bank of Scotland, 22 Whitehall, SW1A 2EB. *Club:* Cavalry and Guards.

CROFTON, Denis Hayes, OBE 1948 (MBE 1943); retired Home and Indian Civil Servant; Member, Panel of Inspectors, Department of the Environment, 1969–79; President, Tunbridge Wells and District Branch, Civil Service Retirement Fellowship, since 1985 (Chairman, 1972–85); *b* 14 Dec. 1908; *s* of late Richard Hayes Crofton, Colonial Civil Service and Mabel Annie Crofton (*née* Smith); *m* 1933, Alison Carr, *d* of late Andrew McClure and Ethel McClure; three *s* one *d*. *Educ:* Tonbridge Sch.; Corpus Christi Coll., Oxford (Class. Mods, Lit. Hum., MA). Indian Civil Service, 1932; served in Bihar; subdivisional Magistrate, Giridih, 1934, Jamshedpur, 1935; Under-Sec. to Govt of Bihar, Polit. and Appt Depts, 1936; Under-Sec. to Govt of India, Dept of Labour, 1939; Private Sec. to Indian Mem., Eastern Gp Supply Council, 1941; Dist Mag. and Collector, Shahabad, Bihar, 1942; Sec. to Gov. of Bihar, 1944; apptd to Home Civil Service, 1947; Principal, Min. of Fuel and Power, Petroleum Div. 1948; Asst Sec., Petroleum Div. and Chm., OEEC Oil Cttee, Paris, 1950–53; Asst Sec., Monopolies and Restrictive Practices Commn, 1953; Asst Sec., Min. of Fuel and Power, Electricity Div., 1956; Petroleum Div., 1961; Accountant General and Under-Secretary for Finance, 1962–68. *Publications:* The Children of Edmonstown Park: memoirs of an Irish family, 1981; Andrew Hayes leaves the King's County: some footnotes on a diaspora, 1990; edited: The Surgery at Aberffrwd: some encounters of a colliery doctor, 1982; A GP's Progress to the Black Country, 1984 (both by Francis Maylett Smith). *Recreations:* reading, gardening. *Address:* 26 Vauxhall Gardens, Tonbridge, Kent. *T:* Tonbridge (0732) 353465. *Club:* Commonwealth Trust.

CROFTON, (Sir) Hugh Dennis, (8th Bt *cr* 1801, of Mohill); *S* nephew, 1987, but does not use the title. *Heir: b* Major Edward Morgan Crofton.

CROFTON, Sir John (Wenman), Kt 1977; retired; Professor of Respiratory Diseases and Tuberculosis, University of Edinburgh, 1952–77; *b* 1912; *s* of Dr W. M. Crofton; *m* 1945, Eileen Chris Mercer, MBE 1984; two *s* three *d*. *Educ:* Tonbridge; Sidney Sussex Coll., Cambridge; St Thomas's Hosp. Medical qualification, 1936; War of 1939–45, RAMC; France, Middle East, Germany. Lecturer in Medicine, Postgraduate Medical Sch. of London, 1947–51, Senior Lecturer, 1951; Part-time Tuberculosis Unit, Medical Research Council, Brompton Hosp., 1947–50; Dean of Faculty of Medicine, 1964–66, and Vice-Principal, 1969–70, Univ. of Edinburgh. Vice-Pres., 1972–73, Pres., 1973–76, RCPE. Hon. Mem., Acads of Medicine of Argentina, Catalonia and Singapore. Hon. FRCPE; Hon. FRCPI; Hon. FRACP; Hon. FACP; Hon. FFCM. Weber-Parkes Prize, RCP, 1966. *Publications:* (jtly) Respiratory Diseases, 1969, 3rd edn 1981; (jtly) Clinical Tuberculosis, 1992; contributor to BMJ, Lancet, Thorax, etc. *Recreations:* conversation, family life, mountains. *Address:* 13 Spylaw Bank Road, Edinburgh EH13 0JW. *T:* 031–441 3730. *Club:* University Staff (Edinburgh).

CROFTON, Sir Malby (Sturges), 5th Bt *cr* 1838 (orig. *cr* 1661); Partner, Messrs Fenn & Crosthwaite; Member of the London Stock Exchange, 1957–75; *b* 11 Jan. 1923; *s* of Sir Malby Richard Henry Crofton, 4th Bt, DSO and Bar, and Katharine Beatrix Pollard; *S* father, 1962. *Educ:* Eton (King's Scholar); Trinity Coll., Cambridge (scholar). Served with Life Guards, 1942–46, in Middle East and Italy. Member: Kensington Borough Council, 1962, Leader, 1968–77, Mayor, Kensington and Chelsea, 1978; GLC, 1970–73; ILEA, 1970–73; Ealing N, GLC, 1977–81; Leader, GLC Scrutiny Cttee, 1977–78. Vice-Chm., NW Thames RHA, 1980–85. Hon.Treasurer, Marie Curie Meml Foundn; Dir, St Edward's Housing Assoc.; Chm., Kensington and Chelsea, Age Concern, 1987–. Pres., Ealing N Cons. Assoc. Freeman, Royal Bor. of Kensington and Chelsea, 1983. Hon. Fellow, Chelsea Coll. *Recreations:* tennis, swimming, motoring, planting trees, farming. *Heir: kinsman* Henry Edward Melville Crofton [*b* 15 Aug. 1931; *m* 1955, Brigid, twin *d* of Gerald K. Riddle; two *s* one *d*]. *Address:* 12 Caithness Road, W14; Longford House, Co. Sligo, Eire. *Clubs:* Cavalry and Guards, Hurlingham.

CROHAM, Baron *cr* 1978 (Life Peer), of the London Borough of Croydon; **Douglas Albert Vivian Allen,** GCB 1973 (KCB 1967; CB 1963); Chairman, Guinness Peat Group, 1983–87; Head of the Home Civil Service and Permanent Secretary, Civil Service Department, 1974–77; *b* 15 Dec. 1917; *s* of late Albert Allen; *m* 1941, Sybil Eileen Allegro, *d* of late John Marco Allegro; two *s* one *d*. *Educ:* Wallington County Grammar Sch.; London School of Economics. BSc (Econ.) First Class Hons, 1938. Entered Board of Trade, 1939; Royal Artillery, 1940–45; Cabinet Office, 1947; Treasury, 1948–58; Under-Secretary, Ministry of Health, 1958–60; Under-Secretary, Treasury, 1960–62, Third Secretary, 1962–64; Dept of Economic Affairs: Dep. Under-Sec. of State, 1964–66; Second Permanent Under-Sec. of State, May-Oct. 1966; Permanent Under-Sec. of State, 1966–68; Permanent Sec., HM Treasury, 1968–74. Director: Pilkington plc (formerly Pilkington Bros), 1978–; Guinness Mahon & Co., 1989–; Dep. Chm., 1978–82, Chm., 1982–85, BNOC; Chm., Trinity Insurance, 1988–. An Industrial Adviser to the Governor, Bank of England, 1978–83. President: Inst. for Fiscal Studies, 1979–; British Inst. of Energy Economies, 1985–. A Trustee, Anglo-German Foundn, 1977– (Chm., 1982–). CBIM; FRSA 1975. Hon. Fellow, LSE, 1969; Hon. DSc (Social Sciences) Southampton, 1977. *Recreation:* woodwork. *Address:* 9 Manor Way, South Croydon, Surrey CR2 7BT. *T:* 081–688 0496. *Club:* Reform.

CROKER, Edgar Alfred, CBE 1989; Secretary and Chief Executive of the Football Association, 1973–89; *b* 13 Feb. 1924; *m* 1952, Kathleen Mullins; one *s* two *d*. *Educ:* Kingston Technical Coll. Served War: Flt Lieut, RAF, 1942–46. Flt Lieut, RAFVR, 1947–55. Professional footballer: Charlton Athletic, 1947–51; Headington United, 1951–56. Sales Dir, Douglas Equipment, 1956–61; Chairman and Managing Dir, Liner-Croker Ltd, 1961–73; Chairman: Liner Concrete Machinery Co. Ltd, 1971–73; Harrington Kilbride Ltd, Publishers, 1989–; PEL Stadium Seating PLC. King's commendation for brave conduct, 1946. *Publication:* The First Voice You Will Hear Is . . . (autobiog.), 1987. *Recreations:* golf, tennis, bridge. *Address:* South Court, The Park, Cheltenham, Glos GL50 2SD. *T:* Cheltenham (0242) 224907. *Clubs:* Royal Air Force, The New (Cheltenham).

CROLL, Hon. David Arnold, PC, QC; BA, LLB; Senator; Chairman, Senate Committees on: Poverty, since 1968; Aging, since 1963; Retirement Age Policies, since 1977; *b* Moscow, 12 March 1900; *s* of Hillel and Minnie Croll; *m* 1925, Sarah Levin (*d* 1987); three *d*. *Educ:* public schs and Patterson Collegiate Institute, Windsor; Osgoode Hall, Toronto; University of Toronto. Emigrated to Canada with family, 1906, settling at Windsor, Ont; first and only commercial venture operation of news-stand, which greatly facilitated secondary education; after high school and course articled to solicitor; graduation from Osgoode Hall law sch. followed by practice at Windsor, 1925–30; formerly senior partner with Croll and Croll, Windsor, Ont., and with Croll, Borins and Shiff, later Croll and Godfrey, Toronto, Ont. Mayor of Windsor, Ont., 1930–34 and 1938–41; Mem. for Windsor-Walkerville, Ont. Legislature, 1934–44; Minister of Labour, Public Welfare and Municipal Affairs for the Province of Ont.; was youngest and first Jewish Cabinet Minister and first Jewish Senator, in Canada. Mem. of House of Commons for Toronto Spadina, 1945–55 when appointed to Senate. Served War of 1939–45, with Canadian Army overseas, enlisting as Private in Sept. 1939 and discharged in rank of Col in Sept. 1945. Hon. LLD St Thomas Univ., 1980. *Recreations:* golf and the more strenuous sports. *Address:* 4th Floor, The First City Building, 151 Yonge Street, Toronto, Ont M5C 2W7, Canada. *Club:* Primrose (Toronto).

CROLL, Prof. James George Arthur, FEng 1990; Professor of Structural Engineering, University College London, since 1985; *b* 16 Oct. 1943; *s* of late Keith Waghorn Croll and of Jean Croll; *m* 1966, Elisabeth Joan (*née* Sprackett); one *s* one *d*. *Educ:* Palmerston North Boys' High Sch., NZ; Univ. of Canterbury, NZ (BE 1st cl. Hons, PhD). FIStructE, FIMA, CEng. Asst Engineer, Min. of Works, NZ, 1962–67; University College London: Res. Fellow, 1967–70; Lectr, 1970–81; Reader in Structural Engineering, 1981–85. Vis. Fellow, Princeton, 1979; Visiting Professor: Fed. Univ. of Rio de Janeiro, 1973, 1981, 1984; Univ. of Hong Kong, 1985. *Publications:* Elements of Structural Stability, 1972; Force Systems and Equilibrium, 1974. *Recreations:* singing, piano, painting, drawing, sailing, ski-ing, travel. *Address:* 92 Highgate Hill, Highgate N6 5HE. *T:* 081–348 7731. *Clubs:* Natural Science (UCL); Hayling Island Sailing.

CROLY, Brig. Henry Gray, CBE 1958; JP; *b* 7 June 1910; *s* of late Lt-Col W. Croly, DSO, late RAMC, Ardvarna, Tralee; *m* 1939, Marjorie Rosanne, *er d* of late Major J. S. Knyvett, late R Warwickshire Regt, Clifford Manor Road, Guildford; two *s* two *d*. *Educ:* Sherborne Sch.; RMA Woolwich. 2nd Lieut RA, 1930; served in India: Mohmand Ops, 1935; Waziristan, 1936–37 (despatches); served War of 1939–45, mostly India and Burma; GSO1, British Mil. Mission to France, 1946–47; 2nd-in-Comd 26 Medium Regt RA, 1947–48; jssc 1949; GSO1, WO, 1950–51; Col GS, SHAPE, 1952; OC 26 Field Regt Suez Canal Zone, 1953–55; Dep. Sec., Chiefs of Staff Cttee, 1955–58; UK Nat. Mil. Rep. to SHAPE, 1959–61; retd 1962. Sec., Health Visitor Trng Council and Council for Trng in Social Work, 1963–66; Asst Sec. of Commns, Lord Chancellor's Office, 1966–74; Sec., Wolfenden Cttee on Voluntary Orgns, 1974–78. JP Surrey, 1968. *Recreations:* golf, reading. *Address:* 20 Middle Bourne Lane, Farnham, Surrey GU10 3NH. *T:* Farnham (0252) 714851. *Clubs:* Army and Navy, MCC; Hankley Common Golf.

CROMARTIE, 5th Earl of, *cr* 1861; **John Ruaridh Grant Mackenzie;** Viscount Tarbat, Baron Castlehaven, Baron MacLeod, 1861; Chief of the Clan Mackenzie; MIExpE; explosives engineer; *b* 12 June 1948; *s* of 4th Earl of Cromartie, MC, TD and of Olga, *d* of late Stuart Laurance; *S* father, 1989; *m* 1973, Helen, *d* of John Murray; (one *s* decd); *m* 1985, Janet Clare, *d* of Christopher J. Harley; two *s*. *Educ:* Rannoch School, Perthshire; Strathclyde University. Mem. Council, IExpE. *Publications:* Selected Climbs in Skye, 1982; articles in Classic Rock Climbs and Cold Climbs. *Recreations:* mountaineering, art, astronomy, geology. *Heir: s* Viscount Tarbat, *qv*. *Address:* Castle Leod, Strathpeffer, Ross-shire IV14 9AA. *Clubs:* Army and Navy; Scottish Mountaineering.

CROMBIE, Alistair Cameron, MA, BSc, PhD; FBA 1990; Fellow, 1969–83, garden master, 1971–81, Trinity College, Oxford; Lecturer in History of Science, University of Oxford, 1953–83; *b* 4 Nov. 1915; 2nd *s* of William David Crombie and Janet Wilmina (*née* Macdonald); *m* 1943, Nancy Hey; three *s* one *d* (and one *s* decd). *Educ:* Geelong Grammar Sch.; Trinity Coll., Melbourne Univ.; Jesus Coll., Cambridge. Zoological Lab., Cambridge, 1941–46; Lectr in History and Philosophy of Science, University Coll., London, 1946–53, nominated Reader, resigned; All Soul's Coll., Oxford, 1954–69. Kennedy Prof. in the Renaissance, 1982, Prof. of History of Science and Medicine, 1983–85, Smith Coll., Mass. Visiting Professor: Technische Hochschule, Aachen, 1948; Univ. of Washington, 1953–54; Princeton Univ., 1959–60; Australian Univs (guest of Vice-Chancellors' Cttee), 1963; Tokyo Univ. (guest of Japan Soc. for Promotion of Sci.), 1976; All-India Inst. of Med. Scis, and guest of Indian Nat. Sci. Acad., 1976; Virginia Mil. Inst., 1977; Williams Coll., Mass. (Bernhard Vis. Prof.), 1984; Prof. d'Histoire des Sciences, Sorbonne (Univ. of Paris I), 1982–83; Directeur Associé, Ecole des Hautes Etudes, Paris, 1989. Conseil Scientifique, Dépt d'Hist. et Philosophie de la Médecine, Univ. of Paris XII, 1981–85. Mem. Council, Science Museum, London, 1962–66; Mem., British Nat. Cttee for History of Science, 1963–69. Editor: Brit. Jl Philos. Sci., 1949–54; Hist. Sci., 1961–; Dir, Oxford Univ. Symp. Hist. Sci., 1961; Pres., Brit. Soc. Hist. Sci., 1964–66; Pres., Internat. Acad. Hist. Sci., 1968–71; Member: Internat. Acad. Hist. Med.; Academia Leopoldina; FRHistS. Galileo Prize, 1969. Hon. DLitt Durham, 1979. *Publications:* Augustine to Galileo, 1952, 4th edn 1979; Robert Grosseteste and the Origins of Experimental Science, 1953, 3rd edn 1971; Scientific Change, 1963; The Mechanistic Hypothesis and the Scientific Study of Vision, 1967; Science Optics and Music in Medieval and Early Modern Thought, 1990; Science Art and Nature in Medieval and Modern Thought, 1991; Styles of Scientific Thinking in the European Tradition, 1991; contrib. Annals of Sci., Brit. Jl Hist. Sci., EHR, Isis, Jl Animal Ecol., Physis, Proc. Royal Soc. Lond., Rev. de Synthèse, TLS, Dict. Sci. Biogr., Encyc. Brit., New Cambridge Modern Hist., etc. *Recreations:* literature, travel, landscape gardening. *Address:* Orchardlea, Boars Hill, Oxford. *T:* Oxford (0865) 735692. *Club:* Brooks's.

CROMBIE, Prof. Leslie, FRS 1973; CChem, FRSC; Sir Jesse Boot Professor of Organic Chemistry, University of Nottingham, 1969–88, now Emeritus (Dean of Science, 1980–83); *b* 10 June 1923; *s* of Walter Leslie Crombie and Gladys May Crombie (*née* Clarkson); *m* 1953 Winifred Mary Lovell Wood; two *s* two *d*. *Educ:* Portsmouth Municipal Coll.; King's Coll., London. PhD, DSc, FKC 1978. Admiralty Chemical Lab., Portsmouth Naval Dockyard, 1941–46. Lectr, Imperial Coll., London, SW7, 1950–58; Reader in Organic Chemistry, King's Coll., London Univ., 1958–63, Fellow, 1978; Prof. of Organic Chemistry, University Coll. (Univ. of Wales), Cardiff, 1963–69. Pres., British Association, Section B, 1978; Chm., Phytochemical Soc. of Europe, 1986–88 (Vice-Chm., 1984–86, 1988–90). Member: British Libraries Chemical Inf. Review Panel, 1976–77; UGC Physical Scis Sub-Cttee, 1978–85; Royal Society: Govt Grants Cttee, 1976–77 (Chm., 1978–79); Sect. Cttee 3, 1977–78 (Chm., 1978–80); Chemical Educn Cttee, 1981–82 (Chm., 1983–87); Educn Cttee, 1983–85 (Chm., 1986–); Travelling Expenses Cttee, 1984–86; Council, 1984–86; Science Research Council: Chem. Cttee, 1970–75; Enzyme Cttee, 1973–75; Chemical Society: Council, 1962–64 and 1972–80; Library Cttee, 1959–63; Primary Jls Cttee, 1964–69; Reports and Reviews Cttee, 1964–69 (Chm., 1969–73); Pub. Services Bd, 1969–77; Perkin Div. Council, 1971–85 (Pres., 1976–79); Presidents' Cttee, 1972–74; Tertiary Pub. Cttee, 1974–76; Exec. Cttee, 1976–79; Div. and Annual Congress Cttee, 1976–79; UKCIS Bd, 1972–77; Royal Inst. of Chemistry: Jt Cttee for HNC and HND quals, 1962–84; Council, 1975–78; Exams and Institns Cttee, 1976–78; Quals and Admissions Cttee, 1976–78; Royal Society of Chemistry: Council, 1980–81; Jls Bd, 1981–85; Quals and Exams Bd, 1983–86; Chm., Perkin Jls Editorial Bd, 1981–85. Tilden Lectr, 1970, Simonsen Lectr, 1975, Hugo Müller Lectr, 1977, Chem. Soc.; Natural Products Chemistry award, 1980; Pedler Lectr, 1982, Flintoff Medal, 1984, RSC; Phytochem. Soc. of Europe medal, 1990. Hon. Fellow, Portsmouth Polytechnic, 1983. *Publications:* over 300 original papers in learned chemical jls, especially those of RSC, London. *Recreation:* gardening. *Address:* 153 Hillside Road, Bramcote, Beeston, Nottingham. *T:* (0602) 259412. *Club:* Athenæum.

CROMER, 4th Earl of, *cr* 1901; **Evelyn Rowland Esmond Baring;** Baron Cromer, 1892; Viscount Cromer, 1899; Viscount Errington, 1901; Managing Director: Inchcape (China) Limited (formerly Manager, China Trading Division, Inchcape Far East Ltd) since 1979; Inchcape Vietnam Ltd, since 1990; *b* 3 June 1946; *e s* of 3rd Earl of Cromer, KG, GCMG, MBE, PC and of Hon. Esmé Harmsworth, CVO, *d* of 2nd Viscount Rothermere; *S* father, 1991; *m* 1971, Plern Isarangkun Na Ayudhya, *e d* of late Dr Charanphat Isarangkun Na Ayudhya, Thailand. *Educ:* Eton. Dep. Chm., Land-Ocean Inchcape Container Transport Co. Ltd (China); Director: The Motor Transport Co. of Guangdong & Hong Kong Ltd (China); Cluff Oil (Hong Kong) Ltd. Mem. Council, St John Ambulance Assoc., Hong Kong. *Recreations:* mountain climbing, deep sea diving. *Heir:* *b* Hon. Vivian John Rowland Baring [*b* 12 June 1950; *m* 1974, Lavinia Gweneth, *e d* of Maj. Sir Mark Baring, KCVO; two *s* one *d*]. *Address:* GPO Box 36, Hong Kong; 9C Sutton Court, Harbour City, Kowloon, Hong Kong. *T:* 730–7454; (office) 8424600. *Clubs:* Oriental; Siam Society; Hong Kong, Royal Hong Kong Yacht (Hong Kong).

CROMPTON, Dan, QPM 1990; Chief Constable, Nottinghamshire Constabulary, since 1990; *b* 15 Feb. 1941; *s* of Arthur and Elizabeth Crompton; *m* 1962, Olive Ramsden; one *s*. *Educ:* Didsbury Technical Sch., Manchester. Manchester City Police, 1960–68; Manchester and Salford Police, 1968–74; Greater Manchester Police, 1974–87; Nottinghamshire Constabulary, 1987–. *Recreations:* reading, popular classics, gardening, cricket, Rugby. *Address:* Police HQ, Sherwood Lodge, Arnold, Nottingham NG5 8PP. *T:* Nottingham (0602) 670999.

CROMPTON, Prof. Gareth, FRCP, FFCM; Professor of Public Health Medicine, University of Wales College of Medicine, since 1989; Chief Administrative Medical Officer and Director of Public Health Medicine, South Glamorgan Health Authority, since 1989; *b* 9 Jan. 1937; *s* of late Edward Crompton, Drefach-Felindre, Dyfed; *m* 1965; one *d*. *Educ:* Llandysul Grammar Sch.; Welsh Nat. Sch. of Medicine. MB, BCh Wales, 1960; DObstRCOG 1962; DPH Wales, 1964; FFCM 1976; FRCP 1986 (MRCP 1980). County Med. Officer, County Welfare Officer and Principal Sch. Med. Officer, Anglesey CC, 1966–73; Area Med. Officer, Gwynedd Health Authority, 1974–77; CMO, Welsh Office, 1978–89. Specialty Advr, Health Service Comr for England and Wales, 1974–77; Advr in Wales, Faculty of Community Medicine, 1974–77. Chm., Anglesey Disablement Adv. Cttee, 1969–77; Sec., Fluoridation Study Gp, Soc. of Med. Officers of Health, 1969–73; Mem., Welsh Hosp. Bd, 1970–74. Mem. GMC, 1981–83 and 1987–89. Med. Fellow, Council of Europe, 1971. QHP 1984–87. *Publications:* papers on the effects of fluoridated water supplies on dental caries, and the epidemiology and management of chronic sickness and disablement. *Recreations:* bowls, golf, watching Rugby, reading contemporary Welsh verse. *Address:* Temple of Peace and Health, Cathays Park, Cardiff CF1 3NW. *T:* Cardiff (0222) 231021.

CROMPTON, Ian William; Stipendiary Magistrate for South Yorkshire, since 1983; a Recorder, since 1989; *b* 28 June 1936; *s* of Thomas and Hilda Crompton; *m* 1962, Audrey (*née* Hopewell); two *s*. *Educ:* Manchester Grammar School; Victoria University of Manchester. LLB. Asst Solicitor, County Magistrates' Court, Strangeways, Manchester, 1961–62; Asst Solicitor, O'Collier, Littler & Kilbeg, 1962–65, Partner, 1965–72; Clerk to the Justices: County Magistrates' Court, Strangeways, 1972–74; Eccles Magistrates' Court, 1974–83. *Recreations:* ballroom and Latin American dancing, golf. *Club:* Hallamshire Golf (Sheffield).

CROMPTON, Air Cdre Roy Hartley, OBE 1962; Group Director, Emergency Planning, Civil (formerly Home) Defence College, Easingwold, York, 1976–85, retired; *b* 24 April 1921; *er s* of Frank and Ann Crompton, Bedford; *m* 1961, Rita Mabel Leslie; one *d*. *Educ:* Bedford Sch.; University Coll., London (BA Hons). Chiefs of Staff Secretariat, 1962–64; Stn Comdr No 1 FTS, 1965–67; Dep. Dir Defence Policy Staff, 1968–70; Gp Dir RAF Staff Coll., 1970; Project Officer, Nat. Defence Coll., 1970–71; AOC and Comdt, Central Flying Sch., RAF, 1972–74. Directing Staff, Home Defence Coll., York, 1974–76. Home Office Consultant, 1987–88. *Recreations:* golf, music, horticulture. *Address:* Sharnford Lodge, Huby, York YO6 1HT. *Club:* Royal Air Force.

CROMWELL, 7th Baron *cr* 1375 (called out of abeyance, 1923); **Godfrey John Bewicke-Copley;** *b* 4 March 1960; *s* of 6th Baron Cromwell and of Vivian, *y d* of late Hugh de Lisle Penfold, Isle of Man; *S* father, 1982. *Heir:* *b* Hon. Thomas David Bewicke-Copley, *b* 6 Aug. 1964. *Address:* House of Lords, SW1.

CRONIN, Vincent Archibald Patrick; author; *b* 24 May 1924; *s* of late Archibald Joseph Cronin, MD, MRCP, DPH and of Agnes Mary Gibson, MB, ChB; *m* 1949, Chantal, *d* of Comte Jean de Rolland; two *s* three *d*. *Educ:* Ampleforth; Harvard; Trinity Coll., Oxford. Rifle Bde, 1943–45. *Publications:* The Golden Honeycomb, 1954; The Wise Man from the West, 1955; The Last Migration, 1957; A Pearl to India, 1959; The Letter after Z, 1960; Louis XIV, 1964; Four Women in Pursuit of an Ideal, 1965; The Florentine Renaissance, 1967; The Flowering of the Renaissance, 1970; Napoleon, 1971; Louis and Antoinette, 1974; trans., Giscard d'Estaing, Towards a New Democracy, 1977; Catherine, Empress of all the Russias, 1978; The View from Planet Earth, 1981; Paris on the Eve, 1989. *Address:* Brion, Dragey, 50530 Sartilly, France.

CROOK, family name of **Baron Crook.**

CROOK, 2nd Baron *cr* 1947, of Carshalton, Surrey; **Douglas Edwin Crook,** MICE; *b* 19 Nov. 1926; *s* of 1st Baron Crook and Ida Gertrude (*d* 1985), *d* of Joseph Haddon; *S* father, 1989; *m* 1954, Ellenor, *d* of late Robert Rouse; one *s* one *d*. *Educ:* Whitgift School, Croydon; Imperial Coll., London (BSc Eng, DIC, ACGI). *Heir:* *s* Hon. Robert Douglas Edwin Crook, *b* 19 May 1955. *Address:* Ridge Hill Barn, Etchinghill, Folkestone, Kent CT18 8BP.

CROOK, Arthur Charles William; Consultant to Times Newspapers, since 1974; Editor, The Times Literary Supplement, 1959–74; *b* 16 Feb. 1912; *m* 1948, Sarita Mary Vivien Bushell (marr. diss.); one *s* two *d*. Editorial staff of The Times; Asst Editor, The Times Literary Supplement, 1951–59. Pres. and Chm., Royal Literary Fund, 1984–90. *Recreation:* theatre. *Address:* 70 Regent's Park Road, NW1 7SX. *T:* 071–722 8446. *Club:* Garrick.

CROOK, Colin, FEng; Chairman, Corporate Technology Committee, Citicorp, since 1990; *b* 1 June 1942; *s* of Richard and Ruth Crook; *m* 1965, Dorothy Jean Taylor; two *d*. *Educ:* Harris Coll., Preston; Liverpool Polytechnic (ACT Hons; Dip. Elec. Engrg). FEng 1981 (CEng 1977). MIEE 1976; MIERE 1976; MIEEE 1976; MACM 1977. Electronics Engr, Canadian Marconi, 1962–64; Computer Designer, The Plessey Co., 1964–68; Systems Engr, Eli Lilly Co., 1968–69; sen. appts, Motorola Semiconductor Div., Switzerland and USA, 1969–79; sen. appts, The Rank Organisation, 1979–83, including: Man. Dir, RPI, 1979–81; Man. Dir, Zynar, CEO Nestar Systems, USA, 1981–83; Mem. of Bd, British Telecom, and Man. Dir, BT Enterprises, 1983–84; Sen. Vice Pres., Data General Corp., 1984–89. *Publications:* articles and learned papers on electronics and computers. *Recreations:* photography, walking, reading, wine, sailing. *Address:* The Old School House, Harvest Hill, Hedsor, Bourne End, Bucks SL8 5JJ. *T:* Bourne End (06285) 27479.

CROOK, Frances Rachel; Director, Howard League for Penal Reform, since 1986; *b* 18 Dec. 1952; *d* of Sheila Sibson-Turnbull and Maurice Crook; one *d*. *Educ:* Camden School; Liverpool University (BA Hons History). Historical Researcher, Liverpool, 1977–78; Teacher, 1978–79; Campaign Co-ordinator, Amnesty International, 1980–85. Councillor (Lab) Barnet, 1982–90. *Recreation:* demonstrations. *Address:* The Howard League, 708 Holloway Road, N19 3NL. *T:* 071–281 7722.

CROOK, Maj.-Gen. James Cooper, MD, FRCPath; late RAMC, retired 1981; Civilian Medical Practitioner, Army Blood Supply Depot, Aldershot, 1982–88; *b* 19 March 1923; *s* of late Francis William Crook and late Mary Catherine Perry, *d* of late Sir Edwin Cooper Perry, GCVO, MD, Superintendent of Guy's Hospital and Vice-Chancellor of London Univ.; *m* 1950, Ruth, *d* of late W. A. Bellamy of Santa Cruz, Tenerife; one *s* two *d*. *Educ:* Worksop Coll.; Guy's Hosp. Med. Sch., Univ. of London. MB BS 1946, MD 1953; DTM&H 1952; FRCPath 1968. Guy's and Pembury Hosps, 1946; Commnd RAMC 1946; served Egypt and N Africa, 1946–49; Pathologist, Queen Alexandra's Mil. Hosp., 1950; David Bruce Laboratories, 1953; med. liaison officer to MRC Radiobiology Unit, AERE, Harwell, 1954; Asst Dir of Pathology, Middle East, 1957; Cons. in Pathology, 1958; RAMC Specialist, Chem. Defence Estab., Porton, 1960; Asst Dir of Pathology, Eastern Comd, 1963; ADGMS, 1966; Comd Cons. in Pathology, BAOR, 1969; Prof. of Pathology, Royal Army Med. Coll., 1974; Dir of Army Pathology and Consulting Pathologist to the Army, 1976–81; Hon. Physician to HM The Queen, 1978–81. Hon. Col, 380 Blood Supply Unit RAMC, TAVR, 1982–86. *Publications:* articles in Jl of Clinical Path., Nature, Med. Sci. and the Law, Jl of RAMC, British Jl of Radiology. *Recreations:* gardening, beekeeping. *Address:* Egloshayle, Fore Street, Kingsand, Torpoint, Cornwall PL10 1NB. *T:* Plymouth (0752) 823666.

CROOK, Prof. John Anthony, MA; Professor of Ancient History, University of Cambridge, 1979–84; Fellow of St John's College, Cambridge, since 1951; *b* 5 Nov. 1921; *s* of Herbert Crook and Hilda Naomi (*née* Flower). *Educ:* St Mary's C of E Sch., Balham; Dulwich Coll.; St John's Coll., Cambridge 1939–41 and 1945–47 (John Stewart of Rannoch Scholar); BA 1947, Craven Student, 1947; Research Student of Balliol Coll., Oxford, 1947–48; MA (Cantab) 1949. Served War, Private and Corporal, 9th Royal Fusiliers, 1941–43 (PoW Stalag VIIIB, 1943–45); Sgt, RAEC, 1945. Univ. Asst Lectr in Classics, Reading Univ., 1948, Lectr, 1949–51; St John's Coll., Cambridge: Tutor, 1956–64; President, 1971–75; Univ. Asst Lectr in Classics, Cambridge Univ., 1953, Lectr, 1955–71, Reader in Roman History and Law, 1971–79, and Brereton Reader, 1974–79. FBA 1970–80. *Publications:* Consilium Principis, 1955; Law and Life of Rome, 1967. *Address:* St John's College, Cambridge CB2 1TP. *T:* Cambridge (0223) 338621.

CROOK, Prof. Joseph Mordaunt, FBA 1988; Professor of Architectural History, Royal Holloway and Bedford New College (formerly at Bedford College), University of London, since 1981; *b* 27 Feb. 1937; *e s* of late Austin Mordaunt Crook and late Irene

Woolfenden; *m* 1st, 1964, Margaret, *o d* of late James Mulholland; 2nd, 1975, Susan, *o d* of late F. H. Mayor. *Educ:* Wimbledon Coll.; Brasenose Coll., Oxford. BA (1st cl. Mod. Hist.) 1958; DPhil 1961, MA 1962, Oxon; FSA 1972. Research Fellow: Inst. of Historical Res., 1961–62; Bedford Coll., London, 1962–63; Warburg Inst., London, 1970–71; Asst Lectr, Univ. of Leicester, 1963–65; Lectr, Bedford Coll., London, 1965–75, Reader in Architectural Hist., 1975–81. Slade Prof. of Fine Art, Oxford Univ., 1979–80; Vis. Fellow: Brasenose Coll., Oxford, 1979–80; Humanities Res. Centre, ANU, Canberra, 1985; Waynflete Lectr and Vis. Fellow, Magdalen Coll., Oxford, 1984–85; Vis. Fellow, Gonville and Caius Coll., Cambridge, 1986; Humanities Fellow, Princeton Univ., 1990. Public Orator, Univ. of London, 1988–90. Member: Exec. Cttee, Soc. Architect. Historians of Gt Britain, 1964–77 (Pres., 1980–84); RIBA Drawings Cttee, 1969–75; Exec. Cttee, Georgian Gp, 1970–77; Exec. Cttee, Victorian Soc., 1970–77, Council, 1978–88; Historic Buildings Council for England, 1974–80; Council, Soc. of Antiquaries, 1980–82; Adv. Council, Paul Mellon Centre for Studies in British Art, 1985–90; Gen. Cttee, Incorp. Church Building Soc., 1987–; Council, British Acad., 1989–. Freeman, 1979, Liveryman, 1984, Worshipful Co. of Goldsmiths. Editor, Architectural History, 1967–75. *Publications:* The Greek Revival, 1968; Victorian Architecture: A Visual Anthology, 1971; The British Museum, 1972, 2nd edn 1973; The Greek Revival: Neo-Classical Attitudes in British Architecture 1760–1870, 1972; The Reform Club, 1973; (jtly) The History of the King's Works, Vol. VI, 1782–1851, 1973 (Hitchcock Medallion, 1974), Vol. V, 1660–1782, 1976; William Burges and the High Victorian Dream, 1981; (jtly) Axel Haig and The Victorian Vision of the Middle Ages, 1984; The Dilemma of Style: architectural ideas from the picturesque to the post-modern, 1987, 2nd edn 1989; *edited:* Eastlake, A History of the Gothic Revival, 1970, rev. edn, 1978; Emmet, Six Essays, 1972; Kerr, The Gentleman's House, 1972; The Strange Genius of William Burges, 1981; *contrib. to:* Concerning Architecture, 1967; The Country Seat, 1970; The Age of Neo-Classicism, 1972; The Building of Early America, 1976; Seven Victorian Architects, 1976; The Ruskin Polygon, 1982; In Search of Modern Architecture, 1983; Rediscovering Hellenism, 1989; The University of London and the World of Learning 1836–1986, 1990; numerous articles in Architect. History, Architect. Review, Country Life, History Today, Jl Royal Soc. Arts, RIBA Jl, Antiquaries Jl, TLS, Architect Design, etc. *Recreation:* strolling. *Address:* 55 Gloucester Avenue, NW1 7BA. *T:* 071–485 8280. *Clubs:* Athenæum, Brooks's.

CROOK, Kenneth Roy, CMG 1978; HM Diplomatic Service, retired; Ambassador to Afghanistan, 1976–79; *b* 30 July 1920; *s* of Alexander Crook, Prescot, Lancs, and Margaret Kay Crook; *m* 1943, Freda Joan Vidler; two *d. Educ:* Prescot Grammar Sch., Lancs; Skerry's Coll., Liverpool. Appointed to: Board of Trade, 1937; Min. of War Transport, 1939. Royal Navy, 1941–46. Board of Trade, 1946–49; Commonwealth Relations Office, 1949; Second Sec., Canberra, 1951–54; First Sec., Madras, 1956–59; Deputy High Commissioner: Peshawar, W Pakistan, 1962–64; Dacca, E Pakistan, 1964–67; Counsellor, FCO, 1967; Head of Information Research Dept, FCO, 1969–71; Governor, Cayman Is, 1971–74; Canadian Nat. Defence Coll., 1974–75; Head of Science and Technology Dept, FCO, 1975–76. *Recreations:* walking, gardening. *Address:* 16 Burntwood Road, Sevenoaks, Kent TN13 1PT. *T:* Sevenoaks (0732) 452774.

CROOK, Brig. Paul Edwin, CBE 1965 (OBE 1946); DSO 1957; *b* 19 April 1915; *s* of late Herbert Crook and Christine Crook, Lyme Regis; *m* 1st, 1944, Joan (marr. diss. 1967), *d* of late William Lewis; one *d*; 2nd, 1967, Betty, *d* of late John William Wyles. *Educ:* Uppingham Sch.; Emmanuel Coll., Cambridge. BA 1936, MA 1956. Commnd into QORWK Regt, 1935; served: India and Palestine, 1937–39; War of 1939–45, Africa, NW Europe, Burma; Chief Civil Affairs Officer (Col), Netherlands East Indies, 1946; comd 3rd Bn The Parachute Regt, 1954–57; Suez Ops, 1956; comd Army Airborne Trng and Develt Centre, 1959–62; Comdr and Chief of Staff, Jamaica Defence Force, 1962–65; Security Ops Advisor to High Comr for Aden and S Arabia, 1965–67; Comdr, Rhine Area, 1969–70. Col, 1959; Brig., 1963; retired 1971. ADC to The Queen, 1965. Hon. Col, 16 Lincoln Co. Parachute Regt (VR), 1974–79; Dep. Hon. Col, The Parachute Regt (TAVR): 15th (Scottish) Bn, 1979–83; 4th Bn, 1984–85. Chm., Lincs County Scouts, 1975–88. Bronze Star (US), 1945. *Publication:* Came the Dawn, 1989. *Recreations:* cricket, golf, jazz. *Address:* Frieston House, Frieston, Grantham, Lincs NG32 3DA. *T:* Loveden (0400) 72060. *Clubs:* Naval and Military, MCC; Jamaica (W Indies).

CROOKENDEN, Maj.-Gen. George Wayet Derek; DL; Emeritus Fellow, Peterhouse, Cambridge, since 1989; *b* 11 Dec. 1920; *o s* of late Lt-Col John Crookenden and Iris Margherita Gay; *m* 1948, Elizabeth Mary Angela Bourke; one *s* one *d. Educ:* Winchester Coll.; Christ Church, Oxford. Commnd Royal Artillery, 1941. GSO1, SHAPE, 1961–62; CO, 19 Field Regt, RA, 1962–64; Comdr, 7 Artillery Bde, 1964–67; Exercise Controller, CICC (West), 1969–71; Chief, British Commanders-in-Chief Liaison Mission, 1971–72; C of S, Contingencies Planning, SHAPE, 1972–75. Col Comdt, RA, 1977–82. Fellow and Sen. Bursar, Peterhouse, Cambridge, 1975–88. DL Cambs, 1984. *Address:* c/o Lloyds Bank, 95–97 Regent Street, Cambridge CB2 1BQ. *Club:* Army and Navy.

CROOKENDEN, Lt-Gen. Sir Napier, KCB 1970 (CB 1966); DSO 1945; OBE 1954; DL; Lieutenant, HM Tower of London, 1975–81; *b* 31 Aug. 1915; 2nd *s* of late Col Arthur Crookenden, CBE, DSO; *m* 1948, Patricia Nassau, *d* of 2nd Baron Kindersley, CBE, MC, and of Nancy Farnsworth, *d* of Dr Geoffrey Boyd; two *s* two *d. Educ:* Wellington Coll.; RMC, Sandhurst. Commissioned, Cheshire Regt, 1935; Bde Major, 6th Airlanding Bde, 1943–44; CO, 9th Bn, The Parachute Regt, 1944–46; GSO1 (Plans) to Dir of Ops, Malaya, 1952–54; Comdr, 16th Parachute Bde, 1960–61; idc 1962; Dir, Land/Air Warfare MoD (Army Dept), 1964–66; Commandant, RMCS, Shrivenham, 1967–69; GOC-in-C, Western Comd, 1969–72. Col, The Cheshire Regt, 1969–71; Col Comdt, The Prince of Wales Div., 1971–74. Director: SE Regional Bd, Lloyds Bank Ltd, 1973–86; Flextech Ltd, 1978–86. A Trustee, Imperial War Museum, 1973–83. Chm., SS&AFA, 1974–85; a Vice-Pres., RUSI, 1978–85. DL Kent, 1979. *Publications:* Dropzone Normandy, 1976; Airborne at War, 1978; Battle of the Bulge 1944, 1980. *Address:* Twin Firs, Four Elms, Edenbridge, Kent TN8 6PL. *Club:* Army and Navy.

CROOKS, Air Marshal David Manson, CB 1985; OBE 1969; FRAeS; Chief of Defence Staff, New Zealand Armed Forces, 1986–87, retired; aviation and defence industry consultant, since 1988; *b* 8 Dec. 1931; *s* of James and Gladys Meta Crooks; *m* 1954, Barbara Naismith McDougall; four *d. Educ:* Rangiora, NZ. Joined RNZAF, 1951; Head, NZ Defence Liaison Staff, Singapore, 1967–70; Commanding Officer: RNZAF Base: Ohakea, 1971–72; Wigram, 1973–74; RCDS, UK, 1974–75; AOC RNZAF Ops Gp, 1978–80; DCAS, 1980–83; CAS, RNZAF, 1983–86. Chm., Friends of RNZAF Museum, 1988–; Member: Bd, RNZAF Museum Trust, 1988–; Nat. Admin Cttee, RNZAF Assoc., 1988–; Patriotic Fund Bd, 1991–; Public Adv. Cttee on Arms Control, 1991–; Pres., Air Cadet League of NZ, 1989–. *Recreations:* tramping, gardening, reading, sailing. *Address:* 13 Burrows Avenue, Karori, Wellington 5, New Zealand. *T:* 4764-588. *Club:* Wellington (Wellington, NZ).

CROOKS, Rev. John Robert Megaw; Dean of Armagh and Keeper of the Library, 1979–89; *b* 9 July 1914; *s* of Canon the Rev. Louis Warden Crooks, OBE, MA, and Maria Kathleen Megaw; *m* 1941, Elizabeth Catherine Vance; two *s. Educ:* Campbell College, Belfast; Trinity College Dublin (MA). Deacon, 1938; priest, 1939; Curate Assistant, St Peter's, Dublin, 1938–43; Hon. Vicar Choral, St Patrick's Cathedral, Dublin, 1939–43; Catechist, High School, Dublin, 1939–43; Curate Assistant, Leighlin, 1943–44; Incumbent, Killylea, Dio. Armagh, 1944–56; Vicar Choral, St Patrick's Cathedral, 1956–73; Diocesan Sec., 1963–79; Hon. Clerical Sec., General Synod, 1970–89; Prebendary of Ballymore, 1971, of Mullabrack 1972; Archdeacon of Armagh, 1973–79. *Recreation:* golf. *Address:* 44 Abbey Street, Armagh BT61 7DZ. *T:* Armagh (0861) 522540. *Club:* Kildare Street and University (Dublin).

CROOKS, Air Vice-Marshal Lewis M.; *see* Mackenzie Crooks.

CROOM-JOHNSON, Rt. Hon. Sir David Powell, Kt 1971; DSC 1944; VRD 1953; PC 1984; a Lord Justice of Appeal, 1984–89; *b* 28 Nov. 1914; 3rd *s* of late Hon. Sir Reginald Powell Croom-Johnson, sometime a Judge of the High Court, and late Lady (Ruby) Croom-Johnson; *m* 1940, Barbara Douglas, *y d* of late Erskine Douglas Warren, Toronto; one *d. Educ:* The Hall, Hampstead; Stowe Sch.; Trinity Hall, Cambridge (MA; Hon. Fellow, 1985). RNVR (London Div.) 1936–53; served with Royal Navy, 1939–46. Called to Bar, Gray's Inn, 1938, Master of the Bench, 1964, Treasurer, 1981; Western Circuit. QC 1958; Recorder of Winchester, 1962–71; Judge of Courts of Appeal, Jersey and Guernsey, 1966–71; Judge of High Court of Justice, Queen's Bench Div., 1971–84. Member: Gen. Council of the Bar, 1958–62; Senate of Inns of Court, 1966–70. Conducted Home Office Inquiry concerning amalg. of Lancs Police Areas, 1967–68; Vice-Chm., Home Office Cttee on Mentally Abnormal Offenders, 1972–75; Chm., Crown Agents Tribunal, 1978–82. Mem., Council, Oakdene Sch., 1956–79; Chm., Knightsbridge Assoc., 1965–71. *Recreations:* books, music. *Address:* 59 Coleherne Court, Old Brompton Road, SW5. *Club:* Garrick.

See also H. P. Croom-Johnson, Hon. Sir M. J. Turner.

CROOM-JOHNSON, Henry Powell, CMG 1964; CBE 1954 (OBE 1944); TD 1948; *b* 15 Dec. 1910; *e s* of late Hon. Sir Reginald Croom-Johnson, sometime Judge of High Court, and of late Lady (Ruby) Croom-Johnson; *m* 1947, Jane, *er d* of late Archibald George Mandry; two *s. Educ:* Stowe Sch.; Trinity Hall, Cambridge. Asst Master, Bedford Sch., 1932–34. Joined staff of British Council, 1935. Served with Queen's Westminsters and King's Royal Rifle Corps, 1939–46 (staff Sicily, Italy, Greece; Lt-Col). Rejoined British Council, 1946: Controller Finance Div., 1951; Controller European Div., 1956; Representative in India, 1957–64; Controller, Overseas Div. B, 1964; Asst Dir-Gen., 1966–72, retired 1973. *Recreations:* climbing, books, music. *Address:* 3a Ravenscourt Square, W6. *T:* 081–748 3677. *Club:* Savile.

See also Sir D. P. Croom-Johnson.

CROOME, (John) Lewis, CMG 1957; *b* 10 June 1907; *s* of John and Caroline Croome; *m* 1st, 1931, Honoria Renée Minturn (*née* Scott; as Honor Croome, Editorial Staff of The Economist) (*d* 1960); four *s* one *d* (and one *s* decd); 2nd, 1961, Pamela Siola, *o d* of Lt-Col Tyrrel Hawker, Hurstbourne Priors, Hants; one *s. Educ:* Henry Thornton Sch., Clapham; London Sch. of Economics. Imperial Economic Cttee, 1931–39; Ministry of Food, 1939–48; Deputy (later Head), British Food Mission, Ottawa, 1942–46; HM Treasury (Central Economic Planning Staff), 1948–51; Min. of Food, 1951–54; UK Delegation to OEEC, Paris, 1954–57; Ministry of Agriculture, Fisheries and Food, 1957–58; Chief Overseas Relations Officer, UKAEA, 1958–72, retired. *Recreations:* painting, reading. *Address:* 8 The Holdens, Bosham, West Sussex. *T:* Bosham (0243) 572292.

CROPPER, James Anthony, FCA; Chairman, James Cropper PLC, since 1971; Vice Lord-Lieutenant of Cumbria, since 1991; *b* 22 Dec. 1938; *s* of Anthony Charles Cropper and Philippa Mary Gloria (*née* Clutterbuck); *m* 1967, Susan Rosemary (*née* Davis); one *s* one *d* (and one *s* decd). *Educ:* Eton; Magdalene Coll., Cambridge (BA). FCA 1966. James Cropper, 1966–, Dir, 1967–; Dir, East Lancashire Paper Group, 1982–84. Member: Lancs River Authority, 1968–74; NW Water Authority, 1973–80, 1983–89; Dir, NW Water Group, 1989–90. Dir, Cumbria Rural Enterprise Agency, 1986–; Mem., NW Business Leadership Team, 1991–. Pres., British Paper and Bd Fedn, 1988–90. Chairman: Frieda Scott Charitable Trust, 1981–; Governors, Abbot Hall Art Gall. and Mus., 1983–88. Member (Indep.): S Westmorland RDC, 1967–74; S Lakeland DC, 1974–77. High Sheriff of Westmorland, 1971; DL Cumbria, 1985. *Recreations:* shooting, wind-surfing. *Address:* Tolson Hall, Kendal, Cumbria LA9 5SE. *T:* Kendal (0539) 722011. *Club:* Brooks's.

CROPPER, Peter John, CBE 1988; financial consultant; *b* 18 June 1927; *s* of late Walter Cecil Cropper and Kathleen Cropper; *m* 1965, Rosemary Winning; one *s. Educ:* Hitchin Grammar Sch.; Gonville and Caius Coll., Cambridge (MA). Served Royal Artillery, 1945–48. Conservative Research Dept, 1951–53, 1975–79, Dir, 1982–84; investment analyst, Mem. of London Stock Exchange, 1953–75; Special Adviser: to Chief Sec. to the Treasury, 1979–82; to Chancellor of the Exchequer, 1984–88. *Address:* 77 Hadlow Road, Tonbridge, Kent TN9 1QB. *Club:* Reform.

CROSBIE, Hon. John Carnell; PC (Canada); MP (PC) St John's West, Newfoundland, since 1976; Minister for International Trade, Canada, since 1988; *b* 30 Jan. 1931; *s* of Chesley Arthur Crosbie and Jessie Carnell; *m* 1952, Jane Furneaux; two *s* one *d. Educ:* Bishop Field Coll., St John's, Nfld; St Andrew's Coll., Aurora, Ont.; Queen's Univ., Kingston, Ont. (Pol. Sc. and Econs); Dalhousie Univ., Halifax, NS (Law); LSE, London, Eng. Joined Newfoundland Law Soc. and Newfoundland Bar; entered law practice, St John's, 1957; Mem. City Council, St John's, 1965; Dep. Mayor, 1966; Minister of Municipal Affairs and Housing, Province of Newfoundland, (Lib. Admin), July 1966; MHA, Prov. of Newfoundland, Sept. 1966; Minister of Health, 1967; resigned from Govt, 1968; re-elected Member for St John's West (Progressive Conservative), Provincial election, 1971; Minister of Finance, Pres. of Treasury Bd and Minister of Econ. Develt, 1972–74; Minister of Fisheries, Min. for Intergovtl Affairs and Govt House Leader, 1974–75; Minister of Mines and Energy and Minister for Intergovtl Affairs, 1975–76; resigned from Newfoundland Govt, Sept. 1976; elected to House of Commons, Oct. 1976; Chm. of Progressive Conservative Caucus Cttee on Energy, 1977; PC parly critic for Industry, Trade and Commerce, 1977–79; Minister of Finance, 1979–80; Party Finance Critic, 1980; Party External Affairs Critic, 1981–83; Minister of Justice and Attorney General, 1984–86; Minister of Transport, 1986–88. *Address:* PO Box 9192, Station B, St John's, Newfoundland A1A 2X9, Canada; House of Commons, Ottawa, Ontario.

CROSBIE, William, BA; RSA 1973; RGI 1977; artist; *b* Hankow, China, 31 Jan. 1915; *s* of Archibald Shearer Crosbie, marine engineer, and Mary Edgar, both Scottish; *m* 1st, 1944, M. G. McPhail (decd); one *d* (and one *d* decd); 2nd, 1975, Margaret Anne Roger. *Educ:* Chinese Tutor; Renfrew primary sch.; Glasgow Academy; Glasgow Sch. of Art, Glasgow Univ. (4 yrs under Forrester Wilson). Haldane Travelling Schol., 1935, for 3 yr period of study in British Schs in Athens, Rome and Paris (Beaux Arts); studied history and theory of techniques, in Beaux Arts and Sorbonne, and finally took a post-grad. qualif. in these (continues to acquire craftsmanship); passed into studio of Fernand Leger, Paris, and remained until war declared. Served War of 1939–45: ambulance service, WVS driving pool, and at sea. Has exhibited, on average, every two yrs, 1946–; principally one-man exhibns: Glasgow, Edinburgh, London, etc; also in USA, Brussels, Hamburg, etc. *Works in:* Kelvingrove Galls, Glasgow; Scottish provincial galls; Edinburgh City Arts Centre (mural), 1980; Scottish Gall. of Modern Art, 1980; Sydney State Gall., Australia; Wellington, NZ; Royal collection, UK, etc; also in many private collections. *Recreation:* sailing. *Address:* Rushes House, 10 Winchester Road, Petersfield, Hants GU32 3BY. *Clubs:* Glasgow Art; Royal Northern and Clyde Yacht (Rhu).

CROSBY, Prof. Theo, RA 1990 (ARA 1982); RIBA, FCSD; Professor of Architecture and Design, Royal College of Art, since 1990; Partner, Pentagram Design, since 1972; *b* 3 April 1925; *s* of N. J. Crosby and N. J. A. Goosen; *m* 1st, 1960, Finella Anne Buchanan (marr. diss. 1988); one *d* (one *s* decd); 2nd, 1990, Polly Hope. *Educ:* Univ. of the Witwatersrand (BArch 1947). RIBA 1948; FCSD (FSIAD 1964). Technical Editor, Architectural Design, 1953–62; now engaged in private architectural practice in exhibns, interiors and conservation. Mem., Berlin Acad., 1977–. Triennale of Milan Gran Premio, 1964; 2 Architectural Heritage Year Awards, 1973. *Publications:* Architecture: City Sense, 1965; The Necessary Monument, 1970; How to Play the Environment Game, 1973; Let's Build a Monument, 1987. *Recreation:* art. *Address:* Tower 3, Whitehall Court, SW1A 2EL. *T:* 071–930 0730 and 071–229 3477; Royal College of Art, Kensington Gore, SW7 2EU. *T:* 071–584 5020.

CROSFIELD, Rev. (George) Philip (Chorley), OBE 1990; Provost of St Mary's Cathedral, Edinburgh, 1970–90, retired; *b* 9 Sept. 1924; *s* of James Chorley Crosfield and Marjorie Louise Crosfield; *m* 1956, Susan Mary Jullion (*née* Martin); one *s* two *d*. *Educ:* George Watson's Coll., Edinburgh; Selwyn Coll., Cambridge. Royal Artillery, 1942–46 (Captain). Priest, 1952; Asst Curate: St David's, Pilton, Edinburgh, 1951–53; St Andrew's, St Andrews, 1953–55; Rector, St Cuthbert's, Hawick, 1955–60; Chaplain, Gordonstoun School, 1960–68; subseq. Canon and Vice Provost, St Mary's Cathedral, Edinburgh. *Recreations:* walking, reading, carpentry. *Address:* 21 Biggar Road, Silverburn, Penicuik EH26 9LQ. *T:* Penicuik 76607.

CROSLAND, Susan Barnes; writer; *b* Baltimore, Maryland; *y c* of Susan Owens and Mark Skinner Watson; *m* 1st, Patrick Skene Catling (marr. diss.); two *d*; 2nd, Rt Hon. (Charles) Anthony (Raven) Crosland, PC, MP (*d* 1977). Journalism: Sunday Express, 1960–64; freelance, 1964–; profile-writer and columnist, Sunday Times and various jls. Trustee, Nat. Portrait Gallery, 1978–. *Publications:* Behind the Image, 1974; Tony Crosland, 1982; Looking Out, Looking In, 1987; *novels:* Ruling Passions, 1989; Dangerous Games, 1991. *Recreation:* freedom. *Address:* 16 Stanford Court, 45 Cornwall Gardens, SW7 4AB. *Club:* Academy.

CROSS, family name of **Viscount Cross.**

CROSS, 3rd Viscount, *cr* 1886; **Assheton Henry Cross;** late Lieut Scots Guards; *b* 7 May 1920; *e s* of 2nd Viscount and Maud Evelyn (who *m* 2nd, 1944, Guy Hope Coldwell (*d* 1948), Stoke Lodge, Ludlow, Salop; she *d* 1976), *d* of late Maj.-Gen. Inigo Jones, CVO, CB, Kelston Park, Bath; *S* father, 1932; *m* 1952, Patricia Mary (marr. diss., 1957; she *m* 1960, Comdr G. H. H. Culme-Seymour), *e d* of E. P. Hewetson, JP, The Craig, Windermere, Westmorland; two *d*; *m* 1972, Mrs Victoria Webb (marr. diss. 1977); *m* 1983, Mrs Patricia J. Rossiter (marr. diss. 1988). *Educ:* Shrewsbury; Magdalene Coll., Cambridge. *Heir:* none. *Club:* Cavalry and Guards.

CROSS, Alexander Galbraith, MA, MD, FRCS; Ophthalmic Surgeon; lately Dean of the Medical School, St Mary's Hospital; Civilian Consultant in Ophthalmology, RN, 1946–76; Consultant Surgeon, Moorfields Eye Hospital, 1947–73; Consultant Ophthalmic Surgeon, St Mary's Hospital, 1946–73; Consultant Ophthalmic Surgeon, Royal National Throat, Nose, and Ear Hospital, 1954–73; Ophthalmic Surgeon, St Dunstan's, 1946–84; Hon. Consultant Ophthalmologist, Royal National Institute for the Blind, 1968–82; *b* 29 March 1908; *er s* of late Walter Galbraith Cross and Mary Stewart Cross, Wimbledon; *m* 1939, Eileen Longman, twin *d* of late Dr H. B. Corry, Liss, Hants; one *d*. *Educ:* King's Coll. Sch.; Gonville and Caius Coll., Cambridge; St Mary's Hosp., London (University Scholar). Meadows Prize, 1932, Broadbent and Agnes Cope Prizes, 1933, Cheadle Gold Medallist, 1933, St Mary's Hospital. House Phys. and House Surg., St Mary's, 1933–35; House Surg. and Sen. Res. Officer, Moorfields Eye Hosp., 1937–39; Ophthalmic Surgeon: West Middlesex Hosp., 1938–48; Tite Street Children's Hosp., 1939–48; Princess Beatrice Hosp., 1939–47; Royal Masonic Hosp., 1961–71. Wing Comdr, RAFVR, 1941–46 and Adviser in Ophthalmology, South-East Asia Air Forces. Examiner in Fellowship and in Diploma of Ophthalmology for RCS and in Ophthalmology for Univ. of Bristol; Recognised Teacher of Ophthalmology, University of London. Co-opted Mem. Council RCS, 1963–68. Mem. Bd of Governors: St Mary's Hosp., 1951–60; Moorfields Eye Hosp., 1962–65 and 1968–75. Mem. Paddington Group Hosp. Management Cttee, 1952–60. Pres. Ophthalmological Soc. of UK, 1975–77 (Sec. 1949–51; Vice-Pres., 1963–66); Member: RSocMed (Sec., Ophthalmic Section, 1951; Vice-Pres., 1960; Hon. Mem. 1979); BMA (Sec., Ophthalmic Section, 1948; Vice-Pres., 1957). Chm., Ophthalmic Gp Cttee, 1963–75; Mem. Council, Faculty of Ophthalmologists, 1963–72, Vice-Pres. 1964, Pres. 1968–71; Dean, Inst. of Ophthalmology, 1967–75 (Deputy Dean, 1966–67); Mem., Orthoptists Bd, 1970, Vice-Chm. 1971, Chm. 1972–75. *Publications:* 12th Edn, May and Worth's Diseases of the Eye; articles in British Jl of Ophthalmology, the Lancet, and other med. jls, dealing with ophthalmology. *Recreations:* gardening, lawn tennis, golf, squash racquets. *Address:* 4 Cottenham Park Road, Wimbledon, SW20 0RZ. *T:* 081–946 3491.

CROSS, Alexander Urquhart, TD 1959; JP; Lord Provost of Perth, 1972–75; *b* 24 Dec. 1906; *m* 1936; one *s* one *d*. *Educ:* Univ. of Glasgow (MA). Owner of private school, 1931–70 (except war years, 1939–45). JP 1972, DL 1972–75, Hon. Sheriff, 1974–, Perth. CStJ 1981. *Address:* 6 Craigie Road, Perth PH2 0BH. *T:* Perth (0738) 25013.

CROSS, Prof. Anthony Glenn, FBA 1989; Professor of Slavonic Studies, since 1985, and Fellow of Fitzwilliam College, since 1986, Cambridge University; *b* 21 Oct. 1936; *s* of Walter Sidney Cross and Ada Cross; *m* 1960, Margaret (*née* Elson); two *d*. *Educ:* High Pavement Sch., Nottingham; Trinity Hall, Cambridge (BA 1960, MA 1964, PhD 1966); Harvard Univ. (AM 1961); LittD East Anglia 1981. Frank Knox Fellow, Harvard Univ., 1960–61; Univ. of East Anglia: Lectr in Russian, 1964–69; Sen. Lectr in Russian, 1969–72; Reader, 1972–81; Roberts Prof. of Russian, Univ. of Leeds, 1981–85. Vis. Fellow: Univ. of Illinois, 1969–70; All Souls Coll., Oxford, 1977–78. Pres., British Univs Assoc. of Slavists, 1982–84; Chm., British Academic Cttee for Liaison with Soviet Archives, 1983–. Reviews Editor, Jl of European Studies, 1971–; Editor, Study Group on Eighteenth-Century Russia Newsletter, 1973–. *Publications:* N. M. Karamzin, 1971; Russia Under Western Eyes 1517–1825, 1971; (ed) Russian Literature in the Age of Catherine the Great, 1976; Anglo-Russian Relations in the Eighteenth Century, 1977; (ed) Great Britain and Russia in the Eighteenth Century, 1979; By the Banks of the Thames, 1980; (ed) Russia and the West in the Eighteenth Century, 1981; The Tale of the Russian Daughter and her Suffocated Lover, 1982; (ed jtly) Eighteenth Century Russian Literature, Culture and Thought: a bibliography, 1984; The Russian Theme in English Literature, 1985; (ed jtly) Russia and the World of the Eighteenth Century, 1988; (ed) An English Lady at the Court of Catherine the Great, 1989. *Recreations:* book collecting,

cricket watching. *Address:* Department of Slavonic Studies, University of Cambridge, Sidgwick Avenue, Cambridge CB3 9DA. *T:* Cambridge (0223) 335007.

CROSS, Sir Barry (Albert), Kt 1989; CBE 1981; FRS 1975; President, Corpus Christi College, Cambridge, since 1987; Secretary, Zoological Society of London, since 1988; *b* 17 March 1925; *s* of Hubert Charles and Elsie May Cross; *m* 1949, Audrey Lilian Crow; one *s* two *d*. *Educ:* Reigate Grammar Sch.; Royal Veterinary Coll. London, MRCVS, BSc (Vet Sci); St John's Coll. Cambridge, BA Hons, MA, PhD. ScD 1964. ICI Research Fellow, Physiological Lab., Cambridge, 1949–51, Gedge Prize 1952; Demonstrator, Zoological Lab., Cambridge, 1951–55; Lectr, 1955–58; Rockefeller Fellow at UCLA, 1957–58; Lectr, Dept of Anatomy, Cambridge 1958–67; Supervisor in Physiology at St John's Coll., 1955–67; Corpus Christi College, Cambridge: Fellow, 1962–67, 1974–; Tutor for Advanced Students, 1964–67; Warden of Leckhampton, 1975–80; WHO Consultant, Geneva 1964; Prof. and Head of Dept of Anatomy, Univ. of Bristol, 1967–74, and Chm., Sch. of Preclinical Studies, 1969–73; Dir, AFRC Inst. of Animal Physiology, Babraham, 1974–86; Dir of Animal Physiology and Genetics Res., AFRC, 1986–89. OECD consultant in agricl biotechnology, 1989–91. Lectures: Share Jones, RCVS, 1967; Charnock Bradley, Edinburgh Univ., 1968; Glaxo, 1975; Entwhistle, Cambridge, 1976; McFadyean, London Univ., 1976; Wilmott, 1978, Long Fox, 1980, Bristol Univ.; Hunterian, London Hunterian Soc., 1988. Member: Council, Anatomical Soc., 1968–73 (Vice Pres. 1973–74); Council, Assoc. for Study of Animal Behaviour, 1959–62, 1973–75; Cttee, Soc. for Study of Fertility, 1961–65; Cttee, Physiological Soc., 1971–75 (Chm. 1974–75); Internat. Soc. for Neuroendocrinology (Vice-Pres., 1972–75, Pres., 1976–80); Council, Zoological Soc. of London, 1985–88; Adv. Cttee, Inst. of Zoology, 1982–88; Farm Animals Welfare Adv. Cttee, MAFF, 1975–78; UGC Wkg Party on Veterinary Educn, 1987–89. Governor, Strangeways Lab., Cambridge, 1987–. FIBiol 1975; FRVC 1979. Hon. FRASE 1987; Hon. Mem., BVA, 1986. Bledisloe Veterinary Award, RASE, 1982. Chevalier, Order of Dannebrog, 1968; Comdr d'honneur de l'Ordre du Bontemps de Médoc et des Graves, 1973. *Publications:* sci. papers on neuroendocrine topics in various biol. jls. *Address:* 6 Babraham Road, Cambridge CB2 2RA. *Club:* Athenæum.

CROSS, Beverley; playwright; *b* 13 April 1931; *s* of George Cross, theatrical manager, and Eileen Williams, actress; *m* 1975, Maggie Smith (*see* Dame Maggie Smith). *Educ:* Nautical Coll., Pangbourne; Balliol Coll., Oxford. Mem. Shakespeare Memorial Theatre Company, 1954–56; then began writing plays. One More River, Duke of York's, 1959; Strip the Willow, Arts, Cambridge, 1960 (Arts Council Drama Award for both, 1960); The Singing Dolphin, Oxford, 1960; The Three Cavaliers, Birmingham Rep., 1960; Belle, or The Ballad of Dr Crippen, Strand, 1961; Boeing-Boeing, Apollo, 1962; Wanted On Voyage, Marlowe, Canterbury, 1962; Half A Sixpence, Cambridge, London, 1963; Jorrocks, New, London, 1966; The Owl on the Battlements, Nottingham, 1971; Catherine Howard, York, 1972; The Great Society, Mermaid, 1974; Hans Andersen, Palladium, 1974; Happy Birthday, Apollo, 1979; Haworth, Birmingham Rep., 1981; The Scarlet Pimpernel, Chichester, Her Majesty's, 1985; Miranda, Chichester Fest., 1987. *Libretti:* The Mines of Sulphur, Sadler's Wells, 1965; All the King's Men, 1969; Victory, Covent Garden, 1970; The Rising of the Moon, Glyndebourne, 1970; A Capital Transfer, British Council, London, 1981. *Screen plays of:* Jason and the Argonauts, 1962; The Long Ships, 1963; Genghis Khan, 1965; Half A Sixpence, 1966; (with Carlo Lizzani) Mussolini: Ultimo Atto, 1973; Sinbad and the Eye of the Tiger, 1977; The Clash of the Titans, 1981. *Television plays:* The Nightwalkers, 1960; The Dark Pits of War, 1960; Catherine Howard, 1969; March on, Boys!, 1975; A Bill of Mortality, 1975. *Directed:* Boeing-Boeing, Sydney, 1964; The Platinum Cat, Wyndham's, 1965. *Publications:* Mars in Capricorn, 1955; The Nightwalkers, 1956; Plays For Children, 1960. *Address:* c/o Curtis Brown Ltd, 162 Regent Street, W1R 5TA. *T:* 071–437 9700.

CROSS, Clifford Thomas, CB 1977; Commissioner, Customs and Excise, 1970–79; *b* 1 April 1920; *o s* of late Arthur and Helena Cross; *m* 1942, Ida Adelaide Barker; one *s* two *d*. *Educ:* Latymer Upper Sch., Hammersmith; Univ. of London (LLB). Joined Inland Revenue, 1939; Customs and Excise, 1946; Asst Sec. 1959; Comr 1970. *Recreations:* squash rackets, bonsai culture, watching television, etc. *Address:* Longacre, 101 Histon Road, Cottenham, Cambs CB4 4UQ. *T:* Cottenham (0954) 50757.

CROSS, Dr Dolores Evelyn; President, Chicago State University, since 1990; *b* 29 Aug. 1938; *d* of Ozie Johnson Tucker and Charles Tucker; *m* 1956, Thomas Edwin Cross; one *s* one *d*. *Educ:* Seton Hall Univ. (BS 1963); Hofstra Univ. (MS 1968); Univ. of Michigan (PhD 1971). Teaching posts, NY and Michigan, 1961–71; Asst Prof. in Educn, Northwestern Univ., 1971–74; Associate Prof. in Educn, Claremont Graduate Sch., 1974–78; Vice-Chancellor for student affairs and special programs, City Univ., NY, and Prof. in Educn, Brooklyn Coll., 1978–81; Pres., NY State Higher Educn Services Corp., 1981–88; Associate Provost and Associate Vice-Pres. for Academic Affairs, Univ. of Minnesota, 1988–90. Hon. LLD: Marymount Manhattan, 1984; Skidmore Coll., 1988. NAACP Muriel Silverberg Award, NY, 1987; John Jay Award, NYC Commn of Indep. Colls and Univs, 1989. *Publications:* Influence of Individual Difference on Theories of Instruction, 1974; Teaching in a Multi-Cultural Society, 1977. *Recreations:* jogging, marathon running. *Address:* Chicago State University, 95th Street at King Drive Avenue, Chicago, Ill 60628, USA. *T:* (312) 995–2400.

CROSS, Prof. George Alan Martin, FRS 1984; André and Bella Meyer Professor of Molecular Parasitology, Rockefeller University, New York, since 1982; *b* 27 Sept. 1942; *s* of George Bernard and Beatrice Mary Cross; *m* 1986, Nadia Nogueira; one *d*. *Educ:* Cheadle Hulme Sch.; Downing Coll., Univ. of Cambridge (BA, PhD). ICI Postdoctoral Fellow, Biochemistry, Cambridge, 1967–69; Research Fellow, Fitzwilliam Coll., Cambridge, 1967–70; Scientist, MRC Biochemical Parasitology Unit, Molteno Inst., Cambridge, 1969–77; Head, Dept of Immunochemistry, Wellcome Research Laboratories, 1977–82. Fleming Lectr, Soc. for General Microbiology, 1978. Chalmers Medal, Royal Soc. for Tropical Medicine and Hygiene, 1983; (jtly) Paul Ehrlich and Ludwig Darmstaedter Prize, 1984. *Publications:* in journals of parasitology, biochemistry, microbiology and molecular biology. *Recreations:* sailing, tennis, building projects, observing people. *Address:* Rockefeller University, 1230 York Avenue, New York, NY 10021, USA. *T:* 212–570–7571.

CROSS, Hannah Margaret, (Mrs E. G. Wright); barrister-at-law; *b* 25 April 1908; *o d* of late F. J. K. Cross and Eleanor Mary Cross (née Phillimore); *m* 1936, Edmund Gordon Wright, Barrister-at-Law (*d* 1971); one *s* one *d*. *Educ:* Downe House Sch.; St Hilda's Coll., Oxford. BA 1929. Called to Bar, Lincoln's Inn, 1931; first woman Mem. of Gen. Council of Bar, 1938–45; Civil Defence, 1939–45. *Address:* The Quay House, Sidlesham, near Chichester, West Sussex PO20 7LX. *T:* Sidlesham (0243) 641258.

CROSS, James Richard, (Jasper), CMG 1971; Under-Secretary, Principal Establishment Officer, Department of Energy, 1978–80; *b* 29 Sept. 1921; *s* of J. P. Cross and Dinah Cross (*née* Hodgins); *m* 1945, Barbara Dagg; one *d*. *Educ:* King's Hosp., Dublin; Trin. Coll., Dublin. Scholar, First Cl. Moderatorship Economics and Polit. Science. RE (Lieut) Asst Principal, Bd of Trade, 1947; Private Sec. to Parly Sec., 1947–49; Principal, 1950; Trade Commissioner: New Delhi, 1953–56; Halifax, 1957–60; Winnipeg, 1960–62; Asst Sec.,

1962; Sen. Trade Comr, Kuala Lumpur, 1962–66; Bd of Trade, 1966–67; Under Sec., 1968; Sen. British Trade Comr, Montreal, 1968–70 (kidnapped by terrorists and held for 59 days, Oct.-Dec. 1970); Under-Sec., Export Planning and Develt Div., DTI, 1971–73; Sec., British Overseas Trade Bd, 1972; Coal Div., DTI, later Dept of Energy, 1973–78. *Recreations:* theatre, bridge, the New Forest. *Address:* The Small House, Queen Katherine Road, Lymington, Hants.

CROSS, Joan, CBE 1951; opera singer; *b* Sept. 1900. *Educ:* St Paul's Girls' Sch. Principal soprano, Old Vic and Sadler's Wells, 1924–44; Dir of Opera, Sadler's Wells, 1941–44; subsequently Principal, National Sch. of Opera (Ltd), Morley Coll., London, resigned. Created rôles in The Rape of Lucretia, Albert Herring, Gloriana and The Turn of the Screw. *Address:* Garrett House, Park Road, Aldeburgh, Suffolk.

CROSS, Air Chief Marshal Sir Kenneth (Brian Boyd), KCB 1959 (CB 1954); CBE 1945; DSO 1943; DFC 1940; *b* 4 Oct. 1911; *s* of Pembroke H. C. Cross and Mrs Jean Cross; *m* 1945, Brenda Megan (*d* 1991), *d* of Wing-Comdr F. J. B. Powell; two *s* one *d*. *Educ:* Kingswood Sch., Bath. Pilot Officer, RAF, 1930; Flying Badge, 1931; 25 Fighter Sqdn, 1931; Flying Officer, 1932; Flying Instructor, No 5 FTS Sealand and Cambridge Univ. Air Sqdn, 1934; Flt Lt 1935; Sqdn Ldr 1938; commanded No 46 Fighter Sqdn UK, Norway, 1939–40; Wing Comdr 1940; posted Middle East, 1941; Actg Group Capt. 1941; Actg Air Commodore, 1943; Director Overseas Operations, Air Ministry, 1944; Imperial Defence Coll., 1946; reverted Group Capt., 1946; Group Capt. Operations HQ BAFO Germany, 1947; OC Eastern Sector Fighter Command, 1949; Dir of Weapons, Air Ministry, 1952; subs. Air Cdre, 1953; Dir of Ops, Air Defence, 1954–Dec. 1955; Air Vice-Marshal, 1956; AOC No 3 (Bomber) Group, 1956–59; Air Marshal, 1961; AOC-in-C, Bomber Comd, 1959–63; Air Chief Marshal, 1965; AOC-in-C, Transport Comd, 1963–66, retd, 1967. Director: Suffolk Branch, 1968, London Branch, 1974, British Red Cross Soc. Norwegian War Cross, 1941; USA Legion of Merit, 1944; French Legion of Honour, 1944; French Croix de Guerre, 1944; Dutch Order of Orange Nassau, 1945. *Recreations:* Rugby football and golf (colours RAF). *Address:* 12 Callow Street, Chelsea, SW3. *Club:* Royal Air Force.

CROSS, Dame Margaret Natalie; *see* Smith, Dame Maggie.

CROSS, Prof. Robert Craigie, CBE 1972; MA Glasgow, MA Oxford; FRSE; Regius Professor of Logic, 1953–78, Vice-Principal, 1974–77, University of Aberdeen; *b* 24 April 1911; *s* of Matthew Cross and Margaret Dickson; *m* 1943, Peggy Catherine Elizabeth Vernon; two *d*. *Educ:* Glasgow Univ.; Queen's Coll., Oxford. MA 1st Cl. Hons Classics, Glasgow, 1932; 1st Cl. Hons Classical Mods, Oxford, 1934; 1st Cl. Lit. Hum., Oxford, 1936. Fellow and Tutor in Philsophy, Jesus Coll., Oxford, 1938; served War, 1941–45, Navy and Admiralty; Senior Tutor, Jesus Coll., Oxford, 1948–53. Trustee, Scottish Hospital Endowments Research Trust, 1968–80; Mem., University Grants Cttee, 1965–74; Mem., North Eastern Regional Hospital Bd, 1958–65. *Publications:* (with A. D. Woozley) Plato's Republic: A Philosophical Commentary, 1964; contributions to learned jls. *Address:* Heatherlands, Ancrum, Roxburghshire TD8 6XA. *T:* Ancrum (08353) 282.

CROSSE, Gordon; composer; *b* 1 Dec. 1937; *s* of Percy and Marie Crosse; *m* 1965, Elizabeth Bunch. *Educ:* Cheadle Hulme Sch.; St Edmund Hall, Oxford; Accad. di S Cecilia, Rome. Music Fellow, Essex Univ., 1969–74; Composer in residence, King's Coll., Cambridge, 1974–76; Vis. Lectr, Univ. of Calif at Santa Barbara, 1977–78. Hon. RAM, 1980. *Operas:* Purgatory, 1966; The Grace of Todd, 1967; The Story of Vasco, 1970; Potter Thompson, 1973; *ballets:* Playground, 1979; Wildboy, 1981; *other compositions:* Concerto da Camera, 1962; Meet My Folks, 1963; "Symphonies", 1964; Second Violin Concerto, 1970; Memories of Morning: Night, 1972; Ariadne, 1973; Symphony 2, 1975; Wildboy (clarinet concerto), Play Ground, 1977; Dreamsongs, 1978; Cello Concerto, 1979; String Quartet, 1980; Dreamcanon (chorus), 1981; Trio for piano, violin and cello, 1986; Trumpet Concerto, 1986; Sea Psalms, 1990; much other orchestral, vocal and chamber music. *Address:* Brant's Cottage, Blackheath, Wenhaston, Halesworth, Suffolk IP19 9EX.

CROSSETT, Robert Nelson, (Tom), DPhil; FIFST; Environment Director, National Power plc, since 1990; *b* 27 May 1938; *s* of Robert Crossett and Mary Nelson; *m* 1966, Susan Marjorie Legg; two *s*. *Educ:* British School, Hamburg; Campbell College, Belfast; Queen's Univ., Belfast (BSc, BAgr); Lincoln College, Oxford (DPhil); Univ. of East Anglia. FIFST 1986. Group Leader Environmental Studies, Aust. Atomic Energy Commn, 1966; Sen. Sci. Officer, ARC Letcombe Lab., 1969; Develt Officer (Crops), Scottish Agricl. Develt Council, 1972; PSO, Dept of Agric. and Fisheries for Scotland, 1975; Ministry of Agriculture, Fisheries and Food: Sci. Liaison Officer (Horticulture and Soils), 1978; Head, Food Sci. Div., 1984; Chief Scientist (Fisheries and Food), 1985–89; Head of Envmtl Policy, National Power, 1989–90. Member: NERC, 1985–89; AFRC, 1985–89; UK Delgn, Tripartite Meetings on Food and Drugs, 1985–88; Cttee on Med. Aspects of Food Policy, 1985–89. *Publications:* papers in plant physiology, marine biology and food science. *Recreations:* walking, gardening, orienteering, boats. *Address:* National Power, Sudbury House, 15 Newgate Street, EC1A 7AU.

CROSSLAND, Anthony, FRCO; Organist and Master of the Choristers, Wells Cathedral, since 1971; *b* 4 Aug. 1931; *s* of Ernest Thomas and Frances Elizabeth Crossland; *m* 1960, Barbara Helen Pullar-Strecker; one *s* two *d*. *Educ:* Christ Church, Oxford. MA, BMus (Oxon), FRCO (CHM), ARCM. Asst Organist: Christ Church Cathedral, Oxford, 1957–61; Wells Cathedral, 1961–71. Conductor: Wells Cathedral Oratorio Soc., 1966–; Wells Sinfonietta, 1985–; Organs Advr to dio. of Bath and Wells, 1971–. Pres., Cathedral Organists' Assoc., 1983–85. *Recreations:* reading, photography. *Address:* 15 Vicars' Close, Wells, Somerset BA5 2UJ. *T:* Wells (Somerset) (0749) 73526.

CROSSLAND, Sir Bernard, Kt 1990; CBE 1980; MSc (London); PhD (Bristol); DSc (Nottingham); FRS 1979; FEng 1979; MRIA; FIMechE; FIEI; Emeritus Professor, The Queen's University, Belfast, since 1984 (Professor and Head of Department of Mechanical and Industrial Engineering, 1959–82, Research Professor, 1982–84; Dean, 1964–67; Pro-Vice-Chancellor, 1978–82); *b* 20 Oct. 1923; *s* of R. F. Crossland and K. M. Rudduck; *m* 1946, Audrey Elliott Birks; two *d*. *Educ:* Simon Langton's, Canterbury. Apprentice, Rolls Royce Ltd, 1940–41; Nottingham Univ., 1941–43; Technical Asst, Rolls Royce, 1943–45; Asst Lectr, Lectr and then Senior Lectr in Mechanical Engineering, Univ. of Bristol, 1946–59. Member: AFRC, 1981–87; Engrg Council, 1983–88; Chairman: Bd for Engineers' Registration, 1983–86; Youth Careers Guidance Cttee, N Ireland, 1975–79, 1979–81; NI Manpower Council, 1981–86; Member: NI Training Council, 1964–76, 1977–81; NI Economic Council, 1981–85; NI Industrial Develt Bd, 1982–87. Assessor, King's Cross Fire Investigation, 1988. Institution of Mechanical Engineers: Chm., Engineering Sciences Div., 1980–84; Vice-Pres., 1983–84; Dep. Pres., 1984–86; Pres., 1986–87; Past Pres., 1987–91; Leonardo da Vinci Lectr, 1970; George Stephenson Lectr, 1989; George Stephenson and Thomas Hawksley Medals; Mem. Council and a Vice-Pres., Royal Soc., 1984–86; Mem. Council, Fellowship of Engrg, 1985–88; Pres., Section 6, British Assoc., 1987. Trustee, Mackie Foundn, 1983–. Freeman, City of London, 1987; Liveryman, Worshipful Co. of Engrs, 1988. Hon. MASME, 1987; Hon. FWeldI. Hon. DSc: NUI, 1984; Dublin, 1985; Edinburgh, 1987; QUB 1988; Aston, 1988; Cranfield Inst. of Technology, 1989. *Publications:* An Introduction to the Mechanics of Machines, 1964; Explosive Welding and its Application, 1982; various papers on fatigue of metals and effect of very high fluid pressures on properties of materials; strength of thick-walled vessels, explosive welding, friction welding, design and history of engineering. *Recreation:* walking. *Address:* The Queen's University, Belfast BT7 1NN. *T:* Belfast (0232) 247303; 16 Malone Court, Belfast BT9 6PA. *T:* Belfast (0232) 667495. *Club:* Athenæum.

CROSSLAND, Sir Leonard, Kt 1969; farmer since 1974; Chairman: Eaton Ltd (UK), 1972–88; Ford Motor Co. Ltd, 1968–72; Energy Research and Development Ltd (formerly Sedgeminster Technical Developments Ltd), since 1974; *b* 2 March 1914; *s* of Joseph and Frances Crossland; *m* 1st, 1941, Rhona Marjorie Griffin; two *d*; 2nd, 1963, Joan Brewer. *Educ:* Penistone Grammar Sch. Purchase Dept, Ford Motor Co. Ltd, 1937–39. Royal Army Service Corps, 1939–45 (despatches twice). Ford Motor Co. Ltd: Purchase Dept. 1945–54; Chief Buyer, Tractor and Implement Dept, 1954–57; Chief Buyer, Car and Truck Dept, 1957–59; Asst Purchase Manager, 1959–60; Purchase Manager, 1960–62; Exec. Dir, Supply and Services, 1962–66; Dir, Manufacturing Staff and Services, 1966; Asst Man. Dir, 1966–67; Man. Dir, 1967; Dep. Chm., 1967; Chm., Autolite Motor Products Ltd; Director: Henry Ford & Son Ltd, Cork; Eaton Corp. (US), 1974–81. Farmer. *Recreations:* shooting, fishing, golf. *Address:* Abbotts Hall, Great Wigborough, Colchester, Essex CO5 7RZ. *T:* Peldon (020635) 456. *Clubs:* City Livery, Royal Automobile, British Racing Drivers'; American.

CROSSLAND, Prof. Ronald Arthur, FSA 1982; Professor of Greek, University of Sheffield, 1958–82, now Emeritus (Dean, Faculty of Arts, 1973–75); *b* 31 Aug. 1920; *s* of late Ralph Crossland, BSc, and late Ethel Crossland (*née* Scattergood). *Educ:* Stanley Road Elementary Sch., Nottingham; Nottingham High Sch.; King's Coll., Cambridge. Major Scholar in Classics, King's Coll., Cambridge, 1939–41 and 1945–46. National Service in Royal Artillery, 1941–45. Henry Fellow, Berkeley Coll., Yale Univ., 1946–47; Instructor in Classics, Yale Univ., 1947–48; Senior Student of Treasury Cttee for Studentships in Foreign Languages and Cultures (for research in Hittite Philology and Linguistics), 1948–51; Hon. Lectr in Ancient History, University of Birmingham, 1950–51; Lecturer in Ancient History, King's Coll., University of Durham, Newcastle upon Tyne, 1951–58. Harris Fellow of King's Coll., Cambridge, 1952–56. Vis. Prof., Univ. Texas, 1962; Collitz Vis. Prof., Univ. Michigan, 1967; Vis. Fellow, Victoria Univ. of Wellington, NZ, 1979. Pres., South Shields Archaeological and Historical Soc., 1976–77. *Publications:* Bronze Age Migrations in the Aegean (with A. Birchall), 1973; chapters on: Immigrants from the North, in Cambridge Ancient History, rev. edn, 1967; Linguistic Problems of the Balkan Area, in Cambridge Ancient History, rev. edn, 1982; Early Greek Migrations, in Civilization of the Ancient Mediterranean (ed M. Grant), 1987; articles in Trans Philological Soc., Archivum Linguisticum, Studia Balcanica, Past and Present. *Recreations:* music, travel, pastime with good company. *Address:* 59 Sherlock Close, Cambridge CB3 0HP. *T:* Cambridge (0223) 358085; (enquiries) Sheffield (0742) 768555 ext. 4603.

CROSSLEY, family name of **Baron Somerleyton.**

CROSSLEY, Geoffrey Allan, CMG 1974; HM Diplomatic Service, retired; Director, External Relations, Continuing Education, European Institute of Business Administration, INSEAD, Fontainebleau, 1980–84; *b* 11 Nov. 1920; *s* of Thomas Crossley and Winifred Mary Crossley (*née* Ellis); *m* 1945, Aline Louise Farcy; two *s* one *d*. *Educ:* Penistone; abroad; Gonville and Caius Coll., Cambridge (Scholar). Served War of 1939–45: Min. of Supply, 1941–; Foreign Office, 1942–; in Algeria and France. Foreign Service, 1945–: Second Sec., Paris, 1945–48; FO, 1948–49; Alternate UK Deleg. on UN Balkans Commn, Greece, 1949–52; Dep. Regional Inf. Officer with Commissioner-Gen. for SE Asia, Singapore, 1952–55; FO, 1955–57; Consulate-Gen., Frankfurt, for Saar Transition from France to Germany, 1957–59; Political Office, NE Command, Cyprus (later in charge), 1959–61; Head of Chancery, Berne, 1961–65; on secondment to Min. of Overseas Development, as Head of W and N African Dept, 1965–67; Dep. High Comr, Lusaka, 1967–69; Counsellor, Oslo, 1969–73; Ambassador to Colombia, 1973–77; Envoy to the Holy See, 1978–80. Founder Mem., Cambridge Soc. Mem., French Inst. of Internat. Relations. *Recreations:* various. *Address:* 22 Rue Emeriau, 75015 Paris, France.

CROSSLEY, Harry; DL; Chief Executive, Derbyshire County Council, 1974–79, retired; *b* 2 Sept. 1918; *s* of late Percy Crossley and Nellie McMinnies Crossley, Burnley, Lancs; *m* 1949, Pamela, *e d* of late Ald. E. A. C. Woodcock, Kettering, Northants; two *s*. *Educ:* Burnley Grammar Sch. Solicitor. LAM RTPI. War service, RA, attached Indian Army (Major), 1939–46. Private practice and local govt service as solicitor; Derbyshire CC: Dep. Clerk of Peace and of CC, 1960–69; Clerk of Peace and of CC, 1969–74. Clerk to Derbyshire Lieutenancy, 1969–79; Sec., Lord Chancellor's Adv. Cttee for Derbyshire, 1969–79. Clerk, Peak Park Planning Bd, 1969–74. DL Derbyshire, 1978. *Publications:* articles for legal and local govt jls. *Recreations:* golf, tennis, gardening. *Address:* Alpine, Bracken Lane, Holloway, Matlock DE4 5AS. *T:* Dethick (0629) 534382.

CROSSLEY, Sir Nicholas John, 4th Bt *cr* 1909, of Glenfield, Dunham Massey, Co. Chester; *b* 10 Dec. 1962; *s* of Sir Christopher John Crossley, 3rd Bt and of Carolyne Louise, *d* of late L. Grey Sykes; *S* father, 1989. *Heir: b* Julian Charles Crossley, *b* 11 Dec. 1964. *Address:* 155 South Plymouth Boulevard, Los Angeles, Calif 90004, USA.

CROSSLEY, Paul Christopher Richard; concert pianist; Artistic Director, London Sinfonietta, since 1988; *b* 17 May 1944; *s* of late Frank Crossley and Myra Crossley (*née* Barrowcliffe). *Educ:* Silcoates Sch., Wakefield; Mansfield Coll., Oxford (BA, MA). International concert pianist; recitals and concerts with all major orchestras; numerous recordings and films for TV. *Recreations:* Mah-Jongg, reading. *Address:* c/o Van Walsum Management, 26 Wadham Road, SW15 2LR. *T:* 081–874 6344.

CROSSLEY, Maj.-Gen. Ralph John, CB 1987; CBE 1981; retired; Chairman, Salisbury Health Authority, since 1990; Director, Defence Policy, Avon Rubber plc, since 1987; Director, Select Industries plc; *b* 11 Oct. 1933; *s* of Edward Crossley and Eva Mary Crossley (*née* Farnworth); *m* 1957, Marion Hilary Crossley (*née* Bacon); one *s* one *d*. *Educ:* Quainton Sch., Harrow; Felsted School. FBIM. Commnd 1952 (Nat. Service); Air Observation Post Pilots course, 1953; Regimental Duty: Canal Zone,1954–56; BAOR, 1956–59; Instructor in Gunnery, Larkhill, 1959–63; Technical Staff Course, 1963–65; Regtl Duty, BAOR, 1965–67, 1969–71; Weapons Staff, UK, 1967–69; Gen. Staff, UK, 1971–72; Instructor, RMCS, 1972–74; CO, 94 Locating Regt, 1974–77; Project Manager, 155 Systems, 1977–81; Dep. Comdt, RMCS, 1981–84; Dir. Gen. of Weapons (Army), 1984–86. Lefroy Gold Medal, RA Instn, 1987. *Recreations:* golf, walking, gardening. *Address:* c/o Odstock Hospital, Salisbury, Wilts.

CROSSLEY-HOLLAND, Kevin John William; author; *b* 7 Feb. 1941; *s* of Prof. Peter Charles Crossley-Holland and Joan Mary Crossley-Holland (*née* Cowper), MBE; *m* 1st, 1963, Caroline Fendall, *er d* of Prof. L. M. Thompson; two *s*; 2nd, 1972, Ruth, *er d* of John Marris; 3rd, 1982, Gillian Paula, *er d* of Peter Cook; two *d*. *Educ:* Bryanston Sch.; St Edmund Hall, Oxford (BA Hons). Editor, Macmillan & Co., 1962–69; Gregory Fellow in Poetry, Univ. of Leeds, 1969–71; Talks Producer, BBC, 1972; Editl Dir, Victor Gollancz, 1972–77; Lectr in English: Tufts-in-London Program, 1967–78; Regensburg

Univ., 1978–80; Arts Council Fellow in Writing, Winchester Sch. of Art, 1983 and 1984; Vis. Prof. of English and Fulbright Scholar in Residence, St Olaf Coll., Minnesota, 1987–; Prof. of Humanities, St Thomas Coll., Minnesota, 1991–; Vis Lectr for British Council in Germany, Iceland, India, Yugoslavia. Editl Consultant, Boydell & Brewer, 1983–90. Chm., Literature Panel, Eastern Arts Assoc., 1986–89; Trustee, Wingfield Coll., 1989– (Chm., Friends, 1989–91). Contribs to radio, TV and musical works. *Publications: poetry:* The Rain-Giver, 1972; The Dream-House, 1976; Time's Oriel, 1983; Waterslain, 1986; The Painting-Room, 1988; New and Selected Poems, 1991; *for children:* Havelok the Dane, 1964; King Horn, 1965; The Green Children, 1966 (Arts Council Award); The Callow Pit Coffer, 1968; (with Jill Paton Walsh) Wordhoard, 1969; Storm and Other Old English Riddles, 1970; The Pedlar of Swaffham, 1971; The Sea Stranger, 1973; The Fire-Brother, 1974; Green Blades Rising, 1975; The Earth-Father, 1976; The Wildman, 1976; The Dead Moon, 1982; Beowulf, 1982; Axe-Age, Wolf-Age, 1985; Storm, 1985 (Carnegie Medal); (with Susanne Lugert) The Fox and the Cat, 1985; British Folk Tales, 1987; Wulf, 1988; Piper and Pooka, 1988; Small Tooth Dog, 1988; Boo!, 1988; Dathera Dad, 1989; (with Ian Penney) Under the Sun and Over the Moon, 1989; Sleeping Nanna, 1989; Sea Tongue, 1991; Tales from Europe, 1991; *travel:* Pieces of Land, 1972; *mythology:* The Norse Myths, 1980; *history:* (with Andrew Rafferty) The Stones Remain, 1989; *translations from Old English:* (with Bruce Mitchell) The Battle of Maldon, 1965; (with Bruce Mitchell) Beowulf, 1968; The Exeter Book Riddles, 1978; The Illustrated Beowulf, 1987; The Anglo-Saxon Elegies, 1988; *edited:* Running to Paradise, 1967; Winter's Tales for Children 3, 1967; Winter's Tales 14, 1968; (with Patricia Beer) New Poetry 2, 1976; The Faber Book of Northern Legends, 1977; The Faber Book of Northern Folk-Tales, 1980; The Anglo-Saxon World, 1982; The Riddle Book, 1982; Folk-Tales of the British Isles, 1985; The Oxford Book of Travel Verse, 1986; Northern Lights, 1987; Medieval Lovers, 1988; Medieval Gardens, 1990; Peter Grimes by George Crabbe, 1990; *opera:* (with Nicola LeFanu) The Green Children, 1990. *Recreations:* opera, telephone calls, wine, walks. *Address:* The Old Vicarage, Walsham-le-Willows, Bury St Edmunds, Suffolk.

CROSTHWAIT, Timothy Leland, CMG 1964; MBE 1944; HM Diplomatic Service, retired; *b* 5 Aug. 1915; *s* of Lt-Col L. G. Crosthwait, Survey of India; *m* 1959, Anne Marjorie, *d* of Col T. M. M. Penney. *Educ:* Wellington Coll.; Peterhouse, Cambridge (MA). Appointed to Indian Civil Service, 1937; Asst Private Sec. to Viceroy, 1942–44; Air Min., 1948–55; Commonwealth Relations Office, 1955; British Deputy High Commissioner in Ceylon, 1957–61; Asst Sec., CRO, 1961–63; British High Commissioner, Zanzibar, 1963–64; British Deputy High Commissioner, Malta, 1965–66; British High Commissioner, Guyana, 1966–67; Ambassador, Malagasy Republic, 1970–75. *Address:* 39 Eaton Terrace, SW1W 8TP. *T:* 071–730 9553. *Club:* United Oxford & Cambridge University.

CROUCH, Colin John, DPhil; Fellow and Tutor in Politics, Trinity College, Oxford, since 1985; *b* 1 March 1944; *s* of Charles and Doris Crouch; *m* 1970, Joan Ann Freedman; two *s*. *Educ:* Latymer Upper Sch.; London School of Economics (BASoc; Pres., Students Union, 1968; Hobhouse Prize, 1969); Nuffield Coll., Oxford (MA, DPhil). Lectr 1969–70 and 1973–79, Sen. Lectr 1979–80, Reader 1980–85, in Sociology, London Sch. of Economics and Political Science; Lectr in Sociology, Univ. of Bath, 1972–73; Jun. Proctor, Univ. of Oxford, 1990–91. Mem., Exec. Cttee, Fabian Soc., 1969–78 (Chm., 1976); Dir, Andrew Shonfield Soc., 1989–. Mem., Standing Cttee, Court of Govs, LSE, 1980–84. Joint Editor, The Political Quarterly, 1985–. *Publications:* The Student Revolt, 1970; (ed jtly) Stress and Contradiction in Modern Capitalism, 1975; (ed) British Political Sociology Year Book, vol. III, 1977; Class Conflict and the Industrial Relations Crisis, 1977; (ed jtly) The Resurgence of Class Conflict in Western Europe since 1968, 2 vols, 1978; (ed) State and Economy in Contemporary Capitalism, 1979; The Politics of Industrial Relations, 1979, 2nd edn 1982; Trade Unions: the logic of collective action, 1982; (ed jtly) International Yearbook of Organizational Democracy, vol. I, 1983; (ed jtly) The New Centralism: Britain out of step in Europe?, 1989; (ed jtly) European Industrial Relations: the challenge of flexibility, 1990; (ed jtly) Corporatism and Accountability: organised interests in British public life, 1990; (ed jtly) The Politics of 1992: beyond the single European market, 1990; Invaders of Political Space: workers, employers and the European state traditions, 1991; numerous articles on industrial relns, politics and social structure in Britain and Western Europe. *Recreations:* playing violin, music, gardening, watching and refereeing football matches. *Address:* 109 Southmoor Road, Oxford OX2 6RE. *T:* Oxford (0865) 54688.

CROUCH, Sir David (Lance), Kt 1987; Chairman, David Crouch & Co. Ltd, since 1964; *b* 23 June 1919; *s* of late Stanley Crouch and Rosalind Kate Crouch (*née* Croom); *m* 1947, Margaret Maplesden, *d* of Major Sydney Maplesden Noakes, DSO and Norah Parkyns Maplesden Noakes (*née* Buckland), Shorne, Kent; one *s* one *d*. *Educ:* University Coll. Sch. Served in City of London Yeomanry (TA), 1938–39; served War of 1939–45, Royal Artillery: Major 1943; attached RAF Staff (GSO2), 1944–45. Joined British Nylon Spinners Ltd, 1946; ICI Ltd, 1950; Dir of Publicity, Internat. Wool Secretariat, 1962–64. Formed own co., David Crouch & Co. Ltd, as international marketing and public relations consultants; Director: Pfizer Ltd, 1969–88; Burson Marsteller Ltd, 1972–83; Kingsway Public Relations (Hldgs) Ltd, 1985–89; Westminster Communications Gp Ltd, 1989–. Contested (C) West Leeds, 1959. MP (C) Canterbury, 1966–87. Chairman: British-Egyptian Parly Gp, 1972–87; British-Algerian Gp, 1980–87; All-Party Gp for the Chemical Industry, 1970–85; All-Party Gp for Energy Studies, 1980–85; British Gp, Inter-Parly Union, 1985–87; Vice-Chm., Cons. Middle East Council, 1980–87; Member: Select Cttee for Nationalized Industries, 1966–74; Public Accounts Cttee, 1974–79; Speaker's Panel, 1982–87; Select Cttee for Social Services, 1983–84; Adv. Cttee on the Arts to Mr Speaker, 1970–87 (Chm., 1983–87). Trustee, Theatres Trust, 1977– (Dep. Chm., 1979–87; Chm., 1987–); Chm., Channel Theatre Co., 1984–87. Pres., Kent Soc., 1987–. Member: SE Thames RHA, 1970–85; MRC, 1984–87; Soc. of Chemical Industry; Council, Univ. of Kent, 1971–; Council, RSA, 1974–78 (Fellow, 1971). Hon. DCLKent, 1987. *Publication:* A Canterbury Tale, 1987. *Recreations:* painting, golf. *Address:* The Oast House, Fisher Street, Badlesmere, Faversham, Kent ME13 0LB. *Clubs:* Athenæum, MCC; Kent and Canterbury (Canterbury); Royal St George's Golf.

CROW, Hilary Stephen, FRTPI; FRGS; Chief Planning Inspector, Departments of the Environment, Transport and Welsh Office, since 1988; *b* 2 Sept. 1934; *s* of Aubrey Everard Crow and late Ivy Marion (*née* Warltier); *m* 1958, Margaret Anderson; two *s* one *d*. *Educ:* Leek High Sch.; William Ellis Sch.; St Catharine's Coll., Cambridge (MA). Planning Asst, various grades, with Lancashire CC and Southport CBC, 1957–72; Divl Planning Officer, 1972–74, Prin. Asst County Planning Officer, 1974–76, Herts CC; joined Planning Inspectorate, 1976: Prin. Inspector for Wales, 1982–85; Asst Chief Inspector, 1985–88; Dep. Chief Inspector, 1988. C of E Lay Reader, 1979–. *Recreations:* music, reading, garden. *Address:* Tollgate House, Houlton Street, Bristol BS2 9DJ. *T:* Bristol (0272) 218965.

CROW, Dr Timothy John, FRCP, FRCPsych; Head, Division of Psychiatry, Clinical Research Centre, and Hon. Consultant Psychiatrist, Northwick Park Hospital, since 1974; *b* 7 June 1938; *s* of Percy Arthur Crow and Barbara Bonner Davies; *m* 1966, Julie Carol Carter; one *s* one *d*. *Educ:* Shrewsbury Sch.; London Hosp. Med. Coll. MB BS, PhD, DPM. Maudsley Hosp., 1966; University of Aberdeen: Lectr in Physiology, 1966–70; Lectr in Mental Health, 1970–72; Sen. Lectr in Psychiatry, Univ. of Manchester, 1972–73. Part-time Mem., Sci. Staff, Div. Neurophysiology and Neuropharmacology, Nat. Inst. for Med. Res., 1974–83; Dep. Dir, Clinical Res. Centre, 1984–89. Member: MRC Neuroscis Projects Grants Cttee, 1978–80; Neuroscis Bd, 1986–90; Chm., Biol. Psych. Gp, RCPsych, 1983–88 (Sec., 1980–83). Andrew W. Woods Vis. Prof., Univ. of Iowa, 1980; Lectures: St George's Hosp., 1980; St Louis, 1981; Univ. of Minnesota, 1981; Univ. of Ohio, 1986; RSocMed, 1988; Roche, RCPsych, Dublin, 1988; Stockholm, 1988; Maudsley, RCPsych, 1989; APA Internat. Scholars, 1990; Univ. of Oregon, 1991. A. P. Noyes Award, 1988; US Nat. Alliance Lieber Award, 1989. Editor: Disorders of Neurohumoural Transmission; Recurrent and Chronic Psychoses, 1987. *Publications:* papers on brain reward mechanisms, learning and schizophrenia in sci. and med. jls. *Recreations:* sciolistic archaeology, anthropology. *Address:* 16 Northwick Circle, Kenton, Middx HA3 0EJ. *T:* 081–907 6124. *Club:* Royal Society of Medicine.

CROWDEN, James Gee Pascoe, JP; FRICS, FCIArb; Senior Partner, Grounds & Co., 1974–88, now consultant; Vice Lord-Lieutenant of Cambridgeshire, since 1985; *b* 14 Nov. 1927; *yr s* of late Lt-Col R. J. C. Crowden, MC, and Nina Mary (*née* Gee), Peterborough; *m* 1955, Kathleen Mary (*d* 1989), *widow* of Captain F. A. Grounds and *d* of late Mr and Mrs J. W. Loughlin, Upwell; one *s* decd. *Educ:* Bedford Sch.; Pembroke Coll., Cambridge (MA). Chartered surveyor; FRICS 1959; FCIArb 1977. Commissioned Royal Lincs Regt, 1947. Rowed in Oxford and Cambridge Boat Race, 1951 and 1952 (Pres., 1952); Captain, Great Britain VIII, European Championships, Macon, 1951 (Gold Medallists); also rowed in 1950 European Championships and 1952 Olympics; coached 20 Cambridge crews, 1953–75; Steward and Mem., Cttee of Management, Henley Royal Regatta; Mem. Council, Amateur Rowing Assoc., 1957–77; Mem. of Court and Freeman, Co. of Watermen and Lightermen of the River Thames (Master, 1991–92). Vice-Pres., British Olympic Assoc., 1988–; Chairman: Cambridgeshire Olympic Appeal, 1984 and 1988; Appeal Exec. Cttee, Peterborough Cathedral, 1979–80; Mem., Ely Diocesan Pastoral Cttee, 1969–89; Ely Cathedral Fabric Cttee, 1986–90. Former Pres. Agricl Valuers' Assocs for Cambs, Herts, Beds and Bucks, Lincs, Norfolk, and Wisbech. Governor: King's Sch., Peterborough; St Hugh's Sch., Woodhall Spa. JP Wisbech, 1969; DL Cambridgeshire, 1971; High Sheriff, Cambridgeshire and Isle of Ely, 1970. FRSA. *Recreations:* rowing, shooting. *Address:* 19 North Brink, Wisbech, Cambridgeshire PE13 1JR. *T:* Wisbech (0945) 583320. *Clubs:* East India, Devonshire, Sports and Public Schools, Sette of Odd Volumes; Hawks', University Pitt, Cambridge County (Cambridge); Leander (Henley-on-Thames).

CROWDER, F(rederick) Petre, QC 1964; a Recorder (formerly Recorder of Colchester), since 1967; Barrister-at-Law; *b* 18 July 1919; *s* of late Sir John Ellenborough Crowder; *m* 1948, Hon. Patricia Stourton, *d* of 25th Baron Mowbray, MC (also 26th Baron Segrave and 22nd Baron Stourton); two *s*. *Educ:* Eton; Christ Church, Oxford. Served War of 1939–45; joined Coldstream Guards, 1939, and served in North Africa, Italy, Burma; attained rank of major. Called to the Bar, Inner Temple, 1948 (Master of the Bench, 1971; Reader, 1990; Treasurer, 1991). South Eastern Circuit; North London Sessions. Recorder of Gravesend, 1960–67; Herts QS: Dep. Chm., 1959–63; Chm., 1963–71. Contested (C) North Tottenham, by-elec. 1945; MP (C) Ruislip-Northwood, 1950–74, Hillingdon, Ruislip-Northwood, 1974–79; PPS to Solicitor-Gen., 1952–54; PPS to Attorney General, 1954–62. *Address:* 2 Harcourt Buildings, Temple, EC4. *T:* 071–353 2112; 8 Quarrendon Street, SW6 3SU. *T:* 071–731 6342. *Clubs:* Carlton, Pratt's, Turf.

CROWDER, Ven. Norman Harry; Archdeacon of Portsmouth, since 1985; *b* 20 Oct. 1926; *s* of Laurence Smethurst Crowder and Frances Annie (*née* Hicks); *m* 1971, Pauleen Florence Alison (*née* Styles); one *s*. *Educ:* Nottingham High School; St John's Coll., Cambridge (MA); Westcott House, Cambridge. Curate, St Mary's, Radcliffe-on-Trent, 1952–55; Residential Chaplain to Bishop of Portsmouth, 1955–59; Asst Chaplain, Canford School, 1959–64, Chaplain 1964–72; Vicar, St John's, Oakfield, Ryde, IoW, 1972–75; Dir of Religious Educn, Portsmouth Dio., and Res. Canon of Portsmouth Cathedral, 1975–85. *Recreations:* water colour, travel. *Address:* Victoria Lodge, 36 Osborn Road, Fareham, Hampshire PO16 7DS. *T:* Fareham (0329) 280101. *Club:* MCC.

CROWDY, Maj.-Gen. Joseph Porter, CB 1984; Commandant and Postgraduate Dean, Royal Army Medical College, 1981–84, retired; Hon. Consultant on nutrition to Army, 1985–88; *b* 19 Nov. 1923; *s* of late Lt-Col Charles R. Crowdy and Kate Crowdy (*née* Porter); *m* 1948, Beryl Elisabeth Sapsford; four *d*. *Educ:* Gresham's Sch.; Edinburgh Univ. MB, ChB 1947, DTM&H 1956, DPH 1957, DIH 1957; FFCM 1974; MFOM 1981; FRIPHH 1982. House Surgeon, Norfolk and Norwich Hosp., 1947–48; joined RAMC, 1949; North Africa, 1952–55; Singapore, 1960–62; Head of Applied Physiology, Army Personnel Res. Estabt, 1963–73; Prof. of Army Health, Royal Army Med. Coll., 1973–76; SMO, Land Forces Cyprus, 1976–78; Dir, Army Preventive Medicine, 1978–81. Col Comdt, RAMC, 1985–88. QHP 1981–84. Editor, RAMC Jl, 1978–83. *Publications:* articles in medical jls, on smoking and health, nutrition, physical fitness and obesity. *Recreation:* antique furniture restoration. *Address:* Pepperdon Mine, Lustleigh, Newton Abbot, Devon TQ13 9SN. *T:* Lustleigh (06477) 419.

CROWE, Brian Lee, CMG 1985; HM Diplomatic Service; Ambassador to Austria, since 1989; *b* 5 Jan. 1938; *s* of Eric Crowe and Virginia Crowe; *m* 1969, Virginia Willis; two *s*. *Educ:* Sherborne; Magdalen Coll., Oxford (1st Cl. Hons PPE). Joined FO, 1961; served: Moscow, 1962–64; London, 1965–67; Aden, 1967; Washington, 1968–73; Bonn, 1973–76; Counsellor and Hd of Policy Planning Staff, FCO, 1976–78; Hd of Chancery, UK Perm. Representation to EEC, Brussels, 1979–81; Counsellor and Hd of EEC Dept (External), FCO, 1982–84; Minister, Commercial, Washington, 1985–89. *Recreations:* winter sports, tennis, riding, squash, swimming. *Address:* c/o Foreign and Commonwealth Office, SW1A 2AH.

CROWE, Gerald Patrick, QC 1973; **His Honour Judge Crowe;** a Circuit Judge, since 1980; *b* 3 April 1930; *y s* of Patrick Crowe and Ethel Maud Crowe (*née* Tooth); *m* 1954, Catherine Mary, *d* of Joseph and Rose Murphy, Newry, N Ireland. *Educ:* St Francis Xavier's Coll.; Liverpool Univ. (LLB). Called to Bar, Gray's Inn, 1952; practised Northern Circuit. A Recorder of the Crown Court, 1976–80. Mem., Lord Chancellor's Adv. Cttee on Legal Aid, 1984–. *Recreations:* golf, fishing. *Address:* The Spinney, Long Hey Road, Caldy, Cheshire. *T:* 051–625 8848; Goldsmith Building, Temple, EC4Y 7BL.

CROWE, Rev. Philip Anthony; Principal of Salisbury and Wells Theological College, since 1988; *b* 16 Aug. 1936; *s* of Frederick Francis Crowe and Hilda Crowe; *m* 1963, Freda Maureen Gill; two *s* one *d*. *Educ:* Repton School; Selwyn Coll., Cambridge; Ridley Hall, Cambridge. National service, RA, 1955–57. Tutor in NT Greek and Mission, Oak Hill, 1962–65; Curate at Christchurch, Cockfosters, 1962–65; Editor, Church of England Newspaper, 1967–70; Sec., Bursary Scheme for Overseas Students, 1967–70; Senior Staff Member, St Martin-in-the Bull Ring, Birmingham, 1970–76; Rector of Breadsall, Derby, 1977–88; Derby Diocesan Missioner, 1977–83; Tutor in Ethics, St John's Coll.,

Nottingham, 1986–88. Hon. Canon, Salisbury Cathedral, 1991–. *Publications:* Pastoral Reorganisation, 1978; Christian Baptism, 1980; The Use and Abuse of Alcohol, 1980; (contrib.) Mission in the Modern World, Church and Sacraments. *Recreations:* gardening, music, squash, walking, caravanning. *Address:* The Principal's House, 19a The Close, Salisbury, Wilts SP1 2EE. *T:* Salisbury (0722) 334223.

CROWE, Dame Sylvia, DBE 1973 (CBE 1967); landscape architect in private practice since 1945; *b* 1901; *d* of Eyre Crowe; unmarried. *Educ:* Berkhamsted; Swanley Hort. Coll. Designed gardens, 1927–39. Served FANY and ATS, 1939–45. Since 1945, private practice as landscape architect has included: work as consultant to: Harlow and Basildon New Town Corporations; Wimbleball and Rutland Water reservoirs; Central Electricity Generating Board, for Trawsfynydd and Wylfa Nuclear Power Stations; Forestry Commission; reclamation of land after 1952 floods and design of public gardens at Mablethorpe and Sutton on Sea; gardens for Oxford Univ., various Colls and Commonwealth Inst., London; Sec., Internat. Federation Landscape Architecture, 1948–59; Vice-Pres., 1964; Pres., Inst. Landscape Architects, 1957–59; Corresp. Mem., Amer. Soc. of Landscape Architects, 1960; Hon. Fellow, Aust. Inst. of Landscape Architects, 1978. Chm., Tree Council, 1974–76. Hon. FRIBA, 1969; Hon. FRTPI, 1970. Hon. DLitt: Newcastle, 1975; Heriot-Watt, 1976; Hon. LLD Sussex, 1978. VMH 1990. *Publications:* Tomorrow's Landscape, 1956; Garden Design, 1958, 2nd edn 1981; The Landscape of Power, 1958; Landscape of Roads, 1960; Forestry in the Landscape, 1966; The Landscapes of Forests and Woodlands, 1979; Patterns of Landscape, 1986. *Recreations:* walking and gardening. *Address:* 59 Ladbroke Grove, W11 3AT. *T:* 071–727 7794.

CROWFOOT, Maj.-Gen. Anthony Bernard, CB 1991; CBE 1982 (MBE 1974); General Officer Commanding North West District, 1989–91; *b* 12 Aug. 1936; *s* of Thomas Bernard Crowfoot and Gladys Dorothy Crowfoot; *m* 1960, Bridget Sarah Bunting; three *s* one *d*. *Educ:* King Edward VII Sch., Norfolk; Royal Military Academy, Sandhurst, psc. Commissioned 1956; 1 E Yorks 1PWO: BAOR, UK, Aden, Gibraltar, 1956–60; Instructor, School of Infantry, 1960–62; 1PWO: BAOR, UK, Aden, 1962–66; Army Staff Coll. 1967; Brigade Major, HQ 5 Inf. Bde, 1968–69; Coy Comd 1PWO, Cyprus, 1970–71; DAAG, MoD, 1971–73; CO 1PWO: UK, BAOR, N Ireland, 1973–76; Instructor, Army Staff College, 1976–77; Col GS, MoD, 1977–80; Comd 39 Inf. Bde, N Ireland, 1980–82; Student, US Army War Coll., 1982–83; Dep. Comdr/COS, HQ British Forces Hong Kong, 1983–86; Dir Gen. Army Manning and Recruiting, MoD, 1986–89. Col, PWO Regt of York, 1986–. FBIM 1990. *Recreations:* sailing, philately, golf. *Address:* c/o National Westminster Bank, 45 Park Street, Camberley, Surrey GU15 3PA. *T:* Camberley (0276) 65171. *Club:* Army and Navy.

CROWHURST, Viscount; Mark John Henry Pepys; *b* 11 Oct. 1983; *s* and *heir* of 8th Earl of Cottenham, *qv*.

CROWLEY, Rear-Adm. George Clement, CB 1968; DSC 1942, and Bar 1944; Official Fellow and Domestic Bursar of Corpus Christi College, Oxford University, 1969–75; *b* 9 June 1916; *s* of Charles Edmund Lucas Crowley and Beatrice Cicely Crowley; *m* 1948, Una Margaret Jelf; two *s*. *Educ:* Pangbourne Coll. Cadet, HMS Frobisher, 1933; served in China and New Zealand, 1934–39; served War of 1939–45, destroyers; comdg HMS Walpole, 1943–45; comdg HMS Tenacious, 1945–46 (despatches); RN Staff Course, 1947; Staff appts, 1948–53; Exec. Off., HMS Newfoundland, 1953–55; Drafting Comdr, Chatham, 1955–57; Asst Dir Plans, 1957–59; Capt. (D) 7th Destroyer Sqdn, 1959–61; CO New Entry, Trng Estab. HMS Raleigh, 1961–63; Capt. of Fleet to Flag Off. C-in-C Far East Fleet, 1963–64; Staff of Jt Exercise Unison, 1964–65; Staff of Defence Operational Analysis Estab., W Byfleet, 1965–66; Director-General, Naval Personal Services, 1966–68. Capt. 1957; Rear-Adm. 1966. *Recreations:* fishing, tennis, gardening. *Address:* Windrush, Shroton, Blandford, Dorset.

CROWLEY, Rt. Rev. John, VG; Auxiliary Bishop of Westminster (Bishop in Central London), (RC), since 1986; Titular Bishop of Tala; *b* Newbury, 23 June 1941. Ordained priest, 1965. Chairman, Catholic Fund for Overseas Development, 1988–. *Address:* 73 St Charles Square, W10 6EJ. *T:* 081–960 4029.

CROWLEY, John Desmond, QC 1982; a Recorder of the Crown Court, since 1980; *b* 25 June 1938; *s* of John Joseph Crowley and Anne Marie (*née* Fallon); *m* 1977, Sarah Maria, *er d* of Christopher Gage Jacobs and Joan Zara (*née* Atkinson); two *d*. *Educ:* St Edmund's College, Ware; Christ's College, Cambridge (BA 1961, LLB 1962). National Service, 2/Lieut 6th Royal Tank Regt, 1957–58. Called to the Bar, Inner Temple, 1962, Bencher, 1989. Mem., Criminal Injuries Compensation Bd, 1985–. *Recreations:* tennis, the turf, wine. *Address:* 2 Crown Office Row, Temple, EC4Y 7UJ. *T:* 071–353 9337.

CROWLEY, Niall, FCA; Chairman: Cahill May Roberts Group, since 1989; Allied Irish Banks Ltd Group, 1977–89; *b* 18 Sept. 1926; *s* of Vincent Crowley and Eileen (*née* Gunning); *m* 1953, Una Hegarty; five *s* one *d*. *Educ:* Xavier Sch.; Castleknock Coll. FCA 1955. Entered father's accounting firm, Stokes Kennedy Crowley & Co., as articled clerk, 1944: qualified, 1949; Partner, 1950, subseq. Managing Partner; Consultant to the firm, which also represents KPMG (formerly Peat Marwick Mitchell & Co.) in Ireland, 1977–84. Director: Irish Life Assurance Co. Ltd, 1964–84 (Chm., 1974–83); Alliance & Leicester Building Soc., 1990–; Girobank, 1990–; Cambridge Group, 1990–. President: Inst. of Chartered Accountants in Ireland, 1971–72; Dublin Chamber of Commerce, 1983–84; Irish Bankers Fedn, 1985–87; Inst. of Bankers, 1987–88. Chm., Financial Services Industry Assoc., 1984–88. Mem. Exec. Bd, Anglo-Irish Encounter Gp, 1983–. Member, Company of Goldsmiths of Dublin, 1973–. Hon. LLD NUI, 1982; Hon. DPhil Pontifical Univ., Maynooth, 1988. *Recreations:* bridge, golf. *Address:* (office) 46 Upper Mount Street, Dublin 2. *T:* Dublin 762464; (home) 18 Herbert Park, Ballsbridge, Dublin 4. *T:* Dublin 683637. *Clubs:* Stephens Green; Portmarnock Golf; Milltown Golf; Fitzwilliam Lawn Tennis (Dublin).

CROWLEY-MILLING, Air Marshal Sir Denis, KCB 1973; CBE 1963; DSO 1943; DFC 1941, Bar 1942; Registrar and Secretary, Order of the Bath, 1985–90 (Gentleman Usher of the Scarlet Rod, 1979–85); *b* 22 March 1919; *s* of T. W. and G. M. Crowley-Milling (*née* Chinnery); *m* 1943, Lorna Jean Jeboult (*née* Stuttard); two *d* (one *s* decd). *Educ:* Malvern Coll., Worcs. Rolls Royce apprentice and RAF Volunteer Reserve, 1937–39; Fighters and Fighter Bombers, Nos 615, 242, 610 and 181 Sqdns, 1939–44; Air Ministry Operational Requirements, 1945–47; OC No 6 Sqdn, Middle East, 1947–50; Personal Staff Officer C-in-C Fighter Comd, 1950–52; Wing Comdr Flying, RAF Odiham, 1952–54; Directing Staff, RAF Staff Coll., Bracknell, 1954–57; Flying Coll., RAF Manby, 1957–58; Plans Staff Fighter Comd, 1958–59; Group Capt. Operations Central Fighter Establishment, 1959–62; Station Comdr, RAF Leconfield, 1962–64; AOC RAF Hong Kong, 1964–66; Dir Operational Requirements, MoD (Air), 1966–67; Comdr, RAF Staff and Principal Air Attaché, Washington, 1967–70; AOC No 38 Gp, RAF Odiham, 1970–72; AOC 46 Gp RAF Upavon, 1973; UK Rep., Perm. Mil. Deputies Gp, Cento, 1974–75. Controller, RAF Benevolent Fund, 1975–81, Mem. Council, 1981–; Mem. Council, Malvern Coll., 1972–90. *Recreations:* golf and shooting. *Address:* c/o Barclays Bank, 46 Park Lane, W1A 4EE. *Club:* Royal Air Force.
See also M. C. Crowley-Milling.

CROWLEY-MILLING, Michael Crowley, CMG 1982; CEng, FIEE; consultant on computer control systems; *b* 7 May 1917; *s* of Thomas William Crowley-Milling and Gillian May (*née* Chinnery); *m* 1958, Gee Dickson. *Educ:* Radley Coll.; St John's Coll., Cambridge (MA 1943). CEng, FIEE 1956. R&D on radar systems, Metropolitan-Vickers Electrical Co. Ltd, Manchester, 1938–46; design and develt of electron linear accelerators for physics, medical and irradiation purposes, 1946–63; contrib. to construction of electron synchrotron, Daresbury Nuclear Physics Lab., Warrington, 1963–71; CERN, Geneva: resp. for control system for Super Proton Synchrotron (SPS), 1971–75; SPS Div. Leader, 1977–78; Dir, Accelerator Prog., 1979–80; Consultant, 1982–83; Consultant to: SLAC, Stanford Univ., Calif., 1984–85; Los Alamos Nat. Lab., New Mexico, 1986–; Dir, Crowley Consultants, 1984–. Crompton Premium, IEE, 1959; Glazebrook Medal, Inst. of Physics, 1980. Captain LMBC, 1938. *Publications:* (ed) Accelerator Control Systems, 1986; (ed) Accelerator and Large Experimental Control Systems, 1990; articles and chapters in books on particle accelerators and computer control systems. *Recreations:* vintage cars, sailing. *Address:* Apt 15, Les Ruches II, 1264–St Cergue, Switzerland. *Clubs:* Vintage Sports Car; Llanbedr & Pensarn Yacht.
See also Sir Denis Crowley-Milling.

CROWSON, Richard Borman, CMG 1986; HM Diplomatic Service, retired; High Commissioner in Mauritius, 1985–89, and concurrently Ambassador (non-resident) to Federal Islamic Republic of the Comoros, 1986–89; *b* 23 July 1929; *s* of late Clarence Borman Crowson and Cecilia May Crowson (*née* Ramsden); *m* 1st, 1960, Sylvia Cavalier (marr. diss. 1974); one *s* one *d*; 2nd, 1983, Judith Elaine Turner. *Educ:* Downing Coll., Cambridge (MA). FCIS. HMOCS, Uganda, 1955–62; Foreign Office, 1962–63; First Sec. (Commercial), Tokyo, 1963–68; Dep. High Commissioner, Barbados, 1968–70; FCO, 1970–75; Counsellor (Commercial and Aid), Jakarta, 1975–77; Counsellor for Hong Kong Affairs, Washington, 1977–82; Counsellor and Head of Chancery, Berne, 1983–85. *Recreations:* music, drama, travel. *Address:* 67 Crofton Road, Orpington, Kent BR6 8HU. *T:* Orpington (0689) 891320. *Club:* Commonwealth Trust.

CROWTHER, Prof. Derek, PhD; FRCP; Professor and Director of Medical Oncology, Christie Hospital and Manchester University, since 1974; *s* of Robinson Westgarth Crowther and Gladys Hannah Crowther; *m* 1959, Margaret Frances Dickinson; two *d* (one *s* decd). *Educ:* City of London Sch.; Clare Coll., Cambridge (Foundn Scholar; MB, BChir, MA 1963); Royal Postgraduate Medical Sch., Hammersmith (PhD 1968); Royal Marsden Hosp. MSc Manchester, 1977. FRCP 1976. Sen. Lectr and Dep. Dir of Med. Oncology, St Bartholomew's Hosp., 1972–74. Prizes in medicine, paediatrics, and pathology, and Gold Medal in Obstetrics and Gynaeocology, Univ. of Cambridge, 1963. *Publications:* on the diagnosis and treatment of cancer. *Recreations:* gardening, travel, camping, cosmology, oriental and modern art. *Address:* 52 Barlow Moor Road, Didsbury, Manchester M20 8TR. *T:* 061–435 6685.

CROWTHER, Eric (John Ronald), OBE 1977; Metropolitan Magistrate, 1968–89; a Recorder of the Crown Court, since 1983; *b* 4 Aug. 1924; *s* of Stephen Charles Crowther, company secretary, and Olive Beatrix Crowther (*née* Selby); *m* 1959, Elke Auguste Ottilie Winkelmann; one *s* one *d*. *Educ:* University College Sch., Hampstead. Royal Navy, 1943–47 (Medit. Area of Ops). Awarded Tancred Studentship in Common Law, 1948; Called to Bar, Lincoln's Inn, 1951; winner of Inns of Court Contest in Advocacy, 1951; Lectr and Student Counsellor, British Council, 1951–81; Lecturer: on Elocution and Advocacy for Council of Legal Educn, 1955– (Dir of Studies, Post-Final Gps, 1975–77); on Evidence to RN, 1968–89. Joined Inner Temple *ad eundem*, 1960. Practised at Criminal Bar, 1951–68. Chairman: Inner London Magistrates' Assoc. Trng Sub-Cttee, 1981–89; Prisoners' Wives Service, 1982–85. Mem. Council, British Council, 1985–; Mem., Bd of Academic Studies, St Catherine's, Cumberland Lodge, 1977–82; Trustee, Professional and Academic Regional Visits Organisation, 1977–89. Mem. Cttee, RADA, 1979–84. Hon. Officer, Internat. Students' Hse, 1981–. Editor, Commonwealth Judicial Jl, 1973–77. *Publications:* Advocacy for the Advocate, 1984; Last in the List, 1988; Look What's on the Bench!, 1991. *Recreations:* travel, transport, the theatre, debating, student welfare, Scottish dancing. *Address:* 21 Old Buildings, Lincoln's Inn, WC2.

CROWTHER, (Joseph) Stanley; MP (Lab) Rotherham, since June 1976; *b* 30 May 1925; *s* of Cyril Joseph Crowther and Florence Mildred (*née* Beckett); *m* 1948, Margaret Royston; two *s*. *Educ:* Rotherham Grammar Sch.; Rotherham Coll. of Technology. Royal Signals, 1943–47. Journalist: Rotherham Advertiser, 1941–43 and 1947–50; Yorkshire Evening Post, 1950–51; freelance, 1951–. Mem., Rotherham Borough Council, 1958–59, 1961–76; Mayor of Rotherham, 1971–72, 1975–76; Chm., Yorkshire and Humberside Develt Assoc., 1972–76; Vice-Pres., Town and Country Planning Assoc. *Recreations:* walking, singing, listening to jazz. *Address:* 15 Clifton Crescent South, Rotherham S65 2AR. *T:* Rotherham (0709) 364559. *Clubs:* Central Labour, Eastwood View Working Men's (Rotherham).

CROWTHER, Thomas Rowland; QC 1981; **His Honour Judge Crowther;** a Circuit Judge since 1985; *b* 11 Sept. 1937; *s* of Kenneth Vincent Crowther, MB, BCh, and Winifred Anita Crowther, MPS; *m* 1969, Gillian Jane (*née* Prince); one *s* one *d*. *Educ:* Newport High Sch.: Keble Coll., Oxford (MA). President, Oxford Univ. Liberal Club, 1957; Editor, Oxford Guardian, 1957. Called to the Bar, Inner Temple, 1961; Junior and Wine Steward, Wales and Chester Circuit, 1974. A Recorder, 1980–85. Contested (L) General Elections: Oswestry, 1964 and 1966; Hereford, 1970. Founder Mem., Gwent Area Broadcasting, 1981. *Recreation:* garden. *Address:* Lansor, Llandegfedd, Caerleon, Gwent NP6 1LS. *T:* Tredunnock (0633) 49224. *Clubs:* Cardiff and County; Newport Golf.

CROWTHER, William Ronald Hilton; QC 1980; a Recorder, since 1984; *b* 7 May 1941; *s* of Ronald Crowther and Ann Bourne Crowther; *m* 1964, Valerie Meredith (*née* Richards); one *s*. *Educ:* Oundle Sch.; Univ. of Oxford (BA Jurisprudence). Called to the Bar, Inner Temple, 1963, Bencher, 1985. *Recreations:* bird-watching and all aspects of natural history, scuba diving. *Address:* 83 South End Road, NW3 2RJ. *T:* 071–794 4619.

CROXON, Raymond Patrick Austin, QC 1983; *b* 31 July 1928; *s* of late Randolph Croxon and of Rose Harvey; *m* 1952, Monica Howard; two *s* two *d*. *Educ:* Strand College; King's College London. LLB. Served in RAMC, 1946–49. Called to the Bar, Gray's Inn, 1960. *Recreations:* gardening, fishing, golf, travel. *Address:* 1 Paper Buildings, Temple, EC4. *Club:* Orpington Sports.

CROXTON-SMITH, Claude; Chartered Accountant in public practice, Bristol, 1946–83, retired; President, Institute of Chartered Accountants in England and Wales, 1970–71; *b* 24 Aug. 1901; *m* 1928, Joan Norah Bloss Watling (*d* 1989); two *d*. *Educ:* Dulwich Coll.; Gonville and Caius Coll., Cambridge. The Sales Staff, Anglo American Oil Co. Ltd, 1924–31; Articled Clerk, Inst. of Chartered Accountants in England and Wales, 1932–36; Chartered Accountant, 1936–39. Served War of 1939–45, RAOC (Major). *Recreations:* walking, reading. *Address:* New Cote Rest Home, Cote House Lane, Westbury-on-Trym, Bristol BS9 3UW. *T:* Bristol (0272) 628341.

CROYDON, Bishop Suffragan of, since 1985; **Rt. Rev. Wilfred Denniston Wood;** *b* Barbados, WI, 15 June 1936; *s* of Wilfred Coward and Elsie Elmira Wood; *m* 1966, Ina Eileen, *d* of L. E. Smith, CBE, Barbadian MP; three *s* two *d*. *Educ:* Combermere Sch. and Codrington Coll., Barbados. Lambeth Dip. in Theol., 1962. Ordained deacon, St Michael's Cath., Barbados, 1961; ordained priest, St Paul's Cath., London, 1962. Curate of St Stephen with St Thomas, Shepherd's Bush, 1962–66, Hon. Curate, 1966–74; Bishop of London's Officer in Race Relations, 1966–74; Vicar of St Laurence, Catford, 1974–82; RD of East Lewisham, 1977–82; Archdeacon of Southwark, 1982–85; Hon. Canon of Southwark Cathedral, 1977–85. Mem., General Synod, 1987–. Chairman: Martin Luther King Meml Trust; Cttee on Black Anglican Concerns, 1986–91. Member: Royal Commn on Criminal Procedure, 1978–80; Archbishop of Canterbury's Commn on Urban Priority Areas, 1983–85; Housing Corp. Bd, 1986–. JP Inner London, 1971–85. Hon. DD Gen. Theol Seminary, NY, 1986. *Publications:* (contrib.) The Committed Church, 1966; (with John Downing) Vicious Circle, 1968. *Recreations:* reading, cricket; armchair follower of most sports. *Address:* 53 Stanhope Road, Croydon CR0 5NS. *T:* 081–686 1822.

CROYDON, Archdeacon of; *see* Hazell, Ven F. R.

CROYDON, Rear-Adm. John Edward Kenneth, JP; CEng, FIEE; *b* 25 Feb. 1929; *s* of late Kenneth P. Croydon and Elizabeth V. Croydon; *m* 1953, Brenda Joyce Buss, MA; one *s* two *d*. *Educ:* King Edward's Sch., Birmingham; Selwyn Coll., Cambridge (MA). BA London; CEng, FIEE 1975; jssc 1969. RN Special Entry Cadet (L), 1947; HMS Verulam and HMS Undine, 1954–55; Royal Naval Coll., Dartmouth, 1959–61; HMS Devonshire, 1961–64; HMS London, 1970–72; MoD, 1972–74; Captain Weapon Trials, 1974–77; Dir, Underwater Weapon Projects (Naval), 1978–80; Dir Gen. Weapons (Naval), 1981–83; Dep. Controller, Warships Equipment, MoD (Navy), 1983–84, retd. Rear Cdre (Dinghies), Royal Naval Sailing Assoc., 1980. Gov., Milton Abbey Sch., 1985–. County Comr for Scouts, Dorset, 1986–. JP Weymouth, 1985. *Recreations:* sailing, music, walking. *Clubs:* Royal Naval Sailing Association; Weymouth Sailing.

CROZIER, Brian Rossiter; writer and consultant on international affairs; Columnist, National Review, New York, since 1978; Co-founder Institute for the Study of Conflict, 1970, and Director, 1970–79; *b* 4 Aug. 1918; *s* of R. H. Crozier and Elsa (*née* McGillivray); *m* 1940, Mary Lillian Samuel; one *s* three *d*. *Educ:* Lycée, Montpellier; Peterborough Coll., Harrow; Trinity Coll. of Music, London. Music and art critic, London, 1936–39; reporter-sub-editor, Stoke-on-Trent, Stockport, London, 1940–41; aeronautical inspection, 1941–43; sub-editor: Reuters, 1943–44; News Chronicle, 1944–48; and writer, Sydney Morning Herald, 1948–51; corresp., Reuters-AAP, 1951–52; features editor, Straits Times, 1952–53; leader writer, corresp. and editor, Foreign Report, Economist, 1954–64; commentator, BBC English, French and Spanish overseas services, 1954–66; Chm., Forum World Features, 1965–74; Columnist: Now!, 1979–81; The Times, 1982–83; Freedom Today (formerly The Free Nation), 1982–89. *Publications:* The Rebels, 1960; The Morning After, 1963; Neo-Colonialism, 1964; South-East Asia in Turmoil, 1965 (3rd edn 1968); The Struggle for the Third World, 1966; Franco, 1967; The Masters of Power, 1969; The Future of Communist Power (in USA: Since Stalin), 1970; De Gaulle, vol. 1 1973, vol. 2 1974; A Theory of Conflict, 1974; The Man Who Lost China (Chiang Kai-shek), 1976; Strategy of Survival, 1978; The Minimum State, 1979; Franco: crepúsculo de un hombre (Spanish orig.), 1980; The Price of Peace, 1980, new edn 1983; (jtly) Socialism Explained, 1984; (jtly) This War Called Peace, 1984; (as John Rossiter) The Andropov Deception (novel), 1984 (pubd under own name, NY, 1986); Socialism: dream and reality, 1987; (ed) The Grenada Documents, 1987; The Gorbachev Phenomenon, 1990; Communism: Why Prolong its Death-throes?, 1990; contrib. to jls in many countries. *Recreations:* piano, taping stereo. *Address:* Kulm House, Dollis Avenue, Finchley, N3 1DA. *T:* 081–346 8124. *Club:* Royal Automobile.

CROZIER, Eric John, OBE 1991; writer and lecturer; *b* 14 Nov. 1914; *m* 1949, Nancy Evans (OBE 1991). Play producer for BBC Television Service, 1936–39. Produced plays and operas for Sadler's Wells Opera, Stratford-on-Avon Meml Theatre, Glyndebourne Opera and other theatres, 1944–46. Closely associated with Benjamin Britten as producer or author of his operas, 1945–51, and was co-founder with him of The English Opera Group, 1947, and The Aldeburgh Festival of Music and the Arts, 1948. *Publications:* Christmas in the Market Place (adapted from French of Henri Ghéon), 1944; The Life and Legends of Saint Nicolas, 1949; Noah Gives Thanks, a play, 1950; (with Benjamin Britten): Albert Herring, a comic opera in three acts, 1947; Saint Nicolas, a cantata, 1948; Let's Make an Opera, an entertainment for children, 1949; (with E. M. Forster and Benjamin Britten) Billy Budd, an opera in four acts, 1951; many opera translations. *Recreations:* listening to music, walking, writing verse. *Address:* 4 The Timberyard, Great Glemham, Saxmundham, Suffolk IP17 2DL. *T:* Rendham (072878) 618.

CRUDDAS, Rear-Adm. Thomas Rennison, CB 1974; CEng, FIMechE; engineering consultant; *b* 6 Feb. 1921; *s* of late Thomas Hepple Wheatley Cruddas, MBE, and Lily (*née* Rennison); *m* 1943, Angela Elizabeth Astbury; one *s* one *d*. *Educ:* Queen Elizabeth Grammar Sch., Darlington; RN Engineering College, Keyham. Joined RN 1938; RNEC, 1939–42; served War, 1939–45: in Mediterranean and E Indies, in HM Ships Unicorn and Valiant; HMS Cardigan Bay, 1948–50; specialised aeronautical engrg, 1950; RNAY Donibristle, 1951–53; Comdr, 1953; HMS Ark Royal, 1953–55; RNAY Fleetlands, 1956–58; Admiralty, 1958–61; Staff of Flag Officer Aircraft Carriers, 1961–63; Captain, 1963; Asst Dir Ship Prodn, 1964–66; service with USN, Washington, DC, as Programme Manager UK Phantom Aircraft, 1967–69; Comd Engr Officer, Staff FONAC, 1970–72; Rear-Adm. Engineering, Naval Air Comd, 1972; Dep. Controller Aircraft B, MoD (PE), 1973–76, retired. Dir, Pressure Vessels Quality Assurance Bd, 1977–86. *Recreation:* country living. *Address:* Beeches Close, Bishop's Waltham, Hants SO3 1FZ. *T:* Bishop's Waltham (0489) 892335.

CRUFT, John Herbert; Hon. Treasurer, Royal Society of Musicians, 1976–87; *b* 4 Jan. 1914; *er s* of late Eugene and Winifred Cruft; *m* 1938, Mary Margaret Miriam, *e d* of late Rev. Pat and Miriam McCormick; two *s*. *Educ:* Westminster Abbey Choir Sch.; Westminster Sch.; Royal College of Music (K. F. Boult Conducting Scholar). Oboist in BBC Television, London Philharmonic and Suisse Romande Orchestras, 1936–40. Served with Royal Corps of Signals, 1940–46. London Symphony Orchestra: Oboist, 1946–49; Sec., 1949–59. British Council: Dir of Music Dept, 1959–61; Dir of Drama and Music Dept, 1961–65; Music Dir, Arts Council of GB, 1965–79; a Dir, National Jazz Centre, 1982–87. Member: Council, RCM, 1983–90, Life Gov., 1990; Council for Dance Educn and Trng, 1990–. Trustee: Loan Fund for Musical Instruments, 1980–; Electro-Acoustic Music Trust, 1980–88; Governor: London Festival Ballet Trust Ltd, 1980–84; Contemporary Dance Trust Ltd, 1982–88. FRCM, Hon. RAM. *Publication:* The Royal College of Music: a Centenary Record 1883–1983 (with late H. C. Colles), 1982. *Address:* 11 Broadhinton Road, Clapham, SW4 0LU. *T:* 071–720 2330.

CRUICKSHANK, Alistair Ronald; Principal Finance Officer, Ministry of Agriculture, Fisheries and Food, since 1989; *b* 2 Oct. 1944; *s* of late Francis John Cruickshank and of Kate Cameron Cruickshank (*née* Brittain); *m* 1967, Sandra Mary Noble; three *d*. *Educ:* Aberdeen Grammar School; Aberdeen University (MA). Joined MAFF as Assistant Principal, 1966; Principal, 1970; Head, successively, of Eggs and Poultry Br. and Milk Br.; Asst Secretary, 1978; Head, successively, of Marketing Policy and Potatoes, Meat Hygiene, and Milk Divs; Under Sec. (Animal Health), 1986. *Recreations:* growing vegetables, looking at old buildings. *Address:* c/o Ministry of Agriculture, Fisheries and Food, Whitehall Place, SW1A 2HH.

CRUICKSHANK, Donald Gordon; Chief Executive, National Health Service in Scotland, since 1989; *b* 17 Sept. 1942; *s* of Donald Campbell Cruickshank and Margaret Buchan Cruickshank (*née* Morrison); *m* 1964, Elizabeth Buchan Taylor; one *s* one *d*. *Educ:* Univ. of Aberdeen (MA); Inst. of Chartered Accountants of Scotland (CA); Manchester Business School (MBA). McKinsey & Co., 1972–77; Times Newspapers, 1977–80; Pearson, 1980–84; Man. Dir, Virgin Group, 1984–89. Chm., Wandsworth HA, 1986–89. *Recreations:* sport, golf, opera. *Address:* Scottish Office Home and Health Department, St Andrew's House, Edinburgh EH1 3DE. *T:* 031–244 2410.

CRUICKSHANK, Prof. Durward William John, PhD, ScD; FRS 1979; CChem, FRSC; Professor of Chemistry (Theoretical Chemistry), 1967–83, now Emeritus, and Hon. Professorial Research Fellow, since 1983, University of Manchester Institute of Science and Technology; *b* 7 March 1924; *s* of William Durward Cruickshank, MB, ChB, and Margaret Ombler Meek, MA, MRCS, LRCP; *m* 1953, Marjorie Alice Travis (*d* 1983), MA, PhD; one *s* one *d*. *Educ:* St Lawrence Coll., Ramsgate; Loughborough Coll. (DLC 1944; BScEng 1st Cl. Hons London, 1944); Cambridge Univ. (Wrangler, Math. Tripos, 1949; Dist. Pt III Math. Tripos, 1950; BA 1949, MA 1954, ScD 1961). PhD Leeds, 1952; CChem, FRIC 1971. Engrg Asst, WO and Admiralty (Naval Opl Res.), 1944–46; Leeds University: Res. Asst, Chemistry Dept, 1946–47; Lectr, 1950–57; Reader in Math. Chemistry, 1957–62; Fellow, St John's Coll., Cambridge, 1953–56; Joseph Black Prof. of Chem. (Theor. Chem.), Glasgow Univ., 1962–67; Dep. Principal, UMIST, 1971–72. Hon. Vis. Prof. of Physics, York Univ., 1985–88. Treasurer, 1966–72, and Gen. Sec., 1970–72, Internat. Union of Crystallography. 1977 Chemical Soc. Award for Struct. Chem., 1978; (first) Dorothy Hodgkin Prize, British Crystallographic Assoc., 1991. *Publications:* scientific papers on crystallography, molecular structure determination and theoretical chemistry in Acta Cryst., Proc. Royal Soc., and Jl Chem. Soc. *Recreations:* golf, genealogy. *Address:* 105 Moss Lane, Alderley Edge, Cheshire SK9 7HW. *T:* Alderley Edge (0625) 582656; Chemistry Department, University of Manchester Institute of Science and Technology, Manchester M60 1QD. *T:* 061–236 3311.

CRUICKSHANK, Prof. Eric Kennedy, OBE 1961; MD; FRCP, FRCPGlas; Dean of Postgraduate Medicine, University of Glasgow, 1972–80; retired; *b* 29 Dec. 1914; *s* of John Cruickshank, CBE, and Jessie (*née* Allan); *m* 1st, 1951, Ann Burch; two *s* two *d*; 2nd, 1969, Josephine Williams. *Educ:* Aberdeen Grammar Sch.; Univ. of Aberdeen (MB, ChB Hons, 1937; MD Hons and gold medal, 1948). Fellow, Harvard and Massachusetts Gen. Hosp., USA, 1938–39; Lectr, then Sen. Lectr, Dept of Medicine, Univ. of Aberdeen, 1939–50; Hon. Consultant in Medicine, NHS, 1948–50; First Dean, Medical Faculty, and Prof. of Medicine, Univ. of West Indies, Kingston, Jamaica, 1950–72. Served War of 1939–45: Captain RAMC, Medical Specialist, Changi Prisoner of War Camp, Singapore (despatches twice). WHO Consultant in Medical Educn, 1959–, Nutrition, 1955–; Member: GMC, 1972–80; Inter-Univ. Council, 1972–84; Greater Glasgow Health Bd, 1972–80. Hon. FACP 1969. *Publications:* on nutrition, neurology, medical educn. *Recreations:* tennis, golf, gardening, ornithology. *Address:* Parsonage House, Oare, Wilts SN8 4JA.

CRUICKSHANK, Herbert James, CBE 1969; CEng, FIMechE; FCIOB; retired; *b* 12 July 1912; *s* of late James William Cruickshank and of Dorothy Adeline Cruickshank; *m* 1st, 1939, Jean Alexandra Payne (*d* 1978); no *c*; 2nd, 1985, Susan Elizabeth Bullen. *Educ:* Regent Street Polytechnic (Schol.). Bovis Ltd: Staff Trainee, 1931; Plant and Labour Controller, 1937; Gilbert-Ash Ltd: (formed within Bovis Gp), 1945; Director, 1949; Civil Engineering Works in Nyasaland, 1949–55; Managing Dir, UK, 1960–63; Chm. and Man. Dir, 1964; Dir, Bovis Holdings, 1964–72; Group Man. Dir, 1966, Dep. Chm. 1970–72. Member: Metrication Bd, 1969–73; SE Thames RHA, 1972–78; BSI Quality Assurance Council, 1976–81. FRSA. *Recreations:* travel, photography, sketching. *Address:* 45 Bidborough Ridge, Tunbridge Wells, Kent TN4 0UU. *T:* Tunbridge Wells (0892) 27270. *Clubs:* Oriental, MCC, Lord's Taverners.

CRUICKSHANK, Prof. John; Professor of French, University of Sussex, 1962–89, retired; *b* Belfast, N Ireland, 18 July 1924; *s* of Arthur Cruickshank, parliamentary reporter, and Eva Cruickshank (*née* Shummacher); *m* 1st, 1949, Kathleen Mary Gutteridge; one *s*; 2nd, 1972, Marguerite Doreen Penny. *Educ:* Royal Belfast Academical Institution; Trinity Coll., Dublin. Awarded Mod. Lang. Sizarship, TCD, 1943; Cryptographer in Mil. Intell., 1943–45; 1st class Moderatorship in Mod. Langs (French and German) and 2nd class Moderatorship (Mental and Moral Science), TCD, 1948; Lecteur d'Anglais, Ecole Normale Supérieure, Paris, 1948–49; Asst Lectr in French and German, Univ. of Southampton, 1951; Sen. Lectr in French, Univ. of Southampton, 1961. Mem., UGC, 1970–77. *Publications:* Albert Camus and the Literature of Revolt, 1959; Critical Readings in the Modern French Novel, 1961; The Novelist as Philosopher, 1962; Montherlant, 1964; (ed) French Literature and Its Background: vols 1–6, 1968–70; Aspects of the Modern European Mind, 1969; Benjamin Constant, 1974; Variations on Catastrophe, 1982; Pascal: Pensées, 1983; articles in: French Studies; Modern Language Review; Times Literary Supplement; Times Higher Education Supplement, etc. *Recreations:* bird-watching, watching cricket. *Address:* Woodpeckers, East Hoathly, Sussex BN8 6QL. *T:* Halland (082584) 364.

CRUICKSHANK, Flight-Lieut John Alexander, VC 1944; ED 1947; late RAF; with Grindlay's Bank Ltd, London, 1952–76; retired; Administrator, Northern Division, North West Securities Ltd, 1977–85; *b* 20 May 1920; *s* of James C. Cruickshank, Aberdeen, and Alice Bow, Macduff, Banffshire; *m* 1955, Marion R. Beverley (*d* 1985), Toronto, Canada. *Educ:* Aberdeen Grammar Sch.; Daniel Stewart's Coll., Edinburgh. Entered Commercial Bank of Scotland, 1938; returned to banking, 1946. Mem. of Territorial Army and called for service, Aug. 1939, in RA; transferred to RAF 1941 and commissioned in 1942; all RAF service was with Coastal Command. ADC to Lord High Commissioner to the Gen. Assembly of the Church of Scotland, 1946–48. Hon. Mem., Merchants of Edinburgh Golf Club, Edinburgh. *Address:* 34 Frogston Road West, Edinburgh EH10 7AJ. *T:* 031–445 1215.

CRUMP, Maurice, CBE 1959; *b* 13 Jan. 1908; *s* of William Hamilton Crump and Jean Morris Alan Crump (*née* Esplen); *m* 1946, Mary Arden, *d* of Austin Stead, Montreal, PQ, Canada. *Educ:* Harrow; Oxford. Called to Bar, Inner Temple, 1931, practised Western Circuit. RAF Reserve, 1929–35; recommissioned RAF Volunteer Reserve, 1940; served War of 1939–45, as pilot, 1940–45; Capt. in Command on North Atlantic Return Ferry, 1944–45. In Dept of Dir of Public Prosecutions, 1945; Asst Dir, 1951–58, Deputy Dir, 1958–66. *Recreations:* flying, travelling. *Address:* No 2, 46 Elm Park Road, SW3 6AX. *T:* 071–351 2126. *Club:* Royal Air Force.

CRUMP, Rt. Rev. William Henry Howes; *b* London, Ontario, Canada, 13 March 1903; *m* 1st, 1932, Betty Margaret Dean Thomas; one *s* one *d*; 2nd, 1964. *Educ:* London,

Ontario; University of Western Ontario; Huron College; Trinity College, Toronto. Ordained Deacon, 1926; Curate, Wawanesa, Manitoba, 1926; Priest, 1927. Rector: Glenboro, Manitoba, 1927; Holland, Manitoba, 1931; Boissevain, Manitoba, 1933; St Aidan's, Winnipeg, 1933–44; Christ Church, Calgary, 1944–60; Canon of St Paul, Diocese of Calgary, 1949; Bishop of Saskatchewan, 1960–71. *Address:* Apt 815 Lions Place, 610 Portage Avenue, Winnipeg, Manitoba R3C 0G5, Canada.

CRUMP, William Maurice Esplen; *see* Crump, Maurice.

CRUMPTON, Michael Joseph, PhD; FRS 1979; Deputy Director of Research, Imperial Cancer Research Fund Laboratories, London, since 1979; *b* 7 June 1929; *s* of Charles E. and Edith Crumpton; *m* 1960, Janet Elizabeth Dean; one *s* two *d. Educ:* Poole Grammar Sch., Poole; University Coll., Southampton; Lister Inst. of Preventive Medicine, London. BSc, PhD, London. National Service, RAMC, 1953–55. Member, scientific staff, Microbiological Research Estabt, Porton, Wilts, 1955–60; Visiting Scientist Fellowship, Nat. Insts of Health, Bethesda, Maryland, USA, 1959–60; Research Fellow, Dept of Immunology, St Mary's Hosp. Med. Sch., London, 1960–66; Mem., scientific staff, Nat. Inst. for Med. Research, Mill Hill, 1966–79, Head of Biochemistry Div., 1976–79. Visiting Fellow, John Curtin Sch. for Med. Research, ANU, Canberra, 1973–74. Member: EMBO, 1982–; WHO Steering Cttee for Encapsulated Bacteria, 1984– (Chm., 1988–); Cell Board, MRC, 1979–83; Scientific Adv. Cttee, Lister Inst., 1986–; Sloan Cttee, General Motors Res. Foundn, 1986–88 (Chm., 1988); MRC AIDS Directed Prog. Steering Cttee, 1987–; Scientific Cttee, Swiss Inst. for Experimental Cancer Res., 1989–; DTI/SERC Biotech. Jt Adv. Bd, 1989–. Member Council: Royal Instn, 1986–90 (Mem., Davy Faraday Lab. Cttee, 1985–90, Chm. of Cttee, 1988–90); MRC, 1986–90; Mem. Sci. Council, Celltech Ltd, 1980–89; Chm., Sci. Adv. Bd, Biomed. Res. Centre, Univ. of British Columbia, Vancouver, 1987–. Dir, Imperial Cancer Res. Technol., 1989–; Non-Exec. Dir, Amersham Internat., 1990–. Mem. Governing Body, BPMF, 1987–. Mem. Editorial Board: Biochemical Jl, 1966–73 (Dep. Chm., 1969–72); Eur. Jl of Immunology, 1972–86; Immunochemistry, 1975–79; Immunogenetics, 1979–85; Biochemistry Internat., 1980–86; Molecular Biol. and Medicine, 1983–86; Human Immunology, 1985–; Regional Editor, Molecular Immunology, 1982–86. Biochem. Soc. Vis. Lectr, Australia, 1983. Sen. Treas., Royal Soc. Club, 1988–89. *Publications:* contribs to Biochemical Jl and various other learned scientific jls. *Recreations:* gardening, reading. *Address:* 33 Homefield Road, Radlett, Herts WD7 8PX. *T:* Radlett (092385) 4675.

CRUTCHLEY, Brooke, CBE 1954; Printer of the University of Cambridge, 1946–74; Fellow of Trinity Hall, 1951–73, Emeritus Fellow, 1977 (Vice-Master, 1966–70); Honorary Fellow of St Edmund's College (formerly St Edmund's House), Cambridge, since 1980; *b* 31 July 1907; *yr s* of late Ernest Tristram Crutchley, CB, CMG, CBE, and Anna, *d* of James Dunne; *m* 1936, Diana, *d* of late Lt-Col Arthur Egerton Cotton, DSO, and Beryl Marie (who *m* 2nd, John Lee Booker); two *s* one *d. Educ:* Shrewsbury; Trinity Hall, Cambridge. Editorial Staff of Yorkshire Post, 1929–30; Asst Univ. Printer at Cambridge, 1930–45; Secretary's Dept of the Admiralty, 1941–45. Pres., Inst. of Printing, 1972–74. Hon. Col, Commonwealth of Kentucky, 1974. Bicentenary Medal, RSA, 1977. *Publication:* To be a printer, (autobiog.), 1980. *Address:* 2 Courtyards, Little Shelford, Cambridge CB2 5ER. *T:* Cambridge (0223) 842389. *Club:* Double Crown.

CRUTHERS, Sir James (Winter), Kt 1980; company director; Vice-Chairman and Executive Vice-President, News America Publishing Inc., since 1984 (Director, since 1983); Vice-Chairman, News America Holdings Inc., since 1984 (Director, since 1984); *b* 20 Dec. 1924; *s* of James William and Kate Cruthers; *m* 1950, Alwyn Sheila Della; one *s* one *d. Educ:* Claremont Central State Sch.; Perth Technical College. Started as junior in Perth Daily News, 1939; war service, AIF and RAAF (Pilot), 1942; Journalist, Perth Daily News, 1946; Editor, Weekly Publications, West Australian Newspapers Ltd, 1953; TVW Enterprises Ltd: General Manager, 1958; Managing Director, 1969; Dep. Chm., 1974; Chm., 1976–81; Chm., Australian Film Commn, 1982–83. Director: News Corp. Ltd, 1981–; Satellite Television plc, 1984– (Chm., 1985–88). Western Australian Citizen Of The Year, Industry and Commerce, 1980. *Recreations:* golf, jogging. *Address:* c/o News America Publishing Inc., 1211 Avenue of the Americas, New York, NY 10036, USA; c/o McLaren and Stewart, GPO Box L892, Perth, WA 6001, Australia. *Clubs:* Weld (Perth); Lake Karrinyup Country (Perth); Doubles (New York).

CRUTTWELL, Mrs Geraldine; *see* McEwan, Geraldine.

CRUTTWELL, Hugh (Percival); Principal of Royal Academy of Dramatic Art, 1966–84, retired; *b* 31 Oct. 1918; *s* of Clement Chadwick Cruttwell and Grace Fanny (*née* Robin); *m* 1953, Geraldine McEwan, *qv*; one *s* one *d. Educ:* King's Sch., Bruton; Hertford Coll., Oxford. *Address:* 8 Ranelagh Avenue, Barnes, SW13 0BY.

CRWYS-WILLIAMS, Air Vice-Marshal David Owen, CB 1990; Director-General of RAF Personal Services, Ministry of Defence, since 1989; *b* 24 Dec. 1940; *s* of Gareth Crwys-Williams and Frances Ellen Crwys-Williams (*née* Strange); *m* 1st, 1964, Jennifer Jean (*née* Pearce) (marr. diss. 1971); one *s* one *d*; 2nd, 1973, Irene Thompson (Suzie) (*née* Whan); one *s* two *d. Educ:* Oakham Sch.; RAF Coll., Cranwell. Commnd as pilot, RAF, 1961; served No 30 Sqn, Kenya, 1962–64, No 47 Sqn, Abingdon, 1964–66; ADC to C-in-C RAF Trng Comd, 1966–68; OC 46 Sqn, 1969; RAF Masirah, 1972; Army Staff Coll., 1973; Personal Staff Officer to C-in-C NEAF, 1974–75; OC No 230 Sqn, 1976–77; Air Sec. Dept, MoD, 1977–78; Dep. Dir Air Plans, MoD, 1979–82; Gp Captain 1979; OC RAF Shawbury, 1983–84; RCDS 1985; Dir of Air Support (Air Cdre) and Dir of Air Staff Duties, MoD, 1986–88; Comdr, British Forces Falkland Is, 1988–89. *Recreations:* furniture restoration, walking, building, fishing. *Address:* c/o Barclays Bank, Marcham Road, Abingdon, Oxon OX14 1UB. *Club:* Royal Air Force.

CRYER, (George) Robert; MP (Lab) Bradford South, since 1987; *b* 3 Dec. 1934; *m* 1963, Ann (*née* Place); one *s* one *d. Educ:* Salt High Sch., Shipley; Hull Univ. BSc Econ Hons, Certif. Educn. Secondary Sch. Teacher, Hull, 1959, Bradford, 1961 and Keighley, 1962; Asst Personnel Officer, 1960; Dewsbury Techn. Coll., 1963; Blackburn Coll. of Technology, 1964–65; Keighley Techn. Coll., 1965–74. MP (Lab) Keighley, Feb. 1974–1983; Parly Under-Sec. of State, DoI, 1976–78. Chm., Jt and Select Cttees on Statutory Instruments, 1979–83, and 1987–; Vice-Chairman: PLP Defence Group, 1980–83; PLP Industry Gp, 1982–83; PLP Employment Gp, 1987–. Contested (Lab): Darwen Div. of Lancs, 1964; Keighley, 1983. MEP (Lab) Sheffield, 1984–89. Labour Councillor, Keighley Borough Council, 1971–74. *Publications:* Steam in the Worth Valley, Vol. 1 1969, Vol. 2 1972; Queensbury Lines, 1984. *Recreations:* working on Worth Valley Railway, cinematography, film appreciation. *Address:* 6 Ashfield Avenue, Shipley, Yorks BD18 3AL. *T:* Bradford (0734) 584701. *Club:* North Bierley East Labour.

CRYSTAL, Prof. David; author, lecturer, and broadcaster on language and linguistics; Hon. Professorial Fellow, University College of North Wales, since 1985; *b* 6 July 1941; *s* of Samuel Cyril Crystal and Mary Agnes Morris; *m* 1st, 1964, Molly Irene Stack (*d* 1976); one *s* two *d* (and one *s* decd); 2nd, 1976, Hilary Frances Norman; one *s. Educ:* St Mary's Coll., Liverpool; University Coll. London (BA 1962); London Univ. (PhD 1966). Res. Asst, UCL, 1962–63; Asst Lectr, UCNW, 1963–65; University of Reading: Lectr, 1965–69; Reader, 1969–75; Prof., 1975–85. Vis. Prof., Bowling Green State Univ., 1969. Sec., Linguistics Assoc. of GB, 1965–70. Mem., Academic Bd, Coll. of Speech Therapists, 1972–79. Editor: Language Res. in Progress, 1966–70; Jl of Child Language, 1973–85; The Language Library, 1978–; Applied Language Studies, 1980–84; Child Language Teaching and Therapy, 1985–; Linguistics Abstracts, 1985–; Blackwells Applied Language Studies, 1986–; Consultant Editor, English Today, 1985–; Adv. Editor, Penguin Linguistics, 1968–75; Associate Editor, Jl of Linguistics, 1970–73; Co-Editor, Studies in Language Disability, 1974–. Regular BBC broadcasts on English language and linguistics. FCST 1983; FRSA 1983. *Publications:* Systems of prosodic and paralinguistic features in English (with R. Quirk), 1964; Linguistics, language and religion, 1965; (ed jtly) Proceedings, Modern approaches to language teaching at university level, 1967; What is linguistics?, 1968, 5th edn 1985; Prosodic systems and intonation in English, 1969; (with D. Davy) Investigating English style, 1969; (ed with W. Bolton) The English language, vol. 2, 1969; Linguistics, 1971, 2nd edn 1985; Basic linguistics, 1973; Language acquisition, 1973; The English tone of voice, 1975; (with D. Davy) Advanced conversational English, 1975; (with J. Bevington) Skylarks, 1975; (jtly) The grammatical analysis of language disability, 1976, 2nd edn 1989; Child language, learning and linguistics, 1976, 2nd edn 1987; Working with LARSP, 1979; Introduction to language pathology, 1980, 2nd edn 1988; A first dictionary of linguistics and phonetics, 1980, 3rd edn 1991; (ed) Eric Partridge: in his own words, 1980; Clinical linguistics, 1981; Directions in applied linguistics, 1981; Profiling linguistic disability, 1982; (ed) Linguistic controversies, 1982; Who cares about English usage?, 1984; Language handicap in children, 1984; Linguistic encounters with language handicap, 1984; Listen to your child, 1986; (ed with W. Bolton) The English language, 1987; Cambridge Encyclopaedia of Language, 1987; Rediscover grammar, 1988; The English Language, 1988; Pilgrimage, 1988; (with J. C. Davies) Convent, 1989; Language A to Z, 1991; (with J. L. Foster) Databank series: Heat, Light, Sound, Roads, Railways, Canals, Manors, Castles, Money, Monasteries, Parliament, Newspapers, 1979; The Romans, The Greeks, The Ancient Egyptians, 1981; Air, Food, Volcanoes, 1982; Deserts, Dinosaurs and Electricity, 1983; Motorcycles, Computers, Horses and Ponies, Normans, Vikings, Anglo-Saxons, Celts, 1984; The Stone Age, Fishing, 1985; contributions to: The Library of Modern Knowledge, 1978; A Dictionary of Modern Thought, 1978, 2nd edn 1987; Reader's Digest Great Illustrated Dictionary, 1984; Reader's Digest Book of Facts, 1985; A Comprehensive Grammar of the English Language, 1985; (ed) Cambridge Encyclopedia, 1990; and to numerous volumes on language, style, prosody, communication, religion, handicap, teaching and reading; symposia and proceedings of learned socs; articles and reviews in jls on linguistics, English language, speech pathology and education. *Recreations:* cinema, music, bibliophily. *Address:* Akaroa, Gors Avenue, Holyhead, Anglesey, Gwynedd LL65 1PB. *T:* Holyhead (0407) 762764, *Fax:* Holyhead (0407) 769728.

CRYSTAL, Michael; QC 1984; Honorary Senior Visiting Fellow, Centre for Commercial Law Studies, Queen Mary and Westfield College (formerly Queen Mary College), University of London, since 1987; *b* 5 March 1948; *s* of Dr Samuel Cyril Crystal, OBE, and Rachel Ettel Crystal; *m* 1972, Susan Felicia Sniderman; one *s* one *d. Educ:* Leeds Grammar Sch.; Queen Mary Coll., Univ. of London (LLB Hons); Magdalen Coll., Oxford (BCL). Called to the Bar, Middle Temple, 1970; called to the Bar *ad eundem*, Gray's Inn, 1989; Lecturer in Law, Pembroke Coll., Oxford, 1971–76. DTI Inspector into County NatWest Ltd and County NatWest Securities Ltd, 1988–89. Gov., RSC, 1988–. *Publications:* various legal text books. *Recreations:* travel, music. *Address:* 27 Rosslyn Hill, NW3 5UJ. *T:* 071–435 7290; 3/4 South Square, Gray's Inn, WC1R 5HP. *T:* 071–696 9900. *Clubs:* Royal Automobile, MCC.

CUBBON, Sir Brian (Crossland), GCB 1984 (KCB 1977; CB 1974); Permanent Under Secretary of State, Home Office, 1979–88; *b* 9 April 1928; *m* 1956, Elizabeth Lorin Richardson; three *s* one *d. Educ:* Bury Grammar Sch.; Trinity Coll., Cambridge. Entered Home Office, 1951; Cabinet Office, 1961–63, 1971–75; Private Sec. to Home Sec., 1968–69; Permanent Under-Sec. of State, Northern Ireland Office, 1976–79. *T:* (089283) 2534. *Club:* United Oxford & Cambridge University.

CUBBON, Maj.-Gen. John Hamilton, CB 1962; CBE 1958 (OBE 1940); DL; *b* 15 March 1911; *s* of Joseph Cubbon; *m* 1951, Amelia Margaret Yates; two *s* one *d. Educ:* St Bees Sch.; RMC Sandhurst. 2nd Lieut Ches Regt, 1931; Commanded: 1st Bn The Parachute Regt, 1946–49; 1st Bn The Ches Regt, 1951–54; 18th Infantry Bde, Malaya, 1956–57. Maj.-Gen. 1960; GOC SW Dist, 1960–63; GOC Land Forces, Middle East Command, 1963–65. DL Devon, 1969. *Recreation:* sailing. *Address:* The Hayes, Harpford, Sidmouth, Devon.

CUBIE, George; Clerk of Select Committees, House of Commons, since 1989; *b* 30 Aug. 1943; *s* of Dr Alexander Cubie and of late Elsie B. C. Thorburn; *m* 1966, Kathleen S. Mullan; one *s. Educ:* Dollar Acad.; Edinburgh Univ. (MA Hons). Clerk in H of C, 1966; Clerk of Financial Cttees, H of C, 1987–89; Sec. to Public Accounts Commn, 1987–89. *Recreation:* walking. *Address:* 97 Ember Lane, Esher, Surrey KT10 8EQ. *T:* 081–398 1232.

CUBITT, family name of **Baron Ashcombe.**

CUBITT, Sir Hugh (Guy), Kt 1983; CBE 1977; FRICS; JP; DL; Director, Property Security Investment Trust PLC; Commissioner, and Chairman, London Advisory Committee, English Heritage, since 1988; *b* 2 July 1928; *s* of late Col Hon. (Charles) Guy Cubitt, CBE, DSO, TD, and Rosamond Mary Edith, *d* of Sir Montagu Cholmeley, 4th Bt; *m* 1958, Linda Ishbel, *d* of late Hon. Angus Campbell, CBE; one *s* two *d. Educ:* RNC Dartmouth and Greenwich. Lieut RN, 1949; served in Korea, 1949–51; Flag Lieut to Adm., BJSM Washington, 1952 and to C-in-C Nore, 1953; retd 1953. Qual. Chartered Auctioneer and Estate Agent, 1958; Chartered Surveyor (FRICS) 1970. Partner: Rogers Chapman & Thomas, 1958–67; Cubitt & West, 1962–79. Regl Dir, 1970–77, Dir, 1977–90, Mem., UK Adv. Bd, 1990–91, National Westminster Bank; Chairman: Lombard North Central, 1980–91; The Housing Corp., 1980–90. Mem. Westminster City Council, 1963–78; Leader of Council, 1972–76; Alderman, 1974–78; Lord Mayor and dep. High Steward of Westminster, 1977–78. Pres., London Chamber of Commerce, 1988–91. Chm., Housing Assocs' Charitable Trust, 1991–; Gov., Peabody Trust, 1991–; Chairman of Governors: West Heath Sch., 1978–; Cranleigh Sch., 1981–; Dir and Mem. Governing Body, RAM, 1978–. Hon. Steward, Westminster Abbey, 1978. Mem., Bd of Green Cloth Verge of Palaces, 1980–. FRSA; Hon. FRAM 1985. JP Surrey, 1964; Dep. Chm., 1974–83, 1985–91, Chm., 1991–, Dorking PSD; High Sheriff of Surrey, 1983–84. DL Greater London, 1978. *Recreations:* country sports, travel, photography. *Address:* Chapel House, Westhumble, Dorking, Surrey RH5 6AY. *T:* Dorking (0306) 882994. *Club:* Boodle's.

CUCKNEY, Sir John (Graham), Kt 1978; Chairman: 3i Group plc (formerly Investors in Industry Group plc), since 1987; Royal Insurance Holdings (formerly Royal Insurance) plc, since 1985; Director: Brixton Estate plc, since 1985; Glaxo Holdings plc, since 1990; *b* 12 July 1925; *s* of late Air Vice-Marshal E. J. Cuckney, CB, CBE, DSC; *m* 2nd, 1960, Muriel, *d* of late Walter Scott Boyd. *Educ:* Shrewsbury; St Andrews Univ. (MA). War

Service, Royal Northumberland Fusiliers, King's African Rifles, followed by attachment to War Office (Civil Asst, Gen. Staff), until 1957; subseq. chm. and dir of various industrial and financial cos including: Brooke Bond Group plc, 1978–84; Thomas Cook Group (Chm., 1978–87); Midland Bank plc (Dir, 1978–88); John Brown plc (Chm., 1983–86; Dep. Chm., 1983–85; Dir, 1981–86); Westland Group (Chm., 1985–89); TI Group (Dep. Chm., 1985–90); Lazard Brothers (Dir, 1964–70 and 1988–90). Public appointments include: Chm., Mersey Docks and Harbour Board, 1970–72; Chief Executive (Second Perm. Sec.), Property Services Agency, DoE, 1972–74; Chm., International Military Services Ltd (an MoD company), 1974–85; Sen. Crown Agent and Chm. of Crown Agents, for Oversea Governments and Administrations, 1974–78. Dir, Trinity House Pilotage and Marine Services Ltd, 1987–. Independent Mem., Railway Policy Review Cttee, 1966–67; special Mem., Hops Marketing Bd, 1971–72; Chairman: EDC for Building, 1976–80; Port of London Authority, 1977–79; Internat. Maritime Bureau, Internat. Chamber of Commerce, 1981–85; NEDC Working Party on European Public Sector Procurement, 1991–; Member: Docklands Joint Cttee, 1977–79; Council, British Exec. Service Overseas, 1981–84; Council, Foundn for Science and Technology, 1987–90; Dir, SBAC, 1986–89. Governor, Centre for Internat. Briefing, Farnham Castle, 1974–84; Chm., Understanding Industry Trust, 1988–; Trustee, RAF Mus., 1987–. Elder Brother of Trinity House, 1980. Hon. DSc Bath, 1991. *Address:* 3i Group plc, 91 Waterloo Road, SE1 8XP. *T:* 071–928 3131. *Club:* Athenæum.

CUDLIPP, family name of **Baron Cudlipp.**

CUDLIPP, Baron *cr* 1974 (Life Peer), of Aldingbourne, W Sussex; **Hugh Cudlipp,** Kt 1973; OBE 1945; Chairman: International Publishing Corporation Ltd, 1968–73 (Deputy Chairman, 1964–68); International Publishing Corporation Newspaper Division, 1970–73; Deputy Chairman (editorial), Reed International Board, 1970–73; Director, Associated Television Ltd, 1956–73; *b* 28 Aug. 1913; *s* of William Cudlipp, Cardiff; *m* 2nd, 1945, Eileen Ascroft (*d* 1962); 3rd, 1963, Jodi, *d* of late John L. Hyland, Palm Beach, Fla. and Mrs D. W. Jones, Southport. *Educ:* Howard Gardens Sch., Cardiff. Provincial newspapers in Cardiff and Manchester, 1927–32; Features Ed., Sunday Chronicle, London, 1932–35; Features Ed., Daily Mirror, 1935–37; Ed., Sunday Pictorial, 1937–40. Military Service, 1940–46; CO, British Army Newspaper Unit, CMF, 1943–46. Ed., Sunday Pictorial, 1946–49; Managing Ed., Sunday Express, 1950–52; Editorial Dir, Daily Mirror and Sunday Pictorial, 1952–63; Joint Managing Dir, Daily Mirror and Sunday Pictorial, 1959–63; Chm., Odhams Press Ltd, 1961–63; Chm., Daily Mirror Newspapers Ltd, 1963–68. Mem., Royal Commn on Standards of Conduct in Public Life, 1974–76. Exec. Founder Chm., Chichester Festivities, 1975–80; Mem. Bd, Productions Co., Chichester Fest. Th., 1980–87; Vice-Pres., Chichester Fest. Th. Trust, 1987–. *Publications:* Publish and be Damned!, 1955; At Your Peril, 1962; Walking on the Water, 1976; The Prerogative of the Harlot, 1980. *Recreation:* music. *Address:* 14 Tollhouse Close, Avenue de Chartres, Chichester, West Sussex PO19 1SF. *Club:* Garrick.

CUDLIPP, Michael John; consultant on corporate communications; *b* 24 April 1934; *o s* of late Percy Cudlipp and Mrs Gwendoline May Cudlipp; *m* 1st, 1957, Margaret Susannah Rees (marr. diss. 1975); one *d*; 2nd, 1985, Jane Gale; two *d*. *Educ:* Tonbridge Sch., Kent. Trainee reporter, feature writer, gossip columnist, sub-editor, South Wales Echo, Cardiff, 1953–57; Sub-editor, Evening Chronicle, Manchester (various freelance jobs on daily and Sunday newspapers in Manchester), 1957–58; News Editor and Asst Editor (News), Sunday Times, 1958–67; Asst Editor (Night), Jt Man. Editor and sen. Dep. Editor, The Times, 1967–73; Chief Editor, London Broadcasting Co., 1973–74; Consultant on Public Relations to NI Office (temp. Civil Servant with rank of Under-Sec.), 1974–75; Dir of Information, Nat. Enterprise Bd, 1975–78; Dir, External and Internal Communications, Internat. Thomson Orgn, 1979–85. Gov., History of Advertising Trust, 1984–86. FZS. *Recreations:* Arts, Welsh rugby football. *Address:* c/o Barclays Bank, 27 Soho Square, W1A 4WA.

CUDLIPP, Reginald; consultant and writer on Japan; Director, Anglo-Japanese Economic Institute, London, 1961–86, retired; *b* Cardiff, 11 Dec. 1910; *s* of William and Mrs B. A. Cudlipp, Cardiff; *m* 1945, Rachel Joyce Braham. *Educ:* Cardiff Technical Coll. Began journalistic career on Penarth News, Glamorgan; Sub-Ed., Western Mail, Cardiff; joined News of the World Sub-Editorial Staff, 1938; served War, 1940–46; rejoined News of the World and became Special Correspondent in USA, 1946–47; Features Ed., 1948–50, Dep. Ed., 1950–53, Ed., 1953–59; Dir, News of the World Ltd, 1955–60. Extensive industrial tours and on-the-spot economic study of Japan regularly, 1962–86. Completed 60 years in active journalism, 1926–86. FRSA; Life Mem., NUJ, 1929–. Editor, Japan (quarterly review and monthly survey), and special publications on the Japanese scene, 1961–86. Lecturer and writer on Japan's past, present and future; also first-hand research on developing nations and economic co-operation, especially in Africa and Asia; invited to Japan, 1989, to brief businessmen on the Japan/EEC partnership after 1992. Order of the Sacred Treasure, Japan, 1982. *Publications:* numerous contribs to newspapers and periodicals, on Japan and Anglo-Japanese affairs. *Recreations:* music, travel, and reading, writing and talking about Japan. *Address:* 14 Walberton Park, Walberton, Arundel, West Sussex BN18 0PJ.

CUENOD, Hugues; Swiss tenor; *b* 26 June 1902; *s* of Frank Cuenod and Gabrielle de Meuron. *Educ:* Swiss schools and colleges; Conservatoire Basel; Vienna; with Mme Singer-Burian. First concert, Paris, 1928; gave many performances of classical and light music, incl. musical comedy, in Europe and USA; numerous concerts with Clara Haskil and Nadia Boulanger; taught at Conservatoire de Genève, 1940–46; after returning to Paris, concentrated on sacred and classical music; sang in all major opera houses, incl. Glyndebourne (début 1954) and NY Metropolitan (début 1987); latterly specialised in French songs; many master classes. Commandeur de l'Ordre des Arts et des Lettres (France). *Relevant publications:* Hugues Cuenod: un diable de musicien, by Jerôme Spycket, 1978. *Address:* 21 Place du Marché, 1800 Vevey, Switzerland; Château de Lully sur Morges, Switzerland.

CUEVAS-CANCINO, Francisco, GCVO (Hon.) 1985; Mexican Ambassador to Austria and Permanent Mexican Representative to UNIDO and IAEA, since 1986; *b* 7 May 1921; *s* of José Luis Cuevas and Sofia Cancino; *m* 1946, Ana Hilditch; two *s* one *d*; *m* Cristina Flores de Cuevas. *Educ:* Free School of Law, Mexico (lawyer, 1943); McGill Univ., Montreal (MCL 1946). Entered Mexican Foreign Service, as Vice-Consul, 1946, reaching rank of Ambassador by own merit; Permanent Representative to UN, 1965–70; Mexican Rep. to UNESCO, 1971–75, and Mem. Exec. Council during first four years; Perm. Rep. to UN, 1978–79; Ambassador: to Brazil, 1979–80; to Belgium, 1980–83; to UK and to Republic of Ireland, 1983–85. Chm., Group of 77, Vienna, 1988. Order of the Liberator, 1970, Order Andrés Bello, 1971, (Venezuela); Medal of Mexican For. Service (25 years), 1972; Order Cruzeiro do Sur (Brazil), 1980; Great Cross of Order of the Crown (Belgium), 1983. *Publications:* La nullité des actes juridiques, 1947; La doctrina de Suárez en el derecho natural (award, Madrid), 1952; Roosevelt y la buena vecindad, 1955; Del Congreso de Panamá a la Conferencia de Caracas, 1955, re-ed 1979; Tratado sobre la organización internacional, 1962; (ed) Porvenir de México by Luis G. Cuevas, 1961; (ed) Pacto de Familia (vol. forms part of Hist. Archives of Mexican Diplomatic Service, 2nd series), 1963; (ed) Foro Internacional, 1961–62; contrib. to book of essays in homage to Hans Morgenthau, 1978; several works and articles on Bolivarian theatre, and on Simón Bolívar (The Liberator), incl.: Visión Surrealista del Libertador, (Bogotá) 1980; Homenaje a Bolívar en el Sesquicentenario de su Muerte, (Bogotá) 1980. *Address:* Mexican Embassy, Renngasse 4, 1010 Vienna, Austria. *T:* 535–17–76. *Clubs:* Travellers', Garrick.

CULHAM, Michael John; Assistant Under Secretary of State (Civilian Management (Administrators)), Ministry of Defence, since 1987; *b* 24 June 1933; *s* of Cecil and Constance Culham; *m* 1963, Christine Mary Daish; one *s* two *d*. *Educ:* Reading Sch.; Lincoln Coll., Oxford (MA). National Service, Queen's Own Royal West Kent Regt, RAEC, 1952–54. Exec. Officer, WO, 1957–61; Asst Principal, Air Min., 1962; Private Sec. to Under-Sec. of State for Air, 1962–64; Principal, MoD, 1964–72; Jt Services Staff Coll., 1969; 1st Sec. (Defence), UK Delegn to NATO, Brussels, 1972–74; Asst Sec., MoD, 1974–82; Asst Under-Sec. of State (Adjt-Gen.), MoD, 1982–87. Member: Royal Patriotic Fund Corp., 1983–87; Adv. Council, RMCS, Shrivenham, 1983–87. Commissioner: Duke of York's Royal Mil. Sch., 1982–87; Queen Victoria Sch., 1982–87; Welbeck Coll., 1985–87; Royal Hosp. Chelsea, 1985–88. Chairman: MoD Recreation Assoc., 1985–90; Defence Sports and Recreation Assoc., 1991–; Vice Pres. Farnham Town Boys' FC, 1987– (Chm., 1983–85). Trustee, Nat. Army Mus., 1985–88. *Recreations:* music, sailing, walking, watching cricket. *Address:* c/o Ministry of Defence, Lacon House, Theobalds Road, WC1X 8RY. *Clubs:* Civil Service; Surrey County Cricket.

CULHANE, Prof. John Leonard, FRS 1985; Professor of Physics, since 1981, and Director, Mullard Space Science Laboratory, since 1983, University College London; *s* of late John Thomas Culhane and Mary Agnes Culhane; *m* 1961, Mary Brigid, *d* of James Smith; two *s*. *Educ:* Clongowes Wood College, Co. Kildare; University College Dublin (BSc Phys 1959; MSc Phys 1960); UCL (PhD Phys 1966). Physics Department, University College London: Res. Asst, 1963; Lectr, 1967; Reader, 1976; Prof., 1981. Sen. Scientist, Lockheed Palo Alto Res. Lab., 1969–70. Chairman: SERC/BNSC Space Sci. Prog. Bd, 1989– (UK Deleg. to ESA Sci. Prog. Cttee, 1989–); Royal Soc. Space Res. Cttee, 1990–; Member: Council, RAS, 1975–78; Space Sci. Adv. Cttee, ESA, 1985–89 (Chm., Astrophysics Working Group, 1985–89); SERC/BNSC Earth Obs. Prog. Bd, 1986–88; Vis. Cttee, RGO/ROE, 1987–; SERC Astron. Plan. Sci. Bd, 1989–. Mem. Council, Surrey Univ., 1985–90. Member: IAU; Amer. Astronomical Soc.; IEEE Professional Group on Nuclear Sci. *Publications:* X-ray Astronomy (with P. W. Sanford), 1981; over 200 papers on solar and cosmic X-ray astronomy, X-ray instrumentation and plasma spectroscopy. *Recreations:* music, racing cars. *Address:* Ariel House, Holmbury St Mary, Dorking, Surrey RH5 6NS. *T:* (lab.) Cranleigh (0483) 274111.

CULHANE, Rosalind, (Lady Padmore), LVO 1938; OBE 1949; Treasury Welfare Adviser, 1943–64; *y d* of late F. W. S. Culhane, MRCS, LRCP, Hastings, Sussex; *m* 1964, Sir Thomas Padmore, *qv*. Joined Treasury in 1923 and attached to office of Chancellor of Exchequer; Asst Private Sec. to Mr Chamberlain, 1934, Sir John Simon, 1937, Sir Kingsley Wood, 1940. *Address:* 39 Cholmeley Crescent, N6. *T:* 081–340 6587.

CULLEN, Hon. Lord; (William) Douglas Cullen; a Senator of the College of Justice in Scotland, and Lord of Session, since 1986; *b* 18 Nov. 1935; *s* of late Sheriff K. D. Cullen and Mrs G. M. Cullen; *m* 1961, Rosamond Mary Downer; two *s* two *d*. *Educ:* Dundee High Sch.; St Andrews Univ. (MA); Edinburgh Univ. (LLB). Called to the Scottish Bar, 1960. Standing Jun. Counsel to HM Customs and Excise, 1970–73; QC (Scot.) 1973; Advocate-depute, 1978–81. Chairman: Medical Appeal Tribunal, 1977–86; Court of Inquiry into the Piper Alpha disaster, 1988–90; Mem., Scottish Valuation Adv. Council, 1980–86. Chm. Council, Cockburn Assoc. (Edinburgh Civic Trust), 1984–86. Mem., Royal Commn on Ancient and Historical Monuments of Scotland, 1987–. *Publications:* The Faculty Digest Supplement 1951–60, 1965; non-legal booklets on buildings in Edinburgh. *Recreations:* gardening, natural history. *Address:* The Court of Session, Parliament House, Edinburgh EH1 1R9. *T:* 031–225 2595. *Club:* New (Edinburgh).

CULLEN OF ASHBOURNE, 2nd Baron *cr* 1920; **Charles Borlase Marsham Cokayne,** MBE 1945; a Lord in Waiting (Government Whip), 1979–82; Major, Royal Signals; *b* 6 Oct. 1912; *e s* of 1st Baron and Grace Margaret (*d* 1971), *d* of Rev. Hon. John Marsham; *S* father, 1932; *m* 1942, Valerie Catherine Mary (marr. diss. 1947), *o d* of late W. H. Collbran; one *d*; *m* 1948, Patricia Mary, *er d* of late Col S. Clulow-Gray and late Mrs Clulow-Gray, formerly of Clare Priory, Suffolk. *Educ:* Eton. Served War of 1939–45 (MBE). Amateur Tennis Champion, 1947, 1952. One of HM Lieutenants, City of London, 1976–. Chm., Osteopathic Educnl Foundn; President: Fedn of Ophthalmic & Dispensing Opticians (formerly Fedn of Optical Corporate Bodies), 1983–; Gen. Council and Register of Osteopaths, 1987–89. Dep. Chm. of Cttees, 1982–. Founder Mem., Action Research. *Heir:* *b* Hon. Edmund Willoughby Marsham Cokayne [*b* 18 May 1916; *m* 1943, Janet Manson, *d* of late William Douglas Watson and of Mrs Lauritson, Calgary]. *Address:* 75 Cadogan Gardens, SW3 2RB. *T:* 071–589 1981. *Clubs:* MCC; Swinley Forest Golf.

CULLEN, Prof. Alexander Lamb, OBE 1960; DSc(Eng); FRS 1977; FEng 1977, FIEE, FIEEE, FInstP, FCGI; Emeritus Professor, University of London; Hon. Research Fellow, Department of Electronic and Electrical Engineering, University College London, since 1984 (SERC Senior Research Fellow, 1980–84); *b* 30 April 1920; *s* of Richard and Jessie Cullen, Lincoln; *m* 1940, Margaret, *er d* of late Alexander Lamb, OBE; two *s* one *d*. *Educ:* Lincoln Sch.; City and Guilds Coll., London. Staff of Radio Dept, RAE Farnborough, working on development of radar, 1940–46; Lectr in Electrical Engineering, University Coll., London, 1946–55 (title of Reader conferred 1955); Prof. of Electrical Engineering, University of Sheffield, 1955–67; Pender Prof. of Electrical Engineering, University College London, 1967–80. Hon. Prof., Northwestern Polytechnical Univ., Xian, China, 1981. Mem., IBA, 1982–89. Dir, Quasar Microwave Technology. Instn of Electrical Engineers: Kelvin premium, 1952; Extra premium, 1953 (with Prof. H. M. Barlow and Dr A. E. Karbowiak); Radio Sect. premium, 1954; Ambrose Fleming premium, 1956 (with J. C. Parr), 1975 (with Dr J. R. Forrest), 1988 (with S. P. Yeo); Duddell premium, 1957 (with Dr H. A. French); Electronics and Communications Sect. premium, 1959; Electronics Letters premium, 1985; Faraday Medal, 1984. Microwave Career Award, IEEE, 1989. Chm., Brit. Nat. Cttee, URSI, 1981–85; Vice-Pres., Internat. URSI, 1981–87, Pres., 1987–90; Mem. Council, Royal Soc., 1984–86. Clifford Paterson Lecture, Royal Soc., 1984; Clerk Maxwell Lecture, IERE, 1986. Hon. FIERE 1987. Hon. DSc: Chinese Univ. of Hong Kong, 1981; Kent, 1986. Hon. DEng Sheffield, 1985. Royal Medal, Royal Soc., 1984. *Publications:* Microwave Measurements (jointly with Prof. H. M. Barlow), 1950; a number of papers on electromagnetic waves and microwave measurement techniques in IEE proceedings and elsewhere. *Recreations:* music and reading. *Address:* Department of Electronic and Electrical Engineering, University College London, Torrington Place, WC1E 7JE. *Club:* English-Speaking Union.

CULLEN, Douglas; *see* Cullen, Hon. Lord.

CULLEN, Sir (Edward) John, Kt 1991; PhD; FEng 1987; Chairman, Health and Safety Commission, since 1983; *b* 19 Oct. 1926; *s* of William Henry Pearson Cullen and Ellen Emma Cullen; *m* 1954, Betty Davall Hopkins; two *s* two *d*. *Educ:* Cambridge Univ. (MA 1952, PhD 1956); Univ. of Texas (MS 1953). UKAEA, 1956–58; ICI, 1958–67; Rohm and Haas Co., 1967–83: Eur. Dir for Engrg and Regulatory Affairs, 1981–83; Dep. Chm., Rohm and Haas (UK) Ltd, 1981–83. Mem., Engrg Council, 1990–. Pres., IChemE, 1988–89. MInstD 1978; FRSA. Liveryman, Engineers' Co. *Publications:* articles on gas absorption, in Trans Faraday Soc., Trans IChemE, Chem. Engrg Science; numerous articles on health and safety. *Recreations:* reading (detective stories), photography, swimming, gardening. *Address:* 14 Gloucester Walk, W8 5JH. *T:* 071–937 0709. *Club:* Institute of Directors.

CULLEN, Gordon; *see* Cullen, T. G.

CULLEN, James Reynolds; *b* 13 June 1900; *s* of Rev. James Harris Cullen, London Missionary Society; *m* 1931, Inez (*d* 1980), *e d* of M. G. Zarifi, MBE; one *s* two *d.* *Educ:* Weimar Gymnasium; The School, Bishop's Stortford (Rhodes Schol.); Tonbridge Sch.; Balliol Coll., Oxford (Scholar). Hertford Schol., 1919; Craven Schol., 1920; 1st class Hon. Mods, 1920; 2nd class Lit. Hum. 1922; MA 1925. Asst Master, Winchester Coll., 1922–30; archæological expeditions to Asia Minor, 1925, and Mytilene, 1930; Dir of Education, Cyprus, 1930–45; Dir of Education, Uganda, 1945–52; Asst Master, Oundle Sch., 1953–60, Cranbrook and Benenden Schs, 1960–68. *Address:* Bayleaf Rest Home, 16 Whyke Road, Chichester, W Sussex PO19 2HN. *Club:* Commonwealth Trust.

CULLEN, Sir John; *see* Cullen, Sir E. J.

CULLEN, Raymond; Chairman, The Calico Printers' Association Ltd and subsidiaries, 1964–68; *b* 27 May 1913; *s* of late John Norman Cullen and Bertha (*née* Dearden); *m* 1940, Doris (*d* 1984), *d* of A. W. Paskin; two *d.* *Educ:* King's Sch., Macclesfield; St Catharine's Coll., Cambridge (Scholar, MA). Joined The Calico Printers' Assoc. Ltd Commn Printing, 1934; transf. overseas, 1938; service in India and China. Dir, W. A. Beardsell & Co. (Private) Ltd, Madras, 1946 (Chm. and Man. Dir, 1949–55); Chm. and Man. Dir, Mettur Industries Ltd, 1949–55; Chm. and Man. Dir, Marshall Fabrics Ltd, 1955–62; Director: Calico Printers' Assoc. Ltd, 1962–68; Barclays Bank Ltd Manchester Local Bd, 1965–69. Member: Textile Coun., 1967–69; Coun., Inst. of Directors, 1967–69; NW Economic Planning Coun., 1968–69; Governor, Manchester Grammar Sch., 1968–83. *Recreations:* fishing, golf (Pres., Cheshire Union of Golf Clubs, 1977–78). *Address:* Cranford, Ladybrook Road, Bramhall, Cheshire SK7 3NB. *T:* 061–485 3204.

CULLEN, Terence Lindsay Graham, QC 1978; *b* 29 Oct. 1930; *s* of late Eric Graham Cullen and Jean Morrison Hunter (*née* Bennett); *m* 1958, Muriel Elisabeth Rolfe; three *s.* *Educ:* RNC, Dartmouth. RN, 1948–55; Prestige Group Ltd, 1955–61. Called to the Bar: Lincoln's Inn, 1961 (Bencher, 1986); Singapore, 1978; Malaysia, 1980; Hong Kong, 1986; Bermuda, 1990. *Recreation:* the Turf. *Address:* 13 Old Square, Lincoln's Inn, WC2A 3UA. *T:* 071–404 4800; Calico House, Newnham, Kent ME9 0LN.

CULLEN, (Thomas) Gordon, CBE 1978; RDI 1976; planning consultant, artist and writer; *b* 9 Aug. 1914; *s* of Rev. T. H. Cullen and Mary Anne (*née* Moffatt); *m* 1955, Comtesse Jacqueline de Chabaneix du Chambon; three *d.* *Educ:* Prince Henry's Grammar Sch., Otley, Yorks; Regent Street Polytechnic Sch. of Architecture, London. Fraternal Delegate, Runcorn Trades Council, 1942; Mem. Planning Div., Develt and Welfare, Barbados, 1944–46; Asst Editor, Architectural Rev., 1946–56. Townscape Consultant: with Ford Foundn, New Delhi, 1960, and Calcutta, 1962; Liverpool, Llantrisant, Tenterden, Peterborough and Ware, 1962–76; London Docklands, 1981–82; Glasgow, 1983–84. Dir, Price and Cullen, architects, 1985–. Exhib. drawings, Paris Salon, Royal Acad.; One-Man Exhibn, Sweden and Holland, 1976; London, 1985. Member: Eton RDC, 1963–73; Wraysbury Parish Council, 1960–89. Hon. FRIBA 1972. Hon. LittD Sheffield, 1975; Hon. LLD Strathclyde, 1988; Dr-IngEh Munich, 1973. Amer. Inst. of Architects Gold Medal, 1976. *Publications:* Townscape, 1964; planning reports.

CULLIMORE, Charles Augustine Kaye; HM Diplomatic Service; High Commissioner to Uganda, since 1989; *b* 2 Oct. 1933; *s* of Charles Cullimore and Constance Alicia Kaye Cullimore (*née* Grimshaw); *m* 1956, Val Elizabeth Margot (*née* Willemsen); one *s* one *d.* *Educ:* Portora Royal Sch., Enniskillen; Trinity Coll., Oxford (MA). N Ireland Short Service Commn, 1955–57. HMOCS, Tanganyika, 1958–61; ICI Ltd, 1961–71; joined HM Diplomatic Service, 1971; FCO, 1971–73; Bonn, 1973–77; FCO, 1977–79; Counsellor, New Delhi, 1979–82; Dep. High Comr, Canberra, 1982–86; FCO, 1986–89. *Recreations:* theatre, walking, tennis. *Address:* c/o Foreign and Commonwealth Office, SW1A 2AH. *Clubs:* Commonwealth Trust; Commonwealth (Canberra).

CULLIMORE, Colin Stuart, CBE 1978; Director of External Affairs, Vestey Group; Director, Albion Insurance; *b* 13 July 1931; *s* of Reginald Victor Cullimore and May Maria Cullimore; *m* 1952, Kathleen Anyta Lamming; one *s.* *Educ:* Westminster Sch.; National Coll. of Food Technol. Commnd Royal Scots Fusiliers, 1951; seconded Parachute Regt; transf. when perm. officer cadre formed; Major 1956; 10th Bn Parachute Regt TA, 1960. Gen. Man., Payne & Son (Butchers) Ltd, 1960; Asst Gen. Man., J. H. Dewhurst Ltd, 1965, Gen. Man. 1969, Man. Dir, 1976. Non-Exec. Dir, NAAFI, 1984–; Dir, Airborne Initiative, 1991–. Chairman: Retail Consortium Food Cttee, 1973–74; Multiple Shops Fedn, 1977–78. Vice-Chairman: Multiple Food Retailers Assoc., 1972–74; Governors, Coll. for Distributive Trades, 1976–79, 1984–88; Retail Consortium, 1985–89; Pres., British Retailers Assoc., 1984–89 (Vice Pres., 1978–84); Dep. Chm., Meat Promotion Exec., 1975–78; Vice Pres., Bd of Admin, CECD (European Retailers), 1986–88 (Mem., 1981–85). Member: Distribn and Consumer Cttees, 1969–72, Finance Cttee, 1980–87, Diet and Health Cttee, 1986–88, Meat and Livestock Commn; EDC for Distrib. Trades, 1972–80; Council and Management Cttee, Inst. of Meat (Vice-Chm., 1981–83); Cttee of Commerce and Distribn, EEC, 1984–; Council, Industry & Parlt Trust, 1987–. Gov., Court of London Inst., 1984–87 and 1989–90; Exec. Trustee, Airborne Assault Normandy Trust, 1983–; Exec. Cttee, British Sporting Art Trust, 1991–; Regtl Council, Parachute Regt, 1991–. FRSA 1987. Liveryman, Butchers' Co. FInstD, 1979; CBIM, 1984. Gold Medal: Inst. of Meat, 1956; Butchers' Co., 1956. *Address:* Wyberton Park, Wyberton, Boston, Lincs PE21 7AF. *T:* Boston (0205) 311423; 20 Christchurch House, 5 Caxton Street, SW1H 0PY. *T:* 071–222 4507; Palazzo Gianbattista, Nigret, Zurrieq, Malta GC. *T:* 356–829587. *Clubs:* Naval and Military, Farmers', Institute of Directors.

CULLINAN, Edward Horder, CBE 1987; RA 1991 (ARA 1989); Senior Partner, Edward Cullinan Architects, since 1965; *b* 17 July 1931; *s* of Dr Edward Cullinan and Joy (*née* Horder); *m* 1961, Rosalind Yeates; one *s* two *d.* *Educ:* Ampleforth Coll.; Cambridge Univ. (Anderson and Webb Schol., 1951; BA); Univ. of California at Berkeley (George VI Meml Fellow, 1956). AADip; RIBA. With Denys Lasdun, 1958–65. Bannister Fletcher Prof., UCL, 1978–79; Graham Willis Prof., Univ. of Sheffield, 1985–87; George Simpson Prof., Univ. of Edinburgh, 1987–. Designed and built: Horder House, Hampshire, 1959–60; Marvin House, Calif, 1959–60; Minster Lovell Mill, 1969–72; Parish Ch. of St Mary, Barnes, 1978–84; Lambeth Community Care Centre, 1979–84; RMC Internat. HQ, 1985–90; all have received awards and been published internationally. FRSA. *Publications:* Edward Cullinan, Architects, 1984; contribs to many architectural jls. *Recreations:* horticulture, cycling, surfing, ski-ing, Sahara travel, building, history, geography. *Address:* 57D Jamestown Road, NW1 7DB. *T:* 071–485 2267.

CULLINGFORD, Eric Coome Maynard, CMG 1963; *b* 15 March 1910; *s* of Francis James and Lilian Mabel Cullingford; *m* 1938, Friedel Fuchs; two *s* one *d.* *Educ:* City of London Sch.; St Catharine's Coll., Cambridge (Exhibitioner). Entered Ministry of Labour as Third Class Officer, 1932; Principal, 1942. Served with Manpower Div. of CCG, 1946–50. Asst Sec., Min. of Labour, 1954. Labour Attaché, Bonn, 1961–65, 1968–72. Regional Controller, Eastern and Southern Region, Dept of Employment and Productivity, 1966–68; retired 1973. *Publications:* Trade Unions in West Germany, 1976; Pirates of Shearwater Island, 1983. *Address:* Combermere, Flat 1, 25 Avenue Road, Malvern, Worcs WR14 3AY.

CULLINGWORTH, Prof. (John) Barry; Unidel Professor of Urban Affairs and Public Policy, University of Delaware, since 1983; *b* 11 Sept. 1929; *s* of Sidney C. and Winifred E. Cullingworth; *m* 1951, Betty Violet (*née* Turner); one *s* two *d.* *Educ:* High Pavement Sch., Nottingham; Trinity Coll. of Music, London; London Sch. of Economics. Research Asst, Asst Lectr and Lectr, Univ. of Manchester, 1955–60; Lectr, Univ. of Durham, 1960–63; Sen. Lectr and Reader, Univ. of Glasgow, 1963–66; Dir, Centre for Urban and Regional Studies, Univ. of Birmingham, 1966–72. Dir, Planning Exchange, Scotland, 1972–75; Official Historian, Cabinet Office, 1975–77. Chm., Dept of Urban and Regional Planning, 1977–80, Res. Prof., Centre for Urban and Community Studies, 1980–82, Prof. of Planning, 1982–83, Univ. of Toronto. Vis. Prof., Univ. of Strathclyde, 1980–86. Vice-Chm., Scottish Housing Adv. Cttee; Chairman: Cttee on Community Facilities in Expanding Towns (Report, The Needs of New Communities, 1967); Cttee on Unfit Housing in Scotland (Report, Scotland's Older Houses, 1967); Cttee on Allocation of Council Houses (Report, Council Housing: Purposes, Procedures and Practices, 1968); Adv. Cttee on Rent Rebates and Rent Allowances, 1973–77. Mem., Ont. Council of Health, 1979–83; Vice-Pres., Housing Centre Trust, 1972–. FRSA 1974; Hon. MRTPI. *Publications:* Housing Needs and Planning Policy, 1960; Housing in Transition, 1963; Town and Country Planning in England and Wales, 1964, 10th edn 1988; English Housing Trends, 1965; Housing and Local Government, 1966; Scottish Housing in 1965, 1967; A Profile of Glasgow Housing, 1968; (with V. Karn) Ownership and Management of Housing in New Towns, 1968; Housing and Labour Mobility, (Paris) 1969; Problems of an Urban Society (3 vols), 1973; Environmental Planning—Reconstruction and Land Use Planning, 1975; Essays on Housing Policy, 1979; New Towns Policy, 1980; Canadian Housing Policy Research, 1980; Land Values, Compensation and Betterment, 1981; Rent Control, 1983; Canadian Planning and Public Participation, 1984; Urban and Regional Planning in Canada, 1987; Energy, Land and Public Policy, 1990. *Address:* College of Urban Affairs and Public Policy, University of Delaware, Newark, Delaware 19716, USA.

CULLIS, Prof. Charles Fowler; Professor of Physical Chemistry, City University, 1967–84, now Emeritus (Head, Chemistry Department, 1973–84; Pro-Vice-Chancellor, 1980–84; Saddlers' Research Professor, 1984–87; Leverhulme Emeritus Research Fellow, 1987–89); *b* 31 Aug. 1922; 2nd *s* of late Prof. C. G. Cullis, Prof. of Mining Geology, Univ. of London, and Mrs W. J. Cullis (*née* Fowler); *m* 1958, Marjorie Elizabeth, *er d* of late Sir Austin Anderson and of Lady Anderson; two *s* two *d.* *Educ:* Stowe Sch. (Open Schol.); Trinity Coll., Oxford. BA 1944, BSc 1st Cl. Hons Chem. 1945, DPhil 1948, MA 1948, DSc 1960; FRSC (FRIC 1958); FRSA. ICI Research Fellow in Chem., Oxford, 1947–50; Lectr in Phys. Chem., Imperial Coll., London, 1950–59; Sen. Lectr in Chem. Engrg and Chem. Tech., Imperial Coll., 1959–64; Reader in Combustion Chemistry, Univ. of London, 1964–66. Vis. Prof., College of Chem., Univ. of California, Berkeley, 1966; Vis. Scientist, CSIRO, Sydney, 1970. Mem. Council, Chem. Soc., 1969–72, 1975–78; Hon. Sec., Brit. Sect. of Combustion Inst., 1969–74; Mem., Rockets Sub-cttee, 1968–73, and of Combustion Sub-cttee, 1969–72, Aeronautical Research Council; Member: Navy Dept Fuels and Lubricants Adv. Cttee (Fire and Explosion Hazards Working Gp), 1967–; Safety in Mines Research Adv. Bd, 1973–88 (Chm., 1980–88); Chem. Cttee, Defence Sci. Adv. Council, 1979–82; Chem. Bd, 1982–87, Phys. Sci. Cttee, 1987–89, CNAA. Scientific Editor, Internat. Union of Pure and Applied Chem., 1976–78. Non-exec. Dir, City Technology Ltd, 1977–. Mem., Mid Sussex DC, 1986–. Governor, City of London Polytechnic, 1982–84. Freeman, City of London, 1983; Liveryman, Bakers' Co., 1983. Joseph Priestley Award, 1974, Combustion Chem. Medal and Award, 1978, Chem. Soc. *Publications:* The Combustion of Organic Polymers (jtly with M. M. Hirschler), 1981; numerous sci. papers in Proc. Royal Soc., Trans Faraday Soc., Jl Chem. Soc., etc, mainly concerned with chemistry of combustion reactions. *Recreations:* music, travel. *Address:* Quinces, Courtmead Road, Cuckfield, W Sussex RH17 5LP. *T:* Haywards Heath (0444) 453513; Chemistry Department, City University, Northampton Square, EC1V 0HB. *T:* 071–253 4399, ext. 3500. *Club:* Athenæum.

See also M. F. Cullis.

CULLIS, Michael Fowler, CVO 1955; HM Diplomatic Service, retired; Director, UK Committee, European Cultural Foundation, Amsterdam, since 1983; *b* 22 Oct. 1914; *s* of late Emeritus Prof. Charles Gilbert Cullis, Imperial Coll. of Science and Technology, London Univ., and late Winifred Jefford Cullis (*née* Fowler); *m* Catherine Robertson, Arbroath, Scotland; no *c.* *Educ:* Wellington Coll. (scholar); Brasenose Coll., Oxford (Hulme Open Scholar). MA, classics. Law (Lincoln's Inn), and journalism, 1938–39. Military Intelligence, Gibraltar, 1939–40; served Min. of Economic Warfare (London, Spain and Portugal), 1940–44; joined FO as head of Austrian Section, 1945; Political Adviser on Austrian Treaty negotiations (London, Moscow, Vienna, Paris, New York), 1947–50; Special Asst, Schuman Plan, 1950; First Sec., British Embassy, Oslo, 1951–55; Regional (Information) Counsellor for the five Nordic countries, British Embassy, Copenhagen, 1955–58; Dep. Gov. of Malta, 1959–61; Sen. Research Associate, Atlantic Institute, Paris, 1962–65; writing, lecturing, etc, at various European centres, 1965–66; Dir, Arms Control and Disarmament Res., FO, then FCO, 1967–74; Advr on relations with non-govtl bodies, FCO, 1974–79; consultant for acad. and institutional fund-raising, and European parly affairs, 1980–82; Historical Advr to Royal Mint, 1986–. Unsuccessful candidate (C), European Elections, 1979. Vice-President: Inst. of Linguists, 1984–89; Internat. Eisteddfod 1984–. FRSA. Chevalier (1st cl.) Order of Dannebrog, 1957. *Publications:* (contrib.) The Price of Victory, 1983; (contrib.) Festschrift for Gerald Stourzh, 1990; articles and broadcasts, mainly on international affairs. *Address:* County End, Bushey Heath, Herts WD2 1NY. *T:* 081–950 1057. *Club:* Athenæum.

See also C. F. Cullis.

CULLITON, Hon. Edward Milton, CC 1981; QC 1947; retired; Chief Justice of Saskatchewan, 1962–81; *b* Grand Forks, Minnesota, USA, 9 April 1906; *s* of John J. Culliton and Katherine Mary Kelly, Canadians; *m* 1939, Katherine Mary Hector. *Educ:* Primary educn in towns in Saskatchewan; Univ. of Saskatchewan. BA 1926, LLB 1928. Practised law in Gravelbourg, Sask., 1930–51. Served War: Canadian Armed Forces (active, overseas, Judges' Advocate Br.), 1941–46. MLA for Gravelbourg, 1935–44, re-elected, 1948; Mem. Opposition until 1951; Provincial Sec., 1938–41; Minister without portfolio, 1941–44. Apptd Judge of Court of Appeal for Sask., 1951. Chm., Sask. Jubilee Cttee, 1952–55. Univ. of Sask.: Mem. Bd of Governors, 1955–61; Chancellor, 1963–69; Mem. Bd, Can. Nat. Inst. for the Blind, 1955– (Pres. Sask. Div., 1962–); Chm., Adv. Bd, Martha House (unmarried mothers), 1955–; Chm., Sask. Revision of Statutes Cttee,

1963–65, and again 1974 until completion 1975–76. Mem., Knights of Columbus, 1930–. Hon. DCL Saskatchewan, 1962. Kt Comdr of St Gregory (Papal) 1963. *Recreations:* golf, curling; interested in football. *Address:* 1303–1830 College Avenue, Regina, Saskatchewan S4P 1C2, Canada. *T:* 569–1758. *Clubs:* Wascana Country, Assiniboia, Royal United Services Institute (all Regina, Sask.).

CULME-SEYMOUR, Comdr Sir Michael; *see* Seymour.

CULSHAW, John Douglas; Assistant Chief Scientific Adviser (Capabilities), Ministry of Defence, 1985–87; *b* 22 Oct. 1927; *s* of Alfred Henry Douglas Culshaw and Dorothy Yeats Culshaw (*née* Hogarth); *m* 1951, Hazel Speirs Alexander; one *s* one *d. Educ:* Alderman Smith Grammar Sch., Washington, Co. Durham; University Coll., Nottingham. BSc London 1949; MSc Nottingham 1950. Joined Weapons Dept, Royal Aircraft Estabt, Min. of Supply, Farnborough, 1950; OC (Scientific) 6 Joint Services Trials Unit RAF (UK), 1956; OC (Sci.) 16 JSTU RA Weapons Research Estabt, Salisbury, S Australia, 1961; Co-ordinating Research and Development Authority Technical Project Officer, RAE, 1964; Supt Mine Warfare Br., Royal Armament R&D Estabt, MoD, Sevenoaks, 1967; Director, Scientific Adv. Br., Home Office, 1970; Dept of Chief Scientific Adviser (Army), 1972; Head of Mathematics and Assessment Dept, RARDE, MoD, Sevenoaks, 1974; Head of Defence Science II, MoD, 1975; RCDS 1976; Dep. Dir, Scientific and Technical Intelligence, 1977; Dir, Defence Operational Analysis Estabt and Asst Chief Scientific Advr (Studies), MoD, 1979–84. *Recreations:* war games, wine-making, folk-song collecting, bee-keeping, historical research. *Club:* Civil Service.

CULYER, Prof. Anthony John; Professor of Economics, since 1979, Head of the Department of Economics and Related Studies, since 1986, and Pro-Vice-Chancellor, since 1991, University of York; Professor, University of Toronto, since 1989; *b* 1 July 1942; *s* of late Thomas Reginald Culyer and Betty Ely (*née* Headland); *m* 1966, Sieglinde Birgit; one *s* one *d. Educ:* King's Sch., Worcester; Exeter Univ. (BA Hons); Univ. of California at Los Angeles. Tutor and Asst Lectr, Exeter Univ., 1965–69; Lectr, Sen. Lectr and Reader, Univ. of York, 1969–79; Deputy Director, Inst. of Social and Economic Research, Univ. of York, 1971–82. Sen. Research Associate, Ontario Economic Council, 1976, Vis. Professorial Lectr, Queen's Univ., Kingston, 1976; William Evans Vis. Professor, Otago Univ., 1979; Vis. Fellow, Australian National Univ., 1979; Visiting Professor: Trent Univ., 1985–86; Inst. für Med. Informatik und Systemforschung, Munich, 1990–91; Toronto Univ., 1991. Lectures: Woodward, Univ. of BC, 1986; Perey, McMaster Univ., 1990. Member: Standing Cttee, Conf. of Heads of Univ. Depts of Econs, 1988–; Coll. Cttee, King's Fund Coll., London, 1989–. Chm., York Dist, RSCM, 1984–. Mem., 1982–90, Non-Exec. Mem., 1990–, Northallerton HA. Co-Editor, Jl of Health Econs, 1982–; Mem., Editl Policy Cttee and Editl Bd, Office of Health Econs, 1990–. *Publications:* The Economics of Social Policy, 1973; (ed with M. H. Cooper) Health Economics, 1973; (ed) Economic Policies and Social Goals, 1974; Need and the National Health Service, 1976; (with J. Wiseman and A. Walker) Annotated Bibliography of Health Economics, 1977; (ed with V. Halberstadt) Human Resources and Public Finance, 1977; Measuring Health: Lessons for Ontario, 1978; (ed with K. G. Wright) Economic Aspects of Health Services, 1978; The Political Economy of Social Policy, 1980; (ed) Health Indicators, 1983; (ed with B. Horisberger) Economic and Medical Evaluation of Health Care Technologies, 1983; Economics, 1985; (ed with G. Terny) Public Finance and Social Policy, 1985; (ed with B. Jonsson) Public and Private Health Services: complementarities and conflicts, 1986; (jtly) The International Bibliography of Health Economics: a comprehensive annotated guide to English language sources since 1914, 1986; Canadian Health Care Expenditures: myth and reality, past and future, 1988; (ed) Standards for the Socio-economic Evaluation of Health Care Products and Services, 1990; (ed jtly) Competition in Health Care: reforming the NHS, 1990; (ed) The Economics of Health, 1991; articles in Oxford Econ. Papers, Economica, Scottish Jl of Political Economy, Public Finance, Jl of Public Economics, Kyklos, Qly Jl of Economics, Jl Royal Statistical Soc., and others. *Recreation:* church music. *Address:* The Laurels, Barmby Moor, York YO4 5EJ. *T:* Pocklington (0759) 302639.

CUMBERLEGE, family name of **Baroness Cumberlege**.

CUMBERLEGE, Baroness *cr* 1990 (Life Peer), of Newick in the County of East Sussex; **Julia Frances Cumberlege,** CBE 1985; DL; Chairman, South West Thames Regional Health Authority, since 1988; *b* 27 Jan. 1943; *d* of Dr L. U. Camm and late M. G. G. Camm; *m* 1961, Patrick Francis Howard Cumberlege; three *s. Educ:* Convent of the Sacred Heart, Tunbridge Wells. Mem., East Sussex AHA, 1977–81; Chm., Brighton HA, 1981–88; Mem. Council, NAHA, 1982–88 (Vice-Chm., 1984–87; Chm., 1987–88). Member: Lewes DC, 1966–79 (Leader, 1977–78); East Sussex CC, 1974–85 (Chm., Social Services Cttee, 1979–82). Chm., Review of Community Nursing for England, 1985 (report, Neighbourhood Nursing—a focus for care, 1986). Member: Social Security Adv. Cttee, 1980–82; DHSS Expert Adv. Gp on AIDS, 1987–89; Council, UK Central Council for Nursing, Midwifery and Health Visiting, 1989–; NHS Policy Bd, 1989–. Lay Mem., 1977–83, Mem. Appts Commn, 1984–90, Press Council. Vice President: Age Concern, Brighton, 1984–; RCN, 1989–. Mem. Council, Brighton Poly, 1987–89; Governor: Chailey Comprehensive Sch., 1972–86; Ringmer Comprehensive Sch., 1979–85; Newick Primary Sch., 1977–85; Chailey Heritage Sch. and Hosp., 1982–88. Founder: Newick Playgp; Newick Youth Club. FRSA 1989. DL East Sussex, 1986; JP East Sussex, 1973–85. DUniv Surrey, 1990. *Recreation:* other people's gardens. *Address:* Vuggles Farm, Newick, Lewes, Sussex. *T:* Barcombe (0273) 400453. *Clubs:* New Cavendish, Royal Society of Medicine.

CUMBRAE (Cathedral of the Isles), Provost of; *see* McCubbin, Very Rev. D.

CUMING, Frederick George Rees, RA 1974 (ARA 1969); ARCA 1954; NDD 1948; NEAC 1960; painter; *b* 16 Feb. 1930; *m* Audrey Lee Cuming; one *s* one *d. Educ:* University School, Bexley Heath; Sidcup Art School; Royal College of Art; travelling schol., Italy. Exhbns in Redfern, Walker, New Grafton, Thackeray, Fieldborne Galleries; Group shows at NEAC, RA, Schools' Exhbn, John Moores London Group; One Man exhbns at Thackeray Gall., galls in Chichester, Lewes, Eastbourne, Guildford, Durham, Chester, Folkstone, Canterbury, New York; works in collections: Dept. of Envt; Treasury; Chantrey Bequest; RA; Kendal Mus.; Scunthorpe Mus.; Bradford; Carlisle; Nat. Mus. of Wales; Brighton and Hove Mus.; Maidstone Mus.; Towner Gall., Eastbourne; Monte Carlo Mus.; St John's Coll., Oxford; Worcester Coll., Oxford; Faringdon Trust, Oxon; works in galls in Canada, France, Germany, Greece, Holland. *Address:* The Gables, Iden, near Rye, E Sussex. *T:* Iden (073275) 322.

CUMMING; *see* Gordon Cumming and Gordon-Cumming.

CUMMING, (John) Alan, CBE 1983; CA, FCBSI, CBIM; Director, Woolwich (formerly Woolwich Equitable) Building Society, since 1978; *b* 6 March 1932; *s* of John Cumming; *m* 1958, Isobel Beaumont Sked; three *s. Educ:* George Watson's Coll., Edinburgh. CA 1956; FCBSI 1971; CBIM (FBIM 1976). Woolwich Equitable Building Society, 1958–: Gen. Manager's Asst, 1965; Asst Gen. Man., 1967; Chief Exec., 1969–86; Exec. Vice-Chm., 1986–91. Chairman: Woolwich Homes, 1989–; URC Trust, 1978–; Cavendish Wates 1st Assured, 1988–; Cavendish Wates 3rd Assured, 1989–; Thamesmead Town, 1990–; Director: Value and Income Trust, 1986–; Woolwich (Europe), 1990–. Chairman: Metrop. Assoc. of Bldg Socs., 1977–78; Bldg Socs Assoc., 1981–83 (Mem. Council, 1970–90); President: Bldg Socs Inst., 1973–74; Europ. Community Mortgage Fedn, 1984–87; Internat. Union of Housing Finance Inst., 1990–. *Recreations:* golf, bridge. *Address:* 8 Prince Consort Drive, Chislehurst, Kent BR7 5SB. *T:* 081–467 8382. *Club:* Caledonian.

CUMMING, Valerie Lynn, AMA; Deputy Director, Museum of London, since 1988; *b* 11 Oct. 1946; *d* of John Gunson Carter and Edna Ruth Carter (*née* Willis); *m* 1972, John Lawrence Cumming. *Educ:* Abbey Sch., Reading; Univ. of Leicester (BA); Courtauld Inst. of Art (Courtauld Cert. in History of Dress). Admin. trainee, Univ. of Surrey, 1968–69; Asst, Chertsey Mus., 1971–73; Res. Asst, 1973–75, Sen. Asst Keeper, 1975–78, Mus. of London; Curator, Court Dress Collection, Kensington Palace, 1978–81; Asst Dir, Mus. of London, 1981–88. Trustee, Olive Matthews Collection, Chertsey Mus., Surrey, 1983–. *Publications:* Exploring Costume History 1500–1900, 1981; Gloves, 1982; (contrib.) Tradescant's Rarities, 1983; A Visual History of Costume: the Seventeenth Century, 1984; (with Aileen Ribeiro) The Visual History of Costume, 1989; Royal Dress, 1989; (contrib.) The Late King's Goods, 1989. *Recreations:* gardening, watching cricket. *Address:* Museum of London, London Wall, EC2Y 5HN. *T:* 071–600 3699.

CUMMING-BRUCE, Rt. Hon. Sir (James) Roualeyn Hovell-Thurlow-, PC 1977; Kt 1964; MA; a Lord Justice of Appeal, 1977–85; *b* 9 March 1912; *s* of 6th Baron Thurlow and Grace Catherine, *d* of Rev. Henry Trotter; *m* 1955, Lady (Anne) Sarah Alethea Marjorie Savile (*d* 1991), *d* of 6th Earl of Mexborough; two *s* one *d. Educ:* Shrewsbury; Magdalene Coll., Cambridge (Hon. Fellow, 1977). Barrister, Middle Temple, 1937 (Harmsworth Scholar); Master of the Bench, 1959; Treasurer, 1975. Served War of 1939–45 (Lt-Col RA). Chancellor of Diocese of Ripon, 1954–57; Recorder of Doncaster, 1957–58; Recorder of York, 1958–61; Junior Counsel to the Treasury (Common Law), 1959–64; Judge of the High Court, Family Div. (formerly Probate, Divorce and Admiralty Div.), 1964–77; Judge of the Restrictive Practices Court, 1968; Presiding Judge, North Eastern Circuit, 1971–74. *Address:* 1 Mulberry Walk, Chelsea, SW3. *T:* 071–352 5754. *Clubs:* Pratt's, United Oxford & Cambridge University.
See also Sir A. J. Gore-Booth, Bt, Baron Thurlow.

CUMMINGS, Constance, CBE 1974; actress; *b* Seattle, USA; *d* of Kate Cummings and Dallas Vernon Halverstadt; *m* 1933, Benn Wolfe Levy, MBE (*d* 1973); one *s* one *d. Educ:* St Nicholas Girls Sch., Seattle, Washington, USA. Began stage work, 1932; since then has appeared in radio, television, films and theatre; joined National Theatre Co., 1971. Member: Arts Council, 1965–71; Council, English Stage Co., 1978–; Chm., Young People's Theatre Panel, 1966–70. *Plays include:* Goodbye, Mr Chips, 1938; The Taming of the Shrew, 1938; The Good Natured Man, 1939; St Joan, 1939; Romeo and Juliet, 1939; The Petrified Forest, 1942; Return to Tyassi, 1952; Lysistrata, 1957; The Rape of the Belt, 1957; JB, 1961; Who's Afraid of Virginia Woolf?, 1964; Justice is a Woman, 1966; Fallen Angels, 1967; A Delicate Balance, 1969; Hamlet, 1969; Children, 1974; Stripwell, 1975; All Over, 1976; Wings, 1978 (televised, USA, 1982); Hay Fever, 1980; The Chalk Garden, NY, 1982; Mrs Warren's Profession, Vienna, 1982; Eve, 1984; The Glass Menagerie, USA, then London, 1985; Crown Matrimonial, 1988; Tête à Tête, USA, 1989; *National Theatre:* Coriolanus, Amphitryon 38, 1971; A Long Day's Journey into Night, 1972; The Cherry Orchard, The Bacchae, 1973; The Circle, 1974–75. Fanny Kemble at Home, one woman show, 1986; has appeared Albert Hall, performing with orchestra Peter and the Wolf and Honegger's Jeanne d'Arc au Bûcher. *Recreations:* anthropology and music. *Address:* 68 Old Church Street, SW3. *T:* 071–352 0437.

CUMMINGS, John Scott; MP (Lab) Easington, since 1987; *b* 6 July 1943; *s* of George Scott Cummings and Mary (*née* Cain); unmarried. *Educ:* Murton Council Infants, Jun. and Sen. Schs; Easington Technical Coll. Colliery apprentice electrician, 1958–63, colliery electrician, 1963–87. Vice-Chm., Coalfields Community Campaign, 1985–87; Member: Northumbrian Water Authority, 1977–83; Aycliffe and Peterlee Develt Corp., 1980–87; Easington RDC, 1970–73; Easington DC, 1973–87 (Chm., 1975–76; Leader, 1979–87). *Recreations:* Jack Russell terriers, walking, travel. *Address:* 76 Toft Crescent, Murton, Seaham, Co. Durham SR7 9EB. *T:* 091–526 1142; House of Commons, SW1A 0AA. *Clubs:* Murton Victoria, Democratic, Ex-Servicesman's (Murton); Peterlee Labour; Thornley Catholic.

CUMMINS, Frank; Examinations Liaison Officer, Sandwell Local Education Authority, 1987–89; Headmaster, Thomas Telford High School, Sandwell, West Midlands, 1973–87; *b* 20 Jan. 1924; *s* of Archibald Ernest and Ruth Elizabeth Cummins; *m* 1st, 1943, Joyce Swale (marr. diss.); three *s*; 2nd, 1973, Brenda Valerie Swift. *Educ:* Whitgift Middle Sch., Croydon; London School of Economics and Institute of Education, London Univ. Served Royal Signals, 1943–46. Assistant Teacher, Shireland Boys' Sch., Smethwick, 1949; Dep. Headmaster, 1956, Headmaster, 1961, Sandwell Boys' Sch., Smethwick. W Midlands Examinations Board: Chm., Exams Cttee, 1983–86 (Vice-Chm., 1980–83); Vice-Chm., Council, 1986–89; Chm., Bd, 1989–; Mem. Jt Management Cttee, Midland Examining Gp for GCSE, 1985– (Chm., Council, 1989–). Chairman, Community Relations Councils: Warley, 1969, Sandwell, 1974; part-time Commissioner for Racial Equality, 1977–82; Chm., Schools Council Steering Group on Educn in a Multi-Cultural Soc., 1981–83. *Recreations:* cooking, camping, walking, theatre, City of Birmingham Symphony Orchestra. *Address:* 21 Green Street, Smethwick, Warley, West Midlands B67 7EB. *T:* 021–558 8484.

CUNEO, Terence Tenison, OBE 1987; portrait and figure painter, ceremonial, military and engineering subjects; *b* 1 Nov. 1907; *s* of Cyrus Cuneo and Nell Marion Tenison; *m* 1934, Catherine Mayfield Monro (*d* 1979), *yr d* of Major E. G. Monro, CBE; one *d. Educ:* Sutton Valence Sch.; Chelsea and Slade. Served War of 1939–45: RE, and as War Artist; special propaganda paintings for Min. of Information, Political Intelligence Dept of FO, and War Artists Advisory Cttee; representative of Illustrated London News, France, 1940. Royal Glasgow Inst. of Fine Arts; Pres. of Industrial Painters Group; Exhibitor, RA, RP, ROI Paris Salon (Hon. Mention, 1957). Has painted extensively in North Africa, South Africa, Rhodesia, Canada, USA, Ethiopia and Far East; one-man exhibition, Underground Activities in Occupied Europe, 1941; one-man exhibitions: RWS Galleries, London, 1954 and 1958; Sladmore Gall., 1971, 1972, 1974; Mall Galls, 1988. Best known works include: Meml Paintings of El Alamein and The Royal Engineers, King George VI at The Royal Artillery Mess, Woolwich, King George VI and Queen Elizabeth at The Middle Temple Banquet, 1950; Meml Painting of The Rifle Brigade, 1951; Visit to Lloyd's of Queen Elizabeth II with the Duke of Edinburgh to lay Foundation Stone of Lloyd's New Building, 1952; Queen's Coronation Luncheon, Guildhall, The Duke of Edinburgh at Cambridge, 1953; Portraits of Viscount Allendale, KG, as Canopy Bearer to Her Majesty, 1954; Coronation of Queen Elizabeth II in Westminster Abbey (presented to the Queen by HM's Lieuts of Counties), 1955; Queen's State Visit to Denmark, Engineering Mural in Science Museum, 1957; Queen Elizabeth II at RCOG, 1960; Queen Elizabeth II at Guildhall Banquet after Indian Tour, 1961; Equestrian Portrait of HM the Queen as Col-in-Chief, Grenadier Guards, 1963; Garter Ceremony, 1964; Commonwealth Prime

Ministers' Banquet, Guildhall, 1969; first official portraits of Rt Hon. Edward Heath, 1971, of Field Marshal Viscount Montgomery of Alamein, 1972; HM the Queen as Patron of Kennel Club, 1975; King Hussein of Jordan, 1980; Col H. Jones, VC, 1984; 40th Anniversary of D-Day, 1984. Set of stamps commemorating the 150th anniv. of GWR. *Publications:* (autobiog.) The Mouse and his Master, 1977; The Railway Painting of Terence Cuneo, 1984; Terence Cuneo, Railway Painter of the Century, 1990; articles in the The Studio, The Artist. *Recreations:* writing, sketching, travel, riding. *T:* 081–398 1986. *Club:* Junior Carlton.

CUNINGHAME, Sir John Christopher Foggo M.; *see* Montgomery Cuninghame, Sir J. C. F.

CUNINGHAME, Sir William Henry F.; *see* Fairlie-Cuninghame.

CUNLIFFE, family name of **Baron Cunliffe.**

CUNLIFFE, 3rd Baron *cr* 1914, of Headley; **Roger Cunliffe,** RIBA; MBIM; consulting architect; *b* 12 Jan. 1932; *s* of 2nd Baron and Joan Catherine Lubbock (*d* 1980); *S* father, 1963; *m* 1957, Clemency Ann Hoare; two *s* one *d*. *Educ:* Eton; Trinity Coll., Cambridge (MA); Architectural Association (AA Dipl.); Open Univ. With various architectural firms in UK and USA, 1957–65; Associate, Robert Matthew, Johnson-Marshall & Partners, 1966–69; Dir, Architectural Assoc., 1969–71; Partner, SCP, 1973–78; own practice as architectural, planning and management consultant, 1977–; Dir, Exhibition Consultants Ltd, 1981–; Member: Urban Motorways Cttee, 1969–72; Council, British Consultants Bureau, 1986–. Governor: Lancing Coll., 1967–86; Goldsmiths' Coll., 1972–78. Mem. Ct, Goldsmiths' Co., 1986–. *Publications:* (with Leonard Manasseh) Office Buildings, 1962; contrib. various professional jls. *Recreations:* photography, taxonomy, planting trees. *Heir:* *s* Hon. Henry Cunliffe, *b* 9 March 1962. *Address:* The Broadhurst, Brandeston, Woodbridge, Suffolk IP13 7AG.

CUNLIFFE, Prof. Barrington Windsor, FBA 1979; FSA; Professor of European Archaeology, Oxford University, and Fellow of Keble College, since 1972; *b* 10 Dec. 1939. *Educ:* Portsmouth; St John's Coll., Cambridge (MA, PhD, LittD). Lecturer, Univ. of Bristol, 1963–66; Prof. of Archæology, Univ. of Southampton, 1966–72. O'Donnell Lectr in Celtic Studies, Oxford Univ., 1983–84. Member: Ancient Monuments Bd for England, 1976–84; Historic Bldgs and Monuments Commn for England, 1987– (Mem., Ancient Monuments Adv. Cttee, 1984–); President: Council for British Archaeology, 1976–79; Soc. of Antiquaries, 1991– (Vice-Pres., 1982–86). Hon. DLitt Sussex, 1983; Hon. DSc Bath, 1984. *Publications:* Fishbourne, a Roman Palace and its Garden, 1971; Roman Bath Discovered, 1971, rev. edn 1984; The Cradle of England, 1972; The Making of the English, 1973; The Regni, 1973; Iron Age Communities in Britain, 1974; Rome and the Barbarians, 1975; Hengistbury Head, 1978; Rome and her Empire, 1978; The Celtic World, 1979; Danebury: the anatomy of an Iron Age hillfort, 1984; The City of Bath, 1986; Greeks Romans and Barbarians, 1988; contribs to several major excavation reports and articles to Soc. of Antiquaries, and in other learned jls. *Recreation:* mild self-indulgence. *Address:* Institute of Archaeology, 36 Beaumont Street, Oxford.

CUNLIFFE, His Honour Christopher Joseph; a Circuit Judge (formerly County Court Judge), 1966–82; *b* 28 Feb. 1916; *s* of Lt-Col E. N. Cunliffe, OBE, RAMC, Buckingham Crescent, Manchester, and Harriet Cunliffe (*née* Clegg); *m* 1942, Margaret Hamer Barber; two *d*. *Educ:* Rugby Sch.; Trinity Hall, Cambridge. BA 1937. Called to the Bar, Lincoln's Inn, 1938. Legal Cadet, Br. North Borneo Civil Service. 1939–40. Served RAFVR, 1941–46; Intelligence, Judge Advocate General's Branch. Practised on Northern Circuit, 1946; Dep. Coroner, City of Liverpool, 1953; Chairman: National Insurance Tribunal, Bootle, 1956–; Mental Health Review Tribunal for SW Lancs and W Ches, 1961–. *Recreations:* golf, gardening. *Address:* Field House, Compton, W Sussex PO18 9HE. *T:* Compton (0705) 631270.

CUNLIFFE, Sir David Ellis, 9th Bt *cr* 1759; salesman; *b* 29 Oct. 1957; *s* of Sir Cyril Henley Cunliffe, 8th Bt and of Eileen Lady Cunliffe, *d* of Frederick William and Nora Anne Parkins; *S* father, 1969; *m* 1983, Linda Carol, *d* of John Sidney and Ella Mary Batchelor; two *d*. *Educ:* St Albans Grammar School. *Heir:* *b* Andrew Mark Cunliffe [*b* 17 April 1959; *m* 1980, Janice Elizabeth, *d* of Ronald William Kyle; one *s* two *d*]. *Address:* Sunnyside, Burnthouse Lane, Needham, near Harleston, Norfolk.

CUNLIFFE, Lawrence Francis; MP (Lab) Leigh, since 1979; *b* 25 March 1929; *m* 1950, Winifred (marr. diss. 1985), *d* of William Haslem; three *s* two *d*. *Educ:* St Edmund's RC Sch., Worsley, Manchester. Engr, NCB, 1949–79. Member, Farnworth Borough Council, 1960–74, Bolton MDC, 1974–79; contested (Lab) Rochdale, Oct. 1972 and Feb. 1974. JP 1967–79. *Address:* House of Commons, SW1A 0AA.

CUNLIFFE, Peter Whalley, CBE 1980; Chairman: Pharmaceuticals Division, Imperial Chemical Industries PLC, 1976–87; British Pharma Group, 1987–90; *b* 29 Oct. 1926; *s* of Fred Cunliffe and Lillie Whalley; *m* 1951, Alice Thérèse Emma Brunel; one *d*. *Educ:* Queen Elizabeth's Grammar Sch., Blackburn; Trinity Hall, Cambridge (Scholar; BA 1st Class Hons, 1948). Joined ICI Ltd, Pharmaceuticals Div., 1950; Services Dir, 1968; Overseas Dir, 1970; Dep. Chm., 1971. Pres., Assoc. of British Pharmaceutical Industry, 1981–83; Member: Council, Internat. Fedn of Pharmaceutical Manufrs Assoc., 1979–87 (Vice Pres., 1982–84, Pres. 1984–86); Exec. Cttee, European Fedn of Pharmaceutical Industries Assocs, 1982–85. FRSA 1981. *Recreations:* reading, walking. *Address:* 10 Sandringham Court, Alderley Road, Wilmslow, Cheshire SK9 1PW.

CUNLIFFE, Stella Vivian; consultant statistician; *b* 12 Jan. 1917; *d* of Percy Cunliffe and Edith Blanche Wellwood Cunliffe. *Educ:* privately, then Parsons Mead, Ashtead; London School of Economics (BScEcon). Danish Bacon Co, 1939–44; Voluntary Relief Work in Europe, 1945–47; Arthur Guinness Son and Co. Ltd, 1947–70; Head of Research Unit, Home Office, 1970–72; Dir of Statistics, Home Office, 1972–77. Statistical Adviser to Cttee of Enquiry into Engineering Profession, 1978–80. Pres., Royal Statistical Soc., 1975–77. *Recreations:* work with youth organisations; gardening; prison after-care. *Address:* 69 Harriotts Lane, Ashtead, Surrey. *T:* Ashtead (0372) 272343.

CUNLIFFE, His Honour Thomas Alfred; a Circuit Judge (formerly County Court Judge), 1963–75; *b* 9 March 1905; *s* of Thomas and Elizabeth Cunliffe, Preston; *m* 1938, Constance Isabella Carden; one *s* one *d*. *Educ:* Lancaster Royal Grammar Sch.; Sidney Sussex Coll., Cambridge (Classical Scholar). Inner Temple: Profumo Prize, 1926; Paul Methven Prize, 1926. Called to the Bar, Inner Temple, 1927; Yarborough Anderson Scholar, 1927. Practised Northern Circuit, 1927–63; Dep. Chm., Lancs County Quarter Sessions, 1961–63; Recorder, Barrow-in-Furness, 1962–63. RAFVR (Squadron Leader), 1940–45. *Recreation:* music. *Address:* 30 Red Dale, Dale Avenue, Heswall, Wirrall, Merseyside L60 7TA. *T:* 051–342 3949.

CUNLIFFE-LISTER, family name of **Baroness Masham of Ilton** and **Earl of Swinton.**

CUNLIFFE-OWEN, Sir Hugo Dudley, 3rd Bt *cr* 1920, of Bray; *b* 16 May 1966; *s* of Sir Dudley Herbert Cunliffe-Owen, 2nd Bt, and of Jean, *o d* of late Surg.-Comdr A. N. Forsyth, RN; *S* father, 1983. *Heir:* none.

CUNNANE, Most Rev. Joseph; Archbishop of Tuam, (RC), 1969–87, retired; *b* 5 Oct. 1913; *s* of William and Margaret Cunnane, Knock, Co. Mayo. *Educ:* St Jarlath's Coll., Tuam; St Patrick's Coll., Maynooth. BA 1st Hons, Ancient Classics, 1935; DD 1941; Higher Dip. Educn 1941. Priest, 1939. Prof. of Irish, St Jarlath's Coll., 1941–57; Curate, Balla, Co. Mayo, 1957–67; Curate, Clifden, Co. Galway, 1967–69. Cross of Chaplain Conventual, SMO Malta, 1970. *Publications:* Vatican II on Priests, 1967; contribs to Irish Ecclesiastical Record, Furrow, Doctrine and Life, Studies in Pastoral Liturgy, etc. *Address:* St Jarlath's Presbytery, Knock, Co. Mayo, Ireland.

CUNNINGHAM, Alexander Alan; Executive Vice President, General Motors, 1984–86, retired; *b* Bulgaria, 7 Jan. 1926; naturalised citizen, US; *m* 1976, Mary Helen; one *s* three *d* of former marr. *Educ:* General Motors Inst., Michigan. BSc (Industrial Engrg) 1951. Served War of 1939–45, navigation electronics radar specialist, RAF. General Motors: Jun. Process Engr, Frigidaire Div., 1951; Asst to Frigidaire Man., NY, Gen. Motors Overseas Ops, 1952; Prodn Planning Technician for Adam Opel AG, Germany, 1953; Exec. Asst to Man. Dir, GM Ltd, London, 1956; Master Mechanic, Gen. Motors do Brasil, 1957, Works Man. 1958; Works Man., Gen. Motors Argentina SA, 1962; Man. Dir, Gen. Motors do Brasil, 1963; Man., Adam Opel's Bochum plant, 1964; Asst Gen. Manufrg Man., Adam Opel AG, 1966, Gen. Manufrg Man. 1969; Man. Dir, Adam Opel AG, 1970; Gen. Dir, European Organisations, Gen. Motors Overseas Corp., 1974–76; Vice Pres., Group Exec. Overseas, 1978; Group Exec., Body Assembly, 1980. Exec. Vice-Pres., N American Cars, 1982. Trustee, Detroit SO, 1983–. *Address:* 70–671 Orville Circle, Rancho Mirage, Calif 92270, USA. *T:* 619/328–8671; (summer) 16472 Malden Circle, Huntington Beach, Calif 92649, USA. *Clubs:* Thunderbird Country, Mission Hills Country (Rancho Mirage); Center (Orange County).

CUNNINGHAM, Sir Charles (Craik), GCB 1974 (KCB 1961; CB 1946); KBE 1952; CVO 1941; *b* Dundee, 7 May 1906; *s* of late Richard Yule Cunningham, Abergeldie, Kirriemuir, and Isabella Craik; *m* 1934, Edith Louisa Webster (*d* 1990); two *d*. *Educ:* Harris Acad., Dundee; University of St Andrews. Entered Scottish Office, 1929; Private Sec. to Parliamentary Under Sec. of State for Scotland, 1933–34; Private Sec. to Sec. of State for Scotland, 1935–39; Asst Sec., Scottish Home Dept, 1939–41; Principal Asst Sec., 1941–42; Dep. Sec., 1942–47; Sec., 1948–57; Permanent Under-Sec. of State, Home Office, 1957–66; Dep. Chm., UKAEA, 1966–71; Chm., Radiochemical Centre Ltd, 1971–74. Dir, Securicor Ltd, 1971–81. Chm., Uganda Resettlement Bd, 1972–73. Mem., Nat. Radiological Protection Bd, 1971–74. Hon. LLD St Andrews, 1960. *Address:* 25 Regent Terrace, Edinburgh EH7 5BS. *T:* 031–556 9614. *Clubs:* Reform; New (Edinburgh).

CUNNINGHAM, David, CB 1983; Solicitor to the Secretary of State for Scotland, 1980–84; *b* 26 Feb. 1924; *s* of Robert Cunningham and Elizabeth (*née* Shields); *m* 1955, Ruth Branwell Crawford; one *s* two *d*. *Educ:* High School of Glasgow; Univ. of Glasgow (MA, LLB). Served war, 1942–47: commnd, Cameronians, 1943; Intelligence Corps (Captain), and Control Commission for Germany, 1945–47. Admitted Solicitor, 1951; entered Office of Solicitor to Secretary of State for Scotland as Legal Asst, 1954; Sen. Legal Asst, 1960; Asst Solicitor, 1966; Cabinet Office Constitution Unit, 1975–77; Dep. Solicitor, 1978–80. *Recreations:* hill walking, reading, theatre, motor-cars. *Address:* The Green Gates, Innerleithen, Peeblesshire, Scotland EH44 6NH. *T:* Innerleithen (0896) 830436.

CUNNINGHAM, George, BA, BSc; Chief Executive, Library Association, since 1984; *b* 10 June 1931; *s* of Harry Jackson Cunningham and Christina Cunningham, Dunfermline; *m* 1957, Mavis Walton; one *s* one *d*. *Educ:* Univs of Manchester and London. Nat. Service in Royal Artillery (2nd Lieut), 1954–56; on staff of Commonwealth Relations Office, 1956–63; 2nd Sec., British High Commn, Ottawa, 1958–60; Commonwealth Officer of Labour Party, 1963–66; Min. of Overseas Development, 1966–69. MP South West Islington, 1970–74, Islington South and Finsbury, 1974–83 (Lab, 1970–81, Ind, 1981–82, SDP, 1982–83). Opposition front bench spokesman (Lab) on home affairs, 1979–81. Contested (SDP) Islington South and Finsbury, 1983, 1987. Mem., Parlt of European Community, 1978–79. *Publications:* (Fabian pamphlet) Rhodesia, the Last Chance, 1966; (ed) Britain and the World in the Seventies, 1970; The Management of Aid Agencies, 1974; Careers in Politics, 1984. *Address:* 28 Manor Gardens, Hampton, Middlesex. *T:* 081–979 6221.

CUNNINGHAM, Prof. George John, MBE 1945; Professor and Chairman, Department of Academic Pathology, Virginia Commonwealth University, Richmond, 1974–77, now Emeritus Professor; Conservator of Pathological Collection, Royal College of Surgeons; Consultant Pathologist to South East and South West Regional Health Authorities; *b* 7 Sept. 1906; *s* of George S. Cunningham and Blanche A. Harvey; *m* 1957, Patricia Champion, Brisbane, Australia. *Educ:* Royal Belfast Academical Institution; Dean Close Sch., Cheltenham; St Bartholomew's Hospital Medical Coll. MRCS, LRCP, 1931; MB, BS London, 1933; MD London, 1937; FRCPath 1964. Asst Pathologist, Royal Sussex County Hosp., Brighton, 1934–42. War Service, RAMC, Middle East and Italy (temp. Lt-Col). Senior Lectr in Pathology, St Bartholomew's Hosp., London, 1946–55; Sir William Collins Prof. of Pathology, Univ. of London, at RCS, 1955–68; Prof. of Pathology, Medical Coll. of Virginia, and Chief Laboratory Service, McGuire VA Hosp., Richmond, 1968–74. Dorothy Temple Cross Travelling Fellow in America, 1951–52; Vis. Prof., New York State Univ., 1961; Vis. Prof., Cairo Univ., 1963. Past Pres., Assoc. Clin. Path., Internat. Acad. of Pathology, Quekett Microscopical Club. Freeman, City of London. *Publications:* chap. on Gen. Pathology of Malignant Tumours in Cancer, Vol. 2, 1957; chap. on Microradiography, in Tools of Biological Research, Vol. 2, 1960; and several articles on Pathology, in medical press. *Recreation:* golf. *Address:* 57 Albany Road, St Leonard's-on-Sea, E Sussex TN38 0LJ. *Clubs:* National Liberal; Royal Blackheath Golf.

CUNNINGHAM, Lt-Gen. Sir Hugh (Patrick), KBE 1975 (OBE 1966); Chairman: LL Consultants Ltd, 1984–89; TREND Group, 1986–90; *b* 4 Nov. 1921; *s* of late Sir Charles Banks Cunningham, CSI; *m* 1955, Jill, *d* of J. S. Jeffrey, East Knoyle; two *s* two *d*. *Educ:* Charterhouse. 2nd Lieut, RE, 1942; served War of 1939–45, India, New Guinea, Burma; Greece, 1950–51; Egypt, 1951–53; Instructor, Sch. of Infantry, 1955–57, RMA Sandhurst, 1957–60; Cameroons, 1960–61; CRE 3 Div., Cyprus and Aden, 1963–66; comd 11 Engr Bde, BAOR, 1967–69; comd Mons OCS, 1969–70; Nat. Defence Coll., Canada, 1970–71; GOC SW District, 1971–74; ACGS (OR), 1974–75; DCDS (OR), 1976–78, retired. Lieutenant of Tower of London, 1983–86. Col, Queen's Gurkha Engineers (formerly Gurkha Engrs), 1976–81; Col Comdt, RE, 1976–81; Col, Bristol Univ. OTC, 1977–87. Director: Fairey Holdings Ltd, 1978–86; Fairey Engineering, 1981–86; MEL, 1982–89; TREND Communications Ltd, 1984–86. Pres., Old Carthusian Soc., 1982–87. Master, Glass Sellers' Co., 1981. Chm. of Governors, Port Regis School, 1982–; Gov., Suttons Hosp. in Charterhouse, 1984–. *Recreations:* bird-watching, opera, golf. *Address:* Brickyard

Farm, East Knoyle, Salisbury, Wilts SP3 6BP. *T:* East Knoyle (0747) 830281; 607 Duncan House, Dolphin Square, SW1. *T:* 071–821 7960. *Clubs:* Army and Navy, MCC.

CUNNINGHAM, Group Captain John, CBE 1963 (OBE 1951); DSO 1941; (Bars 1942, 1944); DFC 1941 (Bar); AE 1941; DL; Executive Director, British Aerospace, Hatfield, 1978–80; *b* 27 July 1917; *s* of late A. G. Cunningham and of E. M. Cunningham. *Educ:* Whitgift. Apprenticed to De Havilland Aircraft Co., Hatfield, 1935–38; employed, 1938–Aug. 1939, with De Havillands, Light Aircraft Development and Test Flying. Called up Aug. 1939; joined AAF, 1935; commanded 604 Sqdn, 1941–42; Staff job, 1942–43; commanded 85 Sqdn, 1943–44 (DSO and two bars, DFC and bar); Group Capt. Night Operations HQ 11 Group, 1944. Chief Test Pilot, de Havilland Aircraft Co., 1946–77. Exec. Dir, Hawker Siddeley Aviation, 1963–77. International Record Flight, 16 Oct. 1957: London to Khartoum direct; distance 3,064 statute miles in 5 hrs 51 mins, by Comet 3; average speed 523 statute mph. Derry and Richards Memorial Medal, GAPAN, 1965; Segrave Trophy, 1979; Air League Founders' Medal, 1979. DL: Middx, 1948; Greater London, 1965. Russian Order of Patriotic War 1st cl., 1944; USA Silver Star, 1945. *Address:* Canley, Kinsbourne Green, Harpenden, Herts AL5 3PE.

CUNNINGHAM, Dr John A., (Jack); MP (Lab) Copeland, since 1983 (Whitehaven, Cumbria, 1970–83); *b* 4 Aug. 1939; *s* of Andrew Cunningham; *m* 1964, Maureen; one *s* two *d*. *Educ:* Jarrow Grammar Sch.; Bede Coll., Durham Univ. Hons Chemistry, 1962; PhD Chemistry, 1966. Formerly: Research Fellow in Chemistry, Durham Univ.; School Teacher; Trades Union Officer. PPS to Rt Hon. James Callaghan, 1972–76; Parly Under-Sec. of State, Dept of Energy, 1976–79; Opposition Spokesman on Industry, 1979–83; elected to Shadow Cabinet, 1983; spokesman on the Environment, 1983–89; Shadow Leader, H of C, 1989–. *Recreations:* fell walking, fly-fishing, gardening, classical and folk music, reading, listening to other people's opinions. *Address:* House of Commons, SW1A 0AA.

CUNNINGHAM, Merce; Artistic Director, Merce Cunningham Dance Company, since 1953; *b* 18 April 1919; *s* of Clifford D. Cunningham. *Educ:* Cornish Inst. of Allied Arts, Seattle, Washington. Martha Graham Dance Co., 1939–45; 1st solo concert, NY, 1944; choreographed: The Seasons, for Ballet Society (later NY City Ballet), 1947; Un Jour ou deux, for Ballet of Paris Opéra, 1973; more than 100 works for own company; other works revived for NY City Ballet, American Ballet Theatre, Rambert Dance Co. (formerly Ballet Rambert), Théâtre du Silence, France, Ohio Ballet, Boston Ballet, Pacific Northwest Ballet. Hon. Mem., Amer. Acad. and Inst. of Arts and Letters, 1984. DLitt Univ. of Illinois, 1972. Samuel H. Scripps American Dance Festival Award for lifetime contribs to dance, 1982; Award of Honor for Arts and Culture, NY, 1983; MacArthur Award, 1985; Kennedy Center Honors, 1985; Laurence Olivier Award, 1985; Meadows Award for excellence in the arts, Meadows Sch. of Arts, Southern Methodist Univ., Dallas, 1987; Nat. Medal of Arts, USA, 1989. Comdr, Order of Arts and Letters, France, 1982; Chevalier de la Légion d'Honneur, 1989. *Publications:* Changes: notes on choreography (ed Frances Starr), 1968; Le Danseur et la danse: entretiens avec Jacqueline Lesschaeve, 1980, English edn The Dancer and the Dance, 1985; articles in 7 Arts, trans/formation, TriQuarterly. *Address:* 463 West Street, New York, NY 10014, USA. *T:* 212 255 8240.

CUNNINGHAM, Robert Kerr, CMG 1983; PhD; FIBiol; FRSC; Chief Natural Resources Adviser, Overseas Development Administration, 1976–83, and Head of Natural Resources Department, 1980–83, retired; *b* 7 June 1923; *s* of John Simpson Cunningham and Agnes Stewart Cunningham; *m* 1947, Jean Sinclair (*née* Brown); one *s* one *d*. *Educ:* Bathgate Acad., Scotland; Edinburgh Univ. (BSc); London Univ. (PhD). FRIC 1964. Served War, RAF, 1942–46. Science Teacher, W Lothian County Educn Cttee, 1947–50; Science Lectr and Chemist, Govt of Bahamas, 1950–55; Colonial Res. Fellowship, Rothamsted Experimental Stn, 1955–56; Res. Off., W African Cocoa Res. Inst., Gold Coast and Ghana, 1956–60; Principal Scientific Off., Rothamsted Experimtl Stn, 1960–64; Prof. of Chemistry and Soil Science, Univ. of WI, Trinidad, 1964–67; Adviser on Res. and Nat. Resources, Min. of Overseas Develt, 1967–76. *Publications:* many scientific papers dealing mainly with soil chem. and plant nutrition in jls; several reports on organisation of R&D in developing countries; (co-author) reports on Brit. and internat. aid in natural resources field. *Recreations:* walking, reading, golf. *Address:* 19 Coleridge Court, Milton Road, Harpenden, Herts AL5 5LD. *T:* Harpenden (0582) 460203. *Club:* Royal Air Force.

CUNNINGHAM-JARDINE, Ronald Charles; Vice Lord-Lieutenant, Dumfries and Galloway Region, districts of Nithsdale, Annandale and Eskdale, since 1990; *b* 19 Sept. 1931; *s* of Charles Frederick Cunningham and Dorothy Agnes Jessie Jardine; *m* 1959, Constance Mary Teresa Inglis; one *s* one *d*. *Educ:* Ludgrove; Eton College; RMA Sandhurst. Royal Scots Greys, 1950–58; Edinburgh Agricultural College, 1959–60; farming, 1960–. *Recreations:* fishing, hunting, coursing, shooting. *Address:* Fourmerkland, Lockerbie, Dumfriesshire DG11 1EH. *T:* Lochmaben (0387) 810226. *Clubs:* White's; Muthaiga (Kenya).

CUNYNGHAME, Sir Andrew (David Francis), 12th Bt *cr* 1702; FCA; *b* 25 Dec. 1942; *s* of Sir (Henry) David St Leger Brooke Selwyn Cunynghame, 11th Bt, and of Hon. Pamela Margaret Stanley (*d* 1991), *d* of 5th Lord Stanley of Alderley; *S* father, 1978; *m* 1st, 1972, Harriet Ann, *d* of C. T. Dupont, Montreal; two *d*; 2nd, 1989, Isabella King, *d* of late Edward Everett Watts, Jr and of Isabella Hardy Watts. *Educ:* Eton. *Heir:* *b* John Philip Henry Michael Selwyn Cunynghame [*b* 9 Sept. 1944; *m* 1981, Marjatta, *d* of Martti Markus; one *s* one *d*]. *Address:* 69 Hillgate Place, W8. *Club:* Brooks's.

CUOMO, Mario Matthew; Governor of New York State, since 1983; lawyer; Democrat; *b* 15 June 1932; *s* of Andrea and Immaculata Cuomo; *m* 1954, Matilda M. Raffa; two *s* three *d*. *Educ:* St John's Coll., NY (Latin Amer. Studies, English, Philosophy; BA 1953); St John's Univ. (LLB 1956). Admitted to NY Bar, 1956, US Supreme Court, 1960; Asst to Judge A. P. Burke, NY State Court of Appeals, 1956–58; joined Corner, Weisbrod, Froeb & Charles (later Corner, Finn, Cuomo & Charles), 1958, Partner, 1963–75; Prof., St John's Univ. Law Sch., 1963–73; Sec. of State for NY, 1975–78 (Chm., NY Urban & Rural Affairs, Adv. Council on Disabled; 1st NY Ombudsman); Lt-Governor, NY, 1979–82. *Publications:* The Forest Hills Controversy: a report and comment, 1972; Forest Hills Diary: the crisis of low income housing, 1974; Diaries of Mario M. Cuomo: the campaign for Governor, 1984; (ed jtly) Lincoln on Democracy, 1990; articles in legal jls. *Address:* State Capitol, Albany, NY 12224, USA.

CUPITT, Rev. Don; Dean of Emmanuel College, since 1965 and University Lecturer in Divinity, Cambridge, since 1973; *b* 22 May 1934; *s* of Robert and Norah Cupitt; *m* 1963, Susan Marianne (*née* Day); one *s* two *d*. *Educ:* Charterhouse; Trinity Hall, Cambridge; Westcott House, Cambridge. Curate, St Philip's Church, Salford, 1959–62; Vice-Principal, Westcott House, Cambridge, 1962–65. Hon. DLitt Bristol, 1985. *Publications:* Christ and the Hiddenness of God, 1971; Crisis of Moral Authority, 1972; The Leap of Reason, 1976; The Worlds of Science and Religion, 1976; (with Peter Armstrong) Who Was Jesus?, 1977; Jesus and the Gospel of God, 1979; The Nature of Man, 1979; The Debate about Christ, 1979; Explorations in Theology, 1979; Taking Leave of God, 1980; The World to Come, 1982; The Sea of Faith, 1984 (TV series, 1984); Only Human, 1985; Life Lines, 1986; The Long-Legged Fly, 1987; The New Christian Ethics, 1988; Radicals and the Future of the Church, 1989; Creation Out of Nothing, 1990; What is a Story?, 1991. *Address:* Emmanuel College, Cambridge CB2 3AP. *T:* Cambridge (0223) 334200.

CUREEU, (George) Nigel C.; *see* Capel Cure.

CURE, Kenneth Graham, OBE 1984; Executive Councilman, Amalgamated Engineering Union, 1979–89, retired; Member, Labour Party National Executive, 1981–89; *b* 22 Feb. 1924; *s* of Herbert and Doris Edith Cure; *m* 1949, Kathleen (*née* Taylor); two *s* one *d*. *Educ:* King Edward VI Grammar School, Birmingham. Apprentice, BSA; trained as Universal Miller and draughtsman; served War of 1939–45, RN (Atlantic convoys and combined ops). Joined AEU, 1952; Founder Sec., Castle Vale Birmingham Branch, 1970; held numerous offices in Branch and District; former Mem., W Midlands Regional Labour Party Exec.; former Chm., Disputes Cttee, Lab. Party NEC; former Mem., Gen. Purposes Cttee, TUC. Former Dir, Co-operative Press Ltd. Chm. of Governors, East Birmingham Coll.; Governor, Fircroft Coll. FRSA. Hon. MSc CNAA, 1986. *Recreation:* reading. *Address:* 73 Forster Road, Beckenham, Kent BR3 4LG.

CURIE, Eve, (Mrs Henry R. Labouisse), writer and journalist; *b* Paris, 6 Dec. 1904; *d* of late Marie and Pierre Curie; *m* 1954, Henry Richardson Labouisse (*d* 1987). *Educ:* by governesses, generally Polish; Sévigné College; Bachelor of Science and Bachelor of Philosophy. Accompanied her mother in her tour of the US 1921; devoted several years to the study of the piano and gave her first concert in 1925 in Paris; later she took up musical criticism and under a pseudonym acted for several years as musical critic of the weekly journal Candide; after the death of her mother in 1934 she collected and classified all the papers, manuscripts, and personal documents left by Mme Curie and went to Poland in 1935 to obtain material as to Mme Curie's youth; wrote Mme Curie's biography; went to America again in 1939 and has gone several times since on lecture tours; was a co-ordinator of the women's war activities at the Ministry of Information in Paris at the beginning of the war, until she went on a lecture tour in the USA; came back to Paris 2 May 1940; after the French capitulation went to live in London for six months, then to America for her third lecture tour; Vichy Govt deprived her of French citizenship in April 1941; in 1942, travelled, as a war correspondent to the battlefronts of Libya, Russia, Burma, China; enlisted in the Fighting French corps, Volontaires Françaises, 1943, as a private; received basic training in England; 2nd Lieut 1943; 1st Lieut 1944. Co-publisher of Paris-Presse, an evening paper in Paris, 1944–49. Special Adviser to the Sec. Gen. of NATO, Paris, Aug. 1952–Nov. 1954. *Publications:* Madame Curie (in US), 1937 (trans. into 32 langs); Journey Among Warriors, 1943. *Recreation:* swimming. *Address:* 1 Sutton Place South, New York, NY 10022, USA.

CURLE, James Leonard; Member and Managing Director, Civil Aviation Authority, 1984–87; *b* 14 Nov. 1925; *s* of Leonard and Mary Curle; *m* 1952, Gloria Madaleine Roch; one *s* one *d*. *Educ:* St Joseph's Academy, Blackheath; SE London Technical College; Borough Polytechnic. CEng, MIEE. Royal Signals, 1944–49; joined Telecommunications Div., MTCA, 1957; Dir Telecommunications, ATS, 1976–79; Dir Gen. Telecommunications, NATS, 1979–84. FRSA 1987. *Address:* 6 Nightingale Lane, Bickley, Kent BR1 2QH. *T:* 081–460 8023.

CURLE, Sir John (Noel Ormiston), KCVO 1975 (CVO 1956); CMG 1966; HM Diplomatic Service, retired; *b* 12 Dec. 1915; *s* of Major W. S. N. Curle, MC, Melrose, Scotland; *m* 1st, 1940, Diana Deane; one *s* one *d*; 2nd, 1948, Pauline, *widow* of Capt. David Roberts; two step *d*. *Educ:* Marlborough; New Coll., Oxford. 1st Class Hons, MA, Laming Travelling Fellow of Queen's Coll. Diplomatic Service, 1939; Irish Guards, 1939; War Cabinet Secretariat, 1941–44. Has served in Lisbon, Ottawa, Brussels, Stockholm (Counsellor), Athens (Counsellor); Boston (Consul-Gen., 1962–66); Ambassador to: Liberia, 1967–70 and Guinea, 1968–70; the Philippines, 1970–72; Vice Marshal of Diplomatic Corps, 1972–75; retired 1975; Dir of Protocol, Hong Kong, 1976–85; Advr for coronation of the King of Swaziland, 1986. Liveryman, Masons Company. *Recreations:* skiing (represented Oxford *v* Cambridge, and British Univs *v* Swiss Univs). *Address:* Appletree House, near Aston-le-Walls, Daventry, Northants NN11 6UG. *T:* Chipping Warden (029586) 211. *Clubs:* Cavalry and Guards, Beefsteak; Hong Kong.

CURNOW, Elizabeth Ann Marguerite; QC 1985; a Recorder of the Crown Court, since 1980; *b* 5 June 1935; *d* of Cecil Curnow and Doris Curnow (*née* Behr); *m* 1981, William Neil Denison, *qv*. *Educ:* St Hilda's Sch., Whitby, Yorks; King's Coll., London (LLB). Called to the Bar, Gray's Inn, 1957, Bencher, 1985. Treasury Counsel, Mddx Crown Court, 1972–77; Central Criminal Court: Jun. Treasury Counsel, 1977–81; Sen. Prosecuting Counsel to the Crown, 1981–85. *Recreations:* gardening, listening to music, tapestry, Burmese cats. *Address:* 6 King's Bench Walk, Temple, EC4Y 7DR. *T:* 071–583 0410.

CURRALL, Alexander, CB 1970; CMG 1965; Managing Director, Post Office, 1972–77; *b* 30 Jan. 1917; *s* of late R. T. Currall, Edinburgh; *m* 1940, Madeleine Crombie Saunders; one *s*. *Educ:* George Watson's Coll., Edinburgh; Edinburgh Univ. Min. of Supply, 1939–40; Royal Artillery and Indian Artillery, 1940–46. Successively in Min. of Supply, Min. of Materials and Board of Trade, concerned mainly with internat. economic negotiations, excepting the period 1950–54, when responsible for public trading in non-ferrous metals, and 1954–55, when holding a Commonwealth Fellowship for travel and study in USA. Seconded to Foreign Office as Dep. Consul-Gen., New York, 1960–62; Minister (Commercial), British High Commn, Ottawa, 1962–66; Under-Secretary: Board of Trade, 1966–67; DEA, 1967–68; Dir, Dept for Nat. Savings, 1968–72. Director: Renold, 1977–84; National Counties Building Soc., 1977–87 (Chm., 1984–86); Applied Photophysics Ltd, 1980–86 (Chm., 1981–86); Photophysics Research Ltd, 1980–86 (Chm., 1981–86); Grantham House Ltd, 1980–86 (Chm., 1981–86); The Pryors Ltd, 1983–87. Manager, Royal Instn, 1972–75, 1977–80, 1981–84. *Address:* Fairlawn, Buckden, Skipton, North Yorkshire BD23 5JA. *Club:* Caledonian.

CURRAN, Leo Gabriel Columbanus, CEng, FIMechE, FIMarE; Chairman, Camac Transport Co. Ltd, since 1981; *b* 23 Nov. 1930; *s* of B. L. Curran and R. Fanning; *m* 1957, Margaret Hickey; one *s* two *d*. *Educ:* St Malachy's Coll., Belfast; Dublin Coll. of Higher Technol. CEng 1974, FIMechE 1969; FIMarE 1974; MIProdE 1970. Managing Director: British Silverware Ltd, 1970–71; Delta Electrical (South African Delta Metal Electrical Pty) Ltd, 1971–73; Gen. Man. and Dir, Harland & Wolff Ltd, 1973–76; Man. Dir, Plessey Hydraulics International Ltd, 1976–79; Bd Mem. for Enginebuilding and Gen. Engrg, British Shipbuilders, 1979–80; Dir, Mica & Micanite (Ireland) Ltd, 1987–. *Recreations:* music, walking. *Address:* Camac Transport Co. Ltd, Camac House, John F. Kennedy Park, Bluebell, Dublin 12, Ireland. *T:* Dublin 500777. *Club:* Institute of Directors.

CURRAN, Prof. Robert Crowe, MD; FRSE 1962; Leith Professor of Pathology, Birmingham University, 1966–86, now Emeritus; Hon. Consultant Pathologist, Birmingham Central Health District, 1966–86; *b* 28 July 1921; *s* of John Curran and Sarah Crowe, Netherton, Wishaw, Lanarkshire; *m* 1947, Margaret Marion Park; one *s* one *d*. *Educ:* Glasgow Univ. MB, ChB 1943, MD 1956; FRCPath 1967; FRCP 1969; Hon. FFPath, RCPI, 1983. RAMC, 1945–47. Lectr in Pathology, Glasgow Univ.,

1950–55. Sen. Lectr and Cons. Pathologist, Sheffield Univ., 1955–58; Prof. of Pathology, St Thomas's Hospital Medical Sch., 1958–66. Registrar, Royal Coll. of Pathologists, 1968–73, Vice-Pres., 1977–80, Pres., 1981–84; Mem., GMC, 1979–86; Hon. Sec., Conf. of Med. Royal Colls and their Faculties in UK, 1982–86. *Publications:* Colour Atlas of Histopathology, 1966, 3rd edn 1985; The Pathological Basis of Medicine, 1972; Gross Pathology—a Colour Atlas, 1974; Tumours: Structure and Diagnosis, 1991; scientific papers on lymphoid tissue, disorders of connective tissue, etc. *Recreations:* golf, music. *Address:* 34A Carpenter Road, Edgbaston, Birmingham B15 2JH.

See also Sir S. C. Curran.

CURRAN, Sir Samuel (Crowe), Kt 1970; FRS 1953; FRSE 1947; FEng 1983; Principal and Vice-Chancellor, University of Strathclyde, 1964–80; *b* 23 May 1912; *s* of John Curran, Kinghorn, Fife, and Sarah Owen Crowe, Ballymena, Ulster; *m* 1940, Joan Elizabeth, *yr d* of Charles William Strothers and Margaret Beatrice (*née* Millington); three *s* one *d*. *Educ:* Glasgow Univ. (MA, BSc; PhD 1937; DSc 1950); St John's Coll., Cambridge (PhD Cantab, 1941; Hon. Fellow, 1971). Cavendish Laboratory, 1937–39; RAE, 1939–40; Min. of Aircraft Production and Min. of Supply, 1940–44; Manhattan Project (Min. of Supply), Univ. of California, 1944–45 (Invention of Scintillation Counter, 1944). Natural Philosophy, Glasgow Univ. 1945–55; UK Atomic Energy Authority, 1955–58; Chief Scientist, AWRE, Aldermaston, Berks, 1958–59; Principal, Royal Coll. of Science and Technology, Glasgow, 1959–64. Vis. Prof. in Energy Studies, Univ. of Glasgow, 1980–88. Pres., Scottish Soc. for the Mentally Handicapped, 1954–. Member: Council for Scientific and Industrial Research, 1962–65; Science Research Council, 1965–68; Adv. Council on Technology, 1965–70; Chairman: Adv. Cttee on Med. Research, 1962–75; Adv. Bd on Relations with Univs, 1966–70; Electricity Supply Res. Council, 1978–80 (Dep. Chm., 1980–82); Dep. Chm., Electricity Council, 1977–79; Chief Scientific Adviser to the Sec. of State for Scotland, 1967–77; Member: Oil Develt Council for Scotland, 1973–78; Adv. Cttee on Safety of Nuclear Installations, 1977–80; Radioactive Waste Management Adv. Cttee, 1978–81; Adv. Council of A Power for Good (APG), 1978–; UK Nat. Commn for Unesco, and Educn Adv. Cttee, 1978–; Standing Commn on Scottish Economy, 1987–. Director: Scottish Television, 1964–82; Hall Thermotank Ltd, 1969–76; Cetec Systems Ltd, 1965–77; Internat. Res. & Develt Co. Ltd, 1970–78; Gen. Steels Div., BSC, 1970–73; Nuclear Structures (Protection) Ltd, 1981–. Hon. Pres., Scottish Polish Cultural Assoc., 1972–; Pres., St Andrews' Soc., Glasgow, 1982–88. FRCPS (Hon.) 1964; FIEE (Hon.) 1989. Hon. LLD: Glasgow, 1968; Aberdeen, 1971; Hon. ScD Lodz, 1973; Hon. DSc Strathclyde, 1980; Hon. DEng Nova Scotia, 1982. Freeman: Motherwell and Wishaw, 1966; City of Glasgow, 1980. DL Glasgow, 1969. St Mungo Prize, 1976. Comdr, St Olav (Norway), 1966; Comdr, Order Polish People's Republic, 1976. *Publications:* (with J. D. Craggs) Counting Tubes, 1949; Luminescence and the Scintillation Counter, 1953; Alpha, Beta and Gamma Ray Spectroscopy, 1964; (jt) Energy Resources and the Environment, 1976; (with J. S. Curran) Energy and Human Needs, 1979; Issues in Science and Education, 1988; papers on nuclear researches and education in Proc. Royal Society. *Recreations:* horology, golf. *Address:* 93 Kelvin Court, Glasgow G12 0AH. *T:* 041–334 8329. *Club:* Caledonian.

See also R. C. Curran.

CURREY, Rear-Adm. Edmund Neville Vincent, CB 1960; DSO 1944; DSC 1941; *b* 1 Oct. 1906; *s* of Dr and Mrs E. F. N. Currey, Lismore, Co. Waterford, Ireland; *m* 1941, Rosemary Knight; one *d*. *Educ:* Royal Naval Colls, Osborne and Dartmouth. Joined RNC Osborne 1920; served in submarines and destroyers as junior officer; served War of 1939–45; commanded HM ships Wrestler, Escapade and Musketeer; Comdr, 1942; Capt., 1949; subsequently served with British Naval Mission to Greece; Naval Asst to Adm. Commanding Reserves; in command of HMS Bermuda; Naval Asst to Second Sea Lord; Rear-Adm., 1958; Chief of Staff to C-in-C, Portsmouth, 1958–61, retired. Polish Gold Cross of Merit, with swords, 1943. *Recreation:* golf. *Address:* 75 Great Pulteney Street, Garden Flat, Bath, Avon BA2 4DL. *T:* Bath (0225) 463743.

CURREY, Prof. Harry Lloyd Fairbridge, FRCP; Arthritis and Rheumatism Council Professor of Rheumatology, University of London, 1983–87, now Emeritus Professor of Rheumatology; Director, Bone and Joint Unit, London Hospital Medical College, 1976–87; Consulting Rheumatologist, London Hospital, since 1988; *b* 5 June 1925; *s* of late Ronald Fairbridge Currey and of Dorothy (*née* White); *m* 1st, 1950, Chrystal Komlosy (decd); one *s* two *d*; 2nd, 1973, Jacqueline Harris. *Educ:* Cordwalles, S Africa; Michaelhouse, Natal; Univ. of Cape Town (MB, ChB 1950, MMed 1960). FRCP 1971 (MRCP 1962). Intern, Groote Schuur Hosp., and House Officer, City Hosp. and Peninsular Maternity Hosps, Cape Town, 1951–53; gen. practice, Port Elizabeth, 1953–58; Med. Registrar, Groote Schuur Hosp., Cape Town, 1959–61; Intern, Hammersmith Hosp., London, 1962; Registrar, Dept of Rheumatology, London Hosp., 1963–65; London Hosp. Med. College: Sen. Lectr, 1965–70; Reader in Rheumatol., 1970–74; Prof of Rheumatol., 1974–83; Res. Fellow, Southwestern Med. Sch., Dallas, Texas, 1966. Philip Ellman Lectr, RCP, 1977. Pres., Heberden Soc., 1980–81; Heberden Round presented 1972. Editor, Annals of the Rheumatic Diseases, 1983–88. *Publications:* Mason and Currey's Clinical Rheumatology, 1970, 4th edn 1986; Essentials of Rheumatology, 1983, 2nd edn 1988; (with S. A. Hull) Rheumatology for GPs, 1987; articles on rheumatol topics in learned jls. *Recreations:* gardening, music, golf, fell-walking, inland waterways. *Address:* The Heights, Galloway Road, Bishop's Stortford, Herts CM23 2HS. *T:* Bishop's Stortford (0279) 654717.

CURRIE, Prof. Sir Alastair (Robert), Kt 1979; Professor of Pathology, Edinburgh University, 1972–86, now Emeritus; Pathologist, Royal Infirmary of Edinburgh; Consultant Pathologist, Lothian Health Board; *b* 8 Oct. 1921; *s* of late John Currie and Maggie Mactaggart; *m* 1949, Jeanne Marion Clarke, MB, ChB; three *s* one *d* (and one *d* decd). *Educ:* Port Ellen Public Sch.; High Sch. and Univ. of Glasgow. BSc; MB, ChB Glasgow; FRCPE; FRCP Glasgow; FRCP; FRCPath; FRSE. RAMC 1949–51; Lectr in Pathology, Univ. of Glasgow 1947–54; Sen. Lectr in Pathology, Univ. of Glasgow, and Cons. Pathologist, Royal Infirmary, Glasgow, 1954–59; Head, Div. of Pathology, Imperial Cancer Research Fund, London, 1959–62; Regius Prof. of Pathology, Univ. of Aberdeen, 1962–72. Chairman: Standing Adv. Cttee on Laboratory Services, 1968–72; Biomedical Res. Cttee, 1975–78; Jt MRC and NRPB Cttee on Radiological Protection, 1974–81; MRC/CRC Cttee for Jtly Supported Insts, 1978–80; CRC/MRC Cttee for Inst. of Cancer Research, 1980–83; Co-ordinating Cttee for Cancer Res., 1980–81; Member: MRC, 1964–68 and 1976–80 (Chm., Cell Biology and Disorders Bd, 1976–78); Scottish NE Regional Hosp. Bd, 1966–71; Council, RCPath, 1968–71; Scottish Health Services Council, 1969–72; Chief Scientist's Cttee, Scottish Home and Health Dept, 1974–78; Court, Edinburgh Univ., 1975–78; Bd of Dirs, Inveresk Research International, 1980–89; Sci. Adv. Council, Alberta Heritage Foundn for Med. Res., 1982–88; Assembly, Gen. Motors Cancer Research Foundn, 1982–86; UK Co-ordinating Cttee for Cancer Res., 1984–88; Cancer Research Campaign: Mem. Council, 1976–91; Mem. Exec. Cttee, 1976–88 (Chm., 1983–88); Mem., 1969–83, Chm., 1978–83, Scientific Cttee; Hon. Treasurer, 1988–91; Royal Society of Edinburgh: Mem. Council, 1980–83; a Vice-Pres., 1988–90; Pres., 1991–. Chairman: Bd of Govs, Beatson Inst. for Cancer Res., 1984–91; Council, Paterson Inst. for Cancer Res., 1990–91; Dep. Chm., Caldeonian Res. Foundn, 1989–. Trustee, Islay Museums, 1987–. Hon. DSc: Birmingham, 1983; Aberdeen, 1985; Hon. LLD Glasgow, 1987; Dr *hc* Edinburgh, 1991. *Publications:* papers in scientific and med. jls. *Address:* 42 Murrayfield Avenue, Edinburgh EH12 6AY. *T:* 031–337 3100; Grianan, Strathlachlan, Strachur, Argyll. *T:* Strachur (036986) 769. *Club:* New (Edinburgh).

CURRIE, Austin; *see* Currie, J. A.

CURRIE, Prof. David Anthony; Professor of Economics, Research Dean and Director, Centre for Economic Forecasting, London Business School, since 1988; *b* 9 Dec. 1946; *s* of Kennedy Moir Currie and Marjorie Currie (*née* Thompson); *m* 1975, Shaziye Gazioglu Currie (separated); two *s*. *Educ:* Battersea Grammar Sch.; Univ. of Manchester (BSc 1st cl. Maths); Univ. of Birmingham (MSocSci Econs); PhD Econs London. Economist: Hoare Govett, 1971–72; Economic Models, 1972; Lectr, Reader and Prof. of Economics, Queen Mary College, Univ. of London, 1972–88. Res. Fellow, Centre for Economic Policy Research, 1983–. Houblon-Norman Res. Fellow, Bank of England, 1985–86; Vis. Scholar, IMF, 1987. *Publications:* Advances in Monetary Economics, 1985; (with Charles Goodhart and David Llewellyn) The Operation and Regulation of Financial Markets, 1986; (with David Vines) Macroeconomic Interactions Between North and South, 1988; articles in jls. *Recreations:* music, literature, running. *Address:* London Business School, Sussex Place, NW1 4SA. *T:* 071–262 5050. *Club:* Reform.

CURRIE, Sir Donald Scott, 7th Bt *cr* 1847; Chief of Maintenance, National Park Service, Department of the Interior, since 1976; *b* 16 Jan. 1930; *s* of George Donald Currie (*d* 1980) (*g g s* of 1st Bt) and of Janet K., *d* of late James Scott; *S* cousin, 1987; *m* 1st, 1948, Charlotte (marr. diss. 1951), *d* of Charles Johnstone; one *s* twin *d*; 2nd, 1952, Barbara Lee, *d* of A. P. Garnier; one *s* two *d*. Rancher and farmer, 1949–75. *Heir:* *s* Donald Mark Currie [*b* 1949; *m*; one *s*]. *Address:* 537 Garfield, Las Animas, Colorado 81054, USA. *T:* (719) 456–1422. *Clubs:* American Legion (Colorado, USA); National Rifle Association (USA); North American Hunting.

CURRIE, Edwina; MP (C) Derbyshire South, since 1983; *b* 13 Oct. 1946; *m* 1972, Raymond F. Currie, BA, FCA; two *d*. *Educ:* Liverpool Inst. for Girls; St Anne's Coll., Oxford (MA 1972); London Sch. of Econs and Pol Science (MSc 1972). Teaching and lecturing posts in econs, econ. history and business studies, 1972–81. Birmingham City Council: Mem., 1975–86; Chm., Social Services Cttee, 1979–80; Chm., Housing Cttee, 1982–83. Chm., Central Birmingham HA, 1981–83; Mem., Birmingham AHA, 1975–82. PPS to Sec. of State for Educn and Science, 1985–86; Parly Under-Sec. of State (Health), DHSS, later Dept of Health, 1986–88. Mem., Parly Select Cttee on Social Services, 1983–86. Columnist, Today, 1990–; regular contributor to nat. newspapers and magazines. Speaker of the Year, Assoc. of Speakers' Clubs, 1990. *Publications:* Financing our Cities (Bow Group pamphlet), 1976; Life Lines, 1989; (jtly) What Women Want, 1990. *Recreations:* family, domestic arts, writing. *Address:* House of Commons, SW1A 0AA. *T:* 071–219 3611. *Club:* Swadlincote Conservative (Derbyshire).

CURRIE, James McGill; Chef de Cabinet to Leon Brittan, Commission of European Communities, since 1989; *b* 17 Nov. 1941; *s* of late David Currie and of Mary (*née* Smith); *m* 1968, Evelyn Barbara McIntyre; one *s* one *d*. *Educ:* St Joseph's High Sch., Kilmarnock; Blairs Coll., Aberdeen; Royal Scots Coll., Valladolid; Univ. of Glasgow (MA). Asst Principal, Scottish Home and Health Dept, 1968–72; Principal, Scottish Educn Dept, 1972–75; Secretary, Management Gp, Scottish Office, 1975–77; Scottish Development Dept: Principal, 1977–79; Asst Sec., 1979–81; Asst Sec., Scottish Economic Planning Dept, 1981–82; Counsellor, UK Perm. Representation to EEC, 1982–87; Dir of Regional Policy, EEC, 1987–89. *Recreations:* tennis, guitar, good food. *Address:* Les Bouleaux, Leeuwerikendreef 6, 1900 Overijse, Belgium. *T:* Brussels 657 1156.

CURRIE, (Joseph) Austin; Teachta Dala (TD) (FG) for Dublin West, Dail Eireann (Irish Parliament), since 1989; Adviser to the European Commission, since 1984; *b* 11 Oct. 1939; *s* of John Currie and Mary (*née* O'Donnell); *m* 1968, Anne Ita Lynch; two *s* three *d*. *Educ:* Edendork Sch.; St Patrick's Academy, Dungannon; Queen's Univ., Belfast (BA). MP (Nat) Tyrone, Parlt of N Ireland, 1964–72; Mem. (SDLP), Fermanagh and S Tyrone, NI Assembly, 1973–75, NI Constitutional Convention, 1975–76, NI Assembly, 1982–86; Minister of Housing, Planning and Local Govt, 1974. Contested (FG) Presidency of Ireland, 1990. Mem., Anglo-Irish Parly tier; frontbench spokesperson on communications, 1991–. Only person to have been elected to both Irish Parlts. Res. Fellow, Faculty of Economic and Social Studies, TCD, 1977–78. *Recreations:* Gaelic football, golf, snooker, reading. *Address:* Tullydraw, Donaghmore, Co. Tyrone, N Ireland; 37 Esker Lawns, Lucan, Co. Dublin, Ireland.

CURRIE, Sir Neil (Smith), Kt 1982; CBE 1977; Chairman, Coal & Allied Industries Ltd, since 1988 (Director, since 1987); *b* 20 Aug. 1926; *s* of Sir George Currie; *m* 1951, Geraldine Evelyn; two *s* two *d*. *Educ:* Wesley Coll., Perth, W Australia; Univ. of Western Australia (BA). Department of External Affairs, 1948–59; Dept of Trade and Industry, 1959–71; Secretary: Dept of Supply, 1971–74; Dept of Manufacturing Industry, 1974–76; Dept of Industry and Commerce, 1976–82; Australian Ambassador to Japan, 1982–86. Dep. Chm., Westpac Banking Corp. (Dir, 1987–). Chm., Australia Japan Foundn, 1989– (Mem., 1986–). *Recreations:* golf, tennis. *Address:* c/o Coal and Allied Industries Ltd, 1 York Street, Sydney, NSW 2000, Australia.

CURRIE, Rev. Piers William Edward, MC 1945; Assistant Priest, St Mary in the Marsh, Norwich, since 1990; *b* 26 Feb. 1913; *e c* of late P. A. and Mrs Currie; *m* 1956, Ella Rosaleen, *y c* of late Rev. W. and Mrs Bennett-Hughes; no *c*. *Educ:* Rugby Sch.; Brasenose Coll., Oxford (MA). Solicitor, admitted Dec. 1939. Served War, 1940–45, in 4th Regt RHA. Sen. Legal Asst, Nat. Coal Bd, 1946–53; Asst Sec., 1953–55; Sec., W Midlands Divisional Bd, 1955–60; Sec. and Legal Adviser, 1960–62; Dep. Sec., NCB, 1962–67; Legal Adviser, Land Commission, 1967–71; Deputy Master, Court of Protection, 1971–77. Ordained deacon, 1980; priest, 1981; Hon. Curate of Holt with Edgefield, 1980–82; permanent permission to officiate, dio. Norwich, 1982; Priest in charge of Baconsthorpe and Hempstead by Holt, dio. Norwich, 1983–85; Staff mem., Glaven Assoc. of Parishes, 1986–90. *Recreations:* gardening, natural history. *Address:* 48 The Close, Norwich NR1 4EG.

CURRIE, Rear-Adm. Robert Alexander, CB 1957; DSC 1944, bar 1945; DL; *b* 29 April 1905; 5th *s* of John Currie, Glasgow, and Rachel Thomson, Dundee; *m* 1944, Lady (Edith Margaret) Beevor (*d* 1985), *widow* of Sir Thomas Beevor, 6th Bt, and *d* of Frank Agnew, Eccles, Norfolk; one step *s* (*see* Sir Thomas Beevor, 7th Bt) three step *d*. *Educ:* RN Colleges, Osborne and Dartmouth. Specialised in Gunnery, 1930. Served War, 1939–45: HMS Hood; HMS Warspite, 2nd Battle of Narvik; Plans Division, Admiralty; Convoy Escort Comdr; Assault Gp Comdr, Far East; Captain RN, 1945; Captain (D) Fifth Flotilla, 1948–49; idc 1950; Director, Royal Naval Staff Coll., 1951–52; Comdg Officer, HMS Cumberland, 1953; Rear-Adm., 1954; Chief of Staff to Chairman, British Joint Service Mission, Washington, DC, 1954–57; retired, 1957. Member: Cttee of Enquiry into the Fishing Industry, 1958–60; W Suffolk County Council, 1962–74. DL, Suffolk, 1968.

King Haakon VII Liberty Cross, Norway, 1945. *Recreation:* painting. *Address:* Saffron Pane, Hall Road, Lavenham, Suffolk CO10 9QU.

CURRIE, Prof. Ronald Ian, CBE 1977; FIBiol; FRSE; Professorial Fellow, Grant Institute of Geology, University of Edinburgh, 1988–90; *b* 10 Oct. 1928; *s* of Ronald Wavell Currie and Elizabeth Currie; *m* 1956, Cecilia, *d* of William and Lilian de Garis; one *s* one *d. Educ:* The Univ., Glasgow (BSc 1st Cl. Hons Zool., 1949); Univ. of Copenhagen. FIBiol 1967; FRSE 1969. Joined Royal Naval Scientific Service, 1949; seconded to National Inst. of Oceanography; Head of Biol. Dept, 1962–66; Dir and Sec., Scottish Marine Biological Assoc., 1966–87 (Hon. Mem., 1989). Hon. Prof., Heriot-Watt Univ., 1979–. William Scoresby Expedn, S Africa, 1950; Discovery Expedn, Antarctica, 1951; res. voyages, N Atlantic, 1955–64; Chm., Biol. Planning Cttee, Internat. Indian Ocean Expedn, 1960; Indian Ocean Expedn, 1963 and 1964. Secretary: Internat. Assoc. for Biol Oceanography, 1964–66 (Pres., 1966–70); Scientific Cttee on Oceanic Res., Internat. Council of Scient. Unions, 1972–78. Chm., NERC Adv. Cttee on Internat. Ocean. Affairs, 1981–87; Member: Scottish Cttee, Nature Conservancy Council; Council, N British Hotels Trust; Royal Nat. Mission to Deep Sea Fishermen; Chm., Kilmore Community Council, 1977–86; Hon. Sec., Challenger Soc., 1956–88; Hon. Mem., Challenger Soc. for Marine Sci., 1989. *Publications:* (with T. J. Hart) The Benguela Current (Discovery Report), 1960; scientific papers on organic prodn in the sea and fertility of the ocean. *Recreations:* cooking, hill walking, shooting, local history. *Address:* Kilmore House, Kilmore, by Oban, Argyll PA34 4XT. *T:* Kilmore (063177) 248. *Club:* Royal Over-Seas League.

CURRY, Dr Alan Stewart; retired; Controller, Forensic Science Service, Home Office, 1976–82; *b* 31 Oct. 1925; *s* of late Richard C. Curry and of Margaret Curry; *m* 1973, J. Venise Hewitt; one *s* (by previous marriage). *Educ:* Arnold Sch., Blackpool; Trinity Coll., Cambridge (Scholar). MA, PhD, CChem, FRSC, FRCPath. Served War of 1939–45 with RAF. Joined Home Office Forensic Science Service, 1952; served in NE Region, 1952–64; Dir, Nottingham Forensic Sci. Lab., 1964–66; Dir, Home Office Central Research Estabt, Aldermaston, 1966–76. Pres., Internat. Assoc. of Forensic Toxicologists, 1969–75; UN Consultant in Narcotics, 1972–; Hon. Consultant in Forensic Toxicology to RAF, 1973–; Consultant in Toxicology to British Airways, 1982–. Fellow, Indian Acad. of Forensic Scis; Mem., Amer. Acad. of Forensic Scis; Hon. Mem., Belg. Pharmaceutical Soc. Hon. DSc Ghent, 1986. Stas Gold Medal, Gesellschaft für Toxicologische und Forensische Chemie, 1983. *Publications:* Poison Detection in Human Organs, 1962, 4th edn 1988; (ed) Methods in Forensic Science, vols 3 and 4, 1964–65; Advances in Forensic and Clinical Toxicology, 1973; (ed) Analytical Methods in Human Toxicology, Part 1 1985, Part 2 1986; (ed, with wife) The Biochemistry of Women: Clinical Concepts; Methods for Clinical Investigation, 1974; over 100 papers in med. and sci. and police jls. *Recreations:* sailing, amateur radio. *T:* Reading (0734) 581481. *Club:* Athenæum.

CURRY, David Maurice; MP (C) Skipton and Ripon, since 1987; Parliamentary Secretary, Ministry of Agriculture, Fisheries and Food, since 1989; *b* 13 June 1944; *s* of Thomas Harold Curry and Florence Joan (*née* Tyerman); *m* 1971, Anne Helene Maud Roullet; one *s* two *d. Educ:* Ripon Grammar Sch.; Corpus Christi Coll., Oxford (MA Hons); Kennedy Sch. of Govt, Harvard (Kennedy Scholar, 1966–67). Reporter, Newcastle Jl, 1967–70; Financial Times: Trade Editor, Internat. Cos Editor, Brussels Corresp., Paris Corresp., and European News Editor, 1970–79. Sec., Anglo-American Press Assoc. of Paris, 1978; Founder, Paris Conservative Assoc., 1977. MEP (C) Essex NE, 1979–89; Chm., Agriculture Cttee, 1982–84; Vice-Chm., Budgets Cttee, 1984–85; spokesman on budgetary matters for European Democratic Gp, 1985–89; Gen. Rapporteur for EEC's 1987 budget. *Publication:* The Food War: the EEC, the US and the battle for world food markets, 1982. *Recreations:* digging, windsurfing, bee-keeping. *Address:* Newland End, Arkesden, Essex CB11 4HF. *T:* Saffron Walden (0799) 550368.

CURRY, Dr Gordon Barrett; Royal Society University Research Fellow, Department of Geology and Applied Geology, University of Glasgow, since 1984; *b* 27 June 1954; *s* of Robert and Violet Curry; *m* 1983, Gillian. *Educ:* Masonic Sch., Dublin; Trinity Coll., Dublin (BA Mod.); Imperial Coll. London (PhD, DIC). FGS. Research Asst to Sir Alwyn Williams, Univ. of Glasgow, 1980–84. President's Award, Geolog. Soc., 1985; Clough Award, Edinburgh Geolog. Soc., 1985–86; Wollaston Fund, Geolog. Soc., 1989. *Publications:* numerous contribs to learned jls. *Recreations:* music, swimming, travel. *Address:* Department of Geology and Applied Geology, University of Glasgow, Lilybank Gardens, Glasgow G12 8QQ. *T:* 041–330 5444.

CURRY, John Anthony, OBE 1976; actor; ice skater; *b* 9 Sept. 1949; *s* of Joseph Henry Curry and Rita Agnes Pritchard. *Educ:* Solihull Sch. British, European, World, and Olympic Figure Skating Champion, 1976. Founder and Director: John Curry Theatre of Skating, 1977; John Curry Sch. of Skating, 1978; Artistic Dir, John Curry Skating Co. Appeared in: A Midsummer Night's Dream, Nottingham and Open Air Theatre, Regent's Park; As You Like It, Open Air Theatre, Regent's Park; A Symphony On Ice, Royal Albert Hall, Metropolitan Opera House, NY, 1984; Cinderella, Liverpool Playhouse, 1986; Hard Times, Lyric Theatre, Belfast and King's Head, 1987. Nat. Advr, Nat. Skating Assoc., 1988–. *Publication:* (with photographs by Keith Money) John Curry, 1978. *Recreations:* theatre, reading. *Address:* c/o London Management, 235 Regent Street, W1.

CURRY, John Arthur Hugh; Chairman, ACAL, since 1986; *b* 7 June 1938; *s* of Alfred Robert and Mercia Beatrice Curry; *m* 1962, Anne Rosemary Lewis; three *s* one *d. Educ:* King's College School, Wimbledon; St Edmund Hall, Oxford (MA); Harvard Univ. Graduate College (MBA). FCA. Arthur Andersen, 1962–64; Man. Dir, Unitech, 1966–86. *Publication:* Partners for Profit, 1966. *Recreations:* tennis, Rugby. *Clubs:* All England Lawn Tennis and Croquet (Chm., 1989–, Mem. Cttee, 1979–); International Lawn Tennis.

CURRY, (Thomas) Peter (Ellison), QC 1966, 1973; *s* of Maj. F. R. P. Curry; *m* 1950, Pamela Joyce, *d* of late Group Capt. A. J. Holmes, AFC, JP; two *s* two *d. Educ:* Tonbridge; Oriel Coll., Oxford. BA 1948; MA 1951. Served War of 1939–45; enlisted 1939; commnd, 1941; 17th Indian Div., India and Burma, 1941–45. War Office, 1946. Called to Bar, Middle Temple, 1953, Bencher, 1979. QC 1966. Solicitor, 1968; partner in Freshfields, Solicitors, 1968–70; returned to Bar; re-appointed QC 1973. Pres., Aircraft and Shipbuilding Industries Arbitration Tribunal, 1978–80. Chm., Chancery Bar Assoc., 1980–85; Dep. Chm., Barristers' Benevolent Assoc., 1989– (Hon. Treas., 1964–71, 1984–89). Rep. Army, Oxford and Sussex at Squash Racquets (described as fastest mover in squash, 1947; triple blue, Oxford; twice cross country winner); World Student Games (5000 m), 1947; British Steeplechase champion 1948, Olympic Games, 1948. Served on AAA Cttee of Inquiry, 1967. Holder of French certificate as capitaine-mécanicien for mechanically propelled boats. *Publications:* (Jt Editor) Palmer's Company Law, 1959; (Jt Editor) Crew on Meetings, 1966, 1975. *Recreations:* work, gardening, the Turf. *Address:* Hurlands, Dunsfold, Surrey. *T:* Dunsfold (048649) 356. *Club:* Army and Navy.

CURTEIS, Ian Bayley; television playwright; *b* 1 May 1935; *m* 1st, 1964, Mrs Joan Macdonald (marr. diss.); two *s*; 2nd, 1985, Joanna Trollope; two step *d. Educ:* Iver Council Sch.; Slough Grammar Sch.; Slough Trading Estate; London Univ. Director and actor in theatres all over Great Britain, and BBC-tv script reader, 1956–63; BBC and ATV staff director (drama), directing plays by John Betjeman, John Hopkins, William Trevor and others, 1963–67. Chm., Cttee on Censorship, Writers' Guild of GB, 1981–85. *Television plays:* Beethoven, Sir Alexander Fleming (BBC's entry at 1973 Prague Fest.), Mr Rolls and Mr Royce, Long Voyage out of War (trilogy), The Folly, The Haunting, Second Time Round, A Distinct Chill, The Portland Millions, Philby, Burgess and Maclean (British entry 1978 Monte Carlo Fest., BAFTA nomination), Hess, The Atom Spies, Churchill and the Generals (BAFTA nomination; Grand Prize, Best Programme of 1980, NY Internat. Film and TV Fest.), Suez 1956 (BAFTA nomination), Miss Morison's Ghosts (British entry 1982 Monte Carlo Fest.), The Mitford Girls, BB and Joe (trilogy), Lost Empires (adapted from J. B. Priestley), The Trials of Lady Sackville, Eureka (1st Euroserial simultaneously shown in UK, West Germany, Austria, Switzerland, Italy and France), The Nightmare Years, Cecil Rhodes, 1990, The Zimmerman Telegram, Eastern Approaches (adapted from Fitzroy Maclean). Also originated and wrote numerous popular television drama series; *film screenplays:* Andre Malraux's La Condition humaine, 1982; Graham Greene's The Man Within, 1983; Tom Paine (for Sir Richard Attenborough), 1983; *play:* A Personal Affair, Globe, 1982. *Publications: plays:* Long Voyage out of War (trilogy), 1971; Churchill and the Generals, 1979; Suez 1956, 1980; The Falklands Play, 1987. *Recreation:* dissidence. *Address:* The Mill House, Coln St Aldwyns, Cirencester, Glos. *Clubs:* Beefsteak, Garrick.

CURTIS, Prof. Charles David; Professor of Geochemistry, since 1988 and Head, Department of Geology, since 1989, University of Manchester; *b* 11 Nov. 1939; *s* of Charles Frederick Curtis and Kate Margaret Curtis (*née* Jackson); *m* 1963, Dr Diana Joy Saxty; two *d. Educ:* Imperial College London; Univ. of Sheffield (BSc, PhD). University of Sheffield: Lectr, Sen. Lectr, Reader, 1965–83; Personal Chair in Geochem., 1983–88. Vis. Prof., Dept of Geology and Geophys., UCLA, 1970–71; Res. Associate, British Petroleum Res. Centre, 1987–88. Mem. Council, NERC, 1990–. Murchison Medal, Geological Soc., 1987. *Publications:* numerous articles in learned jls. *Recreations:* mountaineering, gardening, photography. *Address:* Department of Geology, The University, Oxford Road, Manchester M13 9PL. *T:* 061–275 3803.

CURTIS, Colin Hinton Thomson, CVO 1970; ISO 1970; retired; Chairman, Metropolitan Public Abattoir Board, 1971–81; Member, Queensland Meat Industry Authority, 1972–78; *b* 25 June 1920; *s* of A. Curtis, Brisbane; *m* 1943, Anne Catherline Drevesen; one *s. Educ:* Brisbane Grammar School. RANR Overseas Service, 1940–45. Sec. and Investigation Officer to Chm., Sugar Cane Prices Board, 1948–49; Asst Sec. to Central Sugar Cane Prices Board, 1949; Sec. to Premier of Queensland, 1950–64; Mem., Qld Trade Missions to SE Asia, 1963 and 1964; Asst Under-Sec., Premier's Dept, 1961–64; Assoc. Dir and Dir of Industrial Development, 1964–66; Under-Sec., Premier's Dept and Clerk of Exec. Council, 1966–70; State Dir, Royal Visit, 1970; Agent-General for Queensland in London, 1970–71. *Recreations:* squash, yachting, swimming. *Address:* 57 Daru Avenue, Runaway Bay, Gold Coast, Qld, Australia. *Clubs:* RSL Memorial, Rugby League (Queensland).

CURTIS, Prof. David Roderick, FRACP 1987; FRS 1974; FAA 1965; Howard Florey Professor of Medical Research, and Director, John Curtin School of Medical Research, Australian National University, since 1989; *b* 3 June 1927; *s* of E. D. and E. V. Curtis; *m* 1952, Lauri Sewell; one *s* one *d. Educ:* Univ. of Melbourne; Australian National Univ. MB, BS Melbourne 1950, PhD ANU 1957. John Curtin School, ANU: Department of Physiology: Research Scholar, 1954–56; Research Fellow, 1956–57; Fellow, 1957–59; Sen. Fellow, 1959–62; Professorial Fellow, 1962–66; Prof. of Pharmacology, 1966–68; Prof. of Neuropharmacology, 1968–73; Prof. and Foundn Head, Dept of Pharmacology, 1973–88; Chm., Div. of Physiol Sciences, 1988–89. Pres., Aust. Acad. of Sci, 1986–90 (Burnet Medal, 1983). Chm., Inaugural Australia Prize Cttee, 1989–90. *Publications:* papers in fields of neurophysiology, neuropharmacology in Jl Physiology, Jl Neurophysiol., Brain Research, Exper. Brain Research, etc. *Recreations:* tennis, wombling. *Address:* 7 Patey Street, Campbell, Canberra, ACT 2601, Australia. *T:* Canberra (062) 48–5664; John Curtin School of Medical Research, Australian National University, GPO Box 334, ACT 2601, Australia. *T:* Canberra (062) 49–2597.

CURTIS, Sir (Edward) Leo, Kt 1965; Lord Mayor of Melbourne, Australia, 1963–64 and 1964–65; *b* London, 13 Jan. 1907. Joined Melbourne City Council, Dec. 1955; retired March 1975. Past President of Retail Traders Association of Victoria. *Address:* 4 Armadale Street, Armadale, Vic 3143, Australia. *Clubs:* Athenæum, Kelvin (Melbourne); various sporting.

CURTIS, Most Rev. Ernest Edwin, CBE 1976; Hon. Assistant Bishop of Portsmouth, since 1976; *b* 24 Dec. 1906, *s* of Ernest John and Zoe Curtis; *m* 1938, Dorothy Anne Hill (*d* 1965); one *s* one *d*; *m* 1970, Evelyn Mary Josling. *Educ:* Sherborne; Foster's Sch.; Royal College of Science, London. BSc (hons Chem.) London, 1927; ARCSc 1927; Dipl. Educn, London, 1928. Asst Master, Lindisfarne Coll., Westcliff, 1928–31; Wells Theol Coll., 1932–33; Asst Curate, Holy Trinity, Waltham Cross, 1933–36; Chaplain i/c parishes Rose Hill and Bambous, and Principal, St Paul's Theol Coll., Mauritius, 1937–44; Missions to Seamen Chaplain, Port Louis, 1944; Priest i/c St Wilfrid, Portsmouth, 1945–47; Vicar, All Saints, Portsmouth, and Chaplain, Royal Portsmouth Hospital, 1947–55; Priest i/c St Agatha, Portsmouth, 1954–55; Vicar, St John Baptist, Locks Heath, 1955–66; Warden of Readers, Dio. Portsmouth, 1956–66; Rural Dean of Alverstoke, 1964–66; Bishop of Mauritius and Seychelles, 1966–72, of Mauritius, 1973–76; Archbishop of the Indian Ocean, 1973–76; Priest-in-charge of St Mary and St Rhadagunde, Whitwell, 1976–82. *Recreations:* walking, hill-climbing, piano. *Address:* 5 Elizabeth Gardens, Havenstreet, Ryde, Isle of Wight PO33 4DU. *T:* Isle of Wight (0983) 883049.

CURTIS, Frank; *see* Curtis, R. F.

CURTIS, Very Rev. Frank; *see* Curtis, Very Rev. W. F.

CURTIS, Rt. Rev. John Barry; *see* Calgary, Bishop of.

CURTIS, John Edward, PhD; FSA; Keeper of Western Asiatic Antiquities, British Museum, since 1989; *b* 23 June 1946; *yr s* of late Arthur Norman Curtis and of Laura Letitia Ladd (*née* Thomas); *m* 1977, Vesta Sarkhosh; one *s* one *d. Educ:* Collyer's Grammar Sch,, Horsham; Univ. of Bristol (BA); Inst. of Archaeology, Univ. of London (Postgrad. Diploma in Western Asiatic Archaeology; PhD 1979). FSA 1984. Fellow, British Sch. of Archaeology in Iraq, 1969–71; Res. Asst, Dept of Western Asiatic Antiquities, British Museum, 1971–74, Asst Keeper, 1974–89. Hon. Sec., British Assoc. for Near Eastern Archaeol., 1987–; Hon. Sec. and Treas., Cttee for E Arabian and Gulf Studies, 1976–86; Hon. Sec. and Trustee, Vladimir G. Lukonin Meml Fund, 1987–; Member: Governing Council, 1980–, Exec. Cttee, 1982–, British Sch. of Archaeol. in Iraq; Governing Body, Wainwright Fund, 1988–. *Publications:* (ed) Fifty Years of Mesopotamian Discovery, 1982; Nush-i Jan III: the Small Finds, 1984; (ed) Bronzeworking Centres of Western Asia *c* 1000–539 BC, 1988; Excavations at Qasrij Cliff and Khirbet Qasrij, 1989; Ancient Persia, 1989; articles in learned jls. *Recreations:* collecting, local history, geneaology.

Address: 13 St Mary's Road, NW11 9UE. *T:* 081–458 3117; 1 Francis Cottage, Sandy Hill Road, Saundersfoot, Dyfed SA69 9HW.

CURTIS, John Henry, CB 1981; FAIM, FTS; Chairman, Nortel Aust. Pty Ltd, since 1989; *b* 20 March 1920; *s* of K. H. and E. M. Curtis; *m* 1943, Patricia Foote; one *s* one *d. Educ:* Ipswich Grammar Sch.; Queensland Univ. (BE Hons 1950, BSc 1951, BA 1957). FIEAust 1981; FAIM 1970; FTS 1979. Dir of Posts and Telegraphs, Qld, 1971–73; Dep. Dir Gen., Postmaster-Gen.'s Dept, 1973–75; Man. Dir, Australian Telecommunications Commn, 1975–81; Chairman: D. Richardson & Sons, later Richardson Pacific, 1982–90; A. W. A. Nortel, 1986–89. Comr, Overseas Telecommunications Commn (Australia), 1974–87. Pres., Victorian Div., Aust. Inst. of Management, 1979–81. Mem., Bd of Management, Defence Aerospace, 1984–86. Gov., Internat. Council for Computer Communication, 1982–. Hon. Life Mem., IREE, 1982. *Address:* 1/90 Pembroke Road, Coorparoo, Qld 4151, Australia. *T:* (07) 3977160.

CURTIS, Sir Leo; *see* Curtis, Sir E. L.

CURTIS, Michael Howard; Executive Aide to HH The Aga Khan, 1959–86; Director, Aga Khan Health and Education Services, Geneva, since 1985; Chairman, Nation Printers and Publishers, Nairobi, Kenya, 1972–77; Director, Nation Newspapers, since 1959 (Managing Director and Chief Executive, 1959, retired); *b* 28 Feb. 1920; *e s* of late Howard and Doris May Curtis; *m* 1st, 1947, Barbara Winifred Gough; two *s* two *d*; 2nd, 1961, Marian Joan Williams (*d* 1984); two step *s. Educ:* St Lawrence Coll.; Sidney Sussex Coll., Cambridge (MA). Eastern Daily Press, Norwich, 1945; News Chronicle: Leader Writer, 1946; Dep. Editor, 1952; Editor, 1954–57; Dir, News Chronicle Ltd, 1954–57; Personal Aide to HH The Aga Khan, 1957–59. *Address:* La Vieille Maison, Villemétrie, 60300 Senlis, France. *Clubs:* Garrick; Muthaiga (Nairobi).

CURTIS, His Honour Philip; a Circuit Judge (formerly a Judge of County Courts), 1969–80; *b* 29 April 1908; *s* of James William and Emma Curtis; *m* 1937, Marjorie Lillian Sharp; two *s* one *d. Educ:* St Mary's RC, Denton, Lancs; Manchester Grammar; Brasenose Coll., Oxford. Called to the Bar, Gray's Inn, 1944. *Address:* Mottram Hall Farm, Mottram St Andrew, near Macclesfield, Cheshire. *T:* Prestbury (0625) 829509.

CURTIS, Richard Herbert, QC 1977; **His Honour Judge Curtis;** Senior Circuit Judge, Oxford and Midland Circuit, since 1989. *Educ:* Oxford Univ. (MA). Called to Bar, Inner Temple, 1958, Bencher, 1985. A Recorder, 1974–89; Recorder of Birmingham, 1989–; Hon. Recorder, City of Hereford, 1981. *Address:* 1 King's Bench Walk, Temple, EC4. *T:* 071–353 8436.

CURTIS, Prof. (Robert) Frank, CBE 1985; PhD, DSc; FIFST; Professor, University of East Anglia, 1977–88, now Hon. Professor; *b* 8 Oct. 1926; *s* of late William John Curtis, Somerset, and Ethel Irene Curtis, Bath; *m* 1954, Sheila Rose, *y d* of Bruce Rose, Huddersfield; two *s* one *d. Educ:* City of Bath Sch.; Univ. of Bristol (BSc 1949, PhD 1952, DSc 1972). FRIC 1966; FIFST 1977. Johns Hopkins University: W. H. Grafflin Fellow, 1952; Instr in Chemistry, 1953; Technical Officer, ICI Ltd, Manchester, 1954–56; Res. Fellow, Univ. of WI, 1956–57; Lectr in Chem., University Coll., Swansea, 1957–62, Sen. Lectr, 1962–69; Reader, Univ. of Wales, 1969–70; Head, Chem. Div., 1970–77, Dir, 1977–85, ARC Food Res. Inst.; Dir, AFRC Inst. of Food Res., Reading, 1985–88. Chm., Food Adv. Cttee, MAFF, 1983–88 (Chm., Food Standards Cttee, 1979–83); Mem. Management Bd, AFRC, 1987–88. Mem., Norwich HA, 1989–. Hon. ScD UEA, 1988. *Publications:* res. papers on chemistry and food science in jls of learned socs. *Address:* Manor Barn, Colton, Norwich NR9 5BZ. *T:* Norwich (0603) 880379.

CURTIS, Stephen Russell; Chief Executive, Driver and Vehicle Licensing Agency, since 1990; *b* 27 Feb. 1948; *s* of Barry Russell and Joyce Muriel (*née* Smith); *m* 1972, Gillian Mary Pitkin; three *s* one *d. Educ:* Forest Sch., E17; Exeter Univ. (BA Econs and Stats). Asst Statistician, Business Stats Office, 1970–72; DTI, 1972–78, Statistician, Export Stats, 1975–78; Statistician, 1978–83, Chief Statistician, 1983–85, Business Stats Office; Registrar of Companies, 1985–90, and Chief Exec., 1988–90, Companies House. *Recreations:* travel, photography, walking. *Address:* c/o Driver and Vehicle Licensing Agency, Swansea SA6 7JL. *Club:* Civil Service.

CURTIS, Very Rev. (Wilfred) Frank; Provost of Sheffield, 1974–88, Provost Emeritus since 1988; Rural Dean of Okehampton, since 1989; *b* 24 Feb. 1923; *s* of W. A. Curtis, MC and Mrs M. Curtis (*née* Burbidge); *m* 1951, Muriel (*née* Dover); two *s* two *d. Educ:* Bishop Wordsworth's Sch., Salisbury; King's Coll., London (AKC). Served in RA, 1942–47; Major 1946. London Univ., 1947–52; Curate of High Wycombe, 1952–55; staff of Church Missionary Soc., 1955–74: Area Sec., Devon and Cornwall, 1955–65; Adviser in Rural Work, 1957–65; SW Regional Sec., 1962–65; Home Sec., 1965–74. Vice-Pres., Church Missionary Soc., 1977–; Mem., General Synod, 1977–85. Chm., Community Action Panel (S Yorks Police), 1983–86; Mem., Sheffield Council Voluntary Service, 1978–88; Chm., Radio Sheffield Religious Adv. Panel, 1985–88. Chaplain to Master Cutler, 1976, 1978, 1982, 1984; Hon. Fellow, Sheffield City Polytechnic, 1980. Hon. Canon, 1982, and Bishop's Comissary, 1983–, Maseno North Diocese, Kenya; Bishop's Commissary, Nambale, Kenya, 1988–. *Recreations:* walking, photography, nature study. *Address:* Ashplants Fingle Cottage, Drewsteignton, Exeter, Devon EX6 6QX. *T:* Drewsteignton (0647) 21253.

CURTIS, Sir William (Peter), 7th Bt *cr* 1802; *b* 9 April 1935; *s* of Sir Peter Curtis, 6th Bt, and of Joan Margaret, *d* of late Reginald Nicholson; *S* father, 1976. *Educ:* Winchester College; Trinity College, Oxford (MA); Royal Agricultural College, Cirencester. *Heir:* *cousin* Major Edward Philip Curtis, 16th/5th The Queen's Royal Lancers (retd) [*b* 25 June 1940; *m* 1978, Catherine, *d* of H. J. Armstrong, Christchurch, NZ; two *s* two *d. Educ:* Bradfield; RMA Sandhurst]. *Address:* Oak Lodge, Bank Street, Bishop's Waltham, Hants.

CURTIS-RALEIGH, Dr Jean Margaret Macdonald; Consultant Psychiatrist, Queen Mary's University Hospital, Roehampton, since 1979; Member, Broadcasting Standards Council, since 1988; *b* 12 July 1933; *d* of late Dr Harry Hubert Steadman and Janet Gilchrist Steadman (*née* Macdonald); *m* 1964, His Honour Judge Nigel Hugh Curtis-Raleigh (*d* 1986); five *s. Educ:* Convent of the Sacred Heart, Epsom, Surrey; Sutton High Sch. for Girls; Guy's Hospital Med. Sch. (MB BS); MRCPsych; DPM. Psychiatric trng, Maudsley and Bethlem Royal Hosps, 1963–66. *Recreations:* opera, gardening, walking. *Address:* c/o Hoare's Bank, 37 Fleet Street, EC4P 4DQ.

See also J. H. Steadman.

CURTISS, Air Marshal Sir John (Bagot), KCB 1981 (CB 1979); KBE 1982; FRAeS; Military and Policy Advisor, World War Memorial Fund for Disaster Relief, since 1990; Finance Director, Dinghy Ltd, since 1991; *b* 6 Dec. 1924; *s* of Major E. F. B. Curtiss, RFC; *m* 1946, Peggy Drughorn Bowie; three *s* one *d. Educ:* Radley Coll.; Wanganui Collegiate Sch., NZ; Worcester Coll., Oxford. Served War: Oxford Univ. Air Sqdn, 1942–43; Bomber Comd, 578 and 158 sqdns, 1944–45; Transport Comd, 51 and 59 sqdn, 1945–49; Training Comd, 1950–53; Fighter Comd, 29 and 5 sqdns, 1953–64; Dir, RAF Staff Coll., 1967–69; Stn Comdr RAF Bruggen, RAFG, 1970–72; Gp Capt Ops, HQ Strike Comd, 1972–74; SASO, HQ 11 Gp, 1974–75; Dir-Gen. Organisation, RAF, 1975–77; Comdt, RAF Staff Coll., 1977–80; Air Comdr, Falklands Operations, 1982; AOC No 18 Gp, 1980–83, retd. Dir and Chief Exec., SBAC, 1984–89; Sec., Defence Inds Council, 1985–89. Member, Executive Committee: Air League, 1982–; Forces Help Soc., 1984–86; Pres., Aircrew Assoc., 1987–. Chm., Governors, Canford Sch., 1990–. CBIM 1981. FRAeS 1984. *Recreations:* sailing, reading, bicycling. *Address:* c/o Coutts & Co., 1 Old Park Lane, W1Y 4BS. *Clubs:* MCC, Royal Air Force, Pilgrims; Colonels (Pres. and Founder Mem.); Royal Lymington Yacht; Keyhaven Yacht.

CURWEN, Sir Christopher (Keith), KCMG 1986 (CMG 1982); Deputy Secretary, Cabinet Office, since 1989; *b* 9 April 1929; *s* of late Rev. R. M. Curwen and Mrs M. E. Curwen; *m* 1st, 1956, Noom Tai (marr. diss. 1977); one *s* two *d*; 2nd, 1977, Helen Anne Stirling; one *s* one *d. Educ:* Sherborne Sch.; Sidney Sussex Coll., Cambridge (BA). Served HM Forces, 4th Queen's Own Hussars, 1948–49 (despatches). Joined FO, 1952; Bangkok, 1954; Vientiane, 1956; FO, 1958; Bangkok, 1961; Kuala Lumpur, 1963; FO, 1965; Washington, 1968; FCO, 1971; Geneva, 1977; FCO, 1980–88. *Recreations:* books, gardening, motoring. *Address:* c/o Cabinet Office, 70 Whitehall, SW1A 2AS. *Club:* Travellers'.

CURZON; *see* Roper-Curzon, family name of Baron Teynham.

CURZON, family name of **Earl Howe** and **Viscount Scarsdale.**

CURZON, Leonard Henry, CB 1956; *b* 4 Jan. 1912; *s* of late Frederick Henry Curzon; *m* 1935, Greta, *e d* of late Willem and Anny van Praag; one *s. Educ:* Sir Walter St John's Sch.; Jesus Coll., Cambridge (Scholar, BA, LLB). Civil Servant, 1934–72: Import Duties Adv. Cttee; Air Ministry, Ministries of Aircraft Production, Supply, Aviation and Defence. IDC 1947. *Address:* Southease, Derringstone Hill, Barham, Kent CT4 6QD. *T:* Canterbury (0227) 831449.

CUSACK, Henry Vernon, CMG 1955; CBE 1947; HM Overseas Civil Service (retired); Deputy Director General of the Overseas Audit Service, 1946–55; *b* 26 June 1895; 2nd *s* of late Edward Cusack, Bray, Co. Wicklow, and of Constance Louisa Vernon, *e d* of late Col Vernon, DL, JP, Clontarf Castle, Dublin; unmarried. *Educ:* Aravon Sch., Ireland. Served European War, 1914–19 (General Service and Victory medals), France, Belgium and North Russia, as Captain, RASC, attached RGA; entered Colonial Audit Service, 1920; Asst Auditor: Sierra Leone, 1920–22, Nigeria, 1922–28; Sen. Asst Auditor, Nyasaland, 1928–33; Asst Director, Central Office, Colonial Audit Dept London, 1933–37; Auditor, Gold Coast, 1937–46; a Governor of the King's Hospital Sch., Dublin (Chm., 1964–69). FRGS. Coronation Medal, 1953. *Address:* Our Lady's Manor, Bulloch Castle, Dalkey, Co. Dublin. *Clubs:* Naval and Military; Royal St George Yacht (Dun Laoghaire, Co. Dublin).

CUSDIN, Sidney Edward Thomas, OBE 1946; DSc (Hong Kong); FRIBA, AADip; *b* 28 July 1908; *s* of Sidney Herbert Cusdin, London; *m* 1936, Eva Eileen (Peggy), *d* of F. P. Dorizzi, London; no *c. Educ:* Municipal School of Arts and Crafts, Southend-on-Sea, Essex; Architectural Assoc., London. AA Holloway Scholarship, 1927; Fifth Year Travelling Studentship, 1929; joined staff of Stanley Hall & Easton and Robertson: British Pavilions at Brussels Internat. Exhibition and Johannesburg Exhibition; elected Member of AA Council, 1937, and worked on RIBA Cttees. Served War of 1939–45, RAF, on staff of HQ, No. 26 Group (despatches twice, OBE). Re-joined firm of Easton & Robertson, 1946; firm later known as Easton & Robertson, Cusdin, Preston and Smith, until 1965 when this partnership was dissolved; Sen. Partner, Cusdin, Burden and Howitt, until 1976. Pres. AA, 1950–51; Mem. Council RIBA, 1950–51. Awarded Henry Saxon Snell Prize and Theakston Bequest, 1950; Principal works: London: Development of the Hosp. for Sick Children, Great Ormond Street, British Postgraduate Medical Fedn, and London Univ., Inst. of Child Health; Medical Coll. of St Bartholomew's Hosp., New Hostel and Labs; Middlesex Hosp. Medical Sch.; New Sch. Buildings and Astor Coll.; National Inst. for Medical Research Develt, Mill Hill; Cambridge: Dept of Engineering, New Workshops and Laboratories; Univ. Chemistry Laboratories; United Cambridge Hosps, Addenbrooke's Hosp., Hills Rd, New Develt; MRC, extension of Lab. of Molecular Biology; Harlow: Princess Alexandra Hosp.; Belfast: Queen's Univ. of Belfast, Inst. of Clin. Science; Royal Victoria Hosp. Develt; Royal Belfast Hosp. for Sick Children, alterations and additions; Malaya: plans for Develt of Univ. of Malaya; Hong Kong; plans for develt of Univ. of Hong Kong; Cons. Architect for: Queen Elizabeth Hosp., Hong Kong (awarded RIBA Bronze Medal); Faculty of Medicine, Univ. of Riyad, Saudi Arabia. Chm., British Consultants Bureau, 1972–74. Gov., Brendoncare Foundn, 1987– (Dir, 1984–). Hon. Freeman, Apothecaries' Soc., 1981. *Publications:* (with James Crooks) Suggestions and Demonstration Plans for Hospitals for Sick Children, 1947. *Recreations:* theatre, travel, fishing; spending time in believing that "WS" was Shakespeare. *Address:* 27 Devonshire Close, W1N 1LG. *T:* 071–637 1891; 34 Ringshall, Little Gaddesden, near Berkhamsted, Herts. *Clubs:* Savile, Royal Air Force, The Sette of Odd Volumes.

CUSENS, Prof. Anthony Ralph, OBE 1989; PhD; FRSE; FEng 1988; FICE, FIStructE; Professor of Civil Engineering, University of Leeds, since 1979 (Dean, Faculty of Engineering, 1989–91); *b* 24 Sept. 1927; *s* of James Cusens and May Edith (*née* Thomas); *m* 1953, Pauline Shirin German; three *d. Educ:* St John's Coll., Southsea; University Coll. London (BSc Eng; PhD 1955). FICE 1966; FIStructE 1972; FAmSCE 1972; FRSE 1974; FIHT 1986. Res. Engr, British Cast Concrete Fedn, 1952–54; Sen. Lectr, RMCS, Shrivenham, 1954–56; Sen. Lectr, Univ. of Khartoum, Sudan, 1956–60; Prof. of Structl Engrg, Asian Inst. of Technol., Bangkok, 1960–65; Prof. of Civil Engineering: Univ. of St Andrews, 1965–67; Univ. of Dundee, 1967–78. Visitor, Transport and Road Res. Lab., 1982–88; President: Concrete Soc., 1983–84; IStructE, 1991–92; Chm., Jt Bd of Moderators of ICE, IStructE and CIBSE, 1986–89. *Publications:* (jtly) Bridge Deck Analysis, 1975; Finite Strip Method in Bridge Engineering, 1978; res. papers on concrete technol. and structures. *Recreations:* golf, gardening. *Address:* Old Hall Cottage, Bramham, West Yorks LS23 6QR. *Clubs:* East India; Pannal Golf (Harrogate).

CUSHING, David Henry, DPhil; FRS 1977; Deputy Director, Fisheries Research, England and Wales, 1974–80; *b* 14 March 1920; *s* of W. E. W. Cushing and Isobel (*née* Batchelder); *m* 1943, Diana R. C. Antona-Traversi; one *d. Educ:* Duke's Sch., Alnwick; Newcastle upon Tyne Royal Grammar Sch.; Balliol Coll., Oxford (MA, DPhil). RA, 1940–45; 1st Bn, Royal Fusiliers, 1945–46. Fisheries Lab., 1946–80. Rosenstiel Gold Medal for Oceanographic Science, Rosenstiel Inst. for Marine and Atmospheric Scis, Miami, 1980; Albert Medal for Oceanography, Institut Océanographique, Paris, 1984; Award for Excellence, Amer. Fisheries Soc., 1986. *Publications:* The Arctic Cod, 1966; Fisheries Biology, 1968 (USA); Detection of Fish, 1973; Fisheries Resources and their Management, 1974; Marine Ecology and Fisheries, 1975; Science and the Fisheries, 1977; Climate and Fisheries, 1982; The Provident Sea, 1988. *Address:* 198 Yarmouth Road, Lowestoft, Suffolk NR32 4AB. *T:* Lowestoft (0502) 65569.

CUST, family name of **Baron Brownlow.**

CUSTANCE, Michael Magnus Vere, CB 1959; *b* 3 Jan. 1916; *e s* of late Mrs Arthur Long (Marjorie Bowen, novelist); *m*; one *s* one *d. Educ:* St Paul's (schol.); The Queen's Coll., Oxford (open hist. schol., BA Hons, 1st cl., Mod. Hist., 1937). Asst Principal, Board of Trade, 1938; Ministry of Shipping, 1939; Royal Air Force, 1941–45; Principal, Ministry of War Transport, 1943; Asst Sec., Min. of Transport, 1948; Under-Sec., Min. of Transport and Civil Aviation, 1956; Dep. Sec., Min. of Transport and Civil Aviation, 1958; in Ministry of Aviation, 1959–63; in Ministry of Transport, 1963–66; in Min. of Social Security, later DHSS, 1966–75; Chief Advr to Supplementary Benefits Commn, 1968–75. IDC (1952 Course). *Address:* 7 Claremont Way, Midhurst, West Sussex GU29 9QM.

CUSTIS, Patrick James, CBE 1981; FCA, FCMA, FCIS; director of companies; *b* 19 March 1921; *er s* of late Alfred and Amy Custis; *m* 1954, Rita, *yr d* of late Percy and Annie Rayner; one *s. Educ:* The High Sch., Dublin. JDipMA. FCA 1951; FCMA 1950; FCIS 1945. Served articles with Josolyne Miles & Co., Chartered Accountants, Cheapside, London, 1945–51; Asst to Gen. Man., Rio Tinto Co. Ltd, London, 1952–54; Gp Chief Accountant and Dir of subsid. cos, Glynwed Ltd, W Midlands, 1955–66; Guest Keen & Nettlefolds Ltd, W Midlands, 1967–81 (Dir of Finance, 1974–81); various sen. appts prior to 1974. Mem., Midlands and N Wales Reg. Bd (formerly Birmingham and W Midlands Reg. Bd), Lloyds Bank plc, 1979–91; Director: New Court Property Fund Managers Ltd, 1978–91; Associated Heat Services plc, 1981–90; Wolseley plc, 1982–90; Birmingham Technology Ltd, 1983–; Wyko Group PLC, 1985–; Dep. Chm., Leigh Interests plc, 1982–; Chm., MCD Group plc, 1983–86. Member: HM Prisons Bd, Home Office, 1980–85; Bi-Centenary Adv. Bd, Birmingham Gen. Hosp., 1978–90. Co-opted Mem. Council, Inst. of Chartered Accountants in England and Wales, 1979–85; Liveryman, Worshipful Co. of Chartered Accountants in England and Wales; Pres., Wolverhampton Soc. of Chartered Accountants, 1985–86. FRSA 1987. *Recreations:* walking, gardening, reading. *Address:* West Barn, Westmancote, near Tewkesbury, Glos GL20 7ES. *T:* Bredon (0684) 72865. *Clubs:* Royal Over-Seas League, Lansdowne.

See also R. A. Custis.

CUSTIS, Ronald Alfred; Director General, Energy Industries Council, 1981–Feb. 1992; *b* 28 Feb. 1931; *yr s* of late Alfred and Amy Custis, Dublin; *m* 1st, 1957, Enid Rowe (*d* 1984); one *s* one *d*; 2nd, 1986, Mrs Valerie Mackett. *Educ:* The High Sch., Dublin. Joined HM Treasury, 1947; DES, 1964; Min. of Technology, 1964–70: Private Sec. to Permanent Under Sec., 1964–66; Principal, 1967; Sec. to Cttee of Inquiry into the Brain Drain, 1967–68; Min. of Aviation Supply, later MoD (Procurement Exec.), 1970–74: Private Sec. to Sec. of State for Defence, 1971–73; Asst Sec., 1973; Dept of Energy, 1974–81: Private Sec. to successive Secs of State for Energy, 1974–75; Under Sec., 1978; Dir Gen., Offshore Supplies Office, 1980–81. *Recreations:* reading, walking, listening to music, gardening. *Address:* Woodbrook, London Road, Offham, Maidstone, Kent ME19 5AL. *T:* West Malling (0732) 848751.

See also P. J. Custis.

CUTHBERT, Prof. Alan William, PhD; FRS 1982; Sheild Professor of Pharmacology, University of Cambridge, since 1979; Master of Fitzwilliam College, Cambridge, since 1990; *b* 7 May 1932; *s* of late Thomas William Cuthbert and Florence Mary (*née* Griffin); *m* 1957, Harriet Jane Webster; two *s. Educ:* Leicester Coll. of Technol.; St Andrews Univ. (BSc); London Univ. (BPharm, PhD). MA Cantab. Instructor Lieut, RN, 1953–56. Res. Fellow, then Asst Lectr, Dept of Pharmacology, Sch. of Pharmacy, Univ. of London, 1959–63; Demonstrator in Pharmacol., 1963–66, Lectr, 1966–73, and Reader, 1973–79, Dept of Pharmacol., Univ. of Cambridge; Fellow of Jesus Coll., Cambridge, 1968–90. Chm. Editorial Bd, British Jl of Pharmacology, 1974–82. Member: AFRC, 1988–90; Council, Royal Soc., 1986–88; Council, Zool Soc. of London, 1988–. Pereira Medal in Materia Medica, Pharmaceutical Soc. of GB, 1953; Sir James Irvine Medal in Chemistry, St Andrews Univ., 1955. *Publications:* scientific papers in pharmacol and physiol jls. *Recreations:* travel, painting, growing orchids, Duodecimos. *Address:* Master's Lodge, Fitzwilliam College, Cambridge. *T:* Cambridge (0223) 332000.

CUTHBERT, Lady, (Betty Wake), CBE 1946 (OBE 1943); OStJ 1944; *b* 1904; *d* of Guy Shorrock and Emma Wake; *m* 1928, Vice-Adm. Sir John Cuthbert, KBE, CB (*d* 1987); no *c*. Joined Auxiliary Fire Service, London, as driver, 1938; Fire Staff, Home Office, 1941; Chief Woman Fire Officer, National Fire Service, 1941–46. Nat. Chm., Girls' Venture Corps, 1946–67 (Pres. 1967). Mem., Hampshire CC, 1967–74. *Address:* Ibthorpe Manor Farm, Hurstbourne Tarrant, Andover, Hants.

CUTHBERT, Ian Holm; see Holm, Ian.

CUTHBERTSON, Sir Harold (Alexander), Kt 1983; Managing Director, Blundstone Pty Ltd, since 1957; Chairman and Director, Essential Oils of Tasmania Pty Ltd; Director, Tasmania University Research Co. Pty Ltd; *b* 16 Nov. 1911; *s* of Thomas Alexander Cuthbertson and Vera Rose Cuthbertson; *m* 1937, Jean Westbrook; two *d. Educ:* Hutchins Sch., Hobart. Entered family business, Blundstone Pty Ltd, 1932; after tertiary training, became Dir, 1939. Dir of cos, public and private. Pres., Tas Chamber of Manufrs, 1964–67; Vice Pres., Assoc. of Aust. Chambers of Manufrs, 1966–67; Mem., Commonwealth Immigration Planning Council, 1968–75; Warden, Marine Bd of Hobart, 1963–75. *Recreations:* bowls, fishing. *Address:* 3 David Avenue, Sandy Bay, Tas 7005, Australia. *T:* (002) 251619. *Clubs:* Tasmanian, Athenæum (Pres. 1970), Rotary (Pres., 1959–60) (Hobart).

CUTLER, Sir (Arthur) Roden, VC 1941; AK 1981; KCMG 1965; KCVO 1970; CBE 1957; Governor of New South Wales, 1966–81; company director; Chairman, State Bank of New South Wales, 1981–86; *b* 24 May 1916; *s* of Arthur William Cutler and Ruby Daphne (*née* Pope); *m* 1946, Helen Gray Annetta (*née* Morris), AC 1980 (*d* 1990); four *s. Educ:* Sydney High Sch.; University of Sydney (BEc). Public Trust Office (NSW), 1935–42; War of 1939–45 (VC). State Secretary, RSS & AILA (NSW), 1942–43; Mem., Aliens Classification and Adv. Cttee to advise Commonwealth Govt, 1942–43; Asst Dep. Dir, Security Service, NSW, 1943; Asst Comr Repatriation, 1943–46; High Comr for Australia to New Zealand, 1946–52; High Comr for Australia to Ceylon, 1952–55; HM's Australian Minister to Egypt, 1955–56; Secretary General, SEATO Conference, 1957; Chief of Protocol, Dept of External Affairs, Canberra, 1957–58; State President of RSL, formerly RSSAILA (ACT), 1958; Australian High Comr to Pakistan, 1959–61; Australian Representative to Independence of Somali Republic, 1960; Australian Consul-General, New York, 1961–65; Ambassador to the Netherlands, 1965. Delegate to UN General Assembly, and Australian Rep., Fifth Cttee, 1962–63–64. Chairman: Occidental Life Assurance Co. of Australia, 1987–90; Ansett Express (formerly Air New South Wales), 1981–; First Australia Fund, 1985–; First Australia Prime Income Fund, 1986–; First Australia Prime Income Investment Co., 1986–; Rothmans Foundn, 1987–; Director: Rothmans Hldgs Ltd (formerly Rothmans of Pall Mall), 1981–; Permanent Trustee Co., 1981–. Hon. Col, Royal New South Wales Regt, 1966–85; Hon. Col, Sydney Univ. Regt, 1966–85; Hon. Air Cdre RAAF. Hon. LLD, Univ. of Sydney; Hon. DSc: Univ. of New South Wales; Univ. of Newcastle; Hon. DLitt: Univ. of New England; Univ. of Wollongong. KStJ 1965. *Recreations:* swimming, shooting, yachting. *Address:* 22 Ginahgulla Road, Bellevue Hill, NSW 2023, Australia. *T:* Sydney 326 1233. *Clubs:* Australian, Union (Sydney); Royal Sydney Yacht Squadron, Royal Prince Alfred Yacht (Sydney), Royal Sydney Golf.

CUTLER, Hon. Sir Charles (Benjamin), KBE 1973; ED 1960; Director, since 1976, Chairman, since 1978, Sun Alliance (Australia); *b* Forbes, NSW, 20 April 1918; *s* of George Hamilton Cutler and Elizabeth Cutler; *m* 1943, Dorothy Pascoe (OBE 1976); three *s* one *d. Educ:* rural and high schs, Orange, NSW. MLA for Orange, NSW, 1947; Leader of Country Party (NSW), 1959; Dep. Premier and Minister for Educn, 1965; Dep. Premier, 1972–76, Minister for Local Govt, 1972–76, and Minister for Tourism, 1975–76, NSW. Chm., United World Colls (Aust.) Trust, 1977. Hon. DLitt Newcastle Univ., NSW, 1968. *Recreation:* golf. *Address:* 52 Kite Street, Orange, NSW 2800, Australia. *T:* 62–6418. *Clubs:* Royal Automobile, Imperial Service, Union (Sydney); Orange Golf.

CUTLER, Sir Horace (Walter), Kt 1979; OBE 1963; DL; Member of Greater London Council for Harrow West, 1964–86; Chairman, Branch Retirement Homes PLC, since 1985; *b* London, N16, 28 July 1912; *s* of Albert Benjamin and Mary Ann Cutler; *m* 1957, Christiane, *d* of Dr Klaus Muthesius; one *s* three *d* (and one *s* of previous marriage). *Educ:* Harrow Grammar Sch.; Hereford. Served War of 1939–45: RNVR, 1941–46, Lieut. Harrow Borough Council: elected 1952; Chm. Planning Cttee, 1954; Chm. Housing Cttee, 1955–58; Dep. Mayor, 1958; Alderman, 1959; Mayor, 1959–60; Leader of Council, 1961–65; Chm., Gen. Purposes Cttee, 1962–65; Middlesex CC: elected, 1955; Vice-Chm., Estates and Housing Cttee, 1957; Chm. Planning Cttee, 1961–65; Dep. Leader of CC, 1962; Leader, 1963–65; Greater London Council: Dep. Leader of Opposition, 1964–67 and 1973–74; Dep. Leader, 1967–73; Leader of Opposition, 1974–77 and 1981–82; Leader, 1977–81; Chm. Housing Cttee, 1967–70; Policy and Resources Cttee, 1970–73. Chm., Central Milton Keynes Shopping Management Co. Ltd, 1976–89; Member: Milton Keynes New City Develt Corp, 1967–86; Central Housing Adv. Cttee, Min. of Housing and Local Govt, 1967–74; Nat. Housing and Town Planning Exec. Cttee, 1967–74 (Vice-Chm., London Region, 1968); Dir, S Bank Theatre Bd; Mem., Nat. Theatre Bd, 1975–82; Trustee, Nat. Theatre, 1976–83. Contested (C) Willesden East, 1970; Pres., Harrow West Conservative Assoc., 1964– (Chm., 1961–64). Freeman of Harrow, and City of London. DL Greater London, 1981. FRSA. OStJ. *Publication:* The Cutler Files, 1982. *Recreations:* golf, ski-ing, classical music, travel. *Address:* Hawkswood, Hawkswood Lane, Gerrards Cross, Bucks SL9 7BN. *T:* Fulmer (0753) 663182. *Clubs:* Constitutional, United & Cecil.

CUTLER, Ivor; humorist, since 1957; *b* 1923; *s* of Jack and Polly Cutler; two *s. Educ:* Shawlands Academy. *Radio and television:* Monday Night at Home, Radio 4, 1959–63; John Peel, Radio 1, 1969–; 14 radio plays, Radio 3, 1979–88; Prince Ivor (opera), Radio 3, 1983; King Cutler I to VI (with Phyllis King), Radio 3, 1990–; Magical Mystery Tour, TV, 1967; Ivor Cutler has 15, 1990, Cutler the Lax, 1991, Radio 4 (radio archive selections); *stage:* Establishment Club (cabaret), 1961–62; An Evening of British Rubbish, Comedy Th., 1963. Cartoonist, Private Eye and Observer, 1962–63. Pye Radio Award for humour, 1980. *Gramophone records:* Ivor Cutler of Y'hup, 1959; Get Away from the Wall, 1961; Who Tore Your Trousers?, 1961; Ludo, 1967; Dandruff, 1974; Velvet Donkey, 1975; Jammy Smears, 1976; Life in a Scotch Sitting Room, vol. 2, 1978, reissued 1987; Privilege, 1983; Women of the World (single), 1983; Prince Ivor, 1986; Gruts, 1986. *Publications: stories:* Cockadoodle don't, 1967; (illustr. Martin Honeysett): Gruts, 1961, repr. 1986; Life in a Scotch Sitting Room, vol. 2, 1984; Fremsley, 1987; Glasgow Dreamer, 1990; *children's books:* (illustr. Helen Oxenbury): Meal One, 1971; Balooky Klujypop, 1974; The Animal House, 1977; (illustr. Alfreda Benge): Herbert the Chicken, 1984; Herbert the Elephant, 1984; (illustr. M. Honeysett) One and a Quarter, 1987; (illustr. Patrick Benson) Herbert, 1988; (illustr. Jill Barton) Grape Zoo, 1990; (illustr. Claudio Muñoz) Doris the Hen, 1992; *poetry:* Many Flies Have Feathers, 1973; A Flat Man, 1977; Private Habits, 1981; Large et Puffy, 1984; Fresh Carpet, 1986; A Nice Wee Present from Scotland, 1988; (illustr. M. Honeysett) Fly Sandwich and other Menu, 1991. *Recreation:* making fish and houses from clay. *Address:* c/o BBC, Broadcasting House, W1A 1AA.

CUTLER, Robin; see Cutler, T. R.

CUTLER, Sir Roden; see Cutler, Sir A. R.

CUTLER, Timothy Robert, (Robin); Director-General and Deputy Chairman, Forestry Commission, since 1990; *b* 24 July 1934; *s* of Frank Raymond Cutler and Jeannie Evelyn Cutler (*née* Badenoch); *m* 1958, Ishbel Primrose; one *s* one *d. Educ:* Banff Academy; Aberdeen Univ. (BSc Forestry 1956). National Service, Royal Engineers, 1956–58. Colonial Forest Service, Kenya, 1958–64; New Zealand Forest Service: joined 1964; Dir of Forest Management, 1978; Dep. Dir-Gen., 1986; Chief Exec., Min. of Forestry, 1988–90. *Recreations:* tennis, golf, gardening, stamps. *Address:* Forestry Commission, 231 Corstorphine Road, Edinburgh EH12 7AT. *T:* 031–334 0303.

CUTT, Rev. Canon Samuel Robert; Canon Residentiary since 1979 and Treasurer since 1985 of Wells Cathedral (Chancellor, 1979–85); Warden of the Community of St Denys, Warminster, since 1987; *b* 28 Nov. 1925; *er s* of Robert Bush Cutt and Lilian Elizabeth Cutt (*née* Saint); *m* 1972, Margaret Eva (*d* 1975), *yr d* of Norman and Eva McIntyre. *Educ:* Skegness Grammar Sch.; Selwyn Coll., Cambridge; Cuddesdon Coll., Oxford. BA Cantab 1950, MA 1954. Deacon 1953, Priest 1954. Asst Curate, St Aidan, West Hartlepool, 1953–56; Tutor for King's Coll. London at St Boniface Coll., Warminster, 1956–59; Sub-Warden for KCL at St Boniface Coll., 1959–65; Lectr and Tutor of Chichester Theol Coll., 1965–71; Priest Vicar of Chichester Cath., 1966–71; Minor Canon, 1971–79, and Succentor, 1974–79, St Paul's Cathedral, and Warden, Coll. of Minor Canons, 1974–79; part-time Lectr, Theological Dept, KCL, 1973–79; Priest in Ordinary to the Queen, 1975–79. Dio. Dir of Ordinands, Bath and Wells, 1979–86; Examining Chaplain to Bishop of Bath and Wells, 1980–. OStJ 1981. *Recreations:* walking, music, biographical studies, heraldry, cooking. *Address:* 8 The Liberty, Wells, Somerset BA5 2SU. *T:* Wells (0749) 78763.

CUTTER, Prof. Elizabeth Graham, PhD, DSc; FRSE; FLS; George Harrison Professor of Botany, University of Manchester, 1979–89, now Emeritus; *b* 9 Aug. 1929; *d* of Roy Carnegie Cutter and Alexandra (*née* Graham). *Educ:* Rothesay House Sch., Edinburgh; Univ. of St Andrews (BSc, DSc); Univ. of Manchester (PhD). Asst Lecturer in Botany, 1955–57, Lectr in Botany, 1957–64, Univ. of Manchester; Associate Professor of Botany, 1964–68, Professor of Botany, 1968–72, Univ. of California, Davis; Sen. Lectr in Cryptogamic Botany, 1972–74, Reader in Cryptogamic Botany, 1974–79, Univ. of Manchester. *Publications:* Trends in Plant Morphogenesis (principal editor), 1966; Plant Anatomy: Experiment and Interpretation, pt 1, Cells and Tissues, 1969, 2nd edn 1978; pt 2, Organs, 1971. *Recreations:* photography, fishing. *Address:* 8 Huxley Close, Bramhall, Stockport, Cheshire SK7 2PJ. *T:* 061–439 1566. *Club:* Royal Over-Seas League.

CUTTS, Rt. Rev. Richard Stanley; Assistant Bishop, diocese of Lincoln, and Assistant Curate (NSM) in the South Lafford Group, since 1990; *b* 17 Sept. 1919; *s* of Edward Stanley and Gabrielle Cutts; *m* 1960, Irene Adela Sack; one *s* three *d. Educ:* Felsted School, Essex. Asst Curate, SS Peter and Paul, Godalming, 1951–56; Director of St Cyprian's Mission, Etalaneni and Priest-in-Charge Nkandhla Chapelry, Zululand, 1957–63; Director, Kambula Mission District, 1963–65; Rector, St Mary's, Kuruman and Director, Kuruman

Mission District, 1965–71; Archdeacon of Kuruman, 1969–71; Dean of Salisbury, Rhodesia, 1971–75; Bishop in Argentina and Eastern South America, 1975; name of dio. changed to Argentina and Uruguay 1986, to Argentina 1988; retired 1989. *Address:* 1 The Drove, Osbournby, Sleaford, Lincs NG34 0DH.

CYPRUS AND THE GULF, Bishop in, since 1987; **Rt. Rev. John Edward Brown;** Episcopal Canon, St George's Cathedral, Jerusalem, since 1987; *b* 13 July 1930; *s* of Edward and Muriel Brown; *m* 1956, Rosemary (*née* Wood); one *s. Educ:* Wintringham Grammar Sch., Grimsby; Kelham Theological Coll., Notts. BD London. Deacon 1955, priest 1956; Master, St George's School, Jerusalem; Curate, St George's Cathedral, Jerusalem; Chaplain of Amman, Jordan, 1954–57; Curate-in-Charge, All Saints, Reading, 1957–60; Missionary and Chaplain, All Saints Cathedral, Khartoum, Sudan, 1960–64; Vicar: Stewkley, Buckingham, 1964–69; St Luke's, Maidenhead, 1969–73; Bracknell, Berkshire, 1973–77; Rural Dean of Sonning, 1974–77; Archdeacon of Berkshire, 1978–86. *Recreations:* walking; Middle East and African studies. *Address:* PO Box 2075, Nicosia, Cyprus.

CZIFFRA; pianist; *b* Budapest, Hungary; *m* 1942, Madame Soleyka Cziffra; one *s. Educ:* Academy of Music Franz Liszt, Budapest. Has given recitals and taken part in concerts at the Festival Hall, London, and throughout the world: USA, Canada, France, Israel, Benelux, Germany, Italy, Switzerland, Hungary, Austria, Japan, S America, also BBC and BBC Television, London. Records for HMV: Liszt, Grieg, Tchaikowski, Rackmaninof, Beethoven, Schumann, paraphrases by G. Cziffra, Brahms's Hungarian dances, transciption by Cziffra, etc. Founded, 1968, biennial Concours International de Piano, Versailles, for young pianists; Founder, with son, 1966, Festival of La Chaise Dieu; undertook the creation, in the Chapelle Royale Saint Frambourg, Senlis, of an Auditorium Franz Liszt, 1973; first cultural exchanges between France and Hungary (Foundation Cziffra of Budapest), 1983; Pres., Foundation Cziffra, 1975– (created for young artists). Chevalier de la Légion d'Honneur, 1973. Comdr, Ordre des Arts et des Lettres, 1975. Médaille d'or de l'Académie Française, 1981. *Publication:* Des canons et des fleurs, 1977. *Address:* 1 place Saint Pierre, 60300 Senlis, France. *T:* (4)-453–39–99.

D

d'ABO, Jennifer Mary Victoria; Chairman: Moyses Stevens, since 1989; Roffey Brothers Ltd, since 1988; Member of Council, Prince's Youth Business Trust, since 1987; *b* 14 Aug. 1945; *d* of Michael Hammond-Maude and Rosamond Hammond-Maude (*née* Patrick); *m* 1st, David Morgan-Jones; one *d*; 2nd, Peter Cadbury, *qv*; one *s*; 3rd, Robin d'Abo (marr. diss. 1987). *Educ:* Hatherop Castle, Glos. Chairman: Ryman Ltd, 1981–87; Ryman Gp plc, 1986–87; Director: Burlingtons Furniture Co., 1977–80; (non-exec.) Pentos plc, 1987–88; Jean Sorelle, toiletry manufacturing co., 1980–83; Stormgard plc, 1985–86; London Docklands Develt Corp., 1985–88; Channel Four Television, 1986–87. Mem., Doctors' and Dentists' Remuneration Review Body, 1989–. Trustee, BM (Natural History), 1988–. *Address:* 13 Wilton Crescent, SW1X 8RN.

d'ABREU, Francis Arthur, ERD 1954; Surgeon, 1946–69, Consultant Surgeon, since 1969, Westminster Hospital; Surgeon, 1950–69, now Emeritus, Hospital of St John and St Elizabeth; Surgeon to Jockey Club and National Hunt Committee, since 1964; *b* 1 Oct. 1904; *s* of Dr John Francis d'Abreu and Teresa d'Abreu; *m* 1945, Margaret Ann Bowes-Lyon; one *s* two *d*. *Educ:* Stonyhurst Coll.; Birmingham Univ. MB, ChB Birmingham 1929; MRCS, LRCP 1929; FRCS, 1932; ChM Birmingham 1935. House Surgeon, Gen. Hosp., Birmingham, 1929; Res. Surgical Officer, Gen. and Queen's Hosps, Birmingham, 1930–34; Surg. Registrar, St Bartholomew's Hosp., London, and Westminster Hosp., 1934–39. Formerly: Examiner to Soc. of Apothecaries; Examiner to Univs of Cambridge and London; Mem., Ct of Examiners, RCS. Mem. Bd of Management, Inst. of Sports Medicine. Lieut RAMC (Supp. Reserve), 1939. Served War of 1939–45: Major, RAMC, 1939, Lt-Col 1942–45. Kt of Magistral Grace, Sov. and Mil. Order of Malta; Kt Comdr, Order of St Gregory (Holy See), 1977. *Publications:* contrib. to various medical jls. *Recreation:* gardening. *Address:* 36 Cumberland Terrace, Regent's Park, NW1 4HP.

DACCA; *see* Dhaka.

DACIE, Prof. Sir John (Vivian), Kt 1976; FRS 1967; MD, FRCP; Professor of Haematology, Royal Post-graduate Medical School of London, University of London, 1957–77, now Emeritus; *b* 20 July 1912; British; *s* of John Charles and Lilian Maud Dacie, Putney; *m* 1938, Margaret Kathleen Victoria Thynne; three *s* two *d*. *Educ:* King's Coll. Sch., Wimbledon; King's Coll., London: King's Coll. Hospital, London. MB, BS London 1935; MD 1952; MRCP 1936; FRCP 1956; Hon. FRSM 1984; MD (Hon.): Uppsala, 1961; Marseille, 1977; FRCPath (Pres., 1973–75); Pres., RSM, 1977. Various medical appointments, King's Coll. Hospital, Postgraduate Medical Sch. and Manchester Royal Infirmary, 1936–39. Pathologist, EMS, 1939–42; Major, then Lieut-Col, RAMC, 1943–46. Senior Lecturer in Clinical Pathology, then Reader in Haematology, Postgraduate Medical Sch., 1946–56. Chm., Med. and Scientific Adv. Panel, Leukaemia Research Fund, 1975–85. *Publications:* Practical Haematology, 1950, 2nd edn, 1956, 7th edn (jointly), 1991; Haemolytic Anaemias, 1954: 2nd edn, Part I, 1960, Part II, 1962, Parts III and IV, 1967, 3rd edn, Part I, 1985, Part II, 1988; various papers on anaemia in medical journals. *Recreations:* music, entomology, gardening. *Address:* 10 Alan Road, Wimbledon, SW19. *T:* 081–946 6086.

DACOMBE, William John Armstrong; Director, Campbell Lutyens Hudson & Co. Ltd, since 1988; *b* 21 Sept. 1934; *s* of late John Christian Dacombe and of Eileen Elizabeth Dacombe; *m* 1962, Margaretta Joanna (*née* Barrington); two *d*. *Educ:* Felsted School; Corpus Christi College, Oxford (MA). Kleinwort Benson, 1961–65; N. M. Rothschild & Sons, 1965–73 (Dir, 1970–73); Dir, 1973–84, Asst Chief Exec., 1979–82, Williams & Glyn's Bank; Group Exec. Dir, Royal Bank of Scotland Group, 1982–84; Chief Exec. Dir, Rea Brothers Group, 1984–88; Dir, W. A. Tyzack, 1987–89. Mem., Export Guarantee Adv. Council, 1982–86 (Dep. Chm., 1985–86). FRSA. *Recreations:* art, historic buildings, reading. *Address:* Mullion Cottage, Well Lane, SW14 7AJ. *T:* 081–876 4336. *Club:* Brooks's.

da COSTA, Harvey Lloyd, CMG 1962; **Hon. Mr Justice da Costa;** Judge of Appeal, Court of Appeal for Bermuda, since 1982; *b* 8 Dec. 1914; *s* of John Charles and Martha da Costa. *Educ:* Calabar High Sch., Jamaica; St Edmund Hall (Sen. Exhibnr; Rhodes Schol.), Oxford. BA (Hons) London; MA, BLitt Oxon; Practised at Chancery Bar, 1950–52; Crown Counsel, Jamaica, 1952–54; Sen. Crown Counsel, Jamaica, 1954–56; Asst Attorney-Gen., Jamaica, 1956–59; QC Jamaica 1959; Attorney-Gen. of West Indies, 1959–62; practised Private Bar, Jamaica, 1962–77; Puisne Judge 1978–80, Chief Justice, 1980–81, Bahamas Supreme Court; Judge of Appeal, Court of Appeal for Bahamas, 1982–85. Mem., Anguilla, British Virgin Is and Seychelles Commns. Hon. LLD Univ. of W Indies, 1990. *Recreation:* swimming. *Address:* c/o Court of Appeal, Hamilton HM12, Bermuda.

da COSTA, Sergio Corrêa, GCVO; Brazilian diplomat, retired; *b* 19 Feb. 1919; *s* of Dr I. A. da Costa and Lavinia Corrêa da Costa; *m* 1943, Zazi Aranha; one *s* two *d*. *Educ:* Law Sch., Univ. of Brazil; post grad. UCLA; Brazilian War Coll. Career diplomat; Sec. of Embassy, Buenos Ayres, then Washington, 1944–48; Acting Deleg., Council of OAS, Wash., 1946–48; Inter-American Econ. and Social Coun., Washington, 1946–48; Dep. Head, Economic Dept, Min. of Ext. Relations, 1952; Actg Pres., Braz. Nat. Techn. Assistance Commn, 1955–58; Minister-Counsellor, Rome, 1959–62; Permanent Rep. to FAO, Rome, 1960; Mem., Financial Cttee of FAO, 1962–63; Ambassador to Canada, 1962–65; Asst Sec.-Gen. for Internat. Organizations at Min. Ext. Relations, 1966; Sec.-Gen., Min. of Ext. Relations, 1967–68; Acting Minister for External Relations, 1967–68; Ambassador to UK, 1968–75; Permanent Rep. to UN in NY, 1975–83; Ambassador to USA, 1983–86. Member: Brazilian Acad. of Letters; Brazilian Hist. and Geographical Inst.; Brazilian Soc. of Internat. Law; American Soc. of Internat. Law. Grand Officer: Military Order of Aeronautical Merit, Brazil, 1967; Order of Naval Merit, Brazil, 1967; Grand Cross of Victorian Order (Hon. GCVO), Gt Britain, 1968; also numerous Grand Crosses, etc, of Orders, from other countries, 1957–. *Publications:* (mostly in Brazil): As 4 Coroas de Pedro I, 1941; Pedro I e Metternich, 1942; Diplomacia Brasileira na Questao de Leticia, 1943; A Diplomacia do Marechal, 1945; Every Inch a King—A biography of Pedro I, Emperor of Brazil, 1950 (NY 1964, London 1972). *Recreations:* reading, writing, boating. *Address:* 8/10 rue Guynemer, 75006 Paris, France. *Clubs:* White's, Travellers' (London); Rideau, Country (Ottawa); Circolo della Caccia (Rome).

DACRE, Baroness (27th in line), *cr* 1321; **Rachel Leila Douglas-Home;** *b* 24 Oct. 1929; *er* surv. *d* of 4th Viscount Hampden, CMG (*d* 1965) (whose Barony of Dacre was called out of abeyance in her favour, 1970) and of Leila Emily, *o d* of late Lt-Col Frank Evelyn Seely; *m* 1951, Hon. William Douglas-Home, *qv*; one *s* three *d*. *Heir:* *s* Hon. James Thomas Archibald Douglas-Home [*b* 16 May 1952; *m* 1979, Christine (*née* Stephenson); one *d*]. *Address:* Derry House, Kilmeston, near Alresford, Hants.

DACRE OF GLANTON, Baron *cr* 1979 (Life Peer), of Glanton in the County of Northumberland; **Hugh Redwald Trevor-Roper;** Master of Peterhouse, Cambridge, 1980–87 (Hon. Fellow, 1987); *b* 15 January 1914; *er s* of late Dr B. W. E. Trevor-Roper, Glanton and Alnwick, Northumberland; *m* 1954, Lady Alexandra Howard-Johnston, *e d* of late Field-Marshal Earl Haig, KT, GCB, OM. *Educ:* Charterhouse; Christ Church, Oxford. Research Fellow Merton Coll., 1937–39 (Hon. Fellow, 1980). Student of Christ Church, Oxford, 1946–57; Censor 1947–52; Hon. Student, 1979; Regius Prof. of Modern Hist., and Fellow of Oriel Coll., Oxford Univ., 1957–80 (Hon. Fellow, 1980). Dir, Times Newspapers Ltd, 1974–88. Chevalier, Legion of Honour, 1975. *Publications:* Archbishop Laud, 1940; The Last Days of Hitler, 1947; The Gentry, 1540–1640, 1953; (ed) Hitler's Table Talk, 1953; (ed with J. A. W. Bennett) The Poems of Richard Corbett, 1955; Historical Essays, 1957; (ed) Hitler's War Directives, 1939–45, 1964; (ed) Essays in British History Presented to Sir Keith Feiling, 1964; The Rise of Christian Europe, 1965; Religion, The Reformation and Social Change, 1967; (ed) The Age of Expansion, 1968; The Philby Affair, 1968; The European Witch-Craze of the 16th and 17th Centuries, 1970; The Plunder of the Arts in the Seventeenth Century, 1970; Princes and Artists, 1976; A Hidden Life, 1976; (ed) The Goebbels Diaries, 1978; Renaissance Essays, 1985; Catholics, Anglicans and Puritans, 1987. *Address:* The Old Rectory, Didcot, Oxon OX11 7EB. *Clubs:* Beefsteak, United Oxford & Cambridge University.
See also Earl Haig, P. D. Trevor-Roper.

da CUNHA, John Wilfrid, JP; **His Honour Judge da Cunha;** a Circuit Judge (formerly Judge of County Courts), since 1970; *b* 6 Sept. 1922; 2nd *s* of Frank C. da Cunha, MD, DPH, and Lucy (*née* Finnerty); *m* 1953, Janet, MB, ChB, *d* of Louis Savatard, (Hon.) MSc, LSA, and Judith Savatard, MB, BS; one *s* four *d*. *Educ:* Stonyhurst Coll., Lancs; St John's Coll., Cambridge. MA Cantab 1954. Served 1942–47: 23rd Hussars (RAC); wounded Normandy, 1944; Judge Advocate Gen. (War Crimes); Hon. Major. Called to Bar, Middle Temple, 1948; Northern Circuit. Chm., Local Appeal Tribunal, Min. of Social Security (Wigan), 1964–69. Asst Recorder, Oldham County Borough QS, 1966–70; Chm., Industrial Tribunals, 1966–70; Dep. Chm., Lancs County QS, 1968–71. Comr, NI (Emergency Provisions) Act, 1973; Member: Appeals Tribunal; Parole Bd, 1976–78. Pres., Bristol Medico-Legal Soc., 1989–91. Governor, Mount Carmel Sch., Alderley Edge, 1962–78. JP Lancs 1968. *Recreations:* gardening, pottering. *Address:* c/o Circuit Administrator, Western Circuit Office, Bridge House, Clifton Down, Bristol B38 4BN.

D'AETH, Prof. Richard, PhD; President, Hughes Hall, Cambridge, 1978–84; *b* 3 June 1912; *e s* of Walter D'Aeth and Marion Turnbull; *m* 1943, Pamela Straker; two *d*. *Educ:* Bedford Sch.; Emmanuel Coll., Cambridge (Scholar; 1st Cl. Hons Nat. Sci., PhD); Harvard Univ. (Commonwealth Fellow; AM). Served War, RAF, 1941–46 (Wing Comdr). Master, Gresham's Sch., 1938–40; HM Inspector of Schs, 1946–52; Prof. of Education: University Coll. of West Indies, 1952–58; Univ. of Exeter, 1958–77. Mem., Internat. Assoc. for Advancement of Educnl Res. (Pres., Warsaw, 1969); sometime mem. cttees of Schools Council, BBC, Schs Broadcasting Council, RCN and NSPCC. *Publications:* Education and Development in the Third World, 1975; articles in jls. *Address:* 57 Highsett, Cambridge CB2 1NZ.

DAHL, Mildred; *see* Gordon, M.

DAHL, Robert Henry, TD 1950; MA Oxford; Head Master of Wrekin College, 1952–71; *b* 21 April 1910; *y s* of Murdoch Cameron Dahl, London, and Lilian May Edgcumbe; *m* 1936, Lois Helen Allanby; three *s*. *Educ:* Sedbergh Sch.; Exeter Coll., Oxford. Asst Master (Modern Langs) at Merchant Taylors' Sch., 1934–38. Asst Master and Housemaster at Harrow Sch., 1938–52. Served War of 1939–45: Intelligence Corps, Middle East, 1941–43; Major, 1943; Political Intelligence Dept of Foreign Office, 1943–46. FRSA 1969. *Publication:* Joint Editor, Selections from Albert Schweitzer, 1953. *Recreations:* golf, music, painting. *Address:* 72 Eastgate Street, Bury St Edmunds, Suffolk IP33 1YR.

DAHRENDORF, Sir Ralf, KBE 1982; PhD, DrPhil; FBA 1977; Warden of St Antony's College, Oxford, since 1987; *b* Hamburg, 1 May 1929; adopted British nationality, 1988; *s* of Gustav Dahrendorf and Lina Dahrendorf (*née* Witt); *m* 1980, Ellen Joan (*née* Krug). *Educ:* several schools, including Heinrich-Hertz Oberschule, Hamburg; studies in philosophy and classical philology, Hamburg, 1947–52; DrPhil 1952; postgrad. studies at London Sch. of Economics, 1952–54; Leverhulme Research Schol., 1953–54; PhD 1956. Habilitation, and University Lecturer, Saarbrücken, 1957; Fellow at Center for Advanced Study in the Behavioural Sciences, Palo Alto, USA, 1957–58; Prof. of Sociology, Hamburg, 1958–60; Vis. Prof. Columbia Univ., 1960; Prof. of Sociology, Tübingen, 1960–64; Vice-Chm., Founding Cttee of Univ. of Konstanz, 1964–66; Prof. of Sociology, Konstanz, 1966–69; Parly Sec. of State, Foreign Office, W Germany, 1969–70; Mem., EEC, Brussels, 1970–74; Dir, 1974–84, Governor, 1986–, LSE; Prof. of Social Sci.,

Konstanz Univ., 1984–87. Member: Hansard Soc. Commn on Electoral Reform, 1975–76; Royal Commn on Legal Services, 1976–79; Cttee to Review Functioning of Financial Instns, 1977–80. Trustee, Ford Foundn, 1976–. Chm. Bd, Friedrich Naumann Stiftung, 1982–88; Non-Exec. Dir, Glaxo Holdings PLC, 1984–. Vis. Prof. at several Europ. and N American univs. Reith Lecturer, 1974; Jephcott Lectr, RSocMed, 1983. Hon. Fellow: LSE; Imperial Coll. Hon. MRIA 1974; Fellow, St Antony's Coll., Oxford, 1976. Foreign Hon. Member: Amer. Acad. of Arts and Sciences, 1975–; Nat. Acad. of Sciences, USA, 1977; Amer. Philosophical Soc., 1977; FRSA 1977; Hon. FRCS 1982. Hon. DLitt: Reading, 1973; Dublin, 1975; Hon. LLD: Manchester, 1973; Wagner Coll., NY, 1977; York, Ontario, 1979; Columbia, NY, 1989; Hon. DHL: Kalamazoo Coll., 1974; Johns Hopkins, 1982; Hon. DSc: Ulster, 1973; Bath, 1977; Queen's Univ. Belfast, 1984; Birmingham, 1991; DUniv: Open, 1974; Maryland, 1978; Surrey, 1978; Hon. Dr Univ. Catholique de Louvain, 1977. Journal Fund Award for Learned Publication, 1966. Grand Croix de l'Ordre du Mérite du Sénégal, 1971; Grosses Bundesverdienstkreuz mit Stern und Schulterband (Federal Republic of Germany), 1974; Grand Croix de l'Ordre du Mérite du Luxembourg, 1974; Grosses goldenes Ehrenzeichen am Bande für Verdienste um die Republik Österreich (Austria), 1975; Grand Croix de l'Ordre de Léopold II (Belgium), 1975; Comdr's Cross, Order of Civil Merit (Spain), 1990. *Publications include:* Marx in Perspective, 1953; Industrie- und Betriebssoziologie, 1956 (trans. Italian, Spanish, Dutch, Japanese, Chinese); Soziale Klassen und Klassenkonflikt, 1957 (Class and Class Conflict, 1959; also trans. French, Italian, Spanish, Finnish, Japanese); Homo Sociologicus, 1959 (trans. English, Italian, Portuguese, Finnish); Die angewandte Aufklärung, 1963; Gesellschaft und Demokratie in Deutschland, 1965 (Society and Democracy in Germany, 1966; also trans. Italian); Pfade aus Utopia, 1967 (Uscire dall'Utopia, 1971); Essays in the Theory of Society, 1968; Konflikt und Freiheit, 1972; Plädoyer für die Europäische Union, 1973; The New Liberty, 1975 (trans. German, Italian, Urdu, Arabic, Japanese, Korean); Life Chances, 1979 (trans. German, Japanese, Italian); On Britain, 1982; Die Chancen der Krise, 1983; Reisen nach innen und aussen, 1984; Law and Order, 1985; The Modern Social Conflict, 1988; Reflections on the Revolution in Europe, 1990. *Address:* St Antony's College, Oxford OX2 6JF. *Clubs:* PEN, Reform, Political Economy, Garrick, United Oxford & Cambridge University.

DAICHES, David, CBE 1991; MA Edinburgh; MA, DPhil Oxon; PhD Cantab; FRSL; FRSE; Director, Institute for Advanced Studies in the Humanities, Edinburgh University, 1980–86; Professor of English, University of Sussex, 1961–77, and Dean of the School of English Studies, 1961–68; now Emeritus Professor; *b* 2 Sept. 1912; *s* of late Rabbi Dr Salis Daiches and Flora Daiches (*née* Levin); *m* 1st, 1937, Isobel J. Mackay (*d* 1977); one *s* two *d*; 2nd, 1978, Hazel Neville (*née* Newman) (*d* 1986). *Educ:* George Watson's Coll., Edinburgh; Edinburgh Univ. (Vans Dunlop Schol., Elliot Prize); Balliol Coll., Oxford (Elton Exhibnr). Asst in English, Edinburgh Univ., 1935–36; Andrew Bradley Fellow, Balliol Coll., Oxford, 1936–37; Asst Prof. of English, Univ. of Chicago, 1939–43; Second Sec., British Embassy, Washington, 1944–46; Prof. of English, Cornell Univ., USA, 1946–51; University Lecturer in English at Cambridge, 1951–61; Fellow of Jesus Coll., Cambridge, 1957–62. Visiting Prof. of Criticism, Indiana Univ., USA, 1956–57; Hill Foundation Visiting Prof., Univ. of Minnesota, Spring 1966. Lectures: Elliston, Univ. of Cincinnati, 1960; Whidden, McMaster Univ., Canada, 1964; Ewing, Univ. of Calif, 1967; Carpenter Meml, Ohio Wesleyan Univ., 1969; Alexander, Univ. of Toronto, 1980; Gifford, Univ. of Edinburgh, 1983. Hon. Prof., Stirling Univ., 1980; Sen. Mellon Fellow, Nat. Humanities Center, USA, 1987–88. Fellow, Centre for the Humanities, Wesleyan Univ., Middletown, Conn, 1970. Hon. Fellow, Sunderland Polytechnic, 1977. Hon. LittD, Brown Univ; Docteur *hc* Sorbonne; Hon. DLitt: Edinburgh, 1976; Sussex, 1978; Glasgow, 1987; Guelph, 1990; DUniv Stirling, 1980; Dott. *in honorem* Bologna, 1989. Lifetime Achievement Award, 18th Century Scottish Studies Soc., 1988; Fletcher of Saltoun Award for Services to Scotland, 1988. *Publications:* The Place of Meaning in Poetry, 1935; New Literary Values, 1936; Literature and Society, 1938; The Novel and the Modern World, 1939 (new edn, 1960); Poetry and the Modern World, 1940; The King James Bible: A Study of its Sources and Development, 1941; Virginia Woolf, 1942; Robert Louis Stevenson, 1947; A Study of Literature, 1948; Robert Burns, 1950 (new edn 1966); Willa Cather: A Critical Introduction, 1951; Critical Approaches to Literature, 1956; Two Worlds (autobiog.), 1956; Literary Essays, 1956; John Milton, 1957; The Present Age, 1958; A Critical History of English Literature, 1960; George Eliot's Middlemarch, 1963; The Paradox of Scottish Culture, 1964; (ed) The Idea of a New University, 1964; English Literature (Princeton Studies in Humanistic Scholarship), 1965; More Literary Essays, 1968; Some Late Victorian Attitudes, 1969; Scotch Whisky, 1969; Sir Walter Scott and his World, 1971; A Third World (autobiog.), 1971; (ed) The Penguin Companion to Literature: Britain and the Commonwealth, 1971; Robert Burns and his World, 1971; (ed with A. Thorlby) Literature and Western Civilization, vol. I, 1972, vols II and V, 1973, vols III and IV, 1975; vol. VI, 1976; Charles Edward Stuart: the life and times of Bonnie Prince Charlie, 1973; Robert Louis Stevenson and his World, 1973; Was, 1975; Moses, 1975; James Boswell and his World, 1976; Scotland and the Union, 1977; Glasgow, 1977; Edinburgh, 1978; (with John Flower) Literary Landscapes of the British Isles: a narrative atlas, 1979; (ed) Selected Writings and Speeches of Fletcher of Saltoun, 1979; (ed) Selected Poems of Robert Burns, 1979; (ed) A Companion to Scottish Culture, 1981; Literature and Gentility in Scotland, 1982; Robert Fergusson, 1982; Milton's Paradise Lost, 1983; God and the Poets, 1984; Edinburgh, A Travellers' Companion, 1986; A Wee Dram, 1990; Gen. Editor, Studies in English Literature, 1961–85. *Recreations:* talking, music. *Address:* 12 Rothesay Place, Edinburgh EH3 7SQ.

See also L. H. Daiches.

DAICHES, Lionel Henry, QC (Scot) 1956; *b* 8 March 1911; *s* of late Rev. Dr. Salis Daiches, Edinburgh, and Mrs Flora Daiches; *m* 1947, Dorothy Estelle Bernstein (marr. diss. 1973); two *s*. *Educ:* George Watson's Coll., Edinburgh; Edinburgh Univ. (MA, LLB). Pres., Edinburgh Univ. Diagnostic Soc., 1931; Convener of Debates, Edinburgh Univ. Union, 1933; Editor, The Student, 1933. Served 1940–46 in N Stafford Regt and Major, JAG Branch in N Africa and Italy, including Anzio Beach-head. Admitted Scots Bar, 1946. Standing Junior Counsel to Board of Control, Scotland, 1950–56; Sheriff-Substitute of Lanarkshire at Glasgow, 1962–67. Fellow, Internat. Acad. of Trial Lawyers, 1976. Contested (L) Edinburgh South, 1950. *Publication:* Russians at Law, 1960. *Recreations:* walking and talking. *Address:* 10 Heriot Row, Edinburgh EH3 6HU. *T:* 031–556 4144. *Clubs:* New, Puffin's, Scottish Arts (Edinburgh).

See also D. Daiches.

DAIN, Rt. Rev. Arthur John, OBE 1979; Honorary Consultant to Lausanne Committee for World Evangelization, since 1985 (General Co-Ordinator, 1982–85); *b* 13 Oct. 1912; *s* of Herbert John Dain and Elizabeth Dain; *m* 1st, 1939, Edith Jane Stewart, MA, *d* of Dr Alexander Stewart, DD; four *d*; 2nd, 1986, Hester A. Quirk, BSc. *Educ:* Wolverhampton Gram. Sch.; Ridley Coll., Cambridge. Missionary in India, 1935–40; 10th Gurkha Rifles, 1940–41; Royal Indian Navy, 1941–47; Gen. Sec., Bible and Medical Missionary Fellowship, formerly Zenana Bible and Medical Mission, 1947–59; Overseas Sec., British Evangelical Alliance, 1950–59; Federal Sec., CMS of Australia, 1959–65; Hon. Canon of St Andrew's Cathedral, 1963; Asst Bishop, Diocese of Sydney, 1965–82; Sen. Asst Bishop and Chief Executive Officer, 1980–82. *Publications:* Mission Fields To-day, 1956; Missionary Candidates, 1959. *Recreation:* sport. *Address:* 14 Kipling Court, Winnals Park, Haywards Heath, West Sussex RH16 1EX.

DAIN, David John Michael, CMG 1991; HM Diplomatic Service; High Commissioner, Republic of Cyprus, since 1990; *b* 30 Oct. 1940; *s* of late John Gordon Dain and of Gladys Ellen (*née* Connop); *m* 1969, Susan Kathleen Moss; one *s* four *d*. *Educ:* Merchant Taylors' Sch.; St John's Coll., Oxford (MA Lit.Hum.). Entered HM Diplomatic Service, 1963; Third, later Second Sec., Tehran and Kabul, 1964–68; seconded to Cabinet Office, 1969–72; First Sec., Bonn, 1972–75; FCO, 1975–78; Head of Chancery, Athens, 1978–81; Counsellor and Dep. Head of Mission, Nicosia, 1981–85; Head of Western European Dept, FCO, 1985–89; on attachment to CSSB, 1989–90. FIL 1986. Royal Order of Merit, Norway, 1988. *Recreations:* tennis, bridge, walking, natural history. *Address:* c/o Foreign and Commonwealth Office, SW1. *Clubs:* United Oxford & Cambridge University; Oxford Union Society.

DAINTITH, Prof. Terence Charles; Professor of Law and Director, Institute of Advanced Legal Studies, University of London, since 1988; *b* 8 May 1942; *s* of Edward Terence and Irene May Daintith; *m* 1965, Christine Anne Bulport; one *s* one *d*. *Educ:* Wimbledon Coll.; St Edmund Hall, Oxford (BA Jurisp., MA); Univ. of Nancy (Leverhulme European Schol.). Called to the Bar, Lincoln's Inn, 1966. Associate in Law, Univ. of California, Berkeley, 1963–64; Lectr in Constitutional and Admin. Law, Univ. of Edinburgh, 1964–72; University of Dundee: Prof. and Head of Dept of Public Law, 1972–83 (leave of absence, 1981–83); Dir, Centre for Petroleum and Mineral Law Studies, 1977–83; Hon. Vis. Prof., 1983–; European University Institute, Florence: Prof. of Law, 1981–87; Head, Law Dept, 1982, 1986–87; External Prof., 1988–. Vis. Lectr, Coll. d'Europe, Bruges, 1966–68; Vis. Prof., Univ. of Aix-Marseille III, 1975; Parsons Schol., Univ. of Sydney, 1988. Member: Acad. Europaea, 1989–; Conseil d'Admin., Assoc. Internat. de Droit Economique, 1985–. Editor, Jl Energy and Natural Resources Law, 1983–. *Publications:* The Economic Law of the United Kingdom, 1974; (with G. Willoughby) United Kingdom Oil and Gas Law, 1977, 2nd edn 1984; (with L. Hancher) European Energy Strategy: the legal framework, 1986, French edn 1987; (with S. Williams) The Legal Integration of Energy Markets, 1987; Law as an Instrument of Economic Policy, 1988; contribs to UK and foreign law jls. *Recreations:* cycling, curling, carpentry. *Address:* Institute of Advanced Legal Studies, 17 Russell Square, WC1B 5DR. *T:* 071–637 1731. *Club:* Athenæum.

DAINTON, family name of **Baron Dainton.**

DAINTON, Baron *cr* 1986 (Life Peer), of Hallam Moors in South Yorkshire; **Frederick Sydney Dainton;** Kt 1971; FRS 1957; MA, BSc Oxon, PhD, ScD Cantab; Chancellor, Sheffield University, since 1978; *b* 11 Nov. 1914; *y s* of late George Whalley and Mary Jane Dainton; *m* 1942, Barbara Hazlitt, JP, PhD, *o d* of late Dr W. B. Wright, Manchester; one *s* two *d*. *Educ:* Central Secondary Sch., Sheffield; St John's Coll., Oxford; Sidney Sussex Coll., Cambridge. Open Exhibitioner, 1933; Casberd Prizeman, 1934, Casberd Scholar, 1935, Hon. Fellow 1968, St John's Coll., Oxford; Goldsmiths' Co. Exhibitioner, 1935, 1st class Hons Chemistry, 1937, University of Oxford; Research Student, 1937, Goldsmiths' Co. Senior Student, 1939, University Demonstrator in Chemistry, 1944, H. O. Jones Lecturer in Physical Chemistry, 1946, University of Cambridge. Fellow, 1945, Praelector, 1946, Hon. Fellow 1961, St Catharine's Coll., Cambridge. Prof. of Physical Chemistry, University of Leeds, 1950–65; Vice-Chancellor, Nottingham Univ., 1965–70; Dr Lee's Prof. of Chemistry, Oxford University, 1970–73; Chm., UGC, 1973–78. Vis. Prof., Univ. Toronto, 1949; Tilden Lectr, 1950, Faraday Lectr, 1973, Chem. Soc.; Peter C. Reilly Lectr, Univ. of Notre Dame, Ind., USA, 1952; Arthur D. Little Visiting Prof., MIT, 1959. Lectures: Lady Masson, Melbourne, 1959; George Fisher Baker, Cornell Univ., 1961; Boomer, Univ. of Alberta, 1962; Rede, Cambridge, 1981; Crookshank, RCR, 1981; John Snow, Assoc. of Anaesthetists, 1987. Chm., Cttee on Swing away from Science (report published as Enquiry into the Flow of Candidates in Science and Technology into Higher Education, Cmnd 3541, 1968). Chairman: Assoc. for Radiation Research, 1964–66; Nat. Libraries Cttee, 1968–69; Adv. Cttee on Sci. and Tech. Information, 1966–70; Adv. Bd for Res. Councils, 1972–73; British Cttee, Harkness Fellowship, 1977–81 (Mem., 1973–); British Library Bd, 1978–85; Nat. Radiological Protection Bd, 1978–85. President: Faraday Soc., 1965–67; Chemical Soc., 1972–73 (Hon. Fellow, 1983–); Assoc. for Science Education, 1967; Library Assoc., 1977; BAAS, 1980; Soc. of Designer Craftsmen, 1985–; Arthritis and Rheumatism Council for Res., 1988–. Member: Council for Scientific Policy, 1965–79 (Chm. 1969–72); Central Advisory Council for Science and Technology, 1967–70; Council, Foundn for Science and Technol., 1987–; Crafts Council, 1984–88; Museums and Galleries Commn, 1985–; Trustee: Natural Hist. Museum, 1974–84; Wolfson Foundn, 1978–88. Chairman: Edward Boyle Meml Trust, 1982–; Council, Royal Post-grad. Med. Sch., 1979–90 (Pres., 1990–). Prime Warden, Goldsmiths' Co., 1982–83. Foreign Member: Swedish Acad. of Sci., 1968; Amer. Acad. of Arts and Scis, 1972; Acad. of Scis, Göttingen, 1975; Acad. Mediterranae della Scienze, 1982. Hon. Fellow: Goldsmiths' Coll., London, 1985; Queen Mary Coll., London, 1985; Birkbeck Coll., London, 1986; RPMS, 1990; Hon. FRCP 1979; Hon. FRSC 1983; Hon. FRCR 1984; Hon. FLA 1986. Hon. ScD: Łódź, 1966; Dublin, 1968; Hon. DSc: Bath Univ. of Technology, 1970; Loughborough Univ. of Technology, 1970; Heriot-Watt, 1970; Warwick, 1970; Strathclyde, 1971; Exeter, 1971; QUB, 1971; Manchester, 1972; E Anglia, 1972; Leeds, 1973; McMaster, 1975; Uppsala, 1977; Liverpool, Salford, 1979; Kent, 1981; Hon. LLD: Nottingham, 1970; Aberdeen, 1972; Sheffield, Cambridge, 1979; London, 1984; Lancaster, 1989; Hon. DCL Oxford, 1988; Hon. DLitt CNAA, 1991. Sylvanus Thompson Medal, BIR, 1958; Davy Medal, Royal Soc., 1969; Crookshank Medal, RCR, 1981; 1300 Years Bulgaria Medal, 1982; Curie Medal, Poland, 1983. Kt Comdr, Order of Merit (Poland), 1985. *Publications:* Chain Reactions, 1956; (ed and contrib.) Photochemistry and Reaction Kinetics, 1967; Choosing a British University, 1981; (contrib.) The Parliament of Science, 1981; Universities and the National Health Service, 1983; papers on physico-chemical subjects in scientific jls. *Recreations:* walking, colour photography. *Address:* Fieldside, Water Eaton Lane, Oxford OX5 2PR. *T:* Kidlington (08675) 5132. *Club:* Athenæum.

DAINTY, Prof. (John) Christopher, PhD; Pilkington Professor of Applied Optics, Imperial College of Science and Technology, University of London, since 1984; Senior Research Fellow, Science and Engineering Research Council, since 1987; *b* 22 Jan. 1947; *s* of Jack Dainty and Mary Elizabeth (*née* Elbeck); *m* 1978, Janice Hancock; one *d*. *Educ:* George Heriot's, Edinburgh; City of Norwich Sch.; Polytechnic of Central London (Diploma); Imperial Coll. of Science and Technol. (MSc; PhD 1972). Lectr, Queen Elizabeth Coll., Univ. of London, 1974–78; Associate Prof., Inst. of Optics, Univ. of Rochester, NY, USA, 1978–83. Pres., Internat. Commn for Optics, 1990–. Internat. Commn of Optics Prize, 1984. *Publications:* (with R. Shaw) Image Science, 1974; (ed) Laser Speckle and Related Phenomena, 1975, 2nd edn 1984; (ed. with M. Nieto-Vesperinas) Scattering in Volumes and Surfaces, 1989; scientific papers. *Address:* Blackett Laboratory, Imperial College of Science and Technology, SW7 2AZ. *T:* 071–225 8847.

DAKERS, Lionel Frederick, CBE 1983; DMus; FRCO; Director, Royal School of Church Music, 1972–89; (Special Commissioner, 1958–72), Examiner to the Associated

Board of the Royal Schools of Music, since 1958; Director, Hymns Ancient and Modern, since 1976; *b* Rochester, Kent, 24 Feb. 1924; *o s* of late Lewis and Ethel Dakers; *m* 1951, Mary Elisabeth, *d* of Rev. Claude Williams; four *d. Educ:* Rochester Cathedral Choir Sch. Studied with H. A. Bennett, Organist of Rochester Cathedral, 1933–40, with Sir Edward Bairstow, Organist of York Minster, 1943–45, and at Royal Academy of Music, 1947–51. Organist of All Saints', Frindsbury, Rochester, 1939–42. Served in Royal Army Educational Corps, 1943–47. Cairo Cathedral, 1945–47; Finchley Parish Church, 1948–50; Asst Organist, St George's Chapel, Windsor Castle, 1950–54; Asst Music Master, Eton Coll., 1952–54; Organist of Ripon Cathedral, 1954–57; Conductor Ripon Choral Soc. and Harrogate String Orchestra, 1954–57; Hon. Conductor, Exeter Diocesan Choral Association, 1957–72; Lectr in Music, St Luke's Coll., Exeter, 1958–70; Organist and Master of the Choristers, Exeter Cathedral, 1957–72; Conductor: Exeter Musical Soc., 1957–72; Exeter Chamber Orchestra, 1959–65. President: Incorporated Assoc. of Organists, 1972–75; London Assoc. of Organists, 1976–78; ISM, 1990–91; Vice-President: Fedn of Cathedral Old Choristers' Assocs, 1980–; Church Music Soc., 1990–; Mem. Council, Royal Coll. of Organists, 1967– (Pres., 1976–78); Sec., Cathedral Organists' Assoc., 1972–88. Chairman: Organs Adv. Cttee of Council for Care of Churches of C of E, 1974–; Nat. Learn the Organ Year, 1989–90; Friends of the Musicians' Chapel, 1988–; Salisbury Diocesan Adv. Cttee, 1990–. Mem., Archbishops' Commn in Church Music, 1988–. Trustee, Ouseley Trust, 1990–. Hon. Mem., US Assoc. of Anglican Musicians, 1978; Hon. Life Mem., Methodist Church Music Soc., 1990. ARCO, 1944; FRCO, 1945; ADCM, 1952; BMus Dunelm, 1951; ARAM 1955; FRAM, 1962; FRSCM 1969; FRCM 1980. Fellow, St Michael's Coll., Tenbury, 1973. Hon. Fellow, Westminster Choir Coll., USA, 1975. Hon. DMus: Lambeth, 1979; Exeter, 1990. Compositions: church music, etc. *Publications:* Church Music at the Crossroads, 1970; A Handbook of Parish Music, 1976; Making Church Music Work, 1978; (ed) Music and the Alternative Service Book, 1980; (ed) The Choristers Companion, 1980; (ed) The Psalms—their use and performance today, 1980; The Church Musician as Conductor, 1982; Church Music in a Changing World, 1984; Choosing and Using Hymns, 1985. *Recreations:* book collecting, gardening, continental food, travel. *Address:* 6 Harcourt Terrace, Salisbury, Wilts SP2 7SA. *T:* Salisbury (0722) 324880. *Clubs:* Athenæum; St Wilfrid's (NY) (Hon. mem.).

DAKIN, Dorothy Danvers, OBE 1982; JP; Assistant Chaplain, HM Prison and Remand Centre, Pucklechurch, 1984–87; *b* 22 Oct. 1919; *d* of Edwin Lionel Dakin, chartered civil engr and Mary Danvers Dakin (*née* Walker), artist. *Educ:* Sherborne Sch. for Girls; Newnham Coll., Cambridge. MA Geography. 2nd Officer WRNS (Educn), 1943–50; Housemistress, Wycombe Abbey Sch., 1950–60; Headmistress, The Red Maids' School, Bristol, 1961–81; Chm., ISIS Assoc., 1982–84. President: West of England Br., Assoc. of Headmistresses, 1969–71; Assoc. of Headmistresses of Girls' Boarding Schs, 1971–73; Girls' Schs Assoc. (Independent and Direct Grant), 1973–75; Chm. Council, ISIS, 1977–81. Licensed Reader, C of E, 1982–. FRSA 1988. JP Bristol, 1974. *Recreations:* fencing, painting, travel, embroidery. *Address:* 41 Park Grove, Henleaze, Bristol BS9 4LF.

DALAI LAMA; *see* Tenzin Gyatso.

DALAIS, Sir (Adrien) Pierre, Kt 1989; Chairman: Beau Champ Group of Companies (Sugar), Mauritius, since 1984; Floréal Group of Companies (Textile), since 1972; *b* 12 April 1929; *s* of Pierre Adrien Clement Piat Dalais and Simone de la Hogue Rey; *m* 1954, Clotilde Adam; four *s* one *d. Educ:* St Esprit Coll., Mauritius. Certified Secretary at Cape Town, 1952. Developed textile industry in Mauritius, the Floreal Gp employing 11,000 people in wool spinning, dyeing and knitting; succeeded his father as Chm. of Beau Champ Co. Sugar. Chairman: Mauritius Chamber of Agriculture, 1977–87; Mauritius Commercial Bank Ltd, 1986–89; Ireland Blyth Ltd, 1976–80 and 1987–88. *Recreations:* yachting, golf, tennis. *Address:* Forest Lane, Floréal, Mauritius. *T:* 86 49 04. *Clubs:* Mauritius Turf, Grand Baie Yacht, Dodo, Gymkhana (Mauritius).

DALAL, Maneck Ardeshir Sohrab; Vice-Chairman, Tata Ltd, SW1, since 1989 (Managing Director, 1977–88); Director, Tata Industries, Bombay, since 1979; *b* 24 Dec. 1918; *s* of Ardeshir Dalal, OBE and Amy Dalal; *m* 1947, Kathleen Gertrude Richardson; three *d. Educ:* Trinity Hall, Cambridge (MA). Called to the Bar, Middle Temple, 1945. Manager: Air-India New Delhi, 1946–48; Air-India London, 1948–53; Regional Traffic Manager, 1953–59; Regional Director, 1959–77; Minister for Tourism and Civil Aviation, High Commn for India, 1973–77. President: Indian Chamber of Commerce in Great Britain, 1959–62; Indian Management Assoc. of UK, 1960–63; UK Pres., World Conf. on Religions and Peace, UK and Ireland Gp, 1985–; Vice-Pres., Friends of Vellore, 1979–; Chairman: Foreign Airlines Assoc. of UK, 1965–67; Indian YMCA in London, 1972–; Bharatiya Vidhya Bhavan in London (Indian Cultural Inst. of Gt Britain), 1975–; Northbrook Soc., 1985– (Mem. Cttee, 1975–); Indian Women's Educn Assoc., 1985– (Mem. Cttee, 1975–); Vice-Chm., Fest. of India in GB, 1980–81; Member: Sub-Cttee on Transport, Industrial Trng Bd of GB, 1975–77; Assembly, British Council of Churches, 1984–87; Internat. Bd, United World Colls, 1985–; Bd Govs, Nat. Inst. for Social Work, 1986–; Chm. Central Council, Royal Over-Seas League, 1986–89 (Dep. Chm. Central Council, 1982–86; Mem., 1974–; Vice-Pres., 1989–). Patron, Internat. Centre for Child Studies, 1984–. FCIT 1975; FBIM. *Recreations:* reading, walking. *Address:* Tall Trees, Marlborough Road, Hampton, Mddx TW12 3RX. *T:* 081–979 2065. *Clubs:* Hurlingham, Royal Over-Seas League, MCC.

DALBY, Ven. John Mark Meredith; Archdeacon of Rochdale, since 1991; *b* 3 Jan. 1938; *s* of William and Sheila Mary Dalby (*née* Arkell). *Educ:* King George V Sch., Southport; Exeter Coll., Oxford, (MA 1965); Ripon Hall, Oxford; Univ. of Nottingham (PhD 1977). Ordained deacon 1963, priest 1964; Curate: Hambleden, Bucks, 1963–68; Fawley, Fingest, Medmenham and Turville, Bucks, 1965–68; Vicar of St Peter, Spring Hill, Birmingham, 1968–75; Rural Dean of Birmingham City, 1973–75; Sec., Cttee for Theol Educn, and Selection Sec., ACCM, 1975–80; Hon. Curate of All Hallows, Tottenham, 1975–80; Vicar of St Mark, Worsley, 1980–84; Team Rector of Worsley, 1984–91; Rural Dean of Eccles, 1987–91. Examining Chaplain to the Bp of Manchester, 1980–. Member: Gen. Synod of C of E, 1985–; Liturgical Commn, 1986–. *Publications:* Open Communion in the Church of England, 1959; The Gospel and the Priest, 1975; Tottenham Church and Parish, 1979; The Cocker Connection, 1989; Open Baptism, 1989. *Recreations:* travel, family history, philately, liturgy. *Address:* 21 Belmont Way, Rochdale OL12 6HR. *T:* Rochdale (0706) 48640. *Club:* Commonwealth Trust.

DALBY, Dr (Terry) David (Pereira); Reader in West African Languages, School of Oriental and African Studies, University of London, 1967–83, now Emeritus; Directeur, Observatoire linguistique, since 1987; *b* 7 Jan. 1933; *s* of Ernest Edwin Dalby and Rose Cecilia Dalby; *m* 1st, 1957, Winifred Brand (marr. diss.); two *d*; 2nd, 1982, Catherine Jansens; one *s. Educ:* Cardiff High Sch.; Queen Mary Coll., London (BA 1954, PhD 1961; Hon. Life Mem., Queen Mary Coll. Union Soc., 1954). Served to Lieut, Intell. Corps, 1954–56. United Africa Co. Ltd, London and W Africa, 1957–60; Lectr in Mod. Languages, University Coll. of Sierra Leone, 1961–62; Lectr in W African Langs, SOAS, Univ. of London, 1962–67. Hanns Wolff Vis. Prof., Indiana Univ., 1969. Chm., Centre for Afr. Studies, Univ. of London, 1971–74; Dir, Internat. African Inst., 1974–80; Chairman: Internat. Conf. on Manding Studies, 1972, and Drought in Africa Conf., 1973; UK Standing Cttee on Univ. Studies of Africa, 1978–82 (Dep. Chm., 1975–78). Vice-Pres., Unesco Meeting on Cultural Specificity in Africa, Accra, 1980. Member: Governing Body, SOAS, 1969–70; Council, African Studies Assoc. of UK, 1970–73; Cttee of Management, British Inst. in Paris, 1975–82; Conseil Internat. de Recherche et d'Etude en Linguistique Fondamentale et Appliquée, 1980– (Président, 1984); Centre Internat. de Recherche sur le Bilinguisme, Laval Univ., Que, 1981–; Eur. Council on African Studies, 1985–; Hon. Mem., SOAS, 1983. Editor, African Language Review, 1962–72; Co-editor, Africa, 1976–80. *Publications:* Lexicon of the Mediaeval German Hunt, 1965; Black through White: patterns of communication in Africa and the New World, 1970; (ed) Language and History in Africa, 1970; (ed jtly) Drought in Africa, 1st vol. 1973, 2nd vol. 1978; Language Map of Africa and the adjacent islands, 1977; Clavier international de Niamey, 1984; (jtly) Les langues et l'espace du français, 1985; Afrique et la lettre, 1986; (jtly) Thesaurus of African Languages, 1987; articles in linguistic and other jls. *Recreations:* cartography, local history. *Address:* Cressenville, 27440 Ecouis, France. *T:* 32.49.35.60.

DALE, Barry Gordon, FCA; Group Finance Director, Littlewoods Organisation Plc, since 1988; *b* 31 July 1938; *s* of Francis and Catherine Dale; *m* 1963, Margaret (*née* Fairbrother); one *s* one *d. Educ:* Queen Elizabeth Grammar Sch., Blackburn. Coopers Lybrand, Montreal, 1960–62; Pilkington Brothers Glass, St Helens, 1962–65; ICI, 1965–85: Mond Div., Cheshire, 1966–68; Head Office, 1968–72; Dep. Chief Acct, Mond Div., 1972–78; Finance Dir, ICI Latin America (Wilmington, USA), 1978–80; Chief Acct, Organics Div., Manchester, 1980–84; Bd Mem. for Finance, LRT, 1985–88. Director: Ellis & Everard, 1978–81; Magadi Soda Co. (Kenya), 1980–82; London Buses Ltd, 1985–88; London Underground Ltd, 1985–88; LRT Bus Engineering Ltd, 1985–88; Chairman: London Transport Trustee Co., 1985–88; London Transport Pension Fund Trustees, 1985–88; Datanetworks, 1987–88. *Recreations:* golf, fell walking, other sports. *Address:* Tanglewood, Spinney Lane, Knutsford, Cheshire WA16 0NQ. *T:* Knutsford (0565) 50282; The Littlewoods Organisation Plc, J M Centre, Old Hall Street, Liverpool L70 1AB. *T:* 051–235 2181. *Clubs:* Tatton (Knutsford); West Surrey Golf, Knutsford Golf.

DALE, David Kenneth Hay, CBE 1976; Governor, Montserrat, West Indies, 1980–85, retired 1988; *b* 27 Jan. 1927; *s* of Kenneth Hay Dale and Francesca Sussana Hoffman; *m* 1956, Hanna Szydlowska; one *s. Educ:* Dorchester Grammar Sch. Joined Queen's Royal Regt, 1944; 2/Lieut 8th Punjab Regt, 1945; Lieut 4 Bn (PWO) 8th Punjab Regt, 1946; Lieut Royal Regt of Artillery, 1948, Captain 1955: served Kenya and Malaya (despatches); Dist Officer, Kenya, 1960, Dist Comr, 1962; Admin Officer Cl. B, subseq. Cl. A, Anglo-French Condominium, New Hebrides, W Pacific, 1965–73; Perm. Sec., Min. of Aviation, Communications and Works, Seychelles, 1973–75; Dep. Governor, Seychelles, 1975; Sec. to Cabinet, Republic of Seychelles, 1976; FCO, 1977–80. Clerk, Shipwrights' Co., 1986–87. Vice-Chm. Finance, Somerton Frome Constit. Cons. Assoc., 1990. *Recreations:* birdwatching, walking, colonial and military history. *Address:* Chatley Cottage, Batcombe, near Shepton Mallet, Somerset BA4 6AF. *T:* Upton Noble (074985) 449. *Clubs:* East India; Bath and County (Bath).

DALE, Jim; actor, singer, composer, lyricist; *b* 15 Aug. 1935; *m*; three *s* one *d. Educ:* Kettering Grammar School. Music Hall comedian, 1951; singing, compèring, directing, 1951–61; films, 1965–, include: Lock Up Your Daughters, The Winter's Tale, The Biggest Dog in the World, National Health, Adolf Hitler—My Part in his Downfall, Joseph Andrews, Pete's Dragon, Bloodshy, The Spaceman and King Arthur, Scandalous. Joined Frank Dunlop's Pop Theatre for Edinburgh Festival, 1967–68; National Theatre, 1969–71: main roles in National Health, Love's Labour's Lost, Merchant of Venice, Good-natured Man, Captain of Kopenick; also appeared at Young Vic in Taming of the Shrew, Scapino (title rôle and wrote music); title rôle in musical The Card, 1973; Compère of Sunday Night at the London Palladium, 1973–74; Scapino (title rôle), Broadway, 1974–75 (Drama Critics' and Outer Circle Awards for best actor; Tony award nomination for best actor); Privates on Parade, Long Wharf Theatre, New Haven, Conn., 1979; Barnum, Broadway, 1980 (Tony award for best actor in a musical, Drama Desk Award); A Day in the Death of Joe Egg, NY, 1985 (Tony nomination for best actor; Outer Circle Award for best actor); Me and My Girl, NY, 1987–88; Privates on Parade, NY, 1989; television includes: host of Ringling Brothers Barnum and Bailey Circus (TV special), 1985; Adventures of Huckleberry Finn, 1985. Composed film music for: The Winter's Tale, Shaliko, Twinky, Georgy Girl (nominated for Academy Award), Joseph Andrews. *Address:* c/o Gottlieb, Schiff, Bomser & Sendroff, PC, 555 5th Avenue, New York, NYC 10017, USA. *T:* 212 922 1880.

DALE, Robert Alan; Managing Director-Automotive, Lucas Industries plc, since 1987; *b* 31 Oct. 1938; *s* of Horace and Alice Dale; *m* 1963, Sheila Mary Dursley; one *s* one *d. Educ:* West Bromwich Grammar Sch.; Birmingham Univ. (BA Hons). Joined Lucas Industries as graduate apprentice, 1960; first management appt, 1965; first Bd appt, 1971; Dir, Lucas CAV, 1972–77; Dir and Gen. Man., Lucas Batteries, 1978–81; joined Exec. Cttee of Lucas (Joseph Lucas Ltd), 1980; Managing Director: Lucas World Service, 1981–85; Lucas Electrical, 1985–87; Dir, Lucas Industries, 1987–. *Recreations:* sport, photography, travel. *Address:* Lucas Automotive Ltd, International Headquarters, Stratford Road, Shirley, Solihull, W Midlands B90 4LA.

DALE, Sir William (Leonard), KCMG 1965 (CMG 1951); International legal consultant; Director of Studies, Government Legal Advisers Course, since 1976; *b* 17 June 1906; *e s* of late Rev. William Dale, Rector of Preston, Yorks; *m* 1966, Mrs Gloria Spellman Finn, Washington, DC; one *d. Educ:* Hymers Coll., Hull; London (LLB); Barrister, Gray's Inn, 1931. Asst Legal Adviser, Colonial and Dominions Offices, 1935; Min. of Supply, 1940–45; Dep. Legal Adviser, Colonial and Commonwealth Relations Offices, 1945; Legal Adviser, United Kingdom of Libya, 1951–53; Legal Adviser: Min. of Educn, 1954–61; CRO, subseq. CO, 1961–66. Special Asst to the Law Officers, 1967–68; Gen. Counsel, UNRWA, Beirut, 1968–73. Hon. LLD Hull, 1978. *Publications:* Law of the Parish Church, 1932, 6th edn 1989; Legislative Drafting: a new approach, 1977; The Modern Commonwealth, 1983; (ed) Anglo-French Statutory Drafting, 1987; contributions to journals. *Recreation:* music (except Wagner). *Address:* 20 Old Buildings, Lincoln's Inn, WC2A 3UP. *T:* 071–242 9365. *Club:* Travellers'.

DALES, Richard Nigel; HM Diplomatic Service; Head of Central and Southern Africa Department, Foreign and Commonwealth Office, since 1989; *b* 26 Aug. 1942; *s* of late Kenneth Richard Frank Dales and of Olwen Mary (*née* Preedy); *m* 1966, Elizabeth Margaret Martin; one *s* one *d. Educ:* Chigwell Sch.; St Catharine's Coll., Cambridge (BA 1964). Entered FO, 1964; Third Sec., Yaoundé, Cameroon, 1965–67; FCO, 1968–70; Second Sec., later First Sec., Copenhagen, 1970–73; FCO, 1973; Asst Private Sec. to Foreign and Commonwealth Sec., 1974–77; First Sec., Head of Chancery and Consul, Sofia, Bulgaria, 1977–81; FCO, 1981; Counsellor and Head of Chancery, Copenhagen, 1982–86; Dep. High Comr, Harare, 1986–89. *Recreations:* music, walking. *Address:* c/o Foreign and Commonwealth Office, King Charles Street, SW1A 2AH. *Club:* United Oxford & Cambridge University.

DALGARNO, Prof. Alexander, PhD; FRS 1972; Phillips Professor of Astronomy, since 1977, Chairman of Department of Astronomy, 1971–76, Associate Director of Centre for

Astrophysics, 1973–80, Harvard University; Member of Smithsonian Astrophysical Observatory, since 1967; *b* 5 Jan. 1928; *s* of William Dalgarno; *m* 1st, 1957, Barbara Kane (marr. diss. 1972); two *s* two *d*; 2nd, 1972, Emily Izsák (marr. diss. 1987). *Educ:* Southgate Grammar Sch.; University Coll., London (Fellow 1976). BSc Maths, 1st Cl. Hons London, 1947; PhD Theoretical Physics London, 1951; AM Harvard, 1967. The Queen's University of Belfast: Lectr in Applied Maths, 1952; Reader in Maths, 1956; Dir of Computing Lab, 1960; Prof. of Quantum Mechanics, 1961; Prof. of Mathematical Physics, 1966–67; Prof. of Astronomy, Harvard Univ., 1967–77; Acting Dir, Harvard Coll. Observatory, 1971–73. Chief Scientist, Geophysics Corp. of America, 1962–63. Editor, Astrophysical Journal Letters, 1973–. Fellow: Amer. Acad. of Arts and Sciences, 1968; Amer. Geophysical Union, 1972; Amer. Physical Soc., 1980; Mem., Internat. Acad. Astronautics, 1972; Hon. MRIA 1988. Hon. DSc QUB, 1980. Prize of Internat. Acad. of Quantum Molecular Sci., 1969; Hodgkins Medal, Smithsonian Instn, 1977; Davisson-Germer Prize, Amer. Physical Soc., 1980; Gold Medal, Royal Astronomical Soc., 1986; Meggers Prize, Optical Soc. of America, 1986. *Publications:* numerous papers in scientific journals. *Recreations:* squash, books. *Address:* c/o Harvard-Smithsonian Center for Astrophysics, 60 Garden Street, Cambridge, Mass 02138, USA.

DALGETY, Ramsay Robertson; QC (Scot.) 1986; Deputy Traffic Commissioner for Scotland, since 1988; *b* 2 July 1945; *s* of James Robertson Dalgety and Georgia Dalgety (*née* Whyte); *m* 1971, Mary Margaret Bernard; one *s* one *d*. *Educ:* High School of Dundee; Univ. of St Andrews (LLB Hons). Advocate, 1972–; Temp. Sheriff, 1987–91. Councillor, City of Edinburgh, 1974–80. Director/Chairman: Archer Transport Ltd and Archer Transport (London) Ltd, 1982–85; Venture Shipping Ltd, 1983–85. Director: Scottish Opera Ltd, 1980–90; Scottish Opera Theatre Trust Ltd, 1987–90; Deputy Chairman: Opera Singers Pension Fund, 1989– (Trustee, 1983–); Edinburgh Hibernian Shareholders Assoc., 1990–. *Recreations:* golf, boating, opera, travel, cricket, football. *Address:* Apartment–N, 116 Queensferry Road, Edinburgh EH4 2BT. *T:* 031–332 1417. *Club:* Surrey County Cricket.

DALGLISH, Captain James Stephen, CVO 1955; CBE 1963; *b* 1 Oct. 1913; *e s* of late Rear-Adm. Robin Dalglish, CB; *m* 1939, Evelyn Mary, *e d* of late Rev. A. Ll. Meyricke, Vicar of Aislaby, near Whitby; one *s* one *d*. *Educ:* RN Coll., Dartmouth. Commanded HMS Aisne, 1952–53; HM Yacht Britannia, 1954, HMS Woodbridge Haven and Inshore Flotilla, 1958–59; HMS Excellent, 1959–61; HMS Bulwark, 1961–63; jssc 1950; idc 1957; retired from RN, 1963. Welfare Officer, Metropolitan Police, 1963–73. *Recreations:* gardening, painting. *Address:* Park Hall, Aislaby, Whitby, North Yorks YO21 1SW. *T:* Whitby (0947) 810213.

DALHOUSIE, 16th Earl of, *cr* 1633; **Simon Ramsay,** KT 1971; GCVO 1979; GBE 1957; MC 1944; LLD; Baron Ramsay, 1619; Lord Ramsay, 1633; Baron Ramsay (UK), 1875; Lord Chamberlain to the Queen Mother, 1965; Lord-Lieutenant of Angus, 1967–89; Chancellor, Dundee University, since 1977; *b* 17 Oct. 1914; 2nd *s* of 14th Earl (*d* 1928) and Lady Mary Adelaide Heathcote Drummond Willoughby (*d* 1960), *d* of 1st Earl of Ancaster; *S* brother, 1950; *m* 1940, Margaret Elizabeth, *d* of late Brig.-Gen. Archibald and Hon. Mrs Stirling of Keir; three *s* two *d*. *Educ:* Eton; Christ Church, Oxford. Served TA, Black Watch, 1936–39; embodied, 1939. MP (C) for County of Angus, 1945–50; Conservative Whip, 1946–48 (resigned). Governor-General, Fedn of Rhodesia and Nyasaland, 1957–63. Hon. LLD: Dalhousie, 1952; Dundee, 1967. *Heir: s* Lord Ramsay, *qv*. *Address:* Brechin Castle, Brechin. *T:* Brechin (03562) 2176; 5 Margaretta Terrace, SW3. *T:* 071–352 6477. *Club:* White's.

See also J. C. L. Keswick, Earl of Scarbrough.

DALITZ, Prof. Richard Henry, FRS 1960; Professor Emeritus, Oxford University, and Emeritus Fellow of All Souls, since 1990; *b* 28 Feb. 1925; *s* of Frederick W. and Hazel B. Dalitz, Melbourne, Australia; *m* 1946, Valda (*née* Suiter) of Melbourne, Australia; one *s* three *d*. *Educ:* Scotch Coll., Melbourne; Univ. of Melbourne; Trinity Coll., Univ. of Cambridge, PhD Cantab, 1950. Lecturer in Mathematical Physics, Univ. of Birmingham, 1949–55; Research appointments in various Univs, USA, 1953–55; Reader in Mathematical Physics, Univ. of Birmingham, 1955–56; Prof. of Physics, Univ. of Chicago, 1956–66; Royal Soc. Res. Prof., Oxford Univ., 1963–90; Fellow of All Souls Coll., Oxford, 1964–90. Mem. Council, Royal Soc., 1979–81. Corresp. Mem., Australian Acad. of Science, 1978; Foreign Member: Polish Acad. of Sci., 1980; Nat. Acad. of India, 1990. Maxwell Medal and Prize, Institute of Physics and the Physical Soc., 1966; Bakerian Lectr and Jaffe Prize, 1969, Hughes Medal, 1975, Royal Medal, 1982, Royal Soc.; J. Robert Oppenheimer Meml Prize, Univ. of Miami, 1980; Harrie Massey Prize, Inst. of Physics and Aust. Inst. of Physics, 1990. *Publications:* Strange Particles and Strong Interactions, 1962 (India); Nuclear Interactions of the Hyperons, 1965 (India); (ed jtly) High Energy Physics, 1965 (New York); (jtly) Nuclear Energy Today and Tomorrow, 1971; numerous papers on theoretical physics in various British and American scientific jls. *Recreations:* mountain walking, travelling, biographical research, study of the Sorbian (Wendish) people, especially their language and emigration. *Address:* 1 Keble Road, Oxford OX1 3NP. *T:* Oxford (0865) 273966; All Souls College, Oxford.

DALKEITH, Earl of; Richard Walter John Montagu Douglas Scott, DL; *b* 14 Feb. 1954; *s* and *heir* of 9th Duke of Buccleuch, *qv*; *m* 1981, Lady Elizabeth Kerr, *d* of Marquess of Lothian, *qv*; two *s* one *d*. *Educ:* Eton; Christ Church, Oxford. Dir, Border Television, 1989–. Member: Nature Conservancy Council, 1989–91; Nature Conservancy Council for Scotland, 1991–; IBA, 1990; ITC, 1991–. Dist Councillor, Nithsdale, 1984–90. DL Nithsdale and Annandale and Eskdale, 1987. *Heir: s* Lord Eskdaill, *qv*. *Address:* Dabton, Thornhill, Dumfriesshire. *T:* Thornhill (0848) 30467; 24 Lansdowne Road, W11 3LL. *T:* 071–727 6573.

DALLEY, Christopher Mervyn, CMG 1971; MA Cantab; CEng; Director: London and Scottish Marine Oil Co. Ltd, 1979–84; *b* 26 Dec. 1913; *er s* of late Christopher Dalley; *m* 1947, Elizabeth Alice, *yr d* of late Lt-Gen. Sir James Gammell, KCB, DSO, MC; one *s* three *d*. *Educ:* Epsom Coll., Surrey; Queens' Coll., Cambridge. Served in RN, 1939–45. Joined British Petroleum Co., 1946; joined Oil Operating Companies in Iran, 1954: Asst Gen. Managing Dir, 1958; joined Iraq Petroleum Co. and associated companies, 1962, Man. Dir, 1963, Chm., 1970–73; Chm., Oil Exploration Holdings Ltd, 1973–79; Dir, Viking Resources Trust, 1973–84. Pres., Inst. of Petroleum, 1970; Mem. Council, World Petroleum Congress, 1970. Mem., Governing Body, Royal Medical Foundn (Epsom Coll.), 1970. Order of Homoyoun (Iran), 1963. *Address:* Mead House, Woodham Walter, near Maldon, Essex. *T:* Danbury (024541) 2404. *Club:* Athenæum.

DALMENY, Lord; Harry Ronald Neil Primrose; *b* 20 Nov. 1967; *s* and *heir* of 7th Earl of Rosebery, *qv*. *Educ:* Dragon Sch., Oxford; Eton Coll.; Trinity Coll., Cambridge (BA Hons). *Address:* Dalmeny House, South Queensferry, West Lothian EH30 9TQ. *T:* 031–331 1784. *Club:* University Pitt (Cambridge).

DALRYMPLE, family name of **Earl of Stair.**

DALRYMPLE, Viscount; John David James Dalrymple; *b* 4 Sept. 1961; *s* and *heir* of 13th Earl of Stair, *qv*.

DALRYMPLE, Sir Hew (Fleetwood) Hamilton-, 10th Bt, *cr* 1697; KCVO 1985 (CVO 1974); JP; late Major, Grenadier Guards; Lord-Lieutenant of East Lothian, since 1987 (Vice-Lieutenant, 1973–87); Director, Scottish American Investment Company, since 1967 (Chairman, 1985–91); *b* 9 April 1926; *er s* of Sir Hew (Clifford) Hamilton-Dalrymple, 9th Bt, JP; *S* father, 1959; *m* 1954, Lady Anne-Louise Mary Keppel, *d* of 9th Earl of Albemarle, MC, and of (Diana Cicely) Countess of Albemarle, *qv*; four *s*. *Educ:* Ampleforth. Commnd, Grenadier Guards, 1944; Staff Coll., Camberley, 1957; DAAG HQ 3rd Div., 1958–60; Regimental Adjt, Grenadier Guards, 1960–62; retd 1962. Adjt, 1964–85, Pres. of Council, 1988–, and Captain, Queen's Body Guard for Scotland (Royal Company of Archers). Vice-Chm., Scottish & Newcastle Breweries, 1983–86 (Dir, 1967–86). DL 1964, JP 1987, East Lothian. *Heir: e s* Hew Richard Hamilton-Dalrymple [*b* 3 Sept. 1955; *m* 1987, Jane Elizabeth, *yr d* of Lt-Col John Morris; one *s* one *d*. *Educ:* Ampleforth; Corpus Christi Coll., Oxford (MA); Clare Hall, Cambridge (MPhil); Birkbeck Coll., London (MSc). ODI Fellow, Swaziland, 1982–84]. *Address:* Leuchie, North Berwick, East Lothian. *T:* North Berwick (0620) 2903. *Club:* Cavalry and Guards.

DALRYMPLE-HAMILTON of Bargany, Captain North Edward Frederick, CVO 1961; MBE 1953; DSC 1943; JP; DL; Royal Navy; *b* 17 Feb. 1922; *s* of Admiral Sir Frederick Dalrymple-Hamilton of Bargany, KCB; *m* 1st, 1949, Hon. Mary Colville (*d* 1981), *d* of 1st Baron Clydesmuir, PC, GCIE, TD; two *s*; 2nd, 1983, Antoinette, *widow* of Major Rowland Beech, MC. *Educ:* Eton. Entered Royal Navy, 1940; Comdr 1954; Captain 1960. Comdg Officer HMS Scarborough, 1958; Executive Officer, HM Yacht Britannia, 1959; Captain (F) 17th Frigate Squadron, 1963; Dir of Naval Signals, 1965; Dir, Weapons Equipment Surface, 1967; retd, 1970. Ensign, Royal Company of Archers, Queen's Body Guard for Scotland. DL 1973, JP 1980, Ayrshire. *Address:* Lovestone House, Bargany, Girvan, Ayrshire KA26 9RF. *T:* Old Dailly (046587) 227. *Clubs:* Pratt's, MCC; New (Edinburgh).

DALRYMPLE-HAY, Sir James Brian, 6th Bt, *cr* 1798; estate agent, retired; *b* 19 Jan. 1928; *e s* of Lt-Col Brian George Rowland Dalrymple-Hay (*d* on active service, 1943) and Beatrice (*d* 1935), *d* of A. W. Inglis; *S* cousin, 1952; *m* 1958, Helen Sylvia, *d* of late Stephen Herbert Card and of Molly M. Card; three *d*. *Educ:* Hillsbrow Preparatory Sch., Redhill; Blundell's Sch., Tiverton, Devon. Royal Marine, 1946–47; Lieut Royal Marine Commando, 1947–49. Estate Agent and Surveyor's Pupil, 1949; Principal, 1955–67; Partner, Whiteheads PLC, Estate Agents, 1967, Dir, 1983–85; Principal, Dalrymple-Hay Overseas, 1985–87. *Heir: b* John Hugh Dalrymple-Hay [*b* 16 Dec. 1929; *m* 1962, Jennifer, *d* of late Brig. Robert Johnson, CBE; one *s*]. *Address:* The Red House, Church Street, Warnham, near Horsham, W Sussex.

DALRYMPLE-WHITE, Sir Henry Arthur Dalrymple, 2nd Bt, *cr* 1926; DFC 1941 and Bar 1942; *b* 5 Nov. 1917; *o s* of Lt-Col Sir Godfrey Dalrymple-White, 1st Bt, and late Hon. Catherine Mary Cary, *d* of 12th Viscount Falkland; *S* father 1954; *m* 1948, Mary (marr. diss. 1956), *o d* of Capt. Robert H. C. Thomas; one *s*. *Educ:* Eton; Magdalene Coll., Cambridge; London Univ. Formerly Wing Commander RAFVR. Served War of 1939–45. *Heir: s* Jan Hew Dalrymple-White, *b* 26 Nov. 1950. *Address:* c/o Aero Club of East Africa, PO Box 40813, Nairobi, Kenya.

DALSAGER, Poul; Member, Commission of the European Communities, 1981–84; *b* 5 March 1929; *m* 1951, Betty Jørgensen; two *s*. *Educ:* grammar sch. Bank employee, 1945–64; Mem. (Social Democrat), Danish Parliament, 1964–81; Chm., Market Cttee of Parlt, 1971–73; Chm., Social-Democratic Gp in Parlt, 1978–79; Minister for: Agriculture and Fisheries, 1975–77 and 1979–81; Agriculture, 1977–78. Mem. and Vice Pres., European Parlt, 1973 and 1974. Delegate to UN Gen. Assembly, 1969–71. Mayor, Hjørring, 1990– (Dep. Mayor, 1986–90). *Address:* Gram Mikkelsensvej 12, 9800 Hjørring, Denmark.

DALTON, Sir Alan (Nugent Goring), Kt 1977; CBE 1969; DL; Chairman: Devon and Cornwall Development Company, since 1988; British Railways (Western) Board, since 1978; *b* 26 Nov. 1923; *s* of Harold Goring Dalton and Phyllis Marguerite (*née* Ash). *Educ:* Shendish Prep. Sch., King's Langley; King Edward VI Sch., Southampton. Man. Dir, English Clays, Lovering Pochin & Co. Ltd, 1961–84; Dep. Chm., 1968–84, Chm., 1984–89, English China Clays. Member: Sun Alliance & London Assurance Group Bd, 1976–89; Western (formerly SW) Adv. Bd, Nat. Westminster Bank PLC, 1977–; Director, Westland plc (formerly Westland Aircraft), 1980–85. CBIM; FRSA. DL Cornwall, 1982. *Recreations:* sailing, painting, reading.

DALTON, Alfred Hyam, CB 1976; Deputy Chairman, Board of Inland Revenue, 1973–82 (Commissioner of Inland Revenue, 1970–82); *b* 29 March 1922; *m* 1946, Elizabeth Stalker; three *d*. *Educ:* Merchant Taylors' Sch., Northwood; Aberdeen Univ. Served War, REME, 1942–45 (despatches). Entered Inland Revenue, 1947; Asst Sec., 1958; Sec. to Board, 1969. *Address:* 10 Courtmead Close, Burbage Road, SE24 9HW. *T:* 071–733 5395.

DALTON, Vice-Adm. Sir Geoffrey (Thomas James Oliver), KCB 1986; Secretary-General of Mencap, 1987–90; *b* 14 April 1931; *s* of late Jack Rowland Thomas Dalton and Margaret Kathleen Dalton; *m* 1957, Jane Hamilton (*née* Baynes); four *s*. *Educ:* Parkfield, Sussex; Reigate Grammar Sch.; RNC Dartmouth. Midshipman 1950; served in HM Ships Illustrious, Loch Alvie, Cockade, Virago, Flag Lieut to C-in-C The Nore, and HMS Maryton (in comd), 1950–61; served HMS Murray, RN Staff Course and HMS Dido, 1961–66; served HMS Relentless (in Comd), RN Sch. of PT, HMS Nubian (in Comd), Staff of Flag Officers Second in Comd Far East Fleet and Second Flotilla, 1966–72; Asst Dir of Naval Plans, 1972–74; RCDS, 1975; Captain RN Presentation Team, 1976–77; in Comd HMS Jupiter, 1977–79 and HMS Dryad, 1979–81; Asst Chief of Naval Staff (Policy), 1981–84; Dep. SACLANT, 1984–87. Commander, 1966; Captain, 1972; Rear-Adm. 1981; Vice-Adm. 1984. Liveryman, Drapers' Co., 1957. FBIM 1987. *Recreations:* tennis, fishing, gardening, walking. *Address:* Farm Cottage, Catherington, Portsmouth, Hants PO8 0TD. *Club:* Royal Over-Seas League.

DALTON, Irwin, CBE 1986; Executive Vice-Chairman, 1985–88, and Chief Executive (Operations), 1986–88, National Bus Company; *b* 25 July 1932; *s* of Harry Farr Dalton and Bessie Dalton; *m* 1954, Marie Davies; two *d*. *Educ:* Cockburn High Sch., Leeds. FCA 1973; FCIT 1978. Accountancy profession, 1947–62; Asst Company Sec., 1962–67, Company Sec., 1968–70, West Riding Automobile, Wakefield; Company Sec., Crosville Motor Services, 1971–74; Dir and Gen. Manager, Ribble Motor Services, 1974–76; National Bus Company: Regional Dir, 1977–81; Mem. for Personnel Services, 1981–83; Exec. Bd Mem., 1983–84. Dir, Leyland Bus Gp, 1987–88. A Vice-Pres., Bus and Coach Council, 1983–87, Pres., 1987–88. *Recreations:* golf, other sporting activities. *Address:* Westview, 1 Birling Park Avenue, Birling Road, Tunbridge Wells, Kent TN2 5LQ. *T:* Tunbridge Wells (0892) 33459. *Club:* Tunbridge Wells Golf.

DALTON, Vice-Adm. Sir Norman (Eric), KCB 1959 (CB 1956); OBE 1944; *b* 1 Feb. 1904; *s* of late William John Henry Dalton, Portsmouth; *m* 1927, Teresa Elizabeth (*d* 1982), *d* of late Richard Jenkins, Portsmouth; one *s* one *d*. *Educ:* RN Colls Osborne and Dartmouth. Joined RN, 1917; Capt. 1946; Rear-Adm. 1954; Vice-Adm. 1957. Deputy

Engineer-in-Chief of the Fleet, 1955–57; Engineer-in-Chief of the Fleet, 1957–59; Dir-Gen. of Training, 1959–60; retired 1960. *Address:* New Lodge, Peppard Lane, Henley-on-Thames, Oxon. *T:* Henley (0491) 575552. *Club:* Army and Navy.

DALTON, Peter Gerald Fox, CMG 1958; *b* 12 Dec. 1914; *s* of late Sir Robert (William) Dalton, CMG; *m* 1944, Josephine Anne Helyar; one *s* one *d.* *Educ:* Uppingham Sch.; Oriel Coll., Oxford. HM Embassy, Peking 1937–39; HM Consulate-Gen., Hankow, 1939–41; HM Embassy, Chungking, 1941–42; Foreign Office, 1942–46; HM Legation, Bangkok, 1946; HM Embassy, Montevideo, 1947–50; Foreign Office, 1950–53; Political Adviser, Hong Kong, 1953–56; Foreign Office, 1957–60; HM Embassy, Warsaw, 1960–63; HM Consul-General: Los Angeles, 1964–65; San Francisco, 1965–67; Minister, HM Embassy, Moscow, 1967–69; retd from HM Diplomatic Service, 1969. *Address:* North Lodge, North Street, Mayfield, Sussex TN20 6AN. *T:* Mayfield (0435) 873421.

DALY, His Eminence Cardinal Cahal Brendan; *see* Armagh, Archbishop of, (RC).

DALY, Hon. Francis Lenton; His Honour Judge Daly; Judge of District Courts, Queensland, Australia, since 1989; *b* 23 June 1938; *s* of late Sydney Richard Daly and Lilian May Daly (*née* Lindholm); *m* 1964, Joyce Brenda (*née* Nicholls). *Educ:* Forest School; London School of Economics (LLB). Called to Bar, Gray's Inn, 1961 (Lord Justice Holker Exhibn). English Bar, 1961–66; Legal Secretary, Lord Chancellor's Office, 1966; Bermudian Bar, 1966–72; Asst Judge Advocate General to the Forces, UK, 1972–78; Principal Magistrate, Malaita, Solomon Islands, 1978; Attorney General, 1979, Chief Justice, 1980–84, Solomon Islands; Chief Justice, Nauru, 1983; admitted, Qld Bar, 1984. *Publications:* contribs to International and Comparative Law Qly, Commonwealth Judicial Jl. *Recreations:* yachting, rowing, reading. *Address:* Judges' Chambers, Court House, Cairns, Qld 4870, Australia. *T:* 070–52–3408. *Club:* Cairns Yacht.

DALY, Rt. Rev. John Charles Sydney; *b* 13 Jan. 1903; *s* of S. Owen Daly. *Educ:* Gresham's Sch., Holt; King's Coll., Cambridge; Cuddesdon Coll., Oxford. Curate, St Mary's Church, Tyne Dock, South Shields, 1926–29; Vicar, Airedale with Fryston, Yorks, 1929–35; Bishop of Gambia, 1935–51; Bishop of Accra, 1951–55; Bishop in Korea, 1955–65, of Taejon (Korea), 1965–68; Priest-in-charge of Honington with Idlicote and Whatcote, 1968–70; Vicar of Bishop's Tachbrook, 1970–75. *Address:* 32 Rainbow Fields, Shipston-on-Stour, Warwicks CV36 4BU. *T:* Shipston-on-Stour (0608) 62140.

DALY, Lawrence; General Secretary, National Union of Mineworkers, 1968–84, retired; *b* 20 Oct. 1924; *s* of James Daly and late Janet Taylor; *m* 1948, Renée M. Baxter; four *s* one *d.* *Educ:* primary and secondary schools. Glencraig Colliery (underground), 1939; Workmen's Safety Inspector, there, 1954–64. Part-time NUM lodge official, Glencraig, 1946; Chm., Scottish NUM Youth Committee, 1949; elected to Scottish Area NUM Exec. Cttee, 1962; Gen. Sec., Scottish NUM, 1964; National Exec., NUM, 1965. Mem., TUC General Council, 1971–81. TUC Gold Badge, 1981. *Publications:* (pamphlets): A Young Miner Sees Russia, 1946; The Miners and the Nation, 1968. *Recreations:* literature, politics, folk-song. *Address:* Glencraig, 45 Hempstead Lane, Potten End, Berkhamsted, Herts HP4 2RZ.

DALY, Margaret Elizabeth; Member (C) Somerset and Dorset West, European Parliament, since 1984; *b* 26 Jan. 1938; *d* of Robert and Elizabeth Bell; *m* 1964, Kenneth Anthony Edward Daly; one *d.* *Educ:* Methodist Coll., Belfast. Departmental Head, Phoenix Assurance Co., 1956–60; Trade Union Official, Guild of Insurance Officials, later Union of Insurance Staffs, and subseq. merged with ASTMS, 1960–71; Consultant, Cons. Party, 1976–79; Nat. Dir of Cons. Trade Unionists, 1979–84; Vice Chm., Develt Cttee, Eur. Parlt, 1987–89; Vice-Pres., Jt EEC/African Caribbean Pacific Lomé Assembly, 1988–. *Recreations:* swimming, music, travel. *Address:* The Old School House, Aisholt, Spaxton, Bridgwater, Somerset.

DALY, Michael de Burgh, MA, MD, ScD Cambridge; FRCP; Emeritus Professor of Physiology in the University of London, since 1984; Visiting Scientist, Department of Physiology, Royal Free Hospital School of Medicine, London, since 1984; *b* 7 May 1922; *s* of late Dr Ivan de Burgh Daly, CBE, FRS; *m* 1948, Beryl Esmé, *y d* of late Wing Commander A. J. Nightingale; two *s.* *Educ:* Loretto Sch., Edinburgh; Gonville and Caius Coll., Cambridge; St Bartholomew's Hospital. Nat. Science Tripos. Part I, 1943, Part II, 1944, Physiology with Pharmacology. House-physician, St Bartholomew's Hospital, 1947; Asst Lecturer, 1948–50, and Lecturer, 1950–54, in Physiology, University Coll., London. Rockefeller Foundation Travelling Fellowship in Medicine, 1952–53; Locke Research Fellow of Royal Soc., 1955–58; St Bartholomew's Hospital Medical College: Prof. of Physiology, 1958–84; Governor, 1975–; Treas., 1983–84. Vis. Prof. of Physiology, Univ. of NSW, 1966; Vis. Lectr, Swedish Univs, 1959–60; G. L. Brown Lectr, Physiological Soc., 1985–86. Member: Personnel Res. Ethical Cttee, MoD (Navy) (formerly Adv. Panel for Underwater Personnel Res., MoD), 1975– (Chm., 1990–); MRC/RN Personnel Res. Cttee, Underwater Physiology Sub-Cttee, 1975–; Res. Funds Cttee, British Heart Foundn, 1982–85; Chm., Armed Services Consultant Approval Bd in Applied Physiology/Aviation Medicine, MoD, 1989–. Chm., Editorial Bd of Monographs of Physiological Soc., 1981–87; Co-Editor of Journal of Physiology, 1956–63, 1984–89. FRSM 1959. Member: Soc. of Experimental Biol., 1965–; Physiological Soc., 1951–86 (Hon. Mem., 1986); Osler Med. Club, 1974–87; European Underwater Biomed. Soc., 1971–; Undersea Med. Soc. Inc., 1971–88. Schafer Prize in Physiology, University Coll., London, 1953; Thruston Medal, Gonville and Caius Coll., 1957; Sir Lionel Whitby Medal, Cambridge Univ., 1963; Gold Medal (jtly), BMA, 1972. *Publications:* contributor to: Lippold and Winton, Human Physiology; Starling, Principles of Human Physiology; Emslie-Smith, Paterson, Scratcherd and Read, Textbook of Physiology; papers on the integrative control of respiration and the cardiovascular system in Journal of Physiology; contrib. to film on William Harvey and the Circulation of the Blood. *Recreation:* model engineering. *Address:* 7 Hall Drive, Sydenham, SE26 6XL. *T:* 081–778 8773.

DALY, Michael Francis, CMG 1989; HM Diplomatic Service, retired; *b* 7 April 1931; *s* of late William Thomas Daly and of Hilda Frances Daly; *m* 1st, 1963, Sally Malcolm Angwin (*d* 1966); one *d*; 2nd, 1971, Juliet Mary Siragusa (*née* Arning); one step-*d.* *Educ:* Downside; Gonville and Caius Coll., Cambridge (Scholar; BA Hons). Mil. Service, 1952–54: 2nd Lieut, Intell. Corps. E. D. Sassoon Banking Co., London, 1954; Transreef Industrial & Investment Co., Johannesburg, 1955–66; General Electric Co., London, 1966; HM Diplomatic Service: 1st Sec., FCO, 1967; 1st Sec. (Commercial), Rio de Janeiro, 1969; 1st Sec. (Inf.) and Head of Chancery, Dublin, 1973; Asst, Cultural Relations Dept, FCO, 1976; Counsellor, Consul-Gen. and Head of Chancery, Brasilia, 1977–78; Ambassador to Ivory Coast, Upper Volta and Niger, 1978–83; Head of West African Dept, FCO, and Ambassador (non-resident) to Chad, 1983–86; Ambassador: to Costa Rica and (non-resident) to Nicaragua, 1986–89; to Bolivia, 1989–91. Chm., Anglo-Central American Soc., 1991–. *Recreations:* skiing, sailing, theatre, golf. *Address:* 45 Priory Road, Kew, Surrey TW9 3DQ. *T:* 081–940 1272. *Clubs:* Johannesburg Country (S Africa); Andino, La Paz Golf (Bolivia).

DALY, Lt-Gen. Sir Thomas (Joseph), KBE 1967 (CBE 1953; OBE 1944); CB 1965; DSO 1945, Chief of the General Staff, Australia, 1966–71; *b* 19 March 1913; *s* of late Lt-Col T. J. Daly, DSO, VD, Melbourne; *m* 1946, Heather, *d* of late James Fitzgerald, Melbourne; three *d.* *Educ:* St Patrick's Coll., Sale; Xavier Coll., Kew, Vic; RMC, Duntroon (Sword of Honour). 3rd LH, 1934; attached for training 16/5 Lancers, India, 1938; Adj, 2/10 Aust. Inf. Bn, 1939; Bde Major, 18 Inf. Bde, 1940; GSO2 6 Aust. Div., 1941; GSO1 5 Aust. Div., 1942; Instructor, Staff Sch. (Aust.), 1944; CO 2/10 Inf. Bn, AIF, 1944; Instr, Staff Coll., Camberley, UK, 1946; Joint Services Staff Coll., Latimer, 1948; Dir of Mil. Art, RMC Duntroon, 1949; Dir of Infantry, AHQ, 1951; Comd 28 Brit. Commonwealth Inf. Bde, Korea, 1952; Dir, Ops and Plans, AHQ, 1953; IDC, London, 1956; GOC Northern Command, Australia, 1957–60; Adjt Gen., 1961–63; GOC, Eastern Command, Australia, 1963–66. Col Comdt, Royal Australian Regt, and Pacific Is Regt, 1971–75. Director: Jennings Industries Ltd, 1974–85; Fruehauf Australia Ltd, 1974–88; Associated Merchant Bank (Singapore), 1975–77. Mem., Nat. Council, Australian Red Cross, 1972–75; Chm., Council, Australian Nat. War Memorial, 1974–82 (Mem., 1966–74); Councillor, Royal Agricl Soc. of NSW, 1972–85. Legion of Merit (US), 1953. *Recreations:* golf, watching football, cricket, ski-ing. *Address:* 16 Victoria Road, Bellevue Hill, NSW 2023, Australia. *Clubs:* Australian (Sydney); Ski Club of Australia (Thredbo, NSW); Royal Sydney Golf, Melbourne Cricket.

DALYELL, Tam; MP (Lab) Linlithgow, since 1983 (West Lothian, 1962–83); *b* 9 Aug. 1932; *s* of late Gordon and Eleanor Dalyell; *m* 1963, Kathleen, *o d* of Baron Wheatley, PC; one *s* one *d.* *Educ:* Eton; King's Coll., Cambridge; Moray House Teachers' Training Coll., Edinburgh. Trooper, Royal Scots Greys, 1950–52; Teacher, Bo'ness High Sch., 1956–60. Contested (Lab) Roxburgh, Selkirk, and Peebles, 1959. Dep.-Director of Studies on British India ship-school, Dunera, 1961–62. Member Public Accounts Cttee, House of Commons, 1962–66; Secretary, Labour Party Standing Conference on the Sciences, 1962–64; PPS to Rt Hon. Richard Crossman, Minister of Housing, Leader of H of C, Sec. of State for the Social Services, 1964–70; Opposition spokesman on science, 1980–82; Chairman: PLP Education Cttee, 1964–65; PLP Sports Group, 1964–74; PLP Foreign Affairs Gp, 1974–75; Vice-Chairman: PLP Defence and Foreign Affairs Gps, 1972–74; Scottish Labour Group of MPs, 1973–75; Parly Lab. Party, Nov. 1974–; Sub-Cttee on Public Accounts; Mem., Labour Party NEC, 1986–87. Member: European Parlt, 1975–79; European Parlt Budget Cttee, 1976–79; European Parlt Energy Cttee, 1979; Member: House of Commons Select Cttee on Science and Technology, 1967–69; Liaison Cttee between Cabinet and Parly Labour Party, 1974–76; Council, National Trust for Scotland. Mem. Scottish Council for Devlt and Industry Trade Delegn to China, Nov. 1971. Political columnist, New Scientist, 1967–. *Publications:* The Case of Ship-Schools, 1960; Ship-School Dunera, 1963; Devolution: the end of Britain?, 1977; One Man's Falklands, 1982; A Science Policy for Britain, 1983; Thatcher's Torpedo, 1983; Misrule, 1987; Dick Crossman: a portrait, 1989. *Recreations:* tennis, swimming. *Address:* The Binns, Linlithgow, Scotland. *T:* Philipstoun (050683) 4255.

DALZELL PAYNE, Henry Salusbury Legh, (Harry), CBE 1973; *b* 1929; *s* of late Geoffrey Legh Dalzell Payne; *m* 1963, Serena Helen (marr. diss. 1980), *d* of Col Clifford White Gourlay, MC, TD; two *d.* *Educ:* Cheltenham; RMA Sandhurst; Staff Coll.; RCDS. Commissioned, 7th Hussars, 1949; served Queen's Own Hussars, 1957–66; seconded to Sultan of Muscat's Armed Forces, 1959–60; commanded: 3rd Dragoon Guards, 1967–69; 6th Armoured Bde, 1974–75; 3rd Armoured Div., 1979–80; resigned, 1981. *Recreations:* travel, the turf, fine wines. *Clubs:* Cavalry and Guards, Hurlingham, Turf, White's.

DALZIEL, Geoffrey Albert; British Commissioner, Leader of Salvation Army activities in Great Britain, 1974–80; *b* 10 Dec. 1912; *s* of Alexander William and Olive Mary Dalziel; *m* 1937, Ruth Edith Fairbank; two *s* one *d.* *Educ:* Harrow Elementary Sch. Commissioned Salvation Army Officer, 1934; Corps Officer in Gt Britain, to 1946; on Internat. Trng Coll. Staff, 1946–51; Divisional Youth Sec., 1951–59; Trng Coll. Principal, Melbourne, Aust., 1959–64; Chief Side Officer, Internat. Trng Coll., London, 1964–66; Chief Secretary: Sydney, Aust., 1966–68; Toronto, Canada, 1968–70; Territorial Comdr, Kenya, Uganda and Tanzania, E Africa, 1970–74. *Recreations:* walking, gardening, reading.

DALZIEL, Ian Martin; Director, Adam & Co. Group plc, since 1983; *b* 21 June 1947; *s* of late John Calvin Dalziel and of Elizabeth Roy Dalziel, *e d* of Rev. Ian Bain, FRSE and Mrs Christian Stuart Fisher Bain, Gairloch; *m* 1972, Nadia Maria Iacovazzi; four *s.* *Educ:* Daniel Stewart's Coll., Edinburgh; St John's Coll., Cambridge (BA Hons 1968; LLB Hons 1969; MA 1972); Université Libre de Bruxelles (Weiner Anspach Foundation Scholarship, 1970); London Business Sch. Mullens & Co., 1970–72; Manufacturers Hanover Ltd, 1972–83. Mem., Richmond upon Thames Council, 1978–79. Mem. (C) Lothian, European Parlt, 1979–84. Chm., Continental Assets Trust, 1989–; Director: Independent Insurance Co., 1989–91; Amcur-Lepercq Fund NV, 1990–. *Recreations:* golf, shooting. *Address:* 52 Perrymead Street, SW6 3SP. *T:* 071–736 8923; (office) 22 Charlotte Square, Edinburgh EH2 4DF. *T:* 031–225 8484; (office) 42 Pall Mall, SW1Y 5JG. *T:* 071–839 4615. *Clubs:* New (Edinburgh); Royal and Ancient Golf (St Andrews).

DALZIEL, Dr Keith, FRS 1975; Reader in Biochemistry, University of Oxford, 1978–83; Fellow of Wolfson College, 1970–83, now Emeritus; *b* 24 Aug. 1921; *s* of late Gilbert and Edith Dalziel; *m* 1945, Sallie Farnworth; two *d.* *Educ:* Grecian Street Central Sch., Salford; Royal Techn. Coll., Salford; 1st cl. hons BSc London 1944; PhD London; MA Oxon. Lab. Technician, Manchester Victoria Meml Jewish Hosp., 1935–44, Biochemist 1944–45; Asst Biochemist, Radcliffe Infirmary, Oxford, 1945–47; Res. Asst, Nuffield Haematology Res. Fund, Oxford, 1947–58; Rockefeller Trav. Fellowship in Medicine, Nobel Inst., Stockholm, 1955–57; Sorby Res. Fellow of Royal Soc., Sheffield Univ., 1958–63; Univ. Lectr in Biochem., Oxford, 1963–78. Vis. Prof. of Biochemistry, Univ. of Michigan, 1967. Member: Enzyme Chem. and Tech. Cttee, SRC, 1974; Council, Royal Soc., 1979–80; Editorial Bds, European Jl of Biochemistry and Biochimica Biophysica Acta, 1971–74; Adv. Bd, Jl Theor. Biol., 1976–79; an Associate Editor, Royal Soc., 1983–87. *Publications:* sci. papers in Biochem. Jl, European Jl of Biochemistry, etc. *Recreations:* music, golf, walking. *Address:* 25 Hampden Drive, Kidlington, Oxford. *T:* Kidlington (08675) 2623.

DALZIEL, Malcolm Stuart, CBE 1984; international funding consultant, since 1991; Associate Consultant, since 1988, and Director, since 1990, Consultants in Economic Regeneration in Europe Services; *b* 18 Sept. 1936; *s* of late Robert Henderson Dalziel and Susan Aileen (*née* Robertson); *m* 1961, Anne Elizabeth Harvey; one *s* two *d.* *Educ:* Banbury Grammar Sch.; St Catherine's Coll., Oxford (BA 1960, MA 1965). National Service, 2nd Lieut Northamptonshire Regt, 1955–57. The British Council, 1960–87: Asst Educn Officer, Lahore, Pakistan, 1961–63; Regional Dir, Penang, Malaya, 1963–67; Regional Rep., Lahore, 1967–70; Rep., Sudan, 1970–74; Dir, Management Services Dept, and Dep. Controller, Estabs Div., 1975–79; Rep., Egypt, and Counsellor (Cultural) British Embassy, Cairo, 1979–83; Controller, Higher Educn Div., British Council and Sec., IUPC, 1983–87. Affiliate, Internat., Develt Centre, Queen Elizabeth House, Oxford Univ., 1988–. Dep. Chm., Council for Educn in the Commonwealth, 1990– (Mem. Exec. Cttee, 1986–); Mem. Court, Univ. of Essex, 1986–88. *Recreations:* theatre, ballet, walking,

Rugby. *Address:* 368 Woodstock Road, Oxford OX2 8AE. *T:* Oxford (0865) 58969. *Club:* United Oxford & Cambridge University.

DAMER; *see* Dawson-Damer, family name of Earl of Portarlington.

DAMERELL, Derek Vivian; Governor, 1974–88, and Deputy Chairman, 1984–88, BUPA (Chief Executive, 1974–84); *b* 4 Aug. 1921; *s* of William James Damerell (Lt-Col), MBE and Zoe Damerell; *m* 1942, Margaret Isabel Porritt, *d* of Prof. B. D. Porritt; three *s* three *d.* *Educ:* ISC; Edinburgh Univ.; Harvard Business Sch. Parent Bd, BPB Industries, 1953–64; Regional Dir, Internat. Wool Secretariat, 1965–73. Dir, Murrayfield plc, 1982–87. Governor, Nuffield Nursing Homes Trust, 1974–80; Founder, Independ. Hosp. Gp (Chm., 1975–80); Internat. Fedn of Voluntary Health Service Funds: Mem. Council, 1976–; Dep. Pres., 1980–81, Pres., 1981–84; Mem. Bd of Governors, Assoc. Internat. de la Mutualité, 1974–83. *Recreations:* sailing (jt founder, BCYC, 1947); travel. *Address:* The Miller's House, Houghton, near Huntingdon, Cambs PE17 2BQ. *T:* St Ives (0480) 63285. *Clubs:* various yacht.

DAMMERS, Very Rev. Alfred Hounsell, (Horace); Dean of Bristol, 1973–87; *b* 10 July 1921; *s* of late B. F. H. Dammers, MA, JP; *m* 1947, Brenda Muriel, *d* of late Clifford Stead; two *s* two *d.* *Educ:* Malvern Coll. (Schol.); Pembroke Coll., Cambridge (Schol., MA); Westcott House, Cambridge. Served RA (Surrey and Sussex Yeo.), 1941–44. Asst Curate, Adlington, Lancs, 1948; Asst Curate, S Bartholomew's, Edgbaston, Birmingham, and Lectr at Queen's Coll., Birmingham, 1950; Chaplain and Lectr at S John's Coll., Palayamkottai, S India, 1953; Vicar of Holy Trinity, Millhouses, Sheffield, and Examining Chaplain to Bishop of Sheffield, 1957; Select Preacher at Univ. of Cambridge, 1963; Select Preacher at Univ. of Oxford, 1975, 1989; Chairman, Friends of Reunion, 1965; Canon Residentiary and Director of Studies, Coventry Cathedral, 1965. Founder, The Life Style Movement, 1972. Companion, Community of the Cross of Nails, 1975. *Publications:* Great Venture, 1958; Ye Shall Receive Power, 1958; All in Each Place, 1962; God is Light, God is Love, 1963; AD 1980, 1966; Lifestyle: a parable of sharing, 1982; A Christian Life-style, 1986; Lord Make Us One, 1988. *Recreations:* travel (home and abroad); walking, candle making. *Address:* 4 Bradley Avenue, Shirehampton, Bristol BS11 9SL.

DANCE, Brian David, MA; Headmaster, St Dunstan's College, Catford, since 1973; *b* 22 Nov. 1929; *s* of late L. H. Dance and late Mrs M. G. Swain (*née* Shrivelle); *m* 1955, Chloe Elizabeth, *o d* of late J. F. A. Baker, CB, FEng; two *s* two *d.* *Educ:* Kingston Grammar Sch.; Wadham Coll., Oxford. BA 1952, MA 1956. Asst Master, Kingston Grammar Sch., 1953–59; Sen. History Master: Faversham Grammar Sch., 1959–62; Westminster City Sch., 1962–65; Headmaster: Cirencester Grammar Sch., 1965–66; Luton Sixth Form Coll., 1966–73. Member: Cambridge Local Examination Syndicate, 1968–73; Headmasters' Assoc. Council, 1968–76 (Exec. Cttee, 1972–76, Hon. Legal Sec. 1975–76); Chm., London Area, SHA, 1984–85. Chm., Lewisham Environment Trust, 1987–88. *Publications:* articles in: Times Educnl Supp.; Headmasters' Assoc. 'Review'. *Recreations:* watching most ball games (especially cricket and Rugby football), music, philately, theatre. *Address:* Headmaster's House, St Dunstan's College, Catford SE6 4TY. *T:* 081–690 1277. *Club:* East India, Devonshire, Sports and Public Schools.

d'ANCONA, John Edward William; Director General, Offshore Supplies Office of the Department of Energy, since 1981; *b* 28 May 1935; *o s* of late Adolph and late Margaret d'Ancona; *m* 1958, Mary Helen, *o d* of late Sqdn-Ldr R. T. Hunter and late Mrs Hunter; three *s.* *Educ:* St Edward's Coll., Malta; St Cuthbert's Grammar Sch., Newcastle upon Tyne. BA (Hons) Mod. History, DipEd (Durham). Teacher, 1959–61; Civil Service, 1961–: Asst Principal, Dept of Educn and Science, 1961; Private Sec. to Minister of State, DES, 1964–65; Principal: DES, 1965–67; Min. of Technology and DTI, 1967–74; Asst Sec., DoE, 1974; Under Sec., DoE OSO, 1981. *Recreations:* cricket, philately, wine-bibbing. *Address:* c/o Department of Energy, 1 Palace Street, SW1.

DANCY, Prof. John Christopher, MA; Professor of Education, University of Exeter, 1978–84, now Emeritus; *b* 13 Nov. 1920; *e s* of late Dr J. H. Dancy and Dr N. Dancy; *m* 1944, Angela Bryant; two *s* one *d.* *Educ:* Winchester (Scholar); New Coll., Oxford (Scholar, MA). 1st Class, Classical Hon. Mods., 1940; Craven Scholar, 1946; Gaisford Greek Prose Prize, 1947; Hertford Scholar, 1947; Arnold Historical Essay Prize, 1949. Served in Rifle Brigade, 1941–46; Capt. GSO(3)I, 30 Corps, 1945; Major, GSO(2)I, 1 Airborne Corps, 1945–46. Lecturer in Classics, Wadham Coll., 1946–48; Asst Master, Winchester Coll., 1948–53; Headmaster of Lancing Coll., 1953–61; Master, Marlborough Coll., 1961–72; Principal, St Luke's Coll. of Educn, Exeter, 1972–78. Dir, St Luke's Coll. Foundn, 1978–86. Member, Public Schools' Commission, 1966–68. Chm., Higher Educn Foundn, 1981–86. Chm., British Accreditation Council for Independent Further and Higher Educn, 1984–. *Publications:* Commentary on 1 Maccabees, 1954; The Public Schools and the Future, 1963; Commentary on Shorter Books of Apocrypha, 1972. *Address:* Wharf House, Mousehole, Penzance, Cornwall TR19 6RX. *T:* Penzance (0736) 731137.

DANGAN, Viscount; Garret Graham Wellesley, (Jr); money markets, Banque Indosuez; *b* 30 March 1965; *s* and *heir* of 7th Earl Cowley, *qv*; *m* 1990, Claire Lorraine, *d* of P. W. Brighton, Stow Bridge, Norfolk. *Educ:* Franklin Coll., Switzerland (Associate of Arts degree). Traded Options, Hoare Govett. *Address:* c/o Grasmere, Stow Bridge, King's Lynn, Norfolk PE34 3PH.

DANIEL, Gerald Ernest, IPFA, FCA, IRRV; SAT; FRSA; Public Sector Adviser, Pannell Kerr Forster, Chartered Accountants, since 1984; *b* 7 Dec. 1919; *s* of Ernest and Beata May Daniel; *m* 1942, Ecila Roslyn Dillow; one *s* one *d.* *Educ:* Huish's Grammar Sch., Taunton. Served War, 1939–46, Somerset LI. Various appts in Borough Treasurers' Depts at Taunton, Scunthorpe and Bexhill, 1935–50; Cost and machine accountant, subseq. Chief Accountant, City Treasury, Bristol, 1950–60; Dep. Borough Treasurer, Reading, 1960–64; Borough Treasurer, West Bromwich, 1965–68; City Treasurer, Nottingham, 1968–74; County Treasurer, Nottinghamshire CC, 1974–84. Sec., 1971–76, Chm., 1976–81, Officers Side, Jt Negotiating Cttee for Chief Officers in Local Govt. Dir, Horizon Travel, 1975–85. Treasurer: E Midlands Airport, 1968–84; E Midlands Arts Assoc., 1969–84. President: Nottingham Soc. of Chartered Accountants, 1976; Assoc. of Public Service Finance Officers, 1978; Soc. of County Treasurers, 1979; Chartered Inst. of Public Finance and Accountancy, 1983–84 (Mem. Council, 1971–85; Vice-Pres., 1982); Mem. Council, Assoc. of Accounting Technicians, 1981–83. *Recreations:* gardening, music. *Address:* Brookvale, Star Lane, Blackboys, Uckfield, East Sussex TN22 5LD. *T:* Framfield (0825) 890712. *Club:* Royal Over-Seas League.

DANIEL, Sir Goronwy Hopkin, KCVO 1969; CB 1962; DPhil Oxon; HM Lieutenant for Dyfed, 1978–89; *b* Ystradgynlais, 21 March 1914; *s* of David Daniel; *m* 1940, Lady Valerie, *d* of 2nd Earl Lloyd George; one *s* two *d.* *Educ:* Pontardawe Secondary Sch.; Amman Valley County Sch.; University College of Wales, Aberystwyth; Jesus Coll., Oxford (Hon. Fellow, 1979). Fellow of University of Wales; Meyricke Scholar, Jesus Coll.; Oxford Institute of Statistics, 1937–40; Lecturer, Dept of Economics, Bristol Univ., 1940–41; Clerk, House of Commons, 1941–43; Ministry of Town and Country Planning, 1943–47; Ministry of Fuel and Power, Chief Statistician, 1947–55; Under-Sec., Coal Div., 1955–62, Gen. Div., 1962–64; Permanent Under-Sec. of State, Welsh Office, 1964–69; Principal, Aberystwyth UC, 1969–79; Vice-Chancellor, Univ. of Wales, 1977–79; Chm., Welsh Fourth Channel Authority, 1981–86. Chm., British Nat. Conf. on Social Welfare, 1970; Pres., West Wales Assoc. for the Arts, 1971–85; Member: Welsh Language Council, 1974–78; Gen. Adv. Council, BBC, 1974–79; Adv. Council on Energy Conservation, 1977–79; SSRC, 1980–83; Dep. Chm., Prince of Wales Cttee, 1980–86. Dir, Commercial Bank of Wales, 1972–90 (Dep. Chm., 1985–90). Chairman: Home-Grown Timber Adv. Cttee, 1974–81; Cttee on Water Charges in Wales, 1974–75; Welsh Congregational Meml Coll., 1985–90; Working Gp on Powers and Functions of Univ. of Wales, 1988–89. Hon. LLD, Univ. of Wales, 1980. Hon. Freeman, City of London, 1982. *Publications:* papers in statistical, fuel and power, and other journals. *Recreations:* country pursuits, sailing. *Address:* Cae Ffynnon, 67 St Michaels Road, Cardiff. *T:* Cardiff (0222) 553150. *Club:* Travellers'.

DANIEL, Gruffydd Huw Morgan; His Honour Judge Daniel; a Circuit Judge, since 1986; *b* 16 April 1939; *s* of Prof. John Edward Daniel, MA, and Catherine Megan Daniel; *m* 1968, Phyllis Margaret (*née* Bermingham); one *d.* *Educ:* Ampleforth; University College of Wales (LLB); Inns of Court School of Law. Commissioned 2nd Lieut First Bn Royal Welch Fusiliers, 1959; Captain 6/7 Bn Royal Welch Fusiliers (TA), 1965; served MELF, Cyprus. Called to the Bar, Gray's Inn, 1967; Wales and Chester Circuit (Circuit Junior, 1975); Recorder, 1980–86; Asst Liaison Judge, 1983–87, Liaison Judge, 1988–, Gwynedd. Asst Parly Boundary Comr for Wales, 1981–82, 1985–86. *Recreations:* gardening, shooting, fishing, sailing. *Address:* (residence) Rhiwgoch, Halfway Bridge, Bangor, Gwynedd. *Clubs:* Reform; Royal Anglesey Yacht.

DANIEL, Jack; *see* Daniel R. J.

DANIEL, John Sagar, DSc; Vice-Chancellor, Open University, since 1990; *b* 31 May 1942; *s* of John Edward Daniel and Winifred (*née* Sagar); *m* 1966, Kristin Anne Swanson; one *s* two *d.* *Educ:* Oxford Univ. (BA Metallurgy, MA); Univ. of Paris (DSc Metallurgy). Asst Prof., then Associate Prof., Ecole Polytechnique, Montreal, 1969–73; Dir, Etudes Télé-Univ., Univ. of Quebec, 1973–77; Vice Pres., Learning Services, Athabasca Univ., Alberta, 1979–80; Vice-Rector, Academic Affairs, Concordia Univ., Montreal, 1980–84; Pres., Laurentian Univ., Sudbury, Ont., 1984–90. Hon. Fellow, St Edmund Hall, Oxford, 1990. Hon. DLitt Deakin, Aust., 1985; Hon. DSc Royal Mil. Coll., St Jean, Canada, 1988. Chevalier de l'Ordre des Palmes Académiques (France), 1987. *Publications:* Learning at a Distance: a world perspective, 1982; numerous articles to professional pubns. *Address:* The Open University, Walton Hall, Milton Keynes MK7 6AA. *T:* Milton Keynes (0908) 653214.

DANIEL, Norman Alexander, CBE 1974 (OBE 1968); PhD; historian of the Middle Ages and intercultural relations; *b* 8 May 1919; *s* of George Frederick Daniel and Winifred Evelyn (*née* Jones); *m* 1st, 1941, Marion Ruth (*d* 1981), *d* of Harold Wadham Pethybridge; one *s*; 2nd, 1988, Morna Mackenzie Wales, *d* of Ronald Neil Mackenzie Murray, MC. *Educ:* Frensham Heights Sch.; Queen's Coll., Oxford (BA); Edinburgh Univ. (PhD). Asst Dir, British Inst., Basra, 1947; British Council Asst Representative: Baghdad, 1948; Beirut, 1952; Edinburgh, 1953; Dir, Brit. Inst., Baghdad, 1957; Dep. Rep., Brit. Council, Scotland, 1960; Brit. Council Rep., Sudan, 1962; Vis. Fellow, University Coll., Cambridge, 1969–70; Dir, Visitors Dept, Brit. Council, London, 1970; Cultural Attaché, Cairo, 1971; British Council Rep. and Cultural Counsellor, British Embassy, Cairo, 1973–79; Planning Advr, 1979–84, Consultant, 1984–, Hassan Khalifa; Gen. Sec., Coptic Archaeological Soc., Cairo, 1979–83. Green Vis Prof., Univ. of British Columbia, 1982. Egyptian Order of Merit, 2nd class, 1977. *Publications:* Islam and the West: the making of an image, 1960, 3rd edn 1966, repr. 1980; Islam, Europe and Empire, 1966; The Arabs and Mediaeval Europe, 1975, enlarged and rev. edn 1979, 3rd 1986, trans. Italian (Premio Lao Silesu Terzo Mondo, 1981); The Cultural Barrier, 1975; Heroes and Saracens, 1984; contribs to: Islam: Past Influence and Future Challenge (ed Cachia), 1979; History of the Crusades, vol. 6 (ed Zacour and Hazard), 1990; The Iraqi Revolution of 1958 (ed Furnea and Louis), 1991; (contrib.) D'un orient l'autre, 1991; contrib. to learned jls. *Address:* Le Grammont, rue Nationale, St Gingolph, 74500 Evian, France. *T:* 50 76 72 62; 225 Davenport #602, Toronto, Ont M5R 3R2, Canada. *T:* (416) 924 2023.

DANIEL, Prof. Peter Maxwell, MA, MB, BCh Cambridge; MA, DM Oxon; DSc London; FRCP; FRCS; FRCPath (Founder Fellow); FRCPsych (Founder Fellow); FLS; FInstBiol; Senior Research Fellow, Department of Applied Physiology and Surgical Science, Hunterian Institute, Royal College of Surgeons, since 1976; Visiting Senior Research Fellow, St Thomas's Hospital Medical School, since 1981; Emeritus Professor, lately Professor of Neuropathology, University of London, at the Institute of Psychiatry, Maudsley Hospital, 1957–76; Emeritus Physician, Bethlem Royal and Maudsley Hospitals, since 1977; *b* 14 Nov. 1910; *s* of Peter Daniel, FRCS, surgeon to Charing Cross Hospital, and Beatrice Laetitia Daniel; *m* 1st, Sarah Shelford; two *s* three *d*; 2nd, F. Dawn Bosanquet; one *s*; 3rd, Marion F. Bosanquet. *Educ:* Westminster Sch.; St John's Coll., Cambridge; New Coll., Oxford. Hon. Consultant Pathologist, Radcliffe Infirmary, 1948–56; Senior Research Officer, University of Oxford, 1949–56; Hon. Consultant in Neuropathology to the Army at Home, 1952–77; Hon. Consultant Neuropathologist, Bethlem Royal and Maudsley Hosps, 1956–76. Emeritus Fellow, Leverhulme Trust, 1978–80; Hon. Librarian, RCPath, 1981–; Mem., Library Cttee, Linnean Soc., 1987–. John Hunter Medal and Triennial Prize, 1946–48, and Erasmus Wilson Lectr, 1964, RCS. Editorial Board of: Jl of Physiology, 1958–65; Jl of Neurology, Neurosurgery and Psychiatry, 1953–64; Journal of Neuroendocrinology, 1966–77; Brain, 1974–76; Qly Jl Exp. Physiol., 1980–84. President: British Neuropathological Society, 1963–64; Neurological Section, RSM, 1970–71; Harveian Soc. London, 1966 (Trustee, 1971–; Hon. Mem., 1985); Section of Hist. of Med., RSM, 1979–82; Osler Club, 1979–82; Mem. Council: Royal Microscopical Soc., 1968–72; Neonatal Soc., 1959–61; Assoc. of British Neurologists, 1966–69 (Hon. Mem., 1985); Med. Soc. of London, 1981– (Hon. Librarian, 1984–; Pres., 1987–88). Hon. Mem., Physiological Soc., 1981. Member: Bd of Govs, Bethlem Royal and Maudsley Hosps, 1966–75; Council, Charing Cross Hosp. Medical Sch., 1972–85. Chm., Academic Bd, Inst. of Psychiatry, 1966–70; Vice-Chm., Central Academic Council, British Postgrad. Med. Fedn, 1975–76; Mem., Bd of Studies in Physiology, Univ. of London, 1981–. Life Mem., Anatomical Soc. of GB. Liveryman, Soc. of Apothecaries, 1952–. *Publications:* (jointly) Studies of the Renal Circulation, 1947; The Hypothalamus and Pituitary Gland, 1975; papers in various medical and scientific journals. *Recreations:* books, medical history. *Address:* 5 Seaforth Place, Buckingham Gate, SW1E 6AB. *T:* 071–834 3087. *Clubs:* Athenæum, Garrick, Green Room.

DANIEL, (Reginald) Jack, OBE 1958; FEng, FRINA, FIMarE; RCNC; VSEL Canadian Project Director, since 1987; *b* 27 Feb. 1920; *o s* of Reginald Daniel and Florence Emily (*née* Woods); *m* 1st, Joyce Earnshaw (marr. diss.); two *s*; 2nd, 1977, Elizabeth, *o d* of George Mitchell, Long Ashton, Som. *Educ:* Royal Naval Engineering Coll., Keyham; Royal Naval Coll., Greenwich. Grad., 1942; subseq. engaged in submarine design. Served War of 1939–45; Staff of C-in-C's Far East Fleet and Pacific Fleet, 1943–45. Atomic Bomb Tests, Bikini, 1946; Admty, Whitehall, 1947–49; Admty, Bath, Aircraft Carrier

Design, 1949–52; Guided Missile Cruiser design, 1952–56; Nuclear and Polaris Submarine design, 1956–65; IDC, 1966; Materials, R&D, 1967–68; Head of Forward Design, 1968–70; Director, Submarine Design and Production, 1970–74; Dir-Gen. Ships and Head of RCNC, MoD, 1974–79; British Shipbuilders: Bd Mem., 1979; Man. Dir, for Warshipbuilding, 1980–83; Dir (Training, Educn, Safety), 1981–85; Dir of Technology (Warships), British Shipbuilders, 1983–84; Dir, British Shipbuilders Australia Pty, 1983–86. Dep. Chm., Internationale Schiff Studien GmbH Hamburg, 1984–88; Man. Dir, Warship Design Services Ltd, 1984–87; Director: VSEL Australia Pty, 1986–; VSEL Defence Systems Canada Inc., 1987–; Chm., VSEL-CAP, 1987–. Vice Pres., RINA, 1982. Liveryman, Worshipful Co. of Shipwrights, 1980. Hon. Res. Fellow, UCL, 1974; Founder Fellow, Fellowship of Engineering, 1976. *Publications:* Warship Design, New Concepts and New Technology, Parsons Meml Lecture, 1976; papers for RINA, etc. *Recreations:* gardening, motoring, music. *Address:* Meadowland, Cleveland Walk, Bath BA2 6JU.

DANIEL, William Wentworth; Director, Policy Studies Institute, since 1986; *b* 19 Nov. 1938; *s* of late George Taylor Daniel and Margaret Elizabeth Daniel; *m* 1961, Lynda Mary Coles Garrett (marr. diss.); one *s* two *d. Educ:* Shebbear Coll., Devon; Victoria Univ. of Manchester (BA Hons); Univ. of Manchester Inst. of Science and Technology (MSc Tech). Directing Staff, Ashorne Hill Management Coll., 1963–65; Sen. Res. Officer, Research Services Ltd, 1965–67; Senior Research Fellow: Bath Univ., 1967–69; PSI (formerly PEP), 1969–81; Dep. Dir, PSI, 1981–86. *Publications:* Racial Discrimination in England, 1968; Whatever Happened to the Workers in Woolwich?, 1972; The Right to Manage?, 1972; A National Survey of the Unemployed, 1974; Sandwich Courses in Higher Education, 1975; Pay Determination in Manufacturing Industry, 1976; Where Are They Now?: a follow-up survey of the unemployed, 1977; The Impact of Employment Protection Laws, 1978; Maternity Rights: the experience of women, 1980; Maternity Rights: the experience of employers, 1981; Workplace Industrial Relations in Britain, 1983; Workplace Industrial Relations and Technical Change, 1987; The Unemployed Flow, 1989; (with Terence Hogarth) Britain's New Industrial Gypsies, 1989. *Recreations:* golf, lawn tennis. *Address:* Flat 2, 64 Queensway, W2 3RL. *T:* 071–229 6317; Chyvarton, Higher Upton, Bude, N Cornwall. *Clubs:* Reform; Bude & Cornwall Golf, Holsworthy Golf, David Lloyd Slazenger Racquet (Heston).

DANIELL, Brig. Averell John, CBE 1955 (MBE 1939); DSO 1945; *b* 19 June 1903; *s* of late Lt-Col Oswald James Daniell, QO Royal West Kent Regt, and late May Frances Drummond Daniell (*née* Adams); *m* 1934, Phyllis Kathleen Rhona Grove-Annesley; two *s* one *d. Educ:* Wellington Coll.; RM Acad., Woolwich. Commissioned, Royal Field Artillery, 1923; Captain, RA, 1936; Major, 1940; Lt-Col, 1943. Served War of 1939–45; Middle East, Iraq, Burma. Col, 1948; Brig., 1952; retired, 1955. Administrative Officer, Staff Coll., Camberley, 1955–61. Colonel Commandant, Royal Artillery, 1956–66. *Address:* Oak Lodge, 21 Hillside Street, Hythe, Kent CT21 5EJ. *T:* Hythe (0303) 266494.

DANIELL, Sir Peter (Averell), Kt 1971; TD 1950; DL; Senior Government Broker, 1963–73; *b* 8 Dec. 1909; *s* of R. H. A. Daniell and Kathleen Daniell (*née* Monsell); *m* 1935, Leonie M. Harrison; two *s* one *d. Educ:* Eton Coll.; Trinity Coll., Oxford (MA). Joined Mullens & Co., 1932, Partner, 1945; retd 1973. Served KRRC, 1939–45, Middle East and Italy. Master, Drapers' Co., 1980–81. DL Surrey 1976. *Recreations:* shooting, fishing, golf. *Address:* Glebe House, Buckland, Betchworth, Surrey RH3 7BL. *T:* Betchworth (073784) 2320. *Clubs:* Brooks's, Alpine.

DANIELL, Ralph Allen, CBE 1965 (OBE 1958); HM Diplomatic Service, retired; *b* 26 Jan. 1915; 2nd *s* of late Reginald Allen Daniell; *m* 1943, Diana Lesley (*née* Tyndale); one *s* three *d. Educ:* Lancing Coll.; University Coll., Oxford. Appointed to Board of Trade, 1937. Joined HM Forces, 1942; served with Royal Tank Regt in North Africa and Italian campaigns, 1943–45. Appointed to HM Foreign Service as First Sec., 1946; Mexico City, 1946; Rome, 1949; Foreign Office, 1951; Helsinki, 1953; Counsellor, 1958; Washington, 1958; New York, 1959; Cairo, 1962; Wellington, 1967; Consul-Gen., Chicago, 1972–74. *Address:* 1A Collins Lane, Ringwood, Hants BH24 1LD. *T:* Ringwood (0425) 473662.

DANIELL, Roy Lorentz, CBE 1957; Barrister-at-Law; Charity Commissioner, 1953–62; *s* of late Edward Cecil Daniell, Abbotswood, Speen, Bucks; *m* 1936, Sheila Moore-Gwyn, *d* of late Maj. Moore-Gwyn, Clayton Court, Liss, Hants. *Educ:* Gresham's Sch., Holt; New Coll., Oxford. *Address:* Common Side, Russell's Water, Henley on Thames, Oxon RG9 6ER. *T:* Nettlebed (0491) 641696. *Club:* United Oxford & Cambridge University.

DANIELS, George, MBE 1982; FSA, FBHI; author, watch maker, horological consultant; *b* 19 Aug. 1926; *s* of George Daniels and Beatrice (*née* Cadou); *m* 1964, Juliet Anne (*née* Marryat); one *d. Educ:* elementary. 2nd Bn E Yorks Regt, 1944–47. Started professional horology, 1947; restoration of historical watches, 1956–; hand watch making to own designs, 1969–. President: British Horological Inst., 1980 (Fellow, 1951); British Clock and Watchmakers' Benevolent Soc., 1980; Chm., Horological Industries Cttee, 1985–. Worshipful Co. of Clockmakers: Liveryman, 1968; Warden, 1977; Master, 1980; Tompion Gold Medal, 1981; Asst Hon. Surveyor. Freeman, Goldsmiths' Co., 1979; FSA 1976. Arts, Sciences and Learning Award, City Corporation, London, 1974; Victor Kullberg Medal, Stockholm Watch Guild, 1977; Gold Medal, British Horol Inst., 1981; Gold Badge and Hon. Fellow, Amer. Watchmakers Inst., 1985; Hon. CGIA 1986; City and Guilds Gold Medal for Craftsmanship, 1991. *Publications:* Watches (jtly), 1965 (3rd edn 1978); English and American Watches, 1967; The Art of Breguet, 1975 (3rd edn 1985); (jtly) Clocks and Watches of the Worshipful Company of Clockmakers, 1975; Sir David Salomons Collection, 1978; Watchmaking, 1981 (2nd edn 1985). *Recreations:* vintage cars, fast motorcycles, opera, Scotch whisky. *Address:* 34 New Bond Street, W1A 2AA.

DANIELS, Harold Albert; *b* 8 June 1915; *s* of Albert Pollikett Daniels and Eleanor Sarah Maud Daniels (*née* Flahey); *m* 1946, Frances Victoria Jerdan; one *s* decd. *Educ:* Mercers' Sch.; Christ's Coll., Cambridge. BA 1937; Wren Prize 1938; MA 1940. Asst Principal, Post Office, 1938; Admiralty, 1942; Post Office, 1945; Principal, 1946; Asst Sec., 1950; Under-Sec., 1961; Min. of Posts and Telecommunications, 1969. Asst Under Sec. of State, Home Office, 1974–76. *Address:* Lyle Court Cottage, Bradbourne Road, Sevenoaks, Kent TN13 3PZ. *T:* Sevenoaks (0732) 454039.

DANIELS, Prof. Henry Ellis, FRS 1980; Professor of Mathematical Statistics, University of Birmingham, 1957–78, now Emeritus Professor; Senior Research Associate, Statistical Laboratory, University of Cambridge, 1978–81; *b* 2 Oct. 1912; *s* of Morris and Hannah Daniels; *m* 1950, Barbara Edith Pickering; one *s* one *d. Educ:* Sciennes Sch., Edinburgh; George Heriot's Sch., Edinburgh; Edinburgh Univ.; Clare Coll., Cambridge. MA Edinburgh 1933, BA Cantab 1935, PhD Edinburgh 1943, ScD Cantab 1981. Statistician, Wool Industries Research Assoc., 1935–47; Ministry of Aircraft Production, 1942–45; Lecturer in Mathematics, University of Cambridge, 1947–57; Fellow, King's Coll. Cambridge, 1975–76. Pres., Royal Statistical Soc., 1974–75; Fellow Inst. of Mathematical Statistics; elected Mem. Internat. Statistical Inst., 1956. Freeman, Clockmakers' Co., 1981, Liveryman 1984. Guy Medal (Silver) 1957, (Gold) 1984, Royal Statistical Society. *Publications:* papers in Journal of the Royal Statistical Society, Annals of Mathematical Statistics, Biometrika, etc. *Recreations:* playing the English concertina, repairing watches. *Address:* 12 Kimberley Road, Cambridge CB4 1HH. *T:* Cambridge (0223) 313402.

DANIELS, Laurence John, CB 1979; OBE 1970; Secretary, Department of Capital Territory, Australia, 1977–81, retired; *b* 11 Aug. 1916; *s* of Leslie Daniels and Margaret (*née* Bradley); *m* 1943, Joyce Carey; two *s* eight *d. Educ:* Rostrevor Coll., South Australia; Sydney Univ. (BEc 1943). AASA 1939. Commonwealth (Australian) Taxation Office, 1934–53; Commonwealth Dept of Health, 1953–72; Director-General, Dept of Social Security, 1973–77. *Address:* 5 Nares Crest, Forrest, ACT 2603, Australia. *T:* 062–95 1896.

DANIELS, Robert George Reginald, CBE 1984; JP; DL; Chairman, Dartford Tunnel Joint Committee, 1974–88 (Member, 1968–88, Vice-Chairman, 1970–74); *b* 17 Nov. 1916; *s* of Robert Henry Daniels and Edith Daniels; *m* 1940, Dora Ellen Hancock; one *d. Educ:* private and state. Insurance Representative, Prudential Assurance, 1938–76, retd. Mem., Essex CC, 1965–89 (Alderman, 1969; Vice-Chm., 1977–80, Chm. 1980–83). Member: Theydon Bois Parish Council, 1952– (Chm., 1969–); Epping RDC, 1952–55 and Epping and Ongar RDC, 1955–74 (Vice-Chm., 1958–59 and 1964–65; Chm., 1959–60 and 1965–66); Epping Forest District Council, 1974–79. Chm., Gen. Comrs of Income Tax for Epping Div., 1988– (Comr, 1970–). President: Theydon Bois Br., British Legion, 1985– (Chm., 1973–85); Outward Bound Trust, Essex, 1985–; Mem., Chelmsford Engrg Soc., 1980–. JP Essex (Epping and Ongar Bench), 1969; DL Essex, 1980. *Recreation:* reading. *Address:* 42 Dukes Avenue, Theydon Bois, Epping CM16 7HF. *T:* Theydon Bois (037881) 3123. *Club:* Essex (Chelmsford).

DANILOVA, Alexandra; lecturer, teacher and choreographer, actress; *b* Pskoff, Russia, 20 Nov. 1906; *d* of Dionis Daniloff and Claudia Gotovzeffa; *m* 1st, 1931, Giuseppe Massera (*d* 1936); 2nd, 1941, Kazimir Kokic (marr. annulled, 1949). *Educ:* Theatrical Sch., Petrograd. Maryinski Theatre, Leningrad, 1923–24; Diaghileff Company, 1925–29; Waltzes from Vienna, 1931; Colonel de Basil Company, 1933–37; Prima Ballerina, Ballet Russe de Monte Carlo, 1938–58. Teacher (on Faculty) of School of American Ballet. Guest artist Royal Festival Hall, London, 1955; Ballerina in Oh Captain (Musical), New York, 1958. With own Company has toured West Indies, Japan, Philippines, USA, Canada and S Africa. Capezio Award (for outstanding services to Art of the Dance), 1958; Guest Choreographer Metropolitan Opera House, Guest Teacher and Choreographer, Germany (Krefeld Festival of Dance) and Amsterdam, 1959–60; Choreographed Coppelia for La Scala di Milano, 1961; Lecture performances throughout US; Guest Choreographer, Washington Ballet, 1962–64. Choreographed Coppelia (with George Balanchine), NY City Ballet, 1975. Screen acting debut in film, The Turning Point, 1977. Kennedy Center Honors Award, 1989; Handel Medal, New York City, 1989. *Recreations:* needlework, ping-pong, gardening. *Address:* Carnegie House, 100 West 57th Street, New York, NY 10019, USA.

DANINOS, Pierre; French author; *b* Paris, 26 May 1913; *m* 1st, 1942, Jane Marrain; one *s* two *d*; 2nd, 1968, Marie-Pierre Dourneau. *Educ:* Lycée Janson de Sailly, Paris. Began to write for newspapers, 1931; reporter for French press in England, USA, etc. Liaison agent with British Army, Dunkirk, 1940. Published first book in Rio de Janeiro, 1940; returned to France, 1941, from South America, Chronicler for Le Figaro. *Publications:* Les Carnets du Bon Dieu (Prix Interallié 1947); L'Eternel Second, 1949; Sonia les autres et moi (Prix Courteline, 1952) (English trans., Life with Sonia, 1958); Les Carnets du Major Thompson, 1954 (English trans., Major Thompson Lives in France, 1955); Le Secret du Major Thompson, 1956 (English trans., Major Thompson and I, 1957); Vacances à Tous Prix, 1958; Un certain Monsieur Blot, 1960 (English trans., 1961); Le Jacassin, 1962; Snobissimo, 1964; Le 36ème dessous, 1966; Le Major Tricolore, 1968; Ludovic Morateur, 1970; Le Pyjama, 1972; Les Touristocrates, 1974; Made in France, 1977; La Composition d'Histoire, 1979; Le Veuf Joyeux, 1981; La Galérie des Glaces, 1983; La France dans tous ses états, 1985; Profession: écrivain (autobiog.), 1988. *Recreations:* tennis, ski-ing, collecting British hobbies. *Address:* 81 rue de Grenelle, 75007 Paris, France.

DANKERT, Pieter; Kt of Order of Netherlands Lion; Commander, Order of Orange Nassau; State Secretary for European Affairs, Netherlands, since 1989; *b* Jan. 1934; *m* 1962, Paulette Puig; one *s* two *d. Educ:* Amsterdam Free Univ. Mem. (Partij van de Arbeid) Tweede Kamer, Netherlands; formerly: Internat. Sec., Partij van de Arbeid; Mem., NATO Assembly, WEU Assembly and Assembly of Council of Europe, 1971–77; Mem., European Parlt, 1977–89 (Pres., 1982–84). *Address:* Hoogstraat 1, 1135 BZ Edam, Netherlands.

DANKS, Sir Alan (John), KBE 1970; Chairman, New Zealand University Grants Committee, 1966–77; *b* 9 June 1914; *s* of T. E. Danks; *m* 1943, Loma Beryl Hall (*née* Drabble). *Educ:* West Christchurch High Sch.; Canterbury Coll. (MA). Teaching profession, 1931–43; Economics Dept, Univ. of Canterbury (formerly Canterbury University Coll.), 1943–66; Prof., 1962; Pro-Vice Chancellor, 1964. Chm., Information Authy, 1982–88. Hon. LLD Canterbury, 1973. *Address:* 116 Upland Road, Wellington 5, New Zealand.

DANKWORTH, Mrs C. D.; *see* Laine, Cleo.

DANKWORTH, John Philip William, CBE 1974; FRAM 1973; musician; *b* 20 Sept. 1927; British; *m* 1958, Cleo Laine, *qv*; one *s* one *d. Educ:* Monoux Grammar Sch. Studied Royal Academy of Music, 1944–46. ARAM 1969. Closely involved with post-war development of British jazz, 1947–60; formed large jazz orchestra, 1953. Pops Music Dir, LSO, 1985–; Principal Guest Pops Conductor, San Francisco Orch., 1987–89. Composed works for combined jazz and symphonic musicians including: Improvisations (with Matyas Seiber, 1959); Escapade (commissioned by Northern Sinfonia Orch., 1967); Tom Sawyer's Saturday, for narrator and orchestra (commissioned by Farnham Festival), 1967; String Quartet, 1971; Piano Concerto (commissioned by Westminster Festival, 1972); Grace Abounding (for RPO), 1980; The Diamond and the Goose (for City of Birmingham Choir and Orch.), 1981; Reconciliation (commnd for Silver Jubilee of Coventry Cathedral), 1987. Many important film scores (1964–) including: Saturday Night and Sunday Morning, Darling, The Servant, Morgan, Accident; other works include: Palabras, 1970; dialogue and songs for Colette, Comedy, 1980. Numerous record albums, incl. Echoes of Harlem, Misty, Symphonic Fusions. Variety Club of GB Show Business Personality Award (with Cleo Laine), 1977. Hon. MA Open Univ., 1975; Hon. DMus Berklee Sch. of Music, 1982. *Recreations:* driving, household maintenance. *Address:* UK Management, Laurie Mansfield, International Artistes Ltd, 235 Regent Street, W1. *T:* 071–439 8401.

DANN, Mrs Jill; *b* 10 Sept. 1929; *d* of Harold Norman Cartwright and Marjorie Alice Thornton; *m* 1952, Anthony John Dann; two *s* two *d* (and one *s* decd). *Educ:* Solihull High Sch. for Girls, Malvern Hall; Birmingham Univ. (LLB); St Hilda's Coll., Oxford (BCL). Called to the Bar, Inner Temple, 1952. Mayoress of Chippenham, 1964–65. Church Commissioner, 1968–; Member: General Synod of Church of England, and of its Standing Cttee, 1971–90 (Vice-Chm. House of Laity, 1985–90); Crown Appointments Commn, 1977–87; Chairman: House of Laity, Bristol Diocesan Synod, 1982–88; C of E

Evangelical Council, 1985–89; Trustee, Church Urban Fund, 1987–. Vice Chm., Trinity Coll., Bristol; Pres. of Fellows, Cheltenham and Gloucester Coll. of Higher Educn. Dir, Wiltshire Radio, 1981–88. Pres., Inner Wheel, 1978–79. *Recreations:* reading, enjoying being a grandmother. *Address:* The Riverbank, Reybridge, Lacock, Wilts SN15 2PF. *T:* Lacock (024973) 205. *Club:* Commonwealth Trust.

DANN, Most Rev. Robert William; *b* 28 Sept. 1914; *s* of James and Ruth Dann; *m* 1949, Yvonne (*née* Newnham); one *s* two *d*. *Educ:* Trinity Coll., Univ. of Melbourne. BA Hons Melbourne 1946. Deacon, 1945; Priest, 1946. Dir of Youth and Religious Education, Dio. Melbourne, 1946; Incumbent: St Matthew's, Cheltenham, 1951; St George's, Malvern, 1956; St John's, Footscray, 1961; Archdeacon of Essendon, 1961; Dir of Evangelism and Extension, Dio. Melbourne, 1963; Bishop Coadjutor, Dio. Melbourne, 1969–77; Archbishop of Melbourne and Metropolitan of Province of Victoria, 1977–83. *Address:* 1 Myrtle Road, Canterbury, Vic 3126, Australia.

DANNATT, Prof. (James) Trevor, MA; RA 1983 (ARA 1977); FRIBA; Senior Partner, Trevor Dannatt & Partners, Architects; Professor of Architecture: Manchester University, 1975–86; Royal Academy, 1988; *b* 15 Jan. 1920; *s* of George Herbert and Jane Ellen Dannatt; *m* 1953, Joan Howell Davies; one *s* one *d*. *Educ:* Colfes Sch.; Sch. of Architecture, Regent Street Polytechnic (Dip. Arch.). Professional experience in office of Jane B. Drew and E. Maxwell Fry, 1943–48; Architects Dept, LCC (Royal Festival Hall Gp), 1948–52; commenced private practice, 1952. Vis. Prof., Washington Univ., St Louis, 1976 and 1987. Assessor for national and international architectural competitions, Civic Trust; Member: Cathedrals Adv. Commn; Historic Bldgs Adv. Cttee, English Heritage. Editor, Architects' Year Book, 1945–62. Architectural work includes private houses, housing, school buildings (for LCC, Bootham, St Paul's, Colfe's), university buildings (residences, Leicester, Hull; Trinity Hall Combination Room, Cambridge; Vaughan Coll. and Jewry Wall Mus., Leicester; develt plan and extensive works for Thames Polytechnic), welfare buildings (for London boroughs, Lambeth, Southwark, Greenwich), conservation and restoration, interiors for private, corporate and public clients; Architects for British Embassy and Diplomatic Staff housing, Riyadh, 1985; Consultant Architects, Royal Botanic Gardens, Kew, 1989. Won internat. competition for conference complex in Riyadh, Saudi Arabia, completed 1974. Hon. FAIA, 1988. *Publications:* Modern Architecture in Britain, 1959; Trevor Dannatt: Buildings and Interiors 1951–72, 1972; (Editorial Adviser, and foreword) Buildings and Ideas 1933–83 from the Studio of Leslie Martin, 1983; contribs to Architectural Rev., Architects' Jl, and various foreign journals. *Recreations:* the arts, including architecture. *Address:* 115 Crawford Street, W1H 1AG. *T:* 071–486 6844. *Clubs:* Travellers', Arts.

DANSON, Hon. Barnett Jerome, PC (Canada); consultant, since 1984; company director; *s* of Joseph B. Danson and Saidie W. Danson, Toronto; *m* 1943, Isobel, *d* of Robert John Bull, London, England; four *s*. *Educ:* Toronto public and high schs. Served War: enlisted Queen's Own Rifles as Rifleman, 1939; commnd, 1943; wounded in France, 1944; retd 1945, Lieut. Manager, Jos. B. Danson & Sons Ltd, Toronto, 1945–50; Sales Man., Maple Leaf Plastics Ltd, 1950–53; Principal (Pres.), Danson Corp. Ltd, Scarborough, 1953–74; Chairman: CSPG Consultants, 1980–84; de Havilland Aircraft of Canada Ltd, 1981–84; Canadian Consul General, Boston, Mass, 1984–86. Active in Liberal Party, 1946–: MP (L) for York North, 1968–79; Parly Sec. to Prime Minister Trudeau, 1970–72; Minister of State for Urban Affairs, 1974–76; Minister of Nat. Defence, Canada, 1976–79; former Mem., Standing Cttee on Finance, Trade and Econ. Affairs, and Ext. Affairs and National Defence. Chm., GSW Thermoplastics Co.; Director: Ballet Opera Hall Corp., 1986–; Urban Transportation Develt Corp., 1987–; General Steelwares Building Products Co., 1987–; Paintplas Ltd, 1987–; Techplas Ltd, 1987–; Scintrex Ltd, 1987–; Algoma Central Railway Ltd; Winchester Groupe Inc. Chairman: Inst. for Political Involvement, Toronto; Arms Control Centre, Ottawa; Director: Canadian Council of Native Business; Atlantic Council of Canada; Canadian Inst. of Strategic Studies. Former Pres. and first Chm. Bd, Soc. of Plastics Engineers Inc. Former Member: Bd of Trade of Metrop. Toronto; Canadian Manufacturers Assoc.; Canadian Chamber of Commerce. Dir, Canadian Council of Christians and Jews. Former Hon. Lt-Col, Queen's Own Rifles of Canada. *Recreations:* fishing, reading, music. *Address:* 561 Avenue Road, Apt 1104, Toronto, Ontario M4V 2J8, Canada.

DANTZIC, Roy Matthew, CA; Director, Stanhope Properties PLC, since 1989; *b* 4 July 1944; *s* of David and Renee Dantzic; *m* 1969, Diane Clapham; one *s* one *d*. *Educ:* Brighton Coll., Sussex. CA 1968. Coopers & Lybrand, 1962–69; Kleinwort, Benson Ltd, 1970–72; Drayton Corporation Ltd, 1972–74; Samuel Montagu & Co. Ltd, 1974–80 (Exec. Dir, 1975); Mem. for Finance, BNOC, subseq. Finance Dir, Britoil plc, 1980–84; Dir, Pallas SA, 1984–85; Dir, Wood Mackenzie & Co., subseq. County NatWest Wood Mackenzie, 1985–89; Chm., Premier Portfolio Ltd, 1985–; non-executive Director: Moor Park (1958) Ltd, 1980–90; Saxon Oil plc, 1984–85. Pt-time Mem., CEGB, 1984–87; Pt-time Dir, BNFL, 1987–91. Governor, Brighton Coll., 1990–. *Recreations:* theatre, playing golf, watching cricket. *Address:* 12 Bedford Road, Moor Park, Northwood, Mddx HA6 2AZ. *Clubs:* MCC; Moor Park Golf.

DAR-ES-SALAAM, Archbishop of, (RC), since 1969; **HE Cardinal Laurean Rugambwa;** *b* Bukongo, 12 July 1912; *s* of Domitian Rushubirwa and Asteria Mukaboshezi. *Educ:* Rutabo, Rubya Seminary; Katigondo Seminary; Univ. of Propaganda, Rome (DCL 1951). Priest 1943; Bishop of Rutabo, 1952–60; Cardinal 1960; Bishop of Bukoba, 1960–69. Member: Knights of Columbus; Knights of St Peter Claver. Hon. Dr of Laws: Notre Dame, 1961; St Joseph's Coll., Philadelphia, 1961; Rosary Hill Coll., Buffalo, 1965; Hon. DHL New Rochelle, 1961; Hon. Dr Civil and Canon Law, Georgetown Univ. (Jesuits), 1961; Giving of the Scroll, Catholic Univ. of America, 1961. *Address:* Archbishop's House, PO Box 167, Dar-es-Salaam, Tanzania, East Africa.

DARBOURNE, John William Charles, CBE 1977; RIBA; Principal, John Darbourne Partnership (formerly Darbourne & Darke), Architects, Landscape Architects and Planners; *b* 11 Jan. 1935; *s* of late William Leslie Darbourne and Violet Yorke; *m* 1960, Noreen Fifield (marr. diss. 1989); one *s* three *d*. *Educ:* Battersea Grammar Sch.; University Coll., London Univ. (BA Hons Arch. 1958); Harvard (MLA). RIBA 1960; AILA. Asst Architect in private practice, 1958–60; Post-grad. study in landscape arch. and planning, Harvard, 1960, completed degree course, 1964; successful entry in Lillington (Westminster) national architect competition whilst in USA; founded own practice, 1961, inviting Geoffrey Darke into partnership; practice moved to Richmond, 1963, and, 1966–, grew steadily to undertake several large commns, particularly public housing, offices, corporate headquarters, medical and recreational buildings; in recent years practice has expanded into Europe (through internat. competitions), building in Stuttgart, Hannover and Bolzano; partnership of Darbourne & Darke dissolved, 1987; formed John Darbourne Partnership, which continues major work in UK and Europe. Architectural and Landscape Consultant to City of Bath. Involved in professional and local cttees, and national confs. Fritz Schumacher Award, 1979. *Recreations:* working late, the piano, golf, ski-ing. *Address:* 6 The Green, Richmond, Surrey TW9 1PL. *T:* 081–940 7182. *Clubs:* Athenæum, Reform.

DARBY, Prof. Sir Clifford; *see* Darby, Prof. Sir H. C.

DARBY, Dr Francis John, TD 1964; MRCGP; MFOM; *b* 24 Feb. 1920; *o s* of Col John Francis Darby, CBE, late Royal Signals, and Georgina Alice (*née* Dean); *m* 1969, Pamela Lisbeth, *o d* of Sydney Hill, Sutton Coldfield; one *s* by former *m*. *Educ:* Nottingham High Sch.; Edinburgh Acad.; Edinburgh Univ. (MB ChB 1950). MRCGP 1970; DIH 1963; DMJ 1965; MFOM RCP 1982. Commissioned, Royal Signals, 1939–46: N Africa (despatches), Italy and Egypt, 1942–46. Hospital and general practice, 1950–64; Department of Health and Social Security, 1964–82: Dep. Chief Medical Advr, 1978–80; Chief Medical Advr (Social Security), 1980–82; CMO and Consultant Physician, Cayman Is, 1983–85. Mem. BMA, 1950. Mem., Worshipful Soc. of Apothecaries of London, 1978–; Freeman, City of London, 1979. FRSM 1974 (Fellow, Faculty of History and Philosophy of Medicine, 1991). QHP, 1980–84. *Publications:* various papers on drug prescribing and medical administration. *Recreations:* sailing, swimming. *Address:* Ruardean, Captains Row, Lymington, Hants SO41 9RP. *T:* Lymington (0590) 677119. *Clubs:* Army and Navy; Royal Signals Yacht; Royal Lymington Yacht.

DARBY, Rt. Rev. Harold Richard; Bishop Suffragan of Sherwood, 1975–89; an Assistant Bishop, Diocese of Lincoln, since 1989; *b* 28 Feb. 1919; *s* of late William and Miriam Darby; *m* 1949, Audrey Elizabeth Lesley Green; two *s* three *d*. *Educ:* Cathedral School, Shanghai; St John's Coll., Durham (BA). Military service, 1939–45; Durham Univ., 1946–50. Deacon 1950; priest 1951; Curate of Leyton, 1950–51; Curate of Harlow, 1951–53; Vicar of Shrub End, Colchester, 1953–59; Vicar of Waltham Abbey, 1959–70; Dean of Battle, 1970–75. Hon. DD Nottingham, 1988. *Recreation:* vintage cars. *Address:* Sherwood, Main Street, Claypole, Lincs NG23 5BJ.

DARBY, Prof. Sir (Henry) Clifford, Kt 1988; CBE 1978 (OBE 1946); LittD 1960; FBA 1967; Professor of Geography in the University of Cambridge, 1966–76, now Emeritus; Honorary Fellow: St Catharine's College, Cambridge, 1960; King's College, Cambridge, 1983; *b* 7 Feb. 1909; *s* of Evan Darby and Janet Darby (*née* Thomas), Resolven, Glamorgan; *m* 1941, Eva Constance Thomson; two *d*. *Educ:* Neath County Sch.; St Catharine's Coll., Cambridge. 1st Class Geographical Tripos, Parts I, 1926, II, 1928; PhD 1931; MA 1932. Lecturer in Geography, University of Cambridge, 1931–45; Fellow, King's Coll., Cambridge, 1932–45, 1966–81; Intelligence Corps, 1940–41 (Capt.); Admiralty, 1941–45; John Rankin Prof. of Geography, University of Liverpool, 1945–49; Prof. of Geography, University Coll. London, 1949–66; Leverhulme Research Fellow, 1946–48; Visiting Prof. Univ. of Chicago, 1952, Harvard Univ., 1959, 1964–65, and Univ. of Washington, 1963. Member: Royal Commission on Historical Monuments (England), 1953–77; National Parks Commn, 1958–63; Water Resources Board, 1964–68. President: Institute of British Geographers, 1961; Section E British Assoc., 1963; English Place-Name Soc., 1985–86; Chm., British National Cttee for Geography, 1973–78. Carl Sauer Lectr, Univ. of Calif, Berkeley, 1985; Ralph Brown Lectr, Univ. of Minnesota, 1987. Hon. Member: Croatian Geog. Soc., 1957; Royal Netherlands Geog. Soc., 1958; RGS, 1976; Inst. of British Geographers, 1977. Victoria Medal, RGS, 1963. Daly Medal, American Geog. Soc., 1963; Honors Award, Assoc. of Amer. Geographers, 1977. Hon. degrees: Chicago, 1967; Liverpool, 1968; Durham, 1970; Hull, 1975; Ulster, 1977; Wales, 1979; London, 1987. *Publications:* An Historical Geography of England before AD 1800 (ed and contrib.), 1936; (with H. Fullard) The University Atlas, 1937, 22nd edn 1983; (with H. Fullard) The Library Atlas, 1937, 15th edn 1981; The Cambridge Region (ed and contrib.), 1938; The Medieval Fenland, 1940; The Draining of the Fens, 1940, 3rd edn 1968; (with H. Fullard) The New Cambridge Modern History Atlas, 1970; (ed and contrib.) A New Historical Geography of England, 1973, 2 vol. edn 1976; The Changing Fenland, 1983; General Editor and Contributor, The Domesday Geography of England, 7 vols, 1952–77; articles in geographical and historical journals. *Address:* 60 Storey's Way, Cambridge CB3 0DX. *T:* Cambridge (0223) 354745.

DARBY, John Oliver Robertson; Chairman, Ultramar PLC, since 1988; *b* 5 Jan. 1930; *s* of Ralph Darby and Margaret Darby (*née* Robertson); *m* 1955, Valerie Leyland Cole; three *s*. *Educ:* Charterhouse. FCA 1953. Pilot Officer, RAF, 1953–55; Arthur Young, Chartered Accts, 1955–87: Partner, 1959; Chm., 1974–87. Chairman: Nat. Home Loans Hldgs PLC, 1985–; Property Lending Bank (formerly Property Lending Trust) PLC, 1987–; BREL Gp Ltd, 1989–; Dir, British Rail Engineering Ltd, 1986–89. *Recreations:* racing, golf. *Address:* 141 Moorgate, EC2M 6TX. *T:* 071–256 6080; The Tithe Barn, Headley, Bordon, Hants. *Clubs:* Garrick, Royal Thames Yacht; Royal & Ancient Golf (St Andrews); Liphook Golf.

DARBY, Dr Michael Douglas, FRES, FRGS; Surveyor General, Carroll Art Collection; *b* 2 Sept. 1944; *s* of Arthur Douglas Darby and Ilene Doris Darby (*née* Eatwell); *m* 1977, Elisabeth Susan Done. *Educ:* Rugby School; Reading Univ. (PhD). FRES 1977; FRGS 1984; AMA 1990. Asst to Barbara Jones, 1963; Victoria and Albert Museum: Textiles Dept, 1964–72; Prints and Drawings Dept, 1973–76; Exhibitions Officer, 1977–83; Dep. Dir, 1983–87; Hd of Publications, Exhibitions and Design, 1988–89. Member: Crafts Council, 1984–88; IoW Adv. Cttee, English Heritage, 1986–; Council, Royal Entomol Soc., 1988–; Council, National Trust, 1989–. FRSA 1989. *Publications:* Marble Halls, 1973; Early Railway Prints, 1974, 2nd edn 1979; British Art in the Victoria and Albert Museum, 1983; John Pollard Seddon, 1983; The Islamic Perspective, 1983; articles in art, architectural and entomological periodicals. *Recreations:* beetles, books. *Address:* 52 Avenue Gardens, W3 8HB. *T:* 081–992 6332.

DARBY, Sir Peter (Howard), Kt 1985; CBE 1973; QFSM 1970; HM Chief Inspector of Fire Services, 1981–86; *b* 8 July 1924; *s* of William Cyril Darby and Beatrice Colin; *m* 1948, Ellen Josephine Glynn; one *s* one *d*. *Educ:* City of Birmingham Coll. of Advanced Technology. Fire Brigades: Dep. Ch. Officer, Suffolk and Ipswich FB, 1963; Chief Officer, Nottingham FB, 1966; Chief Officer, Lancashire FB, 1967; County Fire Officer, Greater Manchester FB, 1974; Regional Fire Comdr (No 10) NW Region, 1974–76; Regional Fire Adviser (No 5) Greater London Region, 1977; Chief Officer of the London Fire Brigade, 1977–80. Pres., Chief and Asst Chief Fire Officers' Assoc., 1975–76; Mem. Adv. Council, Central Fire Brigades, 1977; Principal Adviser to Sec. of State on Fire Service matters, 1981–86; Chm., Fire Services Central Examinations Bd, 1985. Chm., Certifire Ltd, 1987–; non-exec. Dir, Argus Alarms Ltd, 1987–. Foundation Gov., St James's Catholic High (formerly Secondary Modern) Sch., Barnet, 1985– (Chm. Governors, 1987–). Freeman, City of London; Liveryman, Worshipful Co. of Basketmakers. CStJ 1983. *Recreations:* fell-walking, golf, fishing, sailing. *Address:* 10 Moor Lane, Rickmansworth, Herts WD3 1LG. *Clubs:* City Livery, KSC.

DARCY DE KNAYTH, Baroness (18th in line), *cr* 1332; **Davina Marcia Ingrams** (*née* **Herbert);** *b* 10 July 1938; *d* of late Squadron Leader Viscount Clive (*d* on active service, 1943), and of Vida, *o d* of late Captain James Harold Cuthbert, DSO, Scots Guards (she *m* 2nd, 1945, Brig. Derek Schreiber, MVO (*d* 1972)); *S* to father's Barony, 1943; *m* 1960, Rupert George Ingrams (*d* 1964), *s* of late Leonard Ingrams and of Mrs Ingrams; one *s* two *d*. *Heir:* *s* Hon. Caspar David Ingrams, *b* 5 Jan. 1962. *Address:* Camley Corner, Stubbings, Maidenhead, Berks.

D'ARCY HART, Philip Montagu; *see* Hart, P. M. D'A.

DARELL, Brig. Sir Jeffrey (Lionel), 8th Bt, *cr* 1795; MC 1945; *b* 2 Oct. 1919; *s* of late Lt-Col Guy Marsland Darell, MC (3rd *s* of 5th Bt); *S* cousin, 1959; *m* 1953, Bridget Mary, *e d* of Maj.-Gen. Sir Allan Adair, 6th Bt, GCVO, CB, DSO, MC; one *s* two *d*. *Educ:* Eton; RMC, Sandhurst. Commissioned Coldstream Guards, July 1939; served War of 1939–45: ADC to GOC-in-C, Southern Comd, 1942; Bde Major, Guards Bde, 1953–55; Officer Comdg 1st Bn Coldstream Guards, 1957–59; GSO1, PS12, War Office, 1959; College Comdr RMA Sandhurst, 1961–64; Comdg Coldstream Guards, 1964–65; Comdr, 56 Inf. Brigade (TA), 1965–67; Vice-Pres., Regular Commns Bd, 1968–70; Comdt, Mons OCS, 1970–72; MoD, 1972–74; retd 1974. ADC to HM the Queen, 1973–74. Trustee and Mem., London Law Trust, 1981–. High Sheriff, Norfolk, 1985. *Recreations:* normal. *Heir: s* Guy Jeffrey Adair Darell [*b* 8 June 1961; *m* 1988, Justine Samantha, *d* of Mr Justice T. Reynolds, Quambi Place, Sydney, Australia]. *Address:* 55 Green Street, W1. *T:* 071–629 3860; Denton Lodge, Harleston, Norfolk. *T:* Homersfield (098686) 206. *Club:* Cavalry and Guards.

DARESBURY, 3rd Baron *cr* 1927, of Walton, Co. Chester; **Edward Gilbert Greenall;** Bt 1876; *b* 27 Nov. 1928; *s* of 2nd Baron Daresbury and Josephine (*d* 1958), *y d* of Brig.-Gen. Sir Joseph Laycock, KCMG, DSO; *S* father, 1990; *m* 1st, 1952, Margaret Ada (marr. diss. 1986), *y d* of late C. J. Crawford; three *s* one *d*; 2nd, 1986, Mary Patricia, *d* of late Lewis Parkinson. *Educ:* Eton. Chairman: Randall & Vautier Ltd; Grunhalle Lager Internat. *Heir: s* Hon. Peter Gilbert Greenall [*b* 18 July 1953; *m* 1982, Clare, *d* of Christopher Weatherby; three *s*]. *Address:* Crossbow House, Trinity, Jersey, CI. *T:* Jersey (0534) 63316.

DARGIE, Sir William Alexander, Kt 1970; CBE 1969 (OBE 1960); FRSA 1951; artist; portrait, figure and landscape painter; Chairman, Commonwealth Art Advisory Board, Prime Minister's Department, 1969–73 (Member, 1953–73); *b* 4 June 1912; *s* of Andrew and Adelaide Dargie; *m* 1937, Kathleen, *d* of late G. H. Howitt; one *s* one *d*. *Educ:* Melbourne, and in studio of A. D. Colquhoun. Official War Artist (Capt.) with AIF in Middle East, Burma, New Guinea, India, 1941–46. Dir, National Gallery of Victoria Art Schs, 1946–53. Member: Interim Council of Nat. Gallery Canberra, 1968–72; Nat. Capital Planning Cttee, Canberra, 1970–73; Aboriginal Arts Adv. Cttee, 1970–72; Trustee: Native Cultural Reserve, Port Moresby, Papua-New Guinea, 1970–73; Museum of Papua-New Guinea, 1970–73; Mem. Council, Nat. Museum, Victoria, 1978–83; Chm., Bd of Trustees, McClelland Gall., 1981–87. MA *hc* Footscray Inst. of Technol., 1986. Archibald Prize for portraiture, 1941, 1942, 1945, 1946, 1947, 1950, 1952, 1956; Woodward Award, 1940; McPhillimy Award, 1940; McKay Prize, 1941. Painted portrait of The Queen for Commonwealth of Aust., 1954; the Duke of Gloucester, 1947; the Duke of Edinburgh for City of Melbourne, 1956. Portraits of Sir Macfarlane Burnet, Sir William Ashton, Sir Lionel Lindsay, acquired for Commonwealth Nat. Collection. Rep. in public and private collections in Aust., NZ, England and USA. One-man exhibition, Leger Galls, London, 1958. Exhibits with RA and Royal Soc. of Portrait Painters. *Publication:* On Painting a Portrait, 1956. *Recreations:* books, chess, tennis. *Address:* 19 Irilbarra Road, Canterbury, Victoria 3126, Australia. *T:* 836 3396 Melbourne. *Clubs:* Melbourne, Naval and Military (Melbourne).

DARK, Anthony Michael B.; *see* Beaumont-Dark.

DARKE, Geoffrey James, RIBA; Principal, Geoffrey Darke Associates, Architects and Planners, since 1987; *b* 1 Sept. 1929; *s* of late Harry James Darke and Edith Anne (*née* Rose); *m* 1959, Jean Yvonne Rose, ARCM; one *s* two *d*. *Educ:* Prince Henry's Grammar Sch., Evesham, Worcs; Birmingham School of Architecture (DipArch); ARIBA 1956. National Service, Malaya, commnd RE, 1954–56. Asst Architect, Stevenage Development Corp., 1952–58; private practice, 1958–61; Partner, Darbourne and Darke, Architects and Landscape Planners, 1961–87. Work has included many large commissions, particularly public buildings. Success in national and internat. competitions, in Stuttgart, 1977, Hanover, 1979 and 1980, and in Bolzano, Italy, 1980; numerous medals and awards for architectural work; co-recipient of Fritz Schumacher Award, Hamburg, 1978, for services to architecture and townplanning. Mem. Council, RIBA, 1977–83; Chm., RIBA Competitions Cttee, 1979–84; has served on many professional committees. FRSA 1981. Mem., Aldeburgh Festival Snape Maltings Foundn, 1979–. *Recreation:* music. *Address:* 23 Arundel Gardens, W11 2LB. *Club:* Reform.

DARKE, Marjorie Sheila; writer, since 1962; *b* 25 Jan. 1929; *d* of Christopher Darke and Sarah Ann (*née* Palin); *m* 1952; two *s* one *d*. *Educ:* Worcester Grammar Sch. for Girls; Leicester Coll. of Art and Technol.; Central Sch. of Art, London. Worked in textile studio of John Lewis Partnership, 1950–54. *Publications:* Ride the Iron Horse, 1973; The Star Trap, 1974; A Question of Courage, 1975; The First of Midnight, 1977; A Long Way to Go, 1978; Comeback, 1981; Tom Post's Private Eye, 1982; Messages and Other Shivery Tales, 1984; A Rose from Blighty, 1990; *for young children:* Mike's Bike, 1974; What Can I Do, 1975; Kipper's Turn, 1976; The Big Brass Band, 1976; My Uncle Charlie, 1977; Carnival Day, 1979; Kipper Skips, 1979; Imp, 1985; The Rainbow Sandwich, 1989; Night Windows, 1990. *Recreations:* reading, music, sewing, country walks, jogging. *Address:* c/o Rogers, Coleridge & White Ltd, Literary Agency, 20 Powis Mews, W11 1JN. *Clubs:* Society of Authors; International PEN.

DARLING; *see* Stormonth Darling and Stormonth-Darling.

DARLING, family name of **Baron Darling.**

DARLING, 2nd Baron, *cr* 1924, of Langham; **Robert Charles Henry Darling;** DL; Major retired, Somerset Light Infantry; *b* 15 May 1919; *s* of late Major Hon. John Clive Darling, DSO; *S* grandfather, 1936; *m* 1942, Bridget Rosemary Whishaw, *d* of Rev. F. C. Dickson; one *s* two *d*. *Educ:* Wellington Coll.; RMC Sandhurst. Retired, 1955. Sec., later Chief Executive, Royal Bath and West and Southern Counties Soc., 1961–79, Pres., 1989. DL Somerset 1972, Avon 1974. *Recreations:* fishing, gardening. *Heir: s* Hon. Robert Julian Henry Darling, FRICS [*b* 29 April 1944; *m* 1970, Janet, *yr d* of Mrs D. M. E. Mallinson, Richmond, Yorks; two *s* one *d*]. *Address:* Puckpits, Limpley Stoke, Bath, Avon BA3 6JH. *T:* Limpley Stoke (0225) 722146.

DARLING, Alistair Maclean; MP (Lab) Edinburgh Central, since 1987; advocate; *b* 28 Nov. 1953; *m*; one *s* one *d*. *Educ:* Aberdeen Univ. Admitted to Faculty of Advocates, 1984. Member: Lothian Regl Council, 1982–87 (Chm., Transport Cttee, 1986–87); Lothian and Borders Police Bd, 1982–86. Mem., Apex. Gov., Napier Coll., Edinburgh, 1982–87. *Address:* 26 St Bernard's Crescent, Edinburgh EH4 1NS; House of Commons, SW1A 0AA.

DARLING, Hon. Sir Clifford, Kt 1977; MP (Bahamas); Speaker, House of Assembly, Bahamas, since 1977; *b* Acklins Island, 6 Feb. 1922; *s* of Charles and Aremelia Darling; *m* Igrid Smith. *Educ:* Acklins Public Sch.; several public schs in Nassau. Became taxi-driver (Gen. Sec. Bahamas Taxicab Union for 8 yrs, Pres. for 10 yrs). An early Mem., Progressive Liberal Party; MHA for Englerston; Senator, 1964–67; Dep. Speaker, House of Assembly, 1967–69; Minister of State, Oct. 1969; Minister of Labour and Welfare, Dec. 1971; Minister of Labour and Nat. Insurance, 1974–77. Past Chm., Tourist Advisory Bd; instrumental in introd. of a comprehensive Nat. Insce Scheme in the Bahamas, Oct. 1974. Member: Masonic Lodge; Elks Lodge; Acklins, Crooked Is and Long Cays Assoc. *Address:* House of Assembly, Nassau, Bahamas.

DARLING, Rt. Rev. Edward Flewett; *see* Limerick and Killaloe, Bishop of.

DARLING, Gerald Ralph Auchinleck, RD 1967; DL; QC 1967; MA; Lieutenant-Commander, retired; Judge, Admiralty Court of the Cinque Ports, since 1979; *b* 8 Dec. 1921; *er s* of late Lieut-Col R. R. A. Darling and Moira (*née* Moriarty); *m* 1954, Susan Ann, *d* of late Brig. J. M. Hobbs, OBE, MC; one *s* one *d*. *Educ:* Harrow Sch. (Reginald Pole Schol.); Hertford Coll., Oxford (Baring Schol., Kitchener Schol.; MA 1948). Served with RNVR, 1940–46: Fleet Fighter Pilot with 807 Seafire Sqdn in HM Ships Furious, Indomitable, Battler and Hunter; Test Pilot, Eastern Fleet and Chief Test Pilot, British Pacific Fleet in HMS Unicorn; RNR until 1967. Called to Bar, Middle Temple, 1950 (Harmsworth Law Schol.), Bencher, 1972, Treasurer, 1991; Barrister, Northern Ireland, 1957; QC Hong Kong 1968. Member: Panel of Lloyd's Arbitrators in Salvage Cases, 1967–78, Appeal Arbitrator, 1978–; Panel of Wreck Commissioners, 1967–. Trustee, Royal Naval Museum, 1985–90. DL Co. Tyrone, 1990. Freeman of City of London, 1968. *Publications:* (contrib.) 3rd edn Halsbury's Laws of England (Admiralty and Ship Collisions); (contrib.) International Commercial and Maritime Arbitration, 1988; (with Christopher Smith) LOF90 and the New Salvage Convention, 1991. *Recreations:* fly fishing, shooting. *Address:* Crevenagh House, Omagh, Northern Ireland BT79 0EH; Queen Elizabeth Building, Temple, EC4Y 9BS. *T:* 071–353 9153. *Clubs:* Naval and Military; Tyrone County (Omagh).

DARLING, Henry Shillington, CBE 1967; Director-General, International Centre for Agricultural Research in Dry Areas, 1977–81, retired; Fellow of Wye College, since 1982; *b* 22 June 1914; *s* of late J. S. Darling, MD, FRCS, and Marjorie Shillington Darling, BA, Lurgan, N Ireland; *m* 1940, Vera Thompson Chapman, LDS, Belfast; one *s* two *d*. *Educ:* Watts' Endowed Sch.; Greenmount Agric. Coll., N Ireland; Queen's Univ., Belfast; Imp. Coll. Tropical Agriculture, Trinidad. BSc (1st Hons), 1938, BAgr (1st Hons) 1939, MAgr 1950, Belfast; AICTA 1942; PhD London, 1959. Middle East Anti-Locust Unit, Iran and Arabia, 1942–44; Research Div., Dept of Agriculture: Uganda, 1944–47; Sudan, 1947–49; Faculty of Agriculture, University Coll., Khartoum, 1949–54; Head of Hop Research Dept, Wye Coll., London Univ., 1954–62; Prof. of Agriculture and Dir of Inst. for Agric. Research, Ahmadu Bello Univ., Zaria, Nigeria, 1962–68; Dep. Vice-Chancellor, Ahmadu Bello Univ., 1967–68; Principal, Wye College, Univ. of London, 1968–77. Technical Adviser, Parly Select Cttee for Overseas Develt, 1970–71. Chairman: Agricultural Panel, Intermediate Technology Develt Gp; British Council Agricl Adv. Panel; Member: Senate and Collegiate Council, London Univ. (Chm., Senate European Studies Cttee), and other univ. cttees; Council, Royal Veterinary Coll.; Council, Ahmadu Bello Univ. Exec. Cttee, and Acad. Policy Cttee, Inter-Univ. Council for Higher Educn Overseas (also Chm., W African Gp and Mem., working parties and gps); Kent Educn Cttee; Exec. Cttee East Malling Res. Station; Council S and E Kent Productivity Assoc. Pres., Agricultural Sect., British Assoc., 1971–72. Technical Adviser: Tear Fund; Methodist Missionary Soc.; Pres., Inter-Collegiate Christian Fellowship, 1971–72. FInstBiol 1968. Hon. DSc: Ahmadu Bello Univ., 1968; Queen's Univ. Belfast, 1984. Order of the Hop, 1959. *Publications:* many papers in jls and reports dealing with applied biology, entomology, agricultural science and rural development in the Third World. *Recreations:* reading, Christian dialogue. *Address:* 1A Jemmett Road, Ashford, Kent TN23 2QA. *T:* Ashford (0233) 632982. *Clubs:* Farmers'; Samaru (Nigeria).

DARLING, Sir James Ralph, Kt 1968; CMG 1958; OBE 1953; MA Oxon; Hon. DCL, Hon. LLD; FACE; Headmaster, Geelong Church of England Grammar School, Corio, Victoria, Australia, 1930–61; *b* 18 June 1899; *s* of late Augustine Major Darling and Jane Baird Nimmo; *m* 1935, Margaret Dunlop, *er d* of late John Dewar Campbell; one *s* three *d*. *Educ:* Repton Sch.; Oriel Coll., Oxford (Hon. Fellow, 1986). 2nd Lieut Royal Field Artillery, 1918–19, France and Germany; Asst Master Merchant Taylors' Sch., Crosby, Liverpool, 1921–24; Asst Master Charterhouse Sch., Godalming, 1924–29; in charge of Public Schs Empire Tour to NZ, 1929; Hon. Sec. Headmasters' Conference of Australia, 1931–45, Chm., 1946–48; Member: Melbourne Univ. Council, 1933–71 (Hon. MA Melbourne); Commonwealth Univs Commission, 1942–51; Commonwealth Immigration Advisory Council, 1952–68; Australian Broadcasting Control Board, 1955–61. President: Australian Coll. of Educn, 1959–63 (Hon. Fellow 1970); Australian Road Safety Council, 1961–70; Chairman: Australian Expert Gp on Road Safety, 1970–71; Australian Frontier Commission, 1962–71 (President, 1971–73); Australian Broadcasting Commission, 1961–67; Commonwealth Immigration Publicity Council, 1962–71; Pres., Elizabethan Trust, 1970–82. Mem. Council, Marcus Oldham Agricl Coll., 1961–; Chm. (Victoria), United World Colls, 1972–91. Hon. DCL Oxon, 1948; Hon. LLD Melbourne, 1973; Hon. DLitt Deakin, 1989. *Publications:* The Education of a Civilized Man, 1962; Timbertop (with E. H. Montgomery), 1967; Richly Rewarding, 1978. *Address:* 3 Myamyn Street, Armadale, Victoria 3143, Australia. *T:* 822.6262. *Clubs:* Australian (Sydney); Melbourne (Melbourne).

DARLING, Gen. Sir Kenneth (Thomas), GBE 1969 (CBE 1957); KCB 1963 (CB 1957); DSO 1945; Commander-in-Chief, Allied Forces, Northern Europe, 1967–69, retired; *b* 17 Sept. 1909; *s* of late G. K. Darling, CIE; *m* 1941, Pamela Beatrice Rose Denison-Pender (*d* 1990). *Educ:* Eton; Royal Military College, Sandhurst. Commissioned 7th Royal Fusiliers, 1929; jssc 1946; idc 1953. Served NW Europe, 1944–45: Comd 5th Parachute Bde, 1946; Comd Airborne Forces Depot, 1948; Comd 16th Parachute Bde, 1950; Brig. A/q 1st (Br) Corps, 1954; Chief of Staff 1st (Br) Corps, 1955; Chief of Staff 2nd Corps, 1956. Dep. Dir of Staff Duties (D), WO, 1957–58; GOC Cyprus District and Dir of Ops, 1958–60; Dir of Infantry, 1960–62; GOC 1st (Br) Corps, 1962–63; GOC-in-C, Southern Command, 1964–66. Colonel: The Royal Fusiliers (City of London Regt), 1963–68; The Royal Regt of Fusiliers, 1968–74; Col Comdt, The Parachute Regt, 1965–67. ADC Gen., 1968–69. *Recreation:* riding. *Address:* Vicarage Farmhouse, Chesterton, Bicester, Oxon OX6 8UQ. *T:* Bicester (0869) 252092. *Club:* Army and Navy.

DARLING, Susan; consultant; *b* 5 May 1942; *d* of Eric Francis Justice Darling and Monica Darling (*née* Grant); *m* 1st, 1977, David John Wiseman (marr. diss. 1981); 2nd, 1982, Thomas Stephen Rogerson. *Educ:* Nonsuch County Grammar Sch. for Girls, Cheam; King's Coll., London (BA Hons). Joined BoT as Asst Principal, 1963; transf. to FCO, 1965; Nairobi, 1967–69; Second, later First Sec., Econ. and Social Affairs, UK Mission to UN, 1969–73; FCO, 1973–74; resigned, 1974; reinstated, 1975; FCO, 1975–78; Dep. High Comr and Head of Chancery, Suva, 1981–84; FCO, 1984–87; Consul-Gen., Perth, WA, 1987–88; resigned FCO, 1988. FRGS. *Recreations:* travel, hill-walking, pottering. *Address:* Box 42380, Casuarina, Darwin, NT 5792, Australia. *Club:* University of London Graduate Mountaineering.

DARLING, William Martindale, CBE 1988 (OBE 1972); FRPharmS; Managing Director, J. M. & W. Darling Ltd, since 1957; Chairman, South Tyneside Health Authority, since 1974; *b* 7 May 1934; *s* of William Darling, MPS and Muriel Darling; *m* 1958, Ann Edith Allen; two *s*. *Educ:* Mortimer Road Primary Sch.; Newcastle Royal

Grammar Sch.; Sunderland Polytechnic Sch. of Pharmacy. MPS 1956. Member: Medicines Commn, 1971–79; Health Educn Council, 1971–78; Pharmacy Bd, CNAA, 1972–78; Cttee on Safety of Medicines, 1979–86; Cttee on Review of Medicines, 1986–; Health Services Supply Council, 1978–84 (Chm. and Vice-Chm.); Chairman: Standing Pharmaceutical Adv. Cttee, 1974–; Nat. Pharmaceutical Supplies Gp, 1984–; Head, UK Pharm. Delegn to EEC, 1972–; Pres., Pharm. Gp, EEC, 1985–86; Mem., Comité Consultatif pour formation des pharmaciens, 1988–; Mem. Council, NAHA, 1974–90 (Chm., 1980–82; Hon. Treasurer, 1988–89); first Chm., Nat. Assoc. of Health Authorities and Trusts, 1990–; Member, Council: Pharmaceutical, later Royal Pharmaceutical Soc., 1962– (Vice-Pres., 1969–71; Pres., 1971–73); Internat. Hosp. Fedn, 1991–. Governor, Sunderland Poly., 1989– (Hon. Fellow, 1990). Hon. Life Mem., South Shields and Westoe Club, 1990. Pharm. Soc. Gold Medal, 1985. *Recreations:* horse racing, sunbathing, eating good food, growing prize flowers and vegetables. *Address:* Hartside, 6 Whitburn Road, Cleadon, near Sunderland SR6 7QL. *T:* 091–536 2089. *Club:* Athenæum.

DARLINGTON, Rear-Adm. Sir Charles (Roy), KBE 1965; BSc; Director of the Naval Education Service and Head of Instructor Branch, Royal Navy, Oct. 1960–Oct. 1965, retired; on staff of Haileybury, 1965–75; *b* 2 March 1910; *o s* of C. A. Darlington, Newcastle under Lyme, Staffs; *m* 1935, Nora Dennison Wright, Maulds Meaburn, Westmorland; one *s* one *d*. *Educ:* Orme Sch., Newcastle under Lyme; Manchester Univ. (BSc). Double First in Maths 1931; Sen. Maths Master, William Hulme's Gram. Sch., 1937–40. Entered Royal Navy, 1941 (Instructor Lieut); served in: HM Ships Valiant and Malaya during War, and later in HM Ships Duke of York, Implacable, Vanguard and Tyne. On Staff of C-in-C Home Fleet, 1954–55, as Fleet Meteorological Officer; for various periods in Admty, HMS Excellent and HMS Collingwood. Rear-Adm. 1960. *Recreations:* cricket, hill-walking, mathematics and trying to avoid ignorance of the arts, and particularly of history.

DARLINGTON, Joyce, (Mrs Anthony Darlington); *see* Blow, Joyce.

DARLINGTON, Stephen Mark, FRCO; Organist and Official Student in Music, Christ Church, Oxford, since 1985; *b* 21 Sept. 1952; *s* of John Oliver Darlington and Bernice Constance Elizabeth (*née* Murphy); *m* 1975, Moira Ellen (*née* Hill); three *d*. *Educ:* King's Sch., Worcester; Christ Church, Oxford (Organ Schol.; MA). Asst Organist, Canterbury Cathedral, 1974–78; Master of the Music, St Albans Abbey, 1978–85. Artistic Dir, Internat. Organ Fest., 1979–85. *Recreations:* travel, walking, punting, Italian food. *Address:* Christ Church, Oxford OX1 1DP. *T:* Oxford (0865) 276195.

DARNLEY, 11th Earl of, *cr* 1725; **Adam Ivo Stuart Bligh;** Baron Clifton of Leighton Bromswold, 1608; Baron Clifton of Rathmore, 1721; Viscount Darnley, 1723; *b* 8 Nov. 1941; *s* of 9th Earl of Darnley and of Rosemary, *d* of late Edmund Basil Potter; *S* half-brother, 1980; *m* 1965, Susan Elaine, JP, *y d* of late Sir Donald Anderson; one *s* one *d*. *Educ:* Harrow; Christ Church, Oxford. Dir, City of Birmingham Touring Opera, 1990–. Governor, Cobham Hall Sch., 1981–. *Heir:* *s* Lord Clifton, *qv*. *Address:* Netherwood Manor, Tenbury Wells, Worcs WR15 8RT. *Clubs:* Brooks's, MCC.

DARNLEY-THOMAS, Mrs John; *see* Hunter, Rita.

DARTMOUTH, 9th Earl of, *cr* 1711; **Gerald Humphry Legge;** Baron Dartmouth, 1682; Viscount Lewisham, 1711; *b* 26 April 1924; *s* of 8th Earl of Dartmouth, CVO, DSO; *S* father, 1962; *m* 1948, Raine (marr. diss. 1976), *d* of late Alexander McCorquodale; three *s* one *d*; *m* 1980, Mrs G. M. Seguin. *Educ:* Eton. Served War, 1943–45, Coldstream Guards, Italy (despatches). FCA 1951. Dir, Rea Brothers Group PLC, Bankers, 1958–89. Chairman: Royal Choral Soc.; Anglo-Brazilian Soc. Hon. LLD Dartmouth Coll., USA, 1969. *Heir:* *s* Viscount Lewisham, *qv*. *Address:* The Manor House, Chipperfield, King's Langley, Herts WD4 9BN. *Club:* Buck's.
See also Baron Herschell.

DARTNALL, Gary; Chairman and Chief Executive, Screen Entertainment Ltd, since 1986; *b* 9 May 1937; *s* of Enid and Gordon Dartnall; *m* 1962, Zena Chidiac; two *d*. *Educ:* King's College, Taunton. Asst Overseas Sales Manager, Associated British Pathé, 1958–60; Far East rep., British Lion Films, 1960–64; Pres., Alliance Inc., 1964–68; Man. Dir, Internat. Dept, Walter Reade Organization (USA) Inc., 1968–71; Pres., EMI Films Inc., 1971–76; Vice-Chm., EMI Television Programs Inc., 1976–80; Pres., VHD Programs Inc. and VHD Disc Manufacturing Inc., 1980–83; Chm. and Chief Exec., THORN EMI Screen Entertainment Ltd, 1983–86; Associate Dir, THORN EMI, 1985–. *Recreation:* sailing. *Address:* Flat 3, Green Park House, 90 Piccadilly, W1. *T:* 071–499 5663.

DARVALL, Sir (Charles) Roger, Kt 1971; CBE 1965; former company director; *b* 11 Aug. 1906; *s* of late C. S. Darvall; *m* 1931, Dorothea M., *d* of late A. C. Vautier; two *d*. *Educ:* Burnie, Tasmania. FASA. Gen. Manager, Australia & New Zealand Bank Ltd, Melbourne, 1961–67; former Director: Broken Hill Pty; Rothmans of Pall Mall Aust.; H. C. Sleigh Ltd; Australia New Guinea Corp.; Electrolux Pty; L. M. Ericsson Pty; Munich Re-Insurance Co. of Aust; Australian Eagle Insurance Co. Comr, State Electricity Commn of Vic, 1969–79. *Recreations:* motoring, gardening, outdoors. *Address:* 22 Barton Street, Mont Albert, Vic 3127, Australia. *Club:* Athenæum (Melbourne).

DARVALL, Sir Roger; *see* Darvall, Sir C. R.

DARWEN, 3rd Baron *cr* 1946, of Heys-in-Bowland; **Roger Michael Davies;** *b* 28 June 1938; *s* of 2nd Baron Darwen and of Kathleen Dora, *d* of George Sharples Walker; *S* father, 1988; *m* 1961, Gillian Irene, *d* of Eric G. Hardy, Bristol; two *s* three *d*. *Educ:* Bootham School, York. *Heir:* *s* Hon. Paul Davies, *b* 1962. *Address:* Labourer's Rest, Green Street, Pleshey, Chelmsford CM3 1HT.

DARWENT, Rt. Rev. Frederick Charles; *see* Aberdeen and Orkney, Bishop of.

DARWIN, Henry Galton, CMG 1977; MA; barrister; Second Legal Adviser, Foreign and Commonwealth Office, 1984–89; *b* 6 Nov. 1929; *s* of late Sir Charles Darwin, KBE, FRS; *m* 1958, Jane Sophia Christie; three *d*. *Educ:* Marlborough Coll.; Trinity Coll., Cambridge. Called to Bar, Lincoln's Inn, 1953. Asst Legal Adviser, FO, 1954–60 and 1963–67; Legal Adviser, British Embassy, Bonn, 1960–63; Legal Counsellor: UK Mission to UN, 1967–70; FCO, 1970–73; a Dir-Gen., Legal Service, Council Secretariat, European Communities, Brussels, 1973–76; Dep. Legal Adviser, FCO, 1976–84. *Publications:* contribs in Report of a Study Group on the Peaceful Settlement of International Disputes, 1966 and International Regulation of Frontier Disputes, 1970; notes in British Yearbook of International Law and American Jl of International Law. *Address:* 30 Hereford Square, SW7. *T:* 071–373 1140; 4/5 Gray's Inn Square, WC1R 5AY. *Club:* Athenæum.

DARWIN, Kenneth; Editor, Familia: Ulster Genealogical Review, since 1985; *b* 24 Sept. 1921; *s* of late Robert Lawrence and Elizabeth Darwin (*née* Swain), Ripon, Yorks. *Educ:* Elementary Sch.; Ripon Grammar Sch.; University Coll., Durham; Oflag VIIB (1943–45). BA 1947, MA 1948. Served 2nd Bn Lancs Fus., N Africa, (Captain) POW, 1942–46; TA Captain (Intelligence Corps), 1949–54. Asst Keeper, Public Record Office (NI), 1948; Dep. Keeper of Records of N Ireland, 1955–70; Vis. Lectr in Archives, UC Dublin, 1967–71; Fellow Commoner, Churchill Coll., Cambridge, 1970; Asst Sec., Min. of Commerce (NI), 1970–74; Sen. Asst Sec., Dept of Finance (NI) and Dept of Civil Service (NI), 1974–77; Dep. Sec., Dept of Finance (NI), 1977–81. Member: Irish MSS Commn, Dublin, 1955–70; Adv. Bd for New History of Ireland, Royal Irish Acad., 1968–; Trustee: Ulster Historical Foundn, 1956–87; Ulster Museum, 1982–88 (Vice-Chm., 1984–86); Lyric Th., Belfast, 1966–69. *Publications:* articles on archives, history and genealogy, in jls and Nat. Trust guides. *Recreations:* travel and fine arts; walking, gardening. *Address:* 18 Seymour Road, Bangor, Co. Down BT19 1BL. *T:* Bangor (0247) 460718. *Clubs:* Commonwealth Trust; Royal British Legion (Bangor, Co. Down).

DARYNGTON, 2nd Baron, *cr* 1923, of Witley; **Jocelyn Arthur Pike Pease;** *b* 30 May 1908; *s* of 1st Baron Daryngton, PC and Alice (*d* 1948), 2nd *d* of Very Rev. H. Mortimer Luckock, sometime Dean of Lichfield; *S* father 1949. *Educ:* Eton; privately; Trinity Coll., Cambridge (MA). Member Inner Temple, 1932. *Heir:* none. *Address:* Oldfield, Wadesmill, Ware, Herts.

DASGUPTA, Prof. Partha Sarathi, PhD; FBA 1989; Professor of Economics and of Philosophy, Stanford University, since 1989; Professor of Economics, Cambridge University, and Fellow of St John's College, Cambridge, since 1985 (on leave of absence); *b* 17 Nov. 1942; *s* of Prof. Amiya Dasgupta and Shanti Dasgupta, Santiniketan, India; *m* 1968, Carol Margaret, *d* of Prof. James Meade, *qv*; one *s* two *d*. *Educ:* Univ. of Delhi (BSc Hons 1962); Univ. of Cambridge (BA 1965, PhD 1968; Stevenson Prize, 1967). Res. Fellow, Trinity Hall, Cambridge, 1968–71, Supernumerary Fellow, 1971–74; Lectr, 1971–75, Reader, 1975–78, Prof. of Econs, 1978–84, LSE. Visiting Professor: Stanford Univ., 1974–75 and 1983–84; Delhi Univ., 1978; Harvard Univ., 1987; Princeton Univ., 1988. Consultant: on Proj. Planning, UNIDO, 1969–72; on Resource Management, World Bank, 1977; on Environmental Component of Natural Resource Pricing, UNCTAD, 1977–80; Res. Advr, WIDER (UN Univ., 1989–). Mem., Expert Panel on Environmtl Health, WHO, 1975–85. For. Mem., Amer. Acad. of Arts and Scis, 1991. Fellow, Econometric Soc., 1975. *Publications:* (with S. Marglin and A. K. Sen) Guidelines for Project Evaluation, 1972; (with G. Heal) Economic Theory and Exhaustible Resources, 1979; The Control of Resources, 1982; (with K. Binmore) Economic Organizations as Games, 1986; (with K. Binmore) The Economics of Bargaining, 1987; (with P. Stoneham) Economic Policy and Technological Performance, 1987; articles on devlt planning, optimum population, taxation and trade, welfare and justice, nat. resources, game theory, indust. org. and technical progress, poverty and unemployment, in Econ. Jl, Econometrica, Rev. of Econ. Stud., etc. *Address:* 1 Dean Drive, Holbrook Road, Cambridge. *T:* Cambridge (0223) 212179.

DASHWOOD, Sir Francis (John Vernon Hereward), 11th Bt, *cr* 1707; (Premier Baronet of Great Britain); *b* 7 Aug. 1925; *s* of Sir John Lindsay Dashwood, 10th Bt, CVO, and Helen Moira Eaton (*d* 1989); *S* father, 1966; *m* 1st, 1957, Victoria Ann Elizabeth Gwynne de Rutzen (*d* 1976); one *s* three *d*; 2nd, 1977, Marcella (*née* Scarafia), formerly wife of Giuseppe Sportoletti Baduel and *widow* of Jack Frye, CBE; one step *s* (from wife's first *m*). *Educ:* Eton; Christ Church, Oxford (BA 1948, MA 1953); Henry Fellow, Harvard Business Sch., USA. Foreign Office, 1944–45. Aluminum Company of Canada Ltd, 1950–51; EMI Ltd, 1951–53. Member of Buckinghamshire County Council, 1950–51; Member Lloyd's, 1956. Chm., Octavian Underwriting, 1991–. Contested (C) West Bromwich, 1955, Gloucester, 1957. High Sheriff Bucks, 1976. SBStJ. *Publication:* The Dashwoods of West Wycombe, 1987. *Heir:* *s* Edward John Francis Dashwood [*b* 25 Sept. 1964; *m* 1989, Lucinda, *d* of G. H. F. Miesegaes; one *d*]. *Address:* West Wycombe Park, Buckinghamshire. *T:* High Wycombe (0494) 23720. *Club:* White's.

DASHWOOD, Sir Richard (James), 9th Bt *cr* 1684, of Kirtlington Park; TD 1987; *b* 14 Feb. 1950; *s* of Sir Henry George Massy Dashwood, 8th Bt, and Susan Mary (*d* 1985), *er d* of late Major V. R. Montgomerie-Charrington, Hunsdon House, Herts; *S* father, 1972; *m* 1984, Kathryn Ann, *er d* of Frank Mahon, Eastbury, Berks; one *s*. *Educ:* Maidwell Hall Preparatory Sch.; Eton College. Commissioned 14th/20th King's Hussars, 1969; T&AVR, 1973– (Bt Major 1987). *Heir:* *s* Frederick George Mahon Dashwood, *b* 29 Jan. 1988. *Address:* Ledwell Cottage, Sandford St Martin, Oxfordshire OX5 4AN. *T:* Great Tew (060883) 267.

da SILVA, John Burke, CMG 1969; HM Diplomatic Service, retired; Adviser, Commercial Union Assurance Co., 1973–84; *b* 30 Aug. 1918; *o s* of late John Christian da Silva and Gabrielle Guittard; *m* 1st, 1940, Janice (decd), *d* of Roy Mayor, Shrewsbury, Bermuda; one *d*; 2nd, 1963, Jennifer, *yr d* of late Capt. the Hon. T. T. Parker, DSC, RN, Greatham Moor, Hants; one *s* two *d*. *Educ:* Stowe Sch.; Trinity Coll., Cambridge (MA). Commnd Intell. Corps 1940, served with 1st Airborne Div., N Africa and Italy, GS02 SHAEF, France and Germany (despatches); Control Commn Germany and Austria. Joined Foreign Service, 1948; served Rome, Hamburg, Bahrain, Aden, Washington, FCO; retired 1973. Chm., Governors, Virginia Water Junior Sch., 1973–83; a Vice-Pres., Royal Soc. for Asian Affairs, 1983–86; Mem. Council, Oriental Ceramic Soc., 1977–80, 1984–87. *Publications:* contributor: Oriental Art, Trans OCS, Asian Affairs, etc. *Recreation:* Oriental Art. *Address:* Copse Close, Virginia Water, Surrey. *T:* Wentworth (0344) 842342. *Club:* Travellers'.

DATE, William Adrian, CBE 1973; Chairman, Grenada Public Service Board of Appeal, since 1967; Member, Judicial and Legal Services Commission, Organisation of Eastern Caribbean States, since 1967; Chairman, Tribunal of Income Tax Appeal Commissioners, since 1988; Member, VAT Appeal Tribunal, since 1986; *b* 1 July 1908; *er s* of James C. Date; *m* 1st, 1933, Dorothy MacGregor Grant (*d* 1979); two *d*; 2nd, 1981, Rhoda Elaine Minors (*d* 1989). *Educ:* Queen's Royal Coll., Trinidad; Grenada Boys' Secondary Sch.; Lodge Sch., Barbados; Middle Temple, London. Magistrate and District Govt Officer, St Lucia, 1933–39; Crown Attorney, St Vincent, 1939–44; Legal Draughtsman, Jamaica, 1944–47; Chief Secretary, Windward Islands, 1947–50; Puisne Judge of the Supreme Court of the Windward and Leeward Islands, 1950–56; Puisne Judge of Supreme Court, British Guiana, 1956–64, retd. Vice-Pres., Grenada Building and Loan Assoc., 1976–; Dir, Grenada Co-operative Bank, 1976–. *Recreations:* tennis, bridge. *Address:* PO Box 133, St George's, Grenada, West Indies.

DATTA, Dr Naomi, FRS 1985; Professor Emeritus, London University; *b* 17 Sept. 1922; *d* of Alexander and Ellen Henrietta Goddard; *m* 1943, S. P. Datta; two *d* one *s*. *Educ:* St Mary's Sch., Wantage; University Coll. London; W London Hosp. Med. Sch. MB BS (external); MD London. Junior medical posts, 1946–47; Bacteriologist in PHLS, 1947–57; Lectr, later Prof. of Microbial Genetics, RPMS, London Univ., 1957–84; retired 1984. *Publications:* papers on the genetics and epidemiology of antibiotic resistance in bacteria. *Recreations:* gardening, cooking, sewing, knitting. *Address:* 9 Duke's Avenue, W4 2AA. *T:* 081-995 7562.

DAUBE, Prof. David, MA, DCL, PhD, Dr jur; FBA 1957; Director of the Robbins Hebraic and Roman Law Collections and Professor-in-Residence at the School of Law, University of California, Berkeley, 1970–81, Emeritus Professor of Law, since 1981; Emeritus Regius Professor, Oxford University, since 1970; Member, Academic Board, Institute of Jewish Studies, London, since 1953; *b* Freiburg, 8 Feb. 1909; 2nd *s* of Jakob Daube; *m* 1st, 1936 (marr. diss., 1964); three *s*; 2nd, 1986, Helen Smelser (*née* Margolis).

Educ: Berthold-gymnasium, Freiburg; Universities of Freiburg, Göttingen and Cambridge. Fellow of Caius Coll., 1938–46, Hon. Fellow, 1974; Lecturer in Law, Cambridge, 1946–51; Professor of Jurisprudence at Aberdeen, 1951–55; Regius Prof. of Civil Law, Oxford Univ., and Fellow of All Souls Coll., 1955–70, Emeritus Fellow, 1980. Senior Fellow, Yale Univ., 1962; Delitzsch Lecturer, Münster, 1962; Gifford Lecturer, Edinburgh, for 1962 and 1963 (lectures delivered, 1963–64); Olaus Petri Lecturer, Uppsala, 1963; Ford Prof. of Political Science, Univ. of California, Berkeley, 1964; Riddell Lectr, Newcastle, 1965; Gray Lectr, Cambridge, 1966; Lionel Cohen Lectr, Jerusalem, 1970; inaug. Frosty Gerard Lectr, UC Irvine, 1981; G. Hitchings Terriberry Lectr, Tulane Univ., 1982. Vis. Prof. of History, 1966–78, Hon. Prof., 1980, Univ. of Constance. President: Société d'Histoire des Droits de l'Antiquité, 1957–58; Classical Assoc. of GB, 1976–77; Jewish Law Assoc., 1983–85; Founder-Pres., B'nai B'rith Oxford, 1961. Corresp. Mem., Akad. Wiss., Göttingen, 1964, Bayer. Akad. Wiss., Munich, 1966; Hon. Mem. Royal Irish Acad., 1970; Fellow: Amer. Acad. of Arts and Sciences, 1971; World Acad. of Art and Sci., 1975; Amer. Acad. for Jewish Research, 1979; Amer. Soc. for Legal History, 1983; Hon. Fellow, Oxford Centre for Postgraduate Hebrew Studies, 1973. Hon. LLD: Edinburgh 1960; Leicester 1964; Cambridge 1981; Dr *hc* Paris 1963; Hon. DHL: Hebrew Union Coll., 1971; Graduate Theol Union, Berkeley, 1988; Dr *jur hc* Munich, 1972; Dr *phil hc* Göttingen, 1987. *Publications*: Studies in Biblical Law, 1947; The New Testament and Rabbinic Judaism, 1956; Forms of Roman Legislation, 1956; The Exodus Pattern in the Bible, 1963; The Sudden in the Scriptures, 1964; Collaboration with Tyranny in Rabbinic Law, 1965; He that Cometh, 1966; Roman Law, 1969; Civil Disobedience in Antiquity, 1972; Ancient Hebrew Fables, 1973; Wine in the Bible, 1975; Medical and Genetic Ethics, 1976; Duty of Procreation, 1977; Typologie im Werk des Flavius Josephus, 1977; Ancient Jewish Law, 1981; Geburt der Detektivgeschichte, 1983; Das Alte Testament im Neuen, 1984; Sons and Strangers, 1984; (with C. Carmichael) Witnesses in Bible and Talmud, 1986; Appeasement or Resistance and other essays on New Testament Judaism, 1987; (ed) Studies in memory of F. de Zulueta, 1959; (with W. D. Davies) Studies in honour of C. H. Dodd, 1956, and articles; *Festschriften*: Daube Noster, 1974; Studies in Jewish Legal History in Honour of D.D., 1974; Donum Gentilicium, 1978. *Address*: School of Law, University of California, Berkeley, Calif 94720, USA.

DAUBENY DE MOLEYNS, family name of **Baron Ventry.**

DAULTANA, Mumtaz Mohammad Khan; Ambassador of Pakistan to the Court of St James's, 1972–78; *b* 23 Feb. 1916; *o s* of Nawab Ahmadyar Daultana; *m* 1943, Almas Jehan; one *s* one *d*. *Educ*: St Anthony's Sch., Lahore; Government Coll., Lahore (BA (Hons)); Corpus Christi Coll., Oxford (MA); Called to Bar, Middle Temple, 1940; 1st cl. 1st position in Bar exam. Mem., All India Muslim League, 1942–; unopposed election as Mem. Punjab Legislative Assembly, 1943; Gen. Sec., Punjab Muslim League, 1944; Sec., All India Muslim League Central Cttee of Action, 1945; Elected Member: Punjab Assembly, 1946; Constituent Assembly of India, 1947; Constituent Assembly, Pakistan, 1947; Finance Minister, Punjab, 1947–48; Pres., Punjab Muslim League, 1948–50; Chief Minister of Punjab, 1951–53; Finance Minister, West Pakistan, 1955–56; Defence Minister, Pakistan, 1957; Pres., Pakistan Muslim League, 1967–72. Elected Member: Nat. Assembly of Pakistan, 1970; Constitution Cttee of Nat. Assembly, 1972. *Publications*: Agrarian Report of Pakistan Muslim League, 1950; Thoughts on Pakistan's Foreign Policy, 1956; Kashmir in Present Day Context, 1965. *Recreations*: music, squash. *Address*: 8 Durand Road, Lahore, Pakistan. *T*: 302459 (Lahore), 532387 (Karachi). *Clubs*: United Oxford & Cambridge University; Gymkhana (Lahore).

DAUNCEY, Brig. Michael Donald Keen, DSO 1945; DL; *b* 11 May 1920; *o s* of late Thomas Gough Dauncey and Alice Dauncey (*née* Keen); *m* 1945, Marjorie Kathleen, *d* of H. W. Neep, FCA; one *s* two *d*. *Educ*: King Edward's School, Birmingham; Inter. Exam., Inst. of Chartered Accountants. Commissioned, 22nd (Cheshire) Regt, 1941; seconded to Glider Pilot Regt, 1943; Arnhem, 1944 (wounded three times; taken prisoner, later escaped); MA to GOC-in-C, Greece, 1946–47; seconded to Para. Regt, 1948–49; Staff Coll., 1950; Instructor, RMA, 1957–58; CO, 1st Bn 22nd (Cheshire) Regt, 1963–66, BAOR and UN peace keeping force, Cyprus; DS plans, JSSC, 1966–68; Comdt, Jungle Warfare Sch., 1968–69; Comdt, Support Weapons Wing, Sch. of Infantry, 1969–72; Defence and Military Attaché, Madrid, 1973–75; retired 1976. Col, 22nd (Cheshire) Regt, 1978–85; Hon. Col, 1st Cadet Bn, Glos Regt (ACF), 1981–90. DL Glos 1983. *Recreations*: rough shooting, travelling, tennis; also under-gardener. *Address*: Uley Lodge, Uley, near Dursley, Glos GL11 5SN. *T*: Dursley (0453) 860216. *Club*: Army and Navy.

DAUNT, Maj.-Gen. Brian, CB 1956; CBE 1953; DSO 1943; late RA; *b* 16 March 1900; *s* of Dr William Daunt, Parade House, Hastings; *m* 1938, Millicent Margaret, *d* of Capt. A. S. Balfour, Allermuir House, Colinton, Edinburgh; two *d* (one *s* decd). *Educ*: Tonbridge; RMA, Woolwich. Commissioned RA, 1920; served NW Frontier, India, 1929–30; War of 1939–45: France, 1940, as 2 i/c Regt; CO Anti-Tank Regt, 1941; Italy, as CO 142 Field Regt, RA, Royal Devon Yeo., 1943 (DSO); CRA: 1st Armoured Div., 1944; 46 Div., 1944; 10 Indian Div., 1946; Italy, 1945 (despatches). Has had various Brigadier's appts. Commandant Coast Artillery Sch. and Inspector Coast Artillery, 1950–53; General Officer Commanding Troops, Malta, 1953–Nov. 1956; retired, 1957; Controller, Home Dept, British Red Cross Society, 1957–66. Col Comdt RA, 1960–65. CStJ 1966. *Recreations*: gardening, music, drama. *Address*: 10 Church Lane, Wallingford, Oxon OX10 0DX. *T*: Wallingford (0491) 38111. *Club*: Army and Navy.

DAUNT, Patrick Eldon; Head of Bureau for Action in favour of Disabled People, EEC, 1982–87, retired; international consultant on education and disability; *b* 19 Feb. 1925; *s* of Dr Francis Eldon Daunt and Winifred Doggett Daunt (*née* Wells); *m* 1958, Jean Patricia, *d* of Lt-Col Percy Wentworth Hargreaves and of Joan (*née* Holford); three *s* one *d*. *Educ*: Rugby Sch.; Wadham Coll., Oxford. BA, 1st Cl. Hons Lit. Hum., 1949, MA 1954, Oxon. Housemaster, Christ's Hosp., 1959; Headmaster, Thomas Bennett Comprehensive Sch., Crawley, 1965. Chm., Campaign for Comprehensive Educn, 1971–73; Principal Administrator, EEC, 1974–82. Vis. Fellow, London Inst. of Educn, 1988–91. Chm., ASBAH, 1990–. *Publications*: Comprehensive Values, 1975; Meeting Disability, a European Response, 1991. *Recreations*: books, botany. *Address*: 4 Bourn Bridge Road, Little Abington, Cambridge CB1 6BJ. *T*: Cambridge (0223) 891485. *Club*: United Oxford & Cambridge University.

DAUNT, Sir Timothy Lewis Achilles, KCMG 1989 (CMG 1982); HM Diplomatic Service; Ambassador to Turkey, since 1986; *b* 11 Oct. 1935; *s* of L. H. G. Daunt and Margery (*née* Lewis Jones); *m* 1962, Patricia Susan Knight; one *s* two *d*. *Educ*: Sherborne; St Catharine's Coll., Cambridge. 8th KRI Hussars, 1954–56. Entered Foreign Office, 1959; Ankara, 1960; FO, 1964; Nicosia, 1967; Private Sec. to Permanent Under-Sec. of State, FCO, 1970; Bank of England, 1972; UK Mission, NY, 1973; Counsellor, OECD, Paris, 1975; Head of South European Dept, FCO, 1978–81; Associate at Centre d'études et de recherches internationales, Paris, 1982; Minister and Dep. UK Perm. Rep. to NATO, Brussels, 1982–85; Asst Under-Sec. of State (Defence), FCO, 1985–86. *Address*: c/o Foreign and Commonwealth Office, SW1.

DAUSSET, Prof. Jean Baptiste Gabriel Joachim; Grand Croix de la Légion d'Honneur; Professeur de Médecine Expérimentale au Collège de France, 1977–87; *b* 19 Oct. 1916; *s* of Henri Dausset and Elizabeth Brullard; *m* 1962, Rose Mayoral; one *s* one *d*. *Educ*: Lycée Michelet, Paris; Faculty of Medicine, University of Paris. Associate Professor, 1958–68, Professor of Immunohaematology, 1968–77, University of Paris. Institut Nationale de la Santé et de la Recherche Médicale: Director of Research Unit on Immunogenetics of Human Transplantation, 1968–84; Centre National de la Recherche Scientifique: Co-Director, Oncology and Immuno-haematology Laboratory, 1968–84. Gairdner Foundn Prize, 1977; Koch Foundn Prize, 1978; Wolf Foundn Prize, 1978; Nobel Prize for Physiology or Medicine, 1980. *Publications*: Immuno-hématologie biologique et clinique, 1956; (with F. T. Rapaport) Human Transplantation, 1968; (with G. Snell and S. Nathanson) Histocompatibility, 1976; (with M. Fougereau) Immunology 1980, 1980; (with M. Pla) HLA, 1985. *Recreation*: plastic art. *Address*: 9 rue de Villersexel, 75007 Paris, France. *T*: 42 22 18 82.

DAVENPORT, (Arthur) Nigel; President, British Actors' Equity Association, since 1986; *b* 23 May 1928; *s* of Arthur Henry Davenport and Katherine Lucy (*née* Meiklejohn); *m* 1st, 1951, Helena White (*d* 1978); one *s* one *d*; 2nd, 1972, Maria Aitken (marr. diss.); one *s*. *Educ*: Cheltenham Coll.; Trinity Coll., Oxford (MA). Entered acting profession, 1951; for first ten years worked almost exclusively in theatre; original mem. English Stage Co. at Royal Court Th., 1956; A Taste of Honey, on Broadway, 1960; mainly television and films, 1961–; starred or co-starred in over 30 cinema films, incl. A High Wind in Jamaica, 1964; Man for All Seasons, 1966; Play Dirty, Royal Hunt of the Sun, Virgin Soldiers, 1969; A Last Valley, 1970; Living Free, Mary, Queen of Scots, 1972; Phase IV, 1973; The Island of Dr Moreau, 1977; Night Hawks, Chariots of Fire, 1980; Greystoke, 1982; *television*: South Riding; George III in The Prince Regent; Howard's Way, 1987–88, 1990; Trainer, 1991. Toured England: King Lear (title rôle), 1986; The Old Country, 1989. Mem. Council, British Actors' Equity, 1976; Vice Pres., 1978–82, 1985–86. *Recreations*: gardening, travel. *Club*: Garrick.

DAVENPORT, Brian John; QC 1980; *b* 17 March 1936; *s* of R. C. Davenport, FRCS, and Mrs H. E. Davenport; *m* 1969, Erica Tickell, *yr d* of Prof. E. N. Willmer, *qv*; two *s* one *d*. *Educ*: Bryanston Sch.; Worcester Coll., Oxford (MA). 2 Lieut RE, 1955–56. Called to the Bar, Gray's Inn, 1960 (Atkin Scholar); Bencher, 1983. Junior Counsel: to Export Credit Guarantees Dept, 1971–74; to Dept of Employment, 1972–74; (Common Law), to Bd of Inland Revenue, 1974–80; (Common Law), to the Crown, 1978–80; a Law Comr, 1981–88. Mem., Gen. Council of the Bar, 1969–73. Mem. Cttee of Management, Barristers Benevolent Assoc., 1963–78, Jt Hon. Sec. 1978–87. *Publications*: (ed jtly with F. M. B. Reynolds) 13th and 14th edns of Bowstead on Agency. *Address*: 43 Downshire Hill, NW3 1NU. *T*: 071–435 3332; c/o Norton Rose, Kempson House, Camomile Street, EC3A 7AN. *T*: 071–583 2434.

DAVENPORT, Major (retd) David John Cecil, CBE 1989; DL; Member, Rural Development Commission, 1982–90 (Deputy Chairman, April–Oct. 1988); *b* 28 Oct. 1934; *s* of late Major John Lewes Davenport, DL, JP, and Louise Aline Davenport; *m* 1st, 1959, Jennifer Burness (marr. diss. 1969); two *d*; 2nd, 1971, Lindy Jane Baker; one *s*. *Educ*: Eton College; Royal Military Academy, Sandhurst. Commnd into Grenadier Guards, 1954, retired 1967. RAC, Cirencester, 1968–69. Chairman, Leominster District Council, 1975–76. Chm., CoSIRA, 1982–88. Chm., Regional Adv. Cttee of the Forestry Commn (SW), 1974–87; Member, Forestry Commn's National Adv. Cttee for England, 1974–87; Mem. Council, Country Landowners' Assoc., 1980–88; Pres., Royal Forestry Soc., 1991– (Vice Pres., 1989–91). DL, 1974, High Sheriff, 1989–90, Hereford and Worcester. *Address*: Mansel Lacy House, Hereford HR4 7HQ. *T*: Bridge Sollars (098122) 224. *Clubs*: Boodle's, MCC.

DAVENPORT, Maurice Hopwood, FCIB; Director, First National Finance Corporation plc, since 1985; *b* 19 March 1925; *s* of Richard and Elizabeth Davenport; *m* 1954, Sheila Timms; one *s* two *d*. *Educ*: Rivington and Blackrod Grammar Sch. FIB 1982. Served RN, 1943–46. Joined Williams Deacon's Bank, 1940; Sec., 1960; Asst Gen. Man., 1969; Dir, 1978–85, Man. Dir, 1982–85, Williams & Glyn's Bank; Director: Royal Bank of Scotland Gp and Royal Bank of Scotland, 1982–85; Royal Trust Bank, 1986–. *Recreations*: walking, gardening, reading. *Address*: Pines, Dormans Park, East Grinstead, West Sussex RH19 2LX. *T*: Dormans Park (034287) 439.

DAVENPORT, Nigel; see Davenport, A. N.

DAVENPORT, Walter Arthur B.; see Bromley-Davenport.

DAVENPORT-HANDLEY, Sir David (John), Kt 1980; OBE 1962; JP; DL; Chairman, Clipsham Quarry Co., since 1947; *b* 2 Sept. 1919; *s* of John Davenport-Handley, JP; *m* 1943, Leslie Mary Goldsmith; one *s* one *d*. *Educ*: RNC Dartmouth. RN retd 1947. Chm., Rutland and Stamford Conservative Assoc., 1952–65; Treasurer, East Midlands Area Conservative Assoc., 1965–71; Chm. 1971–77; Vice-Chm., Nat. Union of Conservative & Unionist Assocs, 1977–79, Chm., 1979–80. Member: Consumers' Cttees for GB and for England and Wales, 1956–65; Parole Bd, 1981–84. Chm., Rutland Historic Churches Preservation Trust, 1987–. President: E Midlands Area Cons. Assoc., 1987–; Nat. Union of Cons. and Unionist Assocs, 1990–91. Governor, Swinton Conservative Coll., 1973–77; Chairman: Board of Visitors, Ashwell Prison, 1955–73; Governors, Casterton Community Coll., 1960–78; Trustee, Oakham Sch., 1970–86. JP 1948, High Sheriff 1954, DL 1962, Vice-Lieutenant 1972, Rutland; Chm., Rutland Petty Sessional Div., 1957–84; DL Leicestershire 1974. *Recreations*: gardening, music, travel. *Address*: Clipsham Hall, Oakham, Rutland, Leics LE15 7SE. *T*: Castle Bytham (078081) 204. *Club*: English-Speaking Union.

DAVENTRY, 3rd Viscount *cr* 1943; **Francis Humphrey Maurice FitzRoy Newdegate;** Lord-Lieutenant of Warwickshire, since 1990; *b* 17 Dec. 1921; *s* of Comdr Hon. John Maurice FitzRoy Newdegate, RN (*y s* of 1st Viscountess; he assumed by Royal Licence, 1936, additional surname and arms of Newdegate and *d* 1976) and Lucia Charlotte Susan, OBE (*d* 1982), *d* of Sir Francis Alexander Newdigate Newdegate, GCMG; *S* uncle, 1986; *m* 1959, Hon. Rosemary, *e d* of 1st Baron Norrie, GCMG, GCVO, CB, DSO, MC; two *s* one *d*. *Educ*: Eton. Served War of 1939–45 with Coldstream Guards, N Africa and Italy; Captain 1943. ADC to Viceroy of India, 1946–48. JP 1960, DL 1970, High Sheriff 1970, Vice-Lieut. 1974–90, Warwickshire. *Heir*: *s* Hon. James Edward FitzRoy Newdegate, *b* 27 July 1960. *Address*: Temple House, Arbury, Nuneaton, Warwickshire CV10 7PT. *T*: Nuneaton (0203) 383514. *Club*: Boodle's.

DAVEY, David Garnet, OBE 1949; MSc, PhD; Research Director of Pharmaceuticals Division, Imperial Chemical Industries Ltd, 1969–75; *b* 8 Aug. 1912; *y s* of I. W. Davey, Caerphilly, Glamorgan; *m* 1938, Elizabeth Gale; one *s* two *d*. *Educ*: University Coll., Cardiff (1st cl. Hons Zoology; MSc 1935); Gonville and Caius Coll., Cambridge (PhD 1938). Harvard Univ. Med. Sch. (Research Fellow). Inst. of Animal Pathology, Univ. of Cambridge, 1938; Lectr, University Coll., Cardiff, 1939–40; Min. of Supply (Radar), 1941; joined ICI 1942; Biological Research Manager, Pharmaceuticals Div., 1957–69. Pres., European Soc. for Study of Drug Toxicity, 1964–69; Member: MRC, 1971–75;

Cttee on Review of Medicines, 1975–81; Sub-cttee on Toxicity, Clinical Trials, and Therapeutic Efficacy, Cttee on Safety of Medicines, 1976–81. Chalmers Gold Medal, Royal Soc. Tropical Medicine and Hygiene, 1947; Therapeutics Gold Medal, Apothecaries Soc., 1947. *Publications:* contribs to Annals Trop. Med.; Trans Royal Soc. Tropical Medicine and Hygiene; British Med. Bulletin; Proc. European Soc. for Study of Drug Toxicity, etc. *Recreation:* gardening. *Address:* Aragon Lodge, Star Lane, Morcombelake, Dorset DT6 6DN. *T:* Chideock (0297) 89458.

DAVEY, David Herbert P.; *see* Penry-Davey.

DAVEY, Francis, MA; Headmaster of Merchant Taylors' School, 1974–82; *b* 23 March 1932; *er s* of Wilfred Henry Davey, BSc and Olive (*née* Geeson); *m* 1960, Margaret Filby Lake, MA Oxon, AMA, *o d* of Harold Lake, DMus Oxon, FRCO; one *s* one *d.* *Educ:* Plymouth Coll.; New Coll., Oxford (Hon. Exhibr); Corpus Christi Coll., Cambridge (Schoolmaster Fellow Commoner). 1st cl. Class. Hon. Mods 1953, 2nd cl. Lit. Hum. 1955, BA 1955, MA 1958. RAF, 1950–51; Classical Upper Sixth Form Master, Dulwich Coll., 1955–60; Head of Classics Dept, Warwick Sch., 1960–66; Headmaster, Dr Morgan's Grammar Sch., Bridgwater, 1966–73. *Publications:* articles in Enciclopedia dello Spettacolo and Classical Review. *Recreations:* Rugby, swimming, gardening, travel. *Address:* Crossings Cottage, Dousland, Yelverton, S Devon PL20 6LU. *T:* Yelverton (0822) 853928. *Clubs:* East India, Devonshire, Sports and Public Schools; Union (Oxford).

DAVEY, Geoffrey Wallace; a Recorder of the Crown Court, since 1974; *b* 16 Oct. 1924; *s* of late Hector F. T. Davey and Alice M. Davey; *m* 1964, Joyce Irving Steel; two *s* one *d.* *Educ:* Queen Elizabeth Grammar Sch., Faversham; Wadham Coll., Oxford (MA). Called to Bar, Lincoln's Inn, 1954; admitted Ghana Bar, 1957; resumed practice NE Circuit, 1970. Chm., Med. Appeal Tribunal, 1982–; Dep. Chm., Agricl Land Tribunal, 1982–. *Recreations:* golf, cooking, carpentry. *Address:* 22 Mill Hill Lane, Northallerton, N Yorkshire. *T:* Northallerton (0609) 775943; 19 Baker Street, Middlesbrough, Cleveland. *T:* Middlesbrough (0642) 217037–8; 5 King's Bench Walk, Temple, EC4.

DAVEY, Idris Wyn; Under-Secretary, Welsh Office, 1972–77; Deputy Chairman, Local Government Boundary Commission for Wales, 1979–89; *b* 8 July 1917; *m* 1943, Lilian Lloyd-Bowen; two *d.* Admiralty, 1940–47; Welsh Bd of Health: Asst Principal, 1948; Principal, 1951; Sec. Local Govt Commn for Wales, 1959–62; Welsh Office: Asst Sec. (in Min. of Housing and Local Govt), 1962; Establishment Officer, 1966–72; Under-Sec., 1972; seconded as Sec. and Mem., Local Govt Staff Commn for Wales and NHS Staff Commn for Wales, 1972–73. Mem., Sports Council for Wales, 1978–88. *Recreations:* watching Rugby football, gardening. *Address:* Beechcroft, 4A Southgate Road, Southgate, Swansea SA3 2BT. *T:* Bishopston (044128) 4320.

DAVEY, Jocelyn; *see* Raphael, Chaim.

DAVEY, John Trevor, FCA; Director since 1968, and Deputy Chairman since 1988, Thames Television PLC; *b* 20 March 1923; *s* of Clarence Reginald Davey and Ivy Ellender Davey (*née* Lippiatt); *m* 1962, Margaret June Cobby; two *d.* *Educ:* Richmond (Surrey) County Secondary Sch. Binder Hamlyn & Co., Chartered Accountants, 1939–55 (during which time served under Articles); Gp Accountant, British Lion Films Ltd, 1955–58; Co. Sec. and Financial Controller, Pulsometer Engrg Co. Ltd, 1958–61; British Electric Traction Co., later BET PLC, 1961–88: Chm. and/or Man. Dir, various subsids, and Main Bd Dir, 1978–88. *Address:* c/o Thames Television PLC, 306–316 Euston Road, NW1 3BB.

DAVEY, Jon Colin; Director of Cable, Independent Television Commission, since 1991; *b* 16 June 1938; *s* of Frederick John Davey and late Dorothy Mary Davey; *m* 1962, Ann Patricia Streames; two *s* one *d.* *Educ:* Raynes Park Grammar Sch. Joined Home Office, 1957; served in Civil Defence, Immigration, Criminal Policy, Prison and Criminal Justice Depts; Asst Sec., Broadcasting Dept, 1981–85; Dir-Gen., Cable Authy, 1985–90. Asst Sec., Franks Cttee on Sect. 2 of Official Secrets Act, 1971–72; Secretary: Williams Cttee on Obscenity and Film Censorship, 1977–79; Hunt Inquiry into Cable Expansion and Broadcasting Policy, 1982. Vice-Chm., Media Policy Cttee, Council of Europe, 1983–84; Mem., British Screen Adv. Council, 1990–. *Recreations:* lawnmaking, Bach, English countryside. *Address:* Independent Television Commission, 70 Brompton Road, SW3 1EY. *T:* 071–824 7799.

DAVEY, Keith Alfred Thomas, CB 1973; Solicitor and Legal Adviser, Department of the Environment, 1970–82; *b* 1920; *s* of W. D. F. Davey; *m* 1949, Kathleen Elsie, *d* of Rev. F. J. Brabyn; one *s* one *d.* *Educ:* Cambridge and County High Sch.; Fitzwilliam House, Cambridge (MA). Served War of 1939–45, Middle East (Captain). Called to the Bar, Middle Temple, 1947. Principal Asst Solicitor, DHSS, 1968–70. *Recreations:* looking at churches, reading history, keeping cats and dogs. *Address:* 165 Shelford Road, Trumpington, Cambridge CB2 2ND. *Clubs:* Athenæum, Sette of Odd Volumes.

DAVEY, Peter Gordon, CBE 1986; Managing Director, Oxford Intelligent Machines Ltd, since 1990; Director, Meta Machines Ltd, since 1984 (Managing Director, 1984–87); *b* 6 Aug. 1935; *s* of late Lt-Col Frank Davey, Royal Signals and H. Jean Davey (*née* Robley); *m* 1961; two *s* two *d.* *Educ:* Winchester Coll.; Gonville and Caius Coll., Cambridge (Mech. Scis Tripos, pt 2 Electrical; MA 1961). MIEE; MBCS 1967. Engineer: GEC Applied Electronics Labs, Stanmore, 1958–61; Lawrence Radiation Lab, Berkeley, Calif, 1961–64; Guest Researcher, Heidelberg Univ., 1964–65; Oxford University: Project Engr, Nuclear Physics Lab., 1966–79; Co-ordinator, Indust. Robotics Research Prog., SERC, 1979–84; Head of Inter-active Computing Facility, Rutherford Lab, SRC, 1978–80; of Robot Welding Project, Engrg Sci. Lab., 1979–84; Sen. Res. Fellow, St Cross Coll., 1981–89. Tech. Dir, Electro Pneumatic Equipment Ltd, Letchworth, 1968–. Ed., Open University Press Industrial Robotics Series, 1982–. Hon. Prof., UCW, Aberystwyth, 1988–. Hon. DSc Hull, 1987. *Publications:* (with W. F. Clocksin) A Tutorial Introduction to Industrial Robotics: artificial intelligence skills, 1982; (contrib.) Robot Vision, 1982; contribs to learned jls on robotics and image analysis systems. *Recreations:* buildings restoration, squash, sailing. *Address:* 22 Park Town, Oxford OX2 6SH.

DAVEY, Peter John; Editor, Architectural Review, since 1981; *b* 28 Feb. 1940; *s* of John Davey and Mary (*née* Roberts); *m* 1968, Carolyn Pulford; two *s.* *Educ:* Oundle Sch.; Edinburgh University (BArch). RIBA. News and Features Editor, Architects' Journal, 1974; Managing Editor, Architectural Review, 1980. Mem. Council, RIBA, 1990–. Kt 1st Cl., Order of White Rose (Finland), 1991. *Publications:* Architects' Journal Legal Handbook (ed), 1973; Arts and Crafts Architecture, 1980; numerous articles in architectural jls. *Recreations:* pursuit of edible fungi, fishing, cooking. *Address:* 44 Hungerford Road, N7 9LP. *Club:* Athenæum.

DAVEY, Dr Ronald William; Physician to the Queen, since 1986; *b* 25 Oct. 1943; *s* of Frederick George Davey and Cissy Beatrice Davey (*née* Lawday); *m* 1966, Geraldine Evelyn Maureen Croucher (marr. diss. 1988); one *s* one *d;* *m* 1991, Priscilla Anne Kennedy. *Educ:* Trinity School of John Whitgift; King's College London; King's College Hosp. (MB BS; MFHom; AKC). Gen. med. practice, 1970–77; Private homoeopathic medical practice, 1978–; research into electro-stimulation and drug addiction, 1978–79; Med. Res. Dir, Blackie Foundn Trust, 1980–; Hon. Res. Fellow, Nat. Heart and Lung Inst., Univ. of London, 1990– (Blackie Res. Fellow, 1988–90); former Consultant to Res. Council for Complementary Medicine (Vice-Chm., 1986–87). *Publications:* medical papers. *Recreations:* riding, ski-ing, music, writing. *Address:* 1 Upper Wimpole Street, W1M 7TD. *T:* 071–580 5489. *Club:* Royal Society of Medicine.

DAVEY, Roy Charles; Headmaster, King's School, Bruton, 1957–72; *b* 25 June 1915; *s* of William Arthur Davey and Georgina (*née* Allison); *m* 1940, Kathleen Joyce Sumner; two *d.* *Educ:* Christ's Hospital; Brasenose Coll., Oxford (Open Scholar). Asst Master, Weymouth Coll., 1937–40. War Service, Royal Artillery, 1940–46. Senior Master, 1946–49, Warden, 1949–57, The Village Coll., Impington. FRSA. *Recreations:* poetry, botany, gardening, games. *Address:* Fir Trees, Buckland Newton, Dorchester, Dorset DT2 7BY. *T:* Buckland Newton (03005) 262. *Club:* East India, Devonshire, Sports and Public Schools.

DAVEY, Prof. William, CBE 1978; PhD; FRSC; President, Portsmouth Polytechnic, 1969–82; Honorary Professor, Polytechnic of Central London, since 1979; *b* Chesterfield, Derbyshire, 15 June 1917; *m* 1941, Eunice Battye; two *s.* *Educ:* University Coll., Nottingham; Technical Coll., Huddersfield. BSc, PhD (London, external). Chemist: ICI Scottish Dyes, 1940; Boots, 1941; Shell, 1942–44. Lectr and Sen. Lectr in Organic Chemistry, Acton Techn. Coll., 1944–53; Head of Dept of Chemistry and Biology, The Polytechnic, Regent Street, London, W1, 1953–59; Principal, Coll. of Technology, Portsmouth, 1960–69. FRSA, FRSC, CBIM. *Publications:* Industrial Chemistry, 1961; numerous original papers in: Jl Chem. Soc., Inst. Petroleum, Jl Applied Chem. *Recreations:* motoring, foreign travel. *Address:* 67 Ferndale, Waterlooville, Portsmouth PO7 7PH. *T:* Waterlooville (0705) 263014.

DAVID, family name of **Baroness David.**

DAVID, Baroness *cr* 1978 (Life Peer), of Romsey in the City of Cambridge; **Nora Ratcliff David;** JP; *b* 23 Sept. 1913; *d* of George Blockley Blakesley, JP, and Annie Edith Blakesley; *m* 1935, Richard William David, *qv;* two *s* two *d.* *Educ:* Ashby-de-la-Zouch Girls' Grammar School; St Felix, Southwold; Newnham Coll., Cambridge (MA; Hon. Fellow 1986). Mem. Bd, Peterborough Develt Corp., 1976–78. A Baroness-in-Waiting (Government Whip), 1978–79; Opposition Whip, 1979–82; Dep. Chief Opposition Whip, 1982–87; opposition spokesman on education. Pres., Inst. for Study and Treatment of Delinquency, 1987–. Member: Cambridge City Council, 1964–67, 1968–74; Cambs County Council, 1974–78. Fellow, Anglia Higher Educn Coll., 1989. JP Cambridge City, 1965–. *Recreations:* swimming, theatre. *Address:* 50 Highsett, Cambridge CB2 1NZ. *T:* Cambridge (0223) 350376; Cove, New Polzeath, Cornwall PL27 6UF. *T:* Trebetherick (020886) 3310.

DAVID, Mrs Elizabeth, CBE 1986 (OBE 1976); FRSL 1982; 2nd *d* of Rupert Sackville Gwynne, MP, and Hon. Stella Ridley; *m* 1944, Lt-Col Ivor Anthony David (marr. diss. 1960). DUniv Essex, 1979; Hon. DLitt Bristol, 1990. Chevalier du Mérite Agricole (France), 1977. *Publications:* A Book of Mediterranean Food, 1950, rev. edn 1988; French Country Cooking, 1951, rev. edn 1987; Italian Food, 1954, rev. illus. edn 1987; Summer Cooking, 1955, rev. edn 1988; French Provincial Cooking, 1960; English Cooking, Ancient and Modern: vol. I, Spices, Salt and Aromatics in the English Kitchen, 1970; English Bread and Yeast Cookery, 1977; An Omelette and a Glass of Wine, 1984. *Address:* c/o Penguin Books Ltd, 27 Wright's Lane, W8 5TZ.

DAVID, Sir (Jean) Marc, Kt 1986; CBE 1982; QC (Mauritius) 1969; Barrister, in private practice since 1964; Hon. Professor of Law, University of Mauritius, since 1990; *b* 22 Sept. 1925; *s* of late Joseph Claudius David and Marie Lucresia David (*née* Henrisson); *m* 1948, Mary Doreen Mahoney; three *s* three *d.* *Educ:* Royal Coll., Port Louis; Royal Coll., Curepipe, Mauritius (Laureate (classical side) of English Scholarship, 1945); LSE (LLB Hons). Called to the Bar, Middle Temple, 1949. Barrister in private practice, 1950–54; Dist Magistrate, then Crown Law Officer (Crown Counsel, Sen. Crown Counsel and Actg AAG), 1954–64. Chm., Mauritius Bar Assoc., 1968, 1979. Chairman: various arbitration tribunals, commns of enquiry and cttees apptd by govt, 1958–; Electoral Supervisory and Boundaries Commns, 1973–82 (Mem., 1968–73); Mem., Panel of Conciliators and Arbitrators, Internat. Centre for Settlement of Investment Disputes, 1969–. Visitor, Univ. of Mauritius, 1980–81. *Recreations:* reading, listening to music, horse racing. *Address:* (home) Villa da Mar, Trou-aux-Biches, Triolet, Mauritius. *T:* 423–9382; (chambers) 11 Jules Koenig Street, Port-Louis, Mauritius. *T:* 208–8938. *Clubs:* Royal Over-Seas League; Lions, City (Port Louis), Turf, Racing (Mauritius).

DAVID, Richard (William), CBE 1967; formerly Publisher to the University, Cambridge University Press; Fellow of Clare Hall, Cambridge; *b* 28 Jan. 1912; *e s* of Rev. F. P. and Mary W. David, Winchester; *m* 1935, Nora (*see* Baroness David); two *s* two *d.* *Educ:* Winchester Coll. (Scholar); Corpus Christi Coll., Cambridge (Scholar). Joined editorial staff, CUP, 1936. Served RNVR, 1940–46, in Mediterranean and Western Approaches; qualified navigator, 1944; Lt-Comdr, 1945. Transferred to London Office of CUP, 1946; London Manager, 1948–63; Sec. to the Syndics of the Press, 1963–70. Member of Council of Publishers Assoc., 1953–63; Chairman of Export Research Cttee, 1956–59; President, 1959–61. Pres., Botanical Soc. of British Isles, 1979–81. *Publications:* The Janus of Poets, 1935; Love's Labour's Lost (The Arden Edition of Shakespeare), 1951; Shakespeare in the Theatre, 1978; (ed) Hakluyt's Voyages: a selection, 1981; (jtly) Review of the Cornish Flora, 1981; (ed jtly) John Raven: by his friends, 1981; (jtly) Sedges of the British Isles, 1982; journal articles on the production of Shakespeare plays, and on botanical subjects, especially Carex. *Recreations:* music, botanising, fly-fishing. *Address:* 50 Highsett, Cambridge CB2 1NZ. *Club:* Garrick.

DAVID, Robert Allan; Head of International and Tourism Division, Department of Employment, since 1989; *b* 27 April 1937; *s* of George David and Mabel Edith David; *m* 1961, Brenda Marshall; three *d.* *Educ:* Cathays High Sch., Cardiff. BoT, 1955–71; Dept of Employment, 1971–. *Recreations:* badminton, tennis, gardening. *Address:* The Briars, Ninehams Road, Tatsfield, Westerham, Kent TN16 2AN. *T:* Tatsfield (0959) 77357.

DAVID, Robin (Robert) Daniel George, QC 1968; DL; **His Honour Judge David;** a Circuit Judge (formerly Chairman, Cheshire Quarter Sessions), since 1968; *b* 30 April 1922; *s* of late Alexander Charles Robert David and late Edrica Doris Pole David (*née* Evans); *m* 1944, Edith Mary David (*née* Marsh); two *d.* *Educ:* Christ Coll., Brecon; Ellesmere Coll., Salop. War Service, 1943–47, Captain, Royal Artillery. Called to Bar, Gray's Inn, 1949; joined Wales and Chester Circuit, 1949. Dep. Chairman, Cheshire QS, 1961; Dep. Chairman, Agricultural Land Tribunal (Wales), 1965–68; Commissioner of Assize, 1970; Mem., Parole Bd for England and Wales, 1971–74. DL Cheshire 1972. *Publication:* The Magistrate in the Crown Court, 1982. *Address:* (home) Hallowsgate House, Kelsall, Cheshire. *T:* Kelsall (0829) 51456; (chambers) 4 Paper Buildings, Temple, EC4. *T:* 071–353 8408, 071–353 0196; (chambers) 40 King Street, Chester. *T:* Chester (0244) 323886.

DAVID, Tudor, OBE 1984; freelance journalist and publisher; Executive Editor, Oil and Gas Finance and Accounting (formerly Journal of Oil and Gas Accountancy), since 1986;

Publisher, Langham Publishing, since 1985; *b* 25 April 1921; *s* of Thomas and Blodwen David; *m* 1st, 1943, Nancy Ramsay (*d* 1984); one *s* one *d*; 2nd, 1987, Margaret Dix. *Educ:* Barry Grammar Sch.; Univ. of Manchester (BA Hons); Univ. of Oxford. Technical Officer, RAF, 1942–47; Extra-mural Lectr, Univ. of Newcastle upon Tyne, 1947–49; Careers Officer, 1950–55; Asst Editor, Education, 1955–65; Editor, The Teacher, 1965–69; Managing Editor, Education, 1969–86. Member: Council, Cymmrodorion, 1968–; Welsh Acad., 1969–. FCP 1980. *Publications:* (ed) Scunthorpe and its Families, 1954; Defence and Disarmament, 1959; Church and School, 1963; (jtly) Perspectives in Geographical Education, 1973; (jtly) Education, the wasted years 1973–86, 1988. *Recreations:* Wales, the Isle of Dogs, opera. *Address:* 21 Pointers Close, Isle of Dogs, E14 3AP. *T:* 071–987 8631. *Club:* London Welsh.

DAVID, Wayne; Member (Lab) South Wales, European Parliament, since 1989; *b* 1 July 1957; *s* of D. Haydn David and Edna A. David; *m* 1991, Catherine Thomas. *Educ:* Cynffig Comprehensive Sch.; University Coll., Cardiff (BA Hons History; PGCE); University Coll., Swansea. History teacher, Brynteg Comprehensive Sch., Bridgend, 1983–85; Mid Glam Tutor Organiser, S Wales Dist, WEA, 1985–89. Treas., European Parly Labour Party (formerly British Labour Gp), 1989–91. Vice-Pres., City of Cardiff Br., UNA, 1989–; Mem., Cefn Cribwr Community Council, 1985–91. *Publications:* (contrib.) Oxford Companion to the Literature of Wales, 1986; two pamphlets; contrib. Llafur—Jl of Welsh Labour History. *Recreations:* music, reading. *Address:* Tŷ Cathway, Bryn Rhedyn, (off The Rise), Tonteg, Pontypridd, Mid Glam CF38 1UY. *T:* Pontypridd (0443) 217810.

DAVID-WEILL, Michel Alexandre; Senior Partner, Lazard Frères & Co., New York, since 1977; Chairman, Lazard Brothers & Co., London, since 1990; *b* 23 Nov. 1932; *s* of Bertha Haardt and Pierre David-Weill; *m* 1956, Hélène Lehideux; four *d*. *Educ:* Institut de Sciences Politiques, Paris; Lycée Francais de New York. Brown Brothers Harriman, 1954–55; Lehman Brothers, NY, 1955–56; Lazard Frères & Co., NY, 1956–, Partner, 1961–; Partner, Lazard Frères et Cie, Paris, 1965–; Lazard Brothers & Co., London, Dir, 1965–; Chm., Lazard Partners, 1984–. Officier, Legion of Honour (France), 1990. *Address:* Lazard Frères & Co., One Rockefeller Plaza, New York, NY 10020, USA. *T:* (212) 632 6000. *Clubs:* Knickerbocker, Brook (NY); Creek (Locust Valley).

DAVIDSON, family name of **Viscount Davidson.**

DAVIDSON, 2nd Viscount *cr* 1937, of Little Gaddesden; **John Andrew Davidson;** Captain of the Yeomen of the Guard (Deputy Government Chief Whip), since 1986; *b* 22 Dec. 1928; *er s* of 1st Viscount Davidson, PC, GCVO, CH, CB, and Frances Joan, Viscountess Davidson (Baroness Northchurch), DBE (*d* 1985), *y d* of 1st Baron Dickinson, PC, KBE; *S* father, 1970; *m* 1st, 1956, Margaret Birgitta Norton (marr. diss. 1974); four *d* (including twin *d*); 2nd, 1975, Mrs Pamela Dobb (*née* Vergette). *Educ:* Westminster School; Pembroke College, Cambridge (BA). Served in The Black Watch and 5th Bn KAR, 1947–49. A Lord in Waiting (Govt Whip), 1985–86. Director: Strutt & Parker (Farms) Ltd, 1960–75; Lord Rayleigh's Farms Inc., 1960–75; Member of Council: CLA, 1965–75; RASE, 1973; Chm., Management Committee, Royal Eastern Counties Hospital, 1966–72; Mem., East Anglia Economic Planning Council, 1971–75. *Recreation:* music. *Heir:* *b* Hon. Malcolm William Mackenzie Davidson [*b* 28 Aug. 1934; *m* 1970, Mrs Evelyn Ann Carew Perfect, *yr d* of William Blackmore Storey; one *s* one *d*]. *Address:* House of Lords, SW1A 0PW.

See also Baron Rayleigh.

DAVIDSON, Hon. Lord; Charles Kemp Davidson, FRSE 1985; a Senator of the College of Justice in Scotland, since 1983; Chairman, Scottish Law Commission, since 1988; *b* Edinburgh, 13 April 1929; *s* of Rev. Donald Davidson, DD, Edinburgh; *m* 1960, Mary, *d* of Charles Mactaggart, Campbeltown, Argyll; one *s* two *d*. *Educ:* Fettes Coll., Edinburgh; Brasenose Coll., Oxford; Edinburgh Univ. Admitted to Faculty of Advocates, 1956; QC (Scot.) 1969; Vice-Dean, 1977–79; Dean, 1979–83; Keeper, Advocates' Library, 1972–76. Procurator to Gen. Assembly of Church of Scotland, 1972–83. Dep. Chm., Boundary Commn for Scotland, 1985–. *Address:* 22 Dublin Street, Edinburgh EH1 3PP. *T:* 031–556 2168.

DAVIDSON, Alan Eaton, CMG 1975; author; HM Diplomatic Service, retired; Managing Director, Prospect Books Ltd, since 1982; *b* 30 March 1924; *s* of William John Davidson and Constance (*née* Eaton); *m* 1951, Jane Macatee; three *d*. *Educ:* Leeds Grammar Sch.; Queen's Coll., Oxford. 1st class hons Class. Mods. and Greats. Served in RNVR (Ordinary Seaman, later Lieut) in Mediterranean, N Atlantic and Pacific, 1943–46. Member of HM Foreign Service, 1948; served at: Washington, 1950–53; The Hague, 1953–55; FO, 1955–59; First Secretary, British Property Commission, and later Head of Chancery, British Embassy, Cairo, 1959–61; Head of Chancery and Consul, Tunis, 1962–64; FO, 1964; Counsellor, 1965; Head, Central Dept, FO, 1966–68; Head of Chancery, UK Delegn to NATO, Brussels, 1968–71; seconded, as Vis. Fellow, Centre for Contemporary European Studies, Univ. of Sussex, 1971–72; Head of Defence Dept, FCO, 1972–73; Ambassador to Vientiane, 1973–75. *Publications:* Seafish of Tunisia and the Central Mediterranean, 1963; Snakes and Scorpions Found in the Land of Tunisia, 1964; Mediterranean Seafood, 1972; The Role of the Uncommitted European Countries in East-West Relations, 1972; Fish and Fish Dishes of Laos, 1975; Seafood of South East Asia, 1976; (with Jane Davidson) Dumas on Food, 1978; North Atlantic Seafood, 1979; (with Jennifer Davidson) Traditional Recipes of Laos, 1981; On Fasting and Feasting (annotated anthology), 1988; A Kipper with My Tea, 1988; (with Charlotte Knox) Seafood, 1989; (with Charlotte Knox) Fruit, 1991. *Address:* 45 Lamont Road, World's End, SW10 0HU. *T:* 071–352 4209.

DAVIDSON, Alfred Edward; international lawyer; Vice-President, General Counsel, Technical Studies, 1957–70, and since 1973; *b* New York, 11 Nov. 1911; *s* of Maurice Philip Davidson and Blanche Reinheimer; *m* 1934, Claire H. Dreyfuss (*d* 1981); two *s*. *Educ:* Harvard Univ. (AB); Columbia Law Sch. (LLB). Advocate, Bar of New York, 1936; of Dist of Columbia, 1972; Asst to Gen. Counsel, US Dept of Labour, Wash., 1938–40; review section, Solicitor's Office, 1940–41; Legis. Counsel, Office of Emergency Management, in Exec. Office of President, 1941–43; Asst Gen. Counsel, Lend-Lease Admin. (later Foreign Economic Admin.), 1943–45; Gen. Counsel, 1945–; Gen. Counsel, UNRRA, Nov. 1945; Counsel, Preparatory Commn for Internat. Refugee Org., 1947; Dir, European Headqrs of UNICEF, 1947–51; Advisor, Office of Sec.-Gen. of UN, 1951–52; Gen. Counsel, UN Korean Reconstr. Agency, 1952–54; Exec. Asst to Chm., Bd of Rio Tinto of Canada, 1955–58; European Representative, Internat. Finance Corp., 1970–72; Counsel to Wilmer, Cutler & Pickering, Attorneys at Law, 1972–75. Dir, Channel Tunnel Study Gp, 1960–70; Chm., Democratic Party Abroad. Co-Founder, Assoc. for Promotion of Humor in Internat. Affairs; Co-Chm., Bipartisan Cttees on Medicare Overseas and Absentee Voting; Hon. Chm., Common Cause Overseas. *Publications:* contribs. various periodicals and newspapers. *Recreations:* tennis, bridge, chess, reading. *Address:* 5 rue de la Manutention, 75116 Paris, France. *Clubs:* Lansdowne (London); Standard (France).

DAVIDSON, Arthur; QC 1978; Legal Director, Mirror Group, since 1991; *b* 7 Nov. 1928. *Educ:* Liverpool Coll.; King George V Sch., Southport; Trinity Coll., Cambridge. Served in Merchant Navy. Barrister, Middle Temple, 1953. Trinity Coll., Cambridge, 1959–62; Editor of the Granta. Legal Dir, Associated Newspapers Hldgs, 1987–90. MP (Lab) Accrington, 1966–83; PPS to Solicitor-General, 1968–70; Chm., Home Affairs Gp, Parly Labour Party, 1971–74; Parly Sec., Law Officers' Dept, 1974–79; Opposition spokesman on Defence (Army), 1980–81, on legal affairs, 1981–83, frontbench spokesman, 1982–83; Member: Home Affairs Select Cttee, 1980–83; Armed Forces Bill Select Cttee, 1981–83. Contested (Lab): Blackpool S, 1955; Preston N, 1959; Hyndburn, 1983. Member: Council, Consumers' Association, 1970–74; Exec. Cttee, Soc. of Labour Lawyers, 1981–; Nat. Exec., Fabian Soc.; Council, Nat. Youth Jazz Orchestra; Chm., House of Commons Jazz Club, 1973–83. *Recreations:* lawn tennis, ski-ing, theatre, listening to good jazz and playing bad jazz; formerly Member Cambridge Univ. athletics team. *Address:* 11 South Square, Gray's Inn, WC1R 5EU. *Clubs:* James Street Men's Working (Oswaldtwistle); Free Gardeners (Rishton); King Street, Marlborough Working Men's (Accrington).

DAVIDSON, Basil Risbridger, MC 1945; author and historian; *b* 9 Nov. 1914; *s* of Thomas and Jessie Davidson; *m* 1943, Marion Ruth Young; three *s*. Served War of 1939–45 (despatches twice, MC, US Bronze Star, Jugoslav Zasluge za Narod); British Army, 1940–45 (Balkans, N Africa, Italy); Temp. Lt-Col demobilised as Hon. Major. Editorial staff of The Economist, 1938–39; The Star (diplomatic correspondent, 1939); The Times (Paris correspondent, 1945–47; chief foreign leader-writer, 1947–49); New Statesman (special correspondent, 1950–54); Daily Herald (special correspondent, 1954–57); Daily Mirror (leader-writer, 1959–62). Vis. Prof., Univ. of Ghana, 1964; Vis. Prof., 1965, Regents' Lectr, 1971, Univ. of California; Montagu Burton Vis. Prof. of Internat. Relations, Edinburgh Univ., 1972; Sen. Simon Res. Fellow, Univ. of Manchester, 1975–76; Hon. Res. Fellow, Univ. of Birmingham, 1978–; Agnelli Vis. Prof., Univ. of Turin, 1990. A Vice-Pres., Anti-Apartheid Movement, 1969–. Author/presenter, Africa (8-part TV documentary series), 1984. Freeman of City of Genoa, 1945. DLitt *hc*: Ibadan, 1975; Dar es Salaam, 1985; DUniv: Open, 1980; Edinburgh, 1981. Haile Selassie African Research Award, 1970; Medalha Amílcar Cabral, 1976. *Publications: novels:* Highway Forty, 1949; Golden Horn, 1952; The Rapids, 1955; Lindy, 1958; The Andrassy Affair, 1966; *non-fiction:* Partisan Picture, 1946; Germany: From Potsdam to Partition, 1950; Report on Southern Africa, 1952; Daybreak in China, 1953; The New West Africa (ed.), 1953; The African Awakening, 1955; Turkestan Alive, 1957; Old Africa Rediscovered, 1959; Black Mother, 1961, rev. edn 1980; The African Past, 1964; Which Way Africa?, 1964; The Growth of African Civilisation: West Africa AD 1000–1800, 1965; Africa: History of a Continent, 1966; A History of East and Central Africa to the late 19th Century, 1967; Africa in History: Themes and Outlines, 1968; The Liberation of Guiné, 1969; The Africans, An Entry to Cultural History, 1969; Discovering our African Heritage, 1971; In the Eye of the Storm: Angola's People, 1972; Black Star, 1974; Can Africa Survive?, 1975; Discovering Africa's Past, 1978 (Children's Rights Workshop Award, 1978); Africa in Modern History, 1978; Crossroads in Africa, 1980; Special Operations Europe, 1980; The People's Cause, 1980; No Fist is Big Enough, 1981; Modern Africa, 1982; The Story of Africa, 1984; The Fortunate Isles, 1989. *Address:* Old Cider Mill, North Wootton, Somerset BA4 4HA. *Club:* Savile.

DAVIDSON, Brian, CBE 1965; *b* 14 Sept. 1909; *o s* of late Edward Fitzwilliam Davidson and late Esther Davidson (*née* Schofield); *m* 1935, Priscilla Margaret (*d* 1981), *d* of late Arthur Farquhar and Florence Chilver; one *s* one *d* (and one *s* decd). *Educ:* Winchester Coll. (Scholar); New Coll., Oxford (Scholar). Gaisford Prize for Greek Verse; 1st class Honour Mods.; 2nd class LitHum; President, Oxford Union Society; President OU Conservative Assoc.; BA 1932. Cholmeley Student Lincoln's Inn; Barrister-at-Law, 1933; Law Society Sheffield Prize; Solicitor, 1939; Air Ministry and Ministry of Aircraft Production, 1940. With Bristol Aeroplane Co., 1943–68: Business Manager, 1946; Director, 1950–68; Director, Bristol Siddeley Engines Ltd, 1959–68. Solicitor with Gas Council, later British Gas Corp., 1969–75. Member: Monopolies Commission, 1954–68; Gloucestershire CC (and Chairman Rating Valuation Appeals Cttee), 1953–60; Cttee Wine Society, 1966–83. *Recreations:* fox-hunting, sailing (represented Oxford Univ.), Scottish country dancing, bridge. *Address:* Sands Court, Dodington, Avon BS17 6SE. *T:* Chipping Sodbury (0454) 313077.

DAVIDSON, Charles Kemp; *see* Davidson, Hon. Lord.

DAVIDSON, Charles Peter Morton; Metropolitan Stipendiary Magistrate, since 1984; *b* 29 July 1938; *s* of late William Philip Morton Davidson, MD, and Muriel Maud Davidson (*née* Alderson); *m* 1966, Pamela Louise Campbell-Rose. *Educ:* Harrow; Trinity Coll., Dublin (MA, LLB). Called to the Bar, Inner Temple, 1963; employed by Legal and General Assurance Soc., 1963–65; in practice at Bar, 1966–84. Chairman, London Rent Assessment Panel, 1973–84; part-time Immigration Appeals Adjudicator, 1976–84; a Chm., Inner London Juvenile Courts, 1985–88. Contested (C) North Battersea, 1966 General Election; Councillor, London Boroughs: of Wandsworth, 1964–68, of Merton, 1968–71. *Recreations:* music, gardening. *Address:* c/o Camberwell Green Magistrates' Court, 15 D'Eynsford Road, SE5 7UP.

DAVIDSON, Francis, CBE 1961; Finance Officer, Singapore High Commission, London, 1961–71; *b* 23 Nov. 1905; *s* of James Davidson and Margaret Mackenzie; *m* 1937, Marial Mackenzie, MA; one *s* one *d*. *Educ:* Millbank Public Sch., Nairn; Nairn Academy. Commercial Bank of Scotland Ltd, 1923–29; Bank of British West Africa Ltd, 1929–41; Colonial Service (Treasury), 1941–61; retired from Colonial Service, Nov. 1961, as Accountant-General of Federation of Nigeria. *Recreation:* philately. *Address:* Woolton, Nairn, Scotland. *T:* Nairn (0667) 52187. *Club:* Royal Over-Seas League.

DAVIDSON, Howard William, CMG 1961; MBE 1942; *b* 30 July 1911; *s* of late Joseph Christopher Davidson, Johannesburg, and Helen, *d* of James Forbes; *m* 1st, 1941, Anne Elizabeth, *d* of late Captain R. C. Power; one *d*; 2nd, 1956, Dorothy (marr. diss. 1972), *d* of late Sir Wm Polson, KCMG; one step *s*. *Educ:* King Edward VII Sch., Johannesburg; Witwatersrand Univ.; Oriel Coll., Oxford (1st cl. Greats 1934; MA 1984). Cadet, Colonial Admin. Service, Sierra Leone, 1935; District Commissioner, 1942; Dep. Fin. Secretary, 1949; Fin. Secretary, Fiji, 1952; Fin. Secretary, N Borneo, 1958; State Financial Secretary and Member Cabinet, Sabah, Malaysia, 1963–64; Financial Adviser, 1964–65; Member of Inter-Governmental Cttee which led to establishment of new Federation of Malaysia; retired, 1965. Inspector (part-time) Min. of Housing and Local Government, 1967–70. Consultant with Peat, Marwick Mitchell & Co, to report on finances of Antigua, 1973. Appointed PDK (with title of Datuk) in first Sabah State Honours List, 1963, now SPDK. *Recreations:* cricket, croquet, gardening, learning. *Clubs:* East India; Sussex County Cricket, Sussex County Croquet.

DAVIDSON, Ian Thomas Rollo, QC 1977; **His Honour Judge Ian Davidson;** a Circuit Judge, since 1984; *b* 3 Aug. 1925; *s* of late Robert Davidson and Margaret Davidson; *m* 1954, Gyöngyi (marr. diss. 1982), *d* of Prof. Cs. Anghi; one *s* one *d*; *m* 1984, Barbara Ann Watts; one *s*. *Educ:* Fettes Coll.; Corpus Christi Coll., Oxford (Schol.). MA,

Lit. Hum. Royal Armoured Corps, 1943–47, Lieut Derbs Yeomanry. Called to Bar, Gray's Inn, 1955. Asst Lectr, University Coll., London, 1959–60; Deputy Recorder, Nottingham, 1971; a Recorder of the Crown Court, 1974. *Recreations:* music, golf, photography. *Address:* c/o Crown Court, Canal Street, Nottingham NG1 7EJ.

DAVIDSON, Ivor Macaulay; Chairman, D. O. Sanbiet Ltd, since 1980; *b* 27 Jan. 1924; *s* of late James Macaulay and Violet Alice Davidson; *m* 1948, Winifred Lowes; four *s* one *d. Educ:* Bellahouston Sch.; Univ. of Glasgow. Royal Aircraft Establishment, 1943; Power Jets (R&D) Ltd, 1944; attached RAF, 1945; National Gas Turbine Establishment, 1946: Dep. Dir, 1964; Dir, 1970–74; Dir-Gen. Engines, Procurement Exec., MoD, 1974–79. *Publications:* numerous, scientific and technical. *Recreations:* music, gardening.

DAVIDSON, James Alfred, OBE 1971; retired RN and Diplomatic Service; *b* 22 March 1922; *s* of Lt-Comdr A. D. Davidson and Mrs (Elizabeth) Davidson; *m* 1955, Daphne (*née* While); two *d,* and two step *s. Educ:* Christ's Hospital; RN Coll., Dartmouth. Royal Navy, 1939–60 (war Service Atlantic, Mediterranean and Far East); commanded HM Ships Calder and Welfare; Comdr 1955; retd 1960. Holds Master Mariner's Cert. of Service. Called to the Bar, Middle Temple, 1960. Joined CRO (later FCO) 1960; served Port of Spain, Phnom Penh (periods as Chargé d'Affaires 1970 and 1971); Dacca (Chargé d'Affaires, later Dep. High Comr, 1972–73); Vis. Scholar, Univ. of Kent, 1973–74; British High Comr, Brunei, 1974–78; participated, Sept. 1978, in finalisation of Brunei Independence Treaty; Governor, British Virgin Islands, 1978–81. Vis. Fellow, LSE Centre for Internat. Studies, 1982–84. Legal Mem., Mental Health Review Tribunal, 1982–; a Chm., Pensions Appeals Tribunals, 1984–. *Publications:* Brunei Coinage, 1977; Indo-China: Signposts in the Storm, 1979. *Address:* Little Frankfield, Seal Chart, near Sevenoaks, Kent. *T:* Sevenoaks (0732) 61600. *Club:* Army and Navy.

DAVIDSON, James Duncan Gordon, OBE 1984; MVO 1947; Chief Executive, Royal Highland and Agricultural Society of Scotland, 1970–91; *b* 10 Jan. 1927; *s* of Alastair Gordon Davidson and M. Valentine B. Davidson (*née* Osborne); *m* 1st, 1955, Catherine Ann Jamieson; one *s* two *d;* 2nd, 1973, Janet Stafford; one *s. Educ:* RN Coll., Dartmouth; Downing Coll., Cambridge. Active List, RN, 1944–55. Subseq. farming, and political work; contested (L) West Aberdeenshire, 1964; MP (L) West Aberdeenshire, 1966–70. FRAgS; MIEx. *Recreations:* family, walking, ski-ing, fishing, music. *Address:* Coire Cas, Newtonmore, Inverness-shire. *T:* Newtonmore (05403) 322.

DAVIDSON, James Patton, CBE 1980; *b* 23 March 1928; *s* of Richard Davidson and Elizabeth Ferguson Carnichan; *m* 1st, 1953, Jean Stevenson Ferguson Anderson (marr. diss. 1981); two *s;* 2nd, 1981, Esmé Evelyn Ancill. *Educ:* Rutherglen Acad.; Glasgow Univ. (BL). Mil. service, commissioned RASC, 1948–50. Clyde Navigation Trust, 1950; Asst Gen. Manager, 1958. Clyde Port Authority: Gen. Manager, 1966; Managing Dir, 1974; Dep. Chm. and Man. Dir, 1976; Chm., 1980–83. Chairman: Ardrossan Harbour Co. Ltd, 1976–83; Clydeport Stevedoring Services Ltd, 1977–83; Clyde Container Services Ltd, 1968–83; S. & H. McCall Transport (Glasgow) Ltd, 1972–83; Rhu Marina Ltd, 1976–80; Scotway Haulage Ltd, 1976–81; R. & J. Strang Ltd, 1976–81; Nat. Assoc. of Port Employers, 1974–79; British Ports Assoc., 1980–83 (Dep. Chm., 1978–80); Port Employers' & Registered Dock Workers' Pension Fund Trustee Ltd, 1978–83; Pilotage Commn, 1983– (Mem., 1979–83); UK Dir, 1976–83 and Mem., Exec. Cttee, 1977–83, Hon. Mem., 1983, Internat. Assoc. of Ports and Harbours. Dir, Iron Trades Insurance Gp, 1981–; Chm., Foods & Feeds (UK), 1982–83. FCIT, CBIM; FRSA. *Recreations:* golf, bridge, travel, reading, sailing. *Address:* 44 Guthrie Court, Gleneagles Village, Gleneagles, Perthshire. *Clubs:* Oriental; Cambuslang Golf.

DAVIDSON, Prof. John Frank, FRS 1974; FEng; Shell Professor of Chemical Engineering, University of Cambridge, since 1978 (Professor of Chemical Engineering, 1975–78); *b* 7 Feb. 1926; *s* of John and Katie Davidson; *m* 1948, Susanne Hedwig Ostberg; one *s* one *d. Educ:* Heaton Grammar Sch., Newcastle upon Tyne; Trinity Coll., Cambridge. MA, PhD, ScD; FEng, FIChemE, MIMechE. 1st cl. Mech. Scis Tripos, Cantab, 1946, BA 1947. Engrg work at Rolls Royce, Derby, 1947–50; Cambridge Univ.: Research Fellow, Trinity Coll., 1949; research, 1950–52; Univ. Demonstrator, 1952; Univ. Lectr, 1954; Steward of Trinity Coll., 1957–64; Reader in Chem. Engrg, Univ. of Cambridge, 1964–75. Visiting Professor: Univ. of Delaware, 1960; Univ. of Sydney, 1967. Member: Flixborough Ct of Inquiry, 1974–75; Adv. Cttee on Safety of Nuclear Installations, HSC, 1977–87. Pres., IChemE, 1970–71; Vice Pres. and Mem. Council, Royal Soc., 1988. Founder FEng, 1976. For. Associate, Nat. Acad. of Engrg, US, 1976; For. Fellow, Indian National Science Acad., 1990. Dr *hc* Institut Nat. Polytech. de Toulouse, 1979; Hon. DSc Aston, 1989. Leverhulme Medal, Royal Soc., 1984; Messel Medal, Soc. of Chemical Industry, 1986. *Publications:* (with D. Harrison): Fluidised Particles, 1963; Fluidization, 1971; 2nd edn (with R. Clift and D. Harrison), 1985; (with D. L. Keairns) Fluidization (Conference Procs), 1978. *Recreations:* hill walking, gardening, mending bicycles and other domestic artefacts. *Address:* 5 Luard Close, Cambridge CB2 2PL. *T:* Cambridge (0223) 246104.

DAVIDSON, John Roderick; Clerk of the Senate, since 1989, Director of Administration, since 1991, University of London; *b* 29 Jan. 1937; *yr s* of Alexander Ross Davidson and Jessie Maud (*née* Oakley). *Educ:* Portsmouth Northern Grammar Sch.; Univ. of Manchester (BA). Advr to students, Chelsea Sch. of Art, 1966–68; Asst Sch. Sec., RPMS, 1968–74; Imperial College of Science, Technology and Medicine: Asst Sec., 1974–77; Personnel Sec., 1977–85; Admin. Sec., 1985–89. *Recreations:* theatre, opera, genealogy. *Address:* Senate House, University of London, Malet Street, WC1E 7HU; 10 Lansdowne, Carlton Drive, SW15 2BY. *T:* 081–789 0021.

DAVIDSON, Keith; *see* Davidson, W. K.

DAVIDSON, Very Rev. Prof. Robert, FRSE; Professor of Old Testament Language and Literature, University of Glasgow, since 1972; Principal, Trinity College, Glasgow, since 1982; *b* 30 March 1927; *s* of George Braid Davidson and Gertrude May Ward; *m* 1952, Elizabeth May Robertson; four *s* three *d. Educ:* Univ. of St Andrews (MA 1st Cl Hons Classics, 1949; BD, Distinction in Old Testament, 1952). FRSE 1989. Asst Lectr, then Lectr in Biblical Studies, Univ. of Aberdeen, 1953–60; Lectr in Hebrew and Old Testament, Univ. of St Andrews, 1960–66; Lectr in Old Testament Studies, Univ. of Edinburgh, 1966–69, Sen. Lectr, 1969–72. Edward Cadbury Lectr, Birmingham Univ., 1988–89. Moderator, Gen. Assembly, Church of Scotland, 1990–91. Hon. DD Aberdeen, 1985. *Publications:* The Bible Speaks, 1959; The Old Testament, 1964; (with A. R. C. Leaney) Biblical Criticism (Vol. 3 of Pelican Guide to Modern Theology), 1970; Genesis 1–11 (Cambridge Bible Commentary), 1973; Genesis 12–50 (Cambridge Bible Commentary), 1979; The Bible in Religious Education, 1979; The Courage to Doubt, 1983; Jeremiah 1–20 (Daily Study Bible), 1983; Jeremiah II, Lamentations (Daily Study Bible), 1986; Ecclesiastes and Song of Songs (Daily Study Bible), 1986; Wisdom and Worship, 1990; articles in Vetus Testamentum, Annual Swedish Theol Inst., Expository Times, Scottish Jl of Theol., Epworth Review and The Furrow. *Recreations:* music, gardening. *Address:* 30 Dumgoyne Drive, Bearsden, Glasgow G61 3AP. *T:* 041–942 1810.

DAVIDSON, Sir Robert (James), Kt 1989; Chairman, Balfour Beatty Ltd, since 1991; *b* 21 July 1928; *m* 1953, Barbara Elsie Eagles; two *s* two *d. Educ:* Royal Tech. Coll., Glasgow (DRC 1949); Imperial Coll., London (DIC 1953). FEng 1984; FIMechE. Joined English Electric Co. as grad. apprentice, 1949; Develt Engr, 1951–52; Design Engr, Hydro Electric Project, 1953–55; Project Manager, Priest Rapids Hydro-Electric Power Stn, USA, 1956–61; Manufg Manager, then Gen. Manager, Netherton Works, 1962–69; English Electric taken over by GEC, 1969; Manager, Outside Construction Dept, 1969–72, Manufg Dir, 1972–74, Man. Dir, 1974–88, GEC Turbine Generators Ltd; Dir, GEC plc, 1985–91; Man. Dir, GEC Power Systems Ltd, 1988–89; Vice-Chm. and Chief Exec. Officer, GEC Alsthom NV, 1989–91; Chm. and Man. Dir, GEC ALSTHOM Ltd, 1989–91; Dir, GEC ALSTHOM SA, 1989–91; Chm., NNC, 1988–91. Dir, Coventry and Warwicks TEC, 1990–. Hon. DSc Strathclyde, 1991. *Recreations:* walking, gardening, listening to music. *Address:* Balfour Beatty Ltd, 7 Mayday Road, Thornton Heath, Surrey CR7 7XA.

DAVIDSON, Air Vice-Marshal Rev. Sinclair Melville, CBE 1968; Priest-in-charge, Holy Trinity, High Hurstwood, 1982–88; *b* 1 Nov. 1922; *s* of late James Stewart Davidson and Ann Sinclair Davidson (*née* Cowan); *m* 1944, Jean Irene, *d* of late Edward Albert Flay; one *s* (and one *s* decd). *Educ:* Bousfield Sch., Kensington; RAF Cranwell; RAF Techn. College; Chichester Theol College. CEng, FRAeS, FIEE. War service with 209, 220 and 53 Sqdns RAF, 1941–45 (despatches); Staff RAF Coastal and Fighter Comds, 1946–53; Air Staff, Egypt, Iraq and Cyprus, 1954–55; psa 1956; Air Staff, Air Min., 1957–60; jssc 1960; Dirg Staff, RAF Staff Coll., Bracknell, 1961–63; Asst Comdt, RAF Locking, 1963–64; Chm. Jt Signal Bd (Middle East), 1965; Chief Signal Officer and Comd Electrical Engr, Near East Air Force, 1966–67; idc 1968; Dir of Signals (Air), MoD, 1969–71; AO Wales and Stn Comdr, RAF St Athan, 1972–74; Asst Chief of Defence Staff (Signals), 1974–77. Sec., IERE, 1977–82. Deacon 1981, priest 1982. *Address:* Trinity Cottage, High Hurstwood, E Sussex TN22 4AA. *T:* Buxted (082581) 2151. *Club:* Royal Air Force.

DAVIDSON, Dr (William) Keith, CBE 1982; FRCGP; JP; Chairman, Scottish Health Service Planning Council, since 1984; *b* 20 Nov. 1926; *s* of James Fisher Keith Davidson and Martha Anderson Davidson (*née* Milloy); *m* 1952, Dr Mary Waddell Aitken Davidson (*née* Jamieson); one *s* one *d. Educ:* Coatbridge Secondary Sch.; Glasgow Univ. DPA 1967; FRCGP 1980. MO 1st Bn Royal Scots Fusiliers, 1950; 2nd Command (Major) 14 Field Ambulance, 1950–51; MO i/c Holland, 1952. Gen. Medical Practitioner, 1953–. Chairman: Glasgow Local Medical Cttee, 1971–75; Glasgow Area Medical Cttee, 1975–79; Scottish Gen. Medical Services Cttee, 1972–75; Dep. Chm., Gen. Medical Services Cttee (UK), 1975–79; Member: Scottish Medical Practices Cttee, 1968–80; Scottish Council on Crime, 1972–75; GMC, 1983–; Scottish Health Service Policy Bd, 1985–88; Greater Glasgow Health Bd, 1989–. British Medical Association: Mem. Council, 1972–81; Fellow, 1975; Chm., Scottish Council, 1978–81; Vice-Pres., 1983–. Hon. Pres., Glasgow Eastern Med. Soc., 1984–85; Pres., Scottish Midland and Western Med. Soc., 1985–86; RSocMed. Vice-Chm., Chryston High Sch. Bd, 1990–. Mem., Bonnetmaker Craft. Elder, Church of Scotland, 1956–; Session Clerk, 1983–. JP Glasgow, 1962. SBStJ 1976. *Recreations:* gardening, caravanning. *Address:* Dunvegan, Stepps, Glasgow G33 6DE. *T:* 041–779 2103. *Club:* Royal Scottish Automobile (Glasgow).

DAVIDSON-HOUSTON, Major Aubrey Claud; portrait painter since 1952; *b* 2 Feb. 1906; *s* of late Lt-Col Wilfred Bennett Davidson-Houston, CMG, and Annie Henrietta Hunt; *m* 1938, Georgina Louie Ethel (*d* 1961), *d* of late Capt. H. S. Dobson; one *d. Educ:* St Edward's Sch., Oxford; RMC, Sandhurst; Slade Sch. of Fine Art. 2nd Lieut, Royal Sussex Regt, 1925; ADC to Governor of Western Australia, 1927–30; Nigeria Regt, RWAFF, 1933–37; PoW (Germany), 1940–45; Sch. of Infty, 1946–47; MS Branch, WO, 1948–49; retd, 1949. Slade Sch. of Fine Art, 1949–52 (diploma). *Portraits include:* The Queen, for RWF; The Duke of Edinburgh, for 8th King's Royal Irish Hussars, for Duke of Edinburgh's Royal Regt, for the House of Lords, and for United Oxford & Cambridge University Club; Queen Elizabeth, The Queen Mother, for Black Watch of Canada; The Prince of Wales, for Royal Regt of Wales (twice); Princess Mary, The Princess Royal, for WRAC; Prince Henry, Duke of Gloucester, for Royal Inniskilling Fusiliers, for Scots Guards and for Trinity House; The Duchess of Kent for ACC; also portraits for Lincoln Coll., Keble Coll., and St Cross Coll., Oxford, and for Selwyn Coll., Cambridge; also for a number of other regts and for City Livery cos, schools, etc. Founder Trustee, Jt Educn Trust, 1971–86. *Address:* Hillview, West End Lane, Esher, Surrey KT10 8LA. *T:* Esher (0372) 464769; 4 Chelsea Studios, 412 Fulham Road, SW6 1EB. *T:* 071–385 2569. *Clubs:* Buck's, Naval and Military, MCC.

DAVIE, Alan, CBE 1972; HRSA 1977; painter, poet, musician, silversmith and jeweller; *b* 1920. *Educ:* Edinburgh Coll. of Art. DA. Gregory Fellowship, Leeds Univ., 1956–59. Teaching, Central Sch. of Arts and Crafts, London, 1953–56 and 1959–60, and Emily Carr Coll. of Art, Vancouver, 1982. One-man exhibitions in GB, USA and most European countries and at Gimpel Fils Galleries in London, Zürich and New York, 1946–; Edinburgh Fest., 1972; Brussels, Paris, Athens and London, 1977; London, Florida, Stuttgart, Zürich, Amsterdam, St Andrews and Edinburgh, 1978; Florida, Edinburgh Fest., Belgium, Sydney and Perth, Australia, 1979; New York, Australia, Colchester and Philadelphia, 1980; London, Frankfurt, NY and Toronto, 1981; Toronto, Edinburgh, Basle, Harrogate, Hong Kong, Paris (Foire Internat. d'Art Contemporain) and Vancouver, 1982; Amsterdam, FIAC Paris, Basel, Madrid, Glasgow and London, 1983; New York, Frankfurt, Cologne, Edinburgh, Windsor, Hertford and Bath, 1984; London (Art Fair, Olympia), Edinburgh and Bonn, 1985; London, Arizona and NY, 1986; Gal. Carre and FIAC, Paris, London, Edinburgh, 1987; Paintings 1956–88, touring Scotland, Helsingborg, 1988. Work represented in exhibitions: 4th Internat. Art Exhibn, Japan; Pittsburgh Internat.; Documenta II & III, Kassel, Germany; British Painting 1700–1960, Moscow; Salon de Mai, Paris; Peggy Guggenheim Collection; ROSC Dublin; Peter Styvesant Collection; British Painting and Sculpture 1960–1970, Washington; III Bienal de Arte Coltejer, Colombia; Hannover, 1973; British Paintings, 1974; Hayward Gall., 1974; Paris, 1975; Lausanne, 1975; 25 years of British Art, RA, 1977; South America, 1977; Kassell, 1977; Sydney, 1979; Works on paper, Gimpel Fils, 1989. Works in Public Collections: Tate Gall., Gulbenkian Foundn London, Belfast, Bristol, Durham, Edinburgh, Hull, Leeds, Manchester, Newcastle, Wakefield; Boston, Buffalo, Dallas, Detroit, Yale New Haven, Phoenix, Pittsburgh, Rhode Island, San Francisco; Ottawa, Adelaide, Sydney, Auckland, São Paulo, Tel Aviv, Venice, Vienna, Baden-Baden, Bochum, Munich, Amsterdam, Eindhoven, The Hague, Rotterdam, Oslo, Basle, Stockholm, Gothenburg, St Paul de Vence and Paris. Created mural, Tarot Sculpture Gdn, Garavicchio, Tuscany, 1987. First public recital of music, Gimpel Fils Gall., 1971; music and lecture tour, Sydney, Melbourne, Canberra, 1979. Prize for Best Foreign Painter, VII Bienal de São Paulo, 1963; Saltire Award, 1977. *Relevant Publication:* Alan Davie (ed Alan Bowness), 1967. *Address:* Gamels Studio, Rush Green, Hertford.

DAVIE, Sir Antony Francis F.; *see* Ferguson Davie.

DAVIE, Prof. Donald Alfred, FBA 1987; Andrew W. Mellon Professor of Humanities, Vanderbilt University, 1978–88; *b* 17 July 1922; *s* of George Clarke Davie and Alice (*née*

Sugden); *m* 1945, Doreen John; two *s* one *d*. *Educ:* Barnsley Holgate Gram. Sch.; St Catharine's Coll., Cambridge (Hon. Fellow, 1973). BA 1947; PhD 1951. Served with Royal Navy, 1941–46 (Sub-Lieut RNVR). Lecturer in Dublin Univ., 1950–57; Fellow of Trinity Coll., Dublin, 1954–57, Hon. Fellow, 1978; Visiting Prof., University of Calif., 1957–58; Lecturer, Cambridge Univ., 1958–64; Fellow of Gonville and Caius Coll., Cambridge, 1959–64; George Elliston Lecturer, University of Cincinnati, 1963; Prof. of Literature, University of Essex, 1964–68, and Pro-Vice-Chancellor, 1965–68; Prof. of English, 1968–74, Olive H. Palmer Prof. in Humanities, 1974–78, Stanford Univ. Clark Lectr, Trinity Coll., Cambridge, 1976. Hon. DLitt Univ. of Southern California, 1978. Fellow, Amer. Acad. of Arts and Scis, 1973. *Publications: poetry:* Brides of Reason, 1955; A Winter Talent, 1957; The Forests of Lithuania, 1959; A Sequence for Francis Parkman, 1961; Events and Wisdoms, 1964; Essex Poems, 1969; Six Epistles to Eva Hesse, 1970; Collected Poems, 1972; The Shires, 1975; In the Stopping Train, 1977; Three for Water-Music, 1981; Collected Poems 1971–1983, 1983; To Scorch or Freeze, 1989; Collected Poems, 1990; *criticism and literary history:* Purity of Diction in English Verse, 1952; Articulate Energy, 1957, 2nd edn 1976; The Heyday of Sir Walter Scott, 1961; Ezra Pound: Poet as Sculptor, 1965; Introduction to The Necklace by Charles Tomlinson, 1955; Thomas Hardy and British Poetry, 1972; Pound, 1976; The Poet in the Imaginary Museum: essays of two decades, 1978; A Gathered Church: the literature of the English dissenting interest 1700–1930, 1978; Trying to Explain (essays), 1980; Dissentient Voice, 1982; Czeslaw Milosz and the Insufficiency of Lyric, 1986; Under Briggflatts, 1989; Slavic Excursions, 1990; *anthologies:* The Late Augustans, 1958; (with Angela Livingstone) Modern Judgements: Pasternak, 1969; Augustan Lyric, 1974; The New Oxford Book of Christian Verse, 1981. *Recreations:* verse-translation; literary politics; travel. *Address:* 4 High Street, Silverton, Exeter EX5 4JB. *Club:* Savile.

DAVIE, Rex; *see* Davie, S. R.

DAVIE, Prof. Ronald, PhD; FBPsS; CPsychol; consulting psychologist; Visiting Professor, Oxford Polytechnic, since 1991; *b* 25 Nov. 1929; *s* of late Thomas Edgar Davie and Gladys (*née* Powell); *m* 1957, Kathleen, *d* of William Wilkinson, Westhoughton, Lancs; one *s* one *d*. *Educ:* King Edward VI Grammar Sch., Aston, Birmingham; Univ. of Reading (BA 1954); Univ. of Manchester (PGCE and Dip. Deaf Educn 1955); Univ. of Birmingham (Dip. Educnl Psych. 1961); Univ. of London (PhD 1970). FBPsS 1973. Teacher, schs for normal and handicapped children, 1955–60; Co. Educnl Psychologist, IoW, 1961–64; Nat. Children's Bureau, London: Sen. Res. Officer, 1964; Dep. Dir, 1968; Dir of Res., 1972; Prof. of Educnl Psychology, Dept of Educn, UC Cardiff, 1974–81; Dir, Nat. Children's Bureau, 1982–90. Vis. Fellow, Inst. of Educn, Univ. of London, 1985–. Co-Dir, Nat. Child Develt Study, 1968–77; Scientific Adviser: Local Authority Social Services Res. Liaison Gp. DHSS, 1975–77; Mental Handicap in Wales Res. Unit, 1977–79; Mental Handicap Res. Liaison Gp, DHSS, 1977–81; Prof. Advr, All Party Parly Gp for Children, 1983–; Hon. Consultant: Play Board, 1984–87; 1981 Educn Act Res. Dissemination Project, 1986–89. President: Links Assoc., 1977–90; Child Develt Soc., 1990–91; Vice-Pres., British Assoc. for Early Childhood Educn, 1984–; Chairman: Trng and Educn. Cttee, Nat. Assoc. Mental Health, 1969–72; Assoc. for Child Psychol. and Psychiatry, 1972–73 (Hon. Sec. 1965–70); Standing Conf. of professional assocs in S Wales concerned with children, 1974–84; Working Party, Children Appearing Before Juvenile Courts, Children's Reg. Planning Cttee for Wales, 1975–77; Develt Psychol. Section, Brit. Psychol. Soc., 1975–77 (Treas. 1973–75); Wales Standing Conf. for Internat. Year of the Child, 1978–79; Steering Cttee, Child Health and Educn Study, 1979–84; Adv. Bd, Whitefield Library, 1983–. Member: Council of Management, Nat. Assoc. Mental Health, 1969–77; Working Party, Children at Risk, DHSS, 1970–72; Educn and Employment Cttee, Nat. Deaf Children's Soc., 1972–78; Management Cttee, Craig y Parc Sch., 1974–76; Cttee, Welsh Br., Assoc. for Child Psychol. and Psychiatry, 1975–80; Bd of Assessors, Therapeutic Educn, 1975–82; Council, British Psychol. Soc., 1977–80; Experimental Panel on Children in Care, SSRC, 1978–79; NCSE Internat. Conf. Prog. Cttee, 1982–85; Council, Child Accident Prevention Trust, 1982–88; Evaluation Panel, Royal Jubilee Trusts, 1982–; Steering Cttee on Special Educn Needs Res., DES, 1983–86; Bd of Trustees, Stress Syndrome Foundn, 1983–85; Adv. Bd, Ravenswood Village, 1984–; Bd of Governors, Elizabeth Garrett Anderson Sch. 1985–88; Council, Caldecott Community, 1985–; Research Cttee, Froebel Inst., 1987–88; Nat. Curriculum Council, 1988–90; BBC/IBA Central Appeals Adv. Cttee, 1989–. Hon. Mem., BPA, 1985. Member Editorial Board: Internat. Jl of Adolescence and Youth, 1986–; Children and Society, 1987–90. *Publications:* (co-author) 11,000 Seven-Year Olds, 1966; Directory of Voluntary Organisations concerned with Children, 1969; Living with Handicap, 1970; From Birth to Seven, 1972; Child Sexual Abuse: the way forward after Cleveland, 1989; chapters in books and papers in sci. and other jls on special educn, psychol., child care and health. *Recreations:* photography, antiques. *Address:* 3 Grange Grove, Canonbury, N1 2NP. *T:* 071–226 3761.

DAVIE, (Stephen) Rex; Principal Establishment and Finance Officer (Under Secretary), Cabinet Office, since 1989; *b* 11 June 1933; *s* of late Sydney and Dorothy Davie; *m* 1955, Christine Stockwell; one *s* one *d*. *Educ:* Ilfracombe Grammar Sch. Executive Officer, Inland Revenue, 1951. National Service, RAF, 1952–54. Office of Minister for Science, 1962; NEDO, 1967; CSD, 1970; Asst Sec. 1979; Cabinet Office, 1983; Sen. Sec., Security Commn, 1979–89. *Recreations:* reading, gardening. *Address:* c/o Cabinet Office, Whitehall, SW1P 3AL. *Club:* Civil Service.

DAVIES, family name of **Barons Darwen, Davies** and **Davies of Penrhys.**

DAVIES; *see* Edmund-Davies.

DAVIES; *see* Llewelyn-Davies.

DAVIES; *see* Prys-Davies.

DAVIES, 3rd Baron, *cr* 1932, of Llandinam; **David Davies,** MA; CEng, MICE, MBA; Chairman, Welsh National Opera Company, since 1975; *b* 2 Oct. 1940; *s* of 2nd Baron and Ruth Eldrydd (*d* 1966), 3rd *d* of Major W. M. Dugdale, CB, DSO; *S* father (killed in action), 1944; *m* 1972, Beryl, *d* of W. J. Oliver; two *s* two *d*. *Educ:* Eton; King's Coll., Cambridge. *Heir: s* Hon. David Daniel Davies, *b* 23 Oct. 1975. *Address:* Plas Dinam, Llandinam, Powys.

DAVIES OF PENRHYS, Baron *cr* 1974 (Life Peer), of Rhondda; **Gwilym Elfed Davies;** *b* 9 Oct. 1913; *s* of David Davies and Miriam Elizabeth (*née* Williams); *m* 1940, Gwyneth Rees, *d* of Daniel and Agnes Janet Rees; two *s* one *d*. *Educ:* Tylorstown Boys' Sch. Branch Official Tylorstown Lodge, NUM, 1935–59. Member Glamorgan CC, 1954–61. Chairman Local Government Cttee, 1959–61. MP (Lab) Rhondda East, Oct. 1959–Feb. 1974; PPS to Minister of Labour, 1964–68, to Minister of Power, 1968. Part-time Mem., S Wales Electricity Bd, 1974–80. Mem., Nat. Sports Council for Wales, 1978–84. Freeman, Borough of Rhondda, 1975. *Recreations:* Rugby football and cricket. *Address:* Maes-y-Ffrwd, Ferndale Road, Tylorstown, Rhondda, Glam. *T:* Ferndale (0443) 730254.

DAVIES, Air Marshal Sir Alan (Cyril), KCB 1979 (CB 1974); CBE 1967; Co-ordinator of Anglo-American Relations, Ministry of Defence, since 1984; *b* 31 March 1924; *s* of Richard Davies, Maidstone; *m* Julia Elizabeth Ghislaine Russell; two *s* (and one *s* decd). Enlisted RAF, 1941; commnd 1943; comd Joint Anti-Submarine School Flight, 1952–54; comd Air Sea Warfare Development Unit, 1958–59; comd No 201 Sqdn, 1959–61; Air Warfare Coll., 1962; Dep. Dir, Operational Requirements, MoD, 1964–66; comd RAF Stradishall, Suffolk, 1967–68; idc 1969; Dir of Air Plans, MoD, 1969–72; ACAS (Policy), MoD, 1972–74; Dep. COS (Ops and Intell.), HQ Allied Air Forces Central Europe, 1974–77; Dep. C-in-C, RAF Strike Command, 1977; Dir, Internat. Mil. Staff, NATO, Brussels, 1978–81; Hd, Support Area Economy Review Team, RAF, 1981–83; *Address:* c/o Lloyds Bank, PO Box 119G, 7 Pall Mall, SW1Y 5NA. *Club:* Royal Air Force.

DAVIES, Albert John; Chief Agricultural Officer, Agricultural Development and Advisory Service, Ministry of Agriculture, Fisheries and Food, 1971–79; *b* 21 Jan. 1919; *s* of David Daniel Davies and Annie Hilda Davies; *m* 1944, Winnifred Ivy Caroline Emberton; one *s* one *d*. *Educ:* Amman Valley Grammar Sch.; UCW Aberystwyth. BSc Hons Agric. 1940. FIBiol. Adv. Staff, UCW Aberystwyth, 1940–41; Asst Techn. Adviser, Montgomeryshire War Agricultural Cttee, 1941–44; Farm Supt, Welsh Plant Breeding Stn, 1944–47; Nat. Agricultural Adv. Service: Crop Husbandry Adviser Wales, 1947–51; Grassland Husbandry Adviser Wales, 1951–57 and E Mids, 1957–59; Dep. Dir Wales, 1959–64; Regional Dir SW Region, 1964; Chief Farm Management Adviser, London Headquarters, 1964–67; Sen. Agric. Adviser, 1967–68; Dep. Dir, 1968–71. *Publications:* articles in learned jls and agric. press. *Recreations:* golf, Rugby, gardening. *Address:* Cefncoed, 38A Ewell Downs Road, Ewell, Surrey. *T:* 081–393 0069. *Clubs:* Farmers'; Epsom Golf.

DAVIES, (Albert) Meredith, CBE 1982; Principal, Trinity College of Music, 1979–88; Guest Conductor, Royal Opera House, Covent Garden, and Sadler's Wells, 1960–72; also BBC; *b* 30 July 1922; 2nd *s* of Reverend E. A. Davies; *m* 1949, Betty Hazel, *d* of late Dr Kenneth Bates; three *s* one *d*. *Educ:* Royal College of Music; Stationers' Company's Sch.; Keble Coll., Oxford; Accademia di S. Cecilia, Rome. Junior Exhibitioner, RCM, 1930; Organist to Hurstpierpoint Coll., Sussex, 1939; elected Organ Scholar, Keble Coll., 1940. Served War of 1939–45, RA, 1942–45. Conductor St Albans Bach Choir, 1947; Organist and Master of the Choristers, Cathedral Church of St Alban, 1947–49; Musical Dir, St Albans Sch., 1948–49; Organist and Choirmaster, Hereford Cathedral, and Conductor, Three Choirs' Festival (Hereford), 1949–56; Organist and Supernumerary Fellow of New Coll., Oxford, 1956; Associate Conductor, City of Birmingham Symphony Orchestra, 1957–59; Dep. Musical Dir, 1959–60; Conductor, City of Birmingham Choir, 1957–64; Musical Dir, English Opera Group, 1963–65; Musical Dir, Vancouver Symphony Orchestra, 1964–71; Chief Conductor, BBC Trng Orchestra, 1969–72; Music Dir, Royal Choral Soc., 1972–85; Conductor, Leeds Phil. Soc., 1975–84. Pres., ISM, 1985–86. *Address:* 40 Monmouth Street, Bridgwater, Somerset TA6 5EJ.

DAVIES, Sir (Alfred William) Michael, Kt 1973; a Judge of the High Court of Justice, Queen's Bench Division, 1973–91; *b* 29 July 1921; *er s* of Alfred Edward Davies, Stourbridge; *m* 1947, Margaret, *y d* of Robert Ernest Jackson, Sheffield; one *s* three *d*. *Educ:* King Edward's Sch., Birmingham; University of Birmingham (LLB). Called to Bar, Lincoln's Inn, 1948, Bencher 1972, Treasurer 1991; QC 1964; Dep. Chm. Northants QS, 1962–71; Recorder of: Grantham, 1963–65; Derby, 1965–71; Crown Court, 1972–73. Leader of Midland Circuit, 1968–71, Jt Leader of Midland and Oxford Circuit, 1971–73. Chm. Mental Health Review Tribunal, for Birmingham Area, 1965–71; Comr of Assize (Birmingham), 1970; Chancellor, Dio. of Derby, 1971–73; Mem., Gen. Council of the Bar, 1968–72. Chm., Hospital Complaints Procedure Cttee, 1971–73. *Recreations:* golf and the theatre. *Address:* c/o Child & Co., 1 Fleet Street, EC4Y 1BD. *Club:* Garrick.

DAVIES, Very Rev. Alun Radcliffe; Dean of Llandaff, since 1977; *b* 6 May 1923; *s* of Rev. Rhys Davies and Jane Davies; *m* 1952, Winifred Margaret Pullen; two *s* one *d*. *Educ:* Cowbridge Grammar Sch.; University Coll., Cardiff (BA 1945; Fellow, 1983); Keble Coll., Oxford (BA 1947, MA 1951); St Michael's Coll., Llandaff. Curate of Roath, 1948–49; Lecturer, St Michael's Coll., Llandaff, 1949–53; Domestic Chaplain to Archbishop of Wales, 1952–57, to Bishop of Llandaff, 1957–59; Chaplain RNR, 1953–60; Vicar of Ystrad Mynach, 1959–75; Chancellor of Llandaff Cathedral, 1969–71; Archdeacon of Llandaff, 1971–77; Residentiary Canon of Llandaff Cathedral, 1975–77. *Address:* The Deanery, The Cathedral Green, Llandaff, Cardiff CF5 2YF. *T:* Cardiff (0222) 561545.

DAVIES, Sir Alun Talfan, Kt 1976; QC 1961; MA; LLB; *b* Gorseinon, 22 July 1913; *s* of late Rev. W. Talfan Davies, Presbyterian Minister, Gorseinon; *m* 1942, Eiluned Christopher, *d* of late Humphrey R. Williams, Stanmore, Middx; one *s* three *d*. *Educ:* Gowerton Gram. Sch.; Aberystwyth Univ. Coll. of Wales (LLB), Hon. Professorial Fellow, 1971; Gonville and Caius Coll., Cambridge (MA, LLB). Called to the Bar, Gray's Inn, 1939, Bencher, 1969. Contested (Ind.) University of Wales (by-elec.), 1943; contested (L): Carmarthen Div., 1959 and 1964; Denbigh, 1966. Mem. Court of University of Wales and of Courts and Councils of Aberystwyth and Swansea University Colls. Recorder: of Merthyr Tydfil, 1963–68; of Swansea, 1968–69; of Cardiff, 1969–71; of the Crown Court, 1972–85; Hon. Recorder of Cardiff, 1972–86; Dep. Chm., Cardiganshire QS, 1963–71; Judge of the Courts of Appeal, Jersey and Guernsey, 1969–84. Member: Commn on the Constitution, 1969–73; Criminal Injuries Compensation Bd, 1977–85. President: Court of Nat. Eisteddfod of Wales, 1977–80; Court, Welsh Nat. Opera, 1978–80; Welsh Centre of Internat. Affairs, 1985–89; Wales Internat. Dir, Cardiff World Trade Centre Ltd, 1985–. Chm., Bank of Wales, 1991– (Dep. Chm., Commercial Bank of Wales, 1973–91; Dir, 1971–); Dir, HTV Ltd, 1967–83 (Vice-Chm., and Chm. Welsh Bd, 1978–83); Vice-Chm., HTV (Group) Ltd, 1978–83. Chm. Trustees, Aberfan Fund (formerly Aberfan Disaster Fund), 1969–88. Hon. LLD Wales: Aberystwyth, 1973. *Address:* 10 Park Road, Penarth, South Glam CF6 2BD. *T:* Penarth (0222) 701341. *Club:* Cardiff and County (Cardiff).

DAVIES, Prof. Alwyn George, FRS 1989; Professor of Chemistry, University College London, since 1969; *b* 13 May 1926; *s* of John Lewis and Victoria May Davies; *m* 1956, Margaret Drake; one *s* one *d*. *Educ:* Hamond's Grammar Sch., Swaffham; University College London (BSc, PhD, DSc; Fellow 1991). CChem, FRSC. Lectr, Battersea Polytechnic, 1949; Lectr, 1953, Reader, 1964, UCL. *Publications:* Organic Peroxides, 1959; scientific papers on physical organic chemistry and organometallic chemistry in learned jls. *Address:* Chemistry Department, University College London, 20 Gordon Street, WC1H 0AJ. *T:* 071–387 7050.

DAVIES, Andrew Owen Evan; Senior Partner, Lee Bolton & Lee, since 1987; Registrar and Legal Adviser of the Diocese of Canterbury, since 1982; *b* 1936; *s* of late Ninian Rhys Davies and Gweneth Elizabeth Davies; *m* 1963, G. Margaret Stephens; one *s* two *d*. *Educ:* Shrewsbury Sch. Solicitor, Notary Public. National Service, Royal Fusiliers, 1954–56. Law studies and articles, 1956–62; admitted Solicitor, 1962; Partner, Evan Davies & Co., 1964–80; Evan Davies & Co. amalgamated with Lee Bolton & Lee, 1980; Partner, Lee

Bolton & Lee, 1980–83, Dep. Sen. Partner, 1983–87. *Recreations:* country pursuits, golf, reading, family. *Address:* 1 The Sanctuary, Westminster, SW1P 3JT. *T:* 071–222 5381. *Club:* Boodle's.

DAVIES, Andrew Wynford; writer; *b* Rhiwbina, Cardiff, 20 Sept 1936; *e s* of Wynford and Hilda Davies; *m* 1960, Diana Lennox Huntley; one *s* one *d. Educ:* Whitechurch Grammar Sch., Cardiff; University College London. Teacher: St Clement Danes Grammar Sch., 1958–61; Woodberry Down Comprehensive Sch., 1961–63; Lecturer: Coventry Coll. of Educn, 1963–71; Univ. of Warwick, 1971–87. Guardian Children's Fiction Award, 1979; Boston Globe Horn Award, 1979; BPG Award, 1980, 1990; Pye Colour TV Award, best children's writer, 1981; writer's awards: RTS, 1986–87; BAFTA, 1989. *Television includes:* To Serve Them All My Days, 1979; A Very Peculiar Practice, 1986–87; Mother Love, 1989; House of Cards, 1990; Filipina Dreamers, 1991; *stage plays:* Rose, 1981; Prin, 1990. *Publications: for children:* The Fantastic Feats of Dr Boox, 1972; Conrad's War, 1978; Marmalade and Rufus, 1980; Marmalade Atkins in Space, 1981; Educating Marmalade, 1982; Danger Marmalade at Work, 1983; Marmalade Hits the Big Time, 1984; Alfonso Bonzo, 1987; (with Diana Davies) Poonam's Pets, 1990; *fiction:* A Very Peculiar Practice, 1986; The New Frontier, 1987; Getting Hurt, 1989; Dirty Faxes, 1990. *Recreations:* tennis, food, alcohol. *Address:* c/o Lemon, Unna & Durbridge, 24 Pottery Lane, W11 4LZ.

DAVIES, (Angie) Michael; Chairman: Worth Investment Trust, since 1987; Bredero Properties, since 1986; Perkins Foods (formerly John Perkins Meats), since 1987; Calor Group, since 1988 (Director, since 1987); *b* 23 June 1934; *s* of Angelo Henry and Clarice Mildred Davies; *m* 1962, Jane Priscilla, *d* of Oliver Martin and Kathleen White; one *d* (one *s* decd). *Educ:* Shrewsbury Schools; Queens' College, Cambridge. Director: Ross Group, 1964–82; Fenchurch Insurance Holdings, 1969–76; Brown Brothers Corp., 1976–81; Imperial Group, 1972–82; Chairman: Imperial Foods, 1979–82; Tozer Kemsley & Millbourn (Holdings) plc, 1982–86; Dep. Chm., TI Gp, 1990– (Dir, 1984–); Director: Littlewoods Organisation, 1982–88; Avdel (formerly Newman Industries), 1983–; British Airways, 1983–; TV-am, 1983–89; Broadwell Land (formerly CC Conversions), 1984–; James Wilkes, 1987–88; Blue Arrow, later Manpower, 1987–. *Address:* Little Woolpit, Ewhurst, Cranleigh, Surrey GU6 7NP. *T:* Cranleigh (0483) 277344.

DAVIES, Prof. Anna Elbina, (A. Morpurgo Davies), FBA 1985; Professor of Comparative Philology, Oxford University, since 1971; Fellow of Somerville College, Oxford, since 1971; *b* Milan, 21 June 1937; *d* of Augusto Morpurgo and Maria (*née* Castelnuovo); *m* 1962, J. K. Davies, *qv* (marr. diss. 1978). *Educ:* Liceo-Ginnasio Giulio Cesare, Rome; Univ. of Rome. Dott.lett. Rome, 1959; Libera docente, Rome, 1963; MA Oxford, 1964. Asst in Classical Philology, Univ. of Rome, 1959–61; Junior Research Fellow, Center for Hellenic Studies, Harvard Univ., 1961–62; Univ. Lectr in Classical Philology, Oxford, 1964–71; Fellow of St Hilda's Coll., Oxford, 1966–71, Hon. Fellow, 1972–. Visiting Professor: Univ. of Pennsylvania, 1971; Yale Univ., 1977; Collitz Prof. of Ling. Soc. of America, Univ. of South Florida, 1975; Webster Vis. Prof., Stanford Univ., 1988. Lectures: Semple, Univ. of Cincinnati, 1983; Jackson, Harvard Univ., 1990. Pres., Philological Soc., 1976–80, Hon. Vice-Pres., 1980–. FSA 1974; Foreign Hon. Mem., Amer. Acad. of Arts and Sciences, 1986; Corresp. Mem., Österreichische Akademie der Wissenschaften, Vienna, 1988; Mem., Academia Europaea, 1989. Hon. DLitt St Andrews, 1981. *Publications:* (as A. Morpurgo) Mycenaeae Graecitatis Lexicon, 1963; articles and reviews on comparative and classical philology in Italian, German, British and American jls. *Address:* Somerville College, Oxford OX2 6HD. *T:* Oxford (0865) 270600.

DAVIES, Rear-Adm. Anthony, CB 1964; CVO 1972; Royal Navy, retired; *b* 13 June 1912; *s* of late James Arthur and Margaret Davies; *m* 1940, Lilian Hilda Margaret (*d* 1980), *d* of late Admiral Sir Harold Martin Burrough, GCB, KBE, DSO, and Lady (Nellie Wills) Burrough; two *s* two *d. Educ:* Royal Naval College, Dartmouth; Open Univ. (BA 1983). Midshipman, HMS Danae, 1930–32; Sub-Lieut, HMS Despatch, 1934; Lieut, HMS Duncan, 1935–37; Gunnery course, 1938; HMS Repulse, 1939; HMS Cossack 1940–41; Lieut-Comdr, HMS Indefatigable, 1943–45; Comdr, HMS Triumph, 1950; HMS Excellent, 1951–54; Capt., HMS Pelican, 1954–55; Dep. Dir, RN Staff Coll., 1956–57; Far East Fleet Staff, 1957–59; Dep. Dir, Naval Intelligence, 1959–62; Head of British Defence Liaison Staff, Canberra, Australia, 1963–65. Warden, St George's House, Windsor Castle, 1966–72. *Address:* Witts Piece, 11A South Street, Aldbourne, Marlborough, Wilts SN8 2DW. *T:* Marlborough (0672) 40418.

DAVIES, (Anthony) Roger; Metropolitan Stipendiary Magistrate, since 1985; Chairman, London Juvenile Courts, since 1986; *b* 1 Sept. 1940; *er s* of late R. George Davies and of Megan Davies, Penarth, Glam; *m* 1967, Clare, *e d* of Comdr W. A. Walters, RN; twin *s* one *d. Educ:* Bridgend; King's Coll., London. LLB (Hons); AKC. Called to the Bar, Gray's Inn, 1965 (Lord Justice Holker Sen. Schol.). Practised at Bar, London and SE Circuit, 1965–85. *Recreations:* reading (history, biography), music (especially opera), travel, family life. *Address:* c/o Horseferry Road Magistrates' Court, SW1. *Club:* Travellers'.

DAVIES, Prof. Arthur; Reardon-Smith Professor of Geography, University of Exeter, 1948–71; Deputy Vice-Chancellor, University of Exeter, 1969–71; Dean of the Faculty of Social Studies, 1961–64; *b* 13 March 1906; *s* of Richard Davies, Headmaster, and Jessie Starr Davies, Headmistress; *m* 1933, Lilian Margaret Morris; one *d. Educ:* Cyfarthfa Castle Sch.; University Coll. of Wales, Aberystwyth, 1st cl. Hons in Geography and Anthropology, 1927; MSc Wales 1930; Fellow, University of Wales, 1929–30, Asst Lecturer in Geography, Manchester Univ., 1930–33; Lecturer in Geography, Leeds Univ., 1933–40. Served War of 1939–45, RA 1940–45, Normandy (despatches twice, Major); Mem., High Mil. Tribunal of Hamburg, 1945. Hon. FRGS 1982. *Publications:* Yugoslav Studies, Leplay Soc., London, 1932; Polish Studies, Leplay Soc., London, 1933; numerous papers in learned jls on Great Age of Discovery, Columbus, Drake (resolving California/San Francisco problem), John Lloyd's discovery of America in 1477, etc. *Recreations:* gardening and architecture. *Address:* Morlais, Winslade Park, Clyst St Mary, Devon. *T:* Topsham (0392) 3296.

DAVIES, Dr Arthur Gordon; Director, Medical & Electrical Instrumentation Co. Ltd, since 1965; *b* 6 Nov. 1917; *s* of Louis Bernard Davies and Elizabeth Davies; *m* 1945, Joan (*née* Thompson); two *d. Educ:* Westminster Hosp. (MB, BS 1943). LRCP, MRCS 1943. Called to the Bar, Lincoln's Inn, 1955. Served War, RAMC (Captain). Coroner to the Royal Household, 1959–83; Coroner, Inner South London, 1959–87. *Recreations:* chess, bridge, photography, electronics.

DAVIES, Brian Meredith; *see* Davies, J. B. M.

DAVIES, Bryan; Secretary, Parliamentary Labour Party, since 1979; *b* 9 Nov. 1939; *s* of George William and Beryl Davies; *m* 1963, Monica Rosemary Mildred Shearing; two *s* one *d. Educ:* Redditch High Sch.; University Coll., London; Inst. of Education; London Sch. of Economics. BA Hons History London, Certif. Educn, BScEcons London. Teacher, Latymer Sch., 1962–65; Lectr, Middlesex Polytechnic at Enfield, 1965–74. MP (Lab) Enfield North, Feb. 1974–1979; an Asst Govt Whip, 1979; Member: Select Cttee on Public Expenditure, 1975–79; Select Cttee on Overseas Develt, 1975–79. Contested (Lab)

Newport West, 1983; Prospective Parly Cand., Oldham Central and Royton. Mem., MRC, 1977–79. *Recreations:* sport, literature. *Address:* 28 Churchfields, Broxbourne, Herts. *T:* Hoddesdon (0992) 466427.

DAVIES, Bryn, CBE 1987 (MBE 1978); Member, General Council, Wales Trades Union Congress, since 1974 (Vice-Chairman, 1983–84, Chairman, 1984–85); *b* 22 Jan. 1932; *s* of Gomer and Ann Davies; *m* 1956, Esme Irene Gould (*d* 1988); two *s. Educ:* Cwmlai School, Tonyrefail. Served HM Forces (RAMC), 1949–51; Forestry Commn, 1951–56; South Wales and Hereford Organiser, Nat. Union of Agricultural and Allied Workers, 1956–. Chm., Mid Glamorgan AHA, 1978–; Member: Welsh Council, 1965–81; Development Commn, 1975–81; Nat. Cttee (Wales), Forestry Commn, 1978–; Nat. Water Council, 1982–; Council, British Heart Foundn, 1986–. *Recreations:* cricket and Rugby football. *Address:* Derwendeg, 36 Hall Drive, North Cornelly, Bridgend, Mid Glamorgan. *T:* Bridgend (0656) 740426. *Clubs:* Tonyrefail Rugby (Pres., 1985–88); Glamorgan CC; St Mary's Golf (Chm., 1989–).

DAVIES, Caleb William, CMG 1962; FFPHM; MRCS; LRCP; DPH; retired; Regional Specialist in Community Medicine, 1974–82 (Acting Regional Medical Officer, 1977–78, 1979–80), South Western Regional Health Authority; *b* 27 Aug. 1916; *s* of Caleb Davies, KIH, MB, ChB, and Emily (*née* Platt); *m* 1939, Joan Heath; three *s* one *d. Educ:* Kingswood Sch., Bath; University Coll. and University Coll. Hosp. Med. Sch., London; Edinburgh Univ.; London Sch. of Hygiene and Tropical Med. Kenya: MO, 1941; MOH, Mombasa, 1946; Tanganyika: Sen. MO, 1950; Asst Dir of Med. Services, 1952; Uganda: Dep. Dir of Medical Services, 1958; Permanent Sec. and Chief Medical Officer, Ministry of Health, 1960; retired 1963; South-Western Regional Hosp. Bd: Asst SMO, 1963–66; Principal Asst SMO, 1966–74. *Recreations:* swimming, photography. *Address:* 76 Westwood Green, Cookham, Berks SL6 9DE. *T:* Bourne End (06285) 27980.

DAVIES, Ven. Carlyle W.; *see* Witton-Davies.

DAVIES, Christopher Evelyn K.; *see* Kevill-Davies.

DAVIES, (Claude) Nigel (Byam); *b* 2 Sept. 1920; unmarried. *Educ:* Eton. Studied at Aix en Provence University, 1937, and at Potsdam, 1938. PhD London (archaeology). Entered Sandhurst, 1939, and later commissioned Grenadier Guards. Served Middle East, Italy and Balkans, 1942–46. Formerly Managing Dir of Windolite Ltd from 1947. MP (C) Epping Div. of Essex, 1950–51. *Publications:* Los Señoríos Independientes del Imperio Azteca, 1968; Los Mexicas: Primeras Pasos Hacia el Imperio, 1973; The Aztecs, 1973; The Toltecs, 1977; Voyagers to the New World: fact and fantasy, 1979; The Toltec Heritage, 1980; Human Sacrifice, 1981; The Ancient Kingdoms of Mexico, 1983; The Rampant God, 1984; The Aztec Empire, 1987. *Recreation:* travel. *Address:* Sonora 75, Colonia Chapultepec, Tijuana, Baja California, Mexico. *T:* 86–10–36. *Club:* Carlton.

DAVIES, Colin; architectural journalist; Lecturer, Brighton School of Architecture; *b* 24 March 1948; *s* of John and Hazel Davies; *m* 1973, Diana Lamont; one *s. Educ:* King Henry VIII Sch., Coventry; Oxford Polytechnic; Architectural Assoc.; University College London (MSc). AADip, RIBA. Asst Editor, Building Magazine, 1975–77; Associate Partner, Derek Stow and Partners, 1977–81; freelance journalist, 1981–88; Editor, Architects' Jl, 1989–90. Lectr, Bartlett and Canterbury Schs of Architecture, 1983–88. *Publications:* High Tech Architecture, 1988; contribs to arch. jls. *Recreations:* choral singing, model making. *Address:* 69 Landseer Road, N19 4JR.

DAVIES, Cyril James, CBE 1987; DL; Chief Executive, City of Newcastle upon Tyne, 1980–86; *b* 24 Aug. 1923; *s* of James and Frances Davies; *m* 1948, Elizabeth Leggett; two *s* two *d. Educ:* Heaton Grammar Sch. CIPFA. Served RN, Fleet Air Arm, 1942–46. Entered City Treasurer's Dept, Newcastle upon Tyne, 1940: Dep. City Treas., 1964; City Treas., 1969; Treas., Tyne and Wear Co., 1973–80. Member: Council, Univ. of Newcastle upon Tyne, 1982–; Northern Arts Bd, 1986–; Council, Theatre Royal Trust, 1986–; Council, Tyne Theatre Trust, 1986–; Dir, North Housing Assoc., 1986–. DL Tyne and Wear, 1989. *Recreations:* theatre, walking, music. *Address:* 36 Lindisfarne Close, Jesmond, Newcastle upon Tyne NE2 2HT. *T:* Newcastle upon Tyne (091) 2815402. *Club:* Naval.

DAVIES, Dr David; Director: Elmhirst Trust, since 1987; Open College of the Arts, since 1989 (Administrative Director, 1988–89); *b* 11 Aug. 1939; *s* of Trefor Alun and Kathleen Elsie Davies; *m* 1968, Joanna Rachel Peace; one *s* three *d. Educ:* Nottingham High Sch.; Peterhouse, Cambridge. MA, PhD. Res. Scientist, Dept of Geophysics, Cambridge, 1961–69; Leader, Seismic Discrimination Gp, MIT Lincoln Laboratory, 1970–73; Editor of Nature, 1973–79; Dir, Dartington N Devon Trust, 1980–87. Rapporteur, Seismic Study Gp of Stockholm Internat. Peace Res. Inst. (SIPRI), 1968–73; Chm., British Seismic Verification Res. Project, 1987–. Member: Warnock Cttee on artificial human fertilisation, 1982–84; BMA Working Party on Surrogacy, 1988–89. Chm., Ivanhoe Trust, 1986–. Member Council: Internat. Disaster Inst., 1979; Beaford Arts Centre, 1980–87; Trustee, Bristol Exploratory, 1983–90; Yorks Organiser, Open Coll. of the Arts, 1987–89. Musical Dir, Blackheath Opera Workshop, 1977–79; Conductor, Exmoor Chamber Orchestra, 1980–87. Hon. Lectr, Bretton Hall Coll., 1987–. Hon. Fellow: Univ. of Leicester, 1988; Univ. of Leeds, 1989. *Publications:* Seismic Methods for Monitoring Underground Explosions, 1968; numerous scientific papers. *Recreations:* orchestral and choral conducting. *Address:* The Manor House, 24 Huddersfield Road, West Bretton, Wakefield, Yorks WF4 4JY.

DAVIES, Air Vice-Marshal David Brian Arthur Llewellyn, FRCGP; Principal Medical Officer, Headquarters RAF Support Command, 1989–91; *b* 4 Feb. 1932; *s* of Graham and Iris Davies; *m* 1958, Jean Mary Goate; two *s. Educ:* University Coll. London (BSc); University Coll. Hosp. (MB BS). MFCM, MFOM; DipAvMed. Sen. MO, various RAF units, incl. Brize Norton, Scampton, Gütersloh and HQ AFCENT, 1958–80; Dep. Dir, Medical Personnel, MoD, 1980–82; OC RAF Hosp., Wegberg, 1982–85; Comdt, Central Med. Estabt, 1985–87; Dep. PMO, Strike Command, 1987–88. QHP, 1989–91. *Recreations:* travel, music, theatre, gardening. *Address:* c/o Royal Bank of Scotland, 127–128 High Holborn, WC1. *Club:* Royal Air Force.

DAVIES, David Cyril, BA, LLB; Headmaster, Crown Woods School, 1971–84; *b* 7 Oct. 1925; *s* of D. T. E. Davies and Mrs G. V. Davies, JP; *m* 1952, Joan Rogers, BSc; one *s* one *d. Educ:* Lewis Sch., Pengam; UCW Aberystwyth. Asst Master, Ebbw Vale Gram. Sch., 1951–55; Head, Lower Sch., Netteswell Bilateral Sch., 1955–58; Sen. Master and Dep. Headmaster, Peckham Manor Sch., 1958–64; Headmaster: Greenway Comprehensive Sch., 1964–67; Woodberry Down Sch., 1967–71. Pres., Inverliever Lodge Trust, 1971–84. *Recreations:* reading, Rugby and roughing it. *Address:* 9 Plaxtol Close, Bromley, Kent. *T:* 081–464 4187.

DAVIES, Prof. David Evan Naunton, CBE 1986; PhD, DSc; FRS 1984; FEng 1979; Vice-Chancellor of Loughborough University of Technology, since 1988; *b* 28 Oct. 1935; *s* of David Evan Davies and Sarah (*née* Samuel); *m* 1962, Enid Patilla (*d* 1990); two *s. Educ:* Univ. of Birmingham (MSc 1958; PhD 1960; DSc 1968). FIEE 1969; FIERE 1975. Lectr and Sen. Lectr in Elec. Engrg, Univ. of Birmingham, 1961–67 (also Hon. SPSO, RRE, Malvern, 1966–67); Asst Dir of Elec. Res., BR Bd, Derby, 1967–71; Vis.

Industrial Prof. of Elec. Engrg, Loughborough Univ. of Technol., 1969–71; University College London: Prof. of Elec. Engrg, 1971–88; Pender Prof. and Hd of Dept of Electronic and Electrical Engrg, 1985–88; Vice-Provost, 1986–88. Director: Gaydon Technology (Rover Group), 1986–88; Loughborough Consultants, 1988–; Inst. Consumer Ergonomics, 1988–. Member: SERC, 1985–89; IT Adv. Bd, DTI, 1988–. Rank Prize for Optoelectronics, 1984; Callendar Medal, Inst. of Measurement & Control, 1984; Faraday Medal, IEE, 1987. *Publications:* technical papers and articles on radar, antennae and aspects of fibre optics. *Address:* Loughborough University of Technology, Loughborough, Leics LE11 3TU. *T:* Loughborough (0509) 263171.

DAVIES, (David) Garfield; General Secretary, Union of Shop, Distributive and Allied Workers, since 1986; *b* 24 June 1935; *s* of David John Davies and Lizzie Ann Davies; *m* 1960, Marian (*née* Jones); four *d*. *Educ:* Heolgam Secondary Modern School; Bridgend Tech. Coll. (part time). Served RAF, 1956–58. Junior operative, Electrical Apprentice and Electrician, British Steel Corp., Port Talbot, 1950–69; Area Organiser, USDAW, Ipswich, 1969–73; Dep. Divl Officer, USDAW, London/Ipswich, 1973–78; Nat. Officer, USDAW, Manchester, 1978–85. Mem., Employment Appeal Tribunal, 1991–. JP 1972–79. *Recreations:* most sport, badminton, squash, swimming, jogging; formerly soccer, cricket, Rugby. *Address:* USDAW, Oakley, 188 Wilmslow Road, Fallowfield, Manchester M14 6LJ. *T:* 061–224 2804; 64 Dairyground Road, Bramhall, Stockport, Cheshire SK7 2QW. *T:* 061–439 9548.

DAVIES, Sir David (Henry), Kt 1973; first Chairman, Welsh Development Agency, 1976–79; General Secretary, Iron and Steel Trades Confederation, 1967–75; *b* 2 Dec. 1909; British; *m* 1934, Elsie May Battrick; one *s* one *d* (and one *d* decd). *Educ:* Ebbw Vale, Mon. Organiser, 1950, Asst. Gen. Sec., 1953–66, Iron and Steel Trades Confederation. Chm., Jt Adv. Cttee on Safety and Health in the Iron and Steel Industry, 1965–67; Vice-Chm., Nat. Dock Labour Bd, 1966–68; Hon. Treas. WEA, 1962–69 (Mem. Central Coun. and Central Exec. Cttee, 1954–69); Hon. Treas., British Labour Party, 1965–67 (Chm., 1963; Mem. Nat. Exec., 1954–67); Hon. Sec., Brit. Sect., Internat. Metalworkers Federation, 1960–; Member: Ebbw Vale UDC, 1945–50; Royal Institute of International Affairs, 1954–; Iron and Steel Operatives Course Adv. Cttee, City and Guilds of London Institute Dept of Technology, 1954–68; Iron and Steel Industry Trng Bd, 1964–; Constructional Materials Gp, Economic Development Cttee for the Building and Civil Engrg Industries, 1965–68; Iron and Steel Adv. Cttee, 1967–; English Industrial Estates Corporation, 1971–; Vice-Pres., European Coal and Steel Community Consultative Cttee, 1975– (Pres., 1973–74). Governor: Ruskin Coll., Oxford, 1954–68; Iron and Steel Industry Management Trng Coll., Ashorne Hill, Leamington Spa, 1966–. Mem. TUC Gen. Coun., 1967–75. *Address:* 82 New House Park, St Albans, Herts AL1 1UP. *T:* St Albans (0727) 56513.

DAVIES, Hon. Sir (David Herbert) Mervyn, Kt 1982; MC 1944; TD 1946; **Hon. Mr Justice Mervyn Davies;** a Judge of the High Court of Justice, Chancery Division, since 1982; *b* 17 Jan. 1918; *s* of Herbert Bowen Davies and Esther Davies, Llangunnor, Carms; *m* 1951, Zita Yollanne Angelique Blanche Antoinette, 2nd *d* of Rev. E. A. Phillips, Bale, Norfolk. *Educ:* Swansea Gram. Sch. Solicitor, 1939. 18th Bn Welch Regt and 2nd London Irish Rifles, Africa, Italy and Austria, 1939–45. Called to Bar, Lincoln's Inn, 1947; Bencher, 1974; QC 1967; a Circuit Judge, 1978–82. Mem., Bar Council, 1972; Mem., Senate of Inns of Court, 1975. *Address:* The White House, Great Snoring, Norfolk. *T:* Walsingham (0328) 820575; 7 Stone Buildings, Lincoln's Inn, WC2A 3SZ. *T:* 071–242 8061.

DAVIES, (David) Hywel, MA, PhD; FEng 1988; FIEE; consultant; Deputy Director-General for Science, Research and Development, EEC, Brussels, 1982–86; *b* 28 March 1929; *s* of John and Maggie Davies; *m* 1961, Valerie Elizabeth Nott; one *s* two *d*. *Educ:* Cardiff High Sch.; Christ's Coll., Cambridge. Radar Research Estabt, 1956; Head of Airborne Radar Group, RRE, 1970; Head of Weapons Dept, Admty Surface Weapons Estabt, 1972; Asst Chief Scientific Advr (Projects), MoD, 1976–79; Dir, RARDE, MoD, 1979–80; Dep. Controller, Res. Programmes, MoD, 1980–82. Man. Dir, Topexpress Ltd, 1988–89. *Publications:* papers on electronics, radar and remote sensing, in Proc. IEE, etc. *Recreations:* Europe, computing, knots. *Address:* 52 Brittains Lane, Sevenoaks, Kent TN13 2JP. *T:* Sevenoaks (0732) 456359.

DAVIES, David John; Chairman: Johnson Matthey plc, since 1990; Sketchley PLC, since 1990; *b* 1 April 1940; *s* of late Stanley Kenneth Davies, CBE and Stephanie Davies; *m* 1st, 1967, Deborah Frances Loeb (marr. diss.); one *s*; 2nd, 1985, Linda Wong Lin-Tye; one *d*. *Educ:* Winchester Coll., Winchester; New Coll., Oxford (MA); Harvard Business Sch. (Advanced Management Program). Chase Manhattan Bank, 1963–67; Hill Samuel Group, 1967–73: Dir, Hill Samuel Inc., New York, 1970–73; Dir, Hill Samuel Ltd, London, 1973; Finance Dir, 1973–83, and Vice-Chm., 1977–83, MEPC; Man. Dir, The Hongkong Land Co. Ltd, 1983–86; Dir, 1986–88, Chief Exec. and Exec. Vice Chm., 1987–88, Hill Samuel Gp; Jt Chm., Hill Samuel & Co., 1987–88. Chairman: Mandarin Oriental Hotel Group, 1983–86; Dairy Farm Ltd, 1983–86; Imry Merchant Developers (formerly Imry Internat.), 1987–89; Wire Ropes Ltd, Wicklow, 1979–; Dep. Chm., Charter Consolidated, 1988–89; Director: Jardine Matheson Group, 1983–86; Hong Kong Electric Co., 1983–85; American Barrick Resources Corp., Toronto, 1986–; Delaware North Cos Inc., Buffalo, NY, 1986–; Singapore Land Ltd, 1986–90; Fitzwilton PLC, Dublin, 1987–90; Asia Securities, Hong Kong, 1987–89; Hardwicke Ltd, Dublin, 1987–; TSB Group, 1987–89; First Pacific Co., Hong Kong, 1988–91; Glyndebourne Productions Ltd, 1990–. Trustee, Anglo-Hong Kong Trust, 1989–. *Recreations:* farming, ski-ing, tennis, travel, opera. *Address:* 7 Aigburth Hall, May Road, Hong Kong; 85 Eaton Terrace, SW1W 8TW. *Clubs:* Turf, Oriental; Cardiff and County (Cardiff); Kildare Street and University (Dublin); Hong Kong (Hong Kong).

DAVIES, Rt. Hon. (David John) Denzil; PC 1978; MP (Lab) Llanelli since 1970; *b* 9 Oct. 1938; *s* of G. Davies, Conwil Elfed, Carmarthen; *m* 1963, Mary Ann Finlay (marr. diss. 1988), Illinois; one *s* one *d*. *Educ:* Queen Elizabeth Grammar Sch., Carmarthen; Pembroke Coll., Oxford. Bacon Scholar, Gray's Inn, 1961; BA (1st cl. Law) 1962; Martin Wronker Prize (Law), 1962. Teaching Fellow, Univ. of Chicago, 1963; Lectr in Law, Leeds Univ., 1964; called to Bar, Gray's Inn, 1964. Member: Select Cttee on Corporation Tax, 1971; Jt Select Cttee (Commons and Lords) on Delegated Legislation, 1972; Public Accounts Cttee, 1974–; PPS to the Secretary of State for Wales, 1974–76; Minister of State, HM Treasury, 1975–79; Opposition spokesman on Treasury matters, 1979–81, on foreign affairs, 1981–82, on defence, 1982–83; chief opposition spokesman: on Welsh affairs, 1983; on defence and disarmament, 1983–88. *Address:* House of Commons, SW1.

DAVIES, David Levric, CB 1982; OBE 1962; Under Secretary (Legal), Treasury Solicitor's Office, 1977–82; *b* 11 May 1925; *s* of Benjamin and Elizabeth Davies; *m* 1955, Beryl Justine Hammond. *Educ:* Llanrwst Grammar Sch.; University Coll. of Wales, Aberystwyth (LLB Hons). Called to the Bar, Middle Temple, 1949. Served War, 1943–46: Sub-Lt RNVR. Crown Counsel, Aden, 1950–55; Tanganyika: Asst to Law Officers, 1956–58; Parly Draftsman, 1958–61; Solicitor-Gen., 1961–64; Home Civil Service, 1964–82: seconded to Jamaica as Sen. Parly Draftsman, 1965–69, and to Seychelles as Attorney-Gen., 1970–72; Sen. Legal Asst, Treasury Solicitor's Office, 1972–73; Asst Treasury Solicitor, 1973–77. *Recreations:* gardening, loafing, reading. *Address:* Greystones, Breach Lane, Shaftesbury, Dorset SP7 8LF. *T:* Shaftesbury (0747) 51224.

DAVIES, David Ronald, MB, BS, FRCS; Surgeon, University College Hospital, London, 1946–75, retired; *b* Clydach, Swansea, 11 May 1910; 3rd *s* of late Evan Llewelyn and Agnes Jane Davies; *m* 1940, Alice Christine, 2nd *d* of Rev. John Thomson; three *s*. *Educ:* University Coll. and University Coll. Hosp., London. MRCS, LRCP 1934; MB BS London, 1934; FRCS, 1937. House appts at UCH, Asst, Surgical Unit, UCH, 1937–39; Asst Surg. EMS at UCH and Hampstead Gen. Hosp., 1939–41; served RAMC, Surgical Specialist and Officer-in-Charge Surgical Div., 1941–46; Surgeon: Queen Mary's Hospital, Roehampton, 1947–69; Harrow Hosp., 1946–69. Mem., BMA. Fellow: University Coll. London; Assoc. of Surgeons; RSocMed; British Assoc. of Urological Surgeons; Internat. Assoc. of Urologists. *Publications:* The Operations of Surgery (with A. J. Gardham); various papers on surgical subjects. *Address:* Newland Farm, Withypool, Somerset. *T:* Exford (064383) 352. *Club:* Oriental.

DAVIES, Prof. David Roy, PhD; Professor of Applied Genetics, since 1968, and Dean of School of Biological Sciences, since 1985, University of East Anglia; Deputy Director, John Innes Institute, since 1978; *b* 10 June 1932; *s* of late J. O. Davies and A. E. Davies; *m* 1957, Winifred Frances Davies, JP, BA (*née* Wills); two *s* two *d*. *Educ:* Llandyssul and Grove Park, Wrexham Grammar Schs; Univ. of Wales. BSc, PhD. UK Atomic Energy Authority, 1956–62 and 1963–68; US Atomic Energy Commn, 1962–63. Editor, Heredity, 1975–82. *Publications:* papers on radiobiology and plant genetics in scientific jls. *Address:* 57 Church Lane, Eaton, Norwich NR4 6NY. *T:* Norwich (0603) 51049.

DAVIES, David Theodore Alban; a District Judge (formerly Registrar), Family Division of the High Court of Justice, since 1983; a Recorder, since 1989; *b* 8 June 1940; *s* of late John Rhys Davies, Archdeacon of Merioneth, and Mabel Aeronwy Davies; *m* 1966, Janet Mary, *er d* of late Frank and Barbara Welburn, Cheadle Hulme, Cheshire; one *s* one *d*. *Educ:* Rossall School (Scholar); Magdalen College, Oxford (Exhibnr, 2nd cl. Mods 1960, 1st cl. Lit Hum, 1962, BA 1962; Eldon Law Schol., 1963; MA 1967). Called to the Bar, Gray's Inn, 1964 (Entrance Schol., Arden Atkin and Mould Prize, Lord Justice Holker Sen. Schol.). Practised SE Circuit, 1965–83. Sec., Family Law Bar Assoc., 1976–80, Treasurer, 1980–83; Member: Senate Law Reform Cttee, 1979–83; Civil and Family Cttee, Judicial Studies Bd, 1988–. *Publication:* (ed jtly) Jackson's Matrimonial Finance and Taxation, 2nd edn 1975, 4th edn 1986. *Recreations:* reading, walking, history. *Address:* 134 Court Lane, SE21 7EB. *T:* 081-693 4132.

DAVIES, Rt. Hon. Denzil; *see* Davies, Rt. Hon. David J. D.

DAVIES, Dickie; television sports presenter, since 1964; *s* of Owen John Davies and Ellen Davies; *m* 1962, Elisabeth Ann Hastings Mann; twin *s*. *Educ:* William Ellis Sch., Highgate; Oldershaw Grammar Sch., Wallasey, Cheshire. Purser, Cunard Line, 1953–60; Television Announcer, Southern TV, 1960–63; World of Sport Presenter, 1964–85, Presenter: ITV Sport, 1985–89; Sportsmasters, 1988–; The World of Golf, 1990. *Recreations;* golf, horse-riding, but mostly work. *Address:* Vine Cottage, Over Wallop, Stockbridge, Hampshire SO20 8JX.

DAVIES, Donald, CBE 1978 (OBE 1973); consultant; *b* 13 Feb. 1924; *s* of late Wilfred Lawson Davies and Alwyne Davies; *m* 1948, Mabel (*née* Hellyar); two *d*. *Educ:* Ebbw Vale Grammar Sch.; UC Cardiff (BSc). CEng, FIMinE. Nationl Coal Board: Colliery Man., 1951–55; Gp Man., 1955–58; Dep. Prodn Man., 1958–60; Prodn Man., 1960–61; Area Gen. Man., 1961–67; Area Dir, 1967–73; Bd Mem., 1973–84. FRSA, FBIM. *Recreations:* golf, walking. *Address:* Wendy Cottage, Dukes Wood Avenue, Gerrards Cross, Bucks SL9 7LA. *T:* Gerrards Cross (0753) 85083.

DAVIES, Donald Watts, CBE 1983; FRS 1987; Consultant, Data Security, since 1984; *b* 7 June 1924; *s* of John and Hilda Davies; *m* 1955, Diane Lucy (*née* Burton); two *s* one *d*. *Educ:* Portsmouth Boys' Southern Secondary Sch.; Imperial Coll. of Science and Technology. ARCS, BSc (Physics, 1st cl. hons), 1943, ARCS, BSc (Maths, 1st cl. hons), 1947. Wartime research, 1943–46; Nat. Physical Laboratory, 1947–84: pioneer of digital computing, 1947–50; pioneer of packet switching (data communication), 1965–70; Supt of Computer Science Div., 1966–78; Individual Merit DCSO, 1978–84. Consultant to financial insts for data security, 1976–. Vis. Prof. RHBNC, London Univ., 1987–. Commonwealth Fund Fellow, 1954–55. Dist. Fellow, BCS, 1975. Hon. DSc Salford, 1989. Sir John Lubbock Prize in Maths, 1946; John Player Award, BCS, 1975; John von Neumann Award, J. v. Neumann Soc., Budapest, 1985. *Publications:* Digital Techniques, 1963; Communication Networks for Computers, 1973; Computer Networks and their Protocols, 1979; Security for Computer Networks, 1984, 2nd edn 1989; papers in learned jls. *Recreations:* mathematical games and puzzles, cipher machines of World War II, travel.

DAVIES, Douglas; *see* Davies, Percy D.

DAVIES, Ednyfed Hudson, BA (Wales); MA (Oxon); barrister; *b* 4 Dec. 1929; *s* of Rev. E. Curig Davies and Enid Curig (*née* Hughes); *m* 1972, Amanda Barker-Mill, *d* of Peter Barker-Mill and Elsa Barker-Mill; two *d*. *Educ:* Friars Sch., Bangor; Dynevor Grammar Sch., Swansea; University College of Swansea; Balliol Coll., Oxford. Called to the Bar, Gray's Inn, 1975. Lecturer in Dept of Extra-Mural Studies, University of Wales, Aberystwyth, 1957–61; Lecturer in Political Thought, Welsh Coll. of Advanced Technology, Cardiff, 1961–66. MP: (Lab) Conway, 1966–70; Caerphilly, 1979–83 (Lab, 1979–81, SDP, 1981–83); Mem., H of C Select Cttee on Energy, 1980–83; Sec., H of C All-Party Tourism Cttee, 1979–83. Contested (SDP) Basingstoke, 1983. Part-time TV and Radio Commentator and Interviewer on Current Affairs, 1962–66; on full-time contract to BBC presenting Welsh-language feature programmes on overseas countries, 1970–76; Chm., Wales Tourist Board, 1976–78. Dep. Chm., Ocean Sound Radio, 1989– (Dir, 1986–); Dir, Southern Radio Hldgs, 1989–. Dir, New Forest Butterfly Farm, 1984–; Trustee, 1986–, Vice-Chm., 1988–, New Forest Ninth Centenary Trust. *Address:* 2 King's Bench Walk, Temple, EC4Y 7DE. *Club:* Cardiff and County (Cardiff).

DAVIES, (Edward) Hunter; author, broadcaster, publisher; *b* Renfrew, Scotland, 7 Jan. 1936; *s* of late John Hunter Davies and Marion (*née* Brechin); *m* 1960, Margaret Forster, *qv*; one *s* two *d*. *Educ:* Creighton Sch., Carlisle; Carlisle Grammar Sch.; University Coll., Durham. BA 1957, DipEd 1958; Editor of Palatinate. Reporter: Manchester Evening Chronicle, 1958–59; Sunday Graphic, London, 1959–60; Sunday Times, 1960–84: Atticus, 1965–67; Chief Feature Writer, 1967; Editor, Look pages, 1970; Editor, Scene pages, 1975; Editor, Sunday Times Magazine, 1975–77; Columnist: Punch, 1979–89; Stamp News, 1981–86; Stamps, 1987–; London Evening Standard, 1987; The Independent, 1989–; Presenter, Bookshelf, Radio 4, 1983–86. Mem., British Library Consultative Gp on Newspapers, 1987–89; Dir, Edinburgh Book Festival Bd, 1990–. *Television:* The Playground (play), 1967; The Living Wall, 1974; George Stephenson, 1975; A Walk in the Lakes, 1979. *Publications: fiction:* Here We Go, Round the Mulberry Bush, 1965 (filmed, 1968); The Rise and Fall of Jake Sullivan, 1970; (ed) I Knew Daisy Smuten, 1970; A Very Loving Couple, 1971; Body Charge, 1972; Flossie Teacake's Fur Coat, 1982; Flossie Teacake—Again!, 1983; Flossie Teacake Strikes Back, 1984; Come on Ossie!, 1985; Ossie Goes Supersonic, 1986; Ossie the Millionaire, 1987; Saturday

Night, 1989; S.T.A.R.S (12 books in Penguin series), 1989–90; *non-fiction*: The Other Half, 1966; (ed) The New London Spy, 1966; The Beatles, 1968, 2nd edn 1985; The Glory Game, 1972, 3rd edn 1990; A Walk Along the Wall, 1974, 2nd edn 1984; George Stephenson, 1975; The Creighton Report, 1976; (ed) Sunday Times Book of Jubilee Year, 1977; A Walk Around the Lakes, 1979; William Wordsworth, 1980; The British Book of Lists, 1980; The Grades, 1981; Father's Day, 1981 (television series, 1983); Beaver Book of Lists, 1981; A Walk Along the Tracks, 1982; England!, 1982; (with Frank Herrmann) Great Britain: a celebration, 1982; A Walk Round London Parks, 1983; The Joy of Stamps, 1983; London at its Best, 1984; (also publisher) The Good Guide to the Lakes, 1984, 3rd edn 1989; The Grand Tour, 1986; The Good Quiz Book to the Lakes, 1987; Back in the USSR, 1987; Beatrix Potter's Lakeland, 1988; My Life in Football, 1990; In Search of Columbus, 1991. *Recreations*: collecting stamps, postal history, Lakeland books, Beatles memorabilia, parking fines. *Address*: 11 Boscastle Road, NW5. *T*: 071–485 3785; Grasmoor House, Loweswater, Cumbria.

DAVIES, Elidir (Leslie Wish), FRIBA, FRSA; Chartered Architect in private practice; *b* 3 Jan. 1907; *yr s* of late Rev. Thomas John Landy Davies and Hetty Boucher (*née* Wish); *m* 1st, Vera (*née* Goodwin) (*d* 1974); 2nd, 1976, Kathleen Burke-Collis (*d* 1989). *Educ*: privately; Colchester Sch.; Bartlett Sch. of Architecture, University of London (under Prof. Albert Richardson). Min. of Supply Air Defence, 1939–44; Min. of Town and Country Planning, London and Wales, 1944–47; University Lectr and Cons. to Argentinian and Uruguay Govts on planning and low cost housing, 1947–49; private practice (Devereux and Davies); rebuilding of Serjeants' Inn, Fleet Street; Royal Vet. Coll., London Univ. (Research and Field Labs); King's Coll. Sch., Wimbledon (Jun. Sch. and Sci. Labs); St James's Hosp., Balham (Out-patients' and other Depts); St Benedict's Hosp. (Hydrotherapy Dept), 1950–61. West Indies: 5-year Hospital progr. for Trinidad (incl. new gen. and maternity hosps, trg schs, specialist depts, and hosp. services). Cons. Arch. Hosps to Govts of Guiana, Barbados and Grenada, 1957–63. Private practice (Elidir L. W. Davies & Partners). Architect to: St David's Coll., Lampeter, restoration and new bldgs; London Borough of Camden; Central Library, Shaw Theatre and arts centre; Mermaid Theatre; Dynevor Castle, Carmarthen, Wales; new arts centre for drama and films; Chigwell Central Public Library; church work: The Temple, White Eagle Lodge, Hants; rebuilding of Wren's church, St Michael Paternoster Royal; Burrswood Nursing Home of Healing, Groombridge, Kent; Century House, Waterloo; BP Offices, 100 Euston Road; private houses and housing developments in London and the country. Chm., Soc. of Theatre Consultants, 1969–71; Mem. of Exec., Assoc. of British Theatre Technicians, 1965–71. Bronze Medal, RIBA, 1953. *Publications*: lectures and articles; contrib. to pubn relating to hospital architecture. *Recreations*: theatre, travel, sailing, visual arts. *Address*: St David's, Burrswood, Groombridge, Kent TN3 9PY. *T*: Groombridge (0892) 864810. *Clubs*: Garrick, Art Workers' Guild.

DAVIES, Emlyn Glyndwr, MSc; Chief Scientific Officer, Controller, Forensic Science Service, Home Office, 1974–76; *b* 20 March 1916; *yr s* of late William and Elizabeth Davies; *m* 1940, Edwina, *d* of late Lemuel and Alice Morgan, Blaengarw; two *s*. *Educ*: Bargoed Grammar Sch.; Maesycwmmer Grammar Sch.; University Coll of Wales, Aberystwyth (MSc). Asst Master, Ardwyn Sch., 1939–42; Ministry of Supply, 1942–44; Forensic Science Laboratory, Cardiff, 1944–58; Director, Forensic Science Laboratories: Nottingham, 1958–59; Preston, 1959–63; Forensic Science Adviser, Home Office, 1963–74. Pres., Forensic Science Soc., 1975–77. *Publications*: contribs to scientific jls. *Recreation*: Rugby football. *Address*: 14 Church Hill Close, Llanblethian, Cowbridge, S Glamorgan CF7 7JH. *T*: Cowbridge (0446) 772234.

DAVIES, Emrys Thomas, CMG 1988; HM Diplomatic Service; High Commissioner, Barbados, since 1990; *b* 8 Oct. 1934; *s* of Evan William Davies and Dinah Davies (*née* Jones); *m* 1960, Angela Audrey, *er d* of late Paul Robert Buchan May, ICS and of Esme May; one *s* two *d*. *Educ*: Parmiters Foundation Sch. RAF, 1953–55. Sch. of Slavonic Studies, Cambridge Univ., 1954; Sch. of Oriental and African Studies, London Univ., 1955–56. Served Peking, 1956–59; FO, 1959–60; Bahrain, 1960–62; FO, 1962–63; Asst Political Adviser to Hong Kong Govt, 1963–68; First Sec., British High Commn, Ottawa, 1968–71; FCO, 1972–76; Commercial Counsellor, Peking, 1976–78 (Chargé, 1976 and 1978); Oxford Univ. Business Summer Sch., 1977; NATO Defense Coll., Rome, 1979; Dep. High Comr, Ottawa, 1979–82; Overseas Inspector, FCO, 1982–84; Dep. UK Perm. Rep. to OECD, and Counsellor (Econ. and Financial) to UK Delegn, Paris, 1984–87; Ambassador to Hanoi, 1987–90. *Address*: c/o Foreign and Commonwealth Office, King Charles Street, SW1A 2AH. *Clubs*: Commonwealth Trust; Cambridge Society.

DAVIES, Dr Ernest Arthur, JP; management consultant and lecturer, retired 1987; *b* 25 Oct. 1926; *s* of Daniel Davies and Ada (*née* Smith), Nuneaton; *m* 1st, 1956, Margaret Stephen Tait Gatt (marr. diss. 1967), *d* of H. Gatt, Gamesley, near Glossop; no *c*; 2nd, 1972, Patricia (marr. diss. 1980), *d* of S. Bates, Radford, Coventry; no *c*. *Educ*: Coventry Jun. Techn. Coll.; Westminster Trng Coll., London; St Salvator's Coll., University of St Andrews; St John's Coll., Cambridge. PhD Cantab 1959; MInstP 1959. RAF Aircraft Apprentice, 1942–43 (discharged on med. grounds). Westminster Trng Coll., 1946–48; Teacher, Foxford Sch., Coventry, 1948–50; University of St Andrews, 1950–54 (1st cl. hons Physics, Neil Arnott Prize, Carnegie Schol.); subseq. research in superconductivity, Royal Society Mond Lab., Cambridge; AEI Research Scientist, 1957–63; Lectr in Physics, Faculty of Technology, University of Manchester, 1963–66; Management Selection Consultant, MSL, 1970–81; Lectr in Business Studies, Hammersmith and West London Coll., 1981–87. MP (Lab) Stretford, 1966–70; Parliamentary Private Secretary to: PMG (Mr Edward Short), Nov.-Dec. 1967; Foreign Secretary (Mr George Brown), Jan.-Mar. 1968; Foreign and Commonwealth Sec. (Mr Michael Stewart), 1968–69; Jt Parly Sec., Min. of Technology, 1969–70. Co-Vice-Chm., Parly Labour Party's Defence and Services Group; Mem., Select Cttee on Science and Technology, 1966–67, 1967–68, 1968–69; Parly Deleg. to 24th Gen. Assembly of UN (UK Rep. on 4th Cttee). Councillor: Borough of Stretford, 1961–67; Borough of Southwark, 1974–82. JP Lancs, 1962, Inner London, 1972. *Publications*: contribs to Proc. Royal Society, Jl of Physics and Chem. of Solids. *Recreations*: reading, walking. *Address*: Flat 3, 5 Rye Hill Park, Peckham, SE15 3JN.

DAVIES, Prof. Eurfil Rhys, CBE 1990; FRCR, FRCPE; FDSRCS; Professor of Clinical Radiology (formerly Radiodiagnosis), University of Bristol, since 1981; *b* 18 April 1929; *s* of late Daniel Haydn Davies and Mary Davies; *m* 1962, Zoë Doreen Chamberlain; three *s*. *Educ*: Rhondda Grammar Sch.; Llandovery Coll.; Clare Coll., Cambridge (MB, BChir 1953; MA); St Mary's Hosp., London. FRCR (FFR 1964); FRCPE 1971; FDSRCS 1989. Served RAMC, 1954–56. Sen. Registrar, St Mary's Hosp., 1963–66; Consultant Radiologist, United Bristol Hosps, 1966–81; Clinical Lectr, Univ. of Bristol, 1972–81. Vis. Sen. Lectr, Lagos Univ., 1971; Mayne Vis. Prof., Queensland Univ., 1982. Civilian Cons. Advr to RN, 1989–. Mem., Bristol and Weston DHA, 1983–86. Member: Admin of Radio Active Substances Adv. Cttee, DHSS, 1978–83; GMC, 1989–. Royal Coll. of Radiologists: Sen. Examr, 1973–74; Mem., Fellowship Bd, 1974–76; Registrar, 1976–81; Chm., Examining Bd, 1981–84; Warden of the Fellowship, 1984–86; Pres., 1986–89; Chairman: Nuclear Medicine Cttee, 1972–78; Examng Bd, 1982–84. Pres., Nuclear Medicine Soc., 1974–76; Chm., Inter Collegiate Standing Cttee for Nuclear Medicine, 1982–84 (Sec., 1980–82). Hon. Fellow, Faculty of Radiologists, RCSI, 1978. *Publications*: (contrib.) Textbook of Radiology, ed Sutton, 1969, 5th edn 1990; (contrib.) Textbook of Urology, ed J. P. Blandy, 1974; (jtly) Radioisotopes in Radiodiagnosis, 1976; (contrib.) Radiological Atlas of Biliary and Pancreatic Disease, 1978; Textbook of Radiology by British Authors, 1984; (ed with W. E. G. Thomas) Nuclear Medicine for Surgeons, 1988; papers in Clin. Radiology, British Jl of Radiology, Lancet. *Recreations*: theatre, walking, wine. *Address*: 19 Hyland Grove, Bristol BS9 3NR.

DAVIES, Gareth; Group Chief Executive since 1984, Chairman since 1987, Glynwed International plc; *b* 13 Feb. 1930; *s* of Lewis and Margaret Ann Davies; *m* 1953, Joan Patricia Prosser; one *s*. *Educ*: King Edward's Grammar School, Aston, Birmingham. FCA. Joined Glynwed Group, 1957; Computer Manager, 1964; Financial Dir, 1969; Man. Dir, 1981. Non-Executive Director: Raglan Property Trust, 1985–; W Midlands Region, Barclays Bank, 1987–; Midlands Electricity Plc (formerly Midlands Electricity Bd), 1989–. *Recreations*: music, gardening. *Address*: 4 Beechgate, Roman Road, Little Aston Park, Sutton Coldfield, West Midlands B74 3AR. *T*: 021–353 4780.

DAVIES, Gareth Lewis; His Honour Judge Gareth Davies; a Circuit Judge, since 1990; *b* 8 Sept. 1936; *s* of David Edward Davies and Glynwen Davies; *m* 1962; two *s* two *d*. *Educ*: Brecon County Grammar Sch.; Univ. of Wales (LLB). National Service, RAF, 1954–56. Articled 1959, qualified Solicitor, 1962; Partner, Ottaways', Solicitors, St Albans, 1965–90; a Recorder, 1987. *Recreations*: sailing instructor, ski-ing, cycling. *Address*: Bronllys Castle, Bronllys, Brecon, Powys LD3 0HL. *T*: Brecon (0874) 711930.

DAVIES, Garfield; *see* Davies, D. G.

DAVIES, Gavyn, OBE 1979; Chief UK Economist since 1986, Partner since 1988, Goldman Sachs; *b* 27 Nov. 1950; *s* of W. J. F. Davies and M. G. Davies; *m* 1989, Susan Jane Nye; one *d*. *Educ*: St John's Coll., Cambridge (BA); Balliol Coll., Oxford. Economic Advr, Policy Unit, 10 Downing Street, 1974–79; Economist, Phillips and Drew, 1979–81; Chief UK Economist, Simon & Coates, 1981–86. Vis. Prof. of Economics, LSE, 1988–. *Recreation*: Southampton FC. *Address*: 5 Old Bailey, EC4M 7AH. *T*: 071–248 6464.

DAVIES, George Raymond, (Gerry), OBE 1977; FLA; Director, The Booksellers Association of Great Britain and Ireland, 1964–66 and 1970–81 (Hon. Life Member, 1981); *b* 3 Oct. 1916; *s* of George John Davies and Eva Florence Davies; *m* 1945, Sylvia Newling; one *s* one *d*. *Educ*: East Ham Grammar Sch. FLA 1948. Local govt service, 1934–40; land reclamation, 1940–45; estate under-bailiff, 1945–46; W Suffolk and Cambridge Public Libraries, 1947–54 (Dep. City Librarian, 1953); Gen. Sec., Booksellers Assoc., 1955–64; Man. Dir, Bowker Publishing Co. Ltd, 1966–67; Editor, Publishers Inf. Card Services Ltd, 1968–69; Jt Dep. Editor, The Bookseller, 1969–70. Founder-Mem., Internat. Community of Booksellers Assocs, 1956 (Mem. Council, 1972–78); Mem. Council, Internat. Booksellers Fedn, 1978–85 (Pres. 1978–81); Editor, Booksellers International, 1982–88; Hon. Life Mem., 1989); Chm., BA Service House Ltd, 1977–82; Patron, Book Trade Benevolent Soc., 1989– (Chm., 1974–86; Pres., 1986–89). *Publications*: (ed jtly) Books are Different, 1966; A Mortal Craft, 1980; (contrib.) The Book of Westminster, 1964; (contrib.) Books and Their Prices, 1967; contrib. to Logos, Library Rev., Library World, Year's Work in Librarianship, Canadian Bookseller, American Bookseller, Australian Bookseller and Publisher, and The Bookseller. *Recreations*: estate management, writing words and music. *Address*: Crotchets, Rotherfield Lane, Mayfield, East Sussex TN20 6AS. *T*: Mayfield (0435) 872356. *Club*: Savile.

DAVIES, George William; Managing Director, George Davies Partnership plc, since 1989; *b* 29 Oct. 1941; *s* of George and Mary Davies; *m* 1st, 1964, Anne; three *d*; 2nd, 1985, Liz; two *d*. *Educ*: Netherton Moss Primary Sch.; Bootle Grammar Sch.; Birmingham Univ. Littlewoods, 1967–72; School Care (own business), 1972–75; Pippa Dee (subsid. of Rosgill Hldgs)—Party Plan/Lingerie, 1975–81; J. Hepworth & Son plc (responsible for launch of Next), 1981; Jt Gp Man. Dir, J. Hepworth & Son, 1984; Chief Exec., 1985–88, Chm., 1987–88, Next (name changed from J. Hepworth & Son). Sen. Fellow, RCA, 1988. FRSA. Hon. DBA Liverpool Polytechnic, 1989. Guardian Young Businessman of the Year, 1985; Wood Mackenzie Retailer of the Year, 1987; Marketing Personality of the Year, 1988. *Publication*: What Next? (autobiog.), 1989. *Recreations*: tennis, squash, golf. *Address*: (office) Magna House, Magna Park, Watling Street, Lutterworth, Leicester LE17 4JQ. *Clubs*: Formby Golf; Rothley Park Golf (Leicestershire); Leicester Squash.

DAVIES, Prof. Glyn Arthur Owen, CEng, FRAeS; Professor of Aeronautical Structures, Imperial College of Science, Technology and Medicine, London, since 1985 (Head of Department of Aeronautics, 1982–89); *b* 11 Feb. 1933; *s* of Arthur and Florence Davies; *m* 1959, Helen Rosemary (*née* Boot); two *d*. *Educ*: Liverpool Inst., Univ. of Liverpool (BEng); Cranfield Inst. of Technology (DCAe); PhD Sydney, 1966. Res. Asst, MIT, 1956; Advanced Project Engr, Brit. Aerospace, 1957–59; Lectr, Sen. Lectr, Dept of Aeronautics, Univ. of Sydney, 1959–66; Lectr, Sen. Lectr, Dept of Aeronautics, Imperial Coll. of Sci. and Technol., 1966–72. Consultant to: ARC, 1975–81; MoD, 1980–; Nat. Agency for Finite Element Methods and Standards, 1983–; SERC, 1986–90; The Computer Bd, 1989–91; UFC (IT), 1991–; DTI (Aviation), 1991–. FRAeS 1987. *Publications*: Virtual Work in Structural Analysis, 1982; Mathematical Methods in Engineering, 1984; Finite Element Primer, 1986. *Recreations*: squash, photography, theatre. *Address*: Hedsor School House, Bourne End, Bucks SL8 5DP.

DAVIES, Prof. Graeme John, FEng 1988; DL; Chief Executive, Universities' Funding Council, since 1991; *b* 7 April 1937; *s* of Harry John Davies and Gladys Edna Davies (*née* Pratt); *m* 1959, Florence Isabelle Martin; one *s* one *d*. *Educ*: Mount Albert Grammar School, Auckland, NZ; Univ. of Auckland (BE, PhD); St Catharine's College, Cambridge (MA, ScD). FIM, FIMechE. Junior Lectr, Univ. of Auckland, 1960–62; University of Cambridge: TI Research Fellow, 1962–64; Univ. Demonstrator in Metallurgy, 1964–66; Lectr, 1966–77; Fellow of St Catharine's Coll., 1967–77 (Hon. Fellow 1989); Prof. of Metallurgy, Univ. of Sheffield, 1978–86; Vice Chancellor, Univ. of Liverpool, 1986–91. Visiting Professor: Brazil, 1976–77; Israel, 1978; Argentina, 1980; China, 1981; Hon. Prof., Zhejiang Univ., China, 1985. Mem., Merseyside Enterprise Forum, 1986–. Guardian, Sheffield Assay Office, 1983–86; Member Council: Inst. Metals, 1981–86; Sheffield Metallurgical and Engineering Assoc., 1978–86 (Pres., 1984–85); ACU, 1987–91. Trustee: Bluecoat Soc. of Arts, 1986–; Museums and Galls on Merseyside, 1987–. FRSA 1989; CBIM 1991. Freeman, City of London, 1987; Liveryman, Co. of Ironmongers, 1989. DL Merseyside, 1989. Rosenhain Medal, Inst. of Metals, 1982. *Publications*: Solidification and Casting, 1973; Texture and Properties of Materials, 1976; Solidificacao e Fundicao das Metais e Suas Ligas, 1978; Hot Working and Forming Processes, 1980; Superplasticity, 1981; Essential Metallurgy for Engineers, 1985; papers to learned jls. *Recreations*: cricket, birdwatching, golf. *Address*: Universities' Funding Council, Northavon House, Frenchay, Bristol BS16 1QY. *Clubs*: Athenæum; Athenæum (Liverpool).

DAVIES, Dame Gwen F.; *see* Ffrangcon-Davies.

DAVIES, (Gwilym) E(dnyfed) Hudson; *see* Davies, Ednyfed H.

DAVIES, Rev. Gwynne Henton; Principal, Regent's Park College, Oxford, 1958–72, Emeritus since 1973; *b* 19 Feb. 1906; *m* 1935, Annie Bronwen (*née* Williams), BA Wales; two *d.* *Educ:* Perse Sch., Cambridge; University College of South Wales, Cardiff (BD, MA); St Catherine's and Regent's Park Colls, Oxford Univ. (MLitt, MA); Marburg/Lahn, Germany. Minister West End Baptist Church, London, W6, 1935–38; Tutor Bristol Baptist Coll., 1938–51; special Lecturer in Hebrew, University of Bristol, 1948–51; (First) Prof. of Old Testament Studies, Faculty of Theology, Durham Univ., 1951–58, Dean of Faculty, 1956; Select Preacher to the Universities of Cambridge and Oxford. OT Editor, The Teachers' Commentary (revised 7th edn), 1955. Secretary, Society for Old Testament Study, 1946–62 (President, 1966); Vice-Pres., Baptist Union of GB and Ireland, 1970–71, Pres., 1971–72. OT Lecture, Pantyfedwen Foundn, 1975; Distinguished Visiting Professor: Meredith Coll., USA, 1978, 1979; William Jewell Coll., 1982, 1983. Vice Pres., Pembrokeshire History Soc., 1985–. Hon. DD: Glasgow, 1958; Stetson, 1965. *Publications:* (with A. B. Davies) The Story in Scripture, 1960; Exodus, 1967; Who's Who in the Bible, 1970; Deuteronomy, in Peake's Commentary on the Bible, rev. edn, 1962; 20 articles in The Interpreter's Bible Dictionary, 1962; The Ark in the Psalms, in Promise and Fulfilment (ed F. F. Bruce), 1963; essay in R. Goldman's Breakthrough, 1968; Genesis, in The Broadman Bible Commentary, 1969; Gerhard von Rad, in O.T. Theology in Contemporary Discussion (ed R. Laurin). *Address:* Headlands, Broad Haven, Haverfordwest, Dyfed SA62 3JP. *T:* Broad Haven (0437) 781339.

DAVIES, Handel, CB 1962; MSc; FEng; Hon. FRAeS; FAIAA; aeronautical engineering consultant; *m* 1942, Mary Graham Harris. *Educ:* Aberdare Grammar Sch.; University of Wales. FRAeS 1948, Hon. FRAeS 1982. Royal Aircraft Establishment and Ministry of Aircraft Production, 1936–47; Head of Aerodynamics Flight Division, RAE, 1948–52. Chief Superintendent, Aeroplane and Armament Experimental Establishment, Boscombe Down, 1952–55; Scientific Adviser to Air Ministry, 1955–56; Director-General, Scientific Research (Air), Ministry of Supply, 1957–59; Dep. Director, RAE, Farnborough, 1959–63. Dep. Controller of Aircraft, (R&D), Ministry of Aviation, 1963–67, Ministry of Technology, 1967–69. Tech. Dir, British Aircraft Corp., 1969–77. Pres., RAeS, 1977–78. Chm., Standing Conf. on Schools Sci. and Technology, 1978–82. Fellow, University Coll., Cardiff, 1981. Gold Medal, RAeS, 1974. Wilbur and Orville Wright Meml Lectr, 1979. *Publications:* papers in Reports and Memoranda of Aeronautical Research Council and in Journal of Royal Aeronautical Society. *Recreation:* sailing. *Address:* Keel Cottage, Woodham Road, Horsell, Woking, Surrey GU21 4DL. *T:* Woking (0483) 714192. *Club:* Royal Air Force Yacht (Hamble).

DAVIES, Harry, JP; DL; Member, Greater Manchester County Council, 1973–86 (Chairman, May 1984–85); *b* 5 March 1915; *s* of Herbert Jacob Davies and Mary Elizabeth Johnson; *m* 1941, Elsie Gore; three *d.* *Educ:* Bedford Methodist Primary School; Leigh Grammar School; Padgate Teacher Training College. 6th Royal Tank Regt, 1941–46. Dep. Head, Westleigh C of E School, 1958; Headmaster, Bedford Methodist School, 1964–77. Mem., Leigh Borough Council, 1959; Mayor, Borough of Leigh, 1971–72. JP Leigh, 1969; DL Greater Manchester, 1987. Silver Jubilee Medal, 1977. *Recreations:* gardening, bread baking, wine making. *Address:* 45 Edale Road, Leigh WN7 2BD. *T:* Leigh (0942) 672583.

DAVIES, Howard John; Controller, Audit Commission for Local Authorities and the National Health Service (formerly for Local Authorities) in England and Wales, since 1987; *b* 12 Feb. 1951; *s* of late Leslie Powell Davies and of Marjorie Davies; *m* 1984, Prudence Mary Keely; two *s.* *Educ:* Manchester Grammar Sch.; Memorial Univ., Newfoundland; Merton Coll., Oxford (MA History and Mod. Langs); Stanford Graduate Sch. of Business, USA (MS Management Science). Foreign Office, 1973–74; Private Sec. to HM Ambassador, Paris, 1974–76; HM Treasury, 1976–82; McKinsey & Co. Inc., 1982–87 (Special Adviser to Chancellor of the Exchequer, 1985–86). Dir, GKN plc, 1990–. Sen. Academic Fellow, Leicester Polytechnic, 1988 (Gov., 1988–). *Recreations:* cricket, writing for publication. *Address:* c/o Audit Commission, 1 Vincent Square, SW1P 2PN. *Clubs:* Barnes Common Cricket; Manchester City Supporters.

DAVIES, Rt. Rev. Howell Haydn; Vicar of St Jude's Parish, Wolverhampton, since 1987; *b* 18 Sept. 1927; *s* of Ivor Thomas Davies and Sarah Gladys Davies (*née* Thomas); *m* 1958, Jean Wylam (*née* King); three *s* three *d.* *Educ:* Birmingham. DipArch (Birm.) 1954; ARIBA 1955. Corporal Clerk (Gen. Duties) RAF, Mediterranean and Middle East, 1945–48. Assistant Architect, 1952–56. Deacon 1959, priest 1960; Curate, St Peter's Parish, Hereford, 1959–61; Missionary of Bible Churchmen's Missionary Soc. in Kenya, 1961–79; Archdeacon of Maseno North, 1971–74; Provost of Nairobi, 1974–79; Vicar of Woking, 1979–81; Bishop of Karamoja, Uganda, 1981–87. *Recreations:* walking, reading, d-i-y, building design. *Address:* St Jude's Vicarage, St Jude's Road, Wolverhampton, West Midlands WV6 0EB. *T:* Wolverhampton (0902) 753360.

DAVIES, Hugh Llewelyn; HM Diplomatic Service; Head of Far Eastern Department, Foreign and Commonwealth Office, since 1990; *b* 8 Nov. 1941; *s* of Vincent Davies (formerly ICS), OBE, and Rose (*née* Temple); *m* 1968, Virginia Ann Lucius; one *d* one *s.* *Educ:* Rugby School; Churchill College, Cambridge (Hons History degree). Joined Diplomatic Service, 1965; Chinese Language Studies, Hong Kong, 1966–68; Second Sec., Office of British Chargé d'Affaires, Peking, 1969–71; Far Eastern Dept, FCO, 1971–74; First Sec. (Econ.), Bonn, 1974–77; Head of Chancery, Singapore, 1977–79; Asst Head, Far Eastern Dept, FCO, 1979–82; on secondment, Barclays Bank International, 1982–83; Commercial Counsellor, Peking, 1984–87; Dep. British Permanent Rep., OECD, Paris, 1987–90. *Recreations:* watersports, sketching, tennis, gardens, living. *Address:* c/o Foreign and Commonwealth Office, SW1A 2AH.

See also J. M. Davies.

DAVIES, Humphrey; *see* Davies, Morgan Wynn Humphrey.

DAVIES, Hunter; *see* Davies, E. H.

DAVIES, Huw Humphreys; Director of Television, HTV Group, since 1989; *b* 4 Aug. 1940; *s* of William Davies and Harriet Jane Davies (*née* Humphreys); *m* 1966, Elizabeth Shân Harries; two *d.* *Educ:* Llangynog Primary School; Llandovery College; Penbroke College, Oxford. MA (LitHum) 1964. Director/Producer: Television Wales and West, 1964; HTV 1968; HTV Cymru/Wales: Asst Controller of Programmes, 1978; Controller of Programmes, 1979–81; Dir of Programmes, 1981–87; Chief Exec., 1987–91. Produced and directed many programmes and series in English and Welsh; latterly numerous plays and drama-documentaries. Chm., Regional Controllers, ITV, 1987–88. Mem., Gorsedd of Bards; Governor, Welsh Coll. of Music and Drama. *Recreations:* reading, swimming. *Address:* 2 Walston Close, Wenvoe, Cardiff CF5 6AS. *T:* Cardiff (0222) 593442.

DAVIES, Hywel; *see* Davies, D. H.

DAVIES, Ian Hewitt, TD; **His Honour Judge Ian Davies;** a Circuit Judge, since 1986; *b* 13 May 1931; *s* of late Rev. J. R. Davies; *m* 1962, Molly Cecilia Vaughan Vaughan. *Educ:* Kingswood Sch.; St John's Coll., Cambridge (MA). Nat. Service, commnd KOYLI; served with 3rd Bn Parachute Regt, 1950–51; TA, 1952–71 (Lt-Col). Called to the Bar, Inner Temple, 1958. *Address:* c/o Crown Court, Middlesex Guildhall, SW1. *Clubs:* Boodle's, Lansdowne, MCC, Hurlingham.

DAVIES, Ian Leonard, CB 1983; MA; CEng, FIEE; Director, Admiralty Underwater Weapons Establishment, 1975–84; *b* 2 June 1924; *s* of late H. Leonard Davies and Mrs J. D. Davies; *m* 1951, Hilary Dawson, *d* of late Rear-Adm. Sir Oswald Henry Dawson, KBE; two *s* two *d.* *Educ:* Barry County Sch.; St John's Coll., Cambridge. Mechanical Sciences Tripos, 1944, and Mathematical Tripos Pt 2, 1949. Telecommunications Research Estabt, 1944; Blind Landing Experimental Unit, 1946. TRE (later the Royal Radar Establishment), 1949–69; Imperial Defence Coll., 1970; Asst Chief Scientific Adviser (Projects), MoD, 1971–72; Dep. Controller Electronics, 1973, Dep. Controller Air Systems (D), 1973–75, MoD(PE). Mem. Council, IEE, 1974–77 (Chm., Electronics Div. Bd, 1975–76). *Publications:* papers on information theory, radar, and lasers. *Recreations:* music, walking. *Address:* 37 Bowleaze Coveway, Preston, Weymouth, Dorset DT3 6PL. *T:* Weymouth (0305) 832206. *Club:* Athenæum.

DAVIES, Ven. Ivor Gordon; Archdeacon Emeritus; *b* 21 July 1917; *m* 1946, Kristine Wiley, SRN; one *s* two *d.* *Educ:* University of Wales (BA); Oxford; London (BD). Deacon 1941, Priest 1942, Llandaff; Curate of St Paul's, Cardiff, 1941–44; CF 1944–47; Curate of St John the Baptist, Felixstowe, 1947–49; Vicar of St Thomas', Ipswich, 1950–57; Residentiary Canon of Southwark Cathedral and Diocesan Missioner, 1957–72; Dean of Lewisham, 1970–72; Archdeacon of Lewisham, 1972–85. *Address:* 10 Garfield Road, Felixstowe, Suffolk. *T:* Felixstowe (0394) 271546.

DAVIES, Jack Gale Wilmot, OBE 1946; Executive Director of the Bank of England, 1969–76; *b* 10 Sept. 1911; *s* of Langford George Davies, MD, BCh, MRCS, LRCP, and Lily Barnes Davies; *m* 1949, Georgette O'Dell (*née* Vanson); one *s.* *Educ:* Tonbridge Sch.; St John's Coll., Cambridge. Nat. Institute of Industrial Psychol., 1935–39. Regimental service, The Middlesex Regt, 1940–42; Chief Psychologist, Directorate for Selection of Personnel, War Office, 1942–46. Bureau of Personnel, UN Secretariat, 1946–48; Secretariat, Human Factors Panel, Cttee on Industrial Productivity, 1948–49; Staff Training Section, UN Secretariat, 1950–52; Secretary, Cambridge Univ. Appointments Board, 1952–68; Asst to the Governor, Bank of England, 1968. Director: Portals Holdings Ltd, 1976–83; Portals Water Treatment Ltd, 1983–90. FBPsS 1946. Fellow St John's Coll., Cambridge, 1959–68; Dep. Pro-Chancellor, City Univ., 1984–89. Hon. DLitt City, 1976. *Publications:* articles in Occupational Psychology and similar journals. *Recreations:* cricket, golf, music. *Address:* 31 Wingate Way, Cambridge. *Clubs:* Royal Automobile, MCC (Pres., 1985–86).

DAVIES, Rev. Jacob Arthur Christian; Assistant Director-General, Regional Representative for Africa, FAO, since 1982; *b* 24 May 1925; *s* of Jacob S. Davies and Christiana; *m* Sylvia Onikeh Cole; two *s* two *d.* *Educ:* Univ. of Reading (BSc 1950); Selwyn Coll., Cambridge; Imperial Coll. of Tropical Agriculture. Permanent Secretary, Min. of Agriculture and Natural Resources, Sierra Leone, 1961–63; Chief Agriculturist, 1962–67; Project Co-manager, UNDP, FAO, 1967–69; Chm., Public Service Commn, 1969–71; Ambassador to USA, 1971–72; High Comr for Sierra Leone in London, 1972–74; Non-resident Ambassador to Denmark, Sweden and Norway, 1972–74; Dep. Dir, Agricl Ops Div., 1974–76, Dir, Personnel Div., 1976–82, FAO. *Recreations:* philately, sports. *Address:* FAO Regional Office for Africa, PO Box 1628, Accra, Ghana.

DAVIES, (James) Brian Meredith, MD, DPH, FFCM; Director of Social Services, City of Liverpool, 1971–81; Hon. Lecturer in (Preventive) Paediatrics, University of Liverpool, 1964–84; *b* 27 Jan. 1920; *s* of late Dr G. Meredith Davies and Caroline Meredith Davies; *m* 1944, Charlotte (*née* Pillar); three *s.* *Educ:* Bedford Sch.; Medical Sch., St Mary's Hosp., London Univ. MB, BS (London) 1943 MD (London) 1948, DPH 1948, MFCM 1972, FFCM 1974. Various hosp. appts. Served War, RAMC, Captain, 1944–47. Asst MOH, Lancashire CC, 1948–50; Dep. MOH, City of Oxford, 1950–53; Clin. Asst (infectious Diseases), United Oxford Hosps, 1950–53; Dep. MOH, 1953–69, Dir of Personal Health and Social Services, 1969–71, City of Liverpool; pt-time Lectr in Public Health, Liverpool Univ., 1953–71. Chm., Liverpool div., BMA, 1958–59; Council of Europe Fellowship, to study Elderly: in Finland, Sweden, Norway and Denmark, 1964 (report awarded special prize); Mem. Public Health Laboratory Service Bd, 1966–71. Teaching Gp of Soc. of Community Med. (Sec. of Gp, 1958–72, Pres. Gp, 1972–73). Member: Personal Social Services Council, 1978–80; Mental Health Review Tribunal, Mersey Area, 1982–. Governor, Occupational Therapy Coll., Huyton, Liverpool, 1969–85; Dir of MERIT (Merseyside Industrial Therapy Services Ltd), 1970–75; Mem. Council, Queen's Inst. of District Nursing, 1971–78; Assoc. of Dirs of Social Services: Chm., NW Br., 1971–73; Mem. Exec. Council, 1973–78; Pres. 1976–77; Mem. Exec. Cttee of Central Council for the Disabled, 1972–76; Adviser to Social Services Cttee of Assoc. of Metropolitan Authorities, 1974–81; Member: RCP Cttee on Rheumatism and Rehabilitation, 1974–83; DES Cttee of Enquiry into Special Educn for Disabled Children, 1975–78; Exec. Cttee, Liverpool Personal Services Soc., 1973–81; Adv. Panel Inf. Service, Disabled Living Foundn, 1979–81; UK Steering Cttee, Internat. Year for the Disabled, 1979–80; Jt Cttee on Mobility of Blind and Partially Sighted People, 1980–81; Exec. Cttee, N Regional Assoc. for the Blind, 1980–81. Vice Pres., MIND Appeal, 1978–79. Christopher Kershaw Meml Lectr, London, 1984. Pres., Merseyside Ski Club, 1970–77. Mem. Council, Prospect Hall Coll., 1973–77; Chm., Bd of Governors, William Rathbone Staff Coll., Liverpool, 1961–75. *Publications:* Community Health and Social Services, 1965, 5th edn 1991; Community Health, Preventive Medicine and Social Services, 1966, 6th edn 1992; (contrib.) Going Home (a Guide for helping the patient on leaving hospital), 1981; The Disabled Child and Adult, 1982; (contrib.) Rehabilitation: a practical guide to the management of physical disability in adults, 1988; numerous papers on Public Health, Physically and Mentally Handicapped and various social services, in scientific and other jls. *Recreations:* skiing, golf, fishing, gardening, music. *Address:* Tree Tops, Church Road, Thornton Hough, Wirral, Merseyside. *T:* 051–336 3435. *Clubs:* Royal Over-Seas League; Bromborough Golf; Holyhead Golf.

DAVIES, Janet Mary H.; *see* Hewlett-Davies.

DAVIES, Dame Jean; *see* Lancaster, Dame J.

DAVIES, John; *see* Davies, L. J.

DAVIES, John Alun Emlyn; retired 1977; *b* 4 May 1909; *s* of Robert Emlyn and Mary Davies; *m* 1941, Elizabeth Boshier; three *s.* *Educ:* Ruabon Grammar Sch.; Trinity Coll., Cambridge (Scholar). BA 1st cl. Pts I and II, History Tripos, MA 1984. Called to Bar, Lincoln's Inn, 1936. Served War of 1939–45: DAA&QMG 2nd Parachute Bde, 1943; DAAG 1st Airborne Div., 1944. Joined BoT, 1946; Asst Solicitor, 1963; Principal Asst Solicitor, DTI, 1968–72; Asst Solicitor, Law Commn, 1972–74; part-time Asst, Law Commn, 1974–77. Asst Sec. to Jenkins Cttee on Company Law, 1959–62. *Recreations:* gardening, walking. *Address:* 29 Crescent Road, Sidcup, Kent DA15 7HN. *T:* 081–300 1421. *Club:* Reform.

DAVIES, Prof. John Brian, FEng 1988; FIEE; Professor of Electrical Engineering, University College London, since 1985; *b* 2 May 1932; *s* of John Kendrick Davies and

Agnes Ada Davies; *m* 1956, Shirley June (*née* Abrahart); one *s* two *d*. *Educ:* Jesus Coll., Cambridge (MA); Univ. of London (MSc, PhD, DSc Eng). MIEEE. Research Engineer, Mullard Res. Labs, Redhill, 1955–63; Lectr, Dept of Electrical Engineering, Univ. of Sheffield, 1963; Sen. Lectr 1967, Reader 1970–85, Dean of Engrg, 1989–91, University College London. Vis. Scientist, Nat. Bureau of Standards, Boulder, Colo, 1971–72; Visitor, Univ. of Oxford, 1983; Vis. Prof., Univ. of Colorado, 1988–89. *Publications:* Electromagnetic Theory, vol. 2, 1972; (contrib.) Numerical Techniques for Microwave and Millimeter Wave Passive Structures, 1989. *Recreations:* fell walking, music, ski-ing. *Address:* 14 Gaveston Drive, Berkhamsted, Herts HP4 1JE. *T:* Berkhamsted (0442) 864954.

DAVIES, Rt. Rev. John Dudley; *see* Shrewsbury, Bishop Suffragan of.

DAVIES, John Duncan, OBE 1984; DSc, PhD; Director, Polytechnic of Wales, since 1978; *b* 19 March 1929; *s* of Ioan and Gertrude Davies; *m* 1949, Barbara, *d* of Ivor and Alice Morgan; three *d*. *Educ:* Pontardawe School; Treforest School of Mines. BSc, MSc, PhD, DSc, Univ. of London. Junior Engineer, Consulting Engineers, 1949; Site Engineer, Cleveland Bridge Co., 1950–54; Royal Engineers, 1952–53; Design Engineer, Local Authority, 1955–56; Asst Lectr, Manchester Univ., 1957–58; University College, Swansea: Lecturer, 1959; Senior Lecturer, 1965; Reader, 1968; Professor of Civil Engineering, 1971–76; Dean, 1974–76; Principal, West Glamorgan Inst. of Higher Education, 1976–77. Member: Open University Delegacy, 1978–83; OU Cttee, 1987–90; Manpower Services Cttee (Wales), 1980–83; Wales Adv. Bd for Public Sector Higher Educn, 1982–83, 1986–89; Council, CNAA, 1985–91. *Publications:* contribs to Structural Mechanics. *Address:* Polytechnic of Wales, Treforest, Pontypridd, Mid Glamorgan CF37 1DL. *T:* Pontypridd (0443) 405133.

DAVIES, John Henry Vaughan, CB 1981; Deputy Secretary, Ministry of Agriculture, Fisheries and Food, 1979–81; *b* 15 Sept. 1921; *s* of late Rev. James Henry Davies and Ethel Sarah Davies; *m* 1st, 1950, Dorothy Rosa Mary Levy (marr. diss.); 2nd, 1959, Claire Daphne Bates (marr. diss.); one *d*; 3rd, 1971, Barbara Ann, *o d* of late David L. Davies, Portland, Oregon. *Educ:* Monkton Combe Sch.; Worcester Coll., Oxford (MA). Served Royal Air Force, FO, 1942–46. Entered Ministry of Agriculture and Fisheries as Asst Principal, 1947; Principal, 1951; Asst Sec., 1964; Under Sec., 1970. Chairman, Joint FAO/WHO Codex Alimentarius Commn, 1968–70. *Publications:* contributor to The Country Seat, 1970; articles on architecture. *Recreations:* reading, architecture. *Address:* 17 Cherrywood Drive, SW15 6DS. *T:* 081–789 1529.

DAVIES, Rev. Canon John Howard; Director of Theological and Religious Studies, University of Southampton, since 1981; Canon Theologian of Winchester, since 1981; *b* 19 Feb. 1929; *s* of Jabez Howard and Sarah Violet Davies; *m* 1956, Ina Mary (*d* 1985), *d* of Stanley William and Olive Mary Bubb; three *s* (and one *s* decd). *Educ:* Southall Grammar Sch.; St John's Coll., Cambridge (MA); Westcott House, Cambridge; Univ. of Nottingham (BD); FRCO 1952. Ordained deacon, 1955, priest 1956. Succentor of Derby Cathedral, 1955; Chaplain of Westcott House, 1958; Lectr in Theology, Univ. of Southampton, 1963, Sen. Lectr 1974. *Publication:* A Letter to Hebrews, 1967. *Recreations:* music, architecture, the countryside. *Address:* 13 Glen Eyre Road, Southampton SO2 3GA. *T:* Southampton (0703) 679359.

DAVIES, John Howard Gay; Editorial Director, Thomson Regional Newspapers Ltd, 1972–82; *b* 17 Jan. 1923; *er s* of late E. E. Davies, Nicholaston Hall, Gower, Glamorgan; *m* 1st, 1948, Eira Morgan (marr. dissolved, 1953); 2nd, 1955, Betty Walmsley; one *s*. *Educ:* Bromsgrove Sch.; Wadham Coll., Oxford. Welsh Guards, 1942–46 (despatches). Western Mail, 1950–52; Daily Telegraph, 1952–55; Deputy Editor, Western Mail, 1955–58; an Assistant Editor, Sunday Times, 1958–62; Exec. Assistant to Editorial Director, Thomson Newspapers Ltd, 1962–64; Editor, Western Mail, 1964, 1965. *Address:* 46 Coalecroft Road, SW15 6LP.

DAVIES, John Irfon; MBE (mil.) 1963; Under Secretary, Welsh Office, 1985–90, retired; Director (Wales), Sallingbury Casey Ltd; *b* 8 June 1930; *s* of Thomas M. Davies and late Mary M. Davies (*née* Harris); *m* 1950, Jean Marion Anderson; one *d*. *Educ:* Stanley School; Croydon Polytechnic. psc, awc; Specialist Navigator course. Joined RAF, 1948, commissioned 1950; No 13 Sqn, MEAF, 1951; HQ 205 Gp, 1952; No 24 Sqn, 1953–54; staff and flying appts, 1954–66; Chief Navigation Instructor, Cranwell, 1967; OC Flying, Muharraq, 1967–69; MoD, 1970–72; Cabinet Office, 1972–74; Principal, Welsh Office, 1974, Asst Sec., 1978. Mem., GMC. *Recreations:* golf, piano, fishing, books. *Address:* Friston, 15 Windsor Road, Radyr, Cardiff CF4 8BQ. *T:* Cardiff (0222) 842617. *Clubs:* Royal Air Force, Farmers'; Radyr Golf.

DAVIES, Prof. John Kenyon, MA, DPhil; FSA; FBA 1985; Rathbone Professor of Ancient History and Classical Archaeology, University of Liverpool, since 1977; *b* 19 Sept. 1937; *s* of Harold Edward Davies and Clarice Theresa (*née* Woodburn); *m* 1st, 1962, Anna Elbina Morpurgo (*see* Anna Elbina Davies) (marr. diss. 1978); 2nd, 1978, Nicola Jane, *d* of Dr and Mrs R. M. S. Perrin; one *s* one *d*. *Educ:* Manchester Grammar Sch.; Wadham Coll., Oxford (BA 1959; MA 1962; DPhil 1966). FSA 1986. Harmsworth Sen. Scholar, Merton Coll., Oxford, 1960–61 and 1962–63; Jun. Fellow, Center for Hellenic Studies, Washington, DC, 1961–62; Dyson Jun. Res. Fellow, Balliol Coll., Oxford, 1963–65; Lectr in Ancient History, Univ. of St Andrews, 1965–68; Fellow and Tutor in Ancient History, Oriel Coll., Oxford, 1968–77; Pro-Vice-Chancellor, Univ. of Liverpool, 1986–90. Vis. Lectr, Univ. of Pennsylvania, 1971. Chairman: St Patrick's Isle (IOM) Archaeological Trust Ltd, 1982–86; NW Archaeol Trust, 1982–. FRSA. Editor: Jl of Hellenic Studies, 1972–77; Archaeol Reports, 1972–74. *Publications:* Athenian Propertied Families 600–300 BC, 1971; Democracy and Classical Greece, 1978 (Spanish trans. 1981, German and Italian trans. 1983); Wealth and the Power of Wealth in Classical Athens, 1981; (ed with L. Foxhall) The Trojan War: its historicity and context, 1984; articles and reviews in learned jls. *Recreation:* choral singing. *Address:* 20 North Road, Grassendale Park, Liverpool L19 0LR. *T:* 051–427 2126.

DAVIES, John Michael; Clerk Assistant, and Clerk of Public Bills, House of Lords, since 1991; *b* 2 Aug. 1940; *s* of Vincent Ellis Davies and Rose Trench (*née* Temple); *m* 1971, Amanda Mary Atkinson, JP; two *s* one *d*. *Educ:* The King's Sch., Canterbury; Peterhouse, Cambridge. Joined Parliament Office, House of Lords, 1964; seconded to Civil Service Dept as Private Sec. to Leader of House of Lords and Govt Chief Whip, 1971–74; Establishment Officer and Sec. to Chm. of Cttees, 1974–83; Principal Clerk, Overseas and European Office, H of L, 1983–85; Principal Clerk, Private Bill and Overseas Offices and Examiner of Petitions for Private Bills, H of L, 1985–88; Reading Clerk and Clerk of Public Bills, H of L, 1988–90. Secretary: Soc. of Clerks-at-the-Table in Commonwealth Parlts, and Jt Editor, The Table, 1967–83; Statute Law Cttee, 1974–83. *Address:* 26 Northchurch Terrace, N1 4EG.

See also H. L. Davies.

DAVIES, (John) Quentin; MP (C) Stamford and Spalding, since 1987; *b* 29 May 1944; *e s* of Dr Michael Ivor Davies and Thelma Davies (*née* Butler), Oxford; *m* 1983, Chantal, *e d* of Lt-Col R. L. C. Tamplin, 17/21 Lancers, Military Kt of Windsor, and Claudine Tamplin (*née* Pleis); two *s*. *Educ:* Dragon Sch.; Leighton Park (exhibnr); Gonville and Caius Coll., Cambridge (Open Scholar; BA Hist. Tripos 1st cl. Hons 1966); Harvard Univ. (Frank Know Fellow, 1966–67). HM Diplomatic Service, 1967; 3rd Sec., FCO, 1967–69; 2nd Sec., Moscow, 1969–72; 1st Sec., FCO, 1973–74. Morgan Grenfell & Co.: Manager, later Asst Dir, 1974–78; Rep. in France, later Dir-Gen. and Pres., Morgan Grenfell France SA, 1978–81; Director, 1981–87; Consultant, 1987–. Dir, Dewe Rogerson International, 1987–. Contested (C) Birmingham, Ladywood, Aug. 1977. Parliamentary Private Secretary: to Minister of State for Educn, 1988–90; to Minister of State, Home Office, 1990–. Chm., City in Europe Cttee, 1975. Liveryman, Goldsmiths' Co. Freeman, City of London. *Recreations:* reading, walking, riding, ski-ing, travel, playing bad tennis, looking at art and architecture. *Address:* House of Commons, SW1A 0AA. *Clubs:* Beefsteak, Travellers', Hurlingham; Constitutional (Spalding); South Lincolnshire Conservative (Bourne); Travellers' (Paris).

DAVIES, J(ohn) R(obert) Lloyd, CMG 1953; *b* 24 March 1913; *o s* of late J. R. and Mrs Davies, Muswell Hill; *m* 1st, 1943, Margery (*née* McClelland), Nottingham (*d* 1978); one *s* one *d*; 2nd, 1982, Grace, *widow* of Frederick Reynolds, Bethesda, Md, USA. *Educ:* Highgate Sch.; Oriel Coll., Oxford. Served War of 1939–45: Royal Navy; Lieut RNVR; Asst Sec., Dept of Employment; Labour Counsellor, Paris and Washington, FCO. Part-time Teacher, Working Men's Coll., London, 1970–. *Recreations:* key-board music, reading. *Address:* 59 Elm Park Court, Pinner, Middlesex. *Club:* United Oxford & Cambridge University.

DAVIES, John Thomas, FCIB; Assistant Chief Executive, since 1991, Director since 1990, Lloyds Bank plc; *b* 9 Feb. 1933; *s* of Joseph Robert and Dorothy Mary Davies; *m* 1957, Margaret Ann Johnson; two *s* three *d*. *Educ:* King Edward's Grammar Sch., Camp Hill, Birmingham. FCIB. Joined Lloyds Bank, 1949; served RAF, 1951–53; Lloyds Bank: Manager of branches, 1963–78; Gen. Management, 1978–89; Dir, Internat. Banking Div., 1989–91. *Recreations:* gardening, walking, reading. *Address:* Lloyds Bank plc, 71 Lombard Street, EC3P 3BS.

DAVIES, His Honour Joseph Marie, QC 1962; a Circuit Judge (formerly Judge of County Courts), 1971–91; *b* 13 Jan. 1916; *s* of Joseph and Mary Davies, St Helen's; *m* 1948, Eileen Mary (*née* Dromgoole); two *s* two *d*. *Educ:* Stonyhurst Coll.; Liverpool Univ. Called to Bar, Gray's Inn, Nov. 1938; practice in Liverpool. Recorder of Birmingham, 1970–71; Cumberland Co. QS: Dep. Chm., 1956–63, 1970–71; Chm., 1963–70. Served War of 1939–45; The King's Regt, Nov. 1939–Dec. 1941; RIASC and Staff Allied Land Forces, SE Asia, 1942–46. *Address:* 4 Elm Grove, Eccleston Park, Prescot, Lancs. *T:* 051–426 5415. *Clubs:* Athenæum (Liverpool); Cumberland County.

DAVIES, Keith Laurence M.; *see* Maitland Davies.

DAVIES, Sir Lancelot Richard B.; *see* Bell Davies.

DAVIES, (Lewis) John, QC 1967; **His Honour Judge John Davies;** a Circuit Judge (Official Referee), since 1984; *b* 15 April 1921; *s* of William Davies, JP, and Esther Davies; *m* 1956, Janet Mary Morris; one *s* two *d*. *Educ:* Pontardawe Grammar Sch.; University College of Wales, Aberystwyth; Trinity Hall (Common Law Prizeman, 1943; Scholar, 1943–44), Cambridge. LLB Wales 1942 (1st cl.); BA Cantab (1st cl.); LLB Cantab (1st cl.). Asst Principal, HM Treasury, 1945–46; Senior Law Lecturer, Leeds Univ., 1946–48; Administrative Asst, British Petroleum, 1949–52. Called to the Bar, Middle Temple, 1948, Bencher, 1973; a Recorder, 1974–84. Mem., Bar Council, 1969–71; Mem., Senate, 1976–78. Mem., Council of Legal Educn, 1976–79. Inspector, DoT, 1977. Mem., Gorsedd, 1986–. *Recreations:* gardening, golf. *Address:* Old Manor Cottage, 24 Park Road, Teddington, Mddx. *T:* 081–977 3975. *Club:* Travellers'.

DAVIES, Lewis Mervyn, CMG 1966; CBE 1984 (OBE 1962); HM Overseas Civil Service, retired; *b* 5 Dec. 1922; *s* of late Rev. Canon L. C. Davies; *m* 1st, 1950, Ione Podger (*d* 1973); one *s*; 2nd, 1975, Mona A. Birley; two step *s*. *Educ:* St Edward's Sch., Oxford. Served with Fleet Air Arm, 1941–46: Lieut A, RNVR. District Commissioner, Gold Coast, 1948; Western Pacific: Senior Asst Secretary, 1956–62; Financial Secretary, 1962–65; Chief Secretary, 1965–70; Deputy Governor, Bahamas, 1970–73; Secretary for Security, Hong Kong, 1973–82; Secretary (Gen. Duties), Hong Kong, 1983–85. Lay Canon, Cathedral Church of St Barnabas, Honiara, Solomon Islands, 1965–70. Commandeur de l'Ordre National du Mérite, 1966. *Recreations:* sailing, tennis. *Address:* Apartado 123, Felanitx, Mallorca 07200, Spain. *T:* Mallorca 827109. *Clubs:* Oriental, Commonwealth Trust; Vall D'or Golf (Mallorca); Bosham Sailing, Royal Hong Kong Yacht.

DAVIES, Lloyd; *see* Davies, J. R. L.

DAVIES, Col Lucy Myfanwy, CBE 1968 (OBE 1962); Deputy Controller Commandant, WRAC, 1967–77; *b* 8 April 1913; *d* of late Col A. M. O. Anwyl-Passingham, CBE, DL, JP, and late Margaret Anwyl-Passingham; *m* 1955, Major D. W. Davies, TD, RAMC (*d* 1959); no *c*. *Educ:* Francis Holland Graham Street Sch. Driver FANY, 1939; commnd ATS, 1941; served in Egypt, 1945–48; Asst Director, WRAC Middle East (Cyprus), 1957–59; Comdt WRAC Depot, 1961–64; Dep. Director WRAC, 1964–68; retired, 1968. An underwriting Member of Lloyd's, 1971–. OStJ 1938. *Recreations:* travel, racing, reading. *Address:* 6 Elm Place, SW7 3QH. *T:* 071–373 5731. *Club:* Lingfield Park.

DAVIES, Marcus John A.; *see* Anwyl-Davies.

DAVIES, Meredith; *see* Davies, Albert Meredith.

DAVIES, Hon. Sir Mervyn; *see* Davies, Hon. Sir D. H. M.

DAVIES, Hon. Sir Michael; *see* Davies, Hon. Sir A. W. M.

DAVIES, Michael; *see* Davies, A. M.

DAVIES, Prof. (Morgan Wynn) Humphrey, LLM, DSc; CEng, FIEE; FCGI; Professor of Electrical Engineering, Queen Mary College, University of London, 1956–79, now Emeritus (Fellow of the College, 1984); *b* 26 Dec. 1911; *s* of late Richard Humphrey Davies, CB; *m* 1944, Gwendolen Enid, *d* of late Canon Douglas Edward Morton, Camborne, Cornwall; one *s*. *Educ:* Westminster Sch.; University College of N Wales, Bangor; Charlottenburg Technische Hochschule, Berlin. Grad. Apprentice with Metropolitan-Vickers, 1933; Lecturer in Electrical Engineering, University of Wales, 1935–42; Commonwealth Fellow, Mass Inst. of Technol., 1938–39; Education Officer to Instn of Electrical Engineers, 1944–47; Lecturer, 1947, and University Reader, 1952, in Electrical Engineering, Imperial Coll., University of London, 1947–56; Dean of Engrg, Univ. of London, 1976–79. Member: Council, IEE, 1948–51, 1958–61 (Chm., Science and Gen. Div. 1964–65). Council, City & Guilds of London Inst., 1952–62; Engineering Adv. Cttee, BBC, 1965–71; Computer Bd for Univs and Res. Councils, 1968–71; Council, University Coll. of N Wales, Bangor, 1976– (Chm., Finance and GP Cttee, 1981–); Chm., Bd of Univ. of London Computer Centre, 1968–79. Hon. DSc Wales, 1985. *Publications:* Power System Analysis (with J. R. Mortlock), 1952; papers in Proc. of

Instn of Electrical Engineers. *Recreation:* travel. *Address:* Church Bank, Beaumaris, Anglesey LL58 8AB. *Club:* Athenæum.

DAVIES, Neil; *see* Davies, W. M. N.

DAVIES, Nigel; *see* Davies, Claude N. B.

DAVIES, Rev. Noel Anthony; General Secretary, Cytun, Churches Together in Wales, since 1990; *b* 26 Dec. 1942; *s* of late Rev. Ronald Anthony Davies and of Anne Davies; *m* 1968, Patricia Barter. *Educ:* UCNW, Bangor (BSc Chem. and Biochem.); Mansfield College, Oxford (BA Theol.). Ordained, 1968; Minister, Bryn Seion Welsh Congregational Church, Glanaman, 1968; Gen. Sec., Council of Churches for Wales and Commn of Covenanted Churches in Wales, 1977. Chm., Union of Welsh Independents (Congregational) Council, 1990. *Publications:* articles in ecumenical jls and Welsh language items. *Recreations:* classical music and hi-fi, gardening, West Highland White terriers, oriental cookery. *Address:* First Floor, 21 St Helens Road, Swansea SA1 4AP. *T:* (office) Swansea (0792) 460876.

DAVIES, (Norah) Olwen, MA; Headmistress, St Swithun's School, Winchester, 1973–86; *b* 21 March 1926; *d* of late Rev. and Mrs E. A. Davies. *Educ:* Tregaron County Sch.; Walthamstow Hall, Sevenoaks; Edinburgh Univ. (MA). DipEd Oxon. Staff of Girls' Remand Home, Essex, 1948–50; Russell Hill Sch., Purley, 1950–53; Woodford House, NZ, 1953–57 (Dep. Headmistress); Westonbirt Sch., 1957–65; Headmistress, St Mary's Hall, Brighton, 1965–73. Pres., Girls' Schools Association, 1981–82. Governor: Hurstpierpoint Coll.; Tormead Sch., Guildford; St John's Special Sch., Brighton; St Michael's Sch., Petworth; Godolphin Sch., Salisbury; St Christopher's Sch., Farnham; Lord Mayor Treloar Coll., Alton. *Address:* 28 Arle Gardens, Alresford, Hants.

DAVIES, Col Norman Thomas, MBE 1970; JP; Registrar, General Dental Council, since 1981; *b* 2 May 1933; *s* of late Edward Ernest Davies and of Elsie Davies (*née* Scott); *m* 1961, Penelope Mary, *e d* of Peter Graeme Agnew, *qv*; one *s* one *d*. *Educ:* Holywell; RMA, Sandhurst; Open Univ. (BA 1979). Commnd RA, 1954; Regtl and Staff Appts, Malaya, Germany and UK, 1954–64; ptsc 1966; psc 1967; Mil. Asst to C of S Northern Army Gp, 1968–69; Commanded C Bty RHA and 2IC 3RHA, 1970–72; GSOI (DS), Staff Coll., Camberley, and Canadian Land Forces Comd and Staff Coll., 1972–74; Commanded 4 Field Regt, RA, 1975–77; Mil. Dir of Studies, RMCS, Shrivenham, 1977–80. Mem., EEC Adv. Cttee on the Training of Dental Practitioners, 1983–. Hon. Mem., BDA, 1990. JP Hants, 1984. *Recreations:* golf, gardening, wine. *Address:* Lowfields Cottage, London Road, Hartley Wintney, Hants RG27 8HY. *T:* Hartley Wintney (025126) 3303. *Club:* Royal Society of Medicine.

DAVIES, Olwen; *see* Davies, N. O.

DAVIES, Sir Oswald, Kt 1984; CBE 1973; DCM 1944; JP; Director, AMEC plc (holding company of Fairclough Construction Group and William Press Group), since 1982 (Chairman, 1982–84); *b* 23 June 1920; *s* of George Warham Davies and Margaret (*née* Hinton); *m* 1942, Joyce Eaton; one *s* one *d*. *Educ:* Central Schs, Sale; Manchester Coll. of Technology. FIHT, FCIOB, FFB; CBIM; FRGS; FRSA. Served War of 1939–45: Sapper, bomb disposal squad, RE, Europe and ME, from 1940 (DCM (ME) 1944); returned to Europe, where involved with his unit in clearance of waterways, port, docks and bridge reconstruction. Dir, 1948–, Jt Man. Dir, 1951, Chm., 1965–83, Fairclough Construction Group plc (formerly Leonard Fairclough Ltd). Dir, Fairport Engrg Ltd. JP 1969. *Recreations:* gardening, Rugby football, sport. *Address:* (office) Sandiway House, Northwich, Cheshire CW8 2YA. *T:* Northwich (0606) 883885.

DAVIES, Patrick Taylor, CMG 1978; OBE 1967; HM Overseas Civil Service, retired; *b* 10 Aug. 1927; *s* of Andrew Taylor Davies and Olive Kathleen Mary Davies; *m* 1959, Marjorie Eileen (*née* Wilkinson); two *d*. *Educ:* Shrewsbury Sch.; St John's Coll., Cambridge (BA); Trinity Coll., Oxford. Lieut, RA, Nigeria, 1945–48. Colonial Admin. Service, Nigeria, 1952; Permanent Sec., Kano State, 1970; Chief Inspector, Area Courts, Kano State, 1972–79. *Address:* Rose Cottage, Childs Ercall, Salop TF9 2DB. *T:* Childs Ercall (095278) 255.

DAVIES, (Percy) Douglas, CB 1981; *b* 17 Sept. 1921; *s* of late Mr and Mrs Thomas Davies; *m* 1947, Renée Margaret Billings; one *s* one *d*. *Educ:* Liverpool Collegiate School; Open Univ. (BA 1989). Clerical Officer, Ministry of Transport, 1938; served Royal Armoured Corps, 1941–46; Chief Executive Officer, Min. of Transport, 1963; Asst Secretary, 1966; Principal Establishment Officer, Under Secretary, Property Services Agency, Dept of the Environment, 1972–81. Chm., Council of Management, London Hostels Assoc., 1983–. *Recreations:* gardening, making things work. *Address:* 37 Byron Avenue, Coulsdon, Surrey CR5 2JS. *T:* 081–660 2789.

DAVIES, Peter; *see* Davies, R. P. H.

DAVIES, Peter Douglas Royston; HM Diplomatic Service; Consul-General, Toronto, and Director-General of Trade Promotion in Canada, since 1991; *b* 29 Nov. 1936; *e s* of Douglas and Edna Davies; *m* 1967, Elizabeth Mary Lovett Williams; one *s* two *d*. *Educ:* Brockenhurst County High Sch.; LSE (BSc(Econ)). Joined HM Diplomatic Service, 1964; FO, 1964–66; Second Sec., Nicosia, 1966–67; FO, 1967–68; First Sec., Budapest, 1968–71; FCO, 1971–74; Consul (Commercial), Rio de Janeiro, 1974–78; Counsellor (Commercial): The Hague, 1978–82; Kuala Lumpur, 1982–83; Dep. High Comr, Kuala Lumpur, 1983–85; RCDS 1986; Head of Arms Control and Disarmament Dept, FCO, 1987–91. *Address:* c/o Foreign and Commonwealth Office, SW1A 2AH.

DAVIES, Peter George; Director General, Carroll Institute, since 1989; *b* 7 April 1927; *s* of George Llewellyn Davies and Alicia (*née* Galloway); *m* 1952, Norma Joyce Brown; one *s* two *d*. *Educ:* London School of Economics and Political Science. BSc Econ, 1st Class Hons 1948. Editorial Asst, News Chronicle, 1950–53; Deputy City Editor, The Times, 1953–55; HM Treasury, 1955; Asst Sec., Fiscal Policy Group, 1975–78; Press Sec. to Chancellor of the Exchequer and Head of Information, 1978–80; Under Secretary 1980; seconded to NEDO as Sec. to NEDC and Administrative Dir, 1980–82. Fellow Commoner, Downing College, Cambridge, 1982–83. Dir Gen., Nat. Assoc. of British and Irish Millers, 1984–89. *Recreations:* walking, music, theatre. *Club:* Travellers'.

DAVIES, Sir Peter Maxwell, Kt 1987; CBE 1981; composer and conductor; *b* 8 Sept. 1934; *s* of Thomas and Hilda Davies. *Educ:* Leigh Grammar Sch.; Manchester Univ. (MusB (Hons) 1956); Royal Manchester Coll. of Music. FRNCM 1978. Studied with Goffredo Petrassi in Rome (schol. 1957); Harkness Fellow, Grad. Music Sch., Princetown Univ., NJ, 1962. Dir of Music, Cirencester Grammar Sch., 1959–62; lecture tours in Europe, Australia, NZ, USA, Canada and Brazil; Visiting Composer, Adelaide Univ., 1966; Founder and Co-Dir, with Harrison Birtwistle, of Pierrot Players, 1967–70; Prof. of Composition, Royal Northern Coll. of Music, 1975–80; Founder and Artistic Director: The Fires of London, 1971–87; St Magnus Fest., Orkney Is, 1977–86 (Pres., 1986–); Artistic Dir, Dartington Hall Summer Sch. of Music, 1979–84; Associate Conductor/ Composer, Scottish Chamber Orch., 1985–. Retrospective Festival, South Bank Centre, 1990. President: Schs Music Assoc., 1983–; Composers' Guild of GB, 1986–; Nat. Fedn of Music Socs, 1989–. Series for Schools Broadcasts, BBC Television. Hon. Member: RAM, 1978; Guildhall Sch. of Music and Drama, 1981; Royal Philharmonic Soc., 1987; Hon. DMus: Edinburgh, 1979; Manchester, 1983; Bristol, 1984; Open Univ., 1986; Hon. DL Aberdeen, 1981; Hon. DLitt Warwick, 1986. Cobbett Medal, for services to chamber music, 1989; (first) Award, Assoc. of British Orchs, 1991. Officier de l'Ordre des Arts et des Lettres (France), 1988. *Compositions* (majority published): 1952: Quartet Movement, for string quartet; 1955: Trumpet Sonata; 1956: Five Pieces for Piano; Stedman Doubles, for clarinet and percussion, rev. 1968; 1957: Clarinet Sonata; St Michael Sonata, for wind instruments; Alma Redemptoris Mater, for wind instruments; 1958: Sextet; Prolation, for orch.; 1959: Five Motets, for soloists, double choir and instruments; Ricercar and Doubles on 'To Many a Well', for instrumental ensemble; Five Klee Pictures, for orch., rev. 1976; William Byrd, Three Dances, arranged for orch.; 1960: O Magnum Mysterium, for unaccompanied voices with two instrumental sonatas and organ fantasia; Five Voluntaries, for orch.; 1961: Ave Maria, Hail Blessed Flower (carol); Te Lucis Ante Terminum, for Voices and instrumental ensemble; String Quartet; 1962: First Fantasia on an In Nomine of John Taverner, for orch. (commnd by BBC); Leopardi Fragments, for soloists and instrumental ensemble; Sinfonia, for chamber orch.; The Lord's Prayer, for unaccompanied voices; Four Carols, for unaccompanied voices; 1963: Veni Sancte Spiritus, for soloists, chorus and orch.; 1964: Second Fantasia on John Taverner's In Nomine, for orch.; Shakespeare Music, for chamber ensemble; Ave, Plena Gracia, for voices with optional organ; 1964–65: Seven In Nomine, for instrumental ensemble; 1965: Ecce Manus Tradentis, for soloists, chorus and instrumental ensemble; The Shepherd's Calendar, for young singers and instrumentalists; Revelation and Fall, for soprano and instruments; Shall I Die for Mannis Sake?, carol for soloists and piano; 1966: Five Carols, for unaccompanied soprano and alto; Notre Dame des Fleurs, for soloists and instrumental ensemble; Solita, for flute with musical box; 1967: Hymnos, for clarinet and piano; Antechrist, for chamber ensemble; Five Little Pieces for Piano; 1968: Missa super l'Homme Armé, for speaker or singer and instrumental ensemble, rev. 1971; Stedman Caters, for instrumental ensemble; Purcell, Fantasia on a Ground and Two Pavanes, realisation for instrumental ensemble; 1969: Eight Songs for a Mad King, for male voice and instrumental ensemble; St Thomas Wake, foxtrot for orch. on a pavane by John Bull (commnd by City of Dortmund); Worldes Blis, for och.; Eram Quasi Agnus, instrumental motet; Gabrielli, Canzona realisation for chamber ensemble; Vesalii Icones, for dancer, 'cello and instrumental ensemble; 1970: Taverner (opera); Points and Dances from Taverner, instrumental dances and keyboard pieces from the opera; Sub Tuam Protectionem, for piano; Ut Re Mi, for piano; 1971: From Stone to Thorn, for mezzo-soprano and instrumental ensemble; Bell Tower, for percussion; Buxtehude, Also Hat Gott Die Welt Geliebet, cantata for soprano and instrumental ensemble; Suite from film, The Devils; Suite from film, The Boyfriend; 1972: Blind Man's Buff, masque for voices, mime and orch.; Fool's Fanfare, for speaker and instrumental ensemble; Hymn to St Magnus, for instrumental ensemble with mezzo-soprano obligate; Tenebrae super Gesualdo, for mezzo-soprano, guitar and instrumental ensemble; Canon In Memoriam Igor Stravinsky, puzzle canon for instrumental ensemble; Lullabye for Ilian Rainbow, for guitar; J. S. Bach, Prelude and Fugue in C Sharp Minor, realisation for instrumental ensemble; Dunstable, Veni Sancte Spiritus—Veni Creator Spiritus, realisation for instrumental ensemble; 1973: Stone Litany—Runes from a House of the Dead, for mezzo-soprano and orch.; Renaissance Scottish Dances, for instrumental ensemble; Si Quis Diliget Me, motet arranged for instrumental ensemble; Purcell, Fantasia on One Note, realisation for instrumental ensemble; 1973–74; Fiddlers at the Wedding, for mezzo-soprano and instrumental ensemble; 1974: Dark Angels, for Voice and guitar; Miss Donnithorne's Maggot, for mezzo-soprano and instrumental ensemble; All Sons of Adam, motet arranged for instrumental ensemble; Psalm 124, motet arranged for instrumental ensemble; J. S. Bach, Prelude and Fugue in C Sharp Major, realisation for instrumental ensemble; 1975: The Door of the Sun, for viola; The Kestrel Paced Round the Sun, for flute; The Seven Brightnesses, for clarinet; Three Studies for Percussion; My Lady Lothian's Lilte, for instrumental ensemble with obligato; Stevie's Ferry to Hoy, for piano; Ave Maris Stella, for chamber ensemble; 1976: The Blind Fiddler, for soprano and chamber ensemble; Three Organ Voluntaries; Kinloche his Fantassie, realisation for instrumental ensemble; Anakreontika (Greek songs); The Blind Fiddler, song cycle for soprano and instrumental ensemble; Symphony No 1; The Martyrdom of St Magnus (chamber opera); 1977: Norn Pater Noster, prayer for voices and organ; Westerlings, for unaccompanied voices; Runes from a Holy Island, for instrumental ensemble; A Mirror of Whitening Light, for instrumental ensemble; Ave Rex Angelorum, for unaccompanied voices or with organ; Our Father Which In Heaven Art, motet arranged for instrumental ensemble; 1978: The Two Fiddlers (opera); Le Jongleur de Notre Dame, masque for mime, baritone, chamber ensemble and children's band; Salome (ballet score); Four Lessons, for two clavichords; Dances from The Two Fiddlers, for instrumental ensemble; 1979: Kirkwall Shopping Songs, for young children; Solstice of Light, for soloists, chorus and organ; Black Pentecost, for soloists and orch.; The Lighthouse (opera); Nocturne, for alto flute; 1980: Cinderella, pantomime opera for young people to perform; Symphony No 2; The Yellow Cake Review, for voice and piano; Farewell to Stromness, piano interlude from The Yellow Cake Review; Yesnaby Ground, piano interlude from The Yellow Cake Review; A Welcome to Orkney, for instrumental ensemble; Little Quartet, string quartet for young musicians; 1981: The Medium, monodrama for mezzo-soprano; Piano Sonata; The Rainbow, for young children to perform; Hill Runes, for guitar; The Bairns of Brugh, for chamber ensemble; Little Quartet No 2, string quartet for young musicians; Tenor Arias from The Martyrdom of St Magnus, for tenor, piano or organ; Lullabye for Lucy, for soloists; Brass Quintet; Seven Songs Home, for unaccompanied children's voices; 1982: Songs of Hoy, masque for children's voices and instruments; Sea Eagle, for horn; Image, Reflection, Shadow, for instrumental ensemble; Sinfonia Concertante, for chamber orch.; Organ Sonata; Tallis, Four Voluntaries, arranged for brass quintet (also arranged for brass band); Gesualdo, Two Motets, arranged for brass quintet (also arranged for brass band); The Pole Star, march for brass quintet (also for brass band); 1983: Birthday Music for John, trio for flute, viola and 'cello; Into the Labyrinth, cantata for tenor and chamber orch.; Sinfonietta Accademica, for chamber orch.; 1984: Agnus Dei, for sopranos, viola and 'cello; Sonatine, for violin and cymbalom; Unbroken Circle, for instrumental ensemble; The Number 11 Bus, music theatre work; Guitar Sonata; One Star, At Last, carol for soloists; Symphony No 3; 1985: An Orkney Wedding, With Sunrise, for orch.; First Ferry to Hoy, for chamber ensemble, children's chorus, percussion and recorders; The Peat Cutters, for brass band and youth choir; Violin Concerto; 1986: Jimmack the Postie (concert overture for orch.); House of Winter, for mezzo-soprano and instrumental ensemble; Excuse Me, for voice and instrumental ensemble; Sea Runes, for vocal sextet; Dowland—Farewell a Fancye, for instrumental ensemble; Winterfold, for mezzo-soprano and chamber ensemble; 1987: Strathclyde Concerto No 1 for Oboe and Orchestra; Resurrection, opera in one act with dialogue; 1988: Mishkenot, for chamber ensemble; Strathclyde Concerto No 2 for Cello and Orchestra; Trumpet Concerto; Dances from The Two Fiddlers, for violin and piano; Six Songs for St Andrews, song cycle for children; 1989: The Great Bank Robbery, Jupiter Landing, Dinosaur at Large, Dangerous Errand, music theatre works for children; Symphony no. 4; Hallelujah! The Lord God Almightie, for chorus and organ; Strathclyde Concerto No 3 for Horn, Trumpet and Orchestra;

Threnody for Michael Vyner, for och.; 1990: Strathclyde Concerto No 4 for Clarinet and Orchestra; Caroline Mathilde (ballet); Apple-Basket: Apple-Blossom, for chorus; Hymn to the Word of God, for tenor soli and chorus; 1991, Dangerous Errand. *Address:* c/o Mrs Judy Arnold, 50 Hogarth Road, SW5 0PU.

DAVIES, Maj.-Gen. Peter Ronald; Chief Executive, Royal Society for the Prevention of Cruelty to Animals, since 1991; *b* 10 May 1938; *e s* of Lt-Col Charles Henry Davies and Joyce Davies (*née* Moore); *m* 1960, Rosemary Julia, *er d* of late David Felice of Douglas, IoM; one *s* one *d*. *Educ:* Llandovery College; Welbeck College; RMA Sandhurst; student: RMCS 1969; Staff Coll., 1970; RCDS, 1984. Commissioned Royal Corps of Signals, 1958; service in BAOR, Berlin, Borneo, Cyprus and UK, 1958–68; OC Artillery Bde Sig. Sqn, 1971–72; Bde Maj., 20 Armd Bde, 1973–75; Directing Staff, Staff Coll., Camberley, 1975–76; CO 1 Armd Div. Signal Regt, 1976–79; Col GS SD, HQ UKLF, 1979–82; Brigade Comdr, 12 Armd Brigade, 1982–84; Dep. Comdt and Dir of Studies, Staff College, Camberley, 1985–86; Comdr Communications, BAOR, 1987–90; GOC Wales, 1990–91. Colonel, King's Regt, 1986–; Chm., Regtl Council and King's and Manchester Regts' Assoc., 1986–; Col Comdt, RCS, 1990–. Gov., Welbeck Coll., 1980–81. *Recreations:* music, literature, wine, rugby football. *Address:* c/o RSPCA Headquarters, Causeway, Horsham, Sussex RH12 1HG. *Clubs:* Army and Navy; London Rugby; Cardiff and County (Cardiff).

DAVIES, Ven. Philip Bertram; Archdeacon of St Albans, since 1987; *b* 13 July 1933; *s* of Rev. Bertram Davies and Nancy Jonsson Davies (*née* Nicol); *m* 1963, (Elizabeth) Jane, *d* of late Ven. John Farquhar Richardson; two *s* two *d* (and one *d* decd). *Educ:* Lancing College. Travancore Tea Estates Ltd, 1954–58; Lewis's Ltd, 1959–61. Cuddesdon Theological College, 1961–63. Curate, St John the Baptist, Atherton, 1963–66; Vicar, St Mary Magdalene, Winton, Eccles, 1966–71; Rector, St Philip with St Stephen, Salford, 1971–76; Vicar, Christ Church, Radlett, 1976–87; RD of Aldenham, 1979–87. *Recreations:* gardening, fishing. *Address:* 6 Sopwell Lane, St Albans, Herts AL1 1RR. *T:* St Albans (0727) 57973.

DAVIES, Maj.-Gen. Philip Middleton, OBE 1975; Director, United Aircraft Industries Ltd, 1986–88; *b* 27 Oct. 1932; *s* of Mrs C. H. Allen (*née* Tickler); *m* 1956, Mona Wallace; two *d*. *Educ:* Charterhouse; RMA, Sandhurst. Commnd Royal Scots, 1953; served Korea, Canal Zone, Cyprus, Suez, Berlin, Libya 1st Bn Royal Scots, 1953–63; Staff Coll., 1963; National Defence Coll., 1971; commanded: 1st Bn Royal Scots, 1973–76; 19 Bde/7 Fd Force, 1977–79; RCDS, 1980; Comd Land Forces, Cyprus, 1981–83; GOC NW Dist, 1983–86; retired. *Recreations:* fishing, gardening. *Clubs:* Army and Navy, Ebury Court.

DAVIES, Quentin; *see* Davies, J. Q.

DAVIES, Rhys Everson, QC 1981; **His Honour Judge Rhys Davies;** a Circuit Judge, since 1990; Hon. Recorder of Manchester, since 1990; *b* 13 Jan. 1941; *s* of late Evan Davies and Nancy Caroline Davies; *m* 1963, Katharine Anne Yeates; one *s* one *d*. *Educ:* Cowbridge Grammar School; Neath Grammar School; Victoria University of Manchester. LLB (Hons). Called to the Bar, Gray's Inn, 1964. On Northern Circuit, 1964–90; a Recorder, 1980–90. *Recreations:* music, conversation. *Address:* Crown Court, Crown Square, Manchester M3 3FL. *T:* 061–832 8393.

DAVIES, Sir Richard Harries, KCVO 1984 (CVO 1982); CBE 1962; BSc; CEng, FIEE; an Extra Equerry to the Duke of Edinburgh, since 1984; *b* 28 June 1916; *s* of Thomas Henry Davies and Minnie Oakley (*née* Morgan); *m* 1st, 1944, Hon. Nan (*d* 1976), *e d* of 1st Baron Macpherson of Drumochter; two *s* two *d*; 2nd, 1979, Mrs Patricia P. Ogier. *Educ:* Porth County Sch.; Cardiff Technical Coll. Scientific Civil Service, 1939–46; British Air Commn, Washington, DC, 1941–45; Vice Pres., Ferranti Electric Inc., New York, 1948–63; Dir, Ferranti Ltd, 1970–76. Duke of Edinburgh's Household: Asst Private Sec., 1977–82; Treasurer, 1982–84. Pres., British Amer. Chamber of Commerce, New York, 1959–62; Vice Pres., Manchester Chamber of Commerce, 1976. Pres., Radio Soc. of GB, 1988. *Recreations:* gardening, sailing, amateur radio. *Address:* Haven House, Thorpeness, Suffolk IP16 4NR. *T:* Aldeburgh (0728) 453603. *Clubs:* Athenæum, Pratt's.

DAVIES, Robert David, CB 1982; CVO 1977; RD 1963; JP; Director, Office of the Premier, Department of the Premier and Cabinet, Western Australia, 1983 and Clerk of Executive Council, 1975–83, retired; *b* 17 Aug. 1927; *s* of late William Harold Davies and of Elsie Davies; *m* 1948, Muriel Patricia Cuff; one *s* one *d*. *Educ:* Fremantle Boys High Sch.; Perth Technical Coll. Senior AASA. Defence Service, 1945–47; Asst Commissioner, State Taxation Dept, 1973; Under Sec., Premier's Dept, WA, 1975. Comdr, RANR, 1972. JP 1970. *Recreations:* fishing, sailing. *Address:* 82 Reynolds Road, Mount Pleasant, WA 6153, Australia. *T:* 364–1596.

DAVIES, Rt. Rev. Robert Edward, CBE 1981; MA, ThD; *b* Birkenhead, England, 30 July 1913; *s* of late R. A. Davies, Canberra; *m* 1953, Helen M., *d* of H. M. Boucher; two *d*. *Educ:* Cessnock High School; Queensland University; St John's Theological College, Morpeth, NSW. Assistant Priest, Christ Church Cathedral, Newcastle, NSW, 1937–41. War of 1939–45: Toc H Army Chaplain, 1941–42; Chaplain, Royal Australian Air Force, Middle East and Mediterranean, 1942–46. Vice-Warden, St John's College, University of Queensland, Brisbane, 1946–48; Archdeacon of Canberra and Rector of Canberra, 1949–53; Archdeacon of Wagga Wagga, NSW, 1953–60; Assistant Bishop of Newcastle and Warden of St John's Theological College, Morpeth, NSW, 1960–63; Bishop of Tasmania, 1963–81. *Recreations:* golf, tennis. *Address:* 12 Elboden Street, Hobart, Tasmania 7000, Australia. *Clubs:* Tasmanian, Naval Military and Air Force of Tas. (Tas.).

DAVIES, Prof. Robert Ernest, FRS 1966; Benjamin Franklin Professor of Molecular Biology and University Professor, University of Pennsylvania, 1977–90, now Emeritus, and Chairman, Research Advisory Board, Institute for Environmental Medicine, School of Medicine, 1970–90; *b* 17 Aug. 1919; *s* of William Owen Davies and Stella Davies; *m* 1961, Helen C. (*née* Rogoff); two step *s*. *Educ:* Manchester Grammar Sch.; Univ. of Manchester and Univ. of Sheffield. BSc(Chem.) Manchester, 1941; MSc Manchester 1942; PhD Sheffield 1949; DSc Manchester 1952; MA Oxon 1956; MA Penn 1971. Temp. Asst Lectr in Chemistry, Univ. of Sheffield. Half-time research (Ministry of Supply, Chemical Defence Research Dept), 1942; full-time research on temp. staff, Medical Research Unit for Research in Cell Metabolism, 1945; apptd to Estab. Staff of MRC, 1947; Hon. Lectr in Biochemistry, Univ. of Sheffield, 1948–54; Vis. Prof., Pharmakologisches Inst., Univ. Heidelberg, March-May 1954; University of Pennsylvania, 1955–: Prof. of Biochemistry, Sch. of Medicine, 1955–62, Grad. Sch. of Medicine, 1962–70; Prof. of Molecular Biology, 1970–77; Chm., Dept of Animal Biology, Sch. of Vet. Medicine, 1962–73; Chairman: Grad. Group Cttee on Molecular Biology, 1962–72; Faculty Senate, 1989–90. Chm., Benjamin Franklin Professors, 1978–; Mem., Bd of Dirs, Assoc. for Women in Science Educnl Foundn, 1978–. Hon. Life Mem., NY Acad. of Scis. *Publications:* very many: in chemistry, biochemistry, physiolog. and biology journals concerning secretion, muscle contraction, kidneys, etc. *Recreations:* mountaineering, caving, underwater swimming, white water boating. *Address:* Department of Animal Biology, School of Veterinary Medicine, University of Pennsylvania, Philadelphia, Pa 19104–6046, USA. *T:* 215–898–7861; 7053 McCallum Street, Philadelphia, Pa 19119, USA. *Clubs:* Fell and Rock-climbing Club of the English Lake District; Cave Diving Group; Manchester Univ. Mountaineering; Explorers' (New York).

DAVIES, Robert Henry, MBE 1962; DFC 1943; HM Diplomatic Service, retired; *b* 17 Aug. 1921; *s* of John and Lena Davies; *m* 1st, 1945, Marion Ainsworth (marr. diss. 1973); one *s* one *d*; 2nd, 1973, Maryse Deuson. *Educ:* John Bright County Sch., Llandudno. RAF, 1940–46; flew with S African Air Force, N Africa, 1942–43. Joined Min. of Food, 1946; transf. to CRO, 1954; served in India, 1954–57 and Canada, 1959–62; HM Diplomatic Service, 1965; served in Brussels, 1967–70; Consul-Gen. and Counsellor (Admin), Moscow, 1973–75; FCO, 1975–76; Counsellor, Paris, 1976–81. *Recreations:* golf, birdwatching, reading. *Address:* 16 Beechcroft Drive, Guildford, Surrey. *Club:* Bramley Golf.

DAVIES, Prof. Robert Rees, DPhil; FBA 1987; Professor of History, since 1976, Vice-Principal, since 1988, University College of Wales, Aberystwyth; *b* 6 Aug. 1938; *s* of William Edward Davies and Sarah Margaret Davies; *m* 1966, Carys Lloyd Wynne; one *s* one *d*. *Educ:* University College London (BA); Merton Coll., Oxford (DPhil). FRHistS 1968. Asst Lectr, UC, Swansea, 1961–63; Lectr, UCL, 1963–76. Wiles Lectr, QUB, 1988; James Ford Special Lectr, Univ. of Oxford, 1988. Chm., Nat. Curriculum History Cttee for Wales, 1989–. Convenor, History at Univs Defence Gp, 1991–. Member: Ancient Monuments Bd for Wales, 1977–; Council, Nat. Museum of Wales, 1987–; Council, Historical Assoc., 1991–. Vice Pres., RHistS, 1988– (Mem. Council, 1979–82). Wolfson Literary Award for History, 1987. Asst Editor and Review Editor, History, 1963–73. *Publications:* Lordship and Society in the March of Wales 1282–1400, 1978; (ed) Welsh Society and Nationhood, 1984; Conquest, Co-existence and Change: Wales 1063–1415, 1987; (ed) The British Isles 1100–1500, 1988; Domination and Conquest: the experience of Ireland, Scotland and Wales 1100–1300, 1990; numerous contribs to learned jls. *Recreations:* walking, music. *Address:* Maeshyfryd, Ffordd Llanbadarn, Aberystwyth, Dyfed. *T:* Aberystwyth (0970) 617113.

DAVIES, Prof. Rodney Deane, DSc, PhD; CPhys, FInstP; FRAS; Professor of Radio Astronomy, University of Manchester, since 1976; Director, Nuffield Radio Astronomy Laboratories, Jodrell Bank, since 1988; *b* 8 Jan. 1930; *s* of Holbin James Davies and Rena Irene (*née* March), Mallala, S Australia; *m* 1953, Valda Beth Treasure; one *s* two *d* (and one *s* decd). *Educ:* Adelaide High Sch.; Univ. of Adelaide (BSc Hons, MSc); Univ. of Manchester (PhD, DSc). Research Officer, Radiophysics Div., CSIRO, Sydney, 1951–53; Univ. of Manchester: Asst Lectr, 1953–56; Lectr, 1956–67; Reader, 1967–76. Visiting Astronomer, Radiophysics Div., CSIRO, Australia, 1963. Member: Internat. Astronomical Union, 1958; Org. Cttee and Working Gps of various Commns; Bd and various panels and cttees of Astronomy Space and Radio Bd and Science Bd of Science Research Council; British Nat. Cttee for Astronomy, 1974–77. Royal Astronomical Society: Mem. Council, 1972–75 and 1978–; Sec., 1978–86; Vice-Pres., 1973–75 and 1986–87; Pres., 1987–89. *Publications:* Radio Studies of the Universe (with H. P. Palmer), 1959; Radio Astronomy Today (with H. P. Palmer and M. I. Large), 1963; The Crab Nebula (co-ed with F. G. Smith), 1971; numerous contribs to Monthly Notices of RAS and internat. jls on the galactic and extragalactic magnetic fields, structure and dynamics of the Galaxy and nearby external galaxies, use of radio spectral lines, the early Universe and studies of the Cosmic Microwave Background. *Recreations:* gardening, fell-walking. *Address:* University of Manchester, Nuffield Radio Astronomy Laboratories, Jodrell Bank, Macclesfield, Cheshire SK11 9DL. *T:* Lower Withington (0477) 71321.

DAVIES, Roger; *see* Davies, A. R.

DAVIES, Roger Oliver; Member, Monopolies and Mergers Commission, since 1989; *b* 4 Jan. 1945; *s* of Griffith William Davies and Dorothy Anne Davies; *m* 1973, Adele Biss; one *s*. *Educ:* Reading Sch.; Devonport High Sch.; London School of Economics (BScEcon). Marketing Dir, 1972, Man. Dir, 1977, Thomson Holidays; Man. Dir, 1982, Chm., 1984–90, Thomson Travel Gp. Commandeur de la République (Tunisia), 1987. *Recreations:* walking, ski-ing, reading.

DAVIES, (Roger) Peter (Havard), OBE 1978; Human Rights consultant; Director, Project Mala (India), since 1988; *b* 4 Oct. 1919; *s* of Arthur William Davies and Edith Mary Davies (*née* Mealand); *m* 1956, Ferelith Mary Helen Short; two *s* two *d*. *Educ:* Bromsgrove Sch., Worcs; St Edmund Hall, Oxford (MA). Army service, N Africa, Italy, NW Europe, Captain RA (AOP), 1939–46. Joined British Council, 1949; served Hungary, Israel, Sarawak, Finland, Chile, India (Calcutta); Director: Drama and Music Dept, 1965–69; Information Dept, 1974–75; retired, 1980. Dir, Anti-Slavery Soc., 1980–87. Mem. Exec. Cttee, UNA, 1985–90; Chairman: Human Rights Cttee, UNA, 1985–90; Exec. Council, Internat. Service for Human Rights, Geneva, 1987–; Vice-Chm., Friends of UNESCO, 1990–. *Publications:* (ed) Human Rights, 1988; occasional articles and broadcasts. *Recreations:* family life, music, golf. *Address:* Ley Cottage, Elmore Road, Chipstead, Surrey CR3 5SG. *T:* Downland (07375) 53905. *Clubs:* Commonwealth Trust; Bengal (Calcutta).

DAVIES, Ronald; MP (Lab) Caerphilly, since 1983; *b* 6 Aug. 1946; *s* of late Ronald Davies; *m* 1981, Christina Elizabeth Rees; one *d*. *Educ:* Bassaleg Grammar Sch.; Portsmouth Polytechnic; Univ. Coll. of Wales, Cardiff. Schoolteacher, 1968–70; WEA Tutor/Organiser, 1970–74; Further Educn Adviser, Mid-Glamorgan LEA, 1974–83. Opposition Whip, 1985–87; Opposition spokesman on agriculture and rural affairs, 1987–. Councillor, Rhymney Valley DC (formerly Bedwas and Machen UDC), 1969–84 (Vice-Chm.). *Address:* House of Commons, SW1A 0AA. *T:* 071–219 3000.

DAVIES, Rt. Rev. Roy Thomas; *see* Llandaff, Bishop of.

DAVIES, Rev. Rupert Eric; Warden, John Wesley's Chapel, Bristol, 1976–82, retired; *b* 29 Nov. 1909; *s* of Walter Pierce and Elizabeth Miriam Davies; *m* 1937, Margaret Price Holt; two *s* two *d*. *Educ:* St Paul's Sch.; Balliol Coll., Oxford (Class. Schol.; 1st cl. Hons Mods, Classics, 1930; 2nd cl. Lit. Hum., 1932); Wesley House, Cambridge (1st cl. Theology, Pt II, 1934); BD Cantab 1946; Univ. of Tübingen, Germany, 1934–35 (trav. schol. in Germany). Chaplain, Kingswood Sch., Bath, 1935–47; Methodist Minister, Bristol, 1947–52 and 1973–76; Tutor, Didsbury Coll., Bristol, 1952–67; Principal, Wesley Coll., Bristol, 1967–73. Pres., Methodist Conf., 1970–71. Select Preacher to Univs of: Cambridge, 1962; Oxford, 1969; Mem. Exec. Cttee, World Methodist Council, 1956–76; Mem., Anglican-Methodist Unity Commn, 1965–68; World Council of Churches: Faith and Order Commn, 1965–74; Deleg. to Fourth Assembly, 1968. *Publications:* The Problem of Authority in the Continental Reformers, 1946; Catholicity of Protestantism (ed), 1950; Approach to Christian Education (ed), 1956; John Scott Lidgett (ed), 1957; The Church in Bristol, 1960; Methodists and Unity, 1962; Methodism, 1963, 2nd edn 1985; History of the Methodist Church in Great Britain (ed), vol. I, 1965, vol. II, 1978, vol. III, 1983, vol. IV, 1988; We Believe in God (ed), 1968; Religious Authority in an Age of Doubt, 1968; A Christian Theology of Education, 1974; What Methodists Believe, 1976, 2nd edn 1988; The Church in Our Times, 1979; (with M. P. Davies) Circles of Community, 1982; (ed) The Testing of the Churches 1932–82, 1982;

The Church of England Observed, 1984; (with M. Morgan) Will You Walk a Little Faster?, 1984; Making Sense of the Creeds, 1987; (ed) The Works of John Wesley, vol. 9, 1989; Making Sense of the Commandments, 1990; contrib. Epworth Review, Procs of Wesley Hist Soc. *Recreations:* gardening, theatre. *Address:* 6 Elmtree Drive, Bishopsworth, Bristol, Avon BS13 8LY. *T:* Bristol (0272) 641087.

DAVIES, Ryland; opera singer; tenor; *b* 9 Feb. 1943; *s* of Gethin and Joan Davies; *m* 1st, 1966, Anne Elizabeth Howells (marr. diss. 1981), *qv*; 2nd, 1983, Deborah Rees; one *d*. *Educ:* Royal Manchester College of Music (Fellow, 1971) (studied with Frederic R. Cox, OBE). Début as Almaviva in The Barber of Seville, WNO, 1964; Glyndebourne Fest. Chorus, 1964–66; has since sung with Royal Opera, Sadler's Wells Opera, WNO, Scottish Opera, at Glyndebourne, and in Brussels, Chicago, NY, San Francisco, Paris, Salzburg, Buenos Aires, Hong Kong and Stuttgart; solo rôles include: Belmonte in Il Seraglio, Fenton in Falstaff, Ferrando in Così Fan Tutte, Flamand in Capriccio; Tamino in The Magic Flute; Essex in Britten's Gloriana; Hylas in The Trojans; Don Ottavio in Don Giovanni; Cassio in Otello; Ernesto in Don Pasquale; Lysander in A Midsummer Night's Dream; title rôle in Werther; Prince in L'Amour des Trois Oranges; Nemorino in L'Elisir d'amore; Alfredo in La Traviata, Pelléas in Pelléas et Melisande, Berlin and Hamburg; Eneas in Esclarmonde, Royal Opera; Jack in The Midsummer Marriage, San Francisco. Many concerts at home with all major British orchestras, and abroad with such orchestras as: Boston Symphony, Cleveland Symphony, Chicago Symphony, Philadelphia, San Francisco, Los Angeles, Bavarian Radio and Vienna Symphony. Principal oratorio rôles include: Bach, B minor Mass; Beethoven: Mass in C; Christus am Olberg; Berlioz, narrator in L'Enfance du Christ; Elgar, St John, in The Kingdom; Handel: Acis, in Acis and Galatea; title rôle, Judas Macoabeus; Messiah; Jonathan, in Saul; Haydn: Nelson Mass; The Seasons; Mendelssohn: Obidiah, in Elijah; Hymn of Praise; Rossini, Messe Solenelle; Schubert, Lazarus; Tippett, Child of Our Time. Has sung in all major religious works including: Missa Solemnis, Verdi's Requiem, Dream of Gerontius, St Matthew Passion, The Creation. Many recordings incl. Il Seraglio, The Trojans, Saul, Così Fan Tutte, Thérèse, Monteverdi Madrigals, Idomeneo, Haydn's The Seasons, Messiah, L'Oracolo (Leone), Judas Maccabaeus, Il Matrimonio Segreto (Cimarosa), L'Amore dei Tre Re (Montemezzi), La Navarraise (Massenet), Lucia di Lammermoor (Donizetti). John Christie Award, 1965. *Recreations:* antiques, art, cinema, sport. *Address:* 71 Fairmile Lane, Cobham, Surrey KT11 2DG.

DAVIES, Sam; *see* Davies, Stanley Mason.

DAVIES, Siobhan; *see* Davies, Susan.

DAVIES, Stanley Mason, (Sam Davies), CMG 1971; Director, Alliance International Health Care Fund (formerly Trust), since 1986 (Consultant, 1984–86); *b* 7 Feb. 1919; *s* of late Charles Davies, MBE and Constance Evelyn Davies; *m* 1943, Diana Joan (*née* Lowe); three *d*. *Educ:* Bootle Grammar School. War Service, UK and W Europe, 1939–46; Royal Army Dental Corps, 1939–41 (Sgt); Corps of Royal Engineers, 1941–46 (Staff Captain). Clerical Officer, Min. of Labour, 1936; Exec. Officer, Inland Revenue, 1938; Higher Exec. Officer, Min. of Pensions, 1946–53; Min. of Health, 1953–68; Asst Sec., DHSS, 1968–75; Under Sec., Industries and Exports Div., DHSS, 1975–76. Consultant: Monsanto Health Care, 1977–85; Sterling Winthrop Drug, 1977–86. Mem., NY Acad. of Scis. FSAScot. Croix de Guerre (France), 1944. *Recreations:* reading, archæology, philately. *Address:* 31 Leverstock Green Road, Hemel Hempstead, Herts. *T:* Hemel Hempstead (0442) 254312. *Club:* Savile.

DAVIES, Stuart Duncan, CBE 1968; BSc; FEng; Hon. FRAeS; Past President, Royal Aeronautical Society, 1972–73 (President, 1971–72); *b* 5 Dec. 1906; *s* of William Lewis Davies and Alice Dryden Duncan; *m* 1935, Ethel Rosalie Ann Radcliffe; one *d*. *Educ:* Westminster City Sch.; London Univ. (BSc Eng.). Vickers (Aviation) Ltd, 1925–31; Hawker Aircraft Ltd, 1931–36; A. V. Roe and Co. Ltd, 1938–55, Chief Designer, 1945–55; with Dowty Group Ltd, 1955–58, as Managing Director of Dowty Fuel Systems Ltd; Technical Director: Hawker Siddeley Aviation Ltd, 1958–64; Dowty Rotol Ltd, 1965–72. British Gold Medal for Aeronautics, 1958. *Address:* Sheridans, 4 Arun Way, Aldwick Bay, Bognor Regis, W Sussex PO21 4HF.

DAVIES, Susan, (Siobhan Davies); freelance choreographer; Director, Siobhan Davies Company, since 1988; Associate Choreographer, Rambert Dance Company, 1989; *b* 18 Sept. 1950; *d* of Grahame Henry Wyatt Davies and Tempé Mary Davies (*née* Wallich); lives with David John Buckland; one *s* one *d*. *Educ:* too many schools, ending with Queensgate School for Girls; Hammersmith College of Art and Building. With London Contemporary Dance Theatre, 1967–87: first choreography, 1970; Associate Choreographer, 1971; Associate Dir, 1983. Formed Siobhan Davies and Dancers, 1980; Jt Dir, with Ian Spink, Second Stride, 1981–86. Arts Award, Fulbright Commn, 1987, to travel and study in America. *Recreation:* imagining having more time than I do.

DAVIES, Susan Elizabeth, (Mrs John Davies), OBE 1988; Founder and Director, Photographers' Gallery, 1971–91; freelance consultant; *b* 14 April 1933; *d* of Stanworth Wills Adey and Joan Mary Margaret Adey (*née* Charlesworth); *m* 1954, John Ross Twiston Davies; two *d* (and one *d* decd). *Educ:* Nightingale Bamford Sch., NY; Eothen Sch., Caterham. Municipal Journal, 1952–54; local and voluntary work, 1960–67; Artists Placement Group, 1967–68; ICA, 1968–71. Hon. FRPS (President's Medal, 1982). Photokina Award, 1986; National Artist Karel Plicka Medal, Czechoslovakia, 1989. *Recreations:* jazz live and recorded, reading, walking, sleeping. *Address:* Walnut Tree Cottage, 53 Britwell Road, Burnham, Bucks SL1 8DH. *T:* Burnham (06286) 04811. *Club:* Chelsea Arts.

DAVIES, Thomas Glyn, CBE 1966; *b* 16 Aug. 1905; *s* of Thomas Davies, Gwaelod-y-Garth, Cardiff; *m* 1935, Margaret Berry; one *d*. *Educ:* Pontypridd Grammar Sch.; Univ. of Wales, Cardiff (MA). Asst Master, Howard Gardens High Sch., Cardiff, 1927–37; Warden, Educational Settlement, Pontypridd, 1937–43; Director of Education: Montgomeryshire, 1943–58; Denbighshire, 1958–70, retd. Mem. ITA, later IBA, 1970–75. Mem., Court and Council, UC Bangor. Fellow, UC Cardiff, 1981. *Recreations:* travel, music. *Address:* 42 Park Avenue, Wrexham, Clwyd LL12 7AH. *T:* Wrexham (0978) 352697.

DAVIES, Trevor Arthur L.; *see* Lloyd Davies.

DAVIES, Vivian; *see* Davies, W. V.

DAVIES, Walter, OBE 1966; Secretary-General and Chief Executive of The British Chamber of Commerce for Italy 1961–86, retired; *b* 7 Dec. 1920; *s* of late William Davies and late Frances Poole; *m* 1947, Alda, *d* of Tiso Lucchetta, Padua; two *d*. *Educ:* St Margaret's Higher Grade Sch., Liverpool; Liverpool Coll. of Commerce. Served War: RA, 1940–41; Scots Guards, 1942–47. Commendatore dell'Ordine al Merito della Repubblica Italiana, 1967. *Recreations:* good food, good company, fishing, motoring. *Address:* Via G. Dezza 27, 20144 Milan, Italy. *T:* Milan 4694391.

DAVIES, Prof. Wendy Elizabeth, FRHistS; FSA; Professor of History since 1985, and Head of History Department since 1987, University College London; *b* 28 Aug. 1942; *d* of Douglas Charles Davies and Lucy (*née* Evans). *Educ:* University Coll. London (BA, PhD). FSA 1988. Temporary Lectr 1970, Res. Fellow 1971, Lectr 1972, Univ. of Birmingham; Lectr 1977, Reader 1981, UCL. *Publications:* An Early Welsh Microcosm, 1978; The Llandaff Charters, 1979; Wales in the Early Middle Ages, 1982; (ed with P. Fouracre) Settlement of Disputes in Early Medieval Europe, 1986; Small Worlds: the village community in early medieval Brittany, 1988; Patterns of Power, 1990; papers in Eng. Historical Rev., Past and Present, Francia, Bull. of Bd of Celtic Studies, Etudes Celtiques, Hist. and Anthropology, etc. *Recreation:* gardening. *Address:* Department of History, University College London, Gower Street, WC1E 6BT. *T:* 071–387 7050.

DAVIES, William Llewellyn M.; *see* Monro Davies.

DAVIES, (William Michael) Neil; Member, Inner London Education Authority, 1980–86 (Chairman, 1982–83); *b* 5 Feb. 1931; *s* of William Henry Davies and Hilda Mary (*née* Fielding); *m* 1955, Myra Blanch Clair Smalley (marr. diss. 1981); two *s* one *d*; *m* 1983, Elizabeth Ann Virgin. *Educ:* Neath Technical Coll.; Fircroft Coll.; Birmingham Univ. Probation Officer, Birmingham, Monmouthshire and Somerset, 1962–76; Principal Child Care Adviser, Lambeth Bor. Council, 1976–82. Member: Taunton Bor. Council, 1968–74; London Bor. of Bexley, 1978–82. Greater London Council: Mem. for Woolwich W, 1980–86; Vice-Chm., Public Services and Fire Bde Cttee, 1980–86; Chm., Thames Barrier Sub Cttee, Educn Cttee, and London Youth Cttee, 1980–86; Vice-Chm., Greater London Trng Bd, and Sports Sub Cttee, 1980–86; Mem., Staff Cttee, Arts and Recreation Cttee, Transport Cttee, and Entertainments Licensing Cttee, 1980–86. Member, National Joint Councils: Fire Bde, 1980–86; Probation Service, 1980–86; Local Authority Bldg Trades, 1980–86. Member: Thames Water Authority, 1980–84; NEC National Assoc. of Maternal and Child Welfare, 1980–86. Contested (Lab.) Ripon, 1979. Alcalde, San Antonio, Texas, 1985. *Recreations:* sport, music, cooking, walking, crafts. *Address:* 1 Wingrad House, Jubilee Street, E1 3BJ. *T:* 071–790 1093. *Clubs:* London Welsh Association, Rugby.

DAVIES, Rev. Dr William Rhys; Principal of Cliff College, Sheffield, since 1983; Moderator of the Free Church Federal Council, 1991–92; *b* Blackpool, 31 May 1932; *m* 1955, Barbara; one *s* one *d*. *Educ:* Junior, Central Selective and Grammar schools, Blackpool; Hartley Victoria Methodist Coll., Manchester; Univ. of Manchester. BD London 1955; MA 1959, PhD 1965, Manchester. Junior Rating and Valuation Officer (Clerical), Blackpool Corp., 1950–51. Methodist Circuit Minister: Middleton, Manchester, 1955–60; Fleetwood, 1960–65; Stockton-on-Tees, 1965–66; Sen. Lectr in Religious Studies, Padgate Coll. of Higher Education, and Methodist Minister without pastoral charge on Warrington Circuit, 1966–79; Superintendent Minister, Bradford Methodist Mission, 1979–83. Pres., Methodist Conf., 1987–88. Member of Methodist Committees: Cliff Coll. Gen. Cttee, 1974–77 and 1981–; Faith and Order Cttee, 1975–82; Doctrinal Cttee, 1979–82; Divl Bd for Social Responsibility, 1982–85; Home Mission Bd, 1983–. Co-Editor, Dunamis (renewal magazine for Methodists), 1972–. *Publications:* (with Ross Peart) The Charismatic Movement and Methodism, 1973; Spirit Baptism and Spiritual Gifts in Early Methodism, (USA) 1974; Gathered into One (Archbishop of Canterbury's Lent Book), 1975; (with Ross Peart) What about the Charismatic Movement?, 1980; Rocking the Boat, 1986; (contrib.) A Dictionary of Christian Spirituality, 1983; contribs to jls. *Recreations:* reading, sport (soccer). *Address:* Cliff House, Calver, Sheffield S30 1XG. *T:* (home) Baslow (024688) 583262, (office) Baslow (024688) 582321.

DAVIES, William Rupert R.; *see* Rees-Davies.

DAVIES, (William) Vivian, FSA 1980; Keeper of Egyptian Antiquities, British Museum, since 1988; *b* 14 Oct. 1947; *s* of Walter Percival Davies and Gwenllian Davies (*née* Evans); *m* 1970, Janet Olwen May Foat; one *s* one *d*. *Educ:* Llanelli Grammar Sch.; Jesus Coll., Oxford (BA, MA). Randall-MacIver Student in Archaeology, Queen's Coll., Oxford, 1973–74; Asst Keeper, 1974–81, Dep. Keeper, 1981–88, Dept of Egyptian Antiquities, BM. Vis. Prof. of Egyptology, Univ. of Heidelberg, 1984–85. Hon. Librarian, Egypt Exploration Soc., 1975–85. Reviews Editor, Jl of Egyptian Archaeology, 1975–85. *Publications:* A Royal Statue Reattributed, 1981; (with T. G. H. James) Egyptian Sculpture, 1983; The statuette of Queen Tetisheri: a reconsideration, 1984; (with A. el-Khouli, A. B. Lloyd, A. J. Spencer) Saqqara Tombs, I: The Mastabas of Mereri and Wernu, 1984; (ed with J. Assmann and G. Burkard) Problems and Priorities in Egyptian Archaeology, 1987; Egyptian Hieroglyphs, 1987; Catalogue of Egyptian Antiquities in the British Museum, VII: Tools and Weapons—1: Axes, 1987; (ed) Egypt and Africa: Nubia from prehistory to Islam, 1991; contribs to : Egypt's Golden Age: the art of living in the New Kingdom, 1982; Excavating in Egypt: The Egypt Exploration Society 1882–1982, 1982; Tanis: l'or des pharaons, 1987; reviews and articles in learned jls. *Recreations:* chess, music, real ale. *Address:* Department of Egyptian Antiquities, British Museum, WC1B 3DG. *T:* 071–323 8306.

DAVIES, Zelma Ince, CB 1989; Under Secretary, Department of Health and Social Services, Northern Ireland, 1984–90, retired; *b* 22 Aug. 1930; *d* of Walter Davies and Ena Davies (*née* Ince). *Educ:* Princess Gardens Sch., Belfast; Queen's Univ., Belfast (BA Hons). Entered NICS, 1955; Principal, Min. of Finance, 1965; Asst Sec., CS Management Div., 1971; Asst and Under Sec., Central Secretariat, 1979–81; Under Sec., Office of the Parly Comr for Admin, 1983–84. *Recreations:* music, reading.

DAVIES-SCOURFIELD, Brig. Edward Grismond Beaumont, CBE 1966 (MBE 1951); MC 1945; DL; General Secretary, National Association of Boys Clubs, 1973–82; *b* 2 Aug. 1918; 4th *s* of H. G. Davies-Scourfield and Helen (*née* Newton); *m* 1945, Diana Lilias (*née* Davidson); one *s* one *d*. *Educ:* Winchester Coll.; RMC Sandhurst. Commnd into KRRC, 1938; served War of 1939–45 (despatches 1945); psc; commanded: 3rd Green Jackets (Rifle Bde), 1960–62; Green Jackets Bde, 1962–64; British Jt Services Trng Team (Ghana), 1964–66; British Troops Cyprus and Dhekelia Area, 1966–69; Salisbury Plain Area, 1970–73; retd 1973. DL Hants, 1984. *Recreations:* country pursuits. *Address:* Old Rectory Cottage, Medstead, Alton, Hants GU34 5LX. *T:* Alton (0420) 62133. *Clubs:* Army and Navy, Mounted Infantry.

DAVIGNON, Viscount Etienne; Ambassador of HM the King of the Belgians; Chairman: Société Générale de Belgique, since 1989 (Executive Director, 1984–89); Sibeka, since 1985; Royal Institute for International Relations, since 1987; Foundation P. H. Spaak, since 1983; Director: Alcatel SA, since 1987; Solvay SA, since 1985; Tanks Consolidated Investments PLC, since 1988; ICL, since 1991; Associate, Kissinger Associates; *b* Budapest, 4 Oct. 1932; *m* 1959, Françoise de Cumont; one *s* two *d*. *Educ:* University of Louvain (LLD). Diplomat; Head of Office of Minister for Foreign Affairs, Belgium, 1963; Political Director, Ministry for Foreign Affairs, Belgium, 1969; Chm., Gov. Board, Internat. Energy Agency, 1974. Mem., 1977–84 (with responsibility for internal mkt, customs, union and industl affairs), and Vice-Pres., 1981–84 (with responsibility for industry, energy and research policies), EEC. *Recreations:* tennis, golf, skiing. *Address:* 12 Avenue des Fleurs, 1150 Brussels, Belgium.

DAVIS; *see* Clinton-Davis.

DAVIS; *see* Lovell-Davis.

DAVIS, Alan Roger M.; *see* Maryon Davis.

DAVIS, Sir Allan; *see* Davis, Sir W. A.

DAVIS, Andrew Frank; conductor; Musical Director, Glyndebourne Festival Opera, since 1988; Chief Conductor, BBC Symphony Orchestra, since 1989; *b* 2 Feb. 1944; *m* 1970, Felicity Mary Vincent (marr. diss. 1983); *m* 1984, Nancicarole Monohan. *Educ:* Watford Grammar Sch.; King's Coll., Cambridge (MA, BMus); Accademia di S Cecilia, Rome. Assistant Conductor, BBC Scottish Symphony Orchestra, 1970–72; Asst Conductor, New Philharmonia Orchestra, 1973–77; Artistic Dir and Chief Conductor, Toronto Symphony, 1975–88, now Conductor Laureate. Principal Guest Conductor, Royal Liverpool Philharmonic Orchestra, 1974–77. Has conducted major US orchestras: New York, Boston, Chicago, Cleveland and LA. Particularly noted for interpretations of Strauss operas; conducts at: La Scala, Milan; Metropolitan Opera, NY; Glyndebourne; Royal Opera House, Covent Gdn. Toronto Symphony Orchestra tours: US Centres, China, Japan, 1978; Europe, 1983, 1986, incl. London, Helsinki, Bonn, Paris and Edinburgh Fest. Many commercial recordings include: complete Dvorak Symphonies, Philharmonia Orch.; Mendelssohn Symphonies, Bavarian Radio Symphony; Borodin Cycle, Holst's The Planets and Handel's Messiah, Toronto Symphony; Tippett's The Mask of Time, BBC SO and Chorus (Record of the Year, Gramophone Awards, 1987). *Recreations:* kite flying, the study of mediaeval stained glass. *Address:* c/o Harold Holt Ltd, 31 Sinclair Road, W14 0NS.

DAVIS, Anthony Ronald William James; media consultant, since 1990; *b* 26 July 1931; *e s* of Donald William Davis, Barnes and Mary Josephine Davis (*née* Nolan-Byrne), Templeogue Mill, Co. Dublin; *m* 1960, Yolande Mary June, *o d* of Patrick Leonard, retd civil engr; one *s* two *d* (and one *d* decd). *Educ:* Hamlet of Ratcliffe and Oratory; Regent Street Polytechnic. Joint Services School for Linguists on Russian course as National Serviceman (Army), 1953–55; Architectural Asst, Housing Dept, Mddx County Architect's Dept, 1956–58; Sub-Editor, The Builder, 1959; Editor: Official Architecture and Planning, 1964–70; Building, 1970–74; Director, Building, 1972–77; Editor-in-Chief, New World Publishers Ltd, 1978–83; Editl Dir, New World Publishers Ltd, Middle East Construction and Saudi Arabian Construction, 1983–86; Editor, World Property, 1986–90. Member Board: Architecture and Planning Publications Ltd, 1966; Building (Publishers) Ltd, 1972. Mem. Council, Modular Soc., 1970–71. JP Berkshire, 1973–81. *Publications:* contribs to various, architectural and technical. *Recreations:* collecting porcelain, music and dreaming. *Address:* 8 Blake Close, Dowles Green, Wokingham, Berks RG11 1QH. *T:* Wokingham (0734) 785046. *Club:* Architecture.

DAVIS, (Arthur) John, RD 1967; FCIB; Vice-Chairman, Lloyds Bank, 1984–91 (Chief General Manager, 1978–84); *b* 28 July 1924; *s* of Alan Wilfrid Davis and Emily Davis; *m* 1950, Jean Elizabeth Edna Hobbs; one *s* one *d* (and one *d* decd). *Educ:* grammar schs. FCIB (FIB 1969). Served War, RN, 1942–46. Entered Lloyds Bank, 1941; Jt Gen. Manager, 1973; Asst Chief Gen. Man., 1973; Dep. Chief Gen. Man., 1976. Pres., Chartered Inst. of Bankers, 1985–87. *Recreations:* gardening, music, country pursuits. *Address:* Little Barley End, Aldbury, Tring, Herts. *T:* Aldbury Common (044285) 321. *Clubs:* Naval, Overseas Bankers.

DAVIS, Brian Michael; Chairman and Chief Executive, Mobil Oil Company Ltd, since 1990; *b* 28 May 1937; *s* of Frederick Thomas Davis and Irene Florence (*née* Burgess); *m* 1962, Patricia Ann Wilkinson; three *s*. *Educ:* London Univ., LSE (BSc Econs). ACMA. Joined Mobil Oil Co. Ltd, 1958: various positions in accounting and finance systems, marketing, planning and supply in UK, Europe and USA, 1958–77; Gen. Manager, Mobil Kenya Gp, 1977–79; Strategic/Marketing Planning, Mobil South Inc./Mobil Europe Inc., 1979–84; Pres., Mobil Oil Portuguesa, 1984–86; Area Exec., Mobil Europe, 1986–87; Pres., Mobil Oil Italiana, 1987–90. *Recreations:* golf, tennis, music, theatre. *Address:* Mobil Oil Company Ltd, 54–60 Victoria Street, SW1E 6QB. *T:* 071–828 9777.

DAVIS, Most Rev. Brian Newton; *see* New Zealand, Primate and Archbishop of.

DAVIS, Maj-Gen. Brian William, CB 1985; CBE 1980 (OBE 1974); Head of Public Affairs, Royal Ordnance plc, since 1987 (Director, Product Support Group, 1985–87); *b* 28 Aug. 1930; *s* of late Edward William Davis, MBE, and Louise Jane Davis (*née* Webber); *m* 1954, Margaret Isobel Jenkins; one *s* one *d*. *Educ:* Weston-super-Mare Grammar Sch.; Mons OCS, Aldershot. Commissioned Royal Artillery, 1949; Regtl Duty, 1949–56 and 1960–61, UK/BAOR; Instr-in-Gunnery, 1956–59; Staff Coll. Camberley, 1962; DAA and QMG HQ 7 Armd Bde BAOR, 1963–66; GSO2 SD UN Force, Cyprus, 1966; Regtl Duty, 1967–69; Lt-Col 1969, Directing Staff, Staff Coll. Camberley, 1969–71; CO 32 Lt Regt RA BAOR/England/N Ireland, 1971–74; Col AQ Ops HQ BAOR, 1975; Brig. 1975; CRA 3 Div., 1976–77; RCDS 1978; Chief of Staff N Ireland, 1979–80; Chief of Comdrs-in-Chief Mission to Soviet Forces in Germany, 1981–82; Maj. Gen., 1982; C of S, Logistic Exec. (Army), 1982–83; DGLP (A) (formerly VQMG), MoD, 1983–85, retired. Col Comdt RA, 1987–; Mem., HAC, 1987–. *Recreations:* Rugby (President, RARFC, 1975–78; Dep. Pres., Army Rugby Union, 1984–89), cricket, fishing, ornithology. *Address:* c/o Royal Bank of Scotland, Lawrie House, Victoria Road, Farnborough, Hants. *Clubs:* Army and Navy, Special Forces, Commonwealth Trust, MCC; Somerset County Cricket; Piscatorial Society.

DAVIS, Carl; composer; Associate Conductor, London Philharmonic Orchestra, 1987–88; Principal Conductor, Bournemouth Pops, 1984–87; *b* 28 Oct. 1936; *s* of Isadore and Sara Davis; *m* 1971, Jean Boht; two *d*. *Educ:* New England Conservatory of Music; Bard Coll. (BA). *Major TV credits:* The Snow Goose, 1972; World at War, 1973; The Naked Civil Servant, 1973; Our Mutual Friend, 1976; Marie Curie, 1977; Prince Regent, The Old Curiosity Shop, 1979; Hollywood, Oppenheimer, The Sailor's Return, Fair Stood the Wind for France, 1980; The Commanding Sea, Private Schulz, 1981; The Last Night of the Poms, Home Sweet Home, La Ronde, 1982; The Unknown Chaplin, The Tale of Beatrix Potter, 1983; The Far Pavilions, 1984; The Day the Universe Changed, 1985; Hotel du Lac, 1985; The Accountant, 1989 (BAFTA Award); Flight Termina, 1990; *scores:* for RSC and National Theatre; *musicals:* The Projector, 1971; Pilgrim, 1975; Cranford, 1976; Alice in Wonderland, 1977; The Wind in the Willows, 1986; Kip's War, 1987; *opera:* Peace, 1978; *TV operas:* The Arrangement, 1967; Orpheus in the Underground, 1976; *West End:* Forty Years On, 1969; Habeas Corpus, 1974; *films:* The French Lieutenant's Woman (BAFTA Original Film Score Award), 1981; Champions, 1984; King David, 1985; Girl in a Swing, Scandal, The Rainbow, 1988; Frankenstein Unbound, 1989; *silent films:* Napoleon, 1980; The Crowd, 1981; Flesh and the Devil, Show People, How to Make Movies, 1982; Broken Blossoms, The Wind, The Musketeers of Pig Alley, An Unseen Enemy, 1983; Thief of Baghdad, 1984; The Big Parade, 1985; Greed, 1986; The General, Ben Hur, 1987; Mysterious Lady, Intolerance, City Lights (re-creation of Chaplin score), 1988; Safety Last, Kid Brother, 1989; *ballets:* Dances of Love and Death, 1981; Fire and Ice (ice ballet for Torvill and Dean), 1986; The Portrait of Dorian Gray (for SWRB), 1987; A Simple Man (based on L. S. Lowry, for Northern Ballet Theatre), 1987; Liaisons Amoureuses, 1989; Lipizzaner (Northern Ballet Theatre), 1989; *orchestral compositions:* Lines on London (symphony), 1980 (commnd by Capital Radio); Clarinet Concerto, 1984; Beginners Please!, 1987; (with Paul McCartney) Liverpool Oratorio, 1991. Co-founder and partner with Terry Oates of Sundergrade Music Ltd, 1978–88. Mem. BAFTA, 1979–. First winner, BAFTA Award for Original TV Music, 1981. Chevalier de L'Ordre des Arts et des Lettres, 1983. *Publications:* sheet music of television themes. *Recreations:* reading, gardening, playing chamber music, cooking. *Address:* c/o Paul Wing, 35 Priory Road, N8. *T:* 081–348 6604, *Telex:* 859888, *Fax:* 081–340 8434.

DAVIS, Sir Charles (Sigmund), Kt 1965; CB 1960; Counsel to the Speaker (European Legislation), (formerly Second Counsel), House of Commons, 1974–83; *b* London, 22 Jan. 1909; *y s* of late Maurice Davis (*b* Melbourne, Australia) and Alfreda Regina Davis; *m* 1940, Pamela Mary, *er d* of late J. K. B. Dawson, OBE, and Phyllis Dawson; two *d*. *Educ:* Trinity Coll., Cambridge. Double 1st Cl. Hons, Law Tripos; Sen. Schol., Exhibitioner and Prizeman of Trinity, 1927–30; MA 1934. Called to the Bar, Inner Temple (Studentship and Certif. of Honour), 1930, and in Sydney, Australia, 1931; practised as barrister in London, 1931–34; entered Legal Branch, Ministry of Health, 1934; held legal posts in various public offices, 1938–46 (Corporal, Home Guard, 1940–45); Asst Solicitor, Min. of Agric. and Fisheries, 1946–55; Prin. Asst Solicitor, MAFF, 1955–57; Legal Adviser and Solicitor, MAFF, and Forestry Commission, 1957–74, retired. Vice-Pres., Cancer Relief Macmillan Fund (formerly Nat. Soc. for Cancer Relief), 1989– (Chm. Council, 1983–85; Trustee, 1985–89). *Recreations:* music (LRAM, ARCM) and much else. *Address:* 43 Wolsey Road, East Molesey, Surrey KT8 9EW.

DAVIS, Mrs Chloë Marion, OBE 1975; Chairman, Consumer Affairs Group of National Organisations, 1973–79; Member: Council on Tribunals, 1970–79; Consumer Standards Advisory Committee of British Standards Institution, 1965–78 (Chairman 1970–73); *b* Dartmouth, Devon, 15 Feb. 1909; *d* of Richard Henry Pound and Mary Jane Chapman; *m* 1928, Edward Thomas Davis (*d* 1983), printer and sometime writer; one *s*. *Educ:* limited formal, USA and England. Various part-time voluntary social and public services from 1929; Birth Control Internat. Information Centre, 1931–38; voluntary activity in bombing etc emergencies, also cookery and domestic broadcasting during War of 1939–45; information service for Kreis Resident Officers, Control Commn for Germany, Berlin, 1946–48; regional Citizens Advice Bureaux office, London Council of Social Service, 1949–55; Sen. Information Officer to Nat. Citizens Advice Bureaux Council, 1956–69. Member: Nat. House-Building Council, 1973–76; Consumer Consultative Cttee, EEC, 1973–76; Exec. Cttee, Housewife's Trust, 1970–77. *Recreations:* reading present history in the morning in newspapers and past history in books in the evening; gardening, walking, talking with friends. *Address:* Auberville Cottage, 246 Dover Road, Walmer, Kent CT14 7NP. *T:* Deal (0304) 374038.

DAVIS, Sir Colin (Rex), Kt 1980; CBE 1965; Chief Conductor, Bavarian Radio Symphony Orchestra, since 1983; *b* 25 Sept. 1927; *s* of Reginald George and Lillian Davis; *m* 1949, April Cantelo (marr. diss., 1964); one *s* one *d*; *m* 1964, Ashraf Naini; three *s* two *d*. *Educ:* Christ's Hospital; Royal College of Music. Orchestral Conductor, Freelance wilderness, 1949–57; Asst Conductor, BBC Scottish Orchestra, 1957–59. Conductor, Sadler's Wells, 1959, Principal Conductor, 1960–65, Musical Director, 1961–65; Chief Conductor, BBC Symphony Orchestra, 1967–71, Chief Guest Conductor, 1971–75; Musical Dir, Royal Opera House, Covent Garden, 1971–86; Principal Guest Conductor: Boston SO, 1972–84; LSO, 1974–; Hon. Conductor, Dresden Staatskapelle, 1990. Conducted at: Metropolitan Opera House, New York, 1969, 1970, 1972; Bayreuth Fest., 1977; Vienna State Opera, 1986. Sibelius Medal, Finland Sibelius Soc., 1977; Grosse Schallplattenpreis, 1978; Shakespeare Prize, Hamburg, 1984. Commendatore of Republic of Italy, 1976; Chevalier, Légion d'Honneur (France), 1982; Commander's Cross, Order of Merit (FRG), 1987; Commandeur, l'Ordre des Arts et des Lettres (France), 1990. *Recreations:* anything at all. *Address:* 39 Cathcart Road, SW10 9JG. *Club:* Athenæum.

DAVIS, David; *see* Davis, William Eric.

DAVIS, David Michael; MP (C) Boothferry, since 1987; an Assistant Government Whip, since 1990; *b* 23 Dec. 1948; *s* of Ronald and Elizabeth Davis; *m* 1973, Doreen Margery Cook; one *s* two *d*. *Educ:* Warwick Univ. (BSc); London Business Sch. (MSc); Harvard (AMP). Joined Tate & Lyle, 1974; Financial Dir, Manbré & Garton, 1977; Man. Dir, Tate & Lyle Transport, 1980; Pres., Zymaize, 1982; Strategic Planning Dir, Tate & Lyle plc, 1984–87. PPS to Parly Under-Sec. of State, DTI, 1989–90. Mem., Financial Policy Cttee, CBI, 1977–79; Exec. Mem., Industrial Soc., 1985–87. Chm., Fedn of Cons. Students, 1973–74. *Recreations:* writing, flying, mountaineering. *Address:* House of Commons, SW1A 0AA.

DAVIS, Derek Alan, CEng; Director, World Energy Council, since 1990; *b* 5 Oct. 1929; *s* of Irene Davis (*née* Longstaff) and Sydney George Davis; *m* 1954, Ann Margery Willett; three *s*. *Educ:* private schools; Battersea Polytechnic; London University. BScEng (First Hons) 1950; MIMechE; CBIM. De Havilland Engine Co Ltd: post-graduate apprentice, 1950–52; develt engineer, Gas Turbine Div., 1952–53, Rocket Div., 1953–56; Central Electricity Generating Board: Research Labs, 1956–60; Manager, Mech. and Civil Engineering, 1960–65; Group Head Fuel, 1965, System Econ. Engineer, 1970, System Planning Engineer, 1973–75, Planning Dept; Dir, Resource Planning, later Dir Production, NE Region, 1975–81; Dir Corporate Strategy Dept, 1981–84; Mem., 1984–90. Member: SERC, 1989–; Meteorology Cttee, MoD, 1986–; ACORD, Dept of Energy, 1990–. *Publications:* articles in tech. and engineering jls. *Recreations:* playing, now watching, sport; gardening, DIY, reading. *Address:* New Lodge, c/o Management & Conference Centre, Smug Oak Lane, Bricket Wood, St Albans AL2 3UE. *T:* Watford (0923) 893989.

DAVIS, Derek Richard; Under Secretary, Oil and Gas Division, Department of Energy, since 1987 (Gas Division, 1985–87); *b* 3 May 1945; *s* of Stanley Lewis Davis, OBE and Rita Beatrice Rachel (*née* Rosenheim); *m* 1987, Diana Levinson; one *s* one *d*. *Educ:* Clifton Coll., Bristol; Balliol Coll., Oxford (BA 1967). Asst Principal, BoT, 1967; Pvte Sec. to Perm. Sec., DTI, 1971–72; Principal, 1972; Asst Sec., Dept of Energy, 1977; Secretary: Energy Commn, 1977–79; NEDC Energy Task Force, 1981; seconded to NCB, 1982–83. *Address:* c/o Department of Energy, 1 Palace Street, SW1E 5HE. *T:* 071–238 3099.

DAVIS, Prof. Derek Russell, MD, FRCP; Norah Cooke Hurle Professor of Mental Health, University of Bristol, 1962–79; *b* 20 April 1914; *s* of late Edward David Darelan Davis, FRCS, and of Alice Mildred (*née* Russell); *m* 1939, Marit, *d* of Iver M. Iversen, Oslo, Norway; one *s* one *d*. *Educ:* Stowe Sch., Buckingham; Clare Coll., Cambridge (major entrance and foundn schol.); Middlesex Hosp. Med. Sch. MA, MD; FRCP. Ho. Phys., Mddx Hosp., 1938; Addenbrooke's Hosp., Cambridge, 1939; Asst Physician, Runwell Hosp., 1939; Mem. Scientific Staff, MRC, 1940; Lectr in Psychopathology, Univ. of Cambridge, 1948; Reader in Clinical Psychology, 1950; Dir, Med. Psychology Research Unit, 1958; Consultant Psychiatrist, United Cambridge Hosps, 1948; Editor, Quarterly Jl of Experimental Psychology, 1949–57. Visiting Professor: Univ. of Virginia, 1958; Univ. of Dundee, 1976; Univ. of Otago, 1977. Fellow, Clare Coll., Cambridge, 1961. Dean of Medicine, Univ. of Bristol, 1970–72. Member: Avon AHA (Teaching),

1974–79; Council of Management, MIND, 1975–; Pres., Fedn of Mental Health Workers, 1972. Adolf Meyer Lectr, Amer. Psychiatric Assoc., 1967. FRCPsych, FBPsS. *Publications:* An Introduction to Psychopathology, 1957, 4th edn 1984; many articles in scientific and med. jls. *Recreations:* Ibsen studies, theatre. *Address:* 9 Clyde Road, Bristol BS6 6RJ. *T:* Bristol (0272) 734744.

See also J. D. Russell-Davis.

DAVIS, Hon. Sir (Dermot) Renn, Kt 1981; OBE 1971; **Hon. Mr Justice Davis;** Chief Justice, Supreme Court of the Falkland Islands, since 1987; Judge, Supreme Court of the British Antarctic Territory, since 1988; Judge, Court of Appeal for Gibraltar, since 1989; *b* 20 Nov. 1928; *s* of Captain Eric R. Davis, OBE and Norah A. Davis (*née* Bingham); *m* 1984, Mary, *widow* of William James Pearce and *d* of late Brig. T. F. K. Howard, DSO, RA. *Educ:* Prince of Wales Sch., Nairobi; Wadham Coll., Oxford (BA Hons). Called to the Bar, Inner Temple, 1953; Daly and Figgis, Advocates, Nairobi, 1953–56; Attorney-General's Chambers, Kenya, 1956–62; Attorney-General, British Solomon Islands Protectorate, and Legal Advr, Western Pacific High Commn, 1962–73; British Judge, New Hebrides Condominium, 1973–76; Chief Justice, Solomon Islands, 1976–80 and Chief Justice, Tuvalu, 1978–80; Chief Justice, Gibraltar, 1980–86. *Recreations:* music, walking. *Address:* The Supreme Court, Stanley, Falkland Islands; Ivy House, Shalbourne, near Marlborough, Wilts SN8 3QH. *Clubs:* United Oxford & Cambridge University; Muthaiga Country (Nairobi); Royal Gibraltar Yacht.

DAVIS, Sir (Ernest) Howard, Kt 1978; CMG 1969; OBE 1960; Deputy Governor, Gibraltar, 1971–78; *b* 22 April 1918; *m* 1948, Marie Davis (*née* Bellotti); two *s*. *Educ:* Christian Brothers Schs, Gibraltar and Blackpool; London Univ. (BA 1st cl. hons). Gen. Clerical Staff, Gibraltar, 1936–46; Asst Sec. and Clerk of Councils, 1946–54; seconded Colonial Office, 1954–55; Chief Asst Sec., Estabt Officer and Public Relations Officer (responsible for opening Radio Gibraltar), Gibraltar, 1955–62; Director of Labour and Social Security, 1962–65; Financial and Development Secretary, 1965–71; Acting Governor, various periods, 1971–77. Dir, Gibraltar and Iberian Bank Ltd, 1981–. Chairman, Committee of Enquiry: PWD, 1980–81; Electricity Dept, 1982; Chm., Gibraltar Broadcasting Corp., 1982–83. Chm., Gibraltar Horticultural Soc., 1988–90. Pres., Calpe Rowing Club, 1985. *Recreations:* cricket, gardening, bridge. *Address:* Flat 6, Mount Pleasant, South Barrack Road, Gibraltar. *T:* A.70358.

DAVIS, Godfrey Rupert Carless, CBE 1981; FSA; Secretary, Royal Commission on Historical Manuscripts, 1972–81; *b* 22 April 1917; *s* of late Prof. Henry William Carless Davis and Rosa Jennie Davis (*née* Lindup); *m* 1942, Dorothie Elizabeth Mary Loveband; one *s* two *d*. *Educ:* Highgate Sch.; Balliol Coll., Oxford (MA, DPhil). Rome Scholar in Ancient History, 1938. Army Service, 1939–46, Devon Regt and Intell. Corps, Captain 1942. Dept of MSS, British Museum: Asst Keeper, 1947; Dep. Keeper, 1961–72. FRHistS 1954 (Treas. 1967–74); FSA 1974. *Publications:* Medieval Cartularies of Great Britain, 1958; Magna Carta, 1963; contrib. British Museum Cat. Add. MSS 1926–1950 (6 vols); learned jls. *Address:* 214 Somerset Road, SW19 5JE. *T:* 081–946 7955.

DAVIS, Rt. Hon. Helen Elizabeth; *see* Clark, Rt. Hon. H. E.

DAVIS, Sir Howard; *see* Davis, Sir E. H.

DAVIS, Ivor John Guest, CB 1983; Director, Common Law Institute of Intellectual Property, since 1986; *b* 11 Dec. 1925; *s* of Thomas Henry Davis and Dorothy Annie Davis; *m* 1954, Mary Eleanor Thompson; one *s* one *d*. *Educ:* Devonport High Sch.; HM Dockyard Sch., Devonport. BSc London (ext.). Apprentice, HM Dockyard, Devonport, 1941–45, Draughtsman, 1946–47; Patent Office, Dept of Trade: Asst Examr, 1947; Asst Comptroller, 1973; Comptroller Gen., Patents, Designs and Trade Marks, 1978. Pres., Administrative Council, European Patent Office, 1981–85. Mem. Governing Bd, Centre d'études de la propriété industrielle, Strasbourg, 1979–85. Mem., Editorial Adv. Bd, World Patent Information Journal, 1979–85. *Recreations:* music, gardening. *Address:* 5 Birch Close, Eynsford, Dartford DA4 0EX.

DAVIS, James Gresham, CBE 1988; MA; FCIT; FICS; Chairman: Simpler Trade Procedures Board, since 1987; International Maritime Industries Forum, since 1981; DFDS Ltd, since 1984 (Director, 1975); Bromley Shipping plc, since 1989; TIP Europe plc, since 1990 (Director, 1987); *b* 20 July 1928; *s* of Col Robert Davis, OBE, JP and Josephine Davis (*née* Edwards); *m* 1973, Adriana Johanna Verhoef, Utrecht, Holland; three *d*. *Educ:* Bradfield Coll.; Clare Coll., Cambridge (MA). FCIT 1969. Served RN, 1946–49. P&OSN Co., 1952–72: Calcutta, 1953; Kobe, Japan, 1954–56; Hong Kong, 1956–57; Director: P&O Lines, 1967–72; Kleinwort Benson Ltd, 1973–88; Pearl Cruises of Scandinavia Inc., 1982–86; Rodskog Shipbrokers (Hong Kong) Ltd, 1983–88; Associated British Ports Holdings plc, 1983–; Transport Develt Gp plc, 1984–; Global Ocean Carriers Ltd, 1988–; Sedgwick Marine & Cargo Ltd, 1988–. Mem. Adv. Board: J. Lauritzen A/S, Copenhagen, 1981–85; DFDS A/S, Copenhagen, 1981–85; Adviser, Tjaereborg (UK) Ltd, 1985–87. Mem. (part-time), British Transport Docks Bd, 1981–83; Dir, British Internat. Freight Assoc., 1989–; Chairman: Friends of the World Maritime Univ., 1985–; Marine Soc., 1987–; Anglian Bd, BR, 1988–; Mem. Council, Missions to Seamen, 1981–. President: World Ship Soc., 1969, 1971, 1984–86; CIT, 1981–82; Inst. of Freight Forwarders, 1984–86; National Waterways Transport Assoc., 1986–; Inst. of Supervisory Management, 1989–; Internat. Cttee, Bureau Veritas, 1989–; Inst. of Chartered Shipbrokers, 1990– (Vice-Pres., 1988–90); Harwich Lifeboat, RNLI, 1984–; Vice-Pres., British Maritime League, 1984–88; Member: Baltic Exchange, 1973; Greenwich Forum, 1981. FRSA 1986. Hon. FNI 1985; Hon. FInstFF 1986. Liveryman and Mem., Court of Assts, Worshipful Co. of Shipwrights; Freeman, City of London, 1986. Younger Brother, Trinity House, 1989. Governor, Queenswood Sch. *Recreations:* golf, family, ships. *Address:* 115 Woodsford Square, W14 8DT. *T:* 071–602 0675; Summer Lawn, Dovercourt, Essex, CO12 4EF. *T:* Harwich (0255) 502981. *Clubs:* Brooks's, Hurlingham, Golfers; Fanlingerers; Harwich & Dovercourt Golf, Royal Calcutta Golf; Holland Park Lawn Tennis.

DAVIS, John; *see* Davis, A. J.

DAVIS, Prof. John Allen, MD, FRCP; Professor of Paediatrics, and Fellow of Peterhouse, University of Cambridge, 1979–88, now Professor Emeritus and Fellow Emeritus; *b* 6 Aug. 1923; *s* of Major H. E. Davis, MC, and Mrs M. W. Davis; *m* 1957, Madeleine Elizabeth Vinicombe Ashlin (author with D. Wallbridge of Boundary and Space: introduction to the work of D. W. Winnicott, 1981); three *s* two *d*. *Educ:* Blundells Sch., Tiverton (Scholar); St Mary's Hosp. Med. Sch. (Scholar; MB, BS 1946; London Univ. Gold Medal); MSc Manchester, 1968; MA Cantab; MD Cantab 1988. FRCP 1967. Army Service, BAOR, 1947–49. House Physician: St Mary's Hosp., 1947; Gt Ormond St Hosp. for Sick Children, 1950; Registrar/Sen. Registrar, St Mary's Paediatric Unit and Home Care Scheme, 1951–57; Sen. Asst Resident, Children's Med. Centre, Boston, Mass, and Harvard Teaching Fellow, 1953; Nuffield Res. Fellowship, Oxford, 1958–59; Sen. Lectr, Inst. of Child Health, and Reader, Hammersmith Hosp., 1960–67; Prof. of Paediatrics and Child Health, Victoria Univ. of Manchester, 1967–79. Second Vice Pres., RCP, 1986; Hon. Member: BPA (former Chm., Academic Bd); Assoc. of Physicians; Société française de pédiatrie; Hungarian Acad. Paediatrics; Neonatal Soc.; Pres., Eur. Soc. for Pediatric Research, 1984–85; Patron: Child Psychotherapy Trust, 1987–; Arts for Health, 1989–. Greenwood Lectr, 1981; Sigmund Freud Meml Lectr, Univ. of Exeter, 1988. Dawson Williams Prize, BMA, 1986; James Spence Medal, BPA, 1991. *Publications:* Scientific Foundations of Paediatrics (ed and contrib.), 1974 (2nd edn 1981); Place of Birth, 1978; (ed jtly) Parent-Baby Attachment in Premature Infants, 1984; papers in various medical and scientific jls. *Recreations:* collecting and painting watercolours, gardening, reading, music. *Address:* Four Mile House, 1 Cambridge Road, Great Shelford, Cambridge CB2 5JE.

DAVIS, John Darelan R.; *see* Russell-Davis, J. D.

DAVIS, Sir John (Gilbert), 3rd Bt *cr* 1946; *b* 17 Aug. 1936; *s* of Sir Gilbert Davis, 2nd Bt, and of Kathleen, *d* of Sidney Deacon Ford; *S* father, 1973; *m* 1960, Elizabeth Margaret, *d* of Robert Smith Turnbull; one *s* two *d*. *Educ:* Oundle School; Britannia RNC, Dartmouth. RN, 1955–56. Joined Spicers Ltd, 1956; emigrated to Montreal, Canada, 1957; joined Inter City Papers and progressed through the company until becoming Pres., 1967; transf. to parent co, Abitibi-Price Inc., 1976 and held several exec. positions before retiring as Exec. Vice-Pres., 1989. *Recreations:* sports, golf, tennis, squash; music, reading. *Heir:* *s* Richard Charles Davis, *b* 11 April 1970. *Address:* 5 York Ridge Road, Willowdale, Ont M2P 1R8, Canada. *T:* 222–4916. *Clubs:* Donalda, Toronto (Toronto); Rosedale Golf.

DAVIS, Sir John (Henry Harris), Kt 1971; CVO 1985; Director, The Rank Foundation, since 1953; President, The Rank Organisation plc, Subsidiary and Associated Cos, 1977–83 (Chief Executive, 1962–74; Chairman, 1962–77); Joint President, Rank Xerox, 1972–83 (Joint Chairman 1957–72); *b* 10 Nov. 1906; *s* of Sydney Myering Davis and Emily Harris; *m* 1926, Joan Buckingham; one *s*; *m* 1947, Marion Gavid; two *d*; *m* 1954, Dinah Sheridan (marr. diss. 1965); *m* 1976, Mrs Felicity Rutland. *Educ:* City of London Sch. British Thomson-Houston Group, 1932–38. Joined Odeon Theatres (predecessor of The Rank Organisation Ltd); Chief Accountant, Jan. 1938; Sec., June 1938; Jt Managing Dir, 1942; Man. Dir, 1948–62 and Dep. Chm., 1951–62, The Rank Organisation Ltd. Director: Southern Television Ltd, 1968–76; Eagle Star Insurance Co. Ltd, 1948–82; Chm., Children's Film Foundation, 1951–80; Chm. and Trustee, The Rank Prize Funds, 1972–. Trustee, Westminster Abbey Trust, 1973–85 (Chm., fund raising cttee, Westminster Abbey Appeal, 1973–85). President: The Advertising Assoc., 1973–76; Cinema and Television Benevolent Fund, 1981–83; East Surrey Cons. Assoc., 1982–87. FCIS 1939. Commandeur de l'Ordre de la Couronne (Belgium), 1974; KStJ. Hon. DTech Loughborough, 1975. *Recreations:* farming, gardening, reading, travel, music. *Address:* 4 Selwood Terrace, SW7. *Club:* Royal Automobile.

DAVIS, Prof. John Horsley Russell, FBA 1988; Professor of Social Anthropology, University of Oxford, since 1990; *b* 9 Sept. 1938; *s* of William Russell Davis and Jean (*née* Horsley); *m* 1981, Dymphna Gerarda Hermans; three *s*. *Educ:* University Coll., Oxford (BA); Univ. of London (PhD). University of Kent, 1966–90: progressively, Lectr, Sen. Lectr, Reader, Social Anthropology; Prof., 1982–90. *Publications:* Land and Family in Pisticci, 1973; People of the Mediterranean, 1977; Libyan Politics: tribe and revolution, 1987. *Recreations:* gardens, music. *Address:* Institute of Social Anthropology, 51 Banbury Road, Oxford OX2 6PF.

DAVIS, John Michael N.; *see* Newsom Davis.

DAVIS, Leslie Harold Newsom, CMG 1957; *b* 6 April 1909; *s* of Harold Newsom Davis and Aileen Newsom Davis (*née* Gush); *m* 1950, Judith Anne, *d* of L. G. Corney, CMG; one *s* two *d*. *Educ:* Marlborough; Trinity Coll., Cambridge. Apptd to Malayan Civil Service, 1932; Private Sec. to Governor and High Comr, 1938–40; attached to 22nd Ind. Inf. Bde as Liaison Officer, Dec. 1941; interned by Japanese in Singapore, 1942–45; District Officer, Seremban, 1946–47; British Resident, Brunei, 1948; Asst Adviser, Muar, 1948–50; Sec. to Mem. for Education, Fed. of Malaya, 1951–52. Mem. for Industrial and Social Relations, 1952–53; Sec. for Defence and Internal Security, Singapore, 1953–55; Permanent Sec., Min. of Communications and Works, Singapore, 1955–57; Special Rep., Rubber Growers' Assoc. in Malaya, 1958–63. *Recreation:* golf. *Address:* Berrywood, Heyshott, near Midhurst, West Sussex GU29 0DH. *Club:* United Oxford & Cambridge University.

DAVIS, Madeline; Regional Nursing Officer, Oxford Regional Health Authority, 1973–83; retired; *b* 12 March 1925; *d* of late James William Henry Davis, JP, and Mrs Edith Maude Davis; *m* 1977, Comdr William Milburn Gibson, RN. *Educ:* Haberdashers' Aske's Hatcham Girls' Sch.; Guy's Hosp. (SRN); British Hosp. for Mothers and Babies, Woolwich; Bristol Maternity Hosp. (SCM). Ward Sister, then Dep. Night Supt, Guy's Hosp., 1949–53; Asst Matron, Guy's Hosp., 1953–57; Admin. Sister then Dep. Matron, St Charles' Hosp., London, 1957–61; Asst Nursing Officer, 1962–68, Chief Regional Nursing Officer, 1968–73, Oxford Regional Hosp. Bd. Formerly Mem., Central Midwives Board. *Recreations:* village community work, theatre, golf. *Clubs:* New Cavendish; North Oxford Golf.

DAVIS, Prof. Mark Herbert Ainsworth; Professor of System Theory, Imperial College London, since 1984; *b* 1 May 1945; *s* of Christopher A. Davis and Frances E. Davis (*née* Marsden); *m* 1988, Jessica I. C. Smith. *Educ:* Oundle Sch.; Clare College, Cambridge (BA 1966, MA 1970, ScD 1983); Univ. of California (PhD 1971). FSS 1985. Research Asst, Electronics Res. Lab., Univ. of California, Berkeley, 1969–71; Lectr, 1971–79, Reader, 1979–84, Imperial College, London. Visiting appointments: Polish Acad. of Sciences, 1973; Harvard, 1974; MIT, 1978; Washington Univ., St Louis, 1979; ETH Zurich, 1984; Oslo Univ., 1991. Editor, Stochastics and Stochastics Reports, 1979–; Co-Editor, Mathematical Finance, 1991–. *Publications:* Linear Estimation and Stochastic Control, 1977, Russian edn 1984; (with R. B. Vinter) Stochastic Modelling and Control, 1985; jl articles on probability, stochastic processes, control and filtering theory. *Recreation:* classical music (violin and viola). *Address:* 11 Chartfield Avenue, SW15 6DT. *T:* 081–789 7677.

DAVIS, Hon. Sir Maurice, Kt 1975; OBE 1953; QC 1965; Chief Justice of the West Indies Associated States Supreme Court, and of Supreme Court of Grenada, 1975–80; *b* St Kitts, 30 April 1912; *m* Kathleen; one *s* five *d*. Pres., St Kitts Bar Assoc., 1968–75. Mem. Legislature, St Kitts, 1944–57; Mem., Exec. Council, St Kitts; Dep. Pres., Gen. Legislative Council, and Mem., Fed. Exec. Council, Leeward Is. *Recreations:* cricket, football. *Address:* PO Box 31, Basseterre, St Kitts, West Indies.

DAVIS, Dr Michael; Hon. Director General, Commission of European Communities, Brussels, since 1989; *b* 9 June 1923; *s* of William James Davis and Rosaline Sarah (*née* May); *m* 1951, Helena Hobbs Campbell, *e d* of Roland and Catherine Campbell, Toronto. *Educ:* UC Exeter (BSc); Bristol Univ. (PhD). CEng, FIMM; CPhys, FInstP. Radar Officer, Flagship, 4th Cruiser Sqdn, British Pacific Fleet, Lieut (Sp. Br.) RNVR, 1943–46 (despatches). Res. Fellow, Canadian Atomic Energy Project, Toronto Univ., 1949–51; Sen. Sci. Officer, Services Electronics Res. Lab., 1951–55; UKAEA: Commercial Dir and Techn. Adviser, 1956–73; Dir of Nuclear Energy, Other Primary Sources and Electricity,

EEC, 1973–81; Dir for Energy Saving, Alternative Sources of Energy, Electricity and Heat, EEC, 1981–88. Chm., OECD Cttee on World Uranium Resources, 1969–73; Dir, NATO Advanced Study Inst., 1971; advised NZ Govt on Atomic Energy, 1967. McLaughlin Meml Lectr, Instn of Engineers of Ireland, 1977. *Publications:* (ed jtly) Uranium Prospecting Handbook, 1972; papers in various sci. jls. *Recreation:* sculpture. *Address:* Résidence Cambridge, Boîte 5, Avenue Château de Walzin 12, B-1180 Brussels, Belgium. *T:* (02) 343.38.78. *Club:* United Oxford & Cambridge University.

DAVIS, Michael McFarland; Director for Wales, Property Services Agency, Department of the Environment, 1972–77; *b* 1 Feb. 1919; 2nd *s* of Harold McFarland and Gladys Mary Davis; *m* 1942, Aline Seton Butler; three *d. Educ:* Haberdashers' Aske's, Hampstead. Entered Air Ministry, 1936. Served War, RAF, 1940–45 (PoW, 1942–45). Private Sec. to Chiefs and Vice-Chiefs of Air Staff, 1945–49, and to Under-Secretary of State for Air, 1952–54; Harvard Univ. Internat. Seminar, 1956; Student, IDC, 1965; Command Sec., FEAF, 1966–69; on loan to Cabinet Office (Central Unit on Environmental Pollution), 1970; transf. to Dept of Environment, 1971. Delegate to UN Conf. on Human Environment, Stockholm, 1972. *Recreations:* doing up old things, music, croquet, wine. *Address:* 18 Roselands, Sidmouth, Devon EX10 8PB. *T:* Sidmouth (0395) 577123. *Club:* Sidmouth Croquet.

DAVIS, Nathanael Vining; Chairman, 1947–86, and Chief Executive Officer, 1947–79, Alcan Aluminium Limited; *b* 26 June 1915; *s* of Rhea Reineman Davis and Edward Kirk Davis; *m* 1941, Lois Howard Thompson; one *s* one *d. Educ:* Harvard Coll.; London Sch. of Economics. With Alcan group since 1939 with exception of 3 years on active duty with US Navy. *Director:* Bank of Montreal, 1961–86; Canada Life Assurance Co., Toronto, 1961–86. *Address:* Box 309, Osterville, Mass 02655, USA. *Clubs:* Mount Royal (Montreal); University (New York).

DAVIS, Peter John; Chief Executive, since 1986, and Chairman, since 1990, Reed International PLC; *b* 23 Dec. 1941; *s* of John Stephen Davis and Adriaantje de Baat; *m* 1968, Susan Hillman; two *s* one *d. Educ:* Shrewsbury Sch.; Grad. Inst. of Marketing (Drexler Travelling Schol., 1961). Management trainee and salesman, Ditchburn Orgn, 1959–65; marketing and sales posts, General Foods Ltd, Banbury, 1965–72; Fitch Lovell Ltd; 1973–76: Marketing Dir, Key Markets; Man. Dir, Key Markets and David Greig; joined J. Sainsbury, 1976; Marketing Dir, 1977; Asst Man. Dir, 1979; Mem. Bd, Sava Centre, 1979–83; Dir, then Dep. Chm., Homebase, 1983–86; Dir, Shaws Supermarkets Inc., Mass, 1984–86; Dep. Chief Exec., Reed Internat., 1986. *Director:* Granada Gp, 1987–91; Boots Co., 1991–. Chm., Adult Literacy and Basic Skills Unit, 1989–; Mem., President's Cttee, BITC, 1991–. Dep. Chm., Financial Develt Bd, NSPCC, 1986–. Governor, Duncombe Sch., Hertford, 1976–. FRSA. *Recreations:* sailing, reading, opera, wine. *Address:* Reed House, 6 Chesterfield Gardens, W1A 1EJ. *T:* 071–491 8279. *Club:* Trearddur Bay Sailing (Cdre, 1982–84).

DAVIS, Hon. Sir Renn; see Davis, Hon. Sir D. R.

DAVIS, Air Vice-Marshal Robert Leslie, CB 1984; RAF, retired 1983; *b* 22 March 1930; *s* of Sidney and Florence Davis; *m* 1956, Diana, *d* of Edward William Bryant; one *s* one *d. Educ:* Woolsingham Grammar Sch., Co. Durham; Bede Sch. Collegiate, Sunderland, Co. Durham; RAF Coll., Cranwell. Commnd, 1952; served fighter units, exchange posting, USAF, Staff Coll., OR and Ops appts, MoD, DS Staff Coll., 1953–69; comd No 19 Sqdn, 1970–72; Dep. Dir Ops Air Defence, MoD, 1972–75; comd RAF Leuchars, 1975–77; Comdr RAF Staff, and Air Attaché, British Defence Staff, Washington, DC, 1977–80; Comdr, British Forces Cyprus, and Administrator, Sovereign Base Areas, Cyprus, 1980–83, retired. Man. Dir, Bodenseewerk Geratetechnik/British Aerospace GmbH, 1983–86, retd. *Recreations:* golf, antiques, music. *Address:* c/o Lloyds Bank, 54 Fawcett Street, Sunderland, Tyne and Wear.

DAVIS, Sir Rupert C. H.; see Hart-Davis.

DAVIS, Prof. Stanley Stewart, CChem, FRSC; Lord Trent Professor of Pharmacy, Nottingham University, since 1975; *b* 17 Dec. 1942; *s* of William Stanley and Joan Davis; *m* 1984, Lisbeth Illum; three *s. Educ:* Warwick Sch.; London Univ. (BPharm, PhD, DSc). FPS. Lecturer, London Univ., 1976–80; Sen. Lectr, Aston Univ., 1970–75. Fulbright Scholar, Univ. of Kansas, 1978–79; various periods as visiting scientist to pharmaceutical industry. *Publications:* (co-ed) Radionuclide Imaging in Drug Research, 1982; (co-ed) Microspheres and Drug Therapy, 1984; (co-ed) Site Specific Drug Delivery, 1986; (co-ed) Polymers in Controlled Drug Delivery, 1988; (co-ed) Drug Delivery to the Gastrointestinal Tract, 1989; (co-ed) Pharmaceutical Application of Cell and Tissue Culture to Drug Transport, 1991; over 500 research pubns in various scientific jls. *Recreations:* squash, tennis, ski-ing. *Address:* 19 Cavendish Crescent North, The Park, Nottingham NG7 1BA. *T:* Nottingham (0602) 481866.

DAVIS, Steve, MBE 1988; snooker player; *b* 22 Aug. 1957; *s* of Harry George Davis and Jean Catherine Davis; *m* 1990, Judy Greig; one *s. Educ:* Alexander McLeod Primary School and Abbey Wood School, London. Became professional snooker player, 1978; has won numerous championships in UK and abroad; major titles include: UK Professional Champion, 1980, 1981, 1984, 1985, 1986, 1987; Masters Champion, 1981, 1982, 1988; International Champion, 1981, 1983, 1984; World Professional Champion, 1981, 1983, 1984, 1987, 1988, 1989; BBC Sports Personality of the Year, 1988. *Publications:* Steve Davis, World Champion, 1981; Frame and Fortune, 1982; Successful Snooker, 1982; How to be Really Interesting, 1988. *Recreations:* chess, keep fit, listening to records (jazz/soul), Tom Sharpe books. *Address:* 10 Western Road, Romford, Essex RM1 3JT. *T:* Romford (0708) 730480. *Club:* Matchroom (Romford).

DAVIS, Terence Anthony Gordon, (Terry Davis); MP (Lab) Birmingham, Hodge Hill, since 1983 (Birmingham, Stechford, 1979–83); *b* 5 Jan. 1938; *s* of Gordon Davis and Gladys (*née* Avery), Stourbridge, West Midlands; *m* 1963, Anne, *d* of F. B. Cooper, Newton-le-Willows, Lancs; one *s* one *d. Educ:* King Edward VI Grammar Sch., Stourbridge, Worcestershire; University Coll. London (LLB); Univ. of Michigan, USA (MBA). Company Executive, 1962–71. Motor Industry Manager, 1974–79. Joined Labour Party, 1965; contested (Lab) Bromsgrove, 1970, Feb. and Oct. 1974; Birmingham, Stechford, March 1977. MP (Lab) Bromsgrove, May 1971–Feb. 1974; Opposition Whip, 1979–80; opposition spokesman: on the health service and social services, 1980–83; on Treasury and economic affairs, 1983–86; on industry, 1986–87. Member: Public Accounts Cttee, 1987–; Adv. Council on Public Records, 1989–. Mem., MSF. Member, Yeovil Rural District Council, 1967–68. *Address:* 5 Hodge Hill Court, Bromford Road, Hodge Hill, Birmingham B36 8AN.

DAVIS, Hon. Sir Thomas (Robert Alexander Harries), KBE 1981; Pa Tu Te Rangi Ariki 1979; Prime Minister, Cook Islands, 1978–87; *b* 11 June 1917; *s* of Sidney Thomes Davis and Mary Anne Harries; *m* 1940, Myra Lydia Henderson; three *s*; *m* 1979, Pa Tepaeru Ariki. *Educ:* King's Coll., Auckland, NZ; Otago Univ. Med. Sch. (MB, ChB 1945); Sch. of Tropical Medicine, Sydney Univ., Australia (DTM&H 1950); Harvard Sch. of Public Health (Master of Public Health 1952). FRSTM&H 1949. MO and Surg. Specialist, Cook Islands Med. Service, 1945–48; Chief MO, Cook Is Med. Service,

1948–52; Res. Staff, Dept of Nutrition, Harvard Sch. of Public Health, 1952–55; Chief, Dept of Environmental Medicine, Arctic Aero-medical Lab., Fairbanks, Alaska, 1955–56; Res. Physician and Dir, Div. of Environmtl Med., Army Medical Res. Lab., Fort Knox, Ky, 1956–61; Dir of Res., US Army Res. Inst. of Environmtl Med., Natick, 1961–63; Res. Exec., Arthur D. Little, Inc., 1963–71. Involved in biol aspects of space prog., first for Army, later for NASA, 1957–71. Formed Democratic Party, Cook Islands, 1971; private med. practice, Cook Islands, 1974–78. Mem., RSocMed, 1960; twice Pres., Med. and Dental Assoc., Cook Islands. Silver Jubilee Medal, 1977; Order of Merit, Fed. Republic of Germany, 1978. *Publications:* Doctor to the Islands, 1954; Makutu, 1956; over 80 scientific and other pubns. *Recreations:* deep sea fishing, yacht racing, agriculture/planting, amateur radio. *Address:* Aremango, Rarotonga, Cook Islands. *Clubs:* Harvard (Boston, Mass); Wellington (NZ); Avatiu Sports (patron), Ivans (Pres. 1990), Rarotonga Yacht (patron); Avatiu Cricket (patron).

DAVIS, William; author, publisher, and broadcaster; Editor and Publisher of High Life, since 1973; Chairman: British Tourist Authority, since 1990; English Tourist Board, since 1990; Director: Thomas Cook, since 1988; British Invisibles, since 1990; *b* 6 March 1933; *m* 1967, Sylvette Jouclas. *Educ:* City of London Coll. On staff of Financial Times, 1954–59; Editor, Investor's Guide, 1959–60; City Editor, Evening Standard, 1960–65 (with one year's break as City Editor, Sunday Express); Financial Editor, The Guardian, 1965–68; Editor, Punch, 1968–77; Editor-in-Chief, Financial Weekly, 1977–80. Presenter, Money Programme, BBC TV, 1967–69. Chm., Headway Publications, 1977–90; Dir, Director, Fleet Publishing International, Morgan-Grampian, and Fleet Holdings, 1977–80. Mem., Develt Council, Royal Nat. Theatre, 1990–. *Publications:* Three Years Hard Labour: the road to devaluation, 1968; Merger Mania, 1970; Money Talks, 1972; Have Expenses, Will Travel, 1975; It's No Sin to be Rich, 1976; (ed) The Best of Everything, 1980; Money in the 1980s, 1981; The Rich: a study of the species, 1982; Fantasy: a practical guide to escapism, 1984; The Corporate Infighter's Handbook, 1984; (ed) The World's Best Business Hotels, 1985; The Supersalesman's Handbook, 1986; The Innovators, 1987; Children of the Rich, 1989. *Recreations:* drinking wine, travelling, playing tennis, thinking about retirement. *Address:* British Tourist Authority, Thames Tower, Black's Road, W6 9EL. *Clubs:* Garrick, Hurlingham.

DAVIS, Sir (William) Allan, GBE 1985; CA; Director, Davis Consultancy Ltd, since 1986; Lord Mayor of London, 1985–86; *b* 19 June 1921; *s* of Wilfred Egwin Davis and Annie Helen Davis; *m* 1944, Audrey Pamela Louch; two *s* one *d. Educ:* Cardinal Vaughan Sch., Kensington. Mem., Inst. of Accountants and Actuaries, Glasgow (now Inst. of Chartered Accountants of Scotland), 1949; FCA; FTII; CBIM. FRSA. Served War, Pilot RNVR FAA, 1940–44. Joined Barclays Bank, 1939; Dunn Wylie & Co.: apprentice, 1944; Partner, 1952; Sen. Partner, 1972–76; Armitage & Norton, London: Partner, 1976; Sen. Partner, 1979–86. Director: Catholic Herald Ltd; City of London Heliport Ltd; Crowning Tea Co. Ltd; Dunkelman & Son Ltd; Fiat Auto (UK) Ltd; Internatio-Muller UK Ltd and UK subsidiaries; NRG Victory Holdings Ltd and subsids. Common Councilman, Ward of Queenhithe, 1971–76; Alderman, Ward of Cripplegate, 1976–91; Sheriff, City of London, 1982–83; HM Lieut, City of London, 1986. Chairman: Port and City of London Health Cttee and Social Services Cttee, 1974–77; Management Cttee, London Homes for the Elderly, 1975–88; Res. into ageing, 1987–89 (Vice Pres., 1989–); Winged Fellowship, 1987–89 (Vice-Patron, 1989–); Queenhithe Ward Club, 1976–77; Barbican Youth Club, 1979–82; Mem. Court, HAC, 1976–91; Gov., Honourable The Irish Soc., 1986–91. City of London Centre, St John Ambulance Association: Hon. Treas., 1979–82, 1983–84; Vice-Chm., 1984–88; Chm., 1988–; Mem. Council, Order of St John for London, 1987–89. Hon. Treas., Worshipful Co. of Painter-Stainers, 1962– (Liveryman, 1960; Mem. Court, 1962–); Hon. Liveryman: Co. of Chartered Accountants in England and Wales, 1983; Co. of Launderers, 1987; Co. of Constructors, 1990. Chancellor, 1985–86, Mem. Council, 1986–, City Univ.; Governor: Bridewell Royal Hosp., 1976–; Cripplegate Foundn, 1976– (Chm., 1981–83); Cardinal Vaughan Meml Sch., 1968–81, 1985–88; Lady Eleanor Holles Sch., 1979– (Chm., 1989–91); Trustee, Sir John Soane's Mus., 1979–. Vice Pres., Lancia Motor Club; Dep. Pres., Publicity Club of London, 1987–. Hon. DSc City, 1985. KCSG 1979; KCHS 1977 (Kt, English Lieutenancy, 1972); KStJ 1986. Knight Commander: Order of Isabel the Catholic, Spain, 1986; Order of Merit, German Federal Republic, 1986; Comdr, Order of Orange-Nassau, Netherlands, 1982; Order of Merit (Class I), State of Qatar, 1985. *Recreation:* travel. *Address:* 168 Defoe House, Barbican, EC2Y 8DN. *T:* 071–638 5354. *Clubs:* Oriental, City Livery.

DAVIS, William Eric, (professionally known as **David Davis**), MBE 1969; MA Oxon; LRAM, ARCM; *b* 27 June 1908; *s* of William John and Florence Kate Rachel Davis; *m* 1935, Barbara de Riemer (*d* 1982); one *s* two *d. Educ:* Bishop's Stortford Coll.; The Queen's Coll., Oxford (MA). Schoolmaster, 1931–35; joined BBC as mem. of Children's Hour, 1935. Served with RNVR Acting Temp. Lieut, 1942–46. BBC, 1946–70; Head of Children's Hour, BBC, 1953–61; Head of Children's Programmes (Sound), BBC, 1961–64; Producer, Drama Dept, 1964–70, retired. *Publications:* various songs, etc. including: Lullaby, 1943; Fabulous Beasts, 1948; Little Grey Rabbit Song Book, 1952; *poetry:* A Single Star, 1973; various speech recordings, including: Black Beauty; Just So Stories; The Wind in the Willows (complete text), 1986. *Recreations:* children, cats, growing roses. *Address:* 18 Mount Avenue, W5 2RG. *T:* 081–997 8156. *Club:* Garrick.

DAVIS, Hon. William Grenville, ; PC (Can.) 1982; CC (Canada) 1986; QC (Can.); barrister and solicitor; Counsel to Tory, Tory, DesLauriers & Binnington, Toronto; Member of the Provincial Parliament, Ontario, 1959–85; Premier of Ontario, Canada, and President of the Council, Ontario, 1971–85; Leader, Progressive Conservative Party, 1971–85; *b* Brampton, Ont., 30 July 1929; *s* of Albert Grenville Davis and Vera M. Davis (*née* Hewetson); *m* 1st, 1953, Helen MacPhee (*d* 1962), *d* of Neil MacPhee, Windsor, Ontario; 2nd, 1963, Kathleen Louise, *d* of Dr R. P. Mackay, California; two *s* three *d. Educ:* Brampton High Sch.; University Coll., Univ. of Toronto (BA); Osgoode Hall Law Sch. (grad. 1955). Called to Bar of Ontario, 1955; practised gen. law, Brampton, 1955–59. Elected Mem. (C) Provincial Parlt (MPP) for Peel Riding, 1959, 1963, Peel North Riding, 1967, 1971, Brampton Riding, 1975, 1977, 1981. Minister of Educn, 1962–71; also Minister of Univ. Affairs, 1964–71; Special Envoy on Acid Rain, apptd by Prime Minister of Canada, 1985–86. Director: Ford Motor Co. of Canada; Inter-City Gas Corp.; Magna Internat. Inc.; NIKE Canada; Power Corp. of Canada; Seagram Co.; Cosma Internat. Inc.; ICG Resources Ltd; Canadian Imperial Bank of Commerce; Lawson Marden Gp Ltd; Honeywell Ltd; Bramalea Ltd (Chm. of Bd, 1987–); St Lawrence Cement; Hemlo Gold Mines Inc.; Vice-Chm., Stadium Corp. Holds hon. doctorates in Law from eight Ontario Univs: Waterloo Lutheran, W Ontario, Toronto, McMaster, Queen's, Windsor; Hon. Graduate: Albert Einstein Coll. of Med.; Yeshiva Univ. of NY; NUI; Ottawa; Tel Aviv. Amer. Transit Assoc. Man of the Year, 1973. A Freemason. *Publications:* Education in Ontario, 1965; The Government of Ontario and the Universities of the Province (Frank Gerstein Lectures, York Univ.), 1966; Building an Educated Society 1816–1966, 1966; Education for New Times, 1967. *Address:* 61 Main Street South, Brampton, Ontario L6Y 1M9, Canada; Tory, Tory, DesLauriers & Binnington, IBM Tower, PO Box 270, Toronto-Dominion Centre, Toronto, Ont M5K IN2, Canada. *Clubs:* Kiwanis, Shriners, Masons, Albany (Ont.).

DAVIS, William Herbert, BSc; CEng, FIMechE; former executive with BL and Land Rover Ltd, retired 1983; *b* 27 July 1919; *s* of William and Dora Davis; *m* 1945, Barbara Mary Joan (*née* Sommerfield); one *d*. *Educ:* Waverley Grammar Sch.; Univ. of Aston in Birmingham (BSc). Austin Motor Co.: Engr Apprentice, 1935–39; Mech. Engr and Section Leader, Works Engrs, 1946–51; Supt Engr, 1951; Asst Production Manager, 1954; Production Manager, 1956; Dir and Gen. Works Manager, 1958. British Motor Corp. Ltd: Dir of Production, 1960; Dep. Managing Dir (Manufacture and Supply), 1961; Dep. Managing Dir, British Leyland (Austin-Morris Ltd), 1968; Chairman and Chief Executive, Triumph Motor Co. Ltd, 1970; Managing Dir, Rover Triumph BLUK Ltd, 1972; Dir (Manufacture), British Leyland Motor Corporation, 1973; Dir, Military Contracts and Govt Affairs, Leyland Cars, 1976–81; Consultant, BL and Land Rover Ltd, 1981–83; Dir, Land Rover Santana (Spain), 1976–83. FIIM, FBIM, SME(USA). *Recreations:* riding, motoring, photography; interests in amateur boxing. *Address:* Arosa, The Holloway, Alvechurch, Worcs B48 7QA. *T:* Redditch (0527) 66187.

DAVIS-GOFF, Sir Robert William; *see* Goff.

DAVIS-RICE, Peter; Director of Nursing and Personnel, North Western Regional Health Authority, since 1990; *b* 1 Feb. 1930; *s* of Alfred Davis-Rice and Doris Eva (*née* Bates); *m* 1967, Judith Anne Chatterton; one *s* two *d*. *Educ:* Riley High Sch., Hull; Royal Coll. of Nursing, Edinburgh; Harefield Hosp., Mddx; City Hosp., York. SRN; British Tuberculosis Assoc. Cert.; MBIM; NAdmin(Hosp)Cert. Staff Nurse, Charge Nurse, St Luke's Hosp., Huddersfield, 1954–57; Theatre Supt, Hull Royal Infirmary, 1957–62; Asst Matron (Theatres), Walton Hosp., Liverpool, 1962–66; Matron, Billinge Hosp., Wigan, 1966–69; Chief Nursing Officer, Oldham and District HMC, 1969–73; Regl Nursing Officer, 1973–90, Asst Gen. Manager (Personnel Services), 1985–90, N Western RHA. Nursing Officer, Greater Manchester Br., BRCS, 1990–. *Publications:* contrib. Nursing Times. *Recreations:* walking, music. *Address:* Riencourt, 185 Frederick Street, Oldham OL8 4DH. *T:* 061–624 2485.

DAVISON, family name of **Baron Broughshane.**

DAVISON, Prof. Alan Nelson, PhD, DSc; FRCPath; Professor of Neurochemistry, Institute of Neurology, University of London, at the National Hospital, Queen Square, and Consulting Neurochemist, National Hospital, 1971–90; Emeritus Professor, Hunterian Institute, since 1990; *b* 6 June 1925; *s* of Alfred N. Davison and Ada E. W. Davison; *m* 1948, Patricia Joyce Pickering; one *s* two *d*. *Educ:* Univ. of Nottingham; Univ. of London (BSc Hons, BPharm; PhD 1954; DSc 1962). FRCPath 1979. Staff of MRC Toxicology Unit, 1950–54; MRC Exchange Fellow, Sorbonne, Paris, 1954; Dept of Pathology, 1957–60, Dept of Biochemistry, 1960–65, Guy's Hosp. Med. Sch. (Reader in Biochem., 1962–65); Prof. of Biochem., Charing Cross Hosp. Med. Sch., 1965–71. Sec., Biochemical Soc., 1968. Chief Editor, Jl of Neurochem., 1970–75; Mem. Editorial Boards: Jl of Pharmacy and Pharmacology, 1960–62; Jl of Neurology, Neurosurgery and Psychiatry, 1965–67; Acta Neuropathologica, 1977–; Brain, 1976–81. Dhole-Eddleston Prize (for most deserving publd work of med. res. appertaining to needs of aged people), 1980. *Publications:* (jtly) Applied Neurochemistry, 1968; (jtly) Myelination, 1970; Biochemistry of Neurological Disease, 1976; Biochemical Correlates of Brain Structure and Function, 1977; The Molecular Basis of Neuropathology, 1981; papers on neurochem. of multiple sclerosis and on ageing and senile dementia. *Recreations:* choral singing, painting. *Address:* Drivers, 54 High Street, Stock, Ingatestone, Essex CM4 9BW. *T:* Stock (0277) 840362.

DAVISON, Arthur Clifford Percival, CBE 1974; FRAM; FWCMD; Musical Director and Conductor: Royal Orchestral Society, since 1956; Little Symphony of London, since 1964; Virtuosi of England, since 1970; *b* Montreal, Canada, 1918; *s* of late Arthur Mackay Davison and Hazel Edith Smith; *m* 1st, 1950, Barbara June Hildred (marr. diss.); one *s* two *d*; 2nd, 1978, Elizabeth Blanche. *Educ:* Conservatory of Music, McGill Univ.; Conservatoire de Musique, Montreal; Royal Associated Board Scholar at Royal Acad. of Music, London; later studies in Europe; LRSM 1947; ARCM 1950; FRAM 1966; FWCMD 1991. A Dir and Dep. Leader, London Philharmonic Orch., 1957–65; Guest Conductor, Royal Danish Ballet and Orch., 1964; Asst Conductor, Bournemouth Symphony Orch., 1965–66. Guest Conductor of Orchestras: London Philharmonic; London Symphony; Philharmonia; Royal Philharmonic; BBC Orchs; Birmingham Symphony; Bournemouth Symphony and Sinfonietta; Ulster; Royal Liverpool Philharmonic; New York City Ballet; CBC Radio and Television Orchs; Royal Danish. Founder of Arthur Davison Concerts for Children, subseq. Arthur Davison Family Concerts, 1966; Dir and Conductor, Nat. Youth Orch. of Wales, 1966–90 (conducted Investiture Week Symphony concert in presence of HRH Prince of Wales, 1969; Guild for Promotion of Welsh Music Award for long and distinguished service, 1976); Mus. Dir, Corralls Concerts, Bournemouth Symphony, 1966–; conducted official Silver Jubilee concert, Fairfield Halls, 1977, and in presence of the Queen and HRH Duke of Edinburgh, Poole Arts Centre, Dorset, 1979; conducted Royal Over-Seas League 70th Anniversary concert, St James's Palace, in presence of HRH Princess Alexandra, 1980; conducted concert for Charter centenery of Borough of Croydon, in presence of the Queen, Fairfield Halls, 1983. Conductor and Lectr, London Univ., Goldsmiths' Coll., 1971–85; Conductor, 1971–84, Gov., 1975–89, Welsh Coll. of Music and Drama; Orchestral Dir, Symphony Orchestra, Birmingham Sch. of Music, 1981–83. EMI/CFP award for sale of half a million classical records, 1973, Gold Disc for sale of one million classical records, 1977. Tour of Europe recorded for BBC TV. FRSA 1977. Hon. Master of Music, Univ. of Wales, 1974. *Publications:* various articles in musical jls. *Recreations:* reading, theatre-going, fishing, boating on Thames, antiques. *Address:* Glencairn, Shepherd's Hill, Merstham, Surrey RH1 3AD. *T:* Merstham (0737) 644434, 642206. *Clubs:* Savage, Royal Over-Seas League.

DAVISON, Ian Frederic Hay, FCA; Chairman: Crédit Lyonnais Capital Markets (formerly CL-Alexanders Laing & Cruickshank Holdings), since 1988; Storehouse plc, since 1990; Director: The Independent, since 1986; Chloride plc, since 1988; Cadbury Schweppes, since 1990; *b* 30 June 1931; *s* of late Eric Hay Davison, FCA, and Inez Davison; *m* 1955, Maureen Patricia Blacker; one *s* two *d*. *Educ:* Dulwich Coll.; LSE (BScEcon); Univ. of Mich. ACA 1956, FCA 1966. Managing Partner, Arthur Andersen & Co., Chartered Accountants, 1966–82; Dep. Chm. and Chief Exec., Lloyd's of London, 1983–86; Dir, Midland Bank, 1986–88. Mem. Council, ICA, 1975–; Chm., Accounting Standards Cttee, 1982–84. Indep. Mem., NEDC for Bldg Industry, 1971–77; Member: Price Commn, 1977–79; Audit Commn, 1983–85; Chairman: EDC for Food and Drink Manufg Industry, 1981–83; Securities Review Cttee, Hong Kong, 1987–88. Dept of Trade Inspector, London Capital Securities, 1975–77; Inspector, Grays Building Soc., 1978–79. Trustee, V&A Museum, 1984–; Dir and Trustee, Royal Opera House, 1984–86; Chm., Monteverdi Trust, 1979–84. Governor, LSE, 1982– (Mem., Steering Cttee; Chm., Finance Panel). Councillor and Alderman, London Bor. of Greenwich, 1961–73. *Publication:* A View of the Room: Lloyd's change and disclosure, 1987. *Recreations:* opera, theatre, music, ski-ing, gardening under supervision, bell-ringing. *Address:* 40 Earlham Street, WC2. *Clubs:* Athenæum, Arts, MCC.

DAVISON, (John) Stanley, OBE 1981; Secretary General, World Federation of Scientific Workers, since 1987; *b* 26 Sept. 1922; *s* of George Davison and Rosie Davison (*née* Segger); *m* 1959, Margaret Smith; two *s* one *d*. *Educ:* Timothy Hackworth Sch., Shildon, Co. Durham; Shildon Senior Boys' Sch.; St Helens Tech. Coll. RAF, 1941–46. Civil Servant (Technical), 1946–52; Regional Organiser, 1953–60, Dep. Gen. Sec., 1960–68, Assoc. of Scientific Workers; Dep. Gen. Sec., ASTMS, 1968–87. Member: Engineering Council, 1986–; Heavy Electrical NEDO, 1976–87; Exec. Council, CSEU, 1981–88; Exec. Council, Internat. Metalworkers' Fedn, 1986–87; All Party Energy Cttee, 1982–88; Chm., Trade Union Side, GEC NJC, 1965–87; Governor, Aston CAT, 1955–60; Mem. Council, Brunel Univ., 1989–. *Recreations:* science policy, amateur dramatics, bridge, caravanning. *Address:* 27 Barnfield Avenue, Shirley, Croydon CR0 8SF. *T:* 081–654 7092. *Clubs:* Players' Theatre; Addington Theatre Group; Caravan.

DAVISON, Rt. Hon. Sir Ronald (Keith), GBE 1978; CMG 1975; PC 1978; Chief Justice of New Zealand, 1978–89; *b* 16 Nov. 1920; *s* of Joseph James Davison and Florence May Davison; *m* 1948, Jacqueline May Carr; one *s* one *d* (and one *s* decd). *Educ:* Auckland Univ. (LLB). Admitted as barrister and solicitor, 1948; QC (NZ) 1963. Chairman: Environmental Council, 1969–74; Legal Aid Bd, 1969–78; Member: Council, Auckland Dist Law Soc., 1960–65 (Pres., 1965–66); Council, NZ Law Soc., 1963–66; Auckland Electric Power Bd (13 yrs); Aircrew Indust. Tribunal, 1970–78. Chm., Montana Wines Ltd, 1971–78; Dir, NZ Insurance Co. Ltd, 1975–78. *Recreations:* golf, fishing, bowls. *Address:* 68 Rama Crescent, Wellington, New Zealand. *Clubs:* Wellington; Northern (Auckland, NZ).

DAVISON, Stanley; *see* Davison, J. S.

DAVSON, Sir Geoffrey Leo Simon, 2nd Bt; *see* Glyn, Sir Anthony, 2nd Bt.

DAVY, Humphrey Augustine A.; *see* Arthington-Davy.

DAWBARN, Sir Simon (Yelverton), KCVO 1980; CMG 1976; HM Diplomatic Service, retired; *b* 16 Sept. 1923; *s* of Frederic Dawbarn and Maud Louise Mansell; *m* 1948, Shelby Montgomery Parker; one *s* two *d*. *Educ:* Oundle Sch.; Corpus Christi Coll., Cambridge. Served in HM Forces (Reconnaissance Corps), 1942–45. Reckitt & Colman (Overseas), 1948–49. Joined Foreign Service, 1949. Foreign Office, 1949–53; Brussels, 1953; Prague, 1955; Tehran, 1957; seconded to HM Treasury, 1959; Foreign Office, 1961; Algiers, 1965; Athens, 1968; FCO, 1971–75. Head of W African Dept and concurrently non-resident Ambassador to Chad, 1973–75; Consul-General, Montreal, 1975–78; Ambassador to Morocco, 1978–82. *Address:* 44 Canonbury Park North, N1 2JT. *T:* 071–226 0659.

DAWE, Donovan Arthur; Principal Keeper, Guildhall Library, London, 1967–73, retired; *b* 21 Jan. 1915; *s* of late Alfred Ernest and Sarah Jane Dawe, Wallington, Surrey; *m* 1946, Peggy Marjory Challen; two *d*. *Educ:* Sutton Grammar Sch. Associate, Library Assoc., 1938. Entered Guildhall Library as junior assistant, 1931. Served with Royal West African Frontier Force in Africa and India, 1941–46. Freeman of City of London and Merchant Taylors' Company, 1953. FRHistS 1954. *Publications:* Skilbecks: drysalters 1650–1950, 1950; 11 Ironmonger Lane: the story of a site in the City of London, 1952; The City of London: a select book list, 1972; Organists of the City of London 1666–1850, 1983; contribs professional literature, Connoisseur, Musical Times, Genealogists' Magazine, etc. *Recreations:* the countryside, local history, musicology. *Address:* 46 Green Lane, Purley, Surrey CR8 3PJ. *T:* 081–660 4218.

DAWE, Roger James, CB 1988; OBE 1970; Deputy Secretary, and Director General of Training Enterprise and Education Directorate, Department of Employment, since 1990; *b* 26 Feb. 1941; *s* of Harry James and Edith Mary Dawe; *m* 1965, Ruth Day Jolliffe; one *s* one *d*. *Educ:* Hardyes Sch., Dorchester; Fitzwilliam House, Cambridge. BA Cantab. Entered Min. of Labour, 1962; Dept of Economic Affairs, 1964–65; Private Sec. to Prime Minister, 1966–70; Principal, Dept of Employment, 1970; Private Sec. to Secretary of State for Employment, 1972–74; Asst Sec., Dept of Employment, 1974–81; Under Sec., MSC, 1981; Chief Exec., Trng Div., MSC, 1982–84; Dep Sec., Dept of Employment, 1985–87; Dir Gen., MSC, then Training Commn, subseq. Training Agency, 1988–90. *Recreations:* tennis, Plymouth Argyle supporter, music, theatre. *Address:* c/o Department of Employment, Caxton House, Tothill Street, SW1H 9NF.

DAWES, Prof. Edwin Alfred, CBiol, FIBiol; CChem, FRSC; Reckitt Professor of Biochemistry, University of Hull, 1963–90, now Emeritus; *b* 6 July 1925; *s* of late Harold Dawes and Maude Dawes (*née* Barker); *m* 1950, Amy Rogerson; two *s*. *Educ:* Goole Grammar Sch.; Univ. of Leeds. BSc, PhD, DSc. Asst Lectr, later Lectr, in Biochemistry, Univ. of Leeds, 1947–50; Lectr, later Sen. Lectr, Univ. of Glasgow, 1951–63; Hull University: Head of Biochemistry Dept, 1963–86; Dean of Science, 1968–70; Pro-Vice-Chancellor, 1977–80; Dir, Biomed. Res. Unit, 1981. Visiting Lecturer: Meml Univ., Newfoundland, Dalhousie Univ., 1959; Univ. of Brazil, 1960, 1972; Univ. of S California, 1962; Univ. of Rabat, 1967; Univ. of Göttingen, 1972; Osmania Univ., Hyderabad, 1986; Univ. of Massachusetts, Amherst, 1989; Biochemical Soc. Lectr, Australia and NZ, 1975; Amer. Medical Alumni Lectr, Univ. of St Andrews, 1980–81. Editor, Biochemical Jl, 1958–65; Editor-in-Chief, Jl of Gen. Microbiol., 1976–81; Man. Editor, Fedn of European Microbiol Socs, and Editor-in-Chief, FEMS Microbiology Letters, 1982–90. Dep. Chm., 1987–, Chm., Scientific Adv. Cttee, 1978–, Yorks Cancer Res. Campaign; Mem., Scientific Adv. Cttee, Whyte-Watson-Turner Cancer Res. Trust, 1984–91. President: Hull Lit. Philosophical Soc., 1976–77; British Ring of Internat. Brotherhood of Magicians, 1972–73; Hon. Pres., Scottish Conjurers' Assoc.; Hon. Vice-Pres., Magic Circle (Official Historian, 1987–; Mem., 1959–). Governor, Pocklington Sch., 1965–74; Member, Court: Leeds Univ., 1974–; Bradford Univ., 1985–. Mem., Hall of Fame and H. A. Smith Literary Award, Soc. Amer. Magicians, 1984; Literary Fellowship and Hon. Life Mem., Acad. Magical Arts, USA, 1985; Maskelyne Literary Award, 1988. *Publications:* Quantitative Problems in Biochemistry, 1956, 6th edn 1980; (jtly) Biochemistry of Bacterial Growth, 1968, 3rd edn 1982; The Great Illusionists, 1979; Isaac Fawkes: fame and fable, 1979; The Biochemist in a Microbial Wonderland, 1982; Vonetta, 1982; The Barrister in the Circle, 1983; (ed) Environmental Regulation of Microbial Metabolism, 1985; (ed) Enterobacterial Surface Antigens, 1985; Microbial Energetics, 1985; (jtly) The Book of Magic, 1986; The Wizard Exposed, 1987; (ed) Continuous Culture in Biotechnology and Environment Conservation, 1988; (contrib.) Philip Larkin: the man and his work, 1989; Henri Robin: expositor of science and magic, 1990; (ed) Molecular Biology of Membrane-Bound Complexes in Photosynthetic Bacteria, 1990; (ed) Novel Biodegradable Microbial Polymers, 1990; numerous papers in scientific jls. *Recreations:* conjuring, book-collecting. *Address:* Dane Hill, 393 Beverley Road, Anlaby, N Humberside HU10 7BQ. *T:* Hull (0482) 657998. *Club:* Savage.

DAWES, Prof. Geoffrey Sharman, CBE 1981; FRS 1971; Director of Charing Cross Medical Research Centre, 1984–89; *b* 21 Jan. 1918; *s* of Rev. W. Dawes, Thurlaston Grange, Derbyshire; *m* 1941, Margaret Monk; two *s* two *d*. *Educ:* Repton Sch.; New Coll., Oxford. BA 1939; BSc 1940; BM, BCh 1943; DM 1947. Rockefeller Travelling Fellowship, 1946; Fellow, Worcester Coll., Oxford, 1946–85, Emeritus Fellow, 1985; University Demonstrator in Pharmacology, Oxford, 1947; Foulerton Research Fellow, Royal Society, 1948; Dir, Nuffield Inst. for Medical Research, Oxford, 1948–85. Mem.,

MRC, 1978–82; Chm., Physiological Systems and Disorders Bd, MRC, 1978–80. Chm., Lister Inst. for Preventive Medicine, 1988–. Governor of Repton, 1959–88, Chm., 1971–85. A Vice-Pres., Royal Society, 1976, 1977. FRCOG, FRCP; Hon. FACOG. Max Weinstein Award, 1963; Gairdner Foundation Award, 1966; Maternité Award of European Assoc. Perinatal Medicine, 1976; Virginia Apgar Award, Amer. Acad. of Pediatrics, 1980; Osler Meml Medal, Oxford Univ., 1990. *Publications:* Foetal and Neonatal Physiology, 1968; various publications in physiological and pharmacological journals. *Recreation:* fishing. *Address:* 8 Belbroughton Road, Oxford OX2 6UZ. *T:* Oxford (0865) 58131.

DAWES, Rt. Rev. Peter Spencer; *see* Derby, Bishop of.

DAWICK, Viscount; Alexander Douglas Derrick Haig; farmer; *b* 30 June 1961; *s* and *heir* of 2nd Earl Haig, *qv. Educ:* Stowe School; Royal Agricl Coll., Cirencester. *Address:* Third Farm, Melrose, Scotland. *Club:* New (Edinburgh).

DAWKINS, Dr (Clinton) Richard; Reader in Zoology, University of Oxford, since 1989 (Lecturer, 1970–89); Fellow, New College, Oxford, since 1970; *b* 26 March 1941; *s* of Clinton John Dawkins and Jean Mary Vyvyan (*née* Ladner); *m* 1st, 1967, Marian Ellina Stamp (marr. diss.); 2nd, 1984, Eve Barham (separated); one *d. Educ:* Oundle Sch.; Balliol Coll., Oxford (MA, DPhil, DSc). Asst Prof. of Zoology, Univ. of California, Berkeley, 1967–69. Gifford Lectr, Glasgow Univ., 1988; Sidgwick Meml Lectr, Newnham Coll., Cambridge, 1988; Kovler Vis. Fellow, Univ. of Chicago, 1990; Nelson Lectr, Univ. of California, Davis, 1990; Royal Instn Christmas Lects for Young People, 1991. Presenter, BBC TV Horizon progs, 1985, 1986. Editor: Animal Behaviour, 1974–78; Oxford Surveys in Evolutionary Biology, 1983–86. Hon. Fellow, Regent's Coll., London, 1988. Silver Medal, Zool Soc., 1989; Michael Faraday Award, Royal Soc., 1990. *Publications:* The Selfish Gene, 1976, 2nd edn 1989; The Extended Phenotype, 1982; The Blind Watchmaker, 1986 (RSL Prize 1987; LA Times Lit. Prize 1987). *Recreation:* the Apple Macintosh. *Address:* New College, Oxford OX1 3BN. *T:* Oxford (0865) 271280.

DAWKINS, Douglas Alfred; Associate Director, Bank of England, 1985–87; *b* 17 Sept. 1927; *s* of Arthur Dawkins and Edith Annie Dawkins; *m* 1953, Diana Pauline (*née* Ormes); one *s* one *d. Educ:* Edmonton County Secondary Sch.; University Coll. London (Rosa Morison Scholar; BA Hons). Entered Bank of England, 1950; Bank for Internat. Settlements, 1953–54; Adviser to Governors, Bank of Libya, 1964–65; Asst Chief of Overseas Dept, 1970; First Dep. Chief of Exchange Control, 1972; Chief of Exchange Control, 1979; Asst Dir, 1980. *Address:* c/o Bank of England, Threadneedle Street, EC2R 8AH.

DAWKINS, Richard; *see* Dawkins, C. R.

DAWNAY, family name of **Viscount Downe.**

DAWOOD, Nessim Joseph; Arabist and Middle East Consultant; Managing Director, The Arabic Advertising and Publishing Co. Ltd, London, since 1958; Director, Contemporary Translations Ltd, London, since 1962; *b* Baghdad, 27 Aug. 1927; 4th *s* of late Yousef Dawood, merchant, and Muzli (*née* Tweg); *m* 1949, Juliet, 2nd *d* of M. and N. Abraham, Baghdad and New York; three *s. Educ:* The American Sch. and Shamash Sch., Baghdad; Iraq State Scholar in England, UC Exeter, 1945–49; Univ. of London, BA (Hons). FIL 1959. Dir, Bradbury Wilkinson (Graphics) Ltd, 1975–86. Has written and spoken radio and film commentaries. *Publications:* The Muqaddimah of Ibn Khaldun, 1967 (US, 1969); Penguin Classics: The Thousand and One Nights, 1954; The Koran, 1956, 36th edn 1991, parallel Arabic/English edn, 1990; Aladdin and Other Tales, 1957; Tales from The Thousand and One Nights, 1973, 16th edn 1989; Arabian Nights (illus. children's edn), 1978; Puffin Classics: Aladdin & Other Tales, 1989; Sindbad the Sailor & other Tales, 1989; contribs to specialised and technical English-Arabic dictionaries; translated numerous technical publications into Arabic. *Recreation:* going to the theatre. *Address:* Berkeley Square House, Berkeley Square, W1X 5LE. *T:* 071–409 0953. *Club:* Hurlingham.

DAWS, Dame Joyce (Margaretta), DBE 1975; FRCS, FRACS; Surgeon, Queen Victoria Memorial Hospital, Melbourne, Victoria, Australia, 1958–85; Thoracic Surgeon, Prince Henry's Hospital, Melbourne, since 1975; President, Victorian Branch Council, Australian Medical Association, 1976; *b* 21 July 1925; *d* of Frederick William Daws and Daisy Ethel Daws. *Educ:* Royal School for Naval and Marine Officers' Daughters, St Margaret's, Mddx; St Paul's Girls' Sch., Hammersmith; Royal Free Hosp., London. MB, BS (London) 1949; FRCS 1952, FRACS. Ho. Surg., Royal Free Hosp.; SHMO, Manchester Royal Infirmary; Hon. Surg., Queen Victoria Meml Hosp., Melb., 1958; Asst Thoracic Surg., Prince Henry's Hosp., Melb., 1967–75. Pres., Bd of Management, After-Care Hosp., Melbourne, 1980–85; Chairman: Victorian Nursing Council, 1983–89; Academic and Professional Panel, Victoria, for Churchill Fellowship Awards, 1984; Jt Adv. Cttee on Pets in Society, 1984; Internat. Protea Assoc., 1987–. Hon. Sec., Victorian Br., AMA, 1974. *Recreations:* opera, ballet, theatre, desert travel, protea grower. *Address:* 26 Edwin Street, Heidelberg West, Victoria 3081, Australia. *T:* 4572579. *Clubs:* Lyceum, Soroptimist International (Melbourne).

DAWSON, Anthony Michael, MD, FRCP; Physician to the Queen, since 1982 (to the Royal Household, 1974–82), and Head of HM Medical Household, since 1989; Physician, King Edward VII Hospital for Officers, since 1968; Consulting Physician, St Bartholomew's Hospital, since 1986 (Physician, 1965–86); *b* 8 May 1928; *s* of Leslie Joseph Dawson and Mabel Jayes; *m* 1956, Barbara Anne Baron Forsyth, *d* of late Thomas Forsyth, MB, ChB; two *d. Educ:* Wyggeston Sch., Leicester; Charing Cross Hosp. Med. Sch. MB, BS 1951, MD 1959, London; MRCP 1954, FRCP 1964. Jun. appts, Charing Cross Hosp., Brompton Hosp., Royal Postgrad. Med. Sch., Central Middlesex Hosp., 1951–57; MRC and US Public Health Res. Fellow, Harvard Med. Sch. at Massachusetts Gen. Hosp., 1957–59; Lectr and Sen. Lectr in Medicine, Royal Free Hosp. Med. Sch., 1959–65; formerly Physician, King Edward VII Convalescent Home for Officers, Osborne. Hon. Sec., Assoc. of Physicians of Gt Britain and Ireland, 1973–78, Treasurer 1978–83. Examnr, London and Oxford, MRCP; Censor, RCP, 1977–78, Treasurer, 1985–91; Treasurer, St Bartholomew's Hosp. Med. Coll., 1976–79, Vice-Pres., 1979–84; Vice-Chm., Bd of Management, King Edward's Hosp. Fund for London. *Publications:* contrib. med. books and jls. *Recreations:* music, gardening. *Address:* Flat 1, 11 Adamson Road, NW3 3HX. *Club:* Garrick.

See also J. L. Dawson.

DAWSON, (Archibald) Keith; Headmaster, Haberdashers' Aske's School, Elstree, since 1987; *b* 12 Jan. 1937; *s* of Wilfred Joseph and Alice Marjorie Dawson; *m* 1961, Marjorie Blakeson; two *d. Educ:* Nunthorpe Grammar School for Boys, York; The Queen's College, Oxford. MA, Dip Ed distinction. Ilford County High School for Boys, 1961–63; Haberdasher's Aske's Sch., 1963–71 (Head of History, 1965–71); Headmaster, John Mason Sch., Abingdon, 1971–79; Principal, Scarborough Sixth Form Coll., 1979–84; Principal, King James's College of Henley, 1984–87. FBIM 1984. *Publications:* Society and Industry in 19th Century England (with Peter Wall), 1968; The Industrial Revolution, 1971. *Recreations:* theatre, music, cricket, hill walking. *Address:* Headmaster's House, Haberdashers' Aske's School, Elstree, Borehamwood, Herts WD6 3AF. *T:* 081–207 4323.

DAWSON, Hon. Sir Daryl (Michael), AC 1988; KBE 1982; CB 1980; **Hon. Justice Dawson;** Justice of the High Court of Australia, since 1982; *b* 12 Dec. 1933; *s* of Claude Charles Dawson and Elizabeth May Dawson; *m* 1971, Mary Louise Thomas. *Educ:* Canberra High Sch.; Ormond Coll., Univ. of Melbourne (LLB Hons); LLM Yale. Sterling Fellow, Yale Univ., 1955–56. QC 1971; Solicitor-General for Victoria, 1974–82. Mem. Council, Univ. of Melbourne, 1976–86; Chm. Council, Ormond Coll., Univ. of Melbourne, 1991–. Chm., Australian Motor Sport Appeal Court, 1986–88 (Mem., 1970–86); Mem., Fédération d'Automobile Appeal Court, 1982–. *Recreation:* squash. *Address:* High Court of Australia, Canberra, ACT 2600, Australia. *Clubs:* Melbourne, Savage, RACV, Beefsteaks (Melbourne).

DAWSON, (Edward) John; Undergraduate, Manchester College, University of Oxford, since 1991; Director, Walsingham Community Homes Ltd, since 1990; *b* 14 Oct. 1935; *s* of late Edward Dawson and Kathleen Dawson (*née* Naughton); *m* 1963, Ann Prudence (*née* Hicks); two *s* one *d. Educ:* St Joseph's Coll., Blackpool; London Graduate Sch. of Business Studies (Sloan Fellow, 1969–70). FCIB. Entered Lloyds Bank, 1952; served RAF, 1954–56; General Manager, Lloyds Bank and Exec. Dir, Lloyds Bank International, 1982–84; Asst Chief Gen. Manager, 1985, Dir, UK Retail Banking, 1985–88, Asst Chief Exec., 1989–90, Dir, 1989–91, Lloyd's Bank; Chairman: Lloyds Bowmaker Finance, 1988–90 (Dir, 1985–90); Black Horse Agencies, 1988–89 (Dir, 1985–89). *Recreations:* golf, cricket, choral singing. *Address:* c/o Lloyds Bank, Westminster House, 4 Dean Stanley Street, SW1P 3HU. *Clubs:* MCC; Sandy Lodge Golf.

DAWSON, Sir (Hugh) Michael (Trevor), 4th Bt *cr* 1920, of Edgewarebury; *b* 28 March 1956; *s* of Sir (Hugh Halliday) Trevor Dawson, 3rd Bt; *S* father, 1983. *Heir: b* Nicholas Antony Trevor Dawson, *b* 17 Aug. 1957.

DAWSON, Ian David; Fellow, Center for International Affairs, Harvard, Aug. 1990–91; *b* 24 Nov. 1934; *s* of Harry Newton Dawson and Margaret (*née* Aspinall); *m* 1955, Barbara (*née* Mather); two *s* one *d. Educ:* Hutton Grammar Sch.; Fitzwilliam House, Cambridge (MA). Directorate of Military Survey, 1958–71; Principal, MoD, 1971; Private Sec. to CAS, 1975–77; Asst Sec., Naval Staff, 1977–80; Sec., AWRE, 1980–83; RCDS, 1984; Dir, Defence and Security Agency, WEU, Paris, 1986–88; Asst Under-Sec. of State (Resources), MoD, 1988–90. *Recreations:* music, mountaineering, travel. *Address:* c/o Ministry of Defence, SW1A 2HB.

DAWSON, James Gordon, CBE 1981; FEng, FIMechE, FSAE; Consultant; *b* 3 Feb. 1916; *s* of James Dawson and Helen Mitchell (*née* Tawse); *m* 1941, Doris Irene (*née* Rowe) (*d* 1982); one *s* one *d. Educ:* Aberdeen Grammar Sch.; Aberdeen Univ. (BScEng Hons Mech. Eng, BScEng Hons Elect. Eng). Develt Test Engr, Rolls Royce Ltd, Derby, 1942; Chief Engr, Shell Research Ltd, 1946; Technical Dir, Perkins Engines Ltd, 1955; Dir, Dowty Group Ltd, 1966; Man. Dir, Zenith Carburetter Co. Ltd, 1969, Chm., 1977–81. Pres., IMechE, 1979–80; FIMechE 1957; Hon. FIMechE 1986. *Publications:* technical papers publd in UK and abroad. *Recreation:* golf. *Address:* Mildmay House, Apethorpe, Peterborough PE8 5DP. *T:* Kingscliffe (0780) 470348. *Club:* Caledonian.

DAWSON, John; *see* Dawson, E. J.

DAWSON, Prof. John Alan; Professor of Marketing, University of Edinburgh, since 1990; *b* 19 Aug. 1944; *s* of Alan and Gladys Dawson; *m* 1967, Jocelyn M. P. Barker; one *s* one *d. Educ:* University College London (BSc, MPhil); University of Nottingham (PhD). Lectr, Univ. of Nottingham, 1967–71; Lectr, 1971, Sen. Lectr, 1974, Reader, 1981–83, Univ. of Wales, Lampeter; Fraser of Allander Prof. of Distributive Studies, and Dir, Inst. for Retail Studies, Univ. of Stirling, 1983–90. Vis. Lectr, Univ. of Western Australia, 1973; Vis. Res. Fellow, ANU, 1978; Visiting Professor: Florida State Univ., 1982; Chuo Univ., 1986. Member: Distributive Trades EDC, 1984–87; Board, Cumbernauld Develt Corp., 1987–. Hon. Sec., Inst. of British Geographers, 1985–88. *Publications:* Evaluating the Human Environment, 1973; Man and His World, 1975; Computing for Geographers, 1976; Small Scale Retailing in UK, 1979; Marketing Environment, 1979; Retail Geography, 1980; Commercial Distribution in Europe, 1982; Teach Yourself Geography, 1983; Shopping Centre Development, 1983; Computer Programming for Geographers, 1985; Shopping Centres Policies and Prospects, 1985; Evolution of European Retailing, 1989; Competition and Markets, 1991; Retail Environments in Developing Countries, 1991; articles in geographical, management and marketing jls. *Recreations:* sport, travel. *Address:* Department of Business Studies, University of Edinburgh, Edinburgh EH8 9JY. *T:* 031–650 3830.

DAWSON, John Leonard, MB, MS; FRCS; Surgeon: King's College Hospital, since 1964; Bromley Hospital, since 1967; King Edward VII Hospital for Officers, since 1975; Dean of the Faculty of Clinical Medicine, King's College School of Medicine and Dentistry, since 1988; *b* 30 Sept. 1932; *s* of Leslie Joseph Dawson and Mabel Annie Jayes; *m* 1958, Rosemary Brundle; two *s* one *d. Educ:* Wyggeston Boys' Grammar Sch., Leicester; King's College Hosp., Univ. of London. MB, BS 1955, MS 1964; FRCS 1958. Served RAMC, 1958–60. Surgeon to Royal Household, 1975–83; Surgeon to the Queen, 1983–90, Serjeant Surgeon, 1990–91. Nuffield Scholarship, Harvard Univ., 1963–64; Sir Arthur Sims Travelling Prof., Australasia, 1981. Examiner in Surgery: Univs. of London, 1966–, and Cambridge, 1980–; Soc. of Apothecaries; Primary FRCS, 1974–80; Mem. Ct of Examrs, RCS, 1981–. Mem. Council, Med. Protection Soc., 1979–88. Vice-Chm., British Jl of Surgery, 1981–89. *Publications:* contribs to surgical text-books and jls on abdominal surgery. *Recreations:* theatre, skiing, gardening, reading. *Address:* 107 Burbage Road, Dulwich, SE21 7AF. *T:* 071–733 3668.

See also A. M. Dawson.

DAWSON, (Joseph) Peter; Assistant Secretary (Pensions and Membership Services) and International Representative, National Association of Teachers in Further and Higher Education, since 1989 (General Secretary, 1979–89); *b* 18 March 1940; *s* of Joseph Glyn and Winifred Olwen Dawson; *m* 1964, Yvonne Anne Charlton Smith; one *s* one *d. Educ:* Bishop Gore Grammar Sch., Swansea; University College of Swansea (BSc, DipEd). Assistant Master, Chiswick Grammar Sch., 1962; Field Officer, 1965, Sen. Field Officer, 1966, National Union of Teachers; Asst Sec., 1969, Negotiating Sec., 1974, Assoc. of Teachers in Technical Instns; Negotiating Sec., NATFHE, 1976. Vice-Pres., 1962–64, Sen. Treasurer, 1965–68, National Union of Students. Member: Teachers' Panel, Teachers' Superannuation Working Party, 1969– (Chm., 1979–); Exec. Bd, European Trade Union Cttee for Educn, 1984–90 (Chm., Higher Educn Working Gp, 1989–); Eur. Cttee, World Confedn of Organisations of Teaching Profession, 1983–. Hon. FCP 1984. *Recreations:* football, cricket, theatre. *Address:* NATFHE, 27 Britannia Street, WC1X 9JP. *T:* 071–837 3636. *Club:* Surrey County Cricket.

DAWSON, Keith; *see* Dawson, A. K.

DAWSON, Sir Michael; *see* Dawson, Sir H. M. T.

DAWSON, Peter; *see* Dawson, J. P.

DAWSON, Ven. Peter; Archdeacon of Norfolk, since 1977; *b* 31 March 1929; *s* of late Leonard Smith and Cicely Alice Dawson; *m* 1955, Kathleen Mary Sansome; one *s* three *d*. *Educ:* Manchester Grammar School; Keble Coll., Oxford (MA); Ridley Hall, Cambridge. Nat. service, Army, 1947–49; University, 1949–52; Theological College, 1952–54. Asst Curate, St Lawrence, Morden, Dio. Southwark, 1954–59; Vicar of Barston, Warwicks, Dio. Birmingham, 1959–63; Rector of St Clement, Higher Openshaw, Dio. Manchester, 1963–68; Rector of Morden, Dio. Southwark, 1968–77, and Rural Dean of Merton, 1975–77. *Recreations:* gardening, politics, the rural community, historical studies. *Address:* Intwood Rectory, Norwich NR4 6TG. *T:* Norwich (0603) 51946.

DAWSON, Rev. Peter, OBE 1986; General Secretary, Professional Association of Teachers, since 1980; Methodist Sector Minister, ordained 1985; *b* 19 May 1933; *s* of Richard Dawson and Henrietta Kate Dawson (*née* Trueman); *m* 1957, Shirley Margaret Pentland Johnson; two *d*. *Educ:* Beckenham Technical Sch.; Beckenham Grammar Sch.; London School of Economics (BScEcon); Westminster Coll. (Postgrad. CertEd). Schoolmaster Fellow Commoner, Keble Coll., Oxford, 1969, and Corpus Christi Coll., Cambridge, 1979. Asst Master, Roan Grammar School for Boys, London, 1957–62; Head of Upper School, Sedgehill Sch., London, 1962–67; Second Master, Gateacre Comprehensive Sch., Liverpool, 1967–70; Headmaster, Eltham Green Sch., London, 1970–80. Mem., Burnham Cttee, 1981–87. Asst Minister, Queen's Hall Methodist Mission, Derby, 1984–87. Mem., Econ. and Social Cttee, EC, 1990–. Pres., Council of Managerial and Professional Staffs, 1989–. Chm., Routledge Soc., 1991–. *Publications:* Making a Comprehensive Work, 1981; Teachers and Teaching, 1984. *Recreations:* reading, golf, grandparenthood. *Address:* (office) Professional Association of Teachers, 2 St James's Court, Friar Gate, Derby DE1 1BT. *T:* Derby (0332) 372337; (home) 72 The Ridings, Ockbrook, Derby DE7 3SF. *T:* Derby (0332) 672669.

DAWSON, Rex Malcolm Chaplin, FRS 1981; PhD, DSc; Deputy Director and Head of Biochemistry Department, Institute of Animal Physiology, Babraham, Cambridge, 1969–84, retired (Deputy Chief Scientific Officer, 1969–84); *b* 3 June 1924; *s* of late James Dawson and Ethel Mary Dawson (*née* Chaplin); *m* 1946, Emily Elizabeth Hodder; one *s* one *d*. *Educ:* Hinckley Grammar Sch.; University Coll., London (BSc 1946, DSc 1960); Univ. of Wales (PhD 1951). MRC Fellowship followed by Beit Meml Fellowship, Neuropsychiatric Res. Centre, Whitchurch Hosp., Cardiff, 1947–52; Betty Brookes Fellow, Dept of Biochemistry, Univ. of Oxford, 1952–55. Vis. Res. Fellow, Harvard Univ., 1959; Vis. Prof., Northwestern Univ., Chicago, 1974. International Lipid Prize, Amer. Oil Chemists' Assoc., 1981. *Publications:* Metabolism and Physiological Significance of Lipids, 1964; Data for Biochemical Research, 1959, 3rd edn 1986; Form and Function of Phospholipids, 1973; numerous papers on structure, turnover and role of phospholipids in cell membranes in various scientific jls. *Recreations:* mercantile marine history, sailing, gardening. *Address:* Kirn House, Holt Road, Langham, Norfolk NR25 7BX. *T:* Binham (032830) 396.

DAWSON, Richard Leonard Goodhugh, MB, FRCS; Plastic Surgeon, retired; *b* 24 Aug. 1916; *s* of L. G. Dawson and Freda Hollis; *m* 1945, Betty Marie Freeman-Mathews; two *s*. *Educ:* Bishop's Stortford Coll., Herts; University Coll., London; University College Hospital. MRCS, LRCP 1939; MB London 1940; FRCS 1947; BS London 1948. Royal Army Medical Corps, 1941–46; service in England and Far East (4 years); POW in Japanese hands, 1942–45. Plastic Surgeon: Mt Vernon Centre for Plastic Surgery, Northwood, 1953–82; Royal Free Hosp., London, 1958–76; Royal Nat. Orthopaedic Hosp., Stanmore, 1954–76. Member, British Assoc. Plastic Surgeons (President, 1974). *Publications:* chapters in Operative Surgery, 1957; numerous contributions to Lancet, BMJ, British Journal Plastic Surgery and other journals. *Recreations:* squash, golf, gardening. *Address:* 15 The Willows, Maidenhead Road, Windsor, Berks SL4 5TP. *T:* Windsor (0753) 853554.

DAWSON, Thomas Cordner; QC (Scot.) 1986; *b* 14 Nov. 1948; *s* of Thomas Dawson and Flora Chisholm (*née* Dunwoodie); *m* 1975, Jennifer Richmond Crombie; two *s*. *Educ:* Royal High Sch. of Edinburgh; Edinburgh Univ. (LLB Hons). Advocate, 1973. Lectr, Univ. of Dundee, 1971–74; Advocate Depute, 1983–87. Member: Supreme Court Legal Aid Cttee, 1980–83; Criminal Injuries Compensation Bd, 1988–. *Recreations:* golf, cricket, reading. *Address:* 19 Craiglea Drive, Edinburgh EH10 5PB. *T:* 031–447 4427. *Club:* Caledonian (Edinburgh).

DAWSON, Air Chief Marshal Sir Walter Lloyd, KCB 1954 (CB 1945); CBE 1943; DSO 1948; *b* 6 May 1902; *s* of late W. J. Dawson, Sunderland; *m* 1927, Elizabeth Leslie (*d* 1975), *d* of late D. V. McIntyre, MA, MB, ChB; one *d* (one *s* decd). Enlisted in RAF as boy mechanic, 1919; commissioned from Cranwell, 1922; Station Comdr St Eval, Coastal Command, 1942–43; Dir, Anti-U-Boat Operations, 1943; Dir of Plans, 1944–46; AOC Levant, 1946–48; Commandant, School of Land/Air Warfare, Old Sarum, 1948–50; idc, 1950–51 (RAF Instructor); Asst Chief of the Air Staff (Policy), 1952–53; Deputy Chief of Staff (Plans and Operations), SHAPE, 1953–56; Inspector-General of RAF, 1956–57; Air Member for Supply and Organisation, 1958–60, retired. Chm., Handley Page, 1966–69 (Vice-Chm., 1964–66). Dir, Southern Electricity Bd, 1961–72. *Address:* Woodlands, Heathfield Avenue, Sunninghill, Berks SL5 0AL. *T:* Ascot (0344) 20030. *Club:* Royal Air Force.

DAWSON, William John Richard Geoffrey Patrick, CMG 1980; OBE 1967; HM Diplomatic Service, retired; *b* 21 Sept. 1926; *m* 1956, June Eaton Dangerfield; one *s* one *d*. Served HM Forces, 1942–45; joined FO, 1951; served in British Middle East Office, Tehran, Lomé, Dar es Salaam, 1952–72; FCO, 1972–73; Nairobi, 1973–77; Counsellor, FCO, 1977–86.

DAWSON-DAMER, family name of **Earl of Portarlington.**

DAWSON-MORAY, Edward Bruce, CMG 1969; *b* 30 June 1909; *s* of late Alwyn Bruce Dawson-Moray and late Ada (*née* Burlton); *m* 1st, 1933, Ursula Frances (*née* Woodbridge) (marr. diss.); one *s* one *d*; 2nd, Beryl Barber. *Educ:* Cranbrook Sch.; University of London (BA Hons). Housemaster, Chillon Coll., Switzerland, 1938–42. British Legation, Berne, 1942; 3rd Secretary, 1944; 3rd Secretary and Vice-Consul, Rome, 1947–48; Consul: Leopoldville, 1948–50; Detroit, 1950–51; 1st Secretary and Consul, Rangoon, 1952–54; Information Officer and Consul, Naples, 1954–56; Foreign Office, 1956–60; Consul, Casablanca, 1960–63; Chief Establishment Officer, Diplomatic Wireless Service, 1963–69; Principal, Civil Service Dept, 1969–74; retired. Dir, Pre-retirement Training, CSD, 1975–82. Senior Editor, Foreign Office List, 1957–60. *Recreations:* literature, photography, opera, travel. *Address:* 2 Pennypiece, Cleeve Road, Goring-on-Thames, Reading, Berks RG8 9BY. *T:* Goring-on-Thames (0491) 873314.

DAWTRY, Sir Alan, Kt 1974; CBE 1968 (MBE (mil.) 1945); TD 1948; Chief Executive (formerly Town Clerk), Westminster City Council, 1956–77; Chairman: Sperry Rand Ltd, 1977–86; Sperry Rand (Ireland) Ltd, 1977–86; President, London Rent Assessment Panel, 1979–86; *b* 8 April 1915; *s* of Melancthon and Kate Nicholas Dawtry, Sheffield; unmarried. *Educ:* King Edward VII Sch., Sheffield; Sheffield Univ. (LLB). Served War of 1939–45: commissioned RA; campaigns France, N Africa, Italy (MBE, despatches twice); released with rank of Lt-Col. Admitted Solicitor, 1938; Asst Solicitor, Sheffield, 1938–48; Deputy Town Clerk, Bolton, 1948–52; Deputy Town Clerk, Leicester, 1952–54; Town Clerk, Wolverhampton, 1954–56; Hon. Sec., London Boroughs Assoc., 1965–78. Member: Metrication Bd, 1969–74; Clean Air Council, 1960–75; Council of Management, Architectural Heritage Fund, 1977–89; CBI Council, 1982–86. Pres., Soc. of Local Authority Chief Execs, 1975–76. Vice-Chm., Dolphin Square Trust, 1985–. FBIM 1975; FRSA 1978. Foreign Orders: The Star (Afghanistan); Golden Honour (Austria); Leopold II (Belgium); Rio Branco (Brazil); Merit (Chile); Legion of Honour (France); Merit (W Germany); the Phœnix (Greece); Merit (Italy); Homayoun (Iran); The Rising Sun (Japan); the Star (Jordan); African Redemption (Liberia); Oaken Crown (Luxembourg); Loyalty (Malaysia); the Right Hand (Nepal); Orange-Nassau (Netherlands); the Two Niles (Sudan); the Crown (Thailand); Zaire (Zaire). *Address:* 901 Grenville House, Dolphin Square, SW1V 3LR. *T:* 071–798 8100.

DAY, Prof. Alan Charles Lynn; Professor of Economics, London School of Economics, University of London, since 1964; *b* 25 Oct. 1924; *s* of late Henry Charles Day, MBE, and of Ruth Day; *m* 1962, Diana Hope Bocking (*d* 1980); no *c*; *m* 1982, Dr Shirley E. Jones. *Educ:* Chesterfield Grammar Sch.; Queens' Coll., Cambridge. Asst Lecturer, then Lecturer, LSE, 1949–54; Economic Adviser, HM Treas., 1954–56; Reader in Economics, London Univ., 1956–64. Ed., National Inst. Econ. Review, 1960–62; Econ. Correspondent, The Observer, intermittently, 1957–81. Economic Adviser on Civil Aviation, BoT, later Dept of Trade and Industry, 1968–72; Economic Adviser, Civil Aviation Authority, 1972–78. Member: Council, Consumers' Assoc., 1963–; Board, British Airports Authority, 1965–68; SE Region Econ. Planning Council, 1966–69; Home Office Cttee on the London Taxicab Trade, 1967–70; Layfield Cttee on Local Govt Finance, 1974–76; Air Transport Users' Cttee, CAA, 1978–79; Home Office Adv. Panel on Satellite Broadcasting Standards, 1982. British Acad. Leverhulme Vis. Prof., Graduate Inst. for International Studies, Geneva, 1971. Governor, LSE, 1971–76, 1977–79, Pro-Director, 1979–83; Hon. Fellow, 1988. *Publications:* The Future of Sterling, 1954; Outline of Monetary Economics, 1956; The Economics of Money, 1959; (with S. T. Beza) Wealth and Income, 1960. *Address:* Chart Place, Chart Sutton, Kent. *T:* Maidstone (0622) 842236; 13 Gower Mews Mansions, WC1. *T:* 071–631 3928.

DAY, Bernard Maurice, CB 1987; Panel Chairman, Civil Service Selection Board, since 1988; *b* 7 May 1928; *s* of M. J. Day and Mrs M. H. Day; *m* 1956, Ruth Elizabeth Stansfield; two *s* one *d*. *Educ:* Bancroft's Sch.; London School of Economics (BScEcon). Army service, commnd RA, 1946–48. British Electric Traction Fedn, 1950–51; Asst Principal, Air Ministry, 1951; Private Sec. to Air Mem. for Supply and Organisation, 1954–56; Principal, 1956; Cabinet Secretariat, 1959–61; Asst Sec., 1965; Sec., Meteorological Office, 1965–69; Estabt Officer, Cabinet Office, 1969–72; Head of Air Staff Secretariat, MoD, 1972–74; Asst Under Sec. of State, MoD, 1974; Civilian Staff Management, 1974–76; Operational Requirements, 1976–80; Programmes and Budget, 1980–82; Supply and Orgn, Air, 1982–84; Resident Chm., CSSB, 1984–85; Asst Under-Sec. of State (Fleet Support), MoD, 1985–88. Chairman: MoD Branch, First Div. Assoc., 1983–84; MoD Liaison Cttee with CS Benevolent Fund, 1975–84. *Recreations:* swimming, gardening, Parochial Church Council, Elmbridge Mental Health Association, and change-ringing. *Address:* 2 Farmleigh Grove, Walton-on-Thames, Surrey KT12 5BU. *T:* Walton-on-Thames (0932) 227416. *Club:* Commonwealth Trust.

DAY, Sir Derek (Malcolm), KCMG 1984 (CMG 1973); HM Diplomatic Service, retired; High Commissioner to Canada, 1984–87; *b* 29 Nov. 1927; *s* of late Mr and Mrs Alan W. Day; *m* 1955, Sheila Nott; three *s* one *d*. *Educ:* Hurstpierpoint Coll.; St Catharine's Coll., Cambridge. Royal Artillery, 1946–48. Entered HM Foreign Service, Sept. 1951; Third Sec., British Embassy, Tel Aviv, 1953–56; Private Sec. to HM Ambassador, Rome, 1956–59; Second, then First Sec., FO, 1959–62; First Sec., British Embassy, Washington, 1962–66; First Sec., FO, 1966–67; Asst Private Sec. to Sec. of State for Foreign Affairs, 1967–68; Head of Personnel Operations Dept, FCO, 1969–72; Counsellor, British High Commn, Nicosia, 1972–75; Ambassador to Ethiopia, 1975–78; Asst Under-Sec. of State, 1979, Dep. Under-Sec. of State, 1980, and Chief Clerk, 1982–84, FCO. Dir, Monenco Ltd (Canada), 1988–. Mem., Commonwealth War Graves Commn, 1987–; Vice-Chm. of Council, British Red Cross, 1988–. Chm. Governors, Hurstpierpoint Coll., 1987–; Gov., Bethany Sch., 1987–. *Address:* Etchinghill, Goudhurst, Kent. *Club:* United Oxford & Cambridge University.

DAY, Douglas Henry; QC 1989; a Recorder, since 1987; *b* 11 Oct. 1943; *s* of James Henry Day and Nancy Day; *m* 1970, Elizabeth Margaret (*née* Jarman); two *s* one *d*. *Educ:* Bec Sch.; Selwyn Coll., Cambridge (MA). Called to the Bar, Lincoln's Inn, 1967. *Address:* Farrar's Building, Temple, EC4Y 7BD. *T:* 071–583 9241. *Club:* Bec Old Boys Rugby.

DAY, Sir Graham; *see* Day, Sir J. G.

DAY, John King, TD; MA, BSc; Principal, Elizabeth College, Guernsey, CI, 1958–71; *b* Ipoh, Perak, FMS, 27 Oct. 1909; *s* of Harold Duncan Day, Mining Engineer, and Muriel Edith Day; *m* 1935, Mary Elizabeth Stinton, *er d* of late Tom Stinton, Headmaster of the High Sch., Newcastle-under-Lyme; three *s*. *Educ:* Stamford Sch.; Magdalen Coll., Oxford. Demy 1928–32. Honour School of Natural Science (Chemistry) Class 2. Assistant Master, Kendal Sch., Westmorland, 1932; Asst Master and Housemaster, Gresham's Sch., 1933–57. Served Royal Norfolk Regt (7th Bn) and Military College of Science, 1939–45. *Recreations:* walking, fishing and sketching. *Address:* 1 Pearson's Road, Holt, Norfolk NR25 6EJ. *T:* Holt (0263) 713435.
See also N. E. Day.

DAY, Sir (Judson) Graham, Kt 1989; Chairman: The Rover Group Holdings plc (formerly BL plc), since 1986 (Chief Executive, 1986–88); Cadbury Schweppes plc, since 1989 (Director, since 1988); PowerGen, since 1990 (Director, since 1990); *b* 3 May 1933; *s* of Frank Charles Day and Edythe Grace (*née* Baker); *m* 1958, Leda Ann (*née* Creighton); one *s* two *d*. *Educ:* Queen Elizabeth High Sch., Halifax, NS; Dalhousie Univ., Halifax, NS (LLB). Private practice of Law, Windsor, Nova Scotia, 1956–64; Canadian Pacific Ltd, Montreal and Toronto, 1964–71; Chief Exec., Cammell Laird Shipbuilders Ltd, Birkenhead, Eng., 1971–75; Dep. Chm., Organising Cttee for British Shipbuilders and Dep. Chm. and Chief Exec. designate, British Shipbuilders, 1975–76; Prof. of Business Admin and Dir, Canadian Marine Transportation Centre, Dalhousie Univ., NS, 1977–81; Vice-Pres., Shipyards & Marine Develt, Dome Petroleum Ltd, 1981–83; Chm. and Chief Exec., British Shipbuilders, 1983–86. Dep. Chm., MAI plc, 1989– (Dir, 1988–); Director: The Laird Gp plc, 1985–; DAF bv (Netherlands), 1987–; BAe plc, 1986–; Crolonx Inc. (Canada), 1989–; Bank of Nova Scotia (Canada), 1989–; NOVA Corp. of Alberta, 1990–. Pres., ISBA, 1991–. Member: Nova Scotia Barristers' Soc.; Law Soc. of Upper Canada; Canadian Bar Assoc. Freeman, City of London. ARINA. Hon. Fellow, Univ. of Wales Coll. of Cardiff, 1990. Hon. doctorates: Dalhousie; City; CNAA; Cranfield; Aston; Warwick. *Recreation:* reading. *Address:* c/o The Rover Group Holdings plc, 11 Strand, WC2N 5JT.

DAY, Lance Reginald; Keeper, Science Museum Library, 1976–87; *b* 2 Nov. 1927; *s* of late Reginald and of Eileen Day; *m* 1959, Mary Ann Sheahan; one *s* two *d*. *Educ:* Sherrardswood Sch., Welwyn Garden City; Alleyne's Grammar Sch., Stevenage; Northern Polytechnic and University Coll., London (MSc). Res. Asst, Science Museum Library, 1951–64, Asst Keeper 1964–70; Asst Keeper, Science Museum, Dept of Chemistry, 1970–74; Keeper, Science Museum, Dept of Communications and Electrical Engrg, 1974–76. Sec., Nat. Railway Museum Cttee, 1973–75; Hon. Sec., Newcomen Soc., 1973–82. *Publications:* reviews and articles. *Recreation:* music. *Address:* 12 Rhinefield Close, Brockenhurst, Hants SO42 7SU. *T:* Lymington (0590) 22079.

DAY, Lucienne, RDI 1962; in freelance practice, since 1948; Consultant, with Robin Day, to John Lewis Partnership, 1962–87; *b* 1917; *d* of Felix Conradi and Dulcie Lilian Duncan-Smith; *m* 1942, Robin Day, *qv*; one *d*. *Educ:* Convent Notre Dame de Sion, Worthing; Croydon School of Art; Royal Coll. of Art. ARCA 1940; FSIAD 1955; Mem. Faculty of Royal Designers for Industry, 1962 (Master, 1987–89). Teacher, Beckenham Sch. of Art, 1942–47; began designing full-time, dress fabrics and later furnishing fabrics, carpets, wallpapers, table-linen, 1947 for Edinburgh Weavers, Heal's Fabrics, Cavendish Textiles, Tomkinsons, Wilton Royal, Thos Somerset etc, and firms in Scandinavia, USA and Germany; also china decoration for Rosenthal China, Selb, Bavaria, 1956–68; work for Barbican Art Centre, 1979; currently also designing and making silk wall-hangings (silk mosaics). Work in permanent collections: V&A; Trondheim Museum, Norway; Cranbrook Museum, Michigan, USA; Röhsska Mus., Gothenberg, Sweden (silk mosaics); Musée des Arts Décoratifs, Montreal. Member: Rosenthal Studio-line Jury, 1960–68; Cttee, Duke of Edinburgh's Prize for Elegant Design, 1960–63; Council, RCA, 1962–67; RSA Design Bursaries Juries. First Award, Amer. Inst. of Decorators, 1950; Gold Medal, 9th Triennale di Milano, 1951; Gran Premio, 10th Triennale di Milano, 1954; Design Council Awards, 1957, 1960, 1968. *Recreations:* plant collecting in Mediterranean regions, gardening. *Address:* 49 Cheyne Walk, Chelsea, SW3. *T:* 071–352 1455.

DAY, Michael John, OBE 1981; Chairman, Commission for Racial Equality, since 1988; *b* 4 Sept. 1933; *s* of Albert Day and Ellen Florence (*née* Itter); *m* 1960, June Marjorie, *d* of late Dr John William Mackay; one *s* one *d*. *Educ:* University College Sch., Hampstead; Selwyn Coll., Cambridge (MA); London School of Economics (Cert. Social Work and Social Admin). Probation Officer, Surrey, 1960–64; Sen. Probation Officer, W Sussex, 1964–67; Asst Prin. Probation Officer, 1967–68, Chief Probation Officer, 1968–76, Surrey; Chief Probation Officer, W Midlands, 1976–88. Chm., Chief Probation Officers' Conf., 1974–77; First Chm., Assoc. Chief Officers of Probation, 1982–84. *Publications:* contribs to professional jls and others. *Recreations:* family, gardening, music, the countryside. *Address:* Elliot House, 10–12 Allington Street, SW1E 5EH. *T:* 071–828 7022.

DAY, Prof. Nicholas Edward, PhD; Professor of Public Health, since 1989, and Fellow of Churchill College, since 1986, University of Cambridge; *b* 24 Sept. 1939; *s* of John King Day, *qv*; *m* 1961, Jocelyn Deanne Broughton; one *s* one *d*. *Educ:* Magdalen Coll., Oxford (BA Maths); Aberdeen Univ. (PhD Med. Stats). Res. Fellow, Aberdeen Univ., 1962–66; Fellow, ANU, 1966–69; Statistician, 1969–78, Head, Unit of Biostats and Field Studies, 1979–86, Internat. Agency for Res. on Cancer, Lyon; Cancer Expert, Nat. Cancer Inst., USA, 1978–79; Dir, 1986–89, Hon. Dir, 1989–, MRC Biostats Unit. *Publications:* Statistical Methods in Cancer Research, vol. 1 1980, vol. 2 1988; Screening for Cancer of the Uterine Cervix, 1986; Screening for Breast Cancer, 1988; over 200 articles in scientific jls. *Recreations:* sea fishing, fruit growing. *Address:* Porch House, Haddenham, Ely, Cambs CB6 3TJ. *T:* Ely (0353) 740472.

DAY, Prof. Peter, DPhil; FRS 1986; Director of the Royal Institution, and of the Davy Faraday Research Laboratory, since 1991; Visiting Professor, University College London, since 1991; *b* 20 Aug. 1938; *s* of Edgar Day and Ethel Hilda Day (*née* Russell); *m* 1964, Frances Mary Elizabeth Anderson; one *s* one *d*. *Educ:* Maidstone Grammar School; Wadham College, Oxford (BA 1961; MA, DPhil 1965; Hon. Fellow, 1991). Cyanamid European Research Institute, Geneva, 1962; Jun. Res. Fellow, 1963–65, Official Fellow, 1965–91, St John's College, Oxford; Departmental Demonstrator, 1965–67, Lectr in Inorganic Chemistry, 1967–89, *ad hominem* Prof. of Solid State Chemistry, 1989–91, Oxford Univ. Dir, Inst. Laue-Langevin, Grenoble, 1988–91 (on secondment). Prof. Associé, Univ. de Paris-Sud, 1975; Guest Prof., Univ. of Copenhagen, 1978; Vis. Fellow, ANU, 1980; Senior Research Fellow, SRC, 1977–82. Du Pont Lectr, Indiana Univ., 1988. Science and Engineering Research Council: Member: Neutron Beam Res. Cttee, 1983–88; Chemistry Cttee, 1985–88; Molecular Electronics Cttee, 1987—88; Nat. Cttee on Superconductivity, 1987–88; Materials Commn, 1988–90. Council Member: CNRS Lab. de Cristallographie, Grenoble, 1990–; Inst. for Molecular Scis, Okazaki, Japan, 1991–. Royal Society of Chemistry: Vice-Pres., Dalton Div., 1986–88; Corday-Morgan Medal, 1971; Solid State Chem. Award, 1986. *Publications:* Physical Methods in Advanced Inorganic Chemistry (ed with H. A. O. Hill), 1968; Electronic States of Inorganic Compounds, 1974; Emission and Scattering Techniques, 1980; Electronic Structure and Magnetism of Inorganic Compounds, vols 1–7, 1972–82; (ed with A. K. Cheetham) Solid State Chemistry, 1987; papers in Jl Chem. Soc.; Inorg. Chem. *Recreation:* driving slowly through rural France. *Address:* 16 Blackhall Road, Oxford OX1 3QF. *T:* Oxford (0865) 57662.

DAY, Peter Rodney, PhD; Director, Center for Agricultural Molecular Biology, Rutgers University, New Jersey, since 1987; Secretary, International Genetics Federation, since 1984; *b* 27 Dec. 1928; *s* of Roland Percy Day and Florence Kate (*née* Dixon); *m* 1950, Lois Elizabeth Rhodes; two *s* one *d*. *Educ:* Birkbeck Coll., Univ. of London (BSc, PhD). John Innes Institute, 1946–63; Associate Prof. of Botany, Ohio State Univ., 1963–64; Chief, Dept of Genetics, Connecticut Agricl Experiment Station, 1964–79; Dir, Plant Breeding Inst., Cambridge, 1979–87. Special Prof. of Botany, Nottingham Univ., 1982–88. Commonwealth Fund Fellow, 1954; John Simon Guggenheim Meml Fellow, 1973. *Publications:* Fungal Genetics (with J. R. S. Fincham), 1963, 4th edn 1979; Genetics of Host-Parasite Interaction, 1974; contrib. Genetical Research, Genetics, Heredity, Nature, Proc. Nat. Acad. Sci., Phytopathology, etc. *Recreation:* Scottish country dancing. *Address:* Center for Agricultural Molecular Biology, Rutgers, State University of New Jersey, NJ 08903, USA. *T:* (908) 932–8165.

DAY, Sir Robin, Kt 1981; Television and Radio Journalist; *b* 24 Oct. 1923; *s* of late William and Florence Day; *m* 1965, Katherine Ainslie (marr. diss. 1986); two *s*. *Educ:* Bembridge Sch.; St Edmund Hall, Oxford (Hon. Fellow, 1989). Military service, 1943–47; commd RA, 1944. Oxford, 1947–51: Union debating tour of American universities, 1949; President, Oxford Union, 1950; BA Hons (Jurisprudence), 1951; MA. Middle Temple: Blackstone Entrance Scholar, 1951; Harmsworth Law Scholar, 1952–53; called to Bar, 1952; Hon. Bencher, 1990. British Information Services, Washington, 1953–54; free-lance broadcaster, 1954–55; BBC Talks Producer (radio), 1955; Newscaster and Parliamentary Correspondent, Independent Television News, 1955–59; columnist in News Chronicle, 1959; ITV programmes, 1955–59: Roving Report (ITN); Tell the People (ITN); Under Fire (Granada); since 1959 BBC TV programmes including: Panorama, Gallery, People to Watch, Daytime, 24 Hours, Midweek, To-night, Sunday Debate, Talk-in, Newsday, Question Time. BBC radio programmes: It's Your Line, 1970–76; Election Call, 1974, 1979, 1983, 1987; The World at One, 1979–87. Chm., Hansard Soc., 1981–83. Mem., Phillimore Cttee on Law of Contempt, 1971–74. Trustee, Oxford Literary and Debating Union Trust. Contested (L) Hereford, 1959. Hon. LLD: Exeter, 1986; Keele, 1988; DU Essex, 1988. Guild of TV Producers' Merit Award, Personality of the Year, 1957; Richard Dimbleby Award for factual television, 1974; Broadcasting Press Guild Award, for Question Time, 1980; RTS Judges' Award for 30 yrs TV journalism, 1985. *Publications:* Television: A Personal Report, 1961; The Case for Televising Parliament, 1963; Day by Day, 1975; Grand Inquisitor—memoirs, 1989. *Recreations:* reading, talking, walking. *Clubs:* Athenæum, Garrick, Royal Automobile, MCC.

DAY, Robin, OBE 1983; RDI 1959; FCSD (FSIAD 1948); design consultant and freelance designer; *b* 25 May 1915; *s* of Arthur Day and Mary Shersby; *m* 1942, Lucienne Conradi (*see* Lucienne Day); one *d*. *Educ:* Royal Coll. of Art (ARCA). National scholarship to RCA, 1935–39; teacher and lectr for several yrs; Design Consultant: Hille International, 1948–; John Lewis Partnership, 1962–. Commissions include: seating for Royal Festival Hall, 1951; interior design of Super VC10 and other passenger aircraft for BOAC, 1963–74. Mem., juries for many national and internat. indust. design competitions. Governor, London Coll. of Furniture. Many awards for design work, including: 6 Design Centre awards; Gold Medal, Triennale di Milano, 1951, and Silver Medal, 1954; Designs Medal, SIAD, 1957. *Recreations:* mountaineering, skiing. *Address:* 49 Cheyne Walk, Chelsea, SW3 5LP. *T:* 071–352 1455. *Clubs:* Alpine, Alpine Ski, Climbers'.

DAY, Stephen Peter, CMG 1989; HM Diplomatic Service; Ambassador to Tunisia, since 1987; *b* 19 Jan. 1938; *s* of Frank William and Mary Elizabeth Day; *m* 1965, Angela Doreen (*née* Waudby); one *s* two *d*. *Educ:* Bancroft's School; Corpus Christi Coll., Cambridge. MA. Entered HMOCS as Political Officer, Western Aden Protectorate, 1961, transf. to FO, 1965; Senior Political Officer, South Arabian Federation, 1964–67; FO, 1967–70; First Sec., Office of C-in-C, Far East, Singapore, 1970–71; First Sec. (Press), UK Mission to UN, NY, 1971–75; FCO, 1976–77; Counsellor, Beirut, 1977–78; Consul-Gen., Edmonton, 1979–81; Ambassador to Qatar, 1981–84; Head of ME Dept, FCO, 1984–87; attached to Household of the Prince of Wales, 1986. *Recreations:* walking, family. *Address:* c/o Foreign and Commonwealth Office, SW1A 2AH. *Club:* Athenæum.

DAY, Stephen Richard; MP (C) Cheadle, since 1987; *b* 30 Oct. 1948; *s* of Francis and Anne Day; *m* 1982, Frances (*née* Booth); one *s* by former marriage. *Educ:* Otley Secondary Modern Sch.; Park Lane Coll., Leeds; Leeds Polytechnic. MIEx 1972. Sales Clerk, William Sinclair & Sons, stationary manufrs, Otley, W Yorks, 1965–70, Asst Sales Manager (working in Home and Export Depts), 1970–77; Sales Representative: Larkfield Printing Co. Ltd (part of Hunting Group), Brighouse, W Yorks, 1977–80; A. H. Leach & Co. (part of Hunting Gp), photographic processing lab., Brighouse, 1980–84; Sales Executive: PPL Chromacopy, photographic labs, Leeds and Manchester, 1984–86; Chromogene, photographic lab., Leeds, 1986–87. Vice-Pres., Stockport Chamber of Commerce, 1987–; Mem. Cttee, Stockport and Dist Heart Foundn, 1985–. Chm., Yorks Area Cons. Political Centre, 1983–86; Vice-Chm., NW Leeds Constituency, 1983–86. Town Councillor, Otley, 1975–76 and 1979–83; City Councillor, Leeds, 1975–80. Contested (C) Bradford West, 1983. Mem., Select Cttee on Social Securities, 1990–; Co-Chm., Parly Adv. Council for Transport Safety, 1989–. Sponsor, Private Member's Bill to introduce compulsory wearing of rear car seat belts by children, 1988. *Publications:* pamphlets on Otley and on rate reform. *Recreations:* movies, music, history (particularly Roman). *Clubs:* Cheadle Hulme Conservative (Cheadle Hulme); Royal Wharfedale (Otley).

DAY-LEWIS, Séan; journalist and author; *b* 3 Aug. 1931; *s* of Cecil Day-Lewis, CBE, CLit and Mary Day-Lewis; *m* 1960, Anna Mott; one *s* one *d*. *Educ:* Allhallows Sch., Rousdon, Devon. National Service, RAF, 1949–51. Bridport News, 1952–53; Southern Times, Weymouth, 1953–54; Herts Advertiser, St Albans, 1954–56; Express and Star, Wolverhampton, 1956–60; The Daily Telegraph, 1960–86, TV and Radio Editor, 1970–86; TV Editor, London Daily News, 1987. Arts Editor, Socialist Commentary, 1966–71; Founder-Chm., Broadcasting Press Guild, 1975; Vice Pres., Bulleid Soc., 1970; Member, BAFTA, 1976. *Publications:* Bulleid: last giant of steam, 1964; C. Day-Lewis: an English literary life, 1980; (ed) One Day in the Life of Television, 1989. *Recreations:* being in Devon, listening to J. S. Bach and others, failing at ball games, giving in to temptation. *Address:* 52 Masbro Road, W14 0LT. *T:* 071–602 3221; Restorick Row, Rosemary Lane, Colyton, Devon EX13 6LW. *T:* Colyton (0297) 53039.

DAYKIN, Christopher David, FIA; Government Actuary, since 1989; *b* 18 July 1948; *s* of John Francis Daykin and Mona Daykin; *m* 1977, Kathryn Ruth (*née* Tingey); two *s* one *d*. *Educ:* Merchant Taylors' Sch., Northwood; Pembroke Coll., Cambridge (BA 1970, MA 1973). FIA 1973. Government Actuary's Department, 1970; VSO, Brunei, 1971; Govt Actuary's Dept, 1972–78; Principal (Health and Social Services), HM Treasury, 1978–80; Govt Actuary's Dept, 1980–, Principal Actuary, 1982–84, Directing Actuary (Social Security), 1985–89. Mem., Council, Inst. of Actuaries, 1985– (Hon. Sec., 1988–90). Treasurer, Emmanuel Church, Northwood, 1982–87; Chm., VSO Harrow and Hillingdon, 1976–. *Publications:* articles and papers on pensions, demography, consumer credit, social security and insurance. *Recreations:* travel, photography, languages. *Address:* Government Actuary's Department, 22 Kingsway, WC2B 6LE. *T:* 071–242 6828.

DEACON, Keith Vivian; Under Secretary, since 1988, and Director of Operations, since 1991, Inland Revenue; *b* 19 Nov. 1935; *s* of Vivian and Louisa Deacon; *m* 1960, Brenda Chater; one *s* one *d*. *Educ:* Sutton County Grammar School; Bristol Univ. (BA Hons English Lang. and Litt.). Entered Inland Revenue as Inspector of Taxes, 1962; Regional Controller, 1985; Dir, Technical Div. I until Head Office reorganisation, 1988; Dir, Insce and Specialist Div., 1988–91. Part time work for Civil Service Selection Board: Observer, 1969–72; Chairman, 1985–87. *Recreations:* reading, walking, music, gardening. *Address:* Board of Inland Revenue, New Wing, Somerset House, WC2R 1LB.

DEACON ELLIOTT, Air Vice-Marshal Robert, CB 1967; OBE 1954; DFC 1941; AE 1944 (2 mentions); *b* 20 Nov. 1914; *m* 1948, Grace Joan Willes, Leamington Spa; two *s* one *d*. *Educ:* Northampton. 72 Fighter Sqdn (Dunkirk and Battle of Britain), 1939–41; HQ Fighter Comd, 1942–43; 84 Group 2 ATAF, 1944–46; Air Ministry (OR 5), 1946–48; OC Flying Wing and OC 26 APC in Cyprus, 1948–51; HQ Fighter Comd, Head of Admin. Plans, 1951–54; Army Staff Coll., on Directing Staff, 1954–56; CO, RAF Leconfield, 1956–57; CO, RAF Driffield, 1957–58; Air University USAF, Maxwell AFB, USA, 1958–61; Commandant, Officer and Aircrew Selection Centre, 1962–65; AOC, RAF Gibraltar, 1965–66; AOC, RAF Malta, and Dep. C-in-C (Air), Allied Forces Mediterranean, 1966–68, retd; Bursar, Civil Service Coll., 1969–79. *Recreations:* shooting, photography. *Address:* Thor House, Old Roar Road, St Leonards-on-Sea, E Sussex TN37 7HH. *T:* Hastings (0424) 752699. *Club:* Royal Air Force.

DEAKIN, Maj.-Gen. Cecil Martin Fothergill, CB 1961; CBE 1956; *b* 20 Dec. 1910; *m* 1934, Evelyn (*d* 1984), *e d* of late Sir Arthur Grant, Bt of Monymusk, Aberdeenshire; one *s* one *d*. *Educ:* Winchester Coll. Commissioned into Grenadier Guards, 1931. Served with Regt NW Europe, 1944–45 (despatches). Commanded: 2nd Bn Grenadier Guards,

1945–46; 1st Bn, 1947–50; 32nd Guards Bde, 1953–55; 29th Infantry Bde, 1955–57 (Suez Expedition, despatches); Brigadier, General Staff, War Office, 1957–59; Director of Military Training, 1959; GOC 56th London Div., TA, 1960; Director Territorial Army, Cadets and Home Guard, 1960–62; Commandant of the JSSC, Latimer, 1962–65. Pres., Grenadier Guards Assoc., 1966–81. *Address:* Lettre Cottage, Killearn, Stirlingshire G63 9LE. *Club:* Royal Yacht Squadron.

See also Sir A. B. C. Edmonstone, Bt.

DEAKIN, Sir (Frederick) William (Dampier); *see* Deakin, Sir William.

DEAKIN, Michael; writer, documentary and film maker; Senior Vice-President, Paramount/Revcom, a division of Paramount Pictures, Hollywood and Revcom Television, Paris, since 1987; Director, Griffin Productions Ltd, since 1985; *b* 21 Feb. 1939; *s* of Sir William Deakin, *qv*, and Margaret Hodson (*née* Beatson-Bell). *Educ:* Bryanston; Univ. d'Aix-Marseille; Emmanuel Coll., Cambridge (MA Hons). Founding Partner, Editions Alecto, Fine Art Publishers, 1960–64; Producer, BBC Radio Current Affairs Dept, 1964–68; Producer, then Editor, Yorkshire Television Documentary Unit, 1968–81. Documentary film productions include: Out of the Shadow into the Sun—The Eiger; Struggle for China; The Children on the Hill; Whicker's World—Way Out West; The Japanese Experience; The Good, the Bad and the Indifferent; Johnny Go Home (British Academy Award, 1976); David Frost's Global Village; The Frost Interview—The Shah; Rampton—The Secret Hospital; Painting With Light (co-prodn with BBC); Act of Betrayal, 1987 (TV film); Not a Penny More, Not a Penny Less, 1990 (TV mini series); Secret Weapon, 1990 (film); also many others. Founding Mem., TV-am Breakfast Television Consortium, 1980; Consultant, TV-am, 1984–87 (Dir of Programmes, 1982–84; Bd Mem., 1984–85). *Publications:* Restif de la Bretonne—Les Nuits de Paris (critical edn and trans. with Nicholas Deakin), 1968; Gaetano Donizetti—a biography, 1968; (for children) Tom Grattan's War, 1970, 2nd edn 1971; The Children on the Hill, 1972, 9th edn 1982; (with John Willis) Johnny Go Home, 1976; (with Antony Thomas) The Arab Experience, 1975, 2nd edn 1976; Flame in the Desert, 1976; (with David Frost) I Could Have Kicked Myself, 1982, 2nd US edn 1983; (with David Frost) Who Wants to be a Millionaire, 1983; (with David Frost) If You'll Believe That You'll Believe Anything . . ., 1986. *Recreations:* travel, music, books, pictures, dalmatians, motorcycling. *Address:* 6 Glenhurst Avenue, NW5 1PS. *Club:* British Academy of Film and Television Arts.

See also N. D. Deakin.

DEAKIN, Prof. Nicholas Dampier; Professor of Social Policy and Administration, since 1980, Dean, Faculty of Commerce and Social Science, 1986–89, University of Birmingham; *b* 5 June 1936; *s* of Sir (Frederick) William Deakin, *qv* and Margaret Ogilvy Hodson; *m* 1st, 1961, Rose Albinia Donaldson (marr. diss. 1988), *d* of Baron Donaldson of Kingsbridge, *qv*, and Frances Annesley Donaldson, *qv*; one *s* two *d*; 2nd, 1988, Lucy Moira, *d* of Jack and Moira Gaster. *Educ:* Westminster Sch.; Christ Church Coll., Oxford. BA (1st cl. Hons) 1959, MA 1963, DPhil 1972. Asst Principal, Home Office, 1959–63, Private Sec. to Minister of State, 1962–63; Asst Dir, Nuffield Foundn Survey of Race Relations in Britain, 1963–68; Res. Fellow, subseq. Lectr, Univ. of Sussex, 1968–72; Head of Social Studies, subseq. Head of Central Policy Unit, GLC, 1972–80. Scientific Advr, DHSS, later Dept of Health, 1986–. Vice-Chm., Social Affairs Cttee, ESRC, 1984–86. Chair, Social Policy Assoc., 1989–; Member: Exec. Cttee, NCVO, 1988–90; Council, RIPA, 1984–88; Governing Council, Family Policy Studies Centre, 1987–. *Publications:* (ed and trans.) Memoirs of the Comte de Gramont, 1965; Colour and the British Electorate 1964, 1965; Colour, Citizenship and British Society, 1969; (with Clare Ungerson) Leaving London, 1977; (jtly) Government and Urban Poverty, 1983; (ed) Policy Change in Government, 1986; The Politics of Welfare, 1987; (ed jtly) Consuming Public Services, 1990; contribs to other vols and learned jls. *Recreations:* reading fiction, music. *Address:* Department of Social Policy and Social Work, University of Birmingham, PO Box 363, Birmingham B15 2TT; 55 Estria Road, Birmingham B15 2LG. *T:* 021–440 6251. *Club:* British Academy of Film and Television Arts.

See also M. Deakin.

DEAKIN, Sir William, Kt 1975; DSO 1943; MA; Warden of St Antony's College, Oxford, 1950–68, retired; Hon. Fellow, 1969; *b* 3 July 1913; *e s* of Albert Witney Deakin, Aldbury, Tring, Herts; *m* 1st, 1935, Margaret Ogilvy (marr. diss. 1940), *d* of late Sir Nicholas Beatson Bell, KCSI, KCIE; two *s*; 2nd, 1943, Livia Stela, *d* of Liviu Nasta, Bucharest. *Educ:* Westminster Sch.; Christ Church, Oxford (Hon. Student, 1979). 1st Class, Modern History, 1934; Amy Mary Preston Read Scholar, 1935. Fellow and Tutor, Wadham Coll., Oxford, 1936–49; Research Fellow, 1949; Hon. Fellow, 1961. Served War of 1939–45; with Queen's Own Oxfordshire Hussars, 1939–41; seconded to Special Operations, War Office, 1941; led first British Military Mission to Tito, May 1943. First Secretary, HM Embassy, Belgrade, 1945–46. Hon. FBA, 1980. Russian Order of Valour, 1944; Chevalier de la Légion d'Honneur, 1953; Grosse Verdienstkreuz, 1958; Yugoslav Partisan Star (1st Class), 1969. *Publications:* The Brutal Friendship, 1962; (with G. R. Storry) The Case of Richard Sorge, 1964; The Embattled Mountain, 1971. *Address:* 83330 Le Castellet Village, Var, France. *Clubs:* White's, Brooks's.

See also M. Deakin, N. D. Deakin.

DEAKINS, Eric Petro; international political consultant; *b* 7 Oct. 1932; *er s* of late Edward Deakins and Gladys Deakins; *m* 1990, Sandra Weaver. *Educ:* Tottenham Grammar Sch.; London Sch. of Economics. BA (Hons) in History, 1953. Executive with FMC (Meat) Ltd, 1956; General Manager, Pigs Div., FMC (Meat) Ltd, 1969. Contested (Lab) Walthamstow, 1987. MP (Lab): Walthamstow W, 1970–74; Walthamstow, 1974–87. Parly Under-Sec. of State, Dept of Trade, 1974–76, DHSS, 1976–79. *Publications:* A Faith to Fight For, 1964; You and your MP, 1987; What Future for Labour?, 1988. *Recreations:* writing, cinema, squash, football. *Address:* 36 Murray Mews, NW1 9RJ.

DEALTRY, Prof. (Thomas) Richard; Professor of Strategic Management, International Management Centres, Buckingham, since 1989; Regional Director, Diverco Ltd, since 1985; *b* 24 Nov. 1936; *s* of George Raymond Dealtry and Edith (*née* Gardner); *m* 1962, Pauline (*née* Sedgwick) (marr. diss. 1982); one *s* one *d*. *Educ:* Cranfield Inst. of Advanced Technol.; MBA. CEng, MIMechE; MInstM; FIMCB. National Service Commn, 1959–61: Temp. Captain 1960. Divl Exec., Tube Investments Ltd, 1967–71; Sen. Exec., Guest, Keen & Nettlefold Gp Corporate Staff, 1971–74; Dir, Simpson-Lawrence Ltd, and Man. Dir, BUKO BV, Holland, 1974–77; Under Sec./Industrial Adviser, Scottish Econ. Planning Dept, 1977–78; Director, Gulf Regional Planning, Gulf Org. for Industrial Consulting, 1978–82; Man. Dir, RBA Management Services Ltd, London and Kuwait, 1982–85. *Recreations:* golf, squash. *Address:* 43 Hunstanton Avenue, Harborne, Birmingham B17 8SX.

DEAN, family name of **Baron Dean of Beswick.**

DEAN OF BESWICK, Baron *cr* 1983 (Life Peer), of West Leeds in the County of West Yorkshire; **Joseph Jabez Dean;** *b* 1922. Engineer; formerly Shop Steward, AUEW. Formerly Leader, Manchester City Council. MP (Lab) Leeds West, Feb. 1974–1983; PPS to Minister of State, CSD, 1974–77; an Asst Govt Whip, 1978–79; Labour Party Pairing Whip, 1982–83, 1985–; Labour Party front bench spokesman on employment. Contested (Lab) Leeds West, 1983. *Address:* House of Lords, SW1A 0PW.

DEAN, Anne, (Mrs Stafford Dean); *see* Howells, Anne.

DEAN, Rt Hon. Sir (Arthur) Paul, Kt 1985; PC 1991; MP (C) Woodspring, Avon, since 1983 (Somerset North, 1964–83); Deputy Chairman of Ways and Means and Deputy Speaker, since 1982; Company Director; *b* 14 Sept. 1924; *s* of Arthur Percival Dean and Jessie Margaret Dean (*née* Gaunt); *m* 1st, 1957, Doris Ellen Webb (*d* 1979); 2nd, 1980, Peggy Parker. *Educ:* Ellesmere Coll., Shropshire; Exeter Coll., Oxford (MA, BLitt). Former President Oxford Univ. Conservative Assoc. and Oxford Carlton Club. Served War of 1939–45, Capt. Welsh Guards; ADC to Comdr 1 Corps BAOR. Farmer, 1950–56. Resident Tutor, Swinton Conservative Coll., 1957; Conservative Research Dept, 1957–64, Assistant Director from 1962; a Front Bench Spokesman on Health and Social Security, 1969–70; Parly Under-Sec. of State, DHSS, 1970–74; Member: Exec. Cttee, CPA, UK Branch, 1975–; House of Commons Services Select Cttee, 1979–82; House of Commons Chairman's Panel, 1979–82; Chm., Conservative Health and Social Security Cttee, 1979–82. Formerly, Member Governing Body of Church in Wales. *Publications:* contributions to political pamphlets. *Recreation:* fishing. *Address:* Bowman's Batch, Knightcott, Banwell, Weston-super-Mare, Avon; House of Commons, SW1. *Clubs:* St Stephen's Constitutional, United Oxford & Cambridge University; Bath and County (Bath).

DEAN, Brenda, (Mrs K. D. McDowall); Deputy General Secretary, Graphical, Paper and Media Union, since 1991 (President, 1983–85, General-Secretary, 1985–91, SOGAT '82); *b* 29 April 1943; *d* of Hugh Dean and Lillian Dean; *m* 1988, Keith Desmond McDowall, *qv*. *Educ:* St Andrews Junior Sch., Eccles; Stretford High Sch. for Girls. Admin. Sec., SOGAT, 1959–72; SOGAT Manchester Branch: Asst Sec., 1972–76; Sec., 1976–83; Mem., Nat. Exec. Council, 1977–83. Co-Chm., Women's Nat. Commn, 1985–87; Member: Printing and Publishing Trng Bd, 1974–82; Supplementary Benefits Commn, 1976–80; Price Commn, 1977–79; Occupational Pensions Bd, 1983–87; Gen. Adv. Council, BBC, 1984–88; TUC Gen. Council, 1985–; NEDC, 1989–; Employment Appeal Tribunal, 1991–. Hon. MA Salford, 1986. *Recreations:* sailing, reading, relaxing, thinking! *Address:* SOGAT House, 274/288 London Road, Hadleigh, Essex SS7 2DE.

DEAN, (Cecil) Roy; HM Diplomatic Service, retired; writer and broadcaster; *b* 18 Feb. 1927; *s* of Arthur Dean and Flora Dean (*née* Clare); *m* 1954, Heather Sturtridge; three *s*. *Educ:* Watford Grammar Sch.; London Coll. of Printing and Graphic Arts (diploma); Coll. for Distributive Trades (MIPR). Served RAF, 1945–48, India and Pakistan; Central Office of Information, 1948–58; Second, later First Sec., Colombo, 1958–62; Vancouver, 1962–64; Lagos, 1964–68; FCO, 1968–71; Consul, Houston, 1971, Acting Consul-Gen., 1972–73; FCO, 1973–76; Dir, Arms Control and Disarmament Res. Unit, 1976–83; Dep. High Comr, Accra, 1983–86, Acting High Comr, 1986. Mem., UN Sec.-General's expert group on disarmament instns, 1980–81. Trustee, Urbanaid, 1987–. Editor: Insight, 1964–68; Arms Control and Disarmament, 1979–83; author and presenter, The Poetry of Popular Song (BBC Radio Four series), 1989–. Press Officer: Bromley Chamber Music Soc.; Bromley Art Soc.; Bromley Arts Council; Ravensbourne Labour Party. *Publications:* Peace and Disarmament, 1982; chapter in Ethics and Nuclear Deterrence, 1982; (contrib.) More Christmas Crackers, 1990; numerous research papers; contribs to learned jls. *Recreations:* crosswords (Times national champion, 1970 and 1979); humour; light verse. *Address:* 14 Blyth Road, Bromley, Kent BR1 3RX. *T:* 081–460 8159. *Club:* Bromley Labour.

DEAN, His Honour (Charles) Raymond, QC 1963; a Circuit Judge (formerly Judge of County Courts), 1971–88; Senior Circuit Judge, 1985–88; *b* 28 March 1923; *s* of late Joseph Irvin Gledhill Dean and late Lilian Dean (*née* Waddington); *m* 1948, Pearl Doreen (*née* Buncall); one *s* one *d*. *Educ:* Hipperholme Grammar Sch.; The Queen's Coll., Oxford (1941–42 and 1945–47). RAF Flying Duties, 1942–45 (Flt Lieut). BA (Jurisprudence) 1947, MA 1948; called to Bar, Lincoln's Inn, 1948; Deputy Chairman, West Riding QS, 1961–65; Recorder: of Rotherham, 1962–65; of Newcastle upon Tyne, 1965–70; of Kingston-upon-Hull, 1970–71. *Recreations:* fishing, motoring, reading, Rugby Union (now non-playing), golf. *Address:* Inner Court, 3 Hudson Mews, Boston Spa, West Yorks LS23 6AD. *T:* Boston Spa (0937) 844155. *Club:* Leeds.

DEAN, David Edis; Director, British Architectural Library, Royal Institute of British Architects, 1969–83; *b* 18 June 1922; *y s* of Arthur Edis Dean, CBE, MA, MLitt, and Elsie Georgina Musgrave Wood; *m* 1945, Sylvia Mummery Gray. *Educ:* Bryanston; Wadham Coll., Oxford (MA); Reading Univ. (DipEd). Served War, RAF Photographic Interpretation, 1943–46. Schoolmaster, 1950–54; Cataloguer, then Dep. Librarian, Royal Commonwealth Soc., 1954–60; Dep. Librarian, RIBA, 1960–69. Hon. FRIBA. *Publications:* English Shopfronts, 1970; The Thirties: recalling the English architectural scene, 1983; The Architect as Stand Designer, 1985; articles, reviews. *Recreations:* book collecting, music, birdwatching. *Address:* 181 Morrell Avenue, Oxford OX4 1NG. *T:* Oxford (0865) 247029.

DEAN, Eric Walter, CB 1968; CBE 1958; Chairman Member, Surrey and Sussex Rent Assessment Panel, 1968–78; *b* 5 March 1906; *s* of late Thomas W. Dean, London; *m* 1935, Joan Mary, *d* of late L. A. Stanley, Folkestone; one *d*. *Educ:* Forest Sch.; Exeter Coll., Oxford (MA). Called to Bar, Inner Temple, 1931. Solicitors Dept, Board of Trade, 1935–68; Asst Solicitor, 1947–61; Principal Asst Solicitor, 1961–68, retired. *Recreations:* music, horse-racing. *Address:* 31 Hove Manor, Hove Street, Hove, Sussex BN3 2DG. *T:* Brighton (0273) 721783.

DEAN, (Frederick) Harold, CB 1976; QC 1979; Chairman, Redundant Churches Uses Committee, Diocese of Oxford, since 1983; *b* 5 Nov. 1908; *o c* of late Frederick Richard Dean and Alice Dean (*née* Baron), Manchester; *m* 1st, 1939, Gwendoline Mary Eayrs Williams (marr. diss., 1966; she *d* 1975), 3rd *d* of late Rev. W. Williams, Kingsley, Staffs; one *s* (one *d* decd); 2nd, 1966, Sybil Marshall Dennis (*d* 1977), *o c* of late Col F. B. M. Chatterton, CMG, CBE; 3rd, 1978, Mary-Rose Lester, *y d* of late Comdr F. L. Merriman, RN. *Educ:* Manchester Grammar Sch.; Manchester Univ. LLB 1930; LLM 1932. Called to Bar, Middle Temple, 1933. Practised on Northern Circuit, 1934–40 and 1945–50. Served in RAFVR, 1940–45 in UK, Iraq, Egypt and E Africa (Sqdn Ldr). AJAG, 1950; DJAG: Far East, 1954–57 and 1962–65; Middle East, 1958–61; Germany, 1967–68; Vice JAG, 1968–72; Judge Advocate General, 1972–79. A Comr, Duke of York's Royal Mil. Sch., 1972–79. Chm., Disciplinary Appeal Cttee, ICA, 1980–87. *Publication:* Bibliography of the History of Military and Martial Law (in composite vol., Guide to the Sources of British Military History, 1971, Supplement, 1987); (jtly) Royal Forces in Halsbury's Laws of England, 1983. *Recreations:* travel, music, reading. *Address:* The Old Farmhouse, 13 Lower Street, Quainton, Aylesbury, Bucks HP22 4BL. *T:* Quainton (029675) 263. *Club:* Athenæum.

DEAN, His Honour Joseph (Jolyon); a Circuit Judge, South Eastern Circuit, 1975–87; *b* 26 April 1921; *s* of late Basil Dean, CBE; *m* 1962, Hon. Jenefer Mills, *yr d* of late 5th Baron Hillingdon, MC, TD; one *s* two *d*. *Educ:* Elstree Sch.; Harrow Sch.; Merton Coll.,

Oxford (MA Classics and Law). 51st (Highland) Div., RA, 1942–45. Called to the Bar, Middle Temple, 1947; Bencher 1972. *Publication:* Hatred, Ridicule or Contempt, 1953 (paperback edns 1955 and 1964). *Recreation:* domestic maintenance. *Address:* The Hall, West Brabourne, Ashford, Kent TN25 5LZ.
See also Winton Dean.

DEAN, Katharine Mary Hope, (Mrs Robert Dean); *see* Mortimer, K. M. H.

DEAN, Michael; QC 1981; **His Honour Judge Dean;** a Circuit Judge, since 1991; *b* 2 Feb. 1938; *s* of late Henry Ross Dean and Dorothea Alicia Dean; *m* 1967, Diane Ruth Griffiths. *Educ:* Altrincham Co. Grammar Sch.; Univ. of Nottingham. Lectr in Law, Univ. of Manchester, 1959–62; called to the Bar, Gray's Inn, 1962; Northern Circuit, Manchester, 1962–65; Lectr in Law, LSE, 1965–67; practice at the Bar, London, 1968–; an Asst Recorder, 1986–89; a Recorder, 1989–91. *Publications:* articles in various legal periodicals. *Recreations:* conversation, music, theatre, sailing. *Address:* 7 King's Bench Walk, Temple, EC4. *T:* 071–383 0404.

DEAN, Sir Patrick (Henry), GCMG 1963 (KCMG 1957; CMG 1947); Director, Taylor Woodrow, 1969–86 (Consultant since 1986); International Adviser, American Express, since 1969; *b* 16 March 1909; *o s* of late Professor H. R. Dean and Irene, *d* of Charles Arthur Wilson; *m* 1947, Patricia Wallace, *y d* of late T. Frame Jackson; two *s*. *Educ:* Rugby Sch.; Gonville and Caius Coll., Cambridge. First Class Hons, Classical Tripos Part I; Law Tripos Parts 1 and 2, 1929–32; Fellow of Clare Coll., Cambridge, 1932–35; called to the Bar, 1934; Barstow Law Scholar, Inns of Court, 1934; practised at Bar, 1934–39; Asst Legal Adviser, Foreign Office, 1939–45; Head of German Political Dept, FO, 1946–50; Minister at HM Embassy, Rome, 1950–51; Senior Civilian Instructor at Imperial Defence Coll., 1952–53; Asst Under-Secretary of State, Foreign Office, 1953–56; Dep. Under-Secretary of State, Foreign Office, 1956–60; Permanent Representative of the United Kingdom to the United Nations, 1960–64; Ambassador in Washington, 1965–69. Mem., Departmental Cttee to examine operation of Section 2 of Official Secrets Act, 1971. Chm., Cambridge Petroleum Royalties, 1975–82; Dep. Pres., English-Speaking Union, 1984– (Chm., 1973–83). Trustee, The Economist, 1971–; Mem., Cttee of Award, Harkness Fellowship, 1970–78. Mem., Governing Body, Rugby School, 1939–84 (Chm. 1972–84). Hon. Fellow, Clare Coll. and Gonville and Caius Coll., Cambridge, 1965. Hon. Bencher, Lincoln's Inn, 1965. Hon. LLD Lincoln Wesleyan Univ., 1961, Chattanooga Univ., 1962, Hofstra Univ., 1964, Columbia Univ., 1965, University of South Carolina, 1967, College of William and Mary, 1968. KStJ 1971. *Publications:* various articles and notes in the Law Quarterly Review. *Recreations:* mountains, walking. *Address:* 5 Bentinck Mansions, Bentinck Street, W1M 5RJ. *T:* 071–935 0881. *Club:* Brooks's.
See also Baron Roskill.

DEAN, Rt. Hon. Sir Paul; *see* Dean, Rt. Hon. Sir A. P.

DEAN, Dr Paul, CB 1981; writer and adviser; Director, National Physical Laboratory, 1977–90 (Deputy Director, 1974–76); *b* 23 Jan. 1933; *s* of late Sydney and Rachel Dean; *m* 1961, Sheila Valerie Gamse; one *s* one *d*. *Educ:* Hackney Downs Grammar Sch.; Queen Mary Coll., Univ. of London (Fellow, 1984). BSc (1st cl. Hons Physics), PhD; CPhys; FInstP, FIMA. National Physical Laboratory: Sen. Sci. Officer, Math. Div., 1957; Principal Sci. Officer, 1963; Sen. Principal Sci. Officer (Individual Merit), 1967; Head of Central Computer Unit, 1967; Supt, Div. of Quantum Metrology, 1969; Under-Sec., DoI (Head of Space and Air Res. and R&D Contractors Divs), 1976–77. Part-time Head, Res. Establts Management Div., DoI, 1979–82; Exec. Dep. Chm., Council of Res. Establts, 1979–82. Mem., Internat. Cttee of Weights and Measures, 1985–90; Pres., Comité Consultatif pour les Etalons de Mesure des Rayonnements Ionisants, 1987–90; Founder Pres., British Measurement and Testing Assoc., 1990–; First Chm., EUROMET, 1988–90. *Publications:* papers and articles in learned, professional and popular jls. *Recreations:* mathematics, computing, astronomy, chess, music, bridge. *Address:* Surrey and Dorset.

DEAN, Peter Henry; free-lance business consultant, since 1985; *b* 24 July 1939; *s* of late Alan Walduck Dean and Gertrude (*née* Bürger); *m* 1965, Linda Louise Keating; one *d*. *Educ:* Rugby Sch.; London Univ. (LLB). Admitted Solicitor, 1962. Joined Rio Tinto-Zinc Corp., 1966; Sec., 1972–74; Dir, 1974–85. Dir, Liberty Life Assurance Co., 1986–; Dir, Associated British Ports Holdings, 1982– (Mem., British Transport Docks Bd, 1980–82); Dep. Chm., Monopolies and Mergers Commn, 1990– (Mem., 1982–). Chm., Council of Management, Highgate Counselling Centre, 1991– (Mem., 1985–); Chm., English Baroque Choir, 1985–89. *Recreations:* choral singing, ski-ing. *Address:* 52 Lanchester Road, Highgate, N6 4TA. *T:* 081–883 5417, *Fax:* 081–365 2398.

DEAN, Raymond; *see* Dean, C. R.

DEAN, Roy; *see* Dean, C. R.

DEAN, Winton (Basil), FBA 1975; author and musical scholar; *b* Birkenhead, 18 March 1916; *e s* of late Basil Dean, CBE, and Esther, *d* of A. H. Van Gruisen; *m* 1939, Hon. Thalia Mary Shaw, 2nd *d* of 2nd Baron Craigmyle; one *s* one adopted *d* (and two *d* decd). *Educ:* Harrow; King's Coll., Cambridge (MA). Translated libretto of Weber's opera Abu Hassan (Arts Theatre, Cambridge) 1938. Served War of 1939–45: in Admiralty (Naval Intelligence Div.), 1944–45. Member: Music Panel, Arts Council, 1957–60, Cttee of Handel Opera Society (London), 1955–60; Council, Royal Musical Assoc., 1965– (Vice-Pres., 1970–). Ernest Bloch Prof. of Music, 1965–66, Regent's Lectr, 1977, Universiy of California (Berkeley); Matthew Vassar Lectr, Vassar Coll., Poughkeepsie, NY, 1979. Member: Management Cttee, Halle Handel Soc., 1979–; Kuratorium, Göttingen Handel Fest., 1981–; Corresp. Mem., Amer. Musicological Soc., 1989–. Ed, with Sarah Fuller, Handel's opera Julius Caesar (Barber Inst. of Fine Arts, Birmingham), performed 1977. Hon. RAM 1971. *Publications:* The Frogs of Aristophanes (trans. of choruses to music by Walter Leigh), 1937; Bizet (Master Musicians), 1948 (3rd rev. edn, 1975); Carmen, 1949; Introduction to the Music of Bizet, 1950; Franck, 1950; Hambleden *v* Feathercombe, the Story of a Village Cricket Match, 1951; Handel's Dramatic Oratorios and Masques, 1959; Shakespeare and Opera (Shakespeare in Music), 1964; Georges Bizet, His Life and Work, 1965; Handel and the Opera Seria, 1969; Beethoven and Opera (in The Beethoven Companion), 1971; ed, Handel, Three Ornamented Arias, 1976; (ed) E. J. Dent, The Rise of Romantic Opera, 1976; The New Grove Handel, 1982; (with J. M. Knapp) Handel's Operas 1704–1726, 1987; Essays on Opera, 1990; contributed to Grove's Dictionary of Music and Musicians (5th and 6th edns), New Oxford History of Music and to musical periodicals and learned journals. *Recreations:* cricket, shooting; naval history. *Address:* Hambledon Hurst, Godalming, Surrey. *T:* Wormley (0428) 682644.
See also J. J. Dean.

DEANE, family name of **Baron Muskerry.**

DEANE, Prof. Basil; Professor of Music, University of Birmingham, since 1987; *b* 27 May 1928; *s* of Canon Richard A. Deane and Lorna Deane; *m* 1955, Norma Greig (*d* 1991); two *s*. *Educ:* Armagh Royal School; The Queen's Univ., Belfast (BA, BMus, PhD). FRNCM 1978. Lecturer in Music, Glasgow Univ., 1953–59; Senior Lectr, Melbourne Univ., 1959–65; Lectr, Nottingham Univ., 1966–68; Prof., Sheffield Univ., 1968–74; Prof. of Music, Manchester Univ., 1975–80; Music Dir, Arts Council, 1980–83; Dir, Hongkong Acad. for Performing Arts, 1983–87. Member of Arts Council, 1977–79 (Chairman, Music Advisory Panel, 1977–79); Chairman of Music Board, Council for Nat. Academic Awards, 1978–80. *Publications:* Albert Roussel, 1962; Cherubini, 1965; Hoddinott, 1979; contribs to periodicals. *Address:* Barber Institute of Fine Arts (Department of Music), PO Box 363, Birmingham B15 2TS.

DEANE, Prof. Phyllis Mary, FBA 1980; Professor of Economic History, University of Cambridge, 1981–82, now Emeritus; Fellow of Newnham College, 1961–83, Honorary Fellow, 1983; *b* 13 Oct. 1918; *d* of John Edward Deane and Elizabeth Jane Brooks; single. *Educ:* Chatham County Sch.; Hutcheson's Girls' Grammar Sch., Glasgow; Univ. of Glasgow. MA Hons Econ. Science Glasgow 1940; MA Cantab; FRHistS. Carnegie Research Scholar, 1940–41; Research Officer, Nat. Inst. of Econ. and Social Research, 1941–45; Colonial Research Officer, 1946–48; Research Officer: HM Colonial Office, 1948–49; Cambridge University: Dept of Applied Econs, 1950–61; Lectr, Faculty of Econs and Politics, 1961–71; Reader in Economic History, 1971–81. Vis. Prof., Univ. of Pittsburgh, 1969. Editor, Economic Jl, 1968–75. Pres., Royal Economic Soc., 1980–82. Hon. DLitt Glasgow, 1989. *Publications:* (with Julian Huxley) The Future of the Colonies, 1945; The Measurement of Colonial National Incomes, 1948; Colonial Social Accounting, 1953; (with W. A. Cole) British Economic Growth 1688–1959, 1962; The First Industrial Revolution, 1965; The Evolution of Economic Ideas, 1978; The State and the Economic System, 1989; papers and reviews in econ. jls. *Recreations:* walking, gardening. *Address:* 4 Stukeley Close, Cambridge CB3 9LT.

DEANE, Hon. Sir William (Patrick), AC 1988; KBE 1982; **Hon. Justice Deane;** Justice of the High Court of Australia, since 1982. Called to the Bar of NSW, 1957; QC 1966. Judge, Supreme Court of NSW, 1977, and Judge, Fed. Court of Australia, 1977–82; Pres., Trade Practices Tribunal, 1977–82. *Address:* High Court of Australia, Canberra, ACT 2600, Australia.

DEANE-DRUMMOND, Maj.-Gen. Anthony John, CB 1970; DSO 1960; MC 1942 and Bar, 1945; *b* 23 June 1917; *s* of late Col J. D. Deane-Drummond, DSO, OBE, MC; *m* 1944, Mary Evangeline Boyd; four *d*. *Educ:* Marlborough Coll.; RMA, Woolwich. Commissioned Royal Signals, 1937. War Service in Europe and N Africa; POW, Italy, 1941 (escaped, 1942); Staff Coll., 1945; Bde Major, 3rd Parachute Bde, 1946–47; Instructor, Sandhurst, 1949–51 and Staff Coll., 1952–55; CO, 22 Special Air Service Regt, 1957–60; Bde Comdr, 44 Parachute Bde, 1961–63; Asst Comdt, RMA, Sandhurst, 1963–66; GOC 3rd Division, 1966–68; ACDS (Operations), 1968–70, retired 1971. Col Comdt, Royal Corps of Signals, 1966–71. Director: Paper and Paper Products Industry Trng Bd, 1971–79; Wood Burning Centre, 1980–83. British Gliding Champion, 1957; Pilot, British Gliding Team, 1958, 1960, 1963, 1965. *Publications:* Return Ticket, 1951; Riot Control, 1975; Arrows of Fortune (autobiog.), 1991. *Recreations:* carpentry and carving, antique furniture restoration, refurbishment of houses, shooting. *Address:* c/o Royal Bank of Scotland, Lombard Street, EC3.

DEANS, Rodger William, CB 1977; Regional Chairman, Social Security Appeal Tribunals and Medical Appeal Tribunals (Scotland), 1984–90, retired; *b* 21 Dec. 1917; *s* of Andrew and Elizabeth Deans, Perth; *m* 1943, Joan Radley; one *s* one *d*. *Educ:* Perth Academy; Edinburgh Univ. Qual. Solicitor in Scotland, 1939. Served in RA and REME, 1939–46 (Major); Mil. Prosecutor, Palestine, 1945–46; Procurator Fiscal Depute, Edinburgh, 1946–47; entered Office of Solicitor to Sec. of State for Scotland, 1947; Scottish Office: Legal Asst, 1947–50; Sen. Legal Asst, 1951–62; Asst Solicitor, 1962–71; Solicitor to Secretary of State for Scotland and Solicitor in Scotland to HM Treasury, 1971–80. Consultant Editor, Green & Son, Edinburgh, 1981–82; Sen. Chm., Supplementary Benefit Appeal Tribunals (Scotland), 1982–84. *Recreations:* hill walking, travelling, gardening. *Address:* 25 Grange Road, Edinburgh EH9 1UQ. *T:* 031–667 1893. *Clubs:* Scottish Arts, Edinburgh University Staff (Edinburgh).

DEAR, Geoffrey James, QPM 1982; DL; HM Inspector of Constabulary, since 1990; *b* 20 Sept. 1937; *er s* of Cecil William Dear and Violet Mildred (*née* Mackney); *m* 1958, Judith Ann Stocker; one *s* two *d*. *Educ:* Fletton Grammar Sch., Hunts; University Coll., London (LLB). Joined Peterborough Combined Police after cadet service, 1956; Mid-Anglia (now Cambridgeshire) Constab., 1965; Bramshill Scholarship, UCL, 1965–68 (Fellow, 1990); Asst Chief Constable (Ops), Notts (City and County), 1972–80; seconded as Dir of Comd Training, Bramshill, 1975–77; Metropolitan Police: Dep. Asst Comr, 1980–81; Asst Comr, 1981–85 (Personnel and Trng, 1981–84; Ops, 1984–85); Chief Constable, W Midlands Police, 1985–90. Member: Govt Adv. Cttee on Alcoholism, 1975–78; Council, RUSI, 1982–89 (Mem. Cttee, 1976–). Lecture tour of Eastern USA univs, 1978; visited Memphis, Tenn, USA to advise on reorganisation of Police Dept, 1979. Vice Chm., London and SE Reg., Sports Council, 1984–85. DL W Midlands, 1985. OStJ 1990. Queen's Commendation for Brave Conduct, 1979. *Publications:* (contrib.) The Police and the Community, 1975; articles in Police Jl and other pubns. *Recreations:* field sports, Rugby football (Pres., Met. Police RFC, 1983–85), fell-walking, reading, gardening, music. *Address:* Home Office, Block A, Government Buildings, Whittington Road, Worcester WR5 2PA. *Club:* Naval and Military.

DEARING, Sir Ronald (Ernest), Kt 1984; CB 1979; Chairman: Polytechnics and Colleges Funding Council, since 1988; Financial Reporting Council, since 1990; Post Office Corporation, 1981–87; County Durham Development Co., 1987–90; Northern Development Company, since 1990; *b* 27 July 1930; *s* of E. H. A. Dearing and M. T. Dearing (*née* Hoyle); *m* 1954, Margaret Patricia Riley; two *d*. *Educ:* Doncaster Grammar Sch.; Hull Univ. (BScEcon); London Business Sch. (Sloan Fellow). Min. of Labour and Nat. Service, 1946–49; Min. of Power, 1949–62; HM Treasury, 1962–64; Min. of Power, Min. of Technology, DTI, 1965–72; Regional Dir, N Region, DTI, 1972–74, and Under-Sec., DTI later Dept of Industry, 1972–76; Dep. Sec. on nationalised industry matters, Dept of Industry, 1976–80; Dep. Chm., Post Office, 1980–81; Chm., NICG, 1983–84. Director (non-executive): Whitbread Co. plc, 1987–90; Prudential plc, 1987–; IMI plc, 1988–; British Coal, 1988–; Erisson Ltd, 1988–; English Estates, 1988–90. Chm., Accounting Standards Review Cttee, CCAB, 1987–88. Mem. Council, Industrial Soc., 1985–. CBIM 1981 (Mem. Council, 1985–; Vice-Chm., 1986). Chm., CNAA, 1987–88. Mem. Governing Council, London Business Sch., 1985–89, Fellow, 1988; Mem. Council, Durham Univ., 1988–; Chm., London Educn Business Partnership, 1989–. Hon. DSc Hull, 1986. *Recreations:* gardening, Do it Yourself. *Address:* c/o Financial Reporting Council, 100 Gray's Inn Road, WC1X 8AL.

DEARNLEY, Christopher Hugh, LVO 1990; MA (Oxon), DMus, FRCO; Organist of St Paul's Cathedral, 1968–90; *b* 11 Feb. 1930; 3rd *s* of Rev. Charles Dearnley; *m* 1957, Bridget (*née* Wateridge); three *s* one *d*. *Educ:* Cranleigh Sch., Surrey; Worcester Coll., Oxford. Organ Scholar, Worcester Coll., Oxford, 1948–52. Asst Organist, Salisbury Cathedral, and Music Master, the Cathedral Sch., Salisbury, 1954–57; Organist and Master of the Choristers, Salisbury Cathedral, 1957–67; Acting Dir of Music, Christ Church, St Laurence, Sydney, 1990–91. Pres., Incorporated Assoc. of Organists, 1968–70; Chairman: Friends of Cathedral Music, 1971–90 (Vice-Pres., 1990–); Harwich Festival, 1982–89

(Pres., 1989–); Percy Whitlock Trust, 1982–89 (Pres., 1989–). Dir, English Hymnal Co., 1970–. Patron, Nat. Accordian Orgn, 1989–; Hon. Gov., Corp. of Sons of the Clergy, 1989–. *Publications*: The Treasury of English Church Music, Vol. III, 1965; English Church Music 1650–1750, 1970. *Recreations*: sketching, gardening. *Address*: c/o Cattai PO, NSW 2756, Australia. *T*: 045–750453.

DEAVE, John James; barrister-at-law; a Recorder of the Crown Court, since 1980; *b* 1 April 1928; *s* of Charles John Deave and Gertrude Debrit Deave; *m* 1958, Gillian Mary, *d* of Adm. Sir Manley Power, KCB, CBE, DSO; one *s* one *d*. *Educ*: Charterhouse; Pembroke Coll., Oxford (MA). Served RA, 2nd Lieut, 1946–48; Pembroke Coll., 1948–51; called to the Bar, Gray's Inn, 1952; in practice at Nottingham, 1957–. *Recreations*: history, gardening. *Address*: (chambers) 1 High Pavement, Nottingham NG1 1HF. *T*: Nottingham (0602) 418218. *Club*: Nottinghamshire United Services.

DEAVIN, Stanley Gwynne, CBE 1971 (OBE 1958); FCA; Chartered Accountant; Chairman, North Eastern Gas Board, 1966–71, retired (Dep. Chairman, 1961–66); *b* 8 Aug. 1905; *s* of Percy John Deavin and Annie (*née* Crayton); *m* 1st, 1934, Louise Faviell (*d* 1982); one *s* one *d*; 2nd, 1982, Hilda Jenkins (*née* Grace). *Educ*: Hymer's Coll., Hull. Firm of Chartered Accountants, 1921–33; Secretary and Accountant, Preston Gas Co., 1933–49; North Western Gas Board: Secretary, 1949–61; Member Board, 1960–61. OStJ. *Recreations*: cricket, Rugby football, theatre. *Address*: 18 Harlow Grange Park, Otley Road, Harrogate, North Yorks HG3 1PX. *T*: Harrogate (0423) 531345.

DeBAKEY, Prof. Michael Ellis, MD, MS; Chancellor, Baylor College of Medicine, since 1979 (Professor of Surgery and Chairman of Department of Surgery since 1948, President, 1969–79, Chief Executive Officer, 1968–69, Baylor University College of Medicine; Vice-President for Medical Affairs, Baylor University, 1968–69); Surgeon-in-Chief, Ben Taub General Hospital, Houston, Texas; Director: First National Heart and Blood Vessel Research and Demonstration Center, 1974–84; DeBakey Heart Center, Baylor College of Medicine, since 1985; Consultant in Surgery to various Hospitals etc., in Texas, and to Walter Reed Army Hospital, Washington, DC; *b* 7 Sept. 1908; *s* of Shaker Morris and Raheeja Zorba DeBakey; *m* 1st, 1936, Diana Cooper (*d* 1972); four *s*; 2nd, 1975, Katrin Fehlhaber; one *d*. *Educ*: Tulane Univ., New Orleans, La, USA (Distinguished Alumnus of Year, 1974). Residency in New Orleans, Strasbourg, and Heidelberg, 1933–36; Instructor, Dept of Surgery, Tulane Univ., 1937–40; Asst Prof. of Surgery, 1940–46; Associate Prof. of Surgery, 1946–48. Colonel Army of US (Reserve). In Office of Surgeon-General, 1942–46, latterly Director Surgical Consultant Div. (Meritorious Civilian Service Medal, 1970). Chairman, President's Commission on Heart Disease, Cancer and Stroke, 1964; US Chm., Task for Mechanical Circulatory Assistance, Jt US–USSR Cttee, 1974; Dir, Cardiovascular Res. and Trng Center, Methodist Hosp. (Houston), 1968–75; Adv. Council, Nat. Heart, Lung, Blood Inst., 1982–86; has served on governmental and university cttees, etc., concerned with public health, research and medical education. Mem. Adv. Editorial Bds: Ann. Surg., 1970–; Coeur, 1969–; Biomedical Materials and Artificial Organs, 1971–; Editor, Jl of Vascular Surgery, 1984–88. Member and Hon. Member of medical societies, including: American Assoc. for Thoracic Surgery (Pres. 1959); Hon. Fellow, RCS, 1974; International Cardiovascular Society (Pres. 1959); BMA (Hon. Foreign Corresp. Member 1966); Royal Society Med., London; Acad. of Medical Sciences, USSR; US—China Physicians Friendship Assoc., 1974; Assoc. Internat. Vasc. Surgeons (Pres., 1983); Southern Surgical Assoc. (Pres., 1989–90). Has received numerous awards from American and foreign medical institutions, and also honorary doctorates; Hektoen Gold Medal, Amer. Med. Assoc., 1970; Nat. Medal of Science, 1987; Markowitz Award, Acad. of Surgical Res., 1988; Assoc. of Amer. Med. Colls. Award, 1988; Crile Award, Internat. Platform Assoc., 1988; Thomas Alva Edison Foundn Award, 1988; first Michael DeBakey Medal, American Soc of Mech. Engrs, 1989; Scripps Clinic and Res. Foundn Inaugural Award, 1989. Presidential Medal of Freedom with Distinction, 1969; Merit Order of the Republic, 1st class (Egypt), 1980; The Independence of Jordan Medal, 1st class, 1980; Sovereign Order of the Knights of the Hospital of St John (Denmark), 1980. *Publications*: The Blood Bank and the Technique and Therapeutics of Transfusions, 1942; (with B. M. Cohen) Buerger's Disease, 1962; A Surgeon's Diary of a Visit to China, 1974; The Living Heart, 1977; The Living Heart Diet, 1984; contributions to standard textbooks of medicine and surgery, Current Therapy, and many symposia; Editor, Year Book of General Surgery, etc.; numerous articles in medical journals. *Recreations*: hunting, music. *Address*: Baylor College of Medicine, One Baylor Plaza, Houston, Texas 77030, USA. *T*: (713) 797–9353. *Clubs*: Cosmos, University Federal (Washington, DC); River Oaks Country (Houston, Texas).

de BASTO, Hon. Gerald Arthur; Judge of the High Court of Hong Kong, 1982–89; *b* London, 31 Dec. 1924; *s* of Bernard de Basto and Lucie Marie, *d* of Raoul Melchior Pattard, Paris; *m* 1961, Diana, *d* of Dr Frederick Osborne Busby Wilkinson; two *s*. *Educ*: Riverview Coll., Sydney, Australia; Univ. of Sydney (LLB). Called to the Bar: Supreme Court of New South Wales and High Court of Australia, 1952; Lincoln's Inn, 1955; admitted to the Hong Kong Bar, 1957; Chairman, Hong Kong Bar, 1968–70, 1973; QC 1968; Judge of the District Court of Hong Kong, 1973–82; Pres., Deportation Tribunal, 1986–89. FRSA 1984. *Recreations*: antiques, travel, reading. *Address*: Canterbury Lodge, 21 Canterbury Drive, Bishopscourt, 7700, South Africa. *T*: (021) 762 5626. *Clubs*: Brooks's; Hong Kong, Royal Hong Kong Jockey (Hong Kong).

de BELLAIGUE, Sir Geoffrey, KCVO 1986 (CVO 1976; LVO 1968); FSA; Director of the Royal Collection, since 1988; Surveyor of the Queen's Works of Art, since 1972; *b* 12 March 1931; *s* of Vicomte Pierre de Bellaigue and Marie-Antoinette Ladd; *m* 1971, Sheila, MVO, 2nd *d* of late Rt Rev. J. K. Russell; two *d*. *Educ*: Wellington Coll.; Trinity Coll., Cambridge (BA 1954, MA 1959); Ecole du Louvre. With J. Henry Schroeder & Co., 1954–59; with the National Trust, Waddesdon Manor, 1960–63 (Keeper of the Collection, 1962–63); Dep. Surveyor, the Queen's Work's of Art, 1963–72. Mem., Exec. Cttee, Nat. Art Collections Fund, 1977–. Hon. Pres., French Porcelain Soc., 1985–. *Publications*: The James A. de Rothschild Collection at Waddesdon Manor: furniture, clocks and gilt bronzes, 1974; Sèvres Porcelain in the Collection of HM the Queen, Vol. I, 1986; (with S. Eriksen) Sèvres Porcelain, 1987; articles in art historical jls and exhibn catalogues, principally for The Queen's Gallery. *Address*: Store Tower, Windsor Castle, Windsor, Berks.

DE BENEDETTI, Carlo; Cavaliere del Lavoro, Italy, 1983; Chairman since 1983, and Chief Executive since 1978, Ing. C. Olivetti & Co., SpA; Vice-Chairman/Chief Executive: Compagnie Industriali Riunite, since 1976; Compagnia Finanziaria De Benedetti, since 1985; Chairman, Cerus, since 1986; Société Financière de Genève, since 1986; SOGEFI, since 1981; Vice-Chairman: Euromobiliare, since 1977; Société Générale de Belgique, since 1988; Cofir, since 1987; GAIC, SpA; *b* 14 Nov. 1934; *s* of Rodolfo and Pierina Fumel; *m* 1960, Margherita Crosetti; three *s*. *Educ*: Turin Polytechnic (degree in electrotech. engrg). Chm./Chief Exec., Gilardini, 1972–76; Chief Exec., Fiat, 1976. Vice-Pres., Confindustria, 1982–; Director: Pirelli SpA, 1987–; Shearson Lehman Brothers Hldgs, 1987–; Compagnie Financière de Suez, 1988; SMI, 1983–; Mediobanca, 1988–; Valeo, 1986–; Member: Internat. Adv. Bd, Morgan Guaranty Trust, NY, 1980–; European Adv. Cttee, NY Stock Exchange, 1985–. Dir, Center for Strategic and Internat.

Studies, Washington, 1978–; Gov., Atlantic Inst. for Atlantic Affairs, Paris; Member: Bd of Trustees, Solomon R. Guggenheim Foundn, NY, 1984–; Bd of Roundtable of European Industrialists. Foreign Mem., Royal Swedish Acad. of Engrg Scis, Stockholm, 1987. Hon. LLD Wesleyan, Conn, 1986. Légion d'Honneur (France), 1987. *Publications*: lectures and articles in business jls. *Address*: Ing. C. Olivetti, Via Jervis 77, 10015 Ivrea, Italy. *T*: (0125) 522011.

DEBENHAM, Sir Gilbert Ridley, 3rd Bt, *cr* 1931; *b* 28 June 1906; 2nd *s* of Sir Ernest Ridley Debenham, 1st Bt, JP; *S* brother, Sir Piers Debenham, 2nd Bt, 1964; *m* 1935, Violet Mary, *e d* of late His Honour Judge (George Herbert) Higgins; three *s* one *d*. *Educ*: Eton; Trinity Coll., Cambridge (BA 1928; BChir 1935). DPM 1946; MRCPsych 1971. *Heir*: *g s* Thomas Adam Debenham, *b* 1971. *Address*: Tonerspuddle Farm, Dorchester, Dorset.

DEBENHAM TAYLOR, John, CMG 1967; OBE 1959; TD 1967; HM Diplomatic Service, retired; *b* 25 April 1920; *s* of John Francis Taylor and Harriett Beatrice (*née* Williams); *m* 1966, Gillian May James; one *d*. *Educ*: Aldenham School. Eastern Counties Farmers Assoc. Ltd, Ipswich and Great Yarmouth, 1936–39. Commd in RA (TA), Feb. 1939; served War of 1939–46 in Finland, Middle East, UK and SE Asia (despatches, 1946). Foreign Office, 1946; Control Commn for Germany, 1947–49; 2nd Sec., Bangkok, 1950; Actg Consul, Songkhla, 1951–52; Vice-Consul, Hanoi, 1952–53; FO, 1953–54; 1st Sec., Bangkok, 1954–56; FO, 1956–58; Singapore, 1958–59; FO, 1960–64; Counsellor, 1964; Counsellor: Kuala Lumpur, 1964–66; FCO (formerly FO), 1966–69; Washington, 1969–72; Paris, 1972–73; FCO, 1973–77. *Recreations*: walking, reading, history. *Address*: Hoxne Place, Hoxne, Eye, Suffolk IP21 5DJ. *T*: Hoxne (037975) 494. *Club*: Naval and Military.

de BERNIÈRE-SMART, Major Reginald Piers Alexander; Director, The Shaftesbury Homes and Arethusa, 1988–89, retired (General Secretary, 1971–88); Caseworker, Chichester Division, SSAFA/FHS, since 1990; *b* 3 March 1924; *s* of Kenneth de Bernière-Smart and Audrey (*née* Brown); *m* 1951, Jean Ashton Smithells; one *s* two *d*. *Educ*: Bowden House, Seaford; Bradfield Coll. Commnd The Queen's Bays (2nd Dragoon Guards), 1943; Italian Campaign, 1944–45 (despatches); Staff, RAC OCTU and Mons OCS, 1948–49; GSO 3 7th Armd Bde, 1951; Adjt, The Queen's Bays, 1952–54; Adjt, RAC Centre, Bovington, 1956–58; retired from 1st The Queen's Dragoon Guards, 1959. Exec. Sec., British Diabetic Assoc., 1960–65; joined Shaftesbury Homes and Arethusa exec. staff, 1966. Chm., Management Cttee, Bradfield Club, Peckham, 1990–. Member: IAM, 1959; NCVCCO, 1971–89. Life Governor, ICRF, 1990. *Recreations*: open air activities, photography, steam and model railways, theatre, poetry, militaria. *Address*: 9 The Wad, West Wittering, Chichester, W Sussex PO20 8AH. *T*: Birdham (0243) 511072. *Clubs*: Victoria League for Commonwealth Friendship; West Wittering Sailing.

de BLANK, Justin Robert; Chairman and Managing Director, Justin de Blank Provisions Ltd, since 1968; Chairman, de Blank Restaurants, since 1986; *b* 25 Feb. 1927; *s* of William de Blank and Agnes Frances de Blank (*née* Crossley); *m* 1st, 1972, Mary Jacqueline Christina du Bois Godet (Molly); 2nd, 1977, Melanie Alexandra Margaret Irwin; three *d*. *Educ*: Grenham House School, Birchington-on-Sea; Marlborough College; Corpus Christi College, Cambridge (BA); Royal Acad. Sch. of Architecture. Unilever, 1953–58; J. Walter Thompson, London and Paris, 1958–66; Conran Design Group, 1967; formed own company, 1968. Dir, Kitchen Range Foods Ltd, 1976–. *Recreations*: gardening, golf, food and wine. *Address*: 42 Elizabeth Street, SW1W 9NZ. *T*: 01–730 2607; The Admiral's House, Weasenham St Peter, King's Lynn, Norfolk PE32 2TD. *T*: Weasenham St Peter (032874) 240. *Club*: Annabel's.

de BOER, Anthony Peter, CBE 1982; Vice-Chairman, Royal Automobile Club, 1985–90, retired (Member, Committee, 1984–90); *b* 22 June 1918; *s* of Goffe de Boer and Irene Kathleen (*née* Grist); *m* 1942, Pamela Agnes Norah Bullock; one *s*. *Educ*: Westminster School. Served War of 1939–45: RE (AA), 1939–40; Indian Army, 6th Gurkha Rifles, 1940–43; RIASC, 1944–46; Major 1944. Joined Royal Dutch/Shell Gp, 1937: served in China, Sudan, Ethiopia, Egypt, Palestine, 1946–58; Area Co-ordinator, Africa and Middle East, 1959–63; Chm., Shell Trinidad, 1963–64; Man. Dir, Marketing, Shell Mex & BP, 1964–67; Deputy Chairman: Wm Cory & Son, 1968–71; Associated Heat Services Ltd, 1969–76; Chairman: Anvil Petroleum plc (formerly Attock Oil Co.), 1974–85; Tomatin Distillers plc, 1978–85; Steel Brothers Hldgs, 1980–87 (Dir, 1971–87); Channel Tunnel Develts (1981), 1981–84; British Road Fedn, 1972–87 (Vice-Pres., 1987–); Director: Nat. Bus Co., 1969–83; Tarmac plc, 1971–83; British Transport Advertising, 1973–83; Internat. Road Fedn, 1974–87; Chloride Gp, 1976–85; Burmah Oil plc, 1978–85; Mem. Policy Cttee, Price Waterhouse, 1979–86. Mem., Bd, British Travel Assoc., 1965–67. Chm., Keep Britain Tidy Gp, 1969–79 (Vice-Pres., 1979–). Mem. Council, CBI, 1980–83; Mem. Council, Sussex Univ., 1969–91; Chm., Indep. Schools Careers Org., 1973–88 (Vice-Pres., 1988–); Pres., Fuel Luncheon Club, 1967–69; Dir, Brighton and Hove Albion Football Club, 1969–72. Freeman, City of London; Liveryman, Coach Makers' and Coach Harness Makers' Co. FBIM 1970 (Mem. Council 1974). *Recreations*: racing, theatre, gardening. *Address*: Halletts Barn, Ditchling Common, Hassocks, West Sussex BN6 8TN. *T*: Hassocks (07918) 2442. *Clubs*: Royal Automobile, Garrick.

de BONO, Dr Edward Francis Charles Publius; Lecturer in Medicine, Department of Medicine, University of Cambridge, 1976–83; Director of The Cognitive Research Trust, Cambridge, since 1971; Secretary-General, Supranational Independent Thinking Organisation (SITO), since 1983; *b* 19 May 1933; *s* of late Prof. Joseph de Bono, CBE and of Josephine de Bono; *m* 1971, Josephine Hall-White; two *s*. *Educ*: St Edward's Coll., Malta; Royal Univ. of Malta; Christ Church, Oxford (Rhodes Scholar). BSc, MD Malta; DPhil Oxon; PhD Cantab. Research Asst, Dept of Regius Prof. of Medicine, Univ. of Oxford, 1958–60; Jun. Lectr in Med., Oxford, 1960–61; Asst Dir of Res., Dept of Investigative Medicine, Cambridge Univ., 1963–76. Research Associate: also Hon. Registrar, St Thomas' Hosp. Med. Sch., Univ. of London; Harvard Med. Sch., and Hon. Consultant, Boston City Hosp., 1965–66. TV series: The Greatest Thinkers, 1981; de Bono's Thinking Course, 1982. *Publications*: The Use of Lateral Thinking, 1967; The Five-Day Course in Thinking, 1968; The Mechanism of Mind, 1969; Lateral Thinking: a textbook of creativity, 1970; The Dog Exercising Machine, 1970; Technology Today, 1971; Practical Thinking, 1971; Lateral Thinking for Management, 1971; Beyond Yes and No, 1972; Children Solve Problems, 1972; Eureka!: an illustrated history of inventions from the wheel to the computer, 1974; Teaching Thinking, 1976; The Greatest Thinkers, 1976; Wordpower, 1977; The Happiness Purpose, 1977; The Case of the Disappearing Elephant, 1977; Opportunities: a handbook of business opportunity search, 1978; Future Positive, 1979; Atlas of Management Thinking, 1981; de Bono's Thinking Course, 1982; Tactics: the art and science of success, 1984; Conflicts: a better way to resolve them, 1985; Six Thinking Hats, 1985; Masterthinker's Handbook, 1985; Letters to Thinkers, 1987; I am Right, You are Wrong, 1990; Positive Revolution for Brazil, 1990; Handbook for a Positive Revolution, 1990; contribs to Nature, Lancet, Clinical Science, Amer. Jl of Physiology, etc. *Recreations*: travel, toys, thinking. *Address*: L2 Albany, Piccadilly, W1V 9RR. *Club*: Athenæum.

de BOTTON, Gilbert; Chairman, Global Asset Management Ltd, since 1983; *b* 16 Feb. 1935; *s* of Jacques and Yolande de Botton; *m* 1st, 1962, Jacqueline (*née* Burgauer) (marr. diss. 1988); one *s* one *d*; 2nd, 1990, Hon. Mrs Janet Green. *Educ:* Victoria College, Alexandria, Egypt; Hebrew Univ., Jerusalem (BA Econ 1955); Columbia Univ. (MA 1957). Ufitec SA Union Financière, Zürich, 1960–68; Managing Director, Rothschild Bank AG, Zürich, 1968–82. Trustee, Tate Gallery, 1985–. *Address:* 1 Eaton Close, SW1W 8JX. *T:* 071–730 9305; (office) 071–493 9990. *Club:* Carlton.

DEBRÉ, Michel Jean-Pierre; Membre de l'Académie française, 1988; Deputy from La Réunion, French National Assembly, 1963–86 (re-elected 1967, 1968, 1973, 1978, 1981, 1982) and since 1988; *b* 15 Jan. 1912; *s* of late Prof. Robert Debré and Dr Jeanne Debré (*née* Debat-Ponsan); *m* 1936, Anne-Marie Lemaresquier; four *s*. *Educ:* Lycée Louis-le-Grand; Faculté de Droit de Paris (LLD); Ecole Libre des Sciences Politiques; Cavalry Sch., Saumur. Auditeur, Conseil d'Etat, 1934; French Army, 1939–40; Résistance clandestine, 1941–44; Commissaire de la République, Angers region, 1944–45; Saar Economic Mission, 1947; Secretary-General for German and Austrian Affairs, 1948. Senator from Indre et Loire, 1948, re-elected 1955; Minister of Justice, 1958–59; Prime Minister, 1959–62; Minister of Economic Affairs and Finances, 1966–68; Minister for Foreign Affairs, 1968–69; Minister for National Defence, 1969–73. Member, European Parliament, 1979–80. Mem. from Amboise, Conseil Général of Indre-et-Loire, 1951–70, 1976–82 and 1988; Mayor of Amboise, 1966–89. Member, Rassemblement pour la République. Officer Légion d'Honneur, Croix de Guerre, Rosette of Résistance, Free French Medal, Medal of Escaped Prisoners. *Publications:* La Mort de l'Etat Républicain, 1947; La République et son Pouvoir, 1950; La République et ses Problèmes, 1952; Ces Princes qui nous Gouvernent, 1957; Au Service de la Nation, 1963; Jeunesse, quelle France te faut-il?, 1965; (with Jean-Louis Debré) Le gaullisme, 1967; Une certaine idée de la France, 1972; Combat pour les Elections, 1973; Une Politique pour la Réunion, 1974; Ami ou Ennemi du Peuple, 1975; Français, choisissons l'espoir, 1979; Lettre ouverte aux Français sur la reconquête de la France, 1980; Peut-on lutter contre le chômage?, 1982; Trois Républiques pour une France (mémoires): vol. I, Combattre, 1984; vol. II, Agir, 1988; vol. III, Gouverner, 1988; as de Jacquier (with M. Emmanuel Monick): Refaire la France, 1944; Demain la Paix, 1945. *Recreation:* equitation. *Address:* 20 rue Jacob, 75006 Paris, France.

DEBREU, Prof. Gerard; Professor of Economics, since 1962, Professor of Mathematics, since 1975, and University Professor, since 1985, University of California, Berkeley; *b* 4 July 1921; *s* of Camille Debreu and Fernande (*née* Decharne); *m* 1945, Françoise Bled; two *d*. *Educ:* Ecole Normale Supérieure, Paris; Agrégé de l'Université, Paris, 1946. DSc Univ. de Paris, 1956. Research Associate: Centre National de la Recherche Scientifique, Paris, 1946–48; Cowles Commn for Research in Economics, Univ. of Chicago, 1950–55; Associate Prof. of Economics, Cowles Foundn for Research in Economics, Yale Univ., 1955–61. Fellow, Amer. Acad. of Arts and Sciences, 1970; President: Econometric Soc., 1971; American-Economic Assoc., 1990. Member: Nat. Acad. of Sciences, USA, 1977; Amer. Philos. Soc., 1984; Dist. Fellow, Amer. Economic Assoc., 1982; For. Associate, French Acad. of Scis, 1984. Hon. degrees: Bonn, 1977; Lausanne, 1980; Northwestern, 1981; Toulouse, 1983; Yale, 1987; Université de Bordeaux I, 1988. Nobel Prize in Economic Sciences, 1983. Chevalier de la Légion d'Honneur, 1976; Comdr de l'Ordre National du Mérite, 1984. *Publications:* Theory of Value: an axiomatic analysis of economic equilibrium, 1959, 2nd edn 1971 (trans. into French, Spanish, German and Japanese); Mathematical Economics: twenty papers, 1983; contribs to Econometrica, Procs of Nat. Acad. of Sciences, Review of Economic Studies, Economie Appliquée, Procs of Amer. Math. Soc., Internat. Economic Review, Review of Economic Studies, La Décision, Jl of Mathematical Economics, Amer. Economic Review. *Address:* Department of Economics, 787 Evans Hall, University of California, Berkeley, Calif 94720, USA. *T:* (415) 642–7284.

de BROKE; *see* Willoughby de Broke.

de BRUYNE, Dirk, Hon. CBE 1983; Commander, Order of Orange Nassau, 1982; Knight, Order of Netherlands Lion, 1976; Chairman, since 1987, Director, since 1982, Royal Dutch Petroleum Co., The Hague; Chairman, ABN–AMRO Holding NV, Netherlands, since 1990; Deputy Chairman, Ocean Transport & Trading, since 1983; *b* Rotterdam, Netherlands, 1 Sept. 1920; *s* of Dirk E. de Bruyne and Maria van Alphen, Rotterdam; *m* 1945, Geertje Straub; one *s* one *d*. *Educ:* Erasmus Univ., Rotterdam (Grad. Econ.). Joined Royal Dutch/Shell Gp of Companies, 1945: served in: The Hague, 1945–55; Indonesia, 1955–58; London, 1958–60 (Dep. Gp Treasurer); The Hague, 1960–62 (Finance Manager); Italy, 1962–65 (Exec. Vice-Pres., Shell Italiana); London, 1965–68 (Regional Co-ordinator: Oil, Africa); Germany, 1968–70 (Pres., Deutsche Shell); Dir of Finance, Shell Petroleum Co. Ltd, 1970; Man. Dir, 1971–79, Chm., Cttee of Man. Dirs, 1979–82, Royal Dutch/Shell Gp of Cos; Man. Dir, 1974–77, Pres., 1977–82, Royal Dutch Petroleum Co.; Director: Shell Transport & Trading Co. Ltd, 1971–74; Shell Canada Ltd, 1977–82; Chm., Shell Oil Co., USA, 1977–82. *Recreations:* swimming, reading. *Clubs:* Dutch (London); De Witte (The Hague).

de BRUYNE, Dr Norman Adrian, FRS 1967; FEng 1976; Chairman, Techne Inc., since 1973 (President, 1967–73); *b* 8 Nov. 1904; *s* of Pieter Adriaan de Bruyne and Maud de Bruyne (*née* Mattock); *m* 1940, Elma Lilian Marsh; one *s* one *d*. *Educ:* Lancing Coll.; Trinity Coll., Cambridge. MA 1930, PhD 1930. Fellow of Trinity Coll., Cambridge, 1928–44. Managing Director: Aero Research Ltd, 1934–48; Ciba (ARL) Ltd, 1948–60; Techne (Cambridge) Ltd, 1964–67. Dir, Eastern Electricity Bd, 1962–67. Awarded Simms Gold Medal, RAeS, 1937. FInstP 1944; FRAeS 1955; *Recreation:* inventing. *Address:* 3700 Brunswick Pike, Princeton, New Jersey 08540, USA. *T:* 609–452 9275.

DE BUTTS, Brig. Frederick Manus, CMG 1967; OBE 1961 (MBE 1943); DL; *b* 17 April 1916; *s* of late Brig. F. C. De Butts, CB, DSO, MC, and K. P. M. O'Donnell; *m* 1944, Evelyn Cecilia, *d* of Sir Walter Halsey, 2nd Bt; one *s* one *d*. *Educ:* Wellington Coll.; Oriel Coll., Oxford. Commissioned into Somerset LI, 1937. Served War of 1939–45, in Middle East, Italy, France and Germany. Staff Coll., 1944; Joint Services Staff Coll., 1954; Bt Lieut-Colonel, 1957; Commanded 3rd Bn Aden Protectorate Levies, 1958–60; Bde Colonel, Light Infantry, 1961–64; Comdr, Trucial Oman Scouts, 1964–67; HQ Home Counties District, Shorncliffe, Kent, 1967–68; Defence Attaché, Cairo, 1968–71; retired 1971; employed on contract as COS (Brig.), MoD, United Arab Emirates, 1971–73; Hon. Brig. 1973. Mem., Dacorum DC, 1976–83. Hon. Dir, Herts Soc., 1981–91. County Chm., 1973–76, County Comr, 1976–81, Vice-Pres., 1981–89, Pres., 1989–, Herts Scouts; Vice-Pres., Herts Girl Guides, 1981–; Governor, Abbot's Hill School, 1971– (Chm., 1975–84). DL Herts 1975. *Recreations:* tennis, hill-walking, ski-ing. *Address:* Church Cottage, Hoggeston, Buckingham, Bucks MK18 3LL.

DEBY, John Bedford; QC 1980; a Recorder of the Crown Court, since 1977; *b* 19 Dec. 1931; *s* of Reginald Bedford Deby and Irene (*née* Slater). *Educ:* Winchester Coll.; Trinity Coll., Cambridge (MA). Called to the Bar, Inner Temple, 1954, Bencher, 1986. *Address:* 11 Britannia Road, Fulham, SW6 2HJ. *T:* 071–736 4976.

de CARDI, Beatrice Eileen, OBE 1973; retired 1973, but continuing archæological research in Lower Gulf countries; *b* 5 June 1914; *d* of Edwin Count de Cardi and Christine Berbette Wurrflein. *Educ:* St Paul's Girls' Sch.; University Coll. London (BA). Secretary (later Asst), London Museum, 1936–44; Personal Asst to Representative of Allied Supplies Exec. of War Cabinet in China, 1944–45; Asst UK Trade Comr: Delhi, 1946; Karachi, 1947; Lahore, 1948–49; Asst Sec. (title changed to Sec.), Council for British Archæology, 1949–73. Archæological research: in Kalat, Pakistan Baluchistan, 1948; in Afghanistan, 1949; directed excavations: in Kalat, 1957; at Bampur, Persian Baluchistan, 1966; survey in Ras al-Khaimah (then Trucial States), 1968; Middle East lecture tour for British Council, 1970; survey with RGS's Musandam Expedn (Northern Oman), 1971–72; directed archæological research projects: in Qatar, 1973–74; in Central Oman, 1974–76, 1978; survey in Ras al-Khaimah, 1977, 1982. Winston Churchill Meml Trust Fellowship for work in Oman, 1973. FSA 1950 (Vice-Pres., 1976–80; Dir, 1980–83). Al-Qasimi Medal (UAE), 1989 (for services to Ras al-Khaimah). *Publications:* Excavations at Bampur, a third millennium settlement in Persian Baluchistan, 1966 (Vol. 51, Pt 3, Anthropological Papers of the American Museum of Natural History), 1970; Archaeological Surveys in Baluchistan 1948 and 1957 (Inst. of Archaeology, Occasional Paper No 8), 1983; contribs to Antiquity, Iran, Pakistan Archæology, East and West, Jl of Oman Studies, Oriens Antiquus. *Recreations:* archæological fieldwork, travel, cooking. *Address:* 1a Douro Place, Victoria Road, W8 5PH. *T:* 071–937 9740.

de CARMOY, Hervé Pierre, Comte de Carmoy; Member, Business Advisory Committee, European Bank for Reconstruction and Development, since 1991; Adviser to HR Finance, since 1991; *b* 4 Jan. 1937; *s* of Guy de Carmoy and Marie de Gourcuff; *m* Roseline de Rohan Chabot; two *c*. *Educ:* Institut d'Etudes Politiques, Paris; Cornell Univ. Gen. Man., Western Europe, Chase Manhattan Bank, 1963–78; Chm., Exec. Bd, Midland Bank, Paris, 1978–79; Gen. Man., Europe, Midland Bank, London, 1979–84; Chief Exec., Internat. Midland Bank, London, 1984–86; Dir and Chief Exec., Global Banking Sector, Midland Bank, 1986–88; Chief Exec. Officer, Société Générale de Belgique, 1988–91; Chm. and Chief Exec., Union Minière, 1989–91. Chairman: Cimenteries Belges Réunies, 1989–; Gechem, 1989–; Vice Chm., Générale de Banque, 1989–. Commandeur de la Légion d'Honneur (Côte d'Ivoire), 1978; Chevalier de l'Ordre du Mérite (France), 1987. *Publications:* Third World Debt, 1987; Stratégie Bancaire: le refus de la dérive, 1988. *Recreations:* tennis, music. *Address:* 10 rue Guynemer, 75006 Paris, France. *Clubs:* Knickerbocker (New York); Travellers' (Paris).

de CHAIR, Somerset; *b* 22 Aug. 1911; *s* of late Admiral Sir Dudley de Chair, Governor of NSW; *m* 1st, 1932, Thelma Arbuthnot (marr. diss. 1950); one *s* (and one *s* decd); 2nd, 1950, Carmen Appleton (*née* Bowen) (marr. diss. 1958); two *s*; 3rd, 1958, Mrs Margaret Patricia Manlove (*née* Field-Hart) (marr. diss. 1974); one *d*; 4th, 1974, Juliet, Marchioness of Bristol, *o d* of 8th Earl Fitzwilliam, DSC; one *d*. *Educ:* King's Sch., Paramatta, New South Wales; Balliol Coll., Oxford. MP (Nat C) for S. West Norfolk, 1935–45; Parliamentary Private Secretary to Rt Hon. Oliver Lyttelton MP, Minister of Production, 1942–44; MP (C) South Paddington, 1950–51. 2nd Lieut Supp. Res. RHG, 1938; served with Household Cavalry in the Middle East, during Iraqi and Syrian campaigns (wounded), IO to 4th Cavalry Bde, 1940–41; Captain GS (I), 1942. Chairman National Appeal Cttee of UN Assoc., and member of National Exec., 1947–50; Chm., Kent Assoc. of Boys' Clubs, 1945–48; Governor, Wye Agricl Coll., 1946–48. *Publications: fiction:* Enter Napoleon,, 1934; Red Tie in the Morning, 1936; The Teetotalitarian State, 1947; The Dome of the Rock, 1948; The Story of a Lifetime, 1954; Bring Back the Gods, 1962; Friends, Romans, Concubines, 1973; The Star of the Wind, 1974; Legend of the Yellow River, 1979; *non-fiction:* The Impending Storm, 1930; Divided Europe, 1931; The Golden Carpet, 1943; The Silver Crescent, 1943; A Mind on the March, 1945; edited and translated: The First Crusade, 1945; Napoleon's Memoirs, 1945; Napoleon's Supper at Beaucaire, 1945; Julius Caesar's Commentaries, 1951; Napoleon on Napoleon, 1991; *biography:* (ed) The Sea is Strong (memoirs of Admiral de Chair), 1961; (ed) Getty on Getty, 1989; *autobiography:* Buried Pleasure, 1985; Morning Glory, 1988; *drama:* Peter Public, 1932; *poetry:* The Millennium, 1949; Collected Verse, 1970. *Address:* Bourne Park, Bishopsbourne, near Canterbury, Kent; St Osyth Priory, St Osyth, Essex; The Lake House, 46 Lake Street, Cooperstown, Otsego County, New York, USA. *Club:* Carlton.

de CHASSIRON, Charles Richard Lucien; HM Diplomatic Service; Counsellor (Commercial/Economic), British Embassy, Rome, since 1989; *b* 27 April 1948; *s* of Hugo and Deane de Chassiron; *m* 1974, Britt-Marie Medhammar; one *s* one *d*. *Educ:* Jesus Coll., Univ. of Cambridge (BA Hons 1969, MA 1973); Univ. of Harvard (MPA 1971). Joined Diplomatic Service, 1971; service in: Stockholm, 1972–75; Maputo, 1975–78; Mem., UK Delegn at Lancaster House Conf. on Rhodesia, 1979; FCO, 1980–82; service in Brasilia, 1982–85; Asst Hd, later Hd, S America Dept, FCO, 1985–89. *Recreations:* art history, walking, tennis. *Address:* c/o Foreign and Commonwealth Office, SW1A 2AH.

DECIES, 6th Baron *cr* 1812; **Arthur George Marcus Douglas de la Poer Beresford;** Ex-Flying Officer, RAFVR (DFC, USA); *b* 24 April 1915; *s* of 5th Baron Decies and Helen Vivien (*d* 1931), *d* of late George Jay Gould; *S* father, 1944; *m* 1937, Ann Trevor (*d* 1945); *m* 1945, Mrs Diana Galsworthy; one *s* two *d*. *Heir:* *s* Hon. Marcus Hugh Tristram de la Poer Beresford [*b* 5 Aug. 1948; *m* 1st, 1970, Sarah Jane (marr. diss. 1974), *o d* of Col Basil Gunnell, New Romney, Kent; 2nd, 1981, Edel Jeannette, *d* of late Vincent Hendron; one *s* one *d*]. *Address:* c/o Coutts & Co., 1 Old Park Lane, W1Y 4BS.

DE CLERCQ, Willy; MP; Member (L) European Parliament, 1979–81, and since 1989; Minister of State, Belgium, since 1985; *b* 8 July 1927; *s* of Frans De Clercq; *m* 1953, Fernande Fazzi; three *c*. *Educ:* Ghent Univ. (Dr en droit 1950); Univ. of Syracuse, USA (MA SocSci 1951). Called to Belgian Bar, 1951; Municipal Councillor, Ghent, 1952–79; Dep. Sec.-Gen., Belgian Liberal Party, 1957; MP Ghent-Eeklo, 1958–; Dep. State Sec., Min. of Budget, 1960; Leader, Parly Lib. Party, 1965; Dep. Prime Minister, 1966–68; created separate Flemish wing of Parly Lib. Party (Chm., 1971–81); Dep. Prime Minister, 1973; Minister of Finance, 1974–77 (Chm., Interim Cttee, IMF; Chm., Bd of Governors, EIB; Governor, World Bank); Dep. Prime Minister and Minister of Finance and Foreign Trade, 1981–85; Mem., Commn of European Communities, 1985–88; Chm., External Econ. Relations Cttee, Eur. Parlt, 1989–. Comdr, Order of Leopold; Grand Cross, Order of Leopold II; holds numerous foreign decorations. *Address:* (office) Belliardstraat 97–113, 1040 Brussels, Belgium. *T:* 02/2342743; (home) Cyriel Buyssestraat 12, 9000 Ghent, Belgium.

de CLIFFORD, 27th Baron *cr* 1299; **John Edward Southwell Russell;** *b* 8 June 1928; *s* of 26th Baron de Clifford, OBE, TD, and Dorothy Evelyn (*d* 1987), *d* of late Ferdinand Richard Holmes Meyrick, MD; *S* father, 1982; *m* 1959, Bridget Jennifer, *yr d* of Duncan Robertson, Llangollen, Denbighshire. *Educ:* Eton. *Heir:* *b* Hon. William Southwell Russell [*b* 26 Feb. 1930; *m* 1961, Jean Brodie, *d* of Neil Brodie Henderson; one *s* two *d*]. *Address:* Cliff House, Sheepy, Atherstone, Warwickshire CV9 3RQ. *Club:* Naval and Military.

de COURCY, family name of **Baron Kingsale.**

de COURCY, Kenneth Hugh; (Duc de Grantmesnil); Chancellor, Order of the Three Orders, since 1977; Chairman, Kilbrittain Newspapers, since 1987; *b* 6 Nov. 1909; 2nd *s* of late Stephen de Courcy of Co. Galway and Hollinwood Mission (*s* of 8th Duc de Grantmesnil), and late Minnie de Courcy (*née* Schafer), *d* of late Frederick and Sophia

Schafer-Andres, Schloss Kyburgh, Kirn am Nahe; *m* 1950, Rosemary Catherine (marr. diss. 1973), *o d* of late Comdr H. L. S. Baker, OBE, RN (retired), Co. Roscommon, Eire; two *s* two *d*. *Educ:* King's College Sch. and by travelling abroad. 2nd Lieut, 3rd City of London Regt (Royal Fusiliers) TA (Regular Army Candidate), 1927. 2nd Lieut Coldstream Guards (Supplementary Reserve), 1930; Lieut and resigned, 1931; Hon. Secretary to late Sir Reginald Mitchell-Banks' unofficial cttee on Conservative policy, 1933; 1934, formed with late Earl of Mansfield, late Viscount Clive, late Lord Phillimore, and late Sir Victor Raikes, KBE, Imperial Policy Group and was Hon. Secretary 1934–39; travelled as Group's chief observer of Foreign Affairs in Europe and America, 1935–39; special visit of enquiry to Mussolini, Doctor Beneš, Dr Schuschnigg, 1936; to King Boris of Bulgaria, etc., 1938; to Italy and King Boris, 1939–40; FCO released 45 secret reports from 1936–40 to PRO, 1972; adviser on War Intelligence to United Steel Companies Ltd, 1944–45. Formerly published monthly serial memoranda on Foreign Affairs and Strategy, (1938–); Proprietor of: Intelligence Digest, 1938–76; The Weekly Review, 1951–76; Director, Ringrone Newspapers Ltd, 1966–68. Editor: Bankers Digest, 1969–72; Special Office Brief, 1973–.Trustee, Marquis de Verneuil Trust, 1971–. Lord of the Manors of Stow-on-the-Wold and Maugersbury, Glos. Hon. Citizen of New Orleans, La, USA, 1950; Hon. Life Mem., Mark Twain Soc., 1977; Companion of Western Europe, 1979. Gave collection of historic documents to Hoover Instn, Stanford Univ., 1983. *Publications:* Review of World Affairs (23 vols since 1938); Mayerling, 1983; Secret Reports of Prime Minister Chamberlain 1938–40, 1984; The Carolingian Crown of France, 1984; various articles on Strategy and Foreign Affairs. *Recreation:* climbing. *Address:* Yeomans Cottage, Longborough, Moreton-in-Marsh, Glos GL56 0QG; (office) 52 Merrion Square, Dublin 2, Ireland.

de COURCY-IRELAND, Patrick Gault, CVO 1980; HM Diplomatic Service, retired; Director of Marketing, Alireza Group of Companies, since 1987; Director, Rezayat Europe Ltd, since 1988; *b* 19 Aug. 1933; *e s* of late Lawrence Kilmaine de Courcy-Ireland and Elizabeth Pentland Gault; *m* 1957, Margaret Gallop; one *s* three *d*. *Educ:* St Paul's Sch.; Jesus Coll., Cambridge (MA). HM Forces (2nd Lieut), 1952–54. Joined Foreign Service, 1957; Student, ME Centre for Arab Studies, 1957–59; Third, later Second Sec., Baghdad, 1959–62; Private Sec. to HM Ambassador, Washington, 1963; Consul (Commercial), New York, 1963–67; UN (Polit.) Dept, 1967–69; Asst Head of Amer. Dept, 1969–71; First Sec. and Hd of Chancery, Kuwait, 1971–73; Asst Hd of SW Pacific Dept, 1973–76; Hd of Trng Dept and Dir, Diplomatic Serv. Language Centre, FCO, 1976–80; Consul-Gen., Casablanca, 1980–84; Consul-Gen,. Jerusalem, 1984–87. Chm., British Sch. of Archaeology in Jerusalem, 1990–. Great Comdr, Order of KHS, 1985. *Recreations:* book collecting, opera. *Address:* 51 Bushwood Road, Kew Gardens, Surrey TW9 3BG. *T:* 081–940 5091. *Clubs:* Athenæum; Hurlingham.

de COURCY LING, John, CBE 1990; HM Diplomatic Service, retired; farmer and landowner, since 1978; *b* 14 Oct. 1933; *s* of Arthur Norman Ling and Veronica de Courcy; *m* 1959, Jennifer Haynes; one *s* three *d*. *Educ:* King Edward's Sch., Edgbaston; Clare Coll., Cambridge. 2nd Lieut, Royal Ulster Rifles, 1956; Lieut on active service, Cyprus, 1957–58. FO, 1959; a private sec. to Lord Harlech, 1960–61, to Joseph Godber, 1961–63; 2nd Sec., Santiago, 1963–66; 1st Sec., Nairobi, 1966–69; Chargé d'Affaires, Chad, 1973; Counsellor, HM Embassy, Paris, 1974–77; left FO, 1978. MEP (C) Midlands Central, 1979–89; Conservative Chief Whip, 1979–83; Vice-Chm., Develt Aid Cttee, 1984–87; Chm., EEC Delegn to Israel, 1979–82. Mem., Exec. Cttee of Nat. Union of Conservative Assocs, 1979–83. Mem., Council of Lloyds, 1986–88. Mem. Council, RIIA, 1990–. *Publications:* contribs to The Tablet. *Recreations:* yacht racing, skiing, opera. *Address:* 31 Chapel Street, Belgrave Square, SW1. *T:* 071–235 5655; Lamb House, Bladon, Oxford OX7 1RS. *T:* Woodstock (0993) 811654. *Clubs:* Beefsteak, Travellers'; Leander (Henley-on-Thames); Leamington Conservative; Royal London Yacht (Cowes); Chipping Norton Golf.

See also Sir Alan Wigan, Bt.

de DENEY, Geoffrey Ivor, CVO 1986; Clerk of the Privy Council, since 1984; *b* 8 Oct. 1931; *s* of late Thomas Douglas and Violet Ivy de Deney; *m* 1959, Diana Elizabeth Winrow; two *s*. *Educ:* William Ellis Sch.; St Edmund Hall, Oxford (MA, BCL); Univ. of Michigan. Home Office: joined, 1956; Asst Principal, 1956–61 (Private Sec. to Parly Under Sec. of State, 1959–61); Principal, 1961–69; Sec. to Graham Hall Cttee on maintenance limits in magistrates' courts; Sec. to Brodrick Cttee on Death Certification and Coroners; Private Sec. to Sec. of State, 1968; Asst Sec., 1969–1978; seconded to Cabinet Office, 1975; Asst Under Sec. of State, 1978–84; Community Programmes and Equal Opportunities Dept, 1978–80; General Dept (and Registrar of the Baronetage), 1980–84. *Recreations:* books, walking. *Address:* 17 Ladbroke Terrace, W11 3PG.

de DUVE, Prof. Christian René Marie Joseph, Grand Cross Order of Leopold II 1975; Professor of Biochemistry, Catholic University of Louvain, 1951–85, now Emeritus; President, International Institute of Cellular and Molecular Pathology, Brussels, since 1975; Andrew W. Mellon Professor at Rockefeller University, New York, 1962–88, now Emeritus; *b* England, 2 Oct. 1917; *s* of Alphonse de Duve and Madeleine Pungs; *m* 1943, Janine Herman; two *s* two *d*. *Educ:* Jesuit Coll., Antwerp; Catholic Univ. of Louvain; Med. Nobel Inst., Stockholm; Washington Univ., St Louis. MD 1941, MSc 1946, Agrégé de l'Enseignement Supérieur 1945, Louvain. Lectr, Med. Faculty, Catholic Univ. of Louvain, 1947–51. Vis. Prof. at various univs. Mem. editorial and other bds and cttees; mem. or hon. mem. various learned socs, incl. For. Assoc. Nat. Acad. of Scis (US) 1975, and For. Mem of Royal Soc., 1988. Holds hon. degrees. Awards incl. Nobel Prize in Physiol. or Med., 1974. *Publications:* A Guided Tour of the Living Cell, 1985; numerous scientific. *Recreations:* tennis, ski-ing, bridge. *Address:* Le Pré St Jean, 239 rue de Weert, 5988 Nethen (Grez-Doiceau), Belgium. *T:* (010)-866628; 80 Central Park West, New York, NY 10023, USA. *T:* (212)-724–8048.

DEECH, Ruth Lynn; Principal, St Anne's College, Oxford, since 1991; *b* 29 April 1943; *d* of Josef Fraenkel and Dora (*née* Rosenfeld); *m* 1967, John Stewart Deech; one *d*. *Educ:* Christ's Hosp., Hertford; St Anne's Coll., Oxford (BA 1st Cl. 1965; MA 1969); Brandeis Univ., USA (MA 1966). Called to the Bar, Inner Temple, 1967. Legal Asst, Law Commn, 1966–67; Asst Prof., Faculty of Law, Univ. of Windsor, Canada, 1968–70; Oxford University: Fellow and Tutor in Law, 1970–91, Vice-Principal, 1988–91, St Anne's Coll.; CUF Lectr in Law, 1971–91; Lectr in Law, Hertford Coll., 1973–78; Sen. Proctor, 1985–86; Acad. Advr in Internat. Law, For. Service Prog., 1976–79; Member: Hebdomadal Council, 1986–; Equal Opportunities Cttee, 1990–; Childcare Cttee, 1990–; Ashmolean Visitors, 1987–; Chm., Health and Safety Cttee, 1986–. Mem., Exec. Council, Internat. Soc. on Family Law, 1988–. Vis. Prof., Osgoode Hall Law Sch., York Univ., Canada, 1978. Governor, Carmel Coll., 1980–90. *Publications:* articles on family law and property law. *Recreations:* after-dinner speaking, music, entertaining. *Address:* St Anne's College, Oxford OX2 6HS. *T:* Oxford (0865) 274800.

DEEDES, family name of **Baron Deedes.**

DEEDES, Baron *cr* 1986 (Life Peer), of Aldington in the County of Kent; **William Francis Deedes,** MC 1944; PC 1962; DL; Editor, The Daily Telegraph, 1974–86; *b* 1 June 1913; *s* of (Herbert) William Deedes; *m* 1942, Evelyn Hilary Branfoot; one *s* three *d* (and one *s* decd). *Educ:* Harrow. Journalist with Morning Post, 1931–37; war correspondent on Abyssinia, 1935. Served war of 1939–45, Queen's Westminsters (12 KRRC). MP (C) Ashford Div. of Kent, 1950–Sept. 1974; Parliamentary Sec., Ministry of Housing and Local Government, Oct. 1954–Dec. 1955; Parliamentary Under-Sec., Home Dept., 1955–57; Minister without Portfolio, 1962–64. DL, Kent, 1962. Hon. DCL Kent, 1988. *Address:* New Hayters, Aldington, Kent. *T:* Aldington (023372) 269. *Club:* Carlton.

See also Baron Latymer.

DEEDES, Maj.-Gen. Charles Julius, CB 1968; OBE 1953; MC 1944; *b* 18 Oct. 1913; *s* of General Sir Charles Deedes, KCB, CMG, DSO; *m* 1939, Beatrice Murgatroyd, Brockfield Hall, York; three *s*. *Educ:* Oratory Sch.; Royal Military Coll., Sandhurst. Served War of 1939–45 (despatches); Asst Military Secretary, GHQ Middle East, 1945; Officer Comdg Glider Pilot Regt, 1948; GSO1 War Office, 1950; Officer Comdg 1st Bn KOYLI, 1954 (despatches); Colonel General Staff, War Office, 1956; Comd 146 Infantry Brigade (TA), 1958; Deputy Director, MoD, 1962; C of S, HQ Eastern Comd, 1965; C of S, HQ Southern Comd, 1968. Colonel of the KOYLI, 1966–68. Dep. Colonel, The Light Infantry (Yorks), 1968–72. Military Cross (Norway), 1940. *Recreations:* riding, tennis. *Address:* Lea Close, Brandsby, York YO6 4RW. *T:* Brandsby (03475) 239.

DEEGAN, Joseph William, CMG 1956; CVO 1954; KPM; Inspector-General of Colonial Police, 1966–67; *b* 8 Feb. 1899; *s* of John and Sarah Deegan; *m* 1926, Elinor Elsie Goodson; one *s* two *d*. *Educ:* St Paul's and St Gabriel's Schs, Dublin. Army, 1919–25 (seconded to King's African Rifles, 1922–25); Tanganyika Police, 1925–38; Uganda Police, 1938–56 (Commissioner of Police, 1950–56); Dep. Inspector-Gen. of Colonial Police, 1956–61, 1963–65. Colonial Police Medal, 1942; King's Police Medal, 1950. *Address:* Tuffshard, Cuckmere Road, Seaford, East Sussex. *T:* Seaford (0323) 894180.

DEELEY, Michael; film producer; *b* 6 Aug. 1932; *s* of John Hamilton-Deeley and Anne Deeley; *m* 1955, Teresa Harrison; one *s* two *d*; *m* 1970, Ruth Stone-Spencer. *Educ:* Stowe. Entered film industry as film editor, 1952; Distributor, MCA TV, 1958–60; independent producer, 1961–63; Gen. Man., Woodfall Films, 1964–67; indep. prod., 1967–72; Man. Director: British Lion Films Ltd, 1973–76; EMI Films Ltd, 1976–77; Pres., EMI Films Inc., 1977–79; Chief Exec. Officer, Consolidated Television Inc. (formerly Consolidated Productions Ltd), 1984–; Dep. Chm., British Screen Adv. Council, 1985–. Member: Prime Minister's Film Industry Working Party, 1975–76; Film Industry Interim Action Cttee, 1977–84. Films include: Robbery; The Italian Job; The Knack; Murphy's War; Conduct Unbecoming; The Man who fell to Earth; The Deer Hunter (Academy Award, Best Picture Producer, 1978); Convoy; Blade Runner. *Address:* Little Island, Osterville, Mass 02655, USA; c/o Pickering Kenyon & Company, 23/24 Great James Street, WC1. *Clubs:* Garrick; Wianno Yacht (Mass).

DEER, Sir (Arthur) Frederick, Kt 1979; CMG 1973; Director, The Mutual Life and Citizens' Assurance Co. Ltd, Australia, 1956–83; *b* 15 June 1910; *s* of Andrew and Maude Deer; *m* 1936, Elizabeth Christine (*d* 1990), *d* of G. C. Whitney; one *s* three *d*. *Educ:* Sydney Boys' High Sch.; Univ. of Sydney (BA, LLB, BEc, Hon. DSc Econ). FAII, FAIM. Admitted to Bar of NSW, 1934. The Mutual Life and Citizens' Assurance Co. Ltd: joined Company, 1930; apptd Manager for S Australia, 1943, and Asst to Gen. Manager, 1954; Gen. Man., 1955–74. Chm., Life Offices' Assoc. for Australasia, 1960–61, 1967–68; Pres., Australian Insurance Inst., 1966. Chm., Cargo Movement Co-ordination Cttee, NSW, 1974–82; Member: Cttee Review of Parly Salaries, NSW, 1971; Admin. Review Council, 1976–82; Fellow, Senate of Univ. of Sydney, 1959–83 (Chm. Finance Cttee of the Univ., 1960–83). Nat. Pres., Australia-Britain Soc., 1973–81; Mem., Salvation Army Sydney Adv. Bd, 1970–90 (Chm., 1970–83). *Recreations:* golf, tennis. *Address:* 1179 Pacific Highway, Turramurra, NSW 2074, Australia. *T:* 44 2912. *Clubs:* Union, University, Avondale, Elanora (all in Sydney).

DEER, Prof. William Alexander, MSc Manchester, PhD Cantab; FRS 1962; FGS; Emeritus Professor of Mineralogy and Petrology, Cambridge University; Hon. Fellow of Trinity Hall, Cambridge, 1978; *b* 26 Oct. 1910; *s* of William Deer; *m* 1939, Margaret Marjorie (*d* 1971), *d* of William Kidd; two *s* one *d*; *m* 1973, Rita Tagg. *Educ:* Manchester Central High Sch.; Manchester Univ.; St John's Coll., Cambridge. Graduate Research Scholar, 1932, Beyer Fellow, 1933, Manchester Univ.; Strathcona Studentship, St John's Coll., Cambridge, 1934; Petrologist on British East Greenland Expedition, 1935–36; 1851 Exhibition Senior Studentship, 1938; Fellow, St John's Coll., Cambridge, 1939; served War of 1939–45, RE, 1940–45. Murchison Fund Geological Soc. of London, 1945 (Murchison Medal, 1974); Junior Bursar, St John's Coll., 1946; Leader NE Baffin Land Expedition, 1948; Bruce Medal, Royal Society of Edinburgh, 1948; Tutor, St John's Coll., 1949; Prof. of Geology, Manchester Univ., 1950–61; Fellow of St John's Coll., Cambridge, 1961–66, Hon. Fellow, 1969; Prof. of Mineralogy and Petrology, 1961–78, Vice-Chancellor, 1971–73, Cambridge Univ.; Master of Trinity Hall, Cambridge, 1966–75. Percival Lecturer, Univ. of Manchester, 1953; Joint Leader East Greenland Geological Expedition, 1953; Leader British East Greenland Expedition, 1966. Trustee, British Museum (Natural History), 1967–75. President: Mineralogical Soc., 1967–70; Geological Soc., 1970–72; Member: NERC, 1968–71; Marshall Aid Commemoration Commn, 1973–79. Hon. DSc Aberdeen, 1983. *Publications:* books; papers in Petrology and Mineralogy. *Recreations:* walking, bassoon playing. *Address:* Blenheim, 1 The Orchards, Hinton Way, Great Shelford, Cambridge CB2 5AB.

DEERHURST, Viscount; Edward George William Omar Coventry; *b* 24 Sept. 1957; *s* and *heir* of 11th Earl of Coventry, *qv*.

de FARIA, Antonio Leite, Hon. GCVO 1973; Grand Cross of Christ (Portugal), 1949; Portuguese Ambassador to the Court of St James's, 1968–73; retired; *b* 23 March 1904; *s* of Dr Antonio B. Leite de Faria and Dona Lucia P. de Sequeira Braga Leite de Faria; *m* 1926, Dona Herminia Cantilo de Faria; two *s*. *Educ:* Lisbon University (Faculty of Law). Attaché to Min. of Foreign Affairs, 1926; Sec. to Portuguese Delegn, League of Nations, 1929–30; 2nd Sec., Rio de Janeiro, 1931, Paris, 1933, Brussels, 1934; 1st Sec., London, 1936; Counsellor, London, 1939; Minister to Exiled Allied Govts, London, 1944; Minister to The Hague, 1945; Dir Gen., Political Affairs, and Acting Sec. Gen., Min. of Foreign Affairs, 1947; Ambassador: Rio de Janeiro, 1950; NATO, 1958; Paris, 1959; Rome (Holy See), 1961; London, 1968. Holds many foreign decorations. *Address:* Rua da Horta Seca 11, Lisboa, Portugal. *T:* 342.25.38; Casa do Bom Retiro, S Pedro de Azurem, Guimarães, Portugal. *T:* (053) 416418.

de FERRANTI, Sebastian Basil Joseph Ziani; Chairman, Ferranti plc, 1963–82 (Managing Director, 1958–75; Director 1954); Director, GEC plc, since 1982; *b* 5 Oct. 1927; *er s* of Sir Vincent de Ferranti, MC, and of Dorothy H. C. Wilson; *m* 1st, 1953, Mona Helen, *d* of T. E. Cunningham; one *s* two *d*; 2nd, 1983, Naomi Angela Rae. *Educ:* Ampleforth. 4th/7th Dragoon Guards, 1947–49. Brown Boveri, Switzerland, and Alsthom, France, 1949–50. Director: British Airways Helicopters, 1982–84; Nat. Nuclear Corp., 1984–88. President: Electrical Research Assoc., 1968–69; BEAMA, 1969–70; Centre for Educn in Science, Educn and Technology, Manchester and region, 1972–82.

Chm., Internat. Electrical Assoc., 1970–72. Member: Nat. Defence Industries Council, 1969–77; Council, IEE, 1970–73. Trustee, Tate Gallery, 1971–78; Chm., Civic Trust for the North-West, 1978–83; Comr, Royal Commn for Exhibn of 1851, 1984–. Vice-Pres., RSA, 1980–84. Chm., Hallé Concerts Soc., 1988–. Mem. Bd of Govs, RNCM, 1988–. Lectures: Granada, Guildhall, 1966; Royal Instn, 1969; Louis Blériot, Paris, 1970; Faraday, 1970–71. High Sheriff of Cheshire, 1988–89. Hon. Fellow, Univ. of Manchester Inst. of Science and Technology. Hon. DSc: Salford Univ., 1967; Cranfield Inst. of Technology, 1973. *Address:* Henbury Hall, Macclesfield, Cheshire SK11 9PJ. *Clubs:* Cavalry and Guards, Pratt's.

de FONBLANQUE, John Robert; HM Diplomatic Service; Counsellor (Political and Institutional) UK Representation to European Community, Brussels, since 1988; *b* 20 Dec. 1943; *s* of late Maj.-Gen. E. B. de Fonblanque, CB, CBE, DSO and of Elizabeth de Fonblanque; *m* 1984, Margaret Prest; one *s*. *Educ:* Ampleforth; King's College, Cambridge (MA); London School of Economics (MSc). FCO, 1968; Second Sec., Jakarta, 1969; Second, later First Sec., UK Representation to European Community, Brussels, 1972; Principal, HM Treasury, 1977; FCO, 1980; Asst Sec., Cabinet Office, 1983; Head of Chancery, New Delhi, 1986. *Recreation:* mountain walking. *Address:* c/o Foreign and Commonwealth Office, SW1A 2AH.

de FRANCIA, Prof. Peter Laurent; Professor, School of Painting, Royal College of Art, London, 1973–86; *b* 25 Jan. 1921; *s* of Fernand de Francia and Alice Groom. *Educ:* Academy of Brussels; Slade Sch., Univ. of London. Canadian Exhibition Commn, Ottawa, 1951; American Museum, Central Park West, NY, 1952–53; BBC, Television, 1953–55; Teacher, St Martin's Sch., London, 1955–63; Tutor, Royal College of Art, 1963–69; Principal, Dept of Fine Art, Goldsmiths Coll., 1969–72. Work represented in public collections: Tate Gall.; V&A Mus.; Mus. of Modern Art, NY; Arts Council of GB; British Mus.; Graves Art Gall., Sheffield; Mus. of Modern Art, Prague. *Publications:* Fernand Léger, 1969; Léger, 1983. *Address:* 44 Surrey Square, SE17 2JX. *T:* 071–703 8361.

DE FREYNE, 7th Baron *cr* 1851; Feudal Baron of Coolavin; **Francis Arthur John French;** Knight of Malta; *b* 3 Sept. 1927; *s* of 6th Baron and Victoria (*d* 1974), *d* of Sir J. Arnott, 2nd Bt; *S* father 1935; *m* 1st, 1954 (marr. diss. 1978); two *s* one *d*; 2nd, 1978, Sheelin Deirdre, *widow* of William Walker Stevenson and *y d* of late Lt-Col H. K. O'Kelly, DSO. *Educ:* Ladycross, Glenstal. *Heir:* *s* Hon. Fulke Charles Arthur John French [*b* 21 April 1957; *m* 1986, Julia Mary, *o d* of Dr James H. Wellard; one *s*].

de GREY, family name of **Baron Walsingham.**

de GREY, Sir Roger, KCVO 1991; PRA (RA 1969; ARA 1962); President of the Royal Academy, since 1984; Principal, City and Guilds of London Art School, since 1973; *b* 18 April 1918; *s* of Nigel de Grey, CMG, OBE, and Florence Emily Frances (*née* Gore); *m* 1942, Flavia Hatt (*née* Irwin); two *s* one *d*. *Educ:* Eton Coll.; Chelsea Sch. of Art. Served War of 1939–45: Royal West Kent Yeomanry, 1939–42; RAC, 1942–45 (US Bronze Star, 1945). Lecturer, Dept of Fine Art, King's Coll., Newcastle upon Tyne, 1947–51; Master of Painting, King's Coll., 1951–53; Senior Tutor, later Reader in Painting, Royal Coll. of Art, 1953–73. Treasurer, RA, 1976–84. Trustee, Nat. Portrait Gall., 1984–. Mem., Fabric Cttee, St Paul's and Rochester Cathedrals, 1990–. Pictures in the following public collections: Arts Council; Contemporary Arts Society; Chantrey Bequest; Queensland Gallery, Brisbane; Manchester, Carlisle, Bradford and other provincial galleries. Liveryman: Fishmongers' Co., 1985; Painter–Stainers' Co., 1985. Hon. ARCA, 1959. Hon. DCL Kent, 1989. *Address:* Royal Academy, Piccadilly, W1B 0DS. *T:* 071–439 7438; City and Guilds of London Art School, 124 Kennington Park Road, SE11 4DJ.

de GRUCHY, Nigel Ronald Anthony; General Secretary, National Association of Schoolmasters Union of Women Teachers, since 1990; *b* 28 Jan. 1943; *s* of Robert Philip de Gruchy and Dorothy Louise de Gruchy (*née* Cullinane); *m* 1970, Judith Ann Berglund, USA; one *s*. *Educ:* De La Salle Coll., Jersey; Univ. of Reading (BA Hons (Econs and Philosophy) 1965); PGCE London Univ. 1969; Cert. Pratique de Langue Française, Paris Univ., 1968; Cert. de Française Parlé et du Diplôme de Langue Française, L'Alliance Française, 1968. TEFL, Berlitz Schs, Santander, 1965–66, Versailles, 1966–67; student of French/Tutor in English, Paris, 1967–68; Head of Econs Dept, St Joseph's Acad., ILEA, 1968–78; Asst Sec., 1978–82, Dep. Gen. Sec., 1982–89, NAS UWT. Sec., London Assoc., 1975–78, Mem., Nat. Exec., 1975–78, NAS UWT. Mem., Gen. Council, TUC, 1989–. *Publications:* contribs to Career Teacher. *Recreations:* golf, cricket, football, literature, music, opera, France, Spain. *Address:* 22 Upper Brook Street, W1Y 1PD. *T:* 071–629 3916.

de HAMEL, Christopher Francis Rivers, DPhil; FSA; FRHistS; Director, Western and Oriental Manuscripts, Sotheby's, since 1982; *b* 20 Nov. 1950; *s* of Dr Francis Alexander de Hamel and Joan Littledale de Hamel (*née* Pollock); *m* 1978 (marr. diss. 1989); two *s*. *Educ:* Otago Univ., NZ (BA Hons); Oxford Univ. (DPhil). FSA 1981; FRHistS 1986. Sotheby's: Cataloguer of medieval manuscripts, 1975; Asst Dir, 1977. *Publications:* Book of Hours, 1970; Glossed Books of the Bible and the Origins of the Paris Booktrade, 1984; A History of Illuminated Manuscripts, 1986; (with M. Manion and V. Vines) Medieval and Renaissance Manuscripts in New Zealand Collections, 1989; all of Sotheby's medieval manuscript catalogues, 1975–; (ed with R. A. Linenthal) Festschrift for Alan G. Thomas, 1981; articles, exhibn catalogues, reviews; whimsical verse. *Recreation:* collecting manuscript fragments, however small. *Address:* Sotheby's, 34/35 New Bond Street, W1A 2AA. *T:* 071–408 5330. *Clubs:* Grolier (New York); Association Internationale de Bibliophilie (Paris).

de HAVILLAND, Olivia Mary; actress; *b* Tokyo, Japan, 1 July 1916; *d* of Walter Augustus de Havilland and Lilian Augusta (*née* Ruse) (parents British subjects); *m* 1st, 1946, Marcus Aurelius Goodrich (marr. diss., 1953); one *s*; 2nd, 1955, Pierre Paul Galante (marr. diss. 1979); one *d*. *Educ:* in California; won scholarship to Mills Coll., but career prevented acceptance. Played Hermia in Max Reinhardt's stage production of Midsummer Night's Dream, 1934. *Legitimate theatre* (USA): Juliet in Romeo and Juliet, 1951; Candida, 1951 and 1952; A Gift of Time, 1962. Began film career 1935, Midsummer Night's Dream. Nominated for Academy Award, 1939, 1941, 1946, 1948, 1949; Acad. Award, 1946, 1949; New York Critics' Award, 1948, 1949; San Francisco Critics' Award, 1948, 1949; Hollywood Foreign Press Assoc. Golden Globe Award, 1949, 1986; Women's National Press Club Award for 1950; Belgian Prix Femina, 1957; British Films and Filming Award, 1967; Filmex Tribute, 1978; Amer. Acad. of Achievement Award, 1978. *Important Films:* The Adventures of Robin Hood, 1938; Gone With the Wind, 1939; Hold Back the Dawn, 1941; Princess O'Rourke, 1943; To Each His Own, 1946; The Dark Mirror, 1946; The Snake Pit, 1948; The Heiress, 1949; My Cousin Rachel, 1952; Not as a Stranger, 1955; The Ambassador's Daughter, 1956; Proud Rebel, 1957; The Light in the Piazza, 1961; Lady in a Cage, 1963; Hush . . . Hush, Sweet Charlotte, 1965; The Adventurers, 1969; Pope Joan, 1971; Airport '77, 1976; The Swarm, 1978. *Television includes:* Noon Wine, 1966; The Screaming Woman, 1971; Roots, The Next Generations, 1979; 3 ABC Cable-TV Cultural Documentaries, 1981; Murder is Easy, 1982; Charles & Diana, a Royal Romance, 1982; North and South, Book II, 1986; Anastasia, 1986; The Woman He Loved, 1988. US Lecture tours, 1971, 1972, 1973, 1974, 1975, 1976, 1978, 1979, 1980. Pres. of Jury, Cannes Film Festival, 1965. Took part in narration of France's BiCentennial Gift to US, Son et Lumière, A Salute to George Washington, Mount Vernon, 19 May 1976; read excerpts from Thomas Jefferson at BiCentennial Service, American Cathedral in Paris, 4 July 1976. Amer. Legion Humanitarian Medal, 1967; Freedoms Foundn Exemplar American Award, 1981. *Publications:* Every Frenchman Has One, 1962; (contrib.) Mother and Child, 1975. *Address:* BP 156–16, 75764 Paris, Cedex 16, France.

DEHENNIN, Herman; Hon. Grand Marshal of Belgian Royal Court; Belgian Ambassador to the Court of St James's, since 1991; *b* 20 July 1929; *s* of Alexander Dehennin and Flora Brehmen; *m* 1954, Margareta-Maria Donvil; two *s*. *Educ:* Catholic Univ. of Leuven. Dr in Law 1951. Lieut, Royal Belgian Artillery, 1951–53; entered Belgian Diplomatic Service, 1954; served The Hague, New Delhi, Madrid, the Congo; Ambassador to Rwanda, 1966–70; Economic Minister, Washington, 1970–74; Dir-Gen., Foreign Econ. Relations, Brussels, 1974–77; Ambassador to Japan, 1978–81; Grand Marshal, Belgian Royal Court, 1981–85; Ambassador to USA, 1985–91. Grand Cross, Order of Leopold, 1985; Grand Cross, Order of the Crown, 1983; foreign Orders: France, Greece, Japan, Luxembourg, Mexico, Portugal, Rwanda, Zaire. *Recreations:* jogging, hiking, tennis, fishing, hunting, reading (history, philosophy, 18th and 19th centuries). *Address:* 36 Belgrave Square, SW1X 8QB. *T:* 071–235 1752. *Clubs:* Anglo-Belgian, Anglo-Belgian Society; Prince Albert, University Foundation, Warande, Order of the Prince (Brussels); Royal Golf of Belgium.

DEHMELT, Prof. Hans Georg; Professor of Physics, University of Washington, Seattle, since 1961; *b* 9 Sept. 1922; *s* of Georg Karl Dehmelt and Asta Ella Dehmelt (*née* Klemmt); US Citizen, 1961; *m* 1st; one *s*; 2nd, 1989, Diana Elaine Dundore. *Educ:* Graues Kloster, Berlin; Technische Hochschule, Breslau; Univ. of Göttingen (Dr rer. nat. 1950). Res. Fellow, Inst. Kopfermann, Göttingen, 1950–52; Res. Associate, Duke Univ., USA, 1952–55; Vis. Asst Prof., 1955, Associate Prof., 1957, Univ. of Washington. Consultant, Varian Associates, Palo Alto, Calif, 1956–70. Member: Amer. Acad. of Arts and Scis; Nat. Acad. of Scis; Fellow, Amer. Phys Soc.; FAAAS. Numerous awards and hon. degrees; Nobel Prize for Physics (jtly), 1989. *Publications:* papers on electron and atomic physics, esp. subatomic particles, charged atoms, anti-matter particles, proposed cosmonium world-atom hypothesis of big bang. *Address:* 1600 43rd Avenue East, Seattle, Washington, 98112, USA.

DEHN, Conrad Francis, QC 1968; Barrister; a Recorder of the Crown Court, since 1974; a Deputy High Court Judge, 1988; *b* London, 24 Nov. 1926; *o s* of late C. G. Dehn, Solicitor and Cynthia Dehn (*née* Fuller) painter, as Francyn; *m* 1st, 1954, Sheila (*née* Magan) (marr. diss.); two *s* one *d*; 2nd, 1978, Marilyn, *d* of late Peter Collyer and of Constance Collyer. *Educ:* Charterhouse (Sen. Exhibr); Christ Church, Oxford (Holford Schol.). Served RA, Best Cadet Mons OCTU, 1946, 2nd Lieut 1947. 1st cl. hons PPE Oxon. 1950, MA 1952; Holt Schol., Gray's Inn, 1951; Pres., Inns of Court Students Union, 1951–52. WEA Tutor, 1951–55. Called to Bar, Gray's Inn, 1952; Bencher, 1977; Chm., Management Cttee, 1987. Chairman: Bar Council Working Party on Liability for Defective Products, 1975–77; Planning Cttee, Senate of Inns of Court and Bar, 1980–83; London Univ. Disciplinary Appeals Cttee, 1986–. Dir, Bar Mutual Indemnity Fund Ltd, 1988–. Mem., Foster Cttee of Inquiry into Operators' Licensing, Dept of Transport, 1978. Mem., Council of Legal Educn, 1981–86. Mem. Governing Body, United Westminster Schs, 1953–57. *Publication:* contrib. to Ideas, 1954. *Recreations:* theatre, travel, walking. *Address:* Fountain Court, Temple, EC4Y 9DH. *T:* 071–583 3335. *Club:* Reform.

de HOGHTON, Sir (Richard) Bernard (Cuthbert), 14th Bt *cr* 1611; KM; DL; *b* 26 Jan. 1945; 3rd *s* of Sir Cuthbert de Hoghton, 12th Bt, and of Philomena, *d* of late Herbert Simmons; *S* half-brother, 1978; *m* 1974, Rosanna Stella Virginia (*née* Buratti); one *s* one *d*. *Educ:* Ampleforth College, York; McGill Univ., Montreal (BA Hons); Birmingham Univ. (MA); PhD (USA). Turner & Newall Ltd, 1967–70; international fund management, Vickers Da Costa & Co. Ltd, 1970–77; international institutional brokerage, de Zoete & Bevan & Co., 1977–86 (Partner, 1984–86); estate management, 1978–; Dir, BZW Ltd (Europe), 1986–89; Asst Dir, Brown Shipley, 1989–. DL Lancs, 1988. Constantinian Order of S George (Naples), 1984; Kt SMO, Malta, 1980. *Recreations:* tennis, shooting, travelling. *Heir:* *s* Thomas James Daniel Adam de Hoghton, *b* 11 April 1980. *Address:* Hoghton Tower, Hoghton, Preston, Lancs. *T:* 071–726 4059.

DEHQANI-TAFTI, Rt. Rev. Hassan Barnaba; Hon. Assistant Bishop of Winchester, since 1990 (Assistant Bishop, 1982–90); *b* 14 May 1920; *s* of Muhammad Dehqani-Tafti and Sakinneh; *m* 1952, Margaret Isabel Thompson; three *d* (one *s* decd). *Educ:* Stuart Memorial Coll., Isfahan, Iran; Tehran Univ.; Ridley Hall, Cambridge. Iran Imperial Army, 1943–45; layman in Diocese of Iran, 1945–47; theological coll., 1947–49; Deacon, Isfahan, 1949; Priest, Shiraz, 1950; Pastor: St Luke's Church, Isfahan, 1950–60; St Paul's Church, Tehran, 1960–61; Bishop in Iran, 1961–90, Vicar-Gen., 1990–91; Pres.-Bishop, Episcopal Church in Jerusalem and Middle East, 1976–86; Episcopal Canon, St George's Cathedral, Jerusalem, 1976–90; Commissary to Bishop in Iran, 1991–. Hon. DD, Virginia Theolog. Seminary, USA, 1981. *Publications:* many books in Persian; in English: Design of my World, 1959; The Hard Awakening, 1981. *Recreations:* Persian poetry (primarily mystical); painting in water colours; walking. *Address:* Sohrab, 1 Camberry Close, Basingstoke, Hants RG21 3AG. *T:* Basingstoke (0256) 27457.

DEISENHOFER, Prof. Johann, PhD; Regental Professor and Professor in Biochemistry, University of Texas Southwestern Medical Center at Dallas, since 1988; Investigator, Howard Hughes Medical Institute, since 1988; *b* 30 Sept. 1943; *s* of Johann and Thekla Deisenhofer; *m* 1989, Kirsten Fischer-Lindahl, PhD. *Educ:* Technische Universität München (Physics Diploma 1971; PhD 1974). Max-Planck-Institut für Biochemie: graduate student, 1971–74; Postdoctoral Fellow, 1974–76; Staff Scientist, 1976–88. (Jtly) Biological Physics Prize, Amer. Physical Soc., 1986; (jtly) Otto Bayer Preis, 1988; (jtly) Nobel Prize in Chemistry, 1988. *Publications:* contribs to Acta Crystallographica, Biochemistry, Jl of Molecular Biology, Nature, Methods in Enzymology, etc. *Recreations:* ski-ing, swimming, classical music. *Address:* University of Texas Southwestern Medical Center, 5323 Harry Hines Boulevard, Dallas, Tex 75235–9050, USA. *T:* (214) 689–5089.

DE-JA-GOU; *see* Gowda, Deve Javare.

de KLERK, Frederik Willem; State President of South Africa, since 1989; *b* 18 March 1936; *s* of J. de Klerk; *m* 1959, Marike Willemse; two *s* one *d*. *Educ:* Monument High School, Krugersdorp; Potchefstroom Univ. Law practice, 1961–72; MP (Nat. Party) Vereeniging, 1972–89; Information Officer, Transvaal, Nat. Party, 1975; Minister: of Posts and Telecommunications and Social Welfare and Pensions, 1978; of Posts and Telecommunications and of Sport and Recreation, 1978–79; of Mines, Energy and Environmental Planning, 1979–80; of Mineral and Energy Affairs, 1980–82; of Internal Affairs, 1982–85; of Nat. Educn and Planning, 1984–89; Leader, Nat. Party, 1989 (Transvaal Leader, 1982–89); Chm., Council of Ministers, 1985–89. Hon. LLD Potchefstroom Univ., 1990; Hon. DPhil Stellenbosch Univ., 1990. *Address:* State President's Office, Private Bag X 1000, Cape Town 8000, South Africa.

de LA BARRE de NANTEUIL, Luc; Commandeur de l'Ordre National du Mérite; Officier de la Légion d'Honneur; Chairman, Les Echos Group, since 1991; *b* 21 Sept. 1925; *m* 1st, Philippa MacDonald; one *s*; 2nd, 1973, Hedwige Frerejean de Chavagneux; one *s* one *d*. *Educ:* school in Poitiers; BA, LLB Lyon and Paris; Dip. d'Etudes Supérieures (Econ); Graduate, Ecole Nat. d'Admin, 1949. French Ministry of Foreign Affairs: Economic Affairs Dept, 1950–51; Secrétariat Général, 1951–52; Pacts Service, 1952–53; Econ. Affairs Dept, 1954–59; First Sec., London, 1959–64; Asst Dir, Afr. and ME Affairs Dept, 1964–70; Hd of Econ. Co-operation Service, Directorate of Econ. Affairs, 1970–76; Ambassador to the Netherlands, 1976–77; French Permanent Representative: to EEC, Brussels, 1977–82 and 1985–86; to Security Council and to UN, New York, 1981–84; Diplomatic Adviser, 1986; Ambassador to UK, 1986–91. *Publication:* David (Jacques Louis), 1985. *Address:* Les Echos, 46 rue la Boetie, Paris 75008, France. *T:* 49.53.65.65.

De la BÈRE, Sir Cameron, 2nd Bt *cr* 1953; jeweller, Geneva; *b* 12 Feb. 1933; *s* of Sir Rupert De la Bère, 1st Bt, KCVO, and Marguerite (*d* 1969), *e d* of late Sir John Humphery; *S* father, 1978; *m* 1964, Clairemonde, *o d* of late Casimir Kaufmann, Geneva; one *d*. *Educ:* Tonbridge, and on the Continent. Translator's cert. in Russian. British Army Intelligence Corps, 1951–53. Company director of Continental Express Ltd (subsid. of Hay's Wharf), 1958–64. Engaged in promotion of luxury retail jewellery stores, Switzerland and France, 1965–. Liveryman, Skinners' Co. *Recreations:* riding, swimming, history. *Heir:* *b* Adrian De la Bère, *b* 17 Sept. 1939. *Address:* 1 Avenue Theodore Flournoy, 1207 Geneva, Switzerland. *T:* (022) 786.00.15. *Clubs:* Hurlingham, Société Littéraire (Geneva).

de la BILLIÈRE, Gen. Sir Peter (Edgar de la Cour), KCB 1988; KBE 1991 (CBE 1983); DSO 1976; MC 1959 and Bar 1966; Middle East Adviser to Ministry of Defence, since 1991; *b* 29 April 1934; *s* of Surgeon Lieut Comdr Claude Dennis Delacour de Labillière (killed in action, HMS Fiji, 1941) and of Frances Christine Wright Lawley; *m* 1965, Bridget Constance Muriel Goode; one *s* two *d*. *Educ:* Harrow School; Staff College; RCDS. Joined KSLI 1952; commissioned DLI; served Japan, Korea, Malaya (despatches 1959), Jordan, Borneo, Egypt, Aden, Gulf States, Sudan, Oman, Falkland Is; CO 22 SAS Regt, 1972–74; GSO1 (DS) Staff Coll., 1974–77; Comd British Army Training Team, Sudan, 1977–78; Dir SAS and Comd, SAS Group, 1978–83; Comd, British Forces Falkland Is and Mil. Comr, 1984–85; GOC Wales, 1985–87; GOC SE Dist, and Perm. Peace Time Comdr, Jt Forces Operations Staff, 1987–90; Comdr British Forces, ME, 1990–91. Col Comdt, Light Div., 1986–89. Mem. Council, RUSI, 1975–77. Chm., Jt Services Hang Gliding, 1986–89; Cdre, Army Sailing Assoc., 1989–91. Comr, Duke of York's Mil. Sch., 1988–90. Hon. Mem., Fishmongers' Co. Legion of Merit (USA), 1991. *Recreations:* family, squash, down market apiculture, tennis perhaps, farming, sailing. *Address:* c/o Coutts & Co., 440 Strand, WC2R 0QS. *Clubs:* Farmers', Special Forces.

DELACOMBE, Maj.-Gen. Sir Rohan, KCMG 1964; KCVO 1970; KBE 1961 (CBE 1951; MBE 1939); CB 1957; DSO 1944; Governor of Victoria, Australia, 1963–74; Administrator of the Commonwealth of Australia on four occasions; *b* 25 Oct. 1906; *s* of late Lieut-Col Addis Delacombe, DSO, Shrewton Manor, near Salisbury; *m* 1941, Eleanor Joyce (CStJ), *d* of late R. Lionel Foster, JP, Egton Manor, Whitby; one *s* one *d*. *Educ:* Harrow; RMC Sandhurst. 2nd Lieut The Royal Scots, 1926; served Egypt, N China, India and UK, 1926–37; active service Palestine, 1937–39 (despatches, MBE); France, Norway, Normandy, Italy, 1939–45; Lieut-Col comd 8th Bn and 2nd Bn The Royal Scots, 1943–45; GSO1, 2nd Infantry Div., Far East, 1945–47; Colonel GS, HQ, BAOR, 1949–50; Brig. Comd 5 Inf. Bde, 1950–53, Germany; Dep. Mil. Sec., War Office, 1953–55; Maj.-Gen. 1956. Col The Royal Scots, 1956–64; GOC 52 Lowland Div. and Lowland District, 1955–58; GOC Berlin (Brit. Sector) 1959–62. Mem. Queen's Body Guard for Scotland, Royal Company of Archers, 1957. Pres., Royal British Legion (Wilts), 1974–85. FRAIA. KStJ, 1963; Freeman, City of Melbourne, 1974. Hon. Col 1st Armoured Regt (Australian Army), 1963–74; Hon. Air Cdre RAAF. LLD *hc* Melbourne; LLD *hc* Monash. *Recreations:* normal. *Address:* Shrewton Manor, near Salisbury, Wilts SP3 4DB. *T:* Shrewton (0980) 620253. *Clubs:* Army and Navy, Victoria Racing (Melbourne).

DELACOUR, Jean-Paul; Knight of Legion of Honour; Officer of National Order of Merit; Inspector General of Finance; Board Member and Managing Director, Société Générale, Paris, since 1986; *b* 7 Nov. 1930; *s* of Henri Delacour and Denise Brochet; *m* 1958, Claude Laurence; four *s* one *d*. *Educ:* Inst. of Political Studies, Paris (Dipl.); ENA (Nat. Sch. of Administration). Inspector of Finance, 1955–61; Dep. Dir, Crédit National, 1961–68; Dir, 1969, Dep. Gen. Manager, 1974, Société Générale; Chm. and Chief Exec. Officer, Soc. Gén. Alsacienne de Banque, 1978–82; Chm., Sogebail, 1985–; Vice-Chm., Soc. Gén. Marocaine des Banques; senior functions in internat. banking and financial insts. Chm., Bd of Catholic Inst. Paris, 1984–. *Address:* Société Générale, 29 boulevard Haussmann, 75009 Paris, France. *T:* 40 98 20 00; *Telex:* 212 127 SOGESAC.

DELACOURT-SMITH OF ALTERYN, Baroness *cr* 1974 (Life Peer), of Alteryn, Gwent; **Margaret Delacourt-Smith;** *b* 1916; *d* of Frederick James Hando; *m* 1st, 1939, Charles Smith (subsequently Lord Delacourt-Smith, PC) (*d* 1972); one *s* two *d*; 2nd, 1978, Professor Charles Blackton. *Educ:* Newport High School for Girls; St Anne's College, Oxford (MA). *Address:* House of Lords, SW1A 0PW.

DELAFONS, John, CB 1982; Deputy Secretary, Department of the Environment, 1979–90, retired; Associate, Department of Land Economy, University of Cambridge, since 1990; *b* 14 Sept. 1930; *m* 1957, Sheila Egerton; four *d*. *Educ:* Ardingly; St Peter's College, Oxford. 1st cl. Hons English. Asst Principal, Min. of Housing and Local Govt, 1953; Harkness Fellowship, Harvard, 1959–60; Principal, 1959–66; Principal Private Sec. to Minister, 1965–66; Department of the Environment: Assistant Sec., 1966–72; Under Sec., 1972–77; Under Sec., Cabinet Office, 1977–79. Bd Mem., English Industrial Estates Corp. 1984–85. Leverhulme and Nuffield Fellowship, 1989–90; Res. Associate, Inst. of Urban and Regl Develt, Univ. of California, 1990. Chm., RIPA, 1981–83, Vice Pres., 1985–. *Publications:* Land-Use Controls in the United States, 1962, revd edn 1969; Development Impact Fees, 1990; Aesthetic Control, 1991. *Address:* 34 Castlebar Road, W5 2DD. *Club:* Athenæum.

de la LANNE-MIRRLEES, Robin Ian Evelyn Stuart; *see* Mirrlees.

de la MADRID HURTADO, Miguel; President of Mexico, 1982–88; *b* 12 Dec. 1934; *m* 1959, Paloma Cordero de la Madrid; four *s* one *d*. *Educ:* Nat. Autonomous Univ., Mexico (Law degree with hon. mention for thesis; with master). Legal Dept, Nat. Bank of Foreign Trade, 1953–57; Asst Dir Gen., Credit Mexican, Min. of Treasury, 1960–65; Gen. Dir, Credit Bank of Mexico, 1965–67; Gen. Manager, Credit, 1967–70; Dir of Finance Pemex, 1970–72; Gen. Dir, Credit Pemex, 1972–75; Dep. Sec., Treasury Ministry, 1975–79; Minister, Nat. Planning and Budget, Govt of Mexico, 1979–82. *Publications:* economic and legal essays. *Address:* Los Piños, Puerta 1, Tacubaya, 11870 Mexico DF, Mexico. *T:* 515–37–17.

de la MARE, Prof. Albinia Catherine, FBA 1987; Professor of Palaeography, King's College, London, since 1989; *b* 2 June 1932; *d* of Richard Herbert Ingpen de la Mare and Amy Catherine Donaldson. *Educ:* Queen's Coll., Harley St., W1; Lady Margaret Hall, Oxford (MA); Warburg Inst., London (PhD). FRHistS; FSA. Dept of Western MSS, Bodleian Liby, 1962–88, Asst Librarian, 1964–88. Susette Taylor Fellow, 1964, Hon. Res. Fellow, 1979–, Lady Margaret Hall, Oxford. Mem., Comité Internat. de Paléographie Latine, 1986–. *Publications:* Catalogue of the Italian manuscripts of Major J. R. Abbey (with J. J. G. Alexander), 1969; Catalogue of the Lyell Manuscripts, Bodleian Library, Oxford, 1971; The Handwriting of Italian Humanists, 1973; New Research on Humanistic Scribes in Florence, in Miniatura Fiorentina del Rinascimento, ed A. Garzelli, 1985; articles in learned periodicals, etc. *Recreations:* music, gardening, travel. *Address:* Tithe Barn House, High Street, Cumnor, Oxford OX2 9PE. *T:* Oxford (0865) 863916.

de la MARE, Sir Arthur (James), KCMG 1968 (CMG 1957); KCVO 1972; HM Diplomatic Service, retired; *b* 15 Feb. 1914; *s* of late Walter H. de la Mare, Trinity, Jersey, Channel Islands, and late Laura Vibert Syvret; *m* 1940, Katherine Elisabeth Sherwood; three *d*. *Educ:* Victoria Coll., Jersey; Pembroke Coll., Cambridge. Joined HM Foreign Service, 1936. HM Vice-Consul: Tokyo, 1936–38; Seoul, Korea, 1938–39; USA 1942–43; First Sec., Foreign Service, 1945; HM Consul, San Francisco, 1947–50; HM Embassy, Tokyo, 1951–53; Counsellor, HM Foreign Service, 1953–63; Head of Security Dept, Foreign Office, 1953–56; Counsellor, HM Embassy, Washington, 1956–60; Head of Far Eastern Dept, Foreign Office, 1960–63; Ambassador to Afghanistan, 1963–65; Asst Under-Sec. of State, Foreign Office, 1965–67; High Comr in Singapore, 1968–70; Ambassador to Thailand, 1970–73. Chairman: Anglo-Thai Soc., 1976–82; Royal Soc. for Asian Affairs, 1978–84; Jersey Soc. in London, 1980–86; Pres., Jersey Br., Royal Commonwealth Soc., 1990–. Mem. (cl. 1), Most Exalted Order of the White Elephant (Thailand), 1972. *Recreations:* gardening, promotion of and publications in Norman-French language. *Address:* Havre de Grace, Rue des Fontaines, Trinity, Jersey, CI. *Clubs:* Commonwealth Trust; Tokyo (Tokyo, Japan).

DELAMERE, 5th Baron *cr* 1821; **Hugh George Cholmondeley;** *b* 18 Jan. 1934; *s* of 4th Baron Delamere, and Phyllis Anne (*d* 1978), *e d* of late Lord George Scott, OBE; *S* father, 1979; *m* 1964, Mrs Ann Willoughby Tinne, *o d* of late Sir Patrick Renison, GCMG and Lady Renison, Mayfield, Sussex; one *s*. *Educ:* Eton; Magdalene Coll., Cambridge. MA Agric. *Heir:* *s* Hon. Thomas Patrick Gilbert Cholmondeley, *b* 19 June 1968. *Address:* Soysambu, Elmenteita, Kenya.

DELAMERE, Sir Monita (Eru), KBE 1990; JP; Officiating Minister, Ringate Church, New Zealand, since 1953; Member, Waitangi Tribunal, since 1986; *b* 17 June 1921; *s* of late Paul Delamere and Hannah Delamere; *m* 1943, Mary; four *s* (one *d* decd). *Educ:* Maraenui and Omaio Native Schools (school Proficiency). Farm hand, 1937–42; soldier, 1942–45; farmer, 1945–55; dry cleaner, 1956–77. Borough Councillor, Kawerau, 1971–80; Sec., Whakatohea Trust Board, 1980–85; Treasurer: Kawerau Credit Union, 1968–79; Opotiki Credit Union, 1979, 1990–. *Recreations:* Rugby (NZ Maori Team, 1945–49), tennis. *Address:* 151 Ford Street, Opotiki, Bay of Plenty, New Zealand. *T:* 07656630.

de la MORENA, Felipe; Spanish Ambassador to the Court of St James's, since 1990; *b* 22 Oct. 1927; *s* of Felipe de la Morena and Luisa Calvet; *m* 1958, María Teresa Casado Bach; two *s* two *d*. *Educ:* Univ. Complutense de Madrid; Univs of Grenoble and Oxford; Diplomatic Sch., Madrid. Entered diplomatic service 1957; served Beirut, Berne, Washington and Min. of Foreign Affairs, Madrid; Dir, Technical Office, later Dir-Gen., Territorial Planning, Min. of Develt Planning, 1974–76; Minister Counsellor, Lisbon, 1976; Ambassador to People's Republic of China, 1978; Dir-Gen., Foreign Policy for Latin America, 1982; Ambassador to Syria and Cyprus (residence Damascus), 1983; Ambassador to Tunisia, 1987. Orders: Alfonso X el Sabio, 1965; Mérito Civil, 1973; Isabel la Católica, 1970; Carlos III, 1980; holds foreign decorations. *Recreation:* golf. *Address:* Spanish Embassy, 24 Belgrave Square, SW1X 8QA. *T:* 071–235 8363. *Clubs:* White's, Royal Automobile, Travellers'; Swinley Forest Golf; Puerta de Hierro, Real Automóvil de España (Madrid).

DELANEY, Francis James Joseph, (Frank); writer and broadcaster, since 1972; *b* 24 Oct. 1942; 5th *s* of Edward Delaney and Elizabeth Josephine O'Sullivan; *m* 1st, 1966, Eilish (*née* Kelliher) (marr. diss. 1978); three *s*; 2nd, 1988, Susan Jane Collier. *Educ:* Abbey Schools, Tipperary, Ireland; Rosse Coll., Dublin. Bank of Ireland, 1961–72; journalism, 1972–: includes: broadcasting news with RTE, Dublin; current affairs with BBC Northern Ireland, BBC Radio Four, London, and BBC Television. Chm., NBL, 1984–86. *Publications:* James Joyce's Odyssey, 1981; Betjeman Country, 1983; The Celts, 1986; A Walk in the Dark Ages, 1988; My Dark Rosaleen (fiction), 1989; sundry criticisms and introductions. *Recreations:* reading, conversation, walking. *Address:* 43 Old Town, SW4 0JL. *Club:* Athenæum.

DELANEY, Shelagh; playwright; *b* Salford, Lancs, 1939; one *d*. *Educ:* Broughton Secondary Sch. *Plays:* A Taste of Honey, Theatre Royal, Stratford, 1958 and 1959, Wyndhams, 1959, New York, 1960 and 1961, off-Broadway revival, trans. to Broadway, 1981 (Charles Henry Foyle New Play Award, Arts Council Bursary, New York Drama Critics' Award); The Lion in Love, Royal Court 1960, New York 1962. *Films:* A Taste of Honey, 1961 (British Film Academy Award, Robert Flaherty Award); The White Bus, 1966; Charlie Bubbles, 1968 (Writers Guild Award for best original film writing); Dance with a Stranger, 1985 (Prix Film Jeunesse-Etranger, Cannes, 1985). *TV plays:* St Martin's Summer, LWT, 1974; Find Me First, BBC TV, 1979; *TV series:* The House that Jack Built, BBC TV, 1977 (stage adaptation, NY, 1979). *Radio plays:* So Does the Nightingale, BBC, 1980; Don't Worry About Matilda, 1983. FRSL 1985. *Publications:* A Taste of Honey, 1959 (London and New York); The Lion in Love, 1961 (London and New York); Sweetly Sings the Donkey, 1963 (New York), 1964 (London). *Address:* c/o Tessa Sayle, 11 Jubilee Place, SW3 3TE.

DELANO, Juan Carlos; Director, Icare; *b* Santiago, 14 June 1941; *m* Maria Paz Valenzuela; three *s* one *d*. *Educ:* St George's Coll., Catholic Univ., Chile; OCD, Belgium. Private enterprise: Distribuidora Audicol SA, Commercial Magara Ltd; Pres., Trading Assoc. of Chile, Dir, Chamber of Commerce of Santiago, 1979–83; Pres., Chilean Nat. Chamber of Commerce and Advr to Confedn of Trade and Industry, 1983–85; Minister of Economy, Promotion and Reconstruction, 1985–87; Ambassador to UK, 1987–90. *Address:* Antupiren No 699, Santiago, Chile. *Clubs:* Union, Polo.

de LAROSIÈRE de CHAMPFEU, Jacques (Martin Henri Marie); Officer, Legion of Honour, 1988; Chevalier, National Order of Merit, 1970; Governor, Bank of France, since 1987; Chairman, Committee of Group of Ten, since 1990; *b* 12 Nov. 1929; *s* of Robert de Larosière and Hugayte de Champfeu; *m* 1960, France du Bos; one *s* one *d*. *Educ:* Institut d'Etudes Politiques, Paris (L ès L, licencié en droit); Nat. Sch. of Administration, Paris. Inspecteur des Finances, 1958; Inspecteur Général des Finances, 1980; appointments at: Inspectorate-General of Finance, 1961; External Finance Office, 1963; Treasury 1965; Asst Dir, Treasury, 1967; Dep. Dir then Head of Dept, Min. of Economics and Finance, 1971; Principal Private Sec. to Minister of Economics and Finance, 1974; Dir, Treasury, 1974–78; Man. Dir, IMF, 1978–87. Director: Renault, 1971–74; Banque Nat. de Paris, 1973–78; Air France and French Railways, 1974–78; Société nat. industrielle aérospatiale, 1976–78. Director appointed by Treasury, General Council, Bank of France, 1974–78; Auditor: Crédit national, 1974–78; Comptoir des entrepreneurs, 1973–75; Crédit foncier de France, 1975–78. Vice Pres., Caisse nat. des télécommunications, 1974–78. Chairman: OECD Econ. and Develt Review Cttee, 1967–71; Deputies Group of Ten, 1976–78. *Address:* Bank of France, 3 rue de la Vrillière, 75409 Paris Cedex 01, France.

de la RUE, Sir Andrew (George Ilay), 4th Bt *cr* 1898, of Cadogan Square; company director; farmer; *b* 3 Feb. 1946; *s* of Sir Eric Vincent de la Rue, 3rd Bt and Cecilia (*d* 1963), *d* of late Maj. Walter Waring; *S* father, 1989; *m* 1984, Tessa Ann, *er d* of David Dobson; two *s*. *Educ:* Millfield. With Lloyd's (Insurance), 1966; Dir, Private Company, 1976–. *Recreations:* shooting, coursing, tennis. *Heir: s* Edward Walter de la Rue, *b* 25 Nov. 1986. *Address:* Stragglethorpe Grange, Brant Broughton, Lincolnshire. *T:* Newark (0636) 626505; 27 Kersley Street, SW11 4PR. *T:* 071–585 1254.

de la TOUR, Frances; actress; *b* 30 July 1944; *d* of Charles de la Tour and Moyra (*née* Fessas); one *s* one *d*. *Educ:* Lycée français de Londres; Drama Centre, London. Royal Shakespeare Company, 1965–71: rôles include Audrey in As You Like It, 1967; Hoyden in The Relapse, 1969; Helena in A Midsummer Night's Dream (Peter Brooks's production), 1971 (also USA tour); Belinda in The Man of Mode, 1971; Violet in Small Craft Warnings, Comedy, 1973 (Best Supporting Actress, Plays and Players Award); Ruth Jones in The Banana Box, Apollo, 1973; Isabella in The White Devil, Old Vic, 1976; appearances at Hampstead Theatre, and Half Moon Theatre incl. title rôle in Hamlet, 1979; Stephanie in Duet for One (written by Tom Kempinski), Bush Theatre and Duke of York's, 1980 (Best New Play, and Best Perf. by Actress, Drama Awards, Best Perf. by Actress in New Play, SWET Award, Best Actress, New Standard Award); Jean in Skirmishes, Hampstead, 1982 (also television, 1982); Sonya in Uncle Vanya, Haymarket, 1982; Josie in A Moon for the Misbegotten, Riverside, 1983 (SWET Best Actress award); title rôle in St Joan, Nat. Theatre, 1984; Dance of Death, Riverside, 1985; Sonya and Masha in Chekhov's Women, Lyric, 1985; Brighton Beach Memoirs, NT, 1986; Lillian, Lyric, 1986, Fortune, 1987; Façades, Lyric, Hammersmith, 1988; Regan in King Lear, Old Vic, 1989; Arkadina, Ranyevskaya and Olga Knipper in Chekhov's Women, Moscow Art Theatre, 1990; Lottie in Lettice and Lovage, USA tour 1991 and 1992. *Films:* include Our Miss Fred, 1972; To the Devil a Daughter, 1976; Rising Damp, 1979 (Best Actress, New Standard British Film Award, 1980). *Television:* Crimes of Passion, 1973; Play for Today (twice), 1973–75; Rising Damp (series), 1974, 1976; Cottage to Let, 1976; Flickers, 1980; Murder with Mirrors, 1984; Duet for One, 1985; A Kind of Living, 1987; Bejewelled, 1990. *Address:* c/o James Sharkey Associates, 15 Golden Square, W1. *T:* 071–434 3806.

DE LA WARR, 11th Earl *cr* 1761; **William Herbrand Sackville;** Baron De La Warr, 1299 and 1572; Viscount Cantelupe 1761; Baron Buckhurst 1864; Stockbroker, Credit Lyonnais Laing (formerly CL-Alexanders Laing and Cruickshank, later Laing & Cruickshank) since 1980; *b* 10 April 1948; *s* of 10th Earl De La Warr and of Anne Rachel, *d* of Geoffrey Devas, MC; *S* father, 1988; *m* 1978, Anne, Countess of Hopetoun, *e d* of Arthur Leveson; two *s* and two step *s*. *Educ:* Eton. *Heir: s* Lord Buckhurst, *qv*. *Address:* Buckhurst Park, Withyham, Sussex; 61 Bourne Street, SW1. *Clubs:* White's, Turf.

See also Hon. T. G. Sackville.

DE LA WARR, Sylvia Countess; Sylvia Margaret Sackville, DBE 1957; *d* of William Reginald Harrison, Liverpool; *m* 1st, 1925, David Patrick Maxwell Fyfe (later Earl of Kilmuir, *cr* 1962, PC, GCVO) (*d* 1967); two *d* (and one *d* decd); 2nd, 1968, 9th Earl De La Warr, PC, GBE (*d* 1976). *Address:* Ludshott Manor, Bramshott, Hampshire GU30 7RD.

DELBRIDGE, Richard; Director, Group Finance, Midland Bank, since 1990; *b* 21 May 1942; *s* of late Tom Delbridge and of Vera Kate Delbridge (*née* Lancashire); *m* 1966, Diana Genevra Rose Bowers-Broadbent; one *s* two *d*. *Educ:* Copleston Sch., Ipswich; LSE (BSc Econ); Univ. of California at Berkeley (MBA). FCA. Arthur Andersen & Co., 1963–66 and 1968–76, Partner 1974–76; Morgan Guaranty Trust Co., NY: Vice-Pres., 1976–79; Sen. Vice-Pres. and Comptroller of Morgan Guaranty Trust Co. and J. P. Morgan Inc., 1979–85; Asst Gen. Manager, 1985–87 and Gen. Manager, 1987–89, London offices. Mem. Bd, Securities Assoc. 1988–89. *Recreations:* hill walking, books. *Address:* 48 Downshire Hill, NW3 1NX.

DELFONT, family name of **Baron Delfont.**

DELFONT, Baron *cr* 1976 (Life Peer), of Stepney; **Bernard Delfont,** Kt 1974; Chairman, First Leisure Corp. (formerly Trusthouse Forte Leisure Ltd), since 1988 (Chairman and Chief Executive, 1980–86; Executive Chairman, 1986–88; President, March–Nov. 1988); Director, Bernard Delfont Organisation; *b* Tokmak, Russia, 5 Sept. 1909; *s* of late Isaac and Olga Winogradsky; *m* Carole Lynne; one *s* two *d*. Entered theatrical management, 1941; has presented over 200 shows in London (and NY), including 50 musicals; also presents summer resort shows; converted London Hippodrome into Talk of the Town Restaurant, 1958. Chief Exec., EMI Ltd, May 1979–Dec. 1980. Past Chief Barker (Pres.), Variety Club of GB, (1969); Life Pres., Entertainment Artistes' Benevolent Fund, for which presented annual Royal Variety Performance, 1958–78; Pres., Entertainment Charities Fund, 1983–; Companion, Grand Order of Water Rats; Member, Saints and Sinners; Pres., Printers Charitable Corp., 1979. *Address:* 7 Soho Street, Soho Square, W1V 5FA. *T:* 071–437 9727.

See also Baron Grade.

DELHI, Archbishop of, (RC), since 1967; **Most Rev. Angelo Fernandes;** Founder Member, Planetary Citizens, 1972; President, World Conference of Religion for Peace, 1970–84, Emeritus President since 1984; *b* 28 July 1913; *s* of late John Ligorio and Evelyn Sabina Fernandes. *Educ:* St Patrick's, Karachi; St Joseph's Seminary, Mangalore; Papal University, Kandy, Ceylon (STL). Secretary to Archbishop Roberts of Bombay, 1943–47; Administrator of Holy Name Cathedral, Bombay, 1947–59; Coadjutor Archbishop of Delhi, 1959–67; Sec. Gen., Catholic Bishops' Conf. of India, 1960–72 (Chm., Justice and Peace Commn, 1986). Member: Vatican Secretariat for Non-Believers, 1966–71; Vatican Justice and Peace Commn, 1967–76; Secretariat of Synod of Bishops, 1971–74, 1980–83; Office of Human Develt of Fedn of Asian Bishops' Confs, 1973–78 (Chm., Exec. Cttee for Ecumenism and Inter-Religious Affairs, Asia, 1985). Hon. DD Vatican, 1959. *Publications:* Apostolic Endeavour, 1962; Religion, Development and Peace, 1971; Religion and the Quality of Life, 1974; Religion and a New World Order, 1976; Towards Peace with Justice, 1981; God's Rule and Man's Role, 1982; Summons to Dialogue, 1983; articles in Clergy Monthly, Vidyajyoti, World Justice, Religion and Society, Social Action, Reality, etc. *Recreations:* music, especially classical, and wide travel on the occasion of numerous meetings in many countries of the world. *Address:* Archbishop's House, Ashok Place, New Delhi 110001, India. *T:* 343457.

DELIGHT, Ven. John David; Archdeacon of Stoke, 1982–90, Archdeacon Emeritus, 1990; *b* 24 Aug. 1925. *Educ:* Christ's Hospital, Horsham; Liverpool Univ.; Oak Hill Theolog. Coll.; Open Univ. (BA). RNVR (Fleet Air Arm), 1943–46. Curate: Tooting Graveney, 1952–55; Wallington, 1955–58; Travelling Sec., Inter-Varsity Fellowship, 1958–61; Vicar, St Christopher's, Leicester, 1961–69; Chaplain, Leicester Prison, 1965–67; Rector of Aldridge, 1969–82; RD, Walsall, 1981–82; Prebendary of Lichfield Cathedral, 1980–; volunteer associate of BCMS and CMS, to develop theol educn by extension in dio. of Machakos, Kenya, 1990–. *Publication:* (contrib.) Families, Facts and Frictions, 1976. *Recreations:* walking, music. *Club:* Christ's Hospital.

DE L'ISLE, 2nd Viscount *cr* 1956; **Philip John Algernon Sidney,** MBE 1977; Baron De L'Isle and Dudley 1835; Bt 1806; Bt 1818; *b* 21 April 1945; *s* of 1st Viscount De L'Isle, VC, KG, GCMG, GCVO, PC and Hon. Jacqueline Vereker (*d* 1962), *o d* of Field-Marshal 6th Viscount Gort, VC, GCB, CBE, DSO, MVO, MC; *S* father, 1991; *m* 1980, Isobel Tresyllian, *y d* of Sir Edmond Compton, *qv*; one *s* one *d*. *Educ:* Tabley House; Mons OCS; RMA Sandhurst. Commnd Grenadier Guards, 1966. Served BAOR, UKLF, NI, Belize and Sudan at Regtl Duty; GSO3 Ops/SD HQ 3 Inf. Bde, 1974–76; retired 1979. Farmer and landowner, 1979–. Chm., Kent County Cttee, CLA, 1983–85. Consultant in Rural Enterprise, 1989–. Freeman, City of London; Liveryman, Goldsmiths' Co. *Heir: s* Hon. Philip William Edmund Sidney, *b* 2 April 1985. *Address:* Penshurst Place, Penshurst, Tonbridge, Kent TN11 8DG. *T:* Penshurst (0892) 870223. *Clubs:* White's, Pratt's.

de LISLE, Everard John Robert March Phillipps; stockbroker; Vice Lord-Lieutenant of Leicestershire, since 1990; *b* 8 June 1930; *s* of late Maj. J. A. F. M. P. de Lisle, DL and Elizabeth Muriel de Lisle; *m* 1959, Hon. Mary Rose, *d* of 1st Viscount Ingleby, PC; two *s* one *d*. *Educ:* Eton; RMA Sandhurst. Commnd RHG, 1950; Captain, 1954; Major, 1960; retired 1962. Mem., Stock Exchange, 1965–. High Sheriff, 1974–75, DL 1980, Leics. *Address:* Stockerston Hall, Oakham, Leics LE15 9JD; 4 Hereford Mansions, Hereford Road, W2 5BA.

DELL, David Michael, CB 1986; Deputy Secretary, Department of Trade and Industry, 1983–91; *b* 30 April 1931; *s* of late Montague Roger Dell and Aimée Gabrielle Dell; unmarried. *Educ:* Rugby Sch.; Balliol Coll., Oxford (MA). 2nd Lieut Royal Signals, Egypt and Cyprus, 1954–55. Admiralty, 1955–60; MoD, 1960–65; Min. of Technol., 1965–70; DTI, 1970; DoI, 1974, Under Sec., 1976–83.

DELL, Rt. Hon. Edmund, PC 1970; Chairman, Public Finance Foundation, since 1984; *b* 15 Aug. 1921; *s* of late Reuben and Frances Dell; *m* 1963, Susanne Gottschalk. *Educ:* Elementary schls; Owen's Sch., London; Queen's Coll., Oxford (Open Schol.). 1st Cl. Hons Mod. Hist., BA and MA 1947. War Service, 1941–45, Lieut RA (Anti-tank). Lecturer in Modern History, Queen's Coll., Oxford, 1947–49; Executive in Imperial Chemical Industries Ltd, 1949–63. Mem., Manchester City Council, 1953–60. Contested (Lab) Middleton and Prestwich, 1955. Pres., Manchester and Salford Trades Council, 1958–61. Simon Research Fellow, Manchester Univ., 1963–64. MP (Lab) Birkenhead, 1964–79; Parly Sec., Min. of Technology, 1966–67; Jt Parly Under-Sec. of State, Dept of Economic Affairs, 1967–68; Minister of State: Board of Trade, 1968–69; Dept of Employment and Productivity, 1969–70; Paymaster General, 1974–76; Sec. of State for Trade, 1976–78. Chm., Public Accts Cttee, 1973–74 (Acting Chm., 1972–73). Mem., Cttee of Three apptd by European Council to review procedures of EEC, 1978–79. Chm. and Chief Exec., Guinness Peat Gp, 1979–82; Founder Chm., Channel Four TV Co., 1980–87; Dir, Shell Transport and Trading Co. plc, 1979–. Pres., London Chamber of Commerce and Industry, 1991– (Dep. Chm., 1988–90; Chm., 1990–91; Chm., Commercial Educn Trust, 1989–). Chairman: Hansard Soc. Commn on Financing of Politics, 1980–81; Working Party on Internat. Business Taxation, Inst. for Fiscal Studies, 1982; Wkg Pty on Company Political Donations (apptd by Hansard Soc. and Constitutional Reform Centre), 1985; Canada–UK Dalhousie Colloquium, 1987; Prison Reform Trust, 1988–; Wkg Pty on 1992: Ownership, Productivity and Investment, 1988–89. Dep. Chm., Governing Body, Imperial Coll. of Science, Technology and Medicine, 1988–. Boys' Chess Champion of London, 1936. Hon. Fellow, Fitzwilliam Coll., Cambridge, 1986. *Publications:* (ed with J. E. C. Hill) The Good Old Cause, 1949; Brazil: The Dilemma of Reform (Fabian Pamphlet), 1964; Political Responsibility and Industry, 1973; (with B. Biesheuvel and R. Marjolin) Report on European Institutions, 1979; The Politics of Economic Interdependence, 1987; A Hard Pounding: politics and economic crisis 1974–76, 1991; articles in learned journals. *Recreation:* listening to music. *Address:* 4 Reynolds Close, NW11 7EA.

DELL, Dame Miriam (Patricia), DBE 1980 (CBE 1975); JP (NZ); Hon. President, International Council of Women, 1986–88 (President, 1979–86; Vice-President, 1976–79); Convener, Public Affairs Unit, Anglican Church of New Zealand, since 1988; *b* 14 June 1924; *d* of Gerald Wilfred Matthews and Ruby Miriam Crawford; *m* 1946, Richard Kenneth Dell; four *d*. *Educ:* Epsom Girls Grammar Sch.; Univ. of Auckland (BA); Auckland Teachers' Coll. (Teachers' Cert. (Secondary Sch.)). Teaching, 1945–47, 1957–58 and 1961–71. Nat. Pres., Nat. Council of Women, 1970–74 (Vice-Pres., 1967–70); Chm., Cttee on Women, NZ, 1974–81; Chm., Envmt and Conservation Orgns of NZ, 1989–. Member: Nat. Develt Council, 1969–74; Cttee of Inquiry into Equal Pay, 1971–72; Nat. Commn for UNESCO, 1974–83; Social Security Appeal Authority, 1974–; Project Develt Bd, Mus. of NZ, 1988–; Nat. Convener, Internat. Women's Year, 1975; Co-ordinator, Internat. Council of Women Develt Prog., 1988–; Sec., Inter-Church Council on Public Affairs, 1986– (Chm., 1982–86). JP NZ 1975. Jubilee Medal, 1977; NZ Commemoration Medal, 1990. *Publications:* Role of Women in National Development, 1970; numerous articles in popular and house magazines, on role and status of women. *Recreations:* gardening, reading, handcrafts, beachcombing. *Address:* 98 Waerenga Road, Otaki, New Zealand. *T:* Otaki 47267; (office) PO Box 12–117, Wellington, New Zealand. *T:* 737623.

DELL, Ven. Robert Sydney; Archdeacon of Derby, since 1973; Canon Residentiary of Derby Cathedral, since 1981; *b* 20 May 1922; *s* of Sydney Edward Dell and Lilian Constance Palmer; *m* 1953, Doreen Molly Layton; one *s* one *d*. *Educ:* Harrow County Sch.; Emmanuel Coll., Cambridge (MA); Ridley Hall. Curate of: Islington, 1948; Holy Trinity, Cambridge, 1950; Asst Chaplain, Wrekin Coll., 1953; Vicar of Mildenhall, Suffolk, 1955; Vice-Principal of Ridley Hall, Cambridge, 1957; Vicar of Chesterton, Cambridge, 1966 (Dir, Cambridge Samaritans, 1966–69). Mem., Archbishops' Commn on Intercommunion, 1965–67; Proctor in Convocation and Mem. Gen. Synod of C of E, 1970–85. Vis. Fellow, St George's House, Windsor Castle, 1981. *Publications:* Atlas of Christian History, 1960; contributor to: Charles Simeon, 1759–1836: essays written in commemoration of his bi-centenary, 1959; Jl of Ecclesiastical History. *Recreations:* reading, walking, travelling. *Address:* 72 Pastures Hill, Littleover, Derby DE3 7BB. *T:* Derby (0332) 512700.

DELLAL, Jack; Chairman, Allied Commercial Exporters Ltd; *b* 2 Oct. 1923; *s* of Sulman and Charlotte Dellal; *m* 1952, Zehava Helmer; one *s* four *d*. *Educ:* Heaton Moor Coll., Manchester. Chm., Dalton, Barton & Co. Ltd, 1962–72; Dep. Chm., Keyser Ullman Ltd, 1972–74; Chm., Highland Electronics Group Ltd, 1971–76; Director: Anglo African Finance PLC, 1983–; General Tire & Rubber (SA) Ltd, 1983–87; Williams, Hunt South Africa Ltd, 1983–87. Vice-Pres., Anglo-Polish Conservative Society, 1970–. Officer, Order of Polonia Restituta, 1970. Freeman Citizen of Glasgow, 1971. *Recreations:* lawn tennis, squash, music, art. *Address:* 23 Ilchester Place, W14 8AA. *T:* 071–603 0981; Manor Farm, Brown Candover, Hants. *Clubs:* Royal Thames Yacht, Queen's, Lansdowne, Hurlingham.

DELLOW, Sir John (Albert), Kt 1990; CBE 1985 (OBE 1979); Deputy Commissioner, Metropolitan Police, 1987–91; *b* 5 June 1931; *s* of Albert Reginald and Lily Dellow; *m* 1952, Heather Josephine Rowe; one *s* one *d*. *Educ:* William Ellis Sch., Highgate; Royal Grammar Sch., High Wycombe. Joined City of London Police, 1951; seconded Manchester City Police, 1966; Superintendent, Kent County Constabulary, 1966, Chief Supt, 1968; jssc 1969; Asst Chief Constable, Kent Co. Constabulary, 1969; Metropolitan Police: Deputy Assistant Commissioner: Traffic Planning, 1973; Personnel, 1975; No 2 Area, 1978; 'A' Dept Operations, 1979; Inspectorate, 1980; Assistant Commissioner: 'B' Dept, 1982; Crime, 1984; Asst Comr (Specialist Ops), 1985–87. Pres., ACPO, 1989–90 (Vice-Pres., 1988–89). Trustee, Metropolitan Museum Trust; Chairman: Metropolitan Police History Soc.; Metropolitan Police Climbing, Canoe, Rowing and Heavy Boat Sections; Cdre, Metropolitan Police Sailing Club. *Publications:* contrib. RUSI Defence Studies series and other jls. *Recreations:* walking, history, listening to wireless. *Address:* c/o 21 Bryanston Street, W1A 4NH.

DEL MAR, Norman Rene, CBE 1975; freelance conductor; Conductor and Professor of Conducting, Royal College of Music; *b* 31 July 1919; *m* 1947, Pauline Mann; two *s*. *Educ:* Marlborough; Royal College of Music. Asst Sir Thomas Beecham, Royal Philharmonic Orchestra, 1947; Principal Conductor, English Opera Group, 1949–54; Conductor and Prof. of Conducting, Guildhall Sch. of Music, 1953–60; Conductor: Yorkshire Symphony Orchestra, 1954; BBC Scottish Orchestra, 1960–65; Royal Acad. of Music, 1974–77; Principal Conductor, Acad. of BBC, 1974–77; Artistic Dir and Principal Conductor, Aarhus Symfoniorkester, Denmark, 1985–88, Conductor of Honour, 1989–; Artistic Dir, Norfolk and Norwich Triennial, 1979, 1982. Principal Guest Conductor, Bournemouth Sinfonietta, 1983–85. FRCM; FGSM; Hon. RAM. Hon. DMus: Glasgow, 1974; Bristol, 1978; Edinburgh, 1983; Hon. DLitt Sussex, 1977. Audio Award, 1980. *Publications:* Richard Strauss, 3 vols, 1962–72; Mahler's Sixth Symphony: a study, 1980; Orchestral Variations, 1981; Anatomy of the Orchestra, 1981; Companion to the Orchestra, 1987. *Recreations:* writing, chamber music. *Address:* Witchings, Hadley Common, Herts EN5 5QL. *T:* 081–449 4836.

DELMAS, Jacques Pierre Michel C.; *see* Chaban-Delmas.

DELORS, Jacques Lucien Jean; President, Commission of the European Economic Community, since 1985; *b* 20 July 1925; *s* of Louis and Jeanne Delors; *m* 1948, Marie Lephaille; one *s* one *d*. *Educ:* Paris Univ. Joined Banque de France, 1945; in office of Chief of Securities Dept, 1950–62, and in Sect. for the Plan and Investments, Conseil Economique et Social, 1959–61; Chief of Social Affairs, Gen. Commissariat of Plan Monnet, 1962–69; Gen. Sec., Interministerial Cttee for Professional Educn, 1969–73; Mem., Gen. Council, Banque de France, 1973–79, and Dir, on leave of absence, 1973–. Special Advr on Social Affairs to Prime Minister, 1969–72. Socialist Party Spokesman on internat. econ. matters, 1976–81; Minister of the Economy and Finance, 1981–83; Minister of Economy, Finance and Budget, 1983–84. Mem., European Parlt, 1979–81 (Pres., Econ. and Financial Cttee, 1979–81). Mayor of Clichy, 1983–84. Associate Prof., Univ. of Paris-Dauphine, 1973–79. Dir, Work and Society Res. Centre, 1975–79. Founder, Club Echange et Projets, 1974. *Publications:* Les indicateurs sociaux, 1971; Changer, 1975; (jtly) En sortir ou pas, 1985; essays, articles and UN reports on French Plan. *Address:* 200 rue de la Loi, 1049 Brussels, Belgium.

de los ANGELES, Victoria; Cross of Lazo de Dama of Order of Isabel the Catholic, Spain; Condecoracíon Banda de la Orden Civil de Alfonso X (El Sabio), Spain; Opera and Concert-Artiste (singing in original languages), Lyric-Soprano, since 1944; *b* Barcelona, Spain, 1 Nov. 1923; *m* 1948, Enrique Magriñá (decd); two *s*. *Educ:* Escoles Milà i Fontanals de la Generalitat de Catalunya, Barcelona; Conservatorium of Barcelona; University of Barcelona. Studied until 1944 at Conservatorium, Barcelona; first public concert, in Barcelona, 1944; début at Gran Teatro del Liceo de Barcelona, in Marriage of Figaro, 1945; concert and opera tours in Spain and Portugal, 1945–49; winner of first prize at Concours International of Geneva, 1947; first appearances at Paris Opéra, Stockholm Royal Opera, Copenhagen Royal Opera, and début at the Scala, Milan, also South-American and Scandinavian concert tours, 1949; first appearance at Covent Garden, and Carnegie Hall Début, 1950; first United States concert tour, and Metropolitan Opera of New York season, first appearances at La Monnaie, Brussels, Holland and Edinburgh Festivals, 1951; first appearances at Teatro Colón, Buenos Aires, and Teatro Municipal, Rio de Janeiro, 1952. Since 1952 has appeared at the most important opera theatres and concert halls of Europe, North, South and Central America and Canada; first tour in S Africa, 1953; first tour in Australia and New Zealand, 1956; first appearance, Vienna State Opera, 1957; opening Festival, Bayreuth, with Tannhäuser, 1961; first tour in Japan and Far East, 1964. Gold Medal, Barcelona, 1958; Silver Medal, province of Barcelona, 1959; Premio Nacional de Música, Spain; Medal Premio Roma, 1969, and various French, Italian, Dutch and American awards; Gold Disc for 5 million copies sold, UK; Hon. Dr Univ. of Barcelona. *Address:* Avenida de Pedralbes 57, 08034 Barcelona, Spain.

de LOTBINIÈRE, Lt-Col Sir Edmond; *see* Joly de Lotbinière.

DELVE, Sir Frederick (William), Kt 1962; CBE 1942; Chief Officer, London Fire Brigade, 1948–62, retired; Hon. President, Securicor plc, since 1985 (Director and Vice-Chairman, 1962–82, Vice-President, 1982–85); *b* 28 Oct. 1902; *s* of Frederick John Delve, Master Tailor, Brighton; *m* 1924, Ethel Lillian Morden (*d* 1980); no *c*. *Educ:* Brighton. Royal Navy, 1918–23; Fire Service since 1923; Chief Officer, Croydon Fire Brigade, 1934–41; Dep. Inspector-in-Chief of NFS, 1941–43; Chief Regional Fire Officer, No 5 London Region, National Fire Service, 1943–48. Pres., Institution of Fire Engineers, 1941–42; King's Police and Fire Services Medal, 1940. *Address:* 53 Ashley Court, Grand Avenue, Hove, East Sussex. *T:* Brighton (0273) 774605.

DELVIN, Lord; title borne by eldest son of Earl of Westmeath, *qv*; not at present used.

DELVIN, Dr David George; television and radio broadcaster, writer and doctor; *b* 28 Jan. 1939; *s* of William Delvin, Ayrshire and Elizabeth Falvey, Kerry; *m* 1st, Kathleen Sears, SRN, SCM; two *s* one *d*; 2nd, Christine Webber. *Educ:* St Dunstan's Coll.; King's Coll., Univ. of London; King's Coll. Hosp. (MB, BS 1962; psychol medicine, forensic medicine and public health prizes, 1962). LRCP, MRCS 1962; MRCGP 1974; DObstRCOG 1965; DCH 1966; DipVen, Soc. of Apothecaries, 1977; FPA Cert. 1972; FPA Instructing Cert. 1974. Dir, Hosp. Medicine Film Unit, 1968–69. Vice-Chm., Med. Journalists' Assoc., 1982–87; General Medical Council: Elected Mem., 1979–; Member: Health Cttee 1980–86; Professional Conduct Cttee, 1987–. Mem., Educn Cttee, Back Pain Assoc., 1983–87. Medical Consultant: FPA, 1981–90; Nat. Assoc. of FP Doctors, 1990–; Med. Advisor to various BBC and ITV progs, 1974–. Med. Editor, General Practitioner, 1972–; Chm., Editorial Boards of Medeconomics, Monthly Index of Med. Specialities, and MIMS Magazine, 1988–; Dr Jekyll Columnist in World Medicine, 1973–82. Cert. of Special Merit, Med. Journalists' Assoc., 1974 and (jtly) 1975. American Medical Writers' Assoc. Best Book Award, 1976; Consumer Columnist of the Year Award, 1986. Médaille de la Ville de Paris (échelon argent), 1983. *Publications:* books, articles, TV and radio scripts, short stories, humorous pieces, medical films and videos; papers on hypertension and contraception in BMJ etc. *Recreations:* athletics, opera, orienteering, scuba-diving, hang-gliding (retired hurt). *Address:* c/o Coutts, 2 Harley Street, W1. *Club:* Royal Society of Medicine.

de MAJO, William Maks, (known as **Willy**), MBE (mil.) 1946; FCSD; Chairman and Managing Director, W. M. de Majo Associates, since 1946; Consultant: John Millar & Sons (1844) Ltd, 1953–89; Ti-Well Ltd; *b* 25 July 1917; *s* of Maks de Majo and Josefine (*née* Ganz); *m* 1941, Veronica Mary Booker (separated); three *d*. *Educ:* Commercial Academy, Vienna. Chartered Designer. In practice as graphic and industrial designer on continent, 1935–39; news typist and broadcaster with BBC Overseas Service, 1940–41; war service as pilot and liaison officer, Royal Yugoslav Air Force, UK, Africa, ME, 1941–45 (Actg Chief Air Sect.); transf. to RAF, SO SHAEF and CCG HQ, 1945–46; re-established practice London, on demobilisation, 1946. Cons. designer to various nat. and internat. cos; guest lectr on design; co-ordinating designer, Fest. of Britain, 1951 (Ulster farm and factory); guest speaker: Internat. Design Conf., Aspen, Colo, 1953; Biennale of Graphic Design, Brno, 1988; designer, Baden-Powell Mus., 1961; designer-in-chief and co-ordinator, internat. exhibits, 1950–75; Member Jury: Canada Olympic Coins Comp., 1976; Crystal Design Awards, 1988; work exhibited on 5 continents. Consultant, Charles Letts & Co., 1967–87. Founder and past Pres., Internat. Council of Graphic Design Assocs, 1963–68; First Vice-Pres. IIID, Internat. Inst. for Inf. Design, Vienna. Past Mem., Internat. Relations Bd, SIAD. Hon. Member: Assoc. of Graphic Designers, Netherlands, 1959; Assoc. of Swedish Art Dirs and Designers, 1965; Chambre Belges des Graphistes, 1966; Graphic Design Austria, 1988. SIAD Design Medal, 1969; ZPAP Polish Designers' Assoc. Commemorative Medal, 1983; winner of numerous nat. and internat. design competitions. *Publications:* contrib. Packaging (design of the gift pack), 1959 (Zürich); articles on graphic and industrial design to most leading jls in GB and abroad. *Recreations:* travelling, cooking, fostering good international relations. *Address:* 99 Archel Road, W14 9QL. *T:* 071–385 0394.

DEMARCO, Richard, OBE 1985; RSW, SSA; Director, The Richard Demarco Gallery Ltd, Edinburgh, 1966–91; *b* 9 July 1930; *s* of Carmine Demarco and Elizabeth (*née* Fusco); *m* 1957, Anne Muckle. *Educ:* Holy Cross Academy, Edinburgh; Edinburgh College of Art. National Service, KOSB and RAEC, 1954–56. Art Master, Duns Scotus Academy, Edinburgh, 1956–67; Co-Founder, Traverse Theatre Club; Vice-Chm. and Director, Traverse Art Gall., 1963–67; appointed Dir, Richard Demarco Gall., Melville Crescent, Edinburgh, by co-founders John Martin, Andrew Elliott and James Walker, 1966; introduced contemporary visual arts into official Edinburgh Festival programme with Edinburgh Open 100 Exhibn, 1967; introduced work of 330 internat. artists to UK, mainly through Edinburgh Fest. exhibns, from Canada, 1968, W Germany, 1970, Romania, 1971, Poland, 1972 and 1979, France, 1973, Austria, 1973, Yugoslavia, 1975, Aust. and NZ, 1984, incl. Joseph Beuys, 1970, and Tadeusz Kantor's Cricot Theatre, with prodns of The Water Hen, 1972, Lovelies and Dowdies, 1973, The Dead Class, 1976. Has presented, 1969–, annual programmes of theatre, music and dance prodns, incl. the Freehold Company's Antigone, 1970, the Dublin Project Company's On Baille Strand, 1977. Prod Macbeth for Edinburgh Fest., on Inchcolm Is, 1988 and 1989. Director: Sean Connery's Scottish Internat. Educn Trust, 1972–74; Edinburgh Arts annual summer sch. and expedns, 1972–. Has directed annual exhib. prog. with Special Unit, HM Prison, Barlinnie, with partic. reference to sculpture of James Boyle, 1974–; directed Edinburgh Fest. Internat. Confs, Towards the Housing of Art in the 21st Century, 1983, Art and the Human Environment, 1984 (also at Dublin Fest.). Was subject of film, Walkabout Edinburgh, dir. by Edward McConnell, 1970; acted in feature films: Long Shot, 1978; That Sinking Feeling, 1980; subject of TV film, The Demarco Dimension, 1987. Has broadcast regularly on television and radio, 1966–; has lectured in over 150 univs, art colls, schools, art galls; as water-colour painter and printmaker is represented in over 1600 public and private collections, incl. Nat. Gall. of Modern Art of Scotland, V&A Museum, Scottish Arts Council. Contributing Editor, Studio International, 1982–. SSA 1964; RWSScot 1966. Hon. FRIAS 1991. Gold Order of Merit, Polish People's Republic, 1976; Order of the Cavaliere della Repùbblica d'Italia, 1987. *Publications:* The Artist as Explorer, 1978; The Road to Meikle Seggie, 1978. *Recreations:* exploring: the small and secret spaces in townscape; cathedrals, abbeys, parish churches; coastlines and islands and The Road to Meikle Seggie. *Address:* 23a Lennox Street, Edinburgh EH4 1PY. *Clubs:* Chelsea Arts; Scottish Arts (Hon. Mem.) (Edinburgh).

de MARÉ, Eric, RIBA; writer and photographer; *b* 10 Sept. 1910; *s* of Bror and Ingrid de Maré; *m* 1st, 1936, Vanessa Burrage (*d* 1972); 2nd, 1974, Enid Verity. *Educ:* St Paul's Sch., London; Architectural Assoc., London (Dip.). RIBA 1934. Asst in several arch. practices, 1933–36; in private practice, 1936–40. War Service, survived, with spell in Home Guard designing frondy camouflage. Editor, Architects' Jl, 1942–46; freelance writer and photographer, mostly on architectural, topographical and photographic subjects, 1946–. Has travelled extensively in British Isles, Europe and USA in search of freelance fodder; much lecturing. Hon. Treasurer, Social Credit Party, 1938–46. Hon. Mem., Glos Architectural Assoc., 1986. Photography exhibitions: Architectural Assoc., 1990; Glasgow Sch. of Architecture, 1991. *Publications:* Britain Rebuilt, 1942; The Canals of England, 1950, 2nd edn 1952, repr. 1987; Scandinavia, 1952; Time on the Thames, 1952; The Bridges of Britain, 1954, 3rd edn 1989; Gunnar Asplund, 1955; Penguin Photography, 1957, 7th edn 1980; London's Riverside: past, present and future, 1958; (with Sir James Richards) The Functional Tradition in Early Industrial Buildings, 1958; Photography and Architecture, 1961; Swedish Cross Cut: the story of the Göta Canal, 1964; London's River: the story of a city, 1964, 2nd edn 1975 (Runner-up for 1964 Carnegie Award); The City of Westminster: heart of London, 1968; London 1851: the year of the Great Exhibition, 1972; The Nautical Style, 1973; The London Doré Saw: a Victorian evocation, 1973; Wren's London, 1975; Architectural Photography, 1975; The Victorian Wood Block Illustrators, 1980 (Yorkshire Post Award for best book on art, 1980); A Matter of Life or Debt, 1983, 4th edn 1986; contrib. Arch. Rev., TLS, Illustrated London News, etc. *Recreations:* talking to friends, reading history, philosophizing, looking at trees, preaching Douglas Social Credit and the Age of Leisure. *Address:* The Old Chapel, Tunley, near Sapperton, Cirencester, Glos GL7 6LW. *T:* Frampton Mansell (028576) 382.

de MARGERIE, Emmanuel; Hon. GCVO 1984; Officier de la Légion d'Honneur; Officier de l'Ordre National du Mérite; Commandeur de l'Ordre des Arts et des Lettres; Ambassadeur de France; Chairman, Christie's Europe, and Christie's France, since 1990; *b* 25 Dec. 1924; *s* of late Roland de Margerie, CVO; *m* 1953, Hélène Hottinguer; one *s* one *d*. *Educ:* Lycée Français de Londres; Univ. Aurore, Shanghai; Sorbonne; Institut d'Etudes Politiques, Paris. Ecole Nat. d'Administration, 1949–51; joined Min. of Foreign Affairs, 1951; Sec., French Embassy, London, 1954–59; Moscow, 1959–61; Quai d'Orsay, 1961–67; Minister, Tokyo, 1967–70; Minister, Washington, 1970–72; Dir, European Dept, Quai d'Orsay, 1972–74; Dir Gen. of French Museums, 1975–77; Ambassador: to Madrid, 1978–81; to UK, 1981–84; to Washington, 1984–89. Grand Cross, Order of Isabel la Católica (Spain), 1980, and various other foreign orders. *Address:* Christie's Europe, 6 rue Paul Baudry, 75008 Paris, France.

de MAULEY, 6th Baron, *cr* 1838; **Gerald John Ponsonby;** *b* 19 Dec. 1921; *er s* of 5th Baron de Mauley and Elgiva Margaret (*d* 1987), *d* of late Hon. Cospatrick Dundas and

Lady Cordeaux; *S* father, 1962; *m* 1954, Helen Alice, *d* of late Hon. Charles W. S. Douglas and *widow* of Lieut-Col B. L. L. Abdy Collins, OBE, MC, RE. *Educ:* Eton; Christ Church, Oxford (MA). Served War of 1939–45, France; Lieut Leics Yeo., Captain RA. Called to Bar, Middle Temple, 1949. *Heir: b* Col Hon. Thomas Maurice Ponsonby, TD, late Royal Glos Hussars [*b* 2 Aug. 1930; *m* 1956, Maxine Henrietta, *d* of W. D. K. Thellusson; two *s*]. *Address:* Langford House, Little Faringdon, Lechlade, Glos.

de MAYO, Prof. Paul, FRS 1975; FRSC 1971; Professor of Chemistry, University of Western Ontario, 1959–90, Professor Emeritus, since 1990; *b* 8 Aug. 1924; *s* of Nissim and Anna de Mayo; *m* 1949, Mary Turnbull; one *s* one *d*. *Educ:* Univ. of London. BSc, MSc, PhD London; DèsS Paris. Asst Lectr, Birkbeck Coll., London, 1954–55; Lectr, Univ. of Glasgow, 1955–57; Lectr, Imperial Coll., London, 1957–59; Dir, Photochemistry Unit, Univ. of Western Ontario, 1969–72. Chemical Institute of Canada: Merck Lecture Award, 1966; Medal, 1982; E. W. R. Steacie Award for Photochemistry, 1985. Centennial Medal, Govt of Canada, 1967. *Publications:* Mono-and sesquiterpenoids, 1959; The Higher Terpenoids, 1959; (ed) Molecular Rearrangements, 1963; (ed) Rearrangements in Ground and Excited States, vols 1–3, 1980; numerous papers in learned jls. *Address:* 436 St George Street, London, Ontario N6A 3B4, Canada. *T:* (office) 661–2171, (home) 679–9026.

DEMERITTE, Richard Clifford; Auditor-General, Commonwealth of the Bahamas, 1980–84 and since 1988; *b* 27 Feb. 1939; *s* of R. H. Demeritte and late Miriam Demeritte (*née* Whitfield); *m* 1966, Ruth Smith; one *s* two *d*. *Educ:* Bahamas Sch. of Commerce; Metropolitan Coll., London; Century Univ., USA. Treasury Department, Bahamas: Asst Accountant, 1967; Accountant, 1969–71; Asst Treasurer, Jan.–Dec. 1972; Dep. Treasurer, 1973–79; High Comr, London, 1984–88; Amb. to EEC, 1986–88, and to Belgium, France, FRG, 1987–88. Fellow: Inst. of Admin. Accountants, London, 1969; Corp. of Accountants and Auditors, Bahamas, 1971 (Pres., 1973–84; Hon. Fellow, 1983); Assoc. of Internat. Accountants, 1976 (Pres./Chm. Council, 1985–); Certified Gen. Accountant, Canada, 1982; FBIM 1985; FRSA 1988. Hon. Life Pres.: YMCA (Grand Bahama); Toastmasters Internat. (Grand Bahama). *Recreations:* chess, golf, billiards, weightlifting. *Address:* (office) PO Box N-3027, Nassau, Bahamas; (home) Rurick, Cable Beach, PO Box CB 11001, Nassau, Bahamas.

DEMEURE de LESPAUL, Edouard Henri; Officer, Order of Leopold II; Managing Director and Chief Executive, Fina plc (formerly Petrofina (UK)), since 1989; *b* 6 Jan. 1928; *s* of Charles Demeure de Lespaul and Adrienne Demeure de Lespaul (*née* Escoyez); *m* 1953, Myriam van Cutsem; two *d*. *Educ:* Univ. of Louvain (Mining Engineering); ENSP 1952 (Petroleum Engineering). Petrofina: Exploration and Production Dept, Brussels, 1952–53; Manager, Drilling Activities, Congo, 1955–56; Man. Dir, Egypt, 1956–61; Manager, Exploration and Production, Brussels, 1961–63; Chm. and Man. Dir, Finaneste NV, Belgium, 1963–89. Military Medal, war voluntary. *Recreations:* swimming, history reading, mountain walking. *Address:* Fina plc, Fina House, 1 Ashley Avenue, Epsom, Surrey KT18 5AD. *T:* Epsom (0372) 726226.

de MILLE, Agnes George, (Mrs W. F. Prude); choreographer and author; *b* New York City; *d* of William C. and Anna George de Mille; *m* 1943, Walter F. Prude (*d* 1988); one *s*. *Educ:* University of Calif. (AB *cum laude*). Dance concerts USA, England, Denmark, France, 1929–40; Choreographed: Black Crook, 1929; Nymph Errant, 1933; Romeo and Juliet 1936; Oklahoma, 1943, 1980; One Touch of Venus, 1943; Bloomer Girl, 1944; Carousel, 1945; Brigadoon, 1947; Gentlemen Prefer Blondes, 1949; Paint Your Wagon, 1951; The Girl in Pink Tights, 1954; Oklahoma (film), 1955; Goldilocks, 1958; Juno, 1959; Kwamina, 1961; One Hundred and Ten in the Shade, 1963; Come Summer, 1968. Founded and directed Agnes de Mille Dance Theatre, 1953–54. Directed: Allegro, 1947; The Rape of Lucretia, 1948; Out of This World, 1950; Come Summer, 1968; Ballets composed: Black Ritual, 1940; Three Virgins and a Devil, 1941; Drums Sound in Hackensack, 1941; Rodeo, 1942; Tally-Ho, 1944; Fall River Legend, 1948; The Harvest According, 1952; The Rib of Eve, 1956; The Bitter Wierd, 1963; The Wind in the Mountains, 1965; The Four Marys, 1965; The Golden Age, 1966; A Rose for Miss Emily, 1970; Texas Fourth, 1976; A Bridegroom called Death, 1979; Agnes de Mille Heritage Dance Theater, 1973–74; Inconsequentials, 1982; The Informer, 1988, etc. Television shows, for Omnibus, etc. Mem., Nat. Adv. Council of the Arts, 1965–66; Founding Mem., Soc. for Stage Directors and Choreographers (Pres., 1966–67). Hon. Degrees: Mills Coll., 1952; Russell Sage College, 1953; Smith Coll., 1954; Northwestern Univ., 1960; Goucher Coll., 1961; University of Calif., 1962; Clark Univ., 1962; Franklin and Marshall Coll., 1966; Western Michigan Univ., 1967; Nasson Coll., 1971; Dartmouth Coll., 1974; Duke Univ., 1975; Univ. of North Carolina, 1980; New York Univ., 1981. New York Critics Award, 1943, 1944, 1945; Antoinette Perry Award, 1962; Handel Medallion, 1976; Kennedy Arts Award, 1981; Emmy Award, 1987; and numerous other awards, 1943–58. *Publications:* Dance to the Piper, 1952; And Promenade Home, 1958; To a Young Dancer, 1962; The Book of the Dance, 1963; Lizzie Borden, Dance of Death, 1968; Dance in America, 1970; Russian Journals, 1970; Speak to me, Dance with me, 1973; Where the Wings Grow, 1978; America Dances, 1981; Reprieve, 1981; Portrait Gallery, 1990; articles in Vogue, Atlantic Monthly, Good Housekeeping, New York Times, McCall's, Horizon, Esquire. *Club:* Merriewold Country (NY).

DE MOLEYNS; *see* Daubeny de Moleyns, family name of Baron Ventry.

de MONTEBELLO, (Guy) Philippe (Lannes); Director, Metropolitan Museum of Art, since 1978; *b* 16 May 1936; *s* of Roger Lannes de Montebello and Germaine (*née* Croisset); *m* 1961, Edith Bradford Myles; two *s* one *d*. *Educ:* Harvard Coll. (BA *magna cum laude*); New York Univ., Inst. of Fine Arts (MA). Curatorial Asst, European Paintings, Metropolitan Mus. of Art, 1963; Asst Curator, Associate Curator, MMA, until 1969; Director, Museum of Fine Arts, Houston, Texas, 1969–74; Vice-Director: for Curatorial Affairs, MMA, Jan. 1974–June 1974; for Curatorial and Educnl Affairs, 1974–77; Actg Dir, MMA, 1977–78. Gallatin Fellow, New York Univ., 1981; Hon. LLD: Lafayette Coll., East Pa, 1979; Bard Coll., Annandale-on-Hudson, NY, 1981; Hon. DFA Iona Coll., New Rochelle, NY, 1982. Alumni Achievement Award, New York Univ., 1978. *Publication:* Peter Paul Rubens, 1968. *Address:* 1150 Fifth Avenue, New York, New York 10028, USA. *T:* 289 4475. *Club:* Knickerbocker (New York).

de MONTMORENCY, Sir Arnold (Geoffroy), 19th Bt *cr* 1631; Chairman, Contemporary Review Co. Ltd, since 1962, and Literary Editor 1960–90; *b* 27 July 1908; *s* of Prof. James Edward Geoffrey de Montmorency (*d* 1934) and Caroline Maud Saumarez (*d* 1973), *d* of Maj.-Gen. James de Havilland; *S* cousin, 1979; *m* 1949, Nettie Hay Anderson (marr. annulled 1953, remarried 1972), *d* of late William Anderson and Janet Hay, Morayshire; no *c*. *Educ:* Westminster School (Triplett Exhibn); Peterhouse, Cambridge. BA 1930, LLM 1931, MA 1934. Harmsworth Law Scholar. Called to the Bar, 1932. Served War, RASC and staff in ME, Italy and Yugoslavia, 1940–45. Contested (L) Cambridge, 1959, Cirencester and Tewkesbury, 1964. Chm. (pt-time), Industrial Tribunals, 1975–81. Member, RIIA; Pres., Friends of Peterhouse. *Publication:* Integration of Employment Legislation, 1984. *Heir:* none. *Address:* 2 Garden Court, Temple, EC4Y 9BL. *Club:* National Liberal.

DEMPSEY, Andrew; *see* Dempsey, J. A.

DEMPSEY, (James) Andrew; Assistant Director responsible for the Hayward Gallery, South Bank Centre, since 1987; *b* 17 Nov. 1942; *s* of James Dempsey, Glasgow; *m* 1966, Grace, *d* of Dr Ian MacPhail, Dumbarton; one *s* one *d*. *Educ:* Ampleforth Coll.; Glasgow Univ. Whistler Research Asst, Fine Art Dept, Univ. of Glasgow, 1963–65; exhibn work for art dept of Arts Council, 1966–71; Keeper, Dept of Public Relations, V&A, 1971–75; Asst Dir of Exhibitions, Arts Council of GB, 1975–87. *Address:* Royal Festival Hall, South Bank, SE1.

DEMPSTER, John William Scott; Principal Establishment and Finance Officer, Department of Transport, since 1990; *b* 10 May 1938; *m* 1965, Ailsa Newman (marr. diss. 1972). *Educ:* Plymouth Coll.; Oriel Coll., Oxford (MA(PPE)). HM Inspector of Taxes, Inland Revenue, 1961–65; Ministry of Transport: Asst Principal, 1965–67; Principal, 1967–73; Asst Sec., Property Services Agency, 1973–76; Principal Private Sec. to Sec. of State for the Environment, 1976–77; Asst Sec., Dept of Transport, 1977–80; Principal Estabt and Finance Officer, Lord Chancellor's Dept, 1980–84; Department of Transport: Head of Marine Directorate, 1984–89; Principal Establishment Officer, 1989–90. *Recreations:* mountaineering, sailing, bridge, Munro collecting. *Address:* 2 Marsham Street, SW1P 3EB. *Clubs:* Alpine, Fell and Rock; Royal Southampton Yacht.

DEMPSTER, Nigel Richard Patton; Editorial Executive, Mail Newspapers Plc (formerly Associated Newspapers), since 1973; Editor: Mail Diary, since 1973; Mail on Sunday Diary, since 1986; *b* 1 Nov. 1941; *s* of Eric R. P. Dempster and Angela Grace Dempster (*née* Stephens); *m* 1st, 1971, Emma de Bendern (marr. diss. 1974), *d* of Count John de Bendern and Lady Patricia Douglas, *d* of 11th Marquess of Queensberry; 2nd, 1977, Lady Camilla Godolphin Osborne, *o c* of 11th Duke of Leeds and Audrey (who *m* 1955, Sir David Lawrence, Bt, *qv*); one *d*. *Educ:* Sherborne. Broker, Lloyd's of London, 1958–59; Stock Exchange, 1959–60; PR account exec., Earl of Kimberley Associates, 1960–63; journalist, Daily Express, 1963–71; columnist, Daily Mail, 1971–. London correspondent, Status magazine, USA, 1965–66; contributor to Queen magazine, 1966–70; columnist ('Grovel'), Private Eye magazine, 1969–85. Broadcaster with ABC (USA) and CBC (Canada), 1976–, and with TV-am, 1983–; resident panellist, Headliners, Thames TV, 1987–89. *Publications:* HRH The Princess Margaret—A Life Unfulfilled (biog.), 1981; Heiress: the story of Christina Onassis, 1989; Nigel Dempster's Address Book, 1990. *Recreations:* photography, squash, running marathons, bicycling. *Address:* c/o Daily Mail, Northcliffe House, Derry Street, W8 5TT. *Clubs:* Royal Automobile; Chappaquiddick Beach (Mass, USA).

de NAVARRO, Michael Antony; QC 1990; a Recorder, since 1990; *b* 1 May 1944; *s* of A. J. M. (Toty) de Navarro and Dorothy M. de Navarro; *m* 1975, Jill Margaret Walker; one *s* two *d*. *Educ:* Downside School; Trinity College, Cambridge (BA Hons). Called to the Bar, Inner Temple, 1968; pupil of Hon. Mr Justice Cazalet and Hon. Mr Justice Turner; Mem., Western Circuit. *Recreations:* opera, cricket, gardening, cooking. *Address:* 2 Temple Gardens, Temple, EC4Y 9AY. *T:* 071–583 6041.

DENBIGH, 11th Earl of, *cr* 1622 **AND DESMOND,** 10th Earl of, *cr* 1622; **William Rudolph Michael Feilding;** *b* 2 Aug. 1943; *s* of 10th Earl of Denbigh and Verena Barbara, *d* of W. E. Price; *S* father, 1966; *m* 1965, Caroline Judith Vivienne, *o d* of Lt-Col Geoffrey Cooke; one *s* two *d*. *Educ:* Eton. *Heir: s* Viscount Feilding, *qv*. *Address:* 21 Moore Park Road, SW6 2HU; Newnham Paddox, Monks Kirby, Rugby, Warwickshire CV23 0RX. *T:* Rugby (0788) 832173.

DENBIGH, Prof. Kenneth George, FRS 1965; MA Cantab, DSc Leeds; Principal of Queen Elizabeth College, University of London, 1966–77; Professor Emeritus in the University of London, 1977; Visiting Research Fellow, King's College, London, since 1985; *b* 30 May 1911; *s* of late G. J. Denbigh, MSc, Harrogate; *m* 1935, Kathleen Enoch; two *s*. *Educ:* Queen Elizabeth Grammar Sch., Wakefield; Leeds University. Imperial Chemical Industries, 1934–38, 1945–48; Lecturer, Southampton Univ., 1938–41; Ministry of Supply (Explosives), 1941–45; Lecturer, Cambridge Univ., Chemical Engineering Dept, 1948–55; Professor: of Chemical Technology, Edinburgh, 1955–60, of Chemical Engineering Science, London Univ., 1960–61; Courtauld's Prof., Imperial Coll., 1961–66. Dir, Council for Science and Society, 1977–83. Fellow, Imperial Coll., 1976; FKC, 1985. Hon. DèsSc Toulouse, 1960; Hon. DUniv. Essex, 1967. *Publications:* The Thermodynamics of the Steady State, 1951; The Principles of Chemical Equilibrium, 1955; Science, Industry and Social Policy, 1963; Chemical Reactor Theory, 1965; An Inventive Universe, 1975; Three Concepts of Time, 1981; (with J. S. Denbigh) Entropy in Relation to Incomplete Knowledge, 1985; various scientific papers. *Address:* 19 Sheridan Road, Merton Park, SW19 3HW.

DENBY, Patrick Morris Coventry, CMG 1982; Assistant Director-General (Treasurer and Financial Comptroller), International Labour Office, Geneva, 1976–81; *b* 28 Sept. 1920; *s* of Robert Coventry Denby and Phyllis Denby (*née* Dacre); *m* 1950, Margaret Joy, *d* of Lt-Col C. L. Boyle; two *d* (and one *d* decd). *Educ:* Bradford Grammar Sch.; Corpus Christi Coll., Oxford (Open Scholar) (Honour Mods, Cl. II, MA). War service with Intelligence Corps, as Temp. Lieut RNVR, and with Foreign Office, 1941–46. Unilever Ltd, UK and Australia: management trainee and product manager, 1946–51; joined International Labour Office, 1951: Professional Officer, 1951; Chief of Budget and Control Div., 1959; Chief of Finance and General Services Dept, Treasurer and Financial Comptroller, 1970; Chm., Investments Cttee; Mem., UN Pension Board, 1971–75; Chm., WIPO Appeal Bd, 1985–. *Recreations:* skiing, mountain walking, tennis. *Address:* Fern Side, Fern Lane, Marlow, Bucks SL7 3SD. *Clubs:* United Oxford & Cambridge University; Stoke Poges Lawn Tennis.

DENCH, Dame Judith Olivia, (Dame Judi Dench), DBE 1988 (OBE 1970); actress (theatre, films and television); *b* 9 Dec. 1934; *d* of Reginald Arthur Dench and Eleanora Olave Dench (*née* Jones); *m* 1971, Michael Williams, *qv*; one *d*. *Educ:* The Mount Sch., York; Central Sch. of Speech and Drama. *Theatre:* Old Vic seasons, 1957–61: parts incl.: Ophelia in Hamlet; Katherine in Henry V; Cecily in The Importance of Being Earnest; Juliet in Romeo and Juliet; also 1957–61: two Edinburgh Festivals; Paris-Belgium-Yugoslavia tour; America-Canada tour; Venice (all with Old Vic Co.). Subseq. appearances incl.: Royal Shakespeare Co., 1961–62: Anya in The Cherry Orchard; Titania in A Midsummer Night's Dream; Dorcas Bellboys in A Penny for a Song; Isabella in Measure for Measure; Nottingham Playhouse tour of W Africa, 1963; Oxford Playhouse, 1964–65: Irina in The Three Sisters; Doll Common in The Alchemist; Nottingham Playhouse, 1965: Saint Joan; The Astrakhan Coat (world première); Amanda in Private Lives; Variety London Critics' Best Actress of the Year Award for perf. as Lika in The Promise, Fortune, 1967; Sally Bowles in Cabaret, Palace, 1968; Associate Mem., RSC, 1969–; London Assurance, Aldwych, 1970, and New, 1972; Major Barbara, Aldwych, 1970; Bianca in Women Beware Women, Viola in Twelfth Night, doubling Hermione and Perdita in The Winter's Tale, Portia in The Merchant of Venice, the Duchess in The Duchess of Malfi, Beatrice in Much Ado About Nothing, Lady Macbeth in Macbeth, Adriana in The Comedy of Errors, Regan in King Lear, Imogen in Cymbeline; The Wolf, Oxford and London, 1973; The Good Companions, Her Majesty's, 1974; The Gay Lord Quex, Albery, 1975; Too True to be Good, Aldwych, 1975, Globe, 1976; Pillars of the

Community, The Comedy of Errors, Aldwych, 1977; The Way of the World, 1978; Juno and the Paycock, Aldwych, 1980 (Best Actress award, SWET, Evening Standard, Variety Club, and Plays and Players); The Importance of Being Earnest, A Kind of Alaska, Nat. Theatre, 1982; Pack of Lies, Lyric, 1983 (SWET award); Mother Courage, Barbican, 1984; Waste, Barbican and Lyric, 1985; Mr and Mrs Nobody, Garrick, 1986; Antony and Cleopatra (Best Actress award, SWET, Evening Standard), Entertaining Strangers, Nat. Theatre, 1987; Hamlet, Royal Nat. Theatre, and Dubrovnik Theatre Fest., 1989; The Cherry Orchard, Aldwych, 1989; The Plough and the Stars, Young Vic, 1991; Director, for Renaissance Theatre Co.: Much Ado About Nothing, 1988; Look Back in Anger, 1989; Dir, The Boys from Syracuse, Regent's Park, 1991. Recital tour of W Africa, 1969; RSC tours: Japan and Australia, 1970; Japan, 1972. Films: He Who Rides a Tiger; A Study in Terror; Four in the Morning (Brit. Film Acad. Award for Most Promising Newcomer, 1965); A Midsummer Night's Dream; The Third Secret; Dead Cert; Saigon: Year of the Cat; Wetherby; A Room with a View; 84 Charing Cross Road; A Handful of Dust; Henry V, 1990. Television appearances include, 1957–: Talking to a Stranger (Best Actress of Year award, Guild of Television Dirs, 1967); Major Barbara; Hilda Lessways; Langrishe, Go Down; Macbeth; Comedy of Errors; On Giant's Shoulders; A Village Wooing; Love in a Cold Climate; Saigon; A Fine Romance (BAFTA Award, 1985); The Cherry Orchard; Going Gently; Mr and Mrs Edgehill (Best Actress, Amer. Cable Award, 1988); The Browning Version; Make or Break; Ghosts; Behaving Badly; Absolute Hell; Can You Hear Me Thinking? Mem. Bd, Royal Nat. Theatre, 1988–91. Awards incl. British and foreign, for theatre, films and TV, incl. BAFTA awards: for best television actress, 1981; for best supporting actress (A Room with a View), 1987, and (A Handful of Dust), 1988. Hon. DLitt: Warwick, 1978; Birmingham, 1989; DUniv York, 1983. Recreations: sewing, drawing, catching up with letters.

DENEUVE, Catherine; French film actress; b 22 Oct. 1943; d of Maurice Dorléac and Renée (née Deneuve); one s by Roger Vadim; m 1967, David Bailey, qv (marr. diss.); one d by Marcel Mastroianni. Educ: Lycée La Fontaine, Paris. Pres.-Dir Gen., Films de la Citrouille, 1971–79. Films include: Les petits chats, 1959; Les portes claquent, 1960; Le vice et la vertu, 1962; Les parapluies de Cherbourg, 1963; La Constanza della Ragione, 1964; Repulsion, 1964; Liebes Karusell, 1965; Belle de jour, 1967; Folies d'avril, 1969; Un flic, 1972; Le sauvage, 1975; Âmes perdues, 1976; Hustle, 1976; A nous deux, 1978; Le dernier métro, 1980 (César for best actress, 1981); Le choc, 1982; The Hunger, 1982; Le bon plaisir, 1984; Let's Hope It's A Girl, 1987; Drôle d'Endroit pour une Rencontre (Strange Place to Meet), 1989. Address: c/o Artmedia, 10 avenue George-V, 75008 Paris, France.

DENHAM, 2nd Baron, cr 1937, of Weston Underwood; **Bertram Stanley Mitford Bowyer,** KBE 1991; PC 1981; 10th Bt, cr 1660, of Denham; 2nd Bt, cr 1933 of Weston Underwood; Captain of the Gentlemen at Arms (Government Chief Whip in the House of Lords), 1979–91; b 3 Oct. 1927; s of 1st Baron and Hon. Daphne Freeman-Mitford, 4th d of 1st Baron Redesdale; S father 1948; m 1956, Jean, o d of Kenneth McCorquodale, Fambridge Hall, White Notley, Essex; three s one d. Educ: Eton; King's Coll., Cambridge. Mem. Westminster CC, 1959–61. A Lord-in-Waiting to the Queen, 1961–64 and 1970–71; Captain of the Yeomen of the Guard, 1971–74. Opposition Dep. Chief Whip, 1974–78, Opposition Chief Whip, 1978–79. Publications: The Man who Lost his Shadow, 1979; Two Thyrdes, 1983; Foxhunt, 1988. Recreations: field sports. Heir: s Hon. Richard Grenville George Bowyer [b 8 Feb. 1959; m 1988, Eleanor, o d of A. Sharpe]. Address: The Laundry Cottage, Weston Underwood, Olney, Bucks. T: Bedford (0234) 711535. Clubs: White's, Carlton, Pratt's, Buck's.

DENHAM, Ernest William; Deputy Keeper of Public Records, Public Record Office, 1978–82; b 16 Sept. 1922; s of William and Beatrice Denham; m 1957, Penelope Agatha Gregory; one s one d. Educ: City of London Sch.; Merton Coll., Oxford (Postmaster). MA 1948. Naval Intell., UK and SEAC, 1942–45. Asst Sec., Plant Protection Ltd, 1947–49; Asst Keeper 1949, Principal Asst Keeper 1967, Records Admin. Officer 1973, Public Record Office; Lectr in Palaeography and Diplomatic, UCL, 1957–73. Recreation: armchair criticism. Address: 4 The Ridge, Green Lane, Northwood, Mddx. T: Northwood (09274) 27382.

DENHAM, Captain Henry Mangles, CMG 1945; RN, retired; b 9 Sept. 1897; s of Henry Mangles Denham and Helen Clara Lowndes; m 1924, Estelle Margaret Sibbald Currie; one s two d. Educ: RN Coll., Dartmouth. Went to sea at beginning of European War, serving at Dardanelles in HMS Agamemnon and destroyer Racoon; occupation of the Rhine in HM Rhine Flotilla; round the world cruise with the Prince of Wales in HMS Renown, 1921; served in Mediterranean for long period largely in HMS Queen Elizabeth and Warspite; at Staff Coll., 1935; Comdr of HMS Penelope, 1936–39. Naval Attaché, Scandinavian Countries, 1940; Naval Attaché, Stockholm, 1940–47; retd list, 1947. Publications: The Aegean, 1963, 5th edn, 1983; Eastern Mediterranean, 1964; The Adriatic, 1967; The Tyrrhenian Sea, 1969; The Ionian Islands to Rhodes, 1972; Southern Turkey, the Levant and Cyprus, 1973; Ionian Islands to Anatolian Coast, 1982; Inside the Nazi Ring, 1984. Recreation: yachting. Clubs: Royal Automobile, Royal Cruising; Royal Yacht Squadron (Cowes).

DENHAM, Maurice; actor since 1934; b 23 Dec. 1909; s of Norman Denham and Winifred Lillico; m 1936, Margaret Dunn (d 1971); two s one d. Educ: Tonbridge Sch. Hull Repertory Theatre, 1934–36; theatre, radio and television, 1936–39. Served War of 1939–45: Buffs, 1939–43; Royal Artillery, 1943–45; despatches, 1946. Theatre, films, radio and television, 1946–. Radio includes: ITMA, 1939–40; Much Binding in the Marsh, 1946; Tale of Two Cities, 1988; The Sitter, 1990; Forsyte Chronicles, 1990. Theatre includes: The Andersonville Trial, Mermaid, 1960; Macbeth, King John, Old Vic, 1961; The Apple Cart, Mermaid, 1970; Uncle Vanya, Hampstead, 1979; Incident at Tulse Hill, Hampstead, 1981. Films include: The Purple Plain, 1954; Doctor at Sea, 1955; Day of the Jackal, 1972; 84 Charing Cross Road, 1986. Television includes: Talking to a Stranger, 1968; All Passion Spent, 1986; Klaus Barbie, 1987; Behaving Badly, 1988; Inspector Morse, 1991; La Nonna, 1991. Recreations: conducting gramophone records, golf. Clubs: Garrick, Green Room; Stage Golfing.

DENHAM, Lt-Col Seymour Vivian G.; see Gilbart-Denham.

DENHOLM, Allan; see Denholm, J. A.

DENHOLM, Sir Ian; see Denholm, Sir J. F.

DENHOLM, (James) Allan; Chairman, East Kilbride Development Corporation, since 1983 (Member, since 1979); Director, William Grant & Sons Ltd, since 1975 (Secretary, since 1966); b 27 Sept. 1936; s of James Denholm and Florence Lily Keith (née Kennedy); m 1964, Elizabeth Avril McLachlan, CA; one s one d. Educ: Hutchesons' Boys' Grammar Sch., Glasgow. CA. Apprentice with McFarlane Hutton & Patrick, 1954–60; Chief Accountant, A. & W. Smith & Co. Ltd, 1960–66. Councillor, Eastwood DC, 1962–64. Member: Legal Panel, CBI Scotland, 1986–; Council, Inst. of Chartered Accountants, Scotland, 1978–83 (Sen. Vice-Pres., 1991–92). Director: Scottish Cremation Soc. Ltd, 1980–; Scottish Mutual Assurance Soc., 1987–. Trustee: Queen's Coll. Educnl Trust,

1984–; Scottish Cot Death Trust, 1985–. Elder, New Kilpatrick Parish Church, Bearsden, 1971–. Recreations: golf, shooting. Address: William Grant & Sons Ltd, 208 West George Street, Glasgow G2 2PE. T: 041–248 3101; Greencroft, 19 Colquhoun Drive, Bearsden, Glasgow G61 4NQ. T: 041–942 1773. Club: Royal Scottish Automobile (Glasgow).

DENHOLM, Sir John Ferguson, (Sir Ian), Kt 1989; CBE 1974; JP; DL; Chairman: J. & J. Denholm Ltd, since 1974; Murray Investment Trusts, since 1985; Murray Management Ltd, since 1985; b 8 May 1927; s of Sir William Lang Denholm, TD; m 1952, Elizabeth Murray Stephen; two s two d. Educ: St Mary's Sch., Melrose; Loretto Sch., Musselburgh. Joined J. & J. Denholm Ltd, 1945. Deputy Chairman: P&O, 1980–85 (Dir, 1974–85); Murray Johnstone Ltd, 1985–; Director: Fleming Mercantile Investment Trust, 1985–; Murray Cos and Trusts, 1973–; Mem. London Bd, Bank of Scotland, 1982–. Member: Nat. Ports Council, 1974–77; Scottish Transport Gp, 1975–82. President: Chamber of Shipping of the UK, 1973–74; Gen. Council of British Shipping, 1988–89. Hon. Norwegian Consul in Glasgow, 1975–. DL, 1980, JP, 1984, Renfrewshire. Recreation: fishing. Address: Newton of Belltrees, Lochwinnoch, Renfrewshire PA12 4JL. T: Lochwinnoch (0505) 842406. Clubs: City of London; Western (Glasgow); Royal Thames Yacht, Royal Yacht Squadron, Royal Northern and Clyde Yacht.

DENINGTON, family name of **Baroness Denington.**

DENINGTON, Baroness cr 1978 (Life Peer), of Stevenage in the County of Hertfordshire; **Evelyn Joyce Denington,** DBE 1974 (CBE 1966); Chairman, Stevenage Development Corporation, 1966–80 (Member, 1950–80); Chairman, Greater London Council, 1975–76; b 9 Aug. 1907; d of Phillip Charles Bursill and Edith Rowena Bursill; m 1935, Cecil Dallas Denington. Educ: Blackheath High Sch.; Bedford Coll. London. Journalism, 1927–31; Teacher, 1933–50; Gen. Sec., Nat. Assoc. of Labour Teachers, 1938–47; Member: St Pancras Borough Council, 1945–59; LCC, 1946–65 (Chm. New and Expanding Towns Cttee, 1960–65); GLC, 1964–77 (Chm. Housing Cttee, 1964–67; Dep. Leader (Lab), Opposition, 1967–73; Chm., Transport Cttee, 1973–75); Central Housing Adv. Cttee, 1955–73 (Chm. Sub-Cttee prod. report Our Older Homes); SE Economic Planning Council, 1966–79; Chm., New Towns Assoc., 1973–75. Member: Sutton Dwellings Housing Trust, 1976–82; North British Housing Assoc., 1976–88; Sutton (Hastoe) Housing Assoc. Ltd, 1981–88. Freeman, City of London. Hon. FRIBA; Hon. MRTPI. Address: Flat 3, 29 Brunswick Square, Hove BN3 1EJ.

DENISON, family name of **Baron Londesborough.**

DENISON, Dulcie Winifred Catherine, (Dulcie Gray), CBE 1983; actress, playwright, authoress; b 20 Nov. 1920; d of late Arnold Savage Bailey, CBE, and of Kate Edith (née Clulow Gray); m 1939, Michael Denison, qv. Educ: England and Malaya. In Repertory in Aberdeen, 1st part Sorrel in Hay Fever, 1939; Repertory in Edinburgh, Glasgow and Harrogate, 1940; BBC Serial, Front Line Family, 1941; Shakespeare, Regents Park; Alexandra in The Little Foxes, Piccadilly; Midsummer Night's Dream, Westminster, 1942; Brighton Rock, Garrick; Landslide, Westminster, 1943; Lady from Edinburgh, Playhouse, 1945; Dear Ruth, St James's; Wind is 90, Apollo, 1946; on tour in Fools Rush In, 1946; Rain on the Just, Aldwych, 1948; Queen Elizabeth Slept Here, Strand, 1949; The Four-poster, Ambassadors, 1950 (tour of S Africa, 1954–55); See You Later (Revue), Watergate, 1951; Dragon's Mouth, Winter Garden, 1952; Sweet Peril, St James's, 1952; We Must Kill Toni, Westminster; The Diary of a Nobody, Arts, 1954; Alice Through the Looking Glass, Chelsea Palace, 1955; Ashcroft Theatre, Croydon, 1972; appeared in own play, Love Affair, Lyric Hammersmith, 1956; South Sea Bubble, Cape Town, 1956; Tea and Sympathy, Melbourne and Sydney, 1956; South Sea Bubble, Johannesburg, 1957; Double Cross, Duchess, 1958; Let Them Eat Cake, Cambridge, 1959; Candida, Piccadilly and Wyndham's, 1960; Heartbreak House, Wyndham's, 1961; A Marriage Has Been Arranged, and A Village Wooing (Hong Kong); Shakespeare Recital (Berlin Festival); Royal Gambit for opening of Ashcroft Theatre, Croydon, 1962; Where Angels Fear to Tread, Arts and St Martin's, 1963; An Ideal Husband, Strand, 1965; On Approval, St Martin's, 1966; Happy Family, St Martin's, 1967; Number 10, Strand, 1967; Out of the Question, St Martin's, 1968; Three, Fortune, 1970; The Wild Duck, Criterion, 1970; Clandestine Marriage (tour), 1971; Ghosts, York; Hay Fever (tour), 1972; Dragon Variation (tour), 1973; At the End of the Day, Savoy, 1973; The Sack Race, Ambassadors, 1974; The Pay Off, Comedy, 1974, Westminster, 1975; Time and the Conways (tour), 1976; Ladies in Retirement (tour), 1976; Façade, QEH, 1976; The Cabinet Minister (tour), 1977; A Murder is Announced, Vaudeville, 1977; Bedroom Farce, Prince of Wales, 1979; The Cherry Orchard, Exeter, 1980; Lloyd George Knew my Father (tour), 1980; The Kingfisher, Windsor, 1980, Worthing and on tour, 1981; Relatively Speaking (Dinner Theatre Tour, Near and Far East), 1981; A Coat of Varnish, Haymarket, 1982; Cavell, Chichester Fest., 1982; School for Scandal, Haymarket, transf. to Duke of York's, and British Council 50th Anniversary European Tour, 1983; There Goes the Bride (Dinner Theatre Tour, Near and Far East), 1985; The Living Room, Royalty, 1987; The Chalk Garden, Windsor and tour, 1989; The Best of Friends (tour) 1990, 1991; The Importance of Being Earnest (tour), 1991. Films include: They were Sisters, 1944; Wanted for Murder, 1945; A Man about the House, 1946; Mine Own Executioner, 1947; My Brother Jonathan, 1947; The Glass Mountain, 1948; The Franchise Affair, 1951; Angels One Five, 1952; There was a Young Lady, 1953; A Man Could Get Killed, 1965. Has appeared in television plays and radio serials; television series: Howard's Way, 1985–90. Fellow, Linnean Soc., 1984. FRSA. Queen's Silver Jubilee Medal, 1977. Publications: play: Love Affair; books: Murder on the Stairs; Murder in Melbourne; Baby Face; Epitaph for a Dead Actor; Murder on a Saturday; Murder in Mind; The Devil Wore Scarlet; No Quarter for a Star; The Murder of Love; Died in the Red; The Actor and His World (with Michael Denison); Murder on Honeymoon; For Richer, For Richer; Deadly Lampshade; Understudy to Murder; Dead Give Away; Ride on a Tiger; Stage-Door Fright; Death in Denims; Butterflies on my Mind (TES Senior Information Book Prize, 1978); Dark Calypso; The Glanville Women; Anna Starr; Mirror Image; Looking Forward, Looking Back (autobiog.). Recreations: swimming, butterflies. Address: Shardeloes, Amersham, Bucks HP7 0RL; c/o Ronnie Waters, ICM, 388 Oxford Street, W1N 9HE. T: 071–629 8080. Club: Lansdowne.

DENISON, Elizabeth Ann Marguerite, (Mrs W. N. Denison); see Curnow, E. A. M.

DENISON, John Law, CBE 1960 (MBE 1945); FRCM; Hon. RAM; Hon. GSM; Director, South Bank Concert Halls (formerly General Manager, Royal Festival Hall), 1965–76; Chairman, Arts Educational Schools, 1977–91; b 21 Jan. 1911; s of late Rev. H. B. W. and Alice Dorothy Denison; m 1st, 1936, Annie Claudia Russell Brown (marriage dissolved, 1946); 2nd, 1947, Evelyn Mary Donald (née Moir) (d 1958), d of John and Mary Scott Moir, Edinburgh; one d; 3rd, 1960, Audrey Grace Burnaby (née Bowles) (d 1970); 4th, 1972, Françoise Charlotte Henriette Mitchell (née Garrigues) (d 1985). Educ: Brighton Coll.; Royal Coll. of Music. Played horn in BBC Symphony, London Philharmonic, City of Birmingham, and other orchestras, 1934–39. Served War of 1939–45; gazetted Somerset Light Inf., 1940; DAA and QMG 214 Inf. Bde and various staff appts, 1941–45 (despatches). Asst Dir, Music Dept, British Council, 1946–48; Music Dir, Arts Council of Great Britain, 1948–65. Chairman: Cultural Programme, London

Celebrations Cttee, Queen's Silver Jubilee, 1976–78; Royal Concert Cttee, St Cecilia Fest., 1976–88; Hon. Treasurer, Royal Philharmonic Soc., 1977–89 (Hon. Mem., 1989); Member: Council, RCM, 1975–90; Exec. Cttee, Musicians Benevolent Fund, 1984–91; Trustee, Prince Consort Foundn, 1990–. FRSA. Comdr, Order of Lion (Finland), 1976; Chevalier de l'Ordre des Arts et des Lettres (France), 1988. *Publications:* articles for various musical publications. *Address:* 22 Empire House, Thurloe Place, SW7 2RU. *Club:* Garrick.

DENISON, (John) Michael (Terence Wellesley), CBE 1983; actor; *b* 1 Nov. 1915; *s* of Gilbert Dixon Denison and Marie Louise (*née* Bain); *m* 1939, Dulcie Gray (*see* D. W. C. Denison). *Educ:* Harrow; Magdalen Coll., Oxford (BA). Dramatic Sch., 1937–38; Westminster Theatre, 1938; Aberdeen Repertory, 1939. First film, 1940. Served War of 1939–45, Royal Signals and Intelligence Corps, 1940–46. Has appeared in following plays (in London, unless stated): Ever Since Paradise, 1946; Rain on the Just, 1948; Queen Elizabeth Slept Here, 1949; The Four-poster, 1950; Dragon's Mouth, 1952; Sweet Peril, 1952; The Bad Samaritan, 1953; Alice Through the Looking Glass, 1953, 1955 and 1972; We Must Kill Toni, 1954; tour of S Africa, 1954–55; All's Well That Ends Well, Twelfth Night, Merry Wives of Windsor, Titus Andronicus, Stratford-on-Avon, 1955; prod. and acted in Love Affair, 1956; A Village Wooing and Fanny's First Play (Edinburgh and Berlin festivals), 1956; Meet Me By Moonlight, 1957; Let Them Eat Cake, 1959; Candida, 1960; Heartbreak House, 1961; My Fair Lady (Melbourne); A Village Wooing (Hong Kong); Shakespeare Recital (Berlin Festival), 1962; Where Angels Fear to Tread, 1963; Hostile Witness, 1964; An Ideal Husband, 1965; On Approval, 1966; Happy Family; Number 10, 1967; Out of the Question, 1968; Three, 1970; The Wild Duck, 1970; Clandestine Marriage (tour), 1971; The Tempest, 1972; Twelfth Night, 1972, 1978, 1985; The Dragon Variation (tour), 1973; At the End of the Day, 1973; The Sack Race, 1974; Peter Pan, 1974; The Black Mikado, 1975; The First Mrs Fraser (tour), 1976; The Earl and the Pussycat (tour), 1976; Robert and Elizabeth (tour), 1976; The Cabinet Minister (tour), 1977; The Lady's Not For Burning, Ivanov, 1978; Bedroom Farce, 1979; The Kingfisher (tour), 1980–81; Venus Observed (Windsor), 1980; Relatively Speaking (Far and Near East tour), 1981; A Coat of Varnish, Captain Brassbound's Conversion, 1982; School for Scandal, 1982, 1983; See How They Run, 1984; There Goes the Bride (Near and Far East tour), 1985; Ring Round the Moon, 1985 and 1988; The Apple Cart, 1986; Court in the Act, 1986, 1987; You Never Can Tell, 1987; The Chalk Garden (tour), 1989; Dear Charles (tour), 1990; The Best of Friends (tour), 1990, 1991; The Importance of Being Earnest (tour), 1991. *Films include:* My Brother Jonathan, 1947; The Glass Mountain, 1948; Landfall, 1949; The Franchise Affair, 1950; Angels One Five, The Importance of Being Earnest, 1951; The Truth About Women, 1957. Many television appearances including title role Boyd, QC, 1956–61 and 1963. Director: Allied Theatre Productions, 1966–75; Play Company of London, 1970–74; New Shakespeare Company, 1971–. On Council British Actors Equity Assoc., 1949–76 (Vice-Pres. 1952, 1961–63, 1973); Mem. Drama Panel, Arts Council, 1975–78. FRSA. *Publications:* (with Dulcie Gray) The Actor and His World, 1964; memoirs: vol. 1, Overture and Beginners, 1973, vol. 2, Double Act, 1985. DNB articles on Sir Noël Coward and Sir Peter Daubeny, 1983, Peter Bridge, 1987. *Recreations:* golf, painting, watching cricket, gardening, motoring. *Address:* Shardeloes, Amersham, Bucks HP7 0RL. *Clubs:* Richmond Golf (Richmond); MCC, Middlesex County Cricket.

DENISON, Michael; *see* Denison, J. M. T. W.

DENISON, William Neil; QC 1980; **His Honour Judge Denison;** a Circuit Judge, since 1985; *b* 10 March 1929; *s* of William George Denison and Jean Brodie; *m*; three *s*; *m* 1981, Elizabeth Ann Marguerite Curnow, *qv*. *Educ:* Queen Mary's Sch., Walsall; Univ. of Birmingham (LLB); Hertford Coll., Univ. of Oxford (BCL). Called to the Bar, Lincoln's Inn, 1952. A Recorder of the Crown Court, 1979–85. Liveryman, Wax Chandlers' Co., 1988. *Recreations:* walking, reading rubbish. *Club:* Garrick.

DENISON-PENDER, family name of **Baron Pender.**

DENISON-SMITH, Maj.-Gen. Anthony Arthur, MBE 1973; Commander, 4th Armoured Division, since 1991; *b* 24 Jan. 1942; *s* of late George Denison-Smith and Dorothy Gwendolin Phillips; *m* 1966, Julia Henrietta Scott; three *s*. *Educ:* Harrow; RMA, Sandhurst. Commissioned Grenadier Guards, 1962; Staff Coll., 1974; Brigade Major, 7th Armoured Brigade, 1977–79; Directing Staff, Staff Coll., 1979–81; CO 2nd Bn Grenadier Guards, 1981–83; Chief of Staff, 4th Armoured Div., 1983–85; Comdr, 22nd Armoured Brigade, 1985–87; Chief of Staff, 1 (BR) Corps, 1987–89; Dir Gen. Trng and Doctrine (Army), 1990–91. *Recreations:* cricket, fishing, Hawkwoods. *Address:* c/o RHQ Grenadier Guards, Birdcage Walk, Wellington Barracks, SW1A 6HQ. *Clubs:* Army and Navy, MCC.

DENMAN, family name of **Baron Denman.**

DENMAN, 5th Baron *cr* 1834; **Charles Spencer Denman,** CBE 1976; MC 1942; TD; Bt 1945; *b* 7 July 1916; *e s* of Hon. Sir Richard Douglas Denman, 1st Bt; *S* father, 1957 and to barony of cousin, 1971; *m* 1943, Sheila Anne (*d* 1987), *d* of late Lt-Col Algernon Bingham Anstruther Stewart, DSO, Seaforth Highlanders, of Ornockenoch, Gatehouse of Fleet; three *s* one *d*. *Educ:* Shrewsbury. Served War of 1939–45 with Duke of Cornwall's Light Infantry (TA), India, Middle East, Western Desert and Dodecanese Islands; Major, 1943. Contested (C) Leeds Central, 1945. Chairman: Gold Fields Mahd adh Dhahab Ltd; Arundell House Plc; Cox & Bell Ltd; Director: Close Brothers Group Plc; British Water & Wastewater Ltd; MGM Life Assurance Soc.; Albaraka Internat. Bank Ltd; Arab-British Centre Ltd; New Zealand Holdings (UK) Ltd; formerly Chairman: Marine and General Mutual Life Assurance Soc.; Tennant Guaranty Ltd; formerly Director: C. Tennant Sons & Co. Ltd; Consolidated Gold Fields Plc; British Bank of the Middle East. Saudi British Bank; British Arabian Corp.; Fletcher Challenge Corp. Member: Cttee for ME Trade, 1963– (Chm., 1971–75); Advisory Council of Export Credits Guarantee Department, 1963–68; British National Export Council, 1965; Cttee on Invisible Exports, 1965–67; British Invisible Exports Council; Guild of World Traders in London; Res. Inst. for Study of Conflict and Terrorism; UK/Saudi Jt Cultural Cttee; Lord Kitchener Nat. Meml Fund. President: RSAA, 1984–; NZ–UK Chamber of Commerce and Industry; Vice Pres., ME Assoc.; Chairman: Arab British Chamber Charitable Foundn; Saudi-British Soc.; formerly Chm., Governors of Windlesham House Sch. *Heir: s* Hon. Richard Thomas Stewart Denman [*b* 4 Oct. 1946; *m* 1984, (Lesley) Jane, *d* of John Stevens; two *d*]. *Address:* House of Lords, SW1. *Club:* Brooks's.

DENMAN, Prof. Donald Robert; Professor of Land Economy, 1968–78 and Head of Department of Land Economy, 1962–78, Cambridge University, now Professor Emeritus; Fellow of Pembroke College, Cambridge, 1962–78, now Emeritus; *b* 7 April 1911; 2nd *s* of Robert Martyn Denman and Letitia Kate Denman, Finchley; *m* 1941, Jessica Hope, 2nd *d* of Richard H. Prior, Chichester; two *s*. *Educ:* Christ's Coll., Finchley. BSc 1938; MSc 1940; PhD 1945; MA 1948; Hon. DSc 1979; FRICS 1949; Dep. Exec. Off., Cumberland War Agricultural Exec. Cttee, 1939–46; University Lectr, Cambridge Univ., 1948–68. Land Management Cttee of Agricultural Improvement Coun., 1953–60; Member: Church Assembly, 1957–69; Standing Cttee of Istituto de Diritto Agrario Internazionale e Comparato, Florence, 1960–; Nat. Commn of Unesco, 1972–74; Advisor to Min. of Co-operation and Rural Affairs, Iran, 1968–75; Mem., Commn on Ecology, IUCN, 1987. Mem. Council, University Coll. at Buckingham, 1973–81. Chm., Commonwealth Human Ecology Council, 1984–88; Mem., Land Decade Educnl Council, 1981–. Patron, Small Farmers' Assoc. Hon. Fellow, Ghana Instn of Surveyors, 1970; Fellow, Royal Swedish Acad. of Forestry and Agriculture, 1971. Gold Medal, RICS, 1972. Distinguished Order of Homayoun of the Imperial Court of Persia, 1974. *Publications:* Tenant Right Valuation: In History and Modern Practice, 1942; Tenant Right Valuation and Current Legislation, 1948; Estate Capital: The Contribution of Landownership to Agricultural Finance, 1957; Origins of Ownership: A Brief History of Landownership and Tenure, 1958; Bibliography of Rural Land Economy and Landownership 1900–1957 (*et al*), 1958; Farm Rents: A Comparison of Current and Past Farm Rents in England and Wales, 1959; (ed and contrib.) Landownership and Resources, 1960; (ed and contrib.) Contemporary Problems of Landownership, 1963; Land in the Market, 1964; (jtly) Commons and Village Greens: A Study in Land Use, Conservation and Management, 1967; (ed and contrib.) Land and People, 1967; Rural Land Systems, 1968; Land Use and the Constitution of Property, 1969; Land Use: An Introduction to Proprietary Land Use Analysis, 1971; Human Environment: the surveyor's response, 1972; The King's Vista (Persian Land reform), 1973; Prospects of Co-operative Planning (Warburton Lecture), 1973; Land Economy: an education and a career (British Assoc. lecture), 1975; The Place of Property, 1978; Land in a Free Society, 1980; The Fountain Principle, 1982; Markets under the Sea?, 1984; Survival and Responsibility, 1987; After Government Failure?, 1987; (jtly) Planning Fails the Inner Cities, 1987; numerous monographs, articles and papers in academic and professional jls and nat. press in Britain and abroad. *Recreation:* travel. *Address:* Pembroke College, Cambridge; 12 Chaucer Road, Cambridge. *T:* Cambridge (0223) 357725. *Clubs:* Carlton, Farmers'.

DENMAN, Sir George Roy; *see* Denman, Sir Roy.

DENMAN, Sir Roy, KCB 1977 (CB 1972); CMG 1968; consultant in international trade; *b* 12 June 1924; *s* of Albert Edward and Gertrude Ann Denman; *m* 1966, Moya Lade; one *s* one *d*. *Educ:* Harrow Gram. Sch.; St John's Coll., Cambridge. War Service 1943–46; Major, Royal Signals. Joined BoT, 1948; Asst Private Sec. to successive Presidents, 1950–52; 1st Sec., British Embassy, Bonn, 1957–60; UK Delegn, Geneva, 1960–61; Counsellor, Geneva, 1965–67; Under-Sec., 1967–70, BoT; Deputy Secretary: DTI, 1970–74; Dept of Trade, 1974–75; Second Permanent Sec., Cabinet Office, 1975–77; Dir-Gen. for External Affairs, EEC Commn, 1977–82; Head, Commn of Eur. Communities Delegn in Washington, 1982–89; Business Fellow, John F. Kennedy Sch. of Govt, Harvard, 1989–90. Mem. negotiating delegn with European Communities, 1970–72. Mem., British Overseas Trade Bd, 1972–75. *Address:* c/o Coutts & Co., 2 Lower Sloane Street, SW1W 8BJ. *Club:* United Oxford & Cambridge University.

DENMAN, Sylvia Elaine; Deputy Director of Education, Inner London Education Authority, 1989–90; *b* Barbados; *d* of late Alexander Yarde and Euleen Yarde (*née* Alleyne), Barbados; *m* Hugh Frederick Denman (marr. diss.); one *d*. *Educ:* Queen's College, Barbados; LSE (LLM); called to the Bar, Lincoln's Inn, 1962. Lectr then Sen. Lectr, Oxford Polytechnic, 1965–76; Sen. Lectr and Tutor, Norman Manley Law Sch., Univ. of West Indies, Jamaica, 1977–82; Fulbright Fellow, New York Univ. Sch. of Law, 1982–83; Prin. Equal Opportunities Officer, ILEA, 1983–86; Pro Asst Dir, Polytechnic of South Bank, 1986–89. Member: Oxford Cttee for Racial Integration, 1965–76; Oxford, Bucks and Berks Conciliation Cttee, Race Relations Bd, 1965–70; London Rent Assessment Panel, 1968–76 and 1984–; Race Relations Bd, 1970–76; Equal Opportunities Commission, 1975–76; Lord Chancellor's Adv. Cttee on Legal Aid, 1975–76. Trustee: Runnymede Trust, 1985–; John Hunt Award Trust, 1987–. Governor, Haverstock Sch., 1989–. FRSA. *Recreations:* music, theatre, wandering about in the Caribbean. *Address:* 32 Belsize Park Gardens, NW3 4LH. *T:* 071-586 1734.

DENNAY, Charles William, CEng, FIEE; FIEIE; Director of Engineering, British Broadcasting Corporation, since 1987; *b* 13 May 1935; *s* of Charles Dennay and Elsie May Smith; *m* 1955, Shirley Patricia Johnston; one *s*. *Educ:* Humberston Foundation Sch.; Borough Polytechnic. DipEE; MIERE. Scientific Asst (Govt), 1953; Technician, BBC, 1956; Transmitter Engineer, 1958; Asst Lectr/Lectr, 1961; Head of Ops Transmitters, 1973; Head of Engrg Transmitter Ops, 1976; Asst Chief Engineer, Transmitters, 1978; Chief Engineer, External Broadcasting, 1979; Controller, Ops and Engineering Radio, 1984; Asst Dir of Engineering, 1985. Vice-Pres., IEIE; a Vice-Pres., RTS. *Recreations:* photography, music, civil aviation. *Address:* Junipers, 111 Winchester Street, Overton, Basingstoke, Hants RG25 3HZ. *T:* Basingstoke (0256) 770183.

DENNE, Christopher James Alured, CMG 1991; HM Diplomatic Service; Head of Consular Department, Foreign and Commonwealth Office, since 1989; *b* 20 Aug. 1945; *s* of Lt Comdr John Richard Alured Denne, DSC, RN (retd) and Alison Patricia Denne; *m* 1968, Sarah Longman; two *s* one *d*. *Educ:* Wellington Coll.; Southampton Univ. (BSc Soc. Sci. 1967). Entered Diplomatic Service, 1967; New Delhi, 1969–72; Second Sec., FCO, 1972–74; First Sec. (Information), Lagos, 1974–77; FCO, 1977; resigned, 1978; BBC External Services, 1979–80; reinstated FCO, 1983; First Sec. and Dep. Permanent Rep., UK Mission to UN, Vienna, 1985–89. *Recreations:* photography, Dartmoor. *Address:* c/o Foreign and Commonwealth Office, SW1A 2AH.

DENNING, Baron (Life Peer) *cr* 1957, of Whitchurch; **Alfred Thompson Denning,** PC 1948; Kt 1944; DL; Master of the Rolls, 1962–82; Hon. Fellow: Magdalen College, Oxford, 1948; Nuffield College, Oxford, 1982; Hon. LLD: Ottawa, 1955; Glasgow, 1959; Southampton, 1959; London, 1960; Cambridge, 1963; Leeds, 1964; McGill, 1967; Dallas, 1969; Dalhousie, 1970; Wales, 1973; Exeter, 1976; Columbia, 1976; Tilburg (Netherlands), 1977; W Ontario, 1979; British Columbia, 1979; Sussex, 1980; Buckingham, 1983; Nottingham, 1984; Hon. DCL Oxford, 1965; *b* 23 Jan. 1899; *s* of Charles and Clara Denning; *m* 1st, 1932, Mary Harvey (*d* 1941); one *s*; 2nd, 1945, Joan, *d* of J. V. Elliott Taylor, and *widow* of J. M. B. Stuart, CIE. *Educ:* Andover Grammar Sch.; Magdalen Coll., Oxford (Demy). 1st Class Mathematical Moderations; 1st Class Mathematical Final School; 1st Class Final Sch. of Jurisprudence; Eldon Scholar, 1921; Prize Student Inns of Court; called to the Bar, 1923; KC 1938; Judge of the High Court of Justice, 1944; a Lord Justice of Appeal, 1948–57; a Lord of Appeal in Ordinary, 1957–62. Chancellor of Diocese of London, 1942–44; and of Southwark, 1937–44; Recorder of Plymouth, 1944; Bencher of Lincoln's Inn, 1944; Nominated Judge for War Pensions Appeals, 1945–48; Chm. Cttee on Procedure in Matrimonial Causes, 1946–47; Chm., Royal Commission on Historical MSS, 1962–82. Held enquiry into circumstances of resignation of Mr J. D. Profumo, Sec. of State for War, 1963. Chairman: Cttee on Legal Education for Students from Africa, 1960; British Institute of International and Comparative Law, 1959–86. Pres., Birkbeck Coll., 1952–83; Treas., Lincoln's Inn, 1964. Hon. Bencher: Middle Temple, 1972; Gray's Inn, 1979; Inner Temple, 1982. Dimbleby Lectr, BBC TV, 1980. Hon. FBA 1979. Served in RE 1917–19 (BEF France). DL Hants, 1978. *Publications:* Joint Editor of Smith's Leading Cases, 1929; of Bullen and Leake's Precedents, 1935; Freedom under the Law, (Hamlyn Lectures), 1949; The Changing Law, 1953; The Road to Justice, 1955; The Discipline of Law, 1979; The Due Process of Law, 1980; The Family Story, 1981; What Next in the Law, 1982; The Closing Chapter,

1983; Landmarks in the Law, 1984; Leaves from my Library, 1986. *Address:* The Lawn, Whitchurch, Hants RG28 7AS. *T:* Whitchurch (0256) 892144.

DENNINGTON, Dudley, FEng; FICE; FIStructE; FHKIE; Partner, since 1972, Senior Partner, since 1989, Bullen & Partners; *b* 21 April 1927; *s* of John Dennington and Beryl Dennington (*née* Hagon); *m* 1951, Margaret Patricia Stewart; two *d. Educ:* Clifton Coll., Bristol; Imperial Coll., London Univ. (BSc). National Service, 2nd Lieut, RE, 1947–49; Sandford Fawcett and Partners, Consulting Engineers, 1949–51; D. & C. Wm Press, Contractors, 1951–52; AMICE 1953; Manager, Design Office, George Wimpey & Co., 1952–65; GLC 1965–72: Asst Chief Engineer, Construction, 1965–67; Chief Engineer, Construction, 1967–70; Traffic Comr and Dir of Development, 1970–72. Mem., Bd for Engineers' Registration, Engrg Council, 1983–85. Vis. Prof., King's Coll., London Univ., 1978–81. FICE 1966 (Mem. Council, 1975–78 and 1981–84; Vice-Pres., 1990–Nov. 1992); FHKIE 1982; FCGI 1984; FEng 1985. *Recreations:* mathematics, painting. *Address:* 25 Corkran Road, Surbiton, Surrey. *T:* 081–399 2977. *Club:* Reform.

DENNIS, Maj.-Gen. Alastair Wesley, CB 1985; OBE 1973; Secretary, Imperial Cancer Research Fund, 1985–91; *b* 30 Aug. 1931; *s* of late Ralph Dennis and of Helen (*née* Henderson); *m* 1957, Susan Lindy Elgar; one *s* two *d. Educ:* Malvern Coll.; RMA, Sandhurst. Commanded 16th/5th The Queen's Royal Lancers, 1971–74; Col GS, Cabinet Office, 1974–75; Comd 20 Armoured Bde, 1976–77; Dep. Comdt, Staff Coll., 1978–80; Director of Defence Policy (B), MoD, Whitehall, 1980–82; Dir, Military Assistance Overseas, MoD, 1982–85. Chm., Assoc. of Med. Res Charities, 1987–91. Mem., Malvern Coll. Council, 1988–. *Recreations:* fishing, golf, gardening. *Address:* c/o Barclays Bank, 2 Market Place, Wallingford, Oxon.

DENNIS, Rt. Rev. John; *see* St Edmundsbury and Ipswich, Bishop of.

DENNIS, Maxwell Lewis, CMG 1971; Chairman, South Australia Totalizator Agency Board, 1973–79; *b* 19 April 1909; *s* of Frank Leonard and Ethel Jane Dennis; *m* 1935, Bernice Abell; one *d* (one *s* decd). *Educ:* Gladstone High Sch., South Australia. FCPA. Entered South Australian Public Service, 1924, Public Service Commissioner, 1965; Chm., Public Service Bd, 1968–73; Life Governor, Royal Soc. for the Blind. *Address:* 31 Hill Street, Victor Harbor, SA 5211, Australia.

DENNISON, Brig. Malcolm Gray; Lord-Lieutenant of Orkney, since 1990; *b* 19 March 1924; *s* of John Reid Dennison of Shapinsay and Margaret Gray of Roeberry. *Educ:* Lincoln Sch.; Edinburgh Univ. RAF, 1942–52: Bomber Comd, 1944–45; Sen. Intell. Officer, 219 and 205 Groups, 1946–47; MECAS, 1947–48; HQ Middle East Air Force, 1948–51; retired 1952. Bahrain Petroleum Co., 1953–55; Sultan's Armed Forces, Intelligence, 1955–83. Sultan's Commendation, 1970; DSM (Oman), 1972; Order of Oman (Military), 1974. *Recreation:* book collecting. *Address:* Roeberry House, St Margaret's Hope, Orkney KW17 2TW. *T:* St Margaret's Hope (085683) 228. *Clubs:* Royal Air Force, Special Forces, Royal Over-Seas League.

DENNISON, Mervyn William, CBE 1967; MC 1944; DL; *b* 13 July 1914; *er s* of Reverend W. Telford Dennison and Hester Mary (*née* Coulter); *m* 1944, Helen Maud, *d* of Claud George Spiller, Earley, Berks; one *s* one *d. Educ:* Methodist Coll., Belfast; Queen's Univ., Belfast (BA); Middle Temple. Called to Bar of Northern Ireland, 1945; Middle Temple, 1964. Served War of 1939–45, with Royal Ulster Rifles and Parachute Regt (POW Arnhem, 1944). Crown Counsel, N Rhodesia, 1947; Legal Draftsman, 1952; Senior Crown Counsel and Parliamentary Draftsman, Federal Govt of Rhodesia and Nyasaland, 1953; Federal Solicitor-Gen., 1959; QC (N Rhodesia) 1960; also Chm. Road Service Bd, N Rhodesia, and Mem. Central African Air Authority. High Court Judge, Zambia, 1961–67. Secretary, Fermanagh CC, NI, 1967–73; Chief Comr, Planning Appeals Commn and Water Appeals Commn, 1973–80; Chm., Industrial Tribunals in N Ireland, 1981–84. Mem. Senate, Queen's Univ., Belfast 1979–87. Hon. Col, The Zambia Regt, 1964–66. JP Co. Fermanagh, 1969–73, DL, 1972–. KStJ 1978 (CStJ 1964). *Recreation:* fishing. *Address:* Creevyloughgare, Saintfield, Ballynahinch, Co. Down BT24 7NB. *T:* Saintfield (0238) 510397. *Club:* Harare (Zimbabwe).

DENNISON, Stanley Raymond, CBE 1946; Vice-Chancellor, 1972–79, and Honorary Professor, 1974–79, University of Hull, now Emeritus Professor; Vice-Chairman, Committee of Vice-Chancellors and Principals of the United Kingdom, 1977–79; *b* 15 June 1912; *o s* of late Stanley Dennison and Florence Ann Dennison, North Shields; unmarried. *Educ:* University of Durham; Trinity College, Cambridge. Lecturer in Economics, Manchester University, 1935–39; Professor of Economics, University Coll. of Swansea, 1939–45; Lecturer in Economics, Cambridge Univ., 1945–58; Fellow of Gonville and Caius Coll., 1945–58; Prof. of Economics, Queen's Univ. of Belfast, 1958–61; David Dale Prof. of Economics, Univ. of Newcastle upon Tyne, 1962–72; Pro-Vice-Chancellor, 1966–72. Chief Economic Asst, War Cabinet Secretariat, 1940–46. Member: University Grants Cttee, 1964–68; North Eastern Electricity Board, 1965–72; Review Body on Remuneration of Doctors and Dentists, 1962–70; Verdon Smith Cttee on Marketing and Distribution of Fatstock and Carcase Meat, 1964; Scott Cttee on Land Utilisation in Rural Areas, 1942 (Minority Report); Beaver Cttee on Air Pollution, 1954; Waverley Cttee on Med. Services for the Armed Forces, 1955. Chm. Governors, Royal Grammar Sch., Newcastle upon Tyne, 1969–87. Hon. LLD Hull, 1980. *Publications:* The Location of Industry and the Depressed Areas, 1939; (with Sir Dennis Robertson) The Control of Industry, 1960; Choice in Education, 1984; various articles, etc, on economic questions. *Recreation:* music. *Address:* 22 Percy Gardens, Tynemouth, Tyne and Wear NE30 4HQ. *Club:* Reform.

DENNISON, Stanley Richard, CBE 1990; PhD; FRSC; Group Chief Executive, ECC Group (formerly English China Clays) plc, 1988–90; *b* 28 May 1930; *s* of Arthur and Ellen Dennison; *m* 1955, Margaret Janet Morrison; two *s* two *d. Educ:* Latymer's Sch., Edmonton; University Coll. London (BSc, PhD). CBIM 1988. Chemist, Min. of Supply, 1954; English China Clays: Res. Chemist, 1956; Res. Man., 1970; Res. Dir, Clay Div., 1980; Man. Dir, Clay Div., 1984; Dir, English China Clays PLC, 1984. Dir, Devon and Cornwall TEC, 1990–91. Mem., Cornwall and Is of Scilly DHA, 1990–. *Publications:* on industrial minerals, their technology and application in paper, in a number of pubns. *Recreations:* music, walking. *Address:* Lower Colvreath Farm, Roche, St Austell, Cornwall PL26 8LR.

DENNISS, Gordon Kenneth, CBE 1979; Consultant Chartered Surveyor, Eastman & Denniss, Surveyors, 1983–88 (Senior Partner, 1945–83); Senior Partner, G. K. Denniss Farms; *b* 29 April 1915; *e s* of late Harold W. Denniss; *m* 1939, Violet Fiedler, Montreal; one *s* two *d. Educ:* Dulwich Coll.; Coll. of Estate Management. FRICS. Articled to uncle, Hugh F. Thoburn, Chartered Surveyor, Kent, developing building estates, 1935, professional asst 1938; Eastman & Denniss: Junior Partner, 1943; sole principal, 1945. Crown Estate Comr, 1965–71. Farming 1500 acres in E Sussex and Kent. Pres., Ashurst CC, Kent. *Recreations:* farming, cricket, political economy, golf. *Address:* 6 Belgrave Place, Belgravia, SW1. *T:* 071–235 4858; Evans Leap, Withyham, Hartfield, E Sussex. *T:* Hartfield (0892) 770720. *Clubs:* Farmers', MCC; Surrey County Cricket.

DENNISTON, Rev. Robin Alastair; Non-Stipendiary Minister, West Fife Team Ministry, since 1990; Oxford Publisher and Senior Deputy Secretary to the Delegates, Oxford University Press, 1984–88 (Academic and General Publisher, 1980–84); *b* 25 Dec. 1926; *s* of late Alexander Guthrie Denniston, CMG, CBE, head of Govt code and cipher school, and late Dorothy Mary Gilliat; *m* 1st, 1950, Anne Alice Kyffin Evans (*d* 1985), *y d* of late Dr Geoffrey Evans, MD, FRCP, consulting Physician at St Bartholomew's Hosp., and late Hon. E. M. K. Evans; one *s* two *d*; 2nd, 1987, Dr Rosa Susan Penelope Beddington, *yr d* of Roy Julian Beddington, artist, and late Anna Dorothy Beddington. *Educ:* Westminster Sch. (King's Schol.; Captain of School, 1945); Christ Church, Oxford (Classical Schol.; 2nd cl. Hons Lit. Hum.). National Service: commnd into Airborne Artillery, 1948. Editor at Collins, 1950–59; Man. Dir, Faith Press, 1959–60; Editor, Prism, 1959–61; Promotion Man., Hodder & Stoughton Ltd, 1960–64, Editorial Dir, 1966, Man. Dir, 1968–72; Dir, Mathew Hodder Ltd (and subsid. cos), 1968–72; Dep. Chm., George Weidenfeld & Nicolson (and subsid. cos), 1973–75; Non-exec. Chm., A. R. Mowbray & Co., 1974–88; Dir, Thomson Publications Ltd, 1975–77; also Chm. of Michael Joseph Ltd, Thomas Nelson & Sons (and subsid. cos), George Rainbird Ltd, 1975–77 and Sphere Books, 1975–76; Academic Publisher, OUP, 1978; non-exec. Dir, W. W. Norton, 1989–. Student of Christ Church, 1978–88. Ordained Deacon, 1978, Priest, 1979; Hon. Curate: Clifton-on-Teme, 1978; New with South Hinksey, 1985; NSM, Great with Little Tew, 1987–90. *Publications:* The Young Musicians, 1956; Partly Living, 1967; (ed) Part Time Priests?, 1960. *Recreations:* farming, music. *Address:* 16a Inverleith Row, Edinburgh EH3 5LS; 10 Lesslies Buildings, Kirkton Road, Burntisland, Fife. *Club:* United Oxford & Cambridge University.

DENNY, Sir Alistair (Maurice Archibald), 3rd Bt, *cr* 1913; *b* 11 Sept. 1922; *er s* of Sir Maurice Edward Denny, 2nd Bt, KBE and Lady Denny (*d* 1982), Gateside House, Drymen, Stirlingshire; *S* father, 1955; *m* 1949, Elizabeth, *y d* of Sir Guy Lloyd, 1st Bt, DSO; two *s* (and one *s* decd). *Educ:* Marlborough. Started engineering training with William Denny & Bros. Served War in Fleet Air Arm, 1944–46. Continued engineering training with Alexander Stephen & Sons, Glasgow, and Sulzer Bros., Winterthur, Switzerland; returned to William Denny & Bros, 1948; left, Sept. 1963, when firm went into liquidation. Chm., St Andrews Links Management Cttee, 1980–81. Council Mem., St Leonard's Sch., St Andrews, 1982–89. *Recreations:* golf, gardening, photography. *Heir: s* Charles Alistair Maurice Denny [*b* 7 Oct. 1950; *m* 1981, Belinda, *yr d* of J. P. McDonald, Walkinstown, Dublin; one *s* one *d*]. *Address:* Crombie Cottage, Abercrombie, by St Monans, Fife KY10 2DE. *T:* St Monans (03337) 631. *Club:* Royal and Ancient Golf (St Andrews).

DENNY, Sir Anthony Coningham de Waltham, 8th Bt, *cr* 1782, of Tralee Castle, Co. Kerry, Ireland; designer; Partner in Verity and Beverley, Architects and Designers (offices in London, Tetbury and Lisbon), since 1959; *b* 22 April 1925; *s* of Rev. Sir Henry Lyttleton Lyster Denny, 7th Bt, and Joan Lucy Dorothy, *er d* of Major William A. C. Denny, OBE; *S* father 1953; *m* 1949, Anne Catherine, *e d* of S. Beverley, FRIBA; two *s* one adopted *d. Educ:* Clayesmore Sch. Served War of 1939–45: Middle East, RAF (Aircrew), 1943–47. Anglo-French Art Centre, 1947–50; Mural Painter and Theatrical Designer, 1950–54. Trustee, Waltham Abbey. Hereditary Freeman of City of Cork. FRSA; MCSD. *Recreations:* architecture and painting. *Heir: s* Piers Anthony de Waltham Denny [*b* 14 March 1954; *m* 1987, Ella Jane, *o d* of Peter P. Huhne; two *d*]. *Address:* Daneway House, Sapperton, Cirencester, Glos. *T:* Frampton Mansell (028576) 232.
See also B. L. Denny.

DENNY, Barry Lyttelton, LVO 1979; HM Diplomatic Service, retired; *b* 6 June 1928; *s* of Rev. Sir Henry Lyttelton Lyster Denny, 7th Bt, and Joan Lucy Dorothy, *er d* of Major William A. C. Denny, OBE; *m* 1st, 1951 (marr. diss. 1968); one *s* one *d*; 2nd, 1969, Anne Rosemary Jordon, *o d* of Col James F. White, MC; one *d. Educ:* Clayesmore Sch.; RMA, Sandhurst. Indian Army Cadet, 1946–47; commnd RA, 1949; retd from HM Forces as Captain (Temp. Major), 1960. Joined Foreign Office, 1962; First Sec., Nicosia, 1964; FO, later FCO, 1966; Kaduna, 1969; FCO, 1972; Vientiane, 1973; FCO, 1975; Kuwait, 1977; Counsellor, Oslo, 1980; seconded to MoD, 1984–89. Comdr, Order of St Olav (Norway), 1981. *Recreations:* polo, collecting, photography. *Club:* Army and Navy.
See also Sir A. C. de W. Denny.

DENNY, Margaret Bertha Alice, (Mrs E. L. Denny), OBE 1946; DL; Under Secretary, Ministry of Transport and Civil Aviation, 1957–58; *b* 30 Sept. 1907; *o d* of late Edward Albert Churchard and late Margaret Catherine (*née* Arnold) and step-*d* of late William Ray Lenanton, JP; *m* 1957, Edward Leslie Denny, JP, formerly Chm., William Denny Bros, Shipbuilders, Dumbarton. *Educ:* Dover County Sch.; Bedford Coll. for Women, London Univ. (BA Hons PhD). Entered Civil Service as Principal Ministry of Shipping, 1940; Asst Sec., 1946. Gov., Bedford Coll., University of London. Member: Scottish Adv. Coun. for Civil Aviation, 1958–67; Western Regional Hospital Board, Scotland, 1960–74; Scottish Cttee, Council of Industrial Design, 1961–71; Gen. Advisory Council, BBC, 1962–66; Gen. Nursing Council, Scotland, 1962–78; Board of Management, State Hosp., Carstairs, 1966–76; Exec. Cttee, Nat. Trust for Scotland, 1974– (Mem. Council, 1973–; Vice-Pres, 1981–); Vice-Chm., Argyll and Clyde Health Bd, 1974–77. County Comr, Girl Guides, Dunbartonshire, 1958–68. DL Dunbartonshire, 1973. Officer, Order of Orange Nassau, 1947. *Address:* Gartochraggan Cottage, Gartocharn, by Alexandria, Dunbartonshire G83 8NE. *T:* Gartocharn (038983) 272.

DENNY, Rev. Norwyn Ephraim; Superintendent, Lowestoft and East Suffolk Methodist Church, since 1986; President of the Methodist Conference, 1982–83; *b* 23 Oct. 1924; *s* of Percy Edward James Denny and Dorothy Ann Denny (*née* Stringer); *m* 1950, Ellen Amelia Shaw; three *d. Educ:* City of Norwich School; Wesley College, Bristol. BD (Hons), London Univ. Ordained Methodist Minister, 1951; Methodist Minister in Jamaica, 1950–54; Minister in Peterborough, 1955–61; Member of Notting Hill Group (Ecumenical) Ministry, 1961–75; Chm., Liverpool Dist Methodist Church, 1975–86. *Publications:* (with D. Mason and G. Ainger) News from Notting Hill, 1967; Caring, 1976. *Recreations:* gardening, astronomy, association football. *Address:* 8 Corton Road, Lowestoft, Suffolk NR32 4PL. *T:* Lowestoft (0502) 573048.

DENNY, Ronald Maurice; Director, Electrocomponents, since 1984; *b* 11 Jan. 1927; *s* of Maurice Denny and Ada (*née* Bradley); *m* 1952, Dorothy Hamilton; one *s* two *d. Educ:* Gosport County Sch. CEng, FIEE. BBC Engineering, 1943; served Royal Navy, 1946–49; BBC Engr (TV), 1949–55; ATV Ltd, 1955, Gen. Man., ATV, 1967; Rediffusion Ltd, 1970; Chief Exec., 1979–85, Chm., 1985–89, Rediffusion PLC; Director: (non-exec.) Thames Television, 1981–89; BET, 1983–89. Mem. of Trust, Philharmonia Orch., 1983–. Hon. Mem., RCM, 1984–. FRSA 1985. *Recreations:* music, sport. *Address:* 19 Nichols Green, W5 2QU. *T:* 081–998 3765. *Clubs:* Athenæum, Arts.

DENNY, William Eric, CBE 1984; QC 1975; a Recorder of the Crown Court, since 1974; *b* 2 Nov. 1927; *s* of William John Denny and Elsie Denny; *m* 1960, Daphne Rose Southern-Reddin; one *s* two *d. Educ:* Ormskirk Grammar Sch.; Liverpool Univ. (Pres., Guild of Undergraduates, 1952–53; LLB). Served RAF, 1946–48. Called to the Bar, Gray's Inn, 1953, Bencher, 1985. Lectured at LSE, 1953–58. Chm., Home Secretary's Adv.

Bd on Restricted Patients, 1980–85 (Mem., 1979). *Recreations:* music, sailing, gardening. *Address:* 1 Hare Court, Temple, EC4Y 7BE.

DENNYS, Nicholas Charles Jonathan; QC 1991; *b* 14 July 1951; *m* 1977, Frances Winifred Markham; four *d*. *Educ:* Eton; Brasenose Coll., Oxford (BA 1973). Admitted Middle Temple, 1973; called to the Bar, 1975. *Recreations:* windsurfing, golf, music. *Address:* The Old Rectory, Arborfield, Berks RG2 9HZ. *T:* Reading (0734) 761003.

DENNYS, Rodney Onslow, CVO 1982 (MVO 1969); OBE (mil.) 1943; FSA, FSG; FRSA; Arundel Herald of Arms Extraordinary, since 1982 (Somerset Herald of Arms, 1967–82); *b* 16 July 1911; *s* of late Frederick Onslow Brooke Dennys, late Malayan Civil Service, and Claire (*née* de Paula); *m* 1944, Elisabeth Katharine (served FO 1938–41; GHQ MEF, 1941–44, awarded certificate for outstandingly good service by C-in-C MEF; Allied Forces HQ N Africa, Algiers, 1944, FO 1944–45), *d* of late Charles Henry Greene; one *s* two *d*. *Educ:* Canford Sch.; LSE. Apptd to FO, 1937; HM Legation, The Hague, 1937–40; FO, 1940–41. Commissioned in Intell. Corps, 1941; Lt-Col 1944; RARO, 1946. Reapptd, FO, 1947; 1st Sec. British Middle East Office, Egypt, 1948–50; 1st Sec. HM Embassy: Turkey, 1950–53; Paris, 1955–57; resigned, 1957. Asst to Garter King of Arms, 1958–61; Rouge Croix Pursuivant of Arms, 1961–67. Served on Earl Marshal's Staff for State Funeral of Sir Winston Churchill, 1965, and for the Prince of Wales' Investiture, 1969. Dep. Dir, Heralds' Museum, 1978–83, Dir, 1983–. Advised Queensland Govt on design of first Mace of Qld Leg. Assembly, and in attendance, in Tabard, on Governor of Qld for inauguration of Mace in Qld Parlt, 1978. Mem. Court, Sussex Univ., 1972–77. CPRE, 1972–: Mem., Nat. Exec., 1973–78; Chm., 1972–77, Vice-Pres., 1977, Sussex Br. Dir, Arundel Castle Trustees Ltd, 1977–87; Member: Exec. Cttee, Sussex Historic Churches Trust, 1973–83; Council Harleian Soc. (Chm. 1977–84); Devon Assoc.; Académicien, Académie Internationale d'Héraldique; Mem. Council, Shrievalty Assoc., 1984–. Fellow, Soc. of Genealogists; FRSA. Freeman of City of London; Liveryman and Freeman of Scriveners' Co. (Mem., Ct of Assistants, 1988–). High Sheriff E Sussex, 1983–84. *Publications:* Flags and Emblems of the World; (jt) Royal and Princely Heraldry of Wales, 1969; The Heraldic Imagination, 1975; Heraldry and the Heralds, 1982; articles in jls on heraldry and kindred subjects. *Recreations:* heraldry, ornithology. *Address:* College of Arms, EC4V 4BT. *T:* 071–248 1912. *Clubs:* Garrick, City Livery; Sussex.

DENSON, John Boyd, CMG 1972; OBE 1965; HM Diplomatic Service, retired; *b* 13 Aug. 1926; *o s* of late George Denson and Alice Denson (*née* Boyd); *m* 1957, Joyce Myra Symondson; no *c*. *Educ:* Perse Sch.; St John's Coll., Cambridge. Royal Regt of Artillery, 1944; Intelligence Corps, 1946; Cambridge, 1947–51 (English and Oriental Langs Triposes). Joined HM Foreign (now Diplomatic) Service, 1951. Served in Hong Kong, Tokyo, Peking, London, Helsinki, Washington, Vientiane; Asst Head of Far Eastern Dept, Foreign Office, 1965–68; Chargé d'Affaires, Peking, 1969–71; Royal Coll. of Defence Studies, 1972; Counsellor and Consul-Gen., Athens, 1973–77; Ambassador to Nepal, 1977–83. Pres., Himalayan Communities Trust, 1986; Mem., Exec. Council, Univs China Cttee of London. Gorkha Dakshina Bahu, 1st cl., 1980. *Recreations:* looking at pictures, the theatre, wine. *Address:* Little Hermitage, Pensile Road, Nailsworth, Glos. *T:* Nailsworth (045383) 3829. *Club:* Royal Over-Seas League.

DENT, Harold Collett; *b* 14 Nov. 1894; *s* of Rev. F. G. T. and Susan Dent; *m* 1922, Loveday Winifred Martin; one *s* one *d*. *Educ:* Public elementary schs; Kingswood Sch., Bath; London Univ. (external student). Asst Master in secondary schs, 1911–25 (War Service, 1914–19); Head of Junior Dept, Brighton, Hove and Sussex Grammar Sch., 1925–28; first headmaster, Gateway School, Leicester, 1928–31; freelance journalist, 1931–35; asst ed., Book Dept Odhams Press, 1935–40; Ed., The Times Educational Supplement, 1940–51; Educational Correspondent, The Times, 1952–55; Professor of Education and Dir of the Inst. of Education, University of Sheffield, 1956–60; Senior Research Fellow, Inst. of Education, University of Leeds, 1960–62; Asst Dean, Inst. of Education, University of London, 1962–65; Visiting Prof., University of Dublin, 1966; BA; FRSA; Hon. FCP; Hon. FEIS. *Publications:* A New Order in English Education, 1942; The Education Act 1944, 1944; Education in Transition, 1944; To be a Teacher, 1947; Secondary Education for All, 1949; Secondary Modern Schools, 1958; The Educational System of England and Wales, 1961; Universities in Transition, 1961; British Education, 1962; 1870–1970, Century of Growth in English Education, 1970; The Training of Teachers in England and Wales 1700–1975, 1977; Education in England and Wales, 1977. *Recreation:* reading. *Address:* Barns Croft, Goblin Lane, Cullompton, Devon EX15 1BB. *T:* Cullompton (0884) 32075.

DENT, Sir John, Kt 1986; CBE 1976 (OBE 1968); Chairman, Civil Aviation Authority, 1982–86; *b* 5 Oct. 1923; *s* of Harry F. Dent; *m* 1954, Pamela Ann, *d* of Frederick G. Bailey; one *s*. *Educ:* King's Coll., London Univ. BSc(Eng), FEng, FRAeS, FIMechE, FIEE, CBIM. Admty Gunnery Estabs at Teddington and Portland, 1944–45; Chief Engr, Guided Weapons, Short Bros & Harland Ltd, Belfast, 1955–60; Chief Engr, Armaments Div., Armstrong Whitworth Aircraft, Coventry, 1961–63; Dir and Chief Engr, Hawker Siddeley Dynamics Ltd, Coventry, 1963–67; Director: Engrg Gp, Dunlop Ltd, Coventry, 1968–76; Dunlop Holdings Ltd, 1970–82; Industrie Pirelli SpA, 1978–81; Dunlop AG, 1979–82; Pirelli Gen. plc, 1980–; Pirelli Ltd, 1985–; Man. Dir, Dunlop Ltd, 1978–82. President: Coventry and District Engrg Employers' Assoc., 1971 and 1972; Engrg Employers' Fedn, 1974–76 (1st Dep. Pres., 1972–74); Inst. of Travel Managers, 1986–; Internat. Fedn of Airworthiness, 1987–89; Chm., Nationalized Industries' Chairman's Group, 1984–85. Member: Engineering Industries Council, 1975–76; Review Bd for Government Contracts, 1976–82; Royal Dockyards Policy Bd, 1976–82; NCB, 1980–82. *Recreations:* gardening, fishing, cabinet-making. *Address:* Helidon Grange, Helidon, near Daventry, Northants NN11 6LG.

DENT, Maj.-Gen. Jonathan Hugh Baillie, CB 1984; OBE 1974; Director General, Fighting Vehicles and Engineer Equipment, Ministry of Defence, 1981–85; *b* 19 July 1930; *s* of Joseph Alan Guthrie Dent and Hilda Ina Dent; *m* 1957, Anne Veronica Inglis; one *s* three *d*. *Educ:* Winchester College. Commissioned, Queen's Bays, 1949; regtl and instructional employment in BAOR, UK, Jordan, Libya, 1949–61; Adjt 1958; Adjt Shropshire Yeomanry, 1959–60; Staff trng, RMCS, 1962–63; Staff Coll. Camberley, 1964; Sqdn Comd, Queen's Dragoon Guards, N Ireland and Borneo, 1965–66; MoD (Operational Requirements), 1967–69; Second in Comd, Queen's Dragoon Guards, 1970; Ministry of Defence: MGO Secretariat, 1971–74; Project Manager Chieftain, 1974–76; RCDS 1977; Defence R&D Attaché, British Embassy, Washington, 1978–80. *Recreations:* fishing, bird watching, walking, shooting, classical music.

DENT, Robin John; Chairman, Mase Westpac Ltd, since 1989; *b* 25 June 1929; *s* of late Rear-Adm. John Dent, CB, OBE; *m* 1952, Hon. Ann Camilla Denison-Pender, *d* of 2nd Baron Pender, CBE; two *d*. *Educ:* Marlborough. Bank of England, 1949–51; joined M. Samuel & Co. Ltd, 1951: Director, 1963–65; Dir, Hill Samuel & Co. Ltd, 1965–67; Dir (London Board), Commercial Banking Co. of Sydney Ltd, 1964–82; Man. Dir, Baring Bros & Co. Ltd, 1967–86; Dir, Barings plc, 1985–89. Member, London Adv. Cttee, Hong Kong & Shanghai Banking Corp., 1974–81; Dir, TR City of London Trust PLC, 1977–. Mem., Deposit Protection Bd, 1982–85; Dep. Chm., Export Guarantees Adv. Council, 1983–85; Chm., Executive Cttee, British Bankers' Assoc., 1984–85; Comr, Public Works Loan Bd, 1987– (Dep. Chm., 1988–90; Chm., 1990–). Mem. Council, Cancer Research Campaign, 1967– (Vice-Chm., Exec. Cttee, 1990–); Treasurer, King Edward's Hosp. Fund for London, 1974–; Special Trustee, St Thomas' Hosp., 1988–. *Address:* 44 Smith Street, SW3 4EP. *T:* 071–352 1234. *Club:* White's.

DENT, Ronald Henry; Chairman, Cape Industries Ltd, 1962–79; *b* 9 Feb. 1913; *s* of late Henry Francis Dent, MA, and Emma Bradley; *m* 1939, Olive May, *d* of late George Wilby, FCA; one *s* one *d*. *Educ:* Portsmouth Grammar Sch. Chartered accountant, 1936. Served War, 1939–45: UK, France, India; War Office, 1942–45. Joined Cape Industries, 1947; Man. Dir, 1957–71. Cancer Research Campaign: Mem. Council, 1965–, Vice-Chm. 1975–83; Chm., Finance Cttee, 1969–75; Chm., Exec. Cttee, 1975–83. Dep. Chm., Finance Cttee, Union Internationale contre le Cancer, Geneva, 1978–90; Dir, Internat. Cancer Foundn, 1978–90. British Inst. of Management: Fellow 1965; Mem. Council, 1968–77; Mem., Bd of Fellows, 1971–77; Chm. Finance Cttee, and Vice-Chm. of Inst., 1972–76. Mem. Council, UK S Africa Trade Assoc., 1969–80. FRSA. *Recreations:* golf, gardening. *Address:* Badgers Copse, Birtley Green, Bramley, Surrey GU5 0LE. *T:* Guildford (0483) 893649. *Club:* St George's Hill Golf.

DENTON, family name of **Baroness Denton of Wakefield.**

DENTON OF WAKEFIELD, Baroness *cr* 1991 (Life Peer), of Wakefield in the County of West Yorkshire; **Jean Denton,** CBE 1990; Deputy Chairman, Black Country Development Corporation, since 1987; *d* of late Charles J. Moss and Kathleen Tuke. *Educ:* Rothwell Grammar Sch.; LSE (BScEcon). Procter & Gamble, 1959–61; EIU, 1961–64; IPC, 1964–66; Hotel and Catering Dept, Univ. of Surrey, 1966–69; racing/rally driver, 1969–72; Marketing Director: Huxford Gp, 1972–78; Heron Motor Gp, 1978–80; Man. Dir, Herondrive, 1980–85; External Affairs Dir, Austin Rover, 1985–86. Director: Ordnance Survey, 1985–88; British Nuclear Fuels, 1987–; Burson-Marsteller, 1987–; London & Edinburgh Insce Group, 1989–; Triplex Lloyd, 1990–; Think Green, 1989–. Chairman: Marketing Gp of GB, 1987, 1988; Women on the Move against Cancer, 1979–; Forum UK; Member: Board, UK 2000, 1986–88; Engrg Council, 1986–; Teachers' Pay Review, 1989, 1990 and 1991. Mem. Adv. Bd, Royal Acad., 1986–87; Mem. Council, RSA, 1988–89, and 1990–; Governor, LSE, 1982–; Trustee, Brooklands Museum, 1987–89. CBIM; FCIM; FIMI; FRSA. *Recreation:* talking shop. *Address:* 83 St George's Road, SE1 6ER. *T:* 071–582 3916. *Clubs:* Reform, British Women Racing Drivers.

DENTON, Dame Catherine Margaret Mary; *see* Scott, Dame M.

DENTON, Charles; Chief Executive, Zenith Productions Ltd, since 1984; Chairman: Action Time Ltd, since 1988; Zenith North Ltd, since 1988; *b* 20 Dec. 1937; *s* of Alan Charles Denton and Mary Frances Royle; *m* 1961, Eleanor Mary Player; one *s* two *d*. *Educ:* Reading Sch.; Bristol Univ. BA History (Hons). Deckhand, 1960; advertising trainee, 1961–63; BBC TV, 1963–68; freelance television producer with Granada, ATV and Yorkshire TV, 1969–70; Dir, Tempest Films Ltd, 1969–71; Man. Dir, Black Lion Films, 1979–81; ATV: Head of Documentaries, 1974–77; Controller of Programmes, 1977–81; Dir of Progs, Central Indep. TV, 1981–84; Dir, Central Indep. Television plc, 1981–87. FRSA 1988; FRTS 1988. *Recreations:* walking, music. *Address:* The Garden House, Norman Court, West Tytherley, near Salisbury, Wilts.

DENTON, Sir Eric (James), Kt 1987; CBE 1974; FRS 1964; ScD; Director, Laboratory of Marine Biological Association, Plymouth, 1974–87; Member, Royal Commission on Environmental Pollution, 1973–76; *b* 30 Sept. 1923; *s* of George Denton and Mary Anne (*née* Ogden); *m* 1946, Nancy Emily, *d* of Charles and Emily Jane Wright; two *s* one *d*. *Educ:* Doncaster Grammar Sch.; St John's Coll., Cambridge. Biophysics Research Unit, University Coll., London, 1946–48; Lectr in Physiology, University of Aberdeen, 1948–56; Physiologist, Marine Biological Assoc. Laboratory, Plymouth, 1956–74; Royal Soc. Res. Professor, Univ. of Bristol, 1964–74, Hon. Professor, 1975. Fellow, University Coll., London, 1965. Hon. Sec., Physiological Soc., 1963–69. Hon. DSc: Exeter, 1976; Göteborg, 1978. Royal Medal, Royal Soc., 1987; Frink Medal, Zool Soc. of London, 1987; International Prize for Biology, Japan Soc. for the Promotion of Science, 1989. *Publications:* Scientific papers in Jl of Marine Biological Assoc., etc. *Recreation:* gardening. *Address:* Fairfield House, St Germans, Saltash, Cornwall PL12 5LS. *T:* St Germans (Cornwall) (0503) 30204; The Laboratory, Citadel Hill, Plymouth PL1 2PB. *T:* Plymouth (0752) 222772.

DENTON, John Grant, OBE 1977; General Secretary, Anglican Church of Australia, since 1969 (part time until 1977); *b* 16 July 1929; *s* of Ernest Bengrey Denton and Gladys Leonard Stevenson; *m* 1956, Shirley Joan Wise; two *s* two *d*. *Educ:* Camberwell C of E Grammar School, Melbourne. Personnel and Industrial Relations Dept, Mobil Oil (Aust.), 1950–54; Administrative Sec., Dio. of Central Tanganyika, as CMS missionary, 1954–64; Dir of Information, Dio. of Sydney, 1964–69; Registrar, Dio. of Sydney, 1969–77 (part time). Mem., ACC, 1976–84 (Chm., 1980–84). *Recreation:* boating. *Address:* 8 Grayling Road, West Pymble, NSW 2073, Australia. *T:* 498 5424 area code (02).

DENTON, Dame Margaret; *see* Scott, Dame M.

DENTON-THOMPSON, Aubrey Gordon, OBE 1958; MC 1942; *b* 6 June 1920; *s* of late M. A. B. Denton-Thompson; *m* 1944, Ruth Cecily Isaac (*d* 1959); two *s* (one *d* decd); *m* 1961, Barbara Mary Wells. *Educ:* Malvern Coll. Served in RA 1940–44; seconded to Basutoland Administration, 1944; apptd to HM Colonial Service, 1945; transferred to Tanganyika as Asst District Officer, 1947; seconded to Colonial Office, 1948–50, District Officer; seconded to Secretariat, Dar es Salaam, as Asst Sec., 1950; Colonial Sec., Falkland Islands, 1955–60; Dep. Permanent Sec., Ministry of Agriculture, Tanganyika, 1960–62; retired from Tanganyika Civil Service, 1963. Man. Dir, Tanganyika Sisal Marketing Assoc. Ltd, 1966–68 (Sec. 1963); Sen. Agricl Advr, UNDP, 1968–78, and FAO Country Rep.: Korea, 1970–73, Indonesia, 1973–76, Turkey, 1976–78; Sen. Advr to Director General, FAO, Rome, July-Dec. 1978; retd Jan. 1979. Chm., New Forest Conservative Assoc., 1985–88 (Dep. Chm., 1983–85). *Address:* Octave Cottage, Ramley Road, Pennington, Lymington, Hants SO41 8GZ. *T:* Lymington (0590) 676626.

DENYER, Roderick Lawrence; QC 1990; a Recorder, since 1990; *b* 1 March 1948; *s* of Oliver James Denyer and Olive Mabel Jones; *m* 1973, Pauline (*née* Vann); two *d*. *Educ:* Grove Park Grammar School for Boys, Wrexham; London School of Economics (LLM). Called to the Bar, Inner Temple, 1970; Lectr in Law, Bristol Univ., 1971–73; in practice at Bar, 1973–. *Publications:* various, in legal jls. *Recreations:* cricket, 19th Century history. *Address:* Devereux Chambers, Devereux Court, Temple, WC2R 3JJ.

DENZA, Mrs Eileen, CMG 1984; Second Counsel to Chairman of Committees and Counsel to European Communities Committee, House of Lords, since 1987; *b* 23 July 1937; *d* of Alexander L. Young and Mrs Young; *m* 1966, John Denza; two *s* one *d*. *Educ:* Aberdeen Univ. (MA); Somerville Coll., Oxford (MA); Harvard Univ. (LLM). Called to the Bar, Lincoln's Inn, 1963. Asst Lectr in Law, Bristol Univ., 1961–63; Asst Legal Adviser, FCO (formerly FO), 1963–74; Legal Counsellor, FCO, 1974–80; Counsellor

(Legal Adviser), Office of UK Perm. Rep. to European Communities, 1980–83; Legal Counsellor, FCO, 1983–86. Pupillage and practice at the Bar, 1986–87. *Publications:* Diplomatic Law, 1976; contribs to: Satow's Guide to Diplomatic Practice, 5th edn; Essays in Air Law; Lee's Consular Law and Practice, 2nd edn; articles in British Yearbook of Internat. Law, Revue du Marché Commun, International and Comparative Law Quarterly. *Recreation:* music making.

de OLLOQUI, Dr José Juan; Eminent Ambassador; Director General, Banca Serfin, Mexico, since 1982; Member Board, Master-Card International, since 1985; Chairman, Board of Carnet of Mexico (Master Card), 1984, 1985, 1987, 1988; *b* 5 Nov. 1931; *m*; three *s* one *d*. *Educ:* Autonomous Univ. of Mexico (LLB 1956, LLD 1979); Univ. of George Washington, Washington, DC (MEc 1970). Official, Bank of Mexico (with license at present), 1951–; Head of Dept of Banking, Currency and Investment, Min. of Finance, 1958–66; Exec. Dir, Interamerican Develt Bank, 1966–71 and also Dep. Dir General for Credit, Min. of Finance, 1966–70; Rep. of Mexico to Exec. Permanent Council of Interamerican Econ. and Social Commn, 1970–71; Chm., Nat. Securities Commn, 1970; Ambassador of Mexico to USA and concurrently Ambassador to Govt of Barbados, 1971–76; Under Sec. of State for Foreign Affairs, 1976–79; Ambassador to UK, 1979–82 and to Ireland, 1980–82. Chm., Euro-Latinamerican Bank, 1982; Mem. Bd of Govs, Central Bank, 1984–. Prof. of History of Economic Thought, Faculty of Law, Nat. Autonomous Univ. of Mexico, 1964 (by open competition), Life Prof., 1966 (Mem. Bd of Trustees, 1983–); Prof. of Internat. Law Research, Sch. of Post-Graduate and PhD Candidates, 1983–; Prof., Nat. Autonomous Univ. of Mexico and Universidad Iberoamericana, on Mexico's Econ. Problems, Econ. Theory and History of Econ. Thought. Pres., Mexico's Nat. Assoc. of Banks, 1984–85; Mem., Bd of several credit instns and official bodies in Mexico, and has represented Mexico, Interamerican Develt Bank and Permanent Council of the Interamerican Econ. and Social Commn at various internat. confs. Pres. and Founder, Miner's Assoc. of Zacatecas, Zac. and Parral, Chihuahua, Mexico, 1963–71. A Vice-Pres., World Food Council. Member: Mexican Lawyer's Bar; Acad. of Political Sciences; Nat. Coll. of Economists; Mexican Acad. of Internat. Law. Dr *hc* in Human Letters St Mary's Coll. 1975. Holds numerous foreign decorations and awards. *Publications:* Mexico fuera de Mexico; Financiamiento Externo y Desarrollo en América Latina; Consideraciones Sobre Dos Gestiones: Servicio Exterior y Banca; several books, articles and bibliographical reviews on legal and econ. matters. *Address:* Banca Serfin, Avenida 16 de Septiembre 38, 06069 Mexico DF, Mexico. *T:* 521 9578 and 518 3284.

de PAULA, (Frederic) Clive, CBE 1970; TD 1950 and Clasp 1951; FCA, JDipMA; Chairman: de Paula Ltd, since 1984; Dennys Sanders & Greene Ltd, since 1987; *b* 17 Nov. 1916; 2nd *s* of late F. R. M. de Paula, CBE, FCA. *Educ:* Rugby Sch.; Spain and France. 2nd Lieut, TA, 1939; Liaison Officer, Free French Forces in London and French Equatorial Africa, 1940; Specially employed Middle East and E Africa, 1941; SOE Madagascar, 1942; comd special unit with 11th E African Div., Ceylon and Burma, 1943; Finance Div., Control Commn, Germany, 1945; demobilised as Major, 1946; Captain 21st Special Air Service Regt (Artists) TA, 1947–56. Joined Robson, Morrow & Co., management consultants, 1946; Partner, 1951; seconded to DEA then to Min. of Technology as an Industrial Adviser, 1967; Co-ordinator of Industrial Advisers to Govt, 1969; returned as Sen. Partner, Robson, Morrow & Co., 1970–71; Man. Dir, Agricultural Mortgage Corp. Ltd, 1971–81; Dir, 1972–83, Dep. Chm., 1978–80, Chm., 1980–83, Tecalemit plc; Non-Exec. Dir, Green's Economiser Group plc, 1972–83; Dep. Chm., C. & J. Clark Ltd, 1985–86. Mem., Inst. of Cost & Works Accountants, 1947–72; Member of Council: British Computer Soc., 1965–68; Management Consultants Assoc., 1970–71; BIM, 1971–76; Mem., EDC for Agriculture, 1972–81. Gen. Comr of Income Tax, Winslow Div., Bucks, 1965–82. Vice Pres., Schoolmistresses and Governesses Benevolent Instn, 1982– (Hon. Treas., 1947–81); Chm., Internat. Wine and Food Soc., 1980–83. *Publications:* Accounts for Management, 1954; (ed) P. Tovey, Balance Sheets: how to read and understand them, 4th edn, 1954; (ed) F.R.M. de Paula, The Principles of Auditing, 12th edn 1957 (trans. Sinhalese, 1967), (with F.A. Attwood) 15th edn as Auditing: Principles and Practice, 1976, (with F. A. Attwood and N. D. Stein) 17th edn as de Paula's Auditing, 1986; Management Accounting in Practice, 1959 (trans. Japanese, 1960); (ed with A. G Russell) A.C. Smith, Internal Control and Audit, 2nd edn, 1968; (with A. W. Willsmore) The Techniques of Business Control, 1973; (with F. A. Attwood) Auditing Standards, 1978. *Address:* c/o National Westminster Bank, 5 Market Place, Glastonbury, Somerset BA6 9HB.

de PEYER, David Charles; Director General, Cancer Research Campaign, since 1984; *b* 25 April 1934; *s* of late Charles de Peyer, CMG and of Flora (*née* Collins); *m* 1959, Ann Harbord. *Educ:* Rendcomb Coll., Cirencester; Magdalen Coll., Oxford (BA PPE). Asst Principal, Min. of Health, 1960; Sec., Royal Commn on NHS, 1976–79; Under Sec., DHSS, 1979–84. *Address:* Cancer Research Campaign, 2 Carlton House Terrace, SW1.

de PEYER, Gervase; Solo Clarinettist; Conductor; Founder and Conductor, The Melos Sinfonia; Founder Member, The Melos Ensemble of London; Director, London Symphony Wind Ensemble; Associate Conductor, Haydn Orchestra of London; solo clarinettist, Chamber Music Society of Lincoln Center, New York, since 1969; Resident Conductor, Victoria International Festival, BC, Canada: Co-founder and Artistic Director, Innisfree Music Festival, Pa, USA; *b* London, 11 April 1926; *m* 1980, Katia Perret Aubry. *Educ:* King Alfred's, London; Bedales; Royal College of Music. Served HM Forces, 1945 and 1946. Principal Clarinet, London Symphony Orchestra, 1955–72. ARCM; Hon. ARAM. Gold Medallist, Worshipful Co. of Musicians, 1948; Charles Gros Grand Prix du Disque, 1961, 1962; Plaque of Honour for recording, Acad. of Arts and Sciences of America, 1962. Most recorded solo clarinettist in world. *Recreations:* travel, cooking, kite-flying, sport, theatre. *Address:* Porto Vecchio #109, 1250 S Washington Street, Alexandria, Va 22314, USA. *T:* 703 7390824.

de PIRO, His Honour Alan C. H., QC 1965; FCIArb 1978; a Circuit Judge, 1983–91; *e s* of late J. W. de Piro; *m* 1947, Mary Elliot (deceased); two *s*; *m* 1964, Mona Addington; one step *s* one step *d*. *Educ:* Repton; Trinity Hall, Cambridge (Sen. Scholar). MA 1947 (Nat. Sci. and Law). Royal Artillery, 1940–45 (Capt.); West Africa. Called to Bar, Middle Temple, 1947; Inner Temple, 1962; Bencher, Middle Temple, 1971, Reader, 1988; in practice at the Bar, London and Midlands, 1947–83; Deputy Chairman: Beds QS, 1966–71; Warwicks QS, 1967–71; a Recorder of the Crown Court, 1972–83. Member: Gen. Council of the Bar, 1961–65, 1966–70, 1971–73; Senate of the Inns of Court and the Bar, 1976–81; Council Internat. Bar Assoc., 1967–86 (Chm., Human Rights Cttee, 1979–82); Editorial Advisory Cttee, Law Guardian, 1965–73; Law Panel British Council, 1967–74. Vice-Pres., L'Union Internat. des Avocats, 1968–73, Co-Pres., 1969. Legal Assessor, Disciplinary Cttee, RCVS, 1970–83. *Recreations:* conversation, gardening, inland waterways. *Address:* The Toll House, Bascote Locks, near Leamington, Warwicks CV33 0DT; 23 Birmingham Road, Stoneleigh, Warwicks. *Club:* Hawks (Cambridge).

de POSADAS, Dr Luis María; Associate Professor, University of Bordeaux, 1988–89; Ambassador of Uruguay to the Court of St James's, 1983–87; *b* 25 June 1927; *s* of Dr Gervasio de Posadas Belgrano and Maria Elena Montero; *m* 1952, Sara Mañe-Garzon; one *s* three *d*. *Educ:* Montevideo Univ., Uruguay. Lawyer. Mem., Chamber of Deputies, 1959–63; Sec., National Govt Council, 1963–65; Ambassador to: Spain, 1965–72; USSR, 1972–76; the Argentine, 1978–80; Dir, Dept of Pol Affairs, Min. of Foreign Affairs, Montevideo, 1981–83. Mem., 1981–87, Vice-Pres., 1986–87, Admin Tribunal of UN. Comdr, Legion of Honour, France, 1964; Grand Cross: Order of the Brilliant Star, China, 1962; Order of St Gregory the Great, The Vatican, 1963; Order of Merit, Malta, 1963; Order of Isabel the Catholic, Spain, 1972; Order of May, Argentina, 1978; Grand Officer: Order of the Southern Cross, Brazil, 1963; Order of Merit, Republic of Italy, 1964. *Publications:* works on internat. law. *Recreations:* literature, golf. *Address:* Espronceda 38, Madrid, Spain.

DERAMORE, 6th Baron *cr* 1885; **Richard Arthur de Yarburgh-Bateson,** Bt 1818; Chartered Architect, retired; *b* 9 April 1911; *s* of 4th Baron Deramore and of Muriel Katherine (*née* Duncombe); *S* brother, 1964; *m* 1948, Janet Mary, *d* of John Ware, MD, Askham-in-Furness, Lancs; one *d*. *Educ:* Harrow; St John's Coll., Cambridge. AA Diploma, 1935; MA Cantab 1936; ARIBA 1936. Served as Navigator, RAFVR, 1940–45: 14 Sqdn, RAF, 1942–44 and 1945. County Architect's Dept, Herts, 1949–52. Member: Council, Queen Mary Sch., Duncombe Park, Helmsley, 1977–85; Management Cttee, Purey Cust Nursing Home, York, 1976–84; Governor, Heslington Sch., York, 1965–88. Fellow, Woodard Schs (Northern Div.) Ltd, 1978–84. *Publications:* freelance articles and short stories. *Recreations:* walking, cycling, motoring, water-colour painting. *Heir:* none. *Address:* Heslington House, Aislaby, Pickering, North Yorks YO18 8PE. *Clubs:* Royal Air Force, Royal Automobile.

DE RAMSEY, 3rd Baron *cr* 1887; **Ailwyn Edward Fellowes,** KBE 1974; TD; DL; Captain RA; Lord Lieutenant of Huntingdon and Peterborough, 1965–68 (of Hunts, 1947–65); *b* 16 March 1910; *s* of late Hon. Coulson Churchill Fellowes and Gwendolen Dorothy, *d* of H. W. Jefferson; *S* grandfather, 1925; *m* 1937, Lilah (*d* 1987), *d* of Frank Labouchere, 15 Draycott Avenue, SW; two *s* two *d*. Served War of 1939–45 (prisoner, Far East). Pres. Country Landowners' Assoc., Sept. 1963–65. Awarded KBE 1974 for services to agriculture. DL Hunts and Peterborough, 1973, Cambs 1974. *Heir: s* Hon. John Ailwyn Fellowes [*b* 27 Feb. 1942; *m* 1st, 1973, Phyllida Mary (marr. diss. 1983), *d* of Dr Philip A. Forsyth, Newmarket, Suffolk; one *s*; 2nd, 1984, Alison Mary, *er d* of Archibald Birkmyre, Hebron Cottage, West Ilsley Berks; one *s* two *d*]. *Address:* Abbots Ripton Hall, Huntingdon. *T:* Abbots Ripton 234. *Club:* Buck's.

See also Lord Fairhaven.

DERBY, 18th Earl of *cr* 1485; **Edward John Stanley,** MC 1944; DL; Bt 1627; Baron Stanley 1832; Baron Stanley of Preston, 1886; Major late Grenadier Guards; Constable of Lancaster Castle, since 1972; *b* 21 April 1918; *s* of Lord Stanley, PC, MC (*d* 1938), and Sibyl Louise Beatrix Cadogan (*d* 1969), *e d* of Henry Arthur, late Viscount Chelsea, and Lady Meux; *g s* of 17th Earl of Derby, KG, PC, GCB, GCVO; *S* grandfather, 1948; *m* 1948, Lady Isabel Milles-Lade (*d* 1990), *yr d* of late Hon. Henry Milles-Lade, and sister of 4th Earl Sondes. *Educ:* Eton; Oxford Univ. Left Army with rank of Major, 1946. President: Merseyside Chamber of Commerce, 1972–; Liverpool Chamber of Commerce, 1948–71; NW Area Conservative Assoc., 1969–72. Pro-Chancellor, Lancaster Univ., 1964–71. Lord Lieut and Custos Rotulorum of Lancaster, 1951–68. Alderman, Lancashire CC, 1968–74. Commanded 5th Bn The King's Regt, TA, 1947–51, Hon. Col, 1951–67; Hon. Captain, RNR (Mersey Div., 1955–90); Hon. Colonel: 1st Bn The Liverpool Scottish Regt, TA, 1964–67; Lancastrian Volunteers, 1967–75; 5th/8th (V) Bn The King's Regt, 1975–88; 4th (V) Bn The Queen's Lancashire Regt, 1975–86; Chm., NW of England and IoM TAVR Assoc., 1979–83. President: Rugby Football League, 1948–; Professional Golfers' Assoc., 1964–. DL Lancs 1946. Hon. LLD: Liverpool, 1949; Lancaster, 1972. Hon. Freeman, City of Manchester, 1961. *Heir: nephew* Edward Richard William Stanley, *b* 10 Oct. 1962. *Address:* Knowsley, Prescot, Merseyside L34 4AF. *T:* 051–489 6147; Stanley House, Newmarket, Suffolk. *T:* Newmarket 663011. *Clubs:* White's; Jockey (Newmarket).

DERBY, Bishop of, since 1988; **Rt. Rev. Peter Spencer Dawes;** *b* 1928; *s* of Jason Spencer Dawes and Janet Dawes; *m* 1954, Ethel Marrin; two *s* two *d*. *Educ:* Bickley Hall School; Aldenham School; Hatfield Coll., Durham (BA); Tyndale Hall, Bristol. Assistant Curate: St Andrew's, Whitehall Park, 1954–57; St Ebbe's, Oxford, 1957–60; Tutor, Clifton Theological Coll., 1960–65; Vicar, Good Shepherd, Romford, 1965–80; Archdeacon of West Ham, 1980–88. Examining Chaplain to Bishop of Chelmsford, 1970–. Member, General Synod, 1970–. *Address:* The Bishop's House, 6 King Street, Duffield, Derby DE6 4EU.

DERBY, Provost of; *see* Lewers, Very Rev. B. H.

DERBY, Archdeacon of; *see* Dell, Ven. R. S.

DERBYSHIRE, Sir Andrew (George), Kt 1986; FRIBA, FCSD; Chairman, Robert Matthew, Johnson-Marshall & Partners, London; President, RMJM Ltd; *b* 7 Oct. 1923; *s* of late Samuel Reginald Derbyshire and late Helen Louise Puleston Derbyshire (*née* Clarke); *m*, Lily Rhodes (*née* Binns), *widow* of late Norman Rhodes; three *s* one *d*. *Educ:* Chesterfield Grammar Sch.; Queens' Coll., Cambridge; Architectural Assoc. MA (Cantab), AA Dip. (Hons). Admty Signals Estabt and Bldg Research Station, 1943–46. Farmer & Dark, 1951–53 (Marchwood and Belvedere power stations); West Riding County Architect's Dept, 1953–55 (bldgs for educn and social welfare). Asst City Architect, Sheffield, 1955–61; responsible for co-ord. of central area redevelt. Mem. Research Team, RIBA Survey of Architects' Offices, 1960–62. Since 1961, as Mem. RM, J-M & Partners, later RMJM Ltd, responsible for: develt of Univ. of York, Central Lancs New Town, NE Lancs Impact Study, Univ. of Cambridge, West Cambridge Develt and New Cavendish Laboratory, Preston Market and Guildhall, London Docklands Study, Hillingdon Civic Centre, Cabtrack and Minitram feasibility studies, Suez Master Plan Study; Castle Peak Power Stations, and Harbour Reclamation and Urban Growth Study, Hong Kong. Member: RIBA Council, 1950–72, 1975–81 (Senior Vice-Pres., 1980); NJCC, 1961–65; Bldg Industry Communications Res. Cttee, 1964–66 (Chm. Steering Cttee); DoE Planning and Transport Res. Adv. Council, 1971–76; Standing Commn on Energy and the Environment, 1978–. Pt-time Mem., 1973–84, CEGB; Board Member: Property Services Agency, 1975–79; London Docklands Develt Corp., 1984–88; Construction Industry Sector Group, NEDC, 1988–; Mem., Construction Industry Council, 1990–. Hoffman Wood Prof. of Architecture, Univ. of Leeds, 1978–80; External Prof., Dept of Civil Engineering, Univ. of Leeds, 1981–85; Gresham Prof. of Rhetoric, Gresham Coll., 1990–. FRSA 1981. DUniv York, 1972. *Publication:* (jtly) The Architect and his Office, 1962. *Recreation:* his family. *Address:* 4 Sunnyfield, Hatfield, Herts AL9 5DX. *T:* Hatfield (0707) 265903; 83 Paul Street, EC2A 4NQ. *T:* 071–251 5588.

DERHAM, Sir Peter (John), Kt 1980; FAIM; FPIA; FInstD; Chairman: Robert Bryce & Co. Ltd, since 1982; Circadian Technologies Ltd (formerly Circadian Pharmaceuticals Ltd), since 1984; Leasing Corporation Ltd, since 1987; *b* 21 Aug. 1925; *s* of John and Mary Derham; *m* 1950, Averil C. Wigan; two *s* one *d*. *Educ:* Melbourne Church of England Grammar School; Univ. of Melbourne (BSc 1958); Harvard Univ. (Advanced Management Programme). Served RAAF and RAN, 1944–46. Joined Moulded Products (Australasia) Ltd (later Nylex Corp.), 1943; Dir, 1953–82, Sales Dir, 1960, Gen. Manager,

1967, Man. Dir, 1972–80. Chairman: Internat. Pacific Corp. Ltd, later Rothschild Australia Ltd, 1981–85; Australia New Zealand Foundn, 1978–83; Australian Canned Fruits Corp., 1981–89; Davy McKee Pacific Pty, 1984–90; Dep. Chm., Australian Mutual Provident Soc. State Bd of Advice, 1990– (Dir, Vic Br. Bd, 1974–90); Director: Lucas Industries Aust., 1981–84; Prime Computer of Australia Ltd, 1986–; Station 3XY Pty, 1980–87; Radio 3XY Pty, 1980–87; Advance Australia Foundn, 1983–; Jt Chm., Advance Australia America Cup Challenge Ltd, 1981–83; Councillor Enterprise Australia, 1975–82 (Dep. Chm., 1975–78). Chairman: Nat. Training Council, 1971–80; Adv. Bd, CSIRO, 1981–86; Australian Tourist Commn, 1981–85; Member: Manufg Industries Adv. Council, 1971–74; Victorian Econ. Develt Corp., 1981–82. Federal Pres., Inst. of Directors in Australia, 1980–82 (Mem., 1975–89, Chm., 1975–82, Victorian Council; Life Mem., 1986) Councillor: Yooralla Soc. of Victoria, 1972–79 (Chm. Workshops Cttee, 1972–81); Aust. Industries Develt Assoc., 1975–80; State Councillor, Industrial Design Council, 1967–73, Federal Councillor, 1970–73; Mem. Council, Inst. of Public Affairs, 1971–; Life Mem., Plastics Inst. of Australia Inc. (Victorian Pres., 1964–66; Nat. Pres., 1971–72); Mem. Board of Advisors, Inst. of Cultural Affairs, 1971–81. Member: Rotary Club of Melbourne (Mem., Bd of Dirs, 1974–75, 1975–76); Victorian State Cttee, Child Accident Prevention Foundn of Australia; Appeal Cttee, Royal Victorian Eye and Ear Hosp.; Bd of Management, Alfred Hosp., 1980–87, Amalgamated Alfred, Caulfield and Royal Southern Meml Hosp., 1987–; OStJ Ambulance, 1988– (Chm., State Council, 1991–); Chm., Caulfield Hosp. Cttee, 1984–87 (Dir, 1981–87; Vice Pres., 1989). President: Alcohol and Drug Foundn (formerly Victorian Foundn on Alcoholism and Drug Dependence), 1986– (Appeal Chm., 1981–86); Victorian Soc. for Prevention of Child Abuse and Neglect, 1987–; Dep Chm., Australian Assoc. for Support of Educn, 1983–; Mem., Melbourne C of E Grammar Sch. Council, 1974–75, 1977–80; Pres., Old Melburnians, 1974–75; Governor, Ian Clunies Ross Meml Foundn, 1979–; Chairman: Trade & Industry Cttee, Victoria's 150th Anniv. Celebration; Police Toy Fund for Underprivileged Children; Pres., Somers Area, Boy Scout Assoc. of Australia, 1985–90; Vict. Trustee, Australian Koala Foundn Inc., 1986–; Trustee, H & L Hecht Trust, 1990–; Life Governor, Assoc. for the Blind. *Recreations:* golf, sailing, tennis, gardening, viticulture. *Address:* 2A Ashley Grove, Malvern, Vic 3144, Australia. *T:* (03) 822 0770. *Clubs:* Australian, Melbourne (Melbourne); Royal Melbourne Golf, Flinders Golf, Royal South Yarra Lawn Tennis, Melbourne Cricket.

DERMOTT, William, CB 1984; Under Secretary, Head of Agricultural Science Service, Agricultural Development and Advisory Service, Ministry of Agriculture, Fisheries and Food, 1976–84, retired; *b* 27 March 1924; *s* of William and Mary Dermott; *m* 1946, Winifred Joan Tinney; one *s* one *d*. *Educ:* Univ. of Durham. BSc, MSc. Agricl Chemist, Univ. of Durham and Wye Coll., Univ. of London, 1943–46; Soil Scientist, Min. of Agriculture, at Wye, Bangor and Wolverhampton, 1947–70; Sen. Sci. Specialist, and Dep. Chief Sci. Specialist, MAFF, 1971–76; Actg Dir Gen., ADAS, 1983–84. Pres., British Soc. of Soil Science, 1981–82. *Publications:* papers on various aspects of agricultural chemistry in scientific journals. *Recreations:* gardening, the countryside. *Address:* 22 Chequers Park, Wye, Ashford, Kent TN25 5BB. *T:* Wye (0233) 812694.

de ROS, 28th Baron *cr* 1264 (Premier Barony of England); **Peter Trevor Maxwell;** *b* 23 Dec. 1958; *s* of Comdr John David Maxwell, RN, and late Georgiana Angela Maxwell, 27th Baroness de Ros; *S* mother, 1983; *m* 1987, Siân Ross; one *s* one *d*. *Educ:* Headfort School, Kells, Co. Meath; Stowe School, Bucks; Down High School, Co. Down. Upholsterer furniture maker. *Recreations:* gardening, travel and sailing. *Heir:* *s* Hon. Finbar James Maxwell, *b* 14 Nov. 1988.

de ROTHSCHILD; *see* Rothschild.

DERRETT, Prof. (John) Duncan (Martin), MA, PhD, DCL, LLD, DD; Professor of Oriental Laws in the University of London, 1965–82, now Emeritus; *b* 30 Aug. 1922; *s* of John West Derrett and Fay Frances Ethel Kate (*née* Martin); *m* 1950, Margaret Esmé Griffiths; four *s* one *d*. *Educ:* Emanuel Sch., London; Jesus Coll., Oxford; Sch. of Oriental and Afr. Studies, London; Inns of Court School of Law. MA 1947, DCL 1966 (Oxon); PhD 1949, LLD 1971, DD 1983 (London). Called to the Bar, Gray's Inn, 1953. Lectr in Hindu Law, SOAS, 1949; Reader in Oriental Laws, 1956, Prof. of Oriental Laws, 1965, Univ. of London; Tagore Prof. of Law, Univ. of Calcutta, 1953 (lectures delivered, 1955); Vis. Professor: Univ. of Chicago, 1963; Univ. of Michigan, 1970; Wilde Lectr in Natural and Compar. Religion, Univ. of Oxford, 1978–81; Japan Soc. Prom. Sci. Fellow and Vis. Prof., Oriental Inst., Univ. of Tokyo, 1982. Fellow, Indian Law Inst., Delhi, 1988. Mem., editorial bd, Zeitschrift für vergleichende Rechtswissenschaft, 1954, subseq. of Kannada Studies, Bharata Manisha, Kerala Law Times. Mem. Selection Cttee, Fac. of Law, Univs of Dacca and Rajshahi, 1978–. Mem., Stud. Novi Test. Soc., 1971. Barcelona Prize in Comparative Law, 1954; N. C. Sen-Gupta Gold Medal, Asiatic Soc. (Calcutta), 1977. *Publications:* The Hoysalas, 1957; Hindu Law Past and Present, 1957; Introduction to Modern Hindu Law, 1963; Religion, Law and the State in India, 1968; Critique of Modern Hindu Law, 1970; Law in the New Testament, 1970; Jesus's Audience, 1973; Dharmaśāstra and Juridical Literature, 1973; History of Indian Law (Dharmaśāstra), 1973; Henry Swinburne (?1551–1624) Civil Lawyer of York, 1973; Bhāruci's Commentary on the Manusmrti, 1975; Essays in Classical and Modern Hindu Law, vols I-IV, 1976–79; Studies in the New Testament, vols I-V, 1977–89; The Death of a Marriage Law, 1978; Beiträge zu Indischem Rechtsdenken, 1979; The Anastasis: the Resurrection of Jesus as an Historical Event, 1982; A Textbook for Novices: Jayarakshita's Perspicuous Commentary on the 'Compendium of Conduct', 1983; The Making of Mark, 1985; New Resolutions of Old Conundrums: a fresh insight into Luke's Gospel, 1986; The Ascetic Discourse: an explanation of the Sermon on the Mount, 1989; trans. R. Lingat, Classical Law of India, 1973; ed, Studies in the Laws of Succession in Nigeria, 1965; ed, Introduction to Legal Systems, 1968; ed, (with W. D. O'Flaherty) The Concept of Duty in South Asia, 1978; collab. with Yale Edn, Works of St Thomas More, Société Jean Bodin, Brussels, Max Planck Inst., Hamburg, Fritz Thyssen Stiftung, Cologne, Institut für Soziologie, Heidelberg, and Sekai Kyusei Kyo, Atami. *Festschriften:* Indology and Law, 1982; Novum Testamentum, 24, 1982, fasc. 3 and foll. *Recreations:* listening to music, gardening, clocks. *Address:* Half Way House, High Street, Blockley, Moreton-in-Marsh, Glos GL56 9EX. *T:* Blockley (0386) 700828.

DERRICK, Patricia, (Mrs Donald Derrick); *see* Lamburn, P.

DERRY AND RAPHOE, Bishop of, since 1980; **Rt. Rev. James Mehaffey;** *b* 29 March 1931; *s* of John and Sarah Mehaffey; *m* 1956, Thelma P. L. Jackson; two *s* one *d*. *Educ:* Trinity College, Dublin (MA, BD); Queen's University, Belfast (PhD). Curate Assistant: St Patrick's, Belfast, 1954–56; St John's, Deptford, London, 1956–58; Minor Canon, Down Cathedral, 1958–60; Bishop's Curate, St Christopher's, Belfast, 1960–62; Incumbent: Kilkeel, Diocese of Dromore, 1962–66; Cregagh, Diocese of Down, 1966–80. *Address:* The See House, Culmore Road, Londonderry BT48 8JF. *T:* Londonderry (0504) 351206.

DERRY, Thomas Kingston, OBE 1976; Kt, Order of St Olav, Norway, 1981; MA, DPhil Oxon; *b* 5 March 1905; *y s* of late Rev. W. T. Derry, Wesleyan Minister; *m* 1930, Gudny (*d* 1989), *e d* of late Hjalmar Wesenberg, Commander of Order of Vasa, Oslo, Norway. *Educ:* Kingswood Sch., Bath; Queen's Coll., Oxford (Bible Clerk and Taberdar). 1st Class, Classical Moderations, 1925; 1st Class, Final Sch. of Modern History, 1927; Senior George Webb Medley Scholar, 1927; Gladstone Prizeman, 1928; Sixth Form Master and Chief History Master, Repton Sch., 1929–37; Headmaster, Mill Hill School, 1938–40; Political Intelligence Dept of Foreign Office, 1941–45 (Chief Intelligence Officer, Scandinavia); Asst Master, St Marylebone Grammar Sch., 1945–65; Visiting Prof., Wheaton Coll., Mass, 1961–62. *Publications:* (with T. L. Jarman) The European World, 1950, rev. and extended edn 1975; The Campaign in Norway (official military history), 1952; A Short History of Norway, 1957; (with T. I. Williams) A Short History of Technology, 1960; The United Kingdom Today, 1961; A Short Economic History of Britain, 1965; (with E. J. Knapton) Europe 1815–1914, 1965; Europe 1914 to the Present, 1966; (with T. L. Jarman and M. G. Blakeway) The Making of Britain, 3 vols, 1956–69; A History of Modern Norway, 1814–1972, 1973; A History of Scandinavia, 1979; (with T. L. Jarman) Modern Britain, 1979. *Address:* Nils Lauritssons vei 27, 0854 Oslo 8, Norway. *T:* (02) 231432.

DERVAIRD, Hon Lord; John Murray; Dickson Minto Professor of Company and Commercial Law, Edinburgh University, since 1990; a Senator of the College of Justice in Scotland, 1988–89; *b* 8 July 1935; *o s* of J. H. Murray, farmer, Stranraer; *m* 1960, Bridget Jane, *d* of Sir William Godfrey, 7th Bt, and of Lady Godfrey; three *s*. *Educ:* Stranraer schs; Edinburgh Academy; Corpus Christi Coll., Oxford (BA 1st cl. Lit. Hum., 1959); Edinburgh Univ. (LLB 1962). Advocate, 1962; QC (Scot.) 1974. Mem., Scottish Law Commn, 1979–88. Chairman: Scottish Lawyers' European Gp, 1975–78; Scottish Council of Law Reporting, 1978–88; Scottish Cttee on Law of Arbitration, 1986–; Scottish Council for Arbitration, 1989–; Vice-President: Agricultural Law Assoc., 1985–91 (Chm., 1979–85); Comité Européen de Droit Rural, 1989–. Hon. Pres., Advocates' Business Law Group, 1988–. Dir and Chm., Scottish Ensemble Ltd, 1988–. *Publications:* (contrib.) Festschrift für Dr Pikalo, 1979; (contrib.) Mélanges offert à Jean Megret, 1985; (contrib.) Encyclopedia of Scots Law, 1987; articles in legal and ornithological jls. *Recreations:* farming, gardening, birdwatching, music, curling, field sports. *Address:* 4 Moray Place, Edinburgh EH3 6DS. *T:* 031–225 1881; Fell Cottage, Craigcaffie, Stranraer. *T:* Stranraer 3356; Wood of Dervaird Farm, Glenluce. *T:* Glenluce (05813) 222. *Clubs:* New, Puffins (Edinburgh).

DERWENT, 5th Baron *cr* 1881; **Robin Evelyn Leo Vanden-Bempde-Johnstone,** LVO 1957; Bt 1795; DL; Managing Director, Hutchison Whampoa (Europe) Ltd, since 1985; Director: Tanks Consolidated Investments PLC, since 1983; Genfin Ltd, since 1986; F&C (Pacific) Investment Trust Ltd, since 1989; *b* 30 Oct. 1930; *s* of 4th Baron Derwent, CBE and Marie-Louise (*d* 1985), *d* of Albert Picard, Paris; *S* father, 1986; *m* 1957, Sybille, *d* of late Vicomte de Simard de Pitray and Madame Jeanine Hennessy; one *s* three *d*. *Educ:* Winchester College; Clare Coll., Cambridge (Scholar, MA 1953). 2nd Lieut 1949, 60th Rifles; Lieut 1950, Queen Victoria's Rifles (TA). HM Diplomatic Service, 1954–69; served FO, Paris, Mexico City, Washington. Director, NM Rothschild & Sons, Merchant Bankers, 1969–85. Chm., London & Provincial Antique Dealers' Assoc., 1989–. DL N Yorks, 1991. Chevalier de la Légion d'Honneur (France), 1957; Officier de l'Ordre National du Mérite (France), 1978. *Recreations:* shooting, fishing. *Heir:* *s* Hon. Francis Patrick Harcourt Vanden-Bempde-Johnstone [*b* 23 Sept. 1965; *m* 1990, Cressida, *o d* of Christopher John Bourke, *qv*]. *Address:* Hackness Hall, Hackness, Scarborough; 30 Kelso Place, W8 5QG. *Clubs:* Boodle's, Beefsteak.

DERX, Donald John, CB 1975; non-executive Director, Glaxo Holdings plc, since 1991; *b* 25 June 1928; *s* of John Derx and Violet Ivy Stroud; *m* 1956, Luisa Donzelli; two *s* two *d*. *Educ:* Tiffin Boys' Sch., Kingston-on-Thames; St Edmund Hall, Oxford (BA). Asst Principal, BoT, 1951; seconded to Cabinet Office, 1954–55; Principal, Colonial Office, 1957; Asst Sec., Industrial Policy Gp, DEA, 1965; Dir, Treasury Centre for Admin. Studies, 1968; Head of London Centre, Civil Service Coll., 1970; Under Sec., 1971–72, Dep. Sec., 1972–84, Dept of Employment; Dir, Policy Studies Inst., 1985–86; with Glaxo Holdings plc, 1986–.

DESAI, family name of **Baron Desai**.

DESAI, Baron *cr* 1991 (Life Peer), of St Clement Danes in the City of Westminster; **Meghnad Jagdishchandra Desai,** PhD; Professor of Economics, London School of Economics and Political Science, since 1983; Head of Development Studies Institute, since 1990; *b* 10 July 1940; *s* of late Jagdishchandra and of Mandakini Desai; *m* 1970, Gail Graham Wilson; one *s* two *d*. *Educ:* Univ. of Bombay (BA Hons, MA); Univ. of Pennsylvania (PhD 1964). Associate Specialist, Dept of Agricultural Econs, Univ. of Calif, Berkeley, 1963–65; Dept of Econs, London Sch. of Econs and Pol Science: Lectr, 1965–77; Sen. Lectr, 1977–80; Reader, 1980–83. Pres., Assoc. of Univ. Teachers in Econs, 1987–90; Mem. Council, REconS, 1988. Chm., Islington South and Finsbury Constituency Labour Pty, 1986–. *Publications:* Marxian Economic Theory, 1974; Applied Econometrics, 1976; Marxian Economics, 1979; Testing Monetarism, 1981; (Asst Editor to Prof. Dharma Kumar) The Cambridge Economic History of India 1757–1970, 1983; (ed jtly) Agrarian Power and Agricultural Productivity in South Asia, 1984; (ed) Lenin on Economics, 1987; contrib. Econometrica, Econ. Jl, Rev. of Econ. Studies, Economica, Econ. Hist. Rev. *Address:* London School of Economics and Political Science, Houghton Street, Aldwych, WC2A 2AE.

DESAI, Anita; novelist; *b* 24 June 1937; *d* of Toni Nimé and D. N. Mazumbar; *m* 1958, Ashvin Desai; two *s* two *d*. *Educ:* Queen Mary's Sch., Delhi; Miranda House, Univ. of Delhi (BA Hons). First story published 1946; novelist and book reviewer (freelance), 1963–. Fellow, Girton Coll., Univ. of Cambridge. Elizabeth Drew Prof., Smith Coll., USA, 1987–88; Purington Prof. of English, Mount Holyoke Coll., USA, 1988–. Winifred Holtby Award, RSL, 1978; Guardian Prize for Children's Fiction, 1983; Hadassah Prize, 1989. Padma Sri, 1989. *Publications:* Cry, The Peacock, 1963; Voices in the City, 1965; Bye-Bye Blackbird, 1971; Where Shall We Go This Summer?, 1973; Fire on the Mountain, 1978; Games at Twilight, 1979; Clear Light of Day, 1980; The Village by the Sea, 1983; In Custody, 1984; Baumgartner's Bombay, 1988. *Address:* c/o Deborah Rogers Ltd, 20 Powis Mews, W11 1JN.

DESAI, Shri Morarji Ranchhodji, BA; Prime Minister of India, 1977–79; *b* Bhadeli, Gujarat, 29 Feb. 1896; *e s* of Shri Ranchhodji and Smt. Vajiyaben Desai. *Educ:* Wilson Coll., Bombay; Univ. of Bombay. Entered Provincial Civil Service of Govt of Bombay, 1918; resigned to join the Civil Disobedience Campaign of Mahatma Gandhi, 1930; convicted for taking part in the Movement during 1930–34; Sec., Gujarat Pradesh Congress Cttee, 1931–37 and 1939–46; Minister for Revenue, Co-operation, Agriculture and Forests, Bombay, 1937–39; convicted, 1940–41, and detained in prison, 1942–45; Minister for Home and Revenue, Bombay, 1946–52; Chief Minister of Bombay, 1952–56; Mem., 2nd, 3rd and 4th Lok Sabha, 1957–70; Minister of Commerce and Industry, Government of India, 1956–58; Treasurer, All India Congress Cttee, 1950–58; Minister of Finance, Government of India, 1958–63, resigned from Govt (under plan to strengthen Congress) Aug. 1963; Chm., Administrative Reforms Commn, Govt of India,

1966; Dep. Prime Minister and Minister of Finance, Government of India, 1967–69; Chm., Parly Gp, Congress Party (Opposition), 1969–77; elected to 5th Lok Sabha, 1971–79; detained in solitary confinement, 1975–77, under State of Emergency; Founder-Chairman, Janata Party, 1977. Hon. Fellow, College of Physicians and Surgeons, Bombay, 1956; Hon. LLD Karnatak Univ., 1957. *Publications:* books include: A View of the Gita; In My View; A Minister and His Responsibilities (Jawaharlal Nehru Meml Lectures); The Story of My Life (2 vols), 1978; Indian Unity: From Dream to Reality (Patel Meml Lectures); book on Nature Cure. *Recreations:* spinning on Charkha; follower of sport and classical Indian dancing. *Address:* 1 Safdarjung Road, New Delhi 110001, India; Oceana, Marine Drive, Bombay 400020, India.

DE ST JORRE, Danielle Marie-Madeleine J.; *see* Jorre De St Jorre.

de STE. CROIX, Geoffrey Ernest Maurice, DLitt; FBA 1972; Fellow and Tutor in Ancient History, New College, Oxford, 1953–77, Emeritus Fellow, 1977, Hon. Fellow, 1985; *b* 8 Feb. 1910; *s* of Ernest Henry de Ste Croix and Florence Annie (*née* Macgowan); *m* 1st, 1932, Lucile (marr. diss. 1959); one *d* (decd); 2nd, 1959, Margaret Knight; two *s*. *Educ:* Clifton Coll. (to 1925); University Coll. London (1946–50) (Fellow, 1987). BA 1st cl. Hons History, London, 1949; MA Oxon, 1953; DLitt Oxon, 1978. Solicitor, 1931. Served War, RAF, 1940–46. Asst Lectr in Ancient Economic History, London Sch. of Economics, and Part-time Lectr in Ancient History, Birkbeck Coll., London, 1950–53. Vis. Prof., Univ. of Amsterdam, 1978. Lectures include: J. H. Gray, Cambridge Univ., 1972–73; Gregynog, UCW, Aberystwyth, 1986; Townsend, Cornell Univ., 1988; has given many other lectures in Europe and N America. *Publications:* The Origins of the Peloponnesian War, 1972; The Class Struggle in the Ancient Greek World, from the Archaic Age to the Arab Conquests, 1981 (Isaac Deutscher Meml Prize, 1982; Spanish edn 1988; Greek edn 1991); contributions to: Studies in the History of Accounting, 1956; The Crucible of Christianity, 1969; Studies in Ancient Society, 1974; Debits, Credits, Finance and Profits, 1974; articles and reviews in various learned jls. *Recreations:* listening to music, walking. *Address:* Evenlode, Stonesfield Lane, Charlbury, Oxford OX7 3ER. *T:* Charlbury (0608) 810453.

de SAUMAREZ, 7th Baron *cr* 1831; **Eric Douglas Saumarez;** Bt 1801; farmer; *b* 13 Aug. 1956; *s* of 6th Baron de Saumarez and Joan Beryl, (Julia), *d* of late Douglas Raymond Charlton; *S* father, 1991; *m* 1982, Christine Elizabeth (marr. diss. 1990), *yr d* of B. N. Halliday; two *d*. *Educ:* Milton Abbey; Nottingham Univ.; RAC, Cirencester. *Recreations:* flying, shooting, ski-ing, fishing. *Heir:* *twin b* Hon. Victor Thomas Saumarez, *b* 13 Aug. 1956. *Address:* Shrubland Park, Coddenham, Ipswich, Suffolk.

de SAVARY, Peter John; international entrepreneur; *b* 11 July 1944; *m* 1986, (Lucille) Lana Paton; two *d* (and two *d* by a former marriage). *Educ:* Charterhouse. Activities in the energy, property, finance, maritime and leisure fields. Chm., Victory Syndicate, 1983 British Challenge for America's Cup. Tourism Personality of the Year, English Tourist Bd, 1988. *Recreations:* sailing, riding, carriage driving. *Address:* Littlecote House, Hungerford, Berks. *Clubs:* St James's, Royal Automobile, Royal Thames Yacht; Royal Burnham Yacht, Royal Torbay Yacht, Royal Corinthian Yacht, Port Pendennis Yacht (Cdre).

DESCH, Stephen Conway; QC 1980; a Recorder of the Crown Court, since 1979; *b* 17 Nov. 1939; *o s* of Harold Ernest Desch and Gwendolen Lucy Desch; *m* 1973, Julia Beatrice Little; two *d*. *Educ:* Dauntsey's Sch.; Magdalen Coll., Oxford (BCL, MA); Northwestern Univ., Chicago. Called to the Bar, Gray's Inn, 1962, Bencher, 1989; joined Midland Circuit, 1964. Lectr in Law, Magdalen Coll., Oxford, 1963–65. *Publication:* Legal Notes to H. E. Desch: Structural Surveying, 1970, 2nd edn (with Stephen Mika), 1988. *Recreations:* country pursuits, farming, mountain walking. *Address:* 2 Crown Office Row, Temple, EC4Y 7HJ. *T:* 071–353 9337.

de SILVA, Desmond (George Lorenz); QC 1984; *b* 13 Dec. 1939; *s* of Edmund Frederick Lorenz de Silva, MBE, retired Ambassador, and Esme Gregg Nathanielsz; *m* 1987, HRH Princess Katarina of Yugoslavia, *d* of HRH Prince Tomislav of Yugoslavia and Princess Margarita of Baden. *Educ:* Dulwich College Prep Sch.; Trinity College, Ceylon. Served with 3rd Carabiniers (3rd Dragoon Guards). Called to the Bar: Middle Temple, 1964; Sierra Leone, 1968; The Gambia, 1981. Vice-Chm., Westminster Community Relations Council, 1980–82; Councilman, City of London, 1980–; Main Session Chm., First Internat. Conf. on Human Value, 1981. Member: Home Affairs Standing Cttee, Bow Gp, 1982; Editl Adv. Bd, Crossbow, 1984; Crime and Juvenile Delinquency Study Gp, Centre for Policy Studies, 1983–. Member: Governing Council, Manorial Soc. of GB, 1982–; Nat. Cttee for 900th anniv. of Domesday. Liveryman, Fletchers' Co. Vice-Pres., St John Ambulance London (Prince of Wales's) Dist., 1984–; CStJ 1986 (OStJ 1980). *Publication:* (ed) English Law and Ethnic Minority Customs, 1986. *Recreations:* politics, shooting, travel. *Address:* 2 Paper Buildings, Temple, EC4; 28 Sydney Street, SW3; Villa Taprobane, Taprobane Island, off Weligama, Sri Lanka. *Clubs:* Carlton, City Livery; Orient (Colombo).

DESIO, Prof. Ardito, Dr rer. nat; FRGS; Professor of Geology (and Past Director of Institute of Geology), at the University of Milan, and of Applied Geology, at the Engineering School of Milan, 1931–72, now Emeritus; *b* Palmanova, Frioul, 18 April 1897; *s* of Antonio Desio and Caterina Zorzella; *m* 1932, Aurelia Bevilacqua; one *s* one *d*. *Educ:* Udine and Florence. Grad. Univ. of Florence in Nat. Sciences, 1920. Asst, University of Florence, 1922, and of Pavia, 1923, also Univ. and Engineering Sch., Milan, 1924–25 to 1930–31; Lectr in Geology, Phys. Geography, University of Milan, 1929–30 and in Palaeontology there until 1935. Volunteer, 1st World War, 1915, Lieut, Alpine Troops, 1916–17, POW, 1917–18; Captain, 1924–53; Major, 1954. Geol Consultant, Edison Co. and Public Power Corp. of Greece, 1948–79. Pres., Italian Geological Cttee, 1966–73. Dir., Rivista Italiana di Paleontologia e Stratigrafia, 1942–; Past Dir., Geologia Tecnica. Past Pres., Ital. Geolog. Soc.; Mem. (Hon. Pres.) Ital. Assoc. of Geologists; Past Pres., Ital. Order of Geologists; Mem., Ital. Order of Journalists; Hon. Member: Ital. Paleont. Soc.; Gesellschaft für Erdkunde zu Berlin, 1941; Italian Geog. Soc., 1955; Faculty of Sciences University of Chile, 1964; Geological Soc. of London, 1964; Indian Paleont. Soc.; Soc. Ital. Progresso delle Scienze, 1978; Ist. per il Medio ed Estremo Oriente, 1979; Assoc. Mineraria Subalpina, 1985; Corresp. Member: Soc. Géol. Belgique, 1952; Explorer Club, USA, 1987; Life Mem., Geog. Soc., USA, 1955; Member: Institut d'Egypte, 1936; Accademia Naz. Lincei, 1948; Inst. Lombardo Accad. Scienze Lettere, 1949. In 1938 discovered first deposits of natural oil and gas in subsoil of Libya and Mg-K salt deposit in Marada Oasis; led expedition to K2 (8611 m, 2nd highest peak in the World; reached for 1st time on 31 July 1954), and 18 expeditions in Africa (Libya, Ethiopia) and Asia (Iran, Afghanistan, Pakistan, Nepal, Burma, Philippines, Tibet); in summer 1987 organised expedition which re-measured height of two highest mts in the world, Mt Everest and K2; in summer 1988 expedition visited the northern slope of Karakorum as far as the Kun Lun mountain range; in summers 1989 and 1990 organised a permanent scientific lab. (a glass and aluminium pyramid) in Nepal below the top of Everest at 5000m; also organised eight geodetic, geophysic and geologic expeditions in the Himalaya, Karakorum and Hindu Kush. Santoro Prize, 1931; Royal Prize, 1934, Royal Acad. Lincei; Gold Medal of the Republic of Pakistan, 1954; Gold Medal of the Sciences, Letters and Arts, of Italy, 1956; Patrons medal of Royal Geog. Soc. of London, 1957; USA Antarctic Service Medal, 1974; Gold Lyon of Lion's Club, Udine, 1976; Paul Harris Award, Internat. Rotary Club, 1986; Gold Medal of Ital. Geol. Soc., 1988; Gold Medal of Rotary Club, 1988. Kt Grand Cross, Order of Merit, Italy, 1955. *Publications:* about 435, among them: Le Isole Italiane dell'Egeo, 1931; La spedizione geografica Italiana al Karakoram 1929, 1936; scientific reports of his expedn to Libyan Sahara, 7 vols, 1938–42; Le vie della sete, 1950; Geologia applicata all'ingegneria, 1949, 3rd edn 1973–89; Ascent of K2, 1956 (11 languages, 15 editions); Geology of the Baltoro Basin (Karakorum), 1970; Results of half-a-century investigation on the glaciers of the Ortler-Cevedale, 1973; La Geologia dell'Italia, 1973; Geology of Central Badakhshan (NE Afghanistan), 1975; Geology of the Upper Shaksgam Valley, Sinkiang, China, 1980; L'Antartide, 1985; Sulle Vie della Sete, dei Ghiacci e dell'Oro, 1987; some 250 articles in newspapers and magazines. *Recreation:* alpinist. *Address:* Viale Maino 14, 20129–Milano, Italy. *T:* 76003845; (office) Diparti Scienze della Terra dell 'Univ., via Mangiagalli 34, 20133 Milano. *T:* 236981221. *Clubs:* Italian Alpine; Touring (Italy); Hon. Member: Alpine; Internat. Rotary; Panatlon; Himalayan; Excursionista Carioca (Brazil); Alpin Français.

DESLONGCHAMPS, Prof. Pierre, OC 1989; PhD; FRS 1983; FRSC 1974; FCIC; Professor of Organic Chemistry, Université de Sherbrooke, Canada, since 1972; *b* 8 May 1938; *s* of Rodolphe Deslongchamps and Madeleine Magnan; *m* 1st, 1960, Micheline Renaud (marr. diss. 1975); two *c*; 2nd, 1976, Shirley E. Thomas (marr. diss. 1983); 3rd, 1987, Marie-Marthe Leroux. *Educ:* Univ. de Montréal (BSc Chem., 1959); Univ. of New Brunswick (PhD Chem., 1964). FCIC 1980; FAAAS 1988. Post-doctoral Student with Dr R.B. Woodward, Harvard Univ., USA, 1965; Asst Prof., Univ. de Montréal, 1966; Asst Prof. 1967, Associate Prof. 1968, Univ. de Sherbrooke. Dr *hc:* Univ. Pierre et Marie Curie, Paris, 1983; Bishop's Univ., Univ. de Montréal, and Univ. Laval, 1984; New Brunswick Univ., 1985. A.P. Sloan Fellow, 1970–72; E. W. R. Steacie Fellow, 1971–74. Scientific Prize of Québec, 1971; E. W. R. Steacie Prize (Nat. Scis), NRCC, 1974; Médaille Vincent, ACFAS, 1975; Merck, Sharp and Dohme Lectures Award, CIC, 1976; Canada Council Izaak Walton Killam Meml Scholarship, 1976–77; John Simon Guggenheim Meml Foundn Fellow, 1979; Medáille Pariseau, ACFAS, 1979; Marie-Victorin Prize, Province of Que., 1987. *Publications:* Stereoelectronic Effects in Organic Chemistry, 1983; contrib. Tetrahedron, Jl Amer. Chem. Soc., Canadian Jl of Chem., Pure Applied Chem., Synth. Commun., Nouv. Jl Chim., Heterocycles, Jl Molecular Struct., Interface, Aldrichimica Acta, and Bull. Soc. Chim., France. *Recreations:* fishing, hockey, reading. *Address:* Department of Chemistry, Faculty of Sciences, Université de Sherbrooke, Sherbrooke, PQ J1K 2R1, Canada. *T:* (819) 821–7002; RR 1, 11 McFarland Road, North Hatley, PQ J0B 2C0. *T:* (819) 842–4238.

DESPRÉS, Robert; President, DRM Holdings Inc., since 1987; *b* 27 Sept. 1924; *s* of Adrien Després and Augustine Marmen; *m* 1949, Marguerite Cantin; two *s* two *d*. *Educ:* Académie de Québec (BA 1943); Laval Univ. (MCom 1947); (postgrad. studies) Western Univ. Comptroller, Québec Power Co., 1947–63; Reg. Manager, Administration & Trust Co., 1963–65; Dep. Minister, Québec Dept of Revenue, 1965–69; Pres. and Gen. Man., Québec Health Insurance Bd, 1969–73; Pres., Université du Québec, 1973–78; Pres. and Chief Exec. Officer, National Cablevision Ltd, 1978–80, and Netcom Inc., 1978–89; Chm. of the Bd, Atomic Energy of Canada Ltd, 1978–86. Mem. Board of Directors: Norcen Energy Resources Ltd; Campeau Corporation; Sidbec-Dosco Inc.; Domtar Inc.; Canada Malting Co. Ltd; Manulife Financial; Nat. Trust Co.; Sidbec; Corp. Minnova Inc.; UniMedia; Mitel Corp.; Flakt Canada Ltd; Wajax Ltd; Réseau de télévision Quatre Saisons Inc.; Solivar Consultants; South Shore Industries Ltd; CFCF Inc.; Greyvest Inc.; Grayvest Financial Services Ltd; Canadian Certified General Accountants' Res. Foundn; Council for Canadian Unity; la Soc. du Musée du Séminaire de Québec; Inst de cardiologie de Québec. *Publications:* contrib. Commerce, and Soc. of Management Accountants Revue. *Recreations:* golf, reading. *Address:* 890 rue Dessane, Québec, Québec G1S 3J8, Canada. *T:* (418) 687–2100. *Clubs:* Rideau, Cercle Universitaire; Lorette Golf.

DESTY, Prof. Denis Henry, OBE 1983; FRS 1984; FInstPet; Senior Research Associate, Special Projects, British Petroleum Co. Ltd, 1965–82; *b* 21 Oct. 1923; *s* of Ernest James Desty and Alice Q. R. Desty; *m* 1945, Doreen (*née* Scott); one *s* (one *d* decd). *Educ:* Taunton's Sch., Southampton; University Coll., Southampton (BSc Hons Chemistry, London, 1948). FInstPet 1974. Served War, RAF, 1942–46: Signals Officer, UK and India. Research Centre, British Petroleum Co. Ltd: Physical Chemist, 1948; Gp Leader, 1952; Sen. Chemist, 1962; retd 1982. Research consultant: technical and indust. orgns, 1982–; Janus Consultancy, 1982–. Chm., Gas Chromatography Discussion Gp, 1958–68 (Special Parchment Award, 1970). M. S. Tswett Chromatography Medal, USA 1974 and USSR 1978; Award for Combustion Chemistry, RSC, 1980; MacRobert Award, Fellowship of Engrg, 1982; Merit Award, Chicago Chromatography Disc Gp, 1986; Martin Medal, Chromatographic Soc., 1991. Silver Jubilee Medal, 1977. Editor, Proc. Internat. Gas Chromatography Symposia, 1956 and 1958. *Publications:* about 50 papers and 60 patents. *Recreations:* boating, camping. *Address:* 16 Albury Road, Burwood Park, Walton-on-Thames, Surrey KT12 5DT. *T:* Walton-on-Thames (0932) 229687, *Fax:* Walton-on-Thames (0932) 245848.

de THIER, Jacques; Grand Officer, Order of Léopold II; Commander, Order of Léopold and Order of the Crown, Belgium; Civic Cross (1914–18); Grand Cross of Royal Victorian Order (Hon. GCVO); Director, Compagnie Financière et de Gestion pour l'Etranger (Cometra), Brussels, 1966–73; Counsellor, Cometra Oil Company, 1974–86; *b* Heusy, Belgium, 15 Sept. 1900; *m* 1946, Mariette Negroponte (*d* 1973); three step *s*. *Educ:* University of Liège. Doctor of Laws (University of Liège), 1922; Mem. Bar (Liège and Verviers), 1923–29. Attached to Prime Minister's Cabinet, Brussels, 1929–32; entered Diplomatic Service, 1930; Attaché, Belgian Legation, Berlin, 1933; Chargé d'Affaires in Athens, 1935, Teheran, 1936; First Sec., Berlin, 1937–38; First Sec., then Counsellor, Washington, 1938–44; Chargé d'Affaires, Madrid, 1944–46; Asst to Dir-Gen., Polit. Dept, Min. of Foreign Affairs, Brussels, 1947, then Asst Head of Belgian Mission in Berlin; Consul-Gen. for Belgium, NY, 1948–55; Pres., Soc. of Foreign Consuls in New York, 1954; Belgian Ambassador: to Mexico, 1955–58; in Ottawa, 1958–61; Mem. Belgian Delegns to Gen. Assemblies of UN, 1956, 1957, 1959 and 1960; Belg. Rep. to Security Council, Sept. 1960; Belgian Ambassador to Court of St James's, 1961–65, and concurrently Belgian Perm. Rep. to Council of WEU, 1961–65. Hon. Chairman: Soc. Belgo-Allemande; Belgian Nat. Cttee, United World Colls. Holds foreign decorations. *Publications:* Un diplomate au vingtième siècle; articles in La Revue Générale, Brussels: Dans l'Iran d'autrefois, 1979; Souvenirs d'un diplomate belge, Washington, 1938–44, 1981; Pourquoi l'Espagne de Franco n'a pas livré Degrelle, 1983. *Recreation:* golf. *Address:* 38 avenue des Klauwaerts, 1050 Brussels, Belgium. *Clubs:* Anglo-Belgian; Cercle Royal Gaulois, Cercle du Parc, Royal Golf de Belgique (Brussels).

de TRAFFORD, Sir Dermot Humphrey, 6th Bt *cr* 1841; VRD 1963; Director, 1977–90, Chairman, 1982–90, Low & Bonar plc (Deputy Chairman, 1980–82); Chairman: GHP Group Ltd, 1965–77 (Managing Director, 1961); Calor Gas Holding, 1974–88; *b* 19 Jan. 1925; *s* of Sir Rudolph de Trafford, 5th Bt, OBE and June Lady

Audley (*née* Chaplin), MBE (*d* 1977); *S* father, 1983; *m* 1st, 1946, Patricia Mary Beeley (marr. diss. 1973); three *s* six *d*; 2nd, 1973, Mrs Xandra Caradini Walter. *Educ:* Harrow Sch.; Christ Church, Oxford (MA). Trained as Management Consultant, Clubley Armstrong & Co. Ltd and Orr & Boss and Partners Ltd, 1949–52; Director: Monks Investment Trust; Imperial Continental Gas Assoc., 1963–87 (Dep. Chm., 1972–87); Petrofina SA, 1971–87. Chm. Council, Inst. of Dirs, 1990–. *Recreations:* golf, ski-ing. *Heir:* *s* John Humphrey de Trafford [*b* 12 Sept. 1950; *m* 1975, Anne, *d* of J. Faure de Pebeyre; one *s* one *d*]. *Address:* The Old Vicarage, Appleshaw, Andover, Hants SP11 9BH. *T:* Andover (0264) 772357. *Clubs:* White's, Royal Ocean Racing; Berkshire Golf; Island Sailing.

DEUKMEJIAN, (Courken) George, Jr; Governor of California, since 1983; lawyer; Republican; *b* 6 June 1928; *s* of C. George Deukmejian and Alice (*née* Gairdan); *m* 1957, Gloria M. Saatjian; one *s* two *d*. *Educ:* Watervliet Sch., NY; Siena College (BA 1949); St John's Univ., NY (JD 1952). Admitted to NY State Bar, 1952, Californian Bar, 1956, US Supreme Court Bar, 1970. US Army, 1953–55. Law practice, Calif., 1955; Partner, Riedman, Dalessi, Deukmejian & Woods; Mem., Calif. Assembly, 1963–67; Mem., Calif. Senate (minority leader), 1967–79; Attorney Gen., Calif., 1979–83. *Address:* State Capitol, Sacramento, Calif 95814, USA.

DEUTSCH, André, CBE 1989; President, André Deutsch Ltd, (Chairman and Managing Director, 1951–84; Joint Chairman and Joint Managing Director, 1984–87; Joint Chairman, 1987–89); *b* 15 Nov. 1917; *s* of late Bruno Deutsch and Maria Deutsch (*née* Havas); unmarried. *Educ:* Budapest; Vienna; Zurich. First job in publishing, with Nicholson & Watson, 1942; started publishing independently under imprint of Allan Wingate (Publishers) Ltd, 1945; started André Deutsch Limited, in 1951. Founded: African Universities Press, Lagos, Nigeria, 1962; East Africa Publishing House, Nairobi, Kenya, 1964. *Recreations:* travel preferably by train, ski-ing, publishing, talking. *Address:* 106 Great Russell Street, WC1B 3LJ. *Clubs:* Garrick, Groucho.

de VALOIS, Dame Ninette, CH 1982; DBE 1951 (CBE 1947); Founder and Director of the Royal Ballet, 1931–63 (formerly the Sadler's Wells Ballet, Royal Opera House, Covent Garden, and the Sadler's Wells Theatre Ballet, Sadler's Wells Theatre); Founder of The Royal Ballet School (formerly The Sadler's Wells School of Ballet); *b* Baltiboys, Blessington, Co. Wicklow, 6 June 1898; 2nd *d* of Lieut-Col T. R. A. Stannus, DSO, Carlingford; *m* 1935, Dr A. B. Connell. Prima ballerina the Royal Opera Season Covent Garden (International), May to July 1919 and again in 1928. Première danseuse British National Opera Company, 1918; Mem., The Diaghileff Russian Ballet, 1923–26; choreographic dir to the Old Vic, the Festival Theatre, Cambridge, and The Abbey Theatre, Dublin, 1926–30; Founder of The National Sch. of Ballet, Turkey, 1947. Principal choreographic works: Job, The Rake's Progress, Checkmate, and Don Quixote. Hon. MusDoc London, 1947; Hon. DLitt: Reading, 1951; Oxford, 1955; New Univ. of Ulster, 1979; Hon. DMus: Sheffield, 1955; Durham, 1982; Hon. MusD Trinity Coll., Dublin, 1957; Hon. DFA Smith Coll., Mass, USA, 1957; Hon. LLD: Aberdeen, 1958; Sussex, 1975; FRAD 1963. Chevalier of the Legion of Honour, 1950. Gold Albert Medal, RSA, 1964; (jtly) Erasmus Prize Foundn Award (first woman to receive it), 1974; Irish Community Award, 1980. *Publications:* Invitation to the Ballet, 1937; Come Dance with Me, 1957; Step By Step, 1977. *Address:* c/o Royal Ballet School, 153 Talgarth Road, W14.

DEVENPORT, Rt. Rev. Eric Nash; *see* Dunwich, Bishop Suffragan of.

de VERE, Anthony Charles Mayle, CMG 1986; HM Diplomatic Service; Foreign and Commonwealth Office, since 1986; *b* 23 Jan. 1930; *m* 1st, 1959, Geraldine Gertrude Bolton (*d* 1980); 2nd, 1986, Rosemary Edith Austin. *Educ:* St John's College, Cambridge. Served Army, Malaya, 1950–52; joined Colonial Service (later HMOCS), 1953, Provincial Admin, Tanganyika; Kibondo, 1953–56; in charge Kondoa–Irangi Develt Scheme, 1957–59; Res. Magistrate, Singida, 1959; Dist Comr, Tunduru, 1960–61, Kigoma, 1961–62; Head of local govt, Western Region, 1962–63, retired 1963; joined FO, later FCO, 1963; First Sec., Lusaka, 1967–70, NY, 1972–74; Counsellor, Washington, 1982–86. *Recreations:* riding, most things rural, sculpture, music, books. *Address:* Haddiscoe Hall, Norfolk NR14 6PE; 40 Ashburn Place, SW7 4JR. *Club:* Athenæum.

DEVEREAU, George Michael; Director General, Central Office of Information, since 1989; *b* 10 Nov. 1937; *s* of George Alfred Devereau and Elspeth Mary Duff Devereau; *m* 1961, Sarah Poupart; four *s*. *Educ:* King William's Coll., Isle of Man; University Coll. London. Asst Ed., Architects' Jl, 1962; Information Officer, MPBW, BRE and DoE, 1967–75; Chief Information Officer: Price Commn, 1975; DoE, 1978; Dept of Transport, 1982; Gp Dir, 1985, Dep. Dir Gen., 1987, COI. *Publication:* Architects Working Details, 1964. *Recreations:* house restoration, travel. *Address:* Central Office of Information, Hercules House, Hercules Road, SE1 7DU.

DEVERELL, Sir Colville (Montgomery), GBE 1963 (OBE 1946); KCMG 1957 (CMG 1955); CVO 1953; retired from Government Service, Nov. 1962; Secretary-General, International Planned Parenthood Federation, 1964–69; *b* 21 Feb. 1907; *s* of George Robert Deverell and Maude (*née* Cooke); *m* 1935, Margaret Wynne, *d* of D. A. Wynne Willson; three *s*. *Educ:* Portora Sch., Enniskillen, Ulster; Trinity Coll., Dublin (LLB); Trinity Coll., Cambridge. District Officer, Kenya, 1931; Clerk to Exec. and Legislative Councils, 1938–39; Civil Affairs Branch, E Africa Comd, 1941–46, serving Italian Somaliland, British Somaliland, Ethiopia; Mem. Lord de la Warr's Delegation, Ethiopia, 1944; seconded War Office in connection Italian Peace Treaty, 1946. Sec., Development and Reconstruction Authority, Kenya, 1946; acted as Financial Sec. and Chief Native Comr, 1949; Administrative Secretary, Kenya, 1949; Colonial Sec., Jamaica, 1952–55; Governor and Comdr-in-Chief, Windward Islands, 1955–59; Governor and Comdr-in-Chief, Mauritius, 1959–62. Chm. UN(FP) Mission to India, 1965; Mem., UN Mission on Need for World Population Inst., 1970; Chairman: UN Family Planning Evaluation Mission to Ceylon, 1971; UN Family Planning Assoc. Feasability Mission, Al Azhar Univ., Cairo, 1972. Constitutional Adviser: Seychelles, 1966; British Virgin Islands, 1973. LLD *jure dignitatis,* Dublin, 1964. *Recreations:* cricket, tennis, squash, golf and fishing. *Address:* 123 Greys Road, Henley-on-Thames, Oxon RG9 1TE.

DEVEREUX, family name of **Viscount Hereford.**

DEVEREUX, Alan Robert, CBE 1980; DL; Director, Gleneagles Group, since 1990; Chairman, Quality Scotland Foundation, since 1991; *b* 18 April 1933; *s* of Donald Charles and Doris Devereux; *m* 1st, 1959, Gloria Alma Hair (*d* 1985); one *s*; 2nd, 1987, Elizabeth Tormey Docherty. *Educ:* Colchester School; Clacton County High School; Mid-Essex Technical Coll. CEng, FIProdE; CBIM. Marconi's Wireless Telegraph Co., 1950–56; Halex Div. of British Xylonite Co., 1956–58; Spa Div., Sanitas Trust, 1958–65; Gen. Man., Dobar Engineering, 1965–67; Norcros Ltd, 1967–69; Gp Man. Dir 1969–78, Dep. Chm. 1978–80, Scotcros Ltd; Dir-Gen., Scotcros Europe SA, 1976–79. Director: Scottish Mutual Assurance Soc., 1975–; Walter Alexander PLC, 1980–90; Hambros Scotland Ltd, 1984–; Scottish Advisor, Hambros Bank, 1984–90. Dep. Chm. 1975–77, Chm. 1977–79, CBI Scotland; CBI: Council Mem., 1972–; Mem. President's Adv. Cttee, 1979; UK Regional Chm., 1979; Mem., Finance and Gen. Purposes Cttee, 1982–84. Chairman: Small Industries Council for Rural Areas of Scotland, 1975–77; Scottish Tourist Bd, 1980–90; Member: Scottish Development Agency, 1977–82; BTA, 1980–90. Chm., Police Dependants' Trust, Scotland. Scottish Free Enterprise Award, 1978. DL Renfrewshire, 1985. *Recreations:* reading, work, running for aeroplanes. *Address:* 293 Fenwick Road, Giffnock, Glasgow G46 6UH. *Club:* East India, Devonshire, Sports and Public Schools.

de VERE WHITE, Hon. Mrs; *see* Glendinning, Hon. Victoria.

de VERE WHITE, Terence; *see* White.

de VESCI, 7th Viscount *cr* 1766; **Thomas Eustace Vesey;** Bt 1698; Baron Knapton, 1750; *b* 8 Oct. 1955; *s* of 6th Viscount de Vesci and Susan Anne (*d* 1986), *d* of late Ronald (Owen Lloyd) Armstrong-Jones, MBE, QC, DL, and of the Countess of Rosse; *S* father, 1983; *m* 1987, Sita-Maria, *o c* of late Baron de Breffny; one *s* one *d*. *Educ:* Eton and Oxford. Assistant Trainer to M. V. O'Brien, 1978–80; Bloodstock Agent in Los Angeles, Calif, 1980–83; returned to family home on death of father to continue bloodstock business, also stud farm, forestry and farming. *Address:* Abbey Leix, Ireland. *T:* Abbeyleix 31162. *Club:* White's.

See also Earl of Snowdon.

DEVESI, Sir Baddeley, GCMG 1980; GCVO 1982; Governor-General of the Solomon Islands, 1978–88; *b* 16 Oct. 1941; *s* of Mostyn Tagabasoe Norua and Laisa Otu; *m* 1969, June Marie Barley; four *s* two *d* (and one *d* decd). *Educ:* St Stephen's Sch., Auckland, NZ; Ardmore Teachers' Coll., Auckland, NZ. MLC and Mem. Exec. Council, 1967–69. Headmaster, St Nicholas Sch., Honiara, 1968; Educn Officer and Lectr, 1970–72; Dist. Officer, 1973; District Comr and Clerk to Malaita Council, 1974; Permanent Secretary, 1976. Dep. Chm., Solomon Islands Broadcasting Corp., 1976. Chancellor, Univ. of S Pacific, 1980–83. Captain, Solomon Islands team, 2nd South Pacific Games, 1969. Comr, Boy Scouts Assoc., 1968. Hon. DU, Univ. of the South Pacific, 1981. KStJ 1984. *Recreations:* reading, swimming, lawn tennis, cricket, snooker. *Address:* c/o Government House, Honiara, Solomon Islands.

de VIGIER, William Alphonse, Hon. CBE 1978; formerly: Chairman (also founder), Acrow plc; Chairman: Acrow Corp. of America; Acrow Canada; Acrow Botswana; Acrow Company of China; *b* 22 Jan. 1912; *m* 1939, Betty Kendall; two *d*. *Educ:* La Chataigneraie, Coppet, Switzerland. Board Member: Acrow Peru SA; Acrow Zimbabwe; Poenamo Ltd, Australia. Mem., British Airways Bd, 1973–78; Vigierhof AG, Switzerland. Knight of Star of the North (Sweden); Grand Commander, Order of Star of Africa. *Recreations:* tennis, skiing, swimming. *Address:* Sommerhaus, Solothurn, Switzerland; Tinkers Lodge, Marsh Lane, Mill Hill, NW7. *Clubs:* East India; Metropolitan (New York).

DE VILLE, Sir Harold Godfrey, (Sir Oscar), Kt 1990; CBE 1979; Chairman, Meyer International plc, 1987–91 (Deputy Chairman, 1985–87; Director, 1984–91); *b* Derbyshire, 11 April 1925; *s* of Harold De Ville and Anne De Ville (*née* Godfrey); *m* 1947, Pamela Fay Ellis; one *s*. *Educ:* Burton-on-Trent Grammar Sch.; Trinity Coll., Cambridge (MA). Served RNVR, 1943–46. With Ford Motor Co. Ltd, 1949–65; BICC, 1965–84: Dir, 1971–84; Exec. Vice-Chm., 1978–80; Exec. Dep. Chm., 1980–84; Chm., BICC Pension Funds, 1973–84. Director: Balfour Beatty Ltd, 1971–78; Phillips Cables Ltd, Canada, 1982–84; Metal Manufacturers Ltd, Australia, 1983–84; Scottish Cables Ltd, S Africa, 1983–84. Mem., BRB, 1985–91. Chairman: Iron and Steel EDC, 1984–86; Govt Review of vocational qualifications, 1985–86; NCVQ, 1986–90; Nat. Jt Council for Engrg Construction Industry, 1985–87. Member: Commn on Industrial Relations, 1971–74; Central Arbitration Cttee, 1976–77; Council: Inst. of Manpower Studies, 1971–; ACAS, 1976–; Industrial Soc., 1976–85; BIM, 1982–86 (Mem., Bd of Companions, 1981–); Confederation of British Industry: Member: Employment Policy Cttee, 1971–78; Council, 1977–85; Finance Cttee, 1984–85; Chm., Working Parties on Employee Participation, 1975–78, on Pay Determination, 1976–78. Mem. Council, Reading Univ., 1985–. *Recreations:* genealogy, fell-walking. *Address:* Bexton Cottage, 18 Pound Lane, Sonning on Thames, Berks RG4 0XE.

de VILLIERS, 3rd Baron, *cr* 1910; **Arthur Percy de Villiers;** retired; *b* 17 Dec. 1911; *s* of 2nd Baron and Adelheid, *d* of H. C. Koch, Pietermaritzburg, Natal; *S* father 1934; *m* 1939, Lovett (marr. diss. 1958), *d* of Dr A. D. MacKinnon, Williams Lake, BC; one *s* two *d*. *Educ:* Magdalen Coll., Oxford. Barrister, Inner Temple, 1938. Farming in New Zealand. Admitted as a barrister to the Auckland Surpreme Court, 1949. *Recreations:* gardening, golf. *Heir:* *s* Hon. Alexander Charles de Villiers, *b* 29 Dec. 1940. *Address:* PO Box 66, Kumeu, Auckland, NZ. *T:* Auckland 4118173. *Club:* Royal Commonwealth Society (Auckland).

de VILLIERS, Dawid Jacobus, DPhil; Minister for Mineral and Energy Affairs and Public Enterprises, South Africa, since 1989; *b* 10 July 1940; *m* 1964, Suzaan Mangold; one *s* three *d*. *Educ:* Univ. of Stellenbosch (BA Hons Philosophy, 1963; BTh, DPhil); Rand Afrikaans Univ. (MA Phil., 1972). Abe Bailey Scholar, 1963–64; Markotter Scholar, 1964. Part-time Lectr in Philosophy, Univ. of Western Cape, 1963–64; Minister of Dutch Reformed Church, Wellington, Cape, 1967–69; Lectr in Philosophy, 1969–72, and Pres. Convocation, 1973–, Rand Afrikaans Univ.; MP for Johannesburg W, 1972–79; Chm., Nat. Party's Foreign Affairs Cttee in Parlt; Ambassador of S Africa to London, 1979–80; Minister: of Trade and Industry (formerly Industries, Commerce and Tourism), SA, 1980–86; of Budget and Welfare, 1986–88; for Admin and Privatisation, 1988. Visited: USA on US Leaders Exchange Prog., 1974; UK as guest of Brit. Govt, 1975; Israel as guest of Israeli Govt, 1977. Represented S Africa in internat. Rugby in S Africa, UK, Ireland, Australia, NZ, France and the Argentine, 1962–70 (Captain, 1965–70). State President's Award for Sport, 1968 and 1970; S African Sportsman of the Year, 1968; Jaycee's Outstanding Young Man of the Year Award, 1971; State President's Decoration for Meritorious Service, Gold, 1988. *Recreations:* sports, reading. *Address:* Private Bag X9079, Cape Town, 8000, South Africa.

DEVINE, Hon. (Donald) Grant; MLA for Estevan, since 1982; Premier of Saskatchewan, since 1982; Minister of Agriculture, since 1985; Leader, Progressive Conservative Party of Saskatchewan, since 1979; *b* Regina, 5 July 1944; *m* 1966, (Adeline) Chantal Guillaume; two *s* three *d*. *Educ:* Saskatchewan Univ. (BScA 1967); Alberta Univ. (MSc 1969; MBA 1970); Ohio State Univ. (PhD 1976). Farming, 1962–; marketing specialist, Fed. Govt, Ottawa, 1970–72; Graduate Assistant, Ohio State Univ., 1972–76; Lectr in Agricl Econs, Saskatchewan Univ., 1976–79. Re-elected MLA for Estevan, 1986. Advisor: Food Prices Rev. Bd and Provincial Govts; Sask. Consumers' Assoc. Member: Amer. Econ. Assoc.; Amer. Marketing Assoc.; Amer. Assoc. for Consumer Res.; Canadian Agricl Econs Soc.; Consumers' Assoc. of Canada. *Publications:* contribs to professional jls on retail food pricing and market performance. *Recreations:* golf, ski-ing, baseball. *Address:* Office of the Premier, Legislative Building, 2405 Legislative Drive, Regina, Sask S4S 0B3, Canada.

DEVINE, Rt. Rev. Joseph; *see* Motherwell, Bishop of, (RC).

de VIRION, Tadeusz; Cross of Valour, Cross of the Home Army, Warsaw Uprising Cross, 1944; Polish Ambassador to the Court of St James's, since 1990; *b* 28 March 1926; *s* of Jerzy de Virion (killed in Auschwitz, 1941); *m* 1985, Jayanti; two *d. Educ:* Univ. of Warsaw (LLM). Barrister, 1950–, specialising in criminal law and political cases, incl. Solidarity; Judge of Tribunal of State, elected by Polish Parlt, 1989; Lectr, Warsaw Barristers' Assoc.; Expert of Senate Commn of law and human rights. Cross of Knights of Malta, 1980; Golden Insignia of Barrister's Merit, 1988. *Recreations:* Jayanti, books. *Address:* Polish Embassy, 47 Portland Place, W1N 3AG. *T:* 071–580 4324. *Clubs:* Brooks's, Polish Heart, Travellers', Special Forces.

DE VITO, Gioconda; Violinist; Professor of Corso di Perfezionamento of Violin at Accademia Di Santa Cecilia, Rome, 1946–61; *b* 26 July 1907; *d* of Giacomo and Emilia De Vito (*née* Del Guidice), Martina Franca Puglia, Italy; *m* 1949, (James) David Bicknell (*d* 1988); no *c. Educ:* Conservatorio Di Musica Rossini, Pesaro. Began to play violin at age of 8½; final examinations (distinction), Conservatorio Pesaro, 1921; first concert, 1921; teacher, Instituto Musicale Nicolo Piccinni, Bari, 1924–34; first prize, Internat. Competition, Vienna, 1932. Prof. of Violin, Conservatorio Di Santa Cecilia, Rome, 1935–46. World wide musical activities since debut with London Philharmonic Orchestra, 1948, at concert conducted by Victor de Sabata; Royal Philharmonic Soc., 1950; Edinburgh Festival, 1949, 1951, 1953 (took part, 1953, in Festival of the Violin with Yehudi Menuhin and Isaac Stern), and 1960; played at Bath Fest. and Festival Hall with Yehudi Menuhin, 1955; Jury Tchaikowsky Internat. Violin Competition, Moscow, and recitals Moscow and Leningrad, 1958; Soloist, Adelaide Centenary Fest., and toured Australia, 1960; concerts, Buenos Aires, 1961; retired, 1961. Last concerts, Gt Brit., Swansea Festival, Oct. 1961; Continent, Basle Philharmonic, Nov. 1961. Many recordings. Diploma di Medaglia d'Oro del Ministero della Pubblica Istruzione for services to Art, 1957; Academician, Accademia Nazionale di Santa Cecilia, Rome, 1976. Gold Medal, Premium Amadeas, 1991. *Recreation:* bird watching. *Address:* Flint Cottage, Loudwater, Rickmansworth, Herts. *T:* Rickmansworth (0923) 772865; Via Cassia 595, Rome. *T:* 3660937.

DEVITT, Lt-Col Sir Thomas Gordon, 2nd Bt, *cr* 1916; Partner of Devitt & Moore, Shipbrokers; *b* 27 Dec. 1902; *e s* of Arthur Devitt (*d* 1921) *e s* of 1st Bt and Florence Emmeline (*d* 1951), *e d* of late William Forbes Gordon, Manar, NSW; *S* grandfather, 1923; *m* 1st, 1930, Joan Mary (who obtained a divorce, 1936), 2nd *d* of late Charles Reginald Freemantle, Hayes Barton, Pyrford, Surrey; 2nd, 1937, Lydia Mary (marr. diss. 1953), *o d* of late Edward Milligen Beloe, King's Lynn, Norfolk; two *d*; 3rd, 1953, Janet Lilian, *o d* of late Col H. S. Ellis, CBE, MC; one *s* one *d. Educ:* Sherborne; Corpus Christi Coll., Cambridge. 1939–45 War as Lt-Col, Seaforth Highlanders and OC Raiding Support Regt. Royal Order of Phœnix of Greece with swords. Chm. Macers Ltd, 1961–70. Chairman: Board of Governors, The Devitt and Moore Nautical Coll., Pangbourne, 1948–61; Nat. Service for Seafarers, 1948–77. Governor, Sherborne Sch., 1967–75. *Recreations:* shooting, fishing. *Heir: s* James Hugh Thomas Devitt [*b* 18 Sept. 1956; *m* 1985, Susan Carol, *d* of Dr Michael Duffus; two *s* one *d*]. *Address:* 49 Lexden Road, Colchester, Essex CO3 3PY. *T:* Colchester (0206) 577958. *Club:* MCC.

DEVLIN, family name of **Baron Devlin.**

DEVLIN, Baron (Life Peer) *cr* 1961, of West Wick; **Patrick Arthur Devlin,** PC 1960; Kt 1948; FBA 1963; High Steward of Cambridge University, 1966–91; *b* 25 Nov. 1905; *e s* of W. J. Devlin; *m* 1932, Madeleine, *yr d* of Sir Bernard Oppenheimer, 1st Bt; four *s* twin *d. Educ:* Stonyhurst Coll.; Christ's Coll., Cambridge. President of Cambridge Union, 1926. Called to Bar, Gray's Inn, 1929; KC 1945; Master of the Bench, Gray's Inn, 1947; Treasurer of Gray's Inn, 1963. Prosecuting Counsel to the Mint, 1931–39. Legal Dept, Min. of Supply, 1940–42; Junior Counsel to the Ministries of War Transport, Food and Supply, 1942–45; Attorney-Gen., Duchy of Cornwall, 1947–48; Justice of the High Court, Queen's Bench Div., 1948–60; Pres. of the Restrictive Practices Court, 1956–60; a Lord Justice of Appeal, 1960–61; a Lord of Appeal in Ordinary, 1961–64, retd; Chm. Wiltshire QS, 1955–71. A Judge of the Administrative Tribunal of the ILO, 1964–86; Chm., Commn apptd under constn of ILO to examine complaints concerning observance by Greece of Freedom of Assoc. and similar Conventions, 1969–71. Chairman: Cttee of Inquiry into Dock Labour Scheme, 1955–56; Nyasaland Inquiry Commn, 1959; Cttee of inquiry into the port transport industry, 1964–65; Jt Bd for the Nat. Newspaper Industry, 1965–69; Commn of Inquiry into Industrial Representation, 1971–72; Cttee on Identification in criminal cases, 1974–76. Chm., Press Council, 1964–69. Chm. of Council, Bedford Coll., University of London, 1953–59. Pres., British Maritime Law Assoc., 1962–76; Chm. Assoc. Average Adjusters, 1966–67. Hon. LLD: Glasgow 1962; Toronto 1962; Cambridge 1966; Leicester, 1966; Sussex 1966; Durham, 1968; Liverpool, 1970; St Louis, 1980; Hon. DCL Oxon, 1965. *Publications:* Trial by Jury, 1956 (Hamlyn Lectures); The Criminal Prosecution in England (Sherrill Lectures), 1957; Samples of Lawmaking (Lloyd Roberts and other lectures), 1962; The Enforcement of Morals, (Maccabean and other lectures), 1965; The House of Lords and the Naval Prize Bill, 1911 (Rede Lecture), 1968; Too Proud to Fight: Woodrow Wilson's Neutrality, 1974; The Judge (Chorley and other lectures), 1979; Easing the Passing: the trial of Dr John Bodkin Adams, 1985. *Address:* West Wick House, Pewsey, Wilts SN9 5JZ.

See also Tim Devlin, Sir P. J. M. Kennedy.

DEVLIN, Alexander, OBE 1977; JP; Member, Glenrothes New Town Development Corporation, 1958–78; *b* 22 Dec. 1927; *s* of Thomas Devlin and Jean Gibson; *m* 1949, Annie Scott Gordon. *Educ:* Cowdenbeath St Columba's High Sch.; National Council of Labour Colls (Local Govt and Public Speaking). Member: Fife CC, 1956–74; Fife Regional Council, 1974–78; Chm., Fife Educn Cttee, 1963–78; Vice-Chm., Educn Cttee of Convention of Scottish Local Authorities, 1974–78. Member: Dunning Cttee on Scottish System for Assessment of Pupils after 4 years Secondary Educn, 1974–77; Scottish Sports Council, 1964–74; Manpower Services Commn, 1978–79. JP Fife, 1963. *Address:* 40 Falcon Drive, Glenrothes, Fife KY7 5HP. *T:* Glenrothes (0592) 759883.

DEVLIN, (Josephine) Bernadette; *see* McAliskey, J. B.

DEVLIN, Keith Michael, PhD; **His Honour Judge Devlin;** a Circuit Judge, since 1984; *b* 21 Oct. 1933; *e s* of Francis Michael Devlin and Norah Devlin (*née* Gregory); *m* 1958, Pamela Gwendoline Phillips; two *s* one *d. Educ:* Price's Sch., Fareham; Eaton Hall OCS; King's Coll., London Univ. (LLB 1960, MPhil 1968, PhD 1976). Commnd RAOC, 1953. Called to the Bar, Gray's Inn, 1964; Dep. Chief Clerk, Metropolitan Magistrates' Courts Service, 1964–66; various appts as Dep. Metropolitan Stipendiary Magistrate, 1975–79; a Recorder, 1983–84; Liaison Judge, Bedfordshire, 1990–. Brunel University: Lectr in Law, 1966–71; Reader in Law, 1971–84; Associate Prof. of Law, 1984–; Mem., Court, 1985–88. Fellow, Netherlands Inst. for Advanced Study in the Humanities and Social Sciences, Wassenaar, 1975–76. Mem., Mental Health Review Tribunals, 1991–. Mem., Consumer Protection Adv. Cttee, 1976–81. MRI (Mem., Finance Cttee, 1988–). Magistrates' Association: Mem., 1974–89, Vice-Chm., 1984–89, Legal Cttee; co-opted Mem. Council, 1980–88. JP Inner London (Juvenile Court Panel), 1968–84 (Chm., 1973–84). Liveryman, Feltmakers' Co. (Mem., Ct of Assts, 1991–). FRSA 1989. Jt Founder and Editor, Anglo-Amer. Law Rev., 1972–84. *Publications:* Sentencing Offenders in Magistrates' Courts, 1970; (with Eric Stockdale) Sentencing, 1987; articles in legal jls. *Recreations:* watching cricket, fly-fishing, Roman Britain. *Address:* Luton Crown Court, 7 George Street, Luton, Beds LU1 2AA. *T:* Luton (0582) 488488. *Clubs:* Athenæum, MCC; Hampshire County Cricket.

DEVLIN, Stuart Leslie, AO 1988; CMG 1980; goldsmith, silversmith and designer in London since 1965; Goldsmith and Jeweller by appointment to HM The Queen, 1982; *b* 9 Oct. 1931; *m* 1986, Carole Hedley-Saunders. *Educ:* Gordon Inst. of Technology, Geelong; Royal Melbourne Inst. of Technology; Royal Coll. of Art. DesRCA (Silversmith), DesRCA (Industrial Design/Engrg). Art Teacher, Vic. Educn Dept, 1950–58; Royal Coll. of Art, 1958–60; Harkness Fellow, NY, 1960–62; Lectr, Prahran Techn. Coll., Melbourne, 1962; one-man shows of sculpture, NY and Sydney, 1961–64; Inspr Art in Techn. Schs, Vic. Educn Dept, 1964–65; exhibns of silver and gold in numerous cities USA, Australia, Bermuda, Middle East and UK, 1965–. Executed many commns in gold and silver: designed coins for Australia, Singapore, Cayman Is, Gibraltar, IoM, Burundi, Botswana, Ethiopia and Bhutan; designed and made: cutlery for State Visit to Paris, 1972; Duke of Edinburgh trophy for World Driving Championship, 1973; silver to commemorate opening of Sydney Opera House, 1973; Grand National Trophy, 1975, 1976; Australian Bravery Awards, 1975; Regalia for the Order of Australia, 1975–76; Queen's Silver Jubilee Medal, 1977; Centrepiece for RE to commemorate their work in NI, 1984; Bas-relief portrait of Princess of Wales for Wedgwood, 1986; full set of Defence Awards for Australia, 1989; Whitbread Employee Volunteering Award, 1990. Developed strategy for use of champagne diamonds in jewellery for Argyle Diamond Mines, 1987. Freeman, City of London, 1966; Liveryman, 1972, Mem. Ct of Assts, 1986, Goldsmiths' Co. *Recreations:* work, squash, windsurfing, ham radio. *Address:* Southbourne Court, Copsale, Southwater, Sussex RH13 7DJ. *T:* Southwater (0403) 733000.

DEVLIN, Tim; Founder, Tim Devlin Enterprises, public relations consultancy, 1989; *b* 28 July 1944; 3rd *s* of Rt Hon. Lord Devlin, *qv*; *m* 1967, Angela Denise, *d* of Mr A. J. G. and late Mrs Laramy; two *s* two *d. Educ:* Winchester Coll.; University Coll., Oxford (Hons degree, History). Feature Writer, Aberdeen Press & Journal, 1966; Reporter, Scotsman, 1967; Educn Reporter, Evening Echo, Watford, 1968–69; Reporter, later News Editor, The Times Educnl Supplement, 1969–71; Reporter, The Times, 1971–73, Educn Corresp., 1973–77; Nat. Dir, ISIS, 1977–84; Public Relations Dir, Inst. of Dirs, 1984–86; Assoc. Dir, Charles Barker Traverse-Healy, 1986–89. *Publications:* (with Mary Warnock) What Must We Teach?, 1977; Good Communications Guide, 1980; Independent Schools—The Facts, 1981; Choosing Your Independent School, 1984; (with Brian Knight) Public Relations and Marketing for Schools, 1990. *Recreations:* writing, art, tennis, children. *T:* Staplehurst (0580) 893176.

DEVLIN, Timothy Robert; MP (C) Stockton South, since 1987; *b* 13 June 1959; *e s* of H. Brendan Devlin, FRCS and Anne Elizabeth Devlin, MB BCh; *m* 1986 (marr. diss. 1989). *Educ:* Dulwich Coll.; LSE; City Univ. Called to the Bar, Lincoln's Inn, 1985 (Hardwick and Thomas More Scholar). Mem., Cons. Research Dept, 1981; former Chm., LSE Conservatives; Soc., 1985, Chm., 1986, Islington North Cons. Assoc. Chairman: Parly Panel on Charity Law; Northern Gp of Cons. MPs; Dep. Chm., Foreign Affairs Forum; Member: Stockton on Tees Cons. Assoc.; Soc. of Cons. Lawyers; Franco-British Parly Group; European Standing Cttee, RIIA; All-Party Clubs Group; Yarm Civic Soc.; Yarm-Vernouillet twinning Assoc.; NT; Friends of the RA; Trustee, Cleveland Families Trust; Gov., Yarm Sch. *Recreations:* walking, opera, ski-ing. *Address:* 2 Russell Street, Stockton-on-Tees, Cleveland TS18 1NS. *T:* Stockton-on-Tees (0642) 605035. *Club:* Carlton.

DEVON, 17th Earl of, *cr* 1553; **Charles Christopher Courtenay,** Bt 1644; RARO Lieutenant (W/Captain) Coldstream Guards; *b* 13 July 1916; *o surv. s* of 16th Earl and Marguerite (*d* 1950), *d* of late John Silva; *S* father, 1935; *m* 1939, Venetia, Countess of Cottenham, *d* of Captain J. V. Taylor; one *s* one *d. Educ:* Winchester; RMC, Sandhurst. Served war of 1939–45 (despatches). *Recreations:* shooting and fishing. *Heir: s* Lord Courtenay, *qv. Address:* Stables House, Powderham, Exeter. *T:* Starcross (0626) 890253.

DEVONPORT, 3rd Viscount *cr* 1917, of Wittington, Bucks; **Terence Kearley;** Bt 1908; Baron 1910; architect and landowner; Chairman, Millhouse Developments Ltd, since 1989; *b* 29 Aug. 1944; *s* of 2nd Viscount Devonport and of Sheila Isabel, *e d* of Lt-Col C. Hope Murray; *S* father, 1973; *m* 1968, Elizabeth Rosemary, *d* of late John G. Hopton (marr. diss. 1979); two *d. Educ:* Aiglon Coll., Switzerland; Selwyn Coll., Cambridge (BA, DipArch, MA); Newcastle Univ. (MPhil). Architect: Davis Brody, New York City, 1967–68; London Borough of Lambeth, 1971–72; Barnett Winskell, Newcastle-upon-Tyne, 1972–75; landscape architect, Ralph Erskine, Newcastle, 1977–78; in private practice, 1979–84 (RIBA, ALI); Forestry Manager, 1973–; farmer, 1978–. Member: Lloyds, 1976–; Internat. Dendrology Soc., 1978–; N Adv. Cttee, TGEW, 1978–; N Adv. Cttee, CLA, 1980–85; Nat. Land Use and Envmt Cttee, TGUK, 1984–87. Vice President: Arboricultural Assoc., 1987–; Forestry Commn Reference Panel, 1987–. Man. Dir, Tweedswood Enterprises, 1979–, and dir various other cos, 1984–. MInstD. Order of Mark Twain (USA), 1977. *Recreations:* nature, travel and good food; interests: trees, the arts, country sports. *Heir: cousin* Chester Dagley Hugh Kearley [*b* 29 April 1932; *m* 1974, Josefa Mesquida]. *Address:* Ray Demesne, Kirkwhelpington, Newcastle upon Tyne NE19 2RG. *Clubs:* Royal Automobile, Beefsteak, Farmers', MCC; Northern Counties (Newcastle upon Tyne).

DEVONS, Prof. Samuel; FRS 1955; Professor of Physics, Columbia University, New York, 1960–85, now Emeritus (Chairman, Dept of Physics, 1963–67); Director, History of Physics Laboratory, Barnard College, Columbia University, 1970–85; *b* 1914; *s* of Rev. David I. Devons and E. Edleston; *m* 1938, Celia Ruth Toubkin; four *d. Educ:* Trinity Coll., Cambridge. BA 1935; MA, PhD 1939. Exhibition of 1851 Senior Student, 1939. Scientific Officer, Senior Scientific Officer, Air Ministry, MAP, and Ministry of Supply, 1939–45. Lecturer in Physics, Cambridge Univ., Fellow and Dir of Studies, Trinity Coll., Cambridge, 1946–49; Prof. of Physics, Imperial Coll. of Science, 1950–55; Langworthy Prof. of Physics and Dir of Physical Laboratories, Univ. of Manchester, 1955–60. Royal Soc. Leverhulme Vis. Prof., Andhra Univ., India, 1967–68; Balfour Vis. Prof., History of Science, Weizmann Inst., Rehovot, Israel, 1973; Racah Vis. Prof. of Physics, Hebrew Univ., Jerusalem, 1973–74. Rutherford Meml Lectr, Royal Soc., Australia, 1989. Rutherford Medal and Prize, Inst. of Physics, 1970. *Publications:* Excited States of Nuclei, 1949; (ed) Biology and Physical Sciences, 1969; (ed) High Energy Physics and Nuclear Structure, 1970; contributions to Proc. Royal Society, Proc. Phys. Soc., etc. *Recreations:* plastic arts, travel. *Address:* Nevis Laboratory, Columbia University, PO Box 137, Irvington-on-Hudson, NY 10533, USA. *T:* (914) 591–8100.

DEVONSHIRE, 11th Duke of, *cr* 1694; **Andrew Robert Buxton Cavendish,** PC 1964; MC; Baron Cavendish, 1605; Earl of Devonshire, 1618; Marquess of Hartington, 1694; Earl of Burlington, 1831; Baron Cavendish (UK) 1831; Vice-Lord-Lieutenant of the County of Derby, 1957–87; Chancellor of Manchester University, 1965–86; *b* 2 Jan. 1920; *o surv. s* of 10th Duke of Devonshire, KG, and Lady Mary Cecil, GCVO, CBE (*d*

1988), d of 4th Marquess of Salisbury, KG, GCVO; S father, 1950; m 1941, Hon. Deborah Vivian Freeman-Mitford, d of 2nd Baron Redesdale; one s two d. Educ: Eton; Trinity Coll., Cambridge. Served War of 1939–45, Coldstream Guards (MC). Contested (C) Chesterfield Div. of Derbyshire, 1945 and 1950. Parliamentary Under-Sec. of State for Commonwealth Relations, Oct. 1960–Sept. 1962; Minister of State, Commonwealth Relations Office, Sept. 1962–Oct. 1964 and for Colonial Affairs, 1963–Oct. 1964. Steward of the Jockey Club, 1966–69. Mem., Horserace Totalisator Board, 1977–86; a Trustee, Nat. Gallery, 1960–68; President: The Royal Hosp. and Home, Putney, 1954– ; Derbyshire Boy Scouts Assoc.; Lawn Tennis Assoc., 1955–61; RNIB, 1979–85; Nat Assoc. for Deaf Children, 1978– ; East Midland Area, MENCAP; Building Societies Assoc., 1954–61; Chairman: Grand Council, British Empire Cancer Campaign, 1956–81; Throughbred Breeders' Assoc., 1978–81. Mayor of Buxton, 1952–54. Hon. Col, Manchester and Salford Univs OTC, 1981–85. Hon. LLD: Manchester; Sheffield; Liverpool; Hon. Dr Law, Memorial Univ. of Newfoundland. Publication: Park Top: a romance of the Turf, 1976. Heir: s Marquess of Hartington, qv. Address: Chatsworth, Bakewell, Derbyshire DE4 1PP. T: Baslow (0246) 582204; 4 Chesterfield Street, W1. T: 071-499 5803; Lismore Castle, Co. Waterford, Eire. T: Lismore 54288. Clubs: Brooks's, Jockey, White's.

DEVONSHIRE, Michael Norman, TD 1969; Master of the Supreme Court, Taxing Office, since 1979; a Recorder, since 1987; b 23 May 1930; s of late Norman George Devonshire and late Edith Devonshire (née Skinner); m 1962, Jessie Margaret Roberts. Educ: King's Sch., Canterbury. Military Service, 2nd Lt, RA, served Korea, 1953–55; 4/5 Bn Queen's Own Royal West Kent Regt TA and 8 Bn Queen's Regt TA, 1955–69; retired in rank of Major, 1969. Articled to H. D. Carter, 1948–53; admitted Solicitor, 1953; Partner, Doyle Devonshire Co., 1957–79. Pres., London Solicitors' Litigation Assoc., 1974–76; Mem., Law Soc. Family Law and Contentious Remuneration Cttees, 1969–79. Mem., Recreation and Conservation Cttee, Southern Water Authy, 1984–89. Mem., Council, Royal Yachting Assoc., 1978– (Trustee, Seamanship Foundn, 1981–85); Vice Chm., Internat. Regs Cttee, IYRU, 1991. Publications: (with M. J. Cook and W. H. Elliott) The Taxation of Contentious Costs, 1979; (consultant ed) Greenslade on Costs, 1991. Recreation: sailing. Address: 17 Chestnut Avenue, Southborough, Tunbridge Wells, Kent TN4 0BS. T: Tunbridge Wells (0892) 28672.

DE VRIES, Peter; writer; b Chicago, 27 Feb. 1910; s of Joost and Henrietta (née Eldersveld) de Vries; m 1943, Katinka Loeser; two s one d. Educ: Calvin College, Michigan (AB); Northwestern University. Editor, community newspaper, Chicago, 1931; free lance writer, 1931– ; associate editor Poetry Magazine, 1938; co-editor, 1942; joined editorial staff New Yorker Magazine, 1944. Mem., Amer. Acad. and Inst. of Arts and Letters. Publications: No But I saw the Movie, 1952; The Tunnel of Love, 1954; Comfort Me with Apples, 1956; The Mackerel Plaza, 1958; The Tents of Wickedness, 1959; Through the Fields of Clover, 1961; The Blood of the Lamb, 1962; Reuben, Reuben, 1964 (filmed, 1984); Let Me Count the Ways, 1965; The Vale of Laughter, 1967; The Cat's Pajamas and Witch's Milk, 1968 (filmed as Pete and Tillie, 1982); Mrs Wallop, 1970; Into Your Tent I'll Creep, 1971; Without a Stitch in Time, 1972; Forever Panting, 1973; The Glory of the Hummingbird, 1975; I Hear America Swinging, 1976; Madder Music, 1978; Consenting Adults, 1980; Sauce for the Goose, 1981; Slouching Towards Kalamazoo, 1983; The Prick of Noon, 1985; Peckham's Marbles, 1986.

DEW, Leslie Robert; Member, Bermuda Insurance Advisory Committee, since 1979; President and Managing Director, Britamco Ltd, 1977–84; President, Insco Ltd, Bermuda (Gulf Oil Corporation Insurance Subsidiaries), 1980–84 (Executive Vice President-Underwriter, 1977–80); Chairman, 1971–77 and formerly Non-Marine Underwriter, Roy J. M. Merrett Syndicates; b 11 April 1914; er s of Robert Thomas Dew, RHA and Ellen Dora Frampton; m 1st, 1939, Vera Doreen Wills (marr. diss. 1956); 2nd, 1956, Patricia Landsberg (née Hyde); one s. Educ: privately. Underwriting Member of Lloyd's, 1950– ; Mem. Cttee of Lloyd's, 1969–72, 1974–77; Dep. Chm. of Lloyd's, 1971, 1975, 1977; Mem. Cttee, Lloyd's Non-Marine Assoc., 1957–77 (Dep. Chm. 1963 and 1965, Chm. 1966); Chm., Lloyd's Common Market Working Gp, 1971–77; Dep. Chm., British Insurers' European Cttee, 1972–77. Binney Award for Civilian Bravery, 1975. Recreations: music, reading. Address: Suite No 165, 48 Par-La-Ville Road, Hamilton HM11, Bermuda. Club: Metropolitan (NY).

DEW, Prof. Ronald Beresford; Professor Emeritus, University of Manchester Institute of Science and Technology, since 1980; b 19 May 1916; s of Edwyn Dew-Jones, FCA, and Jean Robertson Dew-Jones, BA, (née McInnes); m 1940, Sheila Mary Smith, BA; one s one d. Educ: Sedbergh; Manchester Univ. (LLB); Cambridge Univ. (MA). Barrister-at-Law, Middle Temple, 1965. Lieut, RNVR, 1940–45. Asst Managing Dir, P-E Consulting Gp, 1952–62; Director: Kurt Salmon & Co., 1955–62; S. Dodd & Co., 1957–59. Visiting Prof. of Industrial Administration, Manchester Univ., 1960–63; Head of Dept of Management Sciences, Univ. of Manchester Inst. of Science and Technology, 1963–70 and 1974–77; Prof. of Industrial Administration, Manchester Univ., 1963–67; Prof. of Management Sciences, 1967–80. Mem. Council, Internat. Univ. Contact for Management Educn, 1966–71; Dir, Centre for Business Research, 1965–69; Dir, European Assoc. of Management Training Centres, 1966–71; Dep. Chm., Manchester Polytechnic, 1970–72; External Examiner, Univs of: Liverpool, 1967–70; Loughborough, 1968–73; Bath, 1970–73; Khartoum (Sudan), 1967–70. Co-Chm., Conf. of Univ. Management Schools (CUMS), 1970–73; Governor: Manchester Coll. of Commerce, 1966–70; Manchester Polytechnic, 1970–76; Member: Council of BIM, 1971–76 (Bd of NW Region, 1966–80); Council of Manchester Business School, 1967–76; Court of Manchester Univ., 1978–80; Trustee, European Foundation for Management Develt, 1975–77. CBIM, FCA. Recreations: archaeology, ornithology, bee-keeping, travel. Address: University of Manchester Institute of Science and Technology, Department of Management Sciences, Sackville Street, Manchester M60 1QD. T: 061–236 3311.

de WAAL, Sir Constant Hendrik, (Sir Henry), KCB 1989 (CB 1977); QC 1988; First Parliamentary Counsel, 1987–91; b 1 May 1931; s of late Hendrik de Waal and Elizabeth von Ephrussi; m 1964, Julia Jessel; two s. Educ: Tonbridge Sch. (scholar); Pembroke Coll., Cambridge (scholar). 1st cl. Law Tripos, 1st cl. LLM. Called to the Bar, Lincoln's Inn, 1953, Bencher 1989; Buchanan Prize, Cassel Scholar. Fellow of Pembroke Coll., Cambridge, and Univ. Asst Lectr in Law, 1958–60. Entered Parliamentary Counsel Office, 1960; with Law Commission, 1969–71; Parly Counsel, 1971–81; Second Parly Counsel, 1981–86. Recreation: remaining (so far as possible) unaware of current events. Address: 62 Sussex Street, SW1V 4RG.
See also Rev. V. A. de Waal.

de WAAL, Rev. Canon Hugo Ferdinand; Principal, Ridley Hall Theological College, Cambridge, since 1978; Hon. Canon of Ely Cathedral, since 1986; b 16 March 1935; s of Bernard Hendrik and Albertine Felice de Waal; m 1960, Brigit Elizabeth Townsend Massingberd-Mundy; one s three d. Educ: Tonbridge School; Pembroke Coll., Cambridge (MA); Münster Univ., Germany; Ridley Hall, Cambridge. Curate, St Martin's-in-the Bull Ring, Birmingham, 1960; Chaplain, Pembroke Coll., Cambridge, 1964–68; Rector of Dry Drayton, Cambs, 1964–73; with Bar Hill Ecumenical Area, 1967–73; Vicar of St John's, Blackpool Parish Church, 1974–78. Recreations: music, tennis and squash, fly-

fishing. Address: The Principal's Lodge, Ridley Hall, Cambridge CB3 9HG. T: Cambridge (0223) 58665.

de WAAL, Rev. Victor Alexander; Dean of Canterbury, 1976–86; b 2 Feb. 1929; s of late Hendrik de Waal and Elizabeth von Ephrussi; m 1960, Esther Aline Lowndes Moir, PhD; four s. Educ: Tonbridge School; Pembroke Coll., Cambridge (MA); Ely Theological College. With Phs van Ommeren (London) Ltd, 1949–50; Asst Curate, St Mary the Virgin, Isleworth, 1952–56; Chaplain, Ely Theological Coll., 1956–59; Chaplain and Succentor, King's Coll., Cambridge, 1959–63; Chaplain, Univ. of Nottingham, 1963–69; Chancellor of Lincoln Cathedral, 1969–76. Hon. DD Nottingham, 1983. Publications: What is the Church?, 1969; The Politics of Reconciliation: Zimbabwe's first decade, 1990; contrib.: Theology and Modern Education, 1965; Stages of Experience, 1965; The Committed Church, 1966; Liturgy Reshaped, 1982; Liturgie et Espace Liturgique, 1987; Vie Ecclesiale—communauté et communautés, 1989. Address: Cwm Cottage, Rowlestone, Pontrilas, Hereford HR2 0DP. T: Golden Valley (0981) 240391.
See also Sir C. H. de Waal.

DEWAR, family name of **Baron Forteviot.**

DEWAR, David Alexander; an Assistant Auditor General, National Audit Office, since 1984; b 28 Oct. 1934; s of James and Isabella Dewar; m 1959, Rosalind Mary Ellen Greenwood; one s one d. Educ: Leith Academy, Edinburgh. Entered Exchequer and Audit Dept, 1953; Chief Auditor, 1966; Deputy Director of Audit, 1973; Director of Audit, 1977; Dep. Sec. of Dept, 1981. Recreations: gardening, golf. Address: Cherries, 58 Linersh Wood Close, Bramley, Guildford, Surrey GU5 0EQ. T: Guildford (0483) 892507.

DEWAR, Donald Campbell; MP (Lab) Glasgow, Garscadden, since April 1978; solicitor, with Ross Harper & Murphy, Glasgow; b 21 Aug. 1937; s of Dr Alasdair Dewar, Glasgow; m 1964, Alison McNair (marr. diss. 1973); one s one d. Educ: Glasgow Acad.; Glasgow Univ. (MA, LLB). MP (Lab) South Aberdeen, 1966–70; PPS to Pres. of Bd of Trade, 1967; Chm., Select Cttee on Scottish Affairs, 1979–81; front bench spokesman on Scottish Affairs, 1981– ; Mem., Shadow Cabinet, 1984– . Address: 23 Cleveden Road, Glasgow G12 0PQ.

DEWAR, George Duncan Hamilton; chartered accountant; Partner, Peat, Marwick, Mitchell & Co., Glasgow, 1949–81; b 11 Sept. 1916; s of George Readman Dewar and Elizabeth Garrioch Sinclair Hamilton; m 1940, Elizabeth Lawson Potts Lawrie; one s one d. Educ: High Sch. of Glasgow. Mem. Inst. Chartered Accountants of Scotland (admitted, 1940; Mem. Coun., 1960–65; Vice-Pres., 1969–70; Pres., 1970–71). Mem., Scottish Tourist Bd, 1977–80. Recreations: golf, gardening. Address: 82 Langside Drive, Glasgow G43 2SX. T: 041–637 1734. Clubs: Western, Royal Scottish Automobile (Glasgow).

DEWAR, Ian Stewart; JP; Member, South Glamorgan County Council, since 1985 (Vice-Chairman, 1990–91); b 29 Jan. 1929; er s of late William Stewart Dewar and of Eileen Dewar (née Godfrey); m 1968, Nora Stephanie House; one s one d. Educ: Penarth County Sch.; UC Cardiff; Jesus Coll., Oxford (MA). RAF, 1947–49. Asst Archivist, Glamorgan County Council, 1952–53. Entered Min. of Labour, 1953; Asst Private Sec. to Minister, 1956–58; Principal, Min. of Labour and Civil Service Commn, 1958–65; Asst Sec., Min. of Labour, Dept of Employment and Commn on Industrial Relations, 1965–70; Asst Sec., 1970–73, and Under-Sec., 1973–83, Welsh Office. Member, Governing Body: Univ. of Wales, 1985– ; Nat. Mus. of Wales, 1985– ; Chm., Museum Schs Service Cttee, 1989– . JP S Glam, 1985. Address: 59 Stanwell Road, Penarth, South Glamorgan CF6 2LR. T: Cardiff (0222) 703255.

DEWAR, Prof. Michael James Steuart, FRS 1960; MA, DPhil Oxon; Robert A. Welch Professor of Chemistry, University of Texas, 1963–90; Graduate Research Professor, University of Florida, since 1990; b 24 Sept. 1918; s of Francis D. Dewar, ICS, and Nan B. Keith; m 1944, Mary Williamson; two s. Educ: Winchester Coll. (First Scholar); Balliol Coll., Oxford (Brackenbury, Frazer and Gibbs Scholar; Hon. Fellow, 1974). ICI Fellow in Chemistry, Oxford, 1945; Courtaulds Ltd, Fundamental Research Laboratory, 1945–51; Reilly Lecturer at Notre Dame Univ., USA, 1951; Prof. of Chemistry and Head of Dept of Chemistry at Queen Mary Coll., University of London, 1951–59; Prof. of Chemistry, University of Chicago, 1959–63. Visiting Professor: Yale Univ., USA, 1957; Arthur D. Little, MIT, 1966; Maurice S. Kharasch, Univ. of Chicago, 1971; Firth, Sheffield, 1972; Dist. Bicentennial, Univ. of Utah, 1976; Pahlavi, Iran, 1977. Hon. Sec. Chemical Soc., 1957–59. Lectures: Tilden, Chem. Soc., 1954; Falk-Plaut, Columbia Univ., 1963; Daines Memorial, Univ. of Kansas, 1963; Glidden Company, Western Reserve Univ., 1964; Marchon Visiting, Univ. of Newcastle upon Tyne, 1966; Glidden Company, Kent State Univ., 1967; Gnehm, Eidg. Tech. Hochschule, Zurich, 1968; Barton, Univ. of Oklahoma, 1969; (first) Kahlbaum, Univ. of Basel, 1970; (first) Benjamin Rush, Univ. of Pennsylvania, 1971; Venable, Univ. of N Carolina, 1971; Foster, State Univ. of NY at Buffalo, 1973; Robinson, Chem. Soc., 1974; Sprague, Univ. of Wisconsin, 1974; Bircher, Vanderbilt Univ., 1976; Faraday, Northern Illinois Univ., 1977; Priestley, Pennsylvania State Univ., 1980; J. Clarence Karcher, Univ. of Oklahoma, 1984; Res. Scholar Lectr, Drew Univ., 1984; (first) Charles O. A. Coulson, Univ. of Georgia, 1988. Fellow, Amer. Acad. of Arts and Sciences, 1966; Mem., Nat. Acad. of Sciences, 1983. Harrison Howe Award of Amer. Chem. Soc., 1961; (first) G. W. Wheland Meml Medal, Univ. of Chicago, 1976; Evans Award, Ohio State Univ., 1977; South West Regional Award, Amer. Chem. Soc., 1978; Davy Medal, Royal Soc., 1982; James Flack Norris Award, Amer. Chem. Soc., 1984; William H. Nichols Award, Amer. Chem. Soc., 1986; Auburn Kosolapoff Award, Amer. Chem. Soc., 1988; Tetrahedron Prize, 1989; World Assoc. of Theoretical Organic Chemistry Medal, 1989; Chemical Pioneer Award, Amer. Inst. of Chemists, 1990. Publications: The Electronic Theory of Organic Chemistry, 1949; Hyperconjugation, 1962; Introduction to Modern Chemistry, 1965; The Molecular Orbital Theory of Organic Chemistry, 1969; Computer Compilation of Molecular Weights and Percentage Compositions, 1970; The PMO Theory of Organic Chemistry, 1975; papers in scientific journals. Address: Department of Chemistry, University of Florida, Gainesville, Fla 32611, USA. T: 904–332–2050.

DEWAR, Robert James, CMG 1969; CBE 1964; World Bank, retired 1984; b 1923; s of late Dr Robert Scott Dewar, MA, MB, ChB, and Mrs Roubaix Dewar, Dumbreck, Glasgow; m 1947, Christina Marianne, d of late Olof August Ljungberger, Stockholm, Sweden; two s one d. Educ: High Sch. of Glasgow; Edinburgh Univ. (BSc, Forestry); Wadham Coll., Oxford. Asst Conservator of Forests, Colonial Forest Service, Nigeria and Nyasaland, 1944–55; Dep. Chief Conservator of Forests, Nyasaland, 1955–60; Chief Conservator of Forests, Dir of Forestry and Game, Nyasaland (now Malawi), 1960–64; Mem. Nyasaland Legislative Council, 1960. Permanent Secretary, Malawi: Min. of Natural Resources, 1964–67 and 1968–69; Min. of Economic Affairs, 1967–68; retd from Malawi CS, 1969; World Bank: Sen. Agriculturalist, 1969–74; Chief of Agricl Div., Regl Mission for Eastern Africa, 1974–84. Mem. Nat. Development Council, Malawi, 1966–69. Recreations: gardening, golf, angling. Address: Hawkshaw, Comrie Road, Crieff, Perthshire PH7 4BJ. T: Crieff (0764) 4830. Club: Commonwealth Trust.

DEWAR, His Honour Thomas; a Circuit Judge (formerly Judge of the County Court), 1962–84; Joint President, Council of Circuit Judges, 1980 (Vice-President, 1979); *b* 5 Jan. 1909; *s* of James Stewart Dewar and Katherine Rose Dewar; *m* 1950, Katherine Muriel Johnson; one *s*. *Educ:* Penarth Intermediate School; Cardiff Technical Coll.; Sch. of Pharmacy, University of London; Birkbeck Coll., University of London. Pharmaceutical Chemist, 1931; BPharm 1931, PhD 1934, BSc (Botany, 1st cl. hons) 1936, London. Called to Bar, Middle Temple, 1939; Blackstone Pupillage Prize, 1939. Admin. staff of Pharmaceutical Soc., 1936–40; Sec., Middx Pharmaceutical Cttee, 1940–41; Asst Dir, Min. of Supply, 1943; Sec., Wellcome Foundation, 1943–45. Mem. of Western Circuit, 1945–62; Judge of the County Court (circuit 59, Cornwall and Plymouth), 1962–65, (circuit 38, Edmonton, etc), 1965–66 (circuit 41, Clerkenwell), 1966–71; Circuit Judge, SE circuit, 1972–84. Presided over inquiry into X-ray accident at Plymouth Hosp., 1962. Mem. Executive Council, Internat. Law Assoc., 1974–89. Governor, Birkbeck Coll., 1944–46 and 1971–82. *Publications:* Textbook of Forensic Pharmacy, 1946 and four subsequent editions; scientific papers in Quarterly Jl of Pharmacy and Pharmacology. *Recreations:* horticulture, travel. *Address:* 1 Garden Court, Temple, EC4Y 9BJ. *T:* 071–353 3326.

de WARDENER, Prof. Hugh Edward, CBE 1982 (MBE (mil.) 1946); MD, FRCP; Professor of Medicine, University of London, Charing Cross Hospital, 1960–81, now Emeritus; Honorary Consultant Physician to the Army, 1975–80; *b* 8 Oct. 1915; *s* of Edouard de Wardener and Becky (*née* Pearce); *m* 1st, 1939, Janet Lavinia Bellis Simon (marr. diss. 1947); one *s*; 2nd, 1947, Diana Rosamund Crawshay (marr. diss. 1954); 3rd, 1954, Jill Mary Foxworthy (marr. diss. 1969); one *d*; 4th, 1969, Josephine Margaret Storey, MBE; two *s*. *Educ:* Malvern Coll. St Thomas's Hosp., 1933–39; RAMC, 1939–45; St Thomas's Hosp., 1945–60, Registrar, Senior Lecturer, Reader. MRCP 1946, MD 1949, FRCP 1958. Hon. MD, Univ. Pierre et Marie Curie, Paris, 1980. President: Internat. Soc. of Nephrology, 1969–72; Renal Assoc., 1973–76; Mem. Council, Imp. Cancer Res. Fund, 1981–88. *Publications:* The Kidney: An Outline of Normal and Abnormal Structure and Function, 1958, 5th edn 1986; papers in various scientific journals. *Recreations:* normal and scything. *Address:* 9 Dungarvan Avenue, Barnes, SW15 5QU. *T:* 081–878 3130.

DEWBERRY, David Albert; HM Diplomatic Service; Deputy High Commissioner, Dar es Salaam, since 1987; *b* 27 Sept. 1941; *s* of Albert Dewberry and Grace Dewberry (*née* Tarsey); *m* 1974, Catherine Mary (*née* Stabback); three *s* one *d*. *Educ:* Cray Valley Sch., Foots Cray, Kent. Joined CRO, 1958; Karachi, 1963; Kingston, 1966; Warsaw, 1970; Brussels, 1971; Second Sec. (Aid), Dhaka, 1972; FCO, 1974; Consul: Mexico City, 1977; Buenos Aires, 1980; FCO, 1982. *Recreations:* reading, walking. *Address:* c/o Foreign and Commonwealth Office, SW1A 2AH.

DEWDNEY, Duncan Alexander Cox, CBE 1968; Director, The Coverdale Organisation, since 1973; *b* 22 Oct. 1911; *o s* of late Claude Felix Dewdney and Annie Ross Cox; *m* 1935, Ann, *d* of Walter Riley and Emily Sterratt; two *d*. *Educ:* Bromgrove Sch., Worcs; University of Birmingham (BSc Hons, Cadman Medallist). Served War of 1939–45; RAF, 1940–45 (Wing Comdr); Air Staff appts, Head RE8 Min. of Home Security (R&D Dept). British Petroleum Co., 1932–36; International Assoc. (Pet. Ind.) Ltd, 1936–40; Research Man., Esso Development Co., 1945–51; joined Esso Petroleum Co., 1951; Dir, 1957; Man. Dir, 1963–67; Vice-Chm., 1968. Seconded to NBPI as Jt Dep. Chm., 1965–66, part-time Mem. Bd, 1967–69. Exec. Dir, Rio Tinto Zinc Corporation, 1968–72; Chairman: Irish Refining Co. Ltd, 1958–65; Anglesey Aluminium, 1968–71; RTZ Britain, 1969–72; RTZ Development Enterprises, 1970–72; Dep. Chm., Manpower Services Commn, 1974–77; Dir, Esso Chemicals SA, 1964. Chairman: National Economic Develt Cttee for the Mechanical Engrg Industry, 1964–68; Welsh Industrial Develt Bd, 1972–75; Underwater Training Centre, 1977–79. Legion of Merit, 1945. *Address:* Salters, Harestock, Winchester, Hants SO22 5JP. *T:* Winchester (0962) 52034. *Club:* Travellers'.

DEWE, Roderick Gorrie; Chairman, Dewe Rogerson Group Ltd, since 1969; *b* 17 Oct. 1935; *s* of Douglas Percy Dewe and Rosanna Clements Gorrie; *m* 1964, Carol Anne Beach Thomas; one *s* one *d*. *Educ:* abroad and University Coll., Oxford (BA Hons). FIPR. Treasury, Fedn of Rhodesia and Nyasaland Govt, 1957–58; Angel Court Consultants, 1960–68; founded Dewe Rogerson, 1969. *Recreations:* golf, travel. *Address:* 55 Duncan Terrace, N1 8AG; The Booking Hall, Southill Station, near Biggleswade, Beds. *T:* Hitchin (0462) 811274. *Club:* City of London.

DEWE MATHEWS, Marina Sarah, (Mrs John Dewe Mathews); *see* Warner, M. S.

de WET, Dr Carel; South African Ambassador to the Court of St James's, 1964–67 and 1972–77; Director of companies; farmer; *b* Memel, OFS, S Africa, 25 May 1924; *g s* of Gen. Christian de Wet; *m* 1949, Catharina Elizabeth (Rina) Maas, BA; one *s* three *d*. *Educ:* Vrede High Sch., OFS; Pretoria Univ. (BSc); University of Witwatersrand (MB, BCh). Served at Nat. Hosp., Bloemfontein; subseq. practised medicine at Boksburg, Transvaal, at Winburg, OFS, and, from 1948, at Vanderbijlpark, Transvaal. Mayor of Vanderbijlpark, 1950–53; MP (Nat. Party) for Vanderbijlpark, 1953–64, for Johannesburg West, 1967–72; Mem. various Parly and Nat. Party Cttees, 1953–64; Minister of Mines and Health, Govt of S Africa, 1967–72. *Recreations:* game farming, golf, rugby, cricket, hunting, deep sea fishing. *Address:* PO Box 6424, Johannesburg 2000, Republic of South Africa. *T:* (office) 726–2903; (home) 706-6202. *Clubs:* Royal Automobile, East India, Institute of Directors, MCC, Les Ambassadeurs, Eccentric, Wentworth; Here XVII (Cape Town); Constantia (Pretoria); New, Rand Park Golf, Country (Johannesburg); Maccauvlei Country (Vereeniging), Emfuleni Golf (Vanderbijlpark).

DEWEY, Sir Anthony Hugh, 3rd Bt, *cr* 1917; JP; *b* 31 July 1921; *s* of late Major Hugh Grahame Dewey, MC (*e s* of 2nd Bt), and Marjorie Florence Isobell (who *m* 2nd, 1940, Sir Robert Bell, KCSI; she *d* 1988), *d* of Lieut-Col Alexander Hugh Dobbs; *S* grandfather, 1948; *m* 1949, Sylvia, *d* of late Dr J. R. MacMahon, Branksome Manor, Bournemouth; two *s* three *d*. JP Somerset, 1961. *Heir: s* Rupert Grahame Dewey [*b* 29 March 1953; *m* 1978, Suzanne Rosemary, *d* of late Andrew Lusk, Perthshire; two *s* one *d*]. *Address:* Rag, Galhampton, Yeovil, Som BA22 7AJ. *T:* North Cadbury (0963) 40213. *Club:* Army and Navy.

DEWEY, Prof. John Frederick, FRS 1985; FGS; Professor of Geology and Fellow of University College, University of Oxford, since 1986; *b* 22 May 1937; *s* of John Edward and Florence Nellie Mary Dewey; *m* 1961, Frances Mary Blackhurst; one *s* one *d*. *Educ:* Bancroft's School; Queen Mary Coll. and Imperial Coll., Univ. of London (BSc, PhD, DIC, MA). Lecturer: Univ. of Manchester, 1960–64; Univ. of Cambridge, 1964–70; Prof., State Univ. of New York at Albany, 1970–82; Prof. of Geology, Durham Univ., 1982–86. Mem., Academia Europaea, 1990. Numerous honours and awards, UK and overseas. *Publications:* contribs to Geol Soc. of America Bulletin, Geol Soc. London Jl, Jl Geophysical Res. and other learned jls. *Recreations:* skiing, cricket, water colour painting, model railways. *Address:* University College, Oxford OX1 4BH.

DEWHURST, Prof. Sir (Christopher) John, Kt 1977; FRCOG, FRCSE; Professor of Obstetrics and Gynaecology, University of London, at Queen Charlotte's Hospital for Women, 1967–85, now Professor Emeritus; *b* 2 July 1920; *s* of John and Agnes Dewhurst; *m* 1952, Hazel Mary Atkin; two *s* one *d*. *Educ:* St Joseph's Coll., Dumfries; Manchester Univ. MB, ChB. Surg. Lieut, RNVR, 1943–46. Sen. Registrar, St Mary's Hosp., Manchester, 1948–51; Lectr, Sen. Lectr and Reader, Sheffield Univ., 1951–67. Pres., RCOG, 1975–78. Hon. FACOG 1976; Hon. FRCSI 1977; Hon. FCOG (SA) 1978; Hon. FRACOG 1985. Hon. DSc Sheffield, 1977; Hon. MD Uruguay, 1980. *Publications:* A Student's Guide to Obstetrics and Gynaecology, 1960, 2nd edn 1965; The Gynaecological Disorders of Infants and Children, 1963; (jtly) The Intersexual Disorders, 1969; (ed) Integrated Obstetrics and Gynaecology for Postgraduates, 1972, 3rd edn 1981; (jtly) A General Practice of Obstetrics and Gynaecology, 1977, 2nd edn 1984; Practical Paediatric and Adolescent Gynaecology, 1980; Royal Confinements, 1980; Female Puberty and its Abnormalities, 1984. *Recreations:* cricket, gardening, music. *Address:* 21 Jack's Lane, Harefield, Middlesex UB9 6HE. *T:* Harefield (089582) 5403.

DEWHURST, Timothy Littleton, MC 1945; Chief Registrar of the High Court of Justice in Bankruptcy, since 1988 (Registrar, since 1981); *b* 4 March 1920; *s* of late Robert Cyril Dewhurst and Rhoda Joan Dewhurst; *m* 1949, Pandora Laetitia Oldfield (*d* 1984); four *d*. *Educ:* Stowe Sch.; Magdalen Coll., Oxford (MA). Called to Bar, Lincoln's Inn, 1950, Bencher, 1988. Served with Rifle Brigade, 1941–46, N Africa and Italy (despatches 1944). Mem. Bar Council, 1977–79; Conveyancing Counsel of the Court, 1980–81. *Address:* Thomas More Building, Royal Courts of Justice, Strand, WC2.

de WINTER, Carl; Secretary General, Federation of British Artists, 1978–84; *b* 18 June 1934; *s* of Alfred de Winter; *m* 1958, Lyndall Bradshaw; one *s* one *d*. *Educ:* Pangbourne. Purser, Orient Line, 1951–60. Art Exhibitions Bureau: PA to Man. Dir, 1961–66; Director, 1967–84; Royal Soc. of Portrait Painters: Asst Sec., 1962–78; Sec., 1978–84; Royal Soc. of Miniature Painters, Sculptors and Gravers: Asst Sec., 1964–67; Sec., 1968–84; Hon. Mem., 1984; Royal Soc. of Marine Artists: Asst Sec., 1964–70; Sec., 1971–78; Royal Soc. of British Artists: Asst Keeper, 1969–73; Keeper, 1974–84; Royal Inst. of Oil Painters: Sec., 1973–84; Royal Inst. of Painters in Watercolours: Sec., 1979–84; National Soc. of Painters, Sculptors and Printmakers: Sec., 1973–84; New English Art Club: Sec., 1973–84; United Soc. of Artists: Sec., 1975–81. *Address:* Holbrook Park House, Holbrook, near Horsham, W Sussex RH12 4PW. *T:* Horsham (0403) 52431.

de WINTON, Michael Geoffrey, CBE 1960 (OBE 1952); MC 1944; Assistant Legal Secretary to the Law Officers, 1972–80; *b* 17 Oct. 1916; *s* of John Jeffreys de Winton and Ida de Winton; *m* 1948, Ursula Mary, *d* of E. E. Lightwood, MB; two *s* one *d*. *Educ:* Monmouth School. Admitted Solicitor, 1939. War service, 1939–46: commnd S Wales Borderers, 1940; Company Comdr 2nd Punjab Regt, Indian Army, in India, Middle East and Burma, 1942–45 (despatches twice). Administrative officer, Nigeria, 1946–48; Crown Counsel, 1948–53; called to the Bar, Gray's Inn, 1953; Principal legal draftsman, W Nigeria, 1954; Solicitor General and Permanent Sec. to Min. of Justice, W Nigeria, 1957–61; retired from HM Overseas CS and re-admitted solicitor, 1961; Asst Legal Adviser, Colonial Office, 1961–66, CRO 1967, FCO 1968; Asst Solicitor, Law Officers Dept (Internat. and Commonwealth affairs), 1969; Under Secretary, 1974; retired, 1980. Legal consultant to overseas govts and internat. organizations; Principal Legal Adviser, British Indian Ocean Territory, 1982–83. *Recreations:* music, art. *Address:* Stable Cottage, Church Walk, Stalbridge, Dorset DT10 2LR. *T:* Stalbridge (0963) 62834.

DE WOLF, Vice-Adm. Harry George, CBE 1946; DSO 1944; DSC 1944; *b* 1903; *s* of late Harry George De Wolf, Bedford, NS; *m* 1931, Gwendolen Fowle, *d* of Thomas St George Gilbert, Somerset, Bermuda; one *s* (one *d* decd). Served War of 1939–45. Asst Chief of Naval Staff, Canada, 1944–47; Sen. Canadian Naval Officer Afloat, 1947–48; Flag Officer, Pacific Coast, 1948–50; Vice-Chief of Naval Staff, 1950–52; Chm. of Canadian Joint Staff, Washington, 1953–55; Chief of Naval Staff, Canada, 1956–60, retired. Hon. DSc (M): Royal Military College of Canada, 1966; Royal Roads Mil. Coll., 1980. *Address:* Apt 1006, 200 Rideau Terrace, Ottawa, Ont, Canada; Old Post Office, Somerset, Bermuda.

DEWS, Peter; Theatre and TV Director; *b* 26 Sept. 1929; *er s* of John Dews and Edna (Bloomfield); *m* 1960, Ann Rhodes. *Educ:* Queen Elizabeth Grammar Sch., Wakefield; University Coll., Oxford (MA). Asst Master, Holgate and District Grammar Sch., Barnsley, 1952–53; BBC Midland Region Drama Producer (Radio and TV), 1953–63; Dir, Ravinia Shakespeare Festival, Chicago, 1963–64; Artistic Director: Birmingham Repertory Theatre, 1966–72; Chichester Fest. Theatre, 1978–80. Directed: TV: An Age of Kings, 1960 (SFTA Award 1960); The Spread of the Eagle, 1963; Theatre: As You Like It, Vaudeville, 1967; Hadrian VII, Mermaid, 1968, Haymarket and NY, 1969 (Tony Award 1969), Edmonton, 1987; Antony and Cleopatra, Chichester, 1969; Vivat Vivat Regina, Chichester, 1970, Piccadilly and NY, 1972; The Alchemist, Chichester, 1970; Crown Matrimonial, Haymarket, 1972, NY 1973; The Director of the Opera, Chichester, 1973; The Waltz of the Toreadors, Haymarket, 1974; King John, Stratford, Ont, 1974; The Pleasure of His Company, Toronto, 1974; Coriolanus, Tel Aviv, 1975; Othello, Chichester, 1975; Equus, Vancouver, 1975; Number Thirteen Rue de l'Amour, Phœnix, 1976; The Circle, Chichester, transf. to Haymarket, 1976; The Pleasure of His Company, Phœnix, 1976; Man and Superman, Don Juan in Hell, When We Are Married, Ottawa, 1977; Julius Caesar, Chichester, 1977; A Sleep of Prisoners, Chichester Cathedral, 1978; Julius Caesar, A Sleep of Prisoners, Hong Kong Festival, 1979; The Devil's Disciple, The Importance of Being Earnest, Chichester, 1979; Terra Nova, Much Ado About Nothing, Chichester, 1980; Plenty, Toronto, 1981; The Taming of the Shrew, The Comedy of Errors, Stratford, Ont, 1981; Cards on the Table, Vaudeville, 1981; 56 Duncan Terrace, Edmonton, A Midsummer Night's Dream, Plymouth, and Terra Nova, Durban, 1982; Pierewaaien, Arnhem, 1983; Time and the Conways, Chichester, 1983; On The Razzle, Durban, 1983; Romeo and Juliet, Stratford, Ont, and Measure for Measure, Tel Aviv, 1984; Waiting for Godot, and Galileo, Scottish Theatre Co., 1985; King Lear, tour, 1986; An Inspector Calls, Clwyd and Westminster, 1987, tour, 1988; She Stoops to Conquer, tour, 1987. Hon. DLitt: Bradford, 1988; De Paul Univ., Chicago, 1989–90. *Recreation:* music. *Address:* c/o Larry Dalzell Associates Ltd, Suite 12, 17 Broad Court, WC2B 5QN.

DEXTER, Edward Ralph; Managing Director, Ted Dexter & Associates, since 1978; *b* 15 May 1935; *m* 1959, Susan Georgina Longfield; one *s* one *d*. *Educ:* Radley College; Jesus College, Cambridge (Captain of cricket). Served 11th Hussars, 1956–57 (Malaya Campaign Medal 1955). Cricketer, 1958–68; Captain of Sussex, 1960–65; Captain of England, 1962–65; freelance journalist, 1965–88; sports promotion consultant, 1978–. Chm., England (Cricket) Cttee, TCCB, 1989–. Contested (C) Cardiff, 1965. *Publications:* Ted Dexter's Cricket Book, 1963; Ted Dexter Declares, 1966; (jtly) Test Kill, 1976; Deadly Putter, 1979; From Bradman to Boycott, 1981; My Golf, 1982. *Recreations:* golf, reading, motor cycling. *Address:* 20A Woodville Gardens, Ealing, W5 2LQ. *T:* 081–998 6863. *Clubs:* MCC; Sunningdale Golf, Royal and Ancient Golf.

DEXTER, Harold; Organist; Professor, Guildhall School of Music and Drama (Head of General Musicianship Department, 1962–85); Organist, St Botolph's, Aldgate; *b* 7 Oct. 1920; *s* of F. H. and E. Dexter; *m* 1942, Faith Grainger; one *d*. *Educ:* Wyggeston Grammar Sch., Leicester; Corpus Christi Coll., Cambridge, 1939–41 and 1946. ARCO 1938; College Organ Scholar, 1939; John Stewart of Rannoch Scholar, 1940; FRCO 1940;

ARCM 1941. BA, MusB 1942; MA 1946; RCO Choirmaster's Diploma; John Brook Prize, 1946; ADCM, 1948. Royal Navy and RNVR, 1941–46. Organist, Louth Parish Church and Music-Master, King Edward VI Grammar Sch., Louth, 1947–49; Organist, Holy Trinity, Leamington Spa, 1949–56; Music Master, Bablake Sch., Coventry, 1952–56; Master of the Music, Southwark Cathedral, 1956–68. FGSM 1962, FRSCM 1964 (Hon. diplomas). *Address:* 8 Prince Edward Road, Billericay, Essex CM11 2HA. *T:* Billericay (0277) 652042.

DEXTER, Prof. Thomas Michael, FRS 1991; Professor of Haematology and Head of Department of Experimental Haematology, Paterson Institute for Cancer Research, since 1982; *b* 15 May 1945; *s* of Thomas Richard Dexter and Agnes Gertrude Deplege; *m* 1966, Frances Ann Sutton (marr. diss. 1978); one *s* one *d* (twins); one *s* one *d* by Dr Elaine Spooncer. *Educ:* Salford Univ. (BSc 1st class Hons 1970; DSc 1982); Manchester Univ. (PhD 1973). MRCPath 1987. Lady Tata Meml Scholar, 1970–73; Res. Scientist, Paterson Inst., 1973; Life Fellow, Cancer Res. Campaign, Manchester, 1978; Personal Chair, Univ. of Manchester, 1985. Visiting Fellow: Sloan Kettering Inst., NY, 1976–77; Weizmann Inst., Israel, 1980. Maximov Lectr, Leningrad, 1990. Pres., Internat. Soc. for Exptl Hematology, 1988. Mem. editl bd of 12 scientific jls. *Publications:* editor of 230 articles in scientific books. *Recreations:* folk singing, gardening, poetry, dominoes. *Address:* Cancer Research Campaign Laboratory of Experimental Haematology, Paterson Institute for Cancer Research, Christie Hospital, Withington, Manchester M20 9BX. *T:* 061–446 2596.

DEXTRAZE, Gen. Jacques Alfred, CC, CBE, CMM, DSO (Bar), CD; President, J. A. Dextraze and Associates, since 1984; *b* 15 Aug. 1919; *s* of Alfred and Amanda Dextraze; *m* 1942, Frances Helena Pare; three *s* (and one *s* decd). *Educ:* St Joseph de Berthier; MacDonald Business Coll., Montreal. With Dominion Rubber Co, 1938–40. Served War of 1939–45: Fusiliers, Mt Royal, 1939–45, Lt-Col and Comdg Officer, 1944–45; Comdg Officer, Hastings and Prince Edward Regt, 1945. With Singer Mfg Co., 1945–50; Manager, Forest Ops, 1947–50. Resumed mil. career as Comdg Officer, 2nd Bn Royal 22e Regt, 1950–52; Chief of Staff HQ, UN ops in Congo, 1963–64; Chief of Personnel, Can. Forces HQ, 1970–72; Chief of Defence Staff, 1972–77, retired. Chm., Canadian Nat. Rlys, 1977–82. Hon. ADC to the Governor-Gen., 1958. Hon. LLD Wilfred Laurier Univ.; Hon. PhD (Business Admin) Sherbrooke Univ. KStJ; KCLJ. Cross of Grand Officer, Order of the Crown (Belgium), 1977. *Address:* 467 Crestview Road, Ottawa, Ontario K1H 5G7, Canada.

de YARBURGH-BATESON, family name of **Baron Deramore.**

DEYERMOND, Prof. Alan David, DLitt; FSA; FBA 1988; Professor of Spanish, Queen Mary and Westfield College, London (formerly Westfield College), since 1969; *b* 24 Feb. 1932; *s* of late Henry Deyermond and Margaret Deyermond (*née* Lawson); *m* 1957, Ann Marie Bracken; one *d. Educ:* Quarry Bank High Sch., Liverpool; Victoria Coll., Jersey; Pembroke Coll., Oxford (MA; BLitt 1957; DLitt 1985). FSA 1987. Westfield College, London: Asst Lectr, 1955; Lectr, 1958; Reader, 1966; Senior Tutor, 1967–72; Dean, Faculty of Arts, 1972–74, 1981–84; Head of Dept of Spanish, 1983–89; Vice-Principal, 1986–89. Visiting Professor, Universities of: Wisconsin, 1972; California LA, 1977; Princeton, 1978–81; Victoria, 1983; N Arizona, 1986; Johns Hopkins, 1987. Pres., Internat. Courtly Literature Soc., 1977–83, Hon. Life Pres., 1983; Vice-Pres., Asociación Internacional de Hispanistas, 1983–89. Corresponding Fellow: Medieval Acad. of America; Real Acad. de Buenas Letras de Barcelona; Mem., Hispanic Soc. of America; Hon. Fellow, Asociación Hispánica de Literatura Medieval. *Publications:* The Petrarchan Sources of La Celestina, 1961, 2nd edn 1975; Epic Poetry and the Clergy, 1969; A Literary History of Spain: The Middle Ages, 1971; Apollonius of Tyre, 1973; Lazarillo de Tormes: a critical guide, 1975; Historia y crítica de la literatura española: Edad Media, 1980; El Cantar de Mio Cid y la épica medieval española, 1987; contribs to Bulletin of Hispanic Studies etc. *Recreations:* dog-walking, psephology, vegetarian cookery. *Address:* 20 Lancaster Road, St Albans, Herts AL1 4ET. *T:* St Albans (0727) 55383.

d'EYNCOURT, Sir Mark Gervais T.; *see* Tennyson-d'Eyncourt.

DHAKA, Archbishop of, (RC), since 1978; **Most Rev. Michael Rozario,** STL; *b* Solepore, Dacca, Bangladesh, 18 Jan. 1926; *s* of Urban Rozario. *Educ:* Little Flower Seminary, Dacca, Bangladesh; St Albert Seminary, Ranchi, India. Jagannath Coll., Dacca, Bangladesh, 1948–50; Univ. of Notre Dame, USA, 1951–53; Urbano Univ., Rome, 1953–57. Ordained priest, 1956; Bishop of Dinajpur, 1968. Pres., Catholic Bishops' Conf. of Bangladesh. *Address:* Archbishop's House, PO Box 3, Dhaka 1000, Bangladesh.

DHAVAN, Shanti Swarup; Member, Law Commission of India, 1972–77; *b* 2 July 1905; *m* Shakuntala Kapur, *d* of Malik, Basant Lal Kapur; two *s* one *d. Educ:* Punjab Univ.; Emmanuel Coll., Cambridge. BA, 1st Cl. Hons History, Punjab Univ., 1925. Hist. Tripos 1931, Law Tripos 1932, Cambridge Univ.; Pres., Cambridge Union, 1932. Called to the Bar, Middle Temple, 1934; Advocate of High Court, Allahabad, 1937, and Senior Advocate of Supreme Court of India, 1958; Lecturer in Commercial Law, Allahabad Univ., 1940–54; Senior Standing Counsel of Govt of Uttar Pradesh, 1956–58; Judge of Allahabad High Court, 1958–67; High Commissioner in UK, 1968–69; Governor of West Bengal, 1969–72. Founder-mem. and Sec., Bernard Shaw Soc., formed 1949. Pres. Indo-Soviet Cultural Soc., Uttar Pradesh Sect., 1965–67. Leader of cultural delegation to Soviet Union, 1966. Lal Bahadur Sastri Meml Lectr, Kerala Univ., Trivandrum, 1973; Pres., All-India Ramayana Conf., Trivandrum, 1973. *Publications:* The Legal system and theory of the State in Ancient India, 1962; Doctrine of sovereignty and colonialism, 1962; Secularism in Indian Jurisprudence, 1964; also papers on Indian Judicial system, UNO and Kashmir, and the Nehru Tradition. *Recreations:* study of Indian jurisprudence, journalism. *Address:* 28 Tashkent Marg, Allahabad, Uttar Pradesh, 210001, India.

DHENIN, Air Marshal Sir Geoffrey (Howard), KBE 1975; AFC 1953 and Bar, 1957; GM 1943; MA, MD, DPH; FFCM 1975; FRAeS 1971; Director-General, Medical Services (RAF), 1974–78; *b* 2 April 1918; *s* of Louis Richard Dhenin and Lucy Ellen Dagg; *m* 1946, Claude Andree Evelyn Rabut; one *s* two *d* (and one *s* decd). *Educ:* Hereford Cathedral Sch.; St John's Coll., Cambridge; Guy's Hosp., London. Joined RAF; various sqdn and other med. appts, Bomber Comd, 2nd TAF, 1943–45 (despatches 1945); pilot trng, 1945–46; various med. officer pilot appts, 1946–58; Staff Coll., Bracknell, 1958–59; comd Princess Mary's RAF Hosp. Akrotiri, Cyprus, 1960–63; comd RAF Hosp. Ely, 1963–66; PMO Air Support Comd, 1966–68; Dir of Health and Research, RAF, 1968–70; Dep. DGMS, RAF, 1970–71; PMO Strike Comd, 1971–73. Fellow, Internat. Acad. of Aerospace Medicine, 1972. CStJ 1974. QHP 1970–78. Adviser to Saudi Arabian Nat. Guard, 1978–79. *Publication:* (ed) Textbook of Aviation Medicine, 1978. *Recreations:* golf, ski-ing, sub-aqua. *Address:* Ruxbury Lodge, St Ann's Hill, Chertsey, Surrey. *T:* Chertsey (0932) 563624. *Clubs:* Royal Air Force, Wentworth.

DHRANGADHARA, Maharaja Sriraj of Halvad-, His Highness Jhaladhipati Maharana Sriraj Meghrajji III, KCIE 1947; 45th Ruler (dynastic salute of 13 guns), Head of Jhalla–Makhvana Clan; MP for Jhalavad (Gujarat State), 1967–70; *b* 3 March 1923; *s* of HH Maharaja Sriraj Ghanashyamsinhji Saheb, GCIE, KCSI, late Ruler, and HH Maharani Srirajni Anandkunvarba Saheba, Rajmata Saheba; *S* father 1942, assumed government 1943 on termination of political minority; *m* 1943, Princess Brijrajkunvarba Saheba, *d* of HH the Maharaja of Marwar-Jodhpur, GCSI, GCIE, KCVO; three *s. Educ:* Dhrangadhara Rajdham Shala (Palace Sch.) which was moved to UK to become Millfield Sch., Som., 1935; Heath Mount Sch.; Haileybury Coll.; St Joseph's Academy, Dehra Dun; Sivaji Military Sch., Poona; acquired administrative experience at Baroda, then at Dhrangadhra; Christ Church, Oxford, 1952–58 (Mem. High Table and Senior Common Room); Philosophy course; Ruskin Sch. of Drawing; Diploma in Social Anthropology (distinction), 1955; research in Indian Sociology, 1956–58 (BLitt Oxon.). FRAS, FRAI; Associate, Royal Historical Soc. As ruler, pursued active policy of social, agrarian and labour reforms, promulgated compulsory free primary educn, fundamental rights and local self-government; liquidated the State's debts; accepted attachment of Lakhtar, Sayla, Chuda and Muli States and the transfer of British suzerainty over them to the Dhrangadhara Darbar, 1943; Mem., Standing Cttee, Chamber of Princes, 1945–47; proposed Confedn of Saurashtra, 1945, carried it in Saurashtra States-General meeting (also Chm.), 1946; first state in W India to accept participation in Constituent Assembly of India; signed Instrument of Accession to India, 1947; Uparajpramukh, Actg Rajpramukh and C-in-C of State Forces of United State of Saurashtra, 1948–52; proclaimed Indian constitution, 1949; Promoter and Intendant General, Consultation of Rulers of Indian States in Concord for India, 1967. Mem. Gujarat Legislative Assembly (from Dhrangadhra), Feb.–March 1967, resigned. Life Member: Indian Council of World Affairs, 1967; Indian Parly Gp, 1967; CPA, 1967; Linguistic Soc. of India; Numismatic Soc. of India; Heraldry Soc.; WWF. Perm. Pres., Srirajman (Educ.) Foundn; Pres., Rajkumar Coll., Rajkot, 1966–; Mem., Ind. Cttee, United World Colls. Patron, Bhandarkar Oriental Res. Inst. *Heir: s* Maharajkumar Shri Sodhsalji, Yuvaraj Saheb of Halvad–Dhrangadhara, *b* 22 March 1944. *Address:* Ajitnivas Palace, Dhrangadhara-Nagar, Jhalavad, Gujarat 363310, India; Dhrangadhara Bhavan, Gokhale Road, Pune 41106, India; India Lodge, 108 Malcha Marg, Chanakyapuri Diplomatic Enclave, New Delhi 110021, India.

DIAMAND, Peter, Hon. CBE 1972; Artistic Adviser, Orchestre de Paris, since 1976; *b* 1913; *m* 1st, 1948, Maria Curcio, pianist (marr. diss. 1971); 2nd, Sylvia Rosenberg, violinist (marr. diss. 1979); one *s. Educ:* Schiller–Realgymnasium, Berlin; Berlin Univ. Studied Law and Journalism. Left Germany, 1933; became Private Sec. to Artur Schnabel, pianist. Personal Asst to Dir of Netherlands Opera, Amsterdam, 1946, subsequently Artistic Adviser until 1965; Gen. Manager of Holland Festival, 1948–65; Dir, Edinburgh Internat. Festival, 1965–78; Dir and Gen. Manager, RPO, 1978–81. Mem. Board of Netherlands Chamber Orchestra, 1955–77. Hon. LLD Edinburgh, 1972. Knight, Order of Oranje Nassau, Holland, 1959; Grosses Ehrenzeichen fuer Verdienste, Austria, 1964; Medal of Merit, Czechoslovakia, 1966; Commander Italian Republic, 1973; Officier, Ordre des Arts et des Lettres, France, 1985. *Address:* 28 Eton Court, Eton Avenue, NW3. *T:* 071-586 1203.

DIAMOND, family name of **Baron Diamond.**

DIAMOND, Baron *cr* 1970 (Life Peer), of the City of Gloucester; **John Diamond,** PC 1965; FCA; Chairman: Royal Commission on Distribution of Income and Wealth, 1974–79; Industry and Parliament Trust, 1976–82; Trustee, Social Democratic Party, 1981–82, Leader of SDP in House of Lords, 1982–88; *b* Leeds, 30 April 1907; *s* of Henrietta and Rev. S. Diamond, Leeds; *m*; two *s* two *d. Educ:* Leeds Grammar Sch. Qualified as Chartered Accountant, 1931, and commenced practice as John Diamond & Co. MP (Lab) Blackley Div. of Manchester, 1945–51, Gloucester, 1957–70; Chief Secretary to the Treasury, 1964–70 (in the Cabinet, 1968–70); formerly PPS to Minister of Works; Deputy Chm. of Cttees, House of Lords, 1974. Chm., Prime Minister's Adv. Cttee on Business Appts of Crown Servants, 1975–88. Chm. of Finance Cttee, Gen. Nursing Council, 1947–53; Dir of Sadler's Wells Trust Ltd, 1957–64; Hon. Treas., Fabian Soc., 1950–64. Hon. LLD Leeds, 1978. *Publications:* Socialism the British Way (jtly), 1948; Public Expenditure in Practice, 1975. *Recreations:* golf, ski-ing, music. *Address:* Aynhoe, Doggetts Wood Lane, Chalfont St Giles, Bucks.

DIAMOND, Anthony Edward John; QC 1974; **His Honour Judge Diamond;** a Circuit Judge, since 1990; *b* 4 Sept. 1929; *s* of late Arthur Sigismund Diamond, former Master of the Supreme Court, and of Gladys Elkah Diamond (*née* Mocatta); m 1965, Joan Margaret Gee; two *d. Educ:* Rugby; Corpus Christi Coll., Cambridge (MA). Served RA, 1947–49. Called to the Bar, Gray's Inn, 1953 (Bencher, 1985). Head of Chambers at 4 Essex Court, EC4, 1984–90. Dep. High Court Judge, 1982–90; a Recorder, 1985–90. Chm., Banking Act Appeals, 1980; Mem., indep. review body under colliery review procedure, 1985. *Publications:* papers on maritime law. *Recreation:* the visual arts. *Address:* 1 Cannon Place, NW3 1EH. *T:* 071–435 6154.

DIAMOND, Prof. Aubrey Lionel; Professor of Law, University of Notre Dame, and Co-Director, London Law Centre, since 1987; Emeritus Professor of Law, University of London; solicitor; *b* 28 Dec. 1923; *s* of Alfred and Millie Diamond, London; *m* 1955, Dr Eva M. Bobasch; one *s* one *d. Educ:* elementary schs; Central Foundation Sch., London; London Sch. of Economics (LLB, LLM; Hon. Fellow, 1984). Clerical Officer, LCC, 1941–48. Served RAF, 1943–47. Admitted a solicitor, 1951. Sen. Lectr, Law Society's Sch. of Law, 1955–57; Asst Lectr, Lectr and Reader, Law Dept, LSE, 1957–66; Prof. of Law, Queen Mary Coll., Univ. of London, 1966–71, Fellow 1984; Law Comr, 1971–76; Prof. of Law and Dir, Inst. of Advanced Legal Studies, Univ. of London, 1976–86, now Emeritus. Partner in Lawford & Co., Solicitors, 1959–71 (consultant, 1986–). Part-time Chm. of Industrial Tribunals, 1984–90; Dep. Chm., Data Protection Tribunal, 1985–; Consultant, DTI, 1986–88. Member: Central London Valuation Court, 1956–73; Consumer Advisory Council, BSI, 1961–63; Council, Consumers' Assoc., 1963–71 (Vice-Pres., 1981–84); Consumer Council, 1963–66, 1967–71; Cttee on the Age of Majority, 1965–67; Council, Law Society, 1976–. Chairman: Social Sciences and the Law Cttee, SSRC, 1977–80; Hamlyn Trust, 1977–88; Advertising Adv. Cttee, IBA, 1980–88. President: Nat. Fedn of Consumer Groups, 1977–81 (Chm., 1963–67); British Insurance Law Assoc., 1988–90; Vice-Pres., Inst. of Trading Standards Administration, 1975–. Visiting Professor: University Coll. Dar es Salaam, Univ. of E Africa, 1966–67; Law Sch., Stanford Univ., 1971; Melbourne Univ., 1977; Univ. of Virginia, 1982; Tulane Univ., 1984; Vis. teacher, LSE, 1984–. Hon. MRCP 1990. *Publications:* The Consumer, Society and the Law (with Sir Gordon Borrie), 1963 (4th edn, 1981); Introduction to Hire-Purchase Law, 1967 (2nd edn. 1971); (ed) Instalment Credit, 1970; (co-ed) Sutton and Shannon on Contracts (7th edn) 1970; Commercial and Consumer Credit: an introduction, 1982; A Review of Security Interests in Property, 1989; articles and notes in legal jls and symposia. *Address:* University of Notre Dame, London Law Centre, 7 Albemarle Street, W1X 3HF. *T:* 071–493 9002. *Club:* Reform.

DIAMOND, Prof. Derek Robin; Professor of Geography with special reference to Urban and Regional Planning, London School of Economics and Political Science, since 1982; *b* 18 May 1933; *s* of John Diamond (Baron Diamond, *qv*) and Sadie Diamond; *m* 1957, Esme Grace Passmore; one *s* one *d. Educ:* Oxford Univ. (MA); Northwestern Univ., Illinois (MSc). Lecturer: in Geography, 1957–65, in Town and Regional Planning, 1965–68, Glasgow Univ.; Reader in Geography, London School of Economics, 1968–82.

Hon. MRTPI, 1989. Hon. Prof. of Human Geography, Inst. of Geography, Beijing. Editor: Progress in Planning, 1973–; Geoforum, 1974–. *Publication:* Regional Policy Evaluation, 1983. *Recreation:* philately. *Address:* 9 Ashley Drive, Walton-on-Thames, Surrey KT12 1JL. *T:* Walton-on-Thames (0923) 223280. *Club:* Geographical.

DIAMOND, (Peter) Michael, MA, FMA; Director, Birmingham City Museums and Art Gallery, since 1980; *b* 5 Aug. 1942; *s* of late William Howard and Dorothy Gladys Diamond; *m* 1968, Anne Marie; one *s* one *d. Educ:* Bristol Grammar Sch.; Queens' Coll., Cambridge (BA Fine Art 1964, MA 1966). Dip. of Museums Assoc. 1968, FMA 1980. Sheffield City Art Galleries: Art Asst, 1965; Keeper, Mappin Art Gall., 1967; Dep. Dir, 1969; City Arts and Museums Officer, Bradford, 1976. Chairman: Gp of Dirs of Museums, 1985–89; Public Art Commns Agency, 1987–88. Member, Executive Committee: Yorks Arts Assoc., 1977–80; Yorks Sculpture Park, 1978– (Chm., 1978–82); Pres., Yorks Fedn of Museums, 1978–80; Member: Crafts Council, 1980–84; Council, Museums Assoc., 1987–; Board, Museums Training Inst., 1990–. Mem. Council, Aston Univ., 1983–90. FRSA. *Publications:* numerous exhibition catalogues incl. Victorian Paintings, 1968; Art and Industry in Sheffield 1850–75, 1975; (contrib.) Manual of Curatorship, 1984; articles in Museums Jl. *Address:* Birmingham City Museums and Art Gallery, Chamberlain Square, Birmingham B3 3DH.

DIBBEN, Michael Alan Charles; HM Diplomatic Service; Ambassador to Paraguay, since 1991; *b* 19 Sept. 1943; *s* of Lt-Col Alan Frank Dibben and Eileen Beatrice Dibben (*née* Donoghue). *Educ:* Dulwich College. With Ottoman Bank, London, 1961–64; CRO 1964; Min. of Overseas Develt, 1965; Protocol Dept, FCO, 1966; served Montreal, Nassau, Stuttgart, Port of Spain, Douala; First Sec., 1981; Nuclear Energy Dept, FCO, 1981–83; Munich and Hamburg, 1983–87; Inf. Dept, FCO, 1987–90. Mem., Horners' Co. *Recreations:* reading, walking, golf, classical music. *Address:* c/o Foreign and Commonwealth Office, King Charles Street, SW1A 2AH; 55 Lackford Road, Chipstead, Surrey CR3 3TB. *Clubs:* National Liberal, City Livery.

DIBELA, Sir Kingsford, GCMG 1983 (CMG 1978); Governor-General of Papua New Guinea, 1983–89; *b* 16 March 1932; *s* of Norman Dibela and Edna Dalauna; *m* 1952, Winifred Tomolarina; two *s* four *d. Educ:* St Paul's Primary Sch., Dogura. Qualified as primary school teacher; teacher, 1949–63. Pres., Weraura Local Govt Council, 1963–77; MP, PNG, 1975–82; Speaker of Nat. Parlt, 1977–80. *Recreations:* golf, cricket. *Address:* c/o Government House, PO Box 79, Port Moresby, Papua New Guinea. *T:* 214466 (BH). *Club:* Port Moresby Golf.

DICE, Brian Charles; Chief Executive, British Waterways Board, since 1986; *b* 2 Sept. 1936; *s* of late Frederic Charles Dice; *m* 1965, Gwendoline Tazeena Harrison; two *d. Educ:* Clare College, Cambridge; Middle Temple. Cadbury Schweppes, 1960–86, Director, 1979; Managing Director, Schweppes, 1983. *Address:* Stratton Wood, Beaconsfield, Bucks HP9 1HS.

DICK, Air Vice-Marshal Alan David, CB 1978; CBE 1968; AFC 1957; FRAeS 1975; *b* 7 Jan. 1924; *s* of late Brig. Alan MacDonald Dick, CBE, IMS(Retd), and Muriel Angela Dick; *m* 1951, Ann Napier Jeffcoat, *d* of late Col A. C. Jeffcoat, CB, CMG, DSO; two *s* two *d. Educ:* Fettes; Aitchison Coll., Lahore; King's Coll., Cambridge. MA. Joined RAF, 1942; SE Asia Command, 1943–45; Fighter Comd, 1945–46. Central Flying Sch., 1950–53; Empire Test Pilots Sch., 1953; Test Pilot, A&AEE, 1954–57; Fighter Comd, 1957–60; RAF Staff Coll., 1960–63; OC 207 Sqdn, Bomber Comd, 1963–64; Supt of Flying, A&AEE, 1964–68; Strike Comd, 1968–69; IDC 1970; MoD Air Staff, 1971–74; Comdt, A&AEE, 1974–75; Dep. Controller Aircraft/C, MoD(PE), 1975–78. Sec., British Assoc. of Occupational Therapists, 1979–84. *Recreations:* photography, walking, bird watching. *Club:* Royal Air Force.

DICK, Gavin Colquhoun; Vice-Chairman, Mobile Radio Training Trust, since 1990; *b* 6 Sept. 1928; *s* of late John Dick and Catherine MacAuslan Henderson; *m* 1952, Elizabeth Frances, *e d* of late Jonathan Hutchinson; two *d. Educ:* Hamilton Academy; Glasgow Univ. (MA 1950); Balliol Coll., Oxford (Snell Exhibnr, 1949, MA 1957); SOAS (Cert. in Turkish, 1986). National Service, 3rd RTR (Lieut), 1952–54. Asst Principal, BoT, 1954, Principal, 1958; UK Trade Comr, Wellington, NZ, 1961–64; Asst Sec., 1967; Jt Sec., Review Cttee on Overseas Representation, 1968–69; Under-Sec., 1975–84, Dept of Industry, 1981–84. Consultant: Office of Telecommunications, 1984–87; DTI Radiocommunications Div., 1987–89. Bd Mem., English Industrial Estates Corp., 1982–84. Governor, Coll. of Air Training (Hamble), 1975–80. *Recreation:* words. *Address:* Fell Cottage, Bayley's Hill, Sevenoaks, Kent TN14 6HS. *T:* Sevenoaks (0732) 453704. *Club:* United Oxford & Cambridge University.

DICK, Prof. George (Williamson Auchinvole), MD (Edinburgh), DSc (Edinburgh), FRCPE, FRCP, FRCPath, MPH (Johns Hopkins); FIMLS, FLA; Emeritus Professor of Pathology, University of London; Chairman, Medical Advisory and Research Consultants Ltd, since 1981; *b* 14 Aug. 1914; *s* of Rev. David Auchinvole Dick and Blanche Hay Spence; *m* 1941, Brenda Marian Cook; two *s* two *d. Educ:* Royal High Sch., Edinburgh; Univ. of Edinburgh; The Johns Hopkins Univ., Baltimore, Md, USA. BSc 1939 (1st Cl. Hons Path.); Vans Dunlop Scholar; Buchanan Medal; MD (Gold Medal) 1949. Asst Pathologist, Royal Infirmary, Edinburgh, 1939–40; Pathologist, RAMC, 1940–46; OC Medical Div. (Lt-Col) (EA Comd), 1945; Pathologist, Colonial Med. Res. Service, 1946–51; Rockefeller Foundn Fellow (Internat. Health Div.), Rockefeller Inst., New York and Johns Hopkins Univ., 1947–48; Res. Fellow, Sch. of Hygiene and Public Health, Johns Hopkins Univ., Baltimore, Md, 1948–49; Scientific Staff, MRC, 1951–54; Prof. of Microbiology, QUB, 1955–65; Dir, Bland-Sutton Inst. and Sch. of Pathology, Middlesex Hosp. Med. Sch., Univ. of London, 1966–73; Bland-Sutton Prof. of Pathology, Univ. of London, 1966–73; Asst Dir, BPMF, and Postgraduate Dean, SW Thames RHA, 1973–81; Prof. of Pathology, Univ. of London, and Hon. Lectr and Hon. Consultant, Inst. of Child Health, 1973–81. Examnr, Med. Schools in UK, Dublin, Nairobi, Kampala, Riyadh, Jeddah; Assessor, HNC and CMS, S London Coll. Pres., Inst. of Med. Laboratory Technology, 1966–76; Member: Mid Downs Health Authority, W Sussex, 1981–84; Jt Bd of Clinical Nursing Studies, 1982–85; Chm., DHSS/Regl Librarians Jt Wking Party. Pres., Rowhook Med. Soc., 1975–. Treasurer, RCPath, 1973–78; Member: RSM; BMA; Internat. Epidemiol. Soc.; Path. Soc. GB and Ireland; Soc. of Scholars, Johns Hopkins Univ., 1979; Alpha Chapter, Delta Omega Hon. Soc., USA, 1981. Liveryman, Worshipful Co. of Apothecaries, 1981. Singapore Gold Medal, Edinburgh Univ., 1952 and 1958; Laurence Biedl Prize for Rehabilitation, 1958; Sims Woodhead Medal, 1976; Outstanding Alumnus in Public Health award, Johns Hopkins Univ., 1986. *Publications:* Immunisation, 1978, re-issued as Practical Immunisation, 1986; Immunology of Infectious Diseases, 1979; Health on Holiday and other Travels, 1982; papers on yellow fever, Uganda S, Zika and other arbor viruses, Mengovirus, Marburgvirus, poliomyelitis; hepatitis (MHV); EHA (rabies) virus; smallpox, poliomyelitis, whooping cough and combined vaccines; vaccine reactions, immunisation policies, subacute sclerosing panencephalitis; multiple sclerosis, travel, etc. *Address:* Waterland, Rowhook, Horsham RH12 3PX. *T:* Slinfold (0403) 790549.

See also Sir J. A. Dick.

DICK, James Brownlee, CB 1977; MA, BSc, FInstP, FCIBS, FIOB; consultant; *b* 19 July 1919; *s* of James Brownlee Dick and Matilda Forrest; *m* 1944, Audrey Moira Shinn; two *s. Educ:* Wishaw High Sch.; Glasgow Univ. Royal Naval Scientific Service, 1940. Building Research Station, later Building Research Establishment: Physics Div., 1947; Head of User Requirements Div., 1960; Head of Production Div., 1963; Asst Dir, 1964; Dep. Dir, 1969; Dir, 1969–79. Pres., Internat. Council for Building Res., 1974–77. *Publications:* papers in professional and scientific journals. *Address:* 4 Murray Road, Berkhamsted, Herts HP4 1JD. *T:* Berkhamsted (0442) 862580.

DICK, Sir John (Alexander), Kt 1987; MC 1944; QC (Scotland) 1963; Sheriff Principal of Glasgow and Strathkelvin, 1980–86; *b* 1 Jan. 1920; *y s* of Rev. David Auchinvole Dick and Blanche Hay Spence; *m* 1951, Rosemary Benzie Sutherland (*d* 1991); no *c. Educ:* Waid Academy, Anstruther; University of Edinburgh. Enlisted in London Scottish, 1940; commissioned Royal Scots, 1942; Italy, 1944; Palestine, 1945–46; released 1946. MA (1st Cl. Hons Economics) 1947, LLB (with distinction) 1949, Univ. of Edinburgh. Called to Scots Bar, 1949; Lecturer in Public Law, Univ. of Edinburgh, 1953–60; Junior Counsel in Scotland to HM Commissioners of Customs and Excise, 1956–63; Comr under Terrorism (N Ireland) Order 1972, 1972–73; Sheriff of the Lothians and Borders at Edinburgh, 1969–78; Sheriff Principal of North Strathclyde, 1978–82. Hon. LLD Glasgow, 1987. *Recreation:* hill-walking. *Address:* 3 St Margaret's Court, North Berwick, East Lothian EH39 4QH. *T:* North Berwick (0620) 5249. *Club:* Royal Scots (Edinburgh).

See also Prof. George Dick.

DICK, John Kenneth, CBE 1972; FCA, FRSA; Director, N. M. Rothschild & Sons Ltd, 1978–90; *b* 5 April 1913; *s* of late John Dick and Beatrice May Dick (*née* Chitty); *m* 1942, Pamela Madge, 3rd *d* of late Maurice Salmon and Katie Salmon (*née* Joseph); two *s* (and one *s* decd). *Educ:* Sedbergh. Qual. with Mann Judd & Co., Chartered Accountants, 1936; Partner, Mann Judd & Co., 1947; Mitchell Cotts Group Ltd: Jt Man. Dir, 1957; Sole Man. Dir, 1959–78; Dep. Chm., 1964; Chm., 1966–78; Chm., Hume Holdings Ltd, 1975–80. Mem., Commonwealth Develt Corp., 1967–80; Gov., City of London Soc.; Member: British Nat. Export Cttee, 1968–71; Covent Gdn Mkt Authority, 1976–82; Chm., Cttee for Middle East Trade, 1968–71; Pres., Middle East Assoc., 1976–81 (a Vice-Pres., 1970–76). *Recreation:* golf. *Address:* Overbye, Church Street, Cobham, Surrey KT11 3EG. *T:* (office) 071–280 5000; (home) Cobham (Surrey) (0932) 64393. *Club:* Caledonian.

DICK, Kay; writer; *b* 29 July 1915; *o d* of Mrs Kate Frances Dick. *Educ:* Geneva, Switzerland; Lycée Français de Londres, S Kensington. Worked in publishing and bookselling; edited (as Edward Lane) 13 issues of magazine, The Windmill. *Publications: fiction:* By the Lake, 1949; Young Man, 1951; An Affair of Love, 1953; Solitaire, 1958; Sunday, 1962; They, 1977 (South-East Arts Literature Prize, 1977); The Shelf, 1984; *non-fiction:* Pierrot, 1960; Ivy and Stevie, 1971; Friends and Friendship, 1974; *edited:* London's Hour: as seen through the eyes of the fire-fighters, 1942; Late Joys at the Players Theatre, 1943; The Mandrake Root, 1946, At Close of Eve, 1947, The Uncertain Element, 1950 (three vols of strange stories); Bizarre and Arabesque (anthology from Edgar Allan Poe), 1967; Writers at Work, 1972. *Recreations:* friends, gardening, walking the dog. *Address:* Flat 5, 9 Arundel Terrace, Brighton, East Sussex BN2 1GA. *T:* Brighton (0273) 697243.

DICK, Air Vice-Marshal Ronald, CB 1988; Head of British Defence Staff, Washington, and Defence Attaché, 1984–88, retired; International Fellow, National Air and Space Museum, Smithsonian Institution, Washington, DC, since 1988; *b* Newcastle upon Tyne, 18 Oct. 1931; *s* of Arthur John Craig Dick and Lilian Dick; *m* 1955, Pauline Lomax; one *s* one *d. Educ:* Beckenham and Penge County Grammar Sch.; RAF Coll., Cranwell. Commnd 1952; served, 1953–69: No 64 Fighter Sqdn; Flying Instr, No 5 FTS; Central Flying Sch. Examg Wing and Type Sqdn; Flt Comdr, 3615th Pilot Trng Sqdn, USAF, and No IX Bomber Sqdn; Trng (Operational) 2a (RAF), MoD; RAF Staff Coll., Bracknell; Ops B2 (RAF), MoD; Jt Services Staff Coll.; OC No IX Bomber Sqdn, RAF Akrotiri, 1970–72; Staff, RCDS, 1972–74; PSO to Dep. SACEUR, SHAPE, 1974–77; OC RAF Honington, 1978–80; Air Attaché, Washington, DC, 1980–83; Dir of Organization and Estabts, 1983–84, of Organization and Quartering, 1984, RAF. Mem., Bd of Trustees, Amer. Airpower Heritage Foundn, 1987–. Consulting Editor, Air & Space Smithsonian Magazine, 1990–. FRAeS 1987. Wright Jubilee Aerobatic Trophy Winner, 1956. *Recreations:* wild life conservation, bird watching, private flying, military history, opera. *Address:* Cherrywood, Jenny Lane, Woodbridge, Va 22192, USA. *Club:* Royal Air Force.

DICK-LAUDER, Sir Piers Robert; *see* Lauder.

DICKEN, Air Vice-Marshal Michael John Charles Worwood, CB 1990; Air Officer Administration and Air Officer Commanding Support Group, RAF Support Command, since 1989; *b* 13 July 1935; *s* of late Air Cdre Charles Worwood Dicken, CBE and Olive Eva Dicken (*née* Eustice); *m* 1962, Jennifer Ann Dore; two *d* (one *s* decd). *Educ:* Sherborne; St Peter's Hall, Oxford; RAF College, Cranwell. Commissioned 1958; served Cyprus, Borneo and UK to 1970; RAF Staff College, 1971; Asst Defence Advr, Canberra, 1972–74; RAF Uxbridge, 1975–76; NDC, 1976; RAF Coningsby, 1977–79; Staff Coll. Directing Staff and Dir, Comd and Staff Training, 1980–82; OC RAF Hereford, 1982–83; HQ 1 Gp, 1984–85; Dir of Personnel Management (Airmen), 1986–88. Hon. Freeman, Chartered Secretaries' and Administrators' Co., 1989. *Recreations:* golf, gliding, light aircraft, field sports. *Address:* c/o Lloyds Bank, 99 High Street, Huntingdon, Cambs. *Club:* Royal Air Force.

DICKENS, Prof. Arthur Geoffrey, CMG 1974; FBA 1966; Director, Institute of Historical Research and Professor of History in the University of London, 1967–77, now Emeritus Professor; *b* 6 July 1910; *er s* of Arthur James Dickens and Gertrude Helen Dickens (*née* Grasby), both of Hull, Yorks; *m* 1936, Molly (*d* 1978), *er d* of Walter Bygott; two *s. Educ:* Hymers Coll., Hull; Magdalen Coll., Oxford. Demy, 1929–32, Senior Demy, 1932–33, of Magdalen Coll.; BA with 1st Class Hons in Mod. Hist., 1932; MA 1936; DLit London, 1965. Fellow and Tutor of Keble Coll., Oxford, 1933–49, Hon. Fellow, 1971; Oxford Univ. Lecturer in Sixteenth Century English History, 1939–49. Served in RA, 1940–45; demobilised as Staff Capt. G. F. Grant Prof. of History, Univ. of Hull, 1949–62; Dep. Principal and Dean of Faculty of Arts, 1950–53; Pro-Vice-Chancellor, 1959–62; Prof. of History, King's Coll., Univ. of London, 1962–67; FKC, 1977. Mem. Senate and Academic Council, Univ. of London, 1974–77. Pres., Ecclesiastical History Soc., 1966–68. Member: Advisory Council on Public Records, 1968–76; Adv. Council on Export of Works of Art, 1968–76; Records Cttee, Essex CC, 1965–71; History of Medicine Adv. Panel, Wellcome Trust, 1974–79; Steering Cttee, Business History Unit, LSE, 1978–85. Chm., Victoria History of the Counties of England, 1967–68. Sec., 1967–73, Chm. and Gen. Sec., 1973–79, British Nat. Cttee of Historical Sciences; Foreign Sec., British Acad., 1969–79 (Vice-Pres., 1971–72); Vice-Pres., British Record Soc., 1978–80; Hon. Vice-President: RHistS, 1977– (Vice-Pres., 1969–73); Historical Assoc., 1977– (Pres., Central London Branch, 1982–); Sec., Anglo-German Group of Historians, 1969–76; Pres., German History Soc., 1979–89. Editor, Bulletin of the Inst. of Historical Research, 1967–77. Visiting Prof., Univ. of Rochester, NY, 1953–54; Birkbeck Lectr,

Trinity Coll., Cambridge, 1969–70. Fellow, 1954, Vis. Prof., 1972, Folger Library, Washington, DC; Strassberg Vis. Prof., Univ. of Western Australia, 1981; Lectures: James Ford Special, Univ. of Oxford, 1974; Neale, UCL, 1977; Bithell, Inst. of Germanic Studies, 1978; Stenton, Reading, 1980. Hon. Professorial Fellow, Univ. of Wales, Aberystwyth, 1979–. Governor, Highgate Sch., 1976–86. FRHistS 1947; FSA 1962. Medlicott Medal, Historical Assoc., 1985 (first recipient). Hon. DLitt: Kent, 1976; Hull, 1977; Leicester, 1978; Sheffield, 1978; Hon. LittD Liverpool, 1977. Comdr's Cross, Order of Merit, Fed. Repub. of Germany, 1980. *Publications:* Lübeck Diary, 1947; The Register of Butley Priory, 1951; The East Riding of Yorkshire, 1954; Lollards and Protestants, 1959; Thomas Cromwell, 1959; Tudor Treatises, 1960; Clifford Letters, 1962; The English Reformation, 1964, 2nd edn 1989; Reformation and Society in 16th Century Europe, 1966; Martin Luther and the Reformation, 1967; (ed jtly) The Reformation in England to the Accession of Elizabeth I, 1967; The Counter-Reformation, 1968; The Age of Humanism and Reformation, 1972, UK edn 1977; The German Nation and Martin Luther, 1974; (ed and contrib.) The Courts of Europe, 1977; Reformation Studies, 1982; (with J. M. Tonkin) The Reformation in Historical Thought, 1985; (Gen. Editor) Documents of Modern History Series, 1966–; (Gen. Editor) A New History of England Series, 1975–; about 60 articles in: English Historical Review, Church Quarterly Review, Yorkshire Archæological Jl, Cambridge Antiquarian Jl, Bodleian Library Record, Archiv für Reformationsgeschichte, Britain and the Netherlands, Victoria County History, York, Trans Royal Hist. Soc., Jl of Ecclesiastical History, Archæological Jl, Encycl. Britannica, Chambers's Encycl., etc. *Festschrift:* Reformation Principle and Practice: essays in honour of A. G. Dickens, ed P. N. Brooks, 1980. *Recreations:* travel, 20th Century British art. *Address:* c/o Institute of Historical Research, Senate House, WC1E 7HU. *Club:* Athenæum.

DICKENS, Geoffrey Kenneth, JP; MP (C) Littleborough and Saddleworth, since 1983 (Huddersfield West, 1979–83); company director, engineering industry; *b* 26 Aug. 1931; *s* of John Wilfred and Laura Avril Dickens; *m* 1956, Norma Evelyn Boothby; two *s*. *Educ:* Park Lane and Byron Court Primary; East Lane Sch., Wembley; Harrow and Acton Technical Colls. Chairman: Sandridge Parish Council, 1968–69; St Albans Rural District Council, 1970–71 (Leader, 1967–70); Councillor, Hertfordshire CC, 1970–75; Hon. Alderman, City and District of St Albans, 1976. Contested (C): Teesside Middlesbrough, Feb. 1974, and Ealing North, Oct. 1974, general elections. Treas., Assoc. of Conservative Clubs; Vice-Pres., NW Conservative Clubs Council. Royal Humane Soc. Testimonial on Vellum for saving lives, 1972. JP St Albans, later Barnsley, then Oldham, 1968. *Address:* c/o House of Commons, SW1A 0AA.

DICKENS, James McCulloch York; Chief Personnel Officer, Agricultural and Food Research Council, since 1983; *b* 4 April 1931; *e s* of A. Y. Dickens and I. Dickens (*née* McCulloch); *m* 1st, 1955, M. J. Grieve (marr. diss. 1965); 2nd, 1969, Mrs Carolyn Casey. *Educ:* Shawlands Academy, Glasgow; Newbattle Abbey Coll., Dalkeith, Midlothian; Ruskin Coll. and St Catherine's Coll., Oxford. Administrative Asst, National Coal Board, 1956–58; Industrial Relations Officer, National Coal Board, 1958–65; Management Consultant, 1965–66; MP (Lab) West Lewisham, 1966–70; Asst Dir of Manpower, Nat. Freight Corp., 1970–76; National Water Council: Asst Dir (Ind. Rel.), Manpower Services Div., 1976–80; Dir of Manpower, 1980–82; Dir of Manpower and Trng, 1982–83. *Recreations:* music, theatre, the countryside. *Address:* 64 Woodbastwick Road, Sydenham, SE26 5LH. *T:* 081–778 7446.

DICKENS, Monica Enid, (Mrs R. O. Stratton), MBE 1981; writer; Founder of The Samaritans, in the USA, Boston, Mass, 1974; *b* 10 May 1915; *d* of late Henry Charles Dickens, Barrister-at-law, and Fanny Runge; *m* 1951, Comdr Roy Olin Stratton (*d* 1985), US Navy; two *d*. *Educ:* St Paul's Girls' Sch., Hammersmith. *Publications:* One Pair of Hands, 1939; Mariana, 1940; One Pair of Feet, 1942; The Fancy, 1943; Thursday Afternoons, 1945; The Happy Prisoner, 1946; Joy and Josephine, 1948; Flowers on the Grass, 1949; My Turn to Make the Tea, 1951; No More Meadows, 1953; The Winds of Heaven, 1955; The Angel in the Corner, 1956; Man Overboard, 1958; The Heart of London, 1961; Cobbler's Dream, 1963; Kate and Emma, 1964; The Room Upstairs, 1966; The Landlord's Daughter, 1968; The Listeners, 1970; The House at World's End, 1970; Summer at World's End, 1971; Follyfoot, 1971; World's End in Winter, 1972; Dora at Follyfoot, 1972; Spring Comes to World's End, 1973; Talking of Horses, 1973; Last Year when I was Young, 1974; The Horse of Follyfoot, 1975; Stranger at Follyfoot, 1976; An Open Book, 1978; The Messenger, 1985; The Ballad of Favour, 1985; Miracles of Courage, 1985; The Haunting of Bellamy 4, 1986; Dear Doctor Lily, 1988; Enchantment, 1989; Closed at Dusk, 1990; Scarred, 1991. *Recreation:* gardening. *Address:* Lavender Cottage, Brightwalton, Berks RG16 0BY.

DICKENSON, Sir Aubrey Fiennes T.; *see* Trotman-Dickenson.

DICKENSON, Lt-Col Charles Royal, CMG 1965; Postmaster-General of Rhodesia, 1964–68, retired; *b* 17 June 1907; *e s* of Charles Roland and Gertrude Dickenson; *m* 1950, Hendrika Jacoba Margaretha Schippers; two *d*. *Educ:* Shaftesbury Grammar Sch., Dorset. Entered British Post Office as Engineering Apprentice, 1923; British Post Office HQ, 1932–39. Served War in Royal Signals, 1939–45, attaining rank of Lieut-Col. BPO NW Regional HQ as Asst Controller of Telecommunications, 1945–47; BPO HQ, London, 1947–50; loaned to S Rhodesia Govt, 1950–54; Controller of Telecommunications. Ministry of Posts, Federation of Rhodesia and Nyasaland, 1954–57; Regional Controller for N Rhodesia, Fedn of Rhodesia and Nyasaland, 1957–61; Dep. Postmaster-Gen., Rhodesia and Nyasaland, 1961–62; Postmaster-Gen., Rhodesia and Nyasaland, 1962–63. Hon. Mem., S Africa Inst. of Electronic and Radio Engineers (Hon. M(SA) IERE), 1966. ICD, OLM, Rhodesia, 1979. *Recreations:* growing orchids, photography. *Address:* 4600 Gatlin Oaks Lane, Orlando, Florida 32806, USA.

DICKENSON, Joseph Frank, PhD, CEng, FIMechE; Director, North Staffordshire Polytechnic, 1969–86, retired; *b* 26 Nov. 1924; *s* of late Frank Brand Dickenson and late Maud Dickenson (*née* Beharrell); *m* 1948, Sheila May Kingston; two *s* one *d*. *Educ:* College of Technology, Hull. BSc (1st Cl. Hons) Engrg, PhD (both London). Engrg apprenticeship and Jun. Engr's posts, 1939–52; Lectr and Sen. Lectr, Hull Coll. of Technology, 1952–59; Head of Dept of Mechanical Engrg and later Vice-Principal, Lanchester Coll. of Technology, 1960–64; Principal, Leeds Coll. of Technology, 1964–69. *Recreation:* motor cars. *Address:* 5 Byron Walk Mews, Harrogate HG2 0LQ. *T:* Harrogate (0423) 525899.

DICKIE, Brian James; General Director, Canadian Opera Company, since 1989; *b* 23 July 1941; *s* of Robert Kelso Dickie and Harriet Elizabeth (*née* Riddell); *m* 1st, 1968, Victoria Teresa Sheldon (*née* Price); two *s* one *d*; 2nd, 1989, Nancy Gustafson. *Educ:* Haileybury; Trinity Coll., Dublin. Admin. Asst, Glyndebourne Opera, 1962–66; Administrator, Glyndebourne Touring Opera, 1967–81; Glyndebourne Festival Opera: Opera Manager, 1970–81; Gen. Administrator, 1981–89. Artistic Dir, Wexford Fest., 1967–73; Artistic Advr, Théâtre Musical de Paris, 1981–87. Chm., London Choral Soc., 1978–85; Vice-Chm., TNC, 1980–85 (Chm., TNC Opera Cttee, 1976–85); Vice-Pres., Theatrical Management Assoc., 1983–85. *Address:* c/o Canadian Opera Co., 227 Front Street E, Toronto, Ont M5A 1E8, Canada. *T:* (416) 363 6671. *Club:* Garrick.

DICKINS, Basil Gordon, CBE 1952 (OBE 1945); BSc, ARCS, DIC, PhD; Deputy Controller of Guided Weapons, Ministry of Technology, 1966–68; *b* 1 July 1908; *s* of late Basil Dickins; *m* 1st, 1935, Molly Aileen (*d* 1969), *d* of late H. Walters Reburn; 2nd, 1971, Edith, *widow* of Warren Parkinson. *Educ:* Royal Coll. of Science, London. Royal Aircraft Establishment, 1932; Air Min., 1936, later Min. of Aircraft Production; Head of Operational Research Section, HQ Bomber Command, 1941; Asst Scientific Adviser, Air Ministry, 1945; Dir of Tech. Personnel Administration, Min. of Supply, 1948; Dep. Scientific Adviser to Air Ministry, 1952; Dir of Guided Weapons Research and Development, Min. of Supply, 1956; Dir-Gen. of Atomic Weapons, Min. of Supply, 1959; Dir-Gen. of Guided Weapons, Ministry of Aviation, 1962. *Publications:* papers in Proc. Royal Society and Reports and Memoranda of Aeronautical Research Council. *Address:* 5 Batisse de la Mielle, Route de la Haule, St Brelade, Jersey; The Penthouse, Cassandra, Victoria Road, Clifton, Cape Town, South Africa.

DICKINS, Mark Frederick Hakon S., *see* Scrase-Dickins.

DICKINSON, family name of **Baron Dickinson.**

DICKINSON, 2nd Baron *cr* 1930, of Painswick; **Richard Clavering Hyett Dickinson;** *b* 2 March 1926; *s* of late Hon. Richard Sebastian Willoughby Dickinson, DSO (*o s* of 1st Baron) and of May Southey, *d* of late Charles Lovemore, Melsetter, Cape Province, S Africa; *S* grandfather, 1943; *m* 1st, 1957, Margaret Ann (marr. diss. 1980), *e d* of late Brig. G. R. McMeekan, CB, DSO, OBE; two *s*; 2nd, 1980, Rita Doreen Moir. *Heir: s* Hon. Martin Hyett Dickinson, *b* 30 Jan. 1961. *Address:* The Stables, Gloucester Road, Painswick, Stroud, Glos. *T:* Painswick (0452) 813204.

See also Very Rev. H. G. Dickinson, Hon. P. M. de B. Dickinson.

DICKINSON, Anne; *see* Dickinson, V. A.

DICKINSON, Basil Philip Harriman; Under Secretary, Department of the Environment (formerly Ministry of Transport), 1959–74; *b* 10 Sept. 1916; *yr s* of F. H. and I. F. Dickinson; *m* 1941, Beryl Farrow; three *s* one *d*. *Educ:* Cheltenham Coll.; Oriel Coll., Oxford. *Address:* c/o Child & Co., 1 Fleet Street, EC4Y 1BD.

DICKINSON, Sir Ben; *see* Dickinson, Sir S. B.

DICKINSON, Brian Henry Baron; Under Secretary, Food Safety Group, Ministry of Agriculture, Fisheries and Food, since 1989; *b* 2 May 1940; *s* of Alan Edgar Frederic Dickinson and Ethel Mary Dickinson (*née* McWilliam); *m* 1971, Sheila Minto Lloyd. *Educ:* Leighton Park School, Reading; Balliol College, Oxford (BA). Ministry of Agriculture, Fisheries and Food, 1964; Dept of Prices and Consumer Protection, 1975; MAFF, 1978; Under Sec., 1984; Principal Finance Officer, 1986. *Recreation:* bird-watching. *Address:* Ministry of Agriculture, Fisheries and Food, 3 Whitehall Place, SW1A 2HH. *T:* 071–270 8459.

DICKINSON, Prof. Christopher John, DM, FRCP; ARCO; Professor of Medicine and Chairman, Department of Medicine, St Bartholomew's Hospital Medical College, since 1975; *b* 1 Feb. 1927; *s* of Reginald Ernest Dickinson and Margaret Dickinson (*née* Petty); *m* 1953, Elizabeth Patricia Farrell; two *s* two *d*. *Educ:* Berkhamsted School; Oxford University (BSc, MA, DM); University College Hospital Medical College. FRCP 1968. Junior med. posts, UCH, 1953–54; RAMC (Junior Med. Specialist), 1955–56; Registrar and Research Fellow, Middlesex Hosp., 1957–60; Rockefeller Travelling Fellow, Cleveland Clinic, USA, 1960–61; Lectr, then Sen. Lectr and Consultant, UCH and Med. Sch., 1961–75. R. Samuel McLoughlin Vis. Prof., McMaster Univ., Canada, 1970; King Edward Fund Vis. Fellow, NZ, 1972. Sec., European Soc. for Clinical Investigation, 1969–72; Censor, 1978–80, Senior Censor and Vice-Pres., 1982–83, Croonian Lectr, 1986, RCP; Chairman: Med. Research Soc., 1983–87; Assoc. of Professors of Medicine, 1983–87; Mem., MRC, 1986–90. ARCO 1987. *Publications:* Electrophysiological Technique, 1950; Clinical Pathology Data, 1951, 2nd edn 1957; (jtly) Clinical Physiology, 1959, 5th edn 1984; Neurogenic Hypertension, 1965; A Computer Model of Human Respiration, 1977; (jtly) Software for Educational Computing, 1980; Neurogenic Hypertension, 1991; papers on hypertension and respiratory physiology. *Recreations:* theatre, opera, playing the organ. *Address:* Griffin Cottage, 57 Belsize Lane, NW3 5AU. *T:* 071-431 1845. *Club:* Garrick.

DICKINSON, Sir Harold (Herbert), Kt 1975; Director: Development Finance Corporation Ltd, since 1979; Australian Fixed Trusts Ltd, since 1979; Chairman, AFT Property Co. Ltd, since 1980; *b* 27 Feb. 1917; *s* of late William James Dickinson and Barwon Venus Clarke; *m* 1946, Elsie May Smith; two *d*. *Educ:* Singleton Public Sch.; Tamworth High Sch.; Univ. of Sydney (LLB, 1st Cl. Hons). Barrister-at-Law. Served War, 2nd AIF HQ 22 Inf. Bde, 1940–45 (despatches); Japanese POW (Sgt). Dept of Lands, NSW, 1933–40; NSW Public Service Bd, 1946–60: Sec. and Sen. Inspector, 1949–60; Chief Exec. Officer, Prince Henry Hosp., 1960–63; NSW Public Service Bd: Mem., 1963–70; Dep. Chm., 1970–71; Chm., 1971–79. Hon. Mem., NSW Univs Bd, 1967–71; Hon. Dir, Prince Henry, Prince of Wales, Eastern Suburbs Teaching Hosps, 1965–75, Chm. of Dirs, 1975–; Governor, NSW Coll. of Law, 1972–77. *Publications:* contribs to administration jls. *Recreation:* sailing. *Address:* 649 Old South Head Road, Rose Bay North, NSW 2030, Australia. *T:* 371–7475. *Clubs:* Union, Rotary (Sydney).

DICKINSON, Prof. Harry Thomas, DLitt; FRHistS; Professor of British History, University of Edinburgh, since 1980; *b* 9 March 1939; *s* of Joseph Dickinson and Elizabeth Stearman Dickinson (*née* Warriner); *m* 1961, Jennifer Elizabeth Galtry; one *s* one *d*. *Educ:* Gateshead Grammar Sch.; Durham Univ. (BA 1960, DipEd 1961, MA 1963); Newcastle Univ. (PhD 1968); DLitt Edinburgh 1986. History Master, Washington Grammar Sch., 1961–64; Earl Grey Fellow, Newcastle Univ., 1964–66; Asst Lectr, Lectr and Reader, Edinburgh Univ., 1966–80. Fulbright Award, 1973; Huntington Library Fellowship, 1973; Folger Shakespeare Library Sen. Fellowship, 1973, Winston Churchill Meml Fellow, 1980; Leverhulme Award, 1986–87; William Andrews Clark Library Fellow, 1987. Vis. Prof., Nanjing Univ., 1980, 1983, Concurrent Prof. of Hist., 1987–; Vis. Lectr to USA, Japan, France and W Germany; Dean, Scottish Univs Summer Sch., 1979–85; Acad. Sponsor, Scotland's Cultural Heritage, 1984–; Anstey Meml Lectr, Kent Univ., 1989. Member Council: Hist. Assoc., 1982–; Royal Hist. Soc., 1986–90; Specialist Advr, CNAA, 1987–; Mem. Cttee on Humanities, CNAA. Mem. Editl Bds, Nineteenth Century Short Title Catalogue and Nineteenth Century Microfiche Series. *Publications:* (ed) The Correspondence of Sir James Clavering, 1967; Bolingbroke, 1970; Walpole and the Whig Supremacy, 1973; (ed) Politics and Literature in the Eighteenth Century, 1974; Liberty and Property, 1977; (ed) The Political Works of Thomas Spence, 1982; British Radicalism and the French Revolution 1789–1815, 1985; Caricatures and the Constitution 1760–1832, 1986; (ed) Britain and the French Revolution 1789–1815, 1989; pamphlets, essays, articles and reviews. *Recreations:* films, watching sports. *Address:* 44 Viewforth Terrace, Edinburgh EH10 4LJ. *T:* 031–229 1379.

DICKINSON, Very Rev. Hugh Geoffrey; Dean of Salisbury, since 1986; *b* 17 Nov. 1929; *s* of late Hon. Richard Sebastian Willoughby Dickinson, DSO (*o s* of 1st Baron Dickinson) and of May Southey, *d* of late Charles Lovemore; *m* 1963, Jean Marjorie

Storey; one *s* one *d*. *Educ:* Westminster School (KS); Trinity Coll., Oxford (MA, DipTh); Cuddesdon Theol Coll. Deacon 1956, priest 1957; Curate of Melksham, Wilts, 1956–58; Chaplain: Trinity Coll., Cambridge, 1958–63; Winchester College, 1963–67; Bishop's Adviser for Adult Education, Diocese of Coventry, 1969–77; Vicar of St Michael's, St Albans, 1977–86. *Recreations:* woodturning, fishing, gardening. *Address:* The Deanery, 7 The Close, Salisbury, Wilts SP1 2EF.

See also Hon. P. M. de B. Dickinson.

DICKINSON, Prof. Hugh Gordon; Sherardian Professor of Botany, Oxford, since 1991; *b* 5 Aug. 1944; *s* of Reginald Gordon Dickinson and Jean Hartley Dickinson; *m* 1980, Alana Gillian Fairbrother; one *s* one *d*. *Educ:* St Lawrence Coll., Ramsgate; Univ. of Birmingham (BSc, PhD, DSc). Postdoctoral Fellow, UCL, 1969–72; University of Reading: Lectr, 1972–79; Reader, 1979–85; Prof. of Plant Cell Genetics, 1985–91. *Publications:* contribs to internat. sci. jls, magazines and newspapers; editor, books on electron microscopy and reproductive biology. *Recreations:* owning and restoring Lancia cars of the '50s and '60s, rock music 1955–75, Mozart operas. *Address:* Magdalen College, Oxford OX1 4AU.

DICKINSON, Rt. Rev. John Hubert, MA; Vicar of Chollerton, 1959–71; Hon. Canon in Newcastle Cathedral, 1947–71; *m* 1937, Frances Victoria (*d* 1991), *d* of late Rev. C. F. Thorp; two *d*. *Educ:* Jesus Coll., Oxford; Cuddesdon Coll. Deacon, 1925; Priest, 1926; Curate of St John, Middlesbrough, 1925–29; SPG Missionary, South Tokyo, 1929–31; Asst Bishop of Melanesia, 1931–37; Vicar of Felkirk-with-Brierley, 1937–42; Vicar of Warkworth, 1942–59.

DICKINSON, John Lawrence, (Bob), CBE 1973; DL; FCA; Chairman: SKF Steel Ltd, 1974–82; Bofors Cos (UK), 1974–83; General Manager, SKF Holding Co. (Holland), 1975–83; *b* 16 Nov. 1913; *s* of Tom Dickinson and Jennie Louise Dickinson; *m* 1937, Bettine Mary Jenkins; two *d*. *Educ:* Taunton Sch. Qual. as Chartered Accountant, 1937; Chief Accountant, Lucas Industries, 1937–44; SKF (UK) Ltd: Finance Dir and Sec., 1944–62; Sales Dir, 1962–66; Man. Dir, 1967–75, retired. Chairman: Sheffield Twist Drill & Steel Co. Ltd, 1978–81 (Dep. Chm., 1974–78); Weyroc Ltd (subsid. of Swedish Match Co.), 1975–82; British Rail (Eastern) Bd, 1970–81; Mem., National Enterprise Bd, 1975–79; Chm., NEDO Industrial Engines Sector Working Party, 1976–79; Mem. Gen. Council, also Finance and Gen. Purposes Cttee, CBI, until 1977; first Chm., Eastern Regional Council. Dep. Chm., Cranfield Inst., retd 1983. Hon. Life Vice-Pres., Luton and District Chamber of Commerce and Industry. High Sheriff, Bedfordshire, 1972–73, DL Beds 1976–. Gold Medal, Royal Patriots Soc. (Sweden), 1975. *Recreations:* gardening, National Hunt racing. *Address:* Arkle House, Upton End, Shillington, Hitchin, Herts SG5 3PG. *T:* Hitchin (0462) 711554.

DICKINSON, Patric Laurence; Richmond Herald of Arms, since 1989; *b* 24 Nov. 1950; *s* of John Laurence Dickinson and April Katherine, *d* of Robert Forgan, MC, MD, sometime MP. *Educ:* Marling Sch.; Exeter Coll., Oxford (Stapledon Schol.; MA). Pres., Oxford Union Soc., 1972. Called to the Bar, Middle Temple, 1979. Res. Asst, College of Arms, 1968–78; Rouge Dragon Pursuivant, 1978–89. Hon. Treasurer: English Genealogical Congress, 1975–; Bar Theatrical Soc., 1978–; Hon. Sec. and Registrar, British Record Soc., 1979–; Vice-Pres., Assoc. of Genealogists and Record Agents, 1988–. *Recreation:* crossing the Channel. *Address:* College of Arms, Queen Victoria Street, EC4V 4BT. *T:* 071–236 9612.

DICKINSON, Patric (Thomas); poet, playwright and freelance broadcaster; *b* 26 Dec. 1914; *s* of Major A. T. S. Dickinson, 51 Sikhs, FF, IA, and Eileen Constance Kirwan; *m* 1945, Sheila Dunbar Shannon; one *s* one *d*. *Educ:* St Catharine's Coll., Cambridge (Crabtree Exhibitioner). Asst Schoolmaster, 1936–39. Artists' Rifles, 1939–40. BBC, 1942–48 (Feature and Drama Dept); Acting Poetry Editor, 1945–48. Sometime Gresham Prof. in Rhetoric at the City University. Libretti: (for Malcolm Arnold) The Return of Odysseus, 1977; (for Stephen Dodgson) The Miller's Secret, 1973; (for Alan Ridout): Creation, 1973; Good King Wenceslas, 1979. Atlantic Award in Literature, 1948; Cholmondeley Award for Poets, 1973. *Publications: poetry:* The Seven Days of Jericho, 1944; Soldier's Verse (anthology), 1945; Theseus and the Minotaur: play and poems, 1946; Stone in the Midst: play and poems, 1949; (ed) Byron (selected anthology), 1949; A Round of Golf Courses, 1951; The Sailing Race, 1952; The Scale of Things, 1955; (ed with Sheila Shannon) Poems to Remember, 1958; The World I See, 1960; This Cold Universe, 1964; (ed with Sheila Shannon) Poets' Choice: an anthology of English poetry from Spenser to the present day, 1967; (ed) C. Day Lewis, Selections from his Poetry, 1967; Selected Poems, 1968; More Than Time, 1970; A Wintering Tree, 1973; The Bearing Beast, 1976; Our Living John, 1979; Poems from Rye, 1980; Winter Hostages, 1980; (ed and introd) Selected Poems Henry Newbolt, 1981; A Rift in Time, 1982; To Go Hidden, 1984; A Sun Dog, 1988; Two into One (with drawings by John Ward, RA), 1989; Not Hereafter, 1991; *translations:* Aristophanes Against War, 1957; The Aeneid of Vergil, 1960; Aristophanes, vols I and II, 1970; *play:* A Durable Fire, 1962; *autobiography:* The Good Minute, 1965. *Recreation:* following golf (Cambridge Blue, 1935). *Address:* 38 Church Square, Rye, East Sussex. *T:* Rye (0797) 222194. *Club:* Savile.

DICKINSON, Prof. Peter; composer, pianist; Professor of Music, Goldsmiths' College, London University, since 1991; *b* 15 Nov. 1934; *s* of late Frank Dickinson, FBOA(Hons), FAAO, DOS, FRSH, contact lens specialist, and of Muriel Porter; *m* 1964, Bridget Jane Tomkinson, *d* of late Lt-Comdr E. P. Tomkinson, DSO, RN; two *s*. *Educ:* The Leys Sch.; Queens' Coll., Cambridge (organ schol., Stewart of Rannoch schol.; MA); Juilliard Sch. of Music, New York (Rotary Foundn Fellow). LRAM, ARCM; FRCO. Teaching and freelance work in New York, 1958–61, London and Birmingham, 1962–74; first Prof. of Music, Keele Univ., 1974–84, subseq. Prof. Emeritus; founded Centre for American Music, Keele Univ. Concerts, broadcasts and records as pianist, mostly with sister Meriel Dickinson, mezzo soprano, incl. French, American and British works, some specially commissioned, 1960–. Member: Bd, Trinity Coll. of Music, 1984–; Royal Soc. of Musicians, 1985–. FRSA 1981. *Publications: compositions include: orchestral:* Monologue for Strings, 1959; Five Diversions, 1969; Transformations, 1970; Organ Concerto, 1971; Piano Concerto, 1984; Violin Concerto, 1986; Jigsaws, 1988; Merseyside Echoes, 1988; *chamber:* String Quartet No 1, 1958; Juilliard Dances, 1959; Fanfares and Elegies, 1967; Translations, 1971; String Quartet No 2, 1975; American Trio, 1985; London Rags, 1986; Sonatas for piano and tape playback, 1987; Auden Studies, 1988; works for solo organ, piano, clavichord, recorder, flute, violin and baryton; *vocal:* Four Auden Songs, 1956; A Dylan Thomas Cycle, 1959; Elegy, 1966; Five Poems of Alan Porter, 1968; Extravaganzas, 1969; An E. E. Cummings Cycle, 1970; Winter Afternoons (Emily Dickinson), 1970; Three Comic Songs (Auden), 1972; Surrealist Landscape (Lord Berners), 1973; Lust (St Augustine), 1974; A Memory of David Munrow, 1977; Reminiscences (Byron), 1979; The Unicorns (John Heath Stubbs), 1982; Stevie's Tunes (Stevie Smith), 1984; Larkin's Jazz (Philip Larkin), 1989; *choral:* Martin of Tours (Thomas Blackburn), 1966; The Dry Heart (Alan Porter), 1967; Outcry, 1969; Late Afternoon in November, 1975; A Mass of the Apocalypse, 1984; Tiananmen 1989 (Dickinson), 1990; *ballet:* Vitalitas, 1959; *musical drama:* The Judas Tree (Thomas Blackburn), 1965; various church music, music for children and for films; (ed) Twenty British Composers, 1975; (ed) Songs and Piano Music by Lord Berners, 1982; The Music of Lennox Berkeley, 1989; contrib. to The New Grove, and various books and periodicals. *Recreation:* book collecting. *Address:* Goldsmith's College, University of London, New Cross, SE14 6NW. *Club:* United Oxford & Cambridge University.

DICKINSON, Hon. Peter Malcolm de Brissac; author; *b* 16 Dec. 1927; *s* of late Hon. Richard Sebastian Willoughby Dickinson and of May Southey (Nancy) Lovemore; *m* 1953, Mary Rose Barnard (*d* 1988); two *d* two *s*. *Educ:* Eton; King's Coll., Cambridge (BA). Asst Editor, Punch, 1952–69. Chm., Management Cttee, Soc. of Authors, 1978–80. *Publications: children's books:* The Weathermonger, 1968; Heartsease, 1969; The Devil's Children, 1970 (trilogy republished 1975 as The Changes); Emma Tupper's Diary, 1970; The Dancing Bear, 1972; The Gift, 1973; The Iron Lion, 1973; Chance, Luck and Destiny, 1975; The Blue Hawk, 1976; Annerton Pit, 1977; Hepzibah, 1978; Tulku, 1979 (Whitbread Prize; Carnegie Medal); The Flight of Dragons, 1979; City of Gold, 1980 (Carnegie Medal); The Seventh Raven, 1981; Healer, 1983; Giant Cold, 1984; (ed) Hundreds and Hundreds, 1984; A Box of Nothing, 1985; Mole Hole, 1987; Merlin Dreams, 1988; Eva, 1988; AK, 1990 (Whitbread Children's Award); *TV series,* Mandog (Mandog, by Lois Lamplugh, 1972, is based on this series); *novels:* Skin Deep, 1968; A Pride of Heroes, 1969; The Seals, 1970; Sleep and His Brother, 1971; The Lizard in the Cup, 1972; The Green Gene, 1973; The Poison Oracle, 1974; The Lively Dead, 1975; King and Joker, 1976; Walking Dead, 1977; One Foot in the Grave, 1979; A Summer in the Twenties, 1981; The Last House-party, 1982; Hindsight, 1983; Death of a Unicorn, 1984; Tefuga, 1986; Perfect Gallows, 1988; Skeleton-in-Waiting, 1989; Play Dead, 1991. *Recreation:* manual labour. *Address:* 61a Ormiston Grove, W12 0JP.

See also Baron Dickinson, Very Rev. H. G. Dickinson.

DICKINSON, Sir Samuel Benson, (Sir Ben Dickinson), Kt 1980; Chairman, Burmine Pty Ltd, 1985–88; Mining Advisor to South Australian Government, 1975–84; Chairman, South Australian Government Uranium Enrichment Committee, 1979–84; *b* 1 Feb. 1912; *s* of Sydney Rushbrook Dickinson and Margaret Dickinson (*née* Clemes); *m* 1960, Dorothy Joan Weidenhofer; three *s* one *d*. *Educ:* Haileybury College, Melbourne; Univ. of Melbourne. MSc. N Australia Aerial Geological and Geophysical Survey, 1935–36; geologist: Electrolytic Zinc, Mt Lyell, Mt Isa, mining cos, 1937–41; S Australian Geological Survey, 1941–42. Dir of Mines, Govt Geologist, Sec. to Minister of Mines, Dep. Controller, Mineral Production, Chm. Radium Hill Mines, 1943–56; Director: Rio Tinto Mining Co. of Australia, 1956–60; Sir Frank Duval's Gp of Cos, 1960–62; Chief Technical Adviser, Pechiney Australia, 1962–65; Project Manager, Clutha Development Ltd and Daniel K. Ludwig Cos Australia, 1965–75. *Publications:* technical reports for Australian Dept of Mines, Inst. of Mining and Metallurgy and mining jls and bulletins. *Recreations:* golf, bowls. *Address:* PO Box 269, Stirling, SA 5152, Australia. *T:* (08) 339 5135. *Clubs:* Athenæum (Melbourne); American National (Sydney); Naval, Military & Air Force (Adelaide).

DICKINSON, (Vivienne) Anne, (Mrs David Phillips); Chairman, Cornerstone Communications; Director, The Birkdale Group plc; *b* 27 Sept. 1931; *d* of F. Oswald Edward Dickinson and M. Ida Ismay Dickinson; *m* 1st, 1951, John Kerr Large (marr. diss.); one *s* decd; 2nd, 1979, David Hermas Phillips (*d* 1989). *Educ:* Nottingham Girls' High School. Account Executive, W. S. Crawford, 1960–64; Promotions Editor: Good Housekeeping, 1964–65; Harpers Bazaar, 1965–67; Dir in charge of Promotions, Nat. Magazine Co., 1967–68; Dir, Benson PR (now Kingsway), 1968–69; Chm. and Chief Exec., Kingsway Rowland, 1969–89; Chm., The Rowland Co., 1989–90. Vice-Chm., PR Consultants' Assoc., 1989– (Chm., Professional Practices Cttee, 1989–). Chm., Family Welfare Assoc., 1990. FIPR 1985; CBIM 1986. PR Professional of the Year, PR Week, 1988–89. *Recreations:* friends, food, horses. *Address:* 26 Bedford Gardens, W8. *T:* 071–243 0522.

DICKINSON, William Michael, MBE 1960; farmer; *b* 13 Jan. 1930; *s* of late Comdr W. H. Dickinson, RN, and Ruth Sandeman Betts; *m* 1971, Enid Joy Bowers; one *s* two *d*. *Educ:* St Edward's Sch., Oxford. Army Service, 1948–51; 2/Lieut, Oxford and Bucks LI, Sept. 1948; seconded Somaliland Scouts; Lieut 1950; Colonial Service Devonshire Course, 1951–52; Somaliland Protectorate: Admin. Officer, 1952; Dist Officer, 1953–54; Asst Sec. (Political), 1955–56; seconded to British Liaison Orgn, Ethiopia, as Sen. Asst Liaison Officer, 1957–59; Brit. Liaison Officer in charge, 1959; transf. N Rhodesia as Dist Officer, 1960; Dist Comr, 1961; seconded to FO as HM Consul-Gen., Hargeisa, 1961–63; Principal, External Affairs Section, Office of Prime Minister, N Rhodesia, during 1964; Sen. Principal, Min. of Foreign Affairs, Govt of Zambia, 1964–65. Man. Dir, Africa Research Ltd, 1966–90. *Address:* Durfold, Blisland, Bodmin, Cornwall PL30 4JL. *T:* Bodmin (0208) 850560.

DICKS, Terence Patrick, (Terry); MP (C) Hayes and Harlington, since 1983; *b* 17 March 1937; *s* of Frank and Winifred Dicks; *m*; one *s* two *d*. *Educ:* London Sch. of Econs and Pol Science (BScEcon); Oxford Univ. (DipEcon). Clerk: Imperial Tobacco Co. Ltd, 1952–59; Min. of Labour, 1959–66; Admin. Officer, GLC, 1971–86. Contested (C) Bristol South, 1979. *Address:* House of Commons, SW1A 0AA.

DICKSON, Alexander Graeme, (Alec), CBE 1967 (MBE 1945); MA Oxon; Hon. President, Community Service Volunteers, since 1982 (Hon. Director, 1962–82); *b* 23 May 1914; *y s* of late Norman Dickson and Anne Higgins; *m* 1951, Mora Hope Robertson, artist, author of numerous travel books and biographies. *Educ:* Rugby; New Coll., Oxford. Private Sec. to late Sir Alec Paterson, 1935; editorial staff: Yorkshire Post, 1936–37; Daily Telegraph, 1937–38, Germany; refugee relief, Czechoslovakia, winter 1938–39. Served War of 1939–45: Cameron Highlanders; 1st KAR (Abyssinian Campaign); led E Africa Comd mobile educn unit. Displaced Persons Directorate, Berlin, 1946–48; introd Mass Educn, Gold Coast, 1948–49; founded Man O' War Bay Training Centre, Cameroons and Nigeria, 1950–54; Chief Unesco Mission, Iraq, 1955–56; refugee relief, Austro-Hungarian frontier, winter 1956–57. Founder and first Dir, Voluntary Service Overseas, 1958–62; founded Community Service Volunteers, 1962, developing concept of 'A Year Between' for students, linking curriculum to human needs, promoting tutoring in schools, involving disadvantaged and unemployed young people in social service. Shared experience with US Peace Corps, 1961, 1969; India, 1968, 1972; Hong Kong, 1968, 1974, 1980; Israel, 1970, 1980; Nigeria, 1970, 1975, 1976; Malta, 1971; Nepal, 1972; New Zealand, 1972; Papua New Guinea, 1973; Bahamas, 1975; US Nat. Student Volunteer Program, Washington DC and Alaska, 1975; Ontario, 1975, 1981, 1982, 1983; Sri Lanka, Australia, 1976; Japan, 1976, 1980, 1983; Univ. of the South Pacific, 1978; W Germany, Denmark, 1979; Finland, 1980; Sweden, 1982; Malaysia, 1983. Hon. Chm., Nat. Youth Leadership Council (US), 1984–. Consultant to Commonwealth Secretariat, 1974–77; Hon. Consultant: Partnership for Service-Learning (US), 1984–; Inst. for Social Inventions (UK), 1984–; Hon. Advr, Internat. Baccalaureate schs, 1984–. Hon. LLD: Leeds, 1970; Bristol, 1980. Niwano Peace Foundn Award, 1982; Kurt Hahn Centenary Award, 1986. *Publications:* (with Mora Dickson) A Community Service Handbook, 1967; School in the Round, 1969; A Chance to Serve, 1976; Volunteers, 1983; articles on community development and youth service. *Recreations:* identical with work - involving young people in community service, at home or overseas.

Address: 19 Blenheim Road, W4. *T:* 071–994 7437; (office) 071–278 6601.
See also M. G. Dickson.

DICKSON, Arthur Richard Franklin, CBE 1974; QC (Belize), 1979; Commissioner for Law Revision, Belize, 1978; *b* 13 Jan. 1913; *m* 1949, Joanna Maria Margaretha van Baardwyk; four *s.* *Educ:* Rusea's Secondary Sch. and Cornwall Coll., Jamaica. Called to the Bar, Lincoln's Inn, 1938. Judicial Service. HM Overseas Judiciary: Jamaica, 1941; Magistrate, Turks and Caicos Islands, 1944–47; Asst to Attorney-Gen., and Legal Draftsman, Barbados, 1947–49; Magistrate, British Guiana, 1949–52; Nigeria, 1952–62: Magistrate, 1952–54; Chief Magistrate, 1954–56; Chief Registrar, High Court, Lagos, 1956–58; Judge of the High Court, Lagos, 1958–62; retired. Temp. appointment, Solicitors Dept, GPO London, 1962–63; served Northern Rhodesia (latterly Zambia), 1964–67; Judge of the High Court, Uganda, 1967–71; Deputy Chm., Middlesex QS, July-Aug., 1971; Chief Justice, Belize, 1973–74; Judge of the Supreme Court, Anguilla (part-time), 1972–76; part-time Chm., Industrial Tribunals, 1972–85. *Publications:* Revised Ordinances (1909–1941) Turks and Caicos Islands, 1944; (ed) Revised Laws of Belize, 1980. *Recreations:* gardening, walking, swimming. *Address:* 14 Meadow Lane, Lindfield, Haywards Heath, West Sussex RH16 2RJ. *T:* Lindfield (0444) 4450. *Club:* Commonwealth Trust.

DICKSON, Rt. Hon. Brian, PC (Can) 1984; Chief Justice of Canada, 1984–90; *b* 25 May 1916; *s* of Thomas and Sarah Elizabeth Dickson (*née* Gibson); *m* 1943, Barbara Melville, *d* of Henry E. Sellers; three *s* one *d.* *Educ:* Regina Collegiate Institute; University of Manitoba; Manitoba Law School. LLB 1938 (Gold Medal). Served with Royal Canadian Artillery, 1940–45 (wounded, despatches); Hon. Lt-Col, 30th Field Regt, Royal Canadian Artillery. Called to the Bar of Manitoba, 1940; practised law with Aikins, MacAulay & Co., 1945–63; Lectr, Manitoba Law Sch., 1948–54; QC (Can) 1953; Court of Queen's Bench, Manitoba, 1963; Manitoba Court of Appeal, 1967; Supreme Court of Canada, 1973; Life Bencher, Law Soc. of Manitoba; Chm., Board of Governors, Univ. of Manitoba, 1971–73; Chancellor of Diocese of Rupert's Land, 1960–71. Hon. Bencher, Lincoln's Inn, 1984. Hon. Prof., Manitoba Univ., 1985; Hon. Fellow, Amer. Coll. of Trial Lawyers, 1985. Hon. degrees: St John's Coll.; Univs of Manitoba, Saskatchewan, Ottawa, Queen's, Dalhousie, York, Laurentian, British Columbia, Toronto, Yeshiva, McGill, Carleton, Mount Allison. KStJ 1985. Order of the Buffalo Hunt, Manitoba, 1961. *Recreation:* riding. *Address:* c/o Supreme Court Building, Wellington Street, Ottawa, Ont K1A 0J1, Canada. *Club:* Rideau (Ottawa).

DICKSON, David John Scott; Editor, New Scientist, since 1990; *b* 30 Aug. 1947; *s* of David and Rachel Mary Dickson; *m* 1973, Prudence Mary, *d* of Michael and Mary Richardson; one *s* one *d.* *Educ:* Westminster Sch. (Queen's scholar); Trinity Coll., Cambridge (Scholarship in Maths). Medical News, 1968–70; Sec., Brit. Soc. for Social Responsibility in Science, 1970–72; science corresp., 1973–75, features editor, 1975–77, THES; Washington corresp., Nature, 1977–82; European corresp., Science, 1982–89; news editor, New Scientist, 1989–90. Lectures organiser, ICA, 1976–77. Visiting Research Fellow: Univ. of Linköping, Sweden, 1981; Open Univ., 1989. *Publications:* Alternative Technology, 1974; The New Politics of Science, 1984; Het verval van de Geest (The Death of the Spirit), 1990; contribs to various jls on science, technology and society. *Recreations:* music, photography, travel. *Address:* c/o New Scientist, King's Reach Tower, Stamford Street, SE1 9LS.

DICKSON, Eileen Wadham, (Mrs C. F. Dickson); *d* of John Edward Latton, Librarian to Inner Temple, and Ethel Letitia Baker; *m* 1931, Charles Frederick Dickson, OBE. *Educ:* Convent of the Sacred Heart, Roehampton; Bruges, Belgium. Served War of 1939–45 with WVS and on Executive Council of Stage Door Canteen. Joined Harper's Bazaar, 1949; Fashion Editor, 1951; Editor, 1953–65. *Recreations:* theatre, reading, racing, gardens. *Address:* Grimsdyke, Aldworth, Reading, Berks RG8 9RY; 4 Stack House, Ebury Street, SW1W 9JS.

DICKSON, George, CBE 1991 (OBE 1974); HM Diplomatic Service, retired; Consul General, Amsterdam, 1987–91; *b* 23 May 1931; *s* of late George James Stark Dickson and of Isobel (*née* Brown). *Educ:* Aberdeen Acad. DSIR, 1952; CRO, 1952–54; Karachi, 1954–56; Penang, 1957–59; Nicosia, 1960–62; Kampala, 1962–66; FCO, 1966–68; Manila, 1968–71; Jakarta, 1971–75; Stuttgart, 1975–76; Beirut, 1976–79; Head of Chancery, Baghdad, 1979–81; Asst Dir, Internat. Affairs Div., Commonwealth Secretariat, 1981–85; Dep. High Comr, Kingston, Jamaica, 1985–87. *Recreations:* friends, travel, walking. *Clubs:* Commonwealth Trust, Royal Over-Seas League.

DICKSON, Prof. Gordon Ross; Professor of Agriculture, University of Newcastle upon Tyne, since 1973; Deputy Chairman, Home-Grown Cereals Authority, since 1982; Chairman, North England Regional Advisory Committee, Forestry Commission, since 1987; *b* 12 Feb. 1932; *s* of T. W. Dickson, Tynemouth; *m* 1956, Dorothy Stobbs (*d* 1989); two *s* one *d.* *Educ:* Tynemouth High Sch.; Durham Univ. BSc (Agric) 1st cl. hons 1953, PhD (Agric) 1958, Dunelm. Tutorial Research Student, Univ. Sch. of Agric., King's Coll., Newcastle upon Tyne, 1953–56; Asst Farm Dir, Council of King's Coll., Nafferton, Stocksfield-on-Tyne, 1956–58; Farms Director for the Duke of Norfolk, 1958–71; Principal, Royal Agric. Coll., Cirencester, 1971–73. Chm., Agricl Wages Bd for England and Wales, 1981–84. *Address:* Faculty of Agriculture, University of Newcastle upon Tyne, Newcastle upon Tyne NE1 7RU; The West Wing, Bolam Hall, Morpeth, Northumberland NE61 3ST.

DICKSON, Jennifer (Joan), (Mrs R. A. Sweetman), RA 1976 (ARA 1970); RE 1965; graphic artist, photographer and painter; *b* 17 Sept. 1936; 2nd *d* of late John Liston Dickson and Margaret Joan Turner, S Africa; *m* 1962, Ronald Andrew Sweetman; one *s.* *Educ:* Goldsmith's College Sch. of Art, Univ. of London; Atelier 17, Paris. Taught at Eastbourne Sch. of Art, 1959–62 (French Govt Schol., to work in Paris under S. W. Hayter). Directed and developed Printmaking Dept, Brighton Coll. of Art, 1962–68; developed and directed Graphics Atelier, Saidye Bronfman Centre, Montreal, 1970–72. Has held appointments of Vis. Artist at following Universities: Ball State Univ., Muncie, Indiana, 1967; Univ. of the West Indies, Kingston, Jamaica, 1968; Univ. of Wisconsin, Madison, 1972; Ohio State Univ., 1973; Western Illinois Univ., 1973; Haystack Mountain Sch. of Crafts, Maine, 1973; Vis. Artist, Queen's Univ., Kingston, Ont., 1977; part-time Instructor of Drawing, 1980–81, 1983, Sessional Instructor, 1980–85, Ottawa Univ.; Vis. Prof., 1987, Hon. LLD 1988, Univ. of Alberta. Founder Mem., Brit. Printmakers' Council. Prix des Jeunes Artistes (Gravure), Biennale de Paris, 1963; Major Prize, World Print Competition, San Francisco, 1974; Norwegian Print Biennale Prize, 1981. *Publications:* suites of original prints and photographs: Genesis, 1965; Alchemic Images, 1966; Aids to Meditation, 1967; Eclipse, 1968; Song of Songs, 1969; Out of Time, 1970; Fragments, 1971; Sweet Death and Other Pleasures, 1972; Homage to Don Juan, 1975; Body Perceptions, 1975; The Secret Garden, 1976; Openings, 1977; Three Mirrors to Narcissus, 1978; Il Paradiso Terrestre, 1980; Il Tempo Classico, 1981; Grecian Odes, 1983; Aphrodite Anadyomene, 1984; The Gardens of Paradise, part 1, 1984, part 2, 1985; Reflected Palaces, 1985; The Gilded Cage, 1986; Water Gardens, 1987; The Hospital for Wounded Angels, 1987; The Gardens of Desire, 1988; Pavane to Spring, 1989; Sonnet to Persephone, 1990; The Gardener's Journal, 1990. *Address:* 20 Osborne Street, Ottawa, Ontario K1S 4Z9, Canada. *T:* 613–236–5602.

DICKSON, John Abernethy, CB 1970; Director-General and Deputy Chairman, Forestry Commission, 1968–76; *b* 19 Sept. 1915; *yr s* of late John and Williamina Dickson; *m* 1942, Helen Drummond, *o d* of Peter Drummond Jardine; two *d.* *Educ:* Robert Gordon's Coll., Aberdeen; Aberdeen Univ. MA 1936; BSc (For.) 1938. Joined Forestry Commn, 1938; District Officer, 1940; seconded to Min. of Supply, Home Grown Timber Production Dept, 1940–46; Divisional Officer, 1951; Conservator, 1956; Dir (Scotland), 1963; Comr Harvesting and Marketing, 1965. Director: Economic Forestry (Scotland), 1977–84; Forest Thinnings Ltd, 1979–86 (Chm., 1981–86). Chm., Standing Cttee on Commonwealth Forestry, 1968–76; Vice-Pres., Commonwealth Forestry Assoc., 1975– (Chm., 1972–75). Hon. LLD Aberdeen, 1969. FBIM 1975. *Recreation:* gardening. *Address:* 56 Oxgangs Road, Edinburgh EH10 7AY. *T:* 031–445 1067.

DICKSON, Leonard Elliot, CBE 1972; MC 1945; TD 1951; DL; Solicitor, Dickson, Haddow & Co., 1947–84; *b* 17 March 1915; *s* of Rev. Robert Marcus Dickson, DD, Lanark, and Cordelia Elliot; *m* 1950, Mary Elisabeth Cuthbertson; one *s* one *d.* *Educ:* Uppingham, Rutland; Univ. of Cambridge (BA 1936); Univ. of Glasgow (LLB 1947). Served War, with 1st Bn Glasgow Highlanders, HLI, 1939–46. Clerk to Clyde Lighthouses Trust, 1953–65. Chm., Lowland TAVR, 1968–70; Vice-Chm. Glasgow Exec. Council, NHS, 1970–74. DL Glasgow, 1963. *Publication:* Historical Sketch of Glasgow Society of Sons of the Clergy, 1990. *Recreations:* travel, gardening. *Address:* Bridge End, Gartmore, by Stirling FK8 3RR. *T:* Aberfoyle (08772) 220. *Club:* Royal Scottish Automobile (Glasgow).

DICKSON, Murray Graeme, CMG 1961; *b* 19 July 1911; *s* of Norman and Anne Dickson. *Educ:* Rugby; New Coll., Oxford. Prison Service (Borstals), 1935–40. Served War of 1939–45, in Force 136. Entered Colonial Service, 1947; Education Officer, Sarawak, 1947, Deputy Dir of Education, 1952, Dir of Education, 1955–66; retd. Unesco adviser on educl planning to Govt of Lesotho, 1967–68. *Publications:* Understanding Kant's Critique of Pure Reason, 1986; Tales from Herodotus, 1989; The Best of Thucydides, 1991. *Address:* 1 Hauteville Court Gardens, Stamford Brook Avenue, W6 0YF.
See also A. G. Dickson.

DICKSON, Prof. Peter George Muir, DPhil; FBA 1988; Professor of Early Modern History, University of Oxford, since 1989; Fellow, St Catherine's College, Oxford, since 1960; *b* 26 April 1929; *s* of William Muir Dickson, and Regina Dowdall-Nicolls; *m* 1964, Ariane Faye; one *d.* *Educ:* St Paul's Sch.; Worcester Coll., Oxford (Schol.; BA (1st Cl. Hons), MA, DPhil). FRHistS. Research Fellow, Nuffield Coll., Oxford, 1954–56; Tutor, St Catherine's Soc., Oxford, 1956–60; Vice-Master, St Catherine's Coll., 1975–77; Reader in Modern Hist., Oxford Univ., 1978–89. *Publications:* The Sun Insurance Office 1710–1960, 1960; The Financial Revolution in England 1688–1756, 1967; Finance and Government under Maria Theresia 1740–1780, 2 vols, 1987. *Recreations:* tennis, swimming, running, cinema. *Address:* Field House, Iffley, Oxford OX4 4EG. *T:* Oxford (0865) 779599.

DICKSON, Prof. Robert Andrew, MA Oxon, MB, ChM; FRCS, FRCSE; Professor and Head of Department of Orthopaedic Surgery, University of Leeds, since 1981; Consultant Surgeon, St James's University Hospital, Leeds, and Leeds General Infirmary, since 1981; *b* 13 April 1943; *s* of Robert Campbell Miller Dickson and late Maude Evelyn Dickson; *m* 1980, Ingrid Irene Sandberg; one *s.* *Educ:* Edinburgh Academy; Edinburgh Univ. (MB, ChB 1967, ChM 1973); MA Oxon 1979. FRCSE 1972; Moynihan Medal (Assoc. of Surgeons of GB and Ire.), 1977; FRCS *ad eund.* 1982. Lecturer, Nuffield Dept of Orthopaedic Surgery, Univ. of Oxford, 1972–75; Fellow in Spinal Surgery, Univ. of Louisville, Kentucky, 1975–76; Reader, Nuffield Dept of Orthopaedic Surgery, Univ. of Oxford, 1976–81. Arris and Gale Lectr, and Hunterian Prof., RCS. Fellow, Brit. Orthopaedic Assoc.; Member: Brit. Soc. for Surgery of the Hand; Brit. Orthopaedic Research Soc.; Brit. Scoliosis Soc. *Publications:* Surgery of the Rheumatoid Hand, 1979; Musculo-skeletal disease, 1984; Management of spinal deformities, 1984; Management of spinal deformities, 1988; papers on scoliosis, spinal surgery, hand surgery, and microsurgery. *Recreations:* squash, music. *Address:* 14A Park Avenue, Leeds LS8 2JH.

DICKSON, Rt. Hon. Robert George Brian; *see* Dickson, Rt Hon. B.

DICKSON, Robert Hamish, WS; Sheriff of South Strathclyde, Dumfries and Galloway, at Airdrie, since 1988; *b* 19 Oct. 1945; *s* of late Sheriff Ian Anderson Dickson, WS, and Mrs Margaret Forbes Ross or Dickson; *m* 1976, Janet Laird, *d* of late Alexander Campbell, Port of Menteith; one *s.* *Educ:* Glasgow Acad.; Drumtochty Castle; Glenalmond; Glasgow Univ. (LLB). WS 1969. Solicitor: Edinburgh, 1969–71; Glasgow, 1971–86 (Partner, Brown Mair Mackintosh, 1973–86); Sheriff of South Strathclyde, Dumfries and Galloway, at Hamilton, 1986–88 (floating). *Publications:* articles in medical legal jls. *Recreations:* golf, music, reading. *Address:* Airdrie Sheriff Court, Airdrie ML6 6EE. *T:* Airdrie (0236) 51121. *Clubs:* Glasgow Golf, Elie Golf House.

DICKSON MABON, Rt. Hon. Jesse; *see* Mabon, Rt Hon. J. D.

DIEHL, John Bertram Stuart; QC 1987; **His Honour Judge Diehl;** a Circuit Judge, since 1990; *b* 18 April 1944; *s* of E. H. S. and C. P. Diehl; *m* 1967, Patricia L. Charman; two *s.* *Educ:* Bishop Gore Grammar Sch., Swansea; University Coll. of Wales, Aberystwyth (LLB 1965). Called to the Bar, Lincoln's Inn, 1968. Asst Lectr and Lectr in Law, Univ. of Sheffield, 1965–69; barrister, in practice on Wales and Chester Circuit, 1969–90; a Recorder, 1984–90.

DIESKAU, Dietrich F.; *see* Fischer-Dieskau.

DIETRICH, Marlene; actress; *b* Berlin, 27 Dec. 1904; *d* of Eduard von Losch and Josephine Felsing; *m* 1924, Rudolph Sieber (*d* 1976); one *d.* *Educ:* Berlin; Weimar; Max Reinhardt Sch. of Theatre; Stage, Berlin and Vienna; First notable film, The Blue Angel; films in America since 1930, incl. Desire, Destry Rides Again, Foreign Affair, Garden of Allah, Golden Earrings, Rancho Notorious, Scarlet Empress, Shanghai Express, Stage Fright, Witness for the Prosecution, Just a Gigolo; naturalised as an American, 1937; numerous stage appearances in Europe, Great Britain, America and all continents; Special Tony Award, 1967–68. Commandeur, Légion d'Honneur, 1990 (Officier, 1972); US Medal of Freedom. *Publications:* Marlene Dietrich's ABC, 1962; My Life (autobiog.), 1989. *Recreation:* tennis.

DIGBY, family name of **Baron Digby.**

DIGBY, 12th Baron (Ire.) *cr* 1620, and 5th Baron (GB) *cr* 1765; **Edward Henry Kenelm Digby,** JP; Lord-Lieutenant, Dorset, since 1984 (Vice Lord-Lieutenant, 1965–84); Captain, late Coldstream Guards; *b* 24 July 1924; *o s* of 11th and 4th Baron Digby, KG, DSO, MC, and Hon. Pamela Bruce, OBE (*d* 1978), *y d* of 2nd Baron Aberdare; *S* father, 1964; *m* 1952, Dione Marian (*see* Lady Digby); two *s* one *d.* *Educ:* Eton; Trinity Coll., Oxford; RMC. Served War of 1939–45. Capt., 1947; Malaya, 1948–50; ADC to C-in-C:

FARELF, 1950–51; BAOR, 1951–52. Director: Brooklyns Westbrick Ltd, 1970–83; Beazer plc, 1983–; Kier Internat., 1986–; Gifford-Hill Inc., 1986–. Dep. Chm., SW Economic Planning Council, 1972–77. Mem. Council, Royal Agricultural Soc. of England, 1954; Chm., Royal Agricultural Soc. of Commonwealth, 1966–77, Hon. Fellow 1977. Pres., 1976, Vice Pres., 1977, Royal Bath and West Soc. Dorchester Rural District Councillor, 1962–68; Dorset County Councillor, 1966–81 (Vice Chm. CC, 1977–81). President: Council, St John, Dorset; Wessex Br., Inst. of Dirs; Patron, Dorset Br., British Red Cross Soc. Churchwarden, St Andrews, Minterne Magna. DL 1957, JP 1959, Dorset. KStJ 1985. *Recreations:* ski-ing, shooting, tennis. *Heir: s* Hon. Henry Noel Kenelm Digby, ACA [*b* 6 Jan. 1954; *m* 1980, Susan, *er d* of Peter Watts; one *s* one *d*]. *Address:* Minterne, Dorchester, Dorset DT2 7AU. *T:* Cerne Abbas (0300) 314370. *Club:* Pratt's.

DIGBY, Lady; Dione Marian Digby, DBE 1991; DL; Member, National Rivers Authority, since 1989 (Chairman, Wessex Regional Advisory Board, since 1989); Director, Western Advisory Board (formerly South West Regional Board), National Westminster Bank, since 1986; *b* 23 Feb. 1934; *d* of Rear-Adm. Robert St Vincent Sherbrooke, VC, CB, DSO, and Rosemary Neville Sherbrooke (*née* Buckley), Oxton, Notts; *m* 1952, Baron Digby, *qv*; two *s* one *d*. *Educ:* Talindert State Sch., Victoria, Australia; Southover Manor Sch., Lewes, Sussex. Chairman: Dorset Assoc. of Youth Clubs, 1966–73; Dorset Community Council, 1977–79; Standing Conf. of Rural Community Councils and Councils of Voluntary Service SW Region, 1977–79. Councillor (Ind.) W Dorset DC, 1976–86; Mem. Dorset Small Industries Cttee, CoSIRA, 1977 (Chm. 1981); Mem., Wessex Water Authority, 1983–89. Mem. BBC/IBA Central Appeals Adv. Cttee, 1975–80; Governor: Dorset Coll. of Agriculture, 1978–83; Sherborne Sch., 1986–; Mem. Council, Exeter Univ., 1981–. Founder Chairman, Hon. Sec., Summer Music Soc. of Dorset, 1963–; Mem. Bath Festival Soc. Council of Management, 1971–81 (Chm. of the Society, 1976–81); Chm. Bath Fest. Friends Trust, 1982–87; Member: SW Arts Management Cttee, 1981–86; Arts Council of GB, 1982–86; South Bank Bd, 1985–88 (Gov., 1988–90); Western Orchestral Soc. Bd of Management, 1989–; Chm., South and West Concerts Bd, 1989– (Mem., 1986–). DL Dorset, 1983. *Recreations:* music and the arts, skiing, sailing, tennis; interest in local government, politics, history, people. *Address:* Minterne, Dorchester, Dorset DT2 7AU. *T:* Cerne Abbas (03003) 370.

DIGBY, Adrian, CBE 1964; MA Oxon; FSA; Keeper, Department of Ethnography, British Museum, 1953–69; excavated Maya site of Las Cuevas, British Honduras, 1957; *b* 13 June 1909; *s* of late William Pollard Digby, FInstP, MIME, MIEE; *m* 1939, Sylvia Mary, *d* of late Arnold Inman, OBE, KC; two *d*. *Educ:* Lancing; Brasenose Coll., Oxford. Entered British Museum as Asst Keeper, 1932. Hon. Asst Sec. of International Congress of Anthropological and Ethnological Sciences, London, 1934; Hon. Sec. of International Congress of Americanists, Cambridge, 1952. Served in Intelligence Division Naval Staff, Admiralty, 1942–44; Hydrographic Dept, Admiralty, 1944–45. Vis. Prof. in Archaeology, Univ. de Los Andes, Bogota, 1970. Pres. Sect. H of The British Association for the Advancement of Science, 1962; Vice-Pres. Royal Anthropological Inst., 1962–66. *Publications:* Ancient American Pottery (with G. H. S. Bushnell), 1955; Maya Jades, 1964; articles on anthropological subjects in Man and in Chambers's Encyclopædia. *Recreation:* sundials. *Address:* Greentrees, Eastcombe, Stroud, Glos GL6 7DR. *T:* Gloucester (0452) 770409.

DIGBY, Very Rev. Richard Shuttleworth W; *see* Wingfield Digby.

DIGBY, Simon Wingfield, TD 1946; DL; MA; *b* 1910; *s* of late Col F. J. B. Wingfield Digby, DSO; *m* 1936, Kathleen Elizabeth, *d* of late Hon. Mr Justice Courtney Kingstone, Toronto, Canada; one *s* one *d*. *Educ:* Harrow Sch.; Trinity Coll., Cambridge. Delegate to International Studies Conference, 1934. Prospective Conservative Candidate for West Dorset, Jan. 1937–June 1941; MP (U) West Dorset, 1941–Feb. 1974; a Conservative Whip, 1948–51. Barrister-at-law, Inner Temple; served in Army (TA), Aug. 1939–June 1945 in UK and NW Europe; Major, 1943; GSO II, 1944. Civil Lord of the Admiralty, 1951–57. Mem. of Empire Parl. Delegn to East Africa, 1948 and Inter-Parliamentary Union Delegation to Chile, 1962. Pres., Wessex Young Conservatives, 1947–50; Sec., Conservative Social Services Cttee, 1947; Chairman: Conservative Forestry Sub-Cttee, 1959–67; Shipping and Shipbuilding Cttee, 1964–74. Member: Coastal Pollution Select Cttee, 1966–68; Select Cttee on Procedure; Public Accounts Cttee. Delegate (C), Council of Europe Assembly and Assembly of WEU, 1968–74 (Leader, 1972–74). Pres., Soc. of Dorset Men, 1972–85. DL Dorset, 1953. Order of Leopold and Order of White Lion. Medal of Council of Europe Assembly, 1974. *Recreations:* fishing, bloodstock breeding. *Address:* Sherborne Castle, Sherborne, Dorset DT9 5NR. *T:* Gillingham (0747) 822650, (office) Sherborne (0935) 813182; Coleshill House, Coleshill, near Birmingham. *Club:* Carlton.

See also Sir Rupert Hardy, Bt.

DIGBY, Ven. Stephen Basil W.; *see* Wingfield-Digby.

DIGGLE, James, LittD; FBA 1985; Reader in Greek and Latin, University of Cambridge, since 1989; University Orator, since 1982; Fellow of Queens' College, since 1966; *b* 29 March 1944; *s* of James Diggle and Elizabeth Alice Diggle (*née* Buckley); *m* 1973, Sedwell Mary Chapman, *d* of late Rev. Preb. F. A. R. Chapman and of K. A. Chapman (*née* Mill); three *s*. *Educ:* Rochdale Grammar School; St John's College, Cambridge (Major Scholar; Classical Tripos Pt I, first cl., 1964, Pt II, first cl. with dist., 1965; Pitt Scholar, Browne Scholar, Hallam Prize, Members' Latin Essay Prize, 1963; Montagu Butler Prize, Browne Medals for Greek Elegy and Latin Epigram, 1964; Porson Prize, First Chancellor's Classical Medal, Craven Student, Allen Scholar, 1965; BA 1965; MA 1969; PhD 1969; LittD 1985). Queens' College, Cambridge: Research Fellow, 1966–67; Official Fellow and Director of Studies in Classics, 1967–; Librarian, 1969–77; Praelector, 1971–73, 1978–; Cambridge University: Asst Lectr in Classics, 1970–75; Lectr, 1975–89; Chm., Faculty Bd of Classics, 1989–90. Hon. Sec., Cambridge Philological Soc., 1970–74 (Jt Editor, Procs, 1970–82); Chm., Classical Jls Bd, 1991– (Hon. Treas., 1979–91); Jt Editor, Cambridge Classical Texts and Commentaries, 1977–. *Publications:* The Phaethon of Euripides, 1970; (jtly) Flavii Cresconii Corippi Iohannidos, Libri VIII, 1970; (ed jtly) The Classical Papers of A. E. Housman, 1972; (ed jtly) Dionysiaca: nine studies in Greek poetry, presented to Sir Denys Page, 1978; Studies on the Text of Euripides, 1981; Euripidis Fabulae (Oxford Classical Texts), vol. ii 1981, vol. i 1984; (ed jtly) Studies in Latin Literature and its Tradition, in honour of C. O. Brink, 1989; The textual tradition of Euripides' Orestes, 1991. *Recreation:* family life. *Address:* Queens' College, Cambridge CB3 9ET. *T:* Cambridge (0223) 335527.

DIGNAN, Maj.-Gen. Albert Patrick, CB 1978; MBE 1952; FRCS, FRCSI; Director of Army Surgery and Consulting Surgeon to the Army, 1973–78; Hon. Consultant Surgeon, Royal Hospital, Chelsea, 1973–78; Hon. Consultant in Radiotherapy and Oncology, Westminster Hospital, 1974–78; *b* 25 July 1920; *s* of Joseph Dignan; *m* 1952, Eileen White; two *s* one *d*. *Educ:* Trinity Coll., Dublin (Med. Schol.). MB, BCh, BAO, BA 1943, MA, MD 1968, FRCSI 1947, FRCS 1976. Prof. of Physiol. Prize, TCD. Posts in Dublin, Belfast and Wigan; subseq. NS Sen. Specialist in Surgery, Major RAMC Malaya; Sen. Registrar in Surgery, Bristol Royal Infirmary and Wanstead Hosp.; Sen. Specialist in Surgery, BAOR Mil. Hosps and Consultant Surg., Brit. Mil. Hosps Singapore and Tidworth, 1953–68; Brig., and Consulting Surg., Farelf, 1969–70; Consultant Surg., Mil. Hosp. Tidworth, 1971–72; Consultant Surgeon, Queen Alexandra Mil. Hosp. Millbank, 1972–73; Consultant in Accident and Emergency, Ealing Dist, DHSS, 1978–79. Fellow, Association of Surgeons of GB and Ireland. QHS, 1974–78. *Publications:* papers in Brit. Jl Surgery, BMJ, Jl of RAMC, Postgrad. Med. Jl, Univ. Singapore Med. Soc. Med. Gazette. *Recreations:* gardening, golf. *Address:* Ramridge Dene, 182 Beckenham Hill Road, Beckenham, Kent BR3 4JJ.

DILHORNE, 2nd Viscount *cr* 1964, of Green's Norton; **John Mervyn Manningham-Buller;** Bt 1866; Baron 1962; Barrister-at-Law; *b* 28 Feb. 1932; *s* of 1st Viscount Dilhorne, PC, and of Lady Mary Lilian Lindsay, 4th *d* of 27th Earl of Crawford, KT, PC; *S* father, 1980; *m* 1955, Gillian Evelyn (marr. diss. 1973), *d* of Colonel George Stockwell; two *s* one *d*; *m* 1981, Dr Eykyn, MB BS, MRCPath. *Educ:* Eton; RMA Sandhurst. Called to the Bar, Inner Temple, 1979. Formerly Lieut, Coldstream Guards. Managing Director, Stewart Smith (LP&M) Ltd, 1970–74. Member, Wilts County Council, 1967–70. Mem., Jt Parly Cttee on Statutory Instruments, 1981–. FTII (Mem. Council, 1967–82). *Heir: s* Hon. James Edward Manningham-Buller, formerly Captain Welsh Guards [*b* 20 Aug. 1956; *m* 1985, Nicola Marion, *e d* of Sven Mackie; one *s*. *Educ:* Harrow; Sandhurst]. *Address:* 2 Paper Buildings, Temple, EC4. *T:* 01–353 5835; 164 Ebury Street, SW1W 8UP. *T:* 071–730 0913. *Clubs:* Pratt's, Buck's, Beefsteak; Swinley Forest Golf.

DILKE; *see* Fetherston-Dilke.

DILKE, Sir John Fisher Wentworth, 5th Bt *cr* 1862; *b* 1906; *e s* of Sir Fisher Wentworth Dilke, 4th Bt, and Ethel Clifford (*d* 1959); *S* father, 1944; *m* 1st, 1934, Sheila (marr. diss. 1949), *d* of late Sir William Seeds, KCMG; two *s*; 2nd, 1951, Iris Evelyn, *d* of late Ernest Clark. *Educ:* Winchester; New Coll., Oxford. Foreign Office (Cairo), 1929; Editorial Staff, The Times (correspondent in Paris and Moscow), 1936; rejoined Foreign Service, 1939; political corresp., COI, 1945; BBC External Service, 1950. *Heir: s* Charles John Wentworth Dilke, *b* 1937. *Address:* Ludpits, Etchingham, Sussex. *Club:* Royal Thames Yacht.

DILKS, Prof. David Neville, FRHistS; FRSL; Vice-Chancellor, University of Hull, since 1991; *b* Coventry, 17 March 1938; *s* of Neville Ernest Dilks and Phyllis Dilks; *m* 1963, Jill Medlicott; one *s*. *Educ:* Royal Grammar Sch., Worcester; Hertford Coll., Oxford (BA Modern Hist., Class II, 1959); St Antony's Coll., Oxford (Curzon Prizeman, 1960). Research Assistant to: Rt Hon. Sir Anthony Eden (later Earl of Avon), 1960–62; Marshal of the RAF Lord Tedder, 1963–65; Rt Hon. Harold Macmillan, 1964–67; Asst Lectr, then Lectr, in International History, LSE, 1962–70; University of Leeds: Prof. of Internat. History, 1970–91; Chm., Sch. of History, 1974–79; Dean, Faculty of Arts, 1975–77. Vis. Fellow, All Souls' Coll., Oxford, 1973. Consultant, Sec.-Gen. of the Commonwealth, 1967–75; Chm., Commonwealth Youth Exchange Council, 1968–73. Member: Adv. Council on Public Records, 1977–85; Central Council, 1982–85, Library Cttee, 1982–, Royal Commonwealth Soc.; British Nat. Cttee for History of Second World War, 1983–; Inst. of Contemporary British History, 1986–; Acad. Adv. Council, Hughenden Foundn, 1986–; UFC, 1989–91. Trustee: Edward Boyle Meml Trust, 1982– (Hon. Sec., 1981–82); Imperial War Museum, 1983–90; Lennox-Boyd Meml Trust, 1984–91; Nathaniel Trust, 1986–90. Pres., Worcester Old Elizabethans' Assoc., 1986–87. FRSL 1986. Liveryman, Goldsmiths' Co., 1984– (Freeman, 1979). Wrote and presented BBC TV series, The Loneliest Job, 1977; interviewer in BBC TV series, The Twentieth Century Remembered, 1982. *Publications:* Curzon in India, Vol. I, 1969, Vol. II, 1970; (ed) The Diaries of Sir Alexander Cadogan, 1971; (contrib.) The Conservatives (ed Lord Butler of Saffron Walden), 1977; (ed and contrib.) Retreat from Power, vol. 1, 1906–1939, Vol. 2, after 1939, 1981; (ed and contrib.) Britain and Canada (Commonwealth Foundn Paper), 1980; (ed and contrib.) The Missing Dimension: governments and intelligence communities in the twentieth century, 1984; Neville Chamberlain, Vol. I: Pioneering and Reform 1869–1929, 1984; reviews and articles in English Historical Rev., Survey, History, Scandinavian Jl of History, etc. *Recreations:* ornithology, painting, railways, Bentley cars. *Address:* University of Hull, Hull HU6 7RX. *T:* Hull (0482) 465131. *Clubs:* Brooks's, Commonwealth Trust.

DILL, Sir (Nicholas) Bayard, Kt 1955; CBE 1951; JP; Senior Partner, Conyers, Dill & Pearman, Barristers-at-Law, since 1948; *b* 28 Dec. 1905; *s* of Thomas Melville and Ruth Rapalje Dill; *m* 1930, Lucy Clare Dill; two *s*. *Educ:* Saltus Grammar Sch., Bermuda; Trinity Hall, Cambridge. Law Tripos Cantab, 1926. Mem. Colonial Parliament (for Devonshire Parish), 1938–68; Mem. HM Exec. Council, 1944–54; Chairman: Board of Trade, 1935–42, also Bd of Educn, 1940, and Board of Works, 1942–48, Bermuda; St David's Island Cttee, 1940–43; Public Works Planning Commn, 1942–49; Board of Civil Aviation, 1944–63; Bermuda Trade Development Bd, 1957–59; Mem., Legislative Council, Bermuda, 1968–73. Served as Capt., Bermuda Volunteer Engs, 1936–44. Chancellor of Diocese of Bermuda, 1950–84. Life Mem., Internat. Biographical Assoc. JP Hamilton, Bermuda, 1949. *Recreations:* sailing, golf. *Address:* Newbold Place, Devonshire, Bermuda. *T:* (809) 292–4463. *Clubs:* Anglo-Belgian; Royal Thames Yacht; Royal Bermuda Yacht (Commodore, 1936–38), Mid-Ocean, Royal Hamilton Amateur Dinghy (Bermuda); India House, Canadian, Cruising of America, Metropolitan (NYC).

DILLAMORE, Ian Leslie, PhD, DSc; FEng 1985; FIM; Group Managing Director, INCO Engineered Products Ltd, since 1987; *b* 22 Nov. 1938; *s* of Arthur Leslie Dillamore and Louise Mary Dillamore; *m* 1962, Maureen Birch; two *s*. *Educ:* Birmingham Univ. (BSc, MSc, PhD, DSc). ICI Research Fellow, Birmingham Univ., 1962–63, Lectr in Physical Metallurgy, 1963–69; Head of Phys. Metallurgy, BISRA, 1969–72; Head of Metals Technology Unit, British Steel Corp., 1972–76; Head of Metallurgy Dept, Aston Univ., 1976–81, Dean of Engineering, 1980–81; Director of Research and Development, INCO Europe, 1981–82; Dir of Technology, INCO Engineered Products, 1982–87. Hon. Professor of Metallurgy, Birmingham Univ., 1981–. Mem. Council: Metals Soc., 1980–84; Instn of Metallurgists, 1981–84; Vice-Pres., Inst. of Metals, 1985–88; Mem. SRC Metallurgy Cttee, 1972–75, Materials Cttee, 1977–82; Chm., Processing Sub-Cttee, SRC, later SERC, 1979–82; Mem., DTI Non Ferrous Metals Exec. Cttee, 1982–85; Pres. Birmingham Metallurgical Assoc., 1980–81. Sir Robert Hadfield Medal and Prize, Metals Soc., 1976. *Publications:* numerous contribs to metallurgical and engrg jls. *Recreation:* industrial archaeology. *Address:* Wilsons Yard, Derby Road, Melbourne, Derbyshire DE7 1FE. *T:* Melbourne (0332) 864900.

DILLISTONE, Rev. Canon Frederick William, DD; Fellow and Chaplain, Oriel College, Oxford, 1964–70, Fellow Emeritus, 1970; Canon Emeritus of Liverpool Cathedral since 1964; *b* 9 May 1903; *s* of late Frederick Dillistone; *m* 1931, Enid Mary, *d* of late Rev. Cecil Francis Ayerst; two *s* one *d*. *Educ:* Brighton Coll.; BNC, Oxford (Scholar). BA 1924; BD 1933; DD 1951. Deacon, 1927; Priest, 1928; Vicar of St Andrew, Oxford, 1934–38; Prof. of Theology, Wycliffe Coll., Toronto, 1938–45; Prof. of Theology, Episcopal Theological Sch., Cambridge, Mass, 1947–52; Canon Residentiary and Chancellor of Liverpool Cathedral, 1952–56; Dean of Liverpool, 1956–63. Hulsean

Preacher, Cambridge, 1953; Select Preacher, Oxford, 1953–55; Select Preacher, Cambridge, 1960; Stephenson Lectr, Univ. of Sheffield, 1966; Bampton Lectr, Univ. of Oxford, 1968; Vis. Fellow, Clare Hall, Cambridge, 1970; Zabriskie Lectr, Virginia Theol. Seminary, 1971. Asst Editor, Theology Today, 1951–61. Hon. DD: Knox Coll., Toronto, 1946; Episcopal Theological Sch., Cambridge, Mass, 1967; Virginia Theol Seminary, 1979. Chaplain OStJ, 1958. *Publications*: The Significance of the Cross, 1945; The Holy Spirit in the Life of To-day, 1946; Revelation and Evangelism, 1948; The Structure of the Divine Society, 1951; Jesus Christ and His Cross, 1953; Christianity and Symbolism, 1955, repr. 1985; Christianity and Communication, 1956; The Novelist and the Passion Story, 1960; The Christian Faith, 1964; Dramas of Salvation, 1967; The Christian Understanding of Atonement, 1968; Modern Answers to Basic Questions, 1972; Traditional Symbols and the Contemporary World, 1972; Charles Raven: a biography, 1975; C. H. Dodd: a biography, 1977; Into all the World: a biography of Max Warren, 1980; Religious Experience and Christian Faith, 1982; Afire for God: the life of Joe Fison, 1983; The Power of Symbols, 1986; Editor, Scripture and Tradition, 1955; Editor, Myth and Symbol, 1966; contributor to: The Doctrine of Justification by Faith, 1954; A Companion to the Study of St Augustine, 1955; Steps to Christian Understanding, 1958; The Ecumenical Era in Church and Society, 1959; Metaphor and Symbol, 1961; The Theology of the Christian Mission, 1961; Christianity and the Visual Arts, 1964; Mansions of the Spirit, 1966; Christianity in its Social Context, 1967; Studies in Christian History and Interpretation, 1967; Christ for us Today, 1968; Grounds of Hope, 1968; Man, Fallen and Free, 1969; Sociology, Theology and Conflict, 1969; Christ and Spirit in the New Testament, 1973; Religion and Art as Communication, 1974; Theolinguistics, 1981; God's Truth, 1988; Language and the Worship of the Church, 1990. *Recreation*: gardening. *Address*: 11 Eyot Place, Iffley Fields, Oxford OX4 1SA. *T*: Oxford (0865) 241324.

DILLON, family name of **Viscount Dillon.**

DILLON, 22nd Viscount *cr* 1622, of Castello Gallen, Co. Mayo, Ireland; **Henry Benedict Charles Dillon;** Count in France, 1711; *b* 6 Jan. 1973; *s* of 21st Viscount Dillon and of Mary Jane, *d* of late John Young, Castle Hill House, Birtle, Lancs; *S* father, 1982. *Heir: uncle* Hon. Richard Arthur Louis Dillon [*b* 23 Oct. 1948; *m* 1975, Hon. Priscilla Frances Hazlerigg, *d* of 2nd Baron Hazlerigg, *qv*; one *s* one *d*].

DILLON, Hon. Sir Brian; *see* Dillon, Hon. Sir G. B. H.

DILLON, C(larence) Douglas; Chairman, US & Foreign Securities Corporation, 1967–84; Managing Director, Dillon, Read & Co. Inc., 1971–83; retired; *b* Geneva, Switzerland, 21 Aug. 1909; *s* of Clarence Dillon; *m* 1st, 1931, Phyllis Ellsworth (*d* 1982); two *d*; 2nd, 1983, Susan Sage. *Educ*: Groton Sch.; Harvard Univ. (AB). Mem., NY Stock Exchange, 1931–36; US and Foreign Securities Corporation and US and International Securities Corporation, 1937–53 (Dir, 1938–53; Pres., 1946–53); Dir, Dillon, Read & Co. Inc., 1938–53 (Chm. of Bd, 1946–53); American Ambassador to France, 1953–57; Under-Sec. of State for Economic Affairs, USA, 1957–59, Under-Sec. of State, USA, 1959–61; Sec. of the Treasury, USA, 1961–65. Served US Naval Reserve, 1941–45 (Lieut-Comdr; Air Medal, Legion of Merit). Dir, Council on Foreign Relations, 1965–78 (Vice-Chm. 1977–78); Pres., Board of Overseers, Harvard Coll., 1968–72; Chm., Rockefeller Foundn, 1971–75; Chm., Brookings Instn, 1971–75. Trustee Emeritus, Metropolitan Museum of Art (President, 1970–77; Chm., 1977–83). Hon. Dr of Laws: New York Univ., 1956; Lafayette Coll., 1957; Univ. of Hartford, Conn, 1958; Columbia Univ., 1959; Harvard Univ., 1959; Williams Coll., 1960; Rutgers Univ., 1961; Princeton Univ., 1961; University of Pennsylvania, 1962; Bradley Univ., 1964; Middlebury Coll., 1965; Tufts Univ., 1982; Marymount Manhattan Coll., 1984. US Presidential Medal of Freedom, 1989. *Address*: Far Hills, New Jersey 07931, USA.

DILLON, Rt. Hon. Sir (George) Brian (Hugh), Kt 1979; PC 1982; **Rt. Hon. Lord Justice Dillon;** a Lord Justice of Appeal, since 1982; *b* 2 Oct. 1925; *s* of late Captain George Crozier Dillon, RN; *m* 1954, Alison, *d* of late Hubert Samuel Lane, MC and Dr Isabella Lane, MB, ChB Edin.; two *s* two *d*. *Educ*: Winchester College; New College, Oxford. Called to the Bar, Lincoln's Inn, 1948; QC 1965; a Judge of the High Court of Justice, Chancery Division, 1979–82. *Address*: Royal Courts of Justice, WC2.

DILLON, Sir John (Vincent), Kt 1980; CMG 1974; Ombudsman for Victoria (Commissioner for Administrative Investigations), 1973–80; *b* 6 Aug. 1908; *s* of Roger Dillon and Ellen (*née* Egan); *m* 1935, Sheila Lorraine D'Arcy; three *s* one *d*. *Educ*: Christian Brothers Coll., Melbourne. AASA. Mem. Public Service Bd, 1941–54; Stipendiary Magistrate City Court, 1947–61; Chm., Medical Salaries Cttee, 1959–62; Under-Sec., Chief Sec.'s Dept, Vic, 1961–73; Chm., Racecourses Licences Bd, 1961–73. Hon. LLD Melbourne, 1982. *Recreations*: racing, golf, reading. *Address*: 25 Kelvin Grove, Armadale, Vic 3143, Australia. *Clubs*: Athenæum, Victoria Racing, Victoria Amateur Turf, Moonee Valley Racing, Melbourne Cricket, Metropolitan Golf (Melbourne).

DILLON, Sir Max, Kt 1979; *b* 30 June 1913; *s* of Cyril and Phoebe Dillon; *m* 1940, Estelle Mary Jones; one *s* one *d*. *Educ*: Wesley Coll., Melbourne; Melbourne Univ. (Faculty of Commerce). AASA (Sen.); ACIS; FAIM. General Manager, Cable Makers Australia Pty Ltd, 1957–70; Dep. Man. Dir, Metal Manufactures Ltd Gp, 1970–75. President: Aust. Council of Employer Fedns, 1967–69; Associated Chambers of Manufactures, 1974–77; Confedn of Aust. Industry, 1977–80; Chairman: Nat. Employers Policy Cttee, 1971–73 and 1975–78; Central Industrial Secretariat Council, 1972–77; Productivity Promotion Council, 1971–74; Member: Nat. Labour Adv. Council, 1966–72; Nat. Labour Consultative Council, 1977–80; Exec. Cttee, Aust. Manufacturing Council, 1978–80. *Recreations*: golf, swimming. *Address*: 33 Church Street, Pymble, NSW 2073, Australia. *T*: 44 3160. *Clubs*: Australian, Elanora Country (Sydney).

DILLON, Thomas Michael; QC 1973; **His Honour Judge Dillon;** a Circuit Judge, since 1985; *b* 29 Nov. 1927; *yr s* of Thomas Bernard Joseph Dillon, Birmingham, and Ada Gladys Dillon (*née* Noyes); *m* 1956, Wendy Elizabeth Marshall Hurrell; two *s* one *d*. *Educ*: King Edward's Sch., Aston, Birmingham; Birmingham Univ. (LLB); Lincoln Coll., Oxford (BCL). Called to Bar, Middle Temple, 1952, Master of the Bench 1981. 2nd Lieut, RASC, 1953–54. In practice as barrister, 1954–85; a Recorder, 1972–85; Part-time Chm. of Industrial Tribunals, 1968–74. *Recreations*: reading, listening to music. *Address*: 1 Fountain Court, Birmingham B4 6DR. *T*: 021–236 5721.

DILLWYN-VENABLES-LLEWELYN, Sir John Michael; *see* Venables-Llewelyn.

DILNOT, Mary, (Mrs Thomas Ruffle), OBE 1982; Director, IPC Women's Magazines Group, 1976–81; Editor, Woman's Weekly, 1971–81; *b* 23 Jan. 1921; 2nd *d* of George Dilnot, author, and Ethel Dilnot; *m* 1974, Thomas Ruffle. *Educ*: St Mary's Coll., Hampton. Joined Woman's Weekly, 1939. *Recreations*: home interests, reading, travel, golf. *Address*: 28 Manor Road South, Hinchley Wood, Esher, Surrey.

DIMBLEBY, Bel, (Mrs Jonathan Dimbleby); *see* Mooney, Bel.

DIMBLEBY, David; freelance broadcaster and newspaper proprietor; Chairman: Dimbleby & Sons Ltd, since 1986 (Managing Director, 1966–86); Wandsworth Borough News Ltd, since 1986 (Managing Director, 1979–86); *b* 28 Oct. 1938; *e s* of (Frederick) Richard and Dilys Dimbleby; *m* 1967, Josceline Rose Gaskell (*see* J. R. Dimbleby); one *s* two *d*. *Educ*: Glengorse Sch.; Charterhouse; Christ Church, Oxford (MA); Univs of Paris and Perugia. News Reporter, BBC Bristol, 1960–61; Presenter and Interviewer on network programmes on: religion (Quest), science for children (What's New?), politics (In My Opinion), Top of the Form, etc, 1961–63; Reporter, BBC2 (Enquiry), and Dir films, incl.: Ku-Klux-Klan, The Forgotten Million, Cyprus: Thin Blue Line, 1964–65; worked as asst to his father in family newspaper business at Richmond, Surrey, 1965, being apptd Managing Dir, 1966, on his father's death. Special Correspondent CBS News, New York; documentary film (Texas-England) and film reports for '60 minutes', 1966–; Reporter, BBC1 (Panorama), 1967–69; Commentator, Current Events; Presenter, BBC1 (24 Hours), 1969–72; Yesterday's Men, 1971; Chairman, The Dimbleby Talk-In, 1971–74; films for Reporter at Large, 1973; Presenter: BBC 1 (Panorama), 1974–77, 1980–82; (Nationwide), 1982; (People and Power), 1982–83; (This Week, Next Week), 1984–86; Election Campaign Report, 1974; BBC Election and Results programmes, 1979, 1983, 1987; film series: The White Tribe of Africa, 1979 (Royal TV Soc. Supreme Documentary Award); An Ocean Apart, 1988. *Publication*: An Ocean Apart (with David Reynolds), 1988. *Address*: 14 King Street, Richmond, Surrey TW9 1NF.
See also J. Dimbleby.

DIMBLEBY, Jonathan; freelance broadcaster, journalist, and author; *b* 31 July 1944; *s* of Richard and Dilys Dimbleby; *m* 1968, Bel Mooney, *qv*; one *s* one *d*. *Educ*: University Coll. London (BA Hons Philosophy). TV and Radio Reporter, BBC Bristol, 1969–70; BBC Radio, World at One, 1970–71; for Thames TV: This Week, 1972–78, 1986–88; TV Eye, 1979; Jonathan Dimbleby in South America, 1979; documentary series, Witness (Editor), 1986–88; for Yorkshire TV: series, Jonathan Dimbleby in Evidence: The Police, 1980; The Bomb, 1980; The Eagle and the Bear, 1981; The Cold War Game, 1982; The American Dream, 1984; Four Years On—The Bomb, 1984; First Tuesday (Associate Editor/Presenter), 1982–86; for TV-am: Jonathan Dimbleby on Sunday (Presenter/ Editor), 1985–86; for BBC TV: On the Record, 1988–; Presenter, Any Questions?, BBC Radio 4, 1987–. Member: Richard Dimbleby Cancer Fund, 1966–; Bd, Internat. Broadcasting Trust, 1981–; Butler Trust, 1985–; VSO; Amnesty International. SFTA Richard Dimbleby Award, for most outstanding contribution to factual TV, 1974. *Publications*: Richard Dimbleby, 1975; The Palestinians, 1979. *Recreations*: music, sailing, tennis. *Address*: c/o David Higham Associates Ltd, 5 Lower John Street, W1R 4HA.
See also D. Dimbleby.

DIMBLEBY, Josceline Rose; Cookery Editor, Sunday Telegraph, since 1982; *b* 1 Feb. 1943; *d* of late Thomas Josceline Gaskell and of Barbara Montagu-Pollock; *m* 1967, David Dimbleby, *qv*; one *s* two *d*. *Educ*: Cranborne Chase Sch., Dorset; Guildhall School of Music. Contributor, Daily Mail, 1976–78; cookery writer for Sainsbury's, 1978–. André Simon Award, 1979. *Publications*: A Taste of Dreams, 1976, 3rd edn 1984; Party Pieces, 1977; Josceline Dimbleby's Book of Puddings, Desserts and Savouries, 1979, 2nd edn 1983; Favourite Food, 1983, 2nd edn 1984; (for Sainsbury's): Cooking for Christmas, 1978; Family Meat and Fish Cookery, 1979; Cooking with Herbs and Spices, 1979; Curries and Oriental Cookery, 1980; Salads for all Seasons, 1981; Marvellous Meals with Mince, 1982; Festive Food, 1982; Sweet Dreams, 1983; First Impressions, 1984; The Josceline Dimbleby Collection, 1984; Main Attractions, 1985; A Traveller's Tastes, 1986; The Josceline Dimbleby Christmas Book, 1987; The Josceline Dimbleby Book of Entertaining, 1988; The Essential Josceline Dimbleby, 1989; The Cook's Companion, 1991. *Recreations*: singing, travel. *Address*: 14 King Street, Richmond, Surrey TW9 1NF. *T*: 081-940 6668.

DIMECHKIÉ, Nadim, GCVO (Hon.) 1978; business and economic consultant, and Honorary Consultant to the Arab Federation of Chambers of Commerce and Industry, since 1980; *b* Lebanon, 5 Dec. 1919; *s* of Badr and Julia Dimechkié; *m* 1946, Margaret Alma Sherlock; two *s*. *Educ*: American Univ. of Beirut (BA, MA Economics). Deleg., Jt Supply Bd for Syria and Lebanon, 1942–44; Dir Gen., Min. of Nat. Economy, 1943–44; Counsellor, Lebanese Embassy, London, 1944–49; Consul-Gen., Ottawa, 1950; Dir, Economic and Social Dept, Min. of Foreign Affairs, 1951–52; Chargé d'Affaires, Cairo, 1952; Minister, 1953–55; Minister, Switzerland, 1955–57; Ambassador to USA, 1958–62; Dir, Economic Affairs, Min. of Foreign Affairs, 1962–66; Ambassador to UK, 1966–78, and Doyen of the Diplomatic Corps, 1977–78; Ambassador at large, and Senior Adviser on foreign affairs to Foreign Sec., Beirut, 1979–80. Board Member and Consultant: Bank de Credit Populaire Union Nationale, 1985–; Union Foncier et Financing, 1985–; Sterling Drugs Internat., 1985–. Lebanese Order of Cedars, UAR Order of Ismail and Order of Merit; Syrian Order of Merit; Tunisian Order of Merit; Greek Order of Phoenix. *Address*: Ministry of Foreign Affairs, Beirut, Lebanon; Apartment 92, Grosvenor House Hotel, Park Lane, W1. *Clubs*: White's, Travellers', Reform; Golf, Aero (Beirut); Cercle Interallié (Paris).

DIMMOCK, Peter, CVO 1968; OBE 1961; Vice-President and Consultant, ABC Video Enterprises Division, Capital Cities/ABC Inc., New York; a UK Director: Entertainment and Sports Cable Network, since 1984; Screen Sport cable tv, since 1984; Ambrotel, since 1984; *b* 6 Dec. 1920; *e s* of late Frederick Dimmock, OBE, and Paula Dimmock (*née* Hudd); *m* 1960, Mary Freya (Polly) (*d* 1987), *e d* of late Hon. Mr Justice Elwes, OBE, TD; three *d*; *m* 1990, Christabel Rosamund, *widow* of James Hinton Scott. *Educ*: Dulwich Coll.; France. TA; RAF pilot, instr, and Air Ministry Staff Officer, 1939–45. After demobilisation became Press Association correspondent; joined BBC as Television Outside Broadcasts Producer and commentator, 1946; produced both studio and outside broadcasts, ranging from documentaries to sporting, theatrical and public events; has produced or commentated on more than 500 television relays, including Olympic Games 1948, Boat Race 1949, first international television relay, from Calais, 1950, King George VI's Funeral, Windsor, 1952. Produced and directed television outside broadcast of the Coronation Service from Westminster Abbey, 1953; first TV State Opening of Parliament, 1958; first TV Grand National, 1960; TV for Princess Margaret's Wedding, 1960. Created BBC Sportsview Unit and introduced new television programme Sportsview, 1954, regular host of this weekly network programme, 1954–64; Gen. Manager and Head of Outside Broadcasts, BBC TV, 1954–72; responsible for Liaison between BBC and Royal Family, 1963–77; Gen. Manager, BBC Enterprises, 1972–77; Vice-Pres., ABC Worldwide Sales and Marketing TV Sports, and Man. Dir, Sports Worldwide Enterprises, later ABC Sports International, 1978–86. Sports Adviser, European Broadcasting Union, 1959–72. Mem., Greater London and SE Sports Council, 1972–77; Chm., Sports Develt Panel, 1976–77. Fellow, Royal Television Soc., 1978. *Publications*: Sportsview Annuals, 1954–65; Sports in View, 1964. *Recreations*: flying, winter sports, golf. *Address*: c/o Coutts & Co., 440 The Strand, WC2R 0QS. *T*: (office) 071–636 7366. *Clubs*: Garrick, Turf; Berkshire; Monte Carlo; New York Athletic.

DIMMOCK, Rear-Adm. Roger Charles, CB 1988; Chairman, Archer Mullins Ltd, since 1989; *b* 27 May 1935; *s* of Frank Dimmock and Ivy Dimmock (*née* Archer); *m*

1958, Lesley Patricia Reid; two *d* (and one *d* decd). *Educ:* Price's School. Entered Royal Navy, 1953; pilot's wings FAA, 1954, USN, 1955; qualified Flying Instructor, 1959; Master Mariner Foreign Going Cert. of Service, 1979. Served RN Air Sqdns and HM Ships Bulwark, Albion, Ark Royal, Eagle, Hermes, Anzio, Messina, Murray, Berwick (i/c), Naiad (i/c), to 1978; CSO to FO Carriers and Amphibious Ships, 1978–80; Comd RNAS Culrose, 1980–82; Comd HMS Hermes, 1982–83; Dir, Naval Air Warfare, MoD, 1983–84; Naval Sec., 1985–87; FONAC, 1987–88. Mem. Cttee of Management, RNLI, 1987– (Pres., Denmead and Hambledon Br., 1981–). Chairman: Trustees, Fleet Air Arm Museum, 1987–88; Fleet Air Arm Benevolent Trust, 1987–88; First of June Appeal, 1987–88; Gov., Royal Naval Benevolent Trust, 1987–88; Chm., Naval Canteen Cttee, 1987–88. President: RN Hockey Assoc., 1985–89; CS Hockey Assoc., 1987–. *Recreations:* hockey (player and umpire), cricket, squash, golf, family, home and garden, RNLI. *Address:* Beverley House, Beverley Grove, Farlington, Portsmouth PO6 1BP. *T:* Portsmouth (0705) 386548. *Clubs:* Commonwealth Trust, Royal Navy of 1765 and 1785, Royal Aero.

DIMSON, Gladys Felicia, (Mrs S. B. Dimson), CBE 1976; Member of GLC for Battersea North, 1973–85; Member, Inner London Education Authority, 1970–85; *o d* of late I. Sieve, BA; *m* 1936, Dr S. B. Dimson (*d* 1991), *e s* of late Rev. Z. Dimson; one *d*. *Educ:* Laurel Bank Sch., Glasgow; Glasgow Univ.; London Sch. of Economics. Voluntary social worker, mainly in E London, 1950–63; Co-opted Mem., Children's Cttee, LCC, 1958–65; Chm., gp of LCC Children's Homes and of a voluntary Hostel for Girls; Educn Counsellor, Marriage Guidance Council. Member: Home Office Advisory Cttee on Juvenile Delinquency, 1963–65 (Chm. Sub-Cttee on Transition from Sch. to Work); a Youth Employment Cttee, 1960–; Hendon Gp Hosp. Management Cttee, 1965–70; Exec., Greater London Labour Party, 1964–74; Toynbee Housing Soc., 1967– (Chm., 1976–87); Council, Toynbee Hall, 1983–90; Bd of Governors, Nat. Hosp. for Nervous Diseases, 1976–79; Board of Management, Shelter, 1976–89 (Trustee, Shelter Housing Aid Centre); London Local Adv. Cttee, IBA, 1979–83; Hampstead DHA, 1981–84; Trustee, Sutton Housing Trust, 1982–90; Chm., East London Housing Assoc., 1979–. Mem., GLC Haringey, 1964–67, Wandsworth, 1970–73; (Vice-Chm.) GLC Ambulance Cttee; GLC Housing Cttee: Mem. (co-opted), 1968–70; Labour Spokesman, 1970–73, and 1977–81; Chm., 1973–75, 1981–82. Contested (Lab) Hendon South, at Gen. Election, 1970. Mem., Nat. and London Councils of Nat. Fedn of Housing Assocs, 1980–83. FRSA 1977. *Recreations:* walking in the country, lazing in the sun; reading (incl. thrillers); theatre; watching TV. *Address:* 22a North Gate, Prince Albert Road, St John's Wood, NW8 7RE.

See also O. W. Baron.

DINES, Peter Munn, CBE 1991; educational consultant; Secretary, School Examinations and Assessment Council, 1988–91; *b* 29 Aug. 1929; *e s* of Victor Edward Dines and Muriel Eleanor Dines (*née* Turner); *m* 1952, Kathleen Elisabeth Jones; two *s* one *d*. *Educ:* Palmer's Sch., Grays, Essex; Imperial Coll. London (ARCS; BSc 1st cl. 1949); Inst. of Education, London (PGCE 1950); Bristol Univ. (MEd 1968). RAF, 1950–53. Teaching maths, 1953–69; Headmaster, Cramlington High Sch., 1969–76; Jt Sec., Schools Council, 1976–78; Headmaster, Sir John Leman High Sch., Beccles, 1978–80; Examinations Officer, Schools Council, 1980–83; Dep. Chief Exec., 1983–87, Chief Exec., 1988, Secondary Examinations Council. Mem., Schools Broadcasting Council, later Educn Broadcasting Council, 1982–; occasional broadcaster on radio and TV. *Recreations:* sailing, esp. on W coast of Scotland; playing croquet and other games to own rules. *Clubs:* Commonwealth Trust; Clyde Cruising.

DINEVOR; *see* Dynevor.

DINGEMANS, Rear-Adm. Peter George Valentin, CB 1990; DSO 1982; Director, Administration, Argosy Asset Management PLC, since 1990; Chief of Staff to Commander-in-Chief Fleet, 1987–90, retired; *b* 31 July 1935; *s* of Dr George Albert and Marjorie Dingemans; *m* 1961, Faith Vivien Bristow; three *s*. *Educ:* Brighton College. Entered RN 1953; served HM Ships Vanguard, Superb, Ark Royal, 1953–57; qualified Torpedo Anti Submarine specialist, 1961; Comd, HMS Maxton, 1967; RAF Staff Course, 1968; Directorate of Naval Plans, 1971–73; Comd, HMS Berwick, HMS Lowestoft, 1973–74; Staff Asst, Chief of Defence Staff, 1974–76; Captain, Fishery Protection, 1977–79; Comd HMS Intrepid, 1980–83 (incl. service South Atlantic, 1982); Commodore, Amphibious Warfare, 1983–85; Flag Officer Gibraltar, 1985–87. FBIM 1990. Freeman, City of London, 1984; Liveryman, Coach Makers and Coach Harness Makers Co., 1984. *Recreations:* family and friends, tennis, shooting. *Address:* c/o Lloyds Bank, Steyning, Sussex. *Clubs:* Naval and Military, City Livery.

DINGLE, John Thomas, PhD, DSc; Director, Strangeways Research Laboratory, Cambridge, since 1979; Fellow, since 1968, and Steward of Estates, since 1987, Corpus Christi College, Cambridge; *b* 27 Oct. 1927; *s* of Thomas Henry and Violet Nora Dingle; *m* 1953, Dorothy Vernon Parsons; two *s*. *Educ:* King Edward Sch., Bath; London Univ. (BSc, DSc); Clare Coll., Cambridge (PhD). Royal National Hosp. for Rheumatic Diseases, Bath, 1951–59; Research Fellowship, Strangeways Research Laboratory, Cambridge, 1959–61; MRC External Staff, 1961–79; Head of Tissue Physiology Dept, Strangeways Research Laboratory, 1966, Dep. Dir of the Laboratory, 1970–79. Bursar of Leckhampton, 1972–80, Warden, 1980–86. Visiting Professor: of Biochemistry, Royal Free Hosp. Med. Sch., 1975–78; of Rheumatology, New York Univ., 1977. Chm., British Connective Tissue Soc., 1980–87. Chm. Editorial Bd, Biochemical Jl, 1975–82. Pres., Cambridge Univ. RFC, 1990– (Treas., 1982–90). Heberden Orator and Medalist, 1978; American Orthopaedic Assoc. Steindler Award, 1980. *Publications:* communications to learned jls. *Recreations:* Rugby football (playing member, Bath, Bristol, Somerset RFCs, 1943–57), sailing. *Address:* Corpus Christi College, Cambridge CB2 1RH. *Clubs:* Farmers'; Hawks (Cambridge).

DINGLE, Prof. Robert Balson, PhD; FRSE; Professor of Theoretical Physics, University of St Andrews, 1960–87, now Emeritus; *b* 26 March 1926; *s* of late Edward Douglas Dingle and Nora Gertrude Balson; *m* 1958, Helen Glenronnie Munro; two *d*. *Educ:* Bournemouth Secondary Sch.; Cambridge University. PhD 1951. Fellow of St John's Coll., Cambridge, 1948–52; Theoretician to Royal Society Mond Lab., 1949–52; Chief Asst in Theoretical Physics, Technical Univ. of Delft, Holland, 1952–53; Fellow, Nat. Research Council, Ottawa, 1953–54; Reader in Theoretical Physics, Univ. of WA, 1954–60. *Publications:* Asymptotic Expansions: their derivation and interpretation, 1973; contribs to learned journals. *Recreations:* music, local history, gastronomy. *Address:* 6 Lawhead Road East, St Andrews, Fife, Scotland KY16 9ND. *T:* St Andrews (0334) 74287.

DINGWALL, Baroness; *see* Lucas of Crudwell and Dingwall.

DINGWALL, John James, OBE 1964; HM Inspector of Constabulary for Scotland, 1966–70; *b* 2 Sept. 1907; *s* of late James Dingwall, Bannockburn, Stirling; *m* 1932, Jane Anne (*d* 1980), *d* of late James K. Halliday, Falkirk; two *d*. *Educ:* Bridge of Allan and Stirling. Stirlingshire Constabulary, 1927–49; Stirling and Clackmannan Police Force, 1949–55; seconded to Directing Staff, Scottish Police Coll., 1953–55; Chief Constable of Angus, 1955–66. *Recreations:* angling, shooting, golf. *Address:* 56 Carlogie Road, Carnoustie, Angus.

DINGWALL-SMITH, Ronald Alfred, CB 1977; Chairman: Hanover (Scotland) Housing Association Ltd, since 1988 (Director, since 1979); Heritage Housing Ltd, since 1988 (Director, since 1982); *b* 24 Feb. 1917; *m* 1946; one *s* one *d*. *Educ:* Alleyn's Sch., Dulwich; London School of Economics (evening classes). Entered Civil Service as Clerical Officer, Ministry of Transport, 1934; Exchequer and Audit Dept, 1935–47; Scottish Educn Dept, 1947–65; Scottish Development Dept, 1965–70; Under-Sec. (Principal Finance Officer), Scottish Office, 1970–78. Sen. Res. Fellow, Glasgow Univ., 1979–81. Dir, St Vincent Drilling Ltd, 1979–80. Mem., Commn for Local Auth. Accts in Scotland, 1980–85. Governor, Moray Hse Coll. of Educn, Edinburgh, 1980–87. *Recreations:* golf, bowls (Pres., Braid Bowling Club, Edinburgh, 1990 (Hon. Sec., 1980–89)), gardening. *Address:* 3 Frogston Terrace, Edinburgh EH10 7AD. *T:* 031–445 2727. *Club:* Commonwealth Trust.

DINKIN, Anthony David; QC 1991; barrister; *b* 2 Aug. 1944; *s* of Hyman Dinkin and Mary (*née* Hine); *m* 1968, Derina Tanya (*née* Green). *Educ:* Henry Thornton Grammar Sch., Clapham; Coll. of Estate Management, London (BSc (Est. Man.)). Called to the Bar, Lincoln's Inn, 1968. A Recorder of the Crown Court, 1989–. Examr in Law, Reading Univ., 1985–. *Recreations:* gardening, theatre, music, travel. *Address:* 8 New Square, Lincoln's Inn, WC2A 3QP. *T:* 071–242 4986. *Club:* Players.

DINSDALE, Richard Lewis; Chairman, West of England Newspapers Ltd, 1969–72; *b* 23 June 1907; *m* 1930, Irene Laverack (*d* 1984); one *d*. *Educ:* Hull Technical Coll. Joined Hull Daily Mail as reporter, 1926; Editorial posts: Newcastle Evening World; Chief Sub-editor, Manchester Evening News; Dep. Chief Sub-editor, Daily Express, Manchester; Evening News, London; Daily Mirror, 1940–42; War Service, 1942–46; Copy-taster, Daily Mirror, 1946, successively Chief Sub-editor, Dep. Night Editor, Night Editor; Dep. Editor, 1955; seconded Daily Herald as Editorial Adviser, 1961; Dep. Editor, Daily Herald, 1962; Dep. Editor, The Sun, 1964, Editor, 1965–69. *Recreation:* strolling. *Address:* 7 Beaulieu Court, Marine Parade, Worthing, W Sussex BN11 3QZ.

DINWIDDY, Thomas Lutwyche; Master of the Supreme Court (Chancery Division), 1958–73; *b* 27 Aug. 1905; *o c* of late Harry Lutwyche Dinwiddy, Solicitor, and late Ethel Maude (*née* McArthur); *m* 1935, Ruth, *d* of late Charles Ernest Rowland Abbott, Barrister-at-Law and Bencher of Lincoln's Inn; three *s*. *Educ:* Winchester; New Coll., Oxford (BA). Solicitor, Dec. 1930; Partner in Frere Cholmeley & Co., 28 Lincoln's Inn Fields, WC2, 1933–57. Council of Law Soc., 1953–57. Served RA (TA), 1939–45; Staff Coll., Camberley, 1943; demobilised as Major. *Address:* Allonsfield House, Campsea Ashe, Woodbridge, Suffolk IP13 0PX.

DIONISOTTI-CASALONE, Carlo, FBA 1972; Professor of Italian, Bedford College (formerly Bedford College for Women), University of London, 1949–70; *b* 9 June 1908; *s* of Eugenio Dionisotti-Casalone and Carla Cattaneo; *m* 1942, Maria Luisa Pinna-Pintor; three *d* (and one *d* decd). *Educ:* Turin, Italy. Dottore in lettere, Univ. of Turin, 1929; Libero Docente di Letteratura Italiana, Univ. of Turin, 1937; Asst di Letteratura Italiana, Univ. of Rome, 1943; Italian Lectr, Univ. of Oxford, 1947; MA Oxon, 1947. *Publications:* Indici del giornale storico della letteratura italiana (Turin), 1945; Guidiccioni-orazione ai nobili di Lucca (Rome), 1946; Bembo-Savorgnan, Carteggio d'amore (Florence), 1950; Oxford Book of Italian Verse (revised edn), 1952; Bembo, Prose e Rime (Turin), 1960; Geografia e storia della letter. ital. (Turin), 1967; Gli Umanisti e il Volgare (Florence), 1968; Machiavellerie (Turin), 1980; Appunti sui moderni (Bologna), 1988. *Address:* 44 West Heath Drive, NW11.

DI PALMA, Vera June, (Mrs Ernest Jones), OBE 1986; FCCA, FTII; Chairman, Mobile Training Ltd (formerly Mobile Training & Exhibitions Ltd), since 1978; *b* 14 July 1931; *d* of late William Di Palma and of Violet Di Palma; *m* 1972, Ernest Jones. *Educ:* Haverstock Central Sch., London. Accountant in public practice, 1947–64; Taxation Accountant, Dunlop Co., 1964–67; Sen. Lectr in Taxation, City of London Polytechnic, 1967–71; taxation consultant, 1971–80. Pres., Assoc. of Certified Accountants, 1980–81 (Dep. Pres., 1979–80); Public Works Loan Comr, 1978–; Dep. Chm., Air Travel Trust Cttee, 1986–; Mem., VAT Tribunals, 1977–. *Publications:* Capital Gains Tax, 1972, 5th edn 1981; Your Fringe Benefits, 1978. *Recreations:* dog-walking, golf, tennis, gardening. *Address:* Temple Close, Sibford Gower, Banbury, Oxon OX15 5RX. *T:* Swalcliffe (029578) 222.

DIPLOCK, Prof. Anthony Tytherleigh; Professor, since 1977, and Chairman of Division of Biochemistry, since 1984, United Medical and Dental Schools of Guy's and St Thomas' Hospitals (formerly Guy's Hospital Medical School); *b* 24 July 1935; *s* of Bernard and Elsie Diplock; *m* 1st, 1957, Elisabeth Anne Price (marr. diss. 1979); one *s* one *d*; 2nd, 1980, Lynn Christine Richards; one *s*. *Educ:* Univ. of Bristol (BSc Physiol/Chemistry); Univ. of London (PhD Biochem.); DSc London 1976. Mem., then Hd, Biochem. Res. Dept, Vitamins Ltd, Tadworth, subseq. Beecham Res. Labs, 1956–67; Sen. Lectr, then Reader in Biochem., Royal Free Hosp. Med. Sch., Univ. of London, 1967–77. University of London: Mem., Senate, 1980–; Mem. Ct, 1989–; Dean, Faculty of Medicine, 1986–91; Chm., Academic Council Med. Cttee, 1984–91; Mem., numerous Univ. of London cttees and wkg parties, 1978–. Member, Council: BPMF, 1988–; Hunterian Inst., RCS, 1989–; Royal Free Hosp. Sch. of Medicine, 1989–; Roedean Sch., 1989–; Mem., Council of Govs, UMDS, 1987–. Hon. Prof. of Biochem., Xi'an Med. Univ., People's Republic of China, 1985–. *Publications:* Fat-Soluble Vitamins, 1985; (solely or jtly) over 150 pubns on fat-soluble vitamins, trace elements, antioxidant nutrients in human health, nutritional prevention of cancer and cardiovascular disease. *Recreations:* renovating an old cottage, sailing, music, building long-case clocks, dogs. *Address:* Division of Biochemistry, United Medical and Dental Schools, Guy's Hospital, SE1 9RT. *T:* 071–955 4521, *Fax:* 071–403 7195.

DISBREY, Air Vice-Marshal William Daniel, CB 1967; CBE 1945 (OBE 1943); AFC 1939; *b* London, 23 Aug. 1912; *s* of Horace William Disbrey; *m* 1939, Doreen Alice, *d* of William Henry Ivory, Stevenage; two *d*. *Educ:* Minchenden Sch. Joined RAF as an Apprentice, 1928; gained Cadetship to RAF Coll., Cranwell, 1931; No 3 Fighter Sqdn, 1933–34; Fleet Air Arm, 1934–37; Engr Specialist Course, Henlow, 1937–39; Engr Officer, No 13 Group HQ, 1940–41; Engr Officer, HQ Fighter Comd, 1941–43; Chief Engr Officer, 2nd TAF, 1943–46; Staff Coll. Course, 1946; CO, No 12 Sch. of Technical Training, 1946–48; Sen. Technical Officer, Royal Indian Air Force, 1948–51; Min. of Supply, 1951–54; Chief Engr Officer, Bomber Comd, 1954–57; Imperial Defence Coll., 1957; Dir of Research and Development, Bombers, Min. of Aviation, 1958–61; Comdt, No 1 Radio Sch., Locking, 1961–64; Dir-Gen. of Engineering (RAF), 1964–67; AO Engineering, Bomber Comd, 1967, Strike Comd, 1968–70, retired. Manager, Tech. Trng Inst., Airwork Services, Saudi Arabia, 1970. CEng; FIMechE; FRAeS. *Recreations:* golf, sailing. *Address:* Old Heatherwode, Buxted, East Sussex TN22 4JW. *T:* Buxted (082581) 2104. *Club:* Royal Air Force.

DISLEY, John Ivor, CBE 1979; Director: London Marathon Ltd, since 1980; Silva UK Ltd; Reebok UK Ltd; *b* Gwynedd, 20 Nov. 1928; *s* of Harold Disley and Marie Hughes; *m* 1957, Sylvia Cheeseman; two *d. Educ:* Oswestry High Sch.; Loughborough Coll. (Hon. DCL). Schoolmaster, Isleworth, 1951; Chief Instructor, CCPR Nat. Mountaineering Centre, 1955; Gen. Inspector of Educn, Surrey, 1958; Dir, Ski Plan, 1971. Member: Adv. Sports Council, 1964–71; Mountain Leadership Trng Bd, 1965–; Canal Adv. Bd, 1965–66; Internat. Orienteering Fedn, 1972–78; Countryside Commn, 1974–77; Water Space Adv. Council, 1976–81; Royal Commn on Gambling, 1976–78. Vice-Chm., Sports Council, 1974–82; Chm., Nat. Jogging Assoc., 1978–80. Mem., British athletics team, 1950–59; Brit. record holder steeplechase, 1950–56; Welsh mile record holder, 1952–57; bronze medal, Olympics, Helsinki, 1952; Sportsman of the Year, 1955; Athlete of the Year, 1955. *Publications:* Tackle Climbing, 1959; Young Athletes Companion, 1961; Orienteering, 1966; Expedition Guide for Duke of Edinburgh's Award Scheme, 1965; Your Way with Map and Compass, 1971. *Recreations:* running games, mountain activities. *Address:* Hampton House, Upper Sunbury Road, Hampton, Mddx TW12 2DW. *T:* 081–979 1707. *Clubs:* Climbers'; Ranelagh Harriers, Southern Navigators.

DISNEY, Harold Vernon, CBE 1956; Manager, Engineering Division, Reactor Group, UK Atomic Energy Authority, 1969–72, retired; *b* 2 July 1907; *s* of Henry Disney and Julia Vernon; *m* 1936, Lucy Quinton; two *d. Educ:* Hallcroft Higher Standard Sch., Ilkeston; Nottingham Univ. Coll. Internat. Combustion, 1931–35; ICI (Alkali), 1935–46. On loan to Min. of Supply (RFF's), 1941–46. Dept of Atomic Energy, 1946–54; UKAEA: Asst Dir, Defence Projects, Industrial Gp, 1954; Dir of Engineering, Industrial Gp, 1958; Man. Dir, Engineering Gp, Risley, 1962. FIMechE 1947. *Recreation:* gardening. *Address:* 63 Vincent Drive, Westminster Park, Chester CH4 7RQ.

DISS, Eileen, (Mrs Raymond Everett), RDI 1978; freelance designer for theatre, film and television, since 1959; *b* 13 May 1931; *d* of Thomas and Winifred Diss; *m* 1953, Raymond Everett; two *s* one *d. Educ:* Ilford County High Sch. for Girls; Central Sch. of Art and Design. MSIAD; FRSA. BBC Television design, 1952–59. *Television* series and plays: Maigret, 1962–63; The Tea Party, 1964; Up the Junction, 1965; Somerset Maugham, 1969; Uncle Vanya, 1970; The Duchess of Malfi, and Candide, 1972; The Importance of Being Earnest, and Pygmalion, 1973; Caesar and Cleopatra, 1974; Moll Flanders, 1975; Ghosts, and The Winslow Boy, 1976; You Never Can Tell, 1977; The Rear Column, Hedda Gabler, 1980; The Potting Shed, 1981; Porterhouse Blue, 1987; Behaving Badly, 1989; Jeeves & Wooster, 1989 and 1990. Television opera: The Merry Widow, 1968; Tales of Hoffmann, 1969; Die Fledermaus, 1971; Falstaff, 1972; The Yeomen of the Guard, 1974; television films: Cider with Rosie, 1971; Robinson Crusoe, 1974. *Theatre:* Exiles, 1969; Butley, 1971; The Caretaker, 1972; Otherwise Engaged, 1975; The Apple-cart, 1977; The Rear Column, The Homecoming, 1978; The Hothouse, 1980; Translations, 1981; Quartermaine's Terms, 1981; Incident at Tulse Hill, 1981; Rocket to the Moon, 1982; The Communication Cord, 1983; The Common Pursuit, 1984; Other Places, 1985; The Seagull, 1985; Sweet Bird of Youth, 1985; Circe and Bravo, 1986; The Deep Blue Sea, 1988; Veterans Day, 1989; The Mikado, 1989; Steel Magnolias, 1989; Burn This, 1990; National Theatre: Blithe Spirit, 1976; The Philanderer, 1978; Close of Play, When We Are Married, 1979; Watch on the Rhine, 1980; The Caretaker, 1980; Measure for Measure, 1981; The Trojan War Will Not Take Place, 1983. *Films:* Joseph Losey's A Doll's House, 1972; Sweet William, 1978; Harold Pinter's Betrayal, 1982; Secret Places, 1984; 84 Charing Cross Road, 1986; A Handful of Dust, 1988. BAFTA Television Design Award, 1962, 1965 and 1974. *Recreations:* music, cinema. *Address:* 4 Gloucester Walk, W8 4HZ. *T:* 071–937 8794.

DIVER, Hon. Sir Leslie Charles, Kt 1975; President, Legislative Council, Western Australia, 1960–74; Member, Legislative Council (Country Party) for Central Province, Western Australia, 1952–74; *b* Perth, Australia, 4 Nov. 1899; *s* of late J. W. Diver; *m* 1st, 1922, Emma J., *d* of late F. Blakiston; one *s* two *d*; 2nd, 1971, Mrs Thelma May Evans. Farmer and grazier. Chairman: Kellerberrin Road Bd, 1940, 1942–46; Hon. Royal Commn on Retailing of Motor Spirits, 1956. Chm., Sixth Aust. Area Conf., Commonwealth Parly Assoc., 1961; Rep. WA Parlt, Town Planning Adv. Cttee. Warden, State War Meml, 1967–68. *Recreations:* bowls, Australian rules football. *Address:* 48 Sulman Avenue, Salter Point, Como, WA 6152, Australia. *Clubs:* Eastern Districts (Kellerberrin); Manning Memorial Bowling.

DIVERRES, Prof. Armel Hugh; Professor of French and Head of Department of Romance Studies, University College of Swansea, 1974–81, now Emeritus; *b* Liverpool, 4 Sept. 1914; *o s* of late Paul Diverres and Elizabeth (*née* Jones); *m* 1945, Ann Dilys, *d* of late James and Enid Williams; one *s* two *d. Educ:* Swansea Grammar Sch.; University Coll., Swansea; Univ. of Rennes; Sorbonne, Paris. MA (Wales), LèsL (Rennes), Docteur de l'Université de Paris. Fellow of Univ. of Wales, 1938–40; served in RA and Int. Corps, 1940–46, Captain. Asst Lectr in French, 1946–49, Lectr, 1949–54, Univ. of Manchester; Sen. Lectr in French, 1954–57, Carnegie Prof., 1958–74, Dean, Faculty of Arts, 1967–70, Univ. of Aberdeen. Governor: Nat. Mus. of Wales, 1978–81; Centre for Information on Language Teaching and Res., 1977–82; Aberdeen Coll. of Education, 1971–74. Member: CNAA Lang. Board, 1965–78, Cttee for Res., 1975–82, Humanities Bd, 1978–81; Welsh Jt Educn Cttee, 1975–81. Pres., British Br., Internat. Arthurian Soc., 1978–80, Internat. Pres., 1979–81; Pres., Soc. French Stud., 1976–78. Officier des Palmes Académiques, 1971; Chevalier de l'Ordre National du Mérite, 1986. *Publications:* Voyage en Béarn by Froissart (ed), 1953; La Chronique métrique attribuée à Geffroy de Paris (ed), 1956; Chatterton by A. de Vigny (ed), 1967; articles and reviews in learned journals. *Recreation:* hill walking. *Address:* 23 Whiteshell Drive, Langland, Swansea, W Glamorgan SA3 4SY. *T:* Swansea (0792) 360322.

DIX, Alan Michael, OBE 1985; Director General, Motor Agents' Association Ltd, 1976–85; *b* 29 June 1922; *s* of late Comdr Charles Cabry Dix, CMG, DSO, RN, and Ebba Sievers; *m* 1955, Helen Catherine McLaren; one *s* one *d. Educ:* Stenhus Kostskole, Denmark. Escaped Nazi occupied Denmark to Scotland, 1943; joined RAF, commissioned 1944. President, Capitol Car Distributors Inc., USA, 1958–67; Gp Vice-Pres., Volkswagen of America, USA, 1967–68; Man. Dir, Volkswagen (GB) Ltd, London, 1968–72; Pres., Mid Atlantic Toyota Inc., USA, 1972–73; Dir Marketing, British Leyland International, 1973–74; Proprietor, Alan M. Dix Associates, 1974–76. Chm., Motor Agents Pensions Administrators Ltd, 1976–85; Dir, Hire Purchase Information Ltd, 1977–85. Freedom and Livery, Coachmakers' and Coach Harness Makers' Co., 1980. FIMI, FInstM, FIMH, FBIM. King Christian X war medal, 1947. *Publications:* contribs to automotive trade jls. *Recreations:* yachting, photography; the study of professional management (internat. speaker on management and organisation). *Address:* Tigh na Failte, Fir Hill, Letham Grange, near Arbroath, Angus DD11 4RL. *T:* Gowanbank (0241) 89421. *Clubs:* Danish, Royal Air Force, Burkes; Royal Air Force Yacht (Hamble).

DIX, Bernard Hubert; Assistant General Secretary, National Union of Public Employees, 1975–82; *b* 30 March 1925; *s* of Thomas Herbert John Dix and Gertrude Turner; *m* 1979, Eileen Veronica Smith; three *s*; two *s* one *d* by prev. *m. Educ:* LCC elem. schs; LSE (TUC Scholar). Engrg industry, 1939–55 (served Army, 1941–47); Deptl Asst, TUC, 1955–63; Res. Officer, NUPE, 1963–75. Member: Health Services Bd, 1976–80; Hotel and Catering Industry EDC, 1973–79; TUC Local Govt Cttee, 1970–81; TUC Hotel and Catering Industry Cttee, 1973–79; Labour Party NEC, 1981; Bd of Tribune, 1975–82. Member: Plaid Cymru, 1983; Cymdeithas yr Iaith Gymraeg. Elected to Llanddarog Community Council, 1987. Governor, Ruskin Coll., 1969–84. Associate Fellow, Warwick Univ., 1982–84. *Publications:* (with Alan W. Fisher) Low Pay and How to End It, 1974; (jtly) The Forward March of Labour Halted?, 1981; (with Stephen Williams) Serving the Public, Building the Union, 1987; contribs to Y Ddraig Goch, Welsh Nation. *Address:* Pant Tawel, Mynydd Cerrig, Dyfed SA15 5BD. *T:* Pontyberem (0269) 870122. *Club:* Mynydd Cerrig Workingmen's.

DIX, Geoffrey Herbert, OBE 1979; Secretary-General, The Institute of Bankers, 1971–82; *b* 1 March 1922; *o s* of late Herbert Walter and Winifred Ada Dix; *m* 1945, Margaret Sybil Outhwaite, MA (Cantab) (*d* 1981); one *s. Educ:* Watford Grammar Sch.; Gonville and Caius Coll., Cambridge. MA (Mod. langs). Served War, 1942–45: commissioned into Royal Devon Yeomanry; later served with HQ 1st Airborne Corps. Inst. of Export, 1946–51; with Inst. of Bankers, 1951–: Asst Sec., 1956; Under-Sec. 1962; Dep. Sec. 1968. Mem., Jt Cttee for National Awards in Business Studies, 1960–76. *Recreations:* Mozart, theatre. *Address:* Tanglewood, Tally Road, Limpsfield Chart, Oxted, Surrey RH8 0TQ. *T:* Oxted (0883) 713163. *Club:* Caterham Players.

DIX, Prof. Gerald Bennett, FRTPI; architect; Lever Professor of Civic Design, University of Liverpool, 1975–88; Professor Emeritus and Hon. Senior Fellow, Liverpool University, since 1988; Hon. Senior Research Fellow, Chinese Research Academy of Environmental Sciences, since 1989; *b* 12 Jan. 1926; *s* of late Cyril Dix and Mabel Winifred (*née* Bennett); *m* 1st, 1956 (marr. diss.); two *s*; 2nd, 1963, Lois Nichols; one *d. Educ:* Altrincham Grammar Sch.; Univ. of Manchester (BA (Hons Arch.), DipTP (dist.)); Harvard Univ. (MLA). Studio Asst, 1950–51, Asst Lectr in Town and Country Planning, 1951–53, Manchester Univ.; Asst Architect, 1954; Chief Architect-Planner, Addis Ababa, and chief asst to Sir Patrick Abercrombie, 1954–56; Planning Officer, Singapore, 1957–59; Acting Planning Adviser, 1959; Sen. Research Fellow, Univ. of Science and Technol., Ghana, 1959–63; UN Planning Mission to Ghana, 1962; Planner, later Sen. Planner, BRS/ODM, 1963–65 (adv. missions to W Indies, W Africa, Aden, Bechuanaland, Swaziland, Cyprus); Nottingham University: Lectr, 1966–68; Sen. Lectr, 1968–70; Prof. of Planning, and Dir, Inst. of Planning Studies, 1970–75; Liverpool University: Chm., Fac. of Social and Environmental Studies, 1983–84; Pro Vice-Chancellor, 1984–87. Dir, Cyprus Planning Project, 1967–71; adv. visits on planning educn, to Uganda 1971, Nigeria 1972, Sudan 1975, Mexico 1978, Egypt 1980; UK Mem., Adv. Panel on planning Canal towns, Egypt, 1974, and Western Desert, 1975; Jt Dir, Alexandria Comprehensive Master Plan Project, 1980–86. Member: Professional Literature Cttee, RIBA, 1966–80, 1981–88 (Chm. 1975–80); Library Management Cttee, 1969–72, 1975–80; Historic Areas Adv. Cttee, English Heritage, 1986–88. Vice-Pres., World Soc. for Ekistics, 1975–79, Pres., 1987–90. Editorial adviser, Ekistics (journal), 1972–; Chm., Bd of Management, Town Planning Rev., 1976–88; (Founder) Editor, Third World Planning Rev., 1978–90. FRSA. *Publications:* ed, C. A. Doxiadis, Ecology and Ekistics, 1977, Boulder, Colo, 1978, Brisbane, 1978; numerous planning reports to govts in various parts of world; articles and reviews in Town Planning Rev., Third World Planning Rev., Ekistics, RIBA Jl, Arch. Rev. *Recreations:* photography, listening to music, travel. *Address:* Department of Civic Design, University of Liverpool, PO Box 147, Liverpool L69 3BX. *T:* 051–794 3121; 13 Friar's Quay, Norwich, Norfolk NR3 1ES. *T:* Norwich (0603) 632433. *Club:* Athenæum.

DIX, Victor Wilkinson, MA, MB, BChir Cantab, FRCS, MRCP; retired; Professor Emeritus, University of London. Assistant Surgeon, The London Hospital, 1930–37; Surgeon, The London Hospital, 1937–64. *Address:* 8 Shandon Close, Tunbridge Wells, Kent. *T:* Tunbridge Wells (0892) 30839.

DIXEY, John, OBE 1976; Development Co-ordinator, Evening Standard Company, since 1987; *b* 29 March 1926; *s* of John Dixey and Muriel Doris Dixey; *m* 1948, Pauline Seaden; one *s* one *d. Educ:* Battersea Grammar Sch. Served Royal Marines and Royal Fusiliers, 1944–47. Press Telegraphist, Yorkshire Post and Glasgow Herald, 1948–59; Asst to Gen. Sec., Nat. Union of Press Telegraphists, 1959; Labour Officer, Newspaper Soc., 1959–63; Labour Adviser, Thomson Organisation Ltd, 1963–64; Asst Gen. Man., Liverpool Daily Post & Echo, 1964–67; Executive Dir, Times Newspapers, 1967–74; Special Adviser to Man. Dir, Thomson Org., 1974; Dir, Newspaper Publishers Assoc. Ltd, 1975–76; Employment Affairs Advr, IPA, 1977–79; Sec., Assoc. of Midland Advertising Agencies, 1977–79; Production Dir and Bd Mem., The Guardian, 1979–84; Asst Man. Dir, Mirror Gp Newspapers, 1985; Newspaper Consultant, 1986. Chm., Advertising Assoc. Trade Union Liaison Group; Mem., TUC New Daily Newspaper Advisory Group. Ward-Perkins Vis. Fellow, Pembroke Coll., Oxford, 1978. Former Mem., Printing and Publishing Industry Trng Bd; former Governor, London Coll. of Printing. *Recreations:* cooking, photography. *Address:* 23 West Hill, Sanderstead, Surrey CR2 0SB. *T:* 081–657 7940.

DIXEY, Paul (Arthur Groser); Chairman of Lloyd's, 1973, 1974 (Deputy Chairman, 1967, 1969, 1972); *b* 13 April 1915; *e s* of late Neville Dixey, JP (Chairman of Lloyd's, 1931, 1934 and 1936), and Marguerite (*née* Groser); *m* 1939, Mary Margaret Baring, JP, 2nd *d* of late Geoffrey Garrod; four *s* one *d. Educ:* Stowe; Trinity Coll., Cambridge. Elected an Underwriting Mem. of Lloyd's, 1938. Served War of 1939–45, Royal Artillery. Member: London Insce market delegn to Indonesia, 1958; Dunmow RDC, 1958–64; Cttee, Lloyd's Underwriters' Assoc., 1962–74; Cttee, Salvage Assoc., 1962–74; Cttee, Lloyd's, 1964–70, 1972–75; Gen. Cttee, Lloyd's Register of Shipping, 1964–90; Chm., Salvage Assoc., 1964–65. Chairman: Paul Dixey Underwriting Agencies Ltd, 1973–76; Pieri Underwriting Agencies Ltd, 1976–; Director, Merrett Dixey Syndicates Ltd, 1976–78. Mem. Council, Morley Coll., 1952–62; Chm. Governors, Vinehall Sch., 1966–73. Leader, Barn Boys' Club, 1949–61. Chm., Essex Hunt Cttee, 1981–. *Recreations:* riding, fly-fishing. *Address:* Little Easton Spring, Dunmow, Essex CM6 2JB. *T:* Great Dunmow (0371) 872840.

DIXIT, Prof. Avinash Kamalakar; John J. F. Sherrerd '52 Professor of Economics, Princeton University, USA, since 1989; (Professor of Economics, 1981–89); *b* 8 June 1944; *s* of Kamalakar Ramchandra Dixit and Kusum Dixit (*née* Phadke). *Educ:* Bombay Univ. (BSc); Cambridge Univ. (BA, MA); Massachusetts Inst. of Technology (PhD). Acting Asst Professor, Univ. of California, Berkeley, 1968–69; Lord Thomson of Fleet Fellow and Tutor in Economics, Balliol Coll., Oxford, 1970–74; Professor of Economics, Univ. of Warwick, 1974–80. Res. Fellow, Centre for Economic Policy Res., 1984–. Fellow, Econometric Society, 1977–. Co-Editor, Bell Journal of Economics, 1981–83. *Publications:* Optimization in Economic Theory, 1976; The Theory of Equilibrium Growth, 1976; (with Victor Norman) Theory of International Trade, 1980; (with Barry Nalebuff) Thinking Strategically, 1991; several articles in professional jls. *Recreations:* listening to music (pre-Schubert only), watching cricket (when possible). *Address:* Department of Economics, Princeton University, Princeton, New Jersey 08544, USA. *T:* (609) 258–4013.

DIXON, family name of **Baron Glentoran.**

DIXON, Anthony Philip G.; *see* Graham-Dixon.

DIXON, Dr Bernard; science writer and consultant; *b* Darlington, 17 July 1938; *s* of late Ronald Dixon and Grace Peirson; *m* 1963, Margaret Helena Charlton (marr. diss. 1988); two *s* one *d*. *Educ:* Queen Elizabeth Grammar Sch., Darlington; King's Coll., Univ. of Durham; Univ. of Newcastle upon Tyne. BSc, PhD. Luccock Res. Fellow, 1961–64, Frank Schon Fellow, 1964–65, Univ. of Newcastle; Asst Editor, 1965–66, Dep. Editor, 1966–68, World Medicine; Editor, New Scientist, 1969–79; European Editor: The Scientist, 1986–89; Bio Technology, 1989–; Editor, Medical Science Research, 1989–; Mem. Editorial Board: Biologist, 1988–; World Jl of Microbiology and Biotechnology, 1988–; Columnist, BMJ. Biotec. Chm., Cttee, Assoc. of British Science Writers, 1971–72; Member: Soc. for General Microbiology, 1962; Amer. Inst. of Biol Sci., 1986–; European Assoc. of Sci. Eds, 1980–; Amer. Assoc. for Advancement of Sci., 1980–; CSS 1982– (Vice-Chm., 1989–); Soc. for Applied Bacteriol., 1989–; Internat Science Writers Assoc., 1988–; Council: BAAS, 1977–83 (Pres., Section X, 1979; Vice-Pres., 1986–); European Envtl Res. Orgn; Panos Inst; Edinburgh Internat. Science Fest. FIBiol 1982; CBiol 1984. *Publications:* (ed) Journeys in Belief, 1968; What is Science For?, 1973; Magnificent Microbes, 1976; Invisible Allies, 1976; Beyond the Magic Bullet, 1978; (with G. Holister) Ideas of Science, 1984; Health and the Human Body, 1986; Engineered Organisms in the Environment, 1986; Recombinant DNA: what's it all about, 1987; The Science of Science: changing the way we think, 1989; The Science of Science: changing the way we live, 1989; (ed) From Creation to Chaos: classic writings in science, 1989; (with A. L. W. F. Eddleston) Interferons in the Treatment of Chronic Virus Infections of the Liver, 1989; (with T. Murray) Genetic Engineering, 1991; contributor to: Animal Rights—A Symposium, 1979; The Book of Predictions, 1980; Development of Science Publishing in Europe, 1980; Medicine and Care, 1981; From Biology to Biotechnology, 1982; Encyclopædia Britannica, 15th edn, 1984; Encyclopædia Britannica Yearbook, 1986–92; Inquiry into Life, 1986; The Domesday Project, 1986; Industrial Biotechnology in Europe: issues for public policy, 1986; Biotechnology Information, 1987; Future Earth, 1989; Harrap's Illustrated Dictionary of Science, 1989; Biotechnology—A Brave New World?, 1989; numerous articles in scientific and general press on microbiology, and other scientific topics; research papers in Jl of General Microbiology, etc, mostly on microbial biochemistry. *Recreation:* playing Scottish traditional music, collecting old books. *Address:* 130 Cornwall Road, Ruislip Manor, Middlesex HA4 6AW. *T:* Ruislip (0895) 632390.

DIXON, Bernard Tunbridge; solicitor; *b* 14 July 1928; *s* of Archibald Tunbridge Dixon and Dorothy Dixon (*née* Cardinal); *m* 1962, Jessie Netta Watson Hastie; one *s* three *d*. *Educ:* Owen's Sch.; University Coll. London (LLB). Admitted Solicitor, 1952 (Edmund Thomas Child Prize); Partner in Dixon & Co., Solicitors, 1952–59; Legal Asst/Sen. Legal Asst with Treasury Solicitor, 1959–67; Sen. Legal Asst with Land Commission, 1967–70; Sen. Legal Asst with Charity Comrs, 1970–74; Dep. Charity Comr, 1975–81; Charity Comr, 1981–84. *Recreation:* photography. *Address:* c/o Maxwell Entwistle & Byrne, 14 Castle Street, Liverpool L2 0SG.

DIXON, (David) Jeremy; architect in private practice; *b* 31 May 1939; *s* of Joseph Lawrence Dixon and Beryl Margaret Dixon (*née* Braund); *m* 1964, Fenella Mary Anne Clemens; one *s* two *d*. *Educ:* Merchant Taylors' School; Architectural Assoc. Sch. of Architecture (AA Dip. (Hons)). RIBA. Private practice with Fenella Dixon; formed partnership of Jeremy Dixon/BDP, with William Jack, 1984, for extensions to Royal Opera House. Other projects include: competition for Northamptonshire County Offices; Tate Gallery Restaurant and coffee shop; shop for Clifton Nurseries; housing in London at St Mark's Road, Lanark Road, Ashmill St, Dudgeon's Wharf, St George's Wharf, Pimlico. *Recreations:* English landscape, opera, playing the piano badly. *Address:* 47 North Hill, Highgate, N6.

DIXON, Donald; MP (Lab) Jarrow, since 1979; Deputy Chief Opposition Whip, since 1987 (an Opposition Whip, since 1984); *b* 6 March 1929; *s* of late Christopher Albert Dixon and Jane Dixon; *m* Doreen Morad; one *s* one *d*. *Educ:* Ellison Street Elementary School, Jarrow. Shipyard Worker, 1947–74; Branch Sec., GMWU, 1974–79. Councillor, South Tyneside MDC, 1963–. Mem. Select Cttee on H of C Services; Chm., PLP Shipbuilding Gp. Freeman of Jarrow, 1972. *Recreations:* football, reading. *Address:* 1 Hillcrest, Jarrow NE32 4DP. *T:* Jarrow (091) 897635. *Clubs:* Jarrow Labour, Ex Servicemens (Jarrow); Hastings (Hebburn).

DIXON, Prof. Gordon Henry, PhD; FRS 1978; FRSC; Professor of Medical Biochemistry, since 1974, and Head of the Department, 1983–88, Faculty of Medicine, University of Calgary; *b* 25 March 1930; *s* of Walter James Dixon and Ruth Nightingale; *m* 1954, Sylvia Weir Gillen; three *s* one *d*. *Educ:* Cambs High Sch. for Boys; Trinity Coll., Cambridge (Open Schol. 1948; BA Hons, MA); Univ. of Toronto (PhD). FRSC 1970. Res. Asst Prof., Dept of Biochem., Univ. of Washington, Seattle, USA, 1954–58; Mem. staff, MRC Unit for res. in cell metabolism, Univ. of Oxford, 1958–59; Univ. of Toronto: Res. Associate, Connaught Med. Res. Lab., 1959–60; Associate Prof., Dept of Biochem., 1960–63; Prof., Dept of Biochem., Univ. of BC, Vancouver, 1963–72; Prof., Biochem. Group, Univ. of Sussex, 1972–74. Vis. Fellow Commoner, Trinity Coll., Cambridge, 1979–80. Mem. Exec., IUB, 1988–; President: Canadian Biochemical Soc., 1982–83; Pan-American Assoc. of Biochemical Socs, 1987–90 (Mem. Council, 1981–84; Vice-Pres., 1984–87). Flavelle Medal, RSC, 1980. *Publications:* over 200 pubns in learned jls, incl. Jl Biol Chem., Proc. Nat. Acad. Sci. (US), Nature, and Biochemistry. *Recreations:* music, reading, gardening.

DIXON, Guy Holford, JP; Barrister-at-Law; Honorary Recorder of Newark-on-Trent, since 1972; *b* 20 March 1902; *s* of late Dr Montague Dixon, Melton Mowbray; unmarried. *Educ:* Abbotsholme Sch., Derbs; Repton Sch.; University Coll., Oxford. BA (History) Oxon, 1925. Called to the Bar, Inner Temple, 1929. Recorder of Newark-on-Trent, 1965–71; Deputy Chairman: Leics QS, 1960–71; Northampton County QS, 1966–71; a Recorder, 1972–75; a Dep. Circuit Judge, 1975–77. Lay Canon, Leicester Cathedral, 1962. JP Leics, 1960. *Recreation:* looking at and collecting pictures. *Address:* The Old Rectory, Brampton Ash, Market Harborough, Leics LE16 8PD. *T:* Dingley (085885) 200. *Club:* Reform.

DIXON, Jack Shawcross, OBE 1969; HM Diplomatic Service, retired 1976; *b* 8 March 1918; *s* of Herbert Dixon and Helen (*née* Woollacott); *m* 1941, Ida Hewkin; one *d*. *Educ:* Oldham Hulme Grammar Sch.; London Sch. of Economics (BScEcon). Served in Royal Welch Fusiliers and RAOC attached Indian Army, 1940–46. Colonial Office, 1948; entered HM Foreign (subseq. Diplomatic) Service, 1949; FO, 1949; HM Political Agency, Kuwait, 1950; Rep. of Polit. Agent, Mina al Ahmadi, 1951; FO, 1952; 1st Sec., Singapore, 1956; HM Consul, Barcelona, 1959; FO, 1962; 1st Sec., Rome, 1966; FCO, 1971; Head of Treaty and Nationality Dept, FCO, 1973–76. *Publications:* contribs to Jl of Imperial and Commonwealth History, Indica Jaipurensia. *Recreation:* art-historical research (India). *Address:* 26 Brook Court, 47 Meads Road, Eastbourne, E Sussex BN20 7PY. *Club:* Commonwealth Trust.

DIXON, Jeremy; *see* Dixon, D. J.

DIXON, Jon Edmund, CMG 1975; Under Secretary, Ministry of Agriculture, Fisheries and Food, 1971–85; *b* 19 Nov. 1928; *e s* of Edmund Joseph Claude and Gwendoline Alice Dixon; *m* 1953, Betty Edith Stone; two *s* one *d* (and one *d* decd). *Educ:* St Paul's Sch., West Kensington; Peterhouse, Cambridge (Natural Sciences Tripos Part I and Part II (Physiology); MA). Asst Principal, Min. of Agric. and Fisheries, 1952; Private Sec. to successive Parliamentary Secretaries, 1955–58; Principal, 1958; Asst Sec., 1966; Under-Sec., 1971; Minister in UK Delegn, subseq. Office of Permanent Rep., to EEC, 1972–75. Founded JOED Music (editing and publishing Renaissance polyphonic choral music), 1988. *Publications:* Calico Pie (suite for vocal sextet), 1988; The Leuven Carols, 1988; The Pobble Who Has No Toes (4 part-songs), 1989; editions of Renaissance choral music by Byrd, Clemens, Lassus, Philips, Tallis and Victoria; contribs to Early Music News. *Recreations:* musical composition (Choral, Organ and String Music: a selection of works by Jon Dixon, 1970–85 (two LPs)), oil painting, building harpsichords, gardening, walking.

DIXON, Sir Jonathan (Mark), 4th Bt *cr* 1919, of Astle, Chelford, Co. Chester; Technical and Development Director, Lawson Mardon Flexible, since 1989; *b* 1 Sept. 1949; *s* of Captain Nigel Dixon, OBE, RN (*d* 1978), and of Margaret Josephine Dixon; *S* uncle, 1990; *m* 1978, Patricia Margaret, *d* of James Baird Smith; two *s* one *d*. *Educ:* Winchester Coll.; University Coll., Oxford (MA). *Recreation:* fishing. *Heir:* *s* Mark Edward Dixon, *b* 29 June 1982. *Address:* 19 Clyde Road, Redland, Bristol BS6 6RJ.

DIXON, Kenneth Herbert Morley, DL; Chairman, Rowntree (formerly Rowntree Mackintosh) plc, 1981–89, retired; Vice-Chairman, Legal & General Group, since 1986 (Director, since 1984); Deputy Chairman, Bass PLC, since 1990; *b* 19 Aug. 1929; *yr s* of Arnold Morley Dixon and Mary Jolly; *m* 1955, Patricia Oldbury Whalley; two *s*. *Educ:* Cathedral Sch., Shanghai; Cranbrook Sch., Sydney, Australia; Manchester Univ. (BA(Econ) 1952); Harvard Business Sch. AMP, 1969. Lieut Royal Signals, 1947–49. Calico Printers Assoc., 1952–56; joined Rowntree & Co. Ltd, 1956; Dir, 1970; Chm., UK Confectionery Div., 1973–78; Dep. Chm., 1978–81. Dep. Chm., Bass, 1990– (Dir, 1988–); Dir, Yorks TV Hldgs, 1989–; Mem., British Railways Bd, 1990–. Member: Council, Incorporated Soc. of British Advertisers, 1971–79; Council, Cocoa, Chocolate and Confectionery Alliance, 1972–79; Council, Advertising Assoc., 1976–79; BIM Econ. and Social Affairs Cttee, 1980–84; Council, CBI, 1981–90 (Mem., Companies Cttee, 1979–84; Mem., Employment Policy Cttee, 1983–90); Governing Council, Business in the Community, 1983–90; Council, Food from Britain, 1986–89; Exec. Cttee, Food and Drink Fedn, 1986–89 (Mem. Council, 1986–87); Council for Industry and Higher Educn, 1986–; Council, Nat. Forum for Management Educn & Develt, 1987–; Chm., Food Assoc., 1986. Mem. Council, York Univ., 1983– (Chm., 1990–), Pro-Chancellor, 1987–; Chm., Vis. Cttee, Open Univ., 1990–. DL N Yorks, 1991. FRSA; CBIM. *Recreations:* reading, music, fell walking. *Address:* c/o Fairfax House, Castlegate, York YO1 1RN. *T:* York (0904) 655543. *Club:* Reform.

DIXON, Margaret Rumer Haynes; *see* Godden, Rumer.

DIXON, Peter Vibart; Director of Planning and Administration, Turner Kenneth Brown, Solicitors, since 1988; *b* 16 July 1932; *s* of late Meredith Vibart Dixon and Phyllis Joan (*née* Hemingway); *m* 1955, Elizabeth Anne Howie Davison; three *s*. *Educ:* Summer Fields; Radley Coll.; King's Coll., Cambridge (BA Classics and Law 1955, MA 1959). Royal Artillery, 1951–52. Asst Principal, HM Treasury, 1955; Office of Lord Privy Seal, 1956; Treasury, 1956–62: Private Sec. to Economic Sec., 1959; Principal, 1960; Colonial Office, 1963; CS Selection Bd, 1964–65; Treasury, 1965–72, Asst Sec., 1969; Counsellor (Economic), HM Embassy, Washington, 1972–75; Treasury, 1975–82: Press Sec., 1975–78; Under Sec., Industrial Policy, 1978–82; Sec., NEDC, 1982–87. Mem., RIPA (Mem. Council, 1976–82). FRSA 1984; FBIM 1988. *Address:* 17 Lauriston Road, Wimbledon SW19 4TJ. *T:* 081–946 8931. *Club:* United Oxford & Cambridge University.

DIXON, Piers; *b* 29 Dec. 1928; *s* of late Sir Pierson Dixon (British Ambassador in New York and Paris) and Lady (Ismene) Dixon; *m* 1st, 1960, Edwina (marr. diss. 1973), *d* of Rt Hon. Lord Duncan-Sandys, CH, PC; two *s*; 2nd, 1976, Janet (marr. diss. 1981), *d* of R. D. Aiyar, FRCS, and *widow* of 5th Earl Cowley; 3rd, 1984, Anne (marr. diss. 1985), *d* of John Cronin; one *s*. *Educ:* Eton (schol.); Magdalene Coll., Cambridge (exhibnr); Harvard Business Sch. Grenadier Guards, 1948. Merchant banking, London and New York, 1954–64; Sheppards and Chase, stockbrokers, 1964–81. Centre for Policy Studies, 1976–78. Contested (C) Brixton, 1966; MP (C) Truro, 1970–Sept. 1974; Sec., Cons. Backbenchers' Finance Cttee, 1970–71, Vice-Chm., 1972–74; sponsor of Rehabilitation of Offenders Act, 1974. *Publications:* Double Diploma, 1968; Cornish Names, 1973. *Recreations:* tennis, modern history. *Address:* 22 Ponsonby Terrace, SW1. *T:* 071–821 6166. *Clubs:* Beefsteak, Brooks's, Pratt's.

DIXON, Prof. Richard Newland, PhD, ScD; FRS 1986; CChem, FRSC; Professor of Theoretical Chemistry, since 1969, Alfred Capper Pass Professor of Chemistry, since 1990, and Pro-Vice-Chancellor, since 1989, University of Bristol; *b* 25 Dec. 1930; *s* of late Robert Thomas Dixon and Lilian Dixon; *m* 1954, Alison Mary Birks; one *s* two *d*. *Educ:* The Judd Sch., Tonbridge; King's Coll., Univ. of London (BSc 1951); St Catharine's Coll., Univ. of Cambridge (PhD 1955; ScD 1976). FRSC 1976. Scientific Officer, UKAEA, 1954–56; Res. Associate, Univ. of Western Ontario, 1956–57; Postdoctoral Fellow, NRCC, Ottawa, 1957–59; ICI Fellow, Univ. of Sheffield, 1959–60, Lectr in Chem., 1960–69; Bristol University: Hd of Dept of Theoretical Chemistry, 1969–90; Dean, Faculty of Science, 1979–82. Sorby Res. Fellow, Royal Soc., 1964–69; Vis. Schol., Stanford Univ., 1982–83. Mem. Council, Faraday Div., RSC, 1985–, Vice-Pres., 1989–; Mem., and Chm. sub-cttee, Laser Facility Cttee, SERC, 1987–90. Corday-Morgan Medal, Chemical Soc., 1966; RSC Award for Spectroscopy, 1984. *Publications:* Spectroscopy and Structure, 1965; Theoretical Chemistry: Vol. 1, 1974, Vol. 2, 1975, Vol. 3, 1978; numerous articles in res. jls of chemistry and physics. *Recreations:* mountain walking, travel, theatre, concerts. *Address:* 22 Westbury Lane, Bristol BS9 2PE. *T:* Bristol (0272) 681691; School of Chemistry, The University, Bristol BS8 1TS. *T:* Bristol (0272) 303683.

DIXON, Maj.-Gen. Roy Laurence Cayley, CB 1977; CVO 1991; MC 1944; Chapter Clerk, College of St George, Windsor Castle, 1981–90; *b* 19 Sept. 1924; *s* of Lt-Col Sidney Frank Dixon, MC and Edith Mary (Sheena) (*née* Clark); *m* 1986, Anne Maureen Aspeslåen (marr. diss. 1988). *Educ:* Haileybury; Edinburgh Univ. Commnd Royal Tank Regt, 1944; served in armd units and on staff; psc 1956; Instructor, Staff Coll., 1961–64; comd 5th Royal Tank Regt, 1966–67; Royal Coll. of Defence Studies, 1971; Comdr Royal Armd Corps, Germany, 1968–70; qual. helicopter pilot, 1973; Dir, Army Air Corps, 1974–76; Chief of Staff, Allied Forces Northern Europe, 1977–80. Col Comdt, RTR, 1978–83. *Address:* c/o Lloyds Bank, Cox's & Kings Branch, PO Box 1190, 7 Pall Mall, SW1Y 5NA. *Club:* Army and Navy.

DIXON, Stanley; Chairman, Midland-Yorkshire Tar Distillers Ltd, 1968–71; *b* 12 Aug. 1900; *m* 1936, Ella Margaret Hogg; two *s*. *Educ:* Leeds Grammar Sch.; Queen's Coll., Oxford. Articled to Leather & Veale, Chartered Accountants in Leeds, 1924–27; Manager,

Leather & Veale (later Peat, Marwick, Mitchell & Co.), Leeds, 1927–35; Sec., Midland Tar Distillers Ltd, 1935–66; Dir, Midland Tar Distillers Ltd (later Midland-Yorkshire Holdings Ltd), 1943–71. Pres., Inst. of Chartered Accountants in England and Wales, 1968–69. Hon. DSocSc Birmingham, 1972. *Publications:* The Case for Marginal Costing, 1967; The Art of Chairing a Meeting, 1975. *Recreations:* Church affairs, gardening and music. *Address:* 83 Norton Road, Stourbridge, West Midlands DY8 2TB. *T:* Stourbridge (0384) 395672.

DIXON, Group Captain William Michael, CBE 1972; DSO 1943; DFC 1941; AFC 1958; Bursar, Summer Fields School, Oxford, 1975–86; *b* 29 July 1920; *s* of late William Michael Dixon; *m* 1st, 1944, Mary Margaret (*d* 1957), *d* of late William Alexander Spence, MC, MM; three *s*; 2nd, 1988, Eileen Margaret Collinson, *d* of late Claud Henry Tucker, OBE. Served War of 1939–45, Bomber Comd; Air Staff, Rhodesian Air Trng Gp, 1946–49; psa 1949; comd No 2 (Bomber) Sqdn RAAF, 1952–55; comd No 192 Sqdn RAF, 1955–58; jssc 1958; comd RAF Feltwell, 1961–63; Sen. Officer Admin No 1 (Bomber) Gp, 1963–66; Sen. Personnel SO HQ Air Support Comd, 1966–68; DCAS, Royal Malaysian Air Force, 1968–73; Dir of Aircraft Projects (RAF), MoD, 1972–75; ADC to the Queen, 1968–73. *Recreation:* natural history. *Address:* Lower Farm, Duck End Lane, Sutton, Oxford OX8 1RX. *T:* Oxford (0865) 881553.

DIXON-WARD, Frank, CBE 1979; Chairman, London Rent Assessment Committees, 1982 and since 1986; Hon. Legal Adviser, Eurogroup for Animal Welfare, since 1986; Member: Board of Directors, World Society for the Protection of Animals, since 1986; Board of Overseers, Massachusetts SPCA, since 1988; *b* 28 June 1922; *s* of late Cecil Ward, LRAM, and Helen Cecilia Ward, Eastbourne; *m* 1960, Claire Collasius (*d* 1985); one *s* one *d*. *Educ:* Eastbourne Grammar School. Solicitor (Hons), 1948. Articled to Town Clerk, Eastbourne, 1940. Served War, Royal Air Force, 1941–46. Solicitor posts, Peterborough, 1948–51, West Ham, 1952–54; Deputy Town Clerk, Hove, 1954–62; Chairman: Local Govt Legal Soc., 1957; Hove Round Table, 1961–62; Mem. Council, Sussex LTA, 1957–62; Town Clerk: Camberwell, 1963–65; Southwark, 1964–70; Chief Exec., Lambeth, 1970–81; Consultant, 1982. Exec. Dir, RSPCA, 1982–87. Hon. Clerk: South London Housing Consortium, 1965–70; Social Service Cttee, London Boroughs Assoc., 1966–82; Hon. Legal Advr, Age Concern (Gtr London), 1965–82; Member official committees: London Welfare Services, 1963–65; NHS Reorganisation, 1969–74; Homelessness, 1970–72; Citizens Advice Bureaux, 1973–74; Jt Approach to Social Policies, 1975–76; Exec. Cttee, SOLACE, 1975–81. Chm., St Dunstan's College Soc., 1975–78. *Recreations:* music, lawn tennis. *T:* 081–650 8312. *Club:* Royal Over-Seas League.

DIXSON, Maurice Christopher Scott, DPhil; FRAeS; FInstPS; Supervisory Managing Director, Electronic Metrology and Components Groups, and Main Board Director, GEC, since 1990; *b* 5 Nov. 1941; *s* of Herbert George Muns Dixson and Elizabeth Eileen Dixson; *m* 1965, Anne Beverley Morris. *Educ:* University Coll., Swansea (BA Jt Hons); Carleton Univ., Ottawa (MA); Pembroke Coll., Oxford (DPhil). Commercial Exec., Hawker Siddeley Aviation, 1969–74; Contracts Man., Export, later Commercial Man., Export, Mil. Aircraft Div., BAC, 1974–80; British Aerospace: Warton Division: Div. Commercial Man., 1980–81; Exec. Dir, Contracts, 1981–83; Divl Commercial Dir, 1983–86; Military Aircraft Division: Dir-in-Charge, Saudi Arabian Ops, March–Aug. 1986; Commercial Dir and Dir-in-Charge, Saudi Arabian Ops, 1986–87; Chief Exec., Royal Ordnance PLC, 1987–88; Man. Dir, British Aerospace (Commercial Aircraft), 1988–90. *Recreations:* played representative soccer at school and university, supporter of Tottenham Hotspur Football Club, golf, fishing, sport, politics and current affairs. *Address:* Cheney Manor, Swindon, Wilts SN2 2QW. *T:* Swindon (0793) 518000. *Clubs:* Royal Automobile; Royal Lytham and St Anne's Golf (Lytham St Anne's); Moor Park Golf.

DOBB, Erlam Stanley, CB 1963; TD; *b* 16 Aug. 1910; *m* 1937, Margaret Williams; no *c*. *Educ:* Ruthin; University Coll. of N Wales. Chartered Surveyor and Land Agent, Anglesey, Denbigh and Merioneth, 1930–35; Asst Land Comr, to Dir, Agricultural Land Service, MAFF, 1935–70; a Dep. Dir-Gen., Agricl Develt and Adv. Service, MAFF, 1971–73; Dir-Gen., 1973–75. Mem., ARC, 1973–75; Vice-Chm., Adv. Council for Agriculture and Horticulture in England and Wales, 1974–75. Trustee, T. P. Price Charity, Markshall Estate, Essex, 1971–84 (Chm. Trustees, 1971–83). Governor, Royal Agricultural College, 1960–75. Royal Welch Fusiliers (TA), 1938–46, Major. FRICS; FRAgS. *Publications:* professional contributions to journals of learned societies. *Recreations:* golf, gardening. *Address:* Churchgate, Westerham, Kent. *T:* Westerham (0959) 62294. *Clubs:* Farmers'; Crowborough Beacon Golf, Limpsfield Chart Golf.

DOBBIE, Dr Robert Charles; Director, Merseyside Task Force, since 1990; *b* 16 Jan. 1942; *s* of Scott U. Dobbie and Isobel M. Dobbie; *m* 1964, Elizabeth Barbour; three *s*. *Educ:* Univ. of Edinburgh (BSc); Univ. of Cambridge (PhD). Res. Fellow, Univ. of Alberta, 1966–67; ICI Res. Fellow, Univ. of Bristol, 1967–68; Lectr in Inorganic Chemistry, Univ. of Newcastle upon Tyne, 1968–76; sabbatical, UCLA, 1974; Tutor, Open Univ., 1975–85; Principal, DTI, 1976–83; Asst Sec., Dept. of Industry, 1983–90; Under Sec., DTI, 1990– (seconded to DoE). *Publications:* on inorganic and organometallic chemistry. *Recreations:* theatre, hill walking, malt whisky. *Address:* Department of Trade and Industry, 1 Victoria Street, SW1H 0ET.

DOBBING, Prof. John, DSc, FRCP, FRCPath; Professor of Child Growth and Development, Department of Child Health, University of Manchester, and Honorary Consultant, United Manchester Hospitals, 1968–84, now Professor Emeritus; *b* 14 Aug. 1922; *s* of Alfred Herbert Dobbing and May Gwendoline (*née* Cattell); *m* Dr Jean Sands. *Educ:* Bootham Sch., York; St Mary's Hosp., London (BSc 1st cl. hons, MB, BS). DSc Manchester, 1981. FRCPath 1976; FRCP 1981. Lectr in Path. and Gull Student, Guy's Hosp., 1954–61; Sen. Lectr in Physiol., London Hosp., 1961–64; Sen. Lectr, Inst. of Child Health, London, and Hon. Consultant, Hosp. for Sick Children, Gt Ormond Street, 1964–68. *Publications:* Applied Neurochemistry, 1968; (ed with J. A. Davis) Scientific Foundations of Paediatrics, 1974 (2nd edn 1981); Maternal Nutrition in Pregnancy: eating for two?, 1981; Prevention of Spina Bifida, 1983; pubns on undernutrition and developing brain in scientific literature. *Recreations:* writing, travel, France and the French. *Address:* Higher Cliff Farm, via Birch Vale, via Stockport, Cheshire SK12 5DL. *T:* New Mills (0663) 743220.

DOBBS, Bernard; *see* Dobbs, W. B. J.

DOBBS, Prof. (Edwin) Roland, PhD, DSc; Hildred Carlile Professor of Physics, University of London, 1973–90, and Head of Department of Physics, Royal Holloway and Bedford New College, 1985–90; Emeritus Professor of Physics, University of London, 1990; *b* 2 Dec. 1924; *s* of late A. Edwin Dobbs, AMIMechE, and Harriet Dobbs (*née* Wright); *m* 1947, Dorothy Helena, *o d* of late Alderman A. F. T. Jeeves, Stamford, Lincs; two *s* one *d*. *Educ:* Ilford County High Sch.; Queen Elizabeth's Sch., Barnet; University College London. BSc (1st cl. Physics) 1943, PhD 1949; DSc London 1977; FInstP 1964; FIOA 1977. Radar research, Admiralty, 1943–46; DSIR Res. Student, UCL, 1946–49; Lectr in Physics, QMC, Univ. of London, 1949–58; Res. Associate in Applied Maths, 1958–59, Associate Prof. of Physics, 1959–60, Brown Univ., USA; Mem., Gonville and Caius Coll., Cambridge, 1960–; AEI Fellow, Cavendish Lab., Univ. of Cambridge, 1960–64; Prof. and Head of Dept of Physics, Univ. of Lancaster, 1964–73; Bedford College, London University: Head of Dept of Physics, 1973–85; Vice-Principal, 1981–82; Dean, Faculty of Science, 1980–82; Chm., Bd of Studies in Physics, Univ. of London, 1982–85; Vice-Dean, 1986–88, Dean, 1988–90, Faculty of Science, Univ. of London. Member: Physics Cttee, SRC, 1970–73, SERC, 1983–86; Nuclear Physics Bd, SRC, 1974–77; Paul Instrument Fund Cttee, 1984–. Visiting Professor: Brown Univ., 1966; Wayne State Univ., 1969; Univ. of Tokyo, 1977; Univ. of Delhi, 1983; Cornell Univ., 1984; Univ. of Florida, 1989; Univ. of Sussex, 1989–. Pres., Inst. of Acoustics, 1976–78; Hon. Sec., Inst. of Physics, 1976–84. Convenor, Standing Conf. of Profs of Physics of GB, 1985–88. Hon. Fellow, Indian Cryogenics Council, 1977. *Publications:* Electricity and Magnetism, 1984; Electromagnetic Waves, 1985; research papers on metals and superconductors in Procs of Royal Soc., on solid state physics and acoustics in Jl of Physics, Physical Rev. Letters, Physical Acoustics, and on superfluid helium 3 in Jl Low Temperature Physics, etc. *Recreations:* travel, theatre, gardening. *Address:* Mill Farm, Ripe, Lewes, E Sussex BN8 6AX. *T:* Ripe (0323) 811232. *Club:* Athenæum.

See also Prof. M. A. Jeeves.

DOBBS, Joseph Alfred, CMG 1972; OBE 1957 (MBE 1945); TD 1945; HM Diplomatic Service, retired; *b* Abbeyleix, Ireland, 22 Dec. 1914; *s* of John L. Dobbs and Ruby (*née* Gillespie); *m* 1949, Marie, *d* of Reginald Francis Catton, Sydney; four *s*. *Educ:* Worksop Coll.; Trinity Hall, Cambridge (Schol.). Pres., Cambridge Union Soc., 1936. Served War of 1939–45, Major, Royal Artillery (despatches). Joined Foreign Office, 1946; served Moscow, 1947–51, 1954–57 and 1965–68; FO, 1951–54; Delhi, 1957–61; Warsaw, 1961–64; Rome, 1964–65; Consul-Gen., Zagreb, 1969–70; Minister, Moscow, 1971–74. *Recreations:* reading, gardening. *Address:* The Coach House, Charlton Musgrove, Wincanton, Somerset BA9 8ES. *T:* Wincanton (0963) 33356.

DOBBS, Mattiwilda; Order of North Star (Sweden), 1954; opera singer (coloratura soprano); Professor, Howard University, Washington, DC, since 1977; *b* Atlanta, Ga, USA; *d* of John Wesley and Irene Dobbs; *m* 1957, Bengt Janzon, retired Dir. of Information, Nat. Ministry of Health and Welfare, Sweden; no *c*. *Educ:* Spelman Coll., USA (BA 1946); Columbia Univ., USA (MA 1948). Studied voice in NY with Lotte Leonard, 1946–50; special coaching Paris with Pierre Bernac, 1950–52. Marian Anderson Schol., 1948; John Hay Whitney Schol., 1950; 1st prize in singing, Internat. Comp., Geneva Conservatory of Music, 1951. Appeared Royal Dutch Opera, Holland Festival, 1952. Recitals, Sweden, Paris, Holland, 1952; appeared in opera at La Scala, Milan, 1953; Concerts, England and Continent, 1953; Glyndebourne Opera, 1953–54, 1956, 1961; Covent Garden Opera, 1953, 1954, 1956, 1958; command performance, Covent Garden, 1954. Annual concert tours: US, 1954–; Australia, New Zealand, 1955, 1959, 1968; Australia, 1972, 1977; Israel, 1957 and 1959; USSR concerts and opera (Bolshoi Theater), 1959; San Francisco Opera, 1955; début Metropolitan Opera, 1956; there annually, 1956–64. Appearances Hamburg State Opera, 1961–63; Royal Swedish Opera, 1957 and there annually, 1957–73; Norwegian and Finnish Operas, 1957–64. Vis. Prof., Univ. of Texas at Austin, 1973–74; Professor: Univ. of Illinois, 1975–76; Univ. of Georgia, 1976–77. Hon. Dr of Music: Spelman Coll., Atlanta, 1979; Emory Univ., Atlanta, 1980. *Address:* 1101 South Arlington Ridge Road, Apt 301, Arlington, Va 22202, USA.

DOBBS, Captain Sir Richard (Arthur Frederick), KCVO 1991; Lord-Lieutenant of County Antrim, 1975 (HM Lieutenant for County Antrim, 1959–75); *b* 2 April 1919; *s* of Senator Major Arthur F. Dobbs, DL, of Castle Dobbs, and Hylda Louisa Dobbs; *m* 1953, Carola Day, *d* of Christopher Clarkson, Old Lyme, Conn, USA; four *s* one *d*. *Educ:* Eton; Magdalene Coll., Cambridge (MA). Served War: 2nd Lieut Irish Guards (Supp. Reserve), 1939; Captain 1943. Called to Bar, Lincoln's Inn, 1947; Member, Midland Circuit, 1951–55. *Address:* Castle Dobbs, Carrickfergus, County Antrim, N Ireland BT38 9BX. *T:* Whitehead (09603) 72238. *Club:* Cavalry and Guards.

DOBBS, Roland; *see* Dobbs, E. R.

DOBBS, (William) Bernard (Joseph); HM Diplomatic Service, retired; Ambassador to Laos (Lao People's Democratic Republic), 1982–85; *b* 3 Sept. 1925; *s* of late William Evelyn Joseph Dobbs and Maud Clifford Dobbs (*née* Bernard); *m* 1952, Brigid Mary Bilitch; one *s* one *d*. *Educ:* Shrewsbury Sch.; Trinity Coll., Dublin (BA Hons Mod. History 1951; MA 1977). Served Rifle Bde/7th Gurkha Rifles, 1943–47 (Captain). Forbes Forbes Campbell and Co. Ltd, 1952–56; Examiner, Patent Office, 1957–61; British Trade Commission, 1961–65: Lagos, 1961–64; Freetown, 1964–66; HM Diplomatic Service: Freetown, London, Rangoon, Milan, Kinshasa, Vientiane, 1965–85. *Recreations:* reading, walking, writing. *Clubs:* Royal Automobile; Kildare Street and University (Dublin).

DOBEREINER, Peter Arthur Bertram; golf correspondent, The Observer, 1965–90; *b* 3 Nov. 1925; *s* of Major Arthur Dobereiner and Dorothy (*née* Hassall); *m* 1951, Betty Evelyn Jacob; two *s* two *d*. *Educ:* King's College, Taunton; Lincoln College, Oxford. RNVR 1942. Asst Manager, Parry & Co. (Madras), 1946; various newspaper appts, 1949–: East Essex Gazette, Oxford Times, News Chronicle, Daily Express, Daily Mail, The Guardian. Hon. Mem., Amer. Soc. of Golf Course Architects. Screen Writers Guild Award (jtly) (That Was the Week That Was), 1962; MacGregor writing awards, 1977, 1981; Donald Ross award, 1985; Irish Golf Fellowship Award, 1987. *Publications:* The Game With a Hole In It, 1970, 3rd edn 1973; The Glorious World of Golf, 1973, 3rd edn 1975; Stroke, Hole or Match?, 1976; Golf Rules Explained, 1980, 6th edn 1985; For the Love of Golf, 1981; Tony Jacklin's Golf Secrets, 1982; Down the Nineteenth Fairway, 1982; The World of Golf, 1982; (ed) The Golfers, 1982; The Book of Golf Disasters, 1983; The Fifty Greatest Post-War Golfers, 1985; Arnold Palmer's Complete Book of Putting, 1986; Preferred Lies, 1987. *Recreation:* golf. *Address:* Chelsfield Hill House, Pratts Bottom, Orpington, Kent BR6 7SL. *T:* Farnborough (Kent) (0689) 853849. *Clubs:* West Kent Golf; Pine Valley Golf; Hon. Ballybunion (Ireland).

DOBLE, Denis Henry; HM Diplomatic Service; Consul-General, Amsterdam, since 1991; *b* 2 Oct. 1936; *s* of Percy Claud Doble and Dorothy Grace (*née* Petley); *m* 1975, Patricia Ann Robinson; one *d* one *s*. *Educ:* Dover Grammar School; New College, Oxford (MA Modern Hist.). RAF, 1955–57. Colonial Office, 1960–64; Asst Private Sec. to Commonwealth and Colonial Sec., 1963–64; HM Diplomatic Service, 1965; First Sec., Brussels, 1966–68, Lagos, 1968–72; S Asian and Defence Depts, FCO, 1972–75; First Sec. (Economic), Islamabad, 1975–78; Head of Chancery, Lima, 1978–82; E African Dept, FCO, 1982–84; Actg Dep. High Comr, Bombay, 1985; Deputy High Commissioner: Calcutta, 1985–87; Kingston, 1987–91. SBStJ. *Recreations:* travel, cinema, cricket, tennis, colonial history. *Address:* c/o Foreign and Commonwealth Office, SW1A 2AH. *Club:* MCC.

DOBLE, John Frederick, OBE 1981; HM Diplomatic Service; Consul General, Johannesburg, since 1990; *b* 30 June 1941; *s* of Comdr Douglas Doble, RN and Marcella (*née* Cowan); *m* 1975, Isabella Margaret Ruth, *d* of Col. W. H. Whitbread, *qv*; one *d*. *Educ:* Sunningdale; Eton (Scholar); RMA Sandhurst; Hertford College, Oxford. 17th/21st Lancers, 1959–69 (Captain); attached Lord Strathcona's Horse (Royal Canadians), 1967–69; joined HM Diplomatic Service, 1969; Arabian Dept, FCO, 1969–72; Beirut,

1972–73; UK deleg. to NATO, Brussels, 1973–77; Commonwealth Coordination Dept, FCO, 1977–78. Maputo, 1978–81; Inf. Dept, FCO, 1981–83; attached Barclays Bank International, 1983–85; Consul General, Edmonton, Canada, 1985–89. *Recreations:* horse and water sports, history, manual labour. *Address:* c/o Foreign and Commonwealth Office, SW1A 2AH. *Clubs:* Commonwealth Trust; Poplar, Blackwall and District Rowing.

DOBREE, John Hatherley, MS, FRCS; Consulting Ophthalmic Surgeon, St Bartholomew's Hospital, London, EC1 (Consultant 1956); Honorary Ophthalmic Surgeon, North Middlesex Hospital, N18 (Senior Ophthalmic Surgeon 1947); *b* 25 April 1914; *s* of Hatherley Moor Dobree, OBE, and Muriel Dobree (*née* Hope); *m* 1941, Evelyn Maud Smyth; two *s*. *Educ:* Victoria Coll., Jersey; St Bartholomew's Hosp. MS London 1947; FRCS 1950. House Physician, Metropolitan Hosp., E8, 1938–39; House Surgeon, Western Ophthalm. Hosp., 1940. Served in RAMC, 1940–46, in MEF, as RMO and Ophthalmic Specialist. Chief Asst, Eye Dept, St Bartholomew's Hosp., 1946–51. FRSocMed (Past Sec., Sect. of Ophthalmology); Vice-Pres. and Past Hon. Sec. Ophthalmological Soc. of UK; Dep. Master, Oxford Ophth. Congress, 1976. *Publications:* The Retina, vol. x, in Sir Stewart Duke-Elder's System of Ophthalmology, 1967; (with E. S. Perkins) Differential Diagnosis of Fundus Conditions, 1971; (with E. Boulter) Blindness and Visual Handicap, the Facts, 1982; Soldiers of the Company, 1988. *Recreations:* archaeology, walking. *Address:* The Rosery, Great Bealings, Woodbridge, Suffolk IP13 6NW.

DOBROSIELSKI, Marian, PhD Zürich; Banner of Labour, 1st Class 1975 (2nd Class 1973); Knight Cross of the Order of Polonia Restituta, 1964; Professor of Philosophy, Warsaw University, since 1974; Ambassador *ad personam*, since 1973; *b* 25 March 1923; *s* of Stanisław and Stefania Dobrosielski; *m* 1950; one *d*. *Educ:* Univ. of Zürich; Univ. of Warsaw. Served in Polish Army in France, War of 1939–45. With Min. of Foreign Affairs, 1948–81; Polish Legation, Bern, 1948–50; Head of Section, Min. of Foreign Affairs, 1950–54; Asst Prof., Warsaw Univ. and Polish Acad. of Sciences, 1954–57; Mem. Polish delegn to UN Gen. Assembly, 1952, 1953, 1958, 1966, 1972, 1976. First Sec., Counsellor, Polish Embassy in Washington, 1958–64; Min. of Foreign Affairs: Counsellor to Minister, 1964–69; Acting Dir, Research Office, 1968–69; Polish Ambassador to London, 1969–71; Dir, Polish Inst. of Internat. Affairs, 1971–80; Dep. Minister of Foreign Affairs, 1978–81. Univ. of Warsaw: Associate Prof., 1966; Vice-Dean of Faculty of Philosophy, 1966–68; Dir, Inst. of Philosophy, 1971–73 (Chm. Scientific Council, 1969). Chm., Editorial Bd of Studia Filozoficzne, 1968–69; Sec., Polish Philos. Soc., 1955–57 and 1965–69. Chm., Polish Cttee for European Security and Co-operation, 1973–79 (Vice-Chm., 1971–73); Vice-Chm., Cttee on Peace Research, Polish Acad. of Scis, 1984–. Hon. Vice-Pres., Scottish-Polish Cultural Assoc., Glasgow, 1969–71; Chm., Polish delegn to: 2nd stage Conf. on Security and Co-operation in Europe, 1973–75; CSCE Belgrade Meeting, 1977–78; CSCE Meeting, Madrid, 1980–81. *Publications:* A Basic Epistemological Principle of Logical Positivism, 1947; The Philosophical Pragmatism of C. S. Peirce, 1967; On some contemporary problems: Philosophy, Ideology, Politics, 1970; (trans. and introd) Selection of Aphorisms of G. C. Lichtenberg, Oscar Wilde, Karl Kraus, M. von Ebner-Eschenbach, Mark Twain, C. Norwid, 1970–85; On the Theory and Practice of Peaceful Coexistence, 1976; Belgrad 77, 1978; Chances and Dilemmas, 1980; The Crisis in Poland, 1984; On Politics and Philosophy, 1988; Philosophy of Reason, 1988; Karl R. Popper's Philosophy of History and Politics, 1991; numerous articles on philosophy and internat. problems in professional jls. *Recreation:* tennis. *Address:* Kozia Street 9–14, Warszawa, Poland.

DOBRY, George Leon Severyn, CBE 1977; QC 1969; **His Honour Judge George Dobry;** a Circuit Judge, since 1980; *b* 1 Nov. 1918; *m* 1st, 1948, Margaret Headley Smith (*d* 1978), *e d* of late Joseph Quartus Smith, JP, Bardfield Saling, Essex; two *d*; 2nd, 1982, Rosemary Anne Alexander (Principal, English Gardening Sch.), *d* of Charles Edward Wilson Sleigh, Bridge of Allan, Stirlingshire. *Educ:* Gimnazium Mikolaja Reya, Warsaw; Warsaw Univ.; Edinburgh Univ. (MA). Served War of 1939–45: Army, 1939–42; Air Force, 1942–46. Called to Bar, Inner Temple, 1946; Bencher 1977. A Recorder of the Crown Court, 1977–80. Legal Sec., Internat. Commn of Jurists at The Hague, 1955–57. Member Council: 'Justice', 1956–68; on Law Reporting, 1984–. Adviser to Sec. of State for Environment and Sec. of State for Wales on Develt Control, 1973–75; Mem., Docklands Jt Cttee, 1974–76; Inspector, Inquiry into M25, 1978–79. Jt Pres., British-Polish Legal Assoc., 1989–. *Publications:* Woodfall's Law of Landlord and Tenant, 25th edition (one of the Editors), 1952; Blundell and Dobry, Town and Country Planning, 1962; Blundell and Dobry Planning Appeals and Inquiries, 1962, 4th edn 1990; Hill and Redman, Landlord and Tenant (Cons. Editor), 16th edn, 1976; Review of the Development Control System (Interim Report), 1974 (Final Report), 1975; (ed jtly) Development Gains Tax, 1975; (Gen. Editor) Encyclopedia of Development Law, 1976. *Address:* 40 Chester Row, SW1W 8JP; Stoneacre, Otham, Kent. *Clubs:* Garrick, Travellers'.

DOBRYNIN, Anatoly Fedorovich, Hero of Socialist Labour; Order of Lenin (five awards); Order of Red Banner of Labour; Secretary, Central Committee, Communist Party of the Soviet Union, since 1986; Deputy, Supreme Soviet of the USSR, since 1986; *b* 16 Nov. 1919; *m* Irina Nikolaevna Dobrynina; one *d*. *Educ:* Moscow Inst. of Aviation, 1942; Higher Sch. of Diplomacy, 1946 (doctorate in History). Asst to Dean of Faculty, Moscow Inst. of Aviation, engr-designer, 1942–44; Official, Min. of For. Affairs, 1946–52; Counsellor, Counsellor-Minister, Embassy to USA, 1952–54; Asst to Minister for For. Affairs, 1955–57; Dep. Sec. Gen., UN, 1957–60; Chief, Dept of Amer. Countries, Min. of For. Affairs, 1960–62; Amb. to USA, 1962–86. Mem., CPSU Central Cttee, 1971– (Candidate Mem., 1966–71); Chief, Internat. Dept, CPSU Central Cttee, 1986–. *Address:* Central Committee for the Communist Party of the Soviet Union, 4 Staraya Plotchad, Moscow, USSR.

DOBSON, Christopher Selby Austin, CBE 1976; FSA; Librarian, House of Lords, 1956–77; *b* 25 Aug. 1916; *s* of late Alban Tabor Austin Dobson, CB, CVO, CBE; *m* 1941, Helen Broughton (*d* 1984), *d* of late Capt. E. B. Turner, Holyhead; one *d* (one *s* decd). *Educ:* Clifton Coll.; Emmanuel Coll., Cambridge (BA). With National Council of Social Service, 1938–39. Served War of 1939–45, Lieut Middx Regt (despatches). Asst Principal (Temp.), Ministry of Education, 1946–47; Asst Librarian, House of Lords, 1947–56. *Publication:* (ed) Oxfordshire Protestation Returns 1641–42, 1955. *Recreations:* collecting books, stamps, etc. *Address:* Swan House, Symonds Lane, Linton, Cambridge CB1 6HY. *T:* Cambridge (0223) 893796. *Clubs:* Roxburghe; (Hon.) Rowfant (Cleveland).

DOBSON, Vice-Adm. David Stuart; Chief of Staff to Commander Allied Naval Forces Southern Europe, since 1991; *b* 4 Dec. 1938; *s* of Walter and Ethel Dobson; *m* 1962, Joanna Mary Counter; two *s* one *d*. *Educ:* English School, Nicosia, Cyprus; RN College, Dartmouth. Joined RN 1956; qualified Observer, 1961; served HM Ships Ark Royal, Protector, Eagle; BRNC Dartmouth, 1968–70; Flight Comdr, HMS Norfolk, 1970–72; Staff of FO Naval Air Comd, 1972–74; CO HMS Amazon, 1975–76; Naval Sec's Dept, MoD, 1976–78; Naval and Air Attaché, Athens, 1980–82; Senior Naval Officer, Falklands, 1982–83; Captain 5th Destroyer Sqdn (HMS Southampton), 1983–85; Captain of the Fleet, 1985–88; Naval Sec., 1988–90. FIPM 1991. *Recreations:* hill walking, bird watching, choral singing. *Address:* c/o Lloyd's Bank, The Square, Petersfield, Hants GU32 3HL. *Club:* Army and Navy.

DOBSON, Sir Denis (William), KCB 1969 (CB 1959); OBE 1945; QC 1971; Clerk of the Crown in Chancery and Permanent Secretary to the Lord Chancellor, 1968–77; *b* 17 Oct. 1908; *s* of late William Gordon Dobson, Newcastle upon Tyne; *m* 1st, 1934, Thelma (marr. diss. 1947), *d* of Charles Swinburne, Newcastle upon Tyne; one *s* one *d*; 2nd, 1948, Mary Elizabeth, *d* of J. A. Allen, Haywards Heath; two *s* one *d*. *Educ:* Charterhouse; Trinity Coll., Cambridge (MA, LLB). Solicitor, 1933. Served in RAF, 1940–45 (Desert Air Force, 1942–45). Called to the Bar, Middle Temple, 1951; Bencher, 1968. Dep. Clerk of the Crown in Chancery and Asst Permanent Sec. to Lord Chancellor, 1954–68. Mem., Adv. Council on Public Records, 1977–83. *Address:* 50 Egerton Crescent, SW3. *T:* 071–589 7990. *Club:* Athenæum.

See also M. W. R. Dobson.

DOBSON, Frank Gordon; MP (Lab) Holborn and St Pancras, since 1983 (Holborn and St Pancras South, 1979–83); *b* 15 March 1940; *s* of James William and Irene Shortland Dobson, York; *m* 1967, Janet Mary, *d* of Henry and Edith Alker; three *c*. *Educ:* Dunnington County Primary Sch., York; Archbishop Holgate's Grammar Sch., York; London School of Economics (BScEcon). Administrative jobs with Central Electricity Generating Bd, 1962–70, and Electricity Council, 1970–75; Asst Sec., Commn for Local Administration (local Ombudsman's office), 1975–79. Member, Camden Borough Council, 1971–76 (Leader of Council, 1973–75); Chm., Coram's Fields and Harmsworth Meml Playground, 1977–. NUR sponsored MP; front bench spokesman on educn, 1981–83, on health, 1983–87; Shadow Leader of the Commons and Party Campaign Co-ordinator, 1987–89; opposition frontbench spokesman on energy, 1989–. Chm., NHS Unlimited, 1981–89. Governor: LSE, 1986–; Inst. of Child Health, 1987–. *Address:* 22 Great Russell Mansions, Great Russell Street, WC1. *T:* 071–242 5760. *Club:* Covent Garden Community Centre.

DOBSON, Keith; *see* Dobson, W. K.

DOBSON, Michael William Romsey; Group Chief Executive, Morgan Grenfell Group plc, since 1989; *b* 13 May 1952; *s* of Sir Denis (William) Dobson, *qv*. *Educ:* Eton; Trinity Coll., Cambridge. Joined Morgan Grenfell, 1973: Morgan Grenfell NY, 1978–80, Man. Dir, 1984–85; Hd, Investment Div., 1987–88; Dep. Chief Exec., 1988–89. *Recreations:* tennis, golf, bridge. *Address:* 61 Onslow Square, SW7 3LS. *Clubs:* Turf, Queen's, Hurlingham; Racquet and Tennis (New York).

DOBSON, Sir Patrick John H.; *see* Howard-Dobson.

DOBSON, Prof. Richard Barrie, FSA; FRHistS; FBA 1988; Professor of Medieval History, and Fellow of Christ's College, University of Cambridge, since 1988; *b* 3 Nov. 1931; *s* of Richard Henry Dobson and Mary Victoria Dobson (*née* Kidd); *m* 1959, Narda Leon; one *s* one *d*. *Educ:* Barnard Castle Sch.; Wadham Coll., Oxford (BA 1st cl. Modern Hist.; MA 1958; DPhil 1963). Senior demy, Magdalen Coll., Oxford, 1957–58; Lectr in Medieval History, Univ. of St Andrews, 1958–64; University of York: Lectr, Sen. Lectr, Reader, Prof. of History, 1964–88; Dep. Vice-Chancellor, 1984–87. British Acad. Fellow, Folger Shakespeare Liby, Washington, 1974; Cornell Vis. Prof., Swarthmore Coll., USA, 1987. FRHistS 1972 (Vice-Pres., 1985–89); FSA 1979; President: Surtees Soc., 1987; Jewish Historical Soc. of England, 1990–91; Ecclesiastical History Soc., 1991–92. Life Mem., Merchant Taylors' Co, York. Gen. Editor, Yorks Archaeol. Soc., Record Series, 1981–86. *Publications:* The Peasants' Revolt of 1381, 1971, 2nd edn 1983; Durham Priory 1400–1450, 1973; The Jews of Medieval York and the Massacre of March 1190, 1974; (with J. Taylor) Rymes of Robyn Hood, 1977; (ed) York City Chamberlains' Accounts 1396–1500, 1980; (ed) The Church, Politics and Patronage in the Fifteenth Century, 1984; contrib. to A History of York Minster, 1977; articles in learned jls. *Recreations:* hill walking, cinema, chess, modern Jazz. *Address:* Christ's College, Cambridge CB2 3BU. *T:* Cambridge (0223) 334900.

DOBSON, Sir Richard (Portway), Kt 1976; President, BAT Industries Ltd, 1976–79; *b* 11 Feb. 1914; *s* of Prof. J. F. Dobson; *m* 1946, Emily Margaret Carver; one step *d*. *Educ:* Clifton Coll.; King's Coll., Cambridge. Flt-Lt, RAF, 1941–45 (Pilot). Joined British American Tobacco Co. Ltd, 1935: served in China, 1936–40; China, Rhodesia and London, 1946–76; Dir, 1955; Dep. Chm., 1962; Vice-Chm., 1968; Chm., 1970–76. Director: Molins Ltd, 1970–84; Commonwealth Development Finance, 1974–79; Exxon Corporation (USA), 1975–84; Davy Corp. Ltd, 1975–85; Foseco Minsep, 1976–85; Lloyds Bank International, 1976–84; Chm., British Leyland Ltd, 1976–77. Chm., British-North American Res. Assoc., 1976–80. *Publication:* China Cycle, 1946. *Recreations:* fly fishing, golf. *Address:* 16 Marchmont Road, Richmond upon Thames, Surrey TW10 6HQ. *T:* 081–940 1504. *Clubs:* United Oxford & Cambridge University; Richmond Golf.

DOBSON, Sue; Editor, Woman and Home, since 1982; *b* 31 Jan. 1946; *d* of Arthur and Nellie Henshaw; *m* 1966, Michael Dobson (marr. diss. 1974). *Educ:* convent schs; BA Hons CNAA. From 1964, a glorious collection of women's magazines, including Femina and Fair Lady in S Africa, working variously as fashion, cookery, beauty, home and contributing editor, editor at SA Institute of Race Relations and editor of Wedding Day and Successful Slimming in London, with breaks somewhere in between in PR and doing research into the language and learning of children. *Publication:* The Wedding Day Book, 1981, 2nd edn 1989. *Recreations:* photography, reading, travelling, exploring. *Address:* IPC Magazines, King's Reach Tower, Stamford Street, SE1 9LS. *T:* 071–261 5423.

DOBSON, (William) Keith, OBE 1988; Director, Europe Division, British Council, since 1990; *b* 20 Sept. 1945; *s* of Raymond Griffin Dobson and Margaret (*née* Wylie); *m* 1972, Valerie Guest; two *d*. *Educ:* King Edward's Grammar School, Camp Hill, Birmingham; Univ. of Keele (BA Internat. Relns 1968); Univ. of Essex (DipSoc 1972). With Clarks Ltd, Shoemakers, 1968–71; joined British Council: Lagos, 1972–75; London, 1975–77; Ankara, 1977–80; Caracas, 1980–84; Budapest, 1984–87; London, 1987–90. *Recreations:* music, cinema, bridge, woodworking. *Address:* British Council, 10 Spring Gardens, SW1A 2BN. *T:* 071–389 4787.

DOCHERTY, Dr Daniel Joseph, JP; General Medical Practitioner, 1949–87, retired; Examining Medical Officer, Department of Social Security (formerly Department of Health and Social Security), since 1982; *b* 24 Oct. 1924; *s* of Michael Joseph Docherty and Ellen Stewart; *m* 1952, Dr Rosemary Catherine Kennedy; eight *s* two *d*. *Educ:* St Aloysius' Coll.; Anderson Coll. of Medicine; Glasgow Univ. LRCP, LRCS, LRFPS. MO, King's Flight, RAF Benson, 1950. Glasgow Town Councillor, 1959–75; Sen. Magistrate, City of Glasgow, 1964–65; Chm. of Police Cttee, 1967–68; Chm. of Educn Cttee, 1971–74. Mem., MSC, 1974–77; Chm. in Scotland, Job Creation Programme, 1975–78. Member: Strathclyde Univ. Ct, 1971–72; Glasgow Univ. Ct, 1972–74; Council, Open Univ., 1972–75. JP Glasgow, 1961. *Recreation:* travel. *Address:* 92 Mansion House Gardens, Glasgow G41 3DN. *T:* 041–649 0307.

DOCKER, Rt. Rev. Ivor Colin; Bishop Suffragan of Horsham, 1975–91; *b* 3 Dec. 1925; *s* of Colonel Philip Docker, OBE, TD, DL, and Doris Gwendoline Docker (*née* Whitehill); *m* 1950, Thelma Mary, *d* of John William and Gladys Upton; one *s* one *d. Educ:* King Edward's High Sch., Birmingham; Univ. of Birmingham (BA); St Catherine's Coll., Oxford (MA). Curate of Normanton, Yorks, 1949–52; Lecturer of Halifax Parish Church, 1952–54; CMS Area Sec., 1954–59; Vicar of Midhurst, Sussex, 1959–64; RD of Midhurst, 1961–64; Vicar and RD of Seaford, 1964–71; Canon and Prebendary of Colworth in Chichester Cathedral, 1966–81; Vicar and RD of Eastbourne, 1971–75; Proctor in Convocation, 1970–75. Chm., C of E Nat. Council for Social Aid, 1987–. *Recreations:* photography, travel, reading. *Address:* Braemar, Bradley Road, Bovey Tracey, Newton Abbot, Devon TQ13 9EU. *T:* Bovey Tracey (0626) 832468.

DOCTOROW, Edgar Lawrence; Glucksman Professor of American and English Letters, New York University, since 1987; *b* 6 Jan. 1931; *s* of David R. Doctorow and Rose Doctorow Buck; *m* 1954, Helen Setzer; one *s* two *d. Educ:* Kenyon College (AB 1952); Columbia Univ. (graduate study). Script-reader, Columbia Pictures, NY, 1956–59; sen. editor, New American Library, 1959–64; editor-in-chief, 1964–69, publisher, 1968–69, Dial Press; writer-in-residence, Univ. of California, Irvine, 1969–70; Mem., Faculty, Sarah Lawrence Coll., NY, 1971–78; Creative Writing Fellow, Yale Sch. of Drama, 1974–75; Vis. Sen. Fellow, Council on Humanities, Princeton, 1980–81. Hon. degrees from Brandeis Univ., Kenyon, Hobart and William Smith Colls. Guggenheim Fellowship, 1972; Creative Arts Service Fellow, 1973–74. *Publications:* Welcome to Hard Times, 1960; Big as Life, 1966; The Book of Daniel, 1971; Ragtime, 1975 (Amer. Acad. Award, Nat. Book Critics Circle Award); Drinks Before Dinner, 1979 (play, 1978); Loon Lake, 1980; Lives of the Poets, 1984; World's Fair, 1985 (American Book Award); Billy Bathgate, 1989 (Howells Medal, Amer. Acad.; PEN/Faulkner and Nat. Books Critics Awards). *Address:* c/o Random House Publishers, 201 East 50th Street, New York, NY 10022, USA. *Club:* Century Association (NY).

DODD, Air Vice-Marshal Frank Leslie, CBE 1968; DSO 1944; DFC 1945; AFC 1944 and Bars, 1955 and 1958; AE 1945; LRPS 1987; Administrator, MacRobert Trusts, 1974–85; *b* 5 March 1919; *s* of Frank H. Dodd and Lilian (*née* Willis); *m* 1942, Joyce L. Banyard; one *s* three *d. Educ:* King Edward VI Sch., Stafford; Reading University. RAFVR, 1938; CFS course and Flying Instructor, 1940–44; No 544 Sqdn (photo-reconnaissance), 1944–46; CO 45 Sqdn (Beaufighters), 1947–48; CFS Staff and HQ Flying Trng Comd, 1948–52; pfc 1952–53; Chief Instructor CFS, 1953–55; psc 1955; CO 230 OCU Waddington (Vulcans), 1955–59; Gp Captain Trng HQ Bomber Comd, 1959–61; CO RAF Coningsby (Vulcans), 1961–63; idc 1964; AOC and Comdt CFS, 1965–68; MoD (Dir Estabs), 1968–70. Dir Gen., Linesman Project, 1970–74, retired. *Recreations:* golf, music, photography. *Address:* c/o Barclays Bank, 15 Market Square, Stafford ST16 2BE. *Club:* Royal Air Force.

DODD, Kenneth Arthur, (Ken Dodd), OBE 1982; entertainer, comedian, singer and actor; *b* 8 Nov. 1931; *s* of late Arthur and Sarah Dodd; unmarried. *Educ:* Holt High School, Liverpool. Made professional début at Empire Theatre, Nottingham, 1954; created record on London Palladium début, 1965, by starring in his own 42 week season; has also starred in more than 20 pantomimes. Now travels widely in quest to play every theatrical venue in British Isles. Shakespearean début as Malvolio, Twelfth Night, Liverpool, 1971. Record, Tears, topped British charts for six weeks; awarded two Gold, one Platinum, many Silver Discs (Love Is Like A Violin, Happiness, etc). *Relevant publication:* How Tickled I Am: Ken Dodd, by Michael Billington, 1977. *Recreations:* racing, soccer, reading, people. *Address:* 76 Thomas Lane, Knotty Ash, Liverpool L14 5NX.

DODD, William Atherton, CMG 1983; *b* 5 Feb. 1923; *s* of Frederick Dodd and Sarah Atherton; *m* 1949, Marjorie Penfold; two *d. Educ:* Chester City Grammar Sch.; Christ's Coll., Cambridge (MA, CertEd). Served War, 1942–45: Captain, 8 Gurkha Rifles. Sen. History Master, Ipswich Sch., 1947–52; Educn Officer, Dept of Educn, Tanganyika, 1952–61; Sen. Educn Officer, Min. of Educn, Tanzania, 1961–65; Lectr, Dept of Educn in Developing Countries, Univ. of London Inst. of Educn, 1965–70; Educn Adviser, ODM, 1970–77; Chief Educn Advr, 1978–83, and Under Sec. (Educn Div.), 1980–83, ODA. Consultant: UC Cardiff, 1983–87; Inst. of Educn, Univ. of London, 1983–91. UK Mem., Unesco Exec. Bd, 1983–85. Chm., Christopher Cox Meml Fund, 1983–. *Publications:* A Mapbook of Exploration, 1965; Primary School Inspection in New Countries, 1968; Education for Self-Reliance in Tanzania, 1969; (with J. Cameron) Society, Schools and Progress in Tanzania, 1970; (ed) Teacher at Work, 1970; (with C. Criper) Report on the Teaching of the English Language in Tanzania, 1985. *Recreations:* walking, music, cricket. *Address:* 20 Bayham Road, Sevenoaks, Kent TN13 3XD. *T:* Sevenoaks (0732) 454238. *Clubs:* MCC; Sevenoaks Vine.

DODDERIDGE, Morris, CBE 1974 (OBE 1962); British Council Representative, Rome, 1970–75, retired; *b* 17 Oct. 1915; *s* of Reginald William Dodderidge and Amy Andrew; *m* 1941, Esme Williams; two *s* one *d. Educ:* Hertford Grammar Sch.; King's Coll., London; Inst. Educn, London. BA 1st cl. hons English 1937; Brewer Prize for Lit.; Teachers Dip. 1938; DipEd 1952. Asst Master, Hele's Sch., Exeter, 1938–40. War of 1939–45, Royal Signals; served N Africa, Italy, Austria (Captain, despatches). Joined British Council, 1946: Dir of Studies, Milan, 1947–53; Rep., Norway, 1953–57; Teaching of English Liaison Officer, 1957–59; Dir, Recruitment Dept, 1959–64; Controller: Recruitment Div., 1964–66; Overseas Div. A, 1966–67; Home Div. I, 1967–68; Appts Div., 1968–70. *Publications:* Man on the Matterhorn, 1940; (with W. R. Lee) Time for a Song, 1965. *Recreations:* golf, swimming. *Address:* River Cottage, Church Street, Presteigne, Powys LD8 2BU. *T:* Presteigne (0544) 267609.

DODDS, Denis George, CBE 1977; LLB (London); CompIEE; Solicitor; Chairman, British Approval Service for Electricity Cables Ltd, since 1982; *b* 25 May 1913; *s* of Herbert Yeaman Dodds and Violet Katharine Dodds; *m* 1937, Muriel Reynolds Smith; two *s* three *d. Educ:* Rutherford Coll., Newcastle upon Tyne; King's Coll., Durham Univ. Asst Solicitor and Asst Town Clerk, Gateshead, 1936–41. Served Royal Navy (Lieut RNVR), 1941–46. Dep. Town Clerk and Dep. Clerk of the Peace, City of Cardiff, 1946–48; Sec., S Wales Electricity Board, 1948–56; Chief Industrial Relations Officer, CEA and Industrial Relations Adviser, Electricity Council, 1957–59; Dep. Chm., 1960–62, Chm., 1962–77, Merseyside and N Wales Electricity Bd; Chairman: Merseyside Chamber of Commerce and Industry, 1976–78; Port of Preston Adv. Bd, 1978; Assoc. of Members of State Industry Boards, 1976–89. Member: CBI Council for Wales, 1960–78; NW Economic Planning Council, 1971; Dir, Development Corporation for Wales, 1970–83. Mem., Nat. Adv. Council for Employment of the Disabled, 1978–. *Recreations:* music and gardening. *Address:* Corners, 28 Grange Park, Westbury on Trym, Bristol BS9 4BP. *T:* Bristol (0272) 621440.

DODDS, George Christopher Buchanan, CMG 1977; Assistant Under-Secretary of State, Ministry of Defence, 1964–76; *b* 8 Oct. 1916; *o s* of George Hepple Dodds and Gladys Marion (*née* Ferguson), Newcastle upon Tyne; *m* 1944, Olive Florence Wilmot Ling; no *c. Educ:* Rugby; Gonville and Caius Coll., Cambridge (BA). Entered Secretary's Dept, Admiralty, 1939; Royal Marines, 1940–41; Private Sec. to Sec. of the Admiralty, 1941–43; Asst Private Sec. to Prime Minister, June-Aug. 1944; Asst Sec., 1951; idc, 1959. *Recreations:* bird-watching, walking, golf, bridge. *Address:* 5 Bryanston Square, W1. *T:* 071–262 2852. *Club:* Royal Mid-Surrey Golf.

DODDS, James Pickering, CB 1954; Under-Secretary, Department of Health and Social Security, 1968–73; *b* 7 Feb. 1913; *s* of James Thompson and Elizabeth Fingland Dodds; *m* 1942, Ethel Mary Gill (*d* 1987); two *d. Educ:* Queen Elizabeth's Grammar Sch., Darlington; Jesus Coll., Cambridge. Entered Ministry of Health, 1935; Nuffield Home Civil Service Travelling Fellowship, 1950; Under-Sec., 1951; Dir of Establishments and Orgn, 1965–68. *Address:* 17 Herne Road, Oundle, Peterborough PE8 4BS.

DODDS, Nigel Alexander; barrister; Lord Mayor of Belfast, 1988–89; *b* 20 Aug. 1958; *s* of Joseph Alexander and Doreen Elizabeth Dodds; *m* 1985, Diana Joan Harris; two *s. Educ:* Portora Royal Sch., Enniskillen; St John's Coll., Cambridge (MA); Inst. of Professional Legal Studies, Belfast (Cert. of Professional Legal Studies). Called to the Bar, NI, 1981. Mem., Belfast City Council, 1985– (Chm., F and GP Cttee, 1985–87); Alderman, Castle Area, 1989–. Vice Pres., Assoc. of Local Authorities of NI, 1988–89. Mem., Senate, QUB, 1987–. *Address:* City Hall, Belfast BT1 5GS.

DODDS, Sir Ralph (Jordan), 2nd Bt *cr* 1964; *b* 25 March 1928; *o s* of Sir (Edward) Charles Dodds, 1st Bt, MVO, FRS, and Constance Elizabeth (*d* 1969), *o d* of late J. T. Jordan, Darlington; *S* father, 1973; *m* 1954, Marion, *er d* of late Sir Daniel Thomas Davies, KCVO; two *d. Educ:* Winchester; RMA, Sandhurst. Regular commission, 13/18th Royal Hussars, 1948; served UK and abroad; Malaya, 1953 (despatches); resigned, 1958. Underwriting Member of Lloyd's, 1964. *Address:* 49 Sussex Square, W2 2SP. *Clubs:* Cavalry and Guards, Hurlingham.

DODDS-PARKER, Sir (Arthur) Douglas, Kt 1973; MA (Oxford); company director since 1946; *b* 5 July 1909; *o s* of A. P. Dodds-Parker, FRCS, Oxford; *m* 1946, Aileen, *d* of late Norman B. Coster and late Mrs Alvin Dodd, Grand Detour, Ill., USA; one *s. Educ:* Winchester; Magdalen Coll., Oxford. BA in Modern History, 1930; MA 1934. Entered Sudan Political Service, 1930; Kordofan Province, 1931–34; Asst Private Sec. to Governor-General, Khartoum, 1934–35; Blue Nile Province, 1935–38; Public Security Dept, Khartoum, 1938–39; resigned 1938; joined Grenadier Guards, 1939; employed on special duties, March 1940; served in London, Cairo, East African campaign, North Africa, Italy and France, 1940–45; Mission Comdr, SOE, Western and Central Mediterranean, 1943–44; Col, 1944 (despatches, French Legion of Honour, Croix de Guerre). MP (C): Banbury Div. of Oxon, 1945–Sept. 1959; Cheltenham, 1964–Sept. 1974; Jt Parly Under-Sec. of State for Foreign Affairs, Nov. 1953–Oct. 1954, Dec. 1955–Jan. 1957; Parly Under-Sec. for Commonwealth Relations, Oct. 1954–Dec. 1955. Chairman: British Empire Producers Organisation; Joint East and Central Africa Board, 1947–50; Conservative Commonwealth Council, 1960–64; Cons. Parly Foreign and Commonwealth Cttee, 1970–73; Europe Atlantic Gp, 1976–79; Delegate to Council of Europe, North Atlantic and W European Assemblies, 1965–72; led Parly Delegn to China, 1972; Mem., British Parly Delegn to European Parlt, Strasbourg, 1973–75. Mem., Regtl Bd, FANY, 1945–. Freeman, City of London, 1983. *Publications:* Setting Europe Ablaze, 1983; Political Eunuch, 1986. *Address:* 9 North Court, Great Peter Street, SW1P 3LL; The Lighthouse, West Port, New York 12993, USA. *Clubs:* Carlton, Special Forces (Pres., 1977–81), Institute of Directors; Vincent's (Oxford); Leander.

DODGE, John V.; Senior Editorial Consultant, Encyclopædia Britannica, since 1972; Chairman, Board of Editors, Encyclopædia Britannica Publishers, since 1977; *b* 25 Sept. 1909; *s* of George Dannel Dodge and Mary Helen Porter; *m* 1935, Jean Elizabeth Plate; two *s* two *d. Educ:* Northwestern Univ., Evanston, Ill., USA; Univ. of Bordeaux, Bordeaux, France. Free-lance writer, 1931–32; Editor, Northwestern Alumni News and official publications of Northwestern Univ., 1932–35; Exec. Sec., Northwestern Univ. Alumni Assoc., 1937–38; Asst Editor, Encyclopædia Britannica, and Associate Editor, Britannica Book of the Year, 1938–43. US Army, 1943–46 (Intelligence). Associate Editor, Ten Eventful Years and Asst Editor, Encyclopædia Britannica, 1946–50; Editor, Britannica World Language Dictionary, 1954; Managing Editor, Encyclopædia, 1950–60; Executive Editor, 1960–64; Senior Vice-Pres., Editorial, 1964–65; Senior Editorial Consultant, 1965–70; Vice-Pres., Editorial, 1970–72. Conseiller Editorial, Encyclopædia Universalis (Paris), 1968–; Editorial Advisor: Britannica Internat. Encyclopædia (in Japanese), Tokyo, 1969–; Enciclopedia Mirador (Rio de Janeiro) and Enciclopedia Barsa (Mexico City), 1974–; Chm., Editl Bd, Enciclopedia Hispánica (Mexico City and Madrid-Barcelona), 1989–. *Address:* 3851 Mission Hills Road, Northbrook, Ill 60062, USA. *T:* (708) 272–0254.

DODSON, family name of **Baron Monk Bretton.**

DODSON, Sir Derek (Sherborne Lindsell), KCMG 1975 (CMG 1963); MC 1945; DL; HM Diplomatic Service, retired; Special Representative of Secretary of State for Foreign and Commonwealth Affairs, since 1981; *b* 20 Jan. 1920; *e* and *o* surv. *s* of late Charles Sherborne Dodson, MD, and Irene Frances Lindsell; *m* 1952, Julie Maynard Barnes; one *s* one *d. Educ:* Stowe; RMC Sandhurst. Commissioned as 2nd Lieut in Royal Scots Fusiliers, 1939, and served in Army until Feb. 1948. Served War of 1939–45 (MC): India, UK, Middle East, and with Partisans in Greece and N Italy. Mil. Asst to Brit. Comr, Allied Control Commn for Bulgaria, July 1945–Sept. 1946; GSO 3, War Office, Oct. 1946–Nov. 1947; apptd a Mem. HM Foreign Service, 1948; 2nd Sec., 1948; Acting Vice-Consul at Salonika, Sept. 1948; Acting Consul Gen. there in 1949 and 1950; Second Sec., Madrid, 1951; promoted First Sec., Oct. 1951; transferred to Foreign Office, Sept. 1953; apptd Private Sec. to Minister of State for Foreign Affairs, 1955; First Sec. and Head of Chancery, Prague, Nov. 1958; Chargé d'Affaires there in 1959, 1960, 1961, 1962; promoted and apptd Consul at Elisabethville, 1962; Transf. FO and apptd Head of the Central Dept, 1963; Counsellor, British Embassy, Athens, 1966–69; Ambassador: to Hungary, 1970–73; to Brazil, 1973–77; to Turkey, 1977–80. Chm., Beaver Guarantee Ltd, 1984–86; Dir, Benguela Rly Co., 1984–. Chm., Anglo-Turkish Soc., 1982–. Mem., Bd of Governors, United World College of the Atlantic, 1982–. DL Lincoln, 1987. Order of the Southern Cross, Brazil. *Recreations:* shooting, fishing, walking. *Address:* 47 Ovington Street, SW3. *T:* 071–589 5055; Gable House, Leadenham, Lincoln. *T:* Loveden (0400) 72212. *Clubs:* Boodle's, Travellers'.

DODSON, Robert North; *see* North, R.

DODSWORTH, Geoffrey Hugh, FCA, JP; Chairman: Dodsworth & Co. Ltd, since 1988; Jorvik Finance Corporation Ltd, since 1986; Director, First International Leasing Corp., since 1990; *b* 7 June 1928; *s* of late Walter J. J. Dodsworth and Doris M. Baxter; *m* 1st, 1949, Isabel Neale (decd); one *d*; 2nd, 1971, Elizabeth Ann Beeston; one *s* one *d. Educ:* St Peter's Sch., York. MP (C) Herts SW, Feb. 1974–Oct. 1979, resigned. Mem. York City Council, 1959–65; JP York 1961, later JP Herts. Dir, Grindlays Bank Ltd, 1976–80; Chief Exec., Grindlay Brandts Ltd, 1977–80; Pres. and Chief Exec., Oceanic Finance Corp., 1980–85, Dep. Chm., 1985–86; Chm., Oceanic Financial Services, 1985–86; Dir,

County Properties Group, 1987–88. *Recreation:* riding. *Address:* Well Hall, Well, Bedale, N Yorks DL8 2PX. *T:* Bedale (0677) 70223. *Club:* Carlton.

DODSWORTH, Prof. (James) Martin; Professor of English, Royal Holloway and Bedford New College, University of London, since 1987; *b* 10 Nov. 1935; *s* of Walter Edward and Kathleen Ida Dodsworth; *m* 1967, Joanna Rybicka; one *s*. *Educ:* St George's Coll., Weybridge; Univ. of Fribourg, Switzerland; Wadham Coll., Oxford (MA). Asst Lectr and Lectr in English, Birkbeck Coll., London, 1961–67; Lectr and Sen. Lectr, Royal Holloway Coll., later Royal Holloway and Bedford New Coll., London, 1967–87. Vis. Lectr, Swarthmore Coll., Pa, 1966. Chairman: English Assoc., 1987–; Cttee for University English, 1988–90. Editor, English, 1976–87. *Publications:* (ed) The Survival of Poetry, 1970; Hamlet Closely Observed, 1985; (ed) English Economis'd, 1989; contribs to The Guardian, Essays in Criticism, The Review, etc. *Recreations:* reading, eating and drinking, short walks. *Address:* 59 Temple Street, Brill, Bucks HP18 9SU. *T:* Brill (0844) 237106.

DODSWORTH, Sir John Christopher S.; *see* Smith-Dodsworth.

DODSWORTH, Martin; *see* Dodsworth, J. M.

DODWELL, Prof. Charles Reginald, MA, PhD, LittD; FBA 1973; FRHistS, FSA; Pilkington Professor of History of Art and Director of Whitworth Gallery, University of Manchester, 1966–89, now Professor Emeritus; *b* 3 Feb. 1922; *s* of William Henry Walter and Blanche Dodwell; *m* 1942, Sheila Juliet Fletcher; one *s* one *d*. *Educ:* Gonville and Caius Coll., Cambridge (MA, PhD, LittD). Served War, Navy, 1941–45. Research Fellow, Caius Coll., 1950–51. Sen. Research Fellow, Warburg Inst., 1950–53; Lambeth Librarian, 1953–58; Fellow, Lectr, Librarian, Trinity Coll., Cambridge, 1958–66. Visiting scholar, Inst. of Advanced Studies, Princeton, USA, 1965–66. *Publications:* The Canterbury School of Illumination, 1954; Lambeth Palace, 1958; The Great Lambeth Bible, 1959; The St Albans Psalter (section 2) 1960; Theophilus: De Diversis Artibus, 1961; Reichenau Reconsidered, 1965; Painting in Europe 800–1200, 1971; Early English Manuscripts in Facsimile, vol. xviii (section 2), 1972; Anglo-Saxon Art: a new perspective, 1982; The Pictorial Arts of the West 800–1200, 1991; articles in Burlington Magazine, Gazette des Beaux Arts, Atti del 18 Congresso Internazionale di studi sull'alto medioevo (Spoleto), Jumièges, Congrès Scientifique du 13 Centenaire, l'Archéologie, etc. *Recreations:* opera, Shakespearean studies. *Address:* The Yews, 37 South Road, Taunton, Somerset TA1 3DU. *T:* Taunton (0823) 323640.

DODWORTH, Air Vice-Marshal Peter, OBE 1982; AFC 1971; Defence Attaché and Head of British Defence Staff (Washington), since 1991; *b* 12 Sept. 1940; *e s* of Eric and Edna Dodworth; *m* 1963, Kay Parry; three *s*. *Educ:* Southport Grammar Sch.; Leeds Univ. (BSc Physics, 1961). MRAeS 1970. Served: 54 Sqn Hunters, 1963–65; 4 FTS Gnats, 1965–67; Central Flying Sch., 1967–68; Harrier Conversion Team, 1969–72; Air Staff RAF Germany, 1972–76; OC Ops, RAF Wittering, 1976–79; ndc 1980; Air Comdr, Belize, 1980–82; staff, RAF Staff Coll., 1982–83; Stn comdr, RAF Wittering, 1983–85; Command Group Exec., HQ AAFCE, Ramstein, 1985–87; RCDS, 1987; Dir of Personnel, MoD, 1988–91. *Recreations:* squash, golf, DIY, reading. *Address:* British Defence Staff, BFPO 2. *T:* (202) 898 4412. *Club:* Royal Air Force.

DOGGART, George Hubert Graham; Headmaster, King's School, Bruton, 1972–85; *b* 18 July 1925; *e s* of late Alexander Graham Doggart and Grace Carlisle Hannan; *m* 1960, Susan Mary, *d* of R. I. Beattie, Eastbourne; one *s* two *d*. *Educ:* Winchester; King's Coll., Cambridge. BA History, 1950; MA 1955. Army, 1943–47 (Sword of Honour, 161 OCTU, Mons, 1944); Coldstream Guards. On staff at Winchester, 1950–72 (exchange at Melbourne C of E Grammar Sch., 1963); Housemaster, 1964–72. HMC Schools rep. on Nat. Cricket Assoc., 1964–75; President: English Schools Cricket Assoc., 1965–; Quidnuncs, 1983–88; Cricket Soc., 1983–; Member: Cricket Council, 1968–71, 1972, 1983–; MCC Cttee, 1975–78, 1979–81, 1982– (Pres., 1981–82; Treas., 1987–). Captain, Butterflies CC, 1986–. *Publications:* (ed) The Heart of Cricket: memoir of H. S. Altham, 1967; (jtly) Lord Be Praised: the story of MCC's bicentenary celebrations, 1988; (jtly) Oxford and Cambridge Cricket, 1989. *Recreations:* literary and sporting (captained Cambridge v Oxford at cricket, Association football, rackets and squash, 1949–50; played in Rugby fives, 1950; played for England v W Indies, two tests, 1950; captained Sussex, 1954). *Address:* 19 Westgate, Chichester, West Sussex PO19 3ET. *Clubs:* MCC, Lord's Taverners', Hawks (Cambridge).

DOHA, Aminur Rahman S.; *see* Shams-ud Doha, A. R.

DOHERTY, Prof. Peter Charles; FRS 1987; FAA 1983; Chairman, Department of Immunology, St Jude Children's Research Hospital, since 1988; *b* 15 Oct. 1940; *s* of Eric C. and Linda M. Doherty; *m* 1965, Penelope Stephens; two *s*. *Educ:* Univ. of Queensland (BVSc, MVSc); Univ. of Edinburgh (PhD). Veterinary Officer, Queensland Dept of Primary Industries, 1962–67; Scientific Officer, Moredun Research Inst., Edinburgh, 1967–71; Research Fellow, Dept of Microbiology, John Curtin Sch. of Med. Research, Canberra, 1972–75; Associate Prof., later Prof., Wistar Inst., Philadelphia, 1975–82; Prof. of Experimental Pathology, John Curtin Sch. of Medical Res., ANU, 1982–88. Paul Ehrlich Prize and Medal for Immunology, 1983; Gairdner Internat. Award for Med. Research, 1987. *Publications:* papers in scientific jls. *Recreations:* walking, reading, ski-ing. *Address:* c/o St Jude Children's Research Hospital, Memphis, Tenn 38101–0318, USA. *T:* 901 522 0473.

DOHMANN, Barbara; QC 1987; a Recorder, since 1990; *b* Berlin; *d* of Paul Dohmann and Dora Dohmann (*née* Thiele). *Educ:* schools in Germany and USA; Univs of Erlangen, Mainz and Paris. Called to the Bar, Gray's Inn, 1971. *Recreations:* gardening, opera, fiction. *Address:* 2 Hare Court, Temple, EC4. *T:* 071–583 1770. *Club:* CWIL.

DOIG, Very Rev. Dr Andrew Beveridge; *b* 18 Sept. 1914; *s* of George and Hannah Doig; *m* 1st, 1940, Nan Carruthers (*d* 1947); one *d*; 2nd, 1950, Barbara Young; one *s* one *d*. *Educ:* Hyndland Secondary Sch., Glasgow; Glasgow Univ. (MA, BD; Hon. DD 1974); Union Theol Seminary, New York (STM). Ordained, 1938; Church of Scotland Missionary to Nyasaland, 1939–63; service included: Dist Missionary and Sec. of Mission Council; Sen. Army Chaplain, E Africa Comd, 1941–45; Mem., Legislative Council; Mem., Adv. Cttee on African Educn, and Coll. Council, Univ. of Rhodesia and Nyasaland; Regional Sec., Nyasaland and N Rhodesia; seconded to represent African interests in Fed. Parlt, Rhodesias and Nyasaland, 1953–58; Gen. Sec., Synod of Ch. of Central Africa (Presbyterian), 1958–63; Minister, St John's and King's Park, Dalkeith, Scotland, 1963–72; Gen. Sec., National Bible Soc. of Scotland, 1972–82; Moderator of the Gen. Assembly of the Church of Scotland, 1981–82. *Address:* The Eildons, Moulin, Pitlochry. *T:* Pitlochry (0796) 2892.

DOIG, Peter Muir; *b* 27 Sept. 1911; *m* 1938, Emily Scott; two *s*. *Educ:* Blackness Sch., Dundee. Served RAF, 1941–46. Sales Supervisor with T. D. Duncan Ltd, Bakers, Dundee, until 1963. Mem., TGWU; joined Labour Party, 1930; Mem. of Dundee Town Council, 1953–63, Hon. Treasurer, 1959–63. Contested (Lab) S Aberdeen, 1959; MP (Lab) Dundee West, Nov. 1963–1979. *Recreation:* chess. *Address:* 2 Westwater Place, Wormit, Fife.

DOIG, Ralph Herbert, CMG 1974; CVO 1954; *b* 24 Feb. 1909; *s* of late William and Rose Doig; *m* 1937, Barbara Crock; two *s* four *d*. *Educ:* Guildford Grammar Sch.; University of Western Australia (BA, DipCom). Entered Public Service of WA, 1926; Private Sec. to various Premiers, 1929–41; Asst Under-Sec., Premier's Dept, 1941; Under-Sec., Premier's Dept, and Clerk of Executive Council, Perth, Western Australia, 1945–65; Public Service Comr, W Australia, 1965–71; Chm., Public Service Board, WA, 1971–74. State Director: visit to Western Australia of the Queen and the Duke of Edinburgh, 1954; visit of the Duke of Edinburgh for British Empire and Commonwealth Games, 1962; visit of the Queen and the Duke of Edinburgh, 1963. *Recreation:* bowls. *Address:* 27 Marine Terrace, Sorrento, WA 6020, Australia. *T:* 448–6843.

DOLBY, Ray Milton, Hon. OBE 1986; PhD; engineering company executive; electrical engineer; Owner and Chairman, Dolby Laboratories Inc., San Francisco and London, since 1965; *b* Portland, Ore, 18 Jan. 1933; *s* of Earl Milton Dolby and Esther Eufemia (*née* Strand); *m* 1966, Dagmar Baumert; two *s*. *Educ:* San Jose State Coll.; Washington Univ.; Stanford Univ. (Beach Thompson award, BS Elec. Engrg); Pembroke Coll., Cambridge (Marshall schol., 1957–60, Draper's studentship, 1959–61, NSF Fellow, 1960–61; PhD Physics 1961; Fellow, 1961–63; research in long-wave length x-rays, 1957–63; Hon. Fellow 1983). Electronic technician/jun. engr, Ampex Corp., Redwood City, Calif, 1949–53. Served US Army 1953–54. Engr, 1955–57; Sen. Engr, 1957; UNESCO Advr, Central Sci. Instruments Org., Punjab, 1963–65; Cons., UKAEA, 1962–63. Inventions, research, pubns in video tape rec., x-ray microanalysis, noise reduction and quality improvements in audio and video systems; 50 UK patents. Trustee, Univ. High Sch., San Francisco, 1978–84; Mem., Marshall Scholarships Selection Cttee, 1979–85; Dir, San Francisco Opera; Governor, San Francisco Symphony. Fellow: Audio Engrg Soc. (Silver Medal, 1971; Governor, 1972–74, 1979–84; Pres., 1980–81); Brit. Kinematograph, Sound, TV Soc.; Soc. Motion Picture, TV Engrs (S. L. Warner award, 1978; Alexander M. Poniatoff Gold Medal, 1982; Progress Medal, 1983); Inst. of Broadcast Sound, 1987. MIEEE; Tau Beta Pi. Other Awards: Emmy, for contrib. to Ampex video recorder, 1957, and for noise reduction systems on video recorder sound tracks, 1989; Trendsetter, Billboard, 1971; Lyre, Inst. High Fidelity, 1972; Emile Berliner Assoc. Maker of Microphone award, 1972; Top 200 Execs Bi-Centennial, 1976; Sci. and Engrg, 1979, Oscar, 1989, Acad. of Motion Picture Arts and Scis; Man of the Yr, Internat. Tape Assoc., 1987; Pioneer Award, Internat. Teleproduction Soc., 1988; Eduard Rhein Ring, Eduard Rhein Foundn, 1988; Life Achievement Award, Cinema Audio Soc., 1989. *Recreations:* yachting, skiing. *Address:* (home) 3340 Jackson Street, San Francisco, Calif 94118, USA. *T:* (415) 563–6947; (office) 100 Potrero Avenue, San Francisco, Calif 94103. *T:* (415) 558–0200.

DOLCI, Danilo; Coordinator, Centro Studi e Iniziative, since 1958 (Founder); *b* Sesana, Trieste, 1924; *s* of Enrico Dolci and Mely Kontely. *Educ:* University of Rome; University of Milan. Came to Sicily to work for improvement of social conditions, 1952; arrested and tried for non-violent "reverse strike" to find work for unemployed, 1958. Mem. Internat. Council of War Resisters' International, 1963. Hon. DPhil, Univ. of Berne, 1968; Lenin Peace Prize, 1958; Gold Medal, Accademia Nazionale dei Lincei, 1969; Sonning Prize, 1971; Etna Taormina Poetry Prize, 1975; Viareggio Internat. Prize, 1979. *Publications:* Banditi a Partinico, 1955; Inchiesta a Palermo, 1956; Spreco, 1960; Racconti siciliani, 1963; Verso un mondo nuovo, 1964 (trans. A New World in the Making, 1965); Chi Gioca Solo, 1966; Chissà se i pesci piangono (documentazione di un'esperienza educativa), 1973; Non esiste il silenzio, 1974; Esperienze e riflessioni, 1974; Creatura di creature, 1983; Palpitare di nessi, 1985; The World is One Creature, 1986; Dal trasmettere al comunicare, 1988; Occhi ancora rimangono sepolti, 1988; Bozza di Manifesto, 1989; Se gli occhi fioriscono, 1990. *Address:* Centro Studi, Largo Scalia 5, Partinico (PA), Italy. *T:* 091/8781905.

DOLE, Bob; *see* Dole, R. J.

DOLE, John Anthony; Controller and Chief Executive of HM Stationery Office, and the Queen's Printer of Acts of Parliament, 1987–89, retired; *b* 14 Oct. 1929; *s* of Thomas Stephen Dole and Winifred Muriel (*née* Henderson); *m* 1952, Patricia Ivy Clements; two *s*. *Educ:* Bideford Grammar Sch.; Berkhamsted Sch. Air Ministry: Exec. Officer, 1950; Higher Exec. Officer, 1959; Principal, 1964; Ministry of Transport: Principal, 1965; Asst Sec. (Roads Programme), 1968; Administrator of Sports Council, 1972–75; Under Sec., Freight Directorate, 1976–78; Dir, Senior Staff Management, Depts of the Environment and Transport, 1978–82; Controller of Supplies, PSA, DoE, 1982–84; Controller of the Crown Suppliers, 1984–86. *Publications: plays:* Cat on the Fiddle, 1964; Shock Tactics, 1966; Lucky for Some, 1968; Once in a Blue Moon, 1972; Top Gear, 1976. *Recreations:* writing, philately.

DOLE, Robert Joseph, (Bob Dole); Purple Heart; United States Senator, since 1968; Senate Republican Leader, United States Senate, since 1985; *b* Russell, Kansas, 22 July 1923; *s* of Doran and Bina Dole; *m* 1975, Elizabeth Hanford; one *d*. *Educ:* Univ. of Kansas (AB); Washburn Municipal Univ. (LLB). Served US Army, 1943–48; Platoon Ldr, 10th Mountain Div., Italy; wounded and decorated twice for heroic achievement; Captain. Kansas Legislature, 1951–53; Russell County Attorney, Kansas, 1953–61; US House of Representatives, 1960–68. *Address:* Office of the Republican Leader, United States Senate, Washington, DC 20510, USA. *T:* (202) 224-3135.

DOLL, Sir Richard; *see* Doll, Sir W. R. S.

DOLL, Prof. Sir (William) Richard (Shaboe), Kt 1971; OBE 1956; FRS 1966; DM, MD, FRCP, DSc; Hon. Consultant, Imperial Cancer Research Fund Cancer Studies Unit, Radcliffe Infirmary, Oxford, since 1983; first Warden, Green College, Oxford, 1979–83; *b* Hampton, 28 Oct. 1912; *s* of Henry William Doll and Amy Kathleen Shaboe; *m* 1949, Joan Mary Faulkner, MB, BS, MRCP, DPH; one *s* one *d*. *Educ:* Westminster Sch. (Hon. Fellow, 1991); St Thomas's Hosp. Med. Sch., London. MB, BS 1937; MD 1945; FRCP 1957; DSc London 1958. RAMC, 1939–45. Appts with Med. Research Council, 1946–69; Mem. Statistical Research Unit, 1948; Dep. Dir, 1959; Dir, 1961–69. Hon. Associate Physician, Central Middlesex Hosp., 1949–69; Teacher in Medical Statistics and Epidemiology, University Coll. Hosp. Med. Sch., 1963–69; Regius Prof. of Medicine, Oxford Univ., 1969–79. Member: MRC, 1970–74; Royal Commn on Environmental Pollution, 1973–79; Standing Commn on Energy and the Environment, 1978–81; Scientific Council of Internat. Cancer Research Agency, 1966–70 and 1975–78; Council, Royal Society, 1970–71 (a Vice-Pres., 1970–71); Chairman: Adverse Reaction Sub-Cttee, Cttee on Safety of Medicines, 1970–77; UK Co-ordinating Cttee on Cancer Research, 1972–77. Hon. Lectr London Sch. of Hygiene and Tropical Med., 1956–62 (Hon. Fellow 1982); Milroy Lectr, RCP, 1953; Marc Daniels Lectr, RCP, 1969; Harveian Orator, RCP, 1982; William Julius Mickle Fellow, Univ. of London, 1955. Hon. Foreign Member: Norwegian Acad. of Scis, Amer. Acad. of Arts and Scis. Hon DSc: Newcastle, 1969; Belfast, 1972; Reading, 1973; Newfoundland, 1973; Stony Brook, 1988; Harvard, 1988; London, 1988; Oxon, 1989; Hon. DM Tasmania, 1976. David Anderson Berry Prize (jt), RSE 1958; Bisset Hawkins Medal, RCP, 1962; UN award for cancer research, 1962; Gairdner Award, Toronto, 1970; Buchanan Medal, Royal Soc., 1972; Presidential award, NY Acad. Sci., 1974; Prix Griffuel, Paris, 1976; Gold Medal, RIPH&H, 1977; Mott Award, Gen. Motors' Cancer Res. Foundn, 1979; Bruce Medal, Amer. Coll. of Physicians, 1981; National Award, Amer. Cancer Soc., 1981; Gold Medal, BMA, 1983; Conrad Röntgen prize, Accademia dei Lincei, 1984; Johann-Georg-Zimmermann Prize, Hanover, 1985; Royal Medal, Royal Soc., 1986. *Publications:* Prevention of Cancer: pointers from epidemiology, 1967; (jtly) Causes of Cancer, 1982; articles in scientific journals on aetiology of lung cancer, leukaemia and other cancers, also aetiology and treatment of peptic ulcer, effects of ionizing radiations, oral contraceptives; author (jt) Med. Research Council's Special Report Series, 1951, 1957, 1964. *Recreations:* food and conversation. *Address:* 12 Rawlinson Road, Oxford OX2 6UE.

DOLLERY, Sir Colin (Terence), Kt 1987; FRCP; Professor of Medicine, since 1987, and Dean, since 1991, Royal Postgraduate Medical School, University of London; *b* 14 March 1931; *s* of Cyril Robert and Thelma Mary Dollery; *m* 1958, Diana Myra (*née* Stedman); one *s* one *d*. *Educ:* Lincoln Sch.; Birmingham Univ. (BSc, MB,ChB); FRCP 1968. House officer: Queen Elizabeth Hosp., Birmingham; Hammersmith Hosp., and Brompton Hosp., 1956–58; Hammersmith Hospital: Med. Registrar, 1958–60; Sen. Registrar and Tutor in Medicine, 1960–62; Consultant Physician, 1962–; Lectr in Medicine, 1962–65, Prof. of Clinical Pharmacology, 1965–87, Royal Postgrad. Med. Sch. Member: MRC, 1982–84; UGC, subseq. UFC, 1984–. Hon. Mem., Assoc. of Amer. Physicians, 1982. Chevalier de l'Ordre National du Mérite (France), 1976. *Publications:* The Retinal Circulation, 1971 (New York); numerous papers in scientific jls concerned with high blood pressure and drug action. *Recreations:* travel, amateur radio, work. *Address:* 101 Corringham Road, NW11 7DL. *T:* 081–458 2616. *Club:* Athenæum.

DOLLEY, Christopher; Chairman, Damis Agencies Ltd, since 1983; *b* 11 Oct. 1931; *yr s* of late Dr Leslie George Francis Dolley and of Jessie, Otford, Kent; *m* 1966, Christine Elizabeth Cooper; three *s*. *Educ:* Bancrofts Sch.; Corpus Christi Coll., Cambridge. Joined Unilever, 1954; with Unilever subsidiaries, 1954–62: G. B. Ollivant Ltd, 1954–59; United Africa Co., 1959–62. Joined Penguin Books Ltd as Export Manager, 1962; became Dir, 1964, Man. Dir, 1970–73, Chm., 1971–73; Dir for Book Develt, IPC, 1973–77. Exec. Vice-Pres., Penguin Books Inc., Baltimore, 1966; Director: Penguin Publishing Co., 1969–73 (Jt Man. Dir, 1969); Pearson Longman Ltd, 1970–73; The Hamlyn Group, 1971–81. Mem., Nat. Film Finance Corp., 1971–81; Dir, Nat. Film Trustee Corp., 1971–81. *Publication:* (ed) The Penguin Book of English Short Stories, 1967. *Recreations:* golf, gardening, collecting. *Address:* Le Bosq, Taminage, 47120 Duras, France. *T:* 53 83 77 88. *Clubs:* Savile; 14 West Hamilton Street (Baltimore, Md).

DOLLING, Francis Robert; Director: Barclays International (Chairman, 1985–86); Barclays Bank PLC (Deputy Chairman, 1983–85); Chairman, Barclays Merchant Bank Ltd, 1980–85; *b* 21 Jan. 1923; *s* of Frederick George Dolling and Edith Lilian Auriel; *m* 1949, Maisie Alice Noquet; two *d*. *Educ:* Tottenham County School. Served RAF, 1940–47. Joined Barclays Bank DCO, 1947; served in various overseas territories; Managing Director, Barclays National Bank Ltd, South Africa, 1974; Director and Sen. General Manager, Barclays Bank Internat. Ltd, and Director, Barclays Bank Ltd, 1976; Vice-Chm., Barclays Bank, 1980–83. *Recreations:* gardening, golf. *Club:* Royal Automobile.

DOLMETSCH, Carl Frederick, CBE 1954; Director of Haslemere Festival since 1940; specialist and authority on early music and instruments; recording artist in England and America; *b* 23 Aug. 1911; *s* of Arnold Dolmetsch and Mabel Johnston; *m*; one *s* two *d* (and one *s* decd). *Educ:* privately. Began studying music with Arnold Dolmetsch at age of 4; first performed in public at 7, first concert tour at 8, first broadcast on violin and viol, 1925, at 14 years of age; virtuoso recorder-player at 15. Toured and broadcast in America, 1935 and 1936; recorder recitals, Wigmore Hall, Feb. and Nov. 1939, and annually, 1946–; toured and broadcast on radio and TV in Holland, 1946; Italy and Switzerland, 1947; Sweden, 1949; New Zealand, 1953; France, 1956; America, 1957; Switzerland, Austria, Germany, Holland, 1958; Belgium, America, 1959; Sweden, Austria, Germany, 1960; Australia, 1965; Colombia, 1966; France, Sweden, 1967; Alaska, Canada and Italy, 1969; Japan, 1974; Denmark, 1983; Colombia, 1984; Italy, 1985; France, 1991; America (yearly), 1961–. Frequent broadcasts in this country and abroad. Chm. and Man. Dir, Arnold Dolmetsch Ltd, 1963–78; Chm., Dolmetsch Musical Instruments, 1982–. Musical Dir of Soc. of Recorder Players, 1937; Musical Dir, Dolmetsch Internat. Summer School, 1970–; Mem. Incorporated Soc. of Musicians; Mem. Art Workers' Guild, 1953 (Master, 1988); Patron Early Music Soc., University of Sydney. Hon. Fellow of Trinity Coll. of Music, 1950. Hon. DLitt University of Exeter, 1960. Hon. Fellow London Coll. of Music, 1963. *Publications:* Recorder Tutors, 1957, 1962, 1970, 1977; edited and arranged numerous publications of 16th-, 17th- and 18th-century music; contrib. to many music jls. *Recreations:* ornithology, natural history. *Address:* Jesses, Haslemere, Surrey GU27 2BS. *T:* Haslemere (0428) 643818.

DOLTON, David John William; management consultant, since 1989; *b* 15 Sept. 1928; *e s* of Walter William and Marie Frances Duval Dolton; *m* 1959, Patricia Helen Crowe (marr. diss. 1985); one *s* one *d*; *m* 1986, Rosalind Jennifer Chivers. *Educ:* St Lawrence Coll., Ramsgate. FCIS, FBIM, FIPM, MInstAM. Various appointments in Delta Metal Co. Ltd, 1950–76, incl. Commercial Director, Extrusion Division, and Director of Administration and Personnel, Rod Division, 1967–76; Chief Exec., Equal Opportunities Commn, 1976–78; Asst Gen. Manager, Nat. Employers Mutual Gen. Insce Assoc. Ltd, 1979–89. Governor, The Queen's Coll., Birmingham, 1974–88. Reader, Dio. Gloucester. Liveryman, Worshipful Co. of Gold and Silver Wyre Drawers. *Recreations:* music, reading, formerly mountaineering, now mountain and hill walking, swimming, travel. *Address:* 85 Corinium Gate, Cirencester, Glos GL7 2PX. *T:* Cirencester (0285) 657739.

DOMB, Prof. Cyril, PhD; FRS 1977; Professor of Physics, Bar-Ilan University, 1981–89, now Emeritus; *m* Shirley Galinsky; three *s* three *d*. *Educ:* Hackney Downs Sch.; Pembroke Coll., Cambridge. Major Open Schol., Pembroke Coll., 1938–41; Radar Research, Admiralty, 1941–46; MA Cambridge, 1945; Nahum Schol., Pembroke Coll., 1946; PhD Cambridge, 1949; ICI Fellowship, Clarendon Laboratory, Oxford, 1949–52; MA Oxon, 1952; University Lecturer in Mathematics, Cambridge, 1952–54; Prof. of Theoretical Physics, KCL, 1954–81; FKC 1978. Max Born Prize, Inst. of Physics and German Physical Soc., 1981. *Publications:* (ed) Clerk Maxwell and Modern Science, 1963; (ed) Memories of Kopul Rosen, 1970; Phase Transitions and Critical Phenomena, (ed with M.S. Green) vols 1 and 2, 1972, vol. 3, 1974, vols 5a, 5b, 6, 1976, (ed with J. L. Lebowitz) vols 7 and 8, 1983, vol. 9, 1984, vol. 10, 1986, vol. 11, 1987, vol. 12, 1988, vol. 13, 1989; (ed with A. Carmell) Challenge, 1976; articles in scientific journals. *Recreations:* walking, swimming. *Address:* Department of Physics, Bar-Ilan University, Ramat-Gan, Israel; 28 St Peter's Court, Queens Road, NW4.

DOMETT, Rear-Adm. Douglas Brian, CB 1989; CBE 1984; Chief of Naval Staff, Royal New Zealand Navy, 1987–89; *b* 12 May 1932; *s* of Samuel and Hazel Marion Domett; *m* 1986, Merrion Ranwell Clark; four *s* one *d* by previous marr. *Educ:* Putaruru High Sch.; Palmerston North Boys' High Sch.; RNC Dartmouth. Joined RNZN 1950; served in HMNZ Ships Black Prince, Pukaki, Hawea, Rotoiti and Endeavour; specialist training, UK, 1959–62; HMNZS Otago; Ops School, Auckland; RNZAF Comd and Staff Coll., 1967; Dep. Dir, Defence Intelligence, 1968–69; US Armed Forces Staff Coll., 1970; Naval Attaché, Washington, 1970–72; in Comd, HMNZ Ships Waikato, 1972–73, Canterbury, 1974; COS to Commodore, Auckland, 1974–76; Dir, Resources Policy, 1976–79; RCDS 1980; ACDS (Personnel), 1981–83; DCNS, 1983–87. US Legion of Merit, 1973; Korean Order of Nat. Security Merit Medal, 1988. *Recreations:* all sports, farming, gardening, fishing. *Address:* Station Road, Paparoa RD1, Northland, New Zealand. *T:* (089) 431 6851. *Club:* Wellesley (Wellington, NZ).

DOMINGO, Placido; tenor singer, conductor; *b* Madrid, 21 Jan. 1941; *s* of Placido Domingo and Pepita (*née* Embil), professional singers; *m* Marta Ornelas, lyric soprano; three *s*. *Educ:* Instituto, Mexico City; Nat. Conservatory of Music, Mexico City. Operatic début, Monterrey, as Alfredo in La Traviata, 1961; with opera houses at Dallas, Fort Worth, Israel, to 1965; NY City Opera, 1965–; débuts: at NY Metropolitan Opera, as Maurizio in Adriana Lecouvreur, 1968; at La Scala, title role in Ernani, 1969; at Covent Garden, Cavaradossi in Tosca, 1971. Has conducted in Vienna, Barcelona, NY and Frankfurt; début as conductor in UK, Covent Garden, 1983. *Films:* La Traviata, 1983; Carmen, 1984; Otello, 1986; appears on TV, makes recordings, throughout USA and Europe. FRCM; FRNCM. Officer, Legion of Honour, 1983; Medal of City of Madrid. *Publication:* My First Forty Years (autobiog.), 1983. *Recreations:* piano, swimming.

DOMINIAN, Dr Jacobus, FRCPEd, FRCPsych; DPM; Hon. Consultant, Central Middlesex Hospital, since 1988 (Senior Consultant Psychiatrist, 1965–88); *b* 25 Aug. 1929; *s* of Charles Joseph Dominian and late Mary Dominian (*née* Scarlatou); *m* 1955, Edith Mary Smith; four *d*. *Educ:* Lycée Leonin, Athens; St Mary's High Sch., Bombay; Stamford Grammar Sch., Lincs; Cambridge Univ.; Oxford Univ. MA, MB BChir (Cantab). Postgraduate work in medicine, various Oxford hosps, 1955–58, Maudsley Hosp. (Inst. of Psychiatry), 1958–64; training as psychiatrist at Maudsley Hosp.; Dir, One Plus One: Marriage and Partnership Research, 1971–. Hon. DSc Lancaster, 1976. *Publications:* Psychiatry and the Christian, 1961; Christian Marriage, 1967; Marital Breakdown, 1968; The Church and the Sexual Revolution, 1971; Cycles of Affirmation, 1975; Depression, 1976; Authority, 1976; (with A. R. Peacocke) From Cosmos to Love, 1976; Proposals for a New Sexual Ethic, 1977; Marriage, Faith and Love, 1981; Make or Break, 1984; The Capacity to Love, 1985; Sexual Integrity: the answer to AIDS, 1987; contribs to Lancet, BMJ, the Tablet, TLS. *Recreations:* enjoyment of the theatre, music, reading and writing. *Address:* Pefka, The Green, Croxley Green, Rickmansworth, Herts WD3 3JA. *T:* Rickmansworth (0923) 720972.

DOMOKOS, Dr Mátyás; General Director, Diplomatic Service Directorate, Ministry of Foreign Affairs, Hungary, since 1989; *b* 28 Oct. 1930; *m* 1956, Irén Beretyán; one *d*. *Educ:* Karl Marx Univ. of Econs, Budapest. Foreign trading enterprises, 1954–57; Commercial Sec., Damascus and Trade Comr, Khartoum, 1958–61; various posts in Ministry for Foreign Trade, Hungary, 1961–74; Ambassador to UN, Geneva, 1974–79; Head of Dept of Internat. Organisations, Ministry of Foreign Affairs, 1979–84; Ambassador to UK, 1984–89. *Recreations:* gardening, chess. *Address:* Ministry of Foreign Affairs, Budapest, Hungary.

DON-WAUCHOPE, Sir Roger Hamilton; *see* Wauchope.

DONALD, Sir Alan (Ewen), KCMG 1988 (CMG 1979); HM Diplomatic Service, retired; Ambassador to People's Republic of China, 1988–91; *b* 5 May 1931; 2nd *s* of Robert Thomson Donald and Louise Turner; *m* 1958, Janet Hilary Therese Blood; four *s*. *Educ:* Aberdeen Grammar Sch.; Fettes Coll., Edinburgh; Trinity Hall, Cambridge. BA, LLM. HM Forces, 1949–50. Joined HM Foreign Service, 1954: Third Sec., Peking, 1955–57; FO, 1958–61: Private Sec. to Parly Under-Sec., FO, 1959–61; Second, later First Sec., UK Delegn to NATO, Paris, 1961–64; First Sec., Peking, 1964–66; Personnel Dept, Diplomatic Service Admin. Office, later FCO, 1967–71; Counsellor (Commercial), Athens, 1971–73; Political Advr to Governor of Hong Kong, 1974–77; Ambassador to: Republics of Zaire, Burundi and Rwanda, 1977–80; People's Republic of the Congo, 1978–80; Asst Under-Sec. of State (Asia and the Pacific), FCO, 1980–84; Ambassador to Republic of Indonesia, 1984–88. *Recreations:* music, military history, water colour sketching, films, gentle golf. *Address:* c/o Foreign and Commonwealth Office, SW1A 2AH. *Clubs:* United Oxford & Cambridge University; Aula (London/Cambridge).

DONALD, Dr Alastair Geoffrey, OBE 1982; FRCGP, FRCPE; General Medical Practitioner, since 1952; Assistant Director, Edinburgh Postgraduate Board for Medicine, since 1970; Regional Adviser in General Practice, SE Scotland, since 1972; *b* 24 Nov. 1926; *s* of Dr Pollok Donald and Henrietta Mary (*née* Laidlaw); *m* 1952, Patricia Ireland; two *s* one *d*. *Educ:* Edinburgh Academy; Corpus Christi Coll., Cambridge (MA); Edinburgh Univ. (MB, ChB); Member: Cambridge and Edinburgh Univs Athletic Teams, RAF Medical Branch, 1952–54; general medical practice, Leith and Cramond (Edin.), 1954–; Lectr, Dept of General Practice, Univ. of Edinburgh, 1960–70. Royal College of General Practitioners: Vice-Chm. of Council, 1976–77, Chm., 1979–82; Chm., Bd of Censors, 1979–80; past Chm. and Provost, SE Scotland Faculty. Chairman: UK Conf. of Postgrad. Advisers in Gen. Practice, 1978–80; Jt Cttee on Postgrad. Trng for Gen. Practice, 1982–85; Armed Services Gen. Practice Approval Bd, 1987–. Specialist Advr, H of C Social Services Select Cttee, 1986–87. Radio Doctor, BBC (Scotland), 1976–78. Chm., Scottish Cttee, ASH, 1985–. Chm. Court of Directors, Edinburgh Acad., 1978–85 (Dir, 1955–); President: Edinburgh Academical Club, 1978–81; Rotary Club of Leith, 1957–58. Lectures: James Mackenzie, RCGP, 1985; David Bruce, RAMC, 1987. James Mackenzie Medal, RCPE, 1983. *Publications:* contribs to medical jls. *Recreations:* golf, family life, reading The Times. *Address:* 30 Cramond Road North, Edinburgh EH4 6JE. *T:* 031–336 3824. *Clubs:* Hawks (Cambridge); University of Edinburgh Staff (Edinburgh).

DONALD, Craig Reid Cantlie, CMG 1963; OBE 1959; *b* 8 Sept. 1914; *s* of Rev. Francis Cantlie and Mary Donald, Lumphanan, Aberdeenshire; *m* 1945, Mary Isabel Speid (*d* 1989); one *d*. *Educ:* Fettes; Emmanuel Coll., Cambridge (Scholar). BA 1937, MA 1947. Administrative Officer, Cyprus, 1937. Military Service, 1940–46, Lieut-Col. Commissioner, Famagusta, 1948. Registrar, Cooperative Societies, 1951; Deputy Financial Sec., Uganda, 1951; Sec. to the Treasury, 1956–63. Bursar, Malvern Coll., 1964–79. *Recreation:* country pursuits. *Address:* 55 Geraldine Road, Malvern WR14 3NU. *T:* Malvern (0684) 561446. *Club:* Travellers'.

See also I. G. Gilbert.

DONALD, Air Marshal Sir John (George), KBE 1985 (OBE 1972); Medical Adviser, AMI Middle East Services Ltd, since 1989; *b* 7 Nov. 1927; *s* of John Shirran Donald and Janet Knox (*née* Napier); *m* 1954, Margaret Jean Walton; one *s* two *d*. *Educ:* Inverurie Acad.; Aberdeen Univ. (MB, ChB 1951); DTM&H Edin 1964; MRCGP 1971, FRCGP 1977; MFCM 1972, FFCM 1985; MFOM 1982 (AFOM 1980); FRCPE 1986. Commnd RAF, 1953; Senior Medical Officer: Colombo, Ceylon, 1954–57; RAF Stafford, 1957–60; RAF Waddington, 1960–63; student, RAF Staff Coll., 1965; SMO, HQ AFCENT, France and Holland, 1966–68; Dep. Dir, Medical Personnel (RAF), 1969–72; OC, The Princess Mary's RAF Hosp., Akrotiri, Cyprus, 1972–76; OC, RAF Hosp., Ely, 1976–78; PMO,

RAF Germany, 1978–81; PMO, RAF Strike Comd, 1981–84; Dir-Gen., RAF Med. Services, 1984–85; Dep. Surg. Gen. (Ops), MoD, and Dir Gen., RAF Med. Services, 1985–86; Med. Dir, Security Forces Hosp., 1986–89. QHS, 1983–86. CStJ 1984. *Recreations:* golf, skiing, camping, ornithology. *Address:* Curzon House, Drews Park, Knotty Green, Beaconsfield, Bucks HP9 2TT. *T:* Beaconsfield (04946) 4621. *Clubs:* Royal Air Force, Royal Society of Medicine.

DONALD, Prof. Kenneth William, OBE 1983; DSC 1940; MA, MD, DSc, FRCP, FRCPE, FRSE; Professor of Medicine, University of Edinburgh, 1959–76, now Emeritus Professor; Senior Physician, Royal Infirmary, Edinburgh; Physician to the Queen in Scotland, 1967–76; *b* 25 Nov. 1911; *s* of Col William Donald, MC, RA and Julia Jane Donald, Sandgate; *m* 1942, Rêthe Pearl, *d* of D. H. Evans, Regents Park. *Educ:* Cambridge Univ.; St Bartholomew's Hosp. Kitchener Scholar and State Scholar, 1930; Senior Scholar, Emmanuel Coll., Cambridge, 1933. Served with Royal Navy, 1939–45: Senior MO, 1st and 5th Flotilla of Destroyers; Senior MO, Admiralty Experimental Diving Unit. Chief Asst, Med. Prof. Unit and Cattlin Research Fellow, St Bartholomew's Hosp., 1946–48; Rockefeller Travelling Research Fellow, Columbia Univ., 1948–49; Senior Lecturer in Medicine, Inst. Diseases of the Chest, Brompton Hosp., 1949–50; Reader in Medicine, Univ. of Birmingham and Physician, Queen Elizabeth Hosp., Birmingham, 1950–59. Scientific Consultant to the Royal Navy. Physician to the Royal Navy in Scotland. Medical Consultant to Scottish Dept of Home and Health; Member: Commonwealth Scholarship Commn; Medical Sub-Cttee, UGC; RN Personnel Research Cttee (Chm.) of MRC; Scottish Adv. Cttee on Med. Research; Council and Scientific Adv. Cttee, British Heart Foundn; Scottish Gen. Nursing Council; Chairman: Under-Water Physiology Sub-Cttee of MRC; Adv. Gp to Sec. of State for Scotland on Health Care Aspects of Industrial Developments in North Sea. Governor, Inst. of Occupational Medicine, Edinburgh. *Publications:* contribs to scientific and medical jls concerning normal and abnormal function of the lungs, the heart and the circulation and high pressure physiology in relation to diving and submarines, drowning, resuscitation. *Recreations:* reading, theatre, fishing. *Address:* Nant-y-Celyn, Cloddiau, Welshpool, Powys SY21 9JE. *T:* Welshpool (0938) 2859. *Club:* Athenæum.

DONALDSON, family name of **Barons Donaldson of Kingsbridge** and **Donaldson of Lymington.**

DONALDSON OF KINGSBRIDGE, Baron *cr* 1967 (Life Peer), of Kingsbridge; **John George Stuart Donaldson,** OBE 1943; retired farmer; *b* 9 Oct. 1907; *s* of Rev. S. A. Donaldson, Master of Magdalene, Cambridge, and Lady Albinia Donaldson (*née* Hobart-Hampden); *m* 1935, Frances Annesley Lonsdale (*see* F. A. Donaldson); one *s* two *d*. *Educ:* Eton; Trinity Coll., Cambridge. Pioneer Health Centre, Peckham, 1935–38; Road Transport, 1938–39. Royal Engineers, 1939–45. Farmed in Glos, and later Bucks. Member: Glos Agric. Exec. Cttee, 1953–60; SE Regional Planning Council, 1966–69. Parly Under-Sec. of State, NI Office, 1974–76; Minister for the Arts, DES, 1976–79. Joined: SDP, 1981; Soc and Lib Dem, 1987. Hon. Secretary: Nat. Assoc. Discharged Prisoners Aid Socs, 1961; All Party Penal Affairs Gp, 1981–; Chairman: Nat. Assoc. for the Care and Resettlement of Offenders, 1966–74; Bd of Visitors, HM Prison, Grendon, 1963–69; Consumer Council, 1968–71; EDC for Hotel and Catering Industry, 1972–74; Nat. Cttee Family Service Units, 1968–74; Cttee of Enquiry into conditions of service for young servicemen, 1969; Assoc. of Arts Instns, 1980–83; Confedn of Art and Design Assocs, 1982–84; British Fedn of Zoos, 1970–74; Pres., RSPB, 1975–80. Director: Royal Opera House, Covent Garden, 1958–74; Sadler's Wells, 1963–74; British Sugar Corp., 1966–74. *Recreations:* music in general, opera in particular. *Address:* 17 Edna Street, SW11 3DP. *Club:* Brooks's.

See also N. D. Deakin.

DONALDSON OF KINGSBRIDGE, Lady; *see* Donaldson, Frances Annesley.

DONALDSON OF LYMINGTON, Baron *cr* 1988 (Life Peer), of Lymington in the County of Hampshire; **John Francis Donaldson;** Kt 1966; PC 1979; Master of the Rolls, since 1982; *b* 6 Oct. 1920; *er s* of late Malcolm Donaldson, FRCS, FRCOG, and late Evelyn Helen Marguerite Maunsell; *m* 1945, Dorothy Mary (*see* Dame Mary Donaldson); one *s* two *d*. *Educ:* Charterhouse; Trinity Coll., Cambridge (Hon. Fellow, 1983); MA Oxon 1982. Sec. of Debates, Cambridge Union Soc., 1940; Chm. Federation of University Conservative and Unionist Assocs, 1940; BA (Hons) 1941; MA 1959. Commissioned Royal Signals, 1941; served with Guards Armoured Divisional Signals, in UK and NW Europe, 1942–45; and with Military Government, Schleswig-Holstein, 1945–46; Hon. Lieut-Col, 1946. Called to Bar, Middle Temple, 1946; Harmsworth Law Scholar, 1946; Bencher 1966; Treas. 1986; Mem. Gen. Council of the Bar, 1956–61, 1962–66, Junior Counsel to Registrar of Restrictive Trading Agreements, 1959–61; QC 1961; Dep. Chm., Hants QS, 1961–66; Mem. Council on Tribunals, 1965–66; Judge of the High Court, Queen's Bench Div., 1966–79; Pres., Nat. Industrial Relations Court, 1971–74; a Lord Justice of Appeal, 1979–82. Pres. Council, Inns of Court, 1987–90. Mem. Croydon County Borough Council, 1949–53. President: Carthusian Soc., 1978–82; British Maritime Law Assoc., 1979– (Vice-Pres., 1969–78); British Insurance Law Assoc., 1979–81 (Dep. Pres., 1978–79); British Records Assoc., 1982–; Chairman: Adv. Council on Public Records, 1982–; Magna Carta Trust, 1982–. FCIArb 1980 (Pres., 1980–83). Hon. Member: Assoc. of Average Adjusters, 1966 (Chm., 1981); Grain and Feed Trade Assoc., 1979; Liverpool Cotton Assoc., 1979. Governor, Sutton's Hosp. in Charterhouse, 1981–84. Visitor: UCL, 1982–; Nuffield Coll., Oxford, 1982–; London Business Sch., 1986–. Hon. Freeman, Worshipful Co. of Drapers, 1984. DU Essex, 1983; Hon. LLD Sheffield, 1984. *Publications:* Jt Ed., Lowndes and Rudolf on General Average and the York-Antwerp Rules (8th edn), 1955, (9th edn), 1964 and (10th edn), 1975; contributor to title Insurance, in Halsbury's Laws of England (3rd edn), 1958. *Recreations:* sailing, do-it-yourself. *Address:* Royal Courts of Justice, Strand, WC2A 2LL. *T:* 071–936 6002; (home) 071–588 6610. *Clubs:* Royal Cruising, Bar Yacht, Royal Lymington Yacht.

DONALDSON OF LYMINGTON, Lady; *see* Donaldson, Dame D. M.

DONALDSON, Dr Alexander Ivan; Head, Pirbright Laboratory, AFRC Institute for Animal Health, since 1989; *b* 1 July 1942; *s* of Basil Ivan Donaldson and Dorothy Cunningham Donaldson; *m* 1966, Margaret Ruth Elizabeth Swan; one *s* one *d*. *Educ:* High Sch., Dublin; Trinity Coll., Univ. of Dublin (BA, MA, ScD); Ontario Veterinary Coll., Univ. of Guelph (PhD). MRCVS. Post-doctoral research, 1969–71, Vet. Res. Officer, 1973–76, Principal Vet. Res. Officer, 1976–89, Animal Virus Res. Inst., subseq. AFRC. Inst. for Animal Health, Pirbright Lab.; Head, World Ref. Lab. for Foot-and-Mouth Disease, 1985–89. Vis. Prof., Ontario Vet. Coll., Univ. of Guelph, 1972–73. Research Medal, RASE, 1988. *Publications:* numerous articles on animal virology in learned jls. *Recreations:* jogging, squash, windsurfing, photography. *Address:* AFRC Institute for Animal Health, Pirbright Laboratory, Ash Road, Pirbright, Woking, Surrey GU24 0NF. *T:* Guildford (0483) 232441.

DONALDSON, Prof. (Charles) Ian (Edward); Regius Professor of Rhetoric and English Literature, University of Edinburgh, since 1991; *b* 6 May 1935; *s* of Dr William Edward Donaldson and Elizabeth Donaldson (*née* Weigall); *m* 1962, Tamsin Jane Procter (marr. diss. 1990); one *s* one *d*; *m* 1991, Grazia Maria Therese Gunn. *Educ:* Melbourne Grammar Sch.; Melbourne Univ. (BA 1st cl. Hons English 1957); Magdalen Coll., Oxford (BA 1st cl. Hons English 1960; MA 1964). Sen. Tutor in English, Univ. of Melbourne, 1958; Oxford University: Harmsworth Sen. Scholar, Merton Coll., 1960–62; Fellow and Lectr in English, Wadham Coll., 1962–69; CUF Lectr in English, 1963–69; Chm., English Faculty, 1968–69; Prof. of English, ANU Canberra, 1969–91; Foundn Dir, Humanities Res. Centre, ANU, 1974–90. Vis. appts, Univ. of California Santa Barbara, Gonville and Caius Coll., Cambridge, Cornell Univ., Melbourne Univ. FAHA 1975; corresp. FBA 1987. *Publications:* The World Upside-Down: comedy from Jonson to Fielding, 1970; (ed) Ben Jonson Poems, 1975; The Rapes of Lucretia, 1982; (ed) Jonson and Shakespeare, 1983; (ed) Transformations in Modern European Drama, 1983; (ed with Tamsin Donaldson) Seeing the First Australians, 1985; (ed) Ben Jonson, 1985. *Address:* Department of English Literature, The University, Edinburgh EH8 9JX. *T:* 031–667 1011. *Club:* Scottish Arts (Edinburgh).

DONALDSON, David Abercrombie, RSA 1962 (ARSA 1951); RP 1964; RGI 1977; Painter; Head of Painting School, Glasgow School of Art, 1967–81; Her Majesty's Painter and Limner in Scotland, since 1977; *b* 29 June 1916; *s* of Robert Abercrombie Donaldson and Margaret Cranston; *m* 1st, 1942, Kathleen Boyd Maxwell; one *s*; 2nd, 1949, Maria Krystyna Mora-Szorc; two *d*. *Educ:* Coatbridge Sec. Sch.; Glasgow Sch. of Art. Travelling Scholarship, 1938. Joined Staff of Glasgow Sch. of Art, 1940. Paintings in private collections in America, Canada, Australia, South Africa and Europe and public collections in Scotland. Sitters include: The Queen, 1968; Sir Hector Hetherington; Dame Jean Roberts; Sir John Dunbar; Lord Binning; Rev. Lord McLeod; Mrs Winifred Ewing; Miss Joan Dickson; Earl of Haddo; Sir Samuel Curran; Roger Ellis; Sir Norman Macfarlane; Rt Hon. Margaret Thatcher; Dr Steven Watson; Rt Hon. David Steel, Sir Alwyn Williams. Hon. LLD Strathclyde, 1971; Hon. DLitt Glasgow, 1988. *Recreations:* music, cooking. *Address:* 5 Cleveden Drive, Glasgow G12 0SU. *T:* 041–334 1029; 7 Chelsea Manor Studios, Flood Street, SW3. *T:* 071–352 1932; St Roman de Malegarde, 84290 France. *T:* 90 28 92 65. *Club:* Art (Glasgow).

DONALDSON, David Torrance; QC 1984; *b* 30 Sept. 1943; *s* of Alexander Walls Donaldson and Margaret Merry Bryce. *Educ:* Glasgow Academy; Gonville and Caius College, Cambridge (Maj. Schol.; MA); University of Freiburg i. Br., West Germany (Dr jur). Fellow, Gonville and Caius College, Cambridge, 1965–69. Called to the Bar, Gray's Inn, 1968. *Address:* 2 Hare Court, Temple, EC4. *T:* 071–583 1770.

DONALDSON, Dame (Dorothy) Mary, GBE 1983; JP; Lord Mayor of London for 1983–84; Alderman, City of London Ward of Coleman Street, 1975–91; *b* 29 Aug. 1921; *d* of late Reginald George Gale Warwick and Dorothy Alice Warwick; *m* 1945, John Francis Donaldson (*see* Baron Donaldson of Lymington); one *s* two *d*. *Educ:* Portsmouth High Sch. for Girls (GPDST); Wingfield Morris Orthopædic Hosp.; Middlesex Hosp., London. SRN 1946. Chairman: Women's Nat. Cancer Control Campaign, 1967–69; Interim Licensing Authy for Human In Vitro Fertilisation and Embryol., 1985–91; Vice-Pres., British Cancer Council, 1970; Member: NE Met. Regional Hosp. Bd, 1970–74; NE Thames RHA, 1976–81. Governor: London Hosp., 1971–74; Gt Ormond Street Hosp. for Sick Children, 1978–80; Member: Cities of London and Westminster Disablement Adv. Cttee, 1974–79; Inner London Educn Authority, 1968–71; City Parochial Foundn, 1969–75; Cttee, Royal Humane Soc., 1968–83; Cttee, AA, 1985–89; Press Complaints Commn, 1991–; Chm. Council, Banking Ombudsman, 1985–; Vice-Pres., Counsel and Care for the Elderly, 1980–; Pres., British Assoc. of Cancer United Patients, 1985–. Governor: City of London Sch. for Girls, 1971–83; Berkhamsted Schools, 1976–80; Mem., Governing Body, Charterhouse Sch., 1980–85; Mem., Court of Common Council, 1966–75, Sheriff, 1981–82, HM Lieutenant, 1983, City of London; Mem. Guild of Freemen, City of London, 1970 (Mem. Court, 1983–86); Liveryman, Gardeners' Co., 1975; Hon. Freeman, Shipwrights' Co., 1985. JP Inner London, 1960; Mem., Inner London Juvenile Court Panel, 1960–65. Hon. Mem., CIArb, 1981; Hon. Fellow: Girton Coll., Cambridge, 1983; FRSH 1984; Hon. FRCOG 1991. Hon. DSc City, 1983. DStJ 1984. Freedom, City of Winnipeg, 1968. Order of Oman, 1982; Order of Bahrain, 1984. Grand Officier, Ordre Nat. du Mérite, 1984. *Recreations:* gardening, sailing, geriatric ski-ing. *T:* (home) 071–588 6610. *Clubs:* Reform; Royal Cruising, Royal Lymington Yacht, Bar Yacht.

DONALDSON, Air Cdre Edward Mortlock, CB 1960; CBE 1954; DSO 1940; AFC 1941 (and bar 1947); Air Correspondent, The Daily Telegraph, 1961–79; *b* 22 Feb. 1912; *s* of C. E. Donaldson, Malay Civil Service; *m* 1st, 1936, Winifred Constant (marr. diss., 1944); two *d*; 2nd, 1944, Estellee Holland (marr. diss., 1956); one *s*; 3rd, 1957, Anne, Sofie Stapleton (marr. diss., 1982). *Educ:* King's Sch., Rochester; Christ's Hosp., Horsham; McGill Univ., Canada. Joined RAF, 1931; 3 Sqdn, Upavon, Kenley and Sudan until 1936; won RAF air firing trophy, 1933 and 1934; Flight Comdr, 1 Sqdn, 1936–38; led flight aerobatic team, Hendon and Zürich, 1937; Flight-Lieut 1936; Sqdn Leader 1938; Comdr, 151 Squdn, 1938–40, Battle of Britain; Chief Instructor, 5 Flying Training Sch., 1941; Wing Comdr, 1940; went to US to build four air Gunnery Schs, 1941, and teach USAF combat techniques; Group Capt., 1942; Mem. USAF Board and Directing Staff at US Sch. of Applied Tactics, 1944; Comdr RAF Station, Colerne, RAF first jet station, 1944; in comd RAF Station, Milfield, 1946; in comd RAF High Speed Flight, 1946; holder of World's Speed Record, 1946; SASO, No. 12 Group, 1946–49; in comd Air Cadet Corps and CCF, 1949–51; in comd RAF Station, Fassberg, Germany, 1951–54; Joint Services Staff Coll., 1954; Dir of Operational Training, Air Ministry, 1954–56; Air Cdre, 1954; Dep. Comdr Air Forces, Arabian Peninsular Command, 1956–58; Commandant, Royal Air Force Flying Coll., Manby, 1958–61; retd. Legion of Merit (US), 1948. *Recreations:* shooting, sailing, golf. *Address:* 3 Fair Oak Court, Tower Close, Alverstoke, Gosport PO12 2TX; Suite Royal 4011, El Palmar, Denia, Alicante, Spain. *Clubs:* Royal Air Force; Island Sailing (Cowes).

DONALDSON, Frances Annesley, (Lady Donaldson of Kingsbridge); *b* 13 Jan. 1907; *d* of Frederick Lonsdale and Leslie Lonsdale (*née* Hoggan); *m* 1935, John George Stuart Donaldson (*see* Lord Donaldson of Kingsbridge); one *s* two *d*. *Publications:* Approach to Farming, 1941, 6th edn 1946; Four Years' Harvest, 1945; Milk Without Tears, 1955; Freddy Lonsdale, 1957; Child of the Twenties, 1959; The Marconi Scandal, 1962; Evelyn Waugh: portrait of a country neighbour, 1967; Actor Managers, 1970; Edward VIII, 1974 (Wolfson History Award, 1975); King George VI and Queen Elizabeth, 1977; Edward VIII: the road to abdication, 1978; P. G. Wodehouse, 1982; The British Council: the First Fifty Years, 1984; The Royal Opera House in the Twentieth Century, 1988; Yours, Plum: the letters of P. G. Wodehouse, 1990. *Address:* 17 Edna Street, SW11 3DP. *T:* 071-223 0259.

See also N. D. Deakin.

DONALDSON, Prof. Gordon, CBE 1988; FRSE 1978; FBA 1976; Professor of Scottish History and Palæography, University of Edinburgh, 1963–79, now Professor Emeritus; Historiographer to HM the Queen in Scotland, since 1979; *b* 13 April 1913; *s* of Magnus Donaldson and Rachel Hetherington Swan. *Educ:* Royal High Sch., Edinburgh; Universities of Edinburgh and London. Asst in HM Gen. Register House, Edinburgh,

1938; Lecturer in Scottish History, University of Edinburgh, 1947, Reader, 1955. Birkbeck Lectr, Cambridge, 1958. Member: Royal Commission on the Ancient and Historical Monuments of Scotland, 1964–82; Scottish Records Adv. Council, 1964–87; President: Scottish Ecclesiological Soc., 1963–65; Scottish Church History Soc., 1964–67; Scottish History Soc., 1968–72; Scottish Record Soc., 1981–; Stair Soc., 1987–. Editor, Scottish Historical Review, 1972–77. Hon. DLitt Aberdeen, 1976; DUniv Stirling, 1988. *Publications:* The Making of the Scottish Prayer Book of 1637, 1954; A Source Book of Scottish History, 1952–61; Register of the Privy Seal of Scotland, vols v-viii, 1957–82; Shetland Life under Earl Patrick, 1958; Scotland: Church and Nation through sixteen centuries, 1960, 2nd edn 1972; The Scottish Reformation, 1960, repr. 1972; Scotland—James V to James VII, 1965, repr. 1971; The Scots Overseas, 1966; Northwards by Sea, 1966, 2nd edn 1978; Scottish Kings, 1967, repr. 1977; The First Trial of Mary Queen of Scots, 1969; Memoirs of Sir James Melville of Halhill, 1969; (comp.) Scottish Historical Documents, 1970; Mary Queen of Scots, 1974; Who's Who in Scottish History, 1974; Scotland: The Shaping of a Nation, 1974, 2nd edn 1980; Dictionary of Scottish History, 1977; All the Queen's Men, 1983; Isles of Home, 1983; Sir William Fraser, 1985; Scottish Church History, 1985; Reformed by Bishops, 1988; The Faith of the Scots, 1990; A Northern Commonwealth: Scotland and Norway, 1990; contribs to Scottish Historical Review, English Historical Review, Transactions of Royal Historical Society, etc. *Address:* 6 Pan Ha', Dysart, Fife KY1 2TL. *T:* Kirkcaldy (0592) 52685.

DONALDSON, Hamish; Chief Executive, Hill Samuel Bank, 1987–91; *b* 13 June 1936; *s* of late James Donaldson and Marie Christine Cormack; *m* 1965, Linda, *d* of late Dr Leslie Challis Bousfield; three *d*. *Educ:* Oundle School; Christ's College, Cambridge (MA). De La Rue Bull, 1960–66; Urwick, Orr & Partners, 1966–73; Hill Samuel & Co., 1973–91; Man. Dir, Hill Samuel Merchant Bank (SA), 1985–86. Director: TSB Bank, 1988–91; TSB Group, 1990–91; Macquarie Bank, 1989–. *Publication:* a Guide to the Successful Management of Computer Projects, 1978. *Recreation:* amateur operatics. *Address:* Edgecombe, Hill Road, Haslemere, Surrey GU27 2JN. *T:* Haslemere (0428) 644473.

DONALDSON, Ian; *see* Donaldson, C. I. E.

DONALDSON, Dame Mary; *see* Donaldson, Dame D. M.

DONALDSON, Patricia Anne; *see* Hodgson, P. A.

DONALDSON, Prof. Simon Kirwan, DPhil; FRS 1986; Wallis Professor of Mathematics, and Fellow of St Anne's College, University of Oxford, since 1985; *b* 20 Aug. 1957; *m* 1986, Ana Nora Hurtado; one *s* one *d*. *Educ:* Sevenoaks Sch., Kent; Pembroke Coll., Cambridge (BA 1979); Worcester Coll., Oxford (DPhil 1983). Jun. Res. Fellow, All Souls Coll., Oxford, 1983–85. *Publications:* papers in mathematical jls. *Recreation:* sailing. *Address:* St Anne's College, Oxford.

DONALDSON, Timothy Baswell, CBE 1973; PhD; Governor, Central Bank of the Bahamas, since 1974; *b* 2 Jan. 1934; *s* of late Rev. Dr T. E. W. Donaldson and of M. B. Donaldson; *m* 1957, Donna Ruth Penn; two *s*. *Educ:* Fisk Univ., Tennessee (BA Hons); Univ. of Minnesota; Columbia Univ.; Pacific Northwestern Univ. (PhD). FIB. Lectr in Maths, Fisk Univ., 1957–58; Sen. Master, Clarendon Coll., Jamaica, 1959–61; Headmaster, Prince Williams High Sch., 1961–63; Sen. Inspector, Bahamas Min. of Educn, 1963–64; Asst Sec., 1964–66, Controller of Exchange, 1966–68, Min. of Finance, Bahamas; Manager, 1968–70, Chm., 1970–74, Bahamas Monetary Authority. Alternate Governor for Bahamas: IMF; Caribbean Develt Bank; Director: Intercontinental Diversified Corp.; Grand Bahama Port Authority; Morgan Guaranty Trust (Bahamas) Ltd; Bahamas Intenational Trust; Chm., Bahamas Hotel Employers Pension Fund. Chm., Duke of Edinburgh Awards Scheme, Nassau; Treasurer, Bahamas Assoc. for Mentally Retarded; Founder Mem., Rotary Club of E Nassau (Past Sec. and Vice Pres.). Mem., Bd of Trustees, Fisk Univ.; Founder Pres., Bahamas Br., Guild of Graduates; Pres., Gym Tennis Club. Pres. and Hon. Fellow, Bahamas Inst. of Bankers; FIB; Associate, Inst. of Dirs. Delta Chapter, Phi Beta Kappa, 1977. Hon. LLD London Inst. for Applied Research, 1972. *Publications:* numerous articles on international finance in periodicals and journals. *Recreations:* tennis, swimming. *Address:* (office) PO Box N 7112, Nassau, Bahamas. *T:* 23880; (home) PO Box ES-5116, Nassau, Bahamas. *T:* 43259.

DONALDSON, Rear-Adm. Vernon D'Arcy; *b* 1 Feb. 1906; *s* of Adm. Leonard Andrew Boyd Donaldson, CB, CMG, and of Mary Mitchell, *d* of Prof. D'Arcy Thompson, Queen's Coll., Galway; *m* 1946, Joan Cranfield Monypenny of Pitmilly, (The Lady Pitmilly) (*d* 1986), *d* of James Egerton Howard Monypenny. *Educ:* RN Colls, Osborne and Dartmouth. Entered Royal Navy, Sept. 1919; Midshipman, 1923; Sub-Lieut 1927, Lieut 1928; specialised in Torpedoes and served as Torpedo Officer in HMS Vernon, 8th Dest. Flot., China Stn, and HMS Glorious; Comdr Dec. 1939, and served in Plans Div. Admlty, as exec. officer HM Ships Birmingham and Frobisher in Eastern Fleet, and on staff of C-in-C Eastern Fleet; Capt. Dec. 1944. Asst-Dir, TASW Div., Naval Staff, 1945–47; Naval Attaché, China, 1948–49; commanded HMS Gambia, 1950–51; Dir TASW div., Naval Staff, 1952–54; ADC to the Queen, 1953–54; Dep. Chief of Supplies and Transport, Admiralty (acting Rear-Adm.), 1955–57; retired, 1957. *Address:* 36 Knox Court, Knox Place, Haddington, East Lothian EH41 4EB.

DONCASTER, Bishop Suffragan of, since 1982; **Rt. Rev. William Michael Dermot Persson;** *b* 27 Sept. 1927; *s* of Leslie Charles Grenville Alan and Elizabeth Mercer Persson; *m* 1957, Ann Davey; two *s* one *d*. *Educ:* Monkton Combe School; Oriel Coll., Oxford (MA); Wycliffe Hall Theological Coll. National service, Army, 1945–48; commissioned, Royal Signals. Deacon 1953, priest 1954; Curate: Emmanuel, South Croydon, 1953–55; St John, Tunbridge Wells, 1955–58; Vicar, Christ Church, Barnet, 1958–67; Rector, Bebington, Cheshire, 1967–79; Vicar, Knutsford with Toft, 1979–82. General Synod: Mem., House of Clergy, 1975–82, House of Bishops, 1985–; Chm., Council for Christian Unity, 1991–. *Recreations:* gardening, writing poetry. *Address:* Bishop's Lodge, Hooton Roberts, Rotherham S65 4PF.

DONCASTER, Archdeacon of; *see* Carnelley, Ven. Desmond.

DONDELINGER, Jean; Member, Commission of the European Communities, since 1989; *b* Luxembourg, 4 July 1930; *m*; one *s*. *Educ:* Nancy Univ.; Paris Univ.; St Antony's Coll., Oxford. Barrister, Luxembourg, 1954–58; Asst to Head, Internat. Economic Relations Service, Dept of Foreign Affairs, 1958–61; Dep. Permanent Rep. of Luxembourg to EEC, 1961–70, Ambassador and Permanent Rep., 1970–84; Sec.-Gen., Min. of Foreign Affairs, 1984. Rep. of Pres. of Govt, Cttee on Institutional Affairs (Dooge Cttee), 1984–85; Chm., Negotiating Gp on Single Act, 1986; Vice-Pres., ITU World Conf. on Fixing of Orbital Frequencies of Satellites, 1988. *Address:* Commission of the European Communities, 200 rue de la Loi, 1049 Brussels, Belgium.

DONEGALL, 7th Marquess of, *cr* 1791; **Dermot Richard Claud Chichester,** LVO 1986; Viscount Chichester and Baron of Belfast, 1625; Earl of Donegall, 1647; Earl of Belfast, 1791; Baron Fisherwick (GB), 1790; Baron Templemore, 1831; Hereditary Lord High Admiral of Lough Neagh; late 7th Queen's Own Hussars; Standard Bearer, Honourable Corps of Gentlemen at Arms, 1984–86 (one of HM Bodyguard, since 1966); *b* 18 April 1916; 2nd *s* of 4th Baron Templemore, PC, KCVO, DSO, and Hon. Clare Meriel Wingfield, 2nd *d* of 7th Viscount Powerscourt, PC Ireland (she *d* 1969); *S* father 1953, and to Marquessate of Donegall, 1975; *m* 1946, Lady Josceline Gabrielle Legge, *y d* of 7th Earl of Dartmouth, GCVO, TD; one *s* two *d*. *Educ:* Harrow; RMC, Sandhurst. 2nd Lt 7th Hussars, 1936; Lt 1939; served War of 1939–45 in Middle East and Italy (prisoner); Major, 1944; retired, 1949. *Recreations:* hunting, shooting, fishing. *Heir:* *s* Earl of Belfast, *qv*. *Address:* Dunbrody Park, Arthurstown, Co. Wexford, Eire. *T:* Waterford 89126. *Clubs:* Cavalry and Guards; Kildare Street and University (Dublin).

DONEGAN, Rt. Rev. Horace W(illiam) B(aden), Hon. CBE 1957; DD; *b* Matlock, Derbyshire, England, 17 May 1900; *s* of Horace George Donegan and Pembroke Capes Hand. *Educ:* St Stephen's, Annandale, NY; Oxford University, England; Harvard Divinity School; Episcopal Theological Seminary, Rector, Christ Church, Baltimore, 1929–33; Rector, St James' Church, NYC, 1933–47; Suffragan Bishop of New York, 1947–49; Bishop Coadjutor of New York, 1949–50. Bishop of New York, 1950–72. Vice-Pres., Pilgrims, USA; President: St Hilda's and St Hugh's Sch., NY; House of Redeemer, NY; Episcopal Actors Guild, NY; Chaplain, Veterans of Foreign Wars; Episcopal Visitor: Sisters of St Helena; Community of the Holy Spirit; Trustee: St Luke's Hosp., NY; Episcopal Sch., NY; Contemporary Club, NY. Award, Conf. of Christians and Jews; Medal of City of New York; Medal of Merit, St Nicholas Society, NY; Citation, NY Hospital Assoc.; Harlem Arts & Culture Award. Churchill Fellow, Westminster Coll., Fulton, Mo. Hon. degrees: DD: New York Univ., 1940; Univ. of South, 1949; Trinity, 1950; Bard, 1957; King's Univ., Halifax, 1958; Berkley Divinity School, New Haven, Conn., 1969; STD: Hobart, 1948; General Theological Seminary, 1949; Columbia Univ., 1960; DCL Nashotah, 1956; Sub Prelate OStJ, 1956; Grand Cross St Joanikije, 1956; Legion of Honour, France, 1957; Silver Medal of Red Cross of Japan, 1959; Holy Pagania from Armenian Church, 1960; Grand Kt, Order of St Denys of Zante (Greece), 1959. *Publications:* articles in religious publications. *Recreations:* golf, swimming, painting. *Address:* Manhattan House, 200 E 66th Street, New York, NY 10021, USA; 3145 Twin Lakes Lane, Sanibel Island, Florida 33957, USA. *Clubs:* Athenæum, Royal Automobile, American, Kennel (London); Union, Union League, Pilgrims, Century Association, Columbia Faculty, Tuxedo Park (all of New York).

DONERAILE, 10th Viscount *cr* 1785 (Ire.); **Richard Allen St Leger;** Baron Doneraile, 1776; Food Marketing Analyst since 1974; *b* 17 Aug. 1946; *s* of 9th Viscount Doneraile and of Melva, Viscountess Doneraile; *S* father, 1983; *m* 1970, Kathleen Mary Simcox, Churchtown, Mallow, Co. Cork; one *s* one *d*. *Educ:* Orange Coast College, California; Mississippi Univ. Served US Army. Air Traffic Control specialist; antiquarian book appraiser, 1970–73. *Recreations:* outdoor sports, skiing, golf, sailing. *Heir:* *s* Hon. Nathaniel Warham Robert St John St Leger, *b* 13 Sept. 1971. *Club:* Yorba Linda Country (California).

DONIACH, Prof. Israel, MD (London); FRCPath 1963; FRCP 1968; Professor of Morbid Anatomy in University of London, London Hospital, 1960–76, now Emeritus Professor; Hon. Lecturer in Histopathology, St Bartholomew's Hospital Medical School, since 1976; *b* 9 March 1911; *yr s* of late Aaron Selig and late Rahel Doniach; *m* 1933, Deborah Abileah; one *s* (one *d* decd). *Educ:* University Coll. and Hosp., London. Asst Pathologist, St Mary's Hosp., London, 1935–37; Clinical Pathologist and Cancer Research Asst, Mount Vernon Hosp., Northwood, 1937–43; Senior Lecturer in Morbid Anatomy, Postgraduate Medical Sch. of London, 1943–59, Reader, 1959–60. Hon. Fellow: RSocMed; Pathol. Soc.; Soc. for Endocrinol. *Publications:* papers in morbid anatomy and experimental pathology in various journals. *Address:* 25 Alma Square, NW8 9PY. *T:* 071–286 1617.

DONKIN, Alexander Sim; HM Diplomatic Service, retired; Counsellor (Administration), UK Mission to United Nations, and Deputy Consul-General, New York, 1977–82; *b* 14 July 1922; *s* of Matthew Henderson Donkin and Margaret Donkin; *m* 1944, Irene Florence (*née* Willis) (*d* 1988); two *d*. *Educ:* Monkwearmouth Sch., Co. Durham. Served War, RAF, 1941–46; Sqdn Ldr. Civil Service, 1947–66; HM Diplomatic Service, 1966; FCO, 1966–70; Washington, 1970–74; FCO, 1974–77. *Recreations:* music, walking, photography. *Address:* 1 Amberley Road, Eastbourne, East Sussex BN22 0EH.

DONKIN, Air Cdre Peter Langloh, CBE 1946; DSO 1944; retired; *b* 19 June 1913; *s* of Frederick Langloh and Phyllis Donkin; *m* 1941, Elizabeth Marjorie Cox; two *d*. *Educ:* Sherborne; RAF Coll., Cranwell. Commissioned RAF, 1933; No. 16 Sqdn, 1933–38; British Mission in Poland, 1939; CO 225 Sqdn, 1940; CO 239 Sqdn, 1941–42; CO 35 Wing, 1943–44; Sch. Land Air Warfare, 1945; HQ, RAF Levant, 1946; RCAF Staff Coll., 1948–49; Exchange USAF, 1950; CO, RAF Chivenor, 1951–53; Air Attaché, Moscow, 1954–57; Asst Chief of Staff, HQ Allied Air Forces, Central Europe, 1957–58; idc, 1959; AOC, RAF, Hong Kong, 1960–62. *Recreations:* shooting, yachting. *Address:* Coombe Cross Cottage, Templecombe, Som. *Club:* Carlton.

DONKIN, Dr Robin Arthur, FBA 1985; Reader in Historical Geography, since 1990, and Fellow of Jesus College, since 1972, University of Cambridge; *b* Morpeth, 28 Oct. 1928; *s* of Arthur Donkin and Elizabeth Jane Kirkup; *m* 1970, Jennifer Gay Kennedy; one *d*. *Educ:* Univ. of Durham (BA 1950; PhD 1953); MA Cantab 1971. Lieut, Royal Artillery, 1953–55 (Egypt). King George VI Meml Fellow, Univ. of California, Berkeley, 1955–56; Asst Lectr, Dept of Geography, Univ. of Edinburgh, 1956–58; Lectr, Dept of Geography, Univ. of Birmingham, 1958–70; Lectr in the Geography of Latin America, Univ. of Cambridge, 1971–90; Tutor, Jesus Coll., Cambridge, 1975–. Leverhulme Research Fellow, 1966; Vis. Associate Prof. of Geography, Univ. of Toronto, 1969; field work in Middle and S America, NW Africa. *Publications:* The Cistercian Order in Europe: a bibliography of printed sources, 1969; Spanish Red: cochineal and the Opuntia cactus, 1977; The Cistercians: studies in the geography of medieval England and Wales, 1978; Agricultural Terracing in the Aboriginal New World, 1979; Manna: an historical geography, 1980; The Peccary, 1985; The Muscovy Duck, 1986; Meleagrides: an historical and ethnogeographical study of the Guinea fowl, 1991; articles in geographical, historical and anthropological jls. *Address:* Jesus College, Cambridge CB5 8BL; 13 Roman Hill, Barton, Cambridge. *T:* Cambridge (0223) 262572.

DONLEAVY, James Patrick; author; *b* 23 April 1926; *m* Valerie Heron (marr. diss.); one *s* one *d*; *m* Mary Wilson Price (marr. diss.); one *s* one *d*. *Educ:* schs in USA; Trinity Coll., Dublin. Evening Standard Drama Critics' Award, 1961; Brandeis Univ. Creative Arts Award, 1962; AAAL Grantee, 1975. *Publications:* The Ginger Man (novel), 1955; Fairy Tales of New York (play), 1960; What They Did In Dublin With The Ginger Man (introd. and play), 1961; A Singular Man (novel), 1963 (play, 1964); Meet My Maker The Mad Molecule (short stories), 1964; The Saddest Summer of Samuel S (novella), 1966 (play, 1967); The Beastly Beatitudes of Balthazar B (novel), 1968 (play, 1981); The Onion Eaters (novel), 1971; The Plays of J. P. Donleavy, 1972; A Fairy Tale of New York (novel), 1973; The Unexpurgated Code: a complete manual of survival and manners, 1975; The Destinies of Darcy Dancer, Gentleman (novel), 1977; Schultz (novel), 1980; Leila (novel), 1983; De Alfonce Tennis: the superlative game of eccentric champions, its history, accoutrements, rules, conduct and regimen (sports manual), 1984;

Ireland, in all her Sins and in some of her Graces, 1986; Are You Listening Rabbi Low (novel), 1987; A Singular Country, 1989; That Darcy, That Dancer, That Gentleman (novel), 1990; contribs to jls etc., incl. The Observer, The Times (London), New York Times, Washington Post, Esquire, Envoy, Punch, Guardian, Saturday Evening Post, Holiday, Atlantic Monthly, Saturday Review, The New Yorker, Queen, Vogue, Penthouse, Playboy, Architectural Digest, Vanity Fair, Rolling Stone. *Address:* Levington Park, Mullingar, Co. Westmeath, Ireland.

DONN, Mary Cecilia, RGN; Regional Nursing Officer, North East Thames Regional Health Authority, since 1990; *b* 20 Sept. 1940; *d* of Francis and Mary Clark; *m* 1961, Robert Donn (marr. diss. 1975). *Educ:* St Vincent's Convent, Cork; Student Nurse, Whipps Cross Hosp. (RGN 1962); DipN London; William Rathbone Coll.; Thames Polytechnic (DMS). Post-graduate Staff Nurse, Charing Cross Hosp., 1962; Theatre Sister, St Mary's Hosp., Paddington, 1963–64; Theatre Sister, Nursing Officer, Sen. Nursing Officer, Bromley AHA, 1964–83; Dir, Nursing Services, Lewisham and N Southwark HA, 1983–84; Chief Nursing Officer and Dir, Consumer Affairs, Brighton HA, 1984–90. Former chm. and mem., nursing, health, editorial and advisory cttees; Chm., Nat. Assoc. of Theatre Nurses, 1975–78; Mem., NHS Training Authy, 1988–91. *Publications:* numerous contribs to professional jls. *Recreations:* horse-racing, cricket, gardening. *Address:* 2 Somerford Close, Maidenhead, Berks SL6 8EJ. *T:* Maidenhead (0628) 75526.

DONNACHIE, Prof. Alexander, FInstP; Professor of Physics since 1969, and Director of the Physical Laboratories since 1989, University of Manchester; *b* 25 May 1936; *s* of John Donnachie and Mary Ramsey Donnachie (*née* Adams); *m* 1960, Dorothy Paterson; two *d. Educ:* Kilmarnock Acad.; Glasgow Univ. (BSc, PhD). DSIR Res. Fellow 1961–63, Lectr 1963–65, UCL; Res. Associate, CERN, Geneva, 1965–67; Sen. Lectr, Univ. of Glasgow, 1967–69; Hd of Theoretical Physics 1975–85, Dean of Faculty of Science 1985–87, Univ. of Manchester. Mem., SERC, 1989– (Chm., Nuclear Phys Bd, 1989–); CERN: Chairman: Super Proton Synchrotron Cttee, 1988–90; Super Proton Synchrotron and LEAR Cttee, 1991–; Member: Res. Bd, 1988–; Sci. Policy Cttee, 1988–; Council, 1989–; Sec., C11 Commn, IUPAP, 1989–. *Publications:* Electromagnetic Interactions of Hadrons, vols I and II, 1978; over 100 articles in learned jls of Particle Physics. *Recreations:* sailing, walking. *Address:* Department of Physics, University of Manchester, Manchester M13 9PL. *T:* 061–273 4200.

DONNE, David Lucas; Chairman: Crest Nicholson PLC, since 1973; Steetley PLC, since 1983 (Deputy Chairman, 1979–83); Argos PLC, since 1990; *b* 17 Aug. 1925; *s* of late Dr Cecil Lucas Donne, Wellington, NZ, and of Marjorie Nicholls Donne; *m* 1st, 1957, Jennifer Margaret Duncan (*d* 1975); two *s* one *d*; 2nd, 1978, Clare, *d* of Maj. F. J. Yates. *Educ:* Stowe; Christ Church, Oxford (MA Nat. Science). Called to the Bar, Middle Temple, 1949. Studied Business Admin, Syracuse Univ., 1952–53; Charterhouse Group, 1953–64; William Baird, 1964–67. Chairman: Dalgety, 1977–86 (Dep. Chm., 1975–77); ASDA Gp, 1986–88; Director: Royal Trust Bank, 1972– (Dep. Chm., 1989–); Sphere Investment Trust, 1982– (Chm., 1989–). Member: Nat. Water Council, 1980–83; Bd, British Coal (formerly NCB), 1984–87; Stock Exchange Listed Cos Adv. Cttee, 1987–. Trustee, The Game Conservancy, 1987–. *Recreations:* shooting, opera, sailing. *Address:* Box 53, Brownsover Road, Rugby CV21 2UT. *Club:* Royal Thames Yacht.

DONNE, Hon. Sir Gaven (John), KBE 1979; Chief Justice: of Nauru, since 1985; of Tuvalu, since 1986; Member, Kiribati Court of Appeal, since 1987; *b* 8 May 1914; *s* of Jack Alfred Donne and Mary Elizabeth Donne; *m* 1946, Isabel Fenwick, *d* of John Edwin Hall; two *s* two *d. Educ:* Palmerston North Boys' High Sch.; Hastings High Sch.; Victoria Univ., Wellington; Auckland Univ. (LLB New Zealand). Called to the Bar and admitted solicitor, 1938. Military Service, 2nd NZEF, Middle East and Italy, 1941–45. Stipendiary Magistrate, NZ, 1958–75; Puisne Judge, Supreme Court of Western Samoa, 1970–71; Chief Justice, Western Samoa, 1972–75, Mem. Court of Appeal of Western Samoa, 1975–82; Judge, High Court of Niue, 1973; Chief Justice of the Cook Islands, 1975–82, and of Niue, 1974–82; Queen's Rep. in the Cook Islands, 1982–84. Hon. Counsellor, Internat. Assoc. of Youth Magistrates, 1974–. Member: Takapuna Bor. Council, 1957–58; Auckland Town Planning Authority, 1958; Bd of Governors, Westlake High Sch., 1957–58. Grand Cross 2nd Cl., Order of Merit of Fed. Republic of Germany, 1978. *Recreations:* golf, fishing, walking. *Address:* Meneng Drive, Nauru, Central Pacific. *T:* 3465; RD4, Otaramarae, Lake Rotoiti, Rotorua, New Zealand. *T:* Rotorua 073–24861. *Club:* University (Auckland).

DONNE, Sir John (Christopher), Kt 1976; Chairman, National Health Service Training Authority, 1983–86; *b* 19 Aug. 1921; *s* of late Leslie Victor Donne, solicitor, Hove, and Mabel Laetitia Richards (*née* Pike); *m* 1945, Mary Stuart (*née* Seaton); three *d. Educ:* Charterhouse. Royal Artillery, 1940–46 (Captain); served Europe and India. Solicitor, 1949; Notary Public; Consultant, Donne Mileham & Haddock; Pres., Sussex Law Soc., 1969–70. Chairman: SE (Metropolitan) Regional Hosp. Bd, 1971–74; SE Thames RHA, 1973–83. Governor, Guy's Hosp., 1971–74, Guy's Hosp. Med. Sch., 1974–82; Dep. Chm., RHA Chairmen, 1976–78 (Chm., 1974–76); Mem., Gen. Council, King Edward's Hosp. Fund for London, 1972– (Mem., Management Cttee, 1978–84); a Governing Trustee, Nuffield Provincial Hosp. Trust, 1975–; Dir, Nuffield Health and Soc. Services Fund, 1976–. Member: Council, Internat. Hosp. Fedn, 1979–85; Council, Inst. for Med. Ethics (formerly Soc. for Study of Medical Ethics), 1980–86; Court of Univ. of Sussex, 1979–87. FRSA 1985; FRSocMed 1985. Mem. Ct of Assts, Hon. Company of Broderers, 1979– (Master, 1983–84). Mem., Editorial Bd, Jl Medical Ethics, 1977–79. *Recreations:* genealogy, gardening, photography, listening to music. *Address:* The Old School House, Acton Burnell, Shrewsbury SY5 7PG. *T:* Acton Burnell (06944) 647. *Clubs:* Army and Navy, Pilgrims, MCC; Butterflies, Sussex Martlets.

DONNELLY, Alan John; Member (Lab) Tyne and Wear, European Parliament, since 1989; *b* 16 July 1957; *s* of John and Josephine Donnelly; *m* 1979 (marr. diss. 1982); one *s. Educ:* Valley View Primary School and Springfield Comprehensive School, Jarrow. GMBATU Northern Region: Health and Safety Officer, 1978–80; Education Officer, 1980–84; Finance and Admin. Officer, 1984–87; GMB Central Finance Manager, 1987–89. Local Govt Councillor, S Tyneside, 1980–84. B Director, Unity Trust Bank, 1987–89. *Recreations:* tennis, swimming, music. *Address:* 1 South View, Jarrow, Tyne and Wear. *T:* 091–489 7643.

DONNELLY, (Joseph) Brian; HM Diplomatic Service; Royal College of Defence Studies, 1991; *b* 24 April 1945; *s* of Joseph Donnelly and Ada Agnes (*née* Bowness); *m* 1966, Susanne Gibb (separated 1987); one *d. Educ:* Workington Grammar Sch.; Queen's Coll., Oxford (Wyndham Scholar, MA); Univ. of Wisconsin (MA). Joined HM Diplomatic Service, 1973; 2nd Sec., FCO, 1973; 1st Sec., UK Mission to UN, NY, 1975–79; Head of Chancery, Singapore, 1979–82; Asst Head, Personnel Policy Dept, FCO, 1982–84; Dep. to Chief Scientific Adviser, Cabinet Office, 1984–87; Counsellor and Consul General, Athens, 1988–91. *Recreations:* MG cars, running, reading, cooking, films. *Address:* c/o Foreign and Commonwealth Office, King Charles Street, SW1A 2AH. *Club:* MG Owners'.

DONNISON, Prof. David Vernon; Professor of Town and Regional Planning, Glasgow University, since 1980; *b* 19 Jan. 1926; *s* of F. S. V. Donnison, *qv*; *m* 1st, Jean Kidger; two *s* two *d*; 2nd, 1987, Catherine McIntosh, (Kay), Carmichael, *qv. Educ:* Marlborough Coll., Wiltshire; Magdalen Coll., Oxford. Asst Lecturer and Lecturer, Manchester Univ., 1950–53; Lecturer, Toronto Univ., 1953–55; Reader, London Sch. of Economics, 1956–61; Prof. of Social Administration, 1961–69; Dir, Centre for Environmental Studies, 1969–75. Chairman: Public Schs Commission, 1968–70; Supplementary Benefits Commn, 1975–80. Hon. Doctorates: Bradford, 1973; Hull, 1980; Leeds, Southampton, 1981. *Publications:* The Neglected Child and the Social Services, 1954; Welfare Services in a Canadian Community, 1958; Housing since the Rent Act, 1961; The Government of Housing, 1967; An Approach to Social Policy, 1975; Social Policy and Administration Revisited, 1975; (with Paul Soto) The Good City, 1980; The Politics of Poverty, 1982; (with Clare Ungerson) Housing Policy, 1982; (ed with Alan Middleton) Regenerating the Inner City: Glasgow's Experience, 1987. *Address:* The Old Manse, Ardentinny, Argyll PA23 8TR. *T:* Ardentinny (036981) 298.

DONNISON, Frank Siegfried Vernon, CBE 1943; Indian Civil Service (retired); *b* 3 July 1898; *s* of Frank Samuel and of Edith Donnison; *m* 1923, Ruth Seruya Singer, MBE, JP (*d* 1968); one *s* one *d. Educ:* Marlborough Coll.; Corpus Christi Coll., Oxford. Served with Grenadier Guards, 1917–19; ICS (Burma), 1922; Chief Sec. to Govt of Burma, 1946; military service, Burma, 1944–45 (despatches). Historian, Cabinet Office, Historical Section, 1949–66. *Publications:* Public Administration in Burma, 1953; British Military Administration in the Far East, 1943–46, 1956; Civil Affairs and Military Government, North-West Europe, 1944–46, 1961; Civil Affairs and Military Government, Central Organization and Planning, 1966; Burma, 1970. *Recreation:* music. *Address:* Lower Cross Farmhouse, East Hagbourne, Didcot OX11 9LD. *T:* Didcot (0235) 3314.

See also Professor D. V. Donnison.

DONNISON, Kay; *see* Carmichael, C. M.

DONOGHUE, Prof. Denis, MA, PhD; literary critic; Henry James Professor of Letters, New York University, since 1979; *b* 1928. *Educ:* University College, Dublin. BA 1949, MA 1952, PhD 1957; MA Cantab 1965. Admin. Office, Dept of Finance, Irish Civil Service, 1951–54. Asst Lectr, Univ. Coll., Dublin, 1954–57; Coll. Lectr, 1957–62; Visiting Schol., Univ. of Pennsylvania, 1962–63; Coll. Lectr, Univ. Coll., Dublin, 1963–64; University Lectr, Cambridge Univ., 1964–65; Fellow, King's Coll., Cambridge, 1964–65; Prof. of Modern English and American Literature, University Coll., Dublin, 1965–79. Mem. Internat. Cttee of Assoc. of University Profs of English. Mem. BBC Commn to monitor the quality of spoken English on BBC Radio, 1979. Reith Lectr, BBC, 1982. *Publications:* The Third Voice, 1959; Connoisseurs of Chaos, 1965; (ed jtly) An Honoured Guest, 1965; The Ordinary Universe, 1968; Emily Dickinson, 1968; Jonathan Swift, 1969; (ed) Swift, 1970; Yeats, 1971; Thieves of Fire, 1974; (ed) W. B. Yeats, Memoirs, 1973; Sovereign Ghost: studies in Imagination, 1978; Ferocious Alphabets, 1981; The Arts without Mystery, 1983; We Irish (selected essays), 1987; contribs to reviews and journals. *Address:* New York University, 19 University Place, New York, NY 10003, USA; Gaybrook, North Avenue, Mount Merrion, Dublin, Ireland.

DONOHOE, Peter Howard; pianist; *b* 18 June 1953; *s* of Harold Donohoe and Marjorie Donohoe (*née* Travis); *m* 1980, Elaine Margaret Burns; one *d. Educ:* Chetham's School of Music, Manchester; Leeds Univ.; Royal Northern Coll. of Music; Paris Conservatoire. BMus; GRNCM, ARCM; Hon. FRNCM 1983. Professional solo pianist, 1974–; London début, 1978; concert tours in Europe, USA, Canada, Australia, Asia, USSR; regular appearances at Royal Festival Hall, Barbican Hall, Queen Elizabeth Hall, Henry Wood Promenade concerts, 1979–; numerous TV and radio broadcasts, UK and overseas; recordings include music by Rachmaninov, Stravinsky, Prokofiev, Britten, Messiaen, Muldowney, Tchaikovsky. Competition finalist: British Liszt, London, 1976; Liszt-Bartok, Budapest, 1976; Leeds International Piano, 1981; winner, Internat. Tschaikovsky competition, Moscow, 1982. Concerto Recording Award, Gramophone, 1988. *Recreations:* jazz, golf, helping young musicians, clock collecting. *Address:* c/o IMG Artists (Europe), Media House, 3 Burlington Lane, W4 2TH.

DONOUGHMORE, 8th Earl of, *cr* 1800; **Richard Michael John Hely-Hutchinson;** Baron Donoughmore, 1783; Viscount Hutchinson (UK), 1821; Chairman, Headline Book Publishing PLC, since 1986; *b* 8 Aug. 1927; *er s* of 7th Earl of Donoughmore and of Dorothy Jean (MBE 1947), *d* of late J. B. Hotham; *S* father, 1981; *m* 1951, Sheila, *o c* of late Frank Frederick Parsons and Mrs Learmond Perkins; four *s. Educ:* Winchester; New College, Oxford (MA; BM, BCh). Chm., St Luke's Nursing Home, Oxford. *Heir: s* Viscount Suirdale, *qv. Address:* The Manor House, Bampton, Oxon OX8 2LQ. *Clubs:* Hurlingham; Kildare Street and University (Dublin); Jockey (Paris).

DONOUGHUE, family name of **Baron Donoughue**.

DONOUGHUE, Baron *cr* 1985 (Life Peer), of Ashton in the County of Northamptonshire; **Bernard Donoughue;** Executive Vice-Chairman, London and Bishopgate International Investment Holdings, since 1988; *b* 1934; *s* of late Thomas Joseph Donoughue and of Maud Violet Andrews; *m* 1959, Carol Ruth Goodman (marr. diss.); two *s* two *d. Educ:* Secondary Modern Sch. and Grammar Sch., Northampton; Lincoln Coll. and Nuffield Coll., Oxford. BA (1st class hons), MA, DPhil (Oxon). FRHistS. Henry Fellow, Harvard, USA. Mem., Editorial Staff: The Economist, Sunday Times, Sunday Telegraph. Sen. Res. Officer, PEP, 1960–63; Lectr, Sen. Lectr, Reader, LSE, 1963–74; Sen. Policy Advr to the Prime Minister, 1974–79; Development Dir, Economist Intelligence Unit, 1979–81; Asst Editor, The Times, 1981–82; Partner, 1983–86, Head of Res. and Investment Policy, 1984–86, Grieveson, Grant & Co; Dir, Kleinwort, Benson Ltd, 1986–88; Head of Res., 1986–87, of Internat. Res. and Investment Policy, 1987–88, Kleinwort Grieveson Securities. Member: Sports Council, 1965–71; Commn of Enquiry into Association Football, 1966–68; Ct of Governors, LSE, 1968–74, 1982–; Civil Service Coll. Adv. Council, 1976–79; Adv. Bd, Wissenschaftzentrum, Berlin, 1978–; Bd, Centre for European Policy Studies, Brussels, 1982–87; Council, Campaign for Freedom of Information, 1984–; Council, Employment Inst., 1985–; London Arts Bd, 1991–. Governor: Northampton Nene Coll., 1982– (Mem. Bd, 1979–); NE London Polytechnic, 1987–; Trustee, Inst. Public Policy Res., 1990–. Chm. Exec., London Symphony Orch., 1979– (Patron, 1989–). Associate Mem., Nuffield Coll., Oxford, 1982–87; Mem., Sen. Common Room, Lincoln Coll., Oxford, 1985– (Hon. Fellow, 1986); Internat. Fellow, Roosevelt Center for Policy Studies, Washington, DC, 1982–83; Patron, Inst. of Contemporary British History, 1988–. Hon. Fellow, LSE, 1989. Hon. LLD Leicester, 1990. *Publications:* (ed jtly) Oxford Poetry, 1956; Wage Policies in the Public Sector, 1962; Trade Unions in a Changing Society, 1963; British Politics and the American Revolution, 1964; (with W. T. Rodgers) The People into Parliament, 1966; (with G. W. Jones) Herbert Morrison: portrait of a politician, 1973; Prime Minister, 1987. *Recreations:* politics, economics, music, the Gay Hussar. *Address:* 11 Bloomfield Terrace, SW1W 8PG.

DONOVAN, Charles Edward; Board Member, since 1981, and Senior Managing Director, Corporate Activities, since 1991, British Gas plc; *b* 28 Jan. 1934; *s* of Charles and Sarah Donovan; *m* 1963, Robina Evelyn (*née* Anderson); three *s*. *Educ:* Camphill Sch., Paisley; Royal Technical Coll., Glasgow. FIPM 1990; CIGasE 1985; CBIM 1991. Personnel Officer: HQ, BEA, 1962; London and SE, Richard Costain Ltd, Constr. and Civil Engrs, 1963; Sen. Personnel Officer, Engrg, W Midlands Gas Bd, 1966; Southern Gas, 1970–77: Personnel Manager, 1973; Personnel Dir, 1975; British Gas: Dir, Indust. Relations, 1977; Man. Dir, Personnel, 1981–91, also Group Services, 1989–91. *Recreations:* sailing, hill walking. *Address:* British Gas plc, Rivermill House, 152 Grosvenor Road, SW1V 3JL.

DONOVAN, Prof. Desmond Thomas; Yates-Goldsmid Professor of Geology and Head of Department of Geology, University College, London, 1966–82; Hon. Curator, Wells Museum, Somerset, 1982–85; *b* 16 June 1921; *s* of T. B. Donovan; *m* 1959, Shirley Louise Saward; two *s* one *d*. *Educ:* Epsom Coll.; University of Bristol. BSc 1942; PhD 1951; DSc 1960. Asst Lectr in Geology, University of Bristol, 1947; Lectr in Geology, Bristol, 1950; Prof. of Geology, University of Hull, 1962. Pres., Palaeontographical Soc., 1979–84. *Publications:* Stratigraphy: An Introduction to Principles, 1966; (ed) Geology of Shelf Seas, 1968; papers on fossil cephalopods, Jurassic stratigraphy, Pleistocene deposits, marine geology. *Address:* 52 Willow Road, NW3 1TP. *T:* 071-794 8626. *Club:* Athenæum.

DONOVAN, Ian Edward, FCMA; Director and Group Controller, Smiths Industries Aerospace & Defence Ltd, since 1988; *b* 2 March 1940; *s* of late John Walter Donovan and Ethel Molyneux; *m* 1969, Susan Betty Harris; two *s*. *Educ:* Leighton Park, Reading. FCMA 1985. Gen. Factory Manager, Lucas CAV, 1969–72; Finance Man., Lucas Girling, 1972–78; Finance Director: Lucas Girling, Koblenz, 1978–81; Lucas Electrical Ltd, 1982–84; Mem., 1985–88, Gp Dir, Finance and Central Services, 1986–88, CAA. *Recreations:* sailing, gardening, music. *Address:* Lawn Farm, Church Lane, Tibberton, Droitwich, Worcs WR9 7NW.

DOOGE, Prof. James Clement Ignatius; Professor of Civil Engineering, University College, Dublin, 1970–84, now Professor Emeritus; research consultant; Consultant: United Nations; Commission of European Community; specialised agencies; President, Royal Irish Academy, 1987–90; *b* 30 July 1922; *s* of Denis Patrick Dooge and Veronica Catherine Carroll; *m* 1946, Veronica O'Doherty; two *s* three *d*. *Educ:* Christian Brothers' Sch., Dun Laoghaire; University Coll., Dublin (BE, BSc 1942, ME 1952); Univ. of Iowa (MSc 1956). FICE; FASCE. Jun. Civil Engr, Irish Office of Public Works, 1943–46; Design Engr, Electricity Supply Bd, Ireland, 1946–58; Prof. of Civil Engrg, UC Cork, 1958–70. Irish Senate: Mem., 1965–77 and 1981–87; Chm., 1973–77; Leader, 1983–87; Minister for Foreign Affairs, Ireland, 1981–82. President: ICEI, 1968–69 (Hon. FICEI; Kettle Premium and Plaque, 1948, 1985; Mullins Medal, 1951, 1962); Internat. Assoc. for Hydrologic Scis, 1975–79; Member: Exec. Bureau, Internat. Union for Geodesy and Geophysics, 1979–87; Gen. Cttee, ICSU, 1980–86, 1988– (Sec. Gen., 1980–82). Fellow, Amer. Geophysical Union (Horton Award, 1959; Bowie Medal, 1986). Hon. DrAgrSc Wageningen, 1978; Hon. DrTech. Lund, 1980; Hon. DSc Birmingham, 1986; Hon. ScD Dublin, 1988. Internat. Prize for Hydrology, 1983. *Address:* Centre for Water Resources Research, University College, Earlsfort Terrace, Dublin 2, Ireland.

DOOKUN, Sir Dewoonarain, Kt 1984; Chairman and Managing Director, Mauritius Cosmetics Ltd, since 1966; *b* 7 Dec. 1929; *s* of Jadoonath Dookun; *m* 1959, Henriette Keupp; two *s*. *Educ:* St Joseph College; Univ. of Edinburgh. Manufacturing, marketing, business administration and accounts, Mainz, West Germany; founder of: Mauritius Cosmetics, 1966; Paper Converting Co., 1967; Jet Industries, 1967; FDG Garments Industries, 1968; Agri-Pac, 1979; Deramann, 1979; Gumboots Manufacturers, 1976; DG Rubber, 1979; Elite Textiles, 1982; Deodan Textile, 1984. *Recreations:* reading, walking, golf. *Address:* Queen Mary Avenue, Floreal, Mauritius. *T:* 86-2361; *telex:* 4239 Dookun IW. *Clubs:* Institute of Directors; Mauritius Gymkhana; Swastika.

DOOLITTLE, Gen. James H.; Hon. KCB 1945; Trustee, 1963–69 (Chairman of Executive Committee and Vice-Chairman, Board of Trustees, 1965–69), Aerospace Corporation; Chairman of Board, Space Technology Laboratories, Inc., 1959–62; Emeritus Director: Mutual of Omaha Insurance Co.; United Benefit Life Insurance Co.; Tele-Trip Co., Inc.; *b* 14 Dec. 1896; *s* of Frank H. Doolittle and Rosa C. Shephard; *m* 1917, Josephine E. Daniels; two *s*. *Educ:* University of California (AB); MIT (MS, ScD). US Army Air Force, 1917–30; Manager, Aviation Dept, Shell Oil Co., 1930–40; USAAF, 1940–45. Dir, Shell Oil Company, 1946–67 (Vice-Pres., 1946–59). *Publications:* various scientific. *Recreations:* shooting, fishing. *Address:* PO Box 566, Pebble Beach, Calif 93953, USA.

DORAN, Frank; MP (Lab) Aberdeen South, since 1987; *b* 13 April 1949; *s* of Francis Anthony Doran and Betty Hedges or Doran; *m* 1967, Patricia Ann Govan or Doran; two *s*. *Educ:* Ainslie Park Secondary Sch.; Leith Acad.; Dundee Univ. (LLB Hons). Admitted Solicitor, 1977. Eur. Parly Cand. (Lab) NE Scotland, 1984. Asst Editor, Scottish Legal Action Group Bulletin, 1975–78. *Recreations:* cinema, art, sports. *Address:* 12 Laurelbank, Dundee. *T:* Dundee (0382) 27086. *Clubs:* Aberdeen Trades Council; Dundee Labour.

DORAN, John Frederick, CEng, FInstGasE, MInstM; Chairman, East Midlands Gas Region, 1974–77; *b* 28 July 1916; *s* of Henry Joseph and Clara Doran; *m* 1940, Eileen Brotherton; two *s*. *Educ:* Wandsworth Technical Coll.; Wimbledon Technical Coll. Served War, Fleet Air Arm, 1943–46. Various appts Gas Light & Coke Co. (subseq. North Thames Gas Bd), 1935–53; Dist Manager, Hornsey Dist, North Thames Gas Bd, 1953; Regional Sales Manager, North Western Div., North Thames Gas Bd, 1955–57. Southern Gas Board: Regional Sales and Service Manager, Southampton Region and Dorset and Bournemouth Regions, 1957–65; Marketing Manager, 1965–67; Commercial Manager, 1968–69; Commercial Dir, 1970–71; Commercial Dir and Bd Mem., 1971–73. Dep. Chm., East Midlands Gas Region, 1973. Founder, John Doran Gas Museum, Leicester. *Publications:* technical papers to Instn Gas Engrs. *Recreations:* golf, gardening. *Address:* 14 Oberfield Road, Brockenhurst, Hants SO42 7QF. *T:* Lymington (0590) 23185.

DORCHESTER, Area Bishop of, since 1988; **Rt. Rev. Anthony John Russell,** DPhil; *b* 25 Jan. 1943; *s* of Michael John William and Beryl Margaret Russell; *m* 1967, Sheila Alexandra, *d* of Alexander Scott and Elizabeth Carlisle Ronald; two *s* two *d*. *Educ:* Uppingham Sch; Univ. of Durham (BA); Trinity Coll., Oxford (DPhil); Cuddesdon Coll., Oxford. Deacon 1970, Priest 1971; Curate, Hilborough Group of Parishes, 1970–73; Rector, Preston on Stour, Atherstone on Stour and Whitchurch, 1973–88; Chaplain, Arthur Rank Centre (Nat. Agricl Centre), 1973–82, Director, 1983–88; Chaplain to the Queen, 1983–88. Canon Theologian, Coventry Cathedral, 1977–88. Mem., Gen. Synod, 1980–88. Chaplain, Royal Agricl Soc., 1982–, Council Mem., 1983–; Hon. Chaplain, RABI, 1983–. *Publications:* Groups and Teams in the Countryside (ed), 1975; The Village in Myth and Reality, 1980; The Clerical Profession, 1980; The Country Parish, 1986. *Address:* Holmby House, Sibford Ferris, Banbury, Oxfordshire OX15 5RG.

DORE, Prof. Ronald Philip, CBE 1989; FBA 1975; Director, Japan–Europe Industry Research Centre, Imperial College of Science, Technology and Medicine, University of London, since 1986; Adjunct Professor, Massachusetts Institute of Technology, since 1989; *b* 1 Feb. 1925; *s* of Philip Brine Dore and Elsie Constance Dore; *m* 1957, Nancy Macdonald; one *s* one *d*. *Educ:* Poole Grammar Sch.; SOAS, Univ. of London (BA). Lectr in Japanese Instns, SOAS, London, 1951; Prof. of Asian Studies, Univ. of BC, 1956; Reader, later Prof. of Sociol., LSE, 1961 (Hon. Fellow, 1980); Fellow IDS, 1969–82; Asst Dir, Technical Change Centre, 1982–86. Vis. Prof., Imperial Coll., London Univ., 1982–86. Mem., Academia Europaea. Hon. Foreign Mem., Amer. Acad. of Arts and Scis, 1978; Hon. Foreign Fellow, Japan Acad., 1986–. Order of the Rising Sun (Third Class), Japan, 1988. *Publications:* City Life in Japan, 1958; Land Reform in Japan, 1959, 2nd edn 1984; Education in Tokugawa Japan, 1963, 2nd edn 1983; (ed) Aspects of Social Change in Modern Japan, 1967; British Factory, Japanese Factory, 1973; The Diploma Disease, 1976; Shinohata: portrait of a Japanese village, 1978; (ed with Zoe Mars) Community Development, Comparative Case Studies in India, The Republic of Korea, Mexico and Tanzania, 1981; Energy Conservation in Japanese Industry, 1982; Flexible Rigidities: structural adjustment in Japan, 1986; Taking Japan Seriously: a Confucian perspective on leading economic issues, 1987; (ed jtly) Japan and World Depression, Then and Now: essays in memory of E. F. Penrose, 1987; (with Mari Sako) How the Japanese Learn to Work, 1988; (ed jtly) Corporatism and Accountability: organized interests in British public life, 1990; Will the 21st Century be the Age of Individualism?, 1991. *Address:* 157 Surrenden Road, Brighton, East Sussex BN1 6ZA. *T:* Brighton (0273) 501370. *Club:* Reform.

DOREY, Graham Martyn; Deputy Bailiff of Guernsey, 1982–92, Bailiff, from Feb. 1992; *b* 15 Dec. 1932; *s* of late Martyn Dorey and Muriel (*née* Pickard); *m* 1962, Penelope Cecile, *d* of Maj. E. A. Wheadon, ED; two *s* two *d*. *Educ:* Kingswood Sch., Bath; Ecole des Roches, Verneuil; Univs of Bristol and Caen. Admitted Solicitor, 1959; Advocate, Royal Court of Guernsey, 1960; People's Deputy, States of Guernsey, 1970; Solicitor Gen., 1973, Attorney Gen., 1977, Guernsey. *Recreation:* sailing. *Address:* La Hougue ès Pies, Vale, Guernsey. *Clubs:* Royal Ocean Racing; Royal Yacht Squadron.

DORIN, Bernard Jean Robert; Officier de la Légion d'Honneur; Officier de l'Ordre National du Mérite; Ambassador of France to the Court of St James's, since 1990; *b* 25 Aug. 1929; *s* of Robert Dorin and Jacqueline Dorin (*née* Goumard); *m* 1971, Christine du Bois de Meyrignac; two *s* two *d*. *Educ:* Inst. d'Etudes Politiques, Paris; Ecole Nat. d'Administration. Attaché, French Embassy, Ottawa, 1957–59; Min. of Foreign Affairs, 1959–64; technical adviser: for sci. research, nuclear and space, 1966–67; to Minister of Nat. Educn, 1967–68; to Minister for sci. research, 1968–69; Harvard Univ., 1969–70; Min. of Foreign Affairs, 1970–71; Ambassador in Port-au-Prince, 1972–75; Head of Francophone Affairs Dept, 1975–78; Ambassador in Pretoria, 1978–81; Dir for America, Min. of Foreign Affairs, 1981–84; Ambassador, Brazil, 1984–87, Japan, 1987–90. *Recreations:* collections of naïve paintings. *Address:* French Embassy, 58 Knightsbridge, SW1X 7JT. *T:* 071–235 8080. *Club:* Richelieu (Paris).

DORKING, Suffragan Bishop of, since 1986; **Rt. Rev. David Peter Wilcox;** *b* 29 June 1930; *s* of John Wilcox and Stella Wilcox (*née* Bower); *m* 1956, Pamela Ann Hedges; two *s* two *d*. *Educ:* Northampton Grammar School; St John's Coll., Oxford (2nd cl. Hons Theol., MA); Lincoln Theological Coll. Deacon 1954, priest 1955; Asst Curate, St Peter's, St Helier, Morden, Surrey, 1954–56; Asst Curate, University Church, Oxford and SCM Staff Secretary in Oxford, 1956–59; on staff of Lincoln Theological Coll., 1959–64; USPG Missionary on staff of United Theological Coll., Bangalore, and Presbyter in Church of S India, 1964–70; Vicar of Great Gransden with Little Gransden, dio. Ely, 1970–72; Canon Residentiary, Derby Cathedral and Warden, E Midlands Joint Ordination Training Scheme, 1972–77; Proctor in Convocation, 1973–77; Principal of Ripon College, Cuddesdon and Vicar of All Saints', Cuddesdon, 1977–85. *Recreations:* walking, music, art, theatre. *Address:* Dayspring, 13 Pilgrims Way, Guildford, Surrey GU4 8AD. *T:* Guildford (0483) 570829.

DORKING, Archdeacon of; *see* Herbert, Ven. C. W.

DORMAN, Lt-Col Sir Charles (Geoffrey), 3rd Bt *cr* 1923; MC 1942; *b* 18 Sept. 1920; *o s* of Sir Bedford Lockwood Dorman, 2nd Bart, CBE and Lady Constance Phelps Dorman (*née* Hay), (*d* 1946); *S* father 1956; *m* 1954, Elizabeth Ann (marr. diss. 1972), *d* of late George Gilmour Gilmour-White, OBE; one *d*. *Educ:* Rugby Sch.; Brasenose Coll., Oxford (MA). Commissioned, 1941; served with 3rd The King's Own Hussars at Alamein (MC) and in Italian Campaign; Commissioned to 13th/18th Royal Hussars (QMO), 1947; GSO1, 1961–70; retired. *Recreation:* gliding. *Heir: cousin* Philip Henry Keppel Dorman [*b* 19 May 1954; *m* 1982, Myriam Jeanne Georgette, *d* of late René Bay; one *d*]. *Address:* Hutton Grange Cottage, Great Rollright, Chipping Norton, Oxon OX7 5SN.

DORMAN, Sir Maurice Henry, GCMG 1961 (KCMG 1957; CMG 1955); GCVO 1961; DL; MA; retired; Governor and Commander-in-Chief, Malta, 1962–64, and after independence, Governor-General, 1964–71; *b* 7 Aug. 1912; *s* of late John Ehrenfried and late Madeleine Louise Dorman; *m* 1937, Florence Monica Churchward Smith, DStJ 1968; one *s* three *d*. *Educ:* Sedbergh Sch.; Magdalene Coll., Cambridge. Administrative Officer, Tanganyika Territory, 1935; Clerk of Councils, Tanganyika, 1940–45; Asst to the Lt-Governor, Malta, 1945; Principal Asst Sec., Palestine, 1947; Seconded to Colonial Office as Asst Sec., Social Services Dept, 1948; Dir of Social Welfare and Community Develt, Gold Coast, 1950; Colonial Sec., Trinidad and Tobago, 1952–56; Actg Governor of Trinidad, 1954, 1955; Governor, Comdr-in-Chief and Vice-Adm., Sierra Leone, 1956–61, after independence, Governor-Gen., 1961–62. Dep. Chm., Pearce Commn on Rhodesia, 1971–72; Chm., British observers of Zimbabwe independence elecns, 1980. Chairman: Swindon HMC, 1972–74; Wilts AHA, 1974–82; Swindon HA, 1982–88. Chm., West of England (formerly Ramsbury) Bldg Soc., 1983–87 (Dir, 1972–87; Vice-Chm., 1981–83). Vice Pres., Badminton Sch., 1966– (Chm. Bd of Govs, 1975–81); Life Governor, Monkton Combe Sch., 1984–. A Trustee, Imperial War Museum, 1972–85; Venerable Order of St John of Jerusalem: Almoner, 1972–75; Chief Comdr, St John Ambulance, 1975–80; Lord Prior, 1980–86; Mem., Chapter-Gen., 1972–. DL Wilts 1978. Hon. DCL Durham, 1962; Hon. LLD Royal Univ. Malta, 1964. GCStJ 1978 (KStJ 1957). Gran Croce Al Merito Melitense (Soc. Ordine Militaire di Malta), 1966. *Recreations:* once sailing and squash, sometimes golf. *Address:* The Old Manor, Overton, Marlborough, Wilts SN8 4ER. *T:* Lockeridge (067286) 600. *Clubs:* Athenæum; Casino Maltese (Valletta).

See also R. B. Dorman.

DORMAN, Richard Bostock, CBE 1984; HM Diplomatic Service, retired; High Commissioner to Vanuatu, 1982–85; Chairman, the British Friends of Vanuatu, since 1986; *b* 8 Aug. 1925; *s* of late John Ehrenfried and late Madeleine Louise Dorman; *m* 1950, Anna Illingworth; one *s* two *d*. *Educ:* Sedbergh Sch.; St John's Coll., Cambridge. Army Service (Lieut, S Staffs Regt), 1944–48; Asst Principal, War Office, 1951; Principal, 1955; transferred to Commonwealth Relations Office, 1958; First Sec., British High Commission, Nicosia, 1960–64; Dep. High Commissioner, Freetown, 1964–66; SE Asia Dept, FO, 1967–69; Counsellor, Addis Ababa, 1969–73; Commercial Counsellor, Bucharest, 1974–77; Counsellor, Pretoria, 1977–82. *Address:* 67 Beresford Road, Cheam, Surrey SM2 6ER. *T:* 081–642 9627. *Club:* Commonwealth Trust.

See also Sir M. H. Dorman.

DORMAND, family name of **Baron Dormand of Easington.**

DORMAND OF EASINGTON, Baron *cr* 1987 (Life Peer), of Easington in the county of Durham; **John Donkin Dormand;** *b* 27 Aug. 1919; *s* of Bernard and Mary Dormand; *m* 1963, Doris Robinson; one step *s* one step *d*. *Educ:* Bede Coll., Durham; Loughborough Coll.; Univs of Oxford and Harvard. Teacher, 1940–48; Education Adviser, 1948–52 and 1957–63; District Education Officer, Easington RDC, 1963–70. MP (Lab) Easington, 1970–87. An Asst Govt Whip, 1974; a Lord Comr of HM Treasury, 1974–79; Chm., PLP, 1981–87. *Recreations:* music, sport.

DORMER, family name of **Baron Dormer.**

DORMER, 16th Baron *cr* 1615; **Joseph Spencer Philip Dormer;** Bt 1615; landowner and farmer; *b* 4 Sept. 1914; *s* of 14th Baron Dormer, CBE, and Caroline May (*d* 1951), *y d* of Sir Robert Cavendish Spencer Clifford, 3rd Bt; *S* brother, 1975. *Educ:* Ampleforth; Christ Church, Oxford. Served World War II, Scots Guards. Consultant, Thomas Comely & Sons Ltd. Pres., Warwick and Leamington Conservative Assoc., 1983–. Formerly Mem. Council, West Midlands Area Conservative Assoc. Hon. Vice-Pres., Worcs Br., Grenadier Gds Assoc. Kt of Honour and Devotion, SMO Malta, 1989. *Heir: cousin* Geoffrey Henry Dormer [*b* 13 May 1920; *m* 1st, 1947, Janet (marr. diss. 1957), *yr d* of James F. A. Readman; two *d*; 2nd, 1958, Pamela, *d* of late Wallace Levick Simpson; two *s*]. *Address:* Grove Park, Warwick CV35 8RF. *Club:* Cavalry and Guards.

DORNHORST, Antony Clifford, CBE 1977; MD, FRCP; Professor of Medicine, St George's Hospital Medical School, 1959–80; Civilian Consultant in Aviation Medicine to RAF, 1973–85; *b* 2 April 1915; *s* of Ernst Dornhorst and Florence, *née* Partridge; *m* 1946, Helen Mary Innes; three *d*. *Educ:* St Clement Danes Sch.; St Thomas's Hosp. Medical Sch. MB BS London 1937; MD London 1939; FRCP 1955. Junior Appointments, St Thomas' Hosp., 1937–39. Served with RAMC, mostly in Mediterranean theatre, 1940–46. Reader in Medicine, St Thomas's Hosp. Medical Sch., 1949–59. Member: MRC, 1973–77; SW Thames RHA, 1974–82. *Publications:* papers in various journals on normal and abnormal physiology. *Recreation:* music. *Address:* 8 Albert Place, W8 5PD. *T:* 071–937 8782.

DORR, Noel; Secretary, Department of Foreign Affairs, Ireland, since 1987; *b* Limerick, 1933; *m* 1983, Caitríona Doran. *Educ:* St Nathy's Coll., Ballaghaderreen; University Coll., Galway (BA, BComm, HDipEd); Georgetown Univ., Washington, DC (MA). Entered Dept of Foreign Affairs, 1960; Third Sec., 1960–62; Third Sec., Brussels, 1962–64; First Sec., Washington, 1964–70; First Sec., Dept of For. Affairs, 1970–72; Counsellor (Press and Inf.), Dept of For. Affairs, 1972–74; Asst Sec., Political Div., and Political Dir, 1974–77, Dep. Sec. and Political Dir, 1977–80; Perm. Rep. of Ireland to UN, New York, 1980–83; Rep of Ireland, Security Council, 1981–82; Ambassador of Ireland to UK, 1983–87. *Address:* Department of Foreign Affairs, 80 St Stephen's Green, Dublin 2, Ireland.

DORRELL, Ernest John; Secretary, Headmasters' Conference, 1975–79; General Secretary, Secondary Heads Association, 1978–79 (Secretary, Incorporated Association of Headmasters, 1975–77); *b* 31 March 1915; *s* of John Henry Whiting Dorrell and Amy Dorrell (*née* Roberts); *m* 1940, Alwen Irvona Jones; one *s* one *d*. *Educ:* Taunton Sch.; Exeter Coll., Oxford (Exhibr). Hon. Mods and Lit. Hum., MA. Served with 71 Field Regt and HQ 46 Div. RA, 1940–46. Asst Master, Dauntsey's Sch., 1937–40 and 1946–47; Admin. Asst, WR Educn Dept, 1947; Dep. Dir of Educn, Oxfordshire CC, 1950; Dir of Educn, Oxfordshire CC, 1970; Report on Educn in St Helena, 1974. *Recreations:* walking, travel, golf. *Address:* Swan Cottage, Shillingford, Wallingford, Oxon OX10 7EW. *T:* Warborough (086732) 8342.

DORRELL, Stephen James; MP (C) Loughborough, since 1979; Parliamentary Under-Secretary of State, Department of Health, since 1990; *b* 25 March 1952; *s* of Philip Dorrell; *m* 1980, Penelope Anne Wears, *y d* of Mr and Mrs James Taylor, Windsor. *Educ:* Uppingham; Brasenose Coll., Oxford. BA 1973. RAFVR, 1971–73. Personal asst to Rt Hon. Peter Walker, MBE, MP, Feb. 1974; contested (C) Kingston-upon-Hull East, Oct. 1974; PPS to the Secretary of State for Energy, 1983–87; Asst Govt Whip, 1987–88; a Lord Comr of HM Treasury (Govt Whip), 1988–90. Sec., Cons. Backbench Trade Cttee, 1980–81. Bd Mem., Christian Aid, 1985–87. *Recreations:* aviation, reading. *Address:* House of Commons, SW1A 0AA.

DORSET, Archdeacon of; *see* Walton, Ven. G. E.

DORWARD, William, OBE 1977; Commissioner for Hong Kong Economic Affairs, United States, 1983–87, retired; *b* 25 Sept. 1929; *s* of Alexander and Jessie Dorward; *m* 1960, Rosemary Ann Smith; one *s*. *Educ:* Morgan Academy, Dundee. Colonial Office, 1951–53; Commerce and Industry Dept, Hong Kong Govt, 1954–74; Counsellor (Hong Kong Affairs) UK Mission, Geneva, 1974–76; Hong Kong Government: Dep. Dir of Commerce and Industry, 1974–77; Comr of Industry and Customs, 1977–79; Dir of Trade, Industry and Customs, 1979–82, Sec. for Trade and Industry, 1982–83; Mem. Legislative Council, 1979–83. *Address:* Waulkmill House, Skirling, by Biggar ML12 6HB. *Clubs:* Carlton, Royal Over-Seas League; Hong Kong.

DOS SANTOS, Sir Errol Lionel, Kt 1946; CBE 1939; Consultant, Alstons Ltd; *b* 1 Sept. 1890; *s* of Solomon and Margaret dos Santos; *m* 1st, 1915; one *s* one *d*; 2nd, 1939, Enid Hilda Jenkin, Bath, England; two *d*. *Educ:* St Mary's Coll., Trinidad. Entered Trinidad Civil Service as a junior clerk in the Treasury; Financial Sec., 1941; Colonial Sec., 1947; retired from Colonial Service, 1948. Dir, Alstons Ltd, 1948, Chm. 1953–61. *Address:* Flat 3, 7 Bryanston Square, W1. *Clubs:* MCC; Union, Queen's Park Cricket, Portuguese (Trinidad).

DOSSER, Prof. Douglas George Maurice; Professor of Economics, University of York, 1965–81; retired, 1981; *b* 3 Oct. 1927; *s* of George William Dosser; *m* 1954, Valerie Alwyne Elizabeth, *d* of Leslie Jack Lindsey; three *d*. *Educ:* Latymer Upper School; London School of Economics. Lecturer in Economics, Univ. of Edinburgh, 1958–62; Vis. Prof. of Economics, Univ. of Washington, Seattle, 1960; Vis. Res. Prof. of Economics, Columbia Univ., NY, 1962; Reader in Economics, Univ. of York, 1963–65. *Publications:* Economic Analysis of Tax Harmonisation, 1967; (with S. Han) Taxes in the EEC and Britain, 1968; (with F. Andic) Theory of Economic Integration for Developing Countries, 1971; European Economic Integration and Monetary Unification, 1973; (with K. Hartley) The Collaboration of Nations, 1981; articles in Economic Jl, Economica, Rev. of Economic Studies. *Recreations:* art and antiques.

DOTRICE, Roy; actor (stage, films and television); *b* 26 May 1925; *m* 1946, Kay Newman, actress; three *d*. *Educ:* Dayton and Intermediate Schs, Guernsey, CI. Served War of 1939–45: Air Gunner, RAF, 1940; PoW, 1942–45. Acted in Repertory, 1945–55; formed and directed Guernsey Theatre Co., 1955; Royal Shakespeare Co., 1957–65 (Caliban, Julius Caesar, Hotspur, Firs, Puntila, Edward IV, etc); World War 2½, New Theatre, London, 1966; Brief Lives, Golden Theatre, New York, 1967; Latent Heterosexual and God Bless, Royal Shakespeare Co., Aldwych, 1968; Brief Lives (one-man play), Criterion, 1969 (over 400 perfs, world record for longest-running solo perf.), toured England, Canada, USA, 1973, Mayfair, 1974 (over 150 perfs); Broadway season, 1974; Australian tour, 1975; Peer Gynt, Chichester Festival, 1970; One At Night, Royal Court, 1971; The Hero, Edinburgh, 1970; Mother Adam, Arts, 1971; Tom Brown's Schooldays, Cambridge, 1972; The Hollow Crown, seasons in USA 1973 and 1975, Sweden 1975; Gomes, Queen's, 1973; The Dragon Variation, Duke of York's, 1977; Australian tour with Chichester Festival, 1978; Passion of Dracula, Queen's, 1978; Oliver, Albery, 1979; Mister Lincoln (one-man play on Abraham Lincoln), Washington, NY and TV special, 1980, Fortune, 1981; A Life, NY, 1980–81; Henry V, and Falstaff in Henry IV, American Shakespeare Theatre, Stratford, Conn, 1981; Murder in Mind, Strand, 1982; Winston Churchill (one-man play), USA 1982 (also CBS TV); Kingdoms, NY, 1982; The Genius, Los Angeles, 1984 (Dramalogue Best Perf. Award); Down an Alley, Dallas, 1984; Great Expectations, Old Vic, 1985; Enemy of the People, NY, 1985; Hay Fever, NY and Washington, 1986; *films include:* Heroes of Telemark, Twist of Sand, Lock up Your Daughters, Buttercup Chain, Tomorrow, One of Those Things, Nicholas and Alexandra, Amadeus, Corsican Brothers, The Eliminators, Camilla, L-Dopa, The Lady Forgets. *Television:* appearances in: Dear Liar, Brief Lives, The Caretaker (Emmy award), Imperial Palace, Misleading Cases, Clochemerle, Dickens of London, Stargazy on Zummerdown, Family Reunion (USA), Tales of the Gold Monkey (USA), The Wizard (USA), A Team (USA), Tales from the Dark-Side (USA), Beauty and the Beast (USA), etc. TV Actor of the Year Award, 1968; Tony Nomination for A Life, 1981. *Recreations:* fishing, riding. *Club:* Garrick.

DOUBLEDAY, John Vincent; sculptor since 1968; *b* 9 Oct. 1947; *s* of Gordon V. and Margaret E. V. Doubleday; *m* 1969, Isobel J. C. Durie; three *s*. *Educ:* Stowe; Goldsmiths' College School of Art. *Exhibitions include:* Waterhouse Gallery, 1968, 1969, 1970, 1971; Galerie Sothmann, Amsterdam, 1969, 1971, 1979; Richard Demarco Gallery, Edinburgh, 1973; Laing Art Gallery, Newcastle, Bowes Museum, Barnard Castle, 1974; Pandion Gallery, NY, Aldeburgh Festival, 1983; *works include:* Baron Ramsey of Canterbury, 1974; King Olav of Norway, 1975; Prince Philip, Duke of Edinburgh, Earl Mountbatten of Burma, Golda Meir, 1976; Ratu Sukuna, 1977; Regeneration, 1978; Maurice Bowra, 1979; Charlie Chaplin (Leicester Square), Lord Olivier, Mary and Child Christ, 1981; Caduceus (Harvard, Mass), Lord Feather (TUC Congress House), Isambard Kingdom Brunel (two works), Charlie Chaplin (Vevey), 1982; Beatles (Liverpool), Dylan Thomas, Phoenix, 1984; Royal Marines Commando Meml, Lympstone, Devon, 1986; Sherlock Holmes (Meiringen), 1988; Arthur Mourant (St Helier Mus.), 1990; *works in public collections:* Ashmolean Mus., British Mus., Herbert F. Johnson Mus., USA, Tate Gall., V & A, Nat. Mus. of Wales. *Recreations:* cross country skiing, fishing. *Address:* Lodge Cottage, Great Totham, Maldon, Essex CM9 8BX. *T:* Maldon (0621) 892085.

DOUCE, Prof. John Leonard, FIEE; Professor of Electrical Science, Warwick University, since 1965 (part-time since 1989); *b* 15 Aug. 1932; *s* of John William and Florrie Douce; *m* 1959, Jean Shanks; one *s* one *d*. *Educ:* Manchester Grammar Sch.; Manchester Univ. (BSc, MSc, PhD, DSc). SMIEEE, CEng. Lectr, Sen. Lectr, Reader, Queen's Univ., Belfast, 1958–65. Member: Technology Sub-Cttee, UGC, 1980–89; Engrg Bd, 1987–, Science Bd, 1989–, SERC. Sir Harold Hartley Silver Medal, Inst. of Measurement and Control, 1989. *Publications:* Introduction to Mathematics of Servomechanisms, 1963, 2nd edn 1972; papers on control engineering. *Recreations:* bridge, boating, home-brewing. *Address:* 259 Station Road, Balsall Common, Coventry CV7 7EG. *T:* Berkswell (0676) 32070.

DOUEK, Ellis Elliot, FRCS; Consultant Otologist since 1970, and Chairman, Hearing Research Group, since 1974, Guy's Hospital; *b* 25 April 1934; *s* of Cesar Douek and Nelly Sassoon; *m* 1964, Nicole Galante; two *s*. *Educ:* English School, Cairo; Westminster Medical School. MRCS, LRCP 1958; FRCS 1967. House appts, St Helier Hosp., 1959, and Whittington Hosp., 1963; nat. service, RAMC, 1960–62; ENT Registrar, Royal Free Hosp., 1966; Sen. Registrar, King's College Hosp., 1968. Mem., MRC working party on Hearing Research, 1975; MRC Rep. to Europ. Communities on Hearing Res., 1980; UK Rep. to Europ. Communities on Indust. Deafness, 1983; Mem., Scientific Cttee, Inst. de Recherche sur la surdité, Paris, 1989–. Dalby Prize for hearing research, RSM, 1978. *Publications:* Sense of Smell—Its Abnormalities, 1974; Eighth Nerve, in Peripheral Neuropathy, 1975; Olfaction, in Scientific Basis of Otolaryngology, 1976; Cochlear Implant, in Textbook of ENT, 1980; papers on hearing and smell. *Recreations:* drawing and painting; studying history. *Address:* (home) 24 Reynolds Close, NW11. *T:* 081–455 6047; 97 Harley Street, W1. *T:* 071–935 7828. *Club:* Athenæum.

DOUGAL, Malcolm Gordon; HM Diplomatic Service; Director, Joint FCO/DTI Directorate of Overseas Trade Services, Foreign and Commonwealth Office, since 1991; *b* 20 Jan. 1938; *s* of Eric Gordon Dougal and Marie (*née* Wildermuth); *m* 1964, Elke (*née* Urban); one *s*. *Educ:* Ampleforth Coll., Yorkshire; The Queen's Coll., Oxford (MA Mod. History). National Service in Korea and Gibraltar with Royal Sussex Regt, 1956–58; Oxford, 1958–61; Contracts Asst, De Havilland Aircraft, Hatfield, 1961–64; Asst to Export Manager, Ticket Equipment Ltd (Plessey), 1964–66; Export Manager, Harris Lebus Ltd, 1967–69; entered HM Diplomatic Service, 1969; Foreign Office, 1969–72; 1st Secretary (Commercial): Paris, 1972–76; Cairo, 1976–79; Foreign Office, 1979–81; Consul Gen., Lille, 1981–85; Dep. High Comr and Head of Chancery, Canberra, 1986–89; RCDS, 1990. *Recreations:* natural history, walking, books, sport, wine. *Address:* c/o Foreign and Commonwealth Office, Whitehall, SW1A 2AH.

DOUGAN, (Alexander) Derek; company director and marketing consultant; *b* 20 Jan. 1938; *s* of John and Josephine Dougan; *m* 1963, Jutta Maria; two *s*. *Educ:* Mersey Street primary sch., Belfast; Belfast Technical High School. Professional footballer with: Distillery, NI, 1953–57; Portsmouth, 1957–59; Blackburn Rovers, 1959–61; Aston Villa, 1961–63; Peterborough, 1963–65; Leicester, 1965–67; Wolverhampton Wanderers, 1967–75. Represented N Ireland at all levels, from schoolboy to full international, more than 50 times. Chm., PFA, 1970–78. Chief Exec., Kettering Town FC, 1975–78; Chm. and Chief Exec., Wolverhampton Wanderers' FC, 1982–85. Sports Presenter, Yorkshire Television. Mem. Council, Co-Operation North, 1987–. *Publications:* Attack! (autobiog.), 1969; The Sash He Never Wore (autobiog.), 1972; The Footballer (novel), 1974; On the Spot (football as a profession), 1974; Doog (autobiog.), 1980; How Not to Run Football, 1981; (with Patrick Murphy) Matches of the Day 1958–83, 1984. *Recreations:* watching football, playing squash. *Address:* Bayern House, 40 Keepers Lane, Codsall, Wolverhampton, West Midlands WV8 2DP.

DOUGAN, Dr David John; Arts Development Officer, Essex County Council, since 1989; Chairman, National Youth Dance Trust, since 1985; *b* 26 Sept, 1936; *s* of William John Dougan and Blanche May; *m* 1st, 1959, Eileen Ludbrook (marr. diss. 1985); one *s*; 2nd, 1986, Barbara Taylor; one *s* one *d*. *Educ:* Durham Univ. (BA, MA); City Univ. (PhD). Reporter, Tyne Tees Television, 1963; presenter, BBC, 1966; Director, Northern Arts, 1970; Dir, Crafts Council, 1984–88. *Publications:* History of North East Shipbuilding, 1966; Great Gunmaker, 1968; Shipwrights Trade Union, 1971. *Recreations:* theatre, crafts, running. *Address:* 23 Effingham Road, Lee, SE12 8NZ. *T:* 081-318 3837.

DOUGHERTY, Maj.-Gen. Sir Ivan Noel, Kt 1968; CBE 1946; DSO 1941 (bar, 1943); ED; *b* Leadville, NSW, 6 April 1907; *m* 1936, Emily Phyllis Lofts; two *s* two *d* (and one *d* decd). *Educ:* Leadville Primary Sch.; Mudgee High Sch.; Sydney Teachers' Coll.; Sydney Univ. (BEc). NSW Education Dept: Asst Teacher, 1928–32; Dep. Headmaster, 1933–39; Headmaster, 1946–47; Dist Inspector of Schs, 1948–53; Staff Inspector 1953–55. Commissioned Sydney Univ. Regt, 1927. Capt. 1931; Unattached List, 1932–34; transf. to 33/41 Bn. 1934; Major, 1938; Command, 33rd Bn, 1938; Lieut-Col 1939. Served War of 1939–45 (DSO and Bar, CBE, despatches thrice); Australian Imperial Force, Second-in-Command, 2/2 Inf. Bn, 1939–40; Commanded 2/4 inf. Bn (Libya, Greece, Crete campaigns), 1940–42; Brig. 1942; commanded 23 Bde, 1942; commanded 21 Bde, South-West Pacific, 1942–45; R of O, 1946–47; commanded 8th Bde, Austr. Mil. Forces, 1948–52; Maj.-Gen., 1952; commanded 2nd Div., 1952–54; Citizen Military Forces Member, Australian Mil. Bd, 1954–57; R of O, 1957–64; Retired List, 1964. Hon. ADC to Governor-Gen. of Australia, 1949–52; Hon. Col, Australian Cadet Corps, Eastern Command, 1964–70; Representative Hon. Col, Australian Cadet Corps, 1967–70. Dir of Civil Defence for NSW, 1955–73. Mem. Council, Nat. Roads and Motorists' Assoc., 1969–79. Mem. Senate, 1954–74, Dep. Chancellor, 1958–66, Hon. LLD 1976, Univ. of Sydney. *Address:* 4 Leumeah Street, Cronulla, NSW 2230, Australia. *T:* 523–5465.

DOUGHTY, George Henry; General Secretary, Technical and Supervisory Section, Amalgamated Union of Engineering Workers, 1971–74, retired; Member, Central Arbitration Committee, 1976–85; *b* 17 May 1911; British; *m* 1941, Mildred Dawson; two *s*. *Educ:* Handsworth Tech. Sch.; Aston Technical Coll. Draughtsman; trained at General Electric Co., Birmingham, 1927–32; employed as Design Draughtsman: English Electric, Stafford 1932–33; GEC Birmingham, 1934–46. With Draughtsmen's & Allied Technician's Assoc., 1946–71, General Secretary, 1952–71. Member: Gen. Council of TUC, 1968–74; Independent Review Cttee, 1976–89; Chm., EDC for Electrical Engrg, 1974–82. Mem., Royal Commn on Distribution of Income and Wealth, 1974–78. Industrial Relns Advr, SIAD, 1977–88. *Publications:* various technical and Trade Union publications. *Recreation:* photography.

DOUGHTY, Sir William (Roland), Kt 1990; Chairman, North West Thames Regional Health Authority, since 1984; Deputy Chairman, Britannia Refined Metals Ltd, since 1982 (Director, since 1978); *b* 18 July 1925; *s* of Roland Gill Doughty and Gladys Maud Doughty (*née* Peto); *m* 1952, Patricia Lorna Cooke; three *s*. *Educ:* Headstone Sch.; Acton Technical Coll.; Trinity Coll., Dublin (MA); Harvard Business Sch. (AMP). Metal Box Co. Ltd, 1953–66; Molins Ltd, 1966–69, Dir, 1967; Cape Industries, 1969–84, Dir, 1972, Man. Dir, 1980–84. Member: SE Economic Planning Council, 1966–79 (Chm., Industry and Employment Cttee, 1972–79); CBI Council, 1975– (Chm., London Region, 1981–83). Founder and Chm., Assoc. for Conservation of Energy, 1981–85, Pres., 1985–. Governor: SE Tech. Coll., 1967–69; Gt Ormond St Hosp. for Sick Children, 1978–90; Mem., Gen. Council, King Edward VII's Hosp. Fund for London, 1984– (Mem., Management Cttee, 1987–); Chm., King's Fund Centre Cttee, 1991–. LHSM 1986. CBIM; FRSA. *Recreations:* cricket, theatre, golf, horse racing. *Address:* Sun Hollow, North Park, Gerrards Cross, Bucks SL9 8JL. *Clubs:* American, MCC, Middlesex County Cricket.

DOUGILL, John Wilson, FEng 1990; FICE; FIStructE; FASCE; Director of Engineering, Institution of Structural Engineers, since 1987; *b* 18 Nov. 1934; *s* of William John Dougill and Emily Firmstone Wilson; *m* 1959, Daphne Maude Weeks; one *s* one *d*. *Educ:* Trinity Sch. of John Whitgift, Croydon; King's Coll., London; Imperial Coll. of Science and Technology. MScEng, DIC, PhD. Engineer with George Wimpey, 1956–58 and 1960–61; Research Asst to Prof. A. L. L. Baker, Imperial Coll., 1961–64; King's College London: Lectr in Civil Engrg, 1964–73; Reader in Engrg Science, 1973–76; Prof. of Engrg Science, 1976–81; Prof. of Concrete Structures and Technology, Imperial Coll., 1981–87. Vis. Res. Engineer, Univ. of California, Berkeley, 1967–68. Chm., SERC Civil Engrg Sub-Cttee, 1982–83; Mem., NEDO Res. Strategy Cttee, 1983–85. Mem. Court of Governors, Whitgift Foundn, 1981–; Governor, Sidney Perry Foundn, 1986–. *Publications:* papers in jls of engrg mech., materials and struct. engrg. *Recreations:* Alfred, an old English sheep dog, travel, good food, walking. *Address:* Ashcroft, Larch Close, The Glade, Kingswood, Surrey KT20 6JF. *T:* Mogador (0737) 833283.

DOUGLAS, family name of **Viscount Chilston, Earl of Morton,** and **Marquess of Queensberry.**

DOUGLAS AND CLYDESDALE, Marquess of; Alexander Douglas-Hamilton; *b* 31 March 1978; *s* and *heir* of Duke of Hamilton, *qv*.

DOUGLAS, Prof. Alexander Stuart; Regius Professor of Medicine, University of Aberdeen, 1970–85, now Emeritus; Leverhulme Emeritus Senior Research Fellow, since 1990; *b* 2 Oct. 1921; *s* of late Dr R. Douglas, MOH for Moray and Nairn; *m* 1954, Christine McClymont Stewart; one *s* one *d*. *Educ:* Elgin Academy, Morayshire. Mil. Service, RAMC, 1945–48 (despatches 1947). Research Fellow, Radcliffe Infirmary, Oxford, and Postgrad. Med. Sch., London, 1951–53; Lectr, Sen. Lectr and Reader in Medicine, Univ. Dept of Med., Royal Infirmary, Glasgow, 1953–64; Hon. Consultant status, 1957; Prof. of Med., Univ. of Glasgow, 1964–70; secondment to Univ. of East Africa with hon. academic rank of Prof., 1965; Hon. Consultant Physician in Administrative Charge of wards, Royal Infirmary, Glasgow, 1968–70. *Publications:* scientific papers on blood coagulation, etc. *Recreations:* curling, travel. *Address:* Department of Medicine, Aberdeen Royal Infirmary, Foresterhill, Aberdeen AB9 2ZB. *T:* Aberdeen (0224) 681818 (ext. 53014).

DOUGLAS, Arthur John Alexander, CMG 1965; OBE 1962; Assistant Secretary, Overseas Development Administration, Foreign and Commonwealth Office, (formerly Ministry of Overseas Development), 1975–80; *b* 31 May 1920; *s* of Alexander and Eileen Douglas; *m* 1948, Christine Scott Dyke; two *d*. *Educ:* Dumfries Academy; Edinburgh Univ. Royal Navy, 1940–45. District Officer, Basutoland, 1946; Seconded Colonial Office, 1957; Administration Sec., Bechuanaland, 1959; Government Sec. and Chief Sec. 1962–65; Dep. Commissioner for Bechuanaland, 1965–66; ODM, then ODA, 1967–80, retired. *Address:* 13 Pickers Green, Lindfield, West Sussex RH16 2BS. *Club:* Commonwealth Trust.

DOUGLAS, Barry; concert pianist; *b* 23 April 1960. *Educ:* Royal College of Music; studied with John Barstow and Maria Curcio. ARCM, LRAM. Gold Medal, Tchaikovsky International Piano Competition, Moscow, 1986; Berlin Philharmonic début, 1987; engagements incl. regular appearances in major European, US and Far East cities. Recordings incl. Tchaikovsky's Concerto No 1, Mussorgsky's Pictures at an Exhibition, Brahms' Piano Quintet in F minor, Brahms' Piano Concerto No 1, Liszt Concertos Nos 1 and 2, Beethoven Sonata Op 106. Hon. DMus QUB, 1986. *Recreations:* driving, reading, food and wine. *Address:* c/o Terry Harrison Artists Management, 9a Penzance Place, W11 4PE.

DOUGLAS, Prof. Charles Primrose, FRCOG; Professor of Obstetrics and Gynæcology, University of Cambridge, 1976–88, now Emeritus; Fellow, Emmanuel College, Cambridge, 1979–88; *b* 17 Feb. 1921; *s* of Dr C. Douglas, Ayr, Scotland; *m* 1948, Angela Francis; three *s* one *d*. *Educ:* Loretto Sch.; Peterhouse; Edinburgh Univ. Surg. Lieut RNVR, 1944–47. Registrar and Sen. Registrar, Victoria Infirmary, Glasgow, 1950–59; William Waldorf Astor Foundn Fellow, 1957; Visiting Fellow, Duke Univ., NC, 1957; Sen. Lectr, Univ. of the West Indies, 1959–65; Prof. of Obst. and Gyn., Royal Free Hosp. Sch. of Medicine, 1965–76. Member: Bd of Governors, Royal Free Hosp., 1972–74; Camden and Islington AHA, 1974–76, Cambridge AHA, 1981–82; Cambridge DHA, 1983–88. Mem., Council, RCOG, 1980–86. Hon. FACOG, 1983. *Publications:* contribs to BMJ, Amer. Heart Jl, Jl of Obst. and Gynæc. of Brit. Commonwealth, etc. *Recreations:* travel, art. *Address:* Old Mill House, Linton Road, Balsham, Cambs CB1 6HA. *Club:* Royal Over-Seas League.

DOUGLAS, Sir Donald (Macleod), Kt 1972; MBE 1943; ChM St Andrews, MS Minn, FRCSE; FRCS; FRSE 1973; Surgeon to the Queen in Scotland, 1965–76; an Extra Surgeon to the Queen in Scotland, since 1977; Professor of Surgery, University of Dundee (formerly Queen's College), 1951–76, Emeritus Professor, 1977; Surgeon, Ninewells Hospital, Dundee, 1951–76; *b* 28 June 1911; *s* of William Douglas and Christina Broom; *m* 1945, Margaret Diana Whitley; two *s* two *d*. *Educ:* Madras Coll.; Universities of St Andrews and Minnesota. Commonwealth Fellow in Surgery, Mayo Clinic, University of Minnesota, USA, 1937–39; First Asst in Surgery, British Postgraduate Medical Sch., 1939–40; RAMC, 1941–45; Reader in Experimental Surgery, University of Edinburgh, 1945–51; Asst Surgeon, Edinburgh Municipal Hospitals, 1945; formerly Surgeon, Royal Infirmary, Dundee. Assoc. Asst Surgeon, Royal Infirmary, Edinburgh. Dean of Faculty of Medicine, Univ. of Dundee, 1969–70. President: RCSE, 1971–73; Assoc. of Surgeons of GB and Ireland, 1964; Surgical Research Soc. of GB, 1966–69; Harveian Soc., 1974. Trustee, Thalidomide Trust, 1973– (Chm., Health and Welfare). Hon. FACS, 1972; Hon. FRCS (SA), 1972; Hon. FRCSI, 1973. Hon. DSc St Andrews, 1972. *Publications:* Wound Healing, 1965; The Thoughtful Surgeon, 1970; Surgical Departments in Hospitals, 1971. *Address:* The Whitehouse of Nevay, Newtyle, Angus. *T:* Newtyle (08285) 315.

DOUGLAS, Sir (Edward) Sholto, Kt 1977; Solicitor of the Supreme Court of Queensland, since 1934; *b* 23 Dec. 1909; *s* of Hon. Mr Justice E. A. Douglas and Annette Eileen Power; *m* 1939, Mary Constance Curr. *Educ:* St Ignatius Coll., Riverview, Sydney. Queensland Law Society Incorporated: Mem. Council, 1954–76; Actg Pres., 1960; Pres., 1962–64; Mem., Statutory Cttee, 1976–81; Member: Legal Assistance Cttee, Qld, 1965–80; Solicitors' Bd, 1969–75; Exec. Mem., Law Council of Aust., 1973–75. President: Taxpayers Assoc. of Qld, 1955–58; Federated Taxpayers of Aust., 1957–58; Mem. Adv. Cttee, Terminating and Permanent Building Socs, 1966–77. Pres., Qld Div., Nat. Heart Foundn, 1976–77 (Vice-Pres., 1966–75); Vice-Pres., RSPCA, 1965–86; Chm., Management Cttee, Currumbin Bird Sanctuary and Wildlife Reserve, 1978–80. *Recreations:* racing, gardening. *Address:* 81 Markwell Street, Hamilton, Brisbane, Qld 4007, Australia. *T:* 268.2759. *Clubs:* Queensland, Brisbane (Pres. 1965), Tattersalls, Royal Queensland Golf, Queensland Turf, Tattersalls Racing, Brisbane Amateur Turf (all Brisbane).

DOUGLAS, Gavin Stuart, RD 1970; QC (Scot.) 1971; *b* 12 June 1932; *y s* of late Gilbert Georgeson Douglas and Rosena Campbell Douglas. *Educ:* South Morningside Sch.; George Heriot's Sch.; Edinburgh Univ. MA 1953, LLB 1955. Qual. as Solicitor, 1955; nat. service with RN, 1955–57. Admitted to Faculty of Advocates, 1958; Sub-editor (part-time), The Scotsman, 1957–61; Mem. Lord Advocate's Dept in London (as Parly Draftsman), 1961–64; returned to practice at Scots Bar, 1964; Junior Counsel to BoT, 1965–71; Counsel to Scottish Law Commn, 1965–; Hon. Sheriff in various sheriffdoms, 1965–71; a Chm. of Industrial Tribunals, 1966–78; Counsel to Sec. of State for Scotland under Private Legislation Procedure (Scotland) Act 1936, 1969–75, Sen. Counsel under that Act, 1975–; Temporary Sheriff, 1990–. Mem., Lothian Health Bd, 1981–85. Mem. Bd, Leith Nautical Coll., 1981–84. Editor, Session Cases, 7 vols, 1976–82. *Recreations:* golf, ski-ing. *Address:* Parliament House, Parliament Square, Edinburgh EH1 1RF. *Clubs:* Army and Navy; University Staff (Edinburgh); Hon. Company of Edinburgh Golfers (Muirfield).

DOUGLAS, Henry Russell, FJI; Legal Manager, News Group Newspapers, 1976–89; *b* Bishopbriggs, Lanarkshire, 11 Feb. 1925; 2nd *s* of late Russell Douglas and Jeanie Douglas Douglas (*née* Drysdale); *m* 1951, Elizabeth Mary, *d* of late Ralph Nowell, CB; two *s* three *d*. *Educ:* various Scottish and English Grammar Schools; Lincoln Coll., Oxford (MA Hons). Served RNVR, 1943–46 (Sub-Lt, submarines). Merchant Navy, 1946–47; Oxford Univ., 1947–50; Liverpool Daily Post, 1950–69; The Sun, 1969–76. Inst of Journalists, 1956: Fellow, 1969; Pres., 1972–73; Chm. of Executive, 1973–76; Member: Press Council, 1972–80; Council, Newspaper Press Fund, 1972–76, 1986– (Chm., 1990–91); Founder Mem., Media Society, 1973, Treas., 1973–86, Vice-Pres., 1987–89. *Recreations:* chess, travel, history. *Address:* Austen Croft, 31 Austen Road, Guildford, Surrey. *T:* Guildford (0483) 576960. *Club:* United Oxford & Cambridge University.

DOUGLAS, James Murray, CBE 1985; Director, Bookers Countryside, since 1990; Public Affairs Consultant, John Kendall Associates, since 1990; Public Affairs Consultant, John Kendall Associates, since 1990; *b* 26 Sept. 1925; *s* of Herbert and Amy Douglas, Brechin; *m* 1950, Julie Kemmner; one *s* one *d*. *Educ:* Morrison's Acad., Crieff; Aberdeen Univ. (MA); Balliol Coll., Oxford (BA). Entered Civil Service, 1950; Treasury, 1960–63; Asst Sec., Min. of Housing and Local Govt, 1964; Sec. to Royal Commn on Local Govt, 1966–69. Dir-Gen., CLA, 1970–90. Vice-Pres., Confedn of European Agriculture, 1971–88 (Chm., Environment Cttee, 1988–90); Mem., Econ. Develt Cttee for Agriculture, 1972–90; Sec., European Landowning Orgns Gp, 1972–87. Mem., Council, CBI, 1986–89. *Publications:* various articles on local govt planning and landowning. *Address:* 1 Oldfield Close, Bickley, Kent. *T:* 081–467 3213. *Club:* United Oxford & Cambridge University.

DOUGLAS, Kenneth, CBE 1991; CEng, FRINA; Managing Director, Austin and Pickersgill Ltd, 1958–69, and 1979–83; Chairman, Kenton Shipping Services, Darlington, 1968–83; Member, Tyne and Wear Residuary Body, Department of the Environment, since 1985; *b* 28 Oct. 1920; British; *m* 1942, Doris Lewer; one *s* two *d*. *Educ:* Sunderland Technical Coll. (Dip. Naval Architecture). CEng, FRINA. Dep. Shipyard Manager, Vickers Armstrong Naval Yard, Newcastle-upon-Tyne, 1946–53; Dir and Gen. Manager, Wm Gray & Co. Ltd, West Hartlepool, 1954–58; Man. Dir, Upper Clyde Shipbuilders Ltd, Chm., Simons Lobnitz Ltd and Chm., UCS Trng Co., 1969–73; Dep. Chm., Govan Shipbuilders, 1971–73; Chm., Douglas (Kilbride) Ltd, 1972–77; Chm. and Man. Dir, Steel Structures Ltd, 1974–76; Shiprepair Marketing Dir, British Shipbuilders, 1978–79; Mem. Bd, PCEF, 1988–. Fellow, Sunderland Poly., 1980 (Chm. of Governors, 1982–). *Recreations:* fishing, golf. *Address:* 7 Birchfield Road, Sunderland, Tyne and Wear; Monks Cottage, Romaldkirk, Barnard Castle, Co. Durham. *Clubs:* Sunderland, Ashbrooke Cricket and Rugby Football (Sunderland).

DOUGLAS, Margaret Elizabeth; Chief Political Adviser, BBC, since 1987; *b* 22 Aug. 1934; *d* of Thomas Mincher Douglas and Dorothy Jones. *Educ:* Parliament Hill Grammar Sch., London. Joined BBC as sec., 1951; subseq. researcher, dir and producer in Current Affairs television, working on Panorama, Gallery, 24 Hours and on special progs with Lord Avon and Harold Macmillan; Editor, Party Conf. coverage, 1972–83; Chief Asst to Dir-Gen., 1983–87. *Recreations:* watching politics and football. *Address:* BBC, Broadcasting House, W1A 1AA. *T:* 071–580 4468.

DOUGLAS, Prof. Mary, FBA 1989; Avalon Foundation Professor in the Humanities, Northwestern University, 1981–85, Professor Emeritus, since 1985; *b* 25 March 1921; *d* of Gilbert Charles Tew and Phyllis Twomey; *m* 1951, James A. T. Douglas, OBE; two *s* one *d. Educ:* Sacred Heart Convent, Roehampton; Univ. of Oxford (MA, BSc, DPhil). Returned to Oxford, 1946, to train as anthropologist; fieldwork in Belgian Congo, 1949–50, 1953 and 1987; Lectr in Anthropology, Univ. of Oxford, 1950; Univ. of London, 1951–78, Prof. of Social Anthropology, UCL, 1970–78. Res. Scholar, Russell Sage Foundn, NY, 1977–81; Vis. Prof., Princeton Univ., 1986–88. Gifford Lectr, Univ. of Edinburgh, 1989. Mem., Academia Europaea, 1988. Hon. Dr of Philosophy, Univ. of Uppsala, 1986; Hon. LLD Univ. of Notre Dame, 1988. *Publications:* The Lele of the Kasai, 1963; Purity and Danger, 1966; Natural Symbols, 1970; Implicit Meanings, 1975; (with Baron Isherwood) The World of Goods: towards an anthropology of consumption, 1979; Evans-Pritchard, 1980; (with Aaron Wildavsky) Risk and Culture, 1982; In the Active Voice, 1982; Risk Acceptability, 1986; How Institutions Think, 1986. *Address:* 22 Hillway, Highgate, N6 6QA. *Club:* United Oxford & Cambridge University.

DOUGLAS, Richard Giles; MP Dunfermline West, since 1983 (Dunfermline, 1979–83) (Lab and Co-op, 1979–90, SNP since 1990); *b* 4 Jan. 1932; *m* 1954, Jean Gray, *d* of Andrew Arnott; two *d. Educ:* Co-operative College, Stanford Hall, Loughborough; Univ. of Strathclyde; LSE. Engineer (Marine); Mem. AUEW. Tutor organiser in Adult Educn, Co-operative movement, 1957; Sectional Educn Officer, Scotland, 1958–61; Lectr in Economics, Dundee Coll. of Technol., 1964–70. Contested (Lab): South Angus, 1964, Edinburgh West, 1966, Glasgow Pollok, March 1967; (Lab and Co-op) Clackmannan and E Stirlingshire, Oct. 1974; MP (Lab and Co-op) Clackmannan and E Stirlingshire, 1970–Feb. 1974. Joined SNP, 1990. Hon. Lectr, Strathclyde, 1980–. *Address:* Braehead House, High Street, Auchtermuchty, Fife KY14 7AR.

DOUGLAS, Sir Robert (McCallum), Kt 1976; OBE 1956; President, Robert M. Douglas Holdings PLC, since 1980 (Director, 1930–88; Chairman, 1952–77); *b* 2 Feb. 1899; *s* of John Douglas and Eugenia McCallum; *m* 1927, Millicent Irene Tomkys Morgan (*d* 1980); one *s* one *d. Educ:* Terregles Sch.; Dumfries Academy. Served Army, 1916–19. Served 10 years with civil engineering contracting co., 1920–30; founded Douglas Group of Companies, 1930. Mem., MPBW Midland Regional Jt Adv. Cttee, 1940–46. Federation of Civil Engineering Contractors: Chm., Midland Section, 1942–43 and 1947–48; Chm. Council, 1948–49; Pres., 1958–60. Patron, Staffs Agric. Soc.; Pres., Burton Graduate Med. Centre, 1988–. Hon. DSc Aston, 1977. *Recreations:* shooting, farming. *Address:* Dunstall Hall, Barton-under-Needwood, Burton-on-Trent, Staffordshire DE13 8BE. *T:* Barton-under-Needwood (0283) 712471. *Club:* Caledonian.

DOUGLAS, Hon. Sir Roger Owen, Kt 1991; MP (Lab) Manurewa, New Zealand, 1969–90; *b* 5 Dec. 1937; *s* of Norman and Jenny Douglas; *m* 1961, Glennis June Anderson; one *s* one *d. Educ:* Auckland Grammar Sch.; Auckland Univ. (Accountancy Degree). Company Sec. and Acct; Cabinet Minister, 1972–75; Minister in Charge of Inland Revenue Dept and Minister in Charge of Friendly Societies, 1984; Minister of Finance, 1984–88; Minister of Immigration and Minister of Police, 1989–90. Dir, Brierley Investments. *Publications:* There's Got to be a Better Way, 1981; papers on NZ economy: An Alternative Budget, 1980; Proposal for Taxation, 1981; Toward Prosperity, 1987. *Recreations:* cricket, rugby, reading. *Address:* 411 Redoubt Road, Papatuetue RD1, Auckland, New Zealand. *T:* 263–9596.

DOUGLAS, Ronald Albert Neale, DFC 1944; JP; Agent General for Western Australia in London, 1982–86; *b* 18 Sept. 1922; *s* of Edwyn William Albert Douglas and Kate Maria Douglas; *m* 1st, 1944 (marr. diss. 1966); one *s* one *d*; 2nd, Pamela Joy Carroll; one *s. Educ:* Albany High Sch., WA. Served War, RAAF, 1941–46 (Sqdn Ldr). Joined Shell Co. of Australia, 1938; sales rep., 1946–50; various appts, incl. Aviation Manager and Dist Manager, WA and NSW, 1950–60; appts with Shell Cos, France and USA, 1960–61; Sales Man., WA, 1961–65; Commercial Man., Shell Malaysia, 1965–66; Marketing Man., Shell Singapore, 1966–67; Retail Man., Vic/Tas, 1967–71; Chm.'s Rep. and Commercial Man., Shell Gp of Cos in WA, 1971–82. JP WA, 1982. *Recreations:* cricket, golf, fishing, farming. *Address:* 12 Jarrad Street, Cottesloe, Perth, WA 6011, Australia. *T:* 384 9986. *Clubs:* Weld, West Australian, Royal Aero (Perth); Lake Karrinyup Country (WA).

DOUGLAS, Prof. Ronald Walter, DSc, FInstP, FSGT; Professor of Glass Technology, University of Sheffield, 1955–75; *b* 28 March 1910; *s* of John H. P. and A. E. Douglas; *m* 1933, Edna Maud Cadle; two *s. Educ:* Latymer Upper Sch.; Sir John Cass Coll., London. Mem., Research Staff, Research Laboratories of General Electric Company, 1927–55. Pres., Internat. Commn on Glass, 1972–75. *Publications:* (with S. Frank) A History of Glassmaking, 1972; many papers on the physics of glass and semiconductors. *Address:* Otter Close, Perrys Gardens, West Hill, Ottery St Mary, Devon EX11 1XA.

DOUGLAS, Sir Sholto; *see* Douglas, Sir E. S.

DOUGLAS, Prof. Thomas Alexander; Professor of Veterinary Biochemistry and Head of Department of Veterinary Biochemistry (Clinical), University of Glasgow, 1977–90; *b* 9 Aug. 1926; *s* of Alexander and Mary Douglas; *m* 1957, Rachel Ishbel McDonald; two *s. Educ:* Battlefield Public Sch.; High Sch. of Glasgow; Glasgow Vet. Coll., Univ. of Glasgow (BSc; Animal Health Schol., 1950–54; PhD). MRCVS. General Veterinary Practice: Ulverston, 1948–49; Lanark, 1949–50; University of Glasgow: Asst Lectr, Biochemistry, 1954–57; Lectr 1957–71, Sen. Lectr 1971–77, in Vet. Biochem., Vet. Sch.; Dean of Faculty of Vet. Medicine, 1982–85. Mem. Council, RCVS, 1982–85. Mem., UGC, 1986–89 (Chm., Agriculture and Veterinary Studies Sub-Cttee, 1986–89). *Publications:* sci. articles in vet. and biochem. jls. *Recreations:* golf, hill walking. *Address:* 77 South Mains Road, Milngavie, Glasgow G62 6DE. *T:* 041–956 2751.

DOUGLAS, Rt. Hon. Sir William (Randolph), KCMG 1983; Kt 1969; PC 1977; Ambassador of Barbados to the United States of America, since 1987; *b* Barbados, 24 Sept. 1921; *e s* of William P. Douglas and Emily Frances Douglas (*née* Nurse); *m* 1951, Thelma Ruth (*née* Gilkes); one *s* one *d. Educ:* Bannatyne Sch. and Verdun High Sch., Verdun, Que., Canada; McGill Univ. (BA, Hons); London Sch. of Economics (LLB). Private Practice at Barbados Bar, 1948–50; Dep. Registrar, Barbados, 1950; Resident Magistrate, Jamaica, 1955; Asst Attorney-Gen., Jamaica, 1959; Solicitor-Gen., Jamaica, 1962; Puisne Judge, Jamaica, 1962; Chief Justice of Barbados, 1965–86. Chm., Commonwealth Caribbean Council of Legal Education, 1971–77; Mem., ILO Cttee of Experts on the Application of Conventions and Recommendations, 1975–; Dep. Judge, ILO Administrative Tribunal, 1982–. *Address:* Embassy of Barbados, 2144 Wyoming Avenue NW, Washington, DC 20008, USA. *T:* (202) 939–9218/9. *Club:* Barbados Yacht.

DOUGLAS, Prof. William Wilton, MD; FRS 1983; Professor of Pharmacology, Yale University School of Medicine, New Haven, USA, since 1968; *b* 15 Aug. 1922; *s* of Thomas Hall James Douglas and Catherine Dorward (*née* Wilton); *m* 1954, Jeannine Marie Henriette Dumoulin; two *s. Educ:* Glasgow Acad.; Univ. of Glasgow (MB, ChB 1946, MD 1949). Resident House Surgeon: Glasgow Western Infirm., 1946; Law Hosp., Carluke, 1947; Demonstr in Physiology, Univ. of Aberdeen, 1948; served RAMC, 1949–50: Chemical Defence Res. Estab., Porton Down, Wilts (Major); Mem. Staff, National Inst. for Med. Res., Mill Hill, 1950–56; Prof. of Pharmacol., Albert Einstein Coll. of Medicine, New York, 1956–68. *Publications:* papers on cellular mechanisms of secretion in Jl of Physiol., Brit. Jl of Pharmacol., Nature, and Science. *Recreations:* yachting, skiing. *Address:* 76 Blake Road, Hamden, Conn 06517, USA. *T:* (203) 776–8696.

DOUGLAS-HAMILTON, family name of **Duke of Hamilton and Brandon** and **Earl of Selkirk.**

DOUGLAS-HAMILTON, Lord James Alexander; MP (C) Edinburgh West since Oct. 1974; Parliamentary Under Secretary of State for Home Affairs and the Environment, Scottish Office, since 1987; *b* 31 July 1942; 2nd *s* of 14th Duke of Hamilton, and *b* of 15th Duke of Hamilton, *qv*; *m* 1974, Hon. Priscilla Susan Buchan, *d* of Baron Tweedsmuir, *qv* and late Baroness Tweedsmuir of Belhelvie, PC; four *s* (incl. twins). *Educ:* Eton College; Balliol Coll., Oxford (MA, Mod. History; Oxford Boxing Blue, 1961; Pres., Oxford Univ. Cons. Assoc., 1963; Pres., Oxford Union Soc., 1964); Edinburgh Univ. (LLB, Scots Law). Advocate at Scots Bar, 1968. Town Councillor, Murrayfield-Cramond, Edinburgh, 1972. Scottish Conservative Whip, 1977; a Lord Comr of HM Treasury, and Govt Whip for Scottish Cons. Mems, 1979–81; PPS to: Foreign Office Minister, 1983–86; Sec. of State for Scotland, 1986–87. Captain Cameronian Co., 2 Bn Low Vols RARO, 1974–87. Hon. Pres., Scottish Amateur Boxing Assoc., 1975–; President: Royal Commonwealth Soc. in Scotland, 1979–87; Scottish Council, UNA, 1981–87. *Publications:* Motive for a Mission: The Story Behind Hess's Flight to Britain, 1971; The Air Battle for Malta: the diaries of a fighter pilot, 1981, 2nd edn 1990; Roof of the World: man's first flight over Everest, 1983. *Recreations:* golf, forestry. *Clubs:* New (Edinburgh); Hon. Company of Edinburgh Golfers.

DOUGLAS-HOME, family name of **Baroness Dacre** and **Baron Home of the Hirsel.**

DOUGLAS-HOME, Hon. David Alexander Cospatrick, CBE 1991; Chairman: Morgan Grenfell (Scotland), since 1986 (Director, since 1978); Morgan Grenfell International Ltd, since 1987; Director, Morgan Grenfell & Co. Ltd, since 1974; *b* 20 Nov. 1943; *o s* of Baron Home of the Hirsel, *qv*; *heir* to Earldom of Home; *m* 1972, Jane Margaret, *yr d* of Col J. Williams-Wynne, *qv*; one *s* two *d. Educ:* Eton College; Christ Church, Oxford (BA 1966). Chm., Morgan Grenfell Export Services, 1984–; Director: Morgan Grenfell Egyptian Finance Co. Ltd, 1975–77; Morgan Grenfell (Asia) Ltd, 1978–82 (Dep. Chm., 1979–82); Arab Bank Investment Co., 1979–87; Agricultural Mortgage Corp., 1979–; Arab-British Chamber of Commerce, 1975–84; Economic Forestry Group, 1981–; Credit for Exports, 1984–; Morgan Grenfell (Hong Kong), 1989–; Morgan Grenfell Asia Holdings Pte, 1989–; Morgan Grenfell Thai Co., 1990–. Chm., Committee for Middle East Trade, 1986– (Mem., 1973–75). Governor: Ditchley Foundn, 1977–; Commonwealth Inst., 1988–. *Recreations:* outdoor sports. *Address:* 99 Dovehouse Street, SW3 6JZ. *T:* 071–352 9060. *Club:* Turf.

DOUGLAS-HOME, Hon. William; *see* Home.

DOUGLAS-MANN, Bruce Leslie Home; Solicitor, in practice since 1954; Chairman, Shelter, since 1990 (Member of the Board, since 1974, Chairman of the Executive Committee, since 1987); Senior Partner, Douglas-Mann & Co.; *b* 23 June 1927; *s* of late Leslie John Douglas-Mann, MC and of Alice Home Douglas-Mann; *m* 1955, Helen Tucker; one *s* one *d. Educ:* Upper Canada Coll., Toronto; Jesus Coll., Oxford. Leading Seaman, RN, 1945–48; Oxford, 1948–51. Admitted solicitor, 1954. Contested (Lab): St Albans, 1964; Maldon, 1966; MP North Kensington, 1970–74, Merton, Mitcham and Morden, 1974–May 1982, resigned (Lab 1970–81, Ind 1981, SDP Jan.-May 1982); contested: Merton, Mitcham and Morden (SDP), June 1982; Mitcham and Morden (SDP), 1983 (SDP/Alliance), 1987. Chairman: PLP Housing and Construction Gp, 1974–79; PLP Environment Gp, 1979–81 (Vice-Chm., 1972–79); Parly Select Cttee on Environment, 1979–82. Member: SDP Council, 1984–88; Steering Cttee, Yes to Unity, 1987–88; Mem., England Co-ordinating Cttee, SLD, 1988–89; Chm., Hammersmith SLD, 1988–89. Vice-Pres., Soc. of Lab. Lawyers, 1980–81 (Chm., 1974–80). Mem., Kensington or Kensington and Chelsea Borough Council, 1962–68. Chairman: Arts Council Trust for Special Funds, 1981–; Common Voice, 1990–. *Publications:* pamphlets: (ed) The End of the Private Landlord, 1973; Accidents at Work—Compensation for All, 1974. *Address:* 33 Furnival Street, EC4A 1JQ. *T:* 071–405 7216.

DOUGLAS-MANN, Keith John Sholto, FRICS; Chairman, Jones Lang Wootton International and of the London Partnership, 1981–90; *b* 19 Oct. 1931; *s* of late Captain Leslie Douglas-Mann and of Lallie Douglas-Mann; *m* 1962, Shirley Mary Westhead (*née* McDonald); one *s* one *d. Educ:* Westminster Sch. Commnd, Royal Dragoons, 1955. Joined Jones Lang Wootton, 1961. *Recreations:* farming, shooting, rowing. *Clubs:* Cavalry and Guards, Queen's; Leander (Henley-on-Thames).

DOUGLAS MILLER, Robert Alexander Gavin; Chairman and Managing Director, Jenners (Princes St Edinburgh) Ltd; Director: Kennington Leasing Ltd; Chamber Developments Ltd; Bain Clarkson Ltd; First Scottish American Investment Trust; Northern American Trust; *b* 11 Feb. 1937; *s* of F. G. Douglas Miller and Mora Kennedy; *m* 1963, Judith Madeleine Smith; three *s* one *d. Educ:* Harrow; Oxford Univ. (MA). 9th Lancers, 1955–57; Oxford, 1958–61. Treasurer, Queen's Body Guard for Scotland (Royal Company of Archers). Pres., Edinburgh Chamber of Commerce & Manufactures, 1985–87. Member, Council: Assoc. of Scottish Salmon Fishery Bds, 1984–; Atlantic Salmon Trust, 1989–; Chm., Game Conservancy (Scotland), 1990–. Chm., Outreach Trust, 1976–. *Recreations:* shooting, fishing. *Address:* Bavelaw Castle, Balerno, Midlothian. *T:* 031–449 3972. *Club:* New (Edinburgh).
See also Ian MacArthur.

DOUGLAS-PENNANT, family name of **Baron Penrhyn.**

DOUGLAS-SCOTT-MONTAGU, family name of **Baron Montagu of Beaulieu.**

DOUGLAS-WILSON, Ian, MD; FRCPE; Editor of the Lancet, 1965–76; *b* 12 May 1912; *o s* of late Dr H. Douglas-Wilson; *m* 1939, Beatrice May, *e d* of late R. P. Bevan; one *s* two *d. Educ:* Marlborough Coll.; Edinburgh Univ. MB ChB 1936; MD (commended) Edinburgh 1938; FRCP Edinburgh 1945. Served with RAMC, 1940–45 (temp. Major). House-physician, Royal Infirmary, Edinburgh, 1937; joined the Lancet staff, 1946; Asst Ed., 1952–62; Dep. Ed., 1962–64. Corresp. Mem., Danish Soc. of Int. Med., 1965. Dr (*hc*) Edinburgh, 1974. *Address:* 10 Homan Court, Friern Watch Avenue, N12 9HW. *T:* 081–446 9047.

DOUGLAS-WITHERS, Maj.-Gen. John Keppel Ingold, CBE 1969; MC 1943; *b* 11 Dec. 1919; *s* of late Lt-Col H. H. Douglas-Withers, OBE, MC, FSA, and late Mrs V. G. Douglas-Withers; *m* 1945, Sylvia Beatrice Dean, Croydon, Surrey; one *s* one *d. Educ:* Shrewsbury Sch.; Christ Church, Oxford. Diploma in French, Univ. of Poitiers, 1938; Associate of Inst. of Linguists, in French and German, 1939. Commissioned into RA, 1940; Service in UK, Iraq, Western Desert, N Africa and Italy, 1940–45. Instr in Gunnery, Sch. of Artillery, Larkhill, 1945–47; service in Canal Zone, 1948–49; attended Staff Coll.,

Camberley, 1950; Staff appt in WO (Mil. Ops), 1951–53; service in The King's Troop, RHA, 1954–55; Instr, Staff Coll., Camberley, 1956–58; Battery Comdr, G Bty, Mercers Troop, RHA, 1959–60; Staff appt in WO (Mil. Sec. Dept), 1961; commanded 49 Field Regt in BAOR and Hong Kong, 1962–64; student at IDC, 1965; Comd 6 Inf. Bde in BAOR, 1966–67; Chief of Staff, 1st Brit. Corps, 1968–69; GOC SW District, 1970–71; Asst Chief of Personnel and Logistics, MoD, 1972–74; retired 1974. Col Comdt, RA, 1974–82. Asst Dir and Gp Personnel Man., Jardine Matheson & Co. Ltd, Hong Kong, 1974–80; Matheson & Co. Ltd, London, 1980–. MPIM (Hong Kong), 1976. *Recreations:* golf, history, military music, gardening. *Address:* Lloyds Bank, 25 High Street, Shipston-on-Stour, Warwickshire. *Clubs:* East India, Devonshire, Sports and Public Schools; MCC.

DOULTON, Alfred John Farre, CBE 1973 (OBE 1946); TD 1954; psc 1943; MA Oxon; Head of Statistical Team and Comptroller, Independent Schools Information Service, 1974–80, Consultant, 1980–81; *b* 9 July 1911; *s* of H. V. Doulton, Housemaster, Dulwich Coll., and Constance Jessie Farre, Dulwich; *m* 1940, Vera Daphne, *d* of A. R. Wheatley, Esher; four *s* one *d*. *Educ:* Dulwich Coll.; Brasenose Coll., Oxford (Classical Scholar). Asst Master, Uppingham School, 1934–40. Served War, 1940–46 (despatches twice); DAAG 11 Army Group, 1944; active service, Burma, Malaya, Java, 1945–46; DAQMG 4 Corps, AA&QMG 23 Indian Division, 1945–46. Burma Star, Far East and GS Medal with Java Clasp. Head of Classics and Housemaster of The Lodge, Uppingham Sch., 1946; Headmaster, Highgate Sch., 1955–74. Vice-Chm., HMC, 1967 (Hon. Treasurer, 1964–74). Alderman, Haringey, 1968–71 (Vice-Chm. Educn Cttee). Mem., Governing Bodies Assoc., 1977–80. Vice-Chm. and Chm. Finance Cttee, Kelly Coll., 1974–86; Trustee, Uppingham Sch., 1966–85. Mem., Indep. Schools Careers Orgn Council, 1978–81. *Publications:* The Fighting Cock, 1951; Highgate School 1938–1944: the story of a wartime evacuation, 1976. *Recreations:* music, cricket, books, dinghy sailing, ornithology. *Address:* Field Cottage, Salcombe, Devon TQ8 8JS. *T:* Salcombe (054884) 2316. *Clubs:* Athenæum, MCC; Salcombe Yacht (Cdre, 1987–90).
See also J. H. F. Doulton.

DOULTON, John Hubert Farre; Principal, Elizabeth College, Guernsey, since 1988; *b* 2 Jan. 1942; *s* of Alfred John Farre, *qv*; *m* 1986, Margaret Anne (*née* Ball); two step *d*. *Educ:* Rugby School; Keble College, Oxford (1st Mods, 2nd Greats). Teacher: Rugby, 1965–66; Radley, 1966–88. *Recreations:*music, walking, boats, foreign travel, carpentry. *Address:* Brantwood, Forest Road, St Martin's, Guernsey. *T:* Guernsey (0481) 38995.

DOUNE, Lord; John Douglas Stuart; *b* 1966; *s* and *heir* of 20th Earl of Moray, *qv*. *Educ:* Loretto School, Musselburgh; University Coll. London (BA Hist. of Art). *Address:* Doune Park, Doune, Perthshire; Darnaway Castle, Forres, Moray.

DOURO, Marquess of; Arthur Charles Valerian Wellesley; Deputy Chairman: Guinness Mahon Holdings plc, since 1988; Dunhill Holdings plc, since 1991; Director: Transatlantic Holdings PLC, since 1983; Global Asset Management Worldwide Inc., since 1984; Sun Life Corporation plc, since 1988; Rothmans International plc, since 1990; *b* 19 Aug. 1945; *s* and *heir* of 8th Duke of Wellington, *qv*; *m* 1977, Antonia von Preussen, *d* of late Prince Frederick of Prussia and of Lady Brigid Ness; one *s* three *d*. *Educ:* Eton; Christ Church, Oxford. Chm., Deltec Securities (UK) Ltd, 1985–89; Deputy Chairman: Thames Valley Broadcasting, 1975–84; Deltec Panamerica SA, 1985–89; Director: Antofagasta and Bolivia Railway Co., 1977–80; Eucalyptus Pulp Mills, 1979–88; Continental and Industrial Trust plc, 1987–90. MEP (C): Surrey, 1979–84, Surrey West, 1984–89; contested (C) Islington N, Oct. 1974; Mem., Basingstoke Borough Council, 1978–79. Kt Comdr, Order of Isabel the Catholic (Spain), 1986. *Heir:* *s* Earl of Mornington, *qv*. *Address:* Apsley House, Piccadilly, W1V 9FA; The Old Rectory, Stratfield Saye, Reading RG7 2DA.

DOVE, Arthur Allan, CEng, FIGasE; Regional Chairman, British Gas plc, North Thames, since 1988; *b* 20 May 1933; *s* of William Joseph Dove and Lucy Frances Dove; *m* 1958, Nancy Iris Powell; two *s* one *d*. *Educ:* Taunton's Sch., Southampton; King's Coll. and London Sch. of Econs and Pol. Science, Univ. of London (BSc; AKC 1954). CEng, FIGasE 1974; MIS 1962. Asst Statistician, 1958, Marketing Officer, 1961, Southern Gas; Controller of Sales and Marketing, Scottish Gas, 1965; Commercial Sales Manager, Gas Council, 1969; Dep. Chm., South Eastern Gas, 1973; Regl Chm., British Gas plc, S Eastern, 1982–87. *Recreations:* photography, walking. *Address:* British Gas plc, North Thames House, London Road, Staines, Middx TW18 4AE.

DOVER, Suffragan Bishop of, since 1980; **Rt. Rev. Richard Henry McPhail Third;** *b* 29 Sept. 1927; *s* of Henry McPhail and Marjorie Caroline Third; *m* 1966, Helen Illingworth; two *d*. *Educ:* Alleyn's Sch.; Reigate Grammar Sch.; Emmanuel Coll., Cambridge (BA 1950, MA 1955); Lincoln Theological Coll. Deacon 1952, priest 1953; Southwark; Curate: S Andrew, Mottingham, 1952–55; Sanderstead (in charge of St Edmund, Riddlesdown), 1955–59; Vicar of Sheerness, 1959–67; Vicar of Orpington, 1967–76; RD of Orpington, 1973–76; Hon. Canon of Rochester, 1974–76; Proctor in Convocation, 1975–76 and 1980–85; Bishop Suffragan of Maidstone, 1976–80. Chm. of Govs, Christ Church Coll., Canterbury, 1986–. Hon. DCL Kent, 1990. *Recreations:* music, walking. *Address:* Upway, St Martin's Hill, Canterbury, Kent CT1 1PR. *T:* Canterbury (0227) 464537.

DOVER, Den; MP (C) Chorley, since 1979; *b* 4 April 1938; *s* of Albert and Emmie Dover; *m* 1959, Anne Marina Wright; one *s* one *d*; *m* 1989, Kathleen Edna Fisher. *Educ:* Manchester Grammar Sch.; Manchester Univ. BSc Hons. CEng, MICE. John Laing & Son Ltd, 1959–68; National Building Agency: Dep. Chief Executive, 1969–70; Chief Exec., 1971–72; Projects Dir, Capital and Counties Property Co. Ltd, 1972–75; Contracts Manager, Wimpey Laing Iran, 1975–77. Director of Housing Construction, GLC, 1977–79. Member, London Borough of Barnet Council, 1968–71. Mem., Commons Select Cttee on Transport, 1979–87. *Recreations:* cricket, hockey, golf; Methodist. *Address:* 166 Furzehill Road, Boreham Wood, Herts WD6 2DS. *T:* 081–953 5945; 30 Countess Way, Euxton, Chorley, Lancs PR7 6PT.

DOVER, Sir Kenneth James, Kt 1977; DLitt; FRSE 1975; FBA 1966; Chancellor, University of St Andrews, since 1981; Professor of Classics (Winter Quarter), Stanford University, since 1988; *b* 11 March 1920; *o s* of P. H. J. Dover, London, Civil Servant; *m* 1947, Audrey Ruth Latimer; one *s* one *d*. *Educ:* St Paul's Sch. (Scholar); Balliol Coll., Oxford (Domus Scholar); Gaisford Prize, 1939; 1st in Classical Hon. Mods., 1940; Ireland Scholar, 1946; Cromer Prize (British Academy), 1946; 1st in Lit. Hum., Derby Scholar, Amy Mary Preston Read Scholar, 1947; Harmsworth Sen. Scholar, Merton Coll., 1947 (Hon. Fellow, 1980); DLitt Oxon 1974. Served War of 1939–45: Army (RA), 1940–45; Western Desert, 1941–43, Italy, 1943–45 (despatches). Fellow and Tutor, Balliol Coll., 1948–55 (Hon. Fellow, 1977); Prof. of Greek, 1955–76, Dean of Fac. of Arts, 1960–63, 1973–75, Univ. of St Andrews; Pres., Corpus Christi Coll., Oxford, 1976–86 (Hon. Fellow, 1986). Vis. Lectr, Harvard, 1960; Sather Prof. of Classical Literature, Univ. of California, 1967; Prof.-at-large, Cornell Univ., 1984–89. President: Soc. for Promotion of Hellenic Studies, 1971–74; Classical Assoc., 1975; Jt Assoc. of Classical Teachers, 1985. Pres., British Acad., 1978–81. For. Hon. Mem., Amer. Acad. of Arts and Sciences, 1979; For. Mem., Royal Netherlands Acad. of Arts and Sciences, 1979. Hon. LLD: Birmingham, 1979; St Andrews, 1981; Hon. DLitt: Bristol, 1980; London, 1980; St Andrews, 1981; Durham, 1984; Hon. LittD Liverpool, 1983; Hon. DHL Oglethorpe, 1984. *Publications:* Greek Word Order, 1960; Commentaries on Thucydides, Books VI and VII, 1965; (ed) Aristophanes' Clouds, 1968; Lysias and the Corpus Lysiacum, 1968; (with A. W. Gomme and A. Andrewes) Historical Commentary on Thucydides, vol. IV, 1970, vol. V, 1981; (ed) Theocritus, select poems, 1971; Aristophanic Comedy, 1972; Greek Popular Morality in the Time of Plato and Aristotle, 1974; Greek Homosexuality, 1978; (ed) Plato, Symposium, 1980; (ed and co-author) Ancient Greek Literature, 1980; The Greeks, 1980 (contrib., The Greeks, BBC TV series, 1980); Greek and the Greeks, 1987; The Greeks and their Legacy, 1989; articles in learned journals; Co-editor, Classical Quarterly, 1962–68. *Recreations:* historical linguistics, country walking. *Address:* 49 Hepburn Gardens, St Andrews, Fife KY16 9LS. *Club:* Athenæum.

DOW, Christopher; *see* Dow, J. C. R.

DOW, Rear-Adm. Douglas Morrison, CB 1991; Director General, Naval Personal Services, 1989–91; *b* 1 July 1935; *s* of George Torrance Dow and Grace Morrison MacFarlane; *m* 1959, Felicity Margaret Mona Napier; two *s*. *Educ:* George Heriot's School; BRNC Dartmouth. Joined RN, 1952; served Staff of C-in-C Plymouth, 1959–61; HMS Plymouth, 1961–63; RN Supply Sch., 1963–65; Staff of Comdr FEF, 1965–67; HMS Endurance, 1968–70; BRNC Dartmouth, 1970–72; Asst Dir, Officer Appointments (S), 1972–74; Sec. to Comdr British Navy Staff, Washington, 1974–76; HMS Tiger, 1977–78; NDC Latimer, 1978–79; CSO(A) to Flag Officer Portsmouth, 1979; Sec. to Controller of the Navy, 1981; Captain, HMS Cochrane, 1983; Commodore, HMS Centurion, 1985; RCDS 1988. FBIM. *Recreations:* Royal Navy Rugby Union (Chairman, 1985–91), fly fishing, golf, gardening. *Address:* Ministry of Defence (Navy), Whitehall, SW1A 2BE.

DOW, Harold Peter Bourner; QC 1971; *b* 28 April 1921; *s* of late Col H. P. Dow and P. I. Dow; *m* 1943, Rosemary Merewether, *d* of late Dr E. R. A. Merewether, CB, CBE, FRCP; two *s* one *d*. *Educ:* Charterhouse; Trinity Hall, Cambridge (MA). Served RAF (Air Crew), 1941–42. Min. of Supply, 1943–45. Barrister, Middle Temple, 1946. *Publications:* Restatement of Town and Country Planning, 1947; National Assistance, 1948; Rights of Way (with Q. Edwards), 1951; ed, Hobsons Local Government, 1951 and 1957 edns. *Recreations:* music, painting. *Address:* The Priory, Brandeston, near Woodbridge, Suffolk IP13 7AU. *T:* Earl Soham (072882) 244.

DOW, (John) Christopher (Roderick), FBA 1982; Visiting Fellow, National Institute of Economic and Social Research, since 1984; *b* 25 Feb. 1916; *s* of Warrender Begernie and Amy Langdon Dow; *m* 1960, Clare Mary Keegan; one *s* three *d*. *Educ:* Bootham Sch., York; Brighton, Hove and Sussex Grammar Sch.; University College London, Fellow 1973. Economic Adviser, later Senior Economic Adviser, HM Treasury, 1945–54; on staff, and Dep. Dir, National Inst. for Economic and Social Research, 1954–62; Treasury, 1962–63; Asst Sec.-Gen., OECD, Paris, 1963–73; Exec. Dir, Bank of England, 1973–81; an Advr to the Governor of the Bank of England, 1981–84. *Publications:* The Management of the British Economy, 1945–1960, 1964; Fiscal Policy for a Balanced Economy (jointly), 1968; (with I. D. Saville) A Critique of Monetary Policy: Theory and British Experience, 1988. Various articles in learned jls. *Club:* Reform.

DOWDALL, John Michael; Under Secretary, Department of Finance and Personnel, Northern Ireland, since 1989; *b* 6 Sept. 1944; *s* of W. Dowdall, MBE, and E. Dowdall; *m* 1964, Aylerie (*née* Houston); three *s* one *d*. *Educ:* King Edward's Sch., Witley, Surrey; Queen's Univ., Belfast (BScEcon). Lectr in Economics, Royal Univ. of Malta, 1966–69; Lectr in Political Econ., King's Coll., Univ. of Aberdeen, 1969–72; Economic Advr, Dept of Commerce, N Ireland, 1972–78, Principal, Dept of Commerce, 1978–82; Asst Sec., Dept of Finance and Personnel, N Ireland, 1982–85; Dep. Chief Exec., Industrial Develt Bd, NI, 1986–89.

DOWDALLS, Hon. Sheriff Edward Joseph; Principal, Coatbridge College (formerly Coatbridge Technical College), 1973–89; *b* 6 March 1926; *s* of late Alexander Dowdalls and Helen Dowdalls; *m* 1953, Sarah Quinn; one *s*. *Educ:* Our Lady's High Sch., Motherwell; Glasgow Univ. (BSc). Member, Coatbridge Town Council, 1958, Provost, 1967. Mem., Scottish Economic Planning Council, 1968–71; Chm., Lanarkshire Area Health Bd, 1977–81 (Mem., 1974–81). Hon. Sheriff, S Strathclyde and Galloway, 1975–. *Recreations:* reading, watching sport. *Address:* 72 Drumpellier Avenue, Coatbridge, Lanarkshire ML5 1JS. *Clubs:* Drumpellier Cricket, Drumpellier Rugby (Coatbridge).

DOWDEN, Richard George; journalist; Africa Editor, The Independent, since 1986; *b* 20 March 1949; *s* of Peter Dowden and Eleanor Dowden; *m* 1976, Penny Mansfield; two *d*. *Educ:* St George's Coll., Weybridge, Surrey; London Univ. (BA History). Volunteer Teacher, Uganda, 1971–72; Asst Sec., Justice and Peace Commn, 1973–76; Editor, Catholic Herald, 1976–79; journalist, The Times, 1980–86. *Address:* 7 Highbury Grange, N5.

DOWDESWELL, Lt-Col (John) Windsor, MC 1943; TD 1947; JP; Chairman, Gateshead Health Authority, since 1984; Vice Lord-Lieutenant of Tyne and Wear, since 1987; *b* 11 June 1920; *s* of Thomas Reginald Dowdeswell and Nancy Olivia Pitt Dowdeswell; *m* 1948, Phyllis Audrey Horsfield; one *s* one *d*. *Educ:* Malvern Coll. Commnd RA (TA), 1938; served War, RA 50 (N) Division: France, 1940; Western Desert, 1941–43; Sicily, 1943; NW Europe, 1944–46; Lt-Col Comdg 272 (N) Field Regt, RA (TA), 1963–66; Hon. Col, 101 (N) Field Regt, RA (TA), 1981–86. Emerson Walker Ltd, 1946–68 (Man. Dir, 1961–68); Clarke Chapman Ltd, 1968–77; NEI plc, 1977–83. JP Gateshead, 1955 (Chm., 1979–86); DL Tyne and Wear, 1976. *Address:* 40 Oakfield Road, Gosforth, Newcastle upon Tyne NE3 4HS. *T:* 091–285 2196. *Club:* Northern Counties (Newcastle upon Tyne).

DOWDING, family name of **Baron Dowding.**

DOWDING, 2nd Baron *cr* 1943, of Bentley Priory; **Derek Hugh Tremenheere Dowding;** Wing Commander, RAF, retired; *b* 9 Jan. 1919; *s* of (Air Chief Marshal) 1st Baron Dowding, GCB, GCVO, CMG, and Clarice Maud (*d* 1920), *d* of Captain John Williams, IA; *S* father, 1970; *m* 1st, 1940, Joan Myrle (marr. diss. 1946), *d* of Donald James Stuart, Nairn; 2nd, 1947, Alison Margaret (marr. diss. 1960), *d* of Dr James Bannerman, Norwich and *widow* of Major R. M. H. Peebles; two *s*; 3rd, 1961, Odette L. M. S. Hughes, *d* of Louis Joseph Houles. *Educ:* Winchester; RAF College, Cranwell. Served War of 1939–45, UK and Middle East; in comd No 49 (B) Sqdn, 1950; Wing Commander, 1951. Gen. Sec., Sea Cadet Assoc. (formerly Navy League), 1977–. *Heir:* *s* Hon. Piers Hugh Tremenheere Dowding, *b* 18 Feb. 1948. *Address:* c/o Lloyds Bank, 6 Pall Mall, SW1.

DOWDING, Hon. Peter M'Callum, MLA; barrister; *b* 6 Oct. 1943; *m*; five *c*. *Educ:* Hale School, Perth; Univ. of Western Australia (LLB 1964). Churchill Fellowship, 1974, UK and Canada. In practice as solicitor and barrister until 1983 and as barrister, 1990–. MLC North Province, WA, 1980–86; MLA (ALP) Maylands, 1986–90; Cabinet Member, 1983–90; Minister for: Mines, Fuel and Energy, 1983; Planning, and

Employment and Training, 1983–84; Consumer Affairs, 1983–86; Minister assisting the Minister for Public Sector Management, 1984–88; Minister for Works and Services, Labour, Productivity and Employment, and assisting the Treasurer, 1987–88; Treasurer, and Minister for Productivity, 1988–89; Leader, WA Parly Lab Party, 1987–90; Premier, WA, 1988–90; Minister, Public Sector Management, and Women's Interests, 1989–90. *Recreations:* sailing, bushwalking. *Address:* Level 31, 52 Martin Place, Sydney, NSW 2000, Australia. *T:* Australia (02) 223 8088.

DOWELL, Anthony (James), CBE 1973; Senior Principal, since 1967, Director, since 1986, Royal Ballet, Covent Garden (Assistant to Director, 1984–85; Associate Director, 1985–86); *b* 16 Feb. 1943; *s* of late Catherine Ethel and Arthur Henry Dowell; unmarried. *Educ:* Hampshire Sch., St Saviour's Hall, Knightsbridge; Royal Ballet Sch., White Lodge, Richmond, Surrey; Royal Ballet Sch., Barons Court. Joined Opera Ballet, 1960; 1st Company, for Russian Tour, 1961; created The Dream, 1964; Italian Tour, 1965; promoted Principal Dancer, 1966; Eastern Europe Tour, 1966; Japanese Tour, 1975; created Shadow Play, 1967; American Tours and Metropolitan Opera House, New York, 1968, 1969, 1972; created: Pavane, 1973; Manon, 1974. *Principal roles with Royal Ballet include:* La Fête Etrange, 1963; Napoli, 1965; Romeo and Juliet, 1965; Song of the Earth, 1966; Card Game, Giselle, Swan Lake, 1967; The Nutcracker, Cinderella, Monotones, Symphonic Variations, new version of Sleeping Beauty, Enigma Variations, Lilac Garden, 1968; Raymonda Act III, Daphnis and Chloe, La Fille Mal Gardée, 1969; Dances at a Gathering, 1970; La Bayadère, Meditation from Thaïs, Afternoon of a Faun, Anastasia, 1971; Triad, Le Spectre de la Rose, Giselle, 1972; Agon, Firebird, 1973; Manon, 1974; Four Schumann Pieces, Les Sylphides, 1975; Four Seasons, 1975; Scarlet Pastorale, 1976; Rhapsody, 1981; A Month in the Country, The Tempest, Varii Capricci, 1983; Sons of Horus, Frankenstein: the modern Prometheus, 1986; Ondine, 1988. Guest Artist with Amer. Ballet Theater, 1977–79; *performed in:* The Nutcracker; Don Quixote; Other Dances; *created:* Contredanses; Solor in Makarova's La Bayadère; Fisherman in Le Rossignol (Ashton's choreography), NY Metropolitan Opera, 1981. Narrator in A Wedding Bouquet (first speaking role), Joffrey Ballet, 1977; guest appearances with Nat. Ballet of Canada (The Dream, Four Schumann Pieces), 1979 and 1981; Anthony Dowell Ballet Gala, Palladium, 1980 (for charity); narrated Oedipus Rex, NY Metropolitan Opera, 1981. *Television performances:* La Bayadère (USA); Swan Lake, Cinderella, Sleeping Beauty, A Month in the Country, The Dream, Les Noces (all BBC); All the Superlatives (personal profile), Omnibus, BBC. Dance Magazine award, NY, 1972. *Recreations:* painting, paper sculpture, theatrical costume design. *Address:* Royal Opera House, Covent Garden, WC2.

DOWELL, Ian Malcolm; Editor, Birmingham Evening Mail, since 1987; *b* 15 Nov. 1940; *s* of late James Mardlin and Lilian Dowell; *m* 1st, 1967, Maureen Kane; two *d*; 2nd, 1980, Pauline Bridget Haughian. *Educ:* Exmouth Grammar Sch., Devon. Reporter, Exmouth and East Devon Journal, 1958; Sub-Editor, Woodrow Wyatt Newspapers, 1960; Editor, Wallingford News, Berks, 1962; Dep. Editor, Birmingham Planet, 1964–66; Birmingham Evening Mail: Sub-Editor, 1966; Dep. Features Editor, 1972; Chief Sub-Editor, 1976; Asst Editor, 1981; Dep. Editor, 1985. Mem., Guild of British Newspaper Editors, 1987–. Mem., Woodland Trust, 1987–; Fellow, RSPB, 1987. *Recreations:* the countryside, gardening. *Address:* The Birmingham Post & Mail Ltd, 28 Colmore Circus, Birmingham B4 6AX. *T:* 021–236 3366.

DOWELL, Prof. John Derek, FRS 1986; Professor of Elementary Particle Physics, University of Birmingham, since 1980; *b* 6 Jan. 1935; *s* of William Ernest Dowell and Elsie Dorothy Dowell (*née* Jarvis); *m* 1959, Patricia Clarkson; one *s* one *d*. *Educ:* Coalville Grammar Sch., Leics; Univ. of Birmingham (BSc, PhD). Research Fellow, Univ. of Birmingham, 1958–60; Res. Associate, CERN, Geneva, 1960–62; Lectr, 1962–70, Sen. Lectr, 1970–75, Reader, 1975–80, Univ. of Birmingham. Vis. Scientist, Argonne Nat. Lab., USA, 1968–69; Scientific Associate, CERN, Geneva, 1973–74, 1985–87 (Mem., Scientific Policy Cttee, 1982–90). Mem., Nuclear Physics Bd, SERC, 1974–77, 1981–85; Chm., Particle Physics Cttee, SERC, 1981–85; Mem., Europ. Cttee for Future Accelerators, 1989–. Rutherford Prize and Medal, InstP, 1988. *Publications:* numerous, in Phys. Letters, Nuovo Cimento, Nuclear Phys., Phys. Rev., Proc. Royal Soc., and related literature. *Recreations:* piano, amateur theatre, squash, ski-ing. *Address:* 57 Oxford Road, Moseley, Birmingham B13 9ES; School of Physics and Space Research, University of Birmingham, Birmingham B15 2TT.

DOWLING, Kenneth, CB 1985; Deputy Director of Public Prosecutions, 1982–85; *b* 30 Dec. 1933; *s* of Alfred and Maria Dowling; *m* 1957, Margaret Frances Bingham; two *d*. *Educ:* King George V Grammar Sch., Southport. Called to the Bar, Gray's Inn, 1960. RAF, 1952–54. Immigration Branch, Home Office, 1954–61; joined DPP Dept: Legal Asst, 1961; Sen. Legal Asst, 1966; Asst Solicitor, 1972; Asst Dir, 1976; Princ. Asst Dir, 1977. *Recreations:* reading, golf.

DOWLING, Rt. Rev. Owen Douglas; *see* Canberra and Goulburn, Bishop of.

DOWLING, Prof. Patrick Joseph, PhD; FEng 1981; British Steel Professor of Steel Structures, Imperial College, University of London, since 1979; Head of Civil Engineering Department, Imperial College, since 1985; Founder Partner, Chapman and Dowling, Consulting Engineers, since 1981; *b* 23 March 1939; *s* of John Dowling and Margaret McKittrick, Dublin; *m* 1966, Grace Carmine Victoria Lobo, *d* of Palladius Lobo and Marcilia Moniz, Zanzibar; one *s* one *d*. *Educ:* Christian Brothers Sch., Dublin; University Coll., Dublin (BE NUI 1960); Imperial Coll. of Science and Technol., London (PhD 1968). DIC 1961; FRINA 1985; FIStructE 1978; FICE 1979; FCGI 1989. Demonstr in Civil Engrg, UC Dublin, 1960–61; Post-grad. studies, Imperial Coll., London, 1961–65; Bridge Engr, British Constructional Steelwork Assoc., 1965–68; Res. Fellow, 1968–74 and Reader in Structural Steelwork, 1974–79, Imperial Coll., London. Chm., Eurocode 3 (Steel Structures) Drafting Cttee, 1981–84. Instn of Structural Engineers: Oscar Faber Award, 1971; Henry Adams Medal, 1976; Guthrie Brown Medal, 1979; Oscar Faber Medal, 1985; Telford Premium, ICE, 1976; Gustave Trasenster Medal, Assoc. des Ingénieurs sortis de l'Univ. de Liège, 1984. Editor, Jl of Constructional Steel Research, 1980–. Mem. Council, RHBNC, 1990–. *Publications:* Steel Plated Structures, 1977; Buckling of Shells in Offshore Structures, 1982; Structural Steel Design, 1988; technical papers on elastic and inelastic behaviour and design of steel and composite land-based and offshore structures. *Recreations:* travelling, sailing, reading, the enjoyment of good company. *Address:* Imperial College of Science, Technology and Medicine, SW7 2BU. T: 071–589 5111. *Clubs:* Athenæum, Chelsea Arts.

DOWN AND CONNOR, Bishop of, (RC), since 1991; **Most Rev. Patrick Joseph Walsh;** *b*9 April 1931; *s* of Michael and Nora Walsh. *Educ:* Queen's Univ. Belfast (MA); Christ's Coll., Cambridge (MA); Pontifical Lateran Univ., Rome (STL). Ordained 1956; Teacher, St MacNissi's Coll., Garron Tower, 1958–64; Chaplain, Queen's Univ., Belfast, 1964–70; Pres., St Malachy's Coll., Belfast, 1970–83; Auxiliary Bishop of Down and Connor, 1983–91. *Recreations:* walking, music, theatre. *Address:* 73 Somerton Road, Belfast BT15 4DE. *T:* Belfast (0232) 776185.

DOWN AND DROMORE, Bishop of, since 1986; **Rt. Rev. Gordon McMullan;** *b* 1934; *m* 1957, Kathleen Davidson; two *s*. *Educ:* Queen's Univ., Belfast (BSc Econ 1961, PhD 1971); Ridley Hall, Cambridge. ACIS 1957. Dipl. of Religious Studies (Cantab) 1978; ThD Geneva Theol Coll., 1988; MPhil TCD, 1990. Deacon 1962, priest 1963, dio. Down; Curate of Ballymacarrett, 1962–67; Central Adviser on Christian Stewardship to Church of Ireland, 1967–70; Curate of St Columba, Knock, Belfast, 1970–71; Rector of St Brendan's, East Belfast, 1971–76; Rector of St Columba, Knock, Belfast, 1976–80; Archdeacon of Down, 1979–80; Bishop of Clogher, 1980–86. *Publications:* A Cross and Beyond, 1976; We are called . . ., 1977; Everyday Discipleship, 1979; Reflections on St Mark's Gospel, 1984; Growing Together in Prayer, 1990. *Address:* The See House, 32 Knockdene Park South, Belfast BT5 7AB.

DOWN, Sir Alastair (Frederick), Kt 1978; OBE 1944 (MBE 1942); MC 1940; TD 1951; Chairman, The Burmah Oil Co. PLC, 1975–83 (Chief Executive, 1975–80); *b* 23 July 1914; *e s* of Frederick Edward Down and Margaret Isobel Down (*née* Hutchison); *m* 1947, Bunny Mellon; two *s* two *d*. *Educ:* Edinburgh Acad.; Marlborough Coll. Commissioned in 7th/9th Bn, The Royal Scots (TA), 1935. CA 1938. Joined British Petroleum Co. Ltd in Palestine, 1938. Served War of 1939–45 (despatches twice, MC, MBE, OBE, Kt Comdr, Order of Orange Nassau, with swords, 1946): Middle East, N Africa, Italy and Holland, with Eighth Army and 1st Canadian Army as Lt-Col and full Col. Rejoined BP, in Iran, 1945–47; Head Office, 1947–54; Canada, 1954–62 (Chief Rep. of BP in Canada, 1954–57; Pres., BP Group in Canada, 1957–62); Pres. BP Oil Corp., 1969–70; Man. Dir, 1962–75 and Dep. Chm., 1969–75, British Petroleum Co. Ltd; Director: TRW Inc., USA, 1977–86; Scottish American Investment Co. Ltd, 1980–85; Royal Bank of Canada, 1981–85; Chairman: British-North American Res. Assoc., 1980–84; London American Energy NV, 1981–85. Member: Review Body for pay of doctors and dentists, 1971–74; Television Adv. Cttee, 1971–72; Council, Marlborough Coll., 1979–87 (Chm. Council, 1982–87); Hon. Treasurer, Field Studies Council, 1977–81. FRSA 1970; FBIM 1972; JDipMA (Hon.), 1966. Hambro British Businessman of the Year Award, 1980; Cadman Meml Medal, Inst. of Petroleum, 1981. *Recreations:* shooting, golf, fishing. *Address:* Brieryhill, Hawick, Roxburghshire TD9 7LL. *Club:* New (Edinburgh).

DOWN, Antony Turnbull L.; *see* Langdon-Down.

DOWN, Barbara Langdon; *see* Littlewood, Lady (Barbara).

DOWN, Rt. Rev. William John Denbigh; *see* Bermuda, Bishop of.

DOWNE, 11th Viscount, *cr* 1680; **John Christian George Dawnay;** Bt 1642; Baron Dawnay of Danby (UK) *cr* 1897; DL; technology manager; *b* Wykeham, 18 Jan. 1935; *s* of 10th Viscount Downe, OBE and Margaret Christine (*d* 1967), *d* of Christian Bahnsen, NJ; *S* father, 1965; *m* 1965, Alison Diana, *d* of I. F. H. Sconce, OBE; one *s* one *d*. *Educ:* Eton Coll.; Christ Church, Oxford. 2nd Lieut, Grenadier Guards, 1954–55. Non-marine broker at Lloyd's, 1958–65. Part-time Mem., Electronics Res. Gp, J. J. Thomson Physical Lab., Univ. of Reading, 1964–78; Brookdeal Electronics Ltd: Man. Dir. 1965–68; Vice-Chm., 1968–71; Chm., 1971–84; Director: Dawnay Faulkner Associated Ltd (Consultants), 1968–; Allen Bradley Electronics Ltd, 1970–81; Copeland and Jenkins, 1973–; Sintrom PLC, 1974–; George Rowney & Co. Ltd, 1978–83; York Ltd (Chm.), 1980–; Yorkshire Bank, 1990–; Dir, Scarborough Theatre Trust, 1981– (Vice-Chm., 1986–); Member: CLA Yorks Br. Cttee, 1966– (Chm., 1988–90); CLA Exec. Cttee, 1990–; N Yorks Moors Nat. Park Cttee, 1969– (Vice-Chm., 1982–85); N Riding/N Yorks County Council, 1969–85; Nat. Railway Mus. Cttee, 1974– (Chm., 1985–); N Yorks Rural Develt Commn Business Cttee, 1978– (Chm., 1986–); President: N York Moors Hist. Railway Trust, 1970–; Yorks Rural Community Council,. 1977–; Aston Martin Owners Club, 1980–; Friends of the Nat. Railway Mus., 1988–; Trustee, Nat. Mus. of Science and Industry, 1985–. Hon. Col, 150 (Northumbrian) Regt RCT(V), 1984–. Liveryman, Co. of Scientific Instrument Makers, 1991–. DL N Yorks, 1981. *Publications:* contributions to various journals. *Recreations:* linear circuit design, railways (selectively). *Heir:* *s* Hon. Richard Henry Dawnay, *b* 9 April 1967. *Address:* Wykeham Abbey, Scarborough, North Yorks YO13 9QS. *T:* Scarborough (0723) 862404; 5 Douro Place, W8 5PH. *T:* 071–937 9449. *Club:* Pratt's.

DOWNER, Prof. Martin Craig; Professor and Head of Department of Dental Health Policy, Hon. Consultant in Dental Public Health, Eastman Institute of Dental Surgery, since 1990; *b* 9 March 1931; *s* of Dr Reginald Lionel Ernest Downer and Mrs Eileen Maud Downer (*née* Craig); *m* 1961, Anne Catherine (*née* Evans); four *d*. *Educ:* Shrewsbury Sch.; Univ. of Liverpool; Univ. of Manchester (PhD 1974; DDS 1989); Univ. of London. LDSRCS 1958; DDPH RCS 1969. Dental Officer, St Helens Local Authority, 1958–59; gen. dental practice, 1959–64; Dental Officer, Bor. of Haringey, 1964–67; Principal Dental Officer, Royal Bor. of Kensington and Chelsea, 1967–70; Res. Fellow in Dental Health, Univ. of Manchester, 1970–74; Area Dental Officer, Salford HA (also Hon. Lectr, Univ. of Manchester), 1974–79; Chief Dental Officer, SHHD (also Hon. Sen. Lectr, Univs of Edinburgh and Dundee), 1979–83; Chief Dental Officer (Under Sec.), Dept of Health (formerly DHSS), 1983–90. *Publications:* contribs to books and papers in learned jls in gen. field of dental public health, incl. epidemiology and biostatistics, clin. trials and trial methodology, inf. systems, health services res., and econs of dental care. *Recreations:* music, reading, cookery, natural history, vintage aviation, walking. *Address:* Institute of Dental Surgery, Eastman Dental Hospital, 256 Gray's Inn Road, WC1X 8LD.

DOWNES, Sir Edward (Thomas), Kt 1991; CBE 1986; Associate Music Director and Principal Conductor, Royal Opera House, Covent Garden, since 1991; *b* 17 June 1924; *m* Joan; one *s* one *d*. FRCM. Royal Opera House, Covent Garden, 1952–69; Music Dir, Australian Opera, 1972–76; Prin. Conductor, BBC Northern Symphony Orch., subseq. BBC Philharmonic Orch., 1980–91. *Address:* c/o Royal Opera House, Covent Garden, WC2E 7QA.

DOWNES, George Robert, CB 1967; Director of Studies, Royal Institute of Public Administration, since 1972; *b* 25 May 1911; *o s* of late Philip George Downes; *m* Edna Katherine Millar; two *d*. *Educ:* King Edward's Grammar School, Birmingham; Grocers', London. Entered GPO, 1928; Assistant Surveyor, 1937; Asst Principal, 1939. Served War of 1939–45: RNVR, in destroyers, 1942–45. Principal, GPO, 1946; Principal Private Sec. to: Lord President of the Council, 1948–50, Lord Privy Seal, 1951; Assistant Secretary, 1951; Imperial Defence College, 1952; Deputy Regional Director, GPO London, 1955; Dir, London Postal Region, 1960–65; Dir of Postal Services, 1965–67; Dir, Operations and Overseas, PO, 1967–71. *Recreations:* music, gardening. *Address:* Orchard Cottage, Frithsden, Berkhamsted, Herts HP4 1NW.

DOWNES, George Stretton, CBE 1976; Deputy Receiver for the Metropolitan Police District, 1973–76; retired; *b* London, 2 March 1914; *e s* of late George and Rosalind S. Downes; *m* 1st, 1939, Sheilah Gavigan (*d* 1986); two *s* two *d*; 2nd, 1991, Barbara (*née* Haydon). *Educ:* Cardinal Vaughan Sch., Kensington. Joined Metropolitan Police Office, 1934; Secretary, 1969. *Recreations:* golf, gardening. *Address:* 9 Browning Road, Fetcham, Leatherhead, Surrey KT22 9HN.

DOWNES, Prof. (John) Kerry, FSA; Professor of History of Art, University of Reading, 1978–91; *b* 8 Dec. 1930; *s* of Ralph William Downes, *qv*; *m* 1962, Margaret Walton. *Educ:* St Benedict's, Ealing; Courtauld Institute of Art. BA, PhD London. Library, Courtauld Inst. of Art, 1954–58; Librarian, Barber Inst. of Fine Arts, Univ. of Birmingham, 1958–66; Lectr in Fine Art, Univ. of Reading, 1966–71, Reader, 1971–78. Vis. Lectr, Yale Univ., 1968. Mem., Royal Commission on Historical Monuments of England, 1981–; Pres., Soc. of Architectural Historians of GB, 1984–88. *Publications:* Hawksmoor, 1959, 2nd edn 1979; English Baroque Architecture, 1966; Hawksmoor, 1969; Christopher Wren, 1971; Whitehall Palace, in Colvin and others, History of the King's Works, V, 1660–1782, 1976; Vanbrugh, 1977; The Georgian Cities of Britain, 1979; Rubens, 1980; The Architecture of Wren, 1982, 2nd edn 1988; Sir John Vanbrugh, a Biography, 1987; Sir Christopher Wren: Design for St Paul's Cathedral, 1988; contribs to Burlington Magazine, Architectural History, Architectural Rev., TLS, etc. *Recreations:* drawing, making music, learning electronics, procrastination. *Address:* c/o Department of History of Art, University of Reading, London Road, Reading RG1 5AQ. *T:* Reading (0734) 318890.

DOWNES, M. P.; *see* Panter-Downes.

DOWNES, Ralph (William), CBE 1969; Organist, Brompton Oratory, 1936–78, now Organist Emeritus; Curator-Organist, Royal Festival Hall, since 1954; *b* 16 Aug. 1904; *s* of James William and Constance Edith Downes; *m* 1929, Agnes Mary (*née* Rix) (*d* 1980); one *s*. *Educ:* Derby Municipal Secondary Sch. (Scholar); Royal College of Music, London (Schol.); Keble Coll., Oxford. ARCM 1925, MA 1931, BMus 1935. Asst Organist, Southwark Cathedral, 1924; Organ Scholar, Keble Coll., 1925–28; Director of Chapel Music and Lecturer, Princeton Univ., USA, 1928–35; Organ Prof., RCM, 1954–75. Organ Curator to LCC, 1949. Consultant to: the Corporation of Croydon, 1960; Cardiff City Council (St David's Hall), 1977; Designer and Supervisor of organs in: Buckfast Abbey, 1952; Royal Festival Hall, 1954; Brompton Oratory, 1954; St John's Cathedral, Valletta, Malta, 1961; St Albans Cathedral, 1963, 1981; Fairfield Halls, 1964; Paisley Abbey, 1968; Gloucester Cathedral, 1971, and others. Recitals and performances in: Aldeburgh, 1948–85, Belgium, France, Germany, Holland, Italy, Switzerland, also radio and TV. Jury mem., organ festivals, Amsterdam, Haarlem, Munich, St Albans, Manchester. External Examiner: Birmingham Sch. of Music; RAM; Univs of Cambridge and Reading. Received into the Catholic Church, 1930. Hon. RAM 1965; Hon. FRCO 1966; FRCM 1969. KSG 1970. *Publications:* Baroque Tricks (Adventures with the Organ Builders), 1983; miscellaneous articles on the organ, compositions for keyboard and chorus. *Address:* 9 Elm Crescent, Ealing, W5 3JW. *T:* 081–567 6330.

See also J. K. Downes.

DOWNEY, Anne Elisabeth; Her Honour Judge Downey; a Circuit Judge, since 1986; *b* 22 Aug. 1936; *d* of John James Downey and Ida May Downey. *Educ:* Notre Dame Convent, Liverpool; Liverpool Univ. LLB (Hons.). Called to the Bar, Gray's Inn, 1958. A Recorder, 1980–86. *Recreations:* antiques, reading. *Address:* Copperfield, 4 Pine Walk, Prenton, Merseyside. *T:* 051–608 2404.

DOWNEY, Sir Gordon (Stanley), KCB 1984 (CB 1980); Comptroller and Auditor General, 1981–87; Chairman, Financial Intermediaries, Managers and Brokers Regulatory Association, since 1990; Readers' Representative, The Independent, since 1990; *b* 26 April 1928; *s* of Stanley William and Winifred Downey; *m* 1952, Jacqueline Goldsmith; two *d*. *Educ:* Tiffin's Sch.; London Sch. of Economics (BSc(Econ)). Served RA, 1946–48. Ministry of Works, 1951; entered Treasury, 1952; Asst Private Sec. to successive Chancellors of the Exchequer, 1955–57; on loan to Ministry of Health, 1961–62; Asst Sec., 1965, Under-Sec., 1972, Head of Central Unit, 1975; Dep. Sec., Treasury, 1976–81; on loan as Dep. Head, Central Policy Review Staff, Cabinet Office, 1978–81. Special Advr, Ernst & Young (formerly Ernst & Whinney), 1988–90; Complaints Comr, The Securities Assoc., 1989–90. Chm., Delegacy, King's College Med. and Dental Sch., 1989–. *Recreations:* reading, visual arts, tennis. *Address:* Chinley Cottage, 1 Eaton Park Road, Cobham, Surrey KT11 2JG. *T:* Cobham (0932) 67878. *Club:* Army and Navy.

DOWNEY, Air Vice-Marshal John Chegwyn Thomas, CB 1975; DFC 1945, AFC; Deputy Controller of Aircraft (C), Ministry of Defence, 1974–75, retired; *b* 26 Nov. 1920; *s* of Thomas Cecil Downey and Mary Evelyn Downey; *m* Diana, (*née* White); one *s* two *d*. *Educ:* Whitgift Sch. Entered RAF 1939; served War of 1939–45 in Coastal Command (DFC 1945 for his part in anti-U-boat ops). Captained Lincoln Aries III on global flight of 29,000 miles, during which London-Khartoum record was broken. RAF Farnborough 1956–58; commanded Bomber Comd Develt Unit 1959–60; head of NE Defence Secretariat, Cyprus, 1960–62; Comd RAF Farnborough, 1962–64; a Dir, Op. Requirements (RAF) MoD, 1965–67; IDC, 1968; Comdt, RAF Coll. of Air Warfare, Manby, Jan./Oct. 1969; Comdr Southern Maritime Air Region, 1969–71; Senior RAF Mem., RCDS, 1972–74. *Publications:* Management in the Armed Forces: an anatomy of the military profession, 1977; (contrib.) Yearbook of World Affairs, 1983. *Recreations:* sailing, ski-ing. *Address:* c/o Lloyds Bank, 7 Pall Mall, SW1. *Club:* Royal Air Force.

DOWNEY, William George, CB 1967; *b* 3 Jan. 1912; *s* of late William Percy Downey; *m* 1936, Iris, *e d* of late Ernest Frederick Pickering; three *d*. *Educ:* Southend Grammar Sch. ACWA 1935, ACA 1937, FCA 1960. Ministry of Aircraft Production, 1940; Ministry of Supply, 1946 (Director of Finance and Administration, Royal Ordnance Factories, 1952–57); Ministry of Aviation, 1959; Under-Secretary, 1961; Chm., Steering Gp, Develt Cost Estimation, 1964–66; Min. of Technology, 1967, Min. of Aviation Supply, 1970; DTI, 1971; Management Consultant to Procurement Exec., MoD, 1972–74; Under Sec., NI Office, 1974–75; Dir, Harland and Wolff, 1975–81; Consultant to CAA, 1976–79, to Dept of Energy, 1980. *Address:* Starvelarks, Dawes Heath Road, Rayleigh, Essex SS6 7NL. *T:* Rayleigh (0268) 774138.

DOWNIE, Prof. Robert Silcock, FRSE 1986; Professor of Moral Philosophy, Glasgow University, since 1969; *b* 19 April 1933; *s* of late Robert Mackie Downie and late Margaret Barlas Downie; *m* 1958, Eileen Dorothea Flynn; three *d*. *Educ:* The High Sch. of Glasgow; Glasgow Univ.; The Queen's Coll., Oxford. MA, first cl. hons, Philosophy and Eng. Lit., Glasgow, 1955; Russian linguist, Intelligence Corps, 1955–57; Ferguson Schol., 1958; BPhil Oxford Univ., 1959. Glasgow University: Lectr in Moral Philosophy, 1959; Sen. Lectr in Moral Philosophy, 1968; Stevenson Lectr in Med. Ethics, 1985–88. Vis. Prof. of Philosophy, Syracuse Univ., NY, USA, 1963–64. *Publications:* Government Action and Morality, 1964; (jtly) Respect for Persons, 1969; Roles and Values, 1971; (jtly) Education and Personal Relationships, 1974; (jtly) Values in Social Work, 1976; (jtly) Caring and Curing, 1980; Healthy Respect, 1987; (jtly) Health Promotion: models and values, 1990; contribs to: Mind, Philosophy, Analysis, Aristotelian Society, Political Studies. *Recreation:* music. *Address:* Department of Moral Philosophy, University of Glasgow G12 8QQ. *T:* 041–339 8855.

DOWNING, Dr Anthony Leighton; Consultant, Binnie & Partners, Consulting Engineers, since 1986 (Partner, 1973–86); *b* 27 March 1926; *s* of Sydney Arthur Downing and Frances Dorothy Downing; *m* 1952, Kathleen Margaret Frost; one *d*. *Educ:* Arnold Sch., Blackpool; Cambridge and London Universities. BA Cantab. 1946; BSc Special Degree 2 (1) Hons. London, 1950; DSc London 1967. Joined Water Pollution Research Lab., 1946; seconded to Fisheries Research Lab., Lowestoft, 1947–48; granted transfer to Govt Chemist's Lab., 1948; returned to WPRL as Scientific Officer, 1950; subsequently worked mainly in field of biochemical engrg; Dir, Water Pollution Res. Lab., 1966–73. Vis. Prof., Imperial Coll. of Science and Technology, 1978–82. FIChemE 1975; FIWPC 1965 (Pres., 1979); FIBiol 1965; Hon. FIPHE 1965; FIWES 1975; Hon. FIWEM 1987. FRSA. Freeman, City of London, 1988. *Publications:* papers in scientific and technical journals. *Recreations:* golf, snooker, gardening. *Address:* 2 Tewin Close, Tewin Wood, Welwyn, Herts. *T:* Bulls Green (043879) 474. *Clubs:* United Oxford & Cambridge University; Knebworth Golf.

DOWNING, David Francis, PhD; Chairman, Science Recruitment Boards, Civil Service Commission; *b* 4 Aug. 1926; *e s* of late Alfred William Downing, ARCO, and Violet Winifred Downing; *m* 1948, Margaret Joan Llewellyn; one *s* one *d*. *Educ:* Bristol Grammar Sch.; Univ. of Bristol (BSc 1952, PhD 1955). Served Coldstream Gds and Royal Welch Fusiliers, 1944–48 (Lieut RWF, 1947). Student Mem. of delegn from Brit. univs to Soviet univs, 1954; Eli Lilley Res. Fellow, Univ. of Calif, LA, and Fulbright Travel Scholarship, 1955–56; Long Ashton Res. Stn, Univ. of Bristol, 1957–58; Chem. Def. Estab., 1958–63; Def. Res. Staff, Washington, 1963–66; Chem. Def. Estab., 1966–68; Counsellor (Scientific), British High Commn, Ottawa, 1968–73; Head, Management Services, RARDE, 1973–75, and Head, Pyrotechnics Br., 1975–78; Counsellor (Scientific), British Embassy, Moscow, 1978–81; Asst Dir, Resources and Programmes B, MoD, 1981–83; Head, Land Systems Group, British Defence Staff, British Embassy, Washington, 1983–87. Lay Chm., Salisbury Cathedral Council, 1990–. Gov., Salisbury and Wells Theological Coll., 1987– (Chm., 1990–). FRSA 1969. *Publications:* scientific papers, mainly in Jl of Chem. Soc., and Qly Revs of Chem. Soc. *Recreations:* cathedral music, Arctic art, travel, bird watching, skiing. *Address:* 13 The Close, Salisbury, Wilts SP1 2EB. *T:* Salisbury (0722) 323910. *Club:* Army and Navy.

DOWNING, Henry Julian; HM Diplomatic Service, retired; *b* 22 March 1919; *o s* of Henry Julian Downing and Kate Avery; *m* 1951, Ruth Marguerite Ambler. *Educ:* Boys' High Sch., Trowbridge; Hertford Coll., Oxford. Indian Civil Service (Madras) 1941–47. Joined HM Foreign Service, 1947; 2nd Secretary, Madras and Dacca, 1947–50; Foreign Office, 1950–52; 1st Secretary (Commercial), Istanbul, 1952–56; Foreign Office, 1956–58; 1st Secretary and Head of Chancery, Kabul, 1958–62; Foreign Office, 1963–65; HM Consul-General, Lourenço Marques, 1965–69; Head of Claims Dept, 1969–71, of Migration and Visa Dept, 1971–73, FCO; Consul-Gen., Cape Town, 1973–77. *Recreations:* swimming, walking, bird watching. *Address:* 8b Greenaway Gardens, Hampstead, NW3. *T:* 071–435 2593. *Club:* United Oxford & Cambridge University.

DOWNPATRICK, Lord; Edward Edmund Maximilian George Windsor; *b* 2 Dec. 1988; *s* and *heir* of Earl of St Andrews, *qv*.

DOWNS, Sir Diarmuid, Kt 1985; CBE 1979; FRS 1985; FEng, FIMechE; Managing Director, 1967–84, Chairman, 1976–87, Ricardo Consulting Engineers plc; *b* 23 April 1922; *s* of John Downs and Ellen McMahon; *m* 1951, Mary Carmel Chillman; one *s* three *d*. *Educ:* Gunnersbury Catholic Grammar Sch.; City Univ., London (BScEng). CEng, FIMechE 1961. Ricardo Consulting Engineers Ltd, 1942–87: Head, Petrol Engine Dept, 1947; Dir, 1957. Mem., Adv. Council for Applied R&D, 1976–80; Member: SERC, 1981–85 (Chm., Engineering Bd); Design Council, 1981–89; Bd of Dirs, Soc. of Automotive Engineers Inc., 1983–86; Bd of British Council, 1987–; Council, Motor Industry Res. Assoc., 1987–89. President: Fédération Internationale des Sociétés d'Ingénieurs des Techniques de L'Automobile, 1978 (Vice-Pres., 1975); IMechE, 1978–79 (Vice-Pres., 1971–78); Assoc. of Indep. Contract Res. Organisations, 1975–77; Section G, British Assoc. for Advancement of Science, 1984; Royal Commn for Exhibn of 1851. Chm., Technology Activities Cttee, Royal Soc., 1989–; Mem., Adv. Bd, Parly Office of Science and Technology, 1988–. Dir, Gabriel Communications (formerly Universe Publications) Ltd, 1986–. Vis. Fellow, Lincoln Coll. Oxford, 1987–88. Hinton Lecture, Fellowship of Engrg, 1987. Foreign Associate, Nat. Acad. of Engrg, USA, 1987; Hon. Mem., Hungarian Acad. of Scis, 1988. Liveryman, Co. of Engineers, 1984–. Mem. Council: City Univ., 1980–82; Surrey Univ., 1983– (Chm., 1989–). Hon. DSc: City, 1978; Cranfield Inst. of Technol., 1981. George Stephenson Research Prize, 1951, Crompton Lanchester Medal, 1951 and Dugald Clerk Prize, 1952, IMechE; James Alfred Ewing Medal, ICE, 1985; Medal, Internat. Fedn of Automobile Engrs' and Technicians' Assocs, 1986. *Publications:* papers on internal combustion engines in British and internat. engrg jls and conf. proc. *Recreation:* theatre. *Address:* The Downs, 143 New Church Road, Hove, East Sussex BN3 4DB. *T:* Brighton (0273) 419357. *Clubs:* St Stephen's Constitutional; Hove (Hove).

DOWNS, Mrs George Wallingford; *see* Tureck, Rosalyn.

DOWNS, Leslie Hall, CBE 1942; MA Cantab; FIMechE; Chairman, 1936–71, Rose, Downs & Thompson Ltd, Old Foundry, Hull, retired; former Chairman, Rose Downs (Holdings) Ltd, Hull; *b* 6 June 1900; *s* of late Charles Downs, Hull and Bridlington; *m* 1930, Kathleen Mary Lewis; three *d*. *Educ:* Abbotsholme Sch., Derbys; Christ's Coll., Cambridge (Scholar, BA, 1922, MA, 1927). European War, Artists' Rifles; served engineering apprenticeship and subsequently employed in various positions with Rose, Downs & Thompson Ltd; former Chm., Barnsley Canister Co. Ltd; former Vice-Chm., Davy-Ashmore Ltd; former Director: Blundell-Permoglaze (Holdings) Ltd; Ashmore Benson Pease & Co. Ltd; Power Gas Corp. Ltd. Past President Hull Chamber of Commerce and Shipping; Custodian Trustee, Hull Trustee Savings Bank; Former Treasurer and Member of Council, Hull Univ., retd 1976. Hon. DSc Hull Univ. *Recreations:* fly-fishing, cabinet making, reading. *Address:* Brierley House, Hutton-le-Hole, N Yorks YO6 6UA. *T:* Lastingham (07515) 580.

DOWNSHIRE, 8th Marquess of, *cr* 1789 (Ire.); **Arthur Robin Ian Hill;** Viscount Hillsborough, Baron Hill 1717; Earl of Hillsborough, Viscount Kilwarlin 1751; Baron Harwich (GB) 1756; Earl of Hillsborough, Viscount Fairford (GB) 1772; Hereditary Constable of Hillsborough Fort; farmer, since 1963; *b* 10 May 1929; *s* of Lord Arthur Francis Henry Hill (*d* 1953) (*yr s* of 6th Marquess) and Sheila (*d* 1961), *d* of Col Stewart MacDougall of Lunga; *S* uncle, 1989; *m* 1st, 1957, Hon. Juliet Mary (*d* 1986), *d* of 7th Baron Forester; two *s* one *d*; 2nd, 1989, Mrs Diana Hibbert (*née* Cross). *Educ:* Eton. 2nd Lieut Royal Scots Greys, 1948–50. Articled clerk, 1950–55; Chartered Accountant (ACA 1959). *Recreations:* shooting, travel. *Heir:* *s* Earl of Hillsborough, *qv*. *Address:* Clifton Castle, Ripon, North Yorks HG4 4AB. *T:* Ripon (0765) 89326. *Club:* White's.

DOWNSIDE, Abbot of; *see* Fitzgerald-Lombard, Rt Rev. Charles.

DOWNWARD, Maj.-Gen. Peter Aldcroft, CB 1979; DSO 1967; DFC 1952; Governor, Military Knights of Windsor, since 1989; *b* 10 April 1924; *s* of late Aldcroft Leonard and Mary Downward; *m* 1st, 1953, Hilda Hinckley Wood (*d* 1976); two *s*; 2nd, 1980, Mrs Mary Boykett Procter (*née* Allwork). *Educ:* King William's Coll., Isle of Man. Enlisted 1942; 2nd Lieut, The South Lancashire Regt (Prince of Wales's Volunteers), 1943; served with 13th Bn (Lancs) Parachute Regt, NW Europe, India, Far East, 1944–46, Greece and

Palestine, 1947; transf. to Glider Pilot Regt, 1948; Berlin Airlift, 1949, Korea, 1951–53; 1st Bn The South Lancs Regt (PWV) in Egypt and UK, 1953–54; instructor at Light Aircraft Sch., 1955–56; RAF Staff Coll., 1958; War Office, 1959–60; BAOR, 1961–63; Brigade Major 127 Bde, 1964; Comd 4th Bn The East Lancs Regt, 1965–66; Comd 1st Bn The Lancs Regt (PWV), Aden, 1966–67; Allied Forces N Europe, Oslo, 1968–69; instructor, Sch. of Infantry, 1970–71; Comd Berlin Inf. Bde. 1971–74; Comdt, Sch. of Infantry, 1974–76; GOC West Midland District, 1976–78; Lt-Governor and Sec., The Royal Hosp., Chelsea, 1979–84. Col, The Queen's Lancashire Regt, 1978–83; Col Comdt, The King's Division, 1979–83; Hon. Col, Liverpool Univ. OTC, 1980–89. Dir, Oxley Develts Co. Ltd, 1984–89. Chm., Museum of Army Flying, 1984–88; President: British Korean Veterans Assoc., 1986–; Assoc. of Service Newspapers, 1986–. *Recreations:* sailing, skiing, shooting. *Address:* The Mary Tudor Tower, Windsor Castle, Berks SL4 1NJ. *Club:* Army and Navy.

DOWNWARD, Sir William (Atkinson), Kt 1977; JP; Lord-Lieutenant of Greater Manchester, 1974–87; Councillor, Manchester City Council, 1946–75; Alderman, Manchester, 1971–74; *b* 5 Dec. 1912; *s* of late George Thomas Downward; *m* 1946, Enid, *d* of late Ald. Charles Wood. *Educ:* Manchester Central High Sch.; Manchester Coll. of Technology. Dir, Royal Exchange Theatre Co., 1976–89; Chairman: Manchester Overseas Students Welfare Conf., 1972–87; Peterloo Gall., 1974–76. Chm., Pat Seed Appeal Fund, 1977–; President: Manchester Opera Soc., 1977–; Gtr Manchester Fedn of Boys' Clubs, 1978–; Broughton House Home for Disabled Ex-Servicemen, 1978–. Mem. Court of Governors: Manchester Univ., 1969–; Salford Univ., 1974–87. Hon. LLD Manchester, 1977. Hon. RNCM 1982; FRSA 1978. Lord Mayor of Manchester, 1970–71; DL Lancs, 1971; JP Manchester, 1973. KStJ 1974. *Address:* 23 Kenmore Road, Northenden, Manchester M22 4AE. *T:* 061–998 4742; 061–834 0490.

DOWSETT, Prof. Charles James Frank, MA, PhD Cantab; FBA 1977; Calouste Gulbenkian Professor of Armenian Studies, University of Oxford, 1965–91, now Emeritus Professor, and Fellow of Pembroke College, Oxford, 1965–91, now Emeritus Fellow; *b* 2 Jan. 1924; *s* of late Charles Aspinall Dowsett and Louise (*née* Stokes); *m* 1949, Friedel (*d* 1984), *d* of Friedrich Lapuner, Kornberg, E Prussia. *Educ:* Owen's Sch.; St Catherine's Society, Oxford, 1942–43; Peterhouse, Cambridge (Thomas Parke Scholar), 1947–50 (Mod. and Mediaeval Languages Tripos, Part I, 1st Class Russian, 1st Class German, 1948, Part II, Comparative Philology, 1st Class with distinction, 1949). Treasury Studentship in Foreign Languages and Cultures, 1949–54. Ecole Nationale des Langues Orientales Vivantes, Univ. de Paris, 1950–52 (diplôme d'arménien); Ecole des Langues Orientales Anciennes, Institut Catholique de Paris, 1950–53 (diplôme de géorgien); Lecturer in Armenian, School of Oriental and African Studies, University of London, 1954; Reader in Armenian, 1965. Vis. Prof., Univ. of Chicago, 1976. Member: Council, RAS, 1972–76; Philological Soc., 1973–77; Marjory Wardrop Fund for Georgian Studies, 1966–. *Publications:* The History of the Caucasian Albanians by Movses Dasxuranci, 1961; The Penitential of David of Ganjak, 1961; (with J. Carswell) Kütahya Armenian Tiles, vol. 1, The Inscribed Tiles, 1972; (contrib.) Iran and Islam: Vladimir Minorsky Memorial Volume, 1971; (contrib.) Hayg Berberian Memorial Volume, 1986; articles in Bulletin of the School of Oriental and African Studies, Le Muséon, Revue des Etudes Arméniennes, Jl of Soc. for Armenian Studies,The Geographical Journal, W. B. Henning Memorial Volume, 1970, Raft, etc; translations from Flemish (Felix Timmermans' Driekoningentryptiek: "A Christmas Triptych", 1955, Ernest Claes' De Witte: "Whitey", 1970); as Charles Downing (children's books): Russian Tales and Legends, 1956; Tales of the Hodja, 1964; Armenian Folktales and Fables, 1972. *Address:* 21 Hurst Rise Road, Cumnor Hill, Oxford OX2 9HE.

DOWSON, Prof. Duncan, CBE 1989; FRS 1987; FEng; Professor of Engineering Fluid Mechanics and Tribology, since 1966, Head of Department of Mechanical Engineering, since 1987, and Dean for International Relations, since 1987, Leeds University; *b* 31 Aug. 1928; *o s* of Wilfrid and Hannah Dowson, Kirkbymoorside, York; *m* 1951, Mabel, *d* of Mary Jane and Herbert Strickland; one *s* (and one *s* decd). *Educ:* Lady Lumley's Grammar Sch., Pickering, Yorks; Leeds Univ. (BSc Mech Eng. 1950; PhD 1952; DSc 1971). FEng 1982; FIMechE; Fellow ASME 1973; Fellow ASLE 1983. Research Engineer, Sir W. G. Armstrong Whitworth Aircraft Co., 1953–54; Univ. of Leeds: Lecturer in Mechanical Engineering, 1954; Sen. Lecturer, 1963; Reader, 1965; Prof. 1966; Dir, Inst. of Tribology, Dept of Mech. Engrg, 1967–87; Pro-Vice-Chancellor, 1983–85. Chm., Tribology Group Cttee, IMechE, 1967–69. Foreign Mem., Royal Swedish Acad. of Engrg Sciences, 1986. James Clayton Fund Prize (jtly), IMechE, 1963; Thomas Hawksley Gold Medal, IMechE, 1966; Gold Medal, British Soc. of Rheology, 1969; Nat. Award, ASLE, 1974; ASME Lubrication Div. Best Paper Awards (jt), 1975, 1976; ASME Melville Medal (jt), 1976; James Clayton Prize, IMechE, 1978; ASME Mayo D. Hersey Award, 1979; Tribology Gold Medal, IMechE, 1979. Hon. DTech Chalmers Univ. of Technology, Göteborg, 1979. *Publications:* Elastohydrodynamic Lubrication—the fundamentals of roller and gear lubrication (jtly), 1966, 2nd edn 1977; History of Tribology, 1979; (jtly) An Introduction to the Biomechanics of Joints and Joint Replacement, 1981; (jtly) Ball Bearing Lubrication: The Elastohydrodynamics of Elliptical Contacts, 1981; papers on tribology and biomedical engrg, published by: Royal Society; Instn of Mech. Engineers; Amer. Soc. of Mech. Engineers; Amer. Soc. of Lubrication Engineers. *Recreations:* travel, photography. *Address:* 23 Church Lane, Adel, Leeds LS16 8DQ. *T:* Leeds (0532) 678933.

DOWSON, Graham Randall; Partner, Graham Dowson and Associates, since 1975; Chairman: Dowson Shurman (formerly Dowson-Salisbury) Associates Ltd, since 1987; Premier Speakers, since 1987; *b* 13 Jan. 1923; *o s* of late Cyril James Dowson and late Dorothy Celia (*née* Foster); *m* 1954, Fay Weston (marr. diss. 1974); two *d*; *m* 1975, Denise Shurman. *Educ:* Alleyn Court Sch.; City of London Sch.; Ecole Alpina, Switzerland. Served War of 1939–45 (1939–43 and Africa Stars, Atlantic and Defence Medals, etc); RAF, 1941–46 (Pilot, Sqdn-Ldr). Sales, US Steel Corporation (Columbia Steel), Los Angeles, 1946–49; Sales and Senior Commentator, Mid South Network (MBS), radio, US, 1949–52; Dir, Rank Organization Ltd, 1960–75, Chief Exec., 1974–75; Chairman: Erskine House Investments, 1975–83; Mooloya Investments, 1975–78; Pincus Vidler Arthur Fitzgerald Ltd, 1979–83; Marinex Petroleum, 1981–83; Nash Industries, 1988–90; Chm. and Chief Exec., Teltech Ltd, 1984–87; Deputy Chairman: Nimslo European Hldgs, 1978–87; Nimslo International Ltd, 1981–87; Nimslo Ltd, 1979– (Dir, 1978); Paravision (UK) Ltd, 1988–; Director: A. C. Nielsen Co., Oxford, 1953–58; Carron Co. (Holdings) Ltd, 1976–; Carron Investments Ltd, 1976–; RCO Holdings PLC (formerly Barrowmill Ltd), 1979–; Nimslo Corp., 1978–87; Filmbond plc, 1985–88; Fairhaven Internat. Ltd, 1988–; Grovewood Securities, 1990–. Chm., 1972–84, Pres., 1984–, European League for Econ. Co-operation (British Section). Vice-Pres., 1974–, Dep. Chm., 1974–, NPFA; Chm., Migraine Trust, 1985–88; Patron, Internat. Centre for Child Studies. Liveryman, Distillers' Co. FInstD 1957; CBIM 1969; FInstM 1971. *Recreation:* sailing. *Address:* 193 Cromwell Tower, Barbican, EC2Y 8DD. *T:* 071–588 0396. *Clubs:* Carlton, City Livery, Royal Air Force, Saints and Sinners, Thirty; Royal London Yacht (Ex-Commodore).

DOWSON, Sir Philip (Manning), Kt 1980; CBE 1969; MA; RA 1986 (ARA 1979); RIBA, FCSD; a Senior Partner, Ove Arup Partnership, since 1969; Founder Partner, Arup Associates; *b* 16 Aug. 1924; *m* 1950, Sarah Crewdson; one *s* two *d*. *Educ:* Gresham's Sch.; University Coll., Oxford; Clare Coll., Cambridge; Architectural Association. AA Dip. Lieut, RNVR, 1943–47. Member: Royal Fine Art Commn, 1971–; Craft Adv. Cttee, 1972–75. Governor, St Martin's Sch. of Art, 1975–82. Trustee: The Thomas Cubitt Trust, 1978–; Royal Botanic Gdns, Kew, 1983–; Royal Armouries, 1984–. Royal Gold Medal for Architecture, RIBA, 1981. *Recreation:* sailing. *Address:* 2–4 Dean Street, W1V 6QB. *T:* 071–734 8494; 1 Pembroke Studios, Pembroke Gardens, W8. *Club:* Garrick.

DOYLE, Bernard; *see* Doyle, F. B.

DOYLE, Brian André; Judge, Botswana Court of Appeal, 1973–79 and since 1988; *b* 10 May 1911; *s* of John Patrick Doyle, ICS and Louise Doyle (*née* Renard); *m* 1937, Nora (*née* Slattery); one *s* one *d*. *Educ:* Douai Sch.; Trinity Coll., Dublin. BA, LLB. British Univs and Hosps Boxing Champion, 1929, 1930, 1931 (Flyweight), 1932 (Bantamweight); Irish Free State Army Boxing Champion, 1930 (Flyweight). Called to Irish Bar, 1932; Magistrate, Trinidad and Tobago, 1937; Resident Magistrate, Uganda, 1942; Solicitor-Gen., Fiji, 1948; Attorney-Gen., Fiji, 1949; KC (Fiji), 1950, later QC; Attorney-Gen., N Rhodesia, 1956; Minister of Legal Affairs and Attorney-Gen., Northern Rhodesia (Zambia, 1964), 1959–65, retired as minister, 1965; Chm., Local Govt Service Commn, Zambia, 1964; Justice of Appeal, 1965; Chief Justice and Pres., Supreme Court of Zambia, 1969–75. Dir, Law Develt Commn, Zambia, 1976–79; Chm., Delimitation Commn, Botswana, 1981–82. *Recreations:* fishing, golf. *Address:* 26 Choumert Square, Peckham Rye, SE15 4RE. *Clubs:* Lusaka, Chainama Hills Golf; Dulwich and Sydenham Hill Golf.

DOYLE, (Frederick) Bernard; Director, Hamptons, since 1991; *b* 17 July 1940; *s* of James Hopkinson Doyle and Hilda Mary Doyle (*née* Spotsworth); *m* 1963, Ann Weston; two *s* one *d*. *Educ:* St Bede's Coll.; Univ. of Manchester (BSc Hons); Harvard Business Sch., 1965–67 (MBA). CEng, FICE, FIWEM (FIWES 1986); CBIM 1987. Resident Civil Engineer with British Rail, 1961–65; Management Consultant with Arthur D. Little Inc., 1967–72; Booker McConnell Ltd: Secretary to Executive Cttee, 1973; Director, Engineering Div., 1973–76; Chairman, General Engineering Div., 1976–78; Chm. and Chief Exec., Booker McConnell Engineering, and Director, Booker McConnell, 1978–81; Chief Executive: SDP, 1981–83; Welsh Water Authy, 1983–87; Dir, Public Sector Operations, MSL Int., 1988–90. FRSA. *Recreations:* sport, theatre, reading, walking, bird watching. *Address:* 15 Oldfield Place, Hotwells, Bristol BS8 4QJ. *T:* Bristol (0272) 227976.

DOYLE, Air Comdt Dame Jean (Lena Annette) C.; *see* Conan Doyle.

DOYLE, Dr Peter; Research and Technology Director, ICI Group, since 1989; *b* 6 Sept. 1938; *s* of late Peter and Joan Penman Doyle; *m* 1962, Anita McCulloch; one *s* one *d*. *Educ:* Univ. of Glasgow (BSc Hons 1st class 1960; PhD 1963). Research Chemist, ICI Pharmaceuticals, 1963; Manager, Quality Control Dept, 1973–75; Manager, Chemistry Dept, 1975–77; Research Dir, ICI Plant Protection, 1977–86; Business Dir, ICI Seeds, 1985–86; Dep. Chm. and Technical Dir, ICI Pharmaceuticals, 1986–88. Member: ACOST, 1969–; MRC, 1990–. Foreign Mem., Royal Swedish Acad. of Engineering Scis, 1990. Mem. Council, UCL, 1984. Liveryman, Salters' Co., 1983. *Publications:* contribs to Chemical Communications and Jl Chem. Soc. *Recreations:* squash, aspiring golfer. *Address:* ICI Group Headquarters, 9 Millbank, SW1P 3JF. *T:* 071–834 4444. *Club:* Royal Ascot Squash.

DOYLE, Sir Reginald (Derek Henry), Kt 1989; CBE 1980; HM Chief Inspector of Fire Services, since 1987; *b* 13 June 1929; *s* of John Henry and Elsie Doyle; *m* 1953, June Margretta (*née* Stringer); two *d*. *Educ:* Aston Commercial College. RN 1947–54. Fire Brigades, 1954–84; Chief Fire Officer: Worcester City and County, 1973; Hereford and Worcester County, 1974; Kent County, 1977; Home Office Fire Service Inspector, 1984–87. *Recreations:* shooting, swimming, badminton, horses. *Address:* Glebecroft, Marley Road, Harrietsham, Kent ME17 1BS. *T:* Maidstone (0622) 859259. *Club:* Rotary (Weald of Kent).

DOYLE, Prof. William, DPhil; FRHistS; Professor of History, University of Bristol, since 1986; *b* 4 March 1942; *s* of Stanley Joseph Doyle and Mary Alice Bielby; *m* 1968, Christine Thomas. *Educ:* Bridlington Sch.; Oriel Coll., Oxford (BA 1964; MA, DPhil 1968). FRHistS 1976. University of York: Asst Lectr, 1967; Lectr, 1969; Sen. Lectr, 1978; Prof. of Modern History, Univ. of Nottingham, 1981–85. Visiting Professor: Univ. of S Carolina, 1969–70; Univ. de Bordeaux III, 1976; Ecole des Hautes Etudes en Sciences Sociales, Paris, 1988. Dr *hc* Bordeaux, 1987. *Publications:* The Parlement of Bordeaux, 1974; The Old European Order 1660–1800, 1978; Origins of the French Revolution, 1980; The Ancien Régime, 1986; (ed jtly) The Blackwell Dictionary of Historians, 1988; The Oxford History of the French Revolution, 1989; contribs to Past and Present, Historical Jl, French Historical Studies, Studies on Voltaire. *Recreations:* books, decorating, travelling about. *Address:* School of History, University of Bristol, 13 Woodland Road, Bristol BS8 1TB. *T:* Bristol (0272) 303429. *Clubs:* Athenæum, United Oxford & Cambridge University.

DOYLE, William Patrick, PhD; CBIM; President, Texaco Middle East/Far East, since 1991; *b* 15 Feb. 1932; *s* of James W. Doyle and Lillian I. Doyle (*née* Kime); *m* 1957, Judith A. Gosha; two *s* one *d* (and one *s* decd). *Educ:* Seattle Univ. (BS 1955); Oregon State Univ. (PhD 1959). CBIM 1981 (FBIM 1980); MInstD 1982. Texaco, USA: Chemist, 1959; Res. Supervisor, 1966; Asst to Vice Pres. of Petrochemicals, 1968; Asst to Sen. Vice Pres. of Supply and Distribn, 1971; Asst Manager, Producing, 1972; Asst Regional Man., Marketing, 1974; Texaco Ltd: Dep. Man. Dir, 1977; Man. Dir, Exploration and Production, 1981; Vice President: Texaco Europe, 1987; Texaco Latin America and Africa, 1989. Pres., UK Offshore Operators Assoc., 1985 (Vice Pres., 1984). *Publications:* contrib. Jl of Amer. Chem. Soc. *Recreations:* tennis, music, theatre. *Address:* 2000 Westchester Avenue, White Plains, New York 10650, USA.

D'OYLY, Sir Nigel Hadley Miller, 14th Bt *cr* 1663, of Shottisham, Norfolk; *b* 6 July 1914; *s* of Sir Hastings Hadley D'Oyly, 11th Bt, and Evelyn Maude, *d* of George Taverner Miller; *S* half-brother, 1986; *m* 1940, Dolores (*d* 1971), *d* of R. H. Gregory; one *s* two *d*. *Educ:* Radley; RMA Sandhurst. Formerly Major, Royal Scots; served War of 1939–45, Hong Kong, France and War Office. *Heir: s* Hadley Gregory D'Oyly [*b* 29 May 1956; *m* 1978, Margaret Mary Dent (marr. diss. 1982); *m* 1991, Annette Frances Elizabeth, *yr d* of Maj. Michael White]. *Address:* Woodcote, Crowhurst, near Battle, East Sussex TN33 9AB.

DRABBLE, Jane; Assistant Managing Director, BBC Network Television, since 1991; *b* 15 Jan. 1947; *d* of Walter Drabble and Molly (*née* Boreham). *Educ:* Bristol Univ. (BA Hons 1968). BBC: Studio Manager, 1968–72; Producer, Radio Current Affairs, 1972–75; Asst Producer, then Producer, TV Current Affairs, 1975–87; Editor, Everyman, 1987–91. *Recreations:* music, theatre, walking, sailing. *Address:* BBC Television Centre, Wood Lane, W12 7RJ. *T:* 081–743 8000.

DRABBLE, Margaret, (Mrs Michael Holroyd), CBE 1980; author; *b* 5 June 1939; 2nd *d* of His Honour J.F. Drabble, QC and late Kathleen Marie Bloor; *m* 1st, 1960, Clive Walter Swift (marr. diss. 1975); two *s* one *d*; 2nd, 1982, Michael Holroyd, *qv*. *Educ:* The Mount Sch., York; Newnham Coll., Cambridge. Lives in London. Chm., Nat. Book League, 1980–82 (Dep. Chm., 1978–80). E. M. Forster Award, Amer. Acad. of Arts and Letters, 1973; Hon. Fellow, Sheffield City Polytechnic, 1989. Hon. DLitt: Sheffield, 1976; Manchester, 1987; Keele, 1988; Bradford, 1988. *Publications:* A Summer Birdcage, 1962; The Garrick Year, 1964; The Millstone, 1966 (filmed, as A Touch of Love, 1969); Wordsworth, 1966; Jerusalem the Golden, 1967; The Waterfall, 1969; The Needle's Eye, 1972; (ed with B. S. Johnson) London Consequences, 1972; Arnold Bennett, a biography, 1974; The Realms of Gold, 1975; (ed) The Genius of Thomas Hardy, 1976; (ed jtly) New Stories 1, 1976; The Ice Age, 1977; For Queen and Country, 1978; A Writer's Britain, 1979; The Middle Ground, 1980; (ed) The Oxford Companion to English Literature, 5th edn, 1985; The Radiant Way, 1987; (ed with Jenny Stringer) The Concise Oxford Companion to English Literature, 1987; A Natural Curiosity, 1989; Safe as Houses, 1989. *Recreations:* walking, dreaming. *Address:* c/o A. D. Peters, Fifth Floor, The Chambers, Chelsea Harbour, Lots Road, SW10 0XF.

DRACE-FRANCIS, Charles David Stephen, CMG 1987; HM Diplomatic Service; *b* 15 March 1943; *m* 1967, Griselda Hyacinthe Waldegrave; two *s* one *d*. *Educ:* Magdalen Coll., Oxford. Third Sec., FO, 1965; Tehran, 1967; Second, later First Sec., FCO, 1971; Asst Political Advr, Hong Kong, 1974; First Sec., Office of UK Rep. to EEC, Brussels, 1978; FCO, 1980; All Souls Coll., Oxford, 1983; Counsellor and Chargé d'affaires, Kabul, 1984; Counsellor, Lisbon, 1987. *Address:* c/o Foreign and Commonwealth Office, SW1A 2AH.

DRAIN, Geoffrey Ayrton, CBE 1981; JP; General Secretary, National and Local Government Officers Association, 1973–83; Visiting Professor, Imperial College of Science and Technology, 1983–88; *b* 26 Nov. 1918; *s* of late Charles Henry Herbert Drain, MBE, and Ann Ayrton; *m* 1950, Dredagh Joan Rafferty (marr. diss. 1959); one *s*. *Educ:* Preston Grammar Sch.; Bournemouth Sch.; Skipton Grammar Sch.; Queen Mary Coll., Univ. of London (BA, LLB; Fellow, QMC, 1980). Called to Bar, Inner Temple, 1955. Served War, 1940–46. Asst Sec., Inst. of Hosp. Administrators, 1946–52; Exec., Milton Antiseptic Ltd, 1952–58; Dep. Gen.-Sec., NALGO, 1958–73; Mem. Gen. Council, TUC, 1973–83; Pres., Nat. Fedn. of Professional Workers, 1973–75; Staff Side Sec., Health Service Admin. and Clerical Staffs Whitley Council, 1962–72; Comr, Crown Prosecution Service Staff Commn, 1985–87. Director: Bank of England, 1978–86; Collins-Wilde, 1985–88 (Dep. Chm.); Ferguson and Partners, 1986–88 (Dep. Chm.); Home Bridging PLC, 1986–89 (Chm.); Bracken Nominees Ltd, 1986–88 (Chm.); Commercial Bridging PLC (Chm.), 1987–89; Corporate Funding Finance Ltd, 1988–89. Member: NW Metropolitan Regional Hosp. Bd and N London Hosp. Management Cttee, 1967–74; Lord Chancellor's Adv. Cttee on Legal Aid, 1974–76; Layfield Cttee of Inquiry into Local Govt Finance, 1974–76; NEDO Sector Working Party for Paper and Board Ind., 1976–88 (Chm.); Insolvency Law Review Cttee, 1976–82; Council, Industrial Soc., 1974–83; Energy Commn, 1977–79; NEDC, 1977–83; Central Arbitration Cttee, 1977–89; Cttee on Finance for Industry, 1978–83; Engrg Council, 1981–83; Exec. Cttee, Public Services Internat., 1981–85; Employment Appeal Tribunal, 1982–89; Audit Commn, 1983–88; Appeals Panel, FIMBRA (formerly NASDIM), 1985–87. Dir, Co-operative Press Ltd, 1983–84. Member: Bd, Volunteer Centre, (Treas.) 1977–; British-North American Cttee, 1978–84; Franco British Council, 1978–88; Trilateral Commn, 1979–; Jt Hon. Treasurer, European Movement, 1979–83, Dep. Chm., 1983–90; Trustee: Community Develt Foundn, 1974–; Trident Trust, 1979–. Mem., Exec. Cttee, Age Endeavour, 1988–; Chm., Norman Hart Meml Fund, 1990–. Mem., Goldsmiths' Coll. Delegacy, 1985–88. Hampstead Borough Councillor, 1956–58; contested (Lab), Chippenham, 1950; JP N Westminster, 1966. Freeman of City of London and Liveryman of Coopers' Company. *Publication:* The Organization and Practice of Local Government, 1966. *Recreations:* cricket, football, walking, studying birds, bridge. *Address:* Flat 3, Centre Heights, Swiss Cottage, NW3 6JG. *T:* 071–722 2081. *Clubs:* Reform, MCC.

DRAKE, Sir (Arthur) Eric (Courtney), Kt 1970; CBE 1952; DL; *b* 29 Nov. 1910; *e s* of Dr A. W. Courtney Drake; *m* 1st, 1935, Rosemary Moore; two *d*; 2nd, 1950, Margaret Elizabeth Wilson; two *s*. *Educ:* Shrewsbury; Pembroke Coll., Cambridge (MA; Hon. Fellow 1976). With The British Petroleum Co. Ltd, 1935–75, Chm., 1969–75, Dep. Chm., P&O Steam Navigation Co., 1976–81. Pres., Chamber of Shipping, 1964; Hon. Mem., General Council of British Shipping, 1975–; Member: Gen. Cttee, Lloyd's Register of Shipping, 1960–81, 1985–87; MoT Shipping Adv. Panel, 1962–64; Cttee on Invisible Exports, 1969–75; Bd of Governors, Pangbourne Nautical Coll., 1958–69; Court of Governors, London Sch. of Economics and Political Science, 1963–74; Governing Body of Shrewsbury Sch., 1969–83; Cttee of Management, RNLI, 1975–85; Life Mem., Court of City Univ., 1969–; Pres., City and Guilds Insignia Award Assoc., 1971–75; Hon. Petroleum Adviser to British Army, 1971–. Hon. Mem., Honourable Co. of Master Mariners, 1972; Elder Brother of Trinity House, 1975–. Vice Pres., Mary Rose Trust, 1984– (Chm., 1979–83). Freeman of City of London, 1974; one of HM Lieutenants, City of London. DL Hants, 1983. Hon. DSc Cranfield, 1971; Hon. Fellow, UMIST, 1974. Hambro British Businessman of the Year award, 1971; Cadman Meml Medal, Inst. of Petroleum, 1976. Comdr, Ordre de la Couronne, Belgium, 1969; Kt Grand Cross of Order of Merit, Italy, 1970; Officier, Légion d'Honneur, 1972; Order of Homayoun, Iran, 1974; Comdr, Ordre de Leopold, Belgium, 1975. *Address:* The Old Rectory, Cheriton, Alresford, Hants. *T:* Bramdean (0962) 771334. *Clubs:* London Rowing; Royal Yacht Squadron, Leander, Royal Cruising.

DRAKE, Sir Eric; *see* Drake, Sir A. E. C.

DRAKE, Hon. Sir (Frederick) Maurice, Kt 1978; DFC 1944; **Hon. Mr Justice Drake;** a Judge of the High Court of Justice, Queen's Bench Division, since 1978; *b* 15 Feb. 1923; *o s* of late Walter Charles Drake and Elizabeth Drake; *m* 1954, (Alison) May, *d* of late W. D. Waterfall, CB; two *s* three *d*. *Educ:* St George's Sch., Harpenden; Exeter Coll., Oxford. MA Hons 1948. Served War of 1939–45, RAF 96 and 255 Squadrons. Called to Bar, Lincoln's Inn, 1950, QC 1968, Bencher, 1976. Dep. Chm., Beds QS, 1966–71; a Recorder of the Crown Court, 1972–78; Dep. Leader, Midland and Oxford Circuit, 1975–78, Presiding Judge, 1979–83. Standing Senior Counsel to RCP, 1972–78. Nominated Judge for appeals from Pensions Appeal Tribunal, 1985–. Vice-Chm., Parole Bd, England and Wales, 1985–86 (Mem., 1984–86). Chm. Governors, Aldwickbury Prep. Sch. (Trust), 1969–80; Governor, St George's Sch., Harpenden, 1975–79. Hon. Alderman, St Albans DC, 1976–. *Recreations:* music, gardening, sea-fishing, countryside. *Address:* The White House, West Common Way, Harpenden, Herts. *T:* Harpenden (0582) 712329; Royal Courts of Justice, Strand, WC2.

DRAKE, Jack Thomas Arthur H.; *see* Howard-Drake.

DRAKE, Brig. Dame Jean Elizabeth R.; *see* Rivett-Drake.

DRAKE, John Gair; Chief Registrar and Chief Accountant, Bank of England, 1983–90; *b* 11 July 1930; *s* of John Nutter Drake and Anne Drake; *m* 1957, Jean Pamela Bishop; one *s* one *d*. *Educ:* University College School; The Queen's College, Oxford. MA. Joined Bank of England, 1953; editor, Quarterly Bulletin, 1971; Asst Chief Cashier, 1973; Management Development Manager, 1974; Dep. Chief, Economic Intell. Dept, 1977; Dep. Chief Cashier and Dep. Chief, Banking Dept, 1980. Governor, South Bank Polytechnic, 1987–. *Address:* 114 Stanstead Road, Caterham, Surrey CR4 6AE. *Club:* Chaldon Cricket.

DRAKE, Hon. Sir Maurice; *see* Drake, Hon. Sir F. M.

DRAKE-BROCKMAN, Hon. Sir Thomas Charles, Kt 1979; DFC 1944; Senator (Country Party) for West Australia, 1958–78; *b* 15 May 1919; *s* of R. J. Drake-Brockman; *m* 1st, 1942, Edith Sykes (marr. diss.); one *s* four *d*; 2nd, 1972, Mary McGinnity. *Educ:* Guildford Grammar School. Farmer, 1938; RAAF 1941. Minister for Air, 1969–72; Minister for Administrative Services and Minister for Aboriginal Affairs, Nov.-Dec. 1975; Dep. Pres. of the Senate, 1965–69, 1976–78. Gen. Pres., Nat. Country Party (WA) Inc., 1978–81; Federal Pres., Nat. Country Party of Aust., 1978–81. Former Wool President and Exec. Mem., WA Farmers' Union; Vice-Pres., Aust. Wool and Meat Producers' Fedn, 1956–57. State Pres., Australia-Britain Soc., 1982–90. *Address:* 80 Basildon Road, Lesmurdie, WA 6076, Australia.

DRAPER, Alan Gregory; Director, Defence Procurement Management Group, Royal Military College of Science, 1988–91; *b* 11 June 1926; *e s* of late William Gregory Draper and Ada Gertrude (*née* Davies); *m* 1st, 1953, Muriel Sylvia Cuss, FRSA (marr. diss.); three *s*; 2nd, 1977, Jacqueline Gubel. *Educ:* Leeds Grammar Sch.; The Queen's Coll., Oxford (Scholar 1944; MA 1951). RNVR, 1945; Sub-Lt, 1946–47. Admiralty: Asst Principal, 1950; Private Sec. to Civil Lord of the Admiralty, 1953–55; MoD, 1957–60; Head of Polit. Sect., Admiralty 1960–64; First Sec., UK Delegn to NATO, 1964–66; Asst Sec., MoD, 1966; Counsellor, UK Delegn to NATO, 1974–77; Chm., NATO Budget Cttees, 1977–81; Royal Ordnance Factories: Personnel Dir, 1982–84; Dir Gen., Personnel, 1984; Dir, Management/Career Develt, Royal Ordnance plc, 1985; Sen. Lectr, Defence Procurement, RMCS, 1986–91. MIPM 1985. *Publications:* British Involvement in Major European Collaborative Defence Projects: 1957–1987, 1990; The Procurement Executive, Rayner to Lekene, 1991. *Recreations:* reading, travel, amateur dramatics, golf, enjoying my three grandchildren. *Address:* c/o Royal Military College of Science, Shrivenham, Swindon SN6 8LA.

DRAPER, Gerald Carter, OBE 1974; Chairman: G. Draper Consultancy, since 1988; Draper Associates Ltd, 1982–88; *b* 24 Nov. 1926; *s* of Alfred Henderson Draper and Mona Violanta (*née* Johnson); *m* 1951, Winifred Lilian Howe; one *s* three *d*. *Educ:* Univ. of Dublin, Trinity Coll. (MA). FInstM, FCIT. Joined Aer Lingus, 1947; Advertising and PR Manager, 1950; Commercial Man., Central Afr. Airways, 1959; British European Airways: Advertising Man., 1964; Asst Gen. Man. (Market Develt), 1966; Gen. Man. and Dir, Travel Sales Div., 1970; British Airways: Dir, Travel Div., 1973; Marketing Dir, 1977; Dir, Commercial Ops, 1978; Mem. Bd, 1978–82; Man. Dir, Intercontinental Services Div., 1982. Chairman: British Air Tours Ltd, 1978–82; Silver Wing Surface Arrangements Ltd, 1971–82; Deputy Chairman: Trust Houses Forte Travel Ltd, 1974–82; ALTA Ltd, 1977–82; Hoverspeed, 1984–87; Member Board: Internat. Aeradio Ltd, 1971–82; British Airways Associated Cos Ltd, 1972–82; British Intercontinental Hotels Ltd, 1976–82; Communications Strategy Ltd, 1984–86; AGB Travel Research Internat. Ltd, 1984–86; Centre for Airline and Travel Marketing Ltd, 1986–; BR (Southern Region), 1990–. Chm., Outdoor Advertising Assoc., 1985–. Master, Co. of Marketors, 1990; Mem., Guild of Freemen, 1991. FRSA 1979. Chevalier de l'Ordre du Tastevin, 1980; Chambellan de l'Ordre des Coteaux de Champagne, 1982. *Recreations:* shooting, golf. *Address:* Old Chestnut, Onslow Road, Burwood Park, Walton-on-Thames, Surrey KT12 5AY; 13B La Frenaie, Cogolin, Var, France. *Clubs:* Livery; Burhill Golf (Weybridge).

DRAPER, (John Haydn) Paul; Senior Planning Inspector, Department of Environment, 1977–86, retired; *b* 14 Dec. 1916; *o c* of late Haydn Draper, clarinet player, and Nan Draper; *m* 1941, Nancy Allum, author and journalist; one *s* one *d* (and one *d* decd). *Educ:* LCC primary sch.; Bancroft's Sch.; University Coll. London. Engr in Post Office, 1939–48; Royal Signals, Signalman to Major, Middle East, N Africa, Sicily, NW Europe (despatches), 1940–46; MoT, 1948–64 and 1968–70; Jt Principal Private Sec. to Minister, 1956–58; Asst Sec., 1959; Counsellor (Shipping), British Embassy, Washington, 1964–67; BoT, 1967–68; Under-Sec., 1968; DoE, 1970–74; Senior Planning Inspector, 1973–74; Resident Chm., Civil Service Selection Bd, 1975–76. *Address:* 24 Gordon Mansions, Huntley Street, WC1E 7HF.

DRAPER, Michael William; Under Secretary, Department of Health and Social Security, 1976–78; *b* 26 Sept. 1928; *s* of late John Godfrey Beresford Draper and Aileen Frances Agatha Draper (*née* Masefield); *m* 1952, Theodora Mary Frampton, *o d* of late Henry James Frampton; one *s* two *d*. *Educ:* St Edward's Sch., Oxford. FCA. Chartered Accountant, 1953; various posts in England, Ireland, Burma, Nigeria, Unilever Ltd, 1953–64; joined Civil Service, 1964; Principal, Min. of Power, 1964; Asst Sec., DHSS, 1972–76. Sec., Diocese of Bath and Wells, 1978–88; mem. of staff team, Lamplugh House, Christian Renewal Conf. Centre, 1988–89; working with Anglican Church in Zambia, 1991. *Recreations:* mountain walking, church affairs. *Address:* 21 Kent Park Avenue, Kendal, Cumbria LA9 5JT.

DRAPER, Paul; *see* Draper, J. H. P.

DRAPER, Peter Sydney; Group Personnel Director, Property Services Agency, Department of the Environment, since 1990; *b* 18 May 1935; *s* of late Sydney George Draper and Norah Draper; *m* 1959, Elizabeth Ann (*née* French); three *s*. *Educ:* Haberdashers' Aske's; Regent Polytechnic Sch. of Management (Dip. in Management Studies). AMBIM 1966. Joined GCHQ, Cheltenham, 1953; Min. of Transport, 1956–70; Principal, 1969; Department of the Environment, 1970–: Directorate of Estate Management Overseas, PSA, 1970; Asst Sec., 1975; Head of Staff Resources Div., 1975–78; Asst Dir, Home Regional Services, 1978–80; RCDS, 1981; Dir, Eastern Reg., 1982–84, Under Sec., Dir of Defence Services II, 1985–87, Principal Establishment Officer, 1987–90, PSA. *Recreations:* gardening, golf, walking. *Address:* c/o 2 Marsham Street, SW1. *Clubs:* Civil Service; Saffron Walden Golf.

DRAPER, Prof. Ronald Philip, PhD; Regius Chalmers Professor of English, University of Aberdeen, since 1986; *b* 3 Oct. 1928; *s* of Albert William and Elsie Draper; *m* 1950, Irene Margaret Aldridge; three *d*. *Educ:* Univ. of Nottingham (BA, PhD). Educn Officer, RAF, 1953–55. Lectr in English, Univ. of Adelaide, 1955–56; Lectr, Univ. of Leicester, 1957–68, Sen. Lectr, 1968–73; Prof., Univ. of Aberdeen, 1973–86. *Dramatic scripts:* (with P. A. W. Collins) The Canker and the Rose, Mermaid Theatre, 1964; (with Richard Hoggart) D. H. L., A Portrait of D. H. Lawrence, Nottingham Playhouse, 1967 (televised 1980). *Publications:* D. H. Lawrence, 1964, 3rd edn 1984; (ed) D. H. Lawrence, The Critical Heritage, 1970, 3rd edn 1986; (ed) Hardy, The Tragic Novels, 1975, 6th edn 1985; (ed) George Eliot, The Mill on the Floss and Silas Marner, 1977, 3rd edn 1984; (ed) Tragedy, Developments in Criticism, 1980; Lyric Tragedy, 1985; The Winter's Tale, Text and Performance, 1985; (ed) Hardy, Three Pastoral Novels, 1987; (ed) The

Literature of Region and Nation, 1989; (with Martin Ray) An Annotated Critical Bibliography of Thomas Hardy, 1989; (ed) The Epic: developments in criticism, 1990; articles and reviews in Critical Qly, Essays in Criticism, Etudes Anglaises, English Studies, Jl of D. H. Lawrence Soc., MLR, New Lit. Hist., Notes and Queries, Revue des Langues Vivantes, Rev. of English Studies, Shakespeare Qly, Studies in Short Fiction, THES, Thomas Hardy Annual, Thomas Hardy Jl. *Recreations:* reading, listening to music. *Address:* 50 Queen's Road, Aberdeen AB1 6YE. *T:* Aberdeen (0224) 318735.

DRAYCOTT, Douglas Patrick, MA Oxon; QC 1965; a Recorder, since 1972 (Recorder of Shrewsbury, 1966–71); *b* 23 Aug. 1918; *s* of George Draycott and Mary Ann Draycott (*née* Burke); *m* Elizabeth Victoria Hall (marr. diss. 1974); two *s* three *d; m* 1979, Margaret Jean Brunton (*née* Speed). *Educ:* Wolstanton Grammar Sch.; Oriel Coll., Oxford (MA). War Service: Royal Tank Regiment and General Staff, 1939–46. Barrister, Middle Temple, 1950, Master of the Bench, 1972. Joined Oxford Circuit, 1950; Leader, Midland and Oxford Circuit, 1979–83. *Recreation:* cruising on inland waterways. *Address:* 4 King's Bench Walk, Temple, EC4Y 7DL. *T:* 071–353 3581; 11 Sir Harry's Road, Edgbaston, Birmingham B15 2UY. *T:* 021–440 1050; 5 Fountain Court, Steelhouse Lane, Birmingham, B4 6DR. *T:* 021–236 5771.

DRAYCOTT, Gerald Arthur; a Recorder of the Crown Court, 1972–86; *b* 25 Oct. 1911; *s* of Arthur Henry Seely Draycott and Maud Mary Draycott; *m* 1939, Phyllis Moyra Evans; two *s* one *d. Educ:* King Edward's Sch., Stratford-on-Avon. FCII. Called to Bar, Middle Temple, 1938. Served in RAF, 1939–46 (Sqdn Ldr; despatches). Practised at Bar, SE Circuit, 1946–; Dep. Recorder, Bury St Edmunds and Great Yarmouth, 1966–72. Chairman: Eastern Rent Assessment Panel, 1965–77; Nat. Insurance Tribunal, Norwich, 1970–84; E Anglia Med. Appeal Tribunal, 1978–84. *Address:* Nethergate House, Saxlingham Nethergate, Norwich NR15 1PB. *T:* Hempnall (050842) 8306; Octagon House, Colegate, Norwich; 5 King's Bench Walk, Temple, EC4Y 7DN. *Club:* Norfolk County (Norwich).

DRAYSON, Robert Quested, DSC 1943; MA; *b* 5 June 1919; *s* of late Frederick Louis Drayson and late Elsie Mabel Drayson; *m* 1943, Rachel, 2nd *d* of Stephen Spencer Jenkyns; one *s* two *d. Educ:* St Lawrence Coll., Ramsgate; Downing Coll., Cambridge. Univ. of Cambridge: 1938–39, 1946–47; History Tripos, BA 1947, MA 1950. Served RNVR, 1939–46; Lieut in command HM Motor Torpedo Boats. Asst Master and Housemaster, St Lawrence Coll., 1947–50; Asst Master, Felsted Sch., 1950–55; Headmaster, Reed's Sch., Cobham, 1955–63; Headmaster of Stowe, 1964–79; Resident Lay Chaplain to Bishop of Norwich, 1979–84; Lay Reader, 1979. Member: HMC Cttee, 1973–75 (Chm., Midland Div., 1974–75); Council, McAlpine Educnl Endowments Ltd, 1979–; Allied Schools Council, 1980–; Gen. Council, S Amer. Missionary Soc. (and Chm. Selection Cttee), 1980–; Scholarship Cttee, Indep. Schs Travel Assoc., 1982–; Martyrs' Meml and C of E Trust, 1983–. Chm. of Govs, Riddlesworth Hall, 1980–84; Governor: Parkside, 1958–63; Beachborough, 1965–79; Bilton Grange, 1966–79; Beechwood Park, 1967–79; Monkton Combe, 1976–85; Felixstowe Coll., 1981–84; St Lawrence Coll., 1977–. FRSA 1968. *Recreations:* formerly hockey (Cambridge Blue, 1946, 1947; Kent XI (Captain), 1947–56; England Final Trial, 1950); now golf, walking, watching cricket. *Address:* Three Gables, Linkhill, Sandhurst, Cranbrook, Kent TN18 5PQ. *T:* Sandhurst (0580) 850447. *Club:* Hawks (Cambridge).

DRESCHFIELD, Ralph Leonard Emmanuel, CMG 1957; *b* 18 March 1911; *s* of late Henry Theodore and Jessie Mindelle Dreschfield; unmarried. *Educ:* Merchiston Castle Sch.; Trinity Hall, Cambridge (BA). Called to Bar, 1933; entered Colonial Service, 1938, and apptd resident Magistrate, Uganda; served in War of 1939–45, in 4th King's African Rifles; Crown Counsel, Uganda, 1948; Solicitor-Gen., Uganda, 1949; QC 1950; Attorney-Gen., Uganda, 1951–62. Chm. Trustees of Uganda National Parks, 1952–62. Sec., Community Council of Essex, 1963–76. Parly Counsel, Law Reform, Bermuda, 1976–79. Sec., Essex Playing Fields Assoc., 1982–90. *Recreation:* yachting. *Address:* 5 Fairhaven Court, West Mersea, Colchester, Essex. *Clubs:* Royal Ocean Racing, Bar Yacht, Little Ship; West Mersea Yacht.

DREVER, James; Principal and Vice-Chancellor, University of Dundee, 1967–78; *b* 29 Jan. 1910; *s* of late Prof. James Drever; *m* 1936, Joan Isabel Mackay Budge; one *s* one *d. Educ:* Royal High Sch., Edinburgh; Universities of Edinburgh (MA Hons Philosophy, 1932) and Cambridge (MA Moral Science Tripos, 1934). LLD Dundee, 1979. FRSE. Asst, Dept of Philosophy, Edinburgh, 1934–38; Lecturer in Philosophy and Psychology, King's Coll., Newcastle, 1938–41; Royal Navy, 1941–45; Prof. of Psychology, Univ. of Edinburgh, 1944–66. Visiting Professor, Princeton Univ., 1954–55. Editor, British Journal of Psychology, 1954–58; President: British Psychological Soc., 1960–61; Internat. Union of Scientific Psychology, 1963–66. Member: Cttee on Higher Education, 1961–63; SSRC, 1965–69; Adv. Council, Civil Service Coll., 1973–; Oil Develt Council for Scotland, 1973–77; Perm. Cttee of Conf. of European Rectors, 1975–78; Chm., Advisory Council on Social Work, in Scotland, 1970–74. Dir, Grampian Television Ltd, 1973–80. *Publications:* papers and reviews. *Address:* East Ardblair, 494 Perth Road, Dundee DD2 1LR.

DREW, Sir Arthur (Charles Walter), KCB 1964 (CB 1958); Chairman, Museum of Empire and Commonwealth, since 1985; *b* 2 Sept. 1912; *er s* of late Arthur Drew, Mexico City, and Louise Schulte-Ummingen; *m* 1943, Rachel, *er d* of late G. W. Lambert, CB; one *s* three *d. Educ:* Christ's Hospital; King's Coll., Cambridge. Asst Principal, War Office, 1936; Private Sec. to successive Secs of State for War, 1944–49; IDC, 1949; International Staff, NATO, 1951–53; Dep. Under Sec. of State, Home Office, 1961–63; last Permanent Under Sec. of State, War Office, 1963–64; Permanent Under-Sec. of State (Army), MoD, 1964–68; Perm. Under-Sec. of State (Administration), MoD, and Mem., Admiralty, Army (from 1964) and Air Force Boards, 1968–72. Administrator, J. Paul Getty Jr Charitable Trust, 1986–88. Chairman: Beacon Hostels Housing Assoc., 1974–88; Voluntary Welfare Work Council, 1979–89. Chairman: Museums and Galls Commn (formerly Standing Commn on Museums and Galls, 1978–84 (Mem., 1973–84); Ancient Monuments Bd for England, 1978–84; Pres., Museums Assoc., 1984–86, Hon. FMA, 1986; Trustee: British Museum (Natural History), 1972–83; British Museum, 1973–86; Imperial War Museum, 1973–84; Nat. Army Museum, 1975–; RAF Museum, 1976–; Member: Council, Nat. Trust, 1974–84; Historic Houses Assoc., 1981–84; Science Mus. Adv. Council, 1981–84; Council, Zool Soc., 1982–87; Historic Buildings Council, 1982–84; Historic Buildings and Monuments Commn, 1984–86. Chm. of Govs, QMC, Univ. of London, 1982–89; Fellow, QMW, 1990. Master, Drapers' Co., 1977–78. JP 1963, 1973–83, Richmond. Coronation Medal, 1953. *Recreation:* following Baedeker. *Address:* 2 Branstone Road, Kew, Surrey TW9 3LB. *T:* 081–940 1210. *Club:* Reform.

DREW, Prof. George Charles, MA; London University Professor of Psychology, University College, 1958–79, now Professor Emeritus; Honorary Fellow, 1979; *b* 10 Dec. 1911; *e s* of George Frederick Drew; *m* 1936, Inez Annie, *d* of F. Hulbert Lewis; one *s* one *d. Educ:* St George's Sch., Bristol; Bristol, Cambridge and Harvard Univs. Viscount Haldane of Cloan studentship, Cambridge, 1935–36; Rockefeller Fellowship, Harvard Univ., 1936–38; Rockefeller Research Fellowship, Cambridge, 1938–42; Psychological Adviser, Air Ministry, 1942–46; Lecturer in Psychology, University of Bristol, 1946–49, Reader, 1949–51, Prof. of Psychology, 1951–58. Mem. Science Research Council, 1965–67. Vis. Prof., University of Calif, Berkeley, USA, 1967–68. C. S. Myers Lectr, 1973. Founder Mem., Exper. Psych. Soc., 1946 (Pres. 1950–51, 1959–60); Pres., British Psych. Soc., 1962–63; Pres. and Chm., Org. Cttee, 19th Internat. Congress of Psychology, 1969. Dean of Science, UCL, 1973–76. *Publications:* articles on animal behaviour, learning, vision, and other psychological problems, in various British and American journals.

DREW, Jane Beverly, FRIBA; architect; Partner in firm of Fry Drew and Partners, since 1946; *b* 24 March 1911; *m* 1st; two *d*; 2nd, 1942, Edwin Maxwell Fry, CBE, RA (*d* 1987). *Educ:* Croydon. Was in partnership with J. T. Alliston, 1934–39; independent practice, 1939–45; in partnership with Maxwell Fry, 1945–. Asst Town Planning Adviser to Resident Minister, West African Colonies, 1944–45; Senior Architect to Capital project of Chandigarh, Punjab, India, 1951–54; Beamis Prof. Mass Inst. of Techn., Jan.-June, 1961; Vis. Prof. of Architecture, Harvard, Feb-March 1970; Bicentennial Prof., Utah Univ., 1976. Completed work includes housing, hospitals, schools, and colleges in UK, West Africa, including Univs in Nigeria, Middle East and India; a section of Festival of Britain, 1951; town planning, housing and amenity buildings in Iran, W Africa and India. Past Pres., Architectural Association (1969). Hon. FAIA 1978; Hon. FNIA 1985. Hon LLD Ibadan, 1966; DUniv Open Univ., 1973; Hon. DLitt Newcastle, 1987. *Publications:* (with Maxwell Fry) Architecture for Children, 1944; (with Maxwell Fry and Harry Ford) Village Housing in the Tropics, 1945; (Founder Editor, 1945–) Architects' Year Book; (with Maxwell Fry) Architecture in the Humid Tropics; Tropical Architecture, 1956; (with Maxwell Fry) Architecture and the Environment, 1976. *Recreations:* reading, writing, friends. *Address:* West Lodge, Cotherstone, Barnard Castle, Co. Durham DH12 9PF. *T:* Teesdale (0833) 50217. *Club:* Institute of Contemporary Arts.

DREW, Joanna Marie, CBE 1985; Director, Hayward and Regional Exhibitions, South Bank Centre, since 1987; *b* Naini Tal, India, 28 Sept. 1929; *d* of Brig. Francis Greville Drew, CBE, and Sannie Frances Sands. *Educ:* Dartington Hall; Edinburgh Univ. (MA Hons Fine Art); Edinburgh Coll. of Art (DA). Arts Council of GB, 1952–88: Asst Dir of Exhibns, 1970; Dir of Exhibns, 1975; Dir of Art, 1978–86. Mem. Council, RCA, 1979–82. Officier, l'Ordre des Arts et Lettres, 1988 (Chevalier, 1979). *Address:* South Bank Centre, Royal Festival Hall, SE1 8XX.

DREW, John Alexander, CB 1957; *b* 19 July 1907; *s* of Charles Edward Drew, Okehampton, Devon, and Ethel Margaret Drew; *m* 1930, Edith Waud Marriott; two *s* (and one *s* decd). *Educ:* Gram. Sch., Okehampton. Entered CS, 1928; Secretaries' Office, HM Customs and Excise, 1935–40; employed on special duties, 1940–45; Asst Sec., Cabinet Office, 1945–48; Bd of Trade, 1948–50; Asst Under-Sec. of State, Ministry of Defence, 1951–67, retired, 1967. US Medal of Freedom with Bronze Palm, 1946. *Address:* 28 Montague Avenue, Sanderstead, Surrey. *T:* 081–657 3264.

DREW, John Sydney Neville; Head of United Kingdom Offices, Commission of the European Communities, since 1987; *b* 7 Oct. 1936; *s* of late John William Henry Drew and of Kathleen Marjorie (*née* Wright); *m* 1962, Rebecca Margaret Amanda (*née* Usher); two *s* one *d. Educ:* King Edward's Sch., Birmingham; St John's Coll., Oxford (MA); Fletcher School of Law and Diplomacy, Tufts Univ. (AM). Sloan Fellow of London Business Sch., 1971. Lieut, Somerset LI, 1955–57. HM Diplomatic Service, 1960–73; Dir of Marketing and Exec. Programmes, London Business Sch., 1973–79; Dir of Corporate Affairs, Rank Xerox, 1979–84; Dir of European Affairs, Touche Ross Internat., 1984–86. Associate Fellow, Templeton Coll., Oxford, 1982–86; Vis. Prof. of European Management, Imperial Coll. of Science and Technology, 1987–. Hon. Editor, European Business Jl, 1987–. *Publications:* Doing Business in the European Community, 1979, 3rd edn 1991 (trans. Spanish and Portuguese 1987); Networking in Organisations, 1986; articles on European integration and management development. *Recreations:* travel, reading, golf, family life. *Address:* (home) 49 The Ridgeway, NW11 8PQ; (office) Jean Monnet House, 8 Storey's Gate, SW1P 3AT. *T:* 071–222 8122. *Club:* United Oxford & Cambridge University.

DREW, Peter Robert Lionel, OBE 1979; Chairman, Taylor Woodrow Group of Companies, since 1990; *b* 4 Sept. 1927; *s* of Edith Mary Drew (*née* Ball) and Sydney Herbert Drew; *m* 1st, 1952, June Durham; one *s* one *d*; 2nd, 1963, Monica Margaret Mary Allman; one *d. Educ:* Kingston College (Dip. Eng., later Architecture). Helicopter research, Don Juan de la Cierva enterprise, 1949; archit. studies and practice, London, 1951; started housing co., Lytham St Anne's, for Sir Lindsay Parkinson & Co., 1954; Willetts and Bernard Sunley Investment Trust, 1962–65; Taylor Woodrow Property Co., 1965, Dir, 1979–; founded St Katharine by the Tower Ltd (pioneer, London Docks redevelt), 1970; founded World Trade Centre, London, 1973. Chm. and Vice-Pres., internat. WTCA movement. Founding Master, Guild of World Traders in London, 1982. CBIM 1990. FRSA. Gov., Sadler's Wells. Church Warden, All Hallows by the Tower. Liveryman, Painter-Stainers' Co.; Freeman, Co. of Watermen and Lightermen. *Publications:* Buy Your Own Home!, 1957; papers on world trade and urban renewal. *Recreations:* water colour painting, sailing, falling off horses. *Address:* Dockmasters House, St Katharine by the Tower, E1 9LB. *T:* 071–481 1392. *Clubs:* Savile, City Livery; Guild of World Traders' Yacht.

DREWITT, (Lionel) Frank; Managing Director, Harrods Ltd, since 1984; *b* 24 Sept. 1932; *s* of William and Jeanne Drewitt; *m* 1959, Doris Else Heybrok; three *d. Educ:* London Univ. (Bsc Econ). FCA. National Service, 1951–53. Wells & Partners, later Thornton Baker, 1956–64; Chartered Accountant, 1961; joined Harrods Store group, 1964; positions incl. Asst Internal Auditor, Chief Accountant, Company Sec., Asst Man. Dir. *Recreation:* cottages. *Address:* 23 Hertford Avenue, East Sheen, SW14. *T:* 081–876 9348.

DREWRY, Dr David John; Director, British Antarctic Survey, since 1987; *b* 22 Sept. 1947; *s* of late Norman Tidman Drewry and of Mary Edwina Drewry (*née* Wray); *m* 1971, Gillian Elizabeth (*née* Holbrook). *Educ:* Havelock School, Grimsby; Queen Mary Coll., Univ. of London (BSc 1st cl. hons 1969); Emmanuel College, Cambridge (PhD 1973). FRGS 1972. Queen Mary Coll. E Greenland Expdn, 1968; UK-US Antarctic Expdns, 1969–70 and 1971–72; Cambridge E Greenland Expdn, 1972; Sir Henry Strakosh Fellow, 1974; UK-US Antarctic Expdns, 1974–75, 1977–78 (leader), 1978–79 (leader); Sen. Res. Asst, Univ. of Cambridge, 1978–83; leader, UK-Norwegian Svalbard Expdns, 1980, 1983, 1985, 1986; Asst Dir of Research, Univ. of Cambridge, 1983; Dir, Scott Polar Res. Inst., Univ. of Cambridge, 1984–87. Member: Transantarctic Assoc., 1982–; RGS Council, 1986–; Council, Internat. Glaciological Soc., 1980–82, 1989–; ESA Experts Team, 1981–87; European Cttee on Ocean and Polar Science, 1989–; Royal Soc. Interdisciplinary Science Cttee on Antarctic Res., 1990–; Royal Soc. Envmtl Res. Cttee, 1990–; Chm., Council of Managers, Nat. Antarctic Programmes, 1988–; Vice-Pres., Comité Arctique International, 1989–. Hon. Sec., Arctic Club, 1976–83; UK alternate deleg., Sci. Cttee on Antarctic Res., 1985–. US Antarctic Service Medal, 1979; Cuthbert Peek Award, RGS, 1979; Polar Medal, 1986. *Publications:* Antarctica: glaciological and geophysical folio, 1983; Glacial Geologic Processes, 1986; papers on polar glaciology, geophysics, remote sensing in learned jls. *Recreations:* music, book collecting, walking. *Address:* British Antarctic Survey, High Cross, Madingley Road, Cambridge CB3 0ET. *Clubs:* Geographical, Antarctic, Arctic.

DREYER, Adm. Sir Desmond (Parry), GCB 1967 (KCB 1963; CB 1960); CBE 1957; DSC; JP; DL; *b* 6 April 1910; *yr s* of late Adm. Sir Frederic Dreyer, GBE, KCB; *m* 1st, 1934, Elisabeth (*d* 1958), *d* of late Sir Henry Chilton, GCMG; one *s* one *d* (and one *s* decd); 2nd, 1959, Marjorie Gordon, *widow* of Hon. R. G. Whiteley. Served War of 1939–45 (DSC). Cdre First Class, 1955. Chief of Staff, Mediterranean, 1955–57; Asst Chief of Naval Staff, 1958–59; Flag Officer (Flotillas) Mediterranean, 1960–61; Flag Officer Air (Home), 1961–62; Comdr, Far East Fleet, 1962–65; Second Sea Lord, 1965–67; Chief Adviser (Personnel and Logistics) to Sec. of State for Defence, 1967–68. Principal Naval ADC to the Queen, 1965–68. Gentleman Usher to the Sword of State, 1973–80. Member: Nat. Bd for Prices and Incomes, 1968–71; Armed Forces Pay Review Body, 1971–79. President: RN Benevolent Trust, 1970–78; Officers' Pension Soc., 1978–84; Regular Forces Employment Assoc., 1978–82; Not Forgotten Assoc., 1973–91. JP 1968, High Sheriff, 1977–78, DL 1985, Hants. *Recreations:* fishing, golf. *Address:* Brook Cottage, Cheriton, near Alresford, Hants SO24 0QA. *T:* Bramdean (0962) 771215. *Club:* Army and Navy.

DREYFUS, John Gustave, FIOP; typographical consultant and historian; *b* 15 April 1918; *s* of late Edmond and Marguerite Dreyfus; *m* 1948, Irène Thurnauer; two *d* (one *s* decd). *Educ:* Oundle Sch.; Trinity Coll., Cambridge (MA). FIOP 1977. Served War, Army, 1939–45. Joined Cambridge University Press as graduate trainee, 1939; Asst Univ. Printer, 1949–56; Typographical Adviser, 1956–82; Typographical Adviser to Monotype Corp., 1955–82; European Consultant to Limited Editions Club, USA, 1956–77; Dir, Curwen Press, 1970–82; Sandars Reader in Bibliography, Univ. of Cambridge, 1979–80. Helped plan exhibn, Printing and the Mind of Man, 1963 (also designed catalogues). President: Assoc. Typographique Internationale, 1968–73 (organised internat. congresses for Assoc.); Printing Historical Soc., 1991 (org. Caxton Internat. Congress, 1976). FRSA. Sir Thomas More Award, Univ. of San Francisco, 1979; Laureate, Amer. Printing Historical Soc., 1984; Frederic W. Goudy Award, Rochester Inst. of Technology, NY, 1984. *Publications:* The Survival of Baskerville's Punches, 1949; The Work of Jan van Krimpen, 1952; (ed series) Type Specimen Facsimiles, 1963–71; Italic Quartet, 1966; (ed with François Richaudeau) La Chose Imprimée (French encyc. on printing), 1977; A History of the Nonesuch Press, 1981; French Eighteenth Century Typography, 1982; A Typographical Masterpiece, 1990; contrib. The Library. *Recreations:* travel, theatre-going. *Address:* 38 Lennox Gardens, SW1X 0DH. *T:* 071–584 3510. *Club:* Garrick.

DREYFUS, Pierre; Grand Officier, Légion d'Honneur; Conseiller à la Présidence de la République, since 1982; *b* Paris, 18 Nov. 1907; *s* of Emmanuel Dreyfus, Banker, and Madeleine (*née* Bernard); *m* 1936, Laure Ullmo; one *d*. *Educ:* Lycée Janson-de-Sailly; Faculty of Law, Univ. of Paris (Dip., Dr of Law). Inspector-Gen. of Industry and Commerce, Chief of Gen. Inspectorate, and Dir of Cabinet to Minister of Industry and Commerce, M Robert Lacoste, 1947–49; Pres., Commn of Energy of the Plan, and Dir of the Cabinet to Minister of Industry and Commerce, M Bourgès-Maunoury, 1954. President: Houillères de Lorraine, 1950–55; Charbonnages de France, 1954; Société des Aciers Fins de l'Est, 1955. President Director-General, Régie Nationale des Usines Renault, 1955–75; Pres., Renault-Finance, 1976–80; Minister for Industry, 1981–82. *Address:* 12 rue Duroc, 75007 Paris, France.

DRIELSMA, Claude Dunbar H.; *see* Hankes Drielsma.

DRING, Richard Paddison; Editor of Official Report (Hansard), House of Commons, 1972–78; *b* 6 Nov. 1913; *s* of late Fred Dring and late Florence Hasleham Dring, East Sheen; *m* 1939, Joan Wilson, St Albans; one *s*. *Educ:* St Paul's School. Commd in British Army during the War, serving in Europe and later in India with IA. Herts Advertiser, 1932; Press Association, 1936; Official Report (Hansard), House of Commons, 1940: Asst Editor, 1954; Dep. Editor, 1970. *Recreation:* golf. *Address:* 24 Vicarage Drive, SW14 8RX. *T:* 081–876 2162. *Club:* Richmond Golf.

DRINKALL, John Kenneth, CMG 1973; HM Diplomatic Service, retired; High Commissioner to Jamaica, and Ambassador (non-resident) to Haiti, 1976–81; *b* 1 Jan. 1922; *m* 1961, Patricia Ellis; two *s* two *d*. *Educ:* Haileybury Coll.; Brasenose Coll., Oxford. Indian Army, 1942–45. Entered HM Foreign Service, 1947; 3rd Sec., Nanking, 1948; Vice-Consul, Tamsui, Formosa, 1949–51; Acting Consul, 1951; Foreign Office, 1951–53; 1st Sec., Cairo, 1953–56; Foreign Office, 1957–60; 1st Sec., Brasilia, 1960–62; Foreign Office, 1962–65. Appointed Counsellor, 1964; Counsellor: Nicosia, Cyprus, 1965–67; British Embassy, Brussels, 1967–70; FCO, 1970–71; Canadian Nat. Defence Coll., 1971–72; Ambassador to Afghanistan, 1972–76. *Recreations:* lawn tennis, golf, racquets and squash. *Address:* Bolham House, Tiverton, Devon EX16 7RA. *Clubs:* Royal Automobile, All England Lawn Tennis.

DRINKROW, John; *see under* Hardwick, Michael.

DRINKWATER, Sir John (Muir), Kt 1988; QC 1972; a Recorder of the Crown Court, since 1972; a Commissioner of Income Tax, since 1983; *b* 16 March 1925; *s* of late Comdr John Drinkwater, OBE, RN (retd); *m* Jennifer Marion (*d* 1990), *d* of Edward Fitzwalter Wright, Morley Manor, Derbs; one *s* four *d*. *Educ:* RNC Dartmouth. HM Submarines, 1943–47; Flag Lieut to C-in-C Portsmouth and First Sea Lord, 1947–50; Lt-Comdr 1952; invalided 1953. Called to Bar, Inner Temple, 1957, Bencher, 1979. Mem., Parly Boundary Commn for England, 1977–80. Mem. Bd, British Airports Authy, 1985–87, Dir, BAA plc, 1987–. Life Mem. Council, SPAB, 1982. Governor, St Mary's Hosp., 1960–64. *Recreations:* swimming, reading, travel. *Address:* Meysey Hampton Manor, Cirencester, Glos GL7 5JS. *T:* Cirencester (0285) 851366; 27 Kilmaine Road, SW6. *T:* 071–381 1279; Lohitzun, 64120 St Palais, France. *Clubs:* Garrick, Pratt's.

DRISCOLL, James; Chairman, Lifecare NHS Trust, since 1990; Policy Adviser, Nationalised Industries' Chairmen's Group, since 1990 (Director, 1976–90); Chairman and Managing Director, since 1980, Senior Partner, since 1990, Woodcote Consultants Ltd; *b* 24 April 1925; *s* of Henry James Driscoll and Honorah Driscoll; *m* 1955, Jeanne Lawrence Williams, BA, CertEd; one *s* one *d*. *Educ:* Coleg Sant Illtyd, Cardiff; University Coll., Cardiff. BA (1st Cl. Hons). Chm., Welsh Young Conservatives, 1948–49; Nat. Dep. Chm., Young Conservatives, 1950; Dep. Chm., Univ. Cons. Fedn, 1949–50; Dep. Chm., NUS, 1951–53. Vice-Chm., European Youth Campaign, 1951–53. Contested (C) Rhondda West, 1950. Asst Lectr, UC Cardiff, 1950–53; Council of Europe Res. Fellowship, 1953. Joined British Iron and Steel Fedn, 1953; various econ. and internat. posts; Econ. Dir and Dep. Dir-Gen., 1963–67; various posts, British Steel Corporation, 1967–80; Man. Dir, Corporate Strategy, 1971–76, Adviser, 1976–80. Member: Grand Council, FBI, 1957–65; CBI Council, 1970–; Observer, NEDC, 1977–. Chm., Econ. Studies Cttee, Internat. Iron and Steel Inst., 1972–74. Mem., Court of Governors, Univ. of Wales Coll. of Cardiff (formerly UC, Cardiff), 1970– (Fellow, 1986). FREconS; FRSA. *Publications:* various articles and pamphlets on econ. and internat. affairs, esp. steel affairs, European integration, wages policy and financing of world steel investment. *Recreations:* travel, reading. *Address:* Foxley Hatch, Birch Lane, Purley, Surrey CR2 3LH. *T:* 081–668 4081.

DRISCOLL, Dr James Philip, CEng; Partner, Coopers & Lybrand Deloitte, since 1990; *b* 29 March 1943; *s* of Reginald Driscoll and Janetta Bridget Driscoll; *m* 1969, Josephine Klapper, BA; two *s* two *d*. *Educ:* St Illtyd's Coll., Cardiff; Birmingham Univ. (BSc 1964; PhD 1972); Manchester Business Sch. MIChemE 1975; MIGasE 1975; MInstF 1975. Taught at St Illtyd's Coll., Cardiff, 1964; res. posts with Joseph Lucas, Solihull, 1968–69; British Steel Corporation: res. posts, 1969–70; Commercial posts, 1971–79, incl. Manager, Divl Supplies, 1973; Reg. Manager, BSC (Industry), 1979–82; Dir, S Wales Workshops, 1980–82; Industrial Dir, Welsh Office, 1982–85; Associate Dir, 1985–87, Dir, 1987–90, Coopers & Lybrand Associates. *Publications:* various technical papers. *Recreations:* family, sport. *Address:* 6 Cory Crescent, Wyndham Park, Peterston-super-Ely, S Glam. *T:* Peterston-super-Ely (0446) 760372. *Clubs:* Cardiff Athletic, Peterston Football (Cardiff).

DRIVER, Sir Antony (Victor), Kt 1986; Chairman, South West Thames Regional Health Authority, 1982–88; *b* London, 20 July 1920; *s* of late Arthur William Driver and Violet Clementina Driver (*née* Browne); *m* 1948, Patricia (née Tinkler); three *s*. *Educ:* King's Coll., Univ. of London (BScEng Hons); Dip., Graduate Sch. of Industrial Admin., Carnegie-Mellon Univ., Pittsburgh. CEng; FIMechE, FInstPet; FBIM. In oil industry with Shell-Mex and BP Ltd, until 1975, and BP Oil Ltd, 1976–80: seconded to British Petroleum Co., as Marketing Manager, N Europe, 1969–71; General Manager, Sales, 1971–78; Director, Personnel and Admin, 1979–80. Non-executive Director: Candles Ltd, 1976–80; Rockwool Ltd, 1978–80; Baxter Fell & Co. Ltd, 1980–85; Chm., Hoogovens (UK) Ltd, 1985–88. Director: Inst. of Cancer Research, 1981–; Oil Industries Club Ltd, 1981–. Liveryman, Tallow Chandlers' Co., 1977–; Freeman, City of London. *Recreations:* travel, gardening, wine, pyrotechnics. *Address:* Winterdown, Holmbury St Mary, Dorking, Surrey RH5 6NL. *T:* Dorking (0306) 730238.

DRIVER, Bryan, FCIT 1976; Director, Operations and Rolling Stock (formerly Operations Director), Transmanche-Link (Channel Tunnel Contractors), since 1988; *b* 26 August 1932; *s* of Fred and Edith Driver; *m* 1955, Pamela Anne (*née* Nelson); two *d*. *Educ:* Wath-upon-Dearne Grammar School. Joined British Railways (Junior Clerk), 1948; Royal Air Force, 1950–52; management training with BR, 1958–59; posts in London, Doncaster, Newcastle, 1959–69; Divisional Operating Manager, Norwich, 1969–71, Liverpool Street, 1971–72; Divisional Manager, West of England, 1972–75, South Wales, 1975–77; Dep. Gen. Manager, Eastern Region, 1977–82; Man. Dir, 1982–87, Chm., 1985–87, Freightliners Ltd. Formed Bryan Driver Associates, Management Consultants, 1987. *Recreations:* cricket, Rugby football, golf. *Address:* Riverds Lea, 4 Shilton Garth Close, Old Earswick, York YO3 9SQ. *T:* York (0904) 762848. *Clubs:* Savile, MCC; Yorkshire CC, York Golf.

DRIVER, Charles Jonathan, MPhil; Master of Wellington College, since 1989; *b* 19 Aug. 1939; *s* of Rev. Kingsley Ernest Driver and Phyllis Edith Mary (*née* Gould); *m* 1967, Ann Elizabeth Hoogewerf; two *s* one *d*. *Educ:* St Andrews Coll., Grahamstown; Univ. of Cape Town (BA Hons, BEd, STD); Trinity Coll., Oxford (MPhil). Pres., National Union of S African Students, 1963–64; Asst Teacher, Sevenoaks Sch., 1964–65 and 1967–68; Housemaster, Internat. Sixth Form Centre, Sevenoaks Sch., 1968–73; Dir of Sixth Form Studies, Matthew Humberstone Sch., 1973–78; Res. Fellow, Univ. of York, 1976; Principal, Island Sch., Hong Kong, 1978–83; Headmaster, Berkhamsted Sch., 1983–89. Member: HMC; Royal Soc. of Arts; FRSA. *Publications:* Elegy for a Revolutionary (novel), 1968; Send War in Our Time, O Lord (novel), 1969; Death of Fathers (novel), 1972; A Messiah of the Last Days (novel), 1974; I Live Here Now (poems), 1979; (with Jack Cope) Occasional Light (poems), 1979; Patrick Duncan (biog.), 1980; Hong Kong Portraits (poems), 1986. *Recreations:* long-distance running, reading, writing, Rugby. *Address:* Wellington College, Crowthorne, Berks RG11 7PU.

DRIVER, Christopher Prout; writer and broadcaster; Personal Page Co-Editor, The Guardian, since 1988; *b* 1 Dec. 1932; *s* of Dr Arthur Herbert Driver and Elsie Kathleen Driver (*née* Shepherd); *m* 1958, Margaret Elizabeth Perfect; three *d*. *Educ:* Dragon Sch., Oxford; Rugby Sch.; Christ Church, Oxford (MA). Friends Ambulance Unit Internat. Service, 1955–57; Reporter, Liverpool Daily Post, 1958–60; Reporter, 1960–64, Features Editor, 1964–68, Food and Drink Ed., 1984–88, The Guardian; Editor, Good Food Guide, 1969–82. Member: Christian Aid Bd, 1972–84; Highgate URC, 1962–. *Publications:* A Future for the Free Churches?, 1962; The Disarmers: a study in protest, 1964; The Exploding University, 1971; The British at Table 1940–1980, 1983; (jtly) Pepys at Table, 1984; Twelve Poems, 1985; (contrib.) More Words, 1977; (publisher and co-ed) Shaftesbury, 1983; contribs on various topics to New Society, Listener, London Rev. of Books, etc. *Recreations:* cooking, playing violin and viola, avoiding cars, accumulating books. *Address:* 6 Church Road, Highgate, N6 4QT; The Book in Hand, 17 Bell Street, Shaftesbury, Dorset; The Guardian, 119 Faringdon Road, EC1R 3ER. *T:* 071–239 9624.

DRIVER, Sir Eric (William), Kt 1979; retired; Chairman, Mersey Regional Health Authority, 1973–82; Chairman, National Staff Committee, (Works), 1979–82; *b* 19 Jan. 1911; *s* of William Weale Driver and Sarah Ann Driver; *m* 1st, 1938, Winifred Bane; two *d*; 2nd, 1972, Sheila Mary Johnson. *Educ:* Strand Sch., London; King's Coll., London Univ. (BSc). FICE. Civil Engr with ICI Ltd, 1938–73, retd as Chief Civil Engr Mond Div. *Recreations:* hill walking, gardening, travel. *Address:* Chapel House, Crowley, Northwich, Cheshire CW9 6NX. *Club:* Budworth Sailing.

DRIVER, Olga Lindholm; *see* Aikin, O. L.

DROGHEDA, 12th Earl of, *cr* 1661 (Ireland); **Henry Dermot Ponsonby Moore;** Baron Moore of Mellifont, 1616; Viscount Moore, 1621; Baron Moore of Cobham (UK), 1954; photographer; *b* 14 Jan. 1937; *o s* of 11th Earl of Drogheda, KG, KBE and of Joan *o d* of late William Henry Carr; *S* father, 1989; *m* 1st, 1968, Eliza Lloyd (marr. diss. 1972), *d* of Stacy Barcroft Lloyd, Jr, and Mrs Paul Mellon; 2nd, 1978, Alexandra, *d* of Sir Nicholas Henderson, *qv*; two *s* one *d*. *Educ:* Eton; Trinity College, Cambridge. *Publications:* (as Derry Moore): (with Brendan Gill) The Dream Come True, Great Houses of Los Angeles, 1980; (with George Plumptre) Royal Gardens, 1981; (with Sybila Jane Flower) Stately Homes of Britain, 1982; (with Henry Mitchell) Washington, Houses of the Capital, 1982; (with Michael Pick) The English Room, 1984; (with Alvilde Lees-Milne) The Englishwoman's House, 1984; (with Alvilde Lees-Milne) The Englishman's Room, 1986. *Heirs:* *s* Viscount Moore, *qv*. *Address:* 40 Ledbury Road, W11 2AB. *Clubs:* Garrick, Brooks's.

DROMGOOLE, Jolyon; MA Oxon; Director (Council Secretariat), Institution of Civil Engineers, since 1985; Deputy Under-Secretary of State (Army), Ministry of Defence, 1984–85; *b* 27 March 1926; 2nd *s* of Nicholas and Violet Dromgoole; *m* 1956, Anthea, *e d* of Sir Anthony Bowlby, 2nd Bt, *qv*; five *d* (incl. triplets). *Educ:* Christ's Hospital; Dulwich Coll.; University Coll., Oxford, 1944. 2nd Cl. Hons (History), MA. Entered HM Forces, 1944; commissioned 14/20 King's Hussars, 1946. University Coll., 1948–50. Entered Administrative Cl., Civil Service; assigned to War Office, 1950; Private Sec. to Permanent Under-Sec., 1953; Principal, 1955; Private Sec. to Sec. of State, 1964–65; Asst

Sec., 1965; Command Sec., HQ FARELF, Singapore, 1968–71; Royal Coll. of Defence Studies, 1972; Under-Sec., Broadcasting Dept, Home Office, 1973–76; Asst Under-Sec. of State, Gen. Staff, 1976–79, Personnel and Logistics, 1979–84, MoD. *Recreations:* polo, literature. *Address:* 13 Gladstone Street, SE1 6EY. *T:* 071–928 2162; Montreal House, Barnsley, Glos. *T:* Bibury (028574) 331. *Clubs:* Athenæum, Commonwealth Trust.
See also P. S. B. F. Dromgoole.

DROMGOOLE, Patrick Shirley Brookes Fleming; Chief Executive, HTV Group plc, 1988–91; *b* 30 Aug. 1930; *s* of Nicholas and Violet Dromgoole; *m* 1960, Jennifer Veronica Jill Davis (separated 1988); two *s* one *d*. *Educ:* Dulwich Coll.; University Coll., Oxford (MA). Actor and various employments in London and Paris, 1947–51; BBC Drama Producer/Dir, 1954–63; freelance theatre, film and television dir (directed first plays in West End of Orton, Wood, Welland, Halliwell and others), 1963–69; directed regularly Armchair Theatre for ABC TV and Thames TV; made number of undistinguished films for cinema; joined HTV Ltd as Programme Controller, 1969; Asst Man. Dir, 1981; Man. Dir, HTV, 1987. Various awards incl. Pye Oscar, RTS, for Thick as Thieves, 1971; Best Play of the Year, for Machinegunner, 1973; Amer. Emmy, for D.P., 1985. FRTS 1978; FRSA 1989. *Recreations:* travel, tennis, swimming, reading. *Address:* Dalriada, Golf Club Road, St Georges Hill, Weybridge, Surrey KT13 0NN. *Clubs:* Savile; Castel's (Paris); Lotos (New York).
See also J. Dromgoole.

DROMORE, Bishop of, (RC), since 1976; **Most Rev. Francis Gerard Brooks,** DD, DCL; *b* Jan. 1924. Priest, 1949. Formerly President, St Colman's Coll., Violet Hill, Newry. *Address:* Bishop's House, Newry, Co. Down, N Ireland BT35 6PN. *T:* Newry (0693) 62444, *Fax:* Newry (0693) 60496.

DRONFIELD, Ronald; Chief Insurance Officer for National Insurance, Department of Health and Social Security, 1976–84, retired; *b* 21 Dec. 1924; *m* 1966, Marie Renie (*née* Price). *Educ:* King Edward VII Sch., Sheffield; Oriel Coll., Oxford. RN, 1943–46. Entered Min. of National Insurance, 1949; Principal Private Sec. to Minister of Pensions and Nat. Insurance, 1964–66; Cabinet Office, 1970–71. *Recreation:* reading, biography. *Address:* 8 Beechrow, Ham Common, Richmond, Surrey TW10 5HE.

DRONKE, Prof. (Ernst) Peter (Michael), FBA 1984; Fellow of Clare Hall, since 1964, and Professor of Medieval Latin Literature, since 1989, University of Cambridge; *b* 30 May 1934; *s* of Senatspräsident A. H. R. Dronke and M. M. Dronke (*née* Kronfeld); *m* 1960, Ursula Miriam (*née* Brown); one *d*. *Educ:* Victoria University, NZ (MA 1st Cl. Hons 1954); Magdalen College, Oxford (BA 1st Cl. Hons 1957; MA 1961); MA Cantab 1961. Research Fellow, Merton Coll., Oxford, 1958–61; Lectr in Medieval Latin, 1961–79, Reader, 1979–89, Univ. of Cambridge. Guest Lectr, Univ. of Munich, 1960; Guest Prof., Centre d'Etudes Médiévales, Poitiers, 1969; Leverhulme Fellow, 1973; Guest Prof., Univ. Autónoma, Barcelona, 1977; Vis. Fellow, Humanities Res. Centre, Canberra, 1978; Vis. Prof. of Medieval Studies, Westfield Coll., 1981–86. W. P. Ker Lectr, Univ. of Glasgow, 1976; Matthews Lectr, Birkbeck Coll., 1983. Corresp. Fellow, Real Academia de Buenas Letras, 1976. Hon. Pres., Internat. Courtly Literature Soc., 1974. Co-Editor, Mittellateinisches Jahrbuch, 1977–. Premio Internazionale Ascoli Piceno, 1988. *Publications:* Medieval Latin and the Rise of European Love-Lyric, 2 vols, 1965–66; The Medieval Lyric, 1968; Poetic Individuality in the Middle Ages, 1970; Fabula, 1974; Abelard and Heloise in Medieval Testimonies, 1976; (with Ursula Dronke) Barbara et antiquissima carmina, 1977; (ed) Bernardus Silvestris, Cosmographia, 1978; Introduction to Francesco Colonna, Hypnerotomachia, 1981; Women Writers of the Middle Ages, 1984; The Medieval Poet and his World, 1984; Dante and Medieval Latin Traditions, 1986; Introduction to Rosvita, Dialoghi drammatici, 1986; (ed) A History of Twelfth-Century Western Philosophy, 1988; Hermes and the Sibyls, 1990; Latin and Vernacular Poets of the Middle Ages, 1991; essays in learned jls and symposia. *Recreations:* music, film, Brittany. *Address:* 6 Parker Street, Cambridge CB1 1JL. *T:* Cambridge (0223) 359942.

DRUCKER, Henry Matthew, PhD; Director, University Development Office, Oxford University, since 1987; Director, Campaign for Oxford, since 1988; *b* 29 April 1942; *s* of Arthur and Frances Drucker; *m* 1975, Nancy Livia Newman. *Educ:* Allegheny Coll., Meadville, Penn (BA Philosophy); London School of Economics (PhD PolPhil). Lectr in Politics 1964–76, Sen. Lectr in Politics 1976–86, Univ. of Edinburgh. Governor, Napier Poly. of Edinburgh, 1989–. *Publications:* Political Uses of Ideology, 1974; (ed with M. G. Clarke) Our Changing Scotland, 1977; Breakaway—The Scottish Labour Party, 1978; (ed with Nancy Drucker) Scottish Government Yearbook, 1978–82; Doctrine and Ethos in the Labour Party, 1979; (ed) Multi-Party Britain, 1979; (with Gordon Brown) The Politics of Nationalism and Devolution, 1980; (ed) John P. Mackintosh on Scotland, 1982; (general ed.) Developments in British Politics, 1983; (general ed.) Developments in British Politics 2, 1986, revd edn 1988. *Recreations:* tennis, walking. *Address:* University Offices, Wellington Square, Oxford OX1 2JD. *T:* Oxford (0865) 270222. *Club:* Reform.

DRUCKER, Prof. Peter (Ferdinand); writer and consultant; Clarke Professor of Social Science, Claremont Graduate School, Claremont, Calif, since 1971; Professorial Lecturer in Oriental Art, Claremont Colleges, since 1980; *b* 19 Nov. 1909; *s* of Adolph B. Drucker and Caroline (*née* Bond); *m* 1937, Doris Schmitz; one *s* three *d*. *Educ:* Austria, Germany, England. Investment banker, London, 1933–36; newspapers, 1937–41; Professor of Philosophy and Politics, Bennington Coll., Bennington, Vt, USA, 1942–49; Prof. of Management, NY Univ., 1950–72. Management Consultant (internat. practice among businesses and govts) (as well as Professorships), 1948–. Has recorded audio-cassettes on management practice. Holds nineteen hon. doctorates from Univs in Belgium, GB, Japan, Spain, Switzerland, USA. Hon. FBIM; FAAAS; Fellow: Amer. Acad. of Management; Internat. Acad. of Management. Order of Sacred Treasure, Japan; Grand Cross, Austria. *Publications:* End of Economic Man, 1939; Future of Industrial Man, 1942; Concept of Corporation, 1946; The New Society, 1950; Practice of Management, 1954; America's Next Twenty Years, 1959; Landmarks of Tomorrow, 1960; Managing for Results, 1964; The Effective Executive, 1966; The Age of Discontinuity, 1969; Technology, Management and Society, 1970; Men, Ideas and Politics, 1971; The New Markets . . . and other essays, 1971; Management: tasks, responsibilities, practices, 1974; The Unseen Revolution: how pension fund socialism came to America, 1976; Adventures of a Bystander, 1979; Managing in Turbulent Times, 1980; Toward the New Economics, 1981; The Changing World of the Executive (essays), 1982; Innovation and Entrepreneurship, 1985; The Frontiers of Management, 1986; The New Realities, 1989; Managing the Non-Profit Organisation, 1990; *novels:* The Last of All Possible Worlds, 1982; The Temptation to Do Good, 1984. *Recreations:* mountaineering; Japanese history and paintings. *Address:* 636 Wellesley Drive, Claremont, Calif 91711, USA. *T:* (714) 621–1488.

DRUMLANRIG, Viscount; Sholto Francis Guy Douglas; *b* 1 June 1967; *s* and *heir* of 12th Marquess of Queensberry, *qv*.

DRUMM, Rt. Rev. Mgr. Walter Gregory; Rector, Pontifical Beda College, Rome, since 1987; *b* 2 March 1940; *s* of Owen and Kathleen Drumm. *Educ:* St Joseph's Sch. and St Aloysius' Coll., Highgate; Balliol Coll., Oxford (MA). Tutor, The Grange, Warlingham, 1962–66; studied at Beda Coll., 1966–70; ordained, Westminster Dio., 1970; Asst Priest, Wood Green, 1970–73; Chaplain, Oxford Univ., 1973–83; Parish Priest, Our Lady of Victories, Kensington, 1983–87. Prelate of Honour to the Pope, 1988. *Address:* Pontifical Beda College, Viale di San Paolo 18, 00146 Roma, Italy. *T:* 556.1700. *Club:* United Oxford & Cambridge University.

DRUMMOND, family name of **Earl of Perth** and **Baroness Strange.**

DRUMMOND, Maj.-Gen. Anthony John D.; *see* Deane-Drummond.

DRUMMOND, David Classon, FIBiol; Deputy Director, Research and Development Service, Agricultural Development Advisory Service, Ministry of Agriculture, Fisheries and Food, 1987–88, retired; *b* 25 July 1928; *s* of Roger Hamilton Drummond and Marjorie Holt Drummond; *m* 1952, Barbara Anne, *d* of late Prof. Alfred Cobban; three *d*. *Educ:* St Peter's Sch., York; University Coll., London (BSc 1952); Pennsylvania State Univ., USA (Kellogg Fellow; MS 1962). FIBiol 1975. Project Manager, FAO, UN, Karachi, 1971–72; Agricultural Science Service, MAFF: Head of Rodent Res. Dept, and Officer i/c Tolworth Lab., 1974–82; Head of Biol. Div., and Officer i/c Slough Lab., 1982–85; Sen. Agricl Scientist with special responsibilities for R&D, 1985–87. Mem., WHO Expert Adv. Panel on Vector Biology and Control, 1980–. *Publications:* scientific papers and reviews mainly concerned with rodent biology and control and develt of agricl and urban rat control programmes. *Recreations:* travel, gardening, history of rat catching. *Address:* 22 Knoll Road, Dorking, Surrey RH4 3EP.

DRUMMOND, John Richard Gray, CBE 1990; writer and broadcaster; Controller of Music, 1985–May 1992, and of Radio 3, 1987–May 1992, BBC; Director, Promenade Concerts, 1992; *b* 25 Nov. 1934; *s* of late Captain A. R. G. Drummond and Esther (*née* Pickering), Perth, WA. *Educ:* Canford; Trinity Coll., Cambridge (MA History). RNVR, 1953–55. BBC Radio and Television, 1958–78, latterly as Asst Head, Music and Arts. Programmes produced incl.: Tortelier Master Classes, 1964; Leeds Piano Comp., 1966 (1st Prize, Prague Fest., 1967); Diaghilev, 1967; Kathleen Ferrier, 1968; Music Now, 1969; Spirit of the Age, 1975; The Lively Arts, 1976–78. Dir, Edinburgh Internat. Fest., 1978–83. Pres., Kensington Soc.; Chm., Nat. Dance Co-ordinating Cttee, 1986–; Vice-Chm., British Arts Fests Assoc., 1981–83; Mem. various adv. councils and cttees concerning music and dance; Governor, Royal Ballet, 1986–; Mem., Theatres Trust, 1989–. Hon. GSM. FRSA. *Publications:* (with Joan Bakewell) A Fine and Private Place, 1977; (with N. Thompson) The Turn of Dance?, 1984. *Recreations:* conversation, looking at architecture, browsing in bookshops. *Address:* 61c Campden Hill Court, W8 7HL. *T:* 071–937 2257. *Club:* New (Edinburgh).

DRUMMOND, Kevin; *see* Drummond, T. A. K.

DRUMMOND, Maldwin Andrew Cyril, OBE 1990; JP; DL; farmer and author; *b* 30 April 1932; *s* of late Maj. Cyril Drummond, JP, DL, and Mildred Joan Quinnell; *m* 1st, 1955, Susan Dorothy Cayley (marr. diss. 1977); two *d*; 2nd, 1978, Gillian Turner Laing; one *s*. *Educ:* Eton Coll.; Royal Agricl Coll., Cirencester; Univ. of Southampton (Cert. in Environmental Sci., 1972). 2nd Lieut, Rifle Bde, 1950–52; Captain, Queen Victoria's, later Queen's, Royal Rifles (TA), retd 1967. Verderer of New Forest, 1961–90; Chairman: Heritage Coast Forum, 1989–; New Forest Cttee, 1990– (Consultative Panel, 1982–); Mem., Countryside Commn, 1980–86. Member: Southampton Harbour Bd, 1967; British Transport Docks Bd, Southampton, 1968–74; Southern Water Authority, 1984–87. Chairman: Sail Training Assoc., 1967–72; Maritime Trust, 1979–89; Cutty Sark Soc., 1979–89; Warrior (formerly Ships) Preservation Trust, 1979–; Vice-Pres., 1983–, and Chm. Boat Cttee, 1983–, RNLI; Trustee, World Ship Trust, 1980–; Chm., Hampshire Bldgs Preservation Trust, 1986–. Mem., New Forest RDC, 1957–66; Hampshire: County Councillor, 1967–75; JP 1964; DL 1975; High Sheriff, 1980–81. *Publications:* Conflicts in an Estuary, 1973; Tall Ships, 1976; Salt-Water Places, 1979; (with Paul Rodhouse) Yachtsman's Naturalist, 1980; (with Philip Allison) The New Forest, 1980; The Riddle, 1985; West Highland Shores, 1990. *Recreations:* cruising under sail and wondering about the sea. *Address:* Cadland House, Fawley, Southampton SO4 1AA. *T:* (office) Fawley (0703) 892039, (home) Fawley (0703) 891543; Wester Kames Castle, Port Bannatyne, Isle of Bute PA20 0QW. *T:* Rothesay (0700) 3983. *Clubs:* White's, Pratt's, Royal Cruising; Royal Yacht Squadron (Cowes); Leander (Henley).

DRUMMOND, Rev. Norman Walker, MA; BD; Headmaster, Loretto School, since 1984; *b* 1 April 1952; *s* of late Edwin Payne Drummond and of Jean (*née* Walker); *m* 1976, Lady Elizabeth Helen Kennedy, *d* of 7th Marquess of Ailsa, *qv*; two *s* two *d*. *Educ:* Merchiston Castle Sch.; Fitzwilliam Coll., Cambridge (MA Law); New Coll., Univ. of Edinburgh (BD). Ordained as Minister of the Church of Scotland, and commnd to serve as Chaplain to HM Forces in the Army, 1976; Chaplain: Depot, Parachute Regt and Airborne Forces, 1977–78; 1st Bn The Black Watch (Royal Highland Regt), 1978–82; to the Moderator of the Gen. Assembly of the Church of Scotland, 1980; Fettes Coll., 1982–84. Chairman: Musselburgh and Dist Council of Social Service; Ronald Selby Wright Christian Leadership Trust; Member: Scottish Council, Duke of Edinburgh's Award Scheme; Court, Heriot-Watt Univ.; Queen's Bodyguard for Scotland (Royal Co. of Archers); Trustee, Scottish Silver Jubilee and Children's Bursary Fund. Cambridge Univ. Rugby Blue, 1971; Captain: Scottish Univs XV, 1974; Army XV and Combined Services XV, 1976–77. *Publication:* The First Twenty-five Years: official history of The Black Watch Kirk Session, 1979. *Recreations:* Rugby football, cricket, golf, curling, traditional jazz, Isle of Skye. *Address:* The Headmaster's House, Loretto School, Musselburgh, East Lothian, Scotland EH21 7RE. *Clubs:* MCC, Free Foresters; New (Edinburgh); Hawks (Cambridge).

DRUMMOND, (Thomas Anthony) Kevin; QC (Scot.) 1987; *b* 3 Nov. 1943; *s* of Thomas Drummond, BSc, and Mary (*née* Hughes); *m* 1966, Margaret Evelyn Broadley; one *d* (and one *d* decd). *Educ:* Blair's Coll., Aberdeen; St Mirin's Acad., Paisley; Edinburgh Univ. (LLB). Estate Duty Office, CS, 1963–70; Solicitor, 1970; admitted Faculty of Advocates, 1974; Advocate-Depute, Crown Office, Edinburgh, 1985–90. Member: Criminal Injuries Compensation Bd, 1990–; Firearms Consultative Cttee, 1990–. Cartoonist, Scots Law Times, 1981–. *Publications:* legal cartoons under name of TAK: The Law at Work, 1982; The Law at Play, 1983. *Recreations:* shooting, hill-walking, under water hang-gliding. *Address:* Pomathorn House, Howgate, Midlothian EH26 8PJ. *T:* Penicuik (0968) 74046.

DRUMMOND, William Norman, CB 1987; Under Secretary (formerly Deputy Secretary), Department of Economic Development (formerly Department of Commerce), Northern Ireland, 1979–87; *b* 10 July 1927; *s* of Thomas and Martha Drummond, Lurgan; *m* 1958, Pamela Joyce Burnham; two *d*. *Educ:* Lurgan Coll.; Queen's Univ. Belfast (BSc (Hons)). Physicist, Iraq Petroleum Co., Kirkuk, Iraq, 1950–54; Reed's Sch., Cobham, 1954–57; Northern Ireland Civil Service, 1957–87; Dep. Sec., Dept of Manpower Services, NI, 1974–79. Chm., Public Service Training Council. Mem., Planning Appeals Commn (NI). *Recreations:* gardening, reading. *Address:* 8 Magheralave Park East, Lisburn, BT28 3BT. *T:* Lisburn (0846) 664104.

DRUMMOND YOUNG, James Edward; QC (Scot.) 1988; *b* 17 Feb. 1950; *s* of Duncan Drummond Young, MBE, DL, Edinburgh, and Annette (*née* Mackay). *Educ:* John Watson's Sch.; Sidney Sussex Coll., Cambridge (BA 1971); Harvard Univ. (Joseph Hodges Choate Meml Fellow, 1971–72; LLM 1972); Edinburgh Univ. (LLB 1974). Admitted to Faculty of Advocates, 1976. Standing Jun. Counsel in Scotland to Bd of Inland Revenue, 1986–88. *Publications:* (with J. B. St Clair) The Law of Corporate Insolvency in Scotland, 1988; (contrib.) Stair Memorial Encyclopaedia of Scots Law, 1989. *Recreations:* music, travel. *Address:* 14 Ainslie Place, Edinburgh EH3 6AS. *T:* 031–225 7031. *Club:* New (Edinburgh).

DRUON, Maurice Samuel Roger Charles, Hon. CBE 1988; Commandeur de la Légion d'Honneur; Commandeur des Arts et Lettres; author; Member of the French Academy since 1966, Permanent Secretary, since 1986; Member: French Parliament (Paris), 1978–81; Assembly of Council of Europe, 1978–81; European Parliament, 1979–80; Franco-British Council, since 1972; *b* Paris, 23 April 1918; *s* of René Druon de Reyniac and Léonilla Jenny Samuel-Cros; *m* 1968, Madeleine Marignac. *Educ:* Lycée Michelet and Ecole des Sciences Politiques, Paris. Ecole de Cavalerie de Saumur, aspirant, 1940; joined Free French Forces, London, 1942; Attaché Commissariat à l'Intérieur et Direction de l'Information, 1943; War Correspondent, 1944–45; Lieut de réserve de cavalerie. Journalist, 1946–47; Minister for Cultural Affairs, France, 1973–74. Awarded Prix Goncourt, 1948, for novel Les Grandes Familles; Prix de Monaco, 1966. Member: Acad. of Morocco, 1980; Athènes' Acad., 1981; Pres., Franco-Italian Assoc., 1985–. Dr *hc* York Univ., Ontario, 1987. Commandeur du Phénix de Grèce; Grand Officer de l'Ordre de l'Honneur de Grèce; Grand Officier du Mérite de l'Ordre de Malte; Commandeur de l'Ordre de la République de Tunisie; Grand Officier du Lion du Sénégal; Grand Croix du Mérite de la République Italienne; Grand Croix de l'Aigle Aztèque du Mexique; Grand Officier Ouissam Alaouite (Morocco); Commandeur du Mérite de Monaco; Commandeur du Cruseiro del Sul (Brazil); Commandeur de l'ordre du Cèdre (Lebanon); Comdr, Ordre de Léopold (Belgium). *Publications:* Lettres d'un Européen, 1944; La Dernière Brigade (The Last Detachment), 1946 (publ. in England 1957); Les Grandes Familles, La Chute des Corps, Rendez-Vous aux Enfers, 1948–51 (trilogy publ. in England under title The Curtain falls, 1959); La Volupté d'Etre (Film of Memory), 1954 (publ. in England 1955); Les Rois Maudits (The Accursed Kings), 1955–60 (six vols: The Iron King, The Strangled Queen, The Poisoned Crown, The Royal Succession, The She-Wolf of France, The Lily and the Lion, publ. in England 1956–61); Tistou les pouces verts (Tistou of the green fingers), 1957 (publ. in England 1958); Alexandre le Grand (Alexander the God), 1958 (publ. in Eng. 1960); Des Seigneurs de la Plaine- (The Black Prince and other stories), 1962 (publ. in Eng. 1962); Les Mémoires de Zeus I (The Memoirs of Zeus), 1963 (in Eng. 1964); Bernard Buffet, 1964; Paris, de César à Saint Louis (The History of Paris from Caesar to St Louis), 1964 (in Eng. 1969); Le Pouvoir, 1965; Les Tambours de la Mémoire, 1965; Le Bonheur des Uns, 1967; Les Mémoires de Zeus II (The Memoirs of Zeus II), 1967; L'Avenir en désarroi, 1968; Vézelay, colline éternelle, 1968; Nouvelles lettres d'un Européen, 1970; Une Eglise qui se trompe de siècle, 1972; La Parole et le Pouvoir, 1974; Oeuvres complètes, 25 vols, 1973–79; Quand un roi perd la France (Les Rois Maudits 7), 1977; Attention la France!, 1981; Réformer la Démocratie, 1982; *plays:* Mégarée, 1942; Un Voyageur, 1953; La Contessa, 1962; *song:* Le Chant des Partisans (with Joseph Kessel and Anna Marly), 1943 (London). *Recreations:* riding, travel. *Address:* 23 quai de Conti, 75006 Paris, France; Abbaye de Faise, Les Artigues de Lussac, 33570 Lussac, France. *Clubs:* Savile, Garrick; Travellers' (Paris).

DRURY, Allen Stuart; Author; *b* Houston, Texas, 2 Sept. 1918; *s* of Alden M. and Flora A. Drury. *Educ:* Stanford Univ. (BA). Served with US Army, 1942–43. Ed., The Tulare (Calif) Bee, 1939–41; county ed., The Bakersfield Californian, Bakersfield, Calif, 1941–42; United Press Senate Staff, Washington, DC, 1943–45; freelance correspondent, 1946; Nation Ed., Pathfinder Magazine, Washington, DC, 1947–53; National Staff, Washington Evening Star, 1953–54; Senate Staff, New York Times, 1954–59. Mem., National Council on the Arts (apptd by Pres. Reagan), 1982–88. Sigma Delta Chi Award for Editorial Writing, 1942; Hon. LitD, Rollins Coll., Winter Park, Fla, 1961. *Publications:* Advise and Consent, 1959 (Pulitzer Prize for Fiction, 1960); A Shade of Difference, 1962; A Senate Journal, 1963; That Summer, 1965; Three Kids in a Cart, 1965; Capable of Honor, 1966; "A Very Strange Society", 1967; Preserve and Protect, 1968; The Throne of Saturn, 1971; Courage and Hesitation: inside the Nixon administration, 1972; Come Nineveh, Come Tyre, 1973; The Promise of Joy, 1975; A God Against the Gods, 1976; Return to Thebes, 1977; Anna Hastings, 1977; Mark Coffin, USS, 1978; Egypt: the eternal smile, 1980; The Hill of Summer, 1981; Decision, 1983; The Roads of Earth, 1984; Pentagon, 1986; Toward What Bright Glory?, 1990. *Address:* The Lantz Office, 888 Seventh Avenue, New York, NY 10106, USA. *Clubs:* Cosmos, University, National Press (Washington, DC); Bohemian (San Francisco).

DRURY, Very Rev. John Henry; Dean of Christ Church, Oxford, since 1991; *b* 23 May 1936; *s* of Henry and Barbara Drury; *m* 1972, (Frances) Clare Nineham, *d* of Rev. Prof. D. E. Nineham, *qv*; two *d*. *Educ:* Bradfield; Trinity Hall and Westcott House, Cambridge. MA (Hist. Pt 1, Cl. 1; Theol. Pt 2, Cl. 2/1). Curate, St John's Wood Church, 1963; Chaplain of Downing Coll., Cambridge, 1966; Chaplain and Fellow of Exeter Coll., Oxford, 1969 (Hon. Fellow, 1991); Res. Canon of Norwich Cathedral and Examining Chaplain to Bp of Norwich, 1973–79; Vice-Dean of Norwich, 1978; Fleck Resident in Religion, Bryn Mawr Coll., USA, 1978; Lectr in Religious Studies, Sussex Univ., 1979–81; Dean, 1981–91, Fellow, 1982–91, King's College, Cambridge. Examining Chaplain to Bp of Chichester, 1980–82. Mem., Doctrine Commn for C of E, 1978–82. Jt Editor, Theology, 1976–86. *Publications:* Angels and Dirt, 1972; Luke, 1973; Tradition and Design in Luke's Gospel, 1976; The Pot and The Knife, 1979; The Parables in the Gospels, 1985; Critics of the Bible 1724–1873, 1989; The Burning Bush, 1990; articles and reviews in Jl of Theol. Studies, Theology, Expository Times, TLS. *Recreations:* drawing, carpentry, reading. *Address:* Christ Church, Oxford OX1 1DP.

DRURY, Sir Michael; *see* Drury, Sir V. W. M.

DRURY, Sir (Victor William) Michael, Kt 1989; OBE 1978; FRCP; FRCGP; FRACGP; Professor of General Practice, University of Birmingham, since 1980; *b* 5 Aug. 1926; *s* of Leslie and Beatrice Drury; *m* 1950, Joan (*née* Williamson); three *s* one *d*. *Educ:* Bromsgrove Sch.; Univ. of Birmingham (MB ChB Hons); MRCS LRCP 1949; FRCGP 1970 (MRCGP 1963); FRCP 1988; FRACGP 1988. Ho. Surg., Birmingham Gen., 1949–50; RSO, Kidderminster, 1950–51; Major, RAMC, 1951–53; Principal in Gen. Practice, Bromsgrove, 1953; Nuffield Trav. Fellow, 1965; Clarkson Sen. Clin. Tutor, Univ. of Birmingham, 1973–80. Lectures: James MacKenzie, 1983, Eli Lilley, 1984; Sir David Bruce, 1985; Gale, 1986. Royal College of General Practitioners: Mem. Council, 1971–85 (Vice-Chm. 1980); Chm., Practice Org., 1966–71, Cttee and Res. Div., 1983–85; Pres., 1985–88. Member: Cttee on Safety of Medicines (Adverse Drug Reaction), 1975–79; Prescription Pricing Authy, 1981–86; DHA, 1981–85; Res. Cttee, RHA, 1982–86; GMC, 1984–; Standing Cttee, Post Grad. Med. Educn, 1988–. Civilian Advr in Gen. Practice to Army, 1984. Mem. Ct, Liverpool Univ., 1980–87. *Publications:* Introduction to General Practice, 1974; (ed) Treatment, 1978–; Medical Secretaries Handbook, 5th edn 1986; Treatment and Prognosis, 1990; The New Practice Manager, 1990; various chapters in books on Drug Safety, Gen. Practice, etc; res. articles in Lancet, BMJ, Brit. Jl of Surgery, Jl RCGP. *Recreations:* gardening, reading, bridge, talking and listening. *Address:* Rossall Cottage, Church Hill, Belbroughton, near Stourbridge DY9 0DT. *T:* Belbroughton (0562) 730229.

DRYDEN, Sir John (Stephen Gyles), 8th and 11th Bt *cr* 1795 and 1733; *b* 26 Sept. 1943; *s* of Sir Noel Percy Hugh Dryden, 7th and 10th Bt, and of Rosamund Mary, *e d* of late Stephen Scrope; *S* father, 1970; *m* 1970, Diana Constance, *o d* of Cyril Tomlinson, Highland Park, Wellington, NZ; one *s* one *d*. *Educ:* Oratory School. *Heir: s* John Frederick Simon Dryden, *b* 26 May 1976. *Address:* Spinners, Fairwarp, Uckfield, Sussex.

DRYSDALE, Thomas Henry, WS; Deputy Keeper of HM Signet, since 1991; *b* 23 Nov. 1942; *s* of Ian Drysdale and Rosalind Marion Drysdale (*née* Gallie); *m* 1967, Caroline, *d* of Dr Gavin B. Shaw; one *s* two *d*. *Educ:* Cargilfield; Glenalmond; Edinburgh Univ. (LLB). Partner, Shepherd & Wedderburn WS, 1967, Managing Partner, 1988–; Dir, Edinburgh Solicitors' Property Centre, 1976–88 (Chm., 1981–88). *Recreations:* ski-ing, walking, reading. *Address:* Shepherd & Wedderburn WS, 16 Charlotte Square, Edinburgh EH2 4YS. *T:* 031–225 8585. *Clubs:* New (Edinburgh); Scottish Ski.

DRYSDALE WILSON, John Veitch, CEng, FIMechE, FCIArb; Deputy Secretary, Institution of Mechanical Engineers, 1979–90; *b* 8 April 1929; *s* of Alexander Drysdale Wilson and Winifred Rose (*née* Frazier); *m* 1954, Joan Lily, *e d* of Mr and Mrs John Cooke, Guildford; one *s* one *d*. *Educ:* Solihull School; Guildford Technical Coll. Dennis Bros Ltd, Guildford: Engineer Apprentice, 1946–50; MIRA Research Trainee, 1949–50; Jun. Designer, 1950–51. National Service Officer, REME, 1951–53, Captain on Staff of CREME, 6th Armd Div. Management Trainee, BET Fedn, 1953–55; Technical Sales Engr, subseq. Head of Mechanical Laboratories, Esso Petroleum Co. Ltd, 1955–66; Chief Engr, R&D, Castrol Ltd, subseq. Burmah Oil Trading Ltd and Edwin Cooper Ltd, 1966–77; Projects and Res. Officer, Instn of Mechanical Engineers, 1977–79. Director: Mechanical Engineering Publications Ltd, 1979–90; Professional Engineers Insurance Bureau Ltd, 1989–90. Freeman, City of London, 1986; Liveryman: Co. of Engineers, 1987; Co. of Arbitrators, 1987. *Publications:* numerous papers to learned societies in USA and Europe on subjects related to engine lubrication. *Recreations:* travel, gardening, horology. *Clubs:* East India, Caravan.

D'SOUZA, Most Rev. Henry Sebastian; *see* Calcutta, Archbishop of, (RC).

DUBLIN, Archbishop of, and Primate of Ireland, since 1985; **Most Rev. Donald Arthur Richard Caird;** *b* Dublin, 11 Dec. 1925; *s* of George Robert Caird and Emily Florence Dreaper, Dublin; *m* 1963, Nancy Ballantyne, *d* of Prof. William Sharpe, MD, and Gwendolyn Hind, New York, USA; one *s* two *d*. *Educ:* Wesley Coll., Dublin, 1935–44; Trinity Coll., Dublin Univ., 1944–50. Sen. Exhibn, TCD, 1946; elected Schol. of the House, TCD, 1948; 1st cl. Moderatorship in Mental and Moral Science, 1949; Prizeman in Hebrew and Irish Language, 1946 and 1947; Lilian Mary Luce Memorial Prize for Philosophy, 1947; BA 1949; MA and BD 1955; HDipEd 1959. Curate Asst, St Mark's. Dundela, Belfast, 1950–53; Chaplain and Asst Master, Portora Royal Sch., Enniskillen, 1953–57; Lectr in Philosophy, University Coll. of St. David's, Lampeter, 1957; Rector, Rathmichael Parish, Shankill, Co. Dublin, 1960–69; Asst Master, St Columba's Coll., Rathfarnham, Co. Dublin, 1960–67; Dept Lectr in Philosophy, Trinity Coll., Dublin, 1962–63; Lectr in the Philosophy of Religion, Church of Ireland Theol Coll., Dublin, 1964–70; Dean of Ossory, 1969–70; Bishop of Limerick, Ardfert and Aghadoe, 1970–76; Bishop of Meath and Kildare, 1976–85. Fellow of St Columba's Coll., Dublin, 1971. Mem., Bord na Gaeilge, 1974. Hon. DD TCD, 1988. *Publication:* The Predicament of Natural Theology since the Criticism of Kant, in Directions, 1970 (Dublin). *Recreations:* swimming, tennis. *Address:* The See House, 17 Temple Road, Milltown, Dublin 6.

DUBLIN, Archbishop of, and Primate of Ireland, (RC), since 1988; **Most Rev. Desmond Connell,** DD; *b* 24 March 1926; *s* of John Connell and Maisie Connell (*née* Lacy). *Educ:* St Peter's National School, Phibsborough; Belvedere College; Clonliffe College; University Coll., Dublin (MA); St Patrick's Coll., Maynooth; Louvain Univ., Belgium (DPhil); DLitt NUI, 1981. University College, Dublin: Dept of Metaphysics, 1953–72; Prof. of General Metaphysics, 1972–88; Dean, Faculty of Philosophy and Sociology, 1983–88. Chaplain: Poor Clares, Donnybrook, 1953–55; Carmelites, Drumcondra, 1955–66; Carmelites, Blackrock, 1966–88. Prelate of Honour, 1984. *Publications:* The Vision in God, 1967; articles in reviews. *Address:* Archbishop's House, Drumcondra, Dublin 9. *T:* Dublin 373732.

DUBLIN, Auxiliary Bishop of, (RC); *see* Dunne, Most Rev. Patrick.

DUBLIN, (Christ Church), Dean of; *see* Paterson, Very Rev. J. T. F.

DUBLIN, (St Patrick's), Dean of; *no new appointment at time of going to press.*

du BOULAY; *see* Houssemayne du Boulay.

DU BOULAY, Prof. (Francis) Robin (Houssemayne), FBA 1980; Emeritus Professor of Mediæval History in the University of London, 1982; *b* 19 Dec. 1920; *er s* of late Philip Houssemayne Du Boulay and Mercy Tyrrell (*née* Friend); *m* 1948, Cecilia Burnell Matthews; two *s* one *d*. *Educ:* Christ's Hospital; Phillip's Academy, Andover, Mass., USA; Balliol Coll., Oxford. Williams Exhibitioner at Balliol Coll., 1939; Friends' Ambulance Unit and subsequently Royal Artillery, 1940–45; MA 1947; Asst lecturer at Bedford Coll., 1947, Lecturer, 1949; Reader in Mediæval History, in University of London, 1955, Prof., 1960–82. Hon. Sec., RHistS, 1961–65. *Publications:* The Register of Archbishop Bourgchier, 2 vols, 1953–55; Medieval Bexley, 1961; Documents Illustrative of Medieval Kentish Society, 1964; The Lordship of Canterbury, 1966; An Age of Ambition, 1970; (ed jtly) The Reign of Richard II, 1972; Germany in the later Middle Ages, 1983; Legion, and other poems, 1983; The England of Piers Plowman, 1991; various essays and papers on late medieval subjects, English and German, in specialist journals and general symposia. *Address:* Broadmead, Riverhead, Sevenoaks, Kent TN13 3DE.

DUBOWITZ, Prof. Victor, MD, PhD; FRCP; Professor of Paediatrics, University of London, at the Royal Postgraduate Medical School, since 1972; Consultant Paediatrician, Hammersmith Hospital, since 1972; Director, Jerry Lewis Muscle Research Centre, Royal Postgraduate Medical School, since 1975; *b* 6 Aug. 1931; *s* of late Charley and Olga Dubowitz (*née* Schattel); *m* 1960, Dr Lilly Magdalena Suzanne Sebok; four *s*. *Educ:* Beaufort West Central High Sch., S Africa; Univ. of Cape Town (BSc, MB, ChB, 1954; MD 1960). PhD Sheffield, 1965; DCH 1958; FRCP 1972. Intern, Groote Schuur Hosp., Cape Town, 1955; Sen. House Officer, Queen Mary's Hosp. for Children, Carshalton, 1957–59; Res. Associate in Histochem., Royal Postgrad. Med. Sch., 1958–59; Lectr in Clin. Path., National Hosp. for Nervous Diseases, Queen Square, London, 1960; Lectr in Child Health, 1961–65, Sen. Lectr, 1965–67, and Reader, 1967–72, Univ. of Sheffield; Res. Associate, Inst. for Muscle Diseases, and Asst Paediatrician, Cornell Med. Coll., New York, 1965–66. Several lectureships and overseas vis. professorships. Comdr, Order of

Constantine the Great, 1980. Arvo Ylppö Gold Medal, Finland, 1982; Baron ver Heyden de Lancey Prize, Med. Art Soc., 1980 and 1982. *Publications:* Developing and Diseased Muscle: a histochemical study, 1968; The Floppy Infant, 1969, 2nd edn 1980; (with M. H. Brooke) Muscle Biopsy: a modern approach, 1973, 2nd edn 1985; (with L. M. S. Dubowitz) Gestational Age of the Newborn: a clinical manual, 1977; Muscle Disorders in Childhood, 1978; (with L. M. S. Dubowitz) The Neurological Assessment of the Preterm and Full-term Newborn Infant, 1981; Colour Atlas of Muscle Disorders in Childhood, 1989; (jtly) A Colour Atlas of Brain Lesions in the Newborn, 1990; chapters in books and articles in learned jls on paediatric topics, partic. muscle disorders and newborn neurology. *Recreation:* sculpting. *Address:* 25 Middleton Road, Golders Green, NW11 7NR. *T:* 081–455 9352.

DuBRIDGE, Lee A(lvin); *b* 21 Sept. 1901; *s* of Frederick A. and Elizabeth Browne DuBridge; *m* 1st, 1925, Doris May Koht (*d* 1973); one *s* one *d*; 2nd, 1974, Arrola B. Cole. *Educ:* Cornell Coll., Mt Vernon, Ia (BA); University of Wisconsin (MA, PhD). Instructor in Physics, University of Wisconsin, 1925–26; Nat. Research Council Fellow at Calif. Inst. Tech., 1926–28; Asst Prof. Physics, Washington Univ. (St Louis, Mo.), 1928–33; Assoc. Prof., Washington Univ., 1933–34; Prof. of Physics and Dep. Chm., University of Rochester (NY), 1934–46; Dean of Faculty, University of Rochester, 1938–42; on leave from University of Rochester, 1940–45, as Dir of Radiation Lab. of Nat. Def. Research Comm. at MIT, Cambridge; Pres., California Inst. of Techn., Pasadena, 1946–69, Pres. Emeritus, 1969–; Science Adviser to President of USA, 1969–70. Hon. ScD: Cornell Coll.; Mt Vernon, Iowa, 1940; Weslyan Univ., Middletown, Conn., 1946; Polytechnic Inst. of Brooklyn, New York, 1946; University of Brit. Columbia, Can., 1947; Washington Univ., St Louis, Mo, 1948; Occidental Coll., 1952; Maryland, 1955; Columbia, 1957; Indiana, 1957; Wisconsin, 1957; Pennsylvania Mil. Coll., Chester, Pa, 1962; DePauw, Indiana, 1962; Pomona Coll., Claremont, Calif., 1965; Carnegie Inst. of Techn., Pittsburgh, 1965; Hon. LLD: California, 1948; Rochester, 1953; Southern California, 1957; Northwestern, 1958; Loyola, Los Angeles, 1963; Notre Dame, Indiana, 1967; Illinois Inst. Technology, 1968; Hon. LHD: University Judaism, Los Angeles, 1958; Redlands, 1958; Hon. DCL, Union Coll., Schenectady, NY, 1961; Hon. DSc: Rockefeller Institute, NY, 1965; Tufts Univ., 1969; Syracuse Univ., 1969; Rensselaer Polytech. Inst., 1970. King's Medal, 1946; Research Corp. Award, 1947; Medal for Merit of US Govt, 1948, Golden Key Award, 1959; Leif Erikson Award, 1959; Arthur Noble Award, 1961; Golden Plate Award, 1973; Vannevar Bush Award, 1982. *Publications:* Photoelectric Phenomena (with A. L. Hughes), 1932; New Theories of Photoelectric Effect (Paris), 1934; Introduction to Space, 1960; articles in various scientific and other journals. *Address:* 1730 Homet Road, Pasadena, Calif 91106, USA. *T:* 818 793–1683. *Clubs:* Sunset (Los Angeles); Bohemian (San Francisco).

DUBS, Alfred; Director, Refugee Council, since 1988; Member, Broadcasting Standards Council, since 1988; *b* Prague, Czechoslovakia, Dec. 1932; *m*; one *s* one *d*. *Educ:* LSE. BSc (Econs). Local govt officer. Mem., Westminster CC, 1971–78; Chm., Westminster Community Relns Council, 1972–77; Mem., Kensington, Chelsea and Westminster AHA, 1975–78. Member: TGWU; Co-operative Party. Contested (Lab): Cities of London and Westminster, 1970; Hertfordshire South, Feb. and Oct. 1974; Battersea, 1987; prospective parly cand. (Lab) Battersea, 1990–. MP (Lab): Wandsworth, Battersea S, 1979–83; Battersea, 1983–87. Mem., Home Affairs Select Cttee, 1981–83 (Mem., Race Relations and Immigration Sub-Cttee, 1981–83); opposition front bench spokesman on home affairs, 1983–87. *Recreation:* walking in the Lake District. *Address:* 56 Westbourne Park Villas, W2 5EB. *T:* 071–727 2149.

DU CANE, John Peter, OBE 1964; Director, Amax Inc., 1966–91; *b* 16 April 1921; *s* of Charles and Mathilde Du Cane; *m* 1945, Patricia Wallace (*née* Desmond); two *s*. *Educ:* Canford Sch., Wimborne. Pilot, Fleet Air Arm, RN, 1941–46. De Beers Consolidated Mines, 1946–54; Sierra Leone Selection Trust, 1955–63; Director: Consolidated African Selection Trust, 1963–81; Selection Trust Ltd, 1966–81 (Man. Dir, 1975–80; Chm., 1978–81); BP International Ltd, 1981; Chief Exec., BP Minerals Internat. Ltd, 1980–81; Director: Australian Consolidated Minerals Pty, 1981–86 (Dep. Chm., 1983–86); Ultramar Plc, 1983–87; Austamax Resources Ltd, 1984–86 (Dep. Chm., 1984–86). FRSA. *Recreations:* sailing, fishing. *Address:* Castel du Prieuré, La Vicomté, 8 avenue de Bizeux, 35800 Dinard, France.

du CANN, Col Rt. Hon. Sir Edward (Dillon Lott), KBE 1985; PC 1964; Chairman, Lonrho Plc, 1984–91 (Director, since 1972; Joint Deputy Chairman, 1983–84); *b* 28 May 1924; *er s* of late C. G. L. du Cann, Barrister-at-Law, and Janet (*née* Murchie); *m* 1st, 1962, Sallie Innes (marr. diss. 1990), *e d* of late James Henry Murchie, Caldy, Cheshire; one *s* two *d*; 2nd, 1990, Jenifer Patricia Evelyn, *yr d* of Evelyn Mansfield King, *qv*, and *widow* of Sir Robert Cooke. *Educ:* Colet Court; Woodbridge Sch.; St John's Coll., Oxford (MA, Law). Served with RNVR, 1943–46 (CO, HMMTB 5010). Vice-Pres., Somerset and Wilts Trustee Savings Bank, 1956–75; Founder, Unicorn Group of Unit Trusts, 1957 (pioneered equity linked life assurance); Chairman: Barclays Unicorn Ltd and associated cos, 1957–72; Keyser Ullman Holdings Ltd, 1970–75; Cannon Assurance Ltd, 1972–80. Chm., Association of Unit Trust Managers, 1961. Contested: West Walthamstow Div., 1951; Barrow-in-Furness Div., 1955. MP (C) Taunton Div. of Somerset, Feb. 1956–1987. Economic Sec. to the Treasury, 1962–63; Minister of State, Board of Trade, 1963–64. Mem., Lord Chancellor's Adv. Cttee on Public Records, 1960–62; Joint Hon. Sec.: UN Parly Group, 1961–62; Conservative Parly Finance Group, 1961–62; Mem., Select Cttee on House of Lords Reform, 1962; Founder Chairman: Select Cttee on Public Expenditure, 1971–73; All-Party Maritime Affairs Parly Gp, 1984–87; Mem., Select Cttee on Privilege, 1972–87; Chairman: Select Cttee on Public Accounts, 1974–79; 1922 Cttee, 1972–84; Liaison Cttee of Select Cttee Chairmen, 1974–83; (founder) Select Cttee on Treasury and Civil Service Affairs, 1979–83; (first) Public Accounts Commn, 1984–87; Cons. Party Organisation, 1965–67; Burke Club, 1968–79. President: (founder) Anglo-Polish Cons. Soc., 1972–74; Nat. Union of Conservative and Unionist Assocs, 1981–82; Cons. Parly European Community Reform Gp, 1985–87; Vice-Chm., British American Parly Gp, 1978–81. Jt Leader, British-American Parly Gp delegns to USA, 1978, 1980; Leader, Jt British Parly Gp delegn to China, IPU, 1982. Dir, James Beattie Ltd, 1965–79. Pres., Inst. of Freight Forwarders Ltd, 1988–89; Vice-Pres., British Insurance Brokers Assoc., 1978–; Patron, Assoc. of Insurance Brokers, 1974–77. Visiting Fellow, Univ. of Lancaster Business School, 1970–82. Member: Panel of Judges, Templeton Foundn, 1984–; Management Council, GB-Sasa Kawa Foundn, 1984–. Patron, Human Ecology Foundn, 1987–; Governor, Hatfield Coll., Durham Univ., 1988–. Commodore, 1962, Admiral, 1974–87, House of Commons Yacht Club. Hon. Col, 155 (Wessex) Regt, RCT (Volunteers), 1972–82, Hon. Life Mem., Instn of RCT, 1983. Lecturer, broadcaster. Mem. Court of Assts, Fruiterers' Co. (Master, 1990); elected first Freeman of Taunton Deane Borough, 1977. FRSA 1986. *Publications:* Investing Simplified, 1959; pamphlets, and articles on financial and international affairs (incl. The Case for a Bill of Rights, How to Bring Government Expenditure within Parliamentary Control, A New Competition Policy). *Recreations:* travel, gardening, sailing. *Address:* 9 Tufton Court, Tufton Street, SW1P 3QH. *T:* 071–222 1922; Cothay Barton, Greenham, Wellington, Somerset TA21 0JR. *Clubs:* Carlton, Pratt's; Royal Thames Yacht, Royal Western Yacht.

See also R. D. L. Du Cann.

Du CANN, Richard Dillon Lott, QC 1975; a Recorder of the Crown Court, since 1982; *b* 27 Jan. 1929; *yr s* of late C. G. L. Du Cann; *m* 1955, Charlotte Mary Sawtell; two *s* two *d*. *Educ:* Steyning Grammar Sch.; Clare Coll., Cambridge. Called to Bar, Gray's Inn, 1953; Bencher, 1980; Treasury Counsel, Inner London QS, 1966–70; Treasury Counsel, Central Criminal Court, 1970–75. Chairman: Criminal Bar Assoc., 1977–80; Bar of England and Wales, 1980–81. *Publications:* (with B. Hayhoe) The Young Marrieds, 1954; The Art of the Advocate, 1964. *Address:* 3 Raymond Buildings, Gray's Inn, WC1R 5BH. *T:* 071–831 3833.

See also Col Rt Hon. Sir E. D. L. du Cann.

DUCAT-AMOS, Air Comdt Barbara Mary, CB 1974; RRC 1971; Matron-in-Chief, Princess Mary's Royal Air Force Nursing Service, 1972–78, and Director of Royal Air Force Nursing Service, 1976–78; Nursing Sister, Medical Department, Cable and Wireless plc, 1978–85; *b* 9 Feb. 1921; *d* of late Captain G. W. Ducat-Amos, Master Mariner, and late Mrs M. Ducat-Amos. *Educ:* The Abbey Sch., Reading; St Thomas's Hosp., London (The Nightingale Trng Sch.). SRN 1943; CMB Pt 1 1948. PMRAFNS, 1944–47: served in RAF Hosps, UK and Aden; further training; nursing in S Africa and SW Africa, 1948–52; rejoined PMRAFNS, 1952: served in RAF Hosps as General Ward and Theatre Sister, UK, Germany, Cyprus, Aden and Changi (Singapore); Matron 1967; Sen. Matron 1968; Principal Matron 1970. QHNS 1972–78. Nat. Chm., Girls' Venture Corps, 1982–91. CStJ 1975. *Recreations:* music, theatre, travel. *Address:* c/o Barclays Bank, Wimbledon Common Branch, 75 High Street, SW19 5EQ. *Club:* Royal Air Force.

DUCCI, Dr Roberto, Grand Cross, Italian Order of Merit; Ambassador of Italy to the Court of St James's, 1975–80; Professor of Political Science, Rome University, since 1982; *b* 8 Feb. 1914; *s* of Gino Ducci and Virginia Boncinelli; *m* 1951, Wanda Matyjewicz; two *s*. *Educ:* Univ. of Rome (Dr of Law). Entered Foreign Service, 1937; served: Ottawa, 1938; Newark, NJ, 1940; Italian Delegn to Peace Conf., 1946; Warsaw, 1947; Rio de Janeiro, 1949; Italian Delegn to NATO and OEEC, 1950–55; Chm., Drafting Cttee, Rome Treaties, 1956–57; Asst Dir, General Economic Affairs, 1955–57; Ambassador to Finland, 1958–62; Head, Italian Delegn to Brussels, UK-EEC Conf., 1961–63; Dep. Dir-Gen. for Political Affairs, 1963–64; Ambassador to: Yugoslavia, 1964–67; Austria, 1967–70; Director-General for Political Affairs, 1970–75. Counsellor of State, 1980–84, Hon. Pres. Sect. Council of State, 1984. Mem. Bd, European Investment Bank, 1958–68; Chm., Press Agency Italia, 1984. *Publications:* Prima Età di Napoleone, 1933; Questa Italia, 1948; L'Europa Incompiuta, 1971; D'Annunzio Vivente, 1973; Contemporanei, 1976; L'Innocenza (poems), 1978; 24 Hours at No 4 Grosvenor Square, 1979; Il Libro di Musica (poems), 1981; I Capintesta, 1982; Candidato a Morte, 1983; numerous political essays and articles. *Recreations:* riding, collecting frail things. *Address:* Via Belsiana 35, 00187 Rome, Italy. *Club:* Circolo della Caccia (Rome).

duCHARME, Gillian Drusilla Brown; Headmistress, Benenden School, since 1985; *b* 23 Jan. 1938; *d* of Alfred Henry Brown and Alice Drusilla Grant; *m* 1969, Jean Louis duCharme (marr. diss.). *Educ:* Girton College, Cambridge. BA 1960, MA 1964. Visitors' Dept, British Council, London and Oxford, 1964–66; Chm., French Dept and Head of Upper Sch., Park Sch., Brookline, Mass, 1969–77; Dir of Admissions, Concord Acad., Concord, Mass, 1977–80; Headmistress, The Town Sch., New York City, 1980–85. *Recreations:* tennis, cross-country skiing, photography, theatre, film, travel. *Address:* Benenden School, Cranbrook, Kent TN17 4AA. *T:* Cranbrook (0580) 240592.

DUCHÊNE, Louis-François; author; *b* 17 Feb. 1927; *s* of Louis Adrien Duchêne and Marguerite Lucienne Duchêne (*née* Lainé); *m* 1952, Anne Margaret Purves; one *d*. *Educ:* St Paul's Sch.; London Sch. of Economics. Leader writer, Manchester Guardian, 1949–52; Press attaché, High Authority, European Coal and Steel Community, Luxembourg, 1952–55; Correspondent of The Economist, Paris, 1956–58; Dir, Documentation Centre of Action Cttee for United States of Europe (Chm. Jean Monnet), Paris, 1958–63; Editorial writer, The Economist, London, 1963–67. Director: Internat. Inst. for Strategic Studies, 1969–74; European Res. Centre, Sussex Univ., 1974–82. *Publications:* (ed) The Endless Crisis, 1970; The Case of the Helmeted Airman, a study of W. H. Auden, 1972; New Limits on European Agriculture, 1985; (ed with G. Shepherd) Managing Industrial Change in Western Europe, 1987. *Address:* 3 Powis Villas, Brighton, East Sussex BN1 3HD. *T:* Brighton (0273) 29258.

DUCIE, 6th Earl of *cr* 1837; **Basil Howard Moreton;** Baron Ducie, 1763; Baron Moreton, 1837; *b* 15 Nov. 1917; *s* of Hon. Algernon Howard Moreton (2nd *s* of 4th Earl) (*d* 1951), and Dorothy Edith Annie, *d* of late Robert Bell; *S* uncle 1952; *m* 1950, Alison May, *d* of L. A. Bates, Pialba, Queensland; three *s* one *d*. *Heir:* *s* Lord Moreton, *qv*. *Address:* Tortworth House, Tortworth, Wotton-under-Edge, Glos.

DUCK, Hywel Ivor; Director of Fisheries, Secretariat General, Council of Ministers of European Communities, since 1987; *b* 12 June 1933; *s* of Dr Ernest Frank Duck and Minnie Isabel Duck (*née* Peake); *m* 1980, Dr Barbara Elisabeth Huwe; one *s* one *d*. *Educ:* King's School, Canterbury; Trinity College, Cambridge (MA); Diplôme d'Etudes Supérieures Européennes, Nancy. Called to the Bar, Gray's Inn, 1956. Foreign Office, 1956; served Warsaw, FO, Cairo, Khartoum, Damascus; Second later First Sec., Bonn, 1964; DSAO, later FCO, 1968; Consul (Commercial), Zürich and Dep. Dir, British Export Promotion in Switzerland, 1970–73; Head of Div., Secretariat Gen., Council of Ministers, EC, 1973–75; Dir of Ops and Translation, 1975–84; Dir, Directorate-Gen. for Agriculture and Fisheries, 1984–87. *Recreation:* classical music. *Address:* 170 rue de la Loi, 1048 Brussels, Belgium. *T:* 322 234 62 67. *Clubs:* United Oxford & Cambridge University; American and Common Market (Brussels).

DUCKER, Herbert Charles, BSc London; NDA; Field Officer Groundnut Research, under the Federal Ministry of Agriculture, Rhodesia and Nyasaland, now retired; *b* 13 May 1900; *s* of Charles Richard and Gertrude Louise Ducker; *m* 1925, Marjorie, *y d* of late Charles Tuckfield, AMICE; two *s* one *d*. *Educ:* Kingston Grammar Sch., Kingston-on-Thames; South-Eastern Agricultural Coll., Wye; Imperial Coll. of Science, South Kensington. British Cotton Industry Research Assoc. Laboratories; Asst Cotton Specialist, Nyasaland, 1922; Cotton Specialist, Empire Cotton Growing Corporation, Nyasaland, 1925–56; Superintendent-Curator of the National Botanic Gardens, Salisbury, Southern Rhodesia, under the Federal Ministry of Agriculture, of Rhodesia and Nyasaland, 1957. *Publications:* Annual Reports on Cotton Research work 1925–55, carried out in Nyasaland; articles on cotton growing. *Recreation:* fishing. *Address:* Pleasant Ways, MP 13, Mount Pleasant, Harare, Zimbabwe. *Club:* Royal Over-Seas League.

DUCKMANTON, Sir Talbot (Sydney), Kt 1980; CBE 1971; General Manager, Australian Broadcasting Commission, 1965–82 (Deputy General Manager, 1964–65); *b* 26 Oct. 1921; *s* of Sydney James Duckmanton; *m* 1947, Florence Simmonds (decd); one *s* three *d*; *m* 1984 (marr. diss.). Joined Australian Broadcasting Commission, 1939. War Service: AIF and RAAF. President: Asia-Pacific Broadcasting Union, 1973–77; Commonwealth Broadcasting Assoc., 1975–82. Pres., Sydney Legacy, 1964–65; Mem. Council, Aust. Administrative Staff Coll., 1967–82. Trustee, Visnews, 1965–82; Hon. Life Trustee, Cttee for Economic Develt of Australia. FAIM. *Address:* PO Box E148, St James, Sydney, NSW 2000, Australia. *Clubs:* Legacy, Australian, Tattersalls (Sydney).

DUCKWORTH, Brian Roy; His Honour Judge Duckworth; a Circuit Judge, since 1983; *b* 26 July 1934; *s* of Roy and Kathleen Duckworth; *m* 1964, Nancy Carolyn Duckworth, JP (*née* Holden); three *s* one *d*. *Educ:* Sedbergh Sch.; Worcester Coll., Oxford (MA). Called to Bar, Lincoln's Inn, 1958; a Recorder of the Crown Court, 1972–83; Member: Northern Circuit; Bar Council, 1979–82. Councillor, Blackburn RDC, 1960–74 (Chm. 1970–72). Liaison Judge and Hon. Pres., South Cumbria Magistracy, 1987–. *Recreations:* golf, gardening, motor sport. *Address:* c/o The Crown Court, Lancaster Road, Preston PR1 2PD. *T:* Preston (0772) 23431. *Clubs:* St James's (Manchester); Pleasington Golf.

DUCKWORTH, Eric; *see* Duckworth, W. E.

DUCKWORTH, John Clifford; FEng 1975; FIEE, FInstP, FInstE; Chairman, Lintott plc, since 1980; *b* 27 Dec. 1916; *s* of late H. Duckworth, Wimbledon, and of Mrs A. H. Duckworth (*née* Woods); *m* 1942, Dorothy Nancy Wills; three *s*. *Educ:* KCS, Wimbledon; Wadham Coll., Oxford (MA). FIEE 1957; FInstP 1957; SFInstE 1957. Telecommunications Research Establishment, Malvern: Radar Research and Development, 1939–46; National Research Council, Chalk River, Ont., 1946–47; Atomic Energy Research Establishment, Harwell, 1947–50; Ferranti Ltd: Chief Engineer, Wythenshawe Laboratories, 1950–54; Nuclear Power Engineer, Brit. Electricity Authority, 1954–58; Central Electricity Authority, 1957–58; Chief Research and Development Officer, Central Electricity Generating Board, 1958–59; Man. Dir., Nat. Research Develt Corp., 1959–70. Pres., Institute of Fuel, 1963–64; Vice-Pres., Parliamentary and Scientific Cttee, 1964–67. Chm., Science Mus. Adv. Council, 1972–84; Trustee, Science Mus., 1984–90. Vice-Pres., IEE, 1974–77. *Recreations:* swimming, colour photography, cartography. *Address:* Huefield, Helford Passage, Falmouth TR11 5LD. *Club:* Athenæum.

DUCKWORTH, Sir Richard Dyce, 3rd Bt, *cr* 1909; *b* 30 Sept. 1918; *s* of Sir Edward Dyce Duckworth, 2nd Bt, and Cecil Gertrude, *y d* of Robert E. Leman; *S* father, 1945; *m* 1942, Violet Alison, *d* of Lieut-Col G. B. Wauchope, DSO; two *s*. *Educ:* Marlborough Coll. Started business in 1937, retired 1969. *Recreations:* sailing, golf, squash, shooting. *Heir: s* Edward Richard Dyce Duckworth [*b* 13 July 1943; *m* 1976, Patricia, *o d* of Thomas Cahill; one *s* one *d*]. *Address:* Dunwood Cottage, Shootash, Romsey, Hants. *T:* Romsey (0794) 513228.

DUCKWORTH, Prof. Roy, CBE 1987; MD; FRCS, FDSRCS, FRCPath; Emeritus Professor of Oral Medicine, University of London; Dean, The London Hospital Medical College, since 1986; *b* Bolton, 19 July 1929; *s* of Stanley Duckworth and Hilda Evelyn Moores; *m* 1953, Marjorie Jean Bowness, Flimby; two *s* one *d*. *Educ:* King George V Sch., Southport; Univ. of Liverpool (BDS; MD 1964); Univ. of London. FDSRCS 1957; FRCPath 1973; FRCS 1986. Served RAF Dental Br., 1953–55. Nuffield Fellow, RPMS and Guy's Hosp. Dental Sch., 1959–61; The London Hosp. Med. College: Sen. Lectr in Oral Medicine, 1961; Reader in Oral Medicine, 1965; Dean of Dental Studies, 1969–75; Prof. and Head, Dept of Oral Medicine, 1968–90. Consultant in Oral Medicine, The London Hosp., 1965–90. Dean, Faculty of Dental Surgery, RCS, 1983–86. Civil Consultant: in Dental Surg., to Army, 1977–90; in Oral Medicine and Oral Path., to RN, 1982–90; Temp. Consultant, WHO, 1973; British Council Visitor, 1977. Vis. Prof. in many countries. President: British Soc. of Periodontology, 1972–73; British Soc. for Oral Medicine, 1986–87; BDA, 1990–91. Chm., Standing Dental Adv. Cttee, Dept of Health, 1988– (Mem., 1984–88); Member: Adv. Council on Misuse of Drugs, 1977–85; Medicines Commn, 1980–83; Council, Fédération Dentaire Internationale, 1981–; GDC, 1984–89. Scientific Adviser, British Dental Jl, 1975–82; Editor, Internat. Dental Jl, 1981–90. *Publications:* contrib. professional jls. *Recreation:* sailing. *Address:* The London Hospital Medical College, Turner Street, E1 2AD. *T:* 071-377 7602.

DUCKWORTH, (Walter) Eric, OBE 1991; PhD; FEng 1980; FIM, FInstP; Managing Director, Fulmer Ltd (formerly Fulmer Research Institute), 1969–90; *b* 2 Aug. 1925; *s* of Albert Duckworth and Rosamund (*née* Biddle); *m* 1949, Emma Evans; one *s*. *Educ:* Cambridge Univ. (MA, PhD). Research Manager, Glacier Metal Co., 1955; Asst Director, BISRA, 1966; Chm., Yarsley Technical Centre, 1973–89; Director: Ricardo Consulting Engineers plc, 1978–85; H. Darnell Ltd, 1982–; Fleming Technol. Investment Trust plc, 1984–90. Chm., Council of Science and Technology Insts, 1977–78; first Charter Pres., Instn of Metallurgists, 1974–75; Pres., Assoc. of Independent Res. and Technol. Organisations (formerly Assoc. of Indep. Contract Res. Organs), 1978–79, 1988–89; Hon. Treas., Metals Soc., 1981–84; Chm., Professional Affairs Bd, Inst. of Metals, 1985–88. Member: Res. and Technol. Cttee, 1979–88, and Indust. Policy Cttee, 1983–88, Council, 1988–89, CBI; Nominations Cttee, 1983–88, Standing Cttee on Industry, 1988–, Engrg Council; Engrg Bd, SERC, 1985–87. Chm., Christian Nationals Evangelism Commn, 1974–; Trustee, Comino Foundn, 1981–; Vice-Pres., St Mary's Hosp. Med. Sch., 1976–88; Mem. Court, Brunel Univ., 1978–85. Liveryman: Worshipful Co. of Scientific Instrument Makers; Co. of Engineers; Freeman, City of London. First Edwin Liddiard Meml Lectr, London Metallurgical Soc. of Inst. of Metals, 1982. Hon. DTech Brunel, 1976; DUniv Surrey, 1980. Editor, 1978–85, Chm., Editorial Bd, 1985–, Materials and Design. *Publications:* A Guide to Operational Research, 1962, 3rd edn 1977; Statistical Techniques in Technological Research, 1968; Electroslag Refining, 1969; Manganese in Ferrous Metallurgy, 1976; *circa* 100 contribs to learned and other jls on many topics. *Recreations:* gardening, photography, changing other people's attitudes. *Address:* Orinda, Church Lane, Stoke Poges, Bucks SL2 4PB. *T:* Fulmer (0753) 645778. *Club:* Stoke Poges Golf.

du CROS, Sir Claude Philip Arthur Mallet, 3rd Bt *cr* 1916; *b* 22 Dec. 1922; *s* of Sir (Harvey) Philip du Cros, 2nd Bt, and of Dita, *d* of late Sir Claude Coventry Mallet, CMG; *S* father, 1975; *m* 1st, 1953, Mrs Christine Nancy Tordoff (marr. diss. 1974), *d* of late F. R. Bennett, Spilsby, Lincs; one *s*; 2nd, Mrs Margaret Roy Cutler (marr. diss. 1982), *d* of late R. J. Frater, Gosforth, Northumberland. *Heir: s* Julian Claude Arthur Mallet du Cros [*b* 23 April 1955; *m* 1984, Patricia, *o d* of Gerald Wyatt, Littlefield School, Liphook; one *s* one *d*]. *Address:* Long Meadow, Ballaugh Glen, IoM.

DUDA, Dr Karel; Ambassador of the Czech and Slovak Federal Republic to the Court of St James's, since 1990; *b* 31 May 1926; *s* of Karel Duda and Marie Dudová; *m* 1952, Danuše Barešová; one *s* two *d*. *Educ:* Charles Univ., Prague (LLD). Ministry of Finance, 1950–54; Min. of Foreign Affairs, 1954–; Ambassador to USA, 1963–69. *Address:* Czechoslovak Embassy, 25 Kensington Palace Gardens, W8 4QY.

DUDBRIDGE, Bryan James, CMG 1961; retired from HM Overseas Civil Service, Nov. 1961; Deputy Director, formerly Associate Director, British Council of Churches Department of Christian Aid, 1963–72; *b* 2 April 1912; *o s* of late W. Dudbridge, OBE, and of Anne Jane Dudbridge; *m* 1943, Audrey Mary, *o d* of late Dr and Mrs Heywood, Newbury; two *s* one *d*. *Educ:* King's Coll. Sch., Wimbledon; Selwyn Coll., Cambridge. Appointed to Colonial Administrative Service as Cadet in Tanganyika, 1935; Asst Dist Officer, 1937; Dist Officer, 1947; Sen. Dist Officer, 1953; Actg Provincial Commr, Southern Province; Administrative Officer (Class IIA), 1955, and Actg Provincial Commissioner (Local Government); Provincial Commissioner, Western Province, 1957; Minister for Provincial Affairs, 1959–60, retd. *Publications:* contrib. Journal of African Administration, and Tanganyika Notes and Records. *Recreations:* natural history, beagling, wildfowl. *Address:* Red Rock Bungalow, Elm Grove Road, Topsham, Exeter EX3 0EJ. *T:* Exeter (0392) 874468. *Club:* Commonwealth Trust.

DUDBRIDGE, Prof. Glen, PhD; FBA 1984; Professor of Chinese and Fellow of University College, Oxford, since 1989; *b* 2 July 1938; *s* of George Victor Dudbridge and Edna Kathleen Dudbridge (*née* Cockle); *m* 1965, Sylvia Lo (Lo Fung-young); one *s* one *d*. *Educ:* Bristol Grammar School; Magdalene College, Cambridge (MA, PhD); New Asia Institute of Advanced Chinese Studies, Hong Kong. MA Oxon. Nat. Service, RAF, 1957–59. Research Fellow, Magdalene College, Cambridge, 1965; Lectr in Modern Chinese, 1965–85 and Fellow, Wolfson Coll., 1966–85, Univ. of Oxford; Prof. of Chinese and Fellow, Magdalene Coll., Univ. of Cambridge, 1985–89. Visiting Professor: Yale Univ., 1972–73; Univ. of California, Berkeley, 1980. *Publications:* The Hsi-yu chi: a study of antecedents to the sixteenth century Chinese novel, 1970; The Legend of Miao-shan, 1978 (Chinese edn, 1990); The Tale of Li Wa: study and critical edition of a Chinese story from the ninth century, 1983; contribs to Asia Major, Harvard Jl of Asiatic Studies, New Asia Jl. *Address:* Oriental Institute, Pusey Lane, Oxford OX1 2LE.

DUNNING, Richard Scarborough; Finance Director, Department of the Environment, since 1990; *b* 29 Nov. 1950; *s* of Sir John Scarborough Dunning and of Lady (Enid Grace) Dunning; *m* 1987, Priscilla Diana Russell; two *s*. *Educ:* Cheltenham Coll.; Jesus Coll., Cambridge (MA 1st Cl. Hons History). Joined DoE, 1972; Private Sec. to John Smith, MP, 1976–78; Principal, 1977; Asst Sec., 1984; Sec., Cttee of Inquiry into Conduct of Local Govt Business, 1985–86; Under Sec., 1990. *Recreations:* gardening, walking. *Address:* 3 Dora Road, SW19 7EZ. *T:* 081-879 7441.

DUDGEON, Air Vice-Marshal Antony Greville, CBE 1955; DFC 1941; *b* 6 Feb. 1916; *s* of late Prof. Herbert William Dudgeon, Guy's Hosp. and Egyptian Government Service; *m* 1942, Phyllis Margaret, *d* of late Group Capt. John McFarlane, OBE, MC, AFC, Lowestoft, Suffolk; one *s* one *d*. *Educ:* Eton; RAF Cranwell; Staff Coll., Flying Coll.; Polytechnic London. RAF Service, 1933–68, in UK, Europe, Near, Middle and Far East, USA; personnel work, training, operations, flight safety, organisation of new formations, liaison with civilian firms and youth organisations; NATO Staff; 6 command appointments; 3,500 hours as pilot. Manager, Professional Staff Services, McKinsey & Co., Paris, 1968–78; representative, France, Grangersol Ltd, 1978–81. *Publications:* A Flying Command (under pen-name Tom Dagger), 1962; *autobiographical works:* The Luck of the Devil (1929–41), 1985; Wings Over North Africa (1941–43), 1987; The War That Never Was (1941), 1991; several stories contributed to Blackwood's Magazine and to aeronautical jls. *Recreations:* writing, photography, swimming; languages (French, Egyptian). *Address:* 43 Winchendon Road, SW6 5DH. *Clubs:* Royal Air Force, Hurlingham.

DUDLEY, 4th Earl of, *cr* 1860; **William Humble David Ward;** Baron Ward, 1644; Viscount Ednam, 1860; *b* 5 Jan. 1920; *e s* of 3rd Earl of Dudley, MC, TD, and Rosemary Millicent, RRC (*d* 1930), *o d* of 4th Duke of Sutherland; *S* father, 1969; *m* 1st, 1946, Stella (marr. diss., 1961), *d* of M. A. Carcano, KCMG, KBE; one *s* twin *d*; 2nd, 1961, Maureen Swanson; one *s* five *d*. *Educ:* Eton; Christ Church, Oxford. Joined 10th Hussars, 1941, Adjt, 1944–45; ADC to Viceroy of India, 1942–43. Served War of 1939–45 (wounded). Pres., Baggeridge Brick Co. Ltd. *Heir: s* Viscount Ednam, *qv*. *Address:* 6 Cottesmore Gardens, W8 5PR; Vention House, Putsborough, N Devon. *Clubs:* White's, Pratt's; Royal Yacht Squadron.

DUDLEY, Baroness (14th in line), *cr* 1439–1440 (called out of abeyance, 1916); **Barbara Amy Felicity Hamilton;** *b* 23 April 1907; *o d* of 12th Baron Dudley and Sybil Augusta (*d* 1958), *d* of late Rev. Canon Henry William Coventry; *S* brother, 1972; *m* 1929, Guy Raymond Hill Wallace (*d* 1967), *s* of late Gen. Hill Wallace, CB, RHA; three *s* one *d*; *m* 1980, Charles Anthony Crosse Hamilton. *Recreations:* floral water-colours (has exhibited Royal Watercolour Society, Conduit St); gardening. *Heir: e s* Hon. Jim Anthony Hill Wallace [*b* 9 Nov. 1930; *m* 1962, Nicola Jane, *d* of Lt-Col Philip William Edward Leslie Dunsterville; two *s*]. *Address:* Hill House, Kempsey, Worcestershire. *T:* Worcester (0905) 820253.

DUDLEY, Bishop Suffragan of, since 1977; **Rt. Rev. Anthony Charles Dumper;** *b* 4 Oct. 1923; *s* of Charles Frederick and Edith Mildred Dumper; *m* 1948, Sibylle Anna Emilie Hellwig; two *s* one *d*. *Educ:* Surbiton Grammar School; Christ's Coll., Cambridge (MA); Westcott House, Cambridge. Relief Worker, Germany, 1946–47; ordained, 1947; Curate, East Greenwich, 1947–49; Vicar of South Perak, Malaya, 1949–57; Archdeacon of North Malaya, 1955–64; Vicar of Penang, Malaya, 1957–64; Dean of St Andrew's Cathedral, Singapore, 1964–70; Vicar of St Peter's, Stockton on Tees, and Rural Dean of Stockton, 1970–77. *Publication:* Vortex of the East, 1963. *Recreations:* walking, gardening. *Address:* Bishop's House, Halesowen Road, Cradley Heath, West Midlands. *T:* 021–550 3407.

DUDLEY, Archdeacon of; *see* Gathercole, Ven. J. R.

DUDLEY, Prof. Hugh Arnold Freeman, CBE 1988; FRCSE, FRCS, FRACS; Professor of Surgery, St Mary's Hospital, London University, 1973–88, now Emeritus; *b* 1 July 1925; *s* of W. L. and Ethel Dudley; *m* 1947, Jean Bruce Lindsay Johnston; two *s* one *d*. *Educ:* Heath Grammar Sch., Halifax; Edinburgh and Harvard Univs. MB, ChB Edin. 1947; ChM (Gold Medal and Chiene Medal) Edin. 1958; FRCSE 1951; FRACS 1965; FRCS 1974. Research Fell., Harvard Univ., 1953–54; Lecturer in Surgery, Edinburgh Univ., 1954–58; Sen. Lectr, Aberdeen Univ., 1958–63; Foundation Prof. of Surgery, Monash Univ., Melbourne, 1963–72. President: Surgical Res. Soc. of Australasia, 1968 (Corresp. Mem.); Biol. Engrg Soc. of GB, 1978–80; Surgical Res. Soc. of GB, 1981. Dir., Cambmac Medical Instruments. Regl Research Co-ordinator, NW Thames RHA, 1989–. Chm., Med. Writers Gp, 1980–83, Mem. Cttee, 1984–87, Soc. of Authors. Corresponding Member: Surgical Res. Soc. of SA; Vascular Soc. of SA; Hon. Mem., Hellenic Soc. of Experimental Medicine; Hon. Fellow: Amer. Surgical Assoc.; Amer. Assoc. for the Surgery of Trauma; S African Coll. of Surgeons. Chm. Editorial Board of Br. Jl of Surgery and of Br. Jl Surgery Soc. Ltd, 1980–88; Associate Editor, BMJ, 1988–91. *Publications:* Principles of General Surgical Management, 1958; (jtly); Access and Exposure in Abdominal Surgery, 1963; (jtly) Guide for House Surgeons in the Surgical Unit, 5th edn 1974, to 8th edn 1988; (ed) Rob and Smith's Operative Surgery, 3rd and 4th edns, 1976–; Hamilton Bailey's Emergency Surgery, 10th edn 1977, 11th edn 1986; Communication in Medicine and Biology, 1977; (ed) Aid to Clinical Surgery, 1978, 4th edn 1988; (jtly) Practical Procedures for House Officers, 1988; (jtly) Clinical Statistics, 1990; papers in med. and sci. jls. *Recreations:* missing pheasants; annoying others; surgical history. *Address:* House of Broombrae, Glenbuchat, Strathdon, Aberdeenshire AB3 8UA. *T:* Glenkindie (09756) 41341.

DUDLEY, Prof. Norman Alfred, CBE 1977; PhD; FEng; Lucas Professor of Engineering Production, 1959–80, Emeritus Professor 1981, University of Birmingham; Head of Department of Engineering Production and Director of Lucas Institute of Engineering Production, 1956–80; Chartered Engineer; *b* 29 Feb. 1916; *s* of Alfred Dudley; *m* 1940, Hilda Florence, *d* of John Miles; one *s* two *d*. *Educ:* Kings Norton Grammar Sch.;

Birmingham Coll. of Technology. BSc London, PhD Birmingham. FEng 1981. Industrial training and appts: H. W. Ward & Co. Ltd, 1932–39; Imperial Typewriter Co. Ltd, 1940–45; Technical Coll. Lectr, 1945–52; Sen. Lectr, Wolverhampton and Staffs, 1948–52; Lectr in Eng. Prod., 1952, Reader, 1956, University of Birmingham. Chm., Manufacturing Processes Div., Birmingham Univ. Inst. for Advanced Studies in Engineering Sciences, 1965–68. Director: Birmingham Productivity Services Ltd; West Midlands Low Cost Automation Centre. Member: SRC Manufacturing Technol. Cttee; SRC and DoI Teaching Company Cttee, 1977–80. Chm., Cttee of Hds of Univ. Depts of Production Studies, 1970–80. Governor: Dudley and Staffs Tech. Coll., and Walsall and Staffs Tech. Coll., 1955–60; Letchworth Coll. of Technol., 1964–66. Member: Council, West Midlands Productivity Assoc.; Council Internat. Univ. Contact for Management Education, 1957; Council, Instn of Prod. Engineers, 1959–61 (Chm., Research Cttee, 1965–66; Viscount Nuffield Meml Lectr, 1969); UK Delegn to UNCSAT Geneva, 1963; W Midlands Economic Planning Council, 1970–78; Adv. Panel on Economic Develt, West Midlands Metropolitan CC, 1976–77; Council, Nat. Materials Handling Centre. Pres., Midlands Operational Research Soc., 1966–80. Mem., Ergonomics Res. Soc.; Emeritus Mem., Internat. Inst. of Production Engrg Research. FBIM; Hon. FIProdE. Hon. Member: Japanese Industrial Management Assoc.; Internat. Foundn of Prodn Research. Hon. DTech Loughborough, 1981. Editor, International Journal of Production Research, 1961–80. J. D. Scaife Medal, 1958. *Publications:* Work Measurement: Some Research Studies, 1968; (co-ed) Production and Industrial Systems, 1978; various papers on Engineering Production. *Address:* 37 Abbots Close, Knowle, Solihull, West Midlands. *T:* Knowle (0564) 775976.

DUDLEY, Rose; *see* Tremain, Rose.

DUDLEY, William Stuart; Associate Designer of the National Theatre, since 1981; *b* 4 March 1947; *s* of William Dudley and Dorothy Stacey. *Educ:* Highbury Sch., London; St Martin's School of Art; Slade School of Art. DipAD, BA Fine Art; UCL Postgrad. Dip. Fine Art. First production, Hamlet, Nottingham Playhouse, 1970; subseq. prodns include: The Duchess of Malfi and Man is Man, Royal Court, 1971; *National Theatre*, 1971–: Tyger, 1974; The Good-Natured Man, 1974; The Passion, 1977; Lavender Blue, 1977; The World Turned Upside Down, Has Washington Legs?, 1978; Dispatches, Lost Worlds, Lark Rise, Candleford, Undiscovered Country (SWET award, Designer of the Year, 1980), 1979; Good Soldier Schweyk, 1982; Cinderella, 1983; The Mysteries, Real Inspector Hound/The Critic, 1985 (Laurence Olivier (formerly SWET) Award, Designer of the Year, 1985); Futurists, 1986; Waiting for Godot, 1987; Cat on a Hot Tin Roof, The Shaugraun, and The Changeling, 1988; Bartholemew Fair, 1988; The Crucible, 1990; *Royal Court:* Live Like Pigs, 1972; Merry-Go-Round, 1973; Magnificence, 1975; The Fool, 1975; Small Change, 1976; Hamlet, 1980; Kafka's Dick, 1986; Etta Jenks, 1990; *RSC:* Twelfth Night, 1974; Ivanov, 1976; That Good Between Us, 1977; Richard III, The Party, Today, 1984; Merry Wives of Windsor, 1985; A Midsummer Night's Dream, Richard II, 1986; Kiss Me Kate, 1987; *West End:* Mutiny, Piccadilly, 1985; *Opera:* WNO: Il barbiere di Siviglia, 1976; Metropolitan, NY: Billy Budd, 1978; Glyndebourne: Die Entführung aus dem Serail, 1980; Il barbiere di Siviglia, 1981; Royal Opera: Les Contes d'Hoffman (sets), 1980, 1986; Don Giovanni, 1981; The Cunning Little Vixen, 1990; Bayreuth: Der Ring des Nibelungen, 1983; Der Rosenkavalier, 1984; Salzburg Festival: Un ballo in maschera, 1989; The Ship, Glasgow, 1990. Designer of the Year, Laurence Olivier Awards, 1986. *Recreation:* playing the concertina. *Address:* Flat D, 30 Crooms Hill, SE10. *T:* 081–858 8711.

DUDLEY-SMITH, Rt. Rev. Timothy; Bishop Suffragan of Thetford, 1981–92; *b* 26 Dec. 1926; *o s* of Arthur and Phyllis Dudley Smith, Buxton, Derbyshire; *m* 1959, June Arlette MacDonald; one *s* two *d. Educ:* Tonbridge Sch.; Pembroke Coll., and Ridley Hall, Cambridge. BA 1947, MA 1951; Certif. in Educn 1948. Deacon, 1950; priest, 1851; Asst Curate, St Paul, Northumberland Heath, 1950–53; Head of Cambridge Univ. Mission in Bermondesy, 1953–55; Hon. Chaplian to Bp of Rochester, 1953–60; Editor, Crusade, and Editorial Sec. of Evangelical Alliance, 1955–59; Asst Sec. of Church Pastoral-Aid Soc., 1959–65, Sec., 1965–73; Archdeacon of Norwich, 1973–81; Commissary to Archbp of Sydney, 1971–; Exam. Chap. to Bp of Norwich, 1971–85. President: Evangelical Alliance, 1987–91; C of E Evangelical Council, 1990–92. *Publications:* Christian Literature and the Church Bookstall, 1963; What Makes a Man a Christian?, 1966; A Man Named Jesus, 1971; Someone who Beckons, 1978; Lift Every Heart, 1984; A Flame of Love, 1987; Songs of Deliverance, 1988; Praying with the English Hymn Writers, 1989; contributor to various hymn books. *Recreations:* reading, verse, woodwork, family and friends. *Address:* 9 Ashlands, Ford, Salisbury, Wilts SP4 6DY. *T:* Salisbury (0722) 326417. *Club:* Norfolk (Norwich).

DUDLEY-WILLIAMS, Sir Alastair (Edgcumbe James), 2nd Bt *cr* 1964, of Exeter; Director, Wildcat Consultants, since 1986; *b* 26 Nov. 1943; *s* of Sir Rolf Dudley Dudley-Williams, 1st Bt and of Margaret Helen, *er d* of F. E. Robinson, OBE; *S* father, 1987; *m* 1972, Diana Elizabeth Jane, twin *d* of R. H. C. Duncan; three *d. Educ:* Pangbourne College. Hughes Tool Co. (Texas), 1962–64; Bay Drilling Corp. (Louisiana), 1964–65; Bristol Siddeley Whittle Tools Ltd, 1965–67; Santa Fe Drilling Co., 1967–72; Inchcape plc, 1972–86. *Recreations:* shooting, fishing. *Heir: b* Malcolm Philip Edgcumbe Dudley-Williams [*b* 10 Aug. 1947; *m* 1973, Caroline Anne Colina, twin *d* of R. H. C. Duncan; two *s* one *d*]. *Address:* The Corner Cottage, Brook, near Godalming, Surrey GU8 5UQ. *Club:* Royal Cornwall Yacht.

DUE, Ole; Kt, Order of Dannebrog 1970; President, Court of Justice of European Communities, since 1988; *b* 10 Feb. 1931; *s* of Stationmaster H. P. Due and Jenny Due (*née* Jensen); *m* 1954, Alice Maud Halkier Nielsen; three *s* one *d. Educ:* Copenhagen Univ. (Law degree, 1955). Ministry of Justice, Copenhagen: civil servant, 1955; Head of Div., 1970; Head of Dept, 1975; Appeal Court Judge *ai*, 1978; Judge, Court of Justice of EC, 1979–88. Legal Counsellor to Danish Delegn, negotiations of adhesion to EC, 1970–72; Mem., Danish Delegn to Hague Conf. on private internat. law, 1964–76. Hon. Member: Gray's Inn; King's Inn, Dublin. *Publications:* (ed jtly) EF-Karnov 1973, 1975; (ed) EF-lovregister, 1973–75; (jtly) Juridisk Grundbog, 1975; (jtly) Kommenteret færdselslov, 1979; articles on community law, private internat. law and legal technique. *Recreation:* hiking. *Address:* Court of Justice of the European Communities, Boulevard C. Adenauer, L-2925 Luxembourg. *T:* 4303–2200.

DUFF, Rt. Hon. Sir (Arthur) Antony, GCMG 1980 (KCMG 1973; CMG 1964); CVO 1972; DSO 1944; DSC; PC 1980; Deputy Secretary, Cabinet Office, 1980–85; *b* 25 Feb. 1920; *s* of late Adm. Sir Arthur Allen Morison Duff, KCB; *m* 1944, Pauline Marion, *d* of Capt. R. H. Bevan, RN, and *widow* of Flt-Lieut J. A. Sword; one *s* two *d* (and one step *s*). *Educ:* RNC, Dartmouth. Served in RN, 1937–46. Mem., Foreign (subseq. Diplomatic) Service, 1946; 3rd Sec., Athens, Oct. 1946; 2nd Sec., 1948; 2nd Sec., Cairo, 1949; 1st Sec., 1952; transferred Foreign Office, Private Sec. to Minister of State, 1952; 1st Sec., Paris, 1954; Foreign Office, 1957; Bonn, 1960; Counsellor, 1962; British Ambassador to Nepal, 1964–65; Commonwealth Office, 1965–68; FCO, 1968–69; Dep. High Comr, Kuala Lumpur, 1969–72; High Comr, Nairobi, 1972–75; Dep. Under-Sec. of State, 1975–80, Dep. to Perm. Under-Sec. of State, 1976–80, FCO. Dep. Governor, Southern Rhodesia, 1979–80. *Address:* c/o National Westminster Bank, 17 The Hard, Portsea, Hants PO1 3DU. *Club:* Army and Navy.

DUFF, Graham; Field Director (Operations), Crown Prosecution Service, since 1990; *b* 7 Jan. 1947; *s* of Norman Alexander Duff and Doris Duff; *m* 1st, 1969, Lalage Ann Ibbotson (marr. diss. 1978); 2nd, 1987, Jacqueline Tremble; one *d. Educ:* Newcastle Royal Grammar Sch.; Univ. of Durham (BA (Hons) Law); Univ. of Newcastle upon Tyne (Grad. Cert Ed). Called to the Bar, Lincoln's Inn, 1976; Court Clerk, Newcastle upon Tyne Magistrates, 1976; Prosecuting Solicitor, Greater Manchester, 1978; Sen. Prosecuting Solicitor, 1981, Area Prosecuting Solicitor, 1985, Lancashire; Asst Dir of Public Prosecutions, 1986; Br. Crown Prosecutor, Inner London, 1986; Chief Crown Prosecutor, Northumbria and Durham, 1987. *Recreations:* breeding foreign birds, old Riley motor cars, riding, target shooting. *Address:* Crown Prosecution Service, 4–12 Queen Anne's Gate, SW1H 9AZ. *T:* 071–273 8146.

DUFF, Patrick Craigmile, CMG 1982; *b* 6 Jan. 1922; *o s* of late Archibald Craigmile Duff, ICS, and Helen Marion (*née* Phillips); *m* 1st, 1947, Pamela de Villeneuve Graham (*osp*); 2nd, 1950, Elizabeth Rachel, *d* of late Rt Rev. R. P. Crabbe (Bishop of Mombasa, 1936–53) and Mrs Crabbe; two *d. Educ:* Wellington Coll., Berks; New Coll., Oxford (MA 1946). War service, 1941–42. HMOCS, 1942–63: Tanganyika; Kenya; CRO, 1964–65; ODM/ODA, 1966–74; Head, West Indian and Atlantic Dept, FCO, 1975–80; Head, British Develt for E Africa, FCO, 1980–82. *Recreations:* making music, fell walking, ball games. *Address:* 6 Christchurch Road, Winchester, Hants SO23 9SR. *T:* Winchester (0962) 865200. *Club:* Commonwealth Trust.

DUFF, Col Thomas Robert G.; *see* Gordon-Duff.

DUFF GORDON, Sir Andrew (Cosmo Lewis), 8th Bt, *cr* 1813; *b* 17 Oct. 1933; *o s* of Sir Douglas Duff Gordon, 7th Bt and Gladys Rosemary (*d* 1933), *e d* of late Col Vivien Henry, CB; *S* father, 1964; *m* 1st, 1967, Grania Mary (marr. diss. 1975), *d* of Fitzgerald Villiers-Stuart, Ireland; one *s*; 2nd, 1975, Eveline Virginia, BA, *d* of S. Soames, Newbury; three *s. Educ:* Repton. Served with Worcs Regiment and 1st Bn Ches Regt, 1952–54. Mem. of Lloyd's, 1962–. *Recreations:* golf, shooting, skiing. *Heir: s* Cosmo Henry Villiers Duff Gordon, *b* 18 June 1968. *Address:* Downton House, Walton, Presteigne, Powys. *T:* New Radnor 223; 27 Cathcart Road, SW10. *Clubs:* City University; Kington Golf; Sunningdale Golf.

DUFFELL, Maj.-Gen. Peter Royson, CBE 1988 (OBE 1981); MC 1966; Commander, British Forces Hong Kong, and Major-General Brigade of Gurkhas, since 1989; *b* 19 June 1939; *s* of late Roy John Duffell, Lenham, Kent, and of Ruth Doris (*née* Gustaffson); *m* 1982, Ann Murray, *d* of late Col Basil Bethune Neville Woodd, Rolvenden, Kent; one *s* one *d. Educ:* Dulwich Coll. psc, rcds. FRGS 1975. Commnd 2nd KEO Gurkha Rifles, 1960; Staff Coll., Camberley, 1971; Bde Major 5 Bde, 1972–74; MA to C-in-C UKLF, 1976–78; Comdt 1st Bn 2nd KEO Gurkha Rifles, 1978–81; Col GS, MoD, 1981–83; Comdr Gurkha Field Force, 1984–85; COS 1 (BR) Corps, 1986–87; RCDS, 1988. *Recreations:* travel, reading, golf, tennis, collecting pictures, photography. *Address:* c/o Drummonds, 49 Charing Cross, SW1A 2DX. *Clubs:* Travellers'; Hong Kong, Royal Hong Kong Jockey, Royal Hong Kong Golf, Shek O Country (Hong Kong).

DUFFERIN AND CLANDEBOYE, 10th Baron *cr* 1800 (Ire.); **Francis George Blackwood;** Bt (Ire.) 1763; Bt (UK) 1814; Retired Chemical Engineer; now in private practice as a Consulting Engineer; *b* 20 May 1916; *s* of Captain Maurice Baldwin Raymond Blackwood, DSO, RN (*d* 1941) (3rd *s* of 4th Bt) and Dorothea (*d* 1967), *d* of Hon. G. Bertrand Edwards, Sydney, NSW; *S* to baronetcy of cousin, 1979 and to barony of kinsman, 5th Marquess of Dufferin and Ava, 1988; *m* 1941, Margaret Alice, *d* of Hector Kirkpatrick, Lindfield, NSW; two *s* one *d. Educ:* Knox Grammar School; Sydney Technical Coll. (ASTC). ARACI, FIEAust. Worked in the chemical industry, mainly for Union Carbide, Australia Ltd (formerly Timbrol Ltd) as a design engineer, 1936–78. *Recreations:* community service and domestic. *Heir: s* Hon. John Francis Blackwood, architect [*b* 18 Oct. 1944; *m* 1971, Kay Greenhill; one *s* one *d*.]. *Address:* 408 Bobbin Head Road, North Turramurra, NSW 2074, Australia. *T:* 44 5189. *Club:* Royal Automobile of Australia.

DUFFETT, Roger Hugh Edward; Secretary, Royal College of Surgeons of England, since 1988; *b* 20 Jan. 1936; *s* of Dr Edward Cecil Duffett and Cicely Duffett (*née* Haw); *m* 1959, Angela Julie Olden; one *s* one *d. Educ:* Sherborne Sch. (Scholar); Peterhouse, Cambridge (Scholar; MA). Commissioned RA (Nat. Service), 1954–56; British Petroleum Co.: joined 1956; refinery process foreman, 1959–60; research, molecular sieve properties of synthetic zeolites and reactions of frozen free radicals, 1960–64; creation of computerised manpower planning models, 1964–68; creation and operation of computerised linear programming models for integrated oil ops, 1968–71; application of mathematical models to corporate planning, 1971–73; planning, internat. ops for lubricants, 1973–78; negotiation and op., crude oil contracts, 1978–79; consultancy for analysis and resolution of orgnl problems: in shipping, research, engrg, marketing and personnel; for management of secondary schools, Cambs; Unicef (UK); employment of secondees to Enterprise Bds, 1979–87; orgn and systems consultant for BP Oil Internat., for Riding for Disabled, 1987–88. Member: Management Cttee, Clare Park, 1979–83; Riding for Disabled, 1990–; Dir, Quinta Nursing Home, Farnham, 1983–88. *Publications:* contribs to learned jls. *Recreations:* golf, coarse gardening, creating brain teasers, writing, reading. *Address:* Royal College of Surgeons, 35–43 Lincoln's Inn Fields, WC2A 3PN. *T:* 071–405 3474.

DUFFUS, Sir Herbert (George Holwell), Kt 1966; *b* 30 Aug. 1908; *e s* of William Alexander Duffus, JP, and Emily Henrietta Mary (*née* Holwell); *m* 1939, Elsie Mary (*née* Hollinsed); no *c. Educ:* Cornwall Coll., Jamaica. Admitted as Solicitor: Jamaica, 1930, England, 1948. Resident Magistrate, Jamaica, 1946–58; Called to the Bar, Lincoln's Inn, 1956; acted as Puisne Judge, Jamaica, 1956–58; Puisne Judge, Jamaica, 1958–62; Judge of Appeal, Jamaica, 1962–64; Pres. Court of Appeal, 1964–67; Chief Justice of Jamaica, 1968–73; Acting Governor General of Jamaica, 1973. Chairman: Commn of Enquiry into Prisons of Jamaica, 1954; Commn of Enquiry into the administration of justice and police brutality in Grenada, WI, 1974; Police Service Commission (Jamaica), 1958–68. Sole Commissioner, Enquiries into: Maffesanti Affair, 1968; Operations of Private Land Developers in Jamaica, 1975–76; Barbados Govt's Private Enterprises, 1977–78; Electoral Malpractices (Jamaican Local Govt Elecns), 1986. Pres., Boy Scouts Assoc., Jamaica, 1967–70. Chm., Western Regl Council, Cheshire Homes, 1975–89. Chancellor of the Church (Anglican) in Jamaica, 1973–76. *Address:* 6 Braywick Road, PO Box 243, Liguanea PO, Kingston 6, Jamaica. *T:* 92–70171; 119 Main Street, Witchford, Ely, Cambs CB6 2HQ. *T:* Ely (0353) 663281.

DUFFY, Sir (Albert Edward) Patrick, Kt 1991; PhD; MP (Lab) Sheffield, Attercliffe, since 1970; *b* 17 June 1920. *Educ:* London Sch. of Economics (BSc(Econ.), PhD); Columbia Univ., Morningside Heights, New York, USA. Served War of 1939–45, Royal Navy, incl. flying duties with FAA. Lecturer, University of Leeds, 1950–63, 1967–70. Visiting Professor: Drew Univ., Madison, NJ, 1966–70; Amer. Grad. Sch. of Internat. Business, 1982–. Contested (Lab) Tiverton Division of Devon, 1950, 1951, 1955. MP

(Lab) Colne Valley Division of Yorks, 1963–66; PPS to Sec. of State for Defence, 1974–76; Parly Under-Sec. of State for Defence (Navy), MoD, 1976–79; opposition spokesman on defence, 1979–80, 1983–84. Chairman: PLP Economic and Finance Gp, 1965–66, 1974–76; Trade and Industry Sub-Cttee of Select Cttee on Expenditure, 1972–74; PLP Defence Cttee, 1984; Vice-Chairman: PLP Defence Gp, 1979–84; Anglo-Irish Gp, 1979–. Pres., N Atlantic Assembly, 1988–90 (Mem. 1979–; Chm., Defence Co-op. sub-cttee, 1983–87). *Publications:* contrib. to Economic History Review, Victorian Studies, Manchester School, Annals of Amer. Acad. of Pol. and Soc. Sci., etc. *Address:* 153 Bennetthorpe, Doncaster, South Yorks. *Clubs:* Naval; Trades and Labour (Doncaster).

DUFFY, Antonia Susan, (Mrs P. J. Duffy); *see* Byatt, A. S.

DUFFY, Daniel; Chairman, Transport and General Workers' Union, since 1988; *b* 3 Oct. 1929; *s* of late William and Mary Duffy; *m* Susan (*née* Salton). *Educ:* St Mungo's Academy. Transport Driver, 1947; joined S. H. & M. Assoc., 1947. Member: Exec. Council, Scottish Commercial Motormen's Union, 1960–71 (Pres., 1969–71); TGWU Exec. Council, 1971–; TUC General Council, 1988–. *Recreation:* bowls. *Address:* TGWU, Transport House, Smith Square, SW1P 3JB. *T:* 071–828 7788.

DUFFY, Most Rev. Joseph; *see* Clogher, Bishop of, (RC).

DUFFY, Joseph Michael; Hon. Mr Justice Duffy; High Court Judge, Hong Kong, since 1987; *b* 6 Dec. 1936; *s* of John Joseph Duffy and Mary Frances Mullaney; *m* 1962, Patricia Ann Scott; one *s* two *d*. *Educ:* St Andrews Univ. (MA, LLB). Solicitor, Scotland, 1965, Hong Kong, 1976; Advocate, Scotland, 1981; QC Hong Kong, 1983. Apprentice, then Solicitor, Dundee, 1963–72; Crown Counsel and Sen. Crown Counsel, Hong Kong, 1972–76 and 1978–80 (Solicitor, Hong Kong, 1976–78); Dep. Dir and Dir of Public Prosecutions, Hong Kong, 1980–86; Solicitor-General, Hong Kong, 1986–87. *Recreations:* golf, tennis, running, music. *Address:* 53 Mount Nicholson Road, Hong Kong. *T:* 8910446; 7 Bonspiel Gardens, Broughty Ferry, Dundee. *T:* Dundee (0382) 75492. *Clubs:* Shek O Country, Ladies Recreation, Royal Hong Kong Jockey (Hong Kong).

DUFFY, Maureen Patricia, FRSL 1985; author; *b* 1933; *o c* of Grace Rose Wright. *Educ:* Trowbridge High Sch. for Girls; Sarah Bonnell High Sch. for Girls; King's College, London (BA). Chairman: Greater London Arts Literature Panel, 1979–81; Authors Lending and Copyright Soc., 1982–; British Copyright Council, 1989– (Vice Chm., 1981–86); Pres., Writers' Guild of GB, 1985–88 (Jt Chm., 1977–78); Co-founder, Writers' Action Group, 1972–79; Vice-Pres., Beauty Without Cruelty, 1975–. *Publications:* That's How It Was, 1962; The Single Eye, 1964; The Microcosm, 1966; The Paradox Players, 1967; Lyrics for the Dog Hour (poetry), 1968; Wounds, 1969; Rites (play), 1969; Love Child, 1971; The Venus Touch, 1971; The Erotic World of Faery, 1972; I want to Go to Moscow, 1973; A Nightingale in Bloomsbury Square (play), 1974; Capital, 1975; Evesong (poetry), 1975; The Passionate Shepherdess, 1977; Housespy, 1978; Memorials of the Quick and the Dead (poetry), 1979; Inherit the Earth, 1980; Gorsaga, 1981 (televised as First Born, 1988); Londoners: an elegy, 1983; Men and Beasts, 1984; Collected Poems 1949–84, 1985; Change (novel), 1987; A Thousand Capricious Chances: Methuen 1889–1989, 1989; Illuminations (novel), 1991; *visual art:* Prop art exhibn (with Brigid Brophy, *qv*), 1969. *Address:* 18 Fabian Road, SW6 7TZ. *T:* 071–385 3598.

DUFFY, Sir Patrick; *see* Duffy, Sir A. E. P.

DUFFY, Peter Clarke, QPM 1979; Director General, Federation Against Copyright Theft, 1985–89; *b* Hamilton, Scotland, 10 May 1927; *s* of Hugh Duffy and Margaret Archibald; *m* 1958, S. M. Joyce (marr. diss.); one *s* two *d*. *Educ:* Our Lady's High Sch., Motherwell. MInstAM 1983. Served Army, Western Arab Corps, Sudan Defence Force, 1945–48 (War Medal). Joined Metropolitan Police, 1949; Criminal Investigation Dept, 1954; Comdr, New Scotland Yard, 1976–83; Dir, Investigations, Fedn Against Copyright Theft, 1983–85. *Recreations:* golf, living. *Club:* Royal Automobile.

DUFTY, (Arthur) Richard, CBE 1971; FSA; Master of the Armouries in HM Tower of London, 1963–76; *b* 23 June 1911; *s* of T. E. Dufty, and Beatrice (*née* Holmes); *m* 1937, Kate Brazley (*née* Ainsworth) (*d* 1991); one *s* two *d*. *Educ:* Rugby; Liverpool School of Architecture. War service in RN. On staff of Royal Commn on Historical Monuments, 1937–73, Sec. and Gen. Editor 1962–73, with responsibility for Nat. Monuments Record, inc. Nat. Buildings Record, 1964–73. Pres., Soc. of Antiquaries, 1978–81; Member: Ancient Monuments Bd for England, 1962–73 and 1977–80; Council for Places of Worship, 1976–81; Council, Nat. Army Museum, 1963–83; Royal Commn on Historical Monuments, 1975–85. Vice-Chm., Cathedrals Advisory Commission, 1981–88. Chairman: Farnham (Buildings Preservation) Trust, 1968– (recipient of The Times Conservation Award, 1986); British Cttee, Corpus Vitrearum Medii Aevi, 1970–84 (sponsored by British Acad.); London Dio. Adv. Cttee, 1973–84; Standing Cttee on Conservation of West Front of Wells Cathedral, 1974–85. Trustee: Coll. of Arms Trust, 1978–; Marc Fitch Fund, 1978–. Directed, for Soc. of Antiquaries, repair and rehabilitation of Kelmscott, William Morris's home in Oxfordshire, 1964–67. Hon. Freeman, Armourers and Brasiers' Co., 1974. Hon. Mem., Art Workers' Guild, 1977. ARIBA 1935–74; FSA 1946. DLitt Lambeth, 1988. London Conservation Award, GLC, 1984. *Publications:* Kelmscott: an illustrated guide, 1970; Morris Embroideries: the prototypes, 1985; Exoticism and a Chair by Philip Webb, 1986; ed 5 RCHM Inventories and 5 occasional publications; Intr. Vol. to Morris's Story of Cupid and Psyche, 1974. *Recreations:* viewing sales; taking pleasure in Victoriana and Art Nouveau; music. *Address:* 46 Trafalgar Court, Farnham, Surrey GU9 7QF. *Clubs:* Athenæum, Arts, Naval.

DUGARD, Arthur Claude, CBE 1969; Chairman, Cooper & Roe Ltd, 1952–79, retired (formerly Joint Managing Director); *b* 1 Dec. 1904; *s* of Arthur Thomas Turner Dugard, Nottingham; *m* 1931, Christine Mary Roe, Nottingham; two *s*. *Educ:* Oundle Sch., Northants. Joined Cooper & Roe Ltd, Knitwear manufacturers, 1923 (Dir, 1936; Man. Dir, 1947). President: Nottingham Hosiery Manufrs Assoc., 1952–53; Nat. Hosiery Manufrs Fedn, 1959–61; Nottingham Chamber of Commerce, 1961–62. First Chm., CBI North Midland Regional Council, 1965–66; Chm. British Hosiery & Knitwear Export Gp, 1966–68; Mem. East Midlands Economic Planning Council, 1967–72. *Recreation:* golf. *Address:* 16 Hollies Drive, Edwalton, Nottingham NG12 4BZ. *T:* Nottingham (0602) 233217.

DUGDALE, family name of **Baron Crathorne.**

DUGDALE, Mrs John; *see* Dugdale, K. E. H.

DUGDALE, John Robert Stratford; Lord-Lieutenant of Salop, since 1975; *b* 10 May 1923; 2nd *s* of Sir William Francis Stratford Dugdale, 1st Bt, and Margaret, 2nd *d* of Sir Robert Gordon Gilmour, 1st Bt; *m* 1956, Kathryn Edith Helen (*see* K. E. H. Dugdale); two *s* two *d*. *Educ:* Eton; Christ Church, Oxford. Chm., Telford Develt Corp., 1971–75. KStJ 1976. *Recreation:* sleeping. *Address:* Tickwood Hall, Much Wenlock, Salop. *T:* Telford (0952) 882644. *Clubs:* Brooks's, White's.
See also Sir William Dugdale, Bt.

DUGDALE, Kathryn Edith Helen, (Mrs John Dugdale), DCVO 1984 (CVO 1973); JP; a Lady-in-Waiting to the Queen, since 1985; *b* 4 Nov. 1923; *d* of Rt Hon. Oliver Stanley, PC, MC, MP and Lady Maureen Vane-Tempest Stewart; *m* 1956, John Robert Stratford Dugdale, *qv*; two *s* two *d*. *Educ:* many and varied establishments. Served with WRNS. Temp. Woman of the Bedchamber to The Queen, 1955–60, Extra Woman of the Bedchamber 1960–72; Woman of the Bedchamber, 1972–85. Pres., Shropshire Community Council. JP Salop, 1964. Employee of Greater London Fund for the Blind. *Recreations:* gardening, reading. *Address:* Tickwood Hall, Much Wenlock, Salop. *T:* Telford (0952) 882644.

DUGDALE, Norman, CB 1974; Chairman, Bryson House (formerly Belfast Voluntary Welfare Society), since 1985; Member of the Board, since 1986, and Chairman, Northern Ireland Advisory Committee, since 1988, British Council; Permanent Secretary, Department (formerly Ministry) of Health and Social Services, Northern Ireland, 1970–84; *b* 6 Feb. 1921; *yr s* of William and Eva Dugdale, Burnley, Lancs; *m* 1949, Mary Whitehead. *Educ:* Burnley Grammar Sch.; Manchester Univ. (BA). Asst Principal, Bd of Trade, 1941; Min. of Commerce, NI, 1948; Asst Sec., Min. of Health and Local Govt, NI, 1955; Sen. Asst Sec., Min. of Health and Local Govt, NI, 1964; Second Sec., Min. of Health and Social Services, 1968. Governor, Nat. Inst. for Social Work, London, 1965–84; Mem. Court, NUU, 1971–84. Hon. DLitt NUU, 1983. *Publications: poems:* The Disposition of the Weather, 1967; A Prospect of the West, 1970; Night-Ferry, 1974; Corncrake in October, 1978; Running Repairs, 1983; Limbo, 1991; contribs to various literary periodicals. *Recreations:* procrastinating; next week-end.

DUGDALE, Peter Robin, CBE 1987; Director, Guardian Royal Exchange, since 1977; Chairman, Trade Indemnity plc, since 1980; *b* 12 Feb. 1928; *s* of Dr James Norman Dugdale and Lilian (*née* Dolman); *m* 1957, Esmé Cyraine, *d* of L. Norwood Brown; three *s*. *Educ:* Canford; Magdalen Coll., Oxford (MA). Joined Union Insurance Soc. of Canton, Hong Kong, 1949; merged with Guardian Assurance, London, 1960; Marine and Aviation Underwriter, 1965; Pres., Guardian Insurance Company of Canada, 1973; Gen. Man., Guardian Royal Exchange, 1976; Man. Dir, Guardian Royal Exchange Assurance, 1978–90; Chm., Aviation and General Insurance Co. Ltd, 1982–84. Chairman: British Insurance Assoc., 1981–82; Assoc. of British Insurers, 1987–89. Master, Worshipful Co. of Insurers, 1989–90; Hon. Life Mem., Inst. of London Underwriters, 1985. Gov., Canford, 1980–. CBIM 1984. *Recreation:* flat-coated retrievers. *Address:* Cherry Copse, Broad Lane, Hambledon, Hants PO7 4QS. *T:* Hambledon (0705) 632462. *Club:* Oriental.

DUGDALE, Sir William (Stratford), 2nd Bt *cr* 1936; CBE 1982; MC 1943; JP; DL; Director and Chairman, General Utilities PLC, since 1988; *b* 29 March 1922; *er s* of Sir William Francis Stratford Dugdale, 1st Bt, and Margaret, 2nd *d* of Sir Robert Gordon Gilmour, 1st Bt, of Liberton and Craigmillar; *S* father, 1965; *m* 1st, 1952, Lady Belinda Pleydell-Bouverie (*d* 1961), 2nd *d* of 6th Earl of Radnor; one *s* three *d*; 2nd, 1967, Cecilia Mary, *e d* of Sir William Malcolm Mount, 2nd Bt, *qv*; one *s* one *d*. *Educ:* Eton; Balliol Coll., Oxford. Served War of 1939–45, Grenadier Guards (Captain), Admitted as Solicitor, 1949. Director: Phoenix Assurance Co., 1968–85; Lee Valley Water Co., 1989–90; North Surrey Water Co., 1989–; Chairman: Severn Trent Water Authority, 1974–83; National Water Council, 1982–83; Birmingham Diocesan Board of Finance, 1979–. Steward, Jockey Club, 1985–87. Chm., Wolverhampton Racecource PLC, 1965–. Governor, Lady Katherine Leveson's Hosp., Temple Balsall. Mem., Warwicks CC, 1964–76; High Steward, Stratford upon Avon, 1977. JP 1951, DL 1955, High Sheriff 1971, Warwicks. *Publications:* contrib. DNB. *Heir: s* William Matthew Stratford Dugdale, *b* 22 Feb. 1959. *Address:* Blyth Hall, Coleshill, near Birmingham B46 2AD. *T:* Coleshill (0675) 462203; Merevale Hall, Atherstone CV9 2HG. *T:* Atherstone (0827) 713143; 24 Bryanston Mews West, W1H 7FR. *T:* 071–262 2510. *Clubs:* Brooks's, White's, MCC; Jockey (Newmarket).
See also J. R. S. Dugdale, Baron Hazlerigg.

DUGGAN, Gordon Aldridge; HM Diplomatic Service; High Commissioner in Singapore, since 1991; *b* 12 Aug. 1937; *s* of late Joseph Nathan Duggan and Elizabeth Aldridge; *m* 1969, Erica Rose Anderssen; one *s* two *d*. *Educ:* Liverpool Collegiate Sch.; Lincoln Coll., Oxford. BA, BPhil. FO, 1963–66; Canberra, 1966–69; FCO, 1969–72; Information Officer, Bonn, 1972–74; Head of Chancery, Jakarta, 1974–76; Canberra, 1976–79; FCO, 1979–80; Commercial and Economic Counsellor, Lagos, 1981–84; Consul-Gen., Zürich, Dir of British Export Promotion in Switzerland, and Consul-Gen., Liechtenstein, 1985–88; Hd of Commercial Management and Exports Dept, FCO, 1988–89; (on secondment) Dir, Project Develt, NEI, 1989–90. *Recreations:* armchair sport, jazz, theatre, walking, countryside. *Address:* c/o Foreign and Commonwealth Office, King Charles Street, SW1A 2AH. *Club:* United Oxford & Cambridge University.

DUGGAN, Rt. Rev. John Coote; *b* 7 April 1918; *s* of Rev. Charles Coote Whittaker Duggan, BD and Ella Thackeray Duggan (*née* Stritch); *m* 1948, Mary Elizabeth Davin; one *s* one *d* (and one *d* decd). *Educ:* High School, Dublin; Trinity Coll., Dublin (Schol.). Moderator (1st cl.)Men. and Moral Sci., 1940; Bernard Prize, Div. Test. (2nd cl.); BA 1940; BD 1946. Deacon 1941; Priest 1942. Curate Asst: St Luke, Cork, 1941–43; Taney, Dublin, 1943–48; Hon. Clerical Vicar, Christ Church Cath., 1944–48; Incumbent: Portarlington Union, Kildare, 1948–55; St Paul, Glenageary, Dublin, 1955–69; Westport and Achill Union, Tuam, 1969–70; Archdeacon of Tuam, 1969–70; Bishop of Tuam, Killala and Achonry, 1970–85. Exam. Chaplain to Archbp of Dublin, 1958–69; Examiner in BD Degree, Univ. of Dublin, 1960–69. Editor, Irish Churchman's Almanack, 1958–69. *Publications:* A Short History of Glenageary Parish, 1968. *Recreation:* fishing. *Address:* 15 Beechwood Lawn, Rochestown Avenue, Dun Laoghaire, Co. Dublin. *Club:* Kildare Street and University (Dublin).

DUGUID, Andrew Alexander; Head of Market Services, Lloyd's of London, since 1988; *b* 22 June 1944; *s* of Wing Comdr (retd) Alexander Gordon Duguid and Dorothy Duguid (*née* Duder); *m* 1967, Janet Hughes; two *s* one *d*. *Educ:* Whitby Dist High Sch.; Ashbury Coll., Ottawa; Sidcot Sch.; LSE (BSc Econs); Univ. of Lancaster (MA Marketing). Res. Assistant, Brunel Univ., 1967–69; Marketing Executive: Interscan Ltd, 1969–72; Ogilvy Benson and Mather, 1972–73; joined DTI as Principal, 1973; Prin. Pvte Sec. to Sec. of State for Industry, 1977–79; Asst Sec., seconded to Prime Minister's Policy Unit, 1979; returned to set up Policy Planning Unit, Dept of Industry, later DTI, 1982; Under Sec., DTI, 1985–86; Head of Regulatory Services, Lloyd's, 1986–88. Non-exec. Dir, Kingsway Public Relations, 1982–85. *Publication:* (with Elliott Jaques) Case Studies in Export Organisation, 1971. *Recreations:* tennis, ski-ing, walking, canoeing. *Address:* 1 Binden Road, W12 9RJ. *T:* 081–743 7435. *Club:* Hartswood.

DUGUID, Prof. James Paris, CBE 1979; MD, BSc; FRCPath; Professor of Bacteriology, University of Dundee, 1967–84; Consultant, Tayside Health Board, 1963–84; *b* 10 July 1919; *s* of late Maj.-Gen. David Robertson Duguid, CB, and Mary Paris; *m* 1944, Isobel Duff; one *s* three *d*. *Educ:* Edinburgh Academy; Univ. of Edinburgh (MB ChB Hons 1942; BSc 1st Cl. Hons 1943; MD (Gold Medal) 1949); FRCPath 1966. Lectr, Sen. Lectr and Reader, Univ. of Edinburgh, 1944–62; Prof. of Bacteriology, Univ. of St Andrews, 1963–67; Director of Postgrad. Medical Educn, Univ. of Dundee, 1968–71, Dean of

Faculty of Medicine, 1971–74, Mem. Univ. Court, 1977–81. Cons. Adviser in Microbiology, Scottish Home and Health Dept, 1967–85, Mem. Adv. Cttee on Medical Research, 1967–71; Member: Eastern Regional and Tayside Health Bds, 1967–77; Adv. Cttee on Laboratory Services, Scottish Health Serv. Council, 1967–74 (Chm., Epidemiology Sub-cttee, 1966–71); Scottish Health Services Planning Council, 1974–77 (Member: Adv. Cttee on New Developments in Health Care, 1976–84; Scientific Services Adv. Gp, 1975–79; Chm., Microbiology and Clin. Immunology Cttees, 1975–77); Jt Cttee on Vaccination and Immunisation, Health Services Councils, 1967–74; GMC, 1975–81; Council for Professions Supp. to Medicine, 1978–86; Independent Adv. Gp on Gruinard Island, 1986–87. Hon. Mem., Pathol Soc. of GB and Ireland, 1985. Asst Editor: Jl of Pathology and Bacteriology, 1959–68; Jl of Medical Microbiology, 1968–71. *Publications:* (co-ed) Mackie and McCartney, Medical Microbiology, 11th edn 1969, 12th edn 1973, 13th edn 1978; (ed) Mackie and McCartney, Practical Medical Microbiology, 1989; scientific papers on bacterial fimbriae, adhesins, biotyping and phylogeny, airborne infection, and the action of penicillin. *Recreations:* grandchildren, gardening, atheism. *Address:* 69 Dalkeith Road, Dundee DD4 7HF. *T:* Dundee (0382) 456956; Hillside, Glenborrodale, Argyll.

DUKAKIS, Michael Stanley; Governor, Commonwealth of Massachusetts, 1975–79, and 1983–90; *b* 3 Nov. 1933; *s* of Panos Dukakis and Euterpe Boukis-Dukakis; *m* 1963, Katharine Dickson; one *s* two *d. Educ:* Brookline High Sch. (Dip. 1951); Swarthmore Coll., Pa (BA 1955); Harvard Law Sch. (JD 1960). Attorney, Hill & Barlow, Boston, Mass, 1960–74; Lectr and Dir, Intergovtl Studies, John F. Kennedy Sch. of Govt, Harvard Univ., 1979–82. Moderator of public television's The Advocates, 1971–73. State Representative, Brookline, Mass, 1963–71; Democratic Candidate for the Presidency of the USA, 1988. *Publication:* (with Rosabeth Moss Kanter) Creating the Future: Massachusetts comeback and its promise for America, 1988. *Recreations:* walking, playing tennis, gardening. *Address:* 85 Perry Street, Brookline, Mass 02146, USA.

DUKE, family name of **Baron Merrivale.**

DUKE, Cecil Howard Armitage; Director of Establishments and Organisation, Ministry of Agriculture, Fisheries and Food, 1965–71; *b* 5 May 1912; *s* of late John William Duke and Gertrude Beatrice (née Armitage); *m* 1939, Eleanor Lucy (née Harvie); one *s* one *d. Educ:* Selhurst Gram. Sch.; LSE. RNVR, 1942–45 (Corvettes). Entered Civil Service, 1929; Asst Princ., 1940; Princ., 1945; Private Sec. to Lord Presidents of the Council, 1951–53; Asst Sec., Land Drainage Div. and Meat Div., 1953; Under-Sec., 1965. *Recreations:* walking, gardening, watching Sussex cricket. *Address:* 22 Fairways Road, Seaford, East Sussex BN25 4EN. *T:* Seaford (0323) 894338.

DUKE, Maj.-Gen. Sir Gerald (William), KBE 1966 (CBE 1945); CB 1962; DSO 1945; DL; *b* 12 Nov. 1910; *e s* of late Lieut-Col A. A. G. Duke, Indian Army; *m* 1946, Mary Elizabeth (*d* 1979), *er d* of late E. M. Burn, Church Stretton; one *s* one *d. Educ:* Dover Coll.; RMA Woolwich; Jesus Coll., Cambridge. Commissioned RE, 1931; served Egypt and Palestine, 1936–39; War of 1939–45, in Western Desert and Italy; BGS Eighth Army, 1944; North West Europe, Brig. Q (Movements), 21st Army Group, 1944; CRE 49th Div., 1945. Chief Engineer, Malaya Comd, 1946; idc 1948; Mil. Attaché, Cairo, 1952–54; Comdt Sch. of Mil. Engineering, 1956–59. Commodore Royal Engineer Yacht Club, 1957–60. DPS, WO, 1959–62; Engineer-in-Chief (Army), 1963–65; retired. Col Comdt, RE, 1966–75. Chm., SS&AFA, Kent, 1973–85; Pres., Scout Assoc., Kent, 1974–86; Vice-Pres., Hockey Assoc., 1965–. Governor of Dover Coll. FICE. DL Kent, 1970. *Recreations:* sailing, golf. *Address:* Little Barnfield, Hawkhurst, Kent TN18 4PX. *T:* Hawkhurst (0580) 753214. *Clubs:* Royal Ocean Racing; Rye Golf.

DUKE, Rt. Rev. Michael Geoffrey H.; see Hare Duke.

DUKE, Neville Frederick, DSO 1943; OBE 1953; DFC and Two Bars, 1942, 1943, 1944; AFC 1948; MC (Czech) 1946; Managing Director, Duke Aviation; Technical Adviser and Consultant Test Pilot; *b* 11 Jan. 1922; *s* of Frederick and Jane Duke, Tonbridge, Kent; *m* 1947, Gwendoline Dorothy Fellows. *Educ:* Convent of St Mary and Judds Sch., Tonbridge, Kent. Joined Royal Air Force (cadet), 1940, training period, 1940; 92 Fighter Sqdn, Biggin Hill, 1941; Desert Air Force: 112 Fighter Sqdn, Western Desert, 1941–42, 92 Fighter Sqdn, Western Desert, 1943, Chief Flying Instructor, 73 Operational Training Unit, Egypt, 1943–44, Commanding 145 Sqdn Italy (Fighter), 1944, 28 enemy aircraft destroyed. Hawker Aircraft Ltd test flying, 1945; Empire Test Pilots Sch., 1946; RAF high speed flight, 1946 (world speed record); test flying Aeroplane and Armament Experimental Estab., Boscombe Down, 1947–48; resigned from RAF as Sqdn Leader, 1948; test flying Hawker Aircraft Ltd, 1948; Commanding 615 (County of Surrey) Sqdn, Royal Auxiliary Air Force, Biggin Hill, 1950; Chief Test Pilot, Hawker Aircraft Ltd, 1951–56 (Asst Chief, 1948–51). FRSA 1970; ARAeS 1948. World records: London-Rome, 1949; London-Karachi, 1949; London-Cairo, 1950. World Speed Record, Sept. 1953. Closed Circuit World Speed Record, 1953. Gold Medal Royal Danish Aero Club, 1953; Gold Medal, Royal Aero Club, 1954; two De la Vaux Medals, FAI, 1954; Segrave Trophy, 1954; Queen's Commendation, 1955. Member: RAF Escaping Soc.; United Service & Royal Aero Club (Associate); Royal Aeronautical Soc. FRSA. *Publications:* Sound Barrier, 1953; Test Pilot, 1953; Book of Flying, 1954; Book of Flight, 1958; The Crowded Sky (anthology), 1959. *Recreations:* sporting flying, yachting. *Address:* Everton Grange, Lymington, Hants SO41 0ZR. *Clubs:* Royal Air Force; Royal Cruising; Royal Naval Sailing, Royal Lymington Yacht.

DUKES, Alan M.; TD (FG) Kildare, since 1981; President, Fine Gael Party, since 1987 (Leader, 1987–90); *b* 22 April 1945; *s* of James and Rita Dukes; *m* 1968, Fionnuala Corcoran; two *d. Educ:* Colaiste Mhuire, Dublin; University College Dublin (MA). Chief Economist, Irish Farmers' Assoc., 1967–72; Dir, Irish Farmers' Assoc., Brussels, 1973–76; Personal Advr to Comr of European Communities, 1977–80. Minister for Agriculture, 1981–82; opposition spokesman on agric., March-Dec. 1982; Minister for Finance, 1982–86; Minister for Justice, 1986–87. Pres., Irish Council of the European Movt, 1987–; Vice-Pres., European People's Party, 1987–; Mem., Council of State. Governor: EIB, 1982–86; IMF. *Address:* (office) Dáil Éireann, Dublin 2.

DUKES, Justin Paul; Chairman, European Communications Industries Consortium, since 1989; *b* 19 Sept. 1941; *s* of late John Alexander Dukes and Agnes Dukes; two *s* one *d; m* 1990, Jane Macallister. *Educ:* King's Coll., Univ. of Durham. Dir, Financial Times Ltd, 1975–81; Chairman: Financial Times (Europe) Ltd and Fintel Ltd, 1978–81; C. S. & P. International Inc., NY, 1980–83; Man. Dir, Channel Four TV Co., 1981–88; Chief-Exec., Galileo Co., 1988–89. Pres., Inst. of Information Scientists, 1982–83; Mem. Council, Foundn for Management Educn, 1979–90. Member: British Screen Adv. Council, 1986–88; Nat. Electronics Council, 1986–. Trustee, Internat. Inst. of Communications, 1986–. FRTS 1986; FRSA 1986; CBIM 1988. Chevalier, Ordre des Arts et des Lettres (France), 1988. *Recreations:* changing institutions, walking. *Address:* 15 St Mark's Crescent, NW1.

DULBECCO, Dr Renato; Distinguished Research Professor, since 1977, Senior Clayton Foundation Investigator, since 1979, The Salk Institute for Biological Studies; *b* Italy, 22 Feb. 1914; USA citizen; *s* of late Leonardo Dulbecco and late Maria Virdia; *m* 1963, Maureen R. Muir; one *d;* and one *d* (one *s* decd) by previous marriage. *Educ:* Univ. of Turin Medical Sch. (MD). Assistente, Univ. of Turin: Inst. Pathology, 1940–46; Anatomical Inst., 1946–47; Res. Assoc., Indiana Univ., 1947–49; Sen. Res. Fellow, 1949–52, Assoc. Prof., 1952–54, Prof. 1954–63, California Inst. Technology; Vis. Prof., Rockefeller Inst., 1962; Royal Soc. Vis. Prof. at Univ. of Glasgow, 1963–64; Resident Fellow, Salk Inst., Calif, 1963–72, Fellow, 1972–77; Imperial Cancer Research Fund: Asst Dir of Res., 1972–74; Dep. Dir of Res., 1974–77; Prof. of Pathology and Medicine, Univ. of Calif San Diego Med. Sch., 1977–81. MNAS; Member: Fedn of Amer. Scientists; Amer. Assoc. for Cancer Research; Cancer Center, Univ. of Calif at San Diego; Bd of Scientific Counselors, Dept of Cancer Etiology, NCI; Amer. Acad. of Arts and Scis; Internat. Physicians for Prevention of Nuclear War, Inc.; Pres., Amer.-Ital. Foundn for Cancer Res. Trustee: Amer.-Italian Foundn for Cancer Res.; La Jolla Country Day School. Foreign Member: Academia dei Lincei, 1969; Royal Society, 1974; Hon. Member: Accademia Ligure di Scienze a Lettere, 1982; Società Medico-Chirugica di Modena, 1985; Tissue Culture Assoc., 1988. Has given many lectures to learned instns. Hon. DSc Yale, 1968; Hon. LLD Glasgow, 1970; *hc* Dr Med., Vrije Universiteit Brussel, Brussels, 1978; Hon. DSc Indiana, 1984. (Jtly) Nobel Prize for Physiology or Medicine, 1975; Premio Fregene, Italy, 1988; numerous other prizes and awards. *Publications:* (jtly) Microbiology, 1967; numerous in sci. jls. *Recreation:* music. *Address:* The Salk Institute, PO Box 85800, San Diego, Calif 92138, USA. *Club:* Athenæum.

DULVERTON, 2nd Baron, *cr* 1929, of Batsford; **Frederick Anthony Hamilton Wills,** CBE 1974; TD; DL; Bt 1897; MA Oxon; *b* 19 Dec. 1915; *s* of 1st Baron Dulverton, OBE, and Victoria May, OBE (*d* 1968), 3rd *d* of Rear-Adm. Sir Edward Chichester, 9th Bt, CB, CMG; *S* father, 1956; *m* 1st, 1939, Judith Betty (marr. diss. 1960; she *d* 1983), *e d* of late Lieut-Col Hon. Ian Leslie Melville, TD; two *s* one *d* (and one *d* decd); 2nd, 1962, Ruth Violet, *o d* of Sir Walter Farquhar, 5th Bt. *Educ:* Eton; Magdalen Coll., Oxford (MA; Waynflete Fellow, 1982). Commissioned Lovat Scouts (TA), 1935; Major, 1943. President: Timber Growers' Orgn Ltd, 1976–78; Bath and West and Southern Counties Agric. Soc., 1973; British Deer Soc., 1973–87; Three Counties Agric. Soc., 1975; Gloucestershire Trust for Nature Conservation, 1979–; Member, Red Deer Commn, 1972–87; Chairman: Forestry Cttee of GB, 1978–80; Dulverton Trust, 1956–; Trustee, Wildfowl Trust; former Trustee, World Wildlife Fund (UK); Hon. Pres., Timber Growers UK, 1983–. Joint Master: N Cotswold Foxhounds, 1950–56; Heythrop Foxhounds, 1967–70. DL Gloucester, 1979. Commander, Order of Golden Ark (Netherlands), 1985. *Heir:* s Hon. (Gilbert) Michael Hamilton Wills [*b* 2 May 1944; *m* 1980, Rosalind van der Velde-Oliver; one *s* one *d*]. *Address:* Batsford Park, Moreton-in-Marsh, Glos. *T:* Moreton-in-Marsh (0608) 50303; Fassfern, Kinlocheil, Fort William, Inverness-shire. *T:* Kinlocheil (039783) 232. *Clubs:* Boodles's, Pratt's, Army and Navy.

DUMAS, Roland; Chevalier de la Légion d'Honneur; Croix de Guerre (1939–45); Croix du Combattant Volontaire; Minister of Foreign Affairs, France, since 1988; *b* Limoges, Haute-Vienne, 23 Aug. 1922; *s* of Georges Dumas and Elisabeth (née Lecanuet); *m* 1964, Anne-Marie Lillet; two *s* one *d. Educ:* Lycée de Limoges; Faculté de Droit de Paris; Univ. of London; Ecole de langues orientales de Paris. LLL; Diplomas: in Advanced Studies in Laws; in Political Science, Paris, and London School of Economics. Counsel, Court of Appeal, Paris; journalist; Sen. Political Dir, Journal Socialiste Limousin; Political Dir of weekly, La Corrèze Républicaine et Socialiste; Deputy: UDSR, Haute Vienne, 1956–58; FGDS, Corrèze, 1967–68; Socialiste de la Dordogne, 1981–83, 1986–88; Minister for European Affairs, 1983–84; Govt spokesman, 1984; Minister for External Relations, 1984–86. Grand Cross, Order of Isabel (Spain), 1982. *Publications:* J'ai vu vivre la Chine, 1960; Les Avocats, 1970; Le Droit de l'Information et de la Presse, 1981; Plaidoyer pour Roger Gilbert Lecomte, 1985; Le droit de la propriété littéraire et artistique, 1986; Le Peuple Assemblé, 1989. *Address:* 28 rue de Bièvre, 75005 Paris, France.

DUMBELL, Dr Keith Rodney; Senior Specialist in Microbiology, Medical School, University of Cape Town, since 1982; *b* 2 Oct. 1922; *s* of late Stanley Dumbell and Dorothy Ellen (née Hewitt); *m* 1st, 1950, Brenda Margaret (née Heathcote) (*d* 1971); two *d;* 2nd, 1972, Susan (née Herd); two *s. Educ:* Wirral Gram. Sch.; University of Liverpool, MB, ChB 1944; MD (Liverpool), 1950. FRCPath 1975. Asst Lecturer, Dept of Bacteriology, University of Liverpool, 1945–47; Mem. of Scientific Staff, MRC, 1947–50; Junior Pathologist, RAF, 1950–52; Asst in Pathology and Microbiology, Rockefeller Inst. for Medical Research (Dr Peyton Rous' laboratory), 1952–53; Lecturer in Bacteriology, University of Liverpool, 1952–58; Senior Lecturer, 1958–64; Prof. of Virology, Univ. of London at St Mary's Hosp. Med. Sch., 1964–81. *Publications:* articles in various medical and scientific journals. *Address:* Department of Medical Microbiology, Medical School, Observatory, Cape, 7925, South Africa.

DUMBUTSHENA, Hon. Enoch; Hon. Mr Justice Dumbutshena; Chief Justice of Zimbabwe, 1984–90; Commissioner, International Commission of Jurists, since 1990; *b* 25 April 1920; *s* of late Job Matabasi Dumbutshena and Sarah Dumbutshena; *m* 1st, 1948, Alphosina (née Mahlangu) (marr. diss.; she *d* 1989); one *s* one *d;* 2nd, 1964, Miriam Masango; one *s* two *d. Educ:* Univ. of South Africa (BA, BEd, UED). Called to the Bar, Gray's Inn, 1963, Hon. Bencher, 1989. Teacher, 1946–56; journalist, 1956–59; barrister, Southern Rhodesia, 1963–67; Zambia: founded Legal Aid Scheme, 1967–70; private practice, 1970–78; Zimbabwe: private practice, 1978–80; Judge of High Court, 1980; Judge President, 1983. Exec. Mem., Centre for the Independence of Judges and Lawyers. Chairman: Modus Publications; Art Printers Employees Trust, Harare; Pres., Boy Scouts; Trustee, Omay Develt Trust, Harare; Chairman: Moleli-Marshall Hartley Trust; Old Age Zimbabwe. Governor: Arundel Sch., Harare; Moleli Secondary Sch. (Chm., Bd of Govs); Trustee, Chisipite Jun. Sch., Harare. Hon. DCL Oxford, 1990. *Publication:* Zimbabwe Tragedy, 1986. *Recreations:* mountain climbing (average height), reading, formerly tennis. *Address:* PO Box CH70, Chisipite, Harare, Zimbabwe. *T:* (office) 724778, (residence) 884147. *Club:* Harare.

DUMFRIES, Earl of; John Colum Crichton-Stuart; *b* 26 April 1958; *s* and *heir* of 6th Marquess of Bute, *qv; m* 1984, Carolyn E. R. M., *d* of late Bryson Waddell; one *s* two *d.* British Formula Three Champion, 1984; European Formula Three Championship runner-up, 1984; Formula One Ferrari test driver, 1985; JPS Lotus Grand Prix Driver, 1986; Works Driver for World Champion Sports Prototype Team Silk Cut Jaguar, 1988 (Jt Winner, Le Mans sports car race, 1988); Lead Driver for Toyota GB, World Sports Prototype Championship, 1989, 1990. *Heir:* s Lord Mountstuart, *qv.*

DUMMETT, (Agnes Margaret) Ann; Consultant (part-time) on European Policies to Commission for Racial Equality, since 1990; *b* 4 Sept. 1930; *d* of Arthur William Chesney and late Kitty Mary Chesney; *m* 1951, Michael Anthony Eardley Dummett, *qv;* three *s* two *d* (and one *s* one *d* decd). *Educ:* Guildhouse Sch., Pimlico; Ware Grammar Sch. for Girls; Somerville Coll., Oxford (MA). Pres., Oxford Univ. Liberal Club, 1949. Community Relations Officer, Oxford, 1966–69; teaching in further education, 1969–71; Research Worker: Inst. of Race Relations, 1971–73; Runnymede Trust, 1975, 1977; Jt Council for the Welfare of Immigrants, 1978–84; Dir, Runnymede Trust, 1984–87. *Publications:* A Portrait of English Racism, 1973; Citizenship and Nationality, 1976; A

New Immigration Policy, 1978; (with Ian Martin) British Nationality: a guide to the new law, 1982; (ed) Towards a Just Immigration Policy, 1986; chapters in: Justice First (with Michael Dummett), 1969; Colloque de la Société Française pour le Droit International, 1979; Moral Philosophy, 1979; (with Andrew Nicol) Subjects, Citizens, Aliens and Others, 1990; numerous articles and pamphlets. *Recreations:* walking about cities, theatregoing, popular music. *Address:* 54 Park Town, Oxford OX2 6SJ. *T:* Oxford (0865) 58698. *Club:* Commonwealth Trust.

DUMMETT, George Anthony, FEng, FIChemE; Chairman, Council of Engineering Institutions, 1976–77 (Vice-Chairman, 1975); *b* 13 Oct. 1907; *s* of George Herbert Dummett and Gertrude (*née* Higgins); *m* 1st, 1931, Peggy Schaeffer; 2nd, 1939, Ursula Margarete Schubert; two *s* one *d. Educ:* Rugby Sch.; Birmingham Univ.; Pembroke Coll., Cambridge. MA. Research in phys. chem., Cambridge Univ., 1930–32; Research Asst, Thorncliffe Coal Distillation Ltd, 1932–35; APV Co. Ltd (then Aluminium Plant and Vessel Co. Ltd): Technical Res. Asst, 1935; Laboratory Man., 1943; Chem. Engrg Dept Man., 1948; Scientific Man., 1949; Res. Dir, 1956; Dep. Man. Dir, 1965–72; Dir, APV (Holdings) Ltd, 1962–72; Dep. Chm., APV Internat., 1965–72. Chm., Res. Cttee, FBI, 1958–65; Pres., IChemE, 1968–69, Hon. Fellow, 1981. Fellow, Fellowship of Engineering, 1977. Chm., European Fedn Chemical Engrng, 1977–78. Hon. Member: Soc. de Chimie Ind., 1969; Dechema, 1976. *Publications:* From Little Acorns: a history of the APV company, 1981; numerous papers on chemical and biochemical engrg, metallurgy, etc. *Recreations:* music, mountaineering, gardening, stamp collecting. *Address:* 10 Priory Crescent, Lewes, East Sussex BN7 1HP. *T:* Lewes (0273) 473731. *Clubs:* Alpine, Climbers.
See also M. A. E. Dummett.

DUMMETT, Michael Anthony Eardley; Wykeham Professor of Logic in the University of Oxford, and Fellow of New College, Oxford, 1979–Sept. 1992; *b* 27 June 1925; *s* of George Herbert Dummett and Iris Dummett (*née* Eardley-Wilmot); *m* 1951, Ann Chesney (*see* A. M. A. Dummett); three *s* two *d* (one *s* one *d* decd). *Educ:* Sandroyd Sch.; Winchester Coll. (1st Schol.); Christ Church, Oxford. Major hist. schol. (Ch. Ch.), 1942. Served in Army, 1943–47: in RA and Intell. Corps (India, 1945, Malaya, 1946–47, Sgt). Ch. Ch., Oxford, 1947–50, First Class Hons, PPE, 1950. Asst Lectr in Philosophy, Birmingham Univ., 1950–51; Commonwealth Fund Fellow, Univ. of California, Berkeley, 1955–56; Reader in the Philosophy of Mathematics, Univ. of Oxford, 1962–74; All Souls College, Oxford: Fellow, 1950–79, Senior Research Fellow, 1974–79; Sub-Warden, 1974–76; Emeritus Fellow, 1980. Vis. Lectr, Univ. of Ghana, 1958; Vis. Professor: Stanford Univ., several occasions, 1960–66; Univ. of Minnesota, 1968; Princeton Univ., 1970; Rockefeller Univ., 1973; William James Lectr in Philosophy, Harvard Univ., 1976; Alex. von Humboldt-Stiftung Vis. Res. Fellow, Münster Univ., 1981. Founder Mem., Oxford Cttee for Racial Integration, 1965 (Chm., Jan.-May 1966); Member: Exec. Cttee, Campaign Against Racial Discrimination, 1966–67; Legal and Civil Affairs Panel, Nat. Cttee for Commonwealth Immigrants, 1966–68; Chairman: Jt Council for the Welfare of Immigrants, 1970–71 (Vice-Chm., 1967–69, 1973–75); unofficial cttee of enquiry into events in Southall 23 April 1979, 1979–80; shadow board, Barclays Bank, 1981–82. FBA 1968–84. Hon. PhD Nijmegen, 1983; For. Hon. Mem., Amer. Acad. of Arts and Scis, 1985. *Publications:* Frege: philosophy of language, 1973, 2nd edn 1981; The Justification of Deduction, 1973; Elements of Intuitionism, 1977; Truth and other Enigmas, 1978; Immigration: where the debate goes wrong, 1978; Catholicism and the World Order, 1979; The Game of Tarot, 1980; Twelve Tarot Games, 1980; The Interpretation of Frege's Philosophy, 1981; Voting Procedures, 1984; The Visconti-Sforza Tarot Cards, 1986; Ursprünge der analytischen Philosophie, 1988; Frege and Other Philosophers, 1991; The Logical Basis of Metaphysics, 1991; Frege: Philosophy of Mathematics, 1991; contributions to: Mind and Language, 1975; Truth and Meaning, 1976; Studies on Frege, 1976; Contemporary British Philosophy, 1976; Meaning and Use, 1979; Perception and Identity, 1979; Perspectives on the Philosophy of Wittgenstein, 1981; Approaches to Language, 1983; Frege: tradition and influence, 1984; Reflections on Chomsky, 1989; Meaning and Method, 1990; contrib. entry on Frege, to Encyclopedia of Philosophy (ed P. Edwards), 1967; (with Ann Dummett) chapter on Rôle of the Government, in Justice First (ed L. Donnelly), 1969; preface to R. C. Zaehner, The City Within the Heart, 1980; articles in: Aristotelian Soc. Proceedings, Philos. Review, Bull. of London Math. Soc., Synthese, Inquiry, Econometrica, Jl of Symbolic Logic, Zeitschrift für mathematische Logik, Dublin Review, New Blackfriars, Clergy Review, Jl of Warburg and Courtauld Insts, Jl of Playing-Card Soc. *Recreations:* listening to the blues, investigating the history of card games, reading science fiction. *Address:* 54 Park Town, Oxford. *T:* Oxford (0865) 58698. *Club:* Commonwealth Trust.
See also G. A. Dummett.

DUMPER, Rt. Rev. Anthony Charles; *see* Dudley, Bishop Suffragan of.

DUNALLEY, 6th Baron *cr* 1800; **Henry Desmond Graham Prittie;** Lt-Col (retired) late The Rifle Brigade; *b* 14 Oct. 1912; *er s* of 5th Baron Dunalley, DSO, and Beatrix Evelyn (*d* 1967), *e d* of late James N. Graham of Carfin, Lanarkshire; *S* father, 1948; *m* 1947, Philippa, *o d* of late Hon. Philip Cary; two *s* one *d. Educ:* Stowe; RMC, Sandhurst. Retd 1953. *Recreation:* fishing. *Heir: s* Hon. Henry Francis Cornelius Prittie [*b* 30 May 1948; *m* 1978, Sally Louise, *er d* of Ronald Vere; one *s* three *d*]. *Address:* Church End House, Swerford, Oxfordshire OX7 4AX. *T:* Hook Norton (0608) 730005. *Clubs:* Kildare Street and University (Dublin); Christchurch (NZ) (Hon. Mem.).

DUNBAR, Alexander Arbuthnott, DL; farmer; *b* 14 March 1929; *yr s* of Sir Edward Dunbar, 9th Bt; *m* 1965, Elizabeth Susannah, *d* of Rev. Denzil Wright; one *s* one *d. Educ:* Wellington Coll., Berks; Pembroke Coll., Cambridge (MA); Edinburgh Sch. of Agriculture, 1980–81. Mil. Service, Lieut QO Cameron Highlanders, 1947–49. Called to the Bar, Inner Temple, 1953. Joined ICI, 1954: Asst Sec., Wilton Works, 1959–63. Joined North Eastern Assoc. for the Arts, 1963, Sec. 1964, Dir 1967; Director: Northern Arts Assoc., 1967–69; UK and British Commonwealth Branch, Calouste Gulbenkian Foundn, 1970–71; Scottish Arts Council, 1971–80. DL Moray, 1987. *Publications:* contribs to various jls. *Recreations:* art, theatre, conservation, history, cycling. *Address:* Pitgaveny, Elgin, Moray IV30 2PQ.

DUNBAR of Northfield, Sir Archibald (Ranulph), 11th Bt *cr* 1700; *b* 8 Aug. 1927; *er s* of Sir (Archibald) Edward Dunbar, 9th Bt (by some reckonings 10th Bt) and Olivia Douglas Sinclair (*d* 1964), *d* of Maj.-Gen. Sir Edward May, KCB, CMG; *S* father, 1969; *m* 1974, Amelia Millar Sommerville, *d* of Horace Davidson; one *s* two *d. Educ:* Wellington Coll.; Pembroke Coll., Cambridge; Imperial Coll. of Tropical Agriculture, Trinidad. Mil. Service, 2nd Lt, Cameron (att. Gordon) Highlanders, 1945–48. Entered Colonial Agricultural Service, Uganda, as Agricultural Officer, 1953; retired, 1970. Hon. Sheriff, Sheriff Court District of Moray, 1989–. Kt of Honour and Devotion, SMO Malta, 1989. *Publications:* A History of Bunyoro-Kitara, 1965; Omukama Chwa II Kabarega, 1965; The Annual Crops of Uganda, 1969; various articles in Uganda Jl. *Recreations:* swimming, military modelling, model railway. *Heir: s* Edward Horace Dunbar, Younger of Northfield, *b* 18 March 1977. *Address:* The Old Manse, Duffus, Elgin, Scotland IV30 2QD. *T:* Hopeman (0343) 830270. *Club:* New (Edinburgh).

DUNBAR, Charles, CB 1964; Director, Fighting Vehicles Research and Development Establishment, Ministry of Defence, 1960–67; *b* 12 Jan. 1907; *s* of John Dunbar, Barrow-in-Furness, Lancs; *m* 1933, Mary Alice (*née* Clarke), Barnes, SW; two *d. Educ:* Grammar Sch., Barrow-in-Furness; Manchester Univ. (MSc). National Physical Laboratory, Dept of Scientific and Industrial Research, 1929–43; Tank Armament Research Establishment, Min. of Supply, 1943–47; Fighting Vehicles Research and Development Establishments, 1947–67, retired. *Publications:* contribs to learned journals. *Recreations:* golf, fishing. *Address:* Cedar Lodge, 2 Freemans Close, Stoke Poges, Bucks.
See also Peter Graham.

DUNBAR, Sir David H.; *see* Hope-Dunbar.

DUNBAR of Durn, Sir Drummond Cospatrick Ninian, 9th Bt, *cr* 1697; MC 1943; Major Black Watch, retired; *b* 9 May 1917; *o s* of Sir George Alexander Drummond Dunbar, 8th Bt and Sophie Kathleen (*d* 1936), *d* of late J. Benson Kennedy; *S* father, 1949; *m* 1957, Sheila Barbara Mary, *d* of John B. de Fonblanque, London; one *s. Educ:* Radley Coll.; Worcester Coll., Oxford. BA 1938. Served War of 1939–45, Middle East, North Africa, Sicily, Normandy (wounded twice, MC). Retired pay, 1958. *Heir: s* Robert Drummond Cospatrick Dunbar, Younger of Durn [*b* 17 June 1958. *Educ:* Harrow; Christ Church, Oxford; BA 1979]. *Address:* Town Hill, Westmount, Jersey, Channel Islands. *Club:* Naval and Military.

DUNBAR of Mochrum, Sir Jean Ivor, 13th Bt *cr* 1694; *b* 4 April 1918; *s* of Sir Adrian Ivor Dunbar of Mochrum, 12th Bt and Emma Marie (*d* 1925), *d* of Jean Wittevrongel; *S* father, 1977; *m* 1944, Rose Jeanne (marr. diss. 1979), *d* of Henry William Hertsch; two *s* one *d.* Formerly Sergeant, Mountain Engineers, US Army. *Recreation:* horsemanship. *Heir: s* Captain James Michael Dunbar, DDS, US Air Force [*b* 17 Jan. 1950; *m* 1978, Margaret Jacobs].

DUNBAR, John Greenwell; Secretary, Royal Commission on the Ancient and Historical Monuments of Scotland, 1978–90; *b* 1 March 1930; *o s* of John Dunbar and Marie Alton; *m* 1974, Elizabeth Mill Blyth. *Educ:* University College Sch., London; Balliol Coll., Oxford (MA). FSA, FSAScot. Joined staff of Royal Commission on the Ancient and Historical Monuments of Scotland, 1953; Mem., Ancient Monuments Board for Scotland, 1978–90. Vice-President: Soc. for Medieval Archaeology, 1981–86; Soc. of Antiquaries of Scotland, 1983–86. Lindsay-Fischer Lectr, Oslo, 1985. Hon. FRIAS. *Publications:* The Historic Architecture of Scotland, 1966, revd edn 1978; (ed with John Imrie) Accounts of the Masters of Works 1616–1649, 1982; numerous articles in archaeological jls, etc. *Address:* Patie's Mill, Carlops, By Penicuik, Midlothian EH26 9NF. *T:* West Linton (0968) 60250. *Club:* New (Edinburgh).

DUNBAR of Hempriggs, Dame Maureen Daisy Helen, (Lady Dunbar of Hempriggs), Btss (8th in line) *cr* 1706 (NS); *b* 19 Aug. 1906; *d* of Courtenay Edward Moore and Janie King Moore (*née* Askins); assumed the name of Dunbar, in lieu of Blake, on claiming succession to the Hempriggs baronetcy after death of kinsman, Sir George Cospatrick Duff-Sutherland-Dunbar, 7th Bt, in 1963; claim established and title recognised by Lyon Court, 1965; *m* 1940, Leonard James Blake (*d* 1989); one *s* one *d. Educ:* Headington Sch.; Royal Coll. of Music. LRAM 1928. Music teacher at: Monmouth Sch. for Girls, 1930–33; Oxford High Sch., 1935–40; Malvern Coll., 1957–68. *Heir:* (to mother's Btcy) *s* Richard Francis Dunbar of Hempriggs, younger [*b* 8 Jan. 1945 (assumed the name of Dunbar, 1965); *m* 1969, Elizabeth Margaret Jane Lister; two *d*]. *Address:* 51 Gloucester Street, Winchcombe, Cheltenham, Glos GL54 5LX. *T:* Cheltenham (0242) 602122.

DUNBAR-NASMITH, Rear-Adm. David Arthur, CB 1969; DSC 1942; retired 1972; Vice-Lord-Lieutenant, Morayshire, since 1980; Chairman, Moray and Nairn Newspaper Co., since 1982; *b* 21 Feb. 1921; *e s* of late Admiral Sir Martin Dunbar-Nasmith, VC, KCB, KCMG, DL, and of late Justina Dunbar-Nasmith, CBE, DStJ; *m* 1951, Elizabeth Bowlby; two *s* two *d. Educ:* Lockers Park; RNC, Dartmouth. To sea as Midshipman, 1939. War Service, Atlantic and Mediterranean, in HM Ships Barham, Rodney, Kelvin and Petard. In comd: HM Ships Haydon 1943, Peacock 1945–46, Moon 1946, Rowena 1946–48, Enard Bay 1951, Alert 1954–56, Berwick, and 5th Frigate Squadron, 1961–63; Commodore, Amphibious Forces, 1966–67. RN and Joint Service Staff Colls, 1948–49; Staff of Flag Officer 1st Cruiser Squadron, 1949–51; NATO HQ, SACLANT, 1952–54 and SACEUR, 1958–60; Dir of Defence Plans, Min. of Defence, 1963–65; Naval Secretary, 1967–70; Flag Officer, Scotland and N Ireland, 1970–72. Comdr 1951; Capt. 1958; Rear-Adm. 1967. Member: Highlands and Islands Develt Bd, 1972–83 (Dep. Chm., 1972–81; Chm., 1981–82); Countryside Commn for Scotland, 1972–76; British Waterways Bd, 1980–87; N of Scotland Hydro-Electric Bd, 1982–85. Mem. Queen's Body Guard for Scotland (Royal Company of Archers), 1974–; Gentleman Usher of the Green Rod to the Order of the Thistle, 1979–. DL Moray, 1974. *Recreations:* sailing, ski-ing and shooting. *Address:* Glen of Rothes, Rothes, Moray. *T:* Rothes (03403) 216. *Club:* New (Edinburgh).
See also J. D. Dunbar-Nasmith.

DUNBAR-NASMITH, Prof. James Duncan, CBE 1976; RIBA; PPRIAS; FRSA, FRSE; Partner, The Law & Dunbar-Nasmith Partnership, architects, Edinburgh and Forres (founded 1957); Professor Emeritus, Heriot-Watt University, since 1988; *b* 15 March 1927; *y s* of late Adm. Sir Martin Dunbar-Nasmith, VC, KCB, KCMG, DL and of late Justina Dunbar-Nasmith, CBE, DStJ. *Educ:* Lockers Park; Winchester. Trinity Coll., Cambridge (BA); Edinburgh Coll. of Art (DA). ARIBA 1954. Lieut, Scots Guards, 1945–48. Prof. and Hd of Dept. of Architecture, Heriot-Watt Univ. and Edinburgh Coll. of Art, 1978–88. President: Royal Incorporation of Architects in Scotland, 1971–73; Edinburgh Architectural Assoc., 1967–69. Member: Council, RIBA, 1967–73 (a Vice-Pres., 1972–73; Chm., Bd of Educn, 1972–73); Council, ARCUK, 1976–84 (Vice-Chm., Bd of Educn, 1977); Royal Commn on Ancient and Historical Monuments of Scotland, 1972–; Ancient Monuments Bd for Scotland, 1969–83 (interim Chm., 1972–73); Historic Buildings Council for Scotland, 1966–; Exec. Cttee, Europa Nostra, 1986–; Dep. Chm., Edinburgh Internat. Festival, 1981–85; Trustee: Scottish Civic Trust, 1971–; Architectural Heritage Fund, 1976–; Theatres Trust, 1983–. *Recreations:* music, theatre, ski-ing, sailing. *Address:* (office) 16 Dublin Street, Edinburgh EH1 3RE. *T:* 031–556 8631. *Clubs:* Royal Ocean Racing; New (Edinburgh).
See also D. A. Dunbar-Nasmith.

DUNBOYNE, 28th Baron by Summons, 18th Baron by Patent; **Patrick Theobald Tower Butler; His Honour The Lord Dunboyne;** VRD; a Circuit Judge, 1972–86; *b* 27 Jan. 1917; *e s* of 27th Baron Dunboyne and Dora Isolde Butler (*d* 1977), *e d* of Comdr F. F. Tower; *S* father, 1945; *m* 1950, Anne Marie, *d* of late Sir Victor Mallet, GCMG, CVO; one *s* three *d. Educ:* Winchester; Trinity Coll., Cambridge (MA). Pres. of Cambridge Union. Lieut Irish Guards (Suppl. Res.); served European War, 1939–44 (King's Badge) (prisoner, then repatriated); Foreign Office, 1945–46. Barrister-at-Law, Middle Temple (Harmsworth Scholar), Inner Temple, South-Eastern Circuit, King's Inns, Dublin. In practice 1949–71. Recorder of Hastings, 1961–71; Dep. Chm., Quarter Sessions: Mddx, 1963–65; Kent, 1963–71; Inner London 1971–72. Legal Aid No 2 Area

Cttee, 1954–64. Commissary Gen., Diocese of Canterbury, 1959–71. Home Sec's Ward-boundaries Comr, 1960–70. Pres., 1971–, Fellow 1982, Irish Genealogical Res. Soc.; Founder Hon. Sec., Bar Lawn Tennis Soc., 1950 (Vice-Pres. 1963–), and of Irish Peers Assoc., 1963–71 (Chm., 1987–90); Pres., Wireless Telegraphy Appeal Tribunal for Eng. and Wales, 1967–70. Council, Friends of Canterbury Cathedral, 1953–71. Lt, RNVR, 1951–58, RNR, 1958–60. *Publications:* The Trial of J. G. Haigh, 1953; (with others) Cambridge Union, 1815–1939, 1953; Butler Family History, 1966, 7th edn 1990. *Recreations:* rowing, lawn tennis, chess. *Heir: s* Hon. John Fitzwalter Butler [*b* 31 July 1951; *m* 1975, Diana Caroline, *yr d* of Sir Michael Williams, KCMG; one *s* three *d*]. *Address:* 36 Ormonde Gate, SW3 4HA. *T:* 071–352 1837. *Clubs:* Irish; International Lawn Tennis of Great Britain (Vice-Pres., Pres. 1973–83) and (hon.) of Australia, France, Germany, Monaco, Netherlands and USA; Forty Five Lawn Tennis (Pres.); All England Lawn Tennis (Wimbledon); Pitt, Union (Cambridge).

DUNCAN, Agnes Lawrie Addie, (Laura); Sheriff of Glasgow and Strathkelvin, since 1982; *b* 17 June 1947; *d* of late William Smith, District Clerk, and of Mary Marshall Smith McClure; *m* 1990, David Cecil Duncan, farmer, cricket coach, *y s* of late Dr and Mrs H. C. Duncan, Edinburgh. *Educ:* Hamilton Acad.; Glasgow Univ. (LLB 1967). Admitted Solicitor, 1969; called to the Scottish Bar, 1976. Solicitor, private practice, 1969–71; Procurator Fiscal Depute, 1971–75; Standing Junior Counsel to Dept of Employment, 1982. RYA dinghy sailing instructor, and racing coach. *Recreations:* sailing, various other sports. *Address:* Glasgow Sheriff Court, 1 Carlton Place, Glasgow G5 9DA.

DUNCAN, Prof. Archibald Alexander McBeth, FBA 1985; Professor of Scottish History and Literature, Glasgow University, since 1962; *b* 17 Oct. 1926; *s* of Charles George Duncan and Christina Helen McBeth; *m* 1954, Ann Hayes Sawyer, *d* of W. E. H. Sawyer, Oxford; two *s* one *d*. *Educ:* George Heriot's Sch.; Edinburgh Univ.; Balliol Coll., Oxford. Lecturer in History, Queen's Univ., Belfast, 1951–53; Lecturer in History, Edinburgh Univ., 1953–61; Leverhulme Research Fellow, 1961–62. Clerk of Senate, Glasgow Univ., 1978–83. Mem., Royal Commn on the Ancient and Historical Monuments of Scotland, 1969–. *Publications:* Scotland: The Making of the Kingdom, 1975; (ed and revised) W. Croft Dickinson's Scotland from the Earliest Times to 1603, 3rd edn 1977; Regesta Regum Scottorum, v, The Acts of Robert I, 1306–29, 1988. *Address:* 17 Campbell Drive, Bearsden, Glasgow G61 4NF.

DUNCAN, Prof. Archibald Sutherland, DSC 1943; FRCSE, FRCPE, FRCOG; Executive Dean of the Faculty of Medicine and Professor of Medical Education, Edinburgh University, 1966–76, now Emeritus; *b* 17 July 1914; *y s* of late Rev. H. C. Duncan, K-i-H, DD and late Rose Elsie Edwards; *m* 1939, Barbara, *d* of late John Gibson Holliday, JP, Penrith, Cumberland. *Educ:* Merchiston Castle Sch.; Edinburgh Univ. MB, ChB Edinburgh, 1936. Resident hosp. appts in Edinburgh and London, 1936–41. Served RNVR Surg. Lieut-Comdr (surg. specialist), 1941–45 (DSC). Temp. Cons. in Obst. and Gynæc., Inverness, 1946; Lectr in Univ. and part-time Cons. Obstetr and Gynæcol., Aberdeen, 1946–50; Sen. Lectr, University of Edinburgh and Obstetr. and Gynæcol. to Western Gen. Hosp., Edinburgh 1950–53; Prof. of Obstetrics and Gynæcology in the Welsh National Sch. of Medicine, Univ. of Wales, 1953–66; Cons. Obstetrician and Gynæcologist, United Cardiff Hosps, 1953–66; Advisor in Obstetrics and Gynæcology to Welsh Hosp. Board, 1953–66. Member: Clin. Res. Bd of MRC, 1965–69; Council, RCSE, 1968–73; GMC, 1974–78; Lothian Health Bd, 1977–83 (Vice-Chm., 1981–83). Chm., Scottish Council on Disability, 1977–80. Vice-Pres., Inst. of Medical Ethics, 1985–. Hon. Pres., Brit. Med. Students Assoc., 1965–66. Mem. Court, Edinburgh Univ., 1979–83; Hon. Pres. (life), Graduates' Assoc., Edinburgh Univ., 1986. Mem., James IV Assoc. of Surgeons; Hon. Mem., Alpha Omega Alpha Honor Med. Soc. Hon. MD Edinburgh, 1984. Associate Editor, British Jl of Medical Education, 1971–75; Consulting Editor, Jl of Medical Ethics, 1975–81. *Publications:* (ed jtly) Dictionary of Medical Ethics, 1977, 2nd edn 1981; contribs on scientific and allied subjects in various med. jls and books. *Recreations:* mountains, photography. *Address:* 1 Walker Street, Edinburgh EH3 7JY. *T:* 031–225 7657. *Club:* New (Edinburgh).

DUNCAN, Brian Arthur Cullum, CB 1972; CBE 1963 (MBE 1949); QC 1972; Judge Advocate General of the Forces, 1968–72; *b* 2 Feb. 1908; *yr s* of late Frank Hubert Duncan, LDS, RCS, and late Edith Jane Duncan (*née* Cullum); *m* 1934, Irene Flora Templeman (*d* 1983), *o c* of late John Frederick Templeman and late Flora Edith Templeman; two *s* two *d*. *Educ:* Queens' Coll., Cambridge (MA). Called to the Bar, Lincoln's Inn, 1931. Practised South Eastern Circuit, Central Criminal Court, North London Sessions, and Herts and Essex Sessions. Commissioned RAF, April 1940; relinqd commn, 1950 (Wing Comdr). Joined JAG's Dept, 1945. Dep. Judge Advocate Gen. (Army and RAF): Middle East, 1950–53; Germany, 1954–57; Far East, 1959–62; Vice Judge Advocate Gen., 1967–68. *Address:* Culverlands, Neville Park, Baltonsborough, Glastonbury, Som BA6 8PY.

DUNCAN, David Francis; HM Diplomatic Service, retired; *b* 22 Feb. 1923; *s* of late Brig. William Edmonstone Duncan, CVO, DSO, MC, and Mrs Magdalene Emily Duncan (*née* Renny-Tailyour). *Educ:* Eton; Trinity Coll., Cambridge. Served War, RA, 1941–46 (despatches). Entered Foreign (later Diplomatic) Service, 1949; Foreign Office, 1949–52; Bogotá, 1952–54; UK Delegn to ECSC, Luxembourg, 1954–55; FO, 1955–58; Baghdad, 1958; Ankara, 1958–60; FO, 1960–62; Quito, 1962–65; Phnom Penh, 1965 (as Chargé d'Affaires); FO (later Foreign and Commonwealth Office), 1965–70; Islamabad, 1970–71; Counsellor, UK Delegn to Geneva Disarm. Conf., 1971–74; Ambassador to Nicaragua, 1974–76; retired 1976. *Recreations:* walking, photography, travel. *Address:* 133 Rivermead Court, Ranelagh Gardens, SW6 3SE. *T:* 071–736 1576.

DUNCAN, Rev. Denis Macdonald, MA, BD; Managing Director, Arthur James Ltd (Publishers), since 1983; *b* 10 Jan. 1920; *s* of late Rev. Reginald Duncan, BD, BLitt and late Clarice Ethel (*née* Hodgkinson); *m* 1942, Henrietta Watson McKenzie (*née* Houston); one *s* one *d*. *Educ:* George Watson's Boys' Coll., Edinburgh; Edinburgh Univ.; New Coll., Edinburgh. Minister of: St Margaret's, Juniper Green, Edinburgh, 1943–49; Trinity Duke Street Parish Church, Glasgow, 1949–57; Founder-editor, Rally, 1956–67; Managing Editor, British Weekly, 1957–70 (Man. Dir, 1967–70); Man. Dir, DPS Publicity Services Ltd, 1967–74; broadcaster and scriptwriter, Scottish Television, 1963–68; concert promotion at Edinburgh Festival and elsewhere, 1966–; Concert series "Communication through the Arts" poetry/music anthologies (with Benita Kyle), 1970–80. Dir, Highgate Counselling Centre, 1969–86; Associate Dir and Trng Supervisor, Westminster Pastoral Foundn, 1971–79; Chm., Internat. Cttee of World Assoc. of Pastoral Care and Counselling, 1977–79; Dir, Churches' Council for Health and Healing, 1982–88; Moderator of the Presbytery of England, Church of Scotland, 1984. FIBA (FIICS) 1976. PhD Somerset Univ., 1989. *Publications:* (ed) Through the Year with William Barclay, 1971; (ed) Through the Year with Cardinal Heenan, 1972; (ed) Daily Celebration, vol. 1, 1972, vol. 2, 1974; Marching Orders, 1973; (ed) Every Day with William Barclay, 1973; (ed) Through the Year with J. B. Phillips, 1974; Marching On, 1974; Here is my Hand, 1977; Creative Silence, 1980; A Day at a Time, 1980; Love, the Word that Heals, 1981; The Way of Love, 1982; Victorious Living, 1982; Health and Healing: a ministry to wholeness, 1988. *Recreations:* cricket, badminton. *Address:* 1 Cranbourne Road, N10 2BT. *T:* 081–883 1831. *Club:* Arts.

DUNCAN, Douglas John Stewart; Scottish Parliamentary Counsel and Senior Assistant Legal Secretary to Lord Advocate, since 1979; *b* 9 March 1945; *o s* of J. M. Duncan and Helen Stewart Collins; *m* 1972, Claire Isobel Callaghan; four *s*. *Educ:* Aberdeen Univ. (LLB Hons 1966). Asst Lectr in Law, Univ. of Sheffield, 1966–68; Lectr, Scots Law, Univ. of Aberdeen, 1968–70; Lectr, Evidence, Univ. of Edinburgh, 1972–74; Advocate, 1972; practice at the Scottish Bar, 1972–75; Lord Advocate's Dept, 1975–; called to the Bar, Inner Temple, 1990. Developed Statlaw system for electronic origination and publication of legislation (with D. C. Macrae), 1983–84; Chm., Statute Law Database Group, 1986–90. *Publications:* professional articles. *Recreations:* painting, racing. *Address:* Lord Advocate's Department, Fielden House, 10 Great College Street, SW1P 3SL. *Clubs:* Hampshire (Winchester); Royal Northern & University (Aberdeen).

DUNCAN, Geoffrey Stuart; General Secretary, General Synod Board of Education and National Society for Promoting Religious Education, since 1990; *b* 10 April 1938; *s* of Alexander Sidney Duncan and Gertude Ruth (*née* Page); *m* 1962, Shirley Bernice Matilda Vanderput; one *s* one *d*. *Educ:* Hemel Hempstead Grammar Sch.; Univ. of London (BScEcon); Univ. of Exeter (MA). Served RAEC, 1960–64. School and technical coll. teaching, 1964–72; LEA Advr and Officer, 1972–82; Schs Sec. and Dep. Sec., Gen. Synod Bd of Educn and Nat. Soc. for Promoting Religious Educn, 1982–90. Part-time WEA Tutor, 1966–70; part-time Open Univ. Counsellor, 1971–72. *Publications:* contributor to: Faith for the Future, 1986; Schools for Tomorrow, 1988; various educn jls. *Recreations:* campanology, travel. *Address:* 17 Carlton Road, Seaford, East Sussex BN25 2LE. *T:* Seaford (0323) 893587. *Club:* Naval and Military.

DUNCAN, George; Chairman: ASW Holdings PLC (formerly Allied Steel and Wire (Holdings) Ltd), since 1986; Household Mortgage Corporation Plc, since 1986; Whessoe PLC, since 1987 (Deputy Chairman, 1986); *b* 9 Nov. 1933; *s* of William Duncan and Catherine Gray Murray; *m* 1965, Frauke Ulrike Schnuhr; one *d*. *Educ:* Holloway County Grammar Sch.; London Sch. of Economics (BSc(Econ)); Wharton Sch.; Univ. of Pennsylvania (MBA). Mem., Inst. of Chartered Accountants (FCA); CBIM. Chief Executive, Truman Hanbury Buxton and Co. Ltd, 1967–71; Chief Executive, Watney Mann Ltd, 1971–72; Vice-Chm., Internat. Distillers and Vintners Ltd, 1972; Chm., Lloyds Bowmaker Finance Ltd (formerly Lloyds and Scottish plc), 1976–86; Dir, Lloyds Bank Plc, 1982–87. Chm., Humberclyde Finance Gp, 1987–89; Director: BET plc, 1981–; Haden plc, 1974–85 (Dep. Chm., 1984–85); TR City of London Trust PLC, 1977–; Associated British Ports PLC, 1986–; Newspaper Publishing plc, 1986–; Laporte plc, 1987–; Crown House PLC, 1987; Dewe Rogerson Gp Ltd, 1987–; Calor Gp, 1990–. Chm., CBI Companies Cttee, 1980–83; Mem., CBI President's Cttee, 1980–83. Freeman, City of London, 1971. *Recreations:* opera, tennis, ski-ing. *Address:* c/o ASW Holdings PLC, Granville House, 132 Sloane Street, SW1X 9AX. *T:* 071–730 0491. *Club:* Brooks's.

DUNCAN, George Alexander; Fellow Emeritus of Trinity College, Dublin, since 1967; *b* 15 May 1902; *s* of Alexander Duncan and Elizabeth Linn; *m* 1932, Eileen Stone, MSc, *d* of William Henry Stone and Sarah Copeland; one *d*. *Educ:* Ballymena Academy; Campbell Coll., Belfast; Trinity Coll., Dublin; University of North Carolina. BA, LLB 1923, MA 1926; Research Fellow on the Laura Spelman Rockefeller Memorial Foundation, 1924–25; Prof. of Political Economy in the University of Dublin, 1934–67; Registrar of TCD, 1951–52, and Bursar, 1952–57; Pro-Chancellor, Univ. of Dublin, 1965–72. Leverhulme Research Fellow, 1950; Visiting Fellow, Princeton Univ., 1963–64. Mem. of IFS Commissions of Inquiry into Banking, Currency and Credit, 1934–38; Agriculture, 1939; Emigration and Population, 1948. Planning Officer (temp.) in Ministry of Production, London, 1943–45; Economic Adviser to British National Cttee of Internat. Chambers of Commerce, 1941–47. Past Vice-Pres., Royal Dublin Society; Life Mem., Mont Pelerin Soc. Formerly Member: Irish National Productivity Cttee; Council Irish Management Inst.; Exec. Bd, Dublin Economic Research Inst.; Internat. Inst. of Statistics; Bd of Visitors, Nat. Mus. of Ireland. *Publications:* numerous papers in the economic periodicals. *Recreations:* travel, walking. *Address:* 7 Braemor Park, Churchtown, Dublin 14. *T:* Dublin 970442. *Club:* Kildare Street and University (Dublin).

DUNCAN, Dr George Douglas; Regional Medical Officer, East Anglian Regional Health Authority, 1973–85; *s* of late George Forman Duncan and of Mary Duncan (*née* Davidson); *m* 1949, Isobel (*née* Reid); two *s* one *d*. *Educ:* Robert Gordon's Coll., Aberdeen; Aberdeen Univ. MB, ChB 1948, DPH 1952, FFCM 1972. Various hosp. appts; Asst MOH Stirlingshire, Divisional MO Grangemouth, 1953–57; Asst Sen. MO, Leeds RHB, 1957–60; Dep. Sen. Admin. MO, Newcastle RHB, 1960–68; Sen. Admin. MO, East Anglian RHB, 1968–73. Member: Nat. Nursing Staff Cttee and Nat. Staff Cttee for Nurses and Midwives, 1970–74; PHLS Bd, 1973–75; Central Cttee for Community Medicine, 1974–81; Chm., English Regl MOs Gp, 1981–83; Vice-Pres., FCM RCP, 1979–83. QHP 1984–87. Hon. Mem., BPA, 1988–. Hon. MA Cambridge, 1986. *Address:* 12 Storey's Way, Cambridge CB3 0DT. *T:* Cambridge (0223) 63427.

DUNCAN, Sir James (Blair), Kt 1981; Chairman, Transport Development Group, since 1975; *b* 24 Aug. 1927; *s* of late John Duncan and Emily MacFarlane Duncan; *m* 1974, Dr Betty Psaltis, San Francisco. *Educ:* Whitehill Sch., Glasgow. Qualified as Scottish Chartered Accountant. Joined Transport Development Group, 1953; Dir, 1960; Chief Exec., 1970–90; Mem., LTE (part-time), 1979–82. Scottish Council: Mem. 1976–, and Chm. 1982–, London Exec. Cttee; Vice Pres., 1983–. Confedn of British Industry: Mem. Council, 1980–82; Mem. 1979–90, and Chm. 1983–88, London Region Roads and Transportation Cttee; Mem., Transport Policy Cttee, 1983–. London Chamber of Commerce: Mem. Council, 1982–; Mem., Gen. Purposes Cttee, 1983–90; Dep. Chm., 1984–86; Chm., 1986–88. Pres., IRTE, 1984–87. FCIT (Pres., 1980–81; Spurrier Meml Lectr, 1972; Award of Merit, 1973; Herbert Crow Medal, 1978); CBIM; FRSA 1977. *Publications:* papers on transport matters. *Recreations:* travel, reading, walking, swimming, theatre. *Address:* 17 Kingston House South, Ennismore Gardens, SW7 1NF. *T:* 071–589 3545. *Clubs:* Caledonian, Royal Automobile.

DUNCAN, Prof. James Playford, ME Adelaide, DSc Manchester; Professor of Mechanical Engineering, University of British Columbia, 1966–84, now Emeritus; Adjunct Professor, University of Victoria, 1985–87; *b* 10 Nov. 1919; *s* of late Hugh Sinclair Duncan and late Nellie Gladys Duncan; *m* 1942, Jean Marie Booth; three *s* one *d*. *Educ:* Scotch Coll., Adelaide; University of Adelaide, S Australia. Executive Engineer, Richards Industries Ltd, Keswick, S Australia, 1941–46; Senior Physics Master, Scotch Coll., Adelaide, 1946–47; Lecturer in Mechanical Engineering, University of Adelaide, 1948–49, Senior Lecturer, 1950–51 and 1953–54; Turbine Engineer, Metropolitan Vickers Electrical Co., Trafford Park, Manchester, 1952; Turner and Newall Research Fellow, University of Manchester, 1955; Lecturer in Mechanical Engineering, University of Manchester, 1956; Prof. of Mechanical Engineering, University of Sheffield, 1956–66. *Publications:* Sculptured Surfaces in Engineering and Medicine, 1983; Computer Aided Sculpture, 1989. *Recreations:* sailing, flautist. *Address:* 3568 Handley Crescent, Port Coquitlam, BC V3B 2Y5, Canada.

DUNCAN, Ven. John Finch, MBE 1991; Archdeacon of Birmingham, since 1985; *b* 9 Sept. 1933; *s* of John and Helen Maud Duncan; *m* 1965, Diana Margaret Dewes; one *s* two *d*. *Educ:* Queen Elizabeth Grammar School, Wakefield; University Coll., Oxford; Cuddesdon Coll. MA (Oxon). Curate, St John, South Bank, Middlesbrough, 1959–61; Novice, Society of St Francis, 1961–62; Curate, St Peter, Birmingham, 1962–65; Chaplain, Univ. of Birmingham, 1965–76; Vicar of All Saints, Kings Heath, Birmingham, 1976–85. Chm., Copec Housing Trust, 1970–. *Recreations:* golf, theatre, convivial gatherings. *Address:* 122 Westfield Road, Edgbaston, Birmingham B15 3JQ. *T:* 021-454 3402. *Club:* Harborne Golf (Birmingham).

DUNCAN, John Spenser Ritchie, CMG 1967; MBE 1953; HM Diplomatic Service, retired; High Commissioner in the Bahamas, 1978–81; *b* 26 July 1921; *s* of late Rev. J. H. Duncan, DD; *m* 1950, Sheila Conacher, MB, ChB, DObstRCOG; one *d*. *Educ:* George Watson's Boys' Coll.; Glasgow Acad.; Dundee High Sch.; Edinburgh Univ. Entered Sudan Political Service, 1941. Served in HM Forces, 1941–43. Private Sec. to Governor-Gen. of the Sudan, 1954; Dep. Adviser to Governor-Gen. on Constitutional and External Affairs, 1955; appointed to Foreign (subseq. Diplomatic) Service, 1956; seconded to Joint Services Staff Coll., 1957; Political Agent, Doha, 1958; Dep. Dir-Gen., British Information Services, New York, 1959–63; Consul-Gen., Muscat, 1963–65; Head of Personnel Dept, Diplomatic Service, 1966–68; Minister, British High Commn, Canberra, 1969–71; High Comr, Zambia, 1971–74; Ambassador to Morocco, 1975–78. *Publications:* The Sudan: A Record of Achievement, 1952; The Sudan's Path to Independence, 1957. *Address:* 9 Blackford Road, Edinburgh EH9 2DT. *Club:* New (Edinburgh).
See also K. P. Duncan.

DUNCAN, Dr Kenneth Playfair, CB 1985; FRCP; FRCPE; Assistant Director (Biomedical Sciences), National Radiological Protection Board, 1985–88; *b* 27 Sept. 1924; *s* of late Dr J. H. Duncan, MA, BPhil, DD, and H. P. Duncan (*née* Ritchie); *m* 1950, Dr Gillian Crow, MB, ChB; four *d*. *Educ:* Kilmarnock Acad.; Glasgow Acad.; Dundee High Sch.; St Andrews Univ. BSc, MB, ChB; DIH. FFOM 1978. House Surg., Dundee Royal Infirmary, 1947; RAMC, 1948–50; Gen. Practice, Brighton, 1950–51; Area MO, British Rail, 1951–54; Chief Medical Officer: SW Gas Bd, 1954–58; UKAEA, 1958–69; Head of Health and Safety, BSC, 1969–75; Dir of Medical Services, HSE, 1975–82; Dep. Dir-Gen., HSE, 1982–84. External Examiner in Occupational Health, Univ. of Dundee, 1970–74; Examiner in Occupational Health, Soc. of Apothecaries, 1974–79. Vis. Prof., London Sch. of Hygiene and Tropical Medicine, 1977–82. Member: Industrial Health Adv. Cttee, Dept of Employment, 1960–74; MRC, 1975–83. Pres., Soc. of Occupational Medicine, 1970. *Publications:* contrib. medical and scientific jls on radiological protection and gen. occupational health topics. *Recreation:* gardening. *Address:* Westfield, Steeple Aston, Oxon OX5 3SD. *T:* Steeple Aston (0869) 40277.
See also J. S. R. Duncan.

DUNCAN, Laura; *see* Duncan, A. L. A.

DUNCAN, Malcolm McGregor, OBE 1987; WS; Chief Executive, City of Edinburgh District Council, 1980–87; *b* 23 Jan. 1922; *s* of Rev. Reginald Duncan, BD, BLitt, and Clarice Ethel (*née* Hodgkinson); *m* 1954, Winifred Petrie (*née* Greenhorn); two *s* one *d*. *Educ:* George Watson's Coll., Edinburgh; Edinburgh Univ. (MA 1942; LLB 1948). Admitted Writer to the Signet, 1949. Served RAFVR, Flt Lieut, 1942–46. Edinburgh Corporation, 1952; Depute Town Clerk, 1971; Director of Administration, City of Edinburgh District Council, 1975–80. *Recreations:* playing golf, watching other sports, listening to music. *Address:* 52 Glendevon Place, Edinburgh EH12 5UJ. *T:* 031-337 2869.
See also Rev. D. M. Duncan.

DUNCAN, Sean Bruce; His Honour Judge Duncan; a Circuit Judge, since 1988; *b* 21 Dec. 1942; *s* of Joseph Alexander Duncan and Patricia Pauline Duncan; *m* 1974, Dr Diana Bowyer Courtney; three *s* one *d*. *Educ:* Shrewsbury Sch.; St Edmund Hall, Oxford (MA). Called to the Bar, Inner Temple, 1966; Northern Circuit (Hon. Sec., Circuit Cttee, 1985–88); a Recorder, 1984–88. Served with Cheshire Yeomanry (TA), 1963–68 (Lieut). Chairman: Old Swan Boys Club, Liverpool, 1974–79; Liverpool Youth Organisations Cttee, 1977–83; Vice-Chm., Liverpool Council of Voluntary Service, 1982–88. *Recreations:* farming, sport, music. *Address:* c/o Queen Elizabeth II Law Courts, Derby Square, Liverpool. *Clubs:* Royal Liverpool Golf; Liverpool Ramblers AFC (Vice Pres.); Royal Chester Rowing.

DUNCAN, Stanley Frederick St Clare, CMG 1983; HM Diplomatic Service, retired; *b* 13 Nov. 1927; *yr s* of late Stanley Gilbert Scott and Louisa Elizabeth Duncan; *m* 1967, Jennifer Jane Bennett; two *d*. *Educ:* Latymer Upper Sch. FRGS. India Office, 1946; CRO, 1947; Private Sec. to Parly Under-Sec. of State, 1954; Second Sec., Ottawa, 1954–55; Brit. Govt Information Officer, Toronto, 1955–57; Second Sec., Wellington, 1958–60; First Sec., CRO, 1960; seconded to Central African Office, 1962–64; Mem., Brit. Delegn to Victoria Falls Conf. on Dissolution of Fedn of Rhodesia and Nyasaland, 1963; First Sec., Nicosia, 1964–67; FCO, 1967–70; FCO Adviser, Brit. Gp, Inter-Parly Union, 1968–70; Head of Chancery and First Sec., Lisbon, 1970–73; Consul-General and subsequently Chargé d'Affaires in Mozambique, 1973–75; Counsellor (Political), Brasilia, 1976–77; Head of Consular Dept, FCO, 1977–80; Canadian Nat. Defence Coll., 1980–81; Ambassador to Bolivia, 1981–85; High Comr in Malta, 1985–87. Officer, Military Order of Christ (Portugal), 1973. *Recreations:* countryside pursuits. *Address:* Tucksmead, Longworth, Oxon OX13 5ET.

DUNCAN MILLAR, Ian Alastair, CBE 1978; MC; CEng, MICE; DL; Director, Macdonald Fraser & Co. Ltd, Perth, 1961–85; Member, Royal Company of Archers (Queen's Body Guard for Scotland), since 1956; *b* 22 Nov. 1914; *s* of late Sir James Duncan Millar and Lady Duncan Millar (*née* Forester Paton); *m* 1945, Louise Reid McCosh; two *s* two *d*. *Educ:* Gresham's Sch., Holt; Trinity Coll., Cambridge (MA). Served with Corps of Royal Engineers, 1940–45 (Major; wounded; despatches): 7th Armoured Div., N Africa and Normandy; 51 (Highland) Div., France and Germany. Contested Parly Elections (L): Banff, 1945; Kinross and W Perthshire, 1949 and 1963. Depute Chm., North of Scotland Hydro-Electric Bd, 1970–72 (Mem., 1957–72). Chm., United Auctions (Scotland) Ltd, 1967–74. Dir, Hill Farming Research Organisation, 1966–78; Chm., Consultative Cttee to Sec. of State for Scotland under 1976 Freshwater and Salmon Fisheries Act, 1981–86; Mem., Tay Dist Salmon Fisheries Bd, 1962–80, 1986–. Vice-Pres., Scottish Landowners Fedn, 1985–90. Mem. Ct, Dundee Univ., 1975–78. Perth CC, 1945–75: Chm. Planning Cttee, 1954–75; Convener, 1970–75; Chm. Jt CC of Perth and Kinross, 1970–75; Tayside Regional Council: Councillor and Chm., 1974–75; Convener, 1975–78. Fellow, Inst. of Fisheries Management, 1988. DL 1963, JP 1952, Perthshire. *Publication:* A Countryman's Log, 1990. *Recreations:* studying and catching salmon, shooting, meeting people. *Address:* Reynock, Remony, Aberfeldy, Perthshire. *T:* Kenmore (08873) 400. *Club:* Royal Golfing Society (Perth).

DUNCOMBE, family name of **Baron Feversham.**

DUNCOMBE, Sir Philip (Digby) Pauncefort-, 4th Bt *cr* 1859; DL; one of HM Body Guard, Honorable Corps of Gentlemen-at-Arms, since 1979; *b* 18 May 1927; *o s* of Sir Everard Pauncefort-Duncombe, 3rd Bt, DSO, and Evelyn Elvira (*d* 1986), *d* of Frederick Anthony Denny; *S* father, 1971; *m* 1951, Rachel Moyra, *d* of Major H. G. Aylmer; one *s* two *d*. *Educ:* Stowe. 2nd Lieut, Grenadier Guards, 1946; served in Palestine, 1947–48; Malaya, 1948–49; Cyprus, 1957–59; Hon. Major, retired 1960, Regular Army Reserve. County Comdt, Buckinghamshire Army Cadet Force, 1967–70. DL Bucks 1971, High Sheriff, 1987–88. *Heir: s* David Philip Henry Pauncefort-Duncombe [*b* 21 May 1956; *m* 1987, Sarah, *d* of late Reginald Battrum and of Mrs Reginald Battrum; one *s* one *d*]. *Address:* Great Brickhill Manor, Milton Keynes, Bucks MK17 9BE. *T:* Great Brickhill (0525) 261205. *Club:* Cavalry and Guards.

DUNCOMBE, Roy, VRD 1957; Chairman, Nationwide Anglia Building Society, 1989–91 (Deputy Chairman, 1987–88; Chairman, Anglia Building Society, 1985–87); *b* 7 June 1925; *s* of Joseph William Duncombe and Gladys May Duncombe (*née* Reece); *m* 1946, Joan Thornley Pickering; one *s* two *d*. *Educ:* Hinckley Grammar School. RNR, 1943–68 (Lt-Comdr (A); Pilot, Fleet Air Arm). Financial Advr, Ferry Pickering Group, 1987– (Financial Dir, 1965–87); Chm., Bosworth Heritage Ltd, 1987–. *Recreations:* walking, swimming, boating, ornithology. *Address:* Westways, Market Bosworth, Nuneaton, Warwickshire CV13 0LQ. *T:* Market Bosworth (0455) 291728. *Club:* Naval and Military.

DUNCUMB, Dr Peter, FRS 1977; Director, Research Centre in Super-conductivity, Cambridge University, 1988–89; *b* 26 Jan. 1931; *s* of late William Duncumb and of Hilda Grace (*née* Coleman); *m* 1955, Anne Leslie Taylor; two *s* one *d*. *Educ:* Oundle Sch.; Clare Coll., Cambridge (BA 1953, MA 1956, PhD 1957). DSIR Res. Fellow, Cambridge Univ., 1957–59; Tube Investments, subseq. TI Group, Research Laboratories: Res. Scientist and Gp Leader, 1959–67, Head, Physics Dept, 1967–72; Asst Dir, 1972–79; Dir and Gen. Manager, 1979–87. Hon. Prof., Warwick Univ., 1990–. Hon. Mem., Microbeam Analysis Soc. of America, 1973. C. V. Boys Prize, Inst. of Physics, 1966. *Publications:* numerous on electron microscopy and analysis in Jl of Inst. of Physics. *Recreations:* hill walking, family genealogy. *Address:* 5 Woollards Lane, Great Shelford, Cambridge CB2 5LZ. *T:* Cambridge (0223) 843064.

DUNDAS, family name of **Viscount Melville,** and of **Marquess of Zetland.**

DUNDAS, Sir Hugh (Spencer Lisle), Kt 1987; CBE 1977; DSO 1944 and Bar 1945; DFC 1941; RAF retired; DL; Chairman, 1982–87, Managing Director, 1973–82, Deputy Chairman, 1981–82, BET Public Limited Company; *b* 22 July 1920; *s* of late Frederick James Dundas and Sylvia Mary (*née* March-Phillipps); *m* 1950, Hon. Enid Rosamond Lawrence, 2nd *d* of 1st Baron Oaksey and 3rd Baron Trevethin; one *s* two *d*. *Educ:* Stowe. Joined 616 (S Yorks) Sqdn AAF 1939; served in UK Fighter Comd Sqdn, 1939–43; N Africa, Malta, Sicily, Italy, 1943–46; perm. commn 1944; comd 244 Wing, Italy, 1944–46 (Gp Captain; despatches 1945); retd 1947. Comd 601 (Co. London) Sqdn RAuxAF, 1947–50. Beaverbrook Newspapers, 1948–60: various editorial and managerial posts; joined Exec. Staff, Rediffusion Ltd, 1961: Dir, 1966; Dep. Man. Dir, 1968; Man. Dir, 1970–74; Chm., 1978–85; Chm., Thames Television Ltd, 1981–87 (Dir, 1968–87). Mem. Council, and F and GP Cttee, RAF Benevolent Fund, 1976–89; Cancer Relief Macmillan Fund (formerly Nat. Soc. for Cancer Relief): Trustee, 1983–89; Chm. Council, 1988– (Mem., 1976–); Chm., Bd of Management, 1989–. Trustee: Prince's Youth Business Trust (Chm. of Trustees, 1987–90); Home Farm Trust Develt Trust, 1987–90. DL 1969, High Sheriff 1989, Surrey. *Publication:* Flying Start (autobiog.), 1988. *Address:* 55 Iverna Court, W8 6TS. *T:* 071–937 0773; The Schoolroom, Dockenfield, Farnham, Surrey. *T:* Frensham (025125) 2331. *Clubs:* White's, Royal Air Force.

DUNDEE, 12th Earl of, *cr* 1660 (Scotland); **Alexander Henry Scrymgeour;** Viscount Dudhope and Lord Scrymgeour, 1641 (Scotland); Lord Inverkeithing, 1660 (Scotland); Lord Glassary (UK), 1954; Hereditary Royal Standard-Bearer for Scotland; *b* 5 June 1949; *s* of 11th Earl of Dundee, PC, and of Patricia Katherine, *d* of late Col Lord Herbert Montagu Douglas Scott; *S* father, 1983; *m* 1979, Siobhan Mary, *d* of David Llewellyn, Gt Somerford, Wilts; one *s* three *d*. *Educ:* Eton; St Andrews Univ. Contested (C) Hamilton, by-election May 1978. A Lord in Waiting (Govt Whip), 1986–89. *Heir: s* Lord Scrymgeour, *qv*. *Address:* Farm Office, Birkhill, Cupar, Fife. *Clubs:* White's; New (Edinburgh).

DUNDEE (St Paul's Cathedral), Provost of; *see* Sanderson, Very Rev. P. O.

DUNDONALD, 15th Earl of, *cr* 1669; **Iain Alexander Douglas Blair Cochrane;** Lord Cochrane of Dundonald, 1647; Lord Cochrane of Paisley and Ochiltree, 1669; Chairman, Duneth Securities and associated companies, since 1986; Director, New Capital and Scottish Properties and associated companies, since 1987; *b* 17 Feb. 1961; *s* of 14th Earl of Dundonald and Aphra Farquhar (*d* 1972), *d* of late Comdr George Fetherstonhaugh; *S* father, 1986; *m* 1987, Beatrice, *d* of Adolphus Russo; one *s*. *Educ:* Wellington College; RAC Cirencester. DipREM. *Recreations:* shooting, fishing, skiing, sailing. *Heir: s* Lord Cochrane, *qv*. *Address:* Lochnell Castle, Ledaig, Argyll.

DUNEDIN, Bishop of, since 1990; **Rt. Rev. Penelope Ann Bansall Jamieson,** PhD; *b* Chalfont St Peter, Bucks, 21 June 1942; *m* 1964, Ian William Andrew Jamieson; three *d*. *Educ:* St Mary's Sch., Gerrards Cross; High Sch., High Wycombe; Edinburgh Univ. (MA 1964); Victoria Univ., Wellington (PhD 1977); Otago Univ. (BD 1983). Deacon 1982; priest 1983; Asst Curate, St James', Lower Hutt, 1982–85; Vicar, Karori West with Makara, dio. Wellington, 1985–90. *Address:* c/o Diocesan Office, PO Box 5445, Dunedin, New Zealand.

DUNGEY, Prof. James Wynne, PhD; Professor of Physics, Imperial College, University of London, 1965–84; *b* 30 Jan. 1923; *s* of Ernest Dungey and Alice Dungey; *m* 1950, Christine Scotland (*née* Brown); one *s* one *d*. *Educ:* Bradfield; Magdalene Coll., Cambridge (MA, PhD). Res. Fellow, Univ. of Sydney, 1950–53; Vis. Asst Prof., Penn State Coll., 1953–54; ICI Fellow, Cambridge, 1954–57; Lectr, King's Coll., Newcastle upon Tyne, 1957–59; Sen. Principal Scientific Officer, AWRE, Aldermaston, 1959–63; Res. Fellow, Imperial Coll., London, 1963–65. Fellow, Amer. Geophysical Union, 1973. Chapman Medal, RAS, 1982; Gold Medal for Geophysics, RAS, 1990; Fleming Medal, Amer. Geophysical Union, 1991. *Publications:* Cosmic Electrodynamics, 1958; papers on related topics. *Recreations:* music, sailing. *Address:* Long Roof, Leverett's Lane, Walberswick, Southwold, Suffolk IP18 6UF. *T:* Southwold (0502) 722242.

DUNGLASS, Lord (courtesy title used by heirs to Earldom of Home before title was disclaimed); *see under* Douglas-Home, Hon. D. A. C.

DUNHAM, Sir Kingsley (Charles), Kt 1972; FRS 1955; FRSE; PhD Dunelm, 1932; SD Harvard, 1935; FGS; FEng; Hon. FIMM; Director, Institute of Geological Sciences, 1967–75; *b* Sturminster Newton, Dorset, 2 Jan. 1910; *s* of Ernest Pedder and Edith Agnes Dunham; *m* 1936, Margaret, *d* of William and Margaret Young, Choppington, Northumberland; one *s*. *Educ:* Durham Johnston Sch.; Hatfield Coll., Durham Univ. (Sen. Fellow, 1990); Adams House, Harvard Univ. Temporary Geologist, New Mexico Bureau of Mines, 1934; HM Geological Survey of Great Britain; Geologist, 1935–45; Senior Geologist 1946; Chief Petrographer, 1948; Prof. of Geology, Univ. of Durham, 1950–66, Emeritus, 1968–; Sub-Warden of Durham Colls, 1959–61. Miller Prof., University of Ill., 1956. Director: Weardale Minerals Ltd, 1982–86; Blackdene Minerals

Ltd, 1983–86. Member: Council, Royal Society, 1965–66 (Foreign Sec., a Vice-Pres., 1971–76; Royal Medal, 1970); Council for Scientific Policy (Min. of Ed. & Sci.), 1965–66. President: Instn Mining and Metallurgy, 1963–64 (Gold Medal, 1968); Yorks Geological Soc., 1958–60 (Sorby Medal, 1964); Internat. Union of Geological Sciences, 1969–72; Geological Soc. of London, 1966–68 (Council 1949–52, 1960–64; Bigsby Medal, 1954; Murchison Medal, 1966; Wollaston Medal, 1976); BAAS, 1972–73; Mineralogical Soc., 1975–77. NE Region, Inst. of Geologists, 1981–. Institution of Geology: Founder Mem., 1976; Fellow, 1985; Aberconway Medal, 1986. Trustee, British Museum (Natural History), 1963–66. Member Geology-Geophysics Cttee (NERC) 1965–70; Chairman: Internat. Geol. Correlation Project (IUGS-UNESCO), 1973–76; Council for Environmental Science and Engineering, 1973–75. Mem. Council and UK Rep., 1972–77, Hon. Scholar, 1977, Internat. Inst. for Applied Systems Analysis, Laxenburg, Vienna. Pres., Durham Univ. Soc., 1973–75. Mem., City, Dunelm and Palatinate Probus. Hon. President: Friends of Killhope, 1985–; Durham Probus clubs, 1986–. Founder Fellow, Fellowship of Engineering, 1976. Hon. Member: Royal Geol Soc. Cornwall (Bolitho Medal 1972); Geol. Soc. of India, 1972; Hon. Foreign Fellow, Geol. Soc. of America; Corr. Foreign Mem., Austrian Acad. of Scis, 1971; Hon. Foreign Member: Société Géologique de Belge, 1974; Bulgarian Geological Soc., 1975. Fellow, Imperial Coll., 1976; Hon. Fellow, St John's Coll., Durham, 1991. Hon. DSc: Dunelm, 1946; Liverpool, 1967; Birmingham, 1970; Illinois, 1971; Leicester, 1972; Michigan, 1973; Canterbury, 1973; Edinburgh, 1974; Exeter, 1975; Hull, 1978; Hon. ScD Cantab, 1973; DUniv Open, 1982. Mitchell Meml Medal, City of Stoke on Trent, 1974; Haidinger Medaille der Geologischen Bundesanstalt, 1976; von Buch Medal, Deutsche Geologische Gesellschaft, 1981. Hon. Citizen of Texas, 1975. *Publications:* Geology of the Organ Mountains, 1935; Geology of the Northern Pennine Orefield, Vol. 1, 1948, 2nd edn 1990, Vol. 2 (with A. A. Wilson), 1985; (as Editor) Symposium on the Geology, Paragenesis and Reserves of the Ores of Lead & Zinc, 2nd edn, 1950; Fluorspar, 1952; Geology of Northern Skye (with F. W. Anderson) 1966; (with W. C. C. Rose) Geology and Hermatite Deposits of South Cumbria, 1977; articles in Quarterly Jl of Geological Soc., Mineralogical Magazine, Geological Magazine, American Mineralogist, etc. *Recreations:* music (organ and pianoforte); gardening. *Address:* Charleycroft, Quarryheads Lane, Durham DH1 3DY. *T:* Durham (091) 348977. *Club:* Geological Society's.

DUNITZ, Prof. Jack David, FRS 1974; Professor of Chemical Crystallography at the Swiss Federal Institute of Technology (ETH), Zürich, 1957–90; *b* 29 March 1923; *s* of William Dunitz and Mildred (*née* Gossman); *m* 1953, Barbara Steuer; two *d. Educ:* Hillhead High Sch., Glasgow; Hutchesons' Grammar Sch., Glasgow; Glasgow Univ. (BSc, PhD). Post-doctoral Fellow, Oxford Univ., 1946–48, 1951–53; California Inst. of Technology, 1948–51, 1953–54; Vis. Scientist, US Nat. Insts of Health, 1954–55; Sen. Res. Fellow, Davy Faraday Res. Lab., Royal Instn, London, 1956–57. Overseas Fellow, Churchill Coll., Cambridge, 1968; Vis. Professor: Iowa State Univ., 1965; Tokyo Univ., 1967; Technion, Haifa, 1970; Hill Vis. Prof., Univ. of Minnesota, 1983; Fairchild Distinguished Scholar, CIT, 1985; Hooker Distinguished Vis. Prof., McMaster Univ., 1987; Alexander Todd Vis. Prof., Cambridge Univ., 1990. Lectures: British Council, 1965; Treat B. Johnson Meml, Yale Univ., 1965; 3M Univ. of Minnesota, 1966; Reilly, Univ. Notre Dame, US, 1971; Kelly, Purdue Univ., 1971; Gerhard Schmidt Meml, Weizmann Inst. of Sci., 1973; George Fisher Baker, Cornell Univ., 1976; Centenary, Chem. Soc., 1977; Appleton, Brown Univ., 1979; H. J. Backer, Gröningen Univ., 1980; Havinga, Leiden Univ., 1980; Karl Folkers, Wisconsin Univ., 1981; A. L. Patterson Meml, Inst. for Cancer Res., Philadelphia, 1983; C. S. Marvel, Illinois Univ., 1987; Birch, Canberra, 1989; Dwyer, Sydney, 1989; Bijvoet, Utrecht Univ., 1989. For. Mem., Royal Netherlands Acad. of Arts and Sciences, 1979; Mem., Leopoldina Acad., 1979; Foreign Associate, US Nat. Acad. of Scis, 1988; Mem., Academia Europaea, 1989; Hon. Mem., Swiss Soc. of Crystallography, 1990; Fellow AAAS, 1981. Hon. DSc Technion, Haifa, 1990. Tishler Award, Harvard Univ., 1985; Paracelsus Prize, Swiss Chem. Soc., 1986; Gregori Aminoff Prize, Swedish Royal Acad., 1990. Jt Editor, Perspectives in Structural Chemistry, 1967–71; Mem. Editorial Bd: Helvetica Chimica Acta, 1971–85; Structure and Bonding, 1971–81. *Publications:* X-ray Analysis and the Structure of Organic Molecules, 1979; papers on various aspects of crystal and molecular structure in Acta Crystallographica, Helvetica Chimica Acta, Jl Chem. Soc., Jl Amer. Chem. Soc., etc. *Recreation:* walking. *Address:* Obere Heslibachstrasse 77, 8700 Küsnacht, Switzerland. *T:* (01) 9101723; (office) ETH, Universitätstrasse 16, CH-8006 Zürich, Switzerland. *T:* (01) 2562892.

DUNKEL, Arthur; Director General, General Agreement on Tariffs and Trade (GATT), since 1980; *b* 28 Aug. 1932; *s* of Walter Dunkel and Berthe Lerch; *m* 1957, Christiane Müller-Serda; one *s* one *d. Educ:* Univ. of Lausanne (LèsSc écon. et comm.). Federal Office for external economic affairs, 1956: successively Head of sections for OECD matters, 1960; for cooperation with developing countries, 1964; for world trade policy, 1971; Permanent Representative of Switzerland to GATT, 1973; Delegate of Federal Council for Trade Agreements, rank of Ambassador, 1976; in this capacity, head of Swiss delegations to multilateral (GATT, UNCTAD, UNIDO, etc) and bilateral negotiations in the fields of trade, development, commodities, transfer of technology, industrialisation, agriculture, etc. Prof. at Univs of Geneva, 1983, and Fribourg, 1987. Dr *hc* rer. pol. Fribourg, 1980. Freedom Prize, Max Schmidheiny Foundn, 1989. *Publications:* various articles and studies in economic, commercial, agricl and development fields. *Address:* GATT, Centre William Rappard, 154 rue de Lausanne, 1211 Geneva 21, Switzerland.

DUNKELD, Bishop of, (RC), since 1981; **Rt. Rev. Vincent Logan;** *b* 30 June 1941; *s* of Joseph Logan and Elizabeth Flannigan. *Educ:* Blairs College, Aberdeen; St Andrew's Coll., Drygrange, Melrose. Ordained priest, Edinburgh, 1964; Asst Priest, St Margaret's, Davidson's Mains, Edinburgh, 1964–66; Corpus Christi Coll., London, 1966–67 (DipRE); Chaplain, St Joseph's Hospital, Rosewell, Midlothian, 1967–77; Adviser in Religious Education, Archdiocese of St Andrews and Edinburgh, 1967; Parish Priest, St Mary's, Ratho, 1977–81; Episcopal Vicar for Education, Archdiocese of St Andrews and Edinburgh, 1978. *Address:* Bishop's House, 29 Roseangle, Dundee DD1 4LS. *T:* Dundee (0382) 24327.

DUNKERLEY, George William, MC 1942; Chairman, Oil and Pipelines Agency, 1985–88; Director: STC plc, 1985–89; Scandinavian Bank Group plc, 1986–89; *b* 14 June 1919; *s* of Harold and Eva Dunkerley; *m* 1947, Diana Margaret Lang; two *s. Educ:* Felsted School, Essex. FCA. War Service, 1940–46, with RA (The Northumberland Hussars) in N Africa, Sicily, Northern Europe; Major. With Peat Marwick Mitchell & Co., 1948–85, Dep. Senior Partner (UK), 1982–85. *Recreations:* gardening, forestry, travel. *Address:* 31 The Priory, Priory Road, Abbots Kerswell, Newton Abbot, Devon TQ12 5PP. *Club:* Lansdowne.

DUNKLEY, Christopher; journalist and broadcaster; Television Critic, Financial Times, since 1973; Presenter, Feedback, Radio 4, since 1986; *b* 22 Jan. 1944; 2nd *s* of late Robert Dunkley and of Joyce Mary Dunkley (*née* Turner); *m* 1967, Carolyn Elizabeth, *e d* of late Col A. P. C. Lyons; one *s* one *d. Educ:* Haberdashers' Aske's (expelled). Various jobs, incl. theatre flyman, cook, hospital porter, 1961–63; general reporter, then cinema and theatre critic, Slough Observer, 1963–65; feature writer and news editor, UK Press Gazette, 1965–68; night news reporter, then mass media correspondent and TV critic, The Times, 1968–73. Frequent radio broadcaster, 1963–, esp. on Kaleidoscope, Critics' Forum, Meridian, LBC. Occasional television presenter/script writer/chairman; series incl. Edition, Real Time, In Vision (all BBC2), Whistle Blowers, and Panorama: The Television Revolution (BBC1). Critic of the Year, British Press Awards, 1976, 1986; Broadcast Journalist of the Year, TV-am Awards, 1989; Judges' Award, 1990. *Publications:* Television Today and Tomorrow: Wall to Wall Dallas?, 1985; many articles in The Listener, Television World, Stills, Electronic Media, Telegraph Magazine, etc. *Recreations:* motorcycling, reading in secondhand bookshops, collecting almost everything, especially dictionaries, tin toys, Victorian boys' books. *Address:* 38 Leverton Street, NW5 2PG. *T:* 071-485 7101.

DUNKLEY, Captain James Lewis, CBE 1970 (OBE 1946); RD 1943; Marine Manager, P&O Lines, 1971–72 (Marine Superintendent, 1968–71); *b* 13 Sept. 1908; *s* of William E. Dunkley, Thurlaston Grange, Warwickshire; *m* 1937, Phyllis Mary Cale; one *d. Educ:* Lawrence Sheriff Sch., Rugby; Thames Nautical Training Coll., HMS Worcester. Junior Officer, P&O Line, 1928; Captain, 1954; Cdre, 1964. RNR: Sub-Lt, 1931; Comdr, 1951; Captain, 1956. Master, Honourable Co. of Master Mariners, 1970. *Recreations:* gardening, collecting. *Address:* 1 Collindale Gardens, Clacton-on-Sea, Essex CO15 5BH. *T:* Clacton-on-Sea (0255) 813950. *Club:* City Livery.

DUNLAP, Air Marshal Clarence Rupert, CBE 1944; CD; RCAF retired; *b* 1 Jan. 1908; *s* of late Frank Burns Dunlap, Truro, Nova Scotia; *m* 1935, Hester, *d* of late Dr E. A. Cleveland, Vancouver, BC; one *s. Educ:* Acadia Univ.; Nova Scotia Technical Coll. Joined RCAF 1928 as Pilot Officer; trained as pilot and specialised in aerial survey; later specialised in armament; Dir of Armament, RCAF HQ Ottawa on outbreak of War; commanded: RCAF Station, Mountain View, Ont., Jan.-Oct. 1942; RCAF Station, Leeming, Yorks, Dec. 1942–May 1943; 331 Wing NASAF, Tunisia, May-Nov. 1943; 139 Wing TAF, Nov. 1943–Feb. 1945; 64 Base, Middleton St George, Feb.-May 1945; Dep., AMAS, AFHQ, Ottawa, 1945–48; Air Mem. for Air Plans, AFHQ, Ottawa, 1948–49; AOC North-West Air Command, Edmonton, Alberta, 1949–51; Commandant of National Defence Coll., Kingston, Ont., 1951–54; Vice Chief of the Air Staff, AFHQ, Ottawa, 1954–58; Dep. Chief of Staff, Operations, SHAPE, Paris, 1958–62; Chief of Air Staff, AFHQ, Ottawa, 1962–64; Dep. C-in-C, N Amer. Air Def. Comd, 1964–67. Hon. DCL Acadia Univ., 1955; Hon. DEng Nova Scotia Technical Coll., 1967. *Address:* 203–1375 Newport Avenue, Victoria, BC V8S 5E8, Canada. *Clubs:* Union (Victoria); Victoria Golf; Royal Ottawa Golf (Ottawa).

DUNLEATH, 4th Baron, *cr* 1892; **Charles Edward Henry John Mulholland,** TD; Chairman: Dunleath Estates Ltd; Ulster & General Holdings Ltd; Vice Lord-Lieutenant of County Down, since 1990; *b* 23 June 1933; *s* of 3rd Baron Dunleath, CBE, DSO, and of Henrietta Grace, *d* of late Most Rev. C. F. D'Arcy, Archbishop of Armagh; *S* father, 1956; *m* 1959, Dorinda Margery, *d* of late Lieut-Gen. A. E. Percival, CB, DSO and Bar, OBE, MC. *Educ:* Eton; Cambridge Univ. Served with 11th Hussars, 1952–53, with N Irish Horse, 1954–69, Lt-Col 1967–69; Captain, Ulster Defence Regt, 1971–73; Lt-Col, NIH, RARO, 1973–88, Hon. Col 1981–86. Member (Alliance): N Down, NI Assembly, 1973–75; N Down, NI Constitutional Convention, 1975–76; resigned from Alliance Party, 1979, rejoined 1981; Mem. (Alliance) for N Down, and Asst Speaker, NI Assembly, 1982–86. Mem., Ards Borough Council, 1977–81 (Independent 1979–81). Chairman: Carreras Rothmans of NI, 1974–84; NI Independent Television Ltd, 1979–83; Dir, Northern Bank Ltd, 1974–. Governor of BBC for N Ireland, 1967–73; Mem. Admin. Council, King George's Jubilee Trust, 1974–75; President: Royal Ulster Agric. Soc., 1973–76; Lagan Coll., 1982–86. DL Co. Down, 1964. *Heir: cousin* Major Sir Michael Mulholland, Bt, *qv. Address:* Ballywalter Park, Newtownards, Co. Down, Northern Ireland. *T:* Ballywalter (02477) 203. *Club:* Cavalry and Guards.

DUNLEAVY, Philip, CBE 1983 (OBE 1978); JP; Leader, Cardiff City Council, 1974–76 and 1979–82; Lord Mayor of Cardiff, 1982–83; *b* 5 Oct. 1915; *s* of Michael and Bridget Dunleavy; *m* 1936, Valerie Partridge; two *s* two *d. Educ:* St Cuthbert's Sch., Cardiff. Served War, TA (Sgt), 1939–46. Post Office, 1930–39 and 1946–75 (Executive Officer, 1960–75). Member: Cardiff City Council, 1962–83; South Glamorgan County Council, 1974–81. JP 1960. *Recreations:* youth, conservation, local historical research, local govt political activity. *Address:* 35 Merches Gardens, Grangetown, Cardiff CF1 7RF.

DUNLOP, Rear-Adm. Colin Charles Harrison, CB 1972; CBE 1963; DL; *b* 4 March 1918; *s* of late Engr Rear-Adm. S. H. Dunlop, CB; *m* 1941, Moyra Patricia O'Brien Gorges; two *s* (and one *s* decd). *Educ:* Marlborough Coll. Joined RN, 1935; served War of 1939–45 at sea in HM Ships Kent, Valiant, Diadem and Orion; subseq. HMS Sheffield, 1957–59; Sec. to 1st Sea Lord, 1960–63; comd HMS Pembroke, 1964–66; Programme Evaluation Gp, MoD, 1966–68; Director, Defence Policy (A), MoD, 1968–69; Comdr, British Navy Staff, Washington, 1969–71; Chief Naval Supply and Secretariat Officer, 1970–74; Flag Officer, Medway, and Port Adm., Chatham, 1971–74, retd 1974. Director General: Cable TV Assoc., 1974–83; Nat. TV Rental Assoc., 1974–83. DL Kent 1976. *Recreations:* cricket, country pursuits. *Address:* Chanceford Farm, Sand Lane, Frittenden, near Cranbrook, Kent TN17 2BA. *T:* Frittenden (058080) 242. *Clubs:* Army and Navy; MCC, I Zingari, Free Foresters, Incogniti, RN Cricket, Band of Brothers.

DUNLOP, Sir (Ernest) Edward, AC 1987; Kt 1969; CMG 1965; OBE 1947; Consultant Surgeon; Consultant, Royal Melbourne Hospital, since 1967; *b* Wangaratta, Australia, 12 July 1907; *s* of James Henry and Alice Emily Maud Dunlop; *m* 1945, Helen Raeburn Ferguson, *d* of Mephan Ferguson; two *s. Educ:* Benalla High Sch.; Victorian Coll. of Pharmacy, Melbourne; Ormond Coll., Melbourne Univ.; St Bartholomew's, London. Qual. in Pharmacy, Gold Medallist, 1928; MB, BS Melbourne Univ., 1st Cl. Hons and Exhibn 1934; MS Melbourne 1937; FRCS 1938; FRACS 1947; FACS 1964. Membre Titulaire, Internat. Soc. of Surgeons, 1963–; Mem., James IV Assoc. of Surgeons, 1971–. Ho. Surg. and Registrar, Royal Melbourne Hosp., 1935–36; Royal Children's, Melbourne, 1937; Brit. Post-Grad. Med. Sch., Hammersmith, 1938; Specialist Surgeon, EMS London, St Mary's, Paddington, 1939. Served War, 1939–46 (despatches, OBE); RAAMC (Capt. to Col), Europe, Middle East and Far East. Hon. Surg. Royal Melbourne Hosp., 1946, Senior Hon. Surg. 1964–67; Hon. Surg. Victorian Eye and Ear Hosp., 1949, Hon. Life Governor, 1967; Cons. Surg., Peter MacCallum Clinic, Cancer and Repatriation Dept. Colombo Plan Adviser, Thailand and Ceylon 1956, India 1960–64; Team Leader, Australian Surgical Team, South Vietnam, 1969; CMO, British Phosphate Commn, 1974–81. Pres., Victorian Anti-Cancer Council, 1980–83 (Vice-Pres., 1966–74, Chm. Executive, 1975–80); Vice-Pres., Internat. Soc. of Surgeons, 1981–83. Mem., Internat. Med. Scis Acad., 1981–. Sir Edward Dunlop Res. Foundn, Heidelberg Repatriation Hosp., launched 1985; Dunlop/Boon Pong Medical Exchange Foundn, Australia–Thailand, launched 1986. Cecil Joll Prize and Lectr, RCS 1960; Gordon Taylor Lectr, Malaysia, 1978; Chapman Meml Lecture and Medal, Australian Instn of Engineers, 1978; Sir Wallace Kyle Meml Oration, Perth, 1989. Pres. Aust.-Asian Assoc., Victoria, 1965–; Pres. Ex-POW and Relatives Assoc., Victoria, 1946–; Hon. Life Mem., RSL, 1979; Chm., Prime Minister's POW Relief Fund; President: Australian Ex-POW Assoc., 1971–73,

1986–88; Scottish Far East POW Assoc., 1991–; Victorian Foundn on Alcoholism and Drug Dependence; Chm., Adv. Cttee on Drug Educn, Victorian Min. of Health, 1970, 1977; Patron, Australian Foundn on Alcoholism and Drug Dependency; Mem., Standing Cttee on Health Problems of Alcohol, Nat. Health and Medical Res. Council, 1973. Hon. Pres., Melbourne Council for Overseas Students, 1987– (Pres., 1982–85); Member: Council, Ormond Coll.; Cttee, Nurses' Meml Centre, Melbourne; Exec., Vict. Red Cross Soc.; Victorian Cttee, Queen's Jubilee Appeal, 1977; Dir, Queen Elizabeth II Silver Jubilee Trust for Young Australians, 1977–; Vice-President: 3rd Asian Pacific Congress of Gastroenterology, 1968; Melbourne Scots Soc., 1974–77. Vice Pres., Victorian Rugby Union, 1946–; Pres., Victorian Schs RU Assoc., 1986–. Gov., Aust. Adv. Council of Elders, 1983–. Paul Harris Fellow, Rotary, 1988; FIC 1991. Hon. Mem., Assoc. of Surgeons of India, 1974. Hon. Fellow: Pharmaceutical Soc. of Victoria, 1946; AMA, 1973; Coll. of Surgeons of Sri Lanka, 1985; Royal Coll. of Surgs of Thailand, 1988. Hon. DSc Punjab, 1966; LLD (hc) Melbourne, 1988. Freedom of City: Wanganui, NZ, 1962; Prahran, 1988. KCSJ 1987. Australian of the Year Award, 1977; Medal for Service, RACS, 1987; World Veterans Fedn Rehabilitation Award, 1988; Dixon Medal, QUB, 1989; Medal of Merit, Internat. Assoc. of Lions Clubs, 1989. Named in 200 Great Australians, Bicentenary, 1988. Publications: Carcinoma of the Oesophagus; Reflections upon Surgical Treatment, 1960; Appendix of Into the Smother, 1963; The War Diaries of Sir Edward ("Weary") Dunlop, 1986; contribs to med. and surg. jls. Recreations: farming, travelling, golf; Rugby Union football (Blue, Aust. Caps 1932–34, British Barbarians 1939); formerly boxing (Blue). Address: (home) 605 Toorak Road, Toorak, Victoria 3142, Australia. T: 822 4749; (professional) 14 Parliament Place, East Melbourne, Victoria 3002, Australia. T: 650 1214. Clubs: Melbourne, Naval and Military, Peninsula Golf, Melbourne Cricket (Melbourne); Barbarian Football.

DUNLOP, Frank, CBE 1977; Director, Edinburgh International Festival, 1983–91; b 15 Feb. 1927; s of Charles Norman Dunlop and Mary Aarons. Educ: Kibworth Beauchamp Grammar Sch.; University Coll., London (Fellow, 1979). BA Hons, English. Postgrad. Sch. in Shakespeare, at Shakespeare Inst., Stratford-upon-Avon; Old Vic Sch., London. Served with RAF before going to University. Director: (own young theatre co.) Piccolo Theatre, Manchester, 1954; Arts Council Midland Theatre Co., 1955; Associate Dir, Bristol Old Vic, 1956; Dir, Théâtre de Poche, Brussels, 1959–60; Founder and Dir, Pop Theatre, 1960; Dir, Nottingham Playhouse, 1961–63; New Nottingham Playhouse, 1963–64; (dir.) The Enchanted, Bristol Old Vic Co., 1955; (wrote and dir.) Les Frères Jaques, Adelphi, 1960; Director: London Première, The Bishop's Bonfire, Mermaid, 1960; Schweyk, Mermaid, 1963; The Taming of the Shrew, Univ. Arts Centre, Oklahoma, 1965; Any Wednesday, Apollo, 1965; Too True to be Good, Edinburgh Fest., also Strand and Garrick, 1965; Saturday Night and Sunday Morning, Prince of Wales, 1966; The Winter's Tale and The Trojan Women, Edin. and Venice Festivals, also Cambridge Theatre, London, 1966; The Burglar, Vaudeville, 1967; Getting Married, Strand, 1967; A Midsummer Night's Dream and The Tricks of Scapin, Edin. Fest. and Saville Theatre, London, 1967; A Sense of Detachment, Royal Court, 1972; Sherlock Holmes, Aldwych, 1974, NY 1974; Habeas Corpus, NY 1975; The New York Idea, The Three Sisters, NY 1977; The Devil's Disciple, LA and NY, 1978; The Play's the Thing, Julius Caesar, NY, 1978; The Last of Mrs Cheyney, USA, 1978; Rookery Nook, Birmingham and Her Majesty's, 1979; Camelot, USA, 1980; Sherlock Holmes, Norwegian Nat. Th., Oslo, 1980; Lolita, NY, 1981; National Theatre: Assoc. Dir, 1967–71 and Admin. Dir, 1968–71; productions: Nat. Theatre: Edward II (Brecht and Marlowe); Home and Beauty; Macrune's Guevara; The White Devil; Captain of Kopenick; Young Vic: Founder, 1969; Mem. Bd, 1969–; Dir, 1969–78 and 1980–83; Consultant, 1978–80; productions: (author and Dir) Scapino 1970, 1977, NY 1974, LA 1975, Australia 1975, Oslo 1975; The Taming of the Shrew, 1970, 1977; The Comedy of Errors, 1971; The Maids, Deathwatch, 1972; The Alchemist, 1972; Bible One, 1972; French Without Tears, 1973; Joseph and the Amazing Technicolor Dreamcoat (Roundhouse and Albery Theatre), 1973, NY 1976; Much Ado About Nothing, 1973; Macbeth, 1975; Antony and Cleopatra, 1976; King Lear, 1980; Childe Byron, 1981; Masquerade, 1982; for Théâtre National de Belgique: Pantagleise, 1970; Antony and Cleopatra, 1971; Pericles, 1972. Mem., Arts Council Young People's Panel, 1968. Governor, Central School of Arts and Crafts, 1970. Hon. Fellow of Shakespeare Inst. Hon. Dr of Theatre, Philadelphia Coll. of Performing Arts, 1978; DUniv Heriot-Watt, 1989; Dr hc Edinburgh, 1990. Chevalier, Order of Arts and Literature (France), 1987. Recreations: reading and looking. Address: c/o Edinburgh International Festival, 107–115 Long Acre, WC2E 9NT.

DUNLOP, Gordon; see Dunlop, N. G. E.

DUNLOP, Rev. Canon Ian Geoffrey David, FSA; Canon and Chancellor of Salisbury Cathedral, since 1972; b 19 Aug. 1925; s of late Walter N. U. Dunlop and Marguerite Irene (née Shakerley); m 1957, Deirdre Marcia, d of late Dr Marcus Jamieson; one s one d. Educ: Winchester Coll.; New Coll., Oxford (MA); Strasbourg Univ. (Diploma); Lincoln Theol Coll. FSA 1965. Served Irish Guards, 1944–46 (Lieut). Curate, Hatfield, 1956–60; Chaplain, Westminster Sch., 1960–62; Vicar of Bures, Suffolk, 1962–72. Member: Gen. Synod, 1975–85; Cathedrals' Adv. Commn, 1981–86. Trustee, Historic Churches Preservation Trust, 1969–. Publications: Versailles, 1956, 2nd edn 1970; Palaces and Progresses of Elizabeth I, 1962; Châteaux of the Loire, 1969; Companion Guide to the Ile de France, 1979, 2nd edn 1985; Cathedrals Crusade, 1981; Royal Palaces of France, 1985; Thinking It Out, 1986; (contrib.) Oxford Companion to Gardens, 1986; Burgundy, 1990; weekly column in Church Times. Recreations: painting, bird watching. Address: 24 The Close, Salisbury, Wilts SP1 2EH. T: Salisbury (0722) 336809. Club: Army and Navy.

DUNLOP, John; b 20 May 1910; s of Martin T. and Agnes Dunlop, Belfast; m 1st, 1936, Ruby Hunter; two s (and one s decd); 2nd, 1970, Joyce Campbell. Educ: primary sch. and techn. college. Apprentice multiple grocers, 1926; assumed management, 1934; acquired own business, 1944. Mem. (VULC), Mid-Ulster, NI Assembly, 1973–74. MP (UUUP) Mid-Ulster, 1974–83. Civil Defence Medal and ribbon 1945. Recreations: music, choral singing, amateur soccer. Address: Turnaface Road, Moneymore, Magherafelt, Co. Londonderry BT45 7YP. T: Moneymore (06487) 48594.

DUNLOP, (Norman) Gordon (Edward), CBE 1989; Chairman: Ferrum Holdings plc, since 1989; Hi Tech Sports plc, since 1990; b 16 April 1928; s of Ross Munn Dunlop, CA and May Dunlop; m 1952, Jean (née Taylor); one s one d. Educ: Trinity Coll., Glenalmond. CA 1951, Scotland. Thomson McLintock & Co., Glasgow, 1945–56; De Havilland and Hawker Siddeley Aviation Companies, 1956–64; Commercial Union Assce Co. Ltd, 1964–77, Chief Exec., 1972–77; Dir, Inchcape Berhad, Singapore, 1979–82; Chief Financial Officer, 1982–83, Finance Dir, 1983–89, British Airways. Mem. Council of Lloyd's, 1990–. Recreations: gardening, fishing, ski-ing, ballet. Address: 28 Brunswick Gardens, W8 4AL. T: 071–221 5059; Bridle Cottage, Horseshoe Lane, Ibthorpe, Hants SP11 0BY. T: Hurstbourne Tarrant (026476) 501. Clubs: Caledonian, Buck's.

DUNLOP, Richard B.; see Buchanan-Dunlop.

DUNLOP, Sir Thomas, 3rd Bt, cr 1916; Partner, Thomas Dunlop & Sons, Ship and Insurance Brokers, Glasgow, 1938–86; b 11 April 1912; s of Sir Thomas Dunlop, 2nd Bt;

S father, 1963; m 1947, Adda Mary Alison, d of T. Arthur Smith, Lindsaylands, Biggar, Lanarks; one s one d (and one d decd). Educ: Shrewsbury; St John's Coll., Cambridge (BA). Chartered Accountant, 1939. Former Chm., Savings Bank of Glasgow. Member: Cttee of Princess Louise Scottish Hosp., Erskine; Vice-Pres., Royal Alfred Seafarers' Soc. OStJ 1965. Recreations: shooting, fishing, golf. Heir: s Thomas Dunlop [b 22 April 1951; m 1984, Eileen, er d of A. H. Stevenson; one s one d]. Address: The Corrie, Kilmacolm, Renfrewshire. T: Kilmacolm (050587) 3239. Club: Western (Glasgow).

DUNLOP, Sir William (Norman Gough), Kt 1975; JP; Managing Director, Dunlop Farms Ltd, retired 1990; b 9 April 1914; s of Norman Matthew Dunlop and Alice Ada Dunlop (née Gough); m 1940, Ruby Jean (née Archie); three s three d. Educ: Waitaki Boys' High Sch. Farmer in Canterbury, NZ. President: Federated Farmers, NZ, 1973–74; Coopworth Sheep Soc., NZ, 1971–74; Member: Agriculture Adv. Council, NZ, 1970–74; Immigration Adv. Council, NZ, 1971–; Transport Adv. Council, NZ, 1971–76; Chm., Neurological Foundn (Canterbury), 1975–88; Dep. Chm., NZ Meat and Wool Board Electoral Coll., 1973; Director: Rural Bank & Finance Corp., NZ, 1974–81; New Zealand Light Leathers, 1973–80. Trustee: Todd Foundn, 1973–81; Lincoln Coll. Foundn, 1977–88 (Chm. Bd). Anniv. Medal, NZ Animal Production Soc., 1991. Internat. Visitors Award, US Dept of State, 1971. JP 1972. Recreations: music, gardening. Address: 242 Main Road, Monks Bay, Christchurch 8, New Zealand. T: Christchurch 849056. Club: Canterbury (Christchurch).

DUNLUCE, Viscount; see under Antrim, 14th Earl of (who succeeded 1977, but is still known as Viscount Dunluce).

DUNMORE, 11th Earl of, cr 1686; **Kenneth Randolph Murray;** Viscount Fincastle, Lord Murray of Blair, Moulin and Tillemett, 1686; retired; b 6 June 1913; s of Arthur Charles Murray (d 1964) (g g s of 4th Earl), and Susan Maud (d 1922), d of Edward Richards, Tasmania; S brother, 1981; m 1938, Margaret Joy (d 1976), d of late P. D. Cousins, Burnie, Tasmania; two s. Educ: Tasmanian State School. Sgt, 12th/50th Bn, AIF, 1939–45. Former Post-master, Tasmania. Past Master, Tamar Valley Masonic Lodge 42 Tasmanian Constitution, 1957–58. Patron: NSW Combined Scottish Soc.; Exeter RSL Bowls Club. JP Beaconsfield, Tasmania, 1963. Recreation: lawn bowls. Heir: s Viscount Fincastle, qv. Address: Gravelly Beach, Tasmania, Australia. T: 944275. Club: Exeter RSL (Exeter, Tasmania).

DUNN, Baroness cr 1990 (Life Peer), of Hong Kong Island in Hong Kong and of Knightsbridge in the Royal Borough of Kensington and Chelsea; **Lydia Selina Dunn,** DBE 1989 (CBE 1983; OBE 1978); JP; MEC; Director, John Swire & Sons (HK) Ltd, since 1978; Executive Director, Swire Pacific Ltd, since 1982; Director: Hong Kong and Shanghai Banking Corporation, since 1981; Hong Kong and Shanghai Banking Corp. Holdings (London), since 1990; Chairman, Hong Kong Trade Development Council, since 1983; b 29 Feb. 1940; d of Yencheun Yeh Dunn and Chen Yin Chu; m 1988, Michael David Thomas, qv. Educ: St Paul's Convent Sch., Hong Kong; Univ. of Calif., Berkeley (BS). Swire & Maclaine: Exec. Trainee, 1963; Dir, 1973; Man. Dir, 1976; Chm., 1982; also chm. and dir of subsid. cos. Chairman: Eagle's Eye Internat., 1988–; Swire Source America, 1988–; Asian American Managers, 1988–; Christie's Swire (Hong Kong), 1989–; Encomium Ltd; Director: Mass Transit Rly Corp., 1979–85; Kowloon-Canton Rly Corp, 1982–84; Cathay Pacific Airways Ltd, 1985–; Hong Kong Seibu Enterprise Co., 1989–; Christie's Swire (Hldg), 1989–; Volvo, 1991– (Mem. Internat. Adv. Bd, 1985–91); Pres., Carroll Reed Internat., 1990–. MLC, 1976–85, Sen. MLC, 1985–88 (Mem., Finance Cttee, 1976–88); MEC, 1982–88, Sen. MEC, 1988–; Dep. Chm. Exec. Cttee, CPA Hong Kong Br., 1985–88. Member: Transport Adv. Cttee, 1977–80; Econ. Review Cttee, 1978–83; Gen. Cttee, Fedn of Hong Kong Industries, 1978–83 (Chm., Textile Cttee, 1980–81); Clothing Inst., Hong Kong, 1974–88; Hong Kong/Japan Business Co-operation Cttee, 1983–87 (Chm., 1988); Hong Kong/US Econ, Co-op. Cttee, 1984–; Land Develt Policy Cttee, 1981–83; Gen. Cttee, Hong Kong Gen. Chamber of Commerce, 1983–85; Chm., Special Cttee on Land Supply, 1980–83. Member Council: Trade Policy Res. Centre, London, 1980–89; Hong Kong Chinese Univ., 1978–90 (Hon. Treasurer, 1982–85; Chm., Finance Cttee, 1983–85). Member: Hong Kong Br., Hong Kong Assoc. UK, 1983–; Internat. Council, Asia Soc., 1986–; WWF Hong Kong, 1982–85. Chm., Prince Philip Dental Hosp., 1981–87. Patron, Assoc. of Chairmen of Tung Wah Gp of Hosps, 1986–87. JP Hong Kong, 1976. Hon. LLD Chinese Univ. of Hong Kong, 1984. Prime Minister of Japan's Trade Award, 1987. Publication: In the Kingdom of the Blind, 1983. Recreation: collection of antiques. Address: John Swire & Sons (HK) Ltd, 5th Floor, Swire House, 9 Connaught Road C, Hong Kong. Clubs: Hong Kong, Hong Kong Country, World Trade Centre, Royal Hong Kong Jockey (Hong Kong).

DUNN, Prof. Douglas Eaglesham, FRSL; poet and short-story writer; Professor of English and Scottish Literature, St Andrews University, since 1991; b 23 Oct. 1942; s of William Douglas Dunn and Margaret McGowan; m 1st, 1964, Lesley Balfour Wallace (d 1981); 2nd, 1985, Lesley Jane Bathgate; one s one d. Educ: Univ. of Hull (BA). Became full-time writer, 1971. Hon. Vis. Prof., Dundee Univ., 1987–; Fellow in Creative Writing, Univ. of St Andrews, 1989–91. FRSL 1981. Hon. Fellow, Humberside Coll., 1987. Hon. LLD Dundee, 1987. Cholmondeley Award, 1989. Publications: Terry Street, 1969 (Somerset Maugham Award, 1972); The Happier Life, 1972; (ed) New Poems, 1972–73, 1973; Love or Nothing, 1974 (Geoffrey Faber Meml Prize, 1976); (ed) A Choice of Byron's Verse, 1974; (ed) Two Decades of Irish Writing, 1975 (criticism); (ed) The Poetry of Scotland, 1979; Barbarians, 1979; St Kilda's Parliament, 1981 (Hawthornden Prize, 1982); Europa's Lover, 1982; (ed) A Rumoured City: new poets from Hull, 1982; (ed) To Build a Bridge: celebration of Humberside in verse, 1982; Elegies, 1985 (Whitbread Poetry Prize, 1985; Whitbread Book of the Year Award, 1986); Secret Villages, 1985 (short stories); Selected Poems 1964–1983, 1986; Northlight, 1988 (poetry); New and Selected Poems 1966–1988, 1989; Andromache, 1990; (ed) The Essential Browning, 1990; (ed) Scotland: an anthology, 1991; (ed) Faber Book of 20th Century Scottish Poetry, 1992; contrib. to Counterblast pamphlet series, Glasgow Herald, New Yorker, TLS, etc. Recreations: playing the clarinet and saxophone, listening to jazz music, gardening. Address: Department of English, St Andrews University, St Andrews, Fife.

DUNN, Air Marshal Sir Eric (Clive), KBE 1983; CB 1981; BEM 1951; b 27 Nov. 1927; s of late W. E. and of K. M. Dunn; m 1951, Margaret Gray; three d. Educ: Bridlington Sch. CEng, FRAeS. RAF aircraft apprentice, 1944–47; commnd Engr Br., 1954; Staff Coll., 1964; Jt Services Staff Coll., 1967; Sen. Engrg Officer, RAF Boulmer, 1968; MoD, 1969–70; Comd Electrical Engr, NEAF, 1971–72; Dir of Engrg Policy (RAF), 1973–75; RCDS, 1976; AO Wales, and Stn Comdr RAF St Athan, 1977; Air Officer Maintenance, RAF Support Comd, 1977–81; Air Officer Engineering, HQ Strike Comd, 1981–83; Chief Engr, RAF, 1983–86. Recreations: golf, sailing. Address: Headland Cottage, Babcary, Somerton, Somerset TA11 7EQ. Club: Royal Air Force.

DUNN, Lt-Col Sir (Francis) Vivian, KCVO 1969 (CVO 1954; MVO 1939); OBE 1960; FRAM; RM Retd; b 24 Dec. 1908; s of Captain William James Dunn, (Paddy),

MVO, MC, Director of Music, Royal Horse Guards, and Beatrice Maud Dunn; *g s* of Sgt Thomas Dunn, Band Sgt, 1st Bn 33rd (W Riding) Regt of Foot (over a century in succession in military music); *m* 1938, Margery Kathleen Halliday; one *s* two *d*. *Educ:* Peter Symonds Coll.; Winchester; Konservatorium der Musik, Cologne; Royal Acad. of Music. ARAM 1932, FRAM 1953. Played with Queen's Hall Prom. Orch., 1927, BBC Symph. Orch., 1930 (founder mem., 1st violin section). Lieut RM and Director of Music, 1931; addtl duties in cypher work, War of 1939–45; with HMS Vanguard for Royal Tour of S Africa, 1947; toured Canada and USA, 1949; Lt-Col and Principal Director of Music, RM, 1953; Royal Tour of Commonwealth countries, 1953; retired 1968. FRSA 1988. Liveryman, 1956, Mem. Court, 1981–, Master, 1988–89, Worshipful Co. of Musicians. Hon. Mem., Amer. Bandmasters' Assoc., 1969; Pres., International Military Music Soc., 1977–. Guest conductor with principal British orchestras and at Univs in Canada and USA; composer and arranger of ceremonial music for RM. EMI Gold Disc Award, 1969; J. P. Sousa Foundn Award of Merit, 1987. *Address:* 16 West Common, Haywards Heath, Sussex RH16 2AH. *T:* Haywards Heath (0444) 412987. *Clubs:* Army and Navy, MCC.

DUNN, Col George Willoughby, CBE 1959; DSO 1943 and Bar 1944; MC 1943; TD 1949; DL; Consultant, Thornton Oliver, WS (formerly Clark Oliver, Solicitors), Arbroath, since 1984 (Partner, 1939–84); former Chairman: The Alliance Trust; The Second Alliance Trust; Member of Queen's Body Guard for Scotland (Royal Company of Archers); *b* 27 March 1914; *s* of Willoughby Middleton Dunn, coal owner, Lanarkshire; *m* 1944, Louise Wilson, *er d* of Alexander Stephen MacLellan, LLD, ship builder and engr, Glasgow; two *d*. *Educ:* Trinity Coll., Glenalmond; Glasgow Univ. BL 1937; Solicitor, 1937. Served War of 1939–45 with 51st Highland Div., Middle East, N Africa, Sicily and NW Europe; Col late TA The Black Watch. Chm., Royal British Legion Scotland, 1971–74. DL Angus 1971. *Recreations:* golf, fishing. *Address:* David's Hill, St Vigeans, Arbroath, Angus DD11 4RG. *T:* Arbroath (0241) 72538. *Clubs:* Naval and Military; New (Edinburgh).

DUNN, John Churchill; broadcaster, host of own daily radio programme; *b* 4 March 1934; *s* of late John Barrett Jackson Dunn and of Dorothy Dunn (*née* Hiscox); *m* 1958, Margaret Jennison; two *d*. *Educ:* Christ Church Cathedral Choir School, Oxford; The King's School, Canterbury. Nat. Service, RAF, 1953–55. Joined BBC as studio manager, External Service, 1956; announcer/newsreader, Gen. Overseas Service, 1958, Domestic Services, 1959; worked all radio networks before joining Light Programme/Radio 2, and subseq. freelance; *radio series include:* Just For You; Housewives' Choice; Music Through Midnight; Roundabout; Jazz at Night; Saturday Sport; Sunday Sport; 4th Dimension; Breakfast Special; It Makes Me Laugh; Nat. and European Brass Band Championships; Light Music Festivals; The John Dunn Show, 1972–; numerous TV appearances. TV and Radio Industries Club Personality of the Year, 1971, 1984, 1986; Variety Club of GB Radio Personality of the Year, 1983; Daily Mail Silver Microphone, 1988. *Publication:* John Dunn's Curious Collection, 1982. *Recreations:* music, skiing, wine. *Address:* c/o Jo Gurnett Personal Management, 45 Queen's Gate Mews, SW7 5QN. *T:* 071–584 7642.

DUNN, Prof. John Montfort, FBA 1989; Professor of Political Theory, University of Cambridge, since 1987; Fellow of King's College, Cambridge, since 1966; *b* 9 Sept. 1940; *s* of Col. Henry George Montfort Dunn and Catherine Mary Dunn; *m* 1st, 1965, Susan Deborah Fyvel (marr. diss. 1971); 2nd, 1973, Judith Frances Bernal (marr. diss. 1987); one *s* (and one *s* decd) by Dr Heather Joan Glen. *Educ:* Winchester Coll.; King's Coll., Cambridge (BA 1962). Harkness Fellow, Graduate Sch. of Arts and Sciences, Harvard Univ., 1964–65; Official Fellow in History, Jesus Coll., Cambridge, 1965–66; Dir of Studies in History, King's Coll., Cambridge, 1966–72; Lectr in Pol Science, 1972–77, Reader in Politics, 1977–87, Cambridge Univ. Vis. Lectr, Dept of Pol Science, Univ. of Ghana, 1968–69; Visiting Professor: Dept of Civics and Politics, Univ. of Bombay, 1979–80; Faculty of Law, Tokyo Metropolitan Univ., 1983–84; Distinguished Vis. Prof., Murphy Inst. of Pol Economy, Tulane Univ., New Orleans, 1986; Benjamin Evans Lippincott Dist. Prof., Minnesota Univ., 1990. *Publications:* The Political Thought of John Locke, 1969; Modern Revolutions, 1972; Dependence and Opportunity: political change in Ahafo, 1973; (ed) West African States: failure and promise, 1978; Western Political Theory in the Face of the Future, 1979; Political Obligation in its Historical Context, 1980; Locke, 1984; The Politics of Socialism, 1984; Rethinking Modern Political Theory, 1985; (ed) The Economic Limits to Modern Politics, 1989; (ed) Contemporary West African States, 1989; Interpreting Political Responsibility, 1990. *Address:* The Merchant's House, 31 Station Road, Swavesey, Cambridge CB4 5QJ. *T:* Swavesey (0954) 31451.

DUNN, Martin; Editor of Today, since 1991; *b* 26 Jan. 1955. *Educ:* Dudley Grammar Sch., Worcs. Dudley Herald, 1974–77; Birmingham Evening Mail, 1977–78; Birmingham Post, 1978–81; Daily Mail, 1981–83; freelance journalist, 1983; New York Correspondent, The Sun, 1983–84; The Sun, London, 1984–88; Deputy Editor: News of the World, 1988–89; The Sun, 1989–91. *Recreations:* squash, running. *Address:* 1 Virginia street, E1 9BS. *T:* 071–782 4600.

DUNN, Air Marshal Sir Patrick Hunter, KBE 1965 (CBE 1950); CB 1956; DFC 1941; FRAeS; *b* 31 Dec. 1912; *s* of late William Alexander Dunn, Ardentinny, Argyllshire; *m* 1939, Diana Ledward Smith; two *d*. *Educ:* Glasgow Academy; Loretto; Glasgow Univ. Commissioned, 1933, Pre-war service in flying boats; as flying instructor 500 (County of Kent) Sqdn, AAF; with the Long Range Development Unit and as instructor at the Central Flying Sch. War service included command of 80 and 274 Fighter Squadrons and 71 OTU, all in Middle East (1940–42); at Air Ministry, and in Fighter Command, Sector Commander, 1945–46. Post-war service in Air Ministry, 1947–48; Malaya, 1949–50; NATO Defence Coll., 1950–52; Fighter Command, 1953–56; ADC to the Queen, 1953–58. AOC and Commandant, RAF Flying Coll., 1956–58; Deputy Air Sec., 1959–61; AOC No. 1 Group, Bomber Command, 1961–64; AOC-in-Chief, Flying Training Command, 1964–66; retired from RAF, 1967. Director i/c Management Services, British Steel Corp., 1967–68; resigned to become Dep. Chm., British Eagle Internat. Airlines Ltd; Chm., Eagle Aircraft Services, 1969; Aviation Consultant, British Steel Corporation, 1969–76. Mem. Council, Air League, 1968–73 and 1975–79 (Dep. Chm., 1972–73; Chm., Defence Cttee, 1968–73); Mem., British Atlantic Cttee, 1976–. Dir, Gloucester, Coventry, Cricklewood and Kingston Industrial Trading Estates, 1969–75 and 1977–81. A Trustee and Governor of Loretto, 1959–81; President: Fettesian-Lorettonian Club, 1972–75; Lorettonian Soc., 1980–81; Mem. Cttee, Assoc. of Governing Bodies of Public Schs, 1976–79. *Recreations:* tennis, sailing, shooting. *Address:* Little Hillbark, Hockett Lane, Cookham Dean, Berks SL6 9UF. *Clubs:* Royal Air Force, Hurlingham.

See also Sir N. J. D. Marsden, Bt.

DUNN, Richard Johann; Chief Executive, Thames Television PLC, since 1985; Chairman: Euston Films Ltd, since 1985; Cosgrove Hall Ltd, since 1985; Thames Television International Ltd, since 1985; Thames Television Inc. (Reeves Entertainment), since 1990; Deputy Chairman, Independent Television News, since 1990 (Director, since 1985); *b* 5 Sept. 1943; *s* of late Major Edward Cadwalader Dunn, MBE, TD, and of Gudlaug Johannesdóttir; *m* 1972, Virginia Gregory Gaynor, USA; two *s* one *d*. *Educ:* Forest Sch.; St John's Coll., Cambridge. Founder and Chm., Lady Margaret Players, 1965; Teacher in Jizan, Saudi Arabia, 1965–66; Eothen Films, 1966–67; Writer and Producer, Associated British Pathe, 1967–70; Exec. Producer, EMI Special Films Unit, 1970–72; Man. Dir, Swindon Viewpoint Ltd, cable community television service, 1972–76; Founder and first Chm., Community Communications Gp, 1976; Asst to Lord Delfont, EMI Film and Th. Corp., 1976–77; joined Thames Television as asst to Jeremy Isaacs, 1978, Dir of Prodn, 1981–85; Director: Ind. TV Publications Ltd, 1985–89; Thames Valley Broadcasting PLC, 1985–89; Broadcasters Audience Research Board Ltd, 1986–88; Channel Four TV, 1988–91. Dir, ITCA, subseq. ITV Assoc., 1985– (Chm., 1988–90). Mem., then Chm., Film and Video Panel, GLAA, 1978–82; Chm., Battersea Arts Centre, 1984–88, Pres., 1989–; Dir, Starstream Ltd, 1986–. Vice-Pres., RTS, 1988–. Director: Internat. Council of Nat. Acad. of Television Arts and Scis, NY, 1985–89 (Vice Chm., 1990–); Société Européenne des Satellites, 1987–; Studienges Business Channel AG, 1987; Association des Télévisions Commerciales en Europe, 1989–91; Vice Chm., Independent Broadcasting Telethon Trust, 1987–; Cinema and Television Benevolent Fund, 1990–. Governor: Forest Sch., 1986–; Nat. Film and TV Sch., 1987–90. FRTS 1991. *Recreations:* theatre, sports, reading. *Address:* 14 Bolingbroke Grove, Wandsworth Common, SW11 6EP. *T:* 081–673 1966. *Clubs:* Royal Automobile; Hawks (Cambridge).

DUNN, Robert John; MP (C) Dartford, since 1979; *b* July 1946; *s* of late Robert and of Doris Dunn, Swinton, Lancs; *m* 1976, Janet Elizabeth Wall, BD, *d* of late Denis Wall, Dulwich; two *s*. *Educ:* State schs. Senior Buyer, J. Sainsbury Ltd, 1973–79. Councillor, London Borough of Southwark, 1974–78 (Opposition Minority Gp spokesman on Housing and Finance Matters). Vice-Pres., Eccles Conservative Assoc., 1974–; contested (C): Eccles, Gen. Elections, Feb. and Oct. 1974; adopted as Parly Candidate (C) Dartford, 1975. PPS to Parly Under-Secs of State at DES, 1981–82, to Paymaster General and Chancellor of the Duchy of Lancaster, 1982–83; Parly Under-Sec. of State, DES, 1983–88. Mem., Parly Select Cttee on the Environment, 1981–82; Jt Sec., Cons backbench Educn Cttee, 1980–81; Chm., Cons. backbench Social Security Cttee, 1988–89; Vice-Chm., Cons. backbench Party Organization, Transport and Envmt Cttees, 1989–; Mem. Exec. Cttee, 1922 Cttee, 1988–. President: Dartford Young Conservatives, 1976–; Kent Gp Young Conservatives, 1982–85; SE Area Educn Adv. Cttee, 1982–; Dartford Soc., 1982–; Dartford branch, Kent Assoc. for the Disabled, 1983–. *Recreations:* canvassing; American politics. *Address:* House of Commons, SW1A 0AA. *T:* 071–219 5209. *Clubs:* Carlton; Dartford Rotary (Hon. Mem.).

DUNN, Rt. Hon. Sir Robin Horace Walford, Kt 1969; MC 1944; PC 1980; a Lord Justice of Appeal, 1980–84; *b* 16 Jan. 1918; *s* of late Brig. K. F. W. Dunn, CBE, and of Ava, *d* of Brig.-Gen. H. F. Kays, CB; *m* 1941, Judith, *d* of late Sir Gonne Pilcher, MC; one *s* one *d* (and one *d* decd). *Educ:* Wellington; Royal Military Academy, Woolwich (Sword of Honour). First Commissioned, RA, 1938; RHA, 1941; Staff Coll., 1946; retired (hon. Major), 1948. Served War of 1939–45; France and Belgium, 1939–40; Western Desert and Libya, 1941–42; Normandy and NW Europe, 1944–45 (wounded thrice, despatches twice, MC); Hon. Col Comdt, RA, 1980–84, Hon. Col 1984–. Called to Bar (Inner Temple), 1948; Master of the Bench, Inner Temple, 1969. Western Circuit, Junior Counsel to Registrar of Restrictive Trading Agreements, 1959–62; QC 1962; Judge of the High Court of Justice, Family Division (formerly Probate, Divorce and Admiralty Division), 1969–80; Presiding Judge, Western Circuit, 1974–78. Treas., Gen. Council of the Bar, 1967–69 (Mem., 1959–63); Chm. Betting Levy Appeal Tribunal, 1964–69; Dep. Chm., Somerset QS, 1965–71; Mem., Lord Chancellor's Cttee on Legal Educn, 1968–69. *Recreation:* hunting. *Address:* Lynch Mead, Allerford, Somerset TA24 8HJ. *T:* Minehead (0643) 862509.

DUNN, Sir Vivian; *see* Dunn, Sir F. V.

DUNN, William Francis N.; *see* Newton Dunn.

DUNN, William Hubert, QC 1982; a Recorder of the Crown Court, since 1980; *b* 8 July 1933; *s* of William Patrick Millar Dunn and Isabel (*née* Thompson); *m* 1971, Maria Henriqueta Theresa d'Arouje Perestrello de Moser; one *s* one *d*. *Educ:* Rockport, Co. Down, N Ireland; Winchester Coll.; New Coll., Oxford (Hons degree PPE) (Half-Blue fencing 1954–55). 2nd Lieut, Life Guards, 1956–57; Household Cavalry Reserve of Officers, 1957–64. Cholmondeley Scholar, Lincoln's Inn, 1958, called to Bar, 1958; Bencher, Lincoln's Inn, 1990. *Recreations:* hunting, travel, literature. *Address:* 19 Clarendon Street, SW1; Tudor Hall, Holywood, Co. Down, N Ireland. *T:* Holywood (02317) 3139. *Club:* Boodle's.

DUNNACHIE, James Francis, (Jimmy), JP; MP (Lab) Glasgow, Pollok, since 1987; *b* 17 Nov. 1930; *s* of William and Mary Dunnachie; *m* 1974, M. Isobel Payne. Councillor, City of Glasgow Corp., 1972–74 (Chm., Clearance and Rehabilitation); District Councillor, City of Glasgow, 1974–77 (Chm., C and R Cttee); Councillor, Strathclyde Regional Council, 1978–87 (Vice-Chm., Social Work Cttee). An Opposition Whip, 1988–, Scottish Whip, 1989–. *Recreations:* gardening, reading, junior football. *Address:* 15 Loganswell Gardens, Glasgow G46 8HU. *T:* 041–638 9756.

DUNNE, Thomas Raymond, JP; HM Lord-Lieutenant, County of Hereford and Worcester, since 1977; *b* 24 Oct. 1933; *s* of Philip Dunne, MC, and Margaret Walker; *m* 1957, Henrietta Crawley; two *s* two *d*. *Educ:* Eton; RMA Sandhurst. Served Army, 1951–59: Royal Horse Guards. Herefordshire CC, 1962–68. President: 3 Counties Agric. Soc., 1977; W Midlands TA Assoc., 1988–; National Vice Pres., Royal British Legion, 1982–89. Dir, West Regional Bd, Central TV, 1981–. Chm., N Hereford Conservative Assoc., 1968–74. Hon. Col, 4th Worcester and Sherwood Foresters (formerly 2nd Mercian Volunteers), 1987–. High Sheriff 1970, DL 1973, Herefordshire; JP Hereford and Worcester, 1977. KStJ 1978. *Address:* c/o County Hall, Spetchley Road, Worcester.

DUNNET, Prof. George Mackenzie, OBE 1986; DSc; Regius Professor of Natural History, University of Aberdeen, since 1974; *b* 19 April 1928; *s* of John George and Christina I. Dunnet; *m* 1953, Margaret Henderson Thomson, MA; one *s* two *d*. *Educ:* Peterhead Academy; Aberdeen Univ. BSc (1st cl. hons) 1949; PhD 1952; DSc 1984. Research Officer, CSIRO, Australia, 1953–58; Lectr in Ecology, Dir Culterty Field Stn, Univ. of Aberdeen, 1958–66, Sen. Lectr 1966–71; Sen. Research Fellow, DSIR, NZ, 1968–69; Prof. of Zoology, Univ. of Aberdeen, 1971–74. Member: Red Deer Commn, 1975–80; NERC, 1975–77; Council, Scottish Marine Biol Assoc., 1979–86; Scottish Adv. Cttee of Nature Conservancy Council, 1979–84; Nature Conservancy Council for Scotland, 1991– (Chm., Sci. R&D Bd, 1991–); Chairman: Shetland Oil Terminal Environment Adv. Gp, 1977–; Adv. Cttees on Protection of Birds, 1979–81; Salmon Adv. Cttee, 1986–; Fish Farming Adv. Cttee, 1990–. Pres., British Ecological Soc., 1980–81. FRSE 1970; FInstBiol 1974; FRSA 1981. *Publications:* contrib. Ibis, Jl Animal Ecology, Jl Applied Ecol., Aust. Jl Zool., CSIRO Wildl. Res. *Recreations:* walking, photography, croquet. *Address:* Whinhill, Inverebrie, Ellon, Aberdeenshire AB41 8PT. *T:* Schivas (03587) 215. *Club:* Commonwealth Trust.

DUNNETT, Alastair MacTavish; *b* 26 Dec. 1908; *s* of David Sinclair Dunnett and Isabella Crawford MacTavish; *m* 1946, Dorothy Halliday; two *s*. *Educ:* Overnewton

Sch.; Hillhead High Sch., Glasgow. Commercial Bank of Scotland, Ltd, 1925; Co-founder of The Claymore Press, 1933–34; Glasgow Weekly Herald, 1935–36; The Bulletin, 1936–37; Daily Record, 1937–40; Chief Press Officer, Sec. of State for Scotland, 1940–46; Editor, Daily Record, 1946–55; Editor, The Scotsman, 1956–72; Man. Dir, The Scotsman Publications Ltd, 1962–70, Chm., 1970–74; Mem. Exec. Bd, The Thomson Organisation Ltd, 1974–78; Director: Scottish Television Ltd, 1975–79; Thomson Scottish Petroleum Ltd, 1979–87 (Chm., 1972–79). Smith-Mundt Scholarship to USA, 1951. Governor, Pitlochry Festival Theatre, 1958–84. Member: Scottish Tourist Board, 1956–69; Press Council, 1959–62; Council of Nat. Trust for Scotland, 1962–69; Council of Commonwealth Press Union, 1964–78; Edinburgh Univ. Court, 1964–66; Edinburgh Festival Council, 1967–80. Hon. LLD Strathclyde, 1978. *Publications:* Treasure at Sonnach, 1935; Heard Tell, 1946; Quest by Canoe, 1950, repr. 1967, as It's Too Late in the Year; Highlands and Islands of Scotland, 1951; The Donaldson Line, 1952; The Land of Scotch, 1953; (as Alec Tavis) The Duke's Day, 1970; (ed) Alistair Maclean Introduces Scotland, 1972; No Thanks to the Duke, 1978; Among Friends (autobiog.), 1984; (with Dorothy Dunnett) The Scottish Highlands, 1988; End of Term, 1989; *plays:* The Original John Mackay, Glasgow Citizens, 1956; Fit to Print, Duke of York's, 1962. *Recreations:* sailing, riding, walking. *Address:* 87 Colinton Road, Edinburgh EH10 5DF. *T:* 031–337 2107. *Clubs:* Caledonian; Scottish Arts, New (Edinburgh).

DUNNETT, Denzil Inglis, CMG 1967; OBE 1962; HM Diplomatic Service, retired; *b* 21 Oct. 1917; *s* of late Sir James Dunnett, KCIE and late Annie (*née* Sangster); *m* 1946, Ruth Rawcliffe (*d* 1974); two *s* one *d*. *Educ:* Edinburgh Acad.; Corpus Christi Coll., Oxford. Served with RA, 1939–45. Diplomatic Service: Foreign Office, 1947–48; Sofia, 1948–50; Foreign Office, 1950–53; UK Delegn to OEEC, Paris, 1953–56; Commercial Sec., Buenos Aires, 1956–60; Consul, Elisabethville, 1961–62; Commercial Counsellor, Madrid, 1962–67; seconded to BoT, 1967–70; Counsellor, Mexico City, 1970–73; Ambassador to Senegal, Mauritania, Mali and Guinea, 1973–76, and to Guinea-Bissau, 1975–76; Diplomatic Service Chm., CS Selection Bd, 1976–77. London Rep., Scottish Develt Agency, 1978–82. *Publication:* Bird Poems, 1989. *Recreations:* golf, music. *Address:* 11 Victoria Grove, W8 5RW. *T:* 071–584 7523. *Club:* Caledonian.

DUNNETT, Jack; President, Football League, 1981–86 and 1988–89 (Member, Management Committee, 1977–89); *b* 24 June 1922; *m* 1951; two *s* three *d*. *Educ:* Whitgift Middle Sch., Croydon; Downing Coll., Cambridge (MA, LLM). Served with Cheshire Regt, 1941–46 (Capt.). Admitted Solicitor, 1949. Middlesex CC, 1958–61; Councillor, Enfield Borough Council, 1958–61; Alderman, Enfield Borough Council, 1961–63; Councillor, Greater London Council, 1964–67. MP (Lab) Central Nottingham, 1964–74, Nottingham East, 1974–83; former PPS to: Minister of State, FCO; Minister of Transport. Mem. FA Council, 1977–89, Vice-Pres., 1981–86, 1988–89; Mem., Football Trust, 1982–89; Chm., Notts County FC, 1968–87; Vice-Chm., Portsmouth FC, 1989–90. *Recreation:* watching professional football. *Address:* Whitehall Court, SW1A 2EP. *T:* 071–839 6962.

DUNNETT, Sir (Ludovic) James, GCB 1969 (KCB 1960; CB 1957); CMG 1948; Permanent Under-Secretary of State, Ministry of Defence, 1966–74; *b* 12 Feb. 1914; *s* of late Sir James Dunnett, KCIE; *m* 1st, 1944, Olga Adair (*d* 1980); no *c*; 2nd, 1984, Lady Clarisse Grover. *Educ:* Edinburgh Acad.; University Coll., Oxford. Entered Air Ministry, 1936; Private Sec. to Permanent Sec., 1937–44; transferred to Ministry of Civil Aviation, 1945; Under Sec., 1948; Under Sec., Min. of Supply, 1951, Deputy Sec., 1953; Deputy Sec., Min. of Transport, 1958; Permanent Secretary: Min. of Transport, 1959–62; Min. of Labour, 1962–66. Mem., SSRC, 1977–82. Visiting Fellow, Nuffield Coll., Oxford, 1964–72. Chm., Internat. Maritime Industries Forum, 1976–79; Pres., Inst. of Manpower Studies, 1977–80. Trustee, Charities Aid Foundn, 1974–88. *Recreation:* golf. *Address:* 85 Bedford Gardens, W8. *T:* 071–727 5286. *Club:* Reform.

DUNNING, John Ernest Patrick, CBE 1973; retired; Director, Rocket Propulsion Establishment, Westcott, 1955–72; *b* 19 Sept. 1912; *s* of late Rev. E. M. Dunning, MA, sometime Rector of Cumberworth and Denby Dale, Yorks; *m* 1939, Mary Meikle Robertson (*d* 1987). *Educ:* Wheelwright Gram. Sch., Dewsbury; Downing Coll., Cambridge (Exhibr, MA). 1st cl. hons Mech. Scis Tripos, 1935. Blackstone Ltd, Stamford, 1935–37; Bristol Aeroplane Co. Ltd (Engines), 1937–38; Armstrong Whitworth Securities Ltd (Kadenacy Dept), 1938–40; RAE, 1940–50; Asst Dir, Min. of Supply, 1950–55; Dir, Engine Research, Min. of Supply, 1955. FRAeS, FIMechE; FRSA. *Publications:* scientific and technical papers. *Address:* 24 Coombe Hill Crescent, Thame, Oxon OX9 2EH. *T:* Thame (084421) 3893. *Club:* North Oxford Golf.

DUNNING, Prof. John Harry, PhD; ICI Research Professor of International Business, University of Reading, since 1988; State of New Jersey Professor of International Business, Rutgers University, US, since 1989; *b* 26 June 1927; *m* 1st, 1948, Ida Teresa Bellamy (marr. diss. 1975); one *s*; 2nd, 1975, Christine Mary Brown. *Educ:* Lower Sch. of John Lyon, Harrow; University Coll. London (BSc (Econ); PhD). Research Asst, University Coll. London, 1951–52; Lectr and Sen. Lectr, Univ. of Southampton, 1952–64; University of Reading: Prof. of Economics, 1964–74; Hd of Dept of Economics, 1964–87; Esmée Fairburn Prof. of Internat. Investment and Business Studies, 1975–87. Visiting Prof.: Univ. of Western Ontario, Canada; Univ. of California (Berkeley), 1968–69; Boston Univ., USA, 1976; Stockholm Sch. of Economics, 1978; HEC, Univ. of Montreal, Canada, 1980; Walker-Ames Prof., Univ. of Washington, Seattle, 1981; Seth Boyden Distinguished Prof., Rutgers Univ., 1987; Univ. of Berkeley, 1987. Consultant to UN, 1974– and OECD, 1975–. Member: SE Economic Planning Council, 1966–68; Chemicals EDC, 1968–77; UN Study Gp on Multinational Corps, 1973–74. Chm., Economists Advisory Gp Ltd. Fellow, Acad. of Internat. Business (Pres., 1987–88). Hon. PhD: Uppsala, 1975; Universidad Autónoma de Madrid, 1990. *Publications:* American Investment in British Manufacturing Industry, 1958; (with C. J. Thomas) British Industry, 1963; Economic Planning and Town Expansion, 1963; Studies in International Investment, 1970; (ed) The Multinational Enterprise, 1971; (with E. V. Morgan) An Economic Study of the City of London, 1971; (ed) International Investment, 1972; (ed) Economic Analysis and the Multinational Enterprise, 1974; US Industry in Britain, 1976; (with T. Houston) UK Industry Abroad, 1976; International Production and the Multinational Enterprise, 1981; (ed with J. Black) International Capital Movements, 1982; (with J. Stopford) Multinationals: Company Performance and Global Trends, 1983; (with R. D. Pearce) The World's Largest Industrial Companies 1962–83, 1985; (ed) Multinational Enterprises, Economic Structure and International Competitiveness, 1985; Japanese Participation in British Industry, 1986; (with J. Cantwell) World Directory of Statistics on International Direct Investment and Production, 1987; Explaining International Production, 1988; Multinationals, Technology and Competitiveness, 1988; (ed with A. Webster) Structural Change in the World Economy, 1990; numerous articles in learned and professional jls. *Address:* University of Reading, Whiteknights Park, Reading, Berks. *T:* Reading (0734) 875123. *Club:* Athenæum.

DUNNING, Joseph, CBE 1977; Chairman, Lothian Health Board, 1983–84; Principal, Napier College of Commerce and Technology, Edinburgh, 1963–81, retired; *b* 9 Oct. 1920; *s* of Joseph and Elizabeth Ellen Dunning; *m* 1948, Edith Mary Barlow (*d* 1972); one *s* one *d*. *Educ:* London University (BSc Hons); Durham University (MEd); Manchester College of Technology (AMCT). Metallurgical Industry and lecturing, 1936–56; Principal, Cleveland Technical College, 1956–63. MA Open Univ.; FEIS. Hon. Fellow, Napier Polytech. of Edinburgh, 1989. Hon. DEd CNAA, 1983. *Recreations:* silversmithing, photography. *Address:* 2 Thorpe Field, Sockbridge, Penrith, Cumbria CA10 2JN. *Club:* New (Edinburgh).

DUNNING, Sir Simon (William Patrick), 3rd Bt, *cr* 1930; *b* 14 Dec. 1939; *s* of Sir William Leonard Dunning, 2nd Bt, and of Kathleen Lawrie, *d* of J. P. Cuthbert, MC; *S* father, 1961; *m* 1975, Frances Deirdre Morton, *d* of Major Patrick Lancaster; one *d*. *Educ:* Eton. *Recreation:* shooting. *Address:* Low Auchengillan, Blanefield, by Glasgow. *T:* Blanefield (0360) 70323. *Clubs:* Turf; Western (Glasgow).

DUNNINGTON-JEFFERSON, Sir Mervyn (Stewart), 2nd Bt *cr* 1958; Company Director, since 1968; *b* 5 Aug. 1943; *s* of Sir John Alexander Dunnington-Jefferson, 1st Bt, DSO, and of Frances Isobel, *d* of Col H. A. Cape, DSO; *S* father, 1979; *m* 1971, Caroline Anna, *o d* of J. M. Bayley; one *s* two *d*. *Educ:* Eton College. Joined Charrington & Co. Ltd (Brewers), 1961; left in 1968 to become joint founder and director of Hatton Builders Ltd, specialising in building contracting and property development. *Recreations:* sport—cricket, skiing, golf, etc. *Heir:* *s* John Alexander Dunnington-Jefferson, *b* 23 March 1980. *Address:* 7 Bolingbroke Grove, SW11 6ES. *T:* 081–675 3395. *Clubs:* MCC, Queen's.

DUNPHIE, Maj.-Gen. Sir Charles (Anderson Lane), Kt 1959; CB 1948; CBE 1942; DSO 1943; *b* 20 April 1902; *s* of late Sir Alfred Dunphie, KCVO, Rotherfield Greys, Oxon; *m* 1st, 1931, Eileen (*d* 1978), *d* of late Lieut-Gen. Sir Walter Campbell, KCB, KCMG, DSO; one *s* one *d*; 2nd, 1981, Susan, *widow* of Col P. L. M. Wright. *Educ:* RN Colls Osborne and Dartmouth; RMA Woolwich. Commissioned into RH and RFA, 1921; served War of 1939–45 (wounded, despatches); Brig. RAC, 1941; Comdr 26 Armoured Bde, 1942–43; Dep. Dir RAC, War Office, 1943–45; Temp. Maj.-Gen., Dir Gen. Armoured Fighting Vehicles 1945–48; retired 1948. Joined Vickers Ltd, 1948; Chm., 1962–67. One of HM's Honourable Corps of Gentlemen-at-Arms, 1952–62. US Legion of Merit (Commander); US Silver Star. *Address:* Roundhill, Wincanton, Somerset BA9 8HH. *Club:* Army and Navy.

DUNRAVEN and MOUNT-EARL, 7th Earl of, *cr* 1822; **Thady Windham Thomas Wyndham-Quin;** Baron Adare, 1800; Viscount Mountearl, 1816; Viscount Adare, 1822; Bt 1871; *b* 27 Oct. 1939; *s* of 6th Earl of Dunraven and Mount-Earl, CB, CBE, MC, and Nancy, *d* of Thomas B. Yuille, Halifax County, Va; *S* father 1965; *m* 1969, Geraldine, *d* of Air Commodore Gerard W. McAleer, CBE, MB, BCh, DTM&H, Wokingham; one *d*. *Educ:* Ludgrove; Le Rosey. *Heir:* none. *Address:* Kilcurly House, Adare, Co. Limerick, Ireland. *T:* Limerick 86201. *Club:* Kildare Street and University (Dublin).

See also Sir F. G. W. Brooke, Bt.

DUNROSSIL, 2nd Viscount, *cr* 1959; **John William Morrison,** CMG 1981; DL; HM Diplomatic Service, retired; Governor and Commander-in-Chief of Bermuda, 1983–88; *b* 22 May 1926; *e s* of William Shepherd Morrison, 1st Viscount Dunrossil, GCMG, MC, PC, QC; *S* father, 1961; *m* 1st, 1951, Mavis (marr. diss. 1969), *d* of A. Ll. Spencer-Payne, LRCP, MRCS, LDS; three *s* one *d*; 2nd, 1969, Diana Mary Cunliffe, *d* of C. M. Vise; two *d*. *Educ:* Fettes; Oxford. Royal Air Force, 1945–48, Flt-Lieut (Pilot). Joined Commonwealth Relations Office, 1951; Asst Private Sec. to Sec. of State, 1952–54; Second Sec., Canberra, 84211954–56; CRO, 1956–58; First Sec. and Acting Deputy High Commissioner, Dacca, East Pakistan, 1958–60; First Sec., Pretoria/Capetown, 1961–64; FO, 1964–68; seconded to Intergovernmental Maritime Consultative Org., 1968–70; Counsellor and Head of Chancery, Ottawa, 1970–74; Counsellor, Brussels, 1975–78; High Comr in Fiji, and High Comr (non-resident) to Republic of Nauru and to Tuvalu, 1978–82; High Comr, Bridgetown, Antigua, Barbuda, Dominica, Grenada, St Vincent and the Grenadines, and British Govt Rep. to WI Associated States, 1982–83. Chm., Bison Books Ltd, 1990–; Dep. Chm., Bank of Bermuda (Luxembourg) SA, 1990–; Dir, Odin Mining & Investment Ltd; Consultant, Bank of Bermuda Ltd. Pres., Kensington Cttee, Friendship for Overseas Students, 1989–. DL Western Isles, 1990. Liveryman, Merchant Taylor's Co., 1984. *Heir:* *s* Hon. Andrew William Reginald Morrison [*b* 15 Dec. 1953; *m* 1986, Carla Brundage; two *d*]. *Address:* 7 Ringmer Avenue, Fulham, SW6 5LP. *T:* 071–736 8896; Dunrossil House, Trunisgarry, by Lochmaddy, North Uist, Hebrides. *T:* Lochmaddy (08763) 213. *Clubs:* Royal Air Force, Commonwealth Trust.

DUNSANY, 19th Baron of, *cr* 1439; **Randal Arthur Henry Plunkett;** Lieut-Col (retd) Indian Cavalry (Guides); *b* 25 Aug. 1906; *o s* of 18th Baron Dunsany, DL, LittD, and Rt Hon. Beatrice, Lady Dunsany (*d* 1970); *S* father, 1957; *m* 1st, 1938, Mrs Vera Bryce (from whom he obtained a divorce, 1947, she *d* 1986), *d* of Señor G. De Sà Sottomaior, São Paulo, Brazil; one *s*; 2nd, 1947, Sheila Victoria Katrin, *widow* of Major John Frederick Foley, Baron de Rutzen, DL, JP, CC, Welsh Guards (killed in action, 1944), *o d* of Sir Henry Philipps, 2nd Bt; one *d*. *Educ:* Eton. Joined the 16th/5th Lancers (SR), 1926; transferred to the Indian Army, 1928, Guides Cavalry, Indian Armoured Corps, retired, 1947. *Heir:* *s* Hon. Edward John Carlos Plunkett [*b* 10 Sept. 1939. *Educ:* Eton; Slade Sch. of Fine Art]. *Address:* (Seat) Dunsany Castle, Co. Meath, Ireland. *T:* 046–25198. *Clubs:* Beefsteak, Cavalry and Guards; Kildare Street and University (Dublin).

DUNSTAN, (Andrew Harold) Bernard, RA 1968 (ARA 1959); RWA; painter; *b* 19 Jan. 1920; *s* of late Dr A. E. Dunstan; *m* 1949, Diana Maxwell Armfield, *qv*; three *s*. *Educ:* St Paul's; Byam Shaw Sch.; Slade Sch. Has exhibited at RA since 1945. Many one-man exhibitions; now exhibits regularly at Agnews, Bond St. Pictures in public collections include London Museum, Bristol Art Gall., Nat. Gall. of NZ, Arts Council, Nat. Portrait Gall., and many in private collections. Mem., New English Art Club; Chm., Artists' General Benevolent Instn, 1987–; Pres., Royal West of England Acad., 1980–84. Trustee, RA, 1989–. *Publications:* Learning to Paint, 1970; Painting in Progress, 1976; Painting Methods of the Impressionists, 1976; (ed) Ruskin, Elements of Drawing, 1991. *Recreations:* music, walking in London. *Address:* 10 High Park Road, Kew, Richmond, Surrey TW9 4BH. *T:* 081–876 6633. *Club:* Arts.

DUNSTAN, Hon. Donald Allan, AC 1979; QC 1965; National President, Australian Freedom from Hunger Campaign, 1982–87, and since 1991 (Chairman, 1987–91); *b* Suva, Fiji, 21 Sept. 1926; *s* of late Francis Vivian Dunstan, MBE, sometime Branch Manager, Morris Hedstrom Ltd, and Ida May Dunstan (*née* Hill); *m* 1st, 1949, Gretel Ellis (marr. diss.); two *s* one *d*; 2nd, 1976, Adele Koh (*d* 1978). *Educ:* Murray Bridge Infant and Primary Schs, SA; Suva Grammar; St Peter's Coll., Adelaide; St Mark's Coll., Univ. of Adelaide (LLB 1948). Admitted to S Australian Bar, 1948, to Fiji Bar, 1949; in practice: Fiji, 1949–50; Adelaide, 1951–. MHA (Labor) South Australia, for Norwood, 1953–79; Attorney-Gen., Minister for Social Welfare, for Aboriginal Affairs, 1965–67; Premier, Treasurer, Attorney-Gen. and Minister for Housing, 1967–68; Leader of Opposition, 1968–70; Premier, Treasurer, 1970–79; Minister for Develt and Mines, 1970–76, for Ethnic Affairs, 1976–79. Dir of Tourism, Victoria, 1982–83; Chm., Victorian Tourism Commn, 1983–86; Dep. Chm., Alpine Resorts Commn, 1983–86; Mem. Bd, Victorian

Econ. Develt Corp., 1983–86. President: Mus. of Chinese Aust. History, 1984–86; Movement for Democracy in Fiji, 1987–; Chairman: Chinatown Statutory Cttee, 1983–86; Mandela Foundn, 1987–; Jam Factory Craft Workshops, 1990–. TV series, Australia: a personal view. DUniv Flinders, 1991. *Publications:* Don Dunstan's Cookbook, 1976; Don Dunstan's Australia, 1978; Felicia: the political memoirs of Don Dunstan, 1981; Australia: a personal view, 1981. *Address:* 15 Clara Street, Norwood, SA 5067, Australia.

DUNSTAN, Lt-Gen. Sir Donald (Beaumont), AC 1991; KBE 1980 (CBE 1969; MBE 1954); CB 1972; Governor of South Australia, 1982–91; *b* 18 Feb. 1923; *s* of late Oscar Reginald Dunstan and Eileen Dunstan; *m* 1948, Beryl June Dunningham; two *s*. *Educ:* Prince Alfred Coll., South Australia; RMC, Duntroon. Served War of 1939–45: Regimental and Staff appts in SW Pacific Area, 1942–45. Served in Korea, 1954; Instructor: RMC Duntroon, 1955–56, 1963; Staff Coll., Queenscliff, 1958; Staff Coll., Camberley, 1959–60; Dep. Comdr 1 Task Force, Vietnam, 1968–69; Comdr, 10th Task Force, Holsworthy, NSW, 1969; idc 1970; Commander Aust. Force, Vietnam, 1971; Chief of Materiel, 1972–74; GOC Field Force Comd, 1974–77; CGS, 1977–82. KStJ 1982. *Recreations:* golf, fishing. *Address:* 52 Martin Court, West Lakes, SA 5021, Australia. *Clubs:* Australian (Sydney); Royal Sydney Golf, Royal Adelaide Golf.

DUNSTAN, Rev. Prof. Gordon Reginald, CBE 1989; F. D. Maurice Professor of Moral and Social Theology, King's College, London, 1967–82, now Emeritus; Honorary Research Fellow, University of Exeter, since 1982; Chaplain to the Queen, 1976–87; *b* 25 April 1917; *yr s* of late Frederick John Menhennet and Winifred Amy Dunstan (*née* Orchard); *m* 1949, Ruby Maud (*née* Fitzer); two *s* one *d*. *Educ:* Plymouth Corp. Gram. Sch.; University of Leeds; College of the Resurrection, Mirfield. BA, 1st cl. Hist., 1938, Rutson Post-Grad. Schol. 1938, MA w dist. 1939, Leeds Univ.; FSA 1957; FKC 1974. Deacon 1941, priest 1942; Curate, King Cross, Halifax, 1941–45; Huddersfield, 1945–46; Sub Warden, St Deiniol's Library, Hawarden, 1945–49; Vicar of Sutton Courtney with Appleford, 1949–55; Lecturer, Wm Temple Coll., 1947–49; Ripon Hall, Oxford, 1953–55; Minor Canon, St George's Chapel, Windsor Castle, 1955–59; Westminster Abbey, 1959–67; Canon Theologian, Leicester Cathedral, 1966–82, Canon Emeritus, 1982–. Sec., C of E Council for Social Work, 1955–63; Sec., Church Assembly Jt Bd of Studies, 1963–66; Editor of Crucible, 1962–66; Editor of Theology, 1965–75; Dep. Priest in Ordinary to the Queen, 1959–64, Priest in Ordinary, 1964–76; Select Preacher: University of Cambridge 1960, 1977; Leeds, 1970; Hulsean Preacher, 1977. Lectures: Prideaux, Univ. of Exeter, 1968; Moorhouse, Melbourne, 1973; Stephenson, Sheffield, 1980. Gresham's Prof. in Divinity, City Univ., 1969–71. Consultant, Lambeth Conf., 1988. Mem. Council, Canterbury and York Soc., 1950–85 (Vice-Pres., 1985–). Mem. or Sec. cttees on social and ethical problems; Vice-Pres., 1965–66, and Chm. Brit. Cttee, of Internat. Union of Family Organizations, 1964–66; Vice-Pres., London Medical Gp and Inst. of Medical Ethics, 1985–; Pres., Tavistock Inst. of Med. Psychology, 1991–; Member: Adv. Gp on Transplant Policy, Dept of Health, 1969; Council of Tavistock Inst. of Human Relations (Vice-Pres., 1977–82), and Inst. of Marital Studies, 1969–88; Adv. Gp on Arms Control and Disarmament, FCO, 1970–74; Adv. Cttee on Animal Experiments, Home Office, 1975–89; Council, Advertising Standards Auth., 1981–; MRC/RCOG Voluntary Licensing Authority, 1985–91; Nuffield Council on Bioethics, 1991–. Hon. FRSM 1985; Hon. MRCP 1987; FRCOG *ad eundem* 1991. Pres., Devon and Cornwall Record Soc., 1984–87; Vice-Pres., UFAW, 1985–. Hon. DD Exeter, 1973; Hon. LLD Leicester, 1986. *Publications:* The Family Is Not Broken, 1962; The Register of Edmund Lacy, Bishop of Exeter 1420–1455, 5 vols, 1963–72; A Digger Still, 1968; Not Yet the Epitaph, 1968; The Sacred Ministry, 1970; The Artifice of Ethics, 1974; A Moralist in the City, 1974; (ed) Duty and Discernment, 1975; (ed with M. J. Seller) Consent in Medicine, 1983; (ed with M. J. Seller) The Status of the Human Embryo: perspectives from moral tradition, 1988; (ed with D. Callahan) Biomedical Ethics: an Anglo-American dialogue, 1988; (ed with E. A. Shinebourne) Doctors' Decisions: ethical conflicts in medical practice, 1989; (ed) The Human Embryo: Aristotle and the Arabic and European Traditions, 1990. . *Recreations:* small islands, *domus* and *rus*. *Address:* 9 Maryfield Avenue, Exeter EX4 6JN. *T:* Exeter (0392) 214691.

DUNSTAN, Ivan, PhD; CChem, FRSC; Director-General, British Standards Institution, since 1986; *b* 27 Aug. 1930; *s* of Edward Ernest and Sarah Kathleen Dunstan; *m* 1955, Monica Jane (*née* Phillips); two *s* one *d*. *Educ:* Falmouth Grammar Sch.; Bristol Univ. (BSc). Joined Scientific Civil Service, working at Explosives Research and Development Estabt, Waltham Abbey, 1954; became Supt of Gen. Chemistry Div., 1967; Warren Spring Laboratory (DTI) as Dep. Dir (Resources), 1972–74; Dir, Materials Quality Assurance, MoD (PE), 1974–79; Dir, Bldg Res. Estabt, DoE, 1979–83; Standards Dir, BSI, 1983–86. President: RILEM, 1988; European Standards Organ, 1990; Vice-Pres., Inst. of Quality Assurance, 1988; Mem., British Bd of Agrément, 1987. CBIM 1986. *Recreations:* golf, badminton, gardening. *Address:* 6 High Oaks Road, Welwyn Garden City, Herts AL8 7BH. *T:* Welwyn Garden (0707) 22272. *Club:* Athenæum.

DUNSTER, (Herbert) John, CB 1979; consultant in radiation protection; *b* 27 July 1922; *s* of Herbert and Olive Grace Dunster; *m* 1945, Rosemary Elizabeth, *d* of P. J. Gallagher; one *s* three *d*. *Educ:* University Coll. Sch.; Imperial College of Science and Technology (ARCS, BSc). FSRP 1988. Scientist, UK Atomic Energy Authority, 1946–71; Asst Dir, Nat. Radiological Protection Bd, 1971–76; Dep. Dir Gen., HSE, 1976–82; Dir, NRPB, 1982–87. Member: Internat. Commn on Radiological Protection, 1977–; Sci. and Tech. Cttee, Euratom, 1982–; Sci. Adv. Cttee, IAEA, 1982–87. *Publications:* numerous papers in technical jls. *Recreations:* music, photography. *Address:* 19 Diamond Court, 153 Banbury Road, Oxford. *T:* Oxford (0865) 510483.

DUNTZE, Sir Daniel (Evans), 8th Bt *cr* 1774, of Tiverton, Devon; graphics art consultant; *b* 4 April 1926; *s* of George Douglas Duntze (*d* 1946) and of Mabel Lillian, *d* of Daniel Evans; *S* cousin, 1987; *m* 1954, Marietta Welsh; one *s* two *d*. *Educ:* Washington Univ. Sch. of Fine Arts, St Louis, Mo. Served in US Army Air Force, World War II. *Heir:* *s* Daniel Evans Duntze, *b* 11 Aug. 1960. *Address:* 8049 Gannon Avenue, University City, Missouri 6313, USA.

But his name does not, at time of going to press, appear on the Official Roll of Baronets.

DUNWICH, Viscount; Robert Keith Rous; *b* 17 Nov. 1961; *s* and *heir* of Earl of Stradbroke, *qv*.

DUNWICH, Bishop Suffragan of, since 1980; **Rt. Rev. Eric Nash Devenport;** *b* 3 May 1926; *s* of Joseph and Emma Devenport; *m* 1954, Jean Margaret Richardson; two *d*. *Educ:* Kelham Theological Coll. BA (Open Univ.). Curate, St Mark, Leicester, 1951–54; St Matthew, Barrow-in-Furness, 1954–56; Succentor, Leicester Cathedral, 1956–59; Vicar of Shepshed, 1959–64; Oadby, 1964–73; Proctor in Convocation, 1964–80; Hon. Canon of Leicester Cathedral, 1973–80; Leader of Mission, Diocese of Leicester, 1973–80. Chairman: Diocesan Communication Officers Cttee, 1986–; C of E Hospital Chaplaincies Council, 1986–91; Jt Hosp. Chaplaincies Cttee, 1988–91; E Anglian Ministerial Trng Course, 1990–. Chaplain, Worshipful Company of Framework Knitters, 1964–80; Area Chaplain, Actors' Church Union, 1980–. Chm., Local Radio Adv. Council for Radio Suffolk, 1990–. *Publication:* Preaching at the Parish Communion: ASB Gospels-Sundays: Year One, Vol. 2, 1989. *Recreation:* theatre. *Address:* The Old Vicarage, Stowupland, Stowmarket, Suffolk IP14 4BQ. *T:* Stowmarket (0449) 678234. *Club:* Commonwealth Trust.

DUNWOODY, Gwyneth (Patricia); MP (Lab) Crewe and Nantwich, since 1983 (Crewe, Feb. 1974–1983); *b* 12 Dec. 1930; *d* of late Morgan Phillips and of Baroness Phillips, *qv*; *m* 1954, Dr John Elliott Orr Dunwoody, *qv* (marr. diss. 1975); two *s* one *d*. MP (Lab) Exeter, 1966–70; Parly Sec. to BoT, 1967–70; Mem., European Parlt, 1975–79; Front Bench Spokesman on Foreign Affairs, 1980, on Health Service, 1980–83, on Transport, 1984–85; Parly Campaign Co-ordinator, 1983–. Mem., Labour Party NEC, 1981–88. Dir, Film Production Assoc. of GB, 1970–74. *Address:* c/o House of Commons, SW1A 0AA.

DUNWOODY, Dr John (Elliott Orr), CBE 1986; general practitioner; Chairman, Bloomsbury District Health Authority, 1982–90; *b* 3 June 1929; *s* of Dr W. O. and late Mrs F. J. Dunwoody; *m* 1st, 1954, Gwyneth Patricia (*née* Phillips), *qv* (marr. diss. 1975); two *s* one *d*; 2nd, 1979, Evelyn Louise (*née* Borner). *Educ:* St Paul's Sch.; King's Coll., London Univ.; Westminster Hosp. Med. Sch. MB, BS London; MRCS, LRCP 1954. House Surgeon, Westminster (Gordon) Hosp., 1954; House Physician, Royal Berks Hosp., 1954–55; Sen. House Physician, Newton Abbot Hosp., 1955–56; Family Doctor and Medical Officer, Totnes District Hosp, 1956–66; MO, Staff Health Service, St George's Hosp., 1976–77. MP (Lab) Falmouth and Camborne, 1966–70; Parly Under-Sec., Dept of Health and Social Security, 1969–70. Vice-Chm., 1974–77, Chm., 1977–82, Kensington, Chelsea and Westminster AHA (T). Member: Exec. Cttee, British Council, 1967–69; Council, Westminster Med. Sch., 1974–82; (co-opted) Social Services Cttee, Westminster City Council, 1975–78; Nat. Exec. Council, FPA, 1979–87 (Dep. Chm., 1980, Chm., 1981–87). Council Mem., UCL, 1982–90. Hon. Dir, Action on Smoking and Health, 1971–73. Governor, Pimlico Sch., 1972–75. *Publication:* (jtly) A Birth Control Plan for Britain, 1972. *Recreations:* travel, cooking. *Address:* 9 Cautley Avenue, SW4 9HX. *T:* 081–673 7471.

DUNWORTH, John Vernon, CB 1969; CBE 1955; President, International Committee of Weights and Measures, Sèvres, France, 1975–85; *b* 24 Feb. 1917; *o c* of late John Dunworth and Susan Ida (*née* Warburton); *m* 1967, Patricia Noel Boston; one *d*. *Educ:* Manchester Grammar Sch.; Clare Coll., Cambridge; Denman Baynes Research Studentship, 1937, Robins Prize, 1937; MA, PhD; Twisden Studentship and Fellowship, Trinity Coll., 1941. War Service: Ministry of Supply on Radar Development, 1939–44; National Research Council of Canada, on Atomic Energy Development, 1944–45. Univ. Demonstrator in Physics, Cambridge, 1945. Joined Atomic Energy Research Establishment, Harwell, 1947; Dir, NPL, 1964–76. Alternate United Kingdom Member on Organising Cttee of UN Atoms for Peace Confs in Geneva, 1955 and 1958. Pres., 1975–85, Vice-Pres., 1968–75, Internat. Cttee of Weights and Measures; Mem., Manx Communications Commn, 1985–. Fellow Amer. Nuclear Soc. 1960. Chm., British Nuclear Energy Soc., 1964–70; Vice-President, Institute of Physics: Physical Soc., 1966–70. CEng 1966. Comdr (with Star), Order of Alfonso X el Sabio, Spain, 1960. *Address:* The Warbuck, Kirk Michael, Isle of Man. *T:* Ramsey (0624) 813003, 878359. *Club:* Athenæum.

DU PLESSIS, Barend Jacobus; Minister of Finance, Republic of South Africa, since 1984; MP (National Party) Florida, since 1974; Leader of National Party of Transvaal, since 1989; *b* 19 Jan. 1940; *s* of late Jan Hendrik and of Martha J. W. (*née* Botha); *m* 1962, Antoinette (*née* Van Den Berg); three *s* one *d*. *Educ:* Potchefstroom Univ. for Christian Higher Educn (BSc); Potchefstroom Teachers' Trng Coll. (THED). Mathematics Teacher, Hoër Seunskool Helpmekaar, Johannesburg and Johannesburg Technical Coll., 1962; Engineering Div., Data Processing and Admin. Sec., SABC, 1962–68; Systems Engineering and Marketing in Banking and Finance, IBM (SA), 1968–74. Dep. Minister of Foreign Affairs and Information, 1982; Minister of Educn and Trng, 1983. *Address:* Private Bag X115, Pretoria, 0001, Republic of S Africa. *T:* (012) 3238911; (021) 357595.

du PLESSIS, Prof. Daniel Jacob, FRCS; Vice-Chancellor and Principal, University of the Witwatersrand, 1978–83; *b* 17 May 1918; *s* of D. J. du Plessis and L. du Plessis (*née* Carstens); *m* 1946, Louisa Susanna Wicht; two *s*. *Educ:* Univ. of Cape Town (MB ChB; Hon. MD, 1986; Hon. Fellow, Smuts Hall, 1986); Univ. of the Witwatersrand (ChM). Served, SA Medical Corps, 1942–46. Postgraduate study, 1947–51; Surgeon and Lectr, Univ. of Cape Town, 1952–58; Prof. of Surgery, Univ. of the Witwatersrand, 1958–77 (Hon. LLD, 1984). Trustee, S African Blood Transfusion Service, 1985–. Dir, Transvaal Bd, Provincial Bldg Soc., 1984–. Pres., S Transvaal Br., Medical Assoc. of S Africa, 1986–87; Chairman of Council: B. G. Alexander Nursing Coll., 1985–; Bonalesedi (formerly Natalspruit) Nursing Coll., 1985–; Member: Council, Med. Univ. of Southern Africa, 1986–; Adv. Council for Univs and Technikons, 1984–; Council, Johannesburg Coll. of Educn; Council, Univ. of Transkei, 1989–. Governor, Amer. Coll. of Surgeons, 1988–91. Hon. FACS 1974; Hon. Fellow: Assoc. of Surgeons of GB and Ireland, 1979; Amer. Surgical Assoc., 1981; Hon. FCSSA 1982. Hon. Life Vice-President: Assoc. of Surgeons of S Africa; Surgical Res. Soc. of Southern Africa. Paul Harris Fellowship, Rotary Club, Orange Grove, Johannesburg, 1984. Hon. Mem., Alpha Omega Alpha Honor Med. Soc. (USA), 1986. Order for Meritorious Service Cl. 1 (Gold), RSA, 1989. *Publications:* Principles of Surgery, 1968, 2nd edn 1976; Synopsis of Surgical Anatomy, 10th edn (with A. Lee McGregor) 1969, 11th edn 1975, 12th edn (with G. A. G. Decker) 1986; numerous articles in learned jls on surgical topics, espec. on diseases of parotid salivary gland and gastric ulcers. *Address:* 17 Chateau Road, Richmond, Johannesburg, 2092, South Africa. *Club:* Country (Johannesburg).

DUPPA-MILLER, John Bryan Peter; *see* Miller, J. B. P. D.

DUPPLIN, Viscount; Charles William Harley Hay, MA; barrister; Fine Art Underwriter, Roberts & Hiscox Ltd, since 1990; *b* 20 Dec. 1962; *s* and *heir* of 15th Earl of Kinnoull, *qv*. *Educ:* Summer Fields; Eton; Christ Church, Oxford (Scholar); City Univ. (Dip. in Law); Inns of Court Sch. of Law. Called to the Bar, Middle Temple, 1990. Associate, Credit Suisse First Boston Ltd, 1985–88. *Publication:* contrib. Jl of Chem. Soc. *Recreations:* cricket, Cresta Run, skiing, night clubs, philately. *Address:* 59 Scarsdale Villas, W8. *T:* 071–938 4265. *Clubs:* Turf, Lansdowne, United Oxford & Cambridge University, MCC.

DUPREE, Sir Peter, 5th Bt *cr* 1921; *b* 20 Feb. 1924; *s* of Sir Victor Dupree, 4th Bt and of Margaret Cross; *S* father, 1976; *m* 1947, Joan, *d* of late Captain James Desborough Hunt. *Heir:* *cousin* Thomas William James David Dupree, *b* 5 Feb. 1930. *Address:* 15 Hayes Close, Chelmsford, Essex CM2 0RN.

DURACK, Dame Mary, (Mrs Horrie Miller), AC 1989; DBE 1978 (OBE 1966); novelist and historian; *b* 20 Feb. 1913; *d* of Michael Patrick Durack and Bessie Ida Muriel (*née* Johnstone); *m* 1938, Captain H. C. Miller (decd); two *s* two *d* (and two *d* decd). *Educ:* Loreto Convent, Perth. Formerly: lived at Argyle and Ivanhoe Stns, E Kimberley; mem. staff, West Australian Newspapers Ltd. Member: Aust. Soc. of Authors; National Trust;

Royal Western Aust. Hist. Soc. Formerly Exec. Mem., Aboriginal Cultural Foundn. Dir, Aust. Stockman's Hall of Fame. Emeritus Fellow, Literature Bd of Australia Council, 1983–86 and 1987–; Foundn Fellow, Curtin Univ. of Technol., 1978. Hon. Life Member: WA Br., Fellowship of Aust. Writers (Pres., 1958–63); Internat. PEN, Australia (Mem., WA Br.). Patron, Friends of Battye Liby of WA. Commonwealth Lit. Grant, 1973, 1977 and Australian Research Grants Cttee Grant, 1980 and 1984. Hon. DLitt Univ. of WA, 1978. Alice Award, Soc. of Women Writers (Australia), 1982. *Publications:* (E Kimberley District stories illus. by sister, Elizabeth Durack): All-about, 1935; Chunuma, 1936; Son of Djaro, 1938; The Way of the Whirlwind, 1941, new edn 1979; Piccaninnies, 1943; The Magic Trumpet, 1944; (with Florence Rutter) Child Artists of the Australian Bush, 1952; (novel) Keep Him My Country, 1955; (family documentary) Kings in Grass Castles, 1959; To Ride a Fine Horse, 1963; The Courteous Savage, 1964 (new edn as Yagan of the Bibbulmun, 1976); Kookanoo and Kangaroo, 1963; An Australian Settler, 1964 (pub. Australia, A Pastoral Emigrant); The Rock and the Sand, 1969; (with Ingrid Drysdale) The End of Dreaming, 1974; To Be Heirs Forever, 1976; Tjakamarra—boy between two worlds, 1977; Sons in the Saddle, 1983; *plays:* The Ship of Dreams, 1968; Swan River Saga, 1972; scripts for ABC drama dept; libretto for opera, Dalgerie (music by James Penberthy), 1966; six dramatised Kookanoo stories on tape and record, 1973. *Address:* 12 Bellevue Avenue, Nedlands, WA 6009, Australia. *T:* 386–1117.

DURAND, Rev. Sir (Henry Mortimer) Dickon (Marion St George), 4th Bt *cr* 1892; Rector, Youghal Union of Parishes, Co. Cork, since 1982; *b* 19 June 1934; *s* of Lt-Comdr Mortimer Henry Marion Durand, RN (*y s* of 1st Bt) (*d* 1969), and late Beatrice Garvan-Sheridan, *d* of Judge Sheridan, Sydney, NSW; *S* uncle, 1971; *m* 1971, Stella Evelyn, *d* of Captain C. C. L'Estrange; two *s* two *d*. *Educ:* Wellington College; Sydney University; Salisbury Theological College. Curate: All Saints, Fulham, 1969–72; St Leonard's, Heston, 1972–74. Curate-in-Charge, St Benedict's, Ashford, Mddx, 1975–79; Bishop's Curate, Kilbixy Union of Parishes, Co. Westmeath, 1979–82. *Recreations:* heraldry, philately, model railways, printing, militaria, painting, poetry, travel. *Heir: s* Edward Alan Christopher David Percy Durand, *b* 21 Feb. 1974. *Address:* The Rectory, Youghal, Co. Cork, Ireland.

DURAND, Victor Albert Charles, QC 1958; *s* of Victor and Blanche Durand; *m* 1935, Betty Joan Kirchner (*d* 1986); one *s* one *d*. *Educ:* Howard High Sch. (Kitchener Scholar). LLB, BSc, AMInstCE. Served War 1939–45 with RE. Called to Bar, Inner Temple, 1939, Bencher, 1985. Dep. Chm., Warwicks QS, 1961. *Address:* Queen Elizabeth Building, Temple, EC4Y 9BS.

DURANT, Sir Anthony; *see* Durant, Sir R. A. B.

DURANT, John Robert, PhD; Assistant Director (Head of Research and Information), Science Museum, since 1989; *b* 8 July 1950; *s* of Kenneth Albert James Durant and Edna Kathleen Durant (*née* Norman); *m* 1977, Nirmala Naidoo; two *s* one *d*. *Educ:* Queens' College, Cambridge (MA Nat. Scis; PhD Hist. of Sci.). Staff Tutor in Biological Scis, Dept of Extramural Studies, UC Swansea, 1976–82; Staff Tutor in Biol Scis, Dept for External Studies, Univ. of Oxford, 1983–89. Vis. Prof. of History and Public Understanding of Science, Imperial College London, 1989–. *Publications:* (ed) Darwinism and Divinity, 1985; (with P. Klopfer and S. Oyama) Aggression: conflict in animals and humans reconsidered, 1988; articles in professional jls. *Recreations:* family, choral music, writing. *Address:* Science Museum Library, South Kensington, SW7 5NH. *T:* 071–938 8201, *Fax:* 071–938 8213.

DURANT, Sir (Robert) Anthony (Bevis), Kt 1991; MP (C) Reading West, since 1983 (Reading North, Feb. 1974–1983); *b* 9 Jan. 1928; *s* of Captain Robert Michael Durant and Mrs Violet Dorothy Durant (*née* Bevis); *m* 1958, Audrey Stoddart; two *s* one *d*. *Educ:* Dane Court Prep. Sch., Pyrford, Woking; Bryanston Sch., Blandford, Dorset. Royal Navy, 1945–47. Coutts Bank, Strand, 1947–52; Cons. Party Organisation, 1952–67 (Young Cons. Organiser, Yorks; Cons. Agent, Clapham; Nat. Organiser, Young Conservatives). PPS to Sec. of State for Transport and to Sec. of State for Employment, 1983–84; Asst Govt Whip, 1984–86; a Lord Comr of HM Treasury, 1986–88; Vice-Chamberlain of HM Household, 1988–90. Mem., Select Cttee Parly Comr (Ombudsman), 1973–83, 1990–; Mem., Council of Europe, 1981–83; Chairman: All Party Gp on Widows and One Parent Families, 1977–85; Cons. Nat. Local Govt Adv. Cttee, 1981–84; British Br., CPA, 1988–; Vice-Chm., Parly Gp for World Govt, 1979–84. Former Consultant: The Film Production Association of Great Britain Ltd; Delta Electrical Div. of Delta Metal Co. Ltd; Allied Industrial Designers. Mem., Inland Waterways Adv. Council, 1975–84. Dir, British Industrial Scientific Film Assoc., 1967–70. *Recreations:* boating, golf. *Address:* House of Commons, SW1A 0AA.

DURANT, Ven. Stanton Vincent; Archdeacon of Liverpool, Canon of Liverpool Cathedral and Vicar of All Saints, Stoneycroft, since 1991; *b* 13 Sept. 1942; *s* of late Alleyne Durant and of Hyacinth Durant. *Educ:* Harrison Coll., Barbados; Southwark Ordination Course (DTh). British Army, Royal Tank Regiment, 1962–68. Ordained: deacon, 1972; priest, 1973; Assistant curate: St Giles. Ickenham, 1972–76; Emmanuel, Paddington, 1976–78; Vicar, Emmanuel, Paddington, 1978–87; Area Dean, Paddington, 1984–87; Team Rector, Hackney Marsh Team Ministry, 1987–91. *Recreations:* playing cricket, general interest in all sports, listening to music. *Address:* All Saints' Vicarage, Oakhill Park, Liverpool L13 4BN. *T:* 051–228 3581.

DURAS, Marguerite; French author and playwright; *b* Gia Dinh, Indochina; *d* of Henri Donnadieu and Marie (*née* Legrand). *Educ:* Lycée de Saigon; Faculté de droit de Paris; Ecole libre des sciences politiques. Sec., Colonies Ministry, 1935–41. *Screenplays:* also directed: Hiroshima, mon Amour, 1960; Jaune le soleil, 1971; India Song, 1973; Nathalie Granger, 1973; La femme du Gange, 1974; Aurélia Steiner, 1979; L'homme assis dans le couloir, 1980; L'homme atlantique, 1981; Agatha et les lectures illimitées, 1981; Dialogue de Rome, 1982; Les Enfants, 1985; directed and appeared in Le Camion, 1977. Grand Prix du théâtre de l'Académie Française, 1983. *Publications:* Les Impudents, 1943; La vie tranquille, 1944; Un barrage contre le Pacifique, 1950; Le marin de Gibraltar, 1952; Les petits chevaux de Tarquinia, 1953; Des journées entières dans les arbres (short stories), 1954 (Prix Jean Cocteau) (adapted for stage, 1964); Le square, 1955; Moderato Cantabile, 1958; Les viaducs de la Seine-et-Oise, 1960; Dix heures et demi du soir en été, 1960 (filmed, 1967); L'après-midi de Monsieur Andesmas, 1962; Le ravissement de Lol V. Stein, 1964; L'amante anglaise, 1967; Détruire, dit-elle, 1969 (filmed), 1970 (also dir)); L'amour, 1972; L'été 80, 1980; Outside, 1981; La Maladie de la mort, 1983; L'amant, 1984 (Prix Goncourt; Ritz Paris Hemingway Award, 1986); La douleur (short stories), 1985; Les yeux bleus cheveux noirs, 1986; La Pute de la côte normande, 1986; Practicalities, 1990; *plays:* Les eaux et les forêts, 1965; Théâtre I, le vice-consul, 1965; Théâtre II (5 plays), 1968; Susanna Andler, 1969; Yes, Peut-être, 1976; Abahn Sabana David, 1976; La Musica, 1976; Baxter Vera Baxter, 1977; L'Eden cinéma, 1977. *Address:* 5 rue le Benoît, 75006 Paris, France.

DURBIN, Prof. James; Professor of Statistics, University of London (London School of Economics), 1961–88, now Emeritus; *b* 30 June 1923; *m* 1958, Anne Dearnley Outhwaite; two *s* one *d*. *Educ:* St John's Coll., Cambridge. Army Operational Research Group, 1943–45. Boot and Shoe Trade Research Assoc., 1945–47; Dept of Applied Economics, Cambridge, 1948–49; Asst Lectr, then Lecturer, in Statistics, London Sch. of Economics, 1950–53; Reader in Statistics, 1953–61. Visiting Professor: Univ. of North Carolina, 1959–60; Stanford Univ., 1960; Johns Hopkins Univ., 1965–66; Univ. of Washington, 1966; ANU, 1970–71; Univ. of Calif, Berkeley, 1971; Univ. of Cape Town, 1978; UCLA, 1984; Univ. of Calif, Santa Barbara, 1989. Member: ESRC, 1983–86 (Chm., Res. Resources and Methods Cttee, 1982–85); Internat. Statistical Inst., 1955 (Pres., 1983–85); Bd of Dirs, Amer. Statistical Assoc., 1980–82 (Fellow, 1960); Fellow, Inst. of Mathematical Statistics, 1958; Fellow, Econometric Soc., 1967; Royal Statistical Society: Vice Pres., 1969–70 and 1972–73; Pres. 1986–87; Guy Medal in Bronze, 1966, in Silver, 1976. *Publications:* Distribution Theory for Tests based on the Sample Distribution Function, 1973; articles in statistical journals, incl. Biometrika, Jl of Royal Statistical Society, etc. *Recreations:* skiing, mountain walking, travel, opera, theatre. *Address:* 31 Southway, NW11. *T:* 081–458 3037.

DURBIN, Leslie, CBE 1976; MVO 1943; silversmith; *b* 21 Feb. 1913; *s* of late Harry Durbin and of Lillian A. Durbin; *m* 1940, Phyllis Ethel Durbin (*see* Phyllis E. Ginger); one *s* one *d*. *Educ:* Central Sch. of Arts and Crafts, London. Apprenticed to late Omar Ramsden, 1929–39; full-time schol., 1938–39, travelling schol., 1939–40, both awarded by Worshipful Co. of Goldsmiths. Started working on own account in workshop of Francis Adam, 1940–41. RAF, Allied Central Interpretation Unit, 1941–45. Commissioned by Jt Cttee of Assay Offices of GB to design Silver Jubilee Hall Mark; designed regional variants of pound coin for Royal Mint, 1983. Retrospective exhibn, Leslie Durbin, 50 years of Silversmithing, Goldsmiths' Hall, 1982. Hon. LLD Cambridge, 1963. Council of Industrial Design Awards for Silver for the 70's. MVO awarded for work on Stalingrad Sword.

DURBRIDGE, Francis (Henry); playwright and author; *b* 25 Nov. 1912; *s* of late Francis and Gertrude Durbridge; *m* 1940, Norah Elizabeth Lawley; two *s*. *Educ:* Bradford Grammar Sch.; Wylde Green Coll.; Birmingham Univ. After period in stockbroker's office, began to write (as always intended); short stories and plays for BBC; many subseq. radio plays, including Promotion, 1933; created character of Paul Temple. Entered Television with The Broken Horseshoe, 1952 (the first adult television serial); other serials followed; Portrait of Alison, 1954; My Friend Charles, 1955; The Other Man, 1956; The Scarf 1960; The World of Tim Frazer (Exec. Prod.), 1960–61; Melissa, 1962; Bat Out of Hell, 1964; Stupid Like a Fox, 1971; The Doll, 1976; Breakaway, 1980. The television serials have been presented in many languages, and are continuing; novels, based on them, have been published in USA, Europe, etc. The European Broadcasting Union asked for a radio serial for an internat. market (La Boutique, 1967, broadcast in various countries); German, French and Italian productions, 1971–72. Films include two for Korda and Romulus, 1954–57. Stage plays: Suddenly at Home, 1971; The Gentle Hook, 1974; Murder With Love, 1976; House Guest, 1980; Nightcap, 1983; Murder Diary, 1986; A Touch of Fear, 1987; The Small Hours, 1989; Sweet Revenge, 1991. *Publications:* include contribs to newspapers and magazines, at home and abroad. *Recreations:* family, reading, travel. *Address:* c/o Harvey Unna and Stephen Durbridge Ltd, 24 Pottery Lane, Holland Park, W11 4LZ. *Club:* Royal Automobile.

DURHAM, 6th Earl of, *cr* 1833; Baron Durham, 1828; Viscount Lambton, 1833; peerages disclaimed, 1970; *see under* Lambton.

DURHAM, Baron; a subsidiary title of Earldom of Durham (disclaimed 1970), used by Hon. Edward Richard Lambton, *b* 19 Oct. 1961, *heir* to disclaimed Earldom.

DURHAM, Bishop of, since 1984; **Rt. Rev. David Edward Jenkins;** *b* 26 Jan. 1925; *er s* of Lionel C. Jenkins and Dora (*née* Page); *m* 1949, Stella Mary Peet; two *s* two *d*. *Educ:* St Dunstan's Coll., Catford; Queen's Coll., Oxford (MA; Hon. Fellow, 1990). EC, RA, 1943–45 (Captain). Priest, 1954. Succentor, Birmingham Cath. and Lectr, Queen's Coll., 1953–54; Fellow, Chaplain and Praelector in Theology, Queen's Coll., Oxford, 1954–69; Dir, Humanum Studies, World Council of Churches, Geneva, 1969–73 (Consultant, 1973–75); Dir, William Temple Foundn, Manchester, 1973–78 (Jt Dir, 1979–); Prof. of Theology, Univ. of Leeds, 1979–84, Emeritus Prof., 1985. Exam. Chaplain to Bps of Lichfield, 1956–69, Newcastle, 1957–69, Bristol, 1958–84, Wakefield, 1978–84, and Bradford, 1979–84; Canon Theologian, Leicester, 1966–82, Canon Emeritus, 1982–. Lectures: Bampton, 1966; Hale, Seabury-Western, USA, 1970; Moorhouse, Melbourne, 1972; Cadbury, Birmingham Univ., 1974; Lindsay Meml, Keele Univ., 1976; Heslington, York Univ., 1980; Drummond, Stirling Univ., 1981; Hibbert, Hibbert Trust, 1985; Hensley Henson, Oxford, 1987; Gore, Westminster Abbey, 1990. Chm., SCM Press, 1987–; Trustee, Trinity Press Internat., 1989–. Hon. Fellow: St Chad's Coll., Durham, 1986; Sunderland Poly., 1986. Hon. DD: Durham, 1987; Trinity Coll., Toronto, 1989; Aberdeen, 1990. Jt Editor, Theology, 1976–82. *Publications:* Guide to the Debate about God, 1966; The Glory of Man, 1967; Living with Questions, 1969; What is Man?, 1970; The Contradiction of Christianity, 1976; God, Miracle and the Church of England, 1987; God, Politics and the Future, 1988; God, Jesus and Life in the Spirit, 1988; Still Living with Questions, 1990; Free to Believe, 1991; contrib. Man, Fallen and Free, 1969, etc. *Recreations:* music, reading, walking. *Address:* Auckland Castle, Bishop Auckland, Co. Durham DL14 7NR.

DURHAM, Dean of; *see* Arnold, Very Rev. J. R.

DURHAM, Archdeacon of; *see* Perry, Ven. M. C.

DURHAM, Sir Kenneth, Kt 1985; Chairman: Unilever, 1982–86; Kingfisher (formerly Woolworth Holdings) plc, 1986–90 (non-executive Deputy Chairman, 1985–86); Deputy Chairman, British Aerospace, 1986–90 (Board Member, 1980–90); *b* 28 July 1924; *s* of late George Durham and Bertha (*née* Aspin); *m* 1946, Irene Markham; one *s* one *d*. *Educ:* Queen Elizabeth Grammar Sch., Blackburn; Univ. of Manchester (Hatfield Schol.; BSc Hons, Physics). Flight Lieut, RAF, 1942–46. ARE, Harwell, 1950; Unilever: joined Res. Lab., Port Sunlight, 1950, Head of Lab., 1961; Head, Res. Lab., Colworth, Bedford, 1965; assumed responsibility for animal feed interests, 1970; Chm., BOCM Silcock Ltd, 1971; Dir, Unilever Ltd, 1974, Vice-Chm., 1978; Dir, Unilever NV, 1974–86. Board Mem., Delta PLC, 1984–; Dir, Morgan Grenfell Hldgs, 1986–90. Chairman: Food, Drink and Packaging Machinery EDC, NEDO, 1981–86; Trade Policy Res. Centre, 1982–89; Industry and Commerce Liaison Cttee, Royal Jubilee Trusts, 1982–87; Economic and Financial Policy Cttee, CBI, 1983–86; Priorities Bd for Govt Agricl Depts and AFRC, 1984–87; Member: British-N America Cttee, 1982–87; British Shippers Council, 1982–86; Bd, British Exec. Service Overseas, 1982–86; Adv. Cttee, CVCP, 1984–; Governing Body, ICC UK, 1984–88; ACARD, 1984–86; European Adv. Council, NY Stock Exchange, 1985–; Council for Industry and Higher Educn, 1985–; Adv. Panel, Science Policy Res. Unit, Sussex Univ., 1985–; Adv. Bd, Industrial Res. Labs, Durham Univ., 1985–; President: ABCC, 1986–87; BAAS, 1986–87. Attended Harvard Advanced Management Program, 1962; Member: Council, PSI, 1978–85; Council, Royal Free Hosp. Sch. of Med., 1984–. Vice-President: Liverpool Sch. of Tropical Medicine, 1982–; Opportunities for the Disabled, 1982–88; Help the Aged, 1986–; Trustee: Leverhulme Trust, 1974–; Civic Trust, 1982–. Governor, NIESR, 1983–. CBIM 1978; FIGD 1983.

Hon. LLD Manchester, 1984; Hon. DSc: Loughborough, 1984; QUB. Comdr, Order of Orange Nassau (Netherlands), 1985. *Publications:* Surface Activity and Detergency, 1960; various scientific papers. *Recreations:* walking, golf. *Club:* Athenæum.

DURIE, Sir Alexander (Charles), Kt 1977; CBE 1973; Vice-President, The Automobile Association, since 1977 (Director-General, 1964–77); *b* 15 July 1915; *er s* of late Charles and Margaret Durie (*née* Gardner), Shepton Mallet, Somerset; *m* 1941, Joyce, *o c* of late Lionel and Helen Hargreaves (*née* Hirst), Leeds and Bridlington, Yorks; one *s* one *d*. *Educ:* Queen's Coll., Taunton. Joined Shell-Mex and BP Ltd, 1933. Served War of 1939–45, Royal Artillery; Gunnery Staff Course (IG), 1941; Lieut-Col 1945. Dir Shell Co. of Australia Ltd, 1954–56; Dir, 1962, Man. Dir, 1963–64, Shell-Mex and BP Ltd; Director: Mercantile Credit Co. Ltd, 1973–80; Thomas Cook Group Ltd, 1974–79; Private Patients Plan Ltd, 1977–87 (a Vice-Pres., 1987–); H. Clarkson (Holdings) Ltd, 1978–85; Chelsea Building Soc., 1979–87. Mem. Council, Motor and Cycle Trades Benevolent Fund, 1959–73; Vice-Pres. British Assoc. of Industrial Editors, 1959–71; Gen. Commissioner of Income Tax, 1960–85; Member Govt Inquiries into: Civilianisation of Armed Forces, 1964; Cars for Cities, 1964; Road Haulage Operators' Licensing, 1978. FBIM, 1959, Council Mem., 1962–73, Chm. Exec. Cttee, 1962–65, Vice-Chm. Council, 1962–67, Chm., Bd of Fellows, 1970–73 (Verulam Medal 1973); Member: Nat. Road Safety Adv. Council, 1965–68; Adv. Council on Road Res., 1965–68; Brit. Road Fedn Ltd, 1962– (Vice-Pres., 1978); Council, Internat. Road Fedn Ltd, London, 1962–64; Marketing Cttee, BTA, 1970–77; Adv. Cttee on Traffic and Safety, TRRL, 1973–77; Vice-Pres., Alliance Internationale de Tourisme, 1965–71, Pres., 1971–77; Chm., Indep. Schs Careers Orgn, 1969–73 (Vice-Pres., 1973–); Governor: Ashridge Coll., 1963–78 (Vice Pres., 1978–); Queen's Coll., Taunton, 1969–83. Chm. Council, Imperial Soc. of Knights Bachelor, 1986–88 (Mem., 1978–); Pres., Surrey CCC, 1984–85 (Mem. Cttee, 1970–80; Vice-Pres., 1980–84, 1985–); Vice-Pres., Hampshire CCC, 1984–. Freeman of City of London and Liveryman, Worshipful Co. of Paviors, 1965. FCIT; Hon. FInstHE 1969. Spanish Order of Touristic Merit Silver Medal, 1977. *Recreations:* cricket, golf, racing. *Address:* The Garden House, Windlesham, Surrey GU20 6AD. *T:* Bagshot (0276) 72035. *Clubs:* MCC; Royal and Ancient; Berkshire Golf.

DURIE, David Robert Campbell; Minister and Deputy UK Permanent Representative to the European Community, Brussels, since 1991; *b* 21 Aug. 1944; *s* of Frederick Robert Edwin Durie and Joan Elizabeth Campbell Durie (*née* Learoyd); *m* 1966, Susan Frances Weller; three *d*. *Educ:* Fettes Coll., Edinburgh; Christ Church, Oxford (MA Physics). Asst Principal, 1966, Pvte Sec. to Perm. Sec., 1970, Min. of Technology; Principal, DTI, 1971; First Sec., UK Delegn to OECD, 1974; Dept of Prices and Consumer Protection, 1977; Asst Sec., 1978; Dept of Trade, 1979; Cabinet Office, 1982; DTI, 1984; Under Sec., 1985–91. *Recreations:* moderately strenuous outdoor exercise, theatre, family. *Address:* c/o Foreign and Commonwealth Office, SW1A 2AH.

DURKIN, Air Marshal Sir Herbert, KBE 1976; CB 1973; MA; CEng, FIEE, FRAeS; Controller of Engineering and Supply (RAF), 1976–78; *b* 31 March 1922; *s* of Herbert and Helen Durkin, Burnley, Lancs; *m* 1951, Dorothy Hope, *d* of Walter Taylor Johnson, Burnley; one *s* two *d*. *Educ:* Burnley Grammar Sch.; Emmanuel Coll., Cambridge (MA). Commissioned into Tech. Br., RAF, Oct. 1941. Served War, with No 60 Gp, until 1945. India, 1945–47, becoming ADC to AOC-in-C India; Central Bomber Estabt, 1947–50; Sqdn Ldr, 1950; Atomic Weapons Research Estabt, 1950–52; RAF Staff Coll., 1953; Chief Signals Officer, AHQ, Iraq, 1954–56; Wing Comdr, Chief Instr of Signals Div. of RAF Tech. Coll., 1956–58; Air Ministry, 1958–60; jssc, 1961; HQ, 2 ATAF, 1961–63; Gp Capt 1962; Sen. Tech. Staff Officer, HQ Signals Command, 1964–65; Comdt, No 2 Sch. of Tech. Trg, Cosford, 1965–67; Air Cdre, 1967; Director of Eng (Policy), MoD, 1967–69; IDC, 1970; AOC No 90 Group, RAF, 1971–73; Dir-Gen. Engineering and Supply Management, 1973–76. Pres., IEE, 1980 (Dep. Pres., 1979). Pres., Assoc. of Lancastrians in London, 1988–90. Freeman, City of London, 1988. *Recreation:* golf. *Address:* Willowbank, Drakes Drive, Northwood, Middlesex HA6 2SL. *T:* Northwood (09274) 23167. *Club:* Royal Air Force.

DURR, Kent Skelton; South African Ambassador to the Court of St James's, since 1991; *b* 28 March 1941; *s* of Dr John Michael Durr and Diana (*née* Skelton); *m* 1966, Suzanne Wiese; one *s* two *d*. *Educ:* South African Coll. Schs; Cape Town Univ. Dir, family publishing co., 1966–68; Founder and later Man. Dir, Durr Estates, 1968–84. Elected to Provincial Council of Cape, 1974; MP for Maitland, SA, 1977–91; Dep. Minister, Trade and Industry, 1984–86, Finance, 1984–88; Minister of Budget and Public Works in Ministers' Council, 1988–89; Cabinet Minister of Trade and Industry and Tourism, 1989–91. Member: Inst. Valuers, SA, 1972; Inst. Estate Agents; MIH. Mem., SA Nat. Foundn for Conservation of Coastal Birds, 1985 (Award of Honour, 1987); Hon. Mem., Vernacular Architecture Soc., 1983. *Publications:* numerous articles in newspapers and jls on econs, foreign affairs, constitutional affairs, urban renewal, conservation and real estate. *Recreations:* reading history, country pursuits, field sports, mountaineering, conservation, chess, yachting. *Address:* South Africa House, Trafalgar Square, WC2N 5DP. *T:* 071–930 4488. *Clubs:* Cavalry and Guards; City and Civil Service, Kelvin Grove (Cape Town, SA).

DURRANDS, Prof. Kenneth James, DGS (Birm), MSc, CEng, FIMechE, FIEE, FIProdE; Rector, The Polytechnic, Queensgate, Huddersfield, since 1970 (Professor, since 1985); *b* 24 June 1929; *s* of A. I. Durrands, Croxton Kerrial; *m* 1956 (marr. diss. 1971), one *s*; *m* 1983, Jennifer Jones; one *s*. *Educ:* King's Sch., Grantham; Nottingham Technical Coll.; Birmingham Univ. Min. of Supply Engrg Apprentice, ROF, Nottingham, 1947–52; Techn. Engr, UKAEA, Risley, 1954–58; Lecturer in Mechanical and Nuclear Engrg, Univ. of Birmingham, 1958–61; Head of Gen. Engrg Dept, Reactor Engrg Lab., UKAEA, Risley, 1961–67; Mem. Council, IMechE, 1963–66; Visiting Lecturer, Manchester Univ., 1962–68; Technical Dir, Vickers Ltd, Barrow Engrg Works, 1967–70. Member: DoI Educn and Training Cttee, 1973–75 (Chm., 1975–80); DoI Garment & Allied Industries Requirements Bd, 1975–79 (Chm. Computer Cttee, 1975–79); BEC Educn Cttee, 1975–79; BEC Business Studies Bd, 1976–79; Inter-Univ. and Polytech. Council, 1978–81; Yorks Consumers' Cttee, Office of Electricity Regulation, 1990–; British Council: Higher Educn Cttee, 1981–; Engrg and Technology Adv. Cttee, 1981–90; CICHE, 1985–; Council for the Accreditation of Teacher Educn, 1991–; Hon. Sec./Treas., Cttee of Dirs of Polytechnics, 1970–79. Educn Comr, MSC, subseq. Training Commn, 1986–89. Member: Council and Court, Leeds Univ., 1970–; Court, Bradford Univ., 1973–. *Publications:* technical and policy papers. *Recreations:* gardening, squash rackets. *Address:* Church Cottage, Croxton Kerrial, Grantham, Lincolnshire. *Club:* Athenæum.

DURRANT, Anthony Harrisson; His Honour Judge Durrant; a Circuit Judge, since 1991; *b* 3 Jan. 1931; *s* of Frank Baston Durrant and Irene Maud Durrant; *m* 1956, Jacqueline Ostroumoff; one *s* two *d*. *Educ:* Sir Joseph Williamson Mathematical Sch., Rochester. Admitted Solicitor, 1956; Partner, 1960, Sen. Partner, 1976–91, Horwood & James, Aylesbury; a Recorder, 1987–91. Dep. Chm., Agricl Land Tribunal, 1987–91. Pres., Berks, Bucks and Oxon Incorp. Law Soc., 1977–78; Chm., Berks, Bucks and Oxon Jt Consultative Cttee of Barristers and Solicitors, 1985–91. *Recreations:* reading, boating. *Club:* Phyllis Court (Henley).

DURRANT, Sir William Henry Estridge, 7th Bt, *cr* 1784; JP (NSW); *b* 1 April 1901; *s* of Sir William Durrant, 6th Bt; *S* father 1953; *m* 1927, Georgina Beryl Gwendoline (*d* 1968), *d* of Alexander Purse, Kircubbin, Co. Down, N Ireland; one *s* one *d*. Served War of 1939–45 (Pacific Area). NSW Registrar, Australian Inst. of Company Dirs, 1959. *Heir:* *s* William Alexander Estridge Durrant [*b* 26 Nov. 1929; *m* 1953, Dorothy (BA), *d* of Ronal Croker, Quirindi, NSW; one *s* one *d*]. *Address:* 1634 Pacific Highway, Wahroonga, NSW 2076, Australia.

DURRELL, Gerald Malcolm, OBE 1983; Zoologist and Writer since 1946; regular contributor to BBC Sound and TV Services; *b* Jamshedpur, India, 7 Jan. 1925; *s* of Lawrence Samuel Durrell, Civil Engineer, and Louisa Florence Dixie; *m* 1st, 1951, Jacqueline Sonia Rasen (marr. diss. 1979); no *c*; 2nd, 1979, Lee Wilson McGeorge. *Educ:* by Private Tutors, in Greece. Student Keeper, Whipsnade, 1945–46; 1st Animal Collecting Expedition, British Cameroons, 1947–48; 2nd Cameroon Expedition, 1948–49; Collecting trip to British Guiana, 1949–50; began writing, script writing and broadcasting, 1950–53; trip with wife to Argentine and Paraguay, 1953–54; filming in Cyprus, 1955; 3rd Cameroon Expedition with wife, 1957; Trans-Argentine Expedition, 1958–59; Expedition in conjunction with BBC Natural History Unit, Sierra Leone, 1965; collecting trip to Mexico, 1968; Aust. Expedn, 1969–70; expedns to Mauritius, 1976 and 1977, Assam, 1978, Mexico, 1979, Madagascar, 1981. Founder and Hon. Director: Jersey Zoological Park, 1958; Jersey Wildlife Preservation Trust, 1964. Founder Chm., Wildlife Preservation Trust Internat. (formerly SAFE Internat. USA), 1972–. FZS; (Life) FIAL; FRGS; FRSL 1972; MBOU; MIBiol. Hon. LHD Yale, 1977; Hon. DSc Durham, 1988. *Films for TV:* 1st series, 1956; Two in the Bush, 1962; Catch Me a Colobus, 1966; Animal People-Menagerie Manor, 1967; Garden of the Gods, 1967; The Stationary Ark, 1976; The Ark on the Move, 1981; The Amateur Naturalist (series), 1983; Durrell in Russia (series), 1986; Ourselves and Other Animals (series), 1987; Durrell's Ark, 1987. *Publications:* The Overloaded Ark, 1953; Three Singles to Adventure, 1954; The Bafut Beagles, 1954; The New Noah, 1955; The Drunken Forest, 1956; My Family and Other Animals, 1956 (televised, 1987); Encounters with Animals, 1958; A Zoo in my Luggage, 1960; The Whispering Land, 1961; Island Zoo, 1961; Look at Zoos, 1961; My Favourite Animal Stories, 1962; Menagerie Manor, 1964; Two in the Bush, 1966; Rosy is My Relative, 1968; The Donkey Rustlers, 1968; Birds, Beasts and Relatives, 1969; Fillets of Plaice, 1971; Catch Me a Colobus, 1972; Beasts in My Belfry, 1973; The Talking Parcel, 1974; The Stationary Ark, 1976; Golden Bats and Pink Pigeons, 1977; The Garden of the Gods, 1978; The Picnic & Suchlike Pandemonium, 1979; The Mockery Bird, 1981; The Amateur Naturalist, 1982; Ark on the Move, 1983; How to Shoot an Amateur Naturalist, 1984; (with Lee Durrell) Durrell in Russia, 1986; The Fantastic Flying Journey, 1987; (ed) Best Dog Stories, 1990; Marrying Off Mother and other stories, 1991; contribs to Zoo Life, etc. *Recreations:* reading, filming, drawing, swimming, study of the History and Maintenance of Zoological Gardens. *Address:* Les Augres Manor, Trinity, Jersey, Channel Isles. *T:* Central 61949.

DURWARD, (Alan) Scott; Director, since 1985, and Group Chief Executive, since 1989, Alliance & Leicester Building Society; Chairman, Girobank, since 1990; *b* 30 Aug. 1935; *o c* of late Prof. Archibald Durward, MD and Dorothy Durward; *m* 1962, Helen Gourlay; two *s*. *Educ:* Stowe; St John's Coll., Cambridge (MA). Imperial Tobacco Co. Ltd, 1958–65; Rowntree & Co. Ltd, 1965–67; Cheltenham & Gloucester Bldg Soc., 1967–75; Leicester Building Society: Dep. Gen. Man., 1975–77; Gen. Man., 1977–81; Dir and Chief Gen. Man., 1981–85; merger with Alliance Bldg Soc. to form Alliance & Leicester Bldg Soc., 1985; Jt Chief Gen. Manager, 1985–86; Chief Gen. Manager, 1986–89. Chm., Midland Assoc. of Bldg Socs, 1984–85; Member: Council, Bldg Socs Assoc., 1981–85 and 1987–; Council, Eur. Fedn of Bldg Socs, 1987–. Underwriting Mem. of Lloyd's. Director: Gourlay Properties, 1985–; John Laing plc, 1987–89; Mem. Bd, BR (London Midland), 1990–. Mem. Council, Loughborough Univ. of Technology, 1984– (Treas., 1991–). *Recreations:* tennis, fishing. *Address:* Alliance & Leicester Building Society, 49 Park Lane, W1Y 4EQ. *T:* 071-629 6661.

du SAUTOY, Peter Francis, CBE 1971 (OBE 1964); *b* 19 Feb. 1912; *s* of late Col E. F. du Sautoy, OBE, TD, DL and Mabel (*née* Howse); *m* 1937, Phyllis Mary (Mollie), *d* of late Sir Francis Floud, KCB, KCSI, KCMG and Phyllis (*née* Ford); two *s*. *Educ:* Uppingham (Foundn Schol.); Wadham Coll., Oxford (Sen. Class. Schol.). MA, 1st cl. Lit. Hum. Dept of Printed Books, British Museum, 1935–36; Asst Educn Officer, City of Oxford, 1937–40; RAF, 1940–45; joined Faber & Faber Ltd, 1946; Dir, Dec. 1946; Vice-Chm., 1960–71; Chm., 1971–77, editorial consultant, 1977–; Chm., Faber and Faber (Publishers) Ltd, 1971–77; Mem. Bd, Faber Music Ltd, 1966–87 (Chm., 1971–77, Vice Chm., 1977–81); Trustee, Yale Univ. Press, London, 1984– (Mem. Bd, 1977–84). Mem. Council, Publishers Assoc., 1957–63, 1965–77 (Pres., 1967–69); Mem. Exec. Cttee, Internat. Publishers Assoc., 1972–76; Pres., Groupe des Editeurs de Livres de la CEE, 1973–75. Official visits on behalf of Publishers Assoc. and British Council to Australia, USSR, Finland, Hungary, Nigeria, China. Vice-Pres., Aldeburgh Foundn Ltd, 1987– (Mem. Council, 1976–87; Vice-Chm., 1977–80; Dep. Chm., 1982–87); Pres., Suffolk Book League, 1986– (Vice-Pres., 1982–85); Hon. Treasurer, The William Blake Trust, 1959–83; Trustee: The James Joyce Estate, 1970–89; The Alison Uttley Estate. Liveryman, Stationers' Co., 1973; Freeman, City of London, 1973. *Publications:* various articles on publishing. *Address:* 31 Lee Road, Aldeburgh, Suffolk IP15 5EY. *T:* Aldeburgh (0728) 452838. *Club:* Garrick.

See also Mrs J. E. Floud.

DUTHIE, Prof. Sir Herbert Livingston, Kt 1987; MD; FRCS, FRCSEd; Provost of the University of Wales College of Medicine (formerly the Welsh National School of Medicine, University of Wales), since 1979; *b* 9 Oct. 1929; *s* of Herbert William Duthie and Margaret McFarlane Livingston; *m* 1959, Maureen McCann; three *s* one *d*. *Educ:* Whitehill Sch., Glasgow; Univ. of Glasgow (MB, ChB 1952; MD Hons 1962; ChM Hons 1959). FRCSEd 1956; FRCS 1957. Served RAMC, 1954–56. Sen. House Officer, Registrar, and Lectr in Surgery, Western Infirmary, Glasgow, 1956–59; Rockefeller Travelling Fellow, Mayo Clinic, Rochester, Minn, USA, 1959–60; Lectr in Surg., Univ. of Glasgow, 1960–61; Sen. Lectr in Surg., Univ. of Leeds, 1961–63, Reader, 1964; Prof. of Surg., Univ. of Sheffield, 1964–79 (Dean, Faculty of Medicine, 1976–78). President: Surgical Res. Soc., 1978–80; Assoc. of Surgeons of GB and Ireland, 1989–90; Mem., GMC, 1976–, Treasurer 1981–. Hon. LLD Sheffield, 1990. *Publications:* articles on gastroenterological topics. *Address:* St Curig, Windsor Road, Radyr, Cardiff CF4 8BQ. *T:* Cardiff (0222) 843472. *Club:* Army and Navy.

DUTHIE, Prof. Robert Buchan, CBE 1984; MA Oxon, MB, ChM; FRCSE, FRCS; Nuffield Professor of Orthopædic Surgery, Oxford University, 1966–Sept. 1992; Professorial Fellow, Worcester College, Oxford, 1966–Sept. 1992; Surgeon, Nuffield Orthopædic Centre, Oxford, 1966–Sept. 1992; Civilian Consultant Adviser in Orthopaedic Surgery to Royal Navy, since 1978; *b* 4 May 1925; 2nd *s* of late James Andrew Duthie and late Elizabeth Jean Duthie, Edinburgh; *m* 1956, Alison Ann Macpherson Kittermaster, MA; two *s* two *d*. *Educ:* Aberdeen Grammar Sch.; King Edward VI Gram. Sch., Chelmsford; Heriot-Watt Coll., Edinburgh; University of

Edinburgh Med. Sch. Robert Jones Prize 1947, MB, ChB 1948, ChM (with dist.) (Gold Medal for Thesis) 1956, University of Edinburgh; FRCSE 1953; Hon. FACS 1987. Ho. Surg. Royal Infirmary, 1948–49; Ho. Phys., Western Gen. Hosp., Edinburgh, 1949. Active service in Malaya, RAMC, 1949–51. Registrar, Royal Infirmary, Edinburgh, 1951–53; David Wilkie Res. Schol. of University of Edinburgh, 1953; Res. Fellow of Scottish Hosps Endowment Research Trust, Edinburgh, 1953–56; Res. Fellow, Nat. Cancer Inst., Bethesda, USA, 1956–57; Extern. Mem. of MRC in Inst. of Orthopædics, London and Sen. Registrar, 1957–58; Prof. of Orthopædic Surg., University of Rochester Sch. of Medicine and Dentistry and Orthopædic Surg.-in-Chief, University of Rochester Med. Centre, 1958–66. Consultant Adviser in Orthopaedics and Accident Surgery to DHSS, 1971–80. Mem., Royal Commn on Civil Liability and Compensation for Personal Injury, 1973–78; Chairman: Adv. Cttee of Res. in Artificial Limbs and Appliances, DHSS, 1975; Working Party on Orthopaedic Services to Sec. of State for Social Services, 1980–81. Governor, Oxford Sch. for Boys. Fellow Brit. Orthopædic Assoc. (Pres., 1983–84); Pres., Internat. Soc. of Research in Orthopaedics and Trauma, 1987–90; Member: Internat. Soc. for Orthopædic Surgery and Traumatology; Orthopædic Research Soc.; Inter-urban Orthopædic Club: Internat. Orthopædic Club. Amer. Rheumatism Assoc.; Hon. Member: Portuguese Soc. of Orthopaedic Surgery and Traumatology; Japanese Orthopaedic Assoc.; Corresponding Member: Assoc. of Orthopaedic Surgery and Traumatology, Yugoslavia; German Soc. of Orthopaedics and Traumatology. Hon. DSc Rochester, NY, 1982. President's Prize, Soc. Internat. de Chirurgie, 1957. Commander, SMO, Malta. *Publications:* (co-author) Textbook of Orthopædic Surgery, 7th edn, 1982; contribs to med. and surg. jls relating to genetics, histochemistry, transplantation, pathology, neoplasia of musculo-skeletal tissues, and clinical subjects. *Recreations:* family, tennis. *Address:* (until Sept. 1992) Nuffield Orthopædic Centre, Headington, Oxford OX3 7LD; Barna Brow, Harberton Mead, Headington, Oxford. *T:* Oxford (0865) 62745.

DUTHIE, Sir Robert Grieve, (Sir Robin), Kt 1987; CBE 1978; CA; Chairman: Insight International Tours Ltd, since 1979; Capital House Investment Management Ltd, since 1987; Tay Residential Investment Ltd, since 1989; Vice Chairman, Advisory Board for Scotland, British Petroleum, since 1990; *b* 2 Oct. 1928; *s* of George Duthie and Mary (*née* Lyle); *m* 1955, Violetta Noel Maclean; two *s* one *d*. *Educ:* Greenock Academy. Apprentice Chartered Accountant with Thomson Jackson Gourlay & Taylor, CA, 1946–51 (CA 1952); joined Blacks of Greenock, 1952: Man. Dir, 1962; Chairman: Black & Edgington Ltd, 1972–83; Bruntons (Musselburgh), 1984–86; Britoil, 1988–90; Director: British Assets Trust, 1977–; Royal Bank of Scotland, 1978–; Investors Capital Trust, 1985–; Carclo Engineering Gp, 1986–; British Polythene Industries, 1989–. Chm., Greenock Provident Bank, 1974; Dir, Greenock Chamber of Commerce, 1967–68; Tax Liaison Officer for Scotland, CBI, 1976–79. Chm., SDA, 1979–88; Member: Scottish Telecommunications Bd, 1972–77; E Kilbride Develt Corp., 1976–78; Clyde Port Authority, 1971–83 (Chm., 1977–80); Council, Inst. of Chartered Accountants of Scotland, 1973–78; Scottish Econ. Council, 1980–; Council, Strathclyde Business Sch., 1986–; Governing Council, Scottish Business in the Community, 1987–. Chm., Made Up Textiles Assoc. of GB, 1972; Pres., Inverkip Soc., 1966; Mem. of Council, Royal Caledonian Curling Club, 1985–88. Commissioner: Queen Victoria Sch., Dunblane, 1972–89; Scottish Congregational Ministers Pension Fund, 1973–; Treasurer, Nelson Street Evangelical Union Congregational Church, Greenock, 1970–. Fellow, Scottish Vocational Council, 1988. CBIM 1976; FRSA 1983. Hon. FRIAS, 1989. Hon. Fellow, Paisley Coll., 1990. Hon. LLD Strathclyde, 1984; Hon. DTech Napier Coll., 1989. *Recreations:* curling, golf. *Address:* Fairhaven, Finnart Street, Greenock PA16 8JA. *T:* Greenock (0475) 22642. *Club:* Greenock Imperial (Greenock).

DUTTON, James Macfarlane; HM Diplomatic Service, retired; *b* 3 June 1922; *s* of late H. St J. Dutton and Mrs E. B. Dutton; *m* 1958, Jean Mary McAvoy; one *s*. *Educ:* Winchester Coll.; Balliol Coll., Oxford. Dominions Office, 1944–46; Private Sec. to Permanent Under Sec., 1945; Dublin, 1946–48; CRO, 1948–50; Asst Private Sec. to Sec. of State, 1948; 2nd Sec., New Delhi, 1950–53; CRO, 1953–55; 1st Sec., Dacca and Karachi, 1955–58, Canberra, 1958–62; Head of Constitutional and Protocol Dept, CRO, 1963–65; Canadian Nat. Defence Coll., 1965–66; Dep. High Comr and Counsellor (Commercial), Colombo, 1966–70; Head of Rhodesia Econ. Dept, FCO, 1970–72; attached CSD, 1972–73; seconded to: British Electrical & Allied Manufacturers Assoc. (Dir, Overseas Affairs), 1973–74; Wilton Park and European Discussion Centre, 1974–75; Consul-Gen., Gothenburg, 1975–78. *Recreations:* golf, trout-fishing. *Address:* Cockerhurst, Tyrrells Wood, Leatherhead, Surrey KT22 8QH.

DUTTON, Prof. Peter Leslie, FRS 1990; Professor of Biochemistry and Biophysics, since 1981, and Director, Johnson Foundation for Molecular Biophysics, since 1990, University of Pennsylvania; *b* 12 March 1941; *s* of Arthur Bramwell Dutton and Mary Dutton; *m* 1965, Dr Julia R. Dwyer; two *s* one *d*. *Educ:* Univ. of Wales (BSc Hons Chem.; PhD Biochem.). PD Fellow, Dept of Biochem. and Soil Science, Univ. of Wales, 1967–68; University of Pennsylvania: PD Fellow, 1968–71, Asst Prof., 1971–76, Johnson Res. Foundn; Associate Prof., Dept of Biochem. and Biophysics, 1976–81; Hon. MA 1976. *Recreations:* painting (several one-man and group shows in Wales and USA), sailing. *Address:* B501 Richards Building, 37th and Hamilton Walk, University of Pennsylvania, Philadelphia, Pa 19104, USA; 654 West Rose Tree Road, Media, Pa 19063, USA. *T:* (215) 565–0863. *Clubs:* Mantoloking Yacht (NJ); Corinthian Yacht (Philadelphia).

DUTTON, Reginald David Ley; *b* 20 Aug. 1916; *m* 1951, Pamela Jean (*née* Harrison); two *s* one *d*. *Educ:* Magdalen Coll. Sch., Oxford. Joined OUP; subseq. joined leading British advertising agency, London Press Exchange (now Lopex plc), 1937. During War of 1939–45 served in Royal Navy. Returned to agency after his service; there, he worked on many of major accounts; Dir, 1954; Man. Dir and Chief Exec., 1964–71; Chm., 1971–76; retired 1976. Pres. Inst. Practitioners in Advertising, 1969–71; Chm., Jt Ind. Council for TV Advertising Research, 1973–75; Mem. Council, BIM, 1970–74; FIPA 1960. Councillor, Canterbury CC, 1976–77. *Recreations:* fishing, amateur radio. *Address:* Butts Fold, Stalham Road, Hoveton, Norwich. *T:* Norwich (0603) 783145.

DUVAL, Sir (Charles) Gaetan, Kt 1981; QC 1975; barrister; Deputy Prime Minister, 1983–88, and Minister of Employment and Tourism, 1986–88, Mauritius; *b* 9 Oct. 1930. *Educ:* Royal Coll., Curepipe; Faculty of Law, Univ. of Paris. Called to the Bar, Lincoln's Inn. Entered politics, 1958; Member: Town Council, Curepipe, 1960, re-elected 1963 (Chm., 1960–61, 1963–68); Legislative Council, Curepipe, 1960, re-elected, 1963; Municipal Council, Port Louis, 1969 (Mayor, 1969–71; Lord Mayor, 1971–74, 1981); Minister of Housing, 1964–65; Leader, Parti Mauritien Social Démocrate, 1966–; first MLA for Grand River NW and Port-Louis West, 1967; Minister of External Affairs, Tourism and Emigration, 1969–73; Leader of Opposition, 1973–76, 1982; Minister of Justice, 1983–86. Comdr, Legion of Honour, France, 1973; Grand Officer, Order of the Lion, Senegal, 1973. *Address:* c/o Place Foch, Port-Louis, Mauritius.

DUVAL, Sir Gaetan; *see* Duval, Sir C. G.

DUXBURY, Air Marshal Sir (John) Barry, KCB 1986; CBE 1981 (MBE 1967); Director and Chief Executive, Society of British Aerospace Companies, since 1990; Secretary, Defence Industries Council, since 1990; *b* 23 Jan. 1934; *s* of Lloyd Duxbury and Hilda Robins; *m* 1954, Joan Leake; one *s*. *Educ:* Lancashire County Grammar Schs. Commnd 1954; served Maritime Sqdns, Aeroplane and Armament Exptl Estab., Canadian Forces Staff Coll., and Central Tactics and Trials Orgn, 1955–70; CO 201 Sqdn, 1971; PSO to CAS, 1971–74; CO RAF St Mawgan, 1976–77; Sec., Chiefs of Staff Cttee, 1978–80; RAF Dir, RCDS, 1982; Air Sec. (RAF), 1983–85; AOC No 18 Gp, RAF, and Comdr Maritime Air Eastern Atlantic and Channel, 1986–89, retd. ADC to the Queen, 1977. FRIN 1989. *Recreations:* painting, photography. *Club:* Royal Air Force.

DUXBURY, Philip Thomas; Chairman, Bradford and Bingley Building Society, 1988–91; *b* 4 Sept. 1928; *s* of Tom Duxbury and Ellen Duxbury (*née* Hargreaves); *m* 1952, Katherine Mary Hagley; three *s*. *Educ:* Bradford Grammar School. Magnet and Southerns plc, 1944–84 (Dir, 1963; Man. Dir, 1975); Dir, Bradford and Bingley Building Soc., 1980–91. *Recreations:* DIY, travel. *Address:* High Court, East Morton, near Keighley BD20 5SE. *T:* Bradford (0274) 564894.

DWEK, Prof. Raymond Allen, DPhil, DSc; Professor of Glycobiology, and Director of Glycobiology Unit, University of Oxford, since 1988; Professorial Fellow, Exeter College, Oxford, since 1988; *b* 10 Nov. 1941; *s* of Victor Joe Dwek and Alice Liniado; *m* 1964, Sandra (*née* Livingstone); two *s* two *d*. *Educ:* Carmel Coll.; Manchester Univ. (BSc 1st Cl. Hons Chemistry and Mercer Scholar, 1963; MSc 1964); Lincoln Coll., Oxford (DPhil 1966); Exeter Coll., Oxford (DSc 1985). Christ Church, Oxford: Res. Lectr in Physical Chemistry, 1966–68, in Biochem., 1975–76; Lectr in Inorganic Chem., 1968–75; Deptl Demonstrator. Biochem. Dept, Oxford, 1969–74; Royal Soc. Locke Res. Fellow, 1974–76; Lectr in Biochem., Trinity Coll., Oxford, 1976–84. Vis. Royal Soc. Res. Fellow, Weizmann Inst., Rehovot, Israel, 1969; Visiting Professor: Duke Univ., NC, seconded to Inst. of Exploratory Res., Fort Monmouth, NJ, 1968; Univ. of Trieste, Italy, 1974; Univ. of Lund, Sweden, 1977; Inst. of Enzymology, Budapest, 1980. Dir and Founding Scientist, Oxford Glycosystems Ltd, 1988–. Member: Oxford Enzyme Gp, 1971–88; MRC AIDS Antiviral Steering Cttee, 1987–; Founder Mem., Oxford Oligosaccharide Gp, 1983. Mem., editl bds. *Publications:* Nuclear Magnetic Resonance (NMR) in Biochemistry, 1973; (jtly) Physical Chemistry Principles and Problems for Biochemists, 1975, 3rd edn 1983; (jtly) NMR in Biology, 1977; (jtly) Biological Spectroscopy, 1984; articles in books and jls on physical chemistry, biochemistry and medicine; various patents. *Recreations:* family, Patent Law, sport, sailing, listening to music. *Address:* Exeter College, Oxford OX1 3DP. *T:* Oxford (0865) 275344; Glycobiology Unit, Department of Biochemistry, University of Oxford, South Parks Road, Oxford OX1 3QU.

DWIGHT, Reginald Kenneth; *see* John, E. H.

DWORKIN, Paul David, FSS; an Assistant Director, Central Statistical Office, 1989–91; *b* 7 April 1937; *s* of Louis and Rose Dworkin; *m* 1959, Carole Barbara Burke; two *s*. *Educ:* Hackney Downs Grammar Sch., London; LSE (BScEcon 1958). FSS 1969. E Africa High Commn, Dar es Salaam, Tanganyika, 1959; E African Common Services Org., Nairobi, Kenya, 1961; Asst Statistician, BoT, 1962, Stat. 1965; Chief Statistician: DTI, 1972; Dept of Employment, 1977; Under Secretary: Depts of Trade and Industry, 1977–81; Central Statistical Office, 1982–83; Dir of Stats, Dept of Employment, 1983–89. *Recreations:* golf, skiing, theatre. *Clubs:* Civil Service; Ski Club of Great Britain; Stanmore Golf.

DWORKIN, Prof. Ronald Myles, FBA 1979; Professor of Jurisprudence, Oxford University, since 1969; Fellow of University College, Oxford, since 1969; *b* 11 Dec. 1931; *s* of David Dworkin and Madeline Talamo; *m* 1958, Betsy Celia Ross; one *s* one *d*. *Educ:* Harvard Coll.; Oxford Univ.; Harvard Law Sch. Legal Sec. to Judge Learned Hand, 1957–58; Associate, Sullivan & Cromwell, New York, 1958–62; Yale Law School: Associate Prof. of Law, 1962–65; Prof. of Law, 1965–68; Wesley N. Hohfeld Prof. of Jurisprudence, 1968–69. Vis. Prof. of Philosophy, Princeton Univ., 1974–75; Prof. of Law, NY Univ. Law Sch., 1975–; Prof.-at-Large, Cornell Univ., 1976–80; Vis. Prof. of Philosophy and Law, Harvard Univ., 1977, Vis. Prof. of Philosophy, 1979–82. Member: Council, Writers & Scholars Educnl Trust, 1982–; Programme Cttee, Ditchley Foundn, 1982–. Co-Chm., US Democratic Party Abroad, 1972–76. Fellow, Amer. Acad. of Arts and Scis, 1979. Hon. LLD: Williams Coll., 1981; John Jay Coll. of Criminal Justice, 1983; Claremont Coll., 1987; Kalamazoo Coll., 1987. *Publications:* Taking Rights Seriously, 1977; (ed) The Philosophy of Law, 1977; A Matter of Principle, 1985; Law's Empire, 1986; Philosophical Issues in Senile Dementia, 1987; A Bill of Rights for Britain, 1990; several articles in legal and philosophical jls. *Address:* University College, Oxford. *Clubs:* Garrick; Oxford American Democrats (Oxford).

DYDE, John Horsfall, CBE 1970 (OBE 1957); Chairman, Eastern Gas Board, 1959–69; *b* 4 June 1905; *m* 1930, Ethel May Hewitt; two *s*. *Educ:* Scarborough High Sch.; University of Leeds (MSc). Engineer and Manager, North Middlesex Gas Co., 1937–42; prior to nationalisation was Engineer and Gen. Manager of Uxbridge, Maidenhead, Wycombe & District Gas Co. and Slough Gas & Coke Co.; also Technical Director of group of undertakings of the South Eastern Gas Corp. Ltd; Dep.-Chm., Eastern Gas Board, 1949. President: Western Junior Gas Assoc., 1935–36; Southern Assoc. of Gas Engineers and Managers, 1949–50; Institution of Gas Engineers, 1951–52; British Road Tar Association. CEng, FIChemE; Hon. FIGasE. *Recreations:* golf, fishing. *Address:* Stable End, Thellusson Lodge, Aldeburgh, Suffolk IP15 5DT. *T:* Aldeburgh (0728) 453148.

DYE, Maj.-Gen. Jack Bertie, CBE 1968 (OBE 1965); MC; Vice Lord-Lieutenant of Suffolk, since 1983; Director, Volunteers, Territorials and Cadets, 1971–74; Major-General late Royal Norfolk Regiment; *b* 1919. Served War of 1939–45 (MC). Brigadier, 1966; psc. Commanded South Arabian Army, 1966–68; GOC Eastern District, 1969–71. Col Comdt, The Queen's Division, 1970–74; Col, Royal Anglian Regt, 1976–82 (Dep. Col, 1974–76). DL Suffolk, 1979.

DYER, Charles; playwright and novelist; actor-director (as Raymond Dyer); *b* 7 July 1928; *s* of James Sidney Dyer and Florence (*née* Stretton); *m* 1959, Fiona Thomson, actress; three *s*. *Educ:* Queen Elizabeth's Sch., Barnet. *Plays:* Clubs Are Sometimes Trumps, 1948; Who On Earth!, 1951; Turtle in the Soup, 1953; The Jovial Parasite, 1954; Single Ticket Mars, 1955; Time, Murderer, Please, and Poison In Jest, 1956; Wanted—One Body!, 1958; Prelude to Fury, 1959 (also wrote theme music); Rattle of A Simple Man, 1962 (also in Berlin, Paris, NY, Rome and London), 1981; Staircase, 1966 (for RSC; also in NY, Paris (1968, 1982 and 1986), Amsterdam, Berlin, Rome); Mother Adam, Paris, Berlin, 1970, London, 1971, 1973, NY, 1974; The Loving Allelujah, 1974; Circling Dancers, 1979; Lovers Dancing, 1981, 1983; Futility Rites, 1981; as R. Kraselchik: Red Cabbage and Kings, 1960 (also wrote theme music); *screenplays:* Rattle, 1964; Insurance Italian Style, 1967; Staircase, 1968; Brother Sun and Sister Moon, 1970. Also directed plays for the stage and television. *Acted in: plays:* Worm's Eye View, 1948; Room For Two, 1955; Dry Rot, 1958; *films:* Cuptie Honeymoon, 1947; Britannia Mews, 1949; Road Sense, 1950; Off The Record, 1952; Pickwick Papers, 1952; Dockland Case, 1953; Strange Case of Blondie, 1953; Naval Patrol, 1959; Loneliness of the Long Distance Runner, 1962; Mouse On The Moon, 1962; Knack, 1964; Rattle of A Simple Man, 1964; How I Won The War, 1967; Staircase, 1968; *television:* Charlie in Staircase, BBC, 1986;

television series: Hugh and I, 1964. *Publications:* (as Charles Dyer): plays: Wanted—One Body!, 1961; Time, Murderer, Please, 1962; Rattle Of A Simple Man, (Fr.) 1963; Staircase, 1966; Mother Adam, 1970; The Loneliness Trilogy, 1972; Hot Godly Wind, 1973; novels: Rattle Of A Simple Man, 1964; Charlie Always Told Harry Almost Everything, 1969 (USA and Europe, 1970); The Rising of our Herbert, 1972. *Recreations:* amateur music and carpentry. *Address:* Old Wob, Gerrards Cross, Bucks SL9 8SF.

DYER, Sir Henry Peter Francis S.; *see* Swinnerton-Dyer.

DYER, Lois Edith, OBE 1984; FCSP; international physiotherapy consultant; (First) Adviser in Physiotherapy, Department of Health and Social Security, 1976–85; *b* 18 March 1925; *d* of Richard Morgan Dyer and Emmeline Agnes (*née* Wells). *Educ:* Middlesex Hospital. FCSP 1986. Variety of posts as physiotherapist in Britain, Southern, Central and North Africa, 1948–71; extensive travel world wide, visiting and lecturing at national and internat. conferences. First Physiotherapist Member, NHS Health Adv. Service, 1971; first non-medical Chm., Chartered Society of Physiotherapy, 1972–75; Founder Mem., Soc. for Res. in Rehabilitation, 1978–; Hon. Life Vice-Pres., S African Soc. of Physiotherapy. Editor-in-Chief, Physiotherapy Practice, 1985–90. *Publications:* Care of the Orthopaedic Patient (jtly), 1977; numerous papers in professional jls. *Recreations:* music, country pursuits, bird watching, bridge, ecology, wildlife, conservation. *Address:* Garden Flat, 6 Belsize Grove, NW3 4UN. *T:* 071–722 1794.

DYER, Mark; His Honour Judge Dyer; a Circuit Judge, since 1977; *b* 20 Nov. 1928; *er s* of late Maj.-Gen. G. M. Dyer, CBE, DSO, and of Evelyn Mary (*née* List); *m* 1953, Diana, *d* of Sir Percy Lancelot Orde, CIE; two *d. Educ:* Ampleforth Coll.; Christ Church, Oxford (MA). 2nd Lieut, Royal Scots Greys, 1948–49; The Westminster Dragoons (2nd CLY) TA, 1950–58, Captain. Called to the Bar, Middle Temple, 1953; Mem., Gen. Council of the Bar, 1965–69. Dep. Chm., Isle of Wight QS, 1971. A Recorder of the Crown Court, 1972–77; Hon. Recorder of Devizes, 1988. Liaison Judge for Wiltshire, 1981. Mem., Judicial Studies Bd, 1986–91. Pres., Council of HM Circuit Judges, 1992 (Hon. Sec., 1989–91). *Address:* Swindon Combined Court Centre, The Law Courts, Islington Street, Swindon, Wiltshire. *Club:* Cavalry and Guards.
See also S. Dyer.

DYER, Simon, MA; FCA; Director General, Automobile Association, since 1987; *b* 19 Oct. 1939; *s* of late Maj.-Gen. G. M. Dyer, CBE, DSO, and of Evelyn Dyer; *m* 1967, Louise Gay Walsh; two *d. Educ:* Ampleforth Coll., Univ. of Paris; Univ. of Oxford (MA Jurisprudence). FCA 1978 (ACA 1967). Coopers and Lybrand, 1963–67; Automobile Association, 1967–: Dir, 1973; Asst Man. Dir, 1977; Man. Dir, 1983. Member: Exec. Cttee, British Road Fedn, 1987–; Management Cttee, Alliance Internationale de Tourisme, 1987–; Council, Inst. of Advanced Motorists, 1989–; Council, CBI, 1989–. Freedom, City of London, 1984; Liveryman, Co. of Coachmakers and Coach Harness Makers, 1984. *Recreations:* gardening, tennis, ski-ing. *Address:* Fanum House, Basingstoke, Hants RG21 2EA. *Club:* Cavalry and Guards.
See also M. Dyer.

DYER-SMITH, Rear-Adm. John Edward, CBE 1972; Director-General Aircraft (Naval), Ministry of Defence, 1970–72, retired; *b* 17 Aug. 1918; *s* of Harold E. Dyer-Smith and Emily Sutton; *m* 1940, Kathleen Powell; four *s* one *d. Educ:* Devonport High Sch.; RN Engineering Coll.; Imperial Coll. of Science. Served War of 1939–45: Engineer Officer, HMS Prince of Wales, 1940–41; Asst Fleet Engr Officer, Eastern Fleet, 1942–43; HMS Illustrious, 1943. Various MAP and Min. of Aviation appts, 1946–54; Head of Naval Air Dept, RAE, 1957–61; Dir of RN Aircraft/Helicopters, Min. of Aviation, 1961–64; Defence and Naval Attaché, Tokyo, 1965–67; Superintendent, RN Aircraft Yard, Belfast, 1968–70. *Recreation:* travel. *Address:* Casa Gomila, Cala Alcaufar, Sant Lluis, Menorca.

DYKE; *see* Hart Dyke.

DYKE, Gregory; Group Chief Executive, London Weekend Television, since 1991; *b* 20 May 1947; *s* of Joseph and Denise Dyke; two *s* two *d. Educ:* Hayes Grammar Sch.; York Univ. (BA Politics). Varied career, 1965–83; Editor in Chief, TV-am, 1983–84; Dir of Programmes, TVS, 1984–87; London Weekend Television: Dir of Progs, 1987–91; Dep. Man. Dir, 1989–90; Man. Dir, 1990–91. Dir, Channel Four Television, 1988–. *Recreations:* football, squash, tennis. *Address:* c/o LWT, South Bank TV Centre, SE1 9LT.

DYKES, David Wilmer, MA, PhD; Director, National Museum of Wales, 1986–89; *b* 18 Dec. 1933; *s* of late Captain David Dykes, OBE and Jenny Dykes; *m* 1967, Margaret Anne George; two *d. Educ:* Swansea Grammar Sch.; Corpus Christi Coll., Oxford (MA); PhD (Wales). FSA 1973; FRHistS 1965; FRNS 1958 (Parkes-Weber Prize, 1954). Commnd RN, 1955–58. Civil Servant, Bd of Inland Revenue, 1958–59; administrative appts, Univ. of Bristol and Univ. Coll. of Swansea, 1959–63; Dep. Registrar, Univ. Coll. of Swansea, 1963–69; Registrar, Univ. of Warwick, 1969–72; Sec., Nat. Museum of Wales, 1972–86, Acting Dir, 1985–86. Hon. Lectr in History, University Coll., Cardiff, later Univ. of Wales Coll. of Cardiff, 1975–. Mem. Council, Royal Instn of S Wales, 1962–69 and 1985–91. FRSA 1990. Liveryman, Worshipful Co. of Tin Plate Workers, 1985; Freeman, City of London, 1985. CStJ 1991 (Chancellor, Priory for Wales, 1991–). *Publications:* Anglo-Saxon Coins in the National Museum of Wales, 1977; (ed and contrib.) Alan Sorrell: Early Wales Re-created, 1980; Wales in Vanity Fair, 1989; articles and reviews in numismatic, historical and other jls. *Recreations:* numismatics, writing, gardening. *Address:* Cherry Grove, Welsh St Donats, near Cowbridge, South Glam CF7 7SS. *Clubs:* Athenæum, United Oxford & Cambridge University; Cardiff and County (Cardiff); Bristol Channel Yacht (Swansea).

DYKES, Hugh John; MP (C) Harrow East since 1970; Associate Member, Quilter, Hilton, Goodison, Stockbrokers, since 1978; *b* 17 May 1939; *s* of Richard Dykes and Doreen Ismay Maxwell Dykes; *m* 1965, Susan Margaret Dykes (*née* Smith); three *s. Educ:* Weston super Mare Grammar Sch.; Pembroke Coll. Cambridge. Partner, Simon & Coates, Stockbrokers, 1968–78. Dir, Dixons Stores Far East Ltd, 1985–. Contested (C) Tottenham, Gen. Elec., 1966. PPS: to three Parly Under-Secs of State for Defence, 1970; to Parly Under-Sec. of State in Civil Service Dept attached to Cabinet Office, 1973; Mem., H of C EEC Select Cttee, 1983–. Mem., European Parlt, Strasbourg, 1974; Chairman: Cons. Parly European Cttee, 1979–80 (Vice-Chm., 1974–79); Commons Euro-Gp, 1988–; Vice-Pres., Cons. Gp for EEC, 1982–86 (Chm., 1978–81). Chm., European Movement, 1990– (Jt Hon. Sec., 1982–87). Research Sec., Bow Gp, 1965; Chm., Coningsby Club, 1969. Governor: Royal Nat. Orthopaedic Hosp., 1975–82; N London Collegiate Sch., 1982–. *Publications:* (ed) Westropp's "Invest £100", 1964, and Westropp's "Start Your Own Business", 1965; many articles and pamphlets on political and financial subjects. *Recreations:* music, theatre, swimming, travel. *Address:* House of Commons, SW1. *T:* 071–219 3000. *Clubs:* Garrick, Carlton, Beefsteak.

DYKES BOWER, S(tephen) E(rnest), MA; FRIBA; FSA; Surveyor of the Fabric of Westminster Abbey, 1951–73, now Emeritus; Consulting Architect, Carlisle Cathedral, 1947–75; *b* 18 April 1903; 2nd *s* of Ernest Dykes Bower, MD; unmarried. *Educ:* Cheltenham Coll.; Merton Coll., Oxford (Organ Schol.); Architectural Assoc. Sch. of Architecture. Private practice as architect since 1931, work chiefly domestic and ecclesiastical. Architect for: New High Altar, Baldachino and American Memorial Chapel, St Paul's Cathedral (with W. Godfrey Allen); enlargement of Bury St Edmunds Cathedral; Cathedral Library and Bishop's Palace, Exeter; completion of Lancing Coll. Chapel; re-building of Gt Yarmouth Parish Church; St Vedast, Foster Lane, EC; and other churches in London and country; work in Canterbury, Winchester, Norwich, Ely, Gloucester, Wells, Oxford, Carlisle, Peterborough and other cathedrals, Oxford and Cambridge Colls, Public Schs, Halls of City Livery Cos, etc. Lay Canon of St Edmundsbury Cathedral, 1979–84. Pres., Ecclesiological Soc., 1983–. Hon. RCO 1986. *Publications:* papers and addresses on architectural subjects. *Address:* Quendon Court, Quendon, near Saffron Walden, Essex CB11 3XJ. *T:* Rickling (079988) 242. *Clubs:* Athenæum, United Oxford & Cambridge University.

DYMOKE, Lt-Col John Lindley Marmion, MBE 1960; Vice Lord-Lieutenant of Lincolnshire, since 1991; 34th Hereditary Queen's Champion, 1946; *b* 1 Sept. 1926; *s* of late Lionel Marmion Dymoke and Rachel, *d* of Hon. Lennox Lindley; *m* 1953, Susan Cicely Fane; three *s. Educ:* Christ's Hosp. Commnd Royal Lincs Regt, 1946; Staff Coll., 1957; Armed Forces Staff Coll., USA, 1964; Coll. Chief Instructor, RMA Sandhurst, 1961–64; Comd 3rd Bn, Royal Anglian Regt, 1966–69; military service included: India, Sumatra, Malaya, Egypt, Jordan, Aden, France, Germany, USA and UK; retired 1972. Farmer and landowner, 1972–. Dist Councillor, 1973–. Chairman: Lincs Br, CLA, 1982–85; Horncastle Grammar Sch., 1979–. Master, Grocers' Co., 1977–78. DL 1976, High Sheriff 1979, Lincs. *Recreation:* care of Scrivelsby Estate. *Address:* Scrivelsby Court, near Horncastle, Lincolnshire LN9 6JA. *T:* Horncastle (0507) 523325. *Club:* Army and Navy.

DYMOKE, Rear-Adm. Lionel Dorian, CB 1974; *b* 18 March 1921; *s* of Henry Lionel Dymoke and Dorothy (*née* Briscoe); *m* 1st, 1952, Patricia Pimlott (*d* 1968); one *s*; 2nd, 1970, Iris Hemsted (*née* Lamplough). *Educ:* Nautical Coll., Pangbourne. Entered Royal Navy, 1938; Comdr 1953; Captain 1961; Rear-Adm. 1971; retired 1976. *Address:* 3 Woodland Place, Bath, Avon BA2 6EH. *T:* Bath (0225) 464228.

DYMOND, Charles Edward, CBE 1967; JP; HM Diplomatic Service, retired; *b* 15 Oct. 1916; *s* of Charles George Dymond and Dora Kate Dymond (*née* Gillingham); *m* 1945, Dorothy Jean Peaker; two *s* two *d. Educ:* Tiverton Grammar Sch.; Exeter Univ. BSc (Econ) London. Royal Artillery, 1939–46; BoT Regional Div., 1946; Trade Commn Service, 1951; Trade Comr, Johannesburg, 1951; Cape Town, 1955; Nairobi, 1957; Sen. Trade Comr, Lagos, 1963–64; Counsellor (Commercial), Lagos, 1965–66; Counsellor i/c, British High Commn, Auckland, 1967–73; Comr for Pitcairn Island, 1970–72; Consul-General, Perth, 1973–76. JP Western Australia, 1980. *Address:* PO Box 15, Sawyers Valley, WA 6074, Australia.

DYNEVOR, 9th Baron *cr* 1780; **Richard Charles Uryan Rhys;** *b* 19 June 1935; *s* of 8th Baron Dynevor, CBE, MC; *S* father, 1962; *m* 1959, Lucy (marr. diss. 1978), *d* of Sir John Rothenstein, *qv*; one *s* three *d. Educ:* Eton; Magdalene Coll., Cambridge. *Heir: s* Hon. Hugo Griffith Uryan Rhys, *b* 19 Nov. 1966. *Address:* House of Lords, SW1.

DYSART, Countess of (11th in line), *cr* 1643; **Rosamund Agnes Greaves;** Baroness Huntingtower, 1643; *b* 15 Feb. 1914; *d* of Major Owain Greaves (*d* 1941), RHG, and Wenefryde Agatha, Countess of Dysart (10th in line); *S* mother, 1975. *Heir: sister* Lady Katherine Grant of Rothiemurchus [*b* 1 June 1918; *m* 1941, Colonel John Peter Grant of Rothiemurchus, MBE (*d* 1987); one *s* one *d*]. *Address:* Bryn Garth, Grosmont, Abergavenny, Gwent.

DYSON, Rev. Anthony Oakley, DPhil; Samuel Ferguson Professor of Social and Pastoral Theology, Manchester University, since 1980; Academic Director, Centre for Social Ethics and Policy, Manchester University, since 1987; *b* 6 Oct. 1935; *s* of Henry Oakley Leslie Dyson and Lilian Dyson; *m* 1960, Edwina Anne Hammett; two *s. Educ:* William Hulme's Grammar Sch., Manchester; Univs of Cambridge (BA 1959, MA 1963) and Oxford (MA, BD 1964, DPhil 1968). 2nd Lieut, West Yorks Regt, 1954–56; Emmanuel Coll., Cambridge, 1956–59; Exeter Coll., Oxford and Ripon Hall, Oxford, 1959–61; Curate of Putney, Dio. Southwark, 1961–63; Chaplain of Ripon Hall, Oxford, 1963–69; Principal of Ripon Hall, 1969–74; Canon of St George's Chapel, Windsor Castle, 1974–77, Custodian, 1975–77; Lectr in Theology, Univ. of Kent, 1977–80. Licensed to Officiate Dio. Oxford, 1965–75, Dio. Canterbury, 1978–80, Dio. Chester, 1980–, Dio. Manchester, 1980–. Examng Chaplain to Bishop of Carlisle; Select Preacher, Univ. of Oxford, 1971; University Preacher, Cambridge, 1985; Lectures: Hensley Henson, Univ. of Oxford, 1972–73; Pollock, Halifax, NS, 1973; Shann, Hong Kong, 1983. Associate Dir, Centre for the Study of Religion and Society, Canterbury, 1978–80. Hon. MA(Theol) Manchester, 1982. Editor: The Teilhard Review, 1966–72; The Modern Churchman, 1982–. *Publications:* Existentialism, 1965; Who is Jesus Christ?, 1969; The Immortality of the Past, 1974; We Believe, 1977; (ed) Experiments on Embryos; contribs to Evolution Marxism and Christianity, 1967; What Kind of Revolution?, 1968; A Dictionary of Christian Theology, 1969, 2nd edn, 1983; The Christian Marxist Dialogue, 1969; Teilhard Reassessed, 1970; Oxford Dictionary of the Christian Church, 2nd edn, 1974; Education and Social Action, 1975; Ernst Troeltsch and the Future of Theology, 1976; The Language of the Church in Higher and Further Education, 1977; England and Germany: studies in theological diplomacy, 1981; The Nature of Religious Man, 1982; A New Dictionary of Christian Theology, 1983; The Church of England and Politics, 1986; A Dictionary of Pastoral Care, 1987; The British and their Religions, 1988; (contrib.) The Nuclear Weapons Debate: theological and ethical issues, 1989; contrib. Theology, The Modern Churchman, Study Encounter, The Month, Contact, TLS, Bull. of John Rylands Library, Studia Theologica, Jl of Med. Ethics, Hist. of Human Scis, etc. *Recreations:* literature, sport. *Address:* Department of Theological Studies, Faculty of Theology, University of Manchester, Manchester M13 9PL. *T:* 061–275 3597 (ext. 3545); 33 Danesmoor Road, West Didsbury, Manchester M20 9JT. *T:* 061–434 5410.

DYSON, Prof. Freeman John, FRS 1952; Professor, School of Natural Sciences, Institute for Advanced Study, Princeton, New Jersey, since 1953; *b* 15 Dec. 1923; *s* of late Sir George Dyson, KCVO; *m* 1st, 1950, Verena Esther (*née* Huber) (marr. diss. 1958); one *s* one *d*; 2nd, 1958, Imme (*née* Jung); four *d. Educ:* Winchester; Cambridge; Cornell University. Operational research for RAF Bomber Command, 1943–45. Fellow of Trinity Coll., Cambridge, 1946–50, Hon. Fellow, 1989; Commonwealth Fund Fellow at Cornell and Princeton, USA, 1947–49; Mem. of Institute for Advanced Study, Princeton, USA, 1949–50; Professor of Physics, Cornell Univ., Ithaca, NY, USA, 1951–53. Mem. of National Academy of Sciences (USA), 1964; For. Associate, Acad. des Scis, Paris, 1989. Gifford Lectr, Aberdeen, 1985; Radcliffe Lectr, Oxford, 1990. Lorentz Medal, Royal Netherlands Acad. of Sciences, 1966; Hughes Medal, Royal Soc., 1968; Max Planck Medal, German Physical Soc., 1969. *Publications:* Disturbing the Universe, 1979; Weapons and Hope, 1984; Origins of Life, 1986; Infinite in All Directions, 1988; From Eros to Gaia, 1991; contrib. to The Physical Review, Annals of Mathematics, etc. *Address:* School of Natural Sciences, Institute for Advanced Study, Olden Lane, Princeton, NJ 08540, USA.

DYSON, John Anthony, QC 1982; a Recorder, since 1986; *b* 31 July 1943; *s* of Richard and Gisella Dyson; *m* 1970, Jacqueline Carmel Levy; one *s* one *d. Educ:* Leeds Grammar Sch.; Wadham Coll., Oxford (Open Classics Scholar; MA). Harmsworth Law Scholar, 1968, called to Bar, Middle Temple, 1968, Bencher, 1990. *Recreations:* piano playing, gardening, walking. *Address:* 2 Garden Court, Temple, EC4Y 9BL. *T:* 071–353 4741.

DYSON, John Michael; Master of the Supreme Court of Judicature (Chancery Division) since 1973; an Assistant Recorder; *b* 9 Feb. 1929; *s* of late Eric Dyson, Gainsborough and Hope Patison (*née* Kirkland). *Educ:* Bradfield Coll.; Corpus Christi Coll., Oxford. 2nd Lieut, Royal Tank Regt, 1948. Admitted Solicitor, 1956; Partner, Field Roscoe & Co., 1957 (subseq. Field Fisher & Co. and Field Fisher & Martineau). *Address:* 20 Keats Grove, NW3 2RS. *T:* 071–794 3389. *Club:* United Oxford & Cambridge University.

DYSON, Prof. Roger Franklin, PhD; Honorary Professor and Director of Clinical Management Unit Centre for Health Planning and Management, University of Keele, since 1989; *b* 30 Jan. 1940; *s* of John Franklin Dyson and Edith Mary Jobson; *m* 1964, Anne Greaves; one *s* one *d. Educ:* Counthill Grammar Sch., Oldham; Keele Univ. (BA Hons 1st cl. Hist. and Econs, 1962); Leeds Univ. (PhD 1971). Asst Lectr, 1963, Lectr, 1966, Adult Educn Dept, Leeds Univ.; Dep. Dir and Sen. Lectr in Ind. Relations, Adult Educn Dept, 1974, Prof. and Dir of Adult and Continuing Educn, 1976–89, Keele Univ. Consultant Advr on Ind. Relations to Sec. of State, DHSS, 1979–81. Chm., N Staffs HA, 1982–86. Mem., RSocMed; FRSA 1980. Editor, Health Manpower Management (formerly Health Services Manpower Review), 1975–. *Publications:* contribs to BMJ. *Recreations:* gardening, gastronomy. *Address:* Elendil, Newcastle Road, Ashley Heath, Market Drayton TF9 4PH. *T:* Ashley (063087) 2906. *Club:* Carlton.

DYVIG, Peter; Comdr, Order of the Dannebrog, 1986; Ambassador of Denmark in Washington, since 1989; *b* 23 Feb. 1934; *m* 1959, Karen Dyvig (*née* Møller); one *s* one *d. Educ:* Copenhagen Univ. (grad. in Law). Entered Danish For. Service, 1959; bursary at Sch. of Advanced Internat. Studies, Washington, 1963–64; First Secretary: Danish Delegn to NATO, Paris, 1965–67; Brussels, 1967–69; Min. of For. Affairs, Copenhagen, 1969–74; Minister Counsellor, Washington, 1974–76; Ambassador, Asst Under-Sec. of State, Min. of For. Affairs, Copenhagen, 1976–79; Dep. Under-Sec. for Pol. Affairs, 1980; Perm. Under-Sec. of State for Pol. Affairs, 1981–86; Ambassador to UK, 1986–89. *Address:* Royal Danish Embassy, 3200 Whitehaven Street, NW, Washington, DC 20008–3683, USA.

E

EABORN, Prof. Colin, PhD, DSc (Wales); FRS 1970; FRSC; Professor of Chemistry, University of Sussex, since 1962; *b* 15 March 1923; *s* of Tom Stanley and Caroline Eaborn; *m* 1949, Joyce Thomas. *Educ:* Ruabon Grammar Sch., Denbighshire; Univ. Coll. of N Wales, Bangor. Asst Lecturer, 1947, Lecturer, 1950, and Reader 1954, in Chemistry, Univ. of Leicester. Research Associate, Univ. of California at Los Angeles, 1950–51; Robert A. Welch Visiting Scholar, Rice Univ., Texas, 1961–62; Erskine Fellow, Univ. of Canterbury (NZ), 1965; Pro-Vice Chancellor (Science), Univ. of Sussex, 1968–72; Dist. Prof., New Mexico State Univ., 1973; Canadian Commonwealth Fellow, Univ. of Victoria, BC, 1976; R. A. Welch Vis. Lectr, Texas, 1983. Hon. Sec., Chemical Society, 1964–71, Vice-Pres., Dalton Div., 1971–75: Mem. Council, Royal Soc., 1978–80, 1988–89; Chm., British Cttee on Chemical Educn, 1967–69; Mem., Italy/UK Mixed Commn, 1972–80. Hon. DSc Sussex, 1990. F. S. Kipping Award, Amer. Chem. Soc., 1964; Organometallic Award, Chem. Soc., 1975; Ingold Lectureship and Medal, Chem. Soc., 1976; Main Gp Award, Chem. Soc., 1989. *Publications:* Organosilicon Compounds, 1960; Organometallic Compounds of the Group IV Elements, Vol. 1, Part 1, 1968; numerous research papers, mainly in Jl of Chem. Soc. and Jl of Organometallic Chemistry (Regional Editor). *Address:* School of Chemistry and Molecular Sciences, University of Sussex, Brighton BN1 9QJ. *T:* Brighton (0273) 606755, *Fax:* Brighton (0273) 677196.

EADEN, Maurice Bryan, CBE 1983; HM Diplomatic Service, retired; Consul General, Amsterdam, 1980–83; *b* 9 Feb. 1923; *s* of William Eaden and Florence Ada Eaden (*née* Hudson); *m* 1947, Nelly Margaretha Dorgelo; three *s*. *Educ:* Bemrose Sch., Derby. Served Army, 1942–47. Foreign Office, 1947; Vice-Consul, Leopoldville, 1955; First Secretary (Commercial): Addis Ababa, 1958; Beirut, 1963; FO, 1967; First Sec. (Commercial), Bombay, 1970; Counsellor (Administration), Brussels, 1972–75; Consul-Gen., Karachi, 1975–79. *Recreations:* walking in Derbyshire; languages. *Address:* New Houses, Cressbrook, Buxton, Derbyshire. *T:* Tideswell (0298) 871404.

EADIE, Alexander, BEM 1960; JP; MP (Lab) Midlothian since 1966; *b* 23 June 1920; *m* 1941; one *s*. *Educ:* Buckhaven Senior Secondary Sch. Coal-miner from 1934. Chm., Fife County Housing Cttee, 9 yrs; Chm., Fife County Educn Cttee, 18 mths; Governor, Moray House Teachers' Training Coll., Edinburgh, 5 years; Exec. Committee: Scottish Council of Labour Party, 9 yrs; NUM Scottish Area, 2 yrs; Mem., Eastern Regional Hosp. Bd (Scotland), 14 yrs. Contested Ayr, 1959 and 1964; Former PPS to Miss M. Herbison, MP, Minister of Social Security, and Mem. of Parly Select Cttee on Scottish Affairs; Opposition Front Bench Spokesman on Energy (incl. N Sea Oil), 1973–74; Parly Under-Sec. of State, Dept of Energy, 1974–79; Shadow Front Bench Spokesman on Energy, 1979–. Chm., Parly Labour Party Power and Steel Gp, 1972–74; Sec., Miners' Parly Gp, 1983–; Vice-Chm., Parly Trade Union Group, 1972–74. JP Fife, 1951. *Recreations:* bowling, gardening. *Address:* Balkerack, The Haugh, East Wemyss, Fife. *T:* Buckhaven (0592) 3636.

EADIE, Douglas George Arnott, FRCS; Consulting Surgeon, The London Hospital (Consultant Surgeon, 1969–87); Consultant Surgeon, King Edward VII Hospital, London, since 1978; *b* 16 June 1931; *s* of Dr Herbert Arnott Eadie and Hannah Sophia (*née* Wingate); *m* 1957, Gillian Carlyon Coates; two *s* two *d*. *Educ:* Epsom Coll.; London Hosp. Med. Coll. (MB BS; MS 1969). Jun. Specialist in Surgery and Captain RAMC, Far East Land Forces, 1957–60; Hugh Robertson Exchange Fellow, Presbyterian St Luke's Hosp., Chicago, 1962; Surgical Registrar, London Hosp., 1963–67. Cons. to Royal Masonic Hosp., 1980–82; Hon. Cons., Osborne House, IoW, 1980. Chm. of Council, Medical Protection Soc., 1976–83 (Mem. Council, 1974; Treasurer, 1986–). Examiner in Surgery: Soc. of Apothecaries of London, 1976–80; Univ. of London, 1976–84. Master, Soc. of Apothecaries, 1990–91 (Mem. Ct of Assts, 1980); rep. on GMC, 1983–88. FRSM 1956. *Publications:* contribs to med. jls on topics relating to vascular disease. *Recreations:* golf, gardening, shooting. *Address:* Cromwell Hospital, Cromwell Road, W8 5JN; 7 Hillsleigh Road, W8 7LH. *T:* 071-229 5242. *Clubs:* Athenæum, MCC.

EADIE, Mrs Ellice (Aylmer), CBE 1966; Standing Counsel to General Synod of Church of England, 1972–80; *b* 30 June 1912; *d* of late Rt Rev. R. T. Hearn, LLD, sometime Bishop of Cork, and of late Dr M. E. T. Hearn, MD, FRCPI; *m* 1946, John Harold Ward Eadie. *Educ:* Cheltenham Ladies' Coll.; St Hugh's Coll., Oxford. Called to Bar, Gray's Inn, 1936. Flt Officer, WAAF, 1941–46. Parliamentary Counsel Office, 1949–72, Parly Counsel, 1968–72. *Address:* 74 Roebuck House, Palace Street, SW1E 5BD. *T:* 071–828 6158.

EADY, family name of **Baron Swinfen.**

EADY, David, QC 1983; a Recorder, since 1986; *b* 24 March 1943; *s* of late Thomas William Eady and of Kate Eady; *m* 1974, Catherine, *yr d* of J. T. Wiltshire, Bath, Avon; one *s* one *d*. *Educ:* Brentwood Sch.; Trinity Coll., Cambridge (Exhibnr; Pt I Moral Science Tripos, Pt II Law Tripos; MA, LLB). Called to the Bar, Middle Temple, 1966, in practice, South Eastern Circuit. Mem., Cttee on Privacy and Related Matters (Calcutt Cttee), 1989–90. *Publication:* The Law of Contempt (with A. J. Arlidge, QC), 1982. *Recreations:* music, watching cricket. *Address:* 1 Brick Court, Temple, EC4Y 9BY. *T:* 071–353 8845; Goodshill House, Tenterden, Kent TN30 6UN. *T:* Tenterden (05806) 3644.

EAGERS, Derek; Under-Secretary, Department of Trade and Industry (formerly Department of Trade), 1975–84; *b* 13 Sept. 1924; *s* of late Horace Eagers and Florence (*née* Green); *m* 1953, Hazel Maureen Henson; two *s*. *Educ:* King Edward VII Sch., Sheffield; Brasenose Coll., Oxford. RNVR, 1943–47. Min. of Fuel and Power, 1949; UK Atomic Energy Authority, 1955–57; British Embassy, Washington, 1958–60; Principal Private Sec. to successive Ministers of Power, 1963–65; Petroleum Counsellor, Washington, 1966–68; Min. of Power (subseq. Min. of Technology, Dept of Trade and Industry), 1969; Dept of Industry, 1974. *Recreation:* concealing his true ignorance of cricket, gardening and railway history. *Address:* Bryniau Golau, Llangower, Bala, Gwynedd LL23 7BT. *T:* Bala (0678) 520517.

EAGGER, Brig. Arthur Austin, CBE 1944 (OBE 1940), TD 1945; *b* 14 March 1898; *s* of Edward and Elsie Eagger; *m* 1st, 1935, Kate Mortimer Hare (*d* 1946); three *s*; 2nd, 1948, Barbara Noel Hare. *Educ:* Aberdeen Univ. (MB ChB 1922). Lieut 6th Bn Gordon Hldrs. Commissioned RAMC (TA), 1928; late DDMS 1 Airborne Corps. Medical Dir, Slough Industrial Health Service, retired 1963, Consultant 1963–79. Bronze Star (USA), 1945. *Publications:* Industrial Resettlement (Proc. RSM), 1952; Health in the Factory (Jl Royal Institute of Public Health and Hygiene), 1953; Venture in Industry, 1965. *Address:* 1 Underwood Close, Dawlish, Devon EX7 9RY. *T:* Dawlish (0626) 864597.

EAGLAND, (Ralph) Martin; Chief Executive, Leeds Development Corporation, since 1988; *b* 1 May 1942; *s* of Norman Albert Eagland and Jessie Eagland; *m* 1963, Patricia Anne Norton; one *s* one *d*. *Educ:* Hipperholme Grammar Sch.; Leeds Sch. of Town Planning; Univ. of Bradford (MSc); Univ. of Birmingham. FRTPI, FBIM, MIHT, SOLACE. Jun. planning posts, Huddersfield, Dewsbury and Halifax, 1959–67; Principal Planning Officer, City of Gloucester, 1967–72; Asst Co. Planning Officer, Northants CC, 1972–74; Chief Planner (Envmt), W Yorks CC, 1974–79, Head of Econ. Develt Unit, 1979–84; Chief Exec., Kettering Borough Council, 1984–88. Mem., W Yorks Cttee, CoSIRA, 1985–88; Sec., Kettering Enterprise Agency, 1986–88. Hon. Public Relns Officer, RTPI (Yorks Br. Exec. Cttee), 1990–. Mem., Yorks Contract Bridge Assoc., Wakefield. *Publications:* contribs to RTPI Jl, Instn of Highways and Transportation Jl and various property jls and publications. *Recreations:* environmental studies, ballroom dancing, bridge, writing, gardening. *Address:* Little Cliff Farm, Cliff Road, Wooldale, Holmfirth, Huddersfield HD7 1YP. *T:* (office) Leeds (0532) 446273. *Club:* Yorkshire Society (Leeds).

EAGLES, Lt-Col (Charles Edward) James, LVO 1988; Member, HM Body Guard of the Honourable Corps of Gentlemen-at-Arms, 1967–88 (Harbinger, 1981–86; Standard Bearer, 1986–88); *b* 14 May 1918; *o s* of late Major C. E. C. Eagles, DSO, RMLI and Esmé Field; *m* 1941, Priscilla May Nicolette, *d* of late Brig. A. F. B. Cottrell, DSO, OBE; one *s* three *d*. *Educ:* Marlborough Coll. 2nd Lieut RM, 1936; served: HMS Sussex, Mediterranean and S Atlantic, 1938–40; Mobile Naval Base Def. Orgn, UK, ME, Ceylon and India, 1940–43; 1 HAA Regt RM, India, UK and NW Europe, 1943–45; Asst Mil. Sec., 1945; Amphibious Trng Wing, 1945–47; Staff of Maj.-Gen. RM, Portsmouth, 1947–50; HMS Devonshire, 1951–52; RN Staff Course, 1952; DS, Amphibious Warfare Sch., 1952–55; HMS Afrikander, SO (Intell.), S Atlantic, 1955–57; Dep. Dir, PRORM, 1957–59; CSO, Plymouth Gp, 1960; AAG, Staff of CGRM, 1960–62; Dir, PRORM, 1962–65; retd 1965; Civil Service, MoD, 1965–83. *Recreations:* shooting, genealogy. *Address:* Fallowfield, Westwell, Ashford, Kent TN25 4LQ. *T:* Charing (023371) 2552. *Club:* Army and Navy.

EAGLETON, Dr Terence Francis, PhD; Lecturer in Critical Theory and Fellow of Linacre College, Oxford University, 1989–Oct. 1992; Thomas Warton Professor of English Literature, and Fellow of St Catherine's College, University of Oxford, from Oct. 1992; *b* 22 Feb. 1943; *s* of Francis Paul Eagleton and Rosaleen (*née* Riley); *m* 1966, Elizabeth Rosemary Galpin; two *s*. *Educ:* Trinity Coll., Cambridge (MA, PhD). Fellow in English, Jesus Coll., Cambridge, 1964–69; Tutorial Fellow, Wadham Coll., Oxford, 1969–89. *Publications:* Criticism and Ideology, 1976; Marxism and Literary Criticism, 1976; Literary Theory: an introduction, 1983; The Function of Criticism, 1984; The Ideology of the Aesthetic, 1990. *Recreation:* Irish music. *Address:* (until Oct. 1992) Linacre College, Oxford OX1 3JA; (from Oct. 1992) St Catherine's College, Oxford OX1 3UJ. *T:* Oxford (0865) 271700. *Club:* Irish.

EAGLING, Wayne John; dancer and choreographer; Artistic Director, Dutch National Ballet, since 1991; *s* of Eddie and Thelma Eagling. *Educ:* P. Ramsey Studio of Dance Arts; Royal Ballet Sch. Sen. Principal, Royal Ballet, 1975–91; has danced lead rôles in major classics including Sleeping Beauty, Swan Lake, Cinderella; first rôle created for him was Young Boy in Triad, 1972; subsequent created rôles include: Solo Boy in Gloria; Ariel in The Tempest; Woyzeck in Different Drummer. Choreographed: The Hunting of the Snark by Michael Batt; (for Royal Ballet) Frankenstein, The Modern Prometheus, 1985, and Beauty and the Beast; The Wall, Berlin, 1990; choreographed, produced and directed various galas. *Publication:* (with Ross MacGibbon and Robert Jude) The Company We Keep, 1981. *Recreations:* golf, scuba diving, tennis, antique cars. *Address:* Dutch National Ballet, Het Muziektheater, Waterlooplein 22, 1011 PG Amsterdam, The Netherlands.

EALES, Victor Henry James, CEng, MIMechE; Founder and Director, Parkultra Ltd, since 1984; Director of Weapons Production and Quality (Naval), 1980–81, and Head of Naval Weapons Professional and Technical Group, 1979–81, Ministry of Defence; *b* 11 Dec. 1922; *s* of William Henry and Frances Jean Eales; *m* 1949, Elizabeth Gabrielle Irene James; two *s* one *d*. *Educ:* Wimbledon Central Sch.; Guildford Technical Coll.; Portsmouth Polytechnic. Ministry of Defence: Asst Director, Weapons Production (Naval), 1970; Dep. Director, Surface Weapons Projects (Naval), 1975; Director, Weapons Production (Naval), 1979. *Recreation:* golf. *Address:* 11 Penrhyn Avenue, East Cosham, Portsmouth, Hants PO6 2AX.

EALING, Abbot of; *see* Soper, Rt Rev. A. L.

EAMES, Eric James, JP; Lord Mayor of Birmingham, 1974–75, Deputy Lord Mayor, 1975–76; *b* Highley, Shropshire, 13 April 1917; *s* of George Eames; *m* (marr. diss.); one *s*. *Educ:* Highley Sch., Highley, Shropshire. Member (Lab): Birmingham City Council, 1949–; W Midlands CC, 1974–77. Mem., Governing Board, Internat. Center for Information Co-operation and Relationship among World's Major Cities. Chm., Assoc.

for Neighbourhood Councils. Governor, Harper Adams Agric. Coll. JP Birmingham, 1972. *Recreations*: gardening, do-it-yourself enthusiast. *Address*: 78 Westley Road, Acocks Green, Birmingham B27 7UH. *T*: 021–706 7629.

EAMES, Most Rev. Robert Henry Alexander; *see* Armagh, Archbishop of, and Primate of All Ireland.

EARDLEY-WILMOT, Sir John (Assheton), 5th Bt *cr* 1821; LVO 1956; DSC 1943; Staff of Monopolies Commission, 1967–82; *b* 2 Jan. 1917; *s* of Commander Frederick Neville Eardley-Wilmot (*d* 1956) (*s* of 3rd Bt) and Dorothy Little (*d* 1959), formerly of Brooksby, Double Bay, Sydney; *S* uncle, 1970; *m* 1939, Diana Elizabeth, *d* of Commander Aubrey Moore, RN, and Mrs O. Bassett; one *s* one *d*. *Educ*: Stubbington; RNC, Dartmouth. Motor Torpedo Boats, 1939–43; served HMS Apollo, 1944; HMS Fencer, 1945–46; RN Staff Course, 1950; Commander 1950; HMS Opossum, 1951–53; Cabinet Office, 1954–57; Admiralty, 1958–67; retired 1967, as Deputy Director Naval Administrative Planning. MBIM 1978; FRSA 1970. Freeman, City of London (by Redemption). Norwegian War Medal. *Recreation*: fishing. *Heir*: *s* Michael John Assheton Eardley-Wilmot [*b* 13 Jan. 1941; *m* 1971, Wendy (marr. diss. 1987), *y d* of A. J. Wolstenholme; two *s* one *d*; *m* 1987, Diana Margaret, *d* of Robert Graham Wallis; one *d*]. *Address*: 41 Margravine Gardens, W6. *T*: 081–748 3723.

EARL, Christopher Joseph, MD, FRCP; Physician to: Neurological Department, Middlesex Hospital, since 1971; National Hospital, Queen Square, since 1958; Moorfields Eye Hospital, since 1959; Consultant Neurologist, King Edward VII Hospital for Officers, since 1966 and Hospital of St John and St Elizabeth, since 1967; Civil Consultant in Neurology, Royal Air Force, since 1976; *b* 20 Nov. 1925; *s* of Christopher and Winifred Earl, Ashbourne, Derbyshire; *m* 1951, Alma Patience Hopkins, Reading; two *s* three *d*. *Educ*: Cotton Coll.; Guy's Hosp. House phys. and house surg., Guy's Hosp., and MO, RAF, 1948–50. Lecturer in Chemical Pathology, Guy's Hosp., 1950–52; Research Fellow, Harvard Med. Sch., and Neurological Unit, Boston City Hosp., 1952–54; Resident MO, Nat. Hosp., Queen Square, 1954–56; Chief Asst, Neurological Dept, Guy's Hosp., 1956–58; Physician, Neurological Dept, London Hosp., 1961–71. Director: Medical Sickness Annuity & Life Assce Soc. Ltd, 1981–; Permanent Insurance Co. Hon. Dir of Photography, Royal Society of Medicine, 1967–73. Hon. Sec., Assoc. British Neurologists, 1968–74. Mem. Council, Med. Defence Union; Chm., Cttee on Neurology, RCP (Censor, 1983–85). Corresp. Mem., Amer. Neurological Assoc. *Publications*: Papers in learned jls on Biochemistry and Neurology. *Recreation*: reading history. *Address*: 23 Audley Road, Ealing, W5 3ES. *T*: 081–997 0380; 149 Harley Street, W1N 1HG. *Club*: Garrick.

EARL, Eric Stafford; Clerk to the Worshipful Company of Fishmongers, 1974–88, retired; *b* 8 July 1928; *s* of late Alfred Henry Earl and Mary Elizabeth Earl; *m* 1951, Clara Alice Alston. *Educ*: SE Essex Technical Coll.; City of London Coll. Served with RA, 1946–48. Joined Fishmongers' Co. 1948: Accountant, 1961–68; Asst Clerk, 1969–73; Actg Clerk, 1973–74; Liveryman, 1977. Clerk to Governors of Gresham's Sch., 1974–88; Hon. Sec., Shellfish Assoc. of GB, 1974–88; Secretary: Atlantic Salmon Research Trust Ltd, 1974–; City and Guilds of London Art School Ltd, 1974–; Jt Hon. Sec., Central Council for Rivers Protection, 1974–88; Hon. Asst River Keeper of River Thames, 1968–88; Chm., Nat. Anglers' Council, 1983–85; Member Council: Anglers' Co-operative Assoc., 1974– (Vice Chm., 1988–); Nat. Anglers' Council, 1974–; Mem. Exec., Salmon and Trout Assoc., 1980– (Mem. Council, 1988–). Director: Hulbert Property Co. Ltd, 1975–88; Hulbert Property Holdings Ltd, 1975–88. FZS 1988. Hon. Freeman, Watermen's Co., 1984. *Recreations*: fishing, gardening, tennis, cricket. *Address*: Dolphins, Watling Lane, Thaxted, Essex CM6 2RA. *T*: Thaxted (0371) 758. *Club*: Flyfishers'.

EARLE, Arthur Frederick; management and economic consultant, since 1983; *b* Toronto, 13 Sept. 1921; *s* of Frederick C. Earle and Hilda M. Earle (*née* Brown); *m* 1946, Vera Domini Lithgow; two *s* one *d*. *Educ*: Toronto; London Sch. of Economics (BSc (Econ.), PhD; Hon. Fellow 1980). Royal Canadian Navy (Rating to Lieut Comdr), 1939–46. Canada Packers Ltd, 1946–48; Aluminium Ltd cos in British Guiana, West Indies and Canada, 1948–53; Treas., Alumina Jamaica Ltd, 1953–55; Aluminium Union, London, 1955–58; Vice-Pres., Aluminium Ltd Sales Inc., New York, 1958–61; Dir, 1961–74, Dep. Chm., 1961–65, Man. Dir, 1963–65, Hoover Ltd; Principal, London Graduate Sch. of Business Studies, 1965–72. Pres., Internat. Investment Corp. for Yugoslavia, 1972–74; Pres., Boyden Consulting Group Ltd, 1974–82; Associate, 1974–82, Vice-Pres., 1975–82, Boyden Associates, Inc.; Advisor to the Pres., Canada Develt Investment Corp., 1983–86; Director: Rio Algom Ltd, 1983–; National Sea Products Ltd, 1984–86; Bathpaul Ltd, UK, 1984–86; Monkwells Ltd, UK, 1984. Sen. Res. Fellow, Nat. Centre for Management R & D, Univ. of Western Ontario, 1987–90. Member: Commn of Enquiry, Jamaican Match Industry, 1953; Consumer Council, 1963–68; NEDC Cttee on Management Educn, Training and Develt, 1967–69; NEDC for Electrical Engineering Industry. Chm., Canadian Assoc. of Friends of LSE, 1975–. Dir, Nat. Ballet of Canada, 1982–85. Governor: Ashridge Management Coll., 1962–65; LSE, 1968; NIESR, 1968–74; Governor and Mem. Council, Ditchley Foundn, 1967. Fellow, London Business Sch., 1988. Thomas Hawksley Lecture, IMechE, 1968. *Publications*: numerous, on economics and management. *Recreations*: hill climbing, model ship building. *Address*: 1234 Rushbrooke Drive, Oakville, Ont L6M 1K9, Canada. *T*: (416) 847–6459. *Club*: National (Toronto).

EARLE, Ven. E(dward) E(rnest) Maples; Archdeacon of Tonbridge, 1953–76, Archdeacon Emeritus since 1977; Vicar of Shipbourne, Kent, 1959–86; *b* 22 Dec. 1900; 2nd *s* of Ernest William Earle and Lilian Geraldine Earle (*née* Hudson); *m* 1966, Mrs Jocelyn Mary Offer, *widow* of Canon C. J. Offer. *Educ*: London Coll. of Divinity; St John's Coll., Durham University (LTh, MA). Vicar of: St John, Bexley, 1936–39; Rainham (Kent), 1939–44; Secretary Rochester Diocesan Reorganisation Cttee, 1944–52, Great Appeal Cttee, etc., 1944–49; Hon. Canon, Rochester Cathedral, 1949; Rector of Chatham, 1950–52; Proctor in Convocation, 1950–53; Rector of Wrotham 1952–59. *Recreations*: artistic and architectural interests. *Address*: Butcher's Cottage, Stumble Hill, Shipbourne, Tonbridge, Kent.

EARLE, Sir George; *see* Earle, Sir H. G. A.

EARLE, Very Rev. George Hughes, SJ; MA; Superior of Jesuit Students in South Africa, since 1989; *b* 20 Sept. 1925; *s* of late Lieut-Col F. W. Earle, DSO, JP, Morestead House, Winchester, and late Marie Blanche Lyne-Stivens. *Educ*: Pilgrims' Sch., Winchester; Westminster Sch.; Peter Symonds' Sch., Winchester; Balliol Coll., Oxford. Served with RAF, 1943–47. Joined Soc. of Jesus, 1950. Taught at Beaumont Coll., 1955–57, and Stonyhurst Coll., 1962–63; Headmaster, Stonyhurst Coll., 1963–72; Superior of Southwell House, 1972–75; Educnl Asst to Provincial, 1972–75; Co-editor, The Way, 1974–78; Rector of St Aloysius, Glasgow, 1978–81; Superior, English Province, SJ, 1981–87. Dean of St Joseph's, Cedara, Natal, 1990–. *Recreations*: none; wasting time. *Address*: 4 Baron Road, Merrivale, Natal, 3291, South Africa.

EARLE, Sir (Hardman) George (Algernon), 6th Bt *cr* 1869; *S* father, 1979; *m*; one *s* one *d*. *Heir*: *s*.

EARLE, Ion, TD 1946; Assistant to the Directors, Clive Discount Co., 1973–81, retired; *b* 12 April 1916; *s* of late Stephen Earle and of E. Beatrice Earle (*née* Blair White); *m* 1946, Elizabeth Stevens, US citizen; one *s* one *d*. *Educ*: Stowe Sch.; University Coll., Oxford; Université de Grenoble. Federation of British Industries, Birmingham, 1938–51, London, 1952–60; Chief Executive, Export Council for Europe, 1960–64; Dep. Dir-Gen., BNEC, 1965–71 (Dir, 1964–65); Head of Personnel, Kleinwort Benson Ltd, 1972. Royal Artillery, TA, 1939–46 (Major). *Recreations*: golf, tennis, gardening. *Address*: 69 Sea Avenue, Rustington, West Sussex BN16 2DP. *T*: Rustington (0903) 773350. *Clubs*: Royal Wimbledon Golf, West Sussex Golf.

EARLE, Joel Vincent, (Joe); exhibitions consultant, since 1990; Head of Public Services, Victoria and Albert Museum, 1987–89; *b* 1 Sept. 1952; *s* of James Basil Foster Earle and Mary Isabel Jessie Weeks; *m* 1980, Sophia Charlotte Knox; two *s*. *Educ*: Westminster Sch.; New Coll., Oxford (BA 1st Cl. Hons Chinese). Far Eastern Department, Victoria & Albert Museum: Res. Asst, 1974–77; Asst Keeper, 1977–82; Keeper, 1982–87. Exhibns Co-ordinator, Japan Fest. 1991, 1990–91. Trustee: Chiddingstone Castle, 1984–; Design Mus., 1988–; Oriental Mus., Durham, 1990–. *Publications*: An Introduction to Netsuke, 1980, 2nd edn 1982; An Introduction to Japanese Prints, 1980; (contrib.) Japan Style, 1980; (contrib.) The Great Japan Exhibition, 1981; (trans.) The Japanese Sword, 1983; The Toshiba Gallery: Japanese art and design, 1986; articles in learned jls. *Address*: c/o Harrison/Parrott, 12 Penzance Place, W11 4PA. *T*: 071–229 9166.

EARLE, Rev. John Nicholas Francis, (Rev. Nick Earle); Headmaster, Bromsgrove School, 1971–85; *b* 14 Nov. 1926; *s* of John William Arthur Earle and Vivien Constance Fenton (*née* Davies); *m* 1959, Ann Veronica Lester; one *s* two *d*. *Educ*: Winchester Coll.; Trinity Coll., Cambridge. 1st cl. Maths Tripos pt 2, 1st cl. Theol. Tripos pt 1; MA. Deacon, 1952; Priest, 1953. Curate, St Matthew, Moorfields, 1952–57; PARS Fellow, Union Theol Seminary, New York, 1957–58; Lectr, St Botolph, Aldgate, 1958–61; Asst Master, Dulwich Coll., 1961–71. *Publications*: What's Wrong With the Church?, 1961; Culture and Creed, 1967; Logic, 1973. *Recreations*: travel, gardening. *Address*: 1 Red Post Hill, Pond Mead, SE21 7BX.

EARLES, Prof. Stanley William Edward, PhD, DScEng; CEng, FIMechE; Professor of Mechanical Engineering, since 1976, and Head of School of Physical Sciences and Engineering, since 1990, King's College, University of London; *b* 18 Jan. 1929; *s* of late William Edward Earles and Winnifred Anne Cook; *m* 1955, Margaret Isabella Brown; two *d*. *Educ*: King's Coll., Univ. of London (BScEng, PhD, DScEng, AKC). CEng, FIMechE 1976. Nuffield Apprentice, Birmingham, 1944–50; King's Coll., Univ. of London, 1950–53; Scientific Officer, Royal Naval Scientific Service, 1953–55; Queen Mary College, University of London: Lectr in Mech. Eng, 1955–69; Reader in Mech. Eng, 1969–75; Prof. of Mech. Eng, 1975–76; Hd of Dept of Mech. Engrg, KCL, 1976–90. James Clayton Fund prize, IMechE, 1967; Engineering Applied to Agriculture Award, IMechE, 1980. *Publications*: papers and articles in Proc. IMechE, Jl of Mech. Eng Science, Jl of Sound and Vibration, Wear, Proc. ASME and ASLE, and Eng. *Recreations*: real tennis, gardening. *Address*: Woodbury, Church Lane, Wormley, Broxbourne, Herts EN10 7QF. *T*: Hoddesdon (0992) 464616.

EARNSHAW, (Thomas) Roy, CBE 1978 (OBE 1971); Director and General Manager of Division, TBA Industrial Products Ltd, Rochdale, 1966–76; retired; *b* 27 Feb. 1917; *s* of Godfrey Earnshaw and Edith Annie (*née* Perry); *m* 1953, Edith Rushworth; two *d*. *Educ*: Marlborough Coll., Liverpool. MIEx; MICS. Served War, Army, 1940–46: Major Lancs Fusiliers. Shipbroking, Liverpool, 1933–39; appts with subsid. cos of Turner & Newall Ltd: Turner Brothers Asbestos Co. Ltd, Rochdale (mainly Export Sales Manager), 1939–40 and 1946–53; Dir, AM&FM Ltd, Bombay, 1954–59; Export Dir, Ferodo Ltd, Chapel-en-le-Frith, 1959–66. British Overseas Trade Board: Mem. Adv. Council, 1975–82; Export Year Advr, 1976–77; Export United Advr, 1978–83. Director: Actair Holdings Ltd, 1979–83; Actair Internat. Ltd, 1979–83; Unico Finance Ltd, 1979–81. Formerly: Pres., Rochdale Chamber of Commerce; Chm., NW Region Chambers of Commerce; UK Delegate to European Chambers of Commerce. London Economic Adviser to Merseyside CC, 1980–82. Vis. Fellow, Henley Management Coll. (formerly ASC), 1981–90. Mem., Bd of Managers, Henley YMCA, 1989–. FRSA. *Recreations*: gardening, oil painting, hill walking, cycling. *Address*: 89 St Andrews Road, Henley-on-Thames, Oxon RG9 1PN. *T*: Henley-on-Thames (0491) 576620. *Club*: Leander (Henley-on-Thames).

EASMON, Prof. Charles Syrett Farrell, MD, PhD; Fleming Professor of Medical Microbiology, St Mary's Hospital Medical School, University of London, since 1984; *b* 20 Aug. 1946; *s* of Dr McCormack Charles Farrell Easmon and Enid Winifred Easmon; *m* 1977, Susan Lynn (*née* Peach). *Educ*: Epsom Coll.; St Mary's Hospital Med. Sch. (Open Schol.; MB BS; MD); PhD London. MRCPath. Pathology trng, St Bartholomew's Hosp., 1970–71; St Mary's Hospital Medical School: Research Asst, 1971; Lectr, 1973; Sen. Lectr, 1976; Reader and Actg Head of Dept, 1980; Personal Chair, 1983. *Publications*: (ed) Medical Microbiology, vol. 1 1982, vols 2 and 3 1983, vol. 4 1984; (ed) Infections in the Immunocompromised Host, 1983; (ed) Staphylococci and Staphylococcal Infections, 1983; numerous papers in learned jls. *Recreations*: music, history, gardening. *Address*: 21 Cranes Park Avenue, Surbiton, Surrey KT5 8BS.

EASON, Henry, CBE 1967; JP; a Vice-President of the Institute of Bankers, 1969–75, and Consultant with special reference to overseas relationships, 1971–74 (Secretary-General, 1959–71); *b* 12 April 1910; *s* of late H. Eason and F. J. Eason; *m* 1939 (at Hexham Abbey), Isobel, *d* of Wm and Dorothy Stevenson; one *s* two *d*. *Educ*: Yarm (Schol.); King's Coll., University of Durham. BCom (with distinction). Barrister-at-law, Gray's Inn. Served Lloyds Bank until 1939; Asst Sec., Institute of Bankers, 1939. Served War of 1939–45 and until 1946, with Royal Air Force (Wing Commander, despatches twice). Asst Dir, Military Gov. (Banking), NW Europe, 1944–46; United Nations Adviser (Banking) to Pakistan Govt, 1952; Deputy Sec., Institute of Bankers, 1956; Governor, City of London Coll., 1958–69; Mem., British National Cttee, Internat. Chamber Commerce, 1959–74. Director: Internat. Banking Summer Sch., Christ Church, Oxford, 1961, 1964, 1970; Cambridge Banking Seminar, Christ's Coll., Cambridge, 1968 and 1969. Editor, Jl Inst. of Bankers, 1959–71. Hon. Fellow, Inst. of Bankers, 1971. JP Bromley 1967. Gen. Comr of Income Tax, Bromley, 1973–76. *Publications*: contributions to professional journals. *Recreations*: golf, walking, gardening, world travel. *Address*: 12 Redgate Drive, Hayes Common, Bromley BR2 7BT. *T*: 081–462 1900. *Clubs*: Gresham, Overseas Bankers; Langley Park Golf.

EASON, His Honour Robert Kinley; HM's First Deemster, Clerk of the Rolls and Deputy Governor of the Isle of Man, 1974–80; *b* 12 April 1908; 2nd *s* of Henry Alexander Eason and Eleanor Jane Eason (*née* Kinley); *m* 1937, Nora Muriel, *d* of Robert Raisbeck Coffey, Douglas, IOM. *Educ*: Douglas High Sch.; King William's Coll., IOM; University Coll. London. LLB (Hons). Called to Bar, Gray's Inn, 1929; Advocate, Manx Bar, 1930. High Bailiff and Chief Magistrate, Isle of Man, 1961–69; HM's Second Deemster, IOM, 1969–74. Retired from practice, 1982. Chairman: Criminal Injuries Compensation Tribunal, IOM, 1969–74; IOM Income Tax Appeal Comrs, 1974–80; IOM Unit Trust

Tribunal, 1968–74; Tourist (IOM) Appeal Tribunal, 1969–74; Tynwald Arrangements Cttee, 1974–80; Chm. of Trustees: Cunningham House Scout and Guide Headquarters, 1964–90; Ellan Vannin Home, 1971–86; Trustee, Manx Marine Soc., 1974–90. President: Ellynyn Ny Gael, 1974–84; IOM Anti-Cancer Assoc., 1969–85; Wireless Telegraphy Appeal Bd for IOM, 1971–80; Legion Players, 1971–81; SS&AFA, IOM Br., 1973–90; Licensing Appeal Court, 1969–74; King William's College Soc., 1978–80; past Pres., IOM Soc. for Prevention of Cruelty to Animals. Queen's Silver Jubilee Medal, 1977. *Recreation:* organ music. *Address:* Greenacres, Highfield Drive, Baldrine, Lonan, Isle of Man. *T:* Laxey (0624) 861622. *Clubs:* Ellan Vannin, Manx Automobile (Douglas).

EAST, David Albert, QPM 1982; Secretary, Welsh Rugby Union, 1989; *b* 5 June 1936; *s* of Albert East and Florence Emily East; *m* 1957, Gloria (*née* Swinden); one *d*. *Educ:* King Alfred Grammar Sch., Wantage, Berks; University Coll. London (LLB Hons). Berks Constabulary, 1958–65 (constable to sergeant); First Special Course, Police Coll., Bramshill, 1962 (Johnson Prize and Cert. of Distinction); Inspector, York City Police, 1965–68; UCL, 1965–68; Metropol. Police Chief Inspector to Chief Supt, 1968–75; Eight Sen. Comd Course, Bramshill, 1971; Asst Chief Constable, Avon and Somerset Constab., 1975–78; RCDS, 1978; Dep. Chief Constable, Devon and Cornwall Constab., 1978–82, Chief Constable, 1982–83; seconded to Cyprus, 1981 and to Singapore, 1982; Chief Constable, S Wales Constab., 1983–88. Chm., British Police Athletic Assoc. OStJ 1985. Police Long Service and Good Conduct Medal, 1980. *Recreations:* Rugby, cricket.

EAST, Frederick Henry, CB 1976; FEng 1984; FIEE, FRAeS; Deputy Secretary, and Chief Weapon System Engineer (Polaris), Ministry of Defence, 1976–80, retired; *b* 15 Sept. 1919; *s* of Frederick Richard East; *m* 1st, 1942, Pauline Isabel Veale Horne (*d* 1972); 2nd, 1990, Christine Grace Veale Horne. *Educ:* Skinners' Company's Sch., Tunbridge Wells; University Coll., Exeter (Visc. St Cyres Schol., Tucker and Franklin Prize, 1939). BSc London 1940; MInstP. Joined Research Dept, Min. of Aircraft Production, 1940; various appts in RAE, 1942–57; Asst Dir of Air Armament Research and Develt, Min. of Supply/Aviation, 1957–62; Head of Weapon Project Gp, RAE, 1962–67; Student, IDC, 1968; Asst Chief Scientific Adviser (Projects), MoD, 1969–70; Dir, Royal Armament Res. and Develt Establishment, 1971–75. Reader, C of E, 1969–; Mem., Candidates Cttee, ACCM, 1981–86. *Publications:* contrib. to: Application of Critical Path Techniques, 1968; official reports, and articles in jls. *Address:* The Folly, Mill Street, Prestbury, Cheltenham GL52 3BG. *T:* Cheltenham (0242) 230749. *Club:* Athenæum.

EAST, Grahame Richard, CMG 1961; Special Commissioner of Income Tax, 1962–73; *b* 1908; 2nd *s* of William Robert and Eleanor East; *m* 1937, Cynthia Mildred, *d* of Adam Louis Beck, OBE; two *s* two *d*. *Educ:* Bristol Grammar Sch.; Corpus Christi Coll., Oxford. Asst Master, Royal Belfast Academical Institution, Belfast, 1929; Inland Revenue Dept, Secretaries Office, 1930, Asst Sec., 1941. *Address:* 22 Ormsby, Stanley Road, Sutton, Surrey SM2 6TJ. *T:* 081–643 3047.

EAST, John Anthony, OBE 1982; Chief Executive, English Tourist Board, since 1985; *b* 25 May 1930; *s* of John East and Jessie Mary East; *m* 1st, 1957, Barbara Collins; two *s* one *d*; 2nd, 1982, Susan Finch; two *d*. *Educ:* Bromley Grammar School. Reuter's, 1954–58; Notley Advertising, 1958–60; Director: French Government Tourist Office, 1960–70; English Tourist Bd, 1970–. *Publications:* History of French Architecture, 1968; Gascony and the Pyrenees, 1969; articles on France and French architecture. *Recreations:* walking, gardening, studying things French. *Address:* English Tourist Board, Thames Tower, Black's Road, Hammersmith W6 9EL.

EAST, Kenneth Arthur, CMG 1971; HM Diplomatic Service, retired; Ambassador to Iceland, 1975–81; *b* 9 May 1921; *s* of H. F. East; *m* 1946, Katherine Blackley; two *s* three *d*. *Educ:* Taunton's Sch; Southampton Univ. Served HM Forces, 1942–46. India Office/Commonwealth Relations Office, 1946–50; Asst Private Sec. to Sec. of State; First Secretary: Ottawa, 1950–53; Colombo, 1956–60; Head of East and General Africa Dept, CRO, 1961–63; Head of Personnel Dept, CRO, 1963–64; Counsellor, Diplomatic Service Administration, 1965; Counsellor and Head of Chancery, Oslo, 1965–70; Minister, Lagos, 1970–74. *Club:* Commonwealth Trust.

EAST, Sir (Lewis) Ronald, Kt 1966; CBE 1951; retired as Chairman, State Rivers and Water Supply Commission, Victoria (1936–65) and as Commissioner, River Murray Commission, Australia (1936–65); *b* 17 June 1899; *s* of Lewis Findlay East, ISO, Evansford, Vic., Australia and Annie Eleanor (*née* Burchett) Brunswick, Vic.; *m* 1927, Constance Lilias Keil, MA, Kilwinning, Ayrshire; three *d*. *Educ:* Scotch Coll., Melbourne; Melbourne Univ. BCE (Melbourne) 1922; MCE (Melbourne) 1924. Mem., Snowy Mountains Coun., until 1965; Pres., Instn of Engrs, Austr., 1952–53; Mem. Coun., Instn of Civil Engrs, 1960–62; Vice-Pres., Internat. Commn on Irrigation and Drainage, 1959–62. Hon. Fellow, Instn of Engineers, Australia, 1969; FRHSV 1983. Coopers Hill War Meml Prize and Telford Premium, ICE, 1932; Kernot Memorial Medal, University of Melbourne, 1949; Peter Nicol Russell Memorial Medal, Instn of Engineers, Australia, 1957. Hon. DEng Melbourne, 1981. *Publications:* River Improvement, Land Drainage and Flood Protection, 1952; A South Australian Colonist of 1836 and his Descendants, 1972; The Kiel Family and related Scottish Pioneers, 1974; More Australian Pioneers: the Burchetts and related families, 1976; (ed) The Gallipoli Diary of Sergeant Lawrence, 1981; many technical papers on water conservation and associated subjects in Proc. Instn Engs, Austr., Proc. Instn Civil Engrs, Amer. Soc. Civil Engrs and other jls. *Recreation:* handicrafts (model engineering). *Address:* 57 Waimarie Drive, Mt Waverley, Victoria 3149, Australia. *T:* Melbourne 277–4315.

EAST, Sir Ronald; *see* East, Sir L. R.

EAST, Ronald Joseph; Director: Kleinwort Charter Investment Trust PLC; Kleinwort Development Fund PLC; *b* 17 Dec. 1931; *s* of Joseph William and Marion Elizabeth Emma East; *m* 1955, Iris Joyce Beckwith; two *d*. *Educ:* Clare Coll., Cambridge Univ. (MA). Engineering Apprenticeship, Ford Trade Sch., Ford Motor Co. Ltd, 1945–52. Troop Comdr, RA (Lieut), 1953–55. Managerial posts in economics, product planning, finance, and engineering areas of Ford Motor Co. Ltd, 1959–65; Guest, Keen & Nettlefolds Ltd: Corporation Staff Dir of Planning, 1965–70; Planning Exec., Automotive and Allied Products Sector, 1972–73; Chairman: GKN Castings Ltd, 1974–77; GKN Kent Alloys Ltd, 1974–77; GKN Shotton Ltd, 1974–77; Dir, GKN (UK) Ltd, 1974–77; Corporate Staff Dir, Group Supplies, GKN Ltd, 1976–77. Dir, Programme Analysis and Review (PAR) and Special Advisor to Chief Sec. to the Treasury, 1971–72. Chairman: Hale Hamilton Hldgs, 1981–89; Hale Hamilton (Valves), 1981–89. *Recreations:* walking, skiing, ethnology, dramatic art. *Address:* The Waldrons, Feckenham, Worcs. *T:* Astwood Bank (052789) 2486.

EAST, William Gordon; Professor of Geography in the University of London at Birkbeck College, 1947–70, now Emeritus Professor; *b* 10 Nov. 1902; *s* of George Richard East and Jemima (*née* Nicoll); *m* 1934, Dorothea Small; two *s* two *d*. *Educ:* Sloane Sch., Chelsea; Peterhouse, Cambridge. Open scholarship in History, 1921, and research studentship, 1924, at Peterhouse. BA (Hons), Cambridge Univ. (History), 1924. MA 1928; Thirlwall Prizeman of Cambridge Univ., 1927. Asst in historical geography, London Sch. of Economics, 1927; temp. administrative officer in Ministry of Economic Warfare and Foreign Office, 1941–45; Reader in Geography in University of London, 1946. Visiting Professor: Univ. of Minnesota, 1952; Univ. of California, Los Angeles, 1959–60; Univ. of Michigan, 1966–67; Univ. of Wisconsin, 1969–70; Univ. of Saskatchewan, 1971. Myres Memorial Lectr, Oxford Univ., 1970–71. Mem., RGS Council, 1956–59; Pres., Inst. of British Geographers, 1959. Murchison Award, RGS, 1972. *Publications:* The Union of Moldavia and Wallachia, 1859, 1929, repr. 1973; An Historical Geography of Europe, 1935; The Geography Behind History, 1938; Mediterranean Problems, 1940; (ed jtly) The Changing Map of Asia, 1950, 1971; (jt) The Spirit and Purpose of Geography, 1951; (ed jtly) The Changing World, 1956; (ed) The Caxton Atlas, 1960; (ed) Regions of The British Isles, 1960–; The Soviet Union, 1963, 2nd edn 1976; (jt) Our Fragmented World, 1975; contributions to journals of geography, history and foreign affairs. *Address:* Wildwood, 17 Danes Way, Oxshott, Surrey KT22 0LU. *T:* Oxshott (0372) 2351.

EAST ANGLIA, Bishop of, (RC), since 1976; **Rt. Rev. Alan Charles Clark;** *b* 9 Aug. 1919; *s* of William Thomas Durham Clark and Ellen Mary Clark (*née* Compton). *Educ:* Westminster Cathedral Choir Sch.; Ven. English Coll., Rome, Italy. Priest, 1945; Curate, St Philip's, Arundel, 1945–46; postgrad. studies, Rome, 1946–48; Doctorate in Theol., Gregorian Univ., Rome, 1948; Tutor in Philosophy, English Coll., Rome, 1948–53, Vice-Rector, 1954–64; Parish Priest, St Mary's, Blackheath, SE3, 1965–69; Auxiliary Bishop of Northampton, 1969–76; Titular Bishop of Elmham, 1969–76. *Peritus* at Vatican Council, 1962–65; Jt Chm., The Anglican/Roman Catholic Internat. Commn, 1969–81 (Lambeth Cross); Chm., Dept for Mission and Unity, Bishops' Conf. of Eng. and Wales, 1984–; Co-Moderator, Jt Working Group of RC Church and WCC, 1984–. Freeman, City of London, 1969. *Recreation:* music. *Address:* The White House, 21 Upgate, Poringland, Norwich NR14 7SH. *T:* Framingham Earl (05086) 2202.

EASTCOTT, Harry Hubert Grayson, MS; FRCS; FRCOG; Consulting Surgeon, St Mary's Hospital; Consultant in Surgery and Vascular Surgery to the Royal Navy, 1957–82, now Emeritus; *b* 17 Oct. 1917; *s* of Harry George and Gladys Eastcott; *m* 1941, Doreen Joy, *e d* of Brenchley Ernest and Muriel Mittell; four *d*. *Educ:* Latymer Sch.; St Mary's Hosp. Medical School and Middlesex Hospital Medical Sch., University of London; Harvard Med. Sch. War of 1939–45, Junior surgical appts and service as Surgeon Lieut, RNVR up till 1946. Surg. Lieut Comdr RNVR, London Div., until 1957. MRCS; LRCP; MB, BS (Hons), 1941; FRCS 1946; MS (London), 1951. Sen. Registrar, 1950 as Hon. Cons. to St Mary's and Asst Dir Surgical Unit; Research Fellow in Surgery, Harvard Med. Sch., and Peter Bent Brigham Hosp., Boston, Mass, 1949–50; recognised teacher, 1953, and Examr, 1959, in surgery, University of London; Cons. Surgeon, St Mary's Hosp. and Lectr in Surgery, St Mary's Hosp. Med. Sch., 1955–82; Surgeon, Royal Masonic Hosp., 1964–80; Cons. Surgeon, King Edward VII Hosp. for Officers, 1965–87; Hon. Surg., RADA, 1959–; External Examr in Surgery: Queen's Univ., Belfast, 1964–67; Cambridge Univ., 1968–84; Univ. of Lagos, Nigeria, 1970–71. Editorial Sec., British Jl of Surgery, 1972–78. Royal College of Surgeons: Hunterian Prof., 1953; Mem. Court of Examrs, 1964–70; Mem. Council, 1971–83; Bradshaw Lectr, 1980; Vice-Pres., 1981–83; Cecil Joll Prize, 1984; RCS Visitor to RCOG Council, 1972–80. FRSocMed (Hon. Sec., Section of Surgery, 1963–65, Vice-President, 1966, Pres., 1977; Pres., United Services Section, 1981–83). Fellow Medical Soc. of London (Hon. Sec., 1962–64, Vice-Pres. 1964, Pres., 1976, Fothergill Gold Medal, 1974, Trustee 1988). Pres., Assoc. of Surgeons of GB and Ireland, 1982–83. Mem., Soc. Apothecaries, 1967. Hon. FACS, 1977; Hon. FRACS, 1978; Hon. Fellow: Amer. Surgical Assoc., 1981; Amer. Heart Assoc.; Stroke Council, 1981; Hon. Mem., Purkinje Med. Soc., Czechoslovakia, 1984. Editor, Brit. Jl of Surg., 1973–79. *Publications:* Arterial Surgery, 1969, 3rd edn 1991; A Colour Atlas of Operations on the Internal Carotid Artery, 1984; various articles on gen. and arterial surgery, Lancet, Brit. Jl of Surg., etc.; contrib. chap. of peripheral vascular disease, Med. Annual, 1961–80; various chaps in textbooks on these subjects. *Recreations:* music, travel, and a lifelong interest in aeronautics. *Address:* 47 Chiltern Court, Baker Street, NW1 5SP; 6 Upper Harley Street, NW1 4PS. *T:* 071–935 2020. *Club:* Garrick.

EASTERLING, Prof. Patricia Elizabeth; Professor of Greek, University College London, since 1987; *b* 11 March 1934; *d* of Edward Wilson Fairfax and Annie Smith; *m* 1956, Henry John Easterling; one *s*. *Educ:* Blackburn High School for Girls; Newnham College, Cambridge (BA 1955, MA 1959). Asst Lectr, Univ. of Manchester, 1957–58; University of Cambridge: Asst Lectr, 1968; Lectr, 1969–87; Newnham College, Cambridge: Asst Lectr, 1958–60; Fellow and Lectr, 1960–87; Dir of Studies in Classics, 1979–87; Vice-Principal, 1981–86; Hon. Fellow, 1987. Townsend Lectr, Cornell Univ., 1990. Pres., Classical Assoc., 1988–89. *Publications:* (with E. J. Kenney) Ovidiana Graeca, 1965; (ed) Sophocles, Trachiniae, 1982; (with B. M. W. Knox, ed and contrib.) Cambridge History of Classical Literature, vol I, 1985; (ed with J. V. Muir) Greek Religion and Society, 1985; articles and reviews in classical jls. *Recreation:* hill walking. *Address:* Department of Greek and Latin, University College London, Gower Street, WC1E 6BT. *T:* 071-387 7050.

EASTHAM, Kenneth; MP (Lab) Manchester, Blackley, since 1979; *b* 11 Aug. 1927; *s* of late James Eastham; *m* 1951, Doris, *d* of Albert Howarth. Planning engr, GEC, Trafford Park. Mem., Manchester CC, 1962–80 (Dep. Leader 1975–79; Chairman: Planning Cttee, 1971–74; Educn Cttee, 1978–79); Mem., NW Econ. Planning Council, 1975–79. *Address:* House of Commons, SW1; 12 Nan Nook Road, Manchester M23 9BZ.

EASTHAM, Hon. Sir (Thomas) Michael, Kt 1978; **Hon. Mr Justice Eastham;** a Judge of the High Court of Justice, Family Division, since 1978; *b* 26 June 1920; *y s* of late His Hon. Sir Tom Eastham, QC; *m* 1942, Mary Pamela, *o d* of late Dr H. C. Billings; two *d* (and one *d* decd). *Educ:* Harrow; Trinity Hall, Cambridge. Served with Queen's Royal Regiment, 1940–46 (Capt.). Called to the Bar, Lincoln's Inn, 1947, Bencher, 1972. QC 1964. Recorder: of Deal, 1968–71; of Cambridge, 1971; Hon. Recorder of Cambridge, 1972; a Recorder of the Crown Court, 1972–78. Inspector, Vehicle and General Insurance Company, 1971. *Address:* 7a Porchester Terrace, W2. *T:* 071–723 0770. *Club:* Garrick.

EASTON, David John; HM Diplomatic Service; Foreign and Commonwealth Office, since 1989; *b* 27 March 1941; *o s* of Air Cdre Sir James Easton, KCMG, CB, CBE, and Anna, *d* of Lt-Col J. A. McKenna, Ottawa; *m* 1964, Alexandra Julie, *er d* of K. W. Clark, London, W8; two *s* two *d*. *Educ:* Stone House, Broadstairs; Stowe (Exhbnr); Balliol Coll., Oxford (Trevelyan Schol.; BA Hons Jurisprudence 1963, MA 1973). Apprentice, United Steel Cos, Workington, 1960. TA, 1959–65; 2nd Lieut, Oxford Univ. OTC, 1962; Lieut, Inns of Court and City Yeo., 1964. Entered Foreign Office, 1963; Third Sec., Nairobi, 1965–66; Second Sec., UK Mission to UN, Geneva, 1967–70; MECAS, Lebanon, 1970–72; First Sec., FCO, 1972–73; First Sec. (Information), Tripoli, 1973–77; Defence Dept, FCO, 1977–80; First Sec. (Chancery), later Political Counsellor, Amman, 1980–83; Counsellor, FCO, 1984–86; Counsellor (Political), New Delhi, 1986–89. Director, Internat. Community Sch. (Jordan) Ltd, 1980–83 (Chm. 1981–83). Pres., Delhi Diplomatic Assoc., 1988–89. *Recreations:* swimming, tennis, travel, antiques and antiquities. *Address:* c/o Foreign and Commonwealth Office, King Charles Street, SW1A 2AH.

EASTON, James, OBE 1986; HM Diplomatic Service, retired; Counsellor (Administration) and Consul-General, Brussels, 1987–89; *b* 1 Sept. 1931; *s* of John Easton and Helen Easton (*née* Whitney); *m* 1960, Rosemary Hobbin; one *s* two *d*. *Educ:* St John Cantius Catholic Sch., Broxburn. Served 3rd Hussars, 1952–55. Admiralty, 1957–60; FO, 1960; Prague, 1960–62; Paris, 1963–65; FO, 1965–68; Vice-Consul: Belgrade, 1968–71; La Paz, 1971–74; Second Sec. (Commercial), New York, 1974–78; FCO, 1978–83; First Sec., Rome, 1983–87. *Recreation:* music. *Address:* 6 Cedar Gardens, Sutton, Surrey SM2 5DD. *T:* 081–643 2432.

EASTON, John Francis; Under-Secretary (Legal), Solicitor's Office, Inland Revenue, 1980–88, retired; Chairman (part-time), VAT Tribunals, since 1988; *b* 20 Aug. 1928; *s* of Rev. Cecil Gordon Easton and Nora Gladys Easton (*née* Hall); *m* 1960, Hon. Caroline Ina Maud, *e d* of 9th Baron Hawke; one *s* one *d*. *Educ:* City of London Sch.; Keble Coll., Oxford (MA). Called to Bar, Middle Temple, 1951. National Service, RASC, 1951–53. Joined Inland Revenue Solicitor's Office, 1955. Member, General Synod of Church of England, 1970–75; Licensed Diocesan Reader, dio. of St Albans, 1969–. *Recreations:* Church affairs, foreign languages, swimming. *Address:* The Old Hall, Barley, Royston, Herts SG8 8JA. *T:* Barkway (0763) 848368.

EASTON, Robert Alexander, PhD; Chief Executive, Delta plc, since 1989; *b* 24 Oct. 1948; *s* of Malcolm Edward George Easton and Violet May Liddell (*née* Taylor); *m* 1983, Lynden Anne Welch; one *d*. *Educ:* St Lawrence Coll.; Univ. of Manchester (BSc Hons); Univ. of Aston (PhD). Delta plc, 1974–: Dir, 1985–; Dep. Chief Exec., 1988–89. Director: G. E. Crane Holdings Pty, 1986–; Harrisons & Crosxfield, 1991–. *Recreations:* golf, travel, medieval art. *Address:* c/o Delta plc, 1 Kingsway, WC2B 6XF. *T:* 071–836 3535.

EASTON, Sir Robert (William Simpson), Kt 1990; CBE 1980; CEng, FIMechE, FIMarE, FRINA; Chairman and Managing Director, Yarrow Shipbuilders Ltd, since 1979; Chairman: Clyde Port Authority, since 1983; GEC Scotland, since 1990; *b* 30 Oct. 1922; *s* of James Easton and Helen Agnes (*née* Simpson); *m* 1948, Jean, *d* of H. K. Fraser and Jean (*née* Murray); one *s* one *d*. *Educ:* Royal Technical Coll., Glasgow. Fairfield Shipbuilding Co., 1939–51; Yarrow Shipbuilders Ltd: Manager, 1951; Director, 1965; Dep. Managing Director, 1970; Managing Director, 1977; Main Board Director, Yarrow & Co. Ltd, 1970–77. Vice Pres., Clyde Shipbuilders, 1972–79; Director: Genships (Canada), 1979–80; Supermarine Consortium Ltd, 1986–90. Chairman: Merchants House of Glasgow, 1989; Incorporation of Hammermen, 1989. Member: Council, RINA, 1983–; Worshipful Company of Shipwrights, 1982–. *Recreations:* walking, sailing, golf, gardening. *Address:* Springfield, Stuckenduff, Shandon, Dunbartonshire G84 8NW. *T:* Rhu (0436) 820677. *Clubs:* Caledonian; RNVR (Glasgow).

EASTWOOD, Basil Stephen Talbot; HM Diplomatic Service; Counsellor (Economic and Commercial), Athens, since 1987; *b* 4 March 1944; *s* of late Christopher Gilbert Eastwood, CMG and Catherine Emma (*née* Peel); *m* 1970, Alison Faith Hutchings; four *d*. *Educ:* Eton (KS); Merton College, Oxford. Entered Diplomatic Service, 1966; Middle East Centre for Arab Studies, 1967; Jedda, 1968; Colombo, 1969; Cairo, 1972; Cabinet Office, 1976; FCO, 1978; Bonn, 1980; Khartoum, 1984. *Recreation:* theatre. *Address:* c/o Foreign and Commonwealth Office, SW1A 2AH.

EASTWOOD, (George) Granville, OBE 1973; General Secretary, Printing and Kindred Trades Federation, 1958–73; *b* 26 June 1906; *s* of George and Anne Eastwood, *m* 1st, 1934, Margaret Lambert (*d* 1967); no *c*; 2nd, 1971, Elizabeth Gore Underwood (*d* 1981). *Educ:* Burnley; Compositor, Burnley, 1927; Asst Sec., Printing and Kindred Trades Fedn, 1943–58. Workpeople's Sec., HMSO Deptl Whitley Council, 1958–73; Jt Secretary: Printing and Allied Trades Jt Industrial Council, 1958–66; Jt Bd for Nat. Newspaper Industry, 1965–67. Member: Council, Printing Industry's Research Assoc., 1958–73; City and Guilds of London Inst., 1958–73; Council, Inst. of Printing, 1961–76; ILO Printing Conf., Geneva, 1963; Econ. Develt Cttee for Printing and Publishing, 1966–72; Printing and Publishing Industry Trng Bd, 1968–74; Industrial Arbitration Bd, 1973–76; Editorial Adv. Bd, Ind. Relns Digest, 1973–; DHSS Community Health Council, 1974–76; Advisory, Conciliation and Arbitration Service Panel, 1976–80; toured USA and Europe with EDC Jt Mission, 1968. Governor: Chelsea Sch. of Art, 1963–71; Nat. Heart Hosp., Brompton Hosp. and London Chest Hosp., 1969–76. *Publications:* George Isaacs, 1952; Harold Laski, 1977. *Recreations:* reading, gardening. *Address:* 16 The Vineries, Enfield, Mddx EN1 3DQ. *T:* 081-363 2502.

EASTWOOD, Sir John (Bealby), Kt 1975; DL; Chairman, Adam Eastwood & Sons Ltd, Builders, since 1946; *b* 9 Jan. 1909; *s* of William Eastwood and Elizabeth Townroe Eastwood (*née* Bealby); *m* 1st, 1929, Constance Mary (*née* Tilley) (*d* 1981); two *d*; 2nd, 1983, Mrs Joan Mary McGowan (*d* 1986). *Educ:* Queen Elizabeth's Grammar Sch., Mansfield. Civil Engr and Contractor, 1925; founded W. & J. B. Eastwood Ltd, 1945. DL Notts, 1981. OStJ 1972. *Recreations:* shooting, horse-racing, golf, cricket. *Address:* Hexgreave Hall, Farnsfield, Newark, Notts. *Club:* Farmers'.

EASTWOOD, John Stephen; a Recorder, 1987–Dec. 1992; Regional Chairman of Industrial Tribunals, Nottingham Region, 1983–Apr. 1992; *b* 27 April 1925; *s* of Rev. John Edgar Eastwood and Elfreda Eastwood; *m* 1949, Nancy (*née* Gretton); one *s* two *d*. *Educ:* Denstone College, Uttoxeter. Solicitor. RN (Coder), 1943–46. Articles, and Asst Sol. to Leics CC, 1946–50; Asst Sol., Salop CC, 1950–53; Sen. Asst Sol., Northants CC, 1953–58; Partner, Wilson & Wilson, Solicitors, Kettering, 1958–76; Chm., Industrial Tribunals, 1976–83; Asst Recorder, 1983–87. *Recreations:* music, painting, photography, walking, gardening, exploring British Isles, grandchildren. *Address:* 20 Gipsy Lane, Kettering, Northants NN16 8TY. *T:* Kettering (0536) 85612.

EASTWOOD, Noel Anthony Michael, MA; CEng, MRAeS; Chairman, InterData Group, since 1981; *b* 7 Dec. 1932; *s* of Edward Norman Eastwood and Irene Dawson; *m* 1965, Elizabeth Tania Gresham Boyd, *d* of Comdr Thomas Wilson Boyd, CBE, DSO, DL and Irene Barbara Gresham; three *s*. *Educ:* The Leys School, Cambridge; Christ's College, Cambridge. Lieut RA, 1951–53; Pilot Officer, RAFVR, 1954–57; de Havilland Aircraft Co., 1956–60; RTZ Group, 1960–61; AEI Group, 1961–64; Director: Charterhouse Development, 1964–69; Charterhouse Japhet, 1969–79 (Pres., Charterhouse Japhet Texas, 1974–77); Charterhouse Middle East, 1975–79; Wharton Crane & Hoist, 1967–70 (Chm.); Daniel Doncaster & Son, 1971–81; The Barden Corp., 1971–82; Hawk Publishing (UAE), 1981–87; Oryx Publishing (Qatar), 1981–87; Falcon Publishing (Bahrain), 1981–84; Caribbean Publishing, 1981–84; IDP InterData (Australia), 1984–; Ergo Communication Services, 1987–; Spearhead Communications, 1988–; Community Trade Advisers, 1989–; SWB Fishing (Falkland Is), 1990–. Mem. London Cttee, Yorkshire & Humberside Development Assoc., 1975–. Sec., RAeS, 1983. *Recreations:* vintage sportscars, family picnics, desert travel. *Address:* Palace House, Much Hadham, Herts SG10 6HW. *T:* Much Hadham (027984) 2409. *Club:* Royal Thames Yacht.

EASTWOOD, Dr Wilfred, PhD; FEng, FICE, FIStructE, FIMechE; Senior Partner, Eastwood and Partners, Consulting Engineers, since 1972; *b* 15 Aug. 1923; *s* of Wilfred Andrew Eastwood and Annice Gertrude Eastwood; *m* 1947, Dorothy Jean Gover; one *s* one *d*. Road Research Laboratory, 1945–46; University of Manchester, 1946–47; University of Aberdeen, 1947–53; University of Sheffield, 1954–70: Head, Dept of Civil Engrg, 1964–70; Dean, Faculty of Engrg, 1967–70. Pres., IStructE, 1976–77; Chairman: CEI, 1983–84; Commonwealth Engrg Council, 1983–85. Hon. DEng Sheffield, 1983. *Publications:* papers in Proc. ICE and Jl IStructE, etc. *Address:* 45 Whirlow Park Road, Sheffield S11 9NN. *T:* Sheffield (0742) 364645. *Club:* Yorkshire County Cricket (Leeds).

EASTY, Prof. David Leohello, MD; FRCS, FCOphth; Professor of Ophthalmology and Head of Department of Ophthalmology, University of Bristol, since 1982; *b* 1933; *s* of Arthur Victor Easty and Florence Margaret (*née* Kennedy); *m* 1963, Božana Martinović; three *d*. *Educ:* King's Sch., Canterbury; Univ. of Manchester. MD 1963; FRCS 1969; FCOphth 1988. Capt., RAMC, 1959; Med. Officer, British Antarctic Survey, 1960. Moorfield's Eye Hospital: Resident, 1966–69; Lectr, 1969–72; Consultant, Bristol Eye Hosp., 1972–82. Dir, Corneal Transplant Service Eye Bank, 1986–. Member: BMA; RSocMed; Internat. Soc. for Eye Res.; Assoc. for Res. in Vision and Ophthalmology; British Soc. for Immunology. Member: Antarctic Club; Piscatorial Soc. *Publications:* Virus Disease of the Eye, 1985; (with G. Smolim) External Eye Disease, 1985; (ed) Current Ophthalmic Surgery, 1990; (with N. Ragge) Immediate Eye Care, 1990. *Recreations:* fishing, squash, running, opera. *Address:* Bristol Eye Hospital, Lower Maudlim Street, Bristol BS1 2LX. *T:* Bristol (0272) 230060. *Clubs:* Army and Navy; Clifton (Bristol).

EATES, Edward Caston, CMG 1968; LVO 1961; QPM 1961; CPM 1956; Commissioner, The Royal Hong Kong Police, 1967–69, retired; re-employed at Foreign and Commonwealth Office, 1971–76; *b* London, 8 April 1916; *o s* of late Edward Eates and Elizabeth Lavinia Issac Eates (*née* Caston); *m* 1941, Maureen Teresa McGee (*d* 1987); no *c*. *Educ:* Highgate Sch.; King's Coll., London (LLB). Asst Examr, Estate Duty Office, 1935. Army, 1939–46 (RAC): Western Desert and NW Europe; Adjt 2nd Derby Yeo., 1943; Temp. Maj. 1944; Staff Coll. Quetta (sc), 1945. Apptd to Colonial Police Service, Nigeria, 1946; Sen. Supt, Sierra Leone, 1954; Comr, The Gambia, 1957; Asst Comr, 1963, Dep. Comr, 1966, Hong Kong. *Recreations:* cricket and association football (inactive); travel, motoring. *Address:* 2 Riverside Court, Colleton Crescent, Exeter EX2 4BZ. *T:* Exeter (0392) 436434. *Clubs:* Commonwealth Trust, East India; Surrey County Cricket.

EATHER, Maj.-Gen. Kenneth William, CB 1947; CBE 1943; DSO 1941; Executive Director, Water Research Foundation of Australia, 1958–79; *b* 1901; *m* 1st, 1924, Adeline Mabel, *d* of Gustavus Lewis; one *s* one *d*; 2nd, 1968, Kathleen, *d* of M. F. Carroll. Served War of 1939–45; AMF, Middle East and SW Pacific (despatches, DSO, CBE). *Club:* Imperial Service (Sydney).

EATOCK TAYLOR, Prof. (William) Rodney, FEng 1990; Professor of Mechanical Engineering, and Fellow of St Hugh's College, Oxford, since 1989; *b* 10 Jan. 1944; *s* of William Taylor, Hadley Wood, Herts and Norah O'Brien Taylor (*née* Ridgeway); *m* 1971, Jacqueline Lorraine Cannon, *d* of late Desmond Cannon Brookes; two *s*. *Educ:* Rugby Sch.; King's Coll., Cambridge (BA, MA); Stanford Univ. (MS, PhD). FRINA 1986; FIMechE 1989. Engineer, Ove Arup and Partners, 1968–70; University College London: Res. Asst, 1970; Lectr, 1972; Reader, 1980; Prof. of Ocean Engineering, 1984–89; Dean, Faculty of Engineering, 1988–89. Dir, Marine Technology Directorate Ltd, 1990–. Member, Editorial Boards: Engineering Structures, 1978–; Applied Ocean Research, 1984–; Jl of Fluids and Structures, 1990–. *Publications:* numerous contribs to learned jls of structural dynamics and marine hydrodynamics. *Recreations:* walking, music. *Address:* St Hugh's College, Oxford OX2 6LE. *T:* Oxford (0865) 274912. *Club:* Athenæum.

EATON, Air Vice-Marshal Brian Alexander, CB 1969; CBE 1959; DSO and Bar, DFC, American Silver Star; *b* Launceston, Tas, 15 Dec. 1916; *s* of S. A. Eaton; *m* 1952, Josephine Rumbles; one *s* two *d*. *Educ:* Carey Grammar Sch., Melbourne; RAAF Coll., Pt Cook. Served war of 1939–45: Co 3 Sqdn N Africa-Medit., 1943, CO 239 Wing RAF Italy, 1944–45. UK, 1945–46; OC 81 Fighter Wing, Japan, 1948; OC BCAIR, 1948–49; OC 78 Wing Malta, 1952–54; Dir of Ops, RAAF HQ, 1955; OC Williamtown RAAF and Comdt Sch. of Land-Air Warfare, 1957–58; Dir Joint Service Plans, 1959–60; Imp. Defence Coll., 1961; Dir-Gen. of Operational Requirements, 1962; Deputy Chief of Air Staff, 1966–67; AOC HQ 224 Mobile Group (RAF) Far East Air Force, Singapore, 1967–68; Chief of Staff HQFEAF, 1968–69; Air Mem. for Personnel, Dept of Air, Canberra, 1969–73; AOC Operational Comd, RAAF, 1973–74. *Recreations:* shooting, fishing. *Address:* 125 Mugga Way, Red Hill, ACT 2603, Australia. *Club:* Commonwealth (Canberra).

EATON, Rt. Rev. Derek Lionel; *see* Nelson, NZ, Bishop of.

EATON, James Thompson, TD 1963; Lord-Lieutenant, City of Londonderry, since 1986; *b* 11 Aug. 1927; *s* of late J. C. Eaton, DL, and Mrs E. A. F. Eaton, MBE; *m* 1954, Lucy Edith Smeeton, OBE 1986; one *s* one *d*. *Educ:* Campbell Coll., Belfast; Royal Technical Coll., Glasgow. Man. Dir, Eaton & Co. Ltd, 1965–80. Mem., Londonderry Develt Commn, 1969–73 (Chm., Educn Cttee, 1969–73); Chm., Londonderry Port and Harbour Comrs, 1989– (Mem., 1977–; Vice Chm., 1985). Served North Irish Horse (TA), 1950–67 (Major, 1961). High Sheriff, Co. Londonderry, 1982. *Recreations:* military history, gardening. *Address:* Ballyowen House, Londonderry, Northern Ireland. *T:* Londonderry (0504) 860372.

EATON, Vice-Adm. Sir Kenneth (John), KCB 1990; CEng, FIEE; Controller of the Navy, since 1989; *b* 12 Aug. 1934; *s* of John and May Eaton; *m* 1959, Sheena Buttle; two *s* one *d*. *Educ:* Borden Grammar Sch.; Fitzwilliam Coll., Cambridge (BA). FIEE 1989. HMS Victorious, 1959–61; ASWE, 1961–65; HM Ships Eagle, Collingwood and Bristol, 1965–71; Defence Communications Network, 1971–72; ASWE, 1972–76; HMS Ark Royal, 1976–78; MoD, 1978–81; ASWE, 1981–83; Dir Torpedoes, 1983–85; Dir-Gen. Underwater Weapons (Navy), 1985–87; Flag Officer, Portsmouth, and Naval Base Comdr, Portsmouth, 1987–89. *Recreations:* countryside, theatre, opera, classical music. *Address:* c/o Naval Secretary, Old Admiralty Building, Spring Gardens, SW1A 2BE.

EATON, Peter; owner of the largest antiquarian bookstore in England; *b* 24 Jan. 1914; *m* 1st, Ann Wilkinson; 2nd, Valerie Carruthers; two *s*; 3rd, Margaret Taylor; two *d*. *Educ:* elementary sch.; Municipal Sch. (later Coll.) of Technology, Manchester Univ. (expelled). Born in London at 8 York Gate, Regent's Park; advertised for adoption in Nursing Times, Feb. 1914; brought up in Rochdale, where became apprentice printer; became a tramp; in London, later helped found now defunct Domestic Workers Union; advised on start of Tribune newspaper; mem. of Labour Party for 40 yrs; Conscientious Objector, tried at Royal Courts of Justice, 1939; voluntarily joined London Rescue Squad for duration of War and helped Bomb Disposal Squad; started bookselling in Portobello Road when it was predominantly a fruit and vegetable market, 1945; bought Queen Victoria's books from Kensington Palace (now in Victoria State Library, Australia); bought part or all of libraries of Bernard Shaw, H. G. Wells, Marie Stopes and R. H. Tawney; formed many important collections of books, incl. world's largest collection of books on the atom (now in Texas Univ.). Pres., Private Libraries Assoc., 1989–Apr. 1992. Travelled in many parts of the world, incl. Alaska, India and African jungles; FRGS 1950. *Publications:* Marie Stopes: a bibliographical list of her books, 1977; History of Lilies, 1982; articles in trade jls. *Recreations:* taking the dog for a walk, watching my wife play tennis. *Address:* Lilies, Weedon, Aylesbury, Bucks HP22 4NS. *T:* Aylesbury (0296) 641393. *Club:* Reform.

EAYRS, Prof. John Thomas, PhD, DSc; Sands Cox Professor of Anatomy, University of Birmingham, 1968–77; *b* 23 Jan. 1913; *e s* of late Thomas William Eayrs, AMICE, and late Florence May (*née* Clough); *m* 1941, Frances Marjorie Sharp; one *s* two *d. Educ:* King Edward's, Birmingham; University of Birmingham. In industry until 1938. War service: Pte Royal Warwicks Regt, 1939–40; 2nd Lieut Manchester Regt, 1940; Lieut 1940; Capt. 1941; Major 1942; Worcester Regt, 1943; sc Staff Coll., Camberley, 1944. University of Birmingham: Peter Thompson Prize, 1947; John Barritt Melson Memorial Gold Medal, 1947; Lectr in Anatomy, 1948; Bertram Windle Prize, 1950; Sen. Lectr 1955; Research Fellow, Calif. Inst. of Technology, 1956–57; Reader in Comparative Neurology, Birmingham, 1958; Henry Head Research Fellow, Royal Society, London, 1957–62; Prof. of Neuroendocrinology, Birmingham, 1961; Fitzmary Prof. of Physiology, London Univ., 1963–68. Governor, King Edward's Foundn, Birmingham, 1968–77. *Publications:* Scientific Papers dealing with developmental neuroendocrinology and behaviour in Jl Endocrin., Jl Anat. (London), Anim. Behav., etc. *Recreations:* cruising, foreign travel and languages. *Address:* 51 Old Street, Upton upon Severn, Worcester WR8 0HN.

EBAN, Abba; a Member of the Knesset, 1959–88; Minister of Foreign Affairs, Israel, 1966–74; *b* 2 Feb. 1915, Cape Town, SA; *s* of Avram and Alida Solomon; *m* 1945, Susan Ambache; one *s* one *d. Educ:* Cambridge Univ. (MA). Res. Fellow and Tutor for Oriental Languages, Pembroke Coll., Cambridge, 1938. Liaison officer of Allied HQ with Jewish population in Jerusalem, 1942–44; Chief Instructor, Middle East Arab Centre, Jerusalem, 1944–46; Jewish Agency, 1946–47; Liaison Officer with UN Special Commn on Palestine, 1947; UN: Representative of provisional govt of Israel, 1948; Permanent rep., 1949–59; Vice-Pres., General Assembly, 1953; Ambassador to USA, 1950–59; Minister without Portfolio, 1959–60; Minister of Educn and Culture, 1960–63; Dep. Prime Minister, 1963–66. Pres., Weizmann Inst. of Science, 1958–66; Vice-Pres., UN Conf. on Science and Technology in Advancement of New States, 1963; Mem., UN Adv. Cttee on Science and Technology for Develt. Fellow: World Acad. of Arts and Sciences; Amer. Acad. of Arts and Sciences; Amer. Acad. of Pol Science. Hon. Doctorates include: New York; Boston; Maryland; Cincinnati; Temple; Brandeis; Yeshiva. *Publications:* The Modern Literary Movement in Egypt, 1944; Maze of Justice, 1946; Social and Cultural Problems in the Middle East, 1947; The Toynbee Heresy, 1955; Voice of Israel, 1957; Tide of Nationalism, 1959; Chaim Weizmann: a collective biography, 1962; Reality and Vision in the Middle East (Foreign Affairs), 1965; Israel in the World, 1966; My People, 1968; My Country, 1972; An Autobiography, 1978; The New Diplomacy: international affairs in the modern age, 1983; Heritage, Civilisation and the Jews, 1985; articles in English, French, Hebrew and Arabic. *Address:* PO Box 394, Herzliya, Israel.

EBERHART, Richard (Ghormley); Professor Emeritus of English and Poet in Residence, Dartmouth College, USA; Florida Ambassador of the Arts, since 1984; *b* Austin, Minn, 5 April 1904; *s* of late Alpha La Rue Eberhart and late Lena Eberhart (*née* Lowenstein); *m* 1941, Helen Elizabeth Butcher, Christ Church, Cambridge, Mass; one *s* one *d. Educ:* Dartmouth Coll., USA (AB); St John's Coll., Cambridge Univ., England (BA, MA; Hon. Fellow, 1986); Harvard Univ. Grad. Sch. of Arts and Sciences. Taught English, 1933–41, also tutor to son of King Prajadhipok of Siam for a year. Served War in USN Reserve finishing as Lieut-Comdr, 1946; subseq. entered Butcher Polish Co., Boston, Mass, as Asst Man., finishing as Vice-Pres. (now Hon. Vice-Pres. and Mem. Bd of Directors). Founder (and first Pres.) Poets' Theatre Inc., Cambridge, Mass, 1950. Called back to teaching, 1952, and has served as Poet in Residence, Prof., or Lecturer at University of Washington, University of Conn., Wheaton Coll., Princeton, and in 1956 was apptd Prof. of English and Poet in Residence at Dartmouth Coll. Class of 1925 Chair, 1968 (being absent as Consultant in Poetry to the Library of Congress, 1959–61). Visiting Professor: Univ. of Washington, 1967, Jan.-June 1972; Columbia Univ., 1975; Distinguished Vis. Prof., Florida Univ., 1974– (President's Medallion, 1977); Regents Prof., Univ. of California, Davis, 1975; First Wallace Stevens Fellow, Timothy Dwight Coll., Yale, 1976. Shelley Memorial Prize; Bollingen Prize, 1962; Pulitzer Prize, 1966; Fellow, Acad. of Amer. Poets, 1969 (Nat. Book Award, 1977). Advisory Cttee on the Arts, for the National Cultural Center (later John F. Kennedy Memorial Center), Washington, 1959; Member: Amer. Acad. and Inst. of Arts and Letters, 1960; Nat. Acad. of Arts and Sciences, 1967; Amer. Acad. of Arts and Letters, 1982; Elliston Lecturer on Poetry, University of Cincinnati, 1961. Poet Laureate of New Hampshire, 1979–84. Apptd Hon. Consultant in American Letters, The Library of Congress, 1963–66, reapptd, 1966–69. Hon. Pres., Poetry Soc. of America, 1972. Participant, Poetry International, London, 1973; Exhibn, Dartmouth Coll. Library, 1984. Hon. LittD: Dartmouth Coll., 1954; Skidmore Coll., 1966; Coll. of Wooster, 1969; Colgate Univ., 1974; St Lawrence Univ., 1985; Hon. DHL, Franklin Pierce, 1978. Phi Beta Kappa poem, Harvard, 1967; Hon. Mem., Alpha Chapter, Mass, 1967; New York Qly Poetry Day Award, 1980; Sarah Josepha Hale Award, Richards Library, Newport, NH, 1982; Robert Frost Medal, Poetry Soc. of America, 1986. Diploma: World Acad. of Arts and Culture, Republic of China, 1981; Internat. Poets Acad., Madras, India, 1987. Richard Eberhart Day: 14 July 1982, RI; 14 Oct. 1982, Dartmouth; Eberhart at Eighty, celebration at Univ. of Florida, 4–6 April 1984. *Publications:* (concurrently in England and America): A Bravery of Earth, 1930; Reading the Spirit, 1936; Selected Poems, 1951; Undercliff, Poems, 1946–53, also Great Praises, 1957; Collected Poems, 1930–60, 1960; Collected Verse Plays, 1962; The Quarry, 1964; Selected Poems, 1930–65, New Directions, 1965; Thirty One Sonnets, 1967; Shifts of Being, 1968; Fields of Grace, 1972 (Nat. Book Award nominee, 1973); Poems to Poets, 1975; Collected Poems 1930–1976, 1976; Collected Poems 1930–86, 1988; To Eberhart from Ginsberg: a letter about 'Howl', 1956, 1976; Of Poetry and Poets (criticism), 1979; Ways of Light, 1980; Survivors, 1980; Four Poems, 1980; New Hampshire/Nine Poems, 1980; Chocorua, 1981; Florida Poems, 1981; The Long Reach, 1984; Maine Poems, 1989; New and Collected Poems, 1990; Recorded Readings of his Poetry, 1961, 1968; four documentary films, 1972, 1975, 1986, 1987; *Festschriften:* (in New England Review, 1980) Richard Eberhart: A Celebration; (in Negative Capability, 1986) Richard Eberhart. *Recreations:* swimming, cruising, tennis, flying 7–ft kites. *Address:* 5 Webster Terrace, Hanover, New Hampshire 03755, USA. *Clubs:* Century (New York); Buck's Harbor Yacht (S Brooksville, Maine); Signet (Harvard).

EBERLE, Adm. Sir James (Henry Fuller), GCB 1981 (KCB 1979); Rear Admiral of the United Kingdom, since 1990; Director, Royal Institute of International Affairs, 1984–90; writer on international affairs and security; *b* 31 May 1927; *s* of late Victor Fuller Eberle and of Joyce Mary Eberle, Bristol; *m* 1950, Ann Patricia Thompson (*d* 1988), Hong Kong; one *s* two *d. Educ:* Clifton Coll.; RNC Dartmouth and Greenwich. Served War of 1939–45 in MTBs, HMS Renown, HMS Belfast; subseq. in Far East; qual. Gunnery Specialist 1951; Guided Missile Develt and trials in UK and USA, 1953–57; Naval Staff, 1960–62; Exec. Officer, HMS Eagle, 1963–65; comd HMS Intrepid, 1968–70; Asst Chief of Fleet Support, MoD (RN), 1971–74; Flag Officer Sea Training, 1974–75; Flag Officer Carriers and Amphibious Ships, 1975–77; Chief of Fleet Support, 1977–79; C-in-C, Fleet, and Allied C-in-C, Channel and Eastern Atlantic, 1979–81; C-in-C, Naval Home Comd, 1981–82, retired 1983. Vice-Pres., RUSI, 1979. Freeman: Bristol, 1946; London, 1982. Hon. LLD Bristol, 1989. *Publications:* Management in the Armed Forces, 1972; Jim, First of the Pack, 1982; Britain's Future in Space, 1988. *Recreations:* hunting (Master of Britannia Beagles), tennis. *Address:* c/o Royal Institute of International Affairs, Chatham House, St James's Square, SW1Y 4LE. *Clubs:* Farmers'; Society of Merchant Venturers (Bristol); All England Lawn Tennis.

EBERT, Peter; producer; *b* 6 April 1918; *s* of Carl Ebert, CBE, and Lucie Oppenheim; *m* 1st, 1944, Kathleen Havinden; two *d*; 2nd, 1951, Silvia Ashmole; five *s* three *d. Educ:* Salem Sch., Germany; Gordonstoun, Scotland. BBC Producer, 1948–51; 1st opera production, Mefistofele, Glasgow, 1951; Mozart and Rossini guest productions: Rome, Naples, Venice, 1951, 1952, 1954, 1955: Wexford Festival: 12 prods, 1952–65; 1st Glyndebourne Fest. prod., Ariecchino, 1954, followed by Seraglio, Don Giovanni, etc.; 1st Edinburgh Fest. prod., Forza del Destino, 1955; Chief producer: Hannover State Opera, 1954–60; Düsseldorf Opera, 1960–62; directed opera class, Hannover State Conservatory, 1954–60; Head of Opera studio, Düsseldorf, 1960–62. Guest productions in Europe, USA, Canada. TV productions of Glyndebourne operas, 1955–64; 1st TV studio prod., 1963; Opera Adviser to BBC TV, 1964–65; Dir of Productions, 1965–77, Gen. Administrator, 1977–80, Scottish Opera Co. First drama prod., The Devils, Johannesburg, 1966; first musical, Houdini, London, 1966. Dir, Opera Sch., University of Toronto, 1967–68; Intendant: Stadttheater, Augsburg, 1968–73; Stadttheater Bielefeld, 1973–75; Staatstheater Wiesbaden, 1975–77. Hon. DMus St Andrews, 1979. *Recreation:* raising a family. *Address:* Col di Mura, Lippiano, 06010 (PG), Italy.

EBERTS, John David, (Jake); Founder, 1985, and Chief Executive, since 1985, Allied Filmmakers; *b* 10 July 1941; *s* of Edmond Howard Eberts and Elizabeth Evelyn MacDougall; *m* 1968, Fiona Louise Leckie; two *s* one *d. Educ:* McGill Univ. (BChemEng 1962); Harvard Univ. (MBA 1966). Project Engr, l'Air Liquide, Paris, 1962–64; Marketing Manager, Cummins Engine Co., Brussels, 1966–68; Vice Pres., Laird Inc., NY, 1968–71; Man. Dir, Oppenheimer and Co. Ltd, London, 1971–76; Founder, 1976, and Chief Exec., 1976–83 and 1985–86, Goldcrest Films and Television Ltd; Pres., Embassy Communications International, 1984–85. Involved in prodn of many BAFTA and Amer. Acad. award-winning films, including: Chariots of Fire; Gandhi; The Dresser; The Killing Fields; The Name of the Rose; Hope and Glory; Driving Miss Daisy; Dances with Wolves. Film Producers' Award of Merit, 1986; Evening Standard Special Award, 1987. *Publication:* (with Terry Ilott) My Indecision is Final, 1990. *Recreations:* tennis, skiing, photography. *Clubs:* Queen's; North Hatley (Quebec).

EBRAHIM, Sir (Mahomed) Currimbhoy, 4th Bt, *cr* 1910; BA, LLB, Advocate, Pakistan; Member, Standing Council of the Baronetage, 1961; *b* 24 June 1935; *o s* of Sir (Huseinali) Currimbhoy Ebrahim, 3rd Bt, and Alhaja Lady Amina Khanum, *d* of Alhaj Cassumali Jairajbhoy; *S* father 1952; *m* 1958, Dur-e-Mariam, *d* of Minuchehir Ahmud Ghulamaly Nana; three *s* one *d. Recreations:* tennis (Karachi University No 1, 1957, No 2, 1958), cricket, table-tennis, squash, reading (literary), art, poetry writing, debate, quotation writing. *Heir: s* Zulfiqar Ali Currimbhoy Ebrahim, *b* 5 Aug. 1960.

EBRINGTON, Viscount; Charles Hugh Richard Fortescue; *b* 10 May 1951; *s* and *heir* of 7th Earl Fortescue, *qv*; *m* 1974, Julia, *er d* of Air Commodore J. A. Sowrey; three *d.*

EBSWORTH, Ann Marian; Her Honour Judge Ebsworth; a Circuit Judge, since 1983; *b* 19 May 1937; *d* of Arthur E. Ebsworth, OBE, BEM, RM (retd) and late Hilda Mary Ebsworth. *Educ:* Notre Dame Convent, Worth, Sussex; Portsmouth High Sch., GPDST; London Univ. BA Hons (History). Called to Bar, Gray's Inn, 1962; a Recorder of the Crown Court, 1978–83. *Recreations:* Italian travel, medieval history, needlework. *T:* 051–639 1579. *Club:* Commonwealth Trust.

EBSWORTH, Prof. Evelyn Algernon Valentine, PhD, ScD; FRCS, FRSE; Vice-Chancellor, Durham University, since 1990; *b* 14 Feb. 1933; *s* of Wilfred Algernon Ebsworth and Cynthia (*née* Blech); *m* 1st, 1955, Mary Salter (*d* 1987); one *s* three *d*; 2nd, 1990, Rose Zuckerman. *Educ:* King's Coll., Cambridge (BA 1st Cl., 1954; PhD 1957; MA 1958; ScD 1967). FRSE 1969. Fellow, King's Coll., Cambridge, 1957–59; Res. Associate, Princeton Univ., 1958–59; Cambridge University: Demonstrator, 1959–63; Lectr, 1963–67; Fellow, 1959–67, Tutor, 1963–67, Christ's Coll.; Crum Brown Prof. of Chemistry, Edinburgh, 1967–90. Corresp. Mem., Acad. of Scis, Göttingen. *Publications:* Volatile Silicon Compounds, 1963; (with S. Cradock and D. W. H. Rankin) Structural Methods in Inorganic Chemistry, 1988; papers in learned jls. *Recreations:* opera, gardening. *Address:* University of Durham, Old Shire Hall, Durham DH1 3HP.

EBURNE, Sir Sidney (Alfred William), Kt 1983; MC 1944; Senior Crown Agent and Chairman of the Crown Agents for Oversea Governments and Administrations, 1978–83; *b* 26 Nov. 1918; *s* of Alfred Edmund Eburne and Ellen Francis Eburne; *m* 1942, Phoebe Freda (*née* Beeton Dilley); one *s* one *d. Educ:* Downhills School. Served War, 1939–46; Captain, RA. Joined Morgan Grenfell & Co. Ltd, 1946; Director: Morgan Grenfell & Co. Ltd, 1968–75; Morgan Grenfell Holdings Ltd, 1971–75; Peachey Property Corp. Ltd, 1983–88. Crown Agents: Dir of Finance, 1975; Man. Dir, 1976. Governor, Peabody Trust, 1984. *Recreations:* golf, travelling. *Address:* Motts Farm, Eridge, East Sussex TN3 9LJ. *Club:* Carlton.

EBURY, 6th Baron, *cr* 1857; **Francis Egerton Grosvenor;** *b* 8 Feb. 1934; *s* of 5th Baron Ebury, DSO and Ann Acland-Troyte; *heir-pres.* to 7th Earl of Wilton, *qv*; *S* father 1957; *m* 1st, 1957, Gillian Elfrida (Elfin) (marr. diss. 1962), *d* of Martin Soames, London; one *s*; 2nd, 1963, Kyra (marr. diss. 1973), *d* of late L. L. Aslin; 3rd, 1974, Suzanne Jean, *d* of Graham Suckling, Christchurch, NZ; one *d. Educ:* Eton. *Recreation:* ornithology. *Heir: s* Hon. Julian Francis Martin Grosvenor [*b* 8 June 1959; *m* 1987, Danielle, sixth *d* of Theo Rossi, Sydney, Australia]. *Address:* 8B Branksome Tower, 3 Tregunter Path, Hong Kong. *Clubs:* Melbourne, Melbourne Savage (Melbourne); Hong Kong.

ECCLES, family name of **Viscount Eccles** and **Baroness Eccles of Moulton.**

ECCLES, 1st Viscount, *cr* 1964; 1st Baron, *cr* 1962; **David McAdam Eccles,** CH 1984; KCVO 1953; PC 1951; MA Oxon; *b* 18 Sept. 1904; *s* of late W. McAdam Eccles, FRCS and Anna Coralie, *d* of E. B. Anstie, JP; *m* 1st, 1928, Sybil (*d* 1977), *e d* of Viscount Dawson of Penn, PC, GCVO, KCB, KCMG; two *s* one *d*; 2nd, 1984, Mrs Donald Hyde, Somerville, NJ. *Educ:* Winchester, New Coll., Oxford. Joined Ministry of Economic Warfare, Sept. 1939; Economic Adviser to HM Ambassadors at Madrid and Lisbon, 1940–42; Ministry of Production, 1942–43. MP (C) Chippenham Div. of Wilts, 1943–62; Minister of Works, 1951–54; Minister of Education, 1954–57; Pres. of the Board of Trade, 1957–59; Minister of Education, Oct. 1959–July 1962; Paymaster-General, with responsibility for the arts, 1970–73. Trustee, British Museum, 1963–, Chm. of Trustees, 1968–70; Chm., British Liby Bd, 1973–78. Dir, Courtaulds, 1962–70. Chm., Anglo-Hellenic League, 1967–70. Pres., World Crafts Council, 1974–78. Hon. Fellow, RIBA; Sen. Fellow, RCA. *Publications:* Half-Way to Faith, 1966; Life and Politics: A Moral Diagnosis, 1967; On Collecting, 1968; By Safe Hand: Letters of Sybil and David Eccles 1939–42, 1983. *Heir: s* Hon. John Dawson Eccles, *qv. Address:* Dean Farm, Chute, near Andover, Hants; *T:* Chute Standen (026470) 210; 6 Barton Street, SW1. *T:* 071–222 1387. *Clubs:* Brooks's, Roxburghe; Knickerbocker, Grolier (New York).

ECCLES OF MOULTON, Baroness *cr* 1990 (Life Peer), of Moulton in the County of North Yorkshire; **Diana Catherine Eccles;** Chairman, Ealing District Health Authority, since 1988; Member, Teesside Urban Development Corporation, since 1987; *b* 4 Oct. 1933; *d* of late Raymond Sturge and of Margaret Sturge; *m* 1955, Hon. John Dawson Eccles, *qv*; one *s* three *d*. *Educ:* St James's Sch., West Malvern; Open Univ. (BA). Voluntary work, Middlesbrough Community Council, 1955–58; Partner, Gray Design Associates, 1963–77. Director: Tyne Tees Television, 1986–; J . Sainsbury, 1986–; Yorkshire Electricity Gp, 1990–; Member: North Eastern Electricity Bd, 1974–85; British Railways Eastern Bd, 1986–; Yorkshire Electricity Bd, 1989–90. Member: Adv. Council for Energy Conservation, 1982–84; Widdicombe Inquiry into Local Govt, 1985–86; Home Office Adv. Panel on Licences for Experimental Community Radio, 1985–86; Unrelated Live Transplant Regulatory Authority, 1990–. Vice Chairman: Nat. Council for Voluntary Orgns, 1981–87; Durham Univ. Council, 1985– (Lay Mem., 1981–85); Chm., Tyne Tees Television Programme Consultative Council, 1982–84. Trustee, Charities Aid Foundn, 1982–89. *Address:* Moulton Hall, Richmond, N Yorks DL10 6QH. *T:* Darlington (0325) 377227; 6 Barton Street, Westminster SW1P 3NG. *T:* 071–222 7559.

ECCLES, Geoffrey, OBE 1986; CEng; Regional Chairman, British Gas plc, Eastern, 1987–90; *b* 25 Dec. 1925; *s* of George William Eccles and Elsie Eccles (*née* Hepworth); *m* 1946, Marjorie Jackson; one *s*. *Educ:* Halifax and Bradford Colls of Technol. MIGasE. West Midlands Gas Board: various technical and managerial appts, incl. Asst Regl Distribution Engr, 1964; Grid Engr, 1967; Dep. Pipelines Engr, Gas Council, 1971; Pipelines Engr, British Gas Corp., 1980; Dep. Chm., Eastern Gas, 1984. *Recreations:* hill walking, reading, music. *Address:* 3 Little Gaddesden House, Little Gaddesden, Berkhamsted, Herts HP4 1PL. *T:* Little Gaddesden (044284) 2731.

ECCLES, (Hugh William) Patrick; QC 1990; a Recorder, since 1987; *b* 25 April 1946; *s* of Gp Captain (retd) Hugh Haslett Eccles and Mary Eccles; *m* 1972, Rhoda Ann Eccles (*née* Moroney); three *d*. *Educ:* Stonyhurst Coll.; Exeter Coll., Oxford (MA). Called to the Bar, Middle Temple, 1968; practising barrister, head of chambers, 1985–. Mem., County Court Rule Cttee, 1986–. *Recreations:* tennis, wine, P. G. Wodehouse. *Address:* Grapevine Cottage, High Street, Long Wittenham, Oxon OX14 4QQ. *T:* Clifton Hampden (086730) 7436.

ECCLES, Jack Fleming, CBE 1980; retired trade union official; *b* 9 Feb. 1922; *s* of Tom and Dora Eccles; *m* 1952, Milba Hartley Williamson; one *s* one *d*. *Educ:* Chorlton High Sch.; Univ. of Manchester. BA (Com). Gen. and Municipal Workers Union: District Organiser, 1948–60; Nat. Industrial Officer, 1960–66; Regional Sec. (Lancs), 1966–86. Trades Union Congress: Gen. Council, 1973–86; Chm., 1984–85; Pres., 1985. Non-Executive Director: Remploy Ltd, 1976–90; English Industrial Estates, 1976–; Plastics Processing ITB, 1982–88 (Chm.); British Steel plc (formerly BSC), 1986–. *Recreations:* motoring, ciné photography. *Address:* Terange, 11 Sutton Road, Alderley Edge, Cheshire SK9 7RB. *T:* Alderley Edge (0625) 583684.

ECCLES, Sir John Carew, AC 1990; Kt 1958; FRS 1941; FRSNZ; FAA; *b* 27 Jan. 1903; *s* of William James and Mary Eccles; *m* 1st, 1928, Irene Frances Miller (marr. diss. 1968); four *s* five *d*; 2nd, 1968, Helena Táboříková. *Educ:* Melbourne Univ.; Magdalen Coll., Oxford. Melbourne University: 1st class Hons MB, BS 1925; Victorian Rhodes Scholar, 1925. Univ. of Oxford: Christopher Welch Scholar; 1st class Hons Natural Science (Physiology), 1927; MA 1929; DPhil 1929; Gotch Memorial Prize, 1927; Rolleston Memorial Prize, 1932. Junior Res. Fellow, Exeter Coll., Oxford, 1927–32; Staines Med. Fellow, Exeter Coll., 1932–34; Fellow and Tutor of Magdalen Coll., and Univ. Lectr in Physiology, 1934–37; Dir, Kanematsu Memorial Inst. of Pathology, Sydney, 1937–44; Prof. of Physiology: Univ. of Otago, Dunedin, NZ, 1944–51; ANU, Canberra, 1951–66; Mem., Inst. for Biomedical Res., Chicago, 1966–68; Dist. Prof. and Head of Res. Unit of Neurobiology, Health Sci. Faculty, State Univ. of NY at Buffalo, 1968–75, now Dist. Prof. Emeritus. Lectures: Waynflete, Magdalen Coll., Oxford, 1952; Herter, Johns Hopkins Univ., 1955; Ferrier, Royal Soc., 1959; Sherrington, Liverpool Univ., 1966; Patten, Indiana Univ., 1972; Pahlavi, Iran, 1976; Gifford, Edinburgh, 1978, 1979; Carroll, Georgetown, 1982; Idreos, Manchester Coll., Oxford, 1990. Pres., Australian Acad. of Science, 1957–61. Member: Pontifical Acad. of Science; Deutsche Akademie der Naturforscher Leopoldina. Foreign Hon. Member: Amer. Acad. of Arts and Sciences; Amer. Philosophical Soc.; Amer. Neurological Soc.; Accademia Nazionale dei Lincei. Hon. Life Mem., New York Acad. of Sciences, 1965; Foreign Associate, Nat. Acad. of Sciences; For. Mem., Max-Planck Soc. Hon. Fellow: Exeter Coll., Oxford, 1961; Magdalen Coll., Oxford, 1964; Amer. Coll. of Physicians, 1967. Hon. ScD Cantab; Hon. DSc: Oxon; Tasmania; British Columbia; Gustavus Adolphus Coll., Minnesota; Marquette Univ., Wisconsin; Loyola, Chicago; Yeshiva, NY; Fribourg; Georgetown, Washington DC; Hon. LLD Melbourne; Hon. MD: Charles Univ., Prague; Torino; Basel. (Jointly) Nobel Prize for Medicine, 1963; Baly Medal, RCP, 1961; Royal Medal, Royal Soc., 1962; Cothenius Medal, Deutsche Akademie der Naturforscher Leopoldina, 1963. Order of the Rising Sun, Gold and Silver Stars (Japan), 1987. *Publications:* (jtly) Reflex Activity of Spinal Cord, 1932; Neuro-physiological Basis of Mind, 1953; Physiology of Nerve Cells, 1957; Physiology of Synapses, 1964; (jtly) The Cerebellum as a Neuronal Machine, 1967; The Inhibitory Pathways of the Central Nervous System, 1969; Facing Reality, 1970; The Understanding of the Brain, 1973; (jtly) Molecular Neurobiology of the Mammalian Brain, 1977, 2nd edn 1987; (jtly) The Self and Its Brain, 1977; The Human Mystery, 1979; (jtly) Sherrington, his Life and Thought, 1979; The Human Psyche, 1980; (jtly) The Wonder of Being Human: our brain, our mind, 1984; Evolution of the Brain: creation of the self, 1989; contrib. to Can Scientists Believe, 1991; papers in Proc. Royal Soc., Jl of Physiology, Jl of Neurophysiology, Experimental Brain Research. *Recreation:* European travel. *Address:* Ca' a la Gra', CH 6646 Contra (Locarno), Ticino, Switzerland. *T:* 093–672931.

ECCLES, Hon. John Dawson, CBE 1985; Chief Executive (formerly General Manager), Commonwealth Development Corporation, since 1985 (Member, 1982–85); Chairman, Board of Trustees, Royal Botanic Gardens, Kew, since 1983; *b* 20 April 1931; *er s* and *heir* of 1st Viscount Eccles, *qv*; *m* 1955, Diana Catherine Sturge (*see* Baroness Eccles of Moulton); one *s* three *d*. *Educ:* Winchester Coll.; Magdalen Coll., Oxford (BA). Director: Glynwed International plc, 1972–; Investors in Industry plc, 1974–88; Chairman: Head Wrightson & Co. Ltd, 1976–77 (Man. Dir, 1968–77); The Nuclear Power Gp Ltd, 1968–74; Davy Internat. Ltd, 1977–81; Chamberlin & Hill plc, 1982–. Member: Monopolies and Mergers Commn, 1976–85 (Dep. Chm., 1981–85); Industrial Develt Adv. Bd, 1989–. Hon DSc Cranfield Inst. of Technology, 1989. *Address:* 6 Barton Street, SW1P 3NG. *T:* 071-222 7559; Moulton Hall, Richmond, N Yorks DL10 6QH. *T:* Darlington (0325) 377227. *Club:* Brooks's.

ECCLES, Patrick; *see* Eccles, H. W. P.

ECCLES-WILLIAMS, Hilary a'Beckett, CBE 1970; Vice-President, West Midlands Conservative Council, since 1985 (Deputy Chairman, 1982–85); *b* 5 Oct. 1917; *s* of late Rev. Cyril Eccles-Williams and Hermione (*née* Terrell); *m* 1941, Jeanne, *d* of W. J. Goodwin; two *s* four *d*. *Educ:* Eton; Brasenose Coll., Oxford (MA). Served War of 1939–45, Major RA (anti-tank), Dunkirk and Normandy (wounded). Consul: for Nicaragua, 1951–59; for Cuba, 1952–60; for Costa Rica, 1964–; for Bolivia, 1965–82. Chairman of companies; Chm., 1978–82, non-exec. Dir, 1982–87, Rabone Petersen; has travelled 900,000 miles on export business. Chairman: Brit. Export Houses Assoc., 1958–59; Guardians of Birmingham Assay Office, 1979–88 (Guardian, 1970–); President: Birmingham Chamber of Commerce, 1965–66; Assoc. of Brit. Ch. of Commerce (93 Chambers), 1970–72. Comr of Income Tax, 1966–70. Chairman: Birmingham Cons. Assoc., 1976–79 (Pres., 1979–84); W Midlands Metropolitan Co. Co-ordinating Cttee, Cons. Party, 1980–86; European Parlt constituency of Birmingham S Cons. Assoc., 1978–82 (Pres., 1982–84); Latin Amer. Gp, Cons. Foreign and Overseas Council, 1986–89; President: Eur. Parlt constituency of Birmingham E Cons. Assoc., 1984–; Sparkbrook Constituency Cons. Assoc., 1988–; Anglo-Asian Cons. Soc., 1984–87; Cons. Party One Nation Forum, 1990–; Mem., National Union Exec. Cttee, Cons. Party, 1975–85. Mem., Brit. Hallmarking Council, 1976–88; Pres., Birmingham Consular Assoc., 1973–74; Chairman: Asian Christian Colls Assoc., 1960–66; Brit. Heart Foundn, Midland Counties, 1973–74; Golden Jubilee Appeal Cttee, Queen Elizabeth Hosp., Birmingham, 1987–90. Governor, Birmingham Univ., 1966–. Liveryman, Worshipful Co. of Glaziers, 1974; Freeman, Goldsmiths' Co., 1988. Hon. Captain, Bolivian Navy, 1969. Numerous TV appearances. *Recreations:* sailing, golf. *Address:* 36 St Bernard's Road, Solihull, West Midlands B92 7BB. *T:* 021–706 0354. *Clubs:* Olton Mere Sailing; North Warwickshire Golf.

ECCLESTON, Harry Norman, OBE 1979; PPRE (RE 1961; ARE 1948); RWS 1975 (ARWS 1964); Artist Designer at the Bank of England Printing Works, 1958–83; *b* 21 Jan. 1923; *s* of Harry Norman Eccleston and Kate Pritchard, Coseley, Staffs; *m* 1948, Betty Doreen Gripton; two *d*. *Educ:* Sch. of Art, Bilston; Coll. of Art, Birmingham; Royal College of Art. ATD 1947; ARCA (1st Class) 1950. Studied painting until 1942. Served in Royal Navy, 1942–46; Temp. Commn, RNVR, 1943. Engraving Sch., Royal College of Art, 1947–51; engraving, teaching, free-lance graphic design, 1951–58. Pres., Royal Soc. of Painter-Etchers and Engravers, 1975–89. Hon. RBSA 1989. *Recreation:* reading. *Address:* 110 Priory Road, Harold Hill, Romford, Essex. *T:* Ingrebourne (04023) 40275. *Club:* Arts.

ECCLESTONE, Jacob Andrew; Deputy General Secretary, National Union of Journalists, since 1981; *b* 10 April 1939; *s* of Alan Ecclestone and late Delia Reynolds Abraham; *m* 1966, Margaret Joan Bassett; two *s* one *d*. *Educ:* High Storrs Grammar Sch., Sheffield; Open Univ. (BA). Journalism: South Yorkshire Times, 1957–61; Yorkshire Evening News, 1961–62; The Times, 1962–66, 1967–81. Member: Nat. Exec., NUJ, 1977 (Vice-Pres. 1978, Pres., 1979); Press Council, 1977–80; Exec., Nat. Council for Civil Liberties, 1982–. *Recreations:* gardening, climbing, music. *Address:* 40 Chatsworth Way, SE27 9HN. *T:* 081–670 8503.

ECHLIN, Sir Norman David Fenton, 10th Bt, *cr* 1721; Captain 14/1st Punjab Regiment, Indian Army; *b* 1 Dec. 1925; *s* of Sir John Frederick Echlin, 9th Bt, and Ellen Patricia (*d* 1971), *d* of David Jones, JP, Dublin; *S* father, 1932; *m* 1953, Mary Christine, *d* of John Arthur, Oswestry, Salop. *Educ:* Masonic Boys' School, Dublin. *Heir:* none. *Address:* Nartopa, 36 Marina Avenue, Appley, Ryde, IoW.

ECKERSLEY, Sir Donald (Payze), Kt 1981; OBE 1977; farmer, since 1946; Inaugural President, National Farmers' Federation of Australia, 1979–81; *b* 1 Nov. 1922; *s* of Walter Roland Eckersley and Ada Gladys Moss; *m* 1949, Marjorie Rae Clarke; one *s* two *d*. *Educ:* Muresk Agricl Coll. (Muresk Diploma in Agriculture). Aircrew, RAAF, 1940–45. Pres., Milk Producers' Assoc., 1947–50; Farmers' Union of WA: Executive, 1962–67; Pres., Milk Sect., 1965–70; Vice-Pres., 1969–72; Gen. Pres., 1972–75; Pres., Australian Farmers' Fedn, 1975–79; Austr. Rep., Internat. Fedn of Agric., 1979–81. Pres., Harvey Shire Council, 1970–79; Director: Chamberlain John Deere, 1980–; Br. Bd. Australian Mutual Provident Soc., 1983–. Chairman: Leschenault Inlet Management Authority, 1977–; Artificial Breeding Bd of WA, 1981–; SW Develt Authority, 1989–; Bd, Muresk Inst. of Agric., 1984–88; Member: WA Waterways Commn, 1977–; Nat. Energy Adv. Cttee, 1979–; Comr, WA State Housing Commn, 1982–. Mem., Senate, Univ. of WA, 1981–. Mem., Harvey Rotary Club. JP WA, 1982–86. Hon. DTech Curtin, 1989. WA Citizen of Year award, 1976; Man of Year, Austr. Agriculture, 1979. *Publication:* (contrib.) Farm Focus: the '80s, 1981. *Recreations:* golf, fishing. *Address:* Korijedale, Harvey, WA 6220, Australia. *T:* 097–291472. *Clubs:* Weld (Perth); Harvey Golf.

ECKERSLEY, Thomas, OBE 1948; RDI 1963; AGI; graphic designer; Head of Department of Design, London College of Printing, 1958–76; *b* Sept. 1914; *s* of John Eckersley and Eunice Hilton; *m* Daisy Eckersley; three *s*; *m* 1966, Mary Kessell, painter. *Educ:* Salford Sch. of Art. Free-lance Graphic Designer for London Transport, Shell Mex, BBC, GPO, MOI, Unicef, CoID and other leading concerns since 1936. Work exhibited in Sweden, USA, Paris, Hamburg, Lausanne, Milan, Amsterdam; permanent collections of work in V&A Museum, Imperial War Museum, London Transport Museum, Nat. Gall. of Australia, Museum of Modern Art, USA, Library of Congress, USA and Die Neue Sammlung Staatliches Museum München. One-man exhibitions: Soc. of Artists and Designers, 1976; Camden Arts Centre, British Arts Centre, Yale, 1980; Peel Park Gall., Salford, Edinburgh, 1981; Newcastle upon Tyne Polytechnic Gall., 1983; London Transport Museum, 1985; Maidstone Coll. of Art, 1985; Oxford Polytechnic, 1986; Emmerich Poster Museum, Germany, 1987. Mem. of Alliance Graphique Internationale; Hon. Fellow: Manchester Coll. of Art and Design; Humberside Coll. of Higher Educn, 1985; FSTD. Medal of CSD, 1990. *Publications:* contribs to Graphis, Gebrauchsgraphik, Form und Technik, Art and Industry, Print Design and Production, Penrose Annual; *relevant publication:* F. H. K. Henrion, Top Graphic Designers, 1983. *Recreation:* cricket. *Address:* 53 Belsize Park Gardens, NW3. *T:* 071–586 3586.

ECKERSLEY-MASLIN, Rear Adm. David Michael, CB 1984; retired, RN; Director General, NATO Communications and Information Systems Agency, Brussels, since 1986; *b* Karachi, 27 Sept. 1929; *e s* of Comdr C. E. Eckersley-Maslin, OBE, RN, Tasmania, and Mrs L. M. Lightfoot, Bedford; *m* 1955, Shirley Ann, *d* of Captain and Mrs H. A. Martin; one *s* one *d*. *Educ:* Britannia Royal Naval Coll. Qual. Navigation Direction Officer, 1954; rcds 1977. Far East Malayan Campaign, 1950–53; Australian Navy, 1954–56; BRNC Dartmouth, 1959–61; commanded HM Ships Eastbourne, Euryalus, Fife and Blake, 1966–76; Captain RN Presentation Team, 1974; Dir, Naval Operational Requirements, 1977–80; Flag Officer Sea Training, 1980–82; ACNS (Operational Planning) (Falklands), 1982; ACDS (CIS), 1982–84; Asst Dir (CIS), IMS, NATO, Brussels, 1984–86. Vice Pres., AFCEA, 1987–90. Naval Gen. Service Decoration, Palestine, 1948, and Malaya, 1951. *Recreations:* tennis, squash, cricket. *Address:* Dunningwell, Hall Court, Shedfield, near Southampton SO3 2HL. *T:* Wickham (0329) 832350. *Clubs:* MCC, Commonwealth Trust.

EDDERY, Patrick James John; jockey (retained by M. V. O'Brien and J. Tree); *b* 18 March 1952; *s* of Jimmy and Josephine Eddery; *m* 1978, Carolyn Jane (*née* Mercer); two *d.* Rode for Peter Walwyn, 1972–80; Champion Jockey, 1974, 1975, 1976, 1977, 1986, 1988, 1989, 1990; Champion Jockey in Ireland, 1982; won the Oaks, 1974, 1979, the Derby, on Grundy, 1975, on Golden Fleece, 1982, on Quest for Fame, 1990; Prix de l'Arc de Triomphe, 1980, 1985, 1986, 1987; St Leger on Moon Madness, 1986. *Recreations:* swimming, golf, snooker. *Address:* Musk Hill Farm, Lower Winchendon, Aylesbury, Bucks HP18 0DT. *T:* Haddenham (0844) 290282. *Club:* The Subscription Rooms (Newmarket).

EDDEY, Prof. Howard Hadfield, CMG 1974; FRCS, FRACS, FACS; Foundation Professor of Surgery, University of Melbourne, at Austin Hospital and Repatriation General Hospital, 1967–75, now Emeritus; also Dean of Austin Hospital and Repatriation General Hospital Clinical School, 1971–75; *b* Melbourne, 3 Sept. 1910; *s* of Charles Howard and Rachel Beatrice Eddey; *m* 1940, Alice Paul (decd); two *s* one *d. Educ:* Melbourne Univ.; St Bartholomew's Hosp. Med. Sch. BSc, MB BS, 1934; FRCS 1938; FRACS 1941; FACS 1964; Hallet Prize of RCS of Eng., 1938. Served War, 1941–45: AAMC, Major and Surgical Specialist; served in PoW camps: Changi (Singapore); Sandakan and Kuching (Borneo). Hon. Surgeon: Prince Henry Hosp., Melbourne, 1946–47; Alfred Hosp., Melbourne, 1947; Royal Melbourne Hosp., 1947–67; Cons. Surg., 1967, Royal Melbourne and Royal Women's Hosps; Peter MacCallum Clinic. Mem. AMA, 1935; Mem., Faculty of Med., Univ. of Melbourne, 1950–75 (Mem. Convocation, 1965–67); Indep. Lectr in Surgical Anatomy, Univ. of Melb., 1950–65; Dean, Royal Melb. Hosp. Clin. Sch., 1965–67; Colombo Plan Visitor to India, 1960–65; Cons. in Surg., Papuan Med. Coll., 1965–68; Mem. Cancer Inst. Bd, 1958–67; Mem. Med. and Sci. Cttee, Anti-Cancer Council of Vic., 1958–67; Chm., Melb. Med. Postgrad. Cttee, 1963–71; Vice-Pres., Aust. Postgrad. Fedn in Med., 1965–71 (Life Governor, 1972). Mem. Council, RACS, 1967–75 (Mem. Bd of Examrs, 1958–75, Chm. Bd, 1968–73; Hon. Librarian, 1968–75). Mem. Med. Bd of Vic., 1968–77; Mem. Austin Hosp. Bd of Management, 1971–77 (Vice-Pres., 1975–77; Life Governor, 1977). Hunterian Prof., RCS, 1960; Vis. Prof. of Surg., 1962, External Examr in Surg., 1970, Univ. of Singapore; Leverhulme Fellow, Univ. of Melb., 1974; Vis. Prof. of Surg., Univ. of Hong Kong, 1974. Howard Eddey Medal, named in 1972 by RACS and awarded to most successful cand., Part I exam (surgery) for FRACS in SE Asia, in recognition of dist. service to RACS. Hon. Surgeon to HRH Prince Charles on his visit to Victoria, 1974. Melbourne and Australian Universities Lacrosse Blue. *Publications:* many, in sci. jls, particularly in relation to diseases of salivary glands and cancer of mouth. *Recreation:* bowls. *Address:* 5/45 Vanessa Avenue, Highton, Geelong, Vic 3216, Australia. *T:* (052) 435645. *Clubs:* Naval and Military (Melbourne), Melbourne Cricket.

EDDINGTON, Paul Clark-, CBE 1987; actor; *b* 18 June 1927; *s* of Albert Clark Eddington and Frances Mary (*née* Roberts); *m* 1952, Patricia Scott; three *s* one *d. Educ:* Holy Child Convent, Cavendish Sq., W1; Friends (Quaker) Sch., Sibford Ferris, Banbury, Oxon; RADA. First appearance on stage with ENSA, 1944; joined Birmingham Repertory Th., 1945; has played with several other rep. theatres during subseq. 30 years; first appearance in West End in The 10th Man, Comedy Th., 1961; first (and only, so far) appearance in New York in A Severed Head, 1964; joined National Theatre to play in revival of Who's Afraid of Virginia Woolf?, 1981; Noises Off, Savoy, 1982; Lovers Dancing, Albery, 1983; Forty Years On, Queen's, 1984; Jumpers, Aldwych, 1985; HMS Pinafore, Victoria State Opera, Australia, 1987 (tour); The Browning Version, and Harlequinade (double-bill), Royalty, 1988, subseq. Australia; London Assurance, Chichester Fest., 1989, transf. Theatre Royal, Haymarket, 1989. Many TV appearances, including series, The Good Life, Yes Minister and Yes, Prime Minister. Member Council: Equity, 1972–75; Howard League for Penal Reform, 1989–; Governor, Bristol Old Vic Theatre Trust, 1975–84. Hon. MA Sheffield, 1987. *Recreations:* listening to music, reading, washing up, lying down and thinking what ought to be done in the garden. *Address:* c/o ICM Ltd, 388/396 Oxford Street, W1N 9HE. *T:* 071–629 8080. *Club:* Garrick.

EDDLEMAN, Gen. Clyde Davis; DSM with oak leaf cluster (US); Silver Star; Legion of Merit; Bronze Star; Philippines Distinguished Service Star; Vice-Chief of Staff, US Army, 1960–62; *b* 17 Jan. 1902; *s* of Rev. W. H. Eddleman and Janie Eddleman (*née* Tureman); *m* 1926, Lorraine Heath; one *s* (and one *s* decd). *Educ:* US Military Academy, West Point, New York. Commissioned 2nd Lieut of Infantry upon graduation from US Military Academy, 1924. Advanced, through the ranks, and reached grade of Gen. 1959. Comdr, Central Army Group (NATO), and C-in-C, US Army, Europe, at Heidelberg, Germany, 1959–60. Knight Commander's Cross, Order of Merit (Germany); Kt Grand Cross of the Sword (Sweden). *Recreations:* hunting, fishing. *Address:* 1101 S Arlington Ridge Road 802, Arlington, Va 22202, USA.

EDDY, Prof. Alfred Alan; Professor of Biochemistry, University of Manchester Institute of Science and Technology since 1959; *b* 4 Nov. 1926; Cornish parentage; *s* of late Alfred and Ellen Eddy; *m* 1954, Susan Ruth Slade-Jones; two *s. Educ:* Devonport High Sch.; Open scholarship Exeter Coll., Oxford, 1944; BA 1st Class Hons, 1949. ICI Research Fellow, 1950; DPhil 1951. Joined Brewing Industry Research Foundation, Nutfield, 1953. *Publications:* various scientific papers. *Address:* Larchfield, Buxton Road, Disley, Cheshire SK12 2LH.

EDE, Ven. Dennis; Archdeacon of Stoke-upon-Trent, since 1990; *b* 8 June 1931; *m* 1956, Angela Horsman; one *s* two *d. Educ:* Univ. of Nottingham (BA Theology 1955); Barnett House, Oxford (Cert. of Social Studies); Ripon Hall, Oxford; MSocSc Birmingham, 1972. Nat. Service, RAF, 1950–52; Pilot Officer, Admin. Branch. Asst Curate, St Giles, Sheldon, dio. Birmingham, 1957–60; Asst Curate-in-charge, St Philip and St James, Hodge Hill, Birmingham, 1960–64, Priest-in-charge 1964–70, Team Rector 1970–76; Part-time Chaplain, East Birmingham Hosp., 1961–76; Vicar of All Saints Parish Church, West Bromwich, dio. Lichfield, 1976–90. Mem., Gen. Synod of C of E, 1975–76, 1980–90. Diocese of Lichfield: Chm. House of Clergy, 1985–; Chm. of Communications, 1983–; Prebendary of Lichfield Cathedral, 1983–; Hon. Canon, 1990–. Chairman: Sandwell Volunteer, 1980–86; Faith in Sandwell, 1986–90. *Recreations:* walking, cycling, squash. *Address:* Archdeacon's House, 39 The Brackens, Clayton, Newcastle-under-Lyme ST5 4JL. *T:* Newcastle-under-Lyme (0782) 663066, *Fax:* Newcastle-under-Lyme (0782) 711165.

EDE, Jeffery Raymond, CB 1978; Keeper of Public Records, 1970–78; *b* 10 March 1918; *e s* of late Richard Arthur Ede; *m* 1944, Mercy, *d* of Arthur Radford Sholl; one *s* one *d. Educ:* Plymouth Coll.; King's Coll., Cambridge (MA). Served War of 1939–45, Intell. Corps (despatches); GSO2 HQ 8 Corps District, BAOR, 1945–46. Asst Keeper, Public Record Office, 1947–59; Principal Asst Keeper, 1959–66; Dep. Keeper, 1966–69. Lectr in Archive Admin., Sch. of Librarianship and Archives, University Coll., London, 1956–61; Unesco expert in Tanzania, 1963–64. Chm., British Acad. Cttee on Oriental Documents, 1972–78; Vice Pres., Internat. Council on Archives, 1976–78. Pres., Soc. of Archivists, 1974–77. FRHistS 1969. Hon. Mem., L'Institut Grand-Ducal de Luxembourg, 1977. Freeman: Goldsmiths' Company, 1979; City of London, 1979. *Publications:* Guide to the Contents of the Public Record Office, Vol. II (major contributor), 1963; articles in archival and other professional jls. *Recreations:* theatre, countryside. *Address:* Palfreys, East Street, Drayton, Langport, Som TA10 0JZ. *T:* Langport (0458) 251314.

EDEL, (Joseph) Leon; Citizens Professor of English, University of Hawaii, 1970–78, now Emeritus; *b* 9 Sept. 1907; *e s* of Simon Edel and Fanny (*née* Malamud), Pittsburgh, Pa; *m* 1st, 1935, Bertha Cohen (marr. diss. 1950); 2nd, 1950, Roberta Roberts (marr. diss. 1979); 3rd, 1980, Marjorie Sinclair; no *c. Educ:* McGill Univ., Montreal (BA 1927, MA 1928); Univ. of Paris (Docteur-ès-Lettres 1932). Served with US Army in France and Germany, 1943–46: Bronze Star Medal (US), 1945; Chief of Information Control, News Agency, US Zone, 1946–47. Asst Prof., Sir George Williams Coll., Montreal, 1932–34; miscellaneous writing and journalism, 1934–43; Christian Gauss Seminar in Criticism, Princeton Univ., 1951–52; New York University: Vis. Prof., 1952–53; Associate Prof., 1953–55; Prof. of English, 1955–66; Henry James Prof. of English and American Letters, 1966–72. Guggenheim Fellow, 1936–38, 1965–66; Alexander Lectures, Toronto, 1956; Vis. Professor: Indiana, 1954; Hawaii, 1955, 1969, 1970; Harvard, 1959–60; Purdue, 1970; Centenary Vis. Prof., Toronto, 1967; Vernon Vis. Prof. in Biography, Dartmouth, 1977. Westminster Abbey Address, Henry James Meml in Poets' Corner, 1976. Educnl Adv. Cttees Guggenheim Foundn, 1968–80. Pres., US Center of PEN, 1957–59. Pres., Hawaii Literary Arts Council, 1978–79. Fellow, Amer. Acad. of Arts and Sciences, 1959; Bollingen Fellow, 1959–61. Member: Nat. Inst. of Arts and Letters, 1964– (Sec., 1965–67); Amer. Acad. of Arts and Letters, 1972; Council, Authors' Guild, 1965–68 (Pres., 1969–70); Soc. of Authors, 1968. FRSL 1970. Hon. Member: W. A. White Psychiatric Inst., 1966; Amer. Acad. Psychoanalysis, 1975; Associate, Amer. Trust in the British Liby. Hon. DLitt: McGill, 1963; Union Coll., Schenectady, 1963; Univ. of Saskatchewan, 1983; Hawaii Loa Coll., Honolulu, 1988. Nat. Inst. of Arts and Letters Award, 1959; US Nat. Book Award for non-fiction, 1963; Pulitzer Prize for biography, 1963; AAAL Gold Medal for biography, 1976; Hawaii Literary Arts Award, 1978; Nat. Arts Club Medal for Literature, 1981; Nat. Book Critics Circle Award (Biography), 1985. *Publications:* Henry James: les années dramatiques, 1932; The Prefaces of Henry James, 1932; James Joyce: The Last Journey, 1947; (with E. K. Brown) Willa Cather, 1953; The Life of Henry James: The Untried Years, 1953, The Conquest of London, 1962, The Middle Years, 1963, The Treacherous Years, 1969, The Master, 1972, rev. edn in 2 vols, 1978, rewritten, rev. into 1 vol., Henry James, a life, 1985; The Psychological Novel, 1955; Literary Biography, 1957; (with Dan H. Laurence) A Bibliography of Henry James, 1957; Thoreau, 1970; Bloomsbury: A House of Lions, 1979; Stuff of Sleep and Dreams (essays), 1982; Writing Lives: Principia Biographica, 1984; *edited:* The Complete Plays of Henry James, 1949; Selected Letters of Henry James, 1956, 1987; (with Godron N. Ray) James and H. G. Wells, Letters, 1958; The Complete Tales of Henry James, 12 vols, 1962–65; The Diary of Alice James, 1964; Literary History and Literary Criticism, 1965; Henry James: Stories of the Supernatural, 1971; Harold Goddard Alphabet of the Imagination, 1975; Henry James Letters: vol. I, 1843–1875, 1975; vol. II, 1875–1883, 1980; vol. III, 1883–1895, 1981; vol. IV, 1895–1916, 1984; Edmund Wilson: The Twenties, 1975; Edmund Wilson: The Thirties, 1980; Edmund Wilson: The Forties, 1983; Edmund Wilson: The Fifties, 1986; (ed with Lyall H. Powers) The Complete Notebooks of Henry James, 1986; Selected Letters of Henry James, 1987. *Recreations:* music, swimming. *Address:* 3817 Lurline Drive, Honolulu, Hawaii 96816, USA. *Clubs:* Athenæum; Century (New York).

EDELL, Stephen Bristow; Building Societies Ombudsman, since 1987; *b* 1 Dec. 1932; *s* of late Ivan James Edell and late Hilda Pamela Edell; *m* 1958, Shirley Ross Collins; two *s* one *d. Educ:* St Andrew's Sch., Eastbourne; Uppingham. LLB London. Legal Mem., RTPI. Commnd RA, 1951. Articled to father, 1953; qual. Solicitor 1958; Partner, Knapp-Fishers (Westminster), 1959–75; Law Comr, 1975–83; Partner, Crossman Block and Keith (Solicitors), 1983–87. Mem. Cttee, 1973–85, Vice-Pres., 1980–82, Pres., 1982–83, City of Westminster Law Soc. Oxfam: Mem., Retailing and Property Cttee, 1984– (Chm., 1989–); Mem. Council, 1985–; Mem., Exec., 1987–. Makers of Playing Cards' Company: Liveryman, 1955–; Mem., Ct of Assts, 1978–; Sen. Warden, 1980–81; Master, 1981–82. FRSA. *Publications:* Inside Information on the Family and the Law, 1969; The Family's Guide to the Law, 1974; articles in Conveyancer, Jl of Planning and Environmental Law, and newspapers. *Recreations:* family life; music, opera, theatre; early astronomical instruments; avoiding gardening; interested in problems of developing countries. *Address:* The Old Farmhouse, Twineham, Haywards Heath, Sussex RH17 5NP. *T:* Hurstpierpoint (0273) 832058. *Club:* City Livery.

EDELMAN, Prof. Gerald Maurice, MD, PhD; Vincent Astor Distinguished Professor of Biochemistry, The Rockefeller University, New York, since 1974; *b* NYC, 1 July 1929; *s* of Edward Edelman and Anna Freedman; *m* 1950, Maxine Morrison; two *s* one *d. Educ:* Ursinus Coll. (BS); University of Pennsylvania (MD); The Rockefeller University (PhD). Med. Hse Officer, Massachusetts Gen. Hosp., 1954–55; Asst Physician, Hosp. of The Rockefeller Univ., 1957–60; The Rockefeller University: Asst Prof. and Asst Dean of Grad. Studies, 1960–63; Associate Prof. and Associate Dean of Grad. Studies, 1963–66; Prof., 1966–74. Trustee, Rockefeller Brothers Fund, 1972–82; Associate, Neurosciences Res. Program, 1965– (Scientific Chm., 1980–; Dir, Neurosciences Inst., 1981–). Mem., Adv. Bd, Basel Inst. Immunology, 1970–77 (Chm., 1975–77); Member Emeritus, Weizmann Inst. of Science, 1986 (Mem., Bd of Governors, 1971–87); non-resident Fellow and Mem. Bd Trustees, Salk Inst. for Biol. Studies, 1973–85; Member: Biophysics and Biophys. Chem. Study Section, Nat. Insts of Health, 1964–67; Sci. Council, Center for Theoretical Studies, 1970–72; Bd of Overseers, Faculty Arts and Scis, Univ. of Pa, 1976–83; Board of Trustees, Carnegie Inst. of Washington (Mem., Adv. Cttee). Member: Nat. Acad. Scis; Amer. Acad. Arts Scis; Amer. Philosophical Soc.; FAAAS; Fellow: NY Acad. Scis; NY Acad. of Medicine; Member: Amer. Soc. Biol Chemists; Amer. Assoc. Immunologists; Genetics Soc. of America; Harvey Soc. (Pres., 1975–76); Amer. Chem. Soc.; Amer. Soc. Cell Biol.; Soc. for Developmental Biol.; Sigma XI; Alpha Omega Alpha; Council of Foreign Relations. Hon. Member: Pharmaceutical Soc. of Japan; Japanese Biochem. Soc.; Foreign Mem., Academie des Sciences, Institut de France. Hon. DSc: Pennsylvania, 1973; Gustavus Adolphus Coll., Minn., 1975; Paris, Cagliari, Georgetown Univ. Sch. of Med., 1989; Univ. degliStudi di Napoli Federico II, 1990; Hon. ScD: Ursinus Coll., 1974; Williams Coll., 1976; Hon. MD Univ. Siena, Italy, 1974. Spencer Morris Award, Univ. of Pennsylvania, 1954; Eli Lilly Award in Biol Chem., Amer. Chem. Soc., 1965; Annual Alumni Award, Ursinus College, 1969; (jtly) Nobel Prize in Physiology or Medicine, 1972; Albert Einstein Commemorative Award, Yeshiva Univ., 1974; Buchman Meml Award, Caltech, 1975; Rabbi Shai Shacknai Meml Prize in Immunology and Cancer Res., Hebrew Univ. Hadassah Med. Sch., 1977; Regents Medal of Excellence, New York State, 1984; Hans Neurath prize, 1986; Sesquicentennial Commem. Award, Nat. Liby of Medicine, 1986; Cécile and Oskar Vogt award, 1988; Dist. Grad. Award, Pennsylvania Univ., 1990; Personnelité de l'année, Paris, 1990. *Publications:* Neural Darwinism, 1987; Topobiology, 1988; The Remembered Present, 1989. *Recreation:* music. *Address:* Department of Developmental and Molecular Biology, The Rockefeller University, 1230 York Avenue, New York, NY 10021, USA.

EDEN, family name of **Barons Auckland, Eden of Winton** and **Henley.**

EDEN OF WINTON, Baron *cr* 1983 (Life Peer), of Rushyford in the County of Durham; **John Benedict Eden;** Bt (E) 1672 and Bt (GB) 1776; PC 1972; Chairman: Wonderworld plc, since 1982; Gamlestaden plc, since 1987; The Bricom Group, since

1990; Director, Lady Eden's Schools Ltd, 1949–70 and since 1974; *b* 15 Sept. 1925; *s* of Sir Timothy Calvert Eden, 8th and 6th Bt and Patricia (*d* 1990), *d* of Arthur Prendergast; *S* father, 1963; *m* 1st, 1958, Belinda Jane (marr. diss. 1974), *o d* of late Sir John Pascoe; two *s* two *d*; 2nd, 1977, Margaret Ann, Viscountess Strathallan. Lieut Rifle Bde, seconded to 2nd KEO Goorkha Rifles and Gilgit Scouts, 1943–47. Contested (C) Paddington North, 1953; MP (C) Bournemouth West, Feb. 1954–1983. Mem. House of Commons Select Cttee on Estimates, 1962–64; Vice-Chm., Conservative Parly Defence Cttee, 1963–66 (formerly: Chm., Defence Air Sub-Cttee; Hon. Sec., Space Sub-Cttee); Vice-Chm., Aviation Cttee, 1963–64; Additional Opposition Front Bench Spokesman for Defence, 1964–66; Jt Vice-Chm., Cons. Parly Trade and Power Cttee, 1966–68; Opposition Front Bench Spokesman for Power, 1968–70; Minister of State, Min. of Technology, June-Oct. 1970; Minister for Industry, DTI, 1970–72; Minister of Posts and Telecommunications, 1972–74; Mem., Expenditure Cttee, 1974–76; Chairman: House of Commons Select Cttee on European Legislation, 1976–79; Home Affairs Cttee, 1981–83. Vice-Chm., Assoc. of Conservative Clubs Ltd, 1964–67, Vice-Pres., 1970–; President: Wessex Area Council, Nat. Union of Conservative and Unionist Assocs, 1974–77; Wessex Area Young Conservatives, 1978–80. UK Deleg. to Council of Europe and to Western European Union, 1960–62; Mem., NATO Parliamentarians' Conf., 1962–66. Chm., Royal Armouries, 1986–. Pres., Independent Schs Assoc., 1969–71; a Vice-Pres., Nat. Chamber of Trade, 1974–86. Hon. Vice-Pres., Nat. Assoc. of Master Bakers, Confectioners & Caterers, 1978–82. *Heir* (to baronetcies only): *s* Hon. Robert Frederick Calvert Eden, *b* 30 April 1964. *Address:* 41 Victoria Road, W8 5RH; Knoyle Place, East Knoyle, Salisbury, Wilts SP3 6AF. *Clubs:* Boodle's, Pratt's.

EDEN, Conrad W., TD; DMus Lambeth 1973; BMus Oxon; Hon. FRCO; retired 1974; *m* 1943, Barbara L., *d* of late Rev. R. L. Jones, Shepton Mallet. *Educ:* Wells Cath. Sch.; Rugby; RCM; St John's Coll., Oxford. Organist, Wells Cathedral, 1933–36; Durham Cathedral, 1936–74. *Address:* The Vale, Highmore Road, Sherborne, Dorset DT9 4BT. *T:* Sherborne (0935) 813488.

EDEN, Prof. Richard John, OBE 1978; Professor of Energy Studies, Cavendish Laboratory, University of Cambridge, 1982–89, now Emeritus; Fellow of Clare Hall, Cambridge, 1966–89, now Emeritus (Vice-President, 1987–89); *b* 2 July 1922; *s* of James A. Eden and Dora M. Eden; *m* 1949, Elsie Jane Greaves; one *s* one *d* and one step *d*. *Educ:* Hertford Grammar Sch.; Peterhouse, Cambridge. BA 1943, MA 1948, PhD 1951. War service, 1942–46, Captain REME, Airborne Forces. Cambridge University: Bye-Fellow, Peterhouse, 1949–50; Stokes Student, Pembroke Coll., 1950–51; Clare College: Research Fellow, 1951–55; Official Fellow, 1957–66; Dir of Studies in Maths, 1951–53, 1957–62; Royal Soc. Smithson Res. Fellow, 1952–55; Sen. Lectr in Physics, Univ. of Manchester, 1955–57; Cambridge University: Lectr in Maths, 1957–64 (Stokes Lectr, 1962); Reader in Theoretical Physics, 1964–82; Head of High Energy Theoretical Physics Gp, 1964–74, Hd of Energy Res. Gp, 1974–89, Cavendish Lab. Mem., Princeton Inst. for Advanced Study, 1954, 1959, 1973; Vis. Scientist: Indiana Univ., 1954–55; Univ. of California, Berkeley, 1960, 1967; Vis. Professor: Univ. of Maryland, 1961, 1965; Columbia Univ., 1962; Scuola Normale Superiore, Pisa, 1964; Univ. of Marseilles, 1968; Univ. of California, 1969. Member: UK Adv. Council on Energy Conservation, 1974–83; Eastern Electricity Bd, 1985–; Energy Adviser to UK NEDO, 1974–75. Syndic, CUP, 1984–. Chm., Cambridge Energy Res. Ltd, subseq. Caminus Energy Ltd, 1985–91. Companion, Inst. of Energy, 1985. Smiths Prize, Univ. of Cambridge, 1949; Maxwell Prize and Medal, Inst. of Physics, 1970; Open Award for Distinction in Energy Economics, BIEE, 1989. *Publications:* (jtly) The Analytic S Matrix, 1966; High Energy Collisions of Elementary Particles, 1967; Energy Conservation in the United Kingdom (NEDO report), 1975; Energy Prospects (Dept of Energy report), 1976; World Energy Demand to 2020 (World Energy Conf. report), 1977; (jtly) Energy Economics, 1981; (jtly) Electricity's Contribution to UK Energy Self Sufficiency, 1984; (jtly) UK Energy, 1984; papers and review articles on nuclear physics and theory of elementary particles. *Recreations:* painting, reading, gardening, travel. *Address:* Cavendish Laboratory, Cambridge CB3 0HE. *T:* Cambridge (0223) 337231; 6 Wootton Way, Cambridge. *T:* Cambridge (0223) 355591.

EDER, (Henry) Bernard; QC 1990; *b* 16 Oct. 1952; *s* of Hans and Helga Eder; *m* 1976, Diana Levin; three *s* one *d*. *Educ:* Haberdashers' Aske's School, Elstree; Downing College, Cambridge (BA 1974). Called to the Bar, Inner Temple, 1975. *Recreations:* tennis, ski-ing. *Address:* 4 Essex Court, Temple, EC4Y 9AJ. *T:* 071–583 9191.

EDES, (John) Michael, CMG 1981; HM Diplomatic Service, retired; Ambassador and Head, UK Delegation to Conventional Arms Control Negotiations, Vienna, 1989–90; *b* 19 April 1930; *s* of late Lt-Col N. H. Edes and Mrs Louise Edes; *m* 1978, Angela Mermagen; two *s*. *Educ:* Blundell's Sch.; Clare Coll., Cambridge (Scholar; BA); Yale Univ. (MA). HM Forces, 1948–49; Mellon Fellow, Yale Univ., 1952–54; FO, 1954; MECAS, 1955; Dubai, 1956–57; FO, 1957–59 (Moscow, 1959); Rome, 1959–61; FO, 1961–62; UK Delegn to Conf. on Disarmament, Geneva, 1962–65 (UK Mission to UN, NY, 1963); FO, 1965–68; Cabinet Office, 1968–69; FCO, 1969–71; Ambassador to Yemen Arab Republic, 1971–73; Mem., UK Delegn to CSCE, Geneva, 1973–74; FCO, 1974–77; RIIA, 1977–78; Paris, 1978–79; Ambassador to Libya, 1980–83; Hd, UK Delegn to Conf. on Confidence and Security Building Measures and Disarmament in Europe, Stockholm, 1983–86; Hd, UK team at conventional arms control mandate talks, 1987–89. Vis. Fellow, IISS, 1987. *Recreations:* listening to music, gardening. *Address:* c/o Lloyds Bank, 7 Pall Mall, SW1Y 5NA. *Clubs:* Athenæum; Hawks (Cambridge).

EDEY, Prof. Harold Cecil, BCom (London), FCA; Professor of Accounting, London School of Economics, University of London, 1962–80, now Emeritus; *b* 23 Feb. 1913; *s* of Cecil Edey and Elsie (*née* Walmsley); *m* 1944, Dilys Mary Pakeman Jones; one *s* one *d*. *Educ:* Croydon High Sch. for Boys; LSE (Hon. Fellow, 1986). Chartered Accountant, 1935. Commnd in RNVR, 1940–46. Lectr in Accounting and Finance, LSE, 1949–55; Reader in Accounting, Univ. of London, 1955–62; Pro-Dir, LSE, 1967–70. Mem., UK Adv. Coun. on Educn for Management, 1961–65; Mem., Academic Planning Bd for London Grad. Sch. of Business Studies, and Governor, 1965–71; Chm., Arts and Social Studies Cttee, CNAA, 1965–71, and Mem. Council, 1965–73; Chm., Bd of Studies in Econs, 1966–71, Mem. Senate, 1975–80, University of London; Mem. Council, Inst. of Chartered Accountants in England and Wales, 1969–80. Hon. Freeman, 1981, Hon. Liveryman, 1986, Co. of Chartered Accountants in England and Wales. Hon. Professor, UCW, Aberystwyth, 1980–; Patron, Univ. of Buckingham, 1984–. Hon. LLD CNAA, 1972. Bard of the Cornish Gorsedd, 1933. Chartered Accountants Founding Socs' Centenary Award, 1987. *Publications:* (with A. T. Peacock) National Income and Social Accounting, 1954; Business Budgets and Accounts, 1959; Introduction to Accounting, 1963; (with B. S. Yamey and H. Thomson) Accounting in England and Scotland 1543–1800, 1963; (with B. V. Carsberg) Modern Financial Management, 1969; (with B. S. Yamey) Debits, Credits, Finance and Profits, 1974; (with L. H. Leigh) The Companies Act 1981, 1981; Accounting Queries, 1982; articles in various jls. *Address:* 10 The Green, Southwick, Brighton BN42 4DA.

EDGAR, David Burman; author and playwright; Chair, MA in Playwriting Studies, University of Birmingham, since 1989, Hon. Senior Research Fellow, since 1988; *b* 26 Feb. 1948; *s* of Barrie Edgar and Joan (*née* Burman); *m* 1979, Eve Brook; two *s*. *Educ:* Oundle Sch.; Univ. of Manchester (BA 1969). Fellow in Creative Writing, Leeds Polytechnic, 1972–74; Resident Playwright, Birmingham Rep. Theatre, 1974–75, Board Mem., 1985–; UK/US Bicentennial Arts Fellow, 1978–79; Literary Consultant, USA, 1984–88, Hon. Associate Artist, 1989, RSC. Hon. Fellow, Birmingham Polytechnic, 1991. Hon. MA Bradford, 1984. *Plays:* The National Interest, 1971; Excuses Excuses, Coventry, 1972; Death, Story, Birmingham Rep., 1972; Baby Love, 1973; The Dunkirk Spirit, 1974; Dick Deterred, Bush Theatre, 1974; O Fair Jerusalem, Birmingham Rep., 1975; Saigon Rose, Edinburgh, 1976; Blood Sports, incl. Ball Boys, Bush Theatre, 1976; Destiny, 1976, Aldwych, 1977; Wreckers, 1977; Our Own People, 1977; (adaptation) The Jail Diary of Albie Sachs, Warehouse Theatre, 1978; (adaptation) Mary Barnes, Birmingham Rep., then Royal Court, 1978–79; (with Susan Todd) Teendreams, 1979; (adaptation) Nicholas Nickleby, Aldwych, 1980, Plymouth Theatre, NY, 1981; Maydays, Barbican, 1983; Entertaining Strangers, 1985, Nat. Theatre, 1987; That Summer, Hampstead, 1987; (with Stephen Bill and Anne Devlin) Heartlanders, Birmingham Rep., 1989; The Shape of the Table, NT, 1990; *TV and radio:* The Eagle has Landed, 1973; Sanctuary, 1973; I know what I meant, 1974; Ecclesiastes, 1977; (with Neil Grant) Vote for Them, 1989; *film:* Lady Jane, 1986. *Publications:* Destiny, 1976; Wreckers, 1977; The Jail Diary of Albie Sachs, 1978; Teendreams, 1979; Mary Barnes, 1979; Nicholas Nickelby, 1982; Maydays, 1983; Entertaining Strangers, 1985; Plays One, 1987; That Summer, 1987; The Second Time as Farce, 1988; Vote for Them, 1989; Heartlanders, 1989; Edgar Shorts, 1990; Plays Two, 1990; The Shape of the Table, 1990; Plays Three, 1991. *Recreation:* cooking. *Address:* c/o Michael Imison Playwrights Ltd, 28 Almeida Street, N1 1TD.

EDGAR, William, FIMechE; Chief Executive, National Engineering Laboratory, since 1990; *b* 16 Jan. 1938; *s* of William Edgar and Alice Anderson McKerrell; *m* 1961, June Gilmour; two *s*. *Educ:* Royal Coll. of Science and Technology (Strathclyde Univ.); ARCST 1961; Birmingham Univ. (MSc 1962). Develt Engr, BSC, Motherwell and Glasgow, 1954–62; Principal Aeromech. Engr, BAC, Warton, 1963–67; Chief Develt Engr, Gen. Manager Sales and Service, Gen. Works Manager, Weir Pumps, Glasgow, 1967–73; Chief Exec., Seaforth Engineering and Corporate Develt Engr, Seaforth Maritime, Aberdeen, 1973–86; Business Develt Dir, Vickers Marine Engineering, Edinburgh, 1986–88; Exec. Chm., Cochrane Shipbuilders, Yorks, 1988–90. *Recreations:* golf, squash, football, walking, reading. *Address:* Rusteph, 7 Glasclune Gardens, North Berwick, East Lothian EH39 4RB. *T:* North Berwick (0620) 4640. *Clubs:* Sloane; Glen Golf.

EDGCUMBE, family name of **Earl of Mount Edgcumbe.**

EDGE, Geoffrey; Senior Associate, P-E Inbucon, since 1987; *b* 26 May 1943; single. *Educ:* London Sch. of Econs (BA); Birmingham Univ. Asst Lectr in Geography, Univ. of Leicester, 1967–70; Lectr in Geog., Open Univ., 1970–74. Bletchley UDC, 1972–74 (Chm. Planning Sub-cttee 1973–74); Milton Keynes District Councillor, 1973–76 (Vice-Chm. Planning Cttee, 1973–75); Mem. Bucks Water Bd, 1973–74. MP (Lab) Aldridge-Brownhills, Feb. 1974–1979; PPS to Minister of State for Educn, Feb.-Oct. 1974, 1976–77, to Minister of State, Privy Council Office, Oct. 1974–76. Research Fellow, Dept of Planning Landscape, Birmingham Polytechnic, 1979–80; Senior Research Fellow: Preston Polytechnic, 1980–81; NE London Polytechnic, 1982–84; Hon. Res. Fellow, Birmingham Polytechnic, 1980–81; New Initiatives Co-ordinator, COPEC Housing Trust, 1984–87. Chm., W Midlands Enterprise Bd; Mem., W Midlands CC, 1981–86 (Chm., Econ. Develt Cttee); Mem., Walsall MBC, 1983– (Leader, 1988–90). *Publications:* (ed jtly) Regional Analysis and Development, 1973; Open Univ. booklets on industrial location and urban development. *Recreations:* music, reading, touring. *Address:* 31 Dudley Road West, Tividale, Warley, W Midlands. *T:* 021–557 3858.

EDGE, Captain (Philip) Malcolm, FNI; Deputy Master and Chairman, Board of Trinity House, since 1988; *b* 15 July 1931; *s* of Stanley Weston Edge and Edith Edge (*née* Liddell); *m* 1967, (Kathleen) Anne Greenwood; one *s* one *d*. *Educ:* Rockferry High School; HMS Conway. Master Mariner. Apprenticed to Shipping subsidiary of British Petroleum, 1949, and served in all ranks; in command, world wide, 1969–78. Elder Brother and Mem. Board, Trinity House, 1978; Mem., PLA, 1980–. Dir, Standard Steamship Owners' Protection & Indemnity Assoc. Ltd, 1988–. Mem. Council, Internat. Assoc. of Lighthouse Authies, 1988– (Pres., 1988–90); Ex officio Mem., Cttee of Management, RNLI, 1988–; Vice-President: Royal Alfred Seafarers Soc., 1988–; Shipwrecked Mariners Royal Benevolent Soc., 1988–. Hon. Mem., London Flotilla, 1989–. Freeman, City of London, 1980; Liveryman, 1980–, Hon. Mem., 1988–, Hon. Co. of Master Mariners; Liveryman, Shipwrights' Co., 1990–. Freeman, Watermen and Lightermen's Co., 1984. *Recreations:* sailing, family. *Address:* Trinity House, Tower Hill, EC3N 4DH. *T:* 071–480 6601. *Clubs:* Royal Thames Yacht; Samuel Pepys (Oxford).

EDGE, Maj.-Gen. Raymond Cyril Alexander, CB 1968; MBE 1945; FRICS 1949; FRGS; Director General, Ordnance Survey, 1965–69, retired; *b* 21 July 1912; *s* of Raymond Clive Edge and Mary (*née* Masters); *m* 1st, 1939, Margaret Patricia (*d* 1982), *d* of William Wallace McKee; one *s* one *d*; 2nd, 1983, Audrey Anne, *d* of Sir Lewis Richardson, 1st Bt, CBE, and *widow* of Jonathan Muers-Raby. *Educ:* Cheltenham Coll.; RMA; Caius Coll., Cambridge (BA). Commissioned in RE, 1932. Served in India, Royal Bombay Sappers and Miners and Survey of India, 1936–39. War Service in India, Burma (despatches), and Malaya. Lt-Col 1951; Col 1954; Dir (Brig.) Ordnance Survey, 1961; Maj.-Gen. 1965. Col Comdt, RE, 1970–75 (Representative Col Comdt, 1974). Mem., Sec. of State for the Environment's Panel of Independent Inspectors, 1971–82. Chairman: Assoc. British Geodesists, 1963–65; Geodesy Sub-Cttee, Royal Soc., 1968–75; Field Survey Assoc., 1968–70. Pres., Section E, British Assoc., 1969. Member: Council, RGS, 1966–69; Council, RICS, 1966–72 (Vice-Pres. 1970–72); Land Surveyors Council (Chm. 1970–72). *Publications:* contrib. A History of the Ordnance Survey, 1980; various papers on geodetic subjects in Bulletin Géodesique and other publications. *Recreation:* music. *Address:* Brook Farm, North Curry, near Taunton, Som TA3 6DJ. *T:* North Curry (0823) 490444. *Club:* Army and Navy.

EDGE, William, (3rd Bt *cr* 1937); *S* father, 1984. *Heir:* *s* Edward Knowles Edge. Does not use the title and his name is not on the Official Roll of Baronets.

EDGEWORTH JOHNSTONE, Robert; *see* Johnstone.

EDIE, His Honour Thomas Ker; a Circuit Judge, South Eastern Circuit, 1972–84; *b* 3 Oct. 1916; *s* of H. S. Ker Edie, Kinloss, Morayshire; *m* 1945, Margaret, *d* of Rev. A. E. Shooter, TD; four *s* one *d*. *Educ:* Clifton; London Univ. Called to Bar, Gray's Inn, 1941. Metropolitan Magistrate, 1961–70; Dep. Chm. Middlesex QS, 1970–71.

EDINBURGH, Bishop of, since 1986; **Rt. Rev. Richard Frederick Holloway;** *b* 26 Nov. 1933; *s* of Arthur and Mary Holloway; *m* 1963, Jean Elizabeth Kennedy, New York; one *s* two *d*. *Educ:* Kelham Theol Coll.; Edinburgh Theol Coll.; Union Theol Seminary, New York (STM); BD (London). Curate, St Ninian's, Glasgow, 1959–63; Priest-in-charge, St Margaret and St Mungo's, Glasgow, 1963–68; Rector, Old St Paul's,

Edinburgh, 1968–80; Rector, Church of the Advent, Boston, Mass, USA, 1980–84; Vicar, St Mary Magdalen's, Oxford, 1984–86. Mem., Human Fertilisation and Embryo Authority, 1991–; Chm., Edinburgh Council of Social Services, 1991–. *Publications*: Let God Arise, 1972; New Vision of Glory, 1974; A New Heaven, 1978; Beyond Belief, 1982; Signs of Glory, 1983; The Killing, 1984; (ed) The Anglican Tradition, 1984; Paradoxes of Christian Faith and Life, 1984; The Sidelong Glance, 1985; The Way of the Cross, 1986; Seven to Flee, Seven to Follow, 1987; Crossfire: faith and doubt in an age of certainty, 1988; Another Country, Another King, 1991. *Recreations*: running, long-distance walking, reading, going to the cinema, listening to music. *Address*: 3 Eglinton Crescent, Edinburgh EH12 5DH. *T*: 031–226 5099. *Club*: New (Edinburgh).

EDINBURGH, Dean of; *no new appointment at time of going to press.*

EDINBURGH, (St Mary's Cathedral), Provost of; *see* Forbes, Very Rev. G. J. T.

EDIS, Richard John Smale; HM Diplomatic Service; *b* 1 Sept. 1943; *s* of Denis Edis and Sylvia (*née* Smale); *m* 1971, Geneviève Cérisoles; three *s*. *Educ*: King Edward's Sch., Birmingham (schol.); St Catharine's Coll., Cambridge (Exhibnr; MA). British Centre, Stockholm, 1965–66; entered HM Diplomatic Service, 1966; FO, 1966–68; Third, later Second Sec., Nairobi, 1968–70; Second, later First Sec., Lisbon, 1971–74; FCO, 1974–77; First Sec., UK Mission to UN, New York, 1977–80; Asst Head of Southern African Dept, FCO, 1981–82; Counsellor 1982; on secondment to Home CS, 1982–84; Dep. Leader, UK Disarmament Delegn, Geneva, 1984–88; Comr, British Indian Ocean Territory, and Head, E Africa Dept, FCO, 1988–91; Vis. Fellow, Centre of Internat. Studies, Univ. of Cambridge, 1991–92. Special Constabulary Medal, 1991. Officer, Military Order of Christ, Portugal, 1973. *Recreations*: sport, reading. *Address*: c/o Foreign and Commonwealth Office, SW1A 2AH. *Clubs*: Travellers'; The Union (Cambridge).

EDMENSON, Sir Walter Alexander, Kt 1958; CBE 1944; shipowner; *b* 1892; 2nd *s* of late Robert Robson Edmenson; *m* 1918, Doris Davidson (*d* 1975); one *d* (and one *s* killed in action, 1940). Served European War, 1914–18, RFA (despatches). Min. of War Transport Rep., N Ireland, 1939–45. President: The Ulster Steamship Co. Ltd; G. Heyn & Sons Ltd; Director: Clyde Shipping Co., 1946–64; The Belfast Banking Co. Ltd, 1946–70; The North Continental Shipping Co. Ltd, 1946–70; The Belfast Bank Executor & Trustee Co. Ltd, 1946–70; Commercial Insurance Co. of Ireland Ltd, 1964–72; Member Board: BEA, 1946–63; Gallaher Ltd, 1946–66. Chm., N Ireland Civil Aviation Adv. Council, 1946–61; Member: Bd, Ulster Transport Authority, 1948–64; Council, Chamber of Shipping, 1943–73; Lloyd's Register of Shipping, 1949–74; Belfast Harbour Comr, 1940–61; Irish Lights Comr, 1949–85. DL Belfast, 1951–87. Amer. Medal of Freedom with Palms, 1945. *Address*: 101 Bryansford Road, Newcastle, Co. Down BT33 0LF. *T*: Newcastle (Co. Down) (03967) 22769.

EDMOND, Prof. John Marmion, PhD; FRS 1986; Professor of Marine Geochemistry, Massachusetts Institute of Technology, since 1970; *b* 27 April 1943; *s* of Andrew John Shields Edmond and late Christina Marmion Edmond; *m* 1978, Massoudeh Vafai; two *s*. *Educ*: Univ. of Glasgow (BSc 1st class Hons, Pure Chemistry, 1965); Univ. of California at San Diego, Scripps Instn of Oceanography (PhD, Marine Chemistry, 1970). Massachusetts Institute of Technology: Asst Prof., 1970; Associate Prof., 1975; Full Prof., 1981. Mackelwane Award, Amer. Geophysical Union, 1976. *Publications*: over 80 scientific papers in professional jls. *Recreations*: reading, gardening. *Address*: 21 Robin Hood Road, Arlington, Mass 02174, USA. *T*: 617 253 5739.

EDMONDS, David Albert; General Manager, Property Management, National Westminster Bank, since 1991; *b* 6 March 1944; *s* of Albert and Gladys Edmonds; *m* 1966, Ruth Beech; two *s* two *d*. *Educ*: Helsby County Grammar School; University of Keele. BA Hons Political Institutions and History. Asst Principal, Min. of Housing and Local Govt, 1966–69; Private Sec. to Parly Sec., MHLG and DoE, 1969–71; Principal, DoE, 1971–73; Observer, CSSB, 1973–74; Vis. Fellow, Centre for Metropolitan Planning and Research, Johns Hopkins Univ., 1974–75; Private Sec. to Perm. Sec., DoE, 1975–77; Asst Sec., DoE, 1977–79; Principal Private Sec. to Sec. of State, DoE, 1979–83; Under Sec., Inner Cities Directorate, DoE, 1983–84; Chief Exec., Housing Corporation, 1984–91. Dir, Housing Finance Corp., 1988–91. Pres., Internat. New Town Assoc., 1987–91. Dep. Chm., New Statesman and Society, 1988–90 (Chm., New Society, 1986–88); Mem. Editl Adv. Bd, Building, 1986–91. *Recreations*: films, theatre, opera, walking, golf. *Address*: National Westminster Bank, 41 Lothbury, EC2P 2BP. *T*: 071–726 1000. *Clubs*: Wimbledon Park Golf; Wimbledon Wanderers Cricket.

EDMONDS, John Christopher, CMG 1978; CVO 1971; HM Diplomatic Service, retired; *b* 23 June 1921; *s* of late Captain A. C. M. Edmonds, OBE, RN, and late Mrs Edmonds; *m* 1st, 1948, Elena Tornow (marr. diss., 1965); two *s*; 2nd, 1966, Armine Williams. *Educ*: Kelly College. Entered Royal Navy, 1939; psc, 1946. Staff: of NATO Defence Coll., Paris, 1953–55; of C-in-C Home Fleet, 1956–57 (Comdr, 1957); of Chief of Defence Staff, 1958–59. Entered Diplomatic Service, 1959; Foreign Office, 1959–60; 1st Secretary (Commercial), Tokyo, 1960–62; FO, 1963–67; 1st Secretary and Head of Chancery, Ankara, 1967–68; Counsellor: Ankara, 1968–71; Paris, 1972–74; Head of Arms Control and Disarmament Dept, FCO, 1974–77; Leader, UK Delegn to Comprehensive Test Ban Treaty Negotiations, Geneva, with personal rank of Ambassador, 1978–81. Chm., Jt SDP-Liberal Alliance Commn on Defence and Disarmament, 1984–86. Vis. Fellow in Internat. Relations, Reading Univ., 1981–. *Recreations*: golf, gardening, travel. *Address*: North Lodge, Sonning, Berks RG4 0ST. *Club*: Army and Navy.

EDMONDS, John Christopher Paul; Board Member and Managing Director, Group Services, British Rail, since 1989; *b* 22 April 1936; *s* of Frank Winston Edmonds and late Phyllis Mary Edmonds; *m* 1962, Christine Elizabeth Seago; one *s* one *d*. *Educ*: Lowestoft Grammar School; Trinity College, Cambridge. Nat. Service Commission, RAF, 1955–57. Joined British Rail, 1960; Chief Freight Manager, London Midland Region, 1981; Nat. Business Manager, Coal, 1982; Dir, Provincial, 1984; Gen. Manager, Anglia Region, 1987. *Recreations*: gardening, music. *Address*: British Railways Board, Euston House, 24 Eversholt Street, PO Box 100, NW1 1DZ; The Old Rectory, Blunham, Bedford MK44 3NJ.

EDMONDS, John Walter; General Secretary, GMB (formerly General, Municipal, Boilermakers and Allied Trade Union), since 1986; *b* 28 Jan. 1944; *s* of Walter and Rose Edmonds; *m* 1967, Linden (*née* Callaby); two *d*. *Educ*: Brunswick Park Primary; Christ's Hosp.; Oriel Coll., Oxford (BA 1965, MA 1968). General and Municipal Workers' Union: Res. Asst, 1966; Dep. Res. Officer, 1967; Reg. Officer, 1968; Nat. Industrial Officer, 1972. Director: National Building Agency, 1978–82; Unity Trust Bank, 1986–. Mem., Royal Commn on Environmental Pollution, 1979–89. Vis. Fellow, Nuffield Coll., Oxford, 1986–. Mem. Council, Consumers' Assoc. Trustee, Inst. of Policy Research, 1988–. Gov., LSE, 1986–. *Recreations*: cricket, carpentry. *Address*: 50 Graham Road, Mitcham, Surrey. *T*: 081–648 9991.

EDMONDS, Robert Humphrey Gordon, CMG 1969; MBE 1944; HM Diplomatic Service, retired; *b* 5 Oct. 1920; *s* of late Air Vice-Marshal C. H. K. Edmonds, CBE, DSO; *m* 1st, 1951, Georgina Combe (marr. diss.); four *s*; 2nd, 1976, Mrs Enid Balint, *widow* of Dr Michael Balint. *Educ*: Ampleforth; Brasenose Coll., Oxford. Pres., Oxford Union, 1940. Served Army, 1940–46; attached to Political Div., Allied Commn for Austria, 1945–46. Entered Foreign Service, Dec. 1946; served Cairo, 1947; FO, 1949; Rome, 1953; Warsaw, 1957; FO, 1959; Caracas, 1962; FO, CO and FCO, 1966–69; Minister, Moscow, 1969–71; High Comr, Nicosia, 1971–72; Vis. Fellow, Glasgow Univ., 1973–74; Asst Under Sec. of State, FCO, 1974–77; Fellow, Woodrow Wilson Internat. Centre for Scholars, Washington, 1977; retd 1978. Adviser, Kleinwort Benson, 1978–83. Mem. Council, RIIA, 1986–. *Publications*: Soviet Foreign Policy: the Brezhnev years, 1983; Setting the Mould: the United States and Britain 1945–1950, 1986; The Big Three, 1990. *Address*: Raven House, Ramsbury, Wilts SN8 2PA. *Club*: Turf.

EDMONDS, Sheila May, MA, PhD; Fellow, and Lecturer in Mathematics, Newnham College, Cambridge, 1945–82 (Vice-Principal, 1960–81); Fellow Emerita, Newnham College, since 1982; *b* 1 April 1916; *d* of Harold Montagu Edmonds and Florence Myra Edmonds (*née* Lilley). *Educ*: Wimbledon High Sch.; Newnham Coll., Cambridge. Research Student of Westfield Coll., 1939–40, and of Newnham Coll., 1940–41; Research Fellow of Newnham Coll., 1941–43; Asst Lecturer, Newnham Coll., 1943–45. *Publications*: papers in mathematical journals. *Recreations*: travel, photography. *Address*: 5 Cross Lane Close, Orwell, Royston, Herts SG8 5QW. *T*: Cambridge (0223) 207789.

EDMONDS, Winston Godward, CBE 1966; ERD 1945; Managing Director, Manchester Ship Canal Co., 1961–70; *b* 27 Nov. 1912; *s* of Wilfred Bell Edmonds and Nina (*née* Godward); *m* 1940, Sheila Mary (*née* Armitage); one *s*. *Educ*: Merchant Taylors'. Joined LNER, first as traffic apprentice and then in various positions, 1930–46; Manchester Ship Canal Co.: Commercial Manager, 1947–58; Manager, 1959–61. *Recreations*: golf, philately. *Address*: Herons Wood, 22 Castlegate, Prestbury, Cheshire SK10 4AZ. *T*: Prestbury (0625) 828966.

EDMONDS-BROWN, (Cedric Wilfred) George; HM Diplomatic Service; First Secretary, Rome, since 1991; *b* 24 April 1939; *s* of late Maj. W. R. E. Edmonds-Brown and E. M. Edmonds-Brown; *m* 1st, 1964, Everild A. V. Hardman (*d* 1988); one *s* two *d*; 2nd, 1990, Teiko Watanabe; one *s*. *Educ*: Dame Allan's Boys' Sch., Newcastle; King's Coll., Durham Univ. Joined CRO, 1962; Lagos, 1963; Karachi, 1964–68; 3rd Sec., Buenos Aires, 1968–73; FCO, 1973–76; 2nd Sec., Bucharest, 1976–80; 1st Sec. and HM Consul, Caracas, 1980–85; ODA, 1985–88; Head of Chancery, Ottawa, 1988; Dep. High Comr, Barbados, 1989–91. *Recreations*: art, travel, cricket. *Address*: c/o Foreign and Commonwealth Office, King Charles Street, SW1A 2AH; 26 Thames Point, Fairways, Teddington, Middx TW11 9PP. *T*: 081–977 9711.

EDMONDSON, family name of **Baron Sandford.**

EDMONDSON, Anthony Arnold; His Honour Judge Edmondson; a Circuit Judge (formerly County Court Judge and Commissioner, Liverpool and Manchester Crown Courts), since 1971; *b* 6 July 1920; *s* of late Arnold Edmondson; *m* 1947, Dorothy Amelia Wilson, Gateshead-on-Tyne; three *s* one *d*. *Educ*: Liverpool Univ. (LLB Hons); Lincoln Coll., Oxford (BCL Hons). Served RA (Adjutant), 1940–44; RAF (Pilot), 1944–46; thereafter RA (TA) and TARO. Called to the Bar, Gray's Inn, 1947; William Shaw Schol. 1948; practised on Northern Circuit, 1948–71; Chairman, Liverpool Dock Labour Bd Appeal Tribunal, 1955–66; Mem. Court of Liverpool Univ., 1960–. Dep. Chm., Lancashire QS, 1970–71; Pres., S Cumbria Magistrates' Assoc., 1977–87; JP Lancs, 1970. *Recreations*: walking, fishing. *Address*: County Sessions House, Preston, Lancs.

EDMONDSON, Leonard Firby; Executive Council Member, Amalgamated Union of Engineering Workers, 1966–77; *b* 16 Dec. 1912; *s* of Arthur William Edmondson and Elizabeth Edmondson; unmarried. *Educ*: Gateshead Central Sch. Served apprenticeship as engr, Liner Concrete Machinery Co. Ltd, Newcastle upon Tyne, 1929–34; worked in a number of engrg, ship-bldg and ship-repairing firms; shop steward and convener of shop stewards in several firms. AUEW: Mem., Tyne Dist Cttee, 1943–53; Tyne Dist Sec., 1953–66. CSEU: Mem., Exec. Council, 1966–78; Pres., 1976–77. Member: Shipbldg Industry Trng Bd, 1966–79; Council, ACAS, 1976–78; Royal Commn on Legal Services, 1976–79; Council on Tribunals, 1978–84; Cttee of Inquiry into Prison Services, 1978–79; Gen. Council of TUC, 1970–78. Mem., Birtley Canine Soc. *Recreation*: exhibiting Shetland sheep dogs. *Address*: 6 Kenwood Gardens, Low Fell, Gateshead, Tyne and Wear NE9 6PN. *T*: 091–487 9167. *Clubs*: Northern Counties Shetland Sheep Dog; Manors Social (Newcastle-upon-Tyne).

EDMONSTONE, Sir Archibald (Bruce Charles), 7th Bt *cr* 1774; *b* 3 Aug. 1934; *o* surv. *s* of Sir Charles Edmonstone, 6th Bt, and Gwendolyn Mary (*d* 1989), *d* of late Marshall Field and Mrs Maldwin Drummond; *S* father, 1954; *m* 1st, 1957, Jane (marr. diss. 1967), *er d* of Maj.-Gen. E. C. Colville, CB, DSO; two *s* one *d*; 2nd, 1969, Juliet Elizabeth, *d* of Maj.-Gen. C. M. F. Deakin, *qv*; one *s* one *d*. *Educ*: St Peter's Court; Stowe Sch. *Heir*: *s* Archibald Edward Charles Edmonstone, *b* 4 Feb. 1961. *Address*: Duntreath Castle, Blanefield, Stirlingshire.

See also Sir A. R. J. B. Jardine, Captain Sir C. E. McGrigor.

EDMONTON, Area Bishop of, since 1984; **Rt. Rev. Brian John Masters;** *b* 17 Oct. 1932; *s* of Stanley William and Grace Hannah Masters; unmarried. *Educ*: Collyers School, Horsham; Queens' Coll., Cambridge (MA 1955); Cuddesdon Theological Coll. Lloyds broker, 1955–62. Asst Curate, S Dunstan and All Saints, Stepney, 1964–69; Vicar, Holy Trinity with S Mary, Hoxton, N1, 1969–82; Bishop Suffragan of Fulham, 1982–84. Chm. Exec. Cttee, Church Union, 1984–88. *Recreations*: theatre, squash. *Address*: 1 Regent's Park Terrace, NW1 7EE. *T*: 071-267 4455, *Fax*: 071–267 4404. *Club*: United Oxford & Cambridge University.

EDMONTON (Alberta), Archbishop of, (RC), since 1973; **Most Rev. Joseph Neil MacNeil;** *b* 15 April 1924; *s* of John Martin MacNeil and Kate MacNeil (*née* MacLean). *Educ*: St Francis Xavier Univ., Antigonish, NS (BA 1944); Holy Heart Seminary, Halifax, NS; Univs of Perugia, Chicago and St Thomas Aquinas, Rome (JCD 1958). Priest, 1948; pastor, parishes in NS, 1948–55; Chancery Office, Antigonish, 1958–59; admin, dio. Antigonish, 1959–60; Rector, Antigonish Cathedral, 1961; Dir of Extension Dept, St Francis Xavier Univ., Antigonish, 1961–69; Vice-Pres., 1962–69; Bishop of St John, NB, 1969–73. Pres., Canadian Conf. of Catholic Bishops, 1979–81 (Vice-Pres., 1977–79; Mem., Commn on Ecumenism, 1985–); Chm., Alberta Bishops' Conf., 1973–. Chancellor, Univ. of St Thomas, Fredericton, NB, 1969. Founding Mem., Inst. for Res. on Public Policy, 1968–80; Mem., Bd of Directors: The Futures Secretariat, 1981–; Centre for Human Develt, Toronto, 1985–. Chairman: Bd, Newman Theol Coll., Edmonton, 1973–; Bd, St Joseph's Coll., Alberta Univ., 1973–. Mem., Bd of Management, Edmonton Gen. Hosp., 1983–. *Address*: 8421–101 Avenue, Edmonton, Alberta T6A 0L1, Canada.

EDMONTON (Alberta), Bishop of, since 1988; **Rt. Rev. Kenneth Lyle Genge;** *b* 25 Oct. 1933; *s* of Nelson Simms Genge and Grace Winifred Genge; *m* 1959, Ruth Louise Bate; two *s* one *d*. *Educ*: Univ of Saskatchewan (BA 1958); Emmanuel Coll., Saskatoon (LTh 1957; BD 1959). Parish priest, 1959–85; Conference Retreat Centre Director, 1985–88. Hon. DD Emmanuel Coll. and St Chad, 1989. *Recreations*: sports, physical fitness, music. *Address*: 12324 52 Avenue, Edmonton, Alberta T6H 0P4.

EDMUND-DAVIES, family name of **Baron Edmund-Davies.**

EDMUND-DAVIES, Baron *cr* 1974 (Life Peer), of Aberpennar, Mid Glamorgan; **Herbert Edmund Edmund-Davies,** PC 1966; Kt 1958; a Lord of Appeal; Life Governor and Fellow, King's College, London University; Hon. Fellow, Exeter College, Oxford; *b* 15 July 1906; 3rd *s* of Morgan John Davies and Elizabeth Maud Edmunds; *m* 1935, Eurwen Williams-James; three *d. Educ:* Mountain Ash Grammar Sch.; King's Coll., London; Exeter Coll., Oxford. LLB (London) and Postgraduate Research Scholar, 1926; LLD London, 1928; BCL (Oxon) and Vinerian Scholar, 1929; called to Bar, Gray's Inn, 1929; QC 1943; Bencher, 1948; Treasurer, 1965; Lecturer and Examiner, London School of Economics, 1930–31; Army Officers' Emergency Reserve, 1938; Infantry OCTU; commissioned in Royal Welch Fusiliers, 1940; later seconded to JAG's Dept; Asst Judge Advocate-General, 1944–45 (Lt-Col 1944); Recorder of Merthyr Tydfil, 1942–44; of Swansea, 1944–53; of Cardiff, 1953–58; Chm., QS for Denbighshire, 1953–64; Judge of High Court of Justice, Queen's Bench Division, 1958–66; a Lord Justice of Appeal, 1966–74; a Lord of Appeal in Ordinary, 1974–81; Foreign Office Observer, Cairo espionage trials, 1957. Chairman: Transport Users' Consultative Cttee for Wales, 1959–61; Lord Chancellor's Cttee on Limitation of Actions, 1961; Tribunal of Inquiry into Aberfan Disaster, 1966; Council of Law Reporting 1967–72; Home Secretary's Criminal Law Revision Cttee, 1969–77; Home Sec's Police Inquiry Cttee, 1977–79; conducted Use of Welsh in Courts Inquiry, 1973. Mem., Royal Commn on Penal Reform, 1964–66. President: London Welsh Trust/London Welsh Assoc., 1982–; University College of Swansea, 1965–75; Hon. Standing Counsel, Univ. of Wales, 1947–57; Pro-Chancellor, Univ. of Wales, 1974–85. Hon. Life Member, Canadian Bar Assoc.; CIBA Foundn Trustee; Hamlyn Trustee, 1969–87; Fellow, Royal Soc. of Medicine. Hon. LLD: Wales, 1959; Buckingham, 1989. *Publications:* Law of Distress for Rent and Rates, 1931; miscellaneous legal writings.

EDNAM, Viscount; William Humble David Jeremy Ward; *b* 27 March 1947; *s* and *heir* of Earl of Dudley, *qv* and of Stella Viscountess Ednam, *d* of M. A. Carcano, KCMG, KBE; *m* 1st, 1972, Sarah (marr. diss. 1976), *o d* of Sir Alastair Coats, Bt, *qv*; 2nd, 1976, Debra Louise (marr. diss. 1980), *d* of George Robert and Marjorie Elvera Pinney; one *d. Educ:* Eton; Christ Church, Oxford.

EDSBERG, John Christian; Director for Execution of the Budget, Directorate General for Budgets, Commission of the European Communities, since 1986; *s* of Flight Lt Jørgen Palle Christian Edsberg and Olivia Alice Mary (*née* Gulland); *m* 1966, Rosalyn (*née* Padfield); two *s. Educ:* Westminster School; Brasenose College, Oxford (MA Hons Maths and Engrg Science). MICE. Civil engineer with Sir Alexander Gibb & Partners, 1961–66; Engineer and Contracts Manager, Soil Mechanics Ltd, 1966–67; Consultant and Senior Consultant, P. A. Management Consultants Ltd, 1967–74; Commission of the European Communities: Principal Administrator, 1974–81; Directorate Gen. for Transport, 1974–81; Directorate Gen. for Develt, 1981–82; Head of Div., Directorate Gen. for Financial Control, 1982–86. *Recreation:* architecture. *Address:* Commission of the European Communities, 200 rue de la Loi, 1049 Brussels, Belgium. *T:* 235–5529; 46 Sydney Street, SW3. *T:* 071–351 0685.

EDWARD, Judge David Alexander Ogilvy, CMG 1981; QC (Scotland) 1974; FRSE; Judge of the Court of First Instance of the European Communities, since 1989; *b* 14 Nov. 1934; *s* of J. O. C. Edward, Travel Agent, Perth; *m* 1962, Elizabeth Young McSherry; two *s* two *d. Educ:* Sedbergh Sch.; University Coll., Oxford; Edinburgh Univ. Sub-Lt RNVR (Nat. Service); HMS Hornet, 1956–57. Admitted Advocate, 1962; Clerk of Faculty of Advocates, 1967–70, Treasurer, 1970–77. Pres., Consultative Cttee of Bars and Law Societies, EC, 1978–80; Salvesen Prof. of European Instns, 1985–89, Hon. Prof., 1990, Univ. of Edinburgh. Trustee, Nat. Library of Scotland, 1966–; Mem. Law Adv. Cttee, British Council, 1974–88; Specialist Advr, H of L Select Cttee on EC, 1985, 1986 and 1987. Mem., Panel of Arbitrators, Internat. Centre for Settlement of Investment Disputes, 1981–89; Chm., Scottish Council for Arbitration, 1988–89 (Hon. Pres. 1989–). Director: Continental Assets Trust plc, 1985–89 (Chm.); Adam & Co. Group plc, 1983–89; Harris Tweed Association Ltd, 1984–89. FRSE 1990. Distinguished Cross, First Class, Order of St Raymond of Penafort, Spain, 1979. *Publications:* The Professional Secret, Confidentiality and Legal Professional Privilege in the EEC, 1976; (with R. C. Lane) European Community Law: an introduction, 1991; articles in legal jls. *Address:* Court of First Instance of the EC, L-2925 Luxembourg; 20 Rue Principale, Flaxweiler, L-6925 Luxembourg; 32 Heriot Row, Edinburgh EH3 6ES; Ardargie Cottage, Forgandenny, Perth PH2 9DJ. *Clubs:* Athenæum; New (Edinburgh); Royal Scottish Automobile (Glasgow).

EDWARDES, family name of **Baron Kensington.**

EDWARDES, Sir Michael (Owen), Kt 1979; Chairman: Charter Consolidated PLC, since 1988; Tryhorn Investments Ltd, since 1987; Flying Pictures Ltd, since 1987; Deputy Chairman, R K Carvill International Holdings Ltd; *b* 11 Oct. 1930; *s* of Denys Owen Edwardes and Audrey Noel (*née* Copeland); *m* 1st, 1958, Mary Margaret (*née* Finlay) (marr. diss. 1988); three *d*; 2nd, 1988, Sheila Ann (*née* Guy). *Educ:* St Andrew's Coll., Grahamstown, S Africa; Rhodes Univ., Grahamstown (BA; Hon. LLD). Chairman: BL Ltd (formerly British Leyland), 1977–82; Mercury Communications Ltd, 1982–83; ICL PLC, 1984; Dunlop Hldgs plc, 1984–85; Exec. Dir, Chloride Gp PLC, 1969–77 and 1986; Minorco SA, 1984–; Director: Hill Samuel Gp, 1980–87; Standard Securities PLC, 1985–87; Delta Motor Corp. (Pty) Ltd, 1986–; Kaye Organisation, 1987–88; Jet Press Hldgs BV, 1990–. Non-Exec. Dir, Internat. Management Develt Inst., Washington, 1978–. Mem., European Adv. Bd, Rockwell Internat. CBIM (a Vice-Chm., 1977–80); Hon. FIMechE, 1981. Pres., Veterans Squash Club of GB. *Publication:* Back From the Brink, 1983. *Recreations:* sailing, squash, water ski-ing, tennis. *Clubs:* Royal Automobile; Jesters; Rand and Country (Johannesburg).

EDWARDS, family name of **Barons Chelmer and Crickhowell.**

EDWARDS, (Alfred) Kenneth, CBE 1989 (MBE 1963); Deputy Director-General, Confederation of British Industry, 1982–88; Chairman, Facilities & Properties Management Plc, since 1989; *b* 24 March 1926; *s* of late Ernest Edwards and Florence Edwards (*née* Branch); *m* 1949, Jeannette Lilian, *d* of David Speeks, MBE; one *s* two *d. Educ:* Latymer Upper Sch.; Magdalene Coll., Cambridge; University Coll. London (BScEcon). Served RAF, 1944–47; RAF Coll., Cranwell, 1945, FO (Pilot). Entered HMOCS, Nigeria, 1952; Provincial Administration, Warri and Benin, 1952–54; Lagos Secretariat, 1954; Sen. Asst Sec., Nigerian Min. of Communications and Aviation, 1959; retired, 1962. Secretary, British Radio Equipment Manufrs' Assoc., 1962; Gp Marketing Manager, Thorn Elec. Industries Ltd, 1965; Internat. Dir, Brookhirst Igranic Ltd (Thorn Gp), 1967; Gp Marketing Dir, Cutler Hammer Europa, 1972; Dep. Chm., BEAMA Overseas Trade Cttee, 1973; Chief Exec., BEAMA, 1976–82. CBI: Member: Council, 1974, 1976–82; Finance and Gen. Purposes Cttee, 1977–82; Vice-Chm., Eastern Reg. Council, 1974; Chm., Working Party on Liability for Defective Products, 1978–82; Mem., President's Cttee, 1979–82. Member: Elec. Engrg EDC, 1976; Council, Elec. Res. Assoc. Ltd, 1976–82; Exec. Cttee, ORGALIME, 1976–82; Management Bd, Eur. Cttee for Develt of Vocational Training, 1988–; BSI Bd, 1978–82, 1984– (Chm., British Electrotechnical Cttee and Electrotechnical Divisional Council, 1981–; Chm., Quality Policy Cttee, 1988–); BOTB, 1982–88; Salvation Army Adv. Bd (London), 1982–; BTEC, 1983–89; BBC Consultative Gp on Indust. and Business Affairs, 1983–88; Bd and Exec. Cttee, Business in the Community, 1987–88; President: CENELEC, 1977–79; Liaison Cttee for Electrical and Electronic Industries, ORGALIME, 1979–82 (Chm., 1980–82); Mem. Exec. Cttee, 1982–, and Chm. Finance Cttee, 1983–, UNICE. Dir, Polar Electronics Ltd, 1989–. Mem. Court, Cranfield Inst. of Technol., 1970–75. *Publications:* contrib. technical jls; lectures and broadcasts on industrial subjects. *Recreations:* music, books, walking. *Address:* 53 Bedford Road, Rushden, Northants NN10 0ND. *Clubs:* Athenæum, Royal Air Force.

EDWARDS, Andrew John Cumming; Deputy Secretary (Public Services), HM Treasury, since 1990; *b* 3 Nov. 1940; *s* of John Edwards and Norah Hope Edwards (*née* Bevan); *m* 1969, Charlotte Anne Chilcot (marr. diss. 1987); one *s* two *d. Educ:* Fettes Coll., Edinburgh; St John's Coll., Oxford (MA); Harvard Univ. (AM, MPA). Asst master, Malvern Coll., 1962–63; HM Treasury: Asst Principal, 1963–67; Pvte Sec. to Jt Perm. Sec., 1966–67; Principal, 1967–75; Harkness Fellow, Harvard Univ., 1971–73; Asst Sec., 1975–83; RCDS, 1979; Asst Sec., DES, 1983–85; Under Sec., HM Treasury, 1985–89. Gov., British Inst. of Recorded Sound, 1974–79; Sec., Bd of Dirs, Royal Opera House, 1988– (Sec., Develt Bd, 1984–87). Conductor, Acad. of St Mary's, Wimbledon, 1980–. *Publications:* Nuclear Weapons, the balance of terror, the quest for peace, 1986; articles on European Community Budget. *Recreations:* music, writing, reading, walking.

EDWARDS, Arthur Frank George; Vice-Chairman, Thames Water Authority, 1973–83; *b* 27 March 1920; *o s* of Arthur Edwards and Mabel (Elsie) Edwards; *m* 1946, Joyce May Simmons; one *s* one *d. Educ:* West Ham Grammar Sch.; Garnett Coll., London; West Ham Coll. of Technology; City of London Polytechnic; King's College London. MSc. CEng, FIChemE, MSE; Hon. FIWM. Various posts with Ever Ready (GB) Ltd, 1936–50; Prodn Man., J. Burns & Co. Ltd, 1950–53; various lectrg posts, 1954–65; Organiser for science and techn. subjects, London Boroughs of Barking and Redbridge, 1965–82. Member: West Ham Co. Borough Council, 1946–65; Newham Council, 1964–86 (Mayor, 1967–68); GLC, 1964–86 (Dep. Chm., 1970–71; Chm., Public Services Cttee, 1973–77); Chm. of Governors, NE London Polytechnic, 1972–87. Mem., Fabian Soc. *Recreations:* reading, Association football (watching West Ham United). *Address:* 18 Wanstead Park Avenue, E12 5EN. *T:* 081–530 6436. *Club:* West Ham Supporters'.

EDWARDS, Brian, CBE 1988; Regional General Manager, Trent Regional Health Authority, since 1984; *b* 19 Feb. 1942; *s* of John Albert Edwards and Ethel Edwards; *m* 1964, Jean (*née* Cannon); two *s* two *d. Educ:* Wirral Grammar Sch. Jun. Administrator, Clatterbridge Hosp., 1958–62; Dep. Hosp. Sec., Cleaver Hosp., 1962–64; National Trainee, Nuffield Centre, Leeds, 1964–66; Administrator, Gen. Infirmary, Leeds, 1966–67; Hosp. Sec., Keighley Victoria Hosp., 1967–68; Administrator, Mansfield HMC, 1969–70; Lectr, Univ. of Leeds, 1970–72; Dep. Gp Sec., Hull A HMC, 1972–74; Nuffield Travelling Fellow, USA, 1973; Dist Administrator, Leeds AHA(T), 1974–76; Area Administrator, Cheshire AHA, 1976–81; Regional Administrator, Trent RHA, 1981–84. Vis. Lectr, Health Care Studies, 1973–, and Associate Fellow, Nuffield Inst., 1987–, Univ. of Leeds; Vis. Prof., Health Care Studies, Univ. of Keele, 1989; Queen Elizabeth Nuffield Fellow, 1991. Adviser to WHO, 1982–; Chairman: NHS Manpower Planning Adv. Gp, 1983–86; Regional Gen. Managers Gp, 1986–87; Member: Steering Cttee on Future of Nursing, 1988; Standing Cttee on Medical Audit, RCP, 1989–. Dir, Mercia Publications Ltd, 1984–. Inst. of Health Service Administrators: Mem., 1964–; Pres., 1982–83; Mem. Editorial Cttee, Health Care in the UK: its organisation and management, 1982–. Jt Editor, Health Services Manpower Review, 1970–91. CBIM 1988. *Publications:* Si Vis Pacem—preparations for change in the NHS, 1973; Profile for Change, 1973; Bridging in Health, Planning the Child Health Services, 1975; Industrial Relations in the NHS: managers and industrial relations, 1979; Manpower Planning in the NHS, 1984; Employment Policies for Health Care, 1985; Distinction Awards for Doctors, 1987; conf. papers presented in UK, Norway, Germany, USA, India, USSR, Czechoslavakia, and Guyana; contrib. prof. jls. *Recreations:* golf, stage management. *Address:* 3 Royal Croft Drive, Baslow, Derbyshire DE4 1SN. *T:* Baslow (0246) 583459, *Fax:* Baslow (0246) 582583. *Clubs:* Baslow Cricket (Vice-Pres.); Bakewell Golf (Captain, 1991).

EDWARDS, Charles Harold, FRCP; Dean of St Mary's Hospital Medical School, Paddington, 1973–79; *b* 1913; *m* 1959; one *s* two *d. Educ:* Blundell's Sch., Tiverton; Guy's Hosp. Med. Sch. MRCS 1937; LRCP 1937; MRCP 1946; FRCP 1961. Formerly: Resident Medical Appts, Guy's Hosp.; Resident Med. Officer, Nat. Hosp., Queen Square; Neurological Registrar, St Mary's Hosp., Paddington; Consultant Physician, Dept Nervous Diseases, St Mary's Hosp., 1954–78; Consultant Neurologist: Royal Nat. Throat, Nose and Ear Hosp., 1955–78; King Edward VII Hosp., Windsor, 1952–78; Canadian Red Cross Meml Hosp., Taplow, 1952–78; Maidenhead Hosp., 1952–78. Co-ordinator, Special Progs, Wellcome Trust, 1979–85. Mem., British Assoc. of Neurologists, 1952–; FRSocMed. *Publications:* Neurology of Ear, Nose and Throat, 1973; Neurological Section: Synopsis of Otolaryngology, 1967; Scott-Brown, Diseases of Ear, Nose and Throat, 1971; contrib. Qly Jl Medicine, Lancet, etc. *Recreations:* words, gardening. *Address:* Cardinal House, The Green, Hampton Court, Surrey. *T:* 081–979 6922. *Club:* Garrick.

EDWARDS, (Charles) Marcus; His Honour Judge Marcus Edwards; a Circuit Judge, since 1986; *b* 10 Aug. 1937; *s* of John Basil Edwards, *qv*; *m* 1st, 1963, Anne Louise Stockdale (*d* 1970), *d* of Sir Edmund Stockdale, 1st Bt; 2nd, 1975, Sandra Wates (*née* Mouroutsos); one *d* and three step *d. Educ:* Dragon Sch., Oxford; Rugby Sch.; Brasenose Coll., Oxford (scholar; BA Jurisprudence). Trooper, RAC, 1955; 2nd Lieut, Intelligence Corps, Cyprus, 1956–57. HM Diplomatic Service, 1960–65; Third Sec., 1960, Spain, 1961, FO, 1961–62, South Africa and High Commn Territories, 1962–63, Laos, 1964; Second Sec., FO, 1965, resigned. Called to the Bar, Middle Temple, 1962; practised, London, 1966–86; Mem., Midland and Oxford Circuit; a Recorder, 1985–86. Chm., Pavilion Opera, 1987–. *Recreations:* gardening, walking, talking, food and drink. *Address:* Melbourne House, South Parade, W4 1JU. *T:* 081-995 9146. *Club:* Beefsteak.

EDWARDS, Sir Christopher (John Churchill), 5th Bt *cr* 1866; Director, Ohmeda, BOC Group, Louisville, Colorado, since 1989; *b* 16 Aug. 1941; *s* of Sir (Henry) Charles (Serrell Priestley) Edwards, 4th Bt and of Lady (Daphne) Edwards (*née* Birt); *S* father, 1963; *m* 1972, Gladys Irene Vogelgesang; two *s. Educ:* Frensham Heights, Surrey; Loughborough, Leics. Gen. Manager, Kelsar Inc., American Home Products, San Diego, Calif, 1979–84; Vice-Pres., Valleylab Inc., Boulder, Colorado, 1981–89. *Heir: s* David Charles Priestley Edwards, *b* 22 Feb. 1974. *Address:* 11637 Country Club Drive, Westminster, Colorado 80234, USA. *T:* (303) 469–3156. *Club:* Ranch Country (Westminster, Colorado).

EDWARDS, Sir Clive; *see* Edwards, Sir J. C. L.

EDWARDS, David; Director, John Laing plc, since 1982; Chairman, Londondome Ltd, since 1988; *b* 27 Oct. 1929; *s* of Col Cyril Edwards, DSO, MC, DL and Jessie Edwards; *m* 1966, Gay Clothier; two *s* one *d. Educ:* Felsted Sch.; Trinity Hall, Cambridge (MA, LLM).

Called to the Bar, Middle Temple, 1952; Harmsworth Scholar, Middle Temple, 1955; admitted Solicitor, 1958. Partner, E. Edwards Son & Noice, 1959–75; Sec., Legal Aid, 1976–86, and Dep. Sec.-Gen., 1982–86, Law Soc. Dir, Laing Properties, 1988–90. Chm., Offshore Racing Council, 1970–78; Dep. Chm., Royal Yachting Assoc., 1976–81. *Recreation:* sailing. *Address:* Olivers, Colchester, Essex CO2 0HJ. *Clubs:* Royal Ocean Racing; Royal Yacht Squadron (Cowes).
See also Baron Chelmer, J. T. Edwards.

EDWARDS, (David) Elgan (Hugh); His Honour Judge Elgan Edwards; a Circuit Judge, since 1989; *b* 6 Dec. 1943; *s* of Howell and Dilys Edwards; *m* 1982, Carol Anne Smalls; two *s* one *d*. *Educ:* Rhyl Grammar Sch.; University Coll. of Wales, Aberystwyth (LLB Hons 1966; Pres., Students Union, 1967). Called to the Bar, Gray's Inn, 1967; a Recorder (Wales and Chester Circuit), 1983–89. Conservative Parly Candidate: Merioneth, 1970; Stockport South, Feb. 1974. Sheriff, City of Chester, 1977–78. *Recreation:* swimming. *Address:* The Crown Court, Chester Castle, Chester. *T:* Chester (0244) 317606. *Club:* Chester City (Chester).

EDWARDS, Very Rev. David Lawrence; Provost of Southwark Cathedral since 1983; *b* 20 Jan. 1929; *s* of late Lawrence Wright and Phyllis Boardman Edwards; *m* 1st, 1960, Hilary Mary (*née* Phillips) (marr. diss. 1984); one *s* three *d;* 2nd, 1984, Sybil, *d* of Michael and Kathleen Falcon. *Educ:* King's Sch., Canterbury; Magdalen Coll., Oxford. Lothian Prize, 1951; 1st cl. hons Mod. Hist., BA 1952; MA 1956. Fellow, All Souls Coll., Oxford, 1952–59. Deacon, 1954; Priest, 1955. On HQ staff of Student Christian Movement of Gt Brit. and Ireland, 1955–66; Editor and Man. Dir, SCM Press Ltd, 1959–66; Gen. Sec. of Movt, 1965–66. Curate of: St John's, Hampstead, 1955–58; St Martin-in-the-Fields, 1958–66; Fellow and Dean of King's College, Cambridge, 1966–70; Asst Lectr in Divinity, Univ. of Cambridge, 1967–70; Rector of St Margaret's, Westminster, 1970–78; Canon of Westminster, 1970–78; Sub-Dean, 1974–78; Speaker's Chaplain, 1972–78; Dean of Norwich, 1978–82. Exam. Chaplain: to Bp of Manchester, 1965–73; to Bp of Durham, 1968–72; to Bp of Bradford, 1972–78; to Bp of London, 1974–78; to Archbishop of Canterbury, 1975–78. Hulsean Lectr, 1967; Six Preacher, Canterbury Cathedral, 1969–76. Chairman: Churches' Council on Gambling, 1970–78; Christian Aid, 1971–78. Hon. Fellow, South Bank Poly., 1990. DD Lambeth, 1990. *Publications:* A History of the King's School, Canterbury, 1957; Not Angels But Anglicans, 1958; This Church of England, 1962; God's Cross in Our World, 1963; Religion and Change, 1969; F. J. Shirley: An Extraordinary Headmaster, 1969; The Last Things Now, 1969; Leaders of the Church of England, 1971; What is Real in Christianity?, 1972; St Margaret's, Westminster, 1972; The British Churches Turn to the Future, 1973; Ian Ramsey, Bishop of Durham, 1973; Good News in Acts, 1974; What Anglicans Believe, 1974; Jesus for Modern Man, 1975; A Key to the Old Testament, 1976; Today's Story of Jesus, 1976; The State of the Nation, 1976; A Reason to Hope, 1978; Christian England: vol 1, Its story to the Reformation, 1981; vol. 2, From the Reformation to the Eighteenth Century, 1983; vol. 3, From the Eighteenth Century to the First World War, 1984; The Futures of Christianity, 1987; Essentials: a Liberal-Evangelical dialogue with John Stott, 1988; The Cathedrals of Britain, 1989; Tradition and Truth, 1989; Christians in a New Europe, 1990; (ed) The Honest to God Debate, 1963; (ed) Collins Children's Bible, 1978; (ed) Christianity and Conservatism, 1990; (ed) Robert Runcie: a portrait by his friends, 1990. *Address:* Provost's Lodging, 51 Bankside, SE1 9JE. *T:* 071–928 6414. *Club:* Athenæum.
See also M. G. Falcon.

EDWARDS, David Michael, CMG 1990; Law Officer (International Law), Hong Kong Government, since 1990; *b* 28 Feb. 1940; *s* of Ernest William Edwards and Thelma Irene Edwards; *m* 1966, Veronica Margaret Postgate; one *s* one *d*. *Educ:* The King's Sch., Canterbury; Univ. of Bristol. LLB Hons. Admitted to Roll of Solicitors, 1964. Solicitor of Supreme Court, 1964–67; Asst Legal Adviser, Foreign Office, 1967; Legal Adviser: British Military Govt, Berlin, 1972; British Embassy, Bonn, 1974; Legal Counsellor, 1977; Dir, Legal Div., IAEA, Vienna (on secondment), 1977–79; Legal Counsellor, FCO, 1979; Agent of the UK Govt in cases before European Commn and Court of Human Rights, 1979–82; Counsellor (Legal Adviser), UK Mission to UN, New York, and HM Embassy, Washington, 1985–88; Legal Counsellor, 1988–89, Dep. Legal Advr, 1989–90, FCO; Sen. Counsel, Bechtel Ltd, 1990. *Recreations:* reading, travel, gardening. *Address:* 3rd Floor, Central Government Offices, Lower Albert Road, Hong Kong. *Club:* Royal Over-Seas League.

EDWARDS, Prof. David Olaf, DPhil; FRS 1988; University Professor of Physics, Ohio State University, since 1988; *b* 27 April 1932; *s* of Robert Edwards and Margaret Edwina (*née* Larsen); *m* 1967, Wendy Lou Townsend; one *s* one *d*. *Educ:* Holt High Sch., Liverpool; Brasenose Coll., Oxford (BA 1st cl. Hons, 1953; Sen. Hulme Schol., 1953–56; MA; DPhil 1957). FAPS. Pressed Steel Co. Res. Fellow, Clarendon Lab., Oxford Univ., 1957–58; Ohio State University: Vis. Asst Prof., 1958–60; Asst Prof., 1960–62; Associate Prof., 1962–65; Prof., 1965–88. Visiting Professor: Imperial Coll., London, 1964; Sussex Univ., 1964, 1968; Technion, Israel, 1971–72; Ecole Normale Supérieure, Paris, 1978, 1982, 1986; Vis. Scientist, Brookhaven Nat. Lab., 1975. Consultant: Brookhaven Nat. Lab., 1975–77; Los Alamos Scientific Lab., 1979–81. Mem. of various cttees in connection with internat. confs and symposia on low temp. physics in USA and Europe, 1964–. Mem., Fritz London Award Cttee, 1982–. Sir Francis Simon Prize, British Inst. of Phys, 1983; Dist. Schol. Award, Ohio State Univ., 1984; Special Creativity Awards, US Nat. Sci. Foundn, 1981, 1986. *Publications:* (ed jtly) Proceedings of the Ninth International Conference on Low Temperature Physics (LT9), 1966; numerous articles on low temp. physics in scientific jls. *Recreations:* beagling (Master, Rocky Fork Beagles, 1975–), snorkeling (Grand Cayman), crossword puzzles, reading detective stories, watching old British TV programs. *Address:* 2345 Dorset Road, Columbus, Ohio 43221, USA. *T:* 614 486–4553; Department of Physics, Ohio State University, 174 W 18th Avenue, Columbus, Ohio 43210, USA. *T:* 614 292–7275.

EDWARDS, Derek; FEng 1986; FIM; Director, since 1974, Industrial Director, since 1987, RTZ Corp. Ltd; *b* 28 March 1931; *s* of L. R. Edwards and M. N. Edwards; *m* 1956, Julia Maureen Wynn; one *s* two *d*. *Educ:* Newport High Sch.; UC Swansea, Univ. of Wales (BSc Metallurgy). RAF, 1952–54. Alcan (UK), 1954–60; Alcan (W Africa), 1960–62; Pillar Ltd, 1962–70; RTZ Pillar, 1970– (Chm., 1981–). Non-executive Director: TI Group, 1984–; Bridon Ltd, 1985–. *Recreations:* sport, music. *Address:* (office) 6 St James's Square, SW1; Kings Lawn, Sandy Lane Road, Charlton Kings, Cheltenham, Glos GL53 9DB. *Clubs:* East India, MCC.

EDWARDS, Douglas John; Consultant, Argyll Foods Ltd (formerly Louis C. Edwards & Sons (Manchester) Ltd), 1979–84 (Joint Chairman and Managing Director, 1966–79); Chairman and Managing Director, Imexport Meats Ltd, since 1979; *b* 18 March 1916; *s* of Louis Edwards and Catherine Edwards; *m* 1st, 1941, Emmeline H. Haslam (*d* 1964); two *s*; 2nd, 1973, Valerie Barlow-Hitchen. *Educ:* De La Salle Coll., Salford. Served in Grenadier Guards, 1940–45. Member of Lloyd's, 1965–: Joined Manchester Conservative Party, 1947; Mem. Manchester City Council, 1951–74; Alderman, 1967–74; Lord Mayor of City of Manchester, 1971–72; Greater Manchester Metropolitan CC, 1974–78; High Sheriff, 1975–76. President: Manchester Cttee, Grenadier Guards Assoc., 1968–81 (Life Mem.); Greater Manchester Youth Assoc., 1973–80; Chairman: Manchester Br., Variety Club of GB, 1969–70; Northern Cttee, Hotel and Catering Benev. Assoc., 1976–81. Governor: De La Salle Teacher Training Coll., Greater Manchester, 1972–81; De La Salle Coll., Salford, 1972–81. DL Greater Manchester, 1979–81. Freeman and Liveryman, Makers of Playing Cards Co., 1974. Polonia Restituta, First Cl., 1972. KHS (Papal knighthood), 1986. *Recreations:* golf, sailing, shooting. *Address:* Apt 10A, The Marbella, 250 South Ocean Boulevard, Boca Raton, Florida 33432, USA. *T:* (407) 392–8203. *Clubs:* Carlton; Royal Thames Yacht; Lloyd's Yacht; Lancs County Cricket (Life Mem.); Cheshire Polo; Altrincham Rifle; Antibes Yacht; St Francis Yacht (USA) (Hon. Mem.).

EDWARDS, Prof. Edward George, PhD, BSc, FRSC; Vice-Chancellor and Principal, University of Bradford, 1966–78, Hon. Professor, since 1978; Principal of Bradford Institute of Technology, 1957–66; *b* 18 Feb. 1914; *m* 1940, Kathleen Hewitt; two *s* two *d*. *Educ:* Cardiff High Sch.; University of South Wales; Cardiff Coll. of Technology. Lecturer in Chemistry, University of Nottingham, 1938–40; Research Chemist (ICI Ltd), 1940–45; Head of Dept of Chemistry and Applied Chemistry, Royal Technical Coll., Salford, 1945–54; Principal, Coll. of Technology, Liverpool, 1954–57. Hon. DTech Bradford, 1980; Fellow, University Coll., Cardiff, 1981. *Publications:* Higher Education for Everyone, 1982; various research papers in chemical jls; articles and papers on higher educn, technological innovation, university planning. *Recreations:* philosophy, music, walking, travel. *Address:* Corner Cottage, Westwood Drive, Ilkley, West Yorks. *T:* Ilkley (0943) 607112.

EDWARDS, Elgan; *see* Edwards, D. E. H.

EDWARDS, Elizabeth Alice; Chief Area Nursing Officer, Tayside Health Board, since 1988; *b* 26 May 1937. *Educ:* Coleraine High Sch.; Univ. of Edinburgh (BSc Soc. Sci.); SRN, SCM. Staff Nurse, Midwife, Ward Sister and nurse management posts, 1958–72; Principal Nursing Officer, Edinburgh Northern Hosps Gp, 1972–74; Dist Nursing Officer, N Lothian, Lothian Health Bd, 1974–80; Chief Area Nursing Officer, Dumfries and Galloway Health Bd, 1980–88. Mem., Nat. Bd for Scotland, 1983– (Dep. Chm., 1985–). *Publications:* papers on nursing. *Address:* Tayside Health Board, PO Box 75, Vernonholme, Riverside Drive, Dundee DD1 9NL. *T:* Dundee (0382) 645151.

EDWARDS, Very Rev. Erwyd; *see* Edwards, Very Rev. T. E. P.

EDWARDS, Frederick Edward, RD 1968 and Clasp, 1977; Director of Social Work, Strathclyde Region, since 1976; *b* 9 April 1931; *s* of Reginal Thomas Edwards and Jessie Howard Simpson; *m* 1957, Edith Jocelyn Price (marr. diss. 1990); two *s* one *d*; *m* 1990, Mary Olds (*née* Ellis). *Educ:* St Edward's Coll., Liverpool; Univ. of Glasgow (Dip. Applied Soc. Studies 1965). BA Open Univ., 1973. FBIM; FISW. Merchant Navy Deck Officer, 1948–58; Perm. Commn, RNR, 1953, Lt-Comdr 1963; sailed Barque Mayflower to USA, 1957. Morgan Refractories, 1958–60; Probation Service, Liverpool, 1960–69; Dir of Social Work: Moray and Nairn, 1969–74; Grampian, 1974–76. Vis. Prof., Dept of Social Admin and Social Work, Univ. of Glasgow, 1988–. MUniv Open, 1988. Member: Scottish Marriage Guidance Council, 1970– (Chm., 1980–83); Scottish Council on Crime, 1972–75; Adv. Council on Social Work, 1976–81. *Publications:* articles in social work jls. *Recreations:* sailing, natural history, reading. *Address:* Social Work Department, Strathclyde House 4, 20 India Street, Glasgow G2 4PF.

EDWARDS, Gareth Owen; QC 1985; **His Honour Judge Gareth Edwards;** a Circuit Judge, since 1991; *b* 26 Feb. 1940; *s* of Arthur Wyn Edwards and Mair Eluned Edwards; *m* 1967, Katharine Pek Har Goh; two *s* one *d*. *Educ:* Herbert Strutt Grammar Sch., Belper; Trinity Coll., Oxford (BA,BCL). Called to the Bar, Inner Temple, 1963; Army Legal Service, 1963–65; Commonwealth Office, 1965–67. Practised, Wales and Chester Circuit, 1967–; Recorder, Crown Court, 1978–91. *Recreations:* climbing, chess. *Address:* 58 Lache Lane, Chester CH4 7LS. *T:* Chester (0244) 677795. *Club:* Army and Navy.

EDWARDS, Gareth Owen, MBE 1975; Welsh Rugby footballer; Director of Engineering Company in S Wales; *b* 12 July 1947; *s* of Granville and Anne Edwards; *m* 1972, Maureen Edwards; two *s*. *Educ:* Pontardawe Tech. Sch.; Millfield Sch.; Cardiff College of Educn. Rugby Football: 1st cap for Wales, 1967 (*v* France); Captain of Wales on 13 occasions; youngest Captain of Wales (at 20 years), 1968; British Lions Tours: 1968, 1971, 1974; Barbarians, 1967–78. Member of Cardiff RFC, 1966–; a record 53 consecutive caps, to 1978; retired, 1978. *Publications:* Gareth: an autobiography, 1978; (jtly) Rugby Skills, 1979; Rugby Skills for Forwards, 1980; Gareth Edwards on Fishing, 1984; Rugby, 1986; Gareth Edwards' 100 Great Rugby Players, 1987. *Recreations:* fishing, golf. *Address:* 211 West Road, Nottage, Porthcawl, Mid-Glamorgan CF36 3RT. *T:* Porthcawl (065671) 5669.

EDWARDS, Geoffrey Francis, CBE 1975 (OBE 1968; MBE 1956); TD; HM Diplomatic Service, retired; *b* 28 Sept. 1917; *s* of late Oliver and Frances Margaret Edwards, Langley, Bucks; *m* 1st, 1949, Joyce Black (*d* 1953); one *d*; 2nd, 1961, Johanna Elisabeth Franziska Taeger. *Educ:* Brighton Coll. Joined Pixley & Abell, Bullion Brokers, 1936. Commissioned RA (TA), June 1939; served with 117 Fd Regt and 59 (Newfoundland) Heavy Regt RA in NW Europe, 1939–45; joined Control Commn for Germany, 1945; joined British Military Govt, Berlin, 1949; Economic Adviser, 1956; Consul-General, Berlin, 1966–75. Ernst Reuter Silver Plaque, Berlin, 1975. *Recreations:* gardening, fishing, golf. *Address:* Am Kurgarten 105, 5485 Sinzig-Bad Bodendorf, Germany. *T:* (02642) 44821.

EDWARDS, Sir George (Robert), OM 1971; Kt 1957; CBE 1952 (MBE 1945); FRS 1968; FEng; DL; now retired; Chairman, British Aircraft Corporation Ltd, 1963–75; Pro-Chancellor, University of Surrey, 1964–79, now Pro-Chancellor Emeritus; *b* 9 July 1908; *m* 1935, Marjorie Annie (*née* Thurgood); one *d*. *Educ:* S West Essex Tech. Coll.; London Univ. (BScEng). Gen. engineering, 1928–35; joined Design Staff, Vickers-Aviation Ltd, Weybridge, 1935; Experimental Manager, Vickers-Armstrongs Ltd, Weybridge Works, 1940. Chief Designer, Weybridge Works, 1945; Dir, Vickers Ltd, 1955–67. Pres., Royal Aeronautical Soc., 1957–58; Vice-Pres., Royal Society of Arts, 1958–61. Mem., Royal Instn, 1971–. Pres., Surrey CCC, 1979 (Vice-Pres., 1974). DL Surrey, 1981. FEng; Hon. Fellow: RAeS 1960; IMechE; Manchester Coll. of Science and Technology; Hon. FAIAA. Hon. DSc: Southampton, 1962; Salford, 1967; Cranfield Inst. of Technology, 1970; City Univ., 1975; Stirling, 1979; Surrey, 1979; Hon. DSc(Eng) London, 1970; Hon. LLD Bristol, 1973. George Taylor Gold Medal, 1948; British Gold Medal for Aeronautics, 1952; Daniel Guggenheim Medal, 1959; Air League Founders Medal, 1969; Albert Gold Medal (RSA), 1972; Royal Medal, Royal Soc., 1974. *Publications:* various papers and lectures in Jl RAeS, Amer. Inst. of Aeronautical Sciences and Amer. Soc. of Automotive Engrs. *Recreation:* painting. *Address:* Albury Heights, White Lane, Guildford, Surrey. *T:* Guildford (0483) 504488. *Clubs:* Athenæum; Royal Air Force Yacht.

EDWARDS, Huw William Edmund; MP (Lab) Monmouth, since May 1991; *b* 12 April 1953; *s* of Rev. Dr Ifor M. Edwards and Esme Edwards. *Educ:* Eastfields High Sch., Mitcham; Manchester Polytechnic; Univ. of York (BA, MA, MPhil). Lecturer in Social Policy: Coventry (Lanchester) Poly., 1980–81; Univ. of Sheffield, 1983–84; Poly. of the

South Bank, 1984–85; Manchester Poly., 1985–88; Sen. Lectr in Social Policy, Brighton Poly., 1988–91. Res. Associate, Low Pay Unit, 1985–; Tutor with Open Univ., 1987. Mem., Boro' Welsh Congregational Chapel, London. *Publications:* Low Pay in South Wales, 1989; articles in professional jls. *Recreations:* sport, football, Rugby, tennis, cricket, Welsh choral music (Member, Gwalia Male Voice Choir). *Address:* House of Commons, SW1A 0AA. *T:* 071–219 3000. *Club:* London Welsh Association.

EDWARDS, Iorwerth Eiddon Stephen, CMG 1973; CBE 1968; MA, LittD; FBA 1962; Keeper of Egyptian Antiquities, British Museum, 1955–74; *b* 21 July 1909; *s* of late Edward Edwards, Orientalist, and Ellen Jane (*née* Higgs); *m* 1938, Elizabeth, *y d* of late Charles Edwards Lisle; one *d* (one *s* decd). *Educ:* Merchant Taylors'; Gonville and Caius Coll., Cambridge (Major Scholar). Merchant Taylors' Sch. Exhibitioner and John Stewart of Rannoch Univ. Scholar, Cambridge, 1928; 1st Cl. Oriental Languages Tripos (Arabic and Hebrew), Parts I and II, 1930–31; Mason Prize, Tyrwhitt Scholarship and Wright Studentship, 1932. Entered Dept of Egyptian and Assyrian Antiquities, British Museum, 1934; seconded to Foreign Office; attached to British Embassies, Cairo and Baghdad, and to Secretariat, Jerusalem, 1942–45. T. E. Peet Prize, Liverpool Univ., 1947. Visiting Prof., Brown Univ., Providence, RI, USA, 1953–54. Glanville Meml Lectr, Cambridge Univ., 1980; Foreign Guest Lectr, Coll. de France, 1982. Pioneered and chose objects for Tutankhamun Exhibition, London, 1972. Member: Archaeol. Cttee for saving monuments of Philae, 1973–80, Cttee for planning, Nat. Mus., Cairo, 1982, Unesco-Egyptian Min. of Culture; Adv. Cttee for re-organizing Egyptian Mus., Cairo, 1985, Cttee to advise on protection of monuments of Giza, 1990, Egyptian Min. of Culture. Vice-Pres. Egypt Exploration Soc., 1962–88; Member: German Archæological Inst.; Austrian Archæol Inst.; Associate Mem., Inst. of Egypt; Mem., Cttee of Visitors of Metropolitan Museum of Art, NY; Corres. Mem., Fondation Egyptologique Reine Elisabeth; Correspondant étranger de L'Institut, Académie des Inscriptions et Belles-Lettres. *Publications:* Hieroglyphic Texts in the British Museum, Vol. VIII, 1939; The Pyramids of Egypt, 1947, 3rd edn 1985; Hieratic Papyri in the British Museum, 4th Series (Oracular Amuletic Decrees of the Late New Kingdom), 1960; The Early Dynastic Period in Egypt, 1964; Joint Editor of The Cambridge Ancient History (3rd edn), vols I-III, 1970–91; Treasures of Tutankhamun (Catalogue of London exhibn), 1972; Treasures of Tutankhamun (Catalogue of US exhibn), 1976; Tutankhamun's Jewelry, 1976; Tutankhamun: his tomb and its treasures, 1976; articles in Journal of Egyptian Archæology and other scientific periodicals. *Recreations:* watching cricket, gardening. *Address:* Dragon House, The Bullring, Deddington, Oxon OX15 0TT. *T:* Deddington (0869) 38481. *Club:* Athenæum.

EDWARDS, Jack Trevor, CBE 1985; CEng, FICE; FCIT; Chairman, Halcrow Fox and Associates, since 1986; Consultant, Freeman Fox & Partners, since 1986 (Senior Partner, 1979–86); *b* 23 June 1920; *s* of late Col Cyril Ernest Edwards, DSO, MC, JP, and Jessie Boyd; *m* 1959, Josephine, (Sally), *d* of late S. W. Williams; one *d. Educ:* Felsted Sch.; City and Guilds Coll., Imperial Coll. London (BScEng, FCGI). RAF Armament and Airfield Construction Branches, Sqdn Ldr, 1941–46. Civil Engr on hydro-electric and thermal power stations, James Williamson and Partners, 1946–50; Freeman Fox & Partners: Engineer, 1951–64; Partner, 1965–79; special field: civil engrg and building works associated with thermal power stations and railways at home and overseas; major projects: Hong Kong Mass Transit Railway, opened 1980; Baghdad and Taipei Metros; Engineer to Dean and Chapter of St Paul's Cathedral, 1969–86. Mem. Council, British Consultants Bureau, 1979–85 (Chm., 1982–83). Liveryman, Worshipful Co. of Painter-Stainers, 1969–. *Publications:* Civil Engineering for Underground Rail Transport, 1990; contrib. Proc. Instn of Civil Engrs. *Recreation:* sailing. *Address:* Keepers, 77 Brentwood Road, Ingrave, Brentwood, Essex CM13 3NU. *T:* Brentwood (0277) 810285. *Clubs:* St Stephen's Constitutional, Royal Cruising, Royal Burnham Yacht.

See also Baron Chelmer, D. Edwards.

EDWARDS, Prof. James Griffith, CBE 1989; DM, DSc, FRCP, FRCPsych; Professor of Addiction Behaviour, Institute of Psychiatry, University of London, since 1979; Principal Investigator, 1967 and Hon. Director, since 1970, Addiction Research Unit; Hon. Consultant, Bethlem and Maudsley Hospitals, since 1967; *b* 3 Oct. 1928; *yr s* of late Dr J. T. Edwards and late Constance Amy (*née* McFadyean); *m* 1st, 1969, Evelyn Morrison (marr. diss. 1981); one *s* one *d* (and one *d* decd); 2nd, 1981, Frances Susan Stables. *Educ:* Andover Grammar Sch.; Balliol Coll., Oxford (BA Physiology 1952; MA; Theodore Williams Schol. in Anatomy); St Bartholomew's Hosp. (Kirkes Schol. and Gold Medal); DM Oxford, 1966; DPM London, 1962; DSc London, 1990; FRCP 1976; FRCPsych 1976. Served RA, 1948–49 (2nd Lieut). Jun. hosp. appts, King George, Ilford, St Bartholomew's, Hammersmith and Maudsley Hosps, 1956–62; Inst. of Psychiatry: res. worker, 1962; Lectr, 1966; Sen. Lectr, 1967; Reader, 1973. Chm., Royal Coll. of Psych. Special Cttee on Drug Dependence, 1983–87 (on Alcohol and Alcoholism, 1975–78); Medical Dir, Alcohol Educn Centre, 1980–83; Member: Home Office Working Party on Drunkenness Offenders, 1967–70; WHO Expert Adv. Cttee on Drug Dependence, 1969–; DoE Cttee on Drinking and Driving, 1974–75; Home Office Adv. Council on Misuse of Drugs, 1972–; DHSS Adv. Cttee on Alcoholism, 1975–78; ESRC (formerly SSRC), 1981–89; Consultant Advr on Alcoholism, DHSS, 1986–; ODA Consultant in Bolivia, 1987. Trustee, Community Drug Proj., 1967–; Patron, Action on Addiction, 1989–; Vice-Patron, Phoenix House, 1990–. Steven's Lectr and Gold Medallist, RSM, 1971; Dent Lectr, King's Coll., 1980; Roche Vis. Prof., Aust. and NZ, 1982; Pollak Lectr, Inst. of Psychiatry, 1988. Jellinek Meml Award, 1980; Evian Award, 1986; Prize, Assoc. for Med. Educn and Res. on Substance Abuse, USA, 1990. Editor, British Jl of Addiction, 1978–. *Publications:* Unreason in an Age of Reason, 1971; (jtly) Alcohol Control Policies, 1975; (ed jtly) Drugs in Socio-Cultural Perspective, 1980; (jtly) Opium and the People, 1981; Treatment of Drinking Problems, 1982 (trans. into 5 langs), 2nd edn 1987; (ed) Drug Scenes, 1987; (ed jtly) Nature of Dependence, 1990; (ed) Personal Influences and Scientific Movements, 1991; articles in jls on scientific and policy aspects of alcohol and drug dependence. *Recreations:* chess, looking at pictures, frequenting junk shops. *Address:* 32 Crooms Hill, SE10 8ER. *T:* 081–858 5631. *Club:* Athenæum.

See also J. M. McF. Edwards.

EDWARDS, James Valentine, CVO 1978; MA; *b* 4 Feb. 1925; *s* of late Captain Alfred Harold Edwards, OBE, and Mrs Eleanor Edwards; *m* 1965, Barbara, Princess Cantacuzene, Countess Speransky, *d* of late Sir John Hanbury-Williams, CVO, and Lady Hanbury-Williams; two *d,* and one step *s* one step *d. Educ:* St Edmund's, Hindhead; Radley; Magdalen Coll., Oxford (MA). Served RN, 1943–47. Oxford, 1943 and 1947–49. *Address:* Long Sutton House, Long Sutton, near Langport, Somerset TA10 9LZ. *T:* Long Sutton (0458) 241284. *Clubs:* MCC, Free Foresters.

EDWARDS, Jeremy John Cary; Group Managing Director, Henderson Administration Group, since 1989; *b* 2 Jan. 1937; *s* of William Philip Neville Edwards, *qv; m* 1st, 1963, Jenifer Graham (*née* Mould) (decd); one *s* one *d*; 2nd, 1974, April Philippa Harding; one *s. Educ:* Ridley Coll, Ontario; Vinehall Sch., Sussex; Haileybury and Imperial Service Coll. Unilever, 1955–57; Hobson Bates & Co., 1957–59; Overseas Marketing and Advertising, 1959–61; Courtaulds, 1961–63; Vine Products, 1963–66; Loewe SA, 1966–68; Jessel Securities, 1968–70; Man. Dir, Vavasseur Unit Trust Management, 1970–74; Henderson Admin Gp, 1974–: Jt Man. Dir, 1983–89. Hon. Treas., WWF, 1984–; Mem. Council, 1987–, Chm., Appeals Cttee, 1989– (Mem., 1983–), C of E Children's Soc. *Recreations:* fishing, walking, swimming, music. *Address:* 37 Oakley Gardens, SW3 5QQ. *T:* 071–351 1953. *Clubs:* Boodle's, City of London.

EDWARDS, John Basil, CBE 1972; JP; Chairman, Magistrates Association, 1976–79; *b* 15 Jan. 1909; *s* of Charles and Susan Edwards; *m* 1935, Molly Patricia Philips (*d* 1979); one *s* two *d. Educ:* King's Sch., Worcester; Wadham Coll., Oxford (BA Hons Jurisprudence, MA). Commnd Royal Warwickshire Regt (RE) TA, 1938. Admitted Solicitor, 1933. Worcester CC, 1936; Mayor of Worcester, 1947–49; Alderman, City of Worcester, 1948. Magistrates Association: Mem. Council, 1960; Chm., Worcestershire Br., 1960–66; Hon. Treasurer, 1968–70; Dep. Chm., 1970–76. Mem., James Cttee on Distribution of Criminal Business, 1973–75. Chm., Worcester Three Choirs Festival, 1947–72. Freeman, City of London. Liveryman: Haberdashers Company; Distillers Company. JP Worcs 1940; Chm., Worcester City Justices, 1951–79. *Recreation:* gardening. *Address:* 21 Britannia Square, Worcester WR1 3DH. *T:* Worcester (0905) 29933.

See also C. M. Edwards.

EDWARDS, John Charles, JP; Lord Mayor of Cardiff, 1980–81; *b* 3 April 1925; *s* of John Robert Edwards and Elsie Florence Edwards; *m* 1946, Cynthia Lorraine Bushell; one *s* two *d. Educ:* Lansdowne Road Sch., Cardiff; Ruskin Coll., Oxford. Served War of 1939–45, RM (1939–45 Star, France and Germany Star, War Medal 1939–45); TA, 1948–62, RASC (TEM). Postal Exec. Officer, GPO. Member: Cardiff CC, 1962–83 (Dep. Lord Mayor, 1978–79); S Glam CC, 1974–78; Associate Mem., Inst. of Transport Admin, 1982. Freeman of City of London, 1981. JP S Glam, 1979. Mem., St John's Council for S Glam; OStJ 1980. *Recreations:* athletics, football. *Address:* 61 Cosmeston Street, Cathays, Cardiff CF2 4LQ. *T:* Cardiff (0222) 221506. *Clubs:* Civil Service; United Services Mess; Cardiff Athletic.

EDWARDS, Sir (John) Clive (Leighton), 2nd Bt *cr* 1921; *b* 1916; *s* of 1st Bt and Kathleen Ermyntrude (*d* 1975) *d* of late John Corfield, JP; *S* father, 1922. *Educ:* Winchester Coll. Volunteered and served in the Army, 1940–46. *Recreations:* motoring, gardening. *Heir:* none. *Address:* Milntown, Lezayre, Ramsey, Isle of Man. *Clubs:* Midland AC (Hon. Life Mem.), Bugatti Owners.

EDWARDS, John Coates, CMG 1989; HM Diplomatic Service; High Commissioner, Lesotho, since 1988; *b* 25 Nov. 1934; *s* of late Herbert John and Doris May Edwards; *m* 1959, Mary Harris; one *s* one *d. Educ:* Skinners' Co. Sch., Tunbridge Wells, Kent; Brasenose Coll., Oxford (MA). Military Service, 1953–55: Lieut, RA. Asst Principal: Min. of Supply, 1958; Colonial Office, 1960; Private Sec. to Parly Under Sec. of State for the Colonies, 1961; Principal: Nature Conservancy, 1962; Min. of Overseas Develt, 1965; First Sec. (Develt), and UK Perm. Rep. to ECAFE, Bangkok, Thailand, 1968; Asst Sec., Min. of Overseas Develt, 1971; Head of E Africa Develt Div., Nairobi, Kenya, 1972; Asst Sec., Min. of Overseas Develt, 1976; Head of British Develt Div. in the Caribbean, Barbados, and UK Dir, Caribbean Develt Bank, 1978; Hd, West Indian and Atlantic Dept, FCO, 1981–84; Dep. High Comr, Kenya, 1984–88. *Address:* c/o Foreign and Commonwealth Office, SW1. *Clubs:* Commonwealth Trust; Muthaiga Country (Nairobi).

EDWARDS, Prof. John Hilton, FRCP; FRS 1979; Professor of Genetics, University of Oxford, since 1979; *b* 26 March 1928; *s* of late Harold Clifford Edwards, CBE, FRCS, FRCOG; *m* 1953, Felicity Clare, *d* of Dr C. H. C. Toussaint; two *s* two *d. Educ:* Univ. of Cambridge (MB, BChir). FRCP 1972. MO, Falkland Islands Dependency Survey, 1952–53; Mem., MRC Unit on Population Genetics, Oxford, 1958–60; Geneticist, Children's Hosp. of Philadelphia, 1960–61; Lectr, Sen. Lectr, and Reader, Birmingham Univ., 1961–67; Hon. Consultant Paediatrician, Birmingham Regional Bd, 1967; Vis. Prof. of Pediatrics, Cornell Univ., and Sen. Investigator, New York Blood Center, 1967–68; Consultant, Human Genetics, Univ. of Iceland, 1967–; Prof. of Human Genetics, Birmingham Univ., 1969–79. *Publications:* Human Genetics, 1978; scientific papers. *Recreations:* gliding, skiing. *Address:* 78 Old Road, Headington, Oxford. *Club:* Athenæum.

EDWARDS, John Lionel; retired civil servant; *b* 29 Aug. 1915; *s* of Rev. Arthur Edwards and Constance Edwards; *m* 1948, Cecily Miller; one *s* two *d. Educ:* Marlborough; Corpus Christi Coll., Oxford. Entered Scottish Office, 1938. Served War, (Army), 1940–45. Min. of Labour, 1945: Principal Private Sec. to Minister of Labour, 1956; Asst Sec., 1956; Sec., NEDC, 1968–71; Under-Sec., Dept of Employment, 1971–75; Certification Officer for Trade Unions and Employers' Assocs, 1976–81. *Address:* Little Bedwyn, The Ridgway, Pyrford, Surrey. *T:* Byfleet (09323) 43459. *Club:* United Oxford & Cambridge University.

EDWARDS, (John) Michael (McFadyean), CBE 1986; QC 1981; Consultant, Bond Corporation Holdings and other Australian companies, since 1990; *b* 16 Oct. 1925; *s* of Dr James Thomas Edwards and Constance Amy Edwards, *yr d* of Sir John McFadyean; *m* 1st, 1952, Morna Joyce Piper (marr. diss.); one *s* one *d*; 2nd, 1964, Rosemary Ann Moore; two *s. Educ:* Andover Grammar Sch. (schol.); University Coll., Oxford (BCL, MA). Called to the Bar, Middle Temple, 1949; Asst Parly Counsel, HM Treasury, 1955–60; Dep. Legal Advr and Dir of certain subsid. cos, Courtaulds Ltd, 1960–67; British Steel Corporation: Dir, Legal Services, 1967–71; Man. Dir, BSC (Internat.) Ltd, 1967–81; Chm. and Man. Dir, BSC (Overseas Services) Ltd, 1973–81; Provost, City of London Polytechnic, 1981–88. Dir, 1982–90, and Man. Dir, 1988–89, Bell Group Internat. Ltd; Dir and Chief Exec., Bond Corp. (UK), 1989–90; Director: Bell Resources Ltd (Australia), 1983–88; Bell Group Ltd (Australia), 1991–; West Australian Newspapers, 1991–. Member: Overseas Projects Bd, 1973–81; E European Trade Council, 1973–81; Educnl Assets Bd, 1988–. Deputy Chairman: Appeal Cttee, Assoc. of Certified Accountants, 1990– (Chm., 1987–90); Independent Appeals Authy for Sch. Exams, 1991–. Member: Bar Council, 1971–79, 1980–83; Senate of Inns of Court and Bar, 1974–79, 1980–83; Gen. Cttee, Bar Assoc. for Commerce, Finance and Industry, 1967– (Vice-Pres., 1980–82; Chm., 1972–74). Mem., Acad. Council, Inst. of Internat. Business Law and Practice, ICC, Paris, 1982–88; Chairman: Eastman Dental Hosp., 1983– (Governor, 1981–83); Management Cttee, Inst. of Dental Surgery, Univ. of London, 1984–; Mem., Governing Body, BPMF, 1988–. Mem., Council, Regional Opera Trust, (Kent Opera), 1981–88 (Chm., 1983–86). CBIM (Mem. Council, 1978–81); FCIArb, 1984. Freeman, City of London; Mem. Court, Ironmongers' Co. *Recreations:* family (numerous), other people. *Address:* 4 Belgrave Mews West, SW1X 8HT. *T:* 071–235 8881, *Fax:* 071–235 0057. *Club:* Garrick.

See also J. G. Edwards.

EDWARDS, Rear Adm. John Phillip, CB 1984; LVO 1972; CEng, FIMechE 1982; Domestic Bursar and Fellow of Wadham College, Oxford, since 1984; *b* 13 Feb. 1927; *s* of Robert Edwards and Dilys (*née* Phillips); *m* 1951, Gwen Lloyd Bonner; three *d. Educ:* Brynhyfryd Sch., Ruthin, Clwyd; HMS Conway; Royal Naval Engrg Colls, Keyham and Manadon. MA 1984. FBIM 1980. Served, 1948–72: HMS Vengeance, Mauritius, Caledonia, Torquay, Lion, Diamond, Defender, HMCS Stadacona, and HMY Britannia; Mechanical Trng Estab., Portsmouth; Personnel Panel; Staff of C-in-C Fleet; SOWC;

Dep. Dir, RN Staff Coll., 1972–74; Asst Dir, Dir Gen. Ships, 1974–76; RCDS, 1977; Captain of Portland Naval Base, 1978–80; Dir Gen., Fleet Support Policy and Services, 1980–83. Comdr 1964, Captain 1971, Rear Adm. 1980. Mem. (non-exec.), Welsh Office Health Policy Bd, 1985–90. President: Oxford Royal Naval Assoc., 1984; Midland Naval Officers Assoc., 1985; Vice-Pres., N Oxfordshire SSAFA, 1984. Freeman: Co. of Engineers, 1984; City of London, 1984. Hon. FISTC 1976. *Recreations:* golf, tennis. *Address:* Wadham College, Oxford OX1 3PN.

EDWARDS, Joseph Robert, CBE 1963; JP; Consultant, Canewdon Consultants plc, Southend-on-Sea, since 1989 (Chairman, 1986–89); Deputy Chairman, Theale Estates Ltd (formerly Martin Electrical Equipment (Theale) Ltd), since 1979; Director, Creative Industries Group Inc., Detroit, since 1985; *b* 5 July 1908; *y s* of late Walter Smith Edwards and Annie Edwards, Gt Yarmouth; *m* 1st, 1936, Frances Mabel Haddon Bourne (*d* 1975); three *s* one *d*; 2nd, 1976, Joan Constance Mary Tattersall. *Educ:* High Sch., Great Yarmouth. Joined Austin Motor Co., Birmingham, 1928; Hercules factory, 1939; rejoined Austin Motor Co., 1941; Gen. Works Manager, 1951; Local Dir, 1953; Works Dir, 1954; Dir of Manufacturing, British Motor Corp., 1955; Managing Director: British Motor Corp., 1966–68; Pressed Steel/Fisher Ltd, 1956–67; Dep. Chm., Harland & Wolff Ltd, 1968–70; Chm. 1970; Dep. Chm., Associated Engrg, 1969–78; Dir, BPC Ltd, 1973–81; Vice-Chm., Lucas (Industries) Ltd, 1976–79; Chm., Penta Motors Ltd, Reading, 1978–87; Dir, CSE Aviation Ltd, 1973–87. Pres., Motor Industry Research Assoc. Mem., Commn on Industrial Relations to 1974. JP Oxford, 1964. Hon. MA Oxon, 1968. *Recreation:* golf. *Address:* Flat 16, Shoreacres, Banks Road, Sandbanks, Poole, Dorset BH13 7QH. *T:* Canford Cliffs (0202) 709315. *Club:* Royal Motor Yacht.

EDWARDS, Julie Andrews; *see* Andrews, J.

EDWARDS, Kenneth; *see* Edwards, A. K.

EDWARDS, Dr Kenneth John Richard; Vice-Chancellor, University of Leicester, since 1987; *b* 12 Feb. 1934; *s* of John and Elizabeth May Edwards; *m* 1958, Janet Mary Gray; two *s* one *d*. *Educ:* Market Drayton Grammar Sch.; Univ. of Reading (BSc 1st class 1958); University Coll. of Wales, Aberystwyth (PhD 1961). Nat. Service, RAF, 1952–54. Fellow, Univ. of California, 1961–62; ARC Fellow, Welsh Plant Breeding Station, Aberystwyth, 1962–63, Sen. Sci. Officer, 1963–66; Cambridge University: Lectr in Genetics, 1966–84; Head of Dept of Genetics 1981–84; Sec. Gen. of Faculties, 1984–87; St John's College: Fellow, 1971–87; Lectr, 1971–84; Tutor, 1980–84. Vis. Lectr in Genetics, Univ. of Birmingham, 1965; Vis. Prof., INTA, Buenos Aires, 1973; Leverhulme Res. Fellow, Univ. of California, 1973. *Publications:* Evolution in Modern Biology, 1977; articles on genetics in sci. jls. *Recreations:* music, gardening. *Address:* Knighton Hall, Leicester LE2 3WG. *T:* Leicester (0533) 706677.

EDWARDS, Hon. Sir Llewellyn (Roy), AC 1989; Kt 1984; FRACMA; Executive Consultant, Jones Lang Wootton, Brisbane, since 1989; *b* 2 Aug. 1935; *s* of Roy Thomas Edwards and Agnes Dulcie Gwendoline Edwards; *m* 1958, Leone Sylvia Burley (decd); two *s* one *d*; *m* 1989, Jane Anne Brumfield. *Educ:* Raceview State Sch.; Silkstone State Sch.; Ipswich Grammar Sch.; Univ. of Queensland (MB, BS 1965). Qualified Electrician, 1955. RMO and Registrar in Surgery, Ipswich Hosp., 1965–68; gen. practice, Ipswich, 1968–74. MLA (L) Ipswich, Qld Parlt, 1972–83; Minister for Health, Qld, 1974–78; Dep. Premier and Treasurer, Qld, 1978–83; Dep. Med. Supt, Ipswich Hosp., 1983–85. Chairman: Ansvar Australia Insurance Ltd, 1984–; Northern Securities Management Ltd, 1984–; World Expo 88 Authority 1984–89; Director: Westpac Banking Corp., 1984–; James Hardie Industries Pty Ltd, 1990–; Spencer Stuart, 1990–. Mem., Senate, Univ. of Queensland, 1984–. FRACMA 1984. Hon. FAIM 1988. Hon. LLD Queensland, 1988. *Recreations:* tennis, walking, cricket, Rugby Union. *Address:* 8 Ascot Street, Ascot, Qld 4007, Australia. *Clubs:* Brisbane (Brisbane, Qld); Cricketers, United Services (Qld); Ipswich (Ipswich, Qld); Brisbane Polo.

EDWARDS, Malcolm John, CBE 1985; Commercial Director, British Coal (formerly National Coal Board), since 1985; Member of the Board, British Coal, since 1986; *b* 25 May 1934; *s* of John J. Edwards and Edith (*née* Riley); *m* 1967, Yvonne, *d* of Mr and Mrs J. A. W. Daniels, Port Lincoln, S Australia; two *s*. *Educ:* Alleyn's Sch., Dulwich; Jesus Coll., Cambridge (MA). Joined NCB as trainee, 1956; Industrial Sales Manager, 1962; Dir of Domestic and Industrial Sales, 1969; Dir Gen. of Marketing, 1973; Jt Chm., Solid Fuel Adv. Service, 1984; responsible for coal utilisation R & D, 1984–; Chm., British Fuels Gp, 1988–; Dep. Chm., Inter Continental Fuels, 1985–. *Publication:* (with J. J. Edwards) Medical Museum Technology, 1959. *Recreations:* book collecting, arts and crafts movement, music, gardening. *Address:* Lodge Farm, Moot Lane, Downton, Salisbury, Wilts SP5 3LN.

EDWARDS, Marcus; *see* Edwards, C. M.

EDWARDS, Michael; *see* Edwards, J. M. McF.

EDWARDS, Norman L.; *see* Lloyd-Edwards.

EDWARDS, Owen; Director, Sianel 4 Cymru (Welsh Fourth Channel Authority), 1981–89; *b* 26 Dec. 1933; *s* of Sir Ifan ab Owen Edwards and Eirys Mary Edwards; *m* 1958; two *d*. *Educ:* Ysgol Gymraeg, Aberystwyth; Leighton Park, Reading; Lincoln Coll., Oxford (MA). Cataloguer, Nat. Library of Wales, 1958–60; BBC Wales: Compère, TV Programme Heddiw, 1961–66; Programme Organiser, 1967–70; Head of Programmes, 1970–74; Controller, 1974–81. Chairman: Assoc. for Film and TV in Celtic Countries, later Celtic Film and TV Assoc., 1983–85, 1989–91; Royal Nat. Eisteddfod of Wales, 1986–89 (Vice-Chm., 1985–86). Hon LLD Wales, 1989. Gold Medal, RTS, 1989. *Recreations:* walking, fishing. *Address:* 2 Riversdale, Llandaff, Cardiff CF5 2QL. *T:* Cardiff 555392.

EDWARDS, Patricia Anne, (Mrs Roger Cox); Principal Assistant Legal Adviser, Home Office, since 1988; *b* 29 May 1944; *d* of late Maurice James Edwards and of Marion Edwards (*née* Lewis); *m* 1970, Roger Charles Cox, *qv*. *Educ:* Barry and Purley County Grammar Schools; King's College London (LLB). Called to the Bar, Middle Temple, 1967; Criminal Appeal Office, 1965–74; Law Officers' Dept, 1974–77; Home Office: Sen. Legal Asst, 1977–80; Asst Legal Adviser, 1980–88. *Recreations:* music, travel, reading, domestic pursuits. *Address:* Home Office, 50 Queen Anne's Gate, SW1. *T:* 071–273 2768.

EDWARDS, Peter Robert; Chief Executive, Secretan, since 1990; *b* 30 Oct. 1937; *s* of Robert and Doris Edith Edwards; *m* 1st, 1967, Jennifer Ann Boys; one *s*; 2nd, 1970, Elizabeth Janet Barrett; one *d*. *Educ:* Christ's Hospital. Chartered Accountant. Ernst & Young (and predecessor firms), 1955–90. *Recreations:* ornithology, gardening. *Address:* Glebe Cottage, Church Lane, Bury, Pulborough, West Sussex RH20 1PB. *T:* Pulborough (0798) 831774. *Club:* Caledonian.

EDWARDS, Prof. Philip Walter, PhD; FBA 1986; King Alfred Professor of English Literature, University of Liverpool, 1974–90, now Emeritus; *b* 7 Feb. 1923; *er s* of late R. H. Edwards, MC, and late Mrs B. Edwards; *m* 1st, 1947, Hazel Margaret (*d* 1950), *d* of late Prof. C. W. and late Mrs E. R. Valentine; 2nd, 1952, Sheila Mary, *d* of late R. S. and

Mrs A. M. Wilkes, Bloxwich, Staffs; three *s* one *d*. *Educ:* King Edward's High Sch., Birmingham; Univ. of Birmingham. MA, PhD Birmingham; MA Dublin. Royal Navy, 1942–45 (Sub-Lieut RNVR). Lectr in English, Univ. of Birmingham, 1946–60; Commonwealth Fund Fellow, Harvard Univ., 1954–55; Prof. of English Lit., TCD, 1960–66; Fellow of TCD, 1962–66; Prof. of Lit., Univ. of Essex, 1966–74; Pro-Vice-Chancellor, Liverpool Univ., 1980–83. Visiting Professor: Univ. of Michigan, 1964–65; Williams Coll., Mass, 1969; Otago Univ., NZ, 1980; Internat. Christian Univ., Tokyo, 1989; Visiting Fellow: All Souls Coll., Oxford, 1970–71; Huntington Liby, Calif., 1977, 1983. *Publications:* Sir Walter Ralegh, 1953; (ed) Kyd, The Spanish Tragedy, 1959; Shakespeare and the Confines of Art, 1968; (ed) Pericles Prince of Tyre, 1976; (ed with C. Gibson) Massinger, Plays and Poems, 1976; Threshold of a Nation, 1979; (ed jtly) Shakespeare's Styles, 1980; (ed) Hamlet Prince of Denmark, 1985; Shakespeare: a writer's progress, 1986; Last Voyages, 1988; numerous articles on Shakespeare and literature of his time in Shakespeare Survey, Proc. British Acad., etc. *Recreations:* walking, gardening. *Address:* High Gillinggrove, Gillinggate, Kendal, Cumbria LA9 4JB.

EDWARDS, Quentin Tytler, QC 1975; **His Honour Judge Quentin Edwards;** a Circuit Judge, since 1982; Chancellor, Diocese of Chichester, since 1978; *b* 16 Jan. 1925; *s* of Herbert Jackson Edwards and Juliet Hester Edwards; *m* 1948, Barbara Marian Guthrie; two *s* one *d*. *Educ:* Bradfield Coll.; Council of Legal Educn. Royal Navy, 1943–46. Called to Bar, Middle Temple, 1948; Bencher, 1972. A Recorder of the Crown Court, 1974–82; Chancellor, Dio. of Blackburn, 1977–90. Licensed Reader, Dio. of London, 1967; Chm., Ecclesiastical Law Soc., 1990–; Member: Legal Adv. Commn of General Synod of Church of England, 1973; Dioceses Commn, 1978–. Pres., Highgate Literary and Scientific Institn, 1988–. Hon. MA (Archbp of Canterbury), 1961. *Publications:* (with Peter Dow) Public Rights of Way and Access to the Countryside, 1951; (with K. Macmorran, et al) Ecclesiastical Law, 3rd edn, Halsbury's Laws of England, 1955; What is Unlawful?, 1959; (with J. N. D. Anderson, et al) Putting Asunder, 1966. *Recreations:* the open air; the table; architecture. *Address:* Bloomsbury County Court, 7 Marylebone Road, NW1 5HY. *Club:* Athenæum.

EDWARDS, Prof. Richard Humphrey Tudor, FRCP; Professor and Head of Department of Medicine, since 1984, Director, Magnetic Resonance Research Centre, since 1985, and Director, Muscle Research Centre, since 1986, University of Liverpool; *b* 28 Jan. 1939; *s* of Hywel Islwyn Edwards and Menna Tudor Edwards (*née* Davies); *m* 1964, Eleri Wyn Roberts; one *d* (one *s* decd). *Educ:* Llangollen Grammar Sch.; Middlesex Hosp. Med. Sch., London (BSc, PhD, MB, BS). Ho. appts, Middlesex, National Heart and Hammersmith Hosps, 1964–65; Res. Fellow, Asst Lectr, then Lectr (Wellcome Sen. Res. Fellow in Clin. Science), Hon. Cons. Physician (Respiratory Med.), Royal Postgrad. Med. Sch., Hammersmith Hosp., 1966–76; Wellcome Swedish Res. Fellow, Karolinska Inst., Stockholm, 1970; Prof. of Human Metabolism, UCH Med. Sch., 1976–84; Hd of Dept of Medicine, UCL, 1982–84; Hon. Consultant Physician: Royal Liverpool Hosp., 1984–; Robert Jones and Agnes Hunt Orthopaedic Hosp., Oswestry, 1979–. *Publications:* Clinical Exercise Testing, 1975; Muscle Weakness and Fatigue, 1980; sci. papers on human muscle in health and disease in Jl of Physiology, Clinical Sci., Clinical Physiol., Muscle and Nerve, etc. *Recreations:* Wales—planting trees, mountain walking, gardening, music. *Address:* Department of Medicine, University of Liverpool, PO Box 147, Liverpool L69 3BX. *T:* 051–706 4072.

EDWARDS, Prof. Robert Geoffrey, CBE 1988; FRS 1984; Professor of Human Reproduction, Cambridge University, 1985–89, now Emeritus; Extraordinary Fellow, Churchill College, Cambridge; *b* 27 Sept. 1925; *s* of Samuel and Margaret Edwards; *m* 1956, Ruth Eileen Fowler; five *d*. *Educ:* Manchester Central High Sch.; Univs of Wales and Edinburgh. PhD (Edin); DSc (Wales); MA (Cantab). Service in British Army, 1944–48; commnd 1946. UC North Wales, Bangor, 1948–51; Univ. of Edinburgh, 1951–57; Res. Fellow at California Inst. of Tech., 1957–58; Scientist at Nat. Inst. of Medical Research, Mill Hill, NW7, 1958–62; Glasgow Univ. 1962–63; in Dept of Physiology, Cambridge Univ., 1963–89; Ford Foundation Reader in Physiology, 1969–85. Scientific Dir, Bourn Hallam Clinics, Cambridgeshire and London, 1988–91. Founder Chm., European Soc. of Human Reproduction and Embryology, 1984–86. Vis. Scientist: in Johns Hopkins Hosp., Baltimore, 1965; Univ. of N Carolina, 1966; Vis. Prof., Free Univ., Brussels, 1984. Hon. Pres., British Fertility Soc., 1988–. Hon. FRCOG 1985. Hon. MRCP 1986. Hon. Mem. French Soc. for Infertility, 1983. Life Fellow, Australian Fertility Soc., 1985. Hon. Citizen of Bordeaux, 1985. Hon. DSc: Hull, 1983; York; Vrije Univ., Brussels. Spanish Fertility Soc. Gold Medal, 1985; King Faisal Award, 1989. Chief Editor, Human Reproduction, 1986–. *Publications:* A Matter of Life (with P. C. Steptoe), 1980; Conception in the Human Female, 1980; (with C. R. Austin) Mechanisms of Sex Differentiation in Animals and Man; (with J. M. Purdy) Human Conception in Vitro, 1982; (with J. M. Purdy and P. C. Steptoe) Implantation of the Human Embryo, 1985; (with M. Seppälä) In Vitro Fertilisation and Embryo Transfer, 1985; Life Before Birth, 1989; editor of several scientific textbooks on reproduction; numerous articles in scientific and medical jls, organiser of conferences, etc. *Recreations:* farming, politics, music. *Address:* Duck End Farm, Dry Drayton, Cambridge CB3 8DB. *T:* Crafts Hill (0954) 780602.

EDWARDS, Robert John, CBE 1986; Deputy Chairman, Mirror Group Newspapers, 1985–86 (Senior Group Editor, 1984–85); *b* 26 Oct. 1925; *m* 1st, 1952, Laura Ellwood (marr. diss. 1972); two *s* two *d*; 2nd, 1977, Brigid Segrave. *Educ:* Ranelagh Sch., Bracknell. Editor, Tribune, 1951–54; Dep. Editor, Sunday Express, 1957–59; Man. Editor, Daily Express, 1959–61; Editor: Daily Express, 1961, 1963–65; Evening Citizen, Glasgow, 1962–63; Sunday People, 1966–72; Sunday Mirror, 1972–84; Dir, Mirror Group Newspapers, 1976–88. Ombudsman to Today newspaper, 1990–. *Publication:* Goodbye Fleet Street (autobiog.), 1988. *Address:* Georgian Wing, Williamscot House, near Banbury, Oxon OX17 1AE. *T:* Banbury (0295) 750809. *Clubs:* Reform, Kennel, Groucho's.

EDWARDS, Robert Septimus Friar, CVO 1964; CBE 1963; *b* 21 Oct. 1910; *y s* of late Augustus C. Edwards and of Amy Edwards; *m* 1946, Janet Mabel Wrigley; one *s* two *d*. *Educ:* Hereford Cathedral Sch. Chief Engineering Asst, Hereford, until 1936; Min. of Transport, Highway Engineering, 1936–43; Principal, Min. of War Transport, 1943; Mem. British Merchant Shipping Mission, Washington, DC, 1944–46. Sec. Gen. Internat. Conf. on Safety of Life at Sea, 1948; Principal Private Sec. to Minister of Transport, 1949–51; Shipping Attaché, British Embassy, Washington, DC, 1951–54; Dir of Sea Transport, 1954–57; Gen. Manager, London Airports, 1957–63; Gen. Manager, 1967–69, Dir-Gen., 1969–71, Mersey Docks and Harbour Board. Chm., Morris & David Jones Ltd, 1973–74. Called to the Bar, Middle Temple, 1941. *Address:* 3 Simon Court, Hoscote Park, West Kirby, Wirral, Merseyside L48 0RX. *T:* 051–625 2629.

EDWARDS, Robin Anthony, CBE 1981; Partner with Dundas & Wilson, CS (formerly Davidson & Syme, WS), since 1965; *b* 7 April 1939; *s* of Alfred Walton Edwards and Ena Annie Ruffell; *m* 1963, Elizabeth Alexandra Mackay; one *s* one *d*. *Educ:* Daniel Stewart's Coll., Edinburgh; Edinburgh Univ. (MA, LLB (distinction), Cl. Medallist). Former Lectr in Conveyancing, Edinburgh Univ.; Admitted Member, WS Society, 1964; Mem. Council, Law Society of Scotland, 1969–84, Vice-Pres., 1978–79, Pres., 1979–80 (youngest

Pres. ever, at that time). *Recreations:* golf, travel. *Address:* 7/6 Rocheid Park, East Settes Avenue, Edinburgh.

EDWARDS, Dr Roger Snowden, CBE 1964; JP; Chairman, Gas Industry Training Board, 1965–74, retired; *b* 19 Dec. 1904; *s* of late Herbert George Edwards and late Margaret Alice Edwards; *m* 1935, Eveline Brunton, MBE (*d* 1986); two *s* one *d. Educ:* Enfield Grammar Sch.; Imperial Coll. of Science. Junior Staff, Imperial Coll. of Science, 1925–28; Physicist, British Xylonite Co., 1928–29; Physicist, Boot Trade Research Association, 1929–39; Dir, Co-operative Wholesale Soc., 1939–49. Chairman: Council of Industrial Design, 1947–52 (Mem., 1944–47); NE Gas Board, 1949–66; Mem., Gas Council, 1966–70. JP Harrogate, 1960; Surrey, 1966. *Recreation:* golf. *Address:* 23 Manor Way, Letchworth, Herts SG6 3NL.

EDWARDS, Prof. Ronald Walter, DSc; FIBiol, FIWEM, FIFM; Professor, School of Pure and Applied Biology, University of Wales, Cardiff (formerly Professor and Head of Department of Applied Biology, University of Wales Institute of Science and Technology), 1968–90, now Emeritus; Member, National Rivers Authority, since 1988; *b* 7 June 1930; *s* of Walter and Violet Edwards. *Educ:* Solihull Sch., Warwicks; Univ. of Birmingham (BSc, DSc). FIBiol 1965; FIWEM (FIWPC 1981). Biologist, Freshwater Biol Assoc., 1953–58; Sen., Principal, and Sen. Principal Scientific Officer, Water Pollution Res. Lab., 1958–68. Chm., Nat. Parks Rev. Panel, 1989–91; Dep. Chm., Welsh Water Authority, 1983– (Mem., 1974–); Member: Natural Environment Res. Council, 1970–73 and 1982–85; Nat. Cttee, European Year of the Environment, 1987–88; Council, RSPB, 1988–. *Publications:* (co-ed) Ecology and the Industrial Society, 1968; (co-ed) Conservation and Productivity of Natural Waters, 1975; (with Dr M. Brooker) The Ecology of the River Wye, 1982; Acid Waters in Wales, 1990; about 90 papers in learned jls. *Recreations:* music, collecting Staffordshire pottery. *Address:* National Rivers Authority, Rivers House, St Mellons Business Park, Cardiff CF3 0LT.

EDWARDS, Prof. Sir Samuel Frederick, (Sir Sam Edwards), Kt 1975; FRS 1966; Cavendish Professor of Physics, Cambridge University, since 1984 (John Humphrey Plummer Professor, 1972–84); Fellow, Caius College, since 1972; *b* 1 Feb. 1928; *s* of Richard and Mary Jane Edwards, Manselton, Swansea; *m* 1953, Merriell E. M. Bland; one *s* three *d. Educ:* Swansea Grammar Sch.; Caius Coll., Cambridge (MA, PhD); Harvard University. Inst. for Advanced Study, Princeton, 1952; Univ. of Birmingham, 1953; Univ. of Manchester, 1958, Prof. of Theoretical Physics, 1963–72. Chief Scientific Adviser, Department of Energy, 1983–88. Chm., SRC, 1973–77. UK Deleg. to NATO Science Cttee, 1974–79; Mem., Planning Cttee, Max-Planck Gesellschaft, 1974–77. Vice-Pres., Institute of Physics, 1970–73 (Mem. Council, 1967–73); Mem. Council, Inst. of Mathematics and its Applications, 1976– (Vice-Pres., 1979, Pres., 1980–81). Member: Physics Cttee, SRC, 1968–73 (Chm. 1970–73); Polymer Cttee, SRC, 1968–73; Science Bd, SRC, 1970–73; Council, European Physical Soc., 1969–71 (Chm., Condensed Matter Div., 1969–71); UGC, 1971–73; Defence Scientific Adv. Council, 1973– (Chm., 1977–80); Metrology and Standards Req. Bd, Dept of Industry, 1974–77; AFRC, 1990–; Chm., Adv. Council on R&D, Dept of Energy, 1983–88 (Mem., 1974–77); Member Council: European R&D (EEC), 1976–80; Royal Soc., 1982–83 (a Vice-Pres., 1982–83); Pres., BAAS, 1988–89 (Chm. Council, 1977–82); Foreign Mem., Académie des Sciences, France, 1989. Non-exec. Director: Lucas Industries, 1981–; Steetley plc, 1985–. FInstP; FIMA; FRSC. Hon. DTech Loughborough, 1975; Hon. DSc: Salford, Edinburgh, 1976; Bath, 1978; Birmingham, 1986; Wales, 1987; Sheffield, 1989; Dublin, 1991; DUniv Strasbourg, 1986. Maxwell Medal and Prize, Inst. of Physics, 1974; High Polymer Physics Prize, Amer. Phys. Soc., 1982; Davy Medal, Royal Soc., 1984; Gold Medal, Inst. of Maths, 1986; Guthrie Medal and Prize, Inst. of Physics, 1987; Gold Medal, Rheological Soc., 1990. *Publications:* Technological Risk, 1980; (with M. Doi) Theory of Polymer Dynamics, 1986; contribs to learned jls. *Address:* 7 Penarth Place, Cambridge CB3 9LU. *T:* Cambridge (0223) 66610. *Club:* Athenæum.

EDWARDS, Stewart Leslie, CMG 1967; Under-Secretary, Department of Trade, retired; *b* 6 Nov. 1914; *s* of late Walter James and Lilian Emma Edwards; *m* 1940, Dominica Jeanne Lavie, *d* of Joseph Lavie and Jeanne Jauréguiberry; two *s. Educ:* King's Sch., Canterbury; Corpus Christi Coll., Cambridge (Foundn Scholar). BA 1936; MA 1943. Appointed to War Office, 1937. Military service, 1942–44. Called to the Bar, Inner Temple, 1947. Seconded from War Office to OEEC, 1948–51; Board of Trade, 1951–65; Minister (Economic), Bonn, 1965–70; Under-Sec., DTI later Dept of Trade, 1970–74. *Recreations:* music, reading, hill-walking, wine. *Address:* B51 Résidence La Pastourelle, Bât. A, 20 Avenue Daniel-Hedde, 17200 Royan, France. *T:* 46392203.

EDWARDS, Very Rev. (Thomas) Erwyd (Pryse); Dean of Bangor, since 1988; *b* 26 Jan. 1933; *s* of Richard and Gwladys Edwards; *m* 1961, Mair (*née* Roberts); two *s. Educ:* St David's University College, Lampeter (BA 1956); St Michael's College, Llandaff. Curate of Caernarfon, 1958–63; Asst Chaplain, St George's Hosp., London, 1963–66; Chaplain, King's College Hosp., London, 1966–72; Vicar: Penmon, Anglesey, 1972–75; Menai Bridge, 1975–61; St David's, Bangor, 1981–85; St David's and St James's, Bangor, 1985–88; Canon of Bangor Cathedral, 1988. *Address:* The Deanery, Cathedral Precinct, Bangor, Gwynedd LL57 1LH. *T:* Bangor (0248) 370693.

EDWARDS, Vero C. W.; *see* Wynne-Edwards.

EDWARDS, William (Henry); solicitor; *b* 6 Jan. 1938; *s* of Owen Henry Edwards and S. Edwards; *m* 1961, Ann Eleri Rogers; one *s* three *d. Educ:* Sir Thomas Jones' Comprehensive Sch.; Liverpool Univ. LLB. MP (Lab) Merioneth, 1966–Feb. 1974; contested (Lab) Merioneth, Oct. 1974; Prospective Parly Cand. (Lab), Anglesey, 1981–83. Mem., Historic Building Council for Wales, 1971–76. Editor, Solicitors Diary. *Recreations:* golf, Association football (from the terraces). *Address:* Hope House, Lombard Street, Dolgellau, Gwynedd.

EDWARDS, William Philip Neville, CBE 1949; *b* 5 Aug. 1904; *s* of late Neville P. Edwards, Orford, Littlehampton, Sussex; *m* 1st, 1931, Hon. Sheila Cary (*d* 1976), 2nd *d* of 13th Viscount Falkland; one *s* (and one *s* decd); 2nd, 1976, Joan, *widow* of Norman Mullins. *Educ:* Rugby Sch.; Corpus Christi Coll., Cambridge; Princeton Univ., USA (Davison Scholar). Joined Underground Electric group of companies, 1927; shortly afterwards appointed Sec. to Lord Ashfield, Chm. of Board; First Sec. of Standing Jt Cttee of Main Line Railway Companies and of LPTB, 1933; Officer of Board as Personal Asst to Gen. Manager of Railways, 1937; Outdoor Supt of Railways, 1938; Public Relations Officer of Board, 1939; Asst to Chm. of Supply Council of Min. of Supply, 1941–42; Head of Industrial Information Div. of Min. of Production and Alternate Dir of Information of British Supply Council in N America, 1943–45; Dir of Overseas Information Div. of BoT, 1945–46; Head of British Information Services in USA, 1946–49. A Dir, Confedn of British Industry (previously FBI), 1949–66; Man. Dir, British Overseas Fairs Ltd, 1959–66, Chm., 1966–68. UK Associate Dir, Business International SA, 1968–75; Chm., Public Relations (Industrial) Ltd, 1970–75. Chevalier (1st class) of Order of Dannebrog (Denmark), 1955; Commander of Order of Vasa (Sweden), 1962. *Recreations:* golf, gardening. *Address:* Four Winds, Kithurst Lane, Storrington, Sussex RH20 4LP. *Club:* Carlton.

See also J. J. C. *Edwards.*

EDWARDS-JONES, Ian, QC 1967; The Banking Ombudsman, 1985–88; *b* 17 April 1923; *o s* of late Col H. V. Edwards-Jones, MC, DL, Swansea, Glam; *m* 1950, Susan Vera Catharine McClintock, *o d* of E. S. McClintock and of Mrs A. MacRossie; three *s. Educ:* Rugby Sch.; Trinity Coll., Cambridge (BA). Capt., RA, N Africa, Italy, Palestine, 1942–47. Called to Bar, Middle Temple, Lincoln's Inn, 1948, Bencher, Lincoln's Inn, 1975. A Social Security (formerly Nat. Insurance) Comr, 1979–85. *Recreations:* fishing, photography, amateur wine growing. *Address:* c/o Ground Floor, 7 Stone Buildings, Lincoln's Inn, WC2A 3SZ. *T:* 071–405 3886/7. *Clubs:* United Oxford & Cambridge University; Bar Yacht.

EDWARDS-MOSS, (Sir) David John, (5th Bt *cr* 1868); *S* father, 1988, but does not use the title.

EDWARDS-STUART, Antony James Cobham; QC 1991; an Assistant Recorder, since 1991; *b* 2 Nov. 1946; *s* of Lt-Col Ivor Arthur James Edwards-Stuart and Mrs Elizabeth Aileen Le Mesurier Edwards-Stuart (*née* Deck); *m* 1973, Fiona Ann, *d* of Paul Weaver, OBE; two *s* two *d. Educ:* Sherborne Sch.; RMA Sandhurst; St Catherine's Coll., Cambridge. Called to the Bar, Gray's Inn, 1976. Commnd 1st RTR, 1966; Adjutant: 1st RTR, 1973–75; Kent and Sharpshooters Sqn, Royal Yeomanry, 1976–77. *Recreations:* woodwork, shooting. *Address:* 4 Aberdeen Park, Highbury, N5 2BN. *T:* 071–359 7224; 2 Crown Office Row, Temple, EC4Y 7HJ.

EELES, Air Cdre Henry, CB 1956; CBE 1943; retired as Director of Administrative Plans, Air Ministry, 1959; *b* 12 May 1910; *yr s* of Henry Eeles, Newcastle upon Tyne; *m* 1st, 1940, Janet (*d* 1960), *d* of Major J. H. Norton; two *s* one *d*; 2nd, 1963, Pamela Clarice, *d* of Comdr G. A. Matthew, Royal Navy. *Educ:* Harrow. Entered RAF Coll., 1929; Commnd Dec. 1930; Sqdn Ldr 1938; Group Capt. 1949; Air Cdre 1955. Comdt RAF Coll. and AOC RAF Cranwell, 1952–56. *Address:* The Cottage, Sutton Veny, Warminster, Wilts BA12 7AU.

EFFINGHAM, 6th Earl of, *cr* 1837; **Mowbray Henry Gordon Howard;** 16th Baron Howard, of Effingham, *cr* 1554; *b* 29 Nov. 1905; *er s* of 5th Earl and Rosamond Margaret, *d* of late E. H. Hudson; *S* father, 1946; *m* 1st, 1938, Manci Maria Malvina Gertler (marr. diss. 1946); 2nd, 1952, Gladys Irene Kerry (marr. diss. 1971); 3rd, 1972, (Mabel) Suzanne Mingay Cragg, *d* of late Maurice Jules-Marie Le Pen, Paris, and *widow* of Wing Comdr Francis Talbot Cragg. *Educ:* Lancing. Served War 1939–45, RA and 3rd Maritime Reg. *Recreations:* shooting, fishing, philately. *Heir: n* Lt-Comdr David Peter Mowbray Algernon Howard, RN [*b* 29 April 1939; *m* 1964, Anne Mary Sayer (marr. diss. 1975); one *s*]. *Address:* House of Lords, SW1.

EFSTATHIOU, Prof. George Petros; Savilian Professor of Astronomy, Oxford, since 1988; Fellow of New College, Oxford, since 1988; *b* 2 Sept. 1955; *s* of Petros Efstathiou and Christina (*née* Parperi); *m* 1976, Helena Jane (*née* Smart); one *s* one *d. Educ:* Somerset Comprehensive Sch.; Keble Coll., Oxford (BA); Univ. of Durham (Dept of Physics) (PhD). Res. Asst, Astronomy Dept, Univ. of California, Berkeley, 1979–80; SERC Res. Asst, Inst. of Astronomy, Univ. of Cambridge, 1980–83; Jun. Res. Fellow, King's Coll., Cambridge, 1980–84; Institute of Astronomy, Cambridge: Sen. Asst in Res., 1984–87; Asst Dir of Res., 1987–88; Sen. Res. Fellow, King's Coll., Cambridge, 1984–88. Maxwell Medal and Prize Inst. of Physics, 1990. *Publications:* articles in astronomical jls. *Recreations:* playing with his children, running. *Address:* Department of Astrophysics, University of Oxford, Keble Road, Oxford OX1 3RH. *T:* Oxford (0865) 273300.

EGAN, Sir John (Leopold), Kt 1986; DL; Chief Executive, BAA plc, since 1990; *b* 7 Nov. 1939; *m* 1963, Julia Emily Treble; two *d. Educ:* Bablake Sch., Coventry; Imperial Coll., London Univ., 1958–61 (BSc Hons; FIC 1985); London Business Sch., London Univ., 1966–68 (MScEcon). Petroleum Engineer, Shell International, 1962–66; General Manager, AC-Delco Replacement Parts Operation, General Motors Ltd, 1968–71; Managing Director, Leyland Cars Parts Div., Parts and Service Director, Leyland Cars, BLMC, 1971–76; Corporate Parts Director, Massey Ferguson, 1976–80; Chm. and Chief Exec., Jaguar Cars Ltd, 1980–85, Jaguar plc, 1985–90. Director: Foreign and Colonial Investment Trust, 1985–; Legal & General Group, 1987–. DL Warwicks, 1988. Sen. Fellow, RCA, 1987; Hon. FCIM 1989. Hon. Fellow: London Business Sch., 1988; Wolverhampton Poly., 1989., Dr *hc* Cranfield Inst. of Technology, 1986; Hon. DTech Loughborough, 1987; Hon. DBA Internat. Business Sch., 1988; Hon. LLD Bath, 1988. Hon. Insignia for Technology, CGLI, 1987. Internat. Distinguished Entrepreneur Award, Univ. of Manitoba, 1989. MBA Award of the Year, 1988. *Recreations:* music, squash, tennis. *Address:* c/o BAA plc, 130 Wilton Road, SW1V 1LQ. *Clubs:* Royal Automobile; Warwick Boat.

EGDELL, Dr John Duncan; Consultant in Public Health Medicine (formerly Community Physician), Clwyd Health Authority, since 1986; *b* 5 March 1938; *s* of late John William Egdell and of Nellie (*née* Thompson); *m* 1963, Dr Linda Mary Flint; two *s* one *d. Educ:* Clifton Coll.; Univ. of Bristol. MB, ChB (Bristol) 1961; DipSocMed (Edin.) 1967; FFPHM 1990 (MFCM 1973; FFCM 1979). Ho. Phys. and Ho. Surg., Bristol Gen. Hosp., 1961–62; gen. practice, 1962–65; Med. Administration: with Newcastle Regional Hosp. Bd, 1966–69; with South Western Regional Hosp. Bd, 1969–74; Regional Specialist in Community Med., South Western Regional Health Authority, 1974–76; Regional Medical Postgrad. Co-ordinator, Univ. of Bristol, 1973–76; Regl MO, Mersey RHA, 1977–86; Hon. Lectr in Community Health, Univ. of Liverpool, 1980–86. *Recreations:* delving into the past, nature conservation. *Address:* Gelli Gynan Lodge, Llanarmon-yn-Ial, near Mold, Clwyd CH7 4QX. *T:* Llanarmon-yn-Ial (08243) 345.

EGELAND, Leif; *b* 19 Jan. 1903; *s* of late J. J. Egeland, Consul for Norway in Natal, and Ragnhild Konsmo; *m* 1942, Marguerite Doreen (*d* 1984), *d* of late W. J. de Zwaan, Waterkloof, Pretoria; one *d. Educ:* Durban High Sch.; Natal University Coll.; Oxford Univ. MA English Lang. and Literature, Natal Univ. Coll.; MA, Hons BA, Jurisprudence, BCL Oxon; Rhodes Scholar (Natal), Trinity Coll., Oxford, 1924–27; official Fellow in Law and Classics, Brasenose Coll., 1927–30 (Hon. Fellow, 1984); Harmsworth Scholar, Middle Temple, 1927–30; Barrister, Middle Temple, 1930, Hon. Bencher, 1948; Hon. LLD Cambridge, 1948. Admitted as Advocate of Supreme Court of S Africa, 1931; Vice-Consul for Norway, Natal, 1931–44; MP (House of Assembly) for Durban (Berea), 1933–38, for Zululand, 1940–43; SA Minister to Sweden, 1943, to Holland and Belgium, 1946. Served War of 1939–45, as AJAG, in UDF, 1940–43; Middle East with 6th Armoured Div. of UDF, 1943. SA Delegate to San Francisco Conf., 1945, to 1st Gen. Assembly of UN, London, 1946, to Final Assembly of League of Nations, 1946; SA delegate and Pres. of Commn on Italian Political and Territorial Questions at Peace Conf., Paris, 1946–47. High Comr in London for the Union of South Africa, 1948–50. Vice-Pres., Royal Commonwealth Soc., 1948–; Hon. Pres., South Africa Inst. of Internat. Affairs; Chm., Smuts Memorial Trust; Life Trustee, South Africa Foundn. Hon. Pres., SA Guide-dogs Assoc. for the Blind. LLd *hc* Univ. of Natal, 1990. FRSA 1948. Knight Commander with Star of St Olav (Norway), 1943; Knight Grand Cross of North Star

(Sweden), 1946; Order of Meritorious Services (Class I) Gold (S Africa), 1987. *Publication:* (autobiog.) Bridges of Understanding, 1978. *Recreations:* tennis, bridge. *Address:* 41 The Guild, 213 Rivonia Road, Morningside, South Africa. *Clubs:* Rand, Inanda, South African International Lawn Tennis (Hon. Mem., 1950) (S Africa).

EGERTON, family name of **Duke of Sutherland** and **Earl of Wilton.**

EGERTON, Maj.-Gen. David Boswell, CB 1968; OBE 1956; MC 1940; *b* 24 July 1914; *s* of Vice-Admiral W. de M. Egerton, DSO, and late Anita Adolphine (*née* David); *m* 1946, Margaret Gillian, *d* of Canon C. C. Inge; one *s* two *d*. *Educ:* Stowe; RMA Woolwich. Commissioned Royal Artillery, Aug. 1934; served in India, 1935–39; ops in Waziristan, 1937; France and Belgium, 1940 (MC); Egypt 1942, Italy 1944 (wounded). Technical Staff course, RMCS, 1946; BJSM, Washington, DC, 1950–52; Asst Chief Engineer in charge of ammunition development, Royal Armament R&D Estabt, 1955–58; idc 1959; Army Mem., Defence Research Policy Staff, 1959–62; Comdt, Trials Estabt Guided Weapons, RA, 1962–63; Army Mem., Air Defence Working Party, 1963–64; Dir-Gen. of Artillery, Army Dept, 1964–67; Vice-Pres., Ordnance Board, 1967–69, President, 1969–70; retired 1970. Col Comdt, RA, 1970–74. Gen. Sec., Assoc. of Recognised Eng. Lang. Schs, 1971–79. *Recreations:* gardening, travel. *Address:* Campion Cottage, Cheselbourne, Dorchester DT2 7NT. *T:* Milborne St Andrew (025887) 641. *Club:* Army and Navy.

EGERTON, Sir John Alfred Roy, (Jack Egerton), Kt 1976; *b* Rockhampton, 11 March 1918; *s* of J. G. Egerton, Rockhampton; *m* 1940, Moya, *d* of W. Jones; one *s*. *Educ:* Rockhampton High Sch.; Mt Morgan High Sch.; Australian Admin. Staff Coll. A Union Exec. Officer, 1941–76; Federal Officer of Boilermakers' Union, 1951–66 (Vice-Pres. Fed. Council; rep. Union in China, 1956); Official, Metal Trades Fedn, 1951–67; Mem., ACTU Interstate Exec., 1969; former Pres., Qld Trades and Labor Council. Aust. Rep. ILO Congresses, Geneva: 1960, 1966, 1968, 1974; Qld Rep. to ACTU Congress and ALP Fed. Conf.; Pres., ALP Qld Exec., 1968–76 (Mem. Qld Central Exec., 1958); Mem., Fed. Exec. of ALP, 1970, Sen. Vice-Pres. 1972. Alderman and Dep. Mayor, Gold Coast City Council. Director: Qantas Airways Ltd, 1973–84; Mary Kathleen Uranium; SGIO Building Soc.; Beenleigh Rum. Member: Duke of Edinburgh Study Conf. Cttee, 1967–74; Griffith Univ. Council. *Recreations:* reading, Rugby League (Vice-Pres. and Dir, Qld), golf, trotting. *Address:* c/o Gold Coast City Centre, Bundall Road, Southport, Qld 4215, Australia. *Clubs:* NSW and Queensland League, Virginia Golf, Albion Park Trotting.

EGERTON, Sir Philip John Caledon G.; *see* Grey Egerton.

EGERTON, Sir Seymour (John Louis), GCVO 1977 (KCVO 1970); Director, Coutts & Co., Bankers, 1947–85 (Chairman, 1951–76); *b* 24 Sept. 1915; *s* of late Louis Egerton and Jane, *e d* of Rev. Lord Victor Seymour; unmarried. *Educ:* Eton. Served War of 1939–45, in Grenadier Guards. Governor, St George's Hosp., 1958–73. Treasurer, Boy Scouts' Assoc., 1953–64; Vice-Pres., Corporation of the Church House, 1954–81. Sheriff of Greater London, 1968. *Address:* Flat A, 51 Eaton Square, SW1. *T:* 071–235 2164. *Clubs:* Boodle's, Beefsteak, Pratt's.

EGERTON, Sir Stephen (Loftus), KCMG 1988 (CMG 1978); HM Diplomatic Service; Ambassador to Italy, 1989–July 1992; *b* 21 July 1932; *o s* of late William le Belward Egerton, ICS, and late Angela Doreen Loftus Bland; *m* 1958, Caroline, *er d* of Major and Mrs E. T. E. Cary-Elwes, Laurel House, Bergh Apton, Norfolk; one *s* one *d*. *Educ:* Summer Fields; Eton; Trinity Coll., Cambridge. BA 1956, MA 1960. 2nd Lieut, 60th Rifles (KRRC), 1952–53. Entered Foreign Service, 1956; Middle East Centre for Arab Studies, Lebanon, 1956–57; Political Officer and Court Registrar, Kuwait, 1958–61; Private Sec. to Parliamentary Under-Secretary, FO, 1961–62; Northern Dept, FO, 1962–63; Oriental Sec. and later also Head of Chancery, Baghdad, 1963–67; First Sec., UK Mission to the UN, New York, 1967–70; Asst Head of Arabian and Near Eastern Depts, FCO, 1970–72; Counsellor and Head of Chancery, Tripoli, 1972–73; Head of Energy Dept, FCO, 1973–77; Consul-Gen., Rio de Janeiro, 1977–80; Ambassador to Iraq, 1980–82; Asst Under-Sec. of State, FCO, 1982–85; Ambassador to Saudi Arabia, 1986–89. Order of King Feisal bin Abdul Aziz, 1st class, 1987; Grand Cross of the Italian Republic, 1990. *Recreations:* topiary, argument. *Address:* c/o Foreign and Commonwealth Office, SW1A 2AH. *Clubs:* Brooks's; Greenjackets, Eton Ramblers.

EGGAR, Timothy John Crommelin, (Tim); MP (C) Enfield North, since 1979; Minister of State, Department of Education and Science, since 1990; *b* 19 Dec. 1951; *s* of late John Drennan Eggar and of Pamela Rosemary Eggar; *m* 1977, Charmian Diana Minoprio; one *s* one *d*. *Educ:* Winchester Coll.; Magdalene Coll., Cambridge (MA). Called to the Bar, Inner Temple, 1976. European Banking Co., 1975–83; Dir, Charterhouse Petroleum, 1984–85. Chm., Cambridge Univ. Cons. Assoc., 1972; Vice-Chm., Fedn of Cons. Students, 1973–74. PPS to Minister for Overseas Develt, 1982–85; Parly Under-Sec. of State, FCO, 1985–89; Minister of State, Dept of Employment, 1989–90. *Recreations:* ski-ing, village cricket, simple gardening. *Address:* House of Commons, SW1. *Clubs:* Bush Hill Park Conservative, Enfield Highway Conservative, Ponders End Conservative, North Enfield Conservative, Enfield Town Conservative.

EGGINGTON, Dr William Robert Owen; Chief Medical Adviser, Department of Social Security (formerly Chief Medical Adviser (Social Security), Department of Health and Social Security), since 1986; *b* 24 Feb. 1932; *s* of Alfred Thomas Eggington and Phyllis Eggington (*née* Wynne); *m* 1961, Patricia Mary Elizabeth, *d* of Henry David and Elizabeth Grant; one *s* one *d*. *Educ:* Kingswood School, Bath; Guy's Hosp. MB, BS 1955, DTM&H 1960, DPH 1962, DIH 1963; MFCM 1970. House Surgeon, Guy's Hosp., 1955; House Physician, St John's Hosp., Lewisham, 1956. RAMC, 1957–73, retired as Lt-Col, Senior Specialist Army Health. DHSS, 1973–. *Recreations:* Goss heraldic china, military history, football spectator. *Address:* Room 213, Friars House, 157–168 Blackfriars Road, SE1. *T:* 071–972 3286.

EGGINTON, Anthony Joseph, CBE 1991; Director Programmes and Deputy Chairman, Science and Engineering Research Council, since 1988; *b* 18 July 1930; *s* of Arthur Reginald Egginton and Margaret Anne (*née* Emslie); *m* 1957, Janet Leta, *d* of late Albert and Florence Herring; two *d*. *Educ:* Selhurst Grammar Sch., Croydon; University Coll., London. BSc 1951. Res. Assoc., UCL, 1951–56; AERE Harwell (Gen. Physics Div.), 1956–61; Head of Beams Physics Gp, NIRNS Rutherford High Energy Lab., 1961–65; DCSO and Head of Machine Gp, SRC Daresbury Nuclear Physics Lab., 1965–72; Head of Engrg Div., 1972–74, Under Sec. and Dir of Engineering and Nuclear Physics, 1974–78, Dir of Science and Engrg Divs, 1978–83, SRC; Dir of Engrg, SERC, 1983–88. Head, UK Delegn, 1978–83, Chm., 1982–83, Steering Cttee, Inst. Laue-Langevin, Grenoble. *Publications:* papers and articles in jls and conf. proceedings on particle accelerators and beams. *Recreations:* sport, cinema, music. *Address:* Witney House, West End, Witney, Oxon OX8 6NQ. *T:* Witney (0993) 3502. *Club:* Lansdowne.

EGGLESTON, Anthony Francis, OBE 1968; Headmaster, Campion School, Athens, 1983–88, retired; *b* 26 Jan. 1928; *s* of late J. F. Eggleston and late Mrs J. M. Barnard, Harrow, Middx; *m* 1957, Jane Morison Buxton, JP, *d* of late W. L. Buxton, MBE and late Mrs F. M. M. Buxton, Stanmore, Middx; one *s* two *d*. *Educ:* Merchant Taylors' Sch., Northwood (Schol.); St John's Coll., Oxford (Sir Thomas White Schol.). BA 1949, MA 1953; 2nd cl. hons Chemistry. National Service, 1950–52; 2nd Lieut, RA, Suez Canal Zone. Asst Master, Cheltenham Coll., 1952–54; Sen. Science Master, English High Sch., Istanbul, 1954–56; Asst Master, Merchant Taylors' Sch., Northwood, 1956–62; Principal, English Sch., Nicosia, 1962–68; Headmaster, Felsted Sch., 1968–82. *Recreation:* looking at buildings. *Address:* Garden House, Chester Place, Norwich NR2 3DG. *T:* Norwich (0603) 616025.

EGGLESTON, Prof. Harold Gordon; Professor Emeritus of Mathematics, London University; *b* 27 Nov. 1921; 2nd *s* of H. T. and E. M. Eggleston, Bents Green, Sheffield; *m* 1955, Elizabeth, *o d* of F. R. and C. A. W. Daglish, Beamish, County Durham; two *s* one *d*. *Educ:* High Storrs Grammar Sch., Sheffield; Trinity Coll., Cambridge. Lecturer and Senior Lecturer, University Coll. of Swansea, 1948–53; Lecturer, University of Cambridge, 1953–58; Prof. of Mathematics, University of London at Bedford Coll., 1958–66, at Royal Holloway Coll., 1966–81. *Publications:* Problems in Euclidean Space, 1957; Convexity, 1958; Elementary Real Analysis, 1962. *Address:* Victoria Cottage, 6 Church Street, Steeple Bumpstead, Haverhill, Suffolk CB9 7DG.

EGGLESTON, Prof. James Frederick; Professor of Education, University of Nottingham, 1972–84, now Emeritus; *b* 30 July 1927; *s* of Frederick James and Anne Margaret Eggleston; *m* 1956, Margaret Snowden; three *s* two *d*. *Educ:* Appleby Grammar Sch.; Durham Univ. (King's Coll., Newcastle upon Tyne). BSc Hons Zoology; DipEd; FIBiol 1975. School teacher, 1953–64, Head of Biol., later Head of Sci., Hinckley Grammar Sch.; Res. Fellow, Res. Unit for Assessment and Curriculum Studies, Leicester Univ. Sch. of Educn, 1964; team leader, later consultant, Nuffield Sci. Teaching Project, 1964–68; Lectr in Educn, Leicester Univ. Sch. of Educn, 1966; apptd to Colls and Curriculum Chair of Educn, Nottingham Univ., 1973, Dean of Educn, 1975–81. *Publications:* A Critical Review of Assessment Procedures in Secondary School Science, 1965; Problems in Quantitative Biology, 1968; (with J. F. Kerr) Studies in Assessment, 1970; (jtly) A Science Teaching Observation Schedule, 1975; (jtly) Processes and Products of Science Teaching, 1976; contributions to: The Disciplines of the Curriculum, 1971; The Art of the Science Teacher, 1974; Frontiers of Classroom Research, 1975; Techniques and Problems of Assessment, 1976; (with Trevor Kerry) Topic Work in the Primary School, 1988; articles in professional jls. *Recreations:* fell walking, golf, photography. *Address:* The Mount, Bown's Hill, Crich, near Matlock, Derbys DE4 5DG. *T:* Ambergate (077385) 2870.

EGGLESTON, Prof. Samuel John, BScEcon, MA, DLitt; Chairman of the Department of Education, University of Warwick, since 1985; *b* 11 Nov. 1926; *s* of Edmund and Josephine Eggleston, Dorchester. *Educ:* Chippenham Grammar Sch.; LSE (BScEcon 1957); Univ. of London Inst. of Educn (MA 1965). DLitt Univ. of Keele, 1977. Teacher, Suffolk and Worcs, 1950–54; Leverhulme Scholarship, LSE, 1954–57; Teacher, Beds, and Headteacher, Oxfordshire, 1957–60; Lectr, Loughborough Coll. of Educn, 1960–63; Lectr, later Sen. Lectr, Leicester Univ., 1963–67; Keele University: Prof. and Head of Dept of Educn, 1967–84; Chm., Bd of Soc. Scis, 1976–79; Chm., Higher Degree and Res. Cttee, 1981–84. Vis. Commonwealth Fellow, Canada, 1973–74. Director: DES Res. Project, Structure and Function of Youth Service, 1968–74; Schs Council Project, Design and Craft Educn, 1968–74; DES Research Projects: Training for Multi-Racial Educn, 1978–80; Minority Gp Adolescence, 1981–84. Chairman: Council of Europe Workshop on Multi-Cultural Higher Educn, 1981–86; Education Cttee, Central Television, 1987–; Member: Council of Europe Working Party, Diversif. of Tertiary Educn, 1972–78; Cheshire Educn Cttee, 1981–83; Council, Eur. Inst. of Educn and Social Policy, 1983–; Educnl Res. Bd, SSRC, 1973–77; Panel on Public Disorder and Sporting Events, SSRC, 1976–77; Assessment of Performance Unit, DES, Consultative Cttee, 1980–88; Res. Consultancy Cttee, DES, 1981–83; Arts Council Cttee on Trng for the Arts, 1982–87; Academic Adv. Cttee, EEC Erasmus Project, 1990–. Hon. FEICDT 1987; Hon. FCP. Editor: Design and Technology Teaching, 1968–; Sociological Rev., 1982– (Chm., Editorial Bd, 1970–82); Chm., Editorial Bd, European Jl of Educn (formerly Paedagogica Europaea), 1976– (Editor in Chief, 1968–76); Founding Chm., Editorial Bd, Multicultural Teaching, 1982–. Hon. FCollH 1968. *Publications:* The Social Context of the School, 1967; (ed) Contemporary Research in the Sociology of Education, 1974; Adolescence and Community, 1976; New Developments in Design Education, 1976; The Sociology of the School Curriculum, 1977; The Ecology of the School, 1977; (ed) Experimental Education in Europe, 1978; Teacher Decision Making in the Classroom, 1979; School Based Curriculum Development, 1980; Work Experience in Secondary Schools, 1982; Education for Some, 1986; Becoming a Teacher, 1991; articles in books and jls, incl. Sociol., Brit. Jl of Sociol., New Soc., Educnl Res. *Recreations:* work in design and craft, skiing, riding, travel, gardening. *Address:* Department of Education, University of Warwick, Coventry CV4 7AL. *T:* Coventry (0203) 524104.

EGGLETON, Anthony, CVO 1970; Federal Director, Liberal Party of Australia, 1975–90; Secretary-General, CARE International, since 1991; *b* 30 April 1932; *s* of Tom and Winifred Eggleton; *m* 1953, Mary Walker, Melbourne; two *s* one *d*. *Educ:* King Alfred's Sch., Wantage. Journalist, Westminster Press Group, 1948–50; Editorial Staff, Bendigo Advertiser, Vic, 1950–51; Australian Broadcasting Commn, 1951–60 (Dir of ABC-TV News Coverage, 1956–60); Dir of Public Relations, Royal Australian Navy, 1960–65; Press Sec. to Prime Ministers of Australia, 1965–71 (Prime Ministers Menzies, Holt, Gorton, McMahon); Commonwealth Dir of Information, London, 1971–74; Special Advr to Leader of Opposition, and Dir of Communications, Federal Liberal Party, 1974–75; Campaign Dir, Federal Elections, 1975, 1977, 1980, 1983, 1984, 1987, 1990. Exec. Sec., Pacific Democrat Union, 1982–84, 1985–87, Dep. Chm., 1987–90. Australian Public Relations Inst.'s 1st Award of Honour, 1968; Distinguished Service Award, Liberal Party of Australia, 1990. *Address:* PO Box 648, Civic Square, ACT 2608, Australia. *Clubs:* (Foundn Pres.) National Press (Canberra), Commonwealth (Canberra).

EGILSSON, Ólafur; Ambassador of Iceland to the Soviet Union, since 1990, and concurrently to Bulgaria, Japan, Mongolia and Romania; *b* 20 Aug. 1936; *s* of Egill Kristjánsson and Anna Margrjet Thuríður Ólafsdóttir Briem; *m* 1960, Ragna Sverrisdóttir Ragnars; one *s* one *d*. *Educ:* Commercial College, Iceland (grad. 1956); Univ. of Iceland, Faculty of Law (grad. 1963). Reporter on Vísir, 1956–58, Morgunblaðið, 1959–62; publishing Exec., Almenna bókafélagið, 1963–64; Head, NATO Regional Inf. Office, Iceland, 1964–66, and Gen. Sec., Icelandic Assoc. for Western Co-operation and Atlantic Assoc. of Young Political Leaders of Iceland; Icelandic Foreign Service, 1966; Foreign Ministry, 1966–69; First Sec., later Counsellor, Icelandic Embassy, Paris, and Dep. Perm. Rep. to OECD, UNESCO, 1969–71, and Council of Europe, Strasbourg, 1969–70; Dep. Perm. Rep., N Atlantic Council and Dep. Head, Icelandic Delegn to EEC, Brussels, 1971–74; Counsellor, later Minister Counsellor, Political Div., Min. of Foreign Affairs, 1974–80; Chief of Protocol, with rank of Ambassador, 1980–83; Acting Principal Private Sec. to Icelandic President, Oct. 1981–June 1982; Dep. Perm. Under Sec. and Dir Gen. for Political Affairs, Min. of Foreign Affairs, 1983–87; Ambassador of Iceland to UK, 1986–89, and concurrently to the Netherlands, Ireland and Nigeria. Chm., Governing Bd, Icelandic Internat. Develt Agency, 1982–87; Sec., Commn revising Foreign Service

Act, 1968–69. President: Nat. Youth Council of Iceland, 1963–64; Acad. Assoc. of Reykjavík, 1967–68; Exec. Mem., Bible Soc., 1977–87, History Soc., 1982–88. Commander, Icelandic Order of the Falcon, 1981; holds numerous foreign orders. *Publications:* (jtly) Iceland and Jan Mayen, 1980; (ed) Bjarni Benediktsson: Contemporaries' views, 1983; (jtly) NATO's Anxious Birth: the prophetic vision of the 1940's, 1985. *Recreations:* walking, ski-ing, music (opera), history. *Address:* Khlebnyi Pereulok 28, Moscow, USSR. *T:* 095–290 4653, *Fax:* 095–200 1264.

EGLINGTON, Charles Richard John; Director, since 1986, Vice-Chairman, since 1990, S. G. Warburg Securities; *b* 12 Aug. 1938; *s* of Richard Eglington and Treena Margaret Joyce Eglington. *Educ:* Sherborne. Dir, Akroyd & Smithers, 1978–86. Mem. Council, Stock Exchange, 1975–86, Dep. Chm., 1981–84 (Chairman: Quotations Cttee, 1978–81; Property and Finance Cttee, 1983–86); Mem., Gp of Thirty Working Cttee on Clearance and Settlement Systems, 1988–89. Governor: Sherborne Sch., 1980–; Twyford Sch., 1984–. *Recreations:* golf, cricket. *Address:* Warburg Securities, 1 Finsbury Avenue, EC2M 2PA. *T:* 071–606 1066. *Clubs:* MCC; Royal and Ancient Golf (St Andrews); Walton Heath Golf; Rye Golf.

EGLINTON and WINTON, 18th Earl of, *cr* 1507; **Archibald George Montgomerie;** Lord Montgomerie, 1448; Baron Seton and Tranent, 1859; Baron Kilwinning, 1615; Baron Ardrossan (UK), 1806; Earl of Winton (UK), 1859; Hereditary Sheriff of Renfrewshire; Managing Director, since 1972, a Deputy Chairman, since 1980, Gerrard & National Holdings plc; *b* 27 Aug. 1939; *s* of 17th Earl of Eglinton and Winton and Ursula (*d* 1987), *er d* of Hon. Ronald Watson, Edinburgh; *S* father, 1966; *m* 1964, Marion Carolina, *o d* of John Dunn-Yarker; four *s*. *Educ:* Eton. *Heir:* *s* Lord Montgomerie, *qv*. *Address:* The Dutch House, West Green, Hartley Wintney, Hants.

EGLINTON, Prof. Geoffrey, PhD, DSc; FRS 1976; Professor of Organic Geochemistry, University of Bristol, since 1973; *b* 1 Nov. 1927; *s* of Alfred Edward Eglinton and Lilian Blackham; *m* 1955, Pamela Joan Coupland; two *s* (one *d*. decd). *Educ:* Sale Grammar Sch.; Manchester Univ. (BSc, PhD, DSc). Post-Doctoral Fellow, Ohio State Univ., 1951–52; ICI Fellow, Liverpool Univ., 1952–54; Lectr, subseq. Sen. Lectr and Reader, Glasgow Univ., 1954–67; Sen. Lectr, subseq. Reader, Bristol Univ., 1967–73. Mem., NERC, 1984–90. Hon. Fellow, Plymouth Polytechnic, 1981. Gold Medal for Exceptional Scientific Achievement, NASA, 1973; Hugo Müller Silver Medal, Chemical Soc., 1974; Alfred Treibs Gold Medal, Geochem. Soc., 1981; Coke Medal, Geol Soc. of London, 1985. *Publications:* Applications of Spectroscopy to Organic Chemistry, 1965; Organic Geochemistry: methods and results, 1969; 'Chemsyn', 1972, 2nd edn 1975; contrib. Nature, Geochim. Cosmochim. Acta, Phytochem., Chem. Geol., Sci. American. *Recreations:* gardening, walking, sailing. *Address:* Oldwell, 7 Redhouse Lane, Bristol BS9 3RY. *T:* Bristol (0272) 683833. *Club:* Rucksack (Manchester).

EGMONT, 11th Earl of, *cr* 1733; **Frederick George Moore Perceval;** Bt 1661; Baron Perceval, 1715; Viscount Perceval, 1722; Baron Lovell and Holland (Great Britain), 1762; Baron Arden, 1770; Baron Arden (United Kingdom), 1802; *b* 14 April 1914; *o s* of 10th Earl and Cecilia (*d* 1916), *d* of James Burns Moore, Montreal; *S* father, 1932; *m* 1932, Ann Geraldine, *d* of D. G. Moodie; one *s* one *d* (and two *s* decd). *Heir:* *s* Viscount Perceval, *qv*. *Address:* Two-dot Ranch, Nanton, Alberta, Canada.

EGREMONT, 2nd Baron *cr* 1963, **AND LECONFIELD,** 7th Baron *cr* 1859; **John Max Henry Scawen Wyndham,** DL; *b* 21 April 1948; *s* of John Edward Reginald Wyndham, MBE, 1st Baron Egremont and 6th Baron Leconfield, and of Pamela, *d* of late Captain the Hon. Valentine Wyndham-Quin, RN; *S* father, 1972; *m* 1978, Caroline, *er d* of A. R. Nelson, Muckairn, Taynuilt, Argyll, and Hon. Lady Musker; one *s* three *d*. *Educ:* Eton; Christ Church, Oxford (MA Modern History). Mem., Royal Commn on Historical MSS, 1989–. Chm., Friends of the Nat. Libraries, 1985–; Trustee: Wallace Collection, 1988–; British Museum, 1990–. DL W Sussex, 1988. *Publications:* The Cousins, 1977 (Yorkshire Post First Book Award); Balfour: a life of Arthur James Balfour, 1980; The Ladies' Man (novel), 1983; Dear Shadows (novel), 1986; Painted Lives (novel), 1989. *Heir:* *s* Hon. George Ronan Valentine Wyndham, *b* 31 July 1983. *Address:* Petworth House, Petworth, West Sussex GU28 0AE. *T:* Petworth (0798) 42447.

EHRMAN, John Patrick William, FBA 1970; historian; *b* 17 March 1920; *o s* of late Albert and Rina Ehrman; *m* 1948, Elizabeth Susan Anne, *d* of late Vice-Adm. Sir Geoffrey Blake, KCB, DSO; four *s*. *Educ:* Charterhouse; Trinity Coll., Cambridge (MA). Served Royal Navy, 1940–45. Fellow of Trinity Coll., Cambridge, 1947–52; Historian, Cabinet Office, 1948–56; Lees Knowles Lectr, Cambridge, 1957–58; James Ford Special Lectr, Oxford, 1976–77. Hon. Treas., Friends of the National Libraries, 1960–77; Trustee of the Nat. Portrait Gall., 1971–85; Member: Reviewing Cttee on Export of Works of Art, 1970–76; Royal Commn on Historical Manuscripts, 1973–; Chairman: Adv. Cttee to British Library Reference Div., 1975–84; Nat. Manuscripts Conservation Trust, 1989–; Panizzi Foundn Selection Council, 1983–89; Vice-Pres., Navy Records Soc., 1968–70, 1974–76. FSA 1958; FRHistS. *Publications:* The Navy in the War of William III, 1953; Grand Strategy, 1943–5 (2 vols, UK Official Military Histories of the Second World War), 1956; Cabinet Government and War, 1890–1940, 1958; The British Government and Commercial Negotiations with Europe, 1783–1793, 1962; The Younger Pitt, vol. 1, The Years of Acclaim, 1969, vol. 2, The Reluctant Transition, 1983. *Address:* The Mead Barns, Taynton, near Burford, Oxfordshire OX8 5UH. *Clubs:* Army and Navy, Beefsteak, Garrick.

See also W. G. Ehrman.

EHRMAN, William Geoffrey; HM Diplomatic Service; Political Adviser, Hong Kong, since 1989; *b* 28 Aug. 1950; *s* of J. P. W. Ehrman, *qv* and Susan (*née* Blake); *m* 1977, Penelope Anne, *d* of late Brig. H. W. Le Patourel, VC and of Babette Le Patourel; one *s* three *d*. *Educ:* Eton; Trinity Coll., Cambridge (MA). Joined Diplomatic Service, 1973; language student, Hong Kong, 1975–76; Third/Second Sec., Peking, 1976–78; First Secretary: UK Mission to UN, NY, 1979–83; Peking, 1983–84; FCO, 1985–89. *Recreations:* sailing, walking, ski-ing. *Address:* c/o Foreign and Commonwealth Office, SW1A 2AH. *Club:* Royal Cruising.

EICHELBAUM, Rt. Hon. Sir (Johann) Thomas, GBE 1989; PC 1989; Chief Justice of New Zealand, since 1989; *b* 17 May 1931; *s* of Dr Walter and Frida Eichelbaum; *m* 1956, Vida Beryl Franz; three *s*. *Educ:* Hutt Valley High School; Victoria University College (LLB). Partner, Chapman Tripp & Co., Wellington, 1958–78; QC 1978; Judge of High Court of NZ, 1982–88. Pres., NZ Law Soc., 1980–82. *Publication:* (Editor in Chief) Mauet's Fundamentals of Trial Techniques, NZ edn, 1989. *Recreations:* reading, music, tennis, beachcombing. *Address:* 17 Cheviot Road, Lowry Bay, Eastbourne, New Zealand. *T:* 04/685-200; Chief Justice's Chambers, High Court, PO Box 1091, Wellington, New Zealand. *Clubs:* Wellington (Wellington); Northern (Auckland).

EIGEN, Manfred; Director at Max-Planck-Institut für biophysikalische Chemie, Göttingen, since 1964; *b* 9 May 1927; *s* of Ernst and Hedwig Eigen; *m* 1952, Elfriede Müller; one *s* one *d*. *Educ:* Göttingen Univ. Dr rer. nat. (Phys. Chem.) 1951. Research Asst, Inst. für physikal. Chemie, Göttingen Univ., 1951–53; Asst, Max-Planck-Institut für physikal. Chemie, 1953; Research Fellow, Max-Planck-Gesellschaft, 1958; Head of separate dept of biochemical kinetics, Max-Planck-Inst., 1962. Andrew D. White Prof. at Large, Cornell Univ., 1965; Hon. Prof., Technische Hochschule Braunschweig, 1965. For. Hon. Mem., Amer. Acad. of Arts and Sciences, 1964; Mem. Leopoldina, Deutsche Akad. der Naturforscher, Halle, 1964; Mem., Akad. der Wissenschaften, Göttingen, 1965; Hon. Mem., Amer. Assoc. Biol Chemists, 1966; For. Assoc., Nat. Acad. of Scis, Washington, 1966; For. Mem., Royal Soc., 1973. Dr of Science *hc*, Washington, Harvard and Chicago Univs, 1966. Has won prizes, medals and awards including Nobel Prize for Chemistry (jointly), 1967. *Publications:* numerous papers in Z. Elektrochem., Jl Phys. Chem., Trans Faraday Soc., Proc. Royal Soc., Canad. Jl Chem., ICSU Rev., and other learned jls. *Address:* Max-Planck-Institut für biophysikalische Chemie, Karl-Friedrich Bonhoeffer Institut, Postfach 2841, D3400 Göttingen-Nikolausberg, Germany.

EILLEDGE, Elwyn Owen Morris, FCA; Senior Partner, Ernst & Young, Chartered Accountants, since 1989; Joint Chairman, Ernst & Young International, since 1989; *b* 20 July 1935; *s* of Owen and Mary Elizabeth Eilledge; *m* 1962, Audrey Ann Faulkner Ellis; one *s* one *d*. *Educ:* Merton College, Oxford (BA, MA). FCA 1968. Articled with Farrow, Bersey, Gain, Vincent & Co. (now Binder Hamlyn), 1959–66; Whinney Murray & Co. (now Ernst & Whinney), Liberia, 1966–68; Ernst & Whinney: Audit Manager, Hamburg, 1968–71; Partner, London, 1972; Managing Partner, London office, 1983–86; Dep. Sen. Partner, 1985; Sen Partner, 1986–89; Chm., Ernst & Whinney Internat., 1988–89. *Recreations:* gardening, swimming, tennis, listening to classical music. *Address:* (office) Becket House, 1 Lambeth Palace Road, SE1 7EU. *T:* 071–931 3000. *Club:* Brooks's.

EILON, Prof. Samuel, FEng; Senior Research Fellow and Emeritus Professor, Imperial College of Science, Technology and Medicine, University of London, since 1989; Member, Monopolies and Mergers Commission, since 1990; industrial consultant on corporate performance and strategy; *b* 13 Oct. 1923; *s* of Abraham and Rachel Eilon; *m* 1946, Hannah Ruth (*née* Samuel); two *s* two *d*. *Educ:* Reali Sch., Haifa; Technion, Israel Inst. of Technology, Haifa; Imperial Coll., London. PhD 1955, DSc(Eng) 1963, London. Founder FEng, FIMechE, FIProdE. Engr, Palestine Electric Co. Ltd, Haifa, 1946–48; Officer, Israel Defence Forces, 1948–52; CO of an Ordnance and workshop base depot (Major); Res. Asst, Imperial Coll., 1952–55; Lectr in Production Engrg, Imperial Coll., 1955–57; Associate Prof. in Industrial Engrg, Technion, Haifa, 1957–59; Imperial College: Head of Section, 1955–57; Reader, 1959–63; Head of Dept, 1959–87; Prof. of Management Sci., 1963–89. Consultant and Lectr, European Productivity Agency, Paris, 1960–62. Professorial Research Fellow, Case Western Reserve Univ., Cleveland, Ohio, 1967–68. Vis. Fellow, University Coll., Cambridge, 1970–71. Dir, Campari International, 1978–80. Past Mem. of several cttees of IProdE and DES. Member: Council, Operational Res. Soc., 1965–67; Council, Inst. of Management Scis, 1970–72, 1980–82; Exec. Cttee, British Acad. of Management, 1985–89. Adviser, P-E Consulting Gp, 1961–71; Principal and Dir, Spencer Stuart and Associates, 1971–74; Dir, Amey Roadstone Corp., 1974–88. Chief Editor, OMEGA, Internat. Jl of Management Science, 1972–; Deptl Editor, Management Science, 1969–77. CBIM; Hon. FCGI 1978. Two Joseph Whitworth Prizes for papers, IMechE, 1960; Silver Medal, ORS, 1982. *Publications:* Elements of Production Planning and Control, 1962; Industrial Engineering Tables, 1962; (jtly) Exercises in Industrial Management, 1966; (jtly) Industrial Scheduling Abstracts, 1967; (jtly) Inventory Control Abstracts, 1968; (jtly) Distribution Management, 1971; Management Control, 1971, 2nd edn 1979; (jtly) Applications of Management Science in Banking and Finance, 1972; (jtly) Applied Productivity Analysis for Industry, 1976; Aspects of Management, 1977, 2nd edn 1979; The Art of Reckoning: analysis of performance criteria, 1984; Management Assertions and Aversions, 1985; (jtly) The Global Challenge of Innovation, 1991; Management Practice and Mispractice, 1991; over 250 papers and articles in the field of management. *Recreations:* theatre, tennis, walking. *Address:* Mechanical Engineering Building, Imperial College, Exhibition Road, SW7 2BX. *T:* 071–589 5111. *Club:* Athenæum.

EKLUND, Dr (Arne) Sigvard; Director General (now Emeritus), International Atomic Energy Agency, Vienna, 1961–81; *b* Kiruna, Sweden, 1911; *m* 1941, Anna-Greta Johansson; one *s* two *d*. *Educ:* Uppsala Univ., Sweden (DSc). Assoc. Prof. in Nuclear Physics, Royal Inst. of Technology, Stockholm, 1946–56; Dir of Research, later Reactor development Div., AB Atomenergi, 1950–61. Conference Sec.-Gen., 2nd Internat. UN Conf. on Peaceful Uses of Atomic Energy, 1958. Fellow, Amer. Nuclear Soc., 1961; Member: Royal Swedish Acad. of Engineering Sciences, 1953; Royal Swedish Acad. of Sciences, 1972; Hon. Member: British Nuclear Energy Soc., 1963; European Nuclear Soc., 1982. For. Associate, Nat. Acad. of Engineering, USA, 1979. Dr *hc*: Univ. of Graz, 1968; Acad. of Mining and Metallurgy, Cracow, 1971; Univ. of Bucarest, 1971; Chalmers Inst. of Technol., Gothenberg, 1974; Buenos Aires, Budapest, Columbia and Moscow Univs, 1977; Dresden Technical and Yon-sei, Seoul Univs, 1978; Nat. Agrarian Univ. of La Molina, Peru, 1979; Royal Inst. of Technol., Stockholm, 1980. (Jointly) Atoms for Peace Award, 1968; Golden Medal of Honour, Vienna, 1971; Henry DeWolf Smyth Nuclear Statesman Award, 1976; Exceptional Service Award, Amer. Nuclear Soc., 1980. Hon. Senator, Univ. of Vienna, 1977. Kt Comdr, Order of North Star, Sweden, 1971; Das Grosse Goldene Ehrenzeichen am Bande für Verdienste, Austria, 1981; Das Grosse Verdienstkreuz mit Stern und Schulterband, FRG, 1981; Aquila Azteca en el Grado de Banda, Mexico, 1981; SPk, 1987. Comdr, Order of St Gregory, bestowed by His Holiness Pope John Paul II, 1982. *Publications:* Studies in Nuclear Physics, 1946 (Sweden); articles on peaceful uses of nuclear energy. *Address:* Krapfenwaldgasse 48, 1190–Vienna, Austria. *T:* 32 24 24. *Club:* Sällskapet (Stockholm).

ELAM, Caroline Mary; Editor, Burlington Magazine, since 1987; *b* 12 March 1945; *d* of John Frederick Elam and Joan Barrington Elam (*née* Lloyd). *Educ:* Colchester County High Sch.; Lady Margaret Hall, Oxford (BA); Courtauld Inst. of Art, Univ. of London. MA London and Cantab. Lectr, Fine Art Dept, Univ. of Glasgow, 1970–72; Jun. Res. Fellow, King's Coll., Cambridge, 1972–76; Lectr, History of Art Dept, Westfield Coll., Univ. of London, 1976–87. Fellow, Harvard Univ. Center for Renaissance Studies, Villa I Tatti, Florence, 1981–82. Mem. Exec. Cttee, Nat. Art Collections Fund, 1988–. *Publications:* articles in Art History, Burlington Magazine, Mitteilungen des Kunsthistorischen Insts in Florenz, Jl of RSA, etc. *Address:* Burlington Magazine, 6 Bloomsbury Square, WC1 2LP. *T:* 071–430 0481.

See also J. N. Elam.

ELAM, His Honour Henry; a Circuit Judge (formerly Deputy Chairman of the Court of Quarter Sessions, Inner London), 1953–76; barrister-at-law; *b* 29 Nov. 1903; *o s* of Thomas Henry Elam, 33 Sackville Street, W1; *m* 1st, 1930, Eunice (*d* 1975), *yr d* of J. G. Matthews, 41 Redington Road, NW3; one *d*; 2nd, 1975, Doris A. Horsford. *Educ:* Charterhouse; Lincoln Coll., Oxford (MA). Called to Bar, Inner Temple, 1927; Western Circuit; Junior Prosecuting Counsel to the Treasury, Central Criminal Court, 1937; late Dep. Judge Advocate, RAF; Recorder of Poole, 1941–46; 2nd Junior Prosecuting Counsel, 1942–45; 1st Junior, 1945–50; 3rd Senior, Jan.-March 1950; 2nd Senior, 1950–53; Recorder of Exeter, 1946–53; Dep. Chm., West Kent QS, 1947–53. *Recreation:* flyfishing. *Address:* Clymshurst, Burwash Common, East Sussex TN19 7NB. *T:* Burwash (0435) 883335.

ELAM, (John) Nicholas; Head of Cultural Relations Department, Foreign and Commonwealth Office, since 1987; *b* 2 July 1939; *s* of John Frederick Elam, OBE and Joan Barrington Elam (*née* Lloyd); *m* 1967, Florence Helen, *d* of P. Lentz; two *s* one *d*. *Educ:* Colchester Royal Grammar Sch.; New Coll., Oxford (schol.). Frank Knox Fellow, Harvard Univ., 1961–62. Entered HM Diplomatic Service, 1962; FO, 1962–64; Pretoria and Cape Town, 1964–68; Treasury Centre for Admin. Studies, 1968–69; FCO, 1969–71; First Sec., Bahrain, 1971; Commercial Sec., Brussels, 1972–76; FCO, 1976–79, Dep. Head of News Dept, 1978–79; Counsellor and Dep. British Govt Rep., Salisbury, 1979; Dep. High Comr, Salisbury (later Harare), 1980–83; Consul-General, Montreal, 1984–87. *Recreations:* travel, the arts. *Address:* c/o Foreign and Commonwealth Office, SW1A 2AH.
See also C. M. Elam.

ELCOAT, Rev. Canon George Alastair; Vicar of Tweedmouth, Berwick-upon-Tweed, 1987–91 (Priest-in-charge, 1981–87); Chaplain to The Queen, 1982–June 1992; Rural Dean of Norham, 1982–91; *b* 4 June 1922; *s* of George Thomas Elcoat and Hilda Gertrude Elcoat. *Educ:* Tynemouth School; Queen's College, Birmingham. Served RAF, 1941–46. Asst Master, Newcastle Cathedral Choir School, 1947–48. Deacon 1951, priest 1952; Asst Curate, Corbridge, 1951–55; Vicar: Spittal, 1955–62; Chatton with Chillingham, 1962–70; Sugley, 1970–81; RD, Newcastle West, 1977–81; Hon. Canon, Newcastle, 1979–. *Recreations:* fell walking, photography, gardening, music. *Address:* 42 Windsor Crescent, Berwick-upon-Tweed, Northumberland TD15 1NT.

ELDER, David Renwick, MC 1940; CA; *b* 4 Jan. 1920; *s* of John Kidd Elder and Mary Kinnear Swanley; *m* 1947, Kathleen Frances Duncan; two *s* two *d*. *Educ:* Dundee High School. Served 1939–46, The Black Watch (RHR) and Sea Reconnaissance Unit (Major). Royal Dutch Shell Group, 1948–71; Ocean Transport & Trading Ltd, 1971–80 (Dep. Chm., 1975–80; Chm., Ocean Inchcape, 1974–80); Director: Letraset International Ltd, 1975; Capital & Counties Property Ltd, 1979; Whessoe Ltd, 1980. *Recreation:* golf. *Clubs:* Wentworth Golf (Virginia Water); Panmure Golf (Carnoustie).

ELDER, Mark Philip, CBE 1989; Music Director, English National Opera, since 1979; Music Director, Rochester Philharmonic Orchestra, USA, since 1989; *b* 2 June 1947; *s* of John and Helen Elder; *m* 1980, Amanda Jane Stein; one *d*. *Educ:* Bryanston Sch.; Corpus Christi Coll., Cambridge (Music Scholar, Choral Scholar; BA, MA). Music staff, Wexford Festival, 1969–70; Chorus Master and Asst Conductor, Glyndebourne, 1970–71; music staff, Covent Garden, 1970–72; Staff Conductor, Australian Opera, 1972–74; Staff Conductor, ENO, 1974, Associate Conductor, 1977; Principal Guest Conductor, London Mozart Players, 1980–83; Principal Guest Conductor, BBC Symphony Orchestra, 1982–85. *Address:* c/o Ingpen and Williams Ltd, 14 Kensington Court, W8 5DN.

ELDER, Prof. Murdoch George, MD; FRCS, FRCOG; Professor of Obstetrics and Gynaecology, University of London, at Institute of Obstetrics and Gynaecology, since 1978, and Dean, Institute of Obstetrics and Gynaecology, since 1985, Royal Postgraduate Medical School; *b* 4 Jan. 1938; *s* of Archibald James and Lotta Annie Elder; *m* 1964, Margaret Adelaide McVicker; two *s*. *Educ:* Edinburgh Acad.; Edinburgh Univ. (MB ChB 1961, MD 1973). FRCS 1968; FRCOG 1978. Junior posts, Edinburgh and Bristol, 1961–68; Lectr, Inst. of Obst. and Gyn. and Royal Univ. of Malta, 1968–71; Sen. Lectr and Reader, Charing Cross Hosp. Med. Sch., Univ. of London, 1971–78. Green Armytage Scholarship, RCOG, 1976; WHO Travelling Scholarship, 1977; Dir, Clinical Res. Centre, WHO, 1980–; Mem., Steering Cttee on Contraception, WHO, 1980–86; Mem., Hammersmith and Queen Charlotte's Special Health Authy, 1982–; Mem. Council, RPMS, 1979–. Silver Medal, Hellenic Obstetrical Soc., 1983. Mem., Editl Bds, Jl of Obst. and Gyn. and Clinical Reproduction, 1985–. *Publications:* Human Fertility Control, 1979; (ed) Preterm Labour, 1980; (ed) Reproduction, Obstetrics and Gynaecology, 1988; chapters in books and learned articles on steroid and prostaglandin biochemistry in reproduction, clinical obstetrics, gynaecology and contraception. *Recreations:* travel, golf. *Address:* 4 Stonehill Road, SW14 8RW. *T:* 081–876 4332. *Clubs:* Roehampton; 1942.

ELDERFIELD, Maurice; Chairman and Chief Executive, Berfield Associates Ltd, since 1980; Chairman: Midland Industrial Leasing Ltd, 1979–90; Saga Ltd, 1979–90; Sheldon & Partners Ltd, since 1981; *b* 10 April 1926; *s* of Henry Elderfield and Kathleen Maud Elderfield; *m* 1953, Audrey June (*née* Knight); one *s* three *d*. *Educ:* Southgate Grammar Sch. FCA. Fleet Air Arm, 1944–47. Thomson, Kingdom & Co., Chartered Accountants (qual. 1949), 1947–49; Personal Asst to Man. Dir, Forrestell, Land, Timber & Railway Co., 1949–57; Group Chief Accountant, Stephens Group, 1957–60; various posts, Segas, culminating in Board Mem. and Dir for Finance, 1960–73; Dir of Finance, Southern Water Authority, 1973–75; PO Board Mem. for Finance and Corporate Planning, 1975–76; Dir of Finance, Ferranti Ltd, 1977; Finance Mem., British Shipbuilders, 1977–80. Director: S. P. International Ltd, Hong Kong, 1987–; PV Ltd, 1987–90. Chairman: Throgmorton Trust, 1972–84; Throgmorton Investment Management, 1981–84; Capital for Industry Ltd, 1980–84. *Recreations:* golf, tennis, squash. *Address:* Hadleigh, Cansiron Lane, Ashurst Wood, Sussex RH19 3SD; (office) The Square, Forest Row, Sussex RH18 5NB. *Club:* Gravetye Manor Country.

ELDON, 5th Earl of, *cr* 1821; **John Joseph Nicholas Scott;** Baron Eldon 1799; Viscount Encombe 1821; *b* 24 April 1937; *s* of 4th Earl of Eldon, GCVO, and Hon. Magdalen Fraser, OBE (*d* 1969), *d* of 16th Baron Lovat; *S* father, 1976; *m* 1961, Comtesse Claudine de Montjoye-Vaufrey et de la Roche, Vienna; one *s* two *d*. *Educ:* Ampleforth; Trinity Coll., Oxford. 2nd Lieut Scots Guards (National Service). Lieut AER. *Heir:* *s* Viscount Encombe, *qv*. *Address:* 2 Coach House Lane, Wimbledon, SW19.

ELDRIDGE, Eric William, CB 1965; OBE 1948; Public Trustee, 1963–71; *b* 15 April 1906; *o s* of late William Eldridge; *m* 1936, Doris Margaret Kerr; one *s* one *d*. *Educ:* Millfields Central Sch.; City of London Coll. Admitted Solicitor (Hons), 1934. Chief Administrative Officer, Public Trustee Office, 1955–60; Asst Public Trustee, 1960–63. Consultant, Lee and Pembertons, solicitors, 1971–88, retd. *Address:* Old Stocks, Gorelands Lane, Chalfont St Giles, Bucks HP8 4HQ. *T:* Chalfont St Giles (02407) 2159.

ELDRIDGE, John Barron; Chairman, Matthews Wrightson Holdings Ltd, 1971–77; *b* 28 May 1919; *s* of William John Eldridge and Jessie Winifred (*née* Bowditch); *m* 1940, Marjorie Potier; one *s* two *d*. *Educ:* Lancing Coll. FIA 1950. Dir, Matthews Wrightson Holdings Ltd, 1964. Croix de Guerre 1944. *Address:* Castleton, Warwicks Bench Road, Guildford, Surrey GU1 3TL. *T:* Guildford (0483) 62687.

ELEK, Prof. Stephen Dyonis, MD, DSc; FRCP; Professor of Medical Microbiology in the University of London, 1957–74, now Emeritus; Consultant Bacteriologist, St George's Hospital, SW1, 1948–73; *b* 24 March 1914; *s* of Dezso and Anna Elek; *m* Sarah Joanna Hall; three *d*. *Educ:* Lutheran High Sch., Budapest, Hungary; St George's Hosp. Med. Sch., Univ. of London. MB, BS 1940; MD 1943; PhD 1948; DPH 1943; DSc 1958; MRCP 1960; FRCPath 1964. Clinical Pathologist, Maida Vale Hosp. for Nervous Diseases, 1946–47; Laking-Dakin Fellow, 1942–43; Fulbright Fellow, Harvard Medical Sch., 1956. Member: Pathological Soc. of Great Britain; American Society for Microbiology; New York Academy of Sciences; Soc. of Gen. Microbiology, etc. Editor, Jl of Medical Microbiology, 1972–74. Introduced immuno-diffusion as a new analytical tool in serology, 1948. *Publications:* Staphylococcus pyogenes and its Relation to Disease, 1959; scientific papers relating to diphtheria, leprosy, vaccination against mental retardation due to CM Virus infection during pregnancy, etc, in Lancet, BMJ, Jl Path. and Bact., Brit. Jl Exper. Path. *Recreations:* sculpting, walking. *Address:* Avenue de Cour 155, 1007 Lausanne, Switzerland. *T:* 26.58.14. *Club:* Athenæum.

ELEY, Prof. Daniel Douglas, OBE 1961; ScD, PhD Cantab; MSc, PhD Manchester; FRS 1964; CChem, FRSC; Professor of Physical Chemistry, University of Nottingham, 1954–80, now Emeritus; Dean of Faculty of Pure Science, 1959–62; *b* 1 Oct. 1914; *s* of Daniel Eley and Fanny Allen Eley, *née* Ross; *m* 1942, Brenda May Williams, MA, MB, BChir (Cantab), 2nd *d* of Benjamin and Sarah Williams, Skewen, Glam; one *s*. *Educ:* Christ's Coll., Finchley; Manchester Univ.; St John's Coll., Cambridge. Manchester Univ.: Woodiwiss Schol. 1933, Mercer Schol. 1934, Darbishire Fellow 1936, DSIR Sen. Award 1937; PhD 1937; PhD 1940, ScD 1954, Cambridge. Bristol Univ.: Lectr in Colloid Chemistry, 1945; Reader in Biophysical Chemistry, 1951. Leverhulme Emeritus Fellow, 1981. Lectures: Reilly, Univ. of Notre Dame (USA), 1950; Royal Aust. Chem. Inst., 1967; Sir Jesse Boot Foundn, Nottingham Univ., 1955, 1981; Sir Eric Rideal, Soc. of Chem. Industry, 1975. Mem. Council of Faraday Soc., 1951–54, 1960–63; Vice-Pres., 1963–66. Corresp. Mem., Bavarian Acad. of Sciences, 1971. Meetings Sec., British Biophysical Soc., 1961–63, Hon. Sec., 1963–65, Hon. Mem., 1983. Scientific Assessor to Sub-Cttee on Coastal Pollutions, House of Commons Select Cttee on Science and Technology, 1967–68. Medal of Liège Univ., 1950. *Publications:* (ed) Adhesion, 1961; papers in Trans Faraday Soc., Proc. Royal Soc., Jl Chem. Soc., Biochem. Jl, etc. *Recreations:* hill walking, gardening, ski-ing. *Address:* Brooklands, 35 Brookland Drive, Chilwell, Nottingham NG9 4BD; Chemistry Department, Nottingham University, University Park, Nottingham NG7 2RD.

ELEY, John L.; *see* Lloyd-Eley.

ELFER, David Francis, QC 1981; a Recorder of the Crown Court, since 1978; *b* 15 July 1941; *s* of George and Joy Elfer; *m* 1968, Karin Ursula Strub; two *s*; *m* 1988, Alexandra Smith-Hughes; one *s*. *Educ:* St Bede's Coll., Manchester; Emmanuel Coll., Cambridge (MA). Called to the Bar, Inner Temple, 1964, Bencher, 1989; Western Circuit. Bar Col rep. for W Circuit, 1987–89. *Recreation:* music. *Address:* (home) Monks Park, Luddington Avenue, Virginia Water, Surrey GU25 4DF. *T:* Wentworth (09904) 3168; (chambers) 1 Paper Building, Temple, EC4Y 7EP.

ELGIN, 11th Earl of, *cr* 1633, **AND KINCARDINE,** 15th Earl of, *cr* 1647; **Andrew Douglas Alexander Thomas Bruce,** KT 1981; CD 1981; JP; Lord Bruce of Kinloss, 1604, Lord Bruce of Torry, 1647; Baron Elgin (UK), 1849; 37th Chief of the Name of Bruce; Lord-Lieutenant of Fife, since 1987; late Scots Guards; Ensign of Royal Company of Archers, HM Body Guard for Scotland; Hon. Colonel, Elgin Regiment, Canada; *b* 17 Feb. 1924; *e s* of 10th Earl of Elgin, KT, CMG, TD and Hon. Katherine Elizabeth Cochrane (DBE 1938) (*d* 1989), *er d* of 1st Baron Cochrane of Cults; *S* father, 1968; *m* 1959, Victoria, *o d* of Dudley Usher, MBE and Mrs Usher of Larach Bhan, Kilchrennan, Argyll; three *s* two *d*. *Educ:* Eton; Balliol College, Oxford (BA Hons, MA Hons). Served War of 1939–45 (wounded). Dir, Royal Highland and Agricultural Soc., 1973–75; Pres., Scottish Amicable Life Assurance Soc., 1975–. Chm., Nat. Savings Cttee for Scotland, 1972–78; Mem., Scottish Post Office Bd (formerly Scottish Postal Bd), 1980–. Chm., Scottish Money Management Assoc., 1981–. Lord High Comr, Gen. Assembly of Church of Scotland, 1980–81. County Cadet Commandant, Fife, 1952–65. Hon. Col, 153(H) Regt RCT(V), TAVR, 1976–86. JP 1951, DL 1955, Fife. Grand Master Mason of Scotland, 1961–65. Brigade Pres. of the Boys' Brigade, 1966–85; Pres., Royal Caledonian Curling Club, 1968–69. Hon. LLD: Dundee, 1977; Glasgow, 1983; Hon. DLitt St Mary's, Halifax, NS. Freeman: Bridgetown, Barbados; Regina; Port Elgin; Winnipeg; St Thomas, Ont; Moose Jaw. *Heir:* *s* Lord Bruce, *qv*. *Address:* Broomhall, Dunfermline KY11 3DU. *T:* Limekilns (0383) 872222. *Clubs:* Beefsteak, Caledonian, Pratt's; New (Edinburgh); Royal Scottish Automobile (Pres.) (Glasgow).

EL HASSAN, Sayed Abdullah; *see* Hassan.

ELIAS, Gerard, QC 1984; a Recorder of the Crown Court, since 1984; *b* 19 Nov. 1944; *s* of Leonard Elias and Patricia Elias, JP; *m* 1970, Elisabeth Kenyon; three *s*. *Educ:* Cardiff High School; Exeter University. LLB; Barrister; called to the Bar, Inner Temple, 1968; Wales and Chester Circuit (Circuit Treasurer, 1990–); Asst Comr, Boundary Commission for Wales, 1981–83, 1985–. Mem., Bar Council, 1985–89; Dir, Bar Mutual Insurance Fund, 1987–. Governor and Mem. Council, Malvern Coll., 1988–; Mem. Exec. Cttee, Glam CCC, 1986–. *Recreations:* music, cricket. *Address:* 13 The Cathedral Green, Llandaff, Cardiff, South Glamorgan CF5 2EB. *T:* Cardiff (0222) 562635. *Club:* Cardiff and County.

ELIAS, Patrick; QC 1990; *b* 28 March 1947; *s* of Leonard and Patricia Mary Elias; *m* 1970, Wendy; three *s* one *d*. *Educ:* Cardiff High Sch.; Univ. of Exeter (LLB 1969); King's Coll., Cambridge (MA; PhD 1973). Fellow of Pembroke Coll., Cambridge, 1973–84; Lectr, Univ. of Cambridge, 1975–84. *Publications:* (jtly) Labour Law: cases and materials, 1979; Editor, Harvey on Industrial Relations and Employment Law, 1976; (with Keith Ewing) Trade Union Democracy, Members' Rights and the Law, 1987. *Recreations:* literature, music, sport. *Address:* 13 Madingley Road, Cambridge CB3 0EG. *T:* Cambridge (0223) 67214.

ELIASSEN, Kjell, Hon. GCMG 1981; Commander with Star, Royal Order of Saint Olav, 1982; Norwegian Ambassador to the Court of St James's, since 1989; *b* 18 Aug. 1929; *s* of Carl August Eliassen and Bergljot (*née* Store); *m* 1953, Vesla Skretting; one *s* one *d*. *Educ:* Oslo Univ. (law degree). Entered Norwegian Foreign Service 1953; served Belgrade, Moscow, London; Counsellor, Min. of Foreign Affairs, 1963–67; Moscow, 1967–70; Dep. Dir-Gen., Min. of Foreign Affairs, 1970–72; Dir-Gen., 1972–77; Ambassador to Yugoslavia, 1977–80; Perm. Under-Sec., Min. of Foreign Affairs, 1980–84; Ambassador to USA, 1984–89. Numerous foreign decorations. *Address:* 10 Palace Green, W8. *T:* 071–937 6449.

ELIBANK, 14th Lord *cr* 1643 (Scotland); **Alan D'Ardis Erskine-Murray;** Bt (Nova Scotia) 1628; personnel consultant; Deminex UK Oil and Gas, 1981–86; *b* 31 Dec. 1923; *s* of Robert Alan Erskine-Murray (*d* 1939) and Eileen Mary (*d* 1970), *d* of late John Percy MacManus; *S* cousin, 1973; *m* 1962, Valerie Sylvia, *d* of late Herbert William Dennis; two *s*. *Educ:* Bedford Sch.; Peterhouse, Cambridge (MA Law). Barrister-at-Law. RE, 1942–47; Cambridge Univ., 1947–49; Practising Barrister, 1949–55; Shell International Petroleum Co., 1955–80. *Recreations:* golf, tennis. *Heir:* *s* Master of Elibank, *qv*. *Address:* The Coach House, Charters Road, Sunningdale, Ascot, Berks SL5 9QB. *T:* Ascot (0344) 22099. *Club:* MCC.

ELIBANK, Master of; Hon. Robert Francis Alan Erskine-Murray; *b* 10 Oct. 1964; *s* and *heir* of 14th Lord Elibank, *qv*. *Educ:* The Grove, Harrow School; Reading Univ. (BA (Hons) History and Politics, 1987). *Recreations:* judo, soccer, tennis and photography. *Address:* 34 Richmond Hill Court, Richmond upon Thames, Surrey TW10 6BD.

ELION, Prof. Gertrude Belle; Research Professor of Pharmacology and Medicine, Duke University, North Carolina, since 1983; *b* 23 Jan. 1918; *d* of Robert and Bertha Elion. *Educ:* Hunter Coll., New York (AB 1937); New York Univ. (MS 1941). Lab. Asst in Biochemistry, NY Hosp. Sch. of Nursing, 1937; Res. Asst in Organic Chem., Denver Chemical Manufg Co., NY, 1938–39; teacher, secondary schs, NYC, 1940–42; Food Analyst, Quaker Maid Co., 1942–43; Res. Asst in Organic Synthesis, Johnson and Johnson, 1943–44; Wellcome Research Laboratories: Biochemist, 1944–50; Sen. Res. Chemist, 1950–55; Asst to the Associate Res. Dir, 1955–63; Asst to Res. Dir (Chemotherapy), 1963–67; Head, Dept of Experimental Therapy, 1967–83; Scientist Emeritus, 1983–. Hon. Mem., Acad. of Pharmaceutical Sciences, 1983. Nat. Acad. of Scis, 1990. Hon. DSc: George Washington Univ., 1969; Univ. of Michigan, 1983; Hunter Coll. (CUNY), New York Univ., Polytechnic Univ., Brooklyn, NC State Univ., and Ohio State Univ., 1989; Univ. of NC, Russell Sage Coll., 1990; Duke Univ., 1991; Hon. DMS Brown Univ., 1969. Garvan Medal, Amer. Chemical Soc., 1968; President's Medal, 1970, Hall of Fame, 1973, Hunter Coll.; Distinguished NC Chemist Award, NC Inst. of Chemists, 1981; Judd Award, Sloan-Kettering Inst., 1983; (jtly) Cain Award, Amer. Assoc. for Cancer Res., 1984; NC Distinguished Chemist Award, NC Section, Amer. Chemical Soc., 1985; (jtly) Nobel Prize in Physiology or Medicine, 1988; Bertner Award, Univ. of Texas, 1989; Medal of Honor, Amer. Cancer Soc., 1990; City of Medicine Award, Durham, NC, 1990; (jtly) Discoverer's Award, Pharmaceutical Manufrs Assoc., 1990; Third Century Award, Foundn for a Creative America, 1990. *Publications:* contribs to scientific jls on chemistry, pharmacology and cancer research. *Recreations:* photography, travel, music. *Address:* 1 Banbury Lane, Chapel Hill, NC 27514, USA. *T:* 919–967–4102.

ELIOT, family name of **Earl of St Germans.**

ELIOT, Lord; Jago Nicholas Aldo Eliot; *b* 24 March 1966; *s* and *heir* of Earl of St Germans, *qv.*

ELIOT, Ven. Canon Peter Charles, MBE 1945; TD 1945; Archdeacon of Worcester, 1961–75; now Archdeacon Emeritus; Residentiary Canon, Worcester Cathedral, 1965–75; now Canon Emeritus; *b* 30 Oct. 1910; *s* of late Hon. Edward Granville Eliot and late Mrs Eliot; *m* 1934, Lady Alethea Constance Dorothy Sydney Buxton, *d* of 1st and last Earl Buxton, PC, GCMG, and late Countess Buxton; no *c. Educ:* Wellington Coll.; Magdalene Coll., Cambridge. Commissioned in Kent Yeomanry (Lt-Col Comdg, 1949–52), 1933. Admitted Solicitor, 1934; Partner in City firm until 1953. Studied at Westcott House, Cambridge, 1953–54; made Deacon to serve in Parish of St Martin-in-the-Fields, London, 1954; Priest, 1955; Vicar of Cockermouth, 1957–61; Rural Dean of Cockermouth and Workington, 1960–61; Vicar of Cropthorne with Charlton, 1961–65. *Recreations:* amateur acting, sketching, sight-seeing, gardening. *Address:* The Old House, Kingsland, Leominster, Herefordshire HR6 9QS. *T:* Kingsland (0568) 708285. *Club:* Travellers'.

ELIOTT OF STOBS, Sir Charles (Joseph Alexander), 12th Bt *cr* 1666 (NS); *b* 9 Jan. 1937; *s* of Charles Rawdon Heathfield Eliott (*d* 1972) and Emma Elizabeth Harris; *S* cousin, 1989; *m* 1959, Wendy Judith, *d* of Henry John Bailey; one *s* four *d* (and one *s* decd). *Educ:* St Joseph's Christian Brothers' College, Rockhampton. *Heir: s* Rodney Gilbert Charles Eliott [*b* 15 July 1966; *m* 1988, Andrea Therese Saunders; one *d*]. *Address:* 27 Cohoe Street, Toowoomba, Queensland 4350, Australia.

ELKAN, Prof. Walter; Professor of Economics, and Head of Economics Department, Brunel University, 1978–88, now Emeritus Professor; *b* Hamburg, 1 March 1923; *s* of Hans Septimus Elkan and Maud Emily (*née* Barden); *m* Susan Dorothea (*née* Jacobs) (marr. diss. 1982); one *s* two *d. Educ:* Frensham Heights; London Sch. of Economics. BSc (Econ), PhD. Army, 1942–47; Research Asst, LSE, 1950–53; Sen. Res. Fellow, E African Inst. of Social Research, 1954–58; Vis. Res. Assoc., MIT and Lectr, N Western Univ., 1958; Lectr in Econs, Makerere UC, 1958–60; Lectr in Econs, Durham Univ., 1960; Prof. of Econs, 1966–78, and rotating Head of Dept, 1968–78, Durham Univ. Vis. Res. Prof., Nairobi Univ., 1972–73. Member: Council, Overseas Develt Inst.; Econ. and Social Cttee, EEC, 1982–86; Bd of Management, Sch. of Hygiene and Trop. Med., 1982–86; Econ. and Social Cttee for Overseas Res., 1977–; Associate, Inst. of Development Studies. Former Pres., African Studies Assoc.; former Member: Northern Economic Planning Council; REconS. Sometime consultant to Govts of Basutoland, Mauritius, Solomon Is, Fiji, Kenya and others. *Publications:* An African Labour Force, 1956; Migrants and Proletarians, 1960; Economic Development of Uganda, 1961; Introduction to Development Economics, 1973; articles mainly on contemp. African econ. history in econ. and other social science jls; ILO, UNESCO, IBRD and British Govt reports. *Recreation:* music. *Address:* 98 Boundary Road, NW8 0RH. *T:* 071–624 5102.

ELKES, Prof. Joel, MD, ChB; FACP, FAPA; Distinguished Service Professor Emeritus, The Johns Hopkins University, since 1975; Professor of Psychiatry, University of Louisville, 1980–84, now Emeritus (Director, Division of Behavioral Medicine, 1982); *b* 12 Nov. 1913; *s* of Dr Elchanan Elkes and Miriam (*née* Malbin); *m* 1943, Dr Charmian Bourne; one *d*; *m* 1975, Josephine Rhodes, MA. *Educ:* private schools; Lithuania and Switzerland; St Mary's Hosp., London; Univ. of Birmingham Med. Sch. (MB, ChB 1947; MD Hons 1949). MRCS, LRCP 1941. University of Birmingham: Sir Halley Stewart Research Fellow, 1942–45; Lectr, Dept of Pharmacology, 1945–48; Senior Lectr and Actg Head of Dept, 1948–50; Prof. and Chm., Dept of Experimental Psychiatry, 1951–57; Clinical Professor of Psychiatry, George Washington Univ. Med. Sch., Washington, 1957–63; Chief of Clinical Neuropharmacology Research Center, Nat. Inst of Mental Health, Washington, 1957–63; Dir, Behavioral and Clinical Studies Center St Elizabeth's Hosp., Washington, 1957–63; Henry Phipps Prof. and Dir, Dept of Psychiatry and Behavioural Scis, Johns Hopkins Univ. Sch. of Medicine, and Psychiatrist-in-Chief, Johns Hopkins Hosp., 1963–74; Samuel McLaughlin Prof.-in-residence, McMaster Univ., 1975; Prof. of Psychiatry, McMaster Univ., 1976–80. Dir, Foundns Fund for Research in Psychiatry, 1964–68; Consultant, WHO, 1957. Vis. Fellow, New York Univ. and New England Med. Center, Boston, 1950; Benjamin Franklin Fellow, RSA, 1974. Lectures: Harvey, 1962; Salmon, 1963; Jacob Bronowski Meml, 1978, etc. President: (first) Amer. Coll. of Neuropsychopharmacology, 1962; Amer. Psychopathological Assoc., 1968; Chm., Foundns Fund Prize Bd for Res. in Psychiatry, 1977–81; Mem. of Bd, Inst. for Advancement of Health, 1982. Formerly Member: Council, Internat. Collegium N Psychopharm; Central Council, Internat. Brain Research Organisation, UNESCO (Chm., Sub-Cttee on Educn); RSM. Life Fellow, Amer. Psych. Assoc.; Charter Fellow, RCPsych, GB; Fellow: Amer. Acad. of Arts and Scis; Amer. Coll. of Psychiatry; Amer. Coll. of Neuropsychopharmacol; Amer. Acad. of Behavioral Medicine Res. and Soc. of Behavioral Medicine; Fetzer Inst., 1990; Fellow and Mem. Exec. Cttee, World Acad. of Art and Sci., 1985; Member: Physiological Soc., GB; Pharmacological Soc., GB; Amer. Soc. for Pharmacology and Experimental Therapeutics; New York Acad. of Science; Sigma Xi; Scientific Assoc.; Acad. of Psychoanalysis. Distinguished Practitioner, Nat. Acads of Practice, 1985. *Publications:* papers to various jls and symposia. *Recreation:* painting. *Address:* Department of Psychiatry, University of Louisville, Louisville, Ky 40292, USA. *Clubs:* Cosmos (Washington); West Hamilton, Johns Hopkins (Baltimore).

ELKIN, Alexander, CMG 1976; international law consultant; *b* St Petersburg (Leningrad), 2 Aug. 1909; *o c* of Boris and Anna Elkin; *m* 1937, Muriel Solomons, Dublin. *Educ:* Grunewald Gymnasium and Russian Academic Sch., Berlin; Univs of Berlin, Kiel and London. DrJur Kiel 1932, LLM London 1935. Called to the Bar, Middle Temple, 1937; practised at English Bar, 1937–39; BBC Monitoring Service, 1939–42; war-time govt service, 1942–45; Associate Chief, Legal Service, UN Interim Secretariat, London, 1945–46; Asst Dir, UN European Office, Geneva, 1946–48; Legal Adviser to UNSCOB, Salonica, 1948; Dep. Legal Adviser, later Legal Adviser, OEEC (OECD 1960–), Paris, 1949–61; UNECA Legal Consultant, formation of African Develt Bank and Econ. Council for Africa, 1962–64; Actg Gen. Counsel of ADB, 1964–65; UNDP Legal Consultant, formation of Caribbean Develt Bank, 1967–68; Special Adviser on European Communities Law, FCO, 1970–79. Legal consultancies for: WHO, 1948; IBRD, 1966; W Afr. Regional Gp, 1968; OECD, 1975. Lectured: on Europ. payments system and OEEC/OECD activs, Univ. of the Saar, 1957–60, and Univ. Inst. of Europ. Studies, Turin, 1957–65; on drafting of treaties, UNITAR Seminars, The Hague, Geneva and NY, for legal advisers and diplomats, 1967–84; on language and law, Univ. of Bath, 1979–; Univ. of Bradford, 1979–84. Hon. Vis. Prof., Bradford Univ., 1982–84. Mem., RIIA. Hon. LLD Bath, 1990. Ford Foundn Leadership Grant, 1960. *Publications:* contrib. European Yearbook, Jl du Droit Internat., Revue Générale de Droit Internat. Public, Survey of Internat. Affairs 1939–1946, Travaux pratiques de L'Institut de Droit Comparé de la Faculté de Droit de Paris, etc. *Recreations:* reading, visiting art collections, travel. *Address:* 70 Apsley House, Finchley Road, NW8 0NZ. *Club:* Travellers'.

ELKIN, Sonia Irene Linda, OBE 1981 (MBE 1966); Director for Regions and Smaller Firms, Confederation of British Industry, since 1985; *b* 15 May 1932; *d* of Godfrey Albert Elkin and Irene Jessamine Archibald. *Educ:* Beresford House Sch., Eastbourne. Association of British Chambers of Commerce, 1950–66: Overseas Director, 1956–66; Lloyds Bank Overseas Dept, 1966–67; Confederation of British Industry, 1967–: Head of West European Dept, 1967–72; Head of Regional and Smaller Firms Dept, 1972–73; Dep. Director, Regions and Smaller Firms, 1973–79; Director: for Smaller Firms, 1979–83; for Regions, 1983–85. Commissioner, Manpower Services Commission, 1982–85. *Publications:* What about Europe?, 1967; What about Europe Now?, 1971. *Address:* Confederation of British Industry, Centre Point, 103 New Oxford Street, WC1A 1DU. *Club:* United Oxford & Cambridge University (Lady Associate).

ELKINGTON, (Reginald) Geoffrey, CB 1962; *b* 24 Dec. 1907; *s* of Harold and Millicent Elkington; *m* 1935, Bertha Phyllis (*d* 1990), *d* of William and Bertha Dyason; one adopted *s* one adopted *d. Educ:* Battersea Grammar Sch.; Fitzwilliam Coll., Cambridge. Inland Revenue, 1929–42; Min. of Supply, 1942–57 (Under-Sec., 1954); Dept of Scientific Res., 1957–64; Principal Establishment Officer, Min. of Technology, 1964–67; retired from Civil Service, 1967; Estabt Officer (part-time), Monopolies Commn, 1968–73. Sec., AERE Harwell, 1948–51. *Address:* Maranwood, Highfield Road, West Byfleet, Surrey KT14 6QT. *T:* Byfleet (0932) 343766.

ELLACOMBE, Air Cdre John Lawrence Wemyss, CB 1970; DFC 1942 (Bar 1944); FBIM; *b* Livingstone, N Rhodesia, 28 Feb. 1920; *s* of Dr Gilbert H. W. Ellacombe; *m* 1951, Wing Officer Mary Hibbert, OBE, WRAF; one *s* two *d. Educ:* Diocesan Coll., Rondebosch, Cape. War of 1939–45: RAF, 1939; Fighter Comd and Two ATA Force, 1940–45 (Pilot, Battle of Britain). Aden, 1946–48; RAF Staff Coll., 1948–49; Fighter Command, 1949–57; BJSM, Washington, 1959. JSSC, 1959–60; Gp Captain, CO RAF Linton on Ouse, to Nov 1962; CFE, to Aug. 1965; Defence Operational Analysis Estabt, West Byfleet, 1965–68; Air Cdre, Commander Air Forces Gulf, 1968–70; Dir of Ops (Air Defence and Overseas), MoD (Air), 1970–73; St Thomas' Hospital: Dir, Scientific Services, 1973–80; Administrator to Special Trustees, 1980–85. *Recreations:* photography, golf, cricket. *Address:* 33 The Drive, Northwood, Middlesex HA6 1HW. *Club:* Royal Air Force.

ELLEN, Eric Frank, QPM 1980; LLB; CBIM; Executive Director, International Chamber of Commerce Business Security Services, since 1988 (First Director: International Maritime Bureau, since 1981; Counterfeiting Intelligence Bureau, since 1985; Corporate Security Services, since 1988); *b* London, 30 Aug. 1930; *s* of late Robert Frank Ellen and of Jane Lydia Ellen; *m* 1949, Gwendoline Dorothy Perkins; one *s* one *d. Educ:* Wakefield Central Sch., East Ham; Holborn Coll. of Law, Univ. of London (LLB Hons, London Univ. Certificate in Criminology). CBIM (FBIM 1978). Joined PLA Police, 1951; Sgt 1956; Inspector 1961; Chief Insp. 1972; Supt and Chief Supt 1973; attended 11th Sen. Comd Course, Bramshill Police Coll., 1974; Dep. Chief Constable 1975; Chief Constable, 1975–80. Adviser on security to Ports Div. of Dept of Environment; advised Barbados Govt on formation of Barbados Port Authy Police Force, 1983; reviewed port security at Jeddah and Dammam. Sec., Internat. Assoc. of Airport and Seaport Police, 1980–88 (Pres., 1977–78 and 1978–79); Founder, Chm. and Life Mem., EEC Assoc. of Airport and Seaport Police, 1975–78; Chm., Panel on Maritime Fraud, Commonwealth Secretariat, 1982–90; Consultant, Commercial Crime Unit. Member: Internat. Assoc. of Ports and Harbours Standing Cttee on Legal Protection of Port Interests, 1977–79 (Chm., Sub-Cttee on Protection of Ports against Sabotage and Terrorism, 1977–79); Cttee of Conservative Lawyers, 1985–; Shipbrokers Cttee on Maritime Fraud; British Acad. of Forensic Sciences; Hon. Soc. of Middle Temple. Police Long Service and Good Conduct Medal, 1974. Freeman of the City of London, 1978. Police Medal Republic of China, 1979. *Publications:* (co-author) International Maritime Fraud, 1981; (ed) Violence at Sea, 2nd edn, 1987; (ed) Piracy at Sea, 1989; Ports at Risk, 1989; professional articles on marine fraud and counterfeiting, terrorism, piracy and port policing (has lectured on these topics at seminars in over 50 countries). *Recreations:* golf, swimming. *Address:* (office) Maritime House, 1 Linton Road, Barking, Essex IG11 8HG. *T:* 081–591 3000. *Club:* Wig and Pen.

ELLEN, Patricia Mae Hayward; *see* Lavers, P. M.

ELLENBOROUGH, 8th Baron *cr* 1802; **Richard Edward Cecil Law;** Director, Towry Law & Co., since 1958; *b* 14 Jan. 1926; *s* of 7th Baron and Helen Dorothy, *o d* of late H. W. Lovatt; *S* father, 1945; *m* 1953, Rachel Mary (*d* 1986), *o d* of late Major Ivor Hedley; three *s. Educ:* Eton Coll.; Magdalene Coll., Cambridge. Pres., Nat. Union of Ratepayers' Associations, 1960–. *Heir: s* Major the Hon. Rupert Edward Henry Law, Coldstream Guards, retd [*b* 28 March 1955; *m* 1981, Hon. Grania, *d* of Baron Boardman, *qv*; one *s* one *d*]. *Address:* Withypool House, Observatory Close, Church Road, Crowborough, East Sussex TN6 1BN. *T:* Crowborough (0892) 63139. *Clubs:* Gresham, Turf.

ELLERTON, Geoffrey James, CMG 1963; MBE 1956; Chairman, Local Government Boundary Commission for England, since 1983; *b* 25 April 1920; *er s* of late Sir Cecil Ellerton; *m* 1946, Peggy Eleanor, *d* of late F. G. Watson; three *s. Educ:* Highgate Sch.; Hertford Coll., Oxford (MA). Military Service, 1940–45. Apptd Colonial Administrative Service as District Officer, Kenya, 1945. Acted as Minister for Internal Security and Defence, 1960 and 1962. Retired as Permanent Sec., Prime Minister's Office and Sec. to the Cabinet, at time of Kenya's Independence, Dec. 1963. Sec. to the Maud and Mallaby Cttees on Management and Staffing in Local Government, 1964. Joined Elder Dempster

Lines, 1965, Chm., 1972–74; an Exec. Dir, Ocean Transport & Trading Ltd, 1972–80; Dir, Overseas Containers Ltd, 1975–80; Chm., Globe Management Ltd, 1981–83; Dir, Globe Investment Trust PLC, 1983–86. Mem. Council, Liverpool Univ., 1974–78; a Vice-Pres., Liverpool Sch. of Tropical Medicine, 1978-87; Hon. Treasurer, Hakluyt Soc., 1986– (Mem. Council, 1984–86). *Recreations:* music, books. *Address:* Briar Hill House, Broad Campden, Chipping Campden, Glos GL55 6XB. *T:* Evesham (0386) 841003. *Clubs:* Brooks's, Beefsteak, MCC; Nairobi.

ELLES, family name of **Baroness Elles.**

ELLES, Baroness *cr* 1972 (Life Peer), of the City of Westminster; **Diana Louie Elles;** *b* 19 July 1921; *d* of Col Stewart Francis Newcombe, DSO and Elisabeth Chaki; *m* 1945, Neil Patrick Moncrieff Elles, *qv*; one *s* one *d*. *Educ:* private Schs, England, France and Italy; London University (BA Hons). Served WAAF, 1941–45. Barrister-at-law. Care Cttee worker in S London, 1956–72. UK Delegn to UN Gen. Assembly, 1972; Mem., UN Sub-Commn on Prevention of Discrimination and Protection of Minorities, 1973–75; UN special rapporteur on Human Rights, 1973–75; Mem., British delegn to European Parlt, 1973–75. Mem., Cripps Cttee on legal discrimination against women; Chm., Sub-cttee of Women's Nat. Adv. Cttee (Conservative Party) on one-parent families (report publ. as Unhappy Families); Internat. Chm., European Union of Women, 1973–79; Chm., Cons. Party Internat. Office, 1973–78; Opposition front bench spokesman on foreign and Eur. affairs, H of L, 1975–79; MEP (C) Thames Valley, 1979–89; EDG spokesman on NI, 1980–87; Vice-Pres., European Parlt, 1982–87; Chm., Legal Affairs Cttee, 1987–89. Vice-Pres., UK Assoc. of European Lawyers, 1985–. Mem. Council, Caldecott Community, 1990–; Trustee: Cumberland Lodge, 1982–; Industry and Parlt Trust, 1985–; Governor: British Inst. Florence, 1986–; Reading Univ., 1986–; Mill Hill Sch., 1990–. *Publications:* The Housewife and the Common Market (pamphlet), 1971; Human Rights of Aliens, 1980; articles, etc. *Address:* 75 Ashley Gardens, SW1; Villa Fontana, Ponte del Giglio, Lucca, Italy.
See also C. J. Lockhart-Mummery.

ELLES, James Edmund Moncrieff; Member (C) Oxford and Buckinghamshire, European Parliament, since 1984; *b* 3 Sept. 1949; *s* of N. P. M. Elles, *qv* and Baroness Elles, *qv*; *m* 1977, Françoise Le Bail; one *s* one *d*. *Educ:* Ashdown House; Eton College; Edinburgh University. External Relations Div., EEC, 1976–80; Asst to Dep. Dir Gen. of Agriculture, EEC, 1980–84. Mem., Budget and External Relations Cttee, European Parlt. *Address:* c/o European Parliament, 97–113 Rue Belliard, 1040 Brussels, Belgium; Conservative Centre, Church Street, Amersham, Bucks HP7 0BD. *Clubs:* Carlton; Royal and Ancient Golf (St Andrews).

ELLES, Neil Patrick Moncrieff; Chairman, Value Added Tax Appeals Tribunal, since 1972; *b* 8 July 1919; *s* of Edmund Hardie Elles, OBE and Ina Katharine Hilda Skene; *m* 1945, Diana Louie Newcombe (*see* Baroness Elles); one *s* one *d*. *Educ:* Eton; Christ Church, Oxford (MA). War Service, RAF, 1939–45. Called to the Bar, Inner Temple, 1947; Sec., Inns of Court Conservative and Unionist Taxation Cttee, 1957–71; Mem., Special Study Gp, Commn on Law of Competition, Brussels, 1962–67. *Publications:* The Law of Restrictive Trade Practices and Monopolies (with Lord Wilberforce and Alan Campbell), 1966; Community Law through the Cases, 1973. *Recreations:* fishing, listening to music, the cultivation of vines. *Address:* 75 Ashley Gardens, SW1. *T:* 071–828 0175; Villa Fontana, Ponte del Giglio, Lucca, Italy. *Clubs:* Flyfishers', MCC.
See also C. J. Lockhart-Mummery.

ELLINGWORTH, Richard Henry; HM Diplomatic Service, retired; *b* 9 March 1926; *s* of Vincent Ellingworth; *m* 1952, Joan Mary Waterfield; one *s* three *d*. *Educ:* Uppingham; Aberdeen Univ.; Magdalen Coll., Oxford (Demy). Served War of 1939–45: RA, and Intelligence Corps, 1944–47. Oxford, 1947–50 (first Lit. Hum.); HM Embassy, Japan, 1951–55; FO, 1955–59; HM Embassy: Belgrade, 1959–63; Japan, 1963–68 (Olympic Attaché, 1964); Head of Oil Dept., FCO, 1969–71; Research Associate, Internat. Inst. for Strategic Studies, 1971–72; Counsellor, Tehran, 1972–75; seconded to Dept of Energy, 1975–77. Course Dir (European Training), Civil Service Coll., 1978–83. Mem., Farningham Parish Council, 1979–83; pt-time Agent, Sevenoaks Liberal Assoc., 1983–84; Hon. Organiser, Farmingham, Royal British Legion, 1982–87. *Publications:* (with A. N. Gilkes) An Anthology of Oratory, 1946; Japanese Economic Policy and Security, 1972. *Recreations:* gardening, music. *Address:* 10 Marine Parade, Budleigh Salterton EX9 6NS. *T:* Budleigh Salterton (03954) 6204.

ELLIOT; *see* Elliot-Murray-Kynynmound, family name of Earl of Minto.

ELLIOT; *see* Scott-Elliot.

ELLIOT, family name of **Baroness Elliot of Harwood.**

ELLIOT OF HARWOOD, Baroness *cr* 1958 (Life Peer); **Katharine Elliot,** DBE 1958 (CBE 1946); JP; *b* 15 Jan. 1903; *d* of Sir Charles Tennant, 1st Bt, Innerleithen, Peeblesshire, and late Mrs Geoffrey Lubbock; *m* 1934, Rt Hon. Walter Elliot, PC, CH, MC, FRS, LLD, MP (*d* 1958); no *c*. *Educ:* Abbot's Hill, Hemel Hempstead; Paris. Chairman: Nat. Assoc. of Mixed Clubs and Girls' Clubs, 1939–49; Adv. Cttee on Child Care for Scotland, 1956–65; Women's Nat. Adv. Cttee of Conservative Party, 1954–57; Nat. Union of Conservative and Unionist Assocs, 1956–67; Consumer Council, 1963–68. Chm., Lawrie & Symington Ltd, Lanark, 1958–85. Member: Women's Consultative Cttee, Dept of Employment and Productivity (formerly Min. of Labour), 1941–51, 1958–70; Home Office Adv. Cttee on Treatment of Offenders, 1946–62; King George V Jubilee Trust, 1936–68; NFU; Trustee and Mem. Council, Carnegie UK Trust (Exec. Trustee, 1940–86). Pres., Royal Highland Agricl Soc., 1986. UK Delegate to Gen. Assembly of UN, New York, 1954, 1956 and 1957. Contested (C) Kelvingrove Div. of Glasgow, March 1958. Roxburghshire: CC 1946–75 (Vice-Convener, 1974); JP 1968–. Farms in Roxburghshire. FRSA 1964. Hon. LLD: Glasgow, 1959; Selly Oak Colls, Birmingham, 1986. Grand Silver Cross, Austrian Order of Merit, 1963. *Publication:* Tennants Stalk, 1973. *Recreations:* foxhunting, golf, music. *Address:* Harwood, Bonchester Bridge, Hawick, Roxburghshire TD9 9TL; 17 Lord North Street, Westminster, SW1P 3LD. *T:* 071–222 3230.

ELLIOT, Sir Gerald (Henry), Kt 1986; FRSE; Chairman, Christian Salvesen plc, 1981–88; *b* 24 Dec. 1923; *s* of late Surg. Captain J. S. Elliot, RN, and Magda Salvesen; *m* 1950, Margaret Ruth Whale; two *s* one *d*. *Educ:* Marlborough Coll.; New Coll., Oxford (BA PPE 1948). FRSE 1978. Captain FF Rifles, Indian Army, 1942–46. Christian Salvesen Ltd, 1948–88, Dep. Chm. and Man. Dir, 1973–81. Dir, Scottish Provident Instn, 1971–89, Chm., 1983–89; Chairman: Chambers and Fargus, 1975–79; Scottish Br., RIIA, 1973–77 (Sec., 1963–73); FAO Fishery Industries Develt Gp, 1971–76; Forth Ports Authority, 1973–79; Scottish Arts Council, 1980–86. Chairman: Scottish Unit Managers Ltd, 1984–88; Martin Currie Unit Trusts, 1988–90; Biotal, 1987–90. Sec., National Whaling Bd, 1953–62; Mem., Nat. Ports Council, 1978–81. Chm., Scottish Div., Inst. of Dirs, 1989–91; Vice-Chm., Scottish Business in the Community, 1987–89. Chairman: Prince's Scottish Youth Business Trust, 1987–; Scottish Opera, 1987–. A Vice-Pres., RSE, 1988–91. Trustee, Nat. Museums of Scotland, 1987–; Chm., Trustees, David Hume Inst., 1985–. Pres., Edinburgh Univ. Develt Trust, 1990–. Member Court: Edinburgh Univ., 1984–; Regents, RCSE, 1990–. Dr *hc* Edinburgh, 1989; Hon. LLD Aberdeen, 1991. Consul for Finland in Edinburgh, 1957–89; Dean, Consular Corps in Edinburgh-Leith, 1986–88. Kt 1st Cl., Order of White Rose of Finland, 1975. *Publications:* papers on control of whaling and fishing, arts administration and economic management. *Address:* 39 Inverleith Place, Edinburgh EH3 5QD.

ELLIOT, Prof. Harry, CBE 1976; FRS 1973; Emeritus Professor of Physics, University of London; Professor of Physics at Imperial College, London, 1960–80 (Assistant Director of Physics Department, 1963–71); *b* 28 June 1920; *s* of Thomas Elliot and Hannah Elizabeth (*née* Littleton), Weary Hall, Cumberland; *m* 1943, Betty Leyman; one *s* one *d*. *Educ:* Nelson Sch., Wigton; Manchester Univ. MSc, PhD. Served War, Signals Branch, RAF, incl. liaison duties with USAAF and USN, 1941–46. Manchester University: Asst Lectr in Physics, 1948–49; Lectr in Physics, 1949–54; Imperial College, London: Lectr in Physics, 1954–56; Sen. Lectr in Physics, 1956–57; Reader in Physics, 1957–60; Sen. Res. Fellow, 1982–87. Member: Science Research Council, 1971–77; Council, Royal Soc., 1978–79; Science Adv. Cttee, ESA, 1979–81. Hon. Prof., Universitad Mayor de San Andres, 1957; Hon. ARCS, 1965. Fellow, World Acad. of Arts and Scis, 1978. Holweck Prize and Medal, Inst. of Physics and Société Française de Physique, 1976. *Publications:* papers on cosmic rays, solar physics and magnetospheric physics in scientific jls; contrib. scientific reviews and magazine articles. *Recreation:* painting. *Address:* Rosan, Broadwater Down, Tunbridge Wells, Kent TN2 5PE.

ELLIOT-MURRAY-KYNYNMOUND, family name of **Earl of Minto.**

ELLIOT-SMITH, Alan Guy, CBE 1957; *b* 30 June 1904; *s* of late F. Elliot-Smith; *m* 1939, Ruth Kittermaster; no *c*. *Educ:* Charterhouse; Oriel Coll., Oxford. Hons Mod. Lang. Sch., 1925; Asst Master, Harrow Sch., 1925–40; Headmaster, Cheltenham Coll., 1940–51; Mem., Harrow UDC, 1933–36; Deleg. to Inst. of Pacific Relations Conf., Calif., 1936; lectured to German teachers on Education, 1947 and 1948; lectured to Service units in the Middle East, 1949; Head-master of Victoria Coll., Cairo, 1952–56; Representative in Nigeria of the West Africa Cttee, 1957–58; Headmaster, Markham Coll., Lima, Peru, 1960–63. *Recreations:* travel, reading. *Address:* Bevois Mount, Rowsley Road, Eastbourne, Sussex BN20 7XS.

ELLIOTT, family name of **Baron Elliott of Morpeth.**

ELLIOTT OF MORPETH, Baron *cr* 1985 (Life Peer), of Morpeth in the County of Northumberland and of the City of Newcastle-upon-Tyne; **Robert William Elliott;** Kt 1974; DL; Vice-Chairman, Conservative Party Organisation, 1970–74; *b* 11 Dec. 1920; *s* of Richard Elliott; *m* 1956, Jane Morpeth; one *s* four *d* (of whom two are twin *d*). *Educ:* Morpeth Grammar Sch. Farmer, 1939–, at Low Heighley, Morpeth, Northumberland. MP (C) Newcastle-upon-Tyne North, March 1957–1983; Parliamentary Private Secretary: to joint Parliamentary Secs, Ministry of Transport and Civil Aviation, April 1958–Oct. 1959; to Under-Sec., Home Office, Nov. 1959–60; to Minister of State, Home Office, Nov. 1960–61; to Sec. for Technical Co-operation, 1961–63; Asst Govt Whip (unpaid), 1963–64; Opposition Whip, 1964–70; Comptroller of the Household, June-Sept. 1970. Chm., Select Cttee on Agric., Fisheries and Food, 1980–83. DL Northumberland, 1985. *Address:* Lipwood Hall, Haydon Bridge, Northumberland NE47 6DY. *T:* Haydon Bridge (043484) 777. *Clubs:* Carlton; Northern Counties (Newcastle upon Tyne).

ELLIOTT, Hon. Lord; Walter Archibald Elliott, MC 1943; Chairman, Scottish Land Court, since 1978; President, Lands Tribunal for Scotland, since 1971; *b* 6 Sept. 1922; 2nd *s* of late Prof. T. R. Elliott, CBE, DSO, FRS, Broughton Place, Broughton, Peeblesshire; *m* 1954, Susan Isobel Mackenzie Ross, Kaimend, North Berwick; two *s*. *Educ:* Eton; Trinity Coll., Cambridge; Edinburgh Univ. Active service in Italy and North West Europe with 2nd Bn Scots Guards, 1943–45; captured and escaped, Salerno landings (MC); demobilised, Staff Capt., 1947. Barrister-at-law, Inner Temple, 1950; Advocate at Scottish Bar, 1950; QC (Scotland) 1963. Standing Junior Counsel to Accountant of Court and later to Minister of Aviation; conducted Edinburgh ring road inquiry, 1967; Chm., Med. Appeal Tribunals, 1971–78. Brigadier, Royal Company of Archers (Queen's Body Guard for Scotland). *Publications:* Us and Them: a study of group consciousness, 1986; articles in legal periodicals. *Recreations:* gardening, travelling. *Address:* Morton House, Fairmilehead, Edinburgh. *T:* 031–445 2548. *Clubs:* New, Arts (Edinburgh).

ELLIOTT, Anthony Michael Manton, (Tony Elliott); Founder, 1968 and Chairman, Time Out Group; *b* 7 Jan. 1947; *s* of Katherine and Alan Elliott; *m* 1st, 1976, Janet Street-Porter (marr. diss. 1978); 2nd, 1989, Jane L. Coke; three *s* (incl. twins). *Educ:* Stowe; Keele Univ. Time Out Group titles include: Time Out; i-D; Modern Painters; annual guides. Time Out Trust formed 1989. *Recreations:* travel, watching television, cinema going, eating out with friends, reading newspapers and magazines, being with family in time left from working. *Address:* Time Out Group, Tower House, Southampton Street, WC2E 7HD. *T:* 071–836 4411, *Fax:* 071–836 7118.

ELLIOTT, Bruce John, CBE 1988; TD 1963; Registrar of Bedfordshire and Hertfordshire County Courts and District Judge (formerly District Registrar), High Court of Justice, since 1961; a Recorder, since 1986; *b* 8 Feb. 1927; *s* of John Thomas Girvan Elliott and Zena Phyllis Elliott; *m* 1st, 1951, Joy Manderson; 2nd, 1955, Joy Redpath; two *s*; 3rd, 1975, Alison Jane Furniss. *Educ:* Charminster Council Sch.; Bournemouth Secondary Sch.; Law Soc. Sch. of Law. Joined Army, 1945; commissioned in India, 1946; served India, Egypt and Palestine to 1948 (Captain, Hampshire Regt). Admitted Solicitor, 1951; Asst Recorder, 1979; former JP; Hon. Sec., Registrars' Assoc., 1969–87. Territorial Army: 14th Bn, Para. Regt, 1951; qualified parachutist; Major, Royal Hampshire Regt, 1955; 5th Bn, Royal Northumberland Fusiliers, 1961; qualified pilot and glider pilot, 1963; RAF Cadet Reserve Instructor; Company Comdr; subseq. Lt-Col comdg 5th Bn Beds and Herts Regt, 1965; Col Comdt, Beds Army Cadet Force, 1967. Various social work. *Recreations:* the simplest outdoor pursuits. *Address:* Luton County Court, Cresta House, Alma Street, Luton, Beds LU1 2PU. *T:* Luton (0582) 35671.

ELLIOTT, Dr Charles Kennedy; Physician to HM the Queen, 1980–86; *b* 1919; *e s* of late Charles Harper Elliott and Martha Elliott; *m* 1949, Elizabeth Margaret Kyle. *Educ:* Campbell Coll., Belfast; Trinity Coll., Dublin (BA, 1941; MA 1970; MB, BCh 1942). MRCGP; MLCO; MFHom; AFOM RCP. Sir Patrick Dun's Hosp., Dublin, 1943; Captain, RAMC, attached SEAC, 1944; General practitioner, Wisbech, 1949–69; Editor, Rural Medicine, 1969–72; Clinical Asst, Royal London Homoeopathic Hosp., 1973–81; Sub Dean, Faculty of Homoeopathy, 1976–79; Area Surgeon, Cambridgeshire St John Ambulance, 1974–81; Chm., Organizing Cttee, VI Internat. Congress Rural Medicine, Cambridge, 1975; Pres., Internat. Assoc. of Agricl Medicine and Rural Health, 1972–78; Trustee: Rehabilitation Trust of Gt Britain, 1977–; Inst. for Complementary Medicine, 1982–. Hon. DLitt Central Sch. of Religion, 1987. SBStJ 1970; Chevalier de l'Ordre Militaire et Hospitalier de St Lazare de Jerusalem, 1975. *Publications:* (ed jtly) Classical Homoeopathy, 1986, rev. edn 1990; articles in internat. med. pubns and nat. jls.

Recreations: heraldry, history. *Address:* West Walton, Wisbech, Cambridgeshire PE14 7EU. *T:* Wisbech (0945) 780269. *Club:* Royal Society of Medicine.

ELLIOTT, Rev. Dr Charles Middleton; Fellow, Dean and Chaplain of Trinity Hall, Cambridge, since 1990; National Co-ordinator, Institute of Contemporary Spirituality, since 1987; *b* 9 Jan. 1939; *s* of Joseph William Elliott and Mary Evelyn Elliott; *m* 1962, Hilary Margaret Hambling; three *s* (one *d* decd). *Educ:* Repton; Lincoln and Nuffield Colls, Oxford (MA, DPhil). Deacon, 1964; priest, 1965. Lectr in Econs, Univ. of Nottingham, 1963–65; Reader in Econs, Univ. of Zambia, 1965–69; Asst Sec., Cttee on Society, Develt and Peace, Vatican and World Council of Churches, 1969–72; Sen. Lectr in Develt Econs, Univ. of E Anglia, 1972–73; Dir, Overseas Develt Gp, UEA, 1973–77; Minor Canon, Norwich Cathedral, 1974–77; Prof. of Develt Policy and Planning, and Dir, Centre of Develt Studies, Univ. of Wales, 1977–82; Director of Christian Aid, 1982–84; Asst Gen. Sec., BCC, 1982–84; Benjamin Meaker Prof., Bristol Univ., 1985–86; Sen. Consultant, ODI, 1986–87. G. E. M. Scott Fellow, Univ. of Melbourne, 1984–85; Hon. Vis. Prof. of Christian Ethics, Univ. of Edinburgh, 1985–; Vis. Prof. in Theology, KCL, 1986–88. Chm., Indep. Gp on British Aid, 1981–. Prebendary of Lichfield Cathedral, 1987–. *Publications:* The Development Debate, 1972; Inflation and the Compromised Church, 1973; Patterns of Poverty in the Third World, 1975; Praying the Kingdom: an introduction to political spirituality, 1985 (Biennial Collins Prize for Religious Lit., 1985); Comfortable Compassion, 1987; Praying through Paradox, 1987; Signs of Our Times, 1988; articles in Jl of Develt Studies, Econ. Hist. Rev., Theology, World Health Forum, World Develt and in Proc. Royal Soc. *Recreations:* sailing, fly-fishing, walking, chatting to rural craftsmen. *Address:* 11 Perowne Street, Cambridge CB2 1TJ.

ELLIOTT, Dr Charles Thomas, FRS 1988; Deputy Chief Scientific Officer, Royal Signals and Radar Establishment, since 1986; *b* 16 Jan. 1939; *s* of Charles Thomas and Mary Jane Elliott; *m* 1962, Brenda Waistell; one *s* two *d*. *Educ:* Washington Grammar Sch.; Manchester Univ. (BSc, PhD). Univ. of Manchester: Research student, 1960–63; Asst Lectr/Lectr, 1963–67 (research on dielectric breakdown); joined RSRE 1967, to study electrical transport in semiconductors; Vis. Scientist, MIT, Lincoln Lab., USA, 1970–71; research into infrared detectors, 1972–. Rank Prize for optoelectronics and IEE Electronics Div. Premium Award, 1982; Churchill Medal, Soc. of Engineers, 1986. *Publications:* numerous papers and patents. *Recreations:* reading, golf. *Address:* Royal Signals and Radar Establishment, St Andrews Road, Malvern, Worcs WR14 3PS. *T:* Malvern (0684) 894820.

ELLIOTT, Sir Clive (Christopher Hugh), 4th Bt *cr* 1917, of Limpsfield, Surrey; Country Projects Officer, Eastern and Southern Africa, Food and Agriculture Organization of the UN, Rome, since 1989; *b* Moshi, Tanganyika, 12 Aug. 1945; *s* of Sir Hugh Elliott, 3rd Bt, OBE and of Elizabeth Margaret, *d* of A. G. Phillipson; *S* father, 1989; *m* 1975, Marie-Thérèse, *d* of H. Rüttimann; two *s*. *Educ:* Dragon Sch., Oxford; Bryanston Sch., Dorset; University Coll., Oxford (BA Hons Zoology); Univ. of Cape Town, S Africa (PhD Zoology 1973). University of Cape Town: Research Officer, FitzPatrick Inst. of Ornithology, 1968–71; first Officer i/c National Unit for Bird-ringing Admin, 1972–75; ornithologist/ecologist, crop protectionist/project manager, FAO: Chad, 1975–78; Tanzania, 1978–86; Kenya, 1986–89. Member: South African Ornithological Soc.; Field Staff Assoc. of FAO (Information Officer, 1990). *Publications:* (ed jtly with R. L. Bruggers) Quelea Quelea: Africa's Bird Pest, 1989; contrib. to books and jls on ornithology. *Recreations:* tennis (Chm. FAO Tennis Club, 1990), fishing, bird-watching, wildlife conservation, everything African. *Heir:* *s* Ivo Antony Moritz Elliott, *b* 9 May 1978. *Address:* FAO/AGOE, Via delle terme di Caracalla, Rome, Italy. *Club:* British Ornithologists' Union.

ELLIOTT, David Murray, CB 1987; Director General (Internal Market), General Secretariat of Council of European Communities, since 1991; *b* 8 Feb. 1930; *s* of late Alfred Elliott, ISM, and Mabel Kathleen Emily Elliott (*née* Murray); *m* 1956, Ruth Marjorie Ingram; one *d* (one *s* decd). *Educ:* Bishopshalt Grammar Sch.; London Sch. of Economics and Political Science (BScEcon); Kitchener Scholar. National Service, RAF, 1951–54; Gen. Post Office, 1954–57; seconded to Federal Ministry of Communications, Nigeria, 1958–62; GPO, 1962–69; Asst Secretary: Min. of Posts and Telecommunications, 1969–74 (Dep. Leader, UK Delegn to Centenary Congress, UPU, Lausanne, 1974); Dept of Industry, 1974–75; Counsellor at UK Representation to the European Communities, Brussels, 1975–78; Under Sec., Cabinet Office, 1978–82; Minister and Dep. UK Perm. Rep., Eur. Communities, Brussels, 1982–91. *Recreation:* reading The Times. *Address:* General Secretariat of Council of European Communities, 170 rue de la Loi, 1048 Brussels, Belgium. *Clubs:* Travellers'; International Château Ste-Anne (Brussels).

ELLIOTT, David Stuart; Director, Museum of Modern Art, Oxford, since 1976; *b* 29 April 1949; *s* of Arthur Elliott and May Elliott; *m* 1974, Julia Alison; two *d*. *Educ:* Loughborough Grammar Sch.; Durham Univ. (BA Hons Mod. Hist.); Univ. of London (MA Hist. of Art, Courtauld Inst.). Asst Stage Manager, Phoenix Theatre, Leicester, 1966; Asst, City Art Gallery, Leicester, 1971; Regional Art Officer, Arts Council, 1973–76. Contribs to radio and TV. NACF Award, 1988. *Publications:* Alexander Rodchenko, 1979; José Clemente Orozco, 1980; New Worlds: Russian Art and Society 1900–1937, 1986; (ed with Ian Christie) Eisenstein at 90, 1988; (ed with Valery Dudakov) 100 Years of Russian Art 1889–1989, 1989; contribs to arts magazines. *Recreations:* keeping fit, walking, reading, travelling, listening to music. *Address:* Museum of Modern Art, 30 Pembroke Street, Oxford OX1 1BP. *T:* Oxford (0865) 722733.

ELLIOTT, Denholm Mitchell, CBE 1988; actor, stage and films; *b* 31 May 1922; *m* 1954, Virginia McKenna (marr. diss. 1957; she *m* 1957, Bill Travers); *m* 1962, Susan Robinson; one *s* one *d*. *Educ:* Malvern. *Plays:* The Guinea-Pig, Criterion, 1946; Venus Observed, St James's, 1949; Ring Round the Moon, Martin Beck, New York, 1950; Sleep of Prisoners, St Thomas's, Regent Street, 1950; Third Person, Criterion, 1951; Confidential Clerk, Lyric, 1954; South, Arts, 1955; Who Cares, Fortune, 1956; Camino Real, Phœnix, 1957; Traveller Without Luggage, Arts, 1958; The Ark, Westminster, 1959; Stratford-on-Avon Season, 1960; Write Me a Murder, Belasco Theatre, New York, 1961; The Seagull, The Crucible, Ring Round the Moon, Nat. Repertory Co., New York, 1963–64; Come as You Are, New, 1970; Chez Nous, Globe, 1974; The Return of A. J. Raffles, Aldwych, 1975; Heaven and Hell, Greenwich, 1976; The Father, Open Space, 1979; A Life in the Theatre, Haymarket, 1989; *films:* Sound Barrier, 1949; The Cruel Sea, 1952; They Who Dare, 1953; Pacific Destiny, 1955; Scent of Mystery, 1959; Station Six Sahara, 1962; Nothing But the Best, 1963; King Rat, 1964; The High Bright Sun, 1964; You Must Be Joking, 1965; Alfie, 1966; Here we go round the Mulberry Bush, 1967; The Seagull, 1968; Too Late the Hero, 1969; Madame Sin, 1972; A Doll's House, 1973; The Apprenticeship of Duddy Kravitz, 1974; Russian Roulette, 1976; Sweeney II, Saint Jack, The Hound of the Baskervilles, Zulu Dawn, A Game for Vultures, Cuba, 1978; Bad Timing, Sunday Lovers, 1980; Trading Places, 1982; The Missionary, The Wicked Lady, 1983; A Private Function, 1984; Defence of the Realm, A Room with a View, 1986; Maurice, September, 1987; Indiana Jones and the Last Crusade, 1988; *television:* series incl. Bleak House, 1987; Bangkok Hilton, 1990; also plays. Has awards, London and New York, incl. BAFTA Best TV Actor, New Standard Best Film Actor, 1981, BAFTA Best Supporting Film Actor, 1984, 1985, 1986. *Recreations:* ski-ing, golf. *Address:* c/o London Management, 235 Regent Street, W1. *Club:* Garrick.

ELLIOTT, Frank Abercrombie, MD, FRCP; Emeritus Professor of Neurology, University of Pennyslvania, since 1979; Consultant, Elliott Neurology Centre, Pennsylvania Hospital, Philadelphia, since 1975; *b* 18 Dec. 1910; *s* of Arthur Abercrombie Elliott and Kathleen Gosselin; *m* 1st, 1940, Betty Kathleen Elkington; two *d*; 2nd, 1970, Mrs Josiah Marvel (*née* Hopkins). *Educ:* Rondebosch; Univ. of Cape Town. Univ. entrance schol., 1928; Lewis Memorial schol., 1930–34; MB, ChB Cape Town, with Hons and Gold Medal; Hiddingh Travelling Fellowship, 1936–39. House Surg. and House Phys. to professorial units, Cape Town; House Physician, British Postgrad. Sch. of Medicine and Nat. Hosp. for Nervous Diseases, London; Resident MO, Nat. Heart Hosp. RAMC, 1943–48, Lt-Col; Adviser in Neurology, India and War Office. FRCP 1948; FACP 1973. Physician to Charing Cross Hosp., 1947–58; to Moorfields Eye Hospital, 1949–58; Prof. of Neurology, Univ. of Pennsylvania, 1963–78. Lecturer and Examiner, London Univ. Member: Assoc. of British Neurologists; Assoc. of British Physicians; Internat. Soc. of Internal Medicine; Am. Acad. of Neurology; Philadelphia Neurological Soc. *Publications:* (ed) Clinical Neurology, 1952; Clinical Neurology, 1964 (2nd edn, 1971); papers on neurological subjects and the origins of aggressive behaviour. *Address:* Pennsylvania Hospital, Philadelphia, Pa 19107, USA. *Club:* Philadelphia.

ELLIOTT, Frank Alan, CB 1991; Permanent Secretary, Department of Health and Social Services, Northern Ireland, since 1987; *b* 28 March 1937; *s* of Frank Elliott and Doreen Allen; *m* 1964, Olive Lucy O'Brien; one *s* two *d*. *Educ:* Royal Belfast Academical Inst.; Trinity Coll., Dublin (BA (Mod.) 1st cl.). Entered NI Civil Service, 1959; Principal, Min. of Health, 1966, Asst Sec., 1971; Sen. Asst Sec., Dept of Health and Social Services, 1975, Under Sec., 1981. Gov., Sullivan Upper Sch., 1982–. *Recreations:* music and the arts, motoring. *Address:* Department of Health and Social Services, Dundonald House, Upper Newtownards Road, Belfast, Northern Ireland BT4 3SF. *T:* Belfast (0232) 650111.

ELLIOTT, George, FRICS; Senior Partner, Edmond Shipway and Partners, since 1985; *b* 20 Aug. 1932; *s* of Harry Elliott and Nellie Elizabeth Elliott; *m* 1958, Winifred Joan (marr. diss. 1990); one *s* one *d*. *Educ:* Sir George Monoux Grammar Sch.; SW Essex Technical Coll. FRICS 1966. Founder Partner, Edmond Shipway, 1963; Chief Exec., British Urban Develt Services Unit, 1975–78. *Recreation:* travel. *Address:* Flat 8.6, Stirling Court, Marshall Street, W1V 1LQ. *T:* 071–437 3133; (office) 41 Buckingham Palace Road, SW1W 0PP. *T:* 071–828 6855.

ELLIOTT, Harold William, CBE 1967; *b* 24 Nov. 1905; *s* of late W. J. Elliott and Ellen Elliott; *m* 1st, 1929, Mary Molyneux (marr. diss. 1935); one *s* one *d*; 2nd, 1937, Betty (*d* 1976), *d* of late C. J. Thumling; one *s*; 3rd, 1978, Helen Bridget, *y d* of Sir Lionel Faudel-Phillips, 3rd Bt, and *widow* of 5th Earl of Kilmorey. *Educ:* Brighton Coll. Apprenticed to Adolf Saurer, AG Arbon, Switz., 1924; joined Pickfords Ltd, 1926. Mem., Road and Rail Central Conf., 1938; Transport Adv. Cttee, Food Defence Plans Dept, BoT, 1939; Asst Divisional Food Officer (Transport), London, 1940; Controller of Road Transport, Min. of Supply, 1941; Mem., Salvage Bd; Dir of Transport, Middle East Supply Centre, Cairo, 1943–44, with responsibility, within this Anglo-Amer. orgn which covered some 16 countries of ME, for adequacy of civilian transport for food disn and other basic needs of wartime economy of area, incl. locust control and Aid to Russia convoys from Persian Gulf; crossed Saudi Arabia via Riyadh, 1943; Mem., Road Haulage Central Wages Bd and Vice-Chm., Meat Transport Organisation Ltd, 1945; Gen. Man., Hay's Wharf Cartage Co. Ltd, Pickfords Ltd and Carter Paterson & Co. Ltd, 1947; Chief Officer (Freight), Road Transport Exec.; Mem., Coastal Shipping Adv. Cttee, 1948; Mem. Bd of Management, Brit. Road Services, and Dir, Atlantic Steam Navigation Co. Ltd, 1959; Man. Dir, Pickfords Ltd, 1963–70, Chm., 1970. Vice-Pres., CIT, 1970–71; Life Mem., Road Haulage Assoc. Trustee, Sutton Housing Trust, 1971–79; Chm., Holmwood Common Management Cttee, 1971–79; Governor, Brighton Coll., 1955 (Chm. Governors, 1974–78; a Vice Patron, 1980). Liveryman, Worshipful Co. of Carmen, 1939–84; Freeman, City of London, 1939. *Address:* Ombla, Moushill Lane, Milford, Godalming, Surrey GU8 5BH. *T:* Godalming (0483) 420723.

ELLIOTT, Hugh Percival, CMG 1959; retired, 1967; *b* 29 May 1911; *s* of late Major P. W. Elliott, IA; *m* 1951, Bridget Rosalie (*d* 1981), *d* of late Rev. A. F. Peterson. *Educ:* St Lawrence Coll., Ramsgate; Hertford Coll., Oxford. Joined Colonial Administrative Service, Nigeria, 1934; seconded Colonial Office, 1946; Supervisor, Colonial Service Courses, London, 1948–50; Senior District Officer, 1954; Permanent Sec., 1956; Adviser, Govt of Eastern Nigeria, 1962–67. Many visits to Ethiopia, Zimbabwe, Kenya, Uganda and Nigeria to support the initiatives for Moral Re-Armament by African friends, 1968–. Companion, Order of the Niger, Nigeria, 1964. *Publications:* Darkness and Dawn in Zimbabwe, 1978; Dawn in Zimbabwe, 1980. *Recreations:* the countryside, watercolour painting, Africa. *Address:* Flat 8, Rosewood Lodge, 79 Wickham Road, Shirley, Croydon CR0 8TB.

ELLIOTT, Prof. James Philip, PhD; FRS 1980; Professor of Theoretical Physics, University of Sussex, since 1969; *b* 27 July 1929; *s* of James Elliott and Dora Kate Smith; *m* 1955, Mavis Rosetta Avery; one *s* two *d*. *Educ:* University College, Southampton; London External degrees: BSc 1949, PhD 1952. Senior Scientific Officer, AERE Harwell, 1951–58; Vis. Associate Prof., Univ. of Rochester, USA, 1958–59; Lecturer in Mathematics, Univ. of Southampton, 1959–62; Reader in Theoretical Physics, Univ. of Sussex, 1962–69. Fellow of former Physical Soc. *Publications:* Symmetry in Physics, 1979; contribs include: The Nuclear Shell Model, Handbuch der Physik, vol 39, 1957; many papers, mostly published in Proc. Roy. Soc. and Nuclear Phys. *Recreations:* gardening, sport and music. *Address:* 36 Montacute Road, Lewes, Sussex BN7 1EP. *T:* Lewes (0273) 474783.

ELLIOTT, John Dorman; Deputy Chairman, Foster's Brewing Group (formerly Elders IXL Ltd), since 1990 (Chairman and Chief Executive, 1985–90); Immediate Past President, Liberal Party of Australia; *b* 3 Oct. 1941; *s* of Frank Faithful Elliott and Anita Caroline Elliott; *m* 1st, 1965, Lorraine Clare (*née* Golder); two *s* one *d*; 2nd, 1987, Amanda Mary Drummond Moray (*née* Bayles); one *d*. *Educ:* Carey Baptist Grammar School, Melbourne; BCom (Hons) 1962, MBA Melbourne 1965. With BHP, Melbourne, 1963–65; McKinsey & Co., 1966–72; formed consortium and raised $30 million to acquire Henry Jones (IXL), and became Man. Dir, 1972; Elder Smith Goldsbrough Mort merged with Henry Jones (IXL) to form Elders IXL, 1981; Elders IXL acquired Carlton & United Breweries, 1983, largest takeover in Aust. history. *Recreations:* football, tennis, Royal tennis. *Address:* 1 Towers Road, Toorak, Vic 3142, Australia. *T:* 670 0855. *Clubs:* Melbourne, Australian, Savage; Royal Melbourne Tennis.

ELLIOTT, Prof. John Huxtable, FBA 1972; Regius Professor of Modern History, and Fellow of Oriel College, Oxford, since 1990; *b* 23 June 1930; *s* of Thomas Charles Elliott and Janet Mary Payne; *m* 1958, Oonah Sophia Butler. *Educ:* Eton College; Trinity College, Cambridge (MA, PhD). Fellow of Trinity Coll., Cambridge, 1954–67, Hon. Fellow, 1991; Asst Lectr in History, Cambridge Univ., 1957–62; Lectr in History, Cambridge Univ., 1962–67; Prof. of History: KCL, 1968–73; Inst. for Advanced Study,

Princeton, NJ, 1973–90. King Juan Carlos Vis. Prof., New York Univ., 1988. Wiles Lectr, QUB, 1969; Trevelyan Lectr, Cambridge Univ., 1982–83. Corresp. Fellow, Real Academia de la Historia, Madrid, 1965; Fellow, Amer. Acad. Arts and Scis, 1977. Mem., Amer. Philosophical Soc., 1982; Corresponding Member: Hispanic Soc. of America, 1975; Real Academia Sevillana de Buenas Letras, 1976. Dr *hc* Universidad Autónoma de Madrid, 1983. Medal of Honour, Universidad Internacional Menéndez y Pelayo, 1987; Medalla de Oro al Mérito en las Bellas Artes, 1990. Visitante Ilustre de Madrid, 1983; Comdr, 1984, Grand Cross, 1988, Order of Alfonso X El Sabio; Comdr, Order of Isabel la Católica, 1987. *Publications:* The Revolt of the Catalans, 1963; Imperial Spain, 1469–1716, 1963; Europe Divided, 1559–1598, 1968; The Old World and the New, 1492–1650, 1970; ed (with H. G. Koenigsberger) The Diversity of History, 1970; (with J. F. de la Peña) Memoriales y Cartas del Conde Duque de Olivares, 2 vols, 1978–80; (with Jonathan Brown) A Palace for a King, 1980; Richelieu and Olivares, 1984 (Leo Gershoy Award, Amer. Hist. Assoc., 1985); The Count-Duke of Olivares, 1986 (Wolfson Lit. Prize for History); Spain and its World 1500–1700, 1989; (ed) The Hispanic World, 1991. *Recreation:* looking at paintings. *Address:* Oriel College, Oxford OX1 4EW; 122 Church Way, Iffley, Oxford OX4 4EG. *T:* Oxford (0865) 716703.

ELLIOTT, Mark, CMG 1988; HM Diplomatic Service; Ambassador to Israel, since 1988; *b* 16 May 1939; *s* of William Rowcliffe Elliott, *qv*, and Karin Tess Elliott (*née* Classen); *m* 1964, Julian Richardson; two *s*. *Educ:* Eton Coll. (King's Scholar); New Coll., Oxford. HM Forces (Intell. Corps), 1957–59. FO, 1963; Tokyo, 1965; FCO, 1970; Private Sec. to Perm. Under-Sec. of State, 1973–74; First Sec. and Head of Chancery, Nicosia, 1975–77; Counsellor, 1977–81, Head of Chancery, 1978–81, Tokyo; Hd of Far Eastern Dept, FCO, 1981–85; Under-Sec. on secondment to N Ireland Office, 1985–88. *Recreations:* photography, walking, music. *Address:* c/o Foreign and Commonwealth Office, SW1.

ELLIOTT, Dr Michael, CBE 1982; FRS 1979; Lawes Trust Senior Fellow, Rothamsted Experimental Station, since 1989; *b* 30 Sept. 1924; *s* of Thomas William Elliott and Isobel Constance (*née* Burnell); *m* 1950, Margaret Olwen James; two *d*. *Educ:* Skinners Co.'s Sch., Tunbridge Wells, Kent; The Univ., Southampton (BSc, PhD); King's Coll., Univ. of London (DSc; FKC 1984). FRSC. Postgrad. res., University Coll., Southampton, 1945–46, and King's Coll., Univ. of London, 1946–48; Rothamsted Experimental Station: Organic Chemist, Dept of Insecticides and Fungicides, 1948–85; SPSO 1971–79; DCSO 1979–83 (Hd of Dept of Insecticides and Fungicides, 1979–83, and Dep. Dir, 1980–83); Hon. Scientist and Consultant, Chemistry of Insecticides, 1983–85. Vis. Res. Scientist, Div. of Entomology, Univ. of Calif at Berkeley, 1969, 1974 and 1986–88; Vis. Prof., Imperial Coll. of Sci. and Tech., 1978–. Hon. DSc Southampton, 1985. Burdick and Jackson Internat. Award for Res. in Pesticide Chemistry, 1975; Holroyd Medal and Lectureship, Soc. of Chem. Ind., 1977; John Jeyes Medal and Lectureship, Chem. Soc., 1978; Mullard Medal, Royal Soc., 1981; Grande Médaille de la Société Française de Phytiatrie et de Phytopharmacie, 1983; Fine Chemicals and Medicinals Gp Award, RSC, 1984; British Crop Protection Council Award, 1986; Wolf Foundn Prize in Agriculture, 1989; Prix de la Fondation de la Chimie, Paris, 1989. *Publications:* Synthetic Pyrethroids, 1977; papers on chemistry of insecticides and relation of chemical structure with biological activity; chapters in books on insecticides. *Recreations:* photography, designing insecticides. *Address:* 9 Long Ridge, Aston, Stevenage, Herts SG2 7EW. *T:* Stevenage (0438) 88328. *Club:* Camera.

ELLIOTT, Michael Alwyn; arts and business consultant; *b* 15 July 1936; *s* of W. A. Edwards and Mrs J. B. Elliott (assumed stepfather's name); *m* Caroline Margaret McCarthy; two *s* one *d*. *Educ:* Raynes Park Grammar School. AMP INSEAD, 1976. Journalist, 1955–59; Public Relations, Avon Rubber Co. Ltd, 1959–63; Marketing Executive, then Assistant Corporate Planning Manager, CPC International, 1963–68; Kimberly-Clark Ltd: Product Manager, 1968; Marketing Manager, 1969; Marketing and Development Manager, 1975; General Manager, 1976; Director, 1977; Gen. Administrator, Nat. Theatre, 1979–85; Dir of Admin, Denton, Hall, Burgin and Warrens, Solicitors, 1985–88. Mem., Executive Council, Soc. of West End Theatre, 1980–85. *Recreations:* acting, golf, walking. *Address:* 149 Forest Road, Tunbridge Wells, Kent TN2 5EX. *T:* Tunbridge Wells (0892) 30615.

ELLIOTT, Michael Norman; Member (Lab) London West, European Parliament, since 1984; *b* 3 June 1932. *Educ:* Brunel College of Technology. Formerly res. chemist in food industry. Mem., Ealing Borough Council, 1964–86 (former Leader of Council and Chm., Educn Cttee). Vice-Chair, Parly delegn to Sweden, Finland and Iceland; Mem., Parly Cttee of Inquiry into Racism and Xenophobia. Member: CND, 1961–; Friends of the Earth, 1985–. Hon. Fellow, Ealing Coll. of Higher Educn, 1988. *Address:* 358 Oldfield Lane North, Greenford, Middx UB6 8PT. *T:* 081–578 1303.

ELLIOTT, Sir Norman (Randall), Kt 1967; CBE 1957 (OBE 1946); MA; Chairman of the Electricity Council, 1968–72; Chairman, Howden Group, 1973–83; *b* 19 July 1903; *s* of William Randall Elliott and Catherine Dunsmore; *m* 1963, Phyllis Clarke. *Educ:* privately; St Catharine's Coll., Cambridge. Called to the Bar, Middle Temple, 1932 (J. J. Powell Prizeman, A. J. Powell Exhibitioner). London Passenger Transport Board; London and Home Counties Joint Electricity Authority; Yorkshire Electric Power Co.; 21 Army Group: first as CRE (Royal Engineers) then, as Col, Deputy Dir of Works, 21 Army Group (OBE); Chief Engineer and Manager, Wimbledon Borough Council; Gen. Manager and Chief Engineer, London and Home Counties Joint Electricity Authority and sometime Chm. and Dir, Isle of Thanet Electric Supply Co., and Dir, James Howden & Co. Ltd; Chairman: S-E Electricity Bd, 1948–62; S of Scotland Electricity Bd, 1962–67; Member: Brit. Electricity Authority, 1950 and 1951; Central Electricity Authority, 1956 and 1957; Electricity Council, 1958–62; N of Scotland Hydro-Electric Bd, 1965–69. Director: Newarthill & McAlpine Group, 1972–89; Slumberger Ltd, 1977–84. *Publication:* Electricity Statutes, Orders and Regulations, 1947, rev. edn 1951. *Recreations:* ball games and the theatre. *Clubs:* Athenæum; Western (Glasgow); Royal Northern Yacht.

ELLIOTT, Oliver Douglas; British Council Representative in Yugoslavia, 1979–85; *b* 13 Oct. 1925; *y s* of late Walter Elliott and Margherita Elliott, Bedford; *m* 1954, Patience Rosalie Joan Orpen; one *s*. *Educ:* Bedford Modern Sch.; Wadham Coll., Oxford (MA); Fitzwilliam House, Cambridge. Served RNVR (Sub-Lt), 1944–47. Colonial Educn Service, Cyprus, 1953–59; joined British Council, 1959; served Lebanon, 1960–63; Dep. Rep., Ghana, 1963; Dir, Commonwealth I Dept, 1966; Dir, Service Conditions Dept, 1970; Dep. Educn Advr, India, 1973; Representative in Nigeria, 1976–79. *Recreation:* golf.

ELLIOTT, Sir Randal (Forbes), KBE 1977 (OBE 1976); President, New Zealand Medical Association, 1976; *b* 12 Oct. 1922; *s* of Sir James Elliott and Lady (Ann) Elliott (*née* Forbes), MBE; *m* 1949, Pauline June Young; one *s* six *d*. *Educ:* Wanganui Collegiate Sch.; Otago Univ. MB, ChB (NZ), 1947; DO, 1953; FRCS, FRACS. Group Captain, RNZAF. Ophthalmic Surgeon, Wellington Hospital, 1953–. Chm. Council, NZ Med. Assoc. GCStJ 1987 (KStJ 1978). *Publications:* various papers in medical jls. *Recreations:* sailing, skiing, mountaineering. *Address:* Wakefield House, 90 The Terrace, Wellington, New Zealand. *T:* 721–375. *Club:* Wellington (NZ).

ELLIOTT, Robert Anthony K.; *see* Keable-Elliott.

ELLIOTT, Air Vice-Marshal Robert D.; *see* Deacon Elliott.

ELLIOTT, Sir Roger (James), Kt 1987; FRS 1976; Secretary to the Delegates and Chief Executive of Oxford University Press, since 1988; Professor of Physics, Oxford University, since 1989; Fellow of New College, Oxford, since 1974; *b* Chesterfield, 8 Dec. 1928; *s* of James Elliott and Gladys Elliott (*née* Hill); *m* 1952, Olga Lucy Atkinson; one *s* two *d*. *Educ:* Swanwick Hall Sch., Derbyshire; New Coll., Oxford (MA, DPhil). Research Fellow, Univ. of California, Berkeley, 1952–53; Research Fellow, UKAEA, Harwell, 1953–55; Lectr, Reading Univ., 1955–57; Fellow of St John's College, Oxford, 1957–74, Hon. Fellow, 1988; University Reader, Oxford, 1964–74; Wykeham Prof. of Physics, 1974–89; Senior Proctor, 1969; Delegate, Oxford Univ. Press, 1971–88. Chm., Computer Bd for Univs and Research Councils, 1983–87; Vice-Chm., Parly Office of Sci. and Technol., 1990–; Member: Adv. Bd for Res. Councils, 1987–90; (part-time) UKAEA, 1988–. Physical Sec. and Vice-Pres., Royal Soc., 1984–88; Treas., Publishers Assoc., 1990–. Visiting Prof., Univ. of California, Berkeley, 1961; Miller Vis. Prof., Univ. of Illinois, Urbana, 1966; Vis. Dist. Prof., Florida State Univ., 1981. Hon. DSc: Paris, 1983; Bath, 1991. Maxwell Medal, 1968, Guthrie Medal, 1990, Inst. of Physics. *Publications:* Magnetic Properties of Rare Earth Metals, 1973; Solid State Physics and its Applications (with A. F. Gibson), 1973; papers in Proc. Royal Soc., Jl Phys., Phys. Rev., etc. *Address:* 11 Crick Road, Oxford OX2 6QL. *T:* Oxford (0865) 56767. *Club:* Athenæum.

ELLIOTT, Sir Ronald (Stuart), Kt 1981; Director: International Board, Security Pacific National Bank, USA, 1983–91; Security Pacific Australia Ltd, 1985–91; *b* 29 Jan. 1918; *s* of Harold J. W. Elliott and Mercedes E. Manning; *m* 1944, Isabella Mansbridge Boyd; one *s* one *d*. *Educ:* C of E Grammar Sch., Ballarat, Victoria. ABIA; FAIM. Commonwealth Banking Corporation: Sec., 1960–61; Dep. Manager for Queensland, 1961–63; Chief Manager, Foreign Div., 1963–64; Chief Manager, Queensland, 1964–65; Gen. Manager, Commonwealth Develt Bank of Australia, 1966–75; Dep. Man. Dir, 1975–76, Man. Dir, 1976–81, Commonwealth Banking Corp.; Chm., Australian European Finance Corp. Ltd, 1976–81. Director: Australian Bd, Internat. Commodities Clearing House Ltd, 1981–88; Brambles Industries, 1981–90. Mem., Sci. and Industry Forum, Australian Acad. of Sci., 1978–81. Dir., Australian Opera, 1980–87; Mem., Australian Film Develt Corp., 1970–75. *Recreations:* golf, reading, music, particularly opera. *Address:* PO Box 1401, Armidale, NSW 2350, Australia. *T:* (067) 722387. *Clubs:* Union, Australian Golf (Sydney) (Pres., 1982–87, Capt., 1987–88); Armidale Golf.

ELLIOTT, Walter Archibald; *see* Elliott, Hon. Lord.

ELLIOTT, William Rowcliffe, CB 1969; Senior Chief Inspector, Department of Education and Science, 1968–72, retired; *b* 10 April 1910; *s* of Thomas Herbert Elliott and Ada Elliott (*née* Rowcliffe); *m* 1937, Karin Tess, *d* of Ernest and Lilly Classen; one *s*. *Educ:* St Paul's Sch.; The Queen's Coll., Oxford. Schoolmaster, 1933–36; HM Inspector of Schools: in Leeds, 1936–39; in Leicestershire, 1940–44; in Liverpool, 1944–48; Staff Inspector: for Adult Education, 1948–55; for Secondary Modern Education, 1955–57; Chief Inspector for Educational Developments, 1957–59; for Secondary Educn, 1959–66; Dep. Sen. Chief Insp., 1966–67. Pres., Section L, British Assoc., 1969; Mem., Oxfam Governing Council, 1974–80. Chm. of Governors, Friends' Sch., Saffron Walden, 1982–84. Governor of The Retreat, York, 1984–90. *Publications:* Monemvasia, The Gibraltar of Greece, 1971; Chest-tombs and 'tea caddies' by Cotswold and Severn, 1977. *Recreations:* village life, photography, gardenage. *Address:* Malthus Close, Farthinghoe, Brackley, Northants NN13 5NY. *T:* Banbury (0295) 710388. *Club:* Royal Over-Seas League.

See also Mark Elliott.

ELLIS; *see* Scott-Ellis.

ELLIS, Alice Thomas; *see* Haycraft, A. M.

ELLIS, Andrew Steven, OBE 1984; freelance political affairs and governmental relations consultant; Central and Eastern European Director, GJW Government Relations Ltd; *b* 19 May 1952; *s* of Peter Vernon Ellis and Kathleen Dawe; *m* 1st, 1975, Patricia Ann Stevens (marr. diss. 1987); 2nd, 1990, Helen Prudence Drummond. *Educ:* Trinity Coll., Cambridge (BA Mathematics); Univ. of Newcastle upon Tyne (MSc Statistics); Newcastle upon Tyne Polytechnic (BA Law). Proprietor, Andrew Ellis (Printing and Duplicating), Newcastle upon Tyne, 1973–81; freelance Election Agent/Organizer, 1981–84; Sec.-Gen., Liberal Party, 1985–88; Chief Exec., Social and Liberal Democrats, 1988–89; Consultant Nat. Agent, Welsh Liberal Party, 1984–88. Contested (L): Newcastle upon Tyne Central, Oct. 1974, Nov. 1976, 1979; Boothferry, 1983; Leader, Liberal Gp, Tyne & Wear CC, 1977–81; Vice-Chm., Liberal Party, 1980–86. *Publications:* Algebraic Structure (with Terence Treeby), 1971; Let Every Englishman's Home Be His Castle, 1978. *Recreation:* travel. *Address:* 19 Hayle Road, Maidstone, Kent ME15 6PD. *T:* Maidstone (0622) 678443; Porth House, Powell Street, Aberystwyth, Ceredigion SY23 1QQ. *Club:* National Liberal.

ELLIS, Arthur John, CBE 1986; Chairman since 1984, and Chief Executive Officer since 1969, Fyffes Group Ltd; Chairman, Intervention Board Executive Agency (formerly Intervention Board for Agricultural Produce), since 1986; *b* 22 Aug. 1932; *s* of Arthur Ellis and Freda Jane Ellis; *m* 1956, Rita Patricia Blake; two *s* one *d*. *Educ:* Chingford Jun. High Sch.; South West Essex Technical Coll. FCCA; FCMA; FCIS; MBCS. Joined Fyffes Gp Ltd as qual. accountant in Finance and Admin Dept, 1954; Chief Financial Officer, 1965; Financial Dir, 1967. Chm., Nat. Seed Develt Organisation Ltd, 1982–87. *Recreations:* golf, reading, gardening. *Address:* 12 York Gate, Regent's Park, NW1 4QJ. *T:* 071–487 4472. *Clubs:* Reform, Farmers'.

ELLIS, His Honour Arthur Robert Malcolm, DL; a Circuit Judge (formerly Judge of County Courts), 1971–86; *b* 27 June 1912; *s* of David and Anne Amelia Ellis, Nottingham; *m* 1938, Brenda Sewell (*d* 1983); one *d*. *Educ:* Nottingham High Sch. Admitted Solicitor, 1934; called to the Bar, Inner Temple, 1953. Chm., Nottingham Council of Social Service, 1950–55; Dep. Chm., E Midland Traffic Area, 1955–71; Chm., Ministry of Pensions and National Insurance Tribunal, Sutton-in-Ashfield, Notts, 1961–64, resigned; Chm., Min. of Pensions and Nat. Insce Tribunal, Notts, 1964–71; Chm., Medical Appeals Tribunal, 1971–76. Chm., Notts QS, 1963–71 (Dep.-Chm., 1962–63); Chm., Derbyshire QS, 1966–71 (Dep.-Chm., 1965–66). DL Notts, 1973. *Recreations:* golf, bridge, reading. *Address:* Byways, 5 Manvers Grove, Radcliffe-on-Trent, Notts NG12 2FT. *Club:* United Services (Nottingham).

ELLIS, Bryan James; Under-Secretary, Department of Social Security; *b* 11 June 1934; *s* of late Frank and Renée Ellis; *m* 1960, Barbara Muriel Whiteley; one *s* one *d*. *Educ:* Merchant Taylors' Sch.; St John's Coll., Oxford. Sec., Oxford Union Soc., 1956. Joined Civil Service, entering Min. of Pensions and National Insurance (subseq. Min. of Social

Security and DHSS) as Asst Principal, 1958; Principal 1963; Asst Sec. 1971; Under Sec., 1977; Chm., CSSB, 1986; Dep. Dir, OPCS, 1987–90; DSS, 1990–. Chm., Assoc. of First Div. Civil Servants, 1983–85. Chm., Trustees of Leopardstown Park Hosp., Dublin, 1979–84. *Publication:* Pensions in Britain 1955–75, 1989. *Recreations:* walking, theatre and cinema, bridge. *Address:* Department of Social Security, The Adelphi, John Adam Street, WC2N 6HT. *T:* 071–962 8073. *Club:* MCC.

ELLIS, Carol Jacqueline, (Mrs Ralph Gilmore), QC 1980 (practises as Miss Ellis); JP (sits as Mrs Gilmore); Editor, The Law Reports, since 1976; Consultant Editor, Weekly Law Reports, since 1990; *b* 6 May 1929; *d* of Ellis W. Ellis and Flora Bernstein; *m* 1957, Ralph Gilmore; two *s*. *Educ:* Abbey Sch., Reading; La Ramée, Lausanne; Univ. of Lausanne; University Coll. London (LLB). Called to the Bar, Gray's Inn, 1951; supernumerary law reporter for The Law Reports, The Times, and other legal jls, 1952; law reporter to The Law Reports and Weekly Law Reports, 1954; Asst Editor, Weekly Law Reports, 1969; Managing Editor, The Law Reports and Weekly Law Reports, 1970; Editor, Weekly Law Reports, 1976. JP W Central Div. Inner London, 1972–. *Recreations:* travel, music, theatre. *Address:* 11 Old Square, Lincoln's Inn, WC2A 3TS. *T:* 071–403 0341.

ELLIS, (Dorothy) June; Headmistress, The Mount School, York, 1977–86; Clerk to Central Committee, Quaker Social Responsibility and Education, 1987–90; *b* 30 May 1926; *d* of Robert Edwin and Dora Ellis. *Educ:* La Sagesse, Newcastle upon Tyne; BSc Pure Science, Durham; DipEd Newcastle upon Tyne. Assistant Mistress: Darlington High Sch., 1947–49; Rutherford High Sch., 1949–50; La Sagesse High Sch., 1950–53; Housemistress, 1953–61, Sen. Mistress, 1961–64, St Monica's Sch.; Dep. Head, Sibford Sch., 1964–77. Clerk, Swerford Parish Council, 1986–90. Mem. Council, Woodrooke Coll., 1987–; Governor: Ellerslie Sch., Malvern, 1987–; Friends' Sch., Saffron Walden, 1990–. *Recreations:* walking, gardening, home-making. *Address:* Willowside, Swerford, Oxford OX7 4BQ. *T:* Hook Norton (0608) 737334.

ELLIS, Rear-Adm. Edward William, CB 1974; CBE 1968; *b* 6 Sept. 1918; *s* of Harry L. and Winifred Ellis; *m* 1945, Dilys (*née* Little); two *s*. Joined RN, 1940; War service afloat in HM Ships Broadwater and Eclipse, and liaison duties in USS Wichita and US Navy destroyer sqdn; psc 1952; Staff of Flag Officer Flotillas, Mediterranean, 1954–55; Sec. to 4th Sea Lord, 1956–58; Sec. to C-in-C South Atlantic and South America, 1959–60; HM Ships Bermuda and Belfast, 1960–62; Head of C-in-C Far East Secretariat, 1963–65; Sec. to C-in-C Portsmouth and Allied C-in-C Channel, 1965–66; Sec. to Chief of Naval Staff and 1st Sea Lord, 1966–68; Cdre RN Barracks Portsmouth, 1968–71; Adm. Pres., RNC Greenwich, 1972–74. Comdr 1953; Captain 1963; Rear-Adm. 1972. Private Sec. to Lord Mayor of London, 1974–82. Freeman of the City of London, 1974; Liveryman, Shipwrights' Co., 1980. OStJ 1981. Commander, Royal Order of Danebrog, 1974. *Recreations:* fishing, gardening. *Address:* South Lodge, Minstead, Lyndhurst, Hants SO43 7FR. *Club:* Army and Navy.

ELLIS, Eileen Mary, RDI 1984; freelance textile designer; Design Director, Jamasque Ltd; Director, Tintawn Carpets Ltd; *b* 1 March 1933; *m* 1954, Julian Ellis; one *s* two *d*. *Educ:* Huyton College; Leicester, Central and Royal Colleges of Art. Des RCA 1957; FCSD (FSIAD 1976). Designer of contract and decorative woven and printed furnishing fabrics, carpets and woven wall coverings; designed for Ascher & Co., 1957–59; Partner, Orbit Design Group, 1960–73; formed Weaveplan as design consultancy, 1973–; design consultant: Tintawn Carpets, 1969–; Abbotsford Fabrics, 1982–; Vescom, Holland, 1982–; Botany Weaving Mill, Ireland, 1984–; David Evans, 1986–88; Herman Miller, USA, 1986–; Jamasque, 1983–; Sekers, 1982–86; G. & G. Kynoch, 1982–86; John Orr, 1983–85; John Crowther, 1991–. Lecturer: Hornsey Coll. of Art/Middlesex Polytechnic, 1965–74; RCA, 1974–82. RSA Bursary in Dress Textiles, 1953; RSA Travel Bursary for established designer in textile industry, 1973. Textile Inst. Design Medal, 1985. *Recreations:* country life, riding, cooking, reading. *Address:* Holbeam Farm, Stalisfield, Faversham, Kent ME13 0HS. *T:* Eastling (079589) 602; The Glasshouse, 11/12 Lettice Street, SW6 4EH. *T:* 071–736 3085.

ELLIS, Prof. Harold, CBE 1987; MA, MCh, DM; FRCS; FRCOG; Clinical Anatomist, University of Cambridge, since 1989; Fellow, Churchill College, Cambridge, since 1989; *b* 13 Jan. 1926; *s* of Samuel and Ada Ellis; *m* 1958, Wendy Mae Levine; one *s* one *d*. *Educ:* Queen's Coll. (State Scholar and Open Scholar in Natural Sciences), Oxford; Radcliffe Infirmary, Oxford. BM, BCh, 1948; FRCS, MA, 1951; MCh 1956; DM 1962; FRCOG *ad eundem*, 1987; Hon. FACS 1989. House Surgeon, Radcliffe Infirmary, 1948–49; Hallett Prize, RCS, 1949. RAMC, 1949–51. Res. Surgical Officer, Sheffield Royal Infirm., 1952–54; Registrar, Westminster Hosp., 1955; Sen. Registrar and Surgical Tutor, Radcliffe Infirm., Oxford, 1956–60; Sen. Lectr in Surgery, 1960–62, Hon. Consultant Surgeon, 1962–89, Westminster Hosp.; Prof. of Surgery, Univ. of London, 1962–89. Hon. Consultant Surgeon to the Army, 1978–89. Mem. Council, RCS, 1974–86. Member: Association of Surgeons; British Soc. of Gastroenterol.; Surgical Research Soc.; Council: RSocMed; British Assoc. of Surgical Oncology; Associé étranger, L'Academie de Chirurgie, Paris, 1983. *Publications:* Clinical Anatomy, 1960; Anatomy for Anaesthetists, 1963; Lecture Notes on General Surgery, 1965; Principles of Resuscitation, 1967; History of the Bladder Stone, 1970; General Surgery for Nurses, 1976; Intestinal Obstruction, 1982; Notable Names in Medicine and Surgery, 1983; Famous Operations, 1984; Wound Healing for Surgeons, 1984; Maingot's Abdominal Operations, 1985; Research in Medicine, 1990; numerous articles on surgical topics in medical journals. *Recreation:* medical history. *Address:* 16 Bancroft Avenue, N2. *T:* 081–348 2720; Department of Anatomy, University of Cambridge, Cambridge CB2 3DY.

ELLIS, Herbert; *see* Ellis, W. H. B.

ELLIS, Humphry Francis, MBE 1945; MA; writer; *b* 1907; 2nd *s* of late Dr John Constable Ellis, Metheringham, Lincs and Alice Marion Raven; *m* 1933, Barbara Pauline Hasseldine; one *s* one *d*. *Educ:* Tonbridge Sch.; Magdalen Coll., Oxford (Demy). 1st cl. Hon. Mods, 1928; 1st cl. Lit. Hum., 1930. Asst Master, Marlborough Coll., 1930–31. Contributor to Punch, 1931–68; Editorial staff, 1933; Literary and Dep. Ed., 1949–53. Privilege Mem., RFU, 1952–. Served War of 1939–45 in RA (AA Command). *Publications:* So This is Science, 1932; The Papers of A. J. Wentworth, 1949; Why the Whistle Went (on the laws of Rugby Football), 1947; Co-Editor, The Royal Artillery Commemoration Book, 1950; Editor, Manual of Rugby Union Football, 1952; Twenty Five Years Hard, 1960; Mediatrics, 1961; A. J. Wentworth, BA (Retd), 1962; The World of A. J. Wentworth, 1964 (re-issued as A. J. Wentworth, BA, 1980); Swansong of A. J. Wentworth, 1982; A Bee in the Kitchen, 1983; contribs to The New Yorker. *Recreation:* fishing. *Address:* Hill Croft, Kingston St Mary, Taunton, Somerset TA2 8HT. *T:* Kingston St Mary (0823) 451264. *Clubs:* Garrick, MCC.

ELLIS, John; Steel Worker, British Steel plc, Scunthorpe, 1980–89; *b* Hexthorpe, Doncaster, 22 Oct. 1930; *s* of George and Hilda Ellis; *m* 1953, Rita Butters; two *s* two *d*. *Educ:* Rastrick Gram. Sch., Brighouse. Laboratory technician, Meteorological Office, 1947–63; Vice-Chm., Staff side, Air Min. Whitley Council, 1961–63; Member Relations Offr, Co-op. Retail Services, Bristol/Bath Region, 1971–74. Member: Easthampstead RDC, 1962–66; Bristol City Council, 1971–74; Humberside County Council, 1987–. Vice-Chm., Humberside Social Service Council, 1990–; Member: Scunthorpe HA, 1988–90 (Chm., Jt Consultative Cttee, 1990–); Nat. Rivers Authority (formerly Lincs Land Drainage Cttee), 1988– (Member: Anglian Regl Flood Defence cttee; Lincs Flood Defence cttee). Contested (Lab) Wokingham, 1964; MP (Lab) Bristol North-West, 1966–70, Brigg and Scunthorpe, Feb. 1974–1979; PPS to Minister of State for Transport, 1968–70; an Asst Govt Whip, 1974–76. JP, North Riding Yorks, 1960–61. *Recreations:* gardening, cricket. *Address:* 102 Glover Road, Scunthorpe, South Humberside.

ELLIS, John, CB 1985; independent technical consultant; Head of Royal Armament Research and Development Establishment, Chertsey, 1984–85, retired; *b* 9 Jan. 1925; *s* of Frank William and Alice Ellis; *m* 1958, Susan Doris (*née* Puttock). *Educ:* Leeds Univ. BSc, 1st cl. hons. Mech. Eng; CEng, MIMechE. Hydro-Ballistic Research Estabt, Admty, 1945–47; David Brown & Sons Ltd, Huddersfield, 1948; RAE, Min. of Supply (Structures Dept, Armament Dept, Weapons Dept), 1948–68; MVEE (formerly FVRDE), MoD, 1968–84; Dir, MVEE, Chertsey, 1978–84, when MVEE and RARDE amalgamated. *Recreations:* motoring, golf. *Address:* Foresters, 1 Kitchers Close, Sway, Lymington, Hants SO41 6DS. *T:* Lymington (0590) 682410.

ELLIS, John Norman; General Secretary, The Civil and Public Services Association, since 1987; *b* 22 Feb. 1939; *s* of Margaret and Albert Ellis; *m* 1st; one *s* one *d*; 2nd, Diane Anderson; two step *s*. *Educ:* Osmondthorpe; Leeds Secondary Modern; Leeds College of Commerce. Post Office Messenger and Postman, 1954–58; Clerical Officer and Executive Officer, MPBW, 1958–67; Asst Sec., CPSA, 1968–82, Dep. Gen. Sec., 1982–87. Member: Gen. Council, TUC (Mem. Economic, Social Services, Industrial Welfare and Public Services Cttees); Exec. Cttee, Public Services Internat.; Public Services Cttee, British Health Care Assoc.; Dir, CS Housing Assoc. *Recreations:* reading, badminton, watching sport, gardening, listening to music. *Address:* 26 Hareston Valley Road, Caterham, Surrey CR3 6HD.

ELLIS, Sir John (Rogers), Kt 1980; MBE 1943; MA, MD, FRCP; Physician, 1951–81, Consulting Physician, since 1981, The London Hospital; Chairman: Council of Governors, Institute of Education, University of London, since 1984; Graves Medical Audio-Visual Library; *b* 15 June 1916; 3rd *s* of late Frederick William Ellis, MD, FRCS; *m* 1942, Joan, *d* of late C. J. C. Davenport; two *s* two *d*. *Educ:* Oundle Sch.; Trinity Hall, Cambridge; London Hosp. Served RNVR, 1942–46, Mediterranean and Far East, Surg-Lieut. Gen. Practice, Plymouth, 1946; Sen. Lectr, Med. Unit, London Hosp., 1948–51; Sub-Dean, London Hosp. Med. Coll., 1948–58, Vice-Dean, 1967–68, Dean, 1968–81, Fellow, 1986; Asst Registrar, RCP, 1957–61, Mem. Council 1969–72, Streatfield Schol., 1957; Physician to Prince of Wales Gen. Hosp., 1958–68; PMO (part-time), Min. of Health, 1964–68. Mem., City and E London AHA, 1974–81; Vice-Chm., Newham DHA, 1981–85. Member: UGC's Med. Sub-cttee, 1959–69; WHO Expert Adv. Panel on Health Manpower, 1963–82; Jt Bd of Clinical Nursing Studies, 1969–74; formerly Member: Porritt (Med. Services) Cttee; Royal Commn on Med. Educn; UK Educn Cttee, RCN. Sec., Assoc. for Study of Med. Educn, 1956–71, Vice-Pres., 1971–; Court, Univ. of Essex; Pres., Medical Protection Soc., 1985–88. Lectures: Goulstonian, RCP, 1956; Wood-Jones, Univ. of Manchester, 1960; Porter, Univ. of Kansas, 1960; Sir Charles Hastings, BMA, 1964; Anders, Coll. of Physicians, Pa, 1965; Adams, RCSI, 1965; Shattuck, Massachusetts Med. Soc., 1969; Shorstein, 1979, 1985, Sprawson, 1980, 1985, London Hosp. Med. Coll.; Visiting Lecturer: Assoc. of Amer. Med. Colls, 1957, 1960 and 1963; Ghana Acad. of Sciences, 1967. Former examr in Med., Univs of Birmingham, Bristol, Cambridge, E Africa, London, Nairobi, Ireland, Newcastle upon Tyne, St Andrews. Corr. Mem., Royal Flemish Acad. of Medicine; Hon. Member: Swedish Med. Soc.; AOA Honor Med. Soc., USA; Sect. of Med. Educn, RSocMed (former Pres.). Member Bd of Governors, Atlantic Coll.; formerly Member Board of Governors: Inst. of Psychiatry; Bethlem Royal and Maudsley Hosps; London Hosp.; British Postgrad. Med. Fedn; Queen Mary Coll.; CARE for Mentally Handicapped. Formerly Mem. Court, Univ. of Essex. Editor, British Jl of Medical Education, 1966–75. Hon. Fellow: QMC, 1985; London Hosp. Med. Coll., 1986. Hon. MD Uppsala, 1977. *Publications:* LHMC 1785–1985, 1986; articles on medical education in medical and scientific journals. *Recreations:* painting, gardening. *Address:* Little Monkhams, Monkhams Lane, Woodford Green, Essex IG8 0NP. *T:* 081–504 2292.

ELLIS, Prof. John Romaine; *b* 30 Sept. 1922; *m* 1947, Madelaine Della Blaker; one *s* one *d*. *Educ:* Tiffin Sch., Kingston-on-Thames. Royal Aircraft Establishment, 1944–56; Fairey Aviation Company, 1946–48; Royal Military Coll. of Science, Shrivenham, near Swindon, Wilts, 1949–60; Prof. of Automobile Engrg, 1960–82, and Dir, 1960–76, Sch. of Automotive Studies, Cranfield. *Recreations:* golf, tennis, music. *Address:* Summercourt, Lower Road, Edington, Wilts BA13 4QN.

ELLIS, John Russell; General Manager, Southern Region, British Rail, since 1990; *b* 21 May 1938; *s* of Percy Macdonald Ellis and Winifred Maud (*née* Bunker); *m* 1962, Jean Eileen Taylor; two *d*. *Educ:* Rendcomb Coll., Cirencester; Pembroke Coll., Oxford (BA Hons PPE). Joined BR as Grad. Management Trainee, 1962; various posts, 1963–80; Chief Freight Manager, 1980–83, Divl Manager, 1983–84, Asst Gen. Manager, 1984–85, Eastern Region; Dep. Gen. Manager, Southern Region, 1985–87; Gen. Manager, ScotRail, 1987–90. *Recreations:* hockey, cricket, walking, gardening. *Address:* St Anne's, Chipping Campden, Glos GL55 6AL. *T:* (0386) 841253.

ELLIS, Dr Jonathan Richard, FRS 1985; Leader, Theoretical Studies Division, CERN, Geneva, since 1988; *b* 1 July 1946; *s* of Richard Ellis and Beryl Lilian Ellis (*née* Ranger); *m* 1985, Maria Mercedes Martinez Rengifo; one *s* one *d*. *Educ:* Highgate Sch.; King's Coll., Cambridge. BA; PhD. Postdoctoral research, SLAC, Stanford, 1971–72; Richard Chase Tolman Fellow, Caltech, 1972–73; Staff Mem., CERN, Geneva, 1973–. Maxwell Medal, Inst. of Physics, 1982. *Recreations:* movies, hiking in the mountains, horizontal jogging. *Address:* 5 Chemin du Ruisseau, Tannay, 1295 Mies, Vaud, Switzerland. *T:* (41) (22) 776-48-58.

ELLIS, Joseph Stanley, CMG 1967; OBE 1962; Head of News Department, Commonwealth Office, 1967; retired; *b* 29 Nov. 1907; *m* 1933, Gladys Harcombe (*d* 1983); one *s*. *Educ:* Woodhouse Grove, Bradford; University Coll., University of London. Journalist, Manchester Evening News, 1930–40; Publications Div., Min. of Inf., 1941–45; Seconded to Dominions Office for service in Australia until 1949. Central Office of Information, 1949–51; Regional Information Officer, Karachi, 1952; Dir, British Information Services: Pakistan, 1953–55; Canberra, Australia, 1955–58; Kuala Lumpur, Malaya, 1958–62; Head, Information Services Dept, Commonwealth Office, 1962–66. *Recreation:* cricket. *Address:* Ilford Court, Elmbridge, Cranleigh, Surrey GU6 8TJ.

ELLIS, June; *see* Ellis, D. J.

ELLIS, Laurence Edward, MA; Rector, The Edinburgh Academy, 1977–Aug. 1992; *b* 21 April 1932; *s* of Dr and Mrs E. A. Ellis; *m* 1961, Elizabeth Ogilvie; two *s* one *d*. *Educ:* Winchester Coll.; Trinity Coll., Cambridge (MA). AFIMA. 2/Lieut Rifle Bde, 1950–52. Marlborough Coll., 1955–77 (Housemaster, 1968). FRSA. *Publications:* (part-author) texts on school maths, statistics, computing, and calculating; articles in jls. *Recreations:* Lay

Reader; writing, music, woodwork. *Address:* 50 Inverleith Place, Edinburgh EH3 5QB. *T:* (office) 031–556 4603.

ELLIS, Mary; actress; singer; authoress; *b* New York City, 15 June 1900; *m* 1st, L. A. Bernheimer (decd); 2nd (marr. diss.); 3rd, Basil Sydney (marr. diss.); 4th, J. Muir Stewart Roberts (decd). *Educ:* New York. Studied art for three years; studied singing with Madame Ashforth. First Stage appearance, Metropolitan Opera House, New York, in Sœur Angelica, 1918; with Metropolitan Opera House, 1918–22; first appearance dramatic stage, as Nerissa in Merchant of Venice, Lyceum, New York, 1922; was the original Rose Marie (in the musical play, Rose Marie), Imperial, 1924; The Dybbuk, New York, 1925–26; Taming of the Shrew, 1927, and many New York leads followed; first appearance on London stage, as Laetitia in Knave and Quean, Ambassadors', 1930; after appearance in Strange Interlude in London, remained in London, giving up US citizenship in 1946; London: Strange Interlude, 1932; Double Harness, 1933; Music in the Air, 1934; Glamorous Night, Drury Lane, 1935; Innocent Party, St James's, 1937; 2 years, Hollywood, 1936–37; Dancing Years, Drury Lane, 1939. From 1939–43: doing hospital welfare work and giving concerts for troops. Re-appeared on stage as Marie Foret in Arc de Triomphe, Phœnix, London, 1943; Old Vic (at Liverpool Playhouse), 1944 (Ella Rentheim in John Gabriel Borkman; Linda Valaine in Point Valaine; Lady Teazle in The School for Scandal); Maria Fitzherbert in The Gay Pavilion, Piccadilly, 1945; Season at Embassy: Mrs Dane's Defence, also tour and première of Ian Hay's Hattie Stowe, 1946–47; post-war successes include: Playbill, Phœnix, 1949; Man in the Raincoat, Edinburgh, 1949; If this be Error, Hammersmith, 1950. Stratford-on-Avon Season, 1952: Volumnia in Coriolanus. London: After the Ball (Oscar Wilde-Noel Coward), Globe, 1954–55; Mourning Becomes Electra, Arts, 1955–56; Dark Halo, Arts, 1959; Look Homeward Angel, Pembroke Theatre, Croydon, 1960; Phœnix, 1962. First appeared in films, in Bella Donna, 1934; films, 1935–38; (Hollywood) Paris in the Spring; The King's Horses; Fatal Lady; Glamorous Night; Gulliver's Travels, 1961; Silver Cord (revival), Yvonne Arnaud, Guildford, 1971; Mrs Warren's Profession, Yvonne Arnaud, Guildford, 1972. Has made several major television appearances; Television plays, 1956–: Shaw's Great Catherine, Van Druten's Distaff Side and numerous others. Theatre lectures in USA, 1977. *Publications:* Those Dancing Years (autobiog.), 1982; Moments of Truth, 1986. *Recreations:* painting, travel, writing. *Address:* c/o Chase Manhattan Bank, Woolgate House, Coleman Street, EC2.

ELLIS, Maxwell (Philip), MD, MS, FRCS; retired; Dean of the Institute of Laryngology and Otology, University of London, 1965–71; Consulting Surgeon, Royal National Throat, Nose and Ear Hospital, 1937–71; Consulting Ear, Nose and Throat Surgeon, Central Middlesex Hospital, 1937–74; *b* 28 Feb. 1906; *s* of Louis Ellis; *m* 1st, 1935, Barbara Gertrude Chapman (*d* 1977); 2nd, 1979, Mrs Clarice Adler (*d* 1989). *Educ:* University Coll., London (Exhibitioner), Fellow 1975; University Coll. Hosp. (Bucknill Exhbnr). Liston and Alexander Bruce Gold Medals, Surgery and Pathology, UCH, 1927–29. MB, BS (London), Hons Medicine, 1930; MD 1931; FRCS 1932; MS 1937; Geoffrey Duveen Trav. Student, Univ. of London, 1934–36; Leslie Pearce Gould Trav. Schol., 1934, Perceval Alleyn Schol. (Surg. research), 1936, UCH; Hunterian Prof., RCS, 1938. RAFVR, 1940–45 (Wing-Comdr). FRSM, also Mem. Council; Past Pres., Section of Otology; Trustee, Hon. Fellow and Mem. Council, Med. Soc. London (Hon. Sec. 1961–63; Pres., 1970–71); Hon. Member: Assoc. of Otolaryngologists of India; Salonika Soc. of Otolaryngology; Athens Soc. of Otolaryngology; Corresp. Mem., Société Française d'Oto-Rhino-Laryngologie; Hon. Corresp. Mem., Argentine Soc. of Otolaryngology. Lectr on Diseases of Ear, Nose and Throat, Univ. of London, 1952. *Publications:* Modern Trends in Diseases of the Ear, Nose and Throat (Ed. and part author), 1954, 2nd edn 1971; Operative Surgery (Rob and Smith), Vol. 8 on Diseases of the Ear, Nose and Throat (Ed. and part author), 1958; 2nd edn 1969; Clinical Surgery (Rob and Smith), Vol. 11, Diseases of the Ear, Nose and Throat (Ed. and part author), 1966; Sections in Diseases of the Ear, Nose and Throat (Ed. Scott-Brown), 1952, new edns 1965, 1971; Sections in Cancer, Vol. 4 (Ed. Raven), 1958; Section in Modern Trends in Surgical Materials (Ed. Gillis), 1958; papers in various medical and scientific jls. *Recreations:* golf, gardening; formerly bridge and squash rackets. *Address:* 48 Townshend Road, NW8. *T:* 071–722 2252. *Clubs:* Royal Automobile; Sunningdale Golf.

ELLIS, Norman David; Under Secretary, British Medical Association, since 1980 (Senior Industrial Relations Officer, 1978–82); *b* 23 Nov. 1943; *s* of late George Edward Ellis and late Annie Elsie Scarfe; *m* 1966, Valerie Ann Fenn, PhD; one *s*. *Educ:* Minchenden Sch.; Univ. of Leeds (BA); MA (Oxon), PhD. Research Officer, Dept of Employment, 1969–71; Leverhulme Fellowship in Industrial Relations, Nuffield Coll., Oxford, 1971–74; Gen. Sec., Assoc. of First Division Civil Servants, 1974–78. *Publications:* (with W. E. J. McCarthy) Management by Agreement, 1973; Employing Staff, 1984; various contribs to industrial relations literature; contribs to BMJ. *Recreations:* reading, railways, swimming. *Address:* 33 Foxes Dale, SE3 9BH. *T:* 081–852 6244.

ELLIS, Osian Gwynn, CBE 1971; harpist; Professor of Harp, Royal Academy of Music, London, since 1959; *b* Ffynnongroew, Flints, 8 Feb. 1928; *s* of Rev. T. G. Ellis, Methodist Minister; *m* 1951, Rene Ellis Jones, Pwllheli; two *s*. *Educ:* Denbigh Grammar Sch.; Royal Academy of Music. Has broadcast and televised extensively. Has given recitals/concertos all over the world; shared poetry and music recitals with Dame Peggy Ashcroft, Paul Robeson, Burton, C. Day-Lewis, etc. Mem., Melos Ensemble; solo harpist with LSO. Former Mem., Music and Welsh Adv. Cttees, British Council. Works written for him include Harp Concertos by Hoddinott, 1957 and by Mathias, 1970, Jersild, 1972, Robin Holloway, 1985; chamber works by Gian Carlo Menotti, 1977; William Schuman, 1978; from 1960 worked with Benjamin Britten who wrote for him Harp Suite in C (Op. 83) and (for perf. with Sir Peter Pears) Canticle V, Birthday Hansel, and folk songs; accompanied the late Sir Peter Pears on recital tours, Europe and USA, 1974–; records concertos, recitals, folk songs, etc. Film, The Harp, won a Paris award; other awards include Grand Prix du Disque and French Radio Critics' Award. FRAM 1960. Hon. DMus Wales, 1970. *Publication:* Story of the Harp in Wales, 1991. *Address:* 90 Chandos Avenue, N20. *T:* 081–445 7896.

ELLIS, Raymond Joseph; *b* 17 Dec. 1923; *s* of Harold and Ellen Ellis; *m* 1946, Cynthia (*née* Lax); four *c*. *Educ:* elementary school; Sheffield Univ.; Ruskin Coll., Oxford. Coal miner, 1938–79. National Union of Mineworkers: Branch Secretary, Highmoor, 1959–79; Pres., Derbyshire Area, 1972–79. Councillor, South Yorkshire CC, 1976–79. MP (Lab) Derbyshire NE, 1979–87. *Address:* Oakdene, 3 The Villas, Mansfield Road, Wales Bar, Kiveton, Sheffield S31 8RL.

ELLIS, Prof. Reginald John, PhD; FRS 1983; Professor of Biological Sciences, University of Warwick, since 1976; *b* 12 Feb. 1935; *s* of Francis Gilbert Ellis and Evangeline Gratton Ellis; *m* 1963, Diana Margaret Warren; one *d*. *Educ:* Highbury County Sch.; King's Coll., London (BSc, PhD). ARC Fellow, Univ. of Oxford, 1961–64; Lectr in Botany and Biochemistry, Univ. of Aberdeen, 1964–70; Sen. Lectr, 1970–73, Reader, 1973–76, Dept of Biol Sciences, Univ. of Warwick; SERC Senior Res. Fellow, 1983–88. Mem. EMBO, 1986–. LRPS 1987. Tate & Lyle Award (for contribs to plant biochem.), 1980. *Publications:* 120 papers in biochem. jls. *Recreations:* photography, hill walking. *Address:* 44 Sunningdale Avenue, Kenilworth, Warwicks CV8 2BZ. *T:* Kenilworth (0926) 56382.

ELLIS, Richard Peter; Principal Assistant Treasury Solicitor, Legal Advisory Division, Ministry of Defence, since 1988; *b* 25 Oct. 1931; *s* of late Comdr Thomas Ellis, RN and Kathleen Mary Ellis (*nee* Lewis); *m* 1963, Penelope Jane, *yr d* of late Captain J. B. Hall, RN; two *s* two *d*. *Educ:* Sherborne; RMA Sandhurst. Commissioned Royal Irish Fusiliers, 1952; served 1st Bn, BAOR, Berlin, Korea, Kenya; resigned commission 1957. Called to the Bar, Lincoln's Inn, 1960; Practised Common Law Bar, 1960–65, Oxford Circuit; Treasury Solicitor's Dept, 1965–. *Recreations:* country pursuits, travel, reading. *Address:* c/o Lloyds Bank, 79 Brompton Road, SW3 1DD. *Club:* Army and Navy.

ELLIS, (Robert) Thomas; *b* 15 March 1924; *s* of Robert and Edith Ann Ellis; *m* 1949, Nona Harcourt Williams; three *s* one *d*. *Educ:* Universities of Wales and Nottingham. Works Chemist, ICI, 1944–47; Coal Miner, 1947–55; Mining Engineer, 1955–70; Manager, Bersham Colliery, N Wales, 1957–70. MP Wrexham, 1970–83 (Lab, 1970–81; SDP, 1981–83). Contested: Clywd South West (SDP) 1983, (SDP/Alliance) 1987; Pontypridd (SLD) Feb. 1989. Mem., European Parlt, 1975–79. *Publication:* Mines and Men, 1971. *Recreations:* golf, reading, music. *Address:* 3 Old Vicarage, Ruabon, Clwyd LL14 6LG. *T:* Wrexham (0978) 821128.

ELLIS, Ven. Robin Gareth; Archdeacon of Plymouth, since 1982; *b* 8 Dec. 1935; *s* of Walter and Morva Ellis; *m* 1964, Anne Ellis (*née* Landers); three *s*. *Educ:* Worksop Coll., Notts; Pembroke Coll., Oxford (BCL, MA). Curate of Swinton, 1960–63; Asst Chaplain, Worksop Coll., 1963–66; Vicar of Swaffham Prior and Reach, and Asst Director of Religious Education, Diocese of Ely, 1966–74; Vicar of St Augustine, Wisbech, 1974–82; Vicar of St Paul's, Yelverton, 1982–86. *Recreations:* cricket, theatre, prison reform. *Address:* 33 Leat Walk, Roborough, Plymouth, Devon PL6 7AT. *T:* Plymouth (0752) 793397.

ELLIS, Roger Henry, MA; FSA; FRHistS; Secretary, Royal Commission on Historical Manuscripts, 1957–72; *b* 9 June 1910; *e s* of late Francis Henry Ellis, Debdale Hall, Mansfield; *m* 1939, Audrey Honor, *o d* of late H. Arthur Baker, DL; two *d*. *Educ:* Sedbergh (scholar); King's College, Cambridge (scholar, Augustus Austen Leigh Student). 1st Cl. Class. Tripos, Pts I and II. Asst Keeper, Public Record Office, 1934; Principal Asst Keeper, 1956. Served War of 1939–45: Private, 1939; Major, 5th Fusiliers, 1944; Monuments, Fine Arts and Archives Officer in Italy and Germany, 1944–45. Lectr in Archive Admin, Sch. of Librarianship and Archives, University Coll. London, 1947–57. Mem. London Council, British Inst. in Florence, 1947–55; Hon. Editor, British Records Assoc., and (first) Editor of Archives, 1947–57, Chm. Council, 1967–73, Vice-Pres., 1971–. Vice-Pres., Business Archives Council, 1958–; Member: Adv. Council on Export of Works of Art, 1964–72; Jt Records Cttee of Royal Soc. and Historical MSS Commn, 1968–76; ICA Cttee on Sigillography, 1962–77; Pres., Soc. of Archivists, 1964–73. Chm., Drafting Cttee, British Standard 5454 (The Storage and Exhibition of Archival Documents), 1967–76. A Manager, 1973–76, a Vice-Pres., 1975–76, Royal Instn. Corresp. Mem., Indian Historical Records Commn. *Publications:* The Principles of Archive Repair, 1951; (ed) Manual of Archive Administration by Sir Hilary Jenkinson, 2nd edn 1965; Manuscripts and Men (Royal Commn on Hist. MSS centenary exhibn cat.), 1969; Catalogue of Seals in the Public Record Office: Personal Seals, vol. I, 1978, vol. II, 1981, Monastic Seals, vol. I, 1986; Ode on St Crispin's Day, 1979; (ed jtly) Select Writings of Sir Hilary Jenkinson, 1980; Walking Backwards, 1986; opuscula and articles in British and foreign jls and compilations on care, study and use of archives and MSS. *Recreations:* poetry, travel, the arts, gardening (unskilled). *Address:* Cloth Hill, 6 The Mount, Hampstead, NW3 6SZ. *Club:* Athenæum.

ELLIS, Roger Wykeham, CBE 1984; Graduate Recruitment Manager, Barclays Bank, 1986–91; *b* 3 Oct. 1929; *s* of Cecil Ellis, solicitor, and Pamela Unwin; *m* 1964, Margaret Jean Stevenson; one *s* two *d*. *Educ:* St Peter's Sch., Seaford; Winchester Coll.; Trinity Coll., Oxford (Schol., MA). Royal Navy, 1947–49. Asst Master, Harrow Sch., 1952–67, and Housemaster of the Head Master's House, 1961–67; Headmaster of Rossall Sch., 1967–72; Master of Marlborough College, 1972–86. Member: Harrow Borough Educn Cttee, 1956–60; Wilts County Educn Cttee, 1975–86. Governor: Campion Sch., Athens, 1981–; Cheam Sch., 1975– (Chm. of Govs, 1987–); Hawtreys Sch., 1975–86; Sandroyd Sch., 1982–86; Fettes Coll., 1983–; St Edward's Sch., Oxford, 1985–; Harrow Sch., 1987–. Chm., HMC, 1983. *Recreations:* golf, fishing. *Address:* 18 North Avenue, Ealing, W13 8AP. *Club:* East India.

ELLIS, Sir Ronald, Kt 1978; BSc Tech; FEng, FIMechE; FCIT; Chairman, EIDC Ltd, since 1981; *b* 12 Aug. 1925; *s* of William Ellis and Besse Brownbill; *m* 1st, 1956, Cherry Hazel Brown (*d* 1978); one *s* one *d*; 2nd, 1979, Myra Ann Royle. *Educ:* Preston Grammar Sch.; Manchester Univ. (BScTech Hons 1949). FIMechE 1949; FCIT 1975; FEng 1981. Gen. Man., BUT Ltd, 1954; Gen. Sales and Service Man., 1962, Gen. Man., 1966, Leyland Motors Ltd; Man. Dir, British Leyland Truck and Bus, 1968; Dir, British Leyland Motor Corp. Ltd, 1970. Head of Defence Sales, MoD, 1976–81. Chm., Bus Manufacturers Hldg Co., 1972–76. Dir of corp. develt, Wilkinson Sword Gp, 1981–82; Pres. and Man. Dir, Industrial Div., 1982–85, Dir, Internat. Gp, 1981–86, Allegheny International. Director: Yarrow & Co., 1981–86; Redman Heenan Internat., 1981–86; Bull Thompson Associates, 1987–89; IDRH Ltd, 1987–89; R. L. Holdings Ltd, 1989–. Vice-Pres., SMMT, 1972–73; Dir, ROFs, 1976–81. Mem., Engineering Council, 1988–. Governor, UMIST, 1970–, Vice-Pres., 1983–, Hon. Fellow, 1981. Pres., Manchester Technology Assoc., 1982. Liveryman, Engineers' Co., 1984–; Freeman, City of London, 1984. FRSA; CBIM 1984. *Recreations:* fishing, sailing. *Address:* West Fleet House, Abbotsbury, Dorset DT3 4SF. *Clubs:* Turf, Naval, City Livery, Royal Thames Yacht; Royal Naval Sailing Assoc.

ELLIS, Tom; *see* Ellis, R. T.

ELLIS, Vivian, CBE 1984; Lt-Comdr RNVR; composer, author; President, Performing Right Society, since 1983 (Deputy President, 1975–83); *s* of Harry Ellis and Maud Isaacson. *Educ:* Cheltenham Coll. (Musical Exhibition). Commenced his career as concert pianist after studying under Myra Hess; studied composition at the Royal Academy of Music; first song published when fifteen; his first work for the theatre was the composition of additional numbers for The Curate's Egg, 1922; contributed to The Little Revue and The Punch Bowl Revue, 1924; to Yoicks, Still Dancing, and Mercenary Mary, and composer of By the Way, 1925; to Just a Kiss, Kid Boots, Cochran's Revue, My Son John, Merely Molly and composer of Palladium Pleasures, 1926; to Blue Skies, The Girl Friend, and Clowns in Clover, 1927; to Charlot, 1928; and composer of Peg o' Mine, Will o' The Whispers, Vogues and Vanities, 1928; to A Yankee at the Court of King Arthur, The House that Jack Built, and (with Richard Myers) composer of Mister Cinders, 1929, new production, Fortune Theatre, 1983; part-composer of Cochran's 1930 Revue, and composer of Follow a Star and Little Tommy Tucker, 1930; part-composer of Stand Up and Sing, and Song of the Drum (with Herman Finck), and composer of Folly to be Wise, and Blue Roses, 1931; part-composer of Out of the Bottle, 1932; composer of Cochran's revue Streamline, 1934; Jill Darling, 1935; music and lyrics of Charlot Revue, The Town Talks, 1936; Hide and Seek, 1937; The Fleet's Lit Up, Running Riot, Under Your Hat, 1938; composer (to Sir A. P. Herbert's libretto) Cochran light operas: Big Ben, 1946;

Bless the Bride, 1947 (new prodn, Exeter, 1985; Sadler's Wells, 1987); Tough at the Top, 1949; Water Gipsies, 1955; music and lyrics of And So To Bed, 1951; music for The Sleeping Prince, 1953; music and lyrics of Listen to the Wind, 1954; Half in Earnest (musical adaptation of The Importance of Being Earnest), 1958; composer of popular songs, incl. Spread a Little Happiness, This is My Lovely Day, Ma Belle Marguerite, Other People's Babies and I'm on a See-Saw; many dance items; Coronation Scot; also music for the films Jack's the Boy, Water Gipsies, 1932; Falling for You, 1933; Public Nuisance No 1, 1935; Piccadilly Incident, 1946, etc. Ivor Novello Award for outstanding services to British music, 1973; Ivor Novello Award for Lifetime Achievement in British Music, 1983. Vivian Ellis Prize instituted by PRS in collab. with GSMD, to celebrate his 80th birthday. *Publications: novels:* Zelma; Faint Harmony; Day Out; Chicanery; *travel:* Ellis in Wonderland; *autobiography:* I'm on a See-Saw; *humour:* How to Make your Fortune on the Stock Exchange; How to Enjoy Your Operation; How to Bury Yourself in the Country; How to be a Man-about-Town; Good-Bye, Dollie; contrib: The Rise and Fall of the Matinée Idol; Top Hat and Tails: biography of Jack Buchanan; The Story and the Song; *for children:* Hilary's Tune; Hilary's Holidays; The Magic Baton; *song book:* Vivian Ellis: a composer's jubilee, 1982. *Recreations:* gardening, painting, operations. *Club:* Garrick.

ELLIS, Dr (William) Herbert (Baxter), AFC 1954; Medical Adviser, Department of Health and Social Security; Underwriting Member of Lloyd's; *b* 2 July 1921; *er s* of William Baxter Ellis and Georgina Isabella Ellis (*née* Waller); *m* 1st, 1948, Margaret Mary Limb (marr. diss.); one *s* one *d*; 2nd, 1977, Mollie Marguerite Clarke. *Educ:* Oundle Sch.; Durham Univ. (MD, BS). Royal Navy, 1945–59: Surg. Comdr, Fleet Air Arm Pilot. Motor industry, 1960–71; research into human aspects of road traffic accidents, 1960–71; Dir-Gen., Dr Barnardo's, 1971–73; dir of various companies. Industrial Medical Consultant: Wellworthy, 1979–87; Telephone Manufacturing Co., 1980–87; Plessey Co., 1981–87. Part-time Mem., Employment Medical Adv. Service, 1973–81. St John Ambulance: Chief Comdr, 1989–91; County Surgeon, 1979–87, Comdr, 1987–89, Glos Br. KStJ 1989 (CStJ 1988). Gilbert Blane Medal, RCP, 1954. *Publications:* Physiological and Psychological Aspects of Deck Landings, 1954; Hippocrates, RN—memoirs of a naval flying doctor (autobiog.), 1988; various on the human factor in industrial management. *Recreations:* walking, observing humanity, mending fences. *Address:* Little Dalling, Rocks Lane, High Hurstwood, East Sussex TN22 4BH. *T:* Uckfield (0825) 733139; 7 Honeywood House, Canford Cliffs, Poole, Dorset BH14 8LZ. *T:* Poole (0202) 700421. *Clubs:* Army and Navy, Naval and Military.

ELLIS-REES, Hugh Francis, CB 1986; Regional Director, West Midlands, Departments of the Environment and Transport, 1981–89; Member, Black Country Development Corporation, since 1990; *b* 5 March 1929; *s* of late Sir Hugh Ellis-Rees, KCMG, CB and Lady (Eileen Frances Anne) Ellis-Rees; *m* 1956, Elisabeth de Mestre Gray; three *s* one *d*. *Educ:* Ampleforth Coll.; Balliol Coll., Oxford. Served Grenadier Guards, 1948–49. Joined War Office, 1954; transf. to DoE, 1970; Cabinet Office, 1972–74; Under-Sec., DoE, 1974. Non-exec. Dir, Redland Aggregates Ltd, 1984–87. *Recreation:* squash.

ELLISON, Prof. Arthur James, DSc(Eng); CEng, FIMechE, FIEE; Professor of Electrical and Electronic Engineering, and Head of Department, The City University, London, 1972–85, now Professor Emeritus; *b* 15 Jan. 1920; *s* of late Lawrence Joseph and Elsie Beatrice Ellison, Birmingham; *m* 1st, 1952, Marjorie Cresswell (*d* 1955); 2nd, 1963, Marian Elizabeth Gumbrell; one *s* one *d*. *Educ:* Solihull Sch., Warwicks; Birmingham Central Tech. Coll. (now Univ. of Aston); Northampton Polytechnic (now City Univ.), as ext. student of Univ. of London BSc(Eng) (1st Cl. Hons); DSc(Eng). Sen. MIEEE. Design Engr, Higgs Motors, Birmingham, 1938–43; Tech. Asst, RAE, 1943–46; Graduate apprentice with British Thomson-Houston Co., Rugby, 1946, Design Engr, 1947–58; Lectr, Queen Mary Coll. (Univ. of London), 1958–65, Sen. Lectr, 1965–72. Visiting Prof., MIT, USA, 1959; lecture tour of Latin Amer. for Brit. Council, 1968; Hon. Prof., Nat. Univ. of Engrg, Lima, Peru, 1968; numerous overseas lectures and conf. contribs. Ext. Examiner to many UK and overseas univs and polytechnics; Founder and Chm., biennial Internat. Conf. on Elec. Machines, 1974–84 (Pres. of Honour). Consultant to industrial cos and nationalised industry on elec. machines, noise and vibration problems; Director: Landspeed, 1975–; Landspeed University Consultants, 1975–82; Landspeed International, 1975–83; Cotswold Research, 1983–; Building Health Consultants, 1989–. Pres., Soc. for Psychical Research, 1976–79, 1981–84; Chm., Theosophical Res. Centre, 1976–87. Member: Council, IEE, 1981–84; Bd, Eta Kappa Nu Assoc., USA, 1984–86 (Hon. Mem.); Trustee, Res. Council for Complementary Med., 1983–90. *Publications:* Electromechanical Energy Conversion, 1965, 2nd edn 1970; Generalized Electric Machines, 1967; Generalized Electric Machine Set Instruction Book (AEI), 1963, 2nd edn 1968; (jtly) Machinery Noise Measurement, 1985; The Reality of the Paranormal, 1988; ed, Proc. Queen Mary Coll. Conf., The Teaching of Electric Machinery Theory, 1961; jt ed, Proc. Queen Mary Coll. Conf., Design of Electric Machines by Computer, 1969; contribs to: Psychism and the Unconscious Mind, 1968; Intelligence Came First, 1975; numerous papers in engrg and sci. jls on elec. machines, noise and vibration, future guided land transport (IEE premium, 1964); also papers in Jl Soc. for Psych. Res. *Recreations:* reading, meditation, psychical research, travel. *Address:* 10 Foxgrove Avenue, Beckenham, Kent BR3 2BA. *T:* 081–650 3801; Department of Electrical Engineering, The City University, EC1V 0HB. *T:* 071–253 4399. *Club:* Athenæum.

ELLISON, Rt. Rev. and Rt. Hon. Gerald Alexander, KCVO 1981; PC 1973; *b* 19 Aug. 1910; *s* of late Preb. John Henry Joshua Ellison, CVO, Chaplain in Ordinary to the King, Rector of St Michael's, Cornhill, and of Sara Dorothy Graham Ellison (*née* Crum); *m* 1947, Jane Elizabeth, *d* of late Brig. John Houghton Gibbon, DSO; one *s* two *d*. *Educ:* St George's, Windsor; Westminster Sch.; New Coll., Oxford (Hon. Fellow, 1974); Westcott House, Cambridge. Curate, Sherborne Abbey, 1935–37; Domestic Chaplain to the Bishop of Winchester, 1937–39; Chaplain RNVR, 1940–43 (despatches); Domestic Chaplain to Archbishop of York, 1943–46; Vicar, St Mark's Portsea, 1946–50; Hon. Chaplain to Archbishop of York, 1946–50; Canon of Portsmouth, 1950; Examining Chaplain to Bishop of Portsmouth, 1949–50; Bishop Suffragan of Willesden, 1950–55; Bishop of Chester, 1955–73; Bishop of London, 1973–81; Vicar General of Diocese of Bermuda, 1983–84. Dean of the Chapels Royal, 1973–81; Prelate, Order of the British Empire, 1973–81; Prelate, Imperial Soc. of Knights Bachelor, 1973–85; Episcopal Canon of Jerusalem, 1973–81. Select Preacher: Oxford Univ., 1940, 1961, 1972; Cambridge Univ., 1957. Chaplain, Master Mariners' Company, 1946–73; Chaplain, Glass Sellers' Company, 1951–73; Chaplain and Sub-Prelate, Order of St John, 1973–. Hon. Chaplain, RNR. Mem. Wolfenden Cttee on Sport, 1960; Chairman: Bd of Governors, Westfield Coll., Univ. of London, 1953–67; Council of King's Coll., London, 1973–80 (FKC 1968; Vice-Chm. newly constituted Council, 1980–88); Governor, Sherborne Sch., 1982–85. Chm., Archbishop's Commn on Women and Holy Orders, 1963–66; Mem., Archbishop's Commn on Church and State, 1967; President: Actors' Church Union, 1973–81; Pedestrians Assoc. for Road Safety, 1964–75; Nat. Fedn of Housing Assocs, 1981–. Hon. Bencher Middle Temple, 1976. Freeman, Drapers' Co.; Hon. Liveryman: Merchant Taylors' Co.; Glass Sellers' Co.; Painter Stainers' Co.; Mem., Master Mariners' Co. Chm., Oxford Soc., 1973–85. A Steward of Henley Regatta. *Publications:* The Churchman's

Duty, 1957; The Anglican Communion, 1960. *Recreations:* oarsmanship, walking, music, watching television, tapestry, reading. *Address:* Billeys House, 16 Long Street, Cerne Abbas, Dorset. *T:* Cerne Abbas (0300) 341247. *Clubs:* Army and Navy; Leander.

ELLISON, Rt. Rev. John Alexander; *see* Paraguay, Bishop of.

ELLISON, His Honour John Harold, VRD 1948; a Circuit Judge, 1972–87; Chancellor of the Dioceses of Salisbury and Norwich, since 1955; *b* 20 March 1916; *s* of late Harold Thomas Ellison, MIMechE, and late Mrs Frances Amy Swithinbank, both of Woodspeen Grange, Newbury; *m* 1952, Margaret Dorothy Maud, *d* of late Maynard D. McFarlane, Sun City, Arizona; three *s* one *d*. *Educ:* Uppingham Sch.; King's Coll., Cambridge (MA). Res. Physicist, then Engr, Thos Firth & John Brown Ltd, Sheffield; Lieut, RE, TA (49th WR) Div., 1937–39; Officer in RNVR, 1939–51 (retd as Lt-Comdr): Gunnery Specialist, HMS Excellent, 1940; Sqdn Gunnery Officer, 8 Cruiser Sqdn, 1940–42; Naval Staff, Admty, 1942–44; Staff Officer (Ops) to Flag Officer, Western Mediterranean, 1944–45. Called to Bar, Lincoln's Inn, 1948; practised at Common Law Bar, 1948–71. Pres., SW London Br., Magistrates' Assoc., 1974–87. Former Governor, Forres Sch. Trust, Swanage. FRAS. *Publications:* (ed) titles Allotments and Smallholdings, and Courts, in Halsbury's Law of England, 3rd edn, and Allotments and Smallholdings, 4th edn. *Recreations:* organs and music, sailing, ski-ing, shooting. *Address:* Goose Green House, Egham, Surrey TW20 8PE. *Club:* Bar Yacht; Ski Club of GB, Kandahar Ski.

ELLISON, Sir Ralph Henry C.; *see* Carr-Ellison, Sir R. H.

ELLMAN, Louise Joyce; Leader, Lancashire County Council, since 1981 (Chairman, 1981–85; Leader, Labour Group, since 1977); *b* 14 Nov. 1945; *d* of late Harold and Annie Rosenberg; *m* 1967, Geoffrey David Ellman; one *s* one *d*. *Educ:* Manchester High Sch. for Girls; Hull Univ. (BA Hons); York Univ. (MPhil). Lectr, Salford Coll. of Technology, 1970–73; Counsellor, Open Univ., 1973–76. Member: Lancs CC, 1970–; W Lancs DC, 1974–87; Local Govt Adv. Cttee, Labour Party's NEC, 1977–; Regl Exec., NW Labour Party, 1985–. Contested (Lab) Darwen, 1979. Vice-Chm., Lancashire Enterprises Ltd, 1981–; Founder Mem., NW Co-op. Develt Agency, 1979–. Youngest mem., Lancs CC, 1970; youngest mem. and first woman to be Chm., 1981. *Recreations:* reading, travel. *Address:* 40 Elmers Green, Skelmersdale, Lancs. *T:* Skelmersdale (0695) 23669. *Club:* Upholland Labour (Skelmersdale).

ELLMAN-BROWN, Hon. Geoffrey, CMG 1959; OBE 1945; FCA 1950 (ACA 1934); *b* 20 Dec. 1910; *s* of John and Violet Ellman-Brown; *m* 1936, Hilda Rosamond Fairbrother; two *s* one *d*. *Educ:* Plumtree Sch., S Rhodesia. Articled to firm of Chartered Accountants in London, 1929–34; final Chartered Accountant exam. and admitted as Mem. Inst. of Chartered Accountants of England and Wales, 1934. In Rhodesia Air Force (rising to rank of Group Capt.), 1939–46. Resumed practice as Chartered Accountant, 1946–53. Entered S Rhodesia Parliament holding ministerial office (Portfolios of Roads, Irrigation, Local Government and Housing), 1953–58; re-entered Parliament, 1962, Minister of Finance; re-elected, 1962–65, in Opposition Party. Pres. Rhodesia Cricket Union, 1950–52; Mem. S African Cricket Board of Control, 1951–52. Chairman: The Zimbabwe Sugar Assoc.; Industrial Promotion Corp. Central Africa Ltd; Director: RAL Merchant Bank Ltd; Hippo Valley Estates Ltd; Freight Services Ltd. *Recreations:* cricket, golf, shooting, fishing. *Address:* 42 Steppes Road, Chisipite, Harare, Zimbabwe. *T:* 706381. *Clubs:* Harare, Royal Harare Golf (Harare, Zimbabwe); Ruwa Country.

ELLSWORTH, Robert; President, Robert Ellsworth & Co. Inc., since 1977; Deputy Secretary of Defense, USA, 1976–77; *b* 11 June 1926; *s* of Willoughby Fred Ellsworth and Lucile Rarig Ellsworth; *m* 1956, Vivian Esther Sies; one *s* one *d*. *Educ:* Univs of Kansas (BSME) and Michigan (JD). Active service, US Navy, 1944–46, 1950–53 (Lt-Comdr). Mem. United States Congress, 1961–67; Asst to President of US, 1969; Ambassador and Permanent Representative of US on N Atlantic Council, 1969–71; Asst Sec. of Defense (Internat. Security Affairs), 1974–75. Chm. Council, IISS, 1990– (Mem., 1973–). Licensed Lay Reader, Episcopal Dio. of Washington. Hon. LLD: Ottawa, 1969; Boston, 1970. *Recreations:* single sculling, swimming, music. *Address:* 24120 Old Hundred Road, Dickerson, Md 20842, USA. *Clubs:* Brook (New York); Army and Navy (Washington).

ELLWOOD, Air Marshal Sir Aubrey (Beauclerk), KCB 1949 (CB 1944); DSC; DL; *b* 3 July 1897; *s* of late Rev. C. E. Ellwood, Rector of Cottesmore, Rutland, 1888–1926; *m* 1920, Lesley Mary Joan Matthews (*d* 1982); one *s* one *d* (and one *s* decd). *Educ:* Cheam Sch.; Marlborough Coll. Joined Royal Naval Air Service, 1916; permanent commission RAF 1919. Served India 1919–23 and 1931–36 in RAF; RAF Staff Coll., Air Min., Army Co-operation Comd variously, 1938–42; AOC No. 18 Group RAF, 1943–44; Temp. Air Vice-Marshal, 1943; SASO HQ Coastal Comd RAF, 1944–45; Actg Air Marshal, 1947; a Dir-Gen. of Personnel, Air Ministry, 1945–47. Air Marshal, 1949; AOC-in-C, Bomber Command, 1947–50; AOC-in-C, Transport Command, 1950–52; retired, 1952. Governor and Commandant, The Church Lads' Brigade, 1954–70. DL Somerset, 1960. *Recreations:* riding, fishing, music. *Address:* The Old House, North Perrott, Crewkerne, Somerset. *T:* Crewkerne (0460) 73600. *Club:* Naval and Military.

ELMES, Dr Peter Cardwell; Director, Medical Research Council Pneumoconiosis Unit, Llandough Hospital, Penarth, 1976–81, retired from MRC 1982; Consultant in Occupational Lung Diseases, since 1976; *b* 12 Oct. 1921; *s* of Florence Romaine Elmes and Lilian Bryham (*née* Cardwell); *m* 1957, Margaret Elizabeth (*née* Staley); two *s* one *d*. *Educ:* Rugby; Oxford Univ. (BM, BCh 1945); Western Reserve Univ., Cleveland, Ohio (MD 1943). MRCP 1951. Mil. Service, RAMC, 1946–48. Trng posts, Taunton and Oxford, 1948–50; Registrar, then Sen. Registrar in Medicine, Hammersmith Hosp., 1950–58; Dept of Therapeutics, Queen's Univ., Belfast: Sen. Lectr, 1959–63; Reader, 1963–67; Prof. of Therapeutic Sciences, 1967–71; Whitla Prof. of Therapeutics and Pharmacology, 1971–76. Member: Medicines Commn, 1976–79; Industrial Injuries Adv. Council, 1982–87; Indep. Scientific Cttee on Smoking and Health, 1982–. *Publications:* contrib. med. jls on chronic chest disease, treatment and control of infection, occupational lung disease asbestosis, and mesothelioma. *Recreation:* working on house and garden. *Address:* Dawros House, St Andrews Road, Dinas Powys, South Glamorgan CF6 4HB. *T:* Dinas Powys (0222) 512102; *Fax:* Dinas Powys (0222) 515975.

ELMSLIE, Maj.-Gen. Alexander Frederic Joseph, CB 1959; CBE 1955; psc; CEng; FIMechE; FCIT; *b* 31 Oct. 1905; *er s* of Captain A. W. Elmslie, RAEC and Florence Edith Elmslie (*née* Kirk); *m* 1931, Winifred Allan Wright; one *d* one *s*. *Educ:* Farnham Grammar Sch.; RMC Sandhurst; Staff Coll., Camberley. Commissioned in Royal Army Service Corps, 29 Jan. 1925, and subsequently served in Shanghai, Ceylon, E Africa and Singapore; Lieutenant 1927; Captain 1935; served War of 1939–45 (despatches) in Madagascar, India (Combined Ops) and Europe (SHAEF); Major, 1942; Lt-Col 1948; Temp. Brig. 1943; Brig. 1953; Maj.-Gen. 1958. Dep. Dir of Supplies and Transport, War Office, 1953–55; Dir of Supplies and Transport, GHQ Far East Land Forces, 1956–57; Inspector, RASC, War Office, 1957–60, retired. Chairman Traffic Commissioners: NW Traffic Area, 1962–64; SE Traffic Area, 1965–75. Hon. Col 43 (Wessex) Inf. Div. Coln, RASC, TA, 1960–64; Col Comdt, RASC, 1964–65; Col Comdt, Royal Corps of Transport, 1965–69.

Fellow, Royal Commonwealth Soc. *Address:* 9 Stanmer House, Furness Road, Eastbourne, E Sussex.

ELPHIN, Bishop of, (RC), since 1971; **Most Rev. Dominic Joseph Conway;** *b* 1 Jan. 1918; *s* of Dominic Conway and Mary Hoare. *Educ:* Coll. of the Immaculate Conception, Sligo; Pontifical Irish Coll., Pontifical Lateran Univ., Pontifical Angelicum Univ., Gregorian Univ. (all in Rome); National Univ. of Ireland. BPh, STL, DEcclHist, Higher Diploma Educn. Missionary, Calabar Dio., Nigeria, 1943–48; Professor: All Hallows Coll., Dublin, 1948–49; Summerhill Coll., Sligo, 1949–51; Spiritual Dir, 1951–65, Rector, 1965–68, Irish Coll., Rome; Sec.-Gen., Superior Council of the Propagation of the Faith, Rome, 1968–70; Auxiliary Bishop of Elphin, 1970–71. *Address:* St Mary's, Sligo, Ireland. *T:* 62670.

ELPHINSTONE, family name of **Lord Elphinstone.**

ELPHINSTONE, 18th Lord *cr* 1509; **James Alexander Elphinstone;** Baron (UK) 1885; *b* 22 April 1953; *s* of Rev. Hon. Andrew Charles Victor Elphinstone (*d* 1975) (2nd *s* of 16th Lord) and of Hon. Mrs Andrew Elphinstone (*see* Jean Mary Woodroffe); *S* uncle, 1975; *m* 1978, Willa, 4th *d* of Major David Chetwode, Upper Slaughter, Cheltenham; three *s* one *d*. *Educ:* Eton Coll.; Royal Agricultural Coll., Cirencester. ARICS 1979. *Heir: s* Master of Elphinstone, *qv*. *Address:* Drumkilbo, Meigle, Blairgowrie, Perthshire. *T:* Meigle (08284) 216. *Club:* Turf.

ELPHINSTONE, Master of; Hon. Alexander Mountstuart Elphinstone; *b* 15 April 1980; *s* and *heir* of 18th Lord Elphinstone, *qv*.

ELPHINSTONE, Sir Douglas; *see* Elphinstone, Sir M. D. W.

ELPHINSTONE of Glack, Sir John, 11th Bt *cr* 1701, of Logie Elphinstone and Nova Scotia; Land Agent, retired; *b* 12 Aug. 1924; *s* of Thomas George Elphinston (*d* 1967), and of Gladys Mary Elphinston, *d* of late Ernest Charles Lambert Congdon; *S* uncle, 1970; *m* 1953, Margaret Doreen, *d* of Edric Tasker; four *s*. *Educ:* Eagle House, Sandhurst, Berks; Repton; Emmanuel College, Cambridge (BA). Lieut, Royal Marines, 1942–48. Chartered Surveyor; Land Agent with ICI plc, 1956–83. Past Pres., Cheshire Agricultural Valuers' Assoc.; Past Chm., Land Agency and Agric. Div., Lancs, Cheshire and IoM Branch, RICS; Mem., Lancs River Authority, 1970–74. *Recreations:* shooting, ornithology, cricket. *Heir: s* Alexander Elphinston [*b* 6 June 1955; *m* 1986, Ruth, *er d* of Rev. Robert Dunnett; one *s*]. *Address:* Pilgrims, Churchfields, Sandiway, Northwich, Cheshire CW8 2JS. *T:* Sandiway (0606) 883327.

ELPHINSTONE, Sir (Maurice) Douglas (Warburton), 5th Bt *cr* 1816; TD 1946; retired, 1973; *b* 13 April 1909; *s* of Rev. Canon Maurice Curteis Elphinstone (4th *s* of 3rd Bt) (*d* 1969), and Christiana Georgiana (*née* Almond); *S* cousin, 1975; *m* 1943, Helen Barbara, *d* of late George Ramsay Main; one *s* one *d*. *Educ:* Loretto School, Musselburgh; Jesus Coll., Cambridge (MA). FFA; FRSE. Actuary engaged in Life Assurance companies until 1956 (with the exception of the war); Member of Stock Exchange, London, 1957–74. War service with London Scottish and Sierra Leone Regt, RWAFF, mainly in W Africa and India. *Publications:* technical papers mainly in Trans Faculty of Actuaries and Jl Inst. of Actuaries. *Heir: s* John Howard Main Elphinstone, *b* 25 Feb. 1949. *Address:* 11 Scotby Green Steading, Scotby, Carlisle CA4 8EH. *T:* Scotby (0228) 513141.

ELRINGTON, Christopher Robin, FSA, FRHistS; Editor, Victoria History of the Counties of England, since 1977; *b* 20 Jan. 1930; *s* of Brig. Maxwell Elrington, DSO, OBE, and Beryl Joan (*née* Ommanney); *m* 1951, Jean Margaret (*née* Buchanan), RIBA; one *s* one *d*. *Educ:* Wellington Coll., Berks; University Coll., Oxford (MA); Bedford Coll., London (MA). FSA 1964; FRHistS 1969. Asst to Editor, Victoria County History, 1954; Editor for Glos, 1960; Dep. Editor, 1968. British Acad. Overseas Vis. Fellow, Folger Shakespeare Library, Washington DC, 1976. Mem., Adv. Bd for Redundant Churches, 1982–. Pres., Bristol and Glos Archaeol Soc., 1984–85. Hon. Gen. Editor, 1962–72, Pres., 1983–, Wilts Record Soc. *Publications:* Divers Letters of Roger de Martival, Bishop of Salisbury, 2 vols, 1963, 1972; Wiltshire Feet of Fines, Edward III, 1974; articles in Victoria County History and in learned jls. *Address:* 34 Lloyd Baker Street, WC1X 9AB. *T:* 071–837 4971.

EL SAWI, Amir; retired diplomat; Ambassador of the Democratic Republic of the Sudan to the Court of St James's, 1976–82; *b* 1921; *m* 1946, El Sura Mohamed Bella; three *s* six *d*. *Educ:* University Coll., Khartoum; Univ. of Bristol. Min. of Interior, 1944–49; Admin. Officer, Merowi Dist, Northern Province, 1950–51; Asst Dist Comr, Kosti Dist, Blue Nile Prov., 1951–53; Asst Sudan Agent, Cairo, 1953–55; Dist Comr, Gadaraf Dist, Kassala Prov., 1955–56; Asst Permanent Sec., Min. of Foreign Affairs, 1956–58, Min. of Interior, 1958–59; Dep. Governor, Northern Prov., 1959–60; Dep. Perm. Sec., Min. of Interior, 1960–64, Perm. Sec., 1964–70; Perm. Sec., Min. of Civil Service and Admin. Reform, 1971–73; Dep. Minister and Doyen of Sudan Civil Service, 1973–76. Member: Sudan Nat. Council for Refugees; Nat. Public Records Central Office; Nat. Commn for Relief and Rehabilitation. *Recreations:* swimming, tennis. *Address:* PO Box 718, Khartoum, Sudan.

ELSDEN, Sidney Reuben, BA, PhD (Cambridge); Professor of Biology, University of East Anglia, 1965–85; *b* 13 April 1915; *er s* of late Reuben Charles Elsden, Cambridge; *m* 1st, 1942, Frances Scott Wilson (*d* 1943); 2nd, 1948, Erica Barbara Scott, *er d* of late Grahame Scott Gardiner, Wisbech, Cambs; twin *s*. *Educ:* Cambridge and County High Sch. for Boys; Fitzwilliam House, Cambridge (Exhibn, Goldsmiths' Co.). Lecturer, Biochemistry, University of Edinburgh, 1937–42; Mem. Scientific Staff of ARC Unit for Animal Physiology, 1943–48; Sen. Lectr in Microbiology, 1948–59, West Riding Prof. of Microbiology, 1959–65, Sheffield Univ.; Hon. Dir, ARC Unit for Microbiology, Univ. of Sheffield, 1952–65; Dir, ARC Food Research Inst., 1965–77. Visiting Prof. of Microbiology, Univ. of Illinois, Urbana, Ill, USA, 1956. Pres., Soc. for General Microbiology, 1969–72, Hon. Mem. 1977. Hon. DSc Sheffield, 1985. *Publications:* contribs to scientific jls on metabolism of micro-organisms. *Recreations:* gardening, angling. *Address:* 26a The Street, Costessey, Norwich NR8 5DB.

ELSE, John, MBE 1946; TD 1946; Regional Chairman of Industrial Tribunals, Eastern Region, Bury St Edmunds, 1980–84; *b* 9 Aug. 1911; *s* of late Mr and Mrs A. G. Else; *m* 1937, Eileen Dobson; one *d*. *Educ:* Cowley Sch., St Helens; Liverpool Univ. (LLB 1930). Admitted as solicitor, 1932. Commnd TA, 1932; served War: UK and BEF, 1939–41 (despatches, 1940); Iraq, 1942; India, 1942–45 (ADS GHQ, 1944–45). Practised in St Helens, London and Birmingham, 1932–39; Partner, Beale & Co., London and Birmingham, 1946–61; Mem., Mental Health Review Tribunal, 1960–61; Chm., Traffic Comrs and Licensing Authority for Goods Vehicles, W Midlands Traffic Area, 1961–72; Indust. Tribunals Chm., Birmingham, 1972–76, Cambridge, 1976–80. *Recreations:* photography, gardening. *Address:* The Cottage, Long Lane, Fowlmere, Royston, Herts SG8 7TA. *T:* Fowlmere (0763) 208367.

ELSMORE, Sir Lloyd, Kt 1982; OBE 1977; JP; Mayor of Manukau City, since 1968; *b* 16 Jan. 1913; *s* of George and Minnie Elsmore; *m* 1935, Marie Kirk; two *s* two *d*. *Educ:* Greymouth High Sch. Commenced grocery business on own account, 1933; President: Grocers' Assoc., 1949, 1950, 1952, Life Member, 1954; NZ Grocers' Federation, 1955, Life Member, 1959. Mem., Auckland Harbour Bd, 1971–83. Local Body involvement, 1953–; Mayor of Ellerslie Borough Council, 1956–62. *Recreations:* boating, fishing, gardening. *Address:* 18 Sanctuary Point, Pakuranga, New Zealand. *T:* 567–025. *Club:* Rotary (Pakuranga).

ELSOM, Cecil Harry, CBE 1976; Consultant, EPR Partnership (formerly Elsom Pack & Roberts, Architects), since 1980 (Senior Partner, 1947–80); *b* 17 Jan. 1912; *s* of Julius Israelson and Leah Lazarus; name changed by deed poll to Elsom, 1930; *m* 1940, Gwyneth Mary Buxton Hopkin; two *s*. *Educ:* Upton Cross Elem. Sch.; West Ham Polytechnic; Northern Polytechnic Architectural School. FRIBA. Started practice by winning competition for town hall, Welwyn Garden City, 1933; partner in Lyons Israel & Elsom, 1936; won two more competitions, Town Hall, Consett, Co. Durham and Health Clinic in Bilston, Staffs. Served with Ordnance Corps, RE, 1940–46, ending war as Captain. Began new practice, as Sen. Partner, Elsom Pack & Roberts, 1947. Works include housing, schools and old people's homes for GLC, Lambeth BC and Westminster CC; office buildings and flats for Church Commissioners, Crown Estate Commissioners, BSC, LWT (Eternit Prize for offices, Victoria St, 1977); stores in Wolverhampton, Guildford and London for Army & Navy Stores; town centres in Slough, Chesterfield, Derby and Tamworth (three Civic Trust Awards, four Commendations). Adviser to DoE on Lyceum Club, Liverpool; Assessor for Civic Trust Awards, 1980. Pres., Nightingale House Old People's Home, 1973–. Liveryman, Clockmakers' Co., 1979. FSA 1979; FFOB 1969. *Recreations:* horology, model yacht racing. *Address:* 21 Douglas Street, SW1P 4PE. *T:* 071–834 4411. *Clubs:* Arts, Royal Automobile.

ELSON, Graham Peel; General Secretary, Liberal Democrats, since 1989; *b* 21 Aug. 1949; *s* of George Ernest Elson and Rhoda (*née* Atkinson); *m* 1975, Jane Rosamunde Isaac. *Educ:* Palmers Endowed Sch. for Boys, Grays, Essex; NE London Polytechnic (BA Business Studies). Brand Manager, Rank Hovis McDougall Foods, 1972–74; Gen. Manager, Wilkinson Sword Gp, 1974–85. Councillor and Leader, Oxfordshire CC, 1985–89. *Recreations:* boating, gardening, supporting West Ham United FC. *Address:* 4 Cowley Street, SW1P 3NB. *T:* 071–233 2093. *Club:* National Liberal.

ELSTEIN, David Keith; Director of Programmes, Thames Television PLC, since 1986; *b* 14 Nov. 1944; *s* of late Albert Elstein and Millie Cohen; *m* 1978, Jenny Conway; one *s*. *Educ:* Haberdashers' Aske's; Gonville and Caius Coll., Cambridge (BA, MA). BBC: The Money Programme, Panorama, Cause for Concern, People in Conflict, 1964–68; Thames Television: This Week, The Day Before Yesterday, The World At War, 1968–72; London Weekend Television: Weekend World, 1972; Thames Television, 1972–82: This Week (ed., 1974–78); Exec. Producer, Documentaries; founded Brook Prodns, 1982: Exec. Producer, A Week in Politics, 1982–86; Exec. Producer, Concealed Enemies, 1983; Man. Dir, Primetime Television, 1983–86. *Recreations:* theatre, cinema, bridge, politics, reading. *Address:* Thames Television, 306 Euston Road, NW1 3BB. *T:* 071–387 9494.

ELSTOB, Peter (Frederick Egerton); Vice-President: International PEN, since 1981 (Secretary-General, 1974–81); English PEN, since 1978; Managing Director: Archive Press Ltd, since 1964 (co-founder 1963); Yeast-Pac Co. Ltd, since 1970 (co-founder and Director, 1938–70); writer and entrepreneur; *b* London, 22 Dec. 1915; *e s* of Frederick Charles Elstob, chartered accountant, RFC, and Lillian Page, London; *m* 1st, 1937, Medora Leigh-Smith (marr. diss. 1953); three *s* one *d* (and one *d* decd); 2nd, 1953, Barbara Zacheisz; one *s* one *d*. *Educ:* private schs, London, Paris, Calcutta; state schs, NY and NJ; Univ. of Michigan, 1934–35. Reporter, salesman, tourist guide, 1931–36; volunteer, Spanish Civil War, 1936 (imprisoned and expelled); RTR, 1940–46 (despatches); with A. B. Eiloart: founded Yeast-pac Co. Ltd; bought Arts Theatre Club, London, 1941; founded Peter Arnold Studios (artists' and writers' colony, Mexico), 1951–52, and Archives Designs Ltd, 1954–62; Director: MEEC Prodns (Theatre), 1946–54; Peter Arnold Properties, 1947–61; City & Suffolk Property Ltd, 1962–70; ABC Expedns, 1957–61; Manager, Small World Trans-Atlantic Balloon Crossing, 1958–59. Chm., Dorking Divl Lab. Party, 1949–50. Bulgarian Commemorative Medal, 1982. *Publications:* (autobiog.) Spanish Prisoner, 1939; (with A. B. Eiloart) The Flight of the Small World, 1959; novels: Warriors for the Working Day, 1960; The Armed Rehearsal, 1964; Scoundrel, 1986; military history: Bastogne the Road Block, 1968; The Battle of the Reichswald, 1970; Hitler's Last Offensive, 1971; Condor Legion, 1973; (ed) The Survival of Literature, 1979; (ed series) PEN International Books; PEN Broadsheet, 1977–82. *Recreations:* playing the Stock Exchange, travelling. *Address:* Burley Lawn House, Burley Lawn, Ringwood, Hants BH24 4AR. *T:* Burley (04253) 3406. *Clubs:* Savage, Garrick, PEN, Society of Authors.

ELSTON, Christopher David; Senior Adviser (formerly Adviser) (Asia and Australasia), Bank of England, since 1983; *b* 1 Aug. 1938; *s* of Herbert Cecil Elston and Ada Louisa (*née* Paige); *m* 1964, Jennifer Isabel Rampling; one *s* two *d*. *Educ:* University Coll. Sch., Hampstead; King's Coll., Cambridge (BA Classics, 1960, MA 1980); Yale Univ. (MA Econs, 1967). Bank of England, 1960–; seconded to Bank for Internat. Settlements, Basle, Switzerland, 1969–71; Private Sec. to Governor of Bank of England, 1974–76; Asst to Chief Cashier, 1976–79; seconded to HM Diplomatic Service, as Counsellor (Financial), British Embassy, Tokyo, 1979–83. *Recreations:* serious music, photography, walking, cricket, squash. *Address:* c/o Bank of England, Threadneedle Street, EC2R 8AH. *T:* 071–601 4444.

ELTIS, Walter Alfred, DLitt; Director General, National Economic Development Office, since 1988 (Economic Director, 1986–88); *b* 23 May 1933; *s* of Rev. Martin Eltis and Mary (*née* Schnitzer); *m* 1959, Shelagh Mary, *d* of Rev. Preb. Douglas Owen; one *s* two *d*. *Educ:* Wycliffe Coll.; Emmanuel Coll., Cambridge (BA Econs 1956); Nuffield Coll., Oxford. MA Oxon 1960; DLitt Oxon 1990. Nat. Service, Navigator, RAF, 1951–53. Res. Fellow, Exeter Coll., Oxford, 1958–60; Lectr in Econs, Exeter and Keble Colls, Oxford, 1960–63; Fellow and Tutor in Econs, Exeter Coll., Oxford, 1963–88, Emeritus Fellow, 1988. Vis. Reader in Econs, Univ. of WA, 1970; Visiting Professor: Univ. of Toronto, 1976–77; European Univ., Florence, 1979. Econ. Consultant, NEDO, 1963–66. Mem. Council, 1987–, Chm., Social Scis Cttee, 1987–88, CNAA. Gov., Wycliffe Coll., 1972–88. Gen. Ed., Oxford Economic Papers, 1975–81. *Publications:* Economic Growth: analysis and policy, 1966; Growth and Distribution, 1973; (with R. Bacon) The Age of US and UK Machinery, 1974; (with R. Bacon) Britain's Economic Problem: too few producers, 1976, 2nd edn 1978; The Classical theory of Economic Growth, 1984; (with P. Sinclair) Keynes and Economic Policy, 1988; contribs to econ. jls. *Recreations:* chess, music. *Address:* Danesway, Jarn Way, Boars Hill, Oxford OX1 5JF. *T:* Oxford (0865) 735440. *Clubs:* Reform, Royal Automobile.

ELTON, family name of **Baron Elton.**

ELTON, 2nd Baron *cr* 1934, of Headington; **Rodney Elton,** TD 1970; Deputy Chairman, Andry Montgomery Ltd, since 1987; *b* 2 March 1930; *s* of 1st Baron Elton and of Dedi (*d* 1977), *d* of Gustav Hartmann, Oslo; *S* father, 1973; *m* 1958, Anne Frances (divorced,

1979), *e d* of late Brig. R. A. G. Tilney, CBE, DSO, TD; one *s* three *d*; *m* 1979, S. Richenda Gurney, *y d* of late Sir Hugh Gurney, KCMG, MVO, and Lady Gurney. *Educ:* Eton; New Coll., Oxford (MA). Farming, 1954–74. Assistant Master, Loughborough Grammar Sch., 1962–67; Assistant Master, Fairham Comprehensive School for Boys, Nottingham, 1967–69; Lectr, Bishop Lonsdale College of Education, 1969–72. Contested (C) Leics, Loughborough, 1966, 1970. Cons. Whip, House of Lords, Feb. 1974–76, an Opposition spokesman, 1976–79; Parly Under Sec. of State, NI Office, 1979–81, DHSS, 1981–82, Home Office, 1982–84; Minister of State: Home Office, 1984–85; DoE, 1985–86. Chm., FIMBRA, 1987–90; Mem., Panel on Takeovers and Mergers, 1987–90. Formerly Director: Overseas Exhibition Services Ltd; Building Trades Exhibition Ltd. Dep Chm., Assoc. of Cons. Peers, 1986–. Dep. Sec., Cttee on Internat. Affairs, Synod of C of E, 1976–78. Mem. Boyd Commn to evaluate elections in Rhodesia, 1979; Chm., Cttee of Enquiry into discipline in schools, 1988. Chm., Intermediate Treatment Fund, 1990–; Vice-Pres., Inst. of Trading Standards Administrators, 1990–; Member of Council: City and Guilds of London, 1987–91; Rainer Foundn, 1990–; Pres., Building Conservation Trust, 1990–; Trustee: City Parochial Foundn, 1990–; Trust for London, 1990–. Late Captain, Queen's Own Warwickshire and Worcs Yeo.; late Major, Leics and Derbys (PAO) Yeo. Lord of the Manor of Adderbury, Oxon. *Heir: s* Hon. Edward Paget Elton, *b* 28 May 1966. *Address:* House of Lords, SW1A 0PW. *Clubs:* Pratt's, Beefsteak, Cavalry and Guards.

ELTON, Sir Arnold, Kt 1987; CBE 1982; MS; FRCS; Consultant Surgeon: Northwick Park Hospital and Clinical Research Centre, since 1970; British Airways, since 1981; *b* 14 Feb. 1920; *s* of late Max Elton and of Ada Elton; *m* 1952, Billie Pamela Briggs; one *s*. *Educ:* University Coll. London (exhibnr; MB BS 1943); UCH Med. Sch. (MS 1951); Jun. and Sen. Gold Medal in Surgery. LRCP 1943; MRCS 1943, FRCS 1946. House Surg., House Physician and Casualty Officer, UCH, 1943–45; Sen. Surgical Registrar, Charing Cross Hosp., 1947–51 (Gosse Res. Schol.); Consultant Surgeon: Harrow Hosp., 1951–70; Mount Vernon Hosp., 1960–70. First Chm., Med. Staff Cttee, Chm., Surgical Div. and Theatre Cttee, Mem., Ethical Cttee, Northwick Park Hosp. Mem., Govt Wkg Party on Breast Screening for Cancer, 1985–. Examiner: GNC; RCS, 1971–83; Surgical Tutor, RCS, 1970–82. Nat. Chm., Cons. Med. Soc., 1975–; Mem., Cons. Central Council and Nat. Exec. Cttee, 1976–. Founder Mem., British Assoc. of Surgical Oncology; Mem. Ct of Patrons, RCS, 1986–. Fellow: Assoc. of Surgeons of GB; Hunterian Soc.; FRSocMed; FICS; Associate Fellow, British Assoc. of Urological Surgeons. Liveryman: Apothecaries' Soc.; Carmen's Co. Jubilee Medal, 1977. *Publications:* contribs to med. jls. *Recreations:* tennis, music. *Address:* 58 Stockleigh Hall, Prince Albert Road, NW8; The Consulting Rooms, Wellington Hospital, Wellington Place, NW8 9LR. *T:* 071-935 4101. *Clubs:* Carlton, Royal Automobile, MCC.

ELTON, Benjamin Charles; author and performer; *b* 3 May 1959; *s* of Prof. Lewis Richard Benjamin Elton, *qv*. *Educ:* Godalming Grammar Sch.; S Warwicks Coll. of Further Educn; Manchester Univ. (BA Drama). First professional appearance, Comic Strip Club, 1981; writer for television: Happy Families; Filthy Rich and Catflap; jointly: The Young Ones; Blackadder II, 1987; Blackadder the Third, 1988; Blackadder goes Forth, 1989; writer and performer: Friday Live, Saturday Live; The Man from Auntie; writer and director: Gasping, Theatre Royal, Haymarket, 1990; Silly Cow, Theatre Royal, Haymarket, 1991; numerous tours as a stand-up comic. *Publications: novels:* Stark, 1989; Gridlock, 1991; *plays:* Gasping, 1990; Silly Cow, 1991. *Recreations:* walking, reading, socialising. *Address:* c/o Phil McIntyre, 15 Riversway, Navigation Way, Preston, Lancs PR2 2YP. *Clubs:* Groucho, Globe.

ELTON, Sir Charles (Abraham Grierson), 11th Bt *cr* 1717; *b* 23 May 1953; *s* of Sir Arthur Hallam Rice Elton, 10th Bt, and of Lady Elton; *S* father, 1973; *m* 1990, Lucy Lauris, *d* of late Lukas Heller. *Address:* Clevedon Court, Somerset BS21 6QU.

ELTON, Prof. Sir Geoffrey (Rudolph), Kt 1986; LittD; PhD; FBA 1967; Regius Professor of Modern History, Cambridge, 1983–88; Fellow of Clare College, Cambridge, since 1954; *b* 17 Aug. 1921; changed name to Elton under Army Council Instruction, 1944; *er s* of late Prof. Victor Ehrenberg, PhD; *m* 1952, Sheila Lambert; no *c*. *Educ:* Prague; Rydal Sch. London External BA (1st Cl. Hons) 1943; Derby Student, University Coll. London, 1946–48; PhD 1949; LittD Cantab 1960. Asst Master, Rydal Sch., 1940–43. Service in E Surrey Regt and Int. Corps (Sgt), 1944–46. Asst in History, Glasgow Univ., 1948–49; Univ. Asst Lectr, Cambridge, 1949–53, Lectr, 1953–63, Reader in Tudor Studies, 1963–67, Prof. of English Constitutional History, 1967–83. Visiting Amundson Prof., Univ. of Pittsburgh, Sept.-Dec. 1963; Vis. Hill Prof., Univ. of Minnesota, 1976. Lectures: Ford's, Oxford, 1972; Wiles, Belfast, 1972; Hagey, Waterloo, 1974; Tanner, Utah, 1987. Publications Sec., British Acad., 1981–90. Member: Adv. Council on Public Records, 1977–85; Library and Inf. Services Council, 1986–88. FRHistS 1954 (Pres., 1972–76); Founder and Pres., List & Index Soc., 1965–; President: Selden Soc., 1983–85; Ecclesiastical Hist. Soc., 1983–84. Fellow, UCL, 1978. Hon. DLitt: Glasgow, 1979; Newcastle, 1981; Bristol, 1981; London, 1985; Göttingen, 1987. For. Mem., Amer. Acad. Arts and Scis, 1975; Hon. Mem., American Historical Assoc., 1982. *Publications:* The Tudor Revolution in Government, 1953; England under the Tudors, 1955; (ed) New Cambridge Modern History, vol. 2, 1958, new edn 1975; Star Chamber Stories, 1958; The Tudor Constitution, 1960; Henry VIII: an essay in revision, 1962; Renaissance and Reformation (Ideas and Institutions in Western Civilization), 1963; Reformation Europe, 1963; The Practice of History, 1967; The Future of the Past, 1968; The Sources of History: England 1200–1640, 1969; Political History: Principles and Practice, 1970; Modern Historians on British History 1485–1945: a critical bibliography 1945–1969, 1970; Policy and Police: the enforcement of the Reformation in the age of Thomas Cromwell, 1972; Reform and Renewal, 1973; Studies in Tudor and Stuart Politics and Government: papers and reviews, 1946–1972, 2 vols, 1974, vol. 3, 1973–1981, 1983; Reform and Reformation: England 1509–1558, 1977; The History of England (inaug. lecture), 1984; (with R. W. Fogel) Which Road to the Past?, 1984; F. W. Maitland, 1985; The Parliament of England 1559–1581, 1986; contribs to English Hist. Review, Econ. Hist. Rev., History, Hist. Jl, Times Lit. Supplement, Listener, NY Review of Books, etc; recipient of five festschriften. *Recreations:* squash rackets (now forbidden), joinery, gardening, beer. *Address:* Clare College, Cambridge CB2 1TL; Faculty of History, West Road, Cambridge CB3 9EF. *T:* Cambridge (0223) 335326.

See also L. R. B. Elton.

ELTON, George Alfred Hugh, CB 1983; biochemist; Chief Scientist (Fisheries and Food), Ministry of Agriculture, Fisheries and Food, 1981–85; *b* 27 Feb. 1925; *s* of Horace and Violet Elton; *m* 1951, Theodora Rose Edith Kingham; two *d*. *Educ:* Sutton County Sch.; London Univ. (evening student). BSc 1944, PhD 1948, DSc 1956; CChem 1974, FRSC (FRIC 1951); FIFST 1968; FIBiol 1976; CBiol 1984. Mem. Faculty of Science, and Univ. Examnr in Chemistry, Univ. of London, 1951–58; Dir, Fog Res. Unit, Min. of Supply, 1954–58; Reader in Applied Phys. Chemistry, Battersea Polytechnic, 1956–58; Dir, British Baking Industries Res. Assoc., 1958–66; Dir, Flour Milling and Baking Res. Assoc., 1967–70; Ministry of Agriculture, Fisheries and Food: Chief Sci. Adviser (Food), 1971–85; Head of Food Science Div., 1972–73; Dep. Chief Scientist, 1972; Under-Sec. 1974. Vis. Prof., Surrey Univ., 1982–. Chairman: National Food Survey Cttee, 1978–85; Adv. Bd, Inst. of Food Res. (Bristol), 1985–88; Scientific Advr, BFMIRA, 1986–; Scientific Governor: British Nutrition Foundn, 1971–; Internat. Life Scis Inst. (Europe), 1987–; Vice-Chm., EEC Scientific Cttee for Food, 1987–; Member: Cttee on Medical Aspects of Food Policy, 1971–85; UK Delegn, Tripartite Meetings on Food and Drugs, 1971–85; AFRC (formerly ARC), 1981–85; NERC, 1981–85; Fisheries Res. and Develt Bd, 1982–85; Adv. Bd for Research Councils, 1981–84; Council: Chemical Soc., 1972–75; BIBRA, 1990–. Co-inventor, Chorleywood Bread Process (Queen's Award to Industry 1966); Silver Medallist, Royal Soc. of Arts, 1969. Hon. DSc Reading, 1984; DUniv Surrey, 1991. *Publications:* research papers in jls of various learned societies. *Recreation:* golf. *Address:* Green Nook, Bridle Lane, Loudwater, Rickmansworth, Herts WD3 4JH. *Clubs:* Savage, MCC.

ELTON, John; *see* Elton, P. J.

ELTON, Air Vice-Marshal John Goodenough, CB 1955; CBE 1945; DFC 1940; AFC 1935; *b* 5 May 1905; *s* of late Rev. George G. Elton, MA Oxon; *m* 1st, 1927, Helen Whitfield (marr. diss.); one *s*; 2nd, 1949, Francesca Cavallero. *Educ:* St John's, Leatherhead. Entered RAF, 1926; service in UK, 1926–31; Singapore, 1932–35 (AFC); Irak, 1939. Served War of 1939–45 (despatches twice, DFC, CBE); CO 47 Sqdn, Sudan, 1940; HQ, ME, Cairo, 1941; comd in succession Nos 242, 238 and 248 Wings, N Africa, 1942; CO RAF Turnberry, Scotland, 1943; CO RAF Silloth, Cumberland, 1944; AOA, HQ Mediterranean Allied Coastal Air Force, 1945–46; idc 1947; Dep. Dir, Air Min., 1948; RAF Mem., UK Delegn, Western Union Military Cttee, 1949–50; Comdt, Sch. of Tech. Training, Halton, 1951; Air Attaché, Paris, 1952; Air Officer i/c Administration, HQ Bomber Comd, 1953–56; Chief of Staff to the Head of British Jt Services Mission, Washington, DC, 1956–59; retired, 1959. *Address:* 64 Lexham Gardens, W8. *Club:* Royal Air Force.

ELTON, Prof. Lewis Richard Benjamin, MA, DSc; CPhys; FInstP, FIMA, FSRHE; University Professor of Higher Education, University of Surrey, 1987–90, now Emeritus; Higher Education Adviser to Training, Enterprise and Education Directorate, Department of Employment (formerly to Training Agency), since 1989; *b* 25 March 1923; *yr s* of late Prof. Victor Leopold Ehrenberg, PhD, and Eva Dorothea (*née* Sommer); *m* 1950, Mary, *d* of late Harold William Foster and Kathleen (*née* Meakin); three *s* one *d*. *Educ:* Stepanska Gymnasium, Prague; Rydal Sch., Colwyn Bay; Christ's Coll., Cambridge (Exhibr); Univ. Correspondence Coll., Cambridge, and Regent Street Polytechnic; University Coll. London (Univ. Research Studentship). BA 1945, Certif.Ed 1945, MA 1948, Cantab; BSc (External) 1st Cl. Hons Maths 1947, PhD 1950, London. Asst Master, St Bees Sch., 1944–46; Asst Lectr, then Lectr, King's Coll., London, 1950–57; Head of Physics Dept, Battersea Coll. of Technology, 1958–66; University of Surrey: Prof. of Physics, 1964–71; Head of Physics Dept, 1966–69; Prof. of Sci. Educn, 1971–86; Hd, Inst. of Educnl Develt (formerly Educnl Technol.), 1967–84; Associate Head, Dept of Educnl Studies, 1983–86. Research Associate: MIT, 1955–56; Stanford Univ., 1956; Niels Bohr Inst., Copenhagen, 1962; Vis. Professor: Univ. of Washington, Seattle, 1965; UCL, 1970–77; Univ. of Sydney, 1971; Univ. of Sao Paulo, 1975; Univ. of Science, Malaysia, 1978, 1979; Univ. of Malaya, 1982, 1983; Asian Inst. of Technology, 1985, 1986; Fundaçao Armando Alvares Penteado, São Paulo, 1985–89. Member: Governing Body, Battersea Coll. of Technology, 1962–66; Council, Univ. of Surrey, 1966–67, 1981–83; Council for Educational Technology of UK, 1975–81; Army Educn Adv. Bd, 1976–80; Convener, Standing Conf. of Physics Profs, 1971–74; Chairman: Governing Council, Soc. for Research into Higher Educn, 1976–78. Vice-Pres., Assoc. for Educnl and Trng Technology, 1976–. Fellow, Amer. Physical Soc., 1978. *Publications:* Introductory Nuclear Theory, 1959, 2nd edn 1965 (Spanish edn 1964); Nuclear Sizes, 1961 (Russian edn 1962); Concepts in Classical Mechanics, 1971; (with H. Messel) Time and Man, 1978; Teaching in Higher Education: appraisal and training, 1987 (Japanese edn 1989); contribs to sci. jls on nuclear physics, higher education, science educn and educnl technology. *Recreation:* words. *Address:* 3 Great Quarry, Guildford, Surrey GU1 3XN. *T:* Guildford (0483) 576548.

See also B. C. Elton, Sir G. R. Elton.

ELTON, Michael Anthony; Director General, National Association of Pension Funds, since 1987; *b* 20 May 1932; *s* of late Francis Herbert Norris Elton and of Margaret Helen Elton (*née* Gray); *m* 1955, Isabel Clare, *d* of late Thomas Gurney Ryott and of Clare Isabel Ryott; two *s* two *d*. *Educ:* Peter Symonds Sch.; Brasenose Coll., Oxford (Class. Mods 1952, BA 1st cl. Jurisp. 1954; MA, BCL 1955). Articled to Sir Andrew Wheatley, Clerk of Hants County Council, 1954; solicitor; Cumberland CC, 1958–61; Surrey CC, 1961–65; Asst Clerk, Bucks CC, 1965–70, Dep. Clerk of the Peace, 1967–70; Chief Exec., Assoc. of British Travel Agents, 1970–86; Dir Gen., European Fedn for Retirement Provision, 1987–91. CBIM. *Publications:* (with Gyles Brandreth) Future Perfect: how to profit from your pension planning, 1988; Travelling to Retirement: plus ça change, plus c'est la même chose, 1989; articles in professional jls. *Recreations:* tennis (geriatric mixed doubles), squash (former County player for Hants and Cumberland), music (choral singing, opera and lieder), bridge (friendly), gardening (esp. ponds). *Address:* 80 Old Kennels Lane, Oliver's Battery, Winchester, Hants SO22 4JT. *T:* Winchester (0962) 868470. *Club:* United Oxford & Cambridge University.

ELTON, (Peter) John, MC 1944: Director, British Alcan Aluminium (formerly Alcan Aluminium (UK) Ltd), since 1962; *b* 14 March 1924; 2nd *s* of Sydney George Elton; *m* 1948, Patricia Ann Stephens; two *d*. *Educ:* Eastbourne Coll.; Clare Coll., Cambridge. Indian Army: 14th Punjab Regt, 1942–45 (twice wounded). Hons Degree, Econs and Law, Cambridge. Man. Dir, Alcan Aluminium (UK) Ltd, 1967–74, Exec. Chm. 1974–76, non-Exec. Chm., 1976–78; Chm., Alcan Booth Industries Ltd, 1968–76; Director: Alcan Aluminium Ltd, 1972–77; Hill Samuel Group, 1976–87; Consolidated Goldfields, 1977–88; Spillers, 1978–80; TVS Entertainment, 1988–90. *Recreations:* sailing, shooting. *Address:* Salternshill Farm, Buckler's Hard, Beaulieu, Hants SO42 7XE. *T:* Buckler's Hard (0590) 616206. *Clubs:* Bucks; Royal Yacht Squadron (Cowes).

ELVEDEN, Viscount; Arthur Edward Rory Guinness; *b* 10 Aug. 1969; *s* and *heir* of Earl of Iveagh, *qv*.

ELVIN, Herbert Lionel; Emeritus Professor of Education; Director of the University of London Institute of Education, 1958–73 (Professor of Education in Tropical Areas, 1956–58); Director, Department of Education, UNESCO, Paris, 1950–56; *b* 7 Aug. 1905; *e s* of late Herbert Henry Elvin; *m* 1934, Mona Bedortha, *d* of Dr C. S. S. Dutton, San Francisco; one *s*. *Educ:* elementary schs; Southend High Sch.; Trinity Hall, Cambridge (1st Class Hons, History and English; Hon. Fellow, 1980). Commonwealth Fellow, Yale Univ., USA, Fellow of Trinity Hall, Cambridge, 1930–44; Temporary Civil Servant (Air Min., 1940–42, MOI, 1943–45); Principal, Ruskin Coll., Oxford, 1944–50. Parliamentary candidate (Lab), Cambridge Univ., 1935; Formerly: Pres., English New Education Fellowship; Pres., Council for Education in World Citizenship; Chm., Commonwealth Educn Liaison Cttee. Member: Cttee on Higher Education; Govt of India Educn Commn; University Grants Cttee, 1946–50; Central Advisory Council for Education (England) and Secondary School Examinations Council. *Publications:* Men of

America (Pelican Books), 1941; An Introduction to the Study of Literature (Poetry), 1949; Education and Contemporary Society, 1965; The Place of Commonsense in Educational Thought, 1977; (ed) The Educational Systems in the European Community, 1981; Encounters with Education, 1987. *Recreations:* formerly most games indifferently, athletics (half-mile, Cambridge *v* Oxford, 1927). *Address:* 4 Bulstrode Gardens, Cambridge CB3 0EN. *T:* Cambridge (0223) 358309.

ELVIN, Violetta, (Violetta Prokhorova), (Signora Fernando Savarese); ballerina; a prima ballerina of Sadler's Wells Ballet, Royal Opera House, London (now The Royal Ballet), 1951–56; Director, Ballet Company, San Carlo Opera, Naples, 1985–87; *b* Moscow, 3 Nov. 1925; *d* of Vassilie Prokhorov, engineer, and Irena Grimouzinskaya, former actress; *m* 1st, 1944, Harold Elvin (divorced 1952), of British Embassy, Moscow; 2nd, 1953, Siegbert J. Weinberger, New York; 3rd, 1959, Fernando Savarese, lawyer; one *s. Educ:* Bolshoi Theatre Sch., Moscow. Trained for ballet since age of 8 by: E. P. Gerdt, A. Vaganova, M. A. Kojuchova. Grad, 1942, as soloist; made mem. Bolshoi Theatre Ballet; evacuated to Tashkent, 1943; ballerina Tashkent State Theatre; rejoined Bolshoi Theatre at Kuibishev again as soloist, 1944; left for London, 1945. Joined Sadler's Wells Ballet at Covent Garden as guest-soloist, 1946; later became regular mem. Has danced all principal rôles, notably, Le Lac des Cygnes, Sleeping Beauty, Giselle, Cinderella, Sylvia, Ballet Imperial, etc. Danced four-act Le Lac des Cygnes, first time, 1943; guest-artist Stanislavsky Theatre, Moscow, 1944, Sadler's Wells Theatre, 1947; guest-prima ballerina, La Scala, Milan, Nov. 1952–Feb. 1953 (Macbeth, La Gioconda, Swan Lake, Petrouchka); guest artist, Cannes, July 1954; Copenhagen, Dec. 1954; Teatro Municipal, Rio de Janeiro, May 1955 (Giselle, Swan Lake, Les Sylphides, Nutcracker, Don Quixote and The Dying Swan); Festival Ballet, Festival Hall, 1955; guest-prima ballerina in Giselle, Royal Opera House, Stockholm (Anna Pavlova Memorial), 1956; concluded stage career when appeared in Sleeping Beauty, Royal Opera House, Covent Garden, June 1956. *Appeared in films:* The Queen of Spades, Twice Upon a Time, Melba. Television appearances in Russia and England. Has toured with Sadler's Wells Ballet, France, Italy, Portugal, United States and Canada. *Recreations:* reading, painting, swimming. *Address:* Marina di Equa, 80066 Seiano, Bay of Naples, Italy. *T:* 081 879 8520.

ELWES, Captain Jeremy Gervase Geoffrey Philip; Vice Lord-Lieutenant of Humberside, since 1983; *b* 1 Sept. 1921; *s* of Rev. Rolf Elwes, OBE, MC; *m* 1955, Clare Mary Beveridge; four *s. Educ:* Avisford Sch.; Ampleforth Coll.; RMC Sandhurst. Joined Lincolnshire Regt, 1940; commissioned KRRC 1941; served until 1946, S Africa, Middle East, 8th Army, Yugoslavia, Southern Albania (despatches), Dalmatia and Greece; Moulton Agricultural Coll., 1947; farmer, 1949–; founder Dir, Linvend Ltd, 1960–, later J. S. Linder Ltd; founder Dir, Universal Marine Ltd, 1965–71; founder, Elwes Enterprises, 1970–; founder Dir, Euro-Latin Aviation Ltd, 1975–88. Opened country park to the public, Conservation Year, 1970; Mem., BBC Northern Adv. Council, 1966–69; Vice-Chm., BBC Radio Humberside, 1970–73; founder Chm., Lincs and Humberside Arts and Heritage Assoc., 1964–69; Pres., Lincs Branch, CPRE, 1980–89 (Chm., 1959–80); Mem. Council, Vice-Pres. and Steward, Lincs Agric. Soc., 1964–; Mem., Lincs Branch Exec., CLA, 1966–69; founder Chm., Shrievalty Assoc. of GB, 1971–; joint founder, Scarbank Trust Charity, 1978–; Vice-Chm., Environmental Medicine Foundn, 1987–. Mem., Brigg and Scunthorpe Cons. Assoc. Exec. Cttee, 1948–73; Mem., Brigg RDC, 1957–73, Lindsey CC, 1961–71. High Sheriff, Lincs, 1969; DL Lincs 1970, Humberside 1975. Kt of SMO Malta, 1959. *Recreations:* the arts and countryside. *Address:* Elsham Hall, near Brigg, South Humberside DN20 0QZ. *T:* Barnetby (0652) 688738.

ELWES, Jeremy Vernon, CBE 1984; Personnel Director, Reed Business Publishing Group (formerly Business Press International), since 1982; Director, Sutton Enterprise Agency Ltd, since 1987 (Chairman, 1987–90); Chairman, St Helier National Health Service Trust, since 1990; *b* 29 May 1937; *s* of late Eric Vincent Elwes and of Dorothea Elwes (*née* Bilton); *m* 1963, Phyllis Marion Relf, 2nd *d* of George Herbert Harding Relf and late Rose Jane Relf (*née* Luery); one *s. Educ:* Wirral Grammar Sch.; Bromley Grammar Sch.; City of London Coll. ACIS 1963. Technical Journalist, Heywood & Co., 1958–62; Accountant and Co. Sec., Agricultural Press, 1962–70; Sec. and Dir, East Brackland Hill Farming Development Co., 1967–70; IPC Business Press: Pensions Officer, 1966–70; Divl Personnel Manager, 1970–73; Manpower Planning Manager, 1973–78; Exec. Dir (Manpower), 1978–82. Dir, Periodicals Trng Council, 1986–. Chairman: Cons. Political Centre Nat. Adv. Cttee, 1981–84; Cons. SE Area, 1986–90; Member: Nat. Union Exec. Cttee; Gen. Purposes Cttee; Cons. Group for Europe. Chm. of Governors, Walthamstow Hall; Governor, Eltham College. Member Judge, Internat. Wine and Spirit Competition; Mem., Wine Guild of UK; Chancelier, Ordre des Chevaliers Bretvins (Bailliage de GB). *Recreations:* wine and food, reading, walking, golf. *Address:* Crispian Cottage, Weald Road, Sevenoaks, Kent TN13 1QQ. *T:* Sevenoaks (0732) 454208. *Clubs:* Carlton, St Stephen's Constitutional; Edenbridge Golf and Country.

ELWOOD, Sir Brian (George Conway), Kt 1990; CBE 1985; Chairman, Local Government Commission, New Zealand, since 1985; *b* 5 April 1933; *s* of Jack Philip Elwood and Enid Mary Elwood; *m* 1956, Dawn Barbara Elwood (*née* Ward); one *s* two *d. Educ:* Victoria Univ., Wellington (LLB); Trinity Coll., London (ATCL). Barrister and Solicitor, 1957; Mayor, Palmerston North City, 1971–85. Medal for Distinguished Public Service, Lions Club Internat., 1985. *Recreations:* golf, fishing, gardening. *Address:* 38 Leeward Drive, Whitby, Wellington, New Zealand. *T:* (04) 359 255. *Club:* Wellington.

ELWORTHY, family name of **Baron Elworthy.**

ELWORTHY, Baron *cr* 1972 (Life Peer); **Marshal of the Royal Air Force Samuel Charles Elworthy,** KG 1977; GCB 1962 (KCB 1961; CB 1960); CBE 1946; DSO 1941; LVO 1953; DFC 1941; AFC 1941; *b* 23 March 1911; *e s* of late P. A. Elworthy, Gordon's Valley, Timaru, New Zealand; *m* 1936, Audrey (*d* 1986), *o d* of late A. J. Hutchinson, OBE; three *s* one *d. Educ:* Marlborough; Trinity Coll., Cambridge (MA). Commissioned in RAFO 1933, transferred to Auxiliary Air Force (600 Sqdn), 1934; called to Bar, Lincoln's Inn, 1935, Hon. Bencher 1970; permanent commission in RAF, 1936; War Service in Bomber Comd; Acting Air Cdre, 1944; Air Vice-Marshal, 1957; Air Marshal, 1960; Air Chief Marshal, 1962; Marshal of the RAF, 1967. Comdt RAF Staff Coll., Bracknell, 1957–59; Deputy Chief of Air Staff, 1959–60; C-in-C, Unified Command, Middle East, 1960–63; Chief of Air Staff, 1963–67; Chief of the Defence Staff, 1967–71. Constable and Governor, Windsor Castle, 1971–78; Lord-Lieutenant of Greater London, 1973–78. Chairman: Royal Commn for the Exhibition of 1851, 1971–78; King Edward VII Hospital for Officers, 1971–78; Royal Over-Seas League, 1971–76. Sometime Governor: Bradfield Coll.; Wellington Coll.; Marlborough Coll. Hon. Freeman, Skinners' Co., 1968–, Master 1973–74. KStJ 1976. Retired to live in NZ, 1978. *Address:* Gordon's Valley, RD2, Timaru, South Canterbury, New Zealand. *Clubs:* Royal Air Force; Leander; South Canterbury (NZ); Christchurch (NZ).
See also Air Cdre Hon. T. C. Elworthy.

ELWORTHY, Sir Peter (Herbert), Kt 1988; farmer; *b* 3 March 1935; *s* of Harold Herbert Elworthy and June Mary Elworthy (*née* Batchelor); *m* 1960, Fiona Elizabeth McHardy; two *s* two *d. Educ:* Waihi Prep. Sch.; Christ's Coll.; Lincoln Agric. Coll. Nuffield Scholarship, UK, 1970; McMeekan Meml Award, 1978; Bledisloe Award, Lincoln, 1987. Director: Reserve Bank of NZ, 1985–; Landcorp, 1986–89; BP NZ Ltd, 1986–; Chm., Timaru Port Co., 1988–; Chm., NZ Adv. Cttee on Overseas Aid, 1986–88. President: NZ Deer Farmers, 1974–81; Farmers of NZ, 1984–87; Chairman: Ravensdown Co-op, 1977–82; Electricity Distribution Reform Unit; Southland Electrical Power Supply; Rural Reticulation Council; QEII National Trust, 1987–. NZ Commemoration Medal, 1990. *Recreations:* riding, fishing, flying (licensed pilot), reading. *Address:* Craigmore, 2RD, Timaru, New Zealand. *T:* Maungati (036129) 809. *Clubs:* Farmers'; Christchurch (Canterbury, NZ); Wellington (Wellington).

ELWORTHY, Air Cdre Hon. Timothy Charles, CBE 1986; Captain of The Queen's Flight, since 1989; Extra Equerry to the Queen, since 1991; *b* 27 Jan. 1938; *e s* of Baron Elworthy, *qv*; *m* 1st, 1961, Victoria Ann (marr. diss.), *d* of Lt Col H. C. W. Bowring; two *d*; 2nd, 1971, Anabel, *d* of late Reginald Harding, OBE; one *s. Educ:* Radley; RAF Coll., Cranwell. CO 29 (Fighter) Sqn, 1975 (Wing Comdr); PSO to AO Commanding-in-Chief, Strike Comd, 1979; CO RAF Stn Leuchars, 1983 (Gp Capt.); RCDS, 1986; Dir, Operational Requirements, (Air), MoD, 1987 (Air Cdre). FRGS 1990. Upper Freeman, GAPAN, 1990. QCVSA 1968. *Recreations:* country pursuits, wine, travel. *Address:* The Queen's Flight, RAF Station Benson, Oxon OX10 6AA. *T:* Wallingford (0491) 35055. *Clubs:* Royal Air Force, Boodle's

ELY, 8th Marquess of, *cr* 1801; **Charles John Tottenham;** Bt 1780; Baron Loftus, 1785; Viscount Loftus, 1789; Earl of Ely, 1794; Baron Loftus (UK), 1801; Headmaster, Boulden House, Trinity College School, Port Hope, Ontario, 1941–81; *b* 30 May 1913; *s* of G. L. Tottenham, BA (Oxon), and Cécile Elizabeth, *d* of J. S. Burra, Bockhanger, Kennington, Kent; *g s* of C. R. W. Tottenham, MA (Oxon), Woodstock, Newtown Mount Kennedy, Co. Wicklow, and Plâs Berwyn, Llangollen, N Wales; *S* cousin, 1969; *m* 1st, 1938, Katherine Elizabeth (*d* 1975), *d* of Col W. H. Craig, Kingston, Ont; three *s* one *d*; 2nd, 1978, Elspeth Ann, *o d* of late P. T. Hay, Highgate. *Educ:* Collège de Genève, Internat. Sch., Geneva; Queen's Univ., Kingston, Ont (BA). Career as Schoolmaster. *Recreation:* gardening. *Heir: e s* Viscount Loftus, *qv. Address:* Trinity College School, Port Hope, Ontario L1A 3W2, Canada. *T:* 885 5209; 20 Arundel Court, Jubilee Place, SW3. *T:* 071–352 9172. *Club:* University (Toronto).

ELY, Bishop of, since 1990; **Rt. Rev. Stephen Whitefield Sykes,** MA; *b* 1939; *m* 1962; one *s* two *d. Educ:* St John's Coll., Cambridge. BA (Cantab) 1961; MA (Cantab) 1964. Univ. Asst Lectr in Divinity, Cambridge Univ., 1964–68, Lectr. 1968–74; Fellow and Dean, St John's Coll., Cambridge, 1964–74; Van Mildert Canon Prof. of Divinity, Durham Univ., 1974–85; Regius Prof. of Divinity, and Fellow, St John's College, Cambridge, 1985–90. Mem., Archbishop's Cttee on Religious Educn, 1967. Hon. Canon of Ely Cathedral, 1985–90. Examining Chaplain to Bishop of Chelmsford, 1970–75. Edward Cadbury Lectr, Univ. of Birmingham, 1978; Hensley Henson Lectr, Univ. of Oxford, 1982–83. Chm., North of England Inst. for Christian Educn, 1980–85. Pres., Council of St John's Coll., Durham, 1984–. *Publications:* Friedrich Schleiermacher, 1971; Christian Theology Today, 1971; (ed) Christ, Faith and History, 1972; The Integrity of Anglicanism, 1978; (ed) Karl Barth: studies in his theological method, 1980; (ed) New Studies in Theology, 1980; (ed) England and Germany, Studies in Theological Diplomacy, 1982; The Identity of Christianity, 1984; (ed) Authority in the Anglican Communion, 1987; (ed) The Study of Anglicanism, 1988; (ed) Karl Barth: Centenary Essays, 1989; (ed) Sacrifice and Redemption. *Recreation:* walking. *Address:* The Bishop's House, Ely, Cambs CB7 4DW. *T:* Ely (0353) 662749.

ELY, Dean of; *see* Higgins, Very Rev. M. J.

ELY, Archdeacon of; *see* Walser, Ven. David.

ELY, Keith; *see* Ely, S. K.

ELY, Philip Thomas; Senior Partner, Paris Smith & Randall, Southampton, since 1981 (Partner, since 1961); President of the Law Society, July 1991–92 (Vice-President, 1990–91); *b* 22 March 1936; *s* of Eric Stanley Ely and Rose Josephine Ely; *m* 1966, Diana Mary (*née* Gellibrand); two *s* three *d. Educ:* Douai Sch.; LLB (external) London Univ. Admitted Solicitor, 1958. National Service, RN, 1958–60 (commnd, 1959). Articled Hepherd Winstanley & Pugh, Southampton, 1953–58; joined Paris Smith & Randall, Southampton, as Asst Solicitor, 1960. Mem. Council, Law Soc., 1979–. Hampshire Incorporated Law Society: Asst Hon. Sec., 1961–66; Hon. Sec., 1966–74; Hon. Treasurer, 1974–79; Pres., 1979. *Recreations:* fly-fishing, gardening, music, reading. *Address:* Lansdowne House, Castle Lane, Southampton SO9 4FD. *T:* Southampton (0703) 635191. *Club:* Reform.

ELY, (Sydney) Keith; Editor, Daily Post, Liverpool, since 1989; *b* 17 April 1949; *s* of Charles Rodenhurst Ely and Dorothy Mary Ely (*née* Rowlands); *m* 1970, Patricia Davies; three *d. Educ:* Maghull Grammar Sch.; Open Univ. (BA). Journalist: Liverpool Daily Post & Echo, 1968–78; Reuters, 1978–80; Daily Post, Liverpool: Business Editor, 1980–84; Acting Asst Editor, 1984; Systems Develt, 1985–86; Features Editor, 1987; Dep. Editor, 1987. Dir, Corporate Culture Ltd, 1988. *Recreations:* music, computing. *Address:* 6 Harington Close, Formby, Merseyside L37 1XP. *T:* Formby (07048) 78344.

ELYAN, Prof. Sir (Isadore) Victor, Kt 1970; Professor of Law, and Dean of the Faculty of Law, Durban-Westville University, 1973–77, retired; Chief Justice of Swaziland, 1965–70, retired; *b* 5 Sept. 1909; *s* of Jacob Elyan, PC, JP and Olga Elyan; *m* 1939, Ivy Ethel Mabel Stuart-Weir (*d* 1965); no *c*; *m* 1966, Rosaleen Jeanette O'Shea. *Educ:* St Stephen's Green Sch., Dublin; Trinity Coll., Dublin Univ. BA 1929, LLB 1931, MA 1932, TCD. Admitted a Solicitor of Supreme Court of Judicature, Ireland, 1930; Barrister-at-Law, King's Inns 1949, Middle Temple, 1952. Resident Magistrate, HM Colonial Legal Service, Gold Coast, 1946–54; Senior Magistrate, 1954–55; Judge of Appeal of the Court of Appeal for Basutoland, the Bechuanaland Protectorate and Swaziland, 1955–66; Judge, High Courts of Basutoland and the Bechuanaland Protectorate, 1955–65; on occasions acted as Judge between 1953 and 1955, Gold Coast; as Justice of Appeal, West African Court of Appeal; and as Chief Justice of Basutoland, the Bechuanaland Protectorate and Swaziland, also Pres. Court of Appeal, during 1956, 1961 and 1964; Judge of Appeal: Court of Appeal for Botswana, 1966–70; Court of Appeal for Swaziland, 1967–70; Court of Appeal, Lesotho, 1968–70. Served War, 1942–46; attached to Indian Army, 1944–46; GSO2 Military Secretary's Branch (DAMS), 1945–46 in rank of Major. Mem., Internat. Adv. Bd, The African Law Reports, 1969. *Publications:* Editor, High Commission Territories Law Reports, 1956, 1957, 1958, 1959, 1960. *Recreation:* sailing. *Address:* PO Box 22001, Fish Hoek 7975, Cape, South Africa.

ELYSTAN-MORGAN, family name of Baron Elystan-Morgan.

ELYSTAN-MORGAN, Baron *cr* 1981 (Life Peer), of Aberteifi in the County of Dyfed; **Dafydd Elystan Elystan-Morgan; His Honour Judge Elystan-Morgan;** a Circuit Judge, since 1987; *b* 7 Dec. 1932; *s* of late Dewi Morgan and late Mrs Olwen Morgan; *m* 1959, Alwen, *d* of William E. Roberts; one *s* one *d. Educ:* Ardwyn Grammar Sch., Aberystwyth; UCW, Aberystwyth. LLB Hons Aberystwyth, 1953. Research at

Aberystwyth and Solicitor's Articles, 1953–57; admitted a Solicitor, 1957; Partner in N Wales (Wrexham) Firm of Solicitors, 1958–68; Barrister-at-law, Gray's Inn, 1971; a Recorder, 1983–87. MP (Lab) Cardiganshire, 1966–Feb. 1974; Chm., Welsh Parly Party, 1967–68, 1971–74; Parly Under-Secretary of State, Home Office, 1968–70; front-bench spokesman on Home Affairs, 1970–72, on Welsh Affairs, 1972–74, on Legal and Home Affairs, House of Lords, 1981–. Contested (Lab): Cardigan, Oct. 1974; Anglesey, 1979. Pres., Welsh Local Authorities Assoc., 1967–73. *Address:* Carreg Afon, Dolau, Bow Street, Dyfed.

ELYTIS, Odysseus; Order of the Phoenix, 1965; Grand Commander, Order of Honour, 1979; poet; *b* Crete, 2 Nov. 1911; *y c* of Panayiotis and Maria Alepoudelis. *Educ:* Athens Univ. (Law); Sorbonne (Lettres). First publication, 1940; Broadcasting and Program Director, National Broadcasting Inst., 1945–47 and 1953–54; Administrative Board, Greek National Theatre, 1974–76. President, Admin. Board, Greek Broadcasting and Television, 1974. Hon. DLitt: Salonica, 1976; Sorbonne, 1980; Hon. DLit London, 1981. First National Prize in Poetry, 1960; Nobel Prize for Literature, 1979; Benson Silver Medal, RSL, 1981. Commander de la Légion d'Honneur (France), 1989. *Publications:* Orientations, 1940; Sun the First, 1943; The Axion Esti, 1959; Six, but one remorses for the Sky, 1960; The Light Tree, 1971; The Monogram, 1972; Villa Natacha, 1973; The Painter Theophilos, 1973; The Open Book, 1974; The Second Writing, 1976; Maria Nefeli, 1978; Selected Poems, 1981; Three Poems, 1982; Journal of an Unseen April, 1984; Saphfo, 1984; The Little Mariner, 1985. *Address:* Skoufa Street 23, Athens, Greece. *T:* 3626458.

EMANUEL, Aaron, CMG 1957; Consultant to OECD, 1972–83; *b* 11 Feb. 1912; *s* of Jack Emanuel and Jane (*née* Schaverien); *m* 1936, Ursula Pagel; two *s* one *d*. *Educ:* Henry Thornton Sch., Clapham; London Sch. of Economics (BSc Econ.). Economist at International Institute of Agriculture, Rome, 1935–38; Board of Trade, 1938; Ministry of Food, 1940; Colonial Office, 1943; Ministry of Health, 1961; Dept. of Economic Affairs, 1965; Under Secretary: Min. of Housing and Local Govt, 1969; Dept of the Environment, 1970–72. Chm., West Midlands Econ. Planning Bd, 1968–72; Vis. Sen. Lectr, Univ. of Aston in Birmingham, 1972–75. *Publication:* Issues of Regional Policies, 1973. *Address:* 119 Salisbury Road, Moseley, Birmingham B13 8LA. *T:* 021–449 5553.

EMANUEL, David, FCSD; Joint Partner/Director, Emanuel, since 1977; *b* 17 Nov. 1952; *s* of John Lawrence Morris Emanuel and late Elizabeth Emanuel; *m* 1975, Elizabeth Weiner (*see* E. Emanuel) (separated 1990); one *s* one *d*. *Educ:* Cardiff Coll. of Art (Diploma); Harrow Sch. of Art (Diploma); Royal College of Art (MA). Final Degree show at RCA, 1977. Emanuel (couture business) commenced in Mayfair, W1, 1977; The Emanuel Shop (retail), London, SW3, 1986–90; ready-to-wear business partnership in USA, 1988; David Emanuel Couture, 1990. Designed: wedding gown for the Princess of Wales, 1981; ballet productions, incl. Frankenstein, the Modern Prometheus, Royal Opera House, Covent Garden, 1985 and La Scala, Milan, 1987; prodns for theatre and operatic recitals. FCSD (FSIAD 1984). *Publication:* (with Elizabeth Emanuel) Style for All Seasons, 1983. *Recreations:* horse-riding, jet-ski-ing, tennis, opera. *Address:* 13 Regent's Park Terrace, NW1. *T:* 071–482 6486. *Clubs:* White Elephant; Royal Ascot Tennis (Berks).

EMANUEL, Elizabeth Florence, FCSD; *b* 5 July 1953; *d* of Samuel Charles Weiner and Brahna Betty Weiner; *m* 1975, David Leslie Emanuel, *qv* (separated 1990); one *s* one *d*. *Educ:* City of London Sch. for Girls; Harrow Sch. of Art (Diploma with Hons); Royal Coll. of Art (MA 1977; DesRCA 1977). FCSD 1984. Emanuel (couture) commenced in Mayfair, W1, 1977; The Emanuel Shop (retail), London, SW3, 1986–90; launched internat. fashion label, Elizabeth Emanuel, 1991. Design Consultant, Wensum Corporate, 1990–. Designed: wedding gown for the Princess of Wales, 1981; ballet productions, incl. Frankenstein, the Modern Prometheus, Royal Opera House, Covent Garden, 1985 and La Scala, Milan, 1987; costumes for film Diamond Skulls, 1990; uniforms for Virgin Atlantic Airways, 1990; prodns for theatre and operatic recitals. *Publication:* (with David Emanuel) Style for All Seasons, 1983. *Recreations:* ballet, films, writing. *Address:* Elizabeth Emanuel, 26a Brook Street, W1Y 1AE. *T:* 071–629 5560/5569.

EMANUEL, Richard Wolff, MA, DM Oxon, FRCP; Physician to Department of Cardiology, Middlesex Hospital, since 1963; Lecturer in Cardiology, Middlesex Hospital Medical School since 1963; Physician to National Heart Hospital since 1963; Lecturer to National Heart and Lung Institute (formerly Institute of Cardiology), since 1963; *b* 13 Jan. 1923; *s* of Prof. and Mrs J. G. Emanuel, Birmingham; *m* 1950, Lavinia Hoffmann; three *s*. *Educ:* Bradfield Coll.; Oriel Coll., Oxford; Middlesex Hospital. House Appts at Middx Hospital, 1948 and 1950. Captain RAMC, 1948–50; Med. Registrar, Middx Hosp., 1951–52; Sen. Med. Registrar, Middx Hosp., 1953–55; Sen. Med. Registrar, Nat. Heart Hosp., 1956–58; Fellow in Med., Vanderbilt Univ., 1956–57; Sen. Med. Registrar, Dept of Cardiology, Brompton Hosp., 1958–61; Asst Dir, Inst. of Cardiology and Hon. Asst Physician to Nat. Heart Hosp., 1961–63. Advr in Cardiovascular Disease to Sudan Govt, 1969–; Civil Consultant in Cardiology, RAF, 1979–89. Vis. Lecturer: Univ. of Med. Sciences and Chulalongkorn Univ., Thailand; Univ. of the Philippines; Univ. of Singapore; Univ. of Malaya; Khartoum Univ.; St Cyre's Lectr, London, 1968; Ricardo Molina Lectr, Philippines, 1969. Has addressed numerous Heart Socs in SE Asia. Member: British Cardiac Soc., 1955– (Asst Sec., 1966–68; Sec., 1968–70; Mem. Council, 1981–85); Council, British Heart Foundn, 1967–73, 1979– (Chm., Cardiac Care Cttee, 1987–); Cardiol Cttee, RCP, 1967–85 (Sec., 1972–79; Chm., 1979–85); Brit. Acad. of Forensic Sciences (Med.); Assoc. of Physicians of GB and Ireland; Chest, Heart and Stroke Assoc., 1978–. FACC; Hon. Fellow, Philippine Coll. of Cardiology; Hon. Mem., Heart Assoc. of Thailand. Gov., National Heart and Chest Hosps Bd, 1972–75; Mem. Trustees and Exec. Cttee, Gordon Meml Coll. Trust Fund, 1987–. Mem., Editl Cttee, British Heart Journal, 1964–72. Grand Comdr of Most Distinguished Order of Crown of Pahang, 1990. *Publications:* various articles on diseases of the heart in British and American jls. *Recreations:* XVIIIth century glass, fishing. *Address:* 6 Upper Wimpole Street, W1M 7TD. *T:* 071–935 3243; 6 Lansdowne Walk, W11. *T:* 071–727 6688; Canute Cottage, Old Bosham, near Chichester, West Sussex. *T:* Bosham (0243) 3318. *Club:* Oriental.

EMBLING, John Francis, CB 1967; Deputy Under-Secretary of State, Department of Education and Science, 1966–71; *b* 16 July 1909; *m* 1940, Margaret Gillespie Anderson; one *s*. *Educ:* University of Bristol. Teaching: Dean Close, 1930; Frensham Heights, 1931; Lecturer: Leipzig Univ., 1936; SW Essex Technical Coll., 1938 (Head of Dept, 1942); Administrative Asst, Essex LEA, 1944; Ministry of Education: Principal, 1946; Asst Secretary, 1949; Under-Secretary of State for Finance and Accountant-General, Dept of Education and Science, 1960–66. Research Fellow in Higher Educn, LSE, 1972–73, Univ. of Lancaster, 1974–76. Mem. Council, Klagenfurt Univ., 1972–. Grand Cross, Republic of Austria, 1976.

EMBREY, Derek Morris, OBE 1986; CEng, FIEE, FIMechE, MIGasE; Group Technical Director, AB Electronic Products Group PLC, since 1973; *b* 11 March 1928; *s* of Frederick and Ethel Embrey; *m* 1951, Frances Margaret Stephens; one *s* one *d*. *Educ:* Wolverhampton Polytechnic (Hon. Fellow, 1987). Chief Designer (Electronics), Electric Construction Co. Ltd, 1960–65, Asst Manager Static Plant, 1965–69; Chief Engineer, Abergas Ltd, 1969–73. Member: Engineering Council, 1982–87; Welsh Industrial Develt Adv. Bd, 1982–85; NACCB, 1985–87; Council, IERE, 1984–88 (Vice Pres., 1985–88); National Electronics Council, 1985–; Welsh Adv. Bd, 1986– (Chm., 1987–). Vis. Prof., Univ. of Technology, Loughborough, 1978–84 (External Examr, Dept of Mechanical Engrg, 1984–88); Lectr, 'State of the Art' conferences. Member: Council, UWIST, Cardiff, 1984–88; Bd, Inst. of Transducer Technol., Southampton Univ., 1986–. Freeman, City of London. *Publications:* contribs to various jls. *Recreations:* power flying, gliding, music, archaeology. *Address:* 102 Mill Road, Lisvane, Cardiff CF4 5UG. *T:* Cardiff (0222) 758473. *Clubs:* Royal Air Force; Birmingham Electric.

EMECHETA, Buchi; writer and lecturer, since 1972; *b* 21 July 1944; *d* of Alice and Jeremy Emecheta; *m* 1960, Sylvester Onwordi; two *s* three *d*. *Educ:* Methodist Girls' High Sch., Lagos, Nigeria; London Univ. (BSc Hons Sociol.). Librarian, 1960–69; Student, 1970–74; Youth Worker and Res. Student, Race, 1974–76; Community Worker, Camden, 1976–78. Visiting Prof., 11 Amer. univs, incl. Penn. State, Pittsburgh, UCLA, Illinois at Urbana-Champaign, 1979; Sen. Res. Fellow and Vis. Prof. of English, Univ. of Calabar, Nigeria, 1980–81; lectured: Yale, Spring 1982; London Univ., 1982–. Proprietor, Ogwugwn Afo Publishing Co. Included in twenty 'Best of Young British', 1983. Member: Arts Council of GB, 1982–83; Home Sec.'s Adv. Council on Race, 1979–. *Publications:* In the Ditch, 1972; Second Class Citizen, 1975; The Bride Price, 1976; The Slave Girl, 1977; The Joys of Motherhood, 1979; Destination Biafra, 1982; Naira Power, 1982; Double Yoke, 1982; The Rape of Shavi, 1983; Head Above Water (autobiog.), 1984; Gwendolen, 1989; *for children:* Titch the Cat, 1979; Nowhere to Play, 1980; The Moonlight Bride, 1981; The Wrestling Match, 1981; contribs to New Statesman, TLS, The Guardian, etc. *Recreations:* gardening, going to the theatre, listening to music, reading. *Address:* 7 Briston Grove, Crouch End, N8 9EX. *T:* 081–340 3762. *Club:* Africa Centre.

EMELEUS, Prof. Harry Julius, CBE 1958; FRS 1946; MA, DSc; Professor of Inorganic Chemistry, University of Cambridge, 1945–70; now Professor Emeritus; Fellow of Sidney Sussex College, Cambridge; Fellow of Imperial College, London; *b* 22 June 1903; *s* of Karl Henry Emeleus and Ellen Biggs; *m* 1931, Mary Catherine Horton (*d* 1991); two *s* two *d*. *Educ:* Hastings Grammar Sch.; Imperial Coll., London. 1851 Exhibition Senior Student, Imperial Coll. and Technische Hochschule, Karlsruhe, 1926–29; Commonwealth Fund Fellow, Princeton Univ., 1929–31; Member of Staff of Imperial Coll., 1931–45. President: Chemical Society, 1958; Royal Institute of Chemistry, 1963–65. Trustee, British Museum, 1963–72. Hon. Fellow, Manchester Institute of Science and Technology. Hon. Member: Austrian, Finnish, Indian, Bangladesh and French Chemical Societies; Finnish Scientific Academy; Gesellschaft Deutscher Chemiker; Royal Academy of Belgium; Akad. Naturf. Halle; Akad. Wiss. Göttingen; Austrian Acad. of Scis; Acad. of Scis in Catania; Spanish Royal Society for Physics and Chemistry. Hon. Doctor: Ghent; Kiel; Lille; Paris; Tech. Hoch. Aachen; Marquette; Kent. Lavoisier Medal, French Chem. Society; Stock Medal, Gesellschaft Deutscher Chemiker; Davy Medal, Royal Society, 1962. *Publications:* scientific papers in chemical journals. *Recreation:* fishing. *Address:* 149 Shelford Road, Trumpington, Cambridge CB2 2ND. *T:* Cambridge (0223) 840374.

EMERSON, Michael Ronald, MA; FCA; Ambassador and Head of Delegation of the European Communities to the Soviet Union, since 1991; *b* 12 May 1940; *s* of James and Priscilla Emerson; *m* 1966, Barbara Brierley; one *s* two *d*. *Educ:* Hurstpierpoint Coll.; Balliol Coll., Oxford (MA (PPE)). Price Waterhouse & Co., London, 1962–65; Organisation for Economic Cooperation and Development, Paris: several posts in Develt and Economics Depts, finally as Head of General Economics Div., 1966–73; EEC, Brussels: Head of Division for Budgetary Policy, Directorate-General II, 1973–76; Economic Adviser to President of the Commission, 1977; Dir for Nat. Economies and Economic Trends, 1978–81; Dir for Macroecon. Analyses and Policies, 1981–86; Dir, Economic Evaluation of Community Policies, Directorate-General II, 1987–90. Fellow, Centre for Internat. Affairs, Harvard Univ., 1985–86. *Publications:* (ed) Europe's Stagflation, 1984; What Model for Europe, 1987; The Ecoonomics of 1992, 1988; contribs to various economic jls and edited volumes on internat. and European economics. *Address:* Hotel Mizhdounarodnaya, 12 Nab Kasnopresnenskaia, Moscow, USSR; 128 avenue de Tervuren, 1150 Brussels, Belgium. *T:* 02.736.1283.

EMERSON, Dr Peter Albert, FRCP; Hon. Consultant Physician and Director of the Clinical Information System, Westminster and Charing Cross Hospitals, since 1988; *b* 7 Feb. 1923; *s* of Albert Emerson and Gwendoline (*née* Davy); *m* 1947, Ceris Hood Price; one *s* one *d*. *Educ:* The Leys Sch., Cambridge; Clare Coll., Univ. of Cambridge (MA); St George's Hosp., Univ. of London (MB, BChir 1947; MD 1954). FRCP 1964; Hon. FACP 1975. House Physician, St George's Hosp., 1947; RAF Med. Bd, 1948–52 (Sqdn Leader); Registrar, later Sen. Registrar, St George's Hosp. and Brompton Hosp., London, 1952–57; Asst Prof. of Medicine, Coll. of Medicine, State Univ. of New York, Brooklyn, USA, 1957–58; Consultant Phys., Westminster Hosp., 1959–88; Civilian Consultant Phys. in Chest Diseases to RN, 1974–88; Dean, Westminster Medical Sch., London, 1981–84. Hon. Consultant Phys., King Edward VII Hosp., Midhurst, 1969–88. Royal Coll. of Physicians: Asst Registrar, 1965–71; Procensor and Censor, 1978–80; Vice-Pres. and Sen. Censor, 1985–86; Mitchell Lectr, 1969. *Publications:* Thoracic Medicine, 1981; articles in med. jls and chapters in books on thoracic medicine and the application of decision theory and medical audit to clinical medicine. *Recreations:* tennis, restoring old buildings. *Address:* 3 Halkin Street, SW1X 7DJ. *T:* 071–235 8529. *Club:* Royal Air Force.

EMERTON, Dame Audrey (Caroline), DBE 1989; CStJ; RGN, RM, RNT; Chairman, UK Central Council for Nursing, Midwifery and Health Visiting, since 1985; Regional Nursing Officer, South East Thames Regional Health Authority, 1973–91; Chief Nursing Officer, St John Ambulance, since 1988. Formerly: Chief Nursing Officer, Tunbridge Wells and Leybourne HMC; Principal Nursing Officer, Education, Bromley HMC; Senior Tutor, Experimental 2 year and 1 year Course, St George's Hosp., SW1; Dir, Admin, Personnel and Trng, SE Thames RHA, 1985–88. Kent County Commissioner, St John Ambulance Brigade. Pres., Assoc. of Nurse Administrators, 1979–82. Chm., English Nat. Bd for Nursing, Midwifery and Health Visiting, 1983–85. Hon. DCL Kent, 1989. *Address:* UK Central Council for Nursing, Midwifery and Health Visiting, 23 Portland Place, W1N 3AF.

EMERTON, Rev. Prof. John Adney, FBA 1979; Regius Professor of Hebrew, Cambridge, since 1968; Fellow of St John's College, since 1970; Honorary Canon, St George's Cathedral, Jerusalem, since 1984; *b* 5 June 1928; *s* of Adney Spencer Emerton and Helena Mary Emerton; *m* 1954, Norma Elizabeth Bennington; one *s* two *d*. *Educ:* Minchenden Grammar Sch., Southgate; Corpus Christi Coll., Oxford; Wycliffe Hall, Oxford. BA (1st class hons Theology), 1950; 1st class hons Oriental Studies, 1952; MA 1954. Canon Hall Jun. Greek Testament Prize, 1950; Hall-Houghton Jun. Septuagint Prize, 1951, Senior Prize, 1954; Houghton Syriac Prize, 1953; Liddon Student, 1950; Kennicott Hebrew Fellow, 1952. Corpus Christi Coll., Cambridge, MA (by incorporation), 1955; BD 1960; DD 1973. Deacon, 1952; Priest, 1953. Curate of Birmingham Cathedral, 1952–53; Asst Lecturer in Theology, Birmingham Univ., 1952–53; Lecturer in Hebrew and Aramaic, Durham Univ., 1953–55; Lecturer in Divinity, Cambridge Univ., 1955–62; Reader in Semitic Philology and Fellow of St

Peter's Coll., Oxford, 1962–68. Visiting Professor: of Old Testament and Near Eastern Studies, Trinity Coll., Toronto Univ., 1960; of Old Testament, Utd Theol Coll., Bangalore, 1986; Fellow, Inst. for Advanced Studies, Hebrew Univ. of Jerusalem, 1982–83. Select Preacher before Univ. of Cambridge, 1962, 1971, 1986. Sec., Internat. Orgn for the Study of the Old Testament, 1971–89; Pres., Soc. for OT Study, 1979. Mem. Editorial Bd, Vetus Testamentum, 1971–. Corresp. Mem., Akademie der Wissenschaften, Göttingen, 1990. Hon. DD Edinburgh, 1977. *Publications:* The Peshitta of the Wisdom of Solomon, 1959; The Old Testament in Syriac: Song of Songs, 1966; (ed) Studies in the Historical Books of the Old Testament, 1979; (ed) Prophecy: essays presented to Georg Fohrer, 1980; Editor, Congress Volumes (International Organization for Study of the Old Testament): Edinburgh 1973, 1974; Göttingen 1977, 1978; Vienna 1980, 1981; Salamanca 1983, 1985; Jerusalem 1986, 1988; articles in Journal of Semitic Studies, Journal of Theological Studies, Theology, Vetus Testamentum, Zeitschrift für die Alttestamentliche Wissenschaft. *Address:* 34 Gough Way, Cambridge CB3 9LN.

EMERY, Prof. Alan Eglin Heathcote; MD, PhD, DSc; FRSE, FRCP, FRCPE; FLS; Research Director, European Alliance of Muscular Dystrophy Associations; Professor of Human Genetics, University of Edinburgh and Hon. Consultant Physician, Lothian Health Board, 1968–83, now Emeritus Professor and Hon. University Fellow; Visiting Fellow, Green College, Oxford, since 1986; *b* 21 Aug. 1928; *s* of Harold Heathcote Emery and Alice Eglin. *Educ:* Manchester Univ.; Johns Hopkins Univ., Baltimore (PhD). MD, DSc; FRIPHH 1965; FRCPE 1970; MFCM 1974; FRSE 1972; FLS 1985; FRSSAF 1990. Formerly Resident in Medicine and Surgery, Manchester Royal Infirmary; Fellow in Medicine, Johns Hopkins Hosp., Baltimore, 1961–64; Reader in Medical Genetics, Univ. of Manchester, 1964–68 and Hon. Consultant in Medical Genetics, United Manchester Hosps; Sen. Res. Fellow, Green Coll., Oxford, 1985–86. Visiting Professor: Univ. of NY, 1968; Heidelberg, 1972; Hyderabad, 1975; California (UCLA), 1980; Padua, 1984; Medical Coll., Peking, 1985; RPMS, 1986; Duke Univ. (N Carolina), 1987; Univ. of London (Inst. of Neurology), 1988; St George's Univ., Grenada, 1990. Lectures: Harveian, 1970; Woodhull, Royal Instn, 1972; Boerhaave, 1984. Pres., British Clinical Genetics Soc., 1980–83; Council Mem., British Genetic Soc; Mem., Soc. of Authors. Hon. Fellow, Muscular Dystrophy Assoc. of Brazil, 1982. Nat. Foundn (USA) Internat. Award for Research, 1980; Wilfred Card Medal, 1985. Exec. Editor, Procs B, RSE, 1986–90. *Publications:* Elements of Medical Genetics, 1968, 7th edn 1988; Methodology in Medical Genetics, 1976, 2nd edn 1986; Recombinant DNA—an introduction, 1984; Duchenne Muscular Dystrophy, 1987; editor: Modern Trends in Human Genetics, vol. 1, 1970, vol. 2, 1975; Antenatal Diagnosis of Genetic Disease, 1973; Registers for the Detection and Prevention of Genetic Disease, 1976; Principles and Practice of Medical Genetics, 1983, 2nd edn 1990; Psychological Aspects of Genetic Counselling, 1984; numerous scientific papers. *Recreations:* writing poetry, marine biology, oil painting. *Address:* 1 Eton Terrace, Edinburgh EH4 1QE. *T:* 031–343 2262. *Clubs:* Athenæum; Scottish Arts (Edinburgh).

EMERY, Eleanor Jean, CMG 1975; HM Diplomatic Service, retired; *b* 23 Dec. 1918; *d* of Robert Paton Emery and Nellie Nicol Wilson. *Educ:* Western Canada High Sch., Calgary, Alberta; Glasgow Univ. MA Hons in History, 1941. Dominions Office, 1941–45; Asst Private Sec. to Sec. of State, 1942–45; British High Commn, Ottawa, 1945–48; CRO, 1948–52; Principal Private Sec. to Sec. of State, 1950–52; First Sec., British High Commn, New Delhi, 1952–55; CRO, 1955–58; First Sec., British High Commn, Pretoria/Cape Town, 1958–62; Head of South Asia Dept, CRO, 1962–64; Counsellor, British High Commn, Ottawa, 1964–68; Head of Pacific Dependent Territories Dept, FCO, 1969–73; High Comr, Botswana, 1973–77. Chm., UK Botswana Soc., 1984–88, Vice-Chm., 1988. Governor, Commonwealth Inst., 1980–85. *Recreations:* walking, gardening. *Address:* 17 Winchmore Drive, Cambridge CB2 2LW. *Club:* Commonwealth Trust.

See also J. M. Zachariah.

EMERY, Fred; Presenter, Panorama, BBC TV, 1978–80 and since 1982; *b* 19 Oct. 1933; *s* of Frederick G. L. Emery and Alice May (*née* Wright); *m* 1958, E. Marianne Nyberg; two *s*. *Educ:* Bancroft's Sch.; St John's Coll., Cantab (MA). RAF fighter pilot, 266 & 234 Squadrons, National Service, 1953. Radio Bremen, 1955–56; joined The Times, 1958, Foreign Correspondent, 1961; served in Paris, Algeria, Tokyo, Indonesia, Vietnam, Cambodia, Malaysia and Singapore until 1970; Chief Washington Corresp., 1970–77; Political Editor, 1977–81; Home Editor, 1981–82; Exec. Editor (Home and Foreign), 1982. *Recreations:* skiing, hill walking, tennis. *Address:* 5 Woodsyre, SE26 6SS. *T:* 081–761 0076. *Club:* Garrick.

EMERY, George Edward, CB 1980; Director General of Defence Accounts, Ministry of Defence, 1973–80, retired; *b* 2 March 1920; *s* of late Frederick and Florence Emery; *m* 1946, Margaret (*née* Rice); two *d*. *Educ:* Bemrose Sch., Derby. Admiralty, 1938; Min. of Fuel and Power, 1946; Min. of Supply, 1951; Min. of Aviation, 1959; Min. of Technology, 1967; Principal Exec. Officer, 1967; Asst Sec., Min. of Aviation Supply, 1970; Ministry of Defence: Asst Sec., 1971; Exec. Dir, 1973; Under-Sec., 1973. *Recreations:* amateur dramatics, gardening. *Address:* 3 The Orchard, Freshford, Bath BA3 6EW. *T:* Limpley Stoke (0225) 723561.

EMERY, Joan Dawson, (Mrs Jack Emery); *see* Bakewell, J. D.

EMERY, Joyce Margaret; *see* Zachariah, J. M.

EMERY, Lina, (Mrs Ralph Emery); *see* Lalandi-Emery, L.

EMERY, Sir Peter (Frank Hannibal), Kt 1982; MA; FInstPS; MP (C) Honiton, since 1967 (Reading, 1959–66); *b* 27 Feb. 1926; *s* of late F. G. Emery, Highgate; *m* 1st, 1954 (marr. diss.); one *s* one *d*; 2nd, 1972, Elizabeth, *y d* of late G. J. R. Monnington; one *s* one *d*. *Educ:* Scotch Plains, New Jersey, USA; Oriel Coll., Oxford. Joint Founder and First Secretary of the Bow Group. Parliamentary Private Secretary in Foreign Office, War Dept and Min. of Labour, 1960–64; Jt Hon. Secretary, 1922 Cttee, 1964–65; Opposition Front Bench Spokesman for Treasury, Economics and Trade, 1964–66; Parliamentary Under-Secretary of State: DTI, 1972–74; Dept of Energy, 1974; Member: Select Cttee on Industry and Trade, 1979–87; Select Cttee on Procedure, 1972– (Chm., 1983–). Jt Vice-Chm., Conservative Finance Cttee, 1970–72; Chairman: Cons. Housing and Construction Cttee, 1974–75. Member, Delegation to CPA Conference: Westminster, 1961; Canada, 1962; Fiji, 1981; Leader, Delegn to Kenya, 1977; Delegate: Council of Europe and WEU, 1962–64, 1970–72; North Atlantic Assembly, 1983– (Chm., Science and Technology Cttee, 1985–). Chairman: Shenley Trust Services Ltd; Winglaw Gp; Director: Property Growth Insurance, 1966–72; Phillips Petroleum-UK Ltd, 1963–72; Institute of Purchasing and Supply, 1961–72; Secretary-General, European Federation of Purchasing, 1962–72; Chairman, Consultative Council of Professional Management Organisations, 1968–72. Founding Chm., Nat. Asthma Campaign, 1990–. *Recreations:* sliding down mountains, tennis, cricket, golf and bridge (Capt., H of C team, 1984–). *Address:* Tytherleigh Manor, near Axminster, Devon. *T:* South Chard (0460) 20309; 8 Ponsonby Terrace, SW1. *T:* 071–222 6666; (office) 40 Park Street, W1. *T:* 071–437 6666, *Fax:* 071–493 5096. *Clubs:* Carlton, Portland; Leander (Henley-on-Thames).

EMERY-WALLIS, Frederick Alfred John, DL; FSA; Leader, Hampshire County Council, since 1976 (County Councillor, since 1973; Vice-Chairman, 1975–76); Vice-President, Southern Tourist Board, since 1988 (Chairman, 1976–88); *b* 11 May 1927; *o s* of Frederick Henry Wallis and Lillian Grace Emery Coles; *m* 1960, Solange, *o d* of William Victor Randall, London, and Albertine Beaupère, La Guerche-sur-l'Aubois; two *d*. *Educ:* Blake's Academy, Portsmouth. Royal Signals SCU4 (Middle East Radio Security), 1945–48. Portsmouth City Council, 1961–74; Lord Mayor, 1968–69; Alderman, 1969–74. Chm., ACC Recreation Cttee, 1982–85. Chairman: Portsmouth Develt and Estates Cttee, 1965–74; Portsmouth Papers Editorial Bd, 1966–82; S Hampshire Plan Adv. Cttee, 1969–74; Portsmouth South Cons. and Unionist Assoc., 1971–79, 1982–85; Portsmouth Record Series Adv. Panel, 1982–; Hampshire Archives Trust, 1986–; Exec. Cttee, Hampshire Sculpture Trust, 1988–91; Director: Warrior Preservation Trust, 1988–; WNO, 1990–; Member: Economic Planning Council for the South East, 1969–74; British Library Adv. Council, 1979–84, 1986–91; Council, British Records Assoc., 1979–; Library and Information Services Council, 1980–83; Mary Rose Develt Trust, 1980–90; Arts Council of GB Reg. Adv. Bd, 1984–88; Hampshire Gardens Trust, 1984–. Vice-Chm., Portsmouth Polytechnic, 1967–75; Pres., Hampshire Field Club, 1971–74. Trustee, Royal Naval Mus., Portsmouth, 1987–. Vice-Pres., Mottisfont Soc., 1978–. Pres., Portsmouth YMCA, 1978–88. DL Hants 1988. Hon. Fellow, Portsmouth Polytechnic, 1972. FSA 1980. Hon. FRIBA 1985. *Publications:* various publications concerning history and develt of Portsmouth and Hampshire. *Recreations:* book collecting, music. *Address:* Froddington, Craneswater Park, Portsmouth. *T:* Portsmouth (0705) 731409.

EMLYN, Viscount; Colin Robert Vaughan Campbell; *b* 30 June 1962; *s* and *heir* of Earl Cawdor, *qv*. *Educ:* Eton; St Peter's College, Oxford. Member, James Bridal Meml Soc., London.

EMLYN JONES, John Hubert, CBE 1986 (MBE (mil.) 1941); FRICS; JP; Member of the Lands Tribunal, 1968–86; *b* 6 Aug. 1915; *s* of late Ernest Pearson Jones and Katharine Cole Jones (*née* Nicholas); *m* 1954, Louise Anne Montague, *d* of late Raymond Ralph Horwood Hazell; two *s* one *d*. *Educ:* Dulwich. FRICS 1939. Served War, RE, 1939–46: Major 1943. Partner, Rees-Reynolds and Hunt, and Alfred Savill & Sons, Chartered Surveyors, 1950–68. President: Rating Surveyors Assoc., 1965–66 (Hon. Mem. 1968); Climbers' Club, 1966–69 (Hon. Mem. 1970); Alpine Club, 1980–82. Mem. Council, RICS, 1964–69. Mem. Bureau, 1964–72, Treasurer 1967–69, Fédération Internationale des Géomètres; Mem. Council, Rainer Foundn, 1965–85 (Chm. 1968–71). Mem., expedns to Himalayas: Annapurna, 1950; Ama Dablam, 1959 (Leader). High Sheriff, Bucks, 1967–68, JP 1968. *Publications:* articles and revs in mountaineering jls. *Recreations:* mountaineering, music. *Address:* Ivinghoe Manor, Leighton Buzzard, Beds. *T:* Cheddington (0296) 668202. *Clubs:* Garrick, Alpine.

EMMERSON, Rt. Rev. Ralph; an Assistant Bishop, Diocese of Ripon, since 1986; *b* 7 June 1913; *s* of Thomas and Alys Mary Emmerson; *m* 1942, Ann Hawthorn Bygate (*d* 1982); no *c*. *Educ:* Leeds Grammar Sch.; King's Coll., London (BD, AKC); Westcott House, Cambridge. Leeds Educn Authority Youth Employment Dept, 1930–35; Curate, St George's, Leeds, 1938–41; Priest-in-Charge, Seacroft Estate, 1941–48; Rector of Methley and Vicar of Mickletown, 1949–56; Vicar of Headingley, 1956–66; Hon. Canon of Ripon Cath., 1964; Residentiary Canon and Canon Missioner for Dio. Ripon, 1966–72; Bishop Suffragan of Knaresborough, 1972–79; Asst Bishop, Dio. Wakefield, 1980–86. *Address:* Flat 1, 15 High Saint Agnesgate, Ripon HG4 1QR. *T:* Ripon (0765) 701626.

EMMET, Dorothy Mary, MA Oxon, Cantab and Manchester; *b* 1904; *d* of late Rev. C. W. Emmet, Fellow of University Coll., Oxford, and late Gertrude Julia Emmet (*née* Weir). *Educ:* St Mary's Hall, Brighton; Lady Margaret Hall, Oxford. Classical Exhibitioner, Lady Margaret Hall, Oxford, 1923; Hon. Mods Class I, 1925; Lit. Hum. Class I, 1927. Tutor, Maesyrhaf Settlement, Rhondda Valley, 1927–28 and 1931–32; Commonwealth Fellow, Radcliffe Coll., Cambridge, Mass, USA, 1928–30; Research Fellow, Somerville Coll., Oxford, 1930–31; lecturer in Philosophy, Armstrong Coll., Newcastle upon Tyne, 1932–38 (now Newcastle Univ.); lecturer in Philosophy of Religion, University of Manchester, 1938–45; Reader in Philosophy, 1945–46; Prof. of Philosophy, University of Manchester, 1946–66; Prof. Emeritus, 1966. Stanton Lecturer in Philosophy of Religion, University of Cambridge, 1950–53. Visiting Professor: Barnard Coll., Columbia Univ., New York, 1960–61; Univ. of Ibadan, Nigeria, 1974. President Aristotelian Society, 1953–54. Dean of the Faculty of Arts, University of Manchester, 1962–64. Hon. Fellow, Lady Margaret Hall, Oxford. Fellow, Lucy Cavendish Coll., Cambridge, 1967, Emeritus Fellow, 1981. Hon. DLitt: Glasgow, 1974; Leicester, 1976. *Publications:* Whitehead's Philosophy of Organism, 1932, 2nd edn 1982; Philosophy and Faith, 1936; The Nature of Metaphysical Thinking, 1945; Function, Purpose and Powers, 1958, 2nd edn 1972; Rules, Roles and Relations, 1966; (ed with Alasdair MacIntyre) Sociological Theory and Philosophical Analysis, 1970; The Moral Prism, 1979; The Effectiveness of Causes, 1984; The Passage of Nature, 1991; contributions to philosophical journals. *Recreations:* gardening, reading. *Address:* 11 Millington Road, Cambridge CB3 9HW.

EMMETT, Bryan David; *b* 15 Feb. 1941; *m* 1960, Moira (*née* Miller); one *s*. *Educ:* Tadcaster Grammar Sch. Clerical Officer, Min. of Labour, and National Service, 1958–59; Exec. Officer, War Dept, 1959–64; Asst Principal, MOP, 1965–69 (Asst Private Sec. to Ministers of Power, 1968–69); Principal, Electricity Div., DTI, 1969–74; Department of Energy: Principal, and Private Sec. to Minister of State, 1974–75; Asst Sec., and Principal Private Sec. to Sec. of State for Energy, 1975–76; Asst Sec., Petroleum Engrg Div., 1977–80; Under Sec., and Principal Estab. Officer, 1980–81; Principal Estab. and Finance Officer, 1981–82; Chief Exec., Employment Div., MSC, 1982–85; Department of Energy: Head, Energy Policy Div., 1985–86; Head of Oil Div., 1986–87; Dir Gen., Energy Efficiency Office, 1987–88; seconded as Chief Exec., Educn Assets Bd, Leeds, 1988–90; compulsorily retired, 1991. *Recreations:* National Hunt racing, hacking, golf. *Address:* Hayside Farm, Low Street, Sancton, E Yorks Y04 3QY. *Club:* Leeds (Leeds).

EMMS, David Acfield, MA; Director, London House for Overseas Graduates, since 1987; *b* 16 Feb. 1925; *s* of late Archibald George Emms and Winifred Gladys (*née* Richards); *m* 1950, Pamela Baker Speed; three *s* one *d*. *Educ:* Tonbridge Sch.; Brasenose Coll., Oxford. BA Hons Mod. Langs Oxford, 1950, Diploma in Education, 1951; MA 1954. Rugby football, Oxford *v* Cambridge, 1949, 1950. Served War of 1939–45, RA, 1943–47. Undergraduate, 1947–51; Asst Master, Uppingham Sch. (Head of Mod. Languages Dept, CO, CCF Contingent), 1951–60; Headmaster of: Cranleigh School, 1960–70; Sherborne School, 1970–74; Master, Dulwich Coll., 1975–86. Chm., HMC, 1984; Vice-Pres., ISCO, 1973–. Dep. Chm., E-SU, 1984–89; Chm., Jt Educnl Trust, 1987–90; Mem. Cttee, GBA, 1989–. Vice-Chm. Council and Dep. Pro-Chancellor, City Univ., 1989–; Governor: Bickley Park, 1978–81; Feltonfleet, 1967–86; Brambletye, 1982–88; St Felix Sch., Southwold, 1981–88; Portsmouth Grammar Sch., 1987–; Tonbridge (Chm. Exec. Cttee), 1988–; St. George's, Montreux, 1989–. President: Alleyn Club, 1985; Brasenose Soc., 1987; Vice-Pres., Dulwich Soc. Mem. Council, Fairbridge Soc., 1984–. FRSA 1988. Freeman, City of London; Master, Skinners' Co., 1987–88. Hon. Col, 39th (City of London) Signal Regt (Special Communications) (Volunteers), 1988–91. *Publication:* HMC

Schools and British Industry, 1981. *Recreations:* radical gardening, putting names to faces. *Address:* London House, Mecklenburgh Square, WC1N 2AB. *T:* 071–837 8888; Seaforth, Spinney Lane, Itchenor, W Sussex. *Clubs:* East India, Devonshire, Sports and Public Schools; Vincent's (Oxford); Itchenor Sailing.

EMMS, Peter Fawcett; Regional Director, Eastern Region, Departments of the Environment and Transport, since 1989; *b* 25 April 1935; *s* of late Reginald Emms and of Hetty Emms; *m* 1960, Carola Wayne; three *d. Educ:* Derby Sch., Derby; Magdalen Coll., Oxford, 1956–59 (John Doncaster Open Schol. in Mod. Langs; MA French and German). National Service, Jt Services Russian Course, 1954–56. Assistant Master: Abingdon Sch., 1959–62; Rugby Sch., 1962–74; Vis. Master, Groton Sch., Mass, 1967–68; Hd of Mod. Langs 1969–71, Housemaster of Town House 1971–74, Rugby Sch.; joined DoE as Principal, 1974, with posts in Road Safety, Construction Industries and Housing; Asst Sec., 1979; Hd of Greater London Housing, 1979–81; seconded to DES, Further and Higher Educn Br., 1981–83; Hd of Housing Management Div., and of Estate Action Unit, 1983–87; Nuffield Leverhulme Travelling Fellowship, 1987–88; Hd, Dept of Transport Internat. Transport Div., Mem., Central Rhine Commn, 1988–89; Under Sec., 1989. *Publications:* Social Housing: a European dilemma?, 1990; (contrib.) Changing Housing Finance Systems, 1990. *Recreation:* the civilizations of Europe. *Address:* Heron House, 49–51 Goldington Road, Bedford MK40 3LL. *T:* Bedford (0234) 276109; Vauban, France, 71800.

EMPEY, Reginald Norman Morgan; Member, Belfast City Council, since 1985; Lord Mayor of Belfast, 1989–90; *b* 26 Oct. 1947; *s* of Samuel Frederick Empey and Emily Winifred (*née* Morgan); *m* 1977, Stella Ethna Donnan; one *s* one *d. Educ:* The Royal Sch., Armagh; Queen's Univ., Belfast (BSc (Econ)). Cons. & Unionist Assoc., QUB, 1967; Publicity Officer, 1967–68, Vice-Chm., 1968–72, Ulster Young Unionist Council; Chm., Vanguard Unionist Party, 1974–75; Mem., E Belfast, NI Constitutional Convention, 1975–76. Member: Belfast Harbour Comrs, 1985–89; Eastern Health and Social Services Bd, 1985–86; Ulster Unionist Council, 1987– (Hon. Sec., 1990–). *Recreations:* walking, gardening. *Address:* Knockvale House, 205 Sandown Road, Belfast BT5 6GX. *T:* Belfast (0232) 795569.

EMPEY, Most Rev. Walton Newcombe Francis; *see* Meath and Kildare, Bishop of.

EMPSON, Adm. Sir (Leslie) Derek, GBE 1975; KCB 1973 (CB 1969); Chairman, Roymark Ltd, since 1985; *b* 29 Oct. 1918; *s* of Frank Harold Empson and Madeleine Norah Empson (*née* Burge); *m* 1958, Diana Elizabeth Kelly; one *s* one *d. Educ:* Eastbourne Coll.; Clare Coll., Cambridge (Class. Exhibn). Athletics Blue, 1939; BA 1940. Joined Royal Navy for pilot duties, 1940; commd as Sub-Lieut (A) RNVR, 1940; flew as Fleet Air Arm pilot, 1940–45; perm. commn in RN, 1944; Naval Asst to First Sea Lord, 1957–59; Comd HMS Eagle, 1963–65; Imp. Def. Coll., 1966; Flag Officer, Aircraft Carriers, 1967–68; Asst Chief of Naval Staff (Operations and Air), 1968–69; Comdr, Far East Fleet, 1969–71; Second Sea Lord and Chief of Naval Personnel, 1971–74; C-in-C Naval Home Comd and FO Portsmouth Area, 1974–75; Flag ADC to The Queen, 1974–75. Rear-Adm. of the UK, 1984–86; Vice-Adm. of the UK, 1986–88. Comdr 1952; Captain 1957; Rear-Adm. 1967; Vice-Adm. 1970; Adm. 1972. Consultant: Thorn EMI, 1976–86; Warner Communications, 1987–88; Astra Hldgs, 1987–90. Chm. of Governors, Eastbourne Coll., 1972–88. *Address:* Deepdale, Hambledon, Hants. *Clubs:* MCC, Naval; Hawks (Cambridge), Achilles.

EMSLIE, family name of **Baron Emslie.**

EMSLIE, Baron *cr* 1980 (Life Peer), of Potterton in the District of Gordon; **George Carlyle Emslie,** PC 1972; MBE 1946; FRSE 1987; Lord Justice-General of Scotland and Lord President of the Court of Session, 1972–89; *b* 6 Dec. 1919; *s* of late Alexander and Jessie Blair Emslie; *m* Lilias Ann Mailer Hannington; three *s. Educ:* The High School of Glasgow; The University of Glasgow (MA, LLB). Commissioned A&SH, 1940; served War of 1939–45 (despatches): North Africa, Italy, Greece, Austria, 1942–46; psc Haifa, 1944; Brigade Major (Infantry), 1944–46. Advocate, 1948; Advocate Depute (Sheriff Courts), 1955; QC (Scotland) 1957; Sheriff of Perth and Angus, 1963–66; Dean of Faculty of Advocates, 1965–70; Senator of Coll. of Justice in Scotland and Lord of Session, 1970–72. Chm., Scottish Agricultural Wages Bd, 1969–73; Mem., Council on Tribunals (Scottish Cttee), 1962–70. Hon. Bencher: Inner Temple, 1974; Inn of Court of N Ireland, 1981. Hon. LLD Glasgow, 1973. *Recreation:* golf. *Address:* 47 Heriot Row, Edinburgh EH3 6EX. *T:* 031–225 3657. *Clubs:* New (Edinburgh); The Honourable Company of Edinburgh Golfers.

See also Hon. G. N. H. Emslie.

EMSLIE, Hon. (George) Nigel (Hannington); QC (Scot.) 1986; *b* 17 April 1947; *s* of Lord Emslie, *qv*; *m* 1973, Heather Ann Davis; one *s* two *d. Educ:* Edinburgh Acad.; Trinity Coll., Glenalmond; Gonville and Caius Coll., Cambridge (BA); Edinburgh Univ. (LLB). Admitted to Faculty of Advocates, 1972; Standing Junior Counsel: to Forestry Commn in Scotland and to Dept of Agric. and Fisheries for Scotland, 1981; to Inland Revenue in Scotland, 1982. *Address:* 20 Inverleith Place, Edinburgh EH3 5QB. *T:* 031–552 4091. *Clubs:* Hawks (Cambridge); New (Edinburgh).

EMSLIE, Prof. Ronald Douglas, FDSRCS; Dean of Dental Studies, Guy's Hospital Medical and Dental Schools, 1968–80, retired; Professor of Periodontology and Preventive Dentistry, University of London, 1970–80, now Emeritus; *b* 9 March 1915; *s* of late Alexander G. H. Emslie and Elizabeth Spence; *m* 1951, Dorothy, *d* of William A. Dennis, Paris, Ill, USA; four *s. Educ:* Felsted Sch.; Guy's Hosp. Dental Sch., London (BDS); Univ. of Illinois, Chicago (MSc). FDSRCS Eng., 1950; DRD (Edin), 1978. Served War: Surg. Lt (D) RNVR, 1943–46; Surg. Lt Comdr (D) RNVR, 1946. Half-time Asst in Dept of Preventive Dentistry, Guy's Hosp., 1946–48, also in private practice with Mr E. B. Dowsett; Research Fellow, Univ. of Illinois, Chicago, 1948–49; Head of Dept of Preventive Dentistry, Guy's Hosp., 1949–55; Reader in Preventive Dentistry, Univ. of London (Guy's Hosp. Dental Sch.), 1956–62; Prof. of Preventive Dentistry, Univ. of London (Guy's Hosp. Dental Sch.), 1963–70. Pres., Brit. Soc. of Periodontology, 1959–60; Chm., Dental Health Cttee of BDA, 1963–69; Member: Internat. Dental Fedn; Internat. Assoc. for Dental Research; Dental Educn Adv. Council (Chm., 1978–80); Bd of Faculty of Dental Surgery, RCS, 1966–81 (Vice-Dean, 1976–77); Fluoridation Soc. (Chm. 1970–80); Bd of Studies in Dentistry, Univ. of London (Chm., 1975–77). Past Pres., Odontological Section, RSM; Vis. Lectr, Univ. of Illinois, 1956; Nuffield Grant to study dental aspects of facial gangrene, in Nigeria, Sept.-Dec. 1961; Sci. Advr, Brit. Dental Jl, 1961–80 (Sci. Asst Ed., 1951–61); Consultant in Periodontology to RN, 1971–80. Fellow, BDA. *Publications:* various contribs to dental literature. *Recreations:* tennis, sailing, old motor cars. *Address:* Little Hale, Woodland Way, Kingswood, Surrey KT20 6NW. *T:* Mogador (0737) 832662.

EMSON, Air Marshal Sir Reginald (Herbert Embleton), KBE 1966 (CBE 1946); CB 1959; AFC 1941; Inspector-General of the Royal Air Force, 1967–69; *b* 11 Jan. 1912; *s* of Francis Reginald Emson, Hitcham, Buckinghamshire; *m* 1934, Doreen Marjory, *d* of Hugh Duke, Holyport, Maidenhead, Berkshire; two *s* two *d. Educ:* Christ's Hospital; RAF Coll., Cranwell. Joined RAF, 1931; served War of 1939–45 in Aeroplane Armament Establishment Gunnery Research Unit, Exeter; Fighter Command Headquarters and Central Fighter Establishment. Director, Armament Research and Development (Air), Ministry of Supply, 1950–59; Commander RAF Staff and Air Attaché, British Defence Staffs, Washington, 1961–63; Asst Chief of Air Staff (Operational Requirements), 1963–66; Dep. Chief Air Staff, 1966–67. Group Captain, 1943; Air Commodore, 1958; Air Vice-Marshal, 1962; Air Marshal (Acting), 1966. *Address:* Vor Cottage, Holyport, Maidenhead, Berks. *T:* Maidenhead (0628) 21992. *Club:* Royal Air Force.

ENCOMBE, Viscount; John Francis Thomas Marie Joseph Columba Fidelis Scott; *b* 9 July 1962; *s* and *heir* of 5th Earl of Eldon, *qv*.

ENDERBY, Prof. John Edwin, FRS 1985; H. O. Wills Professor of Physics, University of Bristol, since 1981; *b* 16 Jan. 1931; *s* of late Thomas Edwin Enderby and Rheita Rebecca Hollinshead (*née* Stather); *m* Susan Bowles; one *s* two *d* (and one *d* of previous marriage). *Educ:* Chester Grammar Sch.; London Univ. (BSc, PhD). Lecturer in Physics: Coll. of Technology, Huddersfield, 1957–60; Univ. of Sheffield, 1960–67; Reader in Physics, Univ. of Sheffield, 1967–69; Prof. in Physics and Head of the Dept, Univ. of Leicester, 1969–76; Prof. of Physics, Bristol Univ., 1976–; Head of Dept of Physics, and Dir, H. H. Wills Physics Lab., Bristol Univ., 1981–; Directeur-Adjoint, Institut Laue-Langevin, Grenoble, 1985–88. Fellow, Argonne Nat. Lab., Ill., USA, 1989–; Visiting Fellow, Battelle Inst., 1968–69; Visiting Professor: Univ. of Guelph, Ont., 1978; Univ. of Leiden, 1989. Member: Physics Cttee, SRC, 1974–77; Neutron Beam Res. Cttee, SRC, 1974–80 (Chm., 1977–80 and 1988–). Member: Council, Institut Laue-Langevin, Grenoble, 1973–80; Council, Royal Soc., 1990–; Academia Europaea, 1989. FInstP 1970 (Chm., SW Br., 1979–83). Associate Editor, Philosophical Magazine, 1975–81. Editor, Proc. Royal Soc. A, 1989–. *Publications:* (jointly): Physics of Simple Liquids, 1968; Amorphous and Liquid Semiconductors, 1974; many publications on the structure and properties of liquids in: Phil. Mag. Adv. Phys, Jl Phys, Proc. Royal Soc., etc. *Recreations:* gardening, watching Association football. *Address:* H. H. Wills Physics Laboratory, Tyndall Avenue, Bristol BS8 1TL. *T:* Bristol (0272) 303598; 7 Cotham Lawn Road, Bristol BS6 6DU. *T:* Bristol (0272) 733411.

ENDERBY, Kenneth Albert; General Manager, Runcorn Development Corporation, 1978–81; *b* 7 Aug. 1920; *s* of Albert William Enderby and Frances Enderby; *m* 1946, Mary Florence; one *s* two *d. Educ:* Nottingham High Sch.; London Univ. (BSc Econs). IPFA. Served War, Royal Corps of Signals (TA), 1939–46: BEF, MEF, CMF (mentioned in despatches, 1944); Captain. Local Govt Finance: Nottingham, 1936–51; Buckingham, 1951–53; Chief Auditor, City of Sheffield, 1953–56; Dep. City Treasurer, Coventry, 1956–64; Chief Finance Officer, Runcorn Develt Corp., 1964–78. *Recreations:* gardening, camping, fresh air, zymology. *Address:* Four Winds, 2 Helmeth Road, Church Stretton, Salop SY6 7AS. *T:* Church Stretton (0694) 722328.

ENDERBY, Col Samuel, CVO 1977; DSO 1943; MC 1939; JP; *b* 15 Sept. 1907; *s* of Col Samuel Enderby and Mary Cuninghame; *m* 1936, Pamela, *e d* of Major Charles Beck Hornby, DSO; two *s* one *d. Educ:* Uppingham Sch.; RMC Sandhurst. Regular soldier, commissioned 5th Fusiliers, 1928. Served War, 1939–46: MEF, CMF, comd 2/4th KOYLI and 2/5 Leicester Regt; Commandant, Sch. of Infantry: ACRE, 1945–46; Netheravon, 1947–48; comd, 7th Bn Royal Northumberland Fusiliers, 1949; retd 1949. JP 1956; High Sheriff of Northumberland, 1968. Mem., Hon. Corps of Gentlemen at Arms, 1954–77, Standard Bearer, 1976–77. *Address:* The Riding, Hexham, Northumberland NE46 4PF. *T:* Hexham (0434) 2250. *Club:* Army and Navy.

ENFIELD, Viscount; William Robert Byng; Computer programmer, British Gas Northern; *b* 10 May 1964; *s* and *heir* of 8th Earl of Strafford, *qv. Educ:* Winchester Coll.; Durham Univ. *Address:* 11 Hargill Drive, Rickleton, Washington, Tyne and Wear NE38 9EX.

ENGESET, Jetmund, FRCSE; FRCSG; Consultant Surgeon, Grampian Health Board, since 1987; Surgeon to the Queen in Scotland, since 1985; *b* 22 July 1938; *s* of Arne K. Engeset and Marta Engeset; *m* 1966, Anne Graeme (*née* Robertson); two *d. Educ:* Slemdal and Ris Skole, Oslo, Norway; Oslo University; Aberdeen University (MB ChB, ChM Hons). House Officer (Surgical and Medical), Aberdeen Royal Infirmary, 1964–65; Aberdeen University: Res. Assistant, Dept of Surgery, 1965–67; Surgical Registrar, 1967–70; Lectr in Surgery, 1970–74; Sen. Lectr in Surgery, 1974–87; Head of Dept of Surgery, 1982–85 (seconded to Salgrenska Hosp. Surgical Unit, Gothenburg, Sweden, 1972–74). *Publications:* papers on microcirculation, vascular surgery, organ preservation and tissue transplantation. *Recreations:* skiing, angling, squash, gardening. *Address:* Pine Lodge, 315 North Deeside Road, Milltimber, Aberdeen, Aberdeenshire AB1 0DL. *T:* Aberdeen (0224) 733753.

ENGLAND, Frank Raymond Wilton; *b* 24 Aug. 1911; *s* of Joseph and Florence England; *m*; one *d. Educ:* Christ's Coll., Finchley. Served War, Pilot, RAF, 1941–45. Apprenticeship with Daimler Co. Ltd, Hendon, 1927–32; Racing Mechanic to: Sir Henry Birkin, Whitney Straight, ERA Ltd, Richard Seaman, B. Bira, 1932–38; Service Engr, Service Dept Supt, Alvis Limited, 1938–40. Service Manager, Jaguar Cars Ltd, 1946–56; Service Dir, 1956–61; Asst Man. Dir, 1961–66; Dep. Man. Dir, 1966–67; Jt Man. Dir, 1967; Dep. Chm., 1968; Chm. and Chief Executive, 1972; retd as Chm., Jan. 1974. *Recreation:* motor sport. *Address:* Tannachweg 1, A4813 Altmünster, Austria. *T:* 07612 88316. *Clubs:* Royal Air Force, British Racing Drivers'.

ENGLAND, Glyn, BSc(Eng); FEng, FIEE, FIMechE, CBIM; Chairman, Woodlands Initiatives Ltd; Consultant, World Bank; *b* 19 April 1921; *m* 1942, Tania Reichenbach; two *d. Educ:* Penarth County Sch.; Queen Mary Coll., London Univ. (BSc (Eng)); London School of Economics. Department of Scientific and Industrial Research, 1939. War service, 1942–47. Chief Ops Engr, CEGB, 1966–71; Dir-Gen., SW Region, 1971–73; Chm., SW Electricity Bd, 1973–77; part-time Mem., 1975–77, Chm., 1977–82, CEGB. Director: F. H. Lloyd (Hldgs), 1982–87; Triplex Lloyd, 1987–90. Mem., British Nat. Cttee, World Energy Conf., 1977–82; Vice-Pres., Internat. Union of Producers and Distributors of Electrical Energy, 1981–82. Mem., Bd of Dirs, UK Centre for Economic and Environmental Development, 1984–. Chairman: Council for Envmtl Conservation, 1983–88; Bd of Trustees, Silvanus Charitable Trust (formerly Dartington Action Res. Trust), 1985–. Sometime Labour Mem., Herts CC; Mem. Council, Magistrates' Assoc. JP Welwyn, Herts, 1962–71. Hon. DSc Bath, 1981. *Publications:* (with Rex Savidge) Landscape in the Making; papers on: Economic Growth and the Electricity Supply Industry, Security of Electricity Supplies, Planning for Uncertainty, Railways and Power (IMechE Tritton Lecture). *Recreation:* actively enjoying the countryside. *Address:* Woodbridge Farm, Ubley, Bristol BS18 6PX. *T:* Blagdon (0761) 662479.

ENGLE, Sir George (Lawrence Jose), KCB 1983 (CB 1976); QC 1983; First Parliamentary Counsel, 1981–86; *b* 13 Sept. 1926; *o s* of late Lawrence Engle; *m* 1956, Irene, *d* of late Heinz Lachmann; three *d. Educ:* Charterhouse (scholar); Christ Church, Oxford (Marjoribanks and Dixon schols, MA). Served RA, 1945–48 (2nd Lt, 1947). Firsts in Mods and Greats; Cholmeley Schol., Lincoln's Inn, 1952. Called to Bar, Lincoln's Inn,

1953, Bencher, 1984. Joined Parly Counsel Office, 1957; seconded as First Parly Counsel, Fedn of Nigeria, 1965–67; Parly Counsel, 1970–80; Second Parly Counsel, 1980–81; with Law Commn, 1971–73. Pres., Commonwealth Assoc. of Legislative Counsel, 1983–86. *Publications:* Law for Landladies, 1955; (ed jtly) Cross on Statutory Interpretation, 2nd edn 1987; contributor to: Ideas, 1954; O Rare Hoffnung, 1960; The Oxford Companion to English Literature, 1985. *Recreations:* book-hunting, oriental and Islamic pots, bricolage. *Address:* 32 Wood Lane, Highgate, N6 5UB. *T:* 081–340 9750.

ENGLEFIELD, Dermot John Tryal; Librarian, House of Commons, since 1991; *b* 27 Aug. 1927; *o s* of Major Henry Wotton Englefield and Blanchfield Bernardine Englefield (*née* O'Halloran); *m* 1962, Dora, *o d* of Josip and Maca Grahovac, Karlovac, Jugoslavia; one *s* one *d.* *Educ:* Mount St Mary's Coll.; Trinity Coll. Dublin (MA); Sarah Purser Scholarship (Hist. of Art) 1951. ALA 1966. Served RAF, 1946–48. St Marylebone Ref. Liby, 1952–54; House of Commons Liby, 1954–; Asst Librarian (Parly Div.), 1967; Dep. Librarian, 1976. H of C corresp. to European Centre of Parly Res. and Documentation, 1977–; Consultant to: Council of Europe, 1970; European Parlt, 1973; proposed Scottish Assembly, 1978; NI Assembly, 1982; Hong Kong Legislative Council, 1988. Member: Parly Libraries Sect., IFLA (Sec., 1981–85; Chm., 1985–89); Study of Parlt Gp, 1970– (Chm., 1987–90). Gov., Dulwich Coll., 1985–. Editor for Industry and Parlt Trust, 1984–. Silver Jubilee Medal, 1977. *Publications:* The Printed Records of the Parliament of Ireland 1613–1800, 1978; Parliament and Information, 1981; Whitehall and Westminster, 1985; The Study of Parliament Group, 1985; *edited:* (with G. Drewry) Information Sources in Politics and Political Science, 1984; Commons Select Committees, 1984; Today's Civil Service, 1985; Legislative Libraries and Developing Countries, 1986; Local Government and Business, 1987; Parliamentary Libraries and Information Services, 1990; Workings of Westminster, 1991; chapters in books and contribs to jls. *Recreations:* travel, looking, listening, writing. *Address:* c/o House of Commons, SW1A 0AA. *T:* 071–219 3635.

ENGLEHART, Robert Michael; QC 1986; a Recorder, since 1987; *b* 1 Oct. 1943; *s* of G. A. F. and K. P. Englehart; *m* 1971, Rosalind Mary Foster; one *s* two *d.* *Educ:* St Edward's Sch., Oxford; Trinity Coll., Oxford (MA); Harvard Law School (LLM); Bologna Centre (Dip. in Internat. Relns). Assistente, Univ. of Florence, 1968. Called to the Bar, Middle Temple, 1969; practising barrister, 1969–. Chm., London Common Law and Commercial Bar Assoc., 1990. *Publication:* (contrib.) Il Controllo Giudiziario: a comparative study of civil procedure, 1968. *Recreations:* shooting, cricket, windsurfing. *Address:* 2 Hare Court, Temple, EC4Y 7BH. *T:* 071–583 1770. *Club:* MCC.

ENGLISH, Cyril; President, Nationwide Housing Trust, since 1991; Director, Nationwide Anglia (formerly Nationwide) Building Society, 1978–90 (Deputy Chairman, 1989–90); *b* 18 Feb. 1923; *s* of Joseph and Mary Hannah English; *m* 1945, Mary Brockbank; two *d.* *Educ:* Ashton-under-Lyne Grammar School. ALCM; CBIM. Joined Nationwide Building Society, 1939; Asst Secretary, 1961; Asst General Manager, 1967; General Manager, 1971; Deputy Chief General Manager, 1974; Chief Gen. Manager, 1981–85. *Recreations:* golf, music. *Address:* Ashton Grange, Cedar Drive, Pangbourne, Berks RG8 7BH. *T:* Pangbourne (0734) 843841. *Club:* Calcot Park Golf (Reading).

ENGLISH, Sir Cyril (Rupert), Kt 1972; retired; Director-General, City and Guilds of London Institute, 1968–76; *b* 19 April 1913; *m*; two *s.* *Educ:* Northgate Sch., Ipswich. BScEng Ext. London, 1934. Technical teacher, 1935–39. Served Royal Navy, 1939–46, Lieut-Commander (E). HM Inspector of Schools, 1946–55; Staff Inspector (Engineering), 1955–58; Chief Inspector of Further Education, in connection with Industry and Commerce, 1958–65; Senior Chief Inspector, Dept of Education and Science, 1965–67. Member, Anglo-American Productivity Team, 1951; attended Commonwealth Education Conferences, Delhi, 1962, Ottawa, 1964. Chairman: British Assoc. for Commercial and Industrial Educn, 1970–71, 1971–72; RAF Educn Adv. Cttee; Member: Services Colleges Cttee, 1965–66; Adv. Bd, RAF Coll., Cranwell; Academic Adv. Council, Royal Defence Acad.; Bd of Dirs, Industrial Training Service; Central Training Council; CTC Gen. Policy Cttee; Nat. Adv. Council for Educn in Industry and Commerce; Council for Tech. Educn and Training for Overseas Countries (Bd Mem., Chm. Educn Cttee); Reg. Adv. Council for Technol. Educn (London and Home Counties); Schools Science and Technology Cttee; Educn Cttee, IMechE; Associated Examining Bd; Cttee of Inquiry into Training of Teachers (James Cttee); Standing Conf. on Schs' Science and Technology; Cttee on Regular Officer training (Army). Vice-Pres., Soc. Electronic and Radio Technicians, 1972–74, Pres., 1975. Governor, Imperial Coll. FIMechE; FIProdE; FIMarE. Hon. Fellow, Inst. of Road Transport Engrs, 1971. Hon. Fellow, Manchester Polytechnic, 1976. Hon. DTech Brunel, 1970; Hon. DSc Loughborough, 1973; DUniv Open, 1974. *Address:* 12 Pineheath Road, High Kelling, Holt, Norfolk.

ENGLISH, Sir David, Kt 1982; Editor: Daily Mail, since 1971; Mail on Sunday, 1982; Joint Deputy Chairman and Editor in Chief, Associated Newspapers, since 1989 (Vice-Chairman, Associated Newspapers Group, 1986–88); *b* 26 May 1931; *m* 1954, Irene Mainwood; one *s* two *d.* *Educ:* Bournemouth Sch. Daily Mirror, 1951–53; Feature Editor, Daily Sketch, 1956; Foreign Correspondent: Sunday Dispatch, 1959; Daily Express, 1960; Washington Correspdt, Express, 1961–63; Chief American Correspdt, Express, 1963–65; Foreign Editor, Express, 1965–67; Associate Editor, Express, 1967–69; Editor, Daily Sketch, 1969–71. Chairman: Burlington Magazines, 1988–; New Era TV, 1988–. Mem. Bd, Assoc. of British Editors, 1985–. *Publication:* Divided They Stand (a British view of the 1968 American Presidential Election), 1969. *Recreations:* reading, ski-ing, boating. *Address:* Daily Mail, Northcliffe House, 2 Derry Street, W8 5TT. *T:* 071–938 6000. *Clubs:* London Press; Royal Temple Yacht, Ski of Great Britain.

ENGLISH, Rev. Donald; General Secretary, Methodist Church Division of Home Mission, since 1982; Moderator, Free Church Federal Council, 1986–87; President of the Methodist Conference, 1978–79 and 1990–91; *b* 20 July 1930; *s* of Robert and Ena Forster English; *m* 1962, Bertha Forster Ludlow; two *s.* *Educ:* Consett Grammar Sch.; University Coll., Leicester; Wesley House, Cambridge. BA London; DipEd Leicester; MA Cantab. Education Officer, RAF, 1953–55; Travelling Sec., Inter-Varsity Fellowship, 1955–58; Asst Tutor, Wesley Coll., Headingley, 1960–62; ordained into Methodist Ministry, 1962; New Testament Tutor, Trinity Coll., Umuahia, E Nigeria, 1962–66; Circuit Minister, Cullercoats, Northumberland, 1966–72; Tutor in Historical Theology, Hartley Victoria Coll., Manchester (Lord Rank Chair), 1972–73; Tutor in Practical Theol. and Methodism, Wesley Coll., Bristol (Lord Rank Chair), 1973–82. Member: World Methodist Exec., 1976–86; Central Religious Adv. Cttee, 1987–; Vice-Chm., World Methodist Council Exec., 1986–. Hon. Fellow, Roehampton Inst. of Educn, 1989. Hon. DD Asbury, USA, 1979; DUniv Surrey, 1990. *Publications:* Evangelism and Worship, 1971; God in the Gallery, 1975; Christian Discipleship, 1977; Windows on the Passion, 1978; From Wesley's Chair: Presidential Addresses, 1979; Why Believe in Jesus?: evangelistic reflections for Lent, 1986; Evangelistic Counselling, 1987; Evangelism Now, 1987; The Meaning of the Warmed Heart, 1988; Everything in Christ, 1988. *Recreations:* gardening, reading. *Address:* 44 Anne Boleyn's Walk, Cheam, Surrey. *T:* 081–643 3679.

ENGLISH, Gerald; Director, Opera Studio, Victorian College for the Arts, Melbourne, since 1977; *b* 6 Nov. 1925; *m* 1954, Jennifer Ryan; two *s* two *d*; *m* 1974, Linda Jacoby; one *s.* *Educ:* King's Sch., Rochester. After War service studied at Royal College of Music and then began career as lyric tenor; subsequently travelled in USA and Europe, appeared at Sadler's Wells, Covent Garden and Glyndebourne and recorded for major gramophone companies; Professor, Royal Coll. of Music, 1960–77. *Address:* c/o Victorian College for the Arts, 234 St Kilda Road, Melbourne, Vic 3003, Australia.

ENGLISH, Michael; *b* 24 Dec. 1930; *s* of late William Agnew English; *m* 1976, Carol Christine Owen; one *s* one *d.* *Educ:* King George V Grammar Sch., Southport; Liverpool Univ. (LLB). Joined Labour Party, 1949; Rochdale County Borough Council, 1953–65 (Chairman Finance Cttee until 1964). Employed until 1964 as Asst Manager of department concerned with management services in subsidiary of large public company. Contested (Lab) Shipley Div., WR Yorks, 1959; MP (Lab) Nottingham West, 1964–83. Parliamentary Private Secretary, Board of Trade, 1966–67; Chairman: Parly Affairs Gp of Parly Lab. Party, 1970–76; Gen. Sub-Cttee of House of Commons Expenditure Cttee, 1974–79; Chm., E Midlands Gp, PLP, 1976–78; formerly Mem., Chairmen's Panel, Treasury and Civil Service, Procedure (Finance) and Sound Broadcasting Cttees, House of Commons. Mem., Lambeth BC, 1990–. Chm., E Midlands Regional Lab. Party, 1979–80. *Recreation:* reading history. *Address:* 12 Denny Crescent, Kennington, SE11 4UY. *T:* 071–582 9970.

ENGLISH, Sir Terence (Alexander Hawthorne), KBE 1991; FRCS; FRCP; Consultant Cardiothoracic Surgeon, Papworth and Addenbrooke's Hospitals, Cambridge, since 1973; President, Royal College of Surgeons, 1989–July 1992; *b* 3 Oct. 1932; *s* of late Arthur Alexander English and Mavis Eleanor (*née* Lund); *m* 1963, Ann Margaret, *e d* of late Frederick Mordaunt Dicey and Ann Gwendoline (*née* Smartt); two *s* two *d.* *Educ:* Hilton Coll., Natal; Witwatersrand Univ. (BSc(Eng) 1954); Guy's Hosp. Med. Sch. (MB, BS 1962); MA Cantab 1977. FRCSE 1967; FRCS 1967; FRCP 1990. House appointments, Guy's Hosp., 1962–63; Demonstrator, Anatomy Dept, Guy's Hosp., 1964–65; Surgical Registrar: Bolingbroke Hosp., 1966; Brompton Hosp., 1967–68; Res. Fellow, Dept of Surgery, Univ. of Alabama, 1969; Sen. Registrar, Brompton, National Heart and London Chest Hosps, 1968–72; Dir, Papworth Heart Transplant Res. Unit, 1980–88. Chief Med. Advr, BUPA, 1991–. Mem., Specialists Adv. Cttee in Cardiothoracic Surgery, 1980–87. Member: British Cardiac Soc., 1973–; British Transplantation Soc., 1980–; Soc. of Thoracic and Cardiovascular Surgeons, 1972– (Exec. Council, 1975–77); Thoracic Soc., 1971– (Exec. Council, 1978–81). Member Council: RCS, 1981–; British Heart Foundn; Member: GMC, 1983–89; Standing Med. Adv. Cttee, 1989–; Jt Consultants Cttee, 1989–; Supraregional Services Adv. Gp, 1990–. President: Internat. Soc. of Heart Transplantation, 1984–85; Soc. of Perfusionists of GB and Ireland, 1985–86. Upjohn Lectr, Royal Soc., 1988. Capt., Guy's Hosp. RFC, 1959–60. FACC 1986. Hon. FRCSCan 1990; Hon. FRACS 1991; Hon. FCSSA 1991; Hon. FRCS (Thailand); Hon. FRCAnaes, 1991. Man of the Year, RADAR, 1980; Clement Price Thomas Award, RCS, 1986. *Publications:* chapter on Surgery of the Thorax and Heart in Bailey and Love's Short Practice of Thoracic Surgery, 1980; numerous articles in medical jls on matters relating to the practice of heart transplantation and cardiothoracic surgery. *Recreations:* reading, music, walking, tennis. *Address:* 19 Adams Road, Cambridge CB3 9AD. *T:* Cambridge (0223) 68744.

ENGLISH, Terence Michael; a Metropolitan Stipendiary Magistrate, since 1986; Chairman, Inner London Juvenile Court Panel, since 1989; *b* 3 Feb. 1944; *s* of John Robert English and Elsie Letitia English; *m* 1966, Ivy Joan Weatherley; one *s* one *d.* *Educ:* St Ignatius' Coll., London N15; London Univ. (external LLB 1967). Admitted Solicitor of the Supreme Court, 1970. Assistant, Edmonton PSD, 1962–71; Dep. Clerk to Justices, Bullingdon, Bampton E, Henley and Watlington PSDs, 1972–76; Clerk to the Justices: Newbury and Hungerford and Lambourn PSDs, 1977–85; Slough and Windsor PSDs, 1985–86. *Recreations:* golf, philately. *Address:* 3 Beckett Close, Wokingham, Berks RG11 1YZ. *T:* Wokingham (0734) 782888.

ENNALS, family name of **Baron Ennals.**

ENNALS, Baron *cr* 1983 (Life Peer), of Norwich in the County of Norfolk; **David Hedley Ennals;** PC 1970; Chairman: United Nations Association, since 1984; Ockenden Venture; National Association for Mental Health (MIND), since 1984 (Campaign Director, 1970–73); Gandhi Foundation, since 1984; *b* 19 Aug. 1922; *s* of A. F. Ennals, 8 Victoria Terrace, Walsall, Staffs; *m* 1st, 1950, Eleanor Maud Caddick (marr. diss. 1977); three *s* one *d*; 2nd 1977, Katherine Gene Tranoy. *Educ:* Queen Mary's Grammar School, Walsall; Loomis Inst., Windsor, Conn, USA. Served with HM Forces, 1941–46: Captain, RAC. Secretary, Council for Education in World Citizenship, 1947–52; Secretary, United Nations Association, 1952–57; Overseas Sec., Labour Party, 1957–64. MP (Lab): Dover, 1964–70; Norwich North, Feb. 1974–1983; PPS to Minister of Overseas Development, 1964; Parly Under-Sec. of State, Army, 1966–67; Parly Under-Sec., Home Office, 1967–68; Minister of State: DHSS, 1968–70; FCO, 1974–76; Sec. of State for Social Services, 1976–79. Pres., Parly Food and Health Forum, 1985–; Chm., Parly Alternative Medicine Gp, 1989–. Chm., John Bellers Ltd, 1972–74. Chairman: Anti-Apartheid Movement, 1960–64; Campaign for Homeless and Rootless, 1972–74; Peter Bedford Trust, 1984–; Children's Medical Charity, 1984–; Co-Chm., Global Co-operation for a Better World, 1987; Mem. Council, Counsel and Care for the Elderly, 1990–; Pres., Coll. of Occupational Therapy, 1984–; Vice-Pres., UNA. Trustee, Biopolitics Internat. Orgns. Pres., Tibet Soc., 1988. Patron, Nat. Soc. of Non Smokers; Gov., Ditchley Foundn. *Publications:* Strengthening the United Nations, 1957; Middle East Issues, 1958; United Nations Peace Force, 1960; United Nations on Trial, 1962; Out of Mind, 1973. *Address:* 16 Ingram Road, N2 9QA.

See also M. Ennals.

ENNALS, Kenneth Frederick John, CB 1983; Member, Local Government Boundary Commission for England, since 1987; Deputy Secretary, Finance and Local Government, Department of the Environment, 1985–87; *b* 10 Jan. 1932; *s* of Ernest Ennals and Elsie Dorothy Ennals; *m* 1958, Mavis Euphemia; one *s* two *d.* *Educ:* Alleyn's Sch., Dulwich; LSE. Joined Export Credits Guarantee Dept, 1952; Principal, DEA, 1965–69; Min. of Housing and Local Govt, later DoE, 1969; Asst Sec., 1970, Under Sec., 1976–80, DoE; Dir-Gen., Orgn and Estabts, Depts of the Environment and Transport, 1980–84. *Recreations:* reading, painting, dog-walking. *Address:* Skitreadons, Petworth Road, Haslemere, Surrey GU27 3AU. *T:* Haslemere (0428) 2733. *Club:* Commonwealth Trust.

ENNALS, Prof. Martin; Ariel F. Sallows Professor of Human Rights, University of Saskatchewan, 1991–June 1992; *b* 27 July 1927; *s* of A. Ford Ennals and Jessie E. Ennals (*née* Taylor); *m* 1951, Jacqueline B. Ennals (*née* Morris); one *s* one *d.* *Educ:* Queen Mary's Sch., Walsall; London Sch. of Economics. BScEcon (Internat. Relations). UNESCO, 1951–59; Gen. Sec., National Council for Civil Liberties, 1960–66; Information Officer, Nat. Cttee for Commonwealth Immigrants, 1966–68; Sec. Gen., Amnesty International (Nobel Peace Prize, 1977), 1968–80; Head of Police Cttee Support Unit, GLC, 1982–85; Sec.-Gen., International Alert, 1985–91. *Recreations:* escapist television and ski-ing. *Address:* 16 Patterdale, Robert Street, NW1 3QJ; Law Faculty, University of Saskatchewan,

Saskatoon, Saskatchewan, S7N 0W0, Canada.
See also Baron Ennals.

ENNISKILLEN, 7th Earl of, *cr* 1789 (Ire.); **Andrew John Galbraith Cole;** Baron Mountflorence 1760; Viscount Enniskillen 1776; Baron Grinstead (UK) 1815; pilot and company director; Captain Irish Guards, 1965; *b* 28 April 1942; *s* of 6th Earl of Enniskillen, MBE and Sonia (*d* 1982), *d* of Major Thomas Syers, RA; *S* father, 1989; *m* 1964, Sarah, *o d* of Maj.-Gen. J. Keith-Edwards, CBE, DSO, MC, Nairobi; three *d. Educ:* Eton. Man. Dir, Kenya Airways, 1979–81. *Heir: uncle* Arthur Gerald Cole [*b* 15 Nov. 1920; *m* 1949, Prudence Tobina, *d* of late A. R. A. Cartright; three *s* one *d*]. *Address:* c/o Royal Bank of Scotland, 9 Pall Mall, SW1.

ENNISMORE, Viscount; Francis Michael Hare; *b* 28 June 1964; *s* and *heir* of 5th Earl of Listowel, *qv*. *Address:* 10 Downshire Hill, NW3.

ENRICI, Most Rev. Domenico, JCD; former Apostolic Nuncio; *b* 9 April 1909; *s* of late Domenico Enrici and Maria Dalmasso Enrici. *Educ:* Diocesan Seminary, Cuneo; Pontifical Gregorian Univ. and Pontifical Ecclesiastical Academy, Rome. Ordained, 1933; parochial work in Dio. Cuneo, 1933–35. Served at various Apostolic Nunciatures and Delegations: Ireland, 1938–45; Egypt, 1946–48; Palestine and Jordan, 1948–53; Formosa, Free China, 1953–55; apptd Titular Archbp of Ancusa, 1955; Apostolic Internuncio to Indonesia, 1955–58; Apostolic Nuncio to Haiti and Apostolic Delegate to West Indies, 1958–60; Apostolic Internuncio to Japan, 1960–62; Apostolic Delegate to Australia, New Zealand and Oceania, 1962–69; Apostolic Delegate to GB and Gibraltar, 1969–73; Pro-Pres., Pontifical Ecclesiastical Acad., 1974–75; Delegate for Pontifical Representations, 1973–79; retired, 1979. Commander, Order of the Nile (Egypt), 1948; Order of the Sacred Treasure, 1st class (Japan), 1962; Assistant to the Pontifical Throne, Vatican City, 1979. *Publication:* Mistero e Luce (Mystery and Light), 1984. *Address:* Via Senatore Toselli, 8, 12100 Cuneo, Italy. *T:* (0171) 51120.

ENRIGHT, Dennis Joseph, OBE 1991; freelance writer; *b* 11 March 1920; *s* of late George and Grace Enright; *m* 1949, Madeleine Harders; one *d. Educ:* Leamington Coll.; Downing Coll., Cambridge. MA Cantab; DLitt Alexandria. Lecturer in English, University of Alexandria, 1947–50; Organising Tutor, University of Birmingham Extra-Mural Dept, 1950–53; Vis. Prof., Kōnan Univ., Japan, 1953–56; Vis. Lecturer, Free University of Berlin, 1956–57; British Council Professor, Chulalongkorn Univ., Bangkok, 1957–59; Prof. of English, Univ. of Singapore, 1960–70; Hon. Prof. of English, Univ. of Warwick, 1975–80. Dir, Chatto and Windus, 1974–82. Co-Editor, Encounter, 1970–72. FRSL 1961. Cholmondeley Poetry Award, 1974; Queen's Gold Medal for Poetry, 1981. Hon. DLitt Warwick, 1982; DUniv. Surrey, 1985. *Publications: poetry:* The Laughing Hyena, 1953; Bread Rather Than Blossoms, 1956; Some Men Are Brothers, 1960; Addictions, 1962; The Old Adam, 1965; Unlawful Assembly, 1968; Selected Poems, 1969; Daughters of Earth, 1972; The Terrible Shears, 1973; Rhyme Times Rhyme (for children), 1974; Sad Ires, 1975; Paradise Illustrated, 1978; A Faust Book, 1979; Collected Poems, 1981; Instant Chronicles, 1985; Collected Poems 1987, 1987; Selected Poems 1990, 1990; Under the Circumstances, 1991; *novels:* Academic Year, 1955; Heaven Knows Where, 1957; Insufficient Poppy, 1960; Figures of Speech, 1965; *novels for children:* The Joke Shop, 1976; Wild Ghost Chase, 1978; Beyond Land's End, 1979; *criticism:* The Apothecary's Shop, 1957; English Critical Texts (co-editor), 1962; Conspirators and Poets, 1966; Shakespeare and the Students, 1970; Man is an Onion, 1972; (ed) A Choice of Milton's Verse, 1975; Samuel Johnson: Rasselas, 1976; (ed) The Oxford Book of Contemporary Verse 1945–1980, 1980; A Mania for Sentences, 1983; (ed) Fair of Speech: the uses of euphemism, 1985; The Alluring Problem: an essay on irony, 1986; Fields of Vision: essays on literature, language and television, 1988; *travel:* The World of Dew: Japan, 1955; Memoirs of a Mendicant Professor, 1969; *translation:* The Poetry of Living Japan (co-editor), 1957; *anthologies:* (ed) The Oxford Book of Death, 1983; (ed) The Faber Book of Fevers and Frets, 1989; (ed jtly) The Oxford Book of Friendship, 1991; contributor to: Scrutiny, Encounter, London Review of Books, TLS, etc. *Recreations:* reading, writing, television, listening to music. *Address:* 35A Viewfield Road, SW18 5JD.

ENRIGHT, Derek Anthony; Director, Dega '92, since 1987; Special Adviser to EEC on The Third World, since 1988; *b* 2 Aug. 1935; *s* of Lawrence and Helen Enright; *m* 1963, Jane Maureen (*née* Simmons); two *s* two *d. Educ:* St Michael's Coll., Leeds; Wadham Coll., Oxford (BA, DipEd). Head of Classics, John Fisher Sch., Purley, Surrey, 1959–67; Dep. Head of St Wilfrid's, North Featherstone, W Yorks, 1967–79; EEC delegate in Guinea Bissau, 1985–87. Mem. (Lab) Leeds, Eur. Parlt, 1979–84; Brit. Labour Group Spokesman on third world affairs and women's rights, 1979–84. Contested (Lab) Kent East, European elecn, 1984. Order of Merit (Guinea Bissau), 1987. *Publications:* reports on: fishing agreements in West Africa; EEC relations with non ACP developing countries; Namibia after independence. *Recreations:* reading the Guardian, entertaining the family, walking the dogs. *Address:* The Hollies, 112 Carleton Road, Pontefract, W Yorks. *T:* Pontefract (0977) 702096.

ENSOM, Donald, FRICS, FCIArb; Chartered Surveyor; Consultant, Debenham Tewson & Chinnocks, since 1986 (Partner, 1962–86); *b* 8 April 1926; *s* of Charles R. A. W. Ensom and Edith (*née* Young); *m* 1951, Sonia (*née* Sherrard); one *s* one *d. Educ:* Norbury Manor Sch., Croydon. Qualified as Chartered Surveyor, 1951; FRICS 1958; FCIArb 1970. Served RA, 1943–47. Partner, Nightingale, Page & Bennett/Debenham Tewson & Chinnocks (after merger), 1958–86. Chm., Bldg Conservation Trust, 1981–83; Royal Institution of Chartered Surveyors: Pres., Bldg Surveyors Div., 1975–76; Chm., Professional Practice Cttee, 1978–83; Hon. Sec., 1983–90; Vice-Pres., 1988–90. Pres., Land Economy Soc., Univ. of Cambridge, 1990–91. *Recreations:* reading, opera and music, caravanning, canals. *Address:* Saxons, 102 Grange Road, Cambridge CB3 9AA. *Clubs:* East India, Royal Over-Seas League, Chartered Surveyors (1913), Pyramus and Thisbe (Chm. 1987–89).

ENSOR, David, OBE 1986; Managing Director, Croydon Advertiser Ltd, 1979–85; *b* 2 April 1924; *s* of Rev. William Walters and Constance Eva Ensor; *m* 1947, Gertrude Kathleen Brown; two *s. Educ:* Kingswood Sch., Bath; London Coll. of Printing. Served Royal Signals, 1942–46, Captain; ADC to GOC Bengal Dist. Managing Director: George Reveirs, 1947–59; Charles Skipper & East, 1959–69; Knapp Drewett & Sons, 1969–79; Chairman: Methodist Newspaper Co., 1975–; Methodist Publishing House, 1981–. A Vice-Chm., Press Council, 1987–90 (Mem., 1982–90); Mem. Council, Newspaper Soc., 1979–. Pres., London Printing Industries Assoc., 1976. Vice-Pres., Methodist Conf., 1981. *Address:* Milborne Lodge, Dinton Road, Fovant, Salisbury, Wilts SP3 5JW. *T:* Fovant (072270) 521.

ENSOR, George Anthony; Partner, Weightman Rutherfords (formerly Rutherfords), Solicitors, Liverpool, since 1962; a Recorder of the Crown Court, since 1983; *b* 4 Nov. 1936; *s* of George and Phyllis Ensor; *m* 1968, Jennifer Margaret Caile, MB, ChB; two *d. Educ:* Malvern College; Liverpool University (LLB). Solicitor, 1961 (Atkinson Conveyancing Medal, 1962; Rupert Bremner Medal, 1962). Deputy Coroner, City of Liverpool, 1966–; part-time Chairman, Industrial Tribunals, 1975–; Mem., Judicial Studies Bd, 1987–89; President, Liverpool Law Society, 1982. Trustee, Empire Theatre (Merseyside) Trust, Ltd, 1986–. Dir, Liverpool FC, 1985–. *Recreations:* golf, theatre. *Address:* 23 Far Moss Road, Blundellsands, Liverpool L23 8TG. *T:* 051–924 5937. *Clubs:* Artists (Liverpool); Formby Golf; Waterloo Rugby Union.

ENSOR, Michael de Normann, CMG 1980; OBE 1958; Chairman, Overseas Service Pensioners' Benevolent Society, since 1986; *b* 11 June 1919; *s* of Robert Weld Ensor and Dr Beatrice Ensor; *m* 1945, Mona Irene Blackburn; two *s. Educ:* Bryanston School; St. John's Coll., Oxford. Military service, 1940; Colonial Service, Gold Coast/Ghana Civil Service, 1940–58; Secretary, Foundation for Mutual Assistance in Africa South of the Sahara, 1958–64; Dept of Technical Cooperation/Min. of Overseas Development/Overseas Development Administration, 1964–80: Head, East Africa Development Division, 1975–80; Chm., Paragon Management Co., 1983–86. *Address:* Flat 1, 12 The Paragon, Blackheath, SE3 0NZ. *T:* 081–852 5345. *Clubs:* Travellers', Royal Blackheath Golf; Karen (Kenya).

ENSOR WALTERS, P. H. B.; *see* Walters.

ENTWISTLE, Sir (John Nuttall) Maxwell, Kt 1963; Under-writing Member of Lloyd's since 1964; *b* 8 Jan. 1910; *s* of Isaac and Hannah Entwistle; *m* 1940, Jean Cunliffe McAlpine, JP, *d* of late Dr John and Amy Margaret Penman; two *s. Educ:* Merchant Taylors' Sch., Great Crosby. Solicitor, 1931; Notary Public, 1955. Liverpool City: Councillor, 1938; Alderman, 1960; Leader of Liverpool City Council, when initiated preparation of develt plan for City centre. Councillor, Cumbria County, 1979–82. Chairman: Merseyside Development Cttee; Mersey Tunnel Cttee, 1961–63; Abbeyfield Liverpool Soc. Ltd, 1970–75; Council of Management, League of Welldoers, 1972–74. Mem., Liverpool Univ. Court and Council, 1955–64. President: Edge Hill Liverpool Conservative Assoc., 1963–71; Liverpool Clerks Assoc., 1964–78. Merchant Taylors' School: Chm., Appeal Cttee, 1969–74; Pres., Old Boys' Assoc., 1969–70; Governor, 1969–75. *Recreation:* gardening. *Address:* Stone Hall, Sedbergh, Cumbria. *T:* Sedbergh (05396) 20700.

ENTWISTLE, Prof. Kenneth Mercer; Professor of Metallurgy and Materials Science, University of Manchester Institute of Science and Technology, 1962–90, now Emeritus; Engineering Adviser to Chief Executive of Universities' Funding Council, since 1989; *b* 3 Jan. 1925; *s* of William Charles and Maude Elizabeth Entwistle; *m* 1949, Alice Patricia Mary Johnson; two *s* two *d. Educ:* Urmston Grammar Sch.; Univ. of Manchester (BSc Elect. Eng. 1945, MSc 1946, PhD 1948). FIM, CEng. University of Manchester: Lectr in Metallurgy, 1948; Sen. Lectr, 1954; Reader, 1960; Dean, Faculty of Technology, 1976–77; Pro-Vice-Chancellor, 1982–85; Vice-Principal, UMIST, 1972–74. Chairman: Materials Cttee, CNAA, 1972–74; Educn Cttee, Instn of Metallurgists, 1977–79; Metallics Sub-Cttee, SRC, 1979–81; Mem., UGC, 1985–89 (Chm., Technology Sub-Cttee, 1985–89). Comp. UMIST, 1991. Hon. Fellow, Sheffield Polytechnic, 1971. *Publications:* numerous papers in scientific jls. *Recreations:* Scottish dancing, choral singing. *Address:* Greenacre, Bridge End Lane, Prestbury, Macclesfield, Cheshire SK10 4DJ. *T:* Prestbury (0625) 829269. *Club:* Athenæum.

EÖTVÖS, Peter; composer and conductor; *m* 1968, Piroska Molnar; one *s*; *m* 1976, Pi-Hsien Chen; one *d. Educ:* Acad. of Music, Budapest; Musik Hochschule, Cologne. Composer from age 16, chamber music, electronic music, opera and orchestral music; conductor and musical director, Ensemble Intercontemporain, Paris, 1979–9191; principal guest conductor, BBC Symphony Orchestra, 1985–88. *Recreations:* walking, pipe smoking, jazz. *Address:* c/o Allied Artists, 42 Montpelier Square, SW7 1JZ. *T:* 071–589 6243.

EPHRAUMS, Maj.-Gen. Roderick Jarvis, CB 1977; OBE 1965; DL; Major-General Royal Marines, Commando Forces, 1976–78, retired; *b* 12 May 1927; *s* of Hugh Cyril Ephraums and Elsie Caroline (*née* Rowden); *m* 1955, Adela Mary (*née* Forster); two *s* one *d. Educ:* Tonbridge. Commnd 2nd Lieut, RM, 1945; HMS Mauritius, 1946–48; 3 Commando Bde, RM, 1952–54; Staff Coll., Camberley, 1960; Bde Major, 3 Commando Bde, 1962–64; CO, 45 Commando RM, 1969–71; Royal Coll. of Defence Studies, 1972; Comdr, 3 Commando Bde, 1973–74; NATO Defense Coll., Rome, 1975. A Col Comdt, RM, 1985–, Rep. Col Comdt, 1987 and 1988. DL Angus, 1985. OStJ 1987. *Recreations:* painting, gardening. *Club:* Army and Navy.

EPSTEIN, Sir (Michael) Anthony, Kt 1991; CBE 1985; FRS 1979; Fellow, Wolfson College, Oxford, since 1986; Professor of Pathology, 1968–85 (now Emeritus), and Head of Department, 1968–82, University of Bristol; Hon. Consultant Pathologist, Bristol Health District (Teaching), 1968–82; *b* 18 May 1921; *yr s* of Mortimer and Olga Epstein; *m* 1950, Lisbeth Knight; two *s* one *d. Educ:* St Paul's Sch., London; Trinity Coll., Cambridge (Perry Exhibr, 1940); Middlesex Hosp. Medical Sch. MA, MD, DSc, PhD; FRCPath. Ho. Surg., Middlesex Hosp., London, and Addenbrooke's Hosp., Cambridge, 1944; Lieut and Captain, RAMC, 1945–47; Asst Pathologist, Bland Sutton Inst., Mddx Hosp. Med. Sch., 1948–65, with leave as: Berkeley Travelling Fellow, 1952–53; French Govt Exchange Scholar at Institut Pasteur, Paris, 1952–53; Vis. Investigator, Rockefeller Inst., NY, 1956; Reader in Experimental Pathology, Mddx Hosp. Med. Sch., 1965–68; Hon. Consultant in Experimental Virology, Mddx Hosp., 1965–68. Member: Cttee, Pathological Soc. of GB and Ire., 1969–72 (Hon. Mem., 1987); Council, and Vice-Pres., Pathology Section of RSM, 1966–72; Study Gp on Classification of Herpes Viruses, of Internat. Commn for Nomenclature of Viruses, 1971–; Scientific Adv. Bd, Harvard Med. Sch.'s New England Regional Primate Center, 1972–; Cancer Research Campaign MRC Jt Cttee, 1973–77, 1982–87 (Chm. 1983–87); Cttee, British Soc. for Cell Biology, 1974–77; MRC, 1982–86 (Mem. 1979–84, Chm. 1982–84, Cell Bd; Mem., 1984–85, Chm., 1985–88, Tropical Medicine Res. Bd); Council, Royal Soc., 1983–85, 1986–91 (Foreign Sec. and a Vice-Pres., 1986–91; Assessor on MRC, 1987–); Medical and Scientific Panel, Leukaemia Research Fund, 1982–85; Scientific Adv. Cttee, Lister Inst., 1984–87; Expert Working Party on Bovine Spongiform Encephalopathy, DoH, 1988; Exec. Bd, ICSU, 1990–; Exec. Council, ESF, 1990–; Bd of Dirs, European Council for Co-ordinating Cancer Res., 1990–. Discovered in 1964 a new human herpes virus, now known as Epstein-Barr virus, which causes infectious mononucleosis and is also causally implicated in some forms of human cancer (Burkitt's lymphoma and nasopharyngeal carcinoma). Mem., Academia Europaea, 1988. Mem. d'honneur, Belgian Soc. for Cancer Res., 1979. Hon. Professor: Sun Yat-Sen Med. Univ., Guangzhou, 1981; Chinese Acad. of Preventive Medicine, Beijing, 1988. Hon. Fellow, Queensland Inst. of Med. Research, 1983; Hon. FRCP 1986; Hon. MD Edinburgh, 1986. Paul Ehrlich and Ludwig Darmstaedter Prize and Medal, Paul Ehrlich Foundn, W Germany, 1973; Markham Skerrit Prize, 1977; (jtly) Bristol-Myers Award, NY, 1982; Leeuwenhoek Prize Lectr, Royal Soc., 1983; Prix Griffuel, Assoc. pour la recherche sur le cancer, Paris, 1986; Samuel Weiner Distinguished Visitor Award, Univ. of Manitoba, 1988; John H. Lattimer Award, Amer. Urol Assoc., 1988; Internat. Award, Gairdner Foundn, Toronto, 1988. *Publications:* over 215 scientific papers in internat. jls on tumour cell structure, viruses, tumour viruses, Burkitt's lymphoma, and the EB virus. Jt Founder Editor, The Internat. Review of Experimental Pathology (vols 1–28, 1962–86); (ed jtly) The Epstein-Barr Virus, 1979;

(ed jtly) The Epstein-Barr Virus: recent advances, 1986. *Address:* Nuffield Department of Clinical Medicine, University of Oxford, John Radcliffe Hospital, Oxford OX3 9DU. *T:* Oxford (0865) 221334.

ERDMAN, Edward Louis, FSVA; FRSA; Founder, 1934, and Senior Consultant, since 1974, Edward Erdman, Surveyors; *b* 4 July 1906; *s* of David and Pauline Erdman; *m* 1949, Pamela (*née* Mason); one *s*. *Educ:* former Grocers' Co. Sch. Founded practice, 1934. TA KRRC, 1937; war service, N Africa and Italy, 1939–45. Re-opened practice, 1945; Director: Chesterfield Properties Plc, 1960 (Chm., 1979); Warnford Investments Plc, 1962; retired from practice, 1974. WPHT Housing Association (subseq. re-named Sanctuary Housing Association): Mem., Central Council, 1974–; Chm., 1978–87; Pres. 1987–; Dir, Sanctuary Land Co. Ltd, 1978–; Mem., Property Adv. Panel to Treasury, 1975–77. FRSA 1957. *Publication:* People and Property, 1982. *Recreations:* football, cycling, farming. *Address:* (office) 6 Grosvenor Street, W1X 0AD. *T:* 071–629 8191. *Club:* Naval and Military.

EREAUT, Sir (Herbert) Frank (Cobbold), Kt 1976; Bailiff of Jersey, 1975–85; Judge of the Court of Appeal of Guernsey, 1976–89; Director, Standard Chartered Bank (CI), since 1986; *b* 6 May 1919; *s* of Herbert Parker Ereaut and May Julia Cobbold; *m* 1942, Kathleen FitzGibbon; one *d*. *Educ:* Tormore Sch., Upper Deal, Kent; Cranleigh Sch., Surrey; Exeter Coll., Oxford. BA 1946, MA 1966. RASC, 1940–46: N Africa, Italy and NW Europe; 2nd Lieut 1940; Lieut 1941; Captain 1943. Called to Bar, Inner Temple, 1947; Solicitor-General, Jersey, 1958–62, Attorney-General, 1962–69; Dep. Bailiff of Jersey, 1969–74. Chm., TSB Foundn for CI, 1986–90; KStJ 1983 (CStJ 1978). *Recreations:* music, gardening, travel. *Address:* Les Cypres, St John, Jersey, Channel Islands. *T:* Jersey (0534) 22317.

EREMIN, Prof. Oleg, MD, FRCSE, FRACS; Regius Professor of Surgery, University of Aberdeen, since 1985; *b* 12 Nov. 1938; *s* of Theodor and Maria Eremin; *m* 1963, Jennifer Mary Ching; two *s* one *d*. *Educ:* Christian Brothers' Coll., St Kilda, Melbourne; Univ. of Melbourne. MB BS 1964; MD 1985. FRACS 1971; FRCSE 1983. Clinical posts: Royal Melbourne Hosp., 1965–72; Norfolk and Norwich Hosps, 1972–74; Research Asst-Associate, Dept of Pathology, Univ. of Cambridge, 1974–80; Sen. Lectr, Dept Clinical Surgery, Univ. of Edinburgh, 1981–85. *Publications:* articles in surgical, oncological and immunological jls. *Recreations:* music, sport, reading. *Address:* 3 The Chanonry, Old Aberdeen AB2 1RP. *T:* Aberdeen (0224) 484065. *Club:* Royal Northern and University (Aberdeen).

ERI, Sir (Vincent) Serei, GCMG 1990 (CMG 1982); Governor-General of Papua New Guinea, since 1990; *b* 12 Sept 1936; *s* of Eri Haiveta and Morasuru Lafe; *m* Margaret Karulaka Pukari; four *s* two *d*. *Educ:* Terapo and Moveave Catholic Schools; teacher training, Sogeri; Port Moresby Teachers' College; Univ. of Papua New Guinea (BA 1971). Teacher, Sogeri Secondary Sch., 1956–67; Dep. Head Teacher, Ihu Primary Sch., 1959–60; Dep. Headmaster, Coronation High Sch., Kerema, 1961–62; training as Schools Inspector, 1962; served Eastern Highlands and Central Provinces, 1963–64; Port Moresby Teachers' Coll., training then Lectr, 1965–66; Supt of Primary Educn, Dept of Educn, 1971–72 (acting Dir, 1972); Head, Dept of Inf. and Extn Services, 1973–74; Consul, then Consul-Gen., Sydney, 1974–76; PNG High Comr in Canberra, 1976–79; Head, Transport and Civil Aviation, PNG, 1979–80; Sec., Dept of Defence, 1980–82; Harrisons & Crosfield (PNG), 1982–90. Served on internat. bodies on educn matters; Chm., PNG Univ. Finance Cttee, 1984–90; Pres., People's Action Party, 1986–90. *Address:* Government House, PO Box 79, Port Moresby, Papua New Guinea. *T:* 214466 (BH).

ERICKSON, Prof. Charlotte Joanne; Paul Mellon Professor of American History, University of Cambridge, 1983–90, now Professor Emeritus; Fellow of Corpus Christi College, Cambridge, since 1982; MacArthur Fellow, since 1990; *b* 22 Oct. 1923; *d* of Knut Eric Erickson and Lael A. R. Johnson; *m* 1952, G. L. Watt; two *s*. *Educ:* Augustana Coll., Rock Island, Ill (BA 1945); Cornell Univ., Ithaca, NY (MA 1947; PhD 1951). Instructor in History, Vassar Coll., Poughkeepsie, NY, 1950–52; Research Fellow, NIESR, 1952–55; Lillian Gilmore Fellow, Cornell Univ., April–Sept. 1954; Asst Lectr, 1955, Lectr, 1958, Sen. Lectr, 1966, Reader, 1975, Prof., 1979–82, in Economic History, London School of Economics. Guggenheim Fellow, Washington, DC, 1966–67; Sherman Fairchild Distinguished Scholar, Calif Inst. of Technology, 1976–77. Hon. DHumLet Augustana College, 1977. *Publications:* British Industrialists, Steel and Hosiery 1850–1950, 1958; American Industry and the European Immigrant 1860–1885, 1969; Invisible Immigrants, The Adaptation of English and Scottish Immigrants in Nineteenth Century America, 1972; articles in professional jls and collective works. *Recreations:* music, gardening. *Address:* Corpus Christi College, Cambridge CB2 1RH; 8 High Street, Chesterton, Cambridge.

ERICKSON, Prof. John, FRSE 1982; FBA 1985; University Endowment Fellow, and Director, Centre for Defence Studies, University of Edinburgh, since 1988; *b* 17 April 1929; *s* of Henry Erickson and Jessie (*née* Heys); *m* 1957, Ljubica (*née* Petrović); one *s* one *d*. *Educ:* South Shields High Sch.; St John's Coll., Cambridge (MA). Research Fellow, St Anthony's Coll., Oxford, 1956–58; Lectr, Dept of History, St Andrews Univ., 1958–62; Lectr, Sen. Lectr and Reader, Dept of Government, Univ. of Manchester, 1962–67; Edinburgh University: Reader, Lectr in Higher Defence Studies, 1967; Prof. of Politics (Defence Studies), 1969–88. Visiting Professor: Russian Res. Center, Univ. of Indiana, 1967; Texas A&M Univ., 1981; Dept of History, Yale Univ., 1987. Pres., Assoc. of Civil Defence and Emergency Planning Officers, 1981–. FRSA 1991. *Publications:* The Soviet High Command 1918–1941, 1962; Storia dello Stato Maggiore Sovietico, 1963; ed, The Military-Technical Revolution, 1966; ed, The Armed Services and Society, 1970; Soviet Military Power, 1971; The Road to Stalingrad, 1975; (ed) Soviet Military Power and Performance, 1979; The Road to Berlin, 1983. *Recreations:* military models and music. *Address:* 13 Ravelston House Road, Edinburgh EH4 3LP. *T:* 031–332 1787. *Club:* Edinburgh University Staff, Scottish Arts (Edinburgh).

ERKIN, Feridun Cemal, Hon. GBE 1967; Minister of Foreign Affairs, Turkey, 1962–65; *b* 1899; *m* Madame Mukaddes Feridun Erkin (*d* 1955). *Educ:* Galatasaray Lyceum, Istanbul; Faculty of Law, University of Paris. First Sec., London, 1928–29; Chief of Section, Ankara, 1930–33; Counsellor and Chargé d'Affaires, Berlin, 1934–35; Consul-Gen., Beirut, 1935–37; Dir-Gen., Econ. Dept, Min. of Foreign Affairs, 1937; Dir-Gen., Polit. Dept, 1939; Asst Sec.-Gen., 1942; Deleg, UN Conf. San Francisco, 1945; Sec.-Gen. of Min., 1945; Chm. Turkish Delegn, final session of League of Nations, 1946; Ambassador to Italy, 1947–48; to USA, 1948–55; to Spain, 1955–57; to France, 1957–60; to the Court of St James's, 1960–62. Lately Senator. Turkish Governor to Internat. Banks, 1954; Mem. Internat. Diplomatic Academy, 1949–; Mem. Inst. of France, 1959–. Holds Grand Cross of several foreign Orders, including Grand Cross of the Legion of Honour of France. *Publications:* The Turkish-Soviet relations and the Problem of the Straits, 1968 (French and Turkish edns); articles in daily papers and journals. *Recreation:* classical music. *Address:* Ayaspaşa, Sarayarkasi Sok 24/9, Istanbul, Turkey.

ERLEIGH, Viscount; Julian Michael Rufus Isaacs; *b* 26 May 1986; *s* and *heir* of Marquess of Reading, *qv*.

ERNE, 6th Earl of, *cr* 1789; **Henry George Victor John Crichton,** JP; Baron Erne 1768; Viscount Erne (Ireland), 1781; Baron Fermanagh (UK), 1876; Lord Lieutenant of Co. Fermanagh, Northern Ireland, since 1986; *b* 9 July 1937; *s* of 5th Earl and Lady Katharine Cynthia Mary Millicent (Davina) Lytton (who *m* 1945, Hon. C. M. Woodhouse, *qv*), *yr d* of 2nd Earl of Lytton, KG, PC, GCSI, GCIE; *S* father, 1940; *m* 1958, Camilla Marguerite (marr. diss. 1980), *er d* of late Wing-Comdr Owen G. E. Roberts and Mrs Roberts; one *s* four *d*; *m* 1980, Mrs Anna Carin Hitchcock (*née* Bjork). *Educ:* Eton. Page of Honour to the Queen, 1952–54 (to King George VI, 1952). Lieut, North Irish Horse, 1959–66. Member: Royal Ulster Agricultural Society; Royal Forestry Society. JP Co. Fermanagh. *Recreations:* sailing, fishing, shooting. *Heir: s* Viscount Crichton, *qv*. *Address:* Crom Castle, Newtown Butler, Co. Fermanagh. *T:* Newton-butler 208. *Clubs:* White's; Lough Erne Yacht.

ERNSTING, Air Vice-Marshal John, OBE 1959; PhD; FRCP, FRAeS; QHS 1989; Commandant, RAF Institute of Aviation Medicine, since 1988; Senior Consultant (Royal Air Force), since 1991; *b* 21 April 1928; *s* of late Reginald James Ensting and of Phyllis May Josephine Ernsting (*née* Allington); *m* 1st, 1952, Patricia Mary Woolford (decd); two *s* one *d*; 2nd, 1970, Joyce Marion Heppell. *Educ:* Chislehurst and Sidcup County Grammar Sch. for Boys; Guy's Hosp. Med. Sch. (BSc 1949; MB BS 1952; PhD 1964). MFOM 1981; MRCP 1985. Guy's Hosp., 1952–53; Guy's-Maudsley Neurosurgical Unit, 1953–54; RAF Medical Branch, 1954; Lectr in Physiology, Guy's Hosp. Med. Sch., 1961–85; RAF Consultant in Aviation Physiology, 1964; RAF Consultant Adviser in Aviation Medicine, 1971–89; Dep. Dir and Dir of Research, RAF Inst. of Aviation Medicine, 1976–88; Dean of Air Force Medicine, 1990–91. Visiting Professor: Guy's Hosp. Med. Sch., 1985–; KCL, 1987–; Hon. Dir of Studies MSc in Human and Applied Physiology, KCL, 1984–. *Publications:* (ed) Aviation Medicine, 1978, 2nd edn 1988; papers and chapters in books on aviation physiology and aviation medicine. *Recreations:* music, reading, travel. *Address:* Royal Air Force Institute of Aviation Medicine, Farnborough, Hants GU14 6SZ. *T:* Farnborough (0252) 24461, ext. 2279. *Club:* Royal Air Force.

ERRINGTON, Col Sir Geoffrey (Frederick), 2nd Bt *cr* 1963; Chairman, CPM Search (UK) Ltd, since 1990; *b* 15 Feb. 1926; *er s* of Sir Eric Errington, 1st Bt, JP, and Marjorie (*d* 1973), *d* of A. Grant Bennett; *S* father, 1973; *m* 1955, Diana Kathleen Forbes, *o d* of late E. Barry Davenport, Edgbaston, Birmingham; three *s*. *Educ:* Rugby Sch.; New Coll., Oxford. psc 1958. GSO 3 (Int.), HQ 11 Armd Div., 1950–52; GSO 3, MI3 (b), War Office, 1955–57; Bde Major 146 Inf. Bde, 1959–61; Coy Comdr, RMA Sandhurst, 1963–65; Military Assistant to Adjutant-General, 1965–67; CO 1st Bn, The King's Regt, 1967–69; GSO 1, HQ 1st British Corps, 1969–71; Col. GS, HQ NW District, 1971–74; AAG MI (Army), MoD, 1974–75; retired 1975. Col, The King's Regt, 1975–86; Chm., The King's and Manchester Regts Assoc., 1971–86; Dir, Personnel Services, British Shipbuilders, 1977–78; Employer Bd Mem., Shipbuilding ITB, 1977–78. Freeman, City of London, 1980. Liveryman, Coachmakers' and Coach Harness Makers' Co. *Recreations:* travelling, gardening. *Heir: s* Robin Davenport Errington, *b* 1 July 1957. *Address:* Stone Hill Farm, Sellindge, Ashford, Kent TN25 6AJ. *T:* Sellindge (030381) 3191; 203A Gloucester Place, NW1 6BU. *Clubs:* Boodle's, United Oxford & Cambridge University.
See also S. G. Errington.

ERRINGTON, Sir Lancelot, KCB 1976 (CB 1962); Second Permanent Secretary, Department of Health and Social Security, 1973–76; *b* 14 Jan. 1917; *e s* of late Major L. Errington; *m* 1939, Katharine Reine, *o d* of late T. C. Macaulay; two *s* two *d*. *Educ:* Wellington Coll.; Trinity Coll., Cambridge. Entered Home Office, 1939. Served RNVR, 1939–45. Transferred to Ministry of National Insurance, 1945; Principal Private Sec. to Minister of National Insurance, 1951; Asst Sec., 1953; Under-Sec., 1957–65; Cabinet Office, 1965–68; Min. of Social Security, 1968; Asst Under-Sec. of State, DHSS, 1968–71, Dep. Under-Sec. of State, 1971–73. *Recreation:* sailing. *Address:* St Mary's, Fasnacloich, Appin, Argyll. *T:* Appin (063173) 331.

ERRINGTON, Richard Percy, CMG 1955; Chartered Accountant (FCA), retired; *b* 17 May 1904; 2nd *s* of Robert George Errington and Edna Mary Errington (*née* Warr); *m* 1935, Ursula, *d* of Henry Joseph Laws Curtis and Grace Barton Curtis (*née* Macgregor); one *d*. *Educ:* Sidcot Sch. Asst Treasurer, Nigeria Government, 1929–37; Colonial Administrative Service: Nigeria, 1937–46; Nyasaland, 1946–48; Financial Sec. to Govt of Aden Colony (also Mem. Bd of Trustees of Port of Aden), 1948–51; Chm., Aden Port Trust, 1951–60. Mem. Governor's Exec. Council, Aden, 1948–58. Unofficial Mem. Aden Colony Legislative Council, 1951–60 (Official Mem., 1948–51). Chairman: Aden Soc. for the Blind, 1951–60; Aden Lab. Advisory Bd, 1951–57. Area Comr, St John Amb. Bde, 1964–71. SBStJ, 1965. *Recreation:* walking. *Address:* Whitecliffs, Wodehouse Road, Old Hunstanton, Norfolk PE36 6JD. *T:* Hunstanton (0485) 532356.

ERRINGTON, Stuart Grant; JP; Chairman, National Association of Citizens' Advice Bureaux, since 1989; *b* 23 June 1929; *yr s* of Sir Eric Errington, 1st Bt and late Marjorie Lady Errington; *m* 1954, Anne, *d* of late Eric and Eileen Baedeker; two *s* one *d*. *Educ:* Rugby; Trinity College, Oxford (MA). National Service, 2nd Lieut Royal Artillery, 1947–49. Ellerman Lines, 1952–59; Astley Industrial Trust, 1959–70; Exec Dir, 1970, Man. Dir, 1977, Chm., 1985, Mercantile Credit Co., Chm. and Chief Exec., Mercantile Gp, 1988–89. Chairman: Equipment Leasing Assoc., 1976–78; European Fedn of Leasing Assocs, 1978–80; Finance Houses Assoc., 1982–84; Director: Barclays Merchant Bank, Barclays Bank UK, 1979–86; Kleinwort Overseas Investment Trust, 1982–; Municipal Mutual Insurance, 1989–; Northern Electric, 1989–; Nationwide Anglia Building Soc., 1989–. JP Windsor Forest, 1970. *Recreations:* fishing, golf, splitting logs, avoiding telephones. *Address:* Earleywood Lodge, Ascot SL5 9JP. *T:* Ascot (0344) 21977. *Club:* Boodle's.

ERRITT, (Michael) John (Mackey), CB 1991; Deputy Director, Central Statistical Office, 1989–91; *b* 15 Feb. 1931; *s* of late William Albert Erritt, MBE, and Anna Erritt; *m* 1957, Marian Elizabeth Hillock; two *s*. *Educ:* St Andrews Coll., Dublin; Prince of Wales Sch., Nairobi; Queen's Univ., Belfast. BSc(Econ). Research Officer, Science and Industry Cttee, 1953; Asst Statistician, Central Statistical Office, 1955; Statistician: Board of Trade, 1960; Treasury, 1964; Board of Trade, 1967; Chief Statistician: Inland Revenue, 1968; Central Statistical Office, 1973; Depts of Industry, Trade and Prices and Consumer Protection, 1975; MoD, 1979; Asst Under-Sec. of State (Statistics), MoD, 1981; Asst Dir, Central Statistical Office, 1985. *Publications:* articles in official, academic and trade jls. *Address:* Green Tiles, 14 Brook Lane, Lindfield, Sussex RH16 1SG.

ERROLL, 24th Earl of, *cr* 1452; **Merlin Sereld Victor Gilbert Hay;** Lord Hay, 1429; Baron of Slains, 1452; Bt 1685; 28th Hereditary Lord High Constable of Scotland, *cr* 1314; Celtic title, Mac Garadh Mor; 33rd Chief of the Hays (from 1171); Senior Great Officer, Royal Household in Scotland; computer consultant; *b* 20 April 1948; *er s* of 23rd Countess of Erroll and Sir Iain Moncreiffe of that Ilk, 11th Bt, CVO, QC; *S* mother, 1978 (and to baronetcy of father, 1985); *m* 1982, Isabelle Astell, *o d* of late T. S. Astell Hohler, MC; two *s* two *d*. *Educ:* Eton; Trinity College, Cambridge. Page to the Lord Lyon, 1956. Lieut, Atholl Highlanders, 1974. OStJ 1977. Member, Queen's Body Guard for Scotland,

Royal Company of Archers, 1978. *Recreations:* skiing, climbing. *Heir:* s Lord Hay, qv. *Address:* Wolverton Farm, Basingstoke, Hants RG26 5SX. *Clubs:* White's, Pratt's; Puffin's (Edinburgh).

ERROLL OF HALE, 1st Baron, cr 1964; **Frederick James Erroll,** PC 1960; MA, FIEE; FIMechE; Chairman, Bowater Corporation, 1973–84; b 27 May 1914; s of George Murison Erroll, engineer, and Kathleen Donovan Edington, both of Glasgow and London; m 1950, Elizabeth, o d of R. Sowton Barrow, Exmouth, Devon. *Educ:* Oundle Sch.; Trinity Coll., Cambridge. Engineering Apprenticeship, 1931–32; Cambridge Univ., 1932–35; Engineer at Metropolitan-Vickers Electrical Co. Ltd, Manchester, 1936–38; Commissioned into 4th County of London Yeomanry (Sharpshooters), TA, 1939; technical appointments in connection with Tank Construction and Testing, 1940–43; service in India and Burma, 1944–45; Col 1945. MP (C) Altrincham and Sale, 1945–64. A Dir of Engineering and Mining Companies until April 1955; Parly Sec., Min. of Supply, April 1955–Nov. 1956; Parly Sec., BoT, 1956–58; Economic Sec. to the Treasury, Oct. 1958–59; Minister of State, BoT, 1959–61; Pres., BoT, 1961–63; Minister of Power, 1963–64. Mem., H of L Select Cttee on Science and Technology, 1985–. Pres., Consolidated Gold Fields, 1982–89 (Chm., 1976–82); Chairman: Bowater Corporation Ltd; Whessoe plc, 1970–87 (Consultant, 1987–); ASEA Ltd, 1965–84; Fläkt Ltd, 1971–85; Gen. Advr, ASEA, Sweden, 1965–86. Member: Council Inst. Directors, 1949–55, and 1965–87 (Chm. Council, 1973–76, Pres., 1976–84, Chancellor, 1984–87); NEDC, 1962–63. President: Hispanic and Luso-Brazilian Councils, 1969–73; British Export Houses Assoc., 1969–72; British Exec. Service Overseas, 1972–85; UK South Africa Trade Assoc., 1979–84; World Travel Market, 1986–; Vice-President: London Chamber of Commerce, 1969– (Pres., 1966–69); Inst. of Marketing, 1983–; Automobile Assoc., 1986– (Chm., 1974–86). Dep. Chm., Decimal Currency Board, 1966–71; Chm., Cttee on Liquor Licensing, 1971–72; Pres., Electrical Research Assoc., 1971–74. Trustee, Westminster Abbey Trust, 1978–86. FRSA 1971. *Heir:* none. *Address:* House of Lords, SW1A 0PW. *Club:* Carlton.

ERSHAD, Lt-Gen. Hussain Muhammad; President of Bangladesh, 1983–90; President of the Council of Ministers, 1982–90; Minister of Defence, Establishment, Health and Population Control, 1986–90; b 1 Feb. 1930; s of late Makbul Hussain, Advocate, and of Mojida Begum; m 1956, Begum Raushad Ershad; one s one adopted d. *Educ:* Carmichael Coll., Rangpur; Dhaka Univ. (BA 1st Div.). Staff Course, Defence Service Command and Staff Coll., Quetta, Pakistan, 1966; War Course, National Defence Coll., New Delhi, India, 1975. Infantry Regimental Service, 1953–58; Adjt, E Bengal Regimental Centre (Basic Inf. Trng Centre), 1960–62; E Pakistan Rifles, 1962–65; Bde Major/Dep. Asst Adjt and Quarter Master General, 1967–68; CO, Inf. Bn, 1969–71; Adjt General, Bangladesh Army, 1973–74; Dep. Chief of Army Staff, Bangladesh Army, Chm., Coordination and Control Cell for National Security, 1975–78; Chief of Army Staff, Bangladesh Army, 1978–86; C-in-C, Bangladesh Armed Forces, 1982; Chief Martial Law Administrator, Bangladesh, 1982–86. Chm., National Sports Control Bd. *Publications:* poems in Bengali contributed occasionally to literary jls. *Address:* c/o Office of the President, Bangabhaban, Dhaka, Bangladesh. *Club:* Kurmitola Golf (Dhaka).

ERSKINE; *see* St Clair-Erskine.

ERSKINE, family name of **Earls of Buchan** and **Mar and Kellie,** and of **Baron Erskine of Rerrick.**

ERSKINE OF RERRICK, 2nd Baron cr 1964; **Iain Maxwell Erskine;** Bt 1961; professional photographer, management consultant and director of companies; b 22 Jan. 1926; o s of 1st Baron Erskine of Rerrick, GBE, and of Henrietta, d of late William Dunnett, Caithness; S father, 1980; m 1st, 1955, Marie Elisabeth (later Countess of Caledon) (marr. diss. 1964), d of Major Burton Allen; no c; 2nd, 1974, Maria Josephine (marr. diss. 1989), d of late Dr Josef Klupt, Richmond, Surrey; three d. *Educ:* Harrow. Served War of 1939–45; served Regular Army, 1943–65 (2nd Lieut Grenadier Guards, 1944; Temp. Lt-Col (1961); ADC, RMA, Sandhurst, 1951–52; Comptroller to Governor-Gen. of New Zealand, 1960–62; retd as Major, 1963. PRO to Household Bde, 1963–65; Account Exec., CS Services Ltd PR (involved in setting up Advertising Standards Authority, 1965; Higher Exec. Officer, MoD, 1964–66; Advertising and PR Dir, Saward Baker Ltd, 1966–72; attended Ashridges Management Court, 1967; Man. Dir, Lonrho Ltd, Iran, 1972–73; London Manager, Marples Ridgway Construction Ltd, 1974–; Chairman: Strabo Ltd (Trading), 1976; Erskine Associates; Caledonian Commodities Ltd (Trading), 1979–82; DK Financial Services (Dai-Ichi Kangyo), 1988–89; Director: Wansdyke Security Ltd, 1974–85; Bath, Portland and Debenham Gp, 1974–85; Ardil Ltd, 1984–; Crighton Internat. Ltd, 1984–; WSTV Productions Ltd, 1988–; ISICAD (Computers), 1989–; CDA Internat. Ltd. Qualified pilot; Mem. Cttee, De Haviland Aircraft Museum (BAe) (Dir, 1967–88); Trustee: RAF Mus. (Bomber Comd); David Tolkien Trust, Stoke Mandeville Hosp.; Transport Trust; Patron: PHAB (Scot.); Orchestra of the World. Chm., Guards' Flying Club, 1959–65. Col, Confederate States Air Force, 1983. Life Mem. Nat. Trust for Scotland; Mem. Cttee and Life Mem., Royal Photographic Soc.; Mem., RAF Historical Soc. MInstM, MIPR and FInstD, 1967–75. Chevalier, Legion of Honour. OStJ. *Recreations:* fly-fishing, good food, aviation, photography. *Heir:* none. *Address:* House of Lords, SW1A 0PW. *Clubs:* White's, Special Forces.

ERSKINE, Lord; James Thorne Erskine; DL; building technician, since 1989; b 10 March 1949; s and heir of 13th Earl of Mar and 15th Earl of Kellie, qv; m 1974, Mrs Mary Mooney, yr d of Dougal McD. Kirk. *Educ:* Eton; Moray House Coll. of Education, 1968–71; Inverness Coll. (building course, 1987–88). Page of Honour to the Queen, 1962, 1963. Community Service Volunteer, York, 1967–68; Community Worker, Richmond-Craigmillar Parish Church, Edinburgh, 1971–73; Sen. Social Worker, Family and Community Services, Sheffield District Council, 1973–76; Social Worker: Grampian Regional Council, Elgin, 1976–77, Forres, 1977–78; Highland Regional Council, Aviemore, 1979; HM Prison, Inverness, 1979–81; Inverness, Aug.-Dec. 1981; Community Worker, Merkinch Centre, Inverness, Jan.-July 1982; Community Service Supervisor, Inverness, 1983–87. Pilot Officer, RAuxAF, 1979, attached to 2622 Highland Sqdn, RAuxAF Regt; Flying Officer, RAuxAF, 1982–86; RNXS, 1985–89. DL Clackmannan, 1991. *Recreations:* hill walking, railways, gardening, cycling, restoration of Alloa Tower. *Address:* Erskine House, Kirk Wynd, Clackmannan FK10 4JF. *T:* Alloa (0259) 212438. *Club:* New (Edinburgh).

ERSKINE, Sir David; *see* Erskine, Sir T. D.

ERSKINE, Ralph, CBE 1978; architect; own practice (in Sweden since 1939); b 24 Feb. 1914; s of late George and Mildred Erskine; m 1939, Ruth Monica Francis; one s two d. *Educ:* Friends' Sch., Saffron Walden, Essex; Regent Street Polytechnic (architecture). ARIBA 1936; AMTPI 1938; SAR 1965. Won number of prizes in arch. comps in Sweden; one year's study at Academy for Fine Arts, Sweden, 1945. *Work executed:* town plans; workers' houses; co-operative housing and industrial housing; flats; hostels; factories; ski-hotel; shopping centre; school; town hall; hall of residence at Clare Coll., Cambridge; churches; housing estates at Newmarket and Killingworth; clearance scheme,

Byker, Newcastle upon Tyne; design of new town, Resolute Bay, Canada; University Library, Allhuset and Sports Hall, Stockholm Univ. Lecturing: in America, Canada, Japan and many countries in Europe. Hon. Dr, Lund Univ., Sweden, 1975; Hon. DLitt, Heriot-Watt Univ., 1982. For. Mem., Royal Acad. of Arts, Sweden, 1972; Hon. Mem., Bund Deutscher Architekten, 1983. Hon Fellow of AIA, 1966; SAR's Kasper Sahlin prize for 1971 and 1981; Ytong Prize, 1974; Guld medal, Litteris et Artibus, 1980; Canadian Gold Medal, RAIC, 1983; Wolf Prize for Architecture, 1984; Royal Gold Medal, RIBA, 1987. *Publications:* for several arch. magazines, on building in northern climates, etc. *Relevant publication:* Ralph Erskine, by Mats Egelius, 1978. *Recreations:* ski-ing, skating, swimming, yachting, ice yachting. *Address:* Gustav III's väg, Drottningholm, Sweden. *T:* 7590352.

ERSKINE, Sir (Thomas) David, 5th Bt, cr 1821; JP; Vice Lord-Lieutenant, Fife Region, 1981–87; Convener, Fife County Council, 1970–73; b 31 July 1912; o surv. s of Sir Thomas Wilfred Hargreaves John Erskine, 4th Bt, and late Magdalen Janet, d of Sir Ralph Anstruther, 6th Bt of Balcaskie; S father, 1944; m 1947, Ann, er d of late Lt-Col Neil Fraser-Tytler, DSO, MC, and of Christian Helen Fraser-Tytler, CBE, qv; two s (and one d decd). *Educ:* Eton; Magdalene Coll., Cambridge. Employed by Butterfield & Swire, London and China, in 1934 and served with them in China, 1935–41. Joined HM Forces in India and commissioned into Indian Corps of Engineers. Served with them in Mid-East, India and Malaya, being demobilised in 1945 with rank of Major. JP Fife, 1951; DL Fife, 1955–81. *Heir:* s Thomas Peter Neil Erskine [b 28 March 1950; m 1972, Catherine, d of Col G. H. K. Hewlett; two s two d]. *Address:* West Newhall House, Kingsbarns, Fife. *T:* Crail (0333) 50228. *Club:* New (Edinburgh).

ERSKINE, Thomas Ralph, CB 1986; First Legislative Counsel, Northern Ireland, since 1979; b 14 Oct. 1933; m 1966, Patricia Joan Palmer; one s one d. *Educ:* Campbell College; Queen's University, Belfast. Called to the Bar, Gray's Inn, 1962. *Publications:* contribs to Cryptologia, Annals of the History of Computing, legal periodicals, etc. *Recreations:* ski-ing, modern naval history. *Address:* Office of the Legislative Counsel, Parliament Buildings, Belfast BT4 3SW. *T:* Belfast (0232) 63210.

ERSKINE-HILL, Sir (Alexander) Roger, 3rd Bt cr 1945, of Quothquhan, Co. Lanark; b 15 Aug. 1949; s of Sir Robert Erskine-Hill, 2nd Bt and of Christine Alison, o d of late Capt. (A) Henry James Johnstone of Alva, RN; S father, 1989; m 1984, Sarah Anne Sydenham, er d of late Dr R. J. Sydenham Clarke and of Mrs Charles Clarke; one s one d. *Educ:* Eton; Aberdeen Univ. (LLB). Director: Salestrac Ltd; Map Marketing Ltd. *Heir:* s Robert Benjamin Erskine-Hill, b 6 Aug. 1986. *Address:* Great Coleford, Stoodleigh, Tiverton, Devon EX16 9QG.

ERSKINE-HILL, Henry Howard, PhD; FBA 1985; Fellow of Pembroke College, since 1980, and Reader in Literary History, since 1984, Cambridge University; b 19 June 1936; s of Henry Erskine-Hill and Hannah Lilian Poppleton. *Educ:* Ashville Coll.; Nottingham Univ. (BA, PhD); MA Cantab; LittD Cantab 1988. University of Wales, Swansea: Tutor, 1960; Asst Lectr, 1961; Lectr in Eng. Lit., 1962; Sen. Fellow, 1964–65; University of Cambridge: Lectr in English, 1969–84; Fellow, 1969–80, Tutor, 1970–76, Jesus Coll.; Tutor for Graduates, Pembroke Coll., 1983–84. Olin Fellow, Nat. Humanities Center, NC, USA, 1988–89. Taught at British Council seminars in Britain, 1962–69; invited lectr, univs of Alberta, Adelaide, Berkeley (Calif), Bristol, Davis (Calif), Essex, Flinders (S Australia), Liverpool, London, Monash, Nantes, Oxford, Saskatchewan, Stanford, Singapore, Wales (Swansea), Victoria (BC), Warwick, W Australia and York; also at David Nichol Smith Seminar, Canberra, Inter-Univ. Centre, Dubrovnik, Inst. of Hist. Res., London, and Herzog-August Library, Wolfenbüttel. *Publications:* (ed) Alexander Pope: Horatian Satires and Epistles, 1964; Pope: The Dunciad, 1972; The Social Milieu of Alexander Pope, 1975; (ed with Anne Smith) The Art of Alexander Pope, 1978; (ed with Graham Storey) Revolutionary Prose of the English Civil War, 1983; The Augustan Idea, 1983; contributions to: Renaissance and Modern Essays, ed G. R. Hibbard, 1966; English Drama: forms and Development, ed Marie Axton and Raymond Williams, 1977; Ideology and Conspiracy, ed Eveline Cruickshanks, 1982; jls incl. Essays in Criticism, Eighteenth-Century Studies, Jl of the Warburg and Courtauld Insts, Modern Language Review, Rev. of English Studies, Renaissance and Modern Studies. *Recreation:* fell walking. *Address:* Pembroke College, Cambridge CB2 1RF. *T:* Cambridge (0223) 338100. *Club:* United Oxford & Cambridge University.

ERSKINE-HILL, Sir Roger; *see* Erskine-Hill, Sir A. R.

ERSKINE-MURRAY, family name of **Lord Elibank.**

ERVINE-ANDREWS, Lt-Col Harold Marcus, VC 1940; East Lancashire Regiment, retired; b 29 July 1911; s of late C. C. Ervine-Andrews, New Ross, Wexford, Southern Ireland; m 1st, 1939, Betty (decd), er d of R. I. Torrie; one s one d; 2nd, 1981, Margaret Gregory. *Educ:* Stonyhurst Coll.; Royal Military Coll., Sandhurst. 2nd Lieut East Lancs Regt, 1932; Captain 1940; Temp. Major, 1940; War Subst. Major, 1942; Temp. Lieut-Col 1942; served with RAF during North-West Frontier of India Operations, 1936–37 (medal and two clasps, despatches) and NW Frontier, 1938–39; served in France with BEF (VC); attached to RAF in UK, 1940; on loan to Australian Military Forces, 1941; attached RAAF, 1942; GSO 1 Air HQ Allied Land Forces in South-West Pacific Area, 1943; commanding No. 61 Carrier-Borne Army Liaison Section, 1944; SALO in 21st Aircraft Carrier Squadron (East Indies), 1945; Lieut-Col Commanding No. 18 Infantry Holding Bn, 1946; attached to The Army Mobile Information Unit, 1948; Asst Dir of Public Relations to BAOR, 1951, as a Lieut-Col; retired pay, 1952. *Address:* Treveor Cot, Gorran, St Austell, Cornwall PL26 6LW. *T:* Mevagissey (0726) 842140.

ESAKI, Leo; IBM Fellow since 1967; Manager, Quantum Structures (formerly Device Physics), IBM T. J. Watson Research Center, since 1962; b 12 March 1925; s of Soichiro Esaki and Niyoko Ito; m 1986, Masako Kondo (one s two d by previous m). *Educ:* Univ. of Tokyo. MS 1947, PhD 1959. Sony Corp., Japan, 1956–60; IBM Research, 1960–. Director: IBM-Japan, 1976–; Yamada Science Foundn, 1976–. Research in tunnelling in semiconductor junctions which led to the discovery of the tunnel diode, now working on man-made semiconductor superlattice in search of predicted quantum mechanical effect. Sir John Cass sen. vis. res. fellow, London Poly, 1982. Councillor-at-Large, Amer. Phys. Soc., 1971; Dir, Amer. Vacuum Soc., 1972; Member: Japan Academy, 1975; Max-Planck-Ges., 1989; For. Associate, Nat. Acad. of Sciences, USA, 1976; For. Associate, Nat. Acad. of Engineering, USA, 1977; Corresp. Mem., Academia Nacional De Ingenieria, Mexico, 1978. Nishina Meml Award, 1959; Asahi Press Award, 1960; Toyo Rayon Foundn Award, 1961; Morris N. Liebmann Meml Prize, 1961; Stuart Ballantine Medal, Franklin Inst., 1961; Japan Academy Award, 1965; (jtly) Nobel Prize for Physics, 1973; Science Achievement Award, US-Asia Inst., 1983; Centennial Medal, IEEE, 1984; Internat. Prize for New Materials, Amer. Physical Soc., 1985; Distinguished Foreign-born Individual Award, Internat. Center, NY, 1986; IEEE Medal of Honor, 1991. Order of Culture (Japan), 1974. *Publications:* numerous papers in learned jls. *Address:* IBM Thomas J. Watson Research Center, PO Box 218, Yorktown Heights, New York 10598, USA. *T:* (914) 945–2342.

ESCHENBACH, Christoph; pianist and conductor; Music Director, Houston Symphony Orchestra, since 1988; *b* 20 Feb. 1940. *Educ:* Hamburg Conservatory; State Music Conservatory, Cologne. Winner: Internat. Piano Competition, Munich, 1962; Concours Clara Haskil, 1965. Canadian début, Montreal Expo, 1967; US début, Cleveland Orch., 1969; has toured Europe, N and S America, USSR, Israel, Japan; and has performed as pianist with leading orchs incl. Concertgebouw Amsterdam, Orch. de Paris, London Symphony, Berlin Philharmonic, and Cleveland Orch.; festivals incl. Salzburg, Lucerne, Bonn, and Aix-en-Provence. Chief Conductor, Tonhalle Orch., Zürich, and Artistic Dir, Tonhalle-Gesellschaft, Zürich, 1982–86; guest appearances with NY Philharmonic, Boston Symphony, Chicago Symphony, Cleveland Orch., Pittsburgh Symphony, Los Angeles Philharmonic, London Symphony, BBC Philharmonia, Berlin Philharmonic, Bavarian Radio Symphony Munich, Munich Philharmonic, Vienna Symphonic, Czech Philharmonic and New Japan Philharmonic. *Address:* c/o Columbia Artists Management Inc., 165 West 57th Street, New York, NY 10019, USA.

ESCOTT COX, Brian Robert; *see* Cox.

ESCRITT, Maj.-Gen. Frederick Knowles, CB 1953; OBE 1943; MRCS; late RAMC, retired Nov. 1953; *b* 29 Nov. 1893; *s* of Harold Teal Escritt; *m* 1931, Elsa Alfrida, *d* of Director Larssen, Stockholm; one *d*. *Educ:* Dulwich Coll.; Guy's Hosp. MRCS, LRCP, 1918. Joined RAMC, Aug. 1918 (1914–15 Star, British War and Victory Medals). Served War of 1939–45 (Gen. Service Iraq, 1939–45 Star, Burma Star, Defence and War Medals, 1939–45). ADMS Eastern and 14 Armies, 1942–45; DDMS 1 Corps Dist, BAOR, 1945–47; Inspector of Training, AMS, 1950–51; DDMS, Eastern Command, 1951–53. QHS, 1952–53. Order of St John (Officer Brother), 1952.

ESDALE, Mrs G. P. R.; *see* Lindop, Patricia J.

ESER, Prof. Dr Günter Otto; Director General, International Air Transport Association, Montreal/Geneva, since 1985; *b* 10 Sept. 1927; *s* of Ernst Eser and Martha Siering; *m* 1976, Florida Huisman; two *s*. *Educ:* Bonn Univ.; Federal Acad. of Finance, Siegburg; Harvard (Management Programme). Auditor, Fed. German Min. of Finance, 1953–55; Lufthansa German Airlines, 1955–84: Head, Persian subsidiary, Teheran; Head, Munich Dist Office for Southern Germany; Sales Dir, Germany; Gen. Man., N and Central America; Mem., Chief Exec. Bd. Member: Adv. Bd, Europäische Reiseversicherung, 1978–; Adv. Bd, Amer. Univ., 1982–; Bd, Internat. Aviation Management Training Inst., 1987–. Vis. Prof., Pace Univ., NY, 1978–. Bundesverdienstkreuz 1st Class (FRG), 1985; Commendatore Officiale (Italy), 1967. *Recreations:* trekking, ocean-fishing, literature, music. *Address:* c/o IATA, PO Box 672, 1215 Geneva 15 Airport, Switzerland. *T:* Geneva 7992525.

ESHER, 4th Viscount, *cr* 1897; Baron *cr* 1885; **Lionel Gordon Baliol Brett,** CBE 1970; MA; PPRIBA; DistTP; Rector and Vice-Provost, Royal College of Art, 1971–78; *b* 18 July 1913; *o s* of 3rd Viscount Esher, GBE; *S* father, 1963; *m* 1935, Christian, *e d* of late Col Ebenezer Pike, CBE, MC; five *s* one *d*. *Educ:* Eton (Scholar); New Coll., Oxford (Scholar); BA (1st Class), 1935; Hon. Fellow, 1980; RIBA Ashpitel Prizeman, 1939. Served War in RA, 1940–45; France and Germany, 1944–45 (despatches); Major. Architect Planner, Hatfield New Town, 1949–59; major housing projects: Hatfield, Stevenage, Basildon; consultant architect: Downside Abbey; Maidenhead Town Centre; Abingdon Town Centre; Portsmouth City Centre; York City Centre; Santiago, Chile and Caracas, Venezuela (both for UNDP); principal buildings include: (with Francis Pollen): High Comr's House, Lagos; 82 and 190 Sloane St, London; Pall Mall Ct, Manchester; Downside Sch. extensions; Exeter Coll., and Oxenford Hall, Oxford; (with Teggin & Taylor) Civic Offices, Portsmouth. Lecture tours: USA 1953; India, 1954; Australia, 1959; S America, 1970. Governor, Museum of London, 1970–77; Member: Royal Fine Art Commn, 1951–69; Adv. Bd for Redundant Churches (Chm., 1977–83); Advisory Council, Victoria and Albert Museum, 1967–72; Arts Council of GB, 1972–77 (Chm., Art Panel); Environment Panel, British Rail, 1977–85; National Trust (Chm., Thames and Chilterns Reg., 1979–83); Vice-Pres., RIBA, 1962–65; Pres., 1965–67; Trustee, Soane Museum, 1976–. Hon. DLitt Strathclyde Univ., 1967; Hon. DUniv York, 1970; Hon. DSc Edinburgh, 1981. Hon. Fellow: Amer. Inst. of Architects, 1967; Portsmouth Polytechnic, 1984; Chartered Inst. of Designers, 1975. *Publications:* Houses, 1947; The World of Architecture, 1963; Landscape in Distress, 1965; York: a study in conservation, 1969; Parameters and Images, 1970; (with Elisabeth Beazley) Shell Guide to North Wales, 1971; A Broken Wave, 1981; The Continuing Heritage, 1982; Our Selves Unknown (autobiog.), 1985. *Recreation:* landscapes. *Heir: s* Hon. Christopher Lionel Baliol Brett [*b* 23 Dec. 1936; *m* 1st, 1962, Camilla Charlotte (marr. diss. 1970), *d* of Sir (Horace) Anthony Rumbold, 10th Bt, KGMG, KCVO, CB; one *s* two *d*; 2nd, 1971, Valerie Harrington; two *s* twin *d*]. *Address:* Christmas Common Tower, Watlington, Oxford OX9 5HL. *Club:* Arts.

See also Sir Martyn G. Beckett, Sir Evelyn Shuckburgh.

ESKDAILL, Lord; Walter John Francis Montagu Douglas Scott; *b* 2 Aug. 1984; *s* and *heir* of Earl of Dalkeith, *qv*.

ESMONDE, Sir Thomas (Francis Grattan), 17th Bt *cr* 1629 (Ire.), of Ballynastragh, Wexford; Clinical Research Fellow, Department of Neuroscience, Western General Hospital, Edinburgh, since 1990; *b* 14 Oct. 1960; *s* of Sir John Henry Grattan Esmonde, 16th Bt and of Pamela Mary, *d* of late Francis Stephen Bourke, FRCPI; *S* father, 1987; *m* 1986, Pauline Loretto Kearns; one *s*. *Educ:* Sandford Park Secondary School, Ranelagh, Dublin; Medical School, Trinity College, Dublin. MB, BCh, BAO, MRCPI, MRCP (UK). Junior House Officer, Whiteabbey Hosp., 1984–85; SHO, Royal Victoria, Musgrave Park and Whiteabbey Hosps, 1985–87, Altnagelvin Hosp., Londonderry, 1987–88; Med. Registrar, Royal Gwent Hosp., Newport, 1988–89; Registrar in Neurology, Univ. Hosp. of Wales, 1989–90. *Recreations:* chess, judo. *Heir: s* Sean Vincent Grattan Esmonde, *b* 8 Jan. 1989. *Address:* 6 Nutley Avenue, Donnybrook, Dublin 4. *T:* Dublin 693040.

ESPIE, Sir Frank (Fletcher), Kt 1979; OBE 1971; FTS, FIMM, MAIMM, MAIME; company director, retired; *b* 8 May 1917; *s* of late Frank Fancett Espie and Laura Jean Espie; *m* 1st, 1941, Madeline Elizabeth Robertson (decd); one *s* three *d*; 2nd, 1985, Jean Primrose Angove. *Educ:* St Peter's Coll., Adelaide; Univ. of Adelaide (BEng). FTS 1978; FIMM 1958. CRA Ltd: Dir, 1968; Dep. Chm., 1974–79; non-exec. Dir, 1979–85; Bougainville Copper Ltd: Gen. Man., 1965; Man. Dir, 1969; Chm., 1971–79; non-exec. Dir, 1979–85. Director: ICI Aust. Ltd, 1979–87; Tubemakers of Australia, 1980–87; Westpac Banking Corporation, 1981–90; Woodside Petroleum, 1981–89. Chairman: Nat. Petroleum Adv. Cttee, 1979–87; Australian Mineral Foundn Inc., 1988–91. Member: Exec. Cttee, Aust. Mining Industry Council, 1973–81 (Pres., 1978–80); Council: Australasian Inst. of Mining and Metallurgy, 1970–88 (Pres., 1975; Inst. Medal, 1980); Aust. Acad. of Technological Scis, 1980–90. *Recreations:* swimming, golf. *Address:* 31 The Righi, South Yarra, Vic 3141, Australia. *T:* (03) 866.2062. *Clubs:* Melbourne, Athenæum, Royal Melbourne Golf (Melbourne); Union (Sydney); Adelaide (Adelaide).

ESPINOSA, Dr Augusto; Senator of the Republic of Colombia, 1958–74 and since 1978; *b* 5 June 1919; *m* 1944, Myriam de Espinosa; three *s*. *Educ:* Universidad Nacional, Colombia (Dr in Law and Pol Scis, 1942). Manager, Banco de Bogotá, Bucaramanga, 1943–46; Gen. Man., Agriculture, Industrial and Mining Credit Bank, 1959–61. Deputy and Pres., Deptl Assembly of Santander, 1943; Councillor and Pres. of Council of Bucaramanga, 1945–47; Mem., House of Representatives, 1947–51 and 1974–78; Minister of Agriculture, 1958–59; Pres. of Senate, 1963–64; Ambassador to UN and Perm. Colombian Rep., UN, 1970–73; Ambassador to UK, 1982–84. Pres., First Commn of the Senate, 1982. Grand Cross, Order of Merit, France, 1964. *Publications:* El Pensamiento Económico y Político en Colombia (The Economic and Political Thought in Colombia), 1942; essays and articles in leading Colombian newspapers and magazines. *Recreations:* reading, writing; fond of dogs. *Clubs:* Jockey, Country (Bogotá, Colombia).

ESPLEN, (Sir) John Graham, (3rd Bt *cr* 1921, of Hardres Court, Canterbury, but does not use the title); *b* 4 Aug. 1932; *s* of Sir William Graham Esplen, 2nd Bt and of Aline Octavia, *d* of late A. Octavius Hedley; *S* father, 1989; *m* 1956, Valerie Joan, *yr d* of Maj.-Gen. A. P. Lambooy, CB, OBE; one *s* three *d*. *Educ:* Harrow; St Catharine's Coll., Cambridge. *Heir: s* William John Harry Esplen, *b* 24 Feb. 1967. *Address:* The Mill House, Moorlands Road, Merriott, Somerset TA16 5NF.

ESPLIN, Air Vice-Marshal Ian (George), CB 1963; OBE 1946; DFC 1943; retired (voluntarily) 1965; *b* 26 Feb. 1914; *s* of late Donald Thomas Esplin and Emily Freame Esplin; *m* 1944, Patricia Kaleen Barlow; one *s* one *d*. *Educ:* Sydney Univ.; Oxford Univ. BEc 1936; MA 1939. Rowing Blue, 1934 and 1935. NSW Rhodes Schol., 1937. Entered RAF from Oxford, 1939. Served War of 1939–45, as Pilot in Night-Fighters; destroyed three enemy aircraft at night; also served at CFS and in HQ, SEAC; Air Min. (Policy), 1945; Comd RAF Desford, 1947; Dep. Senior Personnel Staff Officer, HQ Reserve Comd, 1948; Directing Staff, RAF Staff Coll., 1950–51; Comd first Jet All Weather Wing, Germany (No 148), 1952–54; Flying Coll. Course, 1954; Dep. Dir of Operational Requirements, Air Min., 1955–58; Comd RAF Wartling, 1958–60; Dir of Operational Reqts, 1960–62; Comdr, RAF Staff and Air Attaché, Washington, DC, 1963–65; Dean, Air Attaché Corps, 1964–65. *Recreations:* golf, tennis, swimming. *Address:* c/o National Westminster Bank, West End Office, 1 St James's Square, SW1. *Clubs:* Vincent's (Oxford); Leander (Henley-on-Thames)

ESQUIVEL, Rt. Hon. Manuel; PC 1986; Member, House of Representatives, Belize, since 1984; Leader of the Opposition, since 1989; Leader, United Democratic Party, since 1982; *b* 2 May 1940; *s* of John and Laura Esquivel; *m* 1971, Kathleen Levy; one *s* two *d*. *Educ:* Loyola Univ., New Orleans (BSc Physics); Bristol Univ. (Cert Ed.). Instructor in Physics, St John's Coll., Belize City, 1967–82; Prime Minister of Belize, 1984–89. Member: Belize City Council, 1974–80; Nat. Senate, 1979–84. Chm., Utd Democratic Party, 1976–82. Hon. DHL Loyola Univ., 1986. *Recreation:* electronics. *Address:* House of Representatives, Belmopan, Belize.

ESSAAFI, M'hamed, Grand Officier, Order of Tunisian Republic, 1963; United Nations Disaster Relief Co-ordinator, since 1982; *b* 26 May 1930; *m* 1956, Hedwige Klat; one *s* one *d*. *Educ:* Sadiki Coll., Tunis; Sorbonne, Paris. Secretariat of State for For. Affairs, 1956; 1st Sec., Tunisian Embassy, London, 1956; 1st Sec., Tunisian Embassy, Washington, 1957; Secretariat of State for For. Affairs, Tunis: Dir of Amer. Dept, 1960; America and Internat. Confs Dept, 1962; Ambassador to London, 1964–69; Ambassador to Moscow, 1970–74; Ambassador to Bonn, 1974–76; Sec.-Gen., Ministry of Foreign Affairs, Tunis, 1969–70 and 1976–78; Ambassador to Belgium and EEC, 1978–79; Permanent Rep. of Tunisia to the UN, and Special Rep. of the Sec.-Gen., 1980–81, Chef de Cabinet 1982. *Address:* United Nations, Room 140, Palais des Nations, CH-1211 Geneva 10, Switzerland.

ESSAME, Enid Mary, MA Cantab; Headmistress of Queenswood School, 1943–71; 2nd *d* of Oliver Essame. *Educ:* Wyggeston Gram. Sch., Leicester; Girls' High Sch., Newark; Newnham Coll., Cambridge (Hist. Tripos, 1928); King's Coll., University of London (Certificate of Education, 1929). Mary Ewart Travelling Scholar, Newnham Coll., 1934–35; AM in Education, American Univ., Washington, DC, USA, 1935. Asst Headmistress Queenswood Sch., 1935–43. British Council lecturer, India and Pakistan, 1953, Nigeria, 1961. Governor, Chorleywood Coll. for Girls with Little or No Sight, 1962. Hon. Sec. Assoc. of Headmistresses of Boarding Schools, Pres. 1962–64. Chm., Assoc. of Ind. and Direct Grant Schools. Bd Mem., Schoolmistresses and Governesses Benevolent Instn, 1974–; Hon. Adviser, Nat. Assoc. for Gifted Children, 1974–. Governor: St Helen's Sch., Northwood; Channing Sch., Highgate; Trustee, Stormont Sch., Potters Bar. Mem., Overseas Grants Cttee, Help the Aged, 1981. JP Herts 1952–76. *Address:* 4 Elmroyd Avenue, Potters Bar, Herts EN6 2ED. *T:* Potters Bar (0707) 53255. *Clubs:* Royal Over-Seas League, Arts Theatre.

ESSAYAN, Michael, QC 1976; *b* 7 May 1927; *s* of late Kevork Loris Essayan and Rita Sirvarte (*née* Gulbenkian); *m* 1956, Geraldine St Lawrence Lee Guinness, *d* of K. E. L. Guinness, MBE; one *s* one *d*. *Educ:* France; Harrow; Balliol Coll., Oxford (1st Cl. Class. Hon. Mods 1949, 1st Cl. Lit. Hum. 1951, MA). Served with RA, 1945–48 (Palestine, 1947–48). Iraq Petroleum Co., London and ME, 1951–56. Called to the Bar, Middle Temple 1957 (Bencher 1983), joined Lincoln's Inn *ad eundem* 1958. Mem., Gen. Council of the Bar, 1987–88. Mem., Bd of Administration, Calouste Gulbenkian Foundn, Lisbon, 1981–. *Publications:* The New Supreme Court Costs (with M. J. Albery, QC), 1960; (ed with Hon. Mr Justice Walton) Adkin's Landlord and Tenant, 15th, 16th, 17th and 18th edns. *Recreations:* wine and wife. *Address:* 6 Chelsea Square, SW3 6LF. *T:* 071–352 6786. *Club:* Brooks's.

ESSEN, Louis, OBE 1959; FRS 1960; DSc, PhD; retired; *b* 6 Sept. 1908; *s* of Fred Essen and Ada (*née* Edson); *m* 1937, Joan Margery Greenhalgh; four *d*. *Educ:* High Pavement Sch., Nottingham; London Univ. (Ext.). BSc 1928, PhD 1941, DSc 1948, London. Joined the National Physical Laboratory, 1929; Senior Principal Scientific Officer, 1956–60; Deputy Chief Scientific Officer, 1960–72. Charles Vernon Boys Prize, Phys. Soc. 1957; Tompion Gold Medal, Clockmakers' Company, 1957; Wolfe Award, 1959; A. S. Popov Gold Medal, USSR Acad. of Sciences, 1959. Hon. FUMIST, 1971. *Publications:* Velocity of Light and Radio Waves, 1969; The Special Theory of Relativity, 1971; scientific papers. *Recreations:* walking, gardening, music. *Address:* High Hallgarth, 41 Durleston Park Drive, Great Bookham, Surrey KT23 4AJ. *T:* Bookham (0372) 454103.

ESSER, Robin Charles; editorial consultant, since 1990; *b* 6 May 1935; *s* of late Charles and Winifred Eileen Esser; *m* 1959, Irene Shirley Clough (decd); two *s* two *d*; 1981, Tui (*née* France); two *s*. *Educ:* Wheelwright Grammar School, Dewsbury; Wadham College, Oxford (BA Hons, MA). Edited Oxford Univ. newspaper, Cherwell, 1954. Commissioned, King's Own Yorkshire Light Infantry, 1956. Freelance reporter, 1957–60; Daily Express: Staff Reporter, 1960; Editor, William Hickey Column, 1963; Features Editor, 1965; New York Bureau, 1969; Northern Editor, 1970; Exec. Editor, 1985; Consultant Editor, Evening News, 1977; Editor, Sunday Express, 1986–89; Gp Editl Consultant, Express Newspapers, 1989–90. *Publications:* The Hot Potato, 1969; The Paper Chase, 1971. *Recreations:* lunching, sailing, talking, reading. *Address:* 34 Elthiron Road, SW6 4BW. *Club:* Buck's.

ESSERY, David James; Under Secretary, Scottish Office Agriculture and Fisheries Department, since 1985; *b* 10 May 1938; *s* of Lawrence and Edna Essery; *m* 1963, Nora Sim; two *s* one *d. Educ:* Royal High Sch., Edinburgh. Entered Dept of Health for Scotland, 1956; Private Sec. to Minister of State, Scottish Office, 1968; Principal, Scottish Develt Dept, 1969; Assistant Secretary: Scottish Economic Planning Dept, 1976; Scottish Develt Dept, 1981–85. *Recreations:* reading, music, cricket, squash. *Address:* (office) Pentland House, 47 Robb's Loan, Edinburgh EH14 1TW. *T:* 031–556 8400. *Club:* Commonwealth Trust.

ESSEX, 10th Earl of, *cr* 1661; **Robert Edward de Vere Capell;** Baron Capell, 1641; Viscount Malden, 1661; *b* 13 Jan. 1920; *s* of Arthur Algernon de Vere Capell (*d* 1924) and Alice Mabel (*d* 1951), *d* of James Currie, Wimbledon; *S* kinsman, 1981; *m* 1942, Doris Margaret, *d* of George Frederick Tomlinson, Morecambe; one *s. Heir: s* Viscount Malden, *qv.*

ESSEX, Francis; author, producer and composer; *b* 24 March 1929; *s* of Harold and Beatrice Essex-Lopresti; *m* 1956, Jeanne Shires; two *s. Educ:* Cotton Coll., N Staffs. Light Entertainment Producer, BBC Television, 1954–60; Sen. Prod., ATV Network Ltd, 1960–65; Controller of Progs, Scottish Television, 1965–69; ATV Network Ltd: Prodn Controller, 1969–76; Mem., Bd of Dirs, 1974; Dir of Production, 1976–81. Chm., Children's Adv. Cttee, TV-am, 1988–90. Chm., Conservatives Abroad, Javea, 1990–. Wrote and presented, The Bells of St Martins, St Martin's Theatre, 1953; devised and directed, Six of One, Adelphi, 1964; *television film scripts include:* Shillingbury Tales; Silent Scream; The Shenachy; Cuffy series; The Night Wind; Waterways; *scores:* Luke's Kingdom; The Seas Must Live; The Lightning Tree; Maddie With Love, etc; writer of plays and songs. Fellow, Royal Television Soc., 1974. British Acad. Light Entertainment Award, 1964, and Leonard Brett Award, 1964, 1981. *Publications:* Shillingbury Tales, 1983; Skerrymor Bay, 1984. *Recreations:* blue-water sailing, gardening. *Address:* Punta Vista, Aldea de las Cuevas, Benidoleig, Prov. de Alicante, Spain.

ESSEX, Francis William, CMG 1959; retired from HMOCS; *b* 29 June 1916; *s* of Frank Essex; *m* 1st, 1947, Marjorie Muriel Joyce Lewis (*d* 1987); two *s*; 2nd, 1987, Mary Frances Payton. *Educ:* Royal Grammar Sch., High Wycombe; Reading Univ.; Exeter Coll., Oxford. Joined Colonial Administrative Service, Sierra Leone, 1939; Asst District Commissioner, 1942; District Commissioner, 1948; Principal, HM Treasury, 1951; Dep. Financial Sec., Sierra Leone, 1953; Financial Sec., British Guiana, 1956–60; Financial Sec. to High Comr for Basutoland, Bechuanaland and Swaziland, 1960–64; Counsellor, British Embassy, South Africa, 1964–65; Sec. for Finance and Development, later Permanent Sec., Min. of Finance, Commerce and Industry, Swaziland, 1965–68; Principal, ODM, 1968–76. Mem., Pearce Commn on Rhodesian opinion, 1971–72. Short term British Technical Co-operation assignments, British Virgin Is, 1977, Tuvalu, 1978 and 1979, Antigua and Barbuda, 1981. *Address:* Cobblestones, Chagford, Devon TQ13 8AW.

ESSEX-CATER, Dr Antony John, LRCP, MRCS; FFPHM; FRAI; Medical Officer of Health, States of Jersey, Channel Islands, 1974–88; Venereologist, General Hospital, Jersey, 1974–88; Vice President, National Association for Maternal and Child Welfare, since 1988 (Chairman, 1975–88); *b* 28 Sept. 1923; *s* of Herbert Stanley Cater and Helen Marjorie Essex; *m* 1947, Jane Mary Binning; three *s* one *d. Educ:* Solihull Sch.; King's Coll., Univ. of London; Charing Cross Hosp.; School of Hyg. and Trop. Med., Univ. of London. Bygott Postgrad. Schol., Univ. of London, 1952–53. DPH, DIH, DCH; FRSH; AFOM. Medical Br., RAF, 1948–50. Dep. MOH, Swansea, 1953–58; Admin. MOH, Birmingham, 1958–61; Dep. MOH, Manchester, 1961–68; County MOH, Monmouthshire, 1968–74. Part-time Lectr in Child Health, Univ. of Birmingham, 1958–61; Council of Europe Medical Fellow, 1968. Short-term Consultant, WHO, 1988–89. Mem. Exec. Cttee 1958, Vice-Chm. 1969, Nat. Assoc. for Maternal and Child Welfare; Member: Public Health Lab. Services Bd, 1969–75; Steering Cttee, Nat. Health Service Reorganization (Wales), 1971–72; Founder Fellow and Mem. First Bd, Fac. of Community Med., Royal Colls of Physicians of UK, 1972–73. Member: BMA; Med. Soc. for Study of Venereal Diseases. *Publications:* Synopsis of Public Health and Social Medicine, 1960, 2nd edn 1967; Manual of Public Health and Community Medicine, 3rd edn 1979; numerous papers on medical and allied subjects. *Recreations:* literary, music, sport. *Address:* Honfleur, La Vallette, Mont Cambrai, St Lawrence, Jersey, CI. *T:* Jersey (0534) 72438. *Club:* Society of Authors.

ESSIG, Philippe Louis Charles Marie; Officier de l'Ordre National du Mérite, 1984; Officier de la Légion d'Honneur, 1988; Chairman, Board of Transmanche-Link, 1988–91; *b* 19 July 1933; *s* of Jean Essig and Germaine Olivier; *m* 1960, Isabelle Lanier; one *s* three *d. Educ:* Lycée Janson-de-Sailly; Ecole Polytechnique; Engineer, Ponts et Chaussées. Engr, Dakar-Niger railway, 1957–59; Asst Dir, Régie du chemin de fer Abidjan-Niger, 1960–61; Dir, Régie des chemins de fer du Cameroun, 1961–66; Régie autonome des transports parisiens (RATP): Chief Engr, Research Dept, 1966–71; Chief Op. Officer, Ops Dept, 1971–73; Man. Dir, Railways, Paris, 1973–81; Gen. Man., 1982–85; Pres., SNCF, 1985–88. Sec. of State for Housing, 1988. Officier de l'Ordre de la Valeur Camerounaise, 1966. *Recreations:* walking, ski-ing, shooting. *Address:* 5 Avenue Fourcault de Pavant, F-78000 Versailles, France.

ESSLIN, Martin Julius, OBE 1972; Professor of Drama, Stanford University, California (for two quarters annually), 1977–88, now Emeritus; *b* 8 June 1918; *s* of Paul Pereszlenyi and Charlotte Pereszlenyi (*née* Schiffer); *m* 1947, Renate Gerstenberg; one *d. Educ:* Gymnasium, Vienna; Vienna Univ.; Reinhardt Seminar of Dramatic Art, Vienna. Joined BBC, 1940; Producer and Scriptwriter, BBC European Services, 1941–55; Asst Head, BBC European Productions Dept, 1955; Asst Head, Drama (Sound), BBC, 1961; Head of Drama (Radio), BBC, 1963–77. Awarded title Professor by Pres. of Austria, 1967; Vis. Prof. of Theatre, Florida State Univ., 1969–76. Hon. DLitt Kenyon Coll., Ohio, 1978. *Publications:* Brecht, A Choice of Evils, 1959; The Theatre of the Absurd, 1962; (ed) Beckett (anthology of critical essays), 1965; Harold Pinter, 1967; The Genius of the German Theatre, 1968; Reflections, Essays on Modern Theatre (NY), 1969 (UK, as Brief Chronicles, 1970); The Peopled Wound: the plays of Harold Pinter, 1970, rev. edn as Pinter: a study of his plays, 1973, 4th edn as Pinter: the Playwright, 1982; (ed) The New Theatre of Europe, 1970; Artaud, 1976; An Anatomy of Drama, 1976; (ed) Illustrated Encyclopaedia of World Theatre, 1977; Mediations, Essays on Brecht, Beckett and the Media, 1981; The Age of Television, 1982; The Field of Drama, 1987; trans. Horváth, Judgement Day, 1986. *Recreations:* reading, book collecting. *Address:* 64 Loudoun Road, NW8. *T:* 071–722 4243; Ballader's Plat, Winchelsea, Sussex. *T:* Rye (0797) 226 392. *Club:* Garrick.

ESSWOOD, Paul Lawrence Vincent; singer (counter-tenor); Professor, Royal Academy of Music, since 1985; *b* West Bridgford, Nottingham, 6 June 1942; *s* of Alfred Walter Esswood and Freda Garratt; *m* 1st, 1966, Mary Lillian Cantrill, ARCM (marr. diss.), two *s*; 2nd, 1990, Aimée Désirée Blattmann. *Educ:* West Bridgford Grammar Sch.; Royal Coll. of Music (ARCM). Lay-Vicar, Westminster Abbey, 1964–71. Prof., RCM, 1973–85; Specialist in baroque performance; first broadcast, BBC, 1965; co-founder: Pro Cantione Antiqua; A Cappella Male Voice Ensemble for Performance of Old Music, 1967; operatic

debut in Cavalli's L'Erismena, Univ. of California, Berkeley, 1968; debut at La Scala, Milan with Zurich Opera in L'Incoronazione di Poppea and Il Ritorno d'Ulisse, 1978; Scottish Opera debut in Dido and Aeneas, 1978; world premieres: Penderecki's Paradise Lost, Chicago Lyric Opera, 1979; Philip Glass's Echnaton, Stuttgart Opera, 1984; performed in major festivals: Edinburgh, Leeds Triennial, English Bach, Vienna, Salzburg, Zurich, Hamburg, Berlin, Naples, Israel, Lucerne, Flanders, Wexford, Holland. Has made over 100 recordings for major cos, incl. solo recitals of Purcell, Schumann and English lute songs. Hon. RAM 1990. *Recreation:* gardening (organic). *Address:* Jasmine Cottage, 42 Ferring Lane, Ferring, West Sussex BN12 6QT. *T:* and *Fax:* Worthing (0903) 504480.

ESTEVE-COLL, Elizabeth Anne Loosemore; Director, Victoria and Albert Museum, since 1988; *b* 14 Oct. 1938; *o d* of P. W. and Nora Kingdon; *m* 1960, José Alexander Timothy Esteve-Coll (*d* 1980). *Educ:* Darlington Girls High Sch.; Birkbeck Coll., London Univ. (BA 1976). Head of Learning Resources, Kingston Polytechnic, 1977; University Librarian , Univ. of Surrey, 1982; Keeper, National Art Library, V&A Museum, 1985. *Recreations:* reading, music, foreign travel. *Address:* c/o Victoria and Albert Museum, South Kensington, SW7 2RL. *T:* 071–938 8501.

ESTEY, Hon. Willard Zebedee, CC 1990; Counsel, McCarthy Tétrault, Toronto; Chancellor, Wilfrid Laurier University, Waterloo, Ont; *b* 10 Oct. 1919; *s* of James Wilfred Estey and Muriel Baldwin Estey; *m* 1946, Marian Ruth McKinnon; three *s* one *d. Educ:* Univ. of Saskatchewan (BA, LLB); Harvard Law Sch. (LLM). Mem., Bar of Sask., 1942 and of Ont, 1947; QC Ont 1960. Prof., Coll. of Law, Univ. of Sask., 1946–47; Lectr, Osgoode Hall Law Sch., 1947–51. Practised law, Toronto, 1947–72. Pres., Canadian Bar Assoc., Ont, 1972. Mem. Court of Appeal, 1973, and Chief Justice of High Court, Supreme Court of Ont, 1975; Chief Justice of Ontario, 1976; Justice of Supreme Court of Canada, 1977–88. Commissioner: Steel Profits Inquiry, Royal Commn of Inquiry, 1974; Air Canada Inquiry, 1975; Inquiry into certain banking operations, 1985–86. Special Advr to Chm., Bank of Nova Scotia. Hon. LLD: Wilfrid Laurier Univ., Waterloo, Ont, 1977; Univ. of Toronto, 1979; Univ. of W Ont, 1980; Law Soc. of Upper Canada, 1981; Univ. of Saskatchewan, 1984; Univ. of Lethbridge, 1985. *Address:* Suite 4700, Toronto Dominion Bank Tower, Toronto Dominion Centre, Toronto, Ont M5K 1E6, Canada.

ETCHELLS, (Dorothea) Ruth, MA, BD; Principal, St John's College with Cranmer Hall, University of Durham, 1979–88; *b* 17 April 1931; *d* of late Walter and Ada Etchells. *Educ:* Merchant Taylor's School for Girls, Crosby, Liverpool; Universities of Liverpool (MA) and London (BD). Head of English Dept, Aigburth Vale High Sch., Liverpool, 1959; Lectr in English, 1963, Sen. Lectr in English and Resident Tutor, 1965, Chester College of Education; Trevelyan College, Univ. of Durham: Resident Tutor and part-time Lectr in English, 1968; Vice Principal, 1972; Sen. Lectr, 1973; Mem. Council, Durham Univ., 1985–88. Examining Chaplain to Bishop of Bath and Wells, 1984–88. Member: Gen. Synod, 1985–; Doctrine Commn, 1986–91; Crown Appointments Commn, 1987–; Bishop's Council and Standing Cttee of Durham Diocesan Synod (Chm., House of Laity, 1988–). Vice-Chm., Durham FHSA, 1990– (Chm., Gen. Med. Cttee, 1990–). Mem., Governing Council, Ridley Coll., Cambridge. Trustee, Anvil, 1983–. *Publications:* Unafraid To Be, 1969; The Man with the Trumpet, 1970; A Model of Making, 1983; (ed) Poets and Prophets, 1988; Praying with the English Poets, 1990. *Recreations:* friends, quiet, country walking, London. *Address:* 12 Dunelm Court, South Street, Durham DH1 4QX. *T:* Durham (091) 3841497.

ETHERINGTON-SMITH, (Raymond) Gordon (Antony), CMG 1962; HM Diplomatic Service, retired; *b* 1 Feb. 1914; *o s* of late T. B. Etherington-Smith and Henriette de Pitner; *m* 1950, Mary Elizabeth Besly (*d* 1989); one *s* three *d. Educ:* Downside; Magdalen Coll., Oxford; Sch. of Oriental and African Studies, London Univ. Entered FO, 1936. Served at: Berlin, 1939; Copenhagen, 1939–40; Washington, 1940–42; Chungking, 1943–45; Kashgar, 1945–46; Moscow, 1947; Foreign Office, 1947–52; Holy See, 1952–54; Counsellor, Saigon, 1954–57; The Hague, 1958–61; Office of UK Commissioner-Gen. for South-East Asia, Singapore, 1961–63; Ambassador to Vietnam, 1963–66; Minister, and Dep. Commandant, Berlin, 1966–70; Ambassador to Sudan, 1970–74. *Recreations:* physical and mental exercise. *Club:* Oriental.

ETHERTON, Terence Michael Elkan Barnet; QC 1990; *b* 21 June 1951; *s* of Alan Kenneth Etherton and Elaine Myrtle (*née* Maccoby). *Educ:* Holmewood House Sch., Tunbridge Wells; St Paul's Sch., London (Sen. Foundn Schol.); Corpus Christi Coll., Cambridge (Open Exhibnr; MA (History and Law); LLM). Called to the Bar, Gray's Inn, 1974 (Uthwatt Schol., 1972; Holker Sen. Award, 1974; Arden Atkin and Mould Prize, 1975); in practice, 1975–; Mem., Gray's Inn and Lincoln's Inn. Mem., Bar Council, 1978–81; Chm., Young Barristers' Cttee of Bar Council, 1980–81; Mem., Lord Rawlinson's Cttee on the Constitution of the Senate of the Inns of Court and the Bar, 1985–86. Captain, Cambridge Univ. Fencing Team, 1971–72; Mem., GB Sen. Internat. Fencing Team (Sabre), 1977–80 (World Championships, 1977, 1978, 1979); England Sabre Team Gold Medal, Commonwealth Fencing Championships, 1978; selected for Moscow Olympics, GB Fencing Team, 1980. *Address:* 3 New Square, Lincoln's Inn, WC2A 3RS. *Club:* Hawks (Cambridge).

ETIANG, Paul Orono, BA London; Minister of Commerce, Uganda, since 1989; *b* 15 Aug. 1938; *s* of late Kezironi Orono and Mirabu Achom Orono; *m* 1967, Zahra Ali Foum; two *s* two *d. Educ:* Makerere Univ. Coll. Uganda Admin. Officer, 1962–64; Asst Sec., Foreign Affairs, 1964–65; 3rd Sec., 1965–66, 2nd Sec., 1966–67, Uganda Embassy, Moscow; 1st Sec., Uganda Mission to UN, New York, 1968; Counsellor, 1968–69, High Commissioner, 1969–71; Uganda High Commission, London; Chief of Protocol and Marshal of the Diplomatic Corps, Uganda, 1971; Permanent Sec., Uganda Min. of Foreign Affairs, 1971–73; Minister of State for Foreign Affairs, 1973; Minister of State in the President's office, 1974; Minister of Transport and Communications, July 1976, of Transport, Communications and Works, Mar. 1977, of Transport and Works, 1978; an Asst. Sec.-Gen., OAU, Addis Ababa, 1978–87; Minister for Regl Co-operation, March–Dec. 1988. *Recreations:* chess, classical music, billiards. *Address:* Ministry of Commerce, PO Box 7000, Kampala, Uganda.

EURICH, Richard Ernst, OBE 1984; RA 1953 (ARA 1942); Artist (Painter); *b* Bradford, 14 March 1903; *s* of late Professor Frederick Wm Eurich; *m* 1934, Mavis Llewellyn Pope; two *d* (one *s* decd). *Educ:* St George's Sch., Harpenden; Bradford Grammar Sch. Studied art at Bradford Sch. of Arts and Crafts, and Slade Sch., London; held One Man Show of drawings at Goupil Gallery in 1929, and several exhibitions of paintings at Redfern Gallery; exhibited at Royal Academy, New English Art Club and London Group; Retrospective Exhibitions: Bradford, 1951; Bradford, Glasgow, London (Fine Art Soc.), Southampton, 1980–81; Imperial War Museum, 1991; works purchased by Contemporary Art Soc. and Chantrey Bequest; Painting, Dunkirk Beach 1940, purchased for Canadian Government; Official War Artist, 1941–45; representative works in various public galleries. Hon. DLitt Bradford, 1989. *Recreations:* music and gardening. *Address:* Appletreewick, Dibden Purlieu, Southampton. *T:* Hythe (Hants) (0703) 842291.

EUSTACE, Dudley Graham, FCA; Finance Director, British Aerospace plc, since 1988; *b* 3 July 1936; *s* of Albert and Mary Eustace; *m* 1964, Carol Diane Zakrajsek; two *d. Educ:*

Cathedral Sch., Bristol; Univ. of Bristol (BA Econ). FCA 1972. John Barritt & Son, Hamilton, Bermuda, 1962; Internat. Resort Facilities, Ont, 1963; Aluminium Securities Ltd, Montreal, 1964–65; Aluminium Co. of Canada Ltd, Vancouver, 1966–69, Montreal, 1969–73; Alcan Aluminio America Latina, Buenos Aires, 1973–76, Rio de Janeiro, 1976–79; Empresa Nacional del Aluminio, Madrid, 1979–83; Alcan Aluminium Ltd, Montreal, 1983–84; British Alcan Aluminium PLC, Gerrards Cross, Bucks, 1984–87; BAe, 1987–. Mem. Council, ECGD, 1988–. *Recreations:* jogging, gardening, reading. *Address:* St Anthony's Cottage, Tylers Green, Penn, Bucks HP10 8EQ. *T:* Penn (049481) 2627. *Clubs:* Royal Automobile; University, Montreal Athletic Association (Montreal, Canada).

EUSTACE, Sir (Joseph) Lambert, GCMG 1985; GCVO 1985; Governor-General, St Vincent and the Grenadines, since 1985; *b* 28 Feb. 1908; *s* of Reynold Lambert Eustace and Beatrice Alexandrine Eustace (*née* St Hilaire); *m* 1945, Faustina Eileen Gatherer; one *s* one *d* (and one *d* decd). *Educ:* St Vincent Grammar School. Founded Intermediate High Sch., 1926; teacher of English, Maths and French, incl. latterly at St Vincent Grammar Sch., 1926–52; Manager, St Vincent Cotton Ginnery, 1952–59; Manager of own factory (oil, soap and feeds), 1959–66; MP South Leeward, 1966–71; Speaker, House of Assembly, 1972–74. Deleg. to overseas confs, 1957–74. *Recreations:* reading, gardening, woodwork. *Address:* Government House, Montrose, St Vincent and the Grenadines, West Indies. *T:* 61401.

EUSTON, Earl of; James Oliver Charles FitzRoy, MA, FCA; *b* 13 Dec. 1947; *s* and *heir* of 11th Duke of Grafton, *qv*; *m* 1972, Lady Clare Kerr, BA, *d* of Marquess of Lothian, *qv*; one *s* four *d*. *Educ:* Eton; Magdalene Coll., Cambridge (MA). Dir, Smith St Aubyn & Co. (Holdings) plc, 1980–86; Executive Director: Enskilda Securities, 1982–87; Jamestown Investments, 1987–; Finance Director: Central Capital Hldgs, 1988–91; Capel-Cure Myers Capital Management, 1988–. *Heir: s* Viscount Ipswich, *qv*. *Address:* 6 Vicarage Gardens, W8; The Racing Stables, Euston, Thetford, Norfolk.

EVAN-COOK, John Edward, JP; *b* 25 Oct. 1902; 2nd *s* of late Evan Cook, JP, of London; *m* 1928, Winifred Elizabeth (*d* 1985), *d* of Joseph Samuel Pointon; no *c*. *Educ:* Westminster City Sch. Served War, 1940–46, Major, RAOC. Adviser on Packaging, War Office, 1940–46. Vice-Chm. London District Rotary, 1950–52; Pres. Rotary Club of Camberwell, 1948. Chairman: Bd of Visitors, HM Prison, Brixton, 1967–73; Evan-Cook Group (retd); Inst. of Packaging (Nat. Chm., 1954, President, 1954–57); Min. of Labour & Nat. Service Local Disablement Cttee, 1959–67. Estates Governor, Dulwich, 1973–90. Chief Scouts' Medal of Merit, 1962; Silver Acorn, 1968. Past Master, Worshipful Company of Paviors; Liveryman: Worshipful Co. of Carmen; Worshipful Co. of Farmers. Sheriff of London, 1958–59; Common Councilman, City of London, 1960–66 and 1972–77. JP City of London, 1950. Order of Homayoun, 3rd Class (Iran); Grand Cross of Merit, Order of Merit (Federal Republic of Germany). *Address:* Deaks Manor, Deaks Lane, Cuckfield, W Sussex RH17 5JA. *T:* Haywards Heath (0444) 452044. *Clubs:* City Livery (Pres., 1964–65), United Wards, Royal Automobile, Bentley Drivers', Institute of Advanced Motorists.

EVANS; *see* Parry-Evans and Parry Evans.

EVANS, family name of **Baroness Blackstone** and **Barons Evans of Claughton** and **Mountevans.**

EVANS OF CLAUGHTON, Baron *cr* 1978 (Life Peer), of Claughton in the County of Merseyside; **(David Thomas) Gruffydd Evans;** JP; DL; President of the Liberal Party, 1977–78; Liberal Party Spokesman in House of Lords on Local Government and Housing; *b* 9 Feb. 1928; *s* of John Cynlais Evans and Nellie Euronwy Evans; *m* 1956, Moira Elizabeth (*née* Rankin); one *s* three *d*. *Educ:* Birkenhead Prep. Sch.; Birkenhead Sch.; Friars Sch., Bangor; Univ. of Liverpool (LLB 1949). Solicitors' final exam., 1952. Pilot Officer, RAF, 1952–54. Hon. Sec., Lancs, Cheshire and N West Liberal Fedn, 1956–60; Chm., Nat. League of Young Liberals, 1960–61. Councillor: Birkenhead CBC, 1957–74; Wirral BC, 1973–78 (Leader Lib. Gp, 1973–77); Merseyside CC, 1973–81 (Leader Lib. Gp, 1977–81); introduced Leasehold Reform Bill, 1981. Chairman: Nat. Exec. 1965–68, Assembly Cttee 1971–74, Gen. Election Cttee of the Liberal Party, 1977–79 and 1983; President: Welsh Liberal Party, 1986–87 (Vice-Pres., 1979–86); Birkenhead & Merseyside Soc & Lib Dem, 1988–. Dir, Granada TV, 1985–. Mem. Court, Liverpool Univ., 1977–83; Governor, Birkenhead Sch., 1974–78, 1988–; Chairman: Birkenhead Council of Voluntary Service, 1964–73; Abbeyfield Soc. (Birkenhead), 1970–74; Liverpool Luncheon Club, 1980–81; Marcher Sound Radio, 1980–. Pres., Oxton CC, 1988–91. JP Wirral, 1960; DL Merseyside, 1989. *Publications:* booklets: Local Finance for Local Government, 1981; Power and Responsibility to Local Government, 1982. *Recreations:* golf; Welsh Rugby; Liverpool FC. *Address:* Sunridge, 69 Bidston Road, Claughton, Birkenhead, Merseyside L43 6TR. *T:* 051–652 3425. *Clubs:* National Liberal, MCC; Oxton Cricket, Birkenhead Squash Racquets, Wirral Ladies' Golf (Birkenhead).

EVANS, A. Briant; Hon. Consulting Gynæcological Surgeon, Westminster Hospital and Chelsea Hospital for Women; Hon. Consulting Obstetric Surgeon, Queen Charlotte's Maternity Hospital; *b* 26 June 1909; *e s* of late Arthur Evans, OBE, MD, MS, FRCS; *m* 1939, Audrey Marie, *er d* of late Roland Eveleigh Holloway; three *s*. *Educ:* Westminster Sch.; Gonville and Caius Coll., Cambridge; Westminster Hosp. MA, MB, BCh Cantab; FRCS; FRCOG. Sometime Examiner in Obstetrics to Univs of Cambridge and London and to Royal College of Obstetricians and Gynæcologists. Temp. Lieut-Col RAMC, served in Egypt, Italy and Austria; OC No. 9 Field Surgical Unit. *Address:* 6 Foxbury Place, Great Bedwyn, Marlborough, Wilts SN8 3PL. *T:* Marlborough (0672) 870094. *Club:* Army and Navy.

EVANS, Alun; *see* Evans, T. A.

EVANS, Alun S.; *see* Sylvester-Evans.

EVANS, Amanda Louise Elliot, (Mrs A. S. Duncan); Editor, Homes & Gardens, since 1986; *b* 19 May 1958; *d* of Brian Royston Elliot Evans and June Annabella (*née* Gilderdale); *m* 1989, Andrew Sinclair Duncan; one *d*. *Educ:* Tonbridge Girls' Grammar Sch. Editorial writer, Interiors magazine, 1981–83; Consultant Editor, Mitchell Beazley Publishers, 1983–84; freelance writer and stylist on A la carte, Tatler, Country Homes & Interiors, Sunday Times, 1984–86; Dep. Editor, Homes & Gardens, April–Oct. 1986. *Recreations:* mountain walking, opera, camping. *Address:* c/o Homes & Gardens, IPC, King's Reach Tower, Stamford Street, SE1 9LS. *T:* 071–261 5678.

EVANS, Anthony; *see* Evans, D. A.

EVANS, Sir Anthony (Adney), 2nd Bt, *cr* 1920; *b* 5 Aug. 1922; *s* of Sir Walter Harry Evans, 1st Bt, and Margaret Mary, *y d* of late Thomas Adney Dickens; *S* father 1954; married; two *s* one *d*. *Educ:* Shrewsbury; Merton Coll., Oxford. *Club:* Leander (Henley).

EVANS, Hon. Sir Anthony (Howell Meurig), Kt 1985; RD 1968; **Hon. Mr Justice Evans;** a Judge of the High Court of Justice, Queen's Bench Division, since 1984; a Judge of the Commercial Court, since 1984; *b* 11 June 1934; *s* of late His Honour David Meurig Evans and Joy Diederické Sander; *m* 1963, Caroline Mary Fyffe Mackie, *d* of late Edwin Gordon Mackie; one *s* two *d*. *Educ:* Bassaleg Sec. Grammar Sch., Mon; Shrewsbury Sch.; St John's Coll., Cambridge. Nat. Service, RNVR, 1952–54 (Lt-Comdr RNR). BA 1957, LLB 1958, Cantab. Called to Bar, Gray's Inn, 1958 (Arden Scholar and Birkenhead Scholar; Bencher, 1979); QC 1971; a Recorder, 1972–84; a Presiding Judge, Wales and Chester Circuit, 1986–88. Mem. Melbourne, Vic, Bar, 1975–84, Hon. Mem., 1985. Dep. Chm., Boundary Commn for Wales, 1989–. Hon. Fellow, Internat. Acad. of Trial Lawyers, 1985; FCIArb 1986. *Publication:* (Jt Editor) The Law of the Air (Lord McNair), 1964. *Recreations:* sailing, music. *Address:* c/o Royal Courts of Justice, Strand, WC2. *Clubs:* Royal Lymington Yacht, Royal Southampton Yacht.

EVANS, Prof. Anthony John, PhD, FLA; University Librarian, since 1964 and Professor in Department of Information and Library Studies (formerly Library and Information Studies), since 1973, Loughborough University of Technology; *b* 1 April 1930; *s* of William John and Marian Audrey (*née* Young); *m* 1954, Anne (*née* Horwell); two *d*. *Educ:* Queen Elizabeth's Hosp., Bristol; Sch. of Pharmacy and University College, Univ. of London. BPharm, PhD. Lectr in Pharm. Eng. Sci., Sch. of Pharmacy, Univ. of London, 1954–58; Librarian, Sch. of Pharmacy, Univ. of London, 1958–63; Dean, Sch. of Educnl Studies, Loughborough Univ. of Technology, 1973–76. Pres., IATUL, 1970–75 (Bd Mem. and Treasurer, 1968–70; Hon. Life Mem., 1976–); Mem. Exec. Bd, IFLA, 1983–89 (Treas., 1985–89; Consultative Cttee, 1968–76; Standing Cttee on Sci. and Tech. Libraries, 1977–87); ASLIB: Vice-Pres., 1985–88; Mem. Council, 1970–80, 1985–88; Internat. Relations Cttee, 1974–85; Annual Lecture, 1985; BSI: Mem. Bd, 1984–86; Chm., Documentation Standards Cttee, 1980–86 (Mem., 1976–86); Member: Inf. Systems Council, 1980–86. Member: Adv. Cttee, Sci. Ref. Library, 1975–83; Vice-Chancellors and Principals Cttee on Libraries, 1972–77; Jt UNESCO/ICSU Cttee for establishment of UNISIST, 1968–71; Internat. Affairs Sub-Cttee, LA, 1985–; Adv. Council to Bd of Dirs of Engineering Information Inc., USA, 1986–; Chm., Adv. Gp on Documentation Standards, ISO, 1983–85; consultancy work for British Council, UNESCO, UNIDO, World Bank in Africa, Asia and Latin America, especially China, Kenya and Mexico. Hon. FLA, 1990. Medal IFLA, 1989. *Publications:* (with D. Train) Bibliography of the tabletting of medicinal substances, 1964, suppl. 1965; (with R. G. Rhodes and S. Keenan) Education and training of users of scientific and technical information, 1977; articles in librarianship and documentation. *Recreations:* travel, sport, model railways. *Address:* 78 Valley Road, Loughborough, Leics LE11 3QA. *T:* Loughborough (0509) 215670. *Club:* Commonwealth Trust.

EVANS, Anthony Thomas; Metropolitan Stipendiary Magistrate, since 1990; *b* 29 Sept. 1943; *s* of Emlyn Roger Evans and late Dorothy Evans; *m* 1965, Gillian Celia Mather (*d* 1988); one *s*. *Educ:* Bishop Gore Grammar Sch., Swansea; Univ. of Manchester (LLB 1965; LLM 1968). Asst Lectr, Univ. of Manchester, 1965–68; admitted Solicitor, 1971; Partner: Haye & Reid, 1971–85; Evans & Co., 1985–89; sole practitioner, 1989–90. *Recreations:* reading, music, theatre. *Address:* Tower Bridge Magistrates Court, Tooley Street, SE1.

EVANS, (Arthur) Mostyn; General Secretary, Transport and General Workers Union, 1978–85; Member, TUC General Council, 1977–85; *b* 13 July 1925; *m* 1947, Laura Bigglestone; two *s* three *d* (and one *s* decd). *Educ:* Cefn Coed Primary Sch., S Wales; Church Road Secondary Modern Sch., Birmingham. District Officer, Birmingham, Chem. and Eng. Industries, 1956; Regional Officer, Midlands, 1960; Nat. Officer, Eng., 1966; National Secretary: Chem., Rubber, and Oil Industries, 1969; Engineering Industries, 1969; (Automotive Section), TGWU, 1969–73; Nat. Organiser, TGWU, 1973–78. Part-time Mem., Nat. Bus Co., 1976–78; Member: BOTB, 1978–79; NEDC, 1978–84; Exec., ITF, 1980–; Council, ACAS, 1982–; Pres., ICEF, 1982– (Vice-Pres., 1980–82). *Recreation:* music. *Address:* Cheney House, Cheney Hill, Heacham, King's Lynn, Norfolk PE31 7BX. *T:* Heacham (0485) 70477.

EVANS, Briant; *see* Evans, A. B.

EVANS, Rt. Rev. Bruce Read; *see* Port Elizabeth, Bishop of.

EVANS, Sir Charles; *see* Evans, Sir R. C.

EVANS, Christina Hambley; *see* Brown, Tina.

EVANS, Rev. Prof. Christopher Francis, FBA 1991; MA; Professor of New Testament Studies, King's College, London, 1962–77, now Emeritus Professor, University of London; *b* 7 Nov. 1909; 2nd *s* of Frank and Beatrice Evans; *m* 1941, Elna Mary (*d* 1980), *d* of Walter and Elizabeth Burt; one *s*. *Educ:* King Edward's Sch., Birmingham; Corpus Christi Coll., Cambridge. Asst Curate, St Barnabas, Southampton, 1934–38; Tutor Schol. Canc. Linc., 1938–44; Chaplain and Divinity Lecturer, Lincoln Training Coll., 1944–48; Chaplain, Fellow and Lecturer in Divinity, Corpus Christi Coll., Oxford, 1948–58, Emeritus Fellow, 1977; Lightfoot Prof. of Divinity in the University of Durham and Canon of Durham Cathedral, 1959–62; Vis. Fellow, Trevelyan Coll., Durham, 1982–83. Select Preacher, University of Oxford, 1955–57; Proctor in Convocation for University of Oxford, 1955–58; Exam. Chaplain: to Bishop of Bristol, 1948–58; to Bishop of Durham, 1958–62; to Archbishop of Canterbury, 1962–74; to Bishop of Lichfield, 1969–75. FKC, 1970. Hon. DLitt Southampton, 1977; Hon. DD Glasgow, 1987. *Publications:* Christology and Theology, 1961; The Lord's Prayer, 1963; The Beginning of the Gospel, 1968; Resurrection and the New Testament, 1970; (ed jtly) The Cambridge History of the Bible: vol. I, From the Beginnings to Jerome, 1970; Is 'Holy Scripture' Christian?, 1971; Explorations in Theology 2, 1977; The Theology of Rhetoric, 1988; Saint Luke, 1990; contribs to Journal of Theological Studies, Theology and Religious Studies, to Studies in the Gospels and to Christian Faith and Communist Faith. *Recreation:* fishing. *Address:* 4 Church Close, Cuddesdon, Oxford OX9 9HD. *T:* Wheatley (08677) 4406; 5 The Square, Clun, Craven Arms, Salop.

EVANS, Air Vice-Marshal Clive Ernest, CBE 1982; Senior Directing Staff (Air), Royal College of Defence Studies, since 1988; *b* 21 April 1937; *s* of Leslie Roberts Evans and Mary Kathleen Butcher; *m* 1963, Therese Goodrich; one *s* one *d*. *Educ:* St Dunstan's Coll., Catford. Flying training, RAF, 1955–56; graduated as pilot, 1956, as qualified flying instr, 1960; served on Vampires, Jet Provosts, Canberras, Lightnings and F111s (exchange tour with USAF), 1960–72; RAF Staff Coll., 1972; PSO to Controller Aircraft, 1973; OC No 24 Sqn (Hercules), 1974–76; Nat. Defence Coll., 1976–77; DS RAF Staff Coll., 1977–79; Head of RAF Presentation Team, 1979–81; OC RAF Lyneham, 1981–83; RCDS, 1984; COS and Dep. Comdr, British Forces Falkland Is, 1985; Dep. Air Sec., 1985–88. *Recreations:* reading, cricket, golf, gardening. *Address:* 43 Purley Bury Close, Purley, Surrey CR8 1HW. *T:* 081–660 8115. *Club:* Royal Air Force.

EVANS, Colin Rodney; Director, Weapon Systems Research Laboratory, Defence Science and Technology Organisation, Adelaide, since 1989; *b* 5 June 1935; *s* of John Evans and Annie (*née* Lawes); *m* 1963, Jennifer MacIntosh; two *d*. *Educ:* Bridlington Sch.; Woolwich Polytechnic; Imperial Coll., London. BSc(Eng); HND; MIMechE. Scientific Officer, ARDE (now RARDE), 1959–60; Lectr, RNC, Greenwich, 1960–61; Scientific Officer, then Sen. Scientific Officer and PSO, ARDE, 1961–69; SO to Chief Scientist (Army),

MoD, 1969–71; British Defence Staff, Washington, 1971–73; SPSO, RARDE, 1973–79; Dep. Dir, Scientific and Technical Intell., MoD, 1979–81; seconded to Sir Derek Rayner's study team on efficiency in govt, 1981; RCDS, 1982; Dep. Dir (1), RARDE, 1983–84; Asst Under Sec. of State, MoD, Dep. Dir (Vehicles) and Hd of RARDE (Chertsey), 1985–89. *Recreations:* squash, tennis, bird watching, stamp collecting. *Address:* DWSRL, PO Box 1700, Salisbury, SA 5108, Australia.

EVANS, David; Director-General, National Farmers' Union, since 1985 (Deputy Director-General, 1984–85); *b* 7 Dec. 1935; *yr s* of William Price Evans and late Ella Mary Evans; *m* 1960, Susan Carter Connal, *yr d* of late Dr John Connal and Antoinette Connal; one *s* one *d*. *Educ:* Welwyn Garden City Grammar Sch.; University Coll. London (BScEcon). Joined Min. of Agriculture, Fisheries and Food, 1959; Private Sec. to Parliamentary Sec. (Lords), 1962–64; Principal, 1964; Principal Private Sec. to Ministers, 1970–71; Asst Sec., 1971; seconded to Cabinet Office, 1972–74; Under-Sec., MAFF, 1976–80; joined NFU as Chief Economic and Policy Adviser, 1981. *Address:* 6 Orchard Rise, Kingston upon Thames, Surrey KT2 7EY. *T:* 081–942 7701.

EVANS, Rev. David; Rector of Heyford with Stowe-Nine-Churches, since 1989; *b* Llanglydwen, Dyfed, 15 Feb. 1937; *o s* of late Rev. W. Noel Evans, JP, and Frances M. Evans; *m* 1962, Jenifer Margaret (*née* Cross); three s. Educ: Sherborne; Keble Coll., Oxford (MA); Wells Theological Coll. (BD London). 2nd Lieut, Royal Signals, 1956–57. Minor Canon, Brecon Cath., and Asst Curate, Brecon St Mary with Battle, 1964–68; Bishop's Chaplain to Students, UC, Swansea, and Asst Curate, Swansea St Mary with Holy Trinity, 1968–71; Bishop of Birmingham's Chaplain for Samaritan and Social Work, 1971–75; Dir, Samaritans of Swansea, 1969–71, of Birmingham, 1971–75; Jt Gen. Sec., 1975–84, Gen. Sec., 1984–89, The Samaritans. Licensed Priest, Dio. of Oxford, 1975–89. Mem., Church in Wales Liturgical Commn, 1969–75. *Recreations:* music, railways. *Address:* The Rectory, Church Lane, Nether Heyford, Northampton NN7 3LQ. *T:* Weedon (0327) 40487.

EVANS, Prof. David Alan Price, FRCP; Director of Medicine, Riyadh Armed Forces Hospital, Saudi Arabia, since 1983; Hon. Professor of Medicine, King Saud University, since 1988; *b* 6 March 1927; *s* of Owen Evans and Ellen (*née* Jones). *Educ:* Univ. of Liverpool (MD, PhD, DSc); Johns Hopkins Univ. RAMC, Jun. Med. Specialist, BMH Kure, Field Hosp. Korea, BMH Singapore and BMH Kinrara, Malaysia, 1953–55; Capt. RAMC, 1954–55. House Physician and House Surg. 1951–52, and Med. Registrar, 1956–58 and 1959–60, United Liverpool Hosps; Res. Fellow, Div. of Med. Genetics, Dept of Medicine, Johns Hopkins Hosp., 1958–59; Lectr 1960–62, Sen. Lectr 1962–68, Personal Chair, 1968–72, Dept of Medicine, Univ. of Liverpool; Prof. and Chm., Dept of Medicine and Dir, Nuffield Unit Medical Genetics, Univ. of Liverpool, 1972–83; Cons. Physician, Royal Liverpool Hosp. (formerly Royal Liverpool Infirmary) and Broadgreen Hosp., Liverpool, 1965–83. Visiting Professor: Karolinska Univ., Stockholm, 1968; Johns Hopkins Univ, 1972. Lectures: Poulson Meml, Oslo Univ., 1972; first Sir Henry Dale, and Medallist, Johns Hopkins Univ., 1972; first Walter Idris Jones, Univ. of Wales, 1974; Watson Smith, RCP, 1976. Member: BMA, 1951; Assoc. of Physicians of GB and Ireland, 1964; Gastroenterological Soc., 1964. University of Liverpool: Roberts Prize, 1959; Samuels Prize, 1965; Thornton Prize, Eastern Psychiatric Assoc., 1964. Life Mem., Johns Hopkins Soc. of Scholars, 1972. Scientific Ed., Saudi Med. Jl, 1983–. *Publications:* medical and scientific, principally concerned with genetic factors determining responses to drugs. *Recreation:* country pursuits. *Address:* 28 Montclair Drive, Liverpool L18 0HA. *T:* 051–722 3112; Pen-yr-Allt, Paradwys, Llangristiolus, Bodorgan, Gwynedd LL62 5PD. *T:* Holyhead (0407) 840346.

EVANS, (David) Anthony; QC 1983; a Recorder of the Crown Court, since 1980; *b* 15 March 1939; *s* of Thomas John Evans, MD and May Evans; *m* 1974, Angela Bewley, *d* of John Clive Bewley, JP and Cynthia Bewley; two *d*. *Educ:* Clifton Coll., Bristol; Corpus Christi Coll., Cambridge (BA). Called to the Bar, Gray's Inn, 1965; practised at the Bar, Swansea, 1965–84. DTI Inspector, 1988–. *Recreations:* sport of all kinds. *Address:* Carey Hall, Neath, W Glamorgan SA10 7AU. *T:* Neath (0639) 643859; 55 Marlborough, 61 Walton Street, SW3. *T:* 071–823 9522. 4 Paper Buildings, Temple, EC4Y 7EX. *T:* 071–583 7765. *Clubs:* Turf, MCC; Cardiff and County (Cardiff); Swansea Cricket and Football (Swansea).

EVANS, Ven. David Eifion; Archdeacon of Cardigan, 1967–79; *b* 22 Jan, 1911; *e s* of John Morris and Sarah Pryse Evans, Borth, Cards, Dyfed; *m* 1st, 1941, Iris Elizabeth Gravelle (*d* 1973); one *s*; 2nd, 1979, Madeleine Kirby. *Educ:* Ardwyn, Aberystwyth; UCW, Aberystwyth; St Michael's Coll., Llandaff. BA 1932; MA 1951. Deacon, 1934; Priest, 1935. Curate: Llanfihangel-ar-Arth, 1934–36; Llanbadarn Fawr, 1936–40; Chaplain to the Forces, 1940–45; Vicar, Llandeloy with Llanrheithan, 1945–48; Penrhyncoch, 1948, with Elerch, 1952–57; St Michael, Aberystwyth, 1957–67; Rural Dean, Llanbadarn Fawr, 1957–67; Chaplain, Anglican Students, 1966–67; Canon of St David's Cathedral (Caerfai), 1963–67; Chaplain, Earl of Lisburne, 1967–69; Vicar: Llanafan with Llanwnnws, 1967–69; Newcastle Emlyn, 1969–79. Member: Governing Body of Church in Wales, 1956–79; Representative Body of Church in Wales, 1967–79; Court of Governors, and Council, UCW, Aberystwyth, 1958–69; Sub-Visitor, St David's Univ. Coll., Lampeter, 1972–79. *Publications:* contributions to: Llên Cymru Yn Y Bedwaredd Ganrif Ar Bymtheg, 1968; Jl of Hist. Soc. of Church in Wales and other Welsh Church periodicals. *Recreation:* reading. *Address:* 31 Bryncastell, Bow Street, Dyfed SY24 5DE. *T:* Aberystwyth (0970) 828747.

EVANS, Prof. (David) Ellis, DPhil; FBA 1983; Jesus Professor of Celtic, University of Oxford, and Fellow of Jesus College, since 1978; *b* Llanfynydd, 23 Sept. 1930; *yr s* of David Evans and Sarah Jane (*née* Lewis); *m* 1957, Sheila Mary, *er d* of David and Evelyn Jeremy; two *d*. *Educ:* Llandeilo Grammar Sch.; University Coll. of Wales, Aberystwyth, and University Coll., Swansea (Hon. Fellow, 1985) (BA Wales, 1952; MA Wales, 1954); Jesus Coll., Oxford (Meyricke Grad. Scholar, 1952–54; DPhil 1962, MA 1978). University College of Swansea: Asst Lectr in Welsh, 1957; Lectr, 1960; Reader, 1968; Prof. of Welsh Lang. and Lit. and Head of Dept of Welsh, 1974; Hon. Prof., 1990; Chm., Faculty of Medieval and Modern Langs, Oxford Univ., 1985–86. Lectures: Sir John Rhys Meml, British Acad., 1977; Rudolf Thurneysen Meml, Univ. of Bonn, 1979; O'Donnell, Univ. of Wales, 1980; G. J. Williams Meml, UC Cardiff, 1986; Sir Thomas Parry-Williams Meml, UCW, Aberystwyth, 1990. Pres. and Organizing Sec., Seventh Internat. Congress of Celtic Studies, Oxford, 1983; President: Cymdeithas Dafydd ap Gwilym, 1978–; Irish Texts Soc., 1983– (Mem. Council, 1978–); Cambrian Archaeol Assoc., 1990–91; Vice President: N Amer. Congress of Celtic Studies, Ottawa, 1986; Nat. Liby of Wales, 1987– (Mem. Court and Council, 1974–). Chairman: Welsh Dialect Studies Group, 1977–80; Council for Name Studies of GB and Ireland, 1980–84 (Mem. Council, 1962–); Member: Bd of Celtic Studies, Univ. of Wales, 1968–; Internat. Cttee of Onomastic Sciences, 1975–; Welsh Arts Council, 1981–87; Royal Commn on Ancient and Hist. Monuments in Wales, 1984–; Court, University of Wales, 1978–; Court, UC Swansea, 1980–; UNESCO Internat. Cttee for the Study of Celtic Cultures, 1984– (Provisional Cttee, 1981–83); Council, Hon. Soc. Cymmrodorion, 1984–; Celtic Commn, Austrian Acad. of Scis, 1987–; Welsh Ctte, UFC, 1989–. Hon. Mem., Druidic Order of Gorsedd of Bards, 1976–; Correspondant étranger, Etudes celtiques, 1982–. Editor, Lang. and Lit. Section, Bull. of Bd of Celtic Studies, 1972– (Editor-in-Chief, 1988–); Mem. Editorial Bd: Geiriadur Prifysgol Cymru/A Dictionary of the Welsh Language, 1973–; Nomina, 1980–85; Welsh Acad. English-Welsh Dictionary, 1981–. *Publications:* Gaulish Personal Names: a study of some continental Celtic formations, 1967; (contrib.) Swansea and its Region, ed W. G. V. Balchin, 1971; (contrib.) Homenaje a Antonio Tovar, 1972; (contrib.) The Anatomy of Wales, ed R. Brinley Jones, 1972; Gorchest y Celtiaid yn yr Hen Fyd, 1975; (ed) Cofiant Agricola, Rheolwr Prydain, 1975; Termau Gwleidyddiaeth, 1976; (contrib.) Indogermanisch und Keltisch, ed K. H. Schmidt, 1977; (contrib.) Aufstieg und Niedergang der römischen Welt, ed H. Temporini and W. Haase, 1983; (contrib.) Proc. 6th Internat. Congress of Celtic Studies, Galway (1979), 1983; (ed) Proc. 7th Internat. Congress of Celtic Studies, Oxford (1983), 1986; (contrib.) Geschichte und Kultur der Kelten, ed K. H. Schmidt, 1986; (ed with R. Brinley Jones) Cofio'r Dafydd, 1987; (contrib.) Y Gwareiddiad Celtaidd, ed Geraint Bowen, 1987; (contrib.) Cell Gymysg o'r Genedlaethol, 1989; (contrib.) Britain 400–600: Language and History; contrib. colloquia; articles and revs in learned journals. *Recreations:* music, walking. *Address:* Jesus College, Oxford OX1 3DW. *T:* Oxford (0865) 279700.

EVANS, Air Chief Marshal Sir David (George), GCB 1979 (KCB 1977); CBE 1967 (OBE 1962); Bath King of Arms, since 1985; Military Adviser to British Aerospace, since 1983; Director: BAe (Military Aircraft) Ltd, since 1989; BAe (Dynamics) Ltd, since 1989; *b* Windsor, Ont, Canada, 14 July 1924; *s* of William Stanley Evans, Clive Vale, Hastings, Sussex; *m* 1949, Denise Marson Williamson-Noble, *d* of late Gordon Till, Hampstead, London; two *d* (and two step *s*). *Educ:* Hodgson Sch., Toronto, Canada; North Toronto Collegiate. Served War, as Pilot, in Italy and NW Europe, 1944–45. Sqdn Pilot, Tactics Officer, Instructor, 1946–52; Sqdn Comdr, Central Flying Sch., 1953–55; RAF Staff Coll. course, 1955; OC No 11 (F) Sqdn, in Germany, 1956–57; Personal Staff Officer to C-in-C, 2nd Allied TAF, 1958–59; OC Flying, RAF, Coltishall, 1959–61; Coll. of Air Warfare course, 1961; Air Plans Staff Officer, Min. of Defence (Air), 1962–63; OC, RAF Station, Gutersloh, Germany, 1964–66; IDC, 1967; AOC, RAF Central Tactics and Trials Organisation, 1968–70; ACAS (Ops), 1970–73; AOC No 1 (Bomber) Group, RAF, 1973–76; Vice-Chief of Air Staff, 1976–77; C-in-C, RAF Strike Command, and UK NATO Air Forces, 1977–80; VCDS (Personnel and Logistics), 1981–83. Non-exec. Dir, NAAFI, 1984– (Pres. Council, 1981–83); Chm., BAe (Canada) Ltd, 1987–; Director: BAe Flying College Ltd, 1987–; Intermin Resource Corp. Ltd, 1986 (Chm., 1989–); Arabian Gold PLC, 1989–. Officers Pensions Society: Vice-Pres., 1983–; Mem. Council, 1988–, Chm., 1990–; Dir, Officers Pensions Soc. Investment Co., 1989–. Queen's Commendation for Valuable Service in the Air (QCVSA), 1955. CBIM 1978 (Mem. Bd of Companions, 1983–; Dep. Chm., 1989–). *Recreations:* rep. RAF at Rugby football and winter sports (President: RAF Winter Sports Assoc.; Combined Services Winter Sports Assoc.); has rep. Gt Brit. at Bobsleigh in World Championships, Commonwealth Games and, in 1964, Olympic Games. *Address:* Royal Bank of Canada, 14/16 Cockspur Street, SW1Y 5BL; British Aerospace, 11 Strand, WC2N 5JT. *T:* 071–389 3902. *Club:* Royal Air Force.

EVANS, David Howard; QC 1991; *b* 27 July 1944; *s* of David Hopkin Evans and Phoebe Dora Evans (*née* Reading); *m* 1973, Anne Celia Segall; two *s*. *Educ:* London Sch. of Economics (BSc Econ 1965; MSc 1967); Wadham Coll., Oxford (BA 1970). Asst Economic Adviser, HM Treasury, 1967–68; called to the Bar, Middle Temple, 1972; Asst Recorder of the Crown Court, 1987. *Recreations:* tennis, swimming, listening to music. *Address:* 24 Pembroke Gardens, W8 6HU. *T:* 071–602 3957; Queen Elizabeth Buildings, Temple, EC4Y 9BS. *T:* 071–583 5766. *Clubs:* Roehampton; Riviera Golf.

EVANS, David John; MP (C) Welwyn, Hatfield, since 1987; *b* 23 April 1935; *s* of Violet Edith Evans and Arthur Thomas Evans; *m* 1956, Janice Hazel (*née* Masters); two *s* one *d*. *Educ:* Raglan Road School; Tottenham Tech. College. Professional cricketer (Glos and Warwicks) and footballer (Aston Villa); founded Exclusive Office Cleaning Ltd, 1960; Chm. and Man. Dir, Brengreen (Holdings), first co. with contract for refuse collection and street cleansing services (Southend-on-Sea Borough Council), 1960–86 (Brengreen (Holdings) acquired by BET plc, 1986); Chairman: Bradnam Enterprises Ltd, 1989–; Broadreach Services Ltd, 1990–. PPS to Minister of State for Industry, DTI, 1990–. Chm., Luton Town Football and Athletic Co. Ltd, 1984–89 (Dir, 1977–90); Mem. Council, Lord's Taverners, 1978– (Chm., 1982–84). *Address:* Little Radley, Mackerye End, Harpenden, Herts AL5 5DS. *T:* Harpenden (0582) 460302. *Clubs:* Carlton; MCC, Lord's Taverners, Middlesex CC; Harpenden Golf; Luton Town Football and Athletic.

EVANS, David Lloyd C.; *see* Carey Evans.

EVANS, David Marshall, QC 1981; **His Honour Judge Marshall Evans;** a Circuit Judge, since 1987; *b* 21 July 1937; *s* of Robert Trevor and Bessie Estelle Evans; *m* 1961, Alice Joyce Rogers; two *s*. *Educ:* Liverpool Coll.; Trinity Hall, Cambridge (MA, LLM); Law Sch., Univ. of Chicago (JD). Called to the Bar, Gray's Inn, 1964. Teaching Fellow, Stanford University Law Sch., 1961–62; Asst Professor, Univ. of Chicago Law Sch., 1962–63; Lectr in Law, University Coll. of Wales, Aberystwyth, 1963–65; joined Northern Circuit, 1965; a Recorder, 1984–87. *Recreations:* walking, photography, visual arts, bird-watching, motorsport. *Address:* Queen Elizabeth II Law Courts, Derby Square, Liverpool L2 1XA. *T:* 051–473 7373. *Club:* Athenæum (Liverpool).

EVANS, David Milne; Cabinet Office, 1977–81; *b* 8 Aug. 1917; *s* of Walter Herbert Evans, MSc and Florence Mary Evans (*née* Milne); *m* 1946, Gwynneth May (*née* Griffiths), BA. *Educ:* Charterhouse (Scholar); Gonville and Caius Coll., Cambridge (Schol.; Wrangler, Math. Tripos). Administrative Class, Home Civil Service (War Office), 1939. Served in Army (Major, RA), 1940–45. Asst Sec., 1954; Imp. Def. Coll., 1954; Asst Under-Sec. of State, MoD, 1967–77 (Under-Sec., CS Dept, 1972). Coronation Medal, 1953; Silver Jubilee Medal, 1977. *Address:* 1 Church Rise, Walston Road, Wenvoe, Cardiff, South Glamorgan CF5 6DE. *T:* Cardiff (0222) 597129.

EVANS, David Philip, CBE 1968; MSc, PhD, FRSC; Principal, Glamorgan Polytechnic, Treforest, Pontypridd, Glam, 1970–72; *b* 28 Feb. 1908; *s* of D. C. and J. Evans, Port Talbot, Glam; *m* 1938, Vura Helena (*née* Harcombe); one *s*. *Educ:* Port Talbot County Grammar Sch.; University Coll., Cardiff (Fellow, 1981). Lectr in Chemistry, Cardiff Technical Coll., 1934–44; Principal: Bridgend Technical Coll., Glam, 1944–52; Glamorgan Coll. of Technology, Treforest, 1952–70. Hon. Fellow, Polytechnic of Wales, 1984. *Publications:* numerous papers in various chemical jls. *Recreations:* fishing, gardening, music. *Address:* Tree Tops, St Bride's Road, Ewenny Cross, Ewenny, Bridgend, Mid Glam CF35 5RG. *T:* Bridgend (0656) 661354.

EVANS, Rt. Rev. David Richard John; Assistant Bishop, Diocese of Bradford, since 1988; *b* 5 June 1938; *s* of William Henry Reginald Evans and Beatrix Catherine Mottram; *m* 1964, Dorothy Evelyn Parsons; one *s* two *d*. *Educ:* Caius College, Cambridge. Hons degree in Mod. Langs and Theology, 1963, MA 1966. Curate, Christ Church, Cockfosters, 1965–68; Missionary Pastor and Gen. Sec., Argentine Inter-Varsity Christian Fellowship, in Buenos Aires, Argentina, 1969–77; Chaplain, Good Shepherd Church, Lima, Peru, 1977–82; Bishop of Peru, 1978–88 (with delegated jurisdiction of Bolivia from 1980).

Internat. Co-ordinator, Evangelical Fellowship of the Anglican Communion, 1989. *Publication:* En Diálogo con Dios, 1976. *Recreations:* golf, philately. *Address:* 30 Grosvenor Road, Shipley, W Yorks BD18 4RN. *T:* Bradford (0274) 582033.

EVANS, (David) Roderick; QC 1989; a Recorder, since 1987; *b* 22 Oct. 1946; *s* of Thomas James and Dorothy Evans; *m* 1971, Kathryn Rebecca Lewis; three *s* one *d. Educ:* Bishop Gore Grammar School, Swansea; University College London (LLB 1967; LLM 1968). Called to the Bar, Gray's Inn, 1970. *Recreations:* reading, walking. *Address:* Angel Chambers, 94 Walter Road, Swansea SA1 5QA. *T:* Swansea (0792) 464623.

EVANS, Eben, OBE 1976; Controller, Books Division, British Council, 1976–80; *b* 1 Nov. 1920; *s* of John Evans and Mary Evans; *m* 1946, Joan Margaret Howells; two *s* two *d. Educ:* Llandovery Grammar Sch.; University Coll. of Wales, Aberystwyth (BA 1948). Served War, 1941–46 (Army, Captain). Appointed to British Council, 1948; Cardiff, 1948–55; Thailand, 1955–59; Gambia, 1959–62; Ghana, 1962–64; Personnel Dept, London, 1964–68; Representative: Algeria, 1968–73; Yugoslavia, 1973–76. *Recreations:* walking, music. *Address:* Gorddinog Isaf, Llanfairfechan, Gwynedd.

EVANS, Rt. Rev. Edward Lewis, BD, MTh; *b* 11 Dec. 1904; *s* of Edward Foley Evans and Mary (*née* Walker). *Educ:* St Anselm's, Croydon; Tonbridge Sch.; Bishops' Coll., Cheshunt. BD London 1935, MTh 1938. Deacon, 1937; priest 1938; Curate of St Mary's, Prittlewell, Essex, 1937–39; Warden of St Peter's, Theological Coll., Jamaica, 1940–49; Rector, Kingston Parish Church, Jamaica, 1949–52; Rector of Woodford and Craigton, 1952–57; Archdeacon of Surrey, Jamaica, 1950–57; Bishop Suffragan of Kingston, 1957–60; Bishop of Barbados, 1960–71. *Publication:* A History of the Diocese of Jamaica, 1977. *Address:* Bungalow 1, Terry's Cross, Woodmancote, Henfield, Sussex BN5 9SX.

EVANS, Edward Stanley Price, FRTPI; City Planning Officer, Liverpool, 1974–84, retired; *b* 13 April 1925; *s* of late Bernard James Reuben Evans and of Nellie Evans; *m* 1948, Eva Magdalena Emma Fry; one *s* (and one *s* decd). *Educ:* Wolverhampton Grammar Sch.; Nottingham Coll. of Art and Crafts (DipTP). FRTPI 1966 (MTPI 1954). Chief Town Planning Officer, Norwich, 1957; City Planning Officer, Nottingham, 1966. Member: DoE Environmental Bd, 1977–79; DoE Panel of Local Plan Inspectors, 1985–. FRSA 1980. *Recreations:* travel, gardening, bridge (social). *Address:* Willow Cottage, The Ridgeway, Heswall, Wirral, Merseyside L60 8NB. *T:* 051–342 4546.

EVANS, Ven. Eifion; *see* Evans, Ven. D. E.

EVANS, Ellis; *see* Evans, D. E.

EVANS, Emrys; *see* Evans, W. E.

EVANS, Ena Winifred; Headmistress, King Edward VI High School for Girls, Birmingham, since 1977; *b* 19 June 1938; *d* of Frank and Leonora Evans. *Educ:* The Queen's Sch., Chester; Royal Holloway Coll., Univ. of London (BSc); Hughes Hall, Cambridge (CertEd). Asst Mistress, Bolton Sch. (Girls' Div.), 1961–65; Bath High School (GPDST): Head of Mathematics Dept, 1965–72; Second Mistress, 1970–72; Dep. Head, Friends' Sch., Saffron Walden, 1972–77. Pres., GSA, 1987–88. Mem., Central Birmingham DHA, 1988–90. Mem. Council, Aston Univ., 1989–. FRSA 1986. *Recreation:* music. *Address:* King Edward VI High School for Girls, Edgbaston Park Road, Birmingham B15 2UB. *T:* 021–472 1834.

EVANS, Very Rev. Eric; *see* Evans, Very Rev. T. E.

EVANS, Fabyan Peter Leaf; His Honour Judge Fabyan Evans; a Circuit Judge, since 1988; *b* 10 May 1943; *s* of Peter Fabyan Evans and Catherine Elise Evans; *m* 1967, Karen Myrtle (*née* Balfour), *g d* of 1st Earl Jellicoe; two *s* one *d. Educ:* Clifton College. Called to the Bar, Inner Temple, 1969. A Recorder, 1985–88. *Recreations:* sailing, singing. *Club:* Brooks's.

EVANS, Sir Francis Loring G.; *see* Gwynne-Evans.

EVANS, Frederick Anthony, CVO 1973; General Secretary, The Duke of Edinburgh's Award Scheme, 1959–72 (Adviser for the Handicapped, 1972–84); *b* 17 Nov. 1907; *s* of Herbert Anthony Evans, mining engineer, and Pauline (*née* Allen); *m* 1934, Nancy (*née* Meakin); two *s* one *d. Educ:* Charterhouse; Corpus Christi, Cambridge. Manager Doondu Coffee Plantation, Kenya, 1927–31; Colonial Service, 1934; Asst District Officer, Nigeria, 1935–39; Provincial Commissioner and Asst Colonial Sec., Gambia, 1940–47; Colonial Sec., Nassau, Bahamas, 1947–51; Acting Governor, 1950; Permanent Sec., Gold Coast (later Ghana), 1951–57. Dir, Anglo-Gambian Archæological Expedition, 1965–66. *Publication:* The State Apartments at Buckingham Palace: a souvenir, 1985. *Recreation:* gardening. *Address:* Bellsfield, South Ridge, Odiham, Hants. *Club:* Commonwealth Trust.

EVANS, Senator Hon. Gareth (John); QC; Senator (Lab) for Victoria, since 1978; Minister for Foreign Affairs and Trade, Australia, since 1988; Deputy Leader of Government in Senate, since 1987; *b* 5 Sept. 1944; *m* 1969, Merran Anderson; one *s* one *d. Educ:* Melbourne Univ. (law and arts); Oxford Univ. (PPE). Lectr in Law, 1971–74, Sen. Lectr, 1974–76, Melbourne Univ.; practising Barrister, 1977–78; Shadow Attorney-General, 1980–83; Attorney-General, 1983–84; Minister for Resources and Energy, 1984–87, for Transport and Communications, 1987–88. *Publications:* (ed) Labor and the Constitution, 1972; (ed) Law, Politics and the Labor Movement, 1980; (ed) Labor Essays, 1980, 1981, 1982; (jtly) Australia's Constitution: Time for Change?, 1983. *Recreations:* reading, writing, tennis, golf, football. *Address:* Parliament House, Canberra, ACT 2600, Australia. *T:* 062 77 7500; 24 Maltravers Road, East Ivanhoe, Vic 3079, Australia.

EVANS, George James; Sheriff of Glasgow and Strathkelvin at Glasgow, since 1983; *b* 16 July 1944; *s* of Colin Evans and Caroline Catherine Kennedy MacPherson Harris; *m* 1973, Lesley Jean Keir Cowie; two *d. Educ:* Ardrossan Acad.; Glasgow Univ. (MA Hons); Edinburgh Univ. (LLB). Advocate, 1973; Standing Jun. Counsel, Dept of Energy, Scotland, 1982. *Publications:* contribs to legal periodicals. *Recreations:* reading, music, Cuban vegetation, swimming, country rambles. *Address:* 14 Dalkeith Avenue, Glasgow G41 5BJ. *T:* 041-427 3709.

EVANS, Sir Geraint Llewellyn, Kt 1969; CBE 1959; retired opera singer; Principal Baritone, Royal Opera House, Covent Garden, 1948–84; *b* 16 Feb. 1922; *m* 1948, Brenda Evans Davies; two *s. Educ:* Guildhall Sch. of Music. Has sung at: Royal Opera House, Covent Garden (since 1948); Glyndebourne Festival Opera; Vienna State Opera; La Scala, Milan; Metropolitan Opera, New York; San Francisco Opera; Lyric Opera, Chicago; Salzburg Festival Opera; Edinburgh Festival Opera; Paris Opera; Teatro Colon, Buenos Aires; Mexico City Opera; Welsh Nat. Opera; Scottish Opera; Berlin Opera; Teatr Wielki, Warsaw. Dir, Harlech Television Ltd. Vice-Pres., Kidney Research Unit for Wales Foundn. Mem., Gorsedd of Bards, Royal Nat. Eisteddfod of Wales; Patron, Churchill Theatre, Bromley; Governor, University Coll. of Wales, Aberystwyth. FGSM 1960; FRNCM 1978; FRCM 1981; FRSA 1984; FTCL 1987; Fellow: University Coll., Cardiff, 1976; Jesus Coll., Oxford, 1979; Aberystwyth, 1988; UC, Swansea, 1990. Freeman, City of London, 1984. Hon. DMus: Wales, 1965; Leicester, 1969; Oxford, 1985; CNAA 1980; London 1982. Hon. RAM 1969. Worshipful Company of Musicians Sir Charles Santley Meml Award, 1963; Harriet Cohen Internat. Music Award (Opera Medal), 1967; Fidelio Medal, Internat. Assoc. of Opera Dirs, 1980; San Francisco Opera Medal, 1981; Soc. of Cymmrodorion Medal, 1984. OStJ 1986. *Publication:* (with Noël Goodwin) Sir Geraint Evans: a knight at the opera, 1984. *Recreations:* rugby, sailing. *Address:* Trelawney, Aberaeron, Dyfed SA46 0BD.

EVANS, Godfrey; *see* Evans, T. G.

EVANS, Gwynfor; Honorary President, Plaid Cymru, since 1982 (President, 1945–81, Vice-President, 1943–45); *b* 1 Sept. 1912; *s* of Dan Evans and Catherine Mary Richard; *m* 1941, Rhiannon Prys Thomas; four *s* three *d. Educ:* Gladstone Road Elementary Sch.; County Sch., Barry; University of Wales, Aberystwyth; St John's Coll., Oxford. Qual. Solicitor, 1939. Hon. Sec. Heddychwyr Cymru (Welsh Pacifist movement), 1939–45; Chm. Union of Welsh Independents, 1954. MP (Plaid Cymru) Carmarthen, July 1966–1970 and Oct. 1974–1979. Contested (Plaid Cymru) Carmarthen, 1979 and 1983. Member: Carmarthen CC, 1949–74; Ct of Govs, UC, Aberystwyth; Council, UC Aberystwyth. Past Mem. Welsh Broadcasting Council. Hon. LLD Wales, 1973; Soc. of Cymmrodorion Medal, 1984. *Publications:* Plaid Cymru and Wales, 1950; Rhagom i Ryddid, 1964; Aros Mae, 1971; Wales can Win, 1973; Land of My Fathers, 1974; A National Future for Wales, 1975; Diwedd Prydeindod, 1981; Bywyd Cymro, 1982; Seiri Cenedl, 1986; Welsh Nation Builders, 1987; Pe Bai Cymru'n Rhydd, 1989; Fighting for Wales, 1990. *Address:* Talar Wen, Pencarreg, Llanybydder, Dyfed. *T:* Llanybydder (0570) 480907.

EVANS, Harold Matthew; Editor-in-Chief, Condé-Nast's Traveler magazine, since 1986; Contributing Editor, US News and World Report, since 1986; *b* 28 June 1928; *s* of late Frederick and late Mary Evans; *m* 1st, 1953, Enid (marr. diss. 1978), *d* of late John Parker and of Susan Parker; one *s* two *d*; 2nd, 1981, Christina Hambley Brown (*see* Tina Brown); one *s* one *d. Educ:* St Mary's Road Central Sch., Manchester; Durham Univ. BA 1952, MA Dunelm 1966. Ashton-under-Lyne, Lancs, Reporter Newspapers, 1944–46 and 1949; RAF, 1946–49; Durham Univ., 1949–52; Manchester Evening News, 1952; Commonwealth Fund Fellow in Journalism, Chicago and Stanford Univs, USA, 1956–57; Asst Ed, Manchester Evening News, 1958–61; Ed., Northern Echo, 1961–66; Editor-in-Chief, North of England Newspaper Co., 1963–66; Sunday Times: Chief Asst to Editor, 1966; Managing Editor, 1966; Editor, 1967–81; Editor, The Times, 1981–82. Member, Executive Board: Times Newspapers Ltd, 1968–82 (Mem. Main Bd, 1978); International Press Inst., 1974–80; Director: The Sunday Times Ltd, 1968–82; Times Newspapers Ltd, 1978–82. Editor-in-Chief, Atlantic Monthly Press, NY, 1984–86; Editl Dir, US News and World Report, Washington, DC, 1984–86; Vice-Pres. and Sen. Editor, Weidenfeld & Nicolson, NY, 1986–87. Writer and Presenter, Evans on Newspapers, BBC TV, 1981. Hon. Vis. Prof. of Journalism, City Univ., 1978–; Vis. Prof., Inst. of Public Affairs, Duke Univ., N Carolina, 1984. Hon. FSIAD. Internat. Editor of the Year, 1975; Gold Medal Award, Inst. of Journalists, 1979; Editor of the Year, 1982. DUniv Stirling, 1982. *Publications:* The Active Newsroom, 1961; Editing and Design (five volumes): vol. 1, Newsman's English, 1972; vol. 5, Newspaper Design, 1973; vol. 2, Newspaper Text, 1974; vol. 3, Newspaper Headlines, 1974; vol. 4, Pictures on a Page, 1977; Good Times, Bad Times, 1983; (jointly): We Learned To Ski, 1974; The Story of Thalidomide, 1978; (ed) Eye Witness, 1981; How We Learned to Ski, 1983; Front Page History, 1984. *Recreations:* running, ski-ing, Sunday in the park with George. *Address:* Condé Nast's Traveler, 360 Madison Avenue, New York, NY 10017, USA. *Clubs:* Garrick, Royal Automobile; Century, Yale (New York).

EVANS, Sir Haydn T.; *see* Tudor Evans.

EVANS, Prof. (Henry) John, PhD; FRCPE; FIBiol; FRSE; Director, Medical Research Council Human Genetics (formerly Clinical and Population Cytogenetics) Unit, Edinburgh, since 1969; *b* 24 Dec. 1930; *s* of David Evans and Gwladys Evans (*née* Jones); *m* 1st, 1957, Gwenda Rosalind (*née* Thomas) (*d* 1974); 2nd, 1976, Roslyn Rose (*née* Angell); four *s. Educ:* Llanelli Boys Grammar Sch.; UCW, Aberystwyth (BSc, PhD 1955). FRSE 1969; FIBiol 1982; FRCPE 1988. Res. Scientist, MRC Radiobiology Unit, Harwell, 1955–65, Head of Cell Biology Section, 1962–65; Vis. Fellow, Brookhaven Nat. Laboratory, Brookhaven, NY, USA, 1960–61; Prof. of Genetics, Univ. of Aberdeen, 1965–69. Chm., Assoc. Radiation Research, 1970–72; Mem., MRC Biological Res. Bd, 1968–72; Council Mem., MRC, 1978–82. Member: Cttee on Biological Effects of Ionizing Radiation, US Nat. Acad. Sci., 1972; Genetic Manipulation Adv. Gp, 1976–80; DHSS Cttee, Mutagenicity of Foods and Chemicals, 1978–; Nat. Radiology Protection Bd, 1982–; Lister Scientific Adv. Council, 1982–90; Sci. Council, Internat. Agency for Research on Cancer, 1982–86 (Chm., 1985–86); Scientific Cttee, CRC, 1983– (Chm., 1990–); Chief Scientist Cttee, SHHD, 1983–87; Council, Imperial Cancer Res. Fund, 1985–90; Cttee on Med. Aspects of Radiation in the Environment, DHSS, 1985–; Scientific Rev. Cttee, Alberta Heritage Foundn for Med. Res., 1986–; Radiation Waste Management Adv. Cttee, DoE, 1988–. Member, Board of Governors: Beatson Inst. Cancer Res., 1985–; Lister Inst. of Preventive Medicine, 1988–; Inveresk Res. Foundn, 1988–89; Caledonian Res. Foundn, 1989–; Inst. Cancer Res., 1990–. Hon. Prof., Univ. of Edinburgh; Vis. Prof., Kyoto Univ., Japan, 1981. Hon. Fellow: UK Clinical Cytogenetics Soc., 1984; UK Environmental Mutagen Soc., 1984. Lilly Prize, 1985, Ballantyne Prize, 1990, RCPE. *Publications:* papers on radiation cytology, mutagenesis, chromosome structure and human cytogenetics in various internat. jls; editor of various books and jls in the field of genetics and radiobiology. *Recreations:* golf, music, fishing. *Address:* 45 Lauder Road, Edinburgh EH9 1UE. *T:* 031-667 2437. *Clubs:* Commonwealth Trust; New (Edinburgh).

EVANS, Huw Prideaux; Deputy Secretary, HM Treasury, since 1989; *b* 21 Aug. 1941; *s* of late Richard Hubert Evans and of Kathleen Annie Evans; *m* 1966, Anne (*née* Bray); two *s. Educ:* Cardiff High Sch.; King's Coll., Cambridge (MA); London Sch. of Econs and Polit. Science (MSc). Economist: HM Treasury, 1964–72; European Commn, 1972–73; Asst Econ. Sec., Hong Kong Govt, 1973–75; Sen. Econ. Adviser (Econ. Forecasting), 1976–79, Under Sec., 1980–89, HM Treasury. *Address:* c/o HM Treasury, Parliament Street, SW1. *T:* 071–270 4430.

EVANS, Hywel Eifion, CB 1974; Welsh Secretary, Ministry of Agriculture, Fisheries and Food, 1968–75; *b* 24 Jan. 1910; *s* of late Gruffydd Thomas and Winnifred Evans, Felin Rhydhir, Pwllheli, Caernarvonshire; *m* 1st, 1939, Mary Elizabeth (*d* 1977), *d* of late Richard and Hannah Jones, Gilfach, Glanywydden, Llandudno; one *s* one *d*; 2nd, 1978, Mrs Mair Lloyd Jones, *d* of late David Lloyd and Amelia Davies, Ceinfan, Narbeth, Dyfed. *Educ:* Pwllheli Grammar Sch.; University Coll. of North Wales, Bangor. BSc (Hons) (Agric.). Research Asst, Dept of Agricultural Economics, UCW, Aberystwyth, 1934–40; Dist and Dep. Exec. Officer, Leicester WAEC, 1940–46; County Advisory Officer: Radnor AEC, 1946–47; Carmarthen AEC, 1947–57; Dep. Regional Dir, Nat. Agricl Advisory Service for Wales, 1957–59, Regional Dir, 1959–66; Dep. Dir, Nat. Agricl Adv. Service (London), 1967–68. FRAgS 1972. *Publications:* articles on agricultural, economic and sociological topics in Welsh Jl of Agriculture, Agriculture, and other jls.

Recreations: idling, fishing, shooting. *Address:* Llawryglyn, Lôn Tyllyd, Llanfarian, Aberystwyth, Wales. *Club:* Farmers'.

EVANS, Dr Ian Philip; Head Master, Bedford School, since 1990; *b* 2 May 1948; *s of* Joseph Emlyn Evans and Beryl Evans; *m* 1972, Sandra Veronica Waggett; two *s. Educ:* Ruabon Boys' Grammar Sch.; Churchill College, Cambridge (BA 1970; MA 1973; 1st cl. hons Nat. Scis Tripos); Imperial College of Science and Technology (PhD, DIC). CChem, MRSC. Post-Doctoral Fellow, Res. Sch. of Chemistry, ANU, 1973–75; Asst Master, St Paul's Sch, 1975–90 (Head of Chemistry Dept, 1984–90). Chief Examr, A-level Chem., Univ. of London Schs Exam. Bd, 1987–90. *Publications:* papers in learned jls. *Recreations:* music, cricket, poetry. *Address:* Bedford School, Burnaby Road, Bedford MK40 2TU. *T:* Bedford (0234) 353436.

EVANS, James; Director, Reuters Holdings, since 1984; *b* 27 Nov. 1932; *s of* Rex Powis Evans and late Louise Evans; *m* 1961, Jette Holmboe; two *d. Educ:* Aldenham School; St Catharine's College, Cambridge (MA). Called to the Bar, Gray's Inn, 1959; admitted Solicitor, 1972. Commissioned 26th Field Regt RA, 1951–53. Legal Dept, Kemsley Newspapers Ltd, 1956–59; practised at Bar, 1959–65; Legal Adviser: Thomson Newspapers Ltd, 1965–73; Times Newspapers Ltd, 1967–73; Sec. and Mem. Exec. Bd, 1973–78, Dir, 1978–86, Thomson Organisation Ltd; Dir, 1977–81, Chm., 1980–81, Times Newspapers Ltd; Chm., Thomson Withy Grove Ltd, 1979–84; International Thomson Organisation plc: Dir, 1978; Jt Dep. Man. Dir, 1982–84; Man. Dir and Chief Exec., 1985–86; Chm., 1986. Chm. and Chief Exec., 1982–84, Dir, 1982–, Thomson Regional Newspapers Ltd. Dir, 1983–90, Chm., 1987–89, Press Assoc. Dir, Press Standards Bd of Finance, 1990. Trustee, Visnews, 1985–. Mem., Monopolies and Mergers Commn, 1989–. Mem. Council, Newspaper Soc., 1984–; Mem., Press Council, 1987–90. Mem., Home Office Deptl Cttee on Official Secrets Act (Franks Cttee), 1971. *Recreations:* various. *Address:* 85 Fleet Street, EC4P 4AJ. *T:* 071–250 1122. *Club:* Garrick.

EVANS, James Donald; retired; Special Correspondent, Westminster Press Ltd, 1983–86; Acting Editor, UK Press Gazette, 1986; *b* 12 Nov. 1926; *yr s of* Arthur Evans and Isabella McKinnon Evans; *m* 1946, Freda Bristow; two *s* three *d. Educ:* Royal Grammar Sch., High Wycombe. Jun. Reporter, Bucks Free Press, 1943–45; Army, 1945–48; Chief Reporter, Maidenhead Advertiser, 1948–50; Northern Echo: District Chief Reporter, 1950–60; Industrial Corresp., 1961–65; Industrial Editor, 1965–66; Editor and Editor-in-Chief, 1966–82; Dir, North of England Newspapers, 1971–82. *Recreations:* driving, reading. *Address:* 11 Onslow Road, Newent, Glos GL18 1TL. *T:* Newent (0531) 822001. *Club:* Presscala.

EVANS, Col J(ames) Ellis, CBE 1973 (OBE 1952); TD 1947; JP; Lord-Lieutenant of Clwyd, 1979–85; *b* 6 Aug. 1910; *s of* James William Evans and Eleanor Evans, MBE, JP; unmarried. *Educ:* Epworth Coll., Rhyl. Chartered Accountant (FCA). Joined TA, 1937; served War of 1939–45, RA: France, 1940; N Africa, 1941–44; Italy, 1944–45; comd 384 Light Regt RA (RWF), TA, 1947–52; Dep. CRA, 53 (Welsh) Div., 1953–57; Chm. Denbigh and Flint TA Assoc., 1961–68; Chm., Wales and Mon TA&VRA, 1971–74 (Vice-Chm., 1968–71); Pres., Wales TA&VRA, 1981–85. Mem., Prestatyn UDC, 1939–74 (Chm. 1947); Mayor, Prestatyn Town Council, 1974–75. Clwyd, formerly Flintshire: JP 1951; DL 1953; High Sheriff, 1970–71; Vice-Lieut, 1970–74, Vice Lord-Lieut, 1977–79. Chm., North Wales Police Authority, 1976–78. *Recreations:* lawn tennis (played for Wales and Lancashire, 1936–48), gardening. *Address:* Trafford Mount, Gronant Road, Prestatyn, Clwyd LL19 9DT. *T:* Prestatyn (0745) 874119. *Club:* City (Chester).

EVANS, James Humphrey R.; *see* Roose-Evans.

EVANS, Jeremy David Agard; Director, Public Affairs, British Rail, since 1990; *b* 20 June 1936; *s of* Arthur Burke Agard Evans and Dorothy (née Osborne); *m* 1964, Alison Mary (née White); one *s* two *d. Educ:* Whitgift Sch.; Christ's Coll., Cambridge (BA Hons). Ministry of Power: Asst Principal, 1960–64 (Private Sec. to Parly Sec., 1963–64); Principal, 1964–69; Sloan Fellow, London Business Sch., 1969–70; Principal, 1970–73, and Private Sec. to Minister for Industry, 1971–73, DTI; Asst Sec., DTI, 1973, Dept of Energy, 1974 (Offshore Supplies Office, 1973); seconded as Sec. to BNOC on its foundn, 1976–78; a Man. Dir, 1978; Man. Dir Corporate Develt, and Sec., 1980–82, Mem. Bd 1981–82; Dir, Britoil plc, 1982–88. Mem., GDC, 1989–. *Recreations:* opera, skiing, walking. *Address:* Dormans House West, Dormans Park, East Grinstead, West Sussex RH19 2LY. *T:* Dormans Park (034287) 518.

EVANS, John; MP (Lab) St Helens, North, since 1983 (Newton, Feb. 1974–1983); Member, National Executive Committee of the Labour Party, since 1982; *b* 19 Oct. 1930; *s of* late James Evans, miner and Margaret (née Robson); *m* 1959, Joan Slater; two *s* one *d. Educ:* Jarrow Central School. Apprentice Marine Fitter, 1946–49 and 1950–52; Nat. Service, Royal Engrs, 1949–50; Engr, Merchant Navy, 1952–55; joined AUEW, 1952; joined Labour Party, 1955; worked in various industries as fitter, ship-building and repairing, steel, engineering, 1955–65, 1968–74. Mem. Hebburn UDC, 1962, Leader 1969, Chm. 1972; Sec./Agent Jarrow CLP, 1965–68. An Asst Govt Whip, 1978–79; Opposition Whip, 1979–80; PPS to Leader of Labour Party, 1980–83; opposition spokesman on employment, 1983–87. Mem., European Parlt, 1975–78; Chm., Regional Policy, Planning and Transport Cttee, European Parlt, 1976–78. Political Sec., Nat. Union of Labour and Socialist Clubs. *Recreations:* watching football, reading, gardening. *Address:* 6 Kirkby Road, Culcheth, Warrington, Cheshire WA3 4BS. *T:* Culcheth (092576) 766322. *Clubs:* Labour (Earlestown); Daten (Culcheth).

EVANS, Prof. John; *see* Evans, Prof. H. J.

EVANS, Dr John; *see* Evans, Dr N. J. B.

EVANS, Maj.-Gen. John Alan Maurice, CB 1989; with GEC Wire and Cables Group, since 1990; *b* 13 Feb. 1936; *s of* John Arthur Mortimer Evans and Margaret (née Lewis); *m* 1958, Shirley Anne May; one *s* one *d. Educ:* Grammar schs in Wales and England; RMA Sandhurst; Trinity Coll., Cambridge (MA). Various Staff and RE appointments; CO, 22 Engr Regt, 1976–78; Comd, Berlin Inf. Bde, 1980–82; RCDS, 1983; Comdt, RMCS, Shrivenham, 1985–87; Sen. Army Mem., RCDS, 1988–90. Col Comdt, RE, 1991–. Pres., Inst. of Royal Engineers, 1990–. *Recreations:* music, reluctant DIY, travel. *Address:* c/o Midland Bank, 29 High Street, Camberley GU15 3RE.

EVANS, John Alfred Eaton; Headmaster, Brentwood School, since 1981; *b* 30 July 1933; *s of* John Eaton Evans and Millicent Jane Evans (née Righton); *m* 1958, Vyvyan Margaret Mainstone; two *s* one *d. Educ:* Bristol Grammar Sch.; Worcester Coll., Oxford. MA (Lit. Hum.). Nat. Service, 1952–54, commnd RAOC. Assistant Master: Blundell's Sch., 1958–63; Rugby Sch., 1963–73; Housemaster: Phillips Acad, Andover, Mass, USA, 1968–69; Rugby Sch., 1973–81. Member selection panels: CMS, 1983–; Admiralty, 1985–; Army Scholarship Bd, 1990–. FRSA 1983. *Publications:* various articles on community service in education. *Recreations:* cricket, Rugby fives, piano, singing, drama, walking. *Address:* Headmaster's House, Brentwood School, Ingrave Road, Brentwood,

Essex CM15 8AS. *T:* Brentwood (0277) 214580. *Clubs:* East India, Devonshire, Sports and Public Schools; Vincent's (Oxford); Jesters; Cryptics Cricket.

EVANS, Prof. John Davies, FBA 1973; Director, University of London Institute of Archæology, and Professor of Archæology in the University of London, 1973–89, now Professor Emeritus; *b* 22 Jan. 1925; *o s of* Harry Evans and Edith Haycocks; *m* 1957, Evelyn Sladdin. *Educ:* Liverpool Institute High Sch. (open schol. in English to Pemb. Coll.); Pembroke Coll., Cambridge. War Service, 1943–47. BA 1948, MA 1950, PhD 1956, LittD 1979; Dr *hc* Lyon 2, 1983. Fellow of British Institute of Archæology at Ankara, 1951–52; Research Fellow of Pembroke Coll., Cambridge, 1953–56; Prof. of Prehistoric Archæology, London Univ., 1956–73. President: Prehistoric Soc., 1974–78; Council for British Archæology, 1979–82; Member: Permanent Council, Internat. Union of Prehistoric and Protohistoric Scis, 1975– (Pres., 1982–86); Royal Commn on Historical Monuments (England), 1985–; Chm., Area Archaeol Adv. Cttee for SE England, 1975–79. FSA 1955 (Dir, 1975–80, 1983–84, Pres., 1984–87); Mem., German Archaeological Inst., 1979– (Corr. Mem., 1968–79). *Publications:* Malta (Ancient Peoples and Places Series), 1959; (with Dr A. C. Renfrew) Excavations at Saliagos, near Antiparos, 1968; The Prehistoric Antiquities of the Maltese Islands, 1971; papers and reports in archæological journals. *Recreations:* walking, listening to music. *Address:* Melbury Cottage, 5 Love Lane, Shaftesbury, Dorset.

EVANS, John Field, QC 1972; **His Honour Judge Evans;** a Circuit Judge, since 1978; *b* 27 Sept. 1928; 2nd *s of* late John David Evans, Llandaff, and Lucy May Evans (née Field). *Educ:* Cardiff High Sch.; Exeter Coll., Oxford (MA). Pilot Officer, RAF, 1948–49. Called to Bar, Inner Temple, 1953; Dep. Chm., Worcestershire QS, 1964–71; a Recorder of the Crown Court, 1972–78. *Recreation:* golf. *Club:* Vincent's (Oxford).

EVANS, John G.; *see* Grimley Evans.

EVANS, John Isaac Glyn; Director of Weapons Production (Naval), Ministry of Defence, 1970–79; *b* 1 April 1919; *s of* William Evans; *m* 1943, Hilda Garratt Evans (née Lee); two *s* one *d. Educ:* Ystalyfera Grammar Sch.; University Coll., Swansea (BSc Physics, BSc Elec. Engineering). Engineer, GEC, 1940–41. Served War, Captain REME, 1941–46. Development Engineer, GEC, 1946–50; Works Group Engineer, Admiralty, 1950–53; main grade, 1953–59; senior grade, 1959–64; superintending grade, 1964–67; Dep. Dir, 1967–70. FIEE. *Recreations:* tennis, badminton, cricket. *Address:* 16 Woodland Grove, Claverton Down, Bath, Avon.

EVANS, John Kerr Q.; *see* Quarren Evans.

EVANS, John Marten Llewellyn, CBE 1956 (MBE 1945); JP; Official Solicitor to the Supreme Court of Judicature, 1950–70; *b* 9 June 1909; *s of* late Marten Llewellyn Evans, Solicitor, and Edith Helena (née Lile); *m* 1943, Winifred Emily, *y d of* late Austin Reed; one *s* one *d. Educ:* Rugby Sch.; Trinity Coll., Oxford. Admitted Solicitor, 1935; Legal Asst to the Official Solicitor, 1937. Served War of 1939–45, Major RA. Senior Legal Asst to the Official Solicitor, 1947; Asst Master in Lunacy, 1950. Vice-Chm., Austin Reed Group Ltd, 1969–77. Master of Worshipful Company of Cutlers, 1967–68. JP City of London, 1969. *Recreations:* the theatre, cricket, golf, tennis. *Address:* The Paddock, Waltham St Lawrence, Reading, Berks.

EVANS, Rev. Canon John Mascal; *b* 17 May 1915; *s of* Rev. Edward Foley Evans and Mary Evans; *m* 1941, Mary Elizabeth (née Rathbone); three *s* two *d. Educ:* St John's Sch., Leatherhead; Brasenose Coll., Oxford; Wells Theological Coll. Asst Curate, St Martin's, Epsom, 1938; Perpetual Curate, Stoneleigh, Epsom, 1942, All Saints, Fleet, 1952; Vicar, St Mary, Walton-on-Thames, 1960–68; Archdeacon of Surrey, 1968–80; Hon. Canon of Guildford, 1963–80, Canon Emeritus, 1980–; Mem. of Ridgeway Team Ministry, Dio. Salisbury, 1980–84. Member: General Synod of C of E, 1977–80; C of E Pensions Bd, 1977–85; Council of Cremation Soc., 1969–80. *Recreations:* outdoor sports, fishing. *Address:* 60 Swan Meadow, Pewsey, Wilts SN9 5HP.

EVANS, John Robert, CC 1978; MD, DPhil, FRCP, FRCP (C); Chairman and Chief Executive Officer, Allelix Inc. (Biotechnology), Mississauga, Ont, since 1983; *b* 1 Oct. 1929; *s of* William Watson Evans and Mary Thompson; *m* 1954, Gay Glassco; four *s* two *d. Educ:* Univ. of Toronto (MD); Oxford Univ. (Rhodes Schol.) (Dphil). MACP; FRCP 1980. Jr interne, Toronto Gen. Hosp., 1952–53; Hon. Registrar, Nat. Heart Hosp., London, 1955; Asst Res.: Sunnybrook Hosp., Toronto, 1956; Toronto Gen. Hosp., 1957; Ontario Heart Foundn Fellow, Hosp. for Sick Children, Toronto, 1958; Chief Res. Physician, Toronto Gen. Hosp., 1959; Research Fellow, Baker Clinic Research Lab., Harvard Med. Sch., 1960; Markle Schol. in Acad. Med., Univ. of Toronto, 1960–65; Associate, Dept of Med., Faculty of Med., Univ. of Toronto, 1961–65; Asst Prof., 1965–66; Dean, Faculty of Med., McMaster Univ., 1965–72, Vice-Pres., Health Sciences, 1967–72; Pres., Univ. of Toronto, 1972–78; Dir, Dept of Population, Health and Nutrition, IBRD, Washington DC, 1979–83. Member: Council RCP (Can.), 1972–78; Inst. of Medicine, Nat. Acad. Sci., USA, 1972– (Mem. Council, 1976–80); Adv. Cttee Med. Res., WHO, 1976–80; Chm. Trustees, Rockefeller Foundn. Director: Dominion Foundries and Steel Ltd; Royal Bank of Canada; Torstar Ltd; Alcan Aluminium Ltd (Montreal). Hon. LLD: McGill, 1972; Dalhousie, 1972; McMaster, 1972; Queen's, 1974; Wilfred Laurier, 1975; York, 1977; Yale, 1978; Toronto, 1980; Hon. DSc: Meml Univ. of Newfoundland, 1973; Montreal, 1977; Hon. DU Ottawa, 1978; Hon. DHL Johns Hopkins, 1978. *Recreations:* ski-ing, fishing, farming. *Address:* 58 Highland Avenue, Toronto, Ontario M4W 2A3, Canada.

EVANS, John Roger W.; *see* Warren Evans.

EVANS, John Stanley, QPM 1990; Chief Constable, Devon and Cornwall Constabulary, since 1989; *b* 6 Aug. 1943; *s of* late William Stanley and of Doris Evans; *m* 1965, Beryl Smith; one *s* one *d. Educ:* Wade Deacon Grammar Sch., Widnes; Liverpool Univ. (LLB Hons 1972). Liverpool City, then Merseyside Police, 1960–80; Asst Chief Constable, Greater Manchester Police, 1980–84; Dep. Chief Constable, Surrey Constabulary, 1984–88. Mem., ACPO (Mem., various cttees; Chm., Gen. Purposes Cttee). Sec., Police Athletic Assoc., 1989–. *Recreations:* most sports (ran London Marathon, 1988, 1989), service and charitable activities. *Address:* Police Headquarters, Middlemoor, Exeter, Devon EX2 7HQ. *T:* Exeter (0392) 52101.

EVANS, (John) Wynford; Chairman, South Wales Electricity plc (formerly South Wales Electricity Board), since 1984; *b* 3 Nov. 1934; *s of* late Gwilym Everton and Margaret Mary Elfreda Evans; *m* 1957, Sigrun Brethfeld; three *s. Educ:* Llanelli Grammar Sch.; St John's Coll., Cambridge (MA). FBCS; FRSA; CBIM; CompIEE. Served RAF (Flying Officer), 1955–57. IBM, 1957–58; NAAFI, W Germany, 1959–62; Kayser Bondor, 1962–63; various posts, inc. Computer and Management Services Manager, S Wales Electricity Bd, 1963–76; ASC, Henley, 1968; Dep. Chm., London Electricity Bd, 1977–84. Dir, Bank of Wales, 1989–. Member: Milton Keynes IT Adv. Panel, 1982–84; Welsh Regional Council, CBI, 1984–; Welsh Language Bd, 1988–89; Dep. Chm., Prince of Wales Cttee, 1989–; Chm., SE Wales Cttee, Industry Year 1986. Director: 1992 Nat. Garden Festival Ltd, 1987–88; Welsh Nat. Opera Ltd, 1988–. Member: Hon. Soc. of

Cymmrodorion, 1978; Court, Cranfield Inst. of Technol., 1980–88; Civic Trust Bd for Wales, 1984–88; Nat. Trust Cttee for Wales, 1985–90; Governor, Polytechnic of Wales, 1987–88. FInstD 1988. *Recreations:* fishing, cross-country ski-ing, golf. *Address:* South Wales Electricity plc, St Mellons, Cardiff CF3 9XW. *T:* Cardiff (0222) 792111. *Clubs:* Flyfishers', London Welsh; Cardiff and County, Radyr Golf (Cardiff).

EVANS, John Yorath Gwynne; Deputy Director (Air), Royal Aircraft Establishment, 1972–76, retired; medical engineering consultant, 1980–88; *b* 10 Feb. 1922; *s* of Randell and Florence Evans, Carms; *m* 1948, Paula Lewis, *d* of late Roland Ford Lewis; two *s* one *d*. *Educ:* UCW Aberystwyth. Royal Aircraft Estabt, 1942; attached to RAF, Germany, 1945–46; Supt Wind Tunnels, RAE Bedford, 1958; Head of Aerodynamics Dept, RAE, 1971. *Publications:* contrib. various sci. and techn. jls. *Recreations:* sailing, travel, reading. *Address:* Rushmoor Cottage, Tilford, Farnham, Surrey GU10 2EP. *T:* Frensham (025125) 2275; 10 West Street, Ditchling, E Sussex BN6 8TS.

EVANS, Rt. Rev. Kenneth Dawson; Assistant Bishop of Guildford, 1986–90; *b* 7 Nov. 1915; *s* of late Dr Edward Victor Evans, OBE; *m* 1939, Margaret, *d* of J. J. Burton; one *s*. *Educ:* Dulwich Coll.; Clare Coll., Cambridge. Ordained, 1938; Curate of: St Mary, Northampton, 1938–41; All Saints', Northampton, 1941–45; Rector of Ockley, 1945–49; Vicar of Dorking, 1949–63; Archdeacon of Dorking and Canon Residentiary of Guildford Cathedral, 1963–68; Bishop Suffragan of Dorking, 1968–85. Hon. Canon of Guildford, 1955–63 and 1979–85. Mem., Bishop's Finance Commn, 1957. *Address:* 3 New Inn Lane, Burpham, Guildford, Surrey GU4 7HN. *T:* Guildford (0483) 67978.

EVANS, Lloyd Thomas; AO 1979; DSc, DPhil; FRS 1976; FAA; Chief Research Scientist, Commonwealth Scientific and Industrial Research Organization Division of Plant Industry, Canberra, Australia; *b* 6 Aug. 1927; *s* of C. D. Evans and G. M. Fraser; *m* 1954, Margaret Honor Newell; two *s* one *d* (and one *d* decd). *Educ:* Wanganui Collegiate Sch., NZ; Univ. of NZ (BSc, MAgrSc, DSc); Univ. of Oxford (DPhil). FAA 1971. Rhodes Scholar, Brasenose Coll., Oxford, 1950–54; Commonwealth Fund Fellow, Calif Inst. of Technol., 1954–56; res. scientist, CSIRO Div. of Plant Industry, Canberra, 1956–. National Acad. of Sciences (USA) Pioneer Fellow, 1963; Overseas Fellow, Churchill Coll., Cambridge, 1969–70; Vis. Fellow, Wolfson Coll., Cambridge, 1978. President: ANZAAS, 1976–77; Aust. Acad. of Science, 1978–82. Member, Board of Trustees: Internat. Foundn for Sci., Stockholm, 1982–87; Internat. Rice Res. Inst., Philippines, 1984–89; Internat. Center for Improvement of Wheat and Maize, 1990–. Mem., Norwegian Acad. of Sci. and Letters, 1990. Hon. Member: Royal Soc., NZ, 1986; RASE, 1987. Hon. LLD Canterbury, 1978. *Publications:* Environmental Control of Plant Growth, 1963; The Induction of Flowering, 1969; Crop Physiology, 1975; Daylength and the Flowering of Plants, 1976; Wheat Science: today and tomorrow, 1981; Policy and Practice, 1987; more than 150 scientific papers in jls. *Recreations:* windsurfing, chopping wood, Charles Darwin. *Address:* 3 Elliott Street, Canberra, ACT 2601, Australia. *T:* Canberra 477815.

EVANS, Mark Armstrong; Director, British Council in Canada, and Cultural Counsellor, British High Commission, Ottawa, since 1988; *b* 5 Aug. 1940; *s* of late Charles Tunstall Evans, CMG, Birmingham, and Kathleen Armstrong, Newcastle; *m* 1965, Katharine, *d* of Alfred Bastable, Brecon; one *s* one *d*. *Educ:* Marlborough Coll.; Clare Coll., Cambridge (BA 1962; MA 1966); Moscow State Univ.; Bristol Univ. (PGCE 1964). Head, Russian and German, Chichester High Sch. for Boys, 1964–69; apptd to British Council, 1969; Bahrain, 1969–71; Frankfurt, 1971–73; MECAS, Lebanon, 1973–74; Dir, UAE in Dubai, 1974–77; temp. posting, Kabul, 1977; Asst Dir, Educnl Contracts, 1977–79; Dep. Rep. and Cultural Attaché, France, 1979–85; Head, Office Services, 1985–88. Mem., RSAA. *Recreations:* building models, gardening, household chores. *Address:* c/o 80 Elgin Street, Ottawa, Ontario K1P 5K7, Canada. *T:* (613) 237 1530. *Club:* Union (Cambridge).

EVANS, Matthew; Managing Director since 1972 and Chairman since 1981, Faber & Faber Ltd; *b* 7 Aug. 1941; *s* of late George Ewart Evans, and of Florence Ellen Evans; *m* 1966, Elizabeth Amanda (*née* Mead); two *s*. *Educ:* Friends' Sch., Saffron Walden; London Sch. of Econs and Polit. Science (BScEcon). Bookselling, 1963–64; Faber & Faber, 1964–. Chairman: National Book League, 1982–84; English Stage Company, 1984–90; Member: Council, Publishers Assoc., 1978–84; Franco-British Soc., 1981–. Governor, BFI, 1982–. FRSA 1990. *Recreation:* cricket. *Address:* c/o Faber & Faber, 3 Queen Square, WC1N 3AU.

EVANS, Michael; *see* Evans, T. M.

EVANS, Michael Nordon, CMG 1964; Permanent Secretary, Ministry of Health and Housing, Kenya, 1960–64, retired; *b* 27 April 1915; *s* of late Christmas and Lilian Margaret Louise Evans, Tunbridge Wells; *m* 1st, 1939, Mary Stockwood; one *d*; 2nd, 1951, Mary Josephine Suzette van Vloten; one *d*. *Educ:* Eastbourne Coll.; Queens' Coll., Cambridge. Apptd District Officer in Colonial Administrative Service, Kenya, 1939; African Courts Officer, Kenya, 1953; Dep. Commissioner for Local Government, 1954; Permanent Sec., 1958. *Recreation:* tennis. *Address:* Hugon Lodge, 13 Hugon Road, Claremont, Cape, 7700, Republic of South Africa. *Clubs:* Hawks (Cambridge); Nairobi (Kenya); Western Province Sports (Cape Town).

EVANS, Mostyn; *see* Evans, Arthur M.

EVANS, Dr (Noel) John (Bebbington), CB 1980; Deputy Secretary, Department of Health and Social Security, 1977–84; *b* 26 Dec. 1933; *s* of William John Evans and Gladys Ellen (*née* Bebbington); *m* 1st, 1960, Elizabeth Mary Garbutt (marr. diss.); two *s* one *d*; 2nd, 1974, Eileen Jane McMullan. *Educ:* Hymers Coll., Hull; Christ's Coll., Cambridge (scholar; 1st cl., Nat. Sci. Tripos); Westminster Medical Sch., London; London Sch. of Hygiene and Tropical Med. (Newsholme prize, Chadwick Trust medal and prize). MA, MB, BChir; FRCP, DPH (Dist.), FFCM. Called to Bar, Gray's Inn, 1965. House officer posts at: Westminster, Westminster Children's, Hammersmith, Central Middlesex and Brompton Hosps, 1958–60; Medical Registrar and Tutor, Westminster Hosp., 1960–61; Asst MoH, Warwickshire CC, 1961–65; Dept of Health and Social Security (formerly Min. of Health), 1965–84, DCMO 1977–82; Sir Wilson Jameson Travelling Fellowship, 1966. Chairman: Welsh Cttee on Drug Misuse, 1986–; Nat. Biological Standards Bd, 1988– (Mem., 1975–); UK Transplant Support Service, 1991–; Member: Welsh Cttee, Countryside Commn, 1985–89; Welsh Health Promotion Authority, 1987–89. Privy Council mem., Council of Royal Pharmaceutical Soc., 1988–. *Publications:* The Organisation and Planning of Health Services in Yugoslavia, 1967; Health and Personal Social Service Research in Wales, 1986; (with P. Benner) Isle of Man Health Services Inquiry, 1986; (with P. Cunliffe) Study of Control of Medicines, 1987; contribs to med. jls. *Recreations:* canals, photography. *Address:* Athelstan, Grosmont, Abergavenny, Gwent NP7 8LW. *T:* Golden Valley (0981) 240616.

EVANS, Ven. Patrick Alexander Sidney; Archdeacon of Maidstone and Director of Ordinands, Diocese of Canterbury, since 1989; *b* 28 Jan. 1943; *m* 1969, Jane Kemp; two *s* one *d*. *Educ:* Clifton College, Bristol; Lincoln Theological Coll. Curate: Holy Trinity, Lyonsdown, Barnet, 1973–76; Royston, 1976–78; Vicar: Gt Gaddesden, 1978–82; Tenterden, 1982–89; RD of West Charing, 1988–89. *Address:* Archdeacon's House, Charing, Kent TN27 0LU. *T:* Charing (023371) 2294.

EVANS, Peter, CBE 1986; National Secretary, General Workers' Trade Group, Transport & General Workers' Union, 1974–90; *b* 8 Nov. 1929; *m* 1st, 1957, Christine Pamela (marr. diss.); one *d*; 2nd, 1975, Gillian Rosemary (decd); two *s* one *d*; 3rd, 1980, Joy Elizabeth. *Educ:* Culvert Road Secondary School, Tottenham. London bus driver, 1955–62; District Officer, TGWU, 1962–66; Regional Trade Group Sec., Public Services, 1966–74. *Recreations:* talking, swimming in deep water. *Address:* 19 Uffington Road, SE27 0RW. *T:* 081–670 5143. *Clubs:* Victoria, Players' Theatre.

EVANS, Prof. Peter Angus, DMus; FRCO; Professor of Music, University of Southampton, 1961–90; *b* 7 Nov. 1929; *y s* of Rev. James Mackie Evans and Elizabeth Mary Fraser; *m* 1953, June Margaret Vickery. *Educ:* West Hartlepool Grammar Sch.; St Cuthbert's Soc., University of Durham. BA (1st cl. hons Music), 1950; BMus, MA 1953; DMus 1958; FRCO 1952. Music Master, Bishop Wordsworth's Sch., Salisbury, 1951–52; Lecturer in Music, University of Durham, 1953–61. Conductor: Palatine Opera Group, 1956–61; Southampton Philharmonic Soc., 1965–90. *Publications:* Sonata for Oboe and Piano, 1953; Three Preludes for Organ, 1955; Edns of 17th Century Chamber Music, 1956–58; The Music of Benjamin Britten, 1979, 2nd edn 1989; contributor to Die Musik, in Geschichte und Gegenwart, to A Concise Encyclopædia of Music, 1958, to New Oxford History of Music, 1974, and to New Grove Dictionary of Music, 1981; writer and reviewer, especially on twentieth century music. *Address:* 9 Bassett Close, Southampton SO2 3FP. *T:* Southampton (0703) 768125.

EVANS, Raymond John Morda, MA, PhD; Headmaster, Silcoates School, 1960–78; *b* 1 Oct. 1917; 2nd *s* of late Rev. J. Morda Evans, Congregational Minister; *m* 1942, Catherine Mair Gernos Davies (*d* 1988), *er d* of late Rev. J. Gernos Davies, Congregational Minister; one *s* two *d* (and one *s* decd). *Educ:* Silcoates Sch., near Wakefield; (Casberd Scholar) St John's Coll., Oxford. BA Oxon (Mod. Langs), 1939, MA 1942; MA, PhD London (Russian Lang. and Lit.), 1959. Dauntsey's Sch., 1939–40; Intelligence Corps (Captain), 1940–46; Leeds Grammar School, 1946–52; Head of Dept of Modern Languages, Royal Naval Coll., Greenwich, 1952–60. JP Wakefield, 1964–87. *Publications:* contrib. to Slavonic and Eastern European Review, and to Mariners' Mirror. *Recreation:* swimming. *Address:* 16 Kepstorn Road, West Park, Leeds LS16 5HL.

EVANS, Prof. Rhydwyn Harding, CBE 1958; MSc, DSc Manchester, PhD Leeds; FICE, FIMechE, FIStructE, MSocCE France, Hon. MIPlantE; Professor of Civil Engineering and Administrative Head of Engineering Departments, University of Leeds, 1946–68, Emeritus Professor, 1968; *b* 9 Oct. 1900; *s* of late David Evans, Tygwyn, Pontardulais, Glam; *m* 1929, Dilys Elizabeth, *o c* of late George Rees, Welsh Poet and Hymnologist, and Kate Ann Rees, London; one *s*. *Educ:* Llanelly Grammar Sch.; University of Manchester. Mercantile Marine, 1918–20. BSc top 1st class Graduate Prizeman, 1923; MSc 1928; PhD 1932; DSc 1943. Demonstrator, Asst Lecturer, Lecturer, Senior Lecturer and later Reader in Civil Engineering, University of Leeds, 1926–46; Dean, Faculty of Tech. University of Leeds, 1948–51; Pro-Vice-Chancellor, University of Leeds, 1961–65. Lectures: Unwin Meml ICE, 1960; first George Hondros Meml, WA, 1970. IStructE: Vice-Pres., 1948–49; Chm., Yorks Br., 1940–41, 1955–56 and 1958–59 (Yorkshire Br. Prize, 1946–47 and 1950–51); ICE: Chm. Yorks Assoc., 1942–43 and 1952–53; Mem. Council, 1949–52; Mem., Joint Matriculation Bd, Manchester, 1949–68; Chm., Leeds Univ. Min. of Labour and NS Bd, 1949–60; first Chm., Trng Consultative Cttee, Cement and Concrete Assoc., 1966–73. Consulting Editor in Civil Engineering: McGraw-Hill Book Co. (UK) Ltd, 1975–; Pitman Ltd, 1978–. Hon. Mem., Concrete Soc., 1970. Hon. DèsSc Ghent, 1953; Hon. DTech Bradford, 1971. Rugby Engrg Soc. Student's Prize, 1925; Telford Premiums, 1942–43–44; Medal, Ghent Univ., 1949, 1953; George Stephenson Gold Medal, 1956; Institution of Water Engineers, Instn Premium, 1953; Reinforced Concrete Assoc. Medal, 1961; Instn of Struct. Engrs: Research Diploma, 1965; Certif. of Commendation, 1970; Henry Adams Award, 1971. *Publications:* Prestressed Concrete (with E. W. Bennett), 1962; Concrete Plain, Reinforced Prestressed, Shell (with C. B. Wilby), 1963; Reinforced and Prestressed Concrete (with F. K. Kong), 1975 (3rd edn. 1987); (jtly) Handbook of Structural Concrete, 1983; papers on elasticity and plasticity of concrete and other building materials; strain and stress distribution in reinforced concrete beams and arches; pre-stressed concrete; extensibility, cracking and tensile stress-strain of concrete; bond stresses; shear stresses; combined bending and shear stresses; torsional stresses; preflexed pre-stressed concrete beams; lightweight aggregate concrete; vibration and pressure moulding of concrete in Journals of Institutions of Civil, Struct. and Water Engineers, Concrete Soc., Philosophical Magazine, Engineer, Engineering, Civil Engineering and Public Works. *Recreations:* motoring, travel, gardening. *Address:* 23 Christopher Rise, Pontlliw, Swansea, West Glamorgan SA4 1EN. *T:* Gorseinon (0792) 891961.

EVANS, Sir Richard (Mark), KCMG 1984 (CMG 1978); KCVO 1986; HM Diplomatic Service, retired; Senior Research Fellow, Wolfson College, Oxford, since 1988; *b* 15 April 1928; *s* of late Edward Walter Evans, CMG; *m* 1973, Rosemary Grania Glen Birkett; two *s*. *Educ:* Dragon Sch., Oxford; Repton Sch.; Magdalen Coll., Oxford. BA (Oxon) 1949. Joined HM Foreign (now Diplomatic) Service: Third Sec., London, 1952–55; Third Sec., Peking, 1955–57; Second Sec., London, 1957–62; First Sec.: Peking, 1962–64; Berne, 1964–68; London, 1968–70; Counsellor, 1970; Head of Near Eastern Dept, FCO, 1970–72, Head of Far Eastern Dept, 1972–74; Fellow, Centre for Internat. Affairs, Harvard Univ., 1974–75; Commercial Counsellor, Stockholm, 1975–77; Minister (Economic), Paris, 1977–79; Asst Under-Sec. of State, 1979–82, Dep. Under-Sec. of State, 1982–83, FCO; Ambassador to People's Republic of China, 1984–88. Internat. Bd of Advice, ANZ Banking Gp, 1988. *Recreations:* travel, reading, music. *Address:* Sevenhampton House, Sevenhampton, near Highworth, Wilts SN6 7QA. *Club:* United Oxford & Cambridge University.

EVANS, Robert, CBE 1987; CEng; FIMechE; Chairman and Chief Executive, British Gas plc, since 1989 (Chief Executive and Member of the Board, 1983–89); *b* 28 May 1927; *s* of Gwilym Evans and Florence May Evans; *m* 1950, Lilian May (*née* Ward); one *s* one *d*. *Educ:* Old Swan Coll., Liverpool; Blackburn Coll.; City of Liverpool Coll. (Tech.). D. Napier & Son Ltd, 1943–49; North Western Gas Bd, 1950–56; Burmah Oil Co., 1956–62; Dir of Engrg, Southern Gas Bd, 1962–70; Dep. Dir (Ops), Gas Council, 1972; Dir of Operations, British Gas, 1972–75; Dep. Chm., North Thames Gas, 1975–77; Chm., E Midlands Gas Region, 1977–82; Man. Dir, Supplies, British Gas Corp., 1982–83. Pres., Instn of Gas Engrs, 1981–82. (Hon. FIGasE 1961). MInstE 1988; CBIM 1983. Freeman, City of London, 1974; Mem., Engineers' Co., 1984. *Recreations:* reading, golf. *Address:* British Gas plc, Rivermill House, 152 Grosvenor Road, SW1V 3JL.

EVANS, Sir (Robert) Charles, Kt 1969; MA, FRCS; Principal, University College of North Wales, 1958–84; Vice-Chancellor, University of Wales, 1965–67, and 1971–73; *b* 19 Oct. 1918; *o s* of late R. C. Evans and Mrs Charles Evans; *m* 1957, Denise Nea Morin; three *s*. *Educ:* Shrewsbury Sch.; University Coll., Oxford. BM, BCh Oxon 1943; MA Oxon 1947; FRCS 1949. RAMC, 1943–46 (despatches). Surgical Registrar, United Liverpool Hosps, and Liverpool Regional Hosps, 1947–57. Hunterian Prof., Royal College

Surg. Eng., 1953. Dep. Leader, Mt Everest Expedition, 1953; Leader, Kangchenjunga Expedition, 1955; Pres., Alpine Club, 1967–70; Mem. Council, Royal Geog. Society, 1960–61. Hon. DSc Wales, 1956. Cullum Medal, American Geog. Soc., 1954; Livingstone Medal, Scottish Geog. Soc., 1955; Founder's Medal, Royal Geog. Society, 1956. *Publications:* Eye on Everest, 1955; On Climbing, 1956; Kangchenjunga—The Untrodden Peak, 1956; articles in Alpine Journal, Geographical Journal, etc. *Address:* Ardincaple, Capel Curig, N Wales LL24 0EU. *Club:* Alpine.

EVANS, Robert John Weston, PhD; FBA 1984; Research Fellow, Brasenose College, since 1968 and University Reader in Modern History of East-Central Europe, since 1990, Oxford; *b* 7 Oct. 1943; *s* of Thomas Frederic and Margery Evans (*née* Weston), Cheltenham; *m* 1969, Kati Róbert; one *s* one *d*. *Educ:* Dean Close School; Jesus College, Cambridge (BA 1st Cl. with distinction 1965, PhD 1968). Lectr, Oxford Univ., 1969–90. Mem., Inst. for Advanced Study, Princeton, 1981–82. Jt Editor, English Historical Review, 1985–. *Publications:* Rudolf II and his World, 1973; The Wechel Presses, 1975; The Making of the Habsburg Monarchy, 1979 (Wolfson Literary Award for History, 1980; Anton Gindely Preis, Austria, 1986); (ed with H. Pogge von Strandmann) The Coming of the First World War, 1988. *Recreations:* music, walking, natural (and unnatural) history. *Address:* Brasenose College, Oxford. *T:* Oxford (0865) 248641; 83 Norreys Road, Cumnor, Oxford.

EVANS, Maj.-Gen. Robert Noel, CB 1981; Postgraduate Dean and Commandant, Royal Army Medical College, 1979–81; *b* 22 Dec. 1922; *s* of William Evans and Norah Moynihan; *m* 1950, Mary Elizabeth O'Brien; four *s* one *d*. *Educ:* Christian Brothers Sch., Tralee, Co. Kerry; National University of Ireland (MB, BCh, BAO 1947). DTM&H 1961; FFARCS 1963. Commnd RAMC 1951; Consultant Anaesthetist, 1963; CO BMH Rinteln, 1969–71; ADMS 4th Div., 1971–73; DDMS HQ BAOR, 1973–75; Comdt, RAMC Trng Centre, 1975–77; DMS, HQ BAOR, 1977–79; QHP 1976–81. Col Comdt, RAMC, 1981–86. MFCM 1978. OStJ 1978. *Recreations:* gardening, walking, music. *Address:* 32 Folly Hill, Farnham, Surrey GU9 0BH. *T:* Farnham (0252) 726938.

EVANS, Roderick; *see* Evans, D. R.

EVANS, Roger W.; *see* Warren Evans.

EVANS, Roy Lyon; General Secretary, Iron and Steel Trades Confederation, since 1985; *b* 13 Aug. 1931; *s* of David Evans and Sarah (*née* Lyon); *m* 1960, Brenda Jones; one *s* two *d*. *Educ:* Gowerton Grammar Sch., Swansea. Employed in Tinplate Section of Steel Industry, 1948. Iron and Steel Trades Confederation: Divl Organiser, NW Area, 1964–69; Divl Organiser, W Wales Area, 1969–73; Asst Gen. Sec., 1973–85. Mem., Gen. Council, TUC, 1985–. Jt Sec., Jt Industrial Council for the Slag Industry, 1975–85; Mem., ECSC Consultative Cttee, 1985– (Pres., 1986–88); Hon. Sec., British Section, IMF, 1985– (Pres., Iron and Steel Dept (World), 1986–). Member: Jt Accident Prevention Adv. Cttee, 1974– (Chm., 1983); NEC of Labour Party, 1981–84. Bd Mem., British Steel (Industry) Ltd, 1986–. *Recreations:* reading, walking. *Address:* Swinton House, 324 Gray's Inn Road, WC1X 8DD. *T:* 071–837 6691.

EVANS, Russell Wilmot, MC 1945; Chairman, Rank Organisation, 1982–83; *b* 4 Nov. 1922; *s* of William Henry Evans and Ethel Williams Wilmot; *m* 1956, Pamela Muriel Hayward (*d* 1989); two *s* one *d*. *Educ:* King Edward's Sch., Birmingham; Birmingham Univ. LLB Hons. Served HM Forces, 1942–47; commnd Durham LI, 1942, Major, 1945. Admitted Solicitor, Birmingham, 1949; Solicitor with Shakespeare & Vernon, Birmingham, 1949–50; Asst Sec., Harry Ferguson, 1951; Sec., Massey-Ferguson (Hldgs) and UK subsids, 1955–62; Dir, gp of private cos in construction industry, 1962–67; joined Rank Organisation, 1967: Dep. Sec., 1967–68; Sec., 1968–72; Dir, 1972–83; Man. Dir, 1975–82; Dep. Chm., 1981; Dir, principal subsid. and associated cos incl. Rank Xerox, 1975–83; Fuji Xerox, 1976–83; Chm., Rank City Wall, 1976–83. Director: Eagle Star Holdings, 1982–87; Oxford Economic Forecasting Ltd, 1986–; Medical Cyclotron Ltd, 1988–. *Recreations:* tennis, golf, photography. *Address:* Walnut Tree, Roehampton Gate, SW15 5JR. *T:* 081–876 2433. *Clubs:* English-Speaking Union, Roehampton (Dir 1971–87, Chm., 1984–87).

EVANS, Simon John; His Honour Judge Simon Evans; a Circuit Judge, since 1991; *b* 18 Jan. 1937; *s* of Dr Thomas Evans and late Dr Enid Allardice Evans (*née* Taylour); *m* 1968, Heather Wendy Champion; one *s* one *d*. *Educ:* Diocesan Coll., Cape Town. Apprentice motor mechanic, Lusaka, Northern Rhodesia, 1954; GCE student,. Guildford, 1955–56; Bar student, London, 1956–59; called to the Bar, Middle Temple, 1959; barrister, Temple, 1959–91; a Recorder, South Eastern Circuit, 1989–91. *Address:* c/o Iselworth Crown Court, 36 Ridgeway Road, Isleworth, Mddx TW7 5LP. *T:* 081–568 8811.

EVANS, (Thomas) Alun; HM Diplomatic Service; Counsellor, Foreign and Commonwealth Office, since 1982; *b* 8 June 1937; *s* of late Thomas Evans and Mabel Elizabeth (*née* Griffiths); *m* 1964, Bridget Elisabeth, *d* of Peter Lloyd, *qv* and Nora Kathleen Williams (*née* Patten); three *s*. *Educ:* Shrewsbury Sch.; University Coll., Oxford (MA). Army, 1956–58. Entered HM Foreign Service, 1961; Third Sec., Rangoon, 1962–64; Second Sec., Singapore, 1964–66; FO, 1966–70; First Sec., Geneva, 1970–74; FCO, 1974–79; Counsellor, Pretoria, 1979–82. *Recreations:* music, fishing. *Address:* c/o Foreign and Commonwealth Office, SW1A 2AH. *Club:* Travellers'.

EVANS, Very Rev. (Thomas) Eric; Dean of St Paul's, since 1988; *b* 1928; *s* of late Eric John Rhys Evans and Florence May Rogers; *m* 1957, Linda Kathleen Budge; two *d*. *Educ:* St David's Coll., Lampeter (BA); St Catherine's Coll., Oxford (MA); St Stephen's House, Oxford. Ordained, 1954; Curate, Margate Parish Church, 1954–58; Sen. Curate, St Peter's, Bournemouth, 1958–62; first Dir, Bournemouth Samaritans; Diocesan Youth Chaplain, dio. Gloucester, 1962–69; Residentiary Canon of Gloucester Cathedral, 1969–88; Archdeacon of Cheltenham, 1975–88. Wing Chaplain, ATC, 1963–69; Hon. Chaplain: Gloucester Coll. of Educn, 1968–75; Gloucestershire Constabulary, 1977–88. Chm., Glos Trng Cttee, 1967–69; Proctor in Convocation and Mem. Gen. Synod of C of E, 1970–; a Church Comr, 1978– (Mem., Bd of Governors, 1978–, Assets Cttee, 1985–88). Canon Missioner, dio. Gloucester, 1969–75; Chairman: House of Clergy, dio. Gloucester, 1979–82; Bd of Social Responsibility, dio. Gloucester, 1982–83; Glos Assoc. for Mental Health, 1983–85 (Vice-Chm., 1965–78); Glos Diocesan Adv. Cttee, 1984–88. Mem. Exec. Cttee, 1975–88, Chm., 1981–88, Council for Places of Worship, subseq. Council for the Care of Churches. Dean, Order of St Michael and St George, 1988–; Dean, Order of the British Empire, 1988–; Chaplain to Guild of Freemen of City of London, 1988–. Dir, Ecclesiastical Insurance Office Ltd, 1979–. Mem. Council, Cheltenham Ladies' College, 1982–. Freeman, City of London, 1988. *Recreation:* travel, esp. Middle East. *Address:* The Deanery, 9 Amen Court, EC4M 7BU. *Clubs:* Carlton, City Livery; Downhill Only (Wengen).

EVANS, (Thomas) Godfrey, CBE 1960; public relations officer; *b* Finchley, 18 Aug. 1920; *s* of A. G. L. Evans; *m* 1973, Angela Peart; one *d*. *Educ:* Kent Coll., Canterbury. Joined Kent County Staff at age of 16. First kept wicket for England in Test *v* India, 1946; first overseas Test tour, Australia and New Zealand, 1946–47; has also played in Test matches in W Indies and S Africa. Has played in 91 Test matches (world record 1959); dismissed 218 batsmen in Test cricket from behind the stumps, 88 more than Oldfield, the previous record-holder, and retained the record until 1976; the first wicket-keeper to have dismissed more than 200 victims and scored over 2000 runs in Test cricket; held world record for not conceding a bye while 1,054 runs were scored in a Test series (Australia, 1946); holds record for longest Test innings without scoring (95 minutes *v* Australia, Adelaide, 1947); holds jointly, with Charles Barnett, record for fastest score before lunch in a Test match (98 *v* India, Lord's, 1952); in making 47 in 29 minutes was three runs off the fastest 50 in Test cricket (*v* Australia, Old Trafford, 1956); first Englishman to tour Australia with MCC four times after War of 1939–45. *Publications:* Behind the Stumps, 1951; Action in Cricket, 1956; The Gloves Are Off, 1960; Wicket Keepers of the World, 1984. *Recreations:* real tennis, golf, squash. *Address:* 51 Delaware Mansions, Delaware Road, W9. *Club:* MCC (Hon. Life Mem.).

EVANS, Thomas Henry, CBE 1957; DL; LLM; Clerk of the Peace, Clerk of the County Council, and Clerk to Lieutenancy for Staffordshire, 1942–72; Clerk of Staffordshire Magistrates Courts Committee, 1952–72; Clerk of Staffordshire County and Stoke-on-Trent Police Authority, 1968–72; *b* 1907; *s* of late Henry Evans, Bootle, Lancs. *Educ:* Merchant Taylors' Sch., Crosby, Lancs; University of Liverpool (LLM). Admitted Solicitor, 1930. Asst Solicitor with Surrey County Council, 1930–35; Asst County Solicitor and later Dep. Clerk of Staffs County Council, 1935–42. Member: Cttee on Consolidation of Highway Law, 1958; Interdepartmental Cttee (Streatfeild) on business of Criminal Courts, 1958; Nat. Advisory Coun. on Training of Magistrates, 1964–73. DL Staffs, 1947. *Publication:* contributor to Macmillan's Local Government Law and Administration. *Address:* 108 Holland Road, Hove, East Sussex.

EVANS, (Thomas) Michael, QC 1973; **His Honour Judge Michael Evans;** a Circuit Judge, since 1979; *b* 7 Sept. 1930; *s* of late David Morgan Evans, Barrister, and of Mary Gwynydd Lloyd; *m* 1957, Margaret Valerie Booker; one *s* four *d*. *Educ:* Brightlands Prep. Sch., Newnham, Glos; Marlborough Coll., Wilts; Jesus Coll., Oxford (MA (Juris.)). Called to the Bar, Gray's Inn, 1954; Wales and Chester Circuit, 1955; a Recorder of the Crown Court, 1972–79. Legal Chm., Mental Health Review Tribunal for Wales, 1970. Chancellor, Diocese of St Davids, 1986–91. *Recreations:* walking, gardening, genealogy. *Address:* The Old Rectory, Reynoldston, Gower, Swansea SA3 1AD. *T:* Gower (0792) 390129.

EVANS, Prof. Trevor, FRS 1988; Personal Professor, University of Reading, since 1968; *b* 26 April 1927; *s* of late Henry and Margaret Evans; *m* Patricia Margaret Booth (*née* Johnson); two *s* and two step *s*. *Educ:* Bridgend Grammar Sch.; Univ. of Bristol (BSc, PhD, DSc). FInstP. Physicist: British Nylon Spinners, 1955–56; Tube Investments Res. Lab., 1956–58; Physics Department, University of Reading, 1958–: Res. Physicist, 1958–61; successively, Lectr, Reader, Personal Prof., 1961–; Hd of Dept, 1984–88; Warden of Wantage Hall, Reading Univ., 1971–84. *Publications:* papers in Proc. Royal Soc. and Phil. Mag., almost entirely concerning synthetic and natural diamond. *Recreation:* pottering in the garden. *Address:* Aston, Tutts Clump, Reading, Berks RG7 6JZ. *T:* Bradfield (0734) 744498.

EVANS, Dr Trevor John; General Secretary, Institution of Chemical Engineers, since 1976; *b* 14 Feb. 1947; *o s* of Evan Alban Evans and Margaret Alice Evans (*née* Hilton); *m* 1973, Margaret Elizabeth (*née* Whitham); three *s* one *d*. *Educ:* King's Sch., Rochester; University Coll., London (BSc (Eng) 1968, PhD 1972); CEng, FIChemE, FBIM. Res. Officer, CSIR, Pretoria, 1968–69; Ford Motor Co., Aveley, Essex, 1972–73; Institution of Chemical Engineers: Asst Sec., Technical, 1973–75; Dep. Sec., 1975–76. Member: Bd, Council of Science and Technology Institutes, 1976–87; Exec. Cttee, Commonwealth Engineers Council, 1976–; Jt Hon. Sec., European Fedn of Chem. Engrg, 1976–. *Publications:* scientific papers and general articles in Chemical Engrg Science, The Chem. Engr, etc. *Recreations:* home renovation, drama. *Address:* The Institution of Chemical Engineers, 12 Gayfere Street, SW1P 3HP. *T:* 071–222 2681.

EVANS, Sir Vincent; *see* Evans, Sir W. V. J.

EVANS, Maj.-Gen. William Andrew; General Officer Commanding Eastern District, 1989–April 1992; *b* 5 Aug. 1939; *s* of late Maj.-Gen. Roger Evans, CB, MC and Eileen (*née* Stanton); *m* 1964, Virginia Susan, *e d* of late William Robert Tomkinson; two *d*. *Educ:* Sherborne; RMA Sandhurst; Christ Church, Oxford (MA). Commnd 5th Royal Inniskilling Dragoon Guards, 1959; served in BAOR, Middle East, Cyprus, Libya, N Ireland; Staff Coll., Bracknell, 1971; Army Instructor, RAF Cranwell, 1974–75; Instructor, Army Staff Coll., 1978–80; CO 5th Royal Inniskilling Dragoon Guards, 1980–82 (despatches, 1981); Col, Asst Dir (Policy), Defence Policy Staff, 1982–83; Comdr 4 Armd Bde, 1983–85; RCDS 1986; DCS, HQ BAOR, 1987–89. *Recreations:* ski-ing, tennis, fishing, birdwatching, cricket (Pres., Army Cricket Assoc., 1989–; Chm., Combined Services Cricket Assoc., 1990). *Address:* c/o National Westminster Bank, North Street, Taunton, Somerset TA1 1NB. *Club:* United Oxford & Cambridge University.

EVANS, Dr William David; Chief Scientist, Department of Energy, since 1989; *b* 20 April 1949; *s* of late Harold Evans and Gladys Evans (*née* Webber); *m* 1980, Elizabeth Crowe; three *s* one *d*. *Educ:* Haberdashers' Aske's School, Elstree; St Catherine's College, Oxford (BA 1971; DPhil 1974; Senior Scholar). FRAS 1975. Dept of Energy, 1974–80; First Sec., Science and Technology, British Embassy, Bonn, 1980–83; Asst Sec., Dept of Energy, 1984–89. Mem., NERC, 1989–; Assessor, SERC, ACORD, 1989–. *Publications:* scientific papers in professional jls. *Recreations:* music, reading, history of technology. *Address:* Department of Energy, 1 Palace Street, SW1E 5HE. *T:* 071–238 3204.

EVANS, (William) Emrys, CBE 1981; Senior Regional Director, Wales, Midland Bank Ltd, 1976–84; *b* 4 April 1924; *s* of late Richard and Mary Elizabeth Evans; *m* 1946, Mair Thomas; one *d*. *Educ:* Llanfair Caereinion County Sch. FCIB. Served War, RN, 1942–46 (despatches 1944). Entered Midland Bank Ltd, 1941; Asst Gen. Manager (Agric.), 1967–72; Reg. Dir, S Wales, 1972–74; Reg. Dir, Wales, 1974–76. Director: Executive Secondment Ltd, 1983–90 (Vice Chm., 1983); Align-Rite Ltd, 1984–; National Welsh Omnibus Services Ltd, 1989–; Chm., Menter a Busnes, 1988–. Chairman: Welsh Cttee for Economic and Industrial Affairs, 1984–; Midland Bank Adv. Council for Wales, 1984–. Director: Develt Corp. for Wales, 1973–77; Welsh Industrial Develt Adv. Bd, 1975–86; Develt Bd for Rural Wales, 1976–89; Royal Welsh Agricl Soc., 1973–; Mem. Council, CBI, Wales, 1975–86 (Chm., 1979–81). Pres., Royal Nat. Eisteddfod of Wales, 1980–83. Vice President: Tenovus Cancer Res. Unit, 1980–; Kidney Res. Unit for Wales Foundn, 1980–; Chm., Dr Barnardo's Centenary in Wales Appeal, 1988; Trustee: Catherine and Lady Grace James Foundn, 1973–; John and Rhys Thomas James Foundn, 1973–; Welsh Sports Aid Trust, 1980– (Vice Chm., 1988–); Llandovery Coll., 1982–; Council for the Protection of Rural Wales, 1991. Chm., Welsh Sports Aid Foundn, 1988– (Gov., 1980–); Member: Council for the Welsh Lang., 1973–78; Design Council Wales Adv. Cttee, 1981–86; Prince of Wales Cttee, 1975–87; Dairy Produce Quota Tribunal, 1984–88. Pres., Welsh Congregational Church in Wales, 1989; Treasurer: Congregational Church in Wales, 1975–86; Mansfield Coll., Oxford, 1977–89 (Trustee, 1989–); Member

Council, and Governor: UC Swansea, 1972– (Chm. Council, 1982–); UC Aberystwyth, 1979–84; Governor, UC Cardiff, 1981–84; Mem., Ct and Council, Univ. of Wales, 1980–. Hon. LLD Wales, 1983. FRSA 1982. High Sheriff, S Glamorgan, 1985–86. *Recreations:* golf, gardening, music. *Address:* Maesglas, Pen-y-turnpike, Dinas Powis, S Glam CF6 4HH. *T:* Cardiff (0222) 512985. *Club:* Cardiff and County (Cardiff).

EVANS, Sir (William) Vincent (John), GCMG 1976 (KCMG 1970; CMG 1959); MBE 1945; QC 1973; Barrister-at-Law; a Judge of the European Court of Human Rights, 1980–91; *b* 20 Oct. 1915; *s* of Charles Herbert Evans and Elizabeth (*née* Jenkins); *m* 1947, Joan Mary Symons; one *s* two *d. Educ:* Merchant Taylors' Sch., Northwood; Wadham Coll., Oxford (Hon. Fellow 1981). 1st Class Hons, Jurisprudence, 1937; BCL, 1938; MA, 1941; elected Cassel Scholar, Lincoln's Inn, 1937; called to Bar, Lincoln's Inn, 1939 (Hon. Bencher, 1983). Served in HM Forces, 1939–46. Legal Adviser (Lt-Col) to British Military Administration, Cyrenaica, 1945–46; Asst Legal Adviser, Foreign Office, 1947–54; Legal Counsellor, UK Permanent Mission to the United Nations, 1954–59; Legal Counsellor, FO, 1959–60; Dep. Legal Adviser, FO, 1960–68; Legal Adviser, FCO, 1968–75, retired. Chm., Bryant Symons & Co. Ltd, 1964–85. Chm., European Cttee on Legal Cooperation, Council of Europe, 1969–71; UK Rep. Council of Europe Steering Cttee on Human Rights, 1976–80 (Chm., 1979–80); Mem., Human Rights Cttee set up under Internat. Covenant on Civil and Political Rights, 1977–84 (Vice-Chm., 1979–80); Mem., Permanent Court of Arbitration, 1987–. Member: Adv. Bd, Centre for Internat. Human Rights Law, Univ. of Essex, 1983–; Council of Management, British Inst. of Internat. and Comparative Law, 1969–; Bd of Govs, British Inst. of Human Rights, 1989–; Diplomatic Service Appeals Bd, 1976–86; Sch. Cttee, Merchant Taylors' Co., 1985–. Pres., Old Merchant Taylors' Soc., 1984–85; Vice-Pres., Hon. Soc. of Cymmrodorion, 1987–. DUniv Essex, 1986. *Recreation:* gardening. *Address:* (home) 4 Bedford Road, Moor Park, Northwood, Mddx. *T:* Northwood (09274) 24085; (office) 2 Hare Court, Temple, EC4. *T:* 071–583 1770. *Club:* Athenæum.

EVANS, Wynford; *see* Evans, J. W.

EVANS-ANFOM, Emmanuel, FRCSE 1955; Commissioner for Education and Culture, Ghana, 1978; Member, Council of State, 1979; Chairman, National Education Commission, since 1984; *b* 7 Oct. 1919; *m* 1952, Leonora Francetta Evans (*d* 1980); three *s* one *d*; *m* 1984, Elise Henkel. *Educ:* Achimota School; Edinburgh University (MB; ChB; DTM&H). House Surgeon, Dewsbury Infirmary, 1948–49; Medical Officer, Gold Coast Medical Service, 1950–56, Specialist Surgeon, 1956–67; Senior Lecturer, Ghana Medical School, 1966–67; Vice-Chancellor, Univ. of Science and Technology, Kumasi, 1967–74. Mem., WHO Expert Panel on Med. and Paramed. Educn, 1972–; Chm., Nat. Council for Higher Educn, 1974–78; Chairman: Med. and Dental Council; Akrofi-Christaller Centre for Mission Res. and Applied Theology, 1986–. Titular Mem., Internat. Assoc. Surgeons; Past President: Ghana Medical Assoc.; Assoc. of Surgeons of W Africa; FICS. Fellow: Ghana Acad. Arts and Sciences, 1971 (Pres., 1987–); African Acad. of Scis, 1986. Chm., Ghana Hockey Assoc. Pres., Ghana Boys' Brigade Council, 1987–. Hon. DSc Salford, 1974. *Publications:* Aetiology and Management of Intestinal Perforations, Ghana Med. Jl, 1963; Traditional Medicine in Ghana: practice problems and prospects, 1986. *Recreations:* hockey, music, art. *Address:* PO Box M135, Accra, Ghana.

EVANS-BEVAN, Sir Martyn Evan, 2nd Bt *cr* 1958; *b* 1 April 1932; *s* of Sir David Martyn Evans-Bevan, 1st Bt, and of Eira Winifred, *d* of late Sidney Archibald Lloyd Glanley; *S* father, 1973; *m* 1957, Jennifer Jane Marion, *d* of Robert Hugh Stevens; four *s. Educ:* Uppingham. Entered family business of Evan Evans Bevan and Evans Bevan Ltd, 1953; High Sheriff of Breconshire, 1967; Liveryman, Worshipful Co. of Farmers; Freeman, City of London. *Recreations:* shooting and fishing. *Heir: s* David Gawain Evans-Bevan; [*b* 16 Sept. 1961; *m* 1987, Philippa, *y d* of Patrick Sweeney; one *d*]. *Address:* Felinnewydd, Llandefalle, Brecon, Powys. *Club:* Carlton.

EVANS-FREKE, family name of **Baron Carbery.**

EVANS-LOMBE, Edward Christopher, QC 1978; a Recorder of the Crown Court, since 1982; *b* 10 April 1937; *s* of Vice-Adm. Sir Edward Evans-Lombe, KCB, and Lady Evans-Lombe; *m* 1964, Frances Marilyn MacKenzie; one *s* three *d. Educ:* Eton; Trinity Coll., Cambridge (MA). National Service, 1955–57: 2nd Lieut Royal Norfolk Regt. Called to the Bar, Inner Temple, 1963, Bencher, 1985. Standing Counsel to Dept of Trade in Bankruptcy matters, 1971. Chm., Agricultural Land Tribunal, S Eastern Region, 1983–. *Recreations:* fishing, falconry, forestry. *Address:* Marlingford Hall, Norwich *T:* Norwich (0603) 880319. *Club:* Norfolk (Norwich).

EVATT, Hon. Justice Elizabeth Andreas, AO 1982; President, Australian Law Reform Commission, since 1988; *b* 11 Nov. 1933; *d* of Clive Raleigh Evatt, QC and Marjorie Hannah (*née* Andreas); *m* 1960, Robert J. Southan, *qv*; one *d* (one *s* decd). *Educ:* Sydney Univ. (LLB); Harvard Univ. (LLM). Called to the Bar: NSW, 1955; Inner Temple, 1958. Chief Judge, Family Court of Australia, 1976–88. Dep. Pres., Australian Conciliation and Arbitration Commn, 1973–89; Chairperson, Royal Commn on Human Relationships, 1974–77; Dep. Pres., Australian Ind. Relns Commn, 1989–. Mem., UN Cttee on Elimination of Discrimination against Women, 1984– (Chairperson, 1989–91). Chancellor, Univ. of Newcastle, 1988–. Hon. LLD: Sydney, 1985; Macquarie, 1989; Hon. Dr Newcastle, 1988. *Publication:* Guide to Family Law, 1986, 2nd edn 1991. *Recreation:* music. *Address:* Law Reform Commission, 99 Elizabeth Street, Sydney, NSW 2000, Australia. *T:* 02 231 1733; GPO Box 3708, Sydney 2001, Australia. *Club:* Royal Corinthian Yacht.

EVE, family name of **Baron Silsoe.**

EVELEIGH, Rt. Hon. Sir Edward Walter, PC 1977; Kt 1968; ERD; MA; a Lord Justice of Appeal, 1977–85; *b* 8 Oct. 1917; *s* of Walter William and Daisy Emily Eveleigh; *m* 1940, Vilma Bodnar; *m* 1953, Patricia Helen Margaret Bury; two *s* (and one *s* decd). *Educ:* Peter Symonds; Brasenose Coll., Oxford (Hon. Fellow 1977). Commissioned in the Royal Artillery (Supplementary Reserve), 1936; served War of 1939–45 (despatches, 1940). Called to Bar, Lincoln's Inn, 1945, Bencher 1968, Treas., 1988; QC 1961. Recorder of Burton-on-Trent, 1961–64, of Gloucester, 1964–68; Chm., QS, County of Oxford, 1968–71 (Dep. Chm., 1963–68); a Judge of the High Court of Justice, Queen's Bench Div., 1968–77; Presiding Judge, SE Circuit, 1971–76. Mem., General Council of the Bar, 1965–67. Mem., Royal Commn on Criminal Procedure, 1978–80; Chm., Statute Law Soc., 1985–89; President: British-German Jurists' Assoc., 1974–85; Bar Musical Soc., 1980–89. Hon. Citizen: Texas, 1980; Austin, 1985; Dallas, 1985. *Address:* Royal Courts of Justice, Strand, WC2 6TW. *Club:* Garrick.

EVELEIGH, Air Vice-Marshal Geoffrey Charles, CB 1964; OBE 1945; RAF retired; *b* 25 Oct. 1912; *s* of Ernest Charles Eveleigh, Henley-on-Thames; *m* 1939, Anthea Josephine, *d* of F. H. Fraser, Ceylon; one *s* one *d. Educ:* Brighton Coll.; RAF Coll., Cranwell. Joined RAF, 1932; served War of 1939–45 in Bomber Command and No 2 Group; Dep. Chief of Air Staff, Royal New Zealand Air Force, 1955–57; Air Commodore, 1957; Dir-Gen. of Signals, Air Ministry, 1959–61; Air Vice-Marshal, 1961; Air Officer, Administration, Fighter Command, 1961–64; retd 1965. *Address:* Cán Tirana, PO Box 32, Puerto de Pollensa, 07470 Mallorca, Spain. *Club:* Royal Air Force.

EVELYN, (John) Michael, CB 1976; Assistant Director of Public Prosecutions, 1969–76, retired (Under-Secretary, 1972); *b* 2 June 1916; *s* of Edward Ernest Evelyn and Kate Rosa Underwood. *Educ:* Charterhouse; Christ Church, Oxford (MA). Called to Bar, 1939. Army service, 1939–46. Dept of Dir of Public Prosecutions, 1946–76. *Publications:* (under pseudonym Michael Underwood): Murder on Trial, 1954; Murder Made Absolute, 1955; Death on Remand, 1956; False Witness, 1957; Lawful Pursuit, 1958; Arm of the Law, 1959; Cause of Death, 1960; Death by Misadventure, 1960; Adam's Case, 1961; The Case against Phillip Quest, 1962; Girl Found Dead, 1963; The Crime of Colin Wise, 1964; The Unprofessional Spy, 1965; The Anxious Conspirator, 1965; A Crime Apart, 1966; The Man who Died on Friday, 1967; The Man who Killed Too Soon, 1968; The Shadow Game, 1969; The Silent Liars, 1970; Shem's Demise, 1970; A Trout in the Milk, 1971; Reward for a Defector, 1973; A Pinch of Snuff, 1974; The Juror, 1975; Menaces, Menaces, 1976; Murder with Malice, 1977; The Fatal Trip, 1977; Crooked Wood, 1978; Anything but the Truth, 1978; Smooth Justice, 1979; Victim of Circumstance, 1979; A Clear Case of Suicide, 1980; Crime upon Crime, 1980; Double Jeopardy, 1981; Hand of Fate, 1981; Goddess of Death, 1982; A Party to Murder, 1983; Death in Camera, 1984; The Hidden Man, 1985; Death at Deepwood Grange, 1986; The Uninvited Corpse, 1987; The Injudicious Judge, 1987; Dual Enigma, 1988; A Compelling Case, 1989; Rosa's Dilemma, 1990; A Dangerous Business, 1990; The Seeds of Murder, 1991. *Recreations:* writing, reading, opera, cinema, travel. *Address:* 100 Ashdown, Eaton Road, Hove, Sussex BN3 3AR. *Clubs:* Garrick, Detection.

EVENNETT, David Anthony; MP (C) Erith and Crayford, since 1983; *b* 3 June 1949; *s* of Norman Thomas Evennett and Irene Evennett; *m* 1975, Marilyn Anne Smith; two *s. Educ:* Buckhurst Hill County High School for Boys; London School of Economics and Political Science. BSc (Econ) Upper Second Hons, MSc (Econ). School Master, Ilford County High School for Boys, 1972–74; Marine Insurance Broker, Lloyd's, 1974–81; Mem., Lloyd's, 1976–; Dir, Lloyd's Underwriting Agency, 1982–. Redbridge Borough Councillor, 1974–78. Contested (C) Hackney South and Shoreditch, 1979. Mem., Select Cttee on Educn, Science and the Arts, 1986–. Mem., Bow Gp, 1971–; Sec., H of C Motor Club, 1985–86. Vice-Pres., Hackney S and Shoreditch Cons. Assoc., 1985–. *Recreations:* my family, reading, history, theatre and cinema. *Address:* House of Commons, SW1A 0AA. *Clubs:* Carlton; Priory Conservative (Belvedere).

EVERARD, Maj.-Gen. Sir Christopher E. W.; *see* Welby-Everard.

EVERARD, Sir Robin (Charles), 4th Bt *cr* 1911; Management Consultant, since 1976; *b* 5 Oct. 1939; *s* of Sir Nugent Henry Everard, 3rd Bt and Frances Audrey (*d* 1975), *d* of J. C. Jesson; *S* father, 1984; *m* 1963, Ariel Ingrid, *d* of late Col Peter Cleasby-Thompson, MBE, MC; one *s* two *d. Educ:* Sandroyd School; Harrow; RMA Sandhurst. Short service commn, Duke of Wellington's Regt, 1958–61. Money Broker; Managing Director, P. Murray-Jones, 1962–76; Consultant, 1976–91. *Heir: s* Henry Peter Charles Everard, *b* 6 Aug. 1970. *Address:* Church Farm, Shelton, Long Stratton, Norwich NR15 2SB.

EVERARD, Timothy John, CMG 1978; HM Diplomatic Service, retired; Secretary General, Order of St John, since 1988; *b* 22 Oct. 1929; *s* of late Charles M. Everard and late Monica M. Everard (*née* Barford); *m* 1955, Josiane Romano; two *s* two *d. Educ:* Uppingham Sch.; Magdalen Coll., Oxford. BA (Mod. Langs). Banking: Barclays Bank DCO, 1952–62, in Egypt, Sudan, Kenya, Zaire. Entered Foreign (later Diplomatic) Service: First Sec., FO, 1962–63; First Sec., Commercial, Bangkok, 1964–66; resigned to take up directorship in Ellis & Everard Ltd, 1966–67. Rejoined Foreign and Commonwealth Office, Oct. 1967: First Sec., FO, 1967–68; Bahrain, 1969–72 (First Sec. and Head of Chancery, HM Political Residency); seconded to Northern Ireland Office, FCO, April-Aug. 1972; Consul-Gen., then Chargé d'Affaires, Hanoi, 1972–73; Economic and Commercial Counsellor, Athens, 1974–78; Commercial Counsellor, Paris, 1978–81; Minister, Lagos, 1981–84; Ambassador to GDR, 1984–88. KStJ 1988. *Recreations:* golf, tennis, sailing. *Address:* 147B Ashley Gardens, SW1P 1HN. *Club:* Reform.

EVERED, David Charles; Second Secretary, Medical Research Council, since 1988; *b* 21 Jan. 1940; *s* of late Thomas Charles Evered and Enid Christian Evered; *m* 1964, Anne Elizabeth Massey Lings, (Kit), *d* of John Massey Lings, Manchester; one *s* two *d. Educ:* Cranleigh Sch., Surrey; Middlesex Hosp. Med. Sch. (BSc 1961, MB 1964, MRCP 1967, MD 1971). Junior hospital appointments, London and Leeds, 1964–70; First Asst in Medicine, Wellcome Sen. Res. Fellow and Consultant Physician, Univ. of Newcastle upon Tyne and Royal Victoria Infirmary, 1970–78; Dir, Ciba Foundn, 1978–88. Member: British Library Medical Information Review Panel, 1978–80; Council, St George's Hosp. Med. Sch. 1983–; Cttee, Assoc. of Med. Res. Charities, 1981–84, 1987–88 (Vice-Chm., 1987–88); Public Understanding of Science Cttee, Royal Soc., 1986–88; Media Resource Service Adv. Cttee, NY, 1986–; NW Thames RHA, 1988–90; Hammersmith & Queen Charlotte's SHA; Council, Internat. Agency for Res. into Cancer (Lyon), 1988–; Vice-Pres., Science Cttee, Louis Jeantet Fondation de Médecine, 1984–91. FRCP 1978; FIBiol 1978; FRSM; Scientific Fellow, Zool Soc. of London (Mem. Council, 1985–89). Member: Soc. for Endocrinology; Eur. Thyroid Assoc. (Mem. Exec. Cttee, 1977–81, Sec.-Treas., 1983–89); Amer. Thyroid Assoc. *Publications:* Diseases of the Thyroid, 1976; (with R. Hall and R. Greene) Atlas of Clinical Endocrinology, 1979, 2nd edn 1990; (with M. O'Connor) Collaboration in Medical Research in Europe, 1981; numerous papers on medicine, education and science policy. *Recreations:* reading, history, tennis, sailing. *Address:* Medical Research Council, 20 Park Crescent, W1N 4AL. *T:* 071–636 5422.

EVEREST, David Anthony, PhD; FRSC; Visiting Research Fellow, University of East Anglia, since 1986; Research Associate, UK Centre for Economic and Environmental Development, since 1987; *b* 18 Sept. 1926; *s* of George Charles and Ada Bertha Everest; *m* 1956, Audrey Pauline (*née* Sheldrick); three *s. Educ:* John Lyon Sch., Harrow; University Coll. London (Bsc, PhD). Lecturer in Chemistry, Battersea Polytechnic, 1949–56; Sen. Scientific Officer, 1956–58, PSO, 1958–64, National Chemical Laboratory; SPSO, 1964–70, Dep. Chief Scientific Officer, 1970–77, National Physical Laboratory; DCSO, RTP Div., Dept of Industry, 1977–79; Chief Scientist, Environmental Protection Gp, 1979–86, and Dir of Sci. Res. Policy, 1983–86, DoE. Editor, Energy and Environment, 1989–. *Publications:* Chemistry of Beryllium, 1962; section on Beryllium in Comprehensive Inorganic Chemistry, 1972; The Greenhouse Effect: issues for policy makers, 1988; The Provision of Expert Advice to Government Matters: the role of advisory committees, 1990; papers in Inorganic Chemistry, Extractive Metallurgy and Material Science. *Recreations:* astronomy, reading, walking. *Address:* Talland, Chorleywood Road, Chorleywood, Herts WD3 4ER. *T:* Rickmansworth (0923) 773253.

EVERETT, Bernard Jonathan; HM Diplomatic Service; Consul-General, Houston, since 1991; *b* 17 Sept. 1943; *s* of Arnold Edwin Everett and Helene May Everett (*née* Heine); *m* 1970, Maria Olinda, *d* of Raul Correia de Albuquerque and Maria de Lourdes Gonçalves de Albuquerque; two *s* one *d* (and one *d* decd). *Educ:* King's Coll. Sch., Wimbledon; Lincoln Coll., Oxford (BA 1965). Researcher, Reader's Digest, 1965; entered HM Diplomatic Service, 1966; Third, later Second Sec., Lisbon, 1967; FCO, 1971;

Consul, Luanda, 1975; FCO, 1976; Head of Chancery, Lusaka, 1978; Consul (Commercial), Rio de Janeiro, 1980; Asst Head, Information Dept, FCO, 1983; on secondment as Head, Sub-Saharan Africa Br., DTI, 1984; Ambassador to Guatemala, 1987–91. *Recreations:* sport, performing arts, numismatics. *Address:* c/o Foreign and Commonwealth Office, SW1.

EVERETT, Christopher Harris Doyle, CBE 1988; MA; Director General and Secretary, Daiwa Anglo-Japanese Foundation, since 1990; *b* 20 June 1933; *s* of late Alan Doyle Everett, MBE, MS, FRCS, and of Annabel Dorothy Joan Everett (*née* Harris); *m* 1955, Hilary (Billy) Anne (*née* Robertson); two *s* two *d.* *Educ:* Winchester College; New College, Oxford. MA (Class. Mods and Lit. Hum.). Grenadier Guards, Nat. Service, 1951–53. HM Diplomatic Service, 1957–70: posts included Beirut, Washington and Foreign Office; Headmaster: Worksop Coll., 1970–75; Tonbridge Sch., 1975–89. Chm., 1986, Vice-Chm., 1987, HMC. JP Tonbridge and W Malling, 1976–89. Hon. FCP 1988. *Recreations:* reading, walking, tennis. *Address:* (office) 5 King William Street, EC4N 7AX. *T:* 071–548 8302; (home) Lavender House, 12 Madeira Park, Tunbridge Wells, Kent TN2 5SX. *T:* Tunbridge Wells (0892) 25624.

EVERETT, Douglas Hugh, MBE 1946; FRS 1980; Leverhulme Professor of Physical Chemistry, University of Bristol, 1954–82, now Emeritus; Dean of Faculty of Science, 1966–68; Pro-Vice-Chancellor, 1973–76; *b* 26 Dec. 1916; *e s* of late Charles Everett and Jessie Caroline; *m* 1942, Frances Elizabeth Jessop; two *d.* *Educ:* Grammar Sch., Hampton-on-Thames; University of Reading; Balliol Coll., Oxford. Wantage Scholar, Reading Univ., 1935–38; Kitchener Scholar, 1936–39; BSc, 1938; Ramsay Fellow, 1939–41; DPhil 1942. Special Scientific Duties, WO, 1942–45. ICI Fellow, Oxford Univ., 1945–47; Chemistry Lecturer, Dundee Univ. Coll., 1947; MA 1947; Fellow, Lecturer and Tutor, Exeter Coll., Oxford, 1947–48; Prof. of Chemistry, Dundee Univ. Coll., University of St Andrews, 1948–54. Chm., Internat. Union of Pure and Applied Chemistry Commn on Colloid and Surface Chemistry, 1969–73. FRSE 1950; DSc 1956. Mem., Building Research Board, DSIR, 1954–61; a Vice-Pres., Faraday Soc., 1958–61, 1963–65, 1968–70, Pres., 1976–78; Mem. Chemical Soc. Council, 1961–64, 1972–74 (Tilden Lectr, 1955; Award in Colloid and Surface Chemistry, 1971); Pres., Section B, BAAS, 1979–80; a Vice-Pres. and Gen. Sec., BAAS, 1983–88; Pres., Internat. Assoc. of Colloid and Interface Scientists, 1988–90. *Publications:* Introduction to Chemical Thermodynamics, 1959, 2nd edn, 1971; Basic Principles of Colloid Science, 1988; papers on Physical Chemistry in scientific jls. *Recreations:* walking, painting. *Address:* School of Chemistry, The University, Bristol BS8 1TS.

EVERETT, Eileen, (Mrs Raymond Everett); *see* Diss, E.

EVERETT, Oliver William, CVO 1991 (LVO 1980); Librarian, Windsor Castle and Assistant Keeper of The Queen's Archives, since 1985; *b* 28 Feb. 1943; *s* of Charles Everett, DSO, MC and Judy Rothwell; *m* 1965, Theffania Vesey Stoney; two *s* two *d.* *Educ:* Felsted Sch.; Christ's Coll., Cambridge; Fletcher Sch. of Law and Diplomacy, Mass, USA. HM Diplomatic Service, 1967–81: First Sec., New Delhi, 1969–73; Head of Chancery, Madrid, 1980–81; Asst Private Sec. to HRH The Prince of Wales, 1978–80; Private Sec. to HRH The Princess of Wales, 1981–83, and Comptroller to The Prince and Princess of Wales, 1981–83; Dep. Librarian, Windsor Castle, 1984. *Recreations:* skiing, real tennis, rackets. *Address:* Garden House, Windsor Castle, Berks. *T:* Windsor (0753) 868286; The East Wing, Kirtlington Park, Oxon. *T:* Bletchington (0869) 50589. *Club:* Ski Club of Great Britain.

EVERETT, Thomas Henry Kemp; Special Commissioner of Income Tax, since 1983; *b* 28 Jan. 1932; *s* of late Thomas Kemp Everett and Katharine Ida Everett (*née* Woodward); *m* 1954, June (*née* Partridge); three *s.* *Educ:* Queen Elizabeth's Hospital, Bristol; Univ. of Bristol. LLB Hons 1957. Solicitor (Hons), admitted 1960; Partner, Meade-King & Co., 1963–83. Clerk to General Commissioners, Bedminster Div., 1965–83. Chairman: Service 9, 1972–75; Bristol Council of Voluntary Service, 1975–80; St Christopher's Young Persons' Residential Trust, 1976–83; Vice-Chm., Governors of Queen Elizabeth's Hosp., 1980–; Mem., Governing Council, St Christopher's School, Bristol, 1983–89; Hon. Treasurer and Vice-Chm., Rowberrow PCC; Mem., Axbridge Deanery Synod. *Recreations:* music, reading, walking. *Address:* Dolebury Cottage, Dolberrow, Churchill, near Bristol BS19 5NS. *T:* Churchill (0934) 852329; 15–17 Bedford Avenue, WC1B 3AS. *T:* 071–631 4242. *Club:* Lansdowne.

EVERITT, Prof. Alan Milner, PhD; FSA; FRHistS; FBA 1989; Hatton Professor and Head of Department of English Local History, University of Leicester, 1968–82, now Professor Emeritus (Associate Professor, 1982–84); *b* 17 Aug. 1926; *s* of Robert Arthur Everitt and Grace Beryl Everitt (*née* Milner); unmarried. *Educ:* Sevenoaks Sch.; Univ. of St Andrews (MA 1951); Inst. of Historical Res., London Univ. (Carnegie Scholar; PhD 1957). FRHistS 1969; FSA 1980. Editorial Assistant, ACU, 1951–54; Department of English Local History, University of Leicester: Res. Assistant, 1957–59; Res. Fellow in Urban Hist., 1960–65; Lectr in Eng. Local Hist., 1965–68. Lectures: Gregynog, Univ. of Wales, 1976; Helen Sutermeister, UEA, 1982; James Ford Special, Univ. of Oxford, 1983. *Publications:* The County Committee of Kent in the Civil War, 1957; Suffolk and the Great Rebellion 1640–1660, 1960; The Community of Kent and the Great Rebellion 1640–60, 1966, 3rd edn 1986; Change in the Provinces: the seventeenth century, 1969; The Pattern of Rural Dissent: the nineteenth century, 1972; Perspectives in English Urban History, 1973; Landscape and Community in England, 1985; Continuity and Colonization: the evolution of Kentish settlement, 1986; contribs to: The Agrarian History of England and Wales; Past and Present, Trans of RHistS, Agricl Hist. Rev., Urban History Yearbook, Jl of Histl Geog., Jl of Transport Hist., Archaeologia Cantiana, Local Historian, TLS, Nomina. *Recreation:* living with the past. *Address:* Fieldedge, Poultney Lane, Kimcote, Lutterworth, Leics LE17 5RX.

EVERITT, Anthony Michael; Secretary-General, Arts Council of Great Britain, since 1990 (Deputy Secretary-General, 1985–90); *b* 31 Jan. 1940; *s* of late Michael Anthony Hamill Everitt and Simone Dolores Cathérine (*née* de Vergriette; she *m* 2nd, John Brunel Cohen). *Educ:* Cheltenham Coll.; Corpus Christi Coll., Cambridge (BA Hons English, 1962). Lectured variously at National Univ. of Iran, Teheran, SE London Coll. of Further Educn, Birmingham Coll. of Art, and Trent Polytechnic, 1963–72; The Birmingham Post: Art Critic, 1970–75; Drama Critic, 1974–79; Features Editor, 1976–79; Director: Midland Gp Arts Centre, Nottingham, 1979–80; E Midlands Arts Assoc., 1980–85. Chairman: Ikon Gall., Birmingham, 1976–79; Birmingham Arts Lab., 1977–79; Vice-Chm., Council of Regional Arts Assocs, 1984–85; Member: Drama Panel, 1974–78, and Regional Cttee, 1979–80, Arts Council of GB; Cttee for Arts and Humanities, 1986–87, Performing Arts Cttee, 1987–, CNAA; General Adv. Council, IBA, 1987–90. *Publications:* Abstract Expressionism, 1974; contribs to Financial Times, Studio Internat., etc. *Address:* 74 Cambray Road, SW12 0EP.

EVERSLEY, David Edward Charles, PhD; social researcher; *b* 22 Nov. 1921; *s* of Dr Otto Eberstadt and Dela Morel; *m* 1st, 1945, Edith Wembridge (*d* 1978); one *s* three *d*; 2nd, 1986, Barbara Rojo (marr. diss. 1990). *Educ:* Goethe-Gymnasium, Frankfurt/Main; Leighton Park Sch., Reading; London Sch. of Economics. BSc (Econ) (London), PhD (Birmingham). Asst Lectr, Lectr, then Reader, in Economic (and then Social) Hist., Univ. of Birmingham, 1949–66. Dir, W Midlands Social and Polit. Res. Unit, 1962–65; Reader in Population and Regional Studies, Univ. of Sussex, 1966; Dir, Social Research Unit, Univ. of Sussex, 1967–69; Prof., 1969. Hon. Sec., Midlands New Towns Soc., 1958–62; Chief Planner (Strategy), Greater London Council, 1969–72; Centre for Environmental Studies, 1972–76; Sen. Res. Fellow, PSI, 1976–81; Vivien Stewart Bursar, Dept of Land Economy, Univ. of Cambridge, 1981–82. Visiting Professor: of Demography, Univ. of California at Berkeley, 1965; Bartlett Sch. of Architecture and Planning, University Coll. London, 1976–79; Dept of Town and Country Planning, QUB, 1984–85; Univ. of Trento, Italy, 1991–92; Vis. Schol., Population Reference Bureau, Washington, 1986. Mem., W Midlands Economic Planning Coun., 1965–66; Corr. Mem., German Acad. for Urban and Regional Planning, 1972–; Pres., Commn sur la Démographie Historique, Internat. Congress of Hist. Sciences, 1965–70. Chm., Regional Studies Assoc., 1972–75, Vice-Chm., 1975–. Chm., Social Responsibility Council, Society of Friends (Quakers), 1972–75; Pres., British Soc. for Population Studies, 1981–83. Hon. Planning Advr, 1988–90, Hon. Dir, 1991–, Herts Soc. Hon. MRTPI 1978, Mem. Council, 1979–88. *Publications:* Rents and Social Policy, 1955; Social Theories of Fertility and the Malthusian Debate, 1959, new US edn 1975; (with D. Keate) The Overspill Problem in the West Midlands, 1958; (ed and contrib. with D. V. Glass) Population in History, 1965; (with Lomas and Jackson) Population Growth and Planning Policy, 1965; (with F. Sukdeo) The Dependants of the Coloured Commonwealth Population of England and Wales, 1969; (ed and contrib. with D. Donnison) London: urban patterns, problems and policies, 1973; The Planner in Society, 1973; A Question of Numbers?, 1973; (ed and contrib. with J. Platts) Public Resources and Private Lives, 1976; (ed and contrib. with Alan Evans) The Inner City, Industry and Employment, 1980; (ed and contrib. with W. Koellmann) Population Change and Social Planning, 1982; Changes in the Composition of Households and the Cycle of Family Life, 1984; Religion and Employment in Northern Ireland, 1989; (with R. Vann) Friends in Life and Death, 1991; numerous chapters in collected vols; contribs to Victoria History of the Counties of England; articles in jls of history, demography and planning. *Recreations:* walking, talking, working. *Address:* Hummerstons, Cottered, Buntingford, Herts SG9 9QP. *T:* Cottered (076381) 354.

EVERSON, Sir Frederick (Charles), KCMG 1968 (CMG 1956); *b* 6 Sept. 1910; *s* of Frederick Percival Everson; *m* 1937, Linda Mary Clark (*d* 1984); two *s* one *d* (and one *s* decd). *Educ:* Tottenham County Sch., Middlesex. BSc (Econ.) London. Entered Civil Service, July 1928; Consular Service, Dec. 1934. Chief Administrative Officer, British Embassy, Bonn, Germany, 1953–56; Ambassador to El Salvador, 1956–60; Commercial Counsellor, British Embassy, Stockholm, 1960–63; Minister (Economic), British Embassy, Paris, 1963–68. *Address:* 8 Gainsborough Court, College Road, Dulwich, SE21 7LT. *T:* 081–693 8125.

EVERSON, John Andrew; HM Chief Inspector of Schools, Teacher Education, Department of Education and Science, since 1990; *b* 26 Oct. 1933; *s* of Harold Leslie Everson and Florence Jane Stone; *m* 1961, Gilda Ramsden; two *s.* *Educ:* Tiffin Boys' Sch., Kingston-upon-Thames; Christ's Coll., Cambridge (MA); King's Coll., London (PGCE). Teacher: Haberdashers' Aske's Sch., Elstree, 1958–65; City of London Sch., 1965–68; Schools Inspectorate, DES, 1968–; Chief Inspector for Secondary Educn, 1981–89; seconded to Peat Marwick McLintock, 1989. *Publications:* (with B. P. FitzGerald) Settlement Patterns, 1968; (with B. P. FitzGerald) Inside the City, 1972. *Recreations:* opera, walking, theatre, chess. *Address:* Department of Education and Science, Sanctuary Buildings, Great Smith Street, SW1. *T:* 071–934 9806. *Club:* Athenæum.

EVERY, Sir Henry (John Michael), 13th Bt *cr* 1641, of Egginton, Derbyshire; Head of Audit Services, BDO Binder Hamlyn, Chartered Accountants, Birmingham, since 1987; *b* 6 April 1947; *s* of Sir John Simon Every, 12th Bt and of Janet Marion, *d* of John Page; *S* father, 1988; *m* 1974, Susan Mary, *er d* of Kenneth Beaton, JP, Eastshotte, Hartford, Cambs; three *s.* *Educ:* Malvern College. FCA. Qualified as Chartered Accountant, 1970; worked in South Africa, 1970–74; Partner with BDO Binder Hamlyn in Birmingham, 1979. Mem. of Cttee, Birmingham and West Midlands Dist Soc. of Chartered Accountants, 1988–. Mem., Egginton Parish Council, 1987–. *Recreations:* tennis, squash, gardening; supporter of Nottingham Forest FC. *Heir:* *s* Edward James Henry Every, *b* 3 July 1975. *Address:* Cothay, Egginton, near Derby DE6 6HJ. *Club:* Speakers' (Burton-on-Trent).

EVES, David Charles Thomas; Deputy Director General, Health and Safety Executive, since 1989; *b* 10 Jan. 1942; *s* of Harold Thomas Eves and Violet Eves (*née* Edwards); *m* 1964, Valerie Ann Carter; one *d.* *Educ:* King's Sch., Rochester; University Coll., Durham. Teacher, Kent CC, 1963–64; HM Inspector of Factories, Min. of Labour, 1964; Under Sec., 1985–89, Dep. Sec., 1989–, Health and Safety Exec., Dept of Employment Gp; HM Chief Inspector of Factories, 1985–88; Dir, Resources and Planning Div., HSE, 1988–89. *Recreations:* sailing, would-be painter. *Address:* Health and Safety Executive, 1 Chepstow Place, W2 4TF. *T:* 071–243 6450. *Club:* Athenæum.

EWANS, Sir Martin Kenneth, KCMG 1987 (CMG 1980); HM Diplomatic Service, retired; Director, Casalee Group SA; Chairman, Civil Service Selection Board, 1989; *b* 14 Nov. 1928; *s* of late John Ewans; *m* 1953, Mary Tooke; one *s* one *d.* *Educ:* St Paul's; Corpus Christi Coll., Cambridge (major scholar, MA). Royal Artillery, 1947–49, 2nd Lt. Joined Commonwealth Relations Office, 1952; Second Sec., Karachi, 1954–55; First Sec.: Ottawa, 1958–61; Lagos, 1962–64; Kabul, 1967–69. Counsellor, Dar-es-Salaam, 1969–73; Head of East African Dept, FCO, 1973–77; Minister, New Delhi, 1978–82; Sen. Civilian Instructor, RCDS, 1982–83; High Commissioner: in Harare, Zimbabwe, 1983–85; Nigeria, 1986–88. *Publication:* Bharatpur, Bird Paradise, 1989. *Recreations:* bird watching, sailing, writing. *Address:* The Barn, Old Hall Farm, South Walsham, Norfolk NR13 6DS. *Club:* Norfolk (Norwich).

EWART, Gavin Buchanan, FRSL; freelance writer (poet), since 1971; *b* 4 Feb. 1916; *s* of George Arthur Ewart and Dorothy Hannah (*née* Turner); *m* 1956, Margaret Adelaide Bennett; one *s* one *d.* *Educ:* Wellington Coll.; Christ's Coll., Cambridge (BA Hons 1937, MA 1942). FRSL 1981. Salesman, Contemporary Lithographs, 1938; served War, Royal Artillery, 1940–46; Production Manager, Editions Poetry, London, 1946; British Council, 1946–52; Advertising copywriter in London advertising agencies, 1952–71. Cholmondeley Award for Poetry, 1971. *Publications:* Poems and Songs, 1939; Londoners, 1964; Pleasures of the Flesh, 1966; The Deceptive Grin of the Gravel Porters, 1968; The Gavin Ewart Show, 1971; Be My Guest!, 1975; No Fool Like An Old Fool, 1976; Or Where a Young Penguin Lies Screaming, 1978; All My Little Ones, 1978; The Collected Ewart 1933–1980, 1980, 2nd edn 1982; The New Ewart, 1982; More Little Ones, 1983; Other People's Clerihews, 1983; The Ewart Quarto, 1984; The Young Pobble's Guide to His Toes, 1985; The Complete Little Ones of Gavin Ewart, 1986; The Learnèd Hippopotamus, 1987; Late Pickings, 1987; Penultimate Poems, 1989; Caterpillar Stew, 1990; Collected Poems 1980–1990, 1991. *Recreations:* reading, listening to music. *Address:* 57 Kenilworth Court, Lower Richmond Road, SW15 1EN. *T:* 081–788 7071.

EWART, Sir (William) Ivan (Cecil), 6th Bt, *cr* 1887; DSC 1945; JP; Administrator, Ngora Freda Carr Hospital, Uganda (Association of Surgeons of East Africa), 1985–89, retired; *b* 18 July 1919; *s* of late Major William Basil Ewart (*y s* of late Frederick William Ewart, 7th *s* of 1st Bt); *S* kinsman (Sir Talbot Ewart, 5th Bt), 1959; *m* 1948, Pauline Chevallier (*d* 1964), *e d* of late Wing Comdr Raphael Chevallier Preston, OBE, AFC, JP, Abbey Flat, Bellapais, Kyrenia, Cyprus; one *s* two *d. Educ:* Radley. Joined Ulster Div., RNVR, 1938. Served War of 1939–45; Lieut, RNVR; service in Coastal Forces (Motor Torpedo-Boats), 1939–42 (DSC); POW, Germany, 1942–45. Chairman: William Ewart & Son Ltd, Linen Manufacturers, 1968–73 (Dir, 1954–73); William Ewart Investments Ltd, Belfast, 1973–77; Ewart New Northern Ltd, Belfast, 1973–77; E Africa Resident Rep., Royal Commonwealth Soc. for the Blind, 1977–84. Pres., NI Chamber of Commerce and Industry, 1974. A Northern Ireland Delegate to the Duke of Edinburgh's Study Conf. on the Human Problems of Industrial Communities within the Commonwealth and Empire, Oxford, 1956; Pres., Church of Ireland's Young Men's Soc., 1951–61 and 1975–77; Chm. Flax Spinners Assoc., 1961–66; Pres., Oldpark Unionist Assoc., 1950–68. Belfast Harbour Comr, 1968–77. High Sheriff for County Antrim, 1976. *Heir: s* William Michael Ewart, *b* 10 June 1953. *Address:* Hill House, Hillsborough, Co. Down BT26 6AE. *T:* Hillsborough (0846) 683000; PO Box 30171, Nairobi, Kenya. *T:* 725726. *Clubs:* Naval; Ulster Reform (Belfast); Nairobi.

EWART-BIGGS, family name of **Baroness Ewart-Biggs.**

EWART-BIGGS, Baroness *cr* 1981 (Life Peer), of Ellis Green in the County of Essex; **(Felicity) Jane Ewart-Biggs;** *d* of Major Basil Randall; *m* 1960, Christopher Ewart-Biggs, CMG, OBE (HM Diplomatic Service) (*d* 1976); one *s* two *d. Educ:* Downe House School, Cold Ash, Newbury, Berks. Lived in Algiers, Brussels, Paris and Dublin, 1960–76, during husband's service overseas. In 1976, established Christopher Ewart-Biggs Memorial Literary Prize. Labour Party spokesman on: home affairs, 1983–; consumer affairs, 1987–; overseas develt, 1987–; an opposition whip, 1988–. Pres., British Cttee, UNICEF, 1984–. Hon. DLitt, New Univ. of Ulster, 1978. *Publications:* autobiography: Pay, Pack and Follow, 1984; A Lady in the Lords, 1988. *Recreations:* travel, discussion and international affairs. *Address:* 31 Radnor Walk, SW3 4BP.

EWBANK, Hon. Sir Anthony (Bruce), Kt 1980; **Hon. Mr Justice Ewbank;** Judge of the High Court of Justice, Family Division, since 1980; *b* 30 July 1925; *s* of late Rev. Harold Ewbank and Gwendolen Ewbank (*née* Bruce); *m* 1958, Moya McGinn; four *s* one *d. Educ:* St John's Sch., Leatherhead; Trinity Coll., Cambridge, Natural Sciences Tripos (MA). Sub Lieut RNVR, 1945–47. Maths Master, Stamford School, 1947–50; Physics Master, Epsom Coll., 1950–53. Permanent RNVR, 1951–56. Called to Bar, Gray's Inn, 1954; Bencher, 1980. Junior Counsel to Treasury in Probate matters, 1969; QC 1972; a Recorder of the Crown Court, 1975–80. Chm., Family Law Bar Assoc., 1978–80. *Address:* Royal Courts of Justice, Strand, WC2.

EWBANK, Prof. Inga-Stina; Professor of English Literature, University of Leeds, since 1985; *b* 13 June 1932; *d* of Gustav and Ingeborg Ekeblad; *m* 1959, Roger Ewbank; one *s* two *d. Educ:* Högre Allänna Läroverket för Flickor, Gothenburg; Univs of Carleton (BA), Gothenburg (Fil.kand.), Sheffield (MA) and Liverpool (PhD). William Noble Fellow, Univ. of Liverpool, 1955–57; Res. Fellow at Shakespeare Inst., Univ. of Birmingham, 1957–60; Univ. of Liverpool: Asst Lectr, 1960–63; Lectr, 1963–70; Sen. Lectr, 1970–72; Reader in English Literature, Bedford Coll., Univ. of London, 1972–74, Hildred Carlile Prof., 1974–84. Vis. Lectr, Univ. of Munich, 1959–60; Vis. Assoc. Prof., Northwestern Univ., 1966; Visiting Professor: Harvard Univ., 1974; Univ. of Maryland, 1981; Georgetown Univ., 1982; Columbia Univ., 1984. Mem., Univ. and Poly. Grants Cttee, Hong Kong, 1982–. *Publications:* Their Proper Sphere: A Study of the Brontë Sisters as Early-Victorian Female Novelists, 1966; Shakespeare, Ibsen and the Unspeakable (Inaugural Lecture), 1975; chapter in, A New Companion to Shakespeare Studies, 1971; (with Peter Hall) Ibsen's John Gabriel Borkman: An English Version, 1975; (ed with Philip Edwards and G. K. Hunter) Shakespeare's Styles, 1980; chapter in, The Cambridge Companion to Shakespeare Studies, 1986; Strindberg and the Intimate Theatre, 1987; chapters in other books; contrib. Shakespeare Survey, Ibsen Yearbook, Rev. Eng. Studies, Mod. Lang. Rev., English Studies, etc. *Recreations:* same as work: reading, theatre; children. *Address:* 19 Woodfield Road, Ealing, W5. *T:* 081–997 2895.

EWBANK, Michael Henry, CBE 1980; Director, Ewbank Preece Group Ltd, 1983–88, retired; *b* 5 May 1930; *s* of Charles Henry Preston Ewbank and Doris Minnie Ewbank; *m* 1959, Julia Ann Bartley (*d* 1986); three *s* one *d. Educ:* Stowe School; City and Guilds Coll., London Univ. BSc, ACGI, CEng, FIChemE. Royal Navy, 1951–53; S/Lt RNR. Technical Engineer, Ewbank and Partners Ltd, 1953–57; Dir, 1957; Dep. Chm. 1965; Chm., 1969. Chairman: British Consultants' Bureau, 1974–76; ME Assoc., 1981–82; Pres., European Cttee of Consulting Firms (CEBI), 1976–78. Director: Associated Nuclear Services, 1984–88; Ewbank Preece Gp Ltd, 1986–88. *Recreations:* riding, skiing. *Address:* Oakwood, Clayhill Road, Leigh, Reigate, Surrey RH2 8PB. *T:* Dawes Green (030678) 354.

EWBANK, Ven. Walter Frederick; Archdeacon Emeritus and Canon Emeritus of Carlisle Cathedral; *b* Poona, India, 29 Jan. 1918; *er s* of late Sir Robert Benson Ewbank, CSI, CIE, and Frances Helen, *d* of Rev. W. F. Simpson; *m* 1st, 1941, Ida Margaret, 3rd *d* of late John Haworth Whitworth, DSO, MC, Inner Temple; three *d*; 2nd, 1976, Mrs Josephine Alice Williamson, MD, ChB, FRCOG. *Educ:* Shrewsbury Sch.; Balliol Coll., Oxford. Classical Scholar of Balliol, 1936; 1st, Classical Hon. Mods, 1938; 2nd, Hon. Sch. of Theology, 1946; BA and MA 1946; Bishops' Coll., Cheshunt, 1946; BD 1952. Friends' Ambulance Unit, 1939–42; Deacon, 1946; Priest, 1947; Asst Curate, St Martin's, Windermere, 1946–49; Dio. Youth Chaplain and Vicar of Ings, 1949–52; Chap. to Casterton Sch. and Vicar of Casterton, 1952–62; Domestic Chap. to Bp of Carlisle and Vicar of Raughtonhead, 1962–66; Vicar of St Cuthbert's, Carlisle, and Chap. to Corporation, 1966–71; Rural Dean of Carlisle, 1970–71; Archdeacon of Westmorland and Furness and Vicar of Winster, 1971–77; Archdeacon of Carlisle, 1977–84; Administrator of Church House, Carlisle and Chm., Diocesan Glebe Cttee, 1977–84; Canon Residentiary of Carlisle Cathedral, 1977–82; Hon. Canon, 1966–77 and 1982–84. Proctor in Convocation and Mem. Ch Assembly, 1957–70; Member: Canon Law Standing Commn, 1968–70; Faculty Jurisdiction Commn, 1979–83; Diocesan Dir: of Ordinands, 1962–70; of Post Ordination Trng, 1962–66; Vice-Chm., Diocesan Synod, 1970–79; Chm., Diocesan Board of Finance, 1977–82. Chm., Carlisle Tithe Barn Restoration Cttee, 1968–70. Winter War Remembrance Medal (Finland), 1940. *Publications:* Salopian Diaries, 1961; Morality without Law, 1969; Charles Euston Nurse-A Memoir, 1982; Thomas Bloomer—A Memoir, 1984; Poems of Cumbria and of the Cumbrian Church, 1985; Ellen Margaret Cartwright—A Memoir, 1991; articles in Church Quarterly Review. *Recreation:* classical studies. *Address:* 7 Castle Court, Castle Street, Carlisle CA3 8TP. *Club:* Royal Over-Seas League.
See also Baron Renfrew of Kaimsthorn.

EWEN, Peter; Chartered Accountant; *b* 4 June 1903; *s* of Alexander H. and Elizabeth Ewen, Liverpool; *m* 1932, Janet Howat (*née* Allan) (*d* 1982); two *d. Educ:* Merchant Taylors, Crosby, Qualified as Chartered Accountant, 1927; after 4 years in India joined Allan Charlesworth & Co., 1931; Partner, 1938; Senior Partner, 1953; retired, 1969. Dir

of companies; Chm., Westinghouse Brake and Signal Co. Ltd, 1962–74. *Address:* Kestor, Moretonhampstead, Devon. *T:* Moretonhampstead (0647) 40307. *Club:* Oriental.

EWENS, John Qualtrough, CMG 1971; CBE 1959; QC 1983; First Parliamentary Counsel, Commonwealth of Australia, 1948–72; *b* 18 Nov. 1907; *er s* of L. J. Ewens, Adelaide; *m* 1935, Gwendoline, *e d* of W. A. Wilson, Adelaide; two *s. Educ:* St Peter's Coll., Adelaide; Univ. of Adelaide. LLB 1929. Barrister and Solicitor, S Australia, 1929. Legal Asst, Attorney-General's Dept, Commonwealth of Australia, 1933; Sen. Legal Officer, 1939; Asst Parly Draftsman, 1945; Principal Asst Parly Draftsman, 1948; First Parly Counsel (formerly called Parly Draftsman), 1948–72; Actg Solicitor-Gen. and Actg Sec., Commonwealth of Australia Attorney-Gen.'s Dept, numerous occasions, 1953–70. Mem. Council: Canberra UC, 1947–60; Australian Nat. Univ., 1960–75; Mem., Australian Law Reform Commn, 1978–80; Consultant (Legislative Drafting): Norfolk Island Admin, 1979–85; Australian Law Reform Commn, 1980–; Constitutional Commn, 1987–88. *Publications:* articles in legal periodicals. *Recreations:* reading, music. *Address:* 8/167 La Perouse Street, Red Hill, ACT 2603, Australia. *T:* Canberra 295 9283. *Club:* University House (Canberra).

EWER, Prof. Tom Keightley, OBE 1978; HDA; BVSc; PhD; MRCVS; Professor of Animal Husbandry, Bristol University, 1961–77, now Emeritus; retired; *b* 21 Sept. 1911; *s* of William Edward Frederick Ewer and Maria Louisa Keightley; *m* 1st, 1937, Iva Rosalind Biddle; three *s*; 2nd, 1959, Margaret June Fischer; three *d* one step *s* two step *d. Educ:* Fowey Grammar Sch.; Sydney Univ. (BVSc); Cambridge Univ. (PhD). Veterinary research with NZ Govt, 1938–45; Senior Lecturer, Univ. of NZ, 1945–47; Wellcome Research Fellow, University of Cambridge, 1947–50; Prof. of Animal Husbandry, University of Queensland, 1950–61; Prof. of Animal Resources, King Faisal Univ., Saudi Arabia, 1978–80. *Publications:* Practical Animal Husbandry, 1982; contrib. to scientific publications, on animal nutrition and veterinary education. *Recreation:* music. *Address:* Oakridge, Winscombe, Avon BS25 1LZ. *T:* Winscombe (093484) 3279.

EWIN, Sir David Ernest Thomas F.; see Floyd Ewin.

EWING; see Orr-Ewing and Orr Ewing.

EWING, Vice-Adm. Sir Alastair; see Ewing, Vice-Adm. Sir R. A.

EWING, Harry; MP (Lab) Falkirk East, since 1983 (Stirling and Falkirk, Sept. 1971–1974, Stirling, Falkirk and Grangemouth, 1974–83); *b* 20 Jan. 1931; *s* of Mr and Mrs William Ewing; *m* 1954, Margaret Greenhill; one *s* one *d. Educ:* Fulford Primary Sch., Cowdenbeath; Beath High Sch., Cowdenbeath. Contested (Lab) East Fife, 1970. Parly Under-Sec. of State, Scottish Office, 1974–79. Jt Chm., Scottish Const. Convention, 1990–. Member: Union of Post Office Workers; UCW. *Recreations:* bowls, gardening. *Address:* House of Commons, SW1A 0AA; Gowanbank, 45 Glenlyon Road, Leven, Fife KY8 4AA. *T:* Leven (0333) 26123.

EWING, Margaret Anne; MP (SNP) Moray, since 1987; *b* 1 Sept. 1945; *d* of John and Peggie McAdam; *m* 1983, Fergus Stewart Ewing, *s* of Stewart Martin Ewing and Winifred Margaret Ewing, *qv. Educ:* Univs of Glasgow and Strathclyde. MA Glasgow 1967, BA Hons Strathclyde 1973. Asst Teacher, Our Lady's High, Cumbernauld, 1968–70; St Modan's High, Stirling: Special Asst Teacher, 1970–73; Principal Teacher, Remedial Educn, 1973–74. MP (SNP) East Dunbartonshire, Oct. 1974–1979; contested (SNP) Strathkelvin and Bearsden, 1983. Sen. Vice-Chm., SNP, 1984–87, Vice-Pres., 1987–; Leader, SNP Parly Gp, 1987–. *Recreations:* the arts in general, folk music in particular. *Address:* Burns Cottage, Tulloch's Brae, Lossiemouth, Morayshire IV31 6QY. *T:* Lossiemouth (034381) 2222.

EWING, Vice-Adm. Sir (Robert) Alastair, KBE 1962; CB 1959; DSC 1942; *b* 10 April 1909; *s* of Major Ian Ewing and Muriel Adèle Child; *m* 1st, 1940, Diana Smeed (*d* 1980), *d* of Major Harry Archer, DSO; one *s*; 2nd, 1984, Anne, *d* of Captain C. G. Chichester, DSO, RN and *widow* of Comdr Henry Wilkin. *Educ:* Royal Naval Coll., Dartmouth. In command of Destroyers during War of 1939–45; NATO Standing Group Staff, 1950–51; Imperial Defence Coll., 1952; in command of HMS Vanguard, 1953–54; Dir of Naval Staff Coll., Greenwich, 1954–56; Naval Sec. to First Lord of the Admiralty, 1956–58; Flag Officer Flotillas (Mediterranean), 1958–60; Adm. Commanding Reserves and Inspector of Recruiting, 1960–62; retd list, 1962. *Address:* 19 Reyntiens View, Odiham, Hants RG25 1AF. *T:* Odiham (0256) 703509. *Clubs:* Army and Navy; Royal Yacht Squadron (Naval Mem.).

EWING, Mrs Winifred Margaret; Member (SNP) European Parliament, since 1975, elected for Highlands and Islands, 1979, 1984 and 1989; *b* 10 July 1929; *d* of George Woodburn and Christina Bell Anderson; *m* 1956, Stewart Martin Ewing; two *s* one *d. Educ:* Queen's Park Sen. Sec. Sch.; University of Glasgow (MA, LLB). Qual. as Solicitor, 1952. Lectr in Law, Scottish Coll. of Commerce, 1954–56; Solicitor, practising on own account, 1956–. Sec., Glasgow Bar Assoc., 1961–67, Pres., 1970–71. MP (SNP): Hamilton, Nov. 1967–70; Moray and Nairn, Feb. 1974–1979; contested (SNP) Orkney and Shetland, 1983. Pres., Scottish National Party; Vice-President: Rainbow Group, 1989; Animal Welfare Intergroup, European Parliament, 1989. Mem., Lomé Assembly, 1981. Mem., Exec. Cttee, Scottish Council for Develt and Industry, 1972–. Pres., Glasgow Central Soroptimist Club, 1966–67. *Address:* 52 Queen's Drive, Glasgow G42 8DD. *T:* 041–423 1765.
See also M. A. Ewing.

EWINS, Prof. David John, CEng; FIMechE; Professor of Vibration Engineering, Mechanical Engineering Department, Imperial College of Science, Technology and Medicine, since 1983; *b* 25 March 1942; *s* of W. J. and P. Ewins; *m* 1964, Brenda Rene (*née* Chalk); three *d. Educ:* Kingswood Grammar Sch., Bristol; Imperial Coll., London (BScEng, ACGI, DScEng); Trinity Coll., Cambridge (PhD). MASME; FIMechE 1990. Res. Asst for Rolls-Royce Ltd, Cambridge Univ., 1966–67; Lectr, then Reader, in Mech. Engrg, Imperial Coll., 1967–83; formed Modal Testing Unit at Imperial Coll., 1981; Dir, Rolls-Royce Centre of Vibration Engrg, Imperial Coll., 1990–. Sen. Lectr, Chulalongkorn Univ., Bangkok, 1968–69; Maître de Conférences, INSA, Lyon, 1974–75; Visiting Professor: Virginia Poly and State Univ., USA, 1981; ETH, Zürich, 1986; Inst. Nat. Polytechnique de Grenoble, 1990. Consultant to: Rolls-Royce, 1969–; MoD, 1977–, and other organisations in Europe and USA. Chm., Dynamic Testing Agency, 1990–. Gov., Cranleigh Sch., 1990–. *Publications:* Modal Testing: Theory and Practice, 1984, 5th edn 1989; papers on vibration engrg in technical jls in UK, USA, France. *Recreations:* music (esp. piano duets), hill walking, travel, good food, French, bridge. *Address:* Imperial College, Exhibition Road, SW7 2BX. *T:* 071–589 5111. *Club:* Executive.

EWINS, Peter David; Managing Director, Maritime Defence Research Agency, since 1991; *b* 20 March 1943; *s* of John Samuel Ewins and Kathleen Ewins; *m* 1968, Barbara Irene Howland; two *s* one *d. Educ:* Imperial College London (BSc Eng); Cranfield Inst. of Technology (MSc). CEng. MRAeS. Joined RAE Farnborough, 1966, research on structl applications of composite materials; section head, 1974; staff of Chief Scientist, RAF, MoD, 1978; Head of Helicopters Res. Div., RAE, 1981; seconded to Cabinet Office (Civil

Service personnel policy), 1984; Dir, Nuclear Projects, MoD, 1987; Dir, ARE, MoD (PE), 1988–91. *Publications:* technical papers on structural composite materials in learned jls. *Recreations:* horticulture, walking, occasional tennis. *Address:* Defence Research Agency (Maritime Division), Portsdown, Cosham, Portsmouth PO6 4AA. *T:* Portsmouth (0705) 219999.

EWUSIE, Prof. Joseph Yanney; Professor of Biology, University of Bophuthatswana, since 1990; *b* 18 April 1927; *s* of Samuel Mainsa Wilson Ewusie and Elizabeth Dickson; *m* 1959, Stella Turkson (*d* 1989); four *s*, and one adopted *d*. *Educ:* Winneba Anglican Sch.; Mfantsipim Sch.; University Coll. of the Gold Coast; Univ. of Cambridge. BSc (London), PhD (Cantab). Lectr in Botany, Univ. of Ghana, 1957–62; Gen. Sec. (Chief Exec.), Ghana Academy of Sciences (highest learned and res. org. in Ghana), 1963–68; Univ. of Cape Coast: Associate Prof. of Botany, 1969–72, Prof., 1973–79; Head, Dept of Botany, 1969–73; Dean, Faculty of Science, 1971–74; Pro-Vice Chancellor, 1971–73; Vice Chancellor, 1973–78; Vis. Prof./Prof., Univs of Nairobi and Ahmadu Bello, Nigeria, 1979–80; Sec.-Gen., Pan African Inst. for Development, 1980–83; Prof. of Biology, Univ. of Swaziland, 1984–90. Mem. Exec. Cttee, ICSU, 1964–67. Founder and First Pres., Bophuthatswana Assoc. for Scientific Advancement, 1990. Member: Bimillenium Foundn, Washington DC, 1984–; NY Acad. of Sciences, 1984–. FWA 1963. Co-Founder and First Editor, Swaziland Jl of Sci. and Technol. Medal (Govt of Hungary) for internat. understanding between Ghana and Hungary, 1964; Dipl. of Merit, Internat. Acad. of Science, Letters and Arts, Rome, 1968; Dipl. of Honour, Internat. Inst. of Community Service, 1975; Ghana Scientist of the Year, Ghana Science Assoc., 1985. *Publications:* School Certificate Biology for Tropical Schools, 1964, 4th edn 1974; Tropical Biological Drawings, 1973; Elements of Tropical Ecology, 1980. *Address:* Department of Biology, University of Bophuthatswana, P/Bag X2046, Mmabotho, Bophuthatswana.

EXETER, 8th Marquess of, *cr* 1801; **William Michael Anthony Cecil;** Baron Burghley 1571; Earl of Exeter 1605; *b* 1 Sept. 1935; *s* of 7th Marquess of Exeter and Edith Lilian Csanady de Telegd (*d* 1954); *S* father, 1988; *m* 1967, Nancy Rose, *d* of Lloyd Arthur Meeker; one *s* one *d*. *Educ:* Eton. Rancher and businessman in 100 Mile House, 1954–. *Publications:* (jtly) Spirit of Sunrise, 1979; The Long View, 1985; The Rising Tide of Change, 1986; Living at the Heart of Creation, 1990. *Heir: s* Lord Burghley, *qv*. *Address:* Box 8, 100 Mile House, BC V0K 2E0, Canada. *T:* 604–395–2767; Mickleton House, Mickleton, Glos GL55 6RY. *T:* Mickleton (0386) 438251.

EXETER, Bishop of, since 1985; **Rt. Rev. (Geoffrey) Hewlett Thompson;** *b* 14 Aug. 1929; *o s* of late Lt-Col R. R. Thompson, MC, RAMC; *m* 1954, Elisabeth Joy Fausitt, BA (Oxon), *d* of late Col G. F. Taylor, MBE and Dr Frances Taylor; two *s* two *d*. *Educ:* Aldenham Sch.; Trinity Hall, Cambridge (MA); Cuddesdon Theol College. 2nd Lieut, Queen's Own Royal West Kent Regt, 1948–49 (Nat. Service). Ordained 1954. Curate, St Matthew, Northampton, 1954; Vicar: St Augustine, Wisbech, 1959; St Saviour, Folkestone, 1966; Bishop Suffragan of Willesden, 1974. Chairman: Community and Race Relations Unit, BCC, 1980–84 (Vice-Chm., 1976–80); Hospital Chaplaincies Council, 1991–. Introduced into House of Lords, 1990. *Recreations:* fell walking, reading, gardening, music. *Address:* The Palace, Exeter EX1 1HY. *T:* Exeter (0392) 72362. *Club:* United Oxford & Cambridge University.

EXETER, Dean of; *see* Eyre, Very Rev. R. M. S.

EXETER, Archdeacon of; *see* Richards, Ven. John.

EXMOUTH, 10th Viscount *cr* 1816; **Paul Edward Pellew;** Bt 1796 (Pellew of Treverry); Baron 1814; *b* 8 Oct. 1940; *s* of 9th Viscount Exmouth and Maria Luisa, Marquesa de Olias (Spain, *cr* 1652; *S* 1940), *d* of late Luis de Urquijo, Marques de Amurrio, Madrid; *S* father, 1970; *m* 1st, 1964 (marr. diss. 1974); one *d*; 2nd, 1975, Rosemary Countess of Burford; twin *s*. *Educ:* Downside. Mem. Cons. Party, House of Lords. Mem., Inst. of Dirs. *Heir: er twin s* Hon. Edward Francis Pellew, *b* 30 Oct. 1978. *Address:* Canonteign, near Exeter, Devon.

EXTON, Clive; scriptwriter and playwright; *b* 11 April 1930; *s* of late J. E. M. Brooks and Marie Brooks (*née* Rolfe); *m* 1951, Patricia Fletcher Ferguson (marr. diss. 1957); two *d*; *m* 1957, Margaret Josephine Reid; one *s* two *d*. *Educ:* Christ's Hospital. *TV plays:* No Fixed Abode, 1959; The Silk Purse; Where I Live; Some Talk of Alexander; Hold My Hand, Soldier; I'll Have You to Remember; The Big Eat; The Trial of Doctor Fancy; Land of my Dreams; The Close Prisoner; The Bone Yard; Conceptions of Murder (series); Are You Ready for the Music?; The Rainbirds; Killers (series); Stigma; Henry Intervenes; (with Tom Stoppard) The Boundary; The Crezz (series); Dick Barton—Special Agent (series); Wolf to the Slaughter, A Guilty Thing Surprised, Shake Hands for Ever (dramatizations of novels by Ruth Rendell); many scripts and script consultant for: Agatha Christie's Poirot; Jeeves and Wooster. *Stage plays:* Have You Any Dirty Washing, Mother Dear?; Twixt. *Films:* Night Must Fall; Isadora; Entertaining Mr Sloane; Ten Rillington Place; Running Scared; Doomwatch; The House in Nightmare Park; The Awakening. *Publications:* No Fixed Abode (in Six Granada Plays, anthol.), 1960; Have You Any Dirty Washing, Mother Dear? (in Plays of the Year, vol. 37), 1970. *Address:* c/o Peters, Fraser & Dunlop, Fifth Floor, The Chambers, Chelsea Harbour, Lots Road, SW10 0XF. *T:* 071–376 7676.

EXTON, Rodney Noel, JP; MA; Deputy Chairman, Johansens Ltd, Cambridge, since 1989; *b* 28 Dec. 1927; *s* of Noel Exton and Winifred (*née* Stokes); *m* 1961, Pamela Sinclair (*née* Hardie); two step *s* two step *d*. *Educ:* Clifton Coll.; Lincoln Coll., Oxford (MA Mod. Langs); Corpus Christi Coll., Cambridge (PGCE). FInstD. Served Royal Hampshire Regt, 1946–48. Asst Master, Eton, 1951–52; Internat. Research Fund Schol. to USA, 1952; Asst Master, Mill Hill Sch., 1953–63; Royal Commonwealth schol. to Australia, 1959–60; Headmaster, Reed's Sch., 1964–77; Walter Hines Page schol. to USA, 1971; Dir, ISCO, 1978–88. Vice-Chm., British Atlantic Educn Cttee, 1972–78; Chm., Exec. Cttee, GAP, 1982–87. Man. Dir, Exton Hotels Co. Ltd, 1966–80; Chm., Kandic Ltd, 1972–82; Dir, Purbeck Properties Ltd, 1986–88. Dir, Vocational Guidance Assoc., 1988–90. Hampshire County Cricket XI, 1946. JP Surrey, 1968. *Recreation:* getting out of bunkers. *Address:* 85 Mount Ararat Road, Richmond, Surrey TW10 6PL. *T:* 081–940 0305. *Clubs:* MCC; Royal Mid-Surrey Golf; Vincent's (Oxford).

EYERS, Patrick Howard Caines, CMG 1985; LVO 1966; HM Diplomatic Service; Ambassador to Jordan, since 1991; *b* 4 Sept. 1933; *s* of late Arthur Leopold Caines Eyers and Nora Lilian Eyers; *m* 1960, Heidi, *d* of Werner Rüsch, Dipl. Ing, and Helene (*née* Feil); two *s* one *d*. *Educ:* Clifton Coll.; Gonville and Caius Coll., Cambridge (BA Hons 1957); Institut Universitaire de Hautes Etudes Internationales, Geneva. RA, 1952–54. Asst Editor, Grolier Soc. Inc., New York, 1957; HM Foreign (now Diplomatic) Service, 1959; ME Centre for Arabic Studies, 1960; Dubai, 1961; Brussels, 1964; FO, 1966; Aden, 1969; Abidjan, 1970; British Mil. Govt, Berlin, 1971; FCO, 1974; Counsellor, Bonn, 1977; Head, Republic of Ireland Dept, FCO, 1981; RCDS, 1984; Ambassador: to Zaire, the Congo, Rwanda and Burundi, 1985–87; to Algeria, 1987–89; to GDR, 1990. Officer, Order of Leopold, Belgium, 1966. *Recreations:* music, skiing, sailing. *Address:* c/o Foreign and Commonwealth Office, SW1. *Clubs:* Ski of GB, Kandahar Ski, Hurlingham.

EYNON, Prof. John Marles, OBE 1990; RIBA; FSA; Professor of Architecture, University of Wales, and Head, Welsh School of Architecture, 1980–87, now Professor Emeritus; *b* 3 Jan. 1923; *s* of Philip Stanley Eynon and Gwendoline Eynon (*née* Marles); *m* 1950, Yvonne Marie, *e d* of Claire Faber (*née* Vermuse) and Vivian Valdemar Faber. *Educ:* Cardiff High Sch.; Welsh Sch. of Architecture, Univ. of Wales (MA, Dip. Arch.) ARIBA 1950, FRIBA 1963, FSA 1974. Military service: Captain RE, regtl duties, wounded, training, staff work. Chartered and Registered Architect, 1950; with Alwyn Lloyd & Gordon, later Alex Gordon & Partners, 1950–70; private practice and consultancy (historic buildings and conservation), 1970–. Lectr, Sen. Lectr, Prof. of Architecture, Welsh Sch. of Architecture, Univ. of Wales, 1956–87. Member: Historic Buildings Council for Wales, 1967–; Welsh Arts Council, 1978–89; Craft Cttee for Wales (Chm.), Craft Council, 1970–89; Cambrian Archaeol. Assoc., 1969–; Assoc. of Artists and Designers in Wales, 1970–; Royal Welsh Agricl Soc., 1977; Llandaff Diocesan Adv. Cttee, Church in Wales, 1988–. Prince of Wales Awards, 1976, 1977; Europa Nostra Award, 1985. *Publications:* contribs to learned jls. *Recreation:* painter (retrospective exhibition, Cardiff, 1976). *Address:* 39 Waterloo Road, Penylan, Cardiff CF3 7BJ. *T:* Cardiff (0222) 485098.

EYRE, Brian Leonard, DSc; CEng; CPhys; Board Member, since 1987, Deputy Chairman, since 1989, and Chief Executive, since 1990, United Kingdom Atomic Energy Authority; *b* 29 Nov. 1933; *s* of Leonard George and Mabel Eyre; *m* 1965, Elizabeth Caroline (*née* Rackham); two *s*. *Educ:* Greenford Grammar Sch.; Univ. of Surrey (BSc, DSc). FIM; FInstP. Research Officer, CEGB, 1959–62; Gp Leader, UKAEA, Harwell, 1962–79; Prof., Materials Science, Univ. of Liverpool, 1979–84; Dir, Fuel and Engrg Technology, UKAEA, Risley, 1984–87. FRSA 1984. *Publications:* over 100 papers in Procs Royal Soc., Philosophical Magazine, Acta Metallurgica, etc. *Recreations:* walking, mountaineering. *Address:* UKAEA, 11 Charles II Street, SW1Y 4QP.

EYRE, Hon. Dean Jack; New Zealand High Commissioner to Canada, 1968–73 and 1976–80; *b* Westport, NZ, 1914; *m*; two *s* one *d*. *Educ:* Hamilton High Sch.; Auckland University Coll. Served War of 1939–45, Lieut in RNVR. Electrical importer and manufacturer. MP (Nat) North Shore, 1949–66; Minister of Customs, Industries and Commerce, 1954–57; Minister of Social Security and Tourist and Health Resorts, 1956–57; Minister of Housing, State Advances and Defence, New Zealand, 1957; Minister in Charge of Police, 1960–63; Minister of Defence, 1960–66; Minister i/c Tourism, 1961–66. *Recreations:* yachting, fishing. *Address:* 517 Wilbrod Street, Ottawa, Ontario K1N 5R4, Canada. *Clubs:* Royal New Zealand Yacht Squadron, Northern, Officers (Auckland); Wellington (Wellington); Royal Ottawa Golf.

EYRE, Sir Graham (Newman), Kt 1989; QC 1970; a Recorder of the Crown Court, since 1975; *b* 9 Jan. 1931; *s* of Newman Eyre; *m* 1954, Jean Dalrymple Walker; one *s* three *d*. *Educ:* Marlborough Coll.; Trinity Coll., Cambridge. BA 1953, LLB 1954, MA 1958. Council Prizewinner, 1954. Called to Bar, Middle Temple, 1954, Harmsworth Law Schol., 1955, Bencher, Middle Temple, 1979; Mem., Lincoln's Inn, 1971; Head of Chambers, 1981. Inspector, The London Airports Inquiries, 1981–84. *Publications:* Rating Law and Valuation, 1963; contrib. Jl Planning Law. *Address:* Walberton House, Walberton, Arundel, West Sussex BN18 0PJ; 8 New Square, Lincoln's Inn, WC2A 3QP. *Club:* Athenæum.

EYRE, Maj.-Gen. Sir James (Ainsworth Campden Gabriel), KCVO 1986 (CVO 1978); CBE 1980 (OBE 1975); Director, Westminster Associates International Ltd, since 1989; *b* 2 Nov. 1930; *s* of Edward Joseph Eyre and Hon. Dorothy Elizabeth Anne Pelline (*née* Lyon-Dalberg-Acton); *m* 1967, Monica Ruth Esther Smyth; one *s* one *d*. *Educ:* Harvard Univ. (BA, LLB). Commissioned RHG, 1955; Commanding Officer, The Blues and Royals, 1970–73; GSO 1 HQ London District, 1973–75; Officer Commanding Household Cavalry and Silver Stick, 1975–78; Col GS HQ Northern Ireland, 1978–80; Sec., Chiefs of Staff Cttee, MoD, 1980–82; Dir of Defence Programmes Staff (Concepts), MoD, 1982–83; GOC London Dist and Maj. Gen. Comdg Household Div., 1983–86. *Recreations:* racing, shooting. *Address:* Somerville House, East Garston, Berks RG16 7EY. *Club:* Turf.

EYRE, Sir Reginald (Edwin), Kt 1984; Chairman: Birmingham Heartlands Ltd (East Birmingham Urban Development Agency), since 1987; Birmingham Cable Corporation Ltd, since 1988; Deputy Chairman, Commission for the New Towns, since 1988; *b* 28 May 1924; *s* of late Edwin Eyre; *m* 1978, Anne Clements; one *d*. *Educ:* King Edward's Camp Hill Sch., Birmingham; Emmanuel Coll., Cambridge (MA). Midshipman and Sub-Lieut, RNVR, War of 1939–45. Admitted a Solicitor, 1950; Senior Partner, Eyre & Co., solicitors, Birmingham, 1951–91. Hon. Consultant, Poor Man's Lawyer, 1948–58. Conservative Political Centre: Chm., W Midlands Area, 1960–63; Chm., National Advisory Cttee, 1964–66. Contested (C) Birmingham (Northfield) 1959; MP (C) Birmingham Hall Green, May 1965–87. Opposition Whip, 1966–70; a Lord Comr of the Treasury, June-Sept. 1970; Comptroller of HM Household, 1970–72; Parliamentary Under-Secretary of State: DoE, 1972–74; Dept of Trade, 1979–82; Dept of Transport, 1982–83. A Vice Chm., Cons. Party Organisation, 1975–79; Founder Chm., Cons. Parly Urban Affairs Cttee, 1974–79. *Publication:* Hope for our Towns and Cities, 1977. *Address:* 45 Aylesford Street, SW1V 3RY; 1041 Stratford Road, Birmingham B28 8AS. *Clubs:* Carlton; Birmingham (Birmingham).

EYRE, Richard Charles Hastings; theatre, film and TV director; Artistic Director, Royal National Theatre, since 1988 (Associate Director, 1981–88); *b* 28 March 1943; *m* 1973, Susan Elizabeth Birtwistle; one *d*. *Educ:* Sherborne Sch.; Peterhouse, Cambridge (BA). Asst Dir, Phoenix Theatre, Leicester, 1966; Lyceum Theatre, Edinburgh: Associate Dir, 1967–70; Dir of Productions, 1970–72; freelance director: Liverpool, 7:84 Co., West End; tours for British Council: W Africa, 1971; SE Asia, 1972; Artistic Dir, Nottingham Playhouse, 1973–78; Prod./Dir, Play for Today, BBC TV, 1978–80; Director: The Churchill Play, Nottingham, 1974; Comedians, Old Vic and Wyndhams, 1976; Touched, Nottingham, 1977; Hamlet, Royal Court, 1980; Edmond, Royal Court, 1985; Kafka's Dick, Royal Court, 1986; National Theatre: Guys and Dolls (SWET Director of the Year, 1982, Standard Best Director, 1982), The Beggar's Opera, and Schweyk in the Second World War, 1982; The Government Inspector, 1985; Futurists, 1986 (Best Production Award, Time Out, 1986); The Changeling, Bartholomew Fair, 1988; Hamlet, The Voysey Inheritance, 1989; Racing Demon, Richard III, 1990; White Chameleon, Napoli Milionaria, 1991. Films: The Ploughman's Lunch (Evening Standard Award for Best Film, 1983), Loose Connections, 1983; Laughterhouse, 1984, released as Singleton's Pluck, USA, 1985 (TV Prize, Venice Film Fest.). Films for TV: The Imitation Game, Pasmore, 1980; Country, 1981; The Insurance Man, 1986 (Special Prize, Tokyo TV Fest., 1986); Past Caring, 1986; Tumbledown, 1988 (BAFTA Award for best single drama, Italia RAI Prize, RTS Award, Press Guild Award, Tokyo Prize); v., 1988 (RTS Award). STV Awards for Best Production, 1969, 1970 and 1971; De Sica Award, Sorrento Film Fest., 1986. *Address:* c/o Royal National Theatre, South Bank, SE1 9PX. *T:* 071–928 2033.

EYRE, Very Rev. Richard Montague Stephens; Dean of Exeter, since 1981; *b* 1929; *s* of Montague Henry and Ethel Mary Eyre; *m* 1963, Anne Mary Bentley; two *d*. *Educ:*

Charterhouse; Oriel Coll. and St Stephen's House, Oxford. MA Oxon. Deacon 1956, priest 1957; Curate, St Mark's Church, Portsea, 1956–59; Tutor and Chaplain, Chichester Theological Coll., 1959–62; Chaplain, Eastbourne Coll., 1962–65; Vicar of Arundel, 1965–73; Vicar of Good Shepherd, Brighton, 1973–75; Archdeacon of Chichester, 1975–81; Treasurer of Chichester Cathedral, 1978–81. Mem., Gen. Synod of C of E, 1985–. *Publication:* Faith in God?, 1990. *Recreations:* golf, music, travel, gardening. *Address:* The Deanery, Exeter, Devon. *T:* Exeter (0392) 72697. *Club:* United Oxford & Cambridge University.

EYRE, Ronald; freelance theatre and television director; writer; *b* 13 April 1929; *s* of Christopher Eyre and Mabel Smith. *Educ:* Queen Elizabeth Grammar Sch., Wakefield, Yorks; University Coll., Oxford (MA English Lang. and Lit.). English Master, Queen Elizabeth Grammar Sch., Blackburn, 1952–54; Sen. English Master, Bromsgrove Sch., 1954–56; Producer, BBC Television, 1956–64. *Theatre Director: RSC:* Much Ado About Nothing, 1971; London Assurance, London, 1972 and New York, 1974; The Marquis of Keith, 1974; Saratoga, 1978; Othello, 1979; The Winter's Tale, 1981; *West End:* Enjoy; Three Months Gone, 1970 (also Royal Court); Voyage Round My Father, 1971; Habeas Corpus, 1973; The Secret Policeman's Other Ball, 1981; Hobson's Choice, 1982; Messiah, 1983; A Patriot for Me, 1983; When We Are Married, 1986; J. J. Farr, 1987; The Sneeze, 1988; A Walk in the Woods, 1988; *Theatre Royal, Stratford East:* Widower's Houses, 1965; *Hampstead Theatre Club:* Events While Guarding the Bofors Gun, 1966; Bakke's Night of Fame, 1968; *Royal Court:* Veterans, 1972; A Pagan Place, 1972; *Chichester Festival Theatre and Haymarket Theatre:* A Patriot for Me, 1983; *National Theatre:* Mrs Warren's Profession, 1970; Saint Joan, 1984; *Stratford, Ontario:* The Government Inspector, 1985; *Shockiku Co., Tokyo:* The Dresser, 1988. *Opera Producer:* Beatrice and Benedict, Buxton, 1980 (also translator); Mussorgsky's Marriage, Nexus Opera, 1981; Falstaff, Los Angeles and Covent Garden, 1982 and Teatro Communale, Florence, 1983, new prodn, Covent Garden, 1984; Jason, Buxton, 1984 (also translator); Curlew River, Nexus Opera and BBC, 1986; Peter Grimes, Opera North, 1989. *Playwright:* theatre: Something's Burning, 1973; television: I'm not Stopping, 1963; A Crack in the Ice, 1964 (theatre, 1966); Bruno, 1965; The Single Passion, 1967; The Glory of Llewellyn Smiley, 1967. Writer and Presenter: The Long Search, BBC, 1977; Seven Ages, BBC, 1987; Midweek, 1988; Frontiers: the Irish border, 1990; Not on Sunday, 1990–91. *Publication:* Ronald Eyre on The Long Search, 1979. *Address:* c/o L. Dalzell, Suite 12, 17 Broad Court, Covent Garden, WC2. *T:* 071–379 0875.

EYRES MONSELL, family name of **Viscount Monsell.**

EYSENCK, Prof. Hans Jürgen, PhD, DSc; Professor of Psychology, University of London, Institute of Psychiatry, 1955–83, Professor Emeritus, since 1983; Director, Psychological Department, Maudsley Hospital, 1946–83; *b* 4 March 1916; *s* of Eduard Anton and Ruth Eysenck; *m* 1st, 1938, Margaret Malcolm Davies (decd); one *s*; 2nd, 1950, Sybil Bianca Giuletta Rostal; three *s* one *d. Educ:* school in Germany, France and England; Univ. of London. BA 1938, PhD 1940, DSc 1964. Senior Research Psychologist, Mill Hill Emergency Hosp., 1942–46; Reader in Psychology, Univ. of London (Inst. of Psychiatry), 1950–54; Visiting Prof., Univ. of Pennsylvania, 1949–50; Visiting Prof., Univ. of California, Berkeley, 1954. Pres., Internat. Soc. for Study of Individual Differences, 1983–85. Dist. Scientist Award, Amer. Psychol Assoc., 1988. *Publications:* Dimensions of Personality, 1947; The Scientific Study of Personality, 1952; The Structure of Human Personality, 1953; Uses and Abuses of Psychology, 1953; The Psychology of Politics, 1954; Sense and Nonsense in Psychology, 1957; Dynamics of Anxiety and Hysteria, 1957; Perceptual Processes and Mental Illness, 1957; (ed) Handbook of Abnormal Psychology, 1960, 2nd edn, 1972; (ed) Behaviour Therapy and the Neuroses, 1960; (ed) Experiments in Personality, 1960; (ed) Experiments with Drugs, 1963; (ed) Experiments in Behaviour Therapy, 1964; (ed) Experiments in Motivation, 1964; Crime and Personality, 1964; Causes and Cures of Neurosis, 1965; Fact and Fiction in Psychology, 1965; Smoking, Health and Personality, 1965; The Biological Basis of Personality, 1968; Personality Structure and Measurement, 1969; Race, Intelligence and Education, 1971; Psychology is about People, 1972; (ed) Readings in Introversion-Extraversion, 3 vols, 1971; (ed) Lexikon der Psychologie, 3 vols, 1972; The Measurement of Intelligence, 1973; The Inequality of Man, 1973; (ed jtly) The Experimental Study of Freudian Theories, 1973; (ed jtly) Encyclopaedia of Psychology, 1973; (with Glenn Wilson) Know Your Own Personality, 1975; (ed) Case Studies in Behaviour Therapy, 1976; Sex and Personality, 1976; (with S. B. G. Eysenck) Psychoticism as a Dimension of Personality 1976; You and Neurosis, 1977; Die Zukunft der Psychologie, 1977; (with D. K. B. Nias) Sex, Violence and the Media, 1978; The Structure and Measurement of Intelligence, 1979; (with Glenn Wilson) The Psychology of Sex, 1979; The Causes and Effects of Smoking, 1980; (with M. W. Eysenck) Mindwatching, 1981; (ed) A Model for Personality, 1981; (with J. Kamin) Intelligence: the battle for the mind, 1981 (US as The Intelligence Controversy, 1981); (with D. K. B. Nias) Astrology: Science or Superstition?, 1982; Personality, Genetics and Behaviour, 1982; (ed) A Model for Intelligence, 1982; (with Carl Sargent) Explaining the Unexplained, 1982; I Do: your guide to happy marriage, 1983; (with Carl Sargent) Know your own psi-Q, 1984; (with M. W. Eysenck) Personality and Individual Differences, 1985; Decline and Fall of the Freudian Empire, 1985; (with L. Eaves and N. Martin) Genes, Culture and Personality, 1989; (with G. Gudjousson) Causes and Cures of Criminality, 1989; Rebel with a Cause (autobiog.), 1990; Smoking, Personality and Stress: environmental factors in the prevention of cancer and coronary disease, 1991; Editor-in-Chief: Behaviour Research and Therapy, 1963–78; Personality and Individual Differences, 1980–; (ed) International Monographs of Experimental Psychology; some 900 articles in British, American, German, Spanish and French Jls of Psychology. *Recreations:* walking, tennis, chess, detective stories, squash. *Address:* 10 Dorchester Drive, SE24.
See also M. W. Eysenck.

EYSENCK, Prof. Michael William; Professor and Head of Department of Psychology, Royal Holloway and Bedford New College, University of London, since 1987; *b* 8 Feb.

1944; *s* of Hans Jürgen Eysenck, *qv* and late Margaret Malcolm Eysenck (*née* Davies); *m* 1975, Mary Christine Kabyn; one *s* two *d. Educ:* Dulwich Coll.; University College London (BA Psych, 1st cl. Hons; Rosa Morrison Medal for outstanding arts graduate, 1965); Birkbeck Coll., London (PhD Psych). Asst Lectr, Lectr and Reader in Psychology, Birkbeck Coll., Univ. of London, 1965–87. Vis. Prof., Univ. of S Florida, Tampa, 1980. Chm., Cognitive Psych. Section, BPsS, 1982–87. Editor, European Jl of Cognitive Psych., 1989–. *Publications:* Human Memory, 1977; (with H. J. Eysenck) Mindwatching, 1981; Attention and Arousal: cognition and performance, 1982; A Handbook of Cognitive Psychology, 1984; (with H. J. Eysenck) Personality and Individual Differences, 1985; (with J. T. Richardson and D. W. Piper) Student Learning: research in education and cognitive psychology, 1987; (with H. J. Eysenck) Mindwatching: why we behave the way we do, 1989; Happiness: facts and myths, 1990; (ed) The Blackwell Dictionary of Cognitive Psychology, 1990; International Review of Cognitive Psychology, 1990; (with M. T. Keane) Cognitive Psychology: a student's handbook, 1990; Anxiety: the cognitive perspective, 1992; numerous book chapters and contribs to Qly Jl of Exptl Psychology, Jl of Exptl Psychology, Jl of Abnormal Psychology, British Jl of Clin. Psychology, Psychol Bull., and others. *Recreations:* travel, tennis, golf, walking, bridge. *Address:* Department of Psychology, Royal Holloway and Bedford New College, University of London, Egham Hill, Egham, Surrey TW20 0EX. *T:* Egham (0784) 434455.

EYTON, Anthony John Plowden, RA 1986 (ARA 1976); RWS 1988 (ARWS 1985); RWA 1984; NEAC 1985; Visiting Teacher, Royal Academy Schools, since 1963; *b* 17 May 1923; *s* of late Captain John Seymour Eyton, ICS, author, and of Phyllis Annie Tyser; *m* 1960, Frances Mary Capell, MA (marr. diss.); three *d. Educ:* Twyford Sch.; Canford Sch.; Dept of Fine Art, Reading Univ.; Camberwell Sch. of Art (NDD). Served War, 1939–45, Cameronians (Scottish Rifles), Hampshire Regt, and Army Educn Corps. Abbey Major Scholarship in Painting, 1950–51. Elected Mem., London Gp, 1958. One Man Exhibitions: St George's Gall., 1955; Galerie de Seine, 1957; New Art Centre, 1959, 1961, 1968; New Grafton Gall., 1973; William Darby Gall., 1975; Newcastle Polytechnic Art Gall., 1978; Browse and Darby, 1978, 1981, 1985, 1987, 1990; Austin Desmond Gall., 1990; Retrospective Exhibn, S London Art Gall., Towner Art Gall., Eastbourne, and Plymouth Art Gall., 1981; Hong Kong and the New Territories exhibn, Imperial War Museum, 1983 (subsequent to commission); work included in British Painting 1945–77, RA. Work in public collections: Tate Gall.; Arts Council; Plymouth Art Gall.; Towner Art Gall., Eastbourne; Carlisle Art Gall.; DoE; RA; Government Picture Coll.; BR; Contemp. Art Soc.; Guildhall Art Gall. Fellowship awarded by Grocers' Co. (for work and travel in Italy), 1974. Hon. Mem., Pastel Soc., 1986; Hon. ROI 1988. Prize, John Moore's Exhibn, Liverpool, 1972; First Prize, Second British Internat. Drawing Biennale, Middlesbrough, 1975; Charles Wollaston Award, RA, 1981. *Recreation:* gardening. *Address:* 166 Brixton Road, SW9 6AU.

EZEILO, Prof. James Okoye Chukuka, CON 1979; PhD; Professor of Mathematics, University of Nigeria; Director, National Mathematical Centre, Abuja, since 1988; *b* 17 Jan. 1930; *s* of Josiah Ezeilo and Janet Ezeilo; *m* 1960, Phoebe Uchechuku; two *s* two *d. Educ:* Dennis Memorial Grammar Sch., Onitsha; University Coll., Ibadan (MSc London); Queens' Coll., Cambridge (PhD). University of Ibadan: Lectr in Maths, 1958–62; Sen. Lectr in Maths, 1962–64; Prof. of Maths, 1964–66; University of Nigeria: Prof. of Maths, 1966–75, 1980–; Vice-Chancellor, 1975–78. Vice-Chancellor, Bayero Univ., Nigeria, 1978–79. Benedict Dist. Prof. of Maths, Carleton Coll., 1979; Vis. Prof. of Maths, Howard Univ., 1979–80. President: Math. Assoc. of Nigeria, 1972–74; Nigerian Math. Soc., 1984–; Mem., Nigerian Council for Science and Technol., 1970–75; Fellow and Foundation Mem., Nigerian Acad. of Science. Hon. DSc Maiduguri, 1989. *Publications:* numerous papers on differential equations in math. jls. *Recreation:* gardening. *Address:* Department of Mathematics, University of Nigeria, Nsukka, Nigeria. *Clubs:* Athenæum; Rotary (Nsukka) (Charter Pres.).

EZRA, family name of **Baron Ezra.**

EZRA, Baron *cr* 1983 (Life Peer), of Horsham in the County of West Sussex; **Derek Ezra;** Kt 1974; MBE 1945; Chairman: Associated Heat Services plc, since 1966; Energy and Technical Services Group Ltd, since 1990; Associated Gas Supplies Ltd, since 1987; *b* 23 Feb. 1919; *s* of David and Lillie Ezra; *m* 1950, Julia Elizabeth Wilkins. *Educ:* Monmouth Sch.; Magdalene Coll., Cambridge (MA, Hon. Fellow, 1977). Army, 1939–47. Joined NCB, 1947; representative of NCB at Cttees of OEEC and ECE, 1948–52; Mem. of UK Delegn to High Authority of European Coal and Steel Community, 1952–56; Dep. Regional Sales Manager, NCB, 1956–58; Regional Sales Manager, 1958–60; Dir-Gen. of Marketing, NCB, 1960–65; NCB Bd Mem., 1965–67; Dep. Chm., 1967–71; Chm., 1971–82. Chairman: J. H. Sankey & Son Ltd, 1977–82; Petrolex PLC, 1982–85; Throgmorton Trust PLC, 1984–91; Director: British Fuel Co., 1966–82; Solvay SA, 1979–90; Redland PLC, 1982–89; Supervisory Bd, Royal Boskalis Westminster NV, 1982–85. Industrial Advr, Morgan Grenfell & Co. Ltd, 1982–88. Chm., NICG, 1972 and 1980–81; President: Nat. Materials Handling Centre, 1979; Coal Industry Soc., 1981–86 (Chm., 1961); W European Coal Producers' Assoc., 1976–79; BSI, 1983–86; Economic Res. Council, 1985–; Inst. of Trading Standards Admin, 1987–; Vice-Pres., BIM, 1978 (Chm., 1976–78); Chm., British Iron and Steel Consumers' Council, 1983–86; Member: BOTB, 1972–82 (Chm., European Trade Cttee); Cons. Cttee, ECSC, 1973–82 (Pres., 1978–79); Adv. Council for Energy Conservation, 1974–79; Adv. Bd, Petrofina SA, 1982–90; Internat. Adv. Bd, Creditanstalt Bankverein, 1982–90; Energy Commn, 1977–79; Ct of Governors, Administrative Staff Coll., 1971–82; Internat. Adv. Bd, Banca Nazionale del Lavoro, 1984–; Governor, London Business Sch., 1973–82. Pres., Keep Britain Tidy Gp, 1985–89 (Chm., 1979–85). Hon. DSc Cranfield, 1979; Hon. LLD Leeds, 1982. Bronze Star (USA), 1945; Grand Officer, Italian Order of Merit, 1979; Comdr, Luxembourg Order of Merit, 1981; Officer of Légion d'Honneur, 1981. *Publications:* Coal and Energy, 1978; The Energy Debate, 1983. *Address:* House of Lords, Westminster, SW1A 0PW. *T:* 071-219 3180.

F

FABER, Julian Tufnell; Chairman: Willis Faber Ltd, 1972–77; Cornhill Insurance plc, 1986–88 (Director, 1972–88); *b* 6 April 1917; *s* of late Alfred and Edith Faber; *m* 1944, Lady (Ann) Caroline, *e d* of 1st Earl of Stockton, OM, PC, FRS, and late Lady Dorothy Macmillan; four *s* one *d*. *Educ:* Winchester; Trinity Coll., Cambridge. Joined Willis, Faber & Dumas Ltd, 1938. Served Welsh Guards (Major 2nd Bn), 1939–45. Director: Willis, Faber & Dumas Ltd, 1952; Willis, Faber & Dumas (Agencies) Ltd, 1965; Taisho Marine & Fire Insurance Co. (UK) Ltd, 1972 (Chm.); Willis Faber (Middle East) SAL, 1973; Morgan Grenfell Ltd, 1974–77; Allianz International Insurance Co., 1974. Mem. Bd of Governors, Summer Fields Sch., Oxford. Member: MCC Cttee, 1981–84; Kent CCC Cttee, 1977–84. *Address:* Fisher's Gate, Withyham, E Sussex; Flat 4, 17 Sloane Court West, SW3. *Clubs:* White's, City of London, MCC.

FABER, Michael Leslie Ogilvie; Professorial Fellow, Institute of Development Studies, Sussex University, since 1982 (Director, 1982–87); *b* 12 Aug. 1929; *s* of George and Kathleen Faber; *m* 1956, Diana Catriona Howard; two *s* twin *d*. *Educ:* Avon Old Farms, USA; Eton; Magdalen Coll., Oxford (MA); Univ. of Michigan. MA Cantab. Served 11th Hussars, PAO, Germany, 1948–49. Merchant Seaman, 1953–54. Claims Adjuster, Amer. Internat. Underwriters, Japan and Korea, 1954; Foreign Correspondent for Sunday Times, Observer, and Economist in FE, ME, N and Central Africa, 1954–60; Lectr in Econs, UCRN, 1958–60; community develt worker with Danilo Dolci in Sicily, 1961; Lectr in Econs, UWI, 1962–63; Sen. Economist and Under-Sec., Govt of Zambia, 1964–67; Dept of Applied Econs, Cambridge, 1968; Overseas Develt Gp, UEA, 1969–78; Dir, Tech. Assistance Gp, Commonwealth Secretariat, 1972–75 and 1978–82. Member: Council, Overseas Develt Inst., 1982–; Bd, Commonwealth Develt Corp., 1988–. Pres., UK Chapter, Soc. for Internat. Develt, 1986–. Leader, UNDP/IBRD Mission to PNG, 1972; specialist negotiator of debt and resource agreements. *Publications:* Economic Structuralism and its Relevance, 1965; (with J. Potter) Towards Economic Independence, 1971; (ed with Dudley Seers) The Crisis in Economic Planning, 1972; (with R. Brown) Mining Agreements: law and policy, 1977; (with R. Brown) Changing the Rules of the Game, 1980; Conciliatory Debt Reduction: why it must come and how it could come, 1988; Beware of Debtspeak, 1988. *Address:* The Combe, Glynde, Lewes, Sussex BN8 6RP. *Clubs:* Brooks's; Lewes Golf.

FABER, Sir Richard (Stanley), KCVO 1980; CMG 1977; FRSL; HM Diplomatic Service, retired; Ambassador to Algeria, 1977–81; *b* 6 Dec. 1924; *er s* of late Sir Geoffrey Faber and of Enid, *d* of Sir Henry Erle Richards, KCSI, KC; unmarried. *Educ:* Westminster Sch.; Christ Church, Oxford (MA). RNVR, 1943–46. 1st cl. Lit. Hum. Oxon; Pres., Oxford Union Soc., 1949. Joined HM Foreign (subseq. Diplomatic) Service, 1950; service in FO and in Baghdad, Paris, Abidjan, Washington; Head of Rhodesia Political Dept, FCO, 1967–69; Counsellor: The Hague, 1969–73; Cairo, 1973–75; Asst Under Sec. of State, FCO, 1975–77. Hon. Treas., RSL, 1986–. *Publications:* Beaconsfield and Bolingbroke, 1961; The Vision and the Need: Late Victorian Imperialist Aims, 1966; Proper Stations: Class in Victorian Fiction, 1971; French and English, 1975; The Brave Courtier (biog. of Sir William Temple), 1983; High Road to England, 1985; Young England, 1987. *Address:* 85B Cherry Drive, Canterbury, Kent CT2 8ER. *T:* Canterbury (0227) 764363. *Club:* Travellers'.

See also T. E. Faber.

FABER, Thomas Erle, PhD; Chairman, Geoffrey Faber Holdings Ltd (formerly Faber & Faber (Publishers) Ltd), since 1977 (Director since 1969); Lecturer in Physics, University of Cambridge, since 1959; Fellow of Corpus Christi College, Cambridge, since 1953; *b* 25 April 1927; *s* of Sir Geoffrey Faber; *m* 1st, 1959, Penelope (*d* 1983), *d* of Clive Morton, actor; two *s* two *d*; 2nd, 1986, Dr Elisabeth van Houts; one *s* one *d*. *Educ:* Oundle Sch.; Trinity Coll., Cambridge (MA, PhD). Univ. of Cambridge: Res. Fellow, Trinity Coll., 1950–53; Univ. Demonstr, 1953–58; Armourers' and Brasiers' Fellow, 1958–59. Treasurer, Corpus Christi Coll., 1963–76. *Publications:* Introduction to the Theory of Liquid Metals, 1972; papers on superconductivity, liquid metals and liquid crystals. *Recreations:* walking, shooting. *Address:* The Old Vicarage, Thompson's Lane, Cambridge CB5 8AQ. *T:* Cambridge (0223) 356685.

See also Sir R. S. Faber.

FABIAN, Prof. Andrew Christopher; Royal Society Research Professor, Institute of Astronomy, University of Cambridge, since 1982; Fellow of Darwin College, Cambridge, since 1983; *b* 20 Feb. 1948; *s* of John Archibald and Daphne Monica Fabian; *m* 1971 (marr. diss. 1991); one *s* one *d*; *m* 1991, Dr Caroline Susan Crawford. *Educ:* Daventry Grammar Sch.; King's Coll., London (BSc Physics); University Coll. London (PhD). SRC post doctoral research asst, University Coll. London, 1972–73; Institute of Astronomy, Cambridge: SRC post doctoral Fellow, 1973–75; SRC PDRA, 1975–77; Radcliffe Fellow in Astronomy, 1977–81. *Publications:* contribs to Monthly Notices RAS, Astrophys. Jl, Nature, etc. *Address:* Institute of Astronomy, Madingley Road, Cambridge CB3 0HA.

FABIAN, (Andrew) Paul; HM Diplomatic Service, retired; Chief Secretary, Turks and Caicos Islands, since 1990; *b* 23 May 1930; *s* of late Andrew Taggart Fabian and Edith Mary Whorwell; *m* 1st, Elisabeth Vivien Chapman; one *s* two *d*; 2nd, 1983, Eryll Francesca Dickinson. *Educ:* Mitcham County School; Reading; St Paul's; Wadham College, Oxford (scholar; MA). Singapore Engineer Regt, 1953–54; Tanganyika, 1955–64 (on secondment to Foreign Office, serving at Usumbura, 1961–64); HM Diplomatic Service, 1964; served Lusaka, Ankara, New Delhi, Islamabad, Karachi; High Comr, Nuku'alofa, Tonga, 1987–90. *Publication:* Delhi Post Bedside Book (ed), 1977. *Recreations:* chess, reading, bird-watching. *Address:* Chief Secretary's Office, Government Secretariat, Grand Turk, Turks and Caicos Islands, WI; La Guionie. *Club:* United Oxford & Cambridge University.

FABIUS, Laurent; President, French National Assembly, since 1988 (Deputy for Seine Maritime, National Assembly, 1978–81, re-elected 1981, 1986); *b* 20 Aug. 1946; *s* of André Fabius and Louise Fabius (*née* Mortimer); *m* 1981, Françoise Castro; two *s*. *Educ:* Lycée Janson-de-Sailly; Lycée Louis-le-Grand; Ecole Normale Supérieure, Paris; Institut d'Etudes Politiques, Paris (Agrégé des lettres); Ecole Nationale d'Administration. Conseil d'Etat, 1973–81; First Deputy Mayor, Grand-Quevilly, 1977–81; Nat. Sec., Parti Socialiste (responsible for the press), 1979–81; Junior Minister, Ministry of Economy and Finance (responsible for the budget), 1981–83; Minister of Industry and Research, 1983–84; Prime Minister of France, 1984–86. Mem., Conseil d'Etat, 1981–. Pres., Regional Council, Haute Normandie, 1981–. *Publications:* La France inégale, 1975; Le Coeur du Futur, 1985; C'est en allant vers la mer, 1990. *Address:* Assemblée Nationale, 128 rue de l'Université, 75007 Paris, France; 15 place du Panthéon, 75005 Paris, France.

FACER, Roger Lawrence Lowe; Deputy Under-Secretary of State, Ministry of Defence, since 1988; *b* 28 June 1933; *s* of late John Ernest Facer and Phyllis Facer; *m* 1960, Ruth Margaret, *o d* of late Herbert Mostyn Lewis, PhD, Gresford, Clwyd; three *d*. *Educ:* Rugby; St John's Coll., Oxford (MA). HM Forces, 2nd Lieut, East Surrey Regt, 1951–53. War Office, 1957; Asst Private Sec. to Secretary of State, 1958; Private Sec. to Permanent Under-Sec., 1958; Principal, 1961; Cabinet Office, 1966; Ministry of Defence, 1968–: Private Sec. to Minister of State (Equipment), 1970; Asst Sec., 1970; Internat. Inst. for Strategic Studies, 1972–73; Counsellor, UK Delegn, MBFR Vienna, 1973–75; Private Sec. to Sec. of State for Defence, 1976–79; Asst Under-Sec. of State, 1979–81; Under Sec., Cabinet Office, 1981–83; Rand Corporation, Santa Monica, USA, 1984; Asst Under-Sec. of State, MoD, 1984–87. *Publications:* Weapons Procurement in Europe—Capabilities and Choices, 1975; Conventional Forces and the NATO Strategy of Flexible Response, 1985; articles in Alpine Garden Soc. Bulletin. *Recreations:* Alpine gardening, hill-walking, opera. *Address:* c/o Ministry of Defence, Whitehall, SW1A 2HB.

FACK, Robbert; Commander, Order of Orange-Nassau, 1979; Chevalier, Order of Netherlands Lion 1971; Netherlands diplomat, retired; Ambassador of the Netherlands to the Court of St James's, 1976–82; also, concurrently, Ambassador to Iceland, 1976–82; *b* 1 Jan. 1917; *m* 1943, Patricia H. Hawkins; four *s*. *Educ:* Univ. of Amsterdam. Military service, 1937–45. Min. of Foreign Affairs, The Hague, 1945–46; New York (UN), 1946–48; Min. of Foreign Affairs, 1948–50; Rome, 1950–54; Canberra, 1954–58; Bonn, 1958–63; Min. of Foreign Affairs, 1963–68; Ambassador-at-large, 1968–70; Perm. Rep. to UN, New York, 1970–74. Holds various foreign decorations. *Publication:* Gedane Zaken (Finished Business), (reminiscences), 1984. *Address:* Widden Hill House, Horton, near Bristol BS17 6QU. *Club:* Dutch.

FAGAN, Maj.-Gen. Patrick Feltrim, CB 1990; MBE (mil.) 1966; FRICS 1971; FRGS 1966; Director General of Military Survey, 1987–90, retired; *b* 8 Dec. 1935; *s* of Air Cdre Thomas Patrick Feltrim Fagan and Hon. Isabel Mairi, *yr d* of 15th Baron Arundell of Wardour; *m* 1967, Veronica Thompson (*née* Lorant), *widow* of Captain C. J. C. Thompson, RE; two *s*. *Educ:* Stonyhurst Coll.; RMA, Sandhurst; University Coll. London (MSc (Hons) 1969). FBIM 1971. Commnd RE, 1955; served in Gibraltar, Germany, Aden and Oman. Internat. Scientific Expedn to Karakoram, 1961–62; UAE-Oman Border Survey, 1964; Jt Services Expedn to S Georgia, 1964–65; Ordnance Survey, 1969–73; Geographic Advr, AFCENT, 1979–83; Chief Geographic Officer, SHAPE, 1983–85; Dir, Survey Operations and Prodn, 1985–87. Member: Council, RGS, 1987– (Vice-Pres., 1990–); Council, BSES, 1987–90; Council, Mt Everest Foundn, 1989– (Dep. Chm., 1990–); Nat. Cttee for Photogrammetry and Remote Sensing, 1987–91; Adv. Bd, Inst. of Engrg, Surveying and Space Geodesy, Nottingham Univ., 1987–; Council, RICS Land Surveyors, 1988–91; RICS Pres's Disciplinary and Appeals Tribunal, 1989–. Dep. Pres., Army RU, 1989–. Col Comdt, RE, 1991–. *Publications:* articles on surveying and mapping in Geographical Jl, Photogrammetric Record, Survey Rev., Chartered Surveyor, and on ski mountaineering in subject jls. *Recreations:* mountain sports, orienteering, boats, cricket, reading, photography, music, travel. *Address:* c/o Lloyds Bank, 7 Pall Mall, SW1Y 5NA. *Clubs:* Alpine, Alpine Ski, Eagle Ski (Pres., 1988–), MCC, Geographical.

FAGE, Prof. John Donnelly, MA, PhD; Professor of African History, 1963–84, now Emeritus, Pro-Vice-Chancellor, 1979–84, and Vice-Principal 1981–84, University of Birmingham; *b* 3 June 1921; *s* of late Arthur Fage, CBE, FRS, and Winifred Eliza Donnelly; *m* 1949, Jean, *d* of late Fred Banister, MBE; one *s* one *d*. *Educ:* Tonbridge Sch.; Magdalene Coll., Cambridge (scholar, MA, PhD). Served War, Pilot with RAFVR (Flt Lt), 1941–45. Bye-Fellow, Magdalene Coll., Cambridge, 1947–49; Lectr and Sen. Lectr, Univ. Coll. of the Gold Coast, 1949–55; Prof. of History, 1955–59, and Dep. Principal, 1957–59; Lectr in African History, SOAS, Univ. of London, 1959–63. Visiting Prof., Univ. of Wisconsin, Madison, 1957, and Smith Coll., Northampton, Mass, 1962; Dir, Centre of West African Studies, Univ. of Birmingham, 1963–82, Dep. Dean, Faculty of Arts, 1973–75, Dean, 1975–78; Founding Hon. Sec., African Studies Assoc. of the UK, 1963–66 (Vice-Pres. 1967–68, Pres. 1968–69); Council Mem., Internat. African Inst., 1965–75, and Consultative Dir, 1975–80; Member: UNESCO Scientific Cttee for Gen. History of Africa, 1971–80; Culture Adv. Cttee of UK Nat. Commn for UNESCO, 1967–85 (Chm., 1978–85); Co-ordinating Council of Area Studies Associations, 1980–86 (Vice-Chm. 1980–84, Chm., 1984–86); Chm., Birmingham Jt Cttee for Adult Educn Inf. and Advice Services, 1985–88. FRHistS. Hon. Fellow, SOAS, Univ. of London. Editor (with Roland Oliver), The Jl of African History, 1960–73; Gen. Editor (with Roland Oliver), The Cambridge History of Africa, 8 vols, 1975–86. *Publications:* An Introduction to the History of West Africa, 1955, 3rd edn 1962; An Atlas of African History, 1958, 2nd edn, 1978; Ghana, a Historical Interpretation, 1959; A Short History of Africa (with Roland Oliver), 1962, 6th edn 1988; A History of West Africa, 1969; (ed) Africa Discovers Her Past, 1970; (ed with Roland Oliver) Papers on African Prehistory, 1970;

A History of Africa, 1978, 2nd edn 1988; A Guide to Sources for Western Africa, 1987; articles in historical and Africanist jls. *Recreations:* doing things to houses and gardens. *Address:* Hafod Awel, Pennal, Machynlleth, Powys SY20 9DP. *T:* Machynlleth (0654) 791207. *Club:* Athenæum.

FAGG, William Buller, CMG 1967; ethnologist, tribal art historian and consultant; Keeper, Ethnography Department (from 1972 the Museum of Mankind), British Museum, 1969–74 (Deputy Keeper, 1955–69); *b* 28 April 1914; *s* of late William Percy Fagg and late Lilian Fagg. *Educ:* Dulwich Coll.; Magdalene Coll., Cambridge. Sir Wm Browne's Medal for Latin Epigram; Montagu Butler Prize for Latin Hexameters; BA Classics, 1936; Archaeology and Anthropology, 1937; MA 1939. Asst Keeper Dept of Ethnography, BM, 1938; seconded to Bd of Trade, Industries and Manufactures Dept, 1940–45. Royal Anthropological Institute: Hon. Sec., 1939–56; Mem. Council, 1966–69, 1972–75, 1976–79; Vice-Pres., 1969–72; Patron's Medal, 1966; Hon. Editor, Man: A Monthly Record of Anthropological Science, 1947–65, Hon. Librarian, 1976–. Chm., UK Cttee for First World Festival of Negro Arts, Dakar, 1966; Trustee: UK African Festival Trust, 1973–77; Chm., African Fine Art Gallery Trust, 1974–; Consulting Fellow in African Art, Museum of Primitive Art, NY, 1957–70. Consultant on Tribal Art to Christies, 1974–. Fieldwork: Nigeria and Congo, 1949–50; Nigeria, 1953, 1958–59, 1971, 1974, 1981; Cameroon, 1966; Mali, 1969. Organised and arranged many loan exhibns including: Nigerian Art (Arts Council), London, Manchester, Bristol, 1960, Munich, Basel, 1961; African Art, Berlin Festival, 1964, Musée des Arts Décoratifs, Paris, 1964–65; African Sculpture, Nat. Gall. of Art, Washington, DC, Kansas City Art Gall., and Brooklyn Museum, 1970. FRSA (Silver-Medallist, 1951). Member: Royal African Soc.; RIIA; Internat. African Inst.; Museums Assoc.; African Studies Assoc.; China Soc.; ICA; Assoc. of Art Historians. Leadership Award, Arts Council of African Studies Assoc., USA, 1986. *Publications:* The Webster Plass Collection of African Art, British Museum, 1953; (with E. Elisofon) The Sculpture of Africa, 1958; Afro-Portuguese Ivories, 1959; Nigerian Images, 1963 (awarded P. A. Talbot Prize, 1964, and grand prize for best work on African art at World Festival of Negro Arts, Dakar, 1966); (with Margaret Plass) African Sculpture: An Anthology, 1964; Tribes and Forms in African Art, 1966; African Tribal Sculptures, 2 vols, 1967; Arts of Western Africa, Arts of Central Africa (UNESCO), 1967; African Tribal Images (The Katherine White Reswick Collection of African Art), 1968; African Sculpture (Washington, DC), 1970; Miniature Wood Carvings of Africa, 1970; The Tribal Image: wooden figure sculpture of the world, 1970; African Sculpture from the Tara Collection, 1971; (ed) The Living Arts of Nigeria, 1971; Eskimo Art in the British Museum, 1972; Yoruba Beadwork, 1980; Masques d'Afrique, 1980; African Majesty: from grassland and forest, 1981; Yoruba Sculpture of West Africa, 1982; Africa and the Renaissance, 1988; numerous exhibn catalogues, articles in Man, etc. *Recreations:* photography (esp. of art, incl. ancient churches), listening to music, cycling, travel, geopolitics. *Address:* 6 Galata Road, Barnes, SW13 9NQ. *T:* 081–748 6620. *Club:* Travellers'.

FAGGE, Sir John William Frederick, 11th Bt, *cr* 1660; *b* 28 Sept. 1910; *s* of late William Archibald Theodore Fagge (*b* of 9th Bt) and Nellie (*d* 1924), *d* of H. T. D. Wise; *S* uncle, 1940; *m* 1940, Ivy Gertrude, *d* of William Edward Frier, 15 Church Lane, Newington, Kent; one *s* one *d*. *Heir:* *s* John Christopher Fagge, *b* 30 April 1942. *Address:* 26 The Mall, Faversham, Kent.

FAINT, John Anthony Leonard; UK Executive Director (on secondment), European Bank for Reconstruction and Development, since 1991; *b* 24 Nov. 1942; *s* of Thomas Leonard Faint and Josephine Rosey Faint (*née* Dunkerley); *m* 1978, Elizabeth Theresa Winter. *Educ:* Chigwell Sch.; Magdalen Coll., Oxford (BA LitHum 1965); MA Development Economics, Fletcher Sch., Mass, 1969. Ministry of Overseas Development (later Overseas Development Administration), London, 1965–71 (study leave in Cambridge, Mass, 1968–69); First Secretary (Aid), Blantyre, Malawi, 1971–73; ODM/ODA, London, 1974–80; Head of SE Asia Develt Div., Bangkok, 1980–83; Head of Finance Dept, ODA, FCO, 1983–86; Alternate Exec. Dir, World Bank, Washington, 1986–89; Head, E Asia Dept, 1989–90, Under Sec., Internat. Div., 1990–91, ODA. *Recreations:* music, bridge, chess, computers. *Address:* Overseas Development Administration, Eland House, Stag Place, SW1E 5DH.

FAIR, Donald Robert Russell, OBE (mil.) 1945; Board Member, Central Electricity Generating Board, 1975–77; *b* 26 Dec. 1916; *s* of Robert Sidney Fair and Mary Louie Fair; *m* 1941, Patricia Laurie Rudland; one *s*. *Educ:* Roan Sch., Blackheath; King's Coll., London Univ. (BSc, AKC). CEng, FInstE; CPhys, FInstP. Served War of 1939–45, RAF (Wing Comdr; despatches 1944; USAAF Commendation 1944). Lectr, RMA Sandhurst, 1948–50; UK AEA, 1950–62; Central Electricity Generating Bd, 1962–77. *Recreations:* sailing, cricket. *Address:* 22 Carlton Leas, The Leas, Folkestone, Kent CT20 2DJ. *T:* Folkestone (0303) 50573. *Club:* Island Sailing.

FAIRBAIRN, Sir Brooke; see Fairbairn, Sir J. B.

FAIRBAIRN, David; Metropolitan Stipendiary Magistrate, 1971–89; Deputy Circuit Judge, 1972–89; *b* 9 Aug. 1924; *s* of Ernest Hulford Fairbairn and late Iva May Fairbairn; *m* 1946, Helen Merriel de la Cour Collingwood, *d* of Harold Lewis Collingwood; two *s* two *d*. *Educ:* Haileybury Coll.; Trinity Hall, Cambridge (MA). Served War of 1939–45, Lieut, RNVR, in Mediterranean. Called to Bar, Middle Temple, 1949; Central Criminal Court Bar Mess; South Eastern Circuit; Herts and Essex QS; Dep. Chm., Surrey QS, 1969–71. Liveryman, Gold and Silver Wyre Drawers' Company, 1957–. *Recreations:* golf, tennis, country life. *Address:* c/o National Westminster Bank, Cranleigh, Surrey GU6 8RH.

FAIRBAIRN, Sir David Eric, KBE 1977; DFC 1944; Australian Ambassador to the Netherlands, 1977–80; grazier, 1939–71; *b* 3 March 1917; *s* of Clive Prell Fairbairn and Marjorie Rose (*née* Jowett); *m* 1945, Ruth Antill (*née* Robertson); three *d*. *Educ:* Geelong Grammar Sch.; Cambridge Univ. (MA). Served RAAF, 1940–45, England and New Guinea. MP (L) Commonwealth of Australia, 1949–75; Minister: for Air, 1962–64; for Nat. Develt, 1964–69; for Educn and Science, March-Aug. 1971; for Defence, 1971–72. *Recreations:* golf, gardening. *Address:* 18 Yarralumla Bay, 51 Musgrave Street, Yarralumla, ACT 2600, Australia. *T:* 2814659. *Clubs:* Melbourne (Melbourne); Commonwealth (Canberra); Royal Canberra Golf.

FAIRBAIRN, David Ritchie, OBE 1990; Group Managing Director, James Martin Associates plc, since 1989; *b* 4 July 1934; *s* of G. F. Fairbairn; *m* 1958, Hon. Susan Hill, *d* of Baron Hill of Luton, PC; one *s* two *d*. *Educ:* Mill Hill Sch.; Gonville and Caius Coll., Cambridge (BAEcon). FBCS; FIDPM, FInstD. President, Cambridge Union Soc. Overseas Marketing Manager, Arthur Guinness Son & Co. Ltd, 1960; President, Guinness-Harp Corp., New York, 1964; Marketing Dir, Guinness Overseas Ltd, 1969; Man. Dir, Dataset Ltd (ICL), 1970; Manager, Retail and Distribution Sector, International Computers Ltd, 1975; Dir of Marketing, EMI Medical Ltd, 1976; Dir, Nat. Computing Centre, 1980–86; Man. Dir, James Martin Associates UK, 1985–89. Pres., Inst. of Data Processing Management, 1982– (Vice-Pres., 1980–82). Vice-Chm., Parly IT Cttee, 1982. Member: Monopolies and Mergers Commn, 1985–; Patent Office Steering Bd, 1989–. Freeman,

City of London. FRSA. *Recreations:* sailing, water-ski-ing, ski-ing. *Address:* 11 Oak Way, West Common, Harpenden, Herts AL5 2RU. *T:* Harpenden (05827) 5820.

FAIRBAIRN, Douglas Foakes, CBE 1971; Director, Town and Commercial Property Services Ltd, since 1986; *b* 9 Oct. 1919; *s* of William and Florence Fairbairn; *m* 1947, Gertrude Betty Buswell; two *s*. *Educ:* John Lyon Sch., Harrow; Royal School of Mines, Imperial Coll., London Univ. BSc (Hons), ARSM. Served War, RAF (Sqdn Ldr), 1940–46. Commonwealth Development Corp., 1949–83; Regional Controller: Central Africa, 1959–66; West Africa, 1966–71. Dir, Bank of Rhodesia and Nyasaland, 1961–63; Chm., Central African Airways, 1964–68; Mem., Central African Power Corp., 1961–77; Co-ordinator of Operations, Commonwealth Develt Corp., 1971–83; Chm., Springwood Cellulose Co. Ltd, 1983–87. *Recreation:* golf. *Address:* 11 Portland Terrace, The Green, Richmond, Surrey TW9 1QQ. *T:* 081–948 1921. *Club:* Richmond Golf.

FAIRBAIRN, Sir (James) Brooke, 6th Bt *cr* 1869, of Ardwick; *b* 10 Dec. 1930; *s* of Sir William Albert Fairbairn, 5th Bt, and of Christine Renée Cotton, *d* of late Rev. Canon Robert William Croft; *S* father, 1972; *m* 1960, Mary Russell, *d* of late William Russell Scott, MB, ChB, FFARCS; two *s* one *d*. *Educ:* Stowe. Proprietor of J. Brooke Fairbairn & Co., textile converters and wholesalers dealing in furnishing fabrics. *Heir:* *s* Robert William Fairbairn [*b* 10 April 1965; *m* 1990, Sarah, *e d* of Roger Griffin]. *Address:* Barkway House, Bury Road, Newmarket, Suffolk CB8 7BT. *T:* Newmarket (0638) 662733; J. Brooke Fairbairn & Co., The Railway Station, Newmarket CB8 9BA. *T:* Newmarket (0638) 665766. *Club:* City Livery.

FAIRBAIRN, John Sydney; Deputy Chairman, M & G Group plc, 1979–89 (non-executive Director, since 1989); *b* 15 Jan. 1934; *s* of late Sydney George Fairbairn, MC and Angela Maude Fairbairn (*née* Fane); *m* 1968, Mrs Camilla Fry, *d* of late G. N. Grinling; one *s* two *d* and two step *s* two step *d*. *Educ:* Eton; Trinity College, Cambridge (BA). FCA. National Service, 2nd Lieut 17/21 Lancers, 1952–54. Monkhouse Stoneham & Co., 1957–60; joined M & G Group, 1961; Dir, 1974. Dep. Chm., Lautro, 1986–89; Chm., Unit Trust Assoc., 1989–91. Chm., Esmée Fairbairn Charitable Trust, 1988– (Trustee, 1965–); Trustee: Wincott Foundn; Monteverdi Trust, 1991–. Council Mem. and Treasurer, King's College London, 1972–84 (FKC 1978); Council Mem., Univ. of Buckingham, 1986–. Mem., Governing Cttee, Dulwich Picture Gall., 1991–. *Address:* Harvest Hill, Cuckfield, West Sussex. *T:* Haywards Heath (0444) 412200. *Clubs:* Brooks's, Beefsteak, MCC.

FAIRBAIRN of Fordell, Sir Nicholas (Hardwick), Kt 1988; QC(Scot.) 1972; MP (C) Perth and Kinross, since 1983 (Kinross and Perthshire West, Oct. 1974–1983); Baron of Fordell; *b* 24 Dec. 1933; *s* of William Ronald Dodds Fairbairn, DPsych, and Mary Ann More-Gordon of Charleton and Kinnaber; *m* 1st, 1962, Hon. Elizabeth Mary Mackay (marr. diss. 1979), *e d* of 13th Baron Reay; three *d* (and one *s* one *d* decd); 2nd, 1983, Suzanne Mary Wheeler. *Educ:* Loretto; Edinburgh Univ.; MA, LLB. Author, forrester, painter, poet, TV and radio broadcaster, journalist, dress-designer, landscape gardener, bon viveur and wit. Called to Scots Bar 1957. Cons. Candidate, Central Edinburgh, 1964, 1966. HM Solicitor Gen. for Scotland, 1979–82. Comr of Northern Lighthouses, 1979–82. Mem., Council of World Population Crisis, 1968–70. Founder and Hon. Pres., Soc. for Preservation of Duddingston Village; Member: Edinburgh Festival Council, 1971–; Bd, Edinburgh Brook Adv. Centre (Chm., 1968–75). Chairman: Traverse Theatre, 1964–72; Waverley Broadcasting Co., 1973–74; Historic Buildings Council for Scotland, 1988–; Dir, Ledlanet Nights, 1960–73. Chm., Scottish Soc. for Defence of Literature and the Arts. President: Dysart and Dundonald Pipe Band; Pres., Edinburgh Brook Adv. Centre (Chm., 1968–75). Vice Pres., Scottish Women's Soc. of Artists, 1988–. Trustee, Scottish Museums, 1987–. Private exhibns throughout Britain since 1960, and in public exhibns. KLJ; KStJ; FSAScot. Hon. Fellow, Internat. Acad. of Trial Lawyers, 1984. Kt Chevalier, Order of Polonia Restituta (Poland), 1988. *Publications:* A Life is Too Short (autobiog.), 1987; contrib., Alistair Maclean Introduces Scotland, 1972. *Recreations:* loving beauty and beautifying love. *Address:* Fordell Castle, By Dunfermline, Fife. *Clubs:* Puffins, Beefsteak, Chatham Dining; New (Edinburgh).

FAIRBANKS, Douglas (Elton), (Jr), KBE 1949; DSC 1944; Captain, USNR, retired; actor, writer, producer, company director; Chairman, Fairtel, Inc. (US), since 1946; formerly Chairman, Douglas Fairbanks Ltd; Director or Special Consultant: Fairbanks Co. Inc.; Norlantic Development; Boltons Trading; Alcoa Inc.; Dougfair Corp. (US); Scripto Pens Ltd (US and UK), 1952–73; Golden Cycle and subsidiaries, 1965–73; Rambagh Palace Hotel, Ltd (Jaipur, India); Cavalcade Film Co. Ltd (UK), etc; *b* New York City, 9 Dec. 1909; *s* of Douglas Elton Fairbanks, Denver, Colorado, and Anna Beth Sully, Providence, RI; *m* 1st, 1929, Lucille Le Sueur (Joan Crawford) (marr. diss. 1933); 2nd, 1939, Mary Lee Epling (*d* 1988), Keystone, W Virginia; three *d*. 3rd, 1991, Vera Shelton. *Educ:* Bovée Sch., Knickerbocker Greys, Collegiate Mil. Sch., NY; Pasadena Polytechnic, Harvard Mil. Sch., Los Angeles; tutored privately in London and Paris. Began career as film actor, 1923, on stage 1927. Organised own producing company, UK, 1935. Studied painting and sculpture, Paris, 1922–24; began writing, professionally, 1928; articles, fiction and essays on public affairs, etc., 1936–. Vice-Pres. Franco-British War Relief and National Vice-Pres. Cttee "Defend America by Aiding the Allies", 1939–40; Presidential Envoy, Special Mission to Latin America, 1940–41; one-time Consultant to Office of the Presidency (Washington, DC); Lieut (jg), USNR, 1941; promoted through grades to Capt., 1954. National Chm., CARE Cttee, 1947–50; Nat. Vice-Pres. Amer. Assoc. for the UN, 1946–60; Pres. Brit-Amer. Alumni Assoc. 1950; Bd Gov., English-Speaking Union of the US, 1949–60; Nat. Chm., Amer. Relief for Korea, 1950–54; Trustee, Edwina Mountbatten Trust; Mem., Bd of Dirs, Mountbatten Meml Trust (US); Mem. Bd of Dirs, Amer. Friends of RSC and RSC Trust; Dir, Shakespeare Globe Theater; Mem. Council, American Museum in Brit.; a Governor and Exec. Cllr, Royal Shakespeare Theatre; Governor: United World Colleges, 1951–; Ditchley Foundations; Co-Chm., US Capitol Bicentenary 1776–1976; Guild of St Bride's Church, Fleet Street, EC; Mem., Council on Foreign Relations (NY); US Naval Mem., US Mil. Delegn, SEATO Conf., 1971; Mem., Bd of Dirs, Pilgrims Soc. of US, 1985–; Vis. Fellow, St Cross Coll., Oxford; MA Oxon; Senior Churchill Fellow, Westminster Coll., Fulton, Mo; Hon. DFA Westminster Coll., Fulton, Mo, USA; Hon. LLD Univ. of Denver, Colo; Silver Star Medal (US); Legion of Merit ("Valor" clasp) (US), Special Naval Commendation (US), KJStJ 1950 (Hon. Dep. Chancellor, Amer. Friends, Order of St John), etc; Officer Legion of Honour (Fr.), Croix de Guerre with Palm (Fr.); Knight Comdr Order of George I (Greece); Knight Grand Officer, Order del Merito (Chile); Grand Officer, Order of Merit (Italy); Comdr Order of Orange Nassau (Neth.); Officer of: Orders of Crown (Belg.), of Star of Italy, Cross of Mil. Valour (Italy), Southern Cross (Brazil); Grand Comdr Order of Merit (West Germany); Murmansk Convoys Campaign (USSR); Hon. Citizen and National Medal of Korea, etc. *Films include:* Stella Dallas; Little Caesar; Outward Bound; Morning Glory; Catherine the Great; The Amateur Gentleman; The Prisoner of Zenda; Gunga Din; The Corsican Brothers; Sinbad the Sailor; The Exile; The Fighting O'Flynn; State Secret; The Young in Heart; Having Wonderful Time; The Rage of Paris; The Joy of Living; L'Athlète Malgré Lui (French); A Woman of Affairs; Lady in Ermine; Stephen Steps Out; The Barker; Chances; The Life of Jimmy Dolan; Mimi; Angels Over

Broadway. *Plays include:* Young Woodley; Romeo and Juliet; The Jest; Man in Possession; The Winding Journey; Moonlight is Silver; My Fair Lady; The Pleasure of his Company; The Secretary Bird; Present Laughter; Sleuth; The Youngest; The Dummy; Towards the Light; produced over 160 TV plays, acted in over 50; also recordings etc. *Publications:* The Salad Days (autobiog.), 1988; short stories, poems, articles, to periodicals; *relevant publications:* Knight Errant, by Brian Connell; The Fairbanks Album, by Richard Schickel; The Fourth Musketeer, by Letitia Fairbanks-Milner. *Recreations:* swimming, tennis, golf, travel. *Address:* The Beekman, 575 Park Avenue, New York, NY 10021, USA; (office) Inverness Corporation, 545 Madison Avenue, New York, NY 10022, USA. *Clubs:* White's, Naval and Military, Garrick, Beefsteak; Puffin's (Edinburgh); Brook, Knickerbocker, Century (NY); Metropolitan (Washington, DC); Racquet (Chicago); Myopia Hunt (Hamilton, Mass) (Hon. Mem.).

FAIRCLOUGH, Anthony John, CMG 1990; Special Adviser and Hon. Director General, Commission of the European Communities, since 1989; Director, Environmental Resources Ltd, since 1989; *b* 30 Aug. 1924; *m* 1957, Patricia Monks; two *s*. *Educ:* St Philip's Grammar Sch., Birmingham; St Catharine's Coll., Cambridge. Scholar 1944, BA Cantab 1945, MA 1950. Ministry of Aircraft Production and Ministry of Supply, 1944–48; Colonial Office, 1948; Secretary, Nyasaland Commn of Inquiry, 1959; Private Secretary to Minister of State for Commonwealth Relations and for the Colonies, 1963–64; Assistant Secretary, 1964; Head of Pacific and Indian Ocean Dept, Commonwealth Office (formerly Colonial Office), 1964–68; Head of W Indian Dept, FCO, 1968–70; Head of New Towns 1 Div., DoE, 1970–72; Under-Sec., 1973; Head of Planning, Minerals and Countryside Directorate, 1973, of Planning, Sport and Countryside Directorate, 1973–74; Dir, Central Unit on Environmental Pollution, 1974–78; Dir, Internat. Transport, Dept of Transport, 1978–81; Dir for the Environment, EEC, 1981–85; Actg Dir Gen. for the Environment, Consumer Protection and Nuclear Safety, EEC, 1985–86; Dep. Dir-Gen. for Develt, EEC, 1986–89. Senior UK Commissioner at Sessions of South Pacific Commn, 1965–67; Minister's Deputy, European Conf. of Mins of Transport, 1978–81; Chm., Environment Cttee, OECD, 1976–79; British Channel Tunnel Co., 1978–81; British Co-Chm., Jt UK/USSR Cttee established under UK/USSR Agreement on cooperation in field of Environmental Protection, 1974–78; Chm., Network for Envmtl Technology Transfer, asbl, Belgium, 1989–; Dir, Groundwork Foundn, 1989–. Advr to European Orgn for Res. and Treatment of Cancer, 1989–. Member: Royal Soc.'s British Nat. Cttee on Problems of Environment, 1974–78; EDC for Internat. Freight Movement, 1978–80; Governing Body, Chiswick Sch., 1973–79. Comp ICE, 1989. FRSA. *Address:* 6 Cumberland Road, Kew, Richmond, Surrey TW9 3HQ; Appt 12, 32 Quai aux Briques, 1000 Brussels, Belgium.

FAIRCLOUGH, Hon. Ellen Louks, PC (Can.) 1957; OC 1979; FCA 1965; Member of Progressive Conservative Party, Canada; *b* Hamilton, Ont, 28 Jan. 1905; *d* of Norman Ellsworth Cook and Nellie Bell Louks; *m* 1931, David Henry Gordon Fairclough; one *s*. *Educ:* Hamilton Public and Secondary Schs. Certified Public Accountant, public practice, 1935–57 (Fellow, Chartered Accountants of Ontario, 1965). Hamilton City Council, Alderman, 1946–49; Controller, 1950. Elected to House of Commons as Progressive Conservative mem. for Hamilton West, 1950; re-elected at gen. elections, 1953, 1957, 1958, 1962, defeated in 1963 election. Sec. of State for Canada, 1957–58; Minister of Citizenship and Immigration, 1958–62; Postmaster-Gen., 1962–63. Patron, Huguenot Soc. of Canada, 1969–; Chancellor, Royal Hamilton College of Music, 1978–80. Mem. Bd, Ontario Bicentennial Commn, 1983–84; Hon. Treas. and Exec. Dir, Chedoke-McMaster Hosps Foundn, 1982–86; Patron, United Empire Loyalists Assoc., Hamilton Br., 1980–. Internat. Treasurer, 1972–76, Hon. Life Mem., Zonta International. Ontario Govt Bldg named Ellen Fairclough Bldg, 1982. LLD (*hc*), McMaster Univ., 1975. *Recreations:* music, reading and photography. *Address:* 25 Stanley Avenue, Hamilton, Ont L8P 2K9, Canada. *T:* Hamilton 522–5248. *Clubs:* Albany (Toronto); Hamilton, Zonta I (Hamilton); Faculty (McMaster).

FAIRCLOUGH, Sir John (Whitaker), Kt 1990; FEng, FIEE, FBCS; Chief Scientific Adviser to Cabinet Office, 1986–90; *b* 23 Aug. 1930; *m* Margaret Ann; two *s* one *d*. *Educ:* Manchester Univ. (BScTech). Ferranti, 1954; IBM: Poughkeepsie Lab., US, 1957; Hursley Lab., UK, 1958; Director of Development, IBM UK Ltd, 1964; Asst Gen. Manager and Dir Data Processing IBM UK, 1968; Dir, Raleigh Development Lab., USA, 1970; System Develt Div. Vice Pres., Raleigh, USA, 1972; System Communication Div. Vice Pres. and Man. Dir, Director of Development, Hursley Lab., UK, 1974; System Product Div. Vice Pres. and Man. Dir, Hursley Lab., UK, 1982; Dir of Manufacturing & Development, IBM UK Ltd, and Chm, IBM UK Laboratories Ltd, 1983. Chairman: Systematica Ltd; Rothschild Ventures Ltd; Non-exec. Director: Oxford Instruments Gp, 1990–; N. M. Rothschild & Sons Ltd; Infolink plc. Chairman: Engineering Council, 1990– (Mem., 1982–90); CEST. Pres., BCS, 1987. Mem., Acad. of Engrg, USA, 1990. Aston, 1990; Hon. DTech Loughborough, 1990. Hon. DSc: Southampton, 1983; Cranfield, 1987; Manchester, 1988–90. *Recreations:* gardening, carpentry. *Address:* The Old Blue Boar, St John's Street, Winchester, Hants SO23 8HF.

FAIRCLOUGH, Wilfred, RE; RWS; ARCA (London); Assistant Director, Kingston Polytechnic, and Head of the Division of Design, 1970–72, retired; Principal of Kingston College of Art, Surrey, 1962–70; *b* 13 June 1907; *s* of Herbert Fairclough and Edith Amy Milton; *m* 1936, Joan Cryer; one *s* one *d*. *Educ:* Royal College of Art, London, 1931–34 (Diploma 1933); British Sch. at Rome, Italy, 1934–37; Rome Scholar in Engraving, 1934–37. Army and Royal Air Force, 1942–46. Rome Scholarships, Faculty of Engraving, 1951 (Chm., 1964–73); Leverhulme Research Award, 1961. RE 1946 (ARE 1934); RWS 1968 (ARWS 1961). Chairman: Assoc. of Art Instns, 1965–66; Assessors, Vocational Courses of Surrey CC. *Work in public and private collections: paintings:* Min. of Supply; Min. of Works; Surrey CC; Scottish Modern Art Assoc.; Beaumont Coll.; *drawings:* British Museum; V&A Museum; Arts Council; Contemporary Art Soc.; Wye Coll., London Univ.; English Electric Co.; Art Galls at Blackburn, Kingston-upon-Thames, Worthing; Graves Art Gall., Sheffield; Atkinson Art Gall., Southport; *prints:* British Museum, V&A Museum; Ashmolean Museum, Oxford; Contemporary Art Soc.; British Sch. at Rome; South London Art Gall.; Stoke Educn Authority; Wye Coll., London Univ.; Gottenburg Museum; Print Collectors Club. *Publications:* The Etchings of Wilfrid Fairclough, 1990; work reproduced: Recording Britain; Londoners' England; Royal Academy Illustrated; Studio; Fine Prints of the Year; Print Collectors Quarterly; illustrated article, Leisure Painter, 1969; paintings, drawings and prints. *Address:* 12 Manorgate Road, Kingston-upon-Thames, Surrey KT2 7AL.

FAIREY, Michael John, CB 1989; Chief Executive, The Royal London Hospital and Associated Community NHS Trust, since 1991; *b* 20 Sept. 1933; *s* of late Ernest John Saunder Fairey and Lily Emily (*née* Pateman); *m* 1st, 1958 (marr. diss. 1989); two *s* one *d*; 2nd, 1990, Victoria Frances Hardman. *Educ:* Queen Elizabeth's Sch., Barnet; Jesus Coll., Cambridge (MA). Served RA, 1952–53. Jun. Administrator, St Thomas' Hosp., 1957–60; Gp Develt Sec., Westminster Hosp., 1960–62; Deputy House Governor, The London Hosp., 1962, House Governor 1972; Regional Administrator, NE Thames RHA, 1973; Dir, Planning and Inf, NHS Management Bd, DHSS, later Dept of Health, 1984–89; Dir of Information Systems, NHS Management Exec., Dept of Health, 1989–91. *Publications:* various articles in med. and computing jls. *Recreations:* church music, history of medieval exploration, Rugby football. *Club:* Athenæum.

FAIRFAX, family name of **Lord Fairfax of Cameron.**

FAIRFAX OF CAMERON, 14th Lord *cr* 1627; **Nicholas John Albert Fairfax;** *b* 4 Jan. 1956; *e s* of 13th Lord and of Sonia, *yr d* of late Capt. Cecil Gunston, MC; *S* father, 1964; *m* 1982, Annabel, *er d* of late Nicholas and of Sarah Gilham Morriss; three *s*. *Educ:* Eton; Downing Coll., Cambridge (LLB in international law subjects, 1981). Called to the Bar, Gray's Inn, 1977. Director, Thomas Miller P and I, and Thomas Miller Defence, 1987–90. *Recreations:* watersports, ski-ing, tennis. *Heir: s* Hon. Edward Nicholas Thomas Fairfax, *b* 20 Sept. 1984. *Address:* 10 Orlando Road, SW4 0LF. *Club:* Queen's.

FAIRFAX, James Oswald; Chairman, John Fairfax Ltd, Sydney, 1977–87; *b* 27 March 1933; *s* of Sir Warwick Oswald Fairfax and Marcie Elizabeth Fairfax (*née* Wilson). *Educ:* Geelong Grammar School; Balliol College, Oxford (MA). Director, John Fairfax, 1957–87; Chm., Amalgamated Television Services Pty Ltd, 1975–87 (Dir, 1958); Chm., David Syme & Co., 1984–87 (Dir, 1977). Member: Bd of Management, Royal Alexandra Hosp. for Children, 1967–85 (Bd, Children's Med. Res. Foundn, 1986–88); Council, International House, Sydney Univ., 1967–79; Internat. Council, Museum of Modern Art, NY, 1971–; Council, Australian Nat. Gallery, 1976–84. *Address:* 5 Lindsay Avenue, Darling Point, NSW 2027, Australia. *Clubs:* Garrick; Union, Australian (Sydney); Melbourne (Melbourne).

FAIRFAX, Sir Vincent Charles, Kt 1971; CMG 1960; Company Director and Pastoralist, Australia; *b* 26 Dec. 1909; *s* of late J. H. F. Fairfax; *m* 1939, Nancy, *d* late Dr C. B. Heald, CBE, FRCP; two *s* two *d*. *Educ:* Geelong Church of England Grammar Sch., Australia; Brasenose Coll., Oxford Univ. (BA). Staff, John Fairfax & Sons Pty Ltd, 1933; Advertising Manager, 1937–38. Major, Australian Imperial Forces, 1940–46. Director: John Fairfax & Sons Pty Ltd, 1946–53; John Fairfax Ltd (Publishers, Sydney Morning Herald), 1956–87; Chm. Australian Sectn, Commonwealth Press Union, 1950–73; Chm., Stanbroke Pastoral Co. Pty Ltd, 1964–82; Director: Bank of NSW, 1953–82; Australian Mutual Provident Soc., 1956–82 (Chm. 1966–82); Chief Comr Scout Assoc., for NSW, 1958–68, for Australia, 1969–73; Pres., Nat. Council, Scout Assoc. of Australia, 1977–86; Dep. Pres., Royal Agric. Society of Commonwealth, 1966–90; Mem. C of E Property Trust, 1950–71; Trustee, Walter and Eliza Hall Trust, 1953–; Mem. Council: Art Gall. Soc. of NSW, 1953–69; Royal Flying Doctor Service, 1954–71; Royal Agric. Society of NSW, 1956 (Pres., 1970–79, Vice-Patron, 1979); Mem., Glebe Administration Bd, 1962–73; Rector's Warden, St Mark's, Darling Point, 1948–71. *Recreations:* tennis, golf, trout fishing. *Address:* Elaine, 550 New South Head Road, Double Bay, Sydney, NSW 2028, Australia. *T:* 327. 1416. *Clubs:* Leander; Commonwealth (Canberra); Melbourne (Melbourne); Union, Royal Sydney Golf (Sydney); Queensland (Brisbane).

FAIRFAX-LUCY, Sir Edmund (John William Hugh Cameron-Ramsay-), 6th Bt *cr* 1836; painter; *b* 4 May 1945; *s* of Sir Brian Fulke Cameron-Ramsay-Fairfax-Lucy, 5th Bt and of Hon. Alice Caroline Helen Buchan, *o d* of 1st Baron Tweedsmuir, PC, GCMG, GCVO, CH; *S* father, 1974; *m* 1986, Lady Lucinda (marr. diss. 1989), *d* of Viscount Lambton, *qv*. *Educ:* City and Guilds of London Art Sch.; Royal Academy Schs of Art. *Heir: cousin* Duncan Cameron Cameron-Ramsay-Fairfax-Lucy, FCA [*b* 18 Sept. 1932; *m* 1964, Janet Barclay, *o d* of P. A. B. Niven; one *s* one *d*]. *Address:* Charlecote Park, Warwick.

FAIRGRIEVE, Sir (Thomas) Russell, Kt 1981; CBE 1974; TD 1959; JP; Chairman, Belwood Nurseries Ltd, 1990; *b* 3 May 1924; *s* of late Alexander Fairgrieve, OBE, MC, JP, and Myma Margaret Fairgrieve; *m* 1954, Millie Mitchell; one *s* three *d*. *Educ:* St Mary's Sch., Melrose; Sedbergh School. Major 8th Gurkha Rifles (Indian Army), 1946. Major, KOSB, 1956. Man. Dir, Laidlaw & Fairgrieve Ltd, 1958; Director: Joseph Dawson (Holdings) Ltd, 1961; William Baird and Co. PLC, 1975–79, 1982–; Bain Dawes (Scotland) Ltd, 1985–. Selkirk County and Galashiels Town Councillor, 1949; Pres., Scottish Conservative Assoc., 1965, Vice-Chm., 1971; Chm., Conservative Party in Scotland, 1975–80. MP (C) Aberdeenshire West, Feb. 1974–83; Parly Under Sec. of State, Scottish Office, 1979–81. JP Selkirkshire, 1962. *Recreation:* golf. *Address:* Pankalan, Boleside, Galashiels, Selkirk TD1 3NX. *T:* Galashiels (0896) 2278. *Clubs:* Carlton; New (Edinburgh); Royal and Ancient (St Andrews).

FAIRHALL, Hon. Sir Allen, KBE 1970; FRSA; Member, House of Representatives, 1949–69; *b* 24 Nov. 1909; *s* of Charles Edward and Maude Fairhall; *m* 1936, Monica Clelland, *d* of James and Ellen Ballantyne; one *s*. *Educ:* East Maitland Primary and High Sch.; Newcastle Tech. Inst. Founded commercial broadcasting stn 2KO, 1931; Supervising Engr, Radio and Signals Supplies Div., Min. of Munitions, 1942–45; Pres., Austr. Fedn of Commercial Broadcasting Stns, 1942–43. Mem. Australian Delegn to UN Gen. Assembly, 1954; Minister for Interior and Works, 1956–58; Minister for Supply, 1961–66; Minister for Defence, 1966–69. Mem. Newcastle CC, 1941. FRSA 1970. Hon. DSc Univ. of Newcastle, 1968. *Recreations:* amateur radio; deep sea fishing. *Address:* 7 Parkway Avenue, Newcastle, NSW 2300, Australia. *T:* 049292295. *Clubs:* Tattersall's, National (Sydney); Newcastle (Newcastle).

FAIRHAVEN, 3rd Baron *cr* 1929 and 1961 (new creation); **Ailwyn Henry George Broughton;** JP; Vice Lord-Lieutenant, Cambridgeshire, 1977–85; *b* 16 Nov. 1936; *s* of 2nd Baron Fairhaven and Hon. Diana Rosamond (*d* 1937), *o d* of late Captain Hon. Coulson Fellowes; *S* father, 1973; *m* 1960, Kathleen Patricia, *d* of Col James Henry Magill, OBE; four *s* two *d*. *Educ:* Eton; RMA, Sandhurst. Royal Horse Guards, 1957–71. Mem., Jockey Club, 1977– (Steward, 1981–82, Sen. Steward, 1985–89). DL Cambridgeshire and Isle of Ely, 1973; JP South Cambridgeshire, 1975. CStJ 1983. *Recreations:* shooting, cooking. *Heir: s* Captain Hon. James Henry Ailwyn Broughton [*b* 25 May 1963; *m* 1990, Sarah Olivia, *d* of H. D. F. Creighton, *qv*]. *Address:* Anglesey Abbey, Cambridge CB5 9EJ. *T:* Cambridge (0223) 811746. *Club:* Turf.

FAIRLIE, Professor Alison (Anna Bowie), FBA 1984; Emeritus Professor of French, University of Cambridge, since 1980 (Professor, 1972–80), and Life Fellow, Girton College, since 1980; *b* 23 May 1917; *e d* of Rev. Robert Paul Fairlie, MA, Minister of the Church of Scotland, and of Florence A. A. Wilson. *Educ:* Ardrossan Acad.; Dumfries Acad.; Penrhos Coll.; St Hugh's Coll. Oxford; Sorbonne. BA 1st Cl. in Final Hons Sch. of Medieval and Mod. Langs, Oxon; MA, DPhil (Oxon). Doctoral Research: in Paris, 1938–40 (interruptions for voluntary war-work); in Oxford, 1940–42; Temp. Admin. Officer, Foreign Office, 1942–44; Girton College, Cambridge: Lectr in French, 1944–67; Staff Fellow, 1946–80; Dir of Studies in Mod. Langs, 1946–67; Professorial Fellow, 1972–80; Univ. Lectr in French, Cambridge, 1948–67, Reader in French, 1967–72. Vice-Pres., Soc. for French Studies, 1965–66 and 1968–69, Pres., 1966–68; Mem. Council, 1969–, Vice Pres., 1983–, Assoc. Internationale des Etudes françaises; Member: Editorial Bd, French Studies, 1972–80, Adv. Bd 1980–; Adv. Bd, Romance Studies, 1982–. Hon. Fellow, St Hugh's Coll., Oxford, 1972. *Publications:* Leconte de Lisle's Poems on the Barbarian Races, 1947; Baudelaire: Les Fleurs du Mal, 1960 (repr. 1975); Flaubert:

Madame Bovary, 1962 (repr. 1976); Imagination and Language, 1981; (ed jtly) Baudelaire, Mallarmé, Valéry—New Essays in honour of Lloyd Austin, 1982; contrib.: to Acta of colloquia, on Baudelaire, Constant, Flaubert, Nerval, etc.; to presentation vols; to learned jls in France, England, Italy, USA, Australia, etc. *Recreations:* reading, travel. *Address:* 11 Parker Street, Cambridge CB1 1JL. *T:* Cambridge (0223) 358465.

FAIRLIE, Hugh, OBE 1984; MA, MEd; *b* 14 Dec. 1919; *s* of Thomas and Joanna Fairlie; *m* 1947, Jemima Peden; two *s*. *Educ:* Univ. of Edinburgh. MA (Hons Maths and NatPhil); MEd (Dist.). FEIS. Teacher, Maybole Carrick Academy, 1947–49; Asst Director of Education: Morayshire, 1949–52; Fife, 1952–57; Depute Dir of Educn, 1957–64, Dir of Educn, 1964–75, Renfrewshire; Lectr, Jordanhill Coll. of Educn, 1975–82. Chairman: Scottish Council for Research in Education, 1978–84; Renfrew District Arts Guild, 1980–. FEIS 1975. *Recreations:* golf, gardens. *Address:* 26 Thornly Park Avenue, Paisley, Scotland PA2 7SE. *T:* 041–884 2494. *Clubs:* Royal Over-Seas League; Paisley Burns; Western Gailes Golf.

FAIRLIE-CUNINGHAME, Sir William Henry, 16th Bt *cr* 1630, of Robertland, Ayrshire; *b* 1 Oct. 1930; *s* of Sir William Alan Fairlie-Cuninghame, 15th Bt, MC, and Irene Alice (*d* 1970), *d* of Henry Margrave Terry; *S* father, 1981; *m* 1972, Janet Menzies, *d* of late Roy Menzies Saddington; one *s*. *Heir:* *s* Robert Henry Fairlie-Cuninghame, *b* 19 July 1974. *Address:* 29A Orinoco Street, Pymble, NSW 2073, Australia.

FAIRTLOUGH, Gerard Howard, CBE 1989; Chief Executive, Celltech Ltd, 1980–90; *b* 5 Sept. 1930; *s* of late Maj.-Gen. Eric V. H. Fairtlough, DSO, MC, and A. Zoë Fairtlough (*née* Barker); *m* 1954, Elizabeth A. Betambeau; two *s* two *d*. *Educ:* Cambridge Univ. (BA Biochemistry, Pt II). Royal/Dutch Shell Group, 1953–78; Managing Director, Shell Chemicals UK Ltd, 1973–78. Divisional Director, NEB, 1978–80. Chm., Coverdale Orgn, 1974–. Mem., SERC, 1989–. Hon. DSc: City, 1987; CNAA, 1990. *Recreations:* walking, Yoga. *Address:* 5 Belmont Grove, SE13 5DW. *T:* 081–852 4904.

FAIRWEATHER, Brig. Claude Cyril, CB 1967; CBE 1965 (OBE 1944); TD 1944; JP; Vice Lord-Lieutenant, County of Cleveland, 1977–82; Chairman, North of England TA&VRA, 1968–71; *b* 17 March 1906; *s* of Nicholas Fairweather, Middlesborough; *m* 1930, Alice Mary, *e d* of late Sir William Crosthwaite; one *s* one *d*. *Educ:* St Peter's Sch., York. 2nd Lieut, Royal Corps of Signals, 1928; Lt-Col 1941; Col 1943; Brig. 1945. Chm., North Riding T&AFA, 1950–53 and 1962–68; Member: TA Advisory Cttee and TA Exec. Cttee, 1968–71. Chm., St John Council, N Yorks (Vice-Pres., N Yorks St John Amb. Bde); Hon. Col, 34 (N) Signal Regt (V), 1967–75; Chairman: N Riding Co. Cadet Cttee, 1947–52; St Luke's Hosp. Man. Cttee, Middlesborough, 1959–74; Cleveland AHA, 1973–76. Retd Company Dir. Hon. Trust Representative for Cleveland, Royal Jubilee Trusts, 1977–81. DL 1949, JP 1963, NR Yorks. KStJ 1978. *Recreations:* golf, cricket, Rugby football. *Address:* The White Lodge, Hutton Rudby, Yarm, Cleveland TS15 0HY. *T:* Stokesley (0642) 700598. *Clubs:* Army and Navy; Cleveland (Middlesborough); Royal and Ancient (St Andrews).

FAIRWEATHER, Prof. Denys Vivian Ivor, MD; FRCOG; Professor and Head of Department of Obstetrics and Gynaecology, 1966–90, and Vice-Provost, 1984–90, University College London; Pro-Vice-Chancellor for Medicine and Dentistry, University of London, since 1989; *b* 25 Oct. 1927; *s* of late Albert James Ivor Fairweather and Gertrude Mary Forbes; *m* 1956, (Gwendolen) Yvonne Hubbard; one *s* two *d*. *Educ:* Forfar Acad.; Websters Seminary, Kirriemuir; St Andrews Univ. (MB, ChB 1949; MD 1966). FRCOG 1967 (MRCOG 1958). Served RAF Med. Br., 1950–55, Sqn Leader. Sen. Lectr, Univ. of Newcastle upon Tyne, 1959–66; Fulbright Scholar, Western Reserve Univ., USA, 1963–64; Dean, Faculty of Clinical Science, UCL, 1982–84; Vice Provost (Medicine) and Head, University Coll. London Sch. of Medicine, later University Coll. and Mddx Sch. of Medicine of UCL, 1984–89; Hon. Fellow, UCL, 1985. Sec.-Gen., FIGO, 1985–. Member: GMC, 1988–; Internat. Med. Adv. Panel, IPPF, 1988–; Vice Pres., FPA, 1985–. Hon. FAARM 1969. Freeman, City of Krakow, 1989. *Publications:* Amniotic Fluid Research and Clinical Applications, 1973, 2nd edn 1978; Labour Ward Manual, 1985; over 160 pubns in scientific jls, on perinatal mortality, rhesus disease, genetics, antenatal diagnosis, very low birthweight, medical education. *Recreations:* gardening, fishing, do-it-yourself. *Address:* c/o Secretariat, International Federation of Gynaecology and Obstetrics, 27 Sussex Place, Regent's Park, NW1 4RG. *T:* 071–723 2951; University of London, Senate House, WC1E 7HU. *T:* 071–636 8000.

FAIRWEATHER, Eric John, FCIB; Corporate Banking Area Manager, Manchester, Midland Bank, since 1987; *b* 9 Nov. 1942; *s* of late John Walter William Fairweather and Lilian Emma Fairweather; *m* 1966, Frances Mary Ewer (marr. diss.); two *d*. *Educ:* Carlisle Grammar Sch. Entered Midland Bank at Carlisle, 1961; Manager, Corporate Finance Div., 1978–81; Sen. Asst Man., Poultry and Princes Street, 1981–84; Dir, Industrial Develt Unit, DTI (Under Sec.), 1984–86; Manager, UK Business Sector, 1986; Manager, Central Management and Planning, 1986–87. *Recreations:* classical music, Association football (Watford and Carlisle United), golf. *Address:* Midland Bank, 56 Spring Gardens, Manchester M60 2RX. *T:* 061–832 9011. *Clubs:* St James's (Manchester); Shaw Hill Golf (Chorley).

FAIRWEATHER, Dr Frank Arthur; Environmental Safety Officer, Research Division, Unilever House, since 1982; *b* 2 May 1928; *s* of Frank and Maud Harriet Fairweather; *m* 1953, Christine Winifred Hobbs; two *s*. *Educ:* City of Norwich Sch.; Middlesex Hospital. MB, BS 1954; MRCPath 1963, FRCPath 1975; FIBiol 1972. Clinical house appts, Ipswich Gp of Hosps, 1955–56; Pathologist, Bland Sutton Inst. of Pathology, and Courtauld Inst. of Biochem., Middlesex Hosp., Soho Hosp. for Women, 1956–60; Jt Sen. Registrar in Histopathology, Middlesex and West Middlesex Hosps, 1961–62; Chief Med. Adviser and Cons. Pathologist, Benger Labs, 1962–63; Chief Pathologist, British Industrial Biological Res. Assoc., Carshalton, and Hon. Sen. Lectr, RCS, 1963–65; Associate Res. Dir, Wyeth Labs, Taplow, 1965–69; Sen. Med. Officer, DHSS, and Principal Med. Officer, Cttee on Safety of Medicines, 1969–72; SPMO, DHSS, 1972–82. Member: Expert Panels on Environmental Pollution, Food Toxicology, and Safety, to WHO; EEC Scientific Cttee for Food, 1976– (Chm., Sci. Cttee for Cosmetology); Consultant Adviser in Toxicology to DHSS, 1978–81; Dir, DHSS Toxicological Lab., St Bartholomew's Hosp., 1978–82, Hon. Dir, 1982–84; Hon. Lectr in Path., Middlesex Hosp., 1972–; Hon. Prof. of Toxicology, Dept of Biochemistry, Univ. of Surrey, 1978–84; Hon. Prof. of Toxicology and Pathology, Sch. of Pharmacy, Univ. of London, 1982. QHP, 1977–80. *Publications:* various toxicological and medical papers. *Recreations:* angling, gardening, painting. *Address:* 394 London Road, Langley, Slough, Berks SL3 7HX.

FAIRWEATHER, Patrick Stanislaus, CMG 1986; HM Diplomatic Service; Deputy Under-Secretary of State, Foreign and Commonwealth Office, since 1990; *b* 17 June 1936; *s* of John George Fairweather and Dorothy Jane (*née* Boanus); *m* 1962, Maria (*née* Merica); two *d*. *Educ:* Ottershaw Sch., Surrey; Trinity Coll., Cambridge (Hons History). National Service in Royal Marines and Parachute Regt, 1955–57. Entered FCO, 1965; 2nd Secretary, Rome, 1966–69; FCO, 1969–70; 1st Secretary (Economic), Paris, 1970–73; FCO, 1973–75; 1st Sec. and Head of Chancery, Vientiane, 1975–76; 1st Sec., UK Representation to EEC, Brussels, 1976–78; Counsellor (Economic and Commercial), Athens, 1978–83; Head of European Community Dept (Internal), FCO, 1983–85; Ambassador to Angola, 1985–87; Asst Under-Sec. of State, FCO, 1987–90. *Recreations:* travel, gardening, photography, dinghy sailing. *Address:* c/o Foreign and Commonwealth Office, SW1A 2AH.

FAITH, (Irene) Sheila; JP; Dental Surgeon; *b* 3 June 1928; *yr d* of late I. Book; *m* 1950, Dennis Faith. *Educ:* Central High School, Newcastle upon Tyne; Durham Univ. LDS 1950. Practised as school dental surgeon, Northumberland. Member: Northumberland CC, 1970–74 (Mem., Health and Social Services Cttees; Rep., S Northumberland Youth Employment Bd); Newcastle City Council, 1975–77 (Mem., Educn Cttee). Vice-Chm., Jt Consultative Cttee on Educn for District of Newcastle during local govt reorganisation, 1973–74. Mem., Parole Bd, 1991–. Contested (C) Newcastle Central, Oct. 1974; MP (C) Belper, 1979–83. Mem., Select Cttee on Health and Social Services, 1979–83; Sec., Conservative backbench Health and Social Services Cttee, 1982–83. MEP (C) Cumbria and Lancs N, 1984–89; Member: Transport Cttee, 1984–87; Cttee on Energy, Res. and Technol., 1987–89. Mem., Exec. Cttee, Cons. Medical Soc., 1981–84; Pres., Cumbria and Lancs N Cons. Euro Constituency Council, 1989–; Dep. Chm., Hampstead and Highgate Cons. Assoc., 1991. Has served as Chm. or Mem. several school governing bodies and Manager of Community Homes and with CAB, Newcastle upon Tyne. JP: Northumberland County, 1972–74; Newcastle upon Tyne, 1974–78; Inner London, 1978–. *Recreations:* reading, music. *Address:* 11 Merlin House, Oak Hill Park, Hampstead, NW3 7LJ. *T:* 071–435 3702.

FAITHFULL, family name of **Baroness Faithfull.**

FAITHFULL, Baroness *cr* 1975 (Life Peer), of Wolvercote, Oxfordshire; **Lucy Faithfull,** OBE 1972; *b* 26 Dec. 1910; *d* of Lt Sydney Leigh Faithfull, RE (killed 1916) and late Elizabeth Adie Faithfull (*née* Algie); unmarried. *Educ:* Talbot Heath Sch. (formerly Bournemouth High Sch.). Social Science Dipl., Birmingham Univ., 1933; Family case work training (Charity Welfare Organisation, now Family Welfare Assoc.), 1936, and Cert. in Child Care, 1969. Club Leader and Sub-Warden, Birmingham Settlement, 1932–35; Asst Organiser, Child Care, LCC Education Dept, 1935–40; Regional Welfare Officer (Evacuation Scheme), Min. of Health, 1940–48; Inspector in Children's Br., Home Office, 1948–58; Oxford City Council: Children's Officer, 1958–70; Director of Social Services, 1970–74; retired, 1974. Chm., All Party Parly Gp for Children. Pres., Nat. Children's Bureau, 1984–; Vice President: Barnardo's, 1989–; Nat. Assoc. of Voluntary Hostels, 1978–; Mem., Nursery and Family Care Assoc. Hon. Member: Council, NSPCC, 1989–; BPA. Mem. Council, Caldecott Community Kent Sch. for Maladjusted Children, 1979–; Trustee and Mem. Cttee, Bessel Leigh Sch. for Maladjusted Children, 1975; Trustee, Gracewell Inst., Birmingham. Patron, Nat. Conciliation Council. Hon. MA Oxford, 1974; Hon. DLitt Warwick, 1978. *Recreations:* friends, travel, garden. *Address:* 303 Woodstock Road, Oxford OX2 7NY. *T:* Oxford (0865) 55389.

FAKLEY, Dennis Charles, OBE 1973; retired; *b* 20 Nov. 1924; *s* of Charles Frederick and Ethel May Fakley; *m* 1976, Louise Grace Swindell. *Educ:* Chatham House Grammar Sch., Ramsgate; Queen Mary Coll., Univ. of London (BSc Special Physics). Royal Naval Scientific Service, 1944–63; Min. of Defence, 1963–84. *Recreations:* reading, cricket. *Address:* 14 Coval Gardens, SW14 7DG. *T:* 081–876 6856.

FALCON, David; Director-General, Royal Institute of Public Administration, since 1988; *b* 3 Jan. 1946; *s* of Arnold and Barbara Falcon; *m* 1967 (marr. diss. 1991); two *s*. *Educ:* Helston County Grammar Sch.; University College London (BSc); Lancaster Univ. (MA); Univ. of Pennsylvania. Research Associate, Univ. of Lancaster, 1969–72; Lectr, Leeds Polytechnic, 1972–74; Sen. Lectr, Sheffield Polytechnic, 1974–76; Asst Dir, Sen. Asst Dir, Dep. Dir of Education, Humberside CC, 1976–85; Dir of Education, ILEA, 1985–88. FRSA; FBIM. *Publications:* articles in educn and management jls. *Recreations:* music, opera, photography, travel. *Address:* Royal Institute of Public Administration, 3 Birdcage Walk, SW1H 9JH. *T:* 071–222 2248.

FALCON, Michael Gascoigne, CBE 1979; JP, DL; Chairman: Norwich Union Insurance Group, since 1981 (Director, since 1963; Vice Chairman, 1979–81); Norwich Winterthur Holdings Ltd, since 1984; Norwich Health Authority, since 1988; *b* 28 Jan. 1928; *s* of late Michael Falcon and Kathleen Isabel Frances Gascoigne; *m* 1954, April Daphne Claire Lambert; two *s* one *d*. *Educ:* Stowe Sch., Bucks; Heriot-Watt Coll., Edinburgh. National Service, Grenadier Gds and Royal Norfolk Regt, 1946–48. Head Brewer and Jt Man. Dir, E. Lacon & Co. Ltd, Great Yarmouth, 1952–68; Exec. Dir, Edgar Watts, Willow Merchants, 1968–73; Chairman: National Seed Develt Orgn Ltd, 1972–82; Pauls & Whites PLC, 1976–85 (Dir, 1973–85); Eastern Counties Regional Bd, Lloyds Bank Plc, 1979–91 (Dir, 1972–91); Director: Securicor (East) Ltd, 1969–72; Lloyds Bank UK Management Ltd, 1979–85; Matthew Brown plc, 1981–87; National Bus Properties Ltd, 1983–86; Greene King & Sons PLC, 1988–; British Railways (Anglia) Bd, 1988–. Trustee, E Anglian Trustee Savings Bank, 1963–75. Chm., Trustees, John Innes Foundn, 1990. Mem., Norwich Prison Bd of Visitors, 1969–82. JP 1967, High Sheriff 1979, DL 1981, Co. of Norfolk; High Steward, Great Yarmouth, 1984–. CStJ 1986. Hon. LLD Nottingham, 1988. *Recreation:* country pursuits. *Address:* Keswick Old Hall, Norwich, Norfolk NR4 6TZ. *T:* Norwich (0603) 54348; Kirkgate, Loweswater, Cockermouth, Cumbria. *Clubs:* Norfolk (Norwich); Royal Norfolk and Suffolk Yacht (Lowestoft).
See also Ven. D. L. Edwards.

FALCON, Norman Leslie, FRS 1960; *b* 29 May 1904; 2nd *s* of late Thomas Adolphus Falcon, MA, RBA; *m* 1938, Dorothy Muriel, 2nd *d* of late F. G. Freeman, HM Consular Service; two *s* one *d*. *Educ:* Exeter Sch.; Trinity Coll., Cambridge (Sen. Exhibitioner 1925, Natural Science Tripos Pt I 1925, 1st cl., Part II 1927, 1st cl.; MA Cantab). Joined Anglo-Persian Oil Company as geologist, 1927; FGS, FRGS, 1927; Geological Exploration in Persia, UK and elsewhere, 1927–40. Served War of 1939–45, Intelligence Corps, 1940–45. Rejoined Anglo-Iranian Oil Company as Geologist on Head Office staff, 1945; Chief Geologist, 1955–65, Geological Adviser, 1965–72, British Petroleum Co Ltd. FInstPet, 1959; Geological Soc. of London: Mem. Council, 1954–58, 1967–71; Foreign Sec. 1967–70; Murchison Medal, 1963; Hon. Mem. 1988; Royal Geographical Society: Mem. Council, 1966–69; Vice-Pres. 1973; Founder's Medal, 1973. Mem., NERC, 1968–71. Hon. Mem., American Assoc. Petroleum Geologists, 1973. Bronze Star Medal (USA), 1945. *Publications:* geological papers. *Recreations:* outdoor pursuits. *Address:* The Downs, Chiddingfold, Surrey GU8 4XJ. *T:* Wormley (042879) 3101.

FALCONER, Alexander, (Alex); Member (Lab) Mid Scotland and Fife, European Parliament, since 1984; *b* Dundee, 1 April 1940; *m*; one *s* one *d*. Former foundry worker; served with RN, 1959–68; insulator, Rosyth dockyard, 1969–84. Shop Steward, TGWU, 1970–84; Chm., Fife Fedn of Trades Councils. Mem., CND. *Address:* 25 Church Street, Inverkeithing, Fife KY11 1LH.

FALCONER, Charles Leslie; QC 1991; *b* 19 Nov. 1951; *s* of John Leslie Falconer and of late Anne Mansel Falconer; *m* 1985, Marianna Catherine Thoroton Hildyard, *d* of Sir D. H. T. Hildyard, *qv*; two *s* one *d*. *Educ:* Trinity Coll., Glenalmond; Queens' Coll.,

Cambridge. Called to the Bar, Inner Temple, 1974. *Address:* Fountain Court, Temple, EC4Y 6DP.

FALCONER, Prof. Douglas Scott, FRS 1973; FRSE 1972; *b* 10 March 1913; *s* of Gerald Scott Falconer and Lillias Harriet Gordon Douglas; *m* 1942, Margaret Duke; two *s*. *Educ:* Edinburgh Academy; Univ. of St Andrews (BSc); Univ. of Cambridge (PhD. ScD). Scientific Staff of Agricultural Research Council, 1947–68; Prof. of Genetics, Univ. of Edinburgh, and Dir, ARC Unit of Animal Genetics, 1968–80. *Publications:* Introduction to Quantitative Genetics, 1960, 3rd edn 1989; Problems on Quantitative Genetics, 1983; papers in scientific jls. *Recreations:* music, walking, sailing. *Address:* Zoology Building, West Mains Road, Edinburgh EH9 3JT.

FALCONER, Hon. Sir Douglas (William), Kt 1981; MBE 1946; a Judge of the High Court of Justice, Chancery Division, 1981–89; *b* 20 Sept. 1914; *s* of late William Falconer, S Shields; *m* 1941, Joan Beryl Argent (*d* 1989), *d* of late A. S. Bishop, Hagley, Worcs; one *s* one *d*. *Educ:* South Shields; King's Coll., Durham Univ.; BSc (Hons) Physics, 1935. Served War of 1939–45 (Hon. Major): commissioned E Yorks Regt, 1939. Called to Bar, Middle Temple, 1950, Bencher 1972; QC 1967. Apptd to exercise appellate jurisdiction of BoT, later DoT, under Trade Marks Act, 1970–81; Member: of Departmental Cttee to review British trade mark law and practice, 1972–73; Standing Adv. Cttee on Patents, 1975–79; Standing Adv. Cttee on Trade Marks, 1975–79; Senate of Four Inns of Court, 1973–74; Senate of Four Inns of Court and the Bar, 1974–77; Chm., Patent Bar Assoc., 1971–80. *Publications:* (Jt Editor) Terrell on the Law of Patents (11th and 12th edns), 1965 and 1971. *Recreations:* music, theatre. *Address:* Ridgwell House, West Street, Reigate, Surrey RH2 9BZ. *T:* Reigate (0737) 244374.

FALCONER, Peter Serrell, FRIBA, FRSA; Founder of The Falconer Partnership, Architects and Consultants, and of Handling Consultants Ltd, Stroud and Johannesburg; *b* 7 March 1916; *s* of Thomas Falconer, FRIBA, and Florence Edith Falconer; presumed heir to the Barony (1206) and Lordship (1646) of Halkerton, vacant since 1966; *m* 1941, Mary Hodson; three *s* one *d*. *Educ:* Bloxham Sch., Banbury. Commenced practice in Stroud, as partner in Ellery Anderson Roiser & Falconer, 1944; Sen. Partner of Peter Falconer and Partners, 1959–82 (with br. office in Adelaide, SA, 1970). Specialist in materials handling and industrial architecture; Mem., Materials Handling Inst. *Publications:* Building and Planning for Industrial Storage and Distribution, 1975; contributor to: Architectural Review; Architects' Jl; Material Handling magazines. *Recreations:* restoring historic buildings, garden planning, motor sport. *Address:* St Francis, Lammas Park, Minchinhampton, Stroud, Glos. *T:* Brimscombe (0453) 882188.

FALDO, Nicholas Alexander, MBE 1988; professional golfer; *b* 18 July 1957; *s* of George and Joyce Faldo; *m* 1st, Melanie (marr. diss.); 2nd, 1986, Gill; one *s* one *d*. *Educ:* Welwyn Garden City. Won English Amateur Golf Championship, 1975; Professional golfer, 1976; Mem., Ryder Cup team, 1977–; many championship titles include: Open, Muirfield, 1987, St Andrews, 1990; US Masters, 1989, 1990; French Open 3 times. *Publication:* Golf: the winning formula, 1989. *Recreations:* fly fishing, DIY, snooker, motor sports. *Address:* c/o IMG, Pier House, Strand on the Green, Chiswick, W4 3NN.

FALETAU, 'Inoke Fotu; Director, Commonwealth Foundation, since 1985; *b* 24 June 1937; 2nd *s* of 'Akau'ola Sateki Faletau and Celia Lyden; *m* 'Evelini Ma'ata Hurrell; three *s* three *d*. *Educ:* St Peter's, Cambridge, NZ; Tonga High Sch.; Auckland Grammar Sch.; UC Swansea (Hon. Fellow 1990); Manchester Univ. Joined Tonga Civil Service, 1958; Asst Sec., Prime Minister's Office, 1965; Sec. to Govt, 1969; seconded to Univ. of South Pacific, 1971; Sec. to Govt, 1972; High Comr, UK, 1972–82; Ambassador to: France, 1972–82; Germany, 1976–82; Belgium, Luxembourg, Netherlands, EEC, 1977–82; USA, 1979–82; USSR, 1980–82; Denmark, 1981–82; Dir. Management Develt Programme, Commonwealth Secretariat, 1983–84. *Recreations:* Rugby, tennis, reading, bridge, fishing. *Address:* Commonwealth Foundation, Marlborough House, Pall Mall, SW1Y 5HY. *Clubs:* Royal Over-Seas League; Nuku'alofa Yacht and Motor Boat.

FALK, Sir Roger (Salis), Kt 1969; OBE (mil.) 1945; Hon. DLitt; CBIM; Vice President, Sadler's Wells Foundation and Trust, since 1986 (Chairman, 1976–86); *b* 22 June 1910; *s* of Lionel David Falk; *m* 1938, Margaret Helen (*née* Stroud) (*d* 1958); one *s* two *d*. *Educ:* Haileybury (Life Governor, 1971–; Council Mem., 1978–); Geneva Univ. Gen. Manager's Office, Rhodesia Railways, Bulawayo, 1931; D. J. Keymer & Co: Manager in Bombay and Calcutta, 1932–35; Dir, 1935–49; Managing Dir, 1945–49; Vice-Chm., 1950; formerly: Dir, P-E International Ltd (Chm., 1973–76); Chm., London Bd, Provincial Insurance Co. Ltd. Shoreditch Borough Council, 1937–45. Dir-Gen. British Export Trade Research Organisation (BETRO) from 1949 until disbandment. Chairman: Furniture Development Council, 1963–82; Central Council for Agric. and Hort. Cooperation, 1967–75; British European Associated Publishers, 1976–79; Action for Dysphasic Adults (ADA), 1982–85 (Vice-Pres., 1985–); Dep. Chm., Gaming Bd, 1978–81; Member: Council of Industrial Design, 1958–67; Monopolies and Mergers Commn, 1965–80; Council, RSA, 1968–74; Council, Imp. Soc. of Knights Bachelor, 1979–; Pres., Design and Industries Assoc., 1971–72. Served War of 1939–45, RAFVR; Wing-Comdr, 1942. Hon. DLitt City Univ. *Publication:* The Business of Management, 1961, 5th rev. edn 1976. *Recreations:* writing, music, reading, theatre. *Address:* 603 Beatty House, Dolphin Square, SW1V 3PL. *T:* 071–828 3752. *Clubs:* Garrick, MCC.

FALKENDER, Baroness *cr* 1974 (Life Peer), of West Haddon, Northants; **Marcia Matilda Falkender,** CBE 1970; Private and Political Secretary to Lord Wilson of Rievaulx, 1956–83 (at 10 Downing Street, 1964–70 and 1974–76); *b* March 1932; *d* of Harry Field. *Educ:* Northampton High School; Queen Mary Coll., Univ. of London. BA Hons Hist. Secretary to Gen. Sec., Labour Party, 1955–56. Member: Prime Minister's Film Industry Working Party, 1975–76; Interim Cttee on Film Industry, 1977–82; British Screen Adv. Council, 1985–. Pres., UN Develt Fund for Women (UK Cttee), 1990–. Chm., Canvasback Productions, 1989–. Director: Peckham Building Soc., 1986–; South London Investment and Mortgage Corp., 1986–; Milford Dock Co., 1986–87. Political columnist, Mail on Sunday, 1982–88. Lay Governor, QMC, London Univ., 1987–. *Publications:* Inside Number 10, 1972; Downing Street in Perspective, 1983. *Address:* 3 Wyndham Mews, Upper Montagu Street, W1H 1RS. *Club:* Reform.

FALKINER, Sir Edmond (Charles), 9th Bt *cr* 1778, of Annemount, Cork; Probation Officer since 1969; *b* 24 June 1938; *s* of Sir Terence Edmond Patrick Falkiner, 8th Bt and Mildred Katherine (*d* 1989), *y d* of Sir John Cotterell, 4th Bt; *S* father, 1987; *m* 1960, Janet Iris, *d* of Arthur E. B. Darby; two *s*. *Educ:* Downside. CQSW. Various jobs, 1956–68. Home Office Probation Training Course, 1968; Hon. Chm., Drugcare (St Albans), 1986–. *Recreations:* jazz, and playing a variety of saxophones. *Heir:* *s* Benjamin Simon Patrick Falkiner, *b* 16 Jan. 1962. *Address:* 111 Wood Street, Barnet, Herts EN5 4BX. *T:* 081–440 2426. *Club:* Ronnie Scott's.

FALKINGHAM, Ven. John Norman; Warden, Community of the Holy Name, 1969–85; *b* 9 Feb. 1917; 2nd *s* of Alfred Richard Falkingham and Amy Grant (*née* Macallister); *m* 1947, Jean Dorothy Thoren; two *d*. *Educ:* Geelong Gram. Sch., Corio, Vic.; Trinity Coll., Univ. of Melbourne. BA (Hons) Melbourne 1940; ThL (1st Cl. Hons), ThD 1978, Australian Coll. of Theol.; prizes for Divinity and Biblical Greek. Deacon, 1941; Priest, 1942. Curate of Holy Trinity, Surrey Hills, Vic., 1941–44; Chaplain, Trinity Coll., Univ. of Melbourne, 1944–50; Incumbent, St Paul's, Caulfield, Vic., 1950–61. Exam. Chaplain to Archbishop of Melbourne, 1947–61; Lectr in Theol. Faculty, Trinity Coll., Melbourne, 1950–60; Canon of St Paul's Cath., Melbourne, 1959–61; Dean of Newcastle, NSW, 1961–75; Rector of St Paul's, Manuka, ACT, 1975–82; Canon of St Saviour's Cath., Goulburn, 1976–81; Archdeacon of Canberra, 1981–82, Archdeacon Emeritus, 1982. Sec., Liturgical Commn of Gen. Synod, 1966–78; Mem. Bd of Delegates, Aust. Coll. of Theology, 1962–88; Lecturer: Canberra Coll. of Ministry, 1975–84; St Mark's Library, Canberra, 1982–87; Chm., Bd of Dirs, Canberra C of E Girls' Grammar Sch., 1983–90. *Publications:* articles in various jls. *Recreation:* walking. *Address:* 4 Serra Place, Stirling, ACT 2611, Australia.

FALKLAND, 15th Viscount *cr* 1620 (Scot.), of Falkland, Co. Fife; **Lucius Edward William Plantagenet Cary;** Lord Cary 1620; *b* 8 May 1935; *s* of 14th Viscount Falkland, and of Constance Mary, *d* of late Captain Edward Berry; *S* father, 1984; *m* 1st, 1962, Caroline Anne (marr. diss. 1990), *o d* of late Lt-Comdr Gerald Butler, DSC, RN, and late Mrs Patrick Parish; one *s* two *d* (and one *d* decd); 2nd, 1990, Nicole, *o d* of late Milburn Mackey. *Educ:* Wellington Coll.; Alliance Française, Paris. Late 2nd Lieut 8th Hussars. Export marketing consultant, formerly Chief Executive, C. T. Bowring Trading (Holdings) Ltd. Mem., H of L Select Cttee on Overseas Trade, 1984–85. Dep. Whip, Lib Dem, H of L, 1989–. *Recreations:* golf, motorcycling, cinema. *Heir:* *s* Master of Falkland, *qv*. *Address:* c/o House of Lords, SW1A 0PW. *Clubs:* Brooks's; Sunningdale Golf.

FALKLAND, Master of; Hon. Lucius Alexander Plantagenet Cary; Captain, 2nd Battalion, Scots Guards; *b* 1 Feb. 1963; *s* and *heir* of 15th Viscount Falkland, *qv*. *Educ:* Loretto School; RMA Sandhurst. *Recreations:* ski-ing, golf. *Address:* Shutelake Farm, Butterleigh, Cullompton, Devon. *Club:* Cavalry and Guards.

FALKNER, Sir (Donald) Keith, Kt 1967; Hon. DMus Oxon, 1969; FRCM; Hon. RAM; Hon. GSM; Hon. FTCL; Hon. FLCM; Director, Royal College of Music, 1960–74, Vice President, since 1984; professional singer; *b* Sawston, Cambs, 1900; *y s* of late John Charles Falkner; *m* 1930, Christabel Margaret (*d* 1990), *o d* of Thomas Fletcher Fullard, MA; two *d*. *Educ:* New Coll. Sch.; Perse Sch.; Royal College of Music; Berlin, Vienna, Paris. Has sung at all principal festivals in England, and many European cities; toured USA eight times, including concerts with Boston Symphony, New York Philharmonic, Cincinnati, St Louis, and Philadelphia Orchestras; toured: South Africa, 1935, 1939, 1955, 1962, 1974; Canada in 1953; New Zealand in 1956; starred in three Warner Bros musicals, 1937–39. British Council Music Officer for Italy, 1946–50. Prof. of the Dept of Music at Cornell Univ., USA, 1950–60. An Artistic Dir, King's Lynn Fest., 1981–83. FRSA 1979. Hon. Mem., Assoc. Européene des Conservatoires de Musique, Académies, et Musikhochschulen, 1976. Served European War, 1914–18, in RNAS, 1917–19; War of 1939–45, RAFVR, 1940–45. Editor, Voice, 1983–. *Recreations:* cricket, golf, lawn tennis, squash rackets, walking. *Address:* Low Cottages, Ilketshall St Margaret, Bungay, Suffolk NR35 1PL. *T:* Bungay (0986) 892573. *Clubs:* Athenæum, Royal Automobile, MCC; Norfolk (Norwich).

FALKUS, Hugh Edward Lance; naturalist, independent writer, film director, broadcaster; now engaged in teaching salmon fishing and speycasting; *b* 15 May 1917; *s* of James Everest Falkus and Alice Musgrove. *Educ:* The East Anglian Sch. (Culford Sch.). Served War of 1939–45 (Fighter Pilot). Films include: Drake's England, 1950; Shark Island, 1952; TV films include: Salmo—the Leaper; (with Niko Tinbergen) Signals for Survival (Italia Prize, 1969; Amer. Blue Ribbon, New York Film Fest., 1971); Highland Story; The Gull Watchers; The Signreaders; The Beachcombers; The Riddle of the Rook (Venice Film Festival, 1972); Tender Trap (Certificate of Merit, BAAS, 1975); Self-Portrait of a Happy Man. Cherry Kearton Medal and Award, RGS, 1982. *Publications:* Sea Trout Fishing, 1962, 2nd edn 1975, revised 2nd edn 1981; The Stolen Years, 1965, 2nd edn 1979; (with Niko Tinbergen) Signals for Survival, 1970; (with Fred Buller) Freshwater Fishing, 1975, 9th edn 1987; (jtly) Successful Angling, 1977; Nature Detective, 1978, 2nd edn 1987; (with Joan Kerr) From Sydney Cove to Duntroon, 1982; Master of Cape Horn, 1982; Salmon Fishing, 1984; The Sea Trout, 1987. *Recreations:* fishing, shooting, sailing, oil painting. *Address:* Cragg Cottage, near Ravenglass, Cumbria CA18 1RT. *T:* Ravenglass (0229) 717247.

FALL, Brian James Proetel, CMG 1984; HM Diplomatic Service; High Commissioner to Canada, since 1989; *b* 13 Dec. 1937; *s* of John William Fall, Hull, Yorkshire, and Edith Juliette (*née* Proetel); *m* 1962, Delmar Alexandra Roos; three *d*. *Educ:* St Paul's Sch.; Magdalen Coll., Oxford; Univ. of Michigan Law Sch. Joined HM Foreign (now Diplomatic) Service, 1962; served in Foreign Office UN Dept, 1963; Moscow, 1965; Geneva, 1968; Civil Service Coll., 1970; FO Eastern European and Soviet Dept and Western Organisations Dept, 1971; New York, 1975; Harvard Univ. Center for Internat. Affairs, 1976; Counsellor, Moscow, 1977–79; Head of Energy, Science and Space Dept, FCO, 1979–80; Head of Eastern European and Soviet Dept, FCO, 1980–81; Prin. Private Sec. to Sec. of State for Foreign and Commonwealth Affairs, 1981–84; Dir, Cabinet, Sec. Gen. of NATO, 1984–86; Asst Under-Sec. of State (Defence), FCO, 1986–88; Minister, Washington, 1988–89. *Address:* c/o Foreign and Commonwealth Office, King Charles Street, SW1A 2AH. *Club:* Travellers'.

FALLA, Paul Stephen; *b* 25 Oct. 1913; *s* of Norris Stephen Falla and Audrey Frances Stock, Dunedin, New Zealand; *m* 1958, Elizabeth Shearer; one *d*. *Educ:* Wellington and Christ's Colls, NZ; Balliol Coll., Oxford (Scholar). Appointed to Foreign Office, 1936; served HM Embassies, Warsaw, 1938–39, Ankara, 1939–43, Tehran, 1943; Foreign Office, 1943–46; UK Delegation to UN, New York, 1946–49; Foreign Office, 1949–67 (Dep. Dir of Research, 1958–67). Member: Exec. Cttee, Translators' Assoc., Soc. of Authors, 1971–73 and 1984–86 (Vice-Chm., 1973); Council, Inst. Linguists, 1975–81 (FIL 1984); Cttee, Translators' Guild, 1975–81. Fellow, Inst. of Translation and Interpreting, 1989. Scott Moncrieff prize, 1972 and 1981; Schlegel-Tieck Prize, 1983. *Publications:* (ed) The Oxford English-Russian Dictionary, 1984; about 50 book translations from Russian, Polish and other languages, 1967–. *Recreations:* reading (history, philosophy, poetry, language matters). *Address:* 63 Freelands Road, Bromley, Kent BR1 3HZ. *T:* 081–460 4995. *Club:* Travellers'.

FALLE, Sir Sam, KCMG 1979 (CMG 1964); KCVO 1972; DSC 1945; HM Diplomatic Service, retired; *b* 19 Feb. 1919; *s* of Theodore and Hilda Falle; *m* 1945, Merete Rosen; one *s* three *d*. *Educ:* Victoria Coll., Jersey, CI. Served Royal Navy, 1937–48; joined Foreign (subseq. Diplomatic) Service, 1948; British Consulate, Shiraz, Iran, 1949–51; British Embassy, Tehran, 1952; British Embassy, Beirut, 1952–55; FO, 1955–57; British Embassy, Baghdad, 1957–61; Consul-Gen., Gothenburg, 1961–63; Head of UN Dept, FO, 1963–67; with Lord Shackleton's mission to Aden 1967; Deputy High Comr, Kuala Lumpur, 1967–69; Ambassador to Kuwait, 1969–70; High Comr, Singapore, 1970–74; Ambassador to Sweden, 1974–77; High Comr in Nigeria, 1977–78; Delegate, Commn of the European Communities, Algiers, 1979–82; carried out evaluation of EEC aid to

Zambia, 1983–84. Kt Grand Cross, Order of Polar Star, Sweden, 1975. *Recreations:* swimming, ski-ing, jogging. *Address:* Slättna, 57030 Mariannelund, Sweden.

FALLON, Hazel Rosemary; *see* Counsell, H. R.

FALLON, Ivan Gregory; Deputy Editor, Sunday Times, since 1984; *b* 26 June 1944; *s* of Padraic and Dorothea Fallon; *m* 1967, Susan Mary Lurring; one *s* two *d*. *Educ:* St Peter's Coll., Wexford; Trinity Coll., Dublin (BBS). Irish Times, 1964–66; Thomson Provincial Newspapers, 1966–67; Daily Mirror, 1967–68; Sunday Telegraph, 1968–70; Deputy City Editor, Sunday Express, 1970–71; Sunday Telegraph, 1971–84: City Editor, 1979–84. Member: Council, Univ. of Buckingham, 1982–; Council of Governors, United Med. and Dental Schs of Guy's and St Thomas's Hosps, 1985–; Trustee: Project Trust, 1984–; Generation Trust, Guy's Hosp., 1985–. FRSA 1989. *Publications:* (with James L. Srodes): DeLorean: the rise and fall of a dream-maker, 1983; Takeovers, 1987; The Brothers: the rise of Saatchi and Saatchi, 1988; Billionaire: the life and times of Sir James Goldsmith, 1991. *Recreations:* squash, tennis. *Address:* Clare Cottage, Mill Street, East Malling, Kent ME19 6BU. *T:* West Malling (0732) 843091. *Clubs:* Beefsteak, Royal Automobile.

FALLON, Martin; *see* Patterson, Harry.

FALLON, Michael; MP (C) Darlington, since 1983; Parliamentary Under-Secretary of State, Department of Education and Science, since 1990; *b* 14 May 1952; *s* of Martin Fallon, OBE, FRCSI and Hazel Fallon; *m* 1986, Wendy Elisabeth, *e d* of Peter Payne, Holme-on-Spalding Moor, Yorks; two *s*. *Educ:* St Andrews Univ. (MA Hons 1974). European Educnl Res. Trust, 1974–75; Opposition Whips Office, House of Lords, 1975–77; EEC Officer, Cons. Res. Dept, 1977–79; Jt Man. Dir, European Consultants Ltd, 1979–81. Sec., Lord Home's Cttee on future of House of Lords, 1977–78; Assistant to Baroness Elles, 1979–83. PPS to Sec. of State for Energy, 1987–88; an Asst Govt Whip, 1988–90; a Lord Comr of HM Treasury, 1990. Pres., Darlington YCs. Lectr on trade and industry, foreign affairs and EEC matters. *Publications:* The Quango Explosion (jtly), 1978; Sovereign Members?, 1982; The Rise of the Euroquango, 1982; contribs to journals. *Recreations:* tennis, swimming, ski-ing. *Address:* House of Commons, SW1A 0AA. *T:* 071-219 3000. *Clubs:* Darlington Conservative, Junior Unionist (Darlington).

FALLON, Peter, QC 1971; **His Honour Judge Fallon;** a Circuit Judge, since 1979, a Senior Circuit Judge, since 1980; *b* 1 March 1931; *s* of Frederick and Mary Fallon; *m* 1st, 1955, Zina Mary (*née* Judd); one *s* two *d*; 2nd, 1980, Hazel Rosemary Counsell, *qv*. *Educ:* Leigh Grammar Sch.; St Joseph's Coll., Blackpool; Bristol Univ. (LLB Hons). Called to Bar, Gray's Inn, 1953. Commissioned in RAF for three years. A Recorder of the Crown Court, 1972–79. *Publications:* Crown Court Practice: Sentencing, 1974; Crown Court Practice: Trial, 1978; contrib. Proc. RSM. *Recreations:* golf, fishing, painting. *Address:* The Crown Court, The Guildhall, Bristol BS1 2HI.

FALLOWS, Albert Bennett, CB 1987; FRICS; Hon. FSVA; Chief Valuer, Inland Revenue Valuation Office and Commissioner of Inland Revenue, 1984–88; *b* 7 Dec. 1928; *s* of Bennett and May Fallows; *m* 1955, Maureen James; two *d*. *Educ:* Leek High School. Private practice, surveying, 1945–56; Stoke City Council, 1956–58; Staffs County Council, 1958–62; District Valuer's Office, Kidderminster, 1962–68; Chief Valuer's Office, 1968–73; District Valuer, Basingstoke, 1973–75; Superintending Valuer, Liaison Officer, DoE/Dept of Transport, 1975–77; Board of Inland Revenue: Superintending Valuer, North West, Preston, 1977–80; Asst Chief Valuer, 1980–83; Dep. Chief Valuer, 1983. Hon. FSVA 1987. *Recreation:* golf. *Address:* 110 Whitedown Lane, Alton, Hants GU34 1QR. *T:* Alton (0420) 82818. *Club:* Blackmoor Golf.

FALLSIDE, Prof. Frank, PhD; CEng, FIWES; Professor of Information Engineering, since 1983, and Fellow of Trinity Hall, since 1962, University of Cambridge; *b* 2 Jan. 1932; *s* of William Thomas Fallside, Leith and Daisy Helen Janet Kinnear Madden, Edinburgh; *m* 1958, Maureen Helen Couttie, Edinburgh; two *s* one *d*. *Educ:* George Heriot's Sch., Edinburgh; Edinburgh Univ. (BSc); PhD Wales; MA Cantab. MIEE 1968; CEng, FIWES 1983. Engr, English Electric Co., 1957–58; Cambridge University: Sen. Asst in Res., 1958–61; Lectr in Engrg, 1961–72; Reader in Electrical Engrg, 1972–83; Tutor for grad. students, Trinity Hall, 1966–72. Director: Cambridge Water Co., 1969–; Cambridge Microprocessor Courses, 1979–; Eastcam Systems, 1983–. *Publications:* (ed with W. A. Woods) Computer Speech Processing, 1985; various tech. papers in engrg and speech science. *Recreations:* sailing, maritime history. *Address:* 37 Earl Street, Cambridge CB1 1JR. *T:* Cambridge (0223) 353966.

FALMOUTH, 9th Viscount, *cr* 1720; **George Hugh Boscawen;** 26th Baron Le Despencer, 1264; Baron Boscawen-Rose, 1720; Lord-Lieutenant of Cornwall, since 1977; *b* 31 Oct. 1919; 2nd but *e* surv. *s* of 8th Viscount; *S* father, 1962; *m* 1953, Elizabeth Price Browne; four *s*. *Educ:* Eton Coll.; Trinity Coll., Cambridge. Served War, 1939–46, Italy. Capt., Coldstream Guards. DL Cornwall, 1968. *Heir: s* Hon. Evelyn Arthur Hugh Boscawen [*b* 13 May 1955; *m* 1977, Lucia Vivian-Neal, *e d* of R. W. Vivian-Neal; one *s* one *d*]. *Clubs:* Athenæum, Army and Navy.

See also Hon. R. T. Boscawen.

FANE, family name of **Earl of Westmorland.**

FANE, Harry Frank Brien, CMG 1967; OBE 1957 (MBE 1945); Department of Employment and Productivity, retired 1968; *b* 21 Aug. 1915; *s* of late Harry Lawson Fane and Edith (*née* Stovold); *m* 1947, Stella, *yr d* of late John Hopwood; two *d*. *Educ:* William Ellis Sch.; Birkbeck Coll., London. Joined Ministry of Labour, 1933. HM Forces, 1940–45: Major, Royal Corps of Signals (despatches); served in N Africa, Italy and Austria. British Embassy, Washington: First Sec. (Labour), 1950–56; Counsellor (Labour), 1960–66. Regional Controller, Dept of Employment and Productivity (formerly Min. of Labour), Birmingham, 1966–68. *Address:* 40 Winterbourne Road, Solihull, West Midlands B91 1LU.

FANE TREFUSIS, family name of **Baron Clinton.**

FANNER, Peter Duncan; His Honour Judge Fanner; a Circuit Judge, since 1986; *b* 27 May 1926; *s* of late Robert William Hodges Fanner, solicitor, and Doris Kitty Fanner; *m* 1949, Sheila Eveline England; one *s* one *d*. *Educ:* Pangbourne Coll. Admitted Solicitor of the Supreme Court, 1951 (holder Justices' Clerks' Society's prize). Served War of 1939–45, Pilot in Fleet Air Arm, Lieut (A) RNVR, 1944–47. Asst Clerk to Bromley Justices, 1947–51; Dep. Clerk to Gore Justices, 1951–56; Clerk to Bath Justices, 1956–72; Metropolitan Stipendiary Magistrate, 1972–86; a Dep. Circuit Judge, 1974–80; a Recorder, 1980–86. Mem. Council of Justices' Clerks' Society, 1966–72; Assessor Mem. of Departmental Cttee on Liquor Licensing, 1971–72. Chm., Bath Round Table, 1963–64. *Publications:* Stone's Justices' Manual; contrib. to Justice of the Peace, The Magisterial Officer, The Lawyer's Remembrancer. *Recreations:* travel, railways. *Address:* Bristol Crown Court, Guildhall, Bristol. *T:* Bristol (0272) 211681.

FANSHAWE OF RICHMOND, Baron *cr* 1983 (Life Peer), of South Cerney in the County of Gloucestershire; **Anthony Henry Fanshawe Royle,** KCMG 1974; *b* 27 March 1927; *s* of Sir Lancelot Royle, KBE; *m* 1957, Shirley Worthington; two *d*. *Educ:* Harrow; Sandhurst. Captain, The Life Guards (Germany, Egypt, Palestine and Transjordan), 1945–48; 21st Special Air Service Regt (TA), 1948–51. MP (C) Richmond, 1959–83; Parliamentary Private Secretary: to Under-Sec. of State for the Colonies, 1960; to Sec. of State for Air, 1960–62; to Minister of Aviation, 1962–64; Vice-Chm., Cons. Parly Foreign Affairs Cttee, 1965–67; Tory Whip, 1967–70; Parly Under-Sec. of State for Foreign and Commonwealth Affairs, 1970–74. Vice-Chm., Cons. Party Orgn, 1979–84 (Chm., Internat. Office, 1979–84). Mem., Assembly of Council of Europe and WEU, 1965. Chm., Wilkinson Sword Gp, 1980–83; Director: Sedgwick Gp, 1984–; Westland Gp, 1985–; Rank Xerox UK, 1988–; TI Group, 1990–. Esteemed Family Order (1st cl.), Brunei, 1975. *Address:* House of Lords, SW1A 0PW. *Clubs:* Pratt's, White's, Brooks's.

See also T. L. F. Royle.

FANSHAWE, Captain Thomas Evelyn, CBE 1971; DSC 1943; RN retd; Captain of the Sea Cadet Corps, 1972–81; *b* 29 Sept. 1918; *s* of Rev. Richard Evelyn Fanshawe and Mrs Isobel Fanshawe (*née* Prosser Hale); *m* 1944, Joan Margaret Moxon; one *s* two *d*. *Educ:* Dover Coll.; Nautical Coll., Pangbourne. FRHS. Served 1939–45 in destroyers and frigates and comdg HMS Clover (DSC, despatches 1943 and 1944); HM Ships Ocean, Constance and Phoenix, 1945–51; comd HM Ships: Zest and Obedient, 1951–54; Loch Insh, 1955–57; Temeraire, 1957–59; Tyne, 1959–61; NATO Defence Coll. and Liaison Officer with C-in-C Southern Europe, 1961–64; comd HMS Plymouth and Captain (D) 29th Escort Sqdn, 1964–66; Sen. Naval Officer Persian Gulf and Comdr Naval Forces Gulf, 1966–68 (Cdre); SBNO and Naval Attaché, S Africa (Cdre), 1969–71; ADC to the Queen, 1970–71; retd 1971. Cmdr 1955; Captain 1961. *Recreations:* gardening, golf, general interest in sport. *Address:* Freshwater House, Stroud, Petersfield, Hants GU32 3PN. *T:* Petersfield (0730) 62430. *Clubs:* Royal Navy of 1765 and 1785, MCC.

FANTONI, Barry Ernest; novelist, broadcaster, cartoonist, jazz musician; Member of editorial staff of Private Eye, since 1963; Diary cartoonist, The Times, since 1983; Director: Barry Fantoni Merchandising Co Ltd, since 1985; Snartz Ltd, since 1988; *b* 28 Feb. 1940; *s* of late Peter Nello Secondo Fantoni and of Sarah Catherine Fantoni; *m* 1972, Teresa Frances, (Tessa), Reidy. *Educ:* Archbishop Temple Sch.; Camberwell Sch. of Arts and Crafts (Wedgwood Scholar). Cartoonist of The Listener, 1968–88; contrib. art criticism to The Times, 1973–77; record reviewer, Punch, 1976–77; designer of film and theatre posters and illustrator of book jackets; mural for Queen Elizabeth II Conf. Centre, London, 1985; film and television actor; presenter and writer, Barry Fantoni's Chinese Horoscopes, BBC Radio 4 series, 1986. One-man shows: Woodstock Gall., London, 1963; Comara Gall., LA, 1964; Brunel Univ., 1974; Times cartoon exhibition, Charlotte Lampard Gall., 1990; retrospective: Cadogan Contemporary Gall., 1991; two-man shows (with Peter Fantoni): Langton Gall., London, 1977; Annexe Gall., London, 1978; Katherine House Gall., 1983; Fulford Cartoon Gall., 1983; New Grafton Gall., 1985; Green & Stone, Cirencester, 1986; work exhibited: AIA Gall., London, 1958, 1961 and 1964; D and AD Annual Exhibn, London, 1964; Royal Acad. Summer Exhibn, 1963 (as Stuart Harris, with William Rushton), 1964, 1975 and 1978 (with Richard Napper); Tate Gall., 1973; Bradford Print Biennale, 1974; National Theatre, 1977; Browse and Darby, 1977; Gillian Jason Gall., 1983; Three Decades of Art Schools, RA, 1983. Musical compositions include: popular songs (also popular songs with Marianne Faithfull and with Stanley Myers); The Cantors Crucifixion (musical improvisation for 13 instruments), 1977; (with John Wells) Lionel (musical), 1977. Male TV Personality of the Year, 1966. Editor, St Martin's Review, 1969–74; weekly columnist on Chinese Horoscopes: Today, 1986–87; Woman, 1987–88; Plus magazine, 1989; The Guardian, 1990. *Publications:* (with Richard Ingrams) Private Pop Eye, 1968; (as Old Jowett, with Richard Ingrams) The Bible for Motorists, 1970; Tomorrow's Nicodemus, 1974; (as Sylvie Krin, with Richard Ingrams) Love in the Saddle, 1974; Private Eye Cartoon Library 5, 1975; (as E. J. Thribb, with Richard Ingrams) So Farewell Then . . . and Other Poems, 1978; Mike Dime, 1980; (as Sylvie Krin, with Richard Ingrams) Born to be Queen, 1981; Stickman, 1982; (ed) Colemanballs, 1982; (ed) Colemanballs 2, 1984; The Times Diary Cartoons, 1984; Barry Fantoni's Chinese Horoscope, 1985, new edn 1991; (ed) Colemanballs 3, 1986; Barry Fantoni Cartoons: a personal selection from The Times and The Listener, 1987; The Royal Family's Chinese Horoscopes, 1988; (ed) Colemanballs 4, 1988; Chinese Horoscope Guide to Love, Marriage and Friendship, 1989; *illustrations for:* How To Be a Jewish Mother, 1966; The BP Festivals and Events in Britain, 1966; (with George Melly) The Media Mob, 1980; The Best of Barry Fantoni Cartoons, 1990. *Recreations:* road running, animal welfare. *Address:* c/o Abner Stein, 10 Roland Gardens, SW7 3PH. *T:* 071-373 0456. *Club:* Chelsea Arts (Chm., 1978–80).

FARINGDON, 3rd Baron *cr* 1916; **Charles Michael Henderson;** Bt 1902; Partner, Cazenove and Company, since 1968; Chairman, Witan Investment Company plc, since 1980; *b* 3 July 1937; *s* of Hon. Michael Thomas Henderson (*d* 1953) (2nd *s* of Col Hon. Harold Greenwood Henderson, CVO, and *g s* of 1st Baron) and Oonagh Evelyn Henderson, *er d* of late Lt-Col Harold Ernest Brassey; *S* uncle, 1977; *m* 1959, Sarah Caroline, *d* of J. M. E. Askew, *qv*; three *s* one *d*. *Educ:* Eton College; Trinity College, Cambridge (BA). Treasurer, Nat. Art Collection Fund, 1984–. Chm. Bd of Governors, Royal Marsden Hosp., 1980–85. *Heir: s* Hon. James Harold Henderson [*b* 14 July 1961; *m* 1986, Lucinda, *y d* of Desmond Hanson, Knipton, Lincs]. *Address:* Buscot Park, Faringdon, Oxon; Barnsley Park, Cirencester, Glos.

FARLEY, Prof. Francis James Macdonald, FRS 1972; Visiting Senior Research Physicist, Yale University, since 1984; Consultant, Centre Antoine Lacassagne, Nice, since 1986; Professor Emeritus, Royal Military College of Science (Dean, 1967–82); *b* 13 Oct. 1920; *er s* of late Brig. Edward Lionel Farley, CBE, MC; *m* 1945, Josephine Maisie Hayden; three *s* one *d*; *m* 1977, Margaret Ann Pearce. *Educ:* Clifton Coll.; Clare Coll., Cambridge. MA 1945; PhD 1950; ScD Cantab 1967; FInstP. Air Defence Research and Development Establishment, 1941–45 (first 3cm ground radar, Doppler radar); Chalk River Laboratories, 1945–46; Research Student, Cavendish Lab., Cambridge, 1946–49; Auckland Univ. Coll., NZ, 1950–57; attached AERE, 1955; CERN, Geneva, 1957–67 (muon g-2 experiment). Vis. Lectr, Univ. of Bristol, 1965–66; Vis. Scientist, CERN, 1967– (muon storage ring, tests of relativity); Vis. Professor: Swiss Inst. of Nuclear Research, 1976–77; Reading, 1982–86. Rep. NZ at UN Conf. on Atomic Energy for Peaceful Purposes, 1955. Governor: Clifton Coll.; Welbeck Coll., 1970–82; Member Court: Univ. of Bath, 1974–82; Cranfield Inst. of Technology, 1989–. Hon. Mem., Instn of Royal Engineers. Hon. Fellow, TCD, 1986. Hughes Medal, Royal Soc., 1980. *Publications:* Elements of Pulse Circuits, 1955; Progress in Nuclear Techniques and Instrumentation, Vol. I, 1966, Vol. II, 1967, Vol. III 1968; scientific papers on nuclear physics, electronics, high energy particle physics, wave energy. *Recreations:* gliding (FAI gold and diamond); ski-ing, windsurfing. *Address:* Le Masage, chemin de Saint Pierre, 06620 Le Bar sur Loup, France. *T:* 93.42.45.12.

FARLEY, Henry Edward, (Rob); Group Deputy Chief Executive, Royal Bank of Scotland Group, 1986–90; Director, Nationwide Anglia Building Society, since 1990; *b* 28 Sept. 1930; *s* of late William and Frances Elizabeth Farley; *m* 1955, Audrey Joyce

Shelvey; one *s* one *d.* *Educ:* Harrow County Sch. for Boys. FCIB (FIB 1966). Entered National Bank, 1947; Head of UK Banking, 1978, Dir, 1981, Williams & Glyn's Bank; Chairman: Williams & Glyn's Bank (IOM) Ltd, 1973–76; Joint Credit Card Co. Ltd, 1982–84; Royal Bank of Scotland Gp Insce, 1988–90; Mem. Bd, Mastercard International Inc., 1982–84; Director: Royal Bank of Scotland Group plc, 1985–90; Royal Bank of Scotland, 1985–90 (Man. Dir, 1985–86); Charterhouse Japhet, 1985–86; Charterhouse Development, 1985–86; Charterhouse plc, 1986–90; Chm., Royscot Finance Gp, 1987–90; Dep. Chm., Supervisory Bd of CC Bank, Germany, 1989–90. Director: EFT-POS (UK) Ltd, 1986–88; A. T. Mays Gp, 1987–90; (Alternate) Citizens Financial Gp (USA), 1989–90; John Maunders Construction Gp, 1989–; Banque Rivaud, Paris, 1990–; High Table Ltd, 1991–. Member: Council, Inst. of Bankers, 1985–90; APACS Council, 1983–90; Exec. Cttee, British Bankers Assoc., 1983–90. Gov. and Mem. Council, UMIST, 1990–. Liveryman, Marketors' Co., 1987. *Publications:* The Clearing Banks and Housing Finance, 1983; Competition and Deregulation: branch networks, 1984; The Role of Branches in a Changing Environment, 1985; Deregulation and the Clearing Banks, 1986. *Recreations:* all forms of rough sport, travel, modern literature. *Address:* 13 Montagu Square, W1H 1RB. *Clubs:* Overseas Bankers', MCC; Pickwick Bicycle; St James (Manchester).

FARLEY, Prof. Martyn Graham, CEng, FRAeS, FIMechE, FIProdE, CBIM; Emeritus Professor, Royal Military College of Science, Shrivenham and Cranfield Institute of Technology, since 1986; Director, Harwell Computer Power Ltd, since 1986; *b* 27 Oct. 1924; *s* of Herbert Booth Farley and Hilda Gertrude (*née* Hendey); *m* 1948, Freda Laugharne; two *s* one *d.* *Educ:* Merchant Venturers Tech. Coll., Bristol; Bristol Aeroplane Co. Tech. Coll. CEng, FRAeS 1968; FIMechE 1969; FIProdE 1975; FSME 1986; FIIM 1988; CBIM 1980. Engine Div., Bristol Aeroplane Co.: Design Apprentice, 1939–45; Engine Design, 1945–46; Develt Engr, 1946–51; Bristol Aero Engines Ltd: Sen. Designer, Gas Turbine Office, 1951–55; Asst Chief Develt Engr, 1955–59; Bristol Siddeley Engines: Asst Chief Mech. Engr, 1959–62; Chief Develt Engr, Small Engines Div., 1962–65, Chief Engr, 1965–67; Small Engines Div., Rolls-Royce: Chief Engr, 1967–68; Gen. Works Manager, 1968–72; Manufg and Prodn Dir, 1972–74; HQ Exec. to Vice-Chm. of Rolls-Royce (1971) Ltd, 1974–75; Prof. and Head of Dept of Management Sciences, RMCS, 1975–84; Vice-Chm., Sch. of Management and Maths, RMCS Faculty of Cranfield Inst. of Technology, 1984–86. Dir, World Tech Ventures, 1984–86; Chm., RECSAM Components Ltd, 1986–89. Royal Aeronautical Society: Mem. Council, 1972–; Vice Pres., 1980–83; Pres., 1983–84; Dir, Aeronautical Trusts, 1975–88; Hon. Treasurer, 1984–88. Vice Pres., Instn of Indust. Engrs, 1981–; Pres., IProdE, 1984–85 (Mem. Council, 1973–; Chm. Council, 1978–80; Vice-Pres., 1982–83); Chm., British Management Data Foundn Ltd, 1978–; Founder Chm., Alliance of Manufg and Management Orgns, 1981–; Member: EEF Manufg Trng Cttee, 1975–; Guggenheim Medal Bd of Award, 1983; Adv. Council, RN Engrg Coll., Manadon, 1988–; Court, Brunel Univ., 1977–80, Loughborough Univ., 1977–, Cranfield Inst. of Technol., 1977–, Bath Univ., 1983–. Mem., Sen. Awards Cttee, 1979–, and Hon. Mem. Council, 1985–, CGLI; Hon. CGIA 1981; Pres., CGIA Assoc., 1984–. Designer and Project Co-ordinator, EITB Manufg Fellowships, 1977–; Hon. Fellow, Indian IProdE, 1979; Hon. FCGI 1990; Hon. Member: Amer. Inst. of Indust. Managers, 1979; Australian Inst. of Indust. Engrs, 1981; Amer. Soc. of Manufg Engrs, 1985 (elected Charter Fellow, 1986). Mem., Co. of Coachmakers and Coach Harness Makers. Internat. Archimedes Award, Amer. Soc. of Prof. Engrs, 1979; Internat. Award, LA Council of Engrs and Scientists, 1981; First Shuttle Contributions Medal, 1981; Educn Award, ASME, 1983; Amer. Instn Advanced Engr Medal, 1984; NASA/Rocketdyne Tech. Award, 1984; California State Engrg Commendation, 1985; NASA Contribs Award, 1985; W. B. Johnson Award, ASME, 1988. *Publications:* articles and technical pubns; procs of conferences. *Address:* Willow End, Vicarage Lane, Shrivenham, Swindon, Wilts SN6 8DT. *T:* Swindon (0793) 782319. *Clubs:* Athenæum; Ariel Rowing (Shrivenham).

FARLEY, Mary-Rose Christine, (Mrs R. D. Farley); *see* Bateman, M.-R. C.

FARLEY, Rob; *see* Farley, H. E.

FARMBROUGH, Rt. Rev. David John; *see* Bedford, Bishop Suffragan of.

FARMER, Bruce; *see* Farmer, E. B.

FARMER, Prof. Edward Desmond; Louis Cohen Professor of Dental Surgery, 1957–82, Director of Post-Graduate Dental Studies, 1972–77, Dean of the Faculty of Medicine, 1977–82, and Pro-Vice-Chancellor, 1967–70, University of Liverpool; *b* 15 April 1917; *s* of late S. R. and L. M. Farmer; *m* 1942, Mary Elwood Little; one *s* two *d.* *Educ:* Newcastle-under-Lyme High Sch.; Univ. of Liverpool (1936–41); Queens' Coll., Cambridge (1948–50). MA Cantab, 1955; MDS Liverpool, 1951; FDSRCS 1952; MRCPath 1967, FRCPath 1968; Hon. FRCR 1981. RNVR, Surgeon Lieut (D), 1942–45; Lectr in Parodontal Diseases, Univ. of Liverpool, 1950–57; Nuffield Fellow, 1948–50. Hon. Cons. Dent. Surg. to Bd of Governors of United Liverpool Hosps and Liverpool AHA (Teaching), formerly Liverpool Regional Hosp. Bd. Member Council: Brit. Soc. of Periodontology, 1954–59 (Pres. 1957–58); RSM, Odonto. Sect., 1965–68. Member: Central Cttee and Exec., Hosp. Dental Service, 1964–76; Negotiating Cttee of Central Cttee for Hosp. Medical Services, 1968–76; Bd of Govs, United Liverpool Hosps, 1968–71; UGC Dental Sect., 1968–77; Conf. and Exec., Dental Post-Grad. Deans, 1972–77; Cttee of Dental Teachers and Res. Workers Gp, BDA, 1974–79; Liverpool AHA(T) (and Chm., Regional Dental Cttee), 1975–77; RHA, 1977–82; Faculty of Dental Surgery, RCS, 1974–82; Dental Cttee of Medical Defence Union; Council, Medical Insurance Agency; Exec., Teaching Hospitals Assoc.; Chm., Commn of Dental Educn, Fedn Dentaire Internat., 1977–79 (Vice-Chm., 1974–77); Alternate, Dental Adv. Cttee to EEC, 1980–83; Vice-Chm., NW Cancer Research Fund, 1987– (Mem. Exec. Cttee, 1982–); President: NW Br. BDA, 1967–68; Hospitals' Gp, BDA, 1972–73; Assoc. for Dental Educn in Europe, 1976–78; British Soc. of Oral Medicine, 1982–83; Pres., Odontological Section, RSM, 1983–84. Chairman: Merseyside Conf. for Overseas Students, 1983–88; Age Concern, Liverpool, 1984–; Member: Council, Liverpool Queen Victoria Dist Nursing Assoc., 1987–; Exec. Cttee, Age Concern England, 1988–. *Publications:* (with F. E. Lawton) Stones' Oral and Dental Diseases, 5th edn, 1966; papers in Proceedings Royal Society Med., Jl of Gen. Microbiology, Brit. Med. Jl, Dental Practitioner; Internat. Dental Jl. *Recreations:* golf, gardening, painting and enjoyment of the countryside. *Address:* Heath Moor, Beacon Lane, Heswall, Merseyside L60 0DG. *T:* 051–342 3179. *Clubs:* Athenæum (Liverpool); Royal Liverpool Golf; Caldy Golf.

FARMER, Dr (Edwin) Bruce; Group Managing Director and Chief Executive, The Morgan Crucible Co., since 1983; *b* 18 Sept. 1936; *s* of Edwin Bruce Farmer and Doris Farmer (*née* Darby); *m* 1962, Beryl Ann, *d* of late William Alfred Griffiths, Birmingham; one *s* one *d.* *Educ:* King Edward's, Birmingham; Univ. of Birmingham (BSc, PhD). Dir and Gen. Manager, Brico Metals, 1967–69; Man. Dir, Brico Engineering, 1970–76; Man. Dir, Wellworthy, 1976–81; The Morgan Crucible Co.: Dir, 1981–83; Chm., Thermal Ceramics Div., 1981–83. CBIM, FRSA. *Recreations:* music, cricket, squash. *Address:* The Morgan Crucible Co., Chariott House, Windsor, Berks SL4 1EP. *T:* Windsor (0753) 850331; Weston House, Bracken Close, Wonersh, Surrey GU5 0QS.

FARMER, Frank Reginald, OBE 1967; FRS 1981; *b* 18 Dec. 1914; *s* of Frank Henry Farmer and Minnie Godson; *m* 1939, Betty Smart; one *s* two *d.* *Educ:* St John's Coll., Cambridge (BA). Kestner Evaporator & Engineering Co., 1936–46; Director, Safety Reliability Directorate, Atomic Energy Authority (formerly Dept of Atomic Energy), 1947–79, retired. Editor, Reliability Engineering, 1980–. FInstP 1965; Hon. FSE 1974; Foreign Associate, Nat. Acad. of Engineers, USA, 1980. Churchill Gold Medal, 1974. *Publication:* Nuclear Reactor Safety, 1977. *Recreations:* golf, books. *Address:* The Long Wood, Lyons Lane, Appleton, Warrington WA4 5ND. *T:* Warrington (0925) 62503.

FARMER, Sir George; *see* Farmer, Sir L. G. T.

FARMER, George Wallace; President, Immigration Appeal Tribunal, since 1991 (Vice President, 1982–91); *b* 4 June 1929; *s* of George Lawrence Farmer and Blanche Amy (*née* Nicholls); *m* 1961, Patricia Mary Joyce; three *d.* *Educ:* The Lodge, Barbados; Harrison Coll., Barbados. Called to the Bar, Middle Temple, 1950. Private practice, Barbados, 1950–52; Magistrate, Barbados, 1952–56; Resident Magistrate, Uganda, 1956–63, Sen. Resident Magistrate, 1963–64; Dir of Public Prosecutions, Uganda, 1964–65; attached to Cottle Catford & Co., Solicitors, Barbados, 1965–67; Legal Manager, Road Transport Industry Trng Bd, 1967–70; Adjudicator, Immigration Appeals, 1970–82. *Recreations:* allotments (Britain), beach cricket (Barbados). *Address:* 40 South Croxted Road, West Dulwich, SE21 8BD. *T:* 081–670 4828.

FARMER, Hugh Robert Macdonald, CB 1967; *b* 3 Dec. 1907; *s* of late Charles Edward Farmer and late Emily (*née* Randolph); *m* 1st, 1934, Penelope Frances (*d* 1963), *d* of late Capt. Evelyn Boothby, RN; one *s* three *d*; 2nd, 1966, Jean (*d* 1988), *widow* of Peter Bluett Winch. *Educ:* Cheam Sch.; Eton Coll.; New Coll., Oxford. House of Commons: Asst Clerk, 1931; Sen. Clerk, 1943; Clerk of Private Bills and Taxing Officer, and Examr of Petitions for Private Bills, 1958–60; Clerk of Cttees, 1960–65; Clerk/Administrator, 1965–72, retired 1972. *Recreations:* golf, gardening. *Address:* The Old Rectory, Iping, Midhurst, West Sussex GU29 0PE. *T:* Midhurst (0730) 815923. *Club:* MCC.

FARMER, Sir (Lovedin) George (Thomas), Kt 1968; LLD, MA, FCA, JDipMA; Coordinator, Rover and Triumph, 1972–73; Chairman: Rover Co. Ltd, 1963–73; Zenith Carburettor Co. Ltd, 1973–77; Deputy Chairman, British Leyland Motor Corporation, 1971–73; *b* 13 May 1908; *m* 1st, 1938, Editha Mary Fisher (*d* 1980); no *c*; 2nd, 1980, Muriel Gwendoline Mercer Pinfold. *Educ:* Oxford High Sch. 2nd Vice-Chm. and Mem. Adv. Cttee, Metalurgica de Santa Ana, Madrid, 1963–74; Director: Empresa Nacional de Automcamiones, 1968–73; ATV Network Ltd, 1968–75; Rea Brothers (Isle of Man) Ltd, 1976–88; Aero Designs (Isle of Man) Ltd, 1979–89. President: Birmingham Chamber of Commerce, 1960–61; Motor and Cycle Trades Benevolent Fund, 1962; SMMT, 1962–64 (Dep. Pres., 1964–65; Chm., Exec. Cttee, 1968–72); Fellowship of Motor Industry, 1965; Member: Midland Regl Bd for Industry, 1961–65; Midland Industrial Adv. Council, 1962; Engrg Adv. Council, 1962–66; Export Council for Europe, 1963; Iron, Steel Bd, 1964–66; Engrg ITB, 1964–66; EDC for Motor Industry, 1967; Past Member: Advisory Council, ECGD (Board of Trade); UK Committee of Federation of Commonwealth and British Chambers of Commerce; Vice-Pres., Inst. of Motor Industry, 1964; Vice-Chm., ABCC, 1964; Past Vice-Pres., West Midlands Engineering Employers' Assoc.; Governor, Chm. Finance Cttee, Dep. Chm. Executive Council (Chm., 1966–75), Royal Shakespeare Theatre; Pres., Loft Theatre, Leamington Spa. Pro-Chancellor, Birmingham Univ., 1966–75; Hon. LLD Birmingham, 1975. Past Pres., Automobile Golfing Soc. Mem., Worshipful Co. of Coach and Coach Harness Makers. *Recreations:* theatre, golf, fishing. *Address:* Longridge, The Chase, Ballakillowey, Colby, Isle of Man. *T:* Port St Mary (0624) 832603. *Club:* Royal and Ancient (St Andrews).

FARMER, Peter John; Public Trustee and Accountant General of the Supreme Court, since 1991; *b* 5 Nov. 1952; *s* of Alec and Norah Farmer; *m* 1986, Christine Ann Tetley. *Educ:* King Edward VI Sch., Southampton; Gonville and Caius College, Cambridge (Maths; MA); London Univ. (Cert. Psych.). Joined HM Customs and Excise, 1975; HM Treasury, 1979; Lord Chancellor's Dept, 1981; Circuit Principal, Leeds, 1983; Asst Sec., 1987; Asst Public Trustee, 1988. MBIM. *Recreations:* English country dancing, hill walking. *Address:* Public Trust Office, 24 Kingsway, WC2B 6JX. *T:* 071–269 7000.

FARMER, Robert Frederick, OBE 1985; General Secretary, Institute of Journalists, 1962–87; Member of Council, Media Society, 1982–90 (Secretary, 1973–82); *b* 19 Aug. 1922; *s* of Frederick Leonard Farmer and Gladys Farmer (*née* Winney); *m* 1958, Anne Walton. *Educ:* Saltley Grammar Sch., Birmingham. FCIS. Served War of 1939–45, Royal Armoured Corps, 1941–52 (commissioned 3rd Carabiniers, despatches, Burma campaign). Secretariat: Instn of Plant Engineers, 1952–59; Instn of Civil Engineers, 1959–62. Consultative Mem., Press Council, 1962–87; Mem., Cttee on Defamation, 1971–75. *Recreations:* cookery, walking, old churches. *Address:* c/o Institute of Journalists, Suite 2, Dock Offices, Surrey Quays, Lower Road, SE16 2XL.

FARNCOMBE, Charles Frederick, CBE 1977; FRAM; Musical Director: Handel Opera Society, 1955–85; Malcolm Sargent Festival Choir, since 1985; *b* 29 July 1919; *o s* of Harold and Eleanor Farncombe, both of London; *m* 1963, Sally Mae (*née* Felps), Riverside, Calif, USA; one *d.* *Educ:* London Univ., 1936–40 (Archibald Dawnay Scholarship in Civil Engrg, 1936) (BSc Hons (Eng) 1940); Royal Sch. of Church Music, 1947–48; Royal Academy of Music, 1948–51 (RAM, Mann Prize). Civil Engr to John Mowlem & Co, 1940–42. Served War, 1942–47, as Captain in REME, in 21st Army Gp. Free Lance Conductor: formed Handel Opera Soc. 1955; Musical Dir, 1968–79, Chief Conductor, 1970–79, Royal Court Theatre, Drottningholm, Sweden; Chief Guest Conductor, 1979–, Chief Conductor, annual Handel Fest., 1985–, Badisches Staatstheater, Karlsruhe, 1979–. AMICE, 1945 (resigned later); FRAM 1963 (ARAM 1962). Hon DMus: Columbus Univ., Ohio, USA, 1959; City Univ., 1988. Gold Medal of the Friends of Drottningholm, 1971; Hon. Fellow Royal Swedish Academy of Music, 1972. Kt Comdr, Order of North Star, Sweden, 1982. *Recreations:* cajoling singers, swimming, cottage on Offa's Dyke. *Address:* c/o Royal Bank of Scotland, Columbia House, 69 Aldwych, WC2B 4JJ.

FARNDALE, Gen. Sir Martin (Baker), KCB 1983 (CB 1980); Master Gunner, St James's Park, since 1988; Director and Senior Defence Adviser, Short Brothers, since 1988; Defence Adviser, Touche Ross, since 1988; *b* Alberta, Canada, 6 Jan. 1929; *s* of Alfred Farndale and Margaret Louise Baker; *m* 1955, Margaret Anne Buckingham; one *s.* *Educ:* Yorebridge Grammar Sch., Yorks. Joined Indian Army, 1946; RMA, Sandhurst, 1947; commnd RA, 1948; Egypt, 1949; 1st RHA, 1950–54 (Germany from 1952); HQ 7 Armoured Div., 1954–57; Staff College, 1959; HQ 17 Gurkha Div., Malaya, 1960–62; MoD, 1962–64; comd Chestnut Troop 1st RHA, Germany and Aden, 1964–66; Instructor, Staff Coll., 1966–69; comd 1st RHA, UK, N Ire., Germany, 1969–71; MoD, 1971–73; comd 7th Armoured Bde, 1973–75. Dir, Public Relations (Army), 1976–78; Dir of Mil. Ops, MoD (Army), 1978–80; Comdr 2nd Armoured Div., BAOR, 1980–83; Comdr 1st (British) Corps, BAOR, 1983–85; C-in-C, BAOR, and Comdr, Northern

Army Gp, 1985–87; retired, 1988. Colonel Commandant: Army Air Corps, 1980–88; RA, 1982–; RHA, 1988–. Hon. Colonel: 3rd Bn Yorkshire Volunteers TA, 1983–90; 1st RHA, 1983–90. Chm., RUSI, 1989–. Chm., RA Historical Affairs Cttee, 1988; Vice-Pres., Royal Patriotic Fund Corp., 1989–. *Publications:* The History of the Royal Artillery France, 1914–18, 1987; Forgotten Fronts and the Home Base 1914–18, 1989; articles for British Army Rev. and Jl RA. *Recreations:* military history, gardening. *Address:* c/o Lloyds Bank, Cox's and King's Branch, 6 Pall Mall, SW1. *Club:* East India, Devonshire, Sports and Public Schools.

FARNELL, Graeme, FMA; Managing Director, Museum Development Company Ltd, since 1989; *b* 11 July 1947; *s* of Wilson Elliot Farnell and Mary Montgomerie Wishart Farnell (*née* Crichton); *m* 1969, Jennifer Gerda (*née* Huddlestone); one *s*. *Educ:* Loughborough Grammar Sch.; Edinburgh Univ. (MA); London Film Sch. (DipFilm Studies). FMA 1989; FSAScot 1976; MBIM. Asst Keeper, Mus. of East Anglian Life, 1973–76; Curator, Inverness Mus. and Art Gall., 1976–79; Dir, Scottish Museums Council, 1979–86; Dir Gen., Museums Assoc., 1986–89. Man. Editor, Museum Development. *Publications:* (ed) The American Museum Experience, 1986; The Handbook of Grants, 1990; contribs to Museums Jl, Internat. Jl of Mus. Management and Curatorship, Museum (Unesco); Industrial Soc. *Recreations:* baroque opera, travel. *Address:* 8 Faraday Drive, Shenley Lodge, Milton Keynes, Bucks MK5 7DA. *T:* Milton Keynes (0908) 660629.

FARNHAM, 12th Baron, *cr* 1756; **Barry Owen Somerset Maxwell;** Bt (Nova Scotia) 1627; Chairman: Brown, Shipley & Co. Ltd (Merchant Bankers), since 1984 (Director, since 1959); Brown Shipley Holdings plc, since 1976; Avon Rubber plc, since 1978 (Director, since 1966); Provident Mutual Life Assurance Association, since 1989 (Director, since 1967; Deputy Chairman, 1987–89); *b* 7 July 1931; *s* of Hon. Somerset Arthur Maxwell, MP (died of wounds received in action, 1942), and Angela Susan (*d* 1953), *o d* of late Capt. Marshall Owen Roberts; *S* grandfather 1957; *m* 1959, Diana Marion, *er d* of Nigel Gunnis; two adopted *d*. *Educ:* Eton; Harvard Univ. Dep. Grand Master, United Grand Lodge of England, 1989–. *Heir:* *b* Hon. Simon Kenlis Maxwell [*b* 12 Dec. 1933; *m* 1964, Karol Anne, *d* of Maj.-Gen. G. E. Prior-Palmer, CB, DSO, and Katherine Edith Bibby; two *s* one *d* (of whom one *s* one *d* are twins)]. *Address:* 11 Earl's Court Gardens, SW5 0TD; Farnham, Co. Cavan. *Clubs:* Boodle's, City of London; Kildare Street and University (Dublin).

FARNINGHAM, Alexander Ian, DSC; Managing Director, Industrial Relations and Personnel, British Shipbuilders, 1977–80; *b* 3 Nov. 1923; *s* of Alexander Farningham and Janet Leask Broadley; *m* 1st, 1949, Lois Elizabeth Halse (marr. diss. 1981); one *s* two *d*; 2nd, 1981, Susan Wyllie. *Educ:* Glebelands Primary Sch., Dundee; Morgan Academy, Dundee; St Andrews Univ. (MA). Mem., RYA. *Recreations:* walking, birdwatching, photography, sailing. *Address:* Ardriach, Lady Ileene Road, Tarbert, Argyll PA29 6TU. *T:* Tarbert (0880) 820343. *Club:* Cruising Association.

FARNWORTH, John David; His Honour Judge Farnworth; a Circuit Judge, since 1991; *b* 20 June 1935; *s* of George Arthur Farnworth and Mary Lilian Farnworth; *m* 1964, Carol Gay Mallett; one *s* two *d*. *Educ:* Bedford Sch.; St Edmund Hall, Oxford (BA). Admitted Solicitor, 1962; a Recorder, 1986–91. *Recreations:* golf, cricket, snooker, art galleries. *Clubs:* MCC; Bedfordshire Golf.

FARQUHAR, Charles Don Petrie, JP; DL; Area Manager, Community Industry, since 1972; engineer; *b* 4 Aug. 1937; *s* of late William Sandeman Farquhar and Annie Preston Young Farquhar; *m*; two *d*. *Educ:* Liff Road and St Michael's Primary Schs, Dundee; Stobswell Secondary Sch., Dundee. Served with Royal Engineers (Trng NCO); subseq. supervisory staff, plant engrg. City Councillor, Dundee, 1965–75 (ex-Convener, Museums, Works and Housing Cttees); Lord Provost and Lord Lieutenant of City of Dundee, 1975–77. Chm., Dundee Dist Licensing Bd, Dundee Dist Licensing Cttee, 1984–. JP Dundee, 1974; DL Dundee, 1977. *Recreations:* fresh-water angling, gardening, caravanning, numismatics, do-it-yourself. *Address:* 15 Sutherland Crescent, Dundee DD2 2HP. *T:* Dundee (0382) 610666/643127, (office) Dundee (0382) 27024.

FARQUHAR, Sir Michael (Fitzroy Henry), 7th Bt *cr* 1796, of Cadogan House, Middlesex; farmer; *b* 29 June 1938; *s* of Sir Peter Walter Farquhar, 6th Bt, DSO, OBE, and Elizabeth Evelyn (*d* 1983), *d* of Francis Cecil Albert Hurt; *S* father, 1986; *m* 1963, Veronica Geraldine Hornidge; two *s*. *Educ:* Eton; Royal Agricultural College. *Recreations:* fishing, shooting. *Heir:* *s* Charles Walter Fitzroy Farquhar, *b* 21 Feb. 1964. *Address:* Manor Farm, West Kington, Chippenham, Wilts SN14 7JG. *T:* Castle Combe (0249) 782671. *Club:* White's.

FARQUHARSON of Invercauld, Captain Alwyne Arthur Compton, MC 1944; JP; Head of Clan Farquharson; *b* 1 May 1919; *er s* of late Major Edward Robert Francis Compton, JP, DL, Newby Hall, Ripon, and Torloisk, Isle of Mull, and Sylvia, *y d* of A. H. Farquharson; recognised by Lord Lyon King of Arms as Laird of Invercauld (16th Baron of Invercauld; *S* aunt 1941), also as Chief of name of Farquharson and Head of Clan, since 1949; assumed (surname) Compton as a third forename and assumed surname of Farquharson of Invercauld, by warrant granted in Lyon Court, Edinburgh, 1949; *m* 1949, Frances Strickland Lovell (*d* 1991), *d* of Robert Pollard Oldham, Seattle, Washington, USA. *Educ:* Eton; Magdalen Coll., Oxford. Joined Royal Scots Greys, 1940. Served War, 1940–45, Palestine, N Africa, Italy, France (wounded); Captain 1943. County Councillor, Aberdeenshire, 1949–75, JP 1951. *Address:* Invercauld, Braemar, Aberdeenshire AB35 5TT. *T:* Braemar (03383) 213.
See also R. E. J. Compton.

FARQUHARSON of Whitehouse, Captain Colin Andrew, FRICS; chartered surveyor and land agent; Lord Lieutenant of Aberdeenshire, since 1987 (Vice Lord Lieutenant, 1983–87); JP; *b* 9 Aug. 1923; *s* of late Norman Farquharson of Whitehouse; *m* 1st, 1948, Jean Sybil Mary (*d* 1985), *d* of late Brig.-Gen. J. G. H. Hamilton of Skene, DSO, JP, DL; two *d* (and one *d* decd); 2nd, 1987, Clodagh, *widow* of Ian Houldsworth of Dallas Lodge, Moray, and *d* of Sir Kenneth Murray of Geanies, Ross-shire; three step *s* two step *d*. *Educ:* Rugby. FLAS 1956, FRICS 1970. Served Grenadier Guards, 1942–48: ADC to Field Marshal Sir Harold Alexander (later (1st) Earl Alexander of Tunis), 1945. Member, Queen's Body Guard for Scotland (Royal Company of Archers), 1964–. Chartered surveyor and land agent in private practice in Aberdeenshire, 1953–; Director, MacRobert Farms (Douneside) Ltd, 1971–87. Member, Bd of Management for Royal Cornhill Hosps, 1962–74; Chm., Gordon Local Health Council, 1975–81; Mem., Grampian Health Bd, 1981–89. DL 1966, JP 1969, Aberdeenshire. *Recreations:* shooting, fishing, farming. *Address:* Whitehouse, Alford, Aberdeenshire AB3 8DP. *Clubs:* MCC; Royal Northern and University (Aberdeen).
See also Master of Arbuthnott.

FARQUHARSON, Rt. Hon. Sir Donald (Henry), Kt 1981; PC 1989; DL; **Rt. Hon. Lord Justice Farquharson;** a Lord Justice of Appeal, since 1989; *b* 1928; *yr s* of Charles Anderson Farquharson, Logie Coldstone, Aberdeenshire, and Florence Ellen Fox; *m* 1960, Helen Mary, *er d* of Comdr H. M. Simpson, RN (retd), Abbots Brow, Kirkby Lonsdale, Westmorland; three *s* (one *d* decd). *Educ:* Royal Commercial Travellers Sch.; Keble Coll., Oxford (MA; Hon. Fellow, 1989). Called to Bar, Inner Temple, 1952; Bencher, 1979. Dep. Chm., Essex QS, 1970; a Recorder of the Crown Court, 1972–81; QC 1972; Judge, High Court of Justice, QBD, 1981–89; Presiding Judge, SE Circuit, 1985–88. A Legal Assessor to GMC and GDC, 1978–81; Chm., Disciplinary Cttee of Bar, 1983–85; Mem., Judicial Studies Bd, 1984–85. DL Essex, 1990. *Recreations:* opera, walking. *Address:* Royal Courts of Justice, Strand, WC2A 2LL.

FARQUHARSON, Sir James (Robbie), KBE 1960 (CBE 1948; OBE 1944); retired, and is now farming; *b* 1 Nov. 1903; *s* of Frank Farquharson, Cortachy, Angus, Scotland, and Agnes Jane Robbie; *m* 1933, Agnes Binny Graham; two *s*. *Educ:* Royal Technical College, Glasgow; Glasgow Univ. BSc Glasgow 1923. Asst Engineer, LMS Railway, 1923–25; Asst Engineer, Kenya and Uganda Railway, 1925–33; Senior Asst Engineer, Kenya and Uganda Railway, 1933–37; Asst to Gen. Manager, Tanganyika Railways, 1937–41; Chief Engineer, Tanganyika Railways, 1941–45; General Manager, Tanganyika Railways, 1945–48; Deputy General Manager, East African Railways, 1948–52; Gen. Manager, Sudan Railways, 1952–57; Gen. Manager, East African Railways and Harbours, 1957–61; Asst Crown Agent and Engineer-in-Chief of Crown Agents for Overseas Governments and Administrations, 1961–65. Chm., Millbank Technical Services Ordnance Ltd, 1973–75. Fellow, Scottish Council for Develt and Industry, 1986–. *Publication:* Tanganyika Transport, 1944. *Recreation:* cricket. *Address:* Kinclune, by Kirriemuir, Angus DD8 5HX. *T:* Kirriemuir (0575) 74710. *Club:* Nairobi (Kenya).

FARQUHARSON, Jonathan; Charity Commissioner, since 1985; *b* 27 Dec. 1937; *s* of Alan George Farquharson and Winifred Mary Farquharson (*née* Wilson); *m* 1963, Maureen Elsie Bright; two *d*. *Educ:* St Albans School; Manchester Univ. (LLB). Solicitor, 1962; with D. Herbert, Banbury, 1962–64; Charity Commission, 1964–. *Recreations:* geology, photography, reading, record collecting. *Address:* Charity Commission, Graeme House, Derby Square, Liverpool L2 7SB. *T:* 051–227 3191.

FARQUHARSON, Robert Alexander, CMG 1975; HM Diplomatic Service, retired; Economic Adviser to Davy McKee International, since 1980; *b* 26 May 1925; *s* of late Captain J. P. Farquharson, DSO, OBE, RN, and late Mrs Farquharson (*née* Prescott-Decie); *m* 1955, Joan Elizabeth, *o d* of Sir (William) Ivo Mallet, GBE, KCMG; two *s* one *d* (and one *s* decd). *Educ:* Harrow; King's Coll., Cambridge. Served with RNVR, 1943–46. Joined Foreign (now Diplomatic) Service, 1949; 3rd Sec., Moscow, 1950; FO, 1952; 2nd Sec., Bonn, 1955; 1st Sec., Panama, 1958; Paris, 1960; FO, 1964; Counsellor, Dir of British Trade Develt, S Africa, 1967; Minister, Madrid, 1971; Consul-Gen., San Francisco, 1973; Ambassador to Yugoslavia, 1977–80. Lord of the Manor of Bockleton. *Address:* The Old Rectory, Tollard Royal, Wilts. *Clubs:* Naval and Military, Flyfishers'.

FARR, Dennis Larry Ashwell, CBE 1991; FMA; Director, Courtauld Institute Galleries, since 1980; *b* 3 April 1929; *s* of late Arthur William Farr and Helen Eva Farr (*née* Ashwell); *m* 1959, Diana Pullein-Thompson (writer), *d* of Captain H. J. Pullein-Thompson, MC, and Joanna (*née* Cannan); one *s* one *d*. *Educ:* Luton Grammar Sch.; Courtauld Inst. of Art, London Univ. (BA, MA). Asst Witt Librarian, Courtauld Inst. of Art, 1952–54; Asst Keeper, Tate Gallery, 1954–64; Curator, Paul Mellon Collection, Washington, DC, 1965–66; Sen. Lectr in Fine Art, and Dep. Keeper, University Art Collections, Univ. of Glasgow, 1967–69; Dir, City Museums and Art Gallery, Birmingham, 1969–80. Fred Cook Meml Lecture, RSA, 1974. Hon. Art Adviser, Calouste Gulbenkian Foundation, 1969–73; Member: British Council Fine Arts Adv. Cttee, 1971–80; Wright Cttee on Provincial Museums and Galleries, 1971–73; Museums Assoc. Council, 1971–74 (Vice-Pres., 1978–79, 1980–81; Pres., 1979–80); Art Panel, Arts Council, 1972–77; ICOM(UK) Exec. Bd, 1976–85; Cttee, Victorian Soc., 1980; Exec. Cttee, Assoc. of Art Historians, 1981–87 (Chm. of Assoc., 1983–86); History of Art and Design Bd, CNAA, 1981–87; Comité Internat. d'Histoire de l'Art, 1983–; Trustee, Birmingham Mus. and Art Gall. Appeal Fund, 1980– (Chm. Trustees, 1978–80); Secretary: Home House Soc. Trustees, 1986–90; Samuel Courtauld Trust, 1990–. FRSA 1970; FMA 1972. Hon. DLitt Birmingham, 1981. JP Birmingham, 1977–80. Gen. Editor, Clarendon Studies in the History of Art, 1985–. *Publications:* William Etty, 1958; Catalogue of the Modern British School Collection, Tate Gallery (with M. Chamot and M. Butlin), 1964; British Sculpture since 1945, 1965; New Painting in Glasgow, 1968; Pittura Inglese 1660–1840, 1975; English Art 1870–1940, 1978, 2nd edn 1984; (contrib.) British Sculpture in the Twentieth Century, 1981; (with W. Bradford) The Courtauld Collection (catalogue for exhibns in Tokyo and Canberra), 1984; (with W. Bradford) The Northern Landscape (catalogue for exhibn in New York), 1986; (contrib.) In Honor of Paul Mellon, Collector and Benefactor, 1986; (jtly) Impressionist and Post-Impressionist Masterpieces: the Courtauld Collection, 1987; (ed and contrib.) 100 Masterpieces from the Courtauld Collections: Bernardo Daddi to Ben Nicholson, 1987; (jtly) The Oxford Dictionary of Art, 1988; (with Eva Chadwick) Lynn Chadwick: Sculptor, a complete catalogue 1947–88, 1990; articles in: Apollo, Burlington Magazine, TLS, etc. *Recreations:* riding, reading, foreign travel. *Address:* 35 Esmond Road, Bedford Park, W4 1JG. *T:* 081–995 6400. *Clubs:* Athenæum, Institute of Contemporary Arts.
See also Denis Cannan.

FARR, Sir John (Arnold), Kt 1984; MP (C) Harborough Division of Leicestershire since 1959; Member of Lloyd's; *b* 25 Sept. 1922; *er s* of late Capt. John Farr, JP, and Mrs M. A. Farr, JP; *m* 1960, Susan Ann, *d* of Sir Leonard Milburn, 3rd Bt, and of Joan Lady Milburn, Guyzance Hall, Acklington, Northumberland; two *s*. *Educ:* Harrow. RN, 1940–46 serving in Mediterranean and S Atlantic; Lieut-Comdr RNVR. Executive Dir, Home Brewery and Apollo Productions Ltd, 1950–55. Contested Ilkeston, General Election, 1955. Sec., Cons. Parly Agric. Cttee, 1970–74, Vice-Chm., 1979–83; Sec., Parly Conservation Cttee, 1972–. Member: Exec. Cttee, UK Branch CPA, 1972–74; UK Delegn to WEU and Council of Europe, 1973–78 (Vice-Chm., Cttee on Agric.); Chairman: Anglo-Irish Parly Gp, 1977–80; Parly Knitwear Ind. Gp, 1980–; British-Zimbabwe Parly Gp, 1980–; British-Korea Parly Gp, 1983–. Vice-Pres., Shooting Sports Trust, 1972–86; Chm., British Shooting Sports Council, 1977–86. *Recreations:* cricket and shooting. *Address:* Shortwood House, Lamport, Northants. *T:* Maidwell (060128) 260; 11 Vincent Square, Westminster, SW1. *Clubs:* Boodle's, MCC.

FARR, Air Vice-Marshal Peter Gerald Desmond, CB 1968; OBE 1952; DFC 1942; retired; Director, Brain Research Trust, 1973–83; *b* 26 Sept. 1917; *s* of late Gerald Farr and Mrs Farr (*née* Miers); *m* 1949, Rosemarie (*d* 1983), *d* of late R. S. Haward; two *s* one *d*. *Educ:* Tonbridge Sch. Commnd in RAF, 1937; served War of 1939–45, Middle East, India and Burma; OC, No. 358 Sqdn, 1944–45; OC, RAF Pegu, 1945–46; OC, 120 Sqdn, 1950–51; Dep. Dir, Jt Anti-Submarine sch., 1952–54; OC, RAF Idris, 1954–55; Directing Staff, Jt Services Staff Coll., 1959; SASO, Malta, 1960–63; OC, RAF Kinloss, 1963–64; Air Officer Administration: RAF Germany, 1964–68; Strike Comd, 1969–72. *Recreations:* golf, fishing, music. *Address:* c/o Lloyds Bank, Great Missenden, Bucks. *Club:* Royal Air Force.

FARRANCE, Roger Arthur, CBE 1988; Chief Executive, Electricity Association, since 1990; Chairman: Electricity Association Services Ltd, since 1991; Electricity Association

Technology Ltd, since 1991; *b* 10 Nov. 1933; *s* of Ernest Thomas Farrance and Alexandra Hilda May (*née* Finch); *m* 1956, Kathleen Sheila (*née* Owen); one *d*. *Educ:* Trinity School of John Whitgift, Croydon; London School of Economics (BScEcon). CIPM; CBIM; CompIEE. HM Inspector of Factories, Manchester, Doncaster and Walsall, 1956–64; Asst Sec., West of England Engineering Employers' Assoc., Bristol, 1964–67; Industrial Relations and Personnel Manager, Foster Wheeler John Brown Boilers Ltd, 1967–68; Dep. Director, Coventry and District Engineering Employers' Assoc., also Coventry Management Trng Centre, 1968–75; Electricty Council: Dep. Industrial Relations Adviser (Negotiating), 1975–76; Industrial Relations Adviser, 1976–79; Mem., 1979–88; Dep. Chm., 1989–90. Member Council: ACAS, 1983–89; CBI, 1983–. Pres., IPM, 1991–. FRSA. OStJ 1983. *Recreations:* photography, music. *Address:* 4 South Ridge Place, The Downs, Wimbledon, SW20 8JQ. *Club:* Royal Automobile.

FARRAND, Julian Thomas, LLD; Insurance Ombudsman, since 1989; *b* 13 Aug. 1935; *s* of J. and E. A. Farrand; *m* 1957, Winifred Joan Charles; one *s* two *d*. *Educ:* Haberdashers' Aske's Sch.; University Coll. London (LLB 1957, LLD 1966). Admitted Solicitor, 1960. Asst Lectr, then Lectr, KCL, 1960–63; Lectr, Sheffield Univ., 1963–65; Reader in Law, QMC, 1965–68; Prof. of Law, 1968–88, Dean of Faculty of Law, 1970–72, 1976–78, Manchester Univ. A Law Comr, 1984–88. Chairman: Gtr Manchester and Lancs Area, 1973–90 (Vice-Pres., 1977–84), London Area, 1984–, Rent Assessment Panel; Supplementary Benefit Appeals Tribunal, 1977–80; Nat. Insce Local Tribunal, 1980–83; Social Security Appeal Tribunal, 1983–88; Govt Conveyancing Cttee, 1984–85. *Publications:* (ed with Dr J. Gilchrist Smith) Emmet on Title, 15th edn 1967 to 19th edn (as sole editor) 1986; Contract and Conveyance, 1963–64, 4th edn 1983; (ed) Wolstenholme and Cherry, Conveyancing Statutes, 13th edn (vols 1–6) 1972; The Rent Acts and Regulations, 1978, 2nd edn (with A. Arden) 1981. *Recreations:* chess, bridge, wine. *Address:* 6 Regent Square, WC1H 8HZ.

FARRANDS, Dr John Law, AO 1990; CB 1982; FTS, CEng; FInstP, FAIP; FIE (Aust); consultant to companies and government, since 1982; *b* 11 March 1921; *s* of Harold Rawlings Farrands and Hilda Elizabeth (*née* Bray); *m* 1946, Jessica (*née* Ferguson); three *s* one *d* (and one *s* decd). *Educ:* Melbourne Univ. (BSc); London Univ. (PhD); Imperial Coll. of Science and Technol. (DIC, CEng). FTS 1976; FInstP 1957; FAIP 1962; FIE(Aust) 1987. Served RAEME, AIF, 1941 (Captain). Scientific Adviser to Mil. Bd, 1957; Chief Supt, Aeronautical Res. Labs, 1967; Chief Def. Scientist, 1971; Permanent Head, Dept of Science and Environment, later Dept of Science and Technol., 1977–82. Chairman: Aust. Inst. of Marine Science, 1982–90; R&D Bd, Overseas Telecommunications Commn, 1983–89. Leader, Aust. Delegn to UNCSTD, 1980. Cllr, Nat. Energy Res., Develt and Demonstration Council, 1978–83. Director: Interscan Australia, 1980–84; Quest Investment, 1986–; SCIRAD, 1987–. *Publications:* (jtly) Changing Disease Patterns and Human Behaviour, 1981; articles in scientific and engrg jls. *Recreations:* fishing, music. *Address:* 20 The Boulevard, Glen Waverley, Vic 3150, Australia. *T:* (03) 232–8195. *Clubs:* Sciences, Naval and Military (Melbourne).

FARRAR, Bernard; City Treasurer, Birmingham City Council, 1986–90; *b* 30 June 1930; *s* of Charles Newton and Edith Ethel Farrar; *m* 1st, 1963, Sheila Mary Moore (*d* 1982); one *d*; 2nd, 1987, Patricia Grace Williams. *Educ:* County Commercial College, Wednesbury. IPFA 1963; FRVA 1986. Borough of Tipton, 1950–58; County Borough of Smethwick, 1958–65; City of Birmingham, 1965–73; W Midlands County Council, 1973–76; Asst City Treasurer, 1976–82, Dep. City Treasurer, 1982–86, City of Birmingham. *Recreations:* visits to theatres and concerts, gardening, walking, DIY.

FARRAR, Rex Gordon, LVO 1975; HM Diplomatic Service, retired; Consul-General and Director of Trade Promotion, Osaka, Japan, 1980–85; *b* 22 Aug. 1925; *s* of late John Percival Farrar and Ethel Florence Farrar (*née* Leader); *m* 1978, Masako (*née* Ikeda); one *s* one *d*. *Educ:* Latymer's Sch., Edmonton; London Univ. (BA Hons History). Served Royal Navy, 1944–47. Joined HM Diplomatic Service, 1947; served, New Orleans, 1953–57; Jakarta, 1960–63; Caracas, 1964–68; San Salvador, 1968–71; Tokyo, 1971–75; Rangoon, 1978–80. *Recreations:* golf, tennis, studying Japanese. *Address:* 2 Lexham Garden Mews, Kensington W8. *T:* 071–370 7729. *Club:* Kobe (Japan).

FARRAR-HOCKLEY, Gen. Sir Anthony Heritage, GBE 1982 (MBE 1957); KCB 1977; DSO 1953 and bar 1964; MC 1944; author (military history), defence consultant and lecturer; Commander-in-Chief Allied Forces Northern Europe, 1979–82; ADC General to the Queen, 1981–83; retired 1983; *b* 8 April 1924; *s* of late Arthur Farrar-Hockley and Agnes Beatrice (*née* Griffin); *m* 1945, Margaret Bernadette Wells (*d* 1981); two *s* (and one *s* decd); *m* 1983, Linda Wood. *Educ:* Exeter Sch. War of 1939–45 (despatches, MC): enlisted under-age in ranks of The Gloucestershire Regt and served until Nov. 1942; commissioned into newly forming 1st Airborne Div., campaigning in Greece, Italy, S France, to 1945 (despatches 1943). Palestine, 1945–46; Korea, 1950–53 (despatches 1954); Cyprus and Port Said, 1956; Jordan, 1958; College Chief Instructor, RMA Sandhurst, 1959–61; commanded parachute bn in Persian Gulf and Radfan campaign, 1962–65; Principal Staff Officer to Dir of Borneo Ops, 1965–66; Comdr, 16 Parachute Bde, 1966–68; Defence Fellowship, Exeter Coll., Oxford, 1968–70 (BLitt); DPR (Army), 1970; Comdr, Land Forces, N Ireland, 1970–71; GOC 4th Div., 1971–73; Dir, Combat Development (Army), 1974–77; GOC SE District, 1977–79. Colonel Commandant: Prince of Wales's Div., 1974–80; Parachute Regt, 1977–83; Col, The Gloucestershire Regt, 1978–84. *Publications:* The Edge of the Sword, 1954; (ed) The Commander, 1957; The Somme, 1964; Death of an Army, 1968; Airborne Carpet, 1969; War in the Desert, 1969; General Student, 1973; Goughie: the Life of General Sir Hubert Gough, GCB, GCMG, KCVO, 1975; Opening Rounds, 1988; The British Part in the Korean War, vol. 1: A Distant Obligation, 1990. *Recreations:* cricket, badminton, sailing, walking. *Address:* c/o National Westminster Bank, 30 Wellington Street, Aldershot, Hants GU11 1EB. *Club:* Savage.

FARRELL, James; Procurator Fiscal, South Strathclyde, Dumfries and Galloway (formerly Lanarkshire) at Airdrie, 1955–75; Solicitor; *s* of Thomas Farrell and Margaret Farrell (*née* Quigley); *m* 1952, Margaret Clare O'Brien; one *s* three *d*. *Educ:* Our Lady's High Sch., Motherwell; St Patrick's Coll., Armagh, N Ireland; Glasgow Univ. (BL). In private practice as a solicitor, prior to joining Procurator Fiscal Service of the Crown. In latter capacity, Prosecutor for the Crown in the Sheriff Court, leading evidence at inquiries, there, into circumstances of death, particularly in suspicious, sudden and unexplained circumstances, fatal accidents, and where the public interest generally is involved; precognition and preparation of cases for High Court of Justiciary, and investigation relating to estates where the Crown may have to intervene as Ultimus Haeres, etc. *Recreations:* golf, bridge, gardening, photography, motoring, walking. *Address:* Clairville, 4 Belleisle Avenue, Uddingston, Glasgow G71 7AP. *T:* Uddingston (0698) 813385. *Club:* St Mungo's Academy FP Centenary (Glasgow).

FARRELL, James Aloysius; Sheriff of Lothian and Borders at Edinburgh, since 1986; *b* 14 May 1943; *s* of James Stoddart Farrell and Harriet Louise McDonnell; *m* 1967, Jacqueline Allen; two *d*. *Educ:* St Aloysius College; Glasgow University (MA); Dundee University (LLB). Admitted to Faculty of Advocates, 1974; Advocate-Depute, 1979–83; Sheriff: Glasgow and Strathkelvin, 1984; S Strathclyde, Dumfries and Galloway, 1985. *Recreations:* sailing, hillwalking, cycling. *Address:* 73 Murrayfield Gardens, Edinburgh. *T:* 031–337 2884.

FARRELL, M. J.; *see* Keane, M. N.

FARRELL, Michael Arthur; General Secretary, Amateur Athletics Association, since 1982; *b* 27 April 1933; *s* of Herbert and Marjorie Farrell; *m* 1st, 1957, Myra Shilton (*d* 1973); two *d*; 2nd, 1976, Beryl Browne. *Educ:* Beverley Grammar Sch., Yorks; Holly Lodge Grammar Sch., Birmingham. Design Draughtsman, 1949–51; Nat. Service, RASC, 1951–53; Planning Engineer, 1953–61; Representative, 1961–74; Sales Manager, Lillywhites Cantabrian, 1974–80; Sales Executive, En-Tout-Cas, 1980–82. *Recreations:* painting, walking, cycling. *Address:* Amateur Athletic Association, Edgbaston House, 3 Duchess Place, Hagley Road, Edgbaston, Birmingham B16 8NM. *T:* 021–456 4050.

FARRELL, Terence, (Terry Farrell), OBE 1978; Chairman, Terry Farrell & Company, since 1987; *b* 12 May 1938; *s* of Thomas and Molly Farrell (*née* Maguire); *m* 1st, 1960, Angela Rosemarie Mallam; two *d*; 2nd, 1973, Susan Hilary Aplin; two *s* one *d*. *Educ:* St Cuthbert's Grammar Sch., Newcastle; Durham Univ. (BArch, 1st class hons); Univ. of Pennsylvania (MArch, MCP). ARIBA 1963; MRTPI 1970; FCSD (FSIAD 1981). Harkness Fellow, Commonwealth Fund, USA, 1962–64. Partner: in Farrell Grimshaw Partnership, 1965–80; in Terry Farrell Partnership, 1980–87. Major projects include: Headquarters and studios for TVam and Limehouse Productions; greenhouses for Clifton Nurseries; Craft Council Galleries; Henley Royal Regatta Headquarters; redevelt of Charing Cross Station. *Exhibitions:* Terry Farrell in the context of London, RIBA Heinz Gall., London, 1987; British Architecture, Japan, 1987. *Publications:* articles in numerous British and foreign jls. *Recreations:* walking, swimming. *Address:* 17 Hatton Street, NW8 8PL.

FARRELL, Timothy Robert Warwick; Organist, Liberal Jewish Synagogue, St John's Wood, since 1975; *b* 5 Oct. 1943; *m* 1975, Penelope Walmsley-Clark; one *s*. *Educ:* Diocesan Coll., Cape Town; Royal Coll. of Music, London; Paris, etc. FRCO, ARCM (piano and organ). Asst Organist, St Paul's, Knightsbridge, 1962–66; Asst Organist, St Paul's Cath., 1966–67; Sub-organist, Westminster Abbey, 1967–74; Organ Tutor at Addington Palace, RSCM, 1966–73; Organist, Choirmaster and Composer, HM Chapels Royal, 1974–79. Broadcaster, gramophone records, electronic and orchestral music, etc. *Recreations:* golf, walking, sailing, flying. *Address:* Liberal Jewish Synagogue, 28 St John's Wood Road, NW8 7HA.

FARRER, Brian Ainsworth; QC 1978; **His Honour Judge Farrer;** a Circuit Judge, since 1985; *b* 7 April 1930; *s* of A. E. V. A. Farrer and Gertrude (*née* Hall); *m* 1960, Gwendoline Valerie (*née* Waddoup), JP; two *s* one *d*. *Educ:* King's Coll., Taunton; University Coll., London (LLB). Called to the Bar, Gray's Inn, 1957. A Recorder, 1974–85. Mem. Cttee, Normid Housing Assoc., 1977–. *Recreations:* golf, music, chess, bridge. *Address:* Shutt Cross House, Walsall Wood Road, Aldridge, West Midlands WS9 8QT; Ardudwy Cottage, Ty Ardudwy, Aberdovey, Gwynedd. *Club:* Aberdovey Golf.

FARRER, Sir (Charles) Matthew, KCVO 1983 (CVO 1973); Private Solicitor to the Queen, since 1965; Partner in Messrs Farrer & Co, Solicitors, since 1959; *b* 3 Dec. 1929; *s* of late Sir (Walter) Leslie Farrer, KCVO, and Hon. Lady Farrer; *m* 1962, Johanna Creszentia Maria Dorothea Bennhold; one *s* one *d*. *Educ:* Bryanston Sch.; Balliol Coll., Oxford (MA). A Trustee, British Museum, 1989–; Comr, Royal Commn on Historical Manuscripts, 1991–. Hon. Treasurer, British Inst. of Archaeology, Ankara. *Recreations:* travel, reading. *Address:* 6 Priory Avenue, Bedford Park, W4 1TX. *T:* 081–994 6052. *Club:* United Oxford & Cambridge University.

FARRER, David John; QC 1986; a Recorder, since 1983; *b* 15 March 1943; *s* of John Hall Farrer and Mary Farrer; *m* 1969, Hilary Jean Bryson; two *s* one *d*. *Educ:* Queen Elizabeth's Grammar Sch., Barnet; Downing Coll., Cambridge (MA, LLB). Called to the Bar, Middle Temple, 1967; in practice, 1968–; Mem., Bar Council, 1986–; Chm., Bar Services Cttee, 1989–. Contested (L): Melton, 1979; Rutland and Melton, 1983. *Recreations:* tennis, cricket, Liberal Party politics. *Address:* The Grange, Hoby, Melton Mowbray, Leics LE14 3DT. *T:* Rotherby (066475) 232. *Club:* National Liberal.

FARRER, Margaret Irene, OBE 1970; Chairman of Central Midwives Board, 1973–79; *b* 23 Feb. 1914; *e d* of Alfred and Emblyn Farrer. *Educ:* Poltimore Coll., Exeter; UCH London. SRN, SCM, DN (London), MTD, RST. Midwifery Tutor, General Lying-in Hosp., 1942–49; Matron: St Mary's Hosp., Croydon, 1949–56; Forest Gate Hosp., 1956–71; Chief Nursing Officer, Thames Gp, 1971–74. Member: Central Midwives Bd, 1952–; Central Health Services Council, 1963–74; NE Metropolitan Regional Hosp. Bd, 1969–74; NE Thames Regional Health Authority, 1973–76; Editorial Bd, Midwife and Health Visitor; Hon. Treas., Royal Coll. of Midwives, 1967–76. *Recreations:* gardening, walking. *Address:* Coombe Brook, Dawlish, South Devon EX7 0QN. *T:* Dawlish (0626) 863323.

FARRER, Sir Matthew; *see* Farrer, Sir C. M.

FARRER, William Oliver, CVO 1991; Senior Partner, Farrer & Co., Solicitors, 1976–91 (Partner, 1955–91); *b* 23 June 1926; *s* of John Oliver Farrer, MC, and Winifred Millicent Farrer; *m* 1st, 1955, Margery Hope Yates (*d* 1976); two *s* one *d*; 2nd, 1979, Hazel Mary Andrew. *Educ:* Eton Coll.; Balliol Coll., Oxford (MA). Lieut, Coldstream Guards, 1945–48. Admitted a Solicitor, 1953; Solicitor to the Duchy of Lancaster, 1984–91; Mem., Solicitors' Disciplinary Tribunal, 1986–91. *Recreations:* golf, music. *Address:* Popmoor, Fernhurst, Haslemere, Surrey GU27 3LL. *T:* Haslemere (0428) 642564. *Clubs:* Brooks's, MCC; Royal and Ancient (St Andrews); Honourable Company of Edinburgh Golfers.

FARRER-BROWN, Leslie, CBE 1960; Consultant; Director: Nuffield Foundation, 1944–64; Alliance Building Society, 1969–83 (Chairman, 1975–81); *b* 2 April 1904; *er s* of late Sydney and Annie Brown; *m* 1928, Doris Evelyn (*d* 1986), *o d* of late Herbert Jamieson; two *s*. *Educ:* LSE (BSc Econ.), Hon. Fellow 1975; Gray's Inn (Barrister-at-Law, 1932). Asst Registrar, LSE, 1927–28; on Administrative Staff, Univ. of London, 1928–36; Sec., Central Midwives Bd, 1936–45; seconded to Min. of Health, 1941–44. Pres., Surrey and Sussex Rent Assessment Panel, 1965–76. Sec., Interdepartmental Cttee on Med. Schs, 1942–44. Chairman: Malta Med. Services Commn, 1956; Highgate Juvenile Court, 1952–61; Highgate Court, 1961–65; Nat. Council of Social Service, 1960–73; Centre for Educational Television Overseas, 1962–70; Overseas Visual Aid Centre, 1958–70; Voluntary Cttee on Overseas Aid and Develt, 1965–76; Centre for Information on Language Teaching, 1966–72; Cttee for Res. and Develt in Modern Languages, 1964–70; Rhodesia Med. Sch. Cttee; Univ. of London Inst. of Child Health, 1966–76; Inst. of Race Relations, 1968–72. Member: Colonial Adv. Med. Cttee, 1946–61; Colonial Social Science Res. Council, 1954–61; Med. Educn Cttee of UGC, 1945–52; Rating of Charities Cttee, 1958–59; Adv. Council, BBC, 1956–65; Court of Governors, LSE; Chm. Council and Sen. Pro-Chancellor, Univ. of Sussex, 1976–80. Trustee, Nuffield Provincial Hospitals Trust, 1955–67; UK Governor, Commonwealth Foundn, 1966–89. JP: Middx, 1947–65;

East Sussex, 1966–81. Hon. FDSRCS. Hon. LLD: Birmingham; Witwatersrand; Sussex; Hon. DSc Keele. *Publication:* (jt) A Short Textbook on Public Health and Social Services. *Recreations:* travel, painting. *Address:* 3 Kennet Court, Woosehill, Wokingham, Berks. *Clubs:* Athenæum, Commonwealth Trust (Life Vice-Pres., 1969).

FARRIMOND, Herbert Leonard, CBE 1977; Adviser, The Associated Octel Company Ltd; Chairman, H. L. Farrimond & Associates Ltd, since 1978; *b* 4 Oct. 1924; *s* of late George and Jane Farrimond, Newcastle upon Tyne; *m* 1951, Patricia Sara (*née* McGrath); one *s*. *Educ:* St Cuthbert's Grammar Sch., Newcastle upon Tyne; Durham Univ. BA (Hons) Politics and Economics. Lieut RM, 1943–46. Australian Dept of Labour and Nat. Service, 1948–50; Imperial Chemical Industries Ltd, and Imperial Metal Industries Ltd, 1950–68; Upper Clyde Shipbuilders Ltd, 1968–69; Dir of Personnel, Dunlop Ltd, 1969–72; Mem., British Railways Bd, 1972–77. Director: British Rail Engineering Ltd; British Rail Shipping and Internat. Services Div.; Transmark Ltd (Chm.); Portsmouth and Sunderland Newspapers Ltd, 1978–80; Chm., British Transport Hotels, 1976–78. Adviser to industrial and commercial cos, 1978–. Mem. Council, Advisory, Conciliation and Arbitration Service, 1974–78. Part-time Mem., British Waterways Bd, 1980–82. Governor, British Transport Staff Coll. Ltd, 1972–77. FCIT; FIPM. *Recreations:* golf, gardening, music. *Address:* 9 Ardgare, Shandon, Helensburgh, Dunbartonshire. *T:* Helensburgh (0436) 820803. *Clubs:* Royal Scottish Automobile (Glasgow); Royal Northern and Clyde Yacht (Rhu).

FARRINGTON, Dr David Philip; Reader in Psychological Criminology, University of Cambridge, since 1988; *b* 7 March 1944; *s* of William Farrington and Gladys Holden (*née* Spurr); *m* 1966, Sally Chamberlain; three *d*. *Educ:* Clare Coll., Cambridge (BA, MA, PhD Psychology). On staff of Cambridge Univ. Inst. of Criminology, 1969–. Chm., Div. of Criminological and Legal Psychology, British Psychological Soc., 1983–85; Pres., British Soc. of Criminology, 1990–. Sellin-Glueck Award, Amer. Soc. of Criminology,1984. *Publications:* Who Becomes Delinquent? 1973; The Delinquent Way of Life, 1977; Behaviour Modification with Offenders, 1979; Psychology, Law and Legal Processes, 1979; Abnormal Offenders, Delinquency and the Criminal Justice System, 1982; Aggression and Dangerousness, 1985; Reactions to Crime, 1985; Prediction in Criminology, 1985; Understanding and Controlling Crime, 1986; Human Development and Criminal Behaviour, 1991. *Address:* Institute of Criminology, 7 West Road, Cambridge CB3 9DT. *T:* Cambridge (0223) 335384.

FARRINGTON, Sir Henry Francis Colden, 7th Bt, *cr* 1818; RA retired; *b* 25 April 1914; *s* of Sir Henry Anthony Farrington, 6th Bt, and of Dorothy Maria (*d* 1969), *o d* of Frank Farrington; *S* father, 1944; *m* 1947, Anne, *e d* of late Major W. A. Gillam, DSO; one *s* one *d*. *Educ:* Haileybury. Retired from Army, 1960 (Major; now Hon. Col). *Heir: s* Henry William Farrington, ARICS [*b* 27 March 1951; *m* 1979, Diana Donne Broughton, *yr d* of Geoffrey Broughton, Somerset; two *s*]. *Address:* Higher Ford, Wiveliscombe, Taunton, Somerset TA4 2RL. *T:* Wiveliscombe (0984) 23219.

FARROW, Christopher John; Director, Kleinwort, Benson Ltd, since 1987; *b* 29 July 1937; *s* of late Thomas and Evangeline Dorothea Farrow; *m* 1961, Alison Brown; one *s* one *d*. *Educ:* Cranleigh Sch.; King's Coll., Cambridge (BA). Board of Trade, 1961; Harkness Fellowship and visiting scholar, Stanford Univ., USA, 1968–69; Private Sec. to Pres. of BoT and Minister for Trade, 1970–72; Dept of Trade and Industry, 1972–74; Cabinet Office, 1975–77; Dept of Industry, 1977–83; Asst Dir, Bank of England, 1983–87. Dir, London Metal Exchange Ltd, 1987–. Mem., Engrg Council, 1984–86. *Recreation:* gardening. *Address:* Kleinwort Benson Ltd, 20 Fenchurch Street, EC3 3DB.

FARROW, Mia (Villiers); actress; *b* 9 Feb. 1945; *d* of John Villiers Farrow and Maureen O'Sullivan; *m* 1970, André Previn (marr. diss. 1979), *qv*; three *s* two *d*; one *s* by Woody Allen, *qv*. *TV series:* Peyton Place, 1965; *films:* Secret Ceremony, 1968; Rosemary's Baby, 1969; John and Mary, 1970; The Public Eye, 1972; The Great Gatsby, 1974; Full Circle, Death on the Nile, A Wedding, 1978; Hurricane, 1980; A Midsummer Night's Sex Comedy, 1982; Zelig, 1983; Broadway Danny Rose, 1984; The Purple Rose of Cairo, 1985; Hannah and her Sisters, 1986; Radio Days, 1987; September, 1988; Another Woman, 1989; Crimes and Misdemeanours, 1990; Alice, 1990; *stage:* The Importance of Being Earnest, NY, 1963; Mary Rose, Shaw, 1973; The Three Sisters, Greenwich, 1974; The House of Bernarda Alba, Greenwich, 1974; Peter Pan, 1975; The Marrying of Ann Leete, RSC, 1975; The Zykovs, Ivanov, RSC, 1976; A Midsummer Night's Dream, Leicester, 1976; Romantic Comedy, NY, 1979. David Donatello Award, Italy, 1969; Best Actress awards: French Academy, 1969; San Sebastian, 1969; Rio de Janeiro, 1970. *Address:* c/o ICM, 8899 Beverly Boulevard, Los Angeles, Calif 90048, USA; Bridgewater, Conn, USA.

FARTHING, (Richard) Bruce (Crosby); Deputy Director-General, General Council of British Shipping, 1980–83; Rapporteur, Sea Transport Commission, International Chamber of Commerce, since 1976; Consultant Director, International Association of Dry Cargo Shipowners, since 1984; *b* 9 Feb. 1926; *s* of late Col Herbert Hadfield Farthing and late Marjorie Cora (*née* Fisher); *m* 1st, 1959, Anne Brenda Williams (marr. diss. 1986), LLB, barrister, *d* of late Thomas Williams, solicitor; one *s* one *d*; 2nd, 1986, Moira Roupell, *o d* of late Lt-Col R. A. Curties and of Mrs Ida Curties. *Educ:* Alleyns Sch., (Dulwich and Rossall) St Catharine's Coll., Cambridge (MA). Commissioned RA and RHA, 1944–48. Called to Bar, Inner Temple, 1954; Govt Legal Service, 1954–59; joined Chamber of Shipping of the United Kingdom, 1959; Asst General Manager, 1966; Secretary, Cttee of European Shipowners and Cttee of European National Shipowners' Assocs, 1967–74; Secretary-General, Council of European and Japanese National Shipowners' Assocs (CENSA), 1974–76; Director, General Council of British Shipping, 1976–80. Trustee, Nautical Museums Trust, 1983–. Chm., King of Norway Reception Cttee, 1988. Freeman, City of London, 1979; Liveryman, Shipwrights' Co., 1982–; Mem. Court of Common Council (Aldgate Ward), 1981–. Pres., Aldgate Ward Club, 1985 (Vice-Pres., 1984); Governor: City of London Sch., 1983– (Dep. Chm., 1988–89, Chm., 1990–); SOAS, 1985–. FBIM. Commander, Royal Norwegian Order of Merit, 1988. *Publications:* ed, Vol. 20, Aspinalls Maritime Law Cases, 1961; International Shipping, 1987. *Recreations:* sailing, music, gardening. *Address:* 44 St George's Drive, SW1V 4BT; Snaylham House, Icklesham, E Sussex TN36 4AJ. *Clubs:* MCC, Incogniti Cricket, Royal Ocean Racing; Rye Golf.

FARVIS, Prof. William Ewart John, CBE 1978 (OBE 1972); BSc, BSc(Eng), CEng, Hon. FIEE; FRSE; engineering consultant; Professor Emeritus of Electrical Engineering, University of Edinburgh (Professor, 1961–77); *b* 12 Dec. 1911; *o s* of late William Henry Farvis and Gertrude Anne Farvis; *m* 1939, Margaret May Edmonstone Martin; one *s* one *d*. *Educ:* Queen Elizabeth's Hosp., Bristol; Bristol and London Univs. Lectr, University Coll., Swansea, 1937–40 and 1945–48; Air Ministry, Telecommunications Res. Estab., 1940–45; Lectr/Sen. Lectr, Edinburgh Univ., 1948–61, Prof. and Head of Dept of Electrical Eng., 1961–77, Chairman, Sch. of Engineering Sci. 1972–75. Mem., British Nat. Cttee for Radio Science, 1960–66; Science Research Council: Mem., Electrical and Systems Cttee, 1968–72; Engineering Board, 1972–75 and 1976–81; Polytechnics Cttee, 1975–78; Chm., Solid-state Devices Panel, 1972–75; Electrical and Systems Cttee 1972–75; Advanced Ground Transport Panel 1975–80; Mem. Council, 1976–81. Mem. Council, IEE, 1972–75 and 1976–79; Hon. FIEE 1987. Editor, Microelectronics Journal, 1976–78. *Recreation:* music. *Address:* 14 Cluny Terrace, Edinburgh EH10 4SW. *T:* 031–447 4939. *Club:* Athenæum.

FASELLA, Prof. Paolo Maria; Director-General for Science, Research and Development, Commission of the European Communities, since 1981; *b* 16 Dec. 1930; *s* of Felice Fasella and Margherita Parazzoli; *m* 1957, Sheila Hauck Dionisi; four *d*. *Educ:* Univ. of Rome. PhD Biolog. Chem. and Applied Biochem. Asst, then Associate Prof. in Biol. Chem., Univ. of Rome, 1959–65; Associate, then Prof. in Biochem., Univ. of Parma, 1965–71; Prof. of Biol. Chem.,Univ. of Rome, 1971–81. Res. Associate, 1961–62, Vis. Scientist (part-time), 1963–64, MIT; Vis. Prof., Dept. of Chem., Cornell Univ., 1966. Mem., Accademia Nazionale delle Scienze—detta dei XL; Hon. Fellow: Inst. of Biology, 1990; Belgian Royal Acad. of Medicine, 1990. Hon. DSc NUI, 1990. *Publications:* numerous papers on protein structure and functions, biological catalysis, biotechnology; articles on sci. res. policy and bioethics. *Address:* Directorate-General for Science, Research and Development, Commission of the European Communities, 200 rue de la Loi, B-1049 Brussels, Belgium. *T:* 32.2.235.35.70.

FASSETT, Kaffe; textile designer; *b* 7 Dec. 1937; *s* of William Elliot Fassett and Madeleine Fassett. Self-educated. *Publications:* Glorious Knitting, 1985; Glorious Needlepoint, 1987; Kaffe Fassett at the V & A, 1988; Family Album, 1989. *Address:* c/o Random Century, 20 Vauxhall Bridge Road, SW1V 2SA.

FATAYI-WILLIAMS, Hon. Atanda, GCON 1983; CFR 1980; Chief Justice of Nigeria, 1979–83; *b* 22 Oct. 1918; *s* of Alhaji Issa Williams and Alhaja Ashakun Williams; *m* 1948, Irene Violet Lofts; three *s*. *Educ:* Methodist Boys' High Sch., Lagos, Nigeria; Trinity Hall, Cambridge (BA 1946, LLM 1947, MA 1949; Hon. Fellow 1983). Called to the Bar, Middle Temple, 1948. Private practice, Lagos, 1948–50; Crown Counsel, Lagos, 1950–55; Dep. Comr for Law Revision, Western Nigeria, 1955–58; Chief Registrar, High Court of Western Nigeria, 1958–60; High Court Judge, 1960–67; Justice of Appeal, Western State Court of Appeal, 1967–69; Justice, Supreme Court of Nigeria, 1969–79. Mem., Council of State, 1983–84, 1990–. Chairman: Ports Arbitration Bd, 1971; All Nigeria Law Reports Cttee, 1972–75; Body of Benchers, 1979–80; Legal Practitioners' Privileges Cttee, 1979–83; Federal Judicial Service Commn, 1979–83; Judiciary Consultative Cttee, 1979–83; National Archives Cttee, 1979–83; Presidential Cttee on Medical Doctors' Remuneration, 1990; Bd of Trustees, The Van Leer Nigerian Educn Trust, 1973–85; Crescent Bearers, Lagos, 1978–84; Council of Legal Educn, 1984–. Member: Nigerian Inst. of Internat. Affairs, 1972–; National Museum Soc., Lagos, 1972–. Trustee, Nigerian Youth Trust, 1979–84. Hon. Fellow, Nigerian Inst. of Advanced Legal Studies, 1983; Life FRSA 1949. *Publications:* (ed) Western Nigeria Law Reports, 1955–58; (with Sir John Verity) Revised Laws of the Western Region of Nigeria, 1959; Sentencing Processes, Practices and Attitudes, as seen by an Appeal Court Judge, 1970; Faces, Cases and Places (autobiog.), 1983. *Recreations:* reading, swimming, walking, speed-boats. *Address:* 8 Adetokunbo Ademola Street, Victoria Island, Lagos, Nigeria. *T:* Lagos 611315. *Clubs:* Athenæum, United Oxford & Cambridge University; Metropolitan, Motor Boat (Lagos).

FATCHETT, Derek John; MP (Lab) Leeds Central, since 1983; *b* 22 Aug. 1945; *s* of Herbert and Irene Fatchett; *m* 1969, Anita Bridgens (*née* Oakes); two *s*. *Educ:* Monks Road Primary School; Lincoln School; Birmingham University (LLB); LSE (MSc). Research Officer, LSE, 1968–70; Research Fellow, University College, Cardiff, 1970–71; Lectr in Industrial Relations, Univ. of Leeds, 1971–83. Labour Whip, 1986–87; Opposition spokesman on education (secondary and tertiary), 1987, on education and training, 1988–; Dep. Campaigns Co-ordinator, 1987–. *Publications:* (jtly) Workers Participation in Management, 1972; (jtly) Worker Participation: industrial control and performance, 1974; (jtly) The Worker Directors, 1976; Trade Unions and Politics in the 1980's: the political fund ballots, 1987; articles in learned jls. *Recreations:* gardening, cricket, jogging. *Address:* 130 Bradford Road, Wakefield, Yorks. *T:* Wakefield (0924) 375291.

FATEH, Abul Fazal Muhammad Abul; Ambassador of Bangladesh at Algiers, 1977–82; *b* 28 Feb. 1926; *s* of Abdul Gafur and Zohra Khatun; *m* 1956, Mahfuza Banu; two *s*. *Educ:* Dacca, Bangladesh. MA (English Lit.); special course, LSE, 1949–50. Carnegie Fellow in Internat. Peace, 1962–63. Entered Pakistan Foreign Service, 1949; 3rd Secretary: Paris, 1951–53; Calcutta, 1953–56; 2nd Sec., Washington, DC, 1956–60; Dir, Min. of Foreign Affairs, Karachi, 1961–65; 1st Sec., Prague, 1965–66; Counsellor, New Delhi, 1966–67; Dep. High Comr for Pakistan, Calcutta, 1968–70; Ambassador of Pakistan, Baghdad, 1971; Adviser to Actg President of Bangladesh, Aug. 1971; Foreign Sec., Bangladesh, Jan. 1972; Ambassador of Bangladesh to France and Spain, 1972–75; Permanent Deleg. to UNESCO, 1972–76; High Comr for Bangladesh in London, 1976–77. Leader, Bangladesh Delegation: Commonwealth Youth Ministers' Conf., Lusaka, 1973; Meeting of UN Council on Namibia, Algiers, 1980; Ministerial Meeting of Non-aligned Countries Co-ordination Bureau on Namibia, Algiers, 1981. Chm., Commonwealth Human Ecology Council Symposium, 1977; Hon. Rep. of Royal Commonwealth Soc. in Bangladesh, 1985–. *Address:* 21 Dhanmondi Residential Area, Road No 8, Dhaka, Bangladesh.

FATT, Prof. Paul, FRS 1969; Emeritus Professor, University of London, since 1989. Professor of Biophysics, University College, London, 1976–89 (Reader, 1956–76); Fellow, UCL, 1973. *Publications:* papers in various scientific jls. *Address:* Department of Protein and Molecular Biology, Royal Free Hospital School of Medicine, Rowland Hill Street, NW3 2PF. *T:* 071–794 0500.

FAULDS, Andrew Matthew William; MP (Lab) Warley East, since 1974 (Smethwick, 1966–74); *b* 1 March 1923; *s* of late Rev. Matthew Faulds, MA, and of Doris Faulds; *m* 1945, Bunty Whitfield; one *d*. *Educ:* George Watson's, Edinburgh; King Edward VI Grammar Sch., Louth; Daniel Stewart's, Edinburgh; High Sch., Stirling; Glasgow Univ. Three seasons with Shakespeare Memorial Co., Stratford-upon-Avon; BBC Repertory Co.: Jet Morgan in Journey into Space (BBC). Has appeared in over 35 films and many TV and radio performances. Parliamentary Private Secretary: to Minister of State for Aviation, Min. of Technology, 1967–68; to Postmaster General, 1968–69; Opposition spokesman for the Arts, 1970–73, 1979–82; Chairman: British br., Parly Assoc. for Euro-Arab Cooperation, 1974–; All-Party Parly Heritage Gp; Member: British Delegn to Council of Europe and WEU, 1975–80, and 1987–; Exec. Cttee, GB China Centre, 1976–; Exec. Cttee, IPU, (British Section), 1983–. *Recreation:* cosseting his constituents. *Address:* 14 Albemarle Street, W1. *T:* 071–499 7589.

FAULKNER OF DOWNPATRICK, Lady; Lucy (Barbara Ethel) Faulkner, CBE 1985; *b* 1 July 1925; *d* of William John Forsythe and Jane Ethel Sewell; *m* 1951, Arthur Brian Deane Faulkner (MP (NI) 1949–73; PC 1959; *cr* Baron Faulkner of Downpatrick, 1977) (killed in a hunting accident, 1977); two *s* one *d*. *Educ:* Aubrey House; Bangor Collegiate Sch.; Trinity College Dublin. BA (Hons History). Journalist, Belfast Telegraph, 1947; Personal Secretary to Sir Basil Brooke, Prime Minister of N Ireland, 1949. Nat. Governor for NI, BBC, 1978–85; Chm., Broadcasting Council for NI, 1981–85; Researcher, 1977, Trustee 1980–, Ulster Historical Foundation; Member: Cttee, Irish Museums Trust, 1984–; NI Tourist Bd, 1985–; Governor, Linenhall Library, 1982–.

Recreations: hunting and dressage, genealogy, book collecting. *Address:* Toberdoney, Farranfad, Downpatrick BT30 8NH. *T:* Seaforde (039687) 712. *Club:* Royal Over-Seas League.

FAULKNER, David Ewart Riley, CB 1985; Deputy Under-Secretary of State and Principal Establishment Officer, Home Office, since 1982; *b* 23 Oct. 1934; *s* of Harold Ewart and Mabel Faulkner; *m* 1961, Sheila Jean Stevenson; one *s* one *d. Educ:* Manchester Grammar Sch.; Merchant Taylors' Sch., Northwood; St John's Coll., Oxford (MA Lit Hum). Home Office: Asst Principal, 1959; Private Sec. to Parly Under-Sec. of State, 1961–63; Principal, 1963; Jt Sec. to Inter-Party Conf. on House of Lords Reform, 1968; Private Sec. to Home Sec., 1969–70; Asst Sec., Prison Dept, 1970, Establishment Dept, 1974, Police Dept, 1976; Asst Under-Sec. of State, 1976; Under Sec., Cabinet Office, 1978–80; Asst Under-Sec. of State, Dir of Operational Policy, Prison Dept, Home Office, 1980–82. Member: UN Cttee on Crime Prevention and Control, 1984–; Adv. Bd, Helsinki Inst. for Crime Prevention and Control, 1988–. *Recreations:* railways, birds. *Address:* Home Office, 50 Queen Anne's Gate, SW1.
   See also R. O. Faulkner.

FAULKNER, Sir Dennis; *see* Faulkner, Sir J. D. C.

FAULKNER, Prof. Douglas, WhSch, BSc, PhD; FEng 1981, FRINA, FIStructE, MSNAME; RCNC; Head of Department of Naval Architecture and Ocean Engineering, University of Glasgow, since 1973; *b* 29 Dec. 1929; *s* of Vincent and Florence Faulkner; *m* 1st, 1954, Jenifer Ann Cole-Adams (marr. diss. 1986); three *d; m* 2nd, 1987, Isobel Parker Campbell. *Educ:* Sutton High Sch., Plymouth; HM Dockyard Technical Coll., Devonport; RNC, Greenwich. Aircraft Carrier Design, 1955–57; Production Engrg, 1957–59; Structural Research at NCRE, Dunfermline, 1959–63; Asst Prof. of Naval Construction, RNC, Greenwich, 1963–66; Structural Adviser to Ship Dept, Bath, 1966–68; Naval Construction Officer att. to British Embassy, Washington DC, 1968–70, and Mem. Ship Research Cttee, Nat. Acad. of Scis, 1968–71; Res. Associate and Defence Fellow, MIT, 1970–71; Structural Adviser to Ship Dept, Bath, and to the Merrison Box Girder Bridge Cttee, 1971–73. UK Rep., Standing Cttee, Internat. Ship Structures Congress, 1973–85. Chm., Conoco-ABS cttee producing a design code for Tension Leg Platforms offshore, 1981–83; Dir, Veritec Ltd, 1985–88; Mem. Bd of Govs, BMT Quality Assessors Ltd, 1990–. FRSA 1983. Consulting Editor, Jl of Marine Structures, 1990– (Editor, 1987–90). *Publications:* (ed jtly) Integrity of Offshore Structures, 1981; Integrity of Offshore Structures—3, 1987; Integrity of Offshore Structures—4, 1990; chapters in Ship Structural Design Concepts (Cornell Maritime Press), 1975; papers related to structural design of ships, in Trans RINA, Jl of Ship Res., Behaviour of Offshore Structures, etc. *Recreations:* hill walking, swimming, music, chess. *Address:* 57 Bellshaugh Place, Glasgow G12 0PF. *T:* 041–357 1748.

FAULKNER, Sir Eric (Odin), Kt 1974; MBE 1945; TD 1945 and Bar 1951; Director, Lloyds Bank Ltd, 1968–84 (Chairman, 1969–77); Advisory Director, Unilever, 1978–84; *b* 21 April 1914; *s* of late Sir Alfred Faulkner, CB, CBE; *m* 1939, Joan Mary (*d* 1991), *d* of Lt-Col F. A. M. Webster; one *s* one *d. Educ:* Bradfield; Corpus Christi Coll., Cambridge (Hon. Fellow, 1975). Joined Glyn, Mills & Co., 1936. Served War of 1939–45, Royal Artillery and Leics Yeomanry; Staff Coll.; Bde Major RA, GSO2; commanded 91 Field Regt RA. Rejoined Glyn, Mills & Co., 1946; Local Dir, 1947–50; Exec. Dir, 1950–68; Dep. Chm., 1959–63; Chm., 1963–68. Chm., Cttee of London Clearing Bankers, 1972–74. Pres., British Bankers' Assoc., 1972–73, 1980–84. Director: Union Discount Co. of London Ltd, 1949–70 (Chm., 1959–70); Hudsons Bay Co., 1950–70 (Dep. Governor, 1952–56); Vickers Ltd, 1957–79. Chairman: Industrial Soc., 1973–76; City Communications Organisation, 1976–79. Warden of Bradfield Coll., 1965–84; Trustee, Winston Churchill Meml Trust, 1973–84. *Recreations:* fishing and walking; formerly cricket and Association football (CUAFC XI 1935). *Address:* Farriers Field, Sevenoaks Road, Ightham, Kent TN15 9AA.

FAULKNER, Hugh (Branston), OBE 1980; charity consultant, since 1989; Director: Asthma Research Council, and Asthma Society, 1983–88; Help the Aged, from formation, 1961–83; *b* Lutterworth, 8 June 1916; *s* of Frank and Ethel Faulkner; *m* 1954, Anne Carlton Milner; one *s* one *d. Educ:* Lutterworth Grammar Sch. FCIS. Educn Administration, City of Leicester, 1936–46; Organising Sec., Fellowship of Reconciliation, 1946–54; business and charity career from 1954. Hon. Dir and later Dir, Voluntary and Christian Service, 1954–79; a Director: Helpage International Ltd, 1966–83; Help the Aged Housing Appeal, 1975–83. Christian peace delegate to USSR, 1952, followed by lecture tour in USA, 1953, on internat. relations; deleg. and speaker, UN World Assembly on Ageing, Vienna, 1982. Mem., Exec. Cttee, Council for Music in Hospitals, 1983–; Trustee: World in Need Trust; Lester Trust; Andrews Pension Trust; Voluntary and Christian Service; Asthma Soc. Training Centre; Advr, Elderly Accommodation Council; Member: Help the Aged Housing Assoc., 1966–; Voluntary Service Housing Assoc. (formerly Voluntary and Christian Service Housing Assoc.), 1980–. *Recreations:* music, gardening. *Address:* Longfield, 4 One Tree Lane, Beaconsfield, Bucks HP9 2BU. *T:* Beaconsfield (0494) 674769. *Club:* National Liberal.

FAULKNER, Dr Hugh Charles, FRCGP; Consultant to Regional Health Authority, Tuscany and to Unità Sanitaria Locale del Chianti; Editorial Board, Salute e Territorio; Hon. Lecturer in Social Medicine, Bedford College, University of London, since 1976; Medical Secretary, Medical Practitioners' Union (ASTMS), and Medical Editor of Medical World, 1971–76; *b* 22 Sept. 1912; *s* of Frank Whitehead Faulkner and Emily Maud Knibb; *m;* one *s* two *d. Educ:* Oundle Sch.; London Hosp. MRCS, LRCP, FRCGP 1979. Boys' Club Manager, 1932–35; qual. MRCS, LRCP, 1943. Served War, RAMC, 1944–46. Gen. Practitioner, 1948–76. Mem. Council of Medical Practitioners' Union, 1948–76. Trustee, Community Health Foundn, 1991–. Mem., Ordine dei Medici (Firenze), 1981. *Publications:* Medicina di Base in due paesi, Gran Bretagna e l'URSS, 1977; Beating the Odds, 1991; articles in Medical World, Lancet, etc. *Recreation:* attacking the Establishment. *Address:* La Galera, Passo del Sugame, Greve-in-Chianti, Firenze, Italy.

FAULKNER, Sir (James) Dennis (Compton), Kt 1991; CBE 1980; VRD 1960; DL; Chairman, Marlowe Cleaners Ltd, since 1973; *b* 22 Oct. 1926; *s* of James and Nora Faulkner; *m* 1952, Janet Cunningham; three *d. Educ:* College of St Columba, Co. Dublin. Served RNVR, 1946–71. Chairman: Belfast Collar Co. Ltd, 1957–63; Belfast Savings Bank, 1960–61; NI Develt Agency, 1978–82; Board Member: Gallaher NI, 1980–89 (Chm., 1982–89); Northern Bank Ltd, 1983–; Chm., Ladybird (NI) Ltd, 1983–88. Farming, 1946–. DL County Down, 1988. *Recreations:* sailing, hunting, shooting, ocean racing. *Address:* Ringhaddy House, Killinchy, Co. Down, Northern Ireland BT23 6TU. *T:* Killinchy (0238) 541114. *Clubs:* Army and Navy, Royal Ocean Racing, Royal Cruising; Cruising Club of America (New York).

FAULKNER, John Richard Hayward; theatre and management consultant; international impresario; *b* 29 May 1941; *s* of Richard Hayward Ollerton and Lilian Elizabeth (*née* Carrigan); *m* 1970, Janet Gill (*née* Cummings); two *d* two step *d. Educ:* Archbishop Holgate's Sch., York; Keble Coll., Oxford (BA). Worked with a number of theatre companies, Prospect Productions, Meadow Players, Century Theatre, Sixty-Nine

Theatre Co., Cambridge Theatre Co., toured extensively, UK, Europe, Indian Sub-Continent, Australia, 1960–72; Drama Director: Scottish Arts Council, 1972–77; Arts Council of GB, 1977–83; Head, Artistic Planning, Nat. Theatre, 1983–88. Mem. Bd, Galactic Smallholdings Ltd, 1985–; Dir, Minotaur Films, 1988–. Trustee: The Arts Educational Schools, 1986–; Performing Arts Labs, The Arts for Nature. Chm., Assoc. of British Theatre Technicians, 1989–. *Recreations:* intricacies and wildernesses. *Address:* 33 Hadley Gardens, Chiswick W4 4NU. *T:* 081–995 3041.

FAULKNER, Most Rev. Leonard Anthony; *see* Adelaide, Archbishop of, (RC).

FAULKNER, Richard Oliver; First Deputy Chairman, Football Trust, 1990; Joint Managing Director, Westminster Communications Group Ltd, since 1989; *b* 22 March 1946; *s* of late Harold Ewart and Mabel Faulkner; *m* 1968, Susan Heyes; two *d. Educ:* Merchant Taylors' Sch., Northwood; Worcester Coll., Oxford (MA PPE). Research asst and journalist, Labour Party, 1967–69; PRO, Construction Ind. Trg Bd, 1969–70; Editor, Steel News, 1971; Account dir, F. J. Lyons (PR) Ltd, 1971–73; Dir, PPR International, 1973–76. Co-founder, parly jl The House Magazine; communications advr (unpaid) to Leader of the Opposition, gen. election, 1987; Govt relations adviser: milling and baking industries, 1972–; Fyffes Gp, 1974–; rly trade unions, 1975–76; C. A. Parsons & Co., 1976–77; Pool Promoters Assoc., 1977–; British Rlys Bd, 1977–; Prudential Assurance Co., 1978–88; British Gas, 1980–; British Hardware Fedn, 1985–; TSB Gp, 1987–; IPU, 1988–90; Southampton City Council, 1989–91; CAMRA, 1989; Barclays de Zoete Wedd, 1990–. Football Trust: Foundn Trustee, 1979–82; Sec., 1983–86; Dep. Chm., 1986–90; Member: Sports Council, 1986–88; Football League enquiry into membership schemes, 1984, anti-hooliganism cttee, 1987–90; former dir, Wimbledon and Crystal Palace Football Clubs; Chm., Women's Football Assoc., 1988–. Vice-Chm., Transport 2000 Ltd, 1986–. Mem., Merton Borough Council, 1971–78; contested (Lab) Devizes 1970, Feb. 1974, Monmouth, Oct. 1974, Huddersfield W, 1979. *Recreations:* collecting Lloyd George memorabilia, tinplate trains, watching Association Football, travelling by railway. *Address:* 7 Buckingham Gate, SW1E 6JS. *T:* 071–630 5454. *Club:* Reform.
   See also D. E. R. Faulkner.

FAULKS, His Honour Peter Ronald, MC 1943; a Circuit Judge, 1980–90; *b* 24 Dec. 1917; *s* of late M. J. Faulks and A. M. Faulks (*née* Ginner); *m* 1949, Pamela Brenda, *d* of Peter Lawless; two *s. Educ:* Tonbridge; Sidney Sussex Coll., Cambridge (MA). Served War of 1939–45, Duke of Wellington's Regt, Dunkirk, N Africa, Anzio, etc; Major 1943; wounded 3 times. Admitted a solicitor, 1949. A Recorder of the Crown Court, 1972–80. Dep. Chm., Agricultural Land Tribunal (SE England), 1972–80; Pres., Berks, Bucks and Oxon Law Soc., 1976–77. *Recreation:* country life. *Address:* Downs Cottage, Westbrook, Boxford, Newbury, Berks. *T:* Boxford (048838) 382. *Clubs:* MCC, Farmers'.
   See also S. C. Faulks.

FAULKS, Sebastian Charles; journalist and author; *b* 20 April 1953; *s* of His Honour Peter Ronald Faulks, *qv; m* 1989, Veronica Youlten; one *s. Educ:* Wellington Coll.; Emmanuel Coll., Cambridge. Editor, New Fiction Society, 1978–81; Daily Telegraph, 1978–82; feature writer, Sunday Telegraph, 1983–86; Literary Editor, Independent, 1986–89; Dep. Editor, 1989–90, Associate Editor, 1990–91, Independent on Sunday. *Publications:* A Trick of the Light, 1984; The Girl at the Lion d'Or, 1989; contribs to newspapers and magazines. *Recreation:* cricket. *Address:* c/o Aitken and Stone, 29 Fernshaw Road, SW10 0TG. *Club:* Guardian Cricket.

FAUVELLE, Major Michael Henry; barrister-at-law; a Recorder of the Crown Court, since 1979; President, Pensions Appeal Tribunals for England and Wales, since 1987 (a Chairman, since 1983 and Deputy President, 1984–87); *b* 12 Aug. 1920; *s* of Victor Edmond Fauvelle and Brigid Mary Fauvelle (*née* Westermann); *m* 1964, Marie-Caroline, *e d* of Count and Countess Stanislas d'Orsetti, Château de la Grènerie, Jarzé, France; one *s* one *d. Educ:* Stonyhurst Coll.; Royal Military Coll., Sandhurst. Commissioned, 2/Lieut The South Lancashire Regt, 1939, T/Major 1944; active service in N Africa, Italy and Palestine (wounded three times, arguably five); Staff employment as GSO 3 (Ops), Gibraltar, 1947; Staff Captain Q HQ Palestine, 1947–48; Staff Captain A HQ BMM to Greece and HQ 2 Inf. Bde, 1948–50; Adjt 1st Bn, 1951; Major 1952; retired, 1953. Called to the Bar, Lincoln's Inn, 1955; Western Circuit and Hampshire Sessions, 1955–; Dep. Recorder, Oxford, Bournemouth and Reading, 1971; Hd of Chambers at 17 Carlton Crescent, Southampton, 1975–82; Lord Chancellor's Legal Visitor, 1983–90. *Recreation:* avoiding stress. *Address:* Tadley Cottage, Wherwell, Hampshire SP11 7JU. *T:* Chilbolton (0264) 860217; 48 Chancery Lane, WC2A 1JR. *T:* 071–936 7031. *Clubs:* Hampshire (Winchester); Home Guard (Wherwell, Hants).

FAVELL, Anthony Rowland; MP (C) Stockport, since 1983; *b* 29 May 1939; *s* of Arnold Rowland Favell and Hildegard Favell; *m* 1966, Susan Rosemary Taylor; one *s* one *d. Educ:* St Bees School, Cumbria; Sheffield University (LLB). Solicitor. *Recreations:* music, gardening, hill walking, squash, windsurfing. *Address:* Skinners Hall, Edale, Sheffield S30 2ZE. *T:* Hope Valley (0433) 670281. *Club:* Lansdowne.

FAWCETT, Colin, QC 1970; *b* 22 Nov. 1923; *s* of late Frank Fawcett, Penrith; *m* 1952, Elizabeth Anne Dickson; one *s* one *d. Educ:* Sedbergh. Commnd Border Regt, 1943. Called to Bar, Inner Temple, 1952, Bencher, 1978. Mem., Criminal Injuries Compensation Bd, 1983–. *Recreations:* fishing, music. *Address:* 6 Hubert Day Close, Beaconsfield, Bucks HP9 1TL. *T:* Beaconsfield (0494) 670755.

FAWCETT, John Harold, CMG 1986; HM Diplomatic Service, retired; *b* 4 May 1929; *yr s* of late Comdr Harold William Fawcett, OBE, RN, and of late Una Isobel Dalrymple Fawcett (*née* Gairdner); *m* 1961, Elizabeth Shaw; one *s. Educ:* Radley (Scholar); University Coll., Oxford (Scholar). 1st cl. Hon. Mods 1951, 2nd cl. Lit. Hum. 1953. Nat. Service, RN (Radio Electrician's Mate), 1947–49. British Oxygen Co., 1954–63 (S Africa, 1955–57). Entered Foreign Service, 1963; FO, 1963–66; 1st Sec. (Commercial), Bombay, 1966–69; 1st Sec. and Head of Chancery, Port-of-Spain, 1969–70; Asst, Caribbean Dept, FCO, 1971–72; Head of Icelandic Fisheries Unit, Western European Dept, FCO, 1973; Amb. to Democratic Republic of Vietnam, 1974; Head of Chancery, Warsaw, 1975–78; Dep. High Comr, Wellington, 1978–86; Counsellor (Commercial and Economic, 1978–83, Political and Economic, 1983–86), and Head of Chancery 1983–86, Wellington; Amb. to Bulgaria, 1986–89. *Recreations:* walking, gardening; collecting books. *Address:* 2 Queen's Square, Dent, Sedbergh, Cumbria LA10 5QL. *Clubs:* Savile; Wellington Racing (Wellington); Royal Bombay Yacht.

FAWCETT, Kay-Tee; *see* Khaw, Kay-Tee.

FAWCUS, Maj.-Gen. Graham Ben, CB 1991; Chief of Staff and Head of UK Delegation, Live Oak, SHAPE, 1989–91; *b* 17 Dec. 1937; *s* of late Col Geoffrey Arthur Ross Fawcus, RE and Helen Sybil Graham (*née* Stronach) *m* 1966, Diana Valerie, *d* of Dr P. J. Spencer-Phillips of Bildeston, Suffolk; two *s* one *d. Educ:* Wycliffe College; RMA Sandhurst (Sword of Honour); King's College, Cambridge (BA 1963, MA 1968). Commissioned RE, 1958; served UK, Cyprus, BAOR, MoD; OC 39 Field Squadron RE, BAOR, 1973–74; MoD, 1975–76; GSO1 (DS), Staff College, 1977–78; CO 25 Engineer Regt, BAOR, 1978–81; Cabinet Office, 1981; Comdt, RSME, 1982–83; ACOS, HQ 1 (Br)

Corps, 1984–85; Chief, Jt Services Liaison Orgn, Bonn, 1986–89. *Recreations:* ski-ing, windsurfing, tennis, Scottish country dancing, furniture restoration. *Address:* c/o Lloyds Bank, Cox & King's Branch, 7 Pall Mall, SW1Y 5NA.

FAWCUS, Sir (Robert) Peter, KBE 1964 (OBE 1957); CMG 1960; Overseas Civil Service, retd; *b* 30 Sept. 1915; *s* of late A. F. Fawcus, OBE; *m* 1943, Isabel Constance (*née* Ethelston); one *s* one *d*. *Educ:* Charterhouse; Clare Coll., Cambridge. Served RNVR, 1939–46 (Lt-Comdr). Joined Colonial Service (District Officer, Basutoland), 1946; Bechuanaland Protectorate: Govt Sec., 1954; Resident Commissioner, 1959; HM Commissioner, 1963–65; retd 1965. *Address:* Dochart House, Killin, Perthshire FK21 8TN.

FAWCUS, Simon James David; His Honour Judge Fawcus; a Circuit Judge, since 1985; *b* 12 July 1938; *s* of late Ernest Augustus Fawcus and of Jill Shaw; *m* 1966, Joan Mary (*née* Oliphant); one *s* four *d*. *Educ:* Aldenham Sch.; Trinity Hall, Cambridge (MA). Called to the Bar, Gray's Inn, 1961; in practice on Northern Circuit, 1962–85; a Recorder, 1980–85. *Recreations:* real tennis and other lesser sporting activities, music (listening). *Address:* Rosehill, Brook Lane, Alderley Edge, Cheshire. *Clubs:* MCC; Manchester Tennis and Racquet, Big Four (Manchester); Circuit Judges Golfing Soc.

FAWKES, Sir Randol (Francis), Kt 1977; Attorney-at-Law, since 1948; *b* 20 March 1924; *s* of Edward Ronald Fawkes and Mildred Fawkes (*née* McKinney); *m* 1951, Jacqueline Fawkes (*née* Bethel); three *s* one *d*. *Educ:* public schools in the Bahamas. Called to the Bar, Bahamas, 1948. A founder: Citizen Cttee, 1949; People's Penny Savings Bank, 1951. Elected Mem. (Progressive Liberal Party), House of Assembly, 1956; promoted law establishing Labour Day as Public Holiday, 1961. Founder, and Pres. 1955–, Bahamas Fedn of Labour (led 19 day general strike which resulted in major labour and political reforms, 1958). Represented Labour Party at constitutional confs in London, 1963 and 1968; addressed UN Cttee of 24 on preparation of Bahamas for independence, 1966. Gen Sec., Bahamas Assoc. of former Mems of Parlt, 1990. *Publications:* You Should Know Your Government, 1949; The Bahamas Government, 1962; The New Bahamas, 1966; The Faith That Moved The Mountain: a memoir of a life and the times, 1977; Majority of One: the first 450 of the PLP–Labour Coalition, 1987. *Recreations:* swimming, music, Bible tract writing. *Address:* PO Box N-7625, John F. Kennedy Drive, Nassau, NP, Bahamas. *T:* (office) 809–32–34053; (home) 809–32–34855.

FAWKES, Wally; cartoonist, since 1945; *b* 21 June 1924; *m* 1st, 1949, Sandra Boyce-Carmichelle; one *s* two *d*; 2nd, 1965, Susan Clifford; one *s* one *d*. *Educ:* Sidcup Central Sch.; Sidcup Sch. of Art; Camberwell Sch. of Art. Came from Vancouver, BC, to England, 1931. Joined Daily Mail, 1945; started Flook strip, 1949, transferred to The Mirror, 1984. Political cartoons for: Spectator, 1959–; Private Eye, and New Statesman, 1965–; Observer, and Punch, 1971–; Today, 1986–87; London Daily News, 1987. Co-Founder, Humphrey Lyttelton Band, 1948. *Publications:* World of Trog, 1977; Trog Shots, 1984; Trog: 40 Graphic Years, 1987; collections of Flook strips. *Recreations:* playing jazz (clarinet and soprano saxophone), cooking, cricket. *Address:* 44 Laurier Road, NW5 1SJ. *T:* 071–267 2979. *Clubs:* MCC, Middlesex County Cricket.

FAY, His Honour Edgar Stewart, QC 1956; FCIArb; a Circuit Judge (formerly an Official Referee of the Supreme Court of Judicature), 1971–80; *b* 8 Oct. 1908; *s* of late Sir Sam Fay; *m* 1st, Kathleen Margaret, *e d* of late C. H. Buell, Montreal, PQ, and Brockville, Ont; three *s*; 2nd, Jenny Julie Henriette (*d* 1990), *yr d* of late Dr Willem Roosegaarde Bisschop, Lincoln's Inn; one *s*. *Educ:* Courtenay Lodge Sch.; McGill Univ.; Pembroke Coll., Cambridge (MA). Called to Bar, Inner Temple, 1932; Master of the Bench, 1962. FCIArb 1981. Recorder: of Andover, 1954–61; of Bournemouth, 1961–64; of Plymouth, 1964–71; Dep. Chm., Hants QS, 1960–71. Member: Bar Council, 1955–59, 1966–70; Senate of Four Inns of Court, 1970–72. Chm., Inquiry into Crown Agents, 1975–77. *Publications:* Why Piccadilly?, 1935; Londoner's New York, 1936; Discoveries in the Statute Book, 1937; The Life of Mr Justice Swift, 1939; Official Referees' Business, 1983. *Address:* Knox End, Ashdon, Saffron Walden, Essex CB10 2HR. *T:* Ashdon (079 984) 275.

FAY, Sir (Humphrey) Michael (Gerard), Kt 1990; Chairman, Fay, Richwhite & Co. Ltd, Merchant Bankers, since 1975; *b* 10 April 1949; *s* of James and Margaret Fay; *m* 1983, Sarah Williams; one *s* two *d*. *Educ:* St Patrick's Coll., Silverstream, Wellington; Victoria Univ., Wellington (LLB 1971). Jt Chief Exec., Capital Markets, 1986–; Dir, Bank of New Zealand, 1989–. Chairman: Australia/NZ Bicentennial Commn, 1988; Expo 1988 Commn, 1987–88; Expo 1992 Commn, 1989–. Chm., NZ Americas Cup Challenges, 1987, 1988, 1992. *Recreations:* yachting, horse breeding and racing, fishing, swimming. *Address:* PO Box 1650, Auckland, New Zealand. *T:* (649) 366 3600. *Clubs:* Northern (Auckland); Royal New Zealand Yacht Squadron, Auckland Racing, Mercury Bay Boating.

FAY, Sir Michael; *see* Fay, Sir H. M. G.

FAYERS, Norman Owen; City Treasurer, Bristol City Council, since 1990; *b* 8 Jan. 1945; *s* of Claude Lance Fayers and Winifred Joyce (*née* Reynolds); *m* 1966, Patricia Ann Rudd; two *s*. *Educ:* Northgate Grammar Sch. for Boys, Ipswich; BA Open Univ. IPFA; IRRV. Ipswich CBC, 1961–66; Eastbourne CBC, 1966–70; Group Accountant (Educn), Royal Borough of Kingston upon Thames, 1970–73; Chief Accountant, RBK & C, 1973–77; Chief Officer, Finance, London Borough of Ealing, 1977–90. Vice-Pres., S Wales and W England Reg., CIPFA, 1991–. *Recreations:* golf, squash, music, bridge. *Address:* The Council House, College Green, Bristol BS99 7BL. *T:* Bristol (0272) 222417.

FAYRER, Sir John (Lang Macpherson), 4th Bt *cr* 1896; research associate; *b* 18 Oct. 1944; *s* of Sir Joseph Herbert Spens Fayrer, 3rd Bt, DSC, and Helen Diana Scott (*d* 1961), *d* of late John Lang; *S* father, 1976. *Educ:* Edinburgh Academy; Scottish Hotel School, Univ. of Strathclyde. *Heir:* none. *Address:* Overhailes, Haddington, East Lothian.

FEA, William Wallace; Director, Guest, Keen & Nettlefolds Ltd, 1958–72 (Deputy Chairman, 1968–72); *b* Cordova, Argentina, 3 Feb. 1907; *s* of Herbert Reginald Fea and Hilda Florence Fea (*née* Norton); *m* 1935, Norah Anne, *d* of Richard Festing; one *s* (and one *s* decd). *Educ:* Cheltenham Coll. (scholar); Brasenose Coll., Oxford (scholar); BA. ACA 1932; FCA. Mem., Council, Inst. of Chartered Accountants, 1953–71; Mem. Council, BIM, 1969–73; Management Cttee, AA, 1971–77. *Recreations:* shooting, listening to music. *Address:* The Lowe, Worfield, near Bridgnorth, Salop WV15 5NS. *T:* Worfield (07464) 241. *Club:* Lansdowne.

FEACHEM, Prof. Richard George Andrew, PhD; FICE; Professor of Tropical Environmental Health, since 1987, and Dean, since 1989, London School of Hygiene and Tropical Medicine; *b* 10 April 1947; *s* of Charles George Paulin Feachem and Margaret Flora Denise Greenhow; *m* 1970, Zuzana Sedlarova; one *s* one *d*. *Educ:* Wellington Coll.; Univ. of Birmingham (BSc 1969); Univ. of NSW (PhD 1974). MICE 1980; FIWEM 1987; FICE 1990. Volunteer, Solomon Is, 1965–66; Research Fellow: Univ. of NSW, 1970–74; Univ. of Birmingham, 1974–76; London School of Hygiene and Tropical Medicine: Lectr and Sen. Lectr, 1976–82; Reader, 1983–87. Consultant, WHO, 1982–83; Principal Public Health Specialist, World Bank, 1988–89. Hon. FFPHM 1990. *Publications:* Water, Wastes and Health in Hot Climates, 1977; Subsistence and Survival: rural ecology in the Pacific, 1977; Water, Health and Development, 1978; Evaluation for Village Water Supply Planning, 1980; Sanitation and Disease, 1983; Environmental Health Engineering in the Tropics, 1983; Evaluating Health Impact, 1986; Disease and Mortality in Sub-Saharan Africa, 1991; over 120 papers in scientific jls. *Recreations:* mountaineering, ski-ing. *Address:* London School of Hygiene and Tropical Medicine, Keppel Street, WC1E 7HT. *T:* 071–636 8636. *Club:* Travellers'.

FEARN, John Martin, CB 1976; Secretary, Scottish Education Department, 1973–76, retired; *b* 24 June 1916; *s* of William Laing Fearn and Margaret Kerr Fearn; *m* 1947, Isobel Mary Begbie, MA, MB, ChB; one *d*. *Educ:* High Sch. of Dundee; Univ. of St Andrews; Worcester Coll., Oxford. Indian Civil Service, Punjab, 1940–47; District Magistrate, Lahore, 1946; Scottish Home Dept, 1947; Asst Sec., 1956; Under-Sec., 1966; Under-Sec., Scottish Educn Dept, 1968. *Recreation:* golf. *Address:* 31 Midmar Gardens, Edinburgh EH10 6DY. *T:* 031–447 5301. *Club:* New (Edinburgh).

FEARN, Sir (Patrick) Robin, KCMG 1991 (CMG 1983); HM Diplomatic Service; Ambassador to Spain, since 1989; *b* 5 Sept. 1934; *s* of Albert Cyprian Fearn and Hilary (*née* Harrison); *m* 1961, Sorrel Mary Lynne Thomas; three *s* one *d*. *Educ:* Ratcliffe Coll.; University Coll., Oxford (BA Hons, Mod. Langs). Nat. Service, Intelligence Corps, 1952–54. Overseas marketing, Dunlop Rubber Co. Ltd, 1957–61; entered Foreign Service, 1961; FO, 1961–62; Third, later Second Sec., Caracas, 1962–64; Havana, 1965; First Sec., Budapest, 1966–68; FCO, 1969–72; Head of Chancery, Vientiane, 1972–75; Asst Head of Science and Technol. Dept, FCO, 1975–76; Counsellor, Head of Chancery and Consul Gen., Islamabad, 1977–79; Head of S America Dept, FCO, 1979–82; Head of Falkland Islands Dept, FCO, 1982; RCDS, 1983; Ambassador to Cuba, 1984–86; Asst Under-Sec. of State (Americas), FCO, 1986–89. *Recreations:* tennis, golf, reading, family life. *Address:* c/o Foreign and Commonwealth Office, SW1A 2AH. *Club:* United Oxford & Cambridge University.

FEARN, Ronald Cyril, (Ronnie), OBE 1985; MP Southport, since 1987 (L 1987–88, Lib Dem since 1988); *b* 6 Feb. 1931; *s* of James Fearn and Martha Ellen Fearn; *m* 1955, Joyce Edna Dugan; one *s* one *d*. *Educ:* King George V Grammar School. FCIB. Banker with Williams Deacons Bank, later Williams & Glyn's Bank, later Royal Bank of Scotland. Lib Dem spokesman on health and tourism, 1988–89, on local govt, transport and tourism, 1989–. Councillor, Sefton MBC, 1974–. *Recreations:* badminton, amateur dramatics, athletics. *Address:* House of Commons, SW1A 0AA. *T:* 071–219 4130; Norcliffe, 56 Norwood Avenue, Southport, Merseyside. *T:* Southport (0704) 28577.

FEATES, Prof. Francis Stanley, CB 1991; PhD; CEng, FIChemE; FRSC; CChem; Professor of Environmental Engineering, University of Manchester Institute of Science and Technology, since 1991; *b* 21 Feb. 1932; *s* of Stanley James Feates and Dorothy Marguerite Jenny Feates (*née* Orford); *m* 1953, Gwenda Grace Goodchild; one *s* three *d*. *Educ:* John Ruskin Sch., Croydon; Birkbeck Coll. London (BSc Special Chem.; PhD). FRSC 1972; FIChemE 1991; CEng 1991. Wellcome Res. Foundn, 1949–52; Chester-Beatty Cancer Res. Inst., Univ. of London, 1952–54. Chemistry Lectr, Goldsmiths' Coll., London, 1954–56; AERE, Harwell, UKAEA, 1956–78; Argonne Nat. Lab., Univ. of Chicago, Illinois, 1965–67; Department of the Environment: Dir, Nuclear Waste Management, 1978–83; Chief Radiochemical Inspector, 1983–86; Chief Inspector, Radioactive Substances, HM Inspectorate of Pollution, 1986–88; Dir and Chief Inspector, HM Inspectorate of Pollution, 1989–91. Director: Sir Alexander Gibb & Partners, 1991–; Siemens Plessey Controls Ltd, 1991–; Grundon Waste Management, 1991–. Expert Mem., Scientific and Technical Cttee, EEC, Brussels, 1989–; Member: Steering Cttee, Nuclear Energy Agency, OECD, Paris, 1988–91; Steering Bd, Lab. of Govt Chemist, 1991–; Observer Mem., NRPB, 1988–91. *Publications:* Hazardous Materials Spills Handbook, 1982; numerous scientific papers on nuclear power, electrochemistry, thermodynamics, waste management, electron microscopy. *Recreations:* walking, cycling, travel. *Address:* The Kilns, Beggarsbush Hill, Benson, Oxon OX10 6PL. *T:* Wallingford (0491) 39276; Department of Chemical Engineering, UMIST, PO Box 88, Manchester M60 1QD.

FEATHER, Prof. John Pliny, FLA; Professor since 1988, and Head of Department of Information and Library Studies, since 1990, Loughborough University; *b* 20 Dec. 1947; *m* 1971, Sarah, *d* of Rev. A. W. Rees and late S. M. Rees. *Educ:* Heath Sch., Halifax; Queen's Coll., Oxford (BLitt, MA); MA Cambridge, PhD Loughborough. FLA 1986. Asst Librarian, Bodleian Liby, Oxford, 1972–79; Munby Fellow in Bibliography, Cambridge Univ., 1977–78; Lectr, then Sen. Lectr, Loughborough Univ., 1979–88. Vis. Prof., UCLA, 1982. Pres., Oxford Bibliographical Soc., 1988–. Mem., many nat. and internat. professional cttees; consultancy, teaching, etc, in USA, Pakistan, Kenya, Sudan, Mexico, Saudi Arabia, Thailand, Aust., NZ, Singapore, and for UNESCO, EEC and British Council, 1977–. *Publications:* The Provincial Book Trade in Eighteenth-Century England, 1985; A Dictionary of Book History, 1987; A History of British Publishing, 1988; Preservation and the Management of Library Collections, 1991; Index to Selected Bibliographical Journals 1971–1985, 1991; articles and reviews in academic and professional jls, conf. procs, etc. *Recreations:* photography, travel, cooking (and eating) good food. *Address:* 36 Farnham Street, Quorn, Leicestershire LE12 8DR. *Clubs:* Savage; Grolier (New York).

FEATHERSTONE, Hugh Robert, CBE 1984 (OBE 1974); FCIS, FCIT; Director-General, Freight Transport Association, 1969–84; *b* 31 March 1926; *s* of Alexander Brown Featherstone and Doris Olive Martin; *m* 1948, Beryl Joan Sly; one *s* one *d*. *Educ:* Minchenden Sch., Southgate, London. FCIS 1956; FCIT 1970. Served War, RNVR, 1943–46 (Sub-Lt). Assistant Secretary: Nat. Assoc. of Funeral Dirs, 1946–48; Brit. Rubber Develt Bd, 1948–58; Asst Sec. 1958–60, Sec. 1960–68, Traders Road Transport Assoc. *Publications:* contrib. to jls concerned with transport and admin. *Recreations:* golf, gardening, languages, travel, bridge. *Address:* 5 Rossdale, Tunbridge Wells, Kent TN2 3PG. *T:* Tunbridge Wells (0892) 30063.

FEAVER, Rt. Rev. Douglas Russell; *b* 22 May 1914; *s* of late Ernest Henry Feaver, Bristol; *m* 1st, 1939, Katharine (*d* 1987), *d* of late Rev. W. T. Stubbs; one *s* two *d*; 2nd, 1988, Mary Frances Clare Harvey, *qv*. *Educ:* Bristol Grammar School; Keble College, Oxford (Scholar; 1st cl. Hons. Mod. History, 1935; 1st Cl. Hons. Theology, 1937; Liddon Student, 1935–37; MA); Wells Theological College. Deacon 1938, priest 1939, St Albans; Curate, St Albans Abbey, 1938–42. Chaplain, RAFVR, 1942–46. Canon and Sub-Dean of St Albans, 1946–58; Chaplain to St Albans School, 1946–58; Proctor in Convocation, 1951–58; Examining Chaplain to Bp of St Albans, 1948–58, to Bp of Portsmouth, 1960–72; Vicar of St Mary's, Nottingham and Rural Dean of Nottingham, 1958–72; Hon. Canon of Southwell, 1958–72; Treasurer, 1959–69; Proctor in Convocation for Southwell, 1970–72; Bishop of Peterborough, 1972–84. Chairman of Trent House Boys' Probation Hostel, 1967–72; Governor of Nottingham Bluecoat School, 1958–72. *Publications:* reviews and articles in Church Times. *Recreation:* conferences not attended.

Address: 6 Mill Lane, Bruton, Somerset BA10 0AT.
See also W. A. Feaver.

FEAVER, William Andrew; art critic, The Observer, since 1975; *b* 1 Dec. 1942; *s* of Rt. Rev. Douglas Russell Feaver, *qv*; *m* 1st, 1964, Victoria Turton (marr. diss.); one *s* three *d*; 2nd, 1985, Andrea Rose; two *d*. *Educ:* St Albans School; Nottingham High School; Keble College, Oxford. South Stanley Boys' Modern Sch., Co. Durham, 1964–65; Newcastle Royal Grammar Sch., 1965–71; Sir James Knott Res. Fellow, Newcastle Univ., 1971–73; art critic: The Listener, 1971–75; Financial Times, 1974–75; art adviser, Sunday Times Magazine, 1974–75. Critic of the Year, UK Press Awards, 1984. *Publications:* The Art of John Martin, 1975; When We Were Young, 1976; Masters of Caricature, 1981; Pitmen Painters, 1988. *Recreation:* painting. *Address:* 1 Rhodesia Road, SW9 9EJ. *T:* 071–737 3386.

FEDIDA, Sam, OBE 1980; independent consultant, information systems; inventor of Prestel, viewdata system (first public electronic information service); *b* 1918; *m* 1942, Joan Iris Druce. Served Royal Air Force, Radar Officer, 1940–46. Became Asst Dir of Research, The English Electric Company; started research for the Post Office, 1970; Prestel first in use 1979, as public service; MacRobert Award, Council of Engineering Instns, 1979; Prestel sold in Europe, USA, Far East. *Address:* Constable Cottage, 23 Brook Lane, Felixstowe, Suffolk IP11 7JP.

FEDRICK, Geoffrey Courtis; HM Diplomatic Service; Counsellor (Management) and Consul-General, Brussels, since 1989; *b* 21 Aug. 1937; *s* of Roy Townsend Fedrick and Vera May Fedrick (*née* Tope); *m* 1st, 1961, Elizabeth Louise Moore; two *s*; 2nd, 1984, Margaret Elizabeth Hearnden (*née* Pawley); one *s*. *Educ:* Plymouth College. HM Forces, 1956–58. Govt Actuary's Dept, 1958–60; CRO, 1960; Salisbury, S Rhodesia, 1961–64; Peshawar, Pakistan, 1965–66; 2nd Sec., Washington, 1967–70; FCO, 1971–75; Consul, Toronto, 1975–79; FCO, 1980–83; First Sec., Lagos, 1983–86; FCO, 1986–88. *Recreations:* golf, bridge, choral singing. *Address:* c/o Foreign and Commonwealth Office, SW1A 2AH. *Club:* Betchworth Park Golf.

FEENY, Max Howard; barrister; *b* 5 Nov. 1928; *s* of late Howard Raymond John Feeny and Frances Kate Feeny (*née* Muspratt); *m* 1952, June Elizabeth (*née* Camplin) (*d* 1986); three *s* four *d*. *Educ:* Stonyhurst Coll.; Oratory Sch.; Univ. of Birmingham (LLB). Called to Bar, Inner Temple, 1953. A Recorder of the Crown Court, 1972–78. Senior Lectr, Inst. of Professional Legal Studies, Queen's Univ. of Belfast, 1982–. Chm. (part-time), Med. Appeals Tribunal, 1987–. Mem., Council of Legal Educn (NI), 1983–87. *Recreations:* gardening, making silage, surf fishing. *Address:* 28 Hampton Grove, Belfast BT7 3DG; Urlee, Lisselton, near Listowel, Co. Kerry, Eire.

FEHR, Basil Henry Frank, CBE 1979; Chairman and Managing Director, Frank Fehr & Co. Ltd London and group of companies, since 1957; Chairman, Fehr Bros Inc. New York and group of companies, since 1970; *b* 11 July 1912; *s* of Frank E. Fehr, CBE and Jane (*née* Poulter); *m* 1st, 1936, Jane Marner (*née* Tallent) (marr. diss. 1951); two *s* one *d*; 2nd, 1951, Greta Constance (*née* Bremner) (marr. diss. 1971); one *d* one step *d*; 3rd, 1974, Anne Norma (*née* Cadman); one *d*. *Educ:* Rugby Sch.; Neûchatel Ecole de Commerce, Switzerland. Served War, 1939–45: HAC, later Instr, Gunnery Sch. of Anti-Aircraft, RA; retd Major. Joined father in family firm, Frank Fehr & Co., 1934; Partner, 1936; Governing Dir, Frank Fehr & Co. London, 1948; Pres., Fehr Bros (Manufactures) Inc. New York, 1949. Chairman: Cocoa Assoc. of London, 1952; London Commodity Exchange, 1954; London Oil and Tallow Trades Assoc., 1955; Copra Assoc. of London, 1957; Inc. Oilseed Assoc., 1958; United Assocs Ltd, 1959. Elected to Baltic Exchange, 1936; Director: Baltic Mercantile and Shipping Exchange, 1963–69 and 1970–77 (Vice Chm. 1973–75, Chm. 1975–77); Colyer Fehr Hldgs Pty, Sydney, 1976– (Chm. 1984–89). Jurat of Liberty of Romney Marsh, 1979. *Recreations:* sports generally, farming. *Address:* Slodden Farm, Dymchurch, Romney Marsh, Kent. *T:* Dymchurch (0303) 872241; 64 Queen Street, EC4R 1ER. *T:* 071–248 5066. *Clubs:* City Livery, Aldgate Ward, MCC, Royal Automobile, Little Ship; Ski Club of Great Britain; West Kent Cricket; Littlestone Golf.

FEIBUSCH, Hans; painter, mural painter, lithographer, sculptor, writer; *b* 15 Aug. 1898; *s* of Dr Carl Feibusch and Marianne Ickelheimer; *m* 1935, Sidonie (*d* 1963), *e d* of D. Gestetner. *Educ:* Frankfurt a/M and Munich Univs. Studied at the Berlin Academy, at Paris Art Schs, in Florence and Rome; received German State award and grant in 1931; pictures in German Public Galleries; work banned and destroyed by Nazis in 1933; since then in London; large mural paintings in churches: St Wilfred's, Brighton; St Elizabeth's, Eastbourne; St Martin's, Dagenham; St John's, Waterloo Road, SE1; St Ethelburga's, Bishopsgate; St Alban's, Holborn; Town Hall, Dudley; Civic Centre, Newport, Mon; Chichester Cathedral; Chichester Palace; Parish Churches, Egham, Goring, Wellingborough, Welling, Preston, Plumstead, Eltham, Portsmouth, Bexley Heath, Wembley, Merton, Southwark, Harrow, Exeter, Battersea, Rotherhithe, Plymouth, Coventry, Christchurch Priory, Bournemouth, Christ Church, St Laurence, Sydney, Portmeirion, Bath; West London Synagogue; statues: St John the Baptist, St John's Wood Church; Christ, Ely Cathedral; Risen Christ, St Alban's Church EC1. 80th birthday exhibn by GLC, Holland Park, 1978; 6 one-man exhibns, incl. Berlin 1980; retrospective exhibn 1925–85, Historisches Museum, Frankfurt, 1986; retrospective exhibns, Frankfurt, 1987, 1988 and Brighton Polytechnic, 1988. Much portrait and figure sculpture, 1975–. Dr of Letters, Lambeth, 1985. German Cross of Merit, 1967, Grand Cross of Merit, 1989. *Publications:* Mural Painting, 1946; The Revelation of Saint John, 1946. *Recreations:* music and poetry. *Address:* 30 Wadham Gardens, NW3 3DP. *T:* 071–586 1456, (studio) 071–286 7420. *Club:* Athenæum.

FEILDEN, Sir Bernard (Melchior), Kt 1985; CBE 1976 (OBE 1969); FRIBA 1968 (ARIBA 1949); Consultant, Feilden and Mawson, Chartered Architects (Partner, 1956–77); Member, Cathedrals Advisory Commission for England, since 1981; *b* 11 Sept. 1919; *s* of Robert Humphrey Feilden, MC, and Olive Feilden (*née* Binyon); *m* 1949, Ruth Mildred Bainbridge; two *s* two *d*. *Educ:* Bedford Sch. Exhibr, Bartlett Sch. of Architecture, 1938 (Hon. Fellow, UCL, 1985). Served War of 1939–45: Bengal Sappers and Miners. AA Diploma (Hons), 1949; Bratt Colbran Schol., 1949. Architect, Norwich Cathedral, 1963–77; Surveyor to the Fabric: York Minster, 1965–77; St Paul's Cathedral, 1969–77; Dir, Internat. Centre for the Preservation and Restoration of Cultural Property, Rome, 1977–81. Hoffman Wood Prof. of Architecture, Leeds Univ., 1973–74. Mem., Ancient Monuments Bd (England), 1964–77; Mem. Council, RIBA, 1972–77; President: Ecclesiastical Architects' and Surveyors' Assoc., 1975–77; Guild of Surveyors, 1976–77. FSA 1969; FRSA 1973; Hon. FAIA 1987. Corresp. Mem., Architectes en Chef, France. DUniv York, 1973; Hon. DLitt: Gothenburg, 1988; East Anglia, 1989. Aga Khan Award for Architecture, 1986. *Publications:* The Wonder of York Minster, 1976; Introduction to Conservation, 1979; Conservation of Historic Buildings, 1982; Between Two Earthquakes, 1987; Guidelines for Conservation, 1989; articles in Architectural Review, Chartered Surveyor, AA Quarterly. *Recreations:* painting, sailing, fishing, photography. *Address:* Stiffkey Old Hall, Stiffkey, near Wells-on-Sea, Norfolk NR23 1QJ. *T:* Binham (Norfolk) (0328) 830585. *Club:* Norfolk (Norwich).
See also G. B. R. Feilden.

FEILDEN, Geoffrey Bertram Robert, CBE 1966; MA Cantab; FRS 1959; Founder FEng 1976, FIMechE, Hon. FIStructE; Hon. FIQA; CBIM; Hon. MIED; Principal Consultant, Feilden Associates Ltd, since 1981; *b* 20 Feb. 1917; *s* of Robert Humphrey Feilden, MC, and Olive Feilden (*née* Binyon); *m* 1st, Elizabeth Ann Gorton; one *s* two *d*; 2nd, Elizabeth Diana Angier (*née* Lloyd). *Educ:* Bedford Sch.; King's Coll., Cambridge (Scholar). Lever Bros. and Unilever Ltd, 1939–40; Power Jets Ltd, 1940–46; Ruston and Hornsby Ltd, 1946–59; Chief Engineer, Turbine Dept, 1949; Engineering Dir, 1954; Man. Dir, Hawker Siddeley Brush Turbines Ltd, and Dir of Hawker Siddeley Industries Ltd, 1959–61; Gp Technical Dir, Davy-Ashmore Ltd, 1961–68; Dep. Dir Gen., British Standards Instn, 1968–70, Dir Gen. 1970–81. Director: Averys Ltd, 1974–79; Plint & Partners Ltd, 1982–. Member: Cttees and Sub-Cttees of Aeronautical Research Council, 1947–62; BTC Res. Adv. Council, 1956–61; Council for Sci. and Indust. Res. of DSIR, 1961–65; Design Council (formerly CoID), 1966–78 (Dep. Chm., 1977–78); Central Adv. Council for Science and Technology, 1970–71; Vis. Cttee to RCA, 1968–84 (Chm., 1977–84); Res. Develt and Engrg Cttee, Industrial Develt Bd for NI, 1983–86; Chm., UK Panel for CODATA (formerly British Nat. Cttee on Data for Sci. and Technol.), 1988– (UK Deleg. to CODATA, 1989–); Pres., European Cttee for Standardisation, 1977–79. Member, Royal Society Delegation: to USSR, 1965; Latin America, 1968; People's Republic of China, 1975; Leader, BSI Delegn to People's Republic of China, 1980. Technical Adviser to Govt of India, 1968. DSIR Visitor to Prod. Engineering Res. Assoc. of Gt Brit., 1957–65, and to Machine Tool Industry Res. Assoc., 1961–65. Member Council: Royal Society (a Vice-Pres., 1967–69); IMechE, 1955–61, 1969–80; Univ. of Surrey, 1977–78. Trustee: Maurice Lubbock Meml Fund, 1973–; Smallpeice Trust, 1981–88. Senior Fellow, RCA, 1986. Hon. DTech Loughborough, 1970; Hon. DSc QUB, 1971. MacRobert Award for innovation (jt winner), 1983. *Publications:* Gas Turbine Principles and Practice (contributor), 1955; First Bulleid Memorial Lecture (Nottingham Univ.), 1959; Report, Engineering Design, 1963 (Chm. of Cttee); numerous papers and articles on engineering subjects. *Recreations:* sailing, ski-ing, driving kitchen and garden machines. *Address:* Verlands, Painswick, Glos GL6 6XP. *T:* Painswick (0452) 812112. *Club:* Athenæum.
See also Sir B. M. Feilden.

FEILDEN, Sir Henry (Wemyss), 6th Bt *cr* 1846; *b* 1 Dec. 1916; *s* of Col Wemyss Gawne Cunningham Feilden, CMG (*d* 1943) (3rd *s* of 3rd Bt) and Winifred Mary Christian (*d* 1980), *d* of Rev. William Cosens, DD; *S* cousin, Sir William Morton Buller Feilden, 5th Bt, 1976; *m* 1943, Ethel May, 2nd *d* of John Atkinson, Annfield Plain, Co. Durham; one *s* two *d*. *Educ:* Canford Sch.; King's Coll., London. Served War, RE, 1940–46. Clerical Civil Service, 1960–79. *Recreations:* watching cricket, reading. *Heir: s* Henry Rudyard Feilden, BVetSc, MRCVS [*b* 26 Sept. 1951; *m* 1982, Anne Shepperd; one *s*]. *Address:* Little Dene, Heathfield Road, Burwash, Etchingham, East Sussex TN19 7HN. *T:* Burwash (0435) 882205. *Club:* MCC.

FEILDING, family name of **Earl of Denbigh.**

FEILDING, Viscount; Alexander Stephen Rudolph Feilding; *b* 4 Nov. 1970; *s* and *heir* of Earl of Denbigh and Desmond, *qv*.

FEINSTEIN, Prof. Charles Hilliard, PhD; FBA 1983; Professor of Economic History, University of Oxford, since 1989; Fellow, All Souls College, since 1989; *b* 18 March 1932; *s* of Louis and Rose Feinstein; *m* 1st, 1958, Ruth Loshak; one *s* three *d*; 2nd, 1980, Anne Digby. *Educ:* Parktown Boys' High Sch., Johannesburg; Univ. of Witwatersrand (BCom 1950); Fitzwilliam Coll., Cambridge (PhD 1958). CA (SA) 1954. Research Officer, Dept of Applied Econs, Univ. of Cambridge, 1958–63; Univ. Lectr in Faculty of Econs, Cambridge, 1963–78; Fellow of Clare Coll., Cambridge, 1963–78; Sen. Tutor, Clare Coll. 1969–78; Prof. of Econ. and Social History, 1978–87, and Head, Dept of Econ. and Related Studies, 1981–86, Univ. of York; Reader in Recent Social and Econ. History, and Professorial Fellow, Nuffield Coll., 1987–89, Univ. of Oxford. Harvard University: Vis. Res. Fellow, Russian Res. Centre, 1967–68; Vis. Scholar, Dept of Econ., 1986–87; Vis. Lectr, Univ. of Delhi, 1972. Mem. Council: Royal Economic Soc., 1980–; Economic History Soc., 1980–; Mem., Economic Affairs Cttee, SSRC, 1982–86 (Chm., 1985–86). Governor, NIESR, 1985–. Man. Editor, The Economic Jl, 1980–86. *Publications:* Domestic Capital Formation in the United Kingdom 1920–1938, 1965; (ed) Socialism, Capitalism and Economic Growth, Essays presented to Maurice Dobb, 1967; National Income, Expenditure and Output of the United Kingdom 1855–1965, 1972; (ed) York 1831–1981, 1981; (jtly) British Economic Growth 1856–1973, 1982; (ed) The Managed Economy: Essays in British Economic Policy and Performance since 1929, 1983; Studies in Capital Formation 1750–1920, 1988. *Recreations:* reading, buying books. *Address:* Treetops, Harberton Mead, Headington, Oxford OX3 0DB.

FELDBERG, Wilhelm Siegmund, CBE 1963; MD Berlin; MA Cantab; FRS 1947; FRCP 1978; Professor Emeritus; Personal Grant Holder, National Institute for Medical Research, London, 1967–91; *b* 19 Nov. 1900; *m* 1925, Katherine (*d* 1976), *d* of late Karl Scheffler; one *d* (and one *s* decd); *m* 1977, Kim O'Rourke (*d* 1981). Reader in Physiology, Cambridge Univ., until 1949; Head of Physiology and Pharmacology Division, National Institute for Medical Research, London, 1949–65 (Hon. Head of Division, 1965–66); Head, Lab. of Neuropharmacology, Nat. Inst. for Med. Res., 1966–74. Hon. Lectr, London Univ., 1950–. Lectures: Dunham, Harvard, 1953; Evarts Graham Meml, Washington Univ., St Louis, USA, 1961; Aschoff Meml, Freiburg Univ., 1961; Dixon Meml, RSM, 1964; William Withering, 1966; Nat. Research Council of Canada/Nuffield Foundn, 1970–71; Ferrier, Royal Soc., 1974; Sherrington, 1980. Hon. Member: Br. Pharmacol. Soc.; RSM; Physiol. Soc.; Soc. française d'allergie; Deutsche Phys. Gesell.; Deutsche Pharm. Gesell.; Berliner Medizinische Gesell.; Berliner Phys. Gesell. Hon. MD: Freiburg, Berlin, Cologne, Würzburg, Heidelberg, Liège; Hon. DSc: Bradford, 1973; London, 1979; Hon. LLD: Glasgow, 1976; Aberdeen, 1977. Grand Cross, Order of Merit of German Federal Republic, 1961. Baly Medal, 1963; Schmiedeberg Plakette, 1969; Stöhr Medal, 1970; Royal Medal, Royal Soc., 1983. *Publications:* Histamin (with E. Schilf); A Pharmacological Approach to the Brain from its Inner and Outer Surface, 1963; articles in med. and scientific jls. *Address:* Lavenham, 74 Marsh Lane, Mill Hill, NW7 4NT. *T:* 081–959 5545.

FELDMAN, Sir Basil, Kt 1982; Chairman: Better Made in Britain Campaign, since 1983; Shopping Hours Reform Council, since 1988; Watchpost Ltd, since 1983; The Quality Mark, since 1987; Chairman: National Union of Conservative Party, 1985–86 (Vice-Chairman, 1982–85; Vice-President, since 1986); National Union Executive Committee, since 1991 (Member, since 1975); *b* 23 Sept. 1926; *s* of late Philip and Tilly Feldman; *m* 1952, Gita Julius; two *s* one *d*. *Educ:* Grocers' School. National Union of Conservative and Unionist Associations, Greater London area: Dep. Chm., 1975–78; Chm., 1978–81; Pres., 1981–85; Vice Pres., 1985–; Jt Nat. Chm., Cons. Party's Impact 80s Campaign, 1982–87; Member: Policy Gp for London, 1975–81, 1984–; Nat. Campaign Cttee, 1976 and 1978; Adv. Cttee on Policy, 1981–86; Cttee for London,

1984–87; Vice-Pres., Greater London Young Conservatives, 1975–77; President: Richmond and Barnes Cons. Assoc., 1976–84; Hornsey Cons. Assoc., 1978–82; Patron, Hampstead Cons. Assoc., 1981–86. Contested GLC Elections, Richmond, 1973; Member: GLC Housing Management Cttee, 1973–77; GLC Arts Cttee, 1976–81. Mem., Free Enterprise Loan Soc., 1977–84. Chairman: Martlet Services Gp Ltd, 1973–81; Solport Ltd, 1980–85; Market Opportunities Adv. Gp, DTI, 1991–; Dir, Young Enterpreneurs Fund, 1985–. Underwriting Mem. of Lloyds, 1979–. Membre Consultatif, Institut Internat. de Promotion et de Prestige, Geneva (affiliated to Unesco), 1978–. Member: Post Office Users National Council, 1978–81 (Mem., Tariffs Sub-Cttee, 1980–81); English Tourist Board, 1986–; Chairman: Clothing EDC (NEDO), 1978–85; Maker/User Working Party (NEDO), 1988–89. Gov., Sports Aid Foundn, 1990–. FRSA 1987. *Publications:* Some Thoughts on Jobs Creation (for NEDO), 1984; Constituency Campaigning: a guide for Conservative Party workers; several other Party booklets and pamphlets. *Recreations:* golf, tennis, theatre, opera, travel. *Club:* Carlton.

FELDSTEIN, Prof. Martin Stuart; Professor, Harvard University, since 1969; *b* 25 Nov. 1939; *m* Kathleen Foley; two *d. Educ:* Harvard Coll. (AB *summa cum laude* 1961); Oxford Univ. (BLitt 1963, MA 1964, DPhil 1967). Nuffield College, Oxford University: Research Fellow, 1964–65; Official Fellow, 1965–67; Lectr in Public Finance, Oxford Univ., 1965–67; Harvard University: Asst Professor, 1967–68; Associate Professor, 1968–69. President, National Bureau of Economic Research, 1977–82 and 1984–; Chm., Council of Economic Advrs, 1982–84. Director: American International Gp; Great Western Financial; TRW. *Publications:* (ed) The American Economy in Transition, 1980; Hospital Costs and Health Insurance, 1981; Inflation, Tax Rules, and Capital Formation, 1983; Capital Taxation, 1983; Effects of Taxation on Capital Formation, 1986; United States in the World Economy, 1988; International Economic Co-operation, 1988. *Address:* National Bureau of Economic Research, 1050 Massachusetts Avenue, Cambridge, Mass 02138, USA.

FELL, Sir Anthony, Kt 1982; *b* 18 May 1914; *s* of Comdr David Mark Fell, RN; *m* 1938, June Warwick; one *s* one *d. Educ:* New Zealand. Contested (C) Brigg, 1948, South Hammersmith, 1949 and 1950. MP (C) Yarmouth, Norfolk, 1951–66 and 1970–83. *Address:* 11 Denny Street, SE11 4UX.

FELL, David, CB 1990; Head of Northern Ireland Civil Service, and Second Permanent Under Secretary of State, Northern Ireland Office, since 1991; *b* 20 Jan. 1943; *s* of Ernest Fell and Jessie (*née* McCreedy); *m* 1967, Sandra Jesse (*née* Moore); one *s* one *d. Educ:* Royal Belfast Academical Instn; The Queen's University of Belfast (BSc: Pure and Applied Mathematics, also (1st Cl. Hons) Physics). Sales Manager, Rank Hovis McDougall Ltd, 1965–66; Teacher, 1966–67; Research Associate, 1967–69; Civil Servant, 1969–: Dept of Agriculture (NI), 1969–72; Dept of Commerce (NI), 1972–82 (Under Secretary, 1981); Under Secretary, Dept of Economic Development (NI), 1982; Dep. Chief Exec., Industrial Develt Bd for NI, 1982–84; Permanent Sec., Dept of Economic Develt (NI), 1984–91. CBIM; FRSA. *Recreations:* music, reading, golf, Rugby Union. *Address:* Stormont Castle, Belfast BT4 3ST. *T:* Belfast (0232) 763011. *Club:* Old Instonians (Belfast).

FELL, Richard Taylor; HM Diplomatic Service; Counsellor (Economic and Commercial), Ottawa, since 1989; *b* 11 Nov. 1948; *s* of late Eric Whineray Fell and Margaret Farrer Fell (*née* Taylor); *m* 1981, Claire Gates; three *s. Educ:* Bootham Sch., York; Bristol Univ. (BSc); Univ. of London (MA). Joined HM Diplomatic Service, 1971; Ottawa, 1972–74; Saigon, 1974–75; Vientiane, 1975; First Sec. and Chargé d'Affaires *ai*, Hanoi, 1979; First Sec., UK Delegn to NATO, 1979–83; First Sec. and Head of Chancery, Kuala Lumpur, 1983–86; FCO, 1986–88; on secondment to Thorn EMI, 1988–89. *Publication:* Early Maps of South-East Asia, 1988. *Recreations:* antiques, reading, sport. *Address:* c/o Foreign and Commonwealth Office, SW1.

FELL, Robert, CB 1972; CBE 1966; Commissioner of Banking, Hong Kong, 1984–87; *b* 6 May 1921; *s* of Robert and Mary Ann Fell, Cumberland; *m* 1946, Eileen Wicks; two *s* one *d. Educ:* Whitehaven Grammar School. War Office, 1939; military service, 1940–46 (despatches); BoT, 1947; Trade Comr, Qld, 1954–59; Asst Sec., Tariff Div., 1961; Commercial Counsellor, Delhi, 1961–66; Under-Sec. i/c export promotion, 1967–71; Sec., ECGD, 1971–74; Chief Exec., The Stock Exchange, 1975–82; Comr for Securities, Hong Kong, 1981–84. Mem., British Overseas Trade Board, 1972–75; Pres., City Branch, BIM, 1976–82. FRSA. *Recreations:* Rugby football (watching), gardening. *Address:* Dalegarth, Guildown Avenue, Guildford, Surrey. *T:* Guildford (0483) 572204. *Club:* Travellers'.

FELLGETT, Prof. Peter Berners, PhD; FRS 1986; Professor of Cybernetics, University of Reading, 1965–87, now Emeritus; *b* 11 April 1922; *s* of Frank Ernest Fellgett and Rose, (Rowena), (*née* Wagstaffe); *m* 1947, Janet Mary, *o d* of late Prof. G. E. Briggs, FRS and Mrs Nora Briggs; one *s* two *d. Educ:* The Leys Sch., Cambridge; Univ. of Cambridge (BA 1943, MA 1947, PhD 1952). Isaac Newton Student, Cambridge Observatories, 1950–51; Lick Observatory, Calif, 1951–52; Cambridge Observatories, 1952–59; Royal Observatory, Edinburgh, 1959–65. *Publications:* approx. 75 pubns in learned jls and 32 gen. articles. *Recreations:* making musical instruments, high quality audio, gardening, fun-running, not being interrupted and not being hurried. *Address:* Little Brighter Farm, St Kew Highway, Bodmin, Cornwall PL30 3DU.

FELLINI, Federico; film director since 1950; *b* 20 Jan. 1920; *s* of late Urbano Fellini and Ida Barbiani; *m* 1943, Giulietta Masina. *Educ:* Bologna, Italy. Journalist, 1937–39; radio-author, scenario writer, etc, 1939–42. Fellow, BAFTA, 1987; has gained many prizes and awards in every part of the world including four "Oscars" (1957, 1958, 1964, 1975) for films La Strada, Le Notti di Cabiria, 8½ and Amarcord. Films include: (as Assistant Director and writer) Quarta Pagina, 1942; Roma Città Aperta, 1944–45; Paisà, 1946; Il Delitto di Giovanni Episcopo, 1947; In Nome della Legge, 1948–49; La Città si Defende, 1951; Il Brigante di Tacca di Lupo, 1953; San Francesco Giullare di Dio, 1954; Fortunella, 1956; (as Director) Luci del Varietà, 1950; Lo Sceicco Bianco, 1952; I Vitelloni, 1953; Agenzia Matrimoniale, 1953; La Strada, 1954; Il Bidone, 1955; Cabiria, 1957; La Dolce Vita, 1960; The Temptation of Dr Antonio, 1962; 8½, 1963 (foreign awards); Giulietta Degli Spiriti, 1965; Never Bet the Devil Your Head, 1968; Director's Blocknotes, 1969; Satyricon, 1969; The Clowns, 1970; Fellini's Roma, 1972; Amarcord, 1974; Casanova, 1976; Orchestra Rehearsal, 1979; La citta delle donne, 1980; E la nave vá, 1983; Ginger and Fred, 1986; Interview, 1987; The Voice of the Moon, 1990. *Publications:* Amarcord (trans. Nina Rootes), 1974; Quattro film, 1975. *Address:* Via Margutta 110, Rome, Italy.

FELLNER, Dr Peter John; Chief Executive and Managing Director, Celltech Group plc, since 1990; *b* 31 Dec. 1943; *s* of Hans Julius Fellner and Jessica (*née* Thompson); *m* 1st, 1969, Sandra Head (*née* Smith); one *d* and one step *s*; 2nd, 1982, Jennifer Mary Zabel (*née* Butler); two step *s. Educ:* Sheffield Univ. (BSc Biochem. 1965); Trinity Coll., Cambridge (PhD 1968). Post-doctoral Res. Fellow, 1968–70, Associate Prof., 1970–73, Strasbourg Univ.; Searle UK Research Laboratories: Sen. Res. Investigator, 1973–77; Dir of Chem., 1977–80; Dir of Res., 1980–84; Dir of Res., Roche UK Res. Centre, 1984–86; Man. Dir, Roche UK, 1986–90; Director: Colborn Dawes Ltd, 1986–90; British Biotechnol. Gp plc, 1988–90. *Recreation:* country walking. *Address:* Celltech Group plc, 216 Bath Road, Slough, Berks SL1 4EN. *T:* Slough (0753) 34655.

FELLOWES, family name of **Baron De Ramsey.**

FELLOWES, Rt. Hon. Sir Robert, KCB 1991 (CB 1987); KCVO 1989 (LVO 1983); PC 1990; Private Secretary to the Queen and Keeper of the Queen's Archives, since 1990; *b* 11 Dec. 1941; *s* of Sir William Fellowes, KCVO; *m* 1978, Lady Jane Spencer, *d* of Earl Spencer, *qv*; one *s* two *d. Educ:* Eton. Scots Guards (short service commission), 1960–63. Director, Allen Harvey & Ross Ltd, Discount Brokers and Bankers, 1968–77; Asst Private Sec. to the Queen, 1977–86, Dep. Private Sec., 1986–90. *Recreations:* golf, shooting, watching cricket. *Clubs:* White's, Pratt's, MCC.

FELLOWS, Derek Edward, FIA; Executive Director, Securities and Investments Board, 1989–91; *b* 23 Oct. 1927; *s* of late Edward Frederick Fellows and of Gladys Fellows; *m* 1948, Mary Watkins; two *d. Educ:* Mercers' Sch. FIA 1956. Entered Prudential Assurance Co. Ltd, 1943; Gp Pensions Manager, 1973–81; Chief Actuary, 1981–88; Man. Dir, Gp Pension Div., 1984–88; Dir, Prudential Corp. plc, 1985–88. Mem., Occupational Pensions Bd, 1974–78. FPMI 1976; Vice Pres., Inst. of Actuaries, 1980–83. *Publications:* contrib. Jl of Inst. of Actuaries. *Recreations:* music, gardening, bridge. *Club:* Actuaries'.

FELLOWS, Edward Frank; Editor, Farmers Weekly, since 1987; *b* 25 Sept. 1930; *s* of Edward Fellows and Gladys Nora Fellows; *m* 1962, Christine Woolmore; three *s. Educ:* Ewell primary and secondary schs; Epsom Sch. of Art (schol.); Merrist Wood Agricl Inst. Nat. Service, CRMP, 1949. Joined editorial staff of Farmer and Stockbreeder, 1957; Editor, Power Farming, 1974; Dep. Editor, Farmers Weekly, 1982; Editor, Crops, 1984. Hon. Mem., Falkland Islands Assoc., 1983–. *Publication:* Tim Chooses Farming, 1962. *Recreations:* Bernese Mountain dogs, walking, photography, gardening, reading. *Address:* Mede Hollow, 3 Crabtree Drive, Givons Grove, Leatherhead, Surrey KT22 8LW. *T:* Leatherhead (0372) 372782. *Club:* Farmers'.

FELLOWS, Jeffrey Keith; Ministry of Defence, London, since 1989; *b* 17 Sept. 1940; *s* of Albert and Hilda May Fellows; *m* 1965, Mary Ewins; one *s. Educ:* Handsworth Grammar Sch.; Birmingham Univ. (BSc (Phys) Hons 1962). Royal Aircraft Establishment: joined Weapons Dept, 1962, Sect. Leader, 1973; Div. Leader, Systems Assessment Dept, 1976; Head of: Combat Mission Systems Div., 1981; Flight Systems Dept, 1983; seconded to BNSC as Dir (Projects and Technol.), 1986; Dep. Dir (Mission Systems), RAE, Farnborough, 1988–89. *Publications:* various, for AGARD, IBA, US Nat. Space Foundn, etc. *Recreations:* tennis, aeromodelling.

FELLOWS, John Walter, FICE, FIHT; Regional Director, South East Region, Departments of the Environment and Transport, since 1990; *b* 27 July 1938; *s* of William Leslie Fellows and Lavinia Keziah (*née* Chilton); *m* 1964, Maureen Joyce Lewis; two *s. Educ:* Dudley Technical High Sch.; Wolverhampton Polytechnic; Birmingham Univ. (MSc). FICE 1990; FIHT 1989. Civil Engineer (pupil), Contractors Wilson Lovatt & Sons Ltd, 1954–59; Civil Engineer: CBs of Wolverhampton, Coventry and Dudley, 1959–69; Department of Transport, 1969–: Asst Sec., Highway Maintenance Div., 1984–88; Dir, SE, 1988–90. *Publications:* papers to ICE and IHT. *Recreations:* boating, sailing, golf, music, theatre. *Address:* Department of the Environment, Charles House, Kensington High Street, W14 8QH. *T:* 071–605 9010.

FELLS, Prof. Ian, FEng; Professor of Energy Conversion, University of Newcastle upon Tyne, since 1975; *b* 5 Sept. 1932; *s* of late Dr Henry Alexander Fells, MBE and Clarice Fells, Sheffield; *m* 1957, Hazel Denton Scott; four *s. Educ:* King Edward VII School, Sheffield; Trinity College, Cambridge. MA, PhD. FInstE, CChem, FRSC, FIChemE; FEng 1979. Chief Wireless Officer, British Troops in Austria, 1951–52; Lectr and Dir of Studies, Dept of Fuel Technology and Chem. Engineering, Univ. of Sheffield, 1958–62; Reader in Fuel Science, King's Coll., Univ. of Durham, 1962; Public Orator, Univ. of Newcastle upon Tyne, 1970–73. Lectures: Brough, Paisley, 1977; Allerdale Wylde, Cumbria Science Socs, 1986; Fawley, Southampton Univ., 1987; Robert Spence, RSC, 1988 and 1990; Charles Parsons' Mem, Royal Soc., 1988. Pres., Inst. of Energy, 1978–79; Scientific Advr, World Energy Council, 1990–; Member: Electricity Supply Res. Council, 1979–90; Sci. Consultative Gp, BBC, 1976–81; Exec., David Davies Inst. of Internat. Affairs, 1975–; CNAA, 1987–; Trustee, Northern Sinfonia Orch., 1984–. Hatfield Meml Prize, 1974; Beilby Meml Medal and Prize, 1976. Participator in TV series: Young Scientist of the Year; The Great Egg Race; Men of Science; Earth Year 2050; Take Nobody's Word For It; QED. *Publications:* Energy for the Future, 1973, 2nd edn 1986; contribs to professional jls. *Recreations:* sailing, guitar, energy conversation. *Address:* Department of Chemical and Process Engineering, The University, Newcastle upon Tyne NE1 7RU. *T:* 091–222 7276; (home) 091–285 5343. *Club:* Naval and Military.

FENBY, Eric William, OBE 1962; Professor of Harmony, Royal Academy of Music, 1964–77; *b* 22 April 1906; *s* of late Herbert Henry and Ada Fenby; *m* 1944, Rowena Clara Teresa Marshall; one *s* one *d. Educ:* Municipal Sch., Scarborough; privately. Amanuensis to Frederick Delius, 1928–34; Mus. Adv. Boosey & Hawkes, 1936–39; début as composer, BBC Promenade Concerts, 1942. Captain, RAEC Sch. of Educn, Cuerdon Hall, 1942–45. Mus. Dir, N Riding Coll. of Educn, 1948–62; Artistic Dir, Delius Centenary Festival, 1962; Pres. Delius Soc., 1964–; Chm., Composers' Guild of Great Britain, 1968, Mem. Council, 1970. Visiting Prof. of Music and Composer in Residence, Jacksonville Univ., Fla, USA, 1968. Mem. Cttee of Management, Royal Philharmonic Soc., 1972. FRCM 1985; Hon. FTCL 1986; Hon. Member: RAM, 1965; Royal Philharmonic Soc., 1984; Hon. DMus Jacksonville, 1978; Hon. DLitt Warwick, 1978; Hon. DLitt Bradford, 1978. *Publications:* Delius as I Knew Him, 1936, rev. edn 1966; a further rev. edn, 1981, packaged with own recordings of all works dictated to him by Delius, known as The Fenby Legacy; Menuhin's House of Music, 1969; Delius, 1971. *Recreations:* walking, chess. *Address:* 1 Raincliffe Court, Stepney Road, Scarborough, N Yorks YO12 5BT. *T:* Scarborough (0723) 372988. *Club:* Royal Academy of Music.

FENDALL, Prof. Neville Rex Edwards, MD; Professor of International Community Health, School of Tropical Medicine, University of Liverpool, 1971–81, now Emeritus Professor; Visiting Professor of Public Health, Boston University, since 1982; Adjunct Professor of Community Health, University of Calgary, since 1983; *b* 9 July 1917; *s* of Francis Alan Fendall and Ruby Inez Matthews; *m* 1942, Margaret Doreen (*née* Beynon). *Educ:* University College Hosp. (MD, BSc); London Sch. of Hygiene and Tropical Med. (DPH); FFPHM. Colonial Medical Service, 1944–64, Nigeria, Malaya, Singapore, Kenya; Brit. Mil. Admin, 1945–46; Dir of Med. Services, Kenya; Staff Mem., Rockefeller Foundn, 1964–66; Regional Dir, Population Council Inc., New York, 1966–71. Mem., Panel of Experts, WHO, 1957–83; Consultant: World Bank; UN Fund for Population Activities; ODM; Cento; Internat. Develt Res. Centre, Canada; APHA; USAID; Overseas govts. Visiting Lecturer: Harvard, 1966–83; Inst. of Tropical Medicine, Marseilles; Univ. of Glasgow; Univ. of Bradford; Vis. Consultant, Univ. of Hawaii; Commonwealth Foundn Travelling Lectr, 1976. Mem., Acad. of Med., Physical and Nat. Scis, Guatemala, 1986–. Gold Medal, Mrigendra Medical Trust, Nepal, 1983. *Publications:* Auxiliaries in Health Care, 1972 (English, French, Spanish edns); (with J. M. Paxman and F. M.

Shattock) Use of Paramedicals for Primary Health Care in the Commonwealth, 1979; (with F. M. Shattock) Restraints and Constraints to Development, 1983; contribs on primary health care, epidemiology, in various jls. *Recreations:* gardening, travel. *Address:* The Coach House, Mill Street, Ludlow, Shropshire SY8 1BB. *Clubs:* Commonwealth Trust; Athenæum (Liverpool).

FENDER, Prof. Brian Edward Frederick, CMG 1985; Vice-Chancellor, University of Keele, since 1985; *b* 15 Sept. 1934; *s* of late George Clements and of Emily Fender; *m* 1st, 1956; one *s* three *d*; 2nd, 1986, Ann Linscott. *Educ:* Carlisle Grammar Sch.; Sale County Grammar Sch.; Imperial College London (ARCS, BSc 1956; DIC, PhD 1959); MA Oxon 1963; CChem, FRSC. Research Instructor, Univ. of Washington, Seattle, 1959–61; Senior Research Fellow, Nat. Chem. Lab. (now NPL), 1961–63; University of Oxford: Dept Demonstrator in Inorganic Chemistry, 1963–65; Lectr, 1965–84; Senior Proctor, 1975–76; Mem., Hebdomadal Council, 1977–80; St Catherine's College: Fellow, 1963–84 (Hon. Fellow 1986); Sen. Tutor, 1965–69; Chm., Management Cttee, Oxford Colls Admissions Office, 1973–80. Inst. Laue-Langevin, Grenoble: Asst Dir, 1980–82; Dir, 1982–85; Mem., Steering Cttee, 1974–77; Mem., Scientific Council, 1977–80. Member: SERC, 1985–90; CERN Review Cttee, 1986–87; Chairman: Science Board, SERC, 1985–90 (Mem., 1974–77); Neutron Beam Res. Cttee, 1974–77 (Mem., 1969–71); Science Planning Group for Rutherford Lab. Neutron Scattering Source, 1977–80; Keele Univ. Science Park, 1985–; Universities' Cttee for Non-teaching Staff, 1987–. Mem. Council, Chem. Soc., 1973–76. Mem. Adv. Cttee, Tate Gall., Liverpool, 1988–. CBIM 1989. *Publications:* scientific articles on neutron scattering and solid state chemistry. *Recreations:* visiting France, modern art. *Address:* The Clock House, University of Keele, Keele, Staffs ST5 5BG. *T:* Newcastle (Staffs) (0782) 628394. *Club:* Athenæum.

FENECH-ADAMI, Hon. Dr Edward; MP Malta, since 1969; Prime Minister of Malta, since 1987 (also Foreign Minister, 1989–90); Leader of Nationalist Party, since 1977; *b* Birkirkara, Malta, 7 Feb. 1934; *s* of late Luigi Fenech-Adami and Josephine (*née* Pace); *m* 1965, Mary (*née* Sciberras); four *s* one *d*. *Educ:* St Aloysius Coll., Malta; Royal Univ. of Malta (BA 1955, LLD 1958). Entered legal practice in Malta, 1959. Mem. Nat. Exec., Nationalist Party, 1961, Asst Gen. Sec., 1962–75, Chm., Gen. Council and Admin. Council, 1975–77; Shadow Minister for Labour and Social Services, 1971–77; Leader of the Opposition, Malta, 1977–81 and 1982–87. Vice-Pres., European Union of Christian Democrat Parties, 1979–. Editor, Il-Poplu, 1962–69. *Address:* Auberge de Castille, Valletta, Malta. *T:* 623026.

FENHALLS, Richard Dorian; Chief Executive, Henry Ansbacher Holdings PLC, since 1985; Chairman, Henry Ansbacher & Co. Ltd, since 1985; *b* 14 July 1943; *s* of Roydon Myers and Maureen Rosa Fenhalls; *m* 1967, Angela Sarah Allen; one *s* one *d*. *Educ:* Hilton Coll., Univ. of Natal (BA); Christ's Coll., Cambridge (MA, LLM). Attorney, S Africa, 1969. Goodricke & Son, Attorney, S Africa, 1969–70; Citibank, 1970–72; Senior Vice President: Marine Midland Bank, 1972–77; American Express Bank, 1977–81; Dep. Chm. and Chief Exec., Guinness Mahon & Co. Ltd, 1981–85. *Recreations:* sailing, ski-ing. *Address:* 15 St James's Gardens, W11 4RE. *Clubs:* Royal Ocean Racing, Royal Thames Yacht, Ski Club of Great Britain; Campden Hill Lawn Tennis; Royal Southern Yacht (Hamble).

FENN, Sir Nicholas (Maxted), KCMG 1989 (CMG 1980); HM Diplomatic Service; High Commissioner in New Delhi, since 1991; *b* 19 Feb. 1936; *s* of Rev. Prof. J. Eric Fenn and Kathleen (*née* Harrison); *m* 1959, Susan Clare (*née* Russell); two *s* one *d*. *Educ:* Kingswood Sch., Bath; Peterhouse, Cambridge (MA). Pilot Officer, RAF, 1954–56. Third Sec., British Embassy, Rangoon, 1959–63; Asst Private Sec. to Sec. of State for Foreign and Commonwealth Affairs, 1963–67; First Secretary: British Interests Sect., Swiss Embassy, Algiers, 1967–69; Public Relations, UK Mission to UN, NY, 1969–72; Dep. Head, Energy Dept, FCO, 1972–75; Counsellor, Peking, 1975–77; Head of News Dept and FCO Spokesman, 1979–82; Spokesman to last Governor of Rhodesia, 1979–80; Ambassador: Rangoon, 1982–86; Dublin, 1986–91. *Recreation:* sailing. *Address:* c/o Foreign and Commonwealth Office, King Charles Street, SW1A 2AH.

FENNELL, Hon. Sir (John) Desmond (Augustine), Kt 1990; OBE 1982; **Hon. Mr Justice Fennell;** a Judge of the High Court of Justice, Queen's Bench Division, since 1990; *b* 17 Sept. 1933; *s* of late Dr A. J. Fennell, Lincoln; *m* 1966, Susan Primrose, *d* of late J. M. Trusted; one *s* two *d*. *Educ:* Ampleforth; Corpus Christi Coll., Cambridge. Served with Grenadier Guards, 1956–58. Called to the Bar, Inner Temple, 1959, Bencher, 1983; Dep. Chm., Bedfordshire QS, 1971; a Recorder of the Crown Court, 1972–89; QC 1974; Leader, Midland and Oxford Circuit, 1983–88; a Judge of the Courts of Appeal of Jersey and Guernsey, 1984–89; a Judge of the Employment Appeal Tribunal, 1991–. Vice-Chm., 1988, Chm., 1989, Gen. Council of the Bar. Inspector, King's Cross Underground fire, 1988. Chm., Buckingham Div. Cons. Assoc., 1976–79 (Pres., 1983–89). *Address:* Royal Courts of Justice, Strand, WC2A 2LL. *Clubs:* Boodle's, Pilgrims.

FENNELL, Prof. John Lister Illingworth, MA, PhD Cantab; FRSL; Professor of Russian, Oxford University, 1967–85; Emeritus Fellow of New College, Oxford, since 1985 (Fellow, 1967); *b* 30 May 1918; *s* of Dr C. H. Fennell and Sylvia Mitchell; *m* 1947, Marina Lopukhin; one *s* one *d*. *Educ:* Radley Coll.; Trinity Coll., Cambridge. FRSL 1980; FRHistS 1985. Served with Army, 1939–45. Asst Lectr, Dept of Slavonic Studies, Cambridge Univ., 1947–52; Reader in Russian and Head of Dept of Slavonic Languages, Nottingham Univ., 1952–56; Lectr in Russian, Oxford Univ., 1956–67, Fellow and Praelector in Russian, University Coll., Oxford, 1964–67. Vis. Lectr, Harvard Univ., 1963–64; Visiting Professor: Univ. of Calif at Berkeley, 1971, 1977; Virginia Univ., 1974; Bonsall and Kratter Vis. Prof., Stanford Univ., 1982–83; Univ. of Texas at Austin, 1986. Organiser, 3rd Internat. Conf. of Historians of Muscovy, Oxford, 1975. Joint Editor: Oxford Slavonic Papers, 1968–86; Russia Mediaevalis. *Publications:* The Correspondence between Prince A. M. Kurbsky and Ivan IV, 1955; Ivan the Great of Moscow, 1961; The Penguin Russian Course, 1961; Pushkin, 1964; Kurbsky's History of Ivan IV, 1965; The Emergence of Moscow, 1968; (ed jtly) Historical Russian Reader, 1969; (ed) Nineteenth Century Russian Literature, 1973; (with A. Stokes) Early Russian Literature, 1974; (ed jtly) The Cambridge Encyclopaedia of Russia and the Soviet Union, 1982; The Crisis of Medieval Russia, 1983; Cambridge Modern History, Vol. II, Chap. 19; articles in Slavonic and East European Review, Jahrbücher für Geschichte Osteuropas, etc. *Recreation:* music. *Address:* 8 Canterbury Road, Oxford OX2 6LU. *T:* Oxford (0865) 56149.

See also J. D. Abell.

FENNER, Prof. Frank John, AC 1989; CMG 1976; MBE 1944; FRCP 1967; FRS 1958; FAA 1954; Visiting Fellow, John Curtin School of Medical Research, Australian National University, since 1983 (University Fellow, 1980–82); *b* 21 Dec. 1914; *s* of Charles and Emma L. Fenner; *m* 1944, Ellen Margaret Bobbie Roberts; one *d* (and one *d* decd). *Educ:* Thebarton Technical High Sch.; Adelaide High Sch.; Univ. of Adelaide. MB, BS (Adelaide) 1938; MD (Adelaide) 1942; DTM (Sydney) 1940. Served as Medical Officer, Hospital Pathologist, and Malariologist, AIF, 1940–46; Francis Haley Research Fellow, Walter and Eliza Hall Inst. for Medical Research, Melbourne, 1946–48; Rockefeller Foundation Travelling Fellow, 1948–49; Prof. of Microbiology, 1949–73, Dir, John Curtin Sch. of Med. Research, 1967–73, Prof. of Environmental Studies and Dir, Centre for Resource and Environmental Studies, 1973–79, ANU; Overseas Fellow, Churchill Coll., Cambridge, 1962–63. Fogarty Schol., Nat. Insts of Health, USA, 1973–74, 1982–83. Chm., Global Commn for Certification of Smallpox Eradication, WHO, 1978–80. For. Associate, Nat. Acad. of Scis, USA, 1977; David Syme Prize, Univ. of Melbourne, 1949; Harvey Lecture, Harvey Soc. of New York, 1957; Royal Society: Leeuwenhoek Lecture, 1961, Florey Lecture, 1983; Australian Acad. of Science: Matthew Flinders Lecture, 1967; Burnet Lecture, 1985. Hon. MD Monash, 1966. Mueller Medal, Australian and New Zealand Assoc. for the Advancement of Science, 1964; Britannica Australia Award for Medicine, 1967; ANZAC Peace Award, 1980; ANZAAS Medal, 1980; Stuart Mudd Award, Internat. Union of Microbiol Socs; 1986; Japan Prize (Preventive Medicine), Sci. & Technol. Foundn of Japan, 1988. *Publications:* The Production of Antibodies (with F. M. Burnet), 1949; Myxomatosis (with F. N. Ratcliffe), 1965; The Biology of Animal Viruses, 1968, 2nd edn 1974; Medical Virology (with D. O. White), 1970, 3rd edn 1986; Classification and Nomenclature of Viruses, 1976; (with A. L. G. Rees) The Australian Academy of Science: the First Twenty-five Years, 1980; (jtly) Veterinary Virology, 1987; (jtly) Smallpox and its Eradication, 1988; (with Z. Jezek) Human Monkeypox, 1988; (with A. Gibbs) Portraits of Viruses: a history of virology, 1988; (jtly) The Orthopoxviruses, 1989; History of Microbiology in Australia, 1990; numerous scientific papers, dealing with virology, epidemiology, bacteriology, and environmental problems. *Recreations:* gardening, tennis. *Address:* 8 Monaro Crescent, Red Hill, Canberra, ACT 2603, Australia. *T:* 295–9176.

FENNER, Dame Peggy, DBE 1986; MP (C) Medway, since 1983 (Rochester and Chatham, 1970–Sept. 1974 and 1979–83); *b* 12 Nov. 1922; *m* 1940, Bernard Fenner; one *d*. *Educ:* LCC School, Brockley; Ide Hill, Sevenoaks. Contested (C) Newcastle-under-Lyme, 1966; Parly Sec., MAFF, 1972–74 and 1981–86; Mem., British Delegn to European Parlt, Strasbourg, 1974; UK rep. to Council of Europe and WEU, 1987–. Member: West Kent Divisional Exec. Educn Cttee, 1963–72; Sevenoaks Urban District Council, 1957–71 (Chairman, 1962 and 1963); Exec. of Kent Borough and Urban District Councils Assoc., 1967–71; a Vice-Pres, Urban District Councils Assoc., 1971. *Recreations:* reading, travel, theatre, gardening. *Address:* 12 Star Hill, Rochester, Kent. *T:* Medway (0634) 42124.

FENNESSY, Sir Edward, Kt 1975; CBE 1957 (OBE 1944); BSc; FIEE, FRIN; *b* 17 Jan. 1912; *m* 1st, 1937, Marion Banks (*d* 1983); one *s* one *d*; 2nd, 1984, Leonora Patricia Birkett, *widow* of Trevor Birkett. *Educ:* Univ. of London. Telecommunications Research, Standard Telephones and Cables, 1934–38; Radar Research, Air Min. Research Station, Bawdsey Manor, 1938. War of 1939–45: commissioned RAFVR, 1940; Group Captain, 1945; staff No 60 Group, RAF, 1940–45; resp. for planning and construction radar systems for defence of UK, and Bomber Ops. Joined Bd of The Decca Navigator Co., 1946; Managing Director: Decca Radar Ltd, 1950–65; The Plessey Electronics Group, 1965–69. Chairman: British Telecommunications Research Ltd, 1966–69; Electronic Engineering Assoc., 1967–68; Man. Dir, Telecommunications, 1969–77, and Dep. Chm., 1975–77, Post Office Corp. Chairman: IMA Microwave Products Ltd, 1979–83; LKB Biochrom, 1978–87; British Medical Data Systems, 1981–91; Dep. Chm., LKB Instruments, 1978–87. Pres., Royal Institute of Navigation, 1975–78. DUniv Surrey, 1971. *Recreations:* sailing, golf. *Address:* Northbrook, Littleford Lane, Shamley Green, Surrey GU5 0RH. *T:* Guildford (0483) 892444. *Clubs:* Royal Air Force; Island Sailing.

FENNEY, Roger Johnson, CBE 1973 (MBE (mil.) 1945); Chairman, Special Trustees, Charing Cross Hospital, 1980–88; *b* 11 Sept. 1916; *s* of James Henry Fenney and Annie Sarah Fenney; *m* 1942, Dorothy Porteus (*d* 1989); two *d*. *Educ:* Cowley Sch., St Helens; Univ. of Manchester (BA Admin 1939). Served War, 1939–46: Gunner to Major, Field Artillery; served N Africa and Italy (mentioned in despatches). Secretary, Central Midwives Board, 1947–82; Governor, Charing Cross Hosp., 1958–74 (Chm., Clinical Res. Cttee, 1970–80; Mem. Council, Med. Sch., 1970–80); Governor, Hammersmith Hosp., 1956–74; Chm., W London Hosp., 1957–68; First Nuffield Fellow for Health Affairs, USA, 1968; Dep. Chm., Kennedy Inst. of Rheumatol., 1970–77. Member: Exec., Arthritis and Rheumatism Council, 1978–; Ealing, Hammersmith and Hounslow AHA, 1974–79; Field Dir, Jt Study Gp (FIGO/ICM), Accra, Yaounde, Nairobi, Dakar, San José and Bogotá, 1972–76. *Address:* 11 Gilray House, Gloucester Terrace, W2 3DF. *T:* 071–262 8313.

FENTEM, Prof. Peter Harold, FRCP; Professor of Physiology, since 1975 and Dean of Medicine, since 1987, University of Nottingham; Hon. Consultant, Clinical Respiratory Physiology, Nottingham Health Authority, since 1976; *b* 12 Sept. 1933; *s* of Harold and Agnes Fentem; *m* 1958, Rosemary Hodson; two *s* two *d*. *Educ:* Bury Grammar Sch.; Univ. of Manchester (BSc 1st cl. hons 1955; MSc 1956; MB ChB Hons 1959). FRCP 1989. Hosp. appts, Manchester Royal Inf., 1959–60; Demonstrator in Path., Univ. of Manchester, 1960–61; Manchester and Cardiff Royal Infs, 1961–64; Lectr in Physiol., St Mary's Hosp. Med. Sch., 1964–68; Sen. Lectr in Physiol., 1968, Reader, 1975, Univ. of Nottingham. Chm., BSI Tech. Sub-Cttee on Compression Hosiery, 1978–89; Sci. Sec., Fitness and Health Adv. Gp, Sports Council, 1981; Civil Consultant to RAF, 1983–; Hon. Consultant to Army, 1989–; Member: Army Personnel Res. Cttee, 1983– (Chm., Applied Physiol. Panel, 1986–); GMC, 1988–; Trent RHA, 1988–90. *Publications:* (jt author): Exercise: the facts, 1981; Work Physiology, in Principles and Practice of Human Physiology, 1981; The New Case for Exercise, 1988; Benefits of Exercise: the evidence, 1990; (Adv. Editor) Physiology Integrated Clinical Science, 1983. *Recreations:* gardening, walking. *Address:* 38 Prestwood Drive, Aspley, Nottingham NG8 3LY. *T:* Nottingham (0602) 293772. *Club:* Royal Society of Medicine.

FENTON, Dr Alexander, CBE 1986; Head of European Ethnological Research Centre, Edinburgh, since 1989; *b* 26 June 1929; *s* of Alexander Fenton and Annie Stirling Stronach; *m* 1956, Evelyn Elizabeth Hunter; two *d*. *Educ:* Turriff Academy; Aberdeen Univ. (MA); Cambridge Univ. (BA); Edinburgh Univ. (DLitt). Senior Asst Editor, Scottish National Dictionary, 1955–59; Asst Keeper, Nat. Museum of Antiquities of Scotland, 1959–75, Dep. Keeper, 1975–78, Director, 1978–85; Res. Dir, Nat. Museums of Scotland, 1985–89. Mem., Ancient Monuments Bd for Scotland, 1979–. Member: Royal Gustav Adolf Acad., Uppsala, Sweden, 1978; Royal Danish Acad. of Scis and Letters, 1979; Jury, Europa Preis für Volkskunst (FVS Foundation, Hamburg) 1975–. Hon. DLitt Aberdeen, 1989. Co-editor, Tools and Tillage (Copenhagen), 1968–; Editor, Review of Scottish Culture, 1984–. *Publications:* The Various Names of Shetland, 1973, 2nd edn 1977; Scottish Country Life, 1976, 2nd edn 1978; (trans.) S. Steensen Blicher, En Landsbydegns Dagbog (The Diary of a Parish Clerk, 1976); The Island Blackhouse, 1978; The Northern Isles: Orkney and Shetland, 1978; (with B. Walker) The Rural Architecture of Scotland, 1981; The Shape of the Past, 2 vols, 1985; (trans.) S. Weöres, Ha a Világ Rigó Lenne (If All the World were a Blackbird), 1985; Wird's an' Work 'e Seasons Roon, 1987; Country Life in Scotland, 1987; The Turra Coo: a legal episode in the populat culture of NE Scotland, 1989; Scottish Country Life, 1989; numerous articles in learned jls. *Address:* 132 Blackford Avenue, Edinburgh EH9 3HH. *T:* 031–667 5456. *Club:* New (Edinburgh).

FENTON, Air Cdre Harold Arthur, CBE 1946; DSO 1943; DFC 1942; BA; AFRAeS; *b* Gallegos, Patagonia, Argentine, 9 Feb. 1909; *s* of Dr E. G. Fenton, FRCSI, DPH, Co.

Sligo and J. Ormsby, Glen Lodge, Ballina, Co. Mayo; *m* 1935, H. de Carteret; no *c*. *Educ:* Sandford Park Sch.; Trinity Coll., Dublin (BA 1927). Joined RAF 1928. Served India, 1930–33. Flying Instructor at Air Service Training Ltd, Hamble, until outbreak of war. During war commanded: Fighter Sqdn, Battle of Britain; Fighter Wing, and Fighter Group, Western Desert and Libya; Fighter Sector, London Area. Finished war as Senior Staff Officer, Germany (83 Group) (despatches thrice). Managing Dir, Deccan Airways Ltd, Hyderabad, Deccan, until 1947; Gen. Manager of Airways Training Ltd, 1947–48; Operations Manager, BOAC, 1949–52; Managing Dir, Peter Jones, 1952–58. *Recreation:* gardening. *Address:* Le Vallon, St Brelade, Jersey, Channel Islands. *T:* Jersey (0534) 41172.

FENTON, James Martin, FRSL; writer; *b* 25 April 1949; *s* of Rev. Canon J. C. Fenton, *qv* and Mary Hamilton (*née* Ingoldby). *Educ:* Durham Choristers Sch.; Repton Sch.; Magdalen Coll., Oxford (MA). FRSL 1983. Asst Literary Editor, 1971, Editorial Asst, 1972, New Statesman; freelance correspondent in Indo-China, 1973–75; Political Columnist, New Statesman, 1976–78; German Correspondent, The Guardian, 1978–79; Theatre Critic, Sunday Times, 1979–84; Chief Book Reviewer, The Times, 1984–86; Far East Corresp., The Independent, 1986–88. *Publications:* Our Western Furniture, 1968; Terminal Moraine, 1972; A Vacant Possession, 1978; A German Requiem, 1980; Dead Soldiers, 1981; The Memory of War, 1982; (trans.) Rigoletto, 1982; You Were Marvellous, 1983; (ed) The Original Michael Frayn, 1983; Children in Exile, 1984; Poems 1968–83, 1985; (trans.) Simon Boccanegra, 1985; The Fall of Saigon, in Granta 15, 1985; The Snap Revolution, in Granta 18, 1986; (ed) Cambodian Witness: the autobiography of Someth May, 1986; (with John Fuller) Partingtime Hall (poems), 1987; All the Wrong Places: adrift in the politics of Asia, 1989. *Address:* 1 Bartlemas Road, Oxford OX4 1XU. *T:* Oxford (0865) 726797; c/o A. D. Peters & Co. Ltd, 10 Buckingham Street, WC2N 6BU.

FENTON, Rev. Canon John Charles; Canon of Christ Church, Oxford, 1978–91, Hon. Canon since 1991; *b* 5 June 1921; *s* of Cornelius O'Connor Fenton and Agnes Claudine Fenton. *Educ:* S Edward's Sch., Oxford; Queen's Coll., Oxford (BA 1943, MA 1947, BD 1953); Lincoln Theol Coll. Deacon 1944, priest 1945. Asst Curate, All Saints, Hindley, Wigan, 1944–47; Chaplain, Lincoln Theol Coll., 1947–51, Sub-Warden, 1951–54; Vicar of Wentworth, Yorks, 1954–58; Principal: Lichfield Theol Coll., 1958–65; S Chad's Coll., Durham, 1965–78. *Publications:* Preaching the Cross, 1958; The Passion according to John, 1961; Crucified with Christ, 1961; Saint Matthew (Pelican Commentaries), 1963; Saint John (New Clarendon Bible), 1970; What was Jesus' Message?, 1971; (with M. Hare Duke) Good News, 1976; Finding the Way through John, 1988; contrib. Theol., and Jl of Theol Studies. *Recreations:* walking, camping, gardening. *Address:* (until July 1992) Christ Church, Oxford OX1 1DP. *T:* Oxford (0865) 276200; (from July 1992) 8 Rowland Close, Wolvercote, Oxford. *T:* Oxford (0865) 54099.

FENWICK, Very Rev. Jeffery Robert; Dean of Guernsey, since 1989; *b* 8 April 1930; *s* of Stanley Robert and Dorothy Fenwick; *m* 1955, Pamela Frances (*née* Galley); one *s* two *d*. *Educ:* Torquay and Selhurst Grammar Schools; Pembroke Coll., Cambridge (MA); Lincoln Theol Coll. Deacon 1955, priest 1956, Liverpool; Curate, St Thomas the Martyr, UpHolland, 1955; Priest-in-charge, Christ the King, Daramombe, Mashonaland, 1958; Secretary, USPG, Oxford, 1964; Rector, Gatooma 1965, Salisbury East 1967, Mashonaland; Dean, Bulawayo, Matabeleland, 1975; Canon Residentiary, Worcester Cathedral, 1978; Librarian and Treasurer, 1978–89. Examining Chaplain, Mashonaland and Matabeleland, 1966–78; Archdeacon of Charter, 1970–75, of Bulawayo 1975–78. Hon. Canon of Winchester Cathedral, 1989–. Chm., Cathedrals Finance Conf. for England, 1983–89. *Publications:* Chosen People, 1971; (contrib.) The Pattern of History, 1973. *Recreations:* painting, music, gardening, walking. *Address:* The Deanery, St Peter Port, Guernsey. *T:* Guernsey (0481) 720036.

FENWICK, John James, DL; Chairman, Fenwick Ltd, since 1979 (Deputy Chairman, 1972–79; Managing Director, 1972–82); Director, Northern Rock Building Society, since 1984; *b* 9 Aug. 1932; *e s* of James Frederick Trevor Fenwick; *m* 1957, Muriel Gillian Hodnett; three *s*. *Educ:* Rugby Sch.; Pembroke Coll., Cambridge (MA). Chairman: Northumberland Assoc. of Youth Clubs, 1966–71; Retail Distributors Assoc., 1977–79; Vice Chm., National Assoc. of Citizens Advice Bureaux, 1971–79; Regional Dir, Northern Bd, Lloyds Bank, 1982–85. Member: Newcastle Diocesan Bd of Finance, 1964–69; Retail Consortium Council, 1976–79; Post Office Users' Nat. Council, 1980–82; Civic Trust for NE, 1979–. Governor: Royal Grammar Sch., Newcastle upon Tyne, 1975– (Chm. of Govs, 1987–); Moorfields Eye Hosp., 1981–86; Royal Shakespeare Theatre, 1985–. DL Tyne and Wear, 1986. *Recreations:* travel, shooting, theatre. *Address:* 27 St Dionis Road, SW6 4UQ; 35 Osborne Road, Newcastle upon Tyne NE2 2AH. *Clubs:* Garrick, MCC.

FERENS, Sir Thomas (Robinson), Kt 1957; CBE 1952; *b* 4 Jan. 1903; *e s* of late J. J. T. Ferens, Hull; *m* 1934, Jessie (*d* 1982), *d* of P. G. Sanderson, Hull and Scarborough; two *d*. *Educ:* Rydal; Leeds Univ. (BSc Eng). *Recreation:* fly-fishing. *Address:* Sunderlandwick, Driffield, North Humberside. *T:* Driffield (0377) 42323.

FERGUSON, Ernest Alexander; Under-Secretary and Accountant-General, Department of Employment, 1973–77; *b* 26 July 1917; *s* of William Henry and Lilian Ferguson; *m* 1940, Mary Josephine Wadsworth; two *s*. *Educ:* Priory Sch., Shrewsbury; Pembroke Coll., Cambridge (Scholar, 1935–39; MA 1944). Served War, RA (Captain), 1940–45. Entered Ministry of Labour, 1945; Principal, 1948; Asst Sec., 1962. Chm., Central Youth Employment Executive, 1967–69; Sec. to NEDC, 1971–73; Dep. Chm., Central Arbitration Cttee, 1977–87. *Recreations:* sport, hill walking, reading. *Address:* 164 Balcombe Road, Horley, Surrey RH6 9DS. *T:* Horley (0293) 785254. *Club:* Civil Service.

FERGUSON, Dr James Brown Provan; Chief Administrative Medical Officer and Director of Public Health, Lanarkshire, since 1988; *b* 23 Oct. 1935; *s* of Peter William Ferguson and Sarah Ferguson (*née* Brown); *m* 1960, Sheila Capstick; three *d*. *Educ:* Univ. of Edinburgh (MB ChB; DipSocMed). FFPHM. Principal SMO, SE Regl Hosp. Bd, 1972–74; Dist MO, N Lothian Dist, 1974–83; SMO, SHHD, 1983–88. W. K. Kellogg Foundn Fellow, 1983; Hon. Lectr, Univ. of Glasgow, 1988. *Publications:* contribs to BMJ, British Jl of Surgery. *Recreations:* walking, cinema, reading, print collecting. *Address:* Lanarkshire Health Board, 14 Beckford Street, Hamilton ML3 0TA. *T:* Hamilton (0698) 281313.

FERGUSON, John Alexander; HM Senior Chief Inspector of Schools in Scotland, 1981–87, retired; *b* 16 Oct. 1927; *s* of George Ferguson and Martha Crichton Dykes; *m* 1953, Jean Stewart; two *s* one *d*. *Educ:* Royal Coll. of Science and Technology, Univ. of Glasgow (BSc Hons, Diploma). Teacher, Airdrie Central Sch., 1950–51; Lectr, 1951–55, Head of Dept of Engrg, 1955–61, Coatbridge Technical Coll.; HM Inspector of Schs, 1961–72, Asst Sec., 1972–75, Scottish Educn Dept; HM Depute Sen. Chief Inspector of Schs, 1975–81. *Recreations:* golf, bridge. *Clubs:* Craigmillar Park Lawn Tennis, Carlton Bridge (Edinburgh); Luffness New Golf.

FERGUSON, John McIntyre, CBE 1976; FEng 1978; FIEE, FIMechE; engineering consultant, 1973, retired 1986; *b* 16 May 1915; *s* of Frank Ferguson and Lilian (*née* Bowen); *m* 1941, Margaret Frances Tayler; three *s*. *Educ:* Armstrong Coll., Durham Univ. BScEng (1st Cl. Hons). English Electric Co., Stafford: Research, 1936; Chief Engr, 1953; Dir Engrg, Heavy Electric Products, 1965; Dir of Engrg, GEC Power Engrg Co., 1969. Member: Metrication Bd, 1969–76; Science Res. Council, 1972–76; UGC, 1977–82. President: IEE, 1977–78; IEETE, 1979–81. Hon. FIEEIE. Hon. DSc Birmingham, 1983. *Recreations:* golf, sailing. *Address:* 11 Appledore Close, Baswich, Stafford ST17 0EW. *T:* Stafford (0785) 664700. *Club:* Commonwealth Trust.

FERGUSON, Sir Neil Edward J.; *see* Johnson-Ferguson.

FERGUSON, Richard; QC 1986; QC (NI) 1973; SC (Ireland) 1983; *b* 22 Aug. 1935; *o s* of late Wesley Ferguson and Edith Ferguson (*née* Hewitt); *m* 1st, Janet Irvine Magowan (marr. diss.); three *s* one *d*; 2nd, Roma Felicity Whelan; one *s*. *Educ:* Methodist Coll., Belfast; Trinity Coll., Dublin (BA); Queen's Univ. of Belfast (LLB). Called to NI Bar, 1956, to Bar of England and Wales, Gray's Inn, 1972, and to Bermuda Bar, 1986. Chm., NI Mental Health Review Tribunal, 1973–84. MP (OU) S Antrim, 1969–70. Chm., NI Mountain Trng Bd, 1974–82; Mem., Irish Sports Council, 1981–83. Governor, Methodist Coll., Belfast, 1978–. FRGS 1980. *Recreations:* playing at being a farmer, drinking Guinness. *Address:* 1 Crown Office Row, EC4Y 7HH. *T:* 071–583 3724; Sandhill House, Derrygonnelly, Co. Fermanagh. *T:* Derrygonnelly (036564) 612. *Club:* Kildare Street and University (Dublin).

FERGUSON DAVIE, Sir Antony (Francis), 6th Bt *cr* 1847, of Creedy, Devonshire; *b* 23 March 1952; *s* of Rev. Sir (Arthur) Patrick Ferguson Davie, 5th Bt, TD, and of Iris Dawn, *d* of Captain Michael Francis Buller; *S* father, 1988. *Educ:* Stanbridge Earls Sch.; London University. BA (History). Ordinand and writer. *Recreations:* art, travel. *Heir:* *cousin* John Ferguson Davie [*b* 1 May 1906; *m* 1942, Joan Zoe (*d* 1987), *d* of late Raymond Hoole; two *s*]. *Address:* c/o National Westminster Bank, North Audley Street, W1. *Club:* Naval and Military.

FERGUSON-SMITH, Prof. Malcolm Andrew, FRS 1983; FRSE 1978; Professor of Pathology and Professorial Fellow, Peterhouse, University of Cambridge, since 1987; Director, East Anglian Regional Clinical Genetics Service, since 1987; *b* 5 Sept. 1931; *s* of John Ferguson-Smith, MA, MD, FRCP and Ethel May (*née* Thorne); *m* 1960, Marie Eva Gzowska; one *s* three *d*. *Educ:* Stowe Sch.; Univ. of Glasgow (MB ChB 1955). MRCPath 1966, FRCPath 1978; MRCPGlas 1972, FRCPGlas 1974. Registrar in Lab. Medicine, Dept of Pathology, Western Infirmary, Glasgow, 1958–59; Fellow in Medicine and Instructor, Johns Hopkins Univ. Sch. of Medicine, 1959–61; Lectr, Sen. Lectr and Reader in Med. Genetics, Univ. of Glasgow, 1961–73, Prof. of Med. Genetics, 1973–87; Hon. Consultant: in Med. Paediatrics, Royal Hosp. for Sick Children, Glasgow, 1966–73; in Clin. Genetics, Yorkhill and Associated Hosps, 1973–87; Dir, W of Scotland Med. Genetics Service, 1973–87. Pres., Clinical Genetics Soc., 1979–81. Bronze Medal, Univ. of Helsinki, 1968; Makdougall-Brisbane Prize, RSE, 1988. Mem., Johns Hopkins Univ. Soc. of Scholars, 1983; Foreign Mem., Polish Acad. of Scis, 1988. Editor, Prenatal Diagnosis, 1980–. *Publications:* (ed) Early Prenatal Diagnosis, 1983; (jtly) Essential Medical Genetics, 1984, 2nd edn 1987; papers on cytogenetics, gene mapping, human genetics and prenatal diagnosis in med. jls. *Recreations:* swimming, sailing, fishing. *Address:* Department of Pathology, University of Cambridge, Tennis Court Road, Cambridge CB2 1QP. *T:* Cambridge (0223) 333691.

FERGUSSON, Adam (Dugdale); consultant on European affairs, since 1989; *b* 10 July 1932; *yr s* of Sir James Fergusson of Kilkerran, 8th Bt, LLD, FRSE, and of Frances Dugdale; *m* 1965, Penelope, *e d* of Peter Hughes, Furneaux Pelham Hall; two *s* two *d*. *Educ:* Eton; Trinity Coll., Cambridge (BA History, 1955). Glasgow Herald, 1956–61: Leader-writer, 1957–58; Diplomatic Corresp., 1959–61; Statist, 1961–67: Foreign Editor, 1964–67; Feature-writer for The Times on political, economic and environmental matters, 1967–77. Special Advr on European Affairs, FCO, 1985–89. European Parliament: Member (C) West Strathclyde, 1979–84; Spokesman on Political Affairs for European Democratic Gp, 1979–82; Vice-Chm., Political Affairs Cttee, 1982–84; Mem., Jt Cttee of ACP/EEC Consultative Assembly, 1979–84; contested (C) London Central, European elecn, 1984. Vice-Pres., Pan-European Union, 1981–; Mem., Scotland Says No Referendum Campaign Cttee, 1978–79. *Publications:* Roman Go Home, 1969; The Lost Embassy, 1972; The Sack of Bath, 1973; When Money Dies, 1975; various pamphlets; articles in national and internat. jls and magazines. *Address:* 15 Warwick Gardens, W14 8PH. *T:* 071–603 7900.

FERGUSSON of Kilkerran, Sir Charles, 9th Bt *cr* 1703; *b* 10 May 1931; *s* of Sir James Fergusson of Kilkerran, 8th Bt, and Frances (*d* 1988), *d* of Edgar Dugdale; *S* father, 1973; *m* 1961, Hon. Amanda Mary Noel-Paton, *d* of Lord Ferrier, *qv*; two *s*. *Educ:* Eton; Edinburgh and East of Scotland Coll. of Agriculture. *Heir:* *s* Captain Adam Fergusson, AAC, *b* 29 Dec. 1962.

FERGUSSON, Sir Ewen Alastair John, KCMG 1987; HM Diplomatic Service; Ambassador to France, since 1987; *b* 28 Oct. 1932; *er s* of late Sir Ewen MacGregor Field Fergusson; *m* 1959, Sara Carolyn, *d* of late Brig-Gen. Lord Esmé Gordon Lennox, KCVO, CMG, DSO and *widow* of Sir William Andrew Montgomery-Cuninghame, 11th Bt; one *s* two *d*. *Educ:* Rugby; Oriel Coll., Oxford (MA; Hon. Fellow, 1988). Played Rugby Football for Oxford Univ., 1952 and 1953, and for Scotland, 1954. 2nd Lieut, 60th Rifles (KRRC), 1954–56. Joined Foreign (now Diplomatic) Service, 1956; Asst Private Sec. to Minister of Defence, 1957–59; British Embassy, Addis Ababa, 1960; FO, 1963; British Trade Development Office, New York, 1967; Counsellor and Head of Chancery, Office of UK Permanent Rep. to European Communities, 1972–75; Private Sec. to Foreign and Commonwealth Sec., 1975–78; Asst Under Sec. of State, FCO, 1978–82; Ambassador to S Africa, 1982–84; Dep. Under-Sec. of State (Middle East and Africa), FCO, 1984–87. Governor, Rugby Sch., 1985–. *Address:* c/o Foreign and Commonwealth Office, SW1. *Clubs:* Royal Automobile; Jockey (Paris).

FERGUSSON, Sir James H. H. C.; *see* Colyer-Fergusson.

FERMAN, James Alan; Secretary, British Board of Film Classification (formerly British Board of Film Censors), since 1975; *b* New York, 11 April 1930; *m* 1956, Monica Sophie (*née* Robinson); one *s* one *d*. *Educ:* Great Neck High Sch., NY; Cornell Univ. (BA Hons); King's Coll., Cambridge (MA Hons). Actor and univ. lectr until 1957; author/adaptor, Zuleika (musical comedy), Saville Theatre, 1957; Television Director: ABC, 1957–59; ATV, 1959–65; freelance, chiefly at BBC, 1965–75; drama series incl.: The Planemakers, Probation Officer, Emergency Ward 10; plays incl.: The Pistol, Who's A Good Boy Then? I Am, Kafka's Amerika, Death of a Private, Before the Party, Chariot of Fire, When the Bough Breaks, Terrible Jim Fitch; documentaries incl.: Decisions of Our Time, The Four Freedoms, CURE; stage productions incl.: Three Sisters, Mooney and His Caravans, This Space Is Mine; wrote and dir., Drugs and Schoolchildren, film series for teachers and social workers. Lectr in Community Studies, Polytechnic of Central London, 1973–76 (Dir and Chm., Community Mental Health Prog. in assoc. with MIND); Educn Adviser, Standing Conf. on Drug Abuse; Vice-Pres., Assoc. for Prevention of Addiction. *Recreations:* reading and hill-walking. *Address:* The Fairhazel Co-operative, Canfield

Gardens, NW6; British Board of Film Classification, 3 Soho Square, W1. *T:* 071–437 2677.

FERMOR, Patrick Michael Leigh, DSO 1944; OBE (mil.) 1943; author; Hon. Citizen of Herakleion, Crete, 1947, Gytheion, Laconia, 1966, and of Kardamyli, Messenia, 1967; *b* 11 Feb. 1915; *s* of late Sir Lewis Leigh Fermor, OBE, FRS, DSc, and Eileen, *d* of Charles Taaffe Ambler; *m* 1968, Hon. Joan Eyres-Monsell, *d* of 1st Viscount Monsell, PC, GBE. *Educ:* King's Sch., Canterbury. After travelling for four years in Central Europe, Balkans and Greece, enlisted in Irish Guards, 1939; "I" Corps, 1940; Lieut, British Mil. Mission, Greece, 1940; Liaison Officer, Greek GHQ, Albania; campaigns of Greece and Crete; 2 years in German occupied Crete with Cretan Resistance, commanded some minor guerilla operations; team-commander in Special Allied Airborne Reconnaissance Force, N Germany, 1945. Dep.-Dir British Institute, Athens, till middle 1946; travelled in Caribbean and Central American republics, 1947–48. Corres. Mem., Athens Acad., 1980. Municipality of Athens Gold Medal of Honour, 1988. *Publications:* The Traveller's Tree (Heinemann Foundation Prize for Literature, 1950, and Kemsley Prize, 1951); trans. Colette, Chance Acquaintances, 1952; A Time to Keep Silence, 1953; The Violins of Saint Jacques, 1953; Mani, 1958 (Duff Cooper Meml Prize; Book Society's Choice); (trans.) The Cretan Runner (George Psychoundakis), 1955; Roumeli, 1966; A Time of Gifts, 1977 (W. H. Smith & Son Literary Award, 1978); Between the Woods and the Water, 1986 (Thomas Cook Travel Book Award, 1986); Internat. PEN/Time Life Silver Pen Award, 1986). *Recreation:* travel. *Address:* c/o Messrs John Murray, 50 Albemarle Street, W1. *Clubs:* White's, Travellers', Pratt's, Beefsteak, Special Forces, Puffins.

FERMOR-HESKETH, family name of **Baron Hesketh.**

FERMOY, 6th Baron *cr* 1856; **Patrick Maurice Burke Roche;** *b* 11 Oct. 1967; *s* of 5th Baron Fermoy and of Lavinia Frances Elizabeth, *o d* of late Captain John Pitman; *S* father, 1984. *Educ:* Eton. Lieutenant, Blues and Royals, commissioned 1987. *Heir: b* Hon. (Edmund) Hugh Burke Roche, *b* 5 Feb. 1972. *Address:* Axford House, Axford, near Marlborough, Wilts.

FERMOY, Dowager Lady; Ruth Sylvia; (Rt. Hon. Ruth Lady Fermoy), DCVO 1979 (CVO 1966); OBE 1952; JP; Woman of the Bedchamber to Queen Elizabeth the Queen Mother since 1960 (an extra Woman of the Bedchamber, 1956–60); *b* 2 Oct. 1908; *y d* of late W. S. Gill, CB, Dalhebity, Bieldside, Aberdeenshire; *m* 1931, Edmund Maurice Burke Roche, 4th Baron Fermoy (*d* 1955); two *d* (one *s* decd). JP Norfolk, 1944. Freedom of King's Lynn, 1963. Hon. RAM 1968; FRCM 1983. Hon. MusD Univ. of East Anglia,1975.

FERNANDES, Most Rev. Angelo; *see* Delhi, Archbishop of, (RC).

FERNANDO, Most Rev. Nicholas Marcus; *see* Colombo, Archbishop of, (RC).

FERNEYHOUGH, Prof. Brian John Peter; composer; Professor of Music, University of California at San Diego, since 1987; *b* 16 Jan. 1943; *s* of Frederick George Ferneyhough and Emily May (*née* Hopwood); *m* 1st, 1967, Barbara Joan Pearson; 2nd, 1980, Elke Schaaf; 3rd, 1984, Carolyn Steinberg. *Educ:* Birmingham Sch. of Music; RAM; Sweelinck Conservatory, Amsterdam; Musikakademie, Basle. Mendelssohn Schol., 1968; Stipend: City of Basle, 1969; Heinrich-Strobel-Stiftung des Südwestfunks, 1972; Composition teacher, Musikhochschule, Freiburg, 1973–86 (Prof., 1978–86); Principal Composition Teacher, Royal Conservatory, The Hague, 1986–87. Guest Artist, Artists' Exchange Scheme, Deutsche Akad. Austauschdienst, Berlin, 1976–77; Lectr, Darmstadt Summer Sch., 1976– (Comp. course co-ordinator, 1984–); Guest Prof., Royal Conservatory, Stockholm, 1981–83, 1985; Vis. Prof., Univ. of Chicago, 1986; Master Class, Civica Scuola di Musica di Milano, 1985–. Mem., ISCM Internat. Jury, 1977, 1988. Prizes, Gaudeamus Internat. Comp., 1968, 1969; First Prize, ISCM Internat. Comp., Rome, 1974; Koussevitsky Prize, 1978. Chevalier, l'Ordre des Arts et des Lettres, 1984. *Compositions include:* Sonatas for String Quartet, 1967; Epicycle, for 20 solo strings, 1968; Firecycle Beta, for large orch. with 5 conductors, 1971; Time and Motion Studies I–III, 1974–76; Unity Capsule, for solo flute, 1975; Funérailles, for 7 strings and harp, 1978; La Terre est un Homme, for orch., 1979; 2nd String Quartet, 1980; Lemma-Icon-Epigram, for solo piano, 1981; Carceri d'Invenzione, for various ensembles, 1981–86; 3rd String Quartet, 1987; Kurze Schatten II, for guitar, 1988; La Chute d'Icare, for clarinet ensemble, 1988; Trittico per G. S., 1989; 4th String Quartet, 1990. *Publications:* collected writings in Quaderni della Civica Scuola di Musica, numero speciale (Italian lang.), 1984; articles in Contrechamps, Musiktexte, and Contemp. Music Rev. *Recreations:* reading, wine, cats. *Address:* 7150-D Calabria Court, San Diego, Calif 92122, USA. *T:* (619) 558 0276.

FERNIE, Prof. Eric Campbell, FSA 1973; Watson Gordon Professor of Fine Art, since 1984, and Dean, Faculty of Arts, since 1989, University of Edinburgh; *b* 9 June 1939; *s* of Sydney Robert and Catherine Reid Fernie; *m* 1964, Margaret Lorraine French; one *s* two *d.* *Educ:* Univ. of the Witwatersrand (BA Hons Fine Arts); Univ. of London (Academic Diploma). Lectr, Univ. of the Witwatersrand, 1963–67; University of East Anglia: Lectr and Sen. Lectr, 1967–84; Dean, Sch. of Fine Art and Music, 1977–81; Public Orator, 1982–84. Chm., Ancient Monuments Bd for Scotland, 1989–. *Publications:* An Introduction to the Communar and Pitcaner Rolls of Norwich Cathedral Priory (with A. B. Whittingham), 1973; The Architecture of the Anglo-Saxons, 1983; contribs to British and overseas architectural jls. *Address:* 17 Buckingham Terrace, Edinburgh EH4 3AD. *T:* 031–332 6858.

FERNS, Prof. Henry Stanley, MA, PhD Cantab; Professor of Political Science, University of Birmingham, 1961–81, now Emeritus Professor; *b* Calgary, Alberta, 16 Dec. 1913; *er s* of Stanley and Janie Ferns; *m* 1940, Helen Maureen, *d* of John and Eleanor Jack; three *s* one *d.* *Educ:* St John's High Sch., Winnipeg; Univ. of Manitoba; Trinity Coll., Cambridge. Research Scholar, Trinity Coll., Cambridge, 1938. Secretarial staff of Prime Minister of Canada, 1940; Asst Prof. of History and Government, Univ. of Manitoba, 1945; Fellow, Canadian Social Science Research Council, 1949; Lectr in Modern History and Government, Univ. of Birmingham, 1950; successively Sen. Lectr, Head of Dept and Prof. of Political Science, Dean, Faculty of Commerce and Social Sci., 1961–65. Pres., Bd of Dirs, Winnipeg Citizens' Cooperative Publishing Co. Ltd, 1946–48; Member of various Conciliation Boards appointed by Minister of Labour of Govt of Manitoba, 1947–49. Past Pres., British Assoc. of Canadian Studies. Hon. DLitt Buckingham, 1983. *Publications:* (with B. Ostry) The Age of McKenzie King: The Rise of the Leader, 1955 (Toronto and London), 2nd edn 1976; Britain and Argentina in the Nineteenth Century, 1960 (Oxford); Towards an Independent University, 1969; Argentina, 1969; The Argentine Republic 1516–1971, 1973; The Disease of Government, 1978; How Much Freedom for Universities?, 1982; Reading from Left to Right, 1983; (with K. W. Watkins) What Politics is About, 1985; articles in learned jls. *Recreations:* journalism, idling and pottering about. *Address:* 1 Kesteven Close, Sir Harry's Road, Birmingham B15 2UT. *T:* 021–440 1016.

FERNYHOUGH, Ven. Bernard; Archdeacon of Oakham, since 1977; Non-Residentiary Canon of Peterborough Cathedral, 1974–77 and since 1989 (Canon Residentiary, 1977–89); *b* 2 Sept. 1932; *s* of Edward and Edith Fernyhough; *m* 1957, Freda Malkin; one *s* one *d.* *Educ:* Wolstanton Grammar Sch.; Saint David's Coll., Lampeter (BA 1953). Precentor, Trinidad Cathedral, 1955–61; Rector of Stoke Bruerne with Grafton Regis and Alderton, 1961–67; Vicar of Ravensthorpe with East Haddon and Holdenby, 1967–77; Rural Dean: Preston, 1965–67; Haddon, 1968–70; Brixworth, 1971–77. *Address:* 18 Minster Precincts, Peterborough PE1 1XX. *T:* Peterborough (0733) 62762.

FERNYHOUGH, Rt. Hon. Ernest, PC 1970; *b* 24 Dec. 1908; British; *m* 1934, Ethel Edwards; one *s* one *d* (and one *s* decd). *Educ:* Wood Lane Council Sch. Full-time official, Union of Shop, Distributive and Allied Workers, 1936–47. MP (Lab) Jarrow, May 1947–1979; PPS to the Prime Minister, 1964–67; Jt Parly Under-Sec. of State, Dept of Employment and Productivity (formerly Min. of Labour), 1967–69. Mem., Council of Europe, 1970–73. Freeman, Borough of Jarrow, 1972. *Address:* 35 Edwards Road, Lache Park, Chester.

FEROZE, Sir Rustam Moolan, Kt 1983; MD; FRCS, FRCOG; retired; (first) President, European Association of Obstetrics and Gynaecology, 1985–88, now Hon. President; Consulting Obstetrician, Queen Charlotte's Maternity Hospital; Consulting Surgeon, Chelsea Hospital for Women; *b* 4 Aug. 1920; *s* of Dr J. Moolan-Feroze; *m* 1947, Margaret Dowsett; three *s* one *d.* *Educ:* Sutton Valence Sch.; King's Coll. and King's Coll. Hospital, London. MRCS, LRCP 1943; MB, BS 1946; MRCOG 1948; MD (Obst. & Dis. Wom.) London 1952; FRCS 1952; FRCOG 1962; Hon. FRCSI 1984; Hon. FRACOG 1985; Hon. FACOG 1986. Surg.-Lt, RNVR, 1943–46. King's Coll. Hosp., 1946; RMO, Samaritan Hosp. for Women, 1948; Sen. Registrar: Hosp. for Women, Soho Sq., and Middlesex Hosp., 1950–53; Chelsea Hosp. for Women, and Queen Charlotte's Maternity Hosp., 1953–54; Consultant Obstetrician and Gynaecologist, King's Coll. Hosp., 1952–85. Dean, Inst. of Obstetrics and Gynaecology, Univ. of London, 1954–67; Dir, Postgrad. Studies, RCOG, 1975–80; Pres., RCOG, 1981–84; Chm., Conf. of Royal Colls and Faculties, 1982–84. McIlrath Guest Prof., Royal Prince Alfred Hosp., Sydney, 1970. Lectures: Soc. of Obstetrics and Gynaecology of Canada, Winnipeg, 1978; Bartholomew Mosse, Dublin, 1982; Shirodkar Meml, Bombay, 1982; Charter Day, National Maternity Hosp., Dublin, 1984. Past Examiner: RCOG; Univs of London, Cambridge, Birmingham and Singapore. *Publications:* contributor: Integrated Obstetrics and Gynaecology for Postgraduates, 1981; Gynaecological Oncology, 1981; Bonney's Gynaecological Surgery, 1986; contribs to med. jls. *Recreations:* gardening, Bonsai, music, swimming. *Address:* 21 Kenwood Drive, Beckenham, Kent BR3 2QX. *Club:* Royal Automobile.

FERRALL, Sir Raymond (Alfred), Kt 1982; CBE 1969; retired; *b* 27 May 1906; *s* of Alfred C. Ferrall and Edith M. Ferrall; *m* 1931, Lorna, *d* of P. M. Findlay; two *s* two *d.* *Educ:* Launceston C of E Grammar Sch. Chairman: Launceston Bank for Savings, 1976–82; Tasmanian Colls of Advanced Educn, 1977–81; Launceston C of E Grammar Sch. Bd, 1956–73; Master Warden, Port of Launceston Authority, 1960–80. Captain, Tasmanian Cricket team, 1934; Vice Captain, Tasmanian Amateur Football team, 1932. Freeman, City of Launceston, 1981. Queen's Silver Jubilee Medal, 1977. *Publications:* Partly Personal, 1976; Idylls of the Mayor, 1978; Notable Tasmanians, 1980; The Age of Chiselry, 1981; The Story of the Port of Launceston, 1984; A Proud Heritage, 1985. *Recreations:* writing, print collecting, sailing. *Address:* Elphin House, 3 Olive Street, Launceston, Tas 7250, Australia. *T:* (003) 317122. *Clubs:* Launceston, Northern, Tamar Yacht (Tasmania).

FERRANTI, Sebastian Basil Joseph Ziani de; *see* de Ferranti.

FERRER, José Vicente; actor, director and producer, USA; *b* 8 Jan. 1912; *s* of Rafael Ferrer and Maria Providencia (*née* Cintrón); *m* 1st, 1938, Uta Hagen (marr. diss. 1948); one *d*; 2nd, 1948, Phyllis Hill (marr. diss. 1953); 3rd, 1953, Rosemary Clooney (marr. diss. 1967); three *s* two *d*; 4th, Stella Daphne Magee. *Educ:* Princeton Univ. AB (architecture), 1933. First appearance, The Periwinkle, Long Island show-boat, 1934; Asst Stage Manager Summer Theatre Stock Co., NY, 1935; first appearance NY stage, 1935; A Slight Case of Murder, 1935; Boy Meets Girl, 1935; Spring Dance, Brother Rat, 1936; In Clover, 1937; Dir Princeton Univ. Triangle Club's Fol-de-Rol, 1937; How To Get Tough About It, Missouri Legend, 1938; Mamba's Daughters, Key Largo, 1939; first star rôle, Lord Fancourt Babberley, Charley's Aunt, 1940; producer and dir, The Admiral Had A Wife, 1941; staged and co-starred, Vickie, 1942; Let's Face It, 1943; played Iago to Paul Robeson's Othello, Theatre Guild, 1943, 1944, 1945; producer and dir Strange Fruit, 1945; Play's The Thing, Richard III, Green Goddess, 1946; producer and star, Cyrano, 1946; Design For Living, Goodbye Again, 1947; Gen. dir to NY Theatre Co., City Centre, 1948; Silver Whistle, Theatre Guild, 1948; produced, directed and appeared in Twentieth Century, 1950; produced, directed, Stalag 17; The Fourposter, 1951; producer, dir and appeared in The Shrike, 1952; The Chase, 1952; staged My 3 Angels, 1953; dir and co-author, Oh Captain, 1958; producer, dir, and starred in, Edwin Booth, 1959; dir, The Andersonville Trial, 1960; starred in, The Girl Who Came to Supper, 1963–64; Man of La Mancha, 1966; dir, Cyrano de Bergerac, Chichester, 1975; British stage début as Messerschmann, Ring Round the Moon, Chichester, 1988; Born Again, Chichester, 1990; *films include:* Joan of Arc, 1947; Whirlpool, 1949; Crisis, Cyrano, 1950; Anything Can Happen, 1951; Moulin Rouge, 1952; Miss Sadie Thompson (Rain), Caine Mutiny, 1953; Deep in My Heart, 1955; Cockleshell Heroes, The Great Man, 1957; The High Cost of Loving, I Accuse, The Shrike (Dir, starred), 1958; Return to Peyton Place (Dir), 1962; State Fair (Dir), 1963; Nine Hours to Rama, Lawrence of Arabia, 1963; Cyrano et D'Artagnan, Train 349 From Berlin, The Greatest Story Ever Told, 1964; Ship of Fools, Enter Laughing, 1966; The Fifth Musketeer, 1976; Fedora, 1977; The Amazing Captain Nemo, 1979; The Big Brawl, 1980; A Midsummer Night's Sex Comedy, 1981; To Be Or Not To Be, Dune, 1983. Pres., Players Club, NY, 1983–. Mem., Acad. of Arts and Scis of Puerto Rico, 1974. Holds hon. degrees. Various awards for acting, etc, since 1944, include American Academy of Arts and Letters Gold Medal, 1949; Academy Award, 1950 (Best Actor, Cyrano); Theatre Hall of Fame, 1981; Ambassador of the Arts, State of Florida, 1983; Hispanic Heritage Festival Don Quixote Award, Florida, 1984; National Medal of Arts, 1985; Florida Prize, New York Times, 1990. *Recreations:* tennis, golf. *Address:* PO Box 616, Miami, Florida 33133, USA.

FERRERS, 13th Earl *cr* 1711; **Robert Washington Shirley;** Viscount Tamworth 1711; Bt 1611; PC 1982; DL; High Steward of Norwich Cathedral, since 1979; Minister of State, Home Office, since 1988; Deputy Leader of the House of Lords, since 1988; *b* 8 June 1929; *o s* of 12th Earl Ferrers and Hermione Morley (*d* 1969); *S* father, 1954; *m* 1951, Annabel Mary, *d* of late Brig. W. G. Carr, CVO, DSO; two *s* three *d.* *Educ:* Winchester Coll. (Fellow, 1988); Magdalene Coll., Cambridge. MA (Agric.). Lieut Coldstream Guards, 1949 (as National Service). A Lord-in-waiting, 1962–64, 1971–74; Parly Sec., MAFF, 1974; Jt Dep. Leader of the Opposition, House of Lords, 1976–79; Dep. Leader of House of Lords, 1979–83; Minister of State, MAFF, 1979–83. Mem., Armitage Cttee on political activities of civil servants, 1976–. Chm., TSB of Eastern England, 1977–79; Mem., TSB Central Bd, 1977–79; Director: Central TSB, 1978–79; TSB Trustcard Ltd, 1978–79; Norwich Union Insurance Group, 1975–79 and 1983–88. Chairman: RCHM(Eng.), 1984–88; British Agricl Export Council, 1984–88; Mem. Council, Food From Britain, 1984–88; Director: Economic Forestry Gp, 1985–88; Chatham Historic Dockyard Trust, 1984–88. Mem. Council, Hurstpierpoint Coll., 1959–68. DL Norfolk,

1983. *Heir*: *s* Viscount Tamworth, *qv*. *Address*: Ditchingham Hall, Bungay, Suffolk NR35 2LE. *Club*: Beefsteak.

FERRIE, Maj.-Gen. Alexander Martin, CBE 1971; RAMC retired; *b* 30 Nov. 1923; *s* of late Archibald Ferrie and Elizabeth Ferrie (*née* Martin). *Educ*: Glasgow Academy; Univ. of Glasgow (MB ChB). MFCM 1974. Commissioned RAMC, 1947; Commanding Officer, Queen Alexandra Military Hospital, Millbank, 1973–75; Director of Medical Supply, Min. of Defence, 1975–77; Dep. Dir of Medical Services, UKLF, and Inspector of Trng, TA Medical Services, 1977–81; QHS 1978–83; DMS, UKLF, 1981–82; Comdt, RAMC Trng Gp, and PMO, UKLF, 1982–83. *Recreation*: gardening. *Address*: c/o Barclays Bank, 47 Church Road, Hove, E Sussex BN3 2BQ.

FERRIER, Baron *cr* 1958, of Culter (Life Peer); **Victor Ferrier Noel-Paton,** ED; DL; *b* Edinburgh, 1900; *s* of late F. Noel-Paton, Dir-Gen. of Commercial Intelligence to the Govt of India; *m* 1932, Joane Mary (*d* 1984), *d* of late Sir Gilbert Wiles, KCIE, CSI; one *s* three *d*. *Educ*: Cargilfield and The Edinburgh Academy. Served RE, 1918–19, Indian Auxiliary Force (Major, ED), 1920–46, and IARO. Commercial and Industrial Management, Bombay, 1920–51; one time Dir and Chm. of a number of Cos in India and UK; Pres., Bombay Chamber of Commerce. Mem., Legislative Council, Bombay, 1936 and Hon. ADC to Governor of Bombay; Past Chairman: Federation of Electricity Undertakings of India; Indian Roads and Transport Develt Assoc., Bombay. A Dep. Speaker and Chm. of Cttees, House of Lords, 1970–73. Mem. of Royal Company of Archers. DL, Lanarks, 1960. *Recreations*: field sports. *Address*: Kilkerran, Maybole, Ayrshire KA19 7SJ. *T*: Crosshill (06554) 515. *Clubs*: Cavalry and Guards, Beefsteak; New (Edinburgh).

See also Sir Charles Fergusson, Bt, Hon. F. R. Noel-Paton.

FERRIER, Prof. Robert Patton, FRSE 1977; Professor of Natural Philosophy, University of Glasgow, since 1973; *b* 4 Jan. 1934; *s* of William McFarlane Ferrier and Gwendoline Melita Edwards; *m* 1961, Valerie Jane Duncan; two *s* one *d*. *Educ*: Glebelands Sch. and Morgan Academy, Dundee; Univ. of St Andrews (BSc, PhD). MA Cantab, FInstP. Scientific Officer, AERE Harwell, 1959–61; Res. Assoc., MIT, 1961–62; Sen. Asst in Res., Cavendish Lab., Cambridge, 1962–66; Fellow of Fitzwilliam Coll., Cambridge, 1965–73; Asst Dir of Res., Cavendish Lab. 1966–71; Lectr in Physics, Univ. of Cambridge, 1971–73; Guest Scientist, IBM Res. Labs San José, Calif, 1972–73. Chm., SERC Semiconductor and Surface Physics Sub-Cttee, 1979–. *Publications*: numerous papers in Phil. Mag., Jl Appl. Physics, Jl Physics, etc. *Recreations*: do-it-yourself, tennis, gardening, reading novels. *Address*: Glencoe, 31 Thorn Road, Bearsden, Glasgow G61 4BS. *T*: 041–942 3592, (office) 041–330 5388.

FERRIS, *see* Grant-Ferris, family name of Baron Harvington.

FERRIS, Hon. Sir Francis (Mursell), Kt 1990; TD 1965; **Hon. Mr Justice Ferris;** Judge of the High Court of Justice, Chancery Division, since 1990; *b* 19 Aug. 1932; *s* of Francis William Ferris and Elsie Lilian May Ferris (*née* Mursell); *m* 1957, Sheila Elizabeth Hester Falloon Bedford; three *s* one *d*. *Educ*: Bryanston Sch.; Oriel Coll., Oxford. BA (Modern History) 1955, MA 1979. Served RA, 1951–52; 299 Field Regt (RBY QOOH and Berks) RA, TA 1952–67, Major 1964. Called to the Bar, Lincoln's Inn, 1956, Bencher, 1987; practice at Chancery Bar, 1958–90; Standing Counsel to Dir Gen. of Fair Trading, 1966–80; QC 1980; a Recorder, 1989–90. Member: Bar Council, 1966–70; Senate of Inns of Court and the Bar, 1979–82. *Recreation*: gardening. *Address*: Royal Courts of Justice, Strand, WC2A 2LL. *Club*: Marlow Rowing.

FERRIS, Paul Frederick; author and journalist; *b* 15 Feb. 1929; *o c* of late Frederick Morgan Ferris and of Olga Ferris; *m* 1953, Gloria Moreton; one *s* one *d*. *Educ*: Swansea Gram. Sch. Staff of South Wales Evening Post, 1949–52; Womans Own, 1953; Observer Foreign News Service, 1953–54. *Publications*: *novels*: A Changed Man, 1958; Then We Fall, 1960; A Family Affair, 1963; The Destroyer, 1965; The Dam, 1967; Very Personal Problems, 1973; The Cure, 1974; The Detective, 1976; Talk to Me About England, 1979; A Distant Country, 1983; Children of Dust, 1988; *non-fiction*: The City, 1960; The Church of England, 1962; The Doctors, 1965; The Nameless: abortion in Britain today, 1966; Men and Money: financial Europe today, 1968; The House of Northcliffe, 1971; The New Militants, 1972; Dylan Thomas, 1977; Richard Burton, 1981; Gentlemen of Fortune: the world's investment bankers, 1984; (ed) The Collected Letters of Dylan Thomas, 1986; Sir Huge: the life of Huw Wheldon, 1990; *television plays*: The Revivalist, 1975; Dylan, 1978; Nye, 1982; The Extremist, 1984; The Fasting Girl, 1984; contribs to The Observer. *Address*: c/o Curtis Brown Ltd, 162–168 Regent Street, W1R 5TB. *T*: 071–872 0331.

FERRIS, Rt. Rev. Ronald Curry; *see* Yukon, Bishop of.

FERRY, Alexander, MBE 1977; General Secretary, Confederation of Shipbuilding and Engineering Unions, since 1978; Member of Board, Harland and Wolff plc, Shipbuilders and Engineers, Belfast, since 1984; *b* 14 Feb. 1931; *s* of Alexander and Susan Ferry; *m* 1958, Mary O'Kane McAlaney; one *s* two *d* (and one *s* decd). *Educ*: St Patrick's High, Senior Secondary, Dunbartonshire. Apprentice Engineer, 1947–52; served Royal Air Force, 1952–54; Engineer, 1954–64; full-time officer, AUEW, 1964–78. Part-time Mem., Monopolies and Mergers Commn, 1986–; Mem., Employment Appeal Tribunal, 1991–. *Publication*: The Red Paper on Scotland (co-author), 1975. *Recreation*: golf. *Address*: 190 Brampton Road, Bexley Heath, Kent DA2 4SY. *T*: 081–303 5338.

FERSHT, Prof. Alan Roy, MA, PhD; FRS 1983; Herchel Smith Professor of Organic Chemistry, and Fellow, Gonville and Caius College, Cambridge since 1988; Director: Cambridge Interdisciplinary Research Centre in Protein Engineering, since 1989; MRC Unit for Protein Function and Design, since 1989; *b* 21 April 1943; *s* of Philip and Betty Fersht; *m* 1966, Marilyn Persell; one *s* one *d*. *Educ*: Sir George Monoux Grammar Sch.; Gonville and Caius Coll., Cambridge (MA, PhD). Res. Fellow, Brandeis Univ., 1968; Scientific Staff, MRC Lab. of Molecular Biology, Cambridge, 1969–77; Fellow, Jesus Coll., Cambridge, 1969–72; Eleanor Roosevelt Fellow, Stanford Univ., 1978; Wolfson Res. Prof. of Royal Society, Dept of Chemistry, Imperial Coll. of Science and Technology, 1978–89. Lectures: Smith Kline & French, Berkeley, 1984; Edsall, Harvard, 1984; B. R. Baker, Univ. of California at Santa Barbara, 1986; Frank Mathers, Univ. of Indiana, 1986; Cornell Biotechnol Program, 1987; Ferdinand Springer, FEBS, 1988–89; Calvin, Berkeley, 1990; Walker, Edinburgh, 1990. Mem., EMBO, 1980–. Hon. For. Mem., Amer. Acad. of Arts and Sci., 1988; Mem., Academia Europaea, 1989. Essex County Jun. Chess Champion, 1961; Pres., Cambridge Univ. Chess Club, 1964 (Half Blue, 1965). FEBS Anniversary Prize, 1980; Novo Biotechnology Prize, 1986; Charmian Medal, RSC, 1986. *Publications*: Enzyme Structure and Mechanism, 1977, 2nd edn 1984; papers in scientific jls. *Recreations*: chess, horology. *Address*: University Chemical Laboratory, Lensfield Road, Cambridge CB2 1EW. *T*: Cambridge (0223) 336341, *Fax*: Cambridge (0223) 336445; 2 Barrow Close, Cambridge CB2 1AT.

FESSEY, Mereth Cecil, CB 1977; Director, Business Statistics Office, 1969–77, retired; *b* Windsor, Berks, 19 May 1917; *s* of late Morton Fessey and Ethel Fessey (*née* Blake), Bristol; *m* 1945, Grace Lilian, *d* of late William Bray, Earlsfield, London; one *s* two *d*. *Educ*: Westminster City Sch.; LSE, Univ. of London. London Transport, 1934; Army, 1940; Min. of Transport, 1947; Board of Trade, 1948; Statistician, 1956; Chief Statistician, 1965. Statistical Adviser to Syrian and Mexican Govts, 1979; Consultant, Statistical Office, Eur. Communities, 1990–. Chm. of Council, Inst. of Statisticians, 1970–73; Vice Pres. and Mem., Council, Royal Statistical Soc., 1974–78; Chm., Cttee of Librarians and Statisticians, LA/Royal Stat. Soc., 1978–. Hon. FLA 1984. *Publications*: articles and papers in: Economic Trends; Statistical News; Jl of Royal Statistical Soc.; The Statistician; Annales de Sciences Economiques Appliquées, Louvain; etc. *Recreations*: chess, walking. *Address*: Undy House, Undy, Gwent NP6 3BX. *T*: Magor (0633) 880478.

FETHERSTON-DILKE, Capt. Charles Beaumont; RN retired; Vice Lord-Lieutenant, Warwickshire, since 1990; *b* 4 April 1921; *s* of late Dr Beaumont Albany Fetherston-Dilke, MBE and Phoebe Stella (*née* Bedford); *m* 1943, Pauline Stanley-Williams; one *s* one *d*. *Educ*: RNC, Dartmouth. Entered RN, 1935; served throughout War of 1939–45 and Korean War, 1952–54 (underwater warfare specialist); Comdr 1955; Danish Naval Staff, 1955–58; staff of C-in-C S Atlantic and S America Station, 1960–61; Captain 1961; Naval Dep. to UK Nat. Mil. Rep., SHAPE, 1962–64; comd HMS St Vincent, 1964–66; Defence Policy Staff, MOD, 1966–68; retired 1968. Warwickshire: JP 1969–91; CC, 1970–81 (Chm., 1978–80); Chm., CLA, 1984–87; High Sheriff 1974; DL 1974. SBStJ 1986. *Publication*: A Short History of Maxstoke Castle, 1985. *Recreations*: country pursuits. *Address*: Keeper's Cottage, Maxstoke, Coleshill, Birmingham B46 2QA. *T*: Coleshill (0675) 465100. *Club*: Army and Navy.

See also M. S. Fetherston-Dilke.

FETHERSTON-DILKE, Mary Stella, CBE 1968; RRC 1966; Organiser, Citizens' Advice Bureau, 1971–83, retired; *b* 21 Sept. 1918; *d* of late B. A. Fetherston-Dilke, MBE. *Educ*: Kingsley Sch., Leamington Spa; St George's Hospital, London (SRN). Joined QARNNS, 1942; Matron-in-Chief, QARNNS, 1966–70, retired. OStJ 1966. *Recreation*: antiques. *Address*: 12 Clareville Court, Clareville Grove, SW7 5AT.

FETTIPLACE, Dr Robert, FRS 1990; Howe Senior Research Fellow, Royal Society, since 1979; *b* 24 Feb. 1946; *s* of George Robert Fettiplace and Maisie Fettiplace (*née* Rolson); *m* 1977, Merriel Cleone Kruse. *Educ*: Nottingham High Sch.; Sidney Sussex Coll., Cambridge (BA 1968; MA 1972; PhD 1974). Research Fellow: Sidney Sussex Coll., Cambridge, 1971–74, Stanford Univ., 1974–76; Elmore Res. Fellow, Cambridge, 1976–79. *Publications*: contribs to Jl Physiology and other learned jls. *Recreations*: bird watching, listening to music. *Address*: Physiological Laboratory, Downing Street, Cambridge CB2 3EG. *T*: Cambridge (0223) 333880.

FEUILLÈRE, Edwige; Officier de la Légion d'Honneur; Commandeur des Arts et Lettres; French actress; *b* 29 Oct.; *m* (divorced). *Educ*: Lycée de Dijon; Conservatoire National de Paris. *Plays include*: La Dame aux camélias, 1940–42, 1952–53; Sodome et Gomorrhe, 1943; L'Aigle a deux têtes, 1946; Partage de midi, Pour Lucrèce, La Parisienne, Phèdre, Lucy Crown, Constance, Rodogune, 1964; La Folle de Chaillot, 1965–66; Delicate Balance; Sweet Bird of Youth; Le bâteau pour Lipaïa, 1971; Leocadia, 1984–85; (with Jean Marais) La Maison du Lac, 1986. *Films include*: L'Idiot, 1946; L'Aigle a deux têtes, 1947; Olivia, 1950; Le Blé en herbe, 1952; En cas de malheur, 1958; La vie à deux, 1958; Les amours célèbres, 1961; Le crime ne paye pas, 1962; La chair de l'orchidée, 1975. *Television series*: Cinema, 1988. *Publications*: Les Feux de la Mémoire, 1977; Moi, La Clairon: biographie romancée de Mlle Clairon, 1984. *Address*: 19 rue Eugène Manuel, 75016 Paris, France.

FEVERSHAM, 6th Baron *cr* 1826; **Charles Antony Peter Duncombe;** free-lance journalist; *b* 3 Jan. 1945; *s* of late Col Antony John Duncombe-Anderson and G. G. V. McNalty; *S* (to barony of) *kinsman*, 3rd Earl of Feversham (the earldom having become extinct), 1963; *m* 1st, 1966, Shannon (*d* 1976), *d* of late Sir Thomas Foy, CSI, CIE; two *s* one *d*; 2nd, 1979, Pauline, *d* of John Aldridge, Newark, Notts; one *s*. *Educ*: Eton; Middle Temple. Chairman: Standing Conf. of Regional Arts Assocs, 1969–76; Trustees, Yorkshire Sculpture Park, 1981–; President: Yorkshire Arts Assoc., 1987– (Chm., 1969–80); Soc. of Yorkshiremen in London, 1974; The Arvon Foundn, 1976–86; Yorks and Cleveland Local Councils Assoc., 1977–; Nat. Assoc. of Local Councils, 1986–. Governor, Leeds Polytechnic, 1969–76. *Publications*: A Wolf in Tooth (novel), 1967; Great Yachts, 1970. *Heir*: *s* Hon. Jasper Orlando Slingsby Duncombe, *b* 14 March 1968. *Address*: Duncombe Park, Helmsley, York Y06 5EB.

FFITCH, George Norman; Managing Director, London Broadcasting Company and Independent Radio News, 1979–85; *b* 23 Jan. 1929; *s* of late Robert George Ffitch; *m* 1958, Pamela Mary Lyle (*d* 1990); one *s* one *d*. *Educ*: state schools and London Univ. Industrial Correspondent, Political Correspondent and Output Editor, Independent Television News, 1955–62; interviewer and presenter, ITV, 1962–67; Political Editor and an Asst Editor, The Economist, 1967–74; Associate Editor, Daily Express, 1974–76; columnist and broadcaster, 1976–79. *Recreation*: playing at playing golf. *Address*: 13 Charlwood Terrace, SW15 1NZ. *T*: 081–785 2460. *Club*: Reform.

FFOLKES, Sir Robert (Francis Alexander), 7th Bt *cr* 1774; OBE 1990; *b* 2 Dec. 1943; *o s* of Captain Sir (Edward John) Patrick (Boschetti) ffolkes, 6th Bt, and Geraldine (*d* 1978), *d* of late William Roffey, Writtle, Essex; *S* father, 1960. *Educ*: Stowe Sch.; Christ Church, Oxford. *Address*: Coast Guard House, Morston, Holt, Norfolk NR25 7BH. *Club*: Turf.

FFORDE, John Standish; Director: Halifax Building Society, since 1984; Credit Lyonnais Capital Markets (formerly CL-Alexanders Laing and Cruickshank Ltd), since 1987; Chairman, The Joint Mission Hospital Equipment Board Ltd, since 1985 (Director, since 1981); *b* 16 Nov. 1921; 4th *s* of late Francis Creswell Fforde, Raughlan, Lurgan, Co. Armagh, and Cicely Creswell; *m* 1951, Marya, *d* of late Joseph Retinger; three *s* one *d*. *Educ*: Rossall Sch.; Christ Church, Oxford (1st cl. Hons PPE). Served RAF, 1940–46. Prime Minister's Statistical Branch, 1951–53; Fellow, Nuffield Coll., Oxford, 1953–56; entered Bank of England, 1957; Dep. Chief, Central Banking Information Dept, 1959–64; Adviser to the Governors, 1964–66; Chief Cashier, 1966–70; Exec. Dir (Home Finance), 1970–82; Advr to the Governors, 1982–84; official historian, 1984–. Dir, Mercantile House Hldgs, 1984–87. *Publications*: The Federal Reserve System, 1945–49, 1953; An International Trade in Managerial Skills, 1957. *Recreations*: travel, walking.

FFOWCS WILLIAMS, Prof. John Eirwyn, FEng 1988; Rank Professor of Engineering (Acoustics), University of Cambridge, and Professorial Fellow, Emmanuel College, Cambridge, since 1972; *b* 25 May 1935; *m* 1959, Anne Beatrice Mason; two *s* one *d*. *Educ*: Friends Sch., Great Ayton; Derby Techn. Coll.; Univ. of Southampton. BSc; MA, ScD Cantab 1986; PhD Southampton. CEng, FRAeS, FInstP, FIMA, FInstAcoust, Fellow Acoustical Soc. of America, FAIAA. Engrg Apprentice, Rolls-Royce Ltd, 1951–55; Spitfire Mitchell Meml Schol. to Southampton Univ., 1955–60 (Pres., Students' Union, 1957–58); Aerodynamics Div., NPL, 1960–62; Bolt, Beranek & Newman Inc., 1962–64; Reader in Applied Maths, Imperial Coll. of Science and Technology, 1964–69; Rolls Royce Prof. of Theoretical Acoustics, Imperial Coll., 1969–72. Chairman: Concorde Noise Panel, 1965–75; Topexpress Ltd, 1979–89; Dir, VSEL Consortium plc, 1987–.

Chm., Noise Research Cttee, ARC, 1969–76. Corresp. Mem., Inst. of Noise Control Engrg, USA, 1986–. FRSA. Foreign Hon. Mem., Amer. Acad. Arts and Scis, 1989. Gov., Felsted Sch., 1980–. AIAA Aero-Acoustics Medal, 1977; Rayleigh Medal, Inst. of Acoustics, 1984; Silver Medal, Société Française d'Acoustique, 1989; Gold Medal, RAeS, 1990. *Publications:* (with A. P. Dowling) Sound and Sources of Sound, 1983; articles in Philosophical Trans Royal Soc., Jl of Fluid Mechanics, Jl IMA, Jl of Sound Vibration, Annual Reviews of Fluid Mechanics, Random Vibration, Financial Times; (jtly) film on Aerodynamic Sound. *Recreations:* friends and cigars. *Address:* 298 Hills Road, Cambridge CB2 2QG. *T:* Cambridge (0223) 248275. *Clubs:* Athenæum, Danish.

FFRANGCON-DAVIES, Dame Gwen, DBE 1991; actress; *b* 25 Jan. 1891; *d* of David Ffrangcon-Davies, the famous singer, and Annie Frances Rayner. *Educ:* South Hampstead High Sch.; abroad. First London success The Immortal Hour, 1922; created the part of Eve in Shaw's Back to Methuselah; principal successes, Tess, in Tess of the D'Urbervilles, Elizabeth Barrett, in The Barretts of Wimpole Street, Anne of Bohemia, in Richard of Bordeaux. Played Lady Macbeth to Macbeth of John Gielgud, Piccadilly, 1942. Appeared, in association with Marda Vanne, in leading parts in various plays in S Africa, 1943–46. Returned to England, 1949; played in Adventure Story, St James's, 1949; Stratford Festival, 1950, as Katherine in King Henry VIII; Portia in Julius Cæsar, Regan in King Lear (again Katherine, Old Vic. 1953); Madame Ranevsky in The Cherry Orchard, Lyric, 1954; Aunt Cleofe in Summertime, Apollo, 1955; Rose Padley in The Mulberry Bush, Royal Court, 1956; Agatha in The Family Reunion, Phoenix, 1956; Miss Madrigal in The Chalk Garden, Haymarket, 1957; Mrs Callifer in The Potting Shed, Globe Theatre, 1958; Mary Tyrone in Long Day's Journey into Night, Edinburgh Fest. and Globe, 1958; Queen Isolde in Ondine, Aldwych, 1961; Queen Mother in Becket, Aldwych, 1961; Hester Bellboys in A Penny for a Song, Aldwych, 1962; Beatrice in Season of Goodwill, Queen's, 1964; Amanda in The Glass Menagerie, Haymarket, 1965; Uncle Vanya, Royal Court, 1970; *Films:* The Burning, 1967; Leo the Last, 1969. Numerous radio and TV plays; Omnibus profile, BBC TV. *Recreation:* gardening. *Address:* c/o Larry Dalzell, Suite 12, 17 Broad Court, WC2B 5QN.

FFRENCH, family name of **Baron ffrench.**

FFRENCH, 8th Baron *cr* 1798; **Robuck John Peter Charles Mario ffrench;** Bt 1779; *b* 14 March 1956; *s* of 7th Baron ffrench and of Sonia Katherine, *d* of late Major Digby Cayley; *S* father, 1986; *m* 1987, Dörthe Marie-Louise, *d* of Captain Wilhelm Schauer. *Educ:* Blackrock, Co. Dublin; Ampleforth College, Yorks. *Heir: uncle* John Charles Mary Joseph Francis ffrench [*b* 5 Oct. 1928; *m* 1963, Sara-Primm, *d* of James A. Turner; three *d*]. *Address:* Castle ffrench, Ballinasloe, Co. Galway, Ireland. *T:* Roscommon 4226.

FFYTCHE, Timothy John, FRCS; Surgeon–Oculist to HM Household, since 1980; Ophthalmic Surgeon to St Thomas's Hospital, since 1973; Consultant Ophthalmologist, Moorfields Eye Hospital, since 1975; Hospital of Tropical Diseases, since 1988; Consultant Ophthalmic Surgeon to King Edward VIIth Hospital for Officers, since 1980; *b* 11 Sept. 1936; *s* of late Louis ffytche and of Margaret (*née* Law); *m* 1961, Bärbl, *d* of late Günther Fischer; two *s*. *Educ:* Lancing Coll.; St George's Hosp., London. MB, BS; DO 1961; FRCS 1968. Registrar, Moorfields Eye Hosp., 1966–69; Wellcome Lectr, Hammersmith Hosp., 1969–70; Sen. Registrar, Middlesex Hosp., 1970–73. Sec., OSUK, 1980–82. Mem., Medical Adv. Bd, LEPRA, 1982–; Vice-Pres., Ophthalmol Sect., RSocMed, 1985–; UK rep. to Internat. Fedn of Ophthalmic Socs, 1985–; Mem., Adv. Cttee to Internat. Council of Ophthalmology, 1985–. Clayton Meml Lectr, LEPRA, 1984. Editorial Committee: Ophthalmic Literature, 1968–; Transactions of OSUK, 1984–89, Eye, 1989–. *Publications:* articles on retinal diagnosis and therapy, retinal photography and the ocular complications of leprosy, in The Lancet, British Jl of Ophthalmol., Trans OSUK, Proc. Roy. Soc. Med., Leprosy Review and other specialist jls. *Recreations:* travel, cricket, occasional fishing. *Address:* 149 Harley Street, W1N 2DE; (home) 1 Wellington Square, SW3 4NJ.

FICKLING, Benjamin William, CBE 1973; FRCS, FDS RCS; Honorary Consultant Dental Surgeon, since 1974, formerly Dental Surgeon: St George's Hospital, SW1, 1936–74; Royal Dental Hospital of London, 1935–74; Mount Vernon Centre for Plastic and Jaw Surgery (formerly Hill End), 1941–74; *b* 14 July 1909; *s* of Robert Marshall Fickling, LDS RCS, and Florence (*née* Newson); *m* 1943, Shirley Dona, *er d* of Albert Latimer Walker, FRCS; two *s* one *d*. *Educ:* Framlingham; St George's Hosp. Royal Dental Hospital. William Brown Senior Exhibition, St George's Hosp., 1929; LDS RCS, 1932; MRCS, LRCP, 1934; FRCS 1938; FDS, RCS 1947, MGDS RCS 1979. Lectures: Charles Tomes, RCS, 1956; Everett Magnus, Melbourne, 1971; Webb-Johnson, RCS, 1978. Examiner (Chm.), Membership in Gen. Dental Surgery, 1979–83; formerly Examiner: in Dental Surgery, RCS; Univ. of London and Univ. of Edinburgh. Dean of Faculty of Dental Surgery, 1968–71, and Mem. Council, Royal College of Surgeons, 1968–71 (Vice-Dean, 1965; Colyer Gold Medal, 1979); Fellow Royal Society of Medicine (Pres. Odontological Section, 1964–65); Pres., British Assoc. of Oral Surgeons, 1967–68; Mem. GDC, 1971–74. Director: Med. Sickness Annuity and Life Assurance Soc. Ltd, 1967–86; Permanent Insurance Co. Ltd, 1974–86; Medical Sickness Finance Corp. Ltd, 1977–86. Civilian Dental Consultant to RN, 1954–76. *Publications:* (joint) Injuries of the Jaws and Face, 1940; (joint) Chapter on Faciomaxillary Injuries and Deformities in British Surgical Practice, 1951. *Address:* 29 Maxwell Road, Northwood, Mddx HA6 2YG. *T:* Northwood (09274) 22035. *Club:* Ski Club of Great Britain.

FIDDES, James Raffan, QC (Scot.) 1965; Sheriff of South Strathclyde, Dumfries and Galloway at Hamilton, 1977–88; *b* 1 Feb. 1919; *er s* of late Sir James Raffan Fiddes, CBE; *m* 1st, 1954, Edith Margaret (*d* 1979), 2nd *d* of late Charles E. Lippe, KC; 2nd, 1985, Jiřina (marr. diss. 1991), *d* of late Jan Kuchař, Brno, Czechoslovakia. *Educ:* Aberdeen Gram. Sch.; Glasgow Univ. (MA, 1942; LLB 1948); Balliol Coll., Oxford, (BA 1944). Advocate, 1948. *Address:* 23 South Learmonth Gardens, Edinburgh EH4 1EZ. *T:* 031–332 1431. *Club:* Scottish Arts (Edinburgh).

FIDDICK, Peter Ronald; journalist and broadcaster; Editor, The Listener, 1989–91; *b* 21 Oct. 1938; *s* of Wing-Comdr Ronald Fiddick and Phyllis (*née* Wherry); *m* 1966, Jane Mary Hodlin; one *s* one *d*. *Educ:* Reading Sch.; Magdalen Coll., Oxford (BA English Lang. and Lit.). Journalist, Liverpool Daily Post, 1962–65; Leader writer, Westminster Press, 1965–66; Asst Editor, Nova, 1968; The Guardian: reporter, 1966–67 and 1969; Asst Features Editor, 1970–75; Television Columnist, 1971–84; Media Editor, 1984–88. Wrote and presented television series: Looking at Television, 1975–76; The Television Programme, 1979–80; Soviet Television—Fact and Fiction, 1985. *Publication:* (with B. Smithies) Enoch Powell on Immigration, 1969. *Recreations:* music, food, Saturdays.

FIDLER, Jan; Ambassador of the Czechoslovak Socialist Republic to the Court of St James's, 1986–90; *b* 14 May 1927; *s* of Marie and Josef Fidler; *m* 1950, Alena (*née* Oulehlová); two *s*. *Educ:* Higher School of Economics. Manager in woollen industry, 1950–60; Min. of Foreign Affairs, 1960–63; Second Sec., Stockholm, 1963–67; Min. of Foreign Affairs, 1967–70; Counsellor, Helsinki, 1970–77; Head, Office of First Dep. Minister, 1977–80; Minister Counsellor, Warsaw, 1980–83; Chief of Diplomatic Protocol, Min. of Foreign Affairs, 1984–86. Holder of State distinctions. *Address:* Sněženkova 3095, Prague 10, Czechoslovakia. *T:* 753440.

FIDLER-SIMPSON, John Cody; *see* Simpson.

FIELD, Brig. Anne, CB 1980; Director, London Regional Board, Lloyds Bank Plc, since 1982 (Deputy Chairman, 1990–91); Deputy Controller Commandant, Women's Royal Army Corps since 1984 (Director, 1977–82); *b* 4 April 1926; *d* of Captain Harold Derwent and Annie Helena Hodgson. *Educ:* Keswick Sch.; St George's, Harpenden; London Sch. of Economics. Joined ATS, 1947; commissioned: ATS, 1948; WRAC, 1949; Lt-Col, 1968; Col, 1971. Hon. ADC to the Queen, 1977–82. Chm., London W Regl Bd, Lloyds Bank, 1985–90. Freeman, City of London, 1981; Liveryman, Spectacle Makers' Co., 1990. CBIM (FBIM 1978). *Address:* c/o Lloyds Bank Plc, 7 Pall Mall, SW1Y 5NA. *Club:* Lansdowne.

FIELD, Arnold, OBE 1965; aerospace consultant/technical journalist; Joint Field Commander, National Air Traffic Services, 1974–77; *b* 19 May 1917; *m* 1943, Kathleen Dulcie Bennett; one *s* one *d*. *Educ:* Sutton Coldfield Royal Sch.; Birmingham Technical Coll. RAF, 1940–46 (Sqdn Ldr). Civil Air Traffic Control Officer, 1946; Centre Supt, Scottish Air Traffic Control Centre, 1954; Centre Supt, London Air Traffic Control Centre, 1957; Divisional Air Traffic Control Officer, Southern Div., 1963; Dir, Civil Air Traffic Ops, 1969. Master, Guild of Air Traffic Control Officers, 1958; Pres., Internat. Fedn of Air Traffic Control Officers, 1970; Mem., Aviation/Space Writers' Assoc., 1986–. Gp Editor, Internat. Defence Newsletter, Law Enforcement Industry Digest, 1988–. *Publications:* The Control of Air Traffic, 1981; International Air Traffic Control, 1985; From Take-off to Touchdown—A Passenger's Guide, 1984; articles in Interavia, Times Supplement, Flight, Controller. *Recreations:* vintage cars, flying. *Address:* Footprints, Stoke Wood, Stoke Poges, Bucks. SL2 4AU. *T:* Farnham Common (0753) 642710. *Club:* Bentley Drivers (Long Crendon).

FIELD, Barry John Anthony, TD 1984; MP (C) Isle of Wight, since 1987; *b* 4 July 1946; *s* of Ernest Field and late Marguerite Eugenie Field; *m* 1969, Jaqueline Anne Miller; one *s* one *d*. *Educ:* Collingwood Boys' Sch.; Mitcham Grammar Sch.; Bembridge Sch.; Victoria Street Coll. Director: Great Southern Cemetery & Crematorium Co. Ltd, 1969–86; J. D. Field & Sons Ltd, 1981–. Mem. of Lloyd's. Councillor, Horsham Dist. Council, 1983–86 (Vice-Chm., Housing, 1984–85, Chm., Housing, 1985–86); Mem., IoW CC, 1986–89. Major RCT TA; Liveryman, Turners' Co.; Mem., Watermen and Lightermen's Co. *Recreations:* sailing, theatre, ski-ing. *Address:* Medina Lodge, 25 Birmingham Road, Cowes, Isle of Wight PO31 7BH. *T:* Cowes (0983) 291787. *Club:* Island Sailing (Cowes).

FIELD, Edward John, CMG 1991; HM Diplomatic Service; Minister, British Embassy, Tokyo, since 1988; *b* 11 June 1936; *s* of Arthur Field, OBE, MC, TD, and late Dorothy Agnes Field; *m* 1960, Irene Sophie du Pont Darden; one *s* one *d*. *Educ:* Highgate Sch.; Corpus Christi Coll., Oxford; Univ. of Virginia. Courtaulds Ltd, 1960–62; FCO, 1963–: 2nd, later 1st Sec., Tokyo, 1963–68; Amer. Dept, FCO, 1968–70; Cultural Attaché, Moscow, 1970–72; 1st Sec. (Commercial), Tokyo, 1973–76; Asst Head, S Asian Dept, FCO, 1976–77; Dept of Trade, 1977–79 (Head, Exports to Japan Unit); Counsellor: (Commercial), Seoul, 1980–83; at Harvard Univ., 1983–84; UK Mission to UN, 1984–87. *Recreations:* tennis, riding, listening to music. *Address:* c/o Foreign and Commonwealth Office, SW1. *Club:* Tokyo (Tokyo).

FIELD, Frank; MP (Lab) Birkenhead, since 1979; *b* 16 July 1942; *s* of late Walter and of Annie Field. *Educ:* St Clement Danes Grammar Sch.; Univ. of Hull (BSc (Econ)). Teacher: at Southwark Coll. for Further Education, 1964–68; at Hammersmith Coll. for Further Education, 1968–69. Director: Child Poverty Action Gp, 1969–79; Low Pay Unit, 1974–80. Mem., Hounslow BC, 1964–68. Contested (Lab) Buckingham S, 1966. Chairman: Select Cttee on Social Services, 1987–90; Select Cttee on Social Security, 1991–. *Publications:* (ed, jtly) Twentieth Century State Education, 1971; (ed, jtly) Black Britons, 1971; (ed) Low Pay, 1973; Unequal Britain, 1974; (ed) Are Low Wages Inevitable?, 1976; (ed) Education and the Urban Crisis, 1976; (ed) The Conscript Army: a study of Britain's unemployed, 1976; (jtly) To Him Who Hath: a study of poverty and taxation, 1976; (with Ruth Lister) Wasted Labour, 1978 (Social Concern Book Award); (ed) The Wealth Report, 1979; Inequality in Britain: freedom, welfare and the state, 1981; Poverty and Politics, 1982; The Wealth Report—2, 1983; (ed) Policies against Low Pay, 1984; The Minimum Wage: its potential and dangers, 1984; Freedom and Wealth in a Socialist Future, 1987; The Politics of Paradise, 1987; Losing Out: the emergence of Britain's underclass, 1989. *Address:* House of Commons, SW1A 0AA. *T:* 071–219 5193.

FIELD, Maj.-Gen. Geoffrey William, OBE 1983 (MBE 1976); Director General Logistic Policy (Army), since 1990; *b* 30 Nov. 1941; *s* of William Edwin Field and Ellen Campbell Field (*née* Forsyth); *m* 1966, Janice Anne Olsen; one *s* two *d*. *Educ:* Daniel Stewart's College, Edinburgh; RMA Sandhurst; RMCS Shrivenham; Australian Staff College; RCDS. Commissioned RE 1961; OC 59 Indep. Cdo Sqn, RE, 1976–78; CO 36 Engr Regt, 1980–83 (served in Falkland Islands campaign); Asst Dir Defence Policy, MoD, 1983–85; Comd 11 Engr Gp, 1986–87; Dir Defence Programmes, MoD, 1989–90. *Recreation:* golf. *Address:* Ministry of Defence, Whitehall, SW1A 2HB. *T:* 071–218 7531.

FIELD, Dr Ian Trevor; Secretary, British Medical Association, since 1989 (Deputy Secretary, 1985–89); *b* 31 Oct. 1933; *s* of late Major George Edward Field, MBE, IA, and Bertha Cecilia Field; *m* 1960, Christine Mary Osman, JP; three *s*. *Educ:* Shri Shivaji School, Poona; Bournemouth School; Guy's Hosp. Med. School. MB, BS; FFPHM; FFOM. Royal Engineers, 1952–54; Med. Sch., 1954–60; house posts, 1960–62; general practice, 1962–64; Asst Sec., later Under Sec., BMA, 1964–75; SMO, 1975–78, SPMO/Under Sec., 1978–85, DHSS, (Internat. Health and Communicable Disease Control, later NHS Regional Orgn); Chief Med. and Health Services Advr, ODA, 1978–83. Member: Council, Liverpool Sch. of Trop. Med., 1979–83; Bd of Management, London Sch. of Hygiene and Trop. Med., 1979–83; Council, Royal Vet. Coll., 1982–88; WHO Global Adv. Cttee on Malaria Control, 1979–82 (Chm., 1981). Liveryman, Soc. of Apothecaries, 1971– (Ct of Assistants, 1986–). *Publications:* contribs to medical jls. *Recreations:* military history, opera, watching cricket and rugby. *Address:* 10 Rockwells Gardens, Dulwich Wood Park, SE19 1HW. *Club:* Athenæum.

FIELD, Brig. Jill Margaret, RRC 1988; QHNS 1989; Matron-in-Chief (Army) and Director of Defence Nursing Services, since 1989; *b* 20 June 1934; *d* of late Major Charles Euston Field, Royal Signals, and of Mrs Eva Gladys Field (*née* Watson). *Educ:* High School for Girls, Southend-on-Sea; St Bartholomew's Hosp., London (SRN). Joined QARANC, 1957; appointments include: service in Mil. Hosps in UK, BAOR, N Africa, Cyprus, Singapore; Instructor, QARANC Trng Centre, 1971–74; Liaison Officer QARANC, MoD, 1980–83; Matron, BMH Hannover, 1984–85; Dep. Medical (Nursing), BAOR, 1985–87; Matron, Cambridge Mil. Hosp., Aldershot and Chief Medical (Nursing) SE and SW Dist, 1987–89. *Recreations:* gardening, reading, music. *Address:* c/o Royal Bank of Scotland, Holt's Farnborough Branch, Lawrie House, Victoria Road, Farnborough, Hants GU14 7NR.

FIELD, Sir Malcolm David, Kt 1991; Group Managing Director, W. H. Smith Group PLC, since 1982; Chairman, NAAFI, since 1986 (Deputy Chairman, 1985–86); *b* 25 Aug. 1937; *s* of Stanley Herbert Raynor Field and Constance Frances (*née* Watson); *m* (marr. diss.); one *d. Educ:* Highgate Sch.; London Business Sch. National Service, commnd Welsh Guards (2nd Lieut), 1955–57 (served in Cyprus and Germany). PA to Dir, ICI (Paints Div.), 1957; joined family wholesale newspaper distributors business, 1960 (taken over by W. H. Smith, 1963); Wholesale Dir, 1970, Man. Dir, Retail Gp, 1978–82, W. H. Smith. Chm., Bd of Management, NAAFI, 1986– (Mem., Bd of Management, 1973–86); Non-exec. Dir, MEPC, 1989–. CBIM 1988; FRSA 1989. *Recreations:* cricket, tennis, golf. *Address:* 47 Cadogan Gardens, SW3 2TH. *T:* 071-581 2576. *Clubs:* Garrick, MCC.

FIELD, Marshall Hayward, CBE 1985; Consultant Partner, Bacon & Woodrow, since 1986; *b* 19 April 1930; *s* of Harold Hayward Field and Hilda Maud Field; *m* 1960, Barbara Evelyn Harris; two *d. Educ:* Dulwich College. FIA 1957. With Pearl Assce, 1948–58; Phoenix Assurance: Actuary, 1964–85; Gen. Manager, 1972–85; Dir, 1980–85. Director: TSB Trust Co. Ltd, 1985–89; TSB Gp Insce and Investment Services Bd, 1989–90; TSB Gp, 1990–. Institute of Actuaries: Hon. Sec., 1975–77; Vice-Pres., 1979–82; Pres., 1986–88; Vice Pres., International Actuarial Assoc., 1984–90; Chm., Life Offices' Assoc., 1983–85. Mem., Fowler Inquiry into Provision for Retirement, 1984; Consultant, Marketing of Investments Bd Organising Cttee, 1985–86. Mem., Dulwich Picture Gall. Cttee, 1985–; Chm., Dulwich College Estates Governors, 1988–90 (Dep. Chm., 1985–88); Governor: Dulwich Coll., 1987–; James Allen's Girls' School, 1981–. Mem., Ct of Assistants, Actuaries' Co., 1989–. *Recreations:* theatre, architecture. *Address:* Low Cross, 35 Woodhall Drive, SE21 7HJ; Bembridge, Isle of Wight.

FIELD, Hon. Michael Walter; Premier of Tasmania, since 1989; MHA (Lab) Braddon, since 1976; *b* 28 May 1948; *s* of William Field and Blanche (*née* Burrows); *m* 1975, Janette Elizabeth Mary Fone; one *s* two *d. Educ:* Railton Primary Sch., Tasmania; Devonport High Sch., Tasmania; Univ. of Tasmania (BA Pol. Sci./History). Teacher, 1971–75; Community Develt Officer, 1975–76. Minister for Transport, Main Roads, Construction and Local Govt, 1979–82; Shadow Minister for: Transport, 1982–83; Education and Ind. Relns, 1982–86; Dep. Leader of Opposition and Shadow Minister for Forestry, Ind. Relns and Energy, 1986–88; Leader of Opposition, 1988–89. *Recreations:* running, reading, music. *Address:* Executive Buildings, Franklin Square, Hobart, Tasmania 7000, Australia. *T:* (002) 30 3464.

FIELD, Richard Alan; QC 1987; *b* 17 April 1947; *s* of Robert Henry Field and Ivy May Field; *m* 1968, Lynne Hauskind; two *s* two *d. Educ:* Ottershaw Sch.; Bristol Univ. (LLB); London School of Economics (LLM with Dist.). Asst Prof., Univ. of British Columbia, 1969–71; Lectr in Law, Hong Kong Univ., 1971–73; Associate Prof., McGill Univ., Montreal, 1973–77; called to the Bar, Inner Temple, 1977. *Publications:* articles and book reviews in UBC Law Rev., Hong Kong Law Jl, McGill Law Jl. *Recreations:* cricket, opera, theatre. *Address:* 11 King's Bench Walk, Temple, EC4Y 7EQ. *Clubs:* Reform, Roehampton.

FIELD, William James; *b* 22 May 1909; *s* of late Frederick William Field, Solicitor; unmarried. *Educ:* Richmond County Sch.; London Univ; abroad. Joined Labour Party, 1935; Parliamentary Private Sec. to Sec. of State for War, May-Oct. 1951 (to Under-Sec. for War, 1950–51); Chm. South Hammersmith Divisional Labour Party, 1945–46; contested Hampstead Div., General Election, 1945; MP (Lab) North Paddington, Nov. 1946–Oct. 1953. Mem. Hammersmith Borough Council, 1945–53, and Leader of that Council, 1946–49; a Vice-Pres. of Assoc. of Municipal Corporations, 1952–53; for several years, mem. Metropolitan Boroughs' Standing Joint Cttee and of many local govt bodies. Volunteered for Army, Sept. 1939 and served in ranks and as officer in Intelligence Corps and RASC.

FIELD-FISHER, Thomas Gilbert, TD 1950; QC 1969; a Recorder of the Crown Court, 1972–87; *b* 16 May 1915; *s* of Caryl Field-Fisher, Torquay; *m* 1945, Ebba, *d* of Max Larsen, Linwood, USA. *Educ:* King's Sch., Bruton; Peterhouse, Cambridge. BA 1937, MA 1942. Called to Bar, Middle Temple, 1942, Bencher, 1976. Served Queen Victoria's Rifles, KRRC, 1939–47; BEF 1940 (POW; despatches). Judge Advocate Gen's Dept, 1945–47 (i/c War Crimes Dept, CMF); joined Western Circuit, 1947. Mem., Bar Council, 1962–66; Deputy Chairman: SW Agricultural Land Tribunal, 1967–82; Cornwall QS, 1968–71; Chm., Maria Colwell Inquiry, 1973–74. Vice-Chm., London Council of Social Service, 1966–79; Vice-Pres., London Voluntary Service Council, 1979–. Mem., Home Secretary's Adv. Cttee on Animal Experiments, 1980–89. Chm., Dogs' Home, Battersea, 1982–; Founder and Chm., Assoc. of British Dogs' Homes, 1985–. Pres., Cornwall Magistrates' Assoc., 1985–. *Publications:* Animals and the Law, 1964; Rent Regulation and Control, 1967; contribs to Halsbury's Laws of England, 3rd, 4th and 5th edns, Law Jl, and other legal publications. *Recreations:* tennis, dogs, collecting watercolours, gardening. *Address:* 38 Hurlingham Court, SW6 3UW. *T:* 071–736 4627; 2 King's Bench Walk, Temple, EC4Y 7DE. *T:* 071–353 1746. *Clubs:* Hurlingham, International Lawn Tennis of Great Britain.

FIELDEN, Frank, MA (Dunelm); Secretary, Royal Fine Art Commission, 1969–79; *b* 3 Oct. 1915; *s* of Ernest and Emma Fielden, Greenfield, Yorks; *m* 1939, Margery Keeler; two *d. Educ:* University of Manchester. Graduated, 1938. Served 1939–45 with Royal Engineers (Special Forces), France, N Africa, Italy, Germany. Town Planning Officer to Nigerian Government, 1945–46; Lecturer and Sen. Lectr, University of Durham, 1946–59; Prof. of Architecture, Univ. of Strathclyde, 1959–69. Mem., Royal Fine Art Commn for Scotland, 1965–69. RIBA Athens Bursar, 1950, Bronze Medallist 1960. Chairman: Soc. of Architectural Historians of Great Britain, 1965–67; Richmond Soc., 1971–74. *Publications:* articles in professional journals and national press. *Recreations:* music, gardening. *Address:* 28 Caledonian Road, Chichester, W Sussex PO19 2LQ.

FIELDHOUSE, family name of **Baron Fieldhouse.**

FIELDHOUSE, Baron *cr* 1990 (Life Peer), of Gosport in the County of Hampshire; **Admiral of the Fleet John David Elliott Fieldhouse,** GCB 1982 (KCB 1980); GBE 1982; Chief of the Defence Staff, 1985–88; retired 1989; *b* 12 Feb. 1928; *s* of Sir Harold Fieldhouse, KBE, CB; *m* 1953, Margaret Ellen Cull; one *s* two *d. Educ:* RNC Dartmouth. MINucE. Midshipman, E Indies Fleet, 1945–46; entered Submarine Service, 1948; comd HMS Acheron, 1955; CO HMS Dreadnought, 1964–66; Exec. Officer, HMS Hermes, 1967; Captain SM10 (Polaris Sqdn), 1968–70; Captain HMS Diomede, 1971; Comdr, Standing Naval Force Atlantic, 1972–73; Dir, Naval Warfare, 1973–74; Flag Officer, Second Flotilla, 1974–76; Flag Officer, Submarines, and Comdr Submarine Force, E Atlantic Area, 1976–78; Controller of the Navy, 1979–81; C-in-C Fleet, and Allied C-in-C, Channel and Eastern Atlantic, 1981–82; Chief of Naval Staff and First Sea Lord, 1982–85. First and Principal Naval ADC to the Queen, 1982–85. Consultant, Vosper Thornycroft (UK) Ltd, 1990–; non-exec. Dir, DESC Ltd, 1991–. Chm., White Ensign Assoc., 1990–. Liveryman: Shipwrights' Co., 1982–; Glovers' Co., 1983–; Freeman, Clockmakers' Co., 1984. Hon. DSc (Eng) London, 1989. *Recreations:* home, family and friends. *Clubs:* Army and Navy; Royal Yacht Squadron.

FIELDHOUSE, Brian; Chief Executive, West Sussex County Council, since 1990; *b* 1 May 1933; *s* of late Harry and Florence Fieldhouse; *m* 1959, Sonia J. Browne; one *s* one *d. Educ:* Barnsley Holgate Grammar Sch.; Keble Coll., Oxford (MA PPE). IPFA 1960. Formerly, Treasurer's Departments: Herts CC; Hants CC; Flints CC; County Treasurer: Lincs parts of Lindsey CC, 1970–73; W Sussex CC, 1973–90. Comr, Public Works Loans Bd, 1988–. Principal Financial Advr, ACC, 1980–85. Pres., Soc. of Co. Treasurers, 1983. FRSA 1984. *Recreations:* hill farming, theatre going. *Address:* County Hall, West Street, Chichester PO19 1RQ. *T:* Chichester (0243) 777100. *Club:* Farmers'.

FIELDHOUSE, Prof. David Kenneth; Vere Harmsworth Professor of Imperial and Naval History, Cambridge University, since 1981; Fellow, Jesus College, Cambridge, since 1981; *b* 7 June 1925; *s* of Rev. Ernest Fieldhouse and Clara Hilda Beatrice Fieldhouse; *m* 1952, Sheila Elizabeth Lyon; one *s* two *d. Educ:* Dean Close Sch., Cheltenham; Queen's Coll., Oxford (MA, DLitt). War Service: RN, Sub-Lt (A), 1943–47. History master, Haileybury Coll., 1950–52; Lectr in Modern History, Univ. of Canterbury, NZ, 1953–57; Beit Lectr in Commonwealth History, Oxford Univ., 1958–81; Fellow, Nuffield Coll., Oxford, 1966–81. *Publications:* The Colonial Empires, 1966, 2nd edn, 1982; The Theory of Capitalist Imperialism, 1967, 2nd edn 1969; Economics and Empire, 1973, 2nd edn 1984; Unilever Overseas, 1978; Colonialism 1870–1945, 1981; Black Africa 1945–80, 1986. *Recreations:* music, farming, golf, writing fiction. *Address:* Jesus College, Cambridge. *T:* Cambridge (0223) 68611.

FIELDING, Sir Colin (Cunningham), Kt 1986; CB 1981; Chairman, Microturbo Ltd, since 1988; consultant in defence systems, information technology and electronics, since 1986; *b* 23 Dec. 1926; *s* of Richard Cunningham and Sadie Fielding; *m* 1953, Gillian Aerona (*née* Thomas); one *d. Educ:* Heaton Grammar Sch., Newcastle upon Tyne; Durham Univ. BSc Hons Physics. British Scientific Instruments Research Assoc., 1948–49; RRE Malvern, 1949–65; Asst Dir of Electronics R&D, Min. of Technology, 1965–68; Head of Electronics Dept, RRE Malvern, 1968–73; RCDS, 1973–74; Dir of Scientific and Technical Intelligence, MoD, 1975–77; Dir, Admiralty Surface Weapons Estabt, 1977–78; Dep. Controller, R&D Estabts and Res. A, and Chief Scientist (RN), MoD, 1978–80; Dep. Chief of Defence Procurement (Nuclear), and Dir, AWRE, MoD, 1980–82; Controller of R&D Estabts, Res. and Nuclear Progs, MoD, 1982–86. Director: Cray Research (UK), 1988–; United Scientific Hldgs plc, 1989–. *Publications:* papers in Proc. IEE, Proc. IERE, Nature. *Recreations:* yachting, tennis, music, golf. *Address:* Cheviots, Rosemount Drive, Bickley, Kent.

FIELDING, Fenella Marion; actress; *b* London, 17 Nov. 1934. *Educ:* North London Collegiate School. Began acting career in 1954; *plays include:* Cockles and Champagne, Saville, 1954; Pay the Piper, Saville, 1954; Jubilee Girl, Victoria Palace, 1956; Valmouth, Lyric, Hammersmith, 1958, Saville, 1959, and Chichester Fest., 1982; Pieces of Eight, Apollo, 1959; Five Plus One, Edinburgh Fest., 1961; Twists, Arts, 1962 (Best Revue Performance of the Year in Variety); Doctors of Philosophy, New Arts, 1962; Luv, New Arts, 1963; So Much to Remember—The Life Story of a Great Lady, Establishment, transf. to Vaudeville, 1963; Let's Get a Divorce, Mermaid, transf. to Comedy, 1966; The Beaux Stratagem and The Italian Straw Hat, Chichester Fest., 1967; The High Bid, Mermaid, 1967; Façade, Queen Elizabeth Hall, 1970; Colette, Ellen Stewart, NY, 1970 (first appearance in NY); Fish Out of Water, Greenwich, 1971; The Old Man's Comforts, Open Space, 1972; The Provok'd Wife, Greenwich, 1973; Absurd Person Singular, Criterion, 1974, transf. to Vaudeville, 1975; Fielding Convertible, Edinburgh Fest., 1976; Jubilee Jeunesse, Royal Opera House, 1977; Look After Lulu, Chichester Fest., transf. to Haymarket, 1978; A personal Choice, Edinburgh Fest., 1978; Fenella on Broadway, W6, Studio, Lyric, Hammersmith, 1979; Valmouth, Chichester, 1982; Wizard of Oz, Bromley, 1983; The Jungle Book, Adelphi, 1984; The Country Wife, Mermaid, 1990; *films include:* Drop Dead, Darling; Lock Up Your Daughters; Carry On Screaming; Carry On Regardless; Doctor in Clover; Doctor in Distress; Doctor in Trouble; No Love for Johnnie; Robin Hood; *television series:* That Was The Week That Was; A Touch of Venus; Ooh La La; Stories from Saki; Dean Martin and the Gold-Diggers; Comedy Tonight; Rhyme and Reason; numerous appearances in UK and USA. *Recreations:* reading, diarising. *Address:* c/o Hamper Neafsey Associates, 4 Great Queen Street, WC2. *T:* 071–734 1827.

FIELDING, Sir Leslie, KCMG 1988; Vice-Chancellor, University of Sussex, 1987–Sept. 1992 *b* 29 July 1932; *o s* of late Percy Archer Fielding and of Margaret (*née* Calder Horry); *m* 1978, Dr Sally P. J. Harvey, FSA, FRHistS, sometime Fellow of St Hilda's Coll., Oxford; one *s* one *d. Educ:* Queen Elizabeth's Sch., Barnet; Emmanuel Coll., Cambridge (1st Cl. Hons, historical tripos pt II; MA; Hon. Fellow 1990); School of Oriental and African Studies, London; St Antony's Coll., Oxford (MA; Vis. Fellow, 1977–78). Served with Royal Regt of Artillery, 1951–53. Entered HM Diplomatic Service, 1956; served in: Tehran, 1957–60; Foreign Office, 1960–64; Singapore, 1964; Phnom Penh (Chargé d'Affaires), 1964–66; Paris, 1967–70; Dep. Head of Planning Staff, FCO, 1970–73. Seconded for service with European Commn in Brussels, 1973; Dir (External Relns Directorate Gen.), 1973–77; permanent transfer 1979; Head of Delegn of Commn in Tokyo, 1978–82; Dir-Gen. for External Relns, 1982–87. UK Mem., High Council of European Univ. Inst. in Florence, 1988–. Chm., Nat. Curriculum Geography Wkg Gp, 1989–90. Hon. Pres., Univ. Assoc. for Contemporary European Studies, 1990–. Mem., Gen. Synod, C of E, 1990–. Admitted to office of Reader by Bishop of Exeter, 1981. FRSA 1989; FRGS 1991. Grand Officer, Order of St Agatha (San Marino), 1987; Knight Commander Order of the White Rose (Finland), 1988; Grosse Silbenes Ehrenzeichen mit dem Stern (Austria), 1989. *Publications:* Europe as a global partner: the external relations of the European Community, 1991; articles on internat. relations, higher educn and ecclesiastical matters. *Recreations:* life in the country, theology. *Address:* University of Sussex, Sussex House, Falmer, Brighton BN1 9RH. *Club:* Travellers'.

FIELDING, Richard Walter; Chairman C. E. Heath PLC, since 1987; *b* 9 July 1933; *s* of Walter Harrison Fielding, MBE, and Marjorie Octavia Adair (*née* Roberts); *m* 1st, 1961, Felicity Ann Jones; one *s* three *d*; 2nd, 1983, Jacqueline Winifred Digby (*née* Hussey). *Educ:* Clifton Coll., Bristol. National Service, Royal Engineers (Lieut), 1951–53. Broker to Dir, Bland Welch & Co. Ltd, 1954–68; Dir to Man. Dir, C. E. Heath & Co. Ltd, 1968–75; Founder and Chm., Fielding and Partners, 1975–86. *Recreations:* hunting, country sports. *Address:* Cuthbert Heath House, 150 Minories, EC3N 1NR. *T:* 071–488 2488.

FIELDS, Terence; MP (Lab) Liverpool, Broad Green, since 1983; *b* 8 March 1937; *s* of late Frank Fields; *m* 1962, Maureen Mongan; two *s* two *d*. Served RAMC, 1955–57. Fireman, Merseyside County Fire Bde, 1957–83. Vice-Chm., Bootle Constit. Lab. Party; former Mem., NW Regl Exec. Cttee, Lab. Party. *Address:* House of Commons, SW1; 20 John Hunter Way, Bootle, Merseyside L30 5RJ.

FIELDSEND, John Charles Rowell; Member, Court of Appeal, St Helena, Falkland Islands and British Antarctic Territory, since 1985; President, Court of Appeal, Gibraltar, since 1991 (Member, since 1986); Chief Justice (non-resident), British Indian Ocean Territory, since 1987 (Principal Legal Adviser, 1984–87); *b* 13 Sept. 1921; *s* of C. E.

Fieldsend, MC, and Phyllis (*née* Brucesmith); *m* 1945, Muriel Gedling; one *s* one *d*. *Educ:* Michaelhouse, Natal; Rhodes University Coll., Grahamstown, SA (BA 1942, LLB 1947). Served RA, 1943–45. Called to the Bar, S Rhodesia, 1947; advocate in private practice, 1947–63; QC S Rhodesia, 1959; Pres., Special Income Tax Court for Fedn of Rhodesia and Nyasaland, 1958–63; High Court Judge, S Rhodesia, 1963, resigned 1968; Asst Solicitor, Law Commn, 1968–78, Sec., 1978–80; Chief Justice: of Zimbabwe, 1980–83; of Turks and Caicos Islands, 1985–87. *Recreations:* home-making, travel. *Address:* Great Dewes, Ardingly, Sussex RH17 6UP.

FIENNES; *see* Twisleton-Wykeham-Fiennes.

FIENNES, family name of **Baron Saye and Sele.**

FIENNES, Sir Maurice (Alberic Twisleton-Wykeham-), Kt 1965; CEng; FIMechE; Engineering and Industrial Consultant; Chairman and Managing Director of Davy-Ashmore Ltd, 1961–69; Associate Consultant, L. H. Manderstam & Partners Ltd, 1977–80; retired; *b* 1 March 1907; *s* of Alberic Arthur Twisleton-Wykeham-Fiennes and Gertrude Theodosia Colley; *m* 1st, 1932, Sylvia Mabel Joan (marr. diss., 1964), *d* of late Major David Finlay, 7th Dragoon Guards. two *s* three *d*; 2nd, 1967, Erika Hueller von Huellenried, *d* of late Dr Herbert Hueller, Vienna. *Educ:* Repton; Armstrong Coll., Newcastle upon Tyne. Apprenticeship with Ransomes and Rapier Ltd, Ipswich; joined Sir W. G. Armstrong, Whitworth & Co Ltd (Engineers), Newcastle-upon-Tyne, 1930; with The United Steel Companies Ltd, 1937, first as Commercial Asst to Managing Dir, then in charge Gun Forgings and Gun Dept at Steel Peech & Tozer; Gen. Works Dir, Brush Electrical Engineering Co. Ltd, 1942; Managing Dir, Davy and United Engineering Co. Ltd, 1945; Managing Dir, Davy-Ashmore Ltd, 1960. Steel Industry Advr for UN Industrial Develt Orgn to Govt of Peru, 1974–75; Engineering Advisor for World Bank to Venezuelan Investment Fund, 1976–77. Mem. Economic Develt Cttee for Mech. Eng, 1964–67; Pres. of Iron and Steel Institute, 1962–63; Chairman: Athlone Fellowships Cttee, 1966–71; Overseas Scholarships Bd, CBI, 1970–76; Mem., Reserve Pension Bd, 1974–75. Governor, Yehudi Menuhin School, 1969–84. *Recreations:* music, grandchildren. *Address:* 11 Heath Rise, Kersfield Road, Putney Hill, SW15 3HF. *T:* 081–785 7489. *Club:* Naval and Military.

FIENNES, Very Rev. Hon. Oliver William Twisleton-Wykeham-; Dean of Lincoln, 1969–89, Dean Emeritus since 1989; *b* 17 May 1926; *yr s* of 20th Baron Saye and Sele, OBE, MC, and Hersey Cecilia Hester, *d* of late Captain Sir Thomas Dacres Butler, KCVO; *m* 1956, Juliet, *d* of late Dr Trevor Braby Heaton, OBE; two *s* two *d*. *Educ:* Eton; New College, Oxford; Cuddesdon College. Asst Curate, New Milton, Hants, 1954; Chaplain, Clifton College, Bristol, 1958; Rector of Lambeth, 1963. Church Comr, 1977–88. Chm., Pilgrims Assoc., 1986–89; World Fellow, Thanksgiving Square, Dallas, 1980; Pres., Lincoln Br., Inst. of Advanced Motorists, 1973–. Governor, Marlborough Coll., 1970–89. Nat Patron, E-SU in USA, 1987. ChStJ 1971. *Recreations:* cricket, travel, country activities. *Address:* Home Farm House, Colsterworth, Grantham, Lincs NG33 5NE. *T:* Grantham (0476) 860811.

FIENNES, Sir Ranulph Twisleton-Wykeham-, 3rd Bt, *cr* 1916; *b* 7 March 1944; *s* of Lieut-Col Sir Ranulph Twisleton-Wykeham-Fiennes, DSO, 2nd Bt (died of wounds, 1943) and Audrey Joan, *yr d* of Sir Percy Newson, 1st Bt; *S* father 1944; *m* 1970, Virginia Pepper (first female member of Antarctic Club, 1985; first woman to be awarded Polar Medal, 1987). *Educ:* Eton. Liveryman, Vintners' Company, 1960. French Parachutist Wings, 1965. Lieut, Royal Scots Greys, 1966, Captain 1968 (retd 1970). Attached 22 SAS Regt, 1966, Sultan of Muscat's Armed Forces, 1968 (Dhofar Campaign Medal, 1969; Sultan's Bravery Medal, 1970). T&AVR 1971, Captain RAC. Leader of British expeditions: White Nile, 1969; Jostedalsbre Glacier, 1970; Headless Valley, BC, 1971; (Towards) North Pole, 1977; Transglobe (first surface journey around the world's polar axis), 1979–82, reached South Pole, 15 Dec. 1980, reached North Pole, 11 April 1982; North Polar Unsupported Expeditions: reached 84°48′N on 16 April 1986; reached 88°58′N on 14 April 1990 (Furthest North Unsupported record). Hon. DSc Loughborough, 1986. Elected to Guinness Hall of Fame, 1987. Livingstone Gold Medal, RSGS, 1983; Explorers' Club of New York Medal (and Hon. Life Membership), 1983; Founder's Medal, RGS, 1984; Polar Medal, 1987; ITN Award, for the Event of the Decade, 1990. *Film:* (cameraman) To the Ends of the Earth, 1983. *Publications:* A Talent for Trouble, 1970; Ice Fall in Norway, 1972; The Headless Valley, 1973; Where Soldiers Fear To Tread, 1975; Hell on Ice, 1979; To the Ends of the Earth, 1983; (with Virginia Fiennes) Bothie, the Polar Dog, 1984; Living Dangerously (autobiog.), 1987. *Recreations:* langlauf, photography. *Heir:* none. *Address:* 10 Belgrave Road, Barnes, SW13 9NS. *T:* 081–741 1494.

FIENNES-CLINTON, family name of **Earl of Lincoln.**

FIFE, 3rd Duke of, *cr* 1900; **James George Alexander Bannerman Carnegie;** *b* 23 Sept. 1929; *o s* of 11th Earl of Southesk, *qv*, and Princess Maud (*d* 1945); *S* aunt, Princess Arthur of Connaught (Dukedom of Fife), 1959; *m* 1956, Hon. Caroline Cicely Dewar (marr. diss. 1966; she *m* 1980, Gen. Sir Richard Worsley), *er d* of 3rd Baron Forteviot, *qv*; one *s* one *d*. *Educ:* Gordonstoun. Nat. Service, Scots Guards (Malayan Campaign), 1948–50. Royal Agricultural College. Clothworkers' Company, and Freeman City of London. Pres. of ABA, 1959–73, Vice-Patron, 1973; a Vice-Patron, Braemar Royal Highland Soc.; a Vice-Pres., British Olympic Assoc. *Heir:* *s* Earl of Macduff, *qv*. *Address:* Elsick House, Stonehaven, Kincardineshire AB3 2NT. *Club:* Turf.

FIFOOT, Erik Richard Sidney, MC 1945; MA; ALA; Bodley's Librarian, and Professorial Fellow of Exeter College, Oxford, 1979–81; *b* 14 June 1925; *s* of Cecil Herbert Stuart Fifoot and Hjördis (*née* Eriksen); *m* 1949, Jean, *o d* of Lt-Col J. S. Thain; two *d*. *Educ:* Berkhamsted Sch.; Oxford Univ. (MA); London Univ. (DipLibr). HM Coldstream Guards, 1943–46. Leeds University Library: Asst Librarian, 1950–52; Sub-Librarian, 1952–58; Dep. Librarian, Nottingham Univ., 1958–60; Librarian, Univ. of Edinburgh, 1960–79. Chm., Standing Conf. of Nat. and Univ. Libraries, 1979–81; Mem., Exec. Bd, Internat. Fedn of Library Assocs and Instns, 1979–83. Founder and dir, Three Rivers Books Ltd, 1981–90. *Publications:* A Bibliography of Edith, Osbert and Sacheverell Sitwell, 1963, 2nd edn 1971; articles and reviews in library, architectural and educnl jls, symposia, and encycl. *Address:* Castle View, Bridge Street, Bampton, Oxon OX8 2HA.

FIFOOT, Paul Ronald Ninnes, CMG 1978; HM Diplomatic Service, retired; *b* 1 April 1928; *o s* of late Ronald Fifoot, Cardiff; *m* 1952, Erica, *er d* of late Richard Alford, DMD; no *c*. *Educ:* Monkton House Sch., Cardiff; Queens' Coll., Cambridge. BA 1948, MA 1952. Military Service, 1948–50. Called to Bar, Gray's Inn, 1953; Crown Counsel, Tanganyika, 1953; Asst to the Law Officers, 1960; Legal Draftsman (later Chief Parliamentary Draftsman), 1961; retd from Tanzania Govt Service, 1966; Asst Legal Adviser, Commonwealth Office, 1966; Legislative Counsel, Province of British Columbia, 1967; Asst Legal Adviser, Commonwealth (later Foreign and Commonwealth) Office, 1968; Legal Counsellor, 1971; Agent of the UK Govt in cases before the European Commn and Court of Human Rights, 1971–76; Counsellor (Legal Advr), UK Mission to UN, NY, 1976–79; Legal Counsellor, FCO, 1979–84; Dep. Leader, UK Delegation to 3rd UN Conference on the Law of the Sea, 1981–82; Leader, UK Delegation to Preparatory Commn for Internat. Sea Bed Authority, 1983–84; Dep. Legal Advr, FCO, 1984–88. Special Legal Advr, FCO, 1988 and 1990; Consultant: Govt of Hong Kong, 1988–89; Council on Tribunals, 1988–89; Constitutional Advr, Lesotho, 1991. *Address:* Zebrato, Lynwood Avenue, Epsom, Surrey KT17 4LQ.

FIGG, Sir Leonard (Clifford William), KCMG 1981 (CMG 1974); HM Diplomatic Service, retired; *b* 17 Aug. 1923; *s* of late Sir Clifford Figg and late Lady (Eileen) Figg (*née* Crabb); *m* 1955, Jane Brown, *d* of late Judge Harold Brown; three *s*. *Educ:* Charterhouse; Trinity Coll., Oxford. RAF, 1942–46 (Flt-Lt). HM Diplomatic Service, 1947; served in: Addis Ababa, 1949–52; FO, 1952–58; Amman, 1958–61; FO, 1961–67; Counsellor, 1965; Deputy Consul-General, Chicago, 1967–69; DTI, 1970–73; Consul General and Minister, Milan, 1973–77; Asst Under Sec. of State, FCO, 1977–80; Ambassador to Ireland, 1980–83. Mem. Council, Cooperation Ireland, 1985–. A Vice-Chm., British Red Cross Soc., 1983–88. President: Aylesbury Divl Conservative Assoc., 1985–; Bucks Assoc. of Youth Clubs, 1987–; Chiltern Soc., 1990–; Chm., Bucks Farming and Wildlife Adv. Gp, 1991–. *Recreations:* field sports. *Address:* c/o Foreign and Commonwealth Office, SW1. *Club:* Brooks's.

FIGGESS, Sir John (George), KBE 1969 (OBE 1949); CMG 1960; a director of Christie, Manson and Woods Ltd, 1973–82; *b* 15 Nov. 1909; *e s* of Percival Watts Figgess and Leonora (*née* McCanlis); *m* 1948, Alette, *d* of Dr P. J. A. Idenburg, The Hague; two *d*. *Educ:* Whitgift Sch. In business in Japan, 1933–38. Commissioned, Intelligence Corps, 1939; Staff Coll., 1941; served with Intelligence Corps, India/Burma Theatre, 1942–45. Attached to UK Liaison Mission, Japan, 1945; Asst Mil. Adviser (Lt-Col), UKLM, Tokyo, 1947–52; GSO1, War Office (MI Directorate), 1953–56; Military Attaché, Tokyo, 1956–61; Information Counsellor, British Embassy, Tokyo, 1961–68; Comr Gen. for Britain, World Exposition, Osaka, Japan, 1968–70. Mem., Expert Adv. Council, Percival David Foundn of Chinese Art, 1984–90; Pres., Oriental Ceramic Soc., 1987–90. Gold and Silver Star, Order of the Sacred Treasure, Japan, 1986. *Publications:* (with Fujio Koyama) Two Thousand Years of Oriental Ceramics, 1960; The Heritage of Japanese Ceramics, 1973; contrib. to Oriental Art, Far Eastern Ceramic Bulletin, etc. *Address:* The Manor House, Burghfield, Berks RG3 3TG. *Club:* Army and Navy.

FIGGIS, Anthony St John Howard; HM Diplomatic Service; Director of Research and Analysis (formerly of Research), Foreign and Commonealth Office, since 1989; *b* 12 Oct. 1940; *s* of Roberts Richmond Figgis and Philippa Maria Young; *m* 1964, Miriam Ellen Hardt; two *s* one *d*. *Educ:* Rugby Sch.; King's Coll., Cambridge (Mod Langs). Joined HM Foreign (later Diplomatic) Service, 1962; Third Sec., Belgrade, 1963–65; Commonwealth Office, 1965–68; Second Sec., Polit. Residency, Bahrain, 1968–70; FCO, 1970–71; First Sec. (Commercial), Madrid, 1971–74; CSCE delegn, Geneva, 1974–75; FCO, 1975–79; Madrid: Head of Chancery, 1979–80; Commercial Counsellor, 1980–82; Counsellor, Belgrade, 1982–85; Head of E European Dept, FCO, 1986–88; Counsellor and Head of Chancery, Bonn, 1988–89. *Recreations:* fly-fishing, tennis, music (piano). *Address:* c/o Foreign and Commonwealth Office, SW1A 2AH. *Club:* Roehampton.

FIGGIS, Arthur Lenox; His Honour Judge Figgis; a Circuit Judge (formerly Judge of County Courts), since 1971; *b* 12 Sept. 1918; *s* of late Frank Fernesley Figgis and late Frances Annie Figgis; *m* 1953, Alison, *d* of late Sidney Bocher Ganthony and late Doris Ganthony; two *s* three *d*. *Educ:* Tonbridge; Peterhouse, Cambridge (MA). Served War, 1939–46, Royal Artillery. Barrister-at-Law, Inner Temple, 1947. *Recreation:* rifle shooting half-blue, 1939, and shot for Ireland (Elcho Shield), 1935–39. *Address:* The Forge, Shamley Green, Guildford, Surrey. *T:* Guildford (0483) 898360.

FIGURES, Sir Colin (Frederick), KCMG 1983 (CMG 1978); OBE 1969; HM Diplomatic Service, retired; Deputy Secretary, Cabinet Office, 1985–89; *b* 1 July 1925; *s* of Frederick and Muriel Figures; *m* 1956, Pamela Ann Timmis; one *s* two *d*. *Educ:* King Edward's Sch., Birmingham; Pembroke Coll., Cambridge (MA). Served Worcestershire Regt, 1943–48. Joined Foreign Office, 1951; attached Control Commn, Germany, 1953–56; Amman, 1956–58; FCO, 1958–59; Warsaw, 1959–62; FCO, 1962–66; Vienna, 1966–69; FCO, 1969–85 (Dep. Sec.). *Recreations:* watching sport, gardening, beachcombing. *Address:* c/o Midland Bank, 130 New Street, Birmingham B2 4JU. *Club:* Old Edwardians (Birmingham).

FILBY, Ven. William Charles Leonard; Archdeacon of Horsham, since 1983; *b* 21 Jan. 1933; *s* of William Richard and Dorothy Filby; *m* 1958, Marion Erica Hutchison; four *s* one *d*. *Educ:* Ashford County Grammar School; London Univ. (BA); Oak Hill Theological Coll. Curate, All Souls, Eastbourne, 1959–62; Curate-in-charge, Holy Trinity, Knaphill, 1962–65; Vicar, Holy Trinity, Richmond-upon-Thames, 1965–71; Vicar, Bishop Hannington Memorial Church, Hove, 1971–79; Rector of Broadwater, 1979–83; RD of Worthing, 1980–83; Hon. Canon of Chichester Cathedral, 1981–83. Proctor in Convocation, 1975–90. Chm., Redcliffe Missionary Trng Coll., Chiswick, 1970–; Mem., Keswick Convention Council, 1973–; Pres., Chichester Diocesan Evangelical Union, 1978–84; Chairman: Diocesan Stewardship Cttee, 1983–; Sussex Churches Broadcasting Cttee, 1984–; Diocesan Cttee for Mission and Renewal, 1989. Bishops Advr for Hosp. Chaplains, 1986–. Governor: St Mary's Hall, Brighton, 1984–; W Sussex Inst. of Higher Educn, 1985–. *Recreations:* sport, music. *Address:* The Archdeaconry, Itchingfield, Sussex RH13 7NX. *T:* Slinfold (0403) 790315.

FILER, Denis Edwin, TD 1965 and 1977; FEng 1985; FIMechE; FIChemE; Director-General, Engineering Council, since 1988; *b* 19 May 1932; *s* of Francis and Sarah Filer; *m* 1957, Pamela Armitage; one *s* two *d*. *Educ:* Manchester Central Grammar Sch.; Manchester Univ. (Hons BSc Mech. Eng.); BA Open 1987. Commissioned REME (Nat. Service); served in Germany; REME TA, 1955–: Col, 1975–77; Hon. Col, 1978–87. ICI: Works Maintenance Engineer, 1960–67; Project Manager, Manchester, 1967–71; Project Manager, Holland (ICI Europa), 1971–73; Div. Maintenance Advisor, Organics Div., 1973; Plastics Div., Wilton Works: Works Engineer, 1973–76; Engineering Manager, 1976–78; Engineering & Production Dir, 1978–81; Dir of Engrg, 1981–88. Chm., Rolinx, 1978–81; Director: Bexford, 1978–80; Engineering Services Wilton, 1978–81; Electra Innvotec Ltd, 1989–; Adwest Gp, 1991–. Member: Council, IMechE, 1983–89 (Vice-Pres., 1987–89; Chm., Process Industries Div. Bd, 1985–87); Board, Lloyd's Register of Quality Assurance, 1986–88, Gen. Cttee, Lloyd's Register, 1988–; Engineering Council, 1986–88 (Chm., Continuous Educn and Trng Cttee; Mem., Standing Cttee for Industry). CBIM. *Recreations:* squash, tennis, Territorial Army. *Address:* Brambles, Watton Green, Watton-at-Stone, Hertford SG14 3RB. *T:* Ware (0920) 830207. *Clubs:* Army and Navy; Wilton Castle (Teesside).

FILKIN, Elizabeth; Assistant Chief Executive, London Docklands Development Corporation, since 1990 (Director of Community Services, 1988–90); *b* 24 Nov. 1940; *d* of Frances Trollope and John Tompkins; *m* 1974, David Geoffrey Nigel Filkin; three *d*. *Educ:* Birmingham Univ. (BSocSci). Organiser, Sparkbrook Assoc., 1961–64; Whyndham Deedes Fellowship, Israel, 1964; Res. Asst, Res. Associate, Lectr, Birmingham Univ., 1964–68; Lectr and Community Worker, Nat. Inst. for Social Work, 1968–71; Community Work Services Officer, London Borough of Brent, 1971–75; Lectr in Social

Studies, Liverpool Univ., 1975–83; Chief Exec., Nat. Assoc. of CABx, 1983–88. *Publications:* The New Villagers, 1968; What a Community Worker Needs to Know, 1974; Community Work and Caring for Children, 1979; Caring for Children, 1979; (ed) Women and Children First, 1984. *Recreations:* walking, swimming. *Address:* London Docklands Development Corporation, Thames Quay, Marsh Wall, E14 9TJ.

FILLEUL, Peter Amy, MA; Head Master, William Hulme's Grammar School, Manchester, 1974–87; *b* 7 Aug. 1929; *s* of J. C. Filleul and L. A. Mundy; *m* 1963, Elizabeth Ann Talbot; one *s* one *d*. *Educ:* Victoria Coll., Jersey; Bedford Sch.; (Exhibnr) Exeter Coll., Oxford (MA, DipEd). Royal Air Force, 1952–55. Portsmouth GS, 1955–65; Stationers' Company's Sch., 1965–68; Cardiff High Sch. (Head Master), 1969–74. *Recreations:* rifle shooting, fishing. *Address:* Kirkliston, Midvale Close, Upper Midvale Road, St Helier, Jersey, Channel Islands JE2 3ZH. *T:* Jersey (0534) 59941.

FILON, Sidney Philip Lawrence, TD; Librarian and Secretary to the Trustees, National Central Library, 1958–71, retired; *b* 20 Sept. 1905; *s* of late Prof. L. N. G. Filon, FRS and late Anne Godet; *m* 1st, 1939, Doris Schelling; one *d*; 2nd, 1959, Liselotte Florstedt; one *d*. *Educ:* Whitgift Sch.; University Coll., London (BSc). Sch. of Librarianship, University Coll., London, 1929–30; FLA 1931. National Central Library, 1930–39. Military service, 1939–45. Dep. Librarian, National Central Library, 1946–58. Mem., Library Advisory Council (England), 1966–71. *Publication:* The National Central Library: an experiment in library cooperation, 1977. *Address:* 107 Littleheath Road, Selsdon, Surrey.

FINCASTLE, Viscount; Malcolm Kenneth Murray; *b* 17 Sept. 1946; *er s* and *heir* of Earl of Dunmore, *qv*; *m* 1970, Joy Anne, *d* of A. Partridge; one *s* one *d*. *Educ:* Launceston Technical High School (Board A Certificate). Electrical Technical Officer, Dept of Aviation. Patron, Scottish Australian Heritage Council's annual Sydney Scottish Week. *Recreation:* flying (Tow Master for Soaring Club of Tasmania). *Address:* PO Box 100E, East Devonport, Tasmania 7310, Australia. *Club:* Soaring Club of Tasmania.

FINCH, Stephen Clark, OBE 1989; independent consultant, since 1989; *b* 7 March 1929; *s* of Frank Finch and Doris Finch (*née* Lloyd), Haywards Heath; *m* 1975, Sarah Rosemary Ann, *d* of Adm. Sir A. T. F. G. Griffin, *qv*; two *d*. *Educ:* Ardingly; Sch. of Signals; RMCS. FInstAM; FBIM. Commnd Royal Signals 1948; served Korea, UK and BAOR; retired 1968. Joined British Petroleum Co. Ltd, 1968: Gp Telecommunications Manager, 1968–81; Sen. Adviser, Regulatory Affairs, 1981–84; Asst Co-ordinator, Inf. Systems Admin, 1984–89. Member: Adv. Panel on Licensing Value Added Network Services, 1982–87; Monopolies and Mergers Commn, 1985–. Member: Inst. of Administrative Management, 1968– (Mem. Council, 1981–84; Medallist, 1985); Telecommunications Managers Assoc., 1968– (Exec. Cttee, 1971–; Chm., 1981–84; Regulatory Affairs Exec., 1984–87; Dir, External Affairs, 1988–); Council, Internat. Telecommunications Users Gp, 1981– (Chm., 1987–89). *Publications:* occasional contribs to learned jls. *Recreations:* sailing, skiing, swimming, opera. *Address:* 97 Englefield Road, Canonbury N1 3LJ. *T:* 071–226 2803. *Club:* National.

FINCH HATTON, family name of **Earl of Winchilsea and Nottingham.**

FINCH-KNIGHTLEY, family name of **Earl of Aylesford.**

FINCHAM, Prof. John Robert Stanley, FRS 1969; FRSE 1978; Arthur Balfour Professor of Genetics, University of Cambridge, 1984–91; Professorial Fellow, Peterhouse, Cambridge, 1984–91; *b* 11 Aug. 1926; *s* of Robert Fincham and Winifred Emily Fincham (*née* Western); *m* 1950, Ann Katherine Emerson; one *s* three *d*. *Educ:* Hertford Grammar Sch.; Peterhouse, Cambridge. BA 1946, PhD 1950, ScD 1964. Bye-Fellow of Peterhouse, 1949–50; Lectr in Botany, University Coll., Leicester, 1950–54; Reader in Genetics, Univ. of Leicester, 1954–60; Head of Dept of Genetics, John Innes Inst., 1960–66; Prof. of Genetics, Leeds Univ., 1966–76; Buchanan Prof. of Genetics, Univ. of Edinburgh, 1976–84. Vis. Associate Prof. of Genetics, Massachusetts Inst. of Technology, 1960–61. Pres., Genetical Soc., 1978–81. Editor, Heredity, 1971–78. *Publications:* Fungal Genetics (with P. R. Day), 1963, 4th edn, 1979; Microbial and Molecular Genetics, 1965; Genetic Complementation, 1966; Genetics, 1983; (jtly) Genetically Engineered Organisms, 1991; papers in Biochemical Jl, Jl Gen. Microbiol., Jl Biol. Chem., Heredity, Jl Molecular Biol., Genet. Res. *Recreations:* listening to music, walking. *Address:* 10 Guest Road, Cambridge CB1 2AL.

FINDLAY, Alastair Donald Fraser; Under Secretary, Scottish Office Industry Department (formerly Industry Department for Scotland), since 1988; *b* 3 Feb. 1944; *s* of late Rev. Donald Fraser Findlay and Isobel Ellis Findlay (*née* Louden); *m* 1969, Morag Cumming Peden; one *s* three *d*. *Educ:* Pitlochry High Sch.; Kelso High Sch.; Univ. of Edinburgh (MA (Hons) Mental Philosophy). Asst Principal, Dept of Agriculture and Fisheries for Scotland, 1966–70; Private Sec. to Jt Parly Under Sec. of State, Scottish Office, 1970–71; Principal, Scottish Office, 1971–74; on loan to FCO as First Sec. (Agric. and Food), The Hague, 1975–78; Asst Sec., Higher Educn Div., Scottish Educn Dept, 1979–82; Fisheries Div., 1982–85, Livestock Products Div., 1985–88, Dept. of Agric. and Fisheries for Scotland. *Recreations:* a garden, motor cars, golf, walking. *Address:* (office) New St Andrew's House, Edinburgh EH1 3TA. *T:* 031–244 4609. *Club:* Commonwealth Trust.

FINDLAY, Donald Russell; QC (Scot.) 1988; *b* 17 March 1951; *s* of James Findlay and Mabel Findlay (*née* Muirhead); *m* 1982, Jennifer Edith (*née* Borrowman). *Educ:* Harris Academy, Dundee; Univ. of Dundee (LLB 1st cl. Hons). Mem., Faculty of Advocates, 1975–; Lectr in Law, Heriot Watt Univ., 1976–77. Mem., Lothian Health Bd, 1987–. Vice Chm., N Cunninghame Cons. and Unionist Assoc., 1989–. Prospective Parly Cand. (C) Cunninghame North, 1989–. *Publications:* contribs to Scots Law Times. *Recreations:* Glasgow Rangers FC, Egyptology, malt whisky, photography, cooking, drinking claret, politics. *Address:* 26 Barnton Park Crescent, Edinburgh EH4 6EP. *T:* 031–336 3734. *Clubs:* Caledonian (Edinburgh); Royal Burgess Golfing Society, Glasgow Rangers Premier.

FINDLAY, Ian Herbert Fyfe; Chairman, Lloyd's, 1978 and 1979 (Deputy Chairman, 1977); *b* 5 Feb. 1918; *s* of Prof. Alexander Findlay, CBE, Aberdeen, and Alice Mary (*née* de Rougement); *m* 1950, Alison Mary Ashby; two *s* one *d*. *Educ:* Fettes Coll., Edinburgh. Served War, Royal Artillery, 1939–46. Mem. of Lloyd's, 1946. Chm., Price Forbes (Holdings) Ltd, 1967; Dep. Chm., Sedgwick Forbes Holdings Ltd, 1972, Chm., 1974–77. Mem. Cttee, Lloyd's Insurance Brokers Assoc., 1961–65 and 1966–69; Chm., Non-Marine Cttee, 1967–68; Chm. of Assoc., 1969–70; Mem., Cttee of Lloyd's, 1971–74, 1976–79; Chm., British Insurance Brokers Assoc., 1980–82. Trustee, St George's English Sch., Rome, 1980–; Chm., Guide Dogs for the Blind, 1981–87; Governor, Brighton Coll., 1981–88. Pres., Senior Golfers' Soc., 1990–. *Recreations:* golf, postal history. *Address:* 24 Forest Ridge, Keston Park, Kent BR2 6EQ. *T:* Farnborough (Kent) (0689) 852993. *Clubs:* City of London; Royal and Ancient Golf (St Andrews); Royal St George's (Sandwich); Addington (Surrey).

FINER, Dr Elliot Geoffrey; Head of Management Development Group, Cabinet Office, since 1990; *b* 30 March 1944; *s* of Reuben and Pauline Finer; *m* 1970, Viviane Kibrit; two *s*. *Educ:* Royal Grammar Sch., High Wycombe; Cheadle Hulme Sch.; East Barnet Grammar Sch.; St Catharine's Coll., Cambridge (BA 1965); Univ. of East Anglia (MSc 1966; PhD 1968). Unilever Research, Welwyn, 1968–75; Dept of Energy, 1975–90; Dir for Industry and Commerce, 1983–86, Dir Gen., 1988–90, Energy Efficiency Office; Under Secretary, 1988. Dir, Spillers Foods Ltd, 1989–. *Publications:* scientific papers and articles on nuclear magnetic resonance spectroscopy and its applications, esp. to phospholipid systems, in learned jls. *Recreations:* home and family, reading, DIY, gardening, computing, music. *Address:* Cabinet Office, Office of the Minister for the Civil Service, Horse Guards Road, SW1P 3AL.

FINER, Prof. Samuel Edward, FBA 1982; Gladstone Professor of Government and Public Administration, University of Oxford, 1974–82, now Professor Emeritus; Emeritus Fellow, All Souls College, Oxford; *b* 22 Sept. 1915; *y s* of Max and Fanny Finer, 210a Green Lanes, N4; *m* 1st, 1949, Margaret Ann (marr. diss. 1975), 2nd *d* of Sir Andrew McFadyean; two *s* one *d*; 2nd, 1977, Dr Catherine J. Jones, 2nd *d* of T. P. Jones, Prestatyn. *Educ:* Holloway Sch., London; Trinity Coll., Oxford. BA (Oxon) 1st Class Hons Mod. Greats, 1937; 1st Cl. Hons Mod. Hist., 1938; MA (Oxon) 1946, DLitt 1979; Sen. George Webb-Medley Schol., 1938–40. Served War, 1940–46; Capt. Royal Signals, 1945. Lecturer in Politics, Balliol Coll., Oxford, 1946–49; Junior Research Fellow, Balliol Coll., Oxford, 1949–50; Prof. of Political Institutions, University of Keele, 1950–66; Prof. of Government, Univ. of Manchester, 1966–74; Dep. Vice-Chancellor, University of Keele, 1962–64. Visiting Prof. and Faculty Mem., Institute of Social Studies, The Hague, Netherlands, 1957–59. Visiting Prof. in Government: Cornell Univ., 1962; Hebrew Univ., Jerusalem, 1969; Simon Fraser Univ., BC, 1976; Europ. Univ. Inst., Florence, 1977; Stanford Univ., 1979; Hong Kong Univ., 1980; Vis. Schweitzer Prof., Columbia Univ., 1982. Chm. Political Studies Assoc. of UK, 1965–69; FRHistS. DU Essex, 1982. *Publications:* A Primer of Public Administration, 1950; The Life and Times of Sir Edwin Chadwick, 1952; (with Sir John Maud) Local Government in England and Wales, 1953; Anonymous Empire—a Study of the Lobby in Britain, 1958, 2nd edn 1966; Private Industry and Political Power, 1958; (with D. J. Bartholomew and H. B. Berrington) Backbench Opinion in the House of Commons, 1955–59, 1961; The Man on Horseback: The Rôle of The Military in Politics, 1962, 2nd edn 1976; Great Britain, in Modern Political Systems: Europe, ed Macridis and Ward, 1963, 1968, 1972, 1980; (ed) Siéyès: What is the Third Estate, 1963; Pareto: Sociological Writings, 1966; Comparative Government, 1970; Adversary Government and Electoral Reform, 1975; Five Constitutions, 1979; Britain's Changing Party System, 1980. *Recreation:* oil-painting. *Address:* All Souls College, Oxford OX1 4AL; 48 Lonsdale Road, Oxford. *T:* Oxford (0865) 58060.

FINESTEIN, His Honour Israel, MA; QC 1970; a Circuit Judge, 1972–87; *b* 29 April 1921; *y c* of late Jeremiah Finestein, Hull; *m* 1946, Marion Phyllis, *er d* of Simon Oster, Hendon, Mddx. *Educ:* Kingston High School, Hull; Trinity Coll., Cambridge (Major Scholar and Prizeman). MA 1946. Called to the Bar, Lincoln's Inn, 1953. President: Jewish Hist. Soc. of England; Bd of Deps of British Jews, 1991–. *Publications:* Short History of the Jews of England, 1956; Sir George Jessel, 1959, etc. *Recreation:* reading history. *Address:* 18 Buttermere Court, Boundary Road, NW8.

FINGERHUT, John Hyman; Consultant to the Pharmaceutical and Allied Industries; *b* 2 Nov. 1910; *s* of late Abraham Fingerhut and Emily (*née* Rowe); *m* 1950, Beatrice Leigh, FCA; two *s* two *d*. *Educ:* Manchester Grammar Sch.; Manchester Univ. FBOA 1931; Hon. FRPharmS (Hon. FPS 1971). Pharmaceutical Chemist, 1932. Served with RAC and Infantry, France, Mauritius and E Africa, 1942–46; commnd Royal Pioneer Corps, transf. to Queen's Royal Regt (seconded King's African Rifles); demobilised as Captain. Merck Sharp & Dohme Ltd: medical rep., 1937–42; Sales Man., 1946; Dep. Man. Dir, 1957; Man. Dir, 1963; Chm., 1967–72; Consultant, 1972–77; Regional Dir, Merck Sharp & Dohme International, 1967–72; Chm., Thomas Morson & Son Ltd, 1967–72; Mem., ABPI Working Party on Resale Price Maintenance, 1970; Associate: Bracken Kelner and Associates Ltd, 1976; Key Pharmaceutical Appointments, 1978–88. Admin. Staff Coll., Henley, 1960. Mem., New Southgate Group Hosp. Management Cttee, 1972–74. Associate Mem., Faculty of Homœopathy, 1974. *Recreations:* music, reading, gardening, washing up. *Address:* 76 Green Lane, Edgware, Mddx HA8 7QA. *T:* 081–958 6163.

FINGLAND, Sir Stanley (James Gunn), KCMG 1979 (CMG 1966); HM Diplomatic Service, retired; High Commissioner to Kenya, 1975–79; UK Permanent Representative to the UN Environment Programme 1975–79, and to UN Centre for Human Settlements, 1979; *b* 19 Dec. 1919; *s* of late Samuel Gunn Fingland and late Agnes Christina (*née* Watson); *m* 1946, Nellie (*née* Lister); one *s* one *d*. *Educ:* Royal High Sch., Edinburgh. TA 1938. War service, 1939–46 as Major, Royal Signals; served N Africa, Sicily, Italy, Egypt. Commonwealth Relations Office, 1948–; British High Commission, India, 1948–51; Australia, 1953–56; Adviser on Commonwealth and External Affairs to Governor-Gen., Nigeria, 1958–60; British High Commission, Nigeria, 1960; Adviser on Commonwealth and External Affairs to Governor-Gen., Fedn of The W Indies, 1960–61, and to the Governor of Trinidad and Tobago, 1962; British Dep. High Commissioner: Trinidad and Tobago, 1962–63; Rhodesia, 1964–66; High Comr, Sierra Leone, 1966–69; Asst Under-Sec. of State, FCO, 1969–72; Ambassador to Cuba, 1972–75. *Recreation:* fishing.

FINGLETON, David Melvin; Metropolitan Stipendiary Magistrate, since 1980; *b* 2 Sept. 1941; *s* of Laurence Fingleton and Norma Phillips (*née* Spiro); *m* 1975, Clare, *yr d* of late Ian Colvin. *Educ:* Aldwickbury Sch., Harpenden; Stowe Sch.; University Coll., Oxford (Exhibnr; BA Hons Modern History, MA). Called to Bar, Middle Temple, 1965; South Eastern Circuit. Mem. of Corp. and Board, Trinity Coll. of Music, 1986–; Trustee, Samuel Butler's Educnl Foundn, 1968–. Music Correspondent, Contemporary Review, 1969–; Opera and Ballet Critic, Tatler and Bystander, 1970–78; Stage Design Corresp., Arts Review, 1976–; Associate Editor, Music and Musicians, 1977–80; Music Critic: Evening News, 1979–80; Daily Express, 1982–. *Publications:* Kiri, 1982; articles in Contemp. Rev., Tatler and Bystander, Music and Musicians, Arts Rev., Evening News, Daily Express. *Recreation:* listening to and writing about music. *Address:* Wells Street Magistrates' Court, 59/65 Wells Street, W1A 3AE. *T:* 071–436 8600. *Clubs:* Garrick, Buck's, MCC.

FINGRET, Peter; Metropolitan Stipendiary Magistrate, since 1985; a Recorder, since 1987; *b* 13 Sept. 1934; *s* of late Iser and Irene Fingret; *m* 1st, 1960, June Moss (marr. diss. 1980); one *s* one *d*; 2nd, 1980, Dr Ann Lilian Mary Hollingworth (*née* Field). *Educ:* Leeds Modern Sch.; Leeds Univ. (LLB Hons); Open Univ. (BA). President, Leeds Univ. Union, 1957–58. Admitted Solicitor, 1960. Partner: Willey Hargrave & Co., Leeds, 1964–75; Fingret, Paterson & Co., Leeds, 1975–82. Stipendiary Magistrate for Co. of Humberside sitting at Kingston-upon-Hull, 1982–85. Councillor, Leeds City Council, 1967–72; Member: Court, Univ. of Leeds, 1975–85; Cttee, Leeds Internat. Piano Competition, 1981–85. *Recreations:* golf, music, theatre. *Address:* Camberwell Green Magistrates' Court, SE5 7UP; 6 Stable Yard, Herring House, Holy Island, Northumberland. *Clubs:* Reform, Royal Society of Medicine.

FINK, Prof. George, FRSE 1989; Director, MRC Brain Metabolism Unit, since 1980, Hon. Professor since 1984, University of Edinburgh; *b* 13 Nov. 1936; *s* of John H. Fink and Therese (*née* Weiss); *m* 1959, Ann Elizabeth Langsam; one *s* one *d*. *Educ:* Melbourne High Sch.; Univ. of Melbourne (MB BS 1960; MD 1978); Hertford Coll., Univ. of Oxford (DPhil 1967). Jun. and sen. house officer, Royal Melbourne and Alfred Hosps, Victoria, Australia, 1961–62; Demonstrator in Anatomy, Monash Unit, Victoria, 1963–64; Nuffield Dominions Demonstrator, Oxford Univ., 1965–67; Sen. Lectr in Anatomy, Monash Univ., 1968–71; Univ. Lectr 1971–80, Official Fellow in Physiology and Med., Brasenose Coll., 1974–80, Oxford Univ. Royal Soc.-Israel Acad. Exchange Fellow, Weizmann Inst., 1979; Walter Cottman Fellow and Vis. Prof., Monash Univ., 1985; Arthur Fishberg Prof., Mt Sinai Med. Sch., NY, 1988. Prosector in Anatomy, Melbourne Univ., 1956; Wolfson Lectr, Univ. of Oxford, 1982; first G. W. Harris Lectr, Physiol Soc., Cambridge, 1987. Member: Council, European Neuroscience Assoc., 1980–82; Mental Health Panel, Wellcome Trust, 1984–89; Steering Cttee, British Neuroendocrine Group, 1984–88 (Trustee, BNG, 1990–); Co-ordinating Cttee, ESF Network on Neuroimmunomodulation, 1990–. Trustee, Jl of Neuroendocrinology, 1990–. *Publications:* (ed with L. J. Whalley) Neuropeptides: Basic and Clinical Aspects, 1982; (ed with A. J. Harmar and K. W. McKerns) Neuroendocrine Molecular Biology, 1986; (ed with A. J. Harmar) Neuropeptides: A Methodology, 1989; numerous scientific publications mainly on neuroendocrinology. *Recreations:* ski-ing, swimming. *Address:* MRC Brain Metabolism Unit, University Department of Pharmacology, 1 George Square, Edinburgh EH8 9JZ. *T:* 031–650 3548.

FINKELSTEIN, Prof. Ludwik, OBE 1990; DSc; FEng 1986; FIEE; CPhys, FInstP; FInstMC; Professor of Measurement and Instrumentation, since 1980, Dean of the School of Engineering, since 1988, Pro-Vice-Chancellor, 1991, The City University; *b* 6 Dec. 1929; *s* of Adolf and Amalia Finkelstein; *m* 1957, Mirjam Emma, *d* of Dr Alfred and Dr Margarethe Wiener; two *s* one *d*. *Educ:* Univ. of London (MSc). DSc City Univ., 1989. Physicist, Technical Staff, Electronic Tubes Ltd, 1951–52; Scientist, Instrument Br., NCB Mining Res. Estabt, 1952–59; Northampton Coll., London, and City University, London: Lectr, 1959–61; Sen. Lectr, 1961–63; Principal Lectr, 1963–67; Reader, 1967–70; Prof. of Instrument and Control Engineering, 1970–80; Head of Dept of Systems Science, 1974–79; Head of Dept of Physics, 1980–88; Dean, Sch. of Electrical Engrg and Applied Physics, 1983–88. Visiting Prof., Delft Univ. of Technology, 1973–74. Pres., Inst. of Measurement and Control, 1980 (Vice-Pres., 1972–75, 1977–79; Hartley Silver Medal, 1980); Chm., Management and Design Div., IEE, 1984–85 (Management and Design Divl Premium (jtly), 1984). Hon. FInstMC 1991. *Publications:* papers in learned jls and conference proc. *Recreations:* books, conversation, Jewish studies. *Address:* The City University, Northampton Square, EC1V 0HB. *T:* 071–253 4399; 9 Cheyne Walk, Hendon NW4 3QH. *T:* 081–202 6966.

FINLAY, Alexander William; retired; *b* 28 Nov. 1921; *s* of late Robert Gaskin Finlay and late Alice Finlay; *m* 1949, Ona Margaret Lewis; no *c*. *Educ:* Tottenham County School. Flt-Lt RAF, 1941–47; various posts, BOAC and British Airways, 1947–78, Planning Dir, 1971–78, retd. Chm., Soc. for Long Range Planning, 1978–79; Mem. Council, Sussex Trust for Nature Conservation, 1982–89; Trustee, Charitable Trust, 1983–. Active interest in support for crime victims, 1989–. FCIT. *Recreations:* conservation, photography, gardening. *Address:* 12 Hunters Way, Chichester, West Sussex PO19 4RB. *Club:* Royal Air Force.

FINLAY, Maj.-Gen. Charles Hector, CB 1966; CBE 1958 (OBE 1942); retired; Trustee, Returned Services League of Australia, since 1985 (Hon. National Treasurer, 1969–84); *b* 6 Oct. 1910; 3rd *s* of Frank J. Finlay and Margaret A. Stephenson; *m* 1935, Helen M., *d* of Arthur P. and Edith M. Adams; two *s*. *Educ:* Sydney; RMC Duntroon, Australia. Graduated RMC, 1931; Light Horse and Cavalry service, 1931–39; ADC to Gov.-Gen., 1932–35; with 14th/20th Hussars, India, 1935–36. Served War of 1939–45; Western Desert, Syria, New Guinea, Philippines, Borneo; Comd 2/24 Inf. Bn, 1942–43. Exchange duty, Canada, 1946–49; DMI, 1950–53; Comd Aust. Component BCFK, 1953–54; attended Imperial Def. Coll., 1955; Aust. Army Rep., London, 1956–57; Quartermaster Gen. AMF, 1957–62; Commandant Royal Military Coll., Duntroon, Australia, 1962–67. Hon. Col, Australian Intelligence Corps, 1973–77. *Recreation:* cricket. *Address:* 89 Buxton Street, Deakin, ACT 2600, Australia. *Clubs:* Naval and Military (Melbourne); Commonwealth (Canberra).

FINLAY, Sir David (Ronald James Bell), 2nd Bt *cr* 1964, of Epping, Co. Essex; Trainee Chartered Accountant; *b* 16 Nov. 1963; *s* of Sir Graeme Bell Finlay, 1st Bt, ERD and of June Evangeline, *y d* of Col Francis Collingwood Drake, OBE, MC, DL; *S* father, 1987. *Educ:* Marlborough College; Bristol Univ. (BSc Hons Economics/Philosophy). Joined Peat Marwick McLintock as trainee chartered accountant, 1986. *Recreation:* ski-ing. *Heir:* none. *Address:* The Garden Flat, 106 Chesterton Road, W10 6EP. *T:* 081–968 3026.

FINLAY, Frank, CBE 1984; actor; *b* Farnworth, Lancs, 6 Aug. 1926; *s* of Josiah Finlay; *m* 1954, Doreen Shepherd; two *s* one *d*. *Educ:* St Gregory the Great, Farnworth; RADA (Sir James Knott Schol.). *Stage:* repertory, 1950–52 and 1954–57; Belgrade, Coventry, 1958; Epitaph for George Dillon, NY, 1958; Royal Court, 1958, 1959–62: Sugar in the Morning; Sergeant Musgrave's Dance; Chicken Soup with Barley, Roots, I'm Talking About Jerusalem; The Happy Haven; Platonov; Chips with Everything, Royal Court, transf. to Vaudeville Theatre, 1962 (Clarence Derwent Best Actor Award); Chichester Festival, 1963: St Joan; The Workhouse Donkey; with National Theatre Co. 1963–70: St Joan, 1963; Willie Mossop in Hobson's Choice, and Iago in Othello (both also Chichester Fest., 1964, Berlin and Moscow, 1965), The Dutch Courtesan (also Chichester Fest.), 1964; Giles Corey in The Crucible, Dogberry in Much Ado About Nothing, Mother Courage, 1965; Joxer Daly in Juno and the Paycock, Dikoy in The Storm, 1966; Bernard in After Haggerty, Aldwych, Criterion, Jesus Christ in Son of Man, Leicester Theatre and Round House (first actor ever to play Jesus Christ on stage in English theatre), 1970; Kings and Clowns (musical), Phoenix, 1978; Filumena, Lyric, 1978, US tour, 1979–80, and NY, 1980; The Girl in Melanie Klein, 1980; The Cherry Orchard, tour and Haymarket, 1983; Mutiny (musical), Piccadilly, 1985–86; Beyond Reasonable Doubt, Queen's, 1987, Australian tour, 1988–89, UK tour, 1989–90; Black Angel, King's Head, Islington, 1990; A Slight Hangover, 1991; *with National Theatre Co.:* Peppino in Saturday, Sunday, Monday, 1973; Sloman in The Party, 1973; Freddy Malone in Plunder, Ben Prosser in Watch It Come Down, Josef Frank in Weapons of Happiness, 1976; Amadeus, 1982; *films include,* 1962–: The Longest Day, Private Potter, The Informers, A Life for Ruth, Loneliness of the Long Distance Runner, Hot Enough for June, The Comedy Man, The Sandwich Man, A Study in Terror, Othello (nominated for Amer. Acad. award; best actor award, San Sebastian, 1966), The Jokers, I'll Never Forget What 'Is Name, The Shoes of the Fisherman, Deadly Bees, Robbery, Inspector Clouseau, Twisted Nerve, Cromwell, The Molly Maguires (in Hollywood), Assault, Victory for Danny Jones, Gumshoe, Shaft in Africa, Van Der Valk and the Girl, Van Der Valk and the Rich; Van Der Valk and the Dead; The Three Musketeers; The Ring of Darkness, The Wild Geese, The Thief of Baghdad, Sherlock Holmes—Murder by Decree; Enigma; Return of the Soldier; The Ploughman's Lunch, 1982; La Chiave (The Key), Italy, 1983; Sakharov, 1983; Christmas Carol, Arch of Triumph, 1919, 1984; Lifeforce, 1985; Casanova, 1986; The Return of the Musketeers, 1988; Cthulhu Mansion, 1991; *TV appearances include:* Julius Caesar, Les Misérables, This Happy Breed, The Lie (SFTA Award), Casanova (series), The Death of Adolf Hitler, Don Quixote (SFTA Award), Voltaire, Merchant of Venice, Bouquet of Barbed Wire (series) (Best Actor Award), 84 Charing Cross Road, Saturday Sunday Monday, Count Dracula, The Last Campaign, Napoleon in Betzi, Dear Brutus, Tales of the Unexpected, Tales from 1001 Nights, Aspects of Love—Mona, In the Secret State, Verdict on Erebus (NZ), King of the Wind, Mountain of Diamonds (series). *Address:* c/o Al Parker Ltd, 55 Park Lane, W1Y 3LB. *Club:* Garrick.

FINLAY, Ian; *see* Finlay, W. I. R.

FINLAY, Rt. Rev. Terence Edward; *see* Toronto, Bishop of.

FINLAY, Thomas Aloysius; Hon. Mr Justice Finlay; Chief Justice of Ireland, since 1985; *b* 17 Sept. 1922; *s* of Thomas A. Finlay and Eva Finlay; *m* 1948, Alice Blayney; two *s* three *d*. *Educ:* Xavier Sch., Dublin; Clongowes Wood Coll.; University Coll. Dublin. BA Legal and Political Science, NUI. Called to the Bar, King's Inns, 1944 (Bencher, 1972); Hon. Bencher: Inn of Court of NI, 1985; Middle Temple, 1986. Mem., Dáil Éireann, 1954–57; Sen. Counsel, 1961; Judge of the High Court, 1972, Pres. of the High Court, 1974. *Recreations:* fishing, shooting, conversation. *Address:* 22 Ailesbury Drive, Dublin 4. *T:* Dublin 693395.

FINLAY, (William) Ian (Robertson), CBE 1965; MA; HRSA; Director of the Royal Scottish Museum, 1961–71 (Keeper of the Department of Art and Ethnography, 1955–61); Professor of Antiquities to the Royal Scottish Academy, since 1971; *b* Auckland, New Zealand, 2 Dec. 1906; *s* of William R. Finlay and Annie M. Somerville; *m* 1933, Mary Scott, *d* of late W. Henderson Pringle, barrister-at-law; two *s* one *d*. *Educ:* Edinburgh Academy; Edinburgh Univ. Joined staff of Royal Scottish Museum, 1932; Deputy Regional Officer for Scotland, Ministry of Information, 1942–44; Vice-Chairman, Scottish Arts Council, 1967; Secretary, Royal Fine Art Commission for Scotland, 1953–61. Guest of State Department in US, 1960. Freeman of City of London; Member of Livery, Worshipful Company of Goldsmiths, London; Mem., Edinburgh Festival Council, 1968–71. FRSA 1971. *Publications:* Scotland, World To-Day Series, 1945; Scottish Art (for British Council), 1945; Art in Scotland, 1948; Scottish Crafts, 1948; The Scottish Tradition in Silver (Saltire booklet), 1948; Scottish Architecture (for schools), 1951; Treasures in Edinburgh, 1951; Scotland, Young Traveller Series, 1953; A History of Scottish Gold and Silver Work, 1956, new edn 1991; Scotland, 1957; The Lothians, 1960; The Highlands, 1963; The Young Robert Louis Stevenson, 1965; The Lowlands, 1967; Celtic Art: an introduction, 1973; The Central Highlands, 1976; Priceless Heritage: the future of museums, 1977; Columba, 1979, new edn 1990; articles, reviews and broadcast talks on art and general subjects. *Address:* Currie Riggs, Balerno, Midlothian. *T:* 031–449 4249.

FINLAY-MAXWELL, David Campbell, PhD; CEng, MIEE; FTI, FSDC; Director, John Gladstone & Co. (Engineering) Ltd (Chairman and Managing Director, 1948–89); Director and President, John Gladstone & Co. Ltd (Managing Director, 1946–86; Chairman, 1960–89); *b* 2 March 1923; *s* of Luke Greenwood Maxwell and of Lillias Maule Finlay; *m* 1954, Constance Shirley Hood; one *s* one *d*. *Educ:* St Paul's; Heriot-Watt Coll. (Edinburgh Univ.) (Electronic and Control Engrg). CEng 1950; MIEE 1950; FTI 1974; FSDC 1985. PhD Leeds, 1983. Major Royal Signals, 1945. Harvard Univ. Advanced Management Programme, 1968. Chairman: Manpower Working Party, NEDO, 1970–73; Wool Industries Res. Assoc., 1974–77; Textile Res. Council, 1977–82; Wool Textile EDC, 1977–79, UK Rep., Consultative Cttee for R&D, Brussels, 1979–84. EEC Reviewer, ESPRIT Prog., 1986–. Dir, Wool Foundn (Internat. Wool Secretariat), 1985–. Member: Council, Textile Inst., 1972–74; British Textile Council, 1977–85; Textile Industry and Dyeing Adv. Cttee, Leeds Univ. Council, 1974–; Soc. of Dyers and Colourists, 1950–. Pres., Comitextil Sci. Res. Cttee, Brussels. Hon. Lectr, Leeds Univ. Dir/Vice-Chm., Sound Recording Bd of Dirs, RNIB (also Mem., Scientific Devel Sub Cttee); Hon. Organiser for UK, Technical Volunteer Helpers for Blind. *Recreations:* radio propagation, satellite tracking. *Address:* John Gladstone & Co. Ltd, Wellington Mills, Huddersfield HD3 3HJ. *T:* Huddersfield (0484) 653437; Folly Hall House, Cross Lane, Kirkburton, Huddersfield HD8 0ST. *T:* Huddersfield (0484) 604546, *Fax:* Huddersfield (0484) 608703. *Clubs:* Special Forces; Royal Scottish Automobile (Glasgow).

FINLAYSON, George; HM Diplomatic Service; Deputy High Commissioner, Dhaka, since 1990; *b* 22 April 1943; *s* of late George Finlayson and Alison Boath (*née* Barclay); *m* 1966, Patricia Grace Ballantine; two *s*. *Educ:* Tynecastle High Sch., Edinburgh. Joined HM Diplomatic Service, 1965; Reykjavik, 1967–69; Prague, 1969–71; Lagos, 1971–75; FCO, 1975–78; 2nd Sec., New Delhi, 1978–81; 1st Sec., FCO, 1981–83; 1st Sec. and Head of Chancery, Montevideo, 1983–87; Consul (Commercial) and Dep. Dir for Trade Promotion, New York, 1987–90. *Recreations:* golf, tennis, drawing, painting. *Address:* c/o Foreign and Commonwealth Office, SW1A 2AH.

FINLAYSON, George Ferguson, CMG 1979; CVO 1983; HM Diplomatic Service, retired; *b* 28 Nov. 1924; *s* of late G. B. Finlayson; *m* 1st, 1951, Rosslyn Evelyn (*d* 1972), *d* of late E. N. James; one *d*; 2nd, 1982, Anthea Judith, *d* of F. D. Perry. *Educ:* North Berwick High Sch. Royal Air Force, 1943–47. Apptd HM Foreign (later Diplomatic) Service, 1949; 2nd Sec. (Inf.), HM Embassy, Rangoon, 1952–54; FO, 1955–59; First Sec., 1959; HM Consul, Algiers, 1959–61; First Sec., HM Embassy, Bamako, 1961–63; HM Consul (Commercial), New York, 1964–68; Counsellor, 1968; Counsellor (Commercial), British High Commn, Singapore, 1969–72; Head of Trade Relations and Exports Dept, FCO, 1972–73; Counsellor (Commercial) Paris, 1973–78; Consul-General: Toronto, 1978–81; Los Angeles, 1981–84. *Recreations:* travel, walking, tennis, swimming. *Address:* 141b Ashley Gardens, SW1. T: 071–834 6227; 49 Westgate, North Berwick, East Lothian. *T:* North Berwick (0620) 2522. *Club:* Oriental.

FINLAYSON, Maj.-Gen. Robert G.; *see* Gordon-Finlayson.

FINLEY, Michael John; Director, International Federation of Periodical Publishers, since 1989; *b* 22 Sept. 1932; *s* of late Walter Finley and of Grace Marie Butler; *m* 1955, Sheila Elizabeth Cole; four *s*. *Educ:* King Edward VII Sch., Sheffield. Editor, 1964–69, Sheffield Morning Telegraph (formerly Sheffield Telegraph); Chief Editorial Dir, 1972–79, and Dir and Gen. Man., 1979–82, Kent Messenger Gp; Exec. Dir, Periodical Publishers Assoc., 1983–88. Hon. Mem. and Past Chm., Parly and Legal Cttee, Guild of British Newspaper Editors. Chm., Inst. of Dirs (Kent branch), 1980–83. Member: BBC Regional Adv. Council, 1967–69; BBC Gen. Adv. Council, 1971–77; Exec. Cttee, Internat. Fedn of Periodical Publishers, 1983–; Bd, Fedn of Periodical Publishers in EEC, 1984–; Bd, Internat. Press Centre, London, 1984–88; Governor: Internat. Press Foundn, 1988–; Cranbrook Sch., 1978–. *Publication:* contrib. Advertising and the Community, 1968. *Recreations:* tennis, rugby (spectator), snooker. *Address:* Sorrento, Staplehurst, Kent TN12 0PZ.

FINLEY, Sir Peter (Hamilton), Kt 1981; OBE 1974; DFC 1944; FCA; Chairman: Boral Ltd, since 1976; Email Ltd, since 1974; Avery Aust. Ltd, since 1972; Custom Credit Corporation Ltd, since 1973; Vice Chairman, National Australia Bank, since 1986 (Director since 1970); *b* 6 Dec. 1919; *s* of Cecil Aubert Finley and Evelyn Finley (*née*

Daniels); *m* 1947, Berenice Mitchell Finley (*née* Armstrong); one *s* one *d*. *Educ:* The King's Sch., Parramatta. Served RAAF with RAF Bomber Command and RAAF SW Pacific Area, 1941–45. With W. V. Armstrong & Co., Chartered Accountants, 1946–48, Peat, Marwick, Mitchell & Co. (formerly Smith Johnson & Co.), 1949–55, P. H. Finley & Co., 1955–72, when virtually ceased practice. Dep. Chm., Cadbury Schweppes Aust. Ltd, 1971–89; Director: Burns Philp & Co. Ltd, 1980–; Sir Robert Menzies Meml Trust, 1979–90; T. R. Services Pty Ltd, 1974–. *Recreations:* cricket, tennis, gardening. *Address:* (business) 6 O'Connell Street, Sydney, NSW 2000, Australia. *T:* 235 1972; (home) 50 Treatts Road, Lindfield, NSW 2070. *T:* 46 5319. *Clubs:* Australian (Sydney); Melbourne (Melbourne).

FINNEY, Albert; actor, stage and film; film director; *m* 1957, Jane Wenham, actress (marr. diss.); one *s*; *m* 1970, Anouk Aimée (marr. diss.). Associate Artistic Dir, English Stage Co., 1972–75; a Dir, United British Artists, 1983–86. *Stage:* London appearance in The Party, New, 1958; Cassio in Othello, and Lysander, Stratford-on-Avon, 1959; subsequently in: The Lily White Boys, Royal Court, 1960; Billy Liar, Cambridge Theatre, 1960; Luther, in Luther: Royal Court Theatre and Phoenix Theatre, 1961–62; New York, 1963; Armstrong in Armstrong's Last Goodnight, Miss Julie and Black Comedy, Chichester, 1965, Old Vic, 1966; A Day in the Death of Joe Egg, NY, 1968; Alpha Beta, Royal Court and Apollo, 1972; Krapp's Last Tape, Royal Court, 1973; Cromwell, Royal Court, 1973; Chez Nous, Globe, 1974; Uncle Vanya, and Present Laughter, Royal Exchange, Manchester, 1977; Orphans, Hampstead, transf. to Apollo, 1986; J. J. Farr, Phoenix, 1987; Another Time, Wyndham's, 1989, Chicago, 1991; *National Theatre:* Love for Love, 1965; Much Ado About Nothing, 1965; A Flea in Her Ear, 1966; Hamlet, 1975; Tamburlaine, 1976; The Country Wife, 1977; The Cherry Orchard, Macbeth, Has "Washington" Legs?, 1978; *Directed for stage:* The Freedom of the City, Royal Court, 1973; Loot, Royal Court, 1975; *Directed for stage and appeared in:* The Biko Inquest, Riverside, 1984; Serjeant Musgrave's Dance, Old Vic, 1984; *Films include:* Saturday Night and Sunday Morning; Tom Jones; Night Must Fall; Two for the Road; Charlie Bubbles (also Director); Scrooge; Gumshoe; Alpha Beta; Murder on the Orient Express; Wolfen; Loophole; Looker; Shoot the Moon; Annie; The Dresser; Under the Volcano; Orphans; Millers Crossing; *TV films:* John Paul II; The Endless Game; The Image; The Green Man (series), 1990. Hon. LittD: Sussex, 1965; Salford, 1979. *Address:* c/o ICM, 388/396 Oxford Street, W1N 9HE.

FINNEY, Prof. David John, CBE 1978; MA, ScD Cantab; FRS 1955; FRSE; Professor of Statistics, University of Edinburgh, 1966–84; Director, Agricultural and Food Research Council (formerly Agricultural Research Council) Unit of Statistics, 1954–84; *b* Latchford, Warrington, 3 Jan. 1917; *e s* of late Robert G. S. Finney and late Bessie E. Whitlow; *m* 1950, Mary Elizabeth Connolly; one *s* two *d*. *Educ:* Lymm and Manchester Grammar Schools; Clare Coll., Cambridge; Galton Laboratory, Univ. of London. Asst Statistician, Rothamsted Experimental Station, 1939–45; Lecturer in the Design and Analysis of Scientific Experiment, University of Oxford, 1945–54; Reader in Statistics, University of Aberdeen, 1954–63, Professor, 1963–66. Dir, ISI Res. Centre, 1987–88. Vis. Prof. of Biomathematics, Harvard Univ., 1962–63; Vis. Scientist, Internat. Rice Res. Inst., 1984–85. United Nations FAO expert attached to Indian Council of Agricultural Research, 1952–53; FAO Key Consultant, Indian Agricl Stats Res. Inst., 1984–90. Scientific Consultant, Cotton Research Corporation, 1959–75. Chm., Computer Bd for Univs and Research Councils, 1970–74 (Mem., 1966–74); Member: Adverse Reactions Sub-Cttee, Cttee on Safety of Medicines, 1963–81; BBC General Adv. Council, 1969–76. President of Biometric Society, 1964–65 (Vice-President, 1963, 1966); Fellow: Royal Statistical Soc. (Pres., 1973–74); American Statistical Assoc.; Mem., Internat. Statistical Inst.; Hon. Fellow Eugenics Society; Hon. Mem., Société Adolphe Quetelet. Weldon Memorial Prize, 1956. Dr *hc*, Faculté des Sciences Agronomiques de l'Etat à Gembloux, Belgium, 1967; Hon. DSc: City, 1976; Heriot-Watt, 1981; Hon. Dr Math Watesloo (Ont), 1989. *Publications:* Probit Analysis, 1947 (3rd edn 1971); Biological Standardization (with J. H. Burn, L. G. Goodwin), 1950; Statistical Method in Biological Assay, 1952 (3rd edn 1978); An Introduction to Statistical Science in Agriculture, 1953 (4th edn 1972); Experimental Design and its Statistical Basis, 1955; Tecnica y Teoria en el diseño de Experimentos, 1957; An Introduction to the Theory of Experimental Design, 1960; Statistics for Mathematicians: An Introduction, 1968; Statistics for Biologists, 1980. Numerous papers in statistical and biological journals. *Recreations:* travel (active), music (passive), and the 3 R's. *Address:* 13 Oswald Court, South Oswald Road, Edinburgh EH9 2HY. *T:* 031–667 0135.

FINNEY, James; Chairman, Staff Commission for Education and Library Boards, 1981–85; Permanent Secretary, Department of Manpower Services for Northern Ireland, 1976–80, retired; *b* 21 Jan. 1920; *s* of James and Ellen Finney, Co. Armagh; *m* 1956, Barbara Ann Bennett, Wargrave, Berks; one *s* three *d*. *Educ:* Royal Belfast Academical Instn; Trinity Coll., Dublin Univ. BA 1st cl. Mods 1942. Royal Engrs, 1943–46. Min. of Educn for N Ireland, 1946–76. *Recreation:* gardening. *Address:* Honeypots, Ballyhanwood Road, Dundonald, Belfast, N Ireland BT16 0XR. *T:* Dundonald (02318) 3428.

FINNEY, Jarlath John; His Honour Judge Finney; a Circuit Judge, since 1986; *b* Hale, Cheshire, 1 July 1930; *s* of late Victor Harold Finney, MA, and Aileen Rose Finney (*née* Gallagher), Dorking, Surrey; *m* 1957, Daisy Emöke, *y d* of late Dr Matyas Veszy, formerly of Budapest; two *s* two *d*. *Educ:* Wimbledon College; Gray's Inn. Served, 2nd Lieut, 8th Royal Tank Regt, 1953–55 (Lieut 1955). Called to Bar, Gray's Inn, 1953; Member, SE Circuit, 1955–86; Member, Panel of Counsel for HM Customs and Excise before VAT Tribunals, 1973–86; a Recorder of the Crown Court, 1980–86. FLS. *Publications:* Gaming, Lotteries, Fundraising and the Law, 1982; (jtly) Sales Promotion Law, 1986; articles. *Recreations:* wild flowers, books, walking in the country, pottering about looking things up. *Address:* The Law Courts, Woodall House, Lordship Lane, Wood Green, N22 5LF. *T:* 081–881 1400. *Club:* Wig and Pen.

FINNEY, Rev. Canon John Thornley; Officer for the Decade of Evangelism, since 1990; *b* 1 May 1932; *s* of Arthur Frederick and Elaine Mary Finney; *m* 1959, Sheila Elizabeth Russell; three *d*. *Educ:* Charterhouse; Hertford College, Oxford (BA Jurisp.; Dip. Theol.). Ordained 1958; Curate, All Saints, Headington, 1958–61; Curate in Charge, Aylesbury, 1961–65; Rector, Tollerton, Notts, 1965–71; Vicar, St Margaret's, Aspley, Nottingham, 1971–80; Adviser in Evangelism to Bishop of Southwell, 1980–89. Manager, Research Project in Evangelism, BCC, 1989–. *Publications:* Saints Alive!, 1983; Understanding Leadership, 1989; The Well Church Book, 1991. *Recreations:* golf, growing old gracefully. *Address:* 14 Devonshire Road, Sherwood, Nottingham NG5 2EW. *T:* Nottingham (0602) 620272.

FINNIS, Prof. John Mitchell, DPhil; FBA 1990; Professor of Law and Legal Philosophy, Oxford University, since 1989; Fellow and Praelector in Jurisprudence, since 1966, Stowell Civil Law Fellow, since 1973, University College, Oxford; *b* 28 July 1940; *s* of Maurice and Margaret Finnis; *m* 1964, Marie Carmel McNally; three *s* three *d* (and one *d* decd). *Educ:* St Peter's Coll., Adelaide, SA; St Mark's Coll., Univ. of Adelaide (LLB 1961); University Coll., Oxford (Rhodes Scholar for SA, 1962; DPhil 1965). Called to the Bar, Gray's Inn, 1970. Associate in Law, Univ. of Calif at Berkeley, 1965–66; Rhodes Reader in Laws of British Commonwealth and United States, Oxford Univ., 1972–89; Prof. and Head of Dept of Law, Univ. of Malaŵi, 1976–78. Special Adviser to Foreign Affairs Cttee, House of Commons, on role of UK Parlt in Canadian Constitution, 1980–82; Consultor, Pontifical Commn, Iustitia et Pax, 1977–89; Member: Pontifical Council de Iustitia et Pace, 1990–; Catholic Bishops' Jt Cttee on Bio-Ethical Issues, 1981–88; Internat. Theol Commn, The Vatican, 1986–. Governor, Linacre Centre, London, 1981– (Vice-Chm., 1987–). *Publications:* Commonwealth and Dependencies, in Halsbury's Laws of England, 4th edn, Vol. 6, 1974, revised 1990; Natural Law and Natural Rights, 1980; Fundamentals of Ethics, 1983; (with Joseph Boyle and Germain Grisez) Nuclear Deterrence, Morality and Realism, 1987; Moral Absolutes, 1991. *Address:* University College, Oxford OX1 4BH. *T:* Oxford (0865) 276602; 12 Gray's Inn Square, WC1R 5JP. *T:* 071-405 8654; 12 Staverton Road, Oxford OX2 6XJ. *T:* Oxford (0865) 58660.

FINSBERG, Sir Geoffrey, Kt 1984; MBE 1959; JP; MP (C) Hampstead and Highgate, since 1983 (Hampstead, 1970–83); *b* 13 June 1926; *o s* of late Montefiore Finsberg, MC, and May Finsberg (*née* Grossman); *m* 1st, 1969, Pamela Benbow Hill (*d* 1989); 2nd, 1990, Yvonne Elizabeth Sarch (*née* Wright). *Educ:* City of London Sch. National Chm., Young Conservatives, 1954–57; Mem., Exec. Cttee, Nat. Union of Cons. and Unionist Assocs, 1953–79 (Mem. Exec. Cttee, 1949–79, Pres., 1986–89, Gtr London Area); a Vice-Chm., Conservative Party Organisation, 1975–79 and 1983–87. Borough Councillor: Hampstead, 1949–65; Camden, 1964–74 (Leader, 1968–70). Chairman: Gtr London Area Cons. Local Govt Cttee, 1972–75. Opposition spokesman on Greater London, 1974–79; Mem. Exec., 1922 Cttee, 1974–75; Member, Select Cttee on Expenditure, 1970–79; Parly Under Sec. of State, DoE, 1979–81, DHSS, 1981–83; Mem., Parly Assembly of Council of Europe and of WEU, 1983–, delegn leader, 1987–. Controller of Personnel and Chief Industrial Relations Adviser, Great Universal Stores, 1968–79; Dep. Chm., South East Reg. Bd, TSB, 1986–89 (Mem., 1983–86). Vice-Pres., Assoc. of Municipal Corporations, 1971–74 (Dep. Chm., 1969–71); Member: Post Office Users Nat. Council, 1970–77; Council, CBI, 1968–79 (Chm., Post Office Panel). FIPM 1975. Patron, Maccabi Assoc. of GB. Governor, Univ. Coll. Sch. JP Inner London, 1962. Order of Merit, (Austria), 1989; Comdr, Order of Isabella the Catholic (Spain), 1990. *Recreations:* bridge, reading. *Address:* House of Commons, SW1A 0AA. *T:* (home) 071–435 5320.

FINTRIE, Lord; James Alexander Norman Graham; *b* 16 Aug. 1973; *s* and *heir* of Marquis of Graham, *qv*.

FIRMSTON-WILLIAMS, Peter, CBE 1987 (OBE 1979); Chairman, Flowers and Plants Association, 1984–89; *b* 30 Aug. 1918; *s* of late Geoffrey and Muriel Firmston-Williams; *m* Margaret Beaulah; one *s* one *d*. *Educ:* Harrow. Served War, Infantry, Green Howards Regt, 1939–45 (Captain). J. Lyons & Co. Ltd, 1945–53; Marketing Director, United Canners Ltd, 1953–55; Associated British Foods Ltd, Director, Store Operations, Fine Fare, 1958–61; Fitch Lovell Ltd, Man. Dir, Key Markets Ltd, 1962–71; Associated Dairies Group Ltd, Man. Dir, ASDA Stores, and Dir, Associated Dairies, 1971–81, retired; Director: Woolworth Hdgs (formerly Paternoster Stores), 1981–85 (non-exec. Dir, 1985–86; Dep. Chm., 1982–85); Bredero Properties Ltd, 1986–; Chm., Bayfleet Hldgs Ltd, 1988–. Chairman: Covent Garden Market Authority, 1982–88; Retail Consortium, 1984–86. *Recreations:* golf, water skiing, gardening. *Address:* Oak House, 12 Pembroke Road, Moor Park, Northwood, Mddx. *T:* Northwood (09274) 23052.

FIRNBERG, David; Director, Eosys Ltd, since 1990 (Managing Director, 1980–88; Chairman, 1989–90); Executive Chairman, The Networking Centre Ltd, since 1990 (Chairman, 1985–90); *b* 1 May 1930; *s* of L. B. Firnberg and K. L. E. Firnberg; *m* 1957, Sylvia Elizabeth du Cros; one *s* three *d*. *Educ:* Merchant Taylors' Sch., Northwood. FBCS; FIInfSc; FAPM. Went West, 1953–56; Television Audience Measurement Ltd, 1956–59; ICT/ICL, 1959–72; David Firnberg Associates Ltd, 1972–74; Dir, Nat. Computing Centre Ltd, 1974–79. President: UK Assoc. of Project Managers, 1978–84; British Computer Soc., 1983–84 (Chm., IT Support for Disabled People project, 1990–); Chairman: UK Council for Computing Develt, 1990–; Steering Cttee, RSA Design Bursaries for Communications and Computing, 1989–; Member: Foundn for Sci. and Technology, 1987–; Council, PITCOM, 1989–. Freeman, City of London, 1987; Mem., Co. of Inf. Technologists. FInstD; FRSA. *Publications:* Computers Management and Information, 1973; Cassell's New Spelling Dictionary, 1976; Cassell's Spelling Dictionary, 1984. *Address:* The Great House, Tring, Herts HP23 6NX. *T:* Cholesbury (024029) 623. *Club:* Wig and Pen.

FIRTH, Andrew Trevor; Regional Chairman, Industrial Tribunals, Yorkshire/Humberside, 1982–88 (Chairman, Industrial Tribunals, 1972–82); *b* 4 June 1922; *s* of Seth Firth and Amy Firth; *m* 1946, Nora Cornforth Armitage; one *s* two *d*. *Educ:* Prince Henry's Grammar Sch.; Leeds Univ. (LLB). Served RA, 6th Airborne Div., Normandy, 1944, Lieut; Intelligence Officer, Potsdam Conf., 1945, Captain; Rhine Army Coll., 1946, Major. Partner, later Sen. Partner, Barret Chamberlain & McDonnell, Solicitors, Harrogate, Otley, Leeds, 1948–72. Pres., Harrogate and Dist Law Soc., 1965–66; Area Chm., Law Soc. Legal Aid Cttee, Yorkshire, 1969–72. Bronze Star Medal, USA, 1945. *Recreations:* Chippendale Soc., golf, grandchildren. *Address:* Chevin Close, Birdcage Walk, Otley, West Yorkshire. *Club:* Otley Golf.

FIRTH, Maj.-Gen. Charles Edward Anson, CB 1951; CBE 1945; DSO 1943; *b* 9 Oct. 1902; *s* of late Major E. W. A. Firth, Indian Army; *m* 1933, Mary Kathleen (*d* 1977), *d* of late Commander W. St J. Fraser, RN; two *s*. *Educ:* Wellington Coll., Berks; RMC Sandhurst. 2nd Lieut The Gloucestershire Regt, 1923; Lieut, 1925; Captain, 1935; Staff Coll., 1936–37; War Office, 1938–40; Major, 1940; Middle East: Temp. Lieut-Colonel; AA and QMG 50 Div., 1941–42; OC 1st Royal Sussex Regt in Middle East, 1942–43; Temp. Brigadier, 7th Indian Infantry Bde, 1943; Comd 167 Infantry Bde, 1943–44 (Italy); Comd 21 Tank Bde, 1944 (N. Africa); Comd 2 Infantry Bde, 1944 (Italy); Comdr and Dep. Comdr British Military Mission to Greece, 1944–45; mentioned in despatches three times, 1941–45. Colonel 1946; War Office, 1946–48; Comd Area Troops, Berlin (British Sector), 1948–50; Maj.-General, 1950; Comd East Anglian Dist, 1950; GOC Salisbury Plain Dist, 1951–53; Director of Personal Services, War Office, 1953–56. Colonel The Gloucestershire Regt, 1954–64; first Colonel Comdt, Military Provost Staff Corps, 1956–61. Chairman: Inter-Services VC Centenary Cttee, 1954–55; Inter-Services Cttee on Resistance to Interrogation, 1955–56. Governor, Dauntsey's Sch., 1961–77 (Vice-Chairman, 1965–77). Grand Commander Order of the Phoenix (Greek), 1946. *Recreations:* gardening, writing, fishing. *Address:* Garden Cottage, Church Street, Great Bedwyn, Marlborough, Wilts SN8 3PF. *T:* Marlborough (0672) 870270. *Club:* Army and Navy.

FIRTH, (David) Colin; Headmaster, Cheadle Hulme School, 1977–89, retired; *b* 29 Jan. 1930; *s* of Jack and Muriel Firth; *m* 1954, Edith Scanlan; three *s* one *d*. *Educ:* Rothwell Grammar Sch.; Sheffield Univ. (BSc, DipEd). Royal Signals, 1952–54; Stand Grammar Sch., 1954–57; East Barnet Grammar Sch., 1957–61; Bristol Grammar Sch., 1961–73; The Gilberd Sch., 1973–77. *Publications:* A Practical Organic Chemistry, 1966; Elementary Thermodynamics, 1969; (jtly) Introductory Physical Science, 1971. *Recreations:* golf, fell walking, talking about gardening. *Address:* Hill House, Fell Lane, Penrith, Cumbria CA11 8BJ.

FIRTH, Edward Michael Tyndall, CB 1951; *b* 17 Feb. 1903; *s* of Edward H. Firth, Sheffield; *m* 1929, Eileen Marie (*d* 1982), *d* of Edward Newman, Hove; two *s*. *Educ:* King Edward VII Sch., Sheffield; University College, Oxford. Classical Scholar, 1922–26. Inland Revenue, 1926; Ministry of Health, 1945; Under Secretary, 1947–58; Registrar General, 1958–63.

FIRTH, Mrs Joan Margaret, PhD; Deputy Director of NHS Finance, Department of Health, since 1990; *b* 25 March 1935; *d* of Ernest Wilson and Ann (*née* Crowther); *m* 1955, Kenneth Firth. *Educ:* Lawnswood High Sch., Leeds; Univ. of Leeds (1st Cl. BSc Colour Chemistry; PhD Dyeing of Wool). Research Asst, Leeds Univ., 1958–60; Head of Science, Selby High Sch., 1960–62; Sen. Lecturer in General Science, Elizabeth Gaskell Coll., Manchester, 1962–66; Lectr in Organic Chemistry, Salford Univ., 1966–67; joined Civil Service as Direct Entry Principal, 1967; Asst Sec., 1974; Under-Sec., DHSS, 1981; Under-Sec., Social Security Div. C, DHSS, later DSS, 1987–90. Member: ESRC, 1988–; Training Bd, 1990–. *Publications:* contrib. Jl Textile Inst., 1958. *Recreations:* wine, walking.

FIRTH, Rt. Rev. Peter James; *see* Malmesbury, Bishop Suffragan of.

FIRTH, Prof. Sir Raymond (William), Kt 1973; MA; PhD; FBA 1949; Professor of Anthropology, University of London, 1944–68, now Emeritus; *b* 25 March 1901; *s* of late Wesley Hugh Bourne Firth and Marie Elizabeth Jane Cartmill; *m* 1936, Rosemary, *d* of late Sir Gilbert Upcott, KCB; one *s*. *Educ:* Auckland Grammar Sch.; Auckland University College; London School of Economics (Hon. Fellow, 1970). Anthropological research in British Solomon Islands, including one year on Tikopia, 1928–29; Lecturer in Anthropology, University of Sydney, 1930–31; Acting Professor of Anthropology, University of Sydney, 1931–32; Lecturer in Anthropology, London School of Economics, 1932–35; Reader, 1935–44; Hon. Secretary Royal Anthropological Institute, 1936–39 (President 1953–55); Research in peasant economics and anthropology in Malaya, as Leverhulme Research Fellow, 1939–40; served with Naval Intelligence Division, Admiralty, 1941–44; Secretary of Colonial Social Science Research Council, Colonial Office, 1944–45; Fellow, Center for Advanced Study in the Behavioral Sciences, Stanford, 1958–59; Prof. of Pacific Anthropology, Univ. of Hawaii, 1968–69. Visiting Professor: British Columbia, 1969; Cornell, 1970; Chicago, 1971; Graduate Center, City Univ. of New York, 1971; Univ. of California, Davis 1974, Berkeley 1977; Auckland, 1978. Life Pres., Assoc. of Social Anthropologists, 1975. Foreign Hon. Member American Academy of Arts and Sciences, 1963; Hon. Member Royal Society, NZ, 1964; Foreign Member: American Philosophical Society, 1965; Royal Soc., NSW; Royal Danish Academy of Sciences and Letters, 1966; Internat. Union of Anthropol and Ethnol Sciences, 1983. Social research surveys: W Africa, 1945; Malaya, 1947; New Guinea, 1951; Tikopia, 1952, 1966; Malaya, 1963. Hon. degrees: DPh Oslo, 1965; LLD Michigan, 1967; LittD East Anglia, 1968; Dr Letters ANU, 1969; DHumLett Chicago, 1968; DSc British Columbia, 1970; DLitt Exeter, 1972; DLit Auckland, 1978; PhD Cracow, 1984; DSc Econ London, 1984. *Publications:* The Kauri Gum Industry, 1924; Primitive Economics of the New Zealand Maori, 1929 (new edn, 1959); Art and Life In New Guinea, 1936; We, The Tikopia: A Sociological Study of Kinship in Primitive Polynesia, 1936; Human Types, 1938 (new edn, 1975); Primitive Polynesian Economy, 1939 (new edn, 1964); The Work of the Gods in Tikopia, 1940 (new edn, 1967); Malay Fishermen: Their Peasant Economy, 1946 (enlarged edn, 1966); Elements of Social Organization, 1951 (new edn 1971); Two Studies of Kinship in London (ed.), 1956; Man and Culture: An Evaluation of the Work of Malinowski (ed.), 1957; Social Change in Tikopia, 1959; History and Traditions of Tikopia, 1961; Essays on Social Organization and Values, 1964; (with B. S. Yamey) Capital Saving and Credit in Peasant Societies, 1964; Tikopia Ritual and Belief, 1967; Rank and Religion in Tikopia, 1970; (with J. Hubert and A. Forge) Families and Their Relatives, 1970; Symbols Public and Private, 1973; Tikopia-English Dictionary, 1985; Tikopia Songs, 1990. *Recreations:* Romanesque art, early music. *Address:* 33 Southwood Avenue, N6 5SA. *Club:* Athenæum.

FIRTH, Tazeena Mary; designer; *b* 1 Nov. 1935; *d* of Denis Gordon Firth and Irene (*née* Morris). *Educ:* St Mary's, Wantage; Chatelard Sch. Theatre Royal, Windsor, 1954–57; English Stage Co., Royal Court, 1957–60; partnership in stage design with Timothy O'Brien estabd 1961; output incl.: The Bartered Bride, The Girl of the Golden West, 1962; West End prodns of new plays, 1963–64; London scene of Shakespeare Exhibn, 1964; Tango, Days in the Trees, Staircase, RSC, and Trafalgar at Madame Tussaud's, 1966; All's Well that Ends Well, As You Like It, Romeo and Juliet, RSC, 1967; The Merry Wives of Windsor, Troilus and Cressida (also Nat. Theatre, 1976), The Latent Heterosexual, RSC, 1968; Pericles (also Comédie Française, 1974), Women Beware Women, Bartholomew Fair, RSC, 1969; 1970: Measure for Measure, RSC; Madame Tussaud's in Amsterdam; The Knot Garden, Royal Opera; 1971: Enemies, Man of Mode, RSC; 1972: La Cenerentola, Oslo; Lower Depths, The Island of the Mighty, RSC; As You Like It, OCSC; 1973: Richard II, Love's Labour's Lost, RSC; 1974: Next of Kin, NT; Summerfolk, RSC; The Bassarids, ENO; 1975: John Gabriel Borkman, NT; Peter Grimes, Royal Opera (later in Paris); The Marrying of Ann Leete, RSC; 1976: Wozzeck, Adelaide Fest.; The Zykovs, RSC; The Force of Habit, NT; 1977: Tales from the Vienna Woods, Bedroom Farce, NT; Falstaff, Berlin Opera; 1978: The Cunning Little Vixen, Göteborg; Evita, London (later in USA, Australia, Vienna); A Midsummer Night's Dream, Sydney Opera House; 1979: Peter Grimes, Göteborg; The Rake's Progress, Royal Opera; Turandot, Vienna State Opera, 1983. Designed independently: The Two Gentlemen of Verona, RSC, 1969; Occupations, RSC, 1971; The Rape of Lucretia, Karlstad, 1982; Katherina Ismailova, Göteborg, 1984; La Traviata, Umeå, The Trojan Woman, Göteborg, and Bluebeard's Castle, Copenhagen, 1985; Il Seraglio, Göteborg, 1986; The Magic Flute, Rigoletto, Umeå, 1987; Romeo and Juliet, Malmö, 1988; The Rake's Progress, Göteborg, and, Dido and Aeneas, Copenhagen, 1989; From the House of the Dead, Göteborg, and, Barbarians, RSC, 1990; Katerina Ismailova, Copenhagen, La Bohème, Malmö, and Il Seraglio, Stockholm, 1991. (Jtly) Gold Medal for Set Design, Prague Quadriennale, 1975. *Recreation:* sailing. *Address:* 33 Lansdowne Gardens, SW8 2EQ. *T:* 071–622 5384.

FISCHER, Annie; Hungarian Pianist; *b* Budapest, 1914; *m* Aladár Toth (decd). *Educ:* Franz Liszt Landemusikhochschule, Budapest. Studied under Arnold Székely and Ernst von Dohnanyi. Concert Début, Budapest, at age of eight (performed Beethoven's C Major Concerto), 1922; began international career as a concert pianist, Zurich, 1926; toured and played in most European Music centres, 1926–39. Concert pianist, Sweden, during War of 1939–45. Returned to Hungary after War and has made concert tours to all parts of the world. Hon. Prof., Acad. of Music, Budapest, 1965. Awarded 1st prize, Internat. Liszt Competition, Budapest, 1933; Kossuth Prizes 1949, 1955, 1965. Eminent Artist; Red Banner, Order of Labour, 1974. *Address:* c/o Terry Harrison Artists Management, 9A Penzance Place, W11 4PE.

FISCHER, Prof. Ernst Otto; Professor of Inorganic Chemistry, Munich University (Techn); *b* Munich, 10 Nov. 1918; *s* of Prof. Karl T. Fischer and Valentine (*née* Danzer); unmarried. *Educ:* Tech. Univ., Munich. Dip. Chem., 1949; Dr rer. nat., 1952, Habilitation 1954. Associate Prof. of Inorganic Chem., Univ. of Munich, 1957, Prof. 1959, Prof. and Dir, Inorganic Chem. Inst., Tech. Univ., Munich, 1964. Member: Bavarian Acad. of Sciences; Akad. deutscher Naturforscher Leopoldina, 1969; Austrian Acad. of Scis, 1976; Accad. dei Lincei, Italy, 1976; Göttingen Akad. der Wissenschaften, 1977; Rheinisch-Westfälische Akad. der Wissenschaften, 1987; Soc. of German Chemists, etc; Centennial For. Fellow, Amer. Chem. Soc., 1976. Hon. Dr rer. nat.: Munich, 1972; Erlangen, 1977; Veszprem, 1983; Hon. DSc Strathclyde, 1975. Has received many prizes and awards including the Nobel Prize for Chemistry, 1973 (jointly with Prof. Geoffrey Wilkinson) for their pioneering work, performed independently, on the chem. of organometallic "sandwich compounds". *Publications:* (with H. Werner) Metall-pi-Komplexe mit di- und oligoolefinischen Liganden, 1963 (trans. as Metal pi-Complexes Vol. 1, Complexes with di- and oligo-olefinic Ligands, 1966–); numerous contribs to learned jls on organometallic chem., etc. *Recreations:* art, history, travel. *Address:* 16 Sohnckestrasse, 8 Munich-Solln, Germany.

FISCHER-DIESKAU, Dietrich; baritone; *b* Berlin, 28 May 1925; *s* of Dr Albert Fischer-Dieskau; *m* 1949, Irmgard Poppen (*d* 1963); three *s*. *Educ:* High Sch., Berlin; Music Academy, Berlin. First Baritone, Städtische Oper, Berlin, 1948–78, Hon. Mem., 1978–; Mem., Vienna State Opera, 1957–63. Extensive Concert Tours of Europe and USA; soloist in Festivals at Edinburgh, Salzburg, Bayreuth, Vienna, Berlin, Munich, Holland, Luzern, Prades, etc. Opera roles include: Wolfram, Jochanaan, Almaviva, Marquis Posa, Don Giovanni, Falstaff, Mandryka, Wozzeck, Danton, Macbeth, Hans Sachs. Many recordings. Prof., Music Acad., Berlin, 1983; Member: Acad. of Arts, Berlin; Acad. of Fine Arts, Munich; Hon. RAM, 1972; Honorary Member: Wiener Konzerthausgesellschaft, 1962; Königlich-Schwedische Akad., 1972; Acad. Santa Cecilia, Rome; Royal Philharmonic Soc., 1985. Hon. DMus Oxford, 1978; Dr *hc*: Sorbonne, 1980; Yale, 1980. Kunstpreis der Stadt Berlin, 1950; Internationaler Schallplattenpreis, since 1955 nearly every year; Orfeo d'oro, 1955 and 1966; Bayerischer Kammersänger, 1959; Edison Prize, 1961, 1964, 1966, 1970; Naras Award, USA, 1962; Mozart-Medaille, Wien, 1962; Berliner Kammersänger, 1963; Electrola Award, 1970; Léonie Sonning Music Prize, Copenhagen, 1975; Golden Gramophone Award, Germany, 1975; Ruckert-Preis, Schweinfurth, 1979; President's Prize, Charles Gros Acad., Paris, 1980; Ernst Von Siemen Prize, 1980; Artist of the Year, Phonoakademie, Germany, 1980; Gold Medal, Royal Philharmonic Soc., 1988. Bundesverdienstkreuz (1st class), 1958, Grosses Verdienstkreuz, 1974, Stern zum Grossen Bundesverdienstkreuz, 1986; Pour le mérite, Deutschland (FRG), 1984; Chevalier de la Légion d'Honneur (France), 1990. *Publications:* Texte Deutscher Lieder, 1968 (The Fischer-Dieskau Book of Lieder, 1976); Auf den Spuren der Schubert-Lieder, 1971; Wagner und Nietzsche, 1974; Robert Schumann—Wort und Musik, 1981; Töne sprechen, Worte klingen, 1985; Nachklang, 1987; Wenn Musik der Liebe Nahrung ist: Künstlerschicksale im 19 Jahrhundert, 1990.

FISH, Prof. Francis, OBE 1989; BPharm, PhD; FRPharmS; Dean, School of Pharmacy, 1978–88, Professor of Pharmacy, 1988, Professor Emeritus, 1989, University of London; *b* 20 April 1924; *s* of William Fish and Phyllis (*née* Griffiths); *m* 1949, Hilda Mary Brown; two *s*. *Educ:* Houghton-le-Spring Grammar Sch.; Technical Coll., Sunderland (now Sunderland Polytechnic). BPharm (London) 1946; PhD (Glasgow) 1955. FPS 1946. Asst Lectr, 1946–48, Lectr, 1948–62, Royal Coll. of Science and Technology, Glasgow; University of Strathclyde: Sen. Lectr, 1962–69; Reader in Pharmacognosy and Forensic Science, 1969–76; Personal Prof., 1976–78; Dean, Sch. of Pharmaceutical Sciences, 1977–78; Supervisor, MSc course in Forensic Science, 1966–78. Mem. Editorial Bd, Jl Pharm. Pharmacol., 1964–70 and 1975–78. Member: Pharm. Soc. Cttee on Pharmacognosy, 1963–74; British Pharm. Codex Pharmacognosy Sub-Cttee A, 1968–73; Brit. Pharm. Conf. Sci. Cttee, 1973–78; Brit. Pharmacopoeia Pharmacognosy Panel, 1974–77; Council, Forensic Science Soc., 1974–77 (Vice-Pres., 1981–82); Professional and Gen. Services Cttee, Scottish Council on Alcoholism, 1976–78; Herbal Sub-Cttee, Cttee on Safety of Medicines, 1978–80; British Pharmacopœia Commn, 1980–; Cttee on Safety of Medicines, 1980–83; Univ. of London Senate, 1981–88; DHSS Standing Pharmaceutical Adv. Cttee, 1982–88; UGC Panel on Studies Allied to Medicine, 1982–89 (Chm., 1984–89); Nuffield Foundn Cttee of Inquiry into Pharmacy, 1983–86; Cttee on Review of Medicines, 1984–91; UGC Medical Subcttee, 1984–89. Chm., Post Qualification Bd for NHS Pharmacists in Scotland, 1989–. Mem., Governing Body, Wye College, 1985–88. Harrison Meml Medal, 1982; Charter Gold Medal, RPSGB, 1987. *Publications:* (with J. Owen Dawson) Surgical Dressings, Ligatures and Sutures, 1967; research pubns and review articles in Pharmaceut., Phytochem. and Forensic Sci. jls. *Recreations:* theatre, winemaking, gardening, golf. *Address:* Trollheim, Connaught Terrace, Crieff, Perthshire PH7 3DJ. *Club:* Crieff Golf.

FISH, Sir Hugh, Kt 1989; CBE 1984 (OBE 1971); Chairman, Water Engineering Ltd, 1988–91; Member, National Rivers Authority, 1989–91; *b* 6 Jan. 1923; *s* of Leonard Mark and Millicent Fish; *m* 1943, Nancy, *o d* of William and Louise Asquith; two *s* one *d*. *Educ:* Rothwell Grammar Sch.; Leeds Univ. (BSc). War Service, 1942–46, RNVR (Lieut). Chemist, W Riding Rivers Bd, 1949–52; Pollution and Fisheries Inspector, Essex River Bd, 1952–65; River Conservator, Essex River Authy, 1965–69; Chief Purification Officer, Thames Conservancy, 1969–74; Thames Water Authority: Dir of Scientific Services, 1974–78; Chief Exec., 1978–84; Mem., 1983–85. Chm., NERC, 1984–88 (Mem., 1976–84). Member: Central Adv. Water Cttee, 1970–72; OGDEN Cttee on Water Authority Management and Structure, 1973; Management Bd, BNSC, 1984–88; Nat. Rivers Authority Adv. Cttee, 1988–89. Pres., Inst. of Fisheries Management, 1987–. Member of Council: IWES, 1975–85 (Pres. 1984); Freshwater Biol Assoc., 1972–74. FRSC, FIWEM. *Publications:* Principles of Water Quality Management, 1973; contribs to various jls on natural science of water. *Recreations:* gardening, water sports, inventions, theatre. *Address:* Red Roofs, Shefford Woodlands, near Newbury, Berks RG16 7AJ. *T:* Great Shefford (048839) 369.

FISH, John; formerly Under-Secretary, Head of Establishment General Services Division, Department of Industry, 1973–80; *b* 16 July 1920; *m* 1948, Frances; two *s*. *Educ:* Lincoln School. BA Open Univ., 1989. Entered Customs and Excise, 1937; Exchequer and Audit Dept, 1939; War service, Pilot in RAF, 1940–46; Exchequer and Audit Dept, 1946; BoT, 1949; Principal, 1950; Min. of Materials, 1951; Volta River Preparatory Commn, Accra, 1953; BoT, 1956; Asst Sec., 1960; Min. of Health, 1962; BoT, 1965; DTI, 1970; Under-Sec., 1973; Dept of Industry, 1974. *Address:* The Green, Stockton, near Rugby, Warwicks CV23 8JF. *T:* Southam (0926) 812833. *Club:* Civil Service.

FISHBURN, (John) Dudley; MP (C) Kensington, since July 1988; *b* 8 June 1946; *s* of John Eskdale Fishburn and Bunting Fishburn; *m* 1981, Victoria, *y d* of Sir Jack Boles, *qv*; two *s* two *d*. *Educ:* Eton Coll.; Harvard Univ. (BA). Exec. Editor, The Economist, 1979–88. Parliamentary Private Secretary: FCO, 1989–90; DTI, 1990. Advr, J. P. Morgan, 1989–; non-exec. Dir, HFC Bank, 1990–. Governor, English National Ballet, 1989–; Trustee, Open Univ., 1982–; Mem., Bd of Overseers, Harvard Univ., 1990–. Editor, The World in 1992. *Recreations:* sailing, cooking. *Address:* House of Commons, SW1A 0AA. *Club:* Brooks's.

FISHER, family name of **Baron Fisher** and **Baroness Fisher of Rednal.**

FISHER, 3rd Baron, *cr* 1909, of Kilverstone; **John Vavasseur Fisher,** DSC 1944; JP; Director, Kilverstone Latin-American Zoo and Wild Life Park, 1973–91; *b* 24 July 1921;

s of 2nd Baron and Jane (*d* 1955), *d* of Randal Morgan, Philadelphia, USA; *S* father, 1955; *m* 1st, 1949, Elizabeth Ann Penelope (marr. diss. 1969), *yr d* of late Herbert P. Holt, MC; two *s* two *d*; 2nd, 1970, Hon. Mrs Rosamund Anne Fairbairn, *d* of 12th Baron Clifford of Chudleigh. *Educ:* Stowe; Trinity Coll., Cambridge. Member: Eastern Gas Bd, 1962–71; East Anglia Economic Planning Council, 1971–77. DL Norfolk, 1968–82; JP Norfolk, 1970. *Heir:* *s* Hon. Patrick Vavasseur Fisher [*b* 14 June 1953; *m* 1977, Lady Karen Carnegie, *d* of Earl of Northesk, *qv*; two *s* three *d*]. *Address:* Kilverstone Hall, Thetford, Norfolk. *T:* Thetford (0842) 2222.

See also Baron Clifford of Chudleigh.

FISHER OF REDNAL, Baroness *cr* 1974 (Life Peer), of Rednal, Birmingham; **Doris Mary Gertrude Fisher,** JP; Member of the European Parliament, 1975–79; Member, Warrington and Runcorn (formerly Warrington) Development Corporation, since 1974; *b* 13 Sept. 1919; *d* of late Frederick J. Satchwell, BEM; *m* 1939, Joseph Fisher (*d* 1978); two *d*. *Educ:* Tinker's Farm Girls Sch.; Fircroft Coll.; Bournville Day Continuation Coll. Member: Birmingham City Council, 1952–74; Labour Party, 1945–; UNESCO study group; Nat. Pres. Co-operative Women's Guild, 1961–62. Contested Ladywood, Birmingham, 1969 by-election; MP (Lab) Birmingham, Ladywood, 1970–Feb. 1974. Member: Gen. Medical Council, 1974–79; New Towns Staff Commn, 1976–79; Birmingham Civic Housing Assoc. Ltd, 1982–; Vice-President: Assoc. of Municipal Authorities, 1980–; Assoc. of Dist Councils, 1982–; Inst. of Trading Standards Admin. Pres., Birmingham Royal Inst. for the Blind, 1980–; Trustee, Sense in the Midlands, 1989–. Guardian, Birmingham Assay Office, 1979–89; Mem., Hallmarking Council, 1989–. Chm. Governors, Baskerville Special Sch., 1981–87; Governor, Hunter's Hill Special Sch., 1988–. JP Birmingham 1961. Hon. Alderman, 1974, Birmingham District Council. *Recreations:* swimming, walking. *Address:* 60 Jacoby Place, Priory Road, Birmingham B5 7UW. *T:* 021–471 2003.

FISHER, Anne; *see* Fisher, Phyllis Anne.

FISHER, Arthur J.; *see* Jeddere-Fisher.

FISHER, Desmond (Michael); Executive Director, Nationalist and Leinster Times, Carlow, since 1989 (Editor and Managing Director, 1984–89); *b* 9 Sept. 1920; *e s* of Michael Louis Fisher and Evelyn Kate Shier; *m* 1948, Margaret Elizabeth Smyth; three *s* one *d*. *Educ:* St Columb's Coll., Derry; Good Counsel Coll., New Ross, Co. Wexford; University Coll., Dublin (BA (NUI)). Asst Editor, Nationalist and Leinster Times, Carlow, 1945–48; Foreign Editor, Irish Press, Dublin, 1948–51; Economic Correspondent, Irish News Agency, Dublin, 1951–54; London Editor, Irish Press, 1954–62; Editor, Catholic Herald, 1962–66; Radio Telefis Eireann: Dep. Head of News, 1967–73; Head of Current Affairs, 1973–75; Dir of Broadcasting Develt, 1975–83. *Publications:* The Church in Transition, 1967; Broadcasting in Ireland, 1978; The Right to Communicate: a status report, 1981; The Right to Communicate: a new human right, 1983; contributor to The Economist, The Furrow, Irish Digest and to various Irish, US and foreign magazines. *Address:* Louvain 22, Dublin 14. *T:* Dublin 884608.

FISHER, Donald, CBE 1987; County Education Officer, Hertfordshire, 1974–90; *b* 20 Jan. 1931; *s* of John Wilfred and Mabel Fisher; *m* 1953, Mavis Doreen (*née* Sutcliffe); one *s* two *d*. *Educ:* Heckmondwike Grammar Sch.; Christ Church, Oxford (MA). Teacher, Hull GS, 1954–59; Admin. Asst, Cornwall LEA, 1959–61; Asst Educn Officer, W Sussex LEA, 1961–64; Headmaster: Helston GS, 1964–67; Midhurst GS, 1967–72; Dep. Educn Officer, W Sussex LEA, 1972–74. Chm., Assoc. of Educn Officers, 1982; Pres., Soc. of Educn Officers, 1984. Chm., Steering Cttee, Educn Policy Inf. Centre, Europe. Formerly Mem., Jt Bd, Certificate of Pre-Vocational Educn; Mem., Schs Curriculum Develt Cttee, 1983–88. Hon. DEd Hatfield Polytechnic, 1989. *Publications:* (contrib.) Educational Administration, 1980, 3rd edn 1989; articles and book reviews in Education. *Recreation:* reading. *Address:* 74 The Ryde, Hatfield, Herts AL9 5DL. *T:* Hatfield (0707) 271428.

FISHER, Doris G.; *b* 1907; *d* of Gathorne John Fisher, Pontypool. *Educ:* Farringtons, Chislehurst; Royal Holloway Coll., University of London (BA Hons (English) 1929, (French) 1931); Sorbonne. Senior English Mistress, Maidenhead County Gram. Sch. 1934–39; Second Mistress, Dover County Grammar Sch., 1945; Headmistress of Farringtons, Chislehurst, Kent, 1946–57, retired. Lecturer at Westminster Training Coll., 1957–59; Lecturer at Avery Hill Training Coll., 1959–62. *Address:* 9 The Ridgeway, Newport, Gwent NP9 5AF.

FISHER, Dudley Henry, CBE 1990; IPFA; Chairman, Wales Region, British Gas Corporation, 1974–87, retired; *b* 22 Aug. 1922; *s* of Arthur and Mary Fisher; *m* 1st, 1946, Barbara Lilian Sexton (*d* 1984); one *s* two *d*; 2nd, Jean Mary Livingstone Miller, *d* of late Dr and Mrs Robert Brown Miller, Cowbridge, S Glam. *Educ:* City of Norwich Sch. Various accountancy positions in Local Govt and Eastern Electricity Bd, 1938–53. War service, RAF, 1942–46 (Flt Lt). Northern Gas Bd, 1953; Wales Gas Board: Asst Chief Accountant, Dep. Chief Accountant, Chief Accountant, Dir of Finance, 1956–69; Dep. Chm., 1970. Member: Adv. Cttee on Local Govt Audit, 1979–82; Audit Commn for Local Authorities in England and Wales, 1983–88; Broadcasting Council for Wales, 1986–90; Hon. Treasurer, British National Cttee, 1980–89, and Chm., Admin. Cttee, 1986–89, World Energy Conf. Chm., Welsh Council, CBI, 1987–89; Dir, Inst. of Welsh Affairs, 1991–. Mem. Council, 1983–88, Treas., 1987–88, UC Cardiff; Mem. Council, Univ. of Wales Coll. of Cardiff, 1988–; Governor, United World Coll. of the Atlantic, 1988–. Trustee, Help the Aged, 1987–. High Sheriff, S Glam, 1988–89. *Recreations:* golf, gardening, reading. *Address:* Norwood Edge, 8 Cyncoed Avenue, Cardiff CF2 6SU. *T:* Cardiff (0222) 757958. *Clubs:* Royal Air Force; Cardiff and County (Cardiff).

FISHER, Rt. Rev. Edward George K.; *see* Knapp-Fisher.

FISHER, Elisabeth Neill; Her Honour Judge Fisher; a Circuit Judge, since 1989; *b* 24 Nov. 1944; *d* of Kenneth Neill Fisher and Lorna Charlotte Honor Fisher. *Educ:* Oxford High Sch. for Girls (GPDST); Cambridge Univ. (MA). Called to the Bar, Inner Temple, 1968. A Recorder, 1982–89. Mem. Senate, 1983–86. *Address:* 69 Christchurch Close, Edgbaston, Birmingham B15 3NE.

FISHER, Francis George Robson, MA Oxon; Deputy Secretary, Headmasters' Conference and Secondary Heads' Association, 1982–86; *b* 9 April 1921; *s* of late John Henry Fisher and Hannah Clayton Fisher; *m* 1965, Sheila Vernon, *o d* of late D. Dunsire and Mrs H. E. Butt; one *s*. *Educ:* Liverpool Coll. (Schol.); Worcester Coll., Oxford (Classical Exhibitioner). Served War of 1939–45; Capt. in Ayrshire Yeomanry, North Africa and Italy, 1942–45. Kingswood Sch., Bath, 1948–59, Housemaster and Sen. English Master, 1950–59; Headmaster, Bryanston Sch., 1959–74; Chief Master, King Edward's Sch., Birmingham, and Head Master, Schs of King Edward VI in Birmingham, 1974–82. Chairman: HMC Direct Grant Sub-Cttee, 1979–80; HMC Assisted Places Sub-Cttee, 1981. Life Governor, Liverpool Coll., 1969–; Governor: Harrow Sch., 1982–87; Bromsgrove Sch., 1985–; Kelly Coll., Tavistock, 1985–. *Recreations:* music, reading, sailing. *Address:* Craig Cottage, Lower Street, Dittisham, S Devon TQ6 0HY. *T:* Dittisham (080422) 309. *Club:* East India, Devonshire, Sports and Public Schools.

FISHER, Fredy; *see* Fisher, M. H.

FISHER, Sir George Read, Kt 1967; CMG 1961; Mining Engineer; President, MIM Holdings Ltd, 1970–75; *b* 23 March 1903; *s* of George Alexander and Ellen Harriett Fisher; *m* 1st, 1927, Eileen Elaine Triggs (*d* 1966); one *s* three *d*; 2nd, 1973, Marie C. Gilbey. *Educ:* Prince Alfred Coll., Adelaide; Adelaide Univ. (BE). Formerly Gen. Manager of Operations for Zinc Corporation Ltd, Broken Hill, NSW; Chm., Mount Isa Mines Ltd, 1953–70. *Recreations:* shooting and bowling. *Address:* GPO Box 1433, Brisbane, Qld 4001, Australia. *Clubs:* Queensland, Brisbane (Brisbane).

FISHER, Harold Wallace; Director, 1959–69, and Vice-President, 1962–69, Exxon Corporation, formerly Standard Oil Company (New Jersey) New York, retired; *b* 27 Oct. 1904; *s* of Dean Wallace Fisher and Grace Cheney Fisher; *m* 1930, Hope Elisabeth Case (*d* 1989); one *s*; *m* 1989, Janet Wilson Sawyer. *Educ:* Massachusetts Institute of Technology (BSc). Joined Standard Oil Company (NJ), 1927; Dir Esso Standard Oil Co. and Pres. Enjay Co. Inc., 1945. Resided in London, 1954–59. UK Rep. for Standard Oil Co. (NJ) and Chm. of its Coordination Cttee for Europe, 1954–57; Joint Managing Dir, Iraq Petroleum Co. Ltd and Associated Companies, 1957–59. Mem., Marine Bd, Nat. Acad. of Engineering, 1971–74; Vice-Chm., Sloan-Kettering Inst. for Cancer Research, 1974–75 (Chm., 1970–74); Mem., MIT Corp. Develt Cttee, 1975–; Vice-Chm., and Chm. Exec. Cttee, Community Blood Council of Greater New York, 1969–71. Hon. DSc 1960, Clarkson Coll. of Technology, Nat. Acad. of Engrg. *Publications:* various patents and technical articles relating to the Petroleum Industry. *Recreations:* golf, photography, horology. *Address:* 68 Goose Point Lane, PO Box 1792, Duxbury, Mass 02331, USA. *Clubs:* Pilgrims, American; University (New York); Duxbury Yacht.

FISHER, Hon. Sir Henry (Arthur Pears), Kt 1968; President, Wolfson College, Oxford, 1975–85, Hon. Fellow, 1985; *b* 20 Jan. 1918; *e s* of late Lord Fisher of Lambeth, PC, GCVO; *m* 1948, Felicity (BA Hons, Open Univ., 1987), *d* of late Eric Sutton; one *s* three *d*. *Educ:* Marlborough; Christ Church, Oxford (Schol.); Gaisford Greek Prose Prize, 1937; 1st Cl. Hon. Mods 1938; BA 1942; MA 1943. Served Leics Regt, 1940–46; Staff Coll., Quetta, 1943; GSO2, 1943–44; GSO1 HQ 14th Army, 1945. Hon. Lieut-Col 1946 (despatches). Fellow of All Souls Coll., 1946–73, Emeritus, 1976–, Estates Bursar, 1961–66, Sub-Warden, 1965–67. Barrister, Inner Temple, 1947, Bencher, 1966; QC 1960; Recorder of Canterbury, 1962–68; a Judge of the High Court of Justice, Queen's Bench Div., 1968–70; Director: J. Henry Schroder Wagg & Co. Ltd, 1970–75; Schroder International Ltd, 1973–75; Thomas Tilling plc, 1970–83; Equity and Law Life Assurance Soc. plc, 1975–87; Equity and Law plc, 1987. Mem., Gen. Council of the Bar, 1959–63, 1964–68, Vice-Chm., 1965–66, Chm., 1966–68; Vice-Pres., Senate of the Four Inns of Court, 1966–68; Vice-Pres., Bar Assoc. for Commerce, Finance and Industry, 1973–. Pres., Howard League, 1983–91; Chairman: Cttee of Inquiry into Abuse of the Social Security System, 1971; City Cttee on Company Law, 1974–76; Cttee of Inquiry into self-regulation at Lloyd's, 1979–80; Appeal Cttee, Panel on Take-overs and Mergers, 1981–87; Jt Commn on the Constitution (set up by Social Democratic and Liberal Parties), 1981–83; Investment Management Regulatory Orgn, 1986–89. Conducted inquiry into Confait case, 1976–77. Member: Private Internat. Law Cttee, 1961–63; Coun. on Tribunals, 1962–65; Law Reform Cttee, 1963–66; Council, Marlborough Coll., 1967–83 (Chm., 1977–82); BBC Programmes Complaints Commn, 1972–79; Governing Body, Imperial Coll., 1973–88 (Chm., 1975–88) (FIC 1974); Trustee, Pilgrim Trust, 1965– (Chm., 1979–83, 1989–). Hon. mem., Lloyd's, 1983. Hon. Fellow, Darwin Coll., Cambridge, 1984. Hon. LLD Hull, 1979. *Recreations:* music, walking. *Address:* Garden End, Marlborough SN8 1AA. *T:* Marlborough (0672) 515420; (professional) 1 Hare Court, Temple, EC4. *T:* 071-353 3171. *Club:* Travellers'.

FISHER, Rev. James Atherton; *b* 1 May 1909; *s* of Rev. Legh Atherton Fisher and Beatrice Edith Fisher; *m* 1938, Joan Gardiner Budden; two *s* one *d*. *Educ:* Haileybury; Sidney Sussex Coll., Cambridge (Scholar); 1st cl. Theological Tripos Pts I and II (Senior Scofield Prize); Cuddesdon Theological Coll; BA 1932, MA 1945; Deacon 1933; Priest, 1934; Asst Curate: St Matthew's, Oxhey, 1933–36; The Priory Church, Dunstable, 1936–39; Chaplain of Bedford Sch., 1939–43; Vicar of St Paul's, Peterborough, 1943–53; Religious Broadcasting Asst, BBC, 1953–58; Chaplain of St Christopher's Coll., Blackheath, 1954–58; Chaplain of Heathfield Sch., Ascot, 1959–64. Canon of St George's, Windsor, 1958–78; Treasurer, 1962–77; Founder Mem., Council of St George's House, Windsor Castle, 1966–78 (resp. for Clergy trng, 1966–74). *Address:* 32 High Lawn, Devizes, Wilts. *T:* Devizes (0380) 4254.

See also P. A. Fisher.

FISHER, James Neil; Partner, Theodore Goddard & Co., Solicitors, 1951–83, Senior Partner, 1980–83; *b* 27 May 1917; *s* of Henry John Fisher and Ethel Marie Fisher; *m* 1953, Elizabeth Mary Preston, *d* of late Bishop Arthur and Mrs Nancy Preston; one *s* two *d*. *Educ:* Harrow Sch.; Balliol Coll., Oxford (MA). Served War, Royal Signals, 1940–46 (Major 1945; despatches). Admitted solicitor, 1949. Chm., Rochester Diocesan Adv. Cttee for the Care of Churches, 1984–90. *Recreations:* the piano, walking, sight-seeing. *Address:* Ridge Lea, Oak Avenue, Sevenoaks, Kent TN13 1PR. *Club:* City University.

FISHER, John Mortimer, CMG 1962; HM Diplomatic Service, retired; *b* 20 May 1915; *yr s* of late Capt. Mortimer Fisher (W Yorks Regt) and Mrs M. S. Fisher (*née* Bailey); *m* 1949, Helen Bridget Emily Caillard; two *s*. *Educ:* Wellington; Trinity Coll., Cambridge. Entered Consular (subseq. Diplomatic) Service, 1937; Probationer Vice-Consul, Bangkok, 1938; served at Casablanca, 1942, Naples, 1944; 1st Sec. in Foreign Office, 1946, Mexico City, 1949; Detroit, Mich., USA, 1952; Counsellor in charge of British Information Services, Bonn, 1955; an Inspector in HM Foreign Service, 1959; Counsellor and Consul-Gen. at Bangkok, 1962; Consul-General, Düsseldorf, 1966–70; part-time Course Dir (Eur. Trng), Civil Service Coll., 1971–85. *Address:* The North Garden, Treyford, Midhurst, West Sussex GU29 0LD. *T:* Harting (0730) 825448.

FISHER, Mrs Margery Lilian Edith; free-lance writer, editor of review journal; *b* 21 March 1913; *d* of late Sir Henry Turner, and late Edith Rose; *m* 1936, James Maxwell McConnell Fisher (*d* 1970); two *s* three *d* (and one *s* decd). *Educ:* Rangi Ruru Sch., Christchurch, NZ; Amberley House Sch., NZ; Somerville Coll., Oxford (1st Cl. Hons English; MA, BLitt). Taught English at Queen Anne's Sch., Caversham, and Oundle Sch., 1939–45; coach for university scholarships and entrance exams; some broadcasting (BBC) of book reviews, free-lance lectr; Editor and proprietor of Growing Point (private jl reviewing children's books). Eleanor Farjeon Award, 1966; May Arbuthnot Award, USA, 1970. *Publications:* (with James Fisher) Shackleton, a biography, 1957; Intent upon Reading (criticism), 1961, rev. edn 1964; Field Day (novel), 1951; Matters of Fact, 1972; Who's Who in Children's Books, 1975; The Bright Face of Danger (criticism), 1986; monographs on: Classics; Henry Treece; John Masefield. *Recreations:* music, gardening. *Address:* Ashton Manor, Northampton NN7 2JL. *T:* Roade (0604) 862277.

FISHER, Mark; MP (Lab) Stoke-on-Trent Central, since 1983; *b* 29 Oct. 1944; *s* of Sir Nigel Fisher, *qv* and Lady Gloria Flower; *m* 1971, Ingrid Geach; two *s* two *d*. *Educ:* Eton College; Trinity College, Cambridge. MA. Documentary film producer and script writer, 1966–75; Principal, Tattenhall Centre of Education, 1975–83. Chairman: PLP Educn

Cttee, 1984–85; PLP Arts Cttee, 1984–85; Vice-Chm., PLP Treasury Cttee, 1983–84; an Opposition Whip, 1985–87; Opposition spokesman on the arts, 1987–. Contested (Lab) Leek, 1979. Staffordshire County Councillor, 1981–85 (Chm., Libraries Cttee, 1981–83). Dep. Pro-Chancellor, Keele Univ., 1989–. Mem. Council, PSI, 1989–. Stage plays: Brave New Town, 1974; The Cutting Room, 1990. *Publication:* City Centres, City Cultures, 1988. *Address:* 8 Bakewell Street, Penkhull, Stoke-on-Trent. *T:* Stoke-on-Trent (0782) 49357.

FISHER, Maurice; RCNC; General Manager, HM Dockyard, Rosyth, 1979–83; retired; *b* 8 Feb. 1924; *s* of William Ernest Fisher and Lily Edith (*née* Hatch); *m* 1955, Stella Leslie Sumsion; one *d. Educ:* St Luke's Sch., Portsmouth; Royal Dockyard Sch., Portsmouth; Royal Naval Coll., Greenwich. Constructor-in-Charge, HM Dockyard, Simonstown, 1956–60; Staff of Director of Naval Construction, 1960–63; Staff of C-in-C Western Fleet, 1963–65; Dep. Supt, Admiralty Experiment Works, Haslar, 1965–68; Dep. Prodn Manager, HM Dockyard, Devonport, 1968–72; Personnel Manager, HM Dockyard, Portsmouth, 1972–74; Planning Manager, 1974–77, Prodn Manager, 1977–79, HM Dockyard, Devonport. *Recreation:* game fishing. *Address:* Waterside, The Street, Chilcompton, Bath BA3 4EN.

FISHER, Max Henry, (Fredy Fisher); Director, S. G. Warburg & Co. Ltd, since 1981; *b* 30 May 1922; *s* of Fritz and Sophia Fischer; *m* 1952, Rosemary Margaret Maxwell; two *s* one *d. Educ:* Fichte-Gymnasium, Berlin; Rendcomb Coll.; Lincoln Coll., Oxford. FO Library, working on German War Documents project, 1949–56; Vis. Lectr, Melbourne Univ., 1956; Financial Times, 1957–80, Editor, 1973–80. Director: Commercial Union Assurance Co., 1981–91; Booker (formerly Booker McConnell), 1981–. Governor, LSE, 1981–. *Publication:* (ed with N. R. Rich) The Holstein Papers. *Recreations:* reading, listening to music. *Address:* 16 Somerset Square, Addison Road, W14 8EE. *T:* 071–603 9841. *Club:* Royal Automobile.

FISHER, Rt. Rev. Brother Michael, SSF, **(Reginald Lindsay Fisher);** Minister-General, Society of Franciscans, 1985–91; Assistant Bishop, Diocese of Ely, since 1985; *b* 6 April 1918; *s* of late Reginald Watson Fisher and Martha Lindsay Fisher. *Educ:* Clapham Central School; Bolt Court; Westcott House, Cambridge. Member, Society of St Francis, 1942. Deacon 1953, priest 1954, dio. Ely; Licence to officiate: Diocese of Ely, 1954–62; Newcastle, 1962–67; Sarum, 1967–79; Bishop Suffragan of St Germans, 1979–85; Bishop to HM Prisons, 1985. Minister Provincial, SSF, 1967–79. MA Lambeth, 1978. *Recreations:* painting, music, cinema, people. *Address:* 15 Botolph Lane, Cambridge, Cambs CB2 3RD. *T:* Cambridge (0223) 353903.

FISHER, Prof. Michael Ellis, FRS 1971; Wilson H. Elkins Professor, Institute for Science and Technology, University of Maryland, since 1987; *b* 3 Sept. 1931; *s* of Harold Wolf Fisher and Jeanne Marie Fisher (*née* Halter); *m* 1954, Sorrel Castillejo; three *s* one *d. Educ:* King's Coll., London. BSc 1951, PhD 1957, FKC 1981. Flying Officer (Educn), RAF, 1951–53; London Univ. Postgraduate Studentship, 1953–56; DSIR Sen. Research Fellow, 1956–58. King's Coll., London: Lectr in Theoretical Physics, 1958–62; Reader in Physics, 1962–64; Prof. of Physics, 1965–66; Cornell University: Prof. of Chemistry and Maths, 1966–73; Horace White Prof. of Chemistry, Physics and Maths, 1973–; Chm., Dept of Chemistry, 1975–78. Guest Investigator, Rockefeller Inst., New York, 1963–64; Vis. Prof. in Applied Physics, Stanford Univ., 1970–71; Walter Ames Prof., Univ. of Washington, 1977; Vis. Prof. of Physics, MIT, 1979; Sherman Fairchild Disting. Scholar, CIT, 1984; Vis. Prof. in Theoretical Physics, Oxford, 1985. Lectures: Buhl, Carnegie-Mellon, 1971; 32nd Richtmyer Meml, 1973; 17th Fritz London Meml, 1975; Morris Loeb, Harvard, 1979; H. L. Welsh, Toronto, 1979; Bakerian, Royal Soc., 1979; Welch Foundn, Texas, 1979; Alpheas Smith, Ohio State Univ., 1982; Laird Meml, Univ. of Western Ontario, 1983; Fries, Rensselaer Polytechnic Inst., NY, 1984; Amos de-Shalit Meml, Weizmann Inst., Rehovoth, 1985; Cherwell-Simon, Oxford, 1985; Marker, Penn. State Univ., 1988. John Simon Guggenheim Memorial Fellow, 1970–71, 1978–79; Fellow, Amer. Acad. of Arts and Scis, 1979; FAAAS 1986; For. Associate, National Acad. of Sciences, USA, 1983. Hon. FRSE 1986. Hon. DSc Yale, 1987. Irving Langmuir Prize in Chemical Physics, Amer. Phys. Soc., 1970; Award in Phys. and Math. Scis, NY Acad. of Scis, 1978; Guthrie Medal, Inst. of Physics, 1980; Wolf Prize in Physics, State of Israel, 1980; Michelson-Morely Award, Case-Western Reserve Univ., 1982; James Murray Luck Award, National Acad. of Sciences, USA, 1983; Boltzmann Medal, Internat. Union of Pure and Applied Physics, 1983. *Publications:* Analogue Computing at Ultra-High Speed (with D. M. MacKay), 1962; The Nature of Critical Points, (Univ. of Colorado) 1964, (Moscow) 1968; contribs to Proc. Roy. Soc., Phys. Rev., Jl Sci. Insts, Jl Math. Phys., Arch. Rational Mech. Anal., Jl Chem. Phys., Rept Prog. Phys., Rev. Mod. Phys., Physica, etc. *Recreations:* Flamenco guitar, travel. *Address:* Institute for Physical Science and Technology, University of Maryland, College Park, Md 20742–2431, USA. *T:* (301) 454 7780.

FISHER, Nancy Kathleen; *see* Trenaman, N. K.

FISHER, Sir Nigel (Thomas Loveridge), Kt 1974; MC 1945; MA (Cambridge); *b* 14 July 1913; *s* of late Comdr Sir Thomas Fisher, KBE, Royal Navy and of late Lady Shakespeare; step *s* of Rt Hon. Sir Geoffrey Shakespeare, 1st Bt; *m* 1935, Lady Gloria Vaughan (marr. diss. 1952), *e d* of 7th Earl of Lisburne; one *s* one *d*; *m* 1956, Patricia, *o d* of late Lieut-Col Sir Walter Smiles, CIE, DSO, DL, MP (*see* Lady Fisher). *Educ:* Eton; Trinity Coll., Cambridge. Served War of 1939–45; volunteered Welsh Guards and commissioned as 2nd Lieut 1939; Hook of Holland, Boulogne, 1940 (despatches); Capt., 1940; Major, 1944; N West Europe, 1945 (wounded, MC). Mem., National Executive Cttee of Conservative Party, 1945–47 and 1973–83; contested Chislehurst (N Kent), Gen. Election, 1945. MP (C): Herts, Hitchin, 1950–55; Surbiton, 1955–74; Kingston-upon-Thames, Surbiton, 1974–83. Mem. British Parl. Deleg. to Sweden, 1950, W Indies 1955, Malta 1966, Canada 1966, Uganda 1967, special mission to St Kitts, Anguilla, 1967. Parly Private Sec. to Minister of Food, 1951–54, to Home Sec., 1954–57; Parly Under-Sec. of State for the Colonies, July 1962–Oct. 1963; Parly Under-Sec. of State for Commonwealth Relations and for the Colonies, 1963–64; Opposition Spokesman for Commonwealth Affairs, 1964–66. Treasurer, CPA, 1966–68 (Vice-Chm., 1975–76; Treasurer, 1977–79, Dep. Chm., 1979–83, UK Branch). Mem. Exec., 1922 Cttee, 1960–62, 1969–83; Pres., Surbiton Cons. Assoc., Pres., British Caribbean Assoc.; Mem., British Bd of African Medical Research Foundn. Freedom of Kingston-upon-Thames, 1983. *Publications:* Iain Macleod, 1973; The Tory Leaders, 1977; Harold Macmillan, 1982. *Recreation:* reading. *Address:* 45 Exeter House, Putney Heath, SW15 3SX. *Clubs:* Boodle's, MCC.
See also M. Fisher.

FISHER, Mrs O. H.; *see* Anderson, Marian.

FISHER, Patricia, (Lady Fisher); Founder and Co-Chairman, Women Caring Trust; *b* 5 April 1921; *d* of late Lieut-Col Sir W. D. Smiles, CIE, DSO, DL, MP for N Down; *m* 1st, 1941, Neville M. Ford (marr. diss., 1956), 2nd *s* of late Dr Lionel Ford, Headmaster of Harrow and Dean of York; two *d*; 2nd, 1956, Sir Nigel Fisher, *qv. Educ:* privately and abroad. MP (UU) North Down (unopposed return), April 1953–55 (as Mrs Patricia Ford). *Recreations:* sailing, travel. *Address:* 45 Exeter House, Putney Heath, SW15 3SX.
See also W. M. J. Grylls.

FISHER, (Phyllis) Anne; Headmistress, Wycombe Abbey School, 1962–74; *b* 8 March 1913; *d* of Rev. L. A. Fisher, Rector of Higham on the Hill, Nuneaton, and Beatrice Fisher (*née* Eustace). *Educ:* Sch. of St Mary and St Anne, Abbots Bromley; Bristol Univ. BA History Hons, 1938. Senior History Mistress: St Helen's, Northwood, 1938–41; St Anne's Coll., Natal, SA, 1941–44; Headmistress, St Winifred's Sch., George, SA, 1944–45; Joint Headmistress, St George's, Ascot, 1946–49; Headmistress, Limuru Girls' Sch., Limuru, Kenya, 1949–57; Headmistress, Arundel Sch., Salisbury, Rhodesia, 1957–61. *Recreations:* study of old churches, the history of painting. *Address:* 7 Selwyn House, Selwyn Road, Eastbourne BN21 2LF. *Clubs:* Commonwealth Trust, Lansdowne.
See also J. A. Fisher.

FISHER, Richard Colomb; HM Diplomatic Service, retired; *b* Hankow, 11 Nov. 1923; *s* of Comdr Richard Fisher, RN and late Phillipa (*née* Colomb), Lee-on-Solent; *m* 1946, Edwine Kempers; two *s. Educ:* RNC Dartmouth. Joined Navy, 1937; to sea as Midshipman, 1941; War Service in submarines, 1943–45, Far East; flying trng, 1946–47; specialised in navigation/direction, 1948; Comdr 1958; retd from RN and joined Diplomatic Service, 1969; 1st Sec., Bonn, 1970–73; Commercial Counsellor, Warsaw, 1973–76, Rome, 1976–79. *Recreations:* history, languages.

FISHER, Roger Anthony, FRCO(CHM); Organist and Master of Choristers, Chester Cathedral, since 1967; *b* 18 Sept. 1936; *s* of Leslie Elgar Fisher and Vera Althea (*née* Salter); *m* 1st, 1967, Susan Mary Green (marr. diss. 1983); one *d*; 2nd, 1985, Gillian Rushforth (*née* Heywood). *Educ:* Bancroft's Sch., Woodford Green, Essex; Royal Coll. Music; Christ Church, Oxford (Organ schol.; MA). FRCO(CHM); ARCM; ATCL. Organist, St Mark's, Regents Park, 1957–62; Asst Organist, Hereford Cathedral, 1962–67; Asst Lectr in Music, Hereford Coll. of Educn, 1963–67. Music Critic, Liverpool Echo, 1976–79. Recital tours, 1967–, incl. USA, Canada, France, Germany, Switzerland, Hungary and Italy, Denmark, Norway and Sweden. Recordings in GB and Europe; BBC broadcasts as organist and with Chester Cathedral Choir. Conductor, choral socs and orchestras; Organ Consultant to churches and cathedrals. Geoffrey Tankard Prize for Solo Organ, RCM, 1959. *Publications:* articles about the organ and related subjects in several periodicals. *Recreations:* railway interests, walking, cycling, motoring. *Address:* 11 Abbey Street, Chester CH1 2JF.

FISHER, Sylvia Gwendoline Victoria; Principal Soprano, Royal Opera House, London; *d* of John Fisher and Margaret Fisher (*née* Frawley); *m* 1954, Ubaldo Gardini (marr. diss.). *Educ:* St Joseph's Coll., Kilmore, Australia; Conservatorium of Music, Melbourne. Won "Sun" Aria Competition, Melbourne, 1936; International Celebrity Concert in Australia, 1947; tour of Australia, 1955. Operatic Debut in Cadmus and Hermione, 1932; Covent Garden Debut in Fidelio (Leonora), 1948. Appeared in: Rome (Sieglinde), 1952; Cagliari (Isolde), 1954; Bologna (Gutrune), 1955; Covent Garden (Brunnhilde), 1956; Frankfurt Opera House (in Der Rosenkavalier), 1957, etc. *Recreations:* gardening and rare books on singing.

FISHER, Thomas Gilbert F.; *see* Field-Fisher.

FISHLOCK, Dr David Jocelyn, OBE 1983; Science Editor, Financial Times, since 1967; *b* 9 Aug. 1932; *s* of William Charles Fishlock and Dorothy Mary Turner; *m* 1959, Mary Millicent Cosgrove; one *s. Educ:* City of Bath Boys' Sch. (now Beechen Cliff Sch.); Bristol Coll. of Technol. FIBiol 1988; Companion, Inst. of Energy, 1987. National Service, REME, 1955–58. Westinghouse Brake & Signal Co. Ltd, 1948–55; McGraw-Hill, 1959–62; New Scientist, 1962–67. Glaxo Travelling Fellow, 1978. Hon. DLitt Salford, 1982. Chemical Writer of the Year Award, BASF, 1982; Worthington Pump Award, 1982; British Press Award, 1986. Silver Jubilee Medal, 1977. *Publications:* The New Materials, 1967; Man Modified, 1969; The Business of Science, 1975; The Business of Biotechnology, 1982; (with Elizabeth Antébi) Biotechnology: strategies for life, 1986. *Recreations:* writing, reading, collecting old medical/pharmaceutical equipment. *Address:* Traveller's Joy, Copse Lane, Jordans, Bucks HP9 2TA. *T:* Chalfont St Giles (02407) 3242. *Club:* Athenæum.

FISHLOCK, Trevor; journalist and author; roving foreign correspondent, The Sunday Telegraph; *b* 21 Feb. 1941; *m* 1978, Penelope Symon. *Educ:* Churcher's Coll., Petersfield; Southern Grammar Sch., Portsmouth. Portsmouth Evening News, 1957–62; freelance and news agency reporter, 1962–68; The Times: Wales and W England staff correspondent, 1968–77; London and foreign staff, 1978–80; S Asia correspondent, Delhi, 1980–83; New York correspondent, 1983–86; roving foreign correspondent, 1986–89; Moscow correspondent, Daily Telegraph, 1989–91. Fellow, World Press Inst., St Paul, Minnesota, 1977–78. Mem., Council for the Welsh Language, 1973–77. David Holden Award for foreign reporting (British Press Awards), 1983; Internat. Reporter of the Year (British Press Awards), 1986. *Publications:* Wales and the Welsh, 1972; Talking of Wales, 1975; Discovering Britain: Wales, 1979; Americans and Nothing Else, 1980; India File, 1983; The State of America, 1986; Indira Gandhi (for children), 1986. *Recreation:* sailing. *Address:* c/o The Sunday Telegraph, Peterborough Court At South Quay, 181 Marsh Wall, E14 9SR. *Clubs:* Travellers', Commonwealth Trust.

FISHWICK, Avril; Vice Lord-Lieutenant of Greater Manchester, since 1988; *b* 30 March 1924; *yr d* of Frank Platt and Charlotte Winifred Young; *m* 1950, Thomas William Fishwick; two *d. Educ:* Woodfield; High Sch. for Girls, Wigan; Liverpool Univ. (LLB 1946; LLM 1947). Admitted Solicitor 1949. War service, Foreign Office, Bletchley Park, 1942–45; Partner, Frank Platt & Fishwick, 1958–. Chm., Tidy Britain Enterprises Ltd; Dir, Northern Adv. Bd, National Westminster Bank, 1984–. Member: Wigan and Leigh HMC, 1960–73 (Mem., Exec. Council, 1966–73); NW RHA, 1985–88; Chm., Wigan AHA, 1973–82. Local President: Civic Trust, 1976; RSPCA, 1974–; Little Theatre, 1985–; Hon. Mem., Soroptimists Internat., 1973–; Mem., Groundwork Trust, Countryside Commn, 1986–. Mem. Court, Manchester Univ., 1984–. DL 1982, High Sheriff 1983–84, Gtr Manchester. *Recreations:* family, natural history. *Address:* Haighlands, Haigh Country Park, Haigh, Wigan WN2 1PB. *T:* Wigan (0942) 831291.

FISK, David John, ScD, PhD; Under Secretary, since 1987, Chief Scientist, since 1988, Department of the Environment; *b* 9 Jan. 1947; *s* of late John Howard Fisk and of Rebecca Elizabeth Fisk (*née* Haynes); *m* 1972, A. Anne Thoday; one *s* one *d. Educ:* Stationers' Company's Sch., Hornsey; St John's Coll., Cambridge (BA, MA, ScD); Univ. of Manchester (PhD). FCIBSE 1983. Joined Building Res. Estabt (traffic noise res.), 1972; Higher Sci. Officer, 1972–73; Sen. Sci. Officer (energy conservation res.), 1973–75; PSO, 1975–78; SPSO, Hd Mechanical and Elec. Engrg Div., 1978–84; Asst Sec., DoE, Central Directorate of Environmental Protection, 1984–87; Dep. Chief Scientist, DoE, 1987–88. Vis. Prof., Univ. of Liverpool, 1988–. *Publications:* Thermal Control of Buildings, 1981; numerous papers on bldg sci., systems theory and economics. *Recreations:* theatre, music. *Address:* c/o Department of the Environment, 43 Marsham Street, SW1.

FISON, Sir (Richard) Guy, 4th Bt *cr* 1905; DSC 1944; Chairman, Fine Vintage Wines PLC, since 1985; *b* 9 Jan. 1917; *er s* of Sir William Guy Fison, 3rd Bt; *S* father, 1964; *m*

1952, Elyn Hartmann (d 1987); one s one d. Educ: Eton; New Coll., Oxford. Served RNVR, 1939–45. Entered Wine Trade, 1948; Master of Wine, 1954; Dir, Saccone & Speed Ltd, 1952–82; Chairman: Saccone & Speed Internat., 1979–82; Percy Fox & Co. Ltd, 1982–83; Wine Develt Bd, 1982–83; Pres., Wine and Spirit Assoc., 1977–78. Hon. Freeman, 1976, Renter Warden, 1981–82, Upper Warden, 1982–83, Master, 1983–84, Vintners' Co. Heir: s Charles William Fison, b 6 Feb. 1954. Address: Medwins, Odiham, Hants RG25 1NE. T: Odiham (0256) 704075. Club: MCC.

FISTOULARI, Anatole; Principal Conductor of London Philharmonic Orchestra, 1943, now guest conductor; b Kiev, Russia, 20 Aug. 1907; obtained British nationality, 1948; s of Gregor and late Sophie Fistoulari; m 1942, Anna Mahler (marr. diss., 1956); one d; 1957, Mary Elizabeth, y d of late James Lockhart, Edinburgh. Educ: Kiev, Berlin, and Paris. Conducted first concert at age of 7 at Opera House in Kiev and later all over Russia; at 13 gave concerts in Germany and Holland; at 24 conducted Grand Opera Russe in Paris at the Châtelet Theatre with Colonne Orchestra and Chaliapine with whom he then toured France and Spain; then conducted the Ballet de Monte-Carlo with Massine in Drury Lane and Covent Garden before the War; toured with same company all over America, France, and Italy; in England in 1941 started opera production of Sorotchinsky Fair by Moussorgsky; March 1942 gave first Symphony Concert with London Symphony Orchestra and later conducted it regularly at Cambridge Theatre; first concert with London Philharmonic Orchestra in Bristol, Jan. 1943; concert engagements in numerous countries, from 1949. Founder, 1946, and Principal Conductor, London Internat. Orch. Guest conductor for Sadler's Wells Ballet, Royal Opera House, Covent Garden and NY Metropolitan Opera House, 1955; on tour with London Philharmonic Orchestra, to Moscow, Leningrad, Paris, 1956. Has made recordings for several firms. Recreation: listening to good concerts. Address: Flat 4, 65 Redington Road, NW3. Club: Savage.

FITCH, Douglas Bernard Stocker, FRICS; FAAV; MRAC; Director, Land and Water Service, Agricultural Development and Advisory Service, Ministry of Agriculture, Fisheries and Food, 1980–87, retired; b 16 April 1927; s of William Kenneth Fitch and Hilda Barrington; m 1952, Joyce Vera Griffiths; three s. Educ: St Albans Sch.; Royal Agricl Coll. (Dip. 1951). FRICS 1977. Served Army, RE, 1944–48. Joined Land Service, MAFF, 1951; Divl Surveyor, Guildford, 1971; Regional Surveyor, SE Reg., 1979. Prof., Rural Planning and Natural Resource Management, European Faculty of Land Use and Develt, 1985–. Royal Institution of Chartered Surveyors: Mem., Agric. Divl Council, 1980–87; Mem., Gen. Council, 1980–86. Internat. Fedn. of Surveyors deleg., 1988–91, and Chm., Standing Conf. on Marine Resource Management, 1985–89. Mem., Bd of Governors, Royal Agricl Coll., 1981–91. Recreation: golf. Address: 71 Oasthouse Crescent, Hale, Farnham, Surrey GU9 0NP. T: Farnham (0252) 716742. Clubs: Farmers', Civil Service.

FITCH, Marcus Felix Brudenell, (Marc), CBE 1977; FSA; b 5 Jan. 1908; s of Hugh Bernard Fitch and Bertha Violet (née James). Educ: Repton; Vienna and Geneva. FSG 1947; FSA 1952. Gold Staff Officer, Coronations of 1937 and 1953. Served Intel. Corps, Belgian Congo, Eritrea and GHQ ME, 1940–46. Chm., Soc. of Genealogists, 1956; founded Marc Fitch Fund, 1956; with Fund founded English Surnames Survey, Leicester Univ., 1965; with Dame Joan Evans estabd Stratigraphical Mus., Knossos, 1966; founded Fitch Archaeological Lab., Athens, 1974; assisted rural re-foundn of St Catherine's British Embassy Sch., Athens, 1974. Master, Tallow Chandlers' Co., 1957. Associate Mem., All Souls Coll., Oxford, 1973. Hon. Fellow, St Cross Coll., Oxford, 1981. Hon. FBA 1978. Hon. DLitt Leicester, 1973; Hon. MA Oxford, 1987. Publications: ed 10 vols for British Record Soc., 1959–86; On Medieval London, 1992. Clubs: Athenæum, Garrick, Royal Automobile.

FITCH, Admiral Sir Richard (George Alison), KCB 1985; Second Sea Lord, Chief of Naval Personnel and Admiral President, Royal Naval College, Greenwich, 1986–88, retired; b 2 June 1929; s of Edward William Fitch and Agnes Jamieson Fitch; m 1969, Kathleen Marie-Louise Igert; one s. Educ: Royal Naval College, Dartmouth. Seagoing appointments, 1946–66; HMS Berwick in Command, 1966–67; Staff of Flag Officer, Second in Command, Far East Fleet, 1967–69; Directorate of Naval Plans, MoD, 1969–71; RCDS 1972; HMS Apollo in Command, 1973–74; Naval Asst to First Sea Lord, 1974–76; HMS Hermes in Command, 1976–78; Dir of Naval Warfare, 1978–80; Naval Secretary, 1980–83; Flag Officer, Third Flotilla and Comdr Anti-Submarine Group Two, 1983–85. Liveryman, Coachmakers' and Coach Harness Makers' Co. CBIM. Recreations: gardening, philately, following sport. Address: West Hay, 32 Sea Lane, Middleton-on-Sea, West Sussex PO22 7RT. T: Middleton-on-Sea (0243) 582361. Clubs: Commonwealth Trust; Royal Yacht Squadron (Cowes); Middleton Sports.

FITCH, Rodney Arthur, CBE 1990; PPCSD (FSIAD 1976); design consultant; Chairman and major shareholder, Fitch-RS (Design Consultants), largest design company in Europe; b 19 Aug. 1938; s of late Arthur and Ivy Fitch; m 1965, Janet Elizabeth, d of Sir Walter Stansfield, CBE, MC, QPM; one s four d. Educ: Willesden Polytechnic, Sch. of Building and Architecture; Central School of Arts and Crafts (Theatre, TV Design); Hornsey School of Art (Interior and Furniture Design). Trainee designer, Hickman Ltd, 1956–58; National Service, RAPC, 1958–60; Charles Kenrick Associates, 1960–62; Conran Design Gp Ltd, 1962–69; C.D.G. (Design Consultants) Ltd, 1969–71; Founder, 1971, Fitch and Company, subseq. Fitch-RS, a multi-discipline design practice engaged on a wide range of UK and overseas projects from offices in Europe, USA and Tokyo. Mem., Design Council, 1988–. Dep. Chm., Court of Govs, London Inst., 1989–; Mem. Council, RCA, 1989–; Trustee, V & A Museum, 1991. CSD (formerly SIAD): Pres., 1988–90; Vice-Pres., 1982–86; Hon. Treas., 1984–87; Past Pres., Designers and Art Dirs Assoc., 1983. FRSA 1976. Publications: (with L. Knobel) Fitch on Retail Design, 1990; regular contributor to design publications. Recreations: cricket, tennis, opera, theatre, his family. Address: 4–6 Soho Square, W1. T: 071–580 3060.

FITCHEW, Geoffrey Edward; Director-General (for Banking, Financial Services and Company Law), Directorate-General XV, European Commission, Brussels, since 1986; b 22 Dec. 1939; s of Stanley Edward Fitchew and Elizabeth Scott; m 1966, Mary Theresa Spillane; two s. Educ: Uppingham School; Magdalen Coll., Oxford (MA); London Sch. of Economics (MScEcon). Asst Principal, HM Treasury, 1964; Private Sec. to Minister of State, 1968–69; Principal, 1969; Gwilym Gibbon Research Fellow, Nuffield Coll., Oxford, 1973–74; Asst Sec., Internat. Finance Div., HM Treasury, 1975–77; Counsellor (Economics and Finance), UK Perm. Rep. to EEC, 1977–80; Asst Sec., HM Treasury, 1980–83; Under Sec., HM Treasury, 1983–86. Recreations: tennis, squash. Address: Directorate-General XV, Commission of the European Community, 200 rue de la Loi, Brussels, Belgium.

FITT, family name of **Baron Fitt**.

FITT, Baron cr 1983 (Life Peer), of Bell's Hill in the County of Down; **Gerard Fitt**; b 9 April 1926; s of George Patrick and Mary Ann Fitt; m 1947, Susan Gertrude Doherty; five d (and one d decd). Educ: Christian Brothers' Sch., Belfast. Merchant Seaman, 1941–53; various positions, 1953–. Councillor, later Alderman, Belfast Corp., 1958–81; MP (Eire Lab), Parlt of N Ireland, Dock Div. of Belfast, 1962–72; Mem. (SDLP), N Belfast, NI

Assembly, 1973–75, NI Constitutional Convention, 1975–76; Dep. Chief Exec., NI Exec., 1974; elected MP (Repub. Lab) Belfast West, 1966, a founder and Leader, Social Democratic and Labour Party, and MP (SDLP), 1970–79, when resigned Leadership; MP (Socialist), 1979–83. Contested (Socialist) Belfast West, 1983. Recreation: full-time politics. Address: House of Lords, SW1A 0PW.

FITT, Robert Louis, CMG 1975; FEng; b 9 Aug. 1905; s of late R. F. Fitt; m 1936, Elsie Ockleshaw, d of late William Ockleshaw, Liverpool; one s. Educ: Launceston and Barnstaple Grammar Schs; City and Guilds Coll., London. BSc; FCGI. Engineer with Sudan Govt, 1927–31; with Mott Hay & Anderson, on Mersey Tunnel and London Underground Extensions, 1931–39. Joined Sir Alexander Gibb & Partners, 1939; Partner, 1946; retired, 1978; responsible for industrial develts, irrigation works, water supplies, thermal and hydro-electric power projects, airports, and economic develt surveys, in countries incl. UK, Iran, Iraq, Sudan, Argentina, Kenya, Tanzania, Swaziland, Rhodesia, Australia and Jamaica. Chm., Assoc. of Consulting Engineers, 1961–62; Vice-Pres., Middle East Assoc., 1972, Pres., Internat. Fedn of Consulting Engrs (FIDIC), 1972–74. FEng, FICE (Vice-Pres., 1976–78). Order of Homayoun, Iran, Third Class, 1955. Recreations: gardening, golf. Address: 27 Longdown Lane North, Ewell, Surrey KT17 3HY. T: 081–393 1727.

FITTALL, Betty Daphne C.; see Callaway-Fittall.

FITTER, Richard Sidney Richmond; author and naturalist; b 1 March 1913; o s of Sidney and Dorothy Fitter; m 1938, Alice Mary (Maisie) Stewart, e d of Dr R. S. Park, Huddersfield; two s one d. Educ: Eastbourne Coll.; LSE. BSc(Econ). Research staff: PEP, 1936–40; Mass-Observation, 1940–42; Operational Research Section, Coastal Command, 1942–45; Sec., Wild Life Cons. Special Cttee of Hobhouse Cttee on Nat. Parks, 1945–46; Asst Editor, The Countryman, 1946–59; Open Air Corresp., The Observer, 1958–66; Dir, Intelligence Unit, Council for Nature, 1959–63; Editor, Kingfisher, 1965–72. Vice-Pres., Fauna and Flora Preservation Soc., 1988– (Hon. Secretary, 1964–81; Chm., 1983–87); Member: Species Survival Commn (formerly Survival Service Commn), Internat. Union for Cons. of Nature, 1963– (Chm., Steering Cttee, 1975–88)); Conservation Adv. Cttee, World Wildlife Fund Internat., 1977–79; Scientific Authority for Animals, DoE, 1965–81; Trustee, World Wildlife Fund, UK, 1977–83; Past Pres., Berks, Bucks and Oxfordshire Naturalists' Trust; Chm., Council for Nature, 1979; Vice/Chm., Falkland Is Foundn, 1986–; Minister's Representative, Southern Council for Sport and Recreation, 1980–82; formerly Hon. Treasurer and Hon. Sec., British Trust for Ornithology; Chm., Gen. Purposes Cttee, Royal Soc. for Protection of Birds; Editor, The London Naturalist; and council or cttee mem. of numerous nat. history and conservation bodies. Scientific FZS. Officier, Order of the Golden Ark, The Netherlands, 1978. Publications: London's Natural History, 1945; London's Birds, 1949; Pocket Guide to British Birds, 1952; Pocket Guide to Nests and Eggs, 1954; (with David McClintock) Pocket Guide to Wild Flowers, 1956; The Ark in Our Midst, 1959; Six Great Naturalists, 1959; Guide to Bird Watching, 1963; Wildlife in Britain, 1963; Britain's Wildlife: rarities and introductions, 1966; (with Maisie Fitter) Penguin Dictionary of Natural History, 1967; Vanishing Wild Animals of the World, 1968; Finding Wild Flowers, 1972; (with H. Heinzel and J. Parslow) Birds of Britain and Europe, with North Africa and the Middle East, 1972; (with A. Fitter and M. Blamey) Wild Flowers of Britain and Northern Europe, 1974; The Penitent Butchers, 1979; (with M. Blamey) Handguide to the Wild Flowers of Britain and Northern Europe, 1979; (with M. Blamey) Gem Guide to Wild Flowers, 1980; (with N. Arlott and A. Fitter) The Complete Guide to British Wildlife, 1981; (ed with Eric Robinson) John Clare's Birds, 1982; (with A. Fitter and J. Wilkinson) Collins Guide to the Countryside, 1984; (with A. Fitter and A. Farrer) Grasses, Sedges, Rushes and Ferns of Britain and Northern Europe, 1984; (ed) The Wildlife of the Thames Counties, 1985; Wildlife for Man, 1986; (with R. Manuel) Field Guide to the Freshwater Life of Britain and NW Europe, 1986; (with A. Fitter) Guide to the Countryside in Winter, 1988. Recreations: botanising, observing wild and human life, exploring new habitats, reading. Address: Drifts, Chinnor Hill, Oxford OX9 4BS. T: Kingston Blount (0844) 51223. Club: Athenæum.

FITZALAN-HOWARD, family name of **Lady Herries of Terregles** and of **Duke of Norfolk**.

FITZALAN-HOWARD, Maj.-Gen. Lord Michael, GCVO 1981 (KCVO 1971; MVO 1952); CB 1968; CBE 1962; MC 1944; DL; Her Majesty's Marshal of the Diplomatic Corps, 1972–81; b 22 Oct. 1916; 2nd s of 3rd Baron Howard of Glossop, MBE, and Baroness Beaumont (11th in line), OBE; b of 17th Duke of Norfolk, qv; granted title and precedence of a Duke's son, 1975; m 1st, 1946, Jean (d 1947), d of Sir Hew Hamilton-Dalrymple, 9th Bt; one d; 2nd, 1950, Margaret, d of Capt. W. P. Meade-Newman; four s one d. Educ: Ampleforth Coll.; Trinity Coll., Cambridge. Joined Scots Guards, 1938. Served in: North West Europe, 1944–45; Palestine, 1945–46; Malaya, 1948–49; Egypt, 1952–53; Germany, 1956–57 and 1961–66; Commander Allied Command Europe Mobile Forces (Land), 1964–66; Chief of Staff, Southern Command, 1967–68; GOC London Dist, and Maj.-Gen. comdg The Household Division, 1968–71. Col: The Lancs Regt (Prince of Wales's Volunteers), 1966–70; The Queen's Lancashire Regiment, 1970–78; Colonel of The Life Guards, 1979–; Gold Stick to the Queen, 1979–; Joint Hon. Col, Cambridge Univ. OTC, 1968–71. Chm. Council, TAVR Assocs, 1973–81, Pres., 1981–84; Patron, Council, TA&VRA, 1984–. DL Wilts, 1974. Freeman, City of London, 1985. Address: Fovant House, Fovant, Salisbury, Wilts SP3 5LA. T: Fovant (072270) 617. Clubs: Buck's, Pratt's.

FITZCLARENCE, family name of **Earl of Munster**.

FITZER, Herbert Clyde, CB 1971; OBE 1958; Head of Royal Naval Engineering Service, 1970–71; Director of Engineering (Ships), Navy Department, Ministry of Defence, 1968–71, retired; b 3 Nov. 1910; s of Herbert John Fitzer; m 1938, Queenie Stent; one d. Educ: Portsmouth Royal Dockyard Sch.; RNC Greenwich; London Univ. 1st cl. hons BSc (Eng) London, 1932; Greenwich Professional Certif. in Electrical Engrg, 1933. CEng, FIEE 1959. Asst Elec. Engr, Admty, 1936; Sheerness Dockyard, 1938; Elec. Engr, Submarine Design, Admty, 1939; Shore Estabs, 1945; Suptg Elec. Engr, Submarine Design, 1950; Asst Dir of Elec. Engrg, Ships Power Systems, 1961; Polaris Project, 1963; Dep. Dir of Elec. Engrg, 1966. Licensed Lay Reader, Dio. Bath and Wells. Publication: Christian Flarepath, 1956. Address: Longacre House, 16 Sharvells Road, Milford-on-Sea, Lymington, Hants SO41 0PE. T: Lymington (0590) 44875.

FitzGEORGE-BALFOUR, Gen. Sir (Robert George) Victor, KCB 1968 (CB 1965); CBE 1945; DSO 1950; MC 1939; DL; Chairman, National Fund for Research into Crippling Diseases, 1975–89; b 15 Sept. 1913; s of Robert S. Balfour and Iris (née FitzGeorge), 47 Wilton Crescent, SW1; m 1943, Mary (Diana), er d of Rear-Adm. Arthur Christian, 3 Sloane Gardens, SW3; one s one d. Educ: Eton; King's Coll., Cambridge (BA). Commissioned 2nd Lieut Coldstream Guards, 1934; Palestine, 1936; Middle East, 1937–43; France and NW Germany, 1944–46; commanded 2nd Bn Coldstream Guards, Malaya, 1948–50; idc 1955; Chief of Staff to Governor of Cyprus, 1956; Commanded 1st Guards Brigade, 1957; Chief of Staff, HQ Southern Comd, 1962–63; Dir of Military

Operations, Ministry of Defence, 1964–66; Senior Army Instructor, IDC, 1966–68; Vice-Chief of the General Staff, 1968–70; UK Mil. Representative, NATO, 1971–73. ADC (Gen.), 1972–73. Col Comdt, HAC, 1976–84. DL West Sussex, 1977. Knight Commander of the Order of Orange Nassau with swords (Netherlands), 1946. *Address:* The Old Rectory, West Chiltington, West Sussex RH20 2QA. *T:* West Chiltington (0798) 812255. *Club:* Army and Navy.

FITZGERALD, family name of **Duke of Leinster.**

FITZGERALD, Charles Patrick; Professor of Far Eastern History, Australian National University, 1953–67, now Emeritus; Visiting Fellow, Department International Relations, Australian National University, 1968–69; *b* 5 March 1902; *s* of Dr H. Sauer; *m* 1941, Pamela Knollys (*d* 1980); two *d* (and one *d* decd). *Educ:* Clifton. China, 1923–27, 1930–32, 1936–38, 1946–50. Leverhulme Fellowship for Anthropological Research in South-West China. DLitt ANU 1968. *Publications:* Son of Heaven, 1932; China, a Cultural History, 1935, rev. edn 1950, repr. 1986; The Tower of Five Glories, 1941; (with George Yeh) Introducing China, 1948; Revolution in China, 1951 (revised version (Penguin) as The Birth of Communist China, 1965); The Empress Wu, 1955; Flood Tide in China, 1958; Barbarian Beds: the origin of the chair in China, 1965; A Concise History of Eastern Asia, 1965; The Third China, Chinese Communities in SE Asia, 1965; Des Mantchous à Mao Tse-tong, 1968; History of China, 1969; Communism Takes China, 1970; The Southern Expansion of the Chinese People: Southern Fields and Southern Ocean, 1972; Mao Tsetung and China, 1976; Ancient China, 1978; Why China?, 1985. *Address:* 4 St Paul's Street, Randwick, NSW 2031, Australia. *Club:* Savile.

FITZGERALD, Rev. (Sir) Daniel Patrick, SSC (4th Bt *cr* 1903, of Geraldine Place, St Finn Barr, Co. Cork, but does not use the title); *b* 28 June 1916; *S* brother, Rev. (Sir) Edward Thomas FitzGerald (3rd Bt), 1988. Roman Catholic priest. *Heir: cousin* John Finnbarr FitzGerald [*b* 1918; *m* 1949, Margaret Hogg; one *s* one *d*].

FITZ-GERALD, Desmond John Villiers, (29th Knight of Glin); Irish Agent, Christie, Manson & Woods Ltd, since 1975; *b* 13 July 1937; *s* of Desmond Windham Otho Fitz-Gerald, 28th Knight of Glin (*d* 1949), and Veronica (who *m* 2nd, 1954, Ray Milner, CC (Canada), QC, Edmonton, Alta, and Qualicum Beach, Vancouver Island, BC), 2nd *d* of late Ernest Amherst Villiers, MP, and of Hon. Elaine Augusta Guest, *d* of 1st Baron Wimborne; *m* 1st, 1966, Louise Vava Lucia Henriette (marr. diss. 1970), *d* of the Marquis de la Falaise, Paris; 2nd, 1970, Olda Ann, *o d* of T. V. W. Willes, 39 Brompton Sq., SW3; three *d*. *Educ:* Stowe Sch.; University of British Columbia (BA 1959); Harvard Univ. (MA 1961). FSA 1970. Asst Keeper, 1965–72, Dep. Keeper, 1972–75, Dept of Furniture and Woodwork, V&A. Director: Irish Georgian Foundn, 1974– (Chm.); Historic Irish Tourist Houses Assoc., 1977– (Chm., 1982–86); Castletown Foundn, 1979–. Vice-Pres., Irish Georgian Soc.; Member: Heritage Gardens Cttee, An Taisce (Irish National Trust), 1978–; Irish Historic Properties Cttee, 1982–. *Publications:* (ed) Georgian Furniture, 1969; (with Maurice Craig) Ireland Observed, a handbook to the buildings and antiquities, 1970; The Music Room from Norfolk House, 1972; (with Edward Malins) Lost Demesnes: Irish Landscape Gardening 1660–1845, 1976; (with Anne Crookshank) The Painters of Ireland, 1978; Irish Furniture, 1978; (jtly) Vanishing Country Houses of Ireland, 1988; *catalogues*, all jointly: Irish Houses and Landscapes, 1963; Irish Architectural Drawings, 1965; Irish Portraits 1660–1860, 1969; Mildred Anne Butler, 1981; articles and reviews on architecture and the decorative arts in many Art periodicals. *Address:* Glin Castle, Glin, Co. Limerick, Ireland. *TA:* Knight Glin. *T:* Listowel (068) 34173 and 34112, *Fax:* (068) 34364; 52 Waterloo Road, Dublin 4. *T:* Dublin 680585, *Fax:* Dublin 680271. *Clubs:* Beefsteak, White's; Kildare Street and University (Dublin).

FITZGERALD, Frank, CBE 1989; PhD; FEng 1977; Managing Director, Technical, since 1981, Director, since 1986, British Steel plc (formerly British Steel Corporation); Chairman: British Steel Consultants Ltd (formerly British Steel Corporation (Overseas Services) Ltd), 1981–89; British Steel Stainless, since 1989; *b* 11 Nov. 1929; *s* of George Arthur Fitzgerald and Sarah Ann (*née* Brook); *m* 1956, Dorothy Eileen Unwin; two *s* one *d*. *Educ:* Barnsley Holgate Grammar Sch.; Univ. of Sheffield (BScTech; PhD). FInstE, FIChemE. Ministry of Supply, RAE, Westcott, Bucks, 1955; United Steel Cos, Swinden Laboratories, Rotherham, 1960–68; British Steel plc (formerly British Steel Corporation), 1968–: Process Res. Manager, Special Steels Div., 1970; Head Corporate Advanced Process Laboratory, 1972; Director, R&D, 1977. Hadfield Medal, Iron and Steel Inst., for work on application of combustion and heat transfer science to industrial furnaces, 1972; Melchett Medal, Inst. of Energy, 1988. *Publications:* papers in learned jls on heat and mass transfer and metallurgical processes. *Recreation:* rock climbing and mountaineering. *Clubs:* Alpine; Climbers'.

FITZGERALD, Garret, PhD; Barrister-at-Law; Member of the Dáil (TD) (FG) for Dublin South East, since 1969; Taoiseach (Prime Minister of Ireland), June 1981–March 1982 and 1982–87; *b* Dublin, 9 Feb. 1926; *s* of late Desmond FitzGerald (Minister for External Affairs, Irish Free State, 1922–27, and Minister for Defence, 1927–32) and Mabel FitzGerald (*née* McConnell); *m* 1947, Joan, *d* of late Charles O'Farrell; two *s* one *d*. *Educ:* St Brigid's Sch., Bray; Coláiste na Rinne, Waterford; Belvedere Coll., University Coll., and King's Inns, Dublin. Called to the Bar, 1947. Aer Lingus (Irish Air Lines), 1947–58; Rockefeller Research Asst, Trinity Coll., Dublin, 1958–59; College Lectr, Dept of Political Economy, University Coll., Dublin, 1959–87. Member: Seanad Eireann (Irish Senate), 1965–69; Dáil Cttee on Public Accounts, 1969–73; Minister for Foreign Affairs, Ireland, 1973–77; Leader and President, Fine Gael Party, 1977–87; Leader of the Opposition, 1977–June 1981, and March–Dec. 1982. President: Council of Ministers, EEC, Jan.–June 1975; European Council, July–Dec. 1984; Irish Council of Eur. Movement, 1977–81 and March–Dec. 1982; Mem., Internat. Exec. Cttee of Eur. Movement, 1972–73 and 1977–81; Vice-Pres., Eur. People's Party, 1979–87. Mem., Oireachtas Library Cttee, 1965–69; Governor, Atlantic Inst. of Internat. Relations, Paris, 1972–73; Mem., Senate of National Univ. of Ireland; 1973–. Formerly: Irish Correspondent of BBC, Financial Times, Economist and other overseas papers; Economic Correspondent, Irish Times; also Past Managing Dir, Economist Intelligence Unit of Ireland; Economic Consultant to Fedn of Irish Industries and Construction Industry Fedn, and Rep. Body for Guards; Past Member: Exec. Cttee and Council, Inst. of Public Admin; Council, Statistical and Social Inquiry, Soc. of Ireland; Senate Electoral Law Commn; Workmen's Compensation Commn; Transport Advisory Cttee for Second Programme; Cttee on Industrial Organisation; Gen. Purposes Cttee of Nat. Industrial Economic Council. Lectures: Radcliffe, Warwick Univ., 1979; Richard Dimbleby, BBC, 1982; Gaitskell, Nottingham Univ., 1988. Hon. LLD: New York, 1974; St Louis, 1974; St Mary's, Halifax, NS, 1985; Keele, 1986; Boston Coll., 1987; Hon. DCh Oxon, 1987. Grand Cordon, Order of Al-Kaubar Al-Undari (Jordan), 1975; Grand Officier, Ordre de la République (Tunisia), 1976; Grand Cross (1st Cl.), Order of Merit (FRG), 1986; Order of Christ (Portugal), 1986; Grand Cordon, Order of Rising Sun (Japan), 1989. *Publications:* State-sponsored Bodies, 1959; Planning in Ireland, 1968; Towards a New Ireland, 1972; Unequal Partners (UNCTAD), 1979; Estimates for Baronies of Minimum Level of Irish Speaking Amongst Successive Decennial Cohorts 1771–1781 to 1861–1871, 1984. *Address:* Leinster House, Kildare Street, Dublin 2, Ireland. *Club:* Royal Irish Yacht (Dun Laoghaire).

FitzGERALD, Sir George (Peter Maurice), 5th Bt *cr* 1880; 23rd Knight of Kerry; MC 1944; Major, Army, retired; *b* 27 Feb. 1917; *s* of Sir Arthur Henry Brinsley FitzGerald, 4th Bt, and Mary Eleanor (*d* 1967), *d* of late Capt. Francis Forester; *S* father 1967; *m* 1939, Angela Dora Mitchell; one *s* one *d*. *Educ:* Harrow; RMC, Sandhurst. Commnd into Irish Guards, 1937; 2nd in comd, 1st Bn, 1944; 2nd in comd, 2nd Bn, 1946; retired, 1948. *Heir: s* Adrian James Andrew Denis FitzGerald, *b* 24 June 1940. *Address:* Colin's Farm House, 55 High Street, Durrington, Salisbury, Wilts SP4 8AQ. *Club:* Army and Navy.

FITZGERALD, Gerald Edward, AC 1991; QC (Australia); Chairman, Australian Heritage Commission, since 1990; *b* 26 Nov. 1941; *m* 1968, Catherine Glynn-Connolly; one *s* two *d*. *Educ:* Univ. of Queensland (LLB). Admitted Queensland Bar, 1964; QC Queensland 1975 and subseq. QC NSW and Victoria; Judge of Federal Court of Australia, 1981–84; Judge of Supreme Court of ACT, 1981–84; Presidential Mem., Administrative Appeals Tribunal, 1981–84; Mem., Australian Law Reform Commn, 1981–84; Chairman, Commission of Inquiry: into possible illegal activities and associated police misconduct, Qld, 1987–89; into the Conservation, Management and Use of Fraser Is. and the Gt Sandy Reg., Qld, 1990. *Recreations:* tennis, reading, music. *Address:* 43 McCaul Street, Taringa East, Brisbane, Qld 4068, Australia. *T:* 07 371 7509. *Clubs:* Queensland, Brisbane (Brisbane).

FITZGERALD, Brig. (retd) Gerald Loftus, CBE 1956; DSO 1945; *b* 5 May 1907; *s* of late Col D. C. V. FitzGerald, MC, Nairobi Kenya; *m* 1937, Mary Stuart, *d* of late Charles E. Mills, Holbrook, Suffolk; one *s* one *d*. *Educ:* Wellington Coll.; Royal Military Academy, Woolwich. Commissioned 2nd Lieut RA, 1926; Regimental duty UK and overseas, 1926–39; staff and regimental duty in UK and NW Europe during War of 1939–45. Brit. Mil. Mission to Greece, 1946–48; Chief Instructor, Officer Cadet Sch., 1949–50; Brit. Joint Services Mission, Washington, USA, 1951–52; Comdr Trg Bde, RA, 1953–55; Dep. Dir, War Office, 1956–58; retired pay, 1959. OStJ 1982. Order of Leopold (with Palm), Belgium, 1945; Croix de Guerre (with Palm), 1945. *Recreations:* field sports, travel. *Club:* Army and Navy.

FitzGERALD, Michael Frederick Clive, QC 1980; *b* 9 June 1936; *s* of Sir William James FitzGerald, MC, QC, and Mrs E. J. Critchley; *m* 1966, Virginia Grace Cave; one *s* three *d*. *Educ:* Downside; Christ's Coll., Cambridge, 1956–59 (MA). 2nd Lieut 9th Queen's Royal Lancers, 1954–56. Called to the Bar, Middle Temple, 1961, Bencher, 1987. *Recreations:* opera, field sports. *Address:* 49 Cheval Place, SW7 1EW. *Clubs:* Athenæum, Special Forces.

FITZGERALD, Prof. Patrick John; Professor of Law, Carleton University, Ottawa, since 1971; *b* 30 Sept. 1928; *s* of Dr Thomas Walter and Norah Josephine Fitzgerald; *m* 1959, Brigid Aileen Judge; two *s* one *d*. *Educ:* Queen Mary's Grammar Sch., Walsall; University Coll., Oxford. Called to the Bar, Lincoln's Inn, 1951; Ontario Bar, 1984. Fellow, Trinity Coll., Oxford, 1956–60. Professor of Law: Leeds Univ., 1960–66; Univ. of Kent at Canterbury, 1966–71. Visiting Prof., University of Louisville, 1962–63. Consultant, Law Reform Commn of Canada, 1973–. *Publications:* Criminal Law and Punishment, 1962; Salmond on Jurisprudence (12th edn), 1966; This Law of Ours, 1977; Looking at Law, 1979; (ed) Crime, Justice and Codification, 1986. *Recreations:* music, golf, bridge. *Address:* 14 Fairbairn Avenue, Ottawa K1S 1T3, Canada.

FITZGERALD, Penelope Mary, (Mrs Desmond Fitzgerald); writer; *b* 1916; *d* of E. V. Knox and Christina Hicks; *m* 1941, Desmond Fitzgerald, MC; one *s* two *d*. *Educ:* Wycombe Abbey; Somerville Coll., Oxford (BA). *Publications:* Edward Burne-Jones, 1975; The Knox Brothers, 1977; The Golden Child, 1977; The Bookshop, 1978; Offshore, 1979 (Booker Prize); Human Voices, 1980; At Freddie's, 1982; (ed) William Morris's unpublished Novel on Blue Paper, 1982; Charlotte Mew and her Friends, 1984 (Rose Mary Crawshay Prize, 1985); Innocence, 1986; The Beginning of Spring, 1988; The Gate of Angels, 1990. *Recreations:* listening, talking, watching grandchildren. *Address:* c/o Wm Collins, 77 Fulham Palace Road, W6.

FITZGERALD-LOMBARD, Rt. Rev. Charles, OSB, **(James Michael Hubert Fitzgerald-Lombard);** Abbot of Downside, since 1990; *b* 29 Jan. 1941; *s* of late Col James C. R. Fitzgerald-Lombard and of Winifred (*née* Woulfe Flanagan). *Educ:* Downside; Collegio Sant Anselmo, Rome; King's Coll., London (MPhil). Monk of Downside Abbey, 1962–; ordained priest, 1968; Teacher and Tutor, Downside Sch., 1968–75; Bursar and Sec. to the Trustees, 1975–90. *Publications:* Prayers and Meditations, 1967, 3rd edn 1974; A Guide to the Church of St Gregory the Great, Downside Abbey, 1981, 2nd edn 1988; English and Welsh Priests 1801–1914, 1991. *Recreations:* electrical and telecommunications engineering, historical research, swimming. *Address:* Downside Abbey, Stratton-on-the-Fosse, Bath BA3 4RH. *T:* Bath (0761) 232226.

FitzGIBBON, Louis Theobald Dillon; Comte Dillon in France; political writer; Honorary Secretary, British Horn of Africa Council, since 1984; *b* 6 Jan. 1925; *s* of Comdr Francis Lee-Dillon FitzGibbon, RN, and Kathleen Clare (*née* Atchison), *widow* of Hon. Harry Lee-Dillon; *m* 1st, 1950, Josephine Miriam Maud (*née* Webb) (marr. diss.); 2nd, 1962, Madeleine Sally (*née* Hayward-Surry) (*d* 1980); one *s* two *d*; 3rd, 1980, Joan Elizabeth Jevons. *Educ:* St Augustine's Abbey Sch.; Royal Naval Coll., Dartmouth. Royal Navy, 1942–54 (incl. War of 1939–45 and service in ex-German U-1171); Polish interpreter's course, 1950–52. Dir, De Leon Properties Ltd, 1954–72. Solicitor's articled clerk, 1960–63; Anglo-Polish Conf., Warsaw, 1963. Personal Asst to the then Rt Hon. Duncan Sandys, MP (later Lord Duncan-Sandys), 1967–68; Gen. Sec., British Council for Aid to Refugees, 1968–72; United Nations (UNHCR) Mission to South Sudan, 1972–73; Dir of a medical charity, 1974–76; Exec. Officer, Nat. Assoc. for Freedom, 1977–78; Gen. Sec. of a trade assoc., 1978–80; missions to: Somalia, 1978, 1980–81; Sudan and Egypt, 1982; Sudan, German Parlt, Somalia and European Parlt, 1984; UN, 1988. Member: RIIA, 1982, 1988; Anglo-Somali Soc. Won first Airey Neave Meml Scholarship (proj. on Somalia), 1981. Hon. Secretary: Jt Cttee for Preservation of Historic Portsmouth, 1956–61; Katyn Memorial Fund, 1971–77; Area Pres., St John Amb. Brigade (Hants East), 1974–76. SMHO Malta, 1985 (Kt of Honour and Devotion and Officer of Merit). Polish Gold Cross of Merit, 1969; Order of Polonia Restituta (Polish Govt in Exile) (Officer, 1971; Comdr, 1972; Kt Comdr, 1976); Officer, Order of Merit (FRG), 1990; Katyn Meml Medal Bronze, USA, 1977; Laureate van de Arbeid, Netherlands, 1982. *Publications:* Katyn—A Crime without Parallel, 1971; The Katyn Cover-up, 1972; Unpitied and Unknown, 1975; Katyn—Triumph of Evil (Ireland), 1975; The Katyn Memorial, 1976; Katyn Massacre (paper) 1977, 3rd edn 1989; Katyn (USA), 1979; Katyn (in German), 1979; The Betrayal of the Somalis, 1982 (commnd by Japan-Somalia Friendship Assoc. in Japanese, 1989); Straits and Strategic Waterways in the Red Sea, 1984; Ethiopia Hijacks the Hijack, 1985; The Evaded Duty, 1985; reports on: Soviet Influence behind the Tripartite Pact of Aden, 1982; Sudan, 1984; contribs to internat. and nat. jls and publications, inc. Sudanow (Khartoum) and Heegan (Mogadishu). *Recreations:* travelling, politics, writing, reading, history, languages, refugee problems, Horn of Africa affairs, Islamic matters, *pro deo*. *Address:* Flat 2, 8 Portland Place, Brighton BN2 1DG. *T:* Brighton (0273) 685661.

FitzHARRIS, Viscount; James Carleton Harris; *b* 19 June 1946; *o s* and *heir* of 6th Earl of Malmesbury, *qv*; *m* 1969, Sally Ann, *yr d* of Sir Richard Newton Rycroft, *qv*; three *s* two *d*. *Educ:* Eton; Queen's Coll., St Andrews (MA). *Heir: s* Hon. James Hugh Carleton Harris, *b* 29 April 1970. *Address:* Greywell Hill, Greywell, Basingstoke, Hants RG25 1DB. *T:* Odiham (0256) 703565.

FITZHERBERT, family name of **Baron Stafford.**

FitzHERBERT, Giles Eden, CMG 1985; HM Diplomatic Service; Ambassador to Venezuela and concurrently Ambassador (non-resident) to the Dominican Republic, since 1988; *b* Dublin, 8 March 1935; *e s* of late Captain H. C. FitzHerbert, Irish Guards, and Sheelah, *d* of J. X. Murphy; *m* 1st, 1962, Margaret Waugh (*d* 1986); two *s* three *d*; 2nd, 1988, Alexandra Eyre; one *s* one *d*. *Educ:* Ampleforth Coll.; Christ Church Oxford; Harvard Business Sch. 2nd Lieut, 8th King's Royal Irish Hussars, 1957–58. Vickers da Costa & Co., 1962–66. First Secretary: Foreign Office, 1966; Rome, 1968–71; FCO, 1972–75; Counsellor: Kuwait, 1975–77; Nicosia, 1977–78; Head of Eur. Community Dept (Ext.), FCO, 1978–82; on sabbatical leave, LSE, 1982; Inspector, FCO, 1983; Minister, Rome, 1983–87. Contested (L) Fermanagh and South Tyrone, Gen. Elect., 1964. *Address:* Cove House, Cove, Tiverton, Devon. *Clubs:* Beefsteak; Kildare Street and University (Dublin).

FitzHERBERT, Sir Richard (Ranulph), 9th Bt *cr* 1784, of Tissington, Derbyshire; *b* 2 Nov. 1963; *s* of Rev. David Henry FitzHerbert, MC (*d* 1976) and of Charmin Hyacinthe, *yr d* of late Samuel Ranulph Allsopp, CBE; *S* uncle, 1989. *Educ:* Eton College. *Recreations:* cricket, shooting, restoring family estate. *Heir: cousin* Arthur William FitzHerbert [*b* 2 Sept. 1922; *m* 1952, Noeline Coral, *d* of Richard Kerkham; one *s* one *d*]. *Address:* Tissington Hall, Ashbourne, Derbys DE6 1RA. *Clubs:* MCC, Bachelors', Flappers'.

FITZHERBERT-BROCKHOLES, Michael John, OBE 1989; JP; Vice Lord-Lieutenant of Lancashire, since 1977; *b* 12 June 1920; *s* of John William Fitzherbert-Brockholes and Eileen Agnes; *m* 1950, Mary Edith Moore; four *s*. *Educ:* The Oratory Sch.; New Coll., Oxford. Scots Guards, 1940–46. Mem., Lancs CC, 1968–89; Chm., Educn Cttee, 1977–81. JP 1960, DL 1975, Lancs. KSG 1978. *Recreation:* gardening. *Address:* Claughton Hall, Garstang, near Preston, Lancs. *T:* Brock (0995) 40286.

FITZ-MAURICE, family name of **Earl of Orkney.**

FITZMAURICE; *see* Mercer Nairne Petty-Fitzmaurice, family name of Marquess of Lansdowne.

FITZMAURICE, Lt-Col Sir Desmond FitzJohn, Kt 1946; CIE 1941; late RE; *b* 17 Aug. 1893; *s* of John Day Stokes Fitzmaurice, ICS, Tralee, Co. Kerry; *m* 1926, Nancy (*d* 1975), *d* of Rev. John Sherlock Leake, Grayswood, Surrey; one *s* three *d*. *Educ:* Bradfield; RMA, Woolwich; Cambridge Univ. Joined RE, 1914. Served in France, Belgium and Italy, European War, 1914–18 (despatches); Instructor, RMA Woolwich, 1918–20; Cambridge Univ., 1920–22; Instructor, Sch. of Military Engineering, Chatham, 1923, 1924; hp list, 1925; Deputy Mint Master, Bombay, 1929–30; Calcutta, 1931–32; Deputy Master, Security Printing, India, 1932; Master Security Printing and Controller of Stamps, India, 1934; retired. *Address:* Lincombe Lodge, Fox Lane, Boars Hill, Oxford OX1 5DN.
See also Sir G. J. Milton-Thompson.

FitzPATRICK, Air Cdre David Beatty, CB 1970; OBE 1953; AFC 1949 and Bar, 1958; *b* 31 Jan. 1920; *s* of late Comdr D. T. FitzPatrick, RN and Beatrice Anne Ward; *m* 1941, Kathleen Mary Miles; one *d*. *Educ:* Kenilworth Coll., Exeter; Midhurst. Commnd RAF, 1938; served War of 1939–45, Atlantic, Mediterranean and Far East theatres; comd No 209 Sqdn (Far East), 1944; (GD Pilot) Sqdn flying duty, 1945–52; cfs, pfc and GW Specialist, RAF Henlow, 1952–57; GW (Trials) Project Officer, Min. of Supply, 1957–59; Base Comdr Christmas Island, 1959–60 (British Nuclear Trials); NATO Def. Coll., and jssc, 1960–61; Dep. Dir (Ops) Air Staff, 1961–64; comd RAF Akrotiri and Nicosia, 1964–66; Dir of (Q) RAF, MoD, 1966–69; attached NBPI for special duty, 1969; Dir, Guided Weapons (Trials and Ranges), Min. of Technology, 1969–72; Dir, Guided Weapons Trials, MoD (PE), 1972–74; retd RAF, 1975; Head, teaching dept of indep. sch., 1975–85, retd. FBIM 1970; FRMetS 1984; MRAeS 1971. *Recreations:* swimming (Life Vice-Pres., Royal Air Force Swimming Assoc.), deep-sea fishing, cricket. *Address:* Whistledown, 38 Courts Mount Road, Haslemere, Surrey GU27 2PP. *T:* Haslemere (0428) 644589.

FITZPATRICK, Gen. Sir (Geoffrey Richard) Desmond, GCB 1971 (KCB 1965; CB 1961); DSO 1945; MBE 1943; MC 1939; *b* 14 Dec. 1912; *o s* of late Brig.-Gen. Sir Richard Fitzpatrick, CBE, DSO, and Lady (G. E.) Fitzpatrick; *m* 1944, Mary Sara, *o d* of Sir Charles Campbell, 12th Bt; one *s* one *d*. *Educ:* Eton; RMC Sandhurst. Commissioned The Royal Dragoons, 1932. Served in Palestine, 1938–39 (MC); War of 1939–45 (despatches, MBE, DSO); in Middle East, Italy, NW Europe. Bt. Lieut-Col 1951; Col 1953; ADC to the Queen, 1959; Maj.-Gen. 1959; Asst Chief of Defence Staff, Ministry of Defence, 1959–61; Dir Mil. Ops, War Office, 1962–64; Chief of Staff, BAOR, 1964–65; Lt-Gen. 1965; GOC-in-C, N Ire., 1965–66; Vice-Chief of Gen. Staff, 1966–68; Gen. 1968; C-in-C, BAOR, and Commander N Army Gp 1968–70; Dep. Supreme Allied Comdr, Europe, 1970–73; ADC (General) to the Queen, 1970–73. Lieutenant-Governor and C-in-C, Jersey, 1974–79. Col, The Royal Dragoons, 1964–69; Dep. Col., 1969–74, Col, 1979–, The Blues and Royals, and Gold Stick to the Queen, 1979–; Col Comdt, RAC, 1971–74. *Address:* Belmont, Otley, Suffolk IP6 9PF. *Clubs:* Cavalry and Guards; Royal Yacht Squadron.

FITZPATRICK, James Bernard, CBE 1983; JP; DL; Chairman, Royal Liverpool University Hospital, since 1991; *b* 21 April 1930; *s* of late B. A. Fitzpatrick and Mrs J. E. Fitzpatrick; *m* 1965, Rosemary, *d* of late Captain E. B. Clark, RD and bar, RNR (Croix de Guerre avec Palme, Polish Golden Cross of Merit with Swords), and late Mrs K. E. Clark, Claughton; one *s* one *d*. *Educ:* Bootle Grammar Sch.; London Univ. (LLB). Admitted Solicitor, 1962; FCIT 1973 (AMInstT 1954); CBIM. Joined Mersey Docks and Harbour Bd, 1951: various management posts from 1965; Personnel and Industrial Relns Dir, 1971, on formation of Mersey Docks and Harbour Co.; Jt Man. Dir, 1974; Dep. Chief Exec., 1975; Man. Dir and Chief Exec., 1977; Chm., 1984–87. Dir, Plan Invest Group plc, 1984–; Mem., 1979–89, Chm., 1988–89, Merseyside Enterprise Forum. Chairman: Nat. Assoc. of Port Employers, 1979–82 (Vice-Chm., 1973–79); Employers' Assoc. of Port of Liverpool, 1974–83; Member: Liverpool Dock Labour Bd, 1974–76 (Chm., 1976); Exec. Council, British Ports Assoc., 1976–87 (Dep. Chm., 1985–87); Nat. Dock Labour Bd, 1978–84. Chm., Liverpool HA, 1986–91. Vice Pres., Inst. of Materials Handling, 1978; Mem. Council, Industrial Soc., 1989. Mem. Council, Liverpool Univ., 1988–89. FIMH; FRSA. JP Liverpool 1977. DL Merseyside, 1985. Hon. Fellow, Liverpool Polytechnic, 1988. *Recreations:* fell walking, gardening, music, reading. *Address:* 57 Hilbre Road, West Kirby, Merseyside L48 3HB. *T:* 051–625 9612; Royal Liverpool Hospital, Prescot Street, Liverpool L7 8XP. *T:* 051–706 2000. *Clubs:* Oriental, Pilgrims; Racquet (Liverpool).

FITZPATRICK, Air Marshal Sir John (Bernard), KBE 1984; CB 1982; Royal Air Force, retired; Independent Panel Inspector, Departments of the Environment and Transport, since 1986; *b* 15 Dec. 1929; *s* of Joseph Fitzpatrick and Bridget Fitzpatrick; *m* 1954, Gwendoline Mary Abbott; two *s* one *d*. *Educ:* St Patrick's School, Dungannon, N Ireland; RAF Apprentice Sch., Halton; RAF Coll. Cranwell. Officer Commanding: No 81 Sqdn, 1966–68; No 35 Sqdn, 1971–72; OC, RAF Scampton, 1974–75; RCDS, 1976; Dir of Ops (Strike), RAF, 1977–79; SASO, HQ Strike Command, 1980–82; Dir Gen. of Organisation, RAF, 1982–83; AOC No 18 Gp, RAF, and Comdr Maritime Air Eastern Atlantic and Channel, 1983–86. *Recreations:* golf, reading, carpentry. *Address:* c/o Lloyds Bank, 23 Market Place, Fakenham, Norfolk NR21 9BT. *Club:* Royal Air Force.

FITZPATRICK, John Ronald; Solicitor and Parliamentary Officer, Greater London Council, 1977–85, Consultant, 1985–86; *b* 22 Sept. 1923; *s* of Henry Fitzpatrick and Mary Lister; *m* 1952, Beryl Mary Newton; two *s* one *d*. *Educ:* St Bede's Coll., Manchester; Univ. of Manchester (LLB). Admitted Solicitor, 1947; LMRTPI 1951. Asst Solicitor: Burnley, 1947; Stockport, 1948–51; Asst/Principal Asst Solicitor, Mddx CC, 1951–65; Asst Clerk/Asst Dir-Gen., GLC, 1965–69; Asst Dir, 1969–72, Dir, 1972–77, Planning and Transportation, GLC. *Recreations:* golf, bridge. *Address:* Courtlands, 2 Langley Grove, New Malden, Surrey. *T:* 081–942 8652.

FitzROY, family name of **Duke of Grafton** and of **Southampton Barony.**

FitzROY NEWDEGATE, family name of **Viscount Daventry.**

FITZSIMMONS, Rt. Hon. William Kennedy, PC (N Ireland) 1965; JP; *b* 31 Jan. 1909; *m* 1935, May Elizabeth Lynd; two *d*. *Educ:* Skegoniell National Sch.; Belfast Techn. Sch. Mem., Belfast City and Dist Water Comrs, 1948–57 (Chm. 1954–55); Pres., Duncairn Unionist Assoc.; N Ireland Parliament: MP, Duncairn Div. of Belfast, 1956–72; Dep. Govt Whip, 1961–63; Parl. Secretary: Min. of Commerce, 1961–65; Min. of Home Affairs, 1963–64; Min. of Develt, 1964–65; Min. of Education, 1965–66 and 1968–69; Minister of Development, 1966–68; Minister of Health and Social Services, 1969–72. JP Belfast, 1951. *Address:* 16 Cleaver Court, Cleaver Avenue, Malone Road, Belfast, Northern Ireland BT9 5JA.

FITZSIMONS, Anthony; *see* Fitzsimons, P. A.

FITZSIMONS, Prof. James Thomas, FRS 1988; Professor of Medical Physiology, University of Cambridge, since 1990; Fellow of Gonville and Caius College, Cambridge, since 1961; *b* 8 July 1928; *s* of Robert Allen Fitzsimons, FRCS and Dr Mary Patricia (*née* McKelvey); *m* 1961, Aude Irène Jeanne, *d* of Gén. Jean Etienne Valluy, DSO and Marie (*née* Bourdillon); two *s* one *d*. *Educ:* St Edmund's Coll., Ware; Gonville and Caius Coll., Cambridge (1st cl. Pts I and II, Nat. Sci. Tripos; BA 1949; MB BChir 1953; MA 1954; PhD 1960; MD 1967, Sir Lionel Whitby Medal; ScD 1979); Charing Cross Hosp. House appts, Leicester Gen. and Charing Cross Hosps, 1954–55; RAF, Inst. of Aviation Medicine, 1955–57 (Flight Lieut); Cambridge University: MRC Scholar, Physiol. Lab., 1957–59; Univ. Demonstrator in Physiol., 1959–64, Lectr, 1964–76, Reader, 1976–90; Gonville and Caius College: Tutor, 1964–72; Coll. Lectr in Physiol, 1964–; Dir of Studies in Medicine, 1978–. Visiting Professor: CNRS Lab. des Régulations Alimentaires, Coll. de France, 1967; Inst. of Neurol Scis, Univ. of Pennsylvania, 1968, 1972; CNRS Lab. de Neurobiol., Coll. de France, 1975; Lectures: Stevenson Meml, Univ. of Western Ontario, 1979; Halliburton, KCL, 1982. Royal Soc. rep., British Nat. Cttee for Physiol. Scis, 1976–82; Mem., Physiol. Soc. Cttee, 1972–76 (Chm., 1975–76); Mem., IUPS Commn on Physiol. of Food and Fluid Intake, 1973–80 (Chm., 1979–80). Member, Editorial Boards: Jl of Physiol., 1977–84; Neuroendocrinology, 1979–84; Editor, Biological Reviews, 1984–. Hon. MD Lausanne, 1978. *Publications:* The Physiology of Thirst and Sodium Appetite, 1979; scientific papers in professional jls. *Recreations:* Irish language and literature, cats, music, photography. *Address:* Physiological Laboratory, Downing Street, Cambridge CB2 3EG. *T:* Cambridge (0223) 333836; 91 Thornton Road, Girton, Cambridge CB3 0NR. *T:* Cambridge (0223) 276874.

FITZSIMONS, P. Anthony; Chief Executive and Managing Director, Bristol & West Building Society, since 1989; *b* 16 March 1946; *m* 1967, Carolann (marr. diss. 1985); two *s*. *Educ:* LSE (BSc Econ.). Rank Xerox: Australia, 1972–75; Southern Europe, 1975–76; Australasia, Middle East, 1976–79; Regional Control Dir, London, 1979–81; Grand Metropolitan: Finance Systems and Strategy Dir, Brewing and Retail Div., 1981–83; Man. Dir, Host Group, 1983–85; Man. Dir, Personal Banking, Citibank, 1985–89. Chm., Avon TEC. *Recreations:* squash, riding, music, sailing. *Address:* Bristol & West Building Society, PO Box 27, Broad Quay, Bristol BS99 7AX. *T:* Bristol (0272) 294271.

FITZWALTER, 21st Baron, *cr* 1295; **(Fitzwalter) Brook Plumptre,** JP; Hon. Captain, The Buffs; *b* 15 Jan. 1914; *s* of late George Beresford Plumptre, Goodnestone, Canterbury, Kent; *S* uncle, 1943 (FitzWalter Barony called out of abeyance in his favour, 1953); *m* 1951, Margaret Melesina, *yr d* of (Herbert) William Deedes, JP, Galt, Hythe, Kent; five *s*. *Educ:* Diocesan Coll., Rondebosch, Cape; Jesus Coll., Cambridge. Served War of 1939–45, with the Buffs (Royal East Kent Regt) in France, Belgium, UK and India; attached RIASC, as Capt. JP Kent, 1949. Landowner and farmer; succeeded to family estate, 1943. *Heir: s* Hon. Julian Brook Plumptre [*b* 18 Oct. 1952; *m* 1988, Sally, *o d* of late I. M. T. Quiney; one *s*]. *Address:* Goodnestone Park, Canterbury, Kent. *T:* Nonington (0304) 840218.

FLACK, Bertram Anthony, CMG 1979; HM Diplomatic Service, retired; *b* 3 Feb. 1924; *y s* of Dr F. H. Flack and Alice Cockshut, Nelson, Lancs; *m* 1948, Jean W. Mellor; two *s* two *d*. *Educ:* Epsom Coll.; Liverpool Univ. (LLB Hons). Enlisted Gren. Gds, 1942; commissioned E Lancashire Regt, 1943; served in NW Europe (Captain). Joined Foreign Service, 1948; served Karachi, 1948–50; Alexandria, 1950–52; Stockholm, 1955–58; Accra, 1958–61; Johannesburg, 1964–67; Dep. High Comr, E Pakistan, 1967–68; Inspector, Diplomatic Service, 1968–70; Head of Communications Dept, FCO, 1971–73; Commercial Counsellor, Stockholm, 1973–75; Canadian Nat. Defence Coll., 1975–76; Dep. High Comr, Ottawa, 1976–79; High Comr, Repub. of Uganda, 1979–80. *Recreations:* cricket, golf. *Address:* Ripple Cottage, Douglas Street, Castletown, Isle of Man.

FLAGG, Rt. Rev. John William Hawkins; General Secretary, South American Missionary Society, since 1986; an Hon. Assistant Bishop of Rochester, since 1986; *b* 16 April 1929; *s* of Wilfred John and Emily Flagg; *m* 1954, Marjorie Lund; two *s* four *d*. *Educ:* All Nations Christian Coll.; Clifton Theological Coll. Agricultural missionary, Chile, 1951; Chaplain and Missionary Superintendent, St Andrew's, Asunción, Paraguay, 1959–64; Archdeacon, N Argentine, 1964–69; Diocesan Bishop of Paraguay and N Argentine, 1969–73; Asst Bishop for Chile, Peru and Bolivia, 1973; Bishop, Diocese of Peru, 1977; Asst Bishop, Diocese of Liverpool, 1978–86; Vicar, St Cyprian's with Christ Church, Edge Hill, 1978–85; Priest-in-Charge of Christ Church, Waterloo, 1985–86. Member of Anglican Consultative Council, 1974–79; Presiding Bishop of Anglican Council of South America (CASA), 1974–77. *Address:* South American Missionary Society, Allen Gardiner House, Pembury Road, Tunbridge Wells, Kent TN2 3QU. *T:* Tunbridge Wells (0892) 38647.

FLANAGAN, Barry, OBE 1991; RA 1991 (ARA 1987); sculptor; *b* 11 Jan. 1941. *Educ:* Birmingham Coll. of Arts and Crafts; St Martin's Sch. of Art. Teacher, St Martin's Sch. of Art and Central Sch. of Art and Design, 1967–71. One-man exhibitions include: Rowan Gall., 1966, 1968, 1970–74; Fischbach Gall., NY, 1969; Galleria del Leone, Venice, 1971; Mus. of Modern Art, NY, Mus. of Modern Art, Oxford, 1974; Hogarth Galls, Sydney, 1975; Centro de Arte y Communicación, Buenos Aires, 1976; Van Abbemuseum, Eindhoven, Arnolfini Gall., Bristol, Serpentine Gall. (tour), 1977–79; Galerie Durand-Dessert, Paris, 1980, 1982, 1988; Waddington Galls, 1980–81, 1983, 1985, 1990; Inst. of Contemporary Arts (prints and drawings), 1981–82; Centre Georges Pompidou, Paris, 1983; Pace Gall., NY, 1983, 1990; Fuji Television Gall., Tokyo, 1985; Tate Gall., 1986; Laing Art Gall., Newcastle upon Tyne, Mus. of Contemporary Art, Belgrade, City Gall., Zagreb, Mus. of Modern Art, Ljubljana (tour), 1987–88. Work includes: Camdonian sculpture, Lincoln's Inn Fields, 1980; bronze sculptures, Baby Elephant and Hare on Bell, Equitable Life Tower West, NY, 1984; bronze sculpture, Kouros horse, Stockley Park, Uxbridge, 1987; two bronze Leaping Hare sculptures for Kawakyo Co., Osaka, 1990. Choreographed two pieces for dance gp, Strider, 1972. Judge, Bath Sculpture Competition, 1985. *Address:* Unit 5E, Fane Street, E14 6PD.

FLANAGAN, Michael Joseph; Chief Executive, Development Board for Rural Wales, since 1990; *b* 21 Nov. 1946; *s* of Daniel and Margaret Constance Flanagan; *m* 1968, Patricia Holland; two *s* one *d. Educ:* St Joseph's Coll., Blackpool; Southampton Coll. of Higher Educn. IPFA 1972; DMS 1983. Trainee Accountant, Lancs CC, 1965–69; Preston County Borough, 1969–70; Southampton City Council, 1970–72; Accountant, 1972, Asst Dir of Finance, 1981–87, Telford Develt Corp.; Dir of Finance and Tech. Services, Develt Bd for Rural Wales, 1987–90. *Recreations:* sport, esp. football, golf, tennis; family activities. *Address:* Tan-y-Fron, Pantyffridd, Berriew, Montgomeryshire.

FLANDERS, Dennis, RWS 1976 (ARWS 1970); RBA 1970; artist: townscapes and landscapes in pencil and water-colour; *b* 2 July 1915; *s* of late Bernard C. Flanders, ARAM (pianist), and Jessie Marguarite Flanders, ARMS (artist); *m* 1952, Dalma J. Darnley, *o d* of late J. Darnley Taylor and of Mrs Joan Darnley Taylor; one *s* one *d. Educ:* Merchant Taylors' Sch.; Regent Street Polytechnic; St Martin's Art Sch.; Central Sch. of Arts and Crafts, Princess Louise Gold Medal at age of 7. Mem. of St Paul's Watch, 1940–42; Royal Engineers, 1942–46. Occasional drawings for Daily Telegraph and other journals; series of drawings for Yorkshire Post, 1949; Birmingham Post, 1950–51; "Famous Streets," Sunday Times, 1952–53; Special artist to the Illustrated London News, 1956–64. Water-colours (reproduced as prints) of: RMA Sandhurst; Police Coll., Bramshill; St Edward's Sch., Oxford; Glencorse Barracks, Midlothian; Hampstead; Nottingham, Loughborough, Essex and Leicester Univs; Somerville, Wadham, Jesus and St Cross Colls, Oxford; Wolfson Coll., Cambridge; prints of City of London Sch. for Boys, Sherborne Sch. Drawings in private collections and Nat. War Collection (1939–45), Guildhall Library, Bank of England, Nat. Library of Wales, and Museums at Exeter, York, Lincoln, Kensington, St Marylebone, Walthamstow, Wolverhampton, and Bury, Lancs. Exhibitor: RA and in provinces: one-man shows: London galleries: Colnaghi's, 1947; J. A. Tooth's, 1951; Coombs & Percival, 1953, 1955; FBA, 1964, 1967; Catto, 1986, 1990; Bedford, 1965, 1966, 1985; Boston (Lincs), 1966; Southport, 1969; Buxton-Lammas, Norfolk, 1972; Worthing, 1972; Cambridge, 1980; York, 1981; Fine Art Soc., London and Edin., 1984; George's Art Bookshop, Bristol, 1985; Bedford, 1986. Member: Art Workers Guild (Master 1975); Soc. for Protection of Ancient Buildings. Freeman: City of London, 1970; Painter Stainers' Co., 1970. Lord Mayor's Art Award, 1966. *Publications: illustrations:* Bolton Abbey, 1947; Chelsea by Richard Edmonds, 1956; Soho for East Anglia by Michael Brander, 1963; A Westminster Childhood by John Raynor, 1973; The Twelve Great Livery Companies of London, 1973; (artist and author) Dennis Flanders' Britannia, 1984. *Recreations:* walking, riding, reading Who's Who. *Address:* 51 Great Ormond Street, WC1N 3HZ. *T:* 071–405 9317; Baker's Cross House, Cranbrook, Kent. *T:* Cranbrook (0580) 712018.

FLANNERY, Martin Henry; MP (Lab) Hillsborough, Sheffield, since Feb. 1974; *b* 2 March 1918; *m* 1949; one *s* two *d. Educ:* Sheffield Grammar Sch.; Sheffield Teachers' Trng College. Served with Royal Scots, 1940–46. Teacher, 1946–74 (Head Teacher, 1969–74). Chairman: Tribune Group, 1980–81; PLP's NI Cttee, 1983–; PLP Consultant MP for NUT, 1974–. *Recreations:* music, rambling. *Address:* 53 Linaker Road, Sheffield S6 5DS.

FLATHER, family name of **Baroness Flather.**

FLATHER, Baroness *cr* 1990 (Life Peer), of Windsor and Maidenhead in the Royal County of Berkshire; **Shreela Flather;** JP; Member, Commission for Racial Equality, 1980–86; Councillor, Royal Borough of Windsor and Maidenhead, 1976–91 (first ethnic minority woman Councillor in UK), Mayor, 1986–87 (first Asian woman to hold this office); Member, Economic and Social Committee, European Community, 1987–90; *b* Lahore, India; *m* Gary Flather, *qv*; two *s. Educ:* University Coll. London (LLB). Called to the Bar, Inner Temple, 1962. Infant Teacher, ILEA, 1965–67; Teacher of English as a second lang., Altwood Comp. Sch., Maidenhead, 1968–74, Broadmoor Hosp., 1974–78. Member: Police Complaints Bd, 1982–85; Lord Chancellor's Legal Aid Adv. Cttee, 1985–88; Social Security Adv. Cttee, 1987–90; Cttee of Inquiry (Rampton, later Swann Cttee) into Educn of Children from Ethnic Minority Gps, 1979–85; Cons. Women's Nat. Cttee (formerly Cons. Women's Nat. Adv. Cttee), 1978–89; Exec. Cttee, Anglo-Asian Cons. Soc., 1979–83; Bd of Visitors, Holloway Prison, 1981–83; Broadmoor Hosp. Bd, 1987–88; HRH Duke of Edinburgh's Inquiry into British Housing, 1984–85; Cttee of Management, Servite Houses Ltd, 1987–; Berks FPC, 1987–88; Thames and Chilterns Tourist Bd, 1987–88; BBC S and E Regional Adv. Council, 1987–89; NEC, Cons. Party, 1989–90; LWT Prog. Adv. Bd, 1990–; Carnegie Inquiry into the Third Age, 1991–; President: Cambs, Chilterns and Thames Rent Assessment Panel, 1983–; Community Council for Berks, 1991–; League of Friends of Broadmoor Hosp., 1991–; Vice-Pres., BSA, 1988–91; Assoc. of DCs, 1990–; Commonwealth Countries League, 1990–; Director: Thames Valley Enterprise, 1990–; Meridian Broadcasting, 1991–. Chm., Maidenhead Community Consultative Council, 1987–90; Vice-Chm., Refugee Council, 1991 (Chm., UK Policy Gp); Trustee: Berks Community Trust, 1978–90; Hillingdon Hosp. Trust, 1990–. Governor: Altwood Comp. Sch., 1978–86; Slough Coll. of Higher Educn, 1984–89. Vice-Chm. and Founder Mem., Maidenhead CRC, 1969–; Vice-Chm., and Mem., Management Cttee, Maidenhead CAB, 1982–88; formerly: Vice-Chairman: Estates and Amenities and Leisure Cttees, Windsor and Maidenhead; Police Consultative Cttee; Maidenhead Volunteer Centre; Sec., Windsor and Maidenhead Cons. Gp; Mem., W Metrop. Conciliation Cttee, Race Relns Bd, 1973–78; Sec./Organiser, Maidenhead Ladies Asian Club, 1968–78; started New Star Boys' Club for Asian Boys and Summer Sch. Project for Asian children, Maidenhead; prepared English Teaching Scheme for Asian adults 'Stepping Stones'. JP Maidenhead, 1971. *Recreations:* travel, cinema. *Address:* House of Lords, SW1A 0PW. *T:* 071–219 5353. *Club:* Oriental.

FLATHER, Gary Denis; QC 1984; a Recorder, since 1986; *s* of Denis and Joan Flather; *m* Shreela Flather (*see* Baroness Flather); two *s. Educ:* Oundle Sch.; Pembroke Coll., Oxford (MA). Called to the Bar, Inner Temple, 1962. National Service, Second Lieut 1st Bn York and Lancaster Regt, 1956–58; Lieut Hallamshire Bn, TA, 1958–61. Asst Parly Boundary Comr, 1982–; Asst Recorder, 1983–86. Mem., Panel of Chairmen: for ILEA Teachers' Disciplinary Tribunal, 1974–90 (Chm., Disciplinary ILEA Tribunal, William Tyndale Jun. Sch. teachers, 1976); for Disciplinary Tribunal for London Polytechnics, 1982–90; a Chm., Police Disciplinary Appeals, 1987–; Legal Mem., Mental Health Review Tribunal (restricted patients), 1987–; a Financial Services Act Inspector, employees of Coutts Bank, 1987–88; a legal assessor, GMC and GDC, 1987–. Chm., Statutory Cttee, RPharmS, 1990–. Pres., Maidenhead Rotary Club, 1990–91. Vice-Pres., Community Council for Berks, 1987–. Escort to the Mayor of the Royal Borough of Windsor and Maidenhead, 1986–87. *Recreations:* travel, music, coping with multiple sclerosis. *Address:* Lamb Building, Temple, EC4Y 7AS. *T:* 071–353 6701. *Club:* Oriental.

FLATLEY, Derek Comedy, MBE 1989; FJI; Public Affairs Correspondent, Southend Evening Echo, since 1970; *b* 16 Oct. 1920; *m* 1959, Valerie Eve Stevens; one *d. Educ:* Grammar sch. Trained West Essex Gazette, 1936. Served War of 1939–45: Household Cavalry, 1945. Army newspaper unit, Southend Standard, 1947; Chief Reporter, 1949. Mem., Press Council, 1968–72; Mem. Council (rep. Essex), Inst. of Journalists, 1957– (Pres. 1966–67); also Chairman: Salaries and Conditions Bd of the Inst., 1958–67; Estabt Cttee, 1963–65; Exec., 1967–70. Fellow, Inst. of Journalists, 1962–. *Recreations:* football, cricket, tennis. *Address:* Windyridge House, 22 Earls Hall Avenue, Southend-on-Sea, Essex SS2 6PD. *T:* Southend-on-Sea (0702) 343485.

FLAVELL, Geoffrey, FRCS; FRCP; Hon. Consulting Thoracic Surgeon to: The Royal London Hospital; Chelmsford and Harlow Districts Health Authorities; Whipps Cross Hospital; *b* 23 Feb. 1913; *o* surviving *s* of late W. A. Flavell, JP, of Wellington, NZ; *m* 1943, Joan Margaret, *o d* of S. Ewart Adams, Hawkwell, Essex; no *c. Educ:* Waitaki; Otago; University of New Zealand; St Bartholomew's Hospital, London. Qualified in medicine, 1937; House appts, St Bartholomew's Hosp., 1937–39; Resident Surgical Officer, Brompton Hosp., 1940–41. Surgeon Specialist, RAF, 1942, O/C Surgical Divs RAF Gen. Hosps, Carthage and Algiers, 1943; RAF Gen. Hosp., Cairo; Adviser in Surgery RAF Med. and Middle East Command, 1944; retired rank of Wing Comdr, 1958. Consultant Thoracic Surgeon, British Legion Hosp., and to LCC, 1946; Senior Registrar to London Hosp., 1947; Sen. Surgeon, Dept of Cardiovascular and Thoracic Surgery, London Hosp., 1950–78 (Chm., Surgical Div., 1974–77); Mem., Faculty of Med., Univ. of London, 1953–; Consultant Thoracic Surgeon, Royal Masonic Hosp., 1957–78; Sen. Thoracic Surgeon, Broomfield Hosp., 1947–78. Visiting Thoracic Surgeon to: Whipps Cross Hosp.; St Margaret's Hosp., Epping; Harold Wood Hosp.; Harts Hosp.; Oldchurch Hosp., Romford. Consultant, Qatar Govt, 1969–. Chm., Adv. Cttee on Cardiothoracic Surgery to NE Thames RHA, 1970–78; Sen. Mem., Soc. of Thoracic Surgeons of GB and Ireland. Touring Lectr for British Council, Middle and Far Eastern Univs, 1961; Ivor Lewis Lectr, N Mddx Hosp., 1978. Liveryman, Hon. Soc. of Apothecaries; Freeman, City of London. *Publications:* Introduction to Chest Surgery, 1957; Basic Surgery (Thoracic section), 1958; The Oesophagus, 1963; many contribs to surgical textbooks and med. jls; various articles on travel, wine and food, in lay periodicals. *Recreations:* history; architecture; literature and art; indulging the senses. *Address:* 9 Camden Crescent, Bath BA1 5HY. *T:* Bath (0225) 444903. *Clubs:* Royal Air Force; Bath and County (Bath).

FLAVELL, Prof. Richard Anthony, PhD; FRS 1984; Chairman and Professor of Immunobiology, and Professor of Biology, Yale University School of Medicine, and Investigator of the Howard Hughes Medical Institute, since 1988; *b* 23 Aug. 1945; *s* of John T. and Iris Flavell; *m* Madlyn (*née* Nathanson); one *d*; two *s* of former *m. Educ:* Dept of Biochemistry, Univ. of Hull (PhD 1970); Univ. of Amsterdam (Royal Soc. Eur. Fellow); Univ of Zürich (Post-doctoral Fellow). Wetenschappelijk Medewerker, Univ. of Amsterdam, 1973–79; Head, Lab. of Gene Structure and Expression, NIMR, Mill Hill, 1979–82; Pres., Biogen Res. Corp., 1982–88; Principal Res. Officer and CSO, Biogen Gp, 1984–88. Mem., EMBO, 1978–. MRI; Mem., Amer. Assoc. of Immunologists. Anniversary Prize, FEBS, 1980; Colworth Medal, Biochem. Soc., 1980. *Publications: chapters in:* Handbook of Biochemistry and Molecular Biology ed Fasman, 3rd edn 1976; McGraw-Hill Yearbook of Science and Technology, 1980; Eukaryotic Genes: their structure, activity and regulation, ed jtly with it Maclean and Gregory, 1983; articles in Biochem. Jl, Biochim. Biophys. Acta, Jl of Cell. Sci., Eur. Jl of Biochem., Jl of Mol. Biol., Nature, Nucl. Acids Res., Gene, Cell, Proc. Nat. Acad. Sci., Biochem. Soc. Trans, Trends in Biochem. Scis, EMBO Jl, Jl Immunol., Jl Exp. Med. Sci.; contrib. Proceedings of symposia. *Recreations:* music, tennis, squash, horticulture. *Address:* Section of Immunobiology, Yale University School of Medicine, 310 Cedar Street, New Haven, Conn 06510, USA; 182 Reservoir Road, Killingworth, Conn 06417, USA.

FLAVELL, Prof. Richard Bailey; Director, John Innes Institute, since 1988; *b* 11 Oct. 1943; *s* of Sidney Flavell and Emily Gertrude Flavell (*née* Bailey); *m* 1966, Hazel New; two *d. Educ:* Univ. of Birmingham (BSc 1964); Univ. of East Anglia (PhD 1967). Research Associate, Univ. of Stanford, California, 1967; Plant Breeding Institute, 1969–88 (Head, Molecular Genetics Dept, 1985–88). Hon. Prof., King's College London, 1986–. Fellow, EMBO, 1990; Dir, Internat. Soc. for Plant Molecular Biology. *Publications:* scientific papers and books. *Recreations:* music, gardening. *Address:* John Innes Institute, John Innes Centre for Plant Science Research, Colney Lane, Norwich NR4 7UH. *T:* Norwich (0603) 52571.

FLAVELLE, Sir (Joseph) David (Ellsworth), 3rd Bt *cr* 1917; *b* 9 Nov. 1921; *s* of Sir (Joseph) Ellsworth Flavelle, 2nd Bt, and of Muriel, *d* of William Norman McEachren; *S* father, 1977; *m* 1942, Muriel Barbara, *d* of Reginald Morton; three *d. Address:* Waterlot, 1420 Watersedge Road, Clarkson, Ontario L5J 1A4, Canada.

FLAXEN, David William; Director of Statistics, Department of Transport, since 1989; *b* 20 April 1941; *s* of late William Henry Flaxen and Beatrice Flaxen (*née* Laidlow); *m* 1969, Eleanor Marie Easton; two *d. Educ:* Manchester Grammar Sch.; Brasenose Coll., Oxford (MA Physics); University Coll. London (DipStat). Teacher, Leyton County High School for Boys, 1963; cadet statistician, 1963–64; statistical posts, Central Statistical Office and Min. of Labour, 1964–71; United Nations Adviser: Swaziland, 1971–72; Ghana, 1985–86; Statistician, Dept of Employment, 1973–75; Chief Statistician: Dept of Employment, 1975–76; Central Statistical Office, 1976–77 and 1981–83; Inland Revenue, 1977–81; Asst Dir (Under Sec.), Central Statistical Office, 1983–89. *Publications:* contribs to articles in Physics Letters, Economic Trends, Dept of Employment Gazette, etc. *Recreations:* bridge, wine, cooking, music. *Address:* 65 Corringham Road, NW11 7BS. *T:* 081–458 5451.

FLECKER, James William, MA; Headmaster, Ardingly College, since 1980; *b* 15 Aug. 1939; *s* of Henry Lael Oswald Flecker, CBE, and Mary Patricia Flecker; *m* 1967, Mary Rose Firth; three *d. Educ:* Marlborough Coll.; Brasenose Coll., Oxford (BA, now MA Lit. Hum., 1962). Asst Master: Sydney Grammar Sch., 1962–63; Latymer Upper Sch., 1964–67; (and later Housemaster), Marlborough Coll., 1967–80. *Recreations:* hockey, cricket, flute playing, children's operas. *Address:* Ardingly College, Haywards Heath, West Sussex RH17 6SQ. *T:* Ardingly (0444) 892577.

FLEET, Kenneth George; journalist; *b* 12 Sept. 1929; *s* of late Fred Major Fleet and Elizabeth Doris Fleet; *m* 1953, (Alice) Brenda, *d* of late Captain H. R. Wilkinson, RD, RNR and Mrs Kathleen Mary Wilkinson; three *s* one *d*. *Educ:* Calday Grange Grammar Sch., Cheshire; LSE (BScEcons). Jl of Commerce, Liverpool, 1950–52; Sunday Times, 1955–56; Dep. City Editor, Birmingham Post, 1956–58; Dep. Financial Editor, Guardian, 1958–63; Dep. City Editor, Daily Telegraph, 1963; City Editor, Sunday Telegraph, 1963–66; City Editor, Daily Telegraph, 1966–77; Editor, Business News, Sunday Times, 1977–78; City Editor, Sunday Express, 1978–82; City Editor-in-Chief, Express Newspapers plc, 1982–83; Exec. Ed. (Finance and Industry), The Times, 1983–87. Dir, TVS Entertainments 1990–. Dir, Young Vic, 1976–83; Chm., Chichester Fest. Theatre, 1985– (Dir, 1984–). Wincott Award, 1974. *Publication:* The Influence of the Financial Press, 1983. *Recreations:* theatre, books, sport. *Address:* PO Box 293, 20 Farringdon Road, EC1M 3NH. *T:* 071–772 1000. *Clubs:* MCC, Lord's Taverners; Piltdown Golf.

FLEET, Stephen George, PhD; FInstP; Registrary, University of Cambridge, since 1983; Professorial Fellow, Downing College, Cambridge, since 1983 (Fellow since 1974; Bursar, 1974–83; President, 1983–85; Vice Master, 1985–88); *b* 28 Sept. 1936; *er s* of late George Fleet and of Elsie Fleet, Lewes, Sussex. *Educ:* Brentwood Sch.; Lewes County Grammar Sch.; St John's Coll., Cambridge (Scholar; MA; PhD 1962). FInstP 1972. Res. Physicist, Mullard Res. Labs, Surrey, 1961–62; Univ. of Cambridge: Demonstr in Mineralogy, 1962–67; Lectr in Mineralogy, 1967–83; Fellow, Fitzwilliam House, 1963–66; Fellow, Fitzwilliam Coll., 1966–73 (Jun. Bursar, 1967–73; Dir of Studies in Physical Sciences, 1971–74); Mem., Council of Senate, 1975–82; Mem., Financial Bd, 1979–83; Chm., Bd of Exams, 1974–83; Chm., Bursars' Cttee, 1980–83; President: Fitzwilliam Soc., 1977; Downing Assoc., 1991. Mem., Finance Cttee, Internat. Union of Crystallography, 1987–. Trustee: Mineralogical Soc. of GB, 1977–87; Foundn of Edward Storey, 1976– (Chm., 1984–88); Treasurer: Cambridge Commonwealth Trust, 1983–; Cambridge Overseas Trust, 1988–; Mem., Cttee of Management, Charities Property Unit Trust, 1983–88. *Publications:* res. pubns in scientific jls. *Recreations:* books, music, history of Sussex. *Address:* Downing College, Cambridge CB2 1DQ. *T:* Cambridge (0223) 334843. *Clubs:* Athenæum, Royal Over-Seas League.

FLEETWOOD, Susan Maureen; actress; Hon. Associate Member, Royal Shakespeare Company, since 1988 (Associate Member, 1980–88); *b* 21 Sept. 1944; *d* of John Joseph Kells Fleetwood and Bridget Maureen (*née* Brereton), St Andrews, Scotland. *Educ:* sixteen schs, incl. Convent of the Nativity, Sittingbourne, Kent; RADA (Bancroft Gold Medal). Rosalind, in As You Like It, and Lady Macbeth, in Macbeth, tour, Arizona, USA, 1964; Founder Mem., Liverpool Everyman, 1965–67: Lady Percy, in Henry IV; Gwendolen, in The Importance of Being Earnest; Alison, in Look Back in Anger; Liz, in Fando and Liz; Margaret, in The Great God Brown; chorus leader, in Murder in the Cathedral; The Woman, in The Four Seasons; Lady Macbeth, in Macbeth; RSC, 1967–68: Regan, in King Lear; Marina/Thaisa, in Pericles; Julia, in The Two Gentlemen of Verona (tour); Beba, in Criminals; Amanda, in The Relapse; RSC, 1972: Portia, in The Merchant of Venice; chorus leader, in Murder in the Cathedral; The Bondwoman, in The Island of the Mighty; RSC, 1975–76: Katharina, in The Taming of the Shrew; Kaleria, in Summerfolk; Princess of France, in Love's Labour's Lost (also US tour); Imogen, in Cymbeline; National Theatre, 1976–78: Pegeen Mike, in Playboy of the Western World; Ophelia, in Hamlet; Jo, in Watch it Come Down; Zenocrate, in Tamburlaine the Great; Nora, in The Plough and the Stars; Clare, in Lavender Blue; Ismene, in The Woman; RSC, 1980–82: Rosalind, in As You Like It; Varya, in The Cherry Orchard; wife, in La Ronde; National Theatre, 1982–83: June Taylor, in Way Upstream; Titania, in A Midsummer Night's Dream; National Theatre, 1988–89: Laura, in The Father; RSC, 1990–91: Beatrice, in Much Ado About Nothing; Madame Arkadina, in The Seagull; other roles: Nina, in The Seagull, Cambridge Theatre Co., 1970; Ophelia, in Hamlet, Prospect Theatre Co., 1970–71; Clara, in I'm NOT Rappaport, Apollo, 1986; Kitty Twombley, in The Cabinet Minister, Royal Exchange, Manchester, 1988. Films include: Clash of the Titans; Heat and Dust; Young Sherlock Holmes; The Sacrifice; White Mischief; Dream Demons; The Krays; television serials include: Eustace and Hilda; The Good Soldier; Strangers and Brothers; Murder of a Moderate Man; Summer's Lease; TV Plays: Watercress Girl; Don't be Silly; Dangerous Corner; Flying in the Branches; many radio plays. *Recreations:* listening to music, going to the theatre, travelling, doing everything I can't do when working. *Address:* c/o Duncan Heath, Paramount House, 162 Wardour Street, W1V 3AT. *T:* 071–439 1471. *Club:* Zanzibar.

FLEISCHMANN, Prof. Martin, FRS 1986; FRSC 1980; Research Professor, Department of Chemistry, University of Southampton, since 1983; *b* 29 March 1927; *s* of Hans Fleischmann and Margarethe Fleischmann (*née* Srb); *m* 1950, Sheila Flinn; one *s* two *d*. *Educ:* Worthing High School; Imperial College of Science and Technology. ARCS 1947; BSc 1948; PhD 1951. ICI Fellow, King's College, Univ. of Durham, 1952–57; Lectr, then Reader, Univ. of Newcastle upon Tyne, 1957–67; Electricity Council Faraday Prof. of Electrochemistry, Univ. of Southampton, 1967–77; Senior Fellowship, SERC, 1977–82. Pres., Internat. Soc. of Electrochemistry, 1970–72; Palladium Medal, US Electrochemical Soc., 1985. *Publications:* numerous papers and chapters in books. *Recreations:* ski-ing, walking, music, cooking. *Address:* Bury Lodge, Duck Street, Tisbury, Wilts SP3 6LJ. *T:* Tisbury (0747) 870384.

FLEMING, Ven. David; Archdeacon of Wisbech, since 1984; Hon. Canon of Ely Cathedral, since 1982; *b* 8 June 1937; *s* of John Frederick Fleming and Emma (*née* Casey); *m* 1966, Elizabeth Anne Marguerite Hughes; three *s* one *d*. *Educ:* Hunstanton County Primary School; King Edward VII Grammar School, King's Lynn; Kelham Theological Coll. National Service with Royal Norfolk Regt, 1956–58. Deacon 1963; Asst Curate, St Margaret, Walton on the Hill, Liverpool, 1963–67; priest 1964; attached to Sandringham group of churches, 1967–68; Vicar of Great Staughton, 1968–76; Chaplain of HM Borstal, Gaynes Hall, 1968–76; RD of St Neots, 1972–76; RD of March, 1977–82; Vicar of Whittlesey, 1976–85; Priest-in-Charge of Pondersbridge, 1983–85; Vicar of Wisbech St Mary, 1985–88. Chm. of House of Clergy, Ely Diocesan Synod, 1982–85. *Recreations:* tennis, chess, extolling Hunstanton. *Address:* 20 Barton Road, Ely CB7 4DE. *T:* Ely (0353) 663632. *Club:* Whittlesey Rotary.

FLEMING, Grahame Ritchie; QC (Scot.) 1990; *b* 13 Feb. 1949; *s* of Ian Erskine Fleming and Helen Ritchie Wallace or Fleming; *m* 1984, Mopsa Dorcas Robbins; one *d*. *Educ:* Forfar Acad.; Univ. of Edinburgh (MA, LLB). Admitted Faculty of Advocates, 1976. Standing Jun. Counsel to Home Office in Scotland, 1986–89. *Recreations:* food, travel, supporting the Scottish Rugby team. *Address:* Advocates' Library, Parliament House, Edinburgh EH1 1RF. *T:* 031–226 5071.

FLEMING, Ian, RSA 1956 (ARSA 1947); RSW 1947; RWA 1975; RGI 1986; Head, Gray's School of Art, Aberdeen, 1954–71, retired; *b* 19 Nov. 1906; *s* of John and Catherine Fleming; *m* 1943, Catherine Margaret Weetch; one *s* two *d*. *Educ:* Hyndland Sch., Glasgow; Glasgow Sch. of Art. Served War, 1941–46 (Normandy, Belgium, Holland, Germany). Lectr, Glasgow Sch. of Art, 1931–48; Warden, Patrick Allan-Fraser Art Coll., Hospitalfield, Arbroath, 1948–54. Chm., Peacock Printmakers Workshop (Aberdeen), 1973–86. Hon. LLD Aberdeen, 1984. *Recreation:* anything Scottish. *Address:* 15 Fonthill Road, Aberdeen. *T:* Aberdeen (0224) 580680.

FLEMING, Rear-Adm. Sir John, KBE 1960; DSC 1944; Director of the Naval Education Service, 1956–60; *b* 2 May 1904; *s* of late James Fleming; *m* 1930, Jean Law (*d* 1986), *d* of late James Stuart Gillitt, South Shields; no *c*. *Educ:* Jarrow Grammar Sch.; St John's Coll., Cambridge. BA 1925, MA 1957. Entered RN as Instructor Lieut, 1925; Instr Lieut-Comdr, 1931; Instr Comdr, 1939; Instr Capt., 1950; Instr Rear-Adm., 1956. Asst Dir Naval Weather Service, 1945, Dep. Dir, 1947; Fleet Instructor Officer and Fleet Meteorological Officer, Home Fleet, 1950; Command Instructor Officer, The Nore, 1951; Education Dept, Admiralty, 1952. *Recreation:* gardening. *Address:* Mullion Cottage, Tanners Lane, Haslemere, Surrey. *T:* Haslemere (0428) 2412.

FLEMING, John, FRSL; writer; *b* 12 June 1919; *s* of Joseph Fleming and Elizabeth Stawart. *Educ:* Rugby Sch.; Trinity Coll., Cambridge (BA). FRSL 1963. Editor of Style & Civilisation, Art in Context, and, Architect and Society, for Penguin Books, 1964–. *Publications:* Robert Adam and his Circle in Edinburgh and Rome, 1962; (with Sir Nikolaus Pevsner and Hugh Honour) The Penguin Dictionary of Architecture, 1966, 4th rev. edn 1991; (with Hugh Honour) The Penguin Dictionary of Decorative Arts, 1977, rev. edn 1989; (with Hugh Honour) A World History of Art, 1982 (Mitchell Prize, 1982), rev. edn 1991 (US edn, The Visual Arts: a history); (with Hugh Honour) The Venetian Hours of Henry James, Whistler and Sargent, 1991. *Recreation:* gardening. *Club:* Travellers'.

FLEMING, John Bryden; retired; *b* 23 June 1918; *s* of W. A. Fleming, advocate, and Maria MacLeod Bryden; *m* 1942, Janet Louise Guthrie (*d* 1981); one *s* three *d*. *Educ:* Edinburgh Academy; Univs of Edinburgh and London. MA Hons Geog. Edinburgh, BScEcon London. Army, 1940–46, RASC and REME. Planning Officer, Dept of Health for Scotland, 1946; Principal, 1956; Asst Sec., Scottish Develt Dept, 1963, Under Sec., 1974–78; Sec., Scottish Special Housing Assoc., 1978–83. *Recreations:* gardening, hill walking. *Address:* 10 Fettes Row, Edinburgh EH3 6SE. *T:* 031–557 4625. *Clubs:* Commonwealth Trust; Scottish Arts (Edinburgh).

FLEMING, John Marley; General Director, Marketing and Product Planning, Cadillac Motor Car Division, General Motors, since 1988; *b* 4 April 1930; *s* of David A. Fleming and Mary L. Fleming (*née* Marley); *m* 1961, Jeanne (*née* Retelle); one *s* two *d*. *Educ:* Harvard Coll., Cambridge, Mass, USA (BA); Harvard Business Sch., Boston, Mass (MBA). Lieut US Navy, 1952–55. Dist Manager, Frigidaire Sales Corp., 1957–63; Sales Promotion Manager, Ford Motor Co., 1963–68; Vice-Pres., J. Walter Thompson Co., 1969; Dir of Marketing, Oldsmobile Div., GMC, 1970–76; Dir of Sales, Adam Opel AG, West Germany, 1977–79; Dir of Commercial Vehicles, 1980–81, and Chm. and Man. Dir, 1982–85, Vauxhall Motors Ltd; Vice Pres., Sales, General Motors, Europe, 1986–87. *Recreations:* ski-ing, sailing, golf. *Address:* 4056 Augusta Court, Bloomfield Hills, Michigan 48302, USA. *Clubs:* Harpenden Golf; Detroit Yacht.

FLEMING, Raylton Arthur; freelance journalist specialising in international affairs, Mallorca, music and restaurants; Liaison Officer, United Nations University, World Institute for Development Economics Research, Helsinki, 1984–86; *b* 1925; *s* of Arthur and Evelyn Fleming; *m* 1967, Leila el Doweini; one *s*. *Educ:* Worksop Coll. Associate Producer, World Wide Pictures Ltd, 1952; Head of Overseas Television Production, Central Office of Information, 1957; Dep. Dir, Films/Television Div., COI, 1961; Asst Controller (Overseas) COI, 1968; Actg Controller (Overseas), 1969; Dir, Exhibns Div. COI, 1971; Controller (Home), COI, 1972–76; Controller (Overseas), COI, 1976–78; Dir of Inf., UN Univ., Japan, 1978–83; Dir, UN Univ. Liaison Office, NY, 1983–84. *Recreations:* music, opera. *Address:* Camino del Castillo, Alaro, Mallorca, Spain.

FLEMING, Robert, (Robin); DL; Chairman, Robert Fleming Holdings, since 1990; *b* 18 Sept. 1932; *s* of late Major Philip Fleming and Joan Cecil Fleming (*née* Hunloke); *m* 1962, Victoria Margaret Aykroyd; two *s* one *d*. *Educ:* Eton College; Royal Military Academy, Sandhurst. Served The Royal Scots Greys, 1951–58. Joined Robert Fleming, 1958; Director: Robert Fleming Trustee Co., 1961 (Chm., 1985–91); Robert Fleming Investment Trust, 1968; Robert Fleming Holdings, 1974 (Dep. Chm., 1986–90). High Sheriff, 1980, DL 1990, Oxfordshire. *Recreations:* most country pursuits, esp. stalking and fishing; most types of music, esp. Scottish traditional. *Address:* Church Farm, Steeple Barton, Bicester, Oxon OX5 3QR. *T:* Bicester (0869) 47177; Black Mount, Bridge of Orchy, Argyll PA36 4AH. *T:* Tyndrum (08384) 237.

FLEMINGTON, Roger; Director, since 1988 and Deputy Group Chief Executive, since 1990, National Westminster Bank; *b* 7 May 1932; *s* of late Walter Harold Flemington and Mary Elizabeth Julia Flemington (*née* Stone); *m* 1955, Doreen Helen Smyter (*d* 1990). *Educ:* Nantwich and Acton Grammar School. FCIB. RAF, 1950–52. National Westminster Bank Group, 1948–: Man. Dir, Diners Club, 1975–77; Sen. Internat. Exec., 1978–79; Chief Internat. Exec., Asia, Australasia and Africa, 1979–81; Asst Gen. Manager, Internat. Banking Div., 1981–84; Dir, Westments, 1984–; Gen. Manager, Premises Div., 1984–86, Domestic Banking Div., 1986–88; Chief Exec., UK Financial Services, 1989–90. Director: Coutts & Co., 1986–; Lombard North Central, 1989–. Pres., CIB, 1991– (Member: Council, 1986–; Gen. Purposes Cttee, 1987–; Dep. Chm., 1990); Member: London & Scottish Bankers Cttee on Private Finance for Housing, 1988–; Exec. Cttee, BBA, 1989– (Chm., Remuneration Sub-Cttee, 1990–); City Adv. Gp, CBI, 1990–. Trustee, Indep. Broadcasting Telethon Trust, 1989–. Freeman, City of London, 1979; Liveryman, Woolmen's Co. FRSA. *Recreations:* music, flyfishing, country pursuits, antiques, travel, reading. *Address:* National Westminster Bank, 41 Lothbury, EC2P 2BP. *T:* 071–726 1266. *Clubs:* Overseas Bankers', MCC.

FLEMMING, John Stanton, FBA 1991; Chief Economist, European Bank for Reconstruction and Development, since 1991; *b* 6 Feb. 1941; *s* of Sir Gilbert Nicolson Flemming, KCB, and of Virginia Coit; *m* 1963, Jean Elizabeth (*née* Briggs); three *s* one *d*. *Educ:* Rugby Sch.; Trinity and Nuffield Colls, Oxon. BA Oxon 1962, MA 1966. Lecturer and Fellow, Oriel Coll., Oxford, 1963–65; Official Fellow in Economics, 1965–80, Emeritus Fellow, 1980, and Bursar, 1970–79, Nuffield Coll., Oxford. Bank of England: Chief Adviser, 1980–84; Economic Adviser to the Governor, 1984–88; Exec. Dir, 1988–91. Member: Nat. Freight Corp., 1978–80; Council, Royal Economic Soc., 1980–; Adv. Bd on Research Councils, 1986–; Chm., Economic Affairs Cttee, SSRC, 1981–84. Associate Editor: Oxford Economic Papers, 1970–73; Review of Economic Studies, 1973–76; Editor, Economic Jl, 1976–80. *Publications:* Inflation, 1976; contrib. economic jls. *Address:* EBRD, 122 Leadenhall Street, EC3.

FLESCH, Michael Charles, QC 1983; *b* 11 March 1940; *s* of Carl and late Ruth Flesch; *m* 1972, Gail Schrire; one *s* one *d*. *Educ:* Gordonstoun Sch.; University College London (LLB 1st Cl. Hons). Called to the Bar, Gray's Inn, 1963 (Lord Justice Holker Sen. Schol.). Bigelow Teaching Fellow, Univ. of Chicago, 1963–64; Lectr (part-time) in Revenue Law, University Coll. London, 1965–82. Practice at Revenue Bar, 1966–. Chm., Taxation and Retirement Benefits Cttee, Bar Council, 1985–. Governor of Gordonstoun Sch., 1976–. *Publications:* various articles, notes and reviews concerning taxation, in legal periodicals. *Recreation:* all forms of sport. *Address:* (home) 38 Farm Avenue, NW2. *T:* 081–452 4547; (chambers) Gray's Inn Chambers, Gray's Inn, WC1. *T:* 071–242 2642. *Clubs:* Arsenal FC, Middlesex CC, Brondesbury Lawn Tennis and Cricket.

FLETCHER; *see* Aubrey-Fletcher.

FLETCHER, Alan Gerard, RDI 1972; FCSD; designer; Partner, Pentagram Design; *b* Nairobi, Kenya, 27 Sept. 1931; *s* of Bernard Fletcher and Dorothy Murphy; *m* 1956, Paola Biagi; one *d.* *Educ:* Christ's Hosp. Sch.; Central Sch. of Arts and Crafts; Royal Coll. of Art (ARCA); Sch. of Architecture and Design, Yale Univ. (Master of Fine Arts). FSIAD 1964. Designer, Fortune Magazine, New York, 1958–59; freelance practice, London, 1959–62; Partner: Fletcher Forbes Gill, 1962–65; Crosby Fletcher Forbes, 1965–72; Partner, Pentagram, 1972–. Pres., Designers and Art Dirs Assoc., 1973; Internat. Pres., Alliance Graphique Internat., 1982–85. Served on design competition juries for: Designers and Art Dirs Assoc. Exhibns, London; Internat. poster Biennale, Warsaw; Annual Awards for Newspaper Design, London; Art Dirs Club, Toronto; European Illustration, London; Common Market EEC symbol, Brussels; Amer. Inst. of Graphic Arts. Sen. Fellow, RCA, 1989. Designers and Art Dirs Assoc. Gold Award for Design, 1974, and President's Award for Outstanding Contribn to Design, 1977; One Show Gold Award for Design, New York, 1974; Design Medal, SIAD, 1983. *Publications:* (jtly) Graphic Design: a visual comparison, 1963; (jtly) A Sign Systems Manual, 1970; (jtly) Identity Kits, 1971; (jtly) Living by Design, 1978; (jtly) Ideas on Design, 1987; (also illus.) Was Ich Sah, 1967. *Address:* Pentagram, 11 Needham Road, W11 2RP. *T:* 071–229 3477.

FLETCHER, Alan Philip; QC 1984; *b* 28 June 1914; *s* of late Philip Cawthorne Fletcher, MC and Edith Maud Fletcher; *m* 1945, Annette Grace Wright; three *s* one *d.* *Educ:* Marlborough College; Trinity College, Oxford. MA; hockey blue, 1936 and 1937. War service, Army, England and India, 1939–45, ending as acting Lt-Col; called to the Bar, Inner Temple, 1940; bencher; Junior Counsel, Inland Revenue (Rating Valuation), 1969–84; Leader, Barnet London Borough Council, 1965–73. *Recreations:* walking, golf, architectural and garden history. *Address:* 26 Hollies Close, Royston, Herts SG8 7DZ. *T:* Royston (0763) 248580.

See also P. J. Fletcher, R. A. Fletcher.

FLETCHER, Hon. Sir Alan (Roy), Kt 1972; Minister for Education and Cultural Activities, Queensland, 1968–74, retired 1975; MLA (Country Party) for Cunningham, Queensland, 1953–74; *b* Pittsworth, 26 Jan. 1907; *s* of Alexander Roy Fletcher, Pittsworth, and Rosina Wilhemina (*née* McIntyre); *m* 1934, Enid Phair, *d* of James Thompson, Ashburton, NZ; two *s* two *d.* *Educ:* Irongate State Sch.; Scots Coll., Warwick, Qld. Pittsworth Shire: Councillor, 1945–57, Chm., 1949–57. Speaker, Legislative Assembly, Qld, 1957–60; Minister for Lands, 1960–68. Dir, Queensland Co-op. Milling Assoc., 1951–65. Member: Presbyterian Schs Council, Warwick, 1951– (Chm., 1958–61); Council, Darling Downs Inst. of Advanced Educn, 1975–. Pres., Old Boys' Assoc., Scots Coll., Warwick, 1948–. *Recreations:* shooting, croquet. *Address:* 3/11 Beresford Street, Pittsworth, Queensland 4356, Australia. *T:* 076–931–091.

FLETCHER, Ann Elizabeth Mary, (Mrs Michael Fletcher); *see* Leslie, A. E. M.

FLETCHER, Col Archibald Ian, OBE 1967; JP; Vice Lord-Lieutenant for Strathclyde Region (District of Argyll and Bute), since 1990; Consultant and Adviser, Dunans Farming & Forestry, since 1987; Director, Argyll and the Islands Enterprise Co. Ltd, since 1990; *b* 9 April 1924; *s* of Ian Archibald Fletcher and Isabelle Douglas-Dick, *widow* of Ralph Gladwin; *m* 1952, Helen Clare de Salis; one *s* two *d.* *Educ:* Ampleforth Coll. Joined Army, Scots Guards, 1942; Guards Depot, commnd 1943 into 3rd Bn; Tank Troop Comdr, NW Europe, 1944–45; served Palestine, Malaya, 1946–51; E Africa, 1961–63; commanded: 1st Bn, 1963–66; Borneo, 1964–65; Regt, 1967–70; retired to farm in Argyllshire. Mem., Nat. Council and Scottish Bd, Timber Growers UK, 1985–91. Chm., Colintraive and Glendaruel Community Council, 1977–91. Hon. Pres., NFU of Scotland, 1985–86. Mem., Argyll CC, 1972–75. JP 1971, DL 1974, Argyll. Chevalier, Mil. Order of Aviz (Portugal), 1955. *Recreations:* country pursuits. *Address:* Dunans, Glendaruel, Argyll PA22 3AD. *Clubs:* New (Edinburgh); Semengo (Sarawak).

FLETCHER, Dr Archibald Peter; Medical Director, IMS International; Director, PMS International; Partner in Documenta Biomedica; *b* 24 Dec. 1930; *s* of Walter Archibald Fletcher and Dorothy Mabel Fletcher; *m* 1972, Patricia Elizabeth (*née* Marr); three *s* two *d.* *Educ:* Kingswood Sch.; London Hosp. Med. Coll.; St Mary's Hosp. Med. Sch., London Univ. MB, BS; PhD (Biochemistry). Sen. Lectr in Chemical Pathology, St Mary's Hosp., London, 1961–69; Head of Biochemistry, American Nat. Red Cross, USA, 1970–73; Med. Dir, Upjohn, Scandinavia; PMO, Medicines Div., DHSS, 1977; Med. Assessor to Cttee on Safety of Medicines; Chief Sci. Officer and SPMO, DHSS, 1978–79; Res. Physician, Upjohn International Inc., Brussels, 1979. *Publications:* numerous papers in scientific and medical journals on glycoproteins, physical chemistry, metabolism of blood cells and safety evaluation of new drugs. *Recreations:* gardening, golf. *Address:* Hall Corner Cottage, Little Maplestead, Halstead, Essex. *T:* Halstead (0787) 475465.

FLETCHER, Augustus James Voisey, OBE 1977; GM 1957; HM Diplomatic Service, retired; Foreign and Commonwealth Office, 1982–89; *b* 23 Dec. 1928; *s* of James Fletcher and Naomi Fletcher (*née* Dudden); *m* 1956, Enyd Gwynne Harries; one *s* one *d.* *Educ:* Weston-super-Mare Grammar Sch.; Oriental Language Institute, Malaya. Colonial Service, Palestine, 1946–48, Malaya, 1948–58; Min. of Defence, 1958–64; FCO, 1964–: Hong Kong (seconded HQ Land Forces), 1966–70; FCO, 1970–73; Hong Kong, 1973–76; FCO, 1976–79; Counsellor, New Delhi, 1979–82. *Recreations:* trout fishing, walking, food/wine, theatre. *Clubs:* Travellers', Commonwealth Trust.

FLETCHER, Charles Montague, CBE 1952; MD, FRCP, FFPHM; Physician to Hammersmith Hospital, 1952–76; Professor of Clinical Epidemiology, University of London at Royal Postgraduate Medical School, 1973–76 (Reader, 1952–73), now Professor Emeritus; *b* 5 June 1911; *s* of late Sir Walter Morley Fletcher, FRS and late Mary Frances Fletcher (*née* Cropper); *m* Louisa Mary Sylvia Seely, *d* of 1st Baron Mottistone; one *s* two *d.* *Educ:* Eton Coll.; Trinity Coll., Cambridge (Sen. Schol.; rowed in Univ. Boat, 1933); St Bartholomew's Hospital. MA 1936, MD 1945, Cantab; MRCP 1942; FRCP 1947; FFPHM (FFCM 1974). Michael Foster Research Student, Trinity Coll., 1934–36; Nuffield Res. Student, Oxford, 1940–42. Asst Phys., EMS, 1943–44; Dir, MRC Pneumoconiosis Res. Unit, 1945–52; Sec., MRC Cttee on Bronchitis Res., 1954–76. Royal Coll. of Physicians: Mem. Council, 1959–62; 2nd Vice Pres., 1975; Sec., Cttee on Smoking and Health, 1961–71; Goulstonian Lectr, 1947; Bissett Hawkins Gold Medal, 1969. WHO Consultant: Pulmonary Heart Disease, 1960; Chronic Bronchitis, 1962; Smoking and Health, 1970. Mem., Central Health Services Council and Standing Med. Adv. Cttee, 1966–76; Vice-Chm., Health Educn Council, 1967; Chairman, Action on Smoking and Health (ASH), 1971–78, Pres., 1979; Member: Exec. Cttee, Asthma Soc., 1980–89; Council, British Diabetic Assoc., 1983–88 (Chm., Educn Sect., 1983–88); Inst. of Med. Ethics Cttee on Assisting Death, 1989–. Introd. many TV med. programmes incl. Hurt Mind, 1955, Your Life in Their Hands, 1958–65, Television Doctor, 1969–70. Consulting Ed. Jl of Med. Ethics, 1975–81. *Publications:* Communication in Medicine, 1973; Natural History of Chronic Bronchitis and Emphysema, 1976; many papers on: first use of penicillin, 1941; dust disease of lungs, 1946–55; bronchitis and emphysema, 1952–76. *Recreations:* music, gardening. *Address:* 24 West Square, SE11 4SN. *T:* 071–735 8753; 2 Coastguard Cottages, Newtown, IoW PO30 4PA. *T:* Calbourne (098378) 321. *Club:* Brooks's.

FLETCHER, Geoffrey Bernard Abbott, MA Cantab; *b* Hampstead, 28 Nov. 1903; *s* of J. Alexander Fletcher and Ursula Constance, *d* of William Richard Rickett and *cousin* of Rt Honourable Sir Joseph Compton-Rickett, MP. *Educ:* Rugby Sch.; King's Coll., Cambridge (Senior Scholar), First Class, Classical Tripos, Part I, 1924; First Class Classical Tripos, Part 2, 1926; Prendergast Student, 1926; Asst Lectr in Classics, University of Leeds, 1927–28; Lectr in Greek, University of Liverpool, 1928–36; Prof. of Classics in the University of Durham, King's Coll., Newcastle upon Tyne, 1937–46, Prof. of Latin, 1946–63; Prof. of Latin, University of Newcastle upon Tyne, 1963–69, now Emeritus Prof. Examiner in Greek, University of Leeds, 1940–42; Examiner in Latin, Queen's Univ., Belfast, 1949–51, University of Wales, 1954–56, Bristol, 1961–63; Dean of Faculty of Arts, University of Durham, 1945–47; Public Orator, University of Durham, 1956–58. *Publications:* an appendix on Housman's Poetry in Housman, 1897–1936, by Grant Richards, 1941; Annotations on Tacitus, 1964; many contributions to classical and other periodicals, British and foreign, and to co-operative works. *Recreations:* music, reading, art galleries. *Address:* Thirlmere Lodge, Elmfield Road, Gosforth, Newcastle upon Tyne NE3 4BB. *T:* 091–285 2873. *Club:* Athenæum.

FLETCHER, Geoffrey Scowcroft; artist and author; *o s* of Herbert Fletcher and Annie Talence Fletcher; *m* Mary Jean Timothy. *Educ:* University Coll., London Univ. (Dip. in Fine Art). Abbey Major Schol., British Sch. at Rome, 1948. Drawings appeared in Manchester Guardian, 1950; London drawings and articles featured in The Daily Telegraph, 1958–. Author of television features on unusual aspects of London; has been instrumental in saving a number of metropolitan buildings from demolition. Drawings and paintings in various public and private collections in England and abroad, incl. exhibn of paintings and drawings in possession of Islington Council, 1972, 1978, and exhibns of drawings and paintings acquired by Bolton Art Gall., 1981, 1986; Geoffrey Fletcher Room, decorated with the artist's drawings, opened Selfridge Hotel, London, 1973. Designed enamel box for St Paul's Cathedral Appeal, 1972; exhibitions of drawings: Miles Gall., St James's, 1980; East End Drawings and Paintings, Limehouse, 1984; London drawings, Guildhall, City of London, 1988; Genoese drawings, for City of Genoa promotion, London, 1988. Drawings and sketchbooks acquired by British Museum, 1990; oil paintings and sketchbooks acquired by Guildhall Art Gall., 1990–91. *Publications:* The London Nobody Knows (filmed, 1968), 1962, 2nd edn 1989; Down Among the Meths Men, 1966; Geoffrey Fletcher's London, 1968; City Sights, 1963; Pearly Kingdom, 1965; London's River, 1966; Elements of Sketching, 1966 (Amer. edn, 1968); London's Pavement Pounders, 1967; London After Dark, 1969; Changing London (Drawings from The Daily Telegraph), 1969; The London Dickens Knew, 1970; London Souvenirs, 1973; Paint It In Water Colour, 1974; Italian Impressions, 1974; Sketch It In Black and White, 1975; The Spitalfields Prints, 1990; Daily Telegraph Series: London Prints, 1975, London Colour Prints, 1978, London Portraits, 1978, London at My Feet, 1979; London Alleys, 1980; London: a private view, 1989. *Address:* c/o Cassell plc, Villiers House, 41–47 Strand, WC2; c/o R. Davis-Poynter, 118 St Pancras, Chichester, W Sussex.

FLETCHER, Sir James Muir Cameron, Kt 1980; FCA; *b* Dunedin, NZ, 25 Dec. 1914; *s* of Sir James Fletcher; *m* 1942, Margery Vaughan, *d* of H. H. Gunthorp; three *s.* *Educ:* Waitaki Boys' High School; Auckland Grammar School. South British Insurance Co., 1931–37; then Fletcher Construction Co. and Fletcher Holdings. *Address:* Fletcher Challenge Ltd, Private Bag, Auckland, New Zealand; 119 St Stephens Avenue, Parnell, Auckland, NZ.

FLETCHER, Major John Antony, MBE (mil.) 1953; RA retired; Secretary, Institute of Road Transport Engineers, 1963–85; *b* 4 May 1918; *s* of Alexander Ernest Fletcher and Abbie (*née* Wheeler); *m* 1st, 1951, Elizabeth Cross (marr. diss. 1979); one *s* three *d*; 2nd, 1980, Susan Mary Brown. *Educ:* Cheltenham Coll. Jun. Sch.; Abingdon Sch.; RMA, Woolwich; Army and RAF Staff Colls (psc, pac). 2nd Lieut, RA, 1938; war service, Malta, Middle East, Malaya and Burma; Korea Commonwealth Div.; retired 1960. Secretariat, Powell Duffryn Gp, 1960–63. Chm., Assoc. of Care-Takers and Care-Seekers, 1985–88. Hon. FIRTE 1985. *Publications:* article in Gunner Jl; eight letters (out of twelve!) to The Times. *Recreations:* being ex!: ex-playing mem., MCC; ex-Stragglers of Asia; ex-United Hunts Club; ex-Sherringham and many other golf clubs. *Address:* Milford Cottage, 10 Cudnall Street, Charlton Kings, Cheltenham, Glos GL53 8HT. *T:* Cheltenham (0242) 522367.

FLETCHER, John Edwin; His Honour Judge Fletcher; a Circuit Judge, since 1986; *b* 23 Feb. 1941; *s* of late Sydney Gerald Fletcher and Cecilia Lane Fletcher. *Educ:* St Bees Sch., Cumbria; Clare Coll., Cambridge (MA). Called to the Bar, Inner Temple, 1964; Midland and Oxford Circuit, 1965–86; a Recorder, 1983–86. Mem. Panel of Chairmen, Medical Appeal Tribunals, 1981–86. *Recreations:* fell walking, philately, music, steam railways.

FLETCHER, Leslie; General Manager (Chief Executive Officer) Williams Deacon's Bank Ltd, 1964–70, Director, 1966–70, retired; *b* 30 Jan. 1906; *s* of late Edward Henry and Edith Howard Fletcher; *m* 1934, Helen, *d* of Frank Turton; one *s* one *d.* *Educ:* City Gram. Sch., Chester; Manchester Univ. (BA Com). Entered Williams Deacon's Bank Ltd 1922; Asst Gen. Man., 1957; Dep. Gen. Man., 1961. Fellow and Mem. Council, Inst. of Bankers. *Recreations:* lawn tennis, golf. *Address:* Mote Cottage, Burley, near Ringwood, Hants. *T:* Burley (04253) 2291.

FLETCHER, Sir Leslie, Kt 1983; DSC 1945; FCA; Chairman, Westland Group plc, since 1989 (Joint Deputy Chairman, 1988–89); *b* 14 Oct. 1922; *s* of Ernest and Lily Fletcher; *m* 1947, Audrey Faviell Jackson; one *s* one *d.* *Educ:* Nether Edge Secondary Sch., Sheffield. FCA 1952. Served War, RNVR (FAA), 1942–46 (Lieut). Helbert Wagg & Co. Ltd (subseq. J. Henry Schroder Wagg & Co. Ltd), 1955–71, Dir 1966–71; Chm., Glynwed Internat., 1971–86; Deputy Chairman: Standard Chartered PLC, 1983–89 (Dir, 1972); RMC Gp, 1991– (Dir, 1983–); Dir, The Rank Organisation, 1984–. Mem. Council, CBI, 1976–86. *Recreations:* gardening, golf, photography. *Address:* 4 Carlton Gardens, Pall Mall, SW1Y 5AB. *T:* 071–839 4061. *Clubs:* Brooks's, MCC, Royal Automobile; Royal & Ancient Golf (St Andrews).

FLETCHER, Comdt Marjorie Helen (Kelsey), CBE 1988; Director, Women's Royal Naval Service, 1986–88; *b* 21 Sept. 1932; *d* of Norman Farler Fletcher and Marie Amelie Fletcher (*née* Adams). *Educ:* Avondale High Sch.; Sutton Coldfield High Sch. for Girls. Solicitor's Clerk, 1948–53; joined WRNS as Telegraphist, 1953; progressively, 3rd Officer to Chief Officer, 1956–76; Supt, 1981; served in Secretarial, Careers Advisor, Intelligence and Staff appts; ndc 1979; Directing Staff, RN Staff Coll., 1980–81; psc 1981; Internat. Mil. Staff, NATO HQ, 1981–84; Asst Dir, Dir Naval Staff Duties, 1984–85. ADC to the Queen, 1986–88. *Publication:* The WRNS, 1989. *Recreations:* reading, needlework, entertaining, cookery, gardening, collecting paintings.

FLETCHER, Neil; Education Officer, National and Local Government Officers' Association, since 1991; *b* 5 May 1944; *s* of Alan and Ruth Fletcher; *m* 1967, Margaret Monaghan; two *s*. *Educ:* Wyggeston Sch., Leicester; City of Leeds Coll. of Educn (Teachers' Cert.); London Univ. (BA Hons). Charter FCP 1990. Schoolteacher, 1966–68; Lectr, 1969–76; NALGO official, 1976–. Member: Camden Bor. Council, 1978–86 (Dep. Leader, 1982–84); ILEA, 1979–90 (Chair, Further and Higher Educn Sub-Cttee, 1981–87; Leader, 1987–90); Chair: Council of Local Educn Authorities, 1987–88, 1989–90; Educn Cttee, AMA, 1987–90 (Vice-Chair, 1986–87). Governor: London Inst., 1986–; LSE, 1990–. FRSA 1989. *Recreations:* cricket, soccer, theatre, cookery, walking. *Address:* 13 Ravenshaw Street, NW6 1NP. *T:* 071–435 5306.

FLETCHER, Paul Thomas, CBE 1959; FEng; Deputy President, British Standards Institution, 1982–89 (Chairman, 1979–82); Consulting Engineer: NNC Ltd, since 1977; BGE Co., Tokyo, since 1986; *b* 30 Sept. 1912; *s* of Stephen Baldwin Fletcher and Jessie Carrie; *m* 1941, Mary Elizabeth King; three *s*. *Educ:* Nicholson Inst., Stornaway, Isle of Lewis; Maidstone Grammar Sch.; Medway Techn. Coll. BSc(Eng); FEng, FICE, FIMechE (Hon. FIMechE 1989), FIEE. Served 3-year apprenticeship with E. A. Gardner & Sons Ltd, Maidstone, remaining for 7 years; joined Min. of Works, 1939, initially in Test Br. of Engrg Div., later with responsibility for variety of engrg services in public bldgs and Govt factories and for plant and equipment for Govt civilian and service res. estabts; Chief Mech. and Elec. Engr, 1951. On formation of UKAEA in 1954, became Dep. Dir of Engrg in Industrial Gp, later Engrg Dir and Dep. Man. Dir; Dir, United Power Co., 1961; Man. Dir, GEC (Process Engrg) Ltd, 1965; Man. Dir, 1971–76, Dep. Chm., 1976–84, Atomic Power Constructions Ltd. Chm., Pressure Vessels Quality Assurance Bd, 1977–84. President: IMechE, 1975–76; ITEME, 1979–81, 1985–88. *Publications:* papers to IMechE. *Recreations:* photography, motoring. *Address:* 26 Foxgrove Avenue, Beckenham, Kent BR3 2BA. *T:* 081–650 5563.

FLETCHER, Air Chief Marshal Sir Peter Carteret, KCB 1968 (CB 1965); OBE 1945; DFC 1943; AFC 1952; FRAeS; aerospace consultant, since 1983; Director, Corporate Strategy and Planning, British Aerospace, 1977–82, retired; Director, Airbus Industry Supervisory Board, 1979–82; *b* 7 Oct. 1916; *s* of F. T. W. Fletcher, Oxford (sometime tobacco farmer, Southern Rhodesia), and Dora Clulee, New Zealand; *m* 1940, Marjorie Isobel Kotze; two *d*. *Educ:* St George's Coll., Southern Rhodesia; Rhodes Univ., S Africa. SR Law Dept, 1937. Served War of 1939–45: SR Air Force, 1939; trans. to RAF, 1941; commanded 135 and 258 Fighter Sqdns and RAF Station Belvedere. Directing Staffs at: RAF Staff Coll., 1945–46; Jt Services Staff Coll., 1946–48; Imp. Defence Coll., 1956–58; Mem. Jt Planning Staff, 1951–53; comdg RAF Abingdon, 1958–60; Dep. Dir Jt Planning Staff, 1960–61; Dir of Opl Requirements (B), Air Min., 1961–63; Asst Chief of Air Staff (Policy and Plans), 1964–66; AOC, No 38 Group, Transport Command, 1966–67; VCAS, 1967–70; Controller of Aircraft, Min. of Aviation Supply (formerly Min. of Technology), 1970–71; Air Systems Controller, Defence Procurement Executive, MoD, 1971–73; Dir, Hawker Siddeley Aviation Ltd, 1974–77. FRAeS 1986. *Recreations:* books, travel. *Address:* 85A Campden Hill Court, Holland Street, Kensington, W8 7HW. *T:* 071–937 1982.

FLETCHER, Philip John; Under Secretary, Planning and Development Control, Department of the Environment, since 1990; *b* 2 May 1946; *s* of Alan Philip Fletcher, *qv*; *m* 1977, Margaret Anne Boys; one *d* (and one *d* decd). *Educ:* Marlborough College; Trinity College, Oxford (MA). Asst Principal, MPBW, 1968; Department of the Environment: Private Sec. to Permanent Sec., 1978; Asst Sec., Private Sector Housebuilding, 1980, local govt expenditure, 1982–85; Under Sec., Housing, Water and Central Finance, 1986–90. *Recreations:* Reader, Church of England; walking. *Address:* Department of the Environment, 2 Marsham Street, SW1P 3EB. *T:* 071–276 3854.

FLETCHER, Robin Anthony, OBE 1984; DSC 1944; DPhil; Warden of Rhodes House, Oxford, 1980–89; Professorial Fellow, Trinity College, Oxford, 1980–89; *b* 30 May 1922; *s* of Philip Cawthorne Fletcher, MC, and Edith Maud Fletcher (*née* Okell); *m* 1950, Jinny May (*née* Cornish); two *s*. *Educ:* Marlborough Coll.; Trinity Coll., Oxford (MA, DPhil). Served Royal Navy (Lieut RNVR), 1941–46. University Lecturer in Modern Greek, 1949–79; Domestic Bursar, Trinity Coll., Oxford, 1950–74; Senior Proctor, 1966–67; Member, Hebdomedal Council, 1967–74. Represented England at hockey, 1949–55 and GB, 1952 Olympic Games (Bronze Medal). *Publications:* Kostes Palamas, Athens, 1984; various articles. *Recreations:* sport, music. *Address:* Binglea, Sandwick, Stromness, Orkney KW16 3LU. *Clubs:* Naval; Vincent's (Oxford).

See also A. P. Fletcher.

FLETCHER, Prof. Ronald Stanley; Professor of Thermal Power, since 1972, Pro-Vice-Chancellor, since 1985, and Head of Cranfield Campus, since 1989, Cranfield Institute of Technology; *b* 12 Dec. 1937; *s* of Reginald and Dorothy Fletcher; *m* 1965, Pamela Alys, *d* of Gwilym and Alys Treharne; one *s* twin *d*. *Educ:* Imperial College, London Univ. (PhD, DIC); UMIST (BSc Tech). Senior Engineer, Northern Research & Engineering Corp., Cambridge, USA, 1965–70; Consultant, Northern Research & Engineering Corp., Herts, 1970–72; Cranfield Institute of Technology: Head of Mechanical Engineering, 1977–87; Dean of Engineering, 1982–85. Visiting Professor: Cairo, 1975; Brazil, 1977; China (Beijing Inst. of Aero. and Astro.), 1979. Bd Mem., Cranfield Conf. Servs Hldgs Ltd. Member: ARC, 1974–77; Governing Body, AFRC Inst. of Engrg Res. (formerly Nat. Inst. of Agricl Engrg), 1978– (Chm., Finance Cttee, 1982–86); Council, British Hydro. Res. Assoc., 1979–89; AGARD (NATO) Propulsion and Energetics Panel, 1980–; Scientific Bd, Univ. de Technologie de Compiègne, 1989–; Scientific Council, Inst. Mediterranéen de Technologie/ESIM, Marseille, 1989–. Governor, Bedford Modern Sch., 1986–89. *Publications:* papers on combustion. *Recreations:* sailing, music. *Address:* 34 Brecon Way, Bedford MK41 8DD. *T:* Bedford (0234) 58483. *Club:* Parkstone Yacht.

FLETCHER-COOKE, Sir Charles (Fletcher), Kt 1981; QC 1958; *b* 5 May 1914; *yr s* of late Capt. C. A. and Gwendolen May Fletcher-Cooke; *m* 1959, Diana Lady Avebury (whom he divorced, 1967), *d* of late Capt. Edward King and of Mrs J. St Vincent Hand; no surv. *c*. *Educ:* Malvern Coll. (Scholar); Peterhouse, Cambridge (Schol., MA 1940). FCIArb 1981. Pres., Cambridge Union, 1936; Editor, The Granta, 1936. Called to Bar through Lincoln's Inn, 1938 (1st Class Hons, Bar Final Examination; Studentship and Certificate of Honour), Bencher 1969. Mem. Senate, Four Inns of Court, 1970–74. Served War of 1939–45, in Naval Intelligence Div. and on Joint Intelligence Staff, with rank of Lieut-Comdr, RNVR. MP (C) Darwen, Lancs, 1951–83; Joint Parly Under-Sec. of State, Home Office, 1961–63; Chm., Select Cttee on Parly Comr for Admin, 1974–77. Legal Adviser to British Delegation, Danube Conf., Belgrade, 1948; Deleg. to Consultative Assembly of Council of Europe, 1954–55; Mem., European Parlt, 1977–79. Mem., Statute Law Cttee, 1955–61, 1970–83. Dato SPMB, Brunei, 1978. *Publications:* (with others) The Rule of Law; (with M. J. Albery) Monopolies and Restrictive Trade Practices. *Recreation:* fishing. *Address:* The Red House, Clifton Hampden, Oxon. *T:* Clifton Hampden (086730) 7754. *Clubs:* Garrick, Pratt's.

FLETCHER-VANE, family name of **Baron Inglewood.**

FLEW, Prof. Antony Garrard Newton; Emeritus Professor, University of Reading, since 1983; *b* 11 Feb. 1923; *o s* of Rev. Dr R. N. Flew; *m* 1952, Annis Ruth Harty; two *d*. *Educ:* St Faiths Sch., Cambridge; Kingswood Sch., Bath; Sch. of Oriental and African Studies, London; St John's Coll., Oxford (John Locke Schol., MA); DLitt Keele, 1974. Lecturer: Christ Church, Oxford, 1949–50; Univ. of Aberdeen, 1950–54; Professor of Philosophy: Univ. of Keele, 1954–71; Univ. of Calgary, 1972–73; Univ. of Reading, 1973–82; (part-time) York Univ., Toronto, 1983–85; Distinguished Res. Fellow (part-time), Social Philosophy and Policy Center, Bowling Green State Univ., Ohio, 1986–90. Many temp. vis. appts. Gavin David Young Lectr, Adelaide, 1963; Gifford Lectr, St Andrews, 1986. A Vice-Pres., Rationalist Press Assoc., 1973–88; Chm., Voluntary Euthanasia Soc., 1976–79. Fellow, Acad. of Humanism, 1983–. *Publications:* A New Approach to Psychical Research, 1953; Hume's Philosophy of Belief, 1961; God and Philosophy, 1966; Evolutionary Ethics, 1967; An Introduction to Western Philosophy, 1971; Crime or Disease?, 1973; Thinking About Thinking, 1975; The Presumption of Atheism, 1976; Sociology, Equality and Education, 1976; A Rational Animal, 1978; Philosophy: an introduction, 1979; The Politics of Procrustes, 1981; Darwinian Evolution, 1984; Thinking About Social Thinking, 1985; Hume, Philosopher of Moral Science, 1986; (with G. Vesey) Agency and Necessity, 1987; The Logic of Mortality, 1987; Power to the Parents, 1987; Equality in Liberty and Justice, 1989; articles in philosophical and other jls. *Recreations:* walking, climbing, house maintenance. *Address:* 26 Alexandra Road, Reading, Berks RG1 5PD. *T:* Reading (0734) 61848. *Club:* Union Society (Oxford).

FLINDALL, Jacqueline; JP; Associate Consultant, PA Management Consultants, since 1986; *b* 12 Oct. 1932; *d* of Henry and Lilian Flindall. *Educ:* St Davids Sch., Ashford, Mddx; University Coll. Hosp., London (DipN). SRN, SCM, UCH, 1950–54; Midwifery, St Luke's Mat. Hosp., Guildford and Watford, 1955; exchange student, Mount Sinai Hosp., NY, 1956; Ward Sister and Clinical Teacher, UCH, 1957–63; Asst Matron, Wexham Park Hosp., 1964–66; Dep. Supt of Nursing, Prince of Wales and St Anne's, 1967–69; Chief Nursing Officer: Northwick Park Hosp., 1969–73; Oxfordshire HA, 1973–83; Regional Nursing Officer, Wessex RHA, 1983–85. Pres., UCH Nurses' League, 1983–. Mem., Hosp. Chaplaincies Council. Gov., St David's Sch., Ashford, Mddx. Professional Organization Mem., RCN; Hon. FRCN 1983. Mem., Most Hon. and Loyal Soc. of Antient Britons. JP Oxford, 1982, Salisbury, 1987. *Publications:* contribs to nursing press. *Recreation:* painting. *Address:* 4 Mill Lane, Romsey, Hants, SO51 8EU. *T:* Romsey (0794) 513926.

FLINT, Prof. Anthony Patrick Fielding, PhD, DSc; FIBiol; Director of Science and Director of the Institute of Zoology, Zoological Society of London, since 1987; *b* 31 Aug. 1943; *s* of Maurice Fielding Flint and Patricia Joan (*née* Ince); *m* 1967, Chan Mun Kwun; two *s*. *Educ:* Hill Crest Sch., Swanage; King's Sch., Bruton; Univ. of St Andrews (Queen's Coll., Dundee) (BSc 1966); Univ. of Bristol (PhD 1969; DSc 1984). FIBiol 1982. Res. Fellow, Univ. of Western Ontario, 1969–72; Sen. Res. Biochemist in Obs and Gyn., Welsh Nat. Sch. of Medicine, Cardiff, 1972–73; Lectr, Nuffield Dept of Obs and Gyn., Oxford Univ., 1973–77; Staff Mem., AFRC Inst. of Animal Physiology and Genetics Res., Cambridge, 1977–87; Dir, MRC/AFRC Comparative Physiology Res. Gp, 1987–90. Special Lectr, 1985–87, Special Prof. in Molecular Biol., 1987–, Univ. of Nottingham Sch. of Agric.; Visiting Professor: Dept of Biology, UCL, 1989–; Biosphere Scis Div., KCL, 1989–. Member: Cttee, Soc. for Study of Fertility, 1981–89 (Sec., 1985–89); Steering Cttee, WHO Task Force on Plants for Fertility Regulation, 1982–87 (Chm., 1985). Member: Council of Management, Journals of Reproduction and Fertility Ltd, 1981–87 (Mem. Exec. Cttee, 1983–87); Bd of Scientific Editors, Jl of Endocrinology, 1983–87. Medal, Soc. for Endocrinology, 1985. *Publications:* (ed jtly) Embryonic Diapause in Mammals, 1981; papers in physiol, endocrinol and biochemical jls. *Recreation:* playing Bach on the organ or cello. *Address:* Zoological Society of London, Regent's Park, NW1 4RY. *Club:* Athenæum.

FLINT, Prof. David, TD, MA, BL, CA; Professor of Accountancy, 1964–85, (Johnstone Smith Chair, 1964–75), and Vice-Principal, 1981–85, University of Glasgow; *b* 24 Feb. 1919; *s* of David Flint, JP, and Agnes Strang Lambie; *m* 1953, Dorothy Mary Maclachlan Jardine; two *s* one *d*. *Educ:* Glasgow High Sch.; University of Glasgow. Served with Royal Signals, 1939–46, Major (despatches). Awarded distinction final examination of Institute of Chartered Accountants of Scotland, 1948. Lecturer, University of Glasgow, 1950–60; Dean of Faculty of Law, 1971–73. Partner, Mann Judd Gordon & Co. Chartered Accountants, Glasgow, 1951–71. Hon. Prof. of Accountancy, Stirling Univ., 1988–. Hon. Pres. Glasgow Chartered Accountants Students Soc., 1959–60; Chm., Assoc. of Univ. Teachers of Accounting (now British Accounting Assoc.), 1969. Mem. Council, Scottish Business Sch., 1971–77; Vice-Pres., Scottish Economic Soc., 1977–; Vice-Pres., Inst. of Chartered Accountants of Scotland, 1973–75, Pres., 1975–76; Pres., European Accounting Assoc., 1983–84; Member: Management and Ind. Rel. Cttee, SSRC, 1970–72 and 1978–80; Commn for Local Authy Accounts in Scotland, 1978–80. FRSA. *Publications:* A True and Fair View in Company Accounts, 1982; Philosophy and Principles of Auditing: an introduction, 1988. *Recreation:* golf. *Address:* 16 Grampian Avenue, Auchterarder, Perthshire PH3 1NY.

FLINT, Michael Frederick, FSA; Chairman, Denton Hall Burgin & Warrens, Solicitors, since 1990; *b* 7 May 1932; *s* of Frederic Nelson La Fargue Flint and Nell Dixon Smith; *m* 1st, 1954, Susan Kate Rhodes (marr. diss.) two *s* one *d*; 2nd, 1984, Phyllida Margaret Medwyn Lindsay Hughes. *Educ:* St Peter's Sch., York; Kingswood Sch., Bath. Admitted Solicitor 1954; Denton Hall & Burgin, now Denton Hall Burgin & Warrens: Articled Clerk, 1951–56; Asst Solicitor, 1956–60; Partner, 1960–66; Paramount Pictures Corporation: Asst Vice-Pres., 1967; Vice-Pres., 1968–70; Consultant, Henry Ansbacher & Co., 1970; Chm., London Screen Enterprises, 1970–72 (Exec. Producer, feature film, Glastonbury Fayre, 1972); Denton Hall Burgin & Warrens: Partner, 1972–; Managing Partner, 1979–82. Founder Mem., Council of Common Law Inst. of Intellectual Property; Chm., Intellectual Property, Entertainment and Telecommunications Cttee, Internat. Bar Assoc., 1985–90. Vice-Pres., Brit. Archaeol Assoc., 1988–. FSA 1965. *Publications:* A User's Guide to Copyright, 1979, 3rd edn 1990; (jtly) Television by Satellite: Legal Aspects, 1987; (jtly) Intellectual Property: The New Law, 1989. *Recreations:* painting, tennis, ski-ing, archaeology, opera. *Address:* Five Chancery Lane, Clifford's Inn, EC4A 1BU. *T:* 071–320 6539. *Clubs:* Savile; Hurlingham.

FLINT, Rachael H.; *see* Heyhoe Flint, R.

FLOOD, David Andrew; Organist, Canterbury Cathedral, since 1988; *b* 10 Nov. 1955; *s* of Frederick Flood and June Flood (*neé* Alexander); *m* 1976, Alayne Nicholas; two *s* two *d*. *Educ:* Royal Grammar School, Guildford; St John's Coll., Oxford (MA); Clare Coll., Cambridge (PGCE). FRCO (CHM). Assistant Organist, Canterbury Cathedral, 1978–86; Organist and Master of Choristers, Lincoln Cathedral, 1986–88. *Recreations:* motoring, cooking, travel. *Address:* 6 The Precincts, Canterbury, Kent CT1 2EE. *T:* Canterbury (0227) 765219.

FLOOD, Prof. John Edward, OBE 1986; DSc, PhD; CEng, FIEE; FInstP; Professor of Electrical Engineering, 1965–90, now Emeritus, and Head of Department of Electrical and Electronic Engineering, 1967–81 and 1983–89, University of Aston in Birmingham; *b* 2 June 1925; *s* of Sydney E. Flood and Elsie G. Flood; *m* 1949, Phyllis Mary Groocock; two *s*. *Educ:* City of London Sch.; Queen Mary Coll., Univ. of London (BSc 1945; PhD 1951; DSc 1965). CEng, FIEE 1959; FIERE 1967; FInstP 1987. Admiralty Signals Estab., 1944–46; Standard Telephone and Cables Ltd, 1946–47; PO Res. Stn, 1947–52; Siemens Brothers Ltd, 1952–57; Chief Engr, Advanced Develt Labs, AEI Telecommunications Div., 1957–65; Dean, Faculty of Engrg, 1971–74, and Sen. Pro-Vice-Chancellor, 1981–83, Univ. of Aston in Birmingham. Chairman: IEE Professional Gp on Telecommunications, 1974–77; IEE S Midland Centre, 1978–79; Univs Cttee on Integrated Sandwich Courses, 1981–82; BSI Cttee on Telecommunications, 1981–; Member: British Electrotechnical Council, 1981–86; Monopolies and Mergers Commn, 1985–. CGIA 1962. *Publications:* Telecommunication Networks, 1975; papers in scientific and technical jls; patents. *Recreations:* swimming, wine-making. *Address:* 60 Widney Manor Road, Solihull, West Midlands B91 3JQ. *T:* 021–705 3604. *Club:* Royal Over-Seas League.

FLOOD, John Martin; Technical Director, Royal Aerospace Establishment, since 1991; *b* 3 Oct. 1939; *s* of Harry Flood and late Rita Flood (*née* Martin); *m* 1962, Irene Edwards; one *s*. *Educ:* Merchant Taylors' School, Crosby; Leeds Univ. (BSc Physics, 1st cl.). Graduate Apprentice, English Electric, Stevenage, 1962; joined RAE, 1963; Asst Dir, Dir Air Guided Weapons and on Army Chief Scientist staff, 1978–83; Supt, air-launched anti-armour weapons, RAE, 1983–85; Head, Attack Weapons and Defensive Systems Depts, RAE, 1985–89; Dep. Dir (Mission Systems), RAE, 1989–91. *Recreations:* bird watching, walking, theatre, reading (political biography), coping with large garden. *Address:* Royal Aerospace Establishment, Farnborough, Hants. *T:* Farnborough (0252) 24461.

FLOOD, Michael Donovan, (Mik); Director, Institute of Contemporary Arts, since 1990; *b* 7 May 1949; *s* of Gp Capt. Donovan John Flood, DFC, AFC and Vivien Ruth (*née* Allison); *m* 1975, Julie Ward (marr. diss. 1989); one *d*. *Educ:* St George's Coll., Weybridge; Llangefni County Sch., Anglesey. Founder and Artistic Dir, Chapter Arts Centre, Cardiff, 1970–81; Develt Dir, Baltimore Theater Project, USA, 1981–82; Administrator, Pip Simmons Theatre Gp, 1982–83; Arts consultancy, 1983–85; Dir, Watermans Arts Centre, Brentford, 1985–90. Producer of large-scale events: Woyzeck, Cardiff, 1976; Deadwood, Kew Gdns, 1986; Offshore Rig, River Thames, 1987. Member: Film Cttee, Welsh Arts Council, 1976–80; Exec. Cttee, SE Wales Arts Assoc., 1980–81; Co-Founder, Nat. Assoc. of Arts Centres, 1976; Bd Dir, Pip Simmons Theatre Gp, 1977–81. Mem., Ct of Govs, RCA, 1990–. Silver Jubilee Medal, 1977. *Publications:* book reviews in nat. newspapers; contribs on arts and cultural politics to British and European periodicals. *Recreations:* sailing, ichthyology, travel. *Address:* 153 Ealing Road, Brentford, Middx TW8 0LF. *T:* 081–560 7033; ICA, The Mall, SW1 5AH. *T:* 071–930 0493.

FLORENCE, Prof. Alexander Taylor, PhD, DSc; FRSE; FRPharmS, FRSC; Dean, School of Pharmacy, University of London, since 1989; *b* 9 Sept. 1940; *s* of late Alexander Charles Gerrard Florence and of Margaret Florence; *m* 1964, Elizabeth Catherine McRae; two *s* one *d*. *Educ:* Royal Coll. of Science and Technology, Glasgow and Univ. of Glasgow (BSc Hons 1962; PhD 1965); DSc Strathclyde, 1984. FRSC 1977; FRPharmS 1987. University of Strathclyde: MRC Jun. Res. Fellow, 1965–66; Lectr in Pharmaceutical Chemistry, 1966–72; Sen. Lectr in Pharm. Chem., 1972–76; J. P. Todd Prof. of Pharmacy, 1976–88. Member: Cttee on Safety of Medicines, 1983– (Mem., Sub-cttee on Chemistry, Pharmacy and Standards of Cttee on Safety of Medicines, 1972–); Nuffield Inquiry into Pharmacy, 1984–86; Standing Pharmaceutical Adv. Cttee, 1989–. FRSE 1987; FRSA 1989. British Pharmaceutical Conf. Science Award, 1972; Harrison Meml Medal, Royal Pharmaceutical Soc., 1986. *Publications:* Solubilization by Surface Active Agents, 1968; Physicochemical Principles of Pharmacy, 1981, 2nd edn 1988; Surfactant Systems, 1983; (ed) Materials Used in Pharmaceutical Formulation, 1985; (ed) Formulation Factors in Adverse Reactions, 1990; pubns on drug delivery and targeting, surfactants and drug absorption, and polymeric systems. *Recreations:* music, writing. *Address:* School of Pharmacy, University of London, 29/39 Brunswick Square, WC1N 1AX. *T:* 071–753 5819.

FLOREY, Prof. Charles du Vé; Professor of Community Medicine, University of Dundee, since 1983; *b* 11 Sept. 1934; *s* of Howard Walter Florey and Mary Ethel Florey; *m* 1966, Susan Jill Hopkins; one *s* one *d*. *Educ:* Univ. of Cambridge (MD); Yale Univ. (MPH). FFCM 1977; FRCPE 1986. Instructor, 1965, Asst Prof., 1966–69, Yale Univ. School of Medicine; Mem. Scientific Staff, MRC, Jamaica, 1969–71; St Thomas's Hospital Medical School, London: Sen. Lectr, 1971–78; Reader, 1978–81; Prof., 1981–83. *Publications:* (with S. R. Leeder) Methods for Cohort Studies of Chronic Airflow Limitation, 1982; (with others) Introduction to Community Medicine, 1983. *Recreations:* photography, sailing, walking, computing. *Address:* Ninewells Hospital and Medical School, Dundee DD1 9SY. *T:* Dundee (0382) 60111.

FLOUD, Mrs Jean Esther, CBE 1976; MA, BSc(Econ); Principal, Newnham College, Cambridge, 1972–83, Hon. Fellow, 1983; *b* 3 Nov. 1915; *d* of Annie Louisa and Ernest Walter McDonald; *m* 1938, Peter Castle Floud, CBE (*d* 1960), *s* of late Sir Francis Floud, KCB, KCSI, KCMG, and formerly Keeper of Circulation, Victoria and Albert Museum; two *d* (one *s* decd). *Educ:* public elementary and selective secondary schools; London School of Economics (BScEcon), Hon. Fellow, 1972. Asst Dir of Educn, City of Oxford, 1940–46; Teacher of Sociology in the University of London (London School of Economics and Inst. of Educn), 1947–62; Official Fellow of Nuffield College, Oxford, 1963–72, Hon. Fellow, 1983; Hon. Fellow, Darwin Coll., Cambridge, 1986. Member: Franks Commission of Inquiry into the University of Oxford, 1964–66; University Grants Cttee, 1969–74; Social Science Research Council, 1970–73; Exec. Cttee, PEP, 1975–77; Adv. Bd for the Res. Councils, 1976–81; Council, Policy Studies Inst., 1979–83. Hon. LittD Leeds, 1973; Hon. DLitt City, 1978. *Publications:* (with A. H. Halsey and F. M. Martin) Social Class and Educational Opportunity, 1956; (with Warren Young) Dangerousness and Criminal Justice, 1981; papers and reviews in sociological jls. *Recreations:* books, music. *Address:* White Lodge, Osler Road, Old Headington, Oxford OX3 9BJ.

See also P. F. du Sautoy.

FLOUD, Prof. Roderick Castle; Provost, City of London Polytechnic, since 1988; *b* 1 April 1942; *s* of late Bernard Francis Castle Floud, MP and Ailsa (*née* Craig); *m* 1964, Cynthia Anne (*née* Smith); two *d*. *Educ:* Brentwood Sch.; Wadham Coll., Oxford; Nuffield Coll., Oxford. MA, DPhil. Asst Lectr in Economic History, UCL, 1966–69; Lectr in Economic History, Univ. of Cambridge and Fellow of Emmanuel Coll., Cambridge, 1969–75; Prof. of Modern History, Birkbeck Coll., Univ. of London, 1975–88. Vis. Prof. of European History and of Economics, Stanford Univ., Calif, 1980–81. Research Associate, Nat. Bureau of Economic Research, USA, 1978–; Research Programme Dir, Centre for Economic Policy Research, 1983–88, Research Fellow, 1988–. Member: Lord Chancellor's Adv. Council on Public Records, 1978–84; Cttee for Humanities, CNAA, 1987–. Treas., Oxford Union Soc., 1966. *Publications:* An Introduction to Quantitative Methods for Historians, 1973, 2nd edn 1980; (ed) Essays in Quantitative Economic History, 1974; The British Machine Tool Industry 1850–1914, 1976; (ed) The Economic History of Britain since 1700, 1981; (ed) The Power of the Past, 1984; (jtly) Height, Health and History, 1990; articles in Economic History Review, Social Science History, etc. *Recreations:* camping, walking, music. *Address:* City of London Polytechnic, 117–119 Houndsditch, EC3A 7BU. *T:* 071–283 1030; 21 Savernake Road, NW3 2JT. *T:* 071–267 2197. *Club:* Athenæum.

FLOWER, family name of **Viscount Ashbrook.**

FLOWER, Antony John Frank, (Tony), MA, PhD; Director, Research Institute for Economic and Social Affairs, since 1982; *b* 2 Feb. 1951; *s* of late Frank Robert Edward Flower and of Dorothy Elizabeth (*née* Williams). *Educ:* Chipping Sodbury Grammar Sch.; Univ. of Exeter (BA Hons Philosophy and Sociology; MA Sociology); Univ. of Leicester (PhD Mass Communications). Graphic Designer, 1973–76; Co-founder with Lord Young of Dartington, and first Gen. Sec., Tawney Soc., 1982–88. Co-ordinator, Argo Venture, 1984–, Dir, Argo Trust, 1986–; Director: Healthline Health Inf. Service, 1986–88; Health Information Trust, 1987–88 (Trustee, 1988–); Environmental Concern Centre in Europe, 1990–. Mem. Bd, Museum of the Earth, 1991–. Associate: Redesign Ltd, 1989–; Nicholas Lacey, Jobst & Partners (Architects), 1989–. Co-ordinator, Campaign for Educnl Choice, 1988–89. Council Mem., Gaia, 1988–. Trustee, Mutual Aid Centre, 1990–. Founder Mem., SDP, 1981; Mem., Council for Social Democracy, 1982–84; Dir of Develt, Green Alliance, 1991–. Associate: Open Coll. of the Arts, 1988–; Inst. for Public Policy Res., 1989. Editor, Tawney Journal, 1982–88; Co-founder and Man. Editor, Samizdat Magazine, 1988–. FRSA 1991. *Publications:* (with Graham Mort) Starting to Write: a course in creative writing, 1990; (ed jtly) The Alternative, 1990. *Recreations:* collecting junk, making and restoring musical instruments. *Address:* (office) 18 Victoria Park Square, E2 9PF. *T:* 081–980 6263.

FLOWER, Desmond John Newman, MC 1944; Chairman, Cassell & Co. Ltd, 1958–71; President, Cassell Australia Ltd, 1965–71; Editorial Consultant, Sheldon Press, 1973–85; *b* London, 25 Aug. 1907; *o s* of late Sir Newman Flower; *m* 1st, 1931, Margaret Cameron Coss (marr. diss., 1952); one *s*; 2nd, 1952, Anne Elizabeth Smith (marr. diss. 1972); one *s* two *d*; 3rd, 1987, Sophie Rombeyko. *Educ:* Lancing; King's Coll., Cambridge. Entered Cassell & Co. 1930; Dir, 1931; Literary Dir, 1938; Dep.-Chm., 1952; Chm. Cassell & Co. (Holdings) Ltd, 1958–70. Served War of 1939–45 (despatches, MC); commissioned 1941, 5 Bn Argyll and Sutherland Highlanders later 91 (A&SH) A/T-Regt. Chm., the Folio Society, 1960–71; Liveryman, Stationers' Co. Président des Comités d'Alliance Française en Grande Bretagne, 1963–72. Officier de la légion d'honneur, 1972 (Chevalier 1950). DLitt (*hc*) University of Caen, 1957. *Publications:* founder and editor (with A. J. A. Symons) Book Collector's quarterly, 1930–34; ed, Complete Poetical Works of Ernest Christopher Dowson, 1934; compiled (with Francis Meynell and A. J. A. Symons) The Nonesuch Century, 1936; (with A. N. L. Munby) English Poetical Autographs, 1938; The Pursuit of Poetry, 1939; Voltaire's England, 1950; History of 5 Bn Argyll and Sutherland Highlanders, 1950; (with James Reeves) The War, 1939–1945, 1960; (with Henry Maas) The Letters of Ernest Dowson, 1967; New Letters of Ernest Dowson, 1984; Fellows in Foolscap (memoirs), 1991; numerous translations, inc. Saint Simon, Voltaire, Maupassant, Morand. *Recreation:* book collecting. *Address:* 26 Grovedale Road, N19 3EQ. *T:* 071–281 0080. *Club:* Royal and Ancient (St Andrews).

FLOWER, Rear-Adm. Edward James William, CB 1980; Director, Post-Design (Ships), Ministry of Defence (Navy), 1977–80, retired; *b* 1923; *m*; three *d*. Joined RN, 1941; served in HM Ships Norfolk, Duke of York, Liverpool, Whitby, Urchin and Tenby; Canadian Nat. Defence Coll., 1966; Fleet Marine Engineering Officer, Western Fleet, 1967–69; commanded RN Nuclear Propulsion Test and Trng Estab., 1970–71; MoD (Navy), 1971–75; Flag Officer Portsmouth, and Port Admiral, Portsmouth, 1975–76; Dir of Engrg (Ships), MoD, 1976–77. *Address:* Fairmount, Hinton Charterhouse, Bath.

FLOWER, Hon. Michael Llowarch Warburton; Partner, Pannone, March Pearson (formerly March Pearson & Skelton), Manchester, since 1986; Vice Lord-Lieutenant, Cheshire, since 1990; *b* 9 Dec. 1935; *s* and *heir* of Viscount Ashbrook, *qv*; *m* 1971, Zoë Mary Engleheart; two *s* one *d*. *Educ:* Eton; Worcester Coll., Oxford (MA Mod. Hist.). 2nd Lieut, Grenadier Guards, 1955. Solicitor, 1963; Partner, Farrer & Co., Solicitors, 1966–76. Landowner. Chm., Taxation Sub-Cttee, 1984–86, Pres., Cheshire Branch, 1990–, CLA. DL 1982, JP 1983, Cheshire. *Recreations:* gardening, the countryside, shooting. *Address:* The Old Parsonage, Arley Green, Northwich, Cheshire CW9 6LZ. *T:* Arley (0565) 777277. *Clubs:* Brooks's; St James's (Manchester).

FLOWERS, family name of **Baron Flowers.**

FLOWERS, Baron *cr* 1979 (Life Peer), of Queen's Gate in the City of Westminster; **Brian Hilton Flowers,** Kt 1969; FRS 1961; Vice-Chancellor, University of London, 1985–90; Chairman, Nuffield Foundation, since 1987 (a Managing Trustee, since 1982); *b* 13 Sept. 1924; *o s* of late Rev. Harold J. Flowers, Swansea; *m* 1951, Mary Frances, *er d* of late Sir Leonard Behrens, CBE; two step *s*. *Educ:* Bishop Gore Grammar Sch., Swansea; Gonville and Caius Coll. (Exhibitioner), Cambridge (MA); Hon. Fellow, 1974; University of Birmingham (DSc). Anglo-Canadian Atomic Energy Project, 1944–46; Research in nuclear physics and atomic energy at Atomic Energy Research Establishment, Harwell, 1946–50; Dept of Mathematical Physics, University of Birmingham, 1950–52; Head of Theoretical Physics Div., AERE, Harwell, 1952–58; Prof. of Theoretical Physics, 1958–61, Langworthy Prof. of Physics, 1961–72, Univ. of Manchester; Rector of Imperial Coll. of Sci. and Technol., 1973–85. Chairman: Science Research Council, 1967–73; Royal Commn on Environmental Pollution, 1973–76; Standing Commn on Energy and the Environment, 1978–81; Univ. of London Working Party on future of med. and dent. teaching resources, 1979–80; Cttee of Vice-Chancellors and Principals, 1983–85; Select Cttee on Science and Technology, H of L, 1989– (Mem., 1980–). President: Inst. of Physics, 1972–74; European Science Foundn, 1974–80; Nat. Soc. for Clean Air, 1977–79. Chm., Computer Bd for Univs and Research Councils, 1966–70. Founding Mem. and Mem. Exec. Council, Academia Europaea, 1988. Founder Mem., SDP, 1981. FInstP 1961; Hon. FCGI, 1975; Hon. MRIA (Science Section), 1976; Hon. FIEE, 1975; Sen. Fellow, RCA, 1983; Hon. Fellow, UMIST, 1985; Corresp. Mem., Swiss Acad. of Engrg Sciences, 1986. MA Oxon, 1956; Hon. DSc: Sussex, 1968; Wales, 1972; Manchester, 1973; Leicester, 1973; Liverpool, 1974; Bristol, 1982; Oxford, 1985; NUI, 1990; Hon. DEng Nova Scotia, 1983; Hon. ScD Dublin, 1984; Hon. LLD: Dundee, 1985; Glasgow, 1987. Rutherford Medal and Prize, 1968, Glazebrook Medal and Prize, 1987, IPPS; Chalmers Medal, Chalmers Univ. of Technol., Sweden, 1980. Officier de la Légion d'Honneur, 1981 (Chevalier, 1975). *Publications:* (with E. Mendoza) Properties of Matter, 1970; contribs to scientific periodicals on structure of the atomic nucleus, nuclear reactions, science policy, energy and the environment. *Recreations:* music, walking, computing, painting, gardening. *Address:* 53 Athenaeum Road, N20 9AL. *T:* 081–446 5993.

FLOYD, Sir Giles (Henry Charles), 7th Bt *cr* 1816; Director, Burghley Estate Farms, since 1958; *b* 27 Feb. 1932; *s* of Sir John Duckett Floyd, 6th Bt, TD, and of Jocelin Evadne (*d* 1976), *d* of late Sir Edmund Wyldbore Smith; *S* father, 1975; *m* 1st, 1954, Lady Gillian Moyra Katherine Cecil (marr. diss. 1978), 2nd *d* of 6th Marquess of Exeter, KCMG; two *s*; 2nd, 1985, Judy Sophia Lane, *er d* of late W. L. Tregoning, CBE, and D. M. E.

Tregoning. *Educ:* Eton College. High Sheriff of Rutland, 1968. *Heir: er s* David Henry Cecil Floyd [*b* 2 April 1956; *m* 1981, Caroline, *d* of John Beckly, Manor Farm, Bowerchalke, Salisbury, Wilts; two *d*]. *Address:* Tinwell Manor, Stamford, Lincs PE9 3UD. *T:* Stamford (0780) 62676. *Clubs:* Turf, Farmers'.

FLOYD, John Anthony; Chairman: Christie Manson & Woods Ltd, 1974–85; Christies International Ltd, 1976–88; *b* 12 May 1923; *s* of Lt-Col Arthur Bowen Floyd, DSO, OBE; *m* 1948, Margaret Louise Rosselli; two *d*. *Educ:* Eton. Served King's Royal Rifle Corps, 1941–46. *Address:* Ecchinswell House, Newbury, Berks. *Clubs:* Boodle's, White's, MCC.

FLOYD EWIN, Sir David Ernest Thomas, Kt 1974; LVO 1954; OBE 1965; MA; Lay Administrator, 1939–44, Registrar and Receiver, 1944–78, Consultant to the Dean and Chapter, since 1978, St Paul's Cathedral; Notary Public; Chairman: Tubular Edgington (formerly Tubular Exhibition) Group PLC, since 1978; Stonebert Ltd and subsidiaries, since 1985; *b* 17 Feb. 1911; 7th *s* of late Frederick P. Ewin and Ellen Floyd; *m* 1948, Marion Irene, *d* of William R. Lewis; one *d*. *Educ:* Eltham. MA (Lambeth) 1962. Freeman, City of London, 1948; Member of Court of Common Council for Ward of Castle Baynard (Dep., 1972–); Vice-Pres., Castle Baynard Ward Club (Chm. 1962 and 1988); Chm., Corp. of London Gresham Cttee, 1975–76; Member: Lord Mayor and Sheriffs Cttee, 1976, 1978, 1984 (Chm., 1987); Court of Assts, Hon. Irish Soc., 1976–79; Surrogate for Province of Canterbury; Trustee: City Parochial Foundn, 1967– (Chm., Pensions Cttee, 1978–); St Paul's Cathedral Trust, 1978–; Temple Bar Trust, 1979–; Dep. Chm., City of London's Endowment Trust for St Paul's Cathedral, 1982–. Hon. Dir, British Humane Assoc.; Governor and Member of Court: Sons of the Clergy Corp.; St Gabriel's Coll., Camberwell, 1946–72. Past Master, Scriveners' Co.; Sen. Past Master, Guild of Freemen of the City of London; Liveryman, Wax Chandlers' Co.; Gold Staff Officer at Coronation of HM Queen Elizabeth, 1953. KStJ 1970 (OStJ 1965). *Publications:* A Pictorial History of St Paul's Cathedral, 1970; The Splendour of St Paul's, 1973; numerous papers and articles. *Recreations:* tennis, gardening, fishing. *Address:* St Augustine's House, 4 New Change, EC4M 9AB. *T:* 071–248 0683; Chapter House, St Paul's Churchyard, EC4. *T:* 071–248 2705; Silver Springs, Stoke Gabriel, South Devon. *T:* Stoke Gabriel (080428) 264. *Clubs:* City Livery, Guildhall.

FLOYER, Prof. Michael Antony, MD; FRCP; Professor of Medicine, The London Hospital Medical College, University of London, 1974–86, now Professor Emeritus; Consulting Physician, The London Hospital, since 1986; *b* 28 April 1920; *s* of Comdr William Antony Floyer, RN and Alice Rosalie Floyer (*née* Whitehead); *m* 1946, Lily Louise Frances Burns; two *s* one *d*. *Educ:* Sherborne Sch.; Trinity Hall, Cambridge; The London Hosp. Med. Coll. MA; MB, BCh; MD; FRCP 1963. RAF Medical Service, Sqdn Leader, RAF Hosps, Karachi and Cawnpore, 1946–48. The London Hospital: House Officer, 1944–45; Registrar in Medicine, 1945–46, Hon. Registrar, 1948–51; Hon. Sen. Registrar, 1951–58; Hon. Consultant Physician, 1958–86; Consultant i/c Emergency and Accident Dept, 1975–86; The London Hospital Medical College: Lectr in Medicine, 1948–51; Sen. Lectr, 1951–67; Asst Dir, Medical Unit, 1953–86; Reader in Medicine, 1967–74; Acting Dean, 1982–83; Dean, 1983–86; Fellow, 1988; seconded to Nairobi Univ., Kenya, as Prof. of Medicine, 1973–75. Oliver-Sharpey Prize, RCP, 1980. *Publications:* chapters in books and papers in scientific jls on the aetiology and mechanism of hypertension and on the physiology of the interstitial fluid space. *Recreations:* wild places and wild things. *Address:* The London Hospital Medical College, E1 2AD. *T:* 071–377 7602; Dukes Cottage, Willingale, Ongar, Essex CM5 0SW. *T:* Willingale (0277) 896270.

FLUTE, Prof. Peter Thomas, TD 1970; MD; FRCP, FRCPath; Postgraduate Medical Dean, South West Thames Regional Health Authority and Assistant Director, British Postgraduate Medical Federation, since 1985; *b* 12 Aug. 1928; *s* of Rev. Richard Prickett Flute and Katie Flute (*née* Click); *m* 1951, Ann Elizabeth Harbroe, *d* of late G. John Wright; two *s* two *d*. *Educ:* Southend High Sch.; King's College London; KCH Med. Sch. (Ware Prize; MB, BS; MRCS). KCH, 1951–52; RAMC, 1952–54; Demonstrator in Pathology, KCH Med. Sch., 1955–56; Elmore Res. Student, Dept of Medicine, Cambridge, 1957–58; Lectr, 1958–62, Sen. Lectr, 1962–68, Reader, 1968–72, Dept of Haematology, KCH Med. Sch.; Hon. Consultant in Haematology, KCH, 1966–72; Prof. of Haematology, St George's Hosp. Med. Sch. and Hon. Consultant, St George's Hosp., 1972–85. RAMC T&AVR: Pathologist, 24 Gen. Hosp., 1955–58, 308 Gen. Hosp., 1958–67; OC 380 Blood Supply Unit, 1967–73, Hon. Col, 1977–82; Hon. Consultant to the Army in Haematology, 1977–87. Mem., Mid-Downs DHA, 1984–90. Royal College of Pathologists: Mem. Council, 1981–84; Exec. Cttee, 1982–84; SW Thames Regional Adviser in Postgraduate Educn, 1975–85; Royal College of Physicians: Mem., Cttee of Haematology, 1981–87; Jt Cttee on Higher Med. Training; Mem., Specialist Adv. Cttee on Haematology, 1977–83; Sec., 1978–83; British Soc. for Haematology: Mem., 1960–; Cttee, 1975–87; Associate Sec., 1977–81; Sec., 1981–83; Pres., 1985–86; Section of Pathology, Royal Society of Medicine: Mem. Council, 1964–68; Sec., 1972–76; Pres., 1978. Mem., Editorial Bd, British Jl of Haematology, 1971–81. *Publications:* chapters and contribs on thrombosis and blood diseases to med. and sci. jls. *Recreations:* mountain walking, reading. *Address:* 17 Church Lane, East Grinstead, West Sussex RH19 3AZ. *T:* East Grinstead (0342) 326288.

FLYNN, Prof. Frederick Valentine, MD (Lond), FRCP, FRCPath; Professor of Chemical Pathology in University of London at University College School of Medicine, 1970–89, now Professor Emeritus, and Consultant Chemical Pathologist to University College Hospital, London, 1960–89; Civil Consultant in Chemical Pathology to Royal Navy, since 1978; *b* 6 Oct. 1924; *e s* of Frederick Walter Flynn and Jane Laing Flynn (*née* Valentine); *m* 1955, Catherine Ann, *o d* of Dr Robert Walter Warrick and Dorothy Ann Warrick (*née* Dimock); one *s* one *d*. *Educ:* University Coll. London; University Coll. Hosp. Med. Sch. (Fellow, UCL, 1974). Obstetric Ho. Surg. and various posts, incl. Research Asst and Registrar, Dept of Clin. Pathology, UCH, 1947–60; Associate in Clin. Path., Pepper Laboratory of Clin. Medicine, Univ. of Pennsylvania, and British Postgrad. Med. Fedn Travelling Fellow, 1954–55. Chairman: Assoc. of Clin. Biochemists Sci. and Technical Cttee, 1968–70; Dept of Health's Adv. Gp on Scientific and Clinical Applications of Computers, 1971–76; Organising Cttee for 1st, 2nd and 3rd Internat. Confs on Computing in Clinical Labs, 1972–80; Research Cttee, NE Thames RHA, 1984–88; Member: Min. of Health Lab. Equipment and Methods Adv. Gp, 1966–71; Min. of Technol. Working Party on Lab. Instrumentation, 1966–67; BMA Working Party on Computers in Medicine, 1968–69; Dept of Health's Adv. Cttee on Med. Computing, 1969–76, and Laboratory Develts Adv. Gp, 1972–75; MRC Working Party on Hypogammaglobulinaemia, 1959–70; MRC Adv. Panel on Applications for Computing Facilities, 1973–77; NW Thames RHA Sci. Cttee, 1973–74; Med. Lab. Techns Bd, Council for Professions Supplementary to Medicine, 1984–88; NHS Supraregional Assay Services Bd, 1990–; Sir Jules Thorn Charitable Trust: Mem. Med. Adv. Cttee, 1983–; Trustee, 1988–; Section of Pathology, RSM: Mem. Council, 1968–72, 1986–; Vice-Pres., 1971–72, 1989–91; Royal Coll. of Pathologists: Mem. Council, 1973–83 and 1984–87; Vice-Pres., 1975–78; Treas., 1978–83; Chm., Panel of Examrs in Chem. Path., 1972–82; Association of Clinical Pathologists: Chm., Working Party on Data Processing in Labs, 1964–67; Mem. Council, 1988–; Pres.-elect, 1988–89; Pres., 1989–90. *Publications:* numerous contribs to med. and sci. books and jls. *Recreations:* photography, carpentry, gardening. *Address:* 20 Oakleigh Avenue, Whetstone, N20 9JH. *T:* 081–445 0882.

FLYNN, John Gerrard; HM Diplomatic Service; Ambassador to Angola, and concurrently non-resident Ambassador to São Tomé and Principe, since 1990; *b* 23 April 1937; *s* of late Thomas Flynn and Mary Chisholm; *m* 1973, Drina Anne Coates; one *s* one *d*. *Educ:* Glasgow Univ. (MA). Foreign Office, 1965; Second Sec., Lusaka, 1966; First Sec., FCO, 1968; seconded to Canning House as Asst Dir-Gen., 1970; First Sec. (Commercial) and Consul, Montevideo, 1971; FCO, 1976; Chargé d'Affaires, Luanda, 1978; Counsellor and Consul-Gen., Brasilia, 1979; Counsellor, Madrid, 1982; High Comr, Swaziland, 1987. *Recreations:* walking, golf. *Address:* c/o Foreign and Commonwealth Office, SW1. *Club:* Travellers'.

FLYNN, Paul Phillip; MP (Lab) Newport West, since 1987; *b* 9 Feb. 1935; *s* of James Flynn and Kathleen Williams; *m* 1st, 1962, Anne Harvey (marr. diss. 1984); one *s* (one *d* decd); 2nd, 1985, Samantha Morgan; one step-*s* one step-*d*. *Educ:* St Illtyd's Coll., Cardiff. Steelworker, 1955–84; Researcher, 1984–87. Mem., Gwent CC, 1974–82. Contested (Lab) Denbigh, Oct. 1974. *Address:* House of Commons, SW1A 0AA. *Club:* Ringland Labour (Newport, Gwent).

FLYNN, Most Rev. Thomas; *see* Achonry, Bishop of, (RC).

FO, Dario; Italian playwright and actor; *b* 24 March 1926; *s* of Felice Fo and Pina (*née* Rota); *m* 1954, Franca Rame; three *c*. *Educ:* Acad. of Fine Arts, Milan. Joined a small theatre gp, 1950; wrote satirical radio series, Poer nano (Poor Dwarf), 1951, and performed selections from it, Teatro Odeon, Milan; appeared in Cocorico, Teatro Odeon, Milan, 1952; jt founder and performer, I Dritti (revue co.), 1953–55 (toured nationally); screenwriter, Rome, 1955–58; performer and writer, theatre gp, Compagnia Fo-Rame, 1958–68; artistic dir, Chi l'ha visto? (TV musical revue), 1959; performer and writer, Canzonissima (TV variety show); returned to theatre work, 1963; jt founder, theatre co-operative, Nuova Scena, 1968 (toured, 1968–69); jt founder, theatre gp, la Commune, 1970; Tricks of the Trade (TV series), 1985; his plays have been translated into many languages and performed in many countries. *Publications:* The Tricks of the Trade, 1991; *plays:* Mistero buffo, 1977; Archangels Don't Play Pinball; Accidental Death of an Anarchist; Hooters, Trumpets and Raspberries; Can't Pay! Won't Pay!; Open Couple – Wide Open Even; Coming Home; History of Masks. *Address:* c/o Methuen, Michelin House, 81 Fulham Road, SW3 6RB.

FOAKES, Prof. Reginald Anthony; Professor of English, University of California at Los Angeles, since 1983; *b* 18 Oct. 1923; 2nd *s* of William Warren Foakes and Frances (*née* Poate); *m* 1951, Barbara, *d* of Harry Garratt, OBE; two *s* two *d*. *Educ:* West Bromwich Grammar Sch.; Birmingham Univ. (MA, PhD). Fellow of the Shakespeare Inst., 1951–54; Lectr in English, Durham Univ., 1954–62; Sen. Lectr, 1963–64; University of Kent at Canterbury: Prof. of Eng. Lit., 1964–82, now Emeritus Prof. of Eng. and Amer. Lit.; Dean, Faculty of Humanities, 1974–77. Commonwealth Fund (Harkness) Fellow, Yale Univ., 1955–56; Visiting Professor: University Coll., Toronto, 1960–62; Univ. of California, Santa Barbara, 1968–69; UCLA, 1981. *Publications:* (ed) Shakespeare's King Henry VIII, 1957; The Romantic Assertion, 1958; (ed with R. T. Rickert) Henslowe's Diary, 1961; (ed) The Comedy of Errors, 1962; (ed) The Revenger's Tragedy, 1966; (ed) Macbeth and Much Ado About Nothing, 1968; Romantic Criticism, 1968; Coleridge on Shakespeare, 1971; Shakespeare, the Dark Comedies to the Last Plays, 1971; (ed) The Henslowe Papers, 2 vols, 1977; Marston and Tourneur, 1978; (ed) A Midsummer Night's Dream, 1984; Illustrations of the English Stage 1580–1642, and Visitor's Guide, 1985; (ed) S. T. Coleridge, Lectures 1808–19: On Literature, 2 vols, 1987. *Address:* Department of English, University of California at Los Angeles, 405 Hilgard Avenue, Los Angeles, Calif 90024, USA.

FOALE, Air Cdre Colin Henry; *b* 10 June 1930; *s* of late William Henry Foale and Frances M. (*née* Muse); *m* 1954, Mary Katherine Harding, Minneapolis, USA; two *s* one *d*. *Educ:* Wolverton Grammar Sch.; RAF Coll., Cranwell. 1951–74: 13 Sqdn Pilot, Egypt; 32 Sqdn Flt Comdr; Fighter Flt, RAF Flying Coll., Manby; Officer and Aircrew Selection, Hornchurch; OC 73 Sqdn, Cyprus (Sqdn Ldr); Staff Coll., Bracknell; Air Staff, HQ RAF Germany (Wing Comdr); Jt Services Staff Coll., Latimer; OC 39 Sqdn, Malta; SO Flying, MoD (PE) (Gp Captain); Stn Comdr, Luqa, Malta, 1974–76; RCDS, 1977 (Air Cdre); Dir of Public Relations (RAF), 1977–79; retired at own request, for business and writing, 1979. Trng Advr to Chm., Conservative Party, 1980–81; Pilot to Cttee for Aerial Photography, Univ. of Cambridge, 1981–90. FBIM, FIWM. *Recreations:* sailing, swimming, flying, travel, music, drama, writing. *Address:* St Catharine's College, Cambridge; 37 Pretoria Road, Cambridge CB4 1HD. *Club:* Royal Air Force.

FOCKE, Paul Everard Justus; QC 1982; a Recorder, since 1986; *b* 14 May 1937; *s* of Frederick Justus Focke and Muriel Focke; *m* 1973, Lady Tana Marie Alexander, *er d* of 6th Earl of Caledon; two *d*. *Educ:* Downside; Exeter Coll., Oxford; Trinity Coll., Dublin. National Service, 1955–57; Territorial Army, 1957–66, Cheshire Yeomanry (Captain). Called to the Bar, Gray's Inn, 1964, to the Bar of NSW and to the NZ Bar, 1982. QC NSW 1984. *Recreations:* travelling, aeroplanes. *Address:* (chambers) 1 Mitre Court Buildings, Temple, EC4. *T:* 071–353 0434; (home) 7 Cheyne Walk, SW3. *T:* 071–351 0299. *Clubs:* Pratt's, Turf, Beefsteak, Cavalry and Guards.

FODEN-PATTINSON, Peter Lawrence; a Deputy Chairman of Lloyd's, 1976; *b* 14 June 1925; *s* of late Hubert Foden-Pattinson; *m* 1956, Joana Pryor (*née* Henderson); one *s*. *Educ:* Downside. Irish Guards, 1943–47. Lloyd's, 1942–: Underwriting Mem., 1956; Mem., Cttee of Lloyd's, 1973–76; Mem., Cttee of Lloyd's Non-Marine Assoc., 1965, Chm. 1971, Dep. Chm. 1970 and 1972. *Recreations:* boating, music. *Address:* 123 Pier House, Cheyne Walk, SW3 5HM. *T:* 071–351 1313. *Club:* Royal Yacht Squadron.

FOËX, Prof. Pierre, DPhil; FFARCS; Nuffield Professor of Anaesthetics, and Fellow of Pembroke College, University of Oxford, since 1991; *b* 4 July 1935; *s* of Georges and Berthe Foëx; *m* 1958, Anne-Lise Schürch; two *s*. *Educ:* Univ. of Geneva (DM); professional qualifying Swiss State Exam. in Medicine and Surgery, 1960; DPhil Oxon 1973. FFARCS 1985. University Hospital, Geneva: Asst, 1961–62 and Chef de Clinique, 1962–63, Dept of Neurology; Asst, 1963–65, Chef de Clinique-adjoint, 1966–68 and Chef de Clinique, 1969–70, Dept of Medicine; Nuffield Department of Anaesthetics, University of Oxford: Res. Fellow, 1970–71; Lectr, 1971–73; Univ. Lectr, 1973–76; Clinical Reader and Hon. Consultant (Clinical Physiology), 1976–91; Fellow, Worcester Coll., Oxford, 1976–91. Mem., Exec. Cttee, Anaesthetic Res. Soc., 1982–86; Senator, European Acad. of Anaesthesiology, 1988–. Vis. Prof., univs in Australia, Canada, Europe, NZ, USA. *Publications:* Anaesthesia for the Compromised Heart, 1989; chapters and papers on cardiac physiology, cardiovascular physiology applied to anaesthesia, myocardial ischaemia, cardiovascular pharmacology, anaesthesia and hypertension. *Recreations:* walking, foreign travel. *Address:* Nuffield Department of Anaesthetics, Radcliffe Infirmary, Woodstock Road, Oxford OX2 6HE. *T:* Oxford (0865) 224770.

FOGARTY, Christopher Winthrop, CB 1973; Deputy Secretary, Overseas Development Administration, Foreign and Commonwealth Office, (formerly Ministry of Overseas Development), 1976–81; *b* 18 Sept. 1921; *s* of late Philip Christopher Fogarty, ICS, and late Hilda Spenser Fogarty; *m* 1961, Elizabeth Margaret Ince (*d* 1972). *Educ:* Ampleforth Coll.; Christ Church, Oxford. War Service (Lieut RA), 1942–45. Asst Principal, 1946, Principal, 1949, HM Treasury; Permanent Sec., Min. of Finance of Eastern Nigeria, 1956; Asst Sec., HM Treasury, 1959, Under-Sec., 1966; Treasury Rep., S Asia and FE, 1967–72; Dep. Sec., HM Treasury, and Dir, European Investment Bank, 1972–76. *Address:* 7 Hurlingham Court, Ranelagh Gardens, SW6 3SH. *Clubs:* Commonwealth Trust, Travellers'; Royal Selangor Golf.
See also M. P. Fogarty.

FOGARTY, Michael Patrick; Director, Institute for Family and Environmental Research, 1981–84; *b* 3 Oct. 1916; *s* of late Philip Christopher Fogarty, ICS, and Mary Belle Pye, Galway; *m* 1939, Phyllis Clark; two *s* two *d*. *Educ:* Ampleforth Coll.; Christ Church, Oxford. Lieut RA, 1940 (wounded, Dunkirk). Nuffield Coll., 1941–51 (Fellow, 1944); Montague Burton Prof. of Industrial Relations, University Coll. of S Wales and Mon, 1951–66; Dir and Prof., Econ. and Social Res. Inst., Dublin, 1968–72; Centre for Studies in Social Policy: Sen. Fellow, 1973; Dep. Dir, 1977–78; Dep. Dir, PSI, 1978–82. Also held posts in Administrative Staff Coll., Oxford Institute of Statistics, Nat. Institute of Economic and Social Research, Ministry of Town and Country Planning, and as Asst Editor, The Economist. Chairman: Cttee on Industrial Relations in the Electricity Supply Bd (Ireland), 1968–69; Banks Inquiry, 1970–71; Member: Commn on the Status of Women (Ireland), 1970–72; Commn on Insurance Industry (Ireland), 1970–72; Cttee on Aid to Political Parties, 1975–76. Pres., Newman Assoc., 1957–59; Chm., Catholic Social Guild, 1959–63; Mem., Social Welfare Commn, RC Bishops' Conf. (E&W); Vice-Pres. Assoc. of University Teachers, 1964–66. Prospective Parly candidate (Lab) Tamworth, 1938–44; Parliamentary Candidate (L): Devizes, 1964 and 1966; Abingdon, Feb. and Oct. 1974. Vice-Pres. of the Liberal Party, 1964–66. Contested (L) Thames Valley, European Parlt, 1979. District Councillor, Vale of White Horse, 1973–87; CC Oxfordshire, 1981–89 (Vice-Chm., 1985–86; Chm., 1986–87). Hon. Dr of Political and Social Science, Louvain, 1963. *Publications:* Prospects of the Industrial Areas of Great Britain, 1945; Plan Your Own Industries, 1947; (ed) Further Studies in Industrial Organisation, 1948; Town and Country Planning, 1948; Economic Control, 1955; Personality and Group Relations in Industry, 1956; Christian Democracy in Western Europe, 1820–1953, 1957; The Just Wage, 1961; Under-Governed and Over-Governed, 1962; The Rules of Work, 1963; Company and Corporation—One Law?, 1965; Companies Beyond Jenkins, 1965; Wider Business Objectives, 1966; A Companies Act 1970?, 1967; (with Allen, Allen and Walters) Women in Top Jobs, 1971; (with Rapoport and Rapoport) Sex, Career and Family, 1971; Women and Top Jobs: the next move, 1972; Irish Entrepreneurs Speak For Themselves, 1974; Forty to Sixty, 1975; Company Responsibility and Participation—A New Agenda, 1975; Pensions—where next?, 1976; (with Eileen Reid) Differentials for Managers and Skilled Manual Workers in the UK, 1980; Retirement Age and Retirement Costs, 1980; (with Allen and Walters) Women in Top Jobs 1968–79, 1981; (ed) Retirement Policy: the next fifty years, 1982; (with Ryan and Lea) Irish Values and Attitudes, 1984. *Recreations:* swimming, walking. *Address:* Red Copse, Boars Hill, Oxford.
See also C. W. Fogarty.

FOGDEN, Michael Ernest George; Chief Executive, The Employment Service, Department of Employment, since 1987; *b* 30 May 1936; *s* of late George Charles Arthur and of Margaret May Fogden; *m* 1957, Rose Ann Diamond; three *s* one *d*. *Educ:* High Sch. for Boys, Worthing. Nat. Service, RAF, 1956–58. Ministry of Pensions and National Insurance, later Department of Health and Social Security: Clerical Officer, 1958–59; Exec. Officer, 1959–67, Private Sec. to Parly Sec., 1967–68; Asst Private Sec. to Sec. of State for Social Services, 1968–70; Principal, 1970–76; Asst Sec., 1976–83; Under Sec., 1983–84; Under Sec., Dept of Employment, 1984–. Chm., First Div. Assoc. of Civil Servants, 1980–83. Chm., London Council, RIPA, 1989–. *Recreations:* gardening, talking, music. *Address:* 59 Mayfield Avenue, Orpington, Kent BR6 0AH. *T:* Orpington (0689) 77395. *Club:* Commonwealth Trust.

FOGEL, Prof. Robert W.; Charles R. Walgreen Professor of American Institutions, University of Chicago, since 1981; *b* 1 July 1926; *s* of Harry G. Fogel and Elizabeth (*née* Mitnik); two *s*. *Educ:* Cornell, Columbia and Johns Hopkins Univs. AB Cornell 1948; AM Columbia 1960; PhD Johns Hopkins 1963. Instructor, Johns Hopkins Univ., 1958–59; Asst Prof., Univ. of Rochester, 1960–64; Assoc. Prof., Univ. of Chicago, 1964–65; Prof., Econs and History, Univ. of Chicago, 1965–75, Univ. of Rochester, 1968–75. Taussig Research Prof., Harvard Univ., 1973–74; Pitt Prof. of Amer. History and Instns, Cambridge Univ., 1975–76; Harold Hitchings Burbank Prof. of Econs and Prof. of History, Harvard Univ., 1975–81. President: Economic History Assoc., 1977–78; Soc. Sci. Hist. Assoc., 1980–81. Fellow: Econometric Soc., 1971; Amer. Acad. of Arts and Scis, 1972; Nat. Acad. of Scis, 1973; FAAAS, 1978; FRHistS 1975; Corresponding FBA, 1991. Hon. DSc Rochester, 1987. Phi Beta Kappa, 1963; Arthur H. Cole Prize, 1968; Schumpeter Prize, 1971; Bancroft Prize, 1975; Gustavus Myers Prize, 1990. *Publications:* The Union Pacific Railroad: a case in premature enterprise, 1960; Railroads and American Economic Growth: essays in econometric history, 1964 (Spanish edn 1972); (jtly) The Reinterpretation of American Economic History, 1971 (Italian edn 1975); (jtly) The Dimension of Quantitative Research in History, 1972; (jtly) Time on the Cross: the economics of American negro slavery, 1974 (Japanese edn 1977, Spanish edn 1981); Ten Lectures on the New Economic History, 1977; (jtly) Which Road to the Past? Two Views of History, 1983; Without Consent or Contract: the rise and fall of American slavery, vol. 1, 1989, vols 2–4 (jtly), 1991; numerous papers in learned jls. *Address:* (home) 5321 S University Avenue, Chicago, Illinois 60615, USA; (office) 1101 E 58th Street, Chicago, Illinois 60637, USA.

FOGG, Alan; Chairman, Royal Philanthropic Society, 1982–90; former Director, PA International; *b* 19 Sept. 1921; *o s* of John Fogg, Dulwich; *m* 1948, Mary Marsh; two *s* one *d*. *Educ:* Repton; Exeter Coll., Oxford (MA, BSc). Served with RN, 1944–47. *Publications:* (with Barnes, Stephens and Titman) Company Organisation: theory and practice, 1970; various papers on management subjects. *Recreations:* travel, gardening, youth charities. *Address:* Albury Edge, Merstham, Surrey RH1 3DB. *T:* Merstham (0737) 642023. *Club:* United Oxford & Cambridge University.

FOGG, Cyril Percival, CB 1973; Director, Admiralty Surface Weapons Establishment, Ministry of Defence (Procurement Executive), 1973–75, retired; *b* 28 Nov. 1914; *s* of Henry Fogg and Mabel Mary (*née* Orton); *m* 1st, 1939, Margaret Amie Millican (*d* 1982); two *d*; 2nd, 1983, June Adele McCoy. *Educ:* Herbert Strutt Sch., Belper; Gonville and Caius Coll., Cambridge (MA, 1st cl. Mechanical Sciences Tripos). Research Staff, General Electric Co., 1936–37; various positions in Scientific Civil Service from 1937 with Air Ministry, Ministries of Aircraft Production, Supply, Aviation and Technology. Head of Ground Radar Dept, RRE Malvern, 1956–58; Dir Electronics R&D (Ground), 1959–63; Imperial Defence Coll., 1961; Dir of Guided Weapons Research, 1963–64; Dir-Gen. of Electronics R&D, Min. of Aviation, 1964–67; Dep. Controller of Electronics, Min. of Technology, later MoD (Procurement Executive), 1967–72. *Address:* 10 Miles Cottages, Taylors Lane, Bosham, Chichester, West Sussex PO18 8QG.

FOGG, Prof. Gordon Elliott, CBE 1983; FRS 1965; Professor and Head of the Department of Marine Biology, University College of North Wales, Bangor, 1971–85, now Professor Emeritus; *b* 26 April 1919; *s* of Rev. L. C. Fogg; *m* 1945, Elizabeth Beryl Llechid-Jones; one *s* one *d*. *Educ:* Dulwich Coll.; Queen Mary Coll., London; St John's Coll., Cambridge. BSc (London), 1939; PhD (Cambridge), 1943; ScD (Cambridge), 1966. Sea-weed Survey of British Isles, 1942; Plant Physiologist, Pest Control Ltd, 1943–45; successively Asst Lectr, Lectr and Reader in Botany, University Coll., London, 1945–60; Rockefeller Fellow, 1954; Prof. of Botany, Westfield Coll., Univ. of London, 1960–71. Trustee: BM (Natural Hist.), 1976–85; Royal Botanic Gardens, Kew, 1983–89. Member: Royal Commn on Environmental Pollution, 1979–85; NERC, 1981–82. Royal Soc. Leverhulme Vis. Prof., Kerala, 1969–70; Leverhulme Emeritus Fellow, 1986. Botanical Sec., Soc. for Experimental Biology, 1957–60; President: British Phycological Soc., 1961–62; International Phycological Soc., 1964; Inst. of Biology, 1976–77; Chm. Council, Freshwater Biol Assoc., 1974–85; Joint Organizing Sec., X International Botanical Congress. Visiting research worker, British Antarctic Survey, 1966, 1974, 1979; Biological Gen. Sec., British Assoc., 1967–72, Pres., Section K, 1973. Fellow, Queen Mary and Westfield Coll., London (formerly QMC), 1976. Hon. LLD Dundee, 1974. *Publications:* The Metabolism of Algae, 1953; The Growth of Plants, 1963; Algal Cultures and Phytoplankton Ecology, 1965, 3rd edn (with B. Thake), 1987; Photosynthesis, 1968; (jointly) The Blue-green Algae, 1973; (with D. Smith) The Explorations of Antarctica, 1990; papers in learned jls. *Recreations:* water colour painting, walking. *Address:* Bodolben, Llandegfan, Menai Bridge, Gwynedd. *T:* Menai Bridge (0248) 712916. *Club:* Athenæum.

FOGGON, George, CMG 1961; OBE 1949 (MBE 1945); Director, London Office, International Labour Organisation, 1976–82, retired; *b* 13 Sept. 1913; *s* of Thomas Foggon, Newcastle upon Tyne; *m* 1st, 1938, Agnes McIntosh (*d* 1968); one *s*; 2nd, 1969, Audrey Blanch. Joined Min. of Labour, 1930. Served War of 1939–45 (MBE), Wing-Comdr, RAFVR, 1941–46. Seconded to FO, 1946; on staff of Mil. Gov., Berlin, 1946–49; Principal, CO, 1949; Asst Sec., W African Inter-Territorial Secretariat, Gold Coast (now Ghana), 1951–53; Comr of Labour, Nigeria, 1954–58; Labour Adviser: to Sec. of State for Colonies, 1958–61; to Sec. for Techn. Co-op., 1962–64; to Min. of Overseas Development, 1965–66; Overseas Labour Advr, FO later FCO, 1966–76, retd. *Recreations:* walking, photography. *Address:* 8 Churton Place, SW1V 2LN. *T:* 071–828 1492. *Clubs:* Athenæum, Oriental.

FOLDES, Andor; international concert pianist since 1933; Head of Piano Master Class, Conservatory, Saarbrücken, 1957–65; *b* Budapest, Hungary, 21 Dec. 1913; *s* of Emil Foldes and Valerie Foldes (*née* Ipolyi); *m* 1940, Lili Rendy (writer); no *c*. *Educ:* Franz Liszt Academy of Music, Budapest. Started piano playing at 5; first appeared with Budapest Philh. Orch. at 8; studied with Ernest von Dohnanyi, received Master Diploma (Fr. Liszt Acad. of Music, Budapest), 1932. Concerts all over Europe, 1933–39; US debut (NBC Orch.), 1940; toured US extensively, 1940–48. US citizen since 1948. Concerts, since, all over the world, incl. three recitals in Peking, 1978. Grand Prix du Disque, Paris, for Bartok Complete Works (piano solo), 1957. Beethoven concerts, Bonn Festival and throughout Europe. Recordings of all Beethoven Sonatas, and works of Mozart and Schubert. Order of Merit, First Class, 1956, Gr. Cross, 1964 (Germany); Commandeur, Mérite Culturel et Artistique (City of Paris), 1968; Medaille d'Argent de la Ville de Paris, 1971. *Publications:* Keys to the Keyboard, 1950; Cadenzas to Mozart Piano Concertos (W Germany); Is there a Contemporary Style of Beethoven-playing?, 1963; various piano compositions. *Relevant publication:* Wolf-Eberhard von Lewinski, Andor Foldes, 1970. *Recreations:* collecting art, reading, writing on musical subjects; swimming, hiking. *Address:* 8704 Herrliberg, Zürich, Switzerland.

FOLDES, Prof. Lucien Paul; Professor of Economics, University of London, at London School of Economics and Political Science, since 1979; *b* 19 Nov. 1930; *s* of Egon and Marta Foldes. *Educ:* Bunce Court Sch.; Monkton Wyld Sch.; London School of Economics (BCom, MScEcon, DBA). National Service, 1952–54. LSE: Asst Lecturer in Economics, 1954–55; Lectr, 1955–61; Reader, 1961–79. Rockefeller Travelling Fellow, 1961–62. *Publications:* articles in Rev. of Economic Studies, Economica, Jl of Mathematical Economics, Stochastics, and others. *Recreation:* mathematical analysis. *Address:* London School of Economics, Houghton Street, WC2A 2AE. *T:* 071–405 7686.

FOLEY, family name of **Baron Foley.**

FOLEY, 8th Baron *cr* 1776; **Adrian Gerald Foley;** *b* 9 Aug. 1923; *s* of 7th Baron and Minoru (*d* 1968), *d* of late H. Greenstone, South Africa; *S* father, 1927; *m* 1st, 1958, Patricia Meek (marr. diss. 1971); one *s* one *d*; 2nd, 1972, Ghislaine Lady Ashcombe. *Heir:* *s* Hon. Thomas Henry Foley, *b* 1 April 1961. *Address:* c/o Marbella Club, Marbella, Malaga, Spain. *Club:* White's.

FOLEY, Rt. Rev. Brian Charles; Former Bishop of Lancaster; *b* Ilford, 25 May 1910. *Educ:* St Cuthbert's Coll., Ushaw; English College and Gregorian Univ., Rome (PhL 1934, STL 1938). Priest, 1937; Assistant Priest, Shoeburyness; subseq. Assistant Priest, Romford; Parish Priest, Holy Redeemer, Harold Hill, and Holy Cross, Harlow. Canon of Brentwood Diocese, 1959. Bishop of Lancaster, 1962–85. President: Catholic Record Society, 1964–80; Catholic Archive Soc., 1979–. *Address:* Nazareth House, Ashton Road, Lancaster LA1 5AQ. *T:* Lancaster (0524) 382748.

FOLEY, Hugh Smith; Principal Clerk of Session and Justiciary, Scotland, since 1989; *b* 9 April 1939; *s* of late John Walker Foley and Mary Hogg (*née* Smith); *m* 1966, Isobel King Halliday; two *s*. *Educ:* Dalkeith High Sch. (Joint Dux). Student Actuary, Standard Life Assce Co., 1956–59; nat. service, RAF, 1959–61; entered Scottish Court Service, Court of Session Br., 1962; Asst Clerk of Session, 1962–71; Depute Clerk of Session, 1972–80; seconded to Sherriff Court, Edinburgh, 1980–81; Prin. Sheriff Clerk Depute, Glasgow, 1981–82; Sheriff Clerk, Linlithgow, 1982; Dep. Prin. Clerk of Session, 1982–86; Sen. Dep. Principal Clerk, 1986–89. Mem., Lord President's Cttee on Procedure in Personal Injuries Litigation in Court of Session, 1978–79. *Recreation:* walking. *Address:* Parliament House, Edinburgh EH1 1RQ. *T:* 031–225 2595.

FOLEY, Johanna Mary, (Jo); Editor, Options, since 1988; *b* 8 Dec. 1945; *d* of John and Monica Foley; *m* 1973, Desmond Francis Conor Quigley. *Educ:* St Joseph's Convent, Kenilworth; Manchester Univ. (BA Jt Hons English and Drama, 1968). Woman's Editor, Walsall Observer, 1968; Reporter, Birmingham Post, 1970; English Teacher, Monkwick Secondary Modern Sch., Colchester, and More House Sch., London, 1972–73; Dep. Beauty Editor, Woman's Own, 1973; launched and edited magazine, Successful Slimming, 1976; Sen. Asst Editor, Woman's Own, 1978; Woman's Editor, The Sun, 1980; Editor, Woman, 1982; Exec. Editor (Features), The Times, 1984–85; Man. Editor, The Mirror, 1985–86; Editor, Observer Magazine, 1986–87. Editor of the Year, British Soc. of Magazine Editors, 1983. *Publication:* The Pick of Woman's Own Diets, 1979. *Recreations:* eating, reading, cinema, opera. *Address:* South Bank Publishing, King's Reach Tower, Stamford Street, SE1 9LS.

FOLEY, Maj.-Gen. John Paul, CB 1991; OBE 1979; MC 1976; Assistant Chief of Defence Staff, Ministry of Defence, since 1989; *b* 22 April 1939; *s* of Henry Thomas Hamilton Foley, MBE and Helen Constance Margaret Foley (*née* Pearson); *m* 1972, Ann Humphries; two *d*. *Educ:* Bradfield College; Mons OCS; Army Staff College (psc). Lieut, Royal Green Jackets, 1959; RMCS and Army Staff Coll., 1970–71; Regimental Duty, 1972–74; Chief of Staff, 51 Inf. Bde, Hong Kong, 1974–76; Instructor, Army Staff Coll., 1976–78; CO 3rd Bn RGJ, 1978–80; Comdt Jun. Div., Staff Coll., 1981–82. Arms Dir, MoD, 1983–85; RCDS 1986; Chief, British Mission to Soviet Forces in Germany, 1987–89. *Recreations:* tennis, walking, shooting, reading. *Address:* Ministry of Defence, Main Building, Whitehall, SW1A 2HB. *Club:* Boodle's.

FOLEY, Maurice (Anthony), CMG 1987; Deputy Director General, Directorate General for Development, Commission of the European Communities, 1973–86; *b* 9 Oct. 1925; *s* of Jeremiah and Agnes Foley; *m* 1952, Catherine, *d* of Patrick and Nora O'Riordan; three *s* one *d*. *Educ:* St Mary's Coll., Middlesbrough. Formerly: electrical fitter, youth organiser, social worker. Member: ETU, 1941–46; Transport and General Workers Union, 1948–; Royal Arsenal Co-operative Soc. MP (Lab), West Bromwich, 1963–73; Joint Parliamentary Under-Sec. of State, Dept of Economic Affairs, 1964–66; Parly Under-Secretary: Home Office, 1966–67; Royal Navy, MoD, 1967–68; FCO, 1968–70. *Address:* Gillingham House, Gillingham Street, SW1.

FOLEY, Sir Noel; *see* Foley, Sir T. J. N.

FOLEY, Rt. Rev. Ronald Graham Gregory; appointed Bishop Suffragan of Reading, 1982, Area Bishop, 1985, retired 1989; Assistant Bishop, Diocese of York, since 1989; *b* 13 June 1923; *s* of Theodore Gregory Foley and Cessan Florence Page; *m* 1944, Florence Redman; two *s* two *d*. *Educ:* King Edward's Grammar Sch., Aston, Birmingham; Wakefield Grammar Sch.; King's Coll., London; St John's Coll., Durham BA Hons Theol., LTh. Curate, South Shore, Blackpool, 1950; Vicar, S Luke, Blackburn, 1954; Dir of Educn, Dio. of Durham, and Rector of Brancepeth, 1960; Chaplain, Aycliffe Approved Sch., 1962; Vicar of Leeds, 1971–82; Chaplain to the Queen, 1977–82. Hon. Canon: Durham Cathedral, 1965–71; Ripon Cath., 1971–82. Dir, Yorks Electricity Bd, 1976–82. Chm. of Trustees, Dorothy Kerin Trust, Burrswood, 1983–89. *Publication:* (jtly) Religion in Approved Schools, 1969. *Recreations:* journalism, reading detective stories, watching other people mow lawns. *Address:* Ramsey Cottage, 3 Poplar Avenue, Kirkbymoorside, York YO6 6ES. *T:* Kirkbymoorside (0751) 32439.

FOLEY, Sir (Thomas John) Noel, Kt 1978; CBE 1967; Chairman: CSR Ltd, 1980–84; Allied Manufacturing and Trading Industries (AMATIL) Ltd, 1955–79 (retired); *b* 1914; *s* of late Benjamin Foley, Brisbane. *Educ:* Brisbane Grammar Sch., Queensland; Queensland Univ. (BA, BCom). Chm., Bank of NSW, 1978–82, Westpac Banking Corp., 1980–87 (Pres., 1982–86). Founding Pres., WWF, Australia, 1978–80. *Address:* c/o Amatil Ltd, 71 Macquarie Street, Sydney, NSW 2000, Australia.

FOLEY, Thomas Stephen; Speaker, House of Representatives, USA, since 1989; *b* 6 March 1929; *s* of Ralph E. Foley and Helen Marie (*née* Higgins); *m* 1968, Heather Strachan. *Educ:* Gonzaga High Sch.; Gonzaga Univ.; Washington Univ. (BA 1951; LLB 1957). Partner, Higgins and Foley, 1957–58; Lectr in Law, Gonzaga Univ., 1958–60; Dep. Prosecuting Attorney, Spokane County, 1958–60; Asst Attorney Gen., Washington State, 1960–61; Special Counsel, Senate Interior and Insular Affairs Cttee, 1961–64; Mem. of 89th–101st Congresses from 5th Dist Washington (Democrat), 1964–. Chm., 1975–80, Vice-Chm., 1981–86, Agriculture Cttee. Chm., House Democratic Caucus, 1976–80; House Majority Whip, 1981–87; Majority Leader, 1987–89. Mem., Bd of Advrs, Yale Univ. Council; Dir, Council on Foreign Relations. *Address:* c/o House of Representatives, H148 Capitol Building, Washington, DC 20515, USA.

FOLEY-BERKELEY, family name of **Baroness Berkeley.**

FOLJAMBE, family name of **Earl of Liverpool.**

FOLKESTONE, Viscount; William Pleydell-Bouverie; *b* 5 Jan. 1955; *s* and *heir* of 8th Earl of Radnor, *qv*. *Educ:* Harrow; Royal Agricultural Coll., Cirencester. *Address:* Round House, Charlton All Saints, Salisbury, Wilts. *T:* Salisbury (0722) 330295.

FOLLETT, Prof. Brian Keith, FRS 1984; Professor of Zoology since 1978, and Chairman, School of Biological Sciences, since 1989, University of Bristol; *b* 22 Feb. 1939; *s* of Albert James Follett and Edith Annie Follett; *m* 1961, Deb (*née* Booth); one *s* one *d*. *Educ:* Bournemouth Sch.; Univ. of Bristol (BSc 1960, PhD 1964); Univ. of Wales (DSc 1975). Res. Fellow, Washington State Univ., 1964–65; Lectr in Zool., Univ. of Leeds, 1965–69; Lectr, subseq. Reader and Prof. of Zool., University Coll. of N Wales, Bangor, 1969–78; Hd of Dept of Zool., Univ. of Bristol, 1978–89. Member: Biol Sci. Cttee, SERC, 1981–84; AFRC, 1984–88 (Mem., Animals Cttee, 1984–88); Biol Sci. Cttee, UGC, 1985–88; UFC, 1989–. Biol Sec. and Vice-Pres., Royal Soc., 1987–. Trustee, BM (Natural Hist.), 1989–. Amoroso Lectr, Soc. for Study of Fertility, 1985. Hon. Fellow, UCNW, Bangor, 1990. Scientific Medal, Zool Soc. of London, 1976; Dale Medal, Soc. of Endocrinology, 1988. *Publications:* papers in physiol, endocrinol, and zool jls. *Address:* 6 Clifton Vale, Bristol BS8 4PT. *T:* Bristol (0272) 262308.

FONTAINE, André Lucien Georges; Editor-in-Chief, le Monde, 1985–91; *b* 30 March 1921; *s* of Georges Fontaine and Blanche Rochon Duvigneaud; *m* 1943, Belita Cavaillé; two *s* one *d*. *Educ:* Paris Univ. (diplomes études supérieures droit public et économie politique, lic.lettres). Joined Temps Présent, 1946; with le Monde from 1947; Foreign Editor, 1951; Chief Editor, 1969. Editorialist, Radio Luxemburg, 1980–. Chm. Adv. Gp, Internat. Strategy for the 9th Plan, 1982–84; Mem. Bd, Institut Français des Relations Internationales. Mem. Bd, Bank Indosuez, 1983–85. Commander: Italian Merit; Greek Phoenix; Officer, Orders of Vasa (Sweden), Leopold (Belgium) and Lion (Finland); Kt, Danebrog (Denmark) and Crown of Belgium; Order of Tudor Vladimirescu (Romania). Atlas' Internat. Editor of the Year, 1976. *Publications:* L'Alliance atlantique à l'heure du dégel, 1960; Histoire de la guerre froide, vol. 1 1965, vol. 2 1966 (English trans., History of the Cold War, 1966 and 1967); La Guerre civile froide, 1969; Le dernier quart du siècle, 1976; La France au bois dormant, 1978; Un seul lit pour deux rêves, 1981; (with Pierre Li) Sortir de l'Hexagonie, 1984. *Address:* 15 rue Falguière, 75501 Paris Cedex 15, France.

FOOKES, Dame Janet (Evelyn), DBE 1989; MP (C) Plymouth, Drake, since 1974 (Merton and Morden, 1970–74); *b* 21 Feb. 1936; *d* of late Lewis Aylmer Fookes and of Evelyn Margery Fookes (*née* Holmes). *Educ:* Hastings and St Leonards Ladies' Coll.; High Sch. for Girls, Hastings; Royal Holloway Coll., Univ. of London (BA Hons). Teacher, 1958–70. Councillor for County Borough of Hastings, 1960–61 and 1963–70 (Chm. Educn Cttee, 1967–70). Mem., Speaker's Panel of Chairmen, 1976–. Sec., Cons. Parly Educn Cttee, 1971–75; Chairman: Educn, Arts and Home Affairs Sub-Cttee of the Expenditure Cttee, 1975–79; Parly Gp for Animal Welfare, 1985– (Sec., 1974–82); Member: Unopposed Bills Cttee, 1973–75; Services Cttee, 1974–76; Select Cttee on Home Affairs, 1984–. Chm., Cons. West Country Mems Cttee, 1976–77, Vice-Chm., 1977. Mem. Council, RSPCA, 1975– (Chm., 1979–81); Member: Nat. Art Collections Fund; Council, SSAFA, 1980–; Council, Stonham Housing Assoc., 1980–; Commonwealth War Graves Commn, 1987–. Mem., RHS. *Recreations:* gardening, gymnasium exercises. *Address:* House of Commons, SW1A 0AA. *Club:* Royal Over-Seas League.

FOOT, family name of **Baron Foot.**

FOOT, Baron *cr* 1967 (Life Peer), of Buckland Monachorum; **John Mackintosh Foot;** Senior Partner, Foot & Bowden, Solicitors, Plymouth; Chairman, United Kingdom Immigrants Advisory Service, 1970–78 (President, 1978–84); *b* 17 Feb. 1909; 3rd *s* of late Rt Hon. Isaac Foot, PC and Eva Mackintosh; *m* 1936, Anne, *d* of Dr Clifford Bailey Farr, Bryn Mawr, Pa; one *s* one *d*. *Educ:* Forres Sch., Swanage; Bembridge Sch., IoW; Balliol Coll., Oxford. Pres., Oxford Union, 1931; Pres., OU Liberal Club, 1931; BA Oxon (2nd cl. hons Jurisprudence), 1931. Admitted Solicitor, 1934. Served in Army, 1939–45 (Hon. Major); jsc 1944. Contested (L); Basingstoke, 1934 and 1935; Bodmin, 1945 and 1950. Member: Dartmoor National Park Cttee, 1963–74; Commn on the Constitution, 1969–73; President: Dartmoor Preservation Assoc., 1976–; Commons, Open Spaces and Footpaths Preservation Soc., 1976–82. Chm. Council, Justice, 1984–89. *Recreations:* chess, crosswords, defending Dartmoor. *Address:* Yew Tree, Crapstone, Yelverton, Devon. *T:* Yelverton (0822) 853417. *Club:* Royal Western Yacht.
See also Rt Hon. Michael Foot.

FOOT, David Lovell, FICFor; Commissioner, Operations, Forestry Commission, since 1986; *b* 20 May 1939; *s* of late John Bartram Lovell Foot, MBE and of Birtha Lilian Foot; *m* 1964, Verena Janine Walton; one *s* one *d*. *Educ:* John Lyon Sch., Harrow; Edinburgh Univ. (BSc Hons 1961). FICFor 1980. Dist Officer, Forestry Commn, 1961–64; Silviculturist, Dept of Forestry and Game, Govt of Malawi, 1964–70; Forestry Commission: various appts in S Scotland, N Wales and E Scotland, 1970–82; Conservator, S Scotland, 1982; Dir, Harvesting and Marketing Div., Edinburgh, 1985. *Recreations:* walking, fishing, photography. *Address:* 36 Coltbridge Terrace, Edinburgh EH12 6AE. *T:* 031–337 3874.

FOOT, Sir Geoffrey (James), Kt 1984; Chairman and Commissioner, Hydro Electric Commission of Tasmania, 1987–89 (Associate Commissioner, 1984–87); *b* 20 July 1915; *s* of James P. Foot and Susan J. Foot; *m* 1940, Mollie W. Snooks; two *s* one *d*. *Educ:* Launceston High Sch. AASA; ACIS. MLC, Tasmania, 1961–72 (Leader for Govt, 1969–72). Chairman: Tasmania Permanent Bldg Soc., 1982–85; Launceston Gas Co., 1982–84; Gas Corp. of Tasmania, 1984–87. Mem., Lilydale Commn—Local Govt, 1983–85. Mem. Council, Univ. of Tas, 1970–85. Freeman, City of Launceston, 1990. Hon. LLD Tasmania, 1988. *Recreations:* reading, music. *Address:* 85 Arthur Street, Launceston, Tas 7250, Australia. *T:* 003–340573. *Club:* Launceston (Launceston).

FOOT, Rt. Hon. Michael, PC 1974; MP (Lab) Blaenau Gwent, since 1983 (Ebbw Vale, Nov. 1960–1983); *b* 23 July 1913; *s* of late Rt Hon. Isaac Foot, PC; *m* 1949, Jill Craigie. *Educ:* Forres Sch., Swanage; Leighton Park Sch., Reading; Wadham Coll., Oxford (Exhibitioner). Pres. Oxford Union, 1933; contested (Lab) Mon, 1935; MP (Lab) Devonport Div. of Plymouth, 1945–55. Sec. of State for Employment, 1974–76; Lord President of the Council and Leader of the House of Commons, 1976–79; Leader of the Opposition, 1980–83. Mem., Labour Party Nat. Exec. Cttee, 1971–83; Deputy Leader of the Labour Party, 1976–80, Leader of the Labour Party 1980–83. Asst Editor, Tribune, 1937–38; Acting Editor, Evening Standard, 1942; Man. Dir, Tribune, 1945–74, Editor, 1948–52, 1955–60; political columnist on the Daily Herald, 1944–64; former Book Critic, Evening Standard. Hon. Fellow, Wadham Coll. 1969. *Publications:* Guilty Men (with Frank Owen and Peter Howard), 1940; Armistice 1918–39, 1940; Trial of Mussolini, 1943; Brendan and Beverley, 1944; Still at Large, 1950; Full Speed Ahead, 1950; Guilty Men (with Mervyn Jones), 1957; The Pen and the Sword, 1957; Parliament in Danger, 1959; Aneurin Bevan: Vol. I, 1897–1945, 1962; Vol. II, 1945–60, 1973; Debts of Honour, 1980; Another Heart and Other Pulses, 1984; Loyalists and Loners, 1986; The Politics of Paradise, 1988. *Recreations:* Plymouth Argyle supporter, chess, reading, walking. *Address:* House of Commons, SW1.
See also Baron Foot.

FOOT, Michael Colin, OBE 1984; Director, British Council Australia, since 1989; *b* 3 Feb. 1935; *s* of William Reginald Foot and Elsie (*née* Collins); *m* 1964, Heather Pearl Foot (*née* Beaton); two *s* two *d*. *Educ:* Taunton's Sch., Southampton; University Coll., Leicester (BA London); Leicester Univ. (PGCE). Lycée Champollion, Grenoble, 1959–60; Ashlyn's Sch., Berkhamsted, 1960–63. Served RAF, 1963–66. British Council: Asst Rep., Chile, 1966–71; Hd of Overseas Recruitment, Personnel Div., 1971–75; Dep. Rep., Nigeria, 1975–78; Dep. Dir, Personnel, 1978–81; Rep., Bangladesh, 1981–83; Dir, Personnel, 1984–85; Controller, Personnel, 1986–89. *Recreations:* reading, theatre, music, botany, swimming. *Address:* c/o Personnel Department, British Council, 10 Spring Gardens, W1A 2BN. *Club:* Royal Air Force.

FOOT, Michael David Kenneth Willoughby; Head, European Division, Bank of England, since 1990; *b* 16 Dec. 1946; *s* of Kenneth Willoughby Foot and Ruth Joan (*née* Cornah); *m* 1972, Michele Annette Cynthia Macdonald; one *s* two *d*. *Educ:* Pembroke Coll., Cambridge (MA); Yale Univ., USA (MA). Joined Bank of England, 1969; manager, 1978; sen. man., 1985; seconded to IMF, Washington, as UK Alternate Exec. Dir, 1985–87; Head, Foreign Exchange Div., 1988–90. *Publications;* contrib. essays on monetary econs to books and jls. *Recreations:* choral singing, voluntary youth work, soccer refereeing. *Address:* Cordons, Windsor Lane, Little Kingshill, Great Missenden, Bucks HP16 0DZ. *T:* Great Missenden (02406) 5806.

FOOT, Michael Richard Daniell; historian; *b* 14 Dec. 1919; *s* of late R. C. Foot and Nina (*née* Raymond); *m* twice; one *s* one *d*; 3rd, 1972, Mirjam Michaela, DLitt, *y d* of late Prof. C. P. M. Romme, Oisterwijk. *Educ:* Winchester (scholar); New Coll., Oxford (scholar). Served in Army, 1939–45 (Major RA, parachutist, wounded). Taught at Oxford, 1947–59; research, 1959–67; Prof of Modern Hist., Manchester, 1967–73; Dir of Studies, European Discussion Centre, 1973–75. French Croix de Guerre, 1945; Officer, Order of Orange Nassau (Netherlands), 1989. *Publications:* Gladstone and Liberalism (with J. L. Hammond), 1952; British Foreign Policy since 1898, 1956; Men in Uniform, 1961; SOE in France, 1966; (ed) The Gladstone Diaries: vols I and II, 1825–1839, 1968; (ed) War and Society, 1973; (ed with Dr H. C. G. Matthew) The Gladstone Diaries: vols III and IV, 1840–1854, 1974; Resistance, 1976; Six Faces of Courage, 1978; (with J. M. Langley) MI9, 1979; SOE: an outline history, 1984; Art and War, 1990; (ed) Holland at war against Hitler, 1990. *Recreations:* reading, talking. *Address:* 45 Countess Road, NW5 2XH. *Clubs:* Savile, Special Forces.

FOOT, Paul Mackintosh; writer; journalist; with The Daily Mirror, since 1979; *b* 8 Nov. 1937; *m*; three *s*. Editor of Isis, 1961; President of the Oxford Union, 1961. TUC delegate from Nat. Union of Journalists, 1967 and 1971. Contested (Socialist Workers Party) Birmingham, Stechford, March 1977. Editor, Socialist Worker, 1974–75. Journalist of the Year, What The Papers Say Awards, 1972, 1989. Campaigning Journalist of the Year, British Press Awards, 1980. *Publications:* Immigration and Race in British Politics,

1965; The Politics of Harold Wilson, 1968; The Rise of Enoch Powell, 1969; Who Killed Hanratty?, 1971; Why You Should Be a Socialist, 1977; Red Shelley, 1981; The Helen Smith Story, 1983; Murder at the Farm: who killed Carl Bridgewater?, 1986; Who Framed Colin Wallace?, 1989; Words as Weapons, 1990; contrib. Counterblasts, 1989. *Address:* c/o The Daily Mirror, Holborn Circus, EC1.

FOOT, Mrs Philippa Ruth, FBA 1976; Griffin Professor, University of California at Los Angeles, 1988–91, now Emeritus (Professor of Philosophy, 1974–91); *b* 3 Oct. 1920; *d* of William Sydney Bence Bosanquet, DSO, and Esther Cleveland Bosanquet, *d* of Grover Cleveland, Pres. of USA; *m* 1945, M. R. D. Foot (marr. diss. 1960), *qv*; no *c*. *Educ:* St George's Sch., Ascot; privately; Somerville Coll., Oxford (BA 1942, MA 1946). Somerville Coll., Oxford: Lectr in philosophy, 1947; Fellow and Tutor, 1950–69; Vice-Principal, 1967–69; Sen. Res. Fellow, 1970–88; Hon. Fellow, 1988. Formerly Vis. Prof., Cornell Univ., MIT, Univ. of California at Berkeley, Princeton Univ., City Univ. of NY; Fellow, Center for Advanced Studies in Behavioral Scis, Stanford, 1981–82. Pres., Pacific Div., Amer. Philos. Assoc., 1982–83. Fellow, Amer. Acad. of Arts and Scis, 1983. *Publications:* Theories of Ethics (ed), 1967; Virtues and Vices, 1978; articles in Mind, Aristotelian Soc. Proc., Philos. Rev., New York Rev., Philosophy and Public Affairs. *Address:* 15 Walton Street, Oxford OX1 2HG. *T:* Oxford (0865) 57130.

FOOTE, Maj.-Gen. Henry Robert Bowreman, VC 1944; CB 1952; DSO 1942; *b* 5 Dec. 1904; *s* of Lieut-Col H. B. Foote, late RA; *m* 1st, 1944, Anita Flint Howard (*d* 1970); 2nd, 1981, Mrs Audrey Mary Ashwell. *Educ:* Bedford Sch. Royal Tank Corps; 2nd Lieut, 1925; Lieut, 1927; Capt., 1936; Staff Coll., 1939; GSO3, WO, 1939; GSO2, WO, 1940; GSO2, Staff Coll., 1940–41; GSO1, 10th Armd Div., 1941–42; OC 7th Royal Tank Regt, 1942; Subst. Major, 1942; GSO1, AFHQ, Italy, 1944; 2i/c, 9th Armd Bde, 1945; Brig. RAC, MELF, 1945–47; Subst. Lieut-Col, 1946; Subst. Col, 1948; OC 2nd Royal Tank Regt, 1947–48; OC Automotive Wing, Fighting Vehicles Proving Establishment, Ministry of Supply, 1948–49; Comd 7th Armd Bde, 1949–50; Maj.-Gen. 1951; Comd 11th Armoured Div., 1950–53; Dir-Gen. of Fighting Vehicles, Min. of Supply, 1953–55; Dir, Royal Armoured Corps, at the War Office, 1955–58; retd. *Address:* Furzefield, West Chiltington Common, Pulborough, West Sussex RH20 2QY. *Club:* Army and Navy.

FOOTE, Prof. Peter Godfrey; Emeritus Professor of Scandinavian Studies, University of London; *b* 26 May 1924; 4th *s* of late T. Foote and Ellen Foote, Swanage, Dorset; *m* 1951, Eleanor Jessie McCaig, *d* of late J. M. McCaig and Margaret H. McCaig; one *s* two *d*. *Educ:* Grammar Sch., Swanage; University Coll., Exeter; Univ. of Oslo; University Coll., London. BA London 1948; MA London 1951; Fil. dr *hc* Uppsala, 1972; dr phil. *hc* Univ. of Iceland, 1987. Served with RNVR, 1943–46. University College London: Asst Lectr, Lectr and Reader in Old Scandinavian, 1950–63; Prof. of Scandinavian Studies, 1963–83; Fellow, 1989. Jt Sec., Viking Soc., 1956–83, Pres., 1974–76, Hon. Life Mem., 1983. Member: Royal Gustav Adolfs Academy, Uppsala, 1967; Kungl. Humanistiska Vetenskapssamfundet, Uppsala, 1968; Vísindafélag Islands, 1969; Vetenskapssocieteten, Lund, 1973; Kungl. Vetenskaps-samhället, Göteborg; Det kongelige Norske Videnskabers Selskab, 1977; Societas Scientiarum Fennica, 1979; Det norske Videnskapsakademi, 1986; Hon. Member: Isl. Bókmenntafélag, 1965; Thjóðvinafélag Ísl. í Vesturheimi, 1975; Corresp. Mem., Kungl. Vitterhets Hist. och Antikvitets Akad., Stockholm, 1971. Crabtree Orator, 1968. Commander with star, Icelandic Order of the Falcon, 1984 (Comdr, 1973); Knight, Order of Dannebrog (Denmark); Comdr, Royal Order of North Star (Sweden), 1977. *Publications:* Gunnlaugs saga ormstungu, 1957; Pseudo-Turpin Chronicle in Iceland, 1959; Laing's Heimskringla, 1961; Lives of Saints: Icelandic manuscripts in fascimile IV, 1962; (with G. Johnston) The Saga of Gisli, 1963; (with D. M. Wilson) The Viking Achievement, 1970, 2nd edn 1980; Aurvandilstá (selected papers), 1984; Jt Editor, Mediæval Scandinavia; Mem. of Ed. Board, Arv, Scandinavica; papers in Saga-Book, Arv, Studia Islandica, Islenzk Tunga, etc. *Recreations:* bell-ringing, walking. *Address:* 18 Talbot Road, N6. *T:* 081–340 1860.

FOOTMAN, Charles Worthington Fowden, CMG 1952; *b* 3 Sept. 1905; *s* of Rev. William Llewellyn and Mary Elizabeth Footman; *m* 1947, Joyce Marcelle Law; one *s* two *d*. *Educ:* Rossall Sch.; Keble Coll., Oxford. Colonial Administrative Service, Zanzibar, 1930; seconded to East African Governors' Conference, 1942; seconded to Colonial Office, 1943–46; Financial Sec., Nyasaland, 1947; Chief Sec., Nyasaland, 1951–60. Retired from HM Overseas Civil Service, 1960. Chm., Public Service Commissions, Tanganyika and Zanzibar, 1960–61; Commonwealth Relations Office, 1962–64; Min. of Overseas Development, 1964–70. *Recreations:* golf and tennis. *Address:* c/o National Westminster Bank, Worthing, West Sussex.

FOOTS, Sir James (William), Kt 1975; mining engineer; Chairman: MIM Holdings Ltd, 1970–83 (Director, 1956–87); Westpac Banking Corporation, 1987–89 (Director, 1971–89); *b* 1916; *m* 1939, Thora H.Thomas; one *s* two *d*. *Educ:* Melbourne Univ. (BME). President: Austr. Inst. Mining and Metallurgy, 1974; Austr. Mining Industry Council, 1974 and 1975; 13th Congress, Council of Mining and Metallurgical Institns, 1986. Fellow, Australian Acad. of Technol Scis. University of Queensland: Mem. Senate, 1970–; Chancellor, 1985–. Hon. DEng Univ. of Qld, 1982. *Address:* PO Box 662, Kenmore, Qld 4069, Australia.

FOOTTIT, Ven. Anthony Charles; Archdeacon of Lynn, since 1987; *b* 28 June 1935; *s* of Percival Frederick and Mildred Foottit; *m* 1977, Rosamond Mary Alyson Buxton; one *s* two *d*. *Educ:* Lancing College; King's Coll., Cambridge (MA). Asst Curate, Wymondham, 1961–64; Vicar, Blakeney Group, 1964–71; Rector, Camelot Group, 1971–81; RD of Cary, 1979–81; St Hugh's Missioner for Lincolnshire, 1981–87; Hon. Canon of Lincoln Cathedral, 1986–87. *Publication:* Mission and Ministry in Rural France, 1967. *Recreations:* gardening, botany, rambling. *Address:* Ivy House, Whitwell Street, Reepham, Norwich NR10 4RA. *T:* Norwich (0603) 870340.

FOPP, Dr Michael Anton; Director, Royal Air Force Museum, since 1988; *b* 28 Oct. 1947; *s* of Sqdn Ldr Desmond Fopp and Edna Meryl (*née* Dodd); *m* 1968, Rosemary Ann Hodgetts; one *s*. *Educ:* Reading Blue Coat Sch.; Metropolitan Police Cadet Coll., Hendon; Metropolitan Police Coll., Peel House, London; City Univ., London (MA 1984; PhD 1989). FBIM; FMA. Metropolitan Police Cadet Corps, 1964–66; Metropolitan Police, 1966–79 (Mounted Br., 1969–79); Dep. Keeper 1979–82, Keeper 1982–85, Battle of Britain Mus.; Co. Sec., Hendon Mus. Trading Co. Ltd, 1983–85; Dir, London Transport Mus., 1985–88. Hon. Sec. 1976–86, Chm. 1986–88, Soc. of Friends of RAF Mus. Pres., London Underground Rly Soc., 1987; Chm., London Transport Flying Club, 1986–. Vis. Lectr, City Univ., 1986–. Freeman: City of London, 1984; Guild of Air Pilots and Navigators, 1987. *Publications:* The Boeing Washington, 1980; The Battle of Britain Museum Guide, 1980; The Bomber Command Museum Guide, 1982; The RAF Museum Guide, 1985; (ed) A Junior Guide to the RAF Museum, 1985; (ed) Battle of Britain Project Book, 1989; various articles on aviation, museums and management, in magazines and jls. *Recreations:* flying, walking, computers, Chinese cookery. *Address:* Royal Air Force Museum, Hendon, NW9 5LL. *T:* 081–205 2266. *Club:* Royal Air Force.

FORBES, family name of **Lord Forbes** and of **Earl of Granard.**

FORBES, 22nd Lord *cr* 1442 or before; **Nigel Ivan Forbes,** KBE 1960; JP, DL; Premier Lord of Scotland; Representative Peer of Scotland, 1955–63; Major (retired) Grenadier Guards; Chairman, Rolawn Ltd, since 1975; *b* 19 Feb. 1918; *o s* of 21st Lord and Lady Mabel Anson (*d* 1972), *d* of 3rd Earl of Lichfield; *S* father, 1953; *m* 1942, Hon. Rosemary Katharine Hamilton-Russell, *o d* of 9th Viscount Boyne; two *s* one *d*. *Educ:* Harrow; RMC Sandhurst. Served War of 1939–45 (wounded); Adjt, Grenadier Guards, Staff Coll. Military Asst to High Comr for Palestine, 1947–48. Minister of State, Scottish Office, 1958–59. Member: Inter-Parly Union Delegn to Denmark, 1956; Commonwealth Parly Assoc. Delegn to Canada, 1961; Parly Delegn to Pakistan, 1962; Inter-Parly Union Delegn to Hungary, 1965; Inter-Parly Union Delegn to Ethiopia, 1971. Director: Grampian Television PLC, 1960–88; Blenheim Travel Ltd, 1981–88; Dep. Chm., Tenant Caledonian Breweries Ltd, 1964–74. Mem., Aberdeen and District Milk Marketing Bd, 1962–72; Mem. Alford District Council, 1955–58; Chm., River Don District Bd, 1962–73. Pres., Royal Highland and Agricultural Society of Scotland, 1958–59; Member: Sports Council for Scotland, 1966–71; Scottish Cttee, Nature Conservancy, 1961–67; Chm., Scottish Br., Nat. Playing Fields Assoc., 1965–80; Pres., Scottish Scout Assoc., 1970–88. JP 1955, DL 1958, Aberdeenshire. *Recreations:* wildlife, travel. *Heir:* *s* Master of Forbes, *qv*. *Address:* Balforbes, Alford, Aberdeenshire AB33 8DR. *T:* Alford (Aberdeen) (09755) 62516. *Club:* Army and Navy.

FORBES, Master of; Hon. Malcolm Nigel Forbes; landowner; *b* 6 May 1946; *s* and heir of 22nd Lord Forbes, *qv*; *m* 1st,1969, Carole Jennifer Andrée (marr. diss. 1982), *d* of N. S. Whitehead, Aberdeen; one *s* one *d*; 2nd, 1988, Jennifer Mary Gribbon, *d* of I. P. Whittington, Tunbridge Wells. *Educ:* Eton; Aberdeen Univ. Director, Instock Disposables Ltd, 1974–. *Address:* Castle Forbes, Alford, Aberdeenshire AB33 8BL. *T:* Alford (09755) 62574; 3 Steeple Close, SW6. *T:* 071–736 0730. *Club:* Royal Northern and University (Aberdeen).

FORBES, Hon. Sir Alastair (Granville), Kt 1960; President, Courts of Appeal for St Helena, Falkland Islands and British Antarctic Territories, 1965–88, and British Indian Ocean Territory, 1986–88; *b* 3 Jan. 1908; *s* of Granville Forbes and Constance Margaret (*née* Davis); *m* 1936, Constance Irene Mary Hughes-White; two *d*. *Educ:* Blundell's Sch.; Clare Coll., Cambridge. Called to the Bar, Gray's Inn, 1932; Magistrate and Govt Officer, Dominica, BWI, 1936; Crown Attorney, Dominica, 1939; Resident Magistrate, Fiji, 1940; Crown Counsel, Fiji, 1942; Solicitor-Gen., Fiji, and Asst Legal Adviser, Western Pacific High Commission, 1945; Legal Draftsman, Federation of Malaya, 1947; Solicitor-Gen., Northern Rhodesia, 1950; Permanent Sec., Ministry of Justice, and Solicitor-Gen., Gold Coast, 1951; Puisne Judge, Kenya, 1956; Justice of Appeal, Court of Appeal for Eastern Africa, 1957; Vice-Pres., Court of Appeal for Eastern Africa, 1958; Federal Justice, Federal Supreme Court of Rhodesia and Nyasaland, 1963–64; Pres., Ct of Appeal: for Seychelles, 1965–76; for Gibraltar, 1970–83. Mem., Panel of Chairmen of Industrial Tribunals (England and Wales), 1965–73; Pres., Pensions Appeal Tribunals for England and Wales, 1973–80 (Chm., 1965–73); Chairman: Constituencies Delimitation Commissions, N Rhodesia, 1962 and 1963, and Bechuanaland, 1964; Gibraltar Riot Inquiry, 1968. *Publications:* Index of the Laws, Dominica, 1940; Revised Edition of Laws of Fiji, 1944. *Recreations:* fishing, shooting. *Address:* Badgers Holt, Church Lane, Sturminster Newton, Dorset DT10 1DH. *T:* Sturminster Newton (0258) 73268. *Club:* Commonwealth Trust.

FORBES, Anthony David Arnold William; Joint Senior Partner, Cazenove & Co., since 1980; *b* 15 Jan. 1938; *s* of late Lt-Col D. W. A. W. Forbes, MC, and Diana Mary (*née* Henderson), later Marchioness of Exeter; *m* 1st, 1962, Virginia June Ropner; one *s* one *d*; 2nd, 1973, Belinda Mary Drury-Lowe. *Educ:* Eton. Served Coldstream Guards, 1956–59. Joined Cazenove & Co., 1960; Member of Stock Exchange, 1965–. Chairman: Hospital and Homes of St Giles, 1975–; Wellesley House Educnl Trust, 1983–; Governor: Cobham Hall, 1975–; Royal Choral Soc., 1979–. *Recreations:* music, shooting, gardening. *Address:* 16 Halsey Street, SW3 2QH. *T:* 071–584 4749.

FORBES, Bryan; *b* 22 July 1926; *m* 1958, Nanette Newman, *qv;* two *d*. *Educ:* West Ham Secondary Sch. Studied at RADA, 1941; entered acting profession, 1942, and (apart from war service) was on West End stage, then in films here and in Hollywood, 1948–60. Formed Beaver Films with Sir Richard Attenborough, 1959; wrote and co-produced The Angry Silence, 1960. Subseq. wrote, dir. and prod. numerous films; *films include:* The League of Gentlemen, Only Two Can Play, Whistle Down the Wind, 1961; The L-Shaped Room, 1962; Séance on a Wet Afternoon, 1963; King Rat (in Hollywood), 1964; The Wrong Box, 1965; The Whisperers, 1966; Deadfall, 1967; The Madwoman of Chaillot, 1968; The Raging Moon, 1970; The Tales of Beatrix Potter, 1971; The Stepford Wives, 1974 (USA); The Slipper and the Rose, 1975 (Royal Film Perf., 1976); International Velvet, 1978; (British segment) The Sunday Lovers, 1980; Better Late Than Never, 1981; The Naked Face, 1983; (narrator) I am a Dancer, 1971. *Stage:* Directed: Macbeth, Old Vic, 1980; Killing Jessica, Savoy, 1986; The Living Room, Royalty, 1987; directed and acted in Star Quality, Th. Royal, Bath, 1983. *Television:* produced and directed: Edith Evans, I Caught Acting Like the Measles, Yorkshire TV, 1973; Elton John, Goodbye Norma Jean and Other Things, ATV 1973; Jessie, BBC, 1980; The Endless Game, C4, 1989; acted in: December Flower, Granada, 1984; First Among Equals, Granada, 1986. Man. Dir and Head of Production, ABPC Studios, 1969–71; Man. Dir and Chief Exec., EMI-MGM, Elstree Studios, 1970–71; Dir, Capital Radio Ltd, 1973–. Member: BBC Gen. Adv. Council, 1966–69; BBC Schs Council, 1971–73; President: Beatrix Potter Soc., 1982–; Nat. Youth Theatre, 1984–; Writers' Guild of GB, 1988–. Won British Acad. Award, 1960; Writers' Guild Award (twice); numerous internat. awards. *Publications:* Truth Lies Sleeping, 1950; The Distant Laughter, 1972; Notes for a Life, 1974; The Slipper and the Rose, 1976; Ned's Girl: biography of Dame Edith Evans, 1977; International Velvet, 1978; Familiar Strangers, 1979; That Despicable Race, 1980; The Rewrite Man, 1983; The Endless Game, 1986; A Song at Twilight, 1989; contribs to: The Spectator, New Statesman, Queen, and other periodicals. *Recreations:* running a bookshop, reading, landscape gardening, photography. *Address:* The Bookshop, Virginia Water, Surrey.

See also Sir John Leon, Bt.

FORBES, Colin, RDI 1974; Partner, Pentagram Design, since 1972; *b* 6 March 1928; *s* of Kathleen and John Forbes; *m* 1961, Wendy Schneider; one *s* two *d*. *Educ:* Sir Anthony Browne's, Brentwood; LCC Central Sch. of Arts and Crafts. Design Asst, Herbert Spencer, 1952; freelance practice and Lectr, LCC Central Sch. of Arts and Crafts, 1953–57; Art Dir, Stuart Advertising, London, 1957–58; Head of Graphic Design Dept, LCC Central Sch. of Arts and Crafts, 1958–61; freelance practice, London, 1961–62; Partner: Fletcher/Forbes/Gill, 1962–65; Crosby/Fletcher/Forbes, 1965–72. Mem., Alliance Graphique Internationale, 1965– (Internat. Pres. 1976–79); Pres., Amer. Inst. Graphic Arts, 1984–86. *Publications:* Graphic Design: visual comparisons, 1963; A Sign Systems Manual, 1970; Creativity and Communication, 1971; New Alphabets A to Z, 1973; Living by Design, 1978. *Address:* 45 East 25th Street, New York, NY 10010, USA. *T:* 212 725 4678.

FORBES, Donald James, MA; Headmaster, Merchiston Castle School, 1969–81; *b* 6 Feb. 1921; *s* of Andrew Forbes; *m* 1945, Patricia Muriel Yeo; two *s* one *d*. *Educ:* Oundle; Clare

Coll., Cambridge (Mod. Lang. Tripos). Capt. Scots Guards, 1941–46; 1st Bn Scots Guards, 1942–46, N Africa, Italy. Asst Master, Dulwich Coll., 1946–55; Master i/c cricket, 1951–55; Headmaster, Dauntsey's Sch., 1956–69. Diploma in Spanish, Univ. of Santander, 1954; Lectr in Spanish, West Norwood Tech. Coll., 1954–55. *Recreations:* cricket, Rugby football, tennis, Rugby fives, curling, golf; history, literature; instrumental and choral music. *Address:* 33 Coates Gardens, Edinburgh EH12 5LG; Breachacha Castle, Isle of Coll. *Clubs:* Hawks (Cambridge); HCEG (Muirfield).

FORBES of Craigievar, Hon. Sir Ewan, 11th Bt *cr* 1630; JP; landowner and farmer; *b* 6 Sept. 1912; 2nd *s* of Sir John Forbes-Sempill, 9th Bt (Forbes) of Craigievar, 18th Lord Sempill; *S* (to Btcy) brother, 1965; *m* 1952, Isabella, *d* of A. Mitchell, Glenrinnes, Banffshire. *Educ:* Dresden; Univ. of Munich; Univ. of Aberdeen. MB, ChB 1944. Senior Casualty Officer, Aberdeen Royal Infirmary, 1944–45; Medical Practitioner, Alford, Aberdeenshire, 1945–55. JP Aberdeenshire, 1969. *Recreations:* shooting, fishing, ski-ing and skating. *Heir: kinsman* John Alexander Cumnock Forbes-Sempill [*b* 29 Aug. 1927; *m* 1st, 1958, Penelope Margaret Ann (marr. diss. 1964), *d* of A. G. Grey-Pennington; 2nd, 1966, Jane Carolyn, *o d* of C. Gordon Evans]. *Address:* Brux, Alford, Aberdeenshire. *T:* Kildrummy (03365) 223.

See also Lady Sempill.

FORBES, Very Rev. Graham John Thomson; Provost, St Mary's Cathedral, Edinburgh, since 1990; *b* 10 June 1951; *s* of J. T. and D. D. Forbes; *m* 1973, Jane T. Miller; three *s.* *Educ:* George Heriot's School, Edinburgh; Univ. of Aberdeen (MA); Univ. of Edinburgh (BD). Curate, Old St Paul's Church, Edinburgh, 1976–82; Provost, St Ninian's Cathedral, Perth, 1982–90. *Recreations:* climbing, running, dry rot. *Address:* 8 Lansdowne Crescent, Edinburgh EH12 5EQ. *T:* (home) 031–225 2978; (office) 031–225 6293.

FORBES, Major Sir Hamish (Stewart), 7th Bt *cr* 1823, of Newe; MBE 1945; MC 1945; Welsh Guards, retired; *b* 15 Feb. 1916; *s* of Lt-Col James Stewart Forbes (*d* 1957) (*g s* of 3rd Bt) and Feridah Frances Forbes (*d* 1953), *d* of Hugh Lewis Taylor; *S* cousin, 1984; *m* 1st, 1945, Jacynthe Elizabeth Mary, *d* of late Eric Gordon Underwood; one *s* three *d;* 2nd, 1981, Mary Christine, MBE, *d* of late Ernest William Rigby. *Educ:* Eton College; Lawrenceville, USA; SOAS. Served Welsh Guards, France, Germany, Turkey, 1939–58. Pres., Church Lads' and Church Girls' Bde Assoc. Patron, Lonach Highland and Friendly Soc. KJStJ 1984. *Recreations:* shooting, sculpture. *Heir: s* James Thomas Stewart Forbes [*b* 28 May 1957; *m* 1986, Kerry Lynne, *o d* of Rev. Lee Toms; one *d*]. *Address:* Brughs, Strathdon, Aberdeenshire AB36 8UT. *Clubs:* Turf, Chelsea Arts.

FORBES, Ian, QPM 1966; Deputy Assistant Commissioner, Metropolitan Police and National Co-ordinator, Regional Crime Squads (England and Wales), 1970–72, retired; *b* 30 March 1914; *y s* of John and Betsy Forbes, Auchlossan, Lumphanan, Aberdeenshire; *m* 1941, Lilian Edith Miller, Edgware, Mddx; two *s.* *Educ:* Lumphanan School, Aberdeenshire. Joined Metropolitan Police, 1939; served in East End, Central London Flying Squad, New Scotland Yard; Detective Superintendent, 1964; served on New Scotland Yard Murder Squad, 1966–69; Commander, No 9 Regional Crime Squad (London area), 1969. *Publication:* Squadman (autobiog.), 1973. *Recreations:* gardening, motoring, reading.

FORBES, James, FCA; Forestry Commissioner, 1982–88; Chairman and Treasurer, Council of Almoners, Christ's Hospital, since 1987; *b* 2 Jan. 1923; *s* of Donald Forbes and Rona Ritchie Forbes (*née* Yeats); *m* 1948, Alison Mary Fletcher Moffat; two *s.* *Educ:* Christ's Hospital; Officers' Training School, Bangalore. Chartered Accountant. Commissioned 15th Punjab Regt, Indian Army, 1942; transf. IAOC, released 1947 (hon. Major); Peat Marwick Mitchell Co., 1952–58; Chief Accountant, L. Rose, 1958; Group Operational Research Manager, Schweppes, 1960, Group Chief Accountant, 1963 (Dir, subsid. cos); Sec. and Financial Adviser, Cadbury Schweppes (on formation), 1969, Main Board Dir, 1971, Group Finance Dir to April 1978; Senior Exec. Dir, Tate & Lyle, 1978, Vice-Chm., 1980–84; Chm., Tate & Lyle Gp Pension Fund, 1978–85. Non-exec. Director: British Transport Hotels, 1978–83; British Rail Investments, 1980–84; Steetley plc, 1984–89; Compass Hotels, 1984–; Lautro Ltd, 1986–90. Mem. Council, Inst. of Chartered Accountants, 1971–88 (Treasurer, 1984–86). Gov., Christ's Hosp., 1983–. Mem., Highland Society. *Recreation:* golf. *Clubs:* Caledonian, Commonwealth Trust.

FORBES, Vice-Adm. Sir John Morrison, KCB 1978; a Chairman, Civil Service Commissioners interview panel, since 1980; Governor of various naval charities; *b* 16 Aug. 1925; *s* of late Lt-Col R. H. Forbes, OBE, and late Gladys M. Forbes (*née* Pollock); *m* 1950, Joyce Newenham Hadden; two *s* two *d.* *Educ:* RNC, Dartmouth. Served War: HMS Mauritius, Verulam and Nelson, 1943–46. HMS Aisne, 1946–49; Gunnery course and staff of HMS Excellent, 1950–51; served in RAN, 1952–54; Staff of HMS Excellent, 1954–56; HMS Ceylon, 1956–58; Staff of Dir of Naval Ordnance, 1958–60; Comdr (G) HMS Excellent, 1960–61; Staff of Dir of Seaman Officers' Appts, 1962–64; Exec. Officer, Britannia RN Coll., 1964–66; Operational Comdr and 2nd in Comd, Royal Malaysian Navy, 1966–68; Asst Dir, Naval Plans, 1969–70; comd HMS Triumph, 1971–72; comd Britannia RN Coll., Dartmouth, 1972–74; Naval Secretary, 1974–76; Flag Officer, Plymouth, Port Adm., Devonport, Comdr, Central Sub Area, Eastern Atlantic, and Comdr, Plymouth Sub Area, Channel, 1977–79. Naval ADC to the Queen, 1974. Kesatria Manku Negara (Malaysia), 1968. *Recreations:* country pursuits. *Address:* c/o National Westminster Bank, Waterlooville, Portsmouth, Hants. *Clubs:* Army and Navy, RN Sailing Association.

FORBES, John Stuart; Sheriff of Tayside, Central and Fife at Dunfermline, since 1980; *b* 31 Jan. 1936; *s* of late John Forbes and Dr A. R. S. Forbes; *m* 1963, Marion Alcock; one *s* two *d.* *Educ:* Glasgow High Sch.; Glasgow Univ. (MA, LLB). Solicitor, 1959–61; Advocate, Scottish Bar, 1962–76; Sheriff of Lothian and Borders, 1976–80. Pres., Glasgow Juridical Soc., 1963–64. Life Trustee, Carnegie, Dunfermline and Hero Fund Trusts, 1985–; Trustee, Carnegie UK Trust, 1990–. *Recreations:* tennis, golf. *Address:* Inglewood, Old Perth Road, Milnathort, Kinross KY13 7YA. *Club:* Edinburgh Sports.

FORBES, Nanette; *see* Newman, N.

FORBES, Thayne John; QC 1984; **His Honour Judge Thayne Forbes;** a Circuit Judge (Official Referee), since 1990; *b* 28 June 1938; *s* of John Thomson Forbes and late Jessie Kay Robertson Stewart; *m* 1960, Celia Joan; two *s* one *d.* *Educ:* Winchester College (Quirister); Wolverton Grammar Sch.; University College London (LLB, LLM). Served Royal Navy (Instructor Lieutenant), 1963–66. Called to Bar, Inner Temple, 1966. A Recorder, 1986–90. *Recreations:* music, reading, sailing, bird watching, astronomy. *Address:* St Dunstan's House, 133–137 Fetter Lane, EC4A 1HD. *T:* 071–936 7437. *Club:* Bar Yacht.

FORBES, Sir William (Daniel) Stuart-, 13th Bt *cr* 1626 (NS), of Pitsligo and of Monymusk, Aberdeenshire; *b* 21 Aug. 1935; *s* of William Kenneth Stuart-Forbes (*d* 1946), 3rd *s* of 10th Bt, and of Marjory Gilchrist; *S* uncle, 1985; *m* 1956, Jannette, *d* of late Hori Toki George MacDonald; three *s* two *d.* *Heir: s* Kenneth Charles Stuart-Forbes [*b* 26 Dec. 1956; *m* 1981, Susan, *d* of Len Murray; one *s* two *d*]. *Address:* Waipuna Street, Blenheim, New Zealand.

FORBES, Captain William Frederick Eustace; Vice Lord-Lieutenant of Stirling and Falkirk, since 1984; Forestry Commissioner, 1982–88; *b* 6 July 1932; *er s* of late Lt-Col W. H. D. C. Forbes of Callendar, CBE and of Elizabeth Forbes; *m* 1956, Pamela Susan, *er d* of Lord McCorquodale of Newton, KCVO, PC; two *d.* *Educ:* Eton. Regular soldier, Coldstream Guards, 1950–59; farmer and company director, 1959–. Chairman: Scottish Woodland Owners' Assoc., 1974–77; Nat. Playing Fields Assoc., Scottish Branch, 1980–90. *Recreations:* country pastimes, golf, cricket, travel. *Address:* Dinning House, Gargunnock, Stirling FK8 3BQ. *T:* Gargunnock (078686) 289. *Clubs:* MCC; New (Edinburgh); Royal and Ancient Golf.

FORBES-LEITH of Fyvie, Sir Andrew (George), 3rd Bt *cr* 1923; landed proprietor; *b* 20 Oct. 1929; *s* of Sir R. Ian A. Forbes-Leith of Fyvie, 2nd Bt, KT, MBE, and Ruth Avis (*d* 1973), *d* of Edward George Barnett; *S* father, 1973; *m* 1962, Jane Kate (*d* 1969), *d* of late David McCall-McCowan; two *s* two *d.* *Heir: s* George Ian David Forbes-Leith, *b* 26 May 1967. *Address:* Dunachton, Kingussie, Inverness-shire. *T:* Kincraig (05404) 226. *Clubs:* Royal Northern (Aberdeen); Highland (Inverness).

FORBES-SEMPILL; *see* Sempill.

FORD, Rev. Adam; Chaplain, since 1976, Head of Lower School, since 1986, St Paul's Girls' School, London; *b* 15 Sept. 1940; *s* of John Ford and Jean Beattie Ford (*née* Winstanley); *m* 1969, Veronica Rosemary Lucia Verey; two *s* two *d.* *Educ:* Minehead Grammar Sch.; King's Coll., Univ. of London (BD Hons, AKC 1964); Lancaster Univ. (MA Indian Religion 1972). Asst, Ecumenical Inst. of World Council of Churches, Geneva, 1964; Curate, Cirencester Parish Church, Glos, 1965–69; Vicar of Hebden Bridge, W Yorkshire, 1969–76; Priest-in-Ordinary to the Queen, 1984–90. Regular contributor to Prayer for the Day, Radio 4, 1978–; writer and narrator, Whose World?, series of TV progs on sci. and religion, 1987. Hon. FRAS 1960. *Publications:* Spaceship Earth, 1981; Weather Watch, 1982; Star Gazers Guide to the Night Sky (audio guide to astronomy), 1982; Universe: God, Man and Science, 1986; The Cuckoo Plant, 1991; articles in The Times and science jls on relationship between science and religion, also on dialogue between religions. *Recreations:* dry stone walling, astronomy, searching for neolithic flints. *Address:* 55 Bolingbroke Road, Hammersmith, W14 0AH. *T:* 071–602 5902.

FORD, Sir Andrew (Russell), 3rd Bt *cr* 1929, of Westerdunes, Co. of East Lothian; Lecturer, Chippenham Technical College, since 1974; *b* 29 June 1943; *s* of Sir Henry Russell Ford, 2nd Bt, TD and of Mary Elizabeth, *d* of late Godfrey F. Wright; *S* father, 1989; *m* 1968, Penelope Anne, *d* of Harry Relph; two *s* one *d.* *Educ:* Winchester; New Coll., Oxford (half-blue, athletics, 1962); Loughborough Coll. (DLC); London Univ. (BA external); Birmingham Univ. (MA external). Schoolmaster: Blairmore Sch., Aberdeens, 1967–71; St Peter's Sch., Cambridge, NZ, 1971–74. *Recreations:* taking exercise, reading. *Heir: s* Toby Russell Ford, *b* 11 Jan. 1973. *Address:* 20 Coniston Road, Chippenham, Wilts SN14 0PX. *T:* Chippenham (0249) 655442.

See also H. F. Ford.

FORD, Anthony; *see* Ford, J. A.

FORD, Antony; HM Diplomatic Service; Consul-General, San Francisco, since 1990; *b* Bexley, 1 Oct. 1944; *s* of late William Ford and Grace Ford (*née* Smith); *m* 1970, Linda Gordon Joy; one *s* one *d.* *Educ:* St Dunstan's Coll., Catford; UCW, Aberystwyth (BA). Joined HM Diplomatic Service, 1967; Third, later Second, Sec., Bonn, 1968–71; Second Sec., Kuala Lumpur, 1971–73; First Secretary: FCO, 1973–77; Washington, 1977–81; FCO, 1981–84; Counsellor: East Berlin, 1984–87; FCO, 1987–90. *Recreations:* reading, gardening, cricket, the Weald of Kent. *Address:* c/o Foreign and Commonwealth Office, King Charles Street, SW1A 2AH.

FORD, Benjamin Thomas; DL; *b* 1 April 1925; *s* of Benjamin Charles Ford and May Ethel (*née* Moorton); *m* 1950, Vera Ada (*née* Fawcett-Fancet); two *s* one *d.* *Educ:* Rowan Road Central Sch., Surrey. Apprenticed as compositor, 1941. War Service, 1943–47, Fleet Air Arm (Petty Officer). Electronic Fitter/Wireman, 1951–64; Convener of Shop Stewards, 1955–64. Pres., Harwich Constituency Labour Party, 1955–63; Mem., Clacton UDC, 1959–62; Alderman Essex CC, 1959–65; JP Essex, 1962–67. MP (Lab) Bradford N, 1964–83; contested (Lab Ind.) Bradford N, 1983. Mem., H of C Select Cttee (Services), 1970–83 (Chm., Accom. and Admin Sub-Cttee, 1979–83); Chairman: British-Portuguese Parly Gp, 1965–83; British-Argentinian Parly Gp, 1974–81; British-Brazilian Parly Gp, 1974–79; British-Malaysian Parly Gp, 1975–83; British-Venezuelan Parly Gp, 1977–83; All-Party Wool Textile Parly Gp, 1974–83; Vice-Chairman: British-Latin American Parly Gp, 1974–79; PLP Defence Cttee, 1979–82; Mem. Exec. Cttee, IPU British Gp, 1971–83 (Chm., 1977–79); Sec., British-Namibian Parly Gp, 1980–83. Chm., Jt Select Cttee on Sound Broadcasting, 1976–77. Bd Mem., Bradford & Northern Housing Assoc., 1975– (Chm., Central and Southern Regl Cttees). Chm., English Shooting Council, 1982–; Mem. Council, Nat. Rifle Assoc., 1970– (Vice-Pres., 1984–); President: Yorks and Humberside Region, Mencap, 1986–; Bradford Civic Soc., 1988–. Freeman, City of London, 1979; Liveryman, Gunmakers' Co., 1978–. DL W Yorks, 1982. Hon. FAIA 1983. Grand Officer, Order of the Southern Cross (Brazil), 1976. *Publication:* Piecework, 1960. *Recreations:* music, shooting, family. *Address:* 9 Wynmore Crescent, Bramhope, Leeds LS16 9DH. *Club:* Idle Working Men's.

FORD, Prof. Boris, MA; Emeritus Professor, University of Bristol; freelance editor and writer; *b* 1 July 1917; *s* of late Brig. G. N. Ford, CB, DSO; *m* 1st, 1950, Noreen; one *s* three *d;* 2nd, 1977, Inge. *Educ:* Gresham's Sch., Holt, Norfolk; Downing Coll., Cambridge. Army Education, finally OC Middle East School of Artistic Studies, 1940–46. Chief Ed. and finally Dir, Bureau of Current Affairs, 1946–51; Information Officer, Technical Assistance Bd, UN (NY and Geneva), 1951–53; Sec., Nat. Enquiry into Liberalising Technical Educn, 1953–55; Editor, Journal of Education, 1955–58; first Head of Sch. Broadcasting, Associated-Rediffusion, 1957–58; Educn Sec., Cambridge Univ. Press, 1958–60; Prof. of Education and Dir of the Inst. of Education, Univ. of Sheffield, 1960–63; Prof. of Education, Univ. of Sussex, 1963–73, Dean, Sch. of Cultural and Community Studies, 1963–71, Chm., Educn Area, and Dir, Sch. of Educn, 1971–73; Prof. of Educn, Univ. of Bristol, 1973–82. Chm., Nat. Assoc. for the Teaching of English, 1963–65; Educational Dir, Pictorial Knowledge, 1968–71. Editor: Pelican Guide to English Literature, 7 Vols, 1954–61; New Pelican Guide to English Literature, 11 Vols, 1982–88; Cambridge Guide to the Arts in Britain, 9 vols, 1988–91; Cambridge Cultural History of Britain, 9 vols, 1992; Editor, Universities Qly, Culture, Education & Society, 1955–86. *Publications:* Discussion Method, 1949; Teachers' Handbook to Human Rights, 1950; Liberal Education in a Technical Age, 1955; Young Readers: Young Writers, 1960; Changing Relationships between Universities and Teachers' Colleges, 1975; Collaboration and Commitment, 1984. *Recreations:* music and living. *Address:* 35 Alma Vale Road, Clifton, Bristol BS8 2HL.

See also R. H. Vignoles.

FORD, Sir Brinsley; *see* Ford, Sir R. B.

FORD, Charles Edmund, FRS 1965; DSc London, FLS, FZS, FIBiol; Member of Medical Research Council's External Staff, Sir William Dunn School of Pathology, Oxford, 1971–78, retired; *b* 24 Oct. 1912; *s* of late Charles Ford and late Ethel Eubornia Ford (*née* Fawcett); *m* 1940, Jean Ella Dowling; four *s. Educ:* Slough Grammar Sch.; King's Coll., University of London. Demonstrator, Dept of Botany, King's Coll., University of London, 1936–38; Geneticist, Rubber Research Scheme, Ceylon, 1938–41 and 1944–45. Lieut Royal Artillery, 1942–43. PSO Dept of Atomic Energy, Min. of Supply, at Chalk River Laboratories, Ont, Canada, 1946–49. Head of Cytogenetics Section, MRC, Radiobiology Unit, Harwell, 1949–71. *Publications:* papers on cytogenetics in scientific journals. *Recreations:* travel, friends. *Address:* 156 Oxford Road, Abingdon, Oxon OX14 2AF. *T:* Abingdon (0235) 520001.

FORD, Colin John; Head of National Museum of Photography, Film and Television, since 1982; lecturer, writer and broadcaster on films, theatre and photography; exhibition organiser; *b* 13 May 1934; *s* of John William and Hélène Martha Ford; *m* 1st, 1961, Margaret Elizabeth Cordwell (marr. diss.); one *s* one *d*; 2nd, 1984, Susan Joan Frances Grayson; one *s. Educ:* Enfield Grammar Sch.; University Coll., Oxford (MA). Manager and Producer, Kidderminster Playhouse, 1958–60; Gen. Man., Western Theatre Ballet, 1960–62; Vis. Lectr in English and Drama, California State Univ. at Long Beach and UCLA (Univ. Extension), 1962–64; Dep. Curator, Nat. Film Archive, 1965–72. Organiser, 30th Anniv. Congress of Internat. Fedn of Film Archives, London, 1968; Dir, Cinema City Exhibn, 1970; Programme Dir, London Shakespeare Film Festival, 1972; Keeper of Film and Photography, Nat. Portrait Gall., 1972–81. Hon. MA Bradford, 1989. *Film:* Masks and Faces, 1966 (BBC TV version, Omnibus, 1968). *Publications:* (with Roy Strong) An Early Victorian Album, 1974, 2nd edn 1977; The Cameron Collection, 1975; (ed) Happy and Glorious: Six Reigns of Royal Photography, 1977; Rediscovering Mrs Cameron, 1979; People in Camera, 1979; (with Brian Harrison) A Hundred Years Ago (Britain in the 1880s), 1983; Portraits (Gallery of World Photography), 1983; (ed) The Story of Popular Photography, 1988; (principal contrib.) Oxford Companion to Film; articles in many jls. *Recreations:* travel, music, small boats. *Address:* National Museum of Photography, Film and Television, Prince's View, Bradford, Yorkshire. *T:* Bradford (0274) 727488.

FORD, Prof. David Frank, PhD; Regius Professor of Divinity and Fellow of Selwyn College, Cambridge University, since 1991; *b* 23 Jan. 1948; *s* of George Ford and Phyllis (*née* Woodman); *m* 1982, Deborah Perrin Hardy, *d* of Rev. Canon Prof. Daniel Wayne Hardy, *qv*; one *s* two *d* (and one *d* decd). *Educ:* Trinity Coll. Dublin (BA (Mod) 1970); St John's Coll., Cambridge (MA 1976; PhD 1977); Yale Univ. (STM 1973); Tübingen Univ. Lectr in Theology, Birmingham Univ., 1976–91. *Publications:* Barth and God's Story: biblical narrative and the theological method of Karl Barth in the Church Dogmatics, 1981; (with Daniel W. Hardy) Jubilate: Theology in praise, 1984; (with Frances M. Young) Meaning and Truth in 2 Corinthians, 1987; (ed) The Modern Theologians, vols I and II, 1989. *Recreations:* gardening, poetry, drama, sports (especially ball games). *Address:* Divinity School, St John's Street, Cambridge CB2 1TW. *T:* Cambridge (0223) 332592.

FORD, Sir David (Robert), KBE 1988 (OBE 1976); LVO 1975; Chief Secretary, Hong Kong, since 1986; *b* 22 Feb. 1935; *s* of William Ewart and Edna Ford; *m* 1st, 1958, Elspeth Anne (*née* Muckart) (marr. diss. 1987); two *s* two *d*; 2nd, 1987, Gillian Petersen (*née* Monsarrat). *Educ:* Tauntons School. National Service, 1953–55; regular commn, RA, 1955; regimental duty, Malta, 1953–58; Lieut, UK, 1958–62; Captain, Commando Regt, 1962–66; active service: Borneo, 1964; Aden, 1966; Staff Coll., Quetta, 1967; seconded to Hong Kong Govt, 1967; retired from Army (Major), 1972. Dep. Dir, Hong Kong Govt Information Service, 1972–74, Dir, 1974–76; Dep. Sec., Govt Secretariat, Hong Kong, 1976; Under Sec., NI Office, 1977–79; Sec. for Information, Hong Kong Govt, 1979–80; Hong Kong Commissioner in London, 1980–81; RCDS, 1982; Dir of Housing, Hong Kong Govt, 1983–84, Sec. for Housing, 1985, Sec. for the Civil Service, 1985–86. *Recreations:* tennis, fishing, photography, theatre. *Address:* c/o Government Secretariat, Hong Kong.

FORD, Rt. Rev. Douglas Albert; Retired Bishop of Saskatoon; *b* 16 July 1917; *s* of Thomas George Ford and Elizabeth Eleanor (Taylor), both English; *m* 1944, Doris Ada (Elborne); two *s* one *d. Educ:* primary and secondary schs, Vancouver; Univ. of British Columbia (BA); Anglican Theological Coll. of BC (LTh); General Synod (BD). Deacon, 1941; Priest, 1942; Curate, St Mary's, Kerrisdale, 1941–42; St George's, Vancouver, 1942–44; Vicar of Strathmore, 1944–49; Rector of: Okotoks, 1949–52; Vermilion, 1952–55; St Michael and All Angels, Calgary, 1955–62; St Augustine, Lethbridge, 1962–66; Dean and Rector, St John's Cath., Saskatoon, 1966–70; Bishop of Saskatoon, 1970–81; Asst Bishop of Calgary, 1981–87; Incumbent of All Saints', Cochrane, dio. Calgary, 1981–85. Hon. DD: Coll. of Emmanuel and St Chad, Saskatoon, 1970; Anglican Theological Coll. of BC, Vancouver, 1971. *Address:* 2212–142 Silvergrove Drive NW, Calgary, Alberta T3B 5H4, Canada.

FORD, Rev. Preb. Douglas William C.; *see* Cleverley Ford.

FORD, Sir Edward (William Spencer), KCB 1967 (CB 1952); KCVO 1957 (MVO 1949); ERD 1987; OStJ 1976; MA; FRSA; DL; Secretary and Registrar of the Order of Merit, since 1975; Secretary to the Pilgrim Trust, 1967–75; *b* 24 July 1910; 4th (twin) *s* of late Very Rev. Lionel G. B. J. Ford, Headmaster of Repton and Harrow and Dean of York, and of Mary Catherine, *d* of Rt Rev. E. S. Talbot, Bishop of Winchester and Hon. Mrs Talbot; *m* 1949, Virginia, *er d* of 1st and last Baron Brand, CMG, and *widow* of John Metcalfe Polk, NY; two *s. Educ:* Eton (King's Schol.); New Coll., Oxford (Open Scholar; Hon. Fellow, 1982). 1st Class Hon. Mods; 2nd Class Lit. Hum. (Greats). Law Student (Harmsworth Scholar) Middle Temple, 1934–35; Tutor to King Farouk of Egypt, 1936–37; called to Bar, Middle Temple, 1937 and practised 1937–39; 2nd Lieut (Supplementary Reserve of Officers) Grenadier Guards, 1936; Lieut 1939; served in France and Belgium, 1939–40 (despatches), and in Tunisia and Italy, 1943–44 (despatches), Brigade Major 10th Infantry and 24th Guards Brigades; Instructor at Staff Coll., Haifa, 1944–45. psc†. Asst Private Secretary to King George VI, 1946–52, and to the Queen, 1952–67; Extra Equerry to the Queen, 1955. Dir, London Life Assoc., 1970–83. Mem., Central Appeals Adv. Cttee, BBC and IBA, 1969–72, 1976–78; Pres., Council, St Christopher's Hospice, Sydenham, 1990– (Mem., 1980–90); Chairman: UK/USA Bicentennial Fellowships Cttee, 1975–80; St John Council for Northamptonshire, 1976–82; Grants Cttee, Historic Churches Preservation Trust, 1977–90. Trustee: York Glaziers' Trust, 1977–; Butler Trust, 1986–90; Hon. Treas., Children's Country Holidays Fund, 1958–73, Vice-Pres., 1973–; Governor, The Ditchley Foundn, 1966–89. Mem. Ct of Assts, Goldsmiths' Co., 1970–, Prime Warden, 1979. High Sheriff Northants 1970, DL 1972. *Address:* Canal House, 23 Blomfield Road, W9 1AD. *T:* 071–286 0028. *Clubs:* White's, Beefsteak, Pratt's, MCC.

FORD, Elbur; *see* Hibbert, Eleanor.

FORD, Air Marshal Sir Geoffrey (Harold), KBE 1979; CB 1974; FEng 1987; Secretary, The Institute of Metals, 1985–88; *b* 6 Aug. 1923; *s* of late Harold Alfred Ford, Lewes,

Sussex; *m* 1951, Valerie, *d* of late Douglas Hart Finn, Salisbury; two *s. Educ:* Lewes County Grammar Sch.; Bristol Univ. (BSc). Served War of 1939–45: commissioned, 1942; 60 Gp, 1943; Italy and Middle East, 1944–46. 90 (Signals) Gp, 1946–49; Bomber Development, 1954–57; Air Ministry, 1958–61; RAF Technical Coll., 1961–62; Min. of Aviation, 1963–64; Chief Signals Officer, RAF Germany, 1965–68; MoD, 1968–72; RCDS, 1972; AO Engineering, Strike Command, 1973–76; Dir-Gen. Engineering and Supply Management, RAF, 1976–78; Chief Engr (RAF), 1978–81. Dir, The Metals Soc., 1981–84. FIEE (Council, 1977–82). *Address:* c/o Barclays Bank, Lewes, East Sussex BN7 2JP. *Club:* Royal Air Force.

FORD, George Johnson, DL; Member, Cheshire County Council, 1962–87 (Chairman, 1976–82); *b* 13 March 1916; *s* of James and Esther Ford; *m* 1941, Nora Helen Brocklehurst; three *s* one *d. Educ:* Chester Coll. Qualified estate agent, 1938. FAI 1938. Member, Runcorn RDC, 1953 (Chm., 1962); Mem. Bd, Warrington and Runcorn Develt Corp., 1981–87 (Runcorn Develt Corp., 1964–81). Mem., West Mercia Cttee, Nat. Trust, 1982. Pres., Frodsham Conservative Assoc., 1962–; Vice Pres., Eddisbury Parly Div., 1984. DL Cheshire, 1979. *Recreations:* horse racing, music and drama. *Address:* Manley Old Hall, Manley, via Warrington, Cheshire WA6 9EA. *T:* Manley (09284) 254. *Club:* City (Chester).

FORD, Gerald Rudolph; President of the United States of America, Aug. 1974–Jan. 1977; lawyer; company director; *b* Omaha, Nebraska, 14 July 1913; (adopted) *s* of Gerald R. Ford and Dorothy Gardner; *m* 1948, Elizabeth (*née* Bloomer); three *s* one *d. Educ:* South High Sch., Grand Rapids; Univ. of Michigan (BA); Law Sch., Yale Univ. (LLB). Served War: US Navy (Carriers), 1942–46. Partner in law firm of Ford and Buchen, 1941–42; Member, law firm of Butterfield, Keeney and Amberg, 1947–49; subseq. with Amberg, Law and Buchen. Member US House of Representatives for Michigan 5th District, 1948–73; Member: Appropriations Cttee, 1951; Dept of Defense Sub-Cttee, etc; House Minority Leader, Republican Party, 1965–73; Vice President of the United States, Dec. 1973–Aug. 1974. Attended Interparly Union meetings in Europe; Mem. US-Canadian Interparly Gp. Director: IDS Mutual Funds, Inc.; Nova Pharmaceutical Corp.; Shearson Lehman Hutton, Inc.; Tesoro Petroleum Corp.; Primerica Corp.; Texas Commerce Bancshares. Holds Amer. Pol. Sci. Assoc.'s Distinguished Congressional Service Award, 1961; several hon. degrees. Delta Kappa Epsilon, Phi Delta Phi. *Publications:* (with John R. Stiles) Portrait of an Assassin, 1965; A Time to Heal, 1979; Humor and the Presidency, 1987. *Recreations:* outdoor sports (formerly football), ski-ing, tennis, golf. *Address:* PO Box 927, Rancho Mirage, Calif 92270, USA.

FORD, Dr Gillian Rachel, (Mrs N. I. MacKenzie), CB 1981; FRCP, FFPHM; Medical Director, Marie Curie Memorial Foundation, since 1990; *b* 18 March 1934; *d* of Cecil Ford and Grace Ford; *m* 1988, Prof. Norman I. MacKenzie. *Educ:* Clarendon Sch., Abergele; St Hugh's Coll., Oxford; St Thomas' Hosp., London. MA, BM, BCh; FFCM 1976; FRCP 1985. Junior hospital posts, St Thomas', Oxford, Reading, 1959–64; Medical Officer, Min. of Health, 1965, Sen. Med. Officer, 1968; SPMO, 1974–77, Dep. Chief MO (Dep. Sec.), 1977–89, DHSS, later Dept of Health; on secondment as Dir of Studies, St Christopher's Hospice, Sydenham, 1985–88. *Publications:* papers on health services research, terminal care and other health subjects in Portfolio for Health, Vol. 1 (Nuffield Provincial Hospitals Trust) and other med. jls. *Recreations:* music, ski-ing, tennis, children's literature. *Address:* 9 Ryecotes Mead, Dulwich Common, SE21. *T:* 081–693 6576.

FORD, Glyn; *see* Ford, J. G.

FORD, Harold Frank; Sheriff at Perth, 1971–80 (Sheriff Substitute at Forfar and Arbroath, 1951–71); *b* 17 May 1915; *s* of Sir Patrick Ford, 1st Bt, and Jessie Hamilton (*d* 1962), *d* of Henry Field, WS; *m* 1948, Lucy Mary, *d* of late Sheriff J. R. Wardlaw Burnet, KC; one *s* three *d. Educ:* Winchester Coll.; University Coll., Oxford (BA); Edinburgh Univ. (LLB). War service with Lothians and Border Yeomanry (Prisoner of War, 1940–45): Hon. Capt. Scottish Bar, 1945; Legal Adviser to UNRRA and IRO in British Zone of Germany, 1947. *Recreations:* golf, gardening. *Address:* Millhill, Meikleour, Perthshire PH2 6EF. *T:* Caputh (073871) 311. *Clubs:* New (Edinburgh); Honourable Company of Edinburgh Golfers, Royal Perth Golfing Society.

See also Sir A. R. Ford, Bt.

FORD, Prof. Sir Hugh, Kt 1975; FRS 1967; FEng 1977; Professor of Mechanical Engineering, 1969–80, Professor Emeritus, since 1980, Pro-Rector, 1978–80, University of London (Imperial College of Science and Technology); Chairman, Sir Hugh Ford & Associates Ltd, since 1982; Director: Air Liquide UK Ltd, since 1979; International Dynamics (formerly RD Projects) Ltd, since 1982; Ford & Dain Research Ltd, since 1972; *b* 16 July 1913; *s* of Arthur and Constance Ford; *m* 1942, Wynyard, *d* of Major F. B. Scholfield; two *d. Educ:* Northampton Sch.; City and Guilds Coll., Univ. of London. DSc (Eng); PhD. Practical trng at GWR Locomotive Works, 1931–36; researches into heat transfer, 1936–39; R&D Engrg, Imperial Chemical Industries, Northwich, 1939–42; Chief Engr, Technical Dept, British Iron and Steel Fedn, 1942–45, then Head of Mechanical Working Div., British Iron and Steel Research Assoc., 1945–47; Reader in Applied Mechanics, Univ. of London (Imp. Coll. of Science and Technology), 1948–51, Prof., 1951–69; Head of Dept of Mech. Engineering, 1965–78. Mem. Bd of Governors, Imperial Coll., 1982–89. Technical Dir, Davy-Ashmore Group, 1968–71; Director: Alfred Herbert Ltd, 1972–79; Ricardo Consulting Engrs Ltd, 1980–88; Chm., Adv. Bd, Prudential Portfolio Managers, 1985–88; Mem., Adv. Bd, Brown and Root (UK), 1983–. John Player Lectr, IMechE, 1973. First Pres., Inst. of Metals, 1985–87 (merger of Inst. of Metallurgists and Metals Soc.); President: Section 6, British Assoc., 1975–76; Welding Inst., 1983–85; Fellow, 1977, Vice-Pres., 1981–84, Fellowship of Engineering; Member: Council, IMechE (Vice-Pres., 1972, 1975, Sen. Vice-Pres., 1976, Pres., 1977–78); SRC, 1968–72 (Chm. Engineering Bd); Council, Royal Soc., 1973–74; ARC, 1976–81. FICE; Whitworth Schol.; FCGI; FIC 1982; Sen. Fellow, RCA, 1987. Hon. MASME, 1980; Hon. FIMechE 1984; Hon. FIChemE 1987. Hon. DSc: Salford, 1976; QUB, 1977; Aston, 1978; Bath, 1978; Sheffield, 1984; Sussex, 1990. Thomas Hawksley Gold Medallist, IMechE, 1948, for researches into rolling of metals; Robertson Medal, Inst. of Metals, 1954; James Alfred Ewing Gold Medal, ICE, 1982; James Watt Internat. Gold Medal, 1985. *Publications:* Advanced Mechanics of Materials, 1963; papers to Royal Soc., IMechE, Iron and Steel Inst., Inst. of Metals, foreign societies, etc. *Recreations:* gardening, music, model engineering. *Address:* 18 Shrewsbury House, Cheyne Walk, SW3; Shamley Cottage, Stroud Lane, Shamley Green, Surrey. *Club:* Athenæum.

FORD, James Allan, CB 1978; MC 1946; *b* 10 June 1920; 2nd *s* of Douglas Ford and Margaret Duncan (*née* Allan); *m* 1948, Isobel Dunnett; one *s* one *d. Educ:* Royal High School, Edinburgh; University of Edinburgh. Served 1940–46, Capt. Royal Scots. Entered Civil Service, 1938; Asst Sec., Dept of Agriculture and Fisheries for Scotland, 1958; Registrar Gen. for Scotland, 1966–69; Principal Establishment Officer, Scottish Office, 1969–79. A Trustee, Nat. Lib. of Scotland, 1981–. *Publications:* The Brave White Flag, 1961; Season of Escape, 1963; A Statue for a Public Place, 1965; A Judge of Men, 1968; The Mouth of Truth, 1972. *Address:* 29 Lady Road, Edinburgh EH16 5PA. *T:* 031–667 4489. *Clubs:* Royal Scots, Scottish Arts (Edinburgh).

FORD, (James) Glyn; Member (Lab) Greater Manchester East, European Parliament, since 1984; Leader, European Parliamentary Labour Party, since 1989; *b* 28 Jan. 1950; *s* of late Ernest Benjamin Ford and Matilda Alberta Ford (*née* James); *m* 1973, Hazel Nancy Mahy (separated); one *d*. *Educ:* Marling; Reading Univ. (BSc Geol. with Soil Sci.); UCL (MSc Marine Earth Sci.); Manchester Univ. Undergraduate Apprentice, BAC, 1967–68; Course Tutor in Oceanography, Open Univ., 1976–78; Teaching Asst, UMIST, 1977–78; Res. Fellow, Sussex Univ., 1978–79; Manchester University: Res. Asst, 1976–77; Res. Fellow, 1979; Lectr, 1979–80; Sen. Res. Fellow, Prog. of Policy Res. in Engrg Sci. and Technol., 1980–84; Hon. Vis. Res. Fellow, 1984–. Vis. Prof., Tokyo Univ., 1983. Tameside Borough Council: Mem., 1978–86; Chairman: Environmental Health and Control Cttee, 1979–80; Educn Services Cttee, 1980–85. Mem., Lab Party NEC, 1989– (Mem., Sci. and Technol. Policy Sub-Cttee, 1981–83). European Parliament: Chm., Cttee of Inquiry into Growth of Racism and Fascism in Europe, 1984–86; Vice-Chm., Sub-Cttee on Security and Disarmament, 1987–89; first Vice-Pres., Socialist Group, 1989–. Contested (Lab), Hazel Grove, 1987. *Publications:* (with C. Niblett and L. Walker) The Future for Ocean Technology, 1987; contribs to learned jls on sci. and technol. policy. *Recreations:* Japan, travel, writing. *Address:* 46 Stanford Road, Mossley, Lancs OL5 0BE. *T:* (home) Mossley (0457) 837892; (office) Mossley (0457) 836276. *Clubs:* Park Bridge Working Mens Institute (Ashton-under-Lyne); Cheadle Labour.

FORD, (John) Anthony; Director, Crafts Council, since 1988 (Deputy Director, 1985–88); *b* 28 April 1938; *s* of Frank Everatt Ford and Dorothy Mary Ford; *m* 1st, 1963, Caroline Rosemary Wharrad (marr. diss.); one *d*; 2nd, 1984, Sandra Edith Williams. *Educ:* Epsom Coll.; St Edmund's Hall, Oxford (MA). Admitted Solicitor, 1963. Dir, Art Services Grants, 1974–79; Crafts Council, 1979–. Vice-Pres. for Europe, World Crafts Council, 1987–. Mem., Fabric Cttee, Rochester Cathedral, 1990. FRSA 1989. *Recreations:* theatre, cinema. *Address:* Crafts Council, 44a Pentonville Road, Islington, N1. *T:* 071–278 7700.

FORD, Sir John (Archibald), KCMG 1977 (CMG 1967); MC 1945; HM Diplomatic Service, retired; *b* 19 Feb. 1922; *s* of Ronald Mylne Ford and Margaret Jesse Coghill, Newcastle-under-Lyme, Staffs; *m* 1956, Emaline Burnette (*d* 1989), Leesville, Virginia; two *d*. *Educ:* St Michael's Coll., Tenbury; Sedbergh Sch., Yorks; Oriel Coll., Oxford. Served in Royal Artillery, 1942–46 (temp. Major); demobilised, 1947. Joined Foreign (subseq. Diplomatic) Service, 1947. Third Sec., British Legation, Budapest, 1947–49; Third Sec. and a Resident Clerk, FO, 1949–52; Private Sec. to Permanent Under-Sec. of State, FO, 1952–54; HM Consul, San Francisco, 1954–56; seconded to HM Treasury, 1956–59; attended Course at Administrative Staff Coll., 1959; First Sec. and Head of Chancery, British Residency, Bahrain, 1959–61; Asst, FO Personnel Dept, 1961–63; Asst, FO Establishment and Organisation Dept, 1963; Head of Diplomatic Service Establishment and Organisation Dept, 1964–66; Counsellor (Commercial), Rome, 1966–70; Asst Under-Sec., FCO, 1970–71; Consul-Gen., New York, and Dir-Gen., British Trade Develt in USA, 1971–75; Ambassador to Indonesia, 1975–78; British High Comr in Canada, 1978–81. Lay Administrator, Guildford Cathedral, 1982–84. Mem., Exec. Cttee, VSO, 1982–87; Chm. of Trustees, Voluntary and Christian Service, 1985–88; Chm., AIDS Care Educn and Trng, 1989–; Trustee, World in Need, 1987–. *Publication:* Honest to Christ, 1988. *Recreations:* walking, gardening, sailing. *Address:* Loquats, Guildown, Guildford, Surrey; Admiral 633, 8750 South Ocean Drive, Jensen Beach, Florida 34957, USA. *Clubs:* Farmers'; Vanbrugh (Guildford).

FORD, (John) Peter, CBE 1969; Chairman and Managing Director, International Joint Ventures Ltd; *b* 20 Feb. 1912; *s* of Ernest and Muriel Ford; *m* 1939, Phoebe Seys, *d* of Herbert McGregor Wood, FRIBA; one *s* two *d*. *Educ:* Wrekin Coll.; Gonville and Caius Coll., Cambridge. BA (Hons Nat. Sci. Tripos) 1934; MA Cantab 1937. Cambridge Univ. Air Sqdn, 1932–35 (Pilot's A Licence, 1933–). Air Ministry (subsequently FO, RAFVR), 1939–40; Coventry Gauge and Tool Co. Ltd (Asst to Chm.), 1941–45; Gen. Man., Brit. Engineers Small Tools and Equipment Co. Ltd, and Gen. Man. Scientific Exports (Gt Brit.) Ltd, 1945–48; Man. Dir, Brush Export Ltd, Associated British Oil Engines (Export) Ltd and National Oil Engines (Export) Ltd, and Dir of other associated cos of The Brush Group, 1949–55; Dir, Associated British Engineering Ltd and subsidiaries, 1957–58; Man. Dir, Coventry Climax International Ltd, 1958–63; Director: Plessey Overseas Ltd, 1963–70; Bryant & May (Latin America) Ltd, 1970–73; Chm., Metra Martech Ltd, 1988–. Chm. Institute of Export, 1954–56, 1965–67; President: Soc. of Commercial Accountants, 1970–74 (Vice-Pres., 1956–70); Soc. of Company and Commercial Accountants, 1974–75; Member: Council, London Chamber of Commerce, 1951–72 (Dep. Chm., 1970–72; Vice-Pres., 1972–); London Ct of Arbitration, 1970–73; FBI, Overseas Trade Policy Cttee, 1952–63; Council, British Internal Combustion Engine Manufacturers Assoc., 1953–55; BNEC Cttee for Exports to Latin America, 1964–71 (Chm. 1968–71); NEDO Cttee for Movement of Exports, 1972–75; British Overseas Trade Adv. Council, 1975–82. Chm., British Shippers' Council, 1972–75 (Dep. Chm., 1971–72). Chm., British Mexican Soc., 1973–77; Vice-Pres., Hispanic and Luso Brazilian Council, 1980–. Freeman of City of London, 1945; Mem. Ct of Assistants, Ironmongers' Co. (Master, 1981); Governor: Wrekin Coll., 1953–57; Oversea Service Coll., 1966–86. CEng, CIMechE, CIMarE, MIEE. Order of Rio Branco (Brazil), 1977. *Publications:* contributor to technical press and broadcaster on international trade subjects. *Recreations:* Athletics (Cambridge Univ. and Internat. Teams, 1932–35; held various county championships, 1932–37; Hon. Treas, 1947–58, Vice-Pres., 1990–, Achilles Club; Pres., London Athletic Club, 1964–66). *Address:* 40 Fairacres, Roehampton Lane, SW15 5LX. *T:* 081–876 2146. *Clubs:* United Oxford & Cambridge University, City Livery, MCC; Hawks (Cambridge).

FORD, Joseph Francis, CMG 1960; OBE 1949; HM Diplomatic Service, retired 1970; *b* 11 Oct. 1912; *s* of J. W. Ford, Chesterfield, Derbs; *m* 1938, Mary Margaret Ford (*née* Taylor); two *s*. *Educ:* Chesterfield Grammar Sch.; Emmanuel Coll., Cambridge (BA). BA (Hons) Modern Chinese, London, 1958. Appointed probationer Vice-Consul to Peking, Nov. 1935; served at Shanghai, Chungking, Washington, Peking, Hanoi, New Orleans and Saigon; Dir, Res. Dept, FCO (formerly Jt Res. Dept, FO/CO), 1967–70; Director: Univs Service Centre, Hong Kong, 1970–72; Great Britain-China Centre, London, 1974–78; Chm., China Soc., 1982–85. *Address:* 10 Raymond Road, Wimbledon, SW19.

FORD, Peter; *see* Ford, J. P.

FORD, Peter; His Honour Judge Ford; a Circuit Judge, since 1990; *b* 30 Sept. 1930; *s* of late Rev. Cecil Henry Ford and Gwyneth Kathleen Ford (*née* Hall); *m* 1961, Jenifer Dekenah, Cape Town; one *d*. *Educ:* Ellesmere Coll.; Univ. of Manchester (LLB). Called to the Bar, Gray's Inn, 1952. In practice as barrister, Northern Circuit, 1952–55; legal advr in industry, 1956–59; in practice as barrister, Patent Bar, 1959–79; Mem., Bds of Appeal, European Patent Office, Munich, 1979–90; Chm., Legal Bd of Appeal, 1985–90; nominated Judge of Patents County Court, 1990. Reader in C of E, 1955–. MRI 1958; FRSA 1953. *Publications:* various articles in legal jls. *Recreations:* music, reading (theology, science), foreign languages, travel. *Address:* The Patents County Court, The Law Courts, Lordship Lane, Wood Green, N22 6LF. *T:* 081–881 1400.

FORD, Peter George Tipping; Secretary, Medical Protection Society, 1983–90; *b* 18 Sept. 1931; *s* of Raymond Eustace Ford, *qv*; *m* 1958, Nancy Elizabeth Procter; four *d*. *Educ:* Epsom College; St Bartholomew's Hosp. Med. Coll., Univ. of London (MB, BS); MRCGP, DObst RCOG. Nat. Service, RAMC, 1957–59. Gen. practice, Hythe, 1960–68; Asst Sec., Med. Protection Soc., 1968–72, Dep. Sec., 1972–83. Sec., Jt Co-ordinating Cttee, UK Defence Organizations, 1985–89. Mem., Soc. of Apothecaries. FRSM. Medal of Honour, Med. Defence Soc. of Queensland, 1984. *Publications:* contribs to medico-legal periodicals. *Recreations:* baroque choral music, gardening, bridge. *Address:* Braeside Cottage, Cannongate Road, Hythe, Kent CT21 5PT. *T:* Hythe (Kent) (0303) 67896. *Club:* Carlton.

FORD, Raymond Eustace, CBE 1963; MD, MRCP; retired as Principal Medical Officer i/c Regional Medical Service, Ministry of Health (1946–63); *b* 24 April 1898; *s* of Rev. George Ford; *m* 1924, Elsie (*née* Tipping); two *s* one *d*. *Educ:* Sheffield Univ. *Recreations:* crosswords and the garden. *Address:* Philbeach, Hythe, Kent CT21 5UE.
See also P. G. T. Ford.

FORD, Sir (Richard) Brinsley, Kt 1984; CBE 1978; FSA; Member of National Art-Collections Fund since 1927 (Member: Executive Committee 1960–88; Vice-Chairman, 1974–75, Chairman 1975–80; Advisory Panel, since 1988); *b* 10 June 1908; *e s* of late Capt. Richard Ford, Rifle Brigade, and Rosamund, *d* of Sir John Ramsden, 5th Bt; *m* 1937, Joan, *d* of late Capt. Geoffrey Vyvyan; two *s* one *d*. *Educ:* Eton; Trinity Coll., Oxford. Joined TA 1939; served for one year as Troop Sergeant Major, RA; commissioned 1941, and transferred to Intelligence Corps (Major 1945). Selected works for Arts Council Festival of Britain and Coronation Exhibitions; a Trustee of the National Gallery, 1954–61; Trustee, Watts Gall., Compton, 1955– (Chm., 1974–84); great-grandson of Richard Ford (1796–1858) who wrote the Handbook for Spain; owner of the Ford Collection of Richard Wilsons. Dir, Burlington Magazine, 1952–86, Trustee, 1988–. Member: Soc. of Dilettanti, 1952– (Sec., 1972–88); Georgian Gp, from foundn, 1937–. Member: Council, Byam Shaw Sch., 1957–73; Exec. Cttee, City and Guilds of London Art Sch., 1976–. President: St Marylebone Soc., 1974–77; Walpole Soc., 1986–; Vice-Pres., Anglo-Spanish Soc. Patron, Attingham Summer Sch. Trust, 1984–. Jt Hon. Adviser on Paintings to Nat. Trust, 1980 (Chm., Nat. Trust Foundn for Art Cttee, 1986–90); Hon. Fellow, Royal Acad., 1981; Companion, NEAC, 1988. Hon. Fellow, Ateneo Veneto, 1988; Corresponding Member: Hispanic Soc. of Amer., 1963; Royal Acad. of San Fernando, Madrid, 1980. Hon. LLD Exeter, 1990. Order of Isabel la Católica of Spain, First Class A, 1986; Officer, Belgian Order of Leopold II, 1945; US Bronze Star, 1946; Médaille d'Argent de la Reconnaissance Française, 1947. *Publications:* The Drawings of Richard Wilson, 1951; contributor to the Burlington Magazine and Apollo. *Address:* 14 Wyndham Place, Bryanston Square, W1H 1AQ. *T:* 071–723 0826. *Club:* Brooks's.

FORD, Gen. Sir Robert (Cyril), GCB 1981 (KCB 1977; CB 1973); CBE 1971 (MBE 1958); Vice-Chairman, Commonwealth War Graves Commission, since 1989 (Commissioner, since 1981); *b* 29 Dec. 1923; *s* of late John Stranger Ford and Gladys Ford, Yealmpton, Devon; *m* 1949, Jean Claudia Pendlebury, *d* of late Gp Capt. Claude Pendlebury, MC, TD, FLAS, FRICS, and Muriel Pendlebury, Yelverton, Devon; one *s*. *Educ:* Musgrave's. War of 1939–45: commissioned into 4th/7th Royal Dragoon Guards, from Sandhurst, 1943; served with Regt throughout NW European campaign, 1944–45 (despatches) and in Egypt and Palestine, 1947–48 (despatches). Instructor, Mons OCS, 1949–50; Training Officer, Scottish Horse (TA), 1952–54; Staff Coll., Camberley, 1955; GSO 2 Mil. Ops, War Office, 1956–57; Sqdn Ldr 4/7 RDG, 1958–59; Bde Major, 20th Armoured Bde, 1960–61; Brevet Lt-Col, 1962; Sqdn Ldr, 4/7 RDG, 1962–63; GSO1 to Chief of Defence Staff, 1964–65; commanded 4/7 RDG in S Arabia and N Ireland, 1966–67; Comdr, 7th Armd Bde, 1968–69; Principal Staff Officer to Chief of Defence Staff, 1970–71; Cmdr Land Forces, N Ireland, 1971–73; Comdt, RMA Sandhurst, 1973–76; Military Secretary, 1976–78; Adjutant-General, 1978–81; ADC General to the Queen, 1980–81; Governor, Royal Hosp., Chelsea, 1981–87. Colonel Commandant: RAC, 1980–82; SAS Regt, 1980–85; Col 4th/7th Royal Dragoon Gds, 1984–88. President: Services Kinema Corp., 1978–81; Army Boxing Assoc., 1978–81. Chm., 1981–87, and Pres., 1986–, Army Benevolent Fund; Chm., Royal Cambridge Home for Soldiers' Widows, 1981–87; Nat. Pres., Forces Help Soc. and Lord Roberts Workshops, 1981–91. Governor, Corps of Commissionaires, 1981–. Freeman, City of London, 1981. CBIM. *Recreations:* cricket, tennis, war studies. *Address:* c/o National Westminster Bank, 45 Park Street, Camberley, Surrey GU15 3PA. *Clubs:* Cavalry and Guards, MCC.

FORD, Robert Stanley; HM Diplomatic Service, retired; *b* 30 Nov. 1929; *s* of late Robert Hempstead Ford and of Janet Mabel Elliot; *m* 1957, Cynthia Valerie Arscott, *d* of late Ronald Prowse Arscott, Bexhill-on-Sea, Sussex; one *s* two *d*. *Educ:* Daniel Stewart's Coll., Edinburgh; Univ. of Edinburgh (MA). Joined HM Diplomatic Service, 1949; HM Forces, 1949; FCO, 1951; Third Sec., Moscow, 1955; Consul, Dakar, 1958; FCO, 1959; Information Officer, NY, 1963; First Sec., Managua, 1965; Consul, Naples, 1968; FCO, 1972; Consul-Gen., Madrid, 1978; FCO, 1982; Counsellor (Admin), Paris, 1984–86. *Recreations:* music, photography, gardening, travel. *Address:* 20 Heatherbank, Haywards Heath, W Sussex RH16 1HY. *T:* Haywards Heath (0444) 455321.

FORD, Robert Webster, CBE 1982; HM Diplomatic Service, retired; *b* 27 March 1923; *s* of late Robert Ford; *m* 1956, Monica Florence Tebbett; two *s*. *Educ:* Alleyne's Sch. Served RAF, 1939–45. Served with British Mission, Lhasa, Tibet and Political Agency in Sikkim and Bhutan, 1945–47; joined Tibetan Govt Service, 1947; advised on and installed Tibet's first radio communication system and broadcasting stn; travelled extensively in Northern and Eastern Tibet, 1947–50; taken prisoner during Chinese Occupation of Tibet, 1950; imprisoned in China, 1950–55; free-lance writer and broadcaster on Chinese and Tibetan affairs, 1955; entered Foreign Service, 1956; 2nd Sec., Saigon, 1957–58; 1st Sec. (Information), Djakarta, 1959; Washington, 1960–62; FO, 1962–67; Consul-Gen., Tangier, 1967–70; Counsellor, 1970; Consul-General; Luanda, 1970–74; Bordeaux, 1974–78; Gothenburg, 1978–80; Geneva, 1980–83. *Publication:* Captured in Tibet, 1956, repr. 1990. *Recreations:* ski-ing, gardening, travelling. *Address:* Cedar Garth, Latimer Road, Monken Hadley, Barnet, Herts EN5 5NU. *Clubs:* Commonwealth Trust, Royal Geographical Society.

FORD, Roy Arthur, MA; Director of Visits, Canterbury Cathedral, 1986–90; *b* 10 May 1925; *s* of Arthur Ford and Minnie Elizabeth Ford; *m* 1965, Christine Margaret Moore; two *s*. *Educ:* Collyer's Sch., Horsham; Corpus Christi Coll., Cambridge (Scholar; 1st Cl. Pts I and II, History Tripos; BA 1949, MA 1971). Asst Master: Uppingham Sch., 1951–54; Tonbridge Sch., 1954–66; Uppingham Sch., (also Head of History and Sixth Form Master), 1966–71; Headmaster: Southwell Minster Grammar Sch., 1971–75; King's Sch., Rochester, 1975–86. *Recreations:* walking, travel, music. *Address:* 28 West Street, Faversham, Kent ME13 7JG. *T:* Faversham (0795) 537614.

FORD, Rev. Wilfred Franklin, CMG 1974; *b* 9 Jan. 1920; *s* of Harold Franklin Ford and Sarah Elizabeth Ford; *m* 1st, 1942, Joan Mary Holland (*d* 1981); three *d*; 2nd, 1982, Hilda Mary Astley. *Educ:* Auckland Univ., NZ (BA); Trinity Theological Coll., NZ. Served War, NZ Army, 1942–44. Entered Methodist Ministry, 1945; Dir, Christian Educn, Methodist Church of NZ, 1956–68; President: Methodist Church of NZ, 1971; NZ Marriage Guidance Council, 1981–84; Life Mem., Wellington Marriage Guidance

Council. *Publications:* contribs to NZ and internat. jls, on Christian educn. *Recreations:* gardening, reading, bowls. *Address:* 122 Totara Drive, Hamilton, New Zealand.

FORD-ROBERTSON, Francis Calder, OBE 1959; *b* 19 March 1901; 3rd *s* of Dr W. Ford Robertson, MD, and Marion Elam; *m* 1928, Cynthia Mary de Courcy Ireland (*d* 1977); two *s*; *m* 1977, Nora Aline de Courcy Chapman (*née* Ireland). *Educ:* Edinburgh Academy; Edinburgh Univ. Appointed to Indian Forest Service as probationer, 1923; IFS, 1924–47; Director: Commonwealth Forestry Bureau, Oxford, 1947–64; Dir-Editor, Multilingual Forestry Terminology Project, at Commonwealth Forestry Inst., Oxford and Washington, DC, USA, 1964–70. Hon. Mem., Soc. of American Foresters, 1970. Hon. MA Oxford, 1952. *Publications:* Our Forests, 1934; (ed) The Terminology of Forest Science, Technology, Practice and Products (English lang. version), 1971; also sundry scientific, mainly bibliographical, articles. *Recreations:* choral singing, gardening, local history and archaeology, Oxford guiding. *Address:* 17 Emden House, Barton Lane, Headington, Oxford. *T:* Oxford (0865) 62431.

FORDE, Hon. Harold McDonald, MD; consultant physician; High Commissioner for Barbados in UK, 1984–86; *b* 10 Jan. 1916; *s* of Gertrude and William McDonald Forde; *m* 1949, Alice Leslie; one *s* two *d*. *Educ:* Harrison College, Barbados; University College London; University College Hospital (MB BS 1942; MD); DPH, DTM&H. MO, Colonial Med. Service, Belize, 1947–52; First Lectr, Dept. of Medicine, Univ. of West Indies, Jamaica, 1952–57; Consultant Physician, Barbados, 1957–78; Med. Supt, Barbados Gen. Hosp., 1961–64; Senior Lectr, Dept of Medicine, Univ. of West Indies, 1967–78 (Associate Dean, 1967–73); Mem. Senate, Univ. of W Indies, 1973–75; Chief Med. Officer, Commonwealth of Bahamas, 1978–79; Consultant Physician, Barbados, 1980–84; Chief Med. Officer, Life of Barbados, 1973–84. Mem. Privy Council, Barbados, 1980–85; Senior Fellow, Commonwealth Fund, 1976; Tech. Expert, Commonwealth Fund for Tech Co-Opn, 1978–79; Governor, Commonwealth Foundn, 1984. Hon. Vice-President: West India Cttee; Commonwealth Inst. Past Dist Gov., Lions Clubs Internat., 1973 (Life Mem., 1988). Hon. FRCPE 1972; Hon. FACP 1975. Silver Jubilee Medal, 1977. *Publications:* articles in WI med. jls. *Recreations:* cricket, soccer, bridge, chess, athletics, music. *Address:* Bethesda Medical Centre, Black Rock, St Michael, Barbados, WI. *Club:* Commonwealth Trust.

FORDER, Ven. Charles Robert; Archdeacon Emeritus, Diocese of York, since 1974; *b* 6 Jan. 1907; *s* of late Henry Forder, Worstead, Norfolk; *m* 1933, Myra, *d* of late Harry Peat, Leeds; no *c*. *Educ:* Paston Sch., North Walsham; Christ's Coll. and Ridley Hall, Cambridge. Exhibitioner of Christ's Coll. and Prizeman, 1926; 1st Cl. Math. Trip. Part I, 1926, BA (Sen. Opt. Part II) 1928, MA 1932; Ridley Hall, 1928. Curate: St Peter's, Hunslet Moor, 1930–33; Burley, 1933–34; Vicar: Holy Trinity, Wibsey, 1934–40; St Clement's, Bradford, 1940–47; Organising Sec., Bradford Church Forward Movement Appeal, 1945–47; Vicar of Drypool, 1947–55; Rector of Routh and Vicar of Wawne, 1955–57; Canon, and Prebendary of Fenton, York Minster, 1957–76; Rector of Sutton-on-Derwent, 1957–63; Rector of Holy Trinity, Micklegate, York, 1963–66; Archdeacon of York, 1957–72. Chaplain to HM Prison, Hull, 1950–53; Proctor in Convocation, 1954–72; Organising Sec., Diocesan Appeal, 1955–76; Church Comr, 1958–73. *Publications:* A History of the Paston Grammar School, 1934, 2nd edn 1975; The Parish Priest at Work, 1947; Synods in Action, 1970; Churchwardens in Church and Parish, 1976; contrib. to Encyclopædia Britannica. *Recreations:* reading and writing. *Address:* Dulverton Hall, St Martin's Square, Scarborough YO11 2DQ. *T:* Scarborough (0723) 373082.

FORDER, Kenneth John; Registrar of the Architects Registration Council of the United Kingdom (established under Architects Registration Acts 1931 to 1969), 1977–90; *b* 11 June 1925; *s* of late James A. Forder and Elizabeth Forder (*née* Hammond); *m* 1948, Dorothy Margôt Burles; two *d*. *Educ:* Westcliff Sch.; Hertford Coll., Oxford (MA); Queen's Coll., Cambridge. Called to Bar, Gray's Inn, 1963. RAF, Flt Lieut, Aircrew Navigator, 1943–47. District Officer, N Rhodesia, 1951–61; District Commissioner, N Rhodesia, 1962–64; General Secretary, National Federation of Meat Traders, 1964–73; Bar Practice, 1973–77. Freeman of the City of London, 1966. *Recreations:* tennis, bridge, chess. *Address:* Napier Cottage, Napier Avenue, SW6 3NJ. *T:* 071–736 3958. *Club:* Hurlingham.

FORDHAM, John Jeremy; His Honour Judge Fordham; a Circuit Judge, since 1986; *b* 18 April 1933; *s* of John Hampden Fordham, CBE and Rowena Langran; *m* 1962, Rose Anita (*née* Brandon), *d* of Philip Brandon, Wellington, New Zealand; one *s* one *d*. *Educ:* Gresham's Sch.; Univ. of New Zealand. LLB (NZ). Merchant Navy, 1950–55 (2nd Mate (Foreign Going) Cert.); labourer, fireman etc, 1955–60; Barrister and Solicitor, New Zealand, 1960–64; called to Bar, Inner Temple, 1965; practised 1965–71, 1976–78; Sen. Magistrate, Gilbert and Ellice Islands, 1971–75; a Metropolitan Stipendiary Magistrate, 1978–86; a Recorder, 1986. *Recreations:* boats, games. *Address:* 9 King's Bench Walk, Temple, EC4. *T:* 071–353 5638. *Club:* Garrick.

FOREMAN, Michael; RDI 1985; AGI; writer and illustrator; *b* 21 March 1938; *s* of Walter and Gladys Mary Foreman; *m* 1st, 1959, Janet Charters (marr. diss. 1966); one *s*; 2nd, 1980, Louise Phillips; two *s*. *Educ:* Notley Road Secondary Modern Sch., Lowestoft; Royal College of Art, London (ARCA 1st Cl. Hons and Silver Medal). Freelance, 1963–; six animated films produced, 1967–68. Awarded Aigle d'Argent, Festival International du Livre, Nice, 1972; (jtly) Kurt Maschler Award, 1982; Graphics Prize, Bologna, 1982; Kate Greenaway Medal, Library Assoc., 1983 and 1989. *Publications:* author and illustrator: The Perfect Present, 1966; The Two Giants, 1966; The Great Sleigh Robbery, 1968; Horatio, 1969; Moose, 1971; Dinosaurs and all that Rubbish, 1972 (Francis Williams Prize, 1972); War and Peas, 1974; All The King's Horses, 1976; Panda and his Voyage of Discovery, 1977 (Francis Williams Prize, 1977); Trick a Tracker, 1980; Panda and the Odd Lion, 1981; Land of Dreams, 1982; Panda and the Bunyips, 1984; Cat and Canary, 1984; Panda and the Bushfire, 1986; Ben's Box, 1986; Ben's Baby, 1987; The Angel and the Wild Animal, 1988; War Boy (autobiog.), 1989; Oneworld, 1990; World of Fairytales, 1990; illustrator of many books by other authors. *Recreations:* football, travelling. *Address:* 5 Church Gate, SW6. *Club:* Chelsea Arts.

FOREMAN, Sir Philip (Frank), Kt 1981; CBE 1972; FEng, FIMechE, FIProdE, CBIM; DL; Member Council, British Standards Institution, since 1986 (Chairman, 1988–91); *b* 16 March 1923; *s* of late Frank and Mary Foreman; *m* 1971, Margaret Cooke; one *s*. *Educ:* Soham Grammar Sch., Cambs; Loughborough Coll., Leics. (DLC (Hons)). Royal Naval Scientific Service, 1943–58. Short Bros, 1958–88: Man. Dir, 1967–88; Chm., 1983–88. Director: Simon Engrg Ltd, 1987–; Renaissance Hldgs, 1987–; Progressive Bldg Soc., 1987– (Chm., 1990–); Ricardo International plc, 1988–; Consultant, Foreman Associates, 1988–. Member: Design Council, 1986–; NI Economic Council, 1972–88; Chm., Teaching Co. Management Cttee, 1987–; Trustee, Scotch-Irish Trust, 1980–. Pres., IMechE, 1985–86. Fellow: Irish Management Inst., 1986; Irish Inst. of Engrs, 1987; MInstD 1987. FRSA 1978. A Freeman, City of London, 1980. Hon. FRAeS 1983. Hon. DSc QUB, 1976; Hon. DTech Loughborough, 1983; DUniv Open, 1985. DL Belfast, 1975. *Publications:* papers to: Royal Aeronautical Soc.; Instn of Mechanical Engineers. *Recreations:* golf, gardening. *Address:* Ashtree House, 26 Ballymenoch Road, Holywood, Co. Down BT18 0HH. *T:* Holywood (02317) 5767.

FORESTER; *see* Weld Forester, family name of Baron Forester.

FORESTER, 8th Baron *cr* 1821; **George Cecil Brooke Weld Forester;** *b* 20 Feb. 1938; *s* of 7th Baron Forester and Marie Louise Priscilla (*d* 1988), *d* of Col Sir Herbert Perrott, 6th Bt, CH, CB; *S* father, 1977; *m* 1967, Hon. Elizabeth Catherine Lyttelton, 2nd *d* of 10th Viscount Cobham, KG, PC, GCMG, GCVO, TD; one *s* three *d*. *Educ:* Eton; Royal Agricultural College, Cirencester (MRAC). *Heir:* *s* Hon. Charles Richard George Weld Forester, *b* 8 July 1975. *Address:* Willey Park, Broseley, Salop TF12 5JJ. *T:* Telford (0952) 882146.

FORESTIER-WALKER, Sir Michael (Leolin), 6th Bt *cr* 1835; Teacher, Feltonfleet School, since 1975; *b* 24 April 1949; *s* of Lt-Col Alan Ivor Forestier-Walker, MBE (*d* 1954) (*g s* of 2nd Bt), and Margaret Joan Forestier-Walker (*née* Marcoolyn) (*d* 1988); *S* cousin, 1983; *m* 1988, Elizabeth Hedley, *d* of Joseph Hedley, Bellingham, Northumberland. *Educ:* Wellington College, Crowthorne; Royal Holloway College, London Univ. (BA Hons). *Recreations:* sailing, electronics. *Heir:* *cousin* Alan David Forestier-Walker [*b* 29 Aug. 1944; *m* 1969, Adela Judith, *d* of late S. P. Davis; one *s* two *d*]. *Address:* 91 Tartar Road, Cobham, Surrey KT11 2AS. *T:* Cobham (0932) 64120.

FORFAR, Prof. John Oldroyd, MC; Professor of Child Life and Health, University of Edinburgh, 1964–82, now Professor Emeritus; *b* 16 Nov. 1916; *s* of Rev. David Forfar, MA and Elizabeth Edith Campbell; *m* 1942, Isobel Mary Langlands Fernback, MB, ChB, DPH, AFOM; two *s* one *d*. *Educ:* Perth Acad.; St Andrews Univ. BSc 1938, MB, ChB 1941, St Andrews; DCH (London) 1948; FRCPE 1953 (MRCPE 1948); MD (Commendation) St Andrews, 1958; FRCP 1964 (MRCP 1947); FRSE 1975; FRCPGlas 1979 (MRCPGlas 1978). House Officer, Perth Royal Infirmary, 1941; RAMC, 1942–46: Med. Off., 47 Royal Marine Commando, 1943–45 (MC 1944; despatches, 1945); Registrar and Sen. Registrar, Dundee Royal Infirmary, 1946–48; Sen. Lectr in Child Health, St Andrews Univ., 1948–50; Sen. Paediatric Phys., Edinburgh Northern Gp of Hosps, and Sen. Lectr in Child Life and Health, Edinburgh Univ., 1950–64. Chairman: Scottish Assoc. of Voluntary Child Care Organisations, 1965–69; Medical Gp, Assoc. of British Adoption Agencies, 1966–76; Jt Paediatric Cttee of Royal Colls of Physicians and British Paediatric Assoc., 1979–85; President: Scottish Paediatric Soc., 1972–74; Assoc. of Clinical Professors and Heads of Departments of Paediatrics, 1980–83; Pres., BPA, 1985–88. Fellow, Amer. Coll. of Nutrition, 1977; Hon. Member: Australian Coll. of Paediatrics, 1986; Faculty of Paediatrics, RCPI, 1986. James Spence Medallist, BPA, 1983. *Publications:* (ed) Textbook of Paediatrics, 1973, 3rd edn 1984; Child Health in a Changing Society, 1988; The British Paediatric Association 1928–1988, 1989; contribs to general medical and to paediatric jls and books. *Recreations:* walking, travelling, gardening. *Address:* 110 Ravelston Dykes, Edinburgh EH12 6HB. *T:* 031–337 7081.

FORGAN, Elizabeth Anne Lucy; Director of Programmes, Channel Four Television, since 1988; *b* 31 Aug. 1944; *d* of Thomas Moinet Forgan and Jean Margaret Muriel. *Educ:* Benenden Sch.; St Hugh's Coll., Oxford (BA). Journalist: Teheran Journal, 1967–68; Hampstead and Highgate Express, 1969–74; Evening Standard, 1974–78; The Guardian, 1978–81; Channel Four TV: Sen. Commissioning Editor, 1981–86; Dep. Dir of Progs, 1987. Member: Scott Trust, 1988–; Bd of Govs, BFI, 1989–91; Vis. Cttee, RCA, 1990–; Human Fertilisation and Embryology Authority, 1990–. FRTS 1988; FRSA. Chevalier de l'ordre des arts et des lettres, 1990. *Recreations:* church music, cheap novels, Scottish Islands. *Address:* 112 Regent's Park Road, NW1 8UG.

FORGE, Andrew Murray; artist, writer; Professor of School of Art, University of Yale, Conn, USA (Dean, 1975–83); *b* Hastingleigh, Kent, 10 Nov. 1923; *s* of Sidney Wallace Forge and late Joanna Ruth Forge (*née* Bliss); *m* 1950, Sheila Deane (marr. diss.); three *d*; *m* 1974, Ruth Miller. *Educ:* Downs Sch.; Leighton Park; Camberwell Sch. of Art (NDD). Sen. Lectr, Slade Sch., UCL, 1950–64; Head of Dept of Fine Art, Goldsmith's Coll., 1964–70. Trustee: Tate Gallery, 1964–71 and 1972–74; National Gallery, 1966–72; Member: Nat. Council for Diplomas in Art and Design, 1964–72; Jt NCDAD/NACEA Cttee, 1968–70; Calouste Gulbenkian Foundn Cttee to report on future of conservation studies in UK, 1970–72; Pres., London Group, 1964–71. Trustee, Amer. Acad. in Rome, 1983–. *Publications:* Klee, 1953; Vermeer, 1954; Soutine, 1965; Rauschenberg, 1972; (with C. Joyes) Monet at Giverny, 1975; (ed) The Townsend Journals, 1976; Monet, 1983; (jtly) The Last Flower Paintings of Manet, 1986; Degas, 1987. *Recreation:* travel. *Address:* Malthouse, Elmsted, near Ashford, Kent.

FORMAN, Sir Denis, Kt 1976; OBE 1956; Deputy Chairman, Granada Group, 1984–90 (Director, 1964–90); *b* 13 Oct. 1917; *s* of late Rev. Adam Forman, CBE, and Flora Smith; *m* 1st, 1948, Helen de Mouilpied (*d* 1987); two *s*; 2nd, 1990, Moni, *widow* of James Cameron, CBE; one step *s* one step *d*. *Educ:* at home; Loretto; Pembroke Coll., Cambridge. Served War, 1940–45: Argyll and Sutherland Highlanders; Commandant, Orkney and Shetland Defences Battle Sch., 1942 (wounded, Cassino, 1944). Chief Production Officer, Central Office of Information Films, 1947; Dir, British Film Inst., 1948–55 (Chm., Bd of Governors, 1971–73); Granada TV Ltd, 1955–87: Dir, 1959; Jt Man. Dir, 1965–81; Chm., 1974–87; Chm., Novello & Co., 1971–88. Dep. Chm., Royal Opera Hse, Covent Gdn, 1983– (Dir, 1981–); Chm., Scottish Film Production Fund, 1990–; Mem. Council, RNCM, 1975–84 (Hon. Mem., RNCM, 1981). Fellow, BAFTA, 1977. DUniv: Stirling, 1982; Keele, 1990; DU Essex, 1986; Hon. LLD: Manchester, 1983; Lancaster, 1989. Ufficiale dell'ordine Al Merito della Repubblica Italiana. *Publications:* Mozart's Piano Concertos, 1971; Son of Adam (autobiog.), 1990; contrib. The Listener. *Recreation:* music. *Address:* Granada Group, 36 Golden Square, W1R 4AH. *Club:* Garrick.
See also M. B. Forman.

FORMAN, (Francis) Nigel; MP (C) Carshalton and Wallington, since 1983 (Carshalton, March 1976–1983); *b* 25 March 1943; *s* of late Brig. J. F. R. Forman and of Mrs P. J. M. Forman; *m*. *Educ:* Dragon Sch., Oxford; Shrewsbury Sch.; New Coll., Oxford; College of Europe, Bruges; Kennedy Sch. of Govt, Harvard; Sussex Univ. Information Officer, CBI, 1970–71; Conservative Research Dept, 1971–76. PPS to Lord Privy Seal, 1979–81 and to Minister of State, FCO, 1979–83, to Chancellor of the Exchequer, 1987–89. Member: Select Cttee on Science and Technology, 1976–79; Select Cttee on Foreign Affairs, 1990–; Vice-Chairman: Cons. Finance Cttee, 1983–87; All Party Social Sci. and Policy Cttee, 1984–; Secretary: Cons. Education Cttee, 1976–79; Cons. Energy Cttee, 1977–79. Mem. Exec., 1922 Cttee, 1990–. Vice-Chm., GB–E Europe Centre; Hon. Treas., Federal Trust; Hon. Dir, Job Ownership Ltd. *Publications:* Towards a More Conservative Energy Policy, 1977; Another Britain, 1979; Mastering British Politics, 1985; (with John Maples) Work to be Done, 1985. *Address:* House of Commons, SW1A 0AA.

FORMAN, Air Vice-Marshal Graham Neil, CB 1989; Director of Legal Services, Royal Air Force, 1982–89; *b* 29 Nov. 1930; *s* of Stanley M. Forman and Eva Forman (*née* Barrett); *m* 1957, Valerie Fay (*née* Shaw); one *s* two *d*. *Educ:* Boston Grammar School; Nottingham Univ. Law School; Law Society's School of Law; admitted solicitor 1953. Commissioned RAF Legal Branch, 1957; served HQ Far East Air Force, Singapore,

1960–63 and 1965–68; Dep. Dir, RAF Legal Services, HQ Near East Air Force, Cyprus, 1971–72 and 1973–76; Dep. Dir, RAF Legal Services, HQ RAF Germany, 1978; Dep. Dir, Legal Services (RAF), 1978–82. *Recreations:* tennis, reading, traditional jazz music, watching cricket. *Address:* c/o Lloyds Bank, High Street, Berkhamsted, Herts. *Clubs:* Royal Air Force; MCC.

FORMAN, Sir John Denis; *see* Forman, Sir Denis.

FORMAN, Michael Bertram, TD 1945; Director of Personnel and Organisation, TI Group plc, 1973–84; retired; *b* 28 March 1921; *s* of late Rev. A. Forman, CBE, and Flora Smith; *m* 1947, Mary Railston-Brown, *d* of Rev. W. R. Railston-Brown; four *d*. *Educ:* Loretto Sch., Musselburgh; Manchester Coll. of Technology. TA commn, 7th KOSB, 1939. War Service in Inf. and Airborne Forces, 1939–46: UK, Holland, Germany (POW), India. Labour Management, Courtaulds Ltd, 1946–53; Dir, Inst. of Personnel Management, 1953–56; Head of Staff Planning, NCB, 1956–59; Chief Staff Officer, SW Div., NCB, 1959–62; TI Group plc (formerly Tube Investments Ltd): Personnel Relations Adviser and Dep. Dir of Personnel, 1962–68; Personnel Dir, Steel Tube Div., 1968–73. Mem. NBPI, 1968–70; Chm., CSAB, 1984–90. CIPM. FRSA. *Recreations:* reading, gardening, fishing, shooting. *Address:* The Priory, Stoke Prior, Bromsgrove, Worcs B60 4LY. *T:* Bromsgrove (0527) 32196. *Club:* Savile.
See also Sir D. Forman.

FORMAN, Miloš; film director; *b* Čáslav, 18 Feb. 1932. *Educ:* Acad. of Music and Dramatic Art, Prague. Director: Film Presentations, Czechoslovak Television, 1954–56; Laterna Magika, Prague, 1958–62. Co-chm. and Prof., Film Div., Columbia Univ. Sch. of Arts, 1978–. Films directed include: Talent Competition; Peter and Pavla, 1963 (Czech. Film Critics' Award; Grand Prix, Locarno, 1964; Prize, Venice Festival, 1965); A Blonde in Love (Grand Prix, French Film Acad., 1966); The Fireman's Ball, 1967; Taking Off, 1971; (co-dir) Visions of Eight, 1973; One Flew Over the Cuckoo's Nest, 1975 (Academy Award, 1976; BAFTA Award, 1977); Hair, 1979; Ragtime, 1982; Amadeus, 1985 (Oscar Award, 1985); Valmont, 1989. *Address:* c/o Robert Lantz, The Lantz Office, 888 Seventh Avenue, New York, NY 10106, USA.

FORMAN, Nigel; *see* Forman, F. N.

FORMAN, Roy; Managing Director and Chief Executive, Private Patients Plan Ltd, since 1985; *b* 28 Dec. 1931; *s* of Leslie and Ena Forman; *m* 1954, Mary (*née* Nelson); three *s* one *d*. *Educ:* Nunthorpe Grammar Sch., York; Nottingham Univ. (BA Hons). RAF, 1953–56. Business economist, 1956–61; electricity supply industry, 1961–80: Chief Commercial Officer, S Wales Elec. Bd, 1972–76; Commercial Adviser, Electricity Council, 1976–80; Gen. Manager, Marketing and Sales, 1980–81, Marketing Dir, 1981–85, PPP. *Recreations:* music, walking, reading. *Address:* Private Patients Plan, PPP House, Crescent Road, Tunbridge Wells, Kent TN1 2PL. *T:* Tunbridge Wells (0892) 512345.

FORMARTINE, Viscount; George Ian Alastair Gordon; *b* 4 May 1983; *s* and *heir* of Earl of Haddo, *qv*.

FORMBY, Myles Landseer, CBE 1962; TD 1946; Consulting Otolaryngologist, retired: Consultant Emeritus to the Army, since 1971; University College Hospital, 1933–66, now Hon. Consulting Surgeon; Royal Masonic Hospital, 1948–66; *b* 13 March 1901; *s* of Arthur Formby, South Australia; *m* 1st, 1931, Dorothy Hussey Essex (marr. diss. 1952; she *d* 1991); one *s* one *d*; 2nd, 1974, Phyllis Mary Helps (*d* 1986), *d* of late Engr-Comdr G. S. Holgate, RN. *Educ:* St Peter's Coll., Adelaide, South Australia; Univ. of Adelaide; Magdalen Coll., Oxford. Elder Scholarship, Univ. of Adelaide, 1920 and 1921, Everard Scholarship, 1924; MB, BS, Adelaide, 1924; Rhodes Scholar for S Australia, 1925; BA Oxford, 1927; BSc Oxford, 1928; FRCS 1930; MA Oxford, 1953. Hon. Asst Surg., Ear, Nose and Throat Hosp., Golden Square, 1931; Hon. Surg., Ear, Nose and Throat, Miller Gen. Hosp., 1932; Hon. Asst Surg., Ear, Nose and Throat Dept, University Coll. Hosp., 1933; Hon. Surg., 1940; Hon. Surg., Ear, Nose and Throat Dept, Royal Masonic Hosp., 1948. RAMC TA, Lieut, 1932; Capt., 1933; Major, 1939; Lieut-Col, 1941; Brig. Consulting Oto-Rhino-Laryngologist to the Army, 1943; served in the Middle East, Italy, North West Europe and India, in War of 1939–45. Hon. Civilian Consultant to War Office, 1946. Mem. Court of Examiners, Royal College of Surgeons, 1947–53, Mem. Council, 1952–57; Royal Society of Medicine: Hon. Dir of Photography, 1958–61; Pres., Section of Laryngology, 1959–60; Hon. Treas., 1962–68; Hon. Fellow, 1970; Hon. Laryngologist to Royal Academy of Music; Pres., British Assoc. of Otolaryngologists. Bronze Star, USA, 1945. *Publications:* Dental Infection in the Aetiology of Maxillary Sinusitis, 1934; Treatment of Otitis Media, 1938; Nasal Allergy, 1943; chapters in Diseases of the Ear, Nose and Throat, 1952; The Maxillary Sinus, 1960; Ultrasonic Destruction of the Labyrinth, 1963. *Recreations:* rowing, lacrosse, golf. *Address:* Thorndene, Kithurst Lane, Storrington, West Sussex RH20 4LP. *T:* Storrington (09066) 2564. *Clubs:* Royal Automobile; Leander.

FORMSTON, Prof. Clifford; Professor of Veterinary Surgery in the University of London, 1943–74, now Emeritus; former Vice-Principal, Royal Veterinary College (1963); *b* 15 Jan. 1907; *s* of Alfred and Annie Formston; *m* 1934, Irene Pembleton (*d* 1973), *d* of Capt. Roland Wood; one *s* one *d*. *Educ:* Chester City Grammar Sch.; Royal Veterinary College, London. MRCVS 1928; FRCVS 1944. Mem. of Royal Veterinary Coll. staff, 1928–74, Fellow, 1974. Member of Council: BVA, 1949–55; RCVS, 1954–62. John Jeyes' Travel Scholarship, 1937; Visiting Professor: Univ. of Cairo, 1960; Univ. of Thessaloniki, 1966; Pahlavi Univ., Iran, 1975; Alfateh Univ., Libya, 1977, 1981; Sir Frederick Hobday Meml Lectr, 1971. Examiner in Veterinary Surgery, Nairobi Univ., 1977. Past President: Royal Counties Veterinary Assoc.; Central Veterinary Soc.; British Equine Veterinary Assoc. Examiner in veterinary surgery to Univs of Bristol, Cambridge, Dublin, Glasgow, Liverpool, London, Edinburgh and Khartoum; Hon. Res. Fellow, Inst. of Ophthalmology; Hon. Cons. Veterinary Surg. to Childe-Beale Trust. Pres., 1975–86, Patron, 1986–, Vet. Benevolent Fund; Life Vice-Pres., Riding for the Disabled Assoc.; Veterinary Patron, Diamond Riding Centre for the Handicapped; Vice-Pres., Battersea Dogs Home. Hon. Fellow, Farriers' Co., 1984. Blaine Award, 1971; John Henry Steel Meml Medallist, 1973; Simon Award, 1974; Victory Medal, Central Vet. Soc., 1975. *Publications:* contrib. scientific jls on general surgery and ophthalmology. *Recreations:* golf, gardening, reading. *Address:* 4 Marlow Court, Chase Side, Southgate, N14 5HR.

FORRES, 4th Baron *cr* 1922; **Alastair Stephen Grant Williamson;** Bt 1909; MARAC; Director: Agriscot Pty Ltd; Jaga Trading Pty Ltd; *b* 16 May 1946; *s* of 3rd Baron Forres and of Gillian Ann Maclean, *d* of Major John Maclean Grant, RA; *S* father, 1978; *m* 1969, Margaret, *d* of late G. J. Mallam, Mullumbimby, NSW; two *s*. *Educ:* Eton. Alderman, Orange City Council, 1987–. Pres., Big Brother Movt, 1986–. Patron, Sydney Scottish Week, 1981–. *Heir:* *s* Hon. George Archibald Mallam Williamson, *b* 16 Aug. 1972. *Address:* Kenso Park, Forest Road, Orange, NSW 2800, Australia. *Clubs:* Union, Australian Jockey, Sydney Turf (Sydney).

FORREST, Prof. Sir (Andrew) Patrick (McEwen), Kt 1986; Regius Professor of Clinical Surgery, University of Edinburgh, 1970–88, now Professor Emeritus; part-time Chief Scientist, Scottish Home and Health Department, 1981–87; Honorary Consultant Surgeon: Royal Infirmary of Edinburgh, until 1988; Royal Prince Alfred Hospital, Sydney; Civilian Consultant to the Royal Navy, 1977–88; *b* 25 March 1923; *s* of Rev. Andrew James Forrest, BD, and Isabella Pearson; *m* 1955, Margaret Beryl Hall (*d* 1961); one *s* one *d*; *m* 1964, Margaret Anne Steward; one *d*. *Educ:* Dundee High Sch.; Univ. of St Andrews. BSc 1942; MB, ChB 1945; ChM hons, University Gold Medal, 1954; MD hons, Rutherford Gold Medal, 1958; FRCSE 1950; FRCS 1952; FRCSGlas 1962; FRSE 1976. Surg.-Lt RNVR, 1946–48. Mayo Foundation Fellow, 1952–53; Lectr and Sen. Lectr, Univ. of Glasgow, 1955–62; Prof. of Surgery, Welsh Nat. Sch. of Medicine, 1962–70. McIlrath Vis. Prof., Royal Prince Alfred Hosp., Sydney, 1969; Nimmo Vis. Prof., Royal Adelaide Hosp., 1973; McLauchlin-Gallie Prof., RCP of Canada, 1974; numerous other visiting professorships; eponymous lectures include: Lister Meml, Canadian Med. Assoc., 1970; Inaugural Bruce Wellesley Hosp., Toronto, 1970; Inaugural Peter Lowe, RCP Glas., 1980. Member: Medical sub-cttee, UGC, 1967–76; MRC, 1974–79; Scientific Adv. Cttee, Cancer Res. Campaign, 1974–83; ABRC, 1982–85. Asst Editor and Editor, Scottish Med. Jl, 1957–61; Hon. Secretary: Scottish Soc. for Experimental Medicine, 1959–62; Surgical Research Soc., 1963–66, Pres., 1974–76; Chairman: British Breast Gp, 1974–77; Working Gp on Breast Cancer Screening (reported, 1986). Member Council: Assoc. of Surgeons of GB and Ireland, 1971–74 (Pres., 1988–89); RCSE, 1976–84, 1986–89; Member: Internat. Surgical Gp, 1963–; James IV Assoc. of Surgeons Inc., 1981–; Scottish Hosp. Endowments Res. Trust, 1990–. Hon. Fellow, Amer. Surgical Assoc., 1981; Hon. FACS, 1978; Hon. FRACS, 1987; Hon. FRCR, 1988; Hon. FRCSCan, 1989. Hon. DSc: Wales, 1981; Chinese Univ. of Hong Kong, 1986; Hon. LLD Dundee, 1986. Lister Medal, RCS, 1987. *Publications:* (ed jtly) Prognostic Factors in Breast Cancer, 1968; (jtly) Principles and Practice of Surgery, 1985; various papers in surgical jls, mainly on gastro-intestinal disease and breast cancer. *Address:* 19 St Thomas Road, Edinburgh EH9 2LR. *T:* 031–667 3203.

FORREST, Geoffrey; Consultant Chartered Surveyor; *b* 31 Oct. 1909; *er s* of late George Forrest, CA, Rossie Lodge, Inverness; *m* 1st, 1951, Marjorie Ridehalgh; two *s*; 2nd, 1974, Joyce Grey. *Educ:* Marlborough Coll. Chartered Surveyor. Served War of 1939–45, in Lovat Scouts. Joined Forestry Commn, 1946; Chief Land Agent for Forestry Commn in Wales, 1958–64; Chief Land Agent for Forestry Commn in Scotland, 1964–65; Sen. Officer of Forestry Commn in Scotland, 1965–69. Scottish Partner, Knight, Frank & Rutley, 1973–76. *Publications:* papers on land use and estate management in professional jls. *Recreations:* fishing, shooting, lawn tennis. *Address:* Harelaw, Lilliesleaf, Melrose TD6 9JW. *Club:* New (Edinburgh).

FORREST, Cdre (Retd) Geoffrey Cornish; Master of P & O vessel Arcadia from her completion in Jan. 1954 until Oct. 1956; Commodore P & O Fleet, 1955–56; *b* 1898. *Educ:* Thames Nautical Training Coll. (the Worcester). *Recreations:* photography, chess, bridge. *Address:* 44 Shirlow Avenue, Faulconbridge, NSW 2776, Australia.

FORREST, Sir James (Alexander), Kt 1967; FAA; Chairman: Chase NBA Group Ltd, 1969–80; Alcoa of Australia Ltd, 1970–78; Director, National Bank of Australasia Ltd, 1950–78 (Chairman, 1959–78); Director, Australian Consolidated Industries Ltd, 1950–77 (Chairman, 1953–77); *b* 10 March 1905; *s* of John and Mary Gray Forrest; *m* 1939, Mary Christina Forrest (*née* Armit); three *s*. *Educ:* Caulfield Grammar Sch.; Melbourne Univ. RAAF and Dept Aircraft Production, 1942–45. Partner, Hedderwick Fookes & Alston, Solicitors, 1933–70, Consultant, 1970–73; Dir, Australian Mutual Provident Society, 1961–77 (Dir, 1945–, Chm., 1955–77, Victoria Branch Bd); Dir, Western Mining Corp. Ltd, 1970–77. Member: Victoria Law Foundn, 1969–75; Council, Royal Children's Hosp. Research Foundn, 1960–78; Scotch Coll. Council, 1959–71; Council, Monash Univ., 1961–71; Council, Boy Scouts Assoc. of Aust., 1949–73; Aust. Scout Educn and Trng Foundn, 1976–; Board, Art Foundn of Victoria, 1977–80. FAA (by Special Election) 1977. Hon. LLD Monash, 1979. *Recreations:* golf, fishing. *Address:* 11 Russell Street, Toorak, Victoria 3142, Australia. *T:* 20–5227. *Clubs:* Melbourne, Australian (Melbourne); Union (Sydney).

FORREST, John Richard, DPhil; FEng 1985, FIEE; Chairman, National Transcommunications Ltd, since 1991; *b* 21 April 1943; *s* of John Samuel Forrest, *qv*; *m* 1973, Jane Patricia Robey Leech; two *s* one *d*. *Educ:* Sidney Sussex Coll., Cambridge (MA); Keble Coll., Oxford (DPhil). Research Associate and Lectr, Stanford Univ., Calif, 1967–70; Lectr, later Prof., Electronic and Elect. Engrg Dept, University Coll. London, 1970–84; Technical Dir, Marconi Defence Systems Ltd, 1984–86; Dir of Engrg, IBA, 1986–90. FRSA; FRTS. Hon. Fellow, BKSTS. Chevalier de l'ordre des arts et des lettres, 1990. *Publications:* papers and contribs to books on phased array radar, satellite communications, broadcasting and optoelectronics. *Recreations:* travel, literature, study of mankind. *Address:* Hilfield Farm House, Hilfield Lane, Aldenham, Herts WD2 8DD. *T:* 081–950 1820.

FORREST, John Samuel, MA, DSc; FRS 1966; FInstP, FEng; Visiting Professor of Electrical Engineering, University of Strathclyde, 1964–90, now Emeritus; *b* 20 Aug. 1907; *m* 1st, 1940, Ivy May Olding (*d* 1976); one *s*; 2nd, 1985, Joan Mary Downie. *Educ:* Hamilton Acad.; Glasgow Univ. Physicist, Central Electricity Board: Glasgow, 1930; London, 1931; i/c of CEB Research Lab., 1934–40; Founder, 1940, Central Electricity Research Labs, Leatherhead, Dir, 1940–73; Sec., Electricity Supply Research Council, 1949–72. Hunter Memorial Lectr, 1961; Baird Memorial Lectr, 1963, 1975, 1979; Faraday Lectures, 1963–64; Kelvin Lecture, Royal Philosophical Soc. of Glasgow, 1971; Maurice Lubbock Meml Lecture, 1975. Mem. Bd, Inst. of Physics, 1945–49; Chm., London Br. Inst. of Physics, 1954–58; Chm., Supply Sect. of IEE, 1961–62; Chm., British Nat. Cttee, Conference Internationale des Grands Réseaux Electriques, 1972–76; Pres., Sect. A, Brit. Assoc., 1963; Member Council: IEE; Royal Meteorological Society, 1945–47; Research Associations; Vice-Pres., Royal Soc., 1972–75. Hon. FIEE. Foreign Associate, Nat. Acad. of Engrg of USA, 1979. Hon. DSc: Strathclyde, 1969; Heriot-Watt, 1972. Coopers Hill War Memorial Prize and Medal, 1941; Willans Medal, 1958. *Publications:* papers on electrical power transmission and insulation. *Address:* Arbores, Portsmouth Road, Thames Ditton, Surrey KT7 0EG. *T:* 081–398 4389.
See also J. R. Forrest.

FORREST, Prof. Sir Patrick; *see* Forrest, Prof. Sir A. P. M.

FORREST, Rear-Adm. Sir Ronald (Stephen), KCVO 1975; JP; DL; *b* 11 Jan. 1923; *s* of Stephen Forrest, MD, and Maud M. McKinstry; *m* 1st, 1947, Patricia (*d* 1966), *e d* of Dr and Mrs E. N. Russell; two *s* one *d*; 2nd, 1967, June (*née* Weaver), *widow* of Lieut G. Perks, RN; one step *s* one step *d*. *Educ:* Belhaven Hill; RNC, Dartmouth. War Service at Sea, Lieut 1943 (despatches 1944); Comdr 1955; CO HMS Teazer, 1956; on loan to Pakistan Navy, 1958–60; Captain 1963; jssc 1963; Chief Staff Officer to Adm. Comdg Reserves, 1964; comd Dartmouth Trng Sqdn, 1966; Dir, Seaman Officers Appointments, 1968; CO, HMS London, 1970; Rear-Adm. 1972; Defence Services Secretary, 1972–75. Pres., Devon Co. Agricl Assoc., 1990–91. County Comr, St John Amb. Bde, Devon, 1976–81, Comdr, 1981–87. Naval Gen. Service Medal, 1949. KStJ 1987 (CStJ 1983). JP

Honiton, 1978; DL Devon, 1985. *Recreation:* gardening. *Address:* Higher Seavington, Millhayes, Stockland, near Honiton, Devon EX14 9DE. *Clubs:* Naval, Army and Navy.

FORREST, Prof. William George Grieve; Wykeham Professor of Ancient History, Oxford University, 1977–Sept. 1992; Fellow of New College, Oxford, 1977–Sept. 1992; *b* 24 Sept. 1925; *s* of William and Ina Forrest; *m* 1956, Margaret Elizabeth Mary Hall; two *d. Educ:* University College Sch., Hampstead; New Coll., Oxford (MA). Served RAF, 1943–47; New Coll., Oxford, 1947–51; Fellow, Wadham Coll., Oxford, 1951–76. Visiting Professor: Trinity and University Colls, Toronto, 1961; Yale, 1968; Vis. Fellow, British Sch. at Athens, 1986. Hon. Dr Univ. of Athens, 1991. *Publications:* Emergence of Greek Democracy, 1966; History of Sparta, 1968, 2nd edn 1980; articles in classical and archaeological periodicals. *Address:* 9 Fyfield Road, Oxford. *T:* Oxford (0865) 56187; (until Sept. 1992) New College, Oxford. *T:* Oxford (0865) 279555.

FORREST, Surgeon Rear-Adm. (D) William Ivon Norman, CB 1970; Director of Naval Dental Services, Ministry of Defence, 1968–71; *b* 8 June 1914; *s* of late Eng. Lt James Forrest; *m* 1942, Mary Margaret McMordie Black; three *s. Educ:* Christ's Hospital. Guy's Hospital, 1931–36. LDS, RCS. Dental House Surgeon, Guy's Hosp., 1936–37. Royal Navy: Surg. Lieut (D), 1937; Surg. Lt-Comdr (D), 1943; Surg. Comdr (D), 1950; Surg. Capt. (D), 1960; Surg. Rear-Adm. (D), 1968. Consultant in Dental Surgery, 1963. *Recreations:* golf, gardening, photography. *Address:* 16 Queen's Road, Waterlooville, Hants PO7 7SB. *T:* Waterlooville (0705) 263139.

FORRESTER, David Michael; Under Secretary, and Head of Schools Branch 4, Department of Education and Science, since 1988; *b* 22 June 1944; *s* of late Reginald Grant Forrester and Minnie Forrester (*née* Chaytow); *m* 1978, Diana Douglas (marr. diss. 1983); one *s* one *d. Educ:* St Paul's Sch.; King's Coll., Cambridge (BA Hons 1st Cl. 1966, MA); Kennedy Sch. of Govt, Harvard Univ. (an inaugural Kennedy Scholar, 1966–67). DES, 1967; Private Sec. to Parly Under Sec., 1971–72; Principal, DES, 1972–76; HM Treasury, 1976–78; Asst Sec., DES, 1979–85; DTI, 1985–87. *Recreations:* cricket, squash, music, esp. opera, mountain walking. *Address:* Department of Education and Science, Sanctuary Buildings, Great Smith Street, SW1. *T:* 071–934 9755. *Club:* Pretenders'.

FORRESTER, Rev. Prof. Duncan Baillie; Professor of Christian Ethics and Practical Theology, since 1978, and Principal of New College, since 1986, University of Edinburgh; Director, Edinburgh University Centre for Theology and Public Issues, since 1984; *b* 10 Nov. 1933; *s* of Rev. Prof. William Forrester and Isobel McColl or Forrester; *m* 1964, Rev. Margaret R. McDonald or Forrester (Minister of St Michael's Parish Church, Edinburgh); one *s* one *d. Educ:* Madras Coll., St Andrews; Univ. of St Andrews (MA Hons Mod. Hist. and Pol. Sci.); Univ. of Chicago (Grad., Dept of Politics); Univ. of Edinburgh (BD); DPhil Sussex. Part-time Asst in Politics, Univ. of Edinburgh, 1957–58; Asst Minister, Hillside Church and Leader of St James Mission, 1960–61; Church of Scotland Missionary to S India, 1962, Lectr, then Prof. of Politics, Madras Christian Coll., Tambaram, 1962–70; ordained as Presbyter of Church of S India, part-time Lectr in Politics, Univ. of Edinburgh, 1966–67; Chaplain and Lectr in Politics and Religious Studies, Sch. of African and Asian Studies, Univ. of Sussex, 1970–78. Lee Lectr, Edinburgh, 1980; Hensley Henson Lectr, Oxford, 1988. Chm., Edinburgh Council of Social Service, 1983–87; Faith and Order Commn, WCC, 1983–. *Publications:* chapters on Luther, Calvin and Hooker, in History of Political Philosophy, ed Strauss and Cropsey, 1963, 3rd edn 1986; Caste and Christianity, 1980; (with J. I. H. McDonald and G. Tellini) Encounter with God, 1983; (ed with D. Murray) Studies in the History of Worship in Scotland, 1984; (ed with D. Skene and co-author) Just Sharing, 1988; Theology and Politics, 1988; Beliefs, Values and Policies: conviction politics in a secular age, 1989; (ed jtly) Worship Now, Book 2, 1989; (ed) Theology and Practice, 1990; articles on Indian politics and religion, ethics and political theology. *Recreations:* hill-walking, ornithology. *Address:* 25 Kingsburgh Road, Edinburgh EH12 6DZ. *T:* 031–337 5646.

FORRESTER, Giles Charles Fielding; His Honour Judge Forrester; a Circuit Judge, since 1986; *b* 18 Dec. 1939; *s* of Basil Thomas Charles Forrester and Diana Florence Forrester (*née* Sandeman); *m* 1966, Georgina Elizabeth Garnett; one *s* one *d. Educ:* Rugby School; Grenoble Univ.; Trinity College, Oxford (MA Jurisp.). Account Exec., Pritchard Wood and Partners (Advertising Agents), 1962–66. Mem., HAC Infantry Bn, 1963–67. Called to the Bar, Inner Temple, 1966; practised, SE Circuit, 1966–86; a Recorder of the Crown Court, 1986. *Recreations:* a wide variety, mainly sporting. *Address:* c/o The Crown Court, Canbury Park Road, Kingston upon Thames, Surrey KT2 6JU. *T:* 081–549 5241. *Clubs:* Roehampton; Royal Western Yacht, St Enedoc Golf; New Zealand Golf.

FORRESTER, Ian Stewart; QC (Scot.) 1988; *b* 13 Jan. 1945; *s* of late Alexander Roxburgh Forrester and Elizabeth Richardson Forrester (*née* Stewart); *m* 1981, Sandra Anne Therese Keegan, Louisiana lawyer; two *s. Educ:* Kelvinside Acad., Glasgow; Univ. of Glasgow (MA 1965; LLB 1967); Tulane Univ. of Louisiana (MCL 1969). Mem., British Univs debating team, 1966; Commonwealth expedn to India, 1967. Admitted Faculty of Advocates, Scots Bar, 1972; admitted Bar of State of NY, following order of NY Court of Appeals, 1977. With Maclay, Murray & Spens, 1968–69; Davis Polk & Wardwell, 1969–72; Cleary, Gottlieb Steen & Hamilton, 1972–81; estab. indep. chambers, Brussels, 1981; co-founder, Forrester & Norall, 1981 (Forrester Norall & Sutton, 1989), practising before European Commn and Court. Chm., British Conservative Assoc., Belgium, 1982–86. Hon. Vis. Prof., European Law, Univ. of Glasgow, 1991–. *Publications:* numerous articles on EEC customs, dumping and trade law, competition law, German civil and commercial codes. *Recreations:* politics, wine, cooking, restoring old houses. *Address:* Forrester Norall & Sutton, 36 rue Joseph II, 1040 Brussels, Belgium; Advocates' Library, Parliament House, Edinburgh EH1 1RF. *Clubs:* Athenæum; International Château Ste-Anne (Brussels); Royal Yacht Club of Belgium.

FORRESTER, John Stuart; *b* 17 June 1924; *s* of Harry and Nellie Forrester; *m* 1945, Gertrude H. Weaver. *Educ:* Eastwood Council Sch.; City Sch. of Commerce, Stoke-on-Trent; Alsager Teachers' Training Coll. Teacher, 1946–66. MP (Lab) Stoke-on-Trent, N, 1966–87. Sec., Constituency Labour Party, 1961–84. Mem., Speaker's Panel of Chairmen, 1982–87; Member: NUT, 1949–87; APEX, 1942–43, 1946–49, 1984–. Councillor, Stoke-on-Trent, 1970–. *Address:* 13 Cadeby Grove, Milton, Stoke-on-Trent ST2 7BY.

FORRESTER, Maj.-Gen. Michael, CB 1969; CBE 1963 (OBE 1960); DSO 1943 and Bar, 1944; MC 1939 and Bar, 1941; retired 1970; *b* 31 Aug. 1917; 2nd *s* of late James Forrester, Chilworth, Hants, and Elsie (*née* Mathwin); *m* 1947, Pauline Margaret Clara (marr. diss. 1960), *d* of late James Fisher, Crossmichael; two *s. Educ:* Haileybury. 2nd Lieut, SRO, Queen's Royal Regt, 1936, Regular Commn, 1938; served in Palestine (Arab Rebellion), 1938–39; served War of 1939–45 in Palestine, Egypt, Greece, Crete, Western Desert, Syria, N Africa, Italy and France; Intell. Officer, GHQ Cairo, 1940; GSO3 (Ops) British Military Mission, Greece, 1940–41; GSO3 (Ops), HQ Western Desert Force and HQ 13 Corps, 1941–42; Staff Coll., Haifa, 1942; Bde Major, 132 Inf. Bde, 1942 (despatches); GSO2 (Ops), HQ 13 Corps and HQ 18 Army Gp, 1943; Comdr, 1st/6th Bn, Queen's Royal Regt, 1943–44; wounded, Normandy; GSO1 (Ops), HQ 13 Corps, 1945–46; Mil. Asst to Supreme Allied Comdr Mediterranean, 1947; Mil. Asst to Comdr Brit. Army Staff and Army Mem., Brit. Jt Services Mission, Washington, DC, 1947–50; Co. Comdr, 2nd Bn Parachute Regt, Cyprus and Canal Zone, 1951–52; Dirg Staff, Staff Coll., Camberley, 1953–55; GSO1 (Ops), GHQ East Africa, 1955–57; transf. to Parachute Regt, 1957; Comdr, 3rd Bn Parachute Regt, 1957–60 (incl. Jordan, 1958); Col, Military Operations (4), War Office, 1960–61; Comdr, 16 Parachute Bde Gp, 1961–63; Imp. Def. Coll., 1964; GOC 4th Div., BAOR, 1965–67; Dir of Infantry, MoD, 1968–70. Col Comdt, The Queen's Division, 1968–70. Lay Co-Chm., Alton Deanery Synod, 1984–88; Mem., Winchester Diocesan Synod, 1988–. Hon. Citizen, Canea, Crete, 1966. *Address:* Hammonds, West Worldham, near Alton, Hants GU34 3BH. *T:* Alton 84470.

FORRESTER, Prof. Peter Garnett, CBE 1981; Director, Faculties Partnership, since 1983; (Chairman, 1983–87); Professor Emeritus, Cranfield Institute of Technology; *b* 7 June 1917; *s* of Arthur Forrester and Emma (*née* Garnett); *m* 1942, Marjorie Hewitt, Berks; two *d. Educ:* Manchester Grammar Sch.; Manchester Univ. (BSc, MSc). Metallurgist, Thomas Bolton & Son Ltd, 1938–40; Research Officer, later Chief Metallurgist, Tin Research Inst., 1940–48; Chief Metallurgist and Research Man., Glacier Metal Co. Ltd, 1948–63; Dep. Principal, Glacier Inst. of Management, 1963–64; Consultant, John Tyzack & Partners, 1964–66; Prof. of Industrial Management, Coll. of Aeronautics, Cranfield, 1966; Dir, Cranfield Sch. of Management, 1967–82, Dean of Faculty, 1972; Pro-Vice-Chancellor, Cranfield Inst. of Technol., 1976–82. Chm., Conf. of Univ. Management Schs, 1976–77. Mem., Bd of Trustees, European Foundation for Management Develt, 1976–82. CBIM. Hon. DSc Cranfield Inst. of Technol., 1983. Burnham Medal, BIM, 1979. *Publications:* The British MBA, 1986; papers and reports on management educn; numerous scientific and technological papers on metallurgy, bearing materials, tribology. *Recreations:* sailing, walking. *Address:* Strawberry Hole Cottage, Ewhurst Lane, Northiam, near Rye, Sussex TN31 6HJ. *T:* Northiam (0797) 252255.

FORRESTER-PATON, His Honour Douglas Shaw; QC 1965; a Circuit Judge (formerly a Judge of County Courts), 1970–86; *b* 1921; 3rd *s* of late Alexander Forrester-Paton, JP; *m* 1948, Agnete, *d* of Holger Tuxen; one *s* two *d. Educ:* Gresham's Sch., Holt; Queen's Coll., Oxford (BA). Called to Bar, Middle Temple, 1947; North East Circuit. Served RAF, 1941–45. Recorder: Middlesbrough, 1963–68; Teesside, 1968–70. *Address:* 24 Kirkby Lane, Great Broughton, Middlesbrough, Cleveland TS9 7HG. *T:* Stokesley (0642) 712301; 5 King's Bench Walk, Temple, EC4.

FORSBERG, (Charles) Gerald, OBE 1955; Comdr RN (Retd); author; Assistant Director of Marine Services, Ministry of Defence (Navy Department), 1972–75 (Deputy Director, 1958–72); *b* Vancouver, 18 June 1912; *s* of Charles G. Forsberg and Nellie (*née* Wallman); *m* 1952, Joyce Whewell Hogarth (*d* 1987), *d* of Dr F. W. Hogarth; one *s* one *d. Educ:* Polytechnic School; Training Ship Mercury; Sir John Cass Coll. Merchant Navy: Cadet to Chief Officer, 1928–38; qual. Master Mariner; transf. RN, 1938. Norwegian campaign, 1940; Malta Convoys, Matapan, Tobruk, Crete, etc, 1940–42; comd HMS Vega as Convoy Escort Comdr, 1943–45 (despatches). Comd HMS Mameluke and HMS Chaplet, 1945–49; comd Salvage Sqdn off Elba in recovery of crashed Comet aircraft in 100 fathoms, 1954. Swam Channel (England-France) in record time, 1957; first person to swim Lough Neagh and Loch Lomond, 1959; British long-distance champion, 1957–58–59; swam Bristol Channel in record time, 1964; many long-distance championships and records, 1951–. Younger Brother of Trinity House, 1958; Civil Service, 1962. President: Channel Swimming Assoc., 1963–; British Long Distance Swimming Assoc., 1982–83. Master of Navy Lodge, 1966; Liveryman, Hon. Co. of Master Mariners. Freeman, City of London, 1968. Hon. Life Mem., Scottish Amateur Swimming Assoc., 1988. Elected to Internat. Marathon Swimming Hall of Fame, 1971; The Observer newspaper's Sports Nut of the Year, 1982. *Publications:* Long Distance Swimming, 1957; First Strokes in Swimming, 1961; Modern Long Distance Swimming, 1963; Salvage from the Sea, 1977; Pocket Book for Seamen, 1981; many short stories, articles, papers, and book reviews for general periodicals, technical jls and encyclopædia; regular monthly contribs to Swimming Times. *Recreations:* motoring, Association football affairs, books. *Address:* c/o Barclays Bank PLC, 19 Euston Road, Morecambe, Lancs LA4 5DE. *Clubs:* Victory Services; Otter Swimming.

FORSHAW, Brig. Peter, CBE 1984 (OBE 1980); FInstPS; Under Secretary, HM Treasury, since 1990 (Head of Purchasing Group and Director, Central Unit on Purchasing); *b* 12 June 1936; *s* of Alfred Ogden Forshaw and Florence Clara Vera (*née* Taylor); *m* 1960, Helen Patricia Talbot Cliff; two *d. Educ:* Wimborne, Dorset; RMCS Shrivenham and Staff Coll., Camberley. FInstPS 1990. National Service, 1954; served Army, 1954–90: Cyprus, 1957–59; Hong Kong, 1965–67; Army Staff Course, 1967; Comd, Germany, 1974–76; on Staff, RMCS, 1976–79; DCS Cyprus, 1982–84; Commander Supply Germany, 1987–89; retired 1990. FBIM 1986. *Recreations:* field sports, glass engraving, water colours. *Address:* HM Treasury, Parliament Street, SW1P 3AG. *T:* 071–270 6464. *Club:* Army and Navy.

FORSTER, Sir Archibald (William), Kt 1987; FEng, FIChemE, FInstPet; Chairman and Chief Executive: Esso UK plc, since 1983; Esso Petroleum Co. Ltd, since 1980; Esso Exploration & Production UK Ltd, since 1983; *b* 11 Feb. 1928; *s* of William Henry and Matilda Forster; *m* 1954, Betty Margaret Channing; three *d. Educ:* Tottenham Grammar Sch.; Univ. of Birmingham (BSc (Hons) ChemEng 1949, Cadman Medallist). Served Royal Air Force, Pilot (FO), 1949–51. Joined Esso Petroleum Co. Ltd, 1951; Refinery Manager, Milford Haven, 1962–63; Supply Manager, London, 1963–64; Refinery Manager, Fawley, 1964–69; Manager, Refining Dept, Esso Europe Inc., 1969–71; Exec. Dir, Esso Petroleum Co. Ltd, 1971–73; Exec. Asst to Chm., Exxon Corp., 1973–74; Manager, Corporate Planning Co-ordination, Exxon Corp., 1974–75; Vice-Pres., Esso Europe Inc., 1975–78; Dir, Exxon Research & Engineering Co., 1975–78; Man. Dir, Esso Petroleum Co. Ltd, 1979–80; Chairman: Exxon Ltd, 1980; Esso Pension Trust, 1980– (Dir, 1979–80); Director: Esso Europe Inc., 1980–87; Esso Africa Inc., 1980–86; Rover Group, 1986–88; Midland Bank, 1986–; Esso Europe-Africa Services Inc., 1987–. Exec. Bd Mem., Lloyd's Register of Shipping, 1981–. Dir, UK CEED 1989–. President: Oil Industries Club, 1982–83; IChemE, 1985; Inst. of Petroleum, 1988–90. Governor, E-SU, 1981–87. FCIM. Hon. DSc: Birmingham, 1981; Loughborough, 1986; Southampton, 1988. *Recreation:* sailing. *Address:* Esso House, Victoria Street, SW1E 5JW. *T:* 071–834 6677. *Club:* Royal Southampton Yacht.

FORSTER, Charles Ian Kennerley, CBE 1964; *b* 18 July 1911; *s* of Douglas Wakefield Forster; *m* 1942, Thelma Primrose Horton (marr. diss. 1974); one *s* one *d*; *m* 1975, Mrs Loraine Huxtable. *Educ:* Rossall Sch. FIA 1936. With Sun Life Assurance Soc., 1928–39, and 1946. Served RA, 1939–45. Statistics Branch, Admty, 1946–54; Ministry of Power, 1954 (Chief Statistician, 1955–65, Dir of Statistics, 1965–69); Min. of Technology, 1969; Under-Sec., Dept of Trade and Industry, 1970–72, retd. Energy consultant to NCB, 1972–81, retd. *Publications:* contribs to Jls of Inst. of Actuaries and Inst. of Actuaries Students Soc., Trans VII World Power Conf., Trans Manchester Statistical Soc., Statistical News. *Recreations:* bridge, stamps. *Address:* 140 Watchfield Court, Chiswick, W4 4NE. *T:* 081–994 3128.

FORSTER, Donald, CBE 1988; Managing Director, 1945–81, and Chairman, 1981–86, B. Forster & Co. Ltd, Leigh (textile manufacturing company); *b* 18 Dec. 1920; *s* of

Bernard and Rose Forster; *m* 1942, Muriel Steinman; one *s* two *d*. *Educ*: N Manchester Grammar School. Served War, RAF pilot (Flt Lieut), 1940–45. Mem., Skelmersdale Develt Corp., 1980–82; Chairman: Warrington/Runcorn Develt Corp., 1982–86; Merseyside Develt Corp., 1984–87. *Recreations*: golf, music, paintings. *Address*: 6 The Dell, South Downs Road, Hale, Cheshire WA14 3HU. *T*: 061-926 9145. *Clubs*: Whitefield Golf; Dunham Forst Country.

FORSTER, His Honour Donald Murray; a Circuit Judge, 1984–90; *b* 18 June 1929; *s* of John Cameron Forster and late Maisie Constance Forster. *Educ*: Hollylea Sch., Liverpool; Merton House Sch., Penmaenmawr; Wrekin Coll., Wellington, Shropshire; St Edmund Hall, Oxford. Honour Sch. of Jurisprudence (2nd Cl. Hons). Called to Bar, Gray's Inn, 1953; Head of Chambers, 1968; a Recorder of the Crown Court, 1978–83. *Recreation*: sport. *Address*: Flat 8, Sutcliffe House, Edmond Castle, Wetheral, Cumbria. *Clubs*: Liverpool Ramblers Association Football (Vice-Pres.); Liverpool Racquet; Mersey Bowmen Lawn Tennis (Liverpool).

FORSTER, Brig. Eric Brown, MBE 1952; General Manager, Potato Marketing Board, 1970–82; *b* 19 May 1917; *s* of late Frank and Agnes Forster; *m* 1943, Margaret Bessie Letitia, *d* of late Lt-Col Arthur Wood, MBE and late Edith Wood; one *s* two *d*. *Educ*: Queen Elizabeth Grammar Sch., Hexham. Commnd from RASC ranks into RAPC, 1941. Dir of Cost and Management Accounting (Army Dept), 1967–68. *Recreations*: philately, gardening. *Address*: Therncroft, Malt Kiln Lane, Appleton Roebuck, York YO5 7DT. *T*: Appleton Roebuck (090484) 393. *Club*: MCC.

FORSTER, Prof. Leonard Wilson, FBA 1976; Schröder Professor of German, University of Cambridge, 1961–79; Fellow of Selwyn College, Cambridge, 1937–50 and since 1961; *b* 30 March 1913; *o s* of Edward James Forster, merchant, and Linda Charlotte (*née* Rogers), St John's Wood, NW8; *m* 1939, Jeanne Marie Louise, *e d* of Dr Charles Otto Billeter, Basel; one *s* two *d*. *Educ*: Marlborough Coll.; Trinity Hall, Cambridge (Thomas Carlyle Student, 1934–35; MA 1938; LittD 1976; Hon. Fellow 1989); Bonn Univ.; Basel Univ. (Dr phil. 1938). English Lektor: Univ. of Leipzig, 1934; Univ. of Königsberg, 1935–36; Univ. of Basel, 1936–38. Naval Staff Admiralty, 1939–41; Foreign Office, 1941–45; Lt-Comdr RNVR (Sp.), 1945–46. Faculty Asst Lectr, 1937, Univ. Lectr in German, 1947–50, Cambridge; Lectr, 1937, Dean and Asst Tutor, 1946–50, Selwyn Coll., Cambridge; Prof. of German, UCL, 1950–61. Pres., Internat. Assoc. for Germanic Studies (IVG), 1970–75. Corresponding Member: Deutsche Akademie für Sprache und Dichtung, 1957; Royal Belgian Academy of Dutch Language and Literature, 1973; Member: Maatschappij der Nederlandse Letterkunde, Leiden, 1966; Royal Netherlands Acad. of Sciences and Letters, 1968. Visiting Professor: Univ. of Toronto, 1957; Univ. of Heidelberg, 1964, 1980; McGill Univ., 1967–68; Univ. of Otago, 1968; Univ. of Utrecht, 1976; Univ. of Kiel, 1980–81; Univ. of Basel, 1985–86. Sen. Consultant: Folger Shakespeare Lib., Washington, 1975; Herzog August Bibliothek, Wolfenbüttel, 1976–83. Co-Editor: German Life and Letters; Daphnis. Hon. DLitt: Leiden, 1975; Bath, 1979; Strasbourg, 1980; Heidelberg, 1986. Gold Medal, Goethe-Institut, Munich, 1966; Friedrich Gundolf-Preis für Germanistik im Ausland, 1981. Grosses Verdienstkreuz (Germany), 1976. *Publications*: G. R. Weckherlin, zur Kenntnis seines Lebens in England, 1944; Conrad Celtis, 1948; German Poetry, 1944–48, 1949; The Temper of Seventeenth Century German Literature, 1952; Penguin Book of German Verse, 1957; Poetry of Significant Nonsense, 1962; Lipsius, Von der Bestendigkeit, 1965; Die Niederlande und die Anfänge der deutschen Barocklyrik, 1967; Janus Gruter's English Years, 1967; The Icy Fire, 1969; The Poet's Tongues: Multilingualism in Literature, 1971; Kleine Schriften zur deutschen Literatur im 17 Jahrhundert, 1977; Literaturwissenschaft als Flucht vor der Literatur?, 1978; Iter Bohemicum, 1980; The Man Who Wanted to Know Everything, 1981; Christian Morgenstern, Sämtliche Galgenlieder, 1985; Christoffel van Sichem in Basel und der frühe deutsche Alexandriner, 1986; articles in British and foreign jls. *Recreation*: foreign travel. *Address*: 49 Maids Causeway, Cambridge CB5 8DE. *T*: Cambridge (0223) 357513; Selwyn College, Cambridge. *Club*: Athenæum.

FORSTER, Margaret; author; *b* 25 May 1938; *d* of Arthur Gordon Forster and Lilian (*née* Hind), *m* 1960, Edward Hunter Davies, *qv*; one *s* two *d*. *Educ*: Carlisle and County High Sch. for Girls; Somerville Coll., Oxford (BA). FRSL. Teacher, Barnsbury Girls' Sch., Islington, 1961–63. Member: BBC Adv. Cttee on Social Effects of Television, 1975–77; Arts Council Literary Panel, 1978–81. Chief non-fiction reviewer, Evening Standard, 1977–80. *Publications*: *non-fiction*: The Rash Adventurer: the rise and fall of Charles Edward Stuart, 1973; William Makepeace Thackeray: memoirs of a Victorian gentleman, 1978; Significant Sisters: grassroots of active feminism 1839–1939, 1984; Elizabeth Barrett Browning: a biography, 1988; (ed, introd. and prefaces) Elizabeth Barrett Browning: selected poems, 1988; *novels*: Dame's Delight, 1964; Georgy Girl, 1965 (filmscript with Peter Nichols, 1966); The Bogeyman, 1965; The Travels of Maudie Tipstaff, 1967; The Park, 1968; Miss Owen-Owen is At Home, 1969; Fenella Phizackerley, 1970; Mr Bone's Retreat, 1971; The Seduction of Mrs Pendlebury, 1974; Mother, can you hear me?, 1979; The Bride of Lowther Fell, 1980; Marital Rites, 1981; Private Papers, 1986; Have the Men Had Enough?, 1989; Lady's Maid, 1990; The Battle for Christabel, 1991. *Recreations*: walking on Hampstead Heath, reading contemporary fiction. *Address*: 11 Boscastle Road, NW5 1EE. *T*: 071–485 3785.

FORSTER, Neil Milward; Chairman, Air UK Group, since 1990; *b* 29 May 1927; *s* of Norman Milward Forster and Olive Christina Forster (*née* Cockrell); *m* 1954, Barbara Elizabeth Smith; one *s* two *d*. *Educ*: Hurstpierpoint College, Sussex; Pembroke College, Cambridge. BA Law and Economics; Fellow Inst. of Transport. Joined Clan Line Steamers, 1952; Chm., Calcutta Liners Conf., 1962–66; Director: Clan Line, 1967; Group and Associated cos, British & Commonwealth Shipping Co., 1974–78; British and Commonwealth Hldgs PLC, 1974–88 (Gp Man. Dir, 1982–86); Chm., Air UK Ltd, 1982–90. Chairman: Europe/SA Shipping Confs, 1977–87; UK S Africa Trade Assoc., 1985–87. Rep. England and GB at hockey, 1951–58. *Recreations*: golf, gardening. *Address*: The Orchard, Upper Slaughter, Cheltenham, Glos. *T*: Bourton-on-the-Water (0451) 22025. *Clubs*: Oriental, MCC.
  See also Sir O. G. Forster.

FORSTER, Norvela; Founder Chairman and Managing Director of consultancy company researching into marketing and management problems in Europe and overseas; *b* 1931; *m* 1981, Michael, *s* of Norman and Margaret Jones. *Educ*: South Wilts Grammar School, Salisbury; London Univ. BSc Hons. Pres., Bedford Coll. Union Soc. Mem. (C) Birmingham South, European Parlt, 1979–84; contested (C) Birmingham East, European Parly elecn, 1984. Past Member: Hampstead Borough Council; Council, Bow Group. Mem. Council, Management Consultancies Assoc. *Publication*: Chambers of Commerce: a comparative study of their role in the UK and in other EEC countries, 1983. *Address*: IAL Consultants Ltd, 14 Buckingham Palace Road, SW1W 0QP. *T*: 071–828 5036; 6 Regency House, Regency Street, SW1. *T*: 071–821 5749. *Clubs*: Royal Ocean Racing; Royal Mid-Surrey Golf.

FORSTER, Sir Oliver (Grantham), KCMG 1983 (CMG 1976); LVO 1961; HM Diplomatic Service, retired; *b* 2 Sept. 1925; 2nd *s* of Norman Milward Forster and Olive

Christina Forster (*née* Cockrell); *m* 1953, Beryl Myfanwy Evans; two *d*. *Educ*: Hurstpierpoint; King's Coll., Cambridge. Served in RAF, 1944–48. Joined Commonwealth Relations Office, 1951. Private Sec. to Parly Under-Sec., 1953–54; Second Sec., Karachi, 1954–56; Principal, CRO, 1956–59; First Sec., Madras, 1959–62; First Sec., Washington, 1962–65; Private Sec. to Sec. of State for Commonwealth Relations, 1965–67; Counsellor, Manila, 1967–70; Counsellor, New Delhi, 1970–75, Minister, 1975; Asst Under-Sec. of State and Dep. Chief Clerk, FCO, 1975–79; Ambassador to Pakistan, 1979–84. HQA 1984. *Address*: 71 Raglan Road, Reigate, Surrey. *Clubs*: United Oxford & Cambridge University, Commonwealth Trust.
  See also N. M. Forster.

FORSTER, Sir William (Edward Stanley), Kt 1982; Judge of the Federal Court of Australia, 1977–89; *b* 15 June 1921; *s* of F. B. Forster; *m* 1950, Johanna B., *d* of Brig. A. M. Forbes; one *s* two *d*. *Educ*: St Peter's Coll., Adelaide; Adelaide Univ. (Stowe Prize; David Murray Scholar; LLB). Served RAAF, 1940–46. Private legal practice, 1950–59; Magistrate, Adelaide Police Court, 1959–61; Master, Supreme Court of SA, and Dist Registrar, High Court of Aust., 1966–71 (Dep. Master, and Dep. Dist Registrar, 1961–66); Sen. Judge, 1971, Chief Judge, 1977, Chief Justice, 1979–85, Supreme Court of NT. Chancellor, dio. of NT, 1975–85. Adelaide University: Lectr in Criminal Law, 1957–58; Lectr in Law of Procedure, 1967–71; Mem., Standing Cttee of Senate, 1967–71. President: NT Div., Australian Red Cross, 1973–85; Aboriginal Theatre Foundn, 1972–75; Chairman: Museum and Art Galls Bd, NT, 1974–85; NT Parole Bd, 1976–85. Air Efficiency Award, 1953. *Address*: 25 River Street, St Peters, SA 5069, Australia. *Clubs*: Adelaide (Adelaide); Darwin Golf.

FORSYTE, Charles; *see* Philo, G. C. G.

FORSYTH OF THAT ILK, Alistair Charles William, JP; FSCA, FSAScot; FInstPet; Baron of Ethie; Chief of the Name and Clan of Forsyth; chairman and director of companies; *b* 7 Dec. 1929; *s* of Charles Forsyth of Strathendry, FCA, and Ella Millicent Hopkins; *m* 1958, Ann, OStJ, *d* of Col P. A. Hughes, IA; four *s*. *Educ*: St Paul's Sch.; Queen Mary Coll., London. FInstPet 1973; FSCA 1976; FSAScot 1979. National Service, 2nd Lieut The Queen's Bays, 1948–50; Lieut The Parachute Regt, TA, 1950–54. Chairman, Caledonian Produce (Holdings) Ltd and subsidiaries, 1984–87; Director: Carritt Moran & Co. Ltd, Calcutta, 1961–63; Strathendry Investments Ltd, 1983–. Convenor of Industrial Develt, Angus DC, 1987–. Trustee, Montrose Harbour Trust, 1990–. Member: Standing Council of Scottish Chiefs, 1978–; Council, 1977–81, Chapter, 1982–, Priory of Scotland of Most Ven. Order of St John of Jerusalem. CStJ 1982 (OStJ 1974). JP NSW, 1965; JP Angus, 1987. *Recreations*: hill walking, Scottish antiquities. *Address*: Ethie Castle, by Arbroath, Angus DD11 5SP. *Club*: New (Edinburgh).

FORSYTH, Bill; film director and script writer; *b* Glasgow, 1947; one *s* one *d*. *Educ*: National Film School. *Films directed*: That Sinking Feeling, 1980; Gregory's Girl, 1981; Local Hero, 1983; Comfort and Joy, 1984; Housekeeping, 1988; Breaking In, 1990. TV film, Andrina, 1981. BAFTA Award: best screenplay, 1982; best dir, 1983. Hon. DLitt Glasgow, 1984; DUniv Stirling, 1989. *Address*: c/o A. D. Peters, The Chambers, Chelsea Harbour, SW10 0XF.

FORSYTH, Bruce; *see* Forsyth-Johnson, B. J.

FORSYTH, Jennifer Mary; Under-Secretary, HM Treasury and Department of Transport, 1975–83, retired; Councillor (Lab) Borough of Kensington and Chelsea, since 1986; *b* 7 Oct. 1924; *o d* of late Matthew Forsyth, theatrical director, and late Marjorie Forsyth. *Educ*: Frensham Heights; London Sch. of Economics and Political Science (Pres. of Students' Union, 1944–45) (BScEcon). Joined Home Finance Div., HM Treasury, 1945; UN Economic Commn for Europe, 1949–51; Information Div., HM Treasury, 1951–53; Principal, Estabts, Overseas Finance and Planning Divs, 1954–62; UK Treasury Delegn, Washington, 1962–64; Assistant Secretary: DEA, 1965–69; Social Services Div., HM Treasury, 1969–75; Under Secretary: Home, Transport and Education Gp, HM Treasury, 1975–80; Dept of Transport (Roads), 1980–83. Governor, Frensham Heights, 1965–76. *Recreations*: going to the theatre and to the Mediterranean. *Address*: Flat 4, One Ladbroke Square, W11 3LX.

FORSYTH, Michael Bruce; MP (C) Stirling, since 1983; Minister of State, Scottish Office, since 1990; *b* 16 Oct. 1954; *s* of John T. Forsyth and Mary Watson; *m* 1977, Susan Jane Clough; one *s* two *d*. *Educ*: Arbroath High School; St Andrews University. MA. Pres., St Andrews Univ. Cons. Assoc., 1972–75; Nat. Chm., Fedn of Cons. Students, 1976–77; PPS to Sec. of State for Foreign and Commonwealth Affairs, 1986–87; Parly Under-Sec. of State, Scottish Office, 1987–90; Chm., Scottish Cons. Party, 1989–90. Mem., Westminster City Council, 1978–83. *Recreations*: photography, mountaineering, amateur astronomy. *Address*: House of Commons, SW1A 0AA.

FORSYTH, William Douglass, OBE 1955; Australian Ambassador, retired 1969; *b* Casterton, Australia, 5 Jan. 1909; of Australian parents; *m* 1935, Thelma Joyce (*née* Sherry); one *s* two *d*. *Educ*: Ballarat High Sch.; Melbourne Univ. (MA, DipEd); Balliol Coll., Oxford (BLitt). Teacher of History, 1931–35; Rockefeller Fellow, Social Studies, Europe, 1936–37 and 1939; Research Fellow, Melbourne Univ., 1940; Editor Austral-Asiatic Bulletin, Melbourne, 1940; Research Sec., Aust. Inst. International Affairs, 1940–41; Australian Dept of Information, 1941–42; Australian Dept of External Affairs, 1942–69: First Sec., 1946; Counsellor, Aust. Embassy, Washington, 1947–48; Aust. rep. Trusteeship Council, 1948 and 1952–55; Sec.-Gen., South Pacific Commission, 1948–51. Australian Member UN Population Commission, 1946–47; Mem., Australian Delegns to UN General Assembly, 1946–48 and 1951–58; San Francisco UN Confs, 1945 and 1955; Minister, Australian Mission to UN, 1951–55; Asst-Sec., Dept of External Affairs, Canberra, 1956–59, 1961–63; Australian Minister to Laos, 1959–60; Australian Ambassador to Viet-Nam, 1959–61; Sec.-Gen., South Pacific Commn, Nouméa, 1963–66; Australian Ambassador to Lebanon, 1967–68. South Pacific Consultant, Dept of Foreign Affairs, 1973–74. Vis. Fellow, ANU, 1975. *Publications*: Governor Arthur's Convict System, 1935, reprinted 1970; The Myth of Open Spaces, 1942; Captain Cook's Australian Landfalls, 1970; articles in Economic Record, etc. *Address*: 88 Banks Street, Yarralumla, Canberra, ACT 2600, Australia.

FORSYTH-JOHNSON, Bruce Joseph, (Bruce Forsyth); entertainer and comedian; *b* 22 Feb. 1928; *m* 1st, 1953, Penny Calvert; three *d*; 2nd, 1973, Anthea Redfern (marr. diss. 1982); two *d*; 3rd, 1983, Wilnelia Merced; one *s*. *Educ*: Higher Latimer Sch., Edmonton. Started stage career as Boy Bruce—The Mighty Atom, 1942; after the war, appeared in various double acts and did a 2 yr spell at Windmill Theatre; first television appearance, Music Hall, 1954; resident compère, Sunday Night at the London Palladium, 1958–60; own revue, London Palladium, 1962; leading role, Little Me, Cambridge Theatre, 1964; début at Talk of the Town (played there 7 times); compèred Royal Variety Show, 1971, and on subseq. occasions; London Palladium Show, 1973 (also Ottawa and Toronto) and 1980; commenced Generation Game, BBC TV series, 1971 (completed 7 series), and 1990–; compèred Royal Windsor to mark BBC Jubilee Celebrations, 1977; One Man Show, Theatre Royal, Windsor, and Lakeside, 1977; Bruce Forsyth's Big Night, ITV,

1978; Play Your Cards Right, ITV, 1980–87; Slinger's Day, ITV, 1986, 1987; You Bet!, 1988. Films include: Star; Can Hieronymous Merkin Ever Forget Mary Humppe and Find True Happiness?; Bedknobs and Broomsticks; The Magnificent 7 Deadly Sins; Pavlova. Numerous records. Show Business Personality of the Year, Variety Club of GB, 1975; TV Personality of the Year, Sun Newspaper, 1976 and 1977; Male TV Personality of the Year, TV Times, 1975, 1976, 1977 and 1978; Favourite Game Show Host, TV Times, 1984. *Recreation:* golf (handicap 10, Wentworth Golf Club). *Address:* Straidarran, Wentworth Drive, Virginia Water, Surrey. *Clubs:* White Elephant, Crockfords, Empress, Tramp.

FORSYTHE, Clifford; MP (UU) Antrim South, since 1983, resigned seat Dec. 1985 in protest against Anglo-Irish Agreement; re-elected Jan. 1986; Member, Antrim South, Northern Ireland Assembly, 1982–86; plumbing and heating contractor; *b* 1929. *Educ:* Glengormley public elementary sch. Formerly professional football player, Linfield and Derry City. Mem., Newtownabbey Borough Council, 1981–85; Mayor, 1983. Dep. Chm., DHSS Cttee, NI Assembly, 1982–86; UU Parly spokesman on transport, communications and local govt. Exec. Mem., Ulster Unionist Council, 1980–83; Chm., S Antrim Official Unionist Assoc., 1981–83. Fellow, Industry and Parlt Trust, 1986. Chm., Glengormley Br., NI Chest, Heart and Stroke Assoc., 1987. *Recreations:* church choir, football, running. *Address:* House of Commons, SW1A 0AA.

FORSYTHE, Air Cdre James Roy, (Paddy), CBE 1966; DFC; Director of Development, 1976–81, Joint Chief Executive, 1981–86, Look Ahead Housing Association Ltd; *b* 10 July 1920; *s* of W. R. and A. M. Forsythe; *m* 1st, 1946, Barbara Mary Churchman (*d* 1983); two *s* two *d*; 2nd, 1989, Mrs W. P. Newbery. *Educ:* Methodist Coll., Belfast; Queen's Univ., Belfast. Bomber Comd, 1944–45; OC, Aberdeen Univ. Air Sqdn, 1952–54; psa 1955; Principal Staff Officer to Dir-Gen. Orgn (RAF), 1956–58; OC, 16 Sqdn, 1958–60; Dirg Staff, Coll. of Air Warfare, Manby, 1960–62; Head of RAF Aid Mission to India, 1963; Stn Comdr, RAF Acklington, 1963–65; Dep. Dir Air Staff Policy, MoD, 1965–68; Dir Public Relations, Far East, 1968–70; Dir Recruiting, RAF, 1971–73; Dir, Public Relations, RAF, 1973–75. MIPR. *Recreations:* Rugby (Chm., RAF RU, 1972, 1973, 1974; Chm., Combined Services RU, 1974; Vice-Pres., 1979, Chm., 1988–90, Pres., 1990–, London Irish RFC), golf. *Address:* 104 Earls Court Road, W8 6EG. *T:* 071–937 5291. *Club:* Royal Air Force.

FORSYTHE, Dr (John) Malcolm; Regional Medical Officer, since 1978, and Regional Director of Public Health and Service Development, since 1989, South East Thames Regional Health Authority; *b* 11 July 1936; *s* of late Dr John Walter Joseph Forsythe and Dr Charlotte Constance Forsythe (*née* Beatty); *m* 1961, Delia Kathleen Moore (marr. diss. 1983); one *s* three *d*; *m* 1984, Patricia Mary Barnes. *Educ:* Repton Sch., Derby; Guy's Hosp. Med. Sch., London Univ. BSc(Hons), MB, BS, MSc; DObstRCOG, FRCP; FFCM. Area Medical Officer, Kent AHA, 1974–78; Dir of Planning, SE Thames RHA, 1985–89. Hon. Consultant, Univ. of Kent Health Services Res. Unit, 1977–. Jack Masur Fellow, Amer. Hosp. Assoc., 1976. Head, UK Deleg., Hospital Cttee, EEC, 1980–85, 1989–90; Consultant, Urwick Orr Ltd; Member: Resource Allocation Wkg Pty and Adv. Gp on Resource Allocation, 1975–78; Technical Sub Gp, Review of Resource Allocation Working Party Formula, 1986–87; DHSS Med. Manpower Planning Review, 1986–88; NHS Computer Policy Cttee, 1981–85; Standing Med. Adv. Cttee to Sec. of State, 1982–86; PHLS Bd, 1986–; Central Council for Postgrad. Med. Educn, 1986–88; Health Services Res. Cttee, MRC, 1988–91; Bd of Governors, United Med. Sch. of Guy's and St Thomas', 1982–; Delegacy, King's Coll. Hosp. Med. and Dental Schs, 1978–. External Examiner to Univ. of London, 1987–89. FRSA 1985. Silver Core Award, IFIP, 1977. *Publications:* (ed jtly) Information Processing of Medical Records, 1969; Proceedings of First World Conference on Medical Informatics, 1975. *Recreations:* squash, music. *Address:* Kapalua, 5 Ryders, Langton Green, Tunbridge Wells, Kent TN3 0DX. *T:* Tunbridge Wells (0892) 863852; (office) Thrift House, Collington Avenue, Bexhill-on-Sea, East Sussex TN39 3NQ. *T:* Bexhill-on-Sea (0424) 730073. *Clubs:* Royal Society of Medicine; Chasers.

FORSYTHE, Air Cdre Paddy; *see* Forsythe, Air Cdre J. R.

FORT, Mrs Jean; Headmistress of Roedean School, Brighton, 1961–70; *b* 1915; *d* of G. B. Rae; *m* 1943, Richard Fort (*d* 1959), MP Clitheroe Division of Lancs; four *s* one *d*. *Educ:* Benenden Sch.; Lady Margaret Hall, Oxford (MA, DipEd). Asst Mistress, Dartford County Sch. for Girls, 1937–39; WVS Headquarters staff, 1939–40; Junior Civil Asst, War Office, 1940–41; Personal Asst to Sir Ernest Gowers, Sen. Regional Comr for Civil Def., London, 1941–44. *Address:* 6 King's Close, Henley-on-Thames, Oxon RG9 2DS.

FORT, Maeve Geraldine, CMG 1990; Ambassador to Mozambique, since 1989; *b* 19 Nov. 1940; *d* of late F. L. Fort. *Educ:* Trinity College, Dublin (MA); Sorbonne, Paris. Joined Foreign Service, 1963; UKMIS, NY, 1964; CRO, 1965; seconded to SEATO, Bangkok, 1966; Bonn, 1968; Lagos, 1971; Second, later First Sec., FCO, 1973; UKMIS, NY, 1978; Counsellor, FCO, 1982; RCDS, 1983; Counsellor, Hd of Chancery and Consul-Gen., Santiago, 1984–86; Head of W African Dept, FCO, 1986–89, and Ambassador (non-resident) to Chad, 1987–89. *Address:* c/o Foreign and Commonwealth Office, King Charles Street, SW1A 2AH.

FORTE, family name of **Baron Forte.**

FORTE, Baron *cr* 1982 (Life Peer), of Ripley in the county of Surrey; **Charles Forte;** Kt 1970; FRSA; Chairman, Trusthouse Forte PLC, since 1982 (Executive Chairman, 1978–81, Deputy Chairman, 1970–78, and Chief Executive, 1971–78); *b* 26 Nov. 1908; *m* 1943, Irene Mary Chierico; one *s* five *d*. *Educ:* Alloa Academy; Dumfries Coll.; Mamiani, Rome. Fellow and Mem. Exec. Cttee, Catering Inst., 1949; Member: Small Consultative Advisory Cttee to Min. of Food, 1946; London Tourist Board. Hon. Consul Gen. for Republic of San Marino. FBIM 1971. Grand Officier, Ordine al Merito della Repubblica Italiana; Cavaliere di Gran Croce della Repubblica Italiana; Cavaliere del Lavoro (Italy). *Publications:* Forte (autobiog.), 1986; articles for catering trade papers. *Recreations:* golf, fishing, shooting, fencing, music. *Address:* 166 High Holborn, WC1V 6TT. *Clubs:* Carlton, Caledonian, Royal Thames Yacht.

FORTE, Hon. Rocco (John Vincent), FCA; Chief Executive, Trusthouse Forte plc, since 1983; *b* 22 Feb. 1945; *s* of Lord Forte, *qv*; *m* 1986, Aliai, *d* of Prof. Giovanni Ricci, Rome; two *d*. *Educ:* Downside Coll.; Pembroke Coll., Oxford (MA). Trusthouse Forte: Dir of Personnel, 1973–78; Dep. Chief Exec., 1978–82; Jt Chief Exec., 1982–83. Vice-Pres., Commonwealth Games Council for England; Mem., BTA. *Address:* Trusthouse Forte, 166 High Holborn, WC1V 6TT.

FORTESCUE, family name of **Earl Fortescue.**

FORTESCUE, 7th Earl *cr* 1789; **Richard Archibald Fortescue,** JP; Baron Fortescue 1746; Viscount Ebrington 1789; *b* 14 April 1922; *s* of 6th Earl Fortescue, MC, TD, and Marjorie (*d* 1964), OBE, *d* of late Col C. W. Trotter, CB, TD; *S* father, 1977; *m* 1st, 1949, Penelope Jane (*d* 1959), *d* of late Robert Evelyn Henderson; one *s* one *d*; 2nd, 1961, Margaret Anne (marr. diss. 1987), *d* of Michael Stratton; two *d*; 3rd, 1989, Carolyn Mary, *d* of Clement Hill. *Educ:* Eton; Christ Church, Oxford. Captain Coldstream Guards (Reserve). JP Oxon, 1964. *Heir:* *s* Viscount Ebrington, *qv*. *Address:* House of Lords, SW1. *Club:* White's.

FORTESCUE, (John) Adrian, LVO 1972; HM Diplomatic Service; on secondment to the Commission of the European Communities, since 1985; *b* 16 June 1941; *s* of T. V. N. Fortescue, *qv*; *m* 1st, 1978, Jillian Sarah Montague-Evans (marr. diss. 1987); one *s*; 2nd, 1989, Marie Wolfcarius. MECAS, 1964; served Amman, FCO and Paris, 1966–72; on loan to EC, 1973–75; FCO, 1976–79; Washington, 1979–81; Head of Presidency Unit, ECD, FCO, 1981–82; on loan to EC, 1982; Counsellor, Budapest, 1983–84. *Address:* c/o Foreign and Commonwealth Office, SW1; 44 Avenue Beau-Séjour, 1180 Brussels, Belgium.

FORTESCUE, Trevor Victor Norman, (Tim), CBE 1984; Secretary-General, Food and Drink Industries Council, 1973–83; *b* 28 Aug. 1916; *s* of Frank Fortescue; *m* 1st, 1939, Margery Stratford (marr. diss. 1975), *d* of Dr G. H. Hunt; two *s* one *d*; 2nd, 1975, Anthea Maureen, *d* of Robert M. Higgins. *Educ:* Uppingham Sch.; King's Coll., Cambridge. BA 1938; MA 1945. Colonial Administrative Service, Hong Kong, 1939–47 and Kenya, 1949–51 (interned, 1941–45); FAO, UN, Washington, DC, 1947–49 and Rome, 1951–54; Chief Marketing Officer, Milk Marketing Bd of England and Wales, 1954–59; Manager, Nestlé Gp of Cos, Vevey, Switz., 1959–63 and London, 1963–66. MP (C) Liverpool, Garston, 1966–Feb. 1974; an Asst Govt Whip, 1970–71; a Lord Comr of HM Treasury, 1971–73. Chairman: Conference Associates Ltd, 1978–87; Standing Cttee, Confedn of Food and Drink Industries of European Community (CIAA), 1982–84; Pres., British Food Manufg Industries Res. Assoc., 1984–; Member: Meat Promotion Rev. Body, 1984; Council, British Industrial Biol. Res. Assoc., 1980–83. Develt Manager (with A. M. Fortescue), Winchester Cathedral, 1989–90; Dir, Winchester Cathedral Enterprises Ltd, 1990–. Trustee, Uppingham Sch., 1957–63; Patron and Trustee, The Quest Community, Birmingham, 1971–85. *Publication:* Lovelines, 1987. *Recreations:* marriage to Anthea; Napoleon. *Address:* Waynflete House, 25 St Swithun Street, Winchester, Hants SO23 9JP. *T:* Winchester (0962) 854693.

See also J. A. Fortescue.

FORTEVIOT, 3rd Baron *cr* 1916; **Henry Evelyn Alexander Dewar,** Bt, *cr* 1907; MBE 1943; DL; Chairman, John Dewar & Sons Ltd, 1954–76; former Director, Distillers Co. Ltd; *b* 23 Feb. 1906; 2nd *s* of 1st Baron Forteviot and Margaret Elizabeth, *d* of late Henry Holland; *S* half-brother 1947; *m* 1933, Cynthia Monica (*d* 1986), *e d* of late Cecil Starkie, Hethe Place, Cowden, Kent; two *s* two *d*. *Educ:* Eton; St John's Coll., Oxford (BA). Served War of 1939–45, with Black Watch (RHR) (MBE). DL Perth, 1961. *Heir:* *s* Hon. John James Evelyn Dewar [*b* 5 April 1938; *m* 1963, Lady Elisabeth Waldegrave, 3rd *d* of 12th Earl Waldegrave, *qv*; one *s* three *d*]. *Address:* Dupplin Castle, Perth, Perthshire. *Club:* Brooks's; Royal (Perth).

See also Duke of Fife, Baroness Strange, Gen. Sir Richard Worsley.

FORTH, Eric; MP (C) Mid Worcestershire, since 1983; Parliamentary Under Secretary of State, Department of Employment, since 1990; *b* 9 Sept. 1944; *s* of William and Aileen Forth; *m* 1967, Linda St Clair; two *d*. *Educ:* Jordanhill Coll. Sch., Glasgow; Glasgow Univ. (MA Hons Politics and Econs). Chm., Young Conservatives', Constituency CPC, 1970–73; Member: Glasgow Univ. Cons. Club, 1962–66; Brentwood UDC, 1968–72. Contested (C) Barking, Feb. and Oct. 1974. Member (C), North Birmingham, European Parlt, 1979–84; Chm., Backbench Cttee, European Democ. Gp, European Parlt, 1979–84. PPS to Minister of State, DES, 1986–87; Parly Under Sec. of State, DTI, 1988–90. Mem., Select Cttee on Employment, 1986; Chm., Cons. Backbench European Affairs Cttee, 1987–88 (Vice-Chm., 1983–86). *Publication:* Regional Policy—A Fringe Benefit?, 1983. *Recreation:* discussion and argument. *Address:* House of Commons, SW1A 0AA. *Club:* Carlton.

FORTIER, Most Rev. Jean-Marie; *see* Sherbrooke, Archbishop of, (RC).

FORTY, Prof. Arthur John, CBE 1991; PhD, DSc; FRSE; FRSA; Principal and Vice-Chancellor, Stirling University, since 1986; *b* 4 Nov. 1928; *s* of Alfred Louis Forty and Elisabeth Forty; *m* 1950, Alicia Blanche Hart Gough; one *s*. *Educ:* Headlands Grammar Sch.; Bristol Univ. (BSc; PhD 1953; DSc 1967). FRSE 1988, FRSA 1989. Served RAF, 1953–56. Sen. Res. Scientist, Tube Investments Ltd, 1956–58; Lectr, Univ. of Bristol, 1958–64; University of Warwick: Foundn Prof. of Physics, 1964–86; Pro-Vice-Chancellor, 1970–86. Visiting scientist: Gen. Electric Co., USA; Boeing Co.; Nat. Bureau of Standards, Washington, USA. Member: SRC Physics Cttee, 1969–73; SRC Materials Cttee, 1970–73; Computer Bd, 1982–85; University Grants Committee: Mem., 1982–86, Vice-Chm., 1985–86; Chairman: Physical Sciences Sub-cttee, 1985–86; Equipment Sub-cttee, 1985–86; Chairman: Jt ABRC, Computer Bd and UGC Working Party on Future Facilities for Advanced Res. Computing (author, Forty Report), 1985; Management Cttee for Res. Councils' Supercomputer Facility, 1986–88; UFC Cttee for Information Systems (formerly Computer Bd for Univs and Res. Councils), 1988–; Jt Policy Cttee for Advanced Res. Computing, 1988–. Mem., British Library Bd, 1987–. Hon. LLD St Andrew's, 1989. *Publications:* papers in Proc. Royal Soc., Phil Magazine and other learned jls. *Recreations:* sailing, gardening, the ancient metallurgy of gold. *Address:* Principal's House, University of Stirling, Stirling FK9 4LA. *Club:* Caledonian.

FORWELL, Dr George Dick, PhD; FRCP; Chief Administrative Medical Officer, since 1973, and Director of Public Health, since 1989, Greater Glasgow Health Board; Hon. Lecturer, since 1973, and Visiting Professor, 1990, Department of Public Health, Glasgow University; *b* 6 July 1928; *s* of Harold C. Forwell and Isabella L. Christie; *m* 1957, Catherine F. C. Cousland; two *d*. *Educ:* George Watson's Coll., Edinburgh; Edinburgh Univ. (MB, ChB 1950; PhD 1955). MRCPE 1957, DIH 1957, DPH 1959, FRCPE 1967, FFCM 1972, FRCPGlas 1974, FRCP 1985. House Officer and Univ. Clin. Asst, Edinburgh Royal Infirm., 1950–52; RAF Inst. of Aviation Med., 1952–54; MRC and RCPE grants, 1954–56; pneumoconiosis field res., 1956–57; Grad. Res. Fellow and Lectr, Edinburgh Univ. Dept of Public Health and Social Med., 1957–60; Asst Dean, Faculty of Med., Edinburgh Univ., 1960–63; Dep. Sen. and Sen. Admin. MO, Eastern Reg. Hosp. Bd, Dundee, 1963–67; PMO, Scottish Home and Health Dept, 1967–73; QHP, 1980–83. Mem., GMC, 1984–89. *Publications:* papers on clin. res. and on health planning and services, in med. and other jls. *Recreation:* running. *Address:* 60 Whittingehame Drive, Glasgow G12 0YQ. *T:* 041–334 7122. *Club:* Royal Air Force.

FORWOOD, Sir Dudley (Richard), 3rd Bt *cr* 1895; Member of Lloyd's; *b* 6 June 1912; *s* of Sir Dudley Baines Forwood, 2nd Bt, CMG, and Norah Isabella (*née* Lockett) (*d* 1962); *S* father, 1961; *m* 1952, Mary Gwendoline (who *m* 1st, Viscount Ratendone, later 2nd Marquis of Willingdon; 2nd, Robert Cullingford; 3rd, Col Donald Croft-Wilcock), *d* of Basil S. Foster. *Educ:* Stowe Sch. Attaché, British Legation, Vienna, 1934–37; Equerry to the Duke of Windsor, 1937–39. Served War of 1939–45, Scots Guards (Major). Master, New Forest Buckhounds, 1956–65; Official Verderer of the New Forest, 1974–82; Chairman: New Forest Consultative Panel, 1970–82; Crufts, 1973–87; Vice Pres., RASE (Hon. Dir, 1973–78). *Recreation:* hunting. *Heir:* *cousin* Peter Noel Forwood [*b* 1925; *m*

1950, Roy Murphy; six *d*]. *Address:* 43 Addison Road, W14. *T:* 071–603 3620; Uppacott, Bagnum, near Ringwood, Hants BH24 3BZ. *T:* Ringwood (0425) 471480.

FORWOOD, Nicholas James; QC 1987; *b* 22 June 1948; *s* of Lt-Col Harry Forwood and Wendy Forwood (*née* French-Smith); *m* 1971, Sally Diane Gerrard, *e d* of His Honour Basil Harding Gerrard, *qv*; one *s* three *d*. *Educ:* Stowe Sch.; St John's Coll., Cambridge (Open Schol., MA, Pt I Mechanical Scis Tripos (1st Cl. Hons), Pt II Law Tripos). Called to the Bar, Middle Temple, 1970. Mem., Law Adv. Cttee, British Council, 1985–. *Recreations:* ski-ing, golf, sailing, opera. *Address:* Brick Court Chambers, 15 Devereux Court, WC2R 3JJ. *T:* 071–583 0777; 11 Avenue Juliette, 1180 Brussels, Belgium. *T:* 375.25.42. *Clubs:* United Oxford & Cambridge University, Ski Club of Gt Britain.

FOSKETT, David Robert; QC 1991; *b* 19 March 1949; *s* of Robert Frederick Foskett and Ruth (*née* Waddington); *m* 1975, Angela Bridget Jacobs; one *d*. *Educ:* Warwick Sch.; King's Coll., London (LLB Hons). King's College, London: Pres., Faculty of Laws, 1969–70; Pres., Union Sec., 1970–71; Mem., Delegacy, 1970–72. Called to the Bar, Gray's Inn, 1972. Mem., Fees Collection Cttee, Bar Council, 1991–. *Publications:* The Law and Practice of Compromise, 1980, 3rd edn 1991; various articles. *Recreations:* theatre, reading poetry and composing verse, bird watching, cricket, golf. *Address:* 1 Crown Office Row, Temple, EC4Y 7HH. *T:* 071–353 1801. *Clubs:* MCC; Woking Golf.

FOSKETT, Douglas John, OBE 1978; FLA; Director of Central Library Services and Goldsmiths' Librarian, University of London, 1978–83; *b* 27 June 1918; *s* of John Henry Foskett and Amy Florence Foskett; *m* 1948, Joy Ada (*née* McCann); one *s* two *d*. *Educ:* Bancroft's Sch.; Queen Mary Coll., Univ. of London (BA 1939); Birkbeck Coll., Univ. of London (MA 1954). Ilford Municipal Libraries, 1940–48; RAMC and Intell. Corps, 1940–46; Metal Box Co. Ltd, 1948–57; Librarian, Univ. of London Inst. of Educn, 1957–78. Chairman of Council, Library Assoc., 1962–63, Vice-Pres., 1966–73, Pres., 1976; Hon. Library Adviser, RNID, 1965–90; Mem., Adv. Cttee on Sci. and Techn. Information, 1969–73; Mem. and Rapporteur, Internat. Adv. Cttee on Documentation, Libraries and Archives, UNESCO, 1968–73; Cons. on Documentation to ILO and to European Packaging Fedn; Cttee Mem., UNISIST/UNESCO and EUDISED/Council of Europe Projects; Member: Army Educn Adv. Bd, 1968–73; Library Adv. Council, 1975–77. Visiting Professor: Univ. of Michigan, 1964; Univ. of Ghana, 1967; Univ. of Ibadan, 1967; Brazilian Inst. for Bibliography and Documentation, 1971; Univ. of Iceland, 1974. FLA 1949, Hon. FLA, 1975; Hon. Fellow, Polytechnic of North London, 1981. *Publications:* Assistance to Readers in Lending Libraries, 1952; (with E. A. Baker) Bibliography of Food, 1958; Information Service in Libraries, 1958, 2nd edn 1967; Classification and Indexing in the Social Sciences, 1963, 2nd edn 1974; Science, Humanism and Libraries, 1964; Reader in Comparative Librarianship, 1977; Pathways for Communication, 1984; contrib. to many professional jls. *Recreations:* books, travel, writing, cricket. *Address:* 1 Daleside, Gerrard's Cross, Bucks SL9 7JF. *T:* Gerrard's Cross (0753) 882835. *Clubs:* MCC; Sussex CCC.

FOSS, Kathleen, (Kate); Member of Board, since 1983 and Chairman, since 1989, Direct Mail Services Standards Board; *b* 17 May 1925; *d* of George Arden and May Elizabeth Arden; *m* 1951, Robert Foss; one *s*. *Educ:* Northampton High Sch.; Whitelands Coll. (Teaching Dip.). Teacher: Northants, 1945–47; Mddx, 1947–53 (Dep. Head); Westmorland, 1953–60 (History specialist). Chairman: Consumers in European Community Gp (UK), 1979–82; Insurance Ombudsman Bureau, 1986– (Mem. Council, 1984–); Member: Nat. Consumer Council, 1980–83; Consumers' Consultative Cttee, Brussels, 1981–86; Law Commn Standing Cttee on Conveyancing, 1985–88; Data Protection Tribunal Panel, 1986–; Council for Licensed Conveyancers, 1986–88. Vice Pres., Keep Britain Tidy Gp, 1982–88 (Vice-Chm., 1979–82); Mem. Exec., National Fedn of Women's Insts, 1969–81 (National Treasurer, 1974–78); Chm., Bd of Dirs, WI Books Ltd, 1981–89. *Recreations:* golf, bridge. *Address:* Merston, 61 Back Lane, Knapton, York YO2 6QJ. *T:* York (0904) 782549.

FOSTER; *see* Hylton-Foster.

FOSTER, Prof. Allan (Bentham); Professor of Chemistry, University of London, 1966–86, now Emeritus; Secretary, British Technology Group, New Cancer Product Development Advisory Board, since 1986; *b* 21 July 1926; *s* of late Herbert and Martha Alice Foster; *m* 1949, Monica Binns; two *s*. *Educ:* Nelson Grammar Sch., Lancs; University of Birmingham. Frankland Medal and Prize, 1947; PhD, 1950; DSc, 1957. University Res. Fellow, University of Birmingham, 1950–53; Fellow of Rockefeller Foundn, Ohio State Univ., 1953–54; University of Birmingham: ICI Res. Fellow, 1954–55; Lectr, 1955–62; Sen. Lectr, 1962–64; Reader in Organic Chemistry, 1964–66; Institute of Cancer Research: Head of Chemistry Div., Chester Beatty Res. Inst., 1966–82; Head, Drug Metabolism Team, Drug Develt Sect., 1982–86. FChemSoc (Mem. Coun., 1962–65, 1967–70); Corresp. Mem., Argentinian Chem. Soc. Editor, Carbohydrate Research. *Publications:* numerous scientific papers mainly in Jl Chem. Soc. and Carbohydrate Research. *Recreations:* golf, gardening. *Address:* 1 Pine Walk, Carshalton Beeches, Surrey SM5 4ES. *T:* 081–642 4102. *Club:* Banstead Downs.

FOSTER, Andrew William; Deputy Chief Executive, NHS Management Executive, since 1991; *b* 29 Dec. 1944; *s* of George William and Gladys Maria Foster; *m* 1967, Christine Marquiss; one *s* one *d*. *Educ:* Abingdon School; Newcastle Polytechnic (BSc Sociol.); LSE (Postgrad. Dip. Applied Social Studies). Social Worker, London, 1966–71; Area Social Services Officer, 1971–75; Asst Dir of Social Services, Haringey, 1975–79; Dir of Social Services, Greenwich, 1979–82, N Yorks, 1982–87; Regional Gen. Manager, Yorks RHA, 1987–91. *Recreations:* golf, squash, walking, travel, theatre, food, wine. *Address:* Brewery House, Thornton-le-Moor, North Yorks DL7 9DS. *T:* Northallerton (0609) 774742.

FOSTER, Brendan, MBE 1976; television athletics commentator, since 1981; Managing Director, Nova International Ltd, since 1987; *b* 12 Jan. 1948; *s* of Francis and Margaret Foster; *m* 1972; one *s* one *d*. *Educ:* St Joseph's Grammar Sch., Hebburn, Co. Durham; Sussex Univ. (BSc); Carnegie Coll., Leeds (DipEd). School Teacher, St Joseph's Grammar Sch., Hebburn, 1970–74; Sports and Recreation Manager, Gateshead Metropolitan Bor. Council, 1974–81; UK Man. Dir, Nike Internat., 1981–87; Chm., Nike (UK), 1981–86; Man. Dir, Nike Europe, 1985–87; Vice Pres. Marketing, Nike Inc. Oregon, USA, 1986–87. Commonwealth Games: Bronze medal: 1500 metres, 1970; 5000 m, 1978; Silver medal, 5000 m, 1974; Gold medal, 10,000 m, 1978; European Games: Bronze medal, 1500 m, 1971; Gold medal, 5000 m, 1974; Olympic Games: Bronze medal, 10,000 m, 1976; World Records: 2 miles, 1973; 3000 metres, 1974. Hon. Fellow, Sunderland Polytechnic, 1977; Hon. MEd, Newcastle, 1978; Hon. DLitt, Sussex, 1982. *Publications:* Brendan Foster, 1978; Olympic Heroes 1896–1984, 1984. *Recreations:* running (now only a recreation), sport (as spectator).

FOSTER, Sir Christopher (David), Kt 1986; MA; Director and Head of Economics Practice, Coopers & Lybrand Deloitte (formerly Coopers & Lybrand Associates), since 1988; *b* 30 Oct. 1930; *s* of George Cecil Foster and Phyllis Joan Foster (*née* Mappin); *m* 1958, Kay Sheridan Bullock; two *s* three *d*. *Educ:* Merchant Taylors' Sch.; King's Coll., Cambridge (Scholar). Economics Tripos 1954; MA 1959. Commnd into 1st Bn Seaforth Highlanders, Malaya, 1949. Hallsworth Research Fellow, Manchester Univ., 1957–59; Senior Research Fellow, Jesus Coll., Oxford, 1959–64; Official Fellow and Tutor, Jesus Coll., 1964–66; Dir-Gen. of Economic Planning, MoT, 1966–70; Head of Unit for Res. in Urban Economics, LSE, 1970–76; Prof. of Urban Studies and Economics, LSE, 1976–78; a Dir and Head of Econ. and Public Policy Div., Coopers & Lybrand Associates, 1978–84; a Dir, Public Sector Practice Leader and Economic Advr, Coopers & Lybrand, 1984–86; Commercial Adviser to British Telecom, 1986–88. Governor, 1967–70, Dir, 1976–78, Centre for Environmental Studies; Visiting Professor: of Economics, MIT, 1970; LSE, 1978–86; Special Economic Adviser (part time), DoE, 1974–77. Member: (part time), PO Bd, 1975–77; Audit Commn, 1983–88; ESRC, 1985–89; Chm., NEDO Construction Industry Sector Gp, 1988–. Chm., Cttee of Inquiry into Road Haulage Licensing, 1977–78; Mem., Cttee of Inquiry into Civil Service Pay, 1981–82; Economic Assessor, Sizewell B Inquiry, 1982–86. Mem., LDDC, 1988–. Vice-Pres., RIPA; Chm., Circle 33 Housing Assoc, 1986–90. *Publications:* The Transport Problem, 1963; Politics, Finance and the Role of Economics: an essay on the control of public enterprise, 1972; (with R. Jackman and M. Perlman) Local Government Finance, 1980; papers in various economic and other journals. *Address:* 6 Holland Park Avenue, W11 3QU. *T:* 071–727 4757. *Clubs:* Reform, Royal Automobile.

FOSTER, Christopher Norman; Deputy Chief Executive, Jockey Club, since 1990 (Secretary, 1983–90); *b* 30 Dec. 1946; *s* of Maj.-Gen. Norman Leslie Foster, *qv*; *m* 1981, Anthea Jane Sammons; two *s*. *Educ:* Westminster Sch. ACA 1969, FCA 1979. Cooper Brothers & Co., Chartered Accountants, 1965–73; Weatherbys, 1973–90. Governor, Westminster Sch. Soc., 1990–. *Recreations:* racing, shooting, fishing, gardening. *Address:* 29 Homefield Road, Chiswick, W4 2LW. *T:* 081–995 9309. *Club:* MCC.

FOSTER, Hon. Dennis (Haley), CVO 1983; CBE 1981; JP; Chief Secretary, Cayman Islands, 1976; retired; *b* 26 March 1931; *s* of late Arnold and Agatha Foster; *m* 1955, Reba Raphael Grant; one *d*. *Educ:* Munro Coll., Kingston, Jamaica. Joined Cayman Is Civil Service, 1950; seconded as Asst Administrator, Turks and Caicos Is, 1959; Dist Comr, Lesser Is, 1960; Asst Administrator, Cayman Is, 1968. *Recreation:* gardening. *Address:* PO Box 860, George Town, Grand Cayman, Cayman Islands, WI. *T:* 9–2236.

FOSTER, Derek; MP (Lab) Bishop Auckland, since 1979; *b* 25 June 1937; *s* of Joseph and Ethel Maud Foster; *m* 1972, Florence Anne Bulmer; three *s* one *d*. *Educ:* Bede Grammar Sch., Sunderland; Oxford Univ. (BA Hons PPE). In industry and commerce, 1960–70; Youth and Community Worker, 1970–73; Further Educn Organiser, Durham, 1973–74; Asst Dir of Educn, Sunderland Borough Council, 1974–79. Councillor: Sunderland Co. Borough, 1972–74; Tyne and Wear County Council, 1973–77 (Chm. Econ. Develt Cttee, 1973–76). Chm., North of England Develt Council, 1974–76. North Regional Whip, 1981–82; PPS to Leader of Opposition, 1983–85; Opposition Chief Whip, 1985–. Mem., Select Cttee on Trade and Industry, 1980–82; opposition front bench spokesman on social security, 1982–83. Vice Chm., Youthaid, 1979–86. *Recreations:* brass bands, choirs, uniformed member Salvation Army. *Address:* 3 Linburn, Rickleton, Washington, Tyne and Wear. *T:* Washington (091) 4171580.

FOSTER, George Arthur C.; *see* Carey-Foster.

FOSTER, Ian Hampden; a Master of the Supreme Court, Queen's Bench Division, since 1991; *b* 27 Feb. 1946; *s* of Eric Hampden Foster and Irene Foster (*née* Warman); *m* 1975, Fiona Jane, *d* of Rev. J. N. Robertson-Glasgow; one *s* one *d*. *Educ:* Battersea Grammar Sch.; Univ. of Exeter (LLB Hons 1968). Called to the Bar, Inner Temple, 1969; practice at common law bar, 1969–91. *Recreations:* gardening, reading. *Address:* Royal Courts of Justice, Strand, WC2.

FOSTER, Joan Mary; Under Secretary, Department of Transport, Highways Planning and Management, 1978–80, retired; *b* 20 January 1923; *d* of John Whitfield Foster and Edith Foster (*née* Levett). *Educ:* Northampton School for Girls. Entered Civil Service (HM Office of Works), Oct. 1939; Ministry of Transport, 1955; Asst Secretary, 1970. *Recreations:* gardening, cooking, good wine. *Address:* 3 Hallfields, Shouldham, King's Lynn, Norfolk PE33 0DN. *T:* Fincham (03664) 7809.

FOSTER, Joanna Katharine; Chair, Equal Opportunities Commission, since 1988; *b* 5 May 1939; *d* of Michael and Lesley Mead; *m* 1961, Jerome Foster; one *s* one *d*. *Educ:* Benenden School; Univ. of Grenoble. Sec. and Editl Asst, Vogue Magazine, London and NY, 1958–59; journalist, San Francisco Chronicle, 1959; Head of Press Dept, Conservative Central Office, 1962–66; Management Adviser, Industrial Soc., 1966–72; Dir, Centre Actif Bilingue, Fontainebleau, 1972–79; Press Attachée and Editor, INSEAD, Fontainebleau, 1972–79; Educn and Trng Dir, Corporate Services Unit, Western Psychiatric Inst. and Clinic, Univ. of Pittsburgh, 1980–82; Management Adviser, 1982–85, Head of Pepperell Unit, 1985–88, Industrial Soc. Member: Council, Industrial Soc., 1990; Council and Exec. Cttee, Duke of Edinburgh's Commonwealth Study Conf., 1990; Pres., European Commn Adv. Cttee on Equal Opportunities, 1991– (Vice Pres., 1990). Dir, WNO, 1990. Hon. Fellow, St Hilda's Coll., Oxford, 1988. *Recreations:* family, friends, food. *Address:* 43 Bainton Road, Oxford OX2 7AG. *T:* Oxford (0865) 514400. *Club:* Reform.

FOSTER, Sir John (Gregory), 3rd Bt *cr* 1930; Consultant Physician, George, Cape Province; *b* 26 Feb. 1927; *s* of Sir Thomas Saxby Gregory Foster, 2nd Bt, and Beryl, *d* of late Dr Alfred Ireland; *S* father, 1957; *m* 1956, Jean Millicent Watts; one *s* three *d*. *Educ:* Michaelhouse Coll., Natal. South African Artillery, 1944–46; Witwatersrand Univ., 1946–51; MB, BCh 1951; Post-graduate course, MRCPE 1955; Medical Registrar, 1955–56; Medical Officer, Cape Town, 1957. DIH London, 1962; FRCPE 1981. *Recreation:* outdoor sport. *Heir:* *s* Saxby Gregory Foster, *b* 3 Sept. 1957. *Address:* 7 Caledon Street, PO Box 1325, George, Cape Province, South Africa. *T:* George 743333. *Club:* Johannesburg Country (S Africa).

FOSTER, (John) Peter, OBE 1990; Surveyor of the Fabric of Westminster Abbey, 1973–88, now Emeritus; *b* 2 May 1919; *s* of Francis Edward Foster and Evelyn Marjorie, *e d* of Sir Charles Stewart Forbes, 5th Bt of Newe; *m* 1944, Margaret Elizabeth Skipper; one *s* one *d*. *Educ:* Eton; Trinity Hall, Cambridge. BA 1940, MA 1946; ARIBA 1949. Commnd RE 1941; served Norfolk Div.; joined Guards Armd Div. 1943, served France and Germany; Captain SORE(2) 30 Corps 1945; discharged 1946. Marshall Sisson, Architect: Asst 1948, later Partner; Sole Principal 1971; Surveyor of Royal Academy of Arts, 1965–80. Partner with John Peters of Vine Press, Hemingford Grey, 1957–63. Art Workers' Guild: Mem., 1971; Master, 1980; Trustee, 1985. Pres., Surveyors Club, 1980. Member: Churches Cttee for Historic Building Council for England, 1977–84; Adv. Bd for Redundant Churches, 1979–91; Exec. Cttee, Georgian Gp, 1983–; Fabric Cttee, Canterbury Cathedral, 1987– (Chm., 1990); Council, Ancient Monuments Soc., 1988–; Fabric Cttee, Ely Cathedral, 1990. Chm., Cathedral Architects Assoc., 1987–90. Governor, Suttons Hosp., Charterhouse, 1982–. FSA 1973. *Recreations:* painting, books, travel, shooting. *Address:* Harcourt, Hemingford Grey, Huntingdon, Cambs PE18 9BJ. *T:* St Ives (0480) 62200. *Club:* Athenæum.

FOSTER, John Robert; National Organiser, Amalgamated Union of Engineering Workers, 1962–81, retired; *b* 30 Jan. 1916; *s* of George Foster and Amelia Ann (*née* Elkington); *m* 1938, Catherine Georgina (*née* Webb); one *s* one *d*. *Educ:* London County Council. Apprentice toolmaker, 1931–36; toolmaker, 1936–47; Amalgamated Engineering Union: Kingston District Sec. (full-time official), 1947–62. In Guyana for ILO, 1982. Lectr on industrial relns and trade union educn, WEA, 1981–. Mem., Industrial Tribunals (England and Wales), 1984–86. Mem., Engrg Industry Trng Bd, 1974–80; Vice-Chm., Electricity Supply Industry Trng Cttee, 1967–81; Mem., Adv. Council on Energy Conservation, 1978–82. Mem., Soc. of Industrial Tutors, 1981–. MRI 1978. *Recreations:* music, photography, angling, 17th Century English Revolution. *Address:* 10 Grosvenor Gardens, Kingston-upon-Thames KT2 5BE.

FOSTER, Very Rev. Canon John William, BEM 1946; Dean of Guernsey, 1978–88; Rector of St Peter Port, Guernsey, 1978–88; Canon Emeritus of Winchester Cathedral since 1988; *b* 5 Aug. 1921; *m* 1943, Nancy Margaret Allen; one *s*. *Educ:* St Aidan's Coll., Birkenhead. Served Leicestershire Yeomanry, 1939–46; Chaplain, Hong Kong Defence Force, 1958–. Reserve of Officers, Hong Kong Defence Force, 1967–73. Priest 1955; Curate of Loughborough, 1954–57; Chaplain, St John's Cathedral, Hong Kong, 1957–60, Precentor, 1960–63; Dean of Hong Kong, 1963–73; Hon. Canon, St John's Cathedral, Hong Kong, 1973; Vicar of Lythe, dio. York, 1973–78; Hon. Canon of Winchester, 1979–88. *Address:* 14 Lightfoots Avenue, Scarborough, N Yorks YO12 5NS. *T:* Scarborough (0723) 379012.

FOSTER, Jonathan Rowe; QC 1989; a Recorder, since 1988; *b* 20 July 1947; *s* of Donald Foster and Hilda Eaton; *m* 1978, Sarah Ann Mary da Cunha; four *s*. *Educ:* Oundle Sch.; Keble Coll., Oxford. Called to the Bar, Gray's Inn, 1970. *Recreations:* children, outdoor pursuits. *Address:* (chambers) 18 St John Street, Manchester M3 4EA. *T:* 061–834 9843. *Clubs:* St James's (Manchester); Hale Golf, Bowdon Lawn Tennis.

FOSTER, Lawrence; conductor; Chief Conductor, Orchestre National of Monte Carlo, since 1978; Music Director, Lausanne Chamber Orchestra, since 1985; *b* Los Angeles, 23 Oct. 1941; *s* of Thomas Foster and Martha Wurmbrandt. *Educ:* Univ. of California, LA; studied under Fritz Zweig, Bruno Walter and Karl Böhm. Asst Conductor, Los Angeles Philharmonic, 1965–68; British début, Royal Festival Hall, 1968; Covent Garden début, Troilus and Cressida, 1976; Chief Guest Conductor, Royal Philharmonic Orchestra, 1969–74; Music Dir and Chief Conductor, Houston Symphony Orchestra, 1971–78; Gen. Music Dir, Duisberg concert series, 1982–86; Prin. Guest. Conductor, Düsseldorf Opera, 1982–. *Recreations:* water skiing, table tennis. *Address:* c/o Harrison/Parrott Ltd, 12 Penzance Place, W11 4PE.

FOSTER, Maj.-Gen. Norman Leslie, CB 1961; DSO 1945; *b* 26 Aug. 1909; *s* of late Col A. L. Foster, Wimbledon; *m* 1937, Joan Constance, *d* of late Canon T. W. E. Drury; two *s*. *Educ:* Westminster; RMA Woolwich. 2nd Lieut, RA, 1929; Served War of 1939–45 in Egypt and Italy; CRA 11th Armoured Division, 1955–56; Deputy Military Sec., War Office, 1958–59; Maj.-Gen., 1959; GOC Royal Nigerian Army, 1959–62; Pres., Regular Commissions Board, 1962–65; retired, 1965. Dir of Security (Army), MoD, 1965–73. Security Advr, CSD, 1974–79. Col Comdt, Royal Regt of Artillery, 1966–74. Pres., Truman and Knightley Educnl Trust Ltd, 1982–87 (Chm., 1976–80). *Address:* Besborough, Heath End, Farnham, Surrey GU9 9AR.
See also C. N. Foster.

FOSTER, Sir Norman (Robert), Kt 1990; RA 1991 (ARA); RDI; RIBA, FCSD, FAIA; architect; Director: Foster Associates Ltd, London; Foster Associates SA, France; Foster Associates Japan; *b* Redditch, 1 June 1935; *s* of late Robert Foster and Lilian Smith; *m* 1964, Wendy Ann Cheesman (*d* 1989); four *s*. *Educ:* Univ. of Manchester Sch. of Architecture (DipArch 1961, CertTP); Yale Univ. Sch. of Architecture (Henry Fellow, Jonathan Edwards Coll., March 1962). Consultancy works on city planning and urban renewal, USA, 1962–63; private practice as Team 4 Architects, London, 1963–67; (with Wendy Foster) founded Foster Associates, 1967; in collab. with Dr Buckminster Fuller, 1968–83; Cons. Architect to Univ. of E Anglia, 1978–87. Mem. Council: AA, 1969–70, 1970–71 (Vice Pres., 1974); RCA, 1981–. Taught at: Univ. of Pennsylvania; AA, London; Bath Acad. of Arts; London Polytechnic. External Examr and Mem. Visiting Bd of Educn, RIBA. Major projects include: IBM Pilot Head Office, Hampshire, 1970; Sainsbury Centre for Visual Arts, Univ. of E Anglia, Norwich, 1977; Technical Park for IBM, Greenford, 1975; Head Office for Willis Faber & Dumas, Ipswich, 1979 (first Trustees' Medal, RIBA, 1990); develt project, Whitney Gall., NY, 1979; Students' Union Project, UCL, 1979; UK headquarters for Renault, 1980; winning design, internat. competition for new headquarters, Hongkong and Shanghai Banking Corp., Hong Kong, 1979 (IStructE Special Award, 1986); Third London Airport Terminal, 1980 and Terminal Zone, Stansted, 1991; winning design, internat. competition for Nat. German Indoor Athletic Stadium, Frankfurt, 1981; limited competition headquarters for Humana, Kentucky, USA, 1981; winner, BBC new Radio Broadcasting Centre, 1983; Stockley Park, UK, 1989; ITN building, 1990; Century Tower, Tokyo, 1991; winner, international competition for: Arts Centre, Nimes, France, 1984; Nomos Furniture System, 1985; Televisa Headquarters, Mexico, 1986; Civic Hall, Nancy, 1986; Esprit Shop, London, 1987; Bilbao Metro System, 1988; Kings Cross London Master Plan, 1988; Millennium Tower, Tokyo, 1990; RA Diploma Galls, 1991; Barcelona Telecoms Tower, 1991. Work exhibited: Mus. of Mod. Art, New York, 1979 and Permanent Exhibn, 1982; Three New Skyscrapers, Museum of Modern Art, NY, 1983; Summer Exhibn RA; Milan, 1983; Barcelona, 1976; Manchester, 1984; Berlin, 1984; Paris, 1985, 1986; Sainsbury Centre, 1985, 1991; Hannover, 1986; Nimes, 1986; RA 1986; Tokyo. IBM Fellow, Aspen Conference, 1980; Hon. FAIA 1980; Hon. Mem., Bund deutscher Architekten, 1983; Member: Internat. Acad. of Architecture, Sofia; French Order of Architects; Associate, Académie Royale de Belgique, 1990. Hon. LittD East Anglia, 1980; Hon. DSc Bath, 1986. ARA 1983; RDI 1988; other awards include: R. S. Reynolds Internat. Awards, USA, 1976, 1979, 1986; RIBA Awards and Commendations, 1969, 1972, 1977, 1978, 1981; Royal Gold Medal for Architecture, 1983; Financial Times Awards for outstanding Industrial Architecture and Commendations, 1967, 1970, 1971, 1974, 1984; Structural Steel Awards, 1972, 1978, 1984, 1986; Internat. Design Award, 1976, 1980; RSA Award, 1976; Ambrose Congreve Award, 1980; Yale Arts Award for Outstanding Achievement, 1985; Constructa-European Award, 1986; Premio Compasso d'Oro Award, 1987; Japan Design Foundn Award, 1987; Annual Interiors Award (USA), 1988; Kunstpreis Award, Berlin, 1989; Trustees Medal, RIBA, 1990; Mies van der Rohe Award, Barcelona, 1991; Gold Medal, French Academy, 1991. *Publications:* contributed to: The Work of Foster Associates, 1979; Norman Foster, 1988; Norman Foster Foster Associates Buildings and Projects, vols 1, 2 and 3, 1989; also to various technical publications. *Recreations:* flying sailplanes, helicopters and light aircraft; running. *Address:* (office) Riverside Three, Albert Wharf, 22 Hester Road, SW11 4AN. *T:* 071–738 0455, *Fax:* 071–738 1107.

FOSTER, Peter; *see* Foster, J. P.

FOSTER, Maj.-Gen. Peter Beaufoy, MC 1944; Major-General Royal Artillery, British Army of the Rhine, 1973–76; retired June 1976; *b* 1 Sept. 1921; *s* of F. K. Foster, OBE, JP, Allt Dinas, Cheltenham; *m* 1947, Margaret Geraldine, *d* of W. F. Henn, sometime Chief Constable of Glos; two *s* one *d* (and one *s* decd). *Educ:* Uppingham School. Commnd RA, 1941; psc 1950; jssc 1958; OC Para. Light Battery, 1958–60; DAMS MS5, WO, 1960–63; Mil. Assistant to C-in-C BAOR, 1963–64; CO 34 Light Air Defence Regt RA, 1964–66; GSO1, ASD5, MoD, 1966–68; BRA Northern Comd, 1968–71; Comdt Royal Sch. of Artillery, 1971–73. Col Comdt, RA, 1977–82; Regimental Comptroller, RA, 1985–86. Chapter Clerk, Salisbury Cathedral, 1978–85. *Recreations:* shooting, gardening, walking. *Address:* Sherborn House, High Street, Chipping Campden, Gloucestershire.

FOSTER, Peter Martin, CMG 1975; HM Diplomatic Service, retired; *b* 25 May 1924; *s* of Frederick Arthur Peace Foster and Marjorie Kathleen Sandford; *m* 1947, Angela Hope Cross; one *s* one *d*. *Educ:* Sherborne; Corpus Christi Coll., Cambridge. Army (Horse Guards), 1943–47; joined Foreign (now Diplomatic) Service, 1948; served in Vienna, Warsaw, Pretoria/Cape Town, Bonn, Kampala, Tel Aviv; Head of Central and Southern Africa Dept, FCO, 1972–74; Ambassador and UK Rep. to Council of Europe, 1974–78; Ambassador to German Democratic Republic, 1978–81. Dir, Council for Arms Control, 1984–86; Chm., Internat. Social Service of GB, 1985–90. *Address:* Rew Cottage, Abinger Lane, Abinger Common, Surrey RH5 6HZ. *T:* Dorking (0306) 730114.

FOSTER, Richard Anthony, FSA, FMA; Director, National Museums and Galleries on Merseyside, since 1986; *b* 3 Oct. 1941; *s* of late Eric Kenneth Foster and of Sylvia Renee Foster (now Westerman); *m* 1964, Mary Browning James; two *s* one *d*. *Educ:* Kingswood Sch.; London Sch. of Economics (BSc Econ 1963); Manchester Univ. (MA 1968). Student Asst, Leicester Museum, 1964–66; Museum Asst, Bowes Museum, Barnard Castle, 1967–68; Keeper in Charge, Durham Light Infantry Museum and Arts Centre, Durham, 1968–70; Dir, Oxford City and County Museum, Woodstock, 1970–74; Dir, Museum Services, Oxfordshire County Museum Service, Woodstock, 1974–78; Dir of Museums, Merseyside County Museums, Liverpool, 1978–86. Member: Merseyside Tourist Board, 1986; Board: NW Museums and Art Galls Service, 1986; Inst. of Popular Music, Univ. of Liverpool, 1987. Advr, Fabric Cttee, Liverpool Cathedral, 1988. Trustee, Boat Mus., Ellesmere Port, 1987. *Recreations:* sailing, watching football. *Address:* National Museums and Galleries on Merseyside, Liverpool Museum, William Brown Street, Liverpool L3 8EN. *T:* 051–207 0001.

FOSTER, Prof. Robert Fitzroy, (Roy), PhD; FRHistS; FBA 1989; Carroll Professor of Irish History, University of Oxford, since 1991; *b* 16 Jan. 1949; *s* of Frederick Ernest Foster and Elizabeth (*née* Fitzroy); *m* 1972, Aisling O'Conor Donelan; one *s* one *d*. *Educ:* Newtown Sch., Waterford; St Andrew's Sch., Middletown, Delaware, USA; Trinity Coll., Dublin (MA; PhD 1975). FRHistS 1979. Lectr, 1974, Reader, 1983, Professor of Modern British Hist., 1988–91, Birkbeck Coll., London Univ. Alistair Horne Fellow, St Antony's Coll., Oxford, 1979–80; British Acad. Res. Reader in the Humanities, 1987–89; Fellow, Inst. for Advanced Study, Princeton, and Vis. Fellow, Dept of English, Princeton Univ., 1988–89. Irish Post Community Award, 1982; Sunday Independent/Irish Life Arts Award, 1988. *Publications:* Charles Stewart Parnell: the man and his family, 1976, 2nd edn 1979; Lord Randolph Churchill: a political life, 1981, 3rd edn 1987; Political Novels and Nineteenth Century History, 1983; Modern Ireland 1600–1972, 1988; (ed) The Oxford Illustrated History of Ireland, 1989; (ed) The Sub-Prefect Should Have Held His Tongue and other essays, by Hubert Butler, 1990; numerous essays and reviews. *Recreation:* recreation. *Address:* Hertford College, Oxford OX1 3BW. *Club:* Academy.

FOSTER, Sir Robert (Sidney), GCMG 1970 (KCMG 1964; CMG 1961); KCVO 1970; Governor-General and Commander-in-Chief of Fiji, 1970–73 (Governor and C-in-C, 1968–70); retired 1973; *b* 11 Aug. 1913; *s* of late Sidney Charles Foster and late Jessie Edith (*née* Fry); *m* 1947, Margaret (*née* Walker); no *c*. *Educ:* Eastbourne Coll.; Peterhouse, Cambridge. MA. Appointed Cadet, Administrative Service, Northern Rhodesia, 1936; District Officer, N Rhodesia, 1938. War Service, 2nd Bn Northern Rhodesia Regt, 1940–43, Major. Provincial Commissioner, N Rhodesia, 1957; Sec., Ministry of Native Affairs, N Rhodesia, 1960; Chief Sec., Nyasaland, 1961–63; Dep. Governor, Nyasaland, 1963–64; High Comr for W Pacific, 1964–68. KStJ 1968. Officer of the Legion of Honour, 1966. *Recreation:* self-help. *Address:* Kenwood, 16 Ardnave Crescent, Southampton SO1 7FJ. *Clubs:* Royal Over-Seas League; Leander (Henley).

FOSTER, Roy; *see* Foster, Robert Fitzroy.

FOSTER, Thomas Ashcroft; social services consultant, since 1990; *b* 27 May 1934; *s* of Thomas Lawrence Foster and Ada May Foster (*née* Ashcroft); *m* 1959, Beryl Wilson; two *d*. *Educ:* Rivington and Blackrod Grammar Sch.; Univ. of Leicester (Dip. Social Studies 1957); University Coll. of South Wales and Momouthshire (Dip. Applied Social Studies 1963). Youth Employment Asst, Derbyshire CC, 1957–59; Child Care Officer, Manchester City Council, 1959–62; Senior Mental Welfare Officer, Carlisle City Council, 1963; Student Supervisor, Children's Dept, Glamorgan CC, 1963–67; Area Children's Officer, Lancs CC, 1967–71; Divl Dir, Social Services, Cheshire CC, 1971–73; Dir, Social Services, Tameside Met. Borough Council, 1973–86; Dir of Social Services, Lancs CC, 1986–90. Mem., Cttee of Inquiry into Mental Handicap Nursing and Care, 1975–79; Social Services Adviser, AMA, 1983–86. Sen. Vice-Pres., Assoc. of Dirs of Social Servs, 1990. Hon. Lectr, Univ. of Lancaster, 1990. *Recreations:* theatre, archaeology, walking.

FOSTER-BROWN, Rear-Adm. Roy Stephenson, CB 1958; RN Retired; *b* 16 Jan. 1904; *s* of Robert Allen Brown and Agnes Wilfreda Stephenson; *m* 1933, Joan Wentworth Foster; two *s*. *Educ:* RNC, Osborne and Dartmouth. Specialised in Submarines, 1924–28; specialised in Signals, 1930. Fleet Signal Officer, Home Fleet, 1939–40; Staff Signal Officer, Western Approaches, 1940–44; Comdr HMS Ajax, 1944–46; Capt., 1946; Capt. Sixth Frigate Sqdn, 1951; Dir Signal Div., Admiralty, 1952–53; Capt. HMS Ceylon, 1954; Rear-Adm. 1955; Flag Officer, Gibraltar, 1956–59; retd 1959. Hon. Comdt, Girls Nautical Trng Corps, 1961–. Master, Armourers and Braziers Co., 1964–65, 1974–75. *Recreations:* sailing, shooting, golf, tennis. *Address:* 13 Ravenscroft Road, Henley on Thames, Oxon RG9 2DH. *Club:* Army and Navy.

FOSTER-SUTTON, Sir Stafford William Powell, KBE 1957 (OBE (mil.) 1945); Kt 1951; CMG 1948; QC (Jamaica, 1938, Fedn Malaya, 1948); *b* 24 Dec. 1898; *s* of late G. Foster Sutton and Mrs Foster Sutton; *m* 1919, Linda Dorothy, *d* of late John Humber Allwood, OBE, and of Mrs Allwood, Enfield, St Ann, Jamaica; one *d* (one *s* decd). *Educ:* St Mary Magdalen Sch.; private tutor. HM Army, 1914–26; served European War, 1914–18, Infantry, RFC and RAF, active service. Called to the Bar, Gray's Inn, 1926; private practice, 1926–36; Solicitor Gen., Jamaica, 1936; Attorney-Gen., Cyprus, 1940; Col Comdg Cyprus Volunteer Force and Inspector Cyprus Forces, 1941–44; Mem. for Law and Order and Attorney-Gen., Kenya, 1944–48; actg Governor, Aug. and Sept. 1947; Attorney-Gen., Malaya, 1948–50; Officer Administering Govt, Malaya, Sept., Dec. 1950; Chief Justice, Fedn of Malaya, 1950–51; Dir of Man-Power, Kenya, 1944–45; Chm. Labour Advisory Board, Kenya, and Kenya European Service Advisory Board, 1944–48; Pres. of the West African Court of Appeal, 1951–55; Chief Justice, Fedn of Nigeria, 1955–58; Actg Governor-Gen., Nigeria, May-June 1957. Pres., Pensions Appeal Tribunals for England and Wales, 1958–73. Chairman: Zanzibar Commn of Inquiry, 1961; Kenya Regional and Electorial Commns, 1962–; Referendum Observers, Malta,

1964; Vice Pres., Britain-Nigeria Assoc., 1982–. Mem. Court, Tallow Chandlers' Co. (Master, 1981). *Address:* 7 London Road, Saffron Walden, Essex.

FOTHERGILL, Dorothy Joan; Director, Postal Pay and Grading, 1974–83, retired; *b* 31 Dec. 1923; *d* of Samuel John Rimington Fothergill and Dorothy May Patterson. *Educ:* Haberdashers' Aske's Sch., Acton; University Coll. London. BA (Hons) History. Entered Civil Service as Asst Principal, 1948; Principal, Overseas Mails branch, GPO, 1953; UPU Congress, Ottawa, 1957; Establishments work, 1958–62; HM Treasury, 1963–65; Asst Sec., Pay and Organisation, GPO, 1965; Director: Postal Personnel, 1970; London Postal Region, 1971. *Recreations:* gardening, walking, theatre. *Address:* 38 Andrewes House, Barbican, EC2Y 8AX.

FOTHERGILL, Richard Humphrey Maclean; Director, The Ceres Trust, since 1988; *b* 21 March 1937; *s* of late Col C. G. Fothergill, RM, and of Mrs E. G. Fothergill; *m* 1962, Angela Cheshire Martin; three *d*. *Educ:* Sandle Manor, Fordingbridge; Clifton Coll., Bristol; Emmanuel Coll., Cambridge (BA Hons Nat. Sci. Tripos, 1958). Commnd RASC, National Service, 1959–61. Contemporary Films Ltd, 1961; Head of Biology, SW Ham Technical Sch., 1961–69; Res. Fellow, Nat. Council for Educnl Technol., 1970–72; Founder and Head of PETRAS (Educnl Develt Unit), Newcastle upon Tyne Polytechnic, 1972–80; Dir, Microelectronics Educn Prog., DES, 1980–86; Dir, CET, 1986–87. Co-founder, Sec. and Treasurer, Standing Conf. on Educnl Develt Services in Polytechnics, 1974–80; Member: London GCE Bd and Schools Council Science Cttee, 1968–72; Standards and Specifications Cttee, CET, 1972–80. *Publications:* A Challenge for Librarians, 1971; Resource Centres in Colleges of Education, 1973; (with B. Williams) Microforms in Education, 1977; Child Abuse: a teaching package, 1978; (with I. Butchart) Non-book Materials in Libraries: a practical guide, 1978, 3rd edn 1990; (with J. S. A. Anderson) Microelectronics Education Programme: policy and guidelines, 1983; Implications of the New Technology for the School Curriculum, 1988; articles in Visual Educn, Educn Libraries Bull., Educnl Media Internat., and Educnl Broadcasting Internat. *Recreations:* reading, television, films, walking. *Address:* 17 Grenville Drive, Brunton Park, Newcastle upon Tyne NE3 5PA. *T:* 091–236 3380. *Club:* National Film Theatre.

FOU TS'ONG; concert pianist; *b* 10 March 1934; *m* 1st, 1960, Zamira Menuhin (marr. diss. 1970); one *s*; 2nd, 1973, Hijong Hyun (marr. diss. 1976); 3rd, 1987, Patsy Toh; one *s*. *Educ:* Shanghai and Warsaw. Debut, Shanghai, 1953. Concerts all over Eastern Europe including USSR up to 1958. Arrived in Great Britain, Dec. 1958; London debut, Feb. 1959, followed by concerts in England, Scotland and Ireland; subsequently has toured all five Continents. Hon. DLitt Hong Kong, 1983. *Recreations:* many different ones. *Address:* c/o Intermusica Artists' Management, 16 Duncan Terrace, N1 8BZ. *T:* 071–278 5455.

FOULDS, (Hugh) Jon; Chairman, Halifax Building Society, since 1990 (Director, since 1986); Deputy Chairman, 3i Group plc (formerly Investors in Industry), since 1988 (Director and Chief Executive, 1976–88); *b* 2 May 1932; *s* of late Dr E. J. Foulds and Helen Shirley (*née* Smith); *m* 1st, 1960, Berry Cusack-Smith (marr. diss. 1970); two *s*; 2nd, 1977, Hélène Senn, *d* of Edouard Senn, Paris. *Educ:* Bootham Sch., York. Director: Brammer plc, 1980– (Chm., 1988–90); London Atlantic Investment Trust, 1983–; Pan-Holding SA, 1986–; Eurotunnel plc, 1988–; Mercury Asset Management Gp plc, 1989–. Hon. MA Salford, 1987. *Recreations:* tennis, ski-ing, shooting, pictures. *Address:* Halifax Building Society, 62 Cornhill, EC3V 3QJ. *T:* 071–839 9011. *Clubs:* Garrick, Hurlingham; Cercle Interallié (Paris).

FOULGER, Keith, BSc(Eng); CEng, MIMechE; FRINA, RCNC; Chief Naval Architect, Ministry of Defence, 1983–85, retired; *b* 14 May 1925; *s* of Percy and Kate Foulger; *m* 1951, Joyce Mary Hart; one *s* one *d*. *Educ:* Univ. of London (Mech. Eng.); Royal Naval Coll., Greenwich. Asst Constructor, 1950; Constructor, 1955; Constructor Commander: Dreadnought Project, 1959; C-in-C Western Fleet, 1965; Chief Constructor, 1967; Asst Director, Submarines, 1973; Deputy Director: Naval Construction, 1979; Naval Ship Production, 1979–81; Submarines, Ship Dept, 1981–83; Asst Under-Sec. of State, 1983. *Recreations:* travel, gardening, local community affairs, restoration of HMS Victory. *Address:* Masons, Grittleton, Chippenham, Wilts SN14 6AP. *T:* Castle Combe (0249) 782308.

FOULIS, Sir Iain (Primrose Liston), 13th Bt, *cr* 1634, of Colinton; Language Tutor, Madrid, since 1966; *b* 9 Aug. 1937; *s* of Lieut-Colonel James Alistair Liston-Foulis, Royal Artillery (killed on active service, 1942), and Mrs Kathleen de la Hogue Moran (*d* 1991), 2nd *d* of Lt-Col. John Moran, Indian Army and Countess Olga de la Hogue, *yr d* of Marquis de la Hogue, Mauritius; *S* cousin, Sir Archibald Charles Liston Foulis, 12th Bt, 1961. *Educ:* Hodder; St Mary's Hall; Stonyhurst Coll.; Cannington Farm Inst., Somerset (Dip. Agr.); Madrid (Dip. in Spanish). National Service, 1957–59; Argyll and Sutherland Highlanders, Cyprus, 1958 (Gen. Service Medal). Landowner, 1961–. Language Teacher, Estremadura and Madrid, 1959–61; Trainee, Bank of London and South America, 1962; Trainee, Bank of London and Montreal (in Nassau, 1963, Guatemala City, 1963–64; Managua, Nicaragua, 1964–65); Toronto (Sales), 1965–66. Life Mem., Nat. Trust for Scotland. Member: Spanish Soc. of the Friends of Castles; Friends of the St James Way. Cert. from Archbishop of Santiago de Compostela for pilgrimage on foot, Somport to Santiago, Jubilee Year, 1971. *Recreations:* long-distance running, swimming, walking, mountaineering, travelling, foreign languages and customs, reading, Spanish medieval history (especially Muslim Spain), car racing and rallies, country pursuits, hunting. *Address:* Edificio Cuzco, Calle Soledad II, Portal 5°, Piso 2° Letra C, San Agustin De Guadalix, 28750 Madrid, Spain. *T:* 91–8418978.

FOULKES, George, JP; MP (Lab Co-op) Carrick, Cumnock and Doon Valley, since 1983 (South Ayrshire, 1979–83); *b* 21 Jan. 1942; *s* of George and Jessie M. A. W. Foulkes; *m* 1970, Elizabeth Anna Hope; two *s* one *d*. *Educ:* Keith Grammar Sch., Keith, Banffshire; Haberdashers' Aske's Sch.; Edinburgh Univ. (BSc 1964). President: Edinburgh Univ. SRC, 1963–64; Scottish Union of Students, 1965–67; Manager, Fund for Internat. Student Cooperation, 1967–68. Scottish Organiser, European Movement, 1968–69; Director: European League for Econ. Cooperation, 1969–70; Enterprise Youth, 1970–73; Age Concern, Scotland, 1973–79. Councillor: Edinburgh Corp., 1970–75; Lothian Regional Council, 1974–79; Chairman: Lothian Region Educn Cttee, 1974–79; Educn Cttee, Convention of Scottish Local Authorities, 1975–78. Jt Chm., All Party Pensioners Cttee, 1983– (Sec./Treasurer 1979–83); Mem., H of C Select Cttee on Foreign Affairs, 1981–83; Opposition spokesman on European and Community Affairs, 1984–85, on Foreign Affairs, 1985–. UK Delegate to Parly Assembly of Council of Europe, 1979–81; Member: UK Exec., CPA, 1987–; Council, Parliamentarians for Global Action, 1987–; IPU, 1989–. Mem., Scottish Exec. Cttee, Labour Party, 1981–89. Rector's Assessor, Edinburgh Univ. Court, 1968–70, Local Authority Assessor, 1971–79. Chm., Scottish Adult Literacy Agency, 1976–79. Mem. Exec., British/China Centre, 1987–. Dir, St Cuthbert's Co-op. Assoc., 1975–79. JP Edinburgh, 1975. *Publication:* Eighty Years On: history of Edinburgh University SRC, 1964. *Recreations:* boating, watching Heart of Midlothian FC. *Address:* 8 Southpark Road, Ayr. *T:* Ayr (0292) 265776. *Clubs:* Commonwealth Trust; Edinburgh University Staff (Edinburgh).

FOULKES, Sir Nigel (Gordon), Kt 1980; Chairman: ECI International Management Ltd, 1987–91; ECI Management (Jersey) Ltd, 1986–91; Equity Capital Trustee Ltd, 1983–90; *b* 29 Aug. 1919; *s* of Louis Augustine and Winifred Foulkes; *m* 1948, Elisabeth Walker, *d* of Ewart B. Walker, Toronto; one *s* one *d* of former marr. *Educ:* Gresham's Sch., Holt; Balliol Coll., Oxford (Schol., MA). RAF, 1940–45. Subsequently executive, consulting and boardroom posts with: H. P. Bulmer; P. E. Consulting Gp; Birfield; Greaves & Thomas; International Nickel; Rank Xerox (Asst Man. Dir 1964–67, Man. Dir 1967–70); Charterhouse Group Ltd (Dir, 1972–83); Dir, Charterhouse J. Rothschild plc, 1984–85; Chm., Equity Capital for Industry, 1983–86 (Vice-Chm., 1982); Dir, Bekaert Gp (Belgium), 1973–85. Chairman: British Airports Authority, 1972–77; Civil Aviation Authority, 1977–82. CBIM; FRSA. *Address:* Westway House, West Adderbury, Banbury, Oxon OX17 3EU. *Club:* Royal Air Force.

FOUNTAIN, Alan; Senior Commissioning Editor, Channel Four TV; *b* 24 March 1946; *s* of Harold Fountain and Winifred Cecily Brown. *Educ:* Nottingham Univ. (BA Hons Philosophy). Film Officer, E Midlands Arts, 1976–79; producer, 1979–81; Channel Four TV, 1981–. *Publications:* (ed) Ruff's Guide to the Turf, 1980; contrib. film and TV pubns. *Recreations:* family, golf, watching sports. *Address:* 23 The Avenue, N10 2QE. *T:* 081–883 1815.

FOURCADE, Jean-Pierre; Officier de l'ordre national du Mérite; Senator, French Republic, for Hauts-de-Seine, since 1977; *b* 18 Oct. 1929; *s* of Raymond Fourcade (Médecin) and Mme Fourcade (*née* Germaine Raynal); *m* 1958, Odile Mion; one *s* two *d*. *Educ:* Collège de Sorèze; Bordeaux Univ. Faculté de Droit, Institut des Etudes politiques (Dip.); Ecole nationale d'administration; higher studies in Law (Dip.). Inspecteur des Finances, 1954–73. Cabinet of M. Valéry Giscard d'Estaing: Chargé de Mission, 1959–61; Conseiller technique, 1962, then Dir Adjoint to chef de service, Inspection gén. des Finances, 1962; Chef de service du commerce, at Direction-Gén. du Commerce intérieur et des Prix, 1968–70; Dir-gén. adjoint du Crédit industriel et commercial, 1970; Dir-gén., 1972, and Administrateur Dir-gén., 1973; Ministre de l'Economie et des Finances, 1974–76; Ministre de l'Equipement et de l'Aménagement du Territoire, 1976–77. Mayor of Saint-Cloud, 1971–; Conseiller général of canton of Saint-Cloud, 1973–89; Conseiller régional d'Ile de France, 1976– (Vice-Président, 1982). Président: Clubs Perspectives et Realités, 1975–82; Comité des Finances Locales, 1980; Commn des Affaires Sociales du Sénat, 1983; Vice-Pres., Union pour la Démocratie Française, 1978–86 (Mem. Bureau, 1986). *Publications:* Et si nous parlions de demain, 1979; La tentation social-démocrate, 1985. *Address:* Palais du Luxembourg, 75006 Paris, France; 8 Parc de Béarn, 92210 Saint-Cloud, France.

FOURNIER, Bernard; Managing Director, Rank Xerox Ltd, since 1989; *b* 2 Dec. 1938; *s* of Jean Fournier and Solange Herview; *m* 1st, 1961, Marie Antoinette Hache; two *s*; 2nd, 1980, Françoise Chavailler; one *s*. *Educ:* Philo Lycée (Baccalauréat); Louis Le Grand, Paris; Ecole des Hautes Etudes Commerciales, Lille. Joined: Publiart SA, 1964; Sanglier SA, 1965; Rank Xerox, 1966: Regional Manager Africa, Eastern Europe, 1980; Gen. Manager, RX France, 1981; Pres., Amer. Ops, Xerox, 1988. *Recreations:* tennis, cooking, oenology, stamps, antiques. *Address:* 37 Brompton Square, SW3.

FOURNIER, Jean, OC 1987; CD 1972; Hon. Director, Royal Trustco Ltd, Toronto; Chairman, Board of Canadian Human Rights Foundation, since 1982; Commissioner of the Metric Commission, Canada, since 1981; *b* Montreal, 18 July 1914; *s* of Arthur Fournier and Emilie Roy; *m* 1942, May Coote; five *s*. *Educ:* High Sch. of Québec; Laval Univ. (BA 1935, LLB 1938). Admitted to Bar of Province of Quebec, 1939. Royal Canadian Artillery (NPAM) (Lieut), 1935; Canadian Active Service Force Sept. 1939; served in Canada and overseas; discharged 1944, Actg Lt-Col. Joined Canadian Foreign Service, 1944; Third Sec., Canadian Dept of External Affairs, 1944; Second Sec., Canadian Embassy, Buenos Aires, 1945; Nat. Defence Coll., Kingston, 1948 (ndc); Seconded: to Privy Council Office, 1948–50; to Prime Minister's Office, Oct. 1950–Feb. 1951; First Sec., Canadian Embassy, Paris, 1951; Counsellor, 1953; Consul Gen., Boston, 1954; Privy Council Office (Asst Sec. to Cabinet), 1957–61; Head of European Division (Political Affairs), Dept of External Affairs, 1961–64; Chm., Quebec Civil Service Commn, 1964–71; Agent Gen. for the Province of Quebec in London, 1971–78. Pres., Inst. of Public Administration of Canada, 1966–67; Vice Pres., Centre Québecois de Relations Internationales; Member: Canadian Inst. of Strategic Studies; Canadian Inst. of Internat. Affairs. Freedom, City of London, 1976. Pres., Canadian Veterans Assoc. of the UK, 1976–77. *Address:* 201 Metcalfe Avenue, Apt 903, Westmount, Québec H3Z 2H7, Canada. *T:* 932–8633. *Clubs:* Canada; St James's, Montreal (Montreal), Royal Canadian Military Institute (Toronto).

FOUYAS, Metropolitan Methodios, of Pisidia; former Archbishop of Thyateira and Great Britain; Greek Orthodox Archbishop of Great Britain, 1979–88; *b* 14 Sept. 1925. BD (Athens); PhD (Manchester), 1962. Vicar of Greek Church in Munich, 1951–54; Secretary-General, Greek Patriarchate of Alexandria, 1954–56; Vicar of Greek Church in Manchester, 1960–66; Secretary, Holy Synod of Church of Greece, 1966–68; Archbishop of Aksum (Ethiopia), 1968–79. Member, Academy of Religious Sciences, Brussels, 1974–. Estabd Foundn for Hellenism in GB, 1982; Editor, Texts and Studies: a review of the Foundn for Hellenism in GB, Vols I–VIII, 1982–91; Founder-Editor, Abba Salama Review of Ethio-Hellenic Studies, 10 Volumes; Editor: Ekklesiastikos Pharos (Prize of Academy of Athens), 11 Volumes; Ecclesia and Theologia, vols I-X, 1980–91. Hon. DD: Edinburgh, 1970; Gr. Th. School of Holy Cross, Boston, 1984. Grand Cordon: Order of Phoenix (Greece); of Sellassie (Ethiopia). *Publications:* Orthodoxy, Roman Catholicism and Anglicanism, 1972; The Person of Jesus Christ in the Decisions of the Ecumenical Councils, 1976; History of the Church in Corinth, 1968; Christianity and Judaism in Ethiopia, Nubia and Meroe, 1st Vol., 1979, 2nd Vol., 1982; Theological and Historical Studies, Vols 1–12, 1979–88; Greeks and Latins, 1990; contrib. to many other books and treatises. *Recreation:* gardening. *Address:* 9 Riga Ferraiou Street, Khalandri, 15232 Athens, Greece. *T:* 6824793.

FOWDEN, Sir Leslie, Kt 1982; FRS 1964; Director of Arable Crops Research, Agricultural and Food Research Council, 1986–88; *b* Rochdale, Lancs, 13 Oct. 1925; *s* of Herbert and Amy D. Fowden; *m* 1949, Margaret Oakes; one *s* one *d*. *Educ:* University Coll., London. PhD Univ. of London, 1948. Scientific Staff of Human Nutrition Research Unit of the MRC, 1947–50; Lecturer in Plant Chemistry, University Coll. London, 1950–55, Reader, 1956–64, Prof. of Plant Chemistry, 1964–73; Dean of Faculty of Science, UCL, 1970–73; Dir, Rothamsted Exptl Station, 1973–86. Rockefeller Fellow at Cornell Univ., 1955; Visiting Prof. at Univ. of California, 1963; Royal Society Visiting Prof., Univ. of Hong Kong, 1967. Consultant Dir, Commonwealth Bureau of Soils, 1973–88. Chm., Agric. and Vet. Adv. Cttee, British Council, 1987–; Member: Advisory Board, Tropical Product Inst., 1966–70; Council, Royal Society, 1970–72; Scientific Adv. Panel, Royal Botanic Gardens, 1977–83 (Trustee, 1983–); Radioactive Waste Management Adv. Cttee, 1983–. Foreign Member: Deutsche Akademie der Naturforscher Leopoldina, 1971; Lenin All-Union Acad. of Agricultural Sciences of USSR, 1978; Acad. of Agricl Scis of GDR, 1986; Corresponding Mem., Amer. Soc. Plant Physiologists, 1981; Hon. Mem., Phytochemical Soc. of Europe, 1985. *Publications:* contribs to scientific journals on topics in plant biochemistry. *Address:* 31 Southdown Road, Harpenden, Herts AL5 1PF. *T:* Harpenden (0582) 764628.

FOWELLS, Joseph Dunthorne Briggs, CMG 1975; DSC 1940; Deputy Director General, British Council, 1976–77, retired; *b* 17 Feb. 1916; *s* of late Joseph Fowells and Maud Dunthorne, Middlesbrough; *m* 1st, 1940, Edith Agnes McKerracher (marr. diss. 1966); two *s* one *d*; 2nd, 1969, Thelma Howes (*d* 1974). *Educ:* Sedbergh Sch.; Clare Coll., Cambridge (MA). School teaching, 1938; service with Royal Navy (Lt-Comdr), 1939–46; Blackie & Son Ltd, Educnl Publishers, 1946; British Council, 1947: Argentina, 1954; Representative Sierra Leone, 1956; Scotland, 1957; Dir Latin America and Africa (Foreign) Dept, 1958; Controller Overseas B Division (foreign countries excluding Europe), 1966; Controller Planning, 1968; Controller European Div., 1970; Asst Dir Gen. (Functional), 1972; Asst Dir Gen. (Regional), 1973–76. *Recreations:* golf, sailing. *Address:* 5/57 Palmeira Avenue, Hove, East Sussex BN3 3GE. *T:* Brighton (0273) 70349.

FOWKE, Sir David (Frederick Gustavus), 5th Bt *cr* 1814, of Lowesby, Leics; *b* 28 Aug. 1950; *s* of Lt-Col Gerrard George Fowke (*d* 1969) (2nd *s* of 3rd Bt) and of Daphne (*née* Monasteriotis); *S* uncle, 1987. *Educ:* Cranbrook School, Sydney; Univ. of Sydney (BA 1971). *Heir:* none.

FOWLER, Prof. Alastair David Shaw, FBA 1974; Professor of English, University of Virginia, since 1990; Regius Professor of Rhetoric and English Literature, University of Edinburgh, 1972–84, now Emeritus (University Fellow, 1985–87); *b* 17 Aug. 1930; *s* of David Fowler and Maggie Shaw; *m* 1950, Jenny Catherine Simpson; one *s* one *d*. *Educ:* Queen's Park Sch., Glasgow; Univ. of Glasgow; Univ. of Edinburgh; Pembroke Coll., Oxford. MA Edin. 1952 and Oxon 1955; DPhil Oxon 1957; DLitt Oxon 1972. Junior Res. Fellow, Queen's Coll., Oxford, 1955–59; Instructor, Indiana Univ., 1957; Lectr, UC Swansea, 1959; Fellow and Tutor in English Lit., Brasenose Coll., Oxford, 1962–71. Visiting Professor: Columbia Univ., 1964; Univ. of Virginia, 1969, 1979, 1985–90; Mem. Inst. for Advanced Study, Princeton, 1966, 1980; Visiting Fellow: Council of the Humanities, Princeton Univ., 1974; Humanities Research Centre, Canberra, 1980; All Souls Coll., Oxford, 1984. Mem., Scottish Arts Council, 1976–77. Adv. Editor, New Literary History, 1972–; Gen. Editor, Longman Annotated Anthologies of English Verse, 1977–80; Mem. Editorial Board: English Literary Renaissance, 1978–; Word and Image, 1984–; The Seventeenth Century, 1986–; Connotations, 1990; Translation and Literature, 1990; English Review, 1990. *Publications:* (trans. and ed) Richard Wills, De re poetica, 1958; Spenser and the Numbers of Time, 1964; (ed) C. S. Lewis, Spenser's Images of Life, 1967; (ed with John Carey) The Poems of John Milton, 1968; Triumphal Forms, 1970; (ed) Silent Poetry, 1970; (ed with Christopher Butler) Topics in Criticism, 1971; Seventeen, 1971; Conceitful Thought, 1975; Catacomb Suburb, 1976; Edmund Spenser, 1977; From the Domain of Arnheim, 1982; Kinds of Literature, 1982; A History of English Literature, 1987; The New Oxford Book of Seventeenth Century Verse, 1991; contribs to jls and books. *Address:* (Jan.–Aug.) Department of English, David Hume Tower, George Square, Edinburgh EH8 9JX; (Sept.–Dec.) Department of English, Wilson Hall, Charlottesville, VA 22903, USA.

FOWLER, Beryl, (Mrs H. Fowler); *see* Chitty, (Margaret) B.

FOWLER, Christopher B.; *see* Brocklebank-Fowler.

FOWLER, Dennis Houston, OBE 1979 (MBE 1963); HM Diplomatic Service, retired; *b* 15 March 1924; *s* of Joseph Fowler and Daisy Lilian Wraith Fowler (*née* Houston); *m* 1944, Lilias Wright Nairn Burnett; two *s* one *d*. *Educ:* Alleyn's Sch., Dulwich. Colonial Office, 1940; RAF, 1942–46; India Office (subseq. CRO), 1947; Colombo, 1951; Second Secretary, Karachi, 1955; CRO, 1959; First Secretary, Dar es Salaam, 1961; Diplomatic Service Administration (subseq. FCO), 1965; First Sec. and Head of Chancery, Reykjavik, 1969; FCO, 1973; First Sec., Head of Chancery and Consul, Kathmandu, 1977; Counsellor and Hd of Claims Dept, FCO, 1980–83. *Recreations:* golf, music, do-it-yourself. *Address:* 25 Dartnell Park Road, West Byfleet, Surrey KT14 6PN. *T:* Byfleet (0932) 341583. *Clubs:* West Byfleet Golf; Royal Nepal Golf (Kathmandu).

FOWLER, Derek, CBE 1979; Chairman, BR Pension Trustee, Co., since 1986; *b* 26 Feb. 1929; *s* of late George Edward Fowler and of Kathleen Fowler; *m* 1953, Ruth Fox; one *d*. *Educ:* Grantham, Lincs. Financial appointments with: Grantham Borough Council, 1944–50; Spalding UDC, 1950–52; Nairobi City Council, 1952–62; Southend-on-Sea CBC, 1962–64. British Railways Board: Internal Audit Manager, 1964–67, and Management Acct, 1967–69, W Region; Sen. Finance Officer, 1969–71; Corporate Budgets Manager, 1971–73; Controller of Corporate Finance, 1973–75; Finance Mem., 1975–78; a Vice-Chm., 1981–90; Dep. Chm., 1990. Dep. Chm., Capita Gp, 1990–; Dir, Beazer, 1990–. Mem., UK Accounting Standards Cttee, 1982–84. Freeman: City of London, 1981; Co. of Information Technologists, 1987; Liveryman, Worshipful Co. of Loriners, 1981. FCCA; IPFA (Mem. Council, 1974–83); JDipMA. *Recreation:* cartophily. *Address:* (office) 55 Old Broad Street, EC2M 1RX.

FOWLER, Sir (Edward) Michael (Coulson), Kt 1981; FNZIA; Mayor of Wellington, New Zealand, 1974–83; Partner, Calder Fowler Styles and Turner, since 1960; company chairman and director; *b* 19 Dec. 1929; *s* of William Coulson Fowler and Faith Agnes Netherclift; *m* 1953, Barbara Hamilton Hall; two *s* one *d*. *Educ:* Christ's Coll., Christchurch, NZ; Auckland Univ. (MArch). ARIBA 1953; FNZIA 1970. Architect, London office, Ove Arup & Partners, 1954–56; own practice, Wellington, 1957–59. Director: Robt Jones Investments Ltd, 1982–; New Zealand Sugar Co., 1983–; Cigna Insurance New Zealand Ltd, 1985–89. Chm., Queen Elizabeth II Arts Council, 1983–87. Wellington City Councillor, 1968–74. Nat. Pres., YHA of NZ, 1984–87. Medal of Honour, NZIA, 1983; Alfred O. Glasse Award, NZ Inst. of Planning, 1984. *Publications:* Wellington Sketches: Folio I, 1971, Folio II, 1974; Country Houses of New Zealand, 1972, 2nd edn 1977; The Architecture and Planning of Moscow, 1980; Eating Houses in Wellington, 1980; Wellington Wellington, 1981; Eating Houses of Canterbury, 1982; Wellington—A Celebration, 1983; The New Zealand House, 1983; Buildings of New Zealanders, 1984. *Recreations:* sketching, reading, writing, history, politics. *Address:* Apartment 1, Michael Fowler Hotel, 51–61 Cable Street, PO Box 400, Wellington, New Zealand. *T:* (04) 856676. *Club:* Wellington (Wellington, NZ).

FOWLER, Prof. Gerald Teasdale; Rector, Polytechnic of East London (formerly North East London Polytechnic), since 1982; *b* 1 Jan. 1935; *s* of James A. Fowler, Long Buckby, Northants, and Alfreda (*née* Teasdale); *m* 1982, Lorna, *d* of William Lloyd, Preston. *Educ:* Northampton Grammar Sch.; Lincoln Coll., Oxford; University of Frankfurt-am-Main. Craven Fellowship, Oxford Univ., 1957–59; part-time Lectr, Pembroke Coll., Oxford, 1958–59; Lectr, Hertford and Lincoln Colls, Oxford, 1959–65; Lectr, Univ. of Lancaster, 1965–66; Asst Dir, The Polytechnic, Huddersfield, 1970–72; Prof. of Educnl Studies, Open Univ., 1972–74; Prof. Associate, Dept of Government, Brunel Univ., 1977–80; Dep. Dir, Preston Polytechnic, 1980–81. Vis. Prof., Dept of Admin, Strathclyde Univ., 1970–74. Chm., Cttee of Dirs of Polytechnics, 1988–90 (Vice Chm., 1986–88). Oxford City Councillor, 1960–64; Councillor, The Wrekin DC, 1973–76, Leader, 1973–74; Councillor, Shropshire CC, 1979–85. Contested (Lab) Banbury, 1964; MP (Lab) The Wrekin, 1966–70, Feb. 1974–1979; Jt Parly Sec., Min. of Technology, 1967–69; Minister of State: Dept of Educn and Science, Oct. 1969–June 1970, March-Oct. 1974 and Jan.-Sept. 1976; Privy Council Office, 1974–76. President: Assoc. for Teaching of Social Science, 1976–79; Assoc. for Recurrent Educn, 1976–78, 1981–85; Assoc. for Liberal Educn, 1977–79; Comparative Educn in Europe Soc. (British Section), 1980; Vice-Pres., Soc. for Research into Higher Educn, 1983–. Chm., Youthaid, 1977–80; Vice Chm., Nat. Parly Youth Lobby, 1978–79. Trustee, Community Projects Foundn, 1978–80. Vice-Chm., Assoc. of Business Executives, 1982– (Pres., 1979–81; Hon. Fellow 1983). FBIM 1984; FRSA 1985. *Address:* Polytechnic of East London, Romford Road, Stratford, E15 4LZ. *T:* 081–590 7722; 4 Princess Road, NW1. *Club:* Reform.

FOWLER, Henry Hamill; investment banker; Limited Partner, Goldman Sachs & Co., New York; *b* 5 Sept. 1908; *s* of Mack Johnson Fowler and Bertha Browning Fowler; *m* 1938, Trudye Pamela Hathcote; two *d* (one *s* decd). *Educ:* Roanoke Coll., Salem, Va; Yale Law Sch. Counsel, Tennessee Valley Authority, 1934–38, Asst Gen. Counsel, 1939; Special Asst to Attorney-Gen. as Chief Counsel to Sub-Cttee, Senate Cttee, Educn and Labor, 1939–40; Special Counsel, Fed. Power Commn, 1941; Asst Gen. Counsel, Office of Production Management, 1941, War Production Board, 1942–44; Econ. Adviser, US Mission Econ. Affairs, London, 1944; Special Asst to Administrator, For. Econ. Administration, 1945; Dep. Administrator, National Production Authority, 1951, Administrator, 1952; Administrator, Defense Prodn Administration, 1952–53; Dir Office of Defense Mobilization, Mem. Nat. Security Coun., 1952–53; Under-Sec. of the Treasury, 1961–64; Secretary of the US Treasury, 1965–68. Sen. Mem. of Fowler, Leva, Hawes & Symington, Washington, 1946–51, 1953–61, 1964–65; Gen. Partner, Goldman Sachs & Co., 1969–80; Chm., Goldman Sachs Internat. Corp., 1969–84. Chairman: Roanoke Coll., 1974–81; Atlantic Council of the US, 1972–77; Inst. of Internat. Educn, 1973–78; US Treasury Adv. Cttee on Reform of Internat. Monetary System, 1973–84; Cttee to Fight Inflation, 1981–89; Bretton Woods Cttee, 1985–; Co-Chairman: Cttee on Present Danger, 1976–; Citizens Network for Foreign Affairs, 1988–.Trustee: Lyndon B. Johnson Foundn; Franklin D. Roosevelt Four Freedoms Foundn; Carnegie Endowment for Peace, 1972–78; Alfred Sloan Foundn, 1970–80. Hon. Degrees: Roanoke Coll., 1961; Wesleyan Univ., 1966; Univ. of William and Mary, 1966. *Recreation:* bridge. *Address:* 85 Broad Street, New York, NY 10004, USA. *Clubs:* Links, River (NYC); Metropolitan (Washington), Bohemian (San Francisco).

FOWLER, Ian; Principal Chief Clerk and Clerk to the Committee of Magistrates for the Inner London area, since 1979; *b* 20 Sept. 1932; *s* of Major Norman William Frederick Fowler, OBE, QPM, and late Alice May (*née* Wakelin); *m* 1961, Gillian Cecily Allchin, JP; two *s* one *d*. *Educ:* Maidstone Grammar Sch.; Skinners Sch., Tunbridge Wells; King's Sch., Canterbury; St Edmund Hall, Oxford (MA). National Service, commnd 2nd Bn The Green Howards, 1951–53. Called to Bar, Gray's Inn, 1957; entered Inner London Magistrates Courts Service, 1959. Dep. Traffic Comr, Eastern Traffic Area, 1987–. Councillor: Herne Bay UDC and Canterbury CC, 1961–83 (Mayor, 1976–77). Mem. Court, Univ. of Kent at Canterbury, 1976–. *Recreation:* reading. *Address:* 3rd Floor, North West Wing, Bush House, Aldwych, WC2B 4PJ. *T:* 071–836 9331; 6 Dence Park, Herne Bay, Kent.

FOWLER, John Francis, DSc, PhD; FInstP; Professor, Department of Human Oncology, University of Wisconsin, USA, since 1988; Director of Cancer Research Campaign's Gray Laboratory, at Mount Vernon Hospital, Northwood, 1970–88; *b* 3 Feb. 1925; *er s* of Norman V. Fowler, Bridport, Dorset; *m* 1953, Kathleen Hardcastle Sutton, MB, BS (marr. diss. 1984); two *s* five *d*. *Educ:* Bridport Grammar Sch.; University Coll. of the South-West, Exeter. BSc 1st class Hons (London) 1944; MSc (London) 1946; PhD (London) 1955; DSc (London) 1974; FInstP 1957. Research Physicist: Newalls Insulation Co., 1944; Metropolitan Vickers Electrical Co., 1947; Newcastle upon Tyne Regional Hosp. Board (Radiotherapy service), 1950; Principal Physicist at King's Coll. Hosp., SE5, 1956; Head of Physics Section in Medical Research Council Radiotherapeutic Res. Unit, Hammersmith Hosp., 1959 (later the Cyclotron Unit); Reader in Physics, London Univ. at Med. Coll. of St Bartholomew's Hosp., 1962; Prof. of Med. Physics, Royal Postgraduate Med. Sch., London Univ., Hammersmith Hosp., 1963–70, Vice-Dean, 1967–70. Vis. Prof. in Oncology, Mddx Hosp. Med. Sch., 1977–. President: Hosp. Physicists Assoc., 1966–67; Europ. Soc. Radiat. Biol., 1974–76; British Inst. Radiol., 1977–78. Hon. Fellow, Amer. Coll. of Radiology, 1981. Hon. MD Helsinki, 1981; Hon. DSc Med. Coll. Wisconsin, 1989. Roentgen Award, BIR, 1965; Röntgen Plakette, Deutsches Röntgen Museum, 1978; Heath Meml Award, Univ. of Texas, Houston, 1981; Breur Medal, European Soc. Therapeutic Radiology and Oncology, 1983; Barclay Medal, BIR, 1985; Marie Sklodowska-Curie Medal, Polish Radiation Res. Soc., 1986. *Publications:* Nuclear Particles in Cancer Treatment, 1981; papers on radiation dosimetry, radio-biology, radioisotopes, in Brit. Jl Radiology, Brit. Jl Cancer, Radiotherapy and Oncology, etc. *Recreations:* theatre, ballroom dancing, getting into the countryside. *Address:* Department of Human Oncology, K4–336, University of Wisconsin Clinical Cancer Centre, Madison, Wis 53792, USA.

FOWLER, Sir Michael; *see* Fowler, Sir E. M. C.

FOWLER, Rt. Hon. Sir Norman; *see* Fowler, Rt Hon. Sir P. N.

FOWLER, Prof. Peter Howard, FRS 1964; DSc; private consultant in the application of physics to industry; Royal Society Research Professor in Physics, University of Bristol, 1964–88, now Emeritus; *b* 27 Feb. 1923; *s* of Sir Ralph Howard Fowler, FRS, and Eileen, *o c* of 1st and last Baron Rutherford; *m* 1949, Rosemary Hempson (*née* Brown); three *d*. *Educ:* Winchester Coll.; Bristol Univ. BSc 1948, DSc 1958. Flying Officer in RAF, 1942–46 as a Radar Technical Officer. Asst Lectr in Physics, 1948, Lectr, 1951, Reader, 1961, Bristol Univ. Visiting Prof., Univ. of Minnesota, 1956–57. Rutherford Meml Lectr, Royal Soc., 1971. Chairman: Jt Cttee on Radiol Protection, MRC, 1983–; Neutron Facilities Review Panel, SERC, 1989; Mem., Meteorol Cttee, 1983–. Gov., King's Sch., Bruton, 1982–. Hughes Medal, Royal Soc., 1974. *Publications:* (with Prof. C. F. Powell and Dr D. H. Perkins) The Study of Elementary Particles by the Photographic Method, 1959; (with Dr V. M. Clapham) Solid State Nuclear Track Detectors, 1981; (with Dr B. Foster) Forty Years of Particle Physics, 1988. *Recreations:* gardening, meteorology. *Address:* 320 Canford Lane, Westbury on Trym, Bristol BS9 3PL.

FOWLER, Peter James, CMG 1990; HM Diplomatic Service; Minister and Deputy High Commissioner, New Delhi, since 1988; *b* 26 Aug. 1936; *s* of James and Gladys Fowler; *m* 1962, Audrey June Smith; one *s* three *d*. *Educ:* Nunthorpe Grammar Sch., York; Trinity Coll., Oxford (BA). Army Service, 1954–56. FCO, 1962–64; Budapest, 1964–65; Lisbon, 1965–67; Calcutta, 1968–71; FCO, 1971–75; East Berlin, 1975–77; Counsellor, Cabinet Office, 1977–80; Comprehensive Test Ban Delegn, Geneva, 1980; Counsellor, Bonn, 1981–85; Head of N America Dept, FCO, 1985–88. *Recreations:* reading, opera. *Address:* c/o Foreign and Commonwealth Office, King Charles Street, SW1A 2AH. *Clubs:* Commonwealth Trust; Gymkhana (Delhi).

FOWLER, Peter Jon, PhD; Professor of Archaeology, University of Newcastle upon Tyne, since 1985; *b* 14 June 1936; *s* of W. J. Fowler and P. A. Fowler; *m* 1959, Elizabeth (*née* Burley); three *d*. *Educ:* King Edward VI Grammar Sch., Morpeth, Northumberland;

Lincoln Coll., Oxford (MA 1961); Univ. of Bristol (PhD 1977). Investigator on staff of RCHM (England), Salisbury office, 1959–65; Staff Tutor in Archaeology, Dept of Extra-Mural Studies, 1965–79, and Reader in Arch., 1972–79, Univ. of Bristol; Sec., Royal Commn on Historical Monuments (England), 1979–85. Member: Historic Bldgs and Ancient Monuments Adv. Cttees, Historic Buildings and Monuments Commn, 1983–86 (Ancient Monuments Bd, 1979–83); Council, National Trust, 1983–; Pres., Council for British Archaeol., 1981–83 (Vice-Pres., 1979–81). Archaeological consultant, Forestry Commn, 1988–; Mem., Landscape Adv. Cttee, DoT, 1990–. *Publications:* Regional Archaeologies: Wessex, 1967; (ed) Archaeology and the Landscape, 1972; (ed) Recent Work in Rural Archaeology, 1975; (ed with K. Branigan) The Roman West Country, 1976; Approaches to Archaeology, 1977; (ed with H. C. Bowen) Early Land Allotment in the British Isles, 1978; (with S. Piggott and M. L. Ryder) Agrarian History of England and Wales, I, pt 1, 1981; The Farming of Prehistoric Britain, 1983; Farms in England, 1983; (with P. Boniface) Northumberland and Newcastle upon Tyne, 1989; (jtly) Who Owns Stonehenge?, 1990; (with M. Sharp) Images of Prehistory, 1990; Then, Now: the past in contemporary society, 1992; contribs to learned jls. *Recreations:* writing, sport. *Address:* Department of Archaeology, The University, Newcastle upon Tyne NE1 7RU.

FOWLER, Rt. Hon. Sir (Peter) Norman, Kt 1990; PC 1979; MP (C) Sutton Coldfield, since Feb. 1974 (Nottingham South, 1970–74); *b* 2 Feb. 1938; *s* of late N. F. Fowler and Katherine Fowler; *m* 1979, Fiona Poole, *d* of John Donald; two *d*. *Educ:* King Edward VI Sch., Chelmsford; Trinity Hall, Cambridge (MA). Nat. Service commn, Essex Regt, 1956–58; Cambridge, 1958–61; Chm., Cambridge Univ. Conservative Assoc., 1960. Joined staff of The Times, 1961; Special Corresp., 1962–66; Home Affairs Corresp., 1966–70; reported Middle East War, 1967. Mem. Council, Bow Group, 1967–69; Editorial Board, Crossbow, 1962–69; Vice-Chm., North Kensington Cons. Assoc., 1967–68; Chm., E Midlands Area, Cons. Political Centre, 1970–73. Chief Opposition spokesman: Social Services, 1975–76; Transport, 1976–79; Opposition spokesman, Home Affairs, 1974–75; PPS, NI Office, 1972–74; Sec. of State for Transport, 1981 (Minister of Transport, 1979–81), for Social Services, 1981–87, for Employment, 1987–90. Mem., Parly Select Cttee on Race Relations and Immigration, 1970–74; Jt Sec., Cons. Parly Home Affairs Cttee, 1971–72, 1974 (Vice-Chm., 1974). *Publications:* After the Riots: the police in Europe, 1979; political pamphlets including: The Cost of Crime, 1973; The Right Track, 1977; Ministers Decide: a memoir of the Thatcher years, 1991. *Address:* House of Commons, SW1A 0AA.

FOWLER, Richard Nicholas; QC 1989; *b* 12 Oct. 1946; 2nd *s* of late Ronald Hugh Fowler and of Winifred Mary Fowler (*née* Hull). *Educ:* Bedford Sch.; Brasenose Coll., Oxford (BA). Called to the Bar, Middle Temple, 1969. Liveryman, Goldsmiths' Co. *Recreations:* walking, opera, dogs. *Address:* 93 Cheyne Walk, SW10 0DQ. *T:* 071–352 4966; 4 Raymond Buildings, Gray's Inn, WC1R 5BP. *T:* 071–405 7211; 28 rue de Toulouse, 1040 Brussels, Belgium. *T:* (02) 230 3545.

FOWLER, Robert Asa; Owner and Chairman, Fowler International, since 1986; Consul General for Sweden, since 1989; *b* 5 Aug. 1928; *s* of Mr and Mrs William Henry Fowler; *m* 1987, Monica Elizabeth Heden; three *s* one *d* by a previous marriage. *Educ:* Princeton Univ. (BA Econs); Harvard Business Sch. (MBA). Lieut USNR, 1950–53. Various appts with Continental Oil, 1955–75; Area Manager, Northwest Europe, Continental Oil Co., 1975–78; Chm. and Man. Dir, Conoco Ltd, 1979–81; Vice-Pres., Internat. Marketing, Conoco Inc., 1981–85. An Hon. Consul Gen. for Sweden. *Recreations:* tennis, skiing. *Address:* 49 Briar Hollow Lane, Houston, Texas 77027, USA. *T:* 713–871–8907. *Clubs:* Hurlingham; River, Knickerbocker (NY); Allegheny Country (Pa); Chagrin Valley Hunt (Ohio).

FOWLER, Ronald Frederick, CBE 1950; *b* 21 April 1910; *e s* of late Charles Frederick Fowler and Amy Beatrice (*née* Hollyoak); *m* 1937, Brenda Kathleen Smith. *Educ:* Bancroft's Sch.; LSE, University of London; Universities of Lille and Brussels. BCom (hons) London, 1931. Sir Ernest Cassel Travelling Scholar, 1929–30; Asst, later Lectr in Commerce, LSE, 1932–40; Central Statistical Office, 1940–50; Dir of Statistics and Under-Sec., Min. of Labour, 1950–68; Dir of Statistical Res., Dept of Employment, 1968–72. Consultant, Prices Div., Statistics Canada, Ottawa, 1971–72; Statistical Consultant, Prices Commn, 1973–77. *Publications:* The Depreciation of Capital, 1934; The Duration of Unemployment, 1968; Some Problems of Index Number Construction, 1970; Further Problems of Index Number Construction, 1973; articles in British and US economic and statistical jls. *Address:* 10 Silverdale Road, Petts Wood, Kent. *Club:* Reform.

FOWLER, Prof. William Alfred, PhD; Institute Professor Emeritus of Physics, California Institute of Technology, since 1982 (Institute Professor of Physics, 1970–82); *b* Pittsburgh, Pa, 9 Aug. 1911; *s* of late John McLeod Fowler and Jennie Summers (*née* Watson); *m* 1st, 1940, Ardiane Foy Olmsted (*d* 1988), Pasadena, Calif.; two *d*; 2nd, 1989, Mary Dutcher, Flushing, NY. *Educ:* Ohio State Univ. (B.Eng. Phys); California Inst. of Technology (PhD Phys). Member: Tau Kappa Epsilon; Tau Beta Pi; Sigma Xi. California Inst. of Technology: Research Fellow in Nuclear Physics, 1936–39; Asst Prof. of Physics, 1939–42; Associate Prof. of Physics, 1942–46; Prof. of Physics, 1946–70. Defense record: Research and develt proximity fuses, rocket ordnance, and atomic weapons; Research staff mem.: Sect. T, NDRC, and Div. 4, NDRC, 1941; Asst Dir of Research, Sect. L. Div. 3, NDRC, 1941–45; Techn. Observer, Office of Field Services and New Develts Div., War Dept, in South and Southwestern Pacific Theatres, 1944; Actg Supervisor, Ord. Div., R&D, NOTS, 1945; Sci. Dir, Project VISTA, Dept Defense, 1951–52. Guggenheim Fellow and Fulbright Lectr, Pembroke Coll. and Cavendish Laboratory, Univ. of Cambridge, Eng., 1954–55; Guggenheim Fellow, St John's Coll., and Dept Applied Math. and Theor. Phys., Univ. of Cambridge, Eng., 1961–62; Walker-Ames Prof. of Physics, Univ. of Washington, 1963; Visitor, The Observatories, Univ. of Cambridge, Summer 1964; Vis. Prof. of Physics, Mass. Inst. of Technology, 1966; Vis. Fellow, Inst. of Theoretical Astronomy, Univ. of Cambridge, Summers 1967–72. Numerous lectureships in USA, 1957–; those given abroad include: Lectr, Internat. Sch. of Physics "Enrico Fermi", Varenna, 1965. Lectr, Advanced Sch. on Cosmic Physics, Erice, Italy, 1969, in addition to past lectures at Cavendish Laboratory, Cambridge; also Lectr at Research Sch. of Physical Sciences, Australian National Univ., Canberra, 1965; Jubilee Lectr, 50th Anniversary, Niels Bohr Inst., Copenhagen, 1970; Scott Lectr, Cavendish Laboratory, Cambridge Univ., Eng., 1971; George Darwin Lectr, RAS, 1973; E. A. Milne Lectr, Milne Soc., 1986; 22nd Liège Internat. Astrophysical Symposium, 1978; Vis. Scholar, Phi Beta Kappa, 1980–81. Member: Nat. Science Bd, Nat. Science Foundation, USA, 1968–74; Space Science Bd, Nat. Academy of Sciences, 1970–73 and 1977–80; Space Program Adv. Council, NASA, 1971–74; Bd of Directors, American Friends of Cambridge Univ., 1970–78; Governing Bd, Amer. Inst. of Physics, 1974–80; Cttee Chm., Nuclear Science Adv. Cttee, Nat. Science Foundn/Dept of Energy, USA, 1977–79; Chm., Off. Phys. Sci., Nat. Acad. Sci., 1981–82; Mem. Review Cttee APS Study: Radionuclide Release in Severe Accidents of Nuclear Power Reactors, 1984. Has attended numerous conferences, congresses and assemblies. Member: Internat. Astro. Union; Amer. Assoc. for Advancement of Science; Amer. Assoc. of Univ. Professors; Nat. Acad. of Sciences; Mem. corres., Soc. Royale des Sciences de Liège; Fellow: Amer. Physical Soc. (Pres., 1976); Amer. Acad. of Arts and Sciences; British Assoc. for Advancement of Science; Benjamin Franklin Fellow, RSA; ARAS. Hon. Member: Mark Twain Soc.; Soc. Amer. Baseball Res., 1980; Naturvetenskapliga Foreningen, 1984. Hon. DSc: Chicago, 1976; Ohio State, 1978; Denison, 1982; Arizona State, 1985; Georgetown, 1986; Massachusetts, 1987; Williams Coll., 1988; Dr *hc*: Liège, 1981; Observatory of Paris, 1981. Various awards and medals for science etc, both at home and abroad, including Medal for Merit, USA, 1948; Vetlesen Prize, 1973; Nat. Medal of Sci., 1974; Eddington Medal, RAS, 1978; Bruce Gold Medal, Astron. Soc. Pacific, 1979; (jtly) Nobel Prize for Physics, 1983; Sullivant Medal, Ohio State Univ., 1985; first William A. Fowler Award for Excellence in Physics, Ohio section, APS, 1986. Légion d'Honneur (France), 1989. *Publications:* contributor to: Physical Review, Astrophysical Jl, Proc. Nat. Acad. of Sciences, Amer. Jl of Physics, Geophysical Jl, Nature, Royal Astronomical Soc., etc. *Address:* Kellogg Radiation Laboratory 106–38, California Institute of Technology, Pasadena, California 91125, USA. *Clubs:* Cosmos (Washington, DC); Athenæum (Pasadena, Calif); Cambridge and District Model Engineering Society.

FOWLER HOWITT, William; *see* Howitt, W. F.

FOWLES, John; writer; *b* 31 March 1926; *s* of Robert John Fowles and Gladys May Richards; *m* 1956, Elizabeth Whitton. *Educ:* Bedford Sch.; New Coll., Oxford. English Centre PEN Silver Pen Award, 1969; W. H. Smith Award, 1970. *Publications:* The Collector, 1963; The Aristos, 1965; The Magus, 1966, rev. edn 1977; The French Lieutenant's Woman, 1969; Poems, 1973; The Ebony Tower, 1974 (televised, 1984); Shipwreck, 1975; Daniel Martin, 1977; Islands, 1978; (with Frank Horvat) The Tree, 1979; (ed) John Aubrey's Monumenta Britannica, parts 1 and 2, 1980, part 3 and Index, 1982; The Enigma of Stonehenge, 1980; Mantissa, 1982; Thomas Hardy's England, 1984; Land, 1985; A Maggot, 1985. *Recreations:* mainly Sabine. *Address:* c/o Anthony Sheil Associates, 43 Doughty Street, WC1N 2LF.

FOX, Dr Alan Martin; Assistant Under Secretary (Ordnance), Ministry of Defence, since 1988; *b* 5 July 1938; *s* of Sidney Nathan Fox and Clarice Solov; *m* 1965, Sheila Naomi Pollard; one *s* two *d*. *Educ:* Bancroft's Sch., Essex; Queen Mary Coll., London (BSc Hons II1, Physics 1959; PhD Math. Phys. 1963). Home Civil Service by Open Competition, 1963; Ministry of Aviation: Private Sec. to Parly Sec., 1965–67; 1st Sec. (Aviation and Defence) on loan to FCO, Paris, 1973–75; MoD 1975–78; RCDS, 1979; MoD, 1980–. *Recreations:* bridge, chess, watching Rugby, cricket, TV. *Address:* Ministry of Defence, Main Building, Horseguards Avenue, SW1A 2HB. *T:* 071–218 7315.

FOX, Dr (Anthony) John; Deputy Director and Chief Medical Statistician, Office of Population Censuses and Surveys, since 1988; *b* 25 April 1946; *s* of Fred Frank Fox, OBE, and Gertrude Price; *m* 1971, Annemarie Revesz; one *s* two *d*. *Educ:* Dauntsey's School; University College London (BSc); Imperial College London (PhD, DIC). Statistician: Employment Medical Adv. Service, 1970–75; OPCS, 1975–79; Prof. of Social Statistics, City Univ., 1980–88. Vis. Prof., LSHTM. *Publications:* Occupational Mortality 1970–72, 1978; Socio-Demographic Mortality Differentials, 1982; Health Inequalities in European Countries, 1989; (jtly) Health and Class: The early years, 1991. *Recreations:* family, tennis, bridge, theatre. *Address:* Office of Population Censuses and Surveys, St Catherine's House, Kingsway, WC2. *T:* 071–242 0262.

FOX, Brian Michael; Principal Establishment and Finance Officer (Grade 3), HM Treasury, since 1989; *b* 21 Sept. 1944; *s* of Walter Frederick and Audrey May Fox; *m* 1966, Maureen Ann Shrimpton; one *d*. *Educ:* East Ham Grammar School for Boys. Joined CS, HM Treasury, 1963–: Private Sec. to Financial Sec., 1967–69; secondment to 3i Gp, 1981–82; Dep. Estabt Officer, 1983–87; Head of Defence Policy and Materiel Div., 1987–89. *Recreations:* table tennis, badminton, soccer. *Address:* HM Treasury, Parliament Street, SW1P 3AG. *T:* 071–270 4410.

FOX, Edward; actor; *b* 13 April 1937; *s* of Robin and Angela Muriel Darita Fox; *m* Tracy (*née* Pelissier); one *d*; and one *d* by Joanna Fox. *Educ:* Ashfold Sch.; Harrow Sch. RADA training, following National Service, 1956–58; entry into provincial repertory theatre, 1958, since when, films, TV films and plays, and in the theatre, have made up the sum of his working life. *Theatre includes:* Knuckle, Comedy, 1973; The Family Reunion, Vaudeville, 1979; Anyone for Denis, Whitehall, 1981; Quartermaine's Terms, Queen's, 1981; Hamlet, Young Vic, 1982; Interpreters, Queen's, 1985; Let Us Go Then, You and I, Lyric, 1987; The Admirable Crichton, Haymarket, 1988; (also dir) Another Love Story, Leicester Haymarket, 1990; The Philanthropist, Wyndham's, 1991. *Films include:* The Go-Between, 1971 (Soc. of Film and Television Arts Award for Best Supporting Actor, 1971); The Day of the Jackal, A Doll's House, 1973; Galileo, 1976; The Squeeze, A Bridge Too Far (BAFTA Award for Best Supporting Actor, 1977), The Duellists, The Cat and the Canary, 1977; Force Ten from Navarone, 1978; The Mirror Crack'd, 1980; Gandhi, 1982; Never Say Never Again, The Dresser, 1983; The Bounty, 1984; The Shooting Party, 1985. *Television series include:* Hard Times, 1977; Edward and Mrs Simpson, 1978 (BAFTA Award for Best Actor, 1978; TV Times Top Ten Award for Best Actor, 1978–79; British Broadcasting Press Guild TV Award for Best Actor, 1978; Royal TV Soc. Performance Award, 1978–79); They Never Slept, 1991. *Recreations:* music, reading, walking. *Clubs:* Garrick, Savile.
See also J. Fox.

FOX, Hazel Mary, (Lady Fox); Editor, British Institute of International and Comparative Law, since 1989 (Director, 1982–89); *b* 22 Oct. 1928; *d* of J. M. B. Stuart, CIE; *m* 1954, Rt Hon. Sir Michael Fox, *qv*; three *s* one *d*. *Educ:* Roedean Sch.; Somerville Coll., Oxford (1st Cl. Jurisprudence, 1949; MA). Called to the Bar, Lincoln's Inn, 1950 (Buchanan Prize; Bencher, 1989); practised at the Bar, 1950–54; Lectr in Jurisprudence, Somerville Coll., Oxford, 1951–58; Lectr, Council of Legal Educn, 1962–76; Fellow of Somerville Coll., 1976–81, Hon. Fellow 1988. Chairman: London Rent Assessment Panel, 1977–; London Leasehold Valuation Tribunal, 1981–; Mem., Home Office Deptl Cttee on Jury Service, 1963–65. JP London, 1959–77; Chm., Tower Hamlets Juvenile Court, 1968–76. General Editor, Internat. and Comparative Law Qly, 1987–. *Publications:* (with J. L. Simpson) International Arbitration, 1959; (ed) International Economic Law and Developing Status, 1988; (ed) Joint Development of Offshore Oil and Gas, vol. I 1989, vol. II 1990. *Address:* c/o British Institute of International and Comparative Law, 17 Russell Square, WC1B 5DR. *T:* 071–636 5802.

FOX, Sir (Henry) Murray, GBE 1974; MA, FRICS; *b* 7 June 1912; *s* of late Sir Sidney Fox and Molly Button; *m* 1941, Helen Isabella Margaret (*d* 1986), *d* of late J. B. Crichton; one *s* two *d*. *Educ:* Malvern; Emmanuel Coll., Cambridge. Chairman: Trehaven Trust Group, 1963–; City of London Sinfonia, 1983–; Pres., City & Metropolitan Building Society, 1985– (Dir, 1972–; Chm., 1976–85); Managing Trustee, Municipal Mutual Insurance Ltd, 1977–. Dir, Toye, Kenning & Spencer Ltd, 1976–. Governor: Christ's Hosp., 1966–82; Bridewell Royal Hosp., 1966 (Vice-Pres. 1976–82); Trustee, Morden Coll., 1976–. Court of Common Council, 1963–82; Past Master: Wheelwrights' Co.; Coopers' Co.; Alderman, Ward of Bread Street, 1966–82; Sheriff, City of London, 1971–72; Lord Mayor of London, 1974–75; one of HM Lieutenants, City of London, 1976–83. Order of Rising Sun and Sacred Treasure (Japan), 1971; Order of Stor

(Afghanistan), 1971; Order of Orange Nassau (Netherlands), 1972. *Recreations:* golf, reading. *Address:* 7 Aldford Street, W1Y 5PQ. *Clubs:* City of London, City Livery (Pres. 1966–67).

FOX, James; actor; *b* 19 May 1939; *s* of Robin and Angela Fox; changed forename from William to James, 1962; *m* 1973, Mary Elizabeth Piper; four *s* one *d*. *Educ:* Harrow Sch.; Central Sch. of Speech and Drama. National Service, 1959–61. Entered acting as child, 1950; left acting to pursue Christian vocation, 1970–79; returned to acting, 1980. Main films include: The Servant, 1963; King Rat, 1964; Thoroughly Modern Millie, 1965; The Chase, 1966; Isadora, 1968; Performance, 1969; A Passage to India, 1984; Runners, 1984; Farewell to the King, 1987; Finding Mawbee (video film as The Mighty Quinn), 1988; She's Been Away, 1989; The Russia House, 1990; Afraid of the Dark, 1991. *Publication:* Comeback: an actor's direction, 1983. *Recreations:* windsurfing, tennis. *Address:* 49 Murray Road, Wimbledon, SW19 4PF. *T:* 081–946 0840.
See also E. Fox.

FOX, John; *see* Fox, A. J.

FOX, Sir (John) Marcus, Kt 1986; MBE 1963; MP (C) Shipley, since 1970; Parliamentary Under Secretary of State, Department of the Environment, 1979–81; *b* 11 June 1927; *s* of late Alfred Hirst Fox; *m* 1954, Ann, *d* of F. W. J. Tindall; one *s* one *d*. *Educ:* Wheelright Grammar Sch., Dewsbury. Mem. Dewsbury County Borough Council, 1957–65; contested (C): Dewsbury, 1959; Huddersfield West, 1966. An Asst Govt Whip, 1972–73; a Lord Comr, HM Treasury, 1973–74; Opposition Spokesman on Transport, 1975–76; Mem., Parly Select Cttee on Race Relations and Immigration, 1970–72; Sec., Cons. Party's Transport Industries Cttee, 1970–72; a Vice-Chairman: Cons. Party Orgn, 1976–79; 1922 Cttee, 1983–; Chm., Cttee of Selection, 1984–. Chm., Nat. Assoc. of Cons. Clubs, 1988–. *Recreations:* reading, tennis, walking. *Address:* House of Commons, SW1A 0AA.

FOX, Kenneth Lambert; public sector consultant, since 1986; *b* 8 Nov. 1927; *s* of J. H. Fox, Grimsby, Lincolnshire; *m* 1959, P. E. Byrne; one *d*. *Educ:* City of London Coll.; Univ. of London. BSc (Hons); FInstPS, MIIM. Plant Man., Rowntree Gp, 1950–63; Supply Man., Ford Motor Co. (UK), 1963–67; Sen. Management Conslt, Cooper & Lybrand Ltd, 1967–70; Man. of Conslts (Europe), US Science Management Corp., 1971–72; Supply Management, British Gas Corp., 1972–75; Dir of Supplies, GLC, 1975–86. *Recreations:* tennis, painting, bird watching, DIY. *Address:* 39 Parkland Avenue, Upminster RM14 2EX. *T:* Upminster (04022) 28927.

FOX, Rt. Rev. Langton Douglas, DD; retired Bishop of Menevia; *b* 21 Feb. 1917; *s* of Claude Douglas Fox and Ethel Helen (*née* Cox). *Educ:* Mark Cross, Wonersh and Maynooth. BA 1938; DD 1945. Priest 1942. Lectr, St John's Seminary, Wonersh, 1942–55; Mem., Catholic Missionary Soc., 1955–59; Parish Priest, Chichester, 1959–65; Auxiliary Bishop of Menevia, 1965–72; Bishop of Menevia, 1972–81. *Address:* Nazareth House, Hillbury Road, Wrexham, Clwyd LL13 7EU.

FOX, Prof. Leslie, DSc Oxon; Professor of Numerical Analysis, Oxford University, and Professorial Fellow, Balliol College, 1963–83, now Emeritus Fellow; Director, Oxford University Computing Laboratory, 1957–82; *b* 30 Sept. 1918; *m* 1st, 1943, Paulene Dennis; 2nd, 1973, Mrs Clemency Clements, *er d* of Thomas Fox. *Educ:* Wheelwright Grammar Sch., Dewsbury; Christ Church, Oxford. Admiralty Computing Service, 1943–45; Mathematics Div., Nat. Physical Laboratory, 1945–56; Associate Prof., Univ. of California, Berkeley, 1956–57; Research Prof., Univ. of Illinois, 1961–62; Vis. Prof., Open Univ., 1970–71. Pres., Math./Phys. Section, BAAS, 1975. Hon. Chm., 10th Canadian Conf. on Applied Mechanics, Univ. of Western Ontario, 1985. Hon. FIMA 1989. DUniv Open, 1986. *Publications:* Numerical Solution of Boundary-value Problems in Ordinary Differential Equations, 1957; (ed) Numerical Solution of Ordinary and Partial Differential Equations, 1962; An Introduction to Numerical Linear Algebra, 1964; (ed) Advances in Programming and Non-Numerical Computation, 1966; Chebyshev Polynomials in Numerical Analysis (with I. J. Parker), 1968; Computing Methods for Scientists and Engineers (with D. F. Mayers), 1968; Numerical Solution of Ordinary Differential Equations for Scientists and Engineers (with D. F. Mayers), 1987; numerous papers in learned journals. *Recreations:* sport, music, literature. *Address:* 2 Elsfield Road, Marston, Oxford OX3 0PR. *T:* Oxford (0865) 722668.

FOX, Sir Marcus; *see* Fox, Sir J. M.

FOX, Rt. Hon. Sir Michael John, Kt 1975; PC 1981; **Rt. Hon. Lord Justice Fox;** a Lord Justice of Appeal, since 1981; *b* 8 Oct. 1921; *s* of late Michael Fox; *m* 1954, Hazel Mary Stuart (*see* Hazel Mary Fox); three *s* one *d*. *Educ:* Drayton Manor Sch., Hanwell; Magdalen Coll., Oxford (BCL, MA). Admiralty, 1942–45. Called to the Bar, Lincoln's Inn, 1949, Bencher, 1975; QC 1968. Judge of the High Court of Justice, Chancery Div., 1975–81. *Address:* Royal Courts of Justice, Strand, WC2. *T:* 071–936 6000.

FOX, Sir Murray; *see* Fox, Sir H. M.

FOX, Sir Paul (Leonard), Kt 1991; CBE 1985; Chairman, Stepgrades Consultants, since 1991; Director, Thames Television Ltd, since 1991; *b* 27 Oct. 1925; *m* 1948, Betty Ruth (*née* Nathan); two *s*. *Educ:* Bournemouth Grammar Sch. Served War, Parachute Regt, 1943–46. Reporter: Kentish Times, 1946; The People, 1947; Scriptwriter, Pathé News, 1947; joined BBC Television, 1950: Scriptwriter, Television Newsreel; Editor, Sportsview, 1953, Panorama, 1961; Head, Public Affairs, 1963, Current Affairs, 1965; Controller, BBC1, 1967–73; Dir of Progs, Yorkshire Television, 1973–84; Man. Dir, BBC Network Television, 1988–91. Chairman: ITV Network Programme Cttee, 1978–80; Council, ITCA, 1982–84; ITN, 1986–88; (Dir, 1980–86); BBC Enterprises Ltd, 1988–91; Director: Trident Television, 1973–80; Channel Four, 1985–88; World Television News, 1986–88. Mem., Royal Commn on Criminal Procedure, 1978–80. Pres., RTS, 1985– Member Committee: Nat. Mus. of Film, Photography and TV, 1985–; Cinema and Television Benevolent Fund, 1986–. BAFTA Fellow, 1990. CBIM 1987. Hon. LLD Leeds, 1984. Cyril Bennett Award, for outstanding television programming, 1984; Founders Award, Internat. Council, US Nat. Acad. of TV Arts and Scis, 1989. *Recreations:* television, attending race meetings. *Address:* c/o Stepgrades Consultants, 317 High Holborn, WC1V 7NL. *Club:* Garrick.

FOX, Prof. Robert, FSA; FRHistS; Professor of the History of Science, University of Oxford, and Fellow of Linacre College, since 1988; *b* 7 Oct. 1938; *s* of Donald Fox and Audrey Hilda Fox (*née* Ramsell); *m* 1964, Catherine Mary Lilian Roper Power; three *d*. *Educ:* Doncaster Grammar Sch.; Oriel Coll., Oxford (BA 1961; MA 1965; DPhil 1967). Asst Master, Tonbridge Sch., 1961–63; Clifford Norton Junior Res. Fellow, Queen's Coll., Oxford, 1965–66; University of Lancaster: Lectr, 1966; Sen. Lectr, 1972; Reader, 1975; Prof. of History of Science, 1988. Mem., Inst. for Advanced Study, Princeton, 1974–75 and 1985; Vis. Prof. and Mem., Davis Center for Historical Studies, Princeton Univ., 1978–79; Dir, Centre de Recherche en Histoire des Sciences et des Techniques, Cité des Sciences et de l'Industrie, Paris, and Dir de recherche associé, Centre Nat. de la Recherche Scientifique, 1986–88; Asst Dir, Science Museum, 1988. *Publications:* The caloric theory of gases from Lavoisier to Regnault, 1971; Sadi Carnot: Réflexions sur la puissance motrice du feu, 1978 (trans. English 1986, German 1987); (ed with George Weisz) The organization of science and technology in France 1808–1914, 1980. *Address:* Modern History Faculty, Broad Street, Oxford OX1 3BD. *T:* Oxford (0865) 277268. *Club:* Athenæum.

FOX, Robin James L.; *see* Lane Fox.

FOX, Roy, CMG 1980; OBE 1967; HM Diplomatic Service, retired; consultant with various companies; *b* 1 Sept. 1920; *s* of J. S. and A. Fox; *m* 1st, 1943, Sybil Verity; two *s* one *d*; 2nd, 1975, Susan Rogers Turner. *Educ:* Wheelwright Grammar Sch., Dewsbury; Bradford Technical Coll. Served in RNVR, 1940–46. Bd of Trade, 1947–58; British Trade Commissioner: Nairobi, 1958–60; Montreal, 1960–62; Winnipeg, 1962–64; Dep. Controller, Bd of Trade Office for Scotland, 1964–65. First Sec. Commercial, Karachi, 1965–68; Deputy High Comr, E Pakistan, 1968–70; Consul-Gen. and Comm. Counsellor, Helsinki, 1970–74; promoted to Minister, 1977; Consul-Gen., Houston, 1974–80. *Recreations:* golf, reading, tennis. *Address:* Beechcroft, Forest Drive, Kingswood, Surrey KT20 6LN. *Club:* Royal Automobile.

FOX, Ruth W.; *see* Winston-Fox.

FOX, Prof. Wallace, CMG 1973; MD, FRCP, FFCM; Professor of Community Therapeutics, Cardiothoracic Institute, Brompton Hospital, 1979–86, now Emeritus; Director, Medical Research Council Tuberculosis and Chest Diseases Unit, Brompton Hospital, 1965–86; Hon. Consultant Physician, Brompton Hospital, 1969–86; WHO Consultant, since 1961; Member of WHO Expert Advisory Panel on Tuberculosis, since 1965; *b* 7 Nov. 1920; *s* of Samuel and Esther Fox; *m* 1956, Gaye Judith Akker; three *s*. *Educ:* Cotham Grammar Sch., Bristol; Guy's Hosp. MB, BS (London) 1943; MRCS, LRCP, 1943; MRCP 1950; MD (Dist.) (London) 1951; FRCP 1962; FFCM 1976. Ho. Phys., Guy's USA Hosp., 1945–46; Resident Phys., Preston Hall Sanatorium, 1946–50; Registrar, Guy's Hosp., 1950–51; Asst Chest Physician, Hammersmith Chest Clinic, 1951–52; Mem. Scientific Staff of MRC Tuberculosis and Chest Diseases Unit, 1952–56, 1961–65; seconded to WHO, to establish and direct Tuberculosis Chemotherapy Centre, Madras, 1956–61; Dir, WHO Collaborating Centre for Tuberculosis Chemotherapy and its Application, 1976–87. Lectures: Marc Daniels, RCP, 1962; First John Barnwell Meml, US Veterans Admin, 1968; Philip Ellman, RSocMed, 1976; Martyrs Meml, Bangladesh Med. Assoc., 1977; first Quezon Meml, Philippine Coll. of Chest Physicians, 1977; Morriston Davies Meml, BTA, 1981; Mitchell, RCP, 1982; E. Merck Oration, Indian Chest Soc., 1983; A. J. S. McFadzean, Univ. of Hong Kong, 1986; Ranbaxy–Robert Koch Oration, Tuberculosis Assoc. of India, 1989. Waring Vis. Prof. in Medicine, Univ. of Colorado and Stanford Univ., 1974. Mem. Tropical Med. Research Bd, 1968–72; Mem., several MRC Cttees; Mem., BCG Vaccination Sub-Cttee, Min. of Health, 1968–; Mem. Council, Chest, Heart & Stroke Assoc., 1974–90; International Union Against Tuberculosis: Mem., later Chm., Cttee of Therapy, 1964–71; Associate Mem., Scientific Cttees, 1973; Mem., Exec. Cttee, 1973–85 (Chm., 1973–77). Chm., Acid Fast Club, 1971–72. Editor, Advances in Tuberculosis Research. Elected Corresp. Mem., Amer. Thoracic Soc., 1962; Mem., Mexican Acad. of Medicine, 1976; Hon. Life Mem., Canadian Thoracic Soc., 1976; Corresp. Mem., Argentine Nat. Acad. of Medicine, 1977; Corresp. For. Member: Argentine Soc. of Phtisiol. and Thoracic Pathol., 1977; Coll. of Univ. Med. Phtisiologists of Argentine, 1978; Hon. Member: Argentine Med. Assoc., 1977; Singapore Thoracic Soc., 1978. Sir Robert Philip Medal, Chest and Heart Assoc., 1969; Weber Parkes Prize, RCP, 1973; Carlo Forlanini Gold Medal, Fedn Ital. contra la Tuberculosi e le Malattie Polmonari Sociali, 1976; Hon. Medal, Czech. Med. Soc., 1980; Robert Koch Centenary Medal, Internat. Union against Tuberculosis, 1982; Presidential Citation Award, Amer. Coll. of Chest Physicians, 1982; Presidential Commendation, Amer. Thoracic Soc., 1989. *Publications:* Reports on tuberculosis services in Hong Kong to Hong Kong Government: Heaf/Fox, 1962; Scadding/Fox, 1975; Fox/Kilpatrick, 1990; contribs to med. jls: on methodology of controlled clinical trials, on epidemiology and on chemotherapy, particularly in tuberculosis, and carcinoma of the bronchus. *Address:* 28 Mount Ararat Road, Richmond, Surrey TW10 6PG. *T:* 081–940 9662.

FOX, William; President, Football League, since 1989; *b* 6 Jan. 1928; *s* of Thomas Fox and Doris Fox (*née* Jones); *m* 1953, Marjorie Hindle; one *s* three *d*. *Educ:* Queen Elizabeth's Grammar Sch., Blackburn. Enlisted 1946, Ballykinlar (Nat. Service), RA; transf. to East Lancs Regt, Corp. 1947, demob. 1948 as small arms instructor. Joined family potato business, 1943; Chm., Wholesale Potato Co., 1968–88, retired. Nat. Fruit and Potato Trades Fedn Rep. on Jt Consultative and Ware Imports Cttees, Potato Marketing Bd; Man. Dir, Fox Commercial Vehicles (Renault main dealers), 1980–88. Bd Mem., Blackburn Rovers FC, 1976– (Vice-Chm., 1979–82; Chm., 1982–); Member: FA (Vice-Pres.); Football League Management Cttee, 1986–. *Recreation:* football only. *Address:* Treetops, Billinge End Road, Blackburn BB2 6PT.

FOX, Winifred Marjorie, (Mrs E. Gray Debros); Under-Secretary, Department of the Environment, 1970–76; *d* of Frederick Charles Fox and Charlotte Marion Ogborn; *m* 1953, Eustachy Gray Debros (*d* 1954); one *d*. *Educ:* Streatham County Sch.; St Hugh's Coll., Oxford. Unemployment Assistance Board, 1937; Cabinet Office, 1942; Ministry of Town and Country Planning, 1944; Ministry of Housing and Local Govt, 1952 (Under-Sec., 1963); Dept of the Environment, 1970; seconded to CSD as Chm., CS Selection Bd, 1971–72. *Address:* The Coach House, Hinton in the Hedges, S Northants. *T:* Brackley (0280) 702100.

FOX-ANDREWS, James Roland Blake; QC 1968; **His Honour Judge James Fox-Andrews;** a Circuit Judge (Official Referee), since 1985; *b* 24 March 1922; step *s* of late Norman Roy Fox-Andrews, QC; *m* 1950, Angela Bridget Swift (*d* 1991); two *s*. *Educ:* Stowe; Pembroke Coll., Cambridge. FCIArb. Called to the Bar, Gray's Inn, 1949, Bencher, 1974. Dep. Chm., Devon QS, 1970–71; Recorder of Winchester, 1971, Hon. Recorder, 1972; a Recorder of Crown Court, 1972–85. Leader, Western Circuit, 1982–84. Member: Gen. Council of the Bar, 1968–72; Senate of Inns of Court and the Bar, 1976–79. *Publications:* (jtly) Leasehold Property (Temporary Provisions) Act, 1951; contrib. Halsbury's Laws of England, 3rd edn, building contracts, architects and engineers; (jtly) Landlord and Tenant Act, 1954; Business Tenancies, 1970, 4th edn 1987; (jtly) Assured Tenancies, 1989. *Address:* 20 Cheyne Gardens, SW3 5QT. *T:* 071–352 9484; Lepe House, Exbury, Hants. *T:* Southampton (0703) 891648.

FOX BASSETT, Nigel; Senior Partner, Clifford Chance, since 1990; *b* 1 Nov. 1929; *s* of Thomas Fox Bassett and Catherine Adriana Wiffen; *m* 1961, Patricia Anne Lambourne; one *s* one *d*. *Educ:* Taunton Sch.; Trinity Coll., Cambridge (MA Hons History and Law). Articled, Coward Chance, 1953; admitted Solicitor, 1956; Partner, 1960. Member: Council, British Inst. of Internat. and Comparative Law, 1977– (Chm., Exec. Cttee, 1986–); Council, British Gp, Internat. Assoc. for Protection of Indust. Property, 1984–89; Council, British Branch, Internat. Law Assoc., 1971–86 (Chm., Cttee on Internat. Securities Regulation, 1989–); Business Section, Internat. Bar Assoc., 1969–; European Gp, Law Soc., 1969–; Cttee, Amer. Bar Assoc., 1979–. Deleg., Banking and Finance Mission to Poland, 1989–. Liveryman, City of London Solicitors' Co. Mem., charitable, sports, opera concerns. *Publications:* (contrib.) Branches and Subsidiaries in the European

Common Market, 1976; (contrib.) Business Law in Europe, 1982, 2nd edn 1990; articles in law professional jls. *Recreations:* shooting, beagling, cricket, art, opera. *Address:* Clifford Chance, Blackfriars House, 19 New Bridge Street, EC4V 6BY. *T:* 071–353 0211. *Clubs:* Garrick, City of London, MCC; Seaview Yacht.

FOX-STRANGWAYS, family name of **Earl of Ilchester.**

FOXALL, Colin; Under Secretary, and Director of the Insurance Services (formerly Comprehensive Guarantee) Group, Export Credits Guarantee Department, since 1986; *b* 6 Feb. 1947; *s* of Alfred George Foxall and Ethel Margaret Foxall; *m* 1980, Diana Gail Bewick; two *s*. *Educ:* Gillingham Grammar Sch., Kent. MIEx; MICM. Joined ECGD, 1966; Dept of Trade, 1974; ECGD, 1975–. *Recreations:* family, home, clay target shooting, trying to lose weight. *Address:* c/o Export Credits Guarantee Department, Crown Building, Cathays Park, Cardiff CF1 3NH.

FOXELL, Clive Arthur Peirson, CBE 1987; FEng 1985; consultant; Managing Director, Engineering and Procurement, and Board Member, British Telecom, 1986–89; *b* 27 Feb. 1930; *s* of Arthur Turner Foxell and Lillian (*née* Ellerman); *m* 1956, Shirley Ann Patey Morris; one *d*. *Educ:* Harrow High Sch.; Univ. of London. BSc; FIEE, FInstP, FInstPS. GEC Res. Labs, 1947; Man., GEC Semiconductor Labs, 1968; Man. Dir, GEC Semiconductors Ltd, 1971; Dep. Dir of Research, PO, 1975; Dep. Dir, PO Procurement Exec., 1978–79; Dir of Purchasing, PO, 1980; British Telecom: Dir of Procurement, 1981, Senior Dir, 1984, Chief Exec., Procurement, 1984; Dir, British Telecommunications Systems Ltd, 1982–89. Chairman: Fulcrum Communications Ltd, 1985–86; TSCR Ltd, 1986–88; Phoneprint Ltd, 1989–; Dir, BT&D Technologies Ltd, 1986–88. Member: Council, IEE, 1975–78, 1982–85, and 1987– (Vice-Chm., Electronics Div., 1980–81, Dep. Chm., 1982–83, Chm., 1983–84); SERC (formerly SRC) Engrg Bd, 1977–80 (Chm., Silicon Working Party, 1980–81; Chm., Microelectronics, 1982–86); SERC, 1986–90; NEDC (electronics), 1987–90; ACARD Working Party on IT, 1981. Pres., IBTE, 1987–90. Bulgin Premium, IERE, 1964. Liveryman, Engineers' Co. *Publications:* Low Noise Microwave Amplifiers, 1968; articles and papers on electronics. *Recreations:* photography, steam railways. *Address:* 4 Meades Lane, Chesham, Bucks HP5 1ND. *T:* Chesham (0494) 785737.

FOXLEE, James Brazier; Under Secretary, Ministry of Agriculture, Fisheries and Food, 1971–81, retired; *b* 20 Nov. 1921; *s* of late Arthur Brazier Foxlee and late Mary Foxlee (*née* Fisher); *m* 1952, Vera June (*née* Guiver); one *s* two *d*. *Educ:* Brentwood Sch. Entered Min. of Agric. and Fisheries (later MAFF) as Clerical Officer, 1938. Served War, RNVR, Ordinary Seaman, 1941; commissioned, 1942; Lieut, in comd Light Coastal Forces craft and mine-sweepers. MAFF: Exec. Officer, 1946; HEO, 1948; SEO, 1950; Principal, 1955 (Welsh Dept, 1955–57; Treas., 1961–62); Asst Sec., 1965 (Regional Controller, Leeds, 1965–69). Hon. Fellow, NIAB, 1982; Hon. Mem., Arable Res. Inst. Assoc., 1990. *Recreations:* watching cricket, camping, oenology. *Address:* Arran, 43 Foxley Lane, Purley, Surrey CR8 3EH. *T:* 081–660 1085. *Club:* Farmers'.

FOXLEY-NORRIS, Air Chief Marshal Sir Christopher (Neil), GCB 1973 (KCB 1969; CB 1966); DSO 1945; OBE 1956; Chairman: Cheshire Foundation, 1974–82, now Chairman Emeritus (Vice-Chairman, 1972–74); Battle of Britain Fighter Association, since 1978; Director, General Portfolio Life Assurance, since 1974; *b* 16 March 1917; *s* of Major J. P. Foxley-Norris and Dorothy Brabant Smith; *m* 1948, Joan Lovell Hughes; no *c*. *Educ:* Winchester; Trinity Coll., Oxford (Hon. Fellow, 1973); Middle Temple. Commissioned RAFO, 1936; France, 1940; Battle of Britain, 1940; various operational tours of duty in wartime. MA 1946. ACDS, 1963; AOC No 224 Gp, FEAF, 1964–67; Dir-Gen., RAF Organization, MoD, 1967–68; C-in-C, RAF Germany and Comdr, NATO 2nd Tactical Air Force, 1968–70; Chief of Personnel and Logistics, MoD, 1971–74; retd. Vice Pres., RUSI, 1979. Chairman: Gardening for the Disabled, 1980–; Trinity Coll. Oxford Soc., 1984–86; Ex RAF and Dependants Severely Disabled Holiday Trust, 1984. Pres., Leonard Cheshire Housing Assoc., 1978–. CBIM. *Publications:* A Lighter Shade of Blue, 1978; various in RUSI and other service jls. *Recreations:* golf, philately. *Address:* Tumble Wood, Northend Common, Henley-on-Thames RG9 6LJ. *T:* Turville Heath (049163) 457. *Clubs:* Royal Air Force; Huntercombe (Oxon).

FOXON, David Fairweather, FBA 1978; Reader in Textual Criticism and Fellow of Wadham College, Oxford, 1968–82, now Emeritus Fellow; *b* 9 Jan. 1923; *s* of late Rev. Walter Foxon and Susan Mary (*née* Fairweather); *m* 1947, Dorothy June (marr. diss. 1963) (*d* 1988), *d* of late Sir Arthur Jarratt, KCVO; one *d*. *Educ:* Kingswood Sch., Bath; Magdalen Coll., Oxford. BA 1948, MA 1953. Foreign Office, 1942–45; Asst Keeper, Dept of Printed Books, British Museum, 1950–65; Harkness Fellow, 1959–61; Professor of English, Queen's Univ., Kingston, Ontario, 1965–67; Guggenheim Fellow, 1967–68. Sen. Res. Fellow, Clark Library, UCLA, 1974–75; Lyell Reader in Bibliography, Oxford, 1975–76; Sandars Reader in Bibliography, Cambridge, 1977–78. Pres., Bibliographical Soc., 1980–81 (Gold Medal, 1985). Hon. Mem., Bibliographical Soc. of America, 1986. John H. Jenkins Award for Bibliography, 1977. *Publications:* T. J. Wise and the Pre-Restoration Drama, 1959; Libertine Literature in England, 1660–1745, 1964; (ed) English Bibliographical Sources, 1964–67; English Verse 1701–1750: a catalogue, 1975; Pope and the Early Eighteenth-century Book Trade, 1991; contribs to bibliographical jls. *Recreation:* music. *Address:* 7 Fane Road, Marston, Oxford OX3 0RZ. *T:* Oxford (0865) 248350.

FOXON, Harold Peter, OBE 1976; Group Managing Director, Inchcape plc, 1981–84 (Director, since 1971; a Managing Director, 1978); *b* 7 April 1919; *s* of William Henry Foxon and Kathleen Avis (*née* Perry); *m* 1948, Elizabeth Mary Butterfield; one *s* three *d*. *Educ:* Bancroft's. Served War, 1939–46, Royal Signals, Captain. Insurance, 1935–39; Smith Mackenzie & Co. Ltd (East Africa), 1946–69; Chm., Mackenzie Dalgety Ltd, 1966–69; Man. Dir, Gilman & Co. Ltd, Hong Kong, and Chm., Inchcape Hong Kong Ltd, 1969–77. Director: Dodwell & Co., Ltd, 1978–81; Anglo-Thai Corpn, 1978–82; Berry Trust Ltd, 1977–88; Member: Hong Kong Trade Adv. Gp, 1978–84; South East Asia Trade Adv. Gp, 1978–82. Master, Barbers' Co., 1986–87. *Recreations:* learning to fly, golf. *Address:* 48 Abingdon Court, Abingdon Villas, W8 6BT. *T:* 071–937 8713; Tanglin, Second Avenue, Frinton-on-Sea, Essex CO13 9LX. *T:* Frinton (0255) 672208. *Clubs:* City of London, Oriental; Muthaiga (Kenya); Hong Kong (Hong Kong).

FOXTON, Maj.-Gen. Edwin Frederick, CB 1969; OBE 1959; MA; Fellow and Domestic Bursar, Emmanuel College, Cambridge, 1969–79; *b* 28 Feb. 1914; *y s* of F. Foxton and T. Wilson; unmarried. *Educ:* Worksop Coll.; St Edmund Hall, Oxford. Commissioned from General List TA, 1937; served: India, 1939–42; Middle East, 1942–45; India, 1945–47 (Chief Educn Officer, Southern Comd, India); War Office, 1948–52; Chief Instructor, Army Sch. of Educn, 1952–55; Dist Educn Officer, HQ Northumbrian District, 1955–57; War Office, 1957–60; Commandant, Army Sch. of Educn, 1961–63; War Office, 1963–65; Chief Educn Officer, FARELF, 1965; Dir of Army Educn, 1965–69. *Address:* South Close, North Dalton, Driffield, East Yorks YO25 9XA.

FOYLE, Christina Agnes Lilian, (Mrs Ronald Batty); Managing Director, W. & G. Foyle Ltd; *d* of late William Alfred Foyle; *m* 1938, Ronald Batty. *Educ:* Aux Villas Unspunnen, Wilderswil, Switzerland. Began Foyle's Literary Luncheons, 1930, where book lovers have been able to see and hear great personalities. Member: Ct, Univ. of Essex; Council, RSA, 1963–69; Chm. East Anglian Region, RSA, 1978; Pres. Chelmsford District, Nat. Trust, 1979. DUniv Essex, 1975. *Publications:* So Much Wisdom, 1984; articles in various books and journals. *Recreations:* bird-watching, gardening, playing the piano. *Address:* Beeleigh Abbey, Maldon, Essex.

FOZARD, Prof. John William, OBE 1981; FRS 1987; FEng, FIMechE; FRAeS, FAIAA; consultant, writer, teacher; *b* 16 Jan. 1928; *s* of John Fozard and Eleanor Paulkit; *m* 1st, 1951, Mary (marr. diss. 1985), *d* of Regtl Sgt-Major C. B. Ward, VC, KOYLI; two *s*; 2nd, 1985, Gloria Ditmars Stanchfield Roberts, *widow* of Alan Roberts, Alexandria, Va, USA. *Educ:* Univ. of London (1st Cl. Hons BScEng 1948); Coll. of Aeronautics, Cranfield (DCAe with distinction 1950). FIMechE 1971; FRAeS 1964; FAIAA 1981; FEng 1984. Hawker Aircraft Ltd: Design Engr, 1950; Head of Proj. Office, 1960; Hawker Siddeley Aviation: Chief Designer, Harrier, 1963–78; Exec. Dir, 1971; Marketing Dir, Kingston Brough Div., BAe, 1978–84; Divl Dir, Special Projects, Mil. Aircraft Div., BAe, 1984–87, retd 1989. Visiting Professor: Sch. of Mechanical, Aeronautical and Production Engrg, Kingston Polytech., 1982–87; Aircraft Design, RMCS, Shrivenham, 1986–87; Lindbergh Prof. of Aerospace Hist., Nat. Air and Space Mus., Smithsonian Instn, Washington, 1988; Vis. Lectr, Univ. of Michigan, 1989; Lectures: 1st J. D. North Meml, RAeS Wolverhampton Br., 1969, and 16th, 1985; 23rd R. J. Mitchell Meml, RAeS Southampton Br., 1976; 32nd Barnwell Meml, RAeS Bristol Br., 1982; 2nd Lindbergh Meml, Nat. Air & Space Museum, Smithsonian Instn, 1978, 12th Lindbergh Meml, 1988; Friday Evening Discourse, Royal Instn, 1986; 9th Sir Sydney Camm Meml, RAeS, 1987; Sir Izaac Newton series to young people around UK, IMechE, 1979–80; over 200 learned soc. lectures in UK, USA, Europe, Australia, China, 1965–. Vice Pres., 1980–85, Pres.-elect, 1985–86, Pres., 1986–87, RAeS. FRSA 1986. Hon. DSc Strathclyde, 1983. Simms Gold Medal, Soc. of Engrs, 1971; British Silver Medal for Aeronautics, 1977; James Clayton Prize, IMechE, 1983; Mullard Award (with R. S. Hooper), Royal Soc., 1983. *Publications:* (ed) Sydney Camm and the Hurricane, 1991; papers in aeronautical jls and in specialist press, 1954–. *Recreations:* music, engineering history. *Address:* 306 North Columbus Street, Alexandria, Va 22314, USA. *T:* 703–549 5142.

FRAENKEL, Peter Maurice, FEng, FICE, FIStructE; Founder and Senior Partner, Peter Fraenkel & Partners, since 1972; Chairman: Peter Fraenkel Group, since 1984; Peter Fraenkel BMT Ltd, since 1990; *b* 5 July 1915; *s* of Ernest Fraenkel and Luise (*née* Tessmann); *m* 1946, Hilda Muriel, *d* of William Norman; two *d*. *Educ:* Battersea Polytechnic; Imperial Coll., London. BSc(Eng). FICE 1954, FIStructE 1954, MConsE 1962; FEng 1984. Asst Engr with London firm of contractors, engaged on design and construction of marine and industrial structures, 1937–40; served in Army, 1941–42; Works Services Br., War Dept, 1942–45; Rendel, Palmer & Tritton, Cons. Engineers: Civil Engr, 1945; Sen. Engr, 1953; Partner, 1961–72. Dir, British Maritime Technology, 1990–. Has been responsible for, or closely associated with, technical and management aspects of many feasibility and planning studies, and planning, design and supervision of construction of large civil engrg projects, incl. ports, docks, offshore terminals, inland waterways, highways, power stations and tunnels in Gt Britain, Middle East, India, Far East and Australia, including: new Oil port at Sullom Voe, Shetland; new Naval Dockyard, Bangkok; Shatin to Tai Po coastal Trunk Road, Hong Kong; comprehensive study for DoE, of maintenance and operational needs of canals controlled by Brit. Waterways Bd (Fraenkel Report), and new port at Limassol, Cyprus. James Watt Medal, 1963, Telford Gold Medal, 1971, ICE. *Publications:* (jtly) papers to Instn of Civil Engrs: Special Features of the Civil Engineering Works at Aberthaw Power Station, 1962; Planning and Design of Port Talbot Harbour, 1970. *Address:* Little Paddock, Oxted, Surrey RH8 0EL. *T:* Oxted (0883) 712927. *Club:* Athenæum.

FRAGA-IRIBARNE, Manuel; Founder-Member, Popular Alliance, Spain, 1976, Leader, 1979–86; Member of the Cortes, since 1977; *b* 23 Nov. 1922; *m* 1948, María del Carmen Estévez; two *s* three *d*. *Educ:* Insts of Coruña, Villalba and Lugo; Univs of Santiago de Compostela and Madrid. Prof. of Polit. Law, Univ. of Valencia, 1945; Prof. of Polit. Sci. and Constit. Law, Univ. of Madrid, 1953; Legal Adviser to the Cortes, 1945; entered Diplomatic Service, 1945; Sec.-Gen., Instituto de Cultura Hispánica, 1951; Sec.-Gen. in Min. of Educn, 1953; Head, Inst. of Polit. Studies, 1961; Minister of Information and Tourism, 1961–69; Ambassador to UK, 1973–75; Interior Minister, Spain, 1975–76; Leader of the Opposition, 1982–86. Holds numerous foreign orders. *Publications:* various books on law, polit. sci., history and sociology, incl. one on British Parlt. *Recreations:* shooting, fishing. *Address:* Joaquín María López 72, Madrid 28015, Spain. *T:* 244 4980. *Clubs:* Athenæum, Travellers'.

FRAME, Sir Alistair (Gilchrist), Kt 1981; MA, BSc; FEng; Chairman: RTZ (formerly Rio Tinto-Zinc) Corporation, 1985–91 (non-executive, 1990–91); Wellcome plc, since 1990; Director, British Steel, since 1991; *b* Dalmuir, Dunbartonshire, 3 April 1929; *s* of Alexander Frame and Mary (*née* Fraser); *m* 1953, Sheila (*née* Mathieson); one *d*. *Educ:* Glasgow and Cambridge Univs (Hon. Fellow, Fitzwilliam Coll., Cambridge, 1985). Director, Reactor and Research Groups, UK Atomic Energy Authority, 1964–68; joined Rio Tinto-Zinc Corp., 1968; appointed to main Board, 1973, Chief Exec. and Dep. Chm., 1978–85. Chm., Davy Corp., 1990–91; Director: Plessey Co., 1978–90; Britoil, 1983–84; Eurotunnel, 1990–. Member: NEB, 1978–79; Engineering Council, 1982–; Chm., Council of Mining and Metall. Instns, 1983–. Hon. DEng Birmingham, 1990; Hon. DSc Glasgow, 1990. *Recreations:* tennis, gardening, walking. *Club:* Royal Automobile.

FRAME, David William; Chairman and Senior Executive, Usborne Grain (formerly Usborne & Son (London)), since 1968; Chief Executive and Deputy Chairman, Usborne plc (formerly Feedex), since 1987; Member, Baltic Exchange, since 1961 (Chairman, 1987–89); *b* 26 July 1934; *s* of William and Ursula Frame; *m* 1963, Margaret Anne Morrison; two *d*. *Educ:* Wellington College. Commissioned Royal Artillery, National Service. Qualified Chartered Accountant, 1960; joined Usborne & Son (London), 1961, Dir 1962; Dir, Usborne and Feedex subsid. cos and other cos. *Recreation:* golf (played for GB and Ireland in Walker Cup, 1961, for England, 1958–63). *Address:* Green Glades, Frensham Vale, Farnham, Surrey. *T:* Frensham (025125) 3272. *Golf Clubs:* Royal and Ancient, Worplesdon, Trevose, Hankley Common, Old Thorns, Plettenberg Bay.

FRAME, Frank Riddell; Director, since 1985, and Adviser to the Board, since 1990, The Hongkong and Shanghai Banking Corporation Ltd; *b* 15 Feb. 1930; *m* 1958, Maureen (*née* Milligan); one *s* one *d*. *Educ:* Hamilton Academy; Univ. of Glasgow (MA, LLB). Solicitor. North of Scotland Hydro-Electric Board, 1955–60; UKAEA, 1960–68; The Weir Group plc, 1968–76 (Dir, 1971–76); joined The Hongkong and Shanghai Banking Corp. Ltd, as Gp Legal Adviser, 1977, Exec. Dir, 1985, Dep. Chm., 1986–90, retired. Chairman: South China Morning Post Ltd, 1981–87; Far Eastern Economic Review Ltd, 1981–87; Director: Marine Midland Banks Inc., 1986–90; British Bank of ME, 1986–91; Swire Pacific Ltd, 1986–90; Securities and Futures Commn, Hong Kong, 1989–90. *Publication:* The Law relating to Nuclear Energy (with Prof. Harry Street), 1966. *Address:*

The Hongkong and Shanghai Banking Corporation Ltd, 99 Bishopsgate, EC2P 2LA. *T*: 071–638 2300, *Fax*: 071–638 2125. *Clubs*: Hong Kong, Shek O Country (Hong Kong).

FRAME, Rt. Rev. John Timothy, DD; Dean of Columbia and Rector of Christ Church Cathedral, Victoria, BC, since 1980; *b* 8 Dec. 1930; *m*; three *d*. *Educ*: Univ. of Toronto. Burns Lake Mission, Dio. Caledonia, 1957; Hon. Canon of Caledonia, 1965; Bishop of Yukon, 1968–80. *Address*: c/o Christ Church Cathedral, 912 Vancouver Street, Victoria, BC V8V 3V7, Canada.

FRANCE, Sir Arnold William, GCB 1972 (KCB 1965; CB 1957); retired; *b* 20 April 1911; *s* of late W. E. France; *m* 1940, Frances Margaret Linton, *d* of late Dr C. J. L. Palmer; four *d*. *Educ*: Bishop's Stortford Coll. District Bank, Ltd, 1929–40. Served War of 1939–45, Army, 1940–43; Deputy Economic and Financial Adviser to Minister of State in Middle East, 1943; HM Treasury, 1945; Asst Sec., 1948; Under Sec., 1952; Third Sec., 1960; Ministry of Health: Dep. Sec., 1963–64; Permanent Sec., 1964–68; Chm., Bd of Inland Revenue, 1968–73. Director: Pilkington Bros, 1973–81; Tube Investments, 1973–81; Rank Organisation, 1973–83. Chm., Central Bd of Finance, C of E, 1973–78. Chm., Bd of Management, Lingfield Hosp. Sch., 1973–81. *Address*: Thornton Cottage, Lingfield, Surrey RH7 6BT. *T*: Lingfield (0342) 832278. *Club*: Reform.
See also J. N. B. Penny.

FRANCE, Sir Christopher (Walter), KCB 1989 (CB 1984); Permanent Secretary, Department of Health (formerly Department of Health and Social Security), since 1987; *b* 2 April 1934; *s* of W. J. and E. M. France; *m* 1961, Valerie (*née* Larman) (*see* V. E. France); one *s* one *d*. *Educ*: East Ham Grammar Sch.; New College, Oxford (BA (PPE), DipEd). CDipAF. HM Treasury, 1959–84: Principal Private Secretary to the Chancellor of the Exchequer, 1973–76; Principal Establishment Officer, 1977–80; on secondment to Electricity Council, 1980–81; Dep. Sec., 1981; on secondment to MoD, 1981–84; Dep. Sec., 1984–86, Second Perm. Sec., 1986, DHSS. *Recreations*: keeping the house up and the garden down. *Address*: Richmond House, 79 Whitehall, SW1A 2NS. *Club*: Reform.

FRANCE, Prof. Peter, DPhil; FBA 1989; Professor of French, University of Edinburgh, since 1980; *b* 19 Oct. 1935; *s* of Edgar France and Doris Woosnam Morgan; *m* 1961, Siân Reynolds; three *d*. *Educ*: Bridlington Sch.; Bradford Grammar Sch.; Magdalen Coll., Oxford (MA; DPhil). Lectr, then Reader, in French, Univ. of Sussex, 1963–80. French Editor, MLR, 1979–85. *Publications*: Racine's Rhetoric, 1965; Rhetoric and Truth in France, 1972; Poets of Modern Russia, 1982; Racine: Andromaque, 1977; Diderot, 1983; Rousseau: Confessions, 1987. *Recreations*: poetry and translation, hill walking. *Address*: 10 Dryden Place, Edinburgh EH9 1RP. *T*: 031–667 1177.
See also Rev. R. T. France.

FRANCE, Rev. Richard Thomas; Principal, Wycliffe Hall, Oxford, since 1989; *b* 2 April 1938; *s* of Edgar and Doris Woosnam France; *m* 1965, Barbara Wilding; one *s* one *d*. *Educ*: Bradford Grammar School; Balliol Coll., Oxford (MA); BD London; PhD Bristol. Asst Curate, St Matthew's Church, Cambridge, 1966–69; Lectr in Biblical Studies, Univ. of Ife, Nigeria, 1969–73; Tyndale House, Cambridge: Librarian, 1973–76; Warden, 1978–81; London Bible College: Senior Lectr, 1981–88; Vice-Principal, 1983–88. *Publications*: Jesus and the Old Testament, 1971; (ed with D. Wenham) Gospel Perspectives, vols 1–3, 1980–83; The Gospel According to Matthew: an introduction and commentary, 1985; The Evidence for Jesus, 1986; Matthew: evangelist and teacher, 1989; Divine Government, 1990. *Recreations*: mountains, wildlife, travel, music. *Address*: Wycliffe Hall, Oxford OX2 6PW. *T*: Oxford (0865) 57539.
See also P. France.

FRANCE, Valerie Edith, (Lady France), MA; Headmistress, City of London School for Girls, since 1986; *b* 29 Oct. 1935; *d* of Neville and Edith Larman; *m* 1961, Sir Christopher Walter France, *qv*; one *s* one *d*. *Educ*: St Hugh's Coll., Oxford (MA); CertEd Cantab. Deputy Headmistress, Bromley High Sch., GPDST, 1984–86. Freeman, City of London, 1988. *Recreations*: family, friends, places. *Address*: City of London School for Girls, Barbican, EC2Y 8BB.

FRANCIS, Clare Mary, MBE 1978; *b* 17 April 1946; *d* of Owen Francis, *qv*; *m* 1977, Jacques Robert Redon (marr. diss. 1985); one *s*. *Educ*: Royal Ballet Sch.; University Coll. London (BScEcon; Hon. Fellow, 1979). Crossed Atlantic singlehanded, Falmouth to Newport, in 37 days, 1973; Round Britain Race, 1974; Azores Race, 1975; L'Aurore Race, 1975, 1976; Observer Transatlantic Singlehanded Race: women's record (29 days), 1976; Whitbread Round the World Race (fully-crewed), first woman skipper, 1977–78. Hon. Fellow, UMIST, 1981. *Television series*: The Commanding Sea (BBC), 1981 (co-writer and presenter). *Publications*: *non-fiction*: Come Hell or High Water, 1977; Come Wind or Weather, 1978; The Commanding Sea, 1981; *novels*: Night Sky, 1983; Red Crystal, 1985; Wolf Winter, 1987; Requiem, 1991. *Recreations*: opera, music. *Address*: c/o John Johnson Agency, 45–47 Clerkenwell Green, EC1R 0HT.

FRANCIS, Dick, (Richard Stanley), OBE 1984; author; *b* 31 Oct. 1920; *s* of George Vincent Francis and Catherine Mary Francis; *m* 1947, Mary Margaret Brenchley; two *s*. *Educ*: Maidenhead County Boys' School. Pilot, RAF, 1940–45 (Flying Officer). Amateur National Hunt jockey, 1946–48; Professional, 1948–57; Champion Jockey, season 1953–54. Racing Correspondent, Sunday Express, 1957–73. Hon. LHD Tufts, 1991. *Publications*: Sport of Queens (autobiog.), 1957, 3rd updated edn, 1982; Dead Cert, 1962; Nerve, 1964; For Kicks, 1965; Odds Against, 1965; Flying Finish, 1966; Blood Sport, 1967; Forfeit, 1968 (Edgar Allan Poe Award, 1970); Enquiry, 1969; Rat Race, 1970; Bonecrack, 1971; Smoke Screen, 1972; Slay-Ride, 1973; Knock Down, 1974; High Stakes, 1975; In the Frame, 1976; Risk, 1977; Trial Run, 1978; Whip Hand, 1979 (Golden Dagger Award, Crime Writers' Assoc., 1980; Edgar Allan Poe Award, 1980); Reflex, 1980; Twice Shy, 1981; Banker, 1982; The Danger, 1983; Proof, 1984; Break In, 1985; Lester, the official biography, 1986; Bolt, 1986; Hot Money, 1987; The Edge, 1988; Straight, 1989; Longshot, 1990; Comeback, 1991; (ed jtly) Great Racing Stories, 1989. *Recreations*: boating, travel. *Address*: 5100 N Ocean Boulevard, #609, Fort Lauderdale, Florida 33308, USA. *T*: (305) 786 0838.

FRANCIS, Prof. Edward Howel, DSc; FRSE; FGS; CGeol; Professor of Earth Sciences, University of Leeds, 1977–89; *b* 31 May 1924; *s* of Thomas Howel Francis and Gwendoline Amelia (*née* Richards); *m* 1952, Cynthia Mary (*née* Williams); one *d*. *Educ*: Port Talbot County Sch.; Univ. of Wales, Swansea (BSc, DSc; Hon. Fellow 1989). FGS 1948; FRSE 1962. Served Army, 1944–47. Geological Survey of Great Britain (now incorporated in British Geol Survey): Field Geologist, Scotland, 1949–62; Dist Geologist, NE England, 1962–67, N Wales, 1967–70; Asst Dir, Northern England and Wales, 1971–77. Geological Society of London: Murchison Fund, 1963; Mem. Council, 1972–74; Pres., 1980–82; Pres., Section C (Geol.), BAAS, 1976; Mem., Inst. of Geol., 1978. Clough Medal, Edinburgh Geol Soc., 1983; Sorby Medal, Yorks Geol Soc., 1983; Major John Sacheverell A'Deane Coke Medal, Geol. Soc. of London, 1989. *Publications*: memoirs, book chapters and papers on coalfields, palaeovolcanic rocks and general stratigraphy, mainly of Britain. *Recreations*: opera, golf. *Address*: Michaelston, 11 Millbeck Green, Collingham, near Wetherby, W Yorks LS22 5AJ. *Club*: Sand Moor Golf.

FRANCIS, Ven. Edward Reginald; Archdeacon of Bromley, since 1979; *b* 31 Jan. 1929; *s* of Alfred John and Elsie Hilda Francis; *m* 1950, Joyce Noreen Atkins; three *s*. *Educ*: Maidstone and Dover Grammar Schools; Rochester Theological College. National Service, RAF, 1947–49. Insurance, including period at Chartered Insurance Inst. (ACII), 1950–59. Ordained, 1961; Chaplain, Training Ship Arethusa, and Curate of All Saints, Frindsbury, 1961–64; Vicar of St William's, Chatham, 1964–73; Vicar and Rural Dean of Rochester, 1973–78. Mem., General Synod of C of E, 1981–. Mem., Kent Industrial Mission, 1979–89; Jt Chm., Council for Social Responsibility, Dioceses of Canterbury and Rochester, 1983–89; Dir of Continuing Ministry Educn, dio. of Rochester, 1989–. *Recreations*: ornithology, walking, music. *Address*: 6 Horton Way, Farningham, Kent DA4 0DQ. *T*: Farningham (0322) 864522.

FRANCIS, Gwyn Jones, CB 1990; Director-General and Deputy Chairman, Forestry Commission, 1986–90, retired; *b* 17 Sept. 1930; *s* of Daniel Brynmor Francis and Margaret Jane Francis; *m* 1st, 1954, Margaretta Meryl Jeremy (*d* 1985); one *s* one *d* (and one *s* decd); 2nd, 1986, Audrey Gertrude (*née* Gill). *Educ*: Llanelli Grammar Sch.; University Coll. of N Wales, Bangor (BSc Hons 1952); Univ. of Toronto (MSc 1965). Served RE, 1952–54. Forestry Commission: Dist Officer, 1954; Principal, Forester Training Sch., 1962; Asst Conservator, 1969; Head, Harvesting and Marketing Div., 1976; Comr, 1983–86. FICFor 1982; FIWSc 1984. *Recreations*: ornithology, gardening, walking. *Address*: 21 Campbell Road, Edinburgh EH12 6DT. *T*: 031–337 5037.

FRANCIS, Sir (Horace) William (Alexander), Kt 1989; CBE 1976; FEng 1977; FICE; Chairman, Black Country Urban Development Corporation, since 1987; Chairman, Thomas Telford Ltd, since 1986; Director: Census Computer Services Ltd, since 1982; Peakbeam Ltd, since 1985; Tysons, since 1988; J. F. Donelan, since 1989; Donelan Tyson, since 1989; *b* 31 Aug. 1926; *s* of Horace Fairie Francis and Jane McMinn Murray; *m* 1949, Gwendoline Maud Dorricott; two *s* two *d*. *Educ*: Royal Technical Coll., Glasgow. Dir, Tarmac Civil Engineering Ltd, 1960; Man. Dir, Tarmac Construction Ltd, 1963; Dir, Tarmac Ltd, 1964, Vice-Chm., 1974–77; Director: Trafalgar House Ltd, 1978–84; Trafalgar House Construction Hldgs, 1979–84, Dep. Chm., 1982–84; Cementation Civil and International Construction Hldgs, 1982–; Cementation Specialist Hldgs, 1982–; Cleveland Redpath Engineering Hldgs, 1982–; Trollope & Colls Hldgs, 1982–. Member: Export Guarantees Adv. Council, 1974–80; British Overseas Trade Bd, 1977–80; Chm., Overseas Projects Bd, 1977–80. Pres., ICE, 1987–88 (Vice-Pres., 1984–87). Lt-Col, Engr and Transport Staff Corps, TA, 1986. FRSA 1989. Hon. LLD Strathclyde, 1988. *Recreations*: golf, shooting, fishing, construction. *Address*: The Firs, Cruckton, near Shrewsbury, Shropshire SY5 8PW. *T*: Shrewsbury (0743) 860796. *Clubs*: Livery, Royal Automobile, Royal Over-Seas League.

FRANCIS, Dr John Michael; Chief Executive, Nature Conservancy Council for Scotland, since 1991; *b* 1 May 1939; *s* of late William Winston Francis and of Beryl Margaret Francis (*née* Savage); *m* 1963, Eileen Sykes, Cyncoed, Cardiff; two *d*. *Educ*: Gowerton County Grammar Sch. for Boys; Royal Coll. of Sci., Imperial Coll. of Sci. and Tech., Univ. of London (BSc, ARCS, PhD, DIC). FRIC 1969; FRSGS 1990. Res. Officer, CEGB, R&D Dept, Berkeley Nuclear Labs, 1963–70; First Dir, Society, Religion and Tech. Project, Church of Scotland, 1970–74: Sen. Res. Fellow in Energy Studies, Heriot-Watt Univ., 1974–76; Scottish Office, Edinburgh, 1976–84; Dir Scotland, Nature Conservancy Council, 1984–91 (Mem., Adv. Cttee for Scotland, 1974–76). Member: Oil Develt Council for Scotland, 1973–76; Indep. Commn on Transport, 1974; Adv. Cttee on Marine Fishfarming Crown Estate Commn, 1989–. Consultant on Sci., Tech. and Social Ethics, WCC, Geneva, 1971–83; Chm., Cttee on Society, Religion and Tech., Church of Scotland, 1980–. Chm., Edinburgh Forum, 1984–. Mem. Council, Nat. Trust for Scotland, 1985–. Mem., St Giles' Cathedral, Edinburgh. Fellow, Inst. for Advanced Studies in the Humanities, Edinburgh Univ., 1988. *Publications*: Scotland in Turmoil, 1973; (jtly) Changing Directions, 1974; (jtly) The Future as an Academic Discipline, 1975; Facing up to Nuclear Power, 1976; (jtly) The Future of Scotland, 1977; contribs to scientific and professional jls and periodicals. *Recreations*: philosophy and ethics of the environment, ecumenical travels, hill walking, theatre. *Address*: Nature Conservancy Council, 12 Hope Terrace, Edinburgh EH9 2AS. *T*: 031–447 4784.

FRANCIS, Sir Laurie (Justice), Kt 1982; New Zealand High Commissioner to Australia, 1976–85; barrister and solicitor, High Court of New Zealand, as Consultant to Farry & Co., Solicitors, Dunedin, since 1985; Commissioner of Oaths for Australian States, including Northern Territory, since 1985; *b* 30 Aug. 1918; *m* 1952, Heather Margaret McFarlane; three *d*. *Educ*: Otago Boys High Sch.; Victoria University of Wellington; Univ. of Otago (LLB). Practised law as Barrister and Solicitor, Winton, Southland, until 1964; Senior Partner, Dunedin firm of Gilbert, Francis, Jackson and Co., Barristers and Solicitors, 1964–76. Hon. Life Mem., RSL, 1984. *Recreations*: golf occasionally, follower of Rugby and cricket, lover of jazz. *Address*: 42 Glengyle Street, Dunedin, New Zealand. *Club*: Dunedin (Fernhill).

FRANCIS, Norman; see Francis, W. N.

FRANCIS, Owen, CB 1960; Chairman, London Electricity Board, 1972–76; *b* 4 Oct. 1912; *yr s* of Sidney and Margaret Francis, The White House, Austwick, Yorks; *m* 1938, Joan St Leger (*née* Norman); two *d*. *Educ*: Giggleswick Sch., Yorks. Joined Govt Actuary's Dept, 1931. *Address*: Meadow Cottage, Stanford Dingley, Berks RG7 6LT. *T*: Bradfield 744394. *Clubs*: Royal Yacht Squadron; Seaview Yacht; St Moritz Tobogganing.
See also C. M. Francis.

FRANCIS, Richard Mark; art historian and consultant; Curator, Tate Gallery, Liverpool, 1986–90; *b* 20 Nov. 1947; *s* of Ralph Lawrence and Eileen Francis; *m* 1976, Tamar Janine Helen Burchill; one *d*. *Educ*: Oakham Sch.; Cambridge Univ.; Courtauld Inst. Walker Art Gall., Liverpool, 1971–72; Arts Council of GB, 1973–80; Asst Keeper, Tate Gall., London, 1980–86. *Publication*: Jasper Johns, 1984. *Recreations*: buying books, riding. *Address*: 64 Hungerford Road, N7 9LP. *T*: 071–609 1022.

FRANCIS, Richard Stanley; see Francis, Dick.

FRANCIS, Sir Richard (Trevor Langford), KCMG 1989; Director-General, British Council, since 1987; *b* 10 March 1934; *s* of Eric Roland Francis and Esther Joy (*née* Todd); *m* 1st, 1958, Beate Ohlhagen (marr. diss.); two *s*; 2nd, 1974, Elizabeth Penelope Anne Fairfax Crone; two *s*. *Educ*: Uppingham Sch.; University Coll., Oxford. BA 1956, MA 1960. Commissioned in RA, 1957. BBC Trainee, 1958–60; TV: Prodn Asst, 1960–62; Producer: Afternoon Programmes, 1962–63; Panorama, 1963–65; Asst Editor: Panorama, 1965–66; 24 Hours, 1966–67; Projects Editor, Current Affairs, TV, 1967–70; Head, EBU Operations for US Elections and Apollo, 1968–69; Head of Special Projects, Current Affairs, TV, 1970–71; Asst Head, Current Affairs Group, TV 1971–73; Head, EBU Operations for US Elections, 1972; Controller, BBC NI, 1973–77; Dir, News and Current Affairs, BBC, 1977–82; Man. Dir, BBC Radio, 1982–86. Visnews: Dir, 1978; Dep. Chm., 1979–82; Member: British Exec., IPI, 1978–82, (Dep. Chm., 1982–86); Press Complaints Commn, 1991–. Hon. Pres., Radio Acad., 1986–. Trustee, Charities Aid Foundn, 1991–. Gov., Westminster Coll., Oxford, 1990–. Hon. Freeman, City of

Freetown, Sierra Leone, 1991. CBIM 1984; FRSA 1988; FKC 1991. *Recreations:* offshore sailing, photography, listening to music 6 miles high. *Address:* c/o British Council, 10 Spring Gardens, SW1A 2BN. *Clubs:* Reform, Garrick, Arts; Chichester Yacht.

FRANCIS, Sir William; *see* Francis, Sir H. W. A.

FRANCIS, William Lancelot, CBE 1961; *b* 16 Sept. 1906; *s* of G. J. Francis and Ethel, *d* of L. G. Reed, Durham; *m* 1st, 1937, Ursula Mary Matthew (*d* 1966); two *s* three *d*; 2nd, 1968, Margaret Morris (*d* 1978). *Educ:* Latymer Upper Sch., Hammersmith; King's Coll., Cambridge. MA, PhD. DSIR Sen. Research Award, Cambridge, 1931–33; Rockefeller Foundn Fellowship in Experimental Zoology, Rockefeller Institute, New York, 1933–34; Science Master, Repton Sch., 1935–40; Radar research and administration in Ministries of Supply and Aircraft Production (TRE Malvern), 1940–45; Dept of Scientific and Industrial Res. Headquarters, 1945–65; Secretary, Science Research Council, 1965–72; Consultant, Civil Service Dept, 1972–75. Member: Nat. Electronics Council, 1965–72; CERN, 1966–70; Advisory Councils: R&D, Fuel and Power, 1966–72; Iron and Steel, 1966–72. Mem. Council, Oxfam, 1975–83. *Publications:* papers on physical chemistry and experimental zoology in scientific jls, 1931–37. *Recreations:* gardening, travel. *Address:* 269 Sheen Lane, SW14. *T:* 081–876 3029. *Club:* Athenæum.

FRANCIS, (William) Norman; His Honour Judge Francis; a Circuit Judge (formerly Judge of County Courts), since 1969; *b* 19 March 1921; *s* of Llewellyn Francis; *m* 1951, Anthea Constance (*née* Kerry); one *s* one *d*. *Educ:* Bradfield; Lincoln Coll., Oxford (BCL, MA). Served War of 1939–45, RA. Called to Bar, Gray's Inn, 1946. Dep. Chm., Brecknock QS, 1962–71. Member: Criminal Law Revision Cttee, 1977–; Policy Adv. Cttee on Sexual Offences, 1977–85; County Court Rule Cttee, 1983–88 (Chm., 1987–88). Pres., Council of HM Circuit Judges, 1987. Trustee, Cardiff Athletic Club. Chancellor, dio. of Llandaff, 1979–. Mem. Representative Body and Governing Body, Church in Wales. Fellow, Woodard Corp. (Western Div.), 1985–91. *Recreations:* hockey, walking. *Address:* 2 The Woodlands, Lisvane, near Cardiff CF4 5SW. *T:* Cardiff (0222) 753070.

FRANCKENSTEIN, Baroness Joseph von; *see* Boyle, Kay.

FRANCKLIN, Comdr (Mavourn Baldwin) Philip, DSC 1940; RN; JP; Lord-Lieutenant of Nottinghamshire, 1972–83 (Vice-Lieutenant, 1968–72); *b* 15 Jan. 1913; *s* of Captain Philip Francklin, MVO, RN (killed in action, 1914); *m* 1949, Xenia Alexandra, *d* of Alexander Davidson, Kilpedder, Co. Wicklow; two *s* one *d* (and one *s* decd). *Educ:* RNC Dartmouth. Joined RN, 1926. Served War of 1939–45: Norway, N and S Atlantic, Indian Ocean (despatches twice); Asst to 5th Sea Lord, 1947–49; Comdr 1950; Korean War, 1950–51; Asst Naval Attaché, Paris, 1952–53. DL, 1963, JP 1958, Notts; High Sheriff of Notts, 1965. KStJ 1973. Croix de Guerre (France). *Address:* Gonalston Hall, Nottingham. *T:* Nottingham (0602) 663635. *Club:* Boodle's.

FRANÇOIS-PONCET, Jean André; Member of the French Senate, since 1983 (Chairman of the Economic Committee, since 1986); Director, FMC Corporation, since 1982; *b* 8 Dec. 1928; *s* of André François-Poncet, Grand'Croix de la Légion d'Honneur, and Jacqueline (*née* Dillais); *m* 1959, Marie-Thérèse de Mitry; two *s* one *d*. *Educ:* Paris Law Sch.; Ecole Nationale d'Administration; Wesleyan Univ.; Fletcher Sch. of Law and Diplomacy. Joined Ministry of Foreign Affairs, 1955; Office of Sec. of State, 1956–58; Sec. Gen. of French delegn to Treaty negotiations for EEC and Euratom, 1956–58; Dep. Head, European Orgns, Ministry of Foreign Affairs, 1958–60; Head of Assistance Mission, Morocco, 1961–63; Dep. Head, African Affairs, 1963–65; Counsellor, Tehran, 1969–71. Professor, Institut d'Etudes Politiques, Paris, 1960–. Chm. 1971, Vice-Pres. 1972, Pres. and Chief Exec. 1973–75, Carnaud SA. Sec. of State for Foreign Affairs, Jan.-July 1976; Sec.-Gen. to Presidency of France, 1976–78; Minister for Foreign Affairs, 1978–81. President: Conseil Général of Lot-et-Garonne, 1978– (Member, from Laplume, 1967–); Comité du bassin Adour-Garonne, 1980–. *Publication:* The Economic Policy of Western Germany, 1970. *Address:* 6 boulevard Suchet, 75116 Paris, France.

FRANCOME, John, MBE 1986; first jockey to F. T. Winter, 1975–85; *b* 13 Dec. 1952; *s* of Norman and Lillian Francome; *m* 1976, Miriam Strigner. *Educ:* Park Senior High School, Swindon. First ride, Dec. 1970; Champion Jockey (National Hunt), 1975–76, 1978–79, 1980–81, 1981–82, 1982–83, 1983–84, 1984–85; record number of jumping winners (1,036), May 1984; retired March 1985 (1138 winners). *Publications:* Born Lucky (autobiog.), 1985; How to Make Money Betting—or at least how not to lose too much, 1986; Twice Lucky: the lighter side of steeplechasing, 1988; *novels* (with James MacGregor): Eavesdropper, 1986; Riding High, 1987; Declared Dead, 1988. *Recreations:* tennis, music. *Address:* Trabbs Farm, Seven Barrows, Lambourn, Berks RG16 7UF.

FRANK, Air Vice-Marshal Alan Donald, CB 1967; CBE 1962; DSO 1943; DFC 1941; Bursar, St Antony's College, Oxford, 1970–74; *b* 27 July 1917; *s* of late Major N. G. Frank and late M. H. Frank (*née* Donald); *m* 1941, Jessica Ann Tyrrell; two *s* two *d*. *Educ:* Eton; Magdalen Coll., Oxford. Commanded 51 Squadron Bomber Command, 1943; RAF Staff Coll., 1944; OC 83 Sqdn, 1957; OC RAF Honington, 1958–60; Group Captain Ops, Bomber Comd, 1960–62; Dir Operational Requirements, MoD, 1962–65; Air Attaché and OC, RAF Staff, Washington, 1965–68; SASO, RAF Air Support Command, 1968–70. *Recreations:* music, gardening. *Address:* Roundway House, Devizes, Wilts SN10 2EG.

FRANK, Sir Andrew; *see* Frank, Sir R. A.

FRANK, Sir Charles; *see* Frank, Sir F. C.

FRANK, Sir Douglas (George Horace), Kt 1976; QC 1964; Deputy Judge of the High Court, Queen's Bench Division, 1976–89; *b* 16 April 1916; *s* of late George Maurice Frank and late Agnes Winifred Frank; *m* 1979, Audrey, BA (Cantab), *yr d* of late Charles Leslie Thomas, Neath, Glam; one *s* four *d* by former marriage. War service in Royal Artillery. Called to the Bar, Gray's Inn, 1946 (Master of the Bench, 1970; Master of Moots, 1978–83; Master of Estate, 1982–84). One time Asst Commissioner, Boundary Commission for England; Pres., Lands Tribunal, 1974–88. Mem., Cttee Public Participation in Planning (Min. Housing and Local Govt), 1968. Mem., Senate of Inns of Court and Bar, 1984–85. Chm., Planning and Local Govt Cttee of the Bar, 1966–73. Hon. Pres., Anglo-American Real Property Inst., 1980–90. *Publications:* various legal. *Recreations:* theatre, music, walking, cooking. *Address:* 1 Verulam Buildings, WC1. *T:* 071–242 5949; La Mayne-Longue-Haute, Sauveterre-La-Lémance, 47500 Fumel, France. *T:* 53–40–68–98.

FRANK, Sir (Frederick) Charles, Kt 1977; OBE 1946; FRS 1954; DPhil; Henry Overton Wills Professor of Physics and Director of the H. H. Wills Physics Laboratory, University of Bristol, 1969–76 (Professor in Physics, 1954–69); now Emeritus Professor; *b* 6 March 1911; *e s* of Frederick and Medora Frank; *m* 1940, Maia Maita Asché, *y d* of late Prof. B. M. Asché; no *c*. *Educ:* Thetford Grammar Sch.; Ipswich Sch.; Lincoln Coll., Oxford. BA, BSc, Oxon. 1933; DPhil Oxon. 1937; Hon. Fellow, Lincoln Coll., 1968. Research: Dyson Perrins Laboratory and Engineering Laboratory, Oxford, 1933–36; Kaiser Wilhelm Institut für Physik, Berlin, 1936–38; Colloid Science Laboratory, Cambridge, 1939–40; Scientific Civil Service (temp.), 1940–46; Chemical Defence Research Establishment, 1940, Air Ministry, 1940–46; Research, H. H. Wills Physical Laboratory, Bristol Univ., 1946–; Research Fellow in Theoretical Physics, 1948; Reader in Physics, 1951–54; Vis. Prof., Univ. of California, San Diego, Inst. of Geophysics and Planetary Physics, and Dept of Physics, 1964–65; Raman Prof., Raman Res. Inst., Bangalore, 1979–80. A Vice-Pres., Royal Society, 1967–69. Foreign Associate: US Nat. Acad. of Engineering, 1980; Royal Soc. of S Africa, 1986; US Nat. Acad. of Sci., 1987. Hon. FIP 1978; Hon. FIASc 1984; Hon. Fellow, Bristol Univ., 1986. Hon. DSc: Ghent, 1955; Bath, 1974; TCD, 1978; Warwick, 1981; DUniv Surrey, 1977. Docteur *hc* Univ. de Paris-Sud, 1986. Holweck Prize, French Physical Soc.; Crystal Growth Award, Amer. Assoc. for Crystal Growth, 1978; Royal Medal, Royal Soc., 1979; Grigori Aminoff Gold Medal, Royal Swedish Acad. of Sciences, 1981; Guthrie Medal and Prize, Inst. of Physics, 1982; Robert Mehl Award, Amer. Metallurgical Soc., 1987; Von Hippel Award, Amer. Materials Res. Soc., 1988. *Publications:* articles in various learned journals, mostly dealing either with dielectrics or the physics of solids, in particular crystal dislocations, crystal growth, mechanical properties of polymers and mechanics of the earth's crust. *Address:* Orchard Cottage, Grove Road, Coombe Dingle, Bristol BS9 2RL. *T:* Bristol (0272) 681708. *Club:* Athenæum.

FRANK, Sir (Robert) Andrew, 4th Bt *cr* 1920, of Withyham, Co. Sussex; producer, since 1986; *b* 16 May 1964; *s* of Sir Robert John Frank, 3rd Bt, FRICS, and of Margaret Joyce, *d* of Herbert Victor Truesdale; *S* father, 1987; *m* 1990, Zoë, *er d* of S. A. Hasan. *Educ:* Ludgrove Prep. School; Eton College. *Recreations:* travel, theatre, cinema. *Heir:* none. *Address:* 50 Under The Wood, Bisham, Marlow, Bucks SL7 1RX. *T:* Marlow (06284) 75298.

FRANKEL, Prof. Herbert; *see* Frankel, Prof. S. H.

FRANKEL, Sir Otto (Herzberg), Kt 1966; DSc; DAgr; FRS 1953; FRSNZ; FAA; Honorary Research Fellow, Division of Plant Industry, CSIRO, Canberra, Australia, since 1966; *b* 4 Nov. 1900; *m* 1939, Margaret Anderson. *Educ:* Vienna; Berlin; Cambridge. Plant Geneticist, 1929–42, and Chief Executive Officer, 1942–49, Wheat Research Institute, NZ; Dir, Crop Research Division, Dept of Scientific and Industrial Research, New Zealand, 1949–51; Chief, Division of Plant Industry, CSIRO, Australia, 1951–62; Member of Executive, Commonwealth Scientific and Industrial Research Organization, Melbourne, Aust, 1962–66. Hon. Mem., Japan Academy, 1983; For. Associate, US Nat. Acad. of Scis, 1988. *Publications:* (ed jtly) Genetic Resources in Plants: their exploration and conservation, 1970; (ed jtly) Crop Genetic Resources for Today and Tomorrow, 1975; (with M. E. Soulé) Conservation and Evolution, 1981; (ed jtly) The Use of Plant Genetic Resources, 1989; numerous articles in British, NZ and Australian scientific journals. *Recreations:* ski-ing, gardening, angling. *Address:* 4 Cobby Street, Campbell, Canberra, ACT 2601, Australia. *T:* 479460.

See also P. H. Frankel.

FRANKEL, Dr Paul Herzberg, CBE 1981; FInstPet; Life President, PEL Group, since 1987; *b* 1 Nov. 1903; *s* of Ludwig and Teresa Herzberg-Frankel; *m* 1931, Helen Spitzer; one *s* four *d*. *Educ:* Vienna Univ. (Dr of Polit. Econ.). FInstPet 1941. Actively engaged in oil industry, mainly in oil refining and marketing, first on Continent and then in UK, mid 1930s-; Dir of Manchester Oil Refinery Ltd and associated cos in UK and on Continent until 1955; founded Petroleum Economics Ltd, the London internat. consulting firm, 1955, Chm., 1955–80, Pres., 1980–87. Chevalier de la Légion d'Honneur, 1976; Grosses Verdienstkreuz des Verdienstordens, Bundesrepublik Deutschland, 1977; Grosses Ehrenzeichen für Verdienste, Republik Osterreich, 1978; Cavaliere Ufficiale dell'Ordine al Merito della Repubblica Italiana, 1988; Goldenes Ehrenzeichen fuer Verdienste um Das Land Wien, 1988. Cadman Medal, Inst. of Petroleum, 1973; Award for outstanding contributions to profession of energy economics and its literature, Internat. Assoc. of Energy Economists, 1985. *Publications:* Essentials of Petroleum, 1946; Oil: the facts of life, 1962; Mattei: oil and power politics, 1966; Paul Frankel: a common carrier of common sense, 1989. *Recreations:* walking, music. *Address:* 30 Dunstall Road, SW20 0HR. *T:* 081–946 5805. *Club:* Reform.

See also Sir O. H. Frankel.

FRANKEL, Prof. (Sally) Herbert, MA Rand, PhD London, DScEcon London, MA Oxon; Emeritus Professor in the Economics of Underdeveloped Countries, University of Oxford, and Emeritus Fellow, Nuffield College, Oxford (Professor, and Professorial Fellow, 1946–71); *b* 22 Nov. 1903; *e s* of Jacob Frankel; *m* 1928, Ilse Jeanette Frankel; one *s* one *d*. *Educ:* St John's Coll., Johannesburg; University of the Witwatersrand; London Sch. of Economics. Prof. of Economics, University of Witwatersrand, Johannesburg, 1931–46; responsible for calculations of National Income of S Africa for the Treasury, 1941–48; Jt Editor of South African Journal of Economics from its inception to 1946; Mem. of Union of South Africa Treasury Advisory Council on Economic and Financial Policy, 1941–45; Mem. of Union of South Africa Miners' Phthisis Commission, 1941–42; Commissioner appointed by Govts of Southern and Northern Rhodesia and the Bechuanaland Protectorate to report upon Rhodesia Railways Ltd, 1942–43; Chm. Commission of Enquiry into Mining Industry of Southern Rhodesia, 1945; Mem. East Africa Royal Commission, 1953–55; Consultant Adviser, Urban African Affairs Commn, Govt of S Rhodesia, 1957–58. Vis. Prof. of Econs, Univ. of Virginia, until 1974. Mem., Mont Pellerin Soc., 1950–. Chm., Bd of Governors, Oxford Centre for Postgrad. Hebrew Studies, 1983–89. Hon. DSc Econ Rhodes Univ., 1969; Hon. DLitt Rand Univ., 1970. *Publications:* Co-operation and Competition in the Marketing of Maize in South Africa, 1926; The Railway Policy of South Africa, 1928; Coming of Age: Studies in South African Citizenship and Politics (with Mr J. H. Hofmeyr and others), 1930; Capital Investment in Africa: Its Course and Effects, 1938; The Economic Impact on Underdeveloped Societies: Essays on International Investment and Social Change, 1953; Investment and the Return to Equity Capital in the South African Gold Mining Industry 1887–1965: An International Comparison, 1967; Gold and International Equity Investment (Hobart Paper 45), 1969; Money: two philosophies, the conflict of trust and authority, 1977; Money and Liberty, 1980. *Recreation:* gardening. *Address:* 62 Cutteslowe House, Park Close, Oxford OX2 8NP. *T:* Oxford (0865) 514748. *Club:* Reform.

FRANKEL, William, CBE 1970; Editor, Jewish Chronicle, 1958–77; *b* 3 Feb. 1917; *s* of Isaac and Anna Frankel, London; *m* 1st, 1939, Gertrude Freda Reed (marr. diss.); one *s* (one *d* decd); 2nd, 1973, Mrs Claire Neuman. *Educ:* elementary and secondary schs in London; London Univ. (LLB Hons). Called to Bar, Middle Temple, 1944; practised on South-Eastern circuit, 1944–55. General Manager, Jewish Chronicle, 1955–58. Special Adviser to The Times, 1977–81. Chm., Jewish Chronicle Ltd, 1991– (Dir, 1959–). Chairman: Mental Health Review Appeal Tribunal, 1978–89; Social Security Appeal Tribunal, 1979–89. Vis. Prof., Jewish Theological Seminary of America, 1968–69. Chm., Inst. of Jewish Affairs, 1990–. Gov., Oxford Centre for Hebrew Studies, 1968–; Trustee, Jewish Youth Fund, 1979–. JP Co. of London, 1963–69. *Publications:* (ed) Friday Nights, 1973; Israel Observed, 1980; (ed) Survey of Jewish Affairs (annual), 1982–. *Address:* 30 Montagu Square, W1H 1RJ. *T:* (office) 071–935 3052; (home) 071–935 1202. *Clubs:* Athenæum, MCC.

FRANKHAM, Very Rev. Harold Edward; Provost of Southwark, 1970–82, now Provost Emeritus; *b* 6 April 1911; *s* of Edward and Minnie Frankham; *m* 1942, Margaret Jean Annear; one *s* two *d* (and one *s* decd). *Educ:* London Coll. of Divinity (LCD). Ordained, 1941; Curate: Luton, 1941–44; Holy Trinity, Brompton, 1944–46; Vicar of Addiscombe, 1946–52; Rector of Middleton, Lancs, 1952–61; Vicar of Luton, 1961–70. Hon. Canon of St Albans, 1967–70. Exec. Sec., Archbishops' Council on Evangelism, 1965–73. *Recreations:* music, travel. *Address:* The Garden Flat, Lambridge House, London Road West, Lambridge, Bath BA1 7HY. *T:* Bath (0225) 333214.

FRANKL, Peter; pianist; *b* 2 Oct 1935; *s* of Laura and Tibor Frankl; *m* 1958, Annie Feiner; one *s* one *d*. *Educ:* Liszt Ferenc Acad. of Music, Budapest. Regular concert tours with leading orchestras and conductors throughout the world; numerous festival appearances, including Edinburgh, Cheltenham, Lucerne, Flanders, Aldeburgh, Adelaide, Windsor. Winner of internat. competitions: Paris, 1957; Munich, 1957; Rio de Janeiro, 1959. Franz Liszt Award, Budapest, 1958. Hon. Citizen, Rio de Janeiro, 1960. Numerous recordings include: complete works for piano by Schumann and Debussy; orchestral and chamber pieces. *Recreations:* football, opera, theatre. *Address:* 5 Gresham Gardens, NW11 8NX. *T:* 081–455 5228.

FRANKLAND, family name of **Baron Zouche.**

FRANKLAND, (Anthony) Noble, CB 1983; CBE 1976; DFC 1944; MA, DPhil; historian and biographer; *b* 4 July 1922; *s* of late Edward Frankland, Ravenstonedale, Westmorland; *m* 1st, 1944, Diana Madeline Fovargue (*d* 1981), *d* of late G. V. Tavernor, of Madras and Southern Mahratta Rly, India; one *s* one *d*; 2nd, 1982, Sarah Katharine, *d* of His Honour the late Sir David Davies, QC and the late Lady Davies (Margaret Kennedy). *Educ:* Sedbergh; Trinity Coll., Oxford. Served Royal Air Force, 1941–45 (Bomber Command, 1943–45). Air Historical Branch Air Ministry, 1948–51; Official Military Historian, Cabinet Office, 1951–58. Rockefeller Fellow, 1953. Deputy Dir of Studies, Royal Institute of International Affairs, 1956–60; Dir, Imperial War Museum (at Southwark, 1960–82, Duxford Airfield, 1976–82, and HMS Belfast, 1978–82). Lees Knowles Lecturer, Trinity Coll., Cambridge, 1963. Historical advisor, Thames Television series, The World At War, 1971–74. Vice-Chm., British Nat. Cttee, Internat. Cttee for Study of Second World War, 1976–82. Biographer of His late Royal Highness The Duke of Gloucester. Mem., Council, Morley Coll., 1962–66; Trustee: Military Archives Centre, KCL, 1963–82; HMS Belfast Trust, 1971–78 (Vice-Chm., 1972–78); HMS Belfast Bd, 1978–82. *Publications:* Documents on International Affairs: for 1955, 1958; for 1956, 1959; for 1957, 1960; Crown of Tragedy, Nicholas II, 1960; The Strategic Air Offensive Against Germany, 1939–1945 (4 vols) jointly with Sir Charles Webster, 1961; The Bombing Offensive against Germany, Outlines and Perspectives, 1965; Bomber Offensive: the Devastation of Europe, 1970; (ed jtly) The Politics and Strategy of the Second World War (8 vols), 1974–78; (ed jtly) Decisive Battles of the Twentieth Century: Land, Sea, Air, 1976; Prince Henry, Duke of Gloucester, 1980; general editor and contributor, Encyclopaedia of 20th Century Warfare, 1989; Historical Chapter in Manual of Air Force Law, 1956; other articles and reviews; broadcasts on radio and TV. *Address:* Thames House, Eynsham, Oxford. *T:* Oxford (0865) 881327.

FRANKLAND, Noble; *see* Frankland, A. N.

FRANKLIN, Albert Andrew Ernst, CVO 1965; CBE 1961 (OBE 1950); HM Diplomatic Service, retired; *b* 28 Nov. 1914; *s* of Albert John Henry Franklin; *m* 1944, Henrietta Irene Barry; two *d*. *Educ:* Merchant Taylors' Sch.; St John's Coll., Oxford. Joined HM Consular Service, 1937; served in Peking, Kunming, Chungking, Calcutta, Algiers, Marseilles, Kabul, Basle, Tientsin, Formosa, Düsseldorf and in the FO; HM Consul-General, Los Angeles, USA, 1966–74. Member of Kitchener Association. FRSA 1971. *Recreation:* chinese ceramics and paintings. *Address:* 5 Dulwich Wood Avenue, SE19 1HB. *T:* 081–670 2769.

FRANKLIN, Sir Eric (Alexander), Kt 1954; CBE 1952; *b* 3 July 1910; *s* of late William John Franklin; *m* 1936, Joy Stella, *d* of late George Oakes Lucas, Cambridge. *Educ:* The English Sch., Maymyo; Emmanuel Coll., Cambridge. Appointed to ICS in 1935 and posted to Burma; Subdivisional Officer, 1936–39. Deputy Registrar, High Court of Judicature at Rangoon, 1939–40; District and Sessions Judge, Arakan, 1941–42; Deputy Sec. to Government of Burma at Simla, 1942–45; Registrar, High Court of Judicature at Rangoon, 1946–47; retired prematurely from ICS, 1948. Appointed on contract as Deputy Sec. to Government of Pakistan. Cabinet Secretariat, 1949; Joint Sec., Cabinet Secretariat, 1952; Establishment Officer and Head of Central Organisation and Methods Office, 1953–55; Establishment Sec. to Government of Pakistan, 1956–57; Chm. Sudan Government Commission on terms of service, 1958–59; Civil Service Adviser to Government of Hashemite Kingdom of Jordan, 1960–63; acting Resident Representative, UN Technical Assistance Board, Jordan, 1961; Senior UN Administrative Adviser to Government of Nepal, 1964–66. Chm., Cambridgeshire Soc. for the Blind, 1969–74, Vice-Pres., 1974. FRSA 1971. El Kawkab el Urdoni (Star of Jordan), 1963. *Recreations:* walking, gardening, music. *Address:* 18 Cavendish Avenue, Cambridge.

FRANKLIN, George Henry, RIBA, FRTPI; Consultant, Third World planning and development; *b* 15 June 1923; *s* of late George Edward Franklin, RN, and Annie Franklin; *m* 1950, Sylvia D. Franklin (*née* Allen); three *s* one *d*. *Educ:* Hastings Grammar Sch.; Hastings Sch. of Art; Architectural Assoc. Sch. of Arch. (AADipl); Sch. of Planning and Research for Regional Develt, London (SPDip). Served War of 1939–45: Parachute Sqdn; RE, Europe; Bengal Sappers and Miners, RIE, SE Asia. Finchley Bor. Council, 1952–54; Architect, Christian Med. Coll., Ludhiana, Punjab, India, 1954–57; Physical Planning Adviser (Colombo Plan) to Republic of Indonesia, 1958–62, and Govt of Malaysia, 1963–64; Physical Planning Adviser, Min. of Overseas Develt, later Overseas Develt Admin, FCO, 1966–83 (Overseas Div., Building Research Station, 1966–73, ODM, later ODA, 1973–83). Hon. Prof., Dept of Town Planning, UWIST, 1982–88; Sen. Advr, Develt Planning Unit, UCL, 1983–. Chm., Overseas Sch., Town and Country Planning Summer Sch., 1970–75. Commonwealth Assoc. of Planners: Mem. Exec. Cttee, 1970–80; Pres., 1980–84; Hon. Sec., 1984–88; Member: Exec. Cttee, Commonwealth Human Ecology Council, 1970–90; Internat. Adv. Bd, Centre for Develt and Environmental Planning, Oxford Polytechnic, 1985–; World Service Cttee, United Bible Socs, 1968–77. Mem., Warminster Council of Churches; Chm., Warminster and Westbury Family Support Service; Co-ordinator, Christian Aid, Warminster Dist. Member Editorial Board: Third World Planning Review, 1979–; Cities, 1983–. FRSA; AIIA, 1955; AITP India, 1956. *Publications:* papers to internat. confs and professional jls concerning planning, building and housing in the Third World. *Recreations:* Third World, Bible Society, environmental issues and interests, fly-fishing. *Address:* The Manse, Sutton Veny, Warminster, Wilts BA12 7AW. *T:* Warminster (0985) 40072. *Clubs:* Commonwealth Trust, Victory Services.

FRANKLIN, Gordon Herbert, CVO 1989 (LVO 1976; MVO 1965); a Serjeant-at-Arms to HM the Queen, since 1990; Personnel Officer, Royal Household, since 1988; *b* 1 Sept. 1933; *s* of late Herbert and of Elsie Franklin; *m* 1959, Gillian Moffett; three *d*. *Educ:* Windsor County Boys' Sch. Barclays Bank, 1950. 2nd ATAF, Germany, 1952–54. Royal Household, 1956–: Chief Clerk, Master of the Household's Dept, 1975; Chief Accountant of Privy Purse, 1982. Member: Central Finance Board and Council of Methodist Church, 1984–. Vice-Pres., Friends of Wesley's Chapel, 1989–. Freeman, City of London, 1982; Liveryman, Painter Stainers' Co., 1983–. *Recreations:* theatre, walking, travel. *Address:* 2 Marlborough House Mews, Pall Mall, SW1Y 5HU. *T:* 071–839 5015.

FRANKLIN, John; *see* Franklin, W. J.

FRANKLIN, Sir Michael (David Milroy), KCB 1983 (CB 1979); CMG 1972; Director: Agricultural Mortgage Corporation, since 1987; Barclays Bank, since 1988; Barclays PLC, since 1988; Whessoe, since 1988; Whitbread & Co., since 1991; *b* 24 Aug. 1927; *o s* of late Milroy Franklin; *m* 1951, Dorothy Joan Fraser; two *s* one *d*. *Educ:* Taunton Sch.; Peterhouse, Cambridge (1st cl. hons Economics). Served with 4th RHA, BAOR. Asst Principal, Min. of Agric. and Fisheries, 1950; Economic Section, Cabinet Office (subseq. Treasury), 1952–55; Principal, Min. of Agric., Fisheries and Food, 1956; UK Delegn to OEEC (subseq. OECD), 1959–61; Private Sec. to Minister of Agric., Fisheries and Food, 1961–64; Asst Sec., Head of Sugar and Tropical Foodstuffs Div., 1965–68; Under-Sec. (EEC Gp), MAFF, 1968–73; a Dep. Dir Gen., Directorate Gen. for Agric., EC, Brussels, 1973–77; Dep. Sec., Head of the European Secretariat, Cabinet Office, 1977–81; Permanent Sec., Dept of Trade, 1982–83; Perm. Sec., MAFF, 1983–87. Pres., West India Cttee, 1987–; Dep. Chm., Europe Cttee, BIEC, 1988–; Mem., Council, Royal Inst. for Internat. Relations, 1988–. Governor, Henley Admin. Staff Coll., 1983. *Publications:* Rich Man's Farming: the crisis in agriculture, 1988; Britain's Future in Europe, 1990. *Address:* 15 Galley Lane, Barnet, Herts EN5 4AR. *Club:* United Oxford & Cambridge University.

FRANKLIN, Prof. Raoul Norman, FInstP, FIMA; FEng, FIEE; CBIM; Vice Chancellor, since 1978, and Professor of Plasma Physics and Technology, since 1986, The City University, London; Fellow, Keble College, Oxford, since 1963; *b* 3 June 1935; *s* of Norman George Franklin and Thelma Brinley Franklin (*née* Davis); *m* 1961, Faith, *d* of Lt-Col H. T. C. Ivens and Eva (*née* Gray); two *s*. *Educ:* Howick District High Sch.; Auckland Grammar Sch., NZ; Univ. of Auckland (ME, DSc); Christ Church, Oxford (MA, DPhil, DSc). FInstP 1968; FIMA 1970; FEng 1990; FIEE 1986; CBIM 1986. Officer, NZ Defence Scientific Corps, 1957–75. Sen. Res. Fellow, RMCS, Shrivenham, 1961–63; Univ. of Oxford: Tutorial Fellow, 1963–78, Dean, 1966–71, Hon. Fellow, 1980, Keble Coll.; Univ. Lectr in Engrg Science, 1966–78; Mem., Gen. Bd, 1967–74 (Vice Chm., 1971–74); Mem., Hebdomadal Council, 1971–74, 1976–78. Consultant, UKAEA Culham, 1968–. Member: UGC Equipment Sub Cttee, 1975–78; Plasma Physics Commn, IUPAP, 1971–79; Science Bd, SERC, 1982–85; Exec. Council, Business in the Community, 1982–; Management Cttee, Spallation Neutron Source, 1983–86; Technology Educn Project, 1986–88; UK–NZ 1990 Cttee, 1988–90. Chairman: Internat. Science Cttee, Phenomena in Ionized Gases, 1976–77; City Techology Ltd, 1978– (Queen's Award for Technol., 1982, 1985, for Export, 1988); Citifluor Ltd, 1984–; OTEC Ltd, 1988–. Mem., London Pensions Fund Authority, 1989–. Trustee: Ruskin School of Drawing, 1975–78; Lloyds Tercentenary Foundn, 1990–. Mem. Council, Gresham Coll., 1981–. Gov., Ashridge Management Coll., 1986–. Liveryman, Curriers' Co., 1984–. FRSA. Freeman, City of London, 1981. Dep. Editor, Jl of Physics D, 1986–90. *Publications:* Plasma Phenomena in Ionized Gases, 1976; papers on plasmas, gas discharges and granular materials. *Recreations:* tennis, walking, gardening. *Address:* The City University, Northampton Square, EC1V 0HB. *T:* 071–253 4399. *Club:* Athenæum.

FRANKLIN, Rt. Rev. William Alfred, OBE 1964; Assistant Bishop (full time), Diocese of Peterborough, and Hon. Canon of the Cathedral, 1978–86, Canon Emeritus since 1986; Hon. Assistant Bishop of Canterbury, since 1987; *b* 16 July 1916; *s* of George Amos and Mary Anne Catherine Franklin; *m* 1945, Winifred Agnes Franklin (*née* Jarvis); one *s* one *d*. *Educ:* schools in London; Kelham Theol Coll. Deacon 1940, priest 1941, London; Curate, St John on Bethnal Green, Chaplain ATC and Univ. Settlements, 1941–43; Curate of St John's, Palmers Green, and Chm. for area Interdenominational Youth Activities, 1943–45; Asst Chaplain, St Saviour's, Belgrano, Buenos Aires, Argentina and teaching duties at Green's School, Buenos Aires, 1945–48; Rector of Holy Trinity, Lomas de Zamora, Buenos Aires, Domestic Chaplain to Bishop in Argentina, Sec. Dio. Bd of Missions, and Chaplain St Alban's Coll., Lomas, 1948–58; Rector, Canon and Sub-Dean of Anglican Cathedral, Santiago, Chaplain Grange School and Founder and Chm. Ecumenical Gp in Chile, 1958–65; Rector of St Alban's, Bogotá, Colombia, 1965–71; Archdeacon of Diocese, 1966–71; consecrated Bishop of Diocese, 1972; resigned, 1978, allowing a national to be elected. Founder and Editor of Revista Anglicana, official magazine of Arensa (Assoc. of Anglican Dioceses in North of S America). *Recreations:* fishing, tennis and cricket. *Address:* 26c The Beach, Walmer, near Deal, Kent CT14 7AJ. *T:* Deal (0304) 361807. *Club:* Anglo-American (Bogotá, Colombia).

FRANKLIN, (William) John, FCA; DL; Deputy Chairman, Chartered Trust plc, since 1986 (Director, since 1982); Chairman, Howells Motors Ltd, 1986–89; Powell Duffryn Wagon, 1986–89; *b* 8 March 1927; *s* of late William Thomas Franklin and Edith Hannah Franklin; *m* 1951, Sally (*née* Davies); one *d*. *Educ:* Monkton House Sch., Cardiff. W. R. Gresty, Chartered Accountants, 1947–50; Peat Marwick Mitchell, Chartered Accountants, 1950–55; Powell Duffryn, 1956–86: Director, Cory Brothers, 1964; Man. Dir, Powell Duffryn Timber, 1967–70; Dir, 1970–86; Man. Dir and Chief Exec., 1976–85; Dep. Chm., Jan.–July 1986. Treas., UC of Swansea, 1989–. DL Mid Glamorgan, 1989. *Recreation:* golf. *Address:* 80 South Road, Porthcawl, Mid Glamorgan CF36 3DA. *Club:* Royal Porthcawl Golf.

FRANKS, family name of **Baron Franks.**

FRANKS, Baron *cr* 1962, of Headington (Life Peer); **Oliver Shewell Franks,** OM 1977; GCMG 1952; KCB 1946; KCVO 1985; CBE 1942; PC 1949; DL; FBA 1960; Provost of Worcester College, Oxford, 1962–76; Chancellor of East Anglia University, 1965–84; Lord Warden of the Stannaries and Keeper of the Privy Seal of the Duke of Cornwall, 1983–85; *b* 16 Feb. 1905; *s* of late Rev. R. S. Franks; *m* 1931, Barbara Mary Tanner (*d* 1987); two *d*. *Educ:* Bristol Grammar Sch.; Queen's Coll., Oxford (MA). Fellow and Praelector in Philosophy, Queen's College, Oxford, 1927–37; University Lecturer in Philosophy, 1935–37; Visiting Prof., Univ. of Chicago, 1935; Prof. of Moral Philosophy, University of Glasgow, 1937–45; temp. Civil Servant, Ministry of Supply, 1939–46; Permanent Sec. Ministry of Supply, 1945–46; Provost of Queen's Coll., Oxford, 1946–48; British Ambassador at Washington, 1948–52; Director: Lloyds Bank Ltd, 1953–75 (Chm., 1954–62); Schroders, 1969–84; Chm., Friends' Provident & Century Life Office, 1955–62; Cttee of London Clearing Bankers, 1960–62. Mem. of Rhodes Trust 1957–73; Chairman: Bd of Governors, United Oxford Hosps, 1958–64; Wellcome Trust, 1965–82 (Trustee, 1963–65); Commission of Inquiry into Oxford Univ., 1964–66; Cttee on Official Secrets Act, Section 2, 1971–72; Cttee on Ministerial Memoirs, 1976; Political Honours Scrutiny Cttee, 1976–; Falkland Is Review Cttee, 1982. Mem., National Economic Development Council, 1962–64. Mem. Council, Duchy of Cornwall, 1966–85. Pres., Kennedy Memorial Cttee, 1963; Trustee: Pilgrim Trust, 1947–79; Rockefeller Foundn, 1961–70. Hon. Fellow: Queen's Coll., Oxford, 1948; St Catharine's Coll.,

Cambridge, 1966; Wolfson Coll., Oxford, 1967; Worcester Coll., Oxford, 1976; Lady Margaret Hall, Oxford, 1978; London Business Sch., 1988; Visiting Fellow, Nuffield Coll., 1959. Hon. DCL, Oxford, and other Honorary Doctorates. DL Oxfordshire, 1978. *Address:* Blackhall Farm, Garford Road, Oxford OX2 6UY. *T:* Oxford (0865) 511286. *Club:* Athenæum.
See also Hon. A. E. Wright.

FRANKS, Sir Arthur Temple, (Sir Dick Franks), KCMG 1979 (CMG 1967); HM Diplomatic Service, retired; *b* 13 July 1920; *s* of late Arthur Franks, Hove; *m* 1945, Rachel Marianne, *d* of late Rev. A. E. S. Ward, DD; one *s* two *d. Educ:* Rugby; Queen's Coll., Oxford. HM Forces, 1940–46 (despatches). Entered Foreign Service, 1949; British Middle East Office, 1952; Tehran, 1953; Bonn, 1962; FCO, 1966–81. *Address:* Roefield, Alde Lane, Aldeburgh, Suffolk. *Clubs:* Travellers', Army and Navy; Aldeburgh Golf.

FRANKS, Cecil Simon; MP (C) Barrow and Furness, since 1983; solicitor; company director; *b* 1 July 1935; *m* (marr. diss. 1978); one *s. Educ:* Manchester Grammar Sch.; Manchester Univ. (LLB). Admitted solicitor, 1958; consultant, Cecil Franks & Co. Member: Salford City Council, 1960–74 (Leader, Cons. Gp); Manchester City Council, 1975–84 (Leader, Cons. Gp). Mem., North West RHA, 1973–75. *Recreations:* ski-ing, tennis, theatre, literature. *Address:* House of Commons, SW1A 0AA. *T:* 071–219 6433; Ivy Cottage, Satterthwaite, Cumbria LA12 8LS. *T:* Satterthwaite (022984) 310.

FRANKS, Desmond Gerald Fergus; His Honour Judge Franks; a Circuit Judge, since 1972; *b* 24 Jan. 1928; *s* of F. Franks, MC, late Lancs Fus., and E. R. Franks; *m* 1952, Margaret Leigh (*née* Daniel); one *d. Educ:* Cathedral Choir Sch., Canterbury; Manchester Grammar Sch.; University Coll., London (LLB). Called to Bar, Middle Temple, 1952; Northern Circuit; Asst Recorder, Salford, 1966; Deputy Recorder, Salford, 1971; a Recorder of the Crown Court, 1972. Pres., SW Pennine Br., Magistrates' Assoc., 1977– . Chm., Selcare (Gtr Manchester) Trust, 1978–84, Vice-Pres., 1984– . *Recreations:* gardening, photography. *Address:* 4 Beathwaite Drive, Bramhall, Cheshire SK7 3NY.

FRANKS, Sir Dick; *see* Franks, Sir A. T.

FRANKS, Air Vice-Marshal John Gerald, CB 1954; CBE 1949; RAF retired, 1960; *b* 23 May 1905; *e s* of late James Gordon Franks, *e s* of Sir John Hamilton Franks, CB, and Margaret, *y d* of Lord Chief Justice Gerald Fitz-Gibbon, Dublin; *m* 1936, Jessica Rae West; two *d. Educ:* Cheltenham Coll.; RAF Coll., Cranwell. RAF; commissioned from Cranwell, 1924; No 56 Fighter Sqdn, Biggin Hill, 1925–26; flying duties with FAA HMS Courageous, Mediterranean, 1928–29; India, 1930–35; Middle East, 1936; RAF Staff Coll., 1939; Air Armament Sch., Manby, 1941; Experimental Establishment, Boscombe Down, 1944; Dir Armament Research and Development, 1945–48; idc 1951; Comdt RAF Technical Coll., Henlow, 1952; Air Officer Commanding No 24 Group, Royal Air Force, 1952–55; Pres. of Ordnance Board, 1959–60. Comdr American Legion of Merit, 1948. *Recreations:* motoring and walking in the west of Ireland. *Address:* The Sextant, Schull, Co. Cork, Ireland.
See also Air Vice-Marshal D. Allison.

FRANZ, Very Rev. Kevin Gerhard; Provost, St Ninian's Cathedral, Perth, since 1990; *b* 16 June 1953; *m* 1976, Veda Fairley; one *s* one *d. Educ:* Univ. of Edinburgh (MA 1974; BD 1979); Edinburgh Theol Coll. Ordained deacon, 1979; priest 1980; Curate, St Martin, Edinburgh, 1979–83; Rector, S Selkirk, 1983–90. *Address:* St Ninian's House, 40 Hay Street, Perth PH1 5HS.

FRASER, family name of **Barons Fraser of Carmyllie, Fraser of Kilmorack,** and **Lovat, Lady Saltoun,** and **Baron Strathalmond.**

FRASER OF CARMYLLIE, Baron *cr* 1989 (Life Peer), of Carmyllie in the District of Angus; **Peter Lovat Fraser;** PC 1989; Lord Advocate since 1989; *b* 29 May 1945; *s* of Rev. George Robson Fraser and Helen Jean Meiklejohn or Fraser; *m* 1969, Fiona Macdonald Mair; one *s* two *d. Educ:* St Andrews Prep. Sch., Grahamstown, S Africa; Loretto Sch., Musselburgh; Gonville and Caius Coll., Cambridge (BA Hons; LLM Hons); Edinburgh Univ. Legal apprenticeship, Edinburgh, 1968; called to Scottish Bar, 1969; QC (Scot.) 1982. Lectr in Constitutional Law, Heriot-Watt Univ., 1972–74; Standing Jun. Counsel in Scotland to FCO, 1979. Hon. Vis. Prof. of Law, Dundee Univ., 1986. Hon. Bencher, Lincoln's Inn, 1989. Chm., Scottish Conservative Lawyers Law Reform Group, 1976. Contested (C): N Aberdeen, Oct. 1974; Angus E, 1987. MP (C): S Angus, 1979–83; Angus E, 1983–87. PPS to Sec. of State for Scotland, 1981–82; Solicitor Gen. for Scotland, 1982–89. *Recreations:* skiing, golf. *Address:* Slade House, Carmyllie, by Arbroath, Angus. *T:* Carmyllie (02416) 215.

FRASER OF KILMORACK, Baron *cr* 1974 (Life Peer), of Rubislaw, Aberdeen; **Richard Michael Fraser,** Kt 1962; CBE 1955 (MBE 1945); Director, Whiteaway Laidlaw Bank Ltd, since 1981; *b* 28 Oct. 1915; *yr s* of late Dr Thomas Fraser, CBE, DSO, TD, DL, LLD, Aberdeen and Maria-Theresia Kayser, Hanover; *m* 1944, Elizabeth Chloë, *er d* of late Brig. C. A. F. Drummond, OBE and Muriel Kyrle Ottley; one *s* (and one *s* decd). *Educ:* Aberdeen Grammar Sch.; Fettes; King's Coll., Cambridge. Begg Exhibition, 1934; James Essay Prize, 1935; BA Hons History, 1937; MA 1945. Served War of 1939–45 (RA); 2nd Lieut 1939; War Gunnery Staff Course, 1940; Capt. Feb. 1941; Major, June 1941; Lieut-Col (GSO1) 1945. Joined Conservative Research Dept, 1946; Head of Home Affairs Sect., 1950–51; Jt Dir, 1951–59, Dir, 1959–64, Chm., 1970–74; Dep. Chm., Cons. Party Orgn, 1964–75; Dep. Chm., Conservative Party's Adv. Cttee on Policy, 1970–75 (Sec., Aug. 1951–Oct. 1964); Sec. to the Conservative Leader's Consultative Cttee (Shadow Cabinet), Oct. 1964–June 1970 and March 1974–75. Director: Glaxo Holdings plc, 1975–85; Glaxo Gp Ltd, 1975–85; Glaxo Trustees Ltd, 1975–86; Glaxo Enterprises Inc., USA, 1983–86. Smith-Mundt Fellowship, USA, 1952. Mem. Council, Imperial Soc. of Knights Bachelor, 1971– . Pres., Old Fettesian Assoc., 1977–80. *Publications:* (contrib.) Ruling Performance: British governments from Attlee to Thatcher, 1987; contribs to political and hist. jls. *Recreations:* reading, music, opera, ballet, travel; collecting and recollecting. *Address:* 18 Drayton Court, Drayton Gardens, SW10 9RH. *T:* 071–370 1543. *Clubs:* Brooks's, Carlton, St Stephen's Constitutional (Hon. Mem.); Coningsby (Hon. Mem., Pres., 1988–).
See also A. S. J. Fraser.

FRASER, Alasdair MacLeod; QC 1989; Director of Public Prosecutions for Northern Ireland, since 1989; *b* 29 Sept. 1946; *s* of Rev. Dr Donald Fraser and late Ellen Hart McAllister; *m* 1975, Margaret Mary Glancy; two *s* one *d. Educ:* Sullivan Upper School, Holywood; Trinity College Dublin (BA (Mod.); LLB); Queen's Univ., Belfast (Dip. Laws). Called to the Bar of Northern Ireland, 1970. Director of Public Prosecutions for Northern Ireland: Court Prosecutor, 1973; Asst Dir, 1974; Senior Asst Dir, 1982; Dep. Dir, 1988. *Address:* Royal Courts of Justice, Belfast, Northern Ireland BT1 3NX. *T:* Belfast (0232) 235111.

FRASER, Alexander Macdonald, AO 1981; PhD; FAIM, FTS; Director, Queensland Institute of Technology, 1966–81, Life Fellow 1981; *b* 11 March 1921; *s* of late John Macdonald Fraser and of Esther Katie Fraser; *m* 1951, Rita Isabel Thomason; one *s. Educ:*

Church of England Grammar Sch., Brisbane; Univ. of Queensland (BE); Imperial Coll. of Science and Technology, Univ. of London (DIC, PhD). MIE(Aust). Military service, 1942–45 (despatches, New Guinea, 1944). Engineer: British Malayan Petroleum Co., 1947–50; Irrigation and Water Supply Commission, Qld, 1951–54 and 1957–65; Research, Imperial Coll. of Science and Technology, 1954–57. *Recreation:* golf. *Address:* 3 Wynyard Street, Indooroopilly, Qld 4068, Australia. *T:* 370.7945. *Club:* Indooroopilly Golf (Brisbane).

FRASER, Sir Angus (McKay), KCB 1985 (CB 1981); TD 1965; Adviser to the Prime Minister on Efficiency and Effectiveness in Government, since 1988; *b* 10 March 1928; *s* of late Thomas Douglas Fraser; *m* 1st, 1955, Margaret Neilson (marr. diss. 1968); one *s* one *d*; 2nd, 1991, Gillian Fenwick (*née* Manning); one step *d.Educ:* Falkirk High Sch.; Glasgow Univ.; Bordeaux Univ. Nat. Service in RA, 1950–52; 44 Parachute Bde (TA), 1953–66. Entered HM Customs and Excise, 1952; HM Treasury, 1961–64; Under-Sec. and Comr of Customs and Excise, 1972; Under-Sec., CSD, 1973; Comr of Customs and Excise, 1976; Dep. Chm., Bd of Customs and Excise, 1978; Dep. Sec., CSD, subseq. MPO, 1980–83; First CS Comr, 1981–83; Chm., Bd of Customs and Excise, 1983–87. Advr, European Patent Office, 1988– . Chm., Civil Service, PO and BT Lifeboat Fund, 1986– ; Mem., Cttee of Management, RNLI, 1986– . President: Electronic Data Interchange Assoc., 1988– ; George Borrow Soc., 1991– ; Vice-Pres., RIPA, 1985– . FSA 1991; FRSA 1985. *Publications:* (ed) A Journey to Eastern Europe in 1844, 1981; (ed) George Borrow's Letters to John Hasfeld 1835–1839, 1982, 1841–1846, 1984; (with M. Collie) George Borrow, a Bibliographical Study, 1984; articles and reviews in jls and encyclopedias, 1950– . *Recreations:* old inns, literary research, book collecting. *Address:* 84 Ennerdale Road, Kew, Richmond, Surrey TW9 2DL. *T:* 081–940 9913. *Clubs:* Reform, Royal Over-Seas League, Caledonian; Norfolk (Norwich).

FRASER, Angus Simon James; Managing Director, Imperial College of Science, Technology and Medicine, since 1989; Chairman, JCT Controls Ltd, since 1989; *b* 28 Feb. 1945; *s* of Baron Fraser of Kilmorack, *qv*; *m* 1970, Jennifer Ann Craig; two *s* one *d. Educ:* Fettes Coll., Edinburgh; Selwyn Coll., Cambridge (MA); European Inst. of Business Admin (INSEAD), France (MBA); Dip. Finance Houses Assoc. Dunlop Co. Ltd, 1968–70; Mercantile Credit Co. Ltd, 1971–76; Chloride Group PLC, 1976– : Gen. Man., Malaysia, 1977–80, France, 1980–82; Man. Dir, Chloride Motive Power, 1982–83; Chm., Chloride Europe, 1983–85; Main Bd Mem., 1984; Exec. Dir, Industrial Operations, 1985–87, Corporate Operations, 1987–88; Non-Exec. Dir, 1988– . Dir, Internat. Dynamics Ltd, 1989. Governor: Kent Coll., Pembury, 1989– ; Imperial Coll., London, 1990– . *Recreations:* music, opera, golf, tennis, fly-fishing, walking, travel, painting. *Address:* Whetstead House, Five Oak Green, Tonbridge, Kent TN12 6SG. *Club:* Royal Automobile.

FRASER, Air Cdre Anthony Walkinshaw; Director, Nissan UK Ltd, since 1989; *b* 15 March 1934; *s* of late Robert Walkinshaw Fraser and Evelyn Elisabeth Fraser; *m* 1955, Angela Mary Graham Shaw (marr. diss. 1990); one *s* three *d*; *m* 1990, Grania Ruth Eleanor Stewart-Smith. *Educ:* Stowe Sch. MIL. RAF Pilot and Flying Instructor, 1952–66; sc Camberley, 1967; MA/VCDS, MoD, 1968–70; Chief Instructor Buccaneer OCU, 1971–72; Air Warfare Course, 1973; Directing Staff, National Defence Coll., 1973; Dep. Dir, Operational Requirements, MoD, 1974–76; Comdt, Central Flying Sch., 1977–79. ADC to the Queen, 1977–79. Dir, SMMT, 1980–88. President: Comité de Liaison de la Construction Automobile, 1980–83; Organisation (formerly Bureau Perm.) Internat. des Constructeurs d'Automobiles, 1983–87 (Vice-Pres., 1981–83). FRSA; FBIM; FIMI. *Recreations:* shooting, golf, fishing, languages. *Address:* Nissan House, Worthing, W Sussex BN13 3HD. *T:* Worthing (0903) 68561. *Clubs:* Boodle's, Royal Air Force, Sunningdale.

FRASER, Lady Antonia, (Lady Antonia Pinter); writer; *b* 27 Aug. 1932; *d* of 7th Earl of Longford, *qv*, and Countess of Longford, *qv*; *m* 1st, 1956, Rt Hon. Sir Hugh Charles Patrick Joseph Fraser, MBE, MP (d 1984) (marr. diss. 1977); three *s* three *d*; 2nd, 1980, Harold Pinter, *qv. Educ:* Dragon School, Oxford; St Mary's Convent, Ascot; Lady Margaret Hall, Oxford (MA). General Editor, Kings and Queens of England series. Mem., Arts Council, 1970–72; Chairman: Soc. of Authors, 1974–75; Crimewriters' Assoc., 1985–86; Vice Pres., English PEN, 1990– (Mem. Cttee, 1979–88; Pres., 1988–89); Chm., Writers in Prison Cttee, 1985–88, 1990). Hon. DLitt: Hull, 1986; Sussex, 1990. *Publications:* (as Antonia Pakenham): King Arthur and the Knights of the Round Table, 1954 (reissued, 1970); Robin Hood: 1955 (reissued, 1971); (as Antonia Fraser): Dolls, 1963; A History of Toys, 1966; Mary Queen of Scots (James Tait Black Memorial Prize, 1969), 1969 (reissued illus. edn, 1978); Cromwell Our Chief of Men, (in USA, Cromwell the Lord Protector), 1973; King James: VI of Scotland, I of England, 1974; (ed) Kings and Queens of England, 1975 (reissued, 1988); (ed) Scottish Love Poems, a personal anthology, 1975 (reissued, 1988); (ed) Love Letters: an anthology, 1976, rev. edn 1989; Quiet as a Nun (mystery), 1977, adapted for TV series, 1978; The Wild Island (mystery), 1978; King Charles II, (in USA, Royal Charles), 1979; (ed) Heroes and Heroines, 1980; A Splash of Red (mystery), 1981 (basis for TV series Jemima Shore Investigates, 1983); (ed) Mary Queen of Scots: poetry anthology, 1981; (ed) Oxford and Oxfordshire in Verse: anthology, 1982; Cool Repentance (mystery), 1982; The Weaker Vessel: woman's lot in seventeenth century England, 1984 (Wolfson History Award, 1984; Prix Caumont-La Force, 1985); Oxford Blood (mystery), 1985; Jemima Shore's First Case (mystery short stories), 1986; Your Royal Hostage (mystery), 1987; Boadicea's Chariot: the Warrior Queens, 1988 (paperback, The Warrior Queens, 1989, in USA The Warrior Queens, 1989); The Cavalier Case (mystery), 1990; Jemima Shore at the Sunny Grave (mystery short stories), 1991; various mystery stories in anthols, incl. Have a Nice Death, 1983 (adapted for TV, 1984); TV plays: Charades, 1977; Mister Clay, Mister Clay (Time for Murder series), 1985. *Recreations:* swimming, life in the garden. *Address:* c/o Curtis Brown, 162–168 Regent Street, W1R 5TB. *Clubs:* PEN, Detection, Vanderbilt.

FRASER, Sir Basil (Malcolm), 2nd Bt, *cr* 1921; *b* 2 Jan. 1920; *s* of Sir (John) Malcolm Fraser, 1st Bt, GBE, and of Irene, *d* of C. E. Brightman of South Kensington; *S* father, 1949. *Educ:* Northaw, Pluckley, Kent; Eton Coll.; Queens' Coll., Cambridge (MA 1950). Served War of 1939–45, RE, 1940–42; Madras Sappers and Miners, 1942–46 (despatches). Mem. AA and RAC. *Recreations:* motoring, music, electronic reproduction of sound. *Heir:* none. *Address:* 175 Beach Street, Deal, Kent CT14 6LE. *Club:* Roadfarers'.

FRASER, Sir Bruce (Donald), KCB 1961 (CB 1956); *b* 18 Nov. 1910; *s* of late Maj.-Gen. Sir Theodore Fraser, KCB and late Constance Ruth Fraser (*née* Stevenson); *m* 1939, Audrey (*d* 1982), *d* of late Lieut-Col E. L. Croslegh; one *s* one *d* decd. *Educ:* Bedford Sch.; Trinity Coll., Cambridge (Scholar); First Class in Classical Tripos Part I, 1930 and in English Tripos Part II, 1932; BA 1932, MA 1964. Ed. the Granta, 1932. Entered Civil Service as Asst Principal, Scottish Office, 1933; transf. to HM Treasury, 1936; Private Sec. to Financial Sec., 1937, and to Permanent Sec., 1941; Asst Sec., 1945; Under Sec., 1951; Third Sec., 1956–60; Dep. Sec., Ministry of Aviation, Jan.-April 1960; Permanent Sec., Ministry of Health, 1960–64; Joint Permanent Under-Sec. of State, Dept of Education and Science, 1964–65; Permanent Sec., Ministry of Land and Natural Resources, 1965–66; Comptroller and Auditor-General, Exchequer and Audit Dept, 1966–71. Hon. DLitt Wales, 1989. *Publication:* Sir Ernest Gowers' The Complete Plain Words, rev. edn 1973. *Address:* Jonathan, St Dogmael's, Cardigan SA43 3LF. *T:* Cardigan (0239) 612387.

FRASER, Sir Campbell; *see* Fraser, Sir J. C.

FRASER, Sir Charles (Annand), KVCO 1989 (CVO 1985; LVO 1968); DL; WS; Partner, W. & J. Burness, WS, Edinburgh; non-executive Vice Chairman, United Biscuits (Holdings), since 1986 (Director, since 1978); *b* 16 Oct. 1928; *o s* of late Very Rev. John Annand Fraser, MBE, TD; *m* 1957, Ann Scott-Kerr; four *s*. *Educ:* Hamilton Academy; Edinburgh Univ. (MA, LLB). Purse Bearer to Lord High Commissioner to General Assembly of Church of Scotland, 1969–88. Chairman: Morgan Grenfell (Scotland), 1985–86; Adam & Co., 1989–90 (Dir, 1983–); Lothian & Edinburgh Enterprise Ltd, 1991–; Director: Scottish Widows' Fund, 1978–; British Assets Trust, 1969–; Scottish Television Ltd, 1979–, and other companies. Trustee, Scottish Civic Trust, 1978–; Mem. Council, Law Society of Scotland, 1966–72; Governor of Fettes, 1976–86; Mem. Court, Heriot-Watt Univ., 1972–78. WS 1959; DL East Lothian, 1984–. *Recreations:* gardening, skiing, squash, piping. *Address:* Shepherd House, Inveresk, Midlothian EH21 7TH. *T:* 031–665 2570. *Clubs:* New, Hon. Co. of Edinburgh Golfers (Edinburgh); Royal and Ancient (St Andrews).

FRASER, Maj.-Gen. Colin Angus Ewen, CB 1971; CBE 1968; General Officer Commanding, Southern Command, Australia, 1971–74; retired March 1974; *b* Nairobi, Kenya, 25 Sept. 1918; *s* of A. E. Fraser, Rutherglen, Vic.; *m* 1942, Dorothy, *d* of A. Champion; two *s* one *d*. *Educ:* Johannesburg; Adelaide High Sch.; RMC, Duntroon (grad. 1938); Melbourne Univ. (BA). Served War of 1939–45: UK, Middle East, Pacific. Staff Coll., Camberley, 1946; Dep. Comdr, Commonwealth Div., Korea, 1955–56; Dir, Military Trng, 1957–58; Services Attaché, Burma, 1960–62; Chief of Staff, Northern Command, Brisbane, 1964–68; Commandant, Royal Military Coll., Duntroon, 1968–69; Commander, Australian Force, Vietnam, 1970–71. *Address:* 107 Orana Road, Ocean Shores, Brunswick Heads, NSW 2483, Australia. *Clubs:* Tasmanian (Hobart); United Services (Qld).

FRASER, Gen. Sir David (William), GCB 1980 (KCB 1973); OBE 1962; retired; Vice Lord-Lieutenant of Hampshire, since 1988; *b* 30 Dec. 1920; *s* of Brig. Hon. William Fraser, DSO, MC, *y s* of 18th Lord Saltoun and Pamela, *d* of Cyril Maude and *widow* of Major W. La T. Congreve, VC, DSO, MC; *m* 1st, 1947, Anne Balfour; one *d*; 2nd, 1957, Julia de la Hey; two *s* two *d*. *Educ:* Eton; Christ Church, Oxford. Commnd into Grenadier Guards, 1941; served NW Europe; comd 1st Bn Grenadier Guards, 1960–62; comd 19th Inf. Bde, 1963–65; Dir, Defence Policy, MoD, 1966–69; GOC 4 Div., 1969–71; Asst Chief of Defence Staff (Policy), MoD, 1971–73; Vice-Chief of the General Staff, 1973–75; UK Mil. Rep. to NATO, 1975–77; Commandant, RCDS, 1978–80; ADC General to the Queen, 1977–80. Col, The Royal Hampshire Regt, 1981–87. DL Hants, 1982. *Publications:* Alanbrooke, 1982; And We Shall Shock Them, 1983; The Christian Watt Papers, 1983; August 1988, 1983; A Kiss for the Enemy, 1985; The Killing Times, 1986; The Dragon's Teeth, 1987; The Seizure, 1988; A Candle for Judas, 1989; In Good Company, 1990; Adam Hardrow, 1990; Codename Mercury, 1991. *Recreation:* shooting. *Address:* Vallenders, Isington, Alton, Hants. *T:* Bentley (0420) 23166. *Clubs:* Turf, Pratt's.

FRASER, Donald Blake, FRCS; FRCOG; Gynæcologist and Obstetrician, St Bartholomew's Hospital, 1946–75; retired 1978; *b* 9 June 1910; *o s* of Dr Thomas B. Fraser, Hatfield Point, NB, Canada; *m* 1939, Betsy, *d* of late Sir James Henderson, KBE; one *s* one *d*. *Educ:* University of New Brunswick; Christ Church, Oxford. Rhodes Scholar, 1930; BA 1st Cl. Hons, 1932, BM, BCh Oxon 1936; MRCS, LRCP, LMCC, 1936; FRCS, 1939; MRCOG, 1940, FRCOG, 1952. Former Examiner: Central Midwives Bd; Universities of Oxford and London; Conjoint Bd; Royal College of Obstetricians and Gynæcologists. *Publications:* (joint) Midwifery (textbook), 1956; articles in medical journals. *Recreation:* philately. *Address:* 13 Stanton Crest, 7 Hale Street, Townsville, Qld 4810, Australia.

FRASER, Donald Hamilton, RA 1985 (ARA 1975); artist; Hon. Fellow, Royal College of Art, 1984; Member, Royal Fine Art Commission, since 1986; *b* 30 July 1929; *s* of Donald Fraser and Dorothy Christiana (*née* Lang); *m* 1954, Judith Wentworth-Sheilds; one *d*. *Educ:* Maidenhead Grammar Sch.; St Martin's Sch. of Art, London; Paris (French Govt Scholarship). Tutor, Royal Coll. of Art, 1958–83, Fellow 1970. Has held 60 one-man exhibitions in Britain, Europe, N America and Japan. Work in public collections includes: Museum of Fine Arts, Boston; Albright-Knox Gall., Buffalo; Carnegie Inst., Pittsburgh; City Art Museum, St Louis; Wadsworth Athenaeum, Hartford, Conn; Hirshhorn Museum, Washington, DC; Yale Univ. Art Museum; Palm Springs Desert Museum; Nat. Gall. of Canada, Ottawa; Nat. Gall. of Vic, Melbourne; many corporate collections and British provincial galleries; Arts Council, DoE, etc. Designed Commonwealth Day issue of postage stamps, 1983. Vice-Pres. Artists Gen. Benevolent Inst., 1981– (Chm., 1981–87); Vice-Pres., Royal Over-Seas League, 1986–. *Publications:* Gauguin's 'Vision after the Sermon', 1969; Dancers, 1989. *Address:* Bramham Cottage, Remenham Lane, Henley-on-Thames, Oxon RG9 2LR. *T:* Henley-on-Thames (0491) 574253. *Club:* Arts.

FRASER, Dame Dorothy (Rita), DBE 1987; QSO 1978; JP; Consultant, Command Pacific Group (formerly ADT Ltd Australasia), since 1988; New Zealand Director, Community Systems Foundation Australasia, 1975–91; *b* 3 May 1926; *d* of Ernest and Kate Tucker; *m* 1947, Hon. William Alex Fraser; one *s* one *d*. *Educ:* Gisborne High Sch. Chm., Otago Hosp. Bd, 1974–86 (Mem., 1953–56, 1962–86); Member: Nursing Council of NZ, 1981–87; Grading Review Cttee (Health Service Personnel Commn), 1984–87; Hosps Adv. Council, 1984–86; NZ Health Service Personnel Commn, 1987–88; Otago Plunket-Karitane Hosp. Bd, 1979–87; NZ Lottery Bd, 1985–90; Vice-Pres., NZ Hosp. Bds Assoc., 1981–86; Chairman: Southern Region Health Services Assoc., 1984–86; Hosp. and Specialist Services Cttee, NZ Bd of Health, 1985–88. Chm., Otago Jt Tertiary Educn Liaison Cttee, 1988; Member: Council, Univ. of Otago, 1974–86; Otago High Schs Bd of Governors, 1964–85. Chm., Dunedin Airport Cttee, 1971–74; Member: Dunedin CC, 1970–74; NZ Exec. Marr. Guidance, 1969–75. Life Mem., NZ Labour Party; Gold Badge for Service to Labour Party. JP 1959. Silver Jubilee Medal, 1977. *Recreations:* gardening, golf, reading. *Address:* 21 Ings Avenue, St Clair, Dunedin, New Zealand. *T:* (03) 455 8663.

FRASER, Edward; *see* Fraser, J. E.

FRASER, George MacDonald; author and journalist; *b* 2 April 1925; *s* of late William Fraser, MB, ChB and Anne Struth Donaldson; *m* 1949, Kathleen Margarette, *d* of late George Hetherington, Carlisle; two *s* one *d*. *Educ:* Carlisle Grammar Sch.; Glasgow Academy. Served in British Army, 1943–47: Infantryman XIVth Army, Lieut Gordon Highlanders. Newspaperman in England, Canada and Scotland from 1947; Dep. Editor, Glasgow Herald, 1964–69. *Publications:* Flashman, 1969; Royal Flash, 1970; The General Danced at Dawn, 1970; The Steel Bonnets, 1971; Flash for Freedom!, 1971; Flashman at the Charge, 1973; McAuslan in the Rough, 1974; Flashman in the Great Game, 1975; Flashman's Lady, 1977; Mr American, 1980; Flashman and the Redskins, 1982; The Pyrates, 1983; Flashman and the Dragon, 1985; The Sheikh and the Dustbin, 1988; The Hollywood History of the World, 1988; Flashman and the Mountain of Light, 1990; *film screenplays:* The Three Musketeers, 1974; The Four Musketeers, 1975; Royal Flash, 1975; The Prince and the Pauper, 1977; Octopussy, 1983; Red Sonja, 1985; Casanova, 1987; The Return of the Musketeers, 1989. *Recreations:* snooker, talking to wife, history, singing. *Address:* Baldrine, Isle of Man.

See also S. W. H. Fraser.

FRASER, Air Marshal Rev. Sir (Henry) Paterson, KBE 1961 (CBE 1945); CB 1953; AFC 1937; RAF, retired; ordained 1977; Concrete Consultant; *b* 15 July 1907; *s* of late Harry Fraser, Johannesburg, South Africa; *m* 1933, Avis Gertrude Haswell; two *s*. *Educ:* St Andrews Coll., Grahamstown, South Africa; Pembroke Coll., Cambridge (MA), RAFO, and Pres. University Air Sqdn, Cambridge; joined RAF, 1929; served in India; RAF Engineering Course, Henlow, 1933–34; Aerodynamic Flight, RAE, Farnborough, 1934–38; RAF Staff Coll., 1938; Directorate of War Organization, Air Ministry, 1939–40; commanded Experimental Flying Section, RAE, Farnborough, 1941; Mem. RAF Element, Combined Chiefs of Staff, Washington DC, 1942; Dep. Dir of War Organization, Air Ministry, 1943; Senior Administrative Planner, 2nd Tactical Air Force, 1943–44, and Dep. Air Officer in Charge of Administration, 2nd TAF, 1944–45; commanded Aircraft and Armament Experimental Establishment, Boscombe Down, 1945–46; Dep. Dir (Air Staff) Policy, Air Ministry, 1947–48; Defence Research Policy Staff, Ministry of Defence, 1948–51; idc 1951; Senior Air Staff Officer, Headquarters Fighter Command, 1952–53; Chief of Staff, Headquarters Allied Air Forces, Central Europe, 1954–56; AOC No. 12 Group, Fighter Command, 1956–58; Dir, RAF Exercise Planning, 1959; UK Representative on Permanent Military Deputies Group of Cento, 1959–62; Inspector-Gen., RAF, 1962–64. Taylor Gold Medal of RAeS, 1937; FRAeS. *Address:* 803 King's Court, Ramsey, Isle of Man. *T:* Ramsey (0624) 813069.

FRASER, Col Hugh Vincent, CMG 1957; OBE 1946; TD 1947; retired 1960; *b* 20 Sept. 1908; *yr s* of William Neilson and Maude Fraser; *m* 1941, Noreen, *d* of Col M. O'C. Tandy; one *s* one *d*. *Educ:* Sherborne Sch. Commissioned into Royal Tank Regt; served War of 1939–45, India and Burma, with 14th Army. Military Attaché, Cairo, 1954–56; NATO, Washington DC, 1957–60. *Recreations:* hunting, shooting; Master Aldershot Command Beagles, 1939. *Address:* Cheyney Holt, Steeple Morden, Herts SG8 0LX.

FRASER, Sir Ian, Kt 1963; DSO 1943; OBE 1940; DL; FRSE, FRCS, FRCSI, FACS; Consulting Surgeon, Belfast; Senior Surgeon: Royal Victoria Hospital, Belfast, 1955–66; Royal Belfast Hospital for Sick Children, 1955–66; Director: Provincial Bank of Ireland; Allied Irish Bank; *b* 9 Feb. 1901; *s* of Robert Moore Fraser, BA, MD, Belfast; *m* 1931, Eleanor Margaret Mitchell; one *s* one *d*. *Educ:* Royal Academical Institution, Belfast; Queen's Univ., Belfast. MB, BCh 1st Cl. Hons 1923; MD 1932; MCh 1927; FRCSI 1926; FRCS 1927; FRSE 1938; FACS 1945. Coulter Schol.; McQuitty Schol.; 1st place in Ire. as FRCSI. Resident Surgical Officer, St Helen's, Lancs; Surgeon: Royal Belfast Hosp. for Sick Children; Royal Victoria Hosp., Belfast, and former Asst Prof. of Surgery. Served War: (overseas) 1940–45: in W Africa, N. Africa, Sicily, Italy (OBE, DSO, Salerno); invasion of France, India; Officer in charge of Penicillin in Research Team, N Africa; Brig, 1945. Hon. Col (TA): No 204 Gen. Hosp., 1961–71; No 4 Field Amb., 1948–71; Surgeon in Ordinary to the Governor of Northern Ireland; Hon. Cons. Surg. to the Army in NI; Chm., Police Authority, Royal Ulster Constabulary, 1970–76; Mem. Adv. Council, Ulster Defence Regt. Past President: RCSI (1956–57); Assoc. of Surgeons GB and Ireland (1957); BMA (1962–63); Irish Med. Graduates Assoc., London, Queen's Univ. Assoc., London; Services Club, QUB; Ulster Med. Soc. President: Ulster Surgical Club; Queen's Univ. Assoc., Belfast; Chm of Convocation and Mem. Senate QUB. Visiting Lecturer: Leicester, Birmingham, Edinburgh, Bradford, London, Sheffield, Dublin, Cheltenham, Rochester, New York, Copenhagen, Glasgow, Manchester, Middlesex Hosp., Bristol, Barnsley, etc; Delegate to various assocs abroad. John Snow Oration, 1967; Downpatrick Hosp. Bi-Centenary Oration, 1967; Bishop Jeremy Taylor Lecture, 1970; Maj.-Gen. Philip Mitchiner Lecture, 1971; Robert Campbell Orator, 1973; David Torrens Lectr, NUU, 1981; Thos Vicary Lecture, RCS, 1983. Visiting Examiner in Surgery: Liverpool, Cambridge, and Manchester Univs; NUI; Apothecaries' Hall, Dublin; TCD; RCS in Ire.; RCS of Glasgow, Councillor, RCSI; Mem. and Trustee, James IV Assoc. of Surgeons; Mem., Health Educn Cttee, Min. of Health, London; Fellow: BMA; Roy. Soc. Med. Lond.; Roy. Irish Acad. of Med.; Hon. FRCPGlas 1972; Hon. FRCSE; Hon. FRCPI 1977; Hon. Fellow: Brit. Assoc. of Paediatric Surgeons; Ulster Med. Soc., 1977; Foreign Mem., L'Académie de Chirurgie, Paris; Hon. Mem., Danish Assoc. of Surgery, Copenhagen; Mem., Internat. Soc. of Surgeons. Hon. Life Governor, Royal Victoria Hosp., Belfast; Governor for GB, Amer. Coll. Surgeons. Hon. DSc: Oxon, 1963; New Univ. of Ulster, 1977. GCStJ 1974 (KStJ 1940); Mem., Chapter General, London, and Knight Commander of Commandery of Ards, Ulster, Order of St John. DL Belfast, 1955. Gold Medal: Ulster Hosp. for Women and Children; Royal Belfast Hosp. for Sick Children. Commander: Ordre de la Couronne (Belgium) 1963; Order of Orange Nassau, 1969; Ordre des Palmes Académiques, 1970; Chevalier de la Legion d'Honneur, France, 1981. *Publications:* various monographs on surgical subjects. *Recreations:* golf, formerly hockey and rugby. *Address:* (residence) 19 Upper Malone Road, Belfast BT9 6TE. *T:* Belfast (0232) 668235.

FRASER, Lt-Comdr Ian Edward, VC 1945; DSC 1943; RD and Bar 1948; JP; (former Managing Director, Universal Divers Ltd, 1947–65 and since 1983 Chairman); *b* 18 Dec. 1920; *s* of S. Fraser, Bourne End, Bucks; *m* 1943, Melba Estelle Hughes; four *s* two *d*. *Educ:* Royal Grammar Sch., High Wycombe; HMS Conway. Merchant Navy, 1937–39; Royal Navy, 1939–47; Lt-Comdr, RNR, 1951–65; Younger Brother of Trinity House, 1980. JP Wallasey, 1957. Officer, American Legion of Merit. *Publication:* Frogman VC, 1957. *Address:* Sigyn, 1 Lyndhurst Road, Wallasey, Merseyside L45 6XA. *T:* 051–639 3355. *Clubs:* Hoylake Sailing (life mem.); New Brighton Rugby (life mem.); Leasowe Golf (life mem.; Captain, 1975).

FRASER, Sir Ian (James), Kt 1986; CBE 1972; MC 1945; Chairman, Lazard Brothers, 1980–85; Deputy Chairman: Vickers Ltd, 1980–89; TSB Group plc, 1985–91; *b* 7 Aug. 1923; 2nd *s* of late Hon. Alastair Thomas Joseph Fraser and Lady Sibyl Fraser (*née* Grimston); *m* 1958, Evelyn Elizabeth Anne Grant (*d* 1984); two *s* two *d*. *Educ:* Ampleforth Coll.; Magdalen Coll., Oxford. Served War of 1939–45: Lieut, Scots Guards, 1942–45 (despatches, MC). Reuter Correspondent, 1946–56; S. G. Warburg & Co. Ltd, 1956–69; Dir-Gen., Panel on Take-overs and Mergers, 1969–72; Part-time Mem., CAA, 1972–74. Chairman, City Capital Markets Cttee, 1974–78; Accepting Houses Cttee, 1981–85; Member: Exec. Cttee, City Communications Centre, 1976–85; Cttee on Finance for Industry, NEDC, 1976–79; President's Cttee, CBI, 1979–81; Exec. Cttee, Jt Disciplinary Scheme of Accountancy Insts, 1979–81. Director: BOC International Ltd, 1972–85; Davy International Ltd, 1972–84; Chloride Gp Ltd, 1976–80; S. Pearson & Son Ltd, 1977–89; EMI Ltd, 1977–80; Eurafrance SA, 1979–85; Pearson-Longman Ltd, 1980–83; Chairman: Rolls-Royce Motors, 1971–80; Datastream Ltd, 1976–77. Mem. Exec., Help the Hospices, 1985–; Vice-Pres., BBA, 1981–85. Trustee, Tablet Trust, 1976– (Chm., Finance Cttee, 1985–). Governor, More House Sch., 1970–75. FRSA 1970; CBIM (FBIM 1974). Kt of Honour and Devotion, SMO of Malta, 1971. *Recreations:* fishing, gardening, Scottish history. *Address:* South Haddon, Skilgate, Taunton, Somerset TA4 2DR. *T:* Bampton (Devon) (0398) 331247. *Club:* White's.

FRASER, Very Rev. Dr Ian Watson, CMG 1973; Minister of St Stephen's Presbyterian Church, Lower Hutt, Wellington, NZ, 1961–73, retired; *b* 23 Oct. 1907; *s* of Malcolm Fraser (*b* Inverness; 1st NZ Govt Statistician) and Caroline (*née* Watson; *b* Napier, NZ); *m* 1932, Alexa Church Stewart; one *s* two *d. Educ:* Scots Coll., Wellington, NZ; Victoria Univ. of Wellington (MA (Hons)); Theol Hall, Dunedin; BD (Melb.); Univ. of Edinburgh; Univ. of Bonn, Germany; Union Theol Seminary, NY (STM, ThD). Minister: St Andrew's Presbyterian Church, Levin, 1933–39; Presbyterian Ch., Wyndham, 1939–42; Chaplain, St Andrew's Coll., Christchurch, 1942–48; Minister, St John's Pres. Ch., Papatoetoe, Auckland, 1948–61. Moderator, Presbyterian Church of NZ, 1968–69. Chm., Nansen Home Cttee, Presbyterian Support Services, 1984–86 (Chm., NZ Refugee Homes Bd, administering Nansen Home, 1962–84). Refugee Award of Nat. Council of Churches, 1970. Compiled biographical register of ministers in Presbyterian Church of NZ, 1840–1990. *Publications:* Understandest Thou? (Introd. to NT), 1946; Understanding the OT, 1958; The Story of Nansen Home, 1984; various booklets. *Recreations:* cabinet making, music, reading. *Address:* 19A Bloomfield Terrace, Lower Hutt 6301, Wellington, New Zealand. *T:* Wellington 697–269.
    See also T. R. C. Fraser.

FRASER, Sir (James) Campbell, Kt 1978; FRSE 1978; Chairman: Scottish Television plc, 1975–91; Green Park Health Care plc, 1985–89; *b* 2 May 1923; *s* of Alexander Ross Fraser and Annie McGregor Fraser; *m* 1950, Maria Harvey (*née* McLaren), JP; two *d. Educ:* Glasgow Univ.; McMaster Univ.; Dundee Sch. of Economics. BCom. Served RAF, 1941–45. Raw Cotton Commn, Liverpool, 1950–52; Economist Intelligence Unit, 1952–57; Dunlop Rubber Co. Ltd, 1957–83: Public Relations Officer, 1958; Group Marketing Controller, 1962; Man. Dir, Dunlop New Zealand Ltd, 1967; Exec. Dir, 1969; Jt Man. Dir, 1971; Man. Dir, 1972; Chm., Dunlop Holdings, 1978–83; Chm. and Man. Dir, Dunlop Ltd, 1977–83; Chm., Dunlop Internat. AG, 1978–83. Director: British Petroleum, 1978–; BAT Industries, 1980–; Charterhouse J. Rothschild, 1982–84; Bridgewater Paper Co., 1984–; Tandem Computers Ltd, 1985–; Alexander Proudfoot PLC, 1987–. Vice-Pres., Scottish Opera, 1986–. Pres., CBI, 1982–84 (Dep. Pres., 1981–82). Founder Mem., Past Chm., and Pres., 1972–84, Soc. of Business Economists; Mem. Exec. Cttee, SMMT, 1973–82. Trustee, The Economist, 1978–. Vis. Professor: Strathclyde Univ., 1980–85; Stirling Univ., 1980–88. Chm., Strathclyde Univ. Business Sch., 1976–81; Mem. Court, St Andrews Univ., 1987–90. CBIM 1971; FPRI 1978. Hon. LLD Strathclyde, 1979; DUniv Stirling, 1979; Hon. DCL Bishop's Univ., Canada. *Publications:* many articles and broadcasts. *Recreations:* reading, theatre, cinema, gardening, walking. *Address:* Silver Birches, 4 Silver Lane, Purley, Surrey. *Club:* Caledonian.

FRASER, Prof. Sir James (David), 2nd Bt, *cr* 1943; Postgraduate Dean, Faculty of Medicine, University of Edinburgh, 1981–89; *b* 19 July 1924; *o s* of Sir John Fraser, 1st Bt, KCVO, MC, and Agnes Govane Herald (*d* 1983), The Manse, Duns, Berwickshire; *S* father 1947; *m* 1950, Maureen, *d* of Rev. John Reay, MC, Bingham Rectory, Nottingham; two *s. Educ:* Edinburgh Academy; Magdalen Coll., Oxford (BA); Edinburgh Univ. (MB, ChB); ChM 1961; FRCSE 1953; FRCS 1973; FRCPE 1980; FRCSI 1984; FRACS 1984. RAMC (Major), 1948–51. Senior Lectr in Clinical Surgery, Univ. of Edinburgh and Hon. Cons. Surgeon, Royal Infirmary, Edinburgh, 1951–70; Prof. of Surgery, Univ. of Southampton, 1970–80, and Hon. Cons. Surgeon, Southampton Univ. Hospital Gp, 1970–80. Pres., RCSEd, 1982–85. *Recreations:* golf, swimming. *Heir: s* Iain Michael Fraser [*b* 27 June 1951; *m* 1982, Sherylle, *d* of Keith Gillespie, New Zealand; one *s* one *d*]. *Address:* 2 Lennox Street, Edinburgh EH4 1QA.

FRASER, (James) Edward, CB 1990; Under Secretary, Scottish Home and Health Department, since 1981; *b* 16 Dec. 1931; *s* of late Dr James F. Fraser, TD, Aberdeen, and late Dr Kathleen Blomfield; *m* 1959, Patricia Louise Stewart; two *s. Educ:* Aberdeen Grammar Sch.; Univ. of Aberdeen (MA); Christ's Coll., Cambridge (BA). FSAScot. RA, 1953; Staff Captain 'Q', Tel-el-Kebir, 1954–55. Asst Principal, Scottish Home Dept, 1957–60; Private Sec. to Permanent Under Sec. of State, 1960–62, and to Parly Under-Sec. of State, 1962; Principal: SHHD, 1962–64; Cabinet Office, 1964–66; HM Treasury, 1966–68; SHHD, 1968–69; Asst Sec., SHHD, 1970–76; Asst Sec., 1976, Under Sec., 1976–81, Local Govt Finance Gp, Scottish Office. Pres., Scottish Hellenic Soc. of Edinburgh and Eastern Scotland, 1987–. *Recreations:* reading, music, walking, Greece ancient and modern. *Address:* St Andrew's House, Edinburgh EH1 3DE. *T:* 031-244 2131. *Club:* Scottish Arts (Edinburgh).

FRASER, James Owen Arthur; a Sheriff of Grampian, Highland and Islands, since 1984; *b* 9 May 1937; *s* of James and Effie Fraser; *m* 1961, Flora Shaw MacKenzie; two *s. Educ:* Glasgow High Sch. (Classical Dux 1954); Glasgow Univ. (MA 1958; LlB 1961). Qualified as Solicitor, 1961; employed as solicitor, Edinburgh, 1961–65, Glasgow, 1965–66; Partner, Bird Son & Semple, later Bird Semple & Crawford Herron, Solicitors, Glasgow, 1967–84. Part-time Lectr in Evidence and Procedure, Glasgow Univ., 1976–83. Temp. Sheriff, 1983–84. *Recreation:* golf. *Address:* Averon Lodge, School Road, Conon Bridge, Ross-shire. *T:* Dingwall (0349) 61556.

FRASER, Hon. John Allen; PC 1979; QC (Can.) 1979; MP (Progressive Conservative) Vancouver South, since 1972; Speaker of the House of Commons, Canada, since 1986; *b* Japan, 1931; *m* Catherine Findlay; three *d. Educ:* Univ. of British Columbia (LLB 1954). Law practice, Vancouver. Opposition environment spokesman, 1972, labour spokesman, 1974; Minister of Environment and Postmaster General, 1979; Opposition spokesman on fisheries, Post Office, and Solicitor-General, 1980–84; Minister of Fisheries and Oceans, 1984–85. *Address:* Office of the Speaker, House of Commons, Ottawa, Ont K1A 0A6, Canada.

FRASER, John Denis; MP (Lab) Norwood, since 1966; *b* 30 June 1934; *s* of Archibald and Frances Fraser; *m* 1960, Ann Hathaway; two *s* one *d. Educ:* Sloane Grammar Sch., Chelsea; Co-operative Coll., Loughborough; Law Soc. Sch. of Law (John Mackrell Prize). Entered Australia & New Zealand Bank Ltd, 1950; Army service, 1952–54, as Sergt, RAEC (educnl and resettlement work). Solicitor, 1960; practised with Lewis Silkin. Mem. Lambeth Borough Coun., 1962–68 (Chm. Town Planning Cttee; Chm. Labour Gp). PPS to Rt Hon. Barbara Castle, 1968–70; Opposition front bench spokesman on Home Affairs, 1972–74; Parly Under-Sec. of State, Dept of Employment, 1974–76; Minister of State, Dept of Prices and Consumer Protection, 1976–79; opposition spokesman on trade, 1979–83, on housing and construction, 1983–87, on legal affairs, 1987–. *Recreations:* walking, music. *Address:* House of Commons, SW1A 0AA.

FRASER, Rt. Hon. (John) Malcolm, AC 1988; CH 1977; PC 1976; MA Oxon; Prime Minister of Australia, 1975–83; *b* 21 May 1930; *s* of late J. Neville Fraser, Nareen, Vic, Australia; *m* 1956, Tamara, *d* of S. R. Beggs; two *s* two *d. Educ:* Melbourne C of E Grammar Sch.; Magdalen Coll., Oxford (MA 1952; Hon. Fellow, 1982). MHR (L) for Wannon, Vic, 1955–83; Mem. Jt Party Cttee on Foreign Affairs, 1962–66; Minister: for the Army, 1966–68; for Educn and Science, 1968–69, 1971–72; for Defence, 1969–71; Leader of Parly Liberal Party, 1975–83; Leader of the Opposition, 1975. Sen. Adjunct Fellow, Center for Strategic and Internat. Studies, Georgetown Univ., Washington, 1983–86. Chairman: UN Sec. Gen's Expert Gp on African Commodity Problems,

1989–90; CARE Australia; Pres., CARE Internat., 1990–. Co-Chm., Commonwealth Eminent Persons Gp on S Africa, 1986. Consultant, Prudential Insurance Co., US; Director: First Australia Fund; First Australia Prime Income Fund; First Australia Prime Income Investment Fund. Member: InterAction Council for Former Heads of Govt; ANZ Internat. Bd of Advice, 1987–. Distinguished Internat. Fellow, Amer. Enterprise Inst. for Public Policy Res., 1984–86; Fellow, Center for Internat. Affairs, Harvard Univ., 1985. Mem. Council, Aust. Nat. Univ., 1964–66. Hon. Vice President: Oxford Soc., 1983; Royal Commonwealth Soc., 1983. Hon. LLD: Univ. of SC, 1981; Deakin Univ., 1989. *Recreations:* fishing, photography, vintage cars. *Address:* ANZ Tower, 55 Collins Street, Melbourne, Vic 3000, Australia. *Club:* Melbourne.

FRASER, John Stewart; Chairman and Chief Executive, Ciba-Geigy plc, since 1990; *b* 18 July 1931; *s* of Donald Stewart Fraser and Ruth (*née* Dobinson); *m* 1955, Diane Louise Witt; two *s* one *d. Educ:* Royal Melbourne Inst. of Technology. ARACI. Technical Rep., Australian Sales Manager and Australian Marketing Manager, Monsanto Australia Ltd, 1953–68; Marketing Manager, Ilford (Australia) Pty Ltd, 1968–73; Ilford Ltd, UK: Marketing Dir, 1973–78; Man. Dir and Chief Exec., 1978–84; Corporate Man. Dir, Ciba-Geigy Plastics and Additives Co., UK, 1982–84; Ciba-Geigy plc, UK: Gp Man. Dir, 1984–87; Gp Man. Dir and Chief Exec., 1987–90. *Recreations:* tennis, golf. *Address:* Ciba-Geigy plc, Hulley Road, Macclesfield, Cheshire SK10 2NX. *T:* Macclesfield (0625) 421933. *Club:* City Livery.

FRASER, Kenneth John Alexander; international marketing consultant; adviser to European Association of Branded Goods Manufacturers; *b* 22 Sept. 1929; *s* of Jack Sears Fraser and Marjorie Winifred (*née* Savery); *m* 1953, Kathleen Grace Booth; two *s* one *d. Educ:* Thames Valley Grammar Sch., Twickenham; London School of Economics (BScEcon Hons). Joined Erwin Wasey & Co. Ltd, 1953, then Lintas Ltd, 1958; Managing Director, Research Bureau Ltd, 1962; Unilever: Head of Marketing Analysis and Evaluation Group, 1965; Head of Marketing Division, 1976–79, 1981–89; Hd of Internat. Affairs, 1985–89; Hd of External Affairs, 1989–90; seconded to NEDO as Industrial Dir, 1979–81. Member: Consumer Protection Adv. Cttee, Dept of Prices and Consumer Protection, 1975; Management Bd, ADAS, MAFF, 1986–; Chairman: CBI Marketing and Consumer Affairs Cttee, 1977; Internat. Chamber of Commerce Marketing Commn, 1978; Vice Chm., Advertising Assoc., 1981–90. FRSA. *Recreations:* canoeing, walking, music, reading. *Address:* 14 Coombe Lane West, Kingston, Surrey KT2 7BX. *T:* 081–949 3760. *Club:* Wig and Pen.

FRASER, Rt. Hon. Malcolm; *see* Fraser, Rt Hon. J. M.

FRASER, Air Marshal Rev. Sir Paterson; *see* Fraser, Air Marshal Rev. Sir H. P.

FRASER, Peter Marshall, MC 1944; MA; FBA 1960; Fellow of All Souls College, Oxford, 1954–87, now Emeritus, and Acting Warden, 1985–87 (Sub-Warden, 1980–82); Lecturer in Hellenistic History, 1948–64, Reader 1964–85; *b* 6 April 1918; *y s* of late Archibald Fraser; *m* 1st, 1940, Catharine, *d* of late Prebendary Heaton-Renshaw (marr. diss.) one *s* three *d*; 2nd, 1955, Ruth Elsbeth, *d* of late F. Renfer, Bern, Switzerland; two *s*; 3rd, 1973, Barbara Ann Stewart, *d* of late L. E. C. Norbury, FRCS. *Educ:* City of London Sch.; Brasenose Coll., Oxford (Hon. Fellow 1977). Seaforth Highlanders, 1941–45; Military Mission to Greece, 1943–45. Sen. Scholar, Christ Church, Oxford, 1946–47; Junior Proctor, Oxford Univ., 1960–61; Domestic Bursar, All Souls Coll., 1962–65. Dir, British Sch. at Athens, 1968–71. Vis. Prof. of Classical Studies, Indiana Univ., 1973–74. Chm., Managing Cttee, Soc. of Afghan Studies, 1972–82; Vice Pres., Soc. for S Asian Studies, 1985–90. Ordinary Mem., German Archaeol. Soc., 1979; Corresp. Fellow, Archaeolog. Soc. of Athens, 1971. Gen. Editor and Chm., British Acad. Cttee, Lexicon of Greek Personal Names, 1973–. Hon. Dr. phil Trier, 1984. *Publications:* (with G. E. Bean) The Rhodian Peraea and Islands, 1954; (with T. Rönne) Boeotian and West Greek Tombstones, 1957; Rostovtzeff, Social and Economic History of the Roman Empire, 2nd edn, revised, 1957; Samothrace, The Inscriptions, (Vol. ii, Excavations of Samothrace), 1960; E. Löfstedt, Roman Literary Portraits, trans. from the Swedish (Romare), 1958; The Wares of Autolycus; Selected Literary Essays of Alice Meynell (ed), 1965; E. Kjellberg and G. Säflund, Greek and Roman Art, trans. from the Swedish (Grekisk och romersk konst), 1968; Ptolemaic Alexandria, 1972; Rhodian Funerary Monuments, 1977; A. J. Butler, Arab Conquest of Egypt, 2nd edn, revised, 1978; (with E. Matthews) A Lexicon of Greek Personal Names, vol. 1, 1987; (ed) Memorial Addresses of All Souls College, 1989. *Address:* All Souls College, Oxford.

FRASER, Ronald Petrie, CB 1972; Secretary, Scottish Home and Health Department, 1972–77; *b* 2 June 1917; *yr s* of late T. Petrie Fraser, Elgin; *m* 1962, Ruth Wright Anderson, Edinburgh; one *d. Educ:* Daniel Stewart's Coll., Edinburgh; University of Edinburgh; The Queen's Coll., Oxford. Joined Dept of Health for Scotland for work on emergency hosp. service, 1940; Asst Private Sec. to Sec. of State for Scotland, 1944; Cabinet Office, 1947; Sec., Scottish Hosp. Endowments Commn, 1950; Asst Sec., Dept of Health for Scotland, 1954; Asst Sec., Scottish Education Dept, 1961; Under-Sec., 1963; Under-Sec., 1968–71; Dep. Sec., 1971, Min. of Agriculture, Fisheries and Food. Chief Counting Officer for Scotland Act Referendum, 1979. *Recreations:* walking, music. *Address:* 40A Lygon Road, Edinburgh EH16 5QA. *T:* 031-667 8298. *Club:* New (Edinburgh).

FRASER, Simon William Hetherington; Sheriff of North Strathclyde at Dumbarton, since 1989; *b* 2 April 1951; *s* of George MacDonald Fraser, *qv*; *m* 1979, Sheena Janet Fraser; one *d. Educ:* Glasgow Acad.; Glasgow Univ. (LLB). Solicitor, 1973–89 (Partner, Flowers & Co., Glasgow, 1976–89). Temp. Sheriff, 1987–89. Pres., Glasgow Bar Assoc., 1981–82. *Recreations:* cricket, snooker. *Address:* Sheriff Court, Church Street, Dumbarton G82 1QR. *T:* Dumbarton (0389) 63266. *Club:* Avizandum (Glasgow).

FRASER, Prof. (Thomas) Russell (Cumming), MD, FRCP; Deputy Director, Medical Research Council, New Zealand, 1975–81, retired; *b* 25 Dec. 1908; *s* of Malcolm Fraser and Caroline (*née* Watson). *Educ:* Otago Univ. Medical School. MB, ChB (distinction) 1932; MRCP 1936; DPM (Eng.) 1937; MD (NZ) 1945; FRCP 1948. Hallett Prize, 1935; NZ University Travel Fellowship, 1935; Rockefeller Travel Fellowship, 1938. Formerly Asst Med. Officer, Maudsley Hosp.; Research Fellow in Medicine, Harvard Univ.; Reader in Medicine, Postgrad. Med. Sch., London; Prof. of Clinical Endocrinology in Univ. of London, RPMS, 1957–74. Member: Assoc. Physicians of Gt Brit.; Med. Research Soc. Hon. DSc, NZ. *Publications:* contribs to medical journals. *Address:* 19B Long Drive, St Heliers, Auckland 5, New Zealand.
    See also Very Rev. Dr I. W. Fraser.

FRASER, Veronica Mary; Diocesan Director of Education, Diocese of Worcester, since 1985; *b* 19 April 1933; *o d* of late Archibald Fraser. *Educ:* Richmond County Sch. for Girls; St Hugh's Coll., Oxford. Head of English Department: The Alice Ottley Sch., Worcester, 1962–65; Guildford County Sch. for Girls, 1965–67 (also Librarian); Headmistress, Godolphin Sch., Salisbury, 1968–80; Adviser on Schools to Bishop of Winchester, 1981–85. *Address:* The Old Palace, Deansway, Worcester WR1 2JE.

FRASER, William James; JP; Lord Provost of Aberdeen, 1977–80; Member, City of Aberdeen District Council; *b* 31 Dec. 1921; *s* of late William and Jessie Fraser; *m* 1961, Mary Ann; three *s* one *d*. *Educ:* York Street Sch., Aberdeen; Frederick Street Sch., Aberdeen. Mem., Scottish Exec., Labour Party, 1949–74 (Chm., 1962–63). Pres., Aberdeen Trades Council, 1952. JP Aberdeen, 1950. *Address:* 79 Salisbury Place, Aberdeen AB1 6QU. *T:* Aberdeen (0224) 51040.

FRASER, Sir William (Kerr), GCB 1984 (KCB 1979; CB 1978); Principal and Vice-Chancellor, University of Glasgow, since 1988; *b* 18 March 1929; *s* of A. M. Fraser and Rachel Kerr; *m* 1956, Marion Anne Forbes; three *s* one *d*. *Educ:* Eastwood Sch., Clarkston; Glasgow Univ. (MA, LLB). Joined Scottish Home Dept, 1955; Private Sec. to Parliamentary Under-Sec., 1959, and to Secretary of State for Scotland, 1966–67; Civil Service Fellow, Univ. of Glasgow, 1963–64; Asst Sec., Regional Development Div., 1967–71; Under Sec., Scottish Home and Health Dept, 1971–75; Dep. Sec., 1975–78, Permanent Under-Sec. of State, 1978–88, Scottish Office. Dir, Scottish Mutual Assce Soc., 1990–. Gov., Caledonian Res. Foundn. FRSE 1985. Hon. LLD: Glasgow, 1982; Strathclyde, 1991. *Address:* The University, Glasgow G12 8QG. *Club:* New (Edinburgh).

FRASER McLUSKEY, Rev. James; *see* McLuskey.

FRASER-TYTLER, Christian Helen, CBE (mil.) 1941; TD; Senior Controller ATS, retired; *b* 23 Aug. 1897; *d* of John Campbell Shairp, Houstoun; *m* 1919, Col Neil Fraser-Tytler, DSO, Croix de Guerre (*d* 1937); two *d*. *Educ:* Home. Foreign Office, 1917–19; War Office, 1939–43; AA Command until 1945 (TD). *Recreation:* fishing. *Address:* Craigmount, The Scores, St Andrews. *T:* St Andrews (0334) 76826.
See also Sir Thomas David Erskine, Bt.

FRAYLING, Prof. Christopher John, MA, PhD; Professor and Head of Department of Cultural History, Royal College of Art, London, since 1979; *b* 25 Dec. 1946; *s* of Arthur Frederick Frayling and Barbara Kathleen (*née* Imhof); *m* 1981, Helen Snowdon. *Educ:* Repton Sch.; Churchill Coll., Cambridge (BA, MA, PhD). Churchill Research Studentship, 1968–71; Lectr in Modern History, Univ. of Exeter, 1971–72; Tutor, Dept of General Studies, Royal College of Art, 1972–73, Vis. Lectr, 1973–79; Research Asst, Dept of Information Retrieval, Imperial War Mus., 1973–74; Lectr in the History of Ideas and European Social History, Univ. of Bath, 1974–79; founded Dept of Cultural History (ex General Studies), RCA, 1979. Historian, lectr, critic; regular contributor, as writer and presenter, to radio (incl. Kaleidoscope, Stop the Week, Meridian, Critics' Forum, Third Opinion, Third Ear; series: The American Cowboy; America: the movie (Silver Medal, NY Internat. Radio Fest., 1989); Britannia: the film) and TV (incl. series Art of Persuasion (Gold Medal, NY Internat. Film and TV Fest., 1985), Busting the Block—or the Art of Pleasing People, Design Classics, Timewatch, and Movie Profiles). Crafts Council: Mem., 1982–85; Mem., Educn Cttee, 1981–85; Chm., Pubns and Inf. Cttee, 1984–85. Arts Council of GB: Mem., 1987–; Mem., Art Panel, 1983– (Dep. Chm., 1984–87; Chm., 1987–); Mem., Photography Adv. Panel, 1983–85; Chm., Art Projects Cttee, 1986–87; Mem., Combined Arts Cttee, 1987–88; Chm., Multidisciplinary Arts Cttee, 1989–. Chm. of Trustees, Crafts Study Centre, Bath, 1982–; Chm., Free Form Arts Trust, 1984–88; Trustee, V&A Museum, 1984– (Member: Adv. Council, 1981–83; Sen. Staff Appts Cttee, 1987–; S Kensington Jt Planning Cttee, 1989–; Educn and Res. Cttees, 1990–). Governor, BFI, 1982–87 (Mem., 1982–86, Chm. 1984–86, Educn Cttee); Member: Art and Design Sect., Leverhulme Team on Arts in Higher Educn, 1982; Working Party on art and design advising NAB, 1985–87. FRSA 1984. Radio play, The Rime of the Bounty (Sony Radio Award, 1990). *Publications:* Napoleon Wrote Fiction, 1972; (ed) The Vampyre—Lord Ruthven to Count Dracula, 1978; Spaghetti Westerns: Cowboys and Europeans, from Karl May to Sergio Leone, 1981; The Schoolmaster and the Wheelwrights, 1983; The Royal College of Art: one hundred and fifty years of art and design, 1987; contribs to: Reappraisals of Rousseau—studies in honour of R. A. Leigh, 1980; Cinema, Politics and Society in America, 1981; Rousseau et Voltaire en 1978, 1981; Rousseau After Two Hundred Years: Proc. of Cambridge Bicentennial Colloquium, 1982; Eduardo Paolozzi: perspectives and themes, 1984; Eduardo Paolozzi—Lost Magic Kingdoms, 1986; Rape: an interdisciplinary study, 1987; 2D/3D—Art and Craft made and designed for the twentieth century, 1987; The Cambridge Guide to the Arts in Britain, Vol. IX (post 1945), 1988; Craft Classics since the 1940s, 1988; Eduardo Paolozzo: Noah's Ark, 1990; Ariel at Bay: reflections on broadcasting and the arts, 1990; articles on film, popular culture and the visual arts/crafts in Cambridge Rev., Cinema, Film, London Magazine, New Society, Crafts, Burlington Magazine, Art and Design, Design Week, Design, TLS, Time Out, Punch, Designer, Craft History, Creative Review, Blueprint, Independent Magazine, Listener, and various learned jls. *Recreation:* finding time. *Address:* Faculty of Humanities, Royal College of Art, Kensington Gore, SW7 2EU. *T:* 071–584 5020.
See also Rev. N. A. Frayling.

FRAYLING, Rev. Canon Nicholas Arthur; Rector of Liverpool, since 1987; Hon. Canon, Liverpool Cathedral, since 1989; *b* 29 Feb. 1944; *s* of Arthur Frederick Frayling, OBE and Barbara Kathleen (*née* Imhof). *Educ:* Repton Sch.; Exeter Univ. (BA Theology 1969); Cuddesdon Theol Coll., Oxford. Management training, retail trade, 1962–64; Temp. Probation Officer (prison welfare), Inner London Probation and After-Care Service, 1965–66, pt-time, 1966–71. Deacon, 1971; priest, 1972; Asst Curate, St John, Peckham, 1971–74; Vicar, All Saints, Tooting Graveney, 1974–83; Canon Residentiary and Precentor, Liverpool Cathedral, 1983–87. Chaplain: St Paul's Eye Hosp., Liverpool, 1987–90; Huyton Coll., 1987–. Chm., Southwark Diocesan Adv. Cttee for Care of Churches, 1980–83. *Recreations:* music, friends. *Address:* 25 Princes Park Mansions, Sefton Park Road, Liverpool L8 3SA. *T:* (home) 051–727 4692, (office) 051–236 5287. *Clubs:* Commonwealth Trust; Athenæum, Lyceum (Hon.), Artists (Hon.) (Liverpool); Liverpool Racquet (Hon.).
See also C. J. Frayling.

FRAYN, Michael; writer; *b* 8 Sept. 1933; *s* of late Thomas Allen Frayn and Violet Alice Lawson; *m* 1960, Gillian Palmer (marr. diss. 1989); three *d*. *Educ:* Kingston Gram. Sch.; Emmanuel Coll., Cambridge (Hon. Fellow, 1985). Reporter, Guardian, 1957–59; Columnist, Guardian, 1959–62; Columnist, Observer, 1962–68. TV: plays: Jamie, 1968; Birthday, 1969; First and Last, 1989 (Internat. Emmy Award, 1990); documentaries: Imagine a City Called Berlin, 1975; Vienna—The Mask of Gold, 1977; Three Streets in the Country, 1979; The Long Straight, 1980; Jerusalem, 1984; stage plays: The Two of Us, 1970; The Sandboy, 1971; Alphabetical Order, 1975 (Evening Standard Drama Award for Best Comedy); Donkeys' Years, 1976 (SWET Best Comedy Award); Clouds, 1976; Liberty Hall, 1980; Make and Break, 1980 (New Standard Best Comedy Award); Noises Off, 1982 (Standard Best Comedy Award; SWET Best Comedy Award); Benefactors, 1984 (Standard Best Play Award; Laurence Olivier (formerly SWET) Award for Play of the Year; Plays and Players London Theatre Critics' Best New Play); Look Look, 1990; filmscript: Clockwise, 1986. Nat. Press Award, 1970. *Publications:* collections of columns: The Day of the Dog, 1962; The Book of Fub, 1963; On the Outskirts, 1964; At Bay in Gear Street, 1967; The Original Michael Frayn, 1983; *non-fiction:* Constructions, 1974; *novels:* The Tin Men, 1965 (Somerset Maugham Award); The Russian Interpreter, 1966 (Hawthornden Prize); Towards the End of the Morning, 1967; A Very Private Life, 1968; Sweet Dreams, 1973; The Trick of It, 1989; *translations:* Tolstoy, The Fruits of Enlightenment, 1979 (prod. 1979); Anouilh, Number One, 1984; Chekhov: The Cherry Orchard, 1978 (prod. 1978, 1989); Three Sisters, 1983 (prod. 1985); Wild Honey, 1984 (prod. 1984); The Seagull, 1986 (prod. 1986); Trifonov, Uncle Vanya, 1988 (prod. 1988); The Sneeze (adapted from one-act plays and short stories), 1989 (prod. 1988); Exchange, 1986 (prod. 1986, 1990). *Address:* c/o Elaine Greene Ltd, 37a Goldhawk Road, W12 8QQ.

FRAZER, Prof. Malcolm John, PhD, FRSC; Director and Chief Executive, Council for National Academic Awards, since 1986; *b* 7 Feb. 1931; *m* 1957, Gwenyth Ida Biggs (marr. diss. 1990), JP, MA; three *s*. *Educ:* Univ. of London; BSc 1952, PhD 1955. Royal Military Coll. of Science, 1956–57; Lecturer and Head of Dept of Chemistry, Northern Polytechnic, London, 1965–72; Prof. of Chemical Educn, 1972–86, and Pro-Vice Chancellor, 1976–81, Univ. of East Anglia, Norwich. Vice-Pres., RSC, 1973–74; Gen. Sec./Vice-Pres., Chm. Council, BAAS, 1978–; Mem. Council, Royal Instn, 1988–. Hon. Fellow: N London Poly., 1988; SCOTVEC, 1990. Hon. FCollP, 1988. Hon. Dr Leuven, 1985. *Publications:* (jointly): Resource Book on Chemical Education in the UK, 1975; Problem Solving in Chemistry, 1982; Problem Solving in the Chemical Industry, 1984; Chemistry, Principles and Applications, 1988; contribs to Jl Chem. Soc., etc; *Address:* Council for National Academic Awards, 344–354 Gray's Inn Road, WC1X 8BP. *Clubs:* Athenæum, National Liberal.

FREARS, Stephen Arthur; film director; *b* 20 June 1941; *s* of Dr Russell E. Frears and Ruth M. Frears; *m* 1968, Mary K. Wilmers (marr. diss. 1974); two *s*; lives with Anne Rothenstein; one *s* one *d*. *Educ:* Gresham's Sch., Holt; Trinity Coll., Cambridge (BA Law). Director: Gumshoe, 1971; Bloody Kids, 1980; Going Gently, 1981; Walter, 1982; Saigon, 1983; The Hit, 1984; My Beautiful Laundrette, 1985; Prick Up Your Ears, 1986; Sammy and Rosie Get Laid, 1987; Dangerous Liaisons, 1989; The Grifters, 1990. *Recreation:* reading. *Address:* Casarotto Co., National House, 60 Wardour Street, W1. *T:* 071–287 4450.

FREDE, Prof. Michael, Dr.phil; Professor of the History of Philosophy, and Fellow of Keble College, Oxford University, since 1991; *b* Berlin, 31 May 1940. *Educ:* Univ. of Göttingen (Dr.phil 1966). Philosophy Res. Assistant, Univ. of Göttingen, 1966–71; Loeb Fellow, Harvard Univ., 1971; University of California at Berkeley: Vis. Lectr, 1968–69; Asst, then Associate, Professor of Philosophy, 1971–74; Prof. of Philosophy, 1974–76; Princeton University: Prof. of Philosophy, 1976–89; Stewart Prof. of Philosophy, 1989–91. *Publication:* Essays in Ancient Philosophy, 1987. *Address:* Keble College, Oxford OX1 3PG.

FREDERICK, Sir Charles Boscawen, 10th Bt *cr* 1723; *b* 11 April 1919; *s* of Sir Edward Boscawen Frederick, 9th Bt, CVO and Edith Katherine (Kathleen) Cortlandt (*d* 1970), *d* of late Col W. H. Mulloy, RE; *S* father, 1956; *m* 1949, Rosemary, *er d* of late Lt-Col R. J. H. Baddeley, MC; two *s* two *d*. *Educ:* Eton. 2nd Lieut Grenadier Guards, 1942; served N Africa and Italy, 1943–45 (despatches); Capt. 1945; Palestine, 1946–47 (despatches); Malaya, 1948–49; Egypt, 1952–53; Major, 1953. Member: London Stock Exchange, 1954–62; Provincial Brokers Stock Exchange, 1962 (Mem. Council, 1966; Dep. Chm. 1972); Stock Exchange Council, and Chm., Provincial Unit, 1973–75. JP 1960. General Commissioner of Income Tax, 1966. *Heir: s* Christopher St John Frederick [*b* 28 June 1950; *m* 1990, Camilla, *o d* of Sir Derek Gilbey, *qv*]. *Address:* Virginia Cottage, Stoke Trister, Wincanton, Somerset BA9 9PQ.

FREDERICTON, Bishop of, since 1989; **Rt. Rev. George Colborne Lemmon;** *b* 20 March 1932; *m* 1957, Lois Jean Foster; two *s* one *d*. *Educ:* Univ. of New Brunswick (BA 1959); Wycliffe Coll., Toronto (LTh 1962; BD 1965). Linotype operator, Globe Print, Telegraph Jl, Toronto Telegram, 1949–62. Deacon 1962, priest 1963; incumbent, Canterbury with Benton, 1962; Rector of: Wilmot with Wicklow and Peel, 1965; Renforth, 1969; Sackville with Dorchester, dio. of Fredericton, 1972–84; Christ Church, Fredericton, 1984–89; Canon of Fredericton. Hon. DD: King's Coll., Halifax, 1990; Wycliffe Coll., Toronto, 1991. *Recreation:* golfing. *Address:* Diocesan Office, 115 Church Street, Fredericton, New Brunswick E3B 4C8, Canada. *T:* (506) 459 1801.

FREEDBERG, Prof. David Adrian; Professor of Art History, Columbia University, since 1984; *b* 1 June 1948; *s* of William Freedberg and Eleonore Kupfer; *m*; one *d*. *Educ:* S African Coll. High Sch., Cape Town; Yale Univ. (BA); Balliol Coll., Oxford (DPhil). Rhodes Scholar, Oxford, 1969–72; Lectr in History of Art: Westfield Coll., Univ. of London, 1973–76; Courtauld Inst. of Art, Univ. of London, 1976–84; Slade Prof. of Fine Art, Univ. of Oxford, 1983–84. Baldwin Prof., Oberlin Coll., Ohio, 1979; Vis. Mem., Inst. for Advanced Study, Princeton, NJ, 1980–81; Gerson Lectr, Univ. of Groningen, 1983; VUB-Leerstoel, Brussels Univ., 1988–89. *Publications:* Dutch Landscape Prints of the Seventeenth Century, 1980; The Life of Christ after the Passion (Corpus Rubenianum Ludwig Burchard, VII), 1983; Iconoclasts and their Motives, 1985; The Power of Images, 1989; (ed) The Prints of Pieter Bruegel the Elder, 1989; articles in Burlington Magazine, Revue de l'Art, Gentse Bijdragen, Münchner Jahrbuch der Bildenden Kunst, Jl of Warburg and Courtauld Insts, Print Quarterly, Quaderni Puteani. *Address:* Department of Art History, Columbia University, Schermerhorn Hall, New York, NY 10027, USA.

FREEDMAN, Amelia, (Mrs Michael Miller), MBE 1989; FRAM 1986; Artistic Director and Founder, Nash Ensemble, since 1964; *b* 21 Nov. 1940; *d* of Miriam Freedman (*née* Claret) and Henry Freedman; *m* 1970, Michael Miller; two *s* one *d*. *Educ:* St George's Sch., Harpenden; Henrietta Barnet, London; RAM. LRAM (piano), ARCM (clarinet). Music teacher, 1961–65: King's Sch., Cambridge; Perse Sch. for Girls, Cambridge; Chorleywood College for the Blind; Sir Philip Magnus Sch., London. Artistic Dir, Bath Internat. Fest., 1984–; Musical Adviser, Israel Fest., 1989–. Chevalier, L'ordre des Arts et des Lettres (France), 1984; Czech Govt Medal for services to Czech music in UK, 1986. *Recreations:* theatre, cinema, ballet, opera; spectator sport—cricket, rugger, football; stamp-collecting, children. *Address:* 14 Cedars Close, Hendon, NW4 1TR. *T:* 081–203 3025.

FREEDMAN, Charles, CB 1983; Commissioner, Customs and Excise, 1972–84; *b* 15 Oct. 1925; *s* of late Solomon Freedman, OBE, and Lilian Freedman; *m* 1949, Sarah Sadie King; one *s* two *d*. *Educ:* Westcliff High Sch.; Cheltenham Grammar Sch.; Trinity Coll., Cambridge (Sen. Schol., BA). Entered HM Customs and Excise, 1947; Asst Sec., 1963. *Address:* 10 Cliff Avenue, Leigh-on-Sea, Essex SS9 1HF. *T:* Southend-on-Sea (0702) 73148. *Club:* Civil Service.

FREEDMAN, Dawn Angela, (Mrs N. J. Shestopal); Her Honour Judge Freedman; a Circuit Judge, since 1991; *b* 9 Dec. 1942; *d* of Julius and Celia Freedman; *m* 1970, Neil John Shestopal. *Educ:* Westcliff High Sch. for Girls; University Coll., London (LLB Hons). Called to the Bar, Gray's Inn, 1966; Metropolitan Stipendiary Magistrate, 1980–91; a Recorder, 1989–91. *Recreations:* theatre, television, cooking. *Address:* 3 Gray's Inn Square, Gray's Inn, WC1R 5AH. *T:* 071–242 0328.

FREEDMAN, Prof. Lawrence David, DPhil; Professor of War Studies, King's College, London, since 1982; *b* 7 Dec. 1948; *s* of late Lt-Comdr Julius Freedman and of Myra

Freedman; *m* 1974, Judith Anne Hill; one *s* one *d*. *Educ:* Whitley Bay Grammar Sch. BAEcon Manchester; BPhil York; DPhil Oxford. Teaching Asst, York Univ., 1971–72; Research Fellow, Nuffield Coll., Oxford, 1974–75; Research Associate, International Inst. for Strategic Studies, 1975–76 (Mem. Council, 1984–); Research Fellow, Royal Inst. of International Affairs, 1976–78; Head of Policy Studies, RIIA, 1978–82. Hon. Dir, Centre for Defence Studies, 1990–. *Publications:* US Intelligence and the Soviet Strategic Threat, 1977, 2nd edn 1986; Britain and Nuclear Weapons, 1980; The Evolution of Nuclear Strategy, 1981; (jtly) Nuclear War & Nuclear Peace, 1983, 2nd edn 1989; (ed) The Troubled Alliance, 1983; The Atlas of Global Strategy, 1985; The Price of Peace, 1986; Britain and the Falklands War, 1988; (jtly) Signals of War, 1990. *Recreations:* tennis, political caricature. *Address:* c/o Department of War Studies, King's College, Strand, WC2R 2LS. *T:* 071–873 2025.

FREEDMAN, Louis, CBE 1978; Proprietor, Cliveden Stud; *b* 5 Feb. 1917; 4th *s* of Sampson and Leah Freedman; *m* 1st, 1944, Cara Kathlyn Abrahamson (marr. diss.); one *s* one *d*; 2nd, 1960, Valerie Clarke; one *s*. *Educ:* University College School. FSVA. TA, RE, 1938; commnd RA, 1943; Devonshire Regt, 1944. Director: Land Securities Investment Trust, 1958–77; GRA Gp, then Wembley PLC, 1985–. Mem., Race Relations Bd, 1968–77. Chm., Nat. Assoc. Property Owners, 1971–72; Pres., Racehorse Owners Assoc., 1972–74. Vice-Chm., NE Thames RHA, 1975–79; Chairman: Camden and Islington AHA, 1979–82; City and Hackney DHA, 1982–84. Governor, Royal Hosp. of St Bartholomew the Great, 1971–; Special Trustee, St Bartholomew's Hosp., 1974– (Chm., 1988–). Owned and bred: Polygamy, winner of the Oaks, 1974; Reference Point, winner of the Derby, King George VI and Queen Elizabeth Stakes, and the St Leger, 1987. *Recreation:* gardening. *Address:* Cliveden Stud House, Taplow, Maidenhead, Berks SL6 0HL. *Clubs:* Garrick; Jockey (Newmarket) (Deputy Senior Steward, 1981–83).

FREEDMAN, Hon. Samuel; Chief Justice of Manitoba, 1971–83; Counsel to Aikins, MacAulay & Thorvaldson; *b* Russia, 1908; *s* of Nathan Freedman and Ada (*née* Foxman); came to Canada, 1911; *m* 1934, Claris Brownie Udow; one *s* two *d*. *Educ:* Winnipeg schs; Univ. of Manitoba. BA 1929, LLB 1933. Called to Manitoba Bar, 1933; KC (Canada) 1944; Judge, Court of Queen's Bench, Manitoba, 1952, Court of Appeal 1960. Chancellor, Univ. of Manitoba, 1959–68; Pres., Manitoba Bar Assoc., 1951–52; Mem. Bd of Governors, Hebrew Univ., Jerusalem, 1955–; Chm., Rhodes Scholarship Selection Cttee, Manitoba, 1956–66; Pres., Medico-Legal Soc. of Manitoba, 1954–55; Mem. Adv. Bd, Centre of Criminology, Univ. of Toronto; Mem. Bd of Dirs, Confedn Centre of the Arts in Charlottetown; one-man Industrial Inquiry Commn, CNR run-throughs, 1964–65. Holds numerous hon. degrees. *Publications:* Report of Industrial Inquiry Commission on Canadian National Railways Run-Throughs, 1965; (chapter) Admissions and Confessions, in, Studies in Canadian Criminal Evidence, ed Salhany and Carter, 1972; contrib. Canadian Bar Review. *Recreations:* walking, golf, reading. *Address:* (office) 30th Floor, Commodity Exchange Tower, Winnipeg, Manitoba R3L 4G1, Canada. *Club:* Glendale Country (Winnipeg).

FREELAND, Sir John Redvers, KCMG 1984 (CMG 1973); QC 1987; HM Diplomatic Service, retired; Judge, Arbitral Tribunal and Mixed Commission for Agreement on German External Debts, since 1988; Judge, European Court of Human Rights, since 1991; *b* 16 July 1927; *o s* of C. Redvers Freeland and Freda Freeland (*née* Walker); *m* 1952, Sarah Mary, *er d* of late S. Pascoe Hayward, QC; one *s* one *d*. *Educ:* Stowe; Corpus Christi Coll., Cambridge. Royal Navy, 1945 and 1948–51. Called to Bar, Lincoln's Inn, 1952, Bencher, 1985; Mem. *ad eundem*, Middle Temple. Asst Legal Adviser, FO, 1954–63, and 1965–67; Legal Adviser, HM Embassy, Bonn, 1963–65; Legal Counsellor, FCO (formerly FO), 1967–70; Counsellor (Legal Advr), UK Mission to UN, NY, 1970–73; Legal Counsellor, FCO, 1973–76; Second Legal Advr, 1976–84, Legal Advr, 1984–87, FCO. Agent of UK govt, cases before European Commn of Human Rights, 1966–70. Mem., US-Chile Internat. Commn of Investigation, 1989–. Member: Exec. Cttee, David Davies Meml Inst. of Internat. Studies, 1974–; Council of Management, British Inst. of Internat. and Comparative Law, 1984–87; Cttee of Management, Inst. of Advanced Legal Studies, 1984–87. *Address:* 1 Point House, 18 West Grove, SE10 8QR. *Club:* Travellers'.

FREELAND, Mary Graham; *see* McGeown, M. G.

FREELING, Nicolas; writer since 1960; *b* 1927, of English parents; *m* 1954, Cornelia Termes; four *s* one *d*. *Educ:* primary and secondary schs. Hotel-restaurant cook, throughout Europe, 1945–60; novelist, 1960–. *Publications:* (numerous trans.) Love in Amsterdam, 1961; Because of the Cats, 1962; Gun before Butter, 1962; Valparaiso, 1963; Double Barrel, 1963; Criminal Conversation, 1964; King of the Rainy Country, 1965; Dresden Green, 1966; Strike Out Where Not Applicable, 1967; This is the Castle, 1968; Tsing-Boum, 1969; Kitchen Book, 1970; Over the High Side, 1971; Cook Book, 1971; A Long Silence, 1972; Dressing of Diamond, 1974; What Are the Bugles Blowing For?, 1975; Lake Isle, 1976; Gadget, 1977; The Night Lords, 1978; The Widow, 1979; Castang's City, 1980; One Damn Thing After Another, 1981; Wolfnight, 1982; Back of the North Wind, 1983; No Part in Your Death, 1984; A City Solitary, 1985; Cold Iron, 1986; Lady Macbeth, 1987; Not as far as Velma, 1989; Sandcastles, 1989; Those in Peril, 1990; The Flanders Sky, 1991. *Address:* Grandfontaine, 67130 Schirmeck, France.

FREEMAN, Catherine; Founder Director, Dove Productions, since 1989; Director, One World Broadcasting Trust, since 1990; *b* 10 Aug. 1931; *d* of Harold Dove and Eileen Carroll; *m* 1st, 1958, Charles Wheeler, *qv*; 2nd, 1962, John Freeman, *qv*; two *s* one *d*. *Educ:* Convent of the Assumption; St Anne's Coll., Oxford (MA Hons). Joined BBC as trainee producer, 1954; Producer/director: Panorama, Brains Trust, Monitor, Press Conference, 1954–58; joined Thames Television as Sen. Producer in Features Dept, 1976; Editor, Daytime progs, 1976–82; originator and series producer of Citizen 2000 for Channel 4; Controller, Documentaries, Features and Religion, 1982–86; Controller, Features and Religion, 1986–89. Member: Devlin Cttee on Identification Procedures, 1974–76; Literature Panel, Arts Council, 1981–84; Broadcasting, Film and Video panel, Arts Council, 1986–88. Dir, ICA, 1983–. *Address:* 2 Chalcot Crescent, NW1 8YD.

FREEMAN, David Charles; Founder/Director of Opera Factory; freelance opera and theatre director; *b* 1 May 1952; *s* of Howard Wilfred Freeman and Ruth Adair Nott; *m* 1985, Marie Angel; one *d*. *Educ:* Sydney Univ., NSW (BA Hons). Opera Factory Sydney, 1973–76; Opera Factory Zürich, 1976–: directed 19 prodns, appearing in 5, writing the text of 3; Opera Factory London, 1981–: directed 15 prodns (7 televised by Channel Four), writing text of one; Associate Artist, ENO, 1981–: prodns include world première of The Mask of Orpheus, 1986; directed: Goethe's Faust, Pts I and II, Lyric, Hammersmith, 1988; (also adapted) Malory's Morte d'Arthur, Lyric, Hammersmith, 1990; opera prodns in New York, Houston, Paris and Germany. Chevalier de l'Ordre des Arts et des Lettres, France, 1985.

FREEMAN, David John; Founder, 1952, and Senior Partner, 1952–March 1992, D. J. Freeman & Co., Solicitors, subseq. Consultant; *b* 25 Feb. 1928; *s* of late Meyer Henry and Rebecca Freeman; *m* 1950, Iris Margaret Alberge; two *s* one *d*. *Educ:* Christ's Coll., Finchley. Lieut, Army, 1946–48. Admitted Solicitor, 1952. Dept of Trade Inspector into the affairs of AEG Telefunken (UK) Ltd, and Credit Collections Ltd, 1977. Governor, Royal Shakespeare Theatre, 1979–. *Recreations:* reading, theatre, gardening. *Address:* 43 Fetter Lane, EC4. *T:* 071-583 4055. *Clubs:* Reform; Huntercombe Golf.

FREEMAN, (Edgar) James (Albert), MC 1945; Regional Chairman of Industrial Tribunals, Bury St Edmunds, 1984–90; *b* 31 Dec. 1917; *yr s* of Horace Freeman and Beatrice Mary Freeman, Cricklewood; *m* 1948, Shirley Lake Whatmough (*d* 1988), *d* of William Henry Whatmough, PhD, and Agnes Caroline Whatmough, Streatham; one *s* two *d*. *Educ:* Westminster Sch.; Trinity Coll., Cambridge (BA). Served in DLI, UK, India and Burma, 1940–46. Called to Bar, Lincoln's Inn, 1947; practised Chancery Bar, 1947–72; Vice-Pres., Value Added Tax Tribunals (England and Wales), 1972–90; full-time Chm. of Industrial Tribunals, 1975–90. *Recreations:* sailing, cycling. *Address:* 45 Nightingale Avenue, Cambridge CB1 4SG. *Clubs:* Royal Cruising, Bar Yacht.

FREEMAN, Dr Ernest Allan, CEng, FIEE, FIMA; Director, Trent Polytechnic, 1981–83; *b* 16 Jan. 1932; *s* of William Freeman and Margaret Sinclair; *m* 1954, Mary Jane Peterson; two *d*. *Educ:* Sunderland Technical Coll.; King's Coll., Univ. of Durham (Mather Scholarship, 1955–57). BSc, PhD, Durham; DSc Newcastle upon Tyne; MA (Oxon) 1972. Sunderland Forge & Engineering Co. Ltd. 1949–55; English Electric Co., 1957–58; Ferranti Ltd (Edinburgh), 1958–59; Sunderland Polytechnic: Dir of Research, 1959–65; Head of Control Engrg Dept, 1965–72; Rector, 1976–80; Tutor and Fellow in Engrg, St Edmund Hall, Oxford Univ., 1972–76. FRSA. *Publications:* contribs mainly in the fields of control engrg, systems theory and computing, to Wireless Engr, Proc. IEE (Heaviside Prize, 1974), Jl of Electronics and Control, Trans AIEE, Electronic Technol., Control, Jl of Optimisation Theory and Application, Trans Soc. of Instrument Technol., Proc. Internat. Fedn for Analogue Computation, Internat. Jl of Control. *Recreations:* swimming, browsing around antique shops. *Address:* 12 Rolfe Place, Headington, Oxford OX3 0DS.

FREEMAN, Prof. Ernest Michael, PhD; FEng 1987; Professor of Applied Electromagnetics, Imperial College of Science, Technology and Medicine, London University, since 1980; *b* 10 Nov. 1937; *s* of Ernest Robert Freeman and Agnes Maud Freeman; *m* 1987, Helen Anne Rigby. *Educ:* Colfe's Grammar Sch., Lewisham; King's Coll., London (BScEng; PhD 1964). Lectr, King's Coll., London, 1960–63 and 1966–70; Engrg Designer, AEI, Rugby, 1964–65; Reader: Brighton Polytechnic, 1970–73; Imperial Coll. of Science and Technology, 1973–80. Chm., Infolytica Ltd, 1978–; Vice Pres., Infolytica Corp., 1978–. *Publications:* papers in learned society jls on magnetics. *Recreations:* photography, military history, art, aristology. *Address:* Electrical Engineering Department, Imperial College of Science, Technology and Medicine, Exhibition Road, SW7 2BT. *T:* 071-584 5413.

FREEMAN, George Vincent; Under-Secretary (Legal), Treasury Solicitor's Department, 1973–76, retired; *b* 30 April 1911; *s* of Harold Vincent Freeman and Alice Freeman; *m* 1945, Margaret Nightingale; one *d*. *Educ:* Denstone Coll., Rocester. Admitted Solicitor, 1934; in private practice Birmingham until 1940. Served RN, 1940–46, Lieut RNVR. Legal Asst, Treasury Solicitor's Dept, 1946; Sen. Legal Asst 1950; Asst Treasury Solicitor 1964. *Recreations:* gardening, photography. *Address:* 8 Shelley Close, Ashley Heath, Ringwood, Hants BH24 2JA. *T:* Ringwood (0425) 477102. *Clubs:* Civil Service; Conservative (Ringwood).

FREEMAN, Harold Webber; Author; *b* 1899; *s* of Charles Albert Freeman and Emma Mary Ann Mills; *m* Elizabeth Boedecker. *Educ:* City of London Sch.; Christ Church, Oxford (classical scholar). 1st class Hon. Mods, 2nd class Lit. Hum. Main background was work on the land, mostly organic gardening; travelled in Europe (foot and bicycle); casual work as linguist (translation, monitoring, travel trade). Has lived mostly in Suffolk, but also, for long periods, in Italy. *Publications:* Joseph and His Brethren, 1928; Down in the Valley, 1930; Fathers of Their People, 1932; Pond Hall's Progress, 1933; Hester and Her Family, 1936; Andrew to the Lions, 1938; Chaffinch's, 1941; Blenheim Orange, 1949; The Poor Scholar's Tale, 1954; Round the Island: Sardinia Re-explored, 1956. *Address:* c/o National Westminster Bank, 2 Tavern Street, Ipswich.

FREEMAN, Hugh Lionel, FRCPsych; FFCM; Hon. Consultant Psychiatrist, Salford Health Authority, University of Manchester School of Medicine, since 1988 (Consultant Psychiatrist, 1961–88); Visiting Fellow, Green College, Oxford, 1986; *b* Salford, 4 Aug. 1929; *s* of late Bernard Freeman, FBOA and Dora Doris Freeman (*née* Kahn); *m* 1957, Sally Joan, MEd, PhD, FBPsS, *er d* of Philip and late Rebecca Casket; three *s* one *d*. *Educ:* Altrincham Grammar Sch.; St John's Coll., Oxford (open schol.; BM BCh 1954; MA; DM 1988); MSc Salford 1980. DPM 1958; FRCPsych 1971; FFCM 1989. Captain, RAMC, 1956–58. House Surg., Manchester Royal Inf., 1955; Registrar, Bethlem Royal and Maudsley Hosps, 1958–60; Sen. Registrar, Littlemore Hosp., Oxford, 1960–61; Consltnt Psychiatrist, Salford Royal Hosp., 1961–70; Hon. Consultant Psychiatrist: Salford Health Dept, 1961–74; Salford Social Services Dept, 1974–88. Hon. Med. Consultant, NAMH, 1963–74. Consultant Psychiatrist, NW Reg., DHSS, 1963–88; Med. Advisor, NW Fellowship for Schizophrenia, 1980–88. Chairman: Psychiatric Sub-Cttee, NW Reg. Med. Adv. Cttee, 1978–83; Area Med. Cttee and Med. Exec. Cttee, Salford AHA, 1974–78. University of Manchester: pt-time Lectr, 1973–88; Mem., Univ. Court, 1989–; Hon. Res. Fellow, UC and Middlesex Sch. of Medicine, 1989. Visiting Professor: Univ. of WI, 1970; Univ. of WA, 1990; Rockefeller Foundn Vis. Fellow, Italy, 1980. Examiner: Univ. of Manchester; RCPsych. Med. Mem., Mental Health Rev. Tribunal, 1982. Member: Sex Educn Panel, Health Educn Council, 1968–72; Working Party on Behaviour Control, Council for Sci. and Society, 1973–76; Minister of State's Panel on Private Practice, DHSS, 1974–75; UK Delgn to EC Conf. on Mental Health in Cities, Milan, 1980; Mental Health Act Commn, 1983–84; Home Sec's Wking Party on Fear of Crime, 1989; Historic Building Panel, City of Manchester, 1981–89. WHO Consultant: Grenada, 1970; Chile, 1978; Philippines, 1979; Bangladesh, 1981; Greece, 1985; Rapporteur: WHO Conf. on Mental Health Services in Pilot Study Areas, Trieste, 1984; WHO Workshop on Nat. Mental Health Progs, Ruanda, 1985; Council of Europe conf. on Health in Cities, 1985. Editor, British Jl of Clin. and Social Psych., 1982–84; Dep. Editor, Internat. Jl of Social Psych., 1980–83; Editor: British Jl of Psych., 1983– (Asst Editor, 1978–83); Current Opinion in Psychiatry, 1988–; Co-Editor, Bull. of RCPsych, 1983; Associate Editor, Internat. Jl of Mental Health, 1981–. Mem. Internat. Res. Seminars, US National Inst. of Mental Health: Washington, 1966; Pisa, 1977; has lectured to and addressed univs, confs and hosps worldwide; advr on and participant in radio and TV progs. Exec. Cttees, Royal Medico-Psychol Assoc., 1965–69; Exec. Cttee, Soc. of Clin. Psychs. Royal College of Psychiatrists: Foundn Mem., 1971; Mem. Council, 1983–; Chm., Journal Cttee; Vice-Chm., Social and Community Gp; External Assessor; FRSH (Hon. Sec., Mental Health Gp, 1973–76; Vice-Chm., 1983–87). Mem., Council, MIND, 1987–91. Corresp. Member: US Assoc. for Clinical Psychosociol Res.; US Assoc. for Behavioral Therapies; Hon. Member: Chilean Soc. of Psych., Neurol. and Neurosurgery; Egyptian Psychiatric Assoc.; Polish Psychiatric Assoc., 1986; Senior Common Room, Pembroke Coll., Oxford, 1981; Hon. Life Mem., Soc. of Clinical Psychiatrists, 1985. Vice-Chm., Manchester Heritage Trust, 1983–89; Mem., Mercian Regional Cttee, NT, 1986–. Hon. Professorial Fellow, Salford Univ., 1986. Freeman, City of London; Liveryman, Soc. of Apothecaries, 1984 (Yeoman, 1979–84). Distinguished Service Commendation, US Nat. Council of Community Mental Health Centers, 1982.

Publications: (ed jtly) Trends in the Mental Health Services, 1963; (ed) Psychiatric Hospital Care, 1965; (ed jtly) New Aspects of the Mental Health Service, 1968; (ed) Progress in Behaviour Therapy, 1969; Mental Health and the Environment, 1985; (jtly) Mental Health Services in Europe, 1985; (ed jtly) Mental Health Services in Britain: the way ahead, 1985; (ed jtly) Interaction between Mental and Physical Illness, 1989; (ed jtly) Community Psychiatry, 1991; (ed jtly) 150 Years of British Psychiatry, 1991; contribs to national press and learned jls. *Recreations:* architecture, travel, music. *Address:* 21 Montagu Square, W1H 1RE. *Clubs:* United Oxford & Cambridge University, Whitefriars.

FREEMAN, James; *see* Freeman, E. J. A.

FREEMAN, Sir James Robin, 3rd Bt *cr* 1945; *S* father, 1981. *Heir:* none.

FREEMAN, Rt. Hon. John, PC 1966; MBE 1943; Visiting Professor of International Relations, University of California, Davis, since 1985. *Educ:* Westminster Sch.; Brasenose College, Oxford (Hon. Fellow, 1968). Active service, 1940–45. MP (Lab) Watford Div. of Herts, 1945–50; Borough of Watford, 1950–55; PPS to Sec. of State for War, 1945–46; Financial Sec., War Office, 1946; Parly Under Sec. of State for War, April 1947; Leader, UK Defence Mission to Burma, 1947; Parly Sec., Min. of Supply, 1947–51, resigned. Asst Editor, New Statesman, 1951–58; Deputy Editor, 1958–60; Editor, 1961–65. British High Commissioner in India, 1965–68; British Ambassador in Washington, 1969–71. Chairman: London Weekend Television Ltd, 1971–84; LWT (Holdings) plc, 1976–84; Page & Moy (Holdings) Ltd, 1976–84; Hutchinson Ltd, 1978–82 (Director till 1984); ITN, 1976–81. Governor, BFI, 1976–82. Vice-Pres., Royal Television Soc., 1975–85 (Gold Medal, 1981). *Address:* c/o Barclay's Bank, 58 Southampton Row, WC1B 4AT.

FREEMAN, John Allen, OBE 1958; PhD; FRES, CBiol, FIBiol; Director, Ministry of Agriculture, Fisheries and Food's Pest Infestation Control Laboratory, 1977–79; *b* 30 Sept. 1912; *s* of Laurence Freeman and Maggie Rentoul Freeman; *m* 1945, Hilda Mary Jackson; one *s* one *d. Educ:* City of London Sch. (Jun. Corp. Scholar, Travers Scholar); Imperial Coll. of Science and Technol., London Univ. (BSc Special 1st Cl. Hons 1933, PhD 1938). ARCS; FRES 1943; FIBiol 1963. Min. of Agric. Scholar in Entomology, 1934–37; Hull University Coll., 1934–35; Rothamsted Exper. Stn, 1936; Cornell Univ., USA, 1936–37; Vineland Exper. Stn, Ont, Canadian Dept of Agric., 1937. Res. Asst, Imp. Coll., London, 1938–40; Jun. Scientific Officer, Dept of Science and Indust. Res. Pest Infestation Lab., 1940; seconded Min. of Food Infest. Control, 1940–47; Chief Entomologist, 1944; Sen. Sci. Officer, 1946; transf. Min. of Agric., 1947; Principal Sci. Off., 1947; seconded OECD, 1954–55, and CENTO, 1957–58; Sen. Principal Sci. Off., 1958; Dep. Chief Sci. Off., and Dep. Dir Pest Infest. Control Lab., 1971; Chief Sci. Off., 1977. Member: British Ecol Soc.; Assoc. of Applied Biol. Treasurer, Royal Entomol Soc. of London, 1977–84; Hon. Treas., Inst. of Biol, 1965–69. Pres., Royal Coll. of Science Union and Imp. Coll. Union, 1934. Has travelled professionally in N and S America, Europe, Africa, ME and Far East. Freeman of City of London, 1947. *Publications:* scientific articles, mainly on pests of stored foods. *Recreations:* gardening, photography, travel, DIY. *Address:* 5 Woodmere Way, Park Langley, Beckenham, Kent BR3 2SJ. *T:* 081–658 6970.

FREEMAN, John Anthony, FCA; Managing Director, Home Service (formerly UK Individual) Division, Prudential Corporation plc, since 1984; *b* 27 May 1937; *o s* of late John Eric Freeman and Dorothy Mabel Freeman; *m* 1st, 1965, Judith Dixon (marr. diss. 1984); one *s* one *d*; 2nd, 1986, Margaret Joyce (*née* Langdon-Ellis). *Educ:* Queen Elizabeth Grammar Sch., Mansfield; Birmingham Univ. (BCom). FCA 1961; FCMA 1974. Mellors Basden & Mellors, Chartered Accountants, 1958–62; Peat Marwick Mitchell, Chartered Accountants, 1962–73; National Freight Corp., 1973–77; Prudential Corp., 1977–. *Recreations:* golf, gardening, music. *Address:* 142 Holborn Bars, EC1N 2NH. *T:* 071-334 6011.

FREEMAN, Joseph William, OBE 1968; Director of Social Service, Leeds, 1970–78; *b* 8 April 1914; *s* of Thomas and Emma Freeman; *m* 1st, 1939, Louise King (*d* 1986); one *s* one *d*; 2nd, 1988, Marilyn Frances Hutchinson (*née* Gamble). *Educ:* Liverpool Univ. (Dip. Soc. Sci.); Toynbee Hall; Open Univ. (BA 1983). CQSW 1970. Qual. social worker; Probation Service, Birmingham, 1938; served War of 1939–45: Army, 1940, commnd RA, 1941; Probation Service, Liverpool, 1946; Children's Officer: Warrington, 1948; Bolton, 1951; Sheffield, 1955. Church organist. *Publications:* papers in social work jls. *Recreations:* music, fell-walking. *Address:* 15 Fairfield Gardens, Crank Road, St Helens WA11 7SL.

FREEMAN, Dr Marie Joyce, FFCM; Health Service Management Consultant, since 1988; *b* 14 April 1934; *d* of Wilfrid George Croxson and Ada Mildred (*née* Chiles); *m* 1958, Samuel Anthony Freeman (decd); one *s. Educ:* Royal Free Hospital Sch. of Medicine (MB BS, DPH). Specialist in Community Medicine, Avon AHA, 1974; District MO, Southmead HA, 1982; Actg Regl MD, SW RHA, 1986–88. *Recreations:* making reproduction antique dolls, embroidery, gardening. *Address:* Hadfield House, Darlington Place, Bath BA2 6BY. *T:* Bath (0225) 466670.

FREEMAN, Michael Alexander Reykers, MD; FRCS; Consultant Orthopaedic Surgeon, The London Hospital, since 1968; *b* 17 Nov. 1931; *s* of Donald George and Florence Julia Freeman; *m* 1st, 1951, Elisabeth Jean; one *s* one *d*; 2nd, 1959, Janet Edith; one *s* one *d*; 3rd, 1968, Patricia; one *d* (and one *s* decd). *Educ:* Stowe Sch.; Corpus Christi Coll., Cambridge (open scholarship and closed exhibn); London Hospital Med. Coll. BA (1st cl. hons), MB BCh, MD (Cantab). FRCS 1959. Trained in medicine and surgery, London Hosp., and in orthopaedic and traumatic surgery, London, Westminster and Middlesex Hosps; co-founder, Biomechanics Unit, Imperial Coll., London, 1964; Cons. Surg. in Orth. and Traum. Surgery, London Hosp., also Res. Fellow, Imperial Coll., 1968; resigned from Imperial Coll., to devote more time to clinical activities, 1979. Special surgical interest in field of reconstructive surgery in lower limb, concentrating on joint replacement; originator of new surgical procedures for reconstruction and replacement of arthritic hip, knee, ankle and joints of foot; has lectured and demonstrated surgery, Canada, USA, Brazil, Japan, China, Australia, S Africa, continental Europe; guest speaker at nat. and internat. profess. congresses. Robert Jones Lectr, RCS, 1989. Member: BMA; Amer. Acad. Orth. Surgs; Orth. Res. Soc.; Soc. Internat. Chirurg. Orth. and Traum.; RSM; Health Unit, IEA; Past Member: Scientific Co-ordinating Cttee, ARC; MRC; Clin. Res. Bd, London Hosp. Bd of Governors; Brent and Harrow AHA; DHSS working parties. President: Internat. Hip Soc., 1982–85; British Hip Soc., 1989–; Vice-Pres., British Orthopaedic Soc., 1990–. Bacon and Cunning Prizes and Copeman Medal, CCC; Andrew Clark and T. A. M. Ross Prize in Clin. Med., London Hosp. Med. Coll.; Robert Jones Medal, Brit. Orth. Assoc. *Publications:* editor and part-author: Adult Articular Cartilage, 1973, 2nd edn 1979; Scientific Basis of Joint Replacement, 1977; Arthritis of the Knee, 1980; chapters in: Bailey and Love's Short Practice of Surgery; Mason and Currey's Textbook of Rheumatology; papers in Proc. Royal Soc., Jl Bone and Joint Surgery, and med. jls. *Recreations:* gardening, reading, surgery. *Address:* 79 Albert Street, NW1. *T:* 071–387 0817.

FREEMAN, Paul, ARCS, DSc (London), FRES; Keeper of Entomology, British Museum (Natural History), 1968–81; *b* 26 May 1916; *s* of Samuel Mellor Freeman and Kate

Burgis; *m* 1942, Audrey Margaret Long; two *d. Educ:* Brentwood Sch., Essex; Imperial Coll., London. Demonstrator in Entomology, Imperial Coll., 1938. Captain, RA and Army Operational Research Group, 1940–45. Lecturer in Entomology, Imperial Coll., 1945–47. Asst Keeper, Dept of Entomology, British Museum (Nat. Hist.), 1947–64, Dep. Keeper, 1964–68, Keeper, 1968. Royal Entomological Soc. of London: Vice-Pres., 1956, 1957; Hon. Sec., 1958–62; Hon. Fellow, 1984. Sec., XIIth Internat. Congress of Entomology, London, 1964. *Publications:* Diptera of Patagonia and South Chile, Pt III-Mycetophilidae, 1951; Simuliidae of the Ethiopian Region (with Botha de Meillon), 1953; numerous papers in learned jls, on taxonomy of Hemiptera and Diptera. *Recreations:* gardening, natural history. *Address:* Briardene, 75 Towncourt Crescent, Petts Wood, Orpington, Kent BR5 1PH. *T:* Orpington (0689) 827296.

FREEMAN, Paul Illife, PhD; Controller and Chief Executive of HM Stationery Office, and the Queen's Printer of Acts of Parliament, since 1989; *s* of late John Percy Freeman and of Hilda Freeman; *m* 1959, Enid Ivy May Freeman; one *s* one *d. Educ:* Victoria University of Manchester (BSc (Hons) Chemistry, PhD). Post Doctoral Fellow, Nat. Research Council of Canada, 1959–61; Research Scientist, Dupont De Nemours Co. Ltd, Wilmington, Del, USA, 1961–64; Nat. Physical Laboratory: Sen. Scientific Officer, 1964–70; Principal Scientific Officer, 1970–74; Exec. Officer, Research Requirements Bds, DoI, 1973–77; Director: Computer Aided Design Centre, 1977–83; National Engrg Lab., 1980–83; Central Computer and Telecommunications Agency, HM Treasury, 1983–88. Member: CS Coll. Adv. Council, 1983–; Bd, NCC, 1983–88; Bd, DVLA, 1990–. Vis. Prof. Univ. of Strathclyde, 1981–86. *Publications:* scientific papers. *Recreations:* reading, walking, gardening. *Address:* 12 Broadway, Wilburton, Ely, Cambridgeshire CB6 3RT. *T:* Ely (0353) 740576.

FREEMAN, Sir Ralph, Kt 1970; CVO 1964; CBE 1952 (MBE (mil.) 1945); FEng; FICE; FASCE; FWeldI; retired consulting engineer; Senior Partner, Freeman, Fox & Partners, 1963–79, (Partner, 1947–79); *b* 3 Feb. 1911; *s* of late Sir Ralph Freeman and late Mary (*née* Lines); *m* 1939, Joan Elizabeth, *er d* of late Col J. G. Rose, DSO, VD, FRIC, Wynberg, Cape, S Africa; two *s* one *d. Educ:* Uppingham Sch.; Worcester Coll., Oxford (MA; Hon. Fellow, 1980). Construction Engineer: Dorman Long & Co., S Africa, Rhodesia and Denmark, 1932–36 and 1937–39; Braithwaite & Co., 1936–37; on staff of Freeman, Fox & Partners, 1939–46, Admty and other war work; served RE, 1943–45 (Temp. Major) at Exp. Bridging Estab. and later seconded as bridging adviser to CE 21 Army Gp HQ, NW Europe campaign. Consulting Engr to the Queen for Sandringham Estate, 1949–76. Past Pres., Instn of Civil Engrs (Mem. Council, 1951–55 and 1957–61, Vice-Pres., 1962–66; Pres., 1966–67); Member: Governing Body, SE London Techn. Coll., 1952–58; Nat. Cons. Council to Min. of Works, 1952–56; Bd of Governors, Westminster Hosp., 1963–69; Council, Worcester Coll. Soc., 1964–87; Adv. Council on Scientific Res. and Develt (MoD), 1966–69; Defence Scientific Adv. Council, 1969–72; Royal Fine Art Commn, 1968–85; Council, Assoc. of Consulting Engrs, 1969–72, 1973–77, Chm., 1975–76; Governing Body, Imp. Coll. of Science and Technology, 1975–83; Chm., Limpsfield Common Local Management Cttee, Nat. Trust, 1972–82; Pres., Welding Inst., 1975–77. Col, Engr and Rly Staff Corps RE (T&AVR), 1963–76, Col comdg 1970–74. DUniv Surrey, 1978. Hon. Mem., Instn Royal Engrs, 1971; Hon. FIMechE, 1971; Hon. Fellow, Zimbabwe (formerly Rhodesian) Instn of Engrs, 1969; FRSA. Kt, Order of Orange Nassau (Netherlands), 1945. *Publications:* several papers in Proc. ICE. *Recreations:* wood and metal work, letter writing. *Address:* Ballards Shaw, Ballards Lane, Limpsfield, Oxted, Surrey RH8 0SN. *T:* Oxted (0883) 723284. *Clubs:* Army and Navy; Leander (Henley-on-Thames).

See also D. L. Pearson.

FREEMAN, Prof. Raymond, MA, DPhil, DSc (Oxon); FRS 1979; John Humphrey Plummer Professor of Magnetic Resonance, and Fellow of Jesus College, Cambridge University, since 1987; *b* 6 Jan. 1932; *s* of late Albert and Hilda Frances Freeman; *m* 1958, Anne-Marie Périnet-Marquet; two *s* three *d. Educ:* Nottingham High Sch. (scholar); Lincoln Coll., Oxford (open scholar). Ingénieur, Centre d'Etudes Nucléaires de Saclay, Commissariat à l'Energie Atomique, France, 1957–59; Sen. Scientific Officer, Nat. Phys. Lab., Teddington, Mddx, 1959–63; Man., Nuclear Magnetic Resonance Research, Varian Associates, Palo Alto, Calif, 1963–73; Lectr in Physical Chemistry, 1973–87, Aldrichian Praelector in Chemistry, 1982–87, and Fellow, Magdalen Coll., 1973–87, Oxford Univ. Chem. Soc. Award in Theoretical Chem. and Spectroscopy, 1978; Leverhulme Medal, Royal Soc., 1990. *Publications:* A Handbook of Nuclear Magnetic Resonance, 1987; articles on nuclear magnetic resonance spectroscopy in various scientific journals. *Recreations:* swimming, traditional jazz. *Address:* Department of Chemistry, University of Cambridge, Lensfield Road, Cambridge CB2 1EW; Jesus College, Cambridge CB5 8BL; 29 Bentley Road, Cambridge CB2 2AW. *T:* Cambridge (0223) 323958.

FREEMAN, His Honour Richard Gavin; a Circuit Judge (formerly County Court Judge), 1968–83; *b* 18 Oct. 1910; *s* of John Freeman, MD, and Violet Alice Leslie Hadden; *m* 1937, Marjorie Pear; one *s* two *d*; *m* 1961, Winifred Ann Bell. *Educ:* Charterhouse; Hertford Coll., Oxford. Called to Bar, Gray's Inn, 1947. Deputy Chairman, Warwick Quarter Sessions, 1963–71. Hon. Major, RA. *Recreations:* cricket, gardening. *Address:* 10 Rees Street, N1. *Club:* Streatley Cricket.

FREEMAN, Roger Norman, MA; FCA; MP (C) Kettering, since 1983; Minister of State, Department of Transport, since 1990; *b* 27 May 1942; *s* of Norman and Marjorie Freeman; *m* 1969, Jennifer Margaret (*née* Watson); one *s* one *d. Educ:* Whitgift Sch., Croydon; Balliol Coll., Oxford (MA PPE). Chartered Accountant, 1969; FCA 1979. Articled with Binder Hamlyn & Co., 1964–69 (Hons Prize, 1968); General Partner, Lehman Brothers, 1969–86. Parliamentary Under-Secretary of State: for the Armed Forces, 1986–88; DoH, 1988–90. *Publications:* Professional Practice, 1968; Fair Deal for Water, 1985. *Address:* House of Commons, SW1A 0AA. *Clubs:* Carlton, Kennel.

FREEMAN-GRENVILLE, family name of **Lady Kinloss.**

FREER, Charles Edward Jesse, DL; *b* 4 March 1901; *s* of late Canon S. Thorold Winckley, FSA and Elizabeth (*née* Freer); changed name to Freer by Deed Poll, 1922; *m* 1st, 1927, Violet Muriel (*d* 1944), *d* of H. P. Gee, CBE, Leicester; two *s* two *d*; 2nd, 1945, Cynthia Lilian, *d* of Leonard R. Braithwaite, FRCS, Leeds; two *d. Educ:* Radley Coll. Solicitor, 1924; served RA (TA) in France, 1940; DJAG in Iceland, 1941–42; at SHAEF, 1943–44, Lt-Col. Chm., Leicestershire QS, 1949–71. Chm. Leicester Diocesan Board of Finance, 1946–56; Chm. Mental Health Tribunal, Sheffield Regional Board, 1961–73. A Chm. of Industrial Tribunals, 1966–73. DL 1946, JP 1946–71, Leics. *Recreations:* reading, walking. *Address:* Elmstead Lodge, 3 Elmstead Road, Canford Cliffs, Poole, Dorset BH13 7EY. *T:* Canford Cliffs (0202) 709490. *Clubs:* East India, Devonshire, Sports and Public Schools; Parkstone Yacht.

FREER, Air Chief Marshal Sir Robert (William George), GBE 1981 (CBE 1966); KCB 1977; Commandant, Royal College of Defence Studies, 1980–82, retired; Director, Pilatus Britten-Norman Ltd, since 1988; *b* Darjeeling, 1 Sept. 1923; *s* of late William Freer, Stretton, Cirencester, Glos; *m* 1950, Margaret, 2nd *d* of late J. W. Elkington and Mrs M. Elkington, Ruskington Manor, near Sleaford, Lincs; one *s* one *d. Educ:* Gosport

Grammar Sch. Flying Instructor, S Africa and UK, 1944–47; RAF Coll., Cranwell, 1947–50; served 54 and 614 Fighter Sqdns, 1950–52; Central Fighter Estabt, 1952–54; commanded 92 Fighter Sqdn, 1955–57 (Queen's Commendation, 1955); Directing Staff, USAF Acad., 1958–60; Staff of Chief of Defence Staff, 1961–63; Station Comdr, RAF Seletar, 1963–66; DD Defence Plans (Air), MoD, 1966–67. Air ADC to the Queen, 1969–71; Dep. Comdt, RAF Staff Coll., 1969–71; SASO, HQ Near East Air Force, 1971–72; AOC 11 Group, 1972–75; Dir-Gen., Organisation (RAF), April-Sept. 1975; AOC No 18 Group, RAF, 1975–78; Dep. C-in-C, Strike Command, 1978–79; psa, 1957; pfc, 1960; IDC, 1968. Director: Rediffusion, 1982–88; British Manufg & Res. Co., 1984–88; Rediffusion Simulation, 1985–88. Pres., RAF LTA, 1975–81; Mem., Sports Council, 1980–82. CBIM (FBIM 1977); FRSA 1988. *Recreations:* golf, tennis. *Address:* c/o Lloyds Bank, Farnham, Surrey. *Clubs:* Royal Air Force; All England Lawn Tennis and Croquet; Hankley Common Golf.

FREESON, Rt. Hon. Reginald, PC 1976; Director, Reg Freeson & Associates, urban renewal consultants, since 1987; *b* 24 Feb. 1926; *m*; one *s* one *d*. *Educ:* Jewish Orphanage, West Norwood. Served in Army, 1944–47. Middle East magazines and newspapers, 1946–48. Joined Labour Party on return to United Kingdom, 1948, Co-operative Party, 1958 and Poale Zion, Labour Zionists, 1964. Journalist, 1948–64: magazines, newspaper agencies and television; Everybody's Weekly, Tribune, News Chronicle, Daily Mirror. Asst Press Officer with Min. of Works, British Railways Board. Some short story writing, research and ghosting of books and pamphlets. Editor: Searchlight, against fascism and racialism, 1964–67; Jewish Vanguard, socialist Zionist qly, 1987–. Radio and television: housing, urban planning, race relations and foreign affairs. Elected Willesden Borough Council, 1952; Alderman, 1955; Leader of Council, 1958–65; Chm. of new London Borough of Brent, 1964–65 (Alderman, 1964–68). MP (Lab): Willesden E, 1964–74; Brent E, Feb. 1974–1987. PPS to Minister of Transport, 1964–67; Parly Secretary: Min. of Power, 1967–69; Min. of Housing and Local Govt, 1969–70; Labour Front-Bench spokesman on housing and urban affairs, 1970–74; Minister for Housing and Construction and Urban Affairs, DoE, 1974–79; responsible for planning, land and local govt, 1976–79; front-bench spokesman on social security, 1979–81; Mem., Select Cttee on the Environment, 1981–84 (Chm., 1982–83). Member: Council of Europe Parly Assembly, 1984–87; Western Eur. Assembly, 1984–87. Dir, JBG Housing Soc., 1981–83; Mem. Exec., Housing Centre Trust, 1987. Mem., Internat. Voluntary Service and UNA International Service. Sponsor, three Willesden housing co-operatives, 1958–60. Founder-Chairman: Willesden (now Brent) Coun. of Social Service, 1960–62; Willesden Social Action, 1961–63; Willesden Internat. Friendship Council (now Brent Community Relns Council), 1959–63 (Vice-Pres., 1967); Chairman: Warsaw Memorial Cttee, 1964–71; Poale Zion, 1984–87; Vice-Pres., Campaign for Democracy in Ulster; Founder/Sponsor, Internat. Centre for Peace in ME; Mem., Jewish Welfare Bd, 1971–74 (Mem. Exec., 1973–74). Life Mem., YHA, 1957. *Recreations:* gardening, music, theatre, reading, country walking. *Address:* 159 Chevening Road, NW6.

FREETH, Denzil Kingson; *b* 10 July 1924; *s* of late Walter Kingson and late Vera Freeth. *Educ:* Highfield Sch., Liphook, Hants; Sherborne Sch. (Scholar); Trinity Hall, Cambridge (Scholar). Served War, 1943–46: RAF (Flying Officer). Pres. Union Soc., Cambridge, 1949; Chm. Cambridge Univ. Conservative Assoc. 1949; debating tour of America, 1949, also debated in Ireland; Mem. Exec. Cttee Nat. Union, 1955. MP (C) Basingstoke Division of Hants, 1955–64. PPS to Minister of State, Bd of Trade, 1956, to Pres. of the Bd of Trade, 1957–59, to Minister of Educn, 1959–60; Parly Sec. for Science, 1961–63. Mem. Parliamentary Cttee of Trustee Savings Bank Assoc., 1956–61. Mem. Select Cttee on Procedure, 1958–59. Employed by and Partner in stockbroking firms, 1950–61 and 1964–89; Mem. of Stock Exchange, 1959–61, 1965–90. Churchwarden, All Saints' Church, Margaret St, W1, 1977–. *Recreations:* good food, wine and conversation. *Address:* 3 Brasenose House, 35 Kensington High Street, W8 5BA. *T:* 071–937 8685. *Clubs:* Carlton; Pitt (Cambridge).

FREETH, Hon. Sir Gordon, KBE 1978; Chairman, Australian Consolidated Minerals, since 1981; *b* 6 Aug. 1914; *s* of late Rt Rev. Robert Evelyn Freeth and Gladys Mary Snashall; *m* 1939, Joan Celia Carew Baker; one *s* two *d*. *Educ:* Sydney Church of England Grammar Sch.; Guildford Grammar Sch.; Univ. of Western Australia. Rowed for Australia in British Empire Games, Sydney, 1938. Admitted as Barrister and Solicitor, WA, 1938; practised Law at Katanning, WA, 1939–49. Served as Pilot, RAAF, 1942–45. Elected to House of Representatives as Member for Forrest, 1949; MP 1949–69; Minister: for Interior and Works, 1958–63; for Shipping and Transport, 1963–68; Assisting Attorney-Gen., 1962–64; for Air, and Minister Assisting the Treasurer, 1968; for External Affairs, 1969; Ambassador to Japan, 1970–73; practised law in Perth, WA, 1973–77; High Comr for Australia in UK, 1977–80. *Recreations:* gardening, golf. *Address:* Tingrith, 25 Owston Street, Mosman Park, WA 6012, Australia. *Club:* Weld (Perth).

FREETH, Peter Stewart, RA 1991 (ARA 1990); Tutor, Etching, Royal Academy Schools, since 1966; *b* 15 April 1938; *s* of Alfred William Freeth and Olive Walker; *m* 1967, Mariolina Meliadò; two *s*. *Educ:* King Edward's Grammar School, Aston; Slade School, London (Dip Fine Art). British Sch., Rome, 1960–62; part-time Tutor, Colchester Sch. of Art, Camden Inst. One man shows, Christopher Mendez Gall., London, 1987–89; represented in collections: British Museum; V&A; Fitzwilliam Mus., Cambridge; Arts Council; Metropolitan Mus., NY; Nat. Gall., Washington. Associate, Royal Soc. of Painter Printmakers. Prix de Rome, Engraving, 1960. *Recreations:* music, books, yet more work. *Address:* 83 Muswell Hill Road, N10 3HT. *T:* 081–444 9907.

FREMANTLE, family name of **Baron Cottesloe.**

FREMANTLE, Comdr Hon. John Tapling, RN (retired); JP; Lord-Lieutenant of Buckinghamshire, since 1984; *b* 22 Jan. 1927; *s* and *heir* of 4th Baron Cottesloe, *qv*, and late Lady Elizabeth Berwick; *m* 1958, Elizabeth Ann, *e d* of late Lt-Col H. S. Barker, DSO; one *s* two *d*. *Educ:* Summer Fields, Hastings; Eton College. Joined RN, 1945; CO HMS Palliser, 1959–61; retired at own request, 1966. High Sheriff, 1969–70, JP, 1984, Bucks. Governor, Stowe School, 1983–89. KStJ 1984. *Recreations:* shooting, stalking, crosswords. *Address:* The Old House, Swanbourne, Milton Keynes, Bucks MK17 0SH. *T:* (home) Mursley (029672) 263; (office) Mursley (029672) 256. *Clubs:* Travellers'; Royal Naval and Royal Albert Yacht (Portsmouth).

FRÉMAUX, Louis Joseph Felix; Principal Guest Conductor, Sydney Symphony Orchestra, 1982–85 (Musical Director and Principal Conductor, 1979–81); *b* 13 Aug. 1921. *Educ:* Conservatoire National Supérieur de Musique de Paris. First concert in England (with Bournemouth SO), 1964; Chef d'orchestre permanent et directeur, l'Orchestre National de l'Opéra de Monte Carlo, 1956–66; Principal Conductor, Orchestre de Lyon, 1968–71; Musical Dir and Principal Conductor, City of Birmingham Symphony Orch., 1969–78. Hon. DMus Birmingham, 1978. Hon. Member, Royal Academy of Music, 1978. Légion d'Honneur; Croix de Guerre (twice). *Recreations:* walking, photography. *Address:* 25 Edencroft, Wheeley's Road, Birmingham B15 2LW.

FRENCH, family name of **Baron De Freyne.**

FRENCH, Prof. Anthony Philip, PhD; Professor of Physics, Massachusetts Institute of Technology, since 1964; *b* 19 Nov. 1920; *s* of Sydney James French and Elizabeth Margaret (*née* Hart); *m* 1946, Naomi Mary Livesay; one *s* one *d*. *Educ:* Varndean Sch., Brighton; Sidney Sussex Coll., Cambridge (major schol.; BA Hons 1942, MA 1946, PhD 1948). British atomic bomb project, Tube Alloys, 1942–44; Manhattan Project, Los Alamos, USA, 1944–46; Scientific Officer, AERE, Harwell, 1946–48; Univ. Demonstrator in Physics, Cavendish Laboratory, Cambridge, 1948–51, Lectr 1951–55; Dir of Studies in Natural Sciences, Pembroke Coll., Cambridge, 1949–55, Fellow of Pembroke, 1950–55; Visiting research scholar: California Inst. of Technology, 1951; Univ. of Michigan, 1954; Prof. of Physics, Univ. of S Carolina, 1955–62 (Head of Dept, 1956–62); Guignard Lectr, 1958; Vis. Prof., MIT, 1962–64; Vis. Fellow of Pembroke Coll., Cambridge, 1975. Member, Internat. Commn on Physics Educn, 1972–84 (Chm., 1975–81); Pres., Amer. Assoc. of Physics Teachers, 1985–86. Hon. ScD Allegheny Coll., 1989. Bragg Medal, Institute of Physics, 1988; Oersted Medal, Amer. Assoc. of Physics Teachers, 1989. *Publications:* Principles of Modern Physics, 1958; Special Relativity, 1968; Newtonian Mechanics, 1971; Vibrations and Waves, 1971; Introduction to Quantum Physics, 1978; Einstein: a centenary volume, 1979; Niels Bohr: a centenary volume, 1985; Introduction to Classical Mechanics, 1986; Physics in a Technological World, 1988. *Recreations:* music, squash, reading, writing. *Address:* c/o Physics Department, Massachusetts Institute of Technology, Cambridge, Mass 02139, USA.

FRENCH, Cecil Charles John, FEng 1982; Group Technology Director, Ricardo International, since 1990; *b* 16 April 1926; *s* of Ernest French and Edith Hannah French (*née* Norris); *m* 1st, 1956, Olive Joyce Edwards (*d* 1969); two *d*; 2nd, 1971, Shirley Frances Outten; one *s* one *d*. *Educ:* King's Coll., Univ. of London (MScEng; DSc Eng 1987); Columbia Univ., New York. FIMechE, FIMarE. Graduate apprentice, CAV Ltd, 1948–50; Marshall Aid scholar, MIT, USA (research into combustion in engines), 1950–52; Ricardo Consulting Engineers, subseq. Ricardo Internat., 1952–, Director, 1969, Vice-Chm., 1982; Man. Dir, 1979–83, Chm., 1984–87, G. Cussons Ltd. President, Instn of Mechanical Engineers, 1988–89 (Vice-Pres, 1981–86, Dep. Pres., 1986–88). *Publications:* numerous articles on diesel engines in learned soc. jls world wide. *Recreations:* folk dancing, photography. *Address:* 303 Upper Shoreham Road, Shoreham-by-Sea, Sussex BN4 5QA. *T:* Shoreham-by-Sea (0273) 452050.

FRENCH, Hon. Sir Christopher James Saunders, Kt 1979; **Hon. Mr Justice French;** Judge of the High Court of Justice, Queen's Bench Division, since 1982 (Family Division, 1979–82); Judge of Employment Appeals Tribunal, since 1985; *b* 14 Oct. 1925; 2nd *s* of late Rev. Reginald French, MC, MA, Hon. Chaplain to the Queen, and Gertrude Emily Mary (*née* Haworth); *m* 1957, Philippa, *d* of Philip Godfrey Price, Abergavenny; one *s* one *d*. *Educ:* Denstone Coll. (scholar); Brasenose Coll., Oxford (scholar). Coldstream Guards, 1943–48 (Capt.). Called to the Bar, Inner Temple, 1950; QC 1966; Master of the Bench, 1975. Dep. Chm., Bucks QS, 1966–71. Recorder of Coventry, 1971–72; a Recorder, and Hon. Recorder of Coventry, 1972–79; Presiding Judge, SE Circuit, 1982–85. Member: Gen. Council of the Bar, 1963–67; Senate of Inns of Court and Bar, 1978–79; Lord Chancellor's Adv. Cttee on Trng Magistrates, 1974–80. *Publication:* (contrib.) Agency, in Halsbury's Laws of England, 4th edn, 1973. *Recreations:* walking, music, painting, fishing. *Address:* Royal Courts of Justice, Strand, WC2. *Clubs:* Garrick, Pilgrims.

FRENCH, David; Director, RELATE: Marriage Guidance (formerly National Marriage Guidance Council), since 1987; *b* 20 June 1947; *s* of late Captain Godfrey Alexander French, CBE, RN, and of Margaret Annis French; *m* 1974, Sarah Anne, *d* of Rt Rev. H. D. Halsey, *qv*; three *s*. *Educ:* Sherborne Sch.; Durham Univ. (BA). MIPM. Nat. Council of Social Service, 1971–74; Hd of Social Services Dept, RNID, 1974–78; Dir of Services, C of E Children's Soc., 1978–87. Chairman: London Corrymeela Venture, 1973–76; St Albans Internat. Organ Fest., 1985–87. Liveryman, Glaziers' Co., 1990–. MRSocMed 1988. *Recreations:* children and families. *Address:* 21 Prospect Road, St Albans, Herts AL1 2AT. *T:* (office) Rugby (0788) 573241.

FRENCH, Douglas Charles; MP (C) Gloucester, since 1987; *b* London, 20 March 1944; *s* of Frederick Emil and Charlotte Vera French; *m* 1978, Sue, *y d* of late Philip Arthur Phillips; two *s* one *d*. *Educ:* Glyn Grammar Sch., Epsom; St Catharine's Coll., Cambridge (MA). Called to the Bar, Inner Temple. Exec., then Dir, P. W. Merkle Ltd, 1966–90. Asst to Rt Hon. Sir Geoffrey Howe, Shadow Chancellor, 1976–79; Special Advr to Chancellor of the Exchequer, 1982–83; PPS to Minister of State, FCO, 1988–89, ODA, 1989–90. Contested (C) Sheffield, Attercliffe, 1979. Chm., Bow Gp, 1978–79. *Publications:* pamphlets, articles and reviews. *Recreations:* gardening, renovating period houses, ski-ing, squash. *Address:* House of Commons, SW1A 0AA. *Clubs:* Royal Automobile, Coningsby.

FRENCH, Henry William, CBE 1971; BSc (London); CEng, FIEE, FInstP; FCP; Senior Chief Inspector (Deputy Secretary), Department of Education and Science, 1972–74; *b* 14 Feb. 1910; *s* of Henry Moxey French and Alice French (*née* Applegate); *m* 1936, Hazel Anne Mary Ainley; two *s*. *Educ:* Varndean School, Brighton; Woolwich Polytechnic. Engineering Technician, 1925–27; Armed Forces (Royal Corps of Signals, Army Educational Corps), 1927–38; Lecturer, Radar Engineering, Mil. Coll. of Science, 1938–46; Dep. Dir, Educn and Training, Electric and Musical Industries, 1946–48; HM Inspector of Schools (Further Education), 1948–56; Regional Staff Inspector (NW), 1956–59; Staff Inspector (Engineering), 1956–65; Chief Inspector for Further Educn for Industry and Commerce, DES, 1965–72. Pro-Chancellor, 1978–86, Sen. Pro-Chancellor and Chm., Council, 1981–86, Loughborough Univ.; Mem. Council, Brighton Polytechnic, 1976–87 (Hon. Fellow, 1987). Fellow, Woolwich Polytechnic, 1966; Hon. Fellow, Sheffield Polytechnic, 1975. Hon. DSc Loughborough Univ. of Technology, 1966. *Publications:* Technician Engineering Drawing 1, 1979; Engineering Technicians: some problems of nomenclature and classification, 1980. *Recreations:* polyphonic music, opera, travel. *Address:* 26 Crossways, Sutton, Surrey SM2 5LB. *T:* 081–642 5277.

FRENCH, Leslie Richard; actor; *b* Kent, 23 April 1904; *s* of Robert Gilbert French and Jetty Sands Leahy; unmarried. *Educ:* London Coll. of Choristers. Began stage work 1914; early Shakespearean training with Sir Philip Ben Greet; parts include Hansel in Hansel and Gretel, Bert in Derby Day; Shakespearean parts include Puck, Ariel, Feste, Costard, etc; The Spirit in Comus; played Feste in the ballet Twelfth Night with the International Ballet at His Majesty's Theatre. Joined the Royal Corps of Signals, 1942; Lord Fancourt Babberly in Charley's Aunt, Christmas 1943. Produced Much Ado About Nothing and The Tempest for OUDS; Everyman as a ballet for the International Ballet Co., Lyric Theatre, 1943; Comus for the International Ballet, London Coliseum, 1946. Productions include: Charles and Mary, Cheltenham Festival, 1948; The Servant of Two Masters; Aladdin (Widow Twanky); Mother Goose (Mother Goose); She Stoops to Conquer for Edinburgh Festival (Tony Lumpkin), 1949; pantomime, Cinderella, 1950; The Dish Ran Away, Whitehall, 1950; Midsummer Night's Dream (Puck), Open Air Theatre during Cheltenham Festival; Open Air Theatre, Regent's Park, 1951; pantomime, Nottingham, 1951–52; The Ghost Train, Huddersfield, 1952; Pisanio in Cymbeline, Attendant Spirit in Comus, Open Air Theatre, 1952; Dyrkin in Out of the Whirlwind, Westminster Abbey, 1953; Open Air Theatre, Cape Town: The Taming of the Shrew, 1956;

Midsummer Night's Dream, 1957; As You Like It (Touchstone), 1958; Johannesburg: The Tempest, 1956; Hamlet, 1957; Shakespearean seasons in Cape Town, 1959, 1960, 1961, 1962, 1963, 1966, 1969; Tempest, E. Oppenheimer Theatre, OFS, 1968; The Tell Tale Heart, 1969; An Evening with Shakespeare (tour), 1969; Twelfth Night, Port Elizabeth, 1970; The Way of the World, S Africa, 1970; Co-dir, Open Air Theatre, Regent's Park, 1958. Prod., Twelfth Night (in Great Hall of Hampton Ct Palace), 1965; Le Streghe (for Visconti), 1966; toured USA, 1969–70 and 1970–71: One Man Shakespearean Recitals, and Shylock in Merchant of Venice; The Chaplain in The Lady's not for Burning, Chichester Festival, 1972; toured USA 1973; recitals and prod Twelfth Night; The Tempest, Cape Town, 1973; As You Like It, Port Elizabeth, 1973; Shakespear (one-man show), Cape Town, Port Elizabeth, 1991; prod Loves Labours Lost, Maynardville Open Air Theatre, 1991; Caroline, Yvonne Arnaud Theatre; Directed: Saturday Sunday Monday, Nat. Arts Council, S Africa, 1976; Romeo and Juliet, Cape Town, 1980; numerous appearances on TV, incl.: Villette (serial), 1970; The Singing Detective, 1986; The Book Liberator, 1988. *Films:* Orders to Kill (M Lafitte), 1957; The Scapegoat (M Lacoste), 1958; The Singer not the Song (Father Gomez); The Leopard (Chevalley), 1963; The Witches, 1966; Happy Ever After, 1966; Joseph of Coppertino, 1966; Death in Venice (Visconti), 1970. First Exhibition of Paintings—oil and water colour, Parsons Gall. Presented with Key to City of Cape Town, Jan. 1963. Gold Medals: Port Elizabeth Shakespeare Society, 1973; 1820 Settlers, 1978; Grahamstown Festival, 1977; Hon. Life Mem., Mark Twain Soc., USA, 1976 (all in recognition of his contribution to art and culture in the theatre in England and overseas). *Recreations:* gardening and painting. *Address:* Flat D, 29 Elsworthy Road, NW3 3BT. *T:* 071–586 5721; 11 Chesterfield Road, Ewell West, Surrey KT19 9QR. *T:* 081–393 1333. *Club:* Garrick.

FRENCH, Neville Arthur Irwin, CMG 1976; LVO 1968; HM Diplomatic Service, retired; *b* Kenya, 28 April 1920; *s* of late Major Ernest French and Alice Irwin (*née* Powell); *m* 1945, Joyce Ethel, *d* of late Henry Robert Greene, Buenos Aires and Montevideo; one *s* two *d. Educ:* London Sch. of Economics (BSc (Econ)). Fleet Auxiliary and Special Duties, Min. of War Transport, 1939–45. Colonial Admin. Service, Tanganyika, 1948, later HMOCS; District Comr, 1949–61; Principal Asst Sec., (External Affairs), Prime Minister's Office, Dar es Salaam, 1961; retd from HMOCS, 1962; Central African Office, 1963–64; 1st Sec., British High Commn, Salisbury, 1964–66; Head of Chancery, British Embassy, Rio de Janeiro, 1966–69; Asst Head of Western Organisations Dept, FCO, 1970–72; Counsellor, and Chargé d'Affaires, Havana, 1972–75; Governor and C-in-C, Falkland Islands, and High Comr, British Antarctic Territory, 1975–77; Dep. High Comr, Madras, 1977–80. Comdr, Order of Rio Branco (Brazil), 1968. *Recreations:* sailing, books. *Address:* c/o Barclays Bank, 84 High Street, Bideford, Devon. *Clubs:* Commonwealth Trust, Naval; Madras.

FRENCH, Philip Neville; writer and broadcaster; Film Critic, The Observer, since 1978; *b* Liverpool, 28 Aug. 1933; *s* of late John and Bessie French; *m* 1957, Kersti Elisabet Molin; three *s. Educ:* Bristol Grammar Sch.; Exeter Coll., Oxford (BA Law) (editor, The Isis, 1956); Indiana Univ. Nat. Service, 2nd Lieut Parachute Regt, 1952–54. Reporter, Bristol Evening Post, 1958–59; Producer, BBC N Amer. Service, 1959–61; Talks Producer, BBC Radio, 1961–67; New Statesman: Theatre Critic, 1967–68; Arts Columnist, 1967–72; Sen. Producer, BBC Radio, 1968–90: editor of The Arts This Week, Critics' Forum and other series, writer-presenter of arts documentaries, Radio 3. Vis. Prof., Univ. of Texas, 1972. Mem., BFI Prodn Bd, 1968–74; Jury Mem., Cannes Film Fest., 1986. *Publications:* Age of Austerity 1945–51 (ed with Michael Sissons), 1963; The Movie Moguls, 1969; Westerns: aspects of a movie genre, 1974, rev. 1977; Three Honest Men: Edmund Wilson, F. R. Leavis, Lionel Trilling, 1980; (ed) The Third Dimension: voices from Radio Three, 1983; numerous articles and essays in magazines, newspapers and anthologies. *Recreations:* woolgathering in England, picking wild strawberries in Sweden. *Address:* 62 Dartmouth Park Road, NW5 1SN. *T:* 071–485 1711.

FREND, Rev. Prof. William Hugh Clifford, TD 1959 (Clasp, 1966); DD, FRSE, FSA; FBA 1983; Priest-in-Charge of Barnwell with Thurning and Luddington, 1984–90; Professor of Ecclesiastical History, 1969–84, now Professor Emeritus, and Dean of Divinity Faculty, 1972–75, Glasgow University; *b* 11 Jan. 1916; 2nd *s* of late Rev. E. G. C. Frend, Shottermill, Surrey and late Edith (*née* Bacon); *m* 1951, Mary Grace, *d* of late E. A. Crook, FRCS; one *s* one *d. Educ:* Fernden Sch.; Haileybury Coll. (Schol.); Keble Coll., Oxford (Schol.). 1st cl. hons Mod. Hist., 1937; Craven Fellow, 1937; DPhil 1940; BD Cantab 1964; DD Oxon 1966. Asst Princ., War Office, 1940; seconded Cabinet Office, 1941; FO, 1942; service in N Africa, Italy and Austria, 1943–46 (Gold Cross of Merit with Swords, Polish Forces); Ed. Bd, German Foreign Min. Documents, 1947–51; Res. Fellow, Nottingham Univ., 1951; S. A. Cook Bye-Fellow, 1952, Fellow, 1956–69, Dir Studies, Archaeology, 1961–69, Gonville and Caius Coll.; University Asst Lectr, 1953, Lectr in Divinity, 1958–69; Birkbeck Lectr in Ecclesiastical History, 1967–68. Lay Mem., CSSB 1970–72. Chm., AUT (Scotland), 1976–78. Vice-Pres., Assoc. internat. d'Etudes patristiques, 1983–87; Président d'Honneur, Internat. Commn for Comparative Study of Ecclesiastical History (CIHEC), 1983 (Vice-Pres. 1975–80, Pres. 1980–83). Assoc. Dir, Egypt Exploration Soc. excavations at Q'asr Ibrim, Nubia, 1963–64; Guest Scholar at Rhodes Univ., 1964 and Peter Ainslie Meml Lecturer; Guest Prof., Univ. of S Africa, 1976; Vis. Prof. of Inter-religious Studies (Walter and Mary Tuohy Chair), John Carroll Univ., Cleveland, 1981; Vis. Fellow, Harvard Univ. Center for Byzantine Studies, Dumbarton Oaks, 1984. Licensed Lay Reader, 1956, Deacon, 1982, Priest, 1983, serving in Aberfoyle parish. Mem., Peterborough Diocesan Synod, 1988–90. Editor, Modern Churchman, 1963–82. Commission Queen's Royal Regt (TA), 1947–67. FSA 1952; FRHistS 1954; FRSE 1979. Hon. DD Edinburgh, 1974. *Publications:* The Donatist Church, 1952; Martyrdom and Persecution in the Early Church, 1965; The Early Church, 1965; (contrib.) Religion in the Middle East, 1968; The Rise of the Monophysite Movement, 1972; Religion Popular and Unpopular in the Early Christian Centuries, 1976; (contrib.) Cambridge History of Africa, vol. ii, 1978; Town and Country in the Early Christian Centuries, 1980; The Rise of Christianity, 1984; Saints and Sinners in the Early Church, 1985; History and Archaeology in the Study of Early Christianity, 1988; (contrib.) Agostino d'Ippona: quaestiones disputatae, 1989; articles in Jl Theol Studies, Jl Roman Studies, Jl Eccles. History, Jahrbuch für Antike und Christentum, etc. *Recreations:* archæology, occasional golf and tennis, writing, collecting old coins and stamps. *Address:* Clerk's Cottage, Little Wilbraham, Cambridge CB1 5LB. *Club:* Authors'.

FRERE, James Arnold, FSA, FRGS; (Marqués de la Unión, Spain, 1808; Marchese de la Unión, Aragón, 1986; Marchese Frere, Aragon, 1989); *b* 20 April 1920; *e s* of late John Geoffrey Frere. *Educ:* Eton Coll.; Trinity Coll., Cambridge. Lieut Intelligence Corps, 1944–47. Regular Army R of O, 1949–67. Bluemantle Pursuivant of Arms, 1948–56; Chester Herald of Arms, 1956–60; an Officer of Supreme Court of Judicature, 1966–70. Member: Surrey Archæological Soc. (Council, 1949–53, 1954–58 and 1959–63); American Soc. of Authors; Council of the Harleian Soc., 1951–66; Hon. Mem. Heraldry Soc. of Southern Africa, 1953–; a Vice-Pres. of Museum of Costume, 1952–60. Press Sec., New Gallery Clinic, 1967–70. Liveryman, Worshipful Co. of Scriveners, 1950 (now Sen. Liveryman). Hon. Consul for Poland (in exile), Powys, 1984–90. Mountjoy King of Arms and Judge-at-Arms, Internat. Coll. of Arms of Noblesse, 1982–; Rey de Armas y Cronista de Perpiñan, 1986; Pres., Real Colegio Heraldicó de Aragona, 1987; Head of Ceremonial and Protocol, Royal House of Aragon, 1988; Grand Master of Ceremonies, Supreme Military Order of Temple of Jerusalem; KM 1959; Knight Grand Cross, and Clairvaux King of Arms, SMO of Temple of Jerusalem, 1981; Kt of Justice of Our Lady of Monteza, 1988; Kt, Royal Order of James I of Aragon, 1989; Kt, Order of St George and the Double Crown, 1990; Knight Grand Cross: Mil. Order of the Collar of St Agatha of Paterno', 1987; Order of the Royal Crown of the Balearics, 1987. Commander's Cross, Polonia Restituta, 1983; Polish Gold Cross of Merit, 1983. *Publications:* The British Monarchy at Home, 1963; (jointly with the Duchess of Bedford) Now ... The Duchesses, 1964. *Recreations:* walking, painting, archæology. *Address:* c/o Society of Antiquaries, Burlington House, Piccadilly, W1. *Club:* City Livery.

FRERE, Rear-Adm. Richard Tobias; Flag Officer Submarines, and Commander Submarines Eastern Atlantic, since 1991; *b* 4 June 1938; *s* of Alexander Stewart Frere and Patricia Frere; *m* 1968, Jane Barraclough; two *d. Educ:* Eton College; Britannia Royal Naval College. Joined RNVR as National Serviceman; transf. RN 1957; commissioned 1958; submarines 1960; served Canada, 1961–62, Australia, 1966–67, 1973; commanded HM Submarines Andrew, Odin and Revenge and Frigate HMS Brazen. JSSC, Canberra, 1973; RCDS London, 1982; Dir Gen. Fleet Support, Policy and Services, 1988–91. *Recreation:* sailing. *Address:* c/o Ministry of Defence (Navy), Main Building, Whitehall, SW1. *Clubs:* Garrick, MCC.

FRERE, Prof. Sheppard Sunderland, CBE 1976; FSA 1944; FBA 1971; Professor of the Archæology of the Roman Empire, and Fellow of All Souls College, Oxford University, 1966–83, now professor Emeritus and Emeritus Fellow; *b* 23 Aug. 1916; *e s* of late N. G. Frere, CMG; *m* 1961, Janet Cecily Hoare; one *s* one *d. Educ:* Lancing Coll.; Magdalene Coll., Cambridge. BA 1938, MA 1944, LittD 1976, DLitt 1977. Master, Epsom Coll., 1938–40. National Fire Service, 1940–45. Master, Lancing Coll., 1945–54; Lecturer in Archæology, Manchester Univ., 1954–55; Reader in Archæology of Roman Provinces, London Univ. Inst. of Archæology, 1955–62; Prof. of the Archæology of the Roman Provinces, London Univ., 1963–66. Dir, Canterbury Excavations, 1946–60; Dir, Verulamium Excavations, 1955–61. Vice-Pres., Soc. of Antiquaries, 1962–66; President: Oxford Architectural and Historical Soc., 1972–80; Royal Archæological Inst., 1978–81; Soc. for Promotion of Roman Studies, 1983–86. Hon. Corr. Mem. German Archæological Inst., 1964, Fellow, 1967; Member: Royal Commn on Hist. Monuments (England), 1966–83; Ancient Monuments Board (England), 1966–82. Hon. LittD: Leeds, 1977; Leicester, 1983; Kent, 1985. Editor, Britannia, 1969–79. *Publications:* (ed) Problems of the Iron Age in Southern Britain, 1961; Britannia, a history of Roman Britain, 1967 (rev. edn 1987); Verulamium Excavations, vol. I, 1972, vol. II, 1983, vol. III, 1984; Excavations on the Roman and Medieval Defences of Canterbury, 1982; Excavations at Canterbury, vol. VII, 1983; (with J. K. St Joseph) Roman Britain from the Air, 1983; (with F. A. Lepper) Trajan's Column, 1988; (with J. J. Wilkes) Strageath: excavations within the Roman fort, 1989; papers in learned jls. *Recreation:* gardening. *Address:* Netherfield House, Marcham, Abingdon, Oxon OX13 6NP.

FRESHWATER, Prof. Donald Cole, FEng 1986; Head of Department of Chemical Engineering, 1957–86, and Dean of Pure and Applied Science, 1982–85, University of Technology, Loughborough, Professor Emeritus, 1987; *b* 21 April 1924; *s* of Thomas and Ethel May Freshwater; *m* 1948, Margaret D. Worrall (marr. diss. 1977); one *s* three *d*; *m* 1980, Eleanor M. Lancashire (*née* Tether). *Educ:* Brewood Grammar Sch.; Birmingham Univ. (BSc, PhD); Sheffield Univ.; Loughborough Coll. (DLC). Fuel Engineer, Min. of Fuel and Power, 1944; Chemical Engr: APV Co. Ltd, 1948; Midland Tar Distillers Co. Ltd, 1950; Lectr, Dept of Chem. Engrg, Univ. of Birmingham, 1952; Prof., Louisiana State Univ., 1986–90. Visiting Professor: Univ. of Delaware, USA, 1962; Georgia Inst. of Technology, 1980–81. Chm., Chem. Engrg Gp, Soc. of Chemical Industry, 1973–75; Mem. Council, IChemE, 1982–87 (Vice Pres., 1985–87). Hon. DSc Loughborough, 1989. *Publications:* Chemical Engineering Data Book, 1959; numerous papers on mass transfer, particle technology and educn in chem. engrg jls. *Recreations:* sailing, collecting watercolours. *Address:* 1817 General Beauregard, Baton Rouge, La 70810, USA. *Club:* Athenæum.

FRETWELL, Elizabeth, OBE 1977; professional adjudicator and vocal coach; operatic and dramatic soprano; *b* Melbourne, Australia; *m* Robert Simmons; one *s* one *d. Educ:* privately. Joined National Theatre, Melbourne, 1950; came to Britain, 1955; joined Sadler's Wells, 1956; Australia, Elizabethan Opera Co., 1963; tour of W Germany, 1963; USA, Canada and Covent Garden, 1964; tour of Europe, 1965; guest soprano with Cape Town and Durban Opera Cos, South Africa, 1970; Australian Opera, 1970–87. Rôles include Violetta in La Traviata, Leonora in Fidelio, Ariadne in Ariadne auf Naxos, Senta in The Flying Dutchman, Minnie in The Girl of the Golden West, Leonora in Il Trovatore, Aida, Ellen Orford in Peter Grimes, Leonora in Forza del Destino, Alice Ford in Falstaff, Amelia in Masked Ball, Georgetta in Il Tabarro, opening season of Sydney Opera Hse, 1973. Has sung in BBC Promenade Concerts and on TV. Mem., music bd, Opera Foundn Australia, 1982–. *Recreation:* rose-growing. *Address:* 47 Kananook Avenue, Bayview, NSW 2104, Australia.

FRETWELL, Sir (Major) John (Emsley), GCMG 1987 (KCMG 1982; CMG 1975); HM Diplomatic Service, retired; Political Director and Deputy to the Permanent Under-Secretary of State, Foreign and Commonwealth Office, 1987–90; *b* 15 June 1930; *s* of late Francis Thomas Fretwell and of Dorothy Fretwell; *m* 1959, Mary Ellen Eugenie Dubois; one *s* one *d. Educ:* Chesterfield Grammar Sch.; Lausanne Univ.; King's Coll., Cambridge (MA). HM Forces, 1948–50. Diplomatic Service, 1953; 3rd Sec., Hong Kong, 1954–55; 2nd Sec., Peking, 1955–57; FO, 1957–59; 1st Sec., Moscow, 1959–62; FO, 1962–67; 1st Sec. (Commercial), Washington, 1967–70; Commercial Counsellor, Warsaw, 1971–73; Head of European Integration Dept (Internal), FCO, 1973–76; Asst Under-Sec. of State, FCO, 1976–79; Minister, Washington, 1980–81; Ambassador to France, 1982–87. Mem., Council of Lloyd's, 1991–. *Recreations:* skiing, walking. *Clubs:* Brooks's; Jockey (Paris).

FREUD, Sir Clement (Raphael), Kt 1987; writer, broadcaster, caterer; *b* 24 April 1924; *s* of late Ernst and Lucie Freud; *m* 1950, Jill, 2nd *d* of H. W. Flewett, MA; three *s* two *d.* Apprenticed, Dorchester Hotel, London. Served War, Royal Ulster Rifles; Liaison Officer, Nuremberg war crimes trials, 1946. Trained, Martinez Hotel, Cannes. Proprietor, Royal Court Theatre Club, 1952–62. Sports writer, Observer, 1956–64; Cookery Editor: Time and Tide, 1961–63; Observer Magazine, 1964–68; Daily Telegraph Magazine, 1968–. Sports Columnist, Sun, 1964–69; Columnist: Sunday Telegraph, 1963–65; News of the World, 1965; Financial Times, 1964–; Daily Express, 1973–75; Times Diarist, 1988–. Consultant: Park Foods, 1987–; THF, 1988–. Contested (L) Cambridgeshire NE, 1987. MP (L): Isle of Ely, July 1973–1983; Cambridgeshire NE, 1983–87. Liberal spokesman on education, the arts and broadcasting; sponsor, Official Information Bill. Chm., Standing Cttee, Liberal Party, 1982–86. Rector, Univ. of Dundee, 1974–80. Pres., Down's Children Assoc., 1988–. £5,000 class winner, Daily Mail London-NY air race, 1969. winning petfood commercial: San Francisco, Tokyo, Berlin, 1967. BBC (sounc Minute, 1968–. MUniv Open, 1989. *Publications:* Grimble, 1968; Grimble at Ch

1973; Freud on Food, 1978; Clicking Vicky, 1980; The Book of Hangovers, 1981; Below the Belt, 1983; No-one Else has Complained, 1988; The Gourmet's Tour of Great Britain and Ireland, 1989; contributor to, New Yorker, etc (formerly to, Punch). *Recreations:* racing, backgammon, pétanque. *Address:* 22 Wimpole Street, W1. *T:* 071–580 2222; Westons, Walberswick, Suffolk; Casa de Colina, Praia da Luz, Algarve. *Clubs:* MCC, Lord's Taverners', Groucho.

See also Lucian Freud.

FREUD, Lucian, CH 1983; painter; *b* 8 Dec. 1922; *s* of late Ernst and Lucie Freud; *m* 1st, 1948, Kathleen Garman Epstein (marr. diss. 1952), *d* of Jacob Epstein; two *d*; 2nd, 1953, Lady Caroline Maureen Blackwood (marr. diss. 1957), *d* of 4th Marquess of Dufferin and Ava. *Educ:* Central Sch. of Art; East Anglian Sch. of Painting and Drawing. Worked on merchant ship SS Baltrover as ordinary seaman, 1942. Teacher, Slade Sch. of Art, 1948–58; Vis. Asst, Norwich Sch. of Art, 1964–65. Painted mostly in France and Greece, 1946–48. Hon. Mem., Amer. Acad. and Inst. of Arts and Letters, 1988. *Exhibitions:* Lefevre Gall., 1944, 1946; London Gall., 1947, 1948; British Council and Galérie René Drouin, Paris, 1948; Hanover Gall., 1950, 1952; British Council and Vancouver Art Gall., 1951; British Council, Venice Biennale, 1954; Marlborough Fine Art, 1958, 1963, 1968; Anthony d'Offay, 1972, 1978 (subseq. Davis & Long, NY), 1982; Nishimura Gall., Tokyo, 1979; Thos Agnew & Sons, 1983; Scottish Nat. Gall. of Modern Art, 1988; *retrospectives:* Hayward Gall., 1974 (subseq. Bristol, Birmingham and Leeds), 1988 (also Washington, Paris and Berlin, 1987–88); Works on Paper, Ashmolean Mus., Oxford, 1988 (subseq. other towns in provinces and in USA). *Works included in public collections:* London: Tate Gall.; Nat. Portrait Gall.; V & A Museum; Arts Council of GB; British Council; British Mus.; DoE; provinces: Cecil Higgins Museum, Bedford; Fitzwilliam Mus., Cambridge; Nat. Mus. of Wales, Cardiff; Scottish Nat. Gall. of Mod. Art, Edinburgh; Hartlepool Art Gall.; Walker Art Gall., Liverpool; Liverpool Univ.; City Art Gall. and Whitworth Gall., Manchester; Ashmolean Mus. of Art, Oxford; Harris Mus. and Art Gall., Preston; Rochdale Art Gall.; Southampton Art Gall.; Australia: Queensland Art Gall., Brisbane; Art Gall. of S Australia, Adelaide; Art Gall. of WA, Perth; France: Musée National d'Art Moderne, Centre Georges Pompidou, Paris; Beaverbrook Foundn, Fredericton, New Brunswick; USA: Art Inst. of Chicago; Mus. of Mod. Art, NY; Cleveland Mus. of Art, Ohio; Mus. of Art, Carnegie Inst., Pittsburgh; Achenbaach Foundn for Graphic Arts and Fine Arts Mus. of San Francisco; Art Mus., St Louis; Hirshhorn Musum and Sculpture Garden, Smithsonian Instn, Washington. *Relevant publications:* Lucian Freud, by Lawrence Gowing, 1982; Lucian Freud, Paintings, by Robert Hughes, 1987; Lucian Freud, works on paper, by Nicholas Penney and Robert Flynn Johnson, 1988. *Address:* c/o James Kirkman, 46 Brompton Square, SW3 2AF.

See also Sir C. R. Freud.

FREYBERG, family name of **Baron Freyberg.**

FREYBERG, 2nd Baron, *cr* 1951, of Wellington, New Zealand, and of Munstead in the Co. of Surrey; **Paul Richard Freyberg,** OBE 1965; MC 1945; *b* 27 May 1923; *s* of 1st Baron Freyberg, VC, GCMG, KCB, KBE, DSO (and 3 bars), and Barbara, GBE (*d* 1973), *d* of Sir Herbert Jekyll, KCMG, and Lady Jekyll, DBE; *S* father, 1963; *m* 1960, Ivry Perronelle Katharine Guild, Aspall Hall, Debenham, Suffolk; one *s* three *d*. *Educ:* Eton Coll. Joined NZ Army, 1940; served with 2nd NZEF: Greece, 1941; Western Desert, 1941–42; transferred to British Army, 1942; Grenadier Guards; North Africa, 1943; Italy, 1943–45 (MC); Palestine, 1947–48; Cyprus, 1956–58; British Cameroons, 1961; Comd HAC Infantry Battalion, 1965–68; Defence Policy Staff, MoD, 1968–71; Dir Volunteers, Territorials and Cadets, 1971–75; Col, Gen. Staff, 1975–78, retired. Staff Coll., 1952; jssc 1958; sowc 1971. *Publication:* Bernard Freyberg, VC, 1991. *Heir: s* Hon. Valerian Bernard Freyberg, *b* 15 Dec. 1970. *Address:* Munstead House, Godalming, Surrey. *T:* Godalming (0483) 416004. *Clubs:* Boodle's, Royal Automobile.

FRICKER, (Anthony) Nigel; QC 1977; **His Honour Judge Fricker;** a Circuit Judge, since 1984; *b* 7 July 1937; *s* of late Dr William Shapland Fricker and of Margaret Fricker; *m* 1960, Marilyn Ann, *d* of A. L. Martin, Pa, USA; one *s* two *d*. *Educ:* King's School, Chester; Liverpool Univ. (LLB 1958). President of Guild of Undergraduates, Liverpool Univ., 1958–59. Called to Bar, Gray's Inn, 1960. Conf. Leader, Ford Motor Co. of Australia, Melbourne, 1960–61. Recorder, Crown Court, 1975–84; Prosecuting Counsel to DHSS, Wales and Chester Circuit, 1975–77; an asst comr, Boundary Commn for Wales, 1981–84. Member: Bar Council, 1966–70; Senate and Bar Council, 1975–78; County Court Rule Cttee, 1988–. Fellow, Internat. Acad. of Trial Lawyers, 1979–. Mem. Court: Liverpool Univ., 1977–; York Univ., 1984–. Confrérie des Chevaliers du Tastevin. *Publications:* (Gen. Ed. and jt author) Family Courts: Emergency Remedies and Procedures, 1990; (with David Bean) Enforcement of Injunctions and Undertakings, 1991; contrib. legal periodicals in UK and USA (Family and Conciliation Courts Rev.). *Address:* 6 Park Square, Leeds LS1 2LW. *T:* Leeds (0532) 459763; Farrar's Building, Temple, EC4Y 7BD. *T:* 071–583 9241. *Club:* Yorkshire (York).

FRICKER, Rt. Rev. Joachim Carl; a Suffragan Bishop of Toronto (Bishop of Credit Valley), since 1985; Canon of Christ's Church Cathedral, Hamilton, since 1964; *b* Zweibrucken, Germany, 1 Dec. 1927; *s* of Carl and Caroline Fricker; *m* 1952, Shirley Joan (*née* Gill); three *s* two *d*. *Educ:* Niagara Falls Public Schools; Univ. of Western Ontario (BA); Huron College (LTh). Ordained deacon and priest, 1952; Rector: St Augustine's, Hamilton, 1952–59; St David's, Welland, 1959–65; St James, Dundas, 1965–73; Dean of Diocese of Niagara and Rector, Christ's Church Cathedral, 1973–85. Chm., Nat. Doctrine and Worship Cttee (Anglican Church of Canada), 1989–June 1992. Hon. DD: Huron Coll., 1974; Trinity Coll., 1987; Hon. DSL, Wycliffe Coll., 1987. *Recreations:* theatre, gardening, reading, walking. *Address:* 2052 Mississauga Road, Mississauga, Ontario L5H 2K6, Canada. *T:* 416–274–5108.

FRIEDBERGER, Maj.-Gen. John Peter William, CB 1991; CBE 1986 (MBE 1975); Administrator, Sovereign Base Areas and Commander, British Forces, Cyprus, 1988–90; *b* 27 May 1937; *s* of late Brig. John Cameron Friedberger, DSO, DL and Phyllis Grace Friedberger, JP; *m* 1966, Joanna Mary, *d* of Andrew Thorne; one *s* two *d*. *Educ:* Red House School, York; Wellington College; RMA Sandhurst. Commissioned, 10th Royal Hussars (PWO), 1956; seconded to Northern Frontier Regt, Sultan's Armed Forces, Oman, 1961–63; Australian Army Staff Coll., 1969; CO The Royal Hussars (PWO), 1975–78; RCDS, 1978–79; Comdr, Royal Brunei Armed Forces, 1982–86; ACOS, HQ Northern Army Group, 1986–88. Hon. Col, Royal Hussars (PWO), 1991–. FRGS. Dato, DPKT (Negara Brunei Darussalam) 1984. *Recreation:* travel. *Address:* c/o Home HQ, The Royal Hussars (PWO), Peninsula Barracks, Winchester, Hants SO23 8TS. *Club:* Cavalry and Guards.

FRIEDLANDER, Frederick Gerard, (Friedrich Gerhart), PhD; FRS 1980; Reader Emeritus, University of Cambridge, since 1982; Hon. Research Fellow, Department of Mathematics, University College London; *b* Vienna, 25 Dec. 1917. *Educ:* Univ. of Cambridge (BA, PhD). Fellow of Trinity Coll., Cambridge, 1940; Temporary Experimental Officer, Admiralty, 1943; Faculty Asst Lectr, Cambridge, 1945; Lecturer: Univ. of Manchester, 1946; Univ. of Cambridge, 1954; Fellow of St John's Coll., Cambridge, 1961; Fellow of Wolfson Coll., Cambridge, 1968; Reader in Partial Differential Equations, Univ. of Cambridge, 1979. *Publications:* Sound Pulses, 1958; The Wave Equation on a Curved Space-Time, 1975; Introduction to the Theory of Distributions, 1982; papers in mathematical jls. *Address:* 43 Narcissus Road, NW6 1TL. *T:* 071–794 8665.

FRIEDMAN, David Peter; QC 1990; *b* 1 June 1944; *s* of Wilfred Emanuel Friedman and Rosa Lees; *m* 1972, Sara Geraldine Linton. *Educ:* Tiffin Boys' School; Lincoln College, Oxford (BCL, MA). Called to the Bar, Inner Temple, 1968. *Recreations:* good food (cooked by others), computer programming, reading. *Address:* 3 Paper Buildings, Temple, EC4Y 7EU. *T:* 071–583 1183. *Club:* Lansdowne.

FRIEDMAN, Prof. Milton, PhD; Economist, USA; Senior Research Fellow, Hoover Institution, Stanford University, since 1976; Professor Emeritus of Economics, University of Chicago, since 1982 (Professor of Economics, 1948–82); Member of Research Staff, National Bureau of Economic Research, 1948–81; Economic Columnist, Newsweek, 1966–84; *b* New York, 31 July 1912; *s* of Jeno Saul and Sarah E. Friedman; *m* 1938, Rose Director; one *s* one *d*. *Educ:* Rutgers (AB), Chicago (AM), and Columbia (PhD) Univs. Associate Economist, Natural Resources Cttee, Washington, 1935–37; Nat. Bureau of Economic Research, New York, 1937–45 (on leave 1940–45). During 1941–45: Principal Economist, Tax Research Div., US Treasury Dept, 1941–43; Associate Dir, Statistical Research Gp, Div. of War Research, Columbia Univ., 1943–45. Fulbright Lecturer, Cambridge Univ., 1953–54; Vis. Prof., Econs, Columbia Univ., 1964–65, etc. Member: President's Commn on an All-Volunteer Armed Force, 1969–70; Commn on White House Fellows, 1971–73. Mem. Bd of Editors, Econometrica, 1957–65; Pres., Amer. Economic Assoc., 1967; Pres., Mont Pelerin Soc., 1970–72. John Bates Clark Medal, Amer. Econ. Assoc., 1951; Member various societies, etc., incl. Royal Economic Soc. (GB). Fellowships and awards, in USA. Holds several Hon. doctorates. Nobel Memorial Prize for Economics, 1976; Nat. Medal of Sci., USA, 1988. Grand Cordon, Sacred Treasure (Japan), 1986; US Presidential Medal of Freedom, 1988. *Publications:* Income from Independent Professional Practice (with Simon Kuznets), 1946; Sampling Inspection (with others), 1948; Essays in Positive Economics, 1953; (ed) Studies in the Quantity Theory of Money, 1956; A Theory of the Consumption Function, 1957; A Program for Monetary Stability, 1960; Capitalism and Freedom, 1962; Price Theory: a Provisional Text, 1962; A Monetary History of the United States 1867–1960 (with Anna J. Schwartz), 1963; Inflation: Causes and Consequences, 1963; The Balance of Payments: Free versus Flexible Exchange Rates (with Robert V. Roosa), 1967; Dollars and Deficits, 1968; Optimum Quantity of Money and Other Essays, 1969; Monetary vs Fiscal Policy (with Walter W. Heller), 1969; Monetary Statistics of the United States (with Anna J. Schwartz), 1970; A Theoretical Framework for Monetary Analysis, 1971; Social Security: Universal or Selective? (with Wilbur J. Cohen), 1972; An Economist's Protest, 1972; Money and Economic Development, 1973; There's No Such Thing as a Free Lunch, 1975; Price Theory, 1976; Free to Choose (with Rose Friedman), 1980; Monetary Trends in the United States and the United Kingdom (with Anna J. Schwahtz), 1982; Bright Promises, Dismal Performance, 1983; (with Rose Friedman) Tyranny of the Status Quo, 1984. *Recreations:* tennis, carpentry. *Address:* Hoover Institution, Stanford, Calif 94305–6010, USA. *Club:* Quadrangle (Chicago).

FRIEDMANN, Jacques-Henri; Officier, Légion d'Honneur, 1988; Chevalier, Ordre du Mérite, 1970; Chairman: SAGI (Housing Society), since 1989; Caisse d'Epargne de Paris, since 1985; *b* Paris, 15 Oct. 1932; *s* of André Friedmann and Marie-Louise Bleiweiss; *m* 1962, Cécile Fleur; two *s* one *d*. *Educ:* Inst. d'Etudes Politiques, Paris (law degree). Student, Ecole Nat. d'Admin, 1957–58; Inspector of Finance, 1959; Lectr, Inst. d'Etudes Politiques, 1964–68; Special Asst 1964, Tech. Advr 1965–66, Deptl Staff of Valéry Giscard d'Estaing, Minister of Finance; Special Asst, Gen Directorate of Domestic Trade and Pricing, 1966; Actg Dep. Sec. Gen., Interministerial Cttee on Europ. Econ. Co-op., 1966–67; Hd, Finance Dept, French Planning Org., 1967–68; Chief Executive Secretary: to Jacques Chirac, Sec. of State for Econ. Affairs and Finance, 1969–70, and Minister responsible for liaison with Parlt, 1971; Hd of Dept of Gen. Inspectorate of Finances and of Central Dept of Gen. Inspectorate for the Nat. Economy, 1971–72; Advr on Econ. and Financial Affairs to Pierre Messmer, Prime Minister, then Chief Exec. Sec., 1972–74; Special Asst to Jacques Chirac, Prime Minister, 1974; Chm., Co. Générale Maritime, 1974–82; Inspector Gen. of Finance, 1980; Chm. and Man Dir, Co. Parisienne de Chauffage Urbaine, 1983–87; Special Asst to Edouard Balladur, Minister of Econ. Affairs, Finance and Privatisation, 1986–87; Chm., Air France, 1987–88. *Address:* SAGI, 4 Place de Rio de Janeiro, 75008 Paris. *T:* (1) 40.75.33.70.

FRIEL, Brian; writer; *b* 9 Jan. 1929; *s* of Patrick Friel and Christina Friel (*née* MacLoone); *m* 1954, Anne Morrison; one *s* four *d*. *Educ:* St Columb's Coll., Derry; St Patrick's Coll., Maynooth; St Joseph's Trng Coll., Belfast. Taught in various schools, 1950–60; writing full-time from 1960. Lived in Minnesota during first season of Tyrone Guthrie Theater, Minneapolis. Member: Irish Acad. of Letters, 1972; Aosdana, 1983–. Hon. DLitt: Chicago, 1979; NUI, 1983; NUU, 1986. *Publications: collected stories:* The Saucer of Larks, 1962; The Gold in the Sea, 1966; *plays:* Philadelphia, Here I Come!, 1965; The Loves of Cass McGuire, 1967; Lovers, 1968; The Mundy Scheme, 1969; Crystal and Fox, 1970; The Gentle Island, 1971; The Freedom of the City, 1973; Volunteers, 1975; Living Quarters, 1976; Aristocrats, 1979; Faith Healer, 1979; Translations, 1981 (Ewart-Biggs Meml Prize, British Theatre Assoc. Award); (trans.) Three Sisters, 1981; The Communication Cord, 1983; (trans.) Fathers and Sons, 1987; Making History, 1988; Dancing at Lughnasa, 1990. *Recreations:* reading, trout-fishing, slow tennis. *Address:* Drumaweir House, Greencastle, Co. Donegal, Ireland.

FRIEND, His Honour Archibald Gordon; a Circuit Judge, 1972–84, retired; *b* 6 July 1912; *m* 1940, Patricia Margaret Smith; no *c*. *Educ:* Dulwich Coll.; Keble Coll., Oxford (MA). Called to the Bar, Inner Temple, 1933. Served War: enlisted RA, Feb. 1940, commnd Nov. 1940; on staff of JAG MEF and PAIFORCE, 1941–44 (Major); released 1945. Dep. Chm., Herts Quarter Sessions, 1963–71, Inner London, later Mddx, QS, 1965–71; Inner London Crown Court, 1972–74; Knightsbridge Crown Court, 1974–84. *Recreation:* gardening. *Address:* 16 Ladbroke Grove, W11 3BQ.

FRIEND, Bernard Ernest, CBE 1986; Chairman: Supervisory Board, Ballast Nedam (Holland), since 1989; Brooke Tool Engineering (Holdings), since 1990 (Director, since 1989); *b* 18 May 1924; *s* of Richard Friend and Ada Florence Friend; *m* 1951, Pamela Florence Amor; one *s* two *d*. *Educ:* Dover Grammar Sch. Chartered Accountant. Flying Officer, RAF, 1943–47. Arthur Young & Co., Chartered Accountants, 1948–55; Comptroller, Esso Petroleum Co. Ltd, 1961–66; Dep. Controller, Esso Europe, 1967–68; Man. Dir, Essoheat, 1968–69; Vice-Pres., Esso Chemicals, Brussels, 1970–73; Chm. and Man. Dir, Esso Chemicals Ltd, 1974–76. Dir, British Aerospace, 1977–89 (Finance Dir, 1977–88). Chm., Graham Rintoul Investment Trust, 1987–. Non-Executive Director: Iron Trades Insurance Gp, 1980–; SD-Scicon, 1988–. *Address:* 27 Archer House, Vicarage Crescent, Battersea, SW11 3LF. *Club:* Royal Air Force.

FRIEND, Lionel; Musical Director: Nexus Opera, since 1981; New Sussex Opera, since 1989; *b* 13 March 1945; *s* of Moya and Norman A. C. Friend; *m* 1969, Jane Hyland; one *s* two *d*. *Educ:* Royal Grammar School, High Wycombe; Royal College of Music; London Opera Centre. LRAM; ARCM. Glyndebourne Opera, 1969–72; Welsh National Opera, 1969–72; Kapellmeister, Staatstheater, Kassel, Germany, 1972–75; Staff Conductor, ENO, 1978–89. Guest Conductor: BBC orchestras; Nash Ensemble, etc. *Recreations:* reading, theatre. *Address:* 136 Rosendale Road, SE21 8LG. *T:* 081–761 7845.

FRIEND, Dame Phyllis (Muriel), DBE 1980 (CBE 1972); Chief Nursing Officer, Department of Health and Social Security, 1972–82; *b* 28 Sept. 1922; *d* of Richard Edward Friend. *Educ:* Herts and Essex High Sch., Bishop's Stortford; The London Hospital (SRN); Royal College of Nursing (RNT). Dep. Matron, St George's Hospital, 1956–59; Dep. Matron, 1959–61, Matron, 1961–68, Chief Nursing Officer 1969–72, The London Hospital. *Address:* Barnmead, Start Hill, Bishop's Stortford, Herts CM22 7TA. *T:* Bishop's Stortford (0279) 654873.

FRINK, Dame Elisabeth, DBE 1982 (CBE 1969); RA 1977 (ARA 1971); sculptor; *b* Thurlow, Suffolk, 14 Nov. 1930; British; *m* 1st, 1955, Michel Jammet (marr. diss. 1963); one *s*; 2nd, 1964, Edward Pool, MC (marr. diss. 1974); 3rd, 1974, Alexander Csáky. *Educ:* Convent of The Holy Family, Exmouth. Guildford Sch. of Art, 1947–49; Chelsea Sch. of Art, 1949–53. Exhibitions: Beaux Arts Gallery, 1952; *one-man exhibitions:* St George's Gallery, 1955; Waddington Galls, 1959, 1961, 1963, 1967, 1968, 1971, 1972, 1976, 1980, 1981; Royal Academy, 1985; Fischer Fine Art, 1989; also in provinces, and NY, Washington (Nat. Museum of Women in the Arts), Los Angeles, Johannesburg, Amsterdam, Montreal, Toronto and Sydney; retrospective, Hong Kong, 1989. Has undertaken many commns worldwide, and illus. various books. Represented in collections in USA, Australia, Holland, Sweden, Germany and Tate Gallery, London. Member: Bd Trustees, British Museum, 1975–89; Royal Fine Art Commn, 1976–81. Hon. Fellow: St Hilda's Coll., Oxford, 1986; Newnham Coll., Cambridge, 1986. Hon. LittD Cambridge, 1988; Hon. Dr RCA, 1982; DU Essex, 1988; Hon. DLitt Oxford, 1989; Dr *hc* Manchester, 1990; Hon. DLit Bristol, 1991. *Address:* PO Box 558, Blandford Forum, Dorset DT11 7XT.

FRIPP, Alfred Thomas, BM; FRCS; *b* 3 July 1899; *s* of late Sir Alfred Fripp, KCVO, and late Lady M. S. Fripp, *d* of late T. B. Haywood; *m* 1931, Kathleen Kimpton, (Jennie) (*d* 1986); one *s* two *d*. *Educ:* Winchester; Christ Church, Oxford. 2nd Lieut 1st Life Guards, 1917–18. Christ Church, Oxford, 1919–21; Guy's Hospital, 1921; Surg., Royal National Orthopædic Hospital, 1934–64. Mem., Pensions Appeal Tribunal, 1966–74. FRCS 1927. Pres. Orthopædic Section, RSocMed, 1950–51. *Recreations:* gardening, rowing. *Address:* Shalesbrook, Forest Row, Sussex RH18 5LS. *Club:* Leander (Henley-on-Thames).

FRISBY, Audrey Mary; *see* Jennings, A. M.

FRISBY, Roger Harry Kilbourne; QC 1969; a Recorder, 1972–78 and since 1986; *b* 11 Dec. 1921; 2nd *s* of late Herbert Frisby and Hylda Mary Frisby; *m* 1961, Audrey Mary (*see* A. M. Jennings) (marr. diss. 1980); two *s* one *d* (and one *s* one *d* by previous marriage). *Educ:* Bablake Sch.; Christ Church, Oxford; King's Coll., Univ. of London. Called to the Bar, Lincoln's Inn, 1950. *Address:* Queen Elizabeth Building, Temple, EC4Y 9BS. *T:* 071–583 5766. *Club:* Hurlingham.

FRISBY, Terence; playwright, actor, producer, director; *b* 28 Nov. 1932; *s* of William and Kathleen Frisby; *m* 1963, Christine Vecchione (marr. diss.); one *s*. *Educ:* Dobwalls Village Sch.; Dartford Grammar Sch.; Central Sch. of Speech Training and Dramatic Art. Substantial repertory acting and directing experience, also TV, films and musicals, 1957–63; appeared in A Sense of Detachment, Royal Court, 1972–73 and X, Royal Court, 1974; Clive Popkiss, in Rookery Nook, Her Majesty's, 1979, and many since. Productions: Once a Catholic (tour), 1980–81; There's a Girl in My Soup (tour), 1982; Woza Albert!, 1983; The Real Inspector Hound/Seaside Postcard (double bill), 1983–84; Comic Cuts, 1984. Has written many TV scripts, incl. series Lucky Feller, 1976; That's Love, 1988–90; film, There's A Girl in My Soup, 1970 (Writers Guild Award, Best British Comedy Screenplay). *Publications: plays:* The Subtopians, 1964; There's a Girl in My Soup, 1966; The Bandwagon, 1970; It's All Right if I Do It, 1977; Seaside Postcard, 1978; Just Remember Two Things: it's not fair and don't be late, 1989 (radio play; Giles Cooper Award, 1988). *Address:* c/o Harvey Unna and Stephen Durbridge Ltd, 24 Pottery Lane, Holland Park, W11 4LZ. *T:* 071–727 1346. *Club:* Richmond Golf.

FRISCHMANN, Wilem William, CBE 1990; PhD; FEng 1985; FIStructE; FCGI; Senior Partner, Pell Frischmann & Partners, Consulting Engineers, since 1968; Chairman: Pell Frischmann Consulting Engineers, since 1985; Pell Frischmann Consultants, since 1986; Pell Frischmann Milton Keynes, since 1988; Pell Frischmann, since 1988; Conseco International, since 1985; Managing Director, Pell Frischmann Water, since 1990; *s* of Lajos Frischmann and Nelly Frischmann; *m* 1957, Sylvia Elvey; one *s* one *d*. *Educ:* Hungary; Hammersmith College of Art and Building; Imperial Coll. of Science and Technology (DIC); City University (PhD). MASCE, MSISdeFr, MConsE. FIStructE 1964; FCGI 1988. Engineering training with F. J. Samuely and Partners and W. S. Atkins and Partners; joined C. J. Pell and Partners, 1958, Partner, 1961. Structural Engineer for Nat. Westminster Tower (ICE Telford Premium Award), Centre Point, Drapers Gardens tower (IStructE Oscar Faber Prize) and similar high buildings, leisure buildings, hotels and hospitals; Engineer for works at Bank of England, Mansion House and Alexandra Palace; particular interest and involvement in tall economic buildings, shear walls and diaphragm floors, large bored piles in London clay, deep basements, lightweight materials for large span bridges, monitoring and quality assurance procedures for offshore structures; advisory appts include: Hong Kong and Shanghai Bank HQ, Malayan Banking Berhad, Kuala Lumpur. *Publications:* The use and behaviour of large diameter piles in London clay (IStructE paper), 1962; papers to learned socs and instns, originator of concepts: English Channel free-trade port; industrial complex based on Varne and Colbart sandbanks; two-mile high vertical city. *Recreations:* ski-ing, tennis, swimming, architecture, work. *Address:* (office) 5 Manchester Square, W1A 1AU; Haversham Grange, Haversham Close, Twickenham, Middx TW1 2JP. *T:* 081–892 8829. *Club:* Arts.

FRITH, Anthony Ian Donald; Board Member: Bristol Waterworks Co., since 1989; Bath District Health Authority, since 1990; consultant, since 1990; *b* 11 March 1929; *s* of Ernest and Elizabeth Frith; *m* 1952, Joyce Marcelle Boyce; one *s* one *d*. *Educ:* various grammar schs and techn. colls. CEng, FIGasE, MInstM. Various appts in North Thames Gas Bd and Gas Light & Coke Co., 1945–65; Sales Man. 1965–67, Dep. Commercial Man. 1967–68, North Thames Gas Bd; Marketing Man., Domestic and Commercial Gas, Gas Council, 1968–72; Sales Dir, British Gas Corp., 1972–73; Chm., SW Region, British Gas, 1973–90. CBIM 1983. *Publications:* various techn. and prof. in Gas Engineering and other jls. *Recreations:* fishing, golf. *Address:* Greenacres, Kingwell Hall, Timsbury, Avon.

FRITH, David Edward John; Editorial Director, Wisden Cricket Monthly, since 1979; *b* 16 March 1937; *s* of Edward Frith and Patricia Lillian Ethel Frith (*née* Thomas); *m* 1957, Debbie Oriel Christina Pennell; two *s* one *d*. *Educ:* Canterbury High Sch., Sydney. First grade cricket, Sydney, 1960–64. Editor, The Cricketer, 1972–78; Founder and Editor, Wisden Cricket Monthly, 1979. Cricket Soc. Literary Award, 1970 and 1987; Cricket Writer of the Year, Wombwell Cricket Lovers Soc., 1984; Magazine Sports Writer of the Year, Sports Council, 1988. *Publications:* Runs in the Family (with John Edrich), 1969; My Dear Victorious Stod, 1977; (ed) Cricket Gallery, 1976; (with Greg Chappell) The Ashes '77, 1977; The Golden Age of Cricket 1890–1914, 1978; The Ashes '79, 1979; Thommo, 1980; The Fast Men, 1981; The Slow Men, 1984; (with Gerry Wright) Cricket's Golden Summer, 1985; (ed) England *v* Australia Test Match Records 1877–1985, 1986; Archie Jackson, 1987; Pageant of Cricket, 1987; Guildford Jubilee 1938–1988, 1988; England *v* Australia: A Pictorial History of the Test Matches since 1877, 1990; By His Own Hand, 1991. *Recreations:* playing cricket, collecting cricketana, watching documentaries, culling Queensland cane toads. *Address:* 6 Beech Lane, Guildford, Surrey GU2 5ES. *T:* Guildford (0483) 32573. *Club:* MCC.

FRITH, Donald Alfred, OBE 1980; MA; Secretary, Headmasters' Conference, and General Secretary, Secondary Heads' Association, 1979–83; *b* 13 May 1918; *yr s* of late Charles Henry Frith and Mabel (*née* Whiting); *m* 1941, Mary Webster Tyler (*d* 1989), *yr d* of late Raymond Tyler and Rosina Mary (*née* Wiles); four *s* one *d*. *Educ:* Whitgift Sch. (schol.); Christ's Coll., Cambridge (schol.). MA Cantab 1944. Served War, 1940–46; commnd RASC; served in Middle East, Italy and at WO. Deme Warden, University College Sch., 1946–52; Headmaster, Richmond Sch., Yorks, 1953–59; Headmaster, Archbishop Holgate's Grammar Sch., York, 1959–78. Asst Dir, Centre for Study of Comprehensive Schs, 1983–88; Chm., N Yorks Forum for Vol. Orgns, 1983–91; Dir, N Yorks TEC, 1990–. Chm., School Curriculum (formerly Schools Council) Industry Project, 1979–86. Additional Mem., N Yorks CC Educn Cttee, 1973–77. Chm., York Community Council, 1971–79. JP York, 1966–79. *Publication:* (gen. ed.) School Management in Practice, 1985. *Recreations:* music, gardening, reading. *Address:* Kilburn, York YO6 4AQ. *Clubs:* Athenæum; Yorkshire (York).

FRITH, Air Vice-Marshal Edward Leslie, CB 1973; *b* 18 March 1919; *s* of late Charles Edward Frith, ISO. *Educ:* Haberdashers' Askes School. Gp Captain, 1961; Air Cdre, 1968; Dir of Personal Services (2) RAF, MoD, 1969–71; Air Vice-Marshal, 1971; Air Officer Administration, Maintenance Comd, later Support Comd, 1971–74. *Recreations:* lawn tennis, bridge. *Clubs:* Roehampton, All England Lawn Tennis and Croquet, International Lawn Tennis of GB.

FRITSCH, Elizabeth; potter; *b* Shropshire, 1940; *d* of Welsh parents; one *s* one *d*. *Educ:* Royal Acad. of Music; Royal College of Art (Silver Medallist, 1970). Established own workshop, E London, 1985. Mem., Crafts Council (Bursary awarded, 1980). *One-woman exhibitions* include: Crafts Council, 1974; CAA, 1976; Leeds City Art Galls, 1978, touring to Glasgow, Bristol, Bolton and Gateshead City Art Galls; V & A, 1980; RCA, 1984; Besson Gall., London, 1989; Royal Mus. of Scotland, 1990; Hetjens Mus., Dusseldorf, 1990; *group exhibitions* include: Oxford Gall., 1974; ICA, 1985; Kunstler Haus, Vienna, 1986; Fischer Fine Art, London, 1987; Kyoto and Tokyo Nat. Museums of Modern Art, 1988; Crafts Council, touring to Amsterdam, 1988; Sotheby's, 1988; 35 Connaught Square, London (Lord Queensberry), 1991; Stuttgart, 1991; Oriel Gall., Cardiff, 1991; *works in public collections:* V & A; Crafts Council; Lotherton Hall, Leeds City Art Galls; Royal Mus. of Scotland; Glasgow, Bolton, Bristol and Birmingham City Art Galls. Judge, Fletcher Challenge Internat. Ceramics Competition, NZ, 1990. Major influences on work: music, fresco painting, topology. Herbert Read Meml Prize, 1970; Winner, Royal Copenhagen Jubilee Competition, 1972; Gold Medal, Internat. Ceramics Competition, Sopot, Poland, 1976. *Recreations:* music, mountains, theatre.

FRODSHAM, Anthony Freer, CBE 1978; company director and management consultant; Chairman of Council, European Business School, since 1986 (Member, since 1983); *b* Peking, China, 8 Sept. 1919; *er s* of late George William Frodsham and Constance Violet Frodsham (*née* Neild); *m* 1953, Patricia Myfanwy, *o c* of late Cmdr A. H. Wynne-Edwards, DSC, RN; two *s*. *Educ:* Ecole Lacordaire, Paris; Faraday House Engineering Coll., London. DFH, CEng, FIMechE, FIMC, CBIM. Served War, 1940–46: Engineer Officer, RN, Asst Fleet Engr Officer on staff of C-in-C Mediterranean, 1944–46 (despatches, 1945). P-E Consulting Group Ltd, 1947–73: Man. Dir and Gp Chief Exec., 1963–72; Group Specialist Adviser, United Dominions Trust Ltd, 1973–74; Dir-Gen., EEF, 1975–82; Director: TACE Ltd, 1973–76; Arthur Young Management Services, 1973–79; F. Pratt Engrg Corp. Ltd, 1982–85; Greyfriars Ltd, 1984–88 (Dep. Chm., 1986–88). Chairman: Management Consultants Assoc., 1968–70; Machine Tools EDC, 1973–79; Independent Chm., Compressed Air and Allied Machinery Cttee, 1976–; Chm., European Business Institute Adv. Cttee, 1982–; Vice-Chm., British Export Finance Adv. Council, 1982–87; President: Inst. of Management Consultants, 1967–68; Inst. of Linguists, 1986–89; Member: CBI Grand Council, 1975–82; CBI President's Cttee, 1979–82; Engineering Industry Training Bd, 1975–79; W European Metal Working Employers' Assoc., 1975–82; Manadon Adv. Council, RNEC, 1988–; Enterprise Counsellor, DTI, 1988–91. A General Commissioner of Tax, 1975–. Conducted MoD Study into Provision of Engineer Officers for Armed Services, 1983. Hon. FIL. Hon. DBA RNEC, 1991. *Publications:* contrib. to technical jls; lectures and broadcasts on management subjects. *Address:* 36 Fairacres, Roehampton Lane, SW15 5LX. *T:* 081–878 9551. *Club:* Carlton.

FROGGATT, Sir Leslie (Trevor), Kt 1981; Chairman, Ashton Mining Ltd, since 1981; *b* 8 April 1920; *s* of Leslie and Mary Helena Froggatt (*née* Brassey); *m* 1945, Jessie Elizabeth Grant; three *s*. *Educ:* Birkenhead Park Sch., Cheshire. Joined Asiatic Petroleum Co. Ltd, 1937; Shell Singapore, Shell Thailand, Shell Malaya, 1947–54; Shell Egypt, 1955–56; Dir of Finance, Gen. Manager, Kalimantan, Borneo, and Dep. Chief Rep., PT Shell Indonesia, 1958–62; Shell International Petroleum Co. Ltd: Area Co-ordinator, S Asia and Australia, 1962–63; assignment in various Shell cos in Europe, 1964–66; Shell Oil Co., Atlanta, 1967–69; Chm. and Chief Exec. Officer, Shell Gp in Australia, 1969–80; non-exec. Dir, Shell Australia Ltd, 1981–87. Chm., Pacific Dunlop, 1986–90 (Vice-Chm., 1981; Dir, 1978–90). Director: Australian Industry Develt Corp., 1978–90; Australian Inst. of Petroleum Ltd, 1976–80, 1982–84 (Chm., 1977–79); Moonee Valley Racing Club Nominees Pty Ltd, 1977–; Tandem Computers Pty Ltd, 1989–. Member: Australian Nat. Airlines Commn (Australian Airlines), 1981–87 (Vice-Chm., 1984–87); Internat. Bd of Advice, ANZ Banking Gp, 1986–; Internat. Adv. Council, Tandem Computers Inc., USA, 1988–. *Recreations:* reading, music, racing, golf. *Address:* 20 Albany Road, Toorak, Vic 3142, Australia. *T:* (03) 822.1357. *Clubs:* Melbourne, Australian, Victoria Racing, Victoria Amateur Turf, Moonee Valley Racing, Commonwealth Golf (Melbourne).

FROGGATT, Sir Peter, Kt 1985; MD; FRCP, FRCPI; Director, AIB Group plc, since 1984; Pro-Chancellor, Dublin University, since 1985; President and Vice-Chancellor, Queen's University of Belfast, 1976–86; *b* 12 June 1928; *s* of Albert Victor and Edith (*née* Curran); *m* 1958, Norma Cochrane; four *s* (and one *s* decd). *Educ:* Royal Belfast Academical Institution; Royal Sch., Armagh (Schol.); Trinity Coll., Dublin (BA; MB; BCh; BAO 1952; MA 1956; MD 1957; Welland Prize; Cunningham Medal; Begley Schol.); Queen's Univ., Belfast (DPH 1956; PhD 1967; Carnwath Prize). MRCPI 1972; FRCPI 1973; FFPHM (FFCM 1973); MRCP 1974; FFOMI 1975; FFCMI 1976; MRIA 1978; FRCP 1980. House Surgeon and Physician, Sir Patrick Dun's Hosp., Dublin, 1952–53; Nuffield Res. Student, 1955–57; Med. Officer, Short Bros and Harland Ltd, 1957–59; Queen's University, Belfast: Lectr, 1959–65; Reader, 1965–68; Prof. of Epidemiology, 1968–76; Dean, Faculty of Medicine, 1971–76; Consultant, Eastern Health and Social Services Board, 1960–76. Hon. Prof., St Bartholemew's Hosp. Med. Sch., 1986–. Rock Carling Fellow, Nuffield Provincial Hosps Trust, 1991–92. Chairman: Independent Scientific Cttee on Smoking and Health, 1980–91 (Mem., 1977–80); Tobacco Products Res. Trust, 1981–; ASME, 1987–; Pres., Biol Scis Section, British Assoc., 1987–88; Member: Bd, 1983–85, Adv. Cttee, NI, 1988–, British Council; Gen. Adv. Cttee, BBC, 1986–88; Supervisory Bd, NHS NI, 1986–. Hon. Member: Soc. for Social Medicine; Soc. of Occupational Medicine. Lectures: Robert Adams, 1977, Kirkpatrick, 1984, Abrahamson, 1986, RCSI; Apothecaries, SOM, 1978; Freyer, NUI, 1984; Bayliss, RCP, 1989; Smiley, FOMI, 1989. Freeman, City of London, 1990. FSS 1963; Hon. FRCSI 1988; Hon. Fellow, Royal Acad. of Medicine in Ireland; CBIM 1986. Hon. LLD: TCD, 1981; QUB, 1991; Hon. DSc NUI, 1982. Dominic Corrigan Gold Medal, RCPI, 1981. *Publications:* (jtly) Causation of Bus-driver Accidents: Epidemiological Study, 1963; (ed jtly) Nicotine, Smoking and the Low Tar Programme, 1988; articles in jls on human genetics, occupational medicine, med. history, med. educn, epidemiology and smoking policies. *Recreations:* golf, music, travel. *Address:* Rathganley, 3 Strangford Avenue, Belfast BT9 6PG.

FRÖHLICH, Prof. Albrecht, PhD; FRS 1976; Professor of Pure Mathematics, King's College, University of London, 1962–81, now Emeritus Professor; Senior Research Fellow, Imperial College, University of London, since 1982; Emeritus Fellow, Robinson College, Cambridge, (Fellow 1982–84); *b* 22 May 1916; *s* of Julius Fröhlich and Frida Fröhlich; *m* 1950, Dr Evelyn Ruth Brooks; one *s* one *d. Educ:* Realgymnasium, Munich; Bristol Univ. (BSc 1948, PhD 1951). Asst Lectr in Maths, University Coll., Leicester, 1950–52; Lectr in Maths, University Coll. of N Staffs, 1952–55; King's College, London: Reader in Pure Maths, 1955–62; Hd, Dept of Maths, 1971–81. Vis. Royal Soc.-Israeli Acad. Research Prof., 1978; George A. Miller Prof., Univ. of Illinois, 1981–82; Gauss Prof., Göttingen Acad. of Scis, 1983; vis. prof. at other univs in USA, Canada, Germany, France and Switzerland. Corres. Mem., Heidelberg Acad. of Scis, 1982. FKC 1977. Hon. DSc Bordeaux, 1986. Senior Berwick Prize, London Math. Soc., 1976. *Publications:* Formal Groups, 1968; Module Structure of Algebraic Integers, 1983; Class Groups and Hermitian Modules, 1984; papers in math. jls. *Recreations:* cooking, eating, walking, music. *Address:* Robinson College, Cambridge.

FROOD, Alan Campbell, CBE 1988; Managing Director, Crown Agents for Oversea Governments and Administrations, 1978–88; Crown Agent, 1980–88; *b* 15 May 1926; *s* of James Campbell Frood, MC and Margaret Helena Frood; *m* 1960, Patricia Ann Cotterell; two *s* two *d. Educ:* Cranleigh Sch.; Peterhouse, Cambridge. Royal Navy, 1944–47 (Sub-Lt RNVR). Bank of England, 1949; Colonial Admin. Service, 1952; Bankers Trust Co., 1962; Dir, Bankers Trust Internat. Ltd, 1967; Gen. Man., Banking Dept, Crown Agents, 1975; Dir of Financial Services, Crown Agents, 1976–78. Hon. Treas., 1973–, and Trustee, 1986–, Queen's Nursing Inst. *Recreations:* sailing, gardening. *Address:* West Orchard, Holmbush Lane, Henfield, West Sussex BN5 9TJ. *T:* Poynings (0273) 857257.

FROSSARD, Sir Charles (Keith), Kt 1983; Bailiff of Guernsey, 1982–92; Judge of the Court of Appeal, Jersey, 1983–92; *b* 18 Feb. 1922; *s* of late Edward Louis Frossard, CBE, MA, Hon. CF, Dean of Guernsey, 1947–67, and Margery Smith Latta; *m* 1950, Elizabeth Marguerite, *d* of late J. E. L. Martel, OBE; two *d. Educ:* Elizabeth Coll., Guernsey; Univ. de Caen (Bachelier en Droit; *Dhc* 1990). Enlisted Gordon Highlanders, 1940; commnd 1941, 17 Dogra Regt, Indian Army; seconded to Tochi Scouts and Chitral Scouts; served India and NW Frontier, 1941–46. Called to Bar, Gray's Inn, 1949; Advocate of Royal Court of Guernsey, 1949; People's Deputy, States of Guernsey, 1958–67; Conseiller, States of Guernsey, 1967–69; HM Solicitor General, Guernsey, 1969–73; HM Attorney General, Guernsey, 1973–76; Dep. Bailiff of Guernsey, 1977–82. Member, Church Assembly and General Synod, Church of England, 1960–82. ACIArb 1987. KStJ 1985. Médaille de Vermeil, Paris, 1984. *Recreations:* hill walking, fishing. *Address:* Les Lierres, Rohais, St Peter Port, Guernsey. *T:* Guernsey (0481) 22076. *Clubs:* Army and Navy, Naval and Military; United (Guernsey).

FROST, Abraham Edward Hardy, CBE 1972; Counsellor, Foreign and Commonwealth Office, 1972–78; *b* 4 July 1918; *s* of Abraham William Frost and Margaret Anna Frost; *m* 1972, Gillian (*née* Crossley); two *d. Educ:* Royal Grammar Sch., Colchester King's Coll., Cambridge (MA); London Univ. (BScEcon). FCIS. RNVR, 1940–46 (Lieut). ILO, Geneva, 1947–48; HM Treasury, 1948–49; Manchester Guardian, City Staff, 1949–51; FO (later FCO), 1951–78. *Publication:* In Dorset Of Course (poems), 1976. *Address:* Hill View, Buckland Newton, Dorset DT2 7BS. *T:* Buckland Newton (03005) 415.

FROST, Albert Edward, CBE 1983; Director, Marks & Spencer Ltd, 1976–87; Chairman, Remploy, 1983–87; *b* 7 March 1914; *s* of Charles Albert Frost and Minnie Frost; *m* 1942, Eugénie Maud Barlow. *Educ:* Oulton Sch., Liverpool; London Univ. Called to the Bar, Middle Temple (1st Cl. Hons). HM Inspector of Taxes, Inland Revenue, 1937; Imperial Chemical Industries Ltd: Dep. Head, Taxation Dept, 1949; Dep. Treasurer, 1957; Treasurer, 1960; Finance Dir, 1968; retd 1976. Director: British Airways Corp., 1976–80; BL Ltd, 1977–80; S. G. Warburg & Co., 1976–83; British Steel, 1980–83 (Chm., Audit and Salaries Cttees); Guinness Peat Gp, 1983–84; Chairman: Guinness Mahon Hldgs Ltd, 1983–84; Guinness Mahon & Co., 1983–84; Billingsgate City Securities, 1989–90. Mem. Council, St Thomas's Med. Sch., London, 1974– (Chm., Finance Cttee, 1978–85); Governor, United Med. Schs of Guy's and St Thomas's Hosps, 1982– (Dep. Chm. of Govs, 1989–; Chm., Finance and Investment Cttees, 1982–85); Member: Council and Finance Cttee, Morley Coll., London, 1975–85; Council, Assoc. for Business Sponsorship of the Arts, 1976– (Jt Dep. Chm.); Exec. Cttee for Develt Appeal, Royal Opera House, Covent Garden, 1975–87; Arts Council of GB, 1982–84; Chairman: Robert Mayer Trust for Youth and Music, 1981–90 (Dir, 1977–90); Jury, and of Org. Cttee, City of London Carl Flesch Internat. Violin Competition. Trustee and Treas., Loan Fund for Mus. Instruments; Dir, City Arts Trust, 1982–. FRSA. *Publications:* (contrib.) Simon's Income Tax, 1952; (contrib.) Gunns Australian Income Tax Law and Practice, 1960; articles on financial matters affecting industry and on arts sponsorship. *Recreations:* violinist (chamber music); swimming (silver medallist, Royal Life Saving Assoc.); athletics (county colours, track and cross country); walking; arts generally. *Address:* Michael House, Baker Street, W1A 1DN. *T:* 071–935 4422. *Club:* Royal Automobile.

FROST, David (Paradine), OBE 1970; author, producer, columnist; star of "The Frost Report", "The Frost Programme", "Frost on Friday", "The David Frost Show", "The Frost Interview", etc; Joint Founder, London Weekend Television; Chairman and Chief Executive, David Paradine Ltd, since 1966; Joint Founder and Director, TV-am; *b* 7 April 1939; *s* of late Rev. W. J. Paradine Frost, Tenterden, Kent; *m* 1983, Lady Carina Fitzalan-Howard, 2nd *d* of Duke of Norfolk, *qv*; three *s. Educ:* Gillingham Grammar Sch.; Wellingborough Grammar Sch.; Gonville and Caius Coll., Cambridge (MA). Sec., The Footlights; Editor, Granta. LLD, Emerson Coll., USA. BBC Television series: That Was the Week That Was, 1962–63 (in USA, 1964–65); A Degree of Frost, 1963, 1973; Not So Much a Programme, More a Way of Life, 1964–65; The Frost Report, 1966–67; Frost Over England, 1967; Frost Over America, 1970; Frost's Weekly, 1973; The Frost Interview, 1974; We British, 1975–76; Forty Years of Television, 1976; The Frost Programme, 1977; The Guinness Book of Records Hall of Fame, 1986, 1987, 1988; Pull the Other One, 1987, 1988, 1990. David Frost at the Phonograph (BBC Sound), 1966, 1972. Frost on Thursday (LBC), 1974. ITV series and programmes: The Frost Programme, 1966–67, 1967–68; Frost on Friday, 1968–69, 1969–70; The Frost Programme, 1972, 1973; The Sir Harold Wilson Interviews, 1976; A Prime Minister on Prime Ministers, 1977–78; Are We Really Going to be Rich?, 1978; David Frost's Global Village, 1979, 1980, 1982; The 25th Anniversary of ITV, The Begin Interview, and Elvis—He Touched Their Lives, 1980; The BAFTA Awards, and Onward Christian Soldiers, 1981; A Night of Knights: a Royal Gala, 1982; The End of the Year Show, 1982, 1983; TV-am, 1983–; David Frost Presents Ultra Quiz, 1984; Twenty Years On, 1985, 1986; Through the Keyhole, 1987, 1988, 1989, 1990. Other programmes include: David Frost's Night Out in London (USA), 1966–67; The Next President (USA), 1968, 1988; Robert Kennedy the Man (USA), 1968; The David Frost Show (USA), 1969–70, 1970–71, 1971–72; The David Frost Revue (USA), 1971–72, 1972–73; That Was the Year That Was (USA), 1973, 1985; David Frost Presents the Guinness Book of Records (USA), 1973, 1974, 1975, 1976; Frost over Australia, 1972, 1973, 1974, 1977; Frost over New Zealand, 1973, 1974; The Unspeakable Crime (USA), 1975; Abortion—Merciful or Murder? (USA), 1975; The Beatles—Once Upon a Time (USA), 1975; David Frost Presents the Best (USA), 1975; The Nixon Interviews with David Frost, 1976–77; The Crossroads of Civilization, 1977–78; Headliners with David Frost, 1978; A Gift of Song—MUSIC FOR UNICEF Concert, The Bee Gees Special, and The Kissinger Interview, 1979; The Shah Speaks, and The American Movie Awards, 1980; Show Business, This Is Your Life 30th Anniversary Special, The Royal Wedding (CBS), 1981; David Frost Presents The Internat. Guinness Book of World Records, annually 1981–; The American Movie Awards, Rubinstein at 95, and Pierre Elliott Trudeau, 1982; Frost over Canada, 1982, 1983; David Frost Live by Satellite from London, 1983; The Search for Josef Mengele, 1985; Spitting Image: Down and Out in the White House, 1986; The Spitting Image Movie Awards, 1987; The Spectacular World of Guinness Records, 1987–88; Entertainment Tonight, 1987, 1988; The Next President with David Frost, 1987–88; ABC Presents a Royal Gala, 1988; The President and Mrs Bush Talking with David Frost, 1989. Produced films: The Rise and Rise of Michael Rimmer, 1970; Charley One-Eye, 1972; Leadbelly, 1974; The Slipper and the Rose, 1975; James A. Michener's Dynasty, 1975; The Ordeal of Patty Hearst, 1978; The Remarkable Mrs Sanger, 1979. Mem., British/USA Bicentennial Liaison Cttee, 1973–76; Pres., Lord's Taverners, 1985, 1986. Golden Rose, Montreux, for Frost Over England, 1967; Royal Television Society's Silver Medal, 1967; Richard Dimbleby Award, 1967; Emmy Award (USA), 1970, 1971; Religious Heritage of America Award, 1970; Albert Einstein Award, Communication Arts, 1971. *Stage:* An Evening with David Frost (Edinburgh Fest.), 1966. *Publications:* That Was the Week That Was, 1963; How to Live under Labour, 1964; Talking with Frost, 1967; To England With Love, 1967; The Presidential Debate 1968, 1968; The Americans, 1970; Whitlam and Frost, 1974; I Gave Them a Sword, 1978; I Could Have Kicked Myself, (David Frost's Book of the World's Worst Decisions), 1982; Who Wants to be a Millionaire?, 1983; (jtly) The Mid-Atlantic Companion, 1986; (jtly) The Rich Tide, 1986; The World's Shortest Books, 1987. *Address:* David Paradine Ltd, 115–123 Bayham Street, NW1 0AG.

FROST, Ven. George; Archdeacon of Salop, since 1987; Vicar of Tong, since 1987; *b* 4 April 1935; *s* of William John Emson Frost and Emily Daisy Frost; *m* 1959, Joyce Pratt; four *s. Educ:* Hatfield Coll., Durham Univ. (BA 1956, MA 1961); Lincoln Theological Coll. Schoolmaster, Westcliff High School, 1956–57; labourer, Richard Thomas and Baldwin Steelworks, Scunthorpe, 1958–59; Asst Curate, St Margaret, Barking Parish Church, 1960–64; Minister, Ecclesiastical District of St Mark, Marks Gate, 1964–70; Vicar: St Matthew, Tipton, 1970–77; St Bartholomew, Penn, Wolverhampton, 1977–87; RD of Trysull, 1984–87; Prebendary of Lichfield Cathedral, 1985–87, Hon. Canon 1987–. *Recreations:* walking, wild flowers, photography. *Address:* Tong Vicarage, Shifnal TF11 8PW. *T:* Albrighton (0902) 372622.

FROST, Jeffrey Michael Torbet; Executive Director, London & Continental Bankers, 1983–89 (Associate Director, 1982–83); *b* 11 June 1938; *s* of late Basil Frost and Dorothy Frost. *Educ:* Diocesan Coll., Cape, South Africa; Radley Coll.; Oriel Coll., Oxford; Harvard Univ. Exec. Dir, Cttee on Invisible Exports, 1976–81. Hon. Sec., Anglo-Brazilian Soc., 1977–84. Liveryman, Worshipful Co. of Clockmakers. FRSA. *Recreations:* bridge, walking, listening to music. *Address:* 34 Paradise Walk, SW3 4JL. *T:* 071–352 8642; The Parish Room, Kintbury, near Newbury, Berks RG15 0UP.

FROST, Maj.-Gen. John Dutton, CB 1964; DSO 1943 and Bar, 1945; MC 1942; DL; farmer; *b* 31 Dec. 1912; *s* of late Brig.-Gen. F. D. Frost, CBE, MC; *m* 1947, Jean MacGregor Lyle; one *s* one *d. Educ:* Wellington Coll.; RMC Sandhurst. Commissioned The Cameronians, Sept. 1932; Capt., Iraq Levies, 1938–41; Major and Lt-Col, Parachute Regt, 1941–45 (Bruneval raid 1942, Oudna 1942, Tunisian campaign, 1942–43, Primosole Bridge, 1943, Italian campaign, 1943, Arnhem Bridge, 1944)); Staff Coll., Camberley, 1946; GSO2, HQ Lowland Dist, 1948–49; GSO2, Senior Officers' Sch., 1949–52; AA and QMG, 17 Gurkha Div., 1952–53; GSO1, 17 Gurkha Div., 1953–55; Comd, Netheravon, 1955–57; Comd, 44 Parachute Bde, 1958–61; Comdr 52nd Lowland Div./District, 1961–64; GOC Troops in Malta and Libya, 1964–66; Comdr Malta Land Force, 1965; retired, 1967. DL West Sussex, 1982. Cross of Grand Officer, SMO, Malta, 1966. *Publications:* A Drop Too Many, 1980; Two Para-Falklands, 1983. *Recreations:* field sports, polo, golf. *Address:* Northend Farm, Milland, Liphook, Hants GU30 7LT. *Club:* Army and Navy.

FROST, Dame Phyllis Irene, DBE 1974 (CBE 1963); Vice-Chairman, Clean World International, since 1980; Chairman, Victorian Relief Committee, since 1979 (Member since 1964); *b* 14 Sept. 1917; *née* Turner; *m* 1941, Glenn Neville Frost (*d* 1987), LDS, BDSc, JP; three *d. Educ:* Croydon Coll., Vic.; St Duthus Coll.; Presbyterian Ladies' Coll.; Univ. of Melbourne. Dip. of Physiotherapy, 1938; studied Criminology, 1939. Chairman: Victorian (formerly Fairlea) Women's Prison Council, 1953–; Aust. Contact Emergency Service, 1984–; Vice-Chairman, Victorian Assoc. for Care and Resettlement of Offenders, 1977–; Member: Internat. Fedn of Abolitionists, 1957–; State Disaster Welfare Cttees, Vic, 1983–. Hon. Life Member: Aust. Freedom from Hunger Campaign, 1972; Aust. Crime Prevention Council, 1972; Nat. Council of Women of Victoria, 1979; Trustee, patron, hon. life mem., hon. convener, and life governor of many community service, health and welfare orgns. Has attended several internat. confs as Aust. delegate or representative, including: Internat. Council of Women; FAO; FFHC (Chm., 4th Session in Rome, 1969; Chm., 3rd Regional Congress for Asia and the Far East, at Canberra, 1970, and Rome, 1971). Chm., Bd of Dirs, Brain Behaviour Res. Inst., La Trobe Univ. JP Croydon, Vic, 1957 (Hon. JP, 1957–84). Freedom, City of Croydon, 1989. Woman of the Year, Sun News Pictorial, 1970; Humanitarian Award, Rosicrucian Order, USA, 1971; Community Service Award, Victorian Employers' Fedn, 1978; Distinguished Service to Children Award, Aust. Parents without Partners, Vic, 1984; Community Service Award, Seventh Day Adventists, 1985. *Address:* Llanberis, 4 Jackson Street, Croydon, Victoria 3136, Australia. *T:* (03) 723 2382. *Club:* Royal Automobile (Vic.).

FROST, Hon. Sir Sydney; *see* Frost, Hon. Sir T. S.

FROST, Terence, (Terry Frost); artist; Professor of Painting, University of Reading, 1977–81 (formerly Reader in Fine Art), Professor Emeritus 1981; *b* Oct. 1915; *m* 1945; five *s* one *d*. *Educ:* Leamington Spa Central Sch. Exhibitions: Leicester Galls, 1952–58; Waddington Galls, 1958–; B. Schaeffer Gallery, New York, 1960–62; Plymouth 1976; Bristol 1976; Serpentine Gall., 1977; Paris, 1978; Norway, 1979; Austin/Desmond Fine Art, 1989. Oil paintings acquired by Tate Gallery, National Gallery of Canada, National Gallery of NSW; also drawing acquired by Victoria and Albert Museum. Other work in public collections; Canada, USA, Germany, Australia, and in Edinburgh, Dublin, Leeds, Hull, Manchester, Birmingham, Liverpool, Bristol, etc. Gregory Fellow in Painting, Univ. of Leeds, 1954–56. Hon. LLD CNAA, 1978. *Publication:* (illus.) 11 Poems by Federico Garcia Lorca, 1989. *Address:* Gernick Field Studio, Tredavoe Lane, Newlyn, Penzance TR18 5DL. *T:* Penzance (0736) 65902.

FROST, Thomas Pearson, FCIB; Director since 1984, and Group Chief Executive since 1987, National Westminster Bank (Deputy Group Chief Executive, 1985–87); *b* 1 July 1933; *s* of James Watterson Frost and Enid Ella Crawte (*née* Pearson); *m* 1958, Elizabeth (*née* Morton); one *s* two *d*. *Educ:* Ormskirk Grammar Sch. FCIB (FIB 1976). Joined Westminster Bank, 1950; Chief Exec. Officer and Vice Chm., NBNA (now National Westminster Bank USA), 1980; Gen. Man., Business Develt Div., National Westminster Bank, 1982. Member: BOTB, 1986–; UK Adv. Bd, British-American Chamber of Commerce, 1987–; Business in the Cities, 1988–; Policy Adv. Cttee, Tidy Britain Gp, 1988–; Chairman: CBI Business & Urban Regeneration Task Force, 1987–88; British Bankers' Assoc., 1991–. Trustee, British Sports Trust, 1988–; Gov., Royal Ballet Sch., 1988–. Fellow, World Scout Foundn, 1984. Freeman, City of London, 1978. CBIM; CompOR 1987. *Recreations:* golf, greenhouse, theatre. *Address:* National Westminster Bank, 41 Lothbury, EC2P 2BP. *T:* 071–726 1212.

FROST, Hon. Sir (Thomas) Sydney, Kt 1975; Chief Justice of Papua New Guinea, 1975–78, retired; *b* 13 Feb. 1916; *s* of late Thomas Frost, Redfern, NSW; *m* 1943, Dorothy Gertrude (*née* Kelly) (*d* 1990); two *s* one *d*. *Educ:* Univ. of Melbourne (Alexander Rushall Meml Scholarship; LLM). Served 2nd AIF, 1941–45. Barrister, Victoria, 1945–64; QC 1961; Judge of the County Court of Victoria, 1964; Judge of Supreme Court of Papua New Guinea, 1964–75. Chairman: Aust. Govt Inquiry into Whales and Whaling, 1978; Royal Commn of Inquiry into Housing Commn Land Purchases and Valuation Matters, Vic., 1979–81; Bd of Accident Inquiry into causes of crash of Beechcraft Super King Air, Sydney, 21 Feb. 1980, 1982. Pres., Medical Services Review Tribunal, 1979–84. *Recreation:* golf. *Address:* Park Tower, 201 Spring Street, Melbourne, Victoria, Australia. *T:* 662 3239. *Clubs:* Australian (Melbourne), Royal Melbourne Golf (Melbourne).

FROY, Prof. Martin; Professor of Fine Art, University of Reading, 1972–91; *b* 9 Feb. 1926; *s* of late William Alan Froy and Helen Elizabeth Spencer. *Educ:* St Paul's Sch.; Magdalene Coll., Cambridge (one year); Slade Sch. of Fine Art. Dipl. in Fine Art (London). Visiting Teacher of Engraving, Slade Sch. of Fine Art, 1952–55; taught at Bath Acad. of Art, latterly as Head of Fine Art, 1954–65; Head of Painting Sch., Chelsea Sch. of Art, 1965–72. Gregory Fellow in Painting, Univ. of Leeds, 1951–54; Leverhulme Research Award, six months study in Italy, 1963; Sabbatical Award, Arts Council, 1965. Mem., Fine Art Panel, 1962–71, Mem. Council, 1969–71, Nat. Council for Diplomas in Art and Design; Trustee: National Gall., 1972–79; Tate Gall., 1975–79. Fellow, UCL, 1978. *One-Artist Exhibitions:* Hanover Gall., London, 1952; Wakefield City Art Gall., 1953; Belgrade Theatre, Coventry, 1958; Leicester Galls, London, 1961; Royal West of England Acad., Bristol, 1964; Univ. of Sussex, 1968; Hanover Gall., London, 1969; Park Square Gall., Leeds, 1970; Arnolfini Gall., Bristol, 1970; City Art Gall., Bristol (seven paintings), 1972; Univ. of Reading, 1979; New Ashgate Gall., Surrey, 1979; Serpentine Gall., 1983. *Other Exhibitions:* Internat. Abstract Artists, Riverside Mus., NY, 1950; ICA, London, 1950; Ten English Painters, Brit. Council touring exhibn in Scandinavia, 1952; Drawings from Twelve Countries, Art Inst. of Chicago, 1952; Figures in their Setting, Contemp. Art Soc. Exhibn, Tate Gall., 1953; Beaux Arts Gall., London, 1953; British Painting and Sculpture, Whitechapel Art Gall., London, 1954; Le Congrès pour la Liberté de la Culture Exhibn, Rome, Paris, Brussels, 1955; Pittsburgh Internat., 1955; Six Young Painters, Arts Council touring Exhibn, 1956; ICA Gregory Meml Exhibn, Bradford City Art Gall., Leeds, 1958; City Art Gall., Bristol, 1960; Malerei der Gegenwart ans Sudwestengland, Kunstverein, Hanover, 1962; Corsham Painters and Sculptors, Arts Council Touring Exhibn, 1965; Three Painters, Bath Fest. Exhibn, 1970; Park Square Gall., Leeds, 1978; Ruskin Sch., Univ. of Oxford, 1978; Newcastle Connection, Newcastle, 1980; Homage to Herbert Read, Canterbury, 1984. *Commissions, etc:* Artist Consultant for Arts Council to City Architect, Coventry, 1953–58; mosaic decoration, Belgrade Th., Coventry, 1957–58; two mural panels, Concert Hall, Morley Coll., London, 1958–59. *Works in Public Collections:* Tate Gall.; Mus. of Mod. Art, NY; Chicago Art Inst.; Arts Council; Contemp. Art Soc.; Royal W of England Acad.; Leeds Univ.; City Art Galls of Bristol, Carlisle, Leeds, Southampton and Wakefield; Reading Mus. and Art Gall. *Address:* Department of Fine Art, University of Reading, Earley Gate, Reading, Berks RG6 2AT.

FRY, Christopher; dramatist; *b* 18 Dec. 1907; *s* of Charles John Harris and Emma Marguerite Hammond, *d* of Emma Louisa Fry; *m* 1936, Phyllis Marjorie Hart (*d* 1987); one *s*. *Educ:* Bedford Modern Sch. Actor at Citizen House, Bath, 1927; Schoolmaster at Hazlewood Preparatory Sch., Limpsfield, Surrey, 1928–31; Dir of Tunbridge Wells Repertory Players, 1932–35; life too complicated for tabulation, 1935–39; The Tower, a pageant-play produced at Tewkesbury Fest., 1939; Dir of Oxford Repertory Players, 1940 and 1944–46, directing at Arts Theatre, London, 1945; Staff dramatist, Arts, 1947. FRSL. Hon. Fellow, Manchester Poly., 1988. DLitt Lambeth, 1988. Queen's Gold Medal (for Poetry), 1962. *Plays:* A Phoenix Too Frequent, Mercury, 1946, St George's Theatre, 1983; The Lady's Not for Burning, Arts, 1948, Globe, 1949, Chichester, 1972; The Firstborn, Edinburgh Festival, 1948; Thor, with Angels, Canterbury Festival, 1949; Venus Observed, St James's, 1950; The Boy with a Cart, Lyric, Hammersmith, 1950; Ring Round the Moon (translated from French of Jean Anouilh), Globe, 1950; A Sleep of Prisoners, produced St Thomas' Church, Regent Street, W1, 1951; The Dark is Light Enough, Aldwych, 1954; The Lark (trans. from French of Jean Anouilh), Lyric, Hammersmith, 1955; Tiger at the Gates (trans. from French of Jean Giraudoux), Apollo, 1955; Duel of Angels (trans. from Pour Lucrèce, of Jean Giraudoux), Apollo, 1958; Curtmantle, Edinburgh Festival, 1962; Judith (trans. from Giraudoux), Her Majesty's, 1962; A Yard of Sun, National, 1970; Peer Gynt (trans.), Chichester, 1970; Cyrano de Bergerac (trans.), Chichester, 1975; One Thing More, or Caedmon Construed, Chelmsford Cathedral, 1986. *TV:* The Brontës of Haworth, four plays, 1973 (also performed on stage, 1985); Sister Dora, 1977; The Best of Enemies, 1977. *Film Commentary* for The Queen is Crowned (Coronation film, 1953); *Film scripts:* (participation) Ben Hur; Barabbas; The Bible; The Beggar's Opera. *Publications:* The Boy with a Cart, 1939; The Firstborn, 1946; A Phoenix Too Frequent, 1946; The Lady's Not for Burning, 1949; Thor, with Angels, 1949; Venus Observed, 1950; (trans.) Ring Round the Moon, 1950; A Sleep of Prisoners, 1951; The Dark is Light Enough, 1954; (trans.) The Lark, 1955; (trans.) Tiger at The Gates, 1955; (trans.) Duel of Angels, 1958; Curtmantle, 1961 (Heinemann Award of RSL); (trans.) Judith, 1962; A Yard of Sun, 1970; (trans.) Peer Gynt, 1970 (this trans. included in The Oxford Ibsen, vol. III, Brand and Peer Gynt, 1972); Four television plays: The Brontës at Haworth, 1954; (trans.) Cyrano de Bergerac, 1975; Can You Find Me: a family history, 1978; (ed and introd) Charlie Hammond's Sketch Book, 1980; Selected Plays, 1985; Genius, Talent and Failure, 1986 (Adam Lecture); One Thing More, or Caedmon Construed, 1987. *Address:* The Toft, East Dean, Chichester, West Sussex. *Club:* Garrick.

FRY, Donald William, CBE 1970; Director, Atomic Energy Establishment, Winfrith, 1959–73; *b* 30 Nov. 1910; *m* 1934, Jessie Florence (*née* Wright); three *s*. *Educ:* Weymouth Gram. Sch.; King's Coll., London. Research Physicist, GEC Laboratories, 1932; RAE Farnborough (Radio Dept), 1936; Air Min. Research Establishment (later the Telecommunications Research Establishment, TRE) Swanage, 1940; moved with the Estab. to Malvern, 1942; joined staff of AERE (still at Malvern), 1946; demonstrated with other mems of group a new Principle for accelerating particles: the travelling wave linear accelerator, 1947. Awarded Duddell Medal of Physical Soc., 1950; Head of Gen. Physics Div. at AERE Harwell, 1950; Chief Physicist, 1954, Dep. Dir, 1958, AERE Harwell. CEng, FIEE 1946; FIEEE 1960; FInstP 1970; Hon. Freeman of Weymouth, 1958. FKC London, 1959. *Publications:* papers in learned journals. *Address:* Coveway Lodge, 25 Bowleaze Coveway, Overcombe, near Weymouth, Dorset DT3 6PL. *T:* Preston (Weymouth) (0305) 833276.

FRY, Dr Ian Kelsey, DM, FRCP, FRCR; Dean, Medical College of St Bartholomew's Hospital, 1981–89; Consultant Radiologist, St Bartholomew's Hospital, 1966–87; *b* 25 Oct. 1923; *s* of Sir William and Lady Kelsey Fry; *m* 1951, Mary Josephine Casey; three *s* (one *d* decd). *Educ:* Radley Coll.; New Coll., Oxford; Guy's Hosp. Medical Sch. BM BCh 1948, DM Oxon 1961; MRCP 1956, FRCP 1972; DMRD 1961; FFR 1963; FRCR 1975. RAF Medical Services, 1949–50 (Sqdn Ldr). Director, Dept of Radiology, BUPA Medical Centre, 1973–86; Mem. Council, Royal College of Radiologists, 1979–82; President, British Institute of Radiology, 1982–83. *Publications:* chapters and articles in books and jls. *Recreations:* golf, walking, racing. *Address:* The Pines, Woodlands Road, Bickley, Bromley, Kent BR1 2AE. *T:* 081–467 4150.

FRY, John, CBE 1988 (OBE 1975); MD, FRCS, FRCGP; general practitioner, since 1947; *b* 16 June 1922; *s* of Ansel and Barbara Fry; *m* 1st, 1944, Joan (*d* 1989), *d* of James and Catherine Sabel; one *s* one *d*; 2nd, 1989, Gertrude A. Amiel (*née* Schwer). *Educ:* Whitgift Middle Sch., Croydon; Guy's Hosp., Univ. of London (MD). FRCS 1947, FRCGP 1967. Hon. Consultant in Gen. Practice to the Army, 1968–87; Consultant to WHO, 1965–83; Trustee, Nuffield Provincial Hosps Trust, 1956– (Queen Elizabeth the Queen Mother Fellowship, 1988). Mem., GMC, 1970– (Sen. Treasurer, 1975–); Councillor, RCGP, 1960–. Guthrie Medal, RAMC, 1987. *Publications:* The Catarrhal Child, 1961; Profiles of Disease, 1966; Medicine in Three Societies, 1969; Common Diseases, 1974, 3rd edn 1983; Textbook of Medical Practice, 1976; Scientific Foundations of Family Medicine, 1978; A New Approach to Medicine, 1978; Primary Care, 1980; Family Good Health Guide, 1982; The Health Care Manual, 1983; Common Dilemmas in Family Medicine, 1983; A History of the Royal College of General Practitioners, 1983; NHS Data Book, 1984; Early Diagnosis, 1985; Disease Data Book, 1985; Primary Health Care: 2000, 1986; GP Data Book, 1988; Primary Medical Care, 1988. *Recreations:* reading, writing, researching, running. *Address:* 138 Croydon Road, Beckenham, Kent BR3 4DG. *T:* 081–650 0568.

FRY, Dame Margaret (Louise), DBE 1989 (OBE 1982); Chairman, National Union of Conservative and Unionist Associations, 1990–91 (a Vice-Chairman, 1987–90); *b* 10 March 1931; *d* of Richard Reed Dawe and Ruth Dora Dawe; *m* 1955, Walter William John Fry; three *s*. *Educ:* Tavistock Grammar School. Conservative Women's Advisory Committee (Western Area): Vice-Chm., 1975–78; Chm., 1978–81; Conservative Women's National Committee: Vice-Chm., 1981–82; Chm., 1984–87; Chm., W Devon Cons. Assoc., 1982–85; Pres., Torridge and W Devon Cons. Women's Cttee, 1988–. Member: Transport Users' Consultative Cttee; SW RHA. *Recreations:* farming, conservation, church, sport (former member, Devon County Hockey XI). *Address:* Thorne Farm, Launceston, Cornwall PL15 9SN. *T:* Launceston (0566) 84308.

FRY, Peter Derek; MP (C) Wellingborough since Dec. 1969; Director, Countrywide Political Communications Ltd, since 1988; *b* 26 May 1931; *s* of Harry Walter Fry and late Edith Fry; *m*; one *s* one *d*; *m* 1982, Helen Claire Mitchell. *Educ:* Royal Grammar School, High Wycombe; Worcester College, Oxford (MA). Tillotsons (Liverpool) Ltd, 1954–56; Northern Assurance Co., 1956–61; Political Education Officer, Conservative Central Office, 1961–63. Member Bucks County Council, 1961–67. Contested (C) North Nottingham, 1964, East Willesden, 1966. Joint Chairman: All Party Roads Study Gp; All Party Midland Main Line Gp; Chairman: Anglo-Bahamian Parly Gp; British Yugoslav Parly Gp; All-Party Footwear and Leather Gp, 1979–87; Hon. Sec., Parly Road Passenger Transport Gp; Mem., Select Cttee on Transport. Played Rugby for Bucks County, 1956–58, Hon. Secretary, 1958–61. *Recreations:* watching Rugby football; reading history and biographies. *Address:* House of Commons, SW1A 0AA. *Club:* Royal Automobile.

FRY, Peter George Robin Plantagenet S.; *see* Somerset Fry.

FRY, Richard Henry, CBE 1965; Financial Editor of The Guardian, 1939–65; *b* 23 Sept. 1900; *m* 1929, Katherine (*née* Maritz); no *c*. *Educ:* Berlin and Heidelberg Univs. *Publications:* Zero Hour, 1936; A Banker's World: the revival of the City, 1957–70, 1970; Bankers in West Africa, 1976. *Address:* 8 Montagu Mews West, W1H 1TF. *T:* 071–262 0817. *Club:* Reform.

FRY, Ronald Ernest, FSS; Director of Economics and Statistics, Departments of the Environment and Transport, 1975–80, retired; *b* 21 May 1925; *s* of Ernest Fry and Lilian (*née* Eveling); *m* 1954, Jeanne Ivy Dawson; one *s* one *d*. *Educ:* Wilson's Grammar Sch., Camberwell; Birkbeck Coll., Univ. of London (BSc (Special)). MIS. Telecommunications Technician, Royal Signals, 1944–47; Scientific Asst, CEGB (London Region), 1948–52; Statistician: Glacier Metal Co., London, 1952–54; CEGB HQ, London, 1954–64; Gen. Register Office, 1965–66; Asst Dir of Research and Intelligence, GLC, 1966–69; Chief Statistician: (Social Statistics) Cabinet Office, 1969–74; (Manpower Statistics) Dept of Employment, 1974–75. *Publications:* various technical publns in statistical and other professional jls. *Recreations:* photography, reading, motoring. *Address:* 39 Claremont Road, Hadley Wood, Barnet, Herts EN4 0HR. *T:* 081–440 1393.

FRY, Stephen John; writer, actor, comedian; *b* 24 Aug. 1957; *s* of Alan John Fry and Marianne Eve (*née* Newman). *Educ:* Uppingham Sch.; Queens' Coll., Cambridge (MA). *TV series:* Blackadder, 1987–89; A Bit of Fry and Laurie, 1989–91; Jeeves in Jeeves and Wooster, 1990–92; *theatre:* Forty Years On, Queen's, 1984; The Common Pursuit, Phoenix, 1988. Columnist: The Listener, 1988–89; Daily Telegraph, 1990–. *Publications:* Me and My Girl, 1984 (musical performed in West End and on Broadway); A Bit of Fry and Laurie: collected scripts, 1990; *novel:* The Liar, 1991. *Recreations:* smoking, drinking, swearing, pressing wild flowers. *Address:* c/o Lorraine Hamilton, 19 Denmark Street, WC2H 8NJ. *T:* 071–836 3941. *Clubs:* Savile, United Oxford & Cambridge University, Groucho, Chelsea Arts.

FRY, Hon. Sir William Gordon, Kt 1980; JP; President, Legislative Council of Victoria, Australia, 1976–79; *b* 12 June 1909; *s* of A. G. Fry, Ballarat; *m* 1936, Lilian G., *d* of A. W. Macrae; four *s*. *Educ:* Ballarat High School; Melbourne Univ. Served War of 1939–45, 2nd AIF (Lt-Col, despatches). Education Dept of Victoria for 40 years; Headmaster of various schools, including Cheltenham East, Windsor, Cheltenham Heights. Councillor, City of Moorabbin; Mayor, 1968; MLC (Lib) for Higinbotham, Vic, 1967–79. Past Chm., Parly Select Cttee, Road Safety. Vice-Pres., Victoria League; Mem., RSL. Formerly Dep. Chm., World Bowls. Life Governor: Melbourne and Dist Ambulance Soc.; Royal Women's Hosp.; Royal Melbourne Hosp.; Gen. Management Cttee, Royal Victoria Eye and Ear Hosp.; Management Bd, Cheltenham-Mordialloc Hosp. (18 years service); Committee Member: Melbourne Family Care Orgn; Richmond Foundn; Legacy Australia; Brighton Tech. Coll. JP Melbourne, 1968. *Recreations:* lawn bowls, golf, swimming. *Address:* 16 Mariemont Avenue, Beaumaris, Victoria 3193, Australia. *Clubs:* West Brighton; Royal Commonwealth Society (Victoria); Returned Services League (Cheltenham-Moorabbin).

FRY, William Norman H.; *see* Hillier-Fry.

FRYBERG, Sir Abraham, Kt 1968; MBE 1941; retired; *b* 26 May 1901; *s* of Henry and Rose Fryberg; *m* 1939, Vivian Greensil Barnard; one *s*. *Educ:* Wesley Coll., Melbourne; Queen's Coll., University of Melbourne. MB, BS (Melbourne) 1928; DPH, DTM (Sydney) 1936; Hon. MD (Qld); Hon. FACMA. Served with 9 Australian Div. (Tobruk, Alamein), 1940–45. Resident Med. Officer, then Registrar, Brisbane Hosp. and Brisbane Children's Hosp., 1929–33; GP, Hughenden, 1934; Health Officer, Qld Health Dept, 1936–46 (except for war service); Dep. Dir-Gen., 1946, Dir-Gen. of Health and Medical Services, Qld, 1947–67, retired. Hon. Col, RAAMC Northern Comd, 1962–67. SBStJ 1958. *Recreation:* racing. *Address:* 19 Dublin Street, Clayfield, Qld 4011, Australia. *T:* Brisbane 2622549. *Club:* United Service (Brisbane).

FRYE, Michael John Ernest; Chairman since 1987 and Chief Executive since 1988, B. Elliott; *b* 2 June 1945; *s* of late Jack Frye, CBE and Daphne Page-Croft; *m* 1st, 1970, Geraldine Elizabeth Kendall; one *s*; 2nd, 1989, Valerie Patricia Harfield-Simpson. *Educ:* Marlborough Coll.; MIT (SB Business Management, Mech. Eng. Minor). B. Elliott and subsidiaries, 1967–; Dir, Goldfields Industrial, 1973–76; Overseas Dir, B. Elliott, 1974–76, non-exec. Dir, 1976–87; Chairman: Rotaflex Group of Cos, 1975–87 (also Chief Exec.); Concord Lighting, 1976–87. Chm. and Founder, Light and Health Res. Council, 1978; Member: NEDC Sub-Cttee, exports for luminaire manufrs, 1980–81; Council, Lighting Industry Fedn, 1980–87 (Vice-Pres., 1987); Illuminating Eng. Soc. of N America, 1979–; Chairman: Cttee to establish nat. lighting award, 1984–87; Lighting Div., CIBSE, 1987–88. Chm. and Mem., numerous technical and arts organisations. Liveryman, Turners' Co. and Lightmongers' Co. Fellow, RSPB; FRSA (Chm., 1991–). Hon. Fellow, RCA. *Recreations:* golf, tennis, chess, bird watching, collecting old or rare bird books. *Address:* B. Elliott, Elliott House, Victoria Road, NW10 6NY. *T:* 081–961 7333. *Clubs:* Boodle's, City Livery, City of London, Royal Automobile; Royal Worlington and Newmarket Golf; Lyford Cay.

FRYER, David Richard; Secretary-General, Royal Town Planning Institute, since 1976; *b* 16 May 1936; *s* of Ernest William Fryer and Gladys Edith Battey; *m* 1961, Carole Elizabeth Hayes; one *s* two *d*. *Educ:* Chesterfield Sch.; New Coll., Oxford (MA, BCL). LMRTPI. Admitted solicitor, 1961. Articled Clerk and Asst Solicitor, Chesterfield Bor. Council, 1958–61; Associate Lawyer, Messrs Jones, Day, Cockley & Reavis, Cleveland, Ohio, 1961–63; Asst Solicitor, N Riding CC, 1963–65; Sen. Asst Solicitor, Bucks CC, 1966–69; Dep. Sec., RICS, 1970–75. Sec., Brit. Chapter, Internat. Real Estate Fedn, 1970–75; Dep. Pres., Internat. Fedn for Housing and Planning, 1984– (Mem., Bureau and Council, 1976–); Sec.-Gen., European Council of Town Planners, 1987–. Member: Exec. Cttee and Council, Public Works Congress and Exhibn Council Ltd, 1976–90; Exec. Cttee, Nat. Council for Social Service, 1976–79 (Chm., Planning and Environment Gp); Council and Standards Cttee, Nat. House-Bldg Council, 1976–; Exec. Cttee, Commonwealth Assoc. of Planners, 1984–88. FRSA 1981. *Recreations:* international affairs, architecture, the countryside. *Address:* Stairways, Portway Road, Hartwell, Aylesbury, Bucks HP17 8RP. *T:* Aylesbury (0296) 748538. *Club:* East India.

FRYER, Dr Geoffrey, FRS 1972; Deputy Chief Scientific Officer, Windermere Laboratory, Freshwater Biological Association, 1981–88; *b* 6 Aug. 1927; *s* of W. and M. Fryer; *m* 1953, Vivien Griffiths Hodgson; one *s* one *d*. *Educ:* Huddersfield College. DSc, PhD London. Royal Navy, 1946–48. Colonial Research Student, 1952–53; HM Overseas Research Service, 1953–60: Malawi, 1953–55; Zambia, 1955–57; Uganda, 1957–60; Sen., then Principal, then Sen. Principal Scientific Officer, Freshwater Biological Assoc., 1960–81. H. R. Macmillan Lectr, Univ. of British Columbia, 1963; Distinguished Vis. Schol., Univ. of Adelaide, 1985; Distinguished Lectr, Biol Scis Br., Dept. Fisheries and Oceans, Canada, 1987; Hon. Prof., Inst. of Environmental and Biol Scis, Lancaster Univ., 1988–. Mem. Council, Royal Soc., 1978–80. Mem., Adv. Cttee on Science, Nature Conservancy Council, 1986–. Frink Medal, Zool Soc. of London, 1983; Linnean Medal for Zoology, Linnean Soc., 1987. *Publications:* (with T. D. Iles) The Cichlid Fishes of the Great Lakes of Africa: their biology and evolution, 1972; numerous articles in scientific jls. *Recreations:* natural history, walking, church architecture, photography. *Address:* Elleray Cottage, Windermere, Cumbria LA23 1AW.

FRYER, Maj.-Gen. (retd) Wilfred George, CB 1956; CBE 1951 (OBE 1941); Chairman, Warminster Press, since 1965; *b* 1 May 1900; *s* of James and Marion Fryer, Kington, Herefordshire; *m* 1931, Jean Eleanore Graham, *d* of Graham Binny, RSW, Edinburgh; two *s* (and one *s* decd). *Educ:* Christ Coll., Brecon; RMA Woolwich. Commissioned 2nd Lieut RE, 1919, Regular Army; served in India, Royal Bombay Sappers and Miners, 1933–38; Major RE, Instructor, Sch. of Mil. Engineering, Chatham, 1938. Served War of 1939–45: Lt-Col RE, ADWE & M, GHQ, Middle East, 1941; SO1 to Chief Engineer, Eighth Army, Western Desert Campaign (OBE), 1941; Col DDWE & M, GHQ, Middle East, 1942; GSO1 to Scientific Adviser to Army Council, 1944; ADWE & M, GHQ and Dep. Chief Engineer, 8 Corps, NW Europe Campaign (despatches), 1944–45; Brig.-Chief Engr, Brit. Army Staff, Washington, DC, 1945; Col E (Equipment), War Office, 1946–48; Brig.-Chief Engr, Singapore Dist, 1948–51; Brig.-Chief Engr, Southern Comd, UK, 1951–53; Maj.-Gen. 1954; Chief Engineer, Middle East Land Forces, 1954–57. "A" Licence air pilot, 1942. MIEE 1952. Nat. Champion, Wayfarer Dinghy, 1960. *Recreations:* ocean racing (Transatlantic Race, 1931), ski-ing (Lauberhorn Cup, 1928), tennis. *Address:* Warminster Press Ltd, Station Road, Warminster BA12 8BR. *Clubs:* Royal Ocean Racing, Hurlingham; Royal Lymington Yacht.

FUAD, Kutlu Tekin; Hon. Mr Justice Fuad; Vice-President, Court of Appeal, Hong Kong, since 1988; *b* 23 April 1926; *s* of Mustafa Fuad Bey, CMG, and Belkis Hilmi; *m* 1952, Inci Izzet; two *s* one *d*. *Educ:* Temple Grove; Marlborough Coll.; St John's Coll., Cambridge (MA). Called to the Bar, Inner Temple, 1952. Mil. Service, Lieut KRRC, 1944–48. Colonial Legal Service, 1953–62: Magistrate, Cyprus; Resident Magistrate, Sen. Crown Counsel, Legal Draftsman, and Dir of Public Prosecutions, Uganda; Judge of the High Court, Uganda, 1963–72 (Pres., Industrial Court; Chm., Law Reform Cttee); Dir, Legal Div., Commonwealth Secretariat, 1972–80; Judge, High Court of Hong Kong, 1980–82; Justice of Appeal, Court of Appeal, Hong Kong, 1982–88. Comr, Supreme Ct of Brunei Darussalam, 1983–86, 1988–. Mem., Law Reform Commn, Hong Kong, 1983–89. Pres., Hong Kong Family Law Assoc., 1986–. Formerly Chm., Visitation Cttee, Makerere University Coll. *Recreations:* music, Rugby football, tennis. *Address:* Supreme Court, Hong Kong; 51 Earl's Court Road, Kensington, W8 6EE. *T:* 071–937 9209. *Club:* Army and Navy.

FUCHS, Sir Vivian (Ernest), Kt 1958; MA, PhD; FRS 1974; Director of the British Antarctic Survey, 1958–73; Leader Commonwealth Trans-Antarctic Expedition, 1955–58; *b* 11 Feb. 1908; *s* of late E. Fuchs, Farnham, Surrey, and late Violet Anne Fuchs (*née* Watson); *m* 1933, Joyce (*d* 1990), 2nd *d* of late John Connell; one *s* one *d* (and one *d* decd); *m* 1991, Mrs Eleanor Honnywill. *Educ:* Brighton Coll.; St John's Coll., Cambridge (Hon. Fellow, 1983). Geologist with: Cambridge East Greenland Expedn, 1929; Cambridge Expdn to E African Lakes, 1930–31; E African Archæological Expdn, 1931–32; Leader Lake Rudolf Rift Valley Expedn, 1933–34; Royal Geog. Society Cuthbert Peek Grant, 1936; Leader Lake Rukwa Expedn, 1937–38. 2nd Lieut Cambs Regt, TA, 1939; served in W Africa, 1942–43; Staff Coll., Camberley, 1943; served NW Europe (despatches), 1944–46; demobilized (Major), 1946. Leader Falkland Islands Dependencies Survey (Antarctica), 1947–50; Dir FIDSc Bureau, 1950–55. President: Internat. Glaciological Soc., 1963–66; British Assoc. for Advancement of Science, 1972; Mem. Council, RGS, 1958–61, Vice-Pres. 1961–64, Pres., 1982–84, Hon. Vice-Pres., 1985–. Founder's Gold Medal, Royal Geog. Soc., 1951; Silver Medal RSA, 1952; Polar Medal, 1953, and Clasp, 1958; Special Gold Medal, Royal Geog. Soc., 1958; Gold Medal Royal Scottish Geog. Society 1958; Gold Medal Geog. Society (Paris), 1958; Richthofen Medal (Berlin), 1958; Kirchenpauer Medal (Hamburg), 1958; Plancius Medal (Amsterdam), 1959; Egede Medal (Copenhagen), 1959; Hubbard Medal, Nat. Geog. Soc. (Washington), 1959; Explorers Club Medal (New York), 1959; Geog. Soc. (Chicago) Gold Medal, 1959; Geol. Soc. of London Prestwich Medal, 1960. Hon. Fellow, Wolfson (formerly University Coll.), Cambridge, 1970. Hon. LLD Edinburgh 1958; Hon. DSc: Durham 1958; Cantab 1959; Leicester 1972; Hon. ScD Swansea, 1971; Hon. LLD Birmingham, 1974. *Publications:* The Crossing of Antarctica (Fuchs and Hillary), 1958; Antarctic Adventure, 1959; (ed) Forces of Nature, 1977; Of Ice and Men, 1982; (ed) The Physical World (Oxford Illustrated Encyclopedia), 1985; A Time to Speak (autobiog.), 1990; geographical and geological reports and papers in scientific jls. *Recreation:* gardening. *Address:* 106 Barton Road, Cambridge CB3 9LH. *T:* Cambridge (0223) 359238. *Club:* Athenæum.

FUENTES, Prof. Carlos; Robert F. Kennedy Professor of Latin American Studies, Harvard University, since 1987; *b* 11 Nov. 1928; *s* of Ambassador Rafael Fuentes and Berta Fuentes; *m* 1st, 1957, Rita Macedo; one *d*; 2nd, 1973, Sylvia Lemus; one *s* one *d*. *Educ:* Law School, Nat. Univ., Mexico; Inst. des Hautes Etudes Internat., Geneva. Sec., Mexican Deleg. to ILO, Geneva, 1950; Under Director of Culture, Nat. Univ., Mexico, 1952–54; Head, Cultural Relations Dept, Min. of Foreign Affairs, Mexico, 1955–58; Ambassador to France, 1975–77; Prof. of English and Romance Languages, Univ. of Pennsylvania, 1978–83; Prof. of Comparative Literature, Harvard, 1984–86; Simón Bolivar Prof., Cambridge, 1986–87. Mem., El Colegio Nacional, Mexico, 1974–; Fellow, Wilson Center, Washington DC, 1974; Mem., Amer. Acad. and Inst. of Arts and Letters, 1986; Trustee, NY Public Library, 1987. Hon. DLitt Wesleyan, 1982; Hon. LLD Harvard, 1983; Hon. LittD Cambridge, 1987; DUniv Essex, 1987. Nat. Prize for Literature, Mexico, 1985; Miguel de Cervantes Prize, 1987. *Publications:* Where the Air is Clear, 1958; The Good Conscience, 1959; The Death of Artemio Cruz, 1962; Aura, 1962; A Change of Skin, 1967 (Biblioteca Breve Prize, Barcelona); Terra Nostra, 1975 (Rómulo Gallegos Prize); Distant Relations, 1980; Burnt Water, 1982; The Old Gringo, 1984 (filmed, 1989); Cristóbal Nonato, 1987; Myself with Others: selected essays, 1988. *Address:* 401 Boylston Hall, Harvard University, Cambridge, Mass 02138, USA. *T:* (617) 495–2543.

FUGARD, Athol; playwright, director, actor; *b* 11 June 1932; *s* of Harold David Fugard and Elizabeth Magdalene Potgieter; *m* 1956, Sheila Meiring; one *d*. *Educ:* Univ. of Cape Town. Directed earliest plays, Nongogo, No Good Friday, Johannesburg, 1960; acted in The Blood Knot, touring S Africa, 1961; Hello and Goodbye, 1965; directed and acted in The Blood Knot, London, 1966; Boesman and Lena, S Africa, 1969; directed Boesman and Lena, London, 1971; directed Serpent Players in various prodns, Port Elizabeth, from 1963, directed co-authors John Kani and Winston Ntshona in Sizwe Bansi is Dead, SA, 1972, The Island, 1973, and London, 1973–74; acted in film, Boesman and Lena, 1972; directed and acted in Statements after an Arrest under the Immorality Act, in SA, 1972, directed in London, 1973; wrote Dimetos for Edinburgh Fest., 1975; directed and acted in, A Lesson from Aloes, SA, 1978, London, 1980 (directed, NY 1981, winning NY Critics Circle Award for Best Play); directed: Master Harold and the Boys, NY, 1982 (Drama Desk Award), Johannesburg, 1983, Nat. Theatre, 1983 (Standard award for Best Play); The Road to Mecca, Yale Repertory Theatre, 1984; (also wrote) My Children! My Africa!, NY, 1990. Hon. DLitt: Natal, 1981; Rhodes, 1983; Cape Town, 1984; Hon. DFA Yale, 1983; Hon. DHL Georgetown, 1984. *Films:* Boesman and Lena, 1973; The Guest, 1977; (acted in) Meetings with Remarkable Men (dir, Peter Brook), 1979; (wrote and acted in) Marigolds in August (Silver Bear Award, Berlin), 1980; (acted in) Gandhi, 1982; (co-dir and acted in) Road to Mecca, 1991. *Publications:* The Blood Knot, 1962; People Are Living There, Hello and Goodbye, 1973; Boesman and Lena, 1973; (jtly) Three Port Elizabeth Plays: Sizwe Bansi is Dead, The Island, Statements after an Arrest under the Immorality Act, 1974; Tsotsi (novel), 1980 (also USA); A Lesson from Aloes, 1981 (also USA); Master Harold and the Boys, US 1982, UK 1983; Notebooks 1960–1977, 1983 (also USA); Road to Mecca, 1985; A Place with the Pigs, 1988. *Recreations:* angling, skin-diving, bird-watching. *Address:* PO Box 5090, Walmer, Port Elizabeth, South Africa.

FUGARD, Maj.-Gen. Michael Teape, CB 1990; an Adjudicator of Immigration Appeals, since 1990; Member, Lord Chancellor's Panel of Independent Inspectors, since 1990; *b* Chester, 27 March 1933; *s* of Rev. Theodore Teape Fugard and Lilian Teape Fugard (*née* Baker); *m* 1961, Theresia Hollensteiner; two *s* two *d*. *Educ:* Chester Cathedral Sch.; Sherborne Sch. Admitted Solicitor, 1957. Enlisted Army, RASC, 1957; commnd, Captain Army Legal Services (now Army Legal Corps), 1958; OC (Major) Army Legal Aid Far East Land Forces, 1960, Lt-Col 1971; Asst Dir Army Legal Services, MoD, 1973–78; Col Legal Staff HQ UKLF, 1979; Comdr Army Law Trng and Pubns Br., 1980; Comdr Army Legal Aid, BAOR, 1982; Comdr (Brig.) Army Legal Gp UK, 1983; Maj.-Gen. 1986; Dir, Army Legal Services, 1986–90. An Asst Recorder, 1986–. Governor, Royal Sch., Bath, 1985–; Chm., Leaden Hall Sch., Salisbury, 1988–. *Address:* Immigration Appeals, Thanet House, 231 Strand, WC2R 1DA.

FUJIYAMA, Naraichi; Order of the Sacred Treasure, First Class, 1987; Senior Consultant to Scottish Development Agency, in Japan, since 1982; *b* 17 Sept. 1915; *m* 1946, Shizuko Takagi. *Educ:* Faculty of Law, Tokyo Univ.; Univ. of NC, USA. Consul, New York, 1953–54; Counsellor, Austria, 1959, Indonesia, 1963; Chief of Protocol, Min. of Foreign Affairs, Tokyo, 1965; Dir-Gen., Public Inf. Bureau, Min. of For. Affairs, 1968; Ambassador to: Austria, 1971–75; Italy, 1975–79, Great Britain, 1979–82. Chm., Bd of Governors, IAEA, Vienna, 1973–74; Press Sec. to the Emperor of Japan for State Visit to USA, 1975. Grand Cross, Order Al Merito, Peru; Kt Grand Cross, Order Al Merito, Italy; Grand Decoration of Honour for Merit in Gold with Sash, Austria. *Recreation:* golf. *Address:* 7–7–19, Koyama, Shinagawa-ku, Tokyo, Japan.

FUKUI, Prof. Dr Kenichi; Order of Culture, Person of Cultural Merits (Japan), 1981; Grand Cordon, Order of the Rising Sun (Japan), 1988; Director, Institute for Fundamental Chemistry, Kyoto, Japan, since 1988; *b* 4 Oct. 1918; *s* of Ryokichi Fukui and Chie Fukui (*née* Sugizawa); *m* 1947, Tomoe Horie; one *s* one *d*. *Educ:* Kyoto Imperial Univ. (AB Engrg, PhD Engrg). Lecturer, 1943–45, Asst Professor, 1945–51, Professor, 1951–82, Kyoto Imperial University; Pres., Kyoto Univ. of Industrial Arts and Textile Fibers, then Kyoto Inst. of Technology, 1982–88. Member: European Acad. of Arts, Sciences and Humanities, 1981–; Japan Acad., 1983–; Pontifical Acad. of Sciences, 1986–. Foreign Associate, Nat. Acad. of Sciences, Washington, 1981–; Foreign Hon. Mem., Amer. Acad. of Arts and Sciences, 1983–; Foreign Mem., Royal Soc., 1989. Nobel Prize in Chemistry (jtly), 1981. *Address:* 23 Kitashirakawahirai-cho, Sakyo-ku, Kyoto-city, Kyoto 606, Japan. *T:* 075–781–5785.

FULBRIGHT, J. William, Hon. KBE 1975; US Senator (Democrat) for Arkansas, 1945–74; *b* Sumner, Mo, 9 April 1905; *s* of Jay Fulbright and Roberta (*née* Waugh); *m* 1932, Elizabeth Kremer Williams (*d* 1985); two *d*; *m* 1990, Harriet Mayor. *Educ:* public schools of Fayetteville, Arkansas; University of Arkansas (AB); (Rhodes Scholar) Pembroke Coll., Oxford Univ. (BA, MA); George Washington Univ. Sch. of Law (LLB). Special Attorney, Dept. of Justice, 1934–35; Lectr in Law, George Washington Univ., 1935–36; Mem. Law Sch. Faculty, University of Arkansas, 1936–39, and Pres. of University, 1939–41. Elected to Congress for 3rd Dist of Arkansas, 1942; Mem. Foreign Affairs Cttee. Elected to Senate, 1945, and subsequently; Mem. US Delegn to Gen. Assembly, UN, 1954; Chm. Banking and Currency Cttee of Senate, 1955–59, resigning to become Chm. Senate Cttee on Foreign Relations, also Mem. Finance Cttee and Jt Economic Cttee. First McCallum Meml Lectr, Oxford, 1975. Hon. Fellow, Pembroke Coll., Oxford, 1949; Fellow, Amer. Acad. of Arts and Sciences (Boston), 1950; Award by Nat. Inst. of Arts and Letters, 1954. Holds over fifty hon. degrees, including DCL Oxford, 1953, and LLD Cantab, 1971. *Publications:* Old Myths and New Realities, 1964; Prospects for the West, 1965; The Arrogance of Power, 1967; The Pentagon Propaganda Machine, 1970; The Crippled Giant, 1972; The Price of Empire, 1989. *Address:* 555 13th Street NW, Washington, DC 20004, USA.

FULCHER, Derick Harold, DSC 1944; Assistant Under-Secretary of State, Department of Health and Social Security, 1969–70; *b* 4 Nov. 1917; *s* of late Percy Frederick Fulcher and Gertrude Lilian Fulcher; *m* 1943, Florence Ellen May Anderson; one *s* one *d*. *Educ:* St Olave's Grammar School. Served in Royal Navy, 1940–46 (Lieut, RNVR). Entered Civil Service (War Office), 1936; Asst Principal, Ministry of National Insurance, 1947; Principal, 1950; Admin. Staff Coll., Henley, 1952; Asst Sec. 1959; seconded to HM Treasury, 1957–59; served on an ILO mission in Trinidad and Tobago, 1967–69. Interviewer for CS Commn, 1971–79. UK Delegate to and Chairman: NATO Management Survey Cttee, 1970–71; Council of Europe Management Survey Cttee, 1971–72. Chm., Supplementary Benefit Appeal Tribunals, 1971–75; Head of UK res. project in W Europe into social security provision for disablement, 1971–72; Res. Consultant, Office of Manpower Econs, 1972–73; served on technical aid mission to Indonesia, 1973; ILO Res. Consultant on Social Security, 1973–80; Consultant to: EEC Statistical Office, 1974; Govt of Thailand on Social Security, 1978–79 and 1981. Fellow, Inst. for European Health Services Research, Leuven Univ., Belgium, 1974–. *Publications:* Medical Care Systems, 1974; Social Security for the Unemployed, 1976. *Recreations:* walking, photography, travel. *Address:* 100 Downs Road, Coulsdon, Surrey CR5 1AF. *T:* Downland (0737) 554231. *Club:* Civil Service.

FULFORD, Robert John; Keeper, Department of Printed Books, British Library (formerly British Museum), 1967–85; *b* 16 Aug. 1923; *s* of John Fulford, Southampton; *m* 1950, Alison Margaret Rees; one *s* one *d*. *Educ:* King Edward VI Sch., Southampton; King's Coll., Cambridge; Charles Univ., Prague. Asst Keeper, Dept of Printed Books, British Museum, 1945–65; Dep. Keeper, 1965–67 (Head of Slavonic Div., 1961–67); Keeper, 1967–85. *Address:* 7 Tulip Tree Close, Tonbridge, Kent TN9 2SH. *T:* Tonbridge (0732) 350356; Maumont, 24390 Hautefort, France. *T:* 53–50–50–07.

FULHAM, Bishop Suffragan of, since 1985; **Rt Rev. Charles John Klyberg;** (first) Archdeacon of Charing Cross, since 1989; *b* 29 July 1931; *s* of Captain Charles Augustine Klyberg, MN and late Ivy Lilian Waddington, LRAM; unmarried. *Educ:* Eastbourne College. ARICS. Asst Estates Manager, Cluttons, 1952–57. Lincoln Theological Coll., 1957–60. Curate, S John's, East Dulwich, 1960–63; Rector of Fort Jameson, Zambia, 1963–67; Vicar, Christ Church and S Stephen, Battersea, 1967–77; Dean of Lusaka Cathedral, Zambia, and Rector of the parish, 1977–85, Dean Emeritus, 1985; Vicar General, 1978–85. UK Commissary for Anglican Church in Zambia, 1985–89. Chm., Church Property Development Gp, 1978–85. *Recreations:* reading, music, travel. *Address:* 4 Cambridge Place, W8 5PB. *T:* 071–937 2560. *Club:* Athenæum.

FULLER, Brian Leslie, CBE 1989; QFSM 1981; Commandant, Fire Service College, since 1990; *b* 18 April 1936; *s* of Walter Leslie Victor Fuller and Eliza May Fuller; *m* 1957, Linda Peters; three *s*. *Educ:* St Albans County Grammar Sch. for Boys. FIFireE 1975. Station Officer: Herts Fire Brigade, 1960–66; Warwicks Fire Brigade, 1966–68; Asst Divl Officer, Notts Fire Brigade, 1968–69; Divl Commander, Essex Fire Brigade, 1969–72; Dep. Chief Fire Officer, Glamorgan Fire Brigade, 1972–74; Chief Fire Officer: Mid Glamorgan Fire Brigade, 1974–80; Notts Fire Brigade, 1980–81; W Midlands Fire Service, 1981–90. *Recreations:* cricket, music, reading. *Address:* Fire Service College, Moreton-in-Marsh, Glos GL56 0RH. *T:* Moreton-in-Marsh (0608) 50831.

FULLER, Geoffrey Herbert, CEng, FRINA, FIMarE; RCNC; defence and maritime consultant; Deputy Chairman, British Maritime Technology Ltd, Teddington, since 1985; *b* 16 Jan. 1927; *s* of late Major Herbert Thomas Fuller and Clarice Christine Fuller; *m* 1952, Pamela-Maria Quarrell; one *d*. *Educ:* Merchant Taylors', Northwood, Mddx; Royal Naval Engrg Coll., Keyham; Royal Naval Coll., Greenwich. FRINA 1965; FIMarE 1974. Constructor Commander: Staff of Flag Officer (Submarines), 1958; British Navy Staff, Washington, 1960; Sen. Officers War Course, 1969; RCDS, 1973; Head of Ship Material Engrg, 1974; Support Manager Submarines, 1976; Dep. Dir, Submarines/Polaris, Ship Dept, MoD, 1979; Dir of Naval Ship Production, 1981–82; Mem. Bd, and Man. Dir, Warship Div., British Shipbuilders, 1983–85; Exec. Chm., 1984–86, Technical Adviser, 1986–87, Vickers Shipbuilding and Engrg Ltd, Barrow. Trustee, Monks Ferry Trng Trust, Birkenhead, 1986–. *Address:* Baytree House, Batcombe, Somerset BA4 6HD. *T:* Shepton Mallet 85711.

FULLER, Hon. Sir John (Bryan Munro), Kt 1974; President: Arthritis Foundation of Australia, since 1980; Barnardo's Australia, since 1985 (Member, Management Committee, 1980–85); *b* 22 Sept. 1917; *s* of late Bryan Fuller, QC; *m* 1940, Eileen, *d* of O. S. Webb; one *s* one *d*. *Educ:* Knox Grammar Sch., Wahroonga. Chm., Australian Country Party (NSW), 1959–64; MLC, NSW, 1961–78; Minister for Decentralisation and Development, 1965–73; NSW Minister for Planning and Environment, 1973–76; Vice-Pres. of Exec. Council and Leader of Govt in Legis. Council, 1968–76; Leader of Opposition, 1976–78. Pres., Assoc. of Former Mems of NSW Parlt, 1988–; Vice-Pres., Graziers Assoc. of NSW, 1965; Member: Council, Univ. of NSW, 1967–78; Cttee, United World Colls Trust, NSW, 1978–; Bd, Foundn for Res. and Treatment Alcohol and Drug Dependence, 1980–85; Council, Nat. Heart Foundn, NSW, 1980–; Federal Pres., Aust. Inst. of Export, 1986– (Pres., NSW, 1985); Leader of various NSW Govt trade missions to various parts of the world. Fellow Australian Inst. of Export 1969. *Recreations:* tennis, bowls. *Address:* 54/8 Fullerton Street, Woollahra, NSW 2025, Australia. *Clubs:* Australian (Sydney); Coolah Bowling, Royal Sydney Golf, Australian Jockey.

FULLER, John Leopold, FRSL 1980; writer; Fellow of Magdalen College, Oxford, and Tutor in English, since 1966; *b* 1 Jan. 1937; *s* of Roy Broadbent Fuller, *qv*; *m* 1960, Cicely Prudence Martin; three *d*. *Educ:* St Paul's School; New Coll., Oxford (BLitt, MA). Vis. Lectr, State Univ. of NY at Buffalo, 1962–63; Asst Lectr, Univ. of Manchester, 1963–66. *Publications:* Fairground Music, 1961; The Tree that Walked, 1967; A Reader's Guide to W. H. Auden, 1970; The Sonnet, 1972; Cannibals and Missionaries, 1972; Epistles to Several Persons, 1973 (Geoffrey Faber Meml Prize, 1974); Squeaking Crust, 1973; The Last Bid, 1975; The Mountain in the Sea, 1975; Lies and Secrets, 1979; The Illusionists (Southern Arts Lit. Prize), 1980; The Extraordinary Wool Mill and other stories, 1980; Waiting for the Music, 1982; Flying to Nowhere (Whitbread Prize for a First Novel), 1983; The Beautiful Inventions, 1983; (ed) The Dramatic Works of John Gay, 1983; Come Aboard and Sail Away, 1983; The Adventures of Speedfall, 1985; Selected Poems 1954–1982, 1985; (with James Fenton) Partingtime Hall, 1986; Tell It Me Again, 1988; The Grey Among the Green, 1988; The Burning Boys, 1989; (ed) The Chatto Book of Love Poetry, 1990; The Mechanical Body, 1991. *Recreations:* printing, correspondence chess, music. *Address:* Magdalen College, Oxford OX1 4AU. *T:* Oxford (0865) 276070.

FULLER, Major Sir John (William Fleetwood), 3rd Bt *cr* 1910; Major, The Life Guards, retired; *b* 18 Dec. 1936; *s* of Major Sir John Gerard Henry Fleetwood Fuller, 2nd Bt, and Fiona, Countess of Normanton, (*d* 1985), *d* of 4th Marquess Camden, GCVO; *S* father, 1981; *m* 1968, Lorna Marian, *o d* of F. R. Kemp-Potter, Findon, Sussex; three *s*. *Heir:* *s* James Henry Fleetwood Fuller, *b* 1 Nov. 1970. *Address:* Neston Park, Corsham, Wilts.

FULLER, Michael John; General Manager, National Bank of Abu Dhabi, since 1991; *b* 20 July 1932; *s* of Thomas Frederick and Irene Emily Fuller; *m* 1955, Maureen Rita Slade (marr. diss. 1989); two *s* two *d*; *m* 1990, Elizabeth Frost. *Educ:* Wallington County Grammar Sch. FCIB 1980. National Service, commnd RAF, 1950–52. Midland Bank, 1948–90: various branch, regl and head office posts; Gp Public Affairs Advr, 1977–79; Regl Dir, Southampton, 1979–81; Gen. Manager, Midland and Wales, 1981–82; Gen. Manager, Business Develt Div., 1982–85; UK Operations Dir, 1985–87; Dep. Chief Exec., 1987–89, Chief Exec., 1989–90, UK Banking Sector. *Recreations:* reading, travelling, rough golf. *Address:* c/o National Bank of Abu Dhabi, PO Box 4, Abu Dhabi, United Arab Republic. *Club:* Royal Air Force.

FULLER, Roy Broadbent, CBE 1970; MA Oxon (by Decree); FRSL; poet and author; solicitor; Professor of Poetry, University of Oxford, 1968–73; *b* 11 Feb. 1912; *e s* of late Leopold Charles Fuller, Oldham; *m* 1936, Kathleen Smith; one *s*. *Educ:* Blackpool High Sch. Admitted a solicitor, 1934; served Royal Navy, 1941–46; Lieut, RNVR, 1944; Asst Solicitor to Woolwich Equitable Building Soc., 1938–58, Solicitor, 1958–69, Director, 1969–87. Vice-Pres., Bldg Socs Assoc., 1969–87 (Chm. Legal Adv. Panel, 1958–69). A Governor of the BBC, 1972–79; Mem., Arts Council, 1976–77 (Chm., Literature Panel, 1976–77); Mem., Library Adv. Council for England, 1977–79. Hon. DLitt Kent, 1986. Queen's Gold Medal for Poetry, 1970. Cholmondeley Award, Soc. of Authors, 1980. *Publications: fiction:* Savage Gold, 1946; With My Little Eye, 1948; The Second Curtain, 1953; Fantasy and Fugue, 1954; Image of a Society, 1956; The Ruined Boys, 1959; The Father's Comedy, 1961; The Perfect Fool, 1963; My Child, My Sister, 1965; Catspaw, 1966; The Carnal Island, 1970; The Other Planet, 1979; Stares, 1990; *non fiction:* Questions and Answers in Building Soc. Law and Practice, 1949; Owls and Artificers: Oxford lectures on poetry, 1971; Professors and Gods: last Oxford lectures on poetry, 1973; (ed with John Lehmann) The Penguin New Writing, 1985; (ed) The Building Societies Act, various dates; *poetry:* Poems, 1939; The Middle of a War, 1942; A Lost Season, 1944; Epitaphs and Occasions, 1949; Counterparts, 1954; Brutus's Orchard, 1957; Collected Poems, 1962; Buff, 1965; New Poems (Duff Cooper Meml Prize), 1968; Off Course, 1969; Seen Grandpa Lately?, 1972; Tiny Tears, 1973; From the Joke Shop, 1975; An Ill-Governed Coast, 1976; Poor Roy, 1977; The Reign of Sparrows, 1980; The Individual and His Times (selected poems), 1982; (with Barbara Giles and Adrian Rumble) Upright Downfall, 1983; New and Collected Poems 1934–84, 1985; Subsequent to Summer, 1985; Consolations, 1987; Available for Dreams (jtly, W. H. Heinemann Award), 1989; The World Through the Window: collected poems for children, 1989; *anthologies:* Byron for Today, 1948; Fellow Mortals: an anthology of animal verse, 1981; *autobiography:* Souvenirs, 1980; Vamp Till Ready, 1982; Home and Dry, 1984; The Strange and the Good: complete memoirs, 1989; Spanner and Pen: post-war memoirs, 1991. *Address:* 37 Langton Way, Blackheath, SE3. *T:* 081–858 2334. *Club:* Athenæum.

See also J. L. Fuller.

FULLER, Simon William John; HM Diplomatic Service; Head of Near East and North African Department, Foreign and Commonwealth Office, since 1990; *b* 27 Nov. 1943; *s* of Rowland William Bevis Fuller and late Madeline Fuller (*née* Bailey); *m* 1984, Eleanor Mary Breedon; three *s*. *Educ:* Wellington College; Emmanuel College, Cambridge (BA Hist.). Served Singapore and Kinshasa, 1969–73; First Sec., Cabinet Office, 1973–75; FCO, 1975–77; UK Mission to UN, New York, 1977–80; FCO, 1980–86 (Counsellor, 1984); Dep. Hd of Mission, Tel Aviv, 1986–90. *Recreations:* cooking and cricket. *Address:* c/o Foreign and Commonwealth Office, SW1A 2AH; 27 Carlisle Mansions, Carlisle Place, SW1P 1EZ. *T:* 071-828 6494. *Clubs:* United Oxford & Cambridge University, MCC.

FULLER-ACLAND-HOOD, Sir (Alexander) William; *see* Hood, Sir William Acland.

FULLERTON, Peter George Patrick Downing; HM Diplomatic Service and Civil Service, retired; *b* 17 Jan. 1930; *s* of late Major R. A. D. Fullerton and Janet Mary Fullerton (*née* Baird); *m* 1962, Elizabeth Evelyn Newman Stevens, *d* of late George Stevens; two *s* two *d*. *Educ:* Radley Coll.; Magdalen Coll., Oxford (MA). HMOCS, Kenya, 1953–63, retd as Dist Comr; joined CRO (later FCO), 1963; Private Sec. to Minister of State, 1963–64; Dar-es-Salaam, 1964–65; Lusaka, 1966–69; seconded to British Leyland Motor Corp., 1970; FCO, 1971; Northern Ireland Office, 1972; FCO, 1973; Canberra, 1974–77; Asst Sec., Dept. of Energy, 1977; Dir, Domestic Programme, Energy Efficiency Office, Dept of Energy, 1985. *Address:* Wellbourne, Cuddesdon, Oxon OX9 9HG. *Clubs:* United Oxford & Cambridge University; Leander.

FULLERTON, William Hugh, CMG 1989; HM Diplomatic Service; Governor, Falkland Islands, Commissioner for South Georgia and South Sandwich Islands, since 1988 (High Commissioner, British Antarctic Territory, 1988–89); *b* 11 Feb. 1939; *s* of late Major Arthur Hugh Theodore Francis Fullerton, RAMC, and of Mary (*née* Parker); *m* 1968, Arlene Jacobowitz; one *d*. *Educ:* Cheltenham Coll.; Queens' Coll., Cambridge (MA Oriental Langs). Shell Internat. Petroleum Co., Uganda, 1963–65; FO, 1965; MECAS, Shemlan, Lebanon, 1965–66; Information Officer, Jedda, 1966–67; UK Mission to UN, New York, 1967; FCO, 1968–70; Head of Chancery, Kingston, Jamaica, 1970–73, and Ankara, 1973–77; FCO, 1977–80; Counsellor (Economic and Commercial), 1980–83 and Consul-Gen., 1981–83, Islamabad; Ambassador to Somalia, 1983–87; on loan to MoD, 1987–88. *Recreations:* travelling in remote areas, sailing, reading, walking. *Address:* c/o Foreign and Commonwealth Office, King Charles Street, SW1. *Club:* Travellers'.

FULTHORPE, Henry Joseph, FRINA; RCNC; General Manager, HM Dockyard, Portsmouth (Deputy Director of Naval Construction), 1967–75; *b* Portsmouth, 2 July 1916; *s* of Joseph Henry and Clarissa Fulthorpe; *m* 1939, Bette May Forshew; two *s* one *d*. *Educ:* Royal Naval Coll., Greenwich. Ship Design and Production, Admiralty, London and Bath, 1939–43; Principal (Ship) Overseer, Vickers, Barrow-in-Furness, 1943–46; Dep. Manager, HM Dockyard, Malta, 1946–49; Sec., Radiological Defence Panel, 1949–52; Staff Constr, first British atom bomb, Montebello Is, 1952–53; Constr i/c Minesweeper Design, Admty, Bath, 1953–54; Chief Constr, Maintenance, Bath, 1954–56; Dep. Manager, HM Dockyard, Portsmouth, 1956–58; Chief Constructor: HM Dockyard, Singapore, 1958–61; Dockyard Dept, Bath, 1961–63; Asst Dir of Naval Construction, Bath, 1963–64; Production Manager, HM Dockyard, Chatham, 1964–67; Manager, Constructive Dept, HM Dockyard, Portsmouth, 1967. *Recreations:* travel, winemaking, cooking. *Address:* Gerard House, 60 Granada Road, Southsea PO4 0RJ. *T:* Portsmouth (0705) 750427.

FULTON, Hon. (Edmund) Davie, PC (Canada) 1957; QC (BC) 1957; Barrister and Solicitor; Associate Counsel, Swinton & Company, Vancouver, 1983–90, retired; Chairman, Canadian Section, International Joint Commission, Ottawa, 1990–July 1992 (a Commissioner, 1986–July 1992); *b* 10 March 1916; *s* of Frederick John Fulton, KC, and Winifred M. Davie; *m* 1946, Patricia Mary, *d* of J. M. Macrae and Christine Macrae (*née* Carmichael), Winnipeg; three *d*. *Educ:* St Michael's Sch., Victoria, BC; Kamloops High Sch.; University of British Columbia; St John's Coll., Oxford. BA (BC), BA Oxon (Rhodes Scholar, elected 1936). Admitted to Bar of British Columbia, 1940. Served in Canadian Army Overseas as Company Comdr with Seaforth Highlanders of Canada and as DAAG 1st Canadian Inf. Div., 1940–45, including both Italian and Northwest Europe campaigns (despatches); transferred to R of O with rank of Major, 1945. Practised law with Fulton, Verchere & Rogers, Kamloops, BC, 1945–68, and with Fulton, Cumming, Richards & Co., Vancouver, 1968–73; Judge, Supreme Court of British Columbia, 1973–81. Elected to House of Commons of Canada, 1945; re-elected in 1949, 1953, 1957, 1958, 1962, 1965. Mem. Senate, University of British Columbia, 1948–57, 1969–75. Acting Minister of Citizenship and Immigration, June 1957–May 1958; Minister of Justice and Attorney Gen., Canada, June 1957–Aug. 1962; Minister of Public Works, Aug. 1962–April, 1963. Mem., Vancouver Adv. Cttee, Guaranty Trust Co. of Canada, 1983–86. Member: Law Soc. of BC, 1940–; Law Soc. of Upper Canada, 1957–; Canadian Bar Assoc., 1940–. Hon. Col, Rocky Mountain Rangers, 1959. Hon. LLD: Ottawa, 1960; Queen's, 1963. Human Relns Award, Canadian Council of Christians and Jews, 1985; Citation for meritorious service to country and profession, Trial Lawyers Assoc. of BC, 1986. *Address:* c/o Canadian Section, International Joint Commission, 18–100 Metcalfe Street, Ottawa, Ont K1P 5M1, Canada; (from Sept. 1992) 1632 West 40th Avenue, Vancouver, BC V6M 1V9, Canada. *Clubs:* Vancouver, Shaughnessy Golf and Country (Vancouver).

FULTON, Prof. John Francis; Director, School of Education, since 1985 and Pro-Vice-Chancellor, since 1987, Queen's University of Belfast; *b* 21 Sept. 1933; *s* of Robert Patrick Fulton and Anne Fulton (*née* McCambridge); *m* 1958, Elizabeth Mary Brennan; one *s* one *d*. *Educ:* St Malachy's College, Belfast; QUB (BA 1954, DipEd 1958, MA 1964); Univ. of Keele (PhD 1975). Lectr and Principal Lectr, St Joseph's Coll. of Educn, Belfast, 1961–73; Lectr, Inst. of Educn, QUB, 1973–76; Prof. and Head of Dept of Educnl Studies, QUB, 1977–85. Mem., IBA, subseq. ITC, 1987–. FRSA. *Publications:* contribs to: Education in Great Britain and Ireland, 1973; Educational Research and Development in Great Britain, 1982; Willingly to School, 1987; articles in learned jls. *Recreations:* golf, music. *Address:* School of Education, Queen's University of Belfast, BT7 1NN. *T:* Belfast (0232) 245133.

FULTON, Robert Andrew; HM Diplomatic Service; Counsellor, UK Mission to the United Nations, New York, since 1989; *b* 6 Feb. 1944; *s* of Rev. Robert M. Fulton and Janet W. Fulton (*née* Mackenzie); *m* 1970, Patricia Mary Crowley; two *s* one *d*. *Educ:* Rothesay Academy; Glasgow University (MA, LLB). Foreign and Commonwealth Office, 1968; Third later Second Secretary, Saigon, 1969; FCO, 1972; First Sec., Rome, 1973; FCO, 1977; First Sec., E Berlin, 1978; FCO, 1981; Counsellor, Oslo, 1984; FCO, 1987. *Recreations:* golf, racing, reading, cinema. *Address:* c/o Foreign and Commonwealth Office, SW1A 2AH.

FUNG, Hon. Sir Kenneth Ping-Fan, Kt 1971; CBE 1965 (OBE 1958); JP; Chairman: Fung Ping Fan Holdings Ltd; Fung Ping Fan & Co. Ltd; Chairman or Director of other companies; Senior Consultant for External Economy of People's Government of Chongqing, since 1985; Director (and Chief Manager, retd), of The Bank of East Asia Ltd, Hong Kong; Chairman, Thomas Cook Travel Services (Hong Kong) Ltd; Director, Hong Kong Macau International Investment Co. Ltd; *b* 28 May 1911; *yr s* of late Fung Ping Shan, JP; *m* 1933, Ivy (*née* Kan) Shiu-Han, OBE, JP, *d* of late Kan Tong-Po, JP; four *s* one *d*. *Educ:* Government Vernacular Sch.; Sch. of Chinese Studies, Univ. of Hong Kong. Unofficial Mem., Urban Council, 1951–60; Unofficial MLC, 1959–65, MEC, 1962–72; Life Mem., Court of Univ. of Hong Kong; Council of Chinese Univ. of Hong Kong; Fourth Pan-Pacific Rehabilitation Conf.; Pres., Chm., etc. of numerous social organisations, both present and past. Chm., Hong Kong Nat. Cttee, United World Colleges; Member: Program for Harvard and East Asia (Mem. Internat. Org. Cttee); Rotary Internat. (Paul Harris Fellow; 50-Year Membership Award, 1985); Bd of Overseers, Univ. of California Med. Sch., San Francisco; The 1001: a Nature Trust; Internat. Council, Asia Soc., NY. Comr St John Ambulance Bde (first Chinese to serve), 1953–58; first Chinese Hon. ADC to 4 successive Governors and Officers Admin. Govt (rep. StJAB). JP Hong Kong, 1952; KStJ 1958. Hon. degrees: LLD, Chinese Univ. of Hong Kong, 1968; DSocSc, Univ. of Hong Kong, 1969. Founder Mem., Royal Asiatic Soc.; Mem. other Socs and Assocs. Silver Acorn, Commonwealth Scout Council (UK), 1976; Gold Dragon, Scout Assoc. of Hong Kong. Order of the Sacred Treasure, II Class (Japan), 1985; Knight Grand Officer, 1984 (Knight Commander, 1979), Internat. Order of St Hubert (Austria). *Recreations:* racing, golf, swimming. *Address:* (home) 14 South Bay Road, Hong Kong. *T:* 5–8122514; (office) Fung Ping Fan & Co. Ltd, Fung House, 2/F 20 Connaught Road C., Hong Kong. *T:* 220311. *Clubs:* Royal Hongkong Jockey (Hon. Steward), Royal Hongkong Golf, Royal Hongkong Yacht, Hongkong Polo Assoc., Sports, Hongkong Country, Hongkong, Shek O Country, Hongkong Squash (Life Mem.), Chinese Recreation (Hon. Pres.), American, Japanese (Pres.), CASAM, Hongkong Automobile Assoc., Rotary (all in Hong Kong); Knickerbocker, Sky, Explorers', Amer. Photographic Soc., Bohemian (all in New York, USA); Hakone Country, Toride Internat. Golf, Hodogaya (Japan).

FUNSTON, G(eorge) Keith; *b* Waterloo, Iowa, USA, 12 Oct. 1910; *s* of George Edwin and Genevieve (Keith) Funston; *m* 1939, Elizabeth Kennedy; one *s* two *d*. *Educ:* Trinity Coll., Hartford, Conn; AB 1932; MBA (*cum laude*), Harvard, 1934. Mem. Research Staff, Harvard Business Sch., 1934–35; Asst to VP Sales, then Asst to Treas., American Radiator & Standard Sanitary, 1935–40; Dir, Purchases & Supplies, Sylvania Electronics, 1940–44; Special Asst to Chm., War Production Bd, 1941–44; Lt-Comdr, US Navy, 1944–46; Pres., Trinity Coll., Hartford, 1944–51; Pres. and Governor, New York Stock Exchange, 1951–67. Chm., Olin Corp., 1967–72; formerly Director: IBM; Metropolitan Life; Republic Steel; AVCO Corp.; Illinois Central Industries; Chemical Bank; Putnam Trust; Hartford Steam Boiler & Insurance Co.; Winn-Dixie Stores; Paul Revere Investors; First Florida Banks. Holds numerous hon. doctorates. *Recreations:* riding, reading, ski-ing, tennis. *Address:* (home) 911 Strangler Fig Lane, Sanibel, Fla 33957, USA. *Clubs:* Round Hill (Greenwich, Conn.); University, The Century Assoc., The Links (New York).

FURBER, (Frank) Robert; retired solicitor; *b* 28 March 1921; *s* of late Percy John Furber and Edith Furber; *m* 1948, Anne Wilson McArthur; three *s* one *d*. *Educ:* Willaston Sch.; Berkhamsted Sch.; University College London. LLB. Articled with Slaughter and May; solicitor 1945; Partner, Clifford-Turner, 1952–86. Mem., Planning Law Cttee, Law Society, 1964–69. Chairman: Blackheath Soc., 1968–89; Blackheath Preservation Trust, 1972–; Film Industry Defence Organization, 1968–89; Governor: Yehudi Menuhin Sch., 1964–91; Live Music Now!, 1977–87; Berkhamsted Sch., and Berkhamsted Sch. for Girls, 1976–91 (Chm., 1986–91); Board Member: Trinity Coll. of Music, 1974–91; Nat. Jazz Centre, 1982–87; Common Law Inst. of Intellectual Property, 1982–87; Chm., Rules of Golf Cttee, Royal and Ancient Golf Club, 1976–80; Trustee, Robert T. Jones Meml Trust, 1982–86; Mem. and Hon. Sec., R & A Golf Amateurism Commn of Inquiry, 1984–85; Mem., CCPR Cttee of Enquiry into Amateurism in Sport, 1986–88. Hon. Fellow, Trinity College, London. *Recreations:* golf, music, books, writing a history of The Moles Golfing Society. *Address:* 8 Pond Road, Blackheath, SE3 9JL. *T:* 081–852 8065. *Clubs:* Buck's; Royal Blackheath Golf, Royal St George's Golf (Captain, 1980–81), Royal and Ancient, Honourable Company of Edinburgh Golfers, Royal Worlington and Newmarket; Pine Valley (USA).

See also Ven. R. S. Brown.

FÜRER-HAIMENDORF, Prof. Christoph von, DPhil Vienna; Emeritus Professor and Hon. Fellow, School of Oriental and African Studies, University of London, since 1976; *b* 27 July 1909; *s* of Rudolf Fürer von Haimendorf und Wolkersdorf; *m* 1938, Elizabeth Barnardo (*d* 1987); one *s*. *Educ:* Theresianische Akademie, Vienna. Asst Lecturer, Vienna Univ., 1931–34; Rockefeller Foundation Fellowship, 1935–37; Lecturer, Vienna University, 1938; Anthropological Fieldwork in Hyderabad and Orissa, 1939–43; Special Officer Subansiri, External Affairs Dept, Govt of India, 1944–45; Adviser to HEH the Nizam's Govt and Prof. of Anthropology in the Osmania Univ., 1945–49; Reader in Anthropology with special reference to India, University of London, 1949–51; Prof. of Asian Anthropology, School of Oriental and African Studies, 1951–76 (Dean of Sch., 1969–74, acting Director, 1974–75). Anthropological Research: in India and Nepal, 1953; in Nepal, 1957, 1962, 1966, 1972, 1976, 1981, 1983; in the Philippines, 1968; in India, 1970, 1976–. Munro Lectr, Edinburgh Univ., 1959; Visiting Prof., Colegio de Mexico, 1964, 1966. Pres., Royal Anthropological Inst., 1975–77. Corresponding Member: Austrian Academy of Science, 1964; Anthropological Soc. of Vienna, 1970. Rivers Memorial Medal of Royal Anthropological Institute, 1949; S. C. Roy Gold Medal, Asiatic Soc., Calcutta, 1964; Sir Percy Sykes Memorial Medal, Royal Central Asian Soc., 1965; King Birendra Prize, Royal Nepal Acad., 1976; Annandale Medal, Asiatic Soc. of Bengal, 1979. Austrian Order of Merit for Art and Science, 1982. *Publications:* The Naked Nagas, 1939; The Chenchus, 1943; The Reddis of the Bison Hills, 1945; The Raj Gonds of Adilabad, 1948; Himalayan Barbary, 1955; The Apa Tanis, 1962; (joint author) Mount Everest, 1963; The Sherpas of Nepal, 1964; (ed and jt author) Caste and Kin in Nepal, India and Ceylon, 1966; Morals and Merit, 1967; The Konyak Nagas, 1969; (ed and jt author) Peoples of the Earth, vol. 12: The Indian Sub-continent, 1973; (ed and jt author) Contributions to the Anthropology of Nepal, 1974; Himalayan Traders, 1975; Return to the Naked Nagas, 1976; The Gonds of Andhra Pradesh, 1979; A Himalayan Tribe, 1980; (ed and jt author) Asian Highland Societies, 1981; Highlanders of Arunachal Pradesh, 1982; Tribes of India, 1982; Himalayan Adventure, 1983; The Sherpas Transformed, 1984; Tribal Populations and Cultures of the Indian Subcontinent, 1985; (jtly) Gonds and their Neighbours, 1987; An Autobiography of an Anthropologist in India, 1989; Exploratory Travels in Nepal, 1989; articles in Journal of Royal Anthropological Inst., Man, Anthropos, Geographical Jl, Man in India. *Recreation:* music. *Address:* 32 Clarendon Road, W11. *T:* 071–727 4520, 071–637 2388.

FURLONG, Mrs Monica; writer; *b* 17 Jan. 1930; *d* of Alfred Gordon Furlong and Freda Simpson; *m* 1953, William John Knights (marr. diss. 1977); one *s* one *d*. *Educ:* Harrow County Girls' Sch.; University College London. Truth, Spectator, Guardian, 1956–61; Daily Mail, 1961–68; Producer, BBC, 1974–78. Moderator, Movement for the Ordination of Women, 1982–85. Hon. DD Gen. Theol Seminary, NY, 1986. *Publications:* Travelling In, 1971; Contemplating Now, 1971; God's A Good Man (poems), 1974; Puritan's Progress, 1975; Christian Uncertainties, 1975; The Cat's Eye (novel), 1976; Merton (biography), 1980; Cousins (novel), 1983; (ed) Feminine in the Church, 1984; Genuine Fake: a biography of Alan Watts, 1986; Thérèse of Lisieux (biog.), 1987; Wise Child (novel), 1987; (ed) Mirror to the Church, 1988; A Year and a Day (novel), 1990. *Address:* c/o Anthony Sheil Associates, 43 Doughty Street, WC1. *T:* 071–405 9351. *Club:* Society of Authors.

FURLONG, Hon. Robert Stafford, MBE (mil.) 1945; Chief Justice of Newfoundland, 1959–79; *b* 9 Dec. 1904; *o s* of Martin Williams Furlong, KC, and Mary Furlong (*née* McGrath). *Educ:* St Bonaventure's Coll., St John's, Newfoundland. Called to the Bar, 1926, appointed KC 1944. Temp. Actg Lt-Comdr (S) RNVR. OStJ 1937; Knight of St Gregory 1958. *Recreations:* golf and motoring. *Address:* 8 Winter Avenue, St John's, Newfoundland. *T:* (709) 726–7228. *Clubs:* Naval (London); Bally Haly Golf and Country, Crow's Nest (all in St John's).

FURLONG, Ronald (John), FRCS; Hon. Consulting Orthopædic Surgeon: St Thomas' Hospital; King Edward VII Hospital for Officers; Queen Victoria Hospital, East Grinstead; and lately to the Army; *s* of Frank Owen Furlong and Elsie Muriel Taffs, Woolwich; *m* 1970, Eileen Mary Watford. *Educ:* Eltham Coll.; St Thomas's Hosp. MB, BS London 1931; MRCS, LRCP, 1931; FRCS 1934. Served with Royal Army Medical Corps, 1941–46. Home Commands, North Africa and Italy; Brigadier, Consulting Orthopædic Surgeon to the Army, 1946, Hon. Consulting Orthopædic Surgeon 1951; Orthopædic Surgeon, St Thomas' Hosp., 1946. *Publications:* Injuries of the Hand, 1957; (trans.) Pauwel's Atlas of the Biomechanics of the Normal and Diseased Hip, 1978; (trans.) Pauwel's Biomechanics of the Locomotor Apparatus, 1980; (trans.) W. Braun, O. Fischer, On the

Centre of Gravity of the Human Body, 1986. *Recreations:* reading, history and archæology. *Address:* 149 Harley Street, W1. *T:* 071–935 4444. *Club:* Athenæum.

FURLONGER, Robert William, CB 1981; retired public servant, Australia; *b* 29 April 1921; *s* of George William Furlonger and Germaine Rose Furlonger; *m* 1944, Verna Hope Lewis; three *s* one *d. Educ:* Sydney High Sch.; Sydney Univ. (BA). Served War, AMF, 1941–45. Australian Dept of External (later Foreign) Affairs, 1945–69 and 1972–77 (IDC, 1960; Dir, Jt Intell. Org., Dept of Def., 1960–72); appointments included: High Comr, Nigeria, 1961; Aust. Perm. Rep. to the European Office of the UN, 1961–64; Minister, Aust. Embassy, Washington, 1965–69; Ambassador to Indonesia, 1972–74, and to Austria, Hungary and Czechoslovakia, 1975–77; Dir-Gen., Office of National Assessments, Canberra, 1977–81. *Recreations:* golf, cricket, music. *Address:* PO Box 548, Belconnen, ACT 2616, Australia. *T:* 2531384. *Clubs:* Canberra; Royal Canberra Golf.

FURMSTON, Bentley Edwin, FRICS; Director of Overseas Surveys, Ordnance Survey, 1984–89; *b* 7 Oct. 1931; *s* of Rev. Edward Bentley Furmston and Mary Furmston (*née* Bennett); *m* 1957, Margaret (*née* Jackson); two *s* one *d. Educ:* The Nelson Sch., Wigton, Cumbria; Victoria Univ., Manchester (BSc Mathematics). Entered Civil Service as Surveyor, Directorate of Overseas Surveys, 1953, with service in Gambia, Swaziland, Basutoland, N Rhodesia; Sen. Surveyor, N Rhodesia, 1960; Sen. Computer, DOS, 1963; seconded to Govt of Malawi as Dep. Commissioner of Surveys, 1965; Principal Survey Officer, DOS, 1968: Overseas Supervisor, Sch. of Military Survey; Regional Survey Officer, W Africa; Asst Director (Survey), 1971; Asst Dir (Cartography), Ordnance Survey, 1973; Dep. Dir, Field Survey, Ordnance Survey, 1974; Dep. Dir (Survey), DOS, 1977; Dir, Overseas Surveys and Survey Advr, Min. of Overseas Develt, 1980. *Publications:* contribs to technical jls. *Recreations:* reading, gardening, hill walking, climbing. *Address:* The Orchards, Carter's Clay Road, Newtown, Romsey, Hants SO51 0GL.

FURMSTON, Prof. Michael Philip, TD 1966; Professor of Law, University of Bristol, since 1978; *b* 1 May 1933; *s* of Joseph Philip Furmston and Phyllis (*née* Clowes); *m* 1964, Ashley Sandra Maria Cope; three *s* seven *d. Educ:* Wellington Sch., Somerset; Exeter Coll., Oxford (BA 1st Cl. Hons Jurisprudence, 1956; BCL 1st Cl. Hons 1957; MA 1960). LlM Birmingham, 1962. Called to the Bar, Gray's Inn, 1960 (1st Cl. Hons), Bencher, 1989. National Service, RA, 1951–53 (2nd Lieut); Major, TA, 1966–78, TAVR. Lecturer: Univ. of Birmingham, 1957–62; QUB, 1962–63; Fellow, Lincoln Coll., Oxford, 1964–78 (Sen. Dean, 1967–68; Sen. Tutor and Tutor for Admissions, 1969–74); Univ. Lectr in Law, 1964–78, Curator, University Chest, 1976–78, Oxford; Lectr in Common Law, Council of Legal Educn, 1965–78; Dean, Faculty of Law, 1980–84, Pro-Vice-Chancellor, 1986–89, Univ. of Bristol. Visiting Professor: City Univ., 1978–82; Katholieke Universiteit, Leuven, 1980 and 1986; Nat. Univ. of Singapore, 1987. Liveryman, Arbitrators' Co. Jt Editor, Construction Law Reports, 1985–. *Publications:* (ed) Cheshire, Fifoot and Furmston's Law of Contract, 8th edn 1972, to 11th edn 1986; Contractors Guide to ICE Conditions of Contract, 1980; Misrepresentation and Fraud, in Halsbury's Law of England, 1980; Croner's Buying and Selling Law, 1982; (ed jtly) The Effect on English Domestic Law of Membership of the European Communities and Ratification of the European Convention on Human Rights, 1983; (jtly) A Building Contract Casebook, 1984, 2nd edn 1990; (jtly) Cases and Materials on Contract, 1985, 2nd edn 1990; (ed) The Law of Tort: policies and trends in liability for damage to property, 1986; (ed) You and the Law, 1987; Croner's Model Business Contracts, 1988; (jtly) 'A' Level Law, 1988; Sale of Goods, 1990. *Recreations:* chess (Member, English team, Postal Olympiads), watching cricket, collecting Austin A35s, dogs. *Address:* The Old Post Office, Shipham, Winscombe, Avon BS25 1TQ. *T:* Winscombe (093484) 2253; Faculty of Law, University of Bristol, Wills Memorial Building, Queen's Road, Bristol BS8 1RJ. *T:* Bristol (0272) 303030, 303373. *Clubs:* Reform, Naval and Military.

FURNELL, Very Rev. Raymond; Provost, St Edmundsbury Cathedral, since 1981; *b* 18 May 1935; *s* of Albert George Edward and Hetty Violet Jane Furnell; *m* 1967, Sherril Witcomb; one *s* three *d. Educ:* Hinchley Wood School, Surrey; Brasted Place Theological Coll.; Lincoln Theol Coll. Thomas Meadows & Co. Ltd, 1951; RAF, 1953; Lummus Co. Ltd, 1955; Geo. Wimpey & Co. Ltd, 1960; Brasted Place, 1961; Lincoln Theol Coll., 1963; Curate, St Luke's, Cannock, 1965; Vicar, St James the Great, Clayton, 1969; Rector, Hanley Team Ministry and RD, Stoke North, 1975–81. Mem., Gen. Synod of C of E, 1988–. *Recreations:* music, drama. *Address:* Provost's House, Bury St Edmunds, Suffolk IP33 1RS.

FURNER, Air Vice-Marshal Derek Jack, CBE 1973 (OBE 1963); DFC 1943; AFC 1954; *b* 14 Nov. 1921; *s* of Vivian J. Furner; *m* 1948, Patricia Donnelly; three *s. Educ:* Westcliff High Sch., Essex. Joined RAF, 1941; commnd as navigator, 1942; Bomber Comd (2 tours), 1942–44; Transport Comd, Far East, 1945–47; Navigation Instructor, 1948–50; trials flying, Boscombe Down, 1951–53 and Wright-Patterson, Ohio, 1953–56; Air Min., 1957; OC Ops Wing, RAF Waddington, 1958–60; Planning Staff, HQ Bomber Comd, 1961–63 and SHAPE, Paris, 1964–65; Dep. Dir Manning, MoD (Air), 1966–67; OC RAF Scampton, 1968; AOC Central Reconnaissance Estab., 1969–70; Sec., Internat. Mil. Staff, NATO, Brussels, 1970–73; Asst Air Secretary, 1973–75. Gen. Manager, 1976–81, Dir, 1977–81, Harlequin Wallcoverings. FIPM 1975; FBIM 1975. Mensa 1989. *Recreations:* mathematical problems, music, computing. *Address:* 1D South Cliff Tower, Bolsover Road, Eastbourne, E Sussex BN20 7JN. *T:* Eastbourne (0323) 33447. *Club:* Royal Air Force.

FURNESS, family name of **Viscount Furness.**

FURNESS, 2nd Viscount, *cr* 1918; **William Anthony Furness;** Baron Furness, *cr* 1910, of Grantley; *b* 31 March 1929; *s* of 1st Viscount and Thelma (*d* 1970), *d* of late Harry Hays Morgan, American Consul-Gen. at Buenos Aires; *S* father, 1940. *Educ:* Downside; USA. Served as Guardsman, Welsh Guards (invalided, 1947). Delegate to Inter-Parliamentary Union Conferences, Washington, 1953, Vienna, 1954, Helsinki, 1955, Warsaw, 1959, Brussels, 1961, Belgrade, 1963. Mem. Council, Hansard Soc. for Parliamentary Govt, 1955–67. Founder Chm., Anglo-Mongolian Soc., 1963; Vice-President: Tibet Soc. of the UK; Catholic Stage Guild. Sovereign Military Order of Malta: joined 1954; Sec., Assoc. of Brit. Members, 1956–65, Sec.-Gen. 1965–78; Regent, Brit. Sub-Priory of Bl. Adrian Fortescue, 1982–; Mem. Sovereign Council, 1960–62; Mem. Board of Auditors, 1979–80; Grand Cross, Order of Merit, 1984, Kt of Justice, 1977 (Solemn Vows, 1982). Grand Officer, Order of Merit, Italy, 1961; KStJ 1971 (CStJ 1964); KCSG 1966. *Heir:* none. *Address:* c/o Midland Bank, 69 Pall Mall, SW1. *Clubs:* Boodle's, Carlton; Travellers' (Paris).

FURNESS, Alan Edwin, CMG 1991; HM Diplomatic Service; Deputy High Commissioner, Bombay, since 1989; *b* 6 June 1937; *s* of late Edwin Furness and Marion Furness (*née* Senton); *m* 1971, Aline Elizabeth Janine Barrett; two *s. Educ:* Eltham Coll.; Jesus Coll., Cambridge (BA, MA). Commonwealth Relations Office, 1961; Private Sec. to Parliamentary Under-Secretary of State, 1961–62; Third, later Second Secretary, British High Commn, New Delhi, 1962–66; First Secretary, DSAO (later FCO), 1966–69; First Sec., UK Delegn to European Communities, Brussels, 1969–72; First Sec. and Head of Chancery, Dakar, 1972–75; First Sec., FCO, 1975–78; Counsellor and Head of Chancery, Jakarta, 1978–81; Counsellor and Head of Chancery, Warsaw, 1982–85; Head of S Pacific Dept., FCO, 1985–88. *Recreations:* music, literature, gardening. *Address:* c/o Foreign and Commonwealth Office, SW1A 2AH. *Club:* United Oxford & Cambridge University.

FURNESS, Robin; *see* Furness, Sir S. R.

FURNESS, Lt-Col Simon John; Vice Lord-Lieutenant of Berwickshire, since 1990; *b* 18 Aug. 1936; 2nd *s* of Sir Christopher Furness, 2nd Bt and Violet Flower Chipchase Furness, OBE (*d* 1988), *d* of Lieut-Col G. C. Roberts, Hollingside, Durham. *Educ:* Charterhouse; RMA Sandhurst; Royal Naval Staff College. Commissioned 2nd Lieut Durham Light Infantry, 1956; served Far East, UK, Germany; active service, Borneo and NI; Comd 5th Bn LI, 1976–78, retired 1978. Dep. Col (Durham), LI, 1989. Mem. Exec., Nat. Trust for Scotland (Chm., Gardens Cttee). DL Berwickshire, 1984. *Recreations:* gardening, country sports, fine arts. *Address:* Nether-byres, Eyemouth, Berwickshire TD14 5SE. *T:* Eyemouth (08907) 50337. *Clubs:* Army and Navy; Durham County.

FURNESS, Sir Stephen (Roberts), 3rd Bt *cr* 1913; farmer and sporting/landscape artist (as Robin Furness); *b* 10 Oct. 1933; *e s* of Sir Christopher Furness, 2nd Bt, and Flower, Lady Furness, OBE (*d* 1988). *d* of late Col G. C. Roberts; *S* father, 1974; *m* 1961, Mary, *e d* of J. F. Cann, Cullompton, Devon; one *s* one *d. Educ:* Charterhouse. Entered RN, 1952; Observer, Fleet Air Arm, 1957; retired list, 1962. NCA, Newton Rigg Farm Inst., 1964. Member: Armed Forces Art Soc.; Darlington Art Soc. *Recreations:* looking at paintings, foxhunting, racing. *Heir:* *s* Michael Fitzroy Roberts Furness, *b* 12 Oct. 1962. *Address:* Otterington Hall, Northallerton, Yorks DL7 9HW. *T:* Northallerton (0609) 772061.
See also S. J. Furness.

FURNISS, Air Vice-Marshal Peter, DFC 1944; TD 1964; Director of Legal Services, RAF, 1978–82; *b* 16 July 1919; *s* of John and Mary Furniss; *m* 1954, Denise Cotet; one *s* two *d. Educ:* Sedbergh School. Commissioned 1st Bn The Liverpool Scottish TA, Queen's Own Cameron Highlanders, 1939; seconded to RAF, 1942; Comd No 73 Fighter Sqdn, 1945–46; demobilised 1946; admitted as Solicitor, 1948; commissioned in Legal Branch, RAF, 1950; Director of Legal Services: HQ Air Forces Middle East, Aden, 1961–63; HQ Far East Air Force, Singapore, 1969–71; HQ RAF Germany, 1973–74; Dep. Dir of Legal Services (RAF), 1975–78. *Recreations:* shooting, gardening, fishing. *Address:* 18 Sevington Park, Loose, Maidstone, Kent ME15 9SB. *T:* Maidstone (0622) 744620. *Club:* Royal Air Force.

FURNIVAL JONES, Sir (Edward) Martin, Kt 1967; CBE 1957; *b* 7 May 1912; *s* of Edward Furnival Jones, FCA; *m* 1955, Elizabeth Margaret, *d* of Bartholomew Snowball, BSc, AMIEE; one *d. Educ:* Highgate Sch.; Gonville and Caius Coll., Cambridge (exhibitioner). MA 1938. Admitted a Solicitor, 1937. Served War of 1939–45: General Staff Officer at Supreme Headquarters, Allied Expeditionary Force, and War Office (despatches, American Bronze Star Medal). Chm. of Bd, Frensham Heights, 1973–76 (Pres. 1977). *Recreation:* birdwatching.

FURNIVALL, Barony *cr* 1295; in abeyance. *Co-heiresses:* Hon. Rosamond Mary Dent (Sister Ancilla, OSB); *b* 3 June 1933; Hon. Patricia Mary Dent [*b* 4 April 1935; *m* 1st, 1956, Captain Thomas Hornsby (marr. diss., 1963; he *d* 1967); one *s* one *d*; 2nd, 1970, Roger Thomas John Bence; one *s* one *d*].

FURSDON, Maj.-Gen. Francis William Edward, CB 1980; MBE (Gallantry) 1958; KStJ 1980; defence consultant and correspondent; Director of Ceremonies, Order of St John, since 1980; *b* 10 May 1925; *s* of late G. E. S. Fursdon and Mrs Fursdon; *m* 1950, Joan Rosemary (*née* Worssam); one *s* one *d. Educ:* Westminster Sch. MLitt (Aberdeen) 1978; DLitt (Leiden) 1979. Passed AMIMechE; FBIM. Enlisted RE, 1942; RE Course, Birmingham Univ., 1943; in ranks until commnd, 1945; 1945–67: Royal W Afr. Frontier Force, India, Burma and Gold Coast; Student RMCS; staff and regtl duty, UK, Singapore, Canal Zone and Cyprus; Staff Coll.; DAA&QMG 19 Inf. Bde, UK and Port Said; GSO2 RE Sch. of Inf.; JSSC; OC 34 Indep. Fd Sqdn, E Africa and Kuwait; Instr, Staff Coll., Camberley; 2 i/c 38 Engr Regt; Admin. Staff Coll., Henley; CO 25 Engr Regt, BAOR, 1967–69; AA&QMG HQ Land Forces, Gulf, 1970–71; Dep. Comd and COS Land Forces, Gulf, 1971; Col Q (Qtg) HQ BAOR, 1972–73; Service Fellow, Aberdeen Univ., 1974; Dir of Def. Policy (Europe and NATO), MoD, 1974–77; Dir, Military Assistance Office, MoD, 1977–80; Mil. Adv. to Governor of Rhodesia, and later Senior British Officer, Zimbabwe, 1980, retired 1980. Defence and Military Correspondent, The Daily Telegraph, 1980–86. Freeman, City of London, 1987. *Publications:* Grains of Sand, 1971; There are no Frontiers, 1973; The European Defence Community: a History, 1980; Falklands Aftermath: picking up the pieces, 1988. *Recreations:* photography (IAC Internat. Award, 1967), gardening, travel. *Address:* c/o National Westminster Bank, 1 St James's Square, SW1Y 4JX. *Clubs:* St John House, Special Forces.

FURST, Stephen Andrew; QC 1991; *s* of Herbert and Viviane Furst; *m* 1979, Bridget Collins; one *s* one *d. Educ:* Edinburgh Academy; St Edmund Hall, Oxford (BA Hons); Leeds Univ. (LLB Hons). Called to the Bar, Middle Temple, 1975. *Address:* 10 Essex Street, WC2A 3AA. *T:* 071–240 6981.

FURTADO, Robert Audley, CB 1970; Special Commissioner, 1946–77, Presiding Commissioner, 1963–77; *b* 20 August 1912; *yr s* of Montague C. Furtado; *m* 1945, Marcelle Elizabeth, *d* of W. Randall Whitteridge; one *s* one *d. Educ:* Whitgift Sch.; University Coll., London. LLB London Univ., 1933; called to Bar, Gray's Inn, 1934. Served War of 1939–45, in Army in India and Burma (Despatches); demobilised rank of Lieut-Col, 1945. *Recreation:* bricolage. *Address:* Hillfold, Langton Herring, Weymouth, Dorset DT3 4JD. *T:* Abbotsbury (0305) 871502.
See also Prof. David Whitteridge and Sir Gordon Whitteridge.

FYFE, Maria; MP (Lab) Glasgow, Maryhill, since 1987; *b* 25 Nov. 1938; *d* of James O'Neill and Margaret Lacey; *m* 1964, James Joseph Fyfe (decd); two *s. Educ:* Strathclyde Univ. (BA Hons. Economic History 1975). Scottish Gas Board, 1959–64; Lectr, later Senior Lecturer in Further Education, Central College of Commerce, Glasgow Trade Union Studies Unit, 1978–87. Mem., Labour Party, 1960–, Scottish Exec., 1981–88 (Chair, Local Govt Sub-Cttee, 1985–87); Mem., Glasgow District Council, 1980–87 (Vice-Convener, Finance Cttee, 1980–84; Convener, Personnel Cttee, 1984–87). Dep. Shadow Minister for Women, 1988–91. *Address:* (office) House of Commons, SW1A 0AA. *T:* 071–219 4430/6819; 1508 Maryhill Road, Glasgow G20 9AB. *T:* 041–945 1495.

FYFE, Prof. William Sefton, CC (Canada) 1989; FRS 1969; Professor of Geology, University of Western Ontario, since 1972 (Dean of Science, 1986–90); *b* 4 June 1927; *s* of Colin and Isabella Fyfe; *m* 1968; two *s* one *d. Educ:* Otago Univ., New Zealand. BSc 1948, MSc 1949, PhD 1952; FRSC 1980. Univ. of California, Berkeley: Lecturer in Chemistry, 1952, Reader, 1958; Prof. of Geology, 1959; Royal Soc. Res. Prof. (Geochemistry), Univ. of Manchester, 1967–72. Guggenheim Fellow, 1983. Hon. Fellow, Geological Soc. Amer.; Corresp. Mem., Brazilian Acad. of Science. Hon. DSc: Meml Univ. of Newfoundland, 1989; Lisbon, 1990; Lakehead, 1990. Mineralogical Soc. of

Amer. Award, 1964; Logan Medal, Geolog. Assoc. of Canada, 1982; Willet G. Miller Medal, Royal Soc. of Canada, 1985; Arthur Holmes Medal, European Union of Geoscientists, 1989; Day Medal, Geol Soc. of America, 1990. Commemoration Medal, New Zealand, 1990. *Publications:* Metamorphic Reactions and Metamorphic Facies, 1958; The Geochemistry of Solids, 1964; Fluids in the Earth's Crust, 1978; also numerous scientific papers. *Address:* Department of Geology, University of Western Ontario, London, Ontario N6A 5B7, Canada.

FYJIS-WALKER, Richard Alwyne, CMG 1980; CVO 1976; HM Diplomatic Service, retired; Chairman, Commonwealth Institute, since 1988; *b* 19 June 1927; *s* of Harold and Marion Fyjis-Walker; *m* 1st, 1951, Barbara Graham-Watson (marr. diss.); one *s*; 2nd, 1972, Gabrielle Josefi; one *s*. *Educ:* Bradfield Coll.; Magdalene Coll., Cambridge (BA). Army (KRRC), 1945–48. Joined Foreign (subseq. Diplomatic) Service, 1955; served: Amman, 1956; FO, 1957–61; Paris, 1961–63; Cairo, 1963–65; FCO, 1966–71; Counsellor, 1970; Ankara, 1971–74; Counsellor (Information), Washington, 1974–78; Counsellor, UK Mission to UN, NY, 1978–79; Ambassador to the Sudan, 1979–84; Ambassador to Pakistan, 1984–87. *Address:* 17 Stonefield Street, N1 0HW.

FYSH, Robert Michael; QC 1989; *b* 2 Aug. 1940; *s* of Dr Leslie Fysh and Margaret Fysh, Ashford, Kent; *m* 1971, Mary Bevan; three *s*. *Educ:* Downside Sch.; Exeter Coll., Oxford (MA). Called to the Bar, Inner Temple, 1965; NI, 1974; NSW, 1975; Ireland, 1975; India, 1982; Pakistan, 1987; SC Trinidad and Tobago Bar, 1990. Editor: Reports of Patent Cases, 1975–; Fleet Street Reports, 1975–. *Publications:* Russell-Clarke on Registered Designs, 4th edn, 1974; The Industrial Property Citator, 1982; (ed) The Spycatcher Cases, 1989. *Recreations:* swimming, travel. *Address:* Francis Taylor Building, Temple, EC4Y 7BY. *T:* 071–353 5657. *Club:* Royal Over-Seas League.

G

GABATHULER, Prof. Erwin, FRS 1990; FInstP; Professor of Experimental Physics, Liverpool University, since 1983; *b* 16 Nov. 1933; *s* of Hans and Lena Gabathuler; *m* 1962, Susan Dorothy Jones, USA; two *s* one *d*. *Educ:* Queen's University Belfast (BSc 1956; MSc 1957); Univ. of Glasgow (PhD 1961). Research Fellow, Cornell Univ., 1961–64; Group Leader, Research, SERC, Daresbury Lab., 1964–73; European Organisation for Nuclear Research: Vis. Scientist, EMC Experiment, 1974–77; Leader, Exp. Physics Div., 1978–80; Dir of Research, 1981–83; Hd of Physics Dept, Liverpool Univ., 1986–91. Dr *hc* Univ. of Uppsala, 1982. *Publications:* articles in research jls. *Recreations:* music, ski-ing, walking. *Address:* 3 Danebank Road, Lymm, Cheshire WA13 9DQ. *T:* Lymm (092575) 2753.

GABB, (William) Harry, CVO 1974 (MVO 1961); DMus (Lambeth), 1974; Organist, Choirmaster and Composer at HM Chapels Royal, 1953–Easter 1974; Sub-Organist, St Paul's Cathedral, London, 1946–Easter 1974; Professor and Examiner of Organ Playing at The Trinity College of Music, London; Special Commissioner for Royal School of Church Music; Member, Council of the Royal College of Organists; Adjudicator and Recitalist; *b* 5 April 1909; *m* 1936, Helen Burnaford Mutton; one *s*. *Educ:* Scholarship at Royal Coll. of Music for Organ and Composition, ARCO 1928; FRCO 1930; ARCM Solo Organ, 1931; Organist, St Jude's, West Norwood, 1925; Organist and Choirmaster, Christ Church, Gypsy Hill, 1928; Sub-Organist, Exeter Cathedral, also Organist, Church of St Leonard's, Exeter and Heavitree Parish Church, 1929–37; Organist and Master of the Choristers, Llandaff Cathedral, 1937; Lectr, St Michael's Theological Coll., Llandaff; Royal Armoured Corps, War of 1939–45. Returned from Army to Llandaff, Jan. 1946. Played organ at the Coronation of Elizabeth II and at many Royal Weddings and Baptisms. Hon. FTCL, 1954. *Address:* St Lawrence Cottage, Bagshot Road, Chobham, Woking, Surrey GU24 8BY. *T:* Chobham (0276) 857879.

GADD, John, CBE 1988; Regional Chairman, British Gas North Thames, 1977–88, retired; *b* 9 June 1925; *s* of late George Gadd and of Winifred Gadd (*née* Bowyer), Dunstable, Bedfordshire; *m* 1959, Nancy Jean, *d* of late Pryce Davies, Henley-on-Thames. *Educ:* Cedars Sch., Leighton Buzzard; Cambridgeshire Technical Coll. FIGasE 1967; MIPM 1975; CBIM 1979. Joined Gas Industry, 1941. Served War, RNVR, 1943–46. Southern Gas Bd, 1946–69: various engineering appts; Personnel Manager, 1962; Dep. Chm., 1969; Chm., Eastern Gas, 1973–77. Administrative Staff Coll., Henley-on-Thames, 1961. FRSA 1985. *Recreations:* gardening, walking. *Address:* The Orchard, Rotherfield Road, Henley-on-Thames, Oxon RG9 1NR. *Clubs:* City Livery; Leander, Phyllis Court (Henley-on-Thames).

GADD, (John) Staffan; Chairman: J. S. Gadd Holdings Ltd, since 1987; SG Investments SA, since 1987; Saga Securities Ltd, since 1985; *b* 30 Sept. 1934; *s* of John Gadd and Ulla Olivecrona; *m* 1958, Margaretha Löfborg; one *s* one *d*; *m* 1990, Kay McGreeghan. *Educ:* Stockholm Sch. of Econs. MBA. Sec., Confedn of Swedish Industries, 1958–61; Skandinaviska Banken, Stockholm, 1961–69 (London Rep., 1964–67); Dep. Man. Dir, Scandinavian Bank Ltd, London, 1969–71, Chief Exec. and Man. Dir, 1971–80; Chief Exec., 1980–84, Chm., 1982–84, Samuel Montagu & Co. Ltd; Chm., Montagu and Co. AB, Sweden, 1982–86; Dir, Guyerzeller Zurmont Bank AG, Switzerland, 1983–84. *Recreations:* shooting, ski-ing, the arts, walking, travel. *Address:* Locks Manor, Hurstpierpoint, West Sussex BN6 9JZ.

GADDES, (John) Gordon; Director General, BEAMA, Federation of British Electrotechnical and Allied Manufacturers' Associations (formerly British Electrical and Allied Manufacturers' Association), since 1982; *b* 22 May 1936; *s* of late James Graham Moscrop Gaddes and of Irene Gaddes (*née* Murray; who married E. O. Kine); *m* 1958, Pamela Jean (*née* Marchbank); one *s* one *d*. *Educ:* Carres Grammar Sch., Sleaford; Selwyn Coll., Cambridge (MA Hons Geography); London Univ. (BScEcon Hons). Joint Services Sch. of Languages, Russian Translator in RAF, 1955–57. Asst Lectr in Business Studies, Peterborough Technical Coll., 1960–64; Lectr in Business Studies, later Head of Business Studies, then Vice-Principal, Dacorum Coll. of Further Educn, Hemel Hempstead, 1964–69; Head of Export Services: British Standards Instn, 1969–72; Quality Assurance Dept, 1972–73; Dir, BSI Hemel Hempstead Centre, 1973–77; Commercial Dir, BSI, 1977–81; Dir, Information, Marketing and Resources, BSI, 1981–82. Secretary, BSI Quality Assurance Council, 1976–80; Member: Council, 1982–, President's Cttee, 1984–86, Production Cttee, 1984–88, CBI; NACCB, 1984–90 (Chm., Assessment Panel, 1985–90); Project Leader for ISO/UNESCO inf. network study, 1974–75; variously, consultant to UNIDO and EC, UK Rep., ORGALIME, 1982– (Chairman: Electrical and Electronic Inds Liaison Cttee, 1982–86; Finance and Admin Cttee, 1986–88; Exec. Cttee, 1988–90); Pres., CENELEC, 1989– (Dep. Pres., 1987–89). Freeman, Glaziers' Co. *Recreation:* swimming. *Address:* Federation of British Electrotechnical and Allied Manufacturers' Associations, Leicester House, 8 Leicester Street, WC2H 7BN. *T:* 071–437 0678. *Club:* Athenæum.

GADSBY, (Gordon) Neville, CB 1972; *b* 29 Jan. 1914; *s* of William George and Margaret Sarah Gadsby; *m* 1938, Jeanne (*née* Harris); two *s* one *d*. *Educ:* King Edward VI Sch., Stratford-upon-Avon; University of Birmingham. BSc 1935, DipEd 1937, Cadbury Prizeman 1937, Birmingham; FRSC, CChem. Princ. Lectr, RMCS, 1946–51; Supt, Army Operational Research Gp, 1951–55; Dep. Sci. Adviser to Army Coun., 1955–59; idc 1960; Dir of Army Operational Science and Research, 1961; Dir, Army Operational Res. Estab., 1961–64; Dir of Biol. and Chem. Defence, MoD, 1965–67; Dep. Chief Scientist (Army), MoD, 1967–68; Dir, Chemical Defence Estabt, Porton, Wilts, 1968–72; Minister, Defence R&D, British Embassy, Washington, 1972–75, retired. *Publications:* Lubrication, 1949; An Introduction to Plastics, 1950. *Recreations:* oil painting, photography. *Address:* Ruan House, Cliff Road, Sidmouth, Devon EX10 8JN. *T:* Sidmouth (0395) 577842.

GADSDEN, Sir Peter (Drury Haggerston), GBE 1979; Hon. AC 1988; MA; FEng; Lord Mayor of London for 1979–80; Company Director; *b* Canada, 28 June 1929; *er s* of late Basil Claude Gadsden, ACT, ThL, and late Mabel Florence Gadsden (*née* Drury); *m* 1955, Belinda Ann, *e d* of late Captain Sir (Hugh) Carnaby de Marie Haggerston, 11th Bt; four *d*. *Educ:* Rockport, Northern Ireland; The Elms, Colwall; Wrekin Coll., Wellington; Jesus Coll., Cambridge (MA; Hon. Fellow, 1988). 2nd Lieut King's Shropshire LI, attached Oxf. and Bucks LI and Durham LI, Germany, 1948–49. Man. Dir, London subsid. of Australian Mineral Sands Producer, 1964–70; Marketing Economist (Mineral Sands) to UN Industrial Development Organisation, 1969; pt-time Mem., Crown Agents for Oversea Govts and Admins, 1981–87. Dep. Chm., W. Canning plc, 1990– (Dir, 1989–); Director: City of London (Arizona) Corp., 1970–88 (Chm., 1985–88); Private Patients Plan Ltd (Chm., 1984–); Wm Jacks PLC, 1984–; World Trade Centre in London Ltd, 1985–; Aitken Hume Internat. PLC, 1986–; Penny & Giles Internat. plc, 1987–. Dir, Clothworkers' Foundn, 1978–; Hon. Mem. London Metal Exchange. President: Nat. Assoc. of Charcoal Manufacturers, 1970–86; City of London Rifle & Pistol Club (formerly Embankment Rifle Club), 1975–87; Leukaemia Res. Fund, City of London Br., 1975–86; Metropolitan Soc. for the Blind; Publicity Club of London, 1983–; Council, London World Trade Centre Assoc., 1980–; St John Ambulance (Eastern Area), 1981–86; British-Australasian Heritage Soc., 1986–. Sheriff London, 1970–71; Common Councilman (Cripplegate Within and Without), 1969–71; Alderman, City of London (Ward of Farringdon Without), 1971–; HM Lieutenant, City of London, 1979–; Founder Master, Engineers' Co., 1983–85; Liveryman: Clothworkers' Co. (Master 1989–90); Plaisterers' Co. (Hon.), 1975–; Marketors Co. (Hon.), 1978–; Hon. Freeman, Actuaries' Co., 1981–; Master, Cripplegate Ward Club, 1982–83; Member: Guild of Freemen, 1963– (Master 1984–85); Guild of World Traders in London, 1985– (Master, 1987–88); Royal Soc. of St George (City of London Br.), 1970–; Council, City Univ., 1985–86 (Chancellor, 1979–80); British Malaysian Soc., 1985–; Council, Britain Australia Soc., 1978– (Chm., 1989–); Bermuda Soc., 1987– (Founder Chm., 1987–89). Chairman: Britain Australia Bicentennial Cttee, 1984–88; Order of Australia Assoc./UK Europe, 1991–. Hon. Freeman, Borough of Islwyn, S Wales, 1983. Vice-President: Sir Robert Menzies Meml Trust; Nuffield Nursing Homes Trust, 1984–; Commonwealth Trust, 1988–; President: Shropshire Soc. in London, 1986–89; Blackwood Little Theatre, 1986–; Governor, Hon. Irish Soc., 1984–87. Fellowship of Engrg Distinction Lectr, 1980; Wm Menelaus Meml Lectr, SW Inst. of Engrs, 1983; paper to MANTECH Symposium, 1983. Trustee: St Bartholomew's and St Mark's Hosps, 1981–88; Britain–Australia Bicentennial Trust, 1986–; Britain-Australia Bicentennial Schooner Trust, 1986–; Britain-Australia Soc. Educnl Trust; Edward King Hse, Lincoln, 1988–; Nat. History Mus. Develt Trust, 1988–; Battle of Britain Meml Trust; Pres., Ironbridge Gorge Museum Develt Trust, 1981–; Member: Management Council, Shakespeare Theatre Trust, 1979–86; Royal Commn for the 1851 Exhibn, 1986–; Chm. and Mem. Council, 1984–88, Vice-Pres., 1988–, Royal Commonwealth Soc.; Patron: Museum of Empire and Commonwealth Trust, 1986–; Guild of Rahere, 1986–. JP, City of London, 1971 (Inner London Area of Greater London, 1969–71). Hon. FCIM; FIMM 1979; CEng 1979, FEng 1980; Hon. Mem., Instn of Royal Engrs, 1986. Hon. Mem. Court, HAC; Hon. Col 5th (Salop and Hereford) Bn LI (Vol.), 1988–. KStJ 1980 (OStJ 1977). Officier de l'Etoile Equatoriale de la République Gabonaise, 1970. Hon. DSc 1979. *Publications:* articles in: InstMM Transactions, 1971; RSM Jl, 1979; Textile Institute and Industry, 1980; articles on titanium, zirconium, and hafnium in Mining Jl Annual Reviews, 1969–86. *Recreations:* ski-ing, sailing, walking, photography, farming, forestry, fishing. *Address:* Harelaw House, Chathill, Northumberland NE67 5HE. *T:* Chathill (066589) 224, 333. *Clubs:* City Livery (Mem. Council), United Wards, Farringdon Ward (patron), City of London, Pilgrims, Light Infantry (Hon.), Mining (Hon.), Presscala (Hon.); Royal London Yacht (Hon.); Birdham Yacht (Hon.).

GAFFNEY; *see* Burke-Gaffney.

GAFFNEY, James Anthony, CBE 1984; FEng; FICE; consulting engineer; *b* Bargoed, Glam, 9 Aug. 1928; *s* of James Francis and Violet Mary Gaffney; *m* 1953, Margaret Mary, 2nd *d* of E. and G. J. Evans, Pontypridd; one *s* two *d*. *Educ:* De La Salle Coll.; St Illtyd's Coll., Cardiff; UWIST; UC, Cardiff (Fellow, 1984). BSc (Eng) London. FEng 1979; FICE 1968; FInstHE 1970. Highway Engr, Glam CC, 1948–60; Asst County Surveyor, Somerset CC, 1960–64; Deputy County Surveyor, Notts CC, 1964–69; County Engr and Surveyor, WR Yorks, 1969–74; Dir Engrg Services, W Yorks MCC, 1974–86. President: County Surveyors' Soc., 1977–78; Instn of Highway Engrs, 1978–79; ICE, 1983–84; Vice-Pres., Fellowship of Engrg, 1989–. Hon. DSc: Wales, 1982; Bradford, 1984. *Recreations:* golf, travel, supporting Rugby. *Address:* Drovers Cottage, 3 Boston Road, Wetherby, W Yorks LS22 5HA. *Clubs:* Royal Automobile; Alwoodley Golf (Leeds).

GAGE, family name of **Viscount Gage.**

GAGE, 7th Viscount *cr* 1720; **George John St Clere Gage;** Bt 1622; Baron Gage (Ire.) 1720; Baron Gage (GB), 1790; *b* 8 July 1932; *s* of 6th Viscount Gage, KCVO, and Hon. Alexandra Imogen Clare Grenfell (*d* 1969), *yr d* of 1st Baron Desborough, KG, GCVO; *S* father, 1982; *m* 1971. *Educ:* Eton. *Heir:* *b* Hon. Henry Nicolas Gage [*b* 9 April 1934; *m* 1974, Lady Diana Adrienne Beatty, *d* of 2nd Earl Beatty; two *s*]. *Address:* Firle Place, Firle, Lewes, East Sussex BN8 6LP.

GAGE, Sir Berkeley (Everard Foley), KCMG 1955 (CMG 1949); Retired; *b* 27 Feb. 1904; *s* of late Brig.-Gen. M. F. Gage, DSO; *m* 1931, Maria von Chapuis (marr. diss. 1954), Liegnitz, Silesia; two *s*; *m* 1954, Mrs Lillian Riggs Miller. *Educ:* Eton Coll.; Trinity Coll., Cambridge. 3rd Sec. Foreign Office or Diplomatic Service, 1928; appointed to Rome, 1928; transferred to Foreign Office, 1931; 2nd Sec., 1933; Private Sec. to Parl.

Under-Sec. of State, 1934; served Peking, 1935; FO 1938; China, 1941; FO 1944; UK Deleg. Dumbarton Oaks Conf., 1944; UK Deleg., San Francisco Conf., April-June 1945; Foreign Service Officer, Grade 5, 1950; Counsellor, British Embassy, The Hague, 1947–50; Chargé d'Affaires, The Hague, in 1947 and 1948; Consul-Gen., Chicago, 1950–54; Ambassador to Thailand, 1954–57; Ambassador to Peru, 1958–63. Chairman: Latin America Cttee, BNEC, 1964–66; Anglo-Peruvian Soc., 1969–71; Member: Council for Volunteers Overseas, 1964–66; Council of Fauna Preservation Soc., 1969–73. Grand Cross, Order of the Sun (Peru), 1964. *Recreation:* swimming. *Address:* 24 Ovington Gardens, SW3 1LE. *T:* 071–589 0361. *Clubs:* Beefsteak (Life Hon. Mem.), Buck's, Saints and Sinners; Tavern (Chicago).

GAGE, William Marcus; QC 1982; a Recorder, since 1985; *b* 22 April 1938; *s* of late His Honour Conolly Gage; *m* 1962, Penelope Mary Groves; three *s*. *Educ:* Repton; Sidney Sussex Coll., Cambridge. MA. National Service, Irish Guards, 1956–58. Called to the Bar, Inner Temple, 1963. Chancellor, diocese of Coventry, 1980–, of Ely, 1989–. Mem., Criminal Injuries Compensation Bd, 1987–. *Recreations:* shooting, fishing, travel. *Address:* Evershaw House, Biddlesden, Brackley, Northants NN13 5TT. *Club:* Beefsteak.

GAINFORD, 3rd Baron *cr* 1917; **Joseph Edward Pease;** *b* 25 Dec. 1921; *s* of 2nd Baron Gainford, TD, and of Veronica Margaret, *d* of Sir George Noble, 2nd Bt; *S* father, 1971; *m* 1953, Margaret Theophila Radcliffe, *d* of late Henry Edmund Guise Tyndale; two *d*. *Educ:* Eton and Gordonstoun. FRGS; Member, Society of Surveying Technicians. RAFVR, 1941–46. Hunting Aerosurveys Ltd, 1947–49; Directorate of Colonial Surveys, 1951–53; Soil Mechanics Ltd, 1953–58; London County Council, 1958–65; Greater London Council, 1965–78. UK Delegate to UN, 1973. Mem., Coll. of Guardians, Nat. Shrine of Our Lady of Walsingham, 1979–. Mem., Plaisterers' Co., 1976. *Recreations:* golf, music, veteran and vintage aviation. *Heir:* *b* Hon. George Pease [*b* 20 April 1926; *m* 1958, Flora Daphne, *d* of late Dr N. A. Dyce Sharp; two *s* two *d*]. *Address:* 1 Dedmere Court, Marlow, Bucks SL7 1PL. *T:* Marlow (0628) 484679. *Clubs:* MCC, Pathfinder.

GAINHAM, Rachel, (Sarah Gainham), (Mrs Kenneth Ames), FRSL 1984; author; *b* 1 Oct. 1922; *d* of Tom Stainer and May Genevieve Gainham; *m* 1964, Kenneth Ames (*d* 1975). *Educ:* Newbury High Sch. for Girls; afterwards largely self educated. From 1947 onwards, travelled extensively in Central and E Europe; Central Europe Correspondent of The Spectator, 1956–66. *Publications:* Time Right Deadly, 1956; Cold Dark Night, 1957; The Mythmaker, 1957; Stone Roses, 1959; Silent Hostage, 1960; Night Falls on the City, 1967 (Book Soc. Choice and US Book of Month Club); A Place in the Country, 1968; Takeover Bid, 1970; Private Worlds, 1971; Maculan's Daughter, 1973; To the Opera Ball, 1975; The Habsburg Twilight, 1979; The Tiger, Life, 1983; contrib. to Encounter, Atlantic Monthly, BBC, etc. *Recreations:* theatre, opera, European history. *Address:* altes Forsthaus, Schlosspark, A2404 Petronell, Austria.

GAINSBOROUGH, 5th Earl of, (2nd) *cr* 1841; **Anthony Gerard Edward Noel,** Bt 1781; Baron Barham, 1805; Viscount Campden, Baron Noel, 1841; JP; *b* 24 Oct. 1923; *s* of 4th Earl and Alice Mary (*d* 1970), *e d* of Edward Eyre, Gloucester House, Park Lane, W1; *S* father 1927; *m* 1947, Mary, *er d* of Hon. J. J. Stourton, *qv* and late Mrs Kathleen Stourton; four *s* three *d*. *Educ:* Georgetown, Garrett Park, Maryland, USA. Chairman: Oakham RDC, 1952–67; Executive Council RDC's Association of England and Wales, 1963 (Vice-Chairman 1962, Pres., 1965); Pres., Assoc. of District Councils, 1974–80; Vice-Chm. Rutland CC, 1958–70, Chm., 1970–73; Chm., Rutland Dist Council, 1973–76. Chm., Bd of Management, Hosp. of St John and St Elizabeth, NW8, 1970–80. Mem. Court of Assistants, Worshipful Co. of Gardeners of London, 1960 (Upper Warden, 1966; Master, 1967). Hon. FIMunE 1969. JP Rutland, 1957, Leics 1974. Knight of Malta, 1948; Bailiff Grand Cross Order of Malta, 1958; Pres. Br. Assoc., SMO, Malta, 1968–74. KStJ 1970. *Recreations:* shooting, sailing. *Heir:* *s* Viscount Campden, *qv*. *Address:* Horn House, Exton Park, Oakham, Leics LE15 7QU. *T:* (office) Empingham (078086) 772. *Clubs:* Brooks's, Pratt's; Royal Yacht Squadron (Cowes), Bembridge Sailing.

See also Earl of Liverpool, Hon. G. E. W. Noel.

GAINSBOROUGH, George Fotheringham, CBE 1973; PhD, FIEE; Barrister-at-law; Secretary, Institution of Electrical Engineers, 1962–80; Director, External Relations, International Electrotechnical Commission, Geneva, 1980–83; *b* 28 May 1915; *o s* of late Rev. William Anthony Gainsborough and of Alice Edith (*née* Fennell); *m* 1937, Gwendoline (*d* 1976), *e d* of John and Anne Berry; two *s*. *Educ:* Christ's Hospital; King's Coll., London; Gray's Inn. Scientific Staff, Nat. Physical Laboratory, 1938–46; Radio Physicist, British Commonwealth Scientific Office, Washington, DC, USA, 1944–45; Administrative Civil Service (Ministries of Supply and Aviation), 1946–62. Imperial Defence College, 1960. Secretary, Commonwealth Engineering Conf., 1962–69; Sec.-General, World Fedn of Engineering Organizations, 1968–76. *Publications:* papers in Proc. Instn of Electrical Engineers. *Address:* 19 Glenmore House, Richmond Hill, Richmond, Surrey TW10 6BQ. *T:* 01–940 8515; Moncorbon, 41360 Savigny-sur-Braye, France. *T:* 54 23 99 25. *Club:* Athenæum.

See also Michael Gainsborough.

GAINSBOROUGH, Michael; Assistant Under-Secretary of State (Adjutant General), Ministry of Defence, since 1987; *b* 13 March 1938; *s* of George Fotheringham Gainsborough, *qv*; *m* 1962, Sally (*née* Hunter); one *s* two *d*. *Educ:* St Paul's Sch.; Trinity Coll., Oxford (MA). Air Ministry, 1959–64; Ministry of Defence, 1964–78; Defence Counsellor, UK Delegn to NATO, Brussels, FCO, 1978–81; Dir, Resources and Programmes (Strategic Systems), MoD, 1981–83; Asst Under-Sec. of State (Naval Staff), 1984, (Programmes), 1985–86, MoD; Center for Internat. Affairs, Harvard Univ., 1986–87. Mem., Royal Patriotic Fund Corp., 1987–. *Recreations:* listening to music, gardening, walking. *Address:* c/o Ministry of Defence, SW1.

GAINSFORD, Ian Derek, FDSRCS; Dean of King's College School of Medicine and Dentistry, King's College London, since 1988; *b* 24 June 1930; *s* of late Rabbi Morris Ginsberg, MA, PhD, AKC, and Anne Freda; *m* 1957, Carmel Liebster; one *s* two *d*. *Educ:* Thames Valley Grammar Sch., Twickenham; King's Coll. and King's College Hosp. Med. Sch., London (BDS; FKC 1984); Toronto Univ., Canada (DDS Hons). Junior Staff, King's College Hosp., 1955–57; Member staff, Dept of Conservative Dentistry, London Hosp. Med. Sch., 1957–70; Sen. Lectr/Consultant, Dept of Conservative Dentistry, King's College Hosp., 1970–; Dep. Dean of Dental Studies, 1973–77; Dir of Clinical Dental Services, KCH, 1977–87 (Dean of Dental Studies, KCHMS, 1977–83); Dean, Faculty of Clinical Dentistry, KCL, 1983–87. President, British Soc. for Restorative Dentistry, 1973–74; Member: Internat. Dental Fedn, 1966–; American Dental Soc. of London, 1960– (Pres., 1982); Amer. Dental Soc. of Europe, 1965– (Hon. Treas. 1971–77; Pres., 1982); Examiner for Membership in General Dental Surgery, RCS, 1979–84 (Chm., 1982–84); External Examiner: Leeds Univ. Dental Sch., 1985–87; Hong Kong Dental Sch., 1988–90; Fellow, and Mem. Odontological Sect., RSM, 1967–. Non-Exec. Dir, SETRHA. Hon. Mem., Amer. Dental Assoc., 1983. Hon. Scientific Advr, British Dental Jl, 1982. FICD 1975; MGDS RCS 1979; FACD 1988. *Publication:* Silver Amalgam in Clinical Practice, 1965, 2nd edn 1976. *Recreations:* theatre, canal cruising. *Address:* 31 York Terrace East, NW1 4PT. *T:* 071–935 8659. *Clubs:* Athenæum, Carlton.

GAIR, Hon. George Frederick, QSO 1988; High Commissioner for New Zealand in the United Kingdom, since 1991, and concurrently High Commissioner in Nigeria and Ambassador to the Republic of Ireland; *b* 13 Oct. 1926; *s* of Frederick James Gair and Roemer Elizabeth Elphege (*née* Boecking); *m* 1951, Esther Mary Fay Levy; one *s* two *d*. *Educ:* Wellington Coll.; Wairarapa Coll.; Victoria and Auckland Univ. Colls (BA 1949). Journalist: NZ Herald, 1945–47; BCON, Japan, 1947–48; Sun News Pictorial, 1949–50; Auckland Star, 1950–52; Auckland PRO, 1952–57; Staff Leader of Opposition, NZ, 1958; Press Officer and Personal Asst to Chief Exec., TEAL (later Air NZ), 1960–66. MP (Nat.) North Shore, 1966–90; Parly Under-Sec. to Minister of Educn, 1969–71; Minister of: Customs, and Associate Minister of Finance, 1972; Housing, and Dep. Minister of Finance, 1975–77; Energy, 1977–78; Health, and of Social Welfare, 1978–81; Transport, Railways, and Civil Aviation, 1981–84; Dep. Leader of Opposition, 1986–87; retd 1990. *Recreation:* walking. *Address:* 43 Chelsea Square, SW3 6LH. *T:* 071–352 5645.

GAIRY, Rt. Hon. Sir Eric Matthew, PC 1977; Kt 1977; Prime Minister of Grenada, 1974–79; also Minister of External Affairs, Planning and Development Lands and Tourism, Information Service, Public Relations and Natural Resources, 1974–79; *b* 18 Feb. 1922; *m* Cynthia Gairy; two *d*. Member of Legislative Council, 1951–52 and 1954–55; Minister of Trade and Production, 1956–57; Chief Minister and Minister of Finance until 1962; Premier, 1967–74; independence of Grenada, 1974.

GAISFORD, Ven. John Scott; Archdeacon of Macclesfield, since 1986; *b* 7 Oct. 1934; *s* of Joseph and Margaret Thompson Gaisford; *m* 1962, Gillian Maclean; one *s* one *d*. *Educ:* Univ. of Durham (Exhibnr, St Chad's Coll., Durham; BA Hons Theol. 1959, DipTh with Distinction 1960, MA 1976). Deacon 1960, priest 1961, Manchester; Assistant Curate: S Hilda, Audenshaw, 1960–62; S Michael, Bramhall, 1962–65; Vicar, S Andrew, Crewe, 1965–86; RD of Nantwich, 1974–85; Hon. Canon of Chester Cathedral, 1980–86. Proctor in Convocation, Mem. Gen. Synod, 1975–; Church Commissioner, 1986–; Mem., Redundant Churches Fund, 1989–. *Recreations:* Scout movement, fell walking, caravanning. *Address:* 2 Lovat Drive, Knutsford, Cheshire WA16 8NS. *T:* Knutsford (0565) 634456. *Club:* Victory Services.

GAIUS, Rev. Sir Saimon, KBE 1988 (OBE 1975); *b* 6 Aug. 1920; *s* of Peni Tovarur and Miriam Ia Pea; *m* 1941, Margaret Ia Kubak; five *s* one *d* (and one *s* one *d* decd). *Educ:* Mission Sch., East New Britain; theological training, PNG and Sydney, Aust. Ordained 1960; worked as United Church Minister; Principal, Pastors' Training Coll., 1967–68; Bishop of New Guinea Island Region, 1968–77; retired as Minister of Religion, 1983. SBStJ 1976. *Recreation:* reading. *Address:* United Church, PO Box 90, Rabaul, East New Britain, Papua New Guinea.

GAJDUSEK, Daniel Carleton, MD; Director of Program for Study of Child Growth and Development and Disease Patterns in Primitive Cultures, and Laboratory of Slow Latent and Temperate Virus Infections, National Institute of Neurological Disorders (formerly of Neurological and Communicative Disorders) and Stroke, National Institutes of Health, Bethesda, Md, since 1958; Chief, Central Nervous System Studies Laboratory, NINDS, since 1970; *b* Yonkers, NY, 9 Sept. 1923; *s* of Karol Gajdusek and Ottilia Dobroczki; forty-four adopted *s* and *d* (all from New Guinea and Micronesia). *Educ:* Marine Biological Lab., Woods Hole, Mass; Univ. of Rochester (BS *summa cum laude*); Harvard Medical Sch. (MD); California Inst. of Technology (Post-Doctoral Fellow). Residencies: Babies Hosp., NY, 1946–47; Children's Hosp., Cincinatti, Ohio, 1947–48; Children's Hosp., Boston, Mass, 1949–51; Sen. Fellow, Nat. Research Council, Calif Inst. of Tech., 1948–49; Children's Hosp., Boston, Mass, 1949–51; Research Fellow, Harvard Univ. and Sen. Fellow, Nat. Foundn for Infantile Paralysis, 1949–52; Walter Reed Army Medical Center, 1952–53; Institut Pasteur, Tehran, Iran and Univ. of Maryland, 1954–55; Vis. Investigator, Nat. Foundn for Infantile Paralysis and Walter and Eliza Hall Inst., Australia, 1955–57. Member: Nat. Acad. of Sciences, 1974; Amer. Philos. Soc., 1978; Amer. Acad. of Arts and Scis, 1978; Amer. Acad. of Neurol.; Infectious Dis. Soc. of America; Amer. Pediatric Soc.; Amer. Epidemiological Soc.; Amer. Soc. for Virology; Deutsche Akademie der Naturforscher Leopoldina, 1982, and many others. Mem., Scientific Council, Fondn pour l'Etude du Système Nerveux, Geneva. Discovered slow virus infections of man; studied child growth and develt and disease patterns in primitive and isolated populations, virus encephalitides, chronic degenerative brain diseases, cerebral amyloidoses, and aging. E. Meade Johnson Award, Amer. Acad. Pediatrics, 1963; DHEW Superior Service Award, 1970; DHEW Distinguished Service Award, 1975; Lucien Dautrebande Prize, Belgium, 1976; shared with Dr Baruch Blumberg Nobel Prize in Physiology or Medicine, for discoveries concerning new mechanisms for the origin and dissemination of infectious diseases, 1976; George Cotzias Meml Prize, Amer. Acad. of Neurol., 1978; Huxley Medal, RAI, 1988. Hon. Curator, Melanesian Ethnography, Peabody Mus., Salem, Mass. Hon. DSc: Univ. of Rochester, 1977; Med. Coll. of Ohio, 1977; Washington and Jefferson Coll., 1980; Harvard Med. Sch. (Bicentennial), 1982; Hahnemann Univ., 1983; Univ. of Medicine and Dentistry of NJ, 1987; Hon. LHD Hamilton Coll., 1977; Docteur *hc* Univ. of Marseille, 1977; Hon. LLD Aberdeen, 1980. *Publications:* Acute Infectious Hemorrhagic Fevers and Mycotoxicoses in the USSR, 1953; ed, with C. J. Gibbs, Jr and M. P. Alpers, Slow, Latent and Temperate Virus Infections, 1965; Journals 1954–87, 41 vols, 1963–87; Smadel-Gajdusek Correspondence 1955–1958; (ed with J. Farquhar) Kuru, 1981; over 750 papers in major jls of medicine, microbiology, immunology, pediatrics, developmental biology, neurobiology, genetics, evolution and anthropology. *Recreations:* mountaineering, linguistics. *Address:* Laboratory of Central Nervous System Studies, NINDS, National Institutes of Health, Bethesda, Md 20892, USA. *T:* 301–496–3281.

GAJE GHALE, VC 1943; Subedar 2/5 Royal Gurkha Rifles FF; *b* 1 July 1922; *s* of Bikram Ghale; *m* 1939, Dhansuba; no *c*. *Educ:* IA 2nd class certificate of education. Enlisted as a Recruit Boy 2nd Bn 5th Royal Gurkha Rifles FF, Feb. 1935; transferred to the ranks, Aug. 1935; Naik, 1941; Acting Havildar, May 1942; War Subst. Havildar, Nov. 1942; Bn Havildar Major June 1943; Jemadar, Aug. 1943. Waziristan operations, 1936–37 (medal with clasp); Burma, 1942–43 (1939–45 Star, VC). *Recreations:* football, basketball, badminton and draughts.

GALBRAITH, family name of **Baron Strathclyde.**

GALBRAITH, James Hunter, CB 1985; Under Secretary, Department of Employment Industrial Relations Division, 1975–85; *b* 16 July 1925; *o s* of late Prof. V. H. Galbraith, FBA, and Dr G. R. Galbraith; *m* 1954, Isobel Gibson Graham; two *s*. *Educ:* Dragon Sch.; Edinburgh Academy; Balliol Coll., Oxford. 1st Cl. Litt Hum. Fleet Air Arm (pilot), 1944–46. Entered Ministry of Labour, 1950; Private Sec. to Permanent Sec., 1953–55; Jun. Civilian Instructor, IDC, 1958–61; Private Sec. to Minister of Labour, 1962–64; Chm. Central Youth Employment Exec., 1964–67; Sen. Simon Research Fellow, Manchester Univ., 1967–68; Asst Under-Sec. of State, Dept of Employment and Productivity (Research and Planning Div.), 1968–71; Dir, Office of Manpower Economics, 1971–73; Under-Sec., Manpower Gen. Div., Dept of Employment, 1973–74; Sec., Manpower Services Commn, 1974–75. Chm., Bd of Govs. Volunteer Centre UK, 1989–. *Recreations:* rugby (Oxford Blue), golf, fishing. *Address:* 27 Sandy Lodge Lane, Moor

Park, Mddx HA6 2HZ. *T:* Northwood (09274) 22458.
See also G. M. Moore.

GALBRAITH, Prof. John Kenneth; Paul M. Warburg Professor of Economics, Harvard University, 1949–75, now Emeritus Professor; *b* Ontario, Canada, 15 Oct. 1908; *s* of William Archibald and Catherine Galbraith; *m* 1937, Catherine M. Atwater; three *s*. *Educ:* Univ. of Guelph; California Univ. BS, MS, PhD. Tutor, Harvard Univ., 1934–39; Social Science Research Fellow, Cambridge Univ., 1937; Asst Prof. of Economics, Princeton Univ., 1939; Asst Administrator, Office of Price Administration, 1941; Deputy Administrator, 1942–43; Dir, State Dept Office of Economic Security Policy, 1945; Mem. Bd of Editors, Fortune Magazine, 1943–48. United States Ambassador to India, 1961–63 (on leave from Professorship). Reith Lecturer, 1966; Vis. Fellow, Trinity Coll., Cambridge, 1970–71 (Hon. Fellow, 1987). TV series, The Age of Uncertainty, 1977. Chm., Americans for Democratic Action, 1967–69; President: Amer. Econ. Assoc., 1972; Amer. Acad. of Arts and Letters, 1984 (Mem., 1982–). LLD Bard, 1958; Miami Univ., 1959; University of Toronto, 1961; Brandeis Univ., 1963; University of Mass, 1963; University of Saskatchewan, 1965; Rhode Island Coll., 1966; Boston Coll., 1967; Hobart and William Smith Colls, 1967; Univ. of Paris, 1975; and others. President's Certificate of Merit; Medal of Freedom. *Publications:* American Capitalism, the Concept of Countervailing Power, 1952; The Great Crash, 1929, 1955, new edn 1979; The Affluent Society, 1958, 4th edn, 1985; Journey to Poland and Yugoslavia, 1958; The Liberal Hour, 1960; Made to Last, 1964; The New Industrial State, 1967, rev. edn, 1978; Indian Painting, 1968; Ambassador's Journal, 1969; Economics, Peace and Laughter, 1971; A China Passage, 1973; Economics and the Public Purpose, 1974; Money: whence it came, where it went, 1975; The Age of Uncertainty, 1977; Almost Everyone's Guide to Economics, 1978; Annals of an Abiding Liberal, 1979; The Nature of Mass Poverty, 1979; A Life in Our Times, 1981; The Anatomy of Power, 1983; China Passage, 1983; A View from the Stands, 1987; A History of Economics, 1987; (with S. Menshikov) Capitalism, Communism and Coexistence, 1989; contribs to learned jls. *Address:* 207 Littauer Center, Harvard University, Cambridge, Mass 02138, USA; 30 Francis Avenue, Cambridge, Mass 02138, USA. *Clubs:* Century (NY); Federal City (Washington).

GALBRAITH, Neil, CBE 1975; QPM 1959; DL; HM Inspector of Constabulary, 1964–76, retired; *b* 25 May 1911; *s* of late Peter and Isabella Galbraith; *m* 1942, Catherine Margaret Thornton; one *s* one *d*. *Educ:* Kilmarnock Academy. Constable to Inspector, Lancs Constabulary, 1931–46. Chief Supt, Herts Constabulary, 1946–51; Asst Chief Constable, Monmouthshire Constabulary, 1951–55; Chief Constable, Leicester City Police, 1956; Chief Constable, Monmouthshire Constabulary, 1957–64. DL Gwent (formerly Monmouth), 1973. *Recreation:* reading. *Address:* Neath House, Trostrey, Usk, Gwent. *T:* Usk (02913) 2779.

GALBRAITH, Samuel Laird; MP (Lab) Strathkelvin and Bearsden, since 1987; *b* 18 Oct. 1945. *Educ:* Glasgow Univ. (BSc Hons 1968; MB ChB Hons 1971; MD 1977); FRCSGlas1975. Consultant in Neurosurgery, Gtr Glasgow Health Bd, 1978–87. Opposition spokesman on Scottish affairs and health, 1988–. *Publication:* An Introduction to Neurosurgery, 1983. *Address:* c/o House of Commons, SW1A 0AA; 48 Woodend Drive, Glasgow G13 1TS.

GALBRAITH, William Campbell, QC 1977; *b* 25 Feb. 1935; *s* of William Campbell Galbraith and Margaret Watson or Galbraith; *m* 1959, Mary Janet Waller; three *s* (and one *s* decd). *Educ:* Merchiston Castle Sch.; Pembroke Coll., Cambridge (BA); Edinburgh Univ. (LLB). Teacher, Turkey, 1959–61; Lectr, Meshed Univ., Iran, 1961–62; admitted to Faculty of Advocates, 1962; in practice at Scottish Bar, 1962–67; Sen. State Counsel, Malaŵi, 1967–70; Parly Draftsman, London, 1970–74; Parly Counsel, Canberra, 1974; returned to practice, 1975. *Recreations:* fishing, music, travel.

GALE, Prof. Ernest Frederick, FRS 1953; BSc London; BA, PhD, ScD Cantab; Professor of Chemical Microbiology, University of Cambridge, 1960–81, now Emeritus; Fellow of St John's College, Cambridge, 1949–88; *b* 15 July 1914; *s* of Nellie Annie and Ernest Francis Edward Gale; *m* 1937, Eiry Mair Jones; one *s*. *Educ:* St John's Coll. Cambridge (Scholar). Research in biochemistry, Cambridge, 1936–83; Senior Student, Royal Commn for Exhibition of 1851, 1939; Beit Memorial Fellow, 1941; Scientific Staff of Med. Research Council, 1943; Reader in Chemical Microbiology, University of Cambridge, 1948–60; Dir, Medical Research Council Unit for Chemical Microbiology, 1948–62. Herter Lecturer, Johns Hopkins Hosp., Baltimore, USA, 1948; Commonwealth Travelling Fellow, Hanna Lecturer, Western Reserve Univ., 1951; Harvey Lectr, New York, 1955; Leeuwenhoek Lectr, Royal Society, London, 1956; Malcolm Lectr, Syracuse Univ., 1967; M. Stephenson Meml Lectr, 1971; Linacre Lectr, St John's Coll., Cambridge, 1973; Squibb Lectr, Nottingham Univ., 1986. Visiting Fellow, ANU, 1964–65. Hon. Mem., Society for General Microbiology, 1978 (Meetings Sec., 1954–58; International Representative, 1963–67; Pres., 1967–69); Mem. Food Investigation Board, 1954–58; Mem. International Union of Biochemistry Commission on Enzymes, 1957–61. *Publications:* Chemical Activities of Bacteria, 1947; The Molecular Basis of Antibiotic Action, 1972, 2nd edn 1981; scientific papers in Biochem. Journal, Journal of General Microbiology, Biochimica et Biophysica Acta, etc. *Recreations:* photography, wood carving. *Address:* 7 Hazeldene, Sandhills Road, Salcombe, Devon TQ8 8JP. *T:* Salcombe (054884) 3426.

GALE, Fay; *see* Gale, G. F.

GALE, Hon. George Alexander, CC 1977; Chief Justice of Ontario, 1967–76; Vice-Chairman, Ontario Law Reform Commission, 1977–81; *b* 24 June 1906; *s* of late Robert Henry and Elma Gertrude Gale; *m* 1934, Hilda Georgina Daly; three *s*. *Educ:* Prince of Wales High Sch., Vancouver; Toronto Univ. (BA); Osgoode Hall Law Sch., Toronto. Called to Ontario Bar, 1932; Partner, Mason, Foulds, Davidson & Gale, 1944; KC (Can.) 1945; Justice, Supreme Court of Ontario, 1946; Justice, Court of Appeal, Ontario, 1963; Chief Justice of High Court of Justice for Ontario, 1964. Formerly Chm. Judicial Council for Provincial Judges; Chm., Cttee on Rules of Practice for Ontario (Mem. 1941–76); former Mem. Canadian Bar Assoc. (formerly Mem. Council); Hon. Mem., Georgia Bar Assoc.; formerly Hon. Lectr, Osgoode Law Sch.; formerly Mem. Exec. Cttee, Canadian Judicial Council. Mem., Ontario Adv. Cttee on Confederation; formerly Chm., Ontario Rhodes Scholarship Selection Cttee; Hon. Mem., Canadian Corps of Commissionaires, 1977. Mem. Bd of Governors: Wycliffe Coll., Toronto Univ.; Ecumenical Foundn of Canada; formerly, Upper Canada Coll., Toronto; Mem. Delta Kappa Epsilon, Phi Delta Phi (Hon.). Anglican; Warden, St John's, York Mills, for 5 years. Hon. Pres., Ontario Curling Assoc. Hon. LLD: McMaster, 1968; York (Toronto), 1969; Windsor, 1980. *Publication:* (ed with Holmested) Practice and Procedure in Ontario, 6th edn. *Recreations:* golf, photography. *Address:* 7700 Bayview Avenue, Thornhill, Ontario L3T 5W1, Canada. *Clubs:* Lawyers, (Hon. Mem.) York (Toronto); Toronto Curling, Chippewa Golf.

GALE, (Gwendoline) Fay, AO 1989; PhD; FASSA; Vice-Chancellor, University of Western Australia, since 1990; *b* 13 June 1932; *d* of Rev. George Jasper Gilding and Kathleen Gertrude Gilding; one *s* one *d*. *Educ:* Adelaide Univ. (BA 1952, Hons I 1954; PhD 1962). University of Adelaide: Lectr, 1966–71; Sen. Lectr, 1972–74; Reader, 1975–77; Prof., 1978–89; Pro-Vice-Chancellor, 1988–89. Elin Wagner Fellow, 1971; Catherine Helen Spence Fellow, 1972. FASSA 1978. British Council Award, 1972. *Publications:* Race Relations in Australia: the Aboriginal situation, 1975; Urban Aborigines, 1972; Poverty among Aboriginal families in Adelaide, 1975; Adelaide Aborigines, a case study of urban life 1966–81, 1982; We are bosses ourselves: the status and role of Aboriginal women today, 1983; Tourists and the National Estate: procedures to protect Australia's heritage, 1987; Aboriginal youth and the criminal justice system: the injustice of justice, 1990. *Recreations:* hiking, camping, music, theatre. *Address:* University of Western Australia, Nedlands, WA 6009, Australia. *T:* (09) 380 2801. *Club:* Karrakatta (Perth, WA).

GALE, John, OBE 1987; Director: Lisden Productions Ltd, since 1975; John Gale Productions Ltd, since 1960; Gale Enterprises Ltd, since 1960; West End Managers Ltd, since 1972; *b* 2 Aug. 1929; *s* of Frank Haith Gale and Martha Edith Gale (*née* Evans); *m* 1950, Liselotte Ann (*née* Wratten); two *s*. *Educ:* Christ's Hospital; Webber Douglas Academy of Dramatic Art. Formerly an actor; presented his first production, Inherit the Wind, London, 1960; has since produced or co-produced, in London, British provinces, USA, Australia, New Zealand and S Africa, over 80 plays, including: Candida, 1960; On the Brighter Side, 1961; Boeing-Boeing, 1962; Devil May Care, 1963; Windfall, 1963; Where Angels Fear to Tread, 1963; The Wings of the Dove, 1963; Amber for Anna, 1964; Present Laughter, 1964, 1981; Maigret and the Lady, 1965; The Platinum Cat, 1965; The Sacred Flame, 1966; An Evening with G. B. S., 1966; A Woman of No Importance, 1967; The Secretary Bird, 1968; Dear Charles, 1968; Highly Confidential, 1969; The Young Churchill, 1969; The Lionel Touch, 1969; Abelard and Héloïse, 1970; No Sex, Please—We're British, 1971; Lloyd George Knew My Father, 1972; The Mating Game, 1972; Parents' Day, 1972; At the End of the Day, 1973; Birds of Paradise, 1974; A Touch of Spring, 1975; Separate Tables, 1977; The Kingfisher, 1977; Sextet, 1977; Cause Célèbre, 1977; Shut Your Eyes and Think of England, 1977; Can You Hear Me at the Back?, 1979; Middle Age Spread, 1979; Private Lives, 1980; A Personal Affair, 1982. The Secretary Bird and No Sex, Please—We're British set records for the longest run at the Savoy and Strand Theatres respectively; No Sex, Please—We're British is the longest running comedy in the history of World Theatre and passed 6,000 performances at the Garrick Theatre in Nov. 1985. Chichester Festival Theatre: Exec. Producer, 1983–84; Director, 1984–89. President, Soc. of West End Theatre Managers, 1972–75; Chm., Theatres National Cttee, 1979–85. Governor and Almoner, Christ's Hospital, 1976–; Member, Amicable Soc. of Blues, 1981–. Liveryman, Gold and Silver Wyredrawers Company, 1974. *Recreations:* travel, Rugby. *Address:* 1 East Dean, near Chichester, W Sussex PO18 0JA. *T:* Chichester (0243) 63407. *Clubs:* Garrick, Green Room; London Welsh Rugby Football (Richmond) (Chairman, 1979–81).

GALE, Michael; QC 1979; a Recorder of the Crown Court, since 1977; *b* 12 Aug. 1932; *s* of Joseph Gale and Blossom Gale; *m* 1963, Joanna Stephanie Bloom; one *s* two *d*. *Educ:* Cheltenham Grammar Sch.; Grocers' Sch.; King's Coll., Cambridge (Exhibnr; BA History and Law, 1954, MA 1958). National Service, Royal Fusiliers and Jt Services Sch. for Linguists, 1956–58. Called to the Bar, Middle Temple, 1957, Bencher, 1988; Harmsworth Law Scholar, 1958. Mem., Gen. Council of the Bar, 1987–. *Recreations:* the arts and country pursuits. *Address:* 6 Pump Court, Temple, EC4Y 7AR. *T:* 071–353 7242. *Clubs:* United Oxford & Cambridge University, MCC.

GALE, Michael Sadler, MC 1945; Assistant Under-Secretary of State, Prison Department, Home Office, 1972–79; *b* 5 Feb. 1919; *s* of Rev. John Sadler and Ethel Gale; *m* 1950, Philippa, *d* of Terence and Betty Ennion; two *s* one *d* (and one *s* decd). *Educ:* Tonbridge Sch.; Oriel Coll., Oxford (Scholar, MA). Served War of 1939–45: enlisted 1939, Royal Fusiliers; commnd 1940, Queen's Own Royal W Kent Regt, Major 1944; served N Africa and NW Europe. Housemaster, HM Borstal, Rochester, 1946–48; Dep. Governor, HM Prison, Durham, 1948–49; Staff Course Tutor, Imperial Trng Sch., Wakefield, 1949–50; Principal, 1950–52; Governor, HM Prison: The Verne, 1952–57; Camp Hill, 1957–62; Wandsworth, 1962–66; Asst Dir, Prison Dept, Home Office, 1966–69; Controller, Planning and Develt, 1969–75; Controller, Operational Administration, 1975–79; Mem. Prisons Board, 1969–79. *Recreations:* walking, reading, gardening. *Address:* 21 Christchurch Road, Winchester, Hants SO23 9SU. *T:* Winchester (0962) 853836.

GALE, Roger James; MP (C) North Thanet, since 1983; *b* Poole, Dorset, 20 Aug. 1943; *s* of Richard Byrne Gale and Phyllis Mary (*née* Rowell); *m* 1st, 1964, Wendy Dawn Bowman (marr. diss. 1967); 2nd, 1971, Susan Sampson (marr. diss.); one *d*; 3rd, 1980, Susan Gabrielle Marks; two *s*. *Educ:* Southbourne Prep. Sch.; Hardye's Sch., Dorchester; Guildhall Sch. of Music and Drama (LGSM). Freelance broadcaster, 1963–72; freelance reporter, BBC Radio, London, 1972–73; Producer, Current Affairs Gp, BBC Radio (progs included Newsbeat and Today), 1973–76; Producer/Dir, BBC Children's Television (progs included Blue Peter and Swap Shop), 1976–79; Producer/Dir, Thames TV, and Editor, teenage unit (progs included White Light, Smith & Goody, CBTV and Crying Out Loud), 1979–83. Joined Conservative Party, 1964; Mem., Cttee, Greater London Young Conservatives, 1964–65. Member: Home Affairs Select Cttee; Special Select Cttee on televising of H of C; All Party Parly Gp, Fund for Replacement of Animals in Med. Experiments; Vice-Chm., All Party Parly Gp for Animal Welfare; Chm., Backbench Media Cttee; Delegate, Council of Europe, 1987–89. Contested Birmingham, Northfield, Oct. 1982 (Lab. majority, 289). Founder Mem., East Kent Development Assoc., 1984–. *Recreations:* swimming, sailing, canoeing. *Address:* House of Commons, Westminster, SW1A 0AA. *Clubs:* Garrick; Kent County Cricket.

GALES, Kathleen Emily, (Mrs Heinz Spitz); Senior Lecturer in Statistics, London School of Economics, 1966–90, retired; *b* 1927; *d* of Albert Henry and Sarah Thomson Gales; *m* 1970, Heinz Spitz. *Educ:* Gateshead Grammar Sch.; Newnham Coll., Cambridge (Exhibr); Ohio Univ. (Schol.). BA Cantab 1950, MA Ohio, 1951. Asst Statistician, Foster Wheeler Ltd, 1951–53; Statistician, Municipal Statistical Office, Birmingham, 1953–55; Res. Asst and part-time Lectr, LSE, 1955–58; Asst Lectr in Statistics, LSE, 1958–60, Lectr, 1960–66. Vis. Assoc. Prof. in Statistics, Univ. of California, 1964–65. Statistical Consultant: Royal Commn on Doctors' and Dentists' Remuneration, 1959; WHO, 1960; Turkish Min. of Health, 1963. Mem. Performing Rights Tribunal, 1974–80. *Publications:* (with C. A. Moser and P. Morpurgo) Dental Health and the Dental Services, 1962; (with B. Abel-Smith) British Doctors at Home and Abroad, 1964; (with T. Blackstone et al.) Students in Conflict: LSE in 1967, 1970; articles in Jl RSS. *Recreations:* badminton, bridge, golf, travel.

GALL, Henderson Alexander, (Sandy), CBE 1988; Foreign Correspondent, Independent Television News, since 1963 (Newscaster, 1968–90); *b* 1 Oct. 1927; *s* of Henderson Gall and Jean Begg; *m* 1958, Eleanor Mary Patricia Ann Smyth; one *s* three *d*. *Educ:* Glenalmond; Aberdeen Univ. (MA). Foreign Correspondent, Reuters, 1953–63, Germany, E Africa, Hungary, S Africa, Congo; joined ITN, 1963, working in Middle East, Africa, Vietnam, Far East, China, Afghanistan; Newscaster on News at Ten, 1970–90; Producer/Presenter/Writer, documentaries on: King Hussein, 1972; Afghanistan, 1982, 1984, 1986; Cresta Run, 1984; George Adamson, 1989. Rector, Aberdeen Univ., 1978–81 (Hon.

LLD, 1981). Sitara-i-Pakistan, 1986; Lawrence of Arabia Medal, RSAA, 1987. *Publications:* Gold Scoop, 1977; Chasing the Dragon, 1981; Don't Worry About the Money Now, 1983; Behind Russian Lines, 1983; Afghanistan: Agony of a Nation, 1988; Salang, 1989; Lord of the Lions, 1991. *Recreations:* golf, gardening, swimming. *Address:* Doubleton Oast House, Penshurst, Kent TN11 8JA. *T:* (office) 071–833 3000. *Clubs:* Turf, Special Forces; St Moritz Tobogganing.

GALL, Sandy; *see* Gall, H. A.

GALLACHER, family name of **Baron Gallacher.**

GALLACHER, Baron *cr* 1982 (Life Peer), of Enfield in Greater London; **John Gallacher;** retired; *b* 7 May 1920; *s* of William Gallacher and Janet Stewart; *m* 1947, Freda Vivian Chittenden; one *s. Educ:* St Patrick's High School, Dumbarton; Co-operative College, Loughborough. Chartered Secretary. President: Enfield Highway Co-operative Soc., 1954–68; Inst. of Meat, 1983–86; Secretary, International Co-operative Alliance, 1963–67; Parliamentary Sec., Co-operative Union, 1974–83; Mem., Select Cttee on the European Communities, 1983–89. Chief opposition spokesman on agriculture and food, 1989–. *Publication:* Service on the Board (a handbook for directors of retail co-operatives), 1974, 2nd edn 1976. *Recreation:* gardening. *Address:* House of Lords, SW1A 0PW. *T:* 071–219 5425.

GALLACHER, Bernard; golf professional, Wentworth Golf Club, since 1975; *b* 9 Feb. 1949; *s* of Bernard and Matilda Gallacher; *m* 1974, Lesley Elizabeth Wearmouth; one *s* two *d. Educ:* St Mary's Academy, Bathgate. Golf tournaments won: Scottish Open Amateur Championship, 1967; PGA Schweppes, W. D. & H. O. Wills Open, 1969; Martini Internat., 1971, 1982; Carrolls Internat., 1974; Dunlop Masters, 1974, 1975; Spanish Open, 1977; French Open, 1979; Tournament Players Championship, 1980; Gtr Manchester Open, 1981; Jersey Open, 1982, 1984. Harry Vardon Trophy, 1969. Scottish Professional Champion , 1971, 1973, 1974, 1977, 1984. Ryder Cup Team, 1969, 1971, 1973, 1975, 1977, 1979, 1981, 1983, European Captain, 1991. *Publication:* (with Mark Wilson) Teach Yourself Golf, 1988. *Recreations:* walking dogs, reading. *Address:* Wentworth Club, Virginia Water, Surrey. *T:* Wentworth (09904) 3353.

GALLACHER, John; HM Diplomatic Service, retired; Group Security Adviser, Gallaher Ltd, since 1985; *b* 16 July 1931; *s* of John Gallacher and Catherine Gallacher (*née* Crilly); *m* 1956, Eileen Agnes (*née* McGuire); one *s. Educ:* Our Lady's High School, Motherwell. Nat. Service, RAF, 1950–52. Kenya Police, 1953–65 (retired as Supt of Police, 1965); Libyan Govt (attached to Min. of Interior), 1965–67; FCO, 1967–70; Lagos, 1970–73; FCO, 1973–74; Kuwait, 1974–77; FCO 1977; Counsellor, FCO, 1983–84. *Recreations:* reading, golf, travel, gardening. *Address:* 1 Clive Road, Strawberry Vale, Twickenham, Mddx TW1 4SQ. *Club:* Royal Over-Seas League.

GALLAGHER, (Francis George) Kenna, CMG 1963; HM Diplomatic Service, retired; *b* 25 May 1917; *er s* of late George and Johanna Gallagher. *Educ:* St Joseph's Coll.; King's Coll., University of London (LLB (Hons)). Clerical officer, Min. of Agric., 1935–38; Asst Examr, Estate Duty Office, 1938–44; served in HM Forces, 1941–45; Examr, Estate Duty Office, 1944–45; apptd a Mem., HM Foreign (subseq. Diplomatic) Service, 1945; Vice-Consul Marseilles, 1946–48; Acting Consul-Gen., there, in 1947; HM Embassy, Paris, 1948–50; FO, 1950–53; First Sec., HM Embassy, Damascus, 1953–55; acted as Chargé d'Affaires, 1953, 1954 and 1955; FO, 1955; appointed Counsellor and Head of European Economic Organisations Dept, 1960; Counsellor (Commercial), HM Embassy, Berne, 1963–65; acted as Chargé d'Affaires (Berne) in 1963 and 1964; Head of Western Economic Dept, CO, 1965–67, of Common Market Dept, 1967–68; Asst Under-Sec. of State, FCO, 1968–71; Ambassador and Head of UK Delegn to OECD, 1971–77. Consultant on Internat. Trade Policy, CBI, 1978–80. *Recreations:* music, chess. *Address:* The Old Courthouse, Kirkwhelpington, Northumberland NE19 2RS. *T:* Otterburn (0830) 40373.

GALLAGHER, Francis Heath, CMG 1957; Coal Industry Tribunal (Australia), 1947; *b* 10 Feb. 1905; *s* of James Gallagher; *m* 1938, Heather Elizabeth Clark; no *c. Educ:* Sydney Grammar Sch.; University of Sydney. BA 1929, LLB 1933, University of Sydney. Admitted as solicitor, Supreme Court of NSW, 1933. Mem. of Industrial Commn of NSW, 1955–57; Presidential Mem., Commonwealth Arbitration Commn, 1957–71. *Recreations:* reading, gardening, sailing, surfing. *Address:* 2 Foam Crest Avenue, Newport Beach, NSW 2106, Australia. *T:* 99–1724. *Clubs:* Australian Jockey, Turf (Sydney).

GALLAGHER, Kenna; *see* Gallagher, F. G. K.

GALLAGHER, Sister Maire Teresa, OBE 1987; SND; Sister Superior, Convent of Notre Dame, Dumbarton, since 1987; *b* 27 May 1933; *d* of Owen Gallagher and Annie McVeigh. *Educ:* Notre Dame High Sch., Glasgow; Glasgow Univ. (MA Hons 1965); Notre Dame Coll. of Educn (Dip. 1953). Principal Teacher of History, Notre Dame High Sch., Glasgow, 1965–72; Lectr in Secondary Educn, Notre Dame Coll., 1972–74; Head Teacher, Notre Dame High Sch., Dumbarton, 1974–87. Chair, Scottish Consultative Council (formerly Scottish Consultative Cttee) on the Curriculum, 1987–91 (Mem., 1976–91; Chair: Secondary Cttee, 1983–87; Main Cttee, 1987–90); Mem., Sec. of State's Cttee of Enquiry into Teachers' Pay and Conditions of Service, 1986; Pres., Scottish Br., Secondary Heads Assoc., 1980–82. Fellow, SCOTVEC, 1989. *Publications:* papers and articles in jls on teaching and management of schools. *Recreations:* homemaking skills, reading. *Address:* Convent of Notre Dame, Cardross Road, Dumbarton G82 4JH. *T:* Dumbarton (0389) 62361.

GALLAGHER, Michael; *b* 1 July 1934; *s* of Michael and Annie Gallagher; *m* 1959, Kathleen Mary Gallagher; two *s* three *d. Educ:* Univ. of Nottingham; Univ. of Wales. Dip. General Studies. Branch Official, NUM, 1967–70; day release, Univ. of Nottingham, 1967–69; TUC scholarship, Univ. of Wales, 1970–72; Univ. of Nottingham, 1972–74. Councillor: Mansfield Borough Council, 1970–74; Nottinghamshire CC, 1973–81. Contested (Lab) Rushcliffe, general election, Feb. 1974; Member (Lab) Nottingham, European Parlt, 1979–83, (SDP) 1983–84; contested (SDP) Lancs Central, European elecn, 1984. *Recreations:* leisure, sports.

GALLAGHER, Dame Monica (Josephine), DBE 1976; *m* 1946, Dr John Paul Gallagher, KCSG, KM; two *s* two *d.* Vice-Chm., Friends of St Mary's Cathedral, Sydney (Chm., 1984–87; Chm., Flower Festival Committee); Pres. Exec. Cttee, Order of British Empire Assoc., NSW (Vice-Pres., 1985–89); Member: Dr Horace Nowland Travelling Scholarship; Australian Church Women, NSW Div.; Nursing Adv. Cttee, Catholic Coll. of Educn, Sydney; Adv. Bd, Festival of Light. Tour Guide, St Mary's Cathedral. State Pres., NSW, and Gen. Pres., Sydney Archdiocese, Catholic Women's League, Aust., 1972–80 (Nat. Pres., 1972–74); Past President: Catholic Central Cttee for Care of Aged; Catholic Women's Club, Sydney; Associated Catholic Cttee; Austcare; Catholic Inst. of Nursing Studies. . Former Member: NSW Div., UNA; UN Status of Women Cttee; Exec. Bd, Mater Misericordiae Hosp., N Sydney; Bd, Gertrude Abbott Nursing Home; Selection Cttee, Queen Elizabeth II Silver Jubilee Trust; former Chm., YWCA Appeal Cttee, Sydney. Good Citizen Award, 1979; Papal Honour, Augustae Crucis Insigne pro Ecclesia et Pontifice, 1981. *Address:* 1 Robert Street, Willoughby, NSW 2068, Australia.

GALLAGHER, Patrick Joseph, DFC 1943; Chairman, Company Solutions Ltd, since 1983; *b* 15 April 1921; *s* of Patrick Gallagher and Mary Bernadine Donnellan; *m* 1950, Veronica Frances Bateman (*d* 1981); one *s. Educ:* Prior Park, Bath. Served War, 1941–46: Flt Lieut; Pilot, RAFVR. Principal, HM Treasury, 1948–58: ASC, 1956; Adviser, Raisman Commn, Nigeria, 1957–58; Consultant, Urwick, Orr & Partners Ltd, 1958–60; Dir, Ogilvy, Benson & Mather, 1960–65; Man. Dir, Glendinning Internat. Ltd, 1965–69; Pres., Glendinning Cos Inc., 1970–74; Managing Director: London Broadcasting Co. Ltd, 1975–79; Independent Radio News Ltd, 1975–79; Chm., Radio Sales & Marketing Ltd, 1976–79. *Recreations:* music, travel. *Address:* 29 Gloucester Place, W1H 3PB. *T:* 071–935 2429. *Club:* Royal Air Force.

GALLEY, Robert Albert Ernest, PhD; FRSC; Director, Shell Research Ltd, Woodstock Agricultural Research Centre, Sittingbourne, Kent, 1960–69; *b* 23 Oct. 1909; *s* of John and Jane A. Galley; *m* 1st 1933, Elsie Marjorie Walton (*d* 1985); one *s* two *d*; 2nd 1988, Ann Louise Grundy (*née* Dale). *Educ:* Colfe's Gram. Sch.; Imperial Coll., London. BSc 1930, PhD 1932, FRIC 1944. Research Chemist, Wool Industries Research Assoc., 1932–34; Chemist, Dept of War Department Chemist, 1934–37; Lectr, Sir John Cass Coll., 1937–39; Prin. Exper. Officer, Min. of Supply, Chemical Inspectorate, 1939–45, Flax Establishment, 1945–46; Sen. Prin. Scientific Officer, Agric. Research Council (Sec. Interdepartmental Insecticides Cttees), 1946–50; seconded to Scientific Secretariat, Office of Lord Pres. of Council, 1950–52; Dir, Tropical Products Institute, Dept of Scientific and Industrial Research (formerly Colonial Products Laboratory), 1953–60. *Publications:* papers in Journal of Chem. Soc., Chemistry and Industry, World Crops, etc. *Recreations:* tennis, gardening, sailing. *Address:* Riversdale, 26 River Reach, Teddington, Middx TW11 9QL.

GALLEY, Roy; Head of Project Control, London Building and Estates Centre, Royal Mail Letters, since 1987; *b* 8 Dec. 1947; *s* of Kenneth Haslam Galley and late Letitia Mary Chapman; *m* 1976, Helen Margaret Butcher; one *s* one *d. Educ:* King Edward VII Grammar Sch., Sheffield; Worcester Coll., Oxford. North-East Postal Bd, 1969–83: started as management trainee; Asst Controller, Projects (regional manager), 1980–83. Councillor, Calderdale Metropolitan Bor. Council, 1980–83. Chm., Kingston and Esher DHA, 1989–. Chm., Yorks Young Conservatives, 1974–76; contested (C): Dewsbury, 1979; Halifax, 1987. MP (C) Halifax, 1983–87. Sec., Cons. Backbench Health Cttee, 1983–87; Mem., Social Services Select Cttee, 1984–87. *Recreations:* history, European literature, theatre, music, gardening, wine-making. *Address:* 12 Selcroft Road, Purley, Surrey CR8 1AD.

GALLIE, Prof. Walter Bryce; Professor of Political Science, and Fellow of Peterhouse, Cambridge University, 1967–78, Professor Emeritus, 1978, Emeritus Fellow 1982; *b* 5 Oct. 1912; 3rd *s* of Walter S. Gallie, structural engineer; *m* 1940, Menna Humphreys (*d* 1990); one *s* one *d. Educ:* Sedbergh Sch.; Balliol Coll., Oxford (Classical Exhibitioner). BA (1st Cl. PPE), 1934, BLitt 1937, MA Oxon, 1947. University Coll. of Swansea; Asst Lectr, Philosophy, 1935; Lectr, 1938; Sen. Lectr, 1948; Prof. of Philosophy, University Coll. of North Staffordshire 1950; Prof. of Logic and Metaphysics, Queen's Univ., Belfast, 1954–67. Visiting Prof., New York Univ., 1962–63; Lectures: Lewis Fry Meml, Bristol Univ., 1964; Wiles, QUB, 1976; J. R. Jones Meml, UC Swansea, 1983; E. H. Carr Meml, UC Aberystwyth, 1987. Pres., Aristotelian Soc., 1970–71. Hon. Professorial Fellow, Univ. of Wales, 1980. Served War, 1940–45, ending with rank of Major, Croix de Guerre, 1945. *Publications:* An English School, 1949; Peirce and Pragmatism, 1952; Free Will and Determinism Yet Again (Inaugural Lecture), 1957; A New University: A. D. Lindsay and the Keele Experiment, 1960; Philosophy and the Historical Understanding, 1964; Philosophers of Peace and War, 1978; Understanding War, 1990; articles in Mind, Aristotelian Soc. Proc., Philosophy, Political Studies, etc. *Recreations:* travelling and reading. *Address:* Cilhendre, Upper Saint Mary Street, Newport, Dyfed SA42 0PS. *T:* Newport (Dyfed) (0239) 820574.

GALLIERS-PRATT, Anthony Malcolm, CBE 1977; *b* 31 Jan. 1926; *s* of George Kenneth and Phyllis Galliers-Pratt; *m* 1950, Angela, *d* of Sir Charles Cayzer, 3rd Bt, and of Lady Cayzer, OBE; three *s. Educ:* Eton. Entered F. Pratt Engineering Corp. Ltd, 1949; Dir, 1951; subseq. Man. Dir and Chm., to 1981. Underwriting Member of Lloyd's. *Recreations:* yachting, shooting. *Address:* The Moorings, The Esplanade, St Peter Port, Guernsey, Channel Islands.

GALLIFORD, Rt. Rev. David George; Bishop Suffragan of Bolton, 1984–91; *b* 20 June 1925; *s* of Alfred Edward Bruce and Amy Doris Galliford; *m* 1st, 1954, Enid May Drax (*d* 1983); one *d*; 2nd, 1987, Claire Margaret Phoenix. *Educ:* Bede Coll., Sunderland; Clare Coll., Cambridge (Organ Scholar, 1942, BA 1949, MA 1951); Westcott House, Cambridge. Served 5th Royal Inniskilling Dragoon Guards, 1943–47. Curate of St John Newland, Hull, 1951–54; Minor Canon of Windsor, 1954–56; Vicar of St Oswald, Middlesborough, 1956–61; Rector of Bolton Percy and Diocesan Training Officer, 1961–70; Canon of York Minster, 1969; Canon Residentiary and Treasurer of York Minster, 1970–75; Bishop Suffragan of Hulme, 1975–84. *Publications:* God and Christian Caring, 1973; Pastor's Post, 1975; (ed) Diocese in Mission, 1968. *Recreations:* pottery, music, painting in oils. *Address:* Bishopsgarth, Maltongate, Thornton-le-Dale, N Yorks YO18 7SA. *T:* Pickering (0751) 74605. *Clubs:* Royal Over-Seas League; Bolton.

GALLINER, Peter; Director, International Press Institute, since 1975; Chairman, Peter Galliner Associates, since 1970; *b* 19 Sept. 1920; *s* of Dr Moritz and Hedwig Galliner; *m* 1st, 1948, Edith Marguerite Goldschmidt; one *d*; 2nd, 1990, Helga Stenschke. *Educ:* Berlin and London. Reuters, 1944–47; Foreign Manager, Financial Times, 1947–60; Chm. and Man. Dir, Ullstein Publishing Co., Berlin, 1960–64; Vice-Chm. and Man. Dir, British Printing Corporation Publishing Gp, 1965–70. Comdr's Cross, Order of Merit (German Federal Republic), 1990; Ecomienda, Orden de Isabel la Católica (Spain). *Recreations:* reading, music. *Address:* 27 Walsingham, St John's Wood Park, NW8 6RH. *T:* 071–722 5502; 8001 Zürich, Untere Zäune 15, Switzerland. *T:* 411–251 8664. *Club:* Reform.

GALLOWAY, 13th Earl of, *cr* 1623; **Randolph Keith Reginald Stewart;** Lord Garlies, 1607; Bt 1627, 1687; Baron Stewart of Garlies (GB), 1796; *b* 14 Oct. 1928; *s* of 12th Earl of Galloway, and Philippa Fendall (*d* 1974), *d* of late Jacob Wendell, New York; *S* father, 1978; *m* 1975, Mrs Lily May Budge, DLJ, *y d* of late Andrew Miller, Duns, Berwickshire. *Educ:* Harrow. KLJ. *Heir: cousin* Andrew Clyde Stewart [*b* 13 March 1949; *m* 1977, Sara, *o d* of Brig. Patrick Pollock; one *s* two *d*]. *Address:* Senwick House, Brighouse Bay, Borgue, Kirkcudbrightshire DG6 4TP.

GALLOWAY, Bishop of, (RC), since 1981; **Rt. Rev. Maurice Taylor,** DD; *b* 5 May 1926; *s* of Maurice Taylor and Lucy Taylor (*née* McLaughlin). *Educ:* St Aloysius Coll., Glasgow; Our Lady's High School, Motherwell; Pontifical Gregorian Univ., Rome (DD). Served RAMC in UK, India, Egypt, 1944–47. Ordained to priesthood, Rome, 1950; lectured in Philosophy, 1955–60, in Theology 1960–65, St Peter's Coll., Cardross; Rector, Royal Scots Coll., Valladolid, Spain, 1965–74; Parish Priest, Our Lady of Lourdes, East

Kilbride, 1974–81. Vice-Pres., Catholic Inst. for Internat. Relations, 1985–. *Publication:* The Scots College in Spain, 1971. *Address:* Candida Casa, 8 Corsehill Road, Ayr KA7 2ST. *T:* Ayr (0292) 266750.

GALLOWAY, Rev. Prof. Allan Douglas; Professor of Divinity, University of Glasgow, 1968–82, now Emeritus Professor; Principal of Trinity College, Glasgow, 1972–82; *b* 30 July 1920; *s* of late William Galloway and Mary Wallace Galloway (*née* Junor); *m* 1948, Sara Louise Phillipp; two *s*. *Educ:* Stirling High Sch.; Univ. of Glasgow; Christ's Coll., Cambridge; Union Theol Seminary, New York. MA, BD, STM, PhD. Ordained, Asst Minister, Clune Park Parish, Port Glasgow, 1948–50; Minister of Auchterhouse, 1950–54; Prof. of Religious Studies, Univ. of Ibadan, Nigeria, 1954–60; Sen. Lectr, Univ. of Glasgow, 1960–66, Reader in Divinity, 1966–68. Hensley Henson Lectr in Theology, Oxford Univ., 1978; Cunningham Lectr, Edinburgh, 1979; Gifford Lectr, Glasgow, 1984. FRSE 1985. *Publications:* The Cosmic Christ, 1951; Basic Readings in Theology, 1964; Faith in a Changing Culture, 1966; Wolfhart Pannenberg, 1973; History of Christian Theology, Vol. 1, Pt III, 1986. *Recreation:* sailing. *Address:* 5 Straid Bheag, Clynder, Helensburgh, Dunbartonshire G84 0QX.

GALLOWAY, George; MP (Lab) Glasgow, Hillhead, since 1987; *b* 16 Aug. 1954; *s* of George and Sheila Galloway; *m* 1979, Elaine Fyffe; one *d*. *Educ:* Charleston Primary Sch.; Harris Acad., Dundee. Engrg worker, 1973; organiser, Labour Party, 1977; Gen. Sec., War on Want, 1983–87. *Recreations:* sport, films, music. *Address:* House of Commons, SW1A 0AA. *T:* 071–219 4084.

GALLOWAY, Maj.-Gen. Kenneth Gardiner, CB 1978; OBE 1960; Director Army Dental Service, 1974–March 1978; *b* 3 Nov. 1917; *s* of David and Helen Galloway, Dundee and Oban; *m* 1949, Sheila Frances (*née* Dunsmor); two *d* (one *s* decd). *Educ:* Oban High Sch.; St Andrews Univ. LDS 1939, BDS 1940. Lieut Army Dental Corps, 1940; Captain 1941; Major 1948; Lt-Col 1955; Col 1963; Brig. 1972; Maj.-Gen. 1974. Served in Egypt, Palestine, Syria and Iraq, 1942–46; Chief Instructor and 2nd in comd, Depot and Training Establishment, RADC, 1956–60; Asst Dir Dental Service, MoD, 1967–71; Dep. Dir Dental Service: Southern Comd, 1971–72; BAOR, 1972–74. QHDS 1971–78. Col Comdt, RADC, 1980–83. OStJ 1960. *Recreations:* tennis, golf, gardening. *Address:* Berwyn Court, Avenue Road, Farnborough, Hants GU14 7BH. *T:* Farnborough (0252) 544948.

GALLWEY, Sir Philip Frankland P.; *see* Payne-Gallwey.

GALPERN, family name of **Baron Galpern.**

GALPERN, Baron *cr* 1979 (Life Peer), of Shettleston in the District of the City of Glasgow; **Myer Galpern,** Kt 1960; DL; JP; *b* 1903. *Educ:* Glasgow Univ. Lord Provost of Glasgow and Lord Lieut for the County of the City of Glasgow, 1958–60. MP (Lab) Glasgow, Shettleston, 1959–79; Second Dep. Chm. of Ways and Means, 1974–76, First Dep. Chm., 1976–79. Mem. of the Court of Glasgow Univ.; Mem., Advisory Cttee on Education in Scotland. Hon. LLD Glasgow, 1961; Hon. FEIS, 1960. DL, Co. of City of Glasgow, 1962; JP Glasgow. *Address:* House of Lords, SW1.

GALPIN, Brian John Francis; His Honour Judge Galpin; a Circuit Judge, since 1978; an Official Referee, Western Circuit, since 1986; *b* 21 March 1921; *s* of late Christopher John Galpin, DSO and late Gladys Elizabeth Galpin (*née* Souhami); *m* 1st, 1947, Ailsa McConnel (*d* 1959); one *d* decd; 2nd, 1961, Nancy Cecilia Nichols; two adopted *s*. *Educ:* Merchant Taylors' Sch.; Hertford Coll., Oxford. MA 1947. RAF Officer, 1941–45. Editor, Isis, 1946. Called to Bar, 1948; a Recorder of the Crown Court, 1972–78. Councillor, Metropolitan Borough of Fulham, 1950–59; Chm., Galpin Soc. for Study of Musical Instruments, 1954–72, Vice-Pres., 1974–; Pres., Madrigal Soc., 1989–91; Mem. Cttee, Bach Choir, 1954–61. Pres., Old Merchant Taylors' Soc., 1988. Trustee, Horniman Mus., 1990–. *Publications:* A Manual of International Law, 1950; Maxwell's Interpretation of Statutes, 10th edn 1953 and 11th edn 1962; Every Man's Own Lawyer, 69th edn 1962, 70th edn 1971, 71st edn 1981; contrib. Halsbury's Laws of England, 3rd and 4th edns, Encycl. of Forms and Precedents, Galpin Soc. Jl. *Recreations:* cricket (retired), music, chess. *Clubs:* Travellers', Pratt's; Hampshire (Winchester).

GALPIN, Rodney Desmond; Chairman and Group Chief Executive: Standard Chartered plc, since 1988; Standard Chartered Bank, since 1988; *b* 5 Feb. 1932; *s* of Sir Albert James Galpin, KCVO, CBE; *m* 1956, Sylvia Craven; one *s* one *d*. *Educ:* Haileybury and Imperial Service Coll. Joined Bank of England, 1952; Sec. to Governor (Lord Cromer), 1962–66; Dep. Principal, Discount Office, 1970–74; Dep. Chief Cashier, Banking and Money Markets Supervision, 1974–78; Chief of Establishments, 1978–80; Chief of Corporate Services, 1980–82; Associate Dir, 1982–84; Exec. Dir, Bank of England, 1984–88. Mem. Council, Foundn for Management Educn, 1984–86; Life Governor and Council Mem., Haileybury, 1973–; Mem. Council, Scout Assoc., 1972–. CBIM 1986 (FBIM 1979). Freeman, City of London, 1981. OStJ. *Recreations:* tennis, gardening, music. *Address:* Standard Chartered plc, 1 Aldermanbury Square, EC2V 7SB.

GALSWORTHY, Anthony Charles, CMG 1985; HM Diplomatic Service; Senior British Representative, Sino-British Joint Liaison Group, Hong Kong, since 1989; *b* 20 Dec. 1944; *s* of Sir Arthur Norman Galsworthy, KCMG, and Margaret Agnes Galsworthy (*née* Hiscocks); *m* 1970, Jan Dawson-Grove; one *s* one *d*. *Educ:* St Paul's Sch.; Corpus Christi Coll., Cambridge (MA). FCO, 1966–67; Hong Kong (language training), 1967–69; Peking, 1970–72; FCO, 1972–77; Rome, 1977–81; Counsellor, Peking, 1981–84; Head of Hong Kong Dept, FCO, 1984–86; Principal Private Sec. to Sec. of State for Foreign and Commonwealth Affairs, 1986–88; seconded to RIIA, 1988–89. *Recreations:* bird-watching, wildlife. *Address:* c/o Foreign and Commonwealth Office, King Charles Street, SW1A 2AH. *Club:* United Oxford & Cambridge University.

GALSWORTHY, (Arthur) Michael (Johnstone); Chairman: Trewithen Estates Management Co. Ltd, since 1979; Probus Garden Estate Co. Ltd, since 1982; a Development Commissioner, since 1988; *b* 10 April 1944; *s* of Sir John Galsworthy, *qv*; *m* 1972, Charlotte Helena Prudence Roberts (*d* 1989); one *s* two *d*. *Educ:* Radley; St Andrews Univ. (MA Hons). International Harvester Corp., 1967–69; Planning Manager, English China Clays PLC, 1970–82; Man. Dir 1982–86, non-Exec. Dir 1986–, Hawkins Wright Associates. Local Adv. Dir, Barclays Bank, 1987–. Mem., Prince of Wales Council, 1985–; Dir, CoSIRA, 1985–88; Trustee, Nat. Agricl Centre Rural Trust, 1986–; Chm., Cornwall Rural Housing Assoc., 1988–; Dir, Devon & Cornwall Develt Co. Ltd, 1991–. Dir, Woodard Corp. (W Region), 1983–88. *Recreations:* gardening, fishing, shooting, walking. *Address:* Trewithen, Grampound Road, near Truro, Cornwall TR2 4DD. *T:* St Austell (0726) 882418. *Clubs:* Brooks's, Farmers'.

GALSWORTHY, Sir John (Edgar), KCVO 1975; CMG 1968; HM Diplomatic Service, retired; *b* 19 June 1919; *s* of Arthur Galsworthy; *m* 1942, Jennifer Ruth Johnstone; one *s* three *d*. *Educ:* Emanuel Sch.; Corpus Christi Coll., Cambridge. HM Forces 1939–41; Foreign Office, 1941–46; Third Sec., Madrid, 1946; Second Sec., Vienna, 1949; First Sec., Athens, 1951; Foreign Office, 1954; Bangkok, 1958; Counsellor, Brussels (UK Delegation to EEC) 1962; Counsellor (Economic), Bonn, 1964–67; Counsellor and subsequently Minister (European Econ. Affairs), Paris, 1967–71; Ambassador to Mexico, 1972–77. Business consultant, 1978–82. UK Observer to El Salvador elections, March 1982. *Recreation:* fishing. *Address:* Lanzeague, St Just in Roseland, Truro, Cornwall TR2 5JD.
See also A. M. J. Galsworthy.

GALSWORTHY, Michael; *see* Galsworthy, A. M. J.

GALTON, Raymond Percy; author and scriptwriter since 1951; *b* 17 July 1930; *s* of Herbert and Christina Galton; *m* 1956, Tonia Phillips; one *s* two *d*. *Educ:* Garth Sch., Morden. *Television:* with Alan Simpson: Hancock's Half Hour, 1954–61 (adaptation and translation, Fleksnes, Scandinavian TV, film and stage); Comedy Playhouse, 1962–63; Steptoe and Son, 1962–74 (adaptations and translations: Sanford and Son, US TV; Stiefbeen and Zoon, Dutch TV; Albert och Herbert, Scandinavian TV, film and stage); Galton-Simpson Comedy, 1969; Clochemerle, 1971; Casanova '74, 1974; Dawson's Weekly, 1975; The Galton and Simpson Playhouse, 1976–77; with Johnny Speight: Tea Ladies, 1979; Spooner's Patch, 1979–80; with John Antrobus: Room at the Bottom, 1986–87 (Banff TV Fest. Award for Best Comedy, 1987); *films* with Alan Simpson: The Rebel, 1960; The Bargee, 1963; The Spy with a Cold Nose, 1966; Loot, 1969; Steptoe and Son, 1971; Steptoe and Son Ride Again, 1973; Den Siste Fleksnes (Scandinavia), 1974; Die Skraphandlerne (Scandinavia), 1975; with Alan Simpson and John Antrobus: The Wrong Arm of the Law, 1963; with Andrew Galton: Camping (Denmark), 1990; *theatre:* with Alan Simpson: Way Out in Piccadilly, 1966; The Wind in the Sassafras Trees, 1968; Albert och Herbert (Sweden), 1981; Fleksnes (Norway), 1983; Mordet pa Skolgatan 15 (Sweden), 1984; with John Antrobus: When Did You Last See Your Trousers?, 1986. Awards, with Alan Simpson: Scriptwriters of the Year, 1959 (Guild of TV Producers and Directors); Best TV Comedy Series, Steptoe and Son, 1962/3/4/5 (Screenwriters Guild); John Logie Baird Award (for outstanding contribution to Television), 1964; Best Comedy Series (Steptoe and Son, Dutch TV), 1966; Best comedy screenplay, Steptoe and Son, 1972 (Screenwriters Guild). *Publications:* (with Alan Simpson): Hancock, 1961; Steptoe and Son, 1963; The Reunion and Other Plays, 1966; Hancock Scripts, 1974; The Best of Hancock, 1986. *Recreations:* reading, worrying. *Address:* The Ivy House, Hampton Court, Mddx. *T:* 081–977 1236.

GALVIN, Bernard Vincent Joseph, CB 1991; Treasurer, Victoria University of Wellington, since 1990; Visiting Fellow, Institute of Policy Studies, since 1989; *b* 15 March 1933; *s* of Eustace Bartholemew Galvin and Margaret Jean (*née* Lenihan); *m* 1st, 1960, Beverly Ann Snook (marr. diss. 1977); three *s* one *d*; 2nd, 1980, Margaret Clark. *Educ:* Univ. of NZ (BSc 1954); Victoria Univ. of Wellington (BA Hons 1959); Harvard Univ. (MPA 1961). Joined Treasury, NZ, 1955; Harkness Fellow, USA, 1960–61; Econ. Counsellor, NZ High Commn, London, 1965–68; Treasury Dir, 1969; Asst Sec., 1972; Dep. Sec., 1974; Perm. Head of PM's Dept, 1975–80; Sec. to Treasury, 1980–86; Chm., Econ. Develt Commn, 1986–89. Alternate Gov., World Bank, 1976–86. Chm., Ministerial Wkg Pty on Disability and Accident Compensation, 1991. Mem. Council, Victoria Univ. of Wellington, 1989–. *Publications:* Policy Co-ordination, Public Sector and Government, 1991; chapters in books on NZ government; articles in public admin jls. *Recreations:* beach house, gardening, reading, walking. *Address:* 10 Jellicoe Towers, 189 The Terrace, Wellington, New Zealand. *T:* (weekdays) (04) 728–143; (weekends) (06) 3643374. *Club:* Wellington (Wellington, NZ).

GALVIN, General John Rogers; General, United States Army; Supreme Allied Commander, Europe, since 1987; *b* 13 May 1929; *s* of John J. Galvin and Josephine Mary Logan; *m* 1961, Virginia Lee Brennan; four *d*. *Educ:* US Mil. Acad. (BS); Columbia Univ. (MA); US Army Command and General Staff Coll.; Univ. of Pennsylvania; US Army War Coll.; Fletcher Sch. of Law and Diplomacy (US Army War Coll. Fellowship). Platoon Leader, I Co., 65 Inf. Regt, Puerto Rico, 1955–56; Instructor, Ranger Sch., Colombia, 1956–58; Co. Comdr, 501 Airborne Battle Group, 101 Airborne Div., 1958–60; Instructor, US Mil. Acad., 1962–65; ACOS, Intell., 1st Cavalry Div., Vietnam, 1966–67; MA and Aide to Sec. of US Army, 1967–69; Comdr, 1st Bn, 8th Cavalry, 1st Cavalry Div., Vietnam, 1969–70; Dep. Sec., Jt Staff, US European Comd, Stuttgart, 1973–74; MA to SACEUR, 1974–75; Comdr, Div. Support Comd, 1975–77; COS, 3rd Inf. Div. (Mechanized), Würzburg, 1977–78; Asst Div. Comdr, 8th Inf. Div. (Mechanized), Mainz, 1978–80; Asst DCOS for Training, US Army Training and Doctrine Comd, 1980–81; Comdg Gen., 24 Inf. Div. (Mechanized), and Fort Stewart, 1981–83; Comdg Gen., VII Corps, Stuttgart, 1983–85; C-in-C, US Southern Comd, Panama, 1985–87; C-in-C, US European Comd, Stuttgart, 1987–. Defense DSM, Army DSM, Silver Star, Legion of Merit (with 2 Oak Leaf Clusters), DFC, Soldier's Medal, Bronze Star (with 2 Oak Leaf Clusters), Combat Infantryman Badge, Ranger Tab, foreign decorations. *Publications:* The Minute Men, 1967; Air Assault: the development of airmobility, 1969; Three Men of Boston, 1975. *Recreations:* walking, jogging. *Address:* Supreme Allied Commander, Europe, Supreme HQ Allied Powers Europe, 7010 SHAPE, Belgium.

GALWAY, 12th Viscount *cr* 1727; **George Rupert Monckton-Arundell;** Baron Killard, 1727; Lieut Comdr RCN, retired; *b* 13 Oct. 1922; *s* of Philip Marmaduke Monckton (*d* 1965) (*g g s* of 5th Viscount) and of Lavender, *d* of W. J. O'Hara; *S* cousin, 1980; *m* 1944, Fiona Margaret, *d* of late Captain P. W. de P. Taylor; one *s* three *d*. *Heir: s* Hon. John Philip Monckton [*b* 8 April 1952; *m* 1980, Deborah Holmes]. *Address:* 583 Berkshire Drive, London, Ontario N6J 3S3, Canada.

GALWAY AND KILMACDUAGH, Bishop of, (RC), since 1976; **Most Rev. Eamonn Casey,** DD; also Apostolic Administrator of Kilfenora, since 1976; *b* Firies, Co. Kerry, 23 April 1927; *s* of late John Casey and late Helena (*née* Shanahan). *Educ:* St Munchin's Coll., Limerick; St Patrick's Coll., Maynooth. LPh 1946; BA 1947. Priest, 1951. Curate, St John's Cath., Limerick, 1951–60; Chaplain to Irish in Slough, 1960–63; set up social framework to re-establish people into new environment; started social welfare scheme; set up lodgings bureau and savings scheme; invited by Cardinal Heenan to place Catholic Housing Aid Soc. on national basis; founded Family Housing Assoc., 1964; Dir, British Council of Churches Housing Trust; Trustee, Housing the Homeless Central Fund; Founder-Trustee of Shelter (Chm. 1968); Mem. Council, Nat. Fedn of Housing Socs; Founder Mem., Marian Employment Agency; Founder Trustee, Shelter Housing Aid Soc., 1963–69; Bishop of Kerry, 1969–76. Exec. Chm., Trocaire, 1973–; Sec., Irish Episcopal Commn for Emigrants. Mem. Bd, Siamsa Tire, Nat. Folk Th. of Ireland. Launched Meitheal, 1982; Pres. Galway Social Service Council; Moderator, Galway Marriage Tribunal; estab. Galway Adult Educn Centre, 1985, Galway Family Guidance Inst., 1986. Chm., Nat. Youth Resource Gp, 1979–86. Member: Commn for Social Welfare, 1971–74; Maynooth Coll. Exec. Council, 1974–84; Episcopal Commn for Univs, 1976–; Governing Body, University Coll., Galway, 1976–. *Publications:* (with Adam Ferguson) A Home of Your Own; Housing—A Parish Solution; contribs to journals, etc. *Recreations:* music, theatre, concerts, films when time, conversation, motoring. *Address:* Mount St Mary's, Galway, Ireland; (office) The Diocesan Office, The Cathedral, Galway. *T:* Galway 63566, 62255, 66553.

GALWAY, James, OBE 1977; FRCM 1983; fluteplayer; *b* 8 Dec. 1939; *s* of James Galway and Ethel Stewart Clarke; *m* 1st, 1965; one *s*; 2nd, 1972; one *s* twin *d*; 3rd, 1984, Jeanne

Cinnante. *Educ:* St Paul's Sch., and Mountcollyer Secondary Modern Sch., Belfast; RCM, and Guildhall Sch. of Music, London; Conservatoire National Supérieur de Musique, Paris. First post in wind band of Royal Shakespeare Theatre, Stratford-upon-Avon; later worked with Sadler's Wells Orch., Royal Opera House Orch. and BBC Symphony Orch.; Principal Flute, London Symphony Orch., 1966, Royal Philharmonic Orch., 1967–69; Principal Solo Flute, Berlin Philharmonic Orch., 1969–75; international soloist, 1975–. Recordings of works by C. P. E. Bach, J. S. Bach, Beethoven, Corigliano, Debussy, Franck, Handel, Khachaturian, Mancini, Mozart, Nielsen, Prokoviev, Reicha, Reincke, Rodrigo, Schubert, Stamitz, Telemann and Vivaldi; also albums of flute showpieces, Australian, Irish and Japanese collections. Grand Prix du Disque, 1976, 1989. Hon. MA Open, 1979; Hon. DMus: QUB, 1979; New England Conservatory of Music, 1980. Officier des Arts et des Lettres, France, 1987. *Publications:* James Galway: an autobiography, 1978; Flute (Menuhin Music Guide), 1982; James Galway's Music in Time, 1983 (TV series, 1983); Masterclass: performance editions of great flute literature, 1987. *Recreations:* music, walking, swimming, films, theatre, TV, chess, backgammon, computing, talking to people. *Address:* c/o Helene Kern, IMG Artists, Media House, 3 Burlington Lane, Chiswick W4 2TH. *T:* 081–747 9977.

GAMBLE, Sir David (Hugh Norman), 6th Bt *cr* 1897; *b* 1 July 1966; *s* of Sir David Gamble, 5th Bt and of Dawn Adrienne, *d* of late David Hugh Gittins; *S* father, 1984. *Educ:* Shiplake College, Henley-on-Thames. *Heir: cousin* Hugh Robert George Gamble, *b* 3 March 1946. *Address:* Keinton House, Keinton Mandeville, Somerton, Somerset. *T:* Charlton Mackrell (045822) 3964.

GAMBLING, Prof. William Alexander, PhD, DSc; FRS 1983; FEng, Hon. FIEE; Professor of Optical Communication, since 1980, and Director, Optoelectronics Research Centre, since 1989, University of Southampton; industrial consultant and company director; *b* 11 Oct. 1926; *s* of George Alexander Gambling and Muriel Clara Gambling; *m* 1952, Margaret Pooley; one *s* two *d*. *Educ:* Univ. of Bristol (BSc, DSc); Univ. of Liverpool (PhD). FIERE 1964; CEng, FIEE 1967; FEng 1979. Lectr in Electric Power Engrg, Univ. of Liverpool, 1950–55; National Res. Council Fellow, Univ. of BC, 1955–57; Univ. of Southampton: Lectr, Sen. Lectr, and Reader, 1957–64; Dean of Engrg and Applied Science, 1972–75; Prof. of Electronics, 1964–80, Hd of Dept, 1974–79. Vis. Professor: Univ. of Colo, USA, 1966–67; Bhabha Atomic Res. Centre, India, 1970; Osaka Univ., Japan, 1977; Hon. Professor: Huazhung Univ. of Sci. and Technol., Wuhan, China, 1986–; Beijing Inst. of Posts and Telecommunications, Beijing, China, 1987–; Hon. Dir, Beijing Optical Fibre Inst., 1987–. Pres., IERE, 1977–78 (Hon. Fellow 1983). Member: Electronics Res. Council, 1977–80 (Mem., Optics and Infra-Red Cttee, 1965–69 and 1974–80); Board, Council of Engrg Instns, 1974–79; National Electronics Council, 1977–78; 1984–; Technol. Sub-Cttee of UGC, 1973–83; British Nat. Cttee for Radio Science, 1978–87; Nat. Adv. Bd for Local Authority Higher Educn, Engrg Working Gp, 1982–84; Engineering Council, 1983–88; British Nat. Cttee for Internat. Engineering Affairs, 1984–88; Chm., Commn D, Internat. Union of Radio Science, 1984–87 (Vice-Chm., 1981–84). FRSA. Selby Fellow, Australian Acad. of Science, 1982; For. Mem., Polish Acad. of Scis, 1985. Member Advisory Boards: Optical and Quantum Electronics; Internat. Jl of Optoelectronics. Freeman, City of London, 1988; Liveryman, Worshipful Co. of Engrs, 1988. Bulgin Premium, IERE, 1961, Rutherford Premium, IERE, 1964, Electronics Div. Premium, IEE, 1976 and 1978, Oliver Lodge Premium, IEE, 1981, Heinrich Hertz Premium, IERE, 1981, for research papers, J. J. Thomson Medal, IEE, 1982, Faraday Medal, IEE, 1983, Churchill Medal, Soc. of Engineers, 1984 and Simms Medal, Soc. of Engineers, 1989, for research innovation and leadership. Academic Enterprise Award, 1982; Micro-optics Award, Japan, 1989; Dennis Gabor Award, USA, 1990; Rank Prize for Optoelectronics, 1991. *Publications:* papers on electronics and optical fibre communications. *Recreations:* music, reading, walking. *Address:* Optoelectronics Research Centre, University of Southampton, Southampton SO9 5NH. *T:* Southampton (0703) 593373.

GAMBON, Michael John, CBE 1990; actor; *b* 19 Oct. 1940; *s* of Edward and Mary Gambon; *m* 1962, Anne Miller; one *s*. *Educ:* St Aloysius School for Boys, Somers Town, London. Served 7 year apprenticeship in engineering; first appeared on stage with Edwards/MácLiammoir Co., Dublin, 1962; Nat. Theatre, Old Vic, 1963–67; Birmingham Rep. and other provincial theatres, 1967–69 (title rôles incl. Othello, Macbeth, Coriolanus); RSC Aldwych, 1970–71; Norman Conquests, Globe, 1974; Otherwise Engaged, Queen's, 1976; Just Between Ourselves, Queen's 1977; Alice's Boys, Savoy, 1978; King Lear and Antony and Cleopatra (title rôles), RSC Stratford and Barbican, 1982–83; Old Times, Haymarket, 1985; Uncle Vanya, Vaudeville, 1988; Veterans Day, Haymarket, 1989; Man of the Moment, Globe, 1990; Othello and Taking Steps, Scarborough, 1990; National Theatre: Galileo, 1980 (London Theatre Critics' Award, Best Actor); Betrayal, 1980; Tales From Hollywood, 1980; Chorus of Disapproval, 1985 (Olivier Award, Best Comedy Performance); Tons of Money, 1986; A View from the Bridge, 1987 (Best Actor, Evening Standard Awards, Olivier Awards, and Plays and Players London Theatre Critics Awards; Best Stage Actor, Variety Club Awards); A Small Family Business, 1987; Mountain Language, 1988. Numerous film and TV appearances, incl. The Singing Detective, 1986 (BAFTA Award, Best Actor, 1987); The Cook, The Thief, His Wife and Her Lover, 1989; The Heat of the Day, 1989; Paris by Night, 1989; A Dry White Season, 1990. *Recreations:* flying, gun collecting, clock making. *Address:* c/o Larry Dalzell Associates, Suite 12, 17 Broad Court, WC2B 5QN.

GAMES, Abram, OBE 1958; RDI 1959; graphic designer; *b* 29 July 1914; *s* of Joseph and Sarah Games; *m* 1945, Marianne Salfeld; one *s* two *d*. *Educ:* Grocers' Company Sch., Hackney Downs. Studio, 1932–36; freelance designer, 1936–40. Infantry, 1940–41; War Office Poster Designer, 1941–46. Freelance, 1946–; Lecturer Royal College of Art, 1947–53. Postage Stamps for Great Britain and Israel, Festival of Britain, BBC Television, Queen's Award to Industry Emblems. One-man shows of graphic design: London and UK, New York, Chicago, Brussels, Stockholm, Jerusalem, Tel Aviv, São Paulo. Rep. Gt Brit. at Museum of Modern Art, New York; first prizes, Poster Competitions: Helsinki, 1957; Lisbon, 1959; New York, 1960; Stockholm, 1962; Barcelona, 1964; Internat. Philatelic Competition, Italy, 1976; Design Medal, Soc. of Industrial Artists, 1960. Silver Medal, Royal Society of Arts, 1962. Inventor of Imagic Copying Processes. *Publication:* Over my Shoulder, 1960. *Recreations:* painting, carpentry. *Address:* 41 The Vale, NW11 8SE. *T:* 081–458 2811.

GAMINARA, Albert William, CMG 1963; HMOCS (retired); *b* 1 Dec. 1913; *s* of late Albert Sidney Gaminara and late Katherine Helen Copeman; *m* 1947, Monica (*née* Watson); one *s* three *d*. *Educ:* City of London Sch.; St John's Coll., Cambridge; Oriel Coll., Oxford. MA Cantab 1943. Appointed to Sierra Leone as Administrative Cadet, 1936; seconded to Colonial Office as Principal, 1947–50; Transferred as Administrative Officer to N Rhodesia, 1950; Mem. of Legislative Council, 1963; Admin. Sec. to Govt of Northern Rhodesia (now Zambia), 1961–63; Sec. to the Cabinet, 1964, Adviser, Cabinet Office, Zambia, 1965. *Address:* Stratton House, Over Stratton, South Petherton, Somerset TA13 5LQ. *Club:* Hawks (Cambridge).

GAMMELL, James Gilbert Sydney, MBE 1944; CA; Chairman, Cairn Energy plc, since 1971; *b* 4 March 1920; *e s* of Lt-Gen. Sir James A. H. Gammell, KCB, DSO, MC; *m* 1944, Susan Patricia Bowring Toms, *d* of late Edward Bowring Toms; five *s* one *d*. *Educ:* Winchester Coll. Chartered Accountant, 1949. Served War, Major Grenadier Guards, 1939–46: France, 1940 and 1944, Russia, 1945. Chm., Ivory & Sime, 1975–85. *Recreation:* farming. *Address:* Foxhall, Kirkliston, West Lothian EH29 9ER. *T:* 031–333 3275. *Club:* New (Edinburgh).

See also J. F. Gammell.

GAMMELL, John Frederick, MC 1943; MA; *b* 31 Dec. 1921; 2nd *s* of Lieut-Gen. Sir James A. H. Gammell, KCB, DSO, MC; *m* 1947, Margaret Anne, *d* of Ralph Juckes, Fiddington Manor, Tewkesbury; two *s* one *d*. *Educ:* Winchester Coll.; Trinity Coll., Cambridge. MA 1953. Asst Master, Horris Hill, Newbury, 1940–41. War Service with KRRC, 1941–44; wounded, 1943; invalided out, 1944. Trinity Coll., Cambridge, 1946–47 (BA); Asst Master, Winchester Coll., 1944–45 and 1947–68; Exchange with Sen. Classics Master, Geelong Grammar Sch., Australia, 1949–50; Housemaster of Turner's, Winchester Coll., 1958–68; Headmaster, Repton Sch., 1968–78; Asst Sec., Cambridge Univ. Careers Service, 1978–83. *Recreation:* friends. *Address:* The Old School House, Seaton, Uppingham LE15 9HR. *T:* Morcott (057287) 835.

See also J. G. S. Gammell.

GAMMIE, Gordon Edward, CB 1981; QC 1989; Counsel to the Speaker (European Legislation etc), House of Commons, since 1983; *b* 9 Feb. 1922; *e s* of Dr Alexander Edward Gammie and Ethel Mary Gammie (*née* Miller); *m* 1949, Joyce Rust; two *s*. *Educ:* St Paul's Sch.; The Queen's Coll., Oxford (MA). War service, 1941–45; Captain, 1st Bn Argyll and Sutherland Highlanders. Called to Bar, Middle Temple, 1948. Entered Govt Legal Service, 1949; Asst Solicitor, Mins of Health and of Housing and Local Govt, 1967; Under-Sec. (Principal Asst Solicitor), Min. of Housing and Local Govt, later DoE, 1969–74; Under-Sec., Cabinet Office, 1975–77; Dep. Treasury Solicitor, 1977–79; Legal Advr and Solicitor to MAFF, 1979–83. *Recreations:* tennis, listening to music. *Address:* Ty Gwyn, 52 Sutton Lane, Banstead, Surrey SM7 3RB. *T:* Burgh Heath (0737) 355287. *Clubs:* Athenæum; St Andrew's (Cheam) Lawn Tennis (Chm., 1987–).

GAMON, Hugh Wynell, CBE 1979; MC 1944; Senior Partner, Sherwood & Co., since 1972; HM Government Agent, since 1970; *b* 31 March 1921; *s* of Judge Hugh R. P. Gamon and E. Margaret Gamon; *m* 1949, June Elizabeth, *d* of William and Florence Temple; one *s* three *d*. *Educ:* St Edward's Sch., Oxford; Exeter Coll., Oxford, 1946–48. MA 1st Cl. Hons Jurisprudence; Law Society Hons; Edmund Thomas Childe Prize. Served War, 1940–46: Royal Corps of Signals, N Africa, Italy and Palestine, with 1st Division. Articled to Clerk of Cumberland CC, 1949–51; Asst Solicitor, Sherwood & Co., 1951; Parly Agent, 1954; Partner, Sherwood & Co., 1955. *Recreations:* gardening, walking. *Address:* Black Charles, Underriver, Sevenoaks, Kent TN15 0RY. *T:* Hildenborough (0732) 833036. *Club:* St Stephen's Constitutional.

GANDAR, Hon. Leslie Walter; JP; Chairman: Social Science Research Council, New Zealand, since 1984; Capital Discovery Place, since 1988; *b* 26 Jan. 1919; *s* of Max Gandar and Doris Harper; *m* 1945, M. Justine, *d* of T. A. Smith and Florence Smith; four *s* one *d* (and one *d* decd). *Educ:* Wellington College; Victoria Univ., Wellington (BSc 1940). FNZIAS, FInstP. Served RNZAF and RAF, 1940–44. Farming, 1945–. MP, Ruahine, 1966–78; Minister of Science, Energy Resources, Mines, Electricity, 1972; Minister of Education, Science and Technology, 1975–78; High Comr for NZ in UK, 1979–82. Chairman, Pohangina County Council, 1954–69. Chancellor, Massey Univ., 1970–76. Chairman: NZ Adv. Council, 1982–87; Queen Elizabeth II Nat. Trust of NZ, 1983–87; NZ Royal Society Prince and Princess of Wales Science Award Liaison Cttee. Pres., Friends of Turnbull Library, 1984–. JP 1958. Hon. DSc Massey, 1977. *Recreations:* music—when not watching cricket; wood-carving; work. *Address:* 34 Palliser Road, Wellington, New Zealand.

GANDEE, John Stephen, CMG 1967; OBE 1958; HM Diplomatic Service, retired; British High Commissioner in Botswana, 1966–69; *b* 8 Dec. 1909; *s* of John Stephen and Constance Garfield Gandee; *m* 1st, May Degenhardt (*d* 1954); one *s* two *d*; 2nd, Junia Henman (*née* Devine); two *d* (and one step *s* one step *d*). *Educ:* Dorking High Sch. Post Office, Dorking, 1923–30; India Office, 1930–47; Private Sec. to Parly Under-Sec. of State, 1946–47; and 1947–49; Asst Private Sec. to Sec. of State, 1947; First Sec., Ottawa, 1952–54; seconded to Bechuanaland Protectorate, 1958–60 and 1961; seconded to Office of High Comr for Basutoland, Bechuanaland Protectorate and Swaziland, 1960–61; Head of Administration Dept, CRO, 1961–64; Head of Office Services and Supply Dept, Diplomatic Service Administration, 1965–66. *Recreations:* walking, gardening. *Address:* Fulbrook, King's Lane, Coldwaltham, Pulborough, W Sussex RH20 1LE. *T:* Pulborough (0798) 873972.

GANDHI, Manmohan Purushottam, MA, FREconS, FSS; Editor, Major Industries of India Annual, since 1951 (vol. 34, 1988); Director: Indian Link Chain Manufacturers Ltd; Zenith Ltd; Orient General Industries Ltd; *b* 5 Nov. 1901; *s* of late Purushottam Kahanji Gandhi, of Limbdi (Kathiawad); *m* 1926, Rambhaben, BA (Indian Women's Univ.), *d* of Sukhlal Chhaganlal Shah of Wadhwan. *Educ:* Bahauddin Coll., Junagad; Gujerat Coll., Ahmedabad; Hindu Univ., Benares. BA (History and Econs), Bombay Univ., 1923; MA (Political Econ. and Political Philosophy), Benares Hindu Univ., 1925; Ashburner Prize of Bombay Univ., 1925. Statistical Asst, Govt of Bombay, Labour Office, 1926; Asst Sec., Indian Currency League, Bombay, 1926; Sec., Indian Chamber of Commerce, Calcutta, 1926–36; Sec., Indian Sugar Mills Assoc., 1932–36; Officer-in-Charge, Credit Dept, National City Bank of New York, Calcutta, 1936–37; Chief Commercial Manager, Rohtas Industries Ltd; Dalmia Cement Ltd, 1937–39; Dir, Indian Sugar Syndicate Ltd, 1937–39; Controller of Supplies, Bengal and Bombay, 1941–43; Sec., Indian Nat. Cttee, Internat. Chamber of Commerce, Calcutta, 1929–31; Sec., Fedn of Indian Chambers of Commerce and Industry, 1928–29. Member: East Indian Railway Adv. Cttee, 1939–40; Bihar Labour Enquiry Cttee, 1937–39; UP and Bihar Power Alcohol Cttee, 1938; UP and Bihar Sugar Control Board, 1938; Western Railway Adv. Cttee, Bombay, 1950–52; Small Scale Industries Export Prom. Adv. Cttee; Technical Adviser, Indian Tariff Board, 1947. Hon. Prof., Sydenham Coll. of Commerce, 1943–50. Member: All India Council of Tech. Educn, 1948–73; All India Bd of Studies in Commerce, 1948–70; All India Bd of Management Studies, 1978–84; Indian Merchants Chamber Cttee, 1945–83; Indian Council of Agriculture Res., 1959–66; Senate and Syndicate, Bombay Univ., 1957–69; Dean, Commerce Faculty, Bombay Univ., 1966–67. Director: E India Cotton Assoc., 1953–73 and 1983–84; Bombay Oils & Oilseeds Exchange, 1972–74; Bombay Yarn Exchange, 1972–75. Member: All-India Handloom Bd, 1952–58; Central Silk Bd, 1954–60; Handloom Export Adv. Council, 1965–68; Small-Scale Industries Bd, 1965–69. National FAO Liaison Cttee, 1974–76. Hon. Metropolitan Magistrate, Bombay, 1947–84; JP 1951–68. Swadeshi Prachar Sanuti, 1930–36. *Publications:* (with a foreword by Mahatma Gandhi) How to Compete with Foreign Cloth, 1931; The Indian Sugar Industry: Its Past, Present and Future, 1934; The Indian Cotton Textile Industry-Its Past, Present and Future, 1937; The Indian Sugar Industry (annually, 1935–64); The Indian Cotton Textile Industry, (annually, 1936–60); Centenary Volume of the Indian Cotton Textile Industry, 1851–1950; Problems of Sugar Industry in India, 1946; Monograph on Handloom Weaving in India, 1953; Some

Impressions of Japan, 1955; What I learnt from the Mahatma including the Twelve Letters of Mahatma Gandhi to M. P. Gandhi, 1930–32, with reminiscences, 1991. *Recreations*: tennis, badminton, billiards, bridge, swimming. *Address*: Giri Kunj, 3rd Floor, 11 Patkar Marg, Bombay 400007, India. *T*: (home) 8228405; 8124235. *Clubs*: Radio, National Sports, Rotary, Fifty-Five Tennis, Garden (Bombay).

GANDY, Christopher Thomas; HM Diplomatic Service, retired; *b* 21 April 1917; *s* of late Dr Thomas H. Gandy and late Mrs Ida Gandy (authoress of A Wiltshire Childhood, Around the Little Steeple, etc); unmarried. *Educ*: Marlborough; King's Coll., Cambridge. On active service with Army and RAF, 1939–45. Entered Foreign Office, Nov. 1945; Tehran, 1948–51; Cairo, 1951–52; FO, 1952–54; Lisbon, 1954–56; Libya, 1956–59; FO, 1960–62; apptd HM Minister to The Yemen, 1962, subsequently Counsellor, Kuwait; Minister (Commercial) Rio de Janeiro, 1966–68. Sen. Associate Mem., St Antony's Coll., Oxford, 1973–. *Publications*: articles in Asian Affairs, Middle East International, The New Middle East, The Annual Register of World Events, Art International, Arts of Asia, Jl of Royal Asiatic Soc., and Financial Times. *Recreations*: music, photography, gardening. *Address*: 60 Ambleside Drive, Headington, Oxford OX3 0AH. *Club*: Travellers'.

GANDY, David Stewart, CB 1989; OBE 1981; Deputy Director of Public Prosecutions and Chief Executive, Crown Prosecution Service, since 1987; *b* 19 Sept. 1932; *s* of Percy Gandy and Elizabeth Mary (*née* Fox); *m* 1956, Mabel Sheldon; one *s* one *d*. *Educ*: Manchester Grammar Sch.; Manchester Univ. Nat. Service, Intell. Corps (Germany and Austria), 1954–56. Admitted Solicitor, 1954; Asst Solicitor, Town Clerk, Manchester, 1956–59; Chief Prosecuting Solicitor: Manchester, 1959–68; Manchester and Salford, 1968–74; Gtr Manchester, 1974–85; Head of Field Management, Crown Prosecution Service, 1985–87. Lect. tour on English Criminal Justice System, for Amer. Bar Assoc., USA and Canada, 1976. Law Society: Mem., Criminal Law Standing Cttee, 1969–; Mem., Council, 1984–; Prosecuting Solicitors' Society of England and Wales: Mem., Exec. Council, 1966–85; Pres., 1976–78; Chm., Heads of Office, 1982–83; President: Manchester Law Soc., 1980–81; Manchester and Dist Medico-Legal Soc., 1982–84; Manchester Trainee Lawyers Gp, 1982–84. Mem. Council, Order of St John, 1978–85. *Recreations*: cricket, theatre, bridge, walking. *Address*: (office) 4–12 Queen Anne's Gate, SW1H 9AZ.

GANDY, Ronald Herbert; Treasurer to the Greater London Council, 1972–77, retired; Hon. Treasurer, UK and Ireland Group, World Conference on Religion and Peace, since 1980; *b* 22 Nov. 1917; *s* of Frederick C. H. Gandy and Olive (*née* Wilson) *m* 1942, Patricia M. Turney; two *s* one *d*. *Educ*: Banister Court Sch. and Taunton's Sch. (now Taunton's Coll.), Southampton. Town Clerk's Dept, Civic Centre, Southampton County Borough Council, 1936; LCC: Admin. Officer, Comptroller's (i.e. Treasurer's) Dept, 1937; Asst Comptroller, 1957; Dep. Comptroller, 1964; Dep. Treasurer, GLC, 1965; Dep. Chief Financial Officer, Inner London Educn Authority, 1967. Mem. CIPFA. *Address*: Braemar, 4 Roughwood Close, Watford, Herts WD1 3HN. *T*: Watford (0923) 224215.

GANE, Barrie Charles, CMG 1988; OBE 1978; HM Diplomatic Service; Counsellor, Foreign and Commonwealth Office, since 1982; *b* 19 Sept. 1935; *s* of Charles Ernest Gane and Margaret Gane; *m* 1974, Jennifer Anne Pitt; two *d* of former marriage. *Educ*: King Edward's School, Birmingham; Corpus Christi College, Cambridge. MA. Foreign Office, 1960; served Vientiane, Sarawak, Kuching and Warsaw; First Sec., Kampala, 1967; FCO, 1970; First Sec., later Counsellor, seconded to HQ British Forces, Hong Kong, 1977. *Recreations*: walking, reading. *Address*: c/o Foreign and Commonwealth Office, SW1A 2AH. *T*: 071–233 3000. *Club*: Brooks's.

GANE, Michael, DPhil, MA; economic and environmental consultant; *b* 29 July 1927; *s* of late Rudolf E. Gane and Helen Gane; *m* 1954, Madge Stewart Taylor; one *d*. *Educ*: Colyton Grammar Sch., Devon; Edinburgh Univ. (BSc Forestry 1948); London Univ. (BSc Econ 1963); Oxford Univ. (DPhil, MA 1967). Asst Conservator of Forests, Tanganyika, 1948–62; Sen. Research Officer, Commonwealth Forestry Inst., Oxford, 1963–69; Dir, Project Planning Centre for Developing Countries, Bradford Univ., 1969–74; Dir, England, Nature Conservancy Council, 1974–81. *Publications*: various contribs to scientific and technical jls. *Recreations*: natural history, gardening. *Address*: Millgreen, Kilmington, Axminster, Devon EX13 7HE.

GANELLIN, Charon Robin, PhD, DSc, FRS 1986; CChem, FRSC; Smith Kline and French Professor of Medicinal Chemistry, University College London, since 1986; *b* 25 Jan. 1934; *s* of Leon Ganellin and Beila Cluer; *m* 1956, Tamara Greene; one *s* one *d*. *Educ*: Harrow County Grammar School for Boys; Queen Mary Coll., London Univ. (BSc, PhD, DSc). Res. Associate, MIT, 1960; Res. Chemist, then Dept Hd in Medicinal Chem., Smith Kline & French Labs Ltd, 1958–59, 1961–75; Smith Kline & French Research Ltd: Dir, Histamine Res., 1975–80; Vice-President: Research, 1980–84; Chem. Res., 1984–86. Hon. Lectr, Dept of Pharmacol., UCL, 1975–; Hon. Prof. of Medicinal Chem., Univ. of Kent at Canterbury, 1979–. Tilden Lectr, RSC, 1982. Chm., Soc. for Drug Res., 1985–87; Hon. Mem., Soc. Española de Quimica Terapeutica, 1982. Medicinal Chem. Award, RSC, 1977; Prix Charles Mentzer, Soc. de Chimie Therap., 1978; Div. of Medicinal Chem. Award, ACS, 1980; Messel Medal, SCI, 1988; Award for Drug Discovery, Soc. for Drug Res., 1989; USA Nat. Inventors' Hall of Fame. 1990. *Publications*: Pharmacology of Histamine Receptors, 1982; Frontiers in Histamine Research, 1985; res. papers and reviews in various jls, incl. Jl Med. Chem., Jl Chem. Soc., Brit. Jl Pharmacol. *Recreations*: music, sailing, walking. *Address*: Department of Chemistry, University College London, 20 Gordon Street, WC1H 0AJ.

GANILAU, Ratu Sir Penaia Kanatabatu, GCMG 1983 (CMG 1968); KCVO 1982 (CVO 1970); KBE 1974 (OBE 1960); DSO 1956; ED 1974; President of the Republic of Fiji, since 1987; *b* 28 July 1918; Fijian; *m* 1st, 1949, Adi Laisa Delaisomosomo Yavaca (decd); five *s* two *d*; 2nd, 1975, Adi Asilina Davila Liliwaimanu Vunivalu (decd); 3rd, 1985, Veniana Bale Cagilaba. *Educ*: Provincial Sch. Northern; Queen Victoria Meml Sch., Fiji. Devonshire Course for Admin. Officers, Wadham Coll., Oxford Univ., 1947. Served with FIR, 1940; demobilised, retained rank of Captain, 1946. Colonial Admin. Service, 1947; District Officer, 1948–53; Mem. Cttee on Fijian Post Primary Educn in the Colony, 1953. Service with Fiji Mil. Forces, 1953–56; demobilised, retained rank of Temp. Lt-Col, 1956; Hon. Col, 2nd Bn (Territorial), FIR, 1973. Seconded to post of Fijian Econ. Develt Officer and Roko Tui Cakaudrove conjoint, 1956; Tour Manager and Govt Rep., Fiji Rugby football tour of NZ, 1957; Dep. Sec. for Fijian Affairs, 1961; Minister for Fijian Affairs and Local Govt, 1965; Leader of Govt Business and Minister for Home Affairs, Lands and Mineral Resources, 1970; Minister for Communications, Works and Tourism, 1972; Dep. Prime Minister, 1973–83; Minister for: Home Affairs, 1975–83; Fijian Affairs and Rural Develt, 1977–83; Governor-Gen., 1983–87. Member: House of Representatives; Council of Ministers; Official Mem., Legislative Council; Chairman: Fijian Affairs Bd; Fijian Develt Fund Bd; Native Land Trust Bd; Great Council of Chiefs. KStJ 1983. *Recreation*: Rugby football (rep. Fiji against Maori All Black, 1938 and during Rugby tour of NZ, 1939). *Address*: Office of the President, Suva, Republic of Fiji. *Clubs*: Fiji, Defence (Suva, Fiji).

GANZ, Prof. Peter Felix; Professor of German, University of Oxford, 1972–85, now Emeritus; *b* 3 Nov. 1920; *s* of Dr Hermann and Dr Charlotte Ganz; *m* 1st, 1949, Rosemary (*née* Allen) (*d* 1986); two *s* two *d*; 2nd, 1987, Prof. Nicolette Mout, Univ. of Leiden. *Educ*: Realgymnasium, Mainz; King's Coll., London. MA 1950; PhD 1954; MA Oxon 1960. Army service, 1940–45. Asst Lectr, Royal Holloway Coll., London Univ., 1948–49; Lectr, Westfield Coll., London Univ., 1949–60; Reader in German, 1960–72; Fellow of Hertford Coll., Oxford Univ., 1963–72 (Hon. Fellow, 1977); Fellow of St Edmund Hall, 1972–85, now Emeritus Fellow; Resident Fellow, Herzog August Bibliothek, Wolfenbüttel, W Germany, 1985–88. Vis. Professor: Erlangen-Nürnberg Univ., 1964–65 and 1971; Munich Univ., 1970 and 1974. Comdr, Order of Merit, Germany, 1973. Jt Editor: Beiträge zur Geschichte der deutschen Sprache und Literatur, 1976–90; Oxford German Studies, 1978–90. *Publications*: Der Einfluss des Englischen auf den deutschen Wortschatz 1740–1815, 1957; Geistliche Dichtung des 12. Jahrhunderts, 1960; Graf Rudolf, 1964; (with F. Norman and W. Schwarz) Dukus Horant, 1964; (with W. Schröder) Probleme mittelalterlicher Überlieferung und Textkritik, 1967; Jacob Grimm's Conception of German Studies, 1973; Gottfried von Strassburgs 'Tristan', 1978; Jacob Burckhardt, Über das Studium der Geschichte, 1981; articles on German medieval literature and language in jls. *Recreations*: music, walking, travel. *Address*: Flat 2, 21 Bardwell Road, Oxford OX2 6SU; Oranje Nassaulaan 27, 2361 LB Warmond, Netherlands.

GANZONI, family name of **Baron Belstead**.

GAON, Dr Solomon; Haham (Chief Rabbi) of the Communities affiliated to the World Sephardi Federation in the Diaspora, since 1978; *b* 15 Dec. 1912; *s* of Isaac and Rachael Gaon; *m* 1944, Regina Hassan; one *s* one *d*. *Educ*: Jesuit Secondary Sch., Travnik, Yugoslavia; Jewish Teachers Seminary, Sarajevo, Yugoslavia; Jews' Coll., London Univ. (BA 1941, PhD 1943; Rabbinic Dip. 1948). Spanish and Portuguese Jews Congregation: Student Minister, 1934–41; Asst Minister, 1941–44; Minister, 1944–46; Sen. Minister, 1946–49; Haham of Spanish and Portuguese Jews Congregation and Associated Sephardi Congregations, 1949–77; Haham (Chief Rabbi), Assoc. of Sephardi Congregations, 1977–80. Pres., Union of Sephardi Communities of England, N America and Canada, 1969–; Vice-Pres., World Sephardi Fedn, 1965–. Prof. of Sephardi Studies, Yeshiva Univ., New York, 1970–, Head of Sephardi Dept, 1977–. Hon. DD Yeshiva Univ., 1974. Alfonso el Sabio (for Cultural Work with and on Spanish Jewry), Spain, 1964. *Publications*: Influence of Alfonso Tostado on Isaac Abravanel, 1944; The Development of Jewish Prayer, 1949; Relations between the Spanish & Portuguese Synagogue in London and its Sister Congregation in New York, 1964; (ed) Book of Prayer of the Spanish & Portuguese Jews' Congregation, London, 1965; Edgar Joshua Nathan, Jr (1891–1965), 1965; Abravanel and the Renaissance, 1974; The Contribution of the English Sephardim to Anglo-Jewry, 1975; Minhath Shelomo, Commentary on Book of Prayer of Spanish & Portuguese Jews, 1990. *Recreations*: walking, tennis, music. *Address*: Barclays Bank, 53 Maida Vale, W9.

GARCIA, Arthur, CBE 1989; Judge of the High Court, Hong Kong, 1979–89; Commissioner for Administrative Complaints, Hong Kong, since 1989; *b* 3 July 1924; *s* of late F. M. Garcia and of Maria Fung; *m* 1948, Hilda May; two *s*. *Educ*: La Salle Coll., Hong Kong; Inns of Court Sch. of Law. Called to the Bar, Middle Temple, 1957. Jun. Clerk, Hong Kong Govt, 1939–41; Staff Mem., British Consulate, Macao, 1942–45; Clerk to Attorney Gen., Hong Kong, 1946–47; Asst Registrar, 1951–54; Colonial Develt and Welfare Scholarship, Inns of Court Sch. of Law, 1954–57; Legal Asst, Hong Kong, 1957–59; Magistrate, 1959; Sen. Magistrate, 1968; Principal Magistrate, 1968; Dist Judge, 1971. *Recreations*: photography, swimming. *Address*: 6th Floor, East Tower, Hennessy Centre, 500 Hennessy Road, Hong Kong. *Club*: Royal Hong Kong Jockey (Hong Kong).

GARCÍA MÁRQUEZ, Gabriel; *see* Márquez.

GARCÍA-PARRA, Jaime; Gran Cruz, Orden de San Carlos, Colombia, 1977; Gran Cruz de Boyacá, Colombia, 1981; Ambassador of Columbia to the United States of America, since 1990; *b* 19 Dec. 1931; *s* of Alfredo García-Cadena and Elvira Parra; *m* 1955, Lillian Duperly; three *s*. *Educ*: Gimnasio Moderno, Bogotá, Colombia; Univ. Javeriana, Bogotá; Univ. la Gran Colombia, Bogotá; Syracuse Univ., USA (MA); LSE, London (MSc). Lawyer. Minister (Colombian Delegn) to Internat. Coffee Org., 1963–66; Finance Vice-Pres., Colombian Nat. Airlines AVIANCA, 1966–69; Consultant in private practice, 1969–74; Actg Labour and Social Security Minister and Minister of Communications, 1974–75; Minister of Mines and Energy, 1975–77; Ambassador of Colombia to UK, 1977–78; Minister of Finance, Colombia, 1978–81; Exec. Dir, World Bank, 1981–82; Senator, Colombia, 1982; Pres. and Chief Exec. Officer, Acerías Paz del Río, steel and cement, 1982–90. Mem., several delegns to UNCTAD and FAO Confs at Geneva, 1964, New Delhi, 1968, Rome, 1970, 1971. Hon. Fellow, LSE, 1980. Gran Cruz, Orden del Baron de Rio Branco, Brasil, 1977. *Publications*: essays: La Inflación y el Desarrollo de América Latina (Inflation and Development in Latin America), 1968; La Estrategia del Desarrollo Colombiano (The Strategy of Colombian Development), 1971; El Problema Inflacionario Colombiano (Colombia's Inflationary Problem), 1972; Petróleo un Problema y una Política (Oil—a Problem and a Policy), 1975; El Sector Eléctrico en la Encrucijada (The Electrical Sector at the Cross-Roads), 1975; Una Política para el Carbón (A Policy for Coal), 1976; La Cuestión Cafetera (The Coffee Dilemma), 1977; Política Agraria (Agrarian Policy), 1977. *Recreations*: walking, reading, poetry, tennis, cooking. *Address*: Apartado Aéreo 12025, Bogotá, Colombia. *Clubs*: Jockey, Country (Bogotá).

GARDAM, David Hill, QC 1968; *b* 14 Aug. 1922; *s* of late Harry H. Gardam, Hove, Sussex; *m* 1954, Jane Mary Gardam, *qv*; two *s* one *d*. *Educ*: Oundle Sch.; Christ Church, Oxford. MA 1948. War Service, RNVR, 1941–46 (Temp. Lieut). Called to the Bar, Inner Temple, 1949; Bencher 1977. *Recreation*: painting. *Address*: 1 Atkin Building, Gray's Inn, WC1R 5BQ. *T*: 071–404 0102; Haven House, Sandwich, Kent.

GARDAM, Jane Mary; novelist; *d* of William Pearson, Coatham Sch., Redcar and Kathleen Mary Pearson (*née* Helm); *m* 1954, David Hill Gardam, *qv*; two *s* one *d*. *Educ*: Saltburn High Sch. for Girls; Bedford Coll., London Univ. Red Cross Travelling Librarian, Hospital Libraries, 1951; Sub-Editor, Weldon's Ladies Jl, 1952; Asst Literary Editor, Time and Tide, 1952–54. FRSL 1976. *Publications*: A Long Way From Verona, 1971; The Summer After The Funeral, 1973; Bilgewater, 1977; God on the Rocks, 1978 (Prix Baudelaire, 1989); The Hollow Land (Whitbread Literary Award), 1981; Bridget and William, 1981; Horse, 1982; Kit, 1983; Crusoe's Daughter, 1985; Kit in Boots, 1986; Swan, 1987; Through the Doll's House Door, 1987; *short stories*: A Few Fair Days, 1971; Black Faces, White Faces (David Highams Award, Winifred Holtby Award), 1975; The Sidmouth Letters, 1980; The Pangs of Love, 1983 (Katherine Mansfield Award, 1984); Showing the Flag, 1989; The Queen of the Tambourine, 1991. *Recreation*: trying to grow roses and lilies. *Address*: Haven House, Sandwich, Kent. *Clubs*: University Women's, Arts, PEN.

GARDEN, Air Vice-Marshal Timothy; Assistant Chief of Air Staff, since 1991; *b* 23 April 1944; *s* of Joseph Garden and Winifred M. Garden (*née* Mayes); *m* 1965, Susan Elizabeth Button; two *d. Educ:* King's Sch., Worcester; St Catherine's Coll., Oxford (MA 1967); Magdalene Coll., Cambridge (MPhil 1982). Joined RAF 1963; Pilot, 3 Sqn, 1967–71; Flying Instructor, 1972–75; Army Staff Coll., 1976; PSO to Air Mem. for Personnel, 1977–79; OC 50 Sqn, 1979–81; Dir Defence Studies RAF, 1982–85; Station Comdr RAF Odiham, 1985–87; Asst Dir, Defence Programmes, 1987–88; Dir Air Force Staff Duties, 1988–90. Mem. Council, RUSI, 1984–87. Governor, King's Sch., Worcester, 1986–. *Publications:* Can Deterrence Last?, 1984; The Technology Trap: science and the military, 1989; contribs to books and jls on defence. *Recreations:* writing, bridge, photography, computing. *Address:* Ministry of Defence, Room 6243, Whitehall, SW1A 2HB. *T:* 071–218 6316. *Club:* Royal Air Force.

GARDINER, Duncan; *see* Gardiner, J. D. B.

GARDINER, Sir George (Arthur), Kt 1990; MP (C) Reigate, since Feb. 1974; *b* 3 March 1935; *s* of Stanley and Emma Gardiner; *m* 1st, 1961, Juliet Wells (marr. diss. 1980); two *s* one *d*; 2nd, 1980, Helen Hackett. *Educ:* Harvey Grammar Sch., Folkestone; Balliol Coll., Oxford. 1st cl. hons PPE. Sec., Oxford Univ. Conservative Assoc., 1957. Chief Political Corresp., Thomson Regional Newspapers, 1964–74. Member: Select Cttee on Home Affairs and its Sub-Cttee on Race Relations and Immigration, 1979–82; Exec., 1922 Cttee, 1987–; Sec., Cons. European Affairs Cttee, 1976–79, Vice-Chm., 1979–80, Chm., 1980–87; Vice-Chm., Cons. For. and Commonwealth Affairs Cttee, 1988–. Editor, Conservative News, 1972–79. Contested (C) Coventry South, 1970. *Publications:* The Changing Life of London, 1973; Margaret Thatcher: from childhood to leadership, 1975. *Address:* House of Commons, SW1.

GARDINER, Dame Helen (Louisa), DBE 1961 (CBE 1952); MVO 1937; *b* 24 April 1901; *y d* of late Henry Gardiner, Bristol. *Educ:* Clifton High School. Formerly in Private Secretary's Office, Buckingham Palace; Chief Clerk, 1946–61. *Recreations:* reading, gardening. *Address:* Higher Courlands, Lostwithiel, Cornwall.

GARDINER, (John) Duncan (Broderick); author and broadcaster; Editor, Western Mail, 1974–81; *b* 12 Jan. 1937; *s* of late Frederick Keith Gardiner and Ruth Dixon; *m* 1965, Geraldine Mallen; one *s* one *d. Educ:* St Edward's School, Oxford. Various editorial positions in Sheffield, Newcastle, Sunday Times, London (1963–64, 1966–73) and Cardiff. *Recreations:* travel, all sport, wine and food, crosswords. *Address:* 145 Pencisely Road, Llandaff, Cardiff.

GARDINER, John Eliot, CBE 1990; conductor; Founder and Artistic Director, English Baroque Soloists, Monteverdi Choir and Monteverdi Orchestra; Chef fondateur, Opéra de Lyon, since 1988 (Musical Director, 1983–88); Principal Conductor, North German Radio Orchestra, since 1991; *b* 20 April 1943; *s* of Rolf Gardiner and late Marabel Gardiner (*née* Hodgkin); *m* 1981, Elizabeth Suzanne Wilcock; three *d. Educ:* Bryanston Sch.; King's Coll., Cambridge (MA History); King's Coll., London (Certif. of Advanced Studies in Music, 1966). French Govt Scholarship to study in Paris and Fontainebleau with Nadia Boulanger, 1966–68. Founded: Monteverdi Choir, following performance of Monteverdi's Vespers of 1610, King's Coll. Chapel, Cambridge, 1964; Monteverdi Orchestra, 1968; English Baroque Soloists (period instruments), 1978; Orchestre Révolutionnaire et Romantique, 1990; Artistic Dir, Göttingen Handel Fest., 1981–90. Youngest conductor of Henry Wood Promenade Concert, Royal Albert Hall, 1968; Début with: Sadler's Wells Opera, London Coliseum, 1969; Royal Opera House, Covent Garden, 1973; Royal Festival Hall, 1972; Guest engagements conducting major European orchestras in Paris, Brussels, Geneva, Frankfurt, Dresden, Leipzig and London; US débuts: Dallas Symphony, 1981; San Francisco Symphony, 1982; Carnegie Hall, NY, 1988; European Music Festivals: Aix-en-Provence, Aldeburgh, Bath, Berlin, Edinburgh, Flanders, Holland, City of London, etc.; concert revivals in London of major dramatic works of Purcell, Handel and Rameau, including world première (staged) of Rameau's opera Les Boréades, Aix-en-Provence, 1982. Principal Conductor, CBC Vancouver Orchestra, 1980–83; Artistic Dir, Veneto Music Fest., 1986. Has made over 100 records ranging from Monteverdi and Mozart to Massenet, Rodrigo and Central American Percussion Music. Dr *hc* Univ. Lumière de Lyon, 1987. Grand Prix du Disque, 1978, 1979, 1980, 1984, 1985; Gramophone Awards for early music and choral music records, 1978, 1980, 1986, 1988, 1989; Prix Caecilia, 1982, 1983, 1985; Edison Award, 1982, 1986, 1987, 1988; Internat. Record Critics Award, 1983; Deutscher Schallplattenpreis, 1986; Arturo Toscanini Music Critics Award, 1985, 1986; IRCA Prize, Helsinki, 1987. Officier, Ordre des Arts et des Lettres (France), 1988. *Publications:* (ed) Claude le Jeune Hélas! Mon Dieu, 1971; contrib. to opera handbook on Gluck's Orfeo, 1980. *Recreations:* forestry, organic farming. *Address:* Gore Farm, Ashmore, Salisbury, Wilts SP5 5AR; 7 Pleydell Avenue, W6 0XX.

GARDINER, John Ralph, QC 1982; *b* 28 Feb. 1946; *s* of late Cyril Ralph Gardiner and of Mary Gardiner; *m* 1976, Pascal Mary Issard-Davies; one *d. Educ:* Bancroft's Sch., Woodford; Fitzwilliam Coll., Cambridge (BA (Law Tripos), MA, LLM). Called to the Bar, Middle Temple, 1968 (Harmsworth Entrance Scholar and Harmsworth Law Scholar); practice at the Bar, 1970–; Mem., Senate of Inns of Court and Bar, 1982–86 (Treasurer, 1985–86); Chm., Taxation and Retirement Benefits Cttee, Bar Council, 1982–85. *Publications:* contributor to Pinson on Revenue Law, 6th to 15th (1982) edns. *Recreations:* tennis, cricket, squash. *Address:* 11 New Square, Lincoln's Inn, WC2. *T:* 071–242 3981; Admiral's House, Admiral's Walk, Hampstead, NW3. *T:* 071–435 0597. *Club:* Cumberland Lawn Tennis.

GARDINER, Patrick Lancaster, FBA 1985; Fellow and Tutor in Philosophy, Magdalen College, Oxford, 1958–89, now Emeritus Fellow; *b* 17 March 1922; *s* of Clive and Lilian Gardiner; *m* 1955, Kathleen Susan Booth; two *d. Educ:* Westminster School; Christ Church, Oxford (MA). Army service (Captain), 1942–45. Lectr, Wadham College, Oxford, 1949–52; Fellow, St Antony's College, Oxford, 1952–58. Vis. Prof., Columbia Univ., NY, 1955. *Publications:* The Nature of Historical Explanation, 1952; (ed) Theories of History, 1959; Schopenhauer, 1963, 2nd edn 1972; (ed) Nineteenth Century Philosophy, 1969; (ed) The Philosophy of History, 1974; Kierkegaard, 1988; articles in philosophical and literary jls, anthologies. *Address:* The Dower House, Wytham, Oxford. *T:* Oxford (0865) 242205.

GARDINER, Peter Dod Robin; First Deputy Head, Stanborough School, Hertfordshire, since 1979; *b* 23 Dec. 1927; *s* of late Brig. R. Gardiner, CB, CBE; *m* 1959, Juliet Wright; one *s* one *d. Educ:* Radley College; Trinity Coll., Cambridge. Asst Master, Charterhouse, 1952–67, and Housemaster, Charterhouse, 1965–67; Headmaster, St Peter's School, York, 1967–79. *Publications:* (ed) Twentieth-Century Travel, 1963; (with B. W. M. Young) Intelligent Reading, 1964; (with W. A. Gibson) The Design of Prose, 1971. *Recreations:* reading, music, walking, acting. *Address:* Stanborough School, Lemsford Lane, Welwyn Garden City, Herts AL8 6YR.

GARDINER, Robert (Kweku Atta); Commissioner for Economic Planning, Ghana, 1975–78; *b* Kumasi, Ghana, 29 Sept. 1914; *s* of Philip H. D. Gardiner and Nancy Torraine Ferguson; *m* 1943, Linda Charlotte Edwards; one *s* two *d. Educ:* Adisadel Coll., Cape Coast, Ghana; Fourah Bay Coll., Sierra Leone; Selwyn Coll., Cambridge (BA); New Coll., Oxford. Lectr in Economics at Fourah Bay Coll., 1943–46; UN Trusteeship Dept, 1947–49; Dir, Extra-Mural Studies, University Coll., Ibadan, 1949–53; Dir, Dept of Social Welfare and Community Development, Gold Coast, 1953–55; Perm. Sec., Min. of Housing, 1955–57; Head of Ghana Civil Service, 1957–59; Dep. Exec. Sec., Economic Commn for Africa, 1959–60; Mem. Mission to the Congo, 1961; Dir Public Admin. Div., UN Dept of Economic and Social Affairs, 1961–62; Officer-in-Charge, UN Operation in the Congo, 1962–63; Exec. Sec., UN Economic Commn for Africa, Addis Ababa, 1962–75. Chm., Commonwealth Foundation, 1970–73. Reith Lectures, 1965; David Livingstone Vis. Prof. of Economics, Strathclyde, 1970–75; Vis. Prof. of Economics, 1974–75, and Consultant, Centre for Development Studies, 1974–77, Univ. of Cape Coast. Lectures: Gilbert Murray Meml, 1969; J. B. Danquah Meml, 1970; Aggrey-Fraser-Guggisberg Meml, 1972. Mem Professional Socs, and activities in internat. affairs. Hon. Fellow: Univ. of Ibadan; Selwyn Coll., Cambridge. Hon. DCL: East Anglia, 1966; Sierra Leone, 1969; Tuskegee Inst., 1969; Liberia, 1972; Hon. LLD: Bristol, 1966; Ibadan, 1967; E Africa, 1968; Haile Sellassie I Univ., 1972; Strathclyde, 1973; Hon. PhD Uppsala, 1966; Hon. DSc: Kumasi, 1968; Bradford, 1969. *Publications:* (with Helen Judd) The Development of Social Administration, 1951, 2nd edn 1959; A World of Peoples (BBC Reith Lectures), 1965. *Recreations:* golf, music, reading, walking. *Address:* PO Box 9274, The Airport, Accra, Ghana.

GARDINER, Victor Alec, OBE 1977; consultant, film and television programme production, facilities and distribution; Director and General Manager, London Weekend Television, 1971–87; *b* 9 Aug. 1929; *m*; one *s* two *d. Educ:* Whitgift Middle Sch., Croydon; City and Guilds (radio and telecommunications). Techn. Asst, GPO Engrg, 1947–49; RAF Nat. Service, 1949–51; BBC Sound Radio Engr, 1951–53; BBC TV Cameraman, 1953–55; Rediffusion TV Sen. Cameraman, 1955–61; Malta TV Trng Man., 1961–62; Head of Studio Prodn, Rediffusion TV, 1962–67; Man. Dir, GPA Productions, 1967–69; Production Controller, London Weekend Television, 1969–71; Director: LWT (Hldgs) Ltd, 1976–87; London Weekend Services Ltd, 1976–87; Richard Price Television Associates, 1981–87; Chairman: Dynamic Technology Ltd, 1972–87; Standard Music Ltd, 1972–87; LWT Internat., 1981–87. Mem., Royal Television Soc., 1970– (Vice-Chm. Council, 1974–75; Chm. Papers Cttee, 1975; Chm. Council, 1976–77; Fellow, 1977). *Recreations:* music, building, gardening.

GARDINER-SCOTT, Rev. William, OBE 1974; MA; Emeritus Minister of Scots Memorial Church and Hospice, Jerusalem; *b* 23 February 1906; *o s* of late William Gardiner Scott, Portsoy, Banffshire; *m* 1953, Darinka Milo, *d* of late Milo Glogovac, Oakland, Calif; one *d. Educ:* Grange School, Bo'ness, West Lothian; Edinburgh University and New College, Edinburgh. In catering business, 1926–30; graduated in Arts, Edin., 1934; Theological Travel Scholarship to Palestine, 1936; travelled as ship's steward to America and India, 1936; ordained to Ministry of Church of Scotland, 1939; Sub-Warden 1939, Deputy Warden 1940, New College Settlement, Edinburgh; enlisted as Army Chaplain, 1941; served in Egypt, 1942–44 and developed community centre at RA Depot, Cairo and initiated publication of weekly Scots newspaper, The Clachan Crack; founded Montgomery House, Alexandria, as community centre for all ranks of allied troops, 1943; served in Palestine as Church of Scotland Chaplain for Galilee and district, 1944–46; Senior Chaplain at Scottish Command, 1946–47; Warden of Student Movement House, London, 1947–49; Chaplain at Victoria Univ. Coll., Wellington, NZ, 1950–54; locum tenens St John's West Church, Leith, 1955; Minister of Church of Scotland, Jerusalem, 1955–60 and 1966–73; Parish of Abernethy, 1960–66. ChStJ. Distinguished Citizen of Jerusalem. *Recreations:* travel, gardening, cooking, walking. *Address:* Scots Memorial Church and Hospice, PO Box 14216, Jerusalem, Israel.

GARDINI, Dr Raul; industrialist and financier; *b* 7 June 1933; *m* Idina Ferruzzi; one *s* two *d.* Chm., Serafino Ferruzzi Srl, controlling Ferruzzi Finanziaria, internat. industrial and service system operating, through Montedison, in chemical, pharmaceutical, energy and agro-industrial sectors worldwide and directly in engineering, construction, insurance and financial services. Mem., European Round Table. Won World Yachts Championship, 1988; America's Cup challenger, 1992; Pres., European America's Cup Class Assoc. *Recreation:* yachting. *Address:* Piazza Belgioioso 2, 20121 Milan, Italy. *T:* (2) 62705210.

GARDNER, family name of **Baroness Gardner of Parkes.**

GARDNER OF PARKES, Baroness *cr* 1981 (Life Peer), of Southgate, Greater London, and of Parkes, NSW; **(Rachel) Trixie (Anne) Gardner;** JP; dental surgeon; Director, Woolwich Building Society, since 1988; *b* Parkes, NSW, 17 July 1927; eighth *c* of late Hon. J. J. Gregory McGirr and late Rachel McGirr, OBE, LC; *m* 1956, Kevin Anthony Gardner, *o s* of George and Rita Gardner, Sydney, Australia; three *d. Educ:* Monte Sant Angelo Coll., N Sydney; East Sydney Technical Coll.; Univ. of Sydney (BDS 1954). Cordon Bleu de Paris, Diplôme 1956. Came to UK, 1955. Member: Westminster City Council, 1968–78 (Lady Mayoress, 1987–88); GLC, for Havering, 1970–73, for Enfield-Southgate, 1977–86. Contested (C) Blackburn, 1970; N Cornwall, Feb. 1974. Vice-Chm., NE Thames RHA, 1990–; Member: Inner London Exec. Council, NHS, 1966–71; Standing Dental Adv. Cttee for England and Wales, 1968–76; Westminster, Kensington and Chelsea Area Health Authority, 1974–82; Industrial Tribunal Panel for London, 1974–; N Thames Gas Consumer Council, 1980–82; Dept of Employment's Adv. Cttee on Women's Employment, 1980–88; Britain–Australia Bicentennial Cttee, 1984–88; London Electricity Bd, 1984–90. British Chm., European Union of Women, 1978–82; UK Rep., UN Status of Women Commn, 1982–88. UK Chm., Plan International Ltd, 1990–; Dir, Gateway Building Soc., 1987–88. Governor: Eastman Dental Hosp., 1971–80; Nat. Heart Hosp., 1974–90. Hon. Pres., War Widows Assoc. of GB, 1984–87. JP North Westminster, 1971. *Recreations:* gardening, reading, travel, needlework. *Address:* House of Lords, SW1A 0PW.

GARDNER, Antony John; Registrar, Central Council for Education and Training in Social Work, since 1988 (Principal Registration Officer, 1970–88); *b* 27 Dec. 1927; *s* of David Gardner, head gardener, and Lillian Gardner; *m* 1956, Eveline A. Burden. *Educ:* Elem. school; Co-operative Coll.; Southampton Univ. Pres. Union, Southampton, 1958–59; BSc (Econ) 1959. Apprentice toolmaker, 1941–45; National Service, RASC, 1946–48; building trade, 1948–53. Tutor Organiser, Co-operative Union, 1959–60; Member and Education Officer, Co-operative Union, 1961–66. Contested (Lab): SW Wolverhampton, 1964; Beeston, Feb. and Oct. 1974; MP (Lab) Rushcliffe, 1966–70. *Recreations:* angling, gardening and the countryside generally. *Address:* 118 Ringwood Road, Parkstone, Poole, Dorset BH14 0RW. *T:* Poole (0202) 676683. *Club:* Parkstone Trades and Labour (Poole).

GARDNER, Prof. David Pierpont, PhD; President, University of California, since 1983; Professor of Education, University of California at Berkeley, since 1983; *b* 24 March 1933; *s* of Reed S. Gardner and Margaret (*née* Pierpont); *m* 1958, Elizabeth Fuhriman (*d* 1991); four *d. Educ:* Brigham Young Univ. (BS 1955); Univ. of Calif, Berkeley (MA 1959, PhD 1966). Dir, Calif Alumni Foundn and Calif Alumni Assoc.,

Univ. of Calif, Berkeley, 1962–64. University of California, Santa Barbara: Asst Prof. of Higher Educn, 1964–69; Associate Prof. of Higher Educn, 1969–70; Prof. of Higher Educn (on leave), 1971–73; Asst to the Chancellor, 1964–67; Asst Chancellor, 1967–69; Vice Chancellor and Exec. Asst, 1969–70; Vice Pres., Univ. of Calif, 1971–73; Pres., and Prof. of Higher Educn, Univ. of Utah, 1973–83, Pres. Emeritus, 1985. Vis. Fellow, Clare Hall, Univ. of Cambridge, 1979 (Associate 1979). Member: Nat. Acad. of Public Administration; Nat. Assoc. of State Univs. and Land Grant Colls; Assoc. of Amer. Univs; Council, Hong Kong Univ. of Sci. and Technology; Business–Higher Educn Forum; Amer. Philosophical Soc.; Nat. Acad. of Educn. Board of Directors: First Security Corp.; Fluor Corp.; George S. and Delores Dore Eccles Foundn; Nature Conservancy; Calif. Chamber of Commerce; Calif. Econ. Develt Corp. Trustee, Tanner Lectures on Human Values. Mem., Editl Bd, Higher Educn Qly. Fulbright 40th Anniversary Distinguished Fellow, Japan, 1986; Fellow, Amer. Acad. of Arts and Scis, 1986. Hon. LLD: Univ. of The Pacific, 1983; Nevada, Las Vegas, 1984; Westminster Coll., 1987; Brown, 1989; Notre Dame, 1989; Hon. DH Brigham Young, 1981; Hon. DLitt Utah, 1983; Hon. HHD Utah State, 1987; Hon. Dr Bordeaux II, 1988; Hon. DHL Internat. Christian Univ. Benjamin P. Cheney Medal, Eastern Washington Univ., 1984; James Bryant Conant Award, Educn Commn of the States, 1985; Hall of Fame Award, Calif. Sch. Bd Res Foundn, 1988. Chevalier, Légion d'Honneur (France), 1985. *Publications*: The California Oath Controversy, 1967; contrib. articles to professional jls. *Address*: (home) 70 Rincon Road, Kensington, Calif 94707, USA; (office) Office of the President, University of California, 300 Lakeside Drive, Oakland, Calif 94612–3550, USA.

GARDNER, Sir Douglas Bruce B.; *see* Bruce-Gardner.

GARDNER, Douglas Frank; Managing Director, Brixton Estate plc, since 1983; *b* 20 Dec. 1943; *s* of Ernest Frank Gardner and of late Mary Gardner; *m* 1978, Adèle (*née* Alexander); one *s* two *d*. *Educ*: Woolverstone Hall; College of Estate Management, London Univ. (BSc). FRICS. Chief Exec., Properties Div., Tarmac plc, 1976–83. *Recreations*: tennis. *Address*: 2 Woodstock Road, Bedford Park, Chiswick, W4 1UE. *T*: 081–994 0152.

GARDNER, Sir Edward (Lucas), Kt 1983; QC 1960; a Recorder of the Crown Court, 1972–85; *b* 10 May 1912; *s* of late Edward Walker Gardner, Fulwood, Preston, Lancs; *m* 1st, 1950, Noreen Margaret (marr. diss. 1962), *d* of late John Collins, Moseley, Birmingham; one *s* one *d*; 2nd, 1963, Joan Elizabeth, *d* of late B. B. Belcher, Bedford; one *s* one *d*. *Educ*: Hutton Grammar Sch. Served War of 1939–45: joined RNVR as ordinary seaman, 1940; served in cruisers, Mediterranean; commnd RNVR; Chief of Naval Information, E Indies, 1945. Journalist (free-lance; Lancashire Daily Post, then Daily Mail) prior to 1940; broadcasting and free-lance journalism, 1946–49; called to Bar, Gray's Inn, 1947; Master of the Bench of Gray's Inn, 1968; admitted to Nigerian and British Guianan Bars, 1962; has also appeared in Courts of Goa, High Court of Singapore, and Supreme Court of India. Deputy Chairman of Quarter Sessions: East Kent, 1961–71; County of Kent, 1962–71; Essex, 1968–71. Contested (C) Erith and Crayford, April 1955; MP (C): Billericay Div. of Essex, 1959–66; S Fylde, 1970–83; Fylde, 1983–87. PPS to Attorney-General, 1962–63. Chm., Select Cttee on Home Affairs, 1984–87. Chairman: Justice Working Party on Bail and Remands in Custody, 1966; Bar Council Cttee on Parly Privilege, 1967; Chm., Soc. of Cons. Lawyers, 1975–85 (Chm. Exec. Cttee, 1969–75; Chm., Cttee responsible for pamphlets, Rough Justice, on future of the Law, 1968, Crisis in Crime and Punishment, 1971, The Proper Use of Prisons, 1978, Who Do We Think We Are?, 1980, on need for new nationality law); Exec. Cttee, Justice, 1968. Member: Departmental Cttee on Jury Service, 1963; Cttee on Appeals in Criminal Cases, 1964; Commonwealth War Graves Commn, 1971–87. A Governor: Thomas Coram Foundn for Children, 1962–; Queenswood Sch., 1975–87. Steward, British Boxing Bd of Control, 1975–84. *Publication*: (part author) A Case for Trial (pamphlet recommending procedural reforms for committal proceedings implemented by Criminal Justice Act, 1967). *Recreation*: walking. *Address*: Sparrows, Hatfield Broad Oak, Bishop's Stortford, Herts CM22 7HN. *T*: Bishop's Stortford (0279) 70265. *Clubs*: Garrick, Pratt's, United and Cecil (Chm. 1970).

GARDNER, Rear-Adm. Herbert, CB 1976; Chartered Engineer; *b* 23 Oct. 1921; *s* of Herbert and Constance Gladys Gardner; *m* 1946, Catherine Mary Roe, Perth, WA. *Educ*: Taunton Sch.; Weymouth Coll. War of 1939–45; joined Dartmouth, 1940; RN Engineering Coll., Keyham, 1940; HMS Nigeria, Cumberland, Adamant, and 4th Submarine Sqdn, 1944; HM S/M Totem, 1945. Dept of Engr-in-Chief, 1947; HM S/M Telemachus, 1949; Admty Develt Establishment, Barrow-in-Furness, 1952; HMS Eagle, 1954; Comdr, 1956; HMS Caledonia, 1956; HMS Blackpool, 1958; Asst to Manager Engrg Dept, Rosyth Dockyard, 1960; HMS Maidstone, 1963; Capt., 1963; Dep. Manager, Engrg Dept, Devonport Dockyard, 1964; Chief Engr and Production Manager, Singapore Dockyard, 1967; Chief Staff Officer (Technical) to Comdr Far East Fleet, 1968; course at Imperial Defence Coll., 1970; Chief of Staff to C-in-C Naval Home Comd, 1971–73; Vice Pres., Ordnance Bd, 1974–76, Pres., 1976–77. *Recreations*: sailing, golf. *Address*: 41 Mayfair Street, Mount Claremont, Perth, WA 6010, Australia. *Club*: Royal Freshwater Bay Yacht (Perth).

GARDNER, James, CBE 1959; RDI 1947; Major RE; industrial designer and consultant; *b* 29 Dec. 1907; *s* of Frederic James Gardner; *m* 1935, Mary Williams; two *s*. *Educ*: Chiswick and Westminster Schools of Art. Jewellery Designer, Cartier Ltd, 1924–31. Served War of 1939–45, Chief Deception Officer, Army Camouflage, 1941–46. Designer, Britain Can Make It Exhibition, 1946; Chief Designer, Festival Gardens, Battersea, 1950; British Pavilion, Brussels, 1958; British Pavilion, Expo '67, Montreal; responsible for: Evoluon Museum, Eindhoven, Netherlands; St Helens Glass Museum, Lancs; main display Geological Museum, London, 1972; visual design of QE2 and sternwheeler Riverboat Mississippi Queen; Mus. of Diaspora, Tel Aviv; Mus. of Natural Sci., Taiwan. Sen. Fellow, RCA, 1987. Minerva Medal, as Designer of the Year, CSD, 1989. *Publication*: Elephants in the Attic, 1983. *Address*: The Studio, 144 Haverstock Hill, Hampstead, NW3 2AY.

GARDNER, James Jesse, CBE 1986; DL; consultant, since 1986; Chairman, North East Television, since 1991; *b* 7 April 1932; *s* of James and Elizabeth Rubina Gardner; *m* 1955, Diana Sotheran; three *s* one *d*. *Educ*: Kirkham Grammar Sch.; Victoria Univ., Manchester (LLB). Nat. Service, 1955–57. Articled to Town Clerk, Preston, 1952–55; Legal Asst, Preston Co. Borough Council, 1955; Crosby Borough Council: Asst Solicitor, 1957–59; Chief Asst Solicitor, 1959–61; Chief Asst Solicitor, Warrington Co. Borough Council, 1961–65; Stockton-on-Tees Borough Council: Dep. Town Clerk, 1966; Town Clerk, 1966–68; Asst Town Clerk, Teesside Co. Borough Council, 1968; Associate Town Clerk and Solicitor, London Borough of Greenwich, 1968–69; Town Clerk and Chief Exec. Officer, Co. Borough of Sunderland, 1970–73; Chief Exec., Tyne and Wear CC, 1973–86; Chm., Tyne and Wear PTE, 1983–86. Chief Exec., Northern Develt Co. Ltd, 1986–87; Chairman: Sunderland DHA, 1988–90; Northumbrian Water Customer Services Cttee, 1990–; Dir, Birtley Enterprise Action Management (BEAM) Ltd, 1989–; Sec., Northern Region Councils Assoc., 1986. Clerk to Lieutenancy, Tyne and Wear, 1974–. Chairman: Prince's Trust, 1986–; Royal Jubilee Trusts, 1989– (former Chm., Northumbria Cttee, Royal Jubilee and Prince's Trusts); Prince's Trust Events Ltd, 1987–; Dir, NE Civic Trust, 1986–; Trustee, Tyne Tees Telethon Trust, 1988–. DL Tyne and Wear, 1976. FRSA 1976; Hon. Fellow, Sunderland Polytechnic, 1986. *Recreations*: golf, music, theatre, food and drink. *Address*: Wayside, 121 Queen Alexandra Road, Sunderland, Tyne and Wear SR2 9HR. *T*: 091–528 2525.

GARDNER, (James) Piers; Director, British Institute of International and Comparative Law, since 1989 (Executive Director, 1987–89); *b* 26 March 1954; *s* of Michael Clement Gardner and Brigitte Elsa Gardner (*née* Ekrut); *m* 1978, Penelope Helen Chloros; two *s* one *d*. *Educ*: Bryanston Sch.; Brasenose Coll., Oxford (MA Jurisp. 1st Class). Articled and in private practice as solicitor, with Stephenson Harwood, London, 1977–80; Secretariat, European Commn of Human Rights, Council of Europe, Strasbourg, 1980–87. *Recreations*: foreign property, arguing. *Address*: British Institute of International and Comparative Law, Charles Clore House, 17 Russell Square, WC1B 5DR. *T*: 071–636 5802. *Club*: Athenæum.

GARDNER, John Linton, CBE 1976; composer; *b* 2 March 1917; *s* of late Dr Alfred Gardner, Ilfracombe, and Muriel (*née* Pullein-Thompson); *m* 1955, Jane, *d* of late N. J. Abercrombie; one *s* two *d*. *Educ*: Eagle House, Sandhurst; Wellington Coll.; Exeter Coll., Oxford (BMus). Served War of 1939–45: RAF, 1940–46. Chief Music Master, Repton Sch., 1939–40. Staff, Covent Garden Opera, 1946–52; Tutor: Morley Coll., 1952–76 (Dir of Music, 1965–69); Bagot Stack Coll., 1955–62; London Univ. (extra-mural) 1959–60; Dir of Music, St Paul's Girls' Sch., 1962–75; Prof. of Harmony and Composition, Royal Acad. of Music, 1956–86. Conductor: Haslemere Musical Soc., 1953–62; Dorian Singers, 1961–62; European Summer Sch. for Young Musicians, 1966–75; Bromley YSO, 1970–76. Brit. Council Lecturer: Levant, 1954; Belgium, 1960; Iberia, 1963; Yugoslavia, 1967. Adjudicator, Canadian Festivals, 1974, 1980. Member: Arts Council Music Panel, 1958–62; Council, Composers' Guild, 1961– (Chm., 1963; Delegate to USSR, 1964); Cttee of Management, Royal Philharmonic Soc., 1965–72; Brit. Council Music Cttee, 1968. Dir, Performing Right Soc., 1965– (Dep. Chm., 1983–88). Worshipful Co. of Musicians: Collard Fellow, 1962–64; elected to Freedom and Livery, 1965. Hon. RAM 1959. Bax Society's Prize, 1958. *Works include*: *orchestral*: Symphony no 1, 1947; Variations on a Waltz of Carl Nielsen, 1952; Piano Concerto no 1, 1957; Sinfonia Piccola (strings), 1960; Occasional Suite, Aldeburgh Festival, 1968; An English Ballad, 1969; Three Ridings, 1970; Sonatina for Strings, 1974; Divertimento, 1977; Symphony no 2, 1984; Symphony no 3, 1989; Concerto for Oboe and Strings, 1990; *chamber*: Concerto da Camera (4 insts), 1968; Partita (solo 'cello), 1968; Chamber Concerto (organ and 11 insts), 1969; English Suite (harpsichord), 1971; Sonata Secolare for organ and brass, 1973; Sonata da Chiesa for two trumpets and organ; String Quartet, 1979; Hebdomade, 1980; Sonatina Lirica for brass, 1983; Triad, 1984; Quartet for Saxes, 1985; Oboe Sonata no 2, French Suite for Sax. 4tet, 1986; String Quartet no 3, 1987; Octad, 1987; Piano Sonata no 3, 1988; Larkin Songs, 1990; *ballet*: Reflection, 1952; *opera*: A Nativity Opera, 1950; The Moon and Sixpence, 1957; The Visitors, 1972; Bel and the Dragon, 1973; The Entertainment of the Senses, 1974; Tobermory, 1976; *musical*: Vile Bodies, 1961; *choral*: Cantiones Sacrae 1973; (sop., chor. and orch.), 1952; Jubilate Deo (unacc. chor.), 1957; The Ballad of the White Horse (bar., chor. and orch.), 1959; Herrick Cantata (ten. solo, chor. and orch.), 1961; A Latter-Day Athenian Speaks, 1962; The Noble Heart (sop., bass, chor. and orch.), Shakespeare Quatercentenary Festival, 1964; Cantor popularis vocis, 18th Schütz Festival Berlin, 1964; Mass in C (unacc. chor.), 1965; Cantata for Christmas (chor. and chamb. orch.), 1966; Proverbs of Hell (unacc. chor.), 1967; Cantata for Easter (soli, chor., organ and percussion), 1970; Open Air (chor. and brass band), 1976; Te Deum for Pigotts, 1981; Mass in D, 1983; many smaller pieces and music for films, Old Vic and Royal Shakespeare Theatres, BBC. *Publications*: contributor to: Dublin Review, Musical Times, Tempo, Composer, Listener, Music in Education, DNB. *Recreations*: jazz, bore-watching. *Address*: 20 Firswood Avenue, Ewell, Epsom, Surrey KT19 0PR. *T*: 081–393 7181.

GARDNER, Prof. John William; Miriam and Peter Haas Professor in Public Service, Stanford University, since 1989; *b* 8 Oct. 1912; *s* of William Frederick and Marie (Flora) Gardner; *m* 1934, Aida Marroquin; two *d*. *Educ*: Stanford Univ. (AB 1935, AM 1936); Univ. of Calif. (PhD 1938). 1st Lt-Captain, US Marine Corps, 1943–46. Teaching Asst in Psychology, Univ. of Calif., 1936–38; Instructor in Psychology, Connecticut Coll., 1938–40; Asst Prof. in Psychology, Mt Holyoke Coll., 1940–42; Head of Latin Amer. Section, Federal Communications Commn, 1942–43. Carnegie Corporation of New York: Staff Mem., 1946–47; Exec. Associate, 1947–49; Vice-Pres., 1949–55; Pres., 1955–67; Pres., Carnegie Foundn for Advancement of Teaching, 1955–67; Sec. of Health, Education and Welfare, 1965–68; Chairman: Urban Coalition, 1968–70; Common Cause, 1970–77; Independent Sector, 1980–83; US Adv. Commn on Internat. Educational and Cultural Affairs, 1962–64; Pres. Johnson's Task Force on Educn, 1964; White House Conf. on Educn, 1965; President's Commn on White House Fellowships, 1977–81. Senior Fellow, Aspen Inst., 1981–. Dir, Amer. Assoc. for Advancement of Science, 1963–65. Director: New York Telephone Co., 1962–65; Shell Oil Co., 1962–65; Time Inc., 1968–71; American Airlines, 1968–71; Rockefeller Brothers Fund, 1968–77; New York Foundn, 1970–76. Trustee: Metropolitan Museum of Art, 1957–65; Stanford Univ., 1968–82. Benjamin Franklin Fellow, RSA, 1964. Holds hon. degrees from various colleges and univs. USAF Exceptional Service Award, 1956; Presidential Medal of Freedom, 1964; Public Welfare Medal, Nat. Acad. of Science, 1967. *Publications*: Excellence, 1961, rev. edn 1984; (ed) Pres. John F. Kennedy's book, To Turn the Tide, 1961; Self-Renewal, 1964, rev. edn 1980; No Easy Victories, 1968; The Recovery of Confidence, 1970; In Common Cause, 1972; Know or Listen to Those who Know, 1975; Morale, 1978; Quotations of Wit and Wisdom, 1980; On Leadership, 1990. *Address*: Graduate School of Business, Stanford University, Stanford, Calif 94305–5015, USA.

GARDNER, Kenneth Burslam; Deputy Keeper of Oriental MSS and Printed Books, The British Library, 1974–86, retired; *b* 5 June 1924; *s* of D. V. Gardner; *m* 1949, Cleone Winifred Adams; two *s* two *d*. *Educ*: Alleyne's Grammar Sch., Stevenage; University College, London; School of Oriental and African Studies, Univ. of London (BA Hons Japanese). War service, Intelligence Corps (Captain), 1943–47. Assistant Librarian, School of Oriental and African Studies, 1949–54; Assistant Keeper, Department of Oriental Printed Books and MSS, British Museum, 1955–57, Keeper, 1957–70; Principal Keeper of Printed Books, British Museum (later The British Library), 1970–74. Order of the Sacred Treasure (3rd class), Japan, 1979. *Publications*: Edo jidai no sashie hangaka-tachi (in Japanese, on book illustration in Japan and related topics), 1977; Descriptive catalogue of Japanese books in the British Library printed before 1700, 1991; contrib. to jls of oriental studies, art and librarianship. *Address*: The Old Stables, 15 Farquhar Street, Bengeo, Hertford SG14 3BN. *T*: Hertford (0992) 583591.

GARDNER, Norman Keith Ayliffe; Senior Consultant, Baxter Eddie Ltd, since 1987; *b* 2 July 1925; *s* of late Charles Ayliffe Gardner and Winifred Gardner; *m* 1951, Margaret Patricia Vinson; one *s* one *d*. *Educ*: Cardiff High Sch.; University Coll., Cardiff (BScEng); College of Aeronautics, Cranfield; Univ. of London Commerce Degree Bureau (BScEcon Hons). CEng. Flight Test Observer, RAE, 1944; Test Observer, Westland Aircraft Ltd, 1946; Development Engr, Handley Page Ltd, 1950; Engr, Min. of Aviation, 1964;

Economic Adviser, Min. of Technology, 1970; Asst Dir (Engrg), DTI, 1973; Sen. Economic Adviser, 1974, Under Secretary: DoI, 1977; Dept of Employment, 1979; DTI, 1984–85. *Publications:* Decade of Discontent: the changing British economy, 1987; A Guide to United Kingdom and European Community Competition Policy, 1990; The Economics of Launching Aid, in The Economics of Industrial Subsidies (HMSO), 1976; papers in Jl Instn Prodn Engrs and other engrg jls. *Recreation:* music. *Address:* 15 Chanctonbury Way, N12 7JB. *T:* 081–445 4162.

GARDNER, Piers; *see* Gardner, J. P.

GARDNER, Ralph Bennett, MM 1944; Under Secretary (Legal), Treasury Solicitor's Department, 1976–82, retired; *b* 7 May 1919; *s* of late Ralph Wilson Gardner and Elizabeth Emma (*née* Nevitt-Bennett); *m* 1950, Patricia Joan Ward (*née* Bartlett); one *s* one *d. Educ:* Worksop Coll. Served War, 1939–46, RA. Admitted a solicitor, 1947; Solicitor, private practice, Chester, 1947–48; Legal Asst, Treasury Solicitor's Dept, 1948; Sen. Legal Asst, 1957; Asst Treas. Solicitor, 1972. Lord of the Manor of Shotwick, County of Chester (by inheritance, 1964). *Recreations:* gardening and local history. *Address:* Wychen, St Mary's Road, Leatherhead, Surrey KT22 8HB. *T:* Leatherhead (0372) 373161. *Club:* East India, Devonshire, Sports and Public Schools.

GARDNER, Prof. Richard Lavenham, PhD; FRS 1979; Hon. Director, Imperial Cancer Research Fund's Developmental Biology Unit, since 1986; Royal Society Henry Dale Research Professor, since 1978; Student of Christ Church, Oxford, since 1974; *b* 10 June 1943; *s* of late Allan Constant and Eileen May Gardner; *m* 1968, Wendy Joy Cresswell; one *s. Educ:* St John's Sch., Leatherhead; North East Surrey Coll. of Technology; St Catharine's Coll., Cambridge (BA 1st Cl. Hons Physiol., 1966; MA; PhD 1971). Res. Asst, Physiological Lab., Cambridge, 1970–73; Lectr in Developmental and Reproductive Biology, Dept of Zoology, Oxford Univ., 1973–77; Res. Student, Christ Church, Oxford, 1974–77. Scientific Medal, Zoological Soc. of London, 1977. *Publications:* contribs to Jl of Embryology and Experimental Morphology, Nature, Jl of Cell Science, and various other jls and symposia. *Recreations:* ornithology, music, sailing, painting, gardening. *Address:* Christ Church, Oxford OX1 1DP.

GARDNER, Robert Dickson Robertson, CBE 1978; Secretary, Greater Glasgow Health Board, 1974–85, retired; *b* 9 May 1924; *s* of Robert Gardner and Isabella McAlonan; *m* 1950, Ada Stewart; two *s* one *d.* Dep. Sec., 1962–66, Sec., 1966–74, Western Regional Hospital Board, Scotland. *Recreations:* swimming, Scottish country dancing, reading. *Address:* 3 Williamwood Drive, Glasgow G44 3TA. *T:* 041–637 8070.

GARDNER, William Maving; designer, craftsman and writer; *b* 25 May 1914; *s* of Robert Haswell Gardner, MIMarE and Lucy (*née* Maving); *m* 1940, Joan Margaret Pollard (*d* 1982); two *s* one *d.* Trained at Royal College of Art, 1935–39 (ARCA 1938, Design Sch. Trav. Schol., Scandinavia, 1939). Served Army, 1939–45. Mem., Royal Mint Panel of Artists, 1938–. Vis. lectr, Central Sch. of Arts and Crafts, 1959–62, Cambridgeshire Coll. of Art and Technology, 1959–62, Hampstead Garden Suburb Inst., 1959–73; Examr in craft subjects AEB City and Guilds of London Inst., 1957–60; served Typography Jury of RSA, Ind. Design Bursary Scheme. FRSA 1955; FCSD (FSIA 1964); Leverhulme Res. Fellow, 1969–70. Vis. Prof. and Fine Art Program Lectr, Colorado State Univ., 1963; Churchill Meml Trav. Fellow, 1966–67 (USA, Polynesia, NZ, Australia, Nepal). External Examr in Lettering, City & Guilds of London Art Sch., 1987–. Hon. Mem., RNS, NZ, 1966. Work exhib. Fort Collins and Denver, Colo, 1963, Monotype House, London, 1965, Portsmouth Coll. of Art, 1965, Hammond Mus., NY, 1970; (with family) Rye Art Gall., 1977. Awarded the Queen's Silver Jubilee Medal, 1977. *Works include:* HM Privy Council Seal 1955, HM Greater and Lesser Royal Signets 1955, Seal of HM Dependencies, 1955; seals for BMA, 1957, RSA, 1966, Univ. of Aston, Birmingham, 1966; *coinage designs and models:* for Jordan 1950, UK 1953, Cyprus 1955 and 1963, Algeria 1964, New Zealand 1967, Guyana 1967, Dominican Republic 1969, UNFAO (Ceylon 1968, Cyprus 1970, Guyana 1970), Falkland Islands 1974, UK 20p coin 1982; *medallic work:* includes Britannia Commemorative Soc. Shakespeare Medal 1967, Churchill Meml Trust's Foundn Medal 1969, Nat. Commemorative Soc. Audubon Medal 1970, Internat. Iron and Steel Inst. Medal 1971, Inst. of Metals Kroll medal 1972, and thirty-six medallic engravings depicting the history of the Royal Arms, completed 1974; participant in series of Commonwealth Silver Jubilee crown pieces, 1977; *calligraphy:* includes Rolls of Honour for House of Commons 1949, LTE 1954, Household Cavalry, Life Guards, RHG, Grenadier, Coldstream, Scots, Irish and Welsh Foot Guards, completed 1956, Warrants of Appointment by Queen Elizabeth the Queen Mother as Lord Warden of the Cinque Ports, 1979, Royal Marines Corps Book of Remembrance, MSS for Canterbury Cath., Eton Coll., 1990, RSA 1991 and elsewhere; *work in other media* for Postmaster Gen. (Jersey definitive stamp 1958), Royal Soc. (Tercentenary stained glass window, 1960), King's College, London, 1971, City of London, 1972—and for Univs, schools, presses, libraries, also privately. *Publications:* Chapter VIII of The Calligrapher's Handbook, 1956; Calligraphy for A Wordsworth Treasury, 1978; Alphabet at Work, 1982; New Calligraphy on an Old Theme, 1984; William Gardner's Book of Calligraphy, 1988. *Address:* Hollingrove Old Chapel, Brightling, near Robertsbridge, East Sussex TN32 5HU.

GARDNER-MEDWIN, Prof. Robert Joseph, RIBA, FRTPI; architect and town planning consultant; Professor Emeritus, Liverpool University, since 1973; *b* 10 April 1907; *s* of late Dr and Mrs F. M. Gardner-Medwin; *m* 1935, Margaret, *d* of late Mr Justice and Mrs Kilgour, Winnipeg; four *s. Educ:* Rossall Sch., Lancashire; School of Architecture, Liverpool Univ. (BArch, Dipl Civ Des). Commonwealth Fund Fellowship in City Planning and Landscape Design, Harvard Univ., 1933–35; private practice, and architectural teaching at Architectural Association and Regent Street Polytechnic, 1936–40. Served War of 1939–45, with Royal Engineers (Major, RE), 1940–43. Adviser in Town Planning and Housing to Comptroller of Development and Welfare in the British West Indies, 1944–47; Chief Architect and Planning Officer to Department of Health for Scotland, 1947–52; Roscoe Prof. of Architecture, Liverpool Univ., 1952–73. President, Liverpool Architectural Society, 1966; Chm., Merseyside Civic Soc., 1972–76, 1979–80. FRSA. Golden Order of Merit, Poland, 1976. *Publications:* (with H. Myles Wright, MA, FRIBA) Design of Nursery and Elementary Schools, 1938; contributions to Town Planning Review, Architects' Journal, Journals of the RIBA and the RTPI, etc. *Address:* 6 Kirby Mount, West Kirby, Wirral, Merseyside.

GARDNER-THORPE, Col and Alderman Sir Ronald (Laurence), GBE 1980; TD 1948 (3 bars); JP; company director; *b* 13 May 1917; *s* of Joseph Gardner and Hannah Coulthurst Thorpe; *m* 1938, Hazel Mary (*née* Dees); one *s. Educ:* De la Salle Coll. Commnd Hants Heavy Regt, 1938; served War, 1939–45: France, Germany, Italy, British Army Staff Washington; 1945–47: AA&QMG 56 London Div., and XIII Corps; Grade 1 SO XIII Corps; GSO 1 GHQ CMF; comd 5th Bn The Buffs, 1956–60; Col 1960. City of London: Alderman, Ward of Bishopsgate, 1972 (Pres., Bishopsgate Ward Club, 1975); Sheriff, 1978–79; Lord Mayor, 1980–81; HM Lieut, 1980–. Vice-Pres., City of London Red Cross, 1977–. Underwriting Mem. of Lloyd's, 1977–. Member: Lord Lieuts Cttee, 1955–; Council, Magistrates' Assoc., 1972–82; London Court of Arbitration, 1975–85; Public Sch. Governing Body, 1963–; Governor: St John's Coll., Southsea, 1963– (Vice-Chm. Governors, 1976–); St Joseph's, Beulah Hill, 1966–76; Christ's Hosp., 1972–; Trustee: United Westminster Schs, 1974–; The Buffs (Royal East Kent Regt) Museum, 1976–; Morden Coll., 1979–89; Rowland Hill Benevolent Fund, 1979–85; Mental Health Foundn, 1981–; Royal Foundn of Greycoat Hosp., 1981–; Duke of Edinburgh's Award, 1982–; President: 25th Anniv. Appeal Fund, The Duke of Edinburgh's Award, 1980–82; David Isaacs Fund, 1982–86 (Vice-Pres., 1973–82); Central London Br., SSAFA, 1983; League of Friends, Hosp. of St John and St Elizabeth, 1983–; Vice-Pres., Variety Club of GB, 1982–86; Chm. Council, Distressed Gentlefolks' Aid Assoc., 1984–87. Chancellor, City Univ., 1980–81; Adm., Port of London, 1980–81. Member: Kent Territorial Assoc., 1954–62 (Mem., Finance Cttee, 1954); City of London T & AVR Assoc., 1977–86; Hon. Col, Kansas Cavalry, 1981–. Hon. Citizen: Baltimore; Kansas City; Arizona; Norfolk, Va; Cuzco, Peru. JP Inner London, 1964 (Dep. Chm. 1968); JP City of London, 1969 (Dep. Chm. 1970); Hon. Treas., Inner London Magistrates, 1972– (Vice Chm., 1977). Freeman, City of London, 1971; Liveryman and Member of Court: Worshipful Co. of Painter Stainers, 1972–; Worshipful Co. of Builders Merchants, 1979–; Mem. Court, Hon. Artillery Co., 1972; Hon. Freeman and Liveryman, Leathersellers' Co., 1986. Hon. FRCP 1986. KStJ 1980; Kt of Magistral Grace, SMO, 1982. Kt Comdr, Royal Order of the Dannebrog, 1960; Kt Comdr, Order of Infant Henri, Portugal, 1979; Kt Comdr, Right Hand of the Ghurka, Nepal, 1980; Kt Comdr, Royal Order of King Abdul Aziz, Saudi Arabia, 1981; Kt Grand Cordon of the Swan, USA, 1984; Kt Grand Cross, Holy Order of the Cross of Jerusalem, USA, 1985; Grand Officer of Merit, Il Melito Melitensi, Italy, 1986. Hon. DCL City, 1980; Hon. DH Lewis, Chicago, 1981. *Publications:* The City and the Buffs, 1985; My Lord Mayor, 1988. *Recreations:* interest in Fine Arts and in City of London tradition. *Address:* 8 Cadogan Square, SW1X 0JU. *Clubs:* Belfry, City Livery, United Wards, Bishopsgate Ward.

GARDOM, Garde Basil; QC (Canada) 1975; Agent General for British Columbia in the United Kingdom and Europe, since 1987; *b* 17 July 1924; *s* of Basil Gardom and Gabrielle Gwladys (*née* Bell); *m* 1956, Theresa Helen Eileen Mackenzie; one *s* four *d. Educ:* Univ. of British Columbia (BA, LlB). Called to Bar of British Columbia, 1949; elected to BC Legislature as Mem. for Vancouver-Point Grey, 1966; re-elected, 1969, 1972, 1975, 1979, 1983; Govt House Leader, 1977–86; Attorney Gen. of BC, 1975–79; Minister of Intergovtl Relns, 1979–86; Chairman: Constitution Cttee, 1975–86; Legislation Cttee, 1975–86; Mem., Treasury Bd and Planning and Priorities Cttee, 1983–86; Minister responsible, Official Visits to Expo '86; Policy Cons., Office of the Premier, 1986–87. Member: Canadian Bar Assoc., 1949–; Vancouver Bar Assoc., 1949–; British Columbia Sports Hall of Fame; Phi Delta Theta Fraternity, 1943. *Recreations:* tennis, fishing, ski-ing. *Address:* British Columbia House, 1 Regent Street, SW1Y 4NS. *T:* 071–930 6857; 1738 Angus Drive, Vancouver, BC V6J 4H5, Canada. *T:* 604–736–1496. *Clubs:* East India, Royal Over-Seas League, Royal Automobile; Union Club of BC, Vancouver Lawn Tennis and Badminton (British Columbia).

GAREL-JONES, (William Armand Thomas) Tristan; MP (C) Watford, since 1979; Minister of State, Foreign and Commonwealth Office, since 1990; *b* 28 Feb. 1941; *s* of Bernard Garel-Jones and Meriel Garel-Jones (*née* Williams); *m* 1966, Catalina (*née* Garrigues); four *s* one *d. Educ:* The King's Sch., Canterbury. Principal, Language Sch., Madrid, Spain, 1960–70; Merchant Banker, 1970–74; worked for Cons. Party, 1974–79 (Personal Asst to Party Chm., 1978–79). Contested (C): Caernarvon, Feb. 1974; Watford, Oct. 1974. PPS to Minister of State, CSD, 1981; Asst Govt Whip, 1982–83; a Lord Comr of HM Treasury, 1983–86; Vice-Chamberlain of HM Household, 1986–88; Comptroller of HM Household, 1988–89; Treasurer of HM Household and Dep. Chief Whip, 1989–90. *Recreation:* collecting books. *Address:* c/o House of Commons, SW1. *Clubs:* Carlton, Beefsteak; Club de Campo (Madrid).

GARFIELD, Leon, FRSL; author; *b* 14 July 1921; *s* of David Garfield and Rose Garfield; *m* 1949, Vivien Dolores Alcock; one *d. Educ:* Brighton Grammar Sch. Served War, RAMC, 1941–46: attained and held rank of Private. Worked in NHS (biochemistry), until 1969; full-time author, 1969–. FRSL 1985. Prix de la Fondation de France, 1984; Swedish Golden Cat, 1985. *Publications:* Jack Holborn, 1964; Devil-in-the-Fog, 1966; Smith, 1967; Black Jack, 1968 (filmed 1979); Mister Corbett's Ghost and Other Stories, 1969; The Boy and the Monkey, 1969; The Drummer Boy, 1970; The Strange Affair of Adelaide Harris, 1971; The Ghost Downstairs, 1972; The Captain's Watch, 1972; Lucifer Wilkins, 1973; Baker's Dozen, 1973; The Sound of Coaches, 1974; The Prisoners of September, 1975; The Pleasure Garden, 1976; The Booklovers, 1976; The House of Hanover, 1976; The Lamplighter's Funeral, 1976; Mirror, Mirror, 1976; Moss and Blister, 1976; The Cloak, 1976; The Valentine, 1977; Labour in Vain, 1977; The Fool, 1977; Rosy Starling, 1977; The Dumb Cake, 1977; Tom Titmarsh's Devil, 1977; The Filthy Beast, 1977; The Enemy, 1977; The Confidence Man, 1978; Bostock & Harris, 1978; John Diamond, 1980 (Whitbread Book of the Year Award, 1980); Mystery of Edwin Drood (completion), 1980; Fair's Fair, 1981; The House of Cards, 1982; King Nimrod's Tower, 1982; The Apprentices, 1982; The Writing on the Wall, 1983; The King in the Garden, 1984; The Wedding Ghost, 1984; Guilt and Gingerbread, 1984; Shakespeare Stories, 1985; The December Rose, 1986; Blewcoat Boy, 1988; with Edward Blishen: The God Beneath the Sea, 1970; The Golden Shadow, 1973; with David Proctor: Child O'War, 1972. *Recreations:* snooker, collecting pictures and china; also wine, women and song. *Address:* c/o John Johnson (Author's Agent) Ltd, Clerkenwell House, 45/47 Clerkenwell Green, EC1R 0HT. *T:* 071–251 0125. *Club:* PEN.

GARFITT, Alan; His Honour Judge Garfitt; a Circuit Judge, since 1977, and Judge, Cambridge County Court and Wisbech County Court, since 1978; *b* 20 Dec. 1920; *s* of Rush and Florence Garfitt; *m* 1st, 1941, Muriel Ada Jaggers; one *s* one *d*; 2nd, 1973, Ivie Maud Hudson; 3rd, 1978, Rosemary Lazell; one *s* one *d. Educ:* King Edward VII Grammar Sch., King's Lynn; Metropolitan Coll. and Inns of Court Sch. of Law. Served War of 1939–45, RAF, 1941–46. LLB London 1947; called to the Bar, Lincoln's Inn, 1948; practising barrister. Hon. Fellow, Faculty of Law, Cambridge, 1978. *Publications:* Law of Contracts in a Nutshell, 4 edns 1949–56; The Book for Police, 5 vols, 1958; jt ed, Roscoe's Criminal Evidence, Practice and Procedure, 16th edn, 1952; contribs to Jl of Planning Law, Solicitors' Jl and other legal pubns. *Recreations:* farming, gardening, DIY activities, horse riding and, as a member since 1961 and President since 1978 of the Association of British Riding Schools (Fellow, 1989), the provision of good teaching and riding facilities for non-horse owners. *Address:* Leap House, Barcham Road, Soham, Ely, Cambs CB7 5TU.

GARING, Air Commodore William Henry, CBE 1943; DFC 1940; *b* Corryong, Victoria, 26 July 1910; *s* of late George Garing, retired grazier, and late Amy Evelyn Garing; *m* 1st, 1940 (marr. diss); one *s* one *d*; 2nd, 1954, Marjorie Irene Smith, Preston, England; two *d. Educ:* Corryong Higher Elementary School; Royal Melbourne Inst. of Technol.; Royal Military Coll., Duntroon, ACT. Began career as Electrical and Mechanical Engineer, 1928; entered RMC, Duntroon, 1929, as specially selected RAAF Cadet; Flying Training: Point Cook, Australia, 1931; Sch. of Air Pilotage and Specialist Navigation Sch., UK 1934–35; Seaplane Flying Instructor and Chief Navigation Instructor, Point

Cook, Victoria, 1936; commanded Seaplane Squadron, Point Cook; conducted first Specialist Air Navigation Course in Australia, 1938; posted to United Kingdom in 1939; served with No 10 Aust. Sunderland Squadron, RAAF, as Flt Commander in Coastal Command, RAF, 1939; operations in N Atlantic, France and Mediterranean (DFC); flew Lord Lloyd to France for discussions with Pétain Government prior to collapse of France, 1940, and subsequently was pilot to the late Duke of Kent and to Mr Eden (later Earl of Avon), and others (Atlantic Star; despatches); arrived Australia, 1941; Senior Air Staff Officer, HQ Northern Area (extended from Neth. Indies through New Guinea, British Solomons to New Caledonia), 1941; commanded No 9 (Operational) Group RAAF, New Guinea, 1942; Milne Bay Campaign, 1942; Buna Campaign, 1942–43 (American DSC, awarded by Gen. MacArthur); 1943 (CBE, awarded for air operations SW Pacific); commanded No 1 Operational Training Unit, E Sale, Victoria, 1943–44; Director Operational Requirements, 1944; SASO to RAAF Rep., Washington, 1945–46, subseq. RAAF Rep. (1939–45 star); OC Western Area, 1947; JSSC, 1948; ADC to the King, 1951; Commandant School Land/Air Warfare, NSW, 1950; AOC Amberley, Qld, 1951; Imperial Defence Coll., London, 1952; AOC Overseas HQ, and RAAF Rep., London, 1953; AOC RAAF, Richmond, NSW, 1953–55; AOC RAAF and Commandant RAAF Staff Coll., Point Cook, Victoria, 1955–60; Air Officer, South Australia, and OC, RAAF, Edinburgh Field, Salisbury, SA, 1960–64, retired. Exec. Dir, Rothmans Nat. Sport Foundn, Sydney, Australia, 1964; Commercial Relations Manager, Alfred Dunhill Ltd, 1971–75. Holds No 1 1st cl. Air Navigators' Certificate (Australia); Air Master Navigator (RAF). Bd, Royal Freemasons Benevolent Assoc.; Co-ordinator, Masonic Internat. Fest., 1977–79. FAIM 1964. *Recreations:* Alpine ski-ing, water ski-ing, yachting, shooting, flying, carpentry, landscape painting, gardening. *Clubs:* Imperial Service, Royal Automobile, New South Wales Leagues (Sydney).

GARLAND, Basil; Registrar, Family Division of High Court of Justice (formerly Probate, Divorce and Admiralty Division), 1969–85; *b* 30 May 1920; *o c* of late Herbert George Garland and Grace Alice Mary Martha Garland; *m* 1942, Dora Mary Sudell Hope; one *s*. *Educ:* Dulwich Coll.; Pembroke Coll., Oxford (MA). Served in Royal Artillery, 1940–46: commnd 1941; Staff Officer, HQ RA, Gibraltar, 1943–45; Hon. Major 1946. Called to Bar, Middle Temple, 1948; Treasury Junior Counsel (Probate), 1965; Registrar, Principal Probate Registry, 1969. *Publications:* articles in Law Jl. *Recreations:* sailing, drama. *Address:* Dalethorpe End, Dedham, Essex CO7 6HW. *T:* Colchester (0206) 322263. *Clubs:* Bar Yacht, Royal Harwich Yacht.

GARLAND, (Frederick) Peter (Collison), CVO 1969; QPM 1965; *b* 4 Sept. 1912; *s* of late Percy Frederick Garland, Southsea, Hants; *m* 1945, Gwendolen Mary, *d* of late Henry James Powell, Putney; three *d*. *Educ:* Bradfield Coll. Joined Metropolitan Police, 1934. Served in RAF (Air Crew), 1941–45. Asst Chief Constable of Norfolk, 1952–56, Chief Constable, 1956–75. CStJ 1961. *Address:* 2 Eaton Road, Norwich NR4 6PY. *T:* Norwich (0603) 53043. *Club:* Royal Air Force.

GARLAND, Nicholas Withycombe; Political Cartoonist, The Daily Telegraph, 1966–86 and since 1991; *b* 1 Sept. 1935; *s* of Tom and Peggy Garland; *m* 1969, Caroline Beatrice Medawar; three *s* one *d*. *Educ:* Slade School of Fine Art. Worked in theatre as stage man. and dir, 1958–64; Political Cartoonist: New Statesman, 1971–78; The Independent, 1986–90; has drawn regularly for The Spectator, 1979–; with Barry Humphries created and drew comic strip, Barry McKenzie, in Private Eye. *Publications:* (illustrated) Horatius, by T. B. Macaulay, 1977; An Indian Journal, 1983; Twenty Years of Cartoons by Garland, 1984; Travels with my Sketchbook, 1987; Not Many Dead, 1990. *Address:* 27 Heath Hurst Road, NW3 2RU.

GARLAND, Patrick Ewart; director and producer of plays, films, television; writer; Artistic Director, Chichester Festival Theatre, 1980–84 and 1991; *b* 10 April 1935; *s* of late Ewart Garland and Rosalind, *d* of Herbert Granville Fell, editor of The Connoisseur; *m* 1980, Alexandra Bastedo. *Educ:* St Mary's Coll., Southampton; St Edmund Hall, Oxford (MA). Actor, Bristol Old Vic, 1959; Age of Kings, BBC TV, 1961; lived in Montparnasse, 1961–62; writing—two plays for ITV, 1962; Research Asst, Monitor, BBC, 1963; Television interviews with: Stevie Smith, Philip Larkin, Sir Noel Coward, Sir John Gielgud, Sir Ralph Richardson, Dame Ninette de Valois, Claire Bloom, Tito Gobbi, Marcel Marceau, 1964–78. Director and Producer, BBC Arts Dept, 1962–74; Stage Director: 40 Years On, 1968, 1984; Brief Lives, 1968; Getting On, 1970; Cyrano, 1971; Hair (Israel), 1972; The Doll's House (New York and London), 1975; Under the Greenwood Tree, 1978; Look After Lulu, 1978; Beecham, 1980 (all West End); York Mystery Plays, 1980; My Fair Lady (US), 1980; Kipling (Mermaid and New York), 1984; Canaries Sometimes Sing, Albery, 1987; The Secret of Sherlock Holmes, Wyndham's, 1988; Victory (adapted from The Dynasts by Thomas Hardy), Chichester, 1989; A Room of One's Own, Hampstead, 1989, New York, 1991; Song in the Night, Lyric, Hammersmith, 1989; The Dressmaker, Windsor and tour, 1990; co-author, Underneath the Arches, Chichester, and Prince of Wales, 1982–83; Artistic Director, Chichester Festival Theatre, 1980–84, 1991: The Cherry Orchard, 1981; The Mitford Girls, 1981 (also London, 1981); On the Rocks, 1982; Cavell, 1982; Goodbye, Mr Chips, 1982; As You Like It, 1983; Forty Years On, Merchant of Venice, 1984; Tovarich, 1991; produced: Fanfare for Elizabeth, the Queen's 60th birthday gala, Covent Garden, 1986; Celebration of a Broadcaster, for Richard Dimbleby Cancer Fund at Westminster Abbey, 1986; thanksgiving service for Lord Olivier, 1989. *Films:* The Snow Goose, 1974; The Doll's House, 1976. Creative Writing Fellowship, Bishop Otter Coll., Chichester, 1984–85. *Publications:* Brief Lives, 1967; The Wings of the Morning (novel), 1989; Oswald the Owl (for children), 1990; poetry in: London Magazine, 1954; New Poems, 1956; Poetry West; Encounter; short stories in: Transatlantic Review, 1976; England Erzählt, Gemini, Light Blue Dark Blue. *Recreations:* reading Victorian novels, walking in Corsica. *Club:* Garrick.

GARLAND, Hon. Sir Patrick Neville, Kt 1985; **Hon. Mr Justice Garland;** a Judge of the High Court, Queen's Bench Division, since 1985; Presiding Judge, South Eastern Circuit, since 1989; a Judge of the Employment Appeal Tribunal, since 1986; *b* 22 July 1929; *s* of Frank Neville Garland and Marjorie Garland; *m* 1955, Jane Elizabeth Bird; two *s* one *d*. *Educ:* Uppingham Sch. (Scholar); Sidney Sussex Coll., Cambridge (Exhibnr and Prizeman; MA, LLM). Called to Bar, Middle Temple, 1953, Bencher, 1979. Asst Recorder, Norwich, 1971; a Recorder, 1972–85; QC 1972; Dep. High Court Judge, 1981–85. Chm., SE Circuit Area Liaison Cttee; President: Central Council of Probation Cttees, 1986–; Official Referees Bar Assoc.; Mem., Parole Bd, 1988– (Vice-Chm., 1989–91). Mem., Lloyd's, 1983–. *Publications:* articles in legal and technical jls. *Recreations:* shooting, gardening, industrial archaeology. *Address:* c/o Royal Courts of Justice, Strand, WC2A 2LL. *Club:* Cumberland Lawn Tennis.

GARLAND, Peter; *see* Garland, F. P. C.

GARLAND, Peter Bryan, PhD; FRSE; Chief Executive, Institute of Cancer Research, since 1989; *b* 1934; *s* of Frederick George Garland and Molly Kate Jones; *m* 1959, Ann Bathurst; one *s* two *d*. *Educ:* Hardye's Sch., Dorchester; Downing Coll., Cambridge (BA 1st Class Hons in Physical Anthropol., 1955; BChir 1958, MB 1959; PhD 1964); King's Coll. Hosp. Med. Sch. (Burney Yeo Schol.). MRC Res. Schol., Chem. Pathol. Dept, KCH Med. Sch., and Biochem. Dept, UCL, 1959–61; British Insulin Manufacturers' Fellow, Biochem. Dept, Cambridge Univ., 1961–64; Lectr, 1964–68, Reader, 1969–70 in Biochem., Bristol Univ.; Prof. of Biochem., Dundee Univ., 1970–84; Principal Scientist and Hd, Biosciences Div., Unilever Research, 1984–87; Dir of Research, Amersham Internat., 1987–89. Vis. Prof., Johnson Res. Foundn, Philadelphia, 1967–69; Vis. Fellow, ANU, 1983. Member: MRC, 1980–84 (Chm., Cell Biol.–Disorders Bd, 1980–82); EMBO, 1981; CRC Scientific Policy Cttee, 1985–; Chm., CRC Technology Ltd, 1988–. FRSE 1977. Colworth Medal, Biochem. Soc., 1970. *Publications:* numerous articles in biochemistry and biophysics. *Recreations:* sport (athletics blue, Cambridge, 1954–55), ski-ing, sailing, windsurfing, reading. *Address:* Institute of Cancer Research, 17A Onslow Gardens, SW7 3AL. *Clubs:* Athenæum; Bosham Sailing.

GARLAND, Hon. Sir (Ransley) Victor, KBE 1982; Chairman, TR Far East Income Trust PLC, since 1990 (Director, since 1984); Company Director: Prudential Corporation plc, since 1984; Throgmorton Trust plc, and associated companies, since 1985; Dunedin Berkeley Development Capitol Ltd, since 1985; Deputy Chairman, South Bank Board, since 1985; *b* Perth, 5 May 1934; *m* Lynette Jamieson, BMus (Melb.); two *s* one *d*. *Educ:* Univ. of Western Australia. BA(Econ); FCA. Practised as Chartered Accountant, 1958–70. MP for Curtin, Australian Federal Parliament, 1969–81; Minister for Supply, 1971–72; Executive Councillor, 1971–; Minister Asstg Treasurer, 1972 and 1975–76; Chief Opposition Whip, 1974–75; Minister for Special Trade Representations, also Minister Asstg Minister for Trade and Resources, 1977–79; Minister for Business and Consumer Affairs, 1979–80; High Comr for Australia in UK, 1981–83. Govt Representative Minister: at Commonwealth Ministerial Meeting for Common Fund, London, 1978; at Ministerial Meetings of ESCAP, New Delhi, 1978; Minister representing Treas., at Ministerial Meeting of OECD, Paris, 1978; Leader, Aust. Delegn to UNCTAD V and Chm. Commonwealth Delegns to UNCTAD V, Manila, 1979; attended, with Premier, Commonwealth Heads of Govt meeting, Lusaka, 1979. Parly Adviser, Aust. Mission to UN Gen. Assembly, New York, 1973; Chairman: House of Reps Expenditure Cttee, 1976–77; Govt Members' Treasury Cttee, 1977. Councillor, Royal Society for the Blind, 1988–. Freeman, City of London, 1982. *Address:* Wilton Place, Knightsbridge, SW1X 8RL. *T:* 071–235 2729. *Clubs:* White's; Weld (Perth).

GARLICK, Prof. George Frederick John, BSc, PhD, DSc, FInstP; *b* 21 Feb. 1919; *s* of George Robert Henry Garlick and Martha Elizabeth (*née* Davies); *m* 1943, Dorothy Mabel Bowsher; one *d*; *m* 1977, Harriet Herta Forster. *Educ:* Wednesbury High Sch.; Univ. of Birmingham (BSc 1940, PhD 1943, DSc 1955). War service: Scientific Officer (Radar Research). In Charge Luminescence Laboratory, Birmingham Univ., 1946–56 (Research Physicist, 1946–49, Lecturer in Physics, 1949–56); Prof. of Physics, Univ. of Hull, 1956–78; Research Prof., Univ. of Southern California, LA, 1978–79; private scientific consultant, 1979–89. FInstP 1949. Jubilee Medal, 1977. *Publications:* Luminescent Materials, 1949; numerous papers in learned scientific journals. *Recreation:* music (organ). *Address:* 267 South Beloit Avenue, Los Angeles, California 90049, USA.

GARLICK, Sir John, KCB 1976 (CB 1973); Permanent Secretary, Department of the Environment, 1978–81; *b* 17 May 1921; *m* 1945, Frances Esther Munday; three *d*. *Educ:* Westcliff High Sch., Essex; University of London. Entered Post Office Engineering Dept, 1937; Ministry of Transport, 1948; Private Secretary to Rt Hon. Ernest Marples, 1959–60; Assistant Secretary, 1960; National Economic Development Office, 1962–64; Under-Sec., Min. of Transport, 1966, later DoE; Dep. Sec., DoE, 1972–73; Dir-Gen., Highways, DoE, 1973–74; Second Permanent Sec., Cabinet Office, 1974–77. Mem., London Docklands Develt Corp., 1981–. Dir, Abbey National plc (formerly Abbey National Building Soc.), 1981–. Chm., Alcohol Concern, 1985–. *Address:* 16 Astons Road, Moor Park, Northwood, Mddx. *T:* Northwood (09274) 24628.

GARLICK, Kenneth John; Keeper of Western Art, Ashmolean Museum, Oxford, 1968–84; Fellow of Balliol College, Oxford, 1968–84, now Emeritus; *b* 1 Oct. 1916; *s* of late D. E. Garlick and Annie Hallifax. *Educ:* Elmhurst Sch., Street; Balliol Coll., Oxford; Courtauld Inst. of Art, London. MA Oxon, PhD Birmingham; FSA, FMA. RAF Signals, 1939–46. Lectr, Bath Academy of Art, 1946–48; Asst Keeper, Dept of Art, City of Birmingham Museum and Art Gallery, 1948–50; Lectr (Sen. Lectr 1960), Barber Inst. of Fine Arts, Univ. of Birmingham, 1951–68. Governor, Royal Shakespeare Theatre, 1978–. *Publications:* Sir Thomas Lawrence, 1954; Walpole Society Vol. XXXIX (Lawrence Catalogue Raisonné), 1964; Walpole Society Vol. XLV (Catalogue of Pictures at Althorp), 1976; (ed with Angus Macintyre) The Diary of Joseph Farington, Vols I-II, 1978, III-VI, 1979; Sir Thomas Lawrence, 1989; numerous articles and reviews. *Recreations:* travel, music. *Address:* 39 Hawkswell House, Hawkswell Gardens, Oxford OX2 7EX. *Club:* Reform.

GARLING, David John Haldane, ScD; Reader in Mathematical Analysis, since 1978, and Fellow of St John's College, since 1963, Cambridge University; *b* 26 July 1937; *s* of Leslie Ernest Garling and Frances Margaret Garling; *m* 1963, Anthea Mary Eileen Dixon; two *s* one *d*. *Educ:* Highgate Sch.; St John's Coll., Cambridge (BA, MA, PhD; ScD 1978). Cambridge University: Asst Lectr, 1963–64; Lectr, 1964–78; Head of Dept of Pure Maths and Math. Stats, 1984–91; Tutor, 1971–78, Pres., 1987–91, St John's Coll. Member: SERC Mathematics Cttee, 1983–86; Council, London Mathematical Soc., 1986–88. *Publications:* A course in Galois Theory, 1987; papers in sci. jls. *Address:* St John's College, Cambridge. *T:* Cambridge (0223) 338600.

GARMOYLE, Viscount; Hugh Sebastian Cairns; *b* 26 March 1965; *s* and *heir* of Earl Cairns, *qv*.

GARNER, Alan; author; *b* 17 Oct. 1934; *s* of Colin and Marjorie Garner; *m* 1st, 1956, Ann Cook; one *s* two *d*; 2nd, 1972, Griselda Greaves; one *s* one *d*. *Educ:* Alderley Edge Council Sch.; Manchester Grammar Sch.; Magdalen Coll., Oxford. Writer and presenter, documentary films: Places and Things, 1978; Images, 1981 (First Prize, Chicago Internat. Film Fest.). *Publications:* The Weirdstone of Brisingamen, 1960; The Moon of Gomrath, 1963; Elidor, 1965; Holly from the Bongs, 1966; The Old Man of Mow, 1967; The Owl Service, 1967 (Library Assoc. Carnegie Medal 1967, Guardian Award 1968); The Hamish Hamilton Book of Goblins, 1969; Red Shift, 1973 (with John Mackenzie, filmed 1978); (with Albin Trowski) The Breadhorse, 1975; The Guizer, 1975; The Stone Book, 1976; Tom Fobble's Day, 1977; Granny Reardun, 1977; The Aimer Gate, 1978; Fairy Tales of Gold, 1979; The Lad of the Gad, 1980; Alan Garner's Book of British Fairy Tales, 1984; A Bag of Moonshine, 1986; Jack and the Beanstalk, 1992; *plays:* Lamaload, 1978; Lurga Lom, 1980; To Kill a King, 1980; Sally Water, 1982; The Keeper, 1983; *dance drama:* The Green Mist, 1970; *libretti:* The Bellybag, 1971 (music by Richard Morris); Potter Thompson, 1972 (music by Gordon Crosse). *Recreation:* work. *Address:* Blackden, Cheshire CW4 8BY. *Club:* Portico Library (Manchester).

GARNER, Sir Anthony (Stuart), Kt 1984; parliamentary and public affairs consultant, since 1988; Director of Organisation, Conservative Central Office, 1976–88; *b* 28 Jan. 1927; *s* of Edward Henry Garner, MC, FIAS, and Dorothy May Garner; *m* 1967, Shirley Doris Taylor; two *s*. *Educ:* Liverpool Coll. Grenadier Guards, 1945–48. Young

Conservative Organiser, 1948–51; Conservative Agent, Halifax, 1951–56; Nat. Organising Sec., Young Conservative Org., 1956–61; Conservative Central Office Agent for: London Area, 1961–64; Western Area, 1964–66; North West Area, 1966–76. Chm., Conservative Agents' Examination Bd, 1976–88. Pres., Conservative Agents' Benevolent Assoc., 1976–88. Director: Anglo-Soviet Develt Corp., 1989–; Carroll Anglo-American Corp., 1989–. Life Governor, Liverpool Coll., 1980–. *Recreations:* sailing, theatre. *Address:* 1 Blomfield Road, W9 1AH. *Clubs:* Carlton, St Stephen's Constitutional.

GARNER, Frederic Francis, CMG 1959; Ambassador to Costa Rica, 1961–67; retired; *b* 9 July 1910; *m* 1946, Muriel (*née* Merrick). *Educ:* Rugby Sch.; Worcester Coll., Oxford. Joined HM Consular Service in China, 1932; served at Peking, Canton, Shanghai, POW in Japan, 1942–45. Consul, Tangier, 1947–50; First Secretary, Bogota, 1950–54; Consul-General, Shanghai, 1954–56; Head of Consular Department, Foreign Office, 1956–58; Ambassador at Phnom Penh, 1958–61. *Address:* c/o National Westminster Bank, 111 Western Road, Brighton, E Sussex BN1 2AF.

GARNER, Frederick Leonard; Chairman, Pearl Assurance Company Ltd, 1977–83, President, and President, Pearl Group, 1983–88, retired; *b* 7 April 1920; *s* of Leonard Frank Garner and Florence Emily Garner; *m* 1953, Giovanna Maria Anzani, Italy. *Educ:* Sutton County Sch., Surrey. Served War, RA, 1940–46. Joined Pearl Assurance Co., 1936; rejoined, 1946; sole employment, 1946–83. Director: Schroder Global Trust, 1971–89; Kleinwort Development Fund, 1981–; Age Concern Insurance Services, 1987–. Mem., Finance Cttee, Age Concern England, 1987–. *Address:* 98 Tudor Avenue, Worcester Park, Surrey KT4 8TU. *T:* 081-337 3313. *Club:* Royal Automobile.

GARNER, John Donald, CMG 1988; CVO 1991 (LVO 1979); HM Diplomatic Service, retired; *b* 15 April 1931; *s* of late Ronald Garner and of Doris Ethel Garner (*née* Norton); *m* Karen Maria Conway; two *d*. *Educ:* Trinity Grammar Sch., N22. Royal Navy, National Service, 1949–51. Foreign Office, 1952–55; Third Secretary: Seoul, 1955; Bangkok, 1957; Foreign Office, 1959–63; Second Secretary: Benghazi and Tripoli, 1963–67; Sydney, 1967–69; First Sec., Tel Aviv, 1969–73; FCO, 1973–76; NDC 1976; Dep. High Commissioner, Lilongwe, 1977–80; Chargé d'affaires, Kabul, 1981–84; High Comr, The Gambia, 1984–87; Consul-Gen., Houston, 1988–91. *Recreation:* golf. *Address:* 30 The Green, N14. *T:* 081-882 6808. *Club:* South Herts Golf.

GARNER, Maurice Richard; specialist in the structure and governmental control of public enterprises; *b* 31 May 1915; *o s* of Jesse H. Garner; *m* 1943, Joyce W. Chapman; one *s* one *d*. *Educ:* Glendale County Sch.; London Sch. of Economics and Political Science. Royal Armoured Corps, 1942–45 (despatches). Inland Revenue (Tax Inspectorate), 1938–46; BoT, Asst Principal and Principal, 1947; Commercial Sec. and UK Trade Comr in Ottawa, 1948–55; transf. to Min. of Power, 1957; Asst Sec. 1960; Under-Sec., Electricity Div., Min. of Technology, 1969, later DTI, retired 1973. Vis. Prof., Dept of Govt, LSE, 1981–85. *Recreations:* reading, oenology. *Address:* New Albany, 33 Sand Hill Lane, Leeds LS17 6AJ. *T:* Leeds (0532) 685115.

GARNER, Michael Scott; His Honour Judge Garner; a Circuit Judge, since 1988; *b* 10 April 1939; *s* of William Garner and Doris Mary (*née* Scott); *m* 1st, 1964, Sheila Margaret (*d* 1981) (*née* Garland); one *s* one *d*; 2nd, 1982, Margaret Anne (*née* Senior). *Educ:* Huddersfield Coll.; Manchester Univ. (LLB). Admitted Solicitor, 1965. Asst Recorder, 1978–85; a Recorder, 1985–88. *Recreations:* motoring, walking. *Address:* 22 Longley Road, Huddersfield HD5 8JL.

GARNETT, John; *see* Garnett, W. J. P. M.

GARNETT, Kevin Mitchell; QC 1991; *b* 22 June 1950; *s* of Frank Raymond Garnett and Cynthia Ruby Eberstein; *m* 1980, Susan Jane Louise (*née* Diboll). *Educ:* Bradfield Coll., Berks; University Coll., Oxford (MA). Called to the Bar, Middle Temple, 1975. *Publications:* (ed jtly) Williams, Mortimer and Sunnucks on Executors, Administrators and Probate, 16th edn 1982, 17th edn 1992; (ed jtly) Copinger and Skone James on Copyright, 13th edn 1991. *Recreations:* tennis, mountain walking. *Address:* Churchbury House, Windmill Road, SW19 5NQ. *T:* 081–946 6486; 5 New Square, Lincoln's Inn, WC2A 3RJ. *T:* 071–404 0404. *Club:* Hurlingham.

GARNETT, Thomas Ronald, MA; Headmaster of Geelong Grammar School, Australia, 1961–73; *b* 1 Jan. 1915; *s* of E. N. Garnett; *m* 1946, Penelope, *d* of Philip Frere; three *s* two *d*. *Educ:* Charterhouse (Scholar); Magdalene Coll., Cambridge (Scholar). BA 1936, MA 1946. Assistant master: Westminster School, 1936–38; Charterhouse, 1938–52; Master of Marlborough College, 1952–61. Served War of 1939–45, RAF, India and Burma, 1941–46, Squadron Leader (despatches). Cricket for Somerset, 1939. *Publications:* Stumbling on Melons, 1984; (ed) A Gardener's Potpourri, 1986; Man of Roses: Alister Clark of Glenara, 1990. *Recreations:* gardening, ornithology. *Address:* Simmons Reef, Blackwood, via Trentham, Vic 3458, Australia. *T:* 053 686514. *Club:* Melbourne (Melbourne).

GARNETT, (William) John (Poulton Maxwell), CBE 1970; MA; Chairman, West Lambeth Health Authority, 1986–90; *b* 6 Aug. 1921; *s* of Dr Maxwell Garnett, CBE, and Margaret Lucy Poulton; *m* 1st, 1943, Barbara Rutherford-Smith (marr. diss.); two *s* two *d*; 2nd, 1986, Julia Cleverdon; two *d*. *Educ:* Rugby Sch.; Kent Sch., USA; Trinity Coll., Cambridge. Royal Navy, 1941–46 (commnd, 1942). ICI Ltd, 1947–62; Dir, Industrial Soc., 1962–86; Dir, 1975–85, Chm., 1979–81, Spencer Stuart & Associates, Management Consultants. Dep. Chm. UNA, 1954–56. Mem., Ct of inquiry into miners' strike, 1972; Arbitrator, Lorry Drivers' Strike, 1979. Mem., Royal Dockyard Policy Bd. Chm., Churches Council on Gambling, 1965–71. DUniv Essex, 1977; Hon. DTech Loughborough, 1978; Hon. LLD, CNAA, 1980. *Publications:* The Manager's Responsibility for Communication, 1964; The Work Challenge, 1973, 1985. *Recreation:* timber construction. *Address:* 8 Alwyne Road, Canonbury, N1. *Club:* Leander (Henley).
See also V. H. B. M. Bottomley.

GARNHAM, Prof. Percy Cyril Claude, CMG 1964; FRS 1964; MD; Professor of Medical Protozoology (now Emeritus Professor), London University, and Head of Department of Parasitology, London School of Hygiene and Tropical Medicine, 1952–68, Hon. Fellow, 1976; Senior Research Fellow, Imperial College of Science and Technology, 1968–79, Hon. Fellow, 1979; Visiting Professor, Department of Biology, University of Strathclyde, 1970–87; *b* 15 Jan. 1901; *s* of late Lieut P. C. Garnham, RN Division, and late Edith Masham; *m* 1924, Esther Long Price, Talley, Carms; two *s* four *d*. *Educ:* privately; St Bartholomew's Hospital. MRCS, LRCP, 1923, MB, BS London, 1923, DPH Eng. 1924, MD London, 1928 (University Gold Medal); Dipl. de Méd. Malariol., University of Paris, 1931; FIBiol 1962; FRCP 1967. Colonial Medical Service, 1925–47; on staff of London School of Hygiene and Tropical Medicine, first as Reader, then as Professor, 1947–68. Heath Clark Lectr, Univ. of London, 1968; Fogarty Internat. Scholar, Nat. Insts of Health, Maryland, 1970, 1972; Manson Orator, 1969, Theobald Smith Orator, 1970; Ross Orator, 1980; Swellengrebel Orator, 1986. Member, Expert Panel of Parasitic Diseases, of WHO; Hon. Pres., European Fedn of Parasitologists; Past President: British Soc. of Parasitologists; Royal Society of Tropical Medicine and Hygiene; Vice-President: World Federation of Parasitologists; International Association against Filariasis; Corresponding Member: Académie Royale des Sciences d'Outre Mer, Belgium; Accad. Lancisiana, Rome; Soc. de Geografia da Lisboa; Hon. Member: Royal Entomol Soc. of London, 1979; Amer. Soc. Tropical Medicine; Société Belge de Médecine Tropicale; Brazilian Soc. Tropical Medicine; Soc. Ital. Medicina Tropicale; Soc. of Protozoologists; Société de Pathologie Exotique (Médaille d'Or, 1971); Acad. Nationale de Médecine, France (Médaille en Vermeil, 1972); Amer. Soc. of Parasitology; Mexican Soc. of Parasitologists; Polish Soc. of Parasitologists; British Soc. of Parasitologists; Groupement des Protistologues de la Langue Française; Foreign Member: Danish Royal Acad. of Sciences and Letters, 1976; Acad. Royale de Médecine, Belgium, 1979. Hon. FRCP Edinburgh, 1966. Freedom, City of London in Farriers Co., 1964. DSc London, 1952; Hon. Dr: Univ. of Bordeaux, 1965; Univ. of Montpellier, 1980; Academician of Pontifical Acad. of Sciences, 1970. KLJ 1979. Darling Medal and Prize, 1951; Bernhard Nocht Medal, 1957; Gaspar Vianna Medal, 1962; Manson Medal, 1965; Emile Brumpt Prize, 1970; Laveran Medal, 1971; Mary Kingsley Medal, 1973; Rudolf Leuckart Medal, 1974; Frink Medal, 1985; Linnean Medal, 1986. *Publications:* Malaria Parasites, 1966; Progress in Parasitology, 1970; numerous papers on parasitology in medical journals. *Recreations:* chamber music and European travel. *Address:* Southernwood, Farnham Common, Bucks. *T:* Farnham Common (02814) 3863. *Club:* Nairobi (Kenya).

GARNIER, Rear-Adm. Sir John, KCVO 1990 (LVO 1965); CBE 1982; Private Secretary to HRH Princess Alexandra, since 1991; Extra Equerry to the Queen, since 1988; *b* 10 March 1934; *s* of Rev. Thomas Vernon Garnier and Helen Stenhouse; *m* 1966, Joanna Jane Cadbury; two *s* one *d*. *Educ:* Berkhamsted School; Britannia Royal Naval College. FIL 1964. Joined RN 1950; served HM Yacht Britannia, 1956–57; HMS Tyne (Suez Operation) 1956; qualified navigation specialist, 1959; Naval Equerry to HM Queen, 1962–65; Comd HMS Dundas, 1968–69; Directorate of Naval Ops and Trade, 1969–71; Comd HMS Minerva, 1972–73; Defence Policy Staff, 1973–75; HMS Intrepid, 1976; Asst Dir, Naval Manpower Planning, 1976–78; RCDS 1979; Comd HMS London, 1980–81; Dir, Naval Ops and Trade, 1982–84; Commodore Amphibious Warfare, 1985; Flag Officer Royal Yachts, 1985–90. Younger Brother of Trinity House, 1974. Freeman of City of London, 1982. *Recreations:* sailing, golf, gardening, opera. *Address:* 22 Friary Court, St James's Palace, SW1A 1BJ.

GARNOCK, Viscount; William James Lindesay-Bethune; *b* 30 Dec. 1990; *s* and *heir* of Earl of Lindsay, *qv*.

GARNONS WILLIAMS, Basil Hugh; Headmaster of Berkhamsted School, 1953–72; *b* 1 July 1906; 5th *s* of Rev. A. Garnons Williams, Rector of New Radnor; *m* 1943, Margaret Olive Shearme (*d* 1981); one *s* two *d*. *Educ:* Winchester Coll. (Scholar); Hertford Coll., Oxford (Scholar). 1st Hon. Classical Moderations 1927; 2nd Lit Hum 1929; BA 1929; BLitt 1933; MA 1938; Classical VI Form Master, Sedbergh Sch., 1930–35; Marlborough Coll., 1935–45; Headmaster of Plymouth Coll., 1945–53. *Publications:* A History of Berkhamsted School, 1541–1972, 1980; Berkhamsted School for Girls, a Centenary History (1888–1988), 1988; articles in Classical Quarterly and Greece and Rome; contributor to History of the World (ed by W. N. Weech), 1944. *Address:* Remenham Place, Remenham Hill, near Henley-on-Thames, Berks RG9 3EU. *T:* Henley-on-Thames (0491) 572875.

GARNSEY, Rt. Rev. David Arthur; *b* 31 July 1909; *s* of Canon Arthur Henry Garnsey and Bertha Edith Frances Garnsey (*née* Benn); *m* 1934, Evangeline Eleanor Wood; two *s* two *d*. *Educ:* Trinity and Sydney Grammar Schs; St Paul's Coll., University of Sydney; New Coll., Oxford. University of Sydney, BA (1st cl. Latin and Greek) 1930; Travelling Sec. Australian SCM, 1930–31; NSW Rhodes Scholar, 1931, New Coll. Oxford, BA (2nd cl. Lit. Hum.) 1933, 2nd cl. Theol. 1934, MA 1937; Ripon Hall, Oxford, 1933. Deacon, 1934; Priest, 1935; Curate, St Mary the Virgin (University Church), and Inter-Collegiate Sec. of SCM, Oxford, 1934–38; St Saviour's Cathedral, Goulburn, NSW, 1938–41; Rector of Young, NSW, 1941–45; Gen. Sec. Australian SCM, 1945–48; Exam. Chap. to Bp of Goulburn, 1939–45, 1948–58; Head Master Canberra Grammar Sch., 1948–58; Canon of St Saviour's Cathedral, Goulburn, 1949–58; Bishop of Gippsland, 1959–74. Pres., Australian Council of Churches, 1970–73. Chm., Bd of Delegates, Aust. Coll. of Theology, 1971–77; Hon. ThD, Australian Coll. of Theology, 1955. Coronation Medal, 1953. *Publications:* A. H. Garnsey: a man for truth and freedom, 1985; booklets for study. *Recreation:* reading. *Address:* 33 Dutton Street, Dickson, Canberra, ACT 2602, Australia. *T:* 062–474786.

GARRARD, Rev. Lancelot Austin, LLD; BD, MA; Professor of Philosophy and Religion, Emerson College, Boston, USA, 1965–71, now Emeritus; *b* 31 May 1904; *s* of late Rev. W. A. Garrard; *m* 1932, Muriel Walsh (*d* 1984); two *s*. *Educ:* Felsted (Scholar); Wadham Coll., Oxford (exhibitioner); Manchester Coll., Oxford; Marburg (Hibbert scholar). 2nd Class, Classical Mods; 2nd Class Lit Hum; Abbot Scholar; BD, MA (Oxon). Asst Master: Edinburgh Acad., 1927; St Paul's Sch., 1928; Unitarian Minister, Dover, 1932–33; Tutor and Bursar, Manchester Coll., Oxford, 1933–43; Minister, Lewins Mead Meeting, Bristol, 1941–43; Liverpool, Ancient Chapel of Toxteth, 1943–52; Tutor, Unitarian Coll., Manchester, 1945–51; Manchester Coll., Oxford, 1952–56; Principal of Manchester Coll., Oxford, 1956–65, Pres., 1980–86; Editor of The Hibbert Journal, 1951–62. Hon. Chief, Chickasaw Nation. Hon. LLD (Emerson Coll, Boston). *Publications:* Duty and the Will of God, 1935; The Interpreted Bible, 1946; The Gospels To-day, 1953; The Historical Jesus: Schweitzer's Quest and Ours, 1956; Athens or Jerusalem?, 1965; Aide-de-Camp to Sir Stamford Raffles: Lt-Col R. C. Garnham, 1985; Index to The Hibbert Journal, 1987. *Address:* 7 Bancroft Court, Reigate, Surrey RH2 7RW. *T:* Reigate (0737) 249672.

GARRARD, Ven. Richard; Archdeacon of Sudbury, since 1991; *b* 24 May 1937; *s* of Charles John Garrard and Marjorie Louise (*née* Pow); *m* 1961, Elizabeth Ann Sewell; one *s* one *d*. *Educ:* Northampton Grammar Sch.; King's Coll., Univ. of London (BD, AKC, MBIM). Ordained deacon, 1961, priest, 1962; Assistant Curate: St Mary's, Woolwich, 1961–66; Great St Mary's, Cambridge, 1966–68; Chaplain/Lectr, Keswick Hall Coll. of Educn, Norwich, 1968–74; Principal, Church Army Training Coll., 1974–79; Canon Chancellor, Southwark Cathedral and Dir of Training, dio. of Southwark, 1979–87; Canon Residentiary, St James's Cathedral, Bury St Edmunds and Advr for Clergy Training, dio. of St Edmundsbury and Ipswich, 1987–91. *Publication:* Picture, Ponder, Pray, Promise, 1991. *Recreations:* cats, crosswords. *Address:* c/o Diocesan House, Tower Street, Ipswich, Suffolk IP1 3BG. *T:* Ipswich (0473) 211028.

GARRELS, John Carlyle; retired; Chairman: Monsanto Chemicals Ltd, 1965–71; Monsanto Textiles Ltd, 1970–71; formerly Director: Forth Chemicals Ltd; Monsanto Australia Ltd; Monsanto Oil Co. of UK, Inc.; British Saccharin Sales Ltd; *b* 5 March 1914; *s* of John C. and Margaret Ann Garrels; *m* 1st, 1938, Valerie Smith; one *s* two *d*; 2nd, 1980, Isabelle Rogers Kehoe. *Educ:* Univ. of Michigan (BS (Chem. Eng.)); Harvard (Advanced Management Programme). Pennsylvania Salt Mfg Co., Production Supervisor, 1936–42; Monsanto Co.: various appts, 1942–54; Asst Gen. Manager, 1955; Monsanto Chemicals Ltd: Dep. Man. Dir, 1960; Man. Dir, 1961; Chm. and Man. Dir, 1965. Pres., British Plastics Fedn, 1970, 1971. Member: National Economic Development Cttee for

Chemical Industry, 1971; Council, Chemical Industries Assoc. *Recreations:* golf, shooting, fishing. *Address:* 3111 SE Fairway West, Stuart, Fla 34997, USA. *T:* 305–283–6132. *Clubs:* American; Sunningdale Golf; Yacht and Country (Stuart, Fla); Fishing of America (New York).

GARRETT, Anthony David; Deputy Master and Comptroller, Royal Mint, since 1988; Director: National Provident Institution, since 1988; Pitney Bowes plc, since 1989; *b* 26 Aug. 1928; *s* of Sir William Garrett, MBE and Lady Garrett; *m* 1952, Monica Blanche Harris; three *s* one *d. Educ:* Ellesmere College; Clare College, Cambridge. MA. National Service, Subaltern IVth QO Hussars, 1946–48; Procter & Gamble Co., 1953–82, Vice-Pres., 1975–82; Bd Mem., 1983–87, and Man. Dir of Parcels, 1986–87, Post Office. FRSA 1991. *Recreations:* golf, bridge, chess, walking. *Address:* Cammock House, Goldsmith Avenue, Crowborough, East Sussex TN6 1RH. *T:* Crowborough (0892) 654557. *Club:* United Oxford & Cambridge University.

GARRETT, Godfrey John, OBE 1982; HM Diplomatic Service; Counsellor, Prague, since 1990; *b* 24 July 1937; *s* of Thomas and May Garrett; *m* 1963, Elisabeth Margaret Hall; four *s* one *d. Educ:* Dulwich Coll.; Cambridge Univ. (MA). Joined FO, 1961; Third Sec., Leopoldville (later Kinshasa), 1963; Second Sec. (Commercial), Prague, 1965; FCO, 1968; First Sec., Buenos Aires, 1971; FCO, 1973; First Sec., later Counsellor, Stockholm, 1981; Counsellor: Bonn, 1983; FCO, 1988; E Berlin, 1990. Order of the Northern Star, Sweden, 1983. *Recreations:* all outdoor activities, especially skiing; travel, gardening, languages. *Address:* c/o Foreign and Commonwealth Office, SW1A 2AH; White Cottage, Henley, Haslemere, Surrey GU27 3HQ. *T:* Haslemere (0428) 652172.

GARRETT, Maj.-Gen. Henry Edmund Melvill Lennox, CBE 1975; Chairman, Forces Help Society and Lord Roberts Workshops, since 1991; *b* 31 Jan. 1924; *s* of John Edmund Garrett and Mary Garrett; *m* 1973, Rachel Ann Beadon; one step *s* one step *d. Educ:* Wellington Coll.; Clare Coll., Cambridge (MA). Commnd 1944; psc 1956; DAAG, HQ BAOR, 1957–60; US Armed Forces Staff Coll., 1960; OC 7 Field Sqdn RE, 1961–63; GSO2 WO, 1963–65; CO 35 Engr Regt, 1965–68; Col GS MoD, 1968–69; Comdr 12 Engr Bde, 1969–71; RCDS, 1972; Chief of Staff HQ N Ireland, 1972–75; Maj.-Gen. i/c Administration, HQ UKLF, 1975–76; Vice Adjutant General, MoD, 1976–78; Dir of Security (Army), MoD, 1978–89. Col Comdt RE, 1982–90. Chm., RE Assoc., 1989–. Chm. Governors, Royal Soldiers' Daughters Sch., 1983–86. *Recreations:* riding, walking. *Address:* c/o National Westminster Bank, 1 Market Street, Bradford, Yorkshire BD1 1EQ. *Club:* Army and Navy.

GARRETT, John Laurence; MP (Lab) Norwich South, since 1987; *b* 8 Sept. 1931; *s* of Laurence and Rosina Garrett; *m* 1959, Wendy Ady; two *d. Educ:* Selwyn Avenue Primary Sch., London; Sir George Monoux Sch., London; University Coll., Oxford (MA, BLitt); Grad. Business Sch. of Univ. of California at Los Angeles (King George VI Fellow). Labour Officer, chemical industry, 1958–59; Head of Market Research, motor industry, 1959–63; Management Consultant, Dir of Public Services, 1963–74, and Associate Dir, 1983–87, Inbucon Ltd. Consultant to Fulton Cttee on CS, 1966–68. MP (Lab) Norwich South, Feb. 1974–1983; PPS to Minister for Civil Service, 1974, to Minister for Social Security, 1977–79; Opposition Treasury spokesman, 1979–80; spokesman: on industry, 1980–83; on energy, 1987–88; on industry, 1988–89; Campaigns Coordinator, Southern and Eastern England, 1989–. Contested (Lab) Norwich South, 1983. *Publications:* Visual Economics, 1966; (with S. D. Walker) Management by Objectives in the Civil Service, 1969; The Management of Government, 1972; Administrative Reform, 1973; Policies Towards People, 1973 (Sir Frederic Hooper Award); Managing the Civil Service, 1980; articles and papers on industry, management and govt. *Recreations:* theatre, dabbling, arguing. *Address:* c/o House of Commons, SW1A 0AA.

GARRETT, Hon. Sir Raymond (William), Kt 1973; AFC, AEA; JP; President, Legislative Council of Victoria, Australia, 1968–76 (Chairman of Committees, 1964–68); Chairman, Parliamentary Library Committee and Vice-Chairman, House Committee, 1968–76; *b* 19 Oct. 1900; *s* of J. J. P. Garrett, Kew, Australia; *m* 1934, Vera H., *d* of C. E. Lugton; one *s* two *d. Educ:* Royal Melbourne Technical Coll.; Univ. of Melbourne. Grad. RAAF Flying Sch., Point Cook, 1926; Citizen Air Force, 1927–37; Commercial Air Pilot, 1927–46. Founded Gliding Club of Vic., and Vic. Gliding Assoc., 1928; British Empire Glider Duration Record, 1931. Served War of 1939–45, RAAF; retd as Gp Captain, 1945 (AFC, AEA). Pres., No 2 Squadron RAAF Assoc. Councillor, Shire of Doncaster and Templestowe, 1954–60; Pres. and Chief Magistrate, 1955–56. Member Legislative Council: for Southern Province, Vic., 1958–70; for Templestowe Province, 1970–76. Member, Statute Law Revision Cttee, 1963–64; Govt Rep. on Council of Monash Univ., 1967–71. Knighted for services in politics, civic affairs and defence, Victoria; Life Governor, Lady Nell Seeing Eye Dog School. Chairman of Directors: Ilford (Aust.) Pty Ltd, 1965–75; Cine Service Pty Ltd. Pres., Victorian Parly Former Members' Assoc; Pres., Baden Powell Guild, Victoria. FInstD. Freeman (first), Doncaster and Templestowe, Vic, 1988. *Recreations:* photography, sports cars. *Address:* Elgar Court, 614 Elgar Road, Box Hill North, Vic 3129, Australia. *Clubs:* Royal Automobile; Air Force (Vic.).

GARRETT, Richard Anthony, CBE 1987; CBIM; company director; Chairman, National Association of Boys' Clubs, 1980–87, retired; *b* 4 July 1918; 3rd *s* of Charles Victor Garrett and Blanche Michell; *m* 1946, Marie Louise Dalglish; one *s* two *d* (and one *d* decd). *Educ:* King's Sch., Worcester. MInstD; CBIM 1979. Served War, 1939–45 (despatches, 1945). Joined W.D. & H.O. Wills, 1936; Chm., ITL, retd 1979; Chm. and Man. Dir, John Player & Sons, 1968–71; Chm., Dataday Ltd, 1978–83; Director: HTV Gp plc, 1976–89 (Vice-Chm., 1978–83); Standard Commercial (formerly Standard Commercial Tobacco) Corp., 1980–. Member: (Founder), Assoc. of Business Sponsorship of the Arts (Dep. Chm., Adv. Council); National Cttee for Electoral Reform. Chm., Bath Festival, 1986–87; Trustee, Glyndebourne Arts Trust, 1976–88. Liveryman, Worshipful Co. of Tobacco Pipe Makers and Tobacco Blenders. *Recreations:* golf, gardening, music, opera, reading. *Address:* Marlwood Grange, Thornbury, Bristol BS12 2JB. *T:* Thornbury (0454) 412630. *Clubs:* Naval and Military, MCC, XL; Bristol and Clifton Golf.

GARRETT, Terence, CMG 1990; CBE 1967; Counsellor (Science and Technology), British Embassy, Moscow, 1987–91; *b* 27 Sept. 1929; *e s* of late Percy Herbert Garrett and Gladys Annie Garrett (*née* Budd); *m* 1960, Grace Elizabeth Bridgeman Braund, *yr d* of Rev. Basil Kelly Braund; two *s* three *d. Educ:* Alleyn's Sch.; Gonville and Caius Coll., Cambridge (Scholar; 1st Cl. Hons, Mathematics). DipMathStat. Instructor Lieut RN, 1952–55. Lecturer, Ewell County Technical Coll., 1955–56; Sen. Lectr, RMCS, Shrivenham, 1957–62; Counsellor (Sci. and Technol.), Moscow, 1962–66 and 1970–74; Programmes Analysis Unit, Min. of Technology, 1967–70; Internat. Technological Collaboration Unit, Dept of Trade, 1974–76; Sec. to Bd of Governors and to Gen. Conf. of Internat. Atomic Energy Agency, Vienna, 1976–78; Counsellor (Science and Technology), Bonn, 1978–82; DCSO, Research and Technology Policy Div., DTI, 1982–87. *Recreation:* travel. *Address:* Lime Tree Farmhouse, Chilton, Didcot, Oxon OX11 0SW. *Club:* Royal Over-Seas League.

GARRETT, Thomas John; Member, Independent Commission for Police Complaints (Northern Ireland), since 1990; Principal, Royal Belfast Academical Institution, 1978–90; *b* 13 Sept. 1927; *s* of late Mr and Mrs T. J. Garrett; *m* 1958, Sheenah Agnew, *o d* of late Mr and Mrs G. Marshall, Drymen, Stirlingshire; one *d. Educ:* Royal Belfast Acad. Instn; QUB (BA); Heidelberg Univ. Asst Master: Royal Belfast Acad. Instn, 1951–54; Nottingham High Sch. for Boys, 1954–56; Sen. German Master, Campbell Coll., Belfast, 1956–73, Housemaster, 1968–73; Headmaster, Portora Royal Sch., Enniskillen, 1973–78. Member: Broadcasting Council for N Ireland, 1982–84; Northern Ireland Partnership, 1987–. *Publications:* Modern German Humour, 1969; Two Hundred Years at the Top—a dramatised history of Portora Royal School, 1977. *Recreations:* writing, hill-walking, ornithology. *Address:* Carnbeg, 44 Dunmore Road, Spa, Ballynahinch, Co. Down BT24 8PR. *T:* Ballynahinch (0238) 562399. *Club:* East India.

GARRETT, William Edward; MP (Lab) Wallsend since 1964; *b* 21 March 1920; *s* of John Garrett, coal miner, and Frances (*née* Barwise); *m* 1st, 1946, Beatrice Kelly (*d* 1978); one *s*; 2nd, 1980, Noel Stephanie Ann Johnson. *Educ:* Prudhoe Elementary Sch.; London Sch. of Economics. Commenced work in coal mines, 1934; served engineering apprenticeship, 1936–40; employed by ICI, 1946–64; Union Organiser at ICI, 1946–64; Mem. of AEU. Member: Prudhoe UDC, 1946–64; Northumberland County Council, 1955–64. Mem. of Labour Party, 1939–; Labour Candidate for Hexham 1953–55, Doncaster 1957–64. Member: Select Cttee on Agriculture, 1966–69; Expenditure Cttee, 1971–79; Sec., All-Party Group for Chem. Industry. Member: Council of Europe, 1979–; WEU, 1979–. Parliamentary Adviser, Machine Tools Trades Assoc. *Recreations:* gardening, walking, reading. *Address:* 84 Broomhill Road, Prudhoe-on-Tyne, Northumberland NE42 5HX. *T:* Prudhoe (0661) 32580. *Club:* Prudhoe Working Men's.

GARRICK, Ronald, CBE 1986; FEng 1984; Managing Director and Chief Executive, Weir Group, since 1982; *b* 21 Aug. 1940; *s* of Thomas Garrick and Anne (*née* McKay); *m* 1965, Janet Elizabeth Taylor Lind; two *s* one *d. Educ:* Royal College of Science and Technology, Glasgow; Glasgow University (BSc MechEng, 1st cl. hons). FIMechE. Joined G. & J. Weir Ltd, 1962; Weir Pumps: Dir, Industrial Div., 1973; Dir Production Div., 1976; Managing Dir, 1981; Dir, Weir Group, 1981. Vis. Prof., Mech. Engrg, Univ. of Strathclyde, 1991. Member: Scottish Council, CBI, 1982–90; Gen. Convocation, 1985–, Court, 1990–, Univ. of Strathclyde; Restrictive Practices Court, 1986–; Scottish Economic Council, 1989–; Offshore Industry Adv. Bd, 1989–; Dep. Chm., Scottish Enterprise Bd, 1991–. Non-Executive Director: Supervisory Bd, NEL, 1989–; Strathclyde Graduate Business Sch., 1990–. *Recreations:* golf, reading. *Address:* 3 Duart Drive, Newton Mearns, Glasgow G77 5DS. *T:* 041–639 3088. *Club:* Caledonian.

GARRIOCH, Sir (William) Henry, Kt 1978; Chief Justice, Mauritius, 1977–78, retired; *b* 4 May 1916; *s* of Alfred Garrioch and Jeanne Marie Madeleine Colin; *m* 1964, Jeanne Louise Marie-Thérèse Desvaux de Marigny. *Educ:* Royal Coll., Mauritius. Called to the Bar, Gray's Inn, 1952. Civil Service (clerical), Mauritius, 1936–48; law student, London, 1949–52; Dist Magistrate, Mauritius, 1955; Crown Counsel, 1958; Sen. Crown Counsel, 1960; Solicitor-Gen., 1964; Dir of Public Prosecutions, 1966; Puisne Judge, 1967; Sen. Puisne Judge, 1970; Actg Governor-Gen., 1977–78. *Recreations:* reading, chess, badminton. *Address:* Lees Street, Curepipe, Mauritius. *T:* 862708.

GARROD, Lt-Gen. Sir (John) Martin (Carruthers), KCB 1988; OBE 1980; Commandant General, Royal Marines, 1987–90; *b* 29 May 1935; *s* of Rev. William Francis Garrod and Isobel Agnes (*née* Carruthers); *m* 1963, Gillian Mary, *d* of late Lt-Col R. G. Parks-Smith, RM; two *d. Educ:* Sherborne School. Joined Royal Marines, 1953; served Malta, Cyprus, DS Officers' Training Wing, RM School of Music, Malaya, Borneo, 1955–66; Staff Coll., Camberley, 1967; HQ 17 Div., Malaya, 1968–69; HQ Farelf, Singapore, 1970–71; 40 Commando RM (Co. Comdr, Plymouth and N Ireland), 1972–73 (despatches); GSO2 Plans, Dept of CGRM, 1973–76; GSO1, HQ Commando Forces RM, 1976–78; CO 40 Commando RM, 1978–79 (OBE operational, NI); Col Ops/Plans, Dept of CGRM, 1980–82; Comdr 3 Commando Bde RM, 1983–84; ADC to the Queen, 1983–84; COS to Comdt Gen. RM, 1984–87. Liveryman, Plaisterers' Co., 1990. *Recreation:* portrait photography. *Address:* c/o Lloyds Bank, 5 The Square, Petersfield, Hants GU32 3HL. *Club:* East India.

GARRY, Robert Campbell, OBE 1976; Regius Professor of Physiology, University of Glasgow, 1947–70, retired; *b* April 1900; *s* of Robert Garry and Mary Campbell; *m* 1928, Flora Macdonald, *d* of Archibald and Helen Campbell; one *s. Educ:* Glasgow Univ. MB, ChB with Hons, Glasgow Univ., 1922; Brunton Memorial Prize; DSc, Glasgow Univ., 1933; continued studies in Freiburg im B, Germany; University Coll., London; Medical Sch., Leeds; Asst and then Lectr, Institute of Physiology, Glasgow Univ.; Head of Physiology Dept, Rowett Research Institute, Aberdeen, 1933–35; Lectr on the Physiology of Nutrition, University of Aberdeen, 1933–35; Prof. of Physiology, University Coll., Dundee, The University of St Andrews, 1935–47; Member: MRC, 1955–59; Sci. Adv. Cttee on Med. Res. in Scotland, 1948–52, 1955–59; Physiol. Sub-Cttee of Flying Personnel Res. Cttee, 1951–75 (Chm., 1967–75); Bd of Management, Hill Farming Res. Orgn, 1963–72. Hon. Mem. Physiol. Soc., 1925; foundn Mem., Nutrition Soc., 1941, Pres., 1950–53, Hon. Mem., 1981. FRSE 1937; FRCPGlas 1948. *Publications:* Papers in scientific periodicals, dealing especially with gastrointestinal physiology and nutrition. *Recreations:* gardening, reading. *Address:* Laich Dyke, Dalginross, Comrie, Crieff, Perthshire PH6 2HB. *T:* Comrie (0764) 70474.

GARSIDE, (Pamela) Jane; JP; Chief Commissioner, Girl Guides Association of the United Kingdom and the Commonwealth, since 1990; *b* 20 Aug. 1936; *d* of Ronald and Nellie Whitwam; *m* 1958, Adrian Fielding Garside; two *s* (two *d* decd). *Educ:* Royds Hall Grammar Sch., Huddersfield; Yorkshire Trng Coll. of Housecraft, Leeds Inst. of Educn (Teaching Dip. 1957). Teacher, Deighton Secondary Sch., 1957–58; Co. Sec. 1959–, Dir 1964–, Highfield Funeral Service Ltd. *Recreations:* reading, gardening, music. *Address:* Girl Guides Association, 17–19 Buckingham Palace Road, SW1W 0PT. *T:* 071–834 6242.

GARSIDE, Roger Ramsay; Chairman, Garside, Miller Associates, advisers to emerging securities markets, since 1990; *b* 29 March 1938; *s* of Capt F. R. Garside and Mrs Peggie Garside; *m* 1969, Evelyne Madeleine Pierrette Guérin; three *d. Educ:* Eton; Clare Coll., Cambridge (BA EngLit, MA); Sloan Fellow in Management, Massachusetts Inst. of Technology. 2nd Lieut, 1/6 QEO Gurkha Rifles, 1958–59; entered HM Foreign Service, 1962; served, Rangoon, 1964–65; Mandarin Chinese Lang. Student, Hong Kong, 1965–67; Second Secretary, Peking, 1968–70; FCO, 1970–71; resigned 1971; World Bank, 1972–74; rejoined Foreign Service, 1975; served FCO, 1975; First Sec., Peking, 1976–79; on leave of absence, as Vis. Professor of East Asian Studies, US Naval Postgrad. Sch., Monterey, Calif, 1979–80; Dep. Head, Planning Staff, FCO, 1980–81; seconded, HM Treasury, 1981–82; Financial and Commercial Counsellor, Paris, 1982–87, resigned 1987; Dir, Public Affairs, Internat. Stock Exchange of UK and Rep. of Ireland, 1987–89. *Publication:* Coming Alive: China after Mao, 1981. *Recreations:* writing, riding, tennis. *Address:* 36 Groveway, SW9 0AR. *T:* 071–582 1577. *Club:* Reform.

GARSON, Greer; actress; *b* Northern Ireland, 29 Sept. 1908; *d* of George Garson and Nina Sophia Greer; *m* 1st, Edward A. Snelson (marr. diss.) (*see* Sir E. A. Snelson); 2nd, 1943, Richard Ney (marr. diss.); 3rd, 1949, Col E. E. Fogelson (*d* 1987), Texas. *Educ:* London and Grenoble Univs. BA Hons London. Birmingham Repertory Theatre, 1932 and 1933; London Theatre debut, Whitehall, 1935; lead roles in 13 London plays; entered films in 1939; *films include:* Goodbye Mr Chips, Pride and Prejudice, When Ladies Meet, Blossoms in the Dust, Mrs Miniver (Academy Award), Random Harvest, Madame Curie, Mrs Parkington, Valley of Decision, That Forsyte Woman, Julius Caesar, The Law and the Lady, Her Twelve Men, Sunrise at Campobello (Golden Globe award), Strange Lady in Town, The Singing Nun, The Happiest Millionaire; *stage appearances include:* Auntie Mame, Tonight at 8.30, Captain Brassbound's Conversion. Appeared in pioneer British TV, on American TV. Hon. DHum, Rollins Coll., Florida, 1950; Hon. Dr in Communication Arts, Coll. of Santa Fe, 1970; Hon. DLitt Ulster, 1977; winner of many internat. awards. Current interests include The Greer Garson Theatre and Fogelson Library Center, Coll. of Santa Fe; Mem. Bd, Dallas Theater Center; adjunct prof. in drama, Southern Methodist Univ., Dallas; Mem., State Commn on the arts in Texas and New Mexico; Principal Founding Donor: Fogelson Forum, Dallas Presbyterian Hosp.; Garson Communications Center, Coll. of Santa Fe; Fogelson Pavilion, Meyerson Symphony Center, Dallas; Fogelson Fountain, Dallas Arboretum; Greer Garson Theatre, Southern Methodist Univ., Dallas. Hon. Alumna, St John's Coll., Santa Fe. Operates Forked Lightning Ranch, Pecos, New Mexico, where Pecos Nat. Monument and Visitors Centre located (with Col E. E. Fogelson, received Conservation Service Award, US Dept of Interior, 1981, for this and other civic projects); also involved in breeding and racing thoroughbred horses (stable includes Ack Ack, horse of the year, 1971). *Recreations:* nature study, music, primitive art. *Address:* Suite 2400, 325 N St Paul, Dallas, Texas 75201, USA.

GARSON, Cdre Robin William, CBE 1978; RN retd; Director of Leisure Services, London Borough of Hillingdon, 1975–86; *b* 13 Nov. 1921; *s* of late Peter Garson and Ada Frances (*née* Newton); *m* 1946, Joy Ligertwood Taylor (*née* Hickman); one *s* one *d*. *Educ:* School of Oriental and African Studies. Japanese Interpreter. Entered Royal Navy, 1937; served War of 1939–45, HM Ships: Resolution, Nigeria, Cyclops, and HM Submarines: Seawolf, H.33, Spark; subsequent principal appointments: In Command HM Submarines: Universal, Uther, Seraph, Saga, Sanguine, Springer, Thule, Astute, 1945–54; Chief Staff Officer Intelligence, Far East, 1966–68; Sen. Polaris UK Rep., Washington, 1969–71; Captain 1st Submarine Sqdn, 1971–73; Commodore, HMS Drake, 1973–75; ADC to the Queen, 1974. Adviser to AMA on Arts and Recreation, 1976–86; Adviser to Sports Council, 1985–86; Mem., Library Adv. Council (England), 1977–83. *Recreations:* golf, ski-ing, tennis. *Address:* Gateways, Hamilton Road West, Old Hunstanton, Norfolk PE36 6JB. *Clubs:* Army and Navy, Royal Navy of 1765 and 1785; Moor Park (Rickmansworth); Hunstanton Golf.

GARSTANG, Walter Lucian, BSc, MA; Headmaster of the Roan School, Greenwich, 1959–68, retired 1968; *b* 2 Sept. 1908; *o s* of late Walter Garstang, MA, DSc; *m* 1933, Barbara Mary, *d* of late Dr S. E. Denyer, CMG, MD; one *s* two *d*. (and one *s* decd). *Educ:* Oundle Sch.; Oxford (Scholar of Trinity Coll., 1927–31). Research chemist, The Gas Light and Coke Co., 1931–37; asst master, Oundle Sch., 1937–44; asst master, Merchant Taylors' Sch., 1944–46; senior science master, Maidstone Grammar Sch., 1946–48; Headmaster, Owen's Sch., 1949–54; Headmaster, Loughborough Grammar Sch., 1955–58. *Address:* 21 Wells Close, Cheltenham GL51 5BX.

GARTHWAITE, Sir William, 2nd Bt, *cr* 1919; DSC 1941 and Bar, 1942; former Chairman, Sir William Garthwaite (Holdings) Ltd; *b* 3 Jan. 1906; *o s* of Sir William Garthwaite, 1st Bt and Francesca Margherita, *d* of James Parfett; *S* father 1956; *m* 1st, 1931, Hon. Dorothy Duveen (marr. diss. 1937) (*d* 1985), *d* of 1st Baron Duveen; 2nd, 1945, Patricia Leonard (marr. diss. 1952); one *s*; 3rd, 1957, Patricia Merriel, *d* of Sir Philip d'Ambrumenil; three *s* (one *d* decd). *Educ:* Bradfield Coll., Berks; Hertford Coll., Oxford. Lloyd's Underwriter and Insur. Broker at Lloyd's, 1926–. Farmer. Contested (C): Hemsworth Div. of W Riding of Yorks, 1931; Isle of Ely, 1935; E Div. of Wolverhampton, 1945; Pres., Royal Tunbridge Wells Cons. Assoc. Served War of 1939–45 as pilot, Fleet Air Arm (DSC and bar, despatches thrice, Air Crew Europe Star, Atlantic Star, Africa Star, 1939–45 Star, Defence Medal). Coronation Medal, 1953. *Recreations:* flying, ski-ing, golf and sailing. *Heir:* *s* William Mark Charles Garthwaite [*b* 4 Nov. 1946; *m* 1979, Mrs Victoria Lisette Hohler, *e d* of Gen. Sir Harry Tuzo, *qv*; one *s* two *d*]. *Address:* Matfield House, Matfield, Kent TN12 7JT. *T:* Brenchley 2454. *Clubs:* Portland, Naval, Royal Thames; Jockey (Paris).

GARTON, George Alan, PhD, DSc; FRSE 1966; FRS 1978; Hon. Research Associate, Rowett Research Institute, Bucksburn, Aberdeen, since 1983; Hon. Research Fellow, University of Aberdeen, since 1987; *b* 4 June 1922; *o s* of late William Edgar Garton, DCM, and late Frances Mary Elizabeth Garton (*née* Atkinson), Scarborough, N Yorks; *m* 1951, Gladys Frances Davison; two *d*. *Educ:* Scarborough High Sch.; Univ. of Liverpool (BSc: (War Service) 1944, (Hons Biochem.) 1946; PhD 1949, DSc 1959). Experimental Asst, Chemical Inspection Dept, Min. of Supply, 1942–45; Johnston Research and Teaching Fellow, Dept of Biochem., Univ. of Liverpool, 1949–50; Rowett Research Inst., Bucksburn, Aberdeen: Biochemist, 1950; Dep. Dir, 1968–83; Head of Lipid Biochem. Dept, 1963–83; Hon. Research Associate, Univ. of Aberdeen, 1966–86. Sen. Foreign Fellow of Nat. Science Foundn (USA), and Vis. Prof. of Biochem., Univ. of N Carolina, 1967. Chm., British Nat. Cttee for Nutritional and Food Sciences, 1982–87; Pres., Internat. Confs on Biochem. Lipids, 1982–89. Scientific Gov., British Nutrition Foundn, 1982–; SBStJ 1985. *Publications:* papers, mostly on aspects of lipid biochemistry, in scientific jls. *Recreations:* gardening, golf, foreign travel. *Address:* Ellerburn, 1 St Devenick Crescent, Cults, Aberdeen AB1 9LL. *T:* Aberdeen (0224) 867012. *Clubs:* Farmers'; Deeside Golf (Aberdeen).

GARTON, Rev. Canon John Henry; Principal of Ripon College, Cuddesdon, since 1986; *b* 3 Oct. 1941; *s* of Henry and Dorothy Garton; *m* 1969, Pauline (*née* George); two *s*. *Educ:* RMA Sandhurst; Worcester Coll., Oxford (MA, DipTh); Cuddesdon Coll., Oxford. Commissioned in Royal Tank Regt, 1962. Ordained, 1969; CF, 1969–73; Lectr, Lincoln Theol Coll., 1973–78; Rector of Coventry East Team Ministry, 1978–86. Hon. Canon of Worcester Cathedral, 1988–. *Address:* The Old Vicarage, High Street, Cuddesdon, Oxford OX9 9HP. *T:* Wheatley (08677) 4368.

GARTON, John Leslie, CBE 1974 (MBE (mil.) 1946); President, Henley Royal Regatta, since 1978; *b* 1 April 1916; *er s* of late C. Leslie Garton and Madeline Laurence; *m* 1939, Elizabeth Frances, *d* of late Sir Walter Erskine Crum, OBE; one *s* (and two *s* decd). *Educ:* Eton; Magdalen Coll., Oxford (MA). Commissioned TA, Royal Berkshire Regt, 1938. Served War, in France, 1940; psc 1943; Gen. Staff Ops Br., First Canadian Army HQ, in Europe, 1944–46; transf. to RARO, Scots Guards, 1951. Chm., Coca-Cola Bottling Co. (Oxford) Ltd, 1951–65, Coca-Cola Western Bottlers Ltd, 1966–71. Henley Royal Regatta: Steward, 1960; Mem. Cttee of Management, 1961–77; Chm., 1966–77. Amateur Rowing Association: Exec. Cttee and Council, 1948–77; Pres., 1969–77; Hon. Life Vice-Pres., 1978. Hon. Sec. and Treas., OUBC Trust Fund, 1959–69; Mem., Finance and Gen. Purposes Cttee, British Olympic Assoc., 1969–77; Thames Conservator, 1970–74; Chm.,

World Rowing Championships, 1975; Pres., Leander Club, 1980–83; Chm., Leander Trust, 1982–. Liveryman, Grocers' Company, 1947–. High Sheriff, Bucks, 1977. *Recreations:* supporting the sport of rowing (rowed in Eton VIII, 1934, 1935, Captain of the Boats, 1935; rowed in the Boat Race for Oxford, 1938, 1939, Pres. OUBC, 1939), shooting (particularly deer-stalking), fishing. *Address:* Mill Green House, Church Street, Wargrave, Berkshire RG10 8EP. *T:* Wargrave (0734) 402944. *Club:* Leander (elected 1936, Life Mem., 1953, Cttee, 1956, Chm. Executive, 1958–59).

GARTON, Prof. William Reginald Stephen, FRS 1969; Professor of Spectroscopy, University of London, Imperial College, 1964–79, now Professor Emeritus; Associate Head, 1970–79, and Senior Research Fellow, since 1979, Department of Physics, Imperial College; *b* Chelsea, SW3, 7 March 1912; *s* of William and Gertrude Emma Caroline Garton; *m* 1st, 1940, Margarita Fraser Callingham (marr. diss. 1976); four *d*; 2nd, 1976, Barbara Lloyd (*née* Jones). *Educ:* Sloane Sch., SW10; Chelsea Polytechnic, SW3; Imperial Coll., (Hon. Fellow 1983). BSc, ARCS 1936; DSc 1958. Demonstrator in Physics, Imperial Coll., 1936–39. Served in RAF, 1939–45. Imperial Coll.: Lectr in Physics, 1946–54; Sen. Lectr, 1954–57; Reader, 1957–64. External Examiner: Univ. of Singapore, 1972–75; Univ. of Malaya, 1986–89. Associate, Harvard Coll. Observatory, 1963–; Nuffield Fellow, Univ. of Western Ontario, 1964; Hertz Fellow, Univ. of Bonn, 1984; Leverhulme Trust Emeritus Fellow, 1987–89. W. F. Meggers Award, 1976, Fellow, 1979, Optical Soc. of America. Hon. DSc York Univ., Toronto, 1972. *Publications:* contrib. on Spectroscopy in Advances in Atomic and Molecular Physics (ed D. R. Bates), 1966 (New York); numerous papers on Spectroscopy and Atomic Physics. *Recreations:* speliology, Oriental history. *Address:* Blackett Laboratory, Imperial College, SW7. *T:* 071–589 5111; Chart House, Great Chart, Ashford, Kent TN23 3AP. *T:* Ashford (0233) 621657; 9 callé Tico Medina, Mojacar (Almeria), Spain.

GARVAGH, 5th Baron *cr* 1818; **Alexander Leopold Ivor George Canning;** Accredited Representative, Trade and Industry, The Cayman Islands, 1981; *b* 6 Oct. 1920; *s* of 4th Baron and Gladys Dora May (*d* 1982), *d* of William Bayley Parker; *S* father 1956; *m* 1st, 1947, Christine Edith (marr. diss. 1974), *d* of Jack Cooper; one *s* two *d*; 2nd, 1974, Cynthia Valerie Mary, *d* of Eric E. F. Pretty, CMG, Kingswood, Surrey. *Educ:* Eton; Christ Church, Oxford. Commissioned Corps of Guides Cavalry, Indian Army, 1940; served Burma (despatches). Mem. Court, Painter Stainers Co. Consultant and contributor, Spanish Property Gazette, 1987–88. *Publications:* contrib. to The Manufacturing Optician, 1949. *Recreations:* travel, motoring, and motor sport; writing articles, short stories, etc. *Heir:* *s* Hon. Spencer George Stratford de Redcliffe Canning [*b* 12 Feb. 1953; *m* 1979, Julia Margery Morison Bye, *er d* of Col F. C. E. Bye, Twickenham; one *d*]. *Address:* Apartado 289, Casa Canning, Calle Mar Menor 17, Costera del Mar, 03724 Moraira, Alicante, Spain. *Club:* Steering Wheel.

GARVEY, Thomas, (Tom); Director, Directorate General 1 (External Relations), European Commission, since 1990; *b* 27 May 1936; *s* of Thomas and Brigid Garvey; *m* 1961, Ellen Devine; two *s* two *d*. *Educ:* University Coll., Dublin (MA Econ). Fellow, Management Inst. Ireland. Various marketing and internal trade appts, 1958–69; Chief Exec., Irish Export Bd, 1969–76; EEC Delegate, Nigeria, 1977–80; Chief Exec., An Post (Irish Postal Service), 1980–84. FRSA. *Publications:* various, in industrial, trade and academic jls. *Recreations:* golf, music. *Club:* United Services (Dublin).

GARVIN, Clifton Canter, Jr; Chairman of the Board and Chief Executive Officer, Exxon Corporation, 1975–86, retired; *b* 22 Dec. 1921; *s* of Clifton C. Garvin, Sr, and Esther Ames; *m* 1943, Thelma Volland; one *s* three *d*. *Educ:* Virginia Polytechnic Inst. and State Univ. MS (ChemEng) 1947. Exxon: Process Engr, subseq. Refining Operating Supt, Baton Rouge, Louisiana Refinery, 1947–59; Asst Gen. Manager, Supply Dept, Exxon Corp., 1959–60; Gen. Manager, Supply Dept, Esso Eastern, 1960–61; Manager, Production, Supply & Distribution Dept, Exxon Co., USA, 1961–62, subseq. Vice-Pres., Central Region, 1963–64; Exec. Asst to Pres. and Chm., Exxon Corp., NY, 1964–65; Pres., Exxon Chemical (US), subseq. Pres. Exxon Chemical (Internat.), 1965–68; Dir, subseq. Exec. Vice-Pres., subseq. Pres., Exxon Corp., 1968–75. Director: Citicorp and Citibank; Hosp. Corp. of America; PepsiCo, Inc.; Johnson & Johnson; J. C. Penney Co., Inc.; TRW Inc.; Americas Soc.; Member: Amer. Inst. of Chem. Engrs; Business Roundtable; Council on Foreign Relns; Business Council; Nat. Associate, White Burkett Miller Center of Public Affairs, Univ. of Virginia; Member: Admin Bd, Lab. of Ornithology, Cornell Univ.; Virginia Polytechnic Institute and State University: Cttee of 100—Coll. of Engrg Corporate Develt; Bd of Visitors. *Recreations:* golf, bird watching. *Address:* Room 1250, One Rockefeller Plaza, New York, NY 10020, USA.

GARY, Lesley; see Blanch, L.

GASCH, Pauline Diana, (Mrs F. O. Gasch); see Baynes, P. D.

GASCOIGNE, Bamber; author and broadcaster; *b* 24 Jan. 1935; *s* of late Derick Gascoigne and Midi (*née* O'Neill); *m* 1965, Christina Ditchburn. *Educ:* Eton (Scholar); Magdalene Coll., Cambridge (Scholar). Commonwealth Fund Fellow, Yale, 1958–59. Theatre Critic, Spectator, 1961–63, and Observer, 1963–64; Co-editor, Theatre Notebook, 1968–74. Founded Saint Helena Press, 1977; Chm., Ackermann Publishing, 1981–85. Trustee, Nat. Gall., 1988–; Member: Bd of Dirs, Royal Opera House, Covent Garden, 1988–; Council, Nat. Trust, 1989–. Theatre: Share My Lettuce, London, 1957–58; Leda Had a Little Swan, New York, 1968; The Feydeau Farce Festival of Nineteen Nine, Greenwich, 1972; Big in Brazil, Old Vic, 1984. Television: presenter of: University Challenge, (weekly) 1962–87; Cinema, 1964; (also author) The Christians, 1977; Victorian Values, 1987; Man and Music, 1987; The Great Moghuls, 1990; deviser and presenter of Connoisseur, 1988–89; author of: The Four Freedoms, 1962; Dig This Rhubarb, 1963; The Auction Game, 1968. FRSL 1976. *Publications:* (many with photographs or watercolour illustrations by Christina Gascoigne): Twentieth Century Drama, 1962; World Theatre, 1968; The Great Moghuls, 1971; Murgatreud's Empire, 1972; The Heyday, 1973; The Treasures and Dynasties of China, 1973; Ticker Khan, 1974; The Christians, 1977; Images of Richmond, 1978; Images of Twickenham, 1981; Why the Rope went Tight, 1981; Fearless Freddy's Magic Wish, 1982; Fearless Freddy's Sunken Treasure, 1982; Quest for the Golden Hare, 1983; Cod Streuth, 1986; How to Identify Prints, 1986; Amazing Facts, 1988. *Address:* Saint Helena Terrace, Richmond, Surrey TW9 1NR.

GASCOIGNE, Stanley, CMG 1976; OBE 1972; Secretary to the Cabinet, Bermuda, 1972–76; Member, Senate, 1976–85, Vice-President, 1980–85; *b* 11 Dec. 1914; *s* of George William Gascoigne and Hilda Elizabeth Gascoigne; *m* 1st, 1941, Sybil Wellspring Outerbridge (*d* 1980); 2nd, 1980, Sandra Alison Lee; two *s*. *Educ:* Mt Allison Univ., Canada (BA 1937): London Univ., England (DipEd 1938): Boston Univ., USA (MEd 1951). Teacher, 1939–51; Inspector of Schools, 1951–59; Director, Marine and Ports Authority, 1959–69; Permanent Sec., Education, 1969–72. Exec. Dir, Inst. of Chartered Accountants of Bermuda, 1976–89. *Recreation:* ornithology. *Address:* Alcyone, Shelly Bay, Hamilton Parish CR BX, Bermuda. *T:* 293–1304. *Clubs:* Royal Bermuda Yacht, Royal Hamilton Amateur Dinghy (Bermuda).

GASH, Prof. Norman, CBE 1989; FBA 1963; FRSL 1973; FRSE 1977; FRHistS; Professor of History, St Salvator's College, University of St Andrews, 1955–80, now Emeritus; *b* 16 Jan. 1912; *s* of Frederick and Kate Gash; *m* 1935, Ivy Dorothy Whitehorn; two *d*. *Educ:* Reading Sch.; St John's Coll., Oxford (Hon. Fellow 1987). Scholar, St John's Coll.; 1st cl. Hons Mod. Hist., 1933; BLitt, 1934; MA 1938. FRHistS 1953. Temp. Lectr in Modern European History, Edinburgh, 1935–36; Asst Lectr in Modern History, University Coll., London, 1936–40. Served War, 1940–46: Intelligence Corps; Capt. 1942; Major (Gen. Staff), 1945. Lectr in Modern British and American History, St Salvator's Coll., University of St Andrews, 1946–53; Prof. of Modern History, University of Leeds, 1953–55; Vice-Principal, 1967–71, Dean of Faculty of Arts, 1978–80, St Andrews Univ. Hinkley Prof. of English History, Johns Hopkins Univ., 1962; Ford's Lectr in English History, Oxford Univ., 1963–64; Sir John Neale Lectr in English Hist., UCL, 1981. Vice-Pres., Hist. Assoc. of Scotland, 1963–64. Hon. DLitt: Strathclyde, 1984; St Andrews, 1985; Southampton, 1988. *Publications:* Politics in the Age of Peel, 1953; Mr Secretary Peel, 1961; The Age of Peel, 1968; Reaction and Reconstruction in English Politics, 1832–1852, 1966; Sir Robert Peel, 1972; Peel, 1976; (jtly) The Conservatives: a history from their origins to 1965, 1978; Aristocracy and People: England 1815–1865, 1979; Lord Liverpool, 1984; Pillars of Government, 1986; (ed) Wellington: studies in the military and political career of the first Duke of Wellington, 1990; articles and reviews in Eng. Hist. Review, Trans. Royal Historical Society, and other learned jls. *Recreations:* gardening, swimming. *Address:* Old Gatehouse, Portway, Langport, Som TA10 0NQ. *T:* Langport (0458) 250334.

GASK, Daphne Irvine Prideaux, (Mrs John Gask), OBE 1976; JP; Member, Inner London Commission of the Peace, 1982–88; *b* 25 July 1920; *d* of Roger Prideaux Selby and Elizabeth May (*née* Stirling); *m* 1945, John Gask, MA, BM, BCh; one *s* one *d*. *Educ:* St Trinnean's, Edinburgh; Tolmers Park, Herts; Collège Brillantmont, Lausanne, Switzerland. BA Open Univ., 1979. CAB worker, 1985–. Member: Shropshire Probation and After-Care Cttee, 1960–80 (Chm., 1978–80); Exec. Cttee, Central Council of Probation and After-Care Cttees, 1964–80 (Vice-Chm., 1977–80); Royal Commn on Criminal Procedure, 1978–80; Council, Magistrates Assoc., 1968–80 (Mem. Exec. Cttee, 1976–80); Sports Council Adv. Gp, 1978–80; NACRO, 1982–; Asst Sec., L'Association Internationale des Magistrats de la Jeunesse et de la Famille, 1979–86 (Hon. Mem., 1986–; Mem. Gen. Purposes Cttee, 1986–). Served on Salop CC, 1965–77; Chm., Leisure Activities Cttee, 1974–77. Mem., W Midland Reg. Sports Council (Vice-Chm., 1970–77). Mem., St Peter's Icthus Soc., Plymouth, 1986– (Chm., Housing Sect., 1987–). JP Salop, 1952. Mello Matlos medal, Brazil, 1986. *Recreations:* tennis, skiing, photography. *Address:* 5 The Old School House, Garrett Street, Cawsand, near Torpoint, Cornwall PL10 1PD. *T:* Plymouth (0752) 822136. *Club:* University Women's.

GASKELL, Dr Colin Simister, CBE 1988; FEng; Group Managing Director, 600 Group, since 1990; *b* 19 May 1937; *s* of James and Carrie Gaskell; *m* 1961, Jill (*née* Haward); one *s* one *d*. *Educ:* Manchester Grammar Sch.; Manchester Univ. (BSc); St Edmund Hall, Oxford (DPhil). CEng, FEng 1989; FIEE, FIElectIE. Research Fellow, Oxford Univ., 1960–61; Central Electricity Res. Labs, 1961–62; Microwave Associates, 1962–67; Chief Engineer, Microwave Div., Marconi Instruments, 1967–71; Technical Dir, Herbert Controls, 1971–74; Marconi Instruments: Technical Management, 1974–77; Technical Dir, 1977–79; Man. Dir, 1979–90. FBIM; FRSA. *Recreations:* reading, riding (as in horse-), family pursuits. *Address:* 28 Pennycroft, Harpenden, Herts AL5 2PB. *T:* Harpenden (0582) 767055.

GASKELL, (John) Philip (Wellesley), MA, PhD, LittD; Fellow of Trinity College, Cambridge, since 1967 (Librarian, 1967–86; Tutor, 1973–83); *b* 6 Jan. 1926; *s* of John Wellesley Gaskell and Olive Elizabeth, *d* of Philip B. Baker; *m* 1st, 1948, Margaret (marr. diss.), *d* of late H. S. Bennett, FBA, and Joan Bennett; two *s* one *d*; 2nd, 1984, Annette Ursula Beighton. *Educ:* Dragon Sch., Oxford; Oundle Sch.; King's Coll., Cambridge. MA, PhD 1956, LittD, 1980. Served War, 1943–47, Lance-Bdr RA: BLA, 1944–45; Radio SEAC, 1946–47. Fellow of King's Coll., Cambridge, 1953–60, Dean, 1954–56, Tutor, 1956–58; Head of English Dept, and Librarian, Oundle Sch., 1960–62; Keeper of Special Collections, Glasgow Univ. Library, 1962–66; Warden of Maclay Hall, 1962–64, of Wolfson Hall, 1964–66, Glasgow Univ. Sandars Reader in Bibliography, Cambridge Univ., 1978–79; Part-time Prof. of Literature, CIT, 1983–88. Editor, The Book Collector, 1952–54. *Publications:* The First Editions of William Mason, 1951; John Baskerville, a bibliography, 1959, rev. edn 1973; Caught!, 1960; A Bibliography of the Foulis Press, 1964, rev. edn 1986; Morvern Transformed, 1968, rev. edn 1980; (with R. Robson) The Library of Trinity College, Cambridge, 1971; A New Introduction to Bibliography, 1972, rev. edns 1974, 1979, 1985; From Writer to Reader, 1978; Trinity College Library, the first 150 years, 1980; (with Clive Hart) Ulysses: a review of three texts, 1989; ed and trans (with P. Bradford) The Orthotypographia of Hieronymus Hornschuch, 1972; contrib. The Library, Jl Printing Historical Soc., etc. *Address:* Primrose Cottage, Mawgan, Helston, Cornwall TR12 6AB. *T:* Mawgan (032622) 314.

GASKELL, Sir Richard (Kennedy Harvey), Kt 1989; Senior Partner, Lawrence Tucketts, solicitors, since 1989 (Partner, 1963–89); President of the Law Society, 1988–89; *b* 17 Sept. 1936; *o s* of late Dr Kenneth Harvey Gaskell, MRCS, LRCP, DMRD and of Jean Winsome Gaskell; *m* 1965, Judith Poland; one *s* one *d*. *Educ:* Marlborough Coll. Admitted solicitor, 1960. Chm., Nat. Cttee, Young Solicitors' Gp, 1964–65; Law Society: Mem. Council, 1969–; Dep. Vice-Pres., 1986–87; Vice Pres., 1987–88; President: Bristol Law Soc., 1978–79; Assoc. of South Western Law Socs, 1980–81. Member: Crown Court Rules Cttee, 1977–83; Security Service Tribunal, 1989–. Director: Law Society Trustees Ltd, 1980–; Bristol Waterworks Co., 1989–. Dir, Wildfowl Trust (Hldgs) Ltd, 1980–; Mem. Council, Wildfowl and Wetlands (formerly Wildfowl) Trust, 1980– (Chm., 1983–87); Dir, SS Great Britain Project Ltd; Mem. Exec. Cttee and Council, SS Great Britain. Trustee: Frenchay and Southmead Med. Trust, 1986–; Laura Ashley Foundn, 1990–; CLIC (UK), 1991–. Mem. Court, 1973–, Convocation, 1989–, Bristol Univ. Hon. LLD Bristol, 1989; Hon. LLM Bristol Polytechnic, 1989. *Address:* Grove Farm, Yatton Keynell, Chippenham, Wilts SN14 7BS. *T:* Castle Combe (0249) 782289; (office) Shannon Court, Corn Street, Bristol BS99 7JZ. *T:* Bristol (0272) 294861. *Club:* Farmers'.

GASKILL, William; freelance stage director; *b* 24 June 1930; *s* of Joseph Linnaeus Gaskill and Maggie Simpson. *Educ:* Salt High Sch., Shipley; Hertford Coll., Oxford. Asst Artistic Dir, English Stage Co., 1957–59; freelance Dir with Royal Shakespeare Co., 1961–62; Assoc. Dir, National Theatre, 1963–65, and 1979; Artistic Director, English Stage Company, 1965–72, Mem. Council, 1978–87; Dir, Joint Stock Theatre Gp, 1973–83. *Publication:* A Sense of Direction: life at the Royal Court (autobiog.), 1988. *Address:* 124A Leighton Road, NW5.

GASKIN, Catherine; author; *b* Co. Louth, Eire, 2 April 1929; *m* 1955, Sol Cornberg. *Educ:* Holy Cross Coll., Sydney, Australia. Brought up in Australia; lived in London, 1948–55, New York, 1955–65, Virgin Islands, 1965–67, Ireland, 1967–81. *Publications:* This Other Eden, 1946; With Every Year, 1947; Dust In Sunlight, 1950; All Else Is Folly, 1951; Daughter of the House, 1952; Sara Dane, 1955; Blake's Reach, 1958; Corporation Wife, 1960; I Know My Love, 1962; The Tilsit Inheritance, 1963; The File on Devlin, 1965; Edge of Glass, 1967; Fiona, 1970; A Falcon for a Queen, 1972; The Property of a Gentleman, 1974; The Lynmara Legacy, 1975; The Summer of the Spanish Woman, 1977; Family Affairs, 1980; Promises, 1982; The Ambassador's Women, 1985; The Charmed Circle, 1988. *Recreations:* music, reading. *Address:* White Rigg, East Ballaterson, Maughold, Isle of Man.

GASKIN, Prof. Maxwell, DFC 1944 (and Bar 1945); Jaffrey Professor of Political Economy, Aberdeen University, 1965–85, now Professor Emeritus; *b* 18 Nov. 1921; *s* of late Albert and Beatrice Gaskin; *m* 1952, Brenda Patricia, *yr d* of late Rev. William D. Stewart; one *s* three *d*. *Educ:* Quarry Bank Sch., Liverpool; Liverpool Univ. (MA). Lever Bros Ltd, 1939–41. Served War, RAF Bomber Comd, 1941–46. Economist, Raw Cotton Commn, 1949–50; Asst Lectr, Liverpool Univ., 1950–51; Lectr and Sen. Lectr, Glasgow Univ., 1951–65; Visiting Sen. Lectr, Nairobi Univ., 1964–65. Consultant to Sec. of State for Scotland, 1965–87. Member, Committee of Inquiry: into Bank Interest Rates (N Ire.), 1965–66; into Trawler Safety, 1967–68; Member and Chairman: Wages Councils, 1967–; Bd of Management for Foresterhill and Associated Hosps, 1971–74; Independent Member: Scottish Agricl Wages Bd, 1972–90; EDC for Civil Engineering, 1978–84; Chm., Industry Strategy Cttee for Scotland (Building and Civil Engrg EDCs), 1974–76. Director: Offshore Med. Support Ltd, 1978–85; Aberdeen Univ. Research & Industrial Services, 1981–85. President: Section F, British Assoc., 1978–79; Scottish Economic Soc., 1981–84. *Publications:* The Scottish Banks, 1965; (co-author and ed) North East Scotland: a survey of its development potential, 1969; (jtly) The Economic Impact of North Sea oil on Scotland, 1978; (ed) The Political Economy of Tolerable Survival, 1981; articles in economic and banking jls; reports on the international coal trade. *Recreations:* music and country life. *Address:* Westfield, Ancrum, Roxburghshire TD8 6XA. *T:* Ancrum (08353) 237.

GASS, Prof. Ian Graham, PhD, DSc; FRS 1983; Professor of Earth Sciences and Head of Discipline, Open University, 1969–82, Personal Chair since 1982; *b* 20 March 1926; *s* of John George and Lillian Robinson Gass; *m* 1955, Florence Mary Pearce; one *s* one *d*. *Educ:* Royal Grammar Sch., Newcastle upon Tyne; Almondbury Grammar Sch.; Leeds Univ. (BSc 1952, MSc 1955, PhD 1960, DSc 1972). Armed Forces, 1944–48. Undergrad., 1948–52; Geologist: Sudan Geol Survey, 1952–55; Cyprus Geol Survey, 1955–60; Asst Lectr, Leicester Univ., 1960–61; Lectr, then Sen. Lectr, Leeds Univ., 1961–69. Mem., NERC, 1985–87. A Vice-Pres., Royal Soc., 1985–86. Led Royal Soc. Expedn to Tristan da Cunha, 1962. Prestwich Medal, Geol Soc., 1979. *Publications:* (ed with T. N. Clifford) African Magmatism and Tectonics, 1970; (ed with P. J. Smith and R. C. L. Wilson) Understanding the Earth, 1971, 2nd edn 1972; articles in scientific jls. *Recreations:* bridge, hill-walking, geology. *Address:* 12 Greenacres, Bedford MK41 9AJ. *T:* Bedford (0234) 352712.

GASS, James Ronald, CMG 1989; Consultant, OECD Forum for the Future, since 1989; *b* 25 March 1924; *s* of Harold Amos Gass and Cherry (*née* Taylor); *m* 1950, Colette Alice Jeanne Lejeune; two *s* one *d*. *Educ:* Birkenhead Park High Sch.; Liverpool Univ. (BA Hons); Nuffield and Balliol Colls, Oxford. Flight Lieut Pilot, RAF, service in US, India and Burma, 1942–46. PSO, DSIR Intelligence Div., 1951–57; Special Asst to Chm., Task Force on Western Scientific Co-operation, NATO, Paris, 1957; OEEC, subsequently OECD, Paris: Head of Div., Scientific and Tech. Personnel, 1958–61; Dep. Dir for Scientific Affairs, 1961–68; Director: Centre for Educnl Res. and Innovation, 1968–89; Social Affairs, Manpower and Educn, 1974–89; retired 1989. *Recreations:* restoration of antiques, gymnastics, philosophy. *Address:* 2 avenue du Vert Bois, Ville d'Avray, 92410 Paris, France. *T:* 47-09-54-81.

GASSMAN, Lewis, JP; a Recorder of the Crown Court, 1972–83; *b* 28 Oct. 1910; 2nd *s* of late Isaac Gassman and Dora Gassman; *m* 1940, Betty Henrietta, *o c* of late H. Jerrold and Mrs A. F. Annenberg; one *d*. Admitted Solicitor, 1933. Borough of Barnes: Councillor and Chm. of Cttees, 1933–41. Contested (Lab): Richmond, Surrey, 1935; Hastings, 1945. War of 1939–45: Army service, Capt. RAOC. JP Surrey, 1948, also SW London; Chm., Mortlake Magistrates, 1953–56 and 1961–71. Consultant in law firm of Kershaw, Gassman & Matthews. A Dep. Chm. of Surrey Quarter Sessions, 1968–71; Chm. of Magistrates, Richmond-upon-Thames, 1971–74. *Recreations:* music, painting, walking. *Address:* 21 Castelnau, Barnes, SW13 9RP. *T:* 081–748 7172. *Club:* Reform.

GASSON, (Gordon) Barry, OBE 1985; ARSA; Principal, Barry Gasson, Architects; Member, Royal Fine Art Commission for Scotland; *b* 27 Aug. 1935; *s* of Gladys Godfrey (previously Gasson) and late Stanley Gasson; *m* Rosemary Mulligan; one *s* two *d*. *Educ:* Solihull Sch.; Birmingham Sch. of Architecture (Dip. Arch. 1958); RIBA (Owen Jones Student); Columbia Univ., NY (MS 1961); Q. W. Boese English Speaking Fellowship; MA Cantab 1963. ARIAS, RIBA. Lectr, Univ. of Cambridge, 1963–73; visiting critic: University Coll., Dublin, 1969–72; California State Poly., 1969; Mackintosh Sch. of Arch., 1978–; Edinburgh Coll. of Art, 1986–; Vis. Prof., Univ. of Manchester, 1987–. Assessor, Civic Trust Awards, RIBA student medals, nat. competitions; Chm., RIBA regional awards. Farmer (biodynamic). FRSA. Designed galleries for Burrell Collection, Glasgow (won in open comp., 1972); awards: Stone Fedn, 1983; Arch. Design; RA Premier Arch., 1984; Museum of the Year; British Tourist Trophy; Sotheby Fine Art; Services in Building; Civic Trust; Eternit Internat., 1985; RIBA 1986; RSA Gold Medal, 1983; World Biennale of Arch. Gold Medal, 1987. *Publication:* contrib. to The Burrell Collection, 1983. *Address:* Wardlaw Farm, Auchentiber, Ayrshire KA13 7RP. *Clubs:* Architecture, Arts.

GASSON, John Gustav Haycraft, CB 1990; Head of Policy and Legal Services Group, Lord Chancellor's Department, 1987–91; *b* 2 Aug. 1931; *s* of late Dr and Mrs S. G. H. Gasson; *m* 1964, Lesley, *d* of L. L. Thomas, Nyamandhlovu, Zimbabwe; two *s* one *d*. *Educ:* Diocesan Coll., Rondebosch, Cape Town; Cape Town Univ. (BA); Pembroke Coll., Oxford (Rhodes Schol. Rhodesia 1953; MA, BCL). Called to the Bar, Gray's Inn, 1957; Advocate of High Court of S Rhodesia, 1959; Lord Chancellor's Dept, 1964; Sec., Law Commn, 1982–87. *Recreations:* cycling, gardening. *Address:* 39 Lawn Crescent, Kew, Surrey TW9 3NS. *Club:* Bulawayo (Zimbabwe).

GATEHOUSE, Graham Gould; Director of Social Services, Surrey County Council, since 1981; *b* 17 July 1935; *s* of G. and G. M. Gatehouse; *m* 1960, Gillian M. Newell; two *s* one *d*. *Educ:* Crewkerne Sch., Somerset; Exeter Univ., Devon (DSA); London School of Economics (Dip. Mental Health). Served Royal Artillery, 1954–56. Somerset County Council, 1957–67; Worcestershire CC, 1967–70; Norfolk CC, 1970–73; West Sussex CC, 1973–81. FRSA 1987. *Recreations:* Rugby football, cricket, theatre. *Address:* Flat 1, 28 St Mary's Road, Long Ditton, Surrey.

GATEHOUSE, Hon. Sir Robert Alexander, Kt 1985; **Hon. Mr Justice Gatehouse;** a Judge of the High Court, Queen's Bench Division, since 1985; *b* 30 Jan. 1924; *s* of late Major-Gen. A. H. Gatehouse, DSO, MC; *m* 1st, 1951, Henrietta Swann; 2nd, 1966, Pamela Fawcett. *Educ:* Wellington Coll.; Trinity Hall, Cambridge. Served War of 1939–45: commissioned into Royal Dragoons; NW Europe. Called to the Bar, Lincoln's Inn, 1950; Bencher, 1977; QC 1969. Governor, Wellington Coll., 1970–. *Recreation:* golf. *Address:* Royal Courts of Justice, Strand, WC2.

GATES, Emeritus Prof. Ronald Cecil, AO 1978; FASSA; Vice-Chancellor, University of New England, 1977–85; *b* 8 Jan. 1923; *s* of Earle Nelson Gates and Elsie Edith (*née* Tucker); *m* 1953, Barbara Mann; one *s* two *d* (and one *s* decd). *Educ:* East Launceston State Sch., Tas; Launceston C of E Grammar Sch., Tas; Univ. of Tas (BCom Econs and Commercial Law); Oxford Univ. (MA PPE). FASSA 1968. Served War, 1942–45: Private, AIF. Clerk, Aust. Taxation Office, Hobart, 1941–42; Rhodes Scholar (Tas), Oxford, 1946–48; Historian, Aust. Taxation Office, Canberra, 1949–52; Univ. of Sydney: Sen. Lectr in Econs, 1952–64; Associate Prof., 1964–65; Rockefeller Fellow in Social Sciences, 1955; Carnegie Travel Grant, 1960; Prof. of Econs, Univ. of Qld, 1966–77 (Pres., Professorial Bd, 1975–77). Pres., Econ. Soc. of Australia and NZ, 1969–72. Chairman: statutory Consumer Affairs Council of Qld, 1971–73; Aust. Inst. of Urban Studies, 1975–77. Comr, Commonwealth Commn of Inquiry into Poverty, 1973–77. Chairman: Aust. Nat. Commn for Unesco, 1981–83 (Vice-Chm., 1979); Adv. Council for Inter-govt Relations, 1979–85; Internat. Relations Cttee, Cttee of Australian Vice-Chancellors, 1981–84; Local Govt Trng Council (formerly Nat. Local Govt Industry Trng Cttee), 1983–. Hon. FRAPI 1976; Hon. Fellow, Aust. Inst. of Urban Studies, 1979. Hon. DEcon Qld, 1978; Hon. DLitt New England, 1987. *Publications:* (with H. R. Edwards and N. T. Drane) Survey of Consumer Finances, Sydney 1963–65: Vol. 2, 1965; Vols 1, 3 and 4, 1966; Vols 5, 6 and 7, 1967; (jtly) The Price of Land, 1971; (jtly) New Cities for Australia, 1972; (jtly) Land for the Cities, 1973; (with P. A. Cassidy) Simulation, Uncertainty and Public Investment Analysis, 1977; La Septaga Murderigmo (detective novel in Esperanto), 1991; chapters in books and articles in learned jls. *Recreations:* music, beef cattle, Esperanto. *Address:* Wangarang, Kelly's Plains Road, Armidale, NSW 2350, Australia.

GATHERCOLE, Ven. John Robert; Archdeacon of Dudley, since 1987; Team Leader and Senior Chaplain, Worcestershire Industrial Mission, since 1985; *b* 23 April 1937; *s* of Robert Gathercole and Winifred Mary Gathercole (*née* Price); *m* 1963, Joan Claire (*née* London); one *s* one *d*. *Educ:* Judd School, Tonbridge; Fitzwilliam Coll., Cambridge (BA 1959, MA 1963); Ridley Hall, Cambridge. Deacon 1962, priest 1963; Curate: St Nicholas, Durham, 1962–66; St Bartholomew, Croxdale, 1966–70; Social and Industrial Adviser to Bishop of Durham, 1967–70; Industrial Chaplain, Redditch, dio. Worcester, 1970–87; RD of Bromsgrove, 1978–85. *Recreations:* vintage sports cars, music. *Address:* 15 Worcester Road, Droitwich, Worcs WR9 8AA. *T:* Droitwich (0905) 773301.

GATHORNE-HARDY, family name of **Earl of Cranbrook.**

GATTY, Trevor Thomas, OBE 1974; HM Diplomatic Service, retired; President, MGT International, since 1989; *b* 8 June 1930; *s* of Thomas Alfred Gatty and Lillian Gatty (*née* Wood); *m* 1st, 1956, Jemima Bowman (marr. diss. 1983); two *s* one *d*; 2nd, 1989, Myrna Saturn; one step *s* one step *d*. *Educ:* King Edward's Sch., Birmingham. Served Army, 1948–50, 2/Lieut Royal Warwickshire Regt, later Lieut Royal Fusiliers (TA), 1950–53. Foreign Office, 1950; Vice-Consul, Leopoldville, 1954; FO, 1958–61; Second (later First) Sec., Bangkok, 1961–64; Consul, San Francisco, 1965–66; Commercial Consul, San Francisco, 1967–68; FCO, 1968–73; Commercial Consul, Zürich, 1973–75; FCO, 1975–76; Counsellor (Diplomatic Service Inspector), 1977–80; Head, Migration and Visa Dept, FCO, 1980–81; Consul-General, Atlanta, 1981–85. *Recreations:* reading, physical fitness, English Springer spaniels. *Address:* 4026 Land O'Lakes Drive, Atlanta, Georgia 30342, USA. *T:* 404 264 9033.

GATWARD, (Anthony) James; Chairman, TVS Television, 1990–91 (Deputy Chairman and Chief Executive, 1984–90); *b* 4 March 1938; *s* of George James Gatward and Lillian Georgina (*née* Strutton); *m* 1969, Isobel Anne Stuart Black, actress; three *d*. *Educ:* George Gascoigne Sch., Walthamstow; South West Essex Technical Coll. and Sch. of Art (drama course). Entered TV industry, 1957; freelance drama producer/director: Canada and USA, 1959–65; BBC and most ITV cos, 1966–70; partner in prodn co., acting as Exec. Prod. and often Dir of many internat. co-prodns in UK, Ceylon, Australia and Germany, 1970–78; Man. Dir, 1979–84, Chief Exec., 1984–91, Television South, subseq. TVS Entertainment; Director: Southstar, Scottish and Global TV, 1971–78; Indep. TV Publications Ltd, 1982–88; Oracle Teletext Ltd, 1982–88; Solent Cablevision Ltd, 1983–89; Channel 4 TV Co., 1984–89; Indep. TV News Ltd, 1986–91; Super Channel Ltd, 1986–88; ITV Super Channel Ltd, 1986–89; Chm., TVS Production, 1984–89; Chm. and Chief Exec., TVS N American Hldgs, 1988–91; Pres., Telso Communications Inc., 1987–90; Chairman: Telso Communications Ltd, 1987–; Telso Overseas Ltd, 1987–; Midem Orgn SA, 1987–89; MTM Entertainment Inc., 1989–91. Instigated and led preparation of application for South and SE England television franchise, 1979–80 (awarded Dec. 1980). Member: Council, Operation Raleigh; Court of the Mary Rose. Governor, S of England Agricl Soc. *Recreations:* farming, sailing, music. *Clubs:* Reform, Royal Thames Yacht.

GAU, John Glen Mackay, CBE 1989; independent producer; Joint Chief Executive, John Gau Productions (Managing Director, 1981–88); *b* 25 March 1940; *s* of Cullis William Gau and Nan Munro; *m* 1966, Susan Tebbs; two *s*. *Educ:* Haileybury and ISC; Trinity Hall, Cambridge; Univ. of Wisconsin. BBC TV: Assistant Film Editor, 1963; Current Affairs Producer, 1965–74; Editor, Nationwide, 1975; Head of Current Affairs Programmes, 1978–81; Dep. Chief Exec. and Dir of Programmes, British Satellite Broadcasting, 1988–90. Dir, Channel 4, 1984–88. Chm., Indep. Programme Producers' Assoc., 1983–86. Chm. Council, RTS, 1986–88. FRTS 1986. *Publication:* (jtly) Soldiers, 1985. *Address:* 4 Queensmere Road, SW19 5NY. *T:* 01–946 4686.

GAUDRY, Roger, CC (Canada) 1968; DSc; FRSC; President, Jules & Paul-Emile Léger Foundation, since 1983; Chairman, Nordic Laboratories, since 1975; *b* 15 Dec. 1913; *m* 1941, Madeleine Vallée; two *s* three *d*. *Educ:* Laval Univ. (BA 1933; BSc 1937; DSc 1940); Rhodes Scholar, Oxford Univ., 1937–39. Organic Chemistry, Laval Univ.: Lectr, 1940; Prof., 1945; Full Prof., 1950. Ayerst Laboratories: Asst Dir of Research, 1954; Dir of Research, 1957; Vice-Pres. and Dir of Research, 1963–65; Rector, Univ. of Montreal, 1965–75; Dir, 1975–, Chm., 1984–88, Bio-Research Labs. Director: Corby Distilleries, 1975–89; Bank of Montreal, 1975–84; Alcan Aluminium, 1976–86; Hoechst Canada, 1977–87; SKW Canada, 1978–88; St Lawrence Starch, 1983–89. Chm., Science Council of Canada, 1972–75; President: Internat. Assoc. of Univs, 1975–80; Sci., Technology and Industry Centre of Montreal, 1988–90. Chm. Bd, UN Univ., 1974–76; Dir, Inst. de recherches cliniques, Montreal, 1975–. Hon. FRCP&S (Canada), 1971. Hon. doctorates: (Laws) Univ. of Toronto, 1966; (Science) RMC of Kingston, 1966; (Science) Univ. of BC, 1967; (Laws) McGill Univ., 1967; Univ. of Clermont-Ferrand, France, 1967; (Laws) St Thomas Univ., 1968; (Laws) Brock Univ., 1969; (Civil Laws) Bishop's Univ., 1969; (Science) Univ. of Saskatchewan, 1970; (Science) Univ. of Western Ontario, 1976; (Laws) Concordia Univ., 1980; Parizeau Medal from Assoc. Canadienne Française pour l'Avancement des Sciences, 1958. Silver Jubilee Medal, 1977. *Publications:* author and co-author of numerous scientific papers in organic and biological chemistry. *Address:* 445 Beverley Avenue, Town of Mount Royal, Montreal, H3P 1L4, Canada.

GAULD, William Wallace; Under-Secretary, Department of Agriculture and Fisheries for Scotland, 1972–79; *b* 12 Oct. 1919; *e s* of late Rev. W. W. Gauld, DD, of Aberdeen, and Charlotte Jane Gauld (*née* Reid); *m* 1943, Jean Inglis Gray; three *d*. *Educ:* Fettes; Aberdeen Univ. MA (1st Cl. Hons Classics). Served Pioneer Corps, 1940–46 (Major 1945). Entered Dept of Agriculture for Scotland, 1947; Private Sec. to Secretary of State for Scotland, 1955–57; Asst Sec., 1958; Scottish Development Dept, 1968–72; Mem. Agricultural Research Council, 1972–79. Pres., Botanical Soc., Edinburgh, 1978–80. *Recreation:* natural history. *Address:* 1 Banks Crescent, Crieff, Perthshire PH7 3SR.

GAULIN, Jean; Group Chief Executive Officer, Ultramar Group, since 1989; *b* 9 July 1942; *m* 1981, Andrée LeBoeuf; two *s* one *d*. *Educ:* Univ. of Montreal (degrees in appl. scis and chem. eng.). Vice-Pres., Ultramar Canada, 1977–79; President: Nouveler Inc., 1980–82; Gaz Metropolitan Inc., 1982–85 (and Chief Exec.); Ultramar Canada, 1985–89. *Address:* Ultramar, 141 Moorgate, EC2M 6TX.

GAULT, Charles Alexander, CBE 1959 (OBE 1947); retired from HM Foreign Service, 1959; *b* 15 June 1908; *o s* of Robert Gault, Belfast, and Sophia Ranken Clark; *m* 1947, Madge, *d* of late William Walter Adams, Blundellsands; no *c*. *Educ:* Harrow; Magdalene Coll., Cambridge. Entered Levant Consular Service, 1931; served in Egypt, Persia, Saudi Arabia, at Foreign Office, India (on secondment to Commonwealth Relations Office), Libya, Israel, Bahrain (HM Political Agent, 1954–59). *Address:* 19 Queens Court, Queens Road, Cheltenham, Glos GL50 2LU. *Club:* Oriental.

GAULT, David Hamilton; Executive Chairman, Gallic Management Co. Ltd, since 1974; *b* 9 April 1928; *s* of Leslie Hamilton Gault and Iris Hilda Gordon Young; *m* 1950, Felicity Jane Gribble; three *s* two *d*. *Educ:* Fettes Coll., Edinburgh. Nat. Service, commnd in RA, 1946–48; Clerk, C. H. Rugg & Co. Ltd, Shipbrokers, 1948–52; H. Clarkson & Co. Ltd, Shipbrokers: Man. 1952–56; Dir 1956–62; Jt Man. Dir 1962–72; Gp Man. Dir, Shipping Industrial Holdings Ltd, 1972–74; Chm., Jebsen (UK) Ltd, 1962–81; Chm., Seabridge Shipping Ltd, 1965–73. *Recreations:* gardening, walking. *Address:* Telegraph House, North Marden, Chichester, West Sussex. *T:* Harting (0730) 825206. *Clubs:* Boodle's, City.

GAULTER, Derek Vivian, CBE 1978; Chairman, Construction Industry Training Board, since 1985; *b* 10 Dec. 1924; *s* of late Jack Rudolf Gaulter, MC and Muriel Gaulter (*née* Westworth); *m* 1949, Edith Irene Shackleton; one *s* three *d*. *Educ:* Denstone College; Peterhouse, Cambridge (MA). RNVR, Sub Lieut MTBs/Minesweepers, 1943–46. Lord Justice Holker Sen. Scholarship, Gray's Inn; called to the Bar, Gray's Inn, 1949; Common Law Bar, Manchester, 1950–55. Federation of Civil Engineering Contractors: Legal Sec., General Sec., Dep. Dir Gen., 1955–86; Dir Gen., 1987. MInstD. *Recreations:* golf, gardening, travel, photography. *Address:* Philips Hill, Old Shire Lane, Chorleywood, Herts WD3 5PW. *T:* Chorleywood (09278) 3004.

GAUNT SUDDARDS, Henry; *see* Suddards.

GAUSDEN, Ronald, CB 1982; nuclear consultant; *b* 15 June 1921; *s* of Jesse Charles William Gausden and Annie Gausden (*née* Durrant); *m* 1st, 1943, Florence May (*née* Ayres) (*d* 1987); two *s* two *d*; 2nd, 1988, Joan Betty (*née* Simcock). *Educ:* Varndean Grammar Sch., Brighton; Brighton Techn. Coll. and Borough Polytechnic. CEng, FIEE. RN Sci. Service, 1943–47; AERE, Harwell, 1947–50; UKAEA Windscale Works, Cumbria: Instrument Engr, 1950–53; Asst Gp Man., 1953–55; Gp Man., 1955–60; Nuclear Installations Inspectorate: Principal Inspector, 1960–63; Asst Chief Inspector, 1963–73; Dep. Chief Inspector, 1973–75; Chief Inspector, 1976–81; Dir, Hazardous Installations Gp, HSE, 1978–81. *Publications:* contrib. Brit. Nuclear Energy Soc. and Inst. Nuclear Engrs. *Recreations:* golf, fishing. *Address:* Granary Cottage, Itchingfield, near Horsham, W Sussex RH13 7NU. *T:* Slinfold (0403) 790646.

GAUTIER-SMITH, Peter Claudius, FRCP; Physician, National Hospitals for Nervous Diseases, Queen Square and Maida Vale, 1962–89; *b* 1 March 1929; *s* of late Claudius Gautier-Smith and Madeleine (*née* Ferguson); *m* 1960, Nesta Mary Wroth; two *d*. *Educ:* Cheltenham Coll. (Exhibnr); King's Coll., Cambridge; St Thomas's Hosp. Med. Sch. MA, MD. Casualty Officer, House Physician, St Thomas' Hosp., 1955–56; Medical Registrar, University Coll. Hosp., 1958; Registrar, National Hosp., Queen Square, 1960–62; Consultant Neurologist, St George's Hosp., 1962–75; Dean, Inst. of Neurology, 1975–82. Mem., Bd of Governors, Nat. Hosps for Nervous Diseases, 1975–89. Hon. Neurologist, Dispensaire Français, London, 1983–89. *Publications:* Parasagittal and Falx Meningiomas, 1970; papers in learned jls on neurology. *Recreations:* literary (twenty-three novels published under a pseudonym); French language; squash (played for Cambridge v Oxford, 1951; Captain, London Univ., 1954); tennis. *Clubs:* MCC; Hawks (Cambridge); Jesters.

GAUTREY, Peter, CMG 1972; CVO 1961; DK (Brunei) 1972; HM Diplomatic Service, retired; High Commissioner in Guyana, 1975–78, concurrently Ambassador (non-resident) to Surinam, 1976–78; *b* 17 Sept. 1918; *s* of late Robert Harry Gautrey, Hindhead, Surrey, and Hilda Morris; *m* 1947, Marguerite Etta Uncles; one *s* one *d*. *Educ:* Abbotsholme Sch., Derbys. Joined Home Office, 1936. Served in Royal Artillery, (Capt.), Sept. 1939–March 1946. Re-joined Home Office; Commonwealth Relations Office, 1948; served in British Embassy, Dublin, 1950–53; UK High Commission, New Delhi, 1955–57 and 1960–63; British Deputy High Commissioner, Bombay, 1963–65; Corps of Diplomatic Service Inspectors, 1965–68; High Commissioner: Swaziland, 1968–71; Brunei, 1972–75. FRSA 1972. *Recreations:* walking, music, art. *Address:* 24 Fort Road, Guildford, Surrey GU1 3TE.

GAUVAIN, Timothy John Lund; Executive Director, St John Ambulance, since 1990; *b* 23 June 1942; *s* of Sqdn Ldr John Henry Percival Gauvain and Barbara Lund (*née* Roberts); *m* 1967, Sandra Gay Duff; one *s*. *Educ:* Stowe Sch.; Magdalene Coll., Cambridge (BA Hons 1964; MA 1969). Served RAF, 1964–82: No 111 Sqdn, Wattisham, 1966–69; ADC to AOC 22 Gp, Market Drayton, 1969–71; Flt Comdr, No 5 Sqdn, Binbrook, 1972–74; Canadian Forces Staff Coll., Toronto, 1974–75; Personal Air Sec. to RAF Minister, MoD, 1975–77; OC No 19 Sqdn, Wildenrath, Germany, 1978–80; Air Warfare Course, RAF Coll., Cranwell, 1981; Forward Policy Directorate (RAF), MoD, 1981–82; retired 1982, Wing Comdr. Dir, Nat. Management Office, BDO Binder Hamlyn, 1985–90. Man. Dir, Eskimo Ice Ltd, 1978–90. *Recreations:* flying, playing the organ, travel. *Address:* 29 Burnaby Gardens, W4 3DR. *T:* 081–994 6587. *Club:* Royal Air Force.

GAVASKAR, Sunil Manohar; Padma Bhushan; cricketer; business executive; *b* 10 July 1949; *s* of Manohar Keshav Gavaskar and Meenal Manohar Gavaskar; *m* 1974, Marshniel Mehrotra; one *s*. *Educ:* St Xavier's High Sch.; St Xavier's Coll.; Bombay Univ. (BA). Represented India in cricket, 1971–88; Captain, Indian Team, 1978, 1979–80, 1980–82 and 1984–85; passed previous world records: no of runs in Test Matches, 1983; no of Test centuries, 1984; first batsman to score over 10,000 Test runs, 1987. *Publications:* Sunny Days, 1976; Idols, 1983; Runs 'n Ruins, 1984. *Address:* 40-A Sir Bhalchandra Road, Dadar, Bombay 400014, India. *T:* (office) 4931611. *Clubs:* Cricket Club of India, Bombay Gymkhana.

GAVIN, Maj.-Gen. James Merricks Lewis, CB 1967; CBE 1963 (OBE 1953); *b* Antofagasta, Chile, 28 July 1911; *s* of Joseph Merricks Gavin; *m* 1942, Barbara Anne Elizabeth, *d* of Group Capt. C. G. Murray, CBE; one *s* two *d*. *Educ:* Uppingham Sch.;

Royal Military Academy; Trinity Coll., Cambridge. 2nd Lieut Royal Engineers, 1931. Mem. Mt Everest Expedn, 1936. Instructor, Royal Military Academy, 1938; Capt. 1939; served War of 1939–45 in Far East, Middle East, Italy, France, including special operations; Brit. Jt Services Mission, Washington, 1948–51; Commanding Officer, 1951–53; Col Staff Coll., Camberley, 1953–55; BAOR, 1956–58; Comdt (Brig.) Intelligence Centre, Maresfield, 1958–61; Maj.-Gen. 1964; Asst Chief of Staff (Intelligence), SHAPE, 1964–67. Technical Dir, BSI, 1967–76. Col Comdt, RE, 1968–73. *Recreations:* mountaineering, sailing, ski-ing. *Address:* Slathurst Farm, Milland, near Liphook, Hants GU30 7ND. *Clubs:* Royal Cruising, Royal Ocean Racing, Alpine; Royal Yacht Squadron (Cowes).

GAVRON, Robert, CBE 1990; Chairman, St Ives plc, since 1964; Chairman and Proprietor, Folio Society Ltd, since 1982; Proprietor, Carcanet Press Ltd, since 1983; *b* 13 Sept. 1930; *s* of Nathaniel and Leah Gavron. *Educ:* Leighton Park Sch., Reading; St Peter's Coll., Oxford (MA). Called to the Bar, Middle Temple, 1955. Entered printing industry, 1955; founded St Ives Gp, 1964 (public co., 1985). Director: Octopus Publishing plc, 1975–87; Electra Management Plc, 1981–. Chm., Open Coll. of the Arts, 1991– (Trustee, 1987–); Member: Literature Panel, Arts Council, 1979–83; Council, Book Trust (formerly NBL), 1982–90; Poetry Soc., 1983–86 (Vice Pres., 1986–); Council, Morley Coll., 1975–85. Hon. Fellow, RCA, 1990. *Address:* St Ives House, Lavington Street, SE1 0NX. *T:* 071–928 8844. *Clubs:* Groucho, MCC.

GAY, Geoffrey Charles Lytton; Consultant, Knight, Frank & Rutley, since 1973; World President, International Real Estate Federation (FIABCI), 1973–75; a General Commissioner for Inland Revenue since 1953; *b* 14 March 1914; *s* of late Charles Gay and Ida, *d* of Sir Henry A. Lytton (famous Savoyard); *m* 1947, Dorothy Ann, *d* of Major Eric Rickman; one *s* two *d*. *Educ:* St Paul's School. FRICS. Joined Knight, Frank & Rutley, 1929. Served War of 1939–45: Durham LI, BEF, 1940; psc; Lt-Col; Chief of Staff, Sind District, India, 1943. Mem. Westminster City Council, 1962–71. Governor: Benenden Sch., 1971–86; Clayesmore Sch. Council; Mem. Council of St John, London, 1971–84; Liveryman, Broderers' Co. Licentiate, RPS, 1983; FRSA 1983. Chevalier de l'Ordre de l'Economie Nationale, 1960. OStJ 1961; KStJ 1979. *Recreations:* photography, fishing, music, theatre. *Address:* Castle View, 122 Newland, Sherborne, Dorset DT9 3DT. *T:* Sherborne (0935) 816676. *Clubs:* Carlton, MCC, Flyfishers'.

GAY, Rear-Adm. George Wilsmore, CB 1969; MBE 1946; DSC 1943; JP; Director-General of Naval Training, 1967–69; retired; *b* 1913; *s* of late Engr Comdr G. M. Gay and late Mrs O. T. Gay (*née* Allen); *m* 1941, Nancy Agnes Clark; two *s* one *d*. *Educ:* Eastman's Sch., Southsea; Nautical Coll., Pangbourne. Entered RN, 1930; Cadet Trng, 1930–32; RNEC, Keyham, 1932–35; HMS Glorious, 1935–37; Engr. Off., HMS Porpoise, 1939–41, HMS Clyde, 1941–43; HMS Dolphin, 1938 and 1943–46; HM Dockyard, Portsmouth, 1946–47; HMS Euryalus, 1947–49; Sqdn Engr Off., 1st Submarine Sqdn, HMS Forth, 1949–50; Trng Comdr, HMS Raleigh, 1951–53; Admiralty Engr Overseer, Vickers Armstrong Ltd, 1953–55; HMS Dolphin, 1956–58; Senior Officer, War Course, Royal Naval Coll., Greenwich, 1958; HM Dockyard, Malta, 1959–60; CO, HMS Sultan, Gosport, 1960–63; Chief Staff Off. Material to Flag Off. Submarines, 1963–66; Admty Interview Bd, 1966. Comdr 1947; Capt. 1958; Rear-Adm. 1967. FIMechE (MIMechE 1958). JP Plymouth 1970. *Recreations:* fishing, sailing, gardening. *Address:* 29 Whiteford Road, Mannamead, Plymouth, Devon PL3 5LU. *T:* Plymouth (0752) 664486. *Club:* Army and Navy.

GAYDON, Prof. Alfred Gordon, FRS 1953; Warren Research Fellow of Royal Society, 1945–74; Professor of Molecular Spectroscopy, 1961–73, now Emeritus, and Fellow, since 1980, Imperial College of Science and Technology, London; *b* 26 Sept. 1911; *s* of Alfred Bert Gaydon and Rosetta Juliet Gordon; *m* 1940, Phyllis Maude Gaze (*d* 1981); one *s* one *d*. *Educ:* Kingston Grammar Sch., Kingston-on-Thames; Imperial Coll., London. BSc (Physics) Imperial Coll., 1932; worked on molecular spectra, and on measurement of high temperatures, on spectra and structure of flames, and shock waves; DSc (London) 1942; Hon. Dr (University of Dijon), 1957. Rumford Medal, Royal Society, 1960; Bernard Lewis Gold Medal, Combustion Inst., 1960. *Publications:* Identification of Molecular Spectra (with Dr R. W. B. Pearse), 1941, 1950, 1963, 1965, 1976; Spectroscopy and Combustion Theory, 1942, 1948; Dissociation Energies and Spectra of Diatomic Molecules, 1947, 1953, 1968; Flames, their Structure, Radiation and Temperature (with Dr H. G. Wolfhard), 1953, 1960, 1970, 1979; The Spectroscopy of Flames, 1957, 1974; The Shock Tube in High-temperature Chemical Physics (with Dr I. Hurle), 1963. *Recreations:* wild-life photography; formerly rowing. *Address:* Dale Cottage, Shellbridge Road, Slindon Common, Sussex BN18 0LT. *T:* Slindon (024365) 277.

GAYRE of Gayre and Nigg, Robert, ERD; Lieutenant-Colonel (late Reserve of Officers); ethnologist and armorist; Editor: The Armorial, since 1959; The Mankind Quarterly, 1960–78 (Hon. Editor in Chief, since 1979), etc; Director of several companies; *s* of Robert Gayre of Gayre and Nigg, and Clara Hull; *m* 1933, Nina Mary (*d* 1983), *d* of Rev. Louis Thomas Terry, MA and Margaret Nina Hill; one *s*. *Educ:* University of Edinburgh (MA); Exeter Coll., Oxford. BEF France, 1939; Staff Officer Airborne HQ, 1942; Educnl Adviser, Allied Mil. Govt, Italy, 1943–44; Dir of Educn, Allied Control Commn for Italy, 1944; Chief of Educn and Religious Affairs, German Planning Unit, SHAEF, 1944; Prof. of Anthropology and head of Dept of Anthropo-geography, University of Saugor, India, 1954–56; Falkland Pursuivant Extraord., 1958; Consultore pro lingua Anglica, Coll. of Heralds, Rome, 1954–; Chamberlain to the Prince of Lippe, 1958–; Grand Bailiff and Comr-Gen. of the English Tongue, Order of St Lazarus of Jerusalem, 1961–69; Grand Referendary, 1969–73; Grand Comdr and Grand Almoner, 1973–; Vicar-Gen., 1985–; Sec.-Gen., VIth Internat. Congress of Genealogy, Edinburgh, 1962. Chm., The Seventeen Forty-Five Association, 1964–80. President: Scottish Rhodesia Soc., to 1968; Aberdeenshire and Banffshire Friends of Rhodesia Assoc., 1969; St Andrew Soc. of Malta, 1968; Ethnological Soc. of Malta; Life Pres., Heraldic Soc. of Malta, 1970–; Hon. Pres., Sicilian Anthropological Soc. Sec.-Gen., Internat. Orders' Commn (Chm., 1978–); Mem. Coun. Internat. Inst. of Ethnology and Eugenics, New York. Mem. Cttee of Honour: Inst. Politicos, Madrid; Cercle Internat. Généalogique, Paris, Mem. Nat. Acad. Sci. of India; Fellow: Collegio Araldico, Rome; Nat. Soc., Naples; Peloritana Acad., Messina; Pontaniana Acad., Naples; Royal Academy, Palermo; F Ist Ital di Geneal. e Arald., Rome; FRSH; MInstBE. Hon. or corr. mem. of heraldic and other socs of many countries. Grand Cross of Merit, SMO Malta, 1963 (Kt Comdr, 1957). Holds knighthoods in international and foreign orders, hon. Doctorates from Italian Univs, and heraldic societies' medals, etc. Hon. Lt-Col, ADC to Governor, Georgia, USA, 1969–; Hon. Lt-Col, ADC, State Militia, Alabama; Hon. Lt-Col, Canadian Arctic Air Force. Hon. Citizen, Commune of Gurro, Italy. *Publications:* Teuton and Slav on the Polish Frontier, 1944; Italy in Transition, 1946; Wassail! In Mazers of Mead, 1948, new edn, USA, 1986; The Heraldry of the Knights of St John, 1956; Heraldic Standards and other Ensigns, 1959; The Nature of Arms, 1961; Heraldic Cadency, 1961, Gayre's Booke, 4 vols 1948–59; Who is Who in Clan Gayre, 1962; A Case for Monarchy, 1962; The Armorial Who is Who, 1961–62, 1963–65, 1966–68, 1969–75, 1976–79; Roll of Scottish Arms (Pt I Vol. I, 1964, Pt I Vol. II, 1969, Vol. III, 1980); Ethnological Elements of Africa, 1966; More Ethnological Elements of Africa, 1972; The Zimbabwean Culture of Rhodesia, 1972; Miscellaneous Racial Studies, 2 vols, 1972; The Knightly Twilight, 1974; Aspects of British and Continental Heraldry, 1974; The Lost Clan, 1974; Syro-Mesopotamian Ethnology, 1974; The Mackay of the Rhinns of Islay, 1979; Minard Castle, 1980; Minard Castle Collection of Pipe Music, 1986; An Autobiography, 1987; The Power Beyond, 1989; contribs Mankind Quarterly, contrib. Encyc. Brit., etc. *Recreations:* yachting, ocean cruising. *Address:* Minard Castle, Minard, by Inveraray, Argyll PA32 8YB; (owns as feudal baron of Lochoreshyre) Lochore Castle, Fife. *Clubs:* Army and Navy, Royal Thames Yacht; Pretoria (Pretoria, SA); Casino Maltese (Valletta); Royal Forth Yacht, Royal Highland Yacht, Royal Malta Yacht, etc.

GAZDAR, Prof. Gerald James Michael, FBA 1988; Professor of Computational Linguistics, since 1985, Dean of School of Cognitive and Computing Sciences, since 1988, University of Sussex; *b* 24 Feb. 1950; *s* of John and Kathleen Gazdar. *Educ:* Heath Mount; Bradfield Coll.; Univ. of East Anglia (BA Phil with Econ); Reading Univ. (MA Linguistics, PhD). Lectr 1975–80, Reader 1980–85, Univ. of Sussex. Fellow, Center for Advanced Study in the Behavioral Sciences, Stanford Univ., California, 1984–85. *Publications:* (with Klein, Pullum) A Bibliography of Contemporary Linguistic Research, 1978; Pragmatics, 1979; (with Klein, Pullum) Order, Concord, and Constituency, 1983; (with Klein, Pullum, Sag) Generalized Phrase Structure Grammar, 1985; (with Coates, Deuchar, Lyons) New Horizons in Linguistics II, 1987; (with Franz, Osborne, Evans) Natural Language Processing in the 1980s, 1987; (with Mellish): Natural Language Processing in Prolog, An Introduction to Computational Linguistics, 1989; Natural Language Processing in LISP, An Introduction to Computational Linguistics, 1989; Natural Language Processing in POP-11, An Introduction to Computational Linguistics, 1989. *Address:* School of Cognitive and Computing Sciences, University of Sussex, Brighton BN1 9QH. *T:* Brighton (0273) 678029.

GAZE, Dr Raymond Michael, FRS 1972; FRSE 1964; Head, Medical Research Council Neural Development and Regeneration Group, Edinburgh University, since 1984, Hon. Professor, since 1986; *b* 22 June 1927; *s* of late William Mercer Gaze and Kathleen Grace Gaze (*née* Bowhill); *m* 1957, Robinetta Mary Armfelt; one *s* two *d*. *Educ:* at home; Sch. of Medicine, Royal Colleges, Edinburgh; Oxford Univ. (MA, DPhil). LRCPE, LRCSE, LRFPSG. House Physician, Chelmsford and Essex Hosp., 1949; National Service, RAMC, 1953–55; Lectr, later Reader, Dept of Physiology, Edinburgh Univ., 1955–70; Alan Johnston, Lawrence and Moseley Research Fellow, Royal Soc., 1962–66; Head, Div. of Developmental Biol., 1970–83, Dep. Dir 1977–83, Nat. Inst. for Med. Research. Visiting Professor: of Theoretical Biology, Univ. of Chicago, 1972; of Biology, Middlesex Hosp. Med. Sch., 1972–74. Member: Physiological Soc.; British Soc. for Develtl Biology; British Soc. for Cell Biology; Brain Res. Assoc.; Scottish Develtl Biology Gp. *Publications:* The Formation of Nerve Connections, 1970; Editor, 1975–88, and contrib., Development (formerly Jl Embryology and Exper. Morphology); various papers on neurobiology in Jl Physiology, Qly Jl Exper. Physiology, Proc. Royal Soc., etc. *Recreations:* drawing, hill-walking, music. *Address:* c/o Institute of Cell, Animal and Population Biology, Ashworth Laboratory, University of Edinburgh, King's Buildings, West Mains Road, Edinburgh EH9 3JT. *T:* 031–667 1081.

GAZZARD, Roy James Albert (Hon. Major); FRIBA; FRTPI; Pro-Director, 1982–84, Director, 1984–86, Centre for Middle Eastern and Islamic Studies, Durham University, now Honorary Fellow; *b* 19 July 1923; *s* of James Henry Gazzard, MBE, and Ada Gwendoline Gazzard (*née* Willis); *m* 1947, Muriel Joy Morgan; one *s* two *d* (and one *s* decd). *Educ:* Stationers' Company's Sch.; Architectural Assoc. Sch. of Architecture (Dip.); School of Planning and Research for Reg. Develt (Dip.). Commissioned, Mddx Regt, 1943; service Palestine and ME. Acting Govt Town Planner, Uganda, 1950; Staff Architect, Barclays Bank Ltd, 1954; Chief Architect, Peterlee Develt Corp., 1960; Dir of Develt, Northumberland CC, 1962; Chief Professional Adviser to Sec. of State's Environmental Bd, 1976; Under Sec., DoE, 1976–79. Prepared: Jinja (Uganda) Outline Scheme, 1954; Municipality of Sur (Oman) Develt Plan, 1975. Renter Warden, Worshipful Co. of Stationers and Newspaper Makers, 1985–86. Govt medals for Good Design in Housing; Civic Trust awards for Townscape and Conservation. *Publications:* Durham: portrait of a cathedral city, 1983; contribs to HMSO pubns on built environment. *Recreations:* travel, writing, broadcasting. *Address:* 13 Dunhelm Court, South Street, Durham DH1 4QX. *T:* Durham (091) 3864067. *Club:* City Livery.

GEACH, Gertrude Elizabeth Margaret; *see* Anscombe, G. E. M.

GEACH, Prof. Peter Thomas, FBA 1965; Professor of Logic, University of Leeds, 1966–81; *b* 29 March 1916; *o s* of Prof. George Hender Geach, IES, and Eleonora Frederyka Adolfina Sgonina; *m* 1941, Gertrude Elizabeth Margaret Anscombe, *qv*; three *s* four *d*. *Educ:* Balliol Coll., Oxford (Domus Schol.; Hon. Fellow, 1979). 2nd cl. Class, Hon. Mods, 1936; 1st cl. Lit. Hum., 1938. Gladstone Research Student, St Deiniol's Library, Hawarden, 1938–39; philosophical research, Cambridge, 1945–51; University of Birmingham: Asst Lectr in Philosophy, 1951; Lectr, 1952; Sen. Lectr, 1959; Reader in Logic, 1961. Vis. Prof., Univ. of Warsaw, 1985. Lectures: Stanton, in the Philosophy of Religion, Cambridge, 1971–74; Hägerström, Univ. of Uppsala, 1975; O'Hara, Univ. of Notre Dame, 1978. Forschungspreis, A. Von Humboldt Stiftung, 1983. *Publications:* Mental Acts, 1957; Reference and Generality, 1962, 3rd rev. edn 1980; (with G. E. M. Anscombe) Three Philosophers, 1961; God and the Soul, 1969; Logic Matters, 1972; Reason and Argument, 1976; Providence and Evil, 1977; The Virtues, 1977; Truth, Love, and Immortality: an introduction to McTaggart's philosophy, 1979; articles in Mind, Philosophical Review, Analysis, Ratio, etc. *Recreations:* reading stories of detection, mystery and horror; collecting and annotating old bad logic texts. *Address:* 3 Richmond Road, Cambridge. *T:* Cambridge (0223) 353950. *Club:* Union Society (Oxford).

GEAR, Ven. Michael Frederick; Archdeacon of Chester, since 1988; *b* 27 Nov. 1934; *s* of Frederick Augustus and Lillian Hannah Gear; *m* 1961, Daphne, *d* of Norman and Millicent Earl; two *d*. *Educ:* St John's College and Cranmer Hall, Durham. BA Social Studies, 1st cl., 1959; DipTh 1961. Assistant Curate: Christ Church, Bexleyheath, 1961–64; St Aldate, Oxford, 1964–67; Vicar of St Andrew, Clubmoor, Liverpool, 1967–71; Rector, Avondale, Salisbury, Rhodesia, 1971–76; Tutor, Wycliffe Hall, Oxford, 1976–80; Team Rector, Macclesfield, 1980–88. *Recreations:* photography, golf, history and contemporary politics of Southern Africa. *Address:* 25 Bartholomew Way, Westminster Park, Chester CH4 7RJ. *T:* Chester (0244) 675417.

GEAR, William, DA (Edinburgh) 1936; RBSA 1966; Painter; Head of Department of Fine Art, Birmingham Polytechnic (formerly Birmingham College of Art and Design), 1964–75; Member London Group, 1953; *b* Methil, Fife, 2 Aug. 1915; *s* of Porteous Gordon Gear; *m* 1949, Charlotte Chertok (*d* 1988); two *s*. *Educ:* Buckhaven High Sch.; Edinburgh Coll. of Art; Edinburgh Univ.; Moray House Training Coll.; Edinburgh Coll. of Art: Post-grad. schol., 1936–37; Travelling schol., 1937–38; Académie Fernand Leger, Paris, 1937; study in France, Italy, Balkans; Moray House Trg Coll., 1938–39. War Service with Royal Corps of Signals, 1940–46, in Middle East, Italy and Germany. Staff Officer, Monuments, Fine Arts and Archives Br., CCG, 1946–47; worked in Paris, 1947–50; Curator, Towner Art Gallery, Eastbourne, 1958–64. Guest lecturer, Nat. Gall.

of Victoria, Melbourne, and University of Western Australia, 1966. Chairman: Fine Art Panel, Nat. Council for Diplomas in Art and Design, 1972; Fine Art Bd, CNAA, 1974; Council Mem., Midlands Arts Centre, 1978. One-man exhibitions since 1944 in various European cities, N and S America, Japan, etc.; London; Gimpel Fils Gall., 1948–; S London Art Gall. (retrospective), 1954; Edinburgh Fest., 1966; (retrospective) Arts Council, N Ireland, 1969; (retrospective) Scottish Arts Council, 1969; Univ. of Sussex, 1964–75; RBSA Birmingham, 1976 (retrospective); Talbot Rice Art Centre, Univ. of Edinburgh, and Ikon Gall., Birmingham (retrospective), 1982; Spacex Gall., Exeter, 1983; Kirkcaldy Art Gall., 1985; Netherbow Art Centre, Edinburgh, 1985; Redfern Gall., London, 1987, 1989; Galerie 1900–2000, Paris, 1988; Karl & Faber, Munich, 1988–89; Galerie Gabriele von Loeper, Hamburg, 1989; England & Co., London, 1989; Kunsthandel Leeman, Amsterdam, 1990. Group exhibitions: with COBRA: Malmö, 1986; Taipeh, Stockholm, 1987; Odense, Oslo, Amsterdam, 1988; Munich, 1989; Berlin, 1990; others: Celtic Vision, Dublin, 1988; Portrait of the Artist, Tate Gall., 1989; 4 Abstract Artists, Redfern Gall., 1989; Scottish Art since 1900, Scottish Nat. Gall. of Modern Art, 1989, Barbican Art Centre, 1990; From Prism to Paintbox, Welsh Arts Council, 1989–90; Scotland's Pictures, Edinburgh Fest., 1990; The Compass Contribution, Glasgow, 1990; The Birmingham School, Birmingham City Art Gall. and tour, 1990–91; The 20th Century Scottish Print, Hunterian Gall., Glasgow, 1990; Avant-Garde British Printmaking 1914–1960, BM, 1990; Galerie la Cité, Luxembourg, 1990; works shown in many exhibitions of contemporary art, also at Royal Acad., 1960, 1961, 1967, 1968, and RSA 1986. Awarded £500 Purchase prize, Fest. of Britain, 1951; David Cargill Award, Royal Glasgow Inst., 1967; Lorne Fellowship, 1976. FIAL, 1960; FRSA 1971. *Works in permanent collections*: Tate Gall.; Arts Council; Brit. Council; Contemp. Art Soc.; Scottish National Gall. of Modern Art; Scottish Arts Council; British Museum; Victoria & Albert Museum; Laing Art Gall., Newcastle; Nat. Gall. of Canada; Bishop Suter Art Gall., NZ; Art Gall., Toronto; City Art Gall., Toledo, Ohio; Museum of Art, Tel Aviv; New Coll., Oxford; Cincinnati Art Gall., Ohio; Nat. Gall. of NSW; Bishop Otter Coll., Chichester; City Art Gall., Manchester; Albright Art Gall., Buffalo, NY; Musée des Beaux Arts, Liège; Inst. of Contemp. Art, Lima, Peru; Towner Art Gall., Eastbourne; Brighton Art Gall.; Pembroke Coll., Cambridge; Chelsea Coll. of Physical Educn; Southampton Art Gall.; Univ. of Glasgow; Arts Council of Northern Ireland; Whitworth Art Gall., Manchester; Univ. of Birmingham; City Museum and Art Gall., Birmingham; Museum of Art, Fort Lauderdale, Fla; Nat. Gall. of Aust.; Karel van Stuÿvenberg Collection, Caracas, Venezuela; Birmingham Polytech.; City Art Centre, Edinburgh; Kirkcaldy Art Gall.; Strathclyde Regl Council; Hereford Liby & Mus.; Dept of Educn, Manchester; Rye Art Gall.; Peir Gall., Orkney; Aberdeen, Dundee and Glasgow Art Galleries, and in numerous private collections in GB, USA, Canada, Italy, France, etc. Furnishing textiles designed for various firms. *Recreations*: cricket, music, gardening. *Address*: 46 George Road, Edgbaston, Birmingham B15 1PL.

GEDDES, family name of **Baron Geddes.**

GEDDES, 3rd Baron *cr* 1942; **Euan Michael Ross Geddes;** Company Director since 1964; *b* 3 Sept. 1937; *s* of 2nd Baron Geddes, KBE, and of Enid Mary, Lady Geddes, *d* of late Clarance H. Butler; *S* father, 1975; *m* 1966, Gillian, *d* of late William Arthur Butler; one *s* one *d*. *Educ*: Rugby; Gonville and Caius Coll., Cambridge (MA 1964); Harvard Business School. *Recreations*: golf, bridge, music, gardening. *Heir*: *s* Hon. James George Neil Geddes, *b* 10 Sept. 1969. *Address*: House of Lords, SW1A 0PW. *T*: Basingstoke (0256) 862105. *Clubs*: Brooks's; Hong Kong (Hong Kong); Aldeburgh Golf, Royal Hong Kong Golf.

GEDDES, Prof. Alexander MacIntosh, (Alasdair), FRCP; FRCPE; Consultant Physician, East Birmingham Hospital, since 1967; Professor of Infectious Diseases, University of Birmingham, since 1982; *b* 14 May 1934; *s* of Angus and Isabella Geddes; *m* 1984, Angela Lewis; two *s*. *Educ*: Fortrose Acad.; Univ. of Edinburgh (MB ChB). Served RAMC, Captain, 1958–60. Med. Registrar, Aberdeen Hosps, 1961–63; Sen. Registrar, City Hosp. and Royal Infirmary, Edinburgh, 1963–67. Examiner: MRCP (UK), 1972–; Final MB, Univs of Birmingham, Glasgow, London, Sheffield, 1975–. Forbes Vis. Fellow, Fairfield Hosp., Melbourne, Aust., 1988; Sir Edward Finch Vis. Prof., Univ. of Sheffield, 1989. Chairman: Sub-Cttee on Communicable and Trop. Diseases, Jt Cttee on Higher Med. Trng, 1984–; Isolation Beds Working Party, DoH, 1989–; Member: Birmingham AHA, 1977–81; Health Educn Authority, 1987–; Sub-Cttee on Efficacy and Adverse Reactions, Cttee on Safety of Medicines, 1978–85; DHSS Expert Adv. Gp on AIDS, 1985–; DoH (formerly DHSS) Jt Cttee on Vaccination and Immunization, 1986–; Trop. Med. Res. Bd, MRC, 1984–88; Ministerial Inquiry into the Public Health Function, 1985–87; Consultant Advr in Infectious Diseases, DoH, 1990–. Chm., Brit. Soc. for Antimicrobial Therapy, 1982–85; Chm., Communicable and Tropical Diseases Cttee, 1983–, Censor, 1987–89, RCP; Mem., Assoc. of Physicians of GB and Ire., 1976–. Lectures: Honeyman-Gillespie, Univ. of Edinburgh, 1975; Public, Univ. of Warwick, 1980; Davidson, RCPE, 1981; Watson-Smith, 1988; Lister, RCPE, 1990. Chm., Editorial Bd, Jl of Antimicrobial Therapy, 1982–85. *Publications*: (ed) Control of Hospital Infection, 1975, 3rd edn 1989; (ed) Recent Advances in Infection, 1975, 3rd edn 1988; (contrib.) Davidson, Principles and Practice of Medicine, 16th edn 1991; papers on infectious diseases, immunology, antibiotic therapy and epidemiology in learned jls. *Recreations*: gardening, reading. *Address*: 34 The Crescent, Solihull, West Midlands B91 1JR. *T*: 021–705 8844, *Fax*: 021–766 8752. *Club*: Athenæum.

GEDDES, Sir (Anthony) Reay (Mackay), KBE 1968 (OBE 1943); President, Charities Aid Foundation (Chairman, 1985–90); *b* 7 May 1912; *s* of late Rt Hon. Sir Eric Geddes, PC, GCB, GBE; *m* 1938, Imogen, *d* of late Captain Hay Matthey, Brixham; two *s* three *d*. *Educ*: Rugby; Cambridge. Bank of England, 1932–35; Dunlop Rubber Company Ltd, 1935, Dir 1947, Chm. 1968–78; Dep. Chm., Midland Bank, 1978–84 (Dir, 1967–84). Director: Shell Transport and Trading Co., 1968–82; Rank Orgn, 1975–84. Pres., Soc. of Motor Manufacturers and Traders, 1958–59; Part-time Mem., UKAEA, 1960–65; Mem. Nat. Economic Develt. Council, 1962–65; Chm., Shipbuilding Inquiry Cttee, 1965–66. Pres., Internat. Chamber of Commerce, 1980. Hon. DSc Aston, 1967; Hon LLD Leicester, 1969; Hon. DTech Loughborough, 1970. *Address*: 49 Eaton Place, SW1X 8DE.

GEDDES, Ford Irvine, MBE 1943; *b* 17 Jan. 1913; *e s* of Irvine Campbell Geddes and Dorothy Jefford Geddes (*née* Fowler); *m* 1945, Barbara Gertrude Vere Parry-Okeden; one *s* four *d*. *Educ*: Loretto Sch.; Gonville and Caius Coll., Cambridge (BA). Joined Anderson Green & Co. Ltd, London, 1934. Served War RE, 1939–45 (Major). Director: Bank of NSW (London Adv. Bd), 1950–81; Equitable Life Assce Soc., 1955–76 (Pres. 1963–71); British United Turkeys Ltd, 1962–69, 1976–78 (Chm., 1976–78); Chairman: P&O Steam Navigation Co., 1971–72 (a Dep. Chm., 1968–71; Dir, 1960–72); British Shipping Federation, 1965–68; Pres., Internat. Shipping Fedn, 1967–69. *Address*: 18 Gordon Place, W8 4JD. *Clubs*: City of London; Union (Sydney).
See also N. L. J. Montagu.

GEDDES, Michael Dawson; Chief Executive, Recruitment and Assessment Services Agency and Civil Service Commissioner, since 1990; *b* 9 March 1944; *s* of David and Audrey Geddes; *m* 1966, Leslie Rose Webb; two *s*. *Educ*: Sherborne Sch., Dorset; Univ. of BC (Goldsmith's Exhibitioner) (BA). Cranfield Institute of Technology: Admin. Asst, 1968–71; Planning Officer, 1971–77; Develt and Estates Officer, 1977–83; Financial Controller, RMCS, 1983–84; Sec., Ashridge (Bonar Law Meml) Trust; Dir, Admin, Ashridge Management Coll. and Dir, Ashridge subsids, 1984–90. *Publications*: (with W. Briner and C. Hastings) Project Leadership, 1990; papers on resource allocation in univs and on project management. *Recreations*: golf, bridge. *Address*: 11 Main Street, Mursley, Bucks MK17 0RT. *T*: Mursley (0296) 720601.

GEDDES, Sir Reay; *see* Geddes, Sir A. R. M.

GEDDES, William George Nicholson, CBE 1979; FRSE; FEng, FICE, FIStructE; Senior Partner, Babtie Shaw and Morton, Consulting Engineers, 1976–79, retired (Partner, 1950–76); *b* 29 July 1913; *s* of William Brydon Geddes and Ina (*née* Nicholson); *m* 1942, Margaret Gilchrist Wilson; one *s* one *d*. *Educ*: Dunbar High Sch.; Univ. of Edinburgh (BSc, 1st Cl. Hons). Engineer: Sir William Arrol & Co., F. A. Macdonald & Partners, Shell Oil Co., ICI, Babtie Shaw and Morton, 1935–79. President: Instn of Structural Engrs, 1971–72; Instn of Engrs and Shipbuilders in Scotland, 1977–79; Instn of Civil Engrs, 1979–80. Visiting Professor, Univ. of Strathclyde, 1978. Pres., Queen's Park Football Club, 1985–88. Hon. DSc Edinburgh, 1980. *Publications*: numerous papers to engrg instns and learned socs both at home and abroad. *Recreations*: fly-fishing, golf, hill-walking. *Address*: 17 Beechlands Avenue, Netherlee, Glasgow G44 3YT. *T*: 041–637 1526. *Clubs*: Caledonian; Royal Scottish Automobile (Glasgow).

GEDLING, Raymond, CB 1969; Deputy Secretary, Department of Health and Social Security, 1971–77; *b* 3 Sept. 1917; *s* of late John and late Mary Gedling; *m* 1956, Joan Evelyn Chapple; one *s*. *Educ*: Grangefield Grammar Sch., Stockton-on-Tees. Entered Civil Service as Executive Officer, Min. of Health, 1936; Asst Principal, 1942, Principal, 1947. Cabinet Office, 1951–52; Principal Private Sec. to Minister of Health, 1952–55; Asst Sec., 1955; Under-Sec., 1961; Asst Under-Sec. of State, Dept of Educn and Science, 1966–68; Dep. Sec., Treasury, 1968–71. *Recreations*: walking, chess. *Address*: 27 Wallace Fields, Epsom, Surrey. *T*: 081–393 9060.

GEE, Anthony Hall; QC 1990; a Recorder of the Crown Court, since 1989; *b* 4 Nov. 1948; *s* of late Harold Stephenson Gee and Marjorie Gee (*née* Hall); *m* 1975, Gillian Pauline Glover, St Annes-on-Sea; one *s* two *d*. *Educ*: Cambs High School for Boys; Chester City Grammar Sch.; Inns of Court School of Law. Called to the Bar, Gray's Inn, 1972; Mem., Northern Circuit, 1972–. *Recreation*: golf. *Address*: (chambers) 28 St John Street, Manchester M3 4DJ. *T*: 061–834 8418. *Club*: Bramhall Golf.

GEE, David Charles Laycock; Director, Friends of the Earth, since 1990; *b* 18 April 1947; *s* of Charles Laycock Gee and Theresa Gee (*née* Garrick); *m* 1974, Vivienne Taylor Gee; three *d*. *Educ*: Thomas Linacre and Wigan Grammar Schs; York Univ. (BA Politics). MIOSH 1985. Res. Dept, AUEW, 1970–73; Educn Service, TUC, 1973–78; Nat. Health/Safety Officer, GMB, 1978–88; Occupational/Environmental Cons., 1988–89. Fellow, Collegium Ramazzini, Italy, 1984; FRSA 1990. *Publications*: (with John Cox and Dave Leon) Cancer and Work, 1982; (with Lesley Doyal et al) Cancer in Britian, 1983; chapter in Radiation and Health—Biological Effects of Low Level Exposure to Ionising Radiation, 1987. *Recreations*: family, swimming, tennis, running, entertaining, theatre, music. *Address*: 24 Broomwood Road, SW11 6HT. *T*: 071–223 0595.

GEE, Prof. Geoffrey, CBE 1958; FRS 1951; Sir Samuel Hall Professor of Chemistry, University of Manchester, 1955–77, now Emeritus Professor; *b* 6 June 1910; *s* of Thomas and Mary Ann Gee; *m* 1934, Marion (*née* Bowden); one *s* two *d*. *Educ*: New Mills Grammar Sch.; Universities of Manchester and Cambridge, BSc 1931, MSc 1932, Manchester; PhD 1936, ScD 1947, Cambridge. ICI (Dyestuffs Group) Research Chemist, 1933–38; British Rubber Producers' Research Association: Research Chemist, 1938–47; Dir, 1947–53. University of Manchester: Prof. of Physical Chemistry, 1953–55; Pro-Vice Chancellor, 1966–68, 1972–77 (full-time, 1975–77). Pres., Faraday Soc., 1969 and 1970. Hon. Fellow, Manchester Polytechnic, 1979. Hon. DSc Manchester, 1983. *Publications*: numerous scientific papers in Transactions of the Faraday Soc., and other journals. *Recreation*: currently interested in relation between science and theology. *Address*: 8 Holmfield Drive, Cheadle Hulme, Cheshire SK8 7DT. *T*: 061–485 3713.

GEE, Richard; His Honour Judge Gee; a Circuit Judge, since 1991; *b* 25 July 1942; *s* of John and Marie Gee; *m* 1965, Jane Frances Ufland; three *s*. *Educ*: Kilburn Grammar School; University College London (LLB Hons). Admitted Solicitor, 1966; Assistant Recorder, 1983; Recorder, 1988. Mem., Main Board and Criminal Law Cttee, Judicial Studies Board, 1988–. *Recreation*: golf.

GEE, Timothy Hugh; HM Diplomatic Service, retired; Consultant, The Entertainment Corporation; *b* 12 Nov. 1936; *s* of Arthur William Gee and Edith (*née* Ingham); *m* 1964, Gillian Eve St Johnston (marr. diss. 1988); two *s* one *d*. *Educ*: Berkhamsted; Trinity Coll., Oxford. 2 Lieut 3rd Regt RHA, 1959–61. Joined British Council, 1961; New Delhi, 1962–66; entered HM Diplomatic Service, 1966; FO, 1966–68; Brussels, 1968–72; FCO, 1972–74; Kuala Lumpur, 1974–79; Counsellor, on secondment to NI Office, 1979–81; Consul-General, Istanbul, 1981–85; Head of Cultural Relations Dept, FCO, 1985–87. *Club*: Travellers'.

GEELONG, Bishop of; *see* Bayton, Rt Rev. J.

GEERING, Ian Walter; QC 1991; *b* 19 July 1947; *s* of late Wilfrid Robert Geering and of Barbara Pearce (*née* James); *m* 1975, (Alison) Diana Burne; two *s* two *d*. *Educ*: Bedford Sch.; Univ. of Edinburgh (BVMS). Called to the Bar, Inner Temple, 1974. *Recreations*: walking, reading, sailing, photography. *Address*: 3 Gray's Inn Place, Gray's Inn, WC1R 5EA.

GEFFEN, Dr Terence John; Medical Adviser, Capsticks Solicitors; *b* 17 Sept. 1921; *s* of late Maximilian W. Geffen and Maia Geffen (later Reid); *m* 1965, Judith Anne Steward; two *s*. *Educ*: St Paul's Sch.; University Coll., London; UCH. MD, FRCP. House Phys., UCH, 1943; RAMC, 1944–47; hosp. posts, Edgware Gen. Hosp., Hampstead Gen. Hosp., UCH, 1947–55; Min. of Health (later DHSS), 1956–82, SPMO, 1972–82; Consultant in Public Health Medicine, NW Thames RHA, 1982–90. FRSM. *Publications*: various in BMJ, Lancet, Clinical Science, etc. *Recreations*: music, reading, bridge. *Address*: 2 Stonehill Close, SW14 8RP. *T*: 081–878 0516.

GEHRELS, Jürgen Carlos; Chief Executive, Siemens plc, since 1986; *b* 24 July 1935; *s* of Hans Gehrels and Ursula (*née* da Rocha); *m* 1963, Sigrid Kausch; one *s* one *d*. *Educ*: Technical Univs, Berlin and Munich (Dipl. Ing.). Siemens AG, Germany, 1965–79; Pres., General Numeric Corp., Chicago, USA, 1979–82; Dir, Factory Automation, Siemens AG, Germany, 1982–86. Chairman: Siemens Communication Systems Ltd, 1986–; Siemens Financial Services Ltd, 1988–; Siemens Controls Ltd, 1990–; Siemens-Nixdorf Inf. Systems Ltd, 1990–; Director: Neve Electronic International Ltd, 1987–; Siemens Domestic Appliances Ltd, 1987–; Comparex Ltd, 1988–; Alfred Engelmann Ltd, 1989–; Plessey UK, 1989–; Plessey Overseas, 1989–; Siemens Holdings plc, 1990–. *Recreations*:

golf, gardening, architecture. *Address:* Siemens plc, Siemens House, Windmill Road, Sunbury-on-Thames, Middx TW16 7HS. *Clubs:* Reform; Burhill Golf (Surrey).

GELDER, Prof. Michael Graham; W. A. Handley Professor of Psychiatry, University of Oxford, since 1969; Fellow of Merton College, Oxford; *b* 2 July 1929; *s* of Philip Graham Gelder and Margaret Gelder (*née* Graham); *m* 1954, Margaret (*née* Anderson); one *s* two *d*. *Educ:* Bradford Grammar Sch.; Queen's Coll., Oxford. Scholar, Theodore Williams Prize 1949 and first class Hons, Physiology finals, 1950; MA, DM Oxon, FRCP, FRCPsych; DPM London (with distinction) 1961. Goldsmit Schol., UCH London, 1951. House Physician, Sen. House Physician, UCH, 1955–57; Registrar, Maudsley Hosp., 1958–61; MRC Fellow in Clinical Research, 1962–63; Sen. Lectr, Inst. of Psychiatry, 1965–67 (Vice-Dean, 1967–68); Physician, Bethlem Royal and Maudsley Hosps, 1967–68. Hon. Consultant Psychiatrist, Oxford RHA, later DHA, 1969–; Mem., Oxford DHA, 1985–. Mem., MRC, 1978–79 (Chm., 1978–79, Mem., 1975–78 and 1987–, Neurosciences Bd). Chm., Wellcome Trust Neuroscience Panel, 1990– (Mem., 1984–88). Chairman: Assoc. of Univ. Teachers of Psychiatry, 1979–82; Jt Cttee on Higher Psychiatric Trng, 1981–85. Europ. Vice-Pres., Soc. for Psychotherapy Research, 1977–82. Mem., Assoc. of Physicians, 1983–. Mem. Council, RCPsych, 1981–90 (Vice Pres. 1982–83; Sen. Vice-Pres., 1983–84; Chm. Res. Cttee, 1986–). Mayne Guest Prof., Univ. of Queensland, 1990. Lectures: Malcolm Millar, Univ. of Aberdeen, 1984; Yap Meml, Hong Kong, 1987. Gold Medal, Royal Medico-Psychol Assoc., 1962. *Publications:* (jtly) Agoraphobia: nature and treatment, 1981; (jtly) The Oxford Textbook of Psychiatry, 1983, 2nd edn 1989; chapters in books and articles in medical jls. *Recreations:* photography, gardening, real-tennis. *Address:* St Mary's, Jack Straw's Lane, Oxford OX3 0DN. *Club:* Athenæum.

GELDOF, Bob, Hon. KBE 1986; singer; songwriter; initiator and organiser, Band Aid, Live Aid and Sport Aid fund-raising events; *b* Dublin, 5 Oct. 1954; *m* 1986, Paula Yates; two *d*. *Educ:* Black Rock Coll. Sometime journalist: Georgia Straight, Vancouver; New Musical Express; Melody Maker. Jt Founder, Boomtown Rats, rock band, 1975. Acted in films: Pink Floyd—The Wall, 1982; Number One, 1985. Organised Band Aid, 1984, to record Do They Know It's Christmas, sales from which raised £8 million for famine relief in Ethiopia; organised simultaneous Live Aid concerts in London and Philadelphia to raise £50 million, 1985; organised Sport Aid to raise further £50 million, 1986. Chm., Band Aid Trust, 1985–; Founder, Live Aid Foundn, USA, 1985–. Freeman: Borough of Swale, 1985; Newcastle. Hon. MA Kent, 1985; Hon. DSc(Econ) London, 1987; Hon. DPh Ghent. TV film: The Price of Progress, 1987. Awards include: UN World Hunger Award, FAO Medal; EEC Gold Medal; Irish Peace Prize; music awards include: Ivor Novello (four times); several gold and platinum discs. Order of Two Niles (Sudan); Cavalier, Order of Leopold II (Belgium). *Publication:* Is That It? (autobiog.), 1986. *Address:* c/o Marsha Hunt, 26 Soho Square, W1.

GELL, Prof. Philip George Houthem, FRS 1969; Professor and Head of Department of Experimental Pathology, Birmingham University, 1968–78; retired; *b* 20 Oct. 1914; *s* of late Major P. F. Gell, DSO, and Mrs E. Lewis Hall; *m* 1941, Albinia Susan Roope Gordon; one *s* one *d*. *Educ:* Stowe Sch.; Trinity Coll., Cambridge; University Coll. Hosp. MRCS, LRCP, 1939; MB, BCh, 1940; FRCPath, 1969. Ho. Phys. to Med. Unit, UCH, 1939; Emergency Public Health Laboratory Service, 1940–43. On staff of Nat. Inst. for Med. Research, 1943–48; Reader in Dept of Exptl Pathology, Birmingham Univ., 1948–60; Prof. (Personal) of Immunological Pathology, Dept of Exptl Pathology, 1960–68. *Publications:* (ed with R. R. A. Coombs and P. J. Lachmann) Clinical Aspects of Immunology, 1968, 3rd edn 1974; contribs to Jl of Experimental Med., Immunology, 1960–. *Recreations:* gardening, painting, philosophy of science. *Address:* Wychwood, Cranes Lane, Kingston, Cambridge. *T:* Cambridge (0223) 262714.

GELL-MANN, Murray; Robert Andrews Millikan Professor of Theoretical Physics at the California Institute of Technology since 1967; *b* 15 Sept. 1929; *s* of Arthur and Pauline Gell-Mann; *m* 1955, J. Margaret Dow (*d* 1981); one *s* one *d*. *Educ:* Yale Univ.; Massachusetts Inst. of Technology. Mem., Inst. for Advanced Study, Princeton, 1951; Instructor, Asst Prof., and Assoc. Prof., Univ. of Chicago, 1952–55; Assoc. Prof. 1955–56, Prof. 1956–66, California Inst. of Technology. Vis. Prof., Collège de France and Univ. of Paris, 1959–60. Overseas Fellow, Churchill Coll., Cambridge, 1966. Mem., President's Science Adv. Cttee, 1969–72. Regent, Smithsonian Instn, 1974–88; Chm. of Bd, Aspen Center for Physics, 1973–79; Dir, J. D. and C. T. MacArthur Foundn, 1979–; Vice-Pres. and Chm. of Western Center, Amer. Acad. of Arts and Sciences, 1970–76; Member: Nat. Acad. of Sciences, 1960–; Sci. and Grants Cttee, Leakey Foundn, 1977–. Santa Fe Institute: Founding Trustee, 1982; Chm., Bd of Trustees, 1982–85; Co-Chm., Sci. Bd, 1985–. Mem. Bd, California Nature Conservancy, 1984–. Foreign Mem., Royal Society, 1978. Hon. ScD: Yale, 1959; Chicago, 1967; Illinois, 1968; Wesleyan, 1968; Utah, 1970; Columbia, 1977; Hon. DSc Cantab, 1980; Hon. Dr, Turin, 1969. Listed on UN Envmtl Program Roll of Honor for Envmtl Achievement (Global 500), 1988. Dannie Heineman Prize (Amer. Phys. Soc.), 1959; Ernest O. Lawrence Award, 1966; Franklin Medal (Franklin Inst., Philadelphia), 1967; John J. Carty Medal (Nat. Acad. Scis), 1968; Research Corp. Award, 1969; Nobel Prize in Physics, 1969. *Publications:* (with Yuval Ne'eman) The Eightfold Way, 1964; various articles in learned jls on topics referring to classification and description of elementary particles of physics and their interactions. *Recreations:* walking in wild country, study of natural history, languages. *Address:* Caltech 452–48, Pasadena, Calif 91125, USA. *T:* 818–356–6686. *Clubs:* Cosmos (Washington) Explorers', Century (New York); Athenæum (Pasadena).

GELLHORN, Peter, FGSM; Conductor and Chorus Master, Glyndebourne Festival Opera, 1954–61, rejoined Glyndebourne Music Staff, 1974 and 1975; Professor, Guildhall School of Music and Drama, since 1981; *b* 24 Oct. 1912; *s* of late Dr Alfred Gellhorn, and late Mrs Else Gellhorn; *m* 1943, Olive Shirley (*née* Layton), 3rd *d* of 1st Baron Layton, CH, CBE; two *s* two *d*. *Educ:* Schiller Realgymnasium, Charlottenburg; University of Berlin; Berlin Music Acad. FGSM 1989. After passing final exams (with dist.) as pianist and conductor, left Germany 1935. Musical Dir, Toynbee Hall, London, E1, 1935–39; Asst Conductor, Sadler's Wells Opera, 1941–43. On industrial war service, 1943–45. Conductor, Royal Carl Rosa Opera (115 perfs), 1945–46; Conductor and Head of Music Staff, Royal Opera House, Covent Garden (over 260 perfs), 1946–53; Dir, BBC Chorus, 1961–72; Conductor, Elizabethan Singers, 1976–80. Has also been working at National Sch. of Opera, annually at Summer Sch. of Music at Dartington Hall; composes; wrote and arranged music for silhouette and puppet films of Lotte Reiniger (at intervals, 1933–57). Mem., Music Staff, London Opera Centre, 1973–78; Conductor: Morley Coll. Opera Gp, 1974–79; Barnes Choir; Associate Conductor, London Chamber Opera, 1982–; Music Dir, Opera Players Ltd; Mem. Staff, Opera Sch., RCM, 1980–88, conducting its opera perfs, 1981. Lectures on Courses arranged by various County Councils and adult colleges; frequently adjudicates at music fests in UK and overseas. Musical Dir, Opera Barga, Italy, from foundn, 1967–69. *Recreations:* reading, walking and going to plays. *Address:* 33 Leinster Avenue, East Sheen, SW14 7JW. *T:* 081–876 3949. *Club:* BBC.

GELLNER, Prof. Ernest André, FBA 1974; William Wyse Professor of Social Anthropology, Cambridge University, since 1984; Professorial Fellow, King's College, Cambridge, since 1984; *b* Paris, 9 Dec. 1925; *s* of Rudolf Gellner and Anna (*née* Fantl), Prague; *m* 1954, Susan Ryan; two *s* two *d*. *Educ:* Prague English Grammar Sch.; St Albans County (now Verulam) Sch.; Balliol Coll., Oxford. MA (Oxon), PhD (Lond). Pte, Czech. Armoured Brig., BLA, 1944–45. On staff of London School of Economics, 1949–84 (Hon. Fellow 1986), Prof. of Philosophy, 1962–84. Visiting Fellow: Harvard, 1952–53; Univ. of California, Berkeley, 1968; Centre de Recherches et d'Études sur les Sociétés Méditerranéens, Aix-en-Provence, 1978–79; Vis. Schol., Inst. of Advanced Studies, Tel Aviv Univ., 1982; Guest of Acad. of Scis of USSR, Moscow, 1988–89. Member: Council, SSRC (later ESRC), 1980–86 (Chm., Internat. Activities Cttee, 1982–84); Council, British Acad., 1981–84; Academia Europaea, 1989. Pres., RAI, 1991; First Pres., for Moroccan Studies, 1990. Tanner Lectr, Harvard Univ., 1990; Memorial Lectures: Frazer; Radcliffe-Brown; Marett; Myers; M. Stuchlík; H. Arendt; A. Little; H. Enayat; E. Westermarck; Marie Curie; B. Blackwood; L. Schapiro; Munro. Hon. For. Mem., Amer. Acad. of Arts and Scis, 1988. Hon. DSc Bristol, 1986; Hon. DLit QUB, 1989. Mem., Editorial or Adv. Boards: British Jl of Sociol.; Amer. Jl of Sociol.; Inquiry; Middle Eastern Studies; Jl of Peasant Studies; Society and Theory; Govt and Opposition; Philosophy of the Social Scis; Cambridge Archæological Jl; Jl of Mediterranean Studies; Co-Editor: Europ. Jl of Sociol., 1966–84; Govt and Opposition, 1980–. *Publications:* Words and Things, 1959; Thought and Change, 1964; Saints of the Atlas, 1969; (ed with G. Ionescu) Populism, 1969; (ed with C. Micaud) Arabs and Berbers, 1973; Cause and Meaning in the Social Sciences, 1973, 2nd edn, as The Concept of Kinship and other essays, 1986; Contemporary Thought and Politics, 1974; The Devil in Modern Philosophy, 1974; Legitimation of Belief, 1975; (ed with J. Waterbury) Patrons and Clients, 1977; Spectacles and Predicaments, 1979; (ed) Soviet and Western Anthropology, 1980; Muslim Society, 1981; Nations and Nationalism, 1983; (ed) Islamic Dilemmas: reformers, nationalists and industrialisation, 1985; The Psychoanalytic Movement, 1985; Culture, Identity and Politics, 1987; State and Society in Soviet Thought, 1988; Plough, Sword and Book, 1988; (ed jtly) Malinowski between Two Worlds, 1988; numerous contributions to learned jls. *Address:* King's College, Cambridge CB2 1ST. *Club:* Reform.

GEM, Dr Richard David Harvey, FSA; Secretary, Cathedrals Fabric Commission for England, since 1991; *b* 10 Jan. 1945. *Educ:* Eastbourne Coll.; Peterhouse, Cambridge (MA, PhD). Inspector of Ancient Monuments, DoE, 1970–80; Res. Officer, Council for Care of Churches, 1981–88; Dep. Sec., then Sec., Cathedrals Adv. Commn for England, 1988–91. Mem., RCHM, 1987–. Pres., British Archaeol Assoc., 1983–89. *Publications:* numerous papers on early medieval architecture in British and foreign learned jls. *Recreations:* gardening, theatre, music, foreign travel, philosphy and theology. *Address:* 83 London Wall, EC2M 5NA. *T:* 071–638 0971; The Bothy, Mentmore, near Leighton Buzzard, Beds LU7 0QG.

GENDERS, Rt. Rev. Roger Alban Marson, (Father Anselm, CR); *b* 15 Aug. 1919; *yr s* of John Boulton Genders and Florence Alice (*née* Thomas). *Educ:* King Edward VI School, Birmingham; Brasenose College, Oxford (Sen. Scholar 1938, BA Lit. Hum. 1946, MA 1946). Served War, Lieut RNVR, 1940–46. Joined Community of the Resurrection, Mirfield, 1948; professed, 1952; ordained, 1952; Tutor, College of the Resurrection, 1952–55; Vice-Principal 1955, and Principal 1957–65, Codrington Coll., Barbados; Exam. Chaplain to Bishop of Barbados, 1957–65; Treasurer of St Augustine's Mission, Rhodesia, 1966–75; Archdeacon of Manicaland, 1970–75; Asst Bursar, Community of the Resurrection, Mirfield, 1975–77; Bishop of Bermuda, 1977–82; Assistant Bishop of Wakefield, 1983–89. *Publications:* contribs to Theology. *Address:* Community of the Resurrection, House of the Resurrection, Mirfield, W Yorks WF14 0BN.

GENGE, Rt. Rev. Kenneth Lyle; *see* Edmonton (Alberta), Bishop of.

GENGE, Rt. Rev. Mark; Bishop of Central Newfoundland, 1976–90; *b* 18 March 1927; *s* of Lambert and Lily Genge; *m* 1959, Maxine Clara (*née* Major); five *d*. *Educ:* Queen's Coll. and Memorial Univ., Newfoundland; Univ. of Durham (MA); BD Gen. Synod of Canada. Deacon, Corner Brook, Newfoundland, 1951; priest, Stephenville, 1952; Durham, 1953–55; Vice-Principal, Queen's Coll., St John's, Newfoundland, 1955–57; Curate, St Mary's Church, St John's, 1957–59; Rector: Foxtrap, 1959–64; Mary's Harbour, 1964–65; Burgeo, 1965–69; Curate, Marbleton, PQ, 1969–71; Rector, South River, Port-de-Grave, 1971–73; District Sec., Canadian Bible Soc., 1973–76. *Recreations:* badminton, swimming. *Address:* c/o Diocesan Office, 34 Fraser Road, Gander, Newfoundland A1V 2E8, Canada.

GENSCHER, Hans-Dietrich; Federal Minister for Foreign Affairs and Deputy Chancellor, Federal Republic of Germany, since May 1974 (in government of Helmut Schmidt, to Oct. 1982, then in government of Helmut Kohl); Chairman of the Free Democratic Party, 1974–85; *b* Reideburg/Saalkreis, 21 March 1927; *m* Barbara; one *d*. *Educ:* Higher Sch. Certif. (Abitur); studied law and economics in Halle/Saale and Leipzig Univs, 1946–49. Served War, 1943–45. Mem., state-level org. of LDP, 1946. Re-settled in W Germany, 1952: practical legal training in Bremen and Mem. Free Democratic Party (FDP); FDP Asst in Parly Group, 1956; Gen. Sec.: FDP Parly Group, 1959–65; FDP at nat. level, 1962–64. Elected Mem., Bundestag, 1965; a Parly Sec., FDP Parly Group, 1965–69; Dep. Chm., FDP, 1969–74; Federal Minister of the Interior, Oct. 1969 (Brandt-Scheel Cabinet); re-apptd Federal Minister of the Interior, Dec. 1972. He was instrumental in maintaining pure air and water; gave a modern structure to the Federal Police Authority; Federal Border Guard Act passed; revised weapons laws, etc.; in promoting relations between West and East, prominent role in CSCE, Helsinki, 1975, Madrid, 1980–83, Stockholm, 1984–86 and in setting up conferences on Conventional Armed Forces, Confidence and Security Building Measures, Vienna, 1989; an initiator of reform process that led to the inclusion of the Single European Act 1986. Co-initiator: 'Eureka' initiative; independence process in Namibia. Promotes co-operation between EC and other regional gps, ASEAN, Central Amer. States, (San José Conferences), Golf Co-operation Council. Hon. Dr: Madras, 1977, Salamanca, 1987, Athens, 1988, Seoul, 1988, Budapest, 1988; Georgetown, Washington, 1990; Hon. Master, German Handicrafts 1975; Hon. citizen Costa Rica, 1987; Grand Fed. Cross of Merit 1973, 1975 with star and sash; Wolfgang-Döring Medal 1976; numerous foreign decorations. *Publications:* Umweltschutz: Das Umweltschutzprogramm der Bundesregierung, 1972; Bundestagsreden, 1972; Aussenpolitik im Dienste von Sicherheit und Freiheit, 1975; Deutsche Aussenpolitik, 1977, 3rd edn 1985; Bundestagsreden und Zeitdokumente, 1979; Zukunftsverantwortung, 1990. *Recreations:* reading, walking, swimming. *Address:* Auswärtiges Amt, Adenauerallee 99–103, 5300 Bonn, Germany.

GENT, (John) David (Wright), FIHT, FIMI; Director General, Retail Motor Industry Federation (formerly Motor Agents Association), since 1985; *b* 25 April 1935; *s* of late Reginald Philip Gent and Stella Eva Parker; *m* 1970, Anne Elaine Hanson. *Educ:* Lancing Coll. Admitted a Solicitor, 1959. Joined Soc. of Motor Manufacturers as Legal Advr, 1961; Asst Sec., 1964; Sec. 1965; Dep. Dir, 1971–80; joined Lucas Industries as Gen. Man., Lucas Service UK, 1981; Gp PR Man., 1982–83; Dir, British Road Fedn, 1983–84. Mem., Road Transport ITB, 1985–. Freeman, City of London, 1985; Liveryman, Coach Makers and Coach Harness Makers' Co., 1985. *Recreations:* farming, gardening. *Address:* 44 Ursula Street, SW11 3DW. *T:* 071–228 8126. *Club:* Royal Automobile.

GENTLEMAN, David (William), RDI 1970; painter and designer; *b* 11 March 1930; *s* of late Tom and Winifred Gentleman; *m* 1st, 1953, Rosalind Dease (marr. diss. 1966); one *d*; 2nd, 1968, Susan, *d* of late George Ewart Evans; two *d* one *s*. *Educ*: Hertford Grammar Sch.; St Albans Sch. of Art; Royal College of Art. Work includes: watercolour painting, graphic design, lithography, book illustration and wood engraving; commissions include mural designs for Charing Cross underground station, 1979; panels for East Cloister, Westminster Abbey, 1986; drawings, engravings and designs for many publishers; postage stamps for the Post Office, including, 1962–89: Shakespeare, Churchill, Darwin, Ely Cathedral (Christmas 1989); posters for London Transport and the National Trust; symbols for British Steel, Bodleian Library, etc. One-man exhibitions at Mercury Gallery: watercolours of: India, 1970; Carolina, 1973; Africa, 1976; Pacific, 1981; Britain, 1982; London, 1985; British coastline, 1988; Paris, 1991. Work in public collections incl. Tate Gall., British Mus. and Nat. Maritime Mus. Member: Nat. Trust Properties Cttee; Alliance Graphique Internat.; Council, Artists' Gen. Benevolent Instn. Master of Faculty, RDI, 1989–91. Hon. Fellow, RCA, 1981. Phillips Gold Medal for Stamp Design, 1969, 1979. *Publications include*: Fenella in Ireland, in Greece, in Spain, in France, 1967; Design in Miniature, 1972; David Gentleman's Britain, 1982; David Gentleman's London, 1985; A Special Relationship, 1987; David Gentleman's Coastline, 1988; David Gentleman's Paris, 1991; (contrib.) Art and Graphics, 1983; *book illustrations include*: Plats du Jour, 1957; The Shepherd's Calendar, 1964; Pattern under the Plough, 1966; covers for New Penguin Shakespeare, 1968–78; Where Beards Wag All, 1970; The Dancing Tigers, 1979; The Strength of the Hills, 1983; Westminster Abbey, 1987; Spoken History, 1987; *limited editions*: Bridges on the Backs, 1961; Swiss Family Robinson, 1963 (USA); Poems of John Keats, 1966 (USA); The Jungle Book, 1968 (USA); Robin Hood, 1977 (USA); edns of lithographs of landscape and buildings, 1967–90. *Address*: 25 Gloucester Crescent, NW1 7DL. *T*: 071–485 8824.

GENTRY, Maj.-Gen. (retd) Sir William George, KBE 1958 (CBE 1950); CB 1954; DSO 1942, and Bar 1945; *b* 20 Feb. 1899; *e s* of late Major F. C. Gentry, MBE and late Mrs F. C. Gentry; *m* 1926, Alexandra Nina Caverhill; one *s* one *d*. *Educ*: Wellington Coll., NZ; RMC of Australia. Commissioned NZ Army, Dec. 1919; attached Indian Army and served in Waziristan, 1921, and Malabar, 1921. Served War of 1939–45 with 2nd NZ Div. (Middle East and Italy): GSO 2 and AA and QMG, 1940; GSO 1, 1941–42; Comd 6 NZ Inf. Bde, 1942–43; DCGS, Army HQ, NZ, 1943–44; Comd 9 NZ Inf. Bde (Italy), 1945. Adjutant Gen., NZ Army, 1949–52; Chief of the Gen. Staff, NZ Army, 1952; retired, 1955. Greek Military Cross, 1941; United States Bronze Star, 1945. *Address*: 52 Kings Crescent, Lower Hutt, New Zealand. *T*: 660208. *Clubs*: Wellington, United Services (Wellington, NZ).

GEORGALA, Prof. Douglas Lindley, CBE 1986; PhD; FIFST; Director of Food Research, Agricultural and Food Research Council, since 1988; Visiting Professor, since 1988: University of East Anglia; University of Leeds; University of Reading; *b* 2 Feb. 1934; *s* of late John Michael Georgala and of Izetta Iris Georgala; *m* 1959, Eulalia Catherina Lochner; one *s* one *d*. *Educ*: South African College Sch., Cape Town; Univ. of Stellenbosch (BScAgric); Univ. of Aberdeen (PhD). FIFST 1987. Research Officer, Fishing Research Inst., Univ. of Cape Town, 1957–60; Research Microbiologist, 1960–69, Division Manager, 1969–72, Head of Laboratory, 1977–86, Unilever Colworth Laboratory; Technical Member, Unilever Meat Products Co-ordination, 1973–77; Mem., Unilever Res. Div., 1987–88; Indust. Consultant, Biotechnology Unit, DTI, 1987–88. Chairman: Fisheries Res. Bd, 1980–84; Adv. Cttee of Food Science Dept, Leeds Univ., 1984–88; Scientific and Technical Cttee, Food and Drink Fedn, 1986–88; Member: ACARD, 1980–83; Food Cttee, AFRC, 1984–88; Co-ordinating Cttee for Marine Science and Technol., 1988–89; Food Adv. Cttee, 1989–; Adv. Cttee on Microbiological Safety of Food, 1991–. FRSA 1984. *Publications*: papers in jls of general microbiology, applied bacteriology, hygiene, etc. *Recreations*: gardening, cycling, recorded music. *Address*: AFRC Institute of Food Research, Shinfield, Reading RG2 9AT.

GEORGE; *see* Lloyd George and Lloyd-George.

GEORGE, Rev. (Alfred) Raymond, MA, BD; Warden, John Wesley's Chapel, Bristol, since 1982; *b* 26 Nov. 1912; *s* of A. H. and G. M. George. *Educ*: Crypt Sch., Gloucester; Balliol Coll., Oxford (1st cl. Hon. Classical Mods, 1st cl. Lit. Hum., BA 1935, MA 1938, BD 1955); Wesley House, Cambridge (1st cl. Theol Tripos, Pt I Sect. B, BA 1937, MA 1962); Marburg University. Asst Tutor, Handsworth Coll., Birmingham, 1938–40; ordained as Methodist minister, 1940; Asst Tutor, Hartley-Victoria Coll., Manchester, 1940–42; Circuit Minister, Manchester, 1942–46; Tutor, Wesley Coll., Headingley, Leeds, 1946–67, Principal, 1961–67; Associate Lectr, Leeds Univ., 1946–67; Actg Head, Theol. Dept, 1967–68; Principal, Richmond Coll., London Univ., 1968–72; Tutor, Wesley College, Bristol, 1972–81. Select Preacher, Cambridge, 1963; Member, World Council of Churches Commn on Faith and Order, 1961–75; Pres. of Methodist Conf., 1975–76; Moderator, Free Church Federal Council, 1979–80; Chm., Jt Liturgical Group, 1984–89. *Publications*: Communion with God in the New Testament, 1953; chapter in vol. I, A History of the Methodist Church in Great Britain, 1965, ed (jtly), vol. II, 1978, and contrib. chapter, ed (jtly), vol. III, 1983; jt Editor of series: Ecumenical Studies in Worship; also articles in jls. *Address*: 40 Knole Lane, Bristol BS10 6SS. *T*: Bristol (0272) 503698.

GEORGE, Rear Adm. Anthony Sanderson, CB 1983; FBIM, CEng, FIIM; Port Manager, Portsmouth, since 1987; *b* 8 Nov. 1928; *s* of Sandys Parker George and Winifred Marie George; *m* 1953, Mary Veronica Frances Bell; two *d*. *Educ*: Royal Naval Coll., Dartmouth; Royal Naval Engrg Coll., Manadon. MIMechE 1957; FBIM 1977; FIIM 1979. Sea-going appts, 1950–62; warship design, Ship Dept of MoD, 1962–64; RN Staff Coll., 1965; British High Commn, Canberra, 1966–67; MEO, HMS Hampshire, 1968–69; Staff of Flag Officer Sea Trng, 1970–71; Dep. Prodn Manager, HM Dockyard, Portsmouth, 1972–75; RCDS, 1976; CSO (Trng) to C-in-C Naval Home Comd, 1977–78; Prodn Manager, HM Dockyard, Portsmouth, 1979–81; Dir, Dockyard Prodn and Support, 1981–82; Chief Exec., Royal Dockyards, 1983–86. Chief Exec., World Energy Business, 1986. Comdr 1965, Captain 1972, Rear Adm. 1981. *Recreations*: sailing, swimming, walking. *Address*: c/o National Westminster Bank, 5 East Street, Chichester, West Sussex PO19 1HH.

GEORGE, Sir Arthur (Thomas), AO 1987; Kt 1972; solicitor and company director; Chairman and Managing Director, George Investment Pty Ltd Group, since 1943; Chairman, Australia Solenoid Holdings Ltd, since 1967; *b* 17 Jan. 1915; *s* of late Thomas George; *m* 1939, Renee, *d* of Anthony Freeleagus; one *d*. *Educ*: Sydney High Sch., NSW. Director: Thomas Nationwide Transport Ltd, 1973–; G & P Hotels Ltd, 1987–. Chm., Assoc. for Classical Archæology, of Sydney Univ., 1966–. Chm., Australian Soccer Fedn., 1969–88; Comr, Australian Sports Commn, 1986–; Member: Exec., FIFA, 1981–; Organising Cttee, 1983 World Youth Championship. Chm. and Founder, The Arthur T. George Foundation Ltd, 1972. Fellow, Confedn of Australian Sport, 1985; Hon. Fellow, Univ. of Sydney, 1985. Coronation Medal; Silver Jubilee Medal. Grand Commander (Keeper of the Laws), Cross of St Marks, and Gold Cross of Mount Athos, Greek Orthodox Church; Order of Phoenix (Greece). *Recreations*: interested in sport, especially Association football, etc. *Address*: 1 Little Queen's Lane, Vaucluse, NSW 2030, Australia.

GEORGE, Bruce Thomas; MP (Lab) Walsall South since Feb. 1974; *b* 1 June 1942. *Educ*: Mountain Ash Grammar Sch.; UCW Swansea; Univ. of Warwick. BA Politics Wales 1964, MA Warwick 1968. Asst Lectr in Social Studies, Glamorgan Polytechnic, 1964–66; Lectr in Politics, Manchester Polytechnic, 1968–70; Senior Lectr, Birmingham Polytechnic, 1970–74. Vis. Lectr, Univ. of Essex, 1985–86. Member: former Select Cttee on Violence in the Family; Select Cttee on Defence; North Atlantic Assembly, 1982– (Rapporteur Gen., Political Cttee); RIIA; IISS; RUSI. Patron, Nat. Assoc. of Widows; Co-founder, Sec., House of Commons FC; Hon. Consultant, Confed. of Long Distance Pigeon Racing Assocs; Vice-Pres., Psoriasis Assoc. Pres., Walsall and District Gilbert and Sullivan Soc. Fellow, Parliament and Industry Trust, 1977–78. *Publications*: numerous articles on defence and foreign affairs. *Recreations*: Association football, snooker, student of American Indians, eating Indian food. *Address*: 42 Wood End Road, Walsall, West Midlands WS5 3BG. *T*: Walsall 27898. *Clubs*: Darlaston Labour, Caldmore Liberal; North Walsall, Pleck and Station Street Working Men's Clubs.

GEORGE, Prof. Donald William, AO 1979; Vice-Chancellor and Principal, University of Newcastle, New South Wales, 1975–86; *b* 22 Nov. 1926; *s* of late H. W. George, Sydney; *m* 1950, Lorna M. Davey, Parkes, NSW; one *s* one *d*. *Educ*: Univ. of Sydney. BSc, BE, PhD, FTS, FIEE, FIMechE, FIEAust, FAIP. Lectr, Elec. Engrg, NSW Univ. of Technology, 1949–53; Exper. Officer, UKAEA, Harwell, 1954–55; Res. Officer, Sen. Res. Officer, AAEC, Harwell and Lucas Heights, 1956–59; Sen. Lectr, Elec. Engrg, Univ. of Sydney, 1960–66; Associate Prof., Elec. Engrg, Univ. of Sydney, 1967–68; P. N. Russell Prof. of Mech. Engrg, Univ. of Sydney, 1969–74. Chairman: Australian-American Educational Foundn, 1977–84; Australian Atomic Energy Commn, 1976–83. Trustee, Asian Inst. of Technology, 1978–. Hon. DEng Newcastle, NSW, 1986. *Publications*: numerous sci. papers and techn. reports. *Address*: Shamley Green, Glenning Road, Berkeley Vale, NSW 2259, Australia. *T*: (043) 883056.

GEORGE, Edward Alan John; Deputy Governor, Bank of England, since 1990; *b* 11 Sept. 1938; *s* of Alan George and Olive Elizabeth George; *m* 1962, Clarice Vanessa Williams; one *s* two *d*. *Educ*: Dulwich Coll.; Emmanuel Coll., Cambridge (BAEcon 2nd Cl. (i); MA). Joined Bank of England, 1962; worked initially on East European affairs; seconded to Bank for International Settlements, 1966–69, and to International Monetary Fund as Asst to Chairman of Deputies of Committee of Twenty on Internat. Monetary Reform, 1972–74; Adviser on internat. monetary questions, 1974–77; Dep. Chief Cashier, 1977–80; Asst Dir (Gilt Edged Div.), 1980–82; Exec. Dir, 1982–90. *Recreations*: family, sailing, bridge. *Address*: Bank of England, EC2R 8AH. *T*: 071–601 4444.

GEORGE, Griffith Owen, TD; DL; a Recorder of the Crown Court, 1972–74; *b* 5 Dec. 1902; *s* of late John and Emiah Owen George, Hirwaun, Glam; *m* 1937, Anne Elinor (*d* 1990), *e d* of late Charles and Anne Edwards, Llandaff; one *s*. *Educ*: Westminster Sch.; Christ Church, Oxford (MA). Beit Prize Essay, 1923; Barrister, Gray's Inn, 1927, Wales and Chester Circuit. Served War of 1939–45, 2nd Lieut RA, 1939; Capt. 1941; Major 1943; on JAG's staff, N Africa, Italy, Middle East, 1943–45. Contested Llanelly (Nat. Con.), 1945. Commissioner in Wales under the National Insurance Acts, 1950–67. Dep. Chm., Glamorgan Quarter Sessions, 1956–66, Chm., 1966–71. JP Glamorgan, 1952–72; DL Glamorgan, 1970. *Address*: Glanyrafon, Ponterwyd, Aberystwyth SY23 3JS. *T*: Ponterwyd (097085) 661.

GEORGE, Henry Ridyard, CBE 1979; FInstPet; oil and gas exploration and production consultant, retired; *b* 14 May 1921; *s* of Charles Herbert George and Mary Ridyard; *m* 1st, 1948, Irene May Myers (*d* 1981); one *s*; 2nd, 1985, Gwen (*née* Gooderham), *widow* of Prof. E. O'Farrell Walsh. *Educ*: George Dixon's Secondary Sch., Birmingham; Univ. of Birmingham (1st Cl. Hons degree, Oil Engrg and Refining and Petroleum Technol., 1941). Served War, REME/IEME, 1941–46 (2nd Lieut, later Captain). Pet. Engr with Royal Dutch/Shell Gp, 1947–68: service in USA, Holland, Brunei, Nigeria and Venezuela in a variety of positions, incl. Chief Pet. Engr in last 3 countries; Dept of Energy, 1968–81, Dir of Pet. Engrg, 1973–81. FRSA 1979. *Recreations*: gardening, golf. *Address*: 39 Lodge Close, Stoke D'Abernon, Cobham, Surrey KT11 2SG. *T*: Cobham (0932) 863878.

GEORGE, Hywel, CMG 1968; OBE 1963; Fellow, Churchill College, Cambridge, since 1971 (Bursar, 1972–90); *b* 10 May 1924; *s* of Rev. W. M. George and Catherine M. George; *m* 1955, Edith Pirchl; three *d*. *Educ*: Llanelli Gram. Sch.; UCW Aberystwyth; Pembroke Coll., Cambridge. RAF, 1943–46. Cadet, Colonial Admin. Service, N Borneo, 1949–52; District Officer, 1952–58; Secretariat, 1959–62; Resident, Sabah, Malaysia, 1963–66; Administrator, 1967–69, Governor, 1969–70, St Vincent; Administrator, British Virgin Is, 1971. Panglima Darjah Kinabalu (with title of Dato), Sabah, 1964; JMN, Malaysia, 1966. CStJ 1969. *Recreation*: walking. *Address*: Churchill College, Cambridge CB3 0DS; Tu Hwnt ir Afon, The Close, Llanfairfechan LL33 0AG.

GEORGE, Most Rev. Ian Gordon Combe; *see* Adelaide, Archbishop of.

GEORGE, Prof. Kenneth Desmond; Professor and Head of Department of Economics, University College of Swansea, since 1988; *b* 11 Jan. 1937; *s* of Horace Avory George and Dorothy Margaret (*née* Hughes); *m* 1959, Elizabeth Vida (*née* Harries); two *s* one *d*. *Educ*: Ystalyfera Grammar Sch.; University Coll. of Wales, Aberstwyth (MA). Res. Asst, then Lectr in Econs, Univ. of Western Australia, 1959–63; Lectr in Econs, University Coll. of N Wales, Bangor, 1963–64; Univ. Asst Lectr, Univ. of Cambridge, 1964–66, Univ. Lectr, 1966–73; Fellow and Dir of Studies in Econs, Sidney Sussex Coll., Cambridge, 1965–73; Prof. and Head of Dept of Econs, 1973–88, and Dep. Principal, 1980–83, UC, Cardiff. Vis. Prof., McMaster Univ., 1970–71. Part-time Mem., Monopolies and Mergers Commn, 1978–86. Editor, Jl of Industrial Economics, 1970–83; Mem. Adv. Bd, Antitrust Law and Econs Rev., 1988–. *Publications*: Productivity in Distribution, 1966; Productivity and Capital Expenditure in Retailing, 1968; Industrial Organisation, 1971, 3rd edn (with C. Joll), 1981; (with T. S. Ward) The Structure of Industry in the EEC, 1975; (ed with C. Joll) Competition Policy in the UK and EEC, 1975; (with J. Shorey) The Allocation of Resources, 1978; (ed with L. Mainwaring) The Welsh Economy, 1988; articles in Econ. Jl, Oxford Econ. Papers, Aust. Econ. Papers, Jl Indust. Econs, Rev. of Econs and Stats, Oxford Bull., Scottish Jl Polit. Econ., and British Jl Indust. Relations. *Recreations*: walking, music, cricket. *Address*: Ein-Tŷ-Ni, 39 St Fagans Drive, St Fagans, Cardiff. *T*: Cardiff (0222) 562801.

GEORGE, Llewellyn Norman Havard; a Recorder of the Crown Court, since 1980; Senior Partner, V. J. G. Johns & Son, Solicitors, since 1972 (Partner, since 1950); *b* 13 Nov. 1925; *s* of Benjamin William George, DSO, RNR, and Annie Jane George; *m* 1950, Mary Patricia Morgan (*née* Davies); one *d*. *Educ*: Cardiff High Sch.; Fishguard Grammar Sch. HM Coroner, 1965–80; Recorder, Wales and Chester Circuit, 1980–. President: West Wales Law Society, 1973–74; Pembrokeshire Law Society, 1981–83; Chairman: (No 5) South Wales Law Society Legal Aid Cttee, 1979; Agricl Land Tribunal (Wales), 1990– (Dep. Chm., 1985–90). Mem., Farrand Cttee, 1984–85. *Recreations*: golf, reading, chess. *Address:* Four Winds, Tower Hill, Fishguard, Dyfed SA65 9LA. *T:* Fishguard (0348) 873894. *Clubs:* Pembrokeshire County; Newport (Pembs) Golf.

GEORGE, Patrick Herbert; artist; Emeritus Professor of Fine Art, University of London, since 1988; *b* 23 July 1923; *s* of A. H. George and N. George (*née* Richards); *m* 1st, 1953, June Griffith (marr. diss. 1980); four *d*; 2nd, 1981, Susan Ward. *Educ:* Downs Sch.; Bryanston Sch.; Edinburgh Coll. of Art; Camberwell Sch. of Art (NDD). Served War, RNVR, 1942–46. Asst, Slade Sch. of Fine Art, London, 1949–. Head, Dept of Fine Art, Nigerian Coll. of Art, Zaria, 1960–62; Slade School of Fine Art: Lectr, 1962; Reader in Fine Art, 1976; Prof. of Fine Art, Univ. of London, 1983; Slade Prof. of Fine Art, 1985–88. Member Committee: Summerson (NCDAD); Arts Council of GB; Eastern Arts. Works in public collections in GB and USA; one-man exhibn, Gainsborough's House, Sudbury, 1975; retrospective exhibn, Serpentine Gall., London, 1980; exhibn, Browse & Darby, 1984 and 1989; dealer, Browse & Darby. *Recreation:* make do and mend. *Address:* 33 Moreton Terrace, SW1 2NS. *T:* 071–828 3302; Grandfathers, Great Saxham, Bury St Edmunds, Suffolk IP29 5JR. *T:* Bury St Edmunds (0284) 810997.

GEORGE, Peter John, OBE 1974; HM Diplomatic Service, retired; Counsellor and Consul General, British Embassy, Manila, 1976–79; Chargé d'Affaires *ai*, 1978; *b* 12 Dec. 1919; *s* of late Cecil John George and Mabel George; *m* 1946, Andrée Louise Pernon; one *d*. *Educ:* Sutton Grammar Sch., Plymouth. Served War, 1939–46: Captain. Home Civil Service, 1936; HM Diplomatic Service, 1966; First Secretary, Commercial: Colombo, 1967–70; Seoul, 1971–73 (Chargé d'Affaires *ai*, 1971 and 1972); Prague, 1973–76. *Recreations:* golf, tennis, ski-ing, bridge. *Address:* St Just, Walton Park, Walton-on-Thames, Surrey.

GEORGE, Rev. Raymond; *see* George, Rev. A. R.

GEORGE, Timothy John Burr, CMG 1991; HM Diplomatic Service; Ambassador to Nepal, since 1990; *b* 14 July 1937; *s* of late Brig. J. B. George, late RAMC, retd and M. Brenda George (*née* Harrison); *m* 1962, Richenda Mary, *d* of late Alan Reed, FRIBA and of Ann Reed (*née* Rowntree); one *s* two *d*. *Educ:* Aldenham Sch.; Christ's Coll., Cambridge (BA). National Service, 2nd Lieut RA, 1956–58; Cambridge Univ., 1958. FCO, 1961; 3rd Secretary: Hong Kong, 1962; Peking, 1963; 2nd, later 1st Sec., FCO, 1966; 1st Sec. (Economic), New Delhi, 1969; Asst Political Adviser, Hong Kong, 1972; Asst European Integration Dept (Internal), FCO, 1974; Counsellor and Head of Chancery, Peking, 1978–80; Res. Associate, IISS, 1980–81; Counsellor and Hd of Chancery, UK Perm. Delegn to OECD, 1982–86; Hd, Republic of Ireland Dept, FCO, 1986–90. *Publication:* (jtly) Security in Southern Asia, 1984. *Address:* c/o Foreign and Commonwealth Office, SW1A 2AH.

GEORGE, Prof. William David, FRCS; Professor of Surgery, University of Glasgow, since 1981; *b* 22 March 1943; *s* of William Abel George and Peggy Eileen George; *m* 1967, Helen Marie (*née* Moran); one *s* three *d*. *Educ:* Reading Bluecoat Sch.; Henley Grammar Sch.; Univ. of London (MB, BS 1966; MS 1977). FRCS 1970. Jun. surgical jobs, 1966–71; Registrar in Surgery, Royal Postgrad. Med. Sch., 1971–73; Lectr in Surg., Univ. of Manchester, 1973–77; Sen. Lectr in Surg., Univ. of Liverpool, 1977–81. *Publications:* articles in BMJ, Lancet, British Jl of Surg. *Recreations:* veteran rowing, fishing, squash. *Address:* 21 Kingsborough Gardens, Glasgow G12 9NH. *T:* 041–339 9546. *Club:* Clyde Amateur Rowing (Glasgow).

GEORGES, Rt. Hon. (Philip) Telford; PC 1986; Law Reform Commissioner, Bahamas, since 1989; Judge of the Court of Appeal: Bermuda, 1975–81 and since 1990; Cayman Islands, since 1984; *b* Dominica, 5 Jan. 1923; *s* of John Georges and Milutine Cox; *m* 1954, Grace Glasgow (marr. diss.); *m* 1981, Joyce Cole. *Educ:* Dominica Grammar Sch.; Toronto Univ. (BA). Called to the Bar, 1949; in private practice, Trinidad and Tobago, 1949–62; Judge of the High Court, Trinidad and Tobago, 1962–74; on secondment as Chief Justice of Tanzania, 1965–71; acting Justice of Appeal, Trinidad and Tobago, 1972; Judge of the Courts of Appeal, Belize, Bahamas, Turks and Caicos Is, 1975–81; Judge of the Supreme Court, 1981–83, Chief Justice, 1983, Zimbabwe; Chief Justice of the Bahamas, 1984–89. Prof. of Law, 1974–81, and Dean of the Faculty of Law, 1977–79, Univ. of WI at Cave Hill. Vice-Chm., Trinidad and Tobago Constitutional Reform Commn, 1971–74; Chm., Crime Commn, Bermuda, 1977–78. Hon. LLD: Toronto; Dar-es-Salaam; West Indies, 1985. *Recreation:* walking. *Address:* Kilimani, 5A The Mount, St George, Barbados.

GERARD, family name of **Baron Gerard.**

GERARD, 4th Baron, *cr* 1876, Bt 1611; **Robert William Frederick Alwyn Gerard;** *b* 23 May 1918; *o s* of 3rd Baron Gerard, MC, and late Mary Frances Emma, *d* of Sir Martin Le Marchant Hadsley Gosselin, GCVO, KCMG, CB; *S* father, 1953. *Heir: cousin* Anthony Robert Hugo Gerard [*b* 3 Dec. 1949; *m* 1976, Kathleen, *e d* of Dr Bernard Ryan, New York, USA; two *s*]. *Address:* Blakesware, Ware, Herts. *T:* Ware (0920) 3665.

GERARD, Geoffrey; *see* Gerard, W. G.

GERARD, Ronald, OBE 1987; Chairman, Ronald Gerard Charitable Trust, since 1983; *b* 30 Oct. 1925; *s* of Samuel and Caroline Gerard; *m* 1952, Patricia Krieger; one *s* one *d*. *Educ:* Regent Street Polytechnic; College of Estate Management. FSVA; FRSH. Royal Engineers, 1943–47, Italy and Egypt; articled to a City Chartered Surveyor, 1947–50; Principal, R. P. Gerard & Co., Surveyors and Valuers, 1952–59; Jt Man. Dir, 1959–87, Chm., 1982–87, London & Provincial Shop Centres Plc (created HQ buildings for many well-known cos incl. Dulux Paints, Honeywell, Calor Gas, Black & Decker, Chubb and Yellow Pages). Underwriting Mem. of Lloyd's, 1976–. Vice-President: English Schools Cricket Assoc., 1981–; Middlesex Colts Assoc., 1986–; Middlesex Cricket Union, 1987–; Mem., Middlesex CCC Cttee, 1972– (Chm., Membership Cttee, 1985–); Trustee, Middlesex CCC Centenary Youth Trust, 1984–; Mem. Council, Lord's Taverners, 1984–. Hon. Mem., Middlesex Assoc. of Cricket Coaches, 1989–. Patron, Brooklands Mus. Trust, and Hon. Mem., Brooklands Club, 1991. Liveryman, Glass Sellers' Co., 1990; Freeman, City of London, 1990. CStJ 1988. FRSA 1985. Granted Arms, 1989. *Clubs:* Athenæum, Carlton, MCC, Lord's Taverners.

GERARD, (William) Geoffrey, CMG 1963; Founder, Gerard Industries Pty Ltd, S Australia (Managing Director, 1930–76; Chairman, 1950–80); *b* 16 June 1907; *s* of late A. E. Gerard; *m* 1932, Elsie Lesetta, *d* of late A. Lowe; one *s* one *d*. *Educ:* Adelaide Technical High Sch. President: Electrical Manufrs' Assoc. of SA, 1949–52; Electrical Develt Assoc. of SA, 1952; SA Chamber of Manufactures, 1953–54; Associated Chambers of Manufactures of Aust., 1955; SA Metal Industries Assoc., 1952 and 1957; Aust.-Amer. Assoc. in SA Incorp., 1961–63; Aust. Metal Industries Assoc., 1962–64; Vice-Chm., Standards Assoc. of Aust., 1956–79; Chm., Nat. Employers' Assoc., 1964–66; Member: SA Industries Adv. Cttee, 1952–53; Commonwealth Immigration Planning Council, 1956–74; Commonwealth Manufg Industries Advisory Coun., 1958–62; Nat. Employers' Policy Cttee, 1964–66; Commonwealth Electrical Industries Adv. Council, 1977–80. Pres., Prince Alfred Coll. Foundn, 1975–80. Pres., Liberal and Country League, SA Div., 1961–64. Rotary Governor's representative in founding Barossa Valley Club, 1956. FAIM. *Recreations:* golf, tennis. *Address:* 9 Robe Terrace, Medindie, SA 5081, Australia. *T:* 44 2560. *Clubs:* Adelaide, Commonwealth (Adelaide), Kooyonga Golf (SA) (Captain, 1953–55, Pres., 1976–78), Rotary (Prospect) (Pres., 1954).

GERARD-PEARSE, Rear-Adm. John Roger Southey, CB 1979; Group Personnel Manager, Jardine Matheson Co. Ltd, Hong Kong, 1980–84; *b* 10 May 1924; *s* of Dr Gerard-Pearse; *m* 1955, Barbara Jean Mercer; two *s* two *d*. *Educ:* Clifton College. Joined RN, 1943; comd HM Ships Tumult, Grafton, Defender, Fearless and Ark Royal; Flag Officer, Sea Training, 1975–76; Asst Chief, Naval Staff (Ops), 1977–79. *Recreations:* sailing, carpentry. *Address:* Enbrook, 170 Offham Road, West Malling, Kent. *T:* West Malling (0732) 842375.

GERE, John Arthur Giles, FBA 1979; FSA; Keeper, Department of Prints and Drawings, British Museum, 1973–81; *b* 7 Oct. 1921; *o s* of Arnold Gere and Carol Giles; *m* 1958, Charlotte Douie; one *s* one *d*. *Educ:* Winchester; Balliol College, Oxford. Assistant Keeper, British Museum, 1946; Deputy Keeper, 1966. *Publications:* (with Robin Ironside) Pre-Raphaelite Painters, 1948; (with Philip Pouncey) Italian Drawings in the British Museum, vol. iii: Raphael and his Circle, 1962; Taddeo Zuccaro: his development studied in his drawings, 1969; I disegni dei maestri: il manierismo a Roma, 1971; (ed with John Sparrow) Geoffrey Madan's Notebooks, 1981; (with Philip Pouncey) Italian Drawings in the British Museum, vol. v: Artists Working in Rome c 1550–c 1640, 1983; (with Nicholas Turner) Drawings by Raphael in English Collections, 1983; various exhibition catalogues; contribs to Burlington Magazine, Master Drawings, etc. *Address:* 21 Lamont Road, SW10. *T:* 071–352 5107. *Club:* Beefsteak.

GERE, Richard; actor; *b* 31 Aug. 1949. *Educ:* Univ. of Massachusetts, Played trumpet, piano, guitar and bass and composed music with various gps; stage performances: with Provincetown Playhouse, Seattle Rep. Theatre; Richard Farina, Long Time Coming and Long Time Gone, Back Bog Beat Bait, off-Broadway; Soon, Habeus Corpus and Grease on Broadway; A Midsummer Night's Dream, Lincoln Center; Taming of the Shrew, Young Vic, London; Bent, on Broadway (Theatre World Award); *films:* Report to the Commissioner, 1975; Baby Blue Marine, 1976; Looking for Mr Goodbar, 1977; Days of Heaven, 1978; Blood Brothers, 1978; Yanks, 1979; American Gigolo, 1979; An Officer and a Gentleman, 1982; Breathless, 1983; Beyond the Limit, 1983; The Cotton Club, 1984; King David, 1985; Power, 1986; No Mercy, 1986; Miles From Home, 1989; Pretty Woman, 1990; Internal Affairs, 1990. Founding Chm. and Pres., Tibet Hse, NY. *Address:* c/o Andrea Jaffe and Associates, 9229 Sunset Boulevard, Suite 414, Los Angeles, Calif 90069, USA.

GERHARD, Dr Derek James (known as **Jeremy**), CB 1986; business consultant; Deputy Master and Comptroller, Royal Mint, 1977–88, retired; *b* 16 Dec. 1927; *s* of late F. J. Gerhard, Banstead; *m* 1952, Dr Sheila Cooper, *d* of late Dr G. K. Cooper; three *s* two *d*. *Educ:* Highgate Sch.; Fitzwilliam Coll., Cambridge (MA; Hon. Fellow 1986); Reading Univ. (PhD). Served 3rd Carabiniers (Prince of Wales DG), 1945–48. Dept of Scientific Adviser, Air Ministry, 1952–57; transf. to DSIR, 1957; Sec., British Commonwealth Scientific Cttee, 1959–60; Asst Sci. Attaché, British Embassy, Washington, 1961–64; transf. to Admin. CS, 1964; Board of Trade, latterly leader UK Delgn to Internat. Consultative Shipping Gp, 1964–69; Head of Management Services, BoT, 1969–71; loaned to CSD (Personnel Management), 1971–73; Dept of Industry, leader UK Delgn to Internat. Tin Council, 1973–75; Air Div., DoI, 1975–77. Pres., Mint Dir's Conf., 1982–84. Mem., Welsh Council, CBI, 1984–87. *Publications:* various scientific papers. *Recreations:* gardening, woodwork. *Address:* Little Dowding, Dorking Road, Walton Heath, Surrey KT20 7TJ. *T:* Tadworth (0737) 813045.

GERKEN, Vice-Adm. Sir Robert William Frank, KCB 1986; CBE 1975; Royal Navy, retired 1987; *b* 11 June 1932; *s* of Francis Sydney and Gladys Gerken; *m* 1st, 1966, Christine Stephenson (*d* 1981); two *d*; 2nd, 1983, Mrs Ann Fermor. *Educ:* Chigwell Sch.; Royal Naval Coll., Dartmouth. Sea service as Lieut and Lt-Comdr, 1953–66; RN Staff Course, 1967; in command HMS Yarmouth, 1968–69; Commander Sea Training, 1970–71; Naval Staff, 1972–73; in command: Sixth Frigate Sqdn, 1974–75; HMS Raleigh, 1976–77; Captain of the Fleet, 1978–81; Flag Officer Second Flotilla, 1981–83; Dir Gen., Naval Manpower and Trng, 1983–85; Flag Officer Plymouth, Port Admiral Devonport, Comdr Central Sub Area Eastern Atlantic, Comdr Plymouth Sub Area Channel, 1985–87. Dir, Corps of Commissionaires, 1988–; Chm., China Fleet Club (UK) Charitable Trust, 1987–. President: British Korean Veterans' Assoc. (Plymouth Br.); Plymouth Lifeboat, RNLI, 1988–. Governor, Chigwell Sch., 1987–. *Recreations:* hearth and home maintenance. *Address:* Faunstone Cottage, Shaugh Prior, Plymouth PL7 5EW. *T:* Shaugh Prior (075539) 445. *Clubs:* Army and Navy; Royal Western Yacht.

GERNSHEIM, Helmut Erich Robert; photo-historian and author; *b* Munich, 1 March 1913; 3rd *s* of Karl Gernsheim, historian of literature at Munich Univ., and Hermine Gernsheim (*née* Scholz); *m* 1942, Alison Eames, London (*d* 1969); no *c*; *m* 1971, Irène Guénin, Geneva. *Educ:* St Anne's Coll., Augsburg; State Sch. of Photography, Munich. Settled in England as free-lance photographer, 1937; became British subject, 1946; during War of 1939–45 made photogr. surveys of historic bldgs and monuments for Warburg Inst. (London Univ.); exhibns of these at Churchill Club and Courtauld Inst., 1945 and 1946, Nat. Gall., 1944; one-man show at Royal Photogr. Society 1948; since 1945 has built up Gernsheim photo-historical collection, since 1964 at University of Texas, Austin; selections were shown at art museums, Europe and America; retrospective exhibn of own photographs 1935–82, Hamburg, 1983, Hanover and Munich, 1984, Freiburg/Breisgau, 1986. Re-discovered world's first photograph (taken in 1826), 1952 and Lewis Carroll's chief hobby, 1948. Co-ed. Photography Yearbook, 1953–55; British Representative World Exhibition of Photography, Lucerne, 1952, Biennale and Unesco Conference on Photography, Paris, 1955, etc. Photographic adviser to Granada TV on first British action still films, 1958–62. Editorial Adviser, Encyclopædia Britannica and several Museums and Universities. Chm., History of Photo. Seminar, Rencontres Internat. de la Photo.: Arles, 1978, Venice, 1979; Frankfurt, 1981. Distinguished Visiting Professor: Univ. of Texas at Austin, 1979; Arizona State Univ., 1981; Regents Prof., Univ. of California, at Riverside, 1984, and at Santa Barbara, 1985, 1989. Dir, Photo-Graphic Editions, London. Trustee: Swiss Foundn for Photography, 1975–81; Alimari Mus., Florence, 1985–. Hon. MSc Brooks Inst., Santa Barbara, Calif., 1984; Hon. Dr Bradford, 1989. Hon. Fellow: Club Daguerre, Frankfurt, 1981; Amer. Photohist. Soc., 1979; Europ. Soc. for History of Photography, 1985. First German cultural prize for photography, 1959; Gold Medal, Accademia Italia delle Belle Arte, Parma, 1980; Hill Medal, German Acad. of Photography, 1983. Cross of Merit, Germany, 1970. *Publications include:* New Photo Vision, 1942; Julia Margaret Cameron, 1948, revd and enlarged edn, 1975; Lewis Carroll-Photographer, 1949, 3rd edn 1969; Beautiful London, 1950; Masterpieces of Victorian Photography, 1951; Those Impossible English, 1952; Churchill, His Life in Photographs, 1955; Creative Photography, 1962, 3rd edn 1990; (with Alison Gernsheim): Roger Fenton, 1954, 2nd edn 1973; The History of Photography, 1955, 3rd edn 1969, enlarged edns, 1983 (Berlin), 1985 (Milan, NY); L. J. M. Daguerre, 1956, 2nd edn 1968; Queen Victoria, a Biography in Word and Picture, 1959; Historic Events, 1960; Edward VII and Queen Alexandra, 1962; Fashion and Reality, 1963, 2nd edn 1981; Concise History of Photography, 1965,

3rd edn, NY, 1987; Alvin Langdon Coburn, photographer, 1966, 2nd edn 1978; The Origins of Photography, 1982; Incunabula of British Photographic Literature, 1984; The Rise of Photography, 1988; contrib. Oxford History of Technology, 19th and 20th century; numerous articles in art and photographic journals in many countries. *Recreations:* travelling, classic music, opera. *Address:* Residenza Tamporiva, Via Tamporiva 28, 6976 Castagnola, Ticino, Switzerland. *T:* Lugano 091 515904.

GEROSA, Peter Norman; Secretary, The Tree Council, 1983–91; *b* 1 Nov. 1928; *s* of late Enrico Cecil and Olive Doris Gerosa; *m* 1955, Dorothy Eleanor Griffin; two *d. Educ:* Whitgift Sch.; London Univ. (Birkbeck). BA (Hons) 1st Cl., Classics. Civil Service, 1945–82; Foreign Office, 1945; Home Office, 1949; HM Customs and Excise, 1953; Min. of Transport, 1966; DoE, 1970; Under Secretary: DoE, 1972; Dept of Transport, 1977; Directorate of Rural Affairs, DoE, 1981–82. *Recreations:* singing, gardening, walking. *Address:* 17 Friths Drive, Reigate, Surrey RH2 0DS. *T:* Reigate (0737) 243771.

GERRARD, Prof. Alfred Horace; Professor of Sculpture in University of London at University College Slade School of Fine Art, 1948–68, now Emeritus; *b* 7 May 1899; *m* 1933, Katherine Leigh-Pemberton (*d* 1970); *m* 1972, Nancy Sinclair. *Educ:* Hartford County Council Sch.; Manchester Sch. of Art; Slade Sch. of Fine Art, University Coll., London. Head of Dept of Sculpture, Slade Sch., UCL, 1925–48. Served European War, 1914–18, Cameron Highlanders, 1916–17; RFC, 1917–19; War of 1939–45, Staff Captain, War Office, attached Royal Engineers, 1939–43; war artist, 1944–45; temp. Head, Slade Sch. of Fine Art, 1948–49. RBS Silver Medal, 1960. Fellow, University Coll. London, 1969. *Recreation:* gardening. *Address:* Dairy House, Leyswood, Groombridge, Tunbridge Wells, Kent. *T:* Groombridge (089276) 268.

GERRARD, His Honour Basil Harding; a Circuit Judge (formerly a Judge of County Courts), 1970–82; *b* 10 July 1919; *s* of late Lawrence Allen Gerrard and Mary (*née* Harding); *m* Sheila Mary Patricia (*née* Coggins), *widow* of Walter Dring, DSO, DFC (killed in action, 1945); one *s* two *d* and one step *d. Educ:* Bryanston Sch.; Caius Coll., Cambridge (BA). Royal Navy, 1940–46. Called to Bar, Gray's Inn, 1947; Recorder of Barrow-in-Furness, 1969–70. Mem., Parole Bd for England and Wales, 1974–76. Chm., Selcare Trust, 1971–78, Vice Pres., 1978–; a Chm., Residential Home Tribunal, 1985–. *Recreation:* gardening. *Address:* Northwood, Toft Road, Knutsford, Cheshire. *Clubs:* Knutsford Golf; Bowdon Croquet.

See also J. J. Rowe, N. J. Forwood.

GERRARD, Ven. David Keith Robin; Archdeacon of Wandsworth, since 1989; *b* 15 June 1939; *s* of Eric Henry and Doris Jane Gerrard; *m* 1963, Jennifer Mary Hartley; two *s* two *d. Educ:* Royal Grammar School, Guildford; St Edmund Hall, Oxford (BA); Lincoln Theol Coll. Curate: St Olave, Woodberry Down, N16, 1963–66; St Mary, Primrose Hill, NW3, 1966–69; Vicar: St Paul, Lorrimore Square, SE17, 1969–79; St Andrew and St Mark, Surbiton, Surrey, 1979–89; RD of Kingston upon Thames, 1983–88. *Publication:* (co-author) Urban Ghetto, 1976. *Recreations:* embroidery, Proust, Yorkshire, statistics. *Address:* 68 North Side, Wandsworth Common, SW18 2QX. *T:* 081–874 5766.

GERRARD, John Henry, CBE 1981 (OBE 1972); MC 1944; QPM 1975; Assistant Commissioner, Metropolitan Police, 1978–81; *b* 25 Nov. 1920; *s* of Archie Reginald and Evelyn Gerrard; *m* 1943, Gladys Hefford; two *s. Educ:* Cordwainers Technical Coll. Served War, Army, 1939–46: Iceland, 1940–42; commissioned 1st Mddx Regt, 1943; NW Europe, 1944–46 (Captain). Constable to Commander, 1946–65; Comdr, West End Central, 1965–68; Comdr 'A' Dept (Public Order/Operations), 1968–70; Deputy Assistant Commissioner: 'A' (Operations), 1970–74; No 1 Area, 1974–78. KStJ 1986; Comr, London Dist, SJAB, 1983–88. *Recreations:* philately, history. *Address:* c/o Edwina Mountbatten House, 63 York Street, W1H 1PS.

GERRARD, Peter Noël, CBE 1991; General Counsel, London Stock Exchange, since 1991; *b* 19 May 1930; *o c* of Sir Denis Gerrard and of Hilda Goodwin (*née* Jones, who *m* 2nd, Sir Joseph Cantley, *qv*); *m* 1957, Prudence Lipson-Ward; one *s* two *d. Educ:* Rugby; Christ Church, Oxford (MA). 2nd Lieut, XII Royal Lancers, Malaya, 1953–54. Solicitor, 1959; Partner, Lovell, White & King, 1960, Sen. Partner, 1980–88; Sen. Partner, Lovell White Durrant, 1988–91. Member: Bd of Banking Supervision, 1990–; City Capital Markets Cttee, 1974–91. Member: Council, Law Society, 1972–82; Bd, Inst. of Advanced Legal Studies, 1985–; Council, St George's Hosp. Med. Sch., 1982–. *Recreations:* music, walking, week-end gardening. *Address:* 40 Canonbury Park North, N1 2JT. *T:* 071–354 0481; Pightle Cottage, Ashdon, Saffron Walden, Essex CB10 2HG. *T:* Ashdon (079984) 374. *Club:* Athenæum.

GERRARD, Ronald Tilbrook, FEng, FICE, FIWEM; Senior Partner, Binnie & Partners, Consulting Engineers, 1974–83, retired; *b* 23 April 1918; *s* of Henry Thomas Gerrard and Edith Elizabeth Tilbrook; *m* 1950, Cecilia Margaret Bremner; three *s* one *d. Educ:* Imperial Coll. of Science and Technology, Univ. of London. BSc(Eng). FCGI; FEng 1979; FICE 1957; FIWE 1965; MEIC. Served War, RE, 1939–45. Resident Engr, sea defence and hydro-electric works, 1947–50; Asst Engr, design of hydro-power schemes in Scotland and Canada, 1951–54; Binnie & Partners: Sen. Engr, 1954; Partner, 1959; resp. for hydro-power, water supply, river engrg, coast protection and indust. works in UK and overseas. Chm., Assoc. of Cons. Engrs, 1969–70; Mem. Council, ICE, 1974–77. Telford Silver Medal, ICE, 1968. *Publications:* (jtly) 4 papers to ICE. *Address:* 6 Ashdown Road, Epsom, Surrey KT17 3PL. *T:* Epsom (0372) 724834. *Club:* Athenæum.

GERRARD-WRIGHT, Maj.-Gen. Richard Eustace John, CB 1985; CBE 1977 (OBE 1971; MBE 1963); *b* 9 May 1930; *s* of Rev. R. L. Gerrard-Wright; *m* 1960, Susan Kathleen Young; two *s* one *d* (and one *d* decd). *Educ:* Christ's Hospital; RMA, Sandhurst. Commnd Royal Lincolnshire Regt, 1949; served Egypt, Germany and UK, 1950–55; Malaya, 1955–58 (despatches, 1958); Instructor, RMA, Sandhurst, 1958–62 (2nd E Anglian Regt, 1960); Staff Coll., India, 1962–63; served Kenya, Aden, Malta, Malaya, 1963–70 (Royal Anglian Regt, 1964); Bn Comdr, UK, Germany, NI, 1970–73 (despatches 1973); Comdr, 39 Inf. Bde, Belfast, 1975–77; Nat. Defence Coll., Canada, 1977–78; Chief of Staff, 1 (Br) Corps, 1978–79; GOC Eastern District, 1980–82; Dir, TA and Cadets, 1982–84; retd 1985. Dep. Col, Royal Anglian Regt, 1975–80; Col Comdt, Queen's Div., 1981–84. *Address:* c/o Lloyds Bank, Minster Place, Ely, Cambs. *Clubs:* MCC; Free Foresters.

GERSHEVITCH, Dr Ilya, FBA 1967; Fellow of Jesus College, Cambridge, since 1962; Reader in Iranian Studies, University of Cambridge, 1965–82, now Emeritus; *b* Zürich, 24 Oct. 1914; *o s* of Arkadi and Mila Gershevitch, Smolensk, Russia; *m* 1951, Lisbeth, *d* of Josef Syfrig, Lucerne; one *d. Educ:* Swiss schools at Locarno and Lugano; Univ. of Rome (classics); Univ. of London (Oriental studies). Dottore in Lettere, Univ. of Rome, 1937; PhD, Univ. of London, 1943; MA Cantab 1948. Monitored foreign broadcasts, London, 1942–47; Lecturer in Iranian Studies, Univ. of Cambridge, 1948–65. First European to penetrate into certain areas of Western Makran (dialect field-work), 1956; Vis. Prof. at Columbia Univ., New York, 1960–61 and 1965–66; Univ. Exchange Visitor, USSR, 1965; Ratanbai Katrak Lecturer, Univ. of Oxford, 1968. Pres., Philological Soc., 1980–84. Mem., Danish Acad., 1982; Foreign Fellow, Accademia dei Lincei, Rome, 1987. Hon. PhD Berne, 1971. *Publications:* A Grammar of Manichean Sogdian, 1954; The Avestan Hymn to Mithra, 1959; Philologia Iranica, 1985; articles in specialist jls, encyclopaedias and collective books. *Recreation:* music. *Address:* 54 Owlstone Road, Cambridge CB3 9JH. *T:* Cambridge (0223) 357996.

GERSON, John Henry Cary; HM Diplomatic Service; Counsellor, on loan to Headquarters British Forces Hong Kong, since 1987; *b* 25 April 1945; *s* of Henry and Benedicta Joan Gerson; *m* 1968, Mary Alison, *d* of late George Ewart Evans; one *s* one *d. Educ:* Bradfield; King's Coll., Cambridge (MA). Third Sec., FCO, 1968; language student, Hong Kong, 1969–71; Second Secretary: Singapore, 1971–73; FCO, 1973–74; First Sec. and HM Consul, Peking, 1974–77; First Sec., FCO, 1978; on loan to Home CS, 1978–79; First Sec., later Counsellor, FCO, 1979–87. Associate Mem., Centre for the Study of Socialist Legal Systems, London Univ., 1986–. *Recreations:* ornithology, sinology, literature. *Address:* c/o Foreign and Commonwealth Office, Private Letter Section, King Charles Street, SW1. *Club:* Athenæum.

GERSTENBERG, Frank Eric, MA; Principal, George Watson's College, Edinburgh, since 1985; *b* 23 Feb. 1941; *s* of late Eric Gustav Gerstenberg and Janie Willis Gerstenberg; *m* 1966, Valerie Myra (*née* MacLellan); one *s* twin *d. Educ:* Trinity College, Glenalmond; Clare College, Cambridge (MA); Inst. of Education, Univ. of London (PGCE). Asst History Teacher, Kelly Coll., Tavistock, 1963–67; Housemaster and Head of History, Millfield School, 1967–74; Headmaster, Oswestry School, 1974–85. *Recreations:* skiing, golf. *Address:* 27 Merchiston Gardens, Edinburgh EH10 5DD. *T:* 031–337 6880. *Clubs:* Public Schools; New (Edinburgh).

GERSTENBERG, Richard Charles; *b* Little Falls, NY, 24 Nov. 1909; *s* of Richard Paul Gerstenberg and Mary Julia Booth; *m* 1934, Evelyn Josephine Hitchingham; one *s* one *d. Educ:* Univ. of Michigan (AB). General Motors Corporation: Asst Comptroller, 1949–55; Treasurer, 1956–60; Vice-Pres., in charge of financial staff, 1960–67; Exec. Vice-Pres. in charge of Finance, 1967–70; Vice-Chm. Bd and Chm. Finance Cttee, 1970–72; Chm., 1972–74; a Director, 1967–79. *Address:* 1024 Stratford Place, Bloomfield Hills, Michigan, USA. *Clubs:* Bloomfield Hills Country; Paradise Valley Country (Scottsdale, Arizona); Mohawk (NY) Fish and Game.

GERTYCH, Dr Zbigniew; Professor, Botanical Garden, Polish Academy of Sciences, Warsaw; *b* 26 Oct. 1922; *s* of Tadeusz Gertych and Maria Gertych (*née* Marecka); *m* 1st, 1945, Roza (*née* Skrochowska) (decd); one *s* two *d*; 2nd, 1970, Zofia (*née* Dobrzanska). *Educ:* Uniw. Jagiellonski, Krakow. MA eng 1946, DAgric 1950. Joined Army as volunteer and participated in September campaign, 1939; during Nazi occupation took part in clandestine activities, was detained in camps and Gestapo prisons; after escape served Home Army (AK) to 1945 (wounded in partisan combat). Polish Academy of Sciences (PAN), 1946–83: Head of Pomology Dept, Dendrology Research Centre, Kórnik, 1947–53; Dir Exp. Fruit Growing Research Centre, Brzeźna, 1953–64; Dir, Research Centre, Agric. and Forestry Econ. Science, 1964–78; Vice-Dir and Dir, Vegetable Growing Inst., Skierniewice, 1964–82; Vice-Sec. and Sec., Agric. and Forestry Scis Dept, 1964–87; First Dep. Gen. Sec., 1981–83; Mem., PAN, 1976; Mem., Presidium of PAN, 1978–86; Asst Prof., 1963, Associate Prof., 1969, Prof., 1979, Jagiellonian Univ., Cracow and Polish Acad. of Scis. MP, Nowy Sacz, 1957–89; Dep. Speaker, Sejm, 1982–85 (Chm., Budget Commn, Social and Economic Council and Main Cttee, Nat. Action for School Assistance); Dep. Chm., Council of Ministers, 1985–87; Ambassador of Poland to the Court of St James's and to Republic of Ireland, 1987–90. Mem., Supreme Council and Exec. Cttee, Internat. Soc. of Hort. Scis. Hon. Dr, Acad. of Agric. Scis, Berlin, 1974; DAgr *hc* Szczecin Univ., 1989. Cross of Valour, 1944; Comdr's Cross, Order of Polonia Restituta, 1984; other Polish decorations; numerous foreign honours and awards. *Publications:* contribs to sci. jls. *Recreations:* music, art, travels. *Address:* Botanical Garden, Polish Academy of Sciences, vl. Prawdziwka 2, POB 84, 02–973 Warsaw 34, Poland. *Club:* Rotary.

GERVIS MEYRICK; *see* Meyrick.

GERY, Sir Robert Lucian W.; *see* Wade-Gery.

GESTETNER, David; President, Gestetner Holdings PLC, since 1987; *b* 1 June 1937; *s* of Sigmund and Henny Gestetner; *m* 1961, Alice Floretta Sebag-Montefiore; one *s* three *d. Educ:* Midhurst Grammar Sch.; Bryanston Sch.; University Coll., Oxford (MA). Gestetner Holdings: Jt Chm., 1972–86; Man. Dir, 1982–86; Jt Pres., 1986–87. *Recreation:* sailing.

See also J. Gestetner.

GESTETNER, Jonathan; Chairman, Marlborough Rare Books Ltd, since 1990; *b* 11 March 1940; *s* of Sigmund and Henny Gestetner; *m* 1965, Jacqueline Margaret Strasmore; two *s* one *d. Educ:* Bryanston Sch.; Massachusetts Institute of Technology (BScMechEngrg). Joined Gestetner Ltd, 1962; Jt Chm., 1972–87, and Jt Pres., 1987–88, Gestetner Hldgs PLC; Director: DRS, USA, 1987–89; Klein Associates, USA, 1987–90. Member: Executive Council, Engineering Employers' London Assoc., 1972–77 (Vice-Pres., 1975–77); Maplin Development Authority, 1973–74; SSRC, 1979–82; Dir, Centre for Policy Studies. Mem., Educnl Council, MIT, 1973–. *Recreation:* the visual arts. *Address:* 7 Oakhill Avenue, NW3 7RD. *T:* 071–435 0905. *Clubs:* Brooks's, MCC.

See also David Gestetner.

GETHIN, Sir Richard (Joseph St Lawrence), 10th Bt *cr* 1665, of Gethinsgrott, Cork; General Manager, Beck & Pollitzer, since 1990; *b* 29 Sept. 1949; *s* of Sir Richard Patrick St Lawrence Gethin, 9th Bt and of Fara, *y d* of late J. H. Bartlett; *S* father, 1988; *m* 1974, Jacqueline Torfrida, *d* of Comdr David Cox; three *d. Educ:* The Oratory School; RMA Sandhurst; RMCS Shrivenham; Cranfield Inst. of Technology (BSc(Eng), MSc). Joined first unit, 1971; served in Germany and UK. *Recreations:* gardening, ski-ing, woodwork. *Heir: cousin* Antony Michael Gethin [*b* 10 Jan. 1939; *m* 1965, Vanse, *d* of late Col C. D. Barlow, OBE, KSLI; two *s* one *d*].

GETHING, Air Commodore Richard Templeton, CB 1960; OBE 1945; AFC 1939; *b* 11 Aug. 1911; *s* of George A. Gething, Wilmslow, Cheshire; *m* 1940, Margaret Helen, *d* of late Sir Herbert Gepp, Melbourne, Australia; one *s* one *d. Educ:* Malvern; Sydney Sussex Coll., Cambridge. Joined RAF, 1933. Served War of 1939–45: Canada; UK; India; Burma. Actg Group Capt., 1943; Group Capt., 1950; Actg Air Commodore, 1956; Dir Operations, Maritime Navigation and Air Traffic, Air Ministry, 1956–60, retired. FRIN (FIN 1956). *Recreation:* gliding. *Address:* Garden Hill, Kangaroo Ground, Victoria 3097, Australia. *Club:* Royal Air Force.

GETTY, Hon. Donald Ross; PC (Can.) 1985; Premier of Alberta, since 1985; MLA Edmonton Whitemud, 1967–79, re-elected 1985; *b* 30 Aug. 1933; *s* of Charles Ross Getty and Beatrice Lillian Getty; *m* 1955, Margaret Inez Mitchell; four *s. Educ:* Univ. of Western Ontario (Business Administration). MLA Alberta 1967; Minister of Federal and Intergovernmental Affairs, 1971; Minister of Energy and Natural Resources, 1975; resigned 1979; re-elected MLA, 1985. Joined Imperial Oil, 1955; Midwestern Industrial Gas, 1961; formed Baldonnel Oil & Gas, 1964 (Pres. and Man. Dir); Partner, Doherty

Roadhouse & McCuaig, 1967; Pres., D. Getty Investments, 1979; Chm., Ipsco, 1981–85; former Chm. and Chief Exec., Nortek Energy Corp.; director of other cos. Played quarterback for Edmonton Eskimos Canadian Football team for 10 years. *Recreations:* horse racing, golf, hunting. *Address:* Legislature Building, Edmonton, Alberta T5K 2B6, Canada.

GHALE, Subedar Gaje; *see* Gaje Ghale.

GHERAIEB, Abdelkrim; Ambassador of Algeria to the Court of St James's, since 1989; *b* 30 July 1935; *m* Fizia Gheraieb; one *s* three *d. Educ:* Univ. of Algiers (LèsL); Inst. of Pol Scis, Univ. of Algiers (Diploma). Hd of Legal Services, First Nat. Assembly, 1962–65; Chm., Assoc. of Algerians in Europe, 1965–79; Ambassador to: Teheran, 1979–82; Peking, 1982–84; Beirut, 1984–86; Saudi Arabia, 1986–89. Member: Assemblée Nationale Populaire, 1977; (nominated) Central Cttee, FLN Party, 1979. Médaille de la Résistance, Algerian war of liberation, 1982. Kt, Order of Cedar (Lebanon), 1986; Order of HM King Abdul Aziz (Saudi Arabia), 1989. *Address:* Embassy of Algeria, 54 Holland Park, W11 3RS. *T:* 071–221 0981.

GHIZ, Joseph Atallah; QC (Can) 1984; MLA (Liberal) 6th Queens, since 1982; Premier of Prince Edward Island, since 1986; *b* 27 Jan. 1945; *s* of Atallah J. and Marguerite Farah (McKarris); *m* 1972, Rose Ellen, *d* of Douglas and Elizabeth McGowan; one *s* one *d. Educ:* Prince of Wales College; Dalhousie Univ. (BCom 1966, LLB 1969). LLM Harvard, 1981. Senior Partner, Scales, Ghiz, Jenkins & McQuaid, 1970–81; Crown Prosecutor, Queen's Co., 1970–72; Federal Narcotics Drug Prosecutor, 1970–79; private practice, 1981–86; Counsel to Commn of Inquiry into Charlottetown Police Force, 1977. Pres., Liberal Party of PEI, 1977–78, Leader, 1981–. Former Lectr, Univ. of Prince Edward Island; Former Governor, Frontier Coll.; Mem., Canadian Council of Multiculturalism (Past Regional Chm.). Hon. LLD Univ. of Prince Edward Island, 1987. *Publications:* Towards a New Canada (jtly), 1978; Constitutional Impasse Over Oil and Gas, 1981. *Address:* 122 North River Road, Charlottetown, PEI C1A 3K8, Canada. *T:* 902–892–3065. *Club:* The Charlottetown.

GHURBURRUN, Sir Rabindrah, Kt 1981; Minister of Economic Planning and Development, Mauritius, 1976–82; *b* 27 Sept. 1929; *s* of Mrs Sookmeen Ghurburrun; *m* 1959; one *s* one *d. Educ:* Keble Coll., Oxford. Called to the Bar, Middle Temple; practised as Lawyer, 1959–68; High Comr for Mauritius in India, 1968–76; MLA 1976; Minister of Justice, 1976. Member: Central Board; Bar Council. Former President: Mauritius Arya Sabha; Mauritius Sugar Cane Planters' Assoc.; Hindu Educn Authority; Nat. Congress of Young Socialists. *Address:* 18 Dr Lesur Street, Cascadelle, Beau Bassin, Mauritius. *T:* 54–6421.

GIAEVER, Prof. Ivar; Institute Professor, Physics Department, Rensselaer Polytechnic Institute, Troy, New York, since 1988; *b* 5 April 1929; *s* of John A. Giaever and Gudrun (*née* Skaarud); *m* 1952, Inger Skramstad; one *s* three *d. Educ:* Norwegian Inst. of Tech.; Rensselear Polytechnical Inst. ME 1952; PhD 1964. Norwegian Army, 1952–53; Norwegian Patent Office, 1953–54; Canadian General Electric, 1954–56; General Electric, 1956–58; Staff Mem., Gen. Electric R&D Center, 1958–88. Fellow, Amer. Phys. Soc.; Member: Nat. Acad. of Sciences; Nat. Acad. of Engineering; Amer. Acad. of Arts and Scis; Norwegian Acad. of Scis; Norwegian Acad. of Technology; Norwegian Profl Engrs; Swedish Acad. of Engrg. Hon. DSc: RPI, 1974; Union Coll., 1974; Clarkson, Potsdam, NY, 1983; Trondheim, Norway; Hon. DEng, Michigan Tech. Univ., 1976; Hon. DPhys: Oslo, 1976; State Univ. of NY, 1984. Oliver E. Buckley Prize, 1964; Nobel Prize for Physics, 1973; Zworykin Award, 1974. *Publications:* contrib. Physical Review, Jl Immunology. *Recreations:* ski-ing, tennis, camping, hiking. *Address:* Physics Department, Rensselaer Polytechnic Institute, Troy, NY 12180-3590, USA. *T:* 518–276–6429.

GIBB, Andrew (McArthur); barrister; *b* 8 Sept. 1927; *s* of late William and of Ruth Gibb; *m* 1956, Olga Mary (*née* Morris); three *d. Educ:* Sedbergh; Queens' Coll., Cambridge (MA). Called to the Bar, Middle Temple, 1952. A Recorder of the Crown Court, 1977–82. Chm., Cttee of Public Inquiry into fire at Wensley Lodge, Hessle, Humberside, 1977. *Recreations:* golf, reading, music. *Address:* 263 Colne Road, Sough, Earby, via Colne, Lancs BB8 6SY. *Clubs:* MCC; Lancashire County Cricket.

GIBB, Andrew Thomas Fotheringham; Partner, Balfour and Manson, Solicitors, Edinburgh, since 1975; President, Law Society of Scotland, 1990–91; *b* 17 Aug. 1947; *s* of Thomas Fotheringham Gibb and Isabel Gow McKenzie or Gibb; *m* 1971, Mrs Patricia Anne Eggo or Gibb; two *s. Educ:* Perth Acad.; Edinburgh Univ. (LLB Hons). Temporary Sheriff, 1989–. Member: Lothian and Borders Legal Aid Cttee, 1977–84; Legal Aid Central Cttee, 1984–86; Council, Law Soc. of Scotland, 1981–. Chm. Management Cttee, Lothian Allellon Soc., 1984–. Elder, St Ninian's Church, Corstorphine, Edinburgh. *Recreations:* music, church organist, golf. *Address:* 39 Braehead Road, Edinburgh EH4 6BD. *Clubs:* New (Edinburgh); Bruntsfield Golf.

GIBB, Sir Francis Ross, (Sir Frank Gibb), Kt 1987; CBE 1982; BSc; FEng; FICE; Chairman and Chief Executive, Taylor Woodrow Group, 1985–89 (Joint Managing Director, 1979–85, and a Joint Deputy Chairman, 1983–85); President, since 1985, Director, since 1990, Taylor Woodrow Construction (Chairman, 1978–85, Joint Managing Director, 1978–84); *b* 29 June 1927; *s* of Robert Gibb and Violet Mary Gibb; *m* 1950, Wendy Marjorie Fowler; one *s* two *d. Educ:* Loughborough Coll. BSc(Eng); CEng. Dir, 1963–70, Man. Dir, 1970, Taylor Woodrow Construction; Director: Taylor Woodrow Internat., 1969–85; Taylor Woodrow plc, 1972–89; Chm., Taywood Santa Fe, 1975–85. Jt Dep. Chm., Seaforth Maritime Ltd, 1986–; Director: Seaforth Maritime Hldgs, 1978–; Eurotunnel plc, 1986–87; (non-exec.), Babcock Internat. Group, 1989–; (non-exec.), Steetley plc, 1990–; (non-exec.), Nuclear Electric plc, 1990–. Member: Construction Industry Adv. Cttee, HSE, 1978–81; Gp of Eight, 1979–81; Board, British Nuclear Associates, 1980–88 (Chm., Agrément Bd, 1980–82); Chm., Nat. Nuclear Corp., 1981–88. Member: Council, CBI, 1979–80, 1985–90; Industrial Policy Cttee, CBI, 1980–85. Dir, Holiday Pay Scheme, 1980–84 and Trustee, Benefits Scheme, 1980–84, Building and Civil Engrg Trustees. Federation of Civil Engineering Contractors: Vice-Chm., 1978–79; Chm., 1979–80; Vice Pres., 1980–84; Pres., 1984–87; Vice-Pres., ICE, 1988–. FRSA; CBIM 1983; Hon. FINucE 1984; Hon. FCGI 1990. Hon. DTech, 1989. *Recreations:* ornithology, gardening, walking, music. *Address:* Ross Gibb Consultants, 18 Latchmoor Avenue, Gerrards Cross, Bucks SL9 8LJ. *Club:* Arts.

GIBB, Ian Pashley; Director of Public Services, Planning and Administration, British Library (Humanities and Social Sciences), 1985–87; *b* 17 April 1926; *s* of late John Pashley Gibb and of Mary (*née* Owen); *m* 1953, Patricia Mary Butler; two *s. Educ:* Latymer Upper Sch.; UCL (BA). ALA. Sen. Library Asst, Univ. of London, 1951–52; Asst Librarian, UCL, 1952–58; Dep. Librarian, National Central Library, 1958–73; British Library: Dep. Dir, Science Reference Library, 1973–75; Head of Divl Office, Reference Div., 1975–77; Dir and Keeper, Reference Div., 1977–85. Part-time Lectr, UCL, 1967–77, Hon. Research Fellow, 1977–85, Examiner, 1985–87. Hon. Treasurer, Bibliographical Soc., 1961–67; Mem., Council, Library Assoc., 1980–82; Dep. Chm., Friends of British Library, 1989–. *Publications:* (ed) Newspaper Preservation and Access, 2 vols, 1988; various articles. *Recreations:* music, watching cricket, walking, wine-tasting, travel especially to Austria. *Address:* The Old Cottage, 16 Tile Kiln Lane, Leverstock Green, Hemel Hempstead, Herts HP3 8ND. *T:* Hemel Hempstead (0442) 256352.

GIBB, Walter Frame, DSO 1945; DFC 1943; Chairman, 1980–84, and Managing Director, 1978–84, British Aerospace, Australia, Ltd; retired; *b* 26 March 1919; British; *m* 1944, Pauline Sylvia Reed; three *d. Educ:* Clifton Coll. Apprentice, Bristol Aero Engines, 1937. RAF, 1940–46. Test Pilot, Bristol Aircraft Ltd, 1946; Asst Chief Test Pilot, 1953; Chief Test Pilot, Bristol Aeroplane Co. Ltd, 1956–60; Product Support Manager, BAC Filton, 1960–78. World Altitude Height Record 63,668 feet in Olympus-Canberra, 1953, and second record 65,890 ft in same machine, 1955. MRAeS. JP Bristol, 1974. *Recreation:* sailing. *Address:* Merlin Haven Lodge, Wotton-Under-Edge, Glos GL12 7BA. *Clubs:* Royal Air Force; Royal Sydney Yacht Squadron.

GIBB, William Eric, MA, DM Oxon; FRCP; Consulting Physician, St Bartholomew's Hospital, since 1976; *b* 30 April 1911; *s* of late James Glenny Gibb, MD, FRCS, and Georgina Henman; *m* 1952, Mary Edith Gertrude Feetham; three *s. Educ:* Rugby Sch.; Oriel Coll., Oxford; St Bartholomew's Hosp. BA Oxon 1st Cl. Hons Final Sch. of Nat. Science; BM, BCh Oxon 1936; MRCP 1940; DM Oxon 1947; FRCP 1949; George Herbert Hunt Travelling Schol. (University of Oxford), 1938. War service with RAFVR Med. Br., 1941–46; Actg Wing-Comdr i/c a Med. Div. Res. House appts, St Bart's Hosp. and Brompton Chest Hosp.; Cattlin Research Scholar, 1947; Physician: St Bart's Hosp., 1947–76; The Metropolitan Hosp., 1952–76. Mem., Pensions Appeal Tribunal, 1976–85. Examiner in Medicine: University of Oxford, 1952–59; Examg Bd of England; RCP; Soc. of Apothecaries. Fellow, Royal Soc. Med. *Publications:* various articles in medical journals. *Recreation:* gardening. *Address:* 1 Bacon's Lane, Highgate, N6 6BL. *Club:* Osler.

GIBBENS, Barnaby John, OBE 1989; Chairman: Callhaven plc; Enterprise Systems Group Ltd; *b* 17 April 1935; *s* of late Dr Gerald Gibbens and Deirdre Gibbens; *m* 1st, 1960, Sally Mary Stephenson (marr. diss. 1990); one *s* two *d*; 2nd, 1990, Kristina de Zabala. *Educ:* Winchester College. FCA 1972. Founder, Computer Analysts & Programmers (later CAP Group, then SEMA Group), 1962; Founding Chm., SEMA Gp, 1988–90. Chairman: Computing Services Industry, Trng Council, 1984–; IT Industry Lead Body, 1987–; IT Trng Accreditation Council, 1991–; a Director: National Computing Centre, 1987–90; UK Skills, 1990–; Member: Nat. Ctte on Computer Networks, 1978; NCVQ, 1989–; NCET, 1991–. Pres., Computing Services Assoc., 1975. Chm. Trustees, Skin Treatment and Res. Trust. Founding Master, Co. of Information Technologists, 1987. *Publications:* articles in national press and jls on computing. *Recreations:* golf, real tennis, music, gardening. *Address:* 12 Kings Road, Wimbledon, SW19 8QN. *T:* 081–542 3878.

GIBBINGS, Sir Peter (Walter), Kt 1989; Chairman, since 1988, and Director, since 1981, Anglia Television Group plc (Deputy Chairman, 1986–88); *b* 25 March 1929; *s* of late Walter White Gibbings and Margaret Russell Gibbings (*née* Torrance); *m* 1st, Elspeth Felicia Macintosh; two *d*; 2nd, Hon. Louise Barbara, *d* of 2nd Viscount Lambert, TD; one *s. Educ:* Rugby; Wadham Coll., Oxford (Scholar). Called to Bar, Middle Temple, 1953 (Garraway Rice Pupillage Prize; Harmsworth Schol.). Served in 9th Queen's Royal Lancers, 1951–52; Dep. Legal Adviser, Trinidad Oil Co. Ltd, 1955–56; Associated Newspapers Ltd, 1956–60; The Observer, 1960–67 (Deputy Manager and Dir, 1965–67); Man. Dir, Guardian Newspapers Ltd, 1967–73; Dir, Manchester Guardian and Evening News Ltd, 1967–73; Chm., Guardian and Manchester Evening News plc, 1973–88. Director: Press Assoc. Ltd, 1982–88 (Chm., 1986–87); Reuters Holdings PLC, 1984–88; The Economist, 1987–. Mem., Press Council, 1970–74; Pres., CPU, 1989–. *Recreations:* sailing, tennis. *Address:* c/o Anglia Television Group plc, Anglia House, Norwich NR1 3JG.

GIBBINS, Elizabeth Mary, BA; Headmistress, St Mary's School, Calne, Wilts, 1946–72; *b* 2 May 1911; *d* of late Kenneth Mayoh Gibbins, MB, BS. *Educ:* Sandecotes Sch., Parkstone; Westfield Coll., University of London; Cambridge Univ. Training Coll. for Women (Postgraduate). History Mistress, St Brandons Clergy Daughters' Sch., Bristol, 1935–38; Headmistress, Diocesan Girls' Sch., Hongkong, 1939–45, Acting Headmistress, Oct. 1972–May 1973. Hon. Sec., Hong Kong Diocesan Assoc., 1974–80. *Address:* 8 Moreton Road, Old Bosham, Chichester, West Sussex PO18 8LL. *T:* Bosham (0243) 573038.

GIBBINS, Rev. Dr Ronald Charles; Methodist Minister; Superintendent Minister, Wesley's Chapel, London, 1978–88; *s* of Charles and Anne Gibbins; *m* 1949, Olive Ruth (*née* Patchett); one *s* two *d. Educ:* London Univ. (BScSociol); Wesley Theological Coll., Bristol; Eden Theological Seminary, US (DMin). Methodist Minister: Bradford, 1948–49; Spennymoor, 1949–50; Middlesbrough, 1950–57; Basildon, 1957–64; East End Mission, London, 1964–78. *Publications:* Mission for the Secular City, 1976; The Lumpen Proletariat, 1979; The Stations of the Resurrection, 1987. *Recreations:* travel, journalism. *Address:* 27 Riverside Close, Kingston upon Thames, Surrey KT1 2JG.

GIBBON, Gen. Sir John (Houghton), GCB 1977 (KCB 1972; CB 1970); OBE 1945 (MBE 1944); Master-General of the Ordnance, 1974–77; ADC (General) to the Queen, 1976–77; *b* 21 Sept. 1917; *er s* of Brigadier J. H. Gibbon, DSO, The Manor House, Little Stretton, Salop; *m* 1951, Brigid Rosamund, *d* of late Dr D. A. Bannerman, OBE, ScD, FRSE, and Muriel, *d* of T. R. Morgan; one *s. Educ:* Eton; Trinity Coll., Cambridge. Commissioned into Royal Artillery, 1939. Served with 2nd Regt RHA: France, 1939–40; Western Desert, 1940–41; Greece, 1941; on staff of HQ 30 Corps; Western Desert, 1941–43; Sicily, 1943; GSO 1, RA, HQ 21 Army Gp, 1944–45; 6 Airborne Div., Palestine, 1946–47; Instructor and Chief Instructor, RMA Sandhurst, 1947–51; GSO 2, War Office, 1951–53; Battery Comdr, 1953–54; AQMG, War Office, 1955–58; CO Field Regt, BAOR, 1959–60; Bde Comdr, Cyprus, 1962; Dir of Defence Plans, Min. of Def., 1962–64; Sec., Chiefs of Staff Cttee, and Dir, Defence Operations Staff, 1966–69; Dir, Army Staff Duties, MoD, 1969–71; Vice-Chief of the Defence Staff, 1972–74. Col Comdt, RA, 1972–82. Chm., Regular Forces Employment Assoc., 1982–85 (Vice-Chm., 1977–82). *Recreations:* rowing, shooting, fishing. *Address:* Beech House, Northbrook Close, Winchester, Hants SO23 8JR. *T:* Winchester (0962) 866155. *Club:* Naval and Military.

GIBBON, Michael, QC 1974; **His Honour Judge Gibbon;** a Circuit Judge, since 1979; *b* 15 Sept. 1930; 2nd *s* of late Frank and Jenny Gibbon; *m* 1956, Malveen Elliot Seager; two *s* one *d. Educ:* Brightlands; Charterhouse; Pembroke Coll., Oxford (MA). Commnd in Royal Artillery, 1949. Called to Bar, Lincoln's Inn, 1954. A Recorder of the Crown Court, 1972–79; Hon. Recorder, City of Cardiff, 1986. Chm., Electoral Adv. Cttee to Home Sec., 1972. Chm., Local Govt Boundary Commn for Wales, 1978–79 (Dep. Chm., 1974–78); a Chm., Bar Disciplinary Tribunal, 1988; Mem., Parole Bd, 1986–88. *Recreations:* music, golf. *Address:* Gellihirion, 3 Cefn-Coed Road, Cardiff CF2 6AN. *T:* Cardiff (0222) 751852. *Clubs:* Cardiff and County (Cardiff); Royal Porthcawl Golf, Cardiff Golf.

GIBBONS, Hon. Sir David; *see* Gibbons, Hon. Sir J. D.

GIBBONS, Prof. Ian Read, FRS 1983; Professor of Biophysics in the University of Hawaii, since 1967; *b* 30 Oct. 1931; *s* of Arthur Alwyn Gibbons and Hilda Read Cake; *m* 1961, Barbara Ruth Hollingworth; one *s* one *d*. *Educ:* Faversham Grammar School; Cambridge Univ. (BA, PhD). Research Fellow, 1958–63, Asst Prof., 1963–67, Harvard Univ.; Associate Prof., 1967–69, Prof., 1969, Univ. of Hawaii. *Publications:* contribs to learned jls. *Recreations:* gardening, computer programming, music. *Address:* Pacific Biomedical Research Center, Kewalo Marine Laboratory, 41 Ahui Street, Honolulu, Hawaii 96813, USA. *T:* (808) 539–7325.

GIBBONS, Hon. Sir (John) David, KBE 1985; JP; Chairman, Bank of N. T. Butterfield & Son Ltd, Bermuda, since 1986; *b* 15 June 1927; *s* of late Edmund G. Gibbons, CBE, and Winifred G. Gibbons, MBE; *m* 1958, Lully Lorentzen; three *s* (and one *d* by former *m*). *Educ:* Saltus Grammar Sch., Bermuda; Hotchkiss Sch., Lakeville, Conn; Harvard Univ., Cambridge, Mass (BA). FBIM. Mem. Govt Boards: Social Welfare Bd, 1949–58; Bd of Civil Aviation, 1958–60; Bd of Educn, 1956–59 (Chm., 1973–74); Trade Develt Bd, 1960–74. MP Bermuda, 1972–84; Minister of Health and Welfare, 1974–75, of Finance, 1975–84; Premier of Bermuda, 1977–82. Chairman: Bermuda Monetary Authy, 1984–86; Economic Council, Bermuda, 1984–86. Mem., Law Reform Cttee, 1969–72. Mem. Governing Body, subseq. Chm., Bermuda Technical Inst., 1956–70. Mem., Bermuda Athletic Assoc. JP Bermuda, 1974. *Recreations:* tennis, golf, skiing, swimming. *Address:* Leeward, 5 Leeside Drive, Pembroke, Bermuda HMO5. *T:* 809–29 52396. *Clubs:* Phoenix (Cambridge, Mass); Harvard (New York); Royal Bermuda Yacht, Royal Hamilton Amateur Dinghy, Mid-Ocean, Riddells Bay Golf, Spanish Point Boat (Bermuda); Lyford Cay (Bahamas).

GIBBONS, Dr John Ernest; Director of Building and Chief Architect, Scottish Office, since 1984; *b* Halesowen, Worcs, 20 April 1940; *s* of late John Howard Gibbons and Lilian Alice Gibbons (*née* Shale); *m* 1963, Patricia Mitchell; one *s* two *d*. *Educ:* Oldbury Grammar Sch.; Birmingham Sch. of Architecture; Edinburgh Univ. PhD; DipArch; DipTP; ARIBA; ARIAS; FSA(Scot). In private practice, 1962–65; Lectr, Birmingham Sch. of Architecture and Univ. of Aston, 1964–66; Res. Fellow, 1967–69, Lectr, 1969–72, Edinburgh Univ.; Scottish Development Department: Prin. Architect, 1972–78; Asst Dir, Building Directorate, 1978–82; Dep. Dir and Dep. Chief Architect, 1982–84. Vis. Res. Scientist, CSIRO, Melbourne, 1974–75. Member, Council: EAA and RIAS, 1977–80; ARCUK, 1984. *Publications:* contribs on architectural and planning matters to professional and technical jls. *Recreations:* reading, photography, music, travel. *Address:* Crichton House, Pathhead, Midlothian EH37 5UX. *T:* Ford (0875) 320085. *Club:* New (Edinburgh).

GIBBONS, Ven. Kenneth Harry; Archdeacon of Lancaster, since 1981; Vicar of St Michael's-on-Wyre, since 1985; *b* 24 Dec. 1931; *s* of Harry and Phyllis Gibbons; *m* 1962, Margaret Ann Tomlinson; two *s*. *Educ:* Blackpool and Chesterfield Grammar Schools; Manchester Univ. (BSc); Cuddesdon Coll., Oxford. RAF, 1952–54. Ordained, 1956; Assistant Curate of Fleetwood, 1956–60; Secretary for Student Christian Movement in Schools, 1960–62; Senior Curate, St Martin-in-the-Fields, Westminster, 1962–65; Vicar of St Edward, New Addington, 1965–70; Vicar of Portsea, 1970–81; RD of Portsmouth, 1973–79; Hon. Canon of Portsmouth, 1974–81; Priest-in-charge of Weeton, 1981–85. Diocesan Dir of Ordinands, 1982–90. Acting Chaplain to HM Forces, 1981–85. *Recreations:* gardening, cinema. *Address:* The Vicarage, St Michael's-on-Wyre, Preston, Lancs PR3 0TQ. *Club:* Reform.

GIBBONS, Sir William Edward Doran, 9th Bt *cr* 1752; JP; transport and management consultant, since 1990; *b* 13 Jan. 1948; *s* of Sir John Edward Gibbons, 8th Bt, and of Mersa Wentworth, *y d* of late Major Edward Baynton Grove Foster; *S* father, 1982; *m* 1972, Patricia Geraldine Archer, *d* of Roland Archer Howse; one *s* one *d*. *Educ:* Pangbourne; RNC Dartmouth; Bristol Univ. (BSc). MCIT. Asst Shipping and Port Manager, Sealink UK, Parkeston Quay, 1979–82; Service Manager (Anglo-Dutch), Sealink UK Ltd, 1982–85; Ferry Line Manager (Harwich–Hook), 1985–87, Gen. Manager, IoW Services, 1987–90, Sealink British Ferries. Non-Exec. Mem., IoW DHA, 1990–. Mem., Manningtree Parish Council, 1981– (Chm., 1985–87). JP Portsmouth, 1990. *Heir:* *s* Charles William Edwin Gibbons, *b* 28 Jan. 1983. *Address:* 5 Yarborough Road, Southsea, Hants.

GIBBS, family name of **Barons Aldenham** and **Wraxall.**

GIBBS, Air Vice-Marshal Charles Melvin, CB 1976; CBE 1966; DFC 1943; RAF retd; Recruiting Consultant with Selleck Associates, Colchester, 1977–86; *b* 11 June 1921; American father, New Zealand mother; *m* 1947, Emma Pamela Pollard; one *d*. *Educ:* Taumarunui, New Zealand. MECI 1980. Joined RNZAF, 1941; service in Western Desert and Mediterranean, 1942–44; Coastal Comd, 1945; India, 1946–47; commanded Tropical Experimental Unit, 1950–52; RAF Staff Coll., 1953; commanded No 118 Squadron, 1954–55; Directing Staff, RAF Staff Coll., 1956–58; Pakistan, 1958–61; Chief Instructor, RAF Chivenor, 1961–63; CO, Wattisham, 1963–66; idc 1967; Defence Policy Staff, 1968–69; Dir of Quartering, 1970–72; AOA, Germany, 1972–74; Dir-Gen. Personal Services, RAF, 1974–76. *Recreations:* fishing, golf. *Address:* 20 Inga Road, Milford, Auckland 9, New Zealand. *T:* 410–4089.

GIBBS, Hon. Sir Eustace Hubert Beilby, KCVO 1986; CMG 1982; HM Diplomatic Service, retired; Vice Marshal of the Diplomatic Corps, 1982–86; *b* 3 July 1929; 2nd surv. *s* of 1st Baron Wraxall, PC; *b* and *heir-pres.* of 2nd Baron Wraxall, *qv*; *m* 1957, Evelyn Veronica Scott; three *s* two *d*. *Educ:* Eton College; Christ Church, Oxford (MA). ARCM 1953. Entered HM Diplomatic Service, 1954; served in Bangkok, Rio de Janeiro, Berlin, Vienna, Caracas, Paris. *Recreations:* music, golf. *Address:* Coddenham House, Coddenham, Ipswich, Suffolk IP6 9TY. *T:* Coddenham (044979) 332. *Clubs:* Pratt's, Beefsteak.

GIBBS, Air Marshal Sir Gerald Ernest, KBE 1954 (CBE 1945); CIE 1946; MC; *b* 3 Sept. 1896; *s* of Ernest William Cecil and Fanny Wilmina Gibbs; *m* 1938, Margaret Jean Bradshaw; one *s* one *d*. Served European War, 1914–18; transferred from Army to RFC 1916, and RAF 1918 (MC and 2 bars, Légion d'Honneur, Croix de Guerre). ADC to Marshal of the Royal Air Force Sir Hugh Trenchard (later 1st Viscount Trenchard), 1927–28; served in Air Staff Plans, Air Ministry, under Gp Capt. C. F. A. Portal (later 1st Viscount Portal of Hungerford), and then Gp Capt. A. T. Harris (later Marshal of the Royal Air Force Sir Arthur Harris, Bt), 1930–34; served various overseas periods with RAF in Iraq, Palestine, Sudan and Kenya between the two wars; commanded No 47 Sqdn RAF Sudan and RAF Kenya. Senior Air Staff Officer of No 11 Group, Fighter Command, 1940–41 during Battle of Britain; Dir of Overseas Operations, Air Ministry, 1942–43; Senior Air Staff Officer, HQ 3rd Tactical Air Force, South-East Asia, 1943–44; Chief Air Staff Officer to Admiral Mountbatten (later Earl Mountbatten of Burma), Supreme HQ, SEAC, 1945–46; Senior Air Staff Officer, HQ, RAF Transport Command, 1946–48; Head of Service Advisers to UK Delegation and Chm. UK Members of Military Staff Cttee, UN, 1948–51; Chief of Air Staff and Commander-in-Chief, Indian Air Force, 1951–54, retired 1954. *Publication:* Survivor's Story, 1956. *Recreations:* golf, ski-ing, sailing. *Address:* Lone Oak, 170 Coombe Lane West, Kingston-upon-Thames, Surrey. *Clubs:* Royal Air Force; Royal Wimbledon Golf (Wimbledon); Seaford Golf (East Blatchington); Trevose Golf (Cornwall).

GIBBS, Rt. Hon. Sir Harry (Talbot), AC 1987; GCMG 1981; KBE 1970; PC 1972; Chief Justice of Australia, 1981–87; *b* 7 Feb. 1917; *s* of late H. V. Gibbs, formerly of Ipswich, Qld; *m* 1944, Muriel Ruth (*née* Dunn); one *s* three *d*. *Educ:* Ipswich Grammar Sch., Qld; Univ. of Queensland (BA, LLM). Served War, Australia and New Guinea, 1939–45, Major (despatches). Admitted as Barrister, Qld, 1939; QC 1957; Judge of Supreme Court of Qld, 1961; Judge of Federal Court of Bankruptcy and of Supreme Court of Australian Capital Territory, 1967; Justice of High Court of Australia, 1970. Hon. Bencher, Lincoln's Inn, 1981. Hon. LLD Queensland, 1980; DUniv Griffith Univ., 1987. *Address:* 30 Lodge Road, Cremorne, NSW 2090, Australia. *T:* 909–1844. *Clubs:* Australian (Sydney); Queensland (Brisbane).

GIBBS, Rt. Rev. John; *b* 15 March 1917; *s* of late A. E. Gibbs, Bournemouth; *m* 1943, G. Marion, *d* of late W. J. Bishop, Poole, Dorset; one *s* one *d*. *Educ:* Univ. of Bristol; Western Coll., Bristol; Lincoln Theological Coll. BA (Bristol); BD (London). In the ministry of the Congregational Church, 1943–49. Student Christian Movement: Inter-Collegiate Sec., 1949–51; Study Sec. and Editor of Student Movement, 1951–55. Curate of St Luke's, Brislington, Bristol, 1955–57; Chaplain and Head of Divinity Dept, Coll. of St Matthias, Bristol, 1957–64, Vice-Principal, 1962–64; Principal, Keswick Hall Coll. of Education, Norwich, 1964–73; Examining Chaplain to Bishop of Norwich, Hon. Canon of Norwich Cathedral, 1968–73; Bishop Suffragan of Bradwell, Dio. Chelmsford, 1973–76; Bishop of Coventry, 1976–85. Hon. Asst to Bps of Gloucester and Bristol, 1985–. Member, Durham Commn on Religious Education, 1967–70; Chairman: C of E Children's Council, 1968–71; C of E Bd of Educn Publications Cttee, 1971–79, Education and Community Cttee, 1974–76; Assoc. of Voluntary Colls, 1985–87; Further and Higher Educn Cttee, General Synod Bd of Educn, 1986–91; BCC Wkg Parties: Chm., The Child in the Church, 1973–76; Chm., Understanding Christian Nurture, 1979–81; Anglican Chm., Anglican–Lutheran European Reg. Commn, 1980–82. Introduced H of L, 1982. *Recreations:* music, bird watching. *Address:* Farthingloe, Southfield, Minchinhampton, Stroud, Glos GL6 9DY.

GIBBS, Sir Martin St John Valentine, KCVO 1991; CB 1958; DSO 1942; TD; JP; Lord-Lieutenant of Gloucestershire, since 1978; *b* 14 Feb. 1917; *er s* of late Major G. M. Gibbs, Parkleaze, Ewen, Cirencester; *m* 1947, Mary Margaret (*widow* of late Captain M. D. H. Wills, MC), *er d* of late Col Philip Mitford; two *d*. *Educ:* Eton. 2nd Lieut, Royal Wilts Yeomanry, 1937; served War of 1939–45 with Royal Wilts Yeo., Major 1942, Lieut-Col 1951, Brevet-Col 1955, Col 1958; Hon. Col: Royal Wilts Yeomanry Sqdn, T&AVR, 1972–82; The Royal Yeomanry, RAC, T&AVR, 1975–82; Col Comdt Yeomanry, RAC, 1975–82. Gloucestershire: JP 1965; High Sheriff, 1958; DL Wilts 1972. *Recreations:* country pursuits. *Address:* Ewen Manor, Ewen, Cirencester, Glos. *T:* Cirencester (0285) 770206. *Clubs:* Cavalry and Guards, MCC.

See also Field Marshal Sir R. C. Gibbs, Sir G. R. Newman, Bt.

GIBBS, Dame Molly (Peel), DBE 1969; (Hon. Lady Gibbs); *b* 13 July 1912; 2nd *d* of John Peel Nelson; *m* 1934, Rt Hon. Sir Humphrey Vicary Gibbs, GCVO, KCMG, OBE, PC (*d* 1990); five *s*. *Educ:* Girls' High School, Barnato Park, Johannesburg. *Address:* 22 Dornie Road, Pomona, PO Borrowdale, Harare, Zimbabwe. *T:* Harare 883281.

GIBBS, Oswald Moxley, CMG 1976; development and trade consultant, since 1990; High Commissioner for Grenada in London, 1974–78 and 1984–90; Ambassador for Grenada to the European Economic Community, 1985–90; *b* St George's, Grenada, 15 Oct. 1927; *s* of Michael Gibbs and Emelda Mary (*née* Cobb); *m* 1955, Dearest Agatha Mitchell (*d* 1989); two *s* two *d*. *Educ:* Happy Hill RC Sch.; St George's RC Sen. Boys' Sch.; Grenada Boys' Secondary Sch.; Christy Trades Sch., Chicago (Technical Drafting Dip.); City of London Coll. BScEcon London. Solicitors' Clerk, Grenada, 1948–51; petroleum refining, Royal Dutch Shell Co., Curaçao, Netherlands Antilles, 1951–55; Civil Servant, Agricl Rehabilitation Dept, Grenada, 1955–57; Transport Worker, London Transport, and Postman, London, 1957–60; Civil Servant, WI Federal Commn, London, 1961–62; Consular Officer, Commn for Eastern Caribbean Govts, London, 1965–75; Welfare Officer, 1965–67; Trade Sec., 1967–72; Dep. Comr, 1972–73; Actg Comr, 1973–75. Rep. Govt of St Kitts-Nevis-Anguilla on London Cttee of Commonwealth Sugar Producing Countries, 1971–75; Consultant, Centre for Industrial Develt, Lomé Convention, Brussels, 1979–80 (signed Lomé III Convention for Grenada, 1984); Deleg., 9th Commonwealth Conf. on Develt and Human Ecology, Univ. of Edinburgh, 1989; Head of Delegn, Commonwealth Heads of Govt Meeting, Kuala Lumpur, 1989; Admin. Dir, N Kensington Family Centre and Unity Assoc., 1980–83; Business Develt Manager, UK Caribbean Chamber of Commerce, 1983–84. Chairman: Civil Service Salaries Revision Commn, Grenada, 1970; Notting Hill Carnival and Arts Cttee, 1981–84. Member: Exec., Commonwealth Human Ecology Council, 1989–; Governing Council, Internat. Fund for Agricl Develt (Rome), 1986–90. Mem., delegns to constitutional, Commonwealth and ACP/EEC meetings and confs. Silver Jubilee Medal, 1977. *Recreations:* development economics, DIY, photography. *Address:* 73A Woodside Green, SE25 5HU.

GIBBS, Dr Richard John; Chief Executive, Kingston and Esher Health Authority, since 1990; *b* 15 May 1943; *s* of Leslie and Mary Gibbs; *m* 1968, Laura Wanda Olasmi; one *d*. *Educ:* Merchant Taylors' Sch., Northwood; Pembroke Coll., Cambridge (BA 1965); Warwick Univ. (PhD 1974). Teacher, City of London Sch. for Boys, 1965; Scientific Officer, Home Office, 1968; Sen. Scientific Officer, 1970, PSO, 1972, DHSS; Res. Schol., Internat. Inst. for Applied Systems Analysis, Austria, 1977; SPSO, DHSS, 1978; Central Policy Review Staff, 1980; Dir of Operational Res. (DCSO), 1982, CSO, 1985, DHSS; Under Sec. and Dir of Stats and Management, DHSS, then DoH, 1986–90. Vis. Prof., UCL, 1985. *Publications:* contribs to Jl of ORS. *Recreations:* windsurfing, cooking. *Address:* Kingston and Esher Health Authority, 17 Upper Brighton Road, Surbiton, Surrey KT6 6LH.

GIBBS, Richard John Hedley, QC 1984; **His Honour Judge Gibbs;** a Circuit Judge, since 1990; *b* 2 Sept. 1941; *s* of Brian Conaway Gibbs and Mabel Joan Gibbs; *m* 1965, Janet (*née* Whittall); one *s* three *d*. *Educ:* Oundle Sch.; Trinity Hall, Cambridge (MA). Called to the Bar, Inner Temple, 1965; a Recorder, 1981–90. Chm., Birmingham Friendship Housing Assoc., 1987–. *Address:* Lord Chancellor's Department, Midland and Oxford Circuit, Stafford Group of Courts, Greyfriars House, Greyfriars, Stafford ST16 2SE.

GIBBS, Roger Geoffrey; Chairman, The Wellcome Trust, since 1989 (Trustee, since 1983); Chairman, Gerrard & National Holdings PLC (formerly Gerrard & National Discount Co. Ltd), 1975–89 (Director, since 1971); *b* 13 Oct. 1934; 4th *s* of Hon. Sir Geoffrey Gibbs, KCMG, and Hon. Lady Gibbs, CBE. *Educ:* Eton; Millfield. Jessel Toynbee & Co. Ltd, 1954–64, Dir 1960; de Zoete & Gorton, later de Zoete & Bevan, Stockbrokers, 1964–71, Partner 1966. Chm., London Discount Market Assoc., 1984–86. Director: Arsenal FC, 1980–; Colville Estate Ltd, 1989–; Howard de Walden Estates Ltd, 1989–. Chm., Arundel Castle Cricket Foundn, 1987–. Member: Council, Royal Nat. Pension

Fund for Nurses, 1975–; Finance Cttee, 1985–, Council, 1989–, ICRF. Ct of Advrs, St Paul's Cathedral, 1990–. Governor, London Clinic, 1983–; Special Trustee, Guy's Hosp., 1983–. Freeman, City of London; Liveryman, Merchant Taylors' Co. Commentator, 10 progs Wide World of Sport, ABC TV, Amer., 1967–85. *Publication:* The Cresta Run 1885–1985. *Recreations:* travel, sport. *Address:* The Wellcome Trust, 1 Park Square West, NW1 4LJ. *T:* 071–486 4902; 23 Tregunter Road, SW10 9LS. *T:* 071–370 3465. *Clubs:* Brooks's, Pratt's; Queen's, MCC (Mem., Finance Sub-Cttee, 1988–); Swinley Forest Golf (Mem. Cttee, 1988–); Vanderbilt.

GIBBS, Field Marshal Sir Roland (Christopher), GCB 1976 (KCB 1972); CBE 1968; DSO 1945; MC 1943; Lord-Lieutenant for Wiltshire, since 1989; Chief of the General Staff, 1976–79; ADC General to the Queen, 1976–79; *b* 22 June 1921; *yr s* of late Maj. G. M. Gibbs, Parkleaze, Ewen, Cirencester; *m* 1955, Davina Jean Merry; two *s* one *d. Educ:* Eton Coll.; RMC Sandhurst. Commnd into 60th Rifles, 1940; served War of 1939–45 in N Africa, Italy and NW Europe. Comd 3rd Bn Parachute Regt, 1960–62; GSO1, Brit. Army Staff, Washington, 1962–63; Comdr 16 Para. Bde, 1963–66; Chief of Staff, HQ Middle East, 1966–67; IDC 1968; Commander, British Forces, Gulf, 1969–71; GOC 1 (British) Corps, 1972–74; C-in-C, UKLF, 1974–76. Colonel Commandant: 2nd Bn The Royal Green Jackets, 1971–78; Parachute Regt, 1972–77. Constable, HM Tower of London, 1985–90. Salisbury Regional Dir, Lloyds Bank, 1979–91. Chm., Nat. Rifle Assoc., 1984–90. DL, 1980, Vice Lord-Lieutenant, 1982–89, Wilts. KStJ 1990. *Recreation:* out-of-door sports. *Address:* Patney Rectory, Devizes, Wilts. *Club:* Turf.

See also Sir M. St J. V. Gibbs.

GIBBS, Stephen, CBE 1981; Chairman: Turner & Newall Ltd, 1979–82; Gibbs Associates Ltd (formerly Gibbs Littlewood Associates), since 1984; *b* 12 Feb. 1920; *s* of Arthur Edwin Gibbs and Anne Gibbs; *m* 1941, Louise Pattison; one *s* one *d. Educ:* Oldbury Grammar Sch.; Birmingham Univ. (part-time). FPRI. British Industrial Plastics Ltd, Oldbury, Warley, W Midlands, 1936–39. Served RASC, 1939–46. British Industrial Plastics Ltd: Technical Dept, 1946–52; General Sales Manager, 1952–56; Director, and Chm. of subsidiary cos, 1956–68; Turner & Newall Ltd, Manchester: Director, 1968–72; Man. Dir, 1972–76; Dep. Chm., 1976–79; Chm., Gascoigne Moody Associates, 1984–87. Chm., Energy Policy Cttee, CBI, 1981–83. *Address:* Corner House, 11 Dodderhill Road, Droitwich, Worcs WR9 8QN.

GIBRALTAR IN EUROPE, Bishop of, since 1980; **Rt. Rev. John Richard Satterthwaite,** CMG 1991; *b* 17 Nov. 1925; *s* of William and Clara Elisabeth Satterthwaite. *Educ:* Millom Grammar Sch.; Leeds Univ. (BA); Coll. of the Resurrection, Mirfield. History Master, St Luke's Sch., Haifa, 1946–48; Curate: St Barnabas, Carlisle, 1950–53; St Aidan, Carlisle, 1953–54; St Michael Paternoster Royal, London, 1955–59, Curate-in-Charge, 1959–65; Guild Vicar, St Dunstan-in-the-West, City of London, 1959–70. Gen. Sec., Church of England Council on Foreign Relations, 1959–70 (Asst Gen. Sec., 1955–59); Gen. Sec., Archbp's Commn on Roman Catholic Relations, 1965–70; Bishop Suffragan of Fulham, 1970; Bishop of Gibraltar, 1970; known as Bishop of Fulham and Gibraltar until creation of new diocese, 1980. Hon. Canon of Canterbury, 1963–; ChStJ 1972 (Asst ChStJ 1963); Hon. Canon of Utrecht, Old Catholic Church of the Netherlands, 1969. Holds decoration from various foreign churches. *Recreations:* fell walking, music. *Address:* 5A Gregory Place, W8 4NG. *T:* 071–937 2796. *Club:* Athenæum.

GIBRALTAR IN EUROPE, Suffragan Bishop of, since 1986; **Rt. Rev. Edward Holland;** *b* 28 June 1936; *s* of Reginald Dick Holland and Olive Holland (*née* Yeoman). *Educ:* New College School; Dauntsey's School; King's College London (AKC). National Service, Worcestershire Regt, 1955–57; worked for Importers, 1957–61; KCL, 1961–65. Deacon 1965, priest 1966, Rochester; Curate, Holy Trinity, Dartford, 1965–69; Curate, John Keble, Mill Hill, 1969–72; Precentor, Gibraltar Cathedral, and Missioner for Seamen, 1972–74; Chaplain at Naples, Italy, 1974–79; Vicar of S Mark's, Bromley, 1979–86. *Recreations:* travel, being entertained and entertaining. *Address:* 11 Lanark Road, W9 1DD. *T:* 071–286 3335.

GIBRALTAR IN EUROPE (Diocese), Auxiliary Bishops of; *see* Capper, Rt Rev. E. M. H.; Pina-Cabral, Rt Rev. D. P. dos S. de.

GIBSON, family name of **Barons Ashbourne** and **Gibson.**

GIBSON, Baron *cr* 1975 (Life Peer), of Penn's Rocks; **Richard Patrick Tallentyre Gibson;** Chairman, National Trust, 1977–86; *b* 5 Feb. 1916; *s* of Thornely Carbutt Gibson and Elizabeth Anne Augusta Gibson; *m* 1945, Elisabeth Dione Pearson; four *s. Educ:* Eton Coll.; Magdalen Coll., Oxford (Hon. Fellow, 1977). London Stock Exchange, 1937. Served with Mddx Yeo, 1939–46; N Africa, 1940–41; POW, 1941–43; Special Ops Exec., 1943–45; Political Intell. Dept, FO, 1945–46. Westminster Press Ltd, 1947–78 (Dir, 1948); Director: Whitehall Securities Corp. Ltd, 1948–60, 1973–83; Financial Times Ltd, 1957–78 (Chm., 1975–77); Economist Newspaper Ltd, 1957–78; Pearson PLC (formerly S. Pearson & Son Ltd), 1960–88 (Dep. Chm., 1969; Exec. Dep. Chm., 1975; Chm., 1978–83); Royal Exchange Assce, 1961–69; Chm., Pearson Longman Ltd, 1967–79. Hon. Treas. Commonwealth Press Union, 1957–67. Chm., Arts Council, 1972–77. Vice-Pres., RSA, 1986–90; Chm., RSA Environment Cttee, 1986–90. Trustee, Historic Churches Preservation Trust, 1958; Member: Exec. Cttee, National Trust, 1963–72; Council, Nat. Trust, 1966–86; Adv. Council, V&A Museum, 1968–75 (Chm., 1970); UK Arts Adv. Commn, Calouste Gulbenkian Foundn, 1969–72; Redundant Churches Fund, 1970–71; Exec. Cttee, Nat. Art Collections Fund, 1970; Bd, Royal Opera House, 1977–87; Treasurer, Sussex Univ., 1983–87; Trustee, Glyndebourne Fest. Opera, 1965–72 and 1977–86. Hon. DLitt Reading, 1980; DUniv Sussex, 1989. *Recreations:* music, gardening, architecture. *Address:* Penn's Rocks, Groombridge, Sussex. *T:* Groombridge (089276) 244. *Clubs:* Garrick, Brooks's.

GIBSON, Sir Alexander (Drummond), Kt 1977; CBE 1967; FRSE 1978; Founder, 1962 and Music Director, 1985–87, Scottish Opera Company (Artistic Director, 1962–85), Conductor Laureate, since 1987; *b* 11 Feb. 1926; *s* of late James McClure Gibson and of Wilhelmina Gibson (*née* Williams); *m* 1959, Ann Veronica Waggett; three *s* one *d. Educ:* Dalziel; Glasgow Univ.; Royal College of Music; Mozarteum, Salzburg, Austria; Accademia Chigiano, Siena, Italy. Served with Royal Signals, 1944–48. Repetiteur and Asst Conductor, Sadler's Wells Opera, 1951–52; Asst Conductor, BBC Scottish Orchestra, Glasgow, 1952–54; Staff Conductor, Sadler's Wells Opera, 1954–57; Musical Dir, Sadler's Wells Opera, 1957–59; Principal Conductor and Musical Dir, Scottish Nat. Orch., 1959–84 (Hon. Pres., 1985–). Principal Guest Conductor, Houston Symphony Orch., 1981–83. FRSA 1980. Hon. RAM 1969; Hon. FRCM, 1973; Hon. FRSAMD, 1973 (Pres., 1991–); Hon. RSA, 1975. Hon. LLD Aberdeen, 1968; Hon. DMus: Glasgow, 1972; Newcastle, 1990; DUniv: Stirling, 1972; Open, 1978; York, 1991. St Mungo Prize, 1970; ISM Distinguished Musician Award, 1976; Sibelius Medal, 1978. *Recreation:* reading. *Address:* 15 Cleveden Gardens, Glasgow G12 0PU. *T:* 041–339 6668. *Clubs:* Garrick, Oriental.

GIBSON, Anne, (Mrs John Bartell); National Officer, (Union for) Manufacturing, Science, Finance, since 1987; Member: TUC General Council, since 1989; Equal Opportunities Commission, since 1991; *b* 10 Dec. 1940; *d* of Harry Tasker and Jessie Tasker (*née* Roberts); *m* 1st, 1962, John Donald Gibson; one *d*; 2nd, 1988, John Bartell. *Educ:* Market Rasen C of E Sch.; Caistor Grammar Sch., Lincs; Chelmsford Coll. of Further Educn, 1970–71; Univ. of Essex, 1972–76 (BA Hons II 1, Govt). Sec., Penney and Porter Engrg Co., Lincoln, 1956; Cashier, Midland Bank, Market Rasen, 1959–62. Organiser, Saffron Walden Labour Party, 1966–70; Asst Sec., Organisation and Industrial Relns Dept, TUC, 1977–87. *Recreations:* Francophile, embroidery, reading, politics. *Address:* Park House, 64/66 Wandsworth Common North Side, SW18 2SH. *T:* 081–871 2100.

GIBSON, Sir Christopher (Herbert), 3rd Bt *cr* 1931; Sales Representative, National Homes Ltd, Abbotsford, BC, Canada; *b* 2 Feb. 1921; *s* of Sir Christopher H. Gibson, 2nd Bt, and Lady Dorothy E. O. Gibson (*née* Bruce); *S* father, 1962; *m* 1941, Lilian Lake Young, *d* of Dr George Byron Young, Colchester; one *s* three *d. Educ:* St Cyprian's, Eastbourne; St George's Coll., Argentina. Served, 1941–45 (5 war medals and stars): 28th Canadian Armd Regt (BCR), Lieut. Sugar Cane Plantation Manager, Leach's Argentine Estates, 1946–51; Manager, Encyclopædia Britannica, 1952–55; Design Draughtsman, Babcock & Wilcox, USA, 1956–57; Tea Plantation Manager, Liebig's, 1958–60; Ranch Manager, Liebig's Extract of Meat Co., 1961–64; Building Inspector, Industrias Kaiser, Argentina, 1964–68; Manager and part-owner, Lakanto Poultry Farms, 1969–76. *Recreations:* shooting, fishing, tennis, cricket. *Heir: s* Rev. Christopher Herbert Gibson, CP, *b* Argentina, 17 July 1948.

GIBSON, Rev. Sir David, 4th Bt *cr* 1926; Catholic Priest; *b* 18 July 1922; *s* of Sir Ackroyd Herbert Gibson, 3rd Bt; *S* father, 1975. Founder of Societas Navigatorum Catholica, 1954. *Address:* The Presbytery, Our Lady and St Neot, West Street, Liskeard, Cornwall PL14 6BW.

GIBSON, David; Under Secretary, Department of Economic Development, Northern Ireland, since 1987; *b* 8 Sept. 1939; *s* of Frank Edward Gibson and Nora Jessie Gibson (*née* Gurnhill); *m* 1963, Roberta Alexandra (*née* McMaster); one *s* two *d. Educ:* King Edward VI Grammar Sch., Retford. FCCA. GPO, 1958–63; MAFF, 1963–68; Belfast City Council, 1968–72; Dept of Commerce, NI, 1972–82; Dir of Accountancy Services, 1982–85, Asst Sec., 1985–87, Dept of Economic Develt, NI. *Recreations:* reading, music, walking. *Address:* Department of Economic Development, Netherleigh, Massey Avenue, Belfast BT4 2JP. *T:* Belfast (0232) 763244.

GIBSON, Vice-Adm. Sir Donald Cameron Ernest Forbes, KCB 1968 (CB 1965); DSC 1941; JP; *b* 17 March 1916; *s* of late Capt. W. L. D. Gibson, Queen's Own Cameron Highlanders, and of Elizabeth Gibson; *m* 1939, Marjorie Alice, *d* of H. C. Harding, Horley, Surrey; one *s. Educ:* Woodbridge Sch., Suffolk. Cadet, Brit. India SN Co. and Midshipman, Royal Naval Reserve, 1933–37; transf. to Royal Navy, 1937; specialised as Pilot, 1938. Served War of 1939–45: HMS Glorious, Ark Royal, Formidable, Audacity; trng Pilots in USA; Empire Central Flying Sch., 1942; Chief Flying Instr, Advanced Flying Sch., 1946–47; HMS Illustrious, 1947–48; Air Gp Comdr, HMS Theseus, 1948–49; Comdr (Air), RNAS Culdrose, 1950–52; RN Staff Course, 1952–53; Comdr (Air) HMS Indomitable and Glory, 1953–54; Capt. RNAS Brawdy, 1954–56, HMS Dainty, 1956–58; Dep. Dir Air Warfare, 1958–60; Canadian Nat. Defence Coll., 1960–61; Capt., HMS Ark Royal, 1961–63; Rear-Adm. 1963; Flag Officer: Aircraft Carriers, 1963–64; Naval Flying Trg, 1964–65; Naval Air Comd, 1965–68; Vice-Adm. 1967. Dir, HMS Belfast Trust, 1971–72; Mem., Gen. Cttee, Devon Community Housing Soc. Ltd, 1983–. JP Barnstaple 1973. *Recreation:* painting. *Address:* Lower Bealy Court, Chulmleigh, North Devon EX18 7EG. *T:* Chulmleigh (0769) 80264.

GIBSON, Sir Donald (Evelyn Edward), Kt 1962; CBE 1951; DCL; MA, FRIBA (Distinction Town Planning), FRTPI; Controller General, Ministry of Public Building and Works, 1967–69, now Consultant; *b* 11 Oct. 1908; *s* of late Prof. Arnold Hartley Gibson; *m* 1st, 1936, Winifred Mary (*née* McGowan) (decd); three *s* one *d*; 2nd, 1978, Grace Haines. *Educ:* Manchester Gram. Sch.; Manchester Univ. BA Hons Architecture; MA. Work in USA, 1931; private practice, 1933; professional Civil Service (Building Research), 1935; Dep. County Architect, Isle of Ely, 1937; City Architect and Town Planning Officer, County and City of Coventry, 1939; County Architect, Notts, 1955; Dir-Gen. of Works, War Office, 1958–62; Dir-Gen., R&D, MPBW, 1962–67; Hoffmann Wood Prof. of Architecture, University of Leeds, 1967–68. Mem. Central Housing Advisory Cttee, 1951, 1953 and 1954. President: RIBA, 1964–65; Dist Heating Assoc., 1971–. Hon. FLI 1968. *Publications:* various publications dealing with housing, planning and architecture in RIBA and RTPI Journals. *Recreation:* model railways. *Address:* Bryn Castell, Llanddona, Beaumaris, Gwynedd LL58 8TR. *T:* Beaumaris (0248) 810399.

GIBSON, Prof. Frank William Ernest, FRS 1976; FAA; Emeritus Professor of Biochemistry, and University Fellow, Australian National University, since 1989; *b* 22 July 1923; *s* of John William and Alice Ruby Gibson; *m* 1st, 1949, Margaret Isabel Nancy (marr. diss. 1979); two *d*; 2nd, 1980, Robin Margaret; one *s. Educ:* Queensland, Melbourne, and Oxford Univs. BSc, DSc (Melb.), DPhil (Oxon). Research Asst, Melbourne and Queensland Univs, 1938–47; Sen. Demonstrator, Melbourne Univ., 1948–49; ANU Scholar, Oxford, 1950–52. Melbourne University: Sen. Lectr, 1953–58; Reader in Chem. Microbiology, 1959–65; Prof. of Chem. Microbiology, 1965–66; Australian National University: Prof. of Biochem., 1967–88; Hd. of Biochem. Dept, 1967–76, Chm., Div. of Biochemical Scis, 1988, John Curtin Sch. of Medical Res.; Howard Florey Prof. of Medical Res., and Dir, John Curtin Sch. of Med. Res., 1977–79. Newton-Abraham Vis. Prof. and Fellow of Lincoln Coll., Oxford Univ., 1982–83. David Syme Research Prize, Univ. of Melb., 1963. FAA 1971. *Publications:* scientific papers on the biochemistry of bacteria, particularly the biosynthesis of aromatic compounds, energy metabolism. *Recreations:* tennis, skiing. *Address:* John Curtin School of Medical Research, PO Box 334, Canberra City, ACT 2601, Australia.

GIBSON, Harold Leslie George, OBE 1978 (MBE 1971); General President, National Union of Hosiery and Knitwear Workers, 1975–82; *b* 15 July 1917; *s* of George Robert and Ellen Millicent Gibson; *m* 1941, Edith Lunt (decd); one *s* one *d. Educ:* elementary and grammar schools, Liverpool. Officer of National Union of Hosiery and Knitwear Workers, 1949; General Secretary, 1962–75. Member: Monopolies and Mergers Commn, 1978–86; Management Cttee, Gen. Fedn of Trade Unions; TUC Textile Cttee; Exec. Cttee, British Textile Confdn; Knitting, Lace & Net Industry Training Board; Strategy Working Party for the Hosiery Industry. Pres., Internat. Textile, Garment and Leather Workers' Fedn, Brussels. Hon. LLM Leicester, 1982. JP 1949–77. *Recreations:* photography, golf, music. *Address:* 15 Links Road, Kibworth Beauchamp, Leicester LE8 0LD. *T:* (private) Kibworth (053753) 2149; (business) Leicester (0533) 556703.

GIBSON, John Peter; consultant; Chief Executive, Seaforth Maritime, 1986–88 (Deputy Chairman, 1978–83; Chairman, 1983–86); *b* 21 Aug. 1929; *s* of John Leighton Gibson and Norah Gibson; *m* 1954, Patricia Anne Thomas; two *s* three *d. Educ:* Caterham Sch.; Imperial Coll., London (BSc (Hons Mech. Engrg), ACGI). Post-grad. apprenticeship Rolls

Royce Derby, 1953–55; ICI (Billingham and Petrochemicals Div.), 1955–69; Man. Dir, Lummus Co., 1969–73; Dir Gen. Offshore Supplies Office, Dept of Energy, 1973–76. Dir, Taylor Woodrow Construction Ltd, 1989–90. *Recreations:* work, gardening, handyman. *Address:* Edbury Farm, Pennymoor, near Tiverton, Devon.

GIBSON, John Sibbald; historian; Under Secretary, Scottish Office, 1973–83, retired; *b* 1 May 1923; *s* of John McDonald Frame Gibson and Marion Watson Sibbald; *m* 1948, Moira Helen Gillespie; one *s* one *d*. *Educ:* Paisley Grammar Sch.; Glasgow Univ. Army, 1942–46, Lieut in No 1 Commando from 1943; Far East. Joined Admin. Grade Home Civil Service, 1947; Asst Principal, Scottish Home Dept, 1947–50; Private Sec. to Parly Under-Sec., 1950–51; Private Sec. to Perm. Under-Sec. of State, Scottish Office, 1952; Principal, Scottish Home Dept, 1953; Asst Sec., Dept of Agriculture and Fisheries for Scotland, 1962; Under Secretary: Scottish Office, 1973; Dept of Agriculture and Fisheries for Scotland, 1979. Mem., Agricl Res. Council, 1979–83. Organiser, Scottish Office Centenary Exhibn, 1985. *Publications:* Ships of the '45: the rescue of the Young Pretender, 1967; Deacon Brodie: Father to Jekyll and Hyde, 1977; The Thistle and the Crown, 1985; Playing the Scottish Card: the Franco-Jacobite invasion of 1708, 1988; (contrib.) The '45: to keep an image whole, 1988; (jtly) The Jacobite Threat: a source book, 1990. *Recreation:* historical research. *Address:* 28 Cramond Gardens, Edinburgh EH4 6PU. *T:* 031–336 2931. *Club:* Scottish Arts (Edinburgh).

GIBSON, John Walter; Chief of Operational Research, SHAPE Technical Centre, 1977–84; *b* 15 Jan. 1922; *s* of late Thomas John Gibson and Catherine Gibson (*née* Gregory), Bamburgh, Northumberland; *m* 1951, Julia, *d* of George Leslie Butler, Buxton, Derbyshire; two *s* one *d*. *Educ:* A. J. Dawson Sch., Durham; Sheffield Univ.; University Coll., London. RNVR, 1942–46. Sheffield Univ., 1940–42, 1946–47 (BSc); University Coll., London, 1947–48; Safety-in-Mines Research Estabt, 1948–53; BJSM, Washington, DC, 1953–56; Royal Armament Research and Develt Estabt, 1957–60; Head of Statistics Div., Ordnance Bd, 1961–64; Supt, Assessment Br., Royal Armament Research and Develt Estabt, 1964–66, Prin. Supt, Systems Div., 1966–69; Asst Chief Scientific Adviser (Studies), MoD, 1969–74; Under-Secretary: Cabinet Office, 1974–76; MoD, 1976–77. FSS 1953. *Address:* 17 Lyndhurst Drive, Sevenoaks, Kent TN13 2HD. *T:* Sevenoaks (0732) 454589.

GIBSON, Joseph, CBE 1980; PhD; CChem, FRSC; FEng, FInstE; consultant; Coal Science Adviser, National Coal Board, 1981–83 (Member for Science, 1977–81); *b* 10 May 1916; *m* 1944, Lily McFarlane Brown; one *s* one *d*. *Educ:* King's Coll. (now Univ. of Newcastle upon Tyne; MSc, PhD). Res., Northern Coke Res. Lab. 1938; Head of Chemistry Dept, Sunderland Technical Coll., and Lectr, Durham Univ., 1946; Chief Scientist, Northern Div., 1958, and Yorks Div., 1964, NCB; Director: Coal Res. Estab., 1968; Coal Utilisation Res., 1975. President: Inst. of Fuel, 1975–76; BCURA, 1977–81 (Chm. 1972–77). Lectures: Cadman Meml, 1980, 1983; Prof. Moore Meml, 1981; Brian H. Morgans Meml, 1983. Coal Science Lecture Medal, 1977; Carbonisation Sci. Medal, 1979. Hon. FIChemE. Hon. DCL Newcastle, 1981. *Publications:* Carbonisation of Coal, 1971; Coal and Modern Coal Processing, 1979; (jtly) Coal Utilisation: technology, economics and policy, 1981; papers on coal conversion and utilisation. *Recreations:* bridge, gardening. *Address:* 31 Charlton Close, Charlton Kings, Cheltenham, Glos. *T:* Cheltenham (0242) 517832.

GIBSON, Joseph David, CBE 1979; Ambassador of Fiji to Japan, 1984–87, retired; *b* 26 Jan. 1928; *s* of late Charles Ivan Gibson and Mamao Lavenia Gibson; *m* Emily Susan Bentley; three *s* two *d*. *Educ:* Levuka Public Sch., Suva; Marist Brothers Secondary Sch.; Auckland Univ., NZ (BA); Auckland Teachers' Coll. (Teachers' Cert.). Asst Teacher, Suva Boys' Grammar Sch., 1952–57; Principal, Suva Educnl Inst., 1957; Principal, Queen Victoria School, Fiji, 1961–62 (Asst Teacher, 1958–59; Sen. Master, 1959; 1st Asst, 1960); Sec. Sch. Inspector, Fiji Educn Dept, 1964–65; Asst Dir of Educn, 1966–69; Dep. Dir of Educn, 1970; Dir of Educn and Permanent Sec. for Educn, 1971–74; Dep. High Comr, London, 1974–76, High Comr, 1976–81; High Comr, New Zealand, 1981–83. Represented Fiji at: Dirs of Educn Conferences, Western Samoa and Pago Pago, 1968, Honolulu, 1970; Commonwealth Ministers of Educn Meeting, Canberra, 1971; Head of Fiji Delegn, Commonwealth Ministers of Educn Meeting, Jamaica, 1974. Member: Fiji Broadcasting Commn, 1971–73; Univ. Council, Univ. of South Pacific, 1971–74. *Recreations:* golf, fishing, represented Auckland and Suva, Fiji, in hockey. *Address:* 15 Naimawi Street, Lami, Suva, Fiji.

GIBSON, Col Leonard Young, CBE (mil.) 1961 (MBE (mil.) 1940); TD 1947; DL; President of Newcastle and District Beagles, since 1983 (Master, 1946–83); *b* 4 Dec. 1911; *s* of late William McLure Gibson and Wilhelmina Mitchell, Gosforth; *m* 1949, Pauline Mary Anthony; one *s* one *d*. *Educ:* Royal Grammar Sch., Newcastle upon Tyne; France and Germany. Service in TA, 1932–61: 72nd (N) Fd Regt RA TA, 1932–39; Staff Coll., Camberley, 1938–39; tsc; Bde Major RA: 50th (N) Div., rearguard Dunkirk, 1939–40 (MBE, despatches); 43rd (W) Div., 1941–42; GSO2, SE Army, 1942; GSO2 (Dirg Staff), Staff Coll., Camberley, 1942–43 (psc†); GSO1 Ops Eastern Comd, 1943–44; 2nd in Comd 107 Med. Regt S Notts Hussars, RHA TA, France, Belgium, Holland, Germany, 1944–45 (despatches; Croix de Guerre with Gold Star, France, 1944); GSO1 Mil. Govt Germany, 1945; Bty Comd, The Elswick Bty, 1947–51; OC 272 (N) Field Regt RA TA, 1956–58; Dep. Comdr RA 50th Inf. Div. TA, 1959–61; Colonel TA, retd. Mem., Northumberland T&AFA, 1958–68. Pres., Masters of Harriers and Beagles Assoc., 1968–69. DL Northumberland, 1971. *Recreations:* hunting, breeding horses and hounds. *Address:* Simonburn Cottage, Humshaugh, Northumberland NE46 4AR. *T:* Hexham (0434) 681402.

GIBSON, Captain Michael Bradford; Managing Director of Racquet Sports International Ltd, since 1975; *b* 20 March 1929; *s* of Lt-Col B. T. Gibson; *m* 1953, Mary Helen Elizabeth Legg; two *s*. *Educ:* Taunton Sch.; RMA Sandhurst; Sidney Sussex Coll., Cambridge (BA). Commnd into RE, 1948, retd 1961. Official Referee to Lawn Tennis Assoc. and All England Lawn Tennis Club, 1961–75. Mem., Inst. of Directors. *Recreations:* hunting, boating. *Address:* Courtyard House, Warnham, Horsham, Sussex. *T:* Horsham (0403) 65589. *Clubs:* All England Lawn Tennis and Croquet; Cottesmore Golf.

GIBSON, Air Vice-Marshal Michael John, OBE 1979; FRAeS; Director General of Policy and Plans, National Air Traffic Services, since 1991; *b* 2 Jan. 1939; *m* 1961, Dorothy Russell; one *s* one *d*. *Educ:* Imperial Coll., London (BSc); Selwyn Coll., Cambridge; National Defense Univ., Washington, DC. ACGI; FRAeS. Commnd RAFVR, 1959; commnd RAF, 1961; various appointments as fighter pilot and instructor; Personal Air Sec. to Air Force Minister, 1972–73; Officer Commanding: 45 Sqdn (Hunter), 1974–76; 20 Sqdn (Jaguar), 1976–79; RAF Brawdy, 1982–84; RAF Stanley, 1984–85; Air Officer Plans, HQ Strike Comd, 1987–88; Dir, Airspace Policy, NATS, 1988–91. *Recreations:* music (singing and church organ playing), boating. *Address:* CAA House, 45–59 Kingsway, WC2B 6TE. *T:* 071–832 5782. *Club:* Royal Air Force.

GIBSON, Paul Alexander; Founder, 1973, and Partner, since 1973, Sidell Gibson Partnership, Architects; *b* 11 Oct. 1941; *s* of Wing-Comdr Leslie Gibson and Betty Gibson (later Betty Stephens); *m* 1969, Julia Atkinson. *Educ:* Kingswood Sch., Bath; King's Coll., London; Canterbury Sch. of Architecture; Regent Street Polytechnic Sch. of Architecture (DipArch 1968). Worked for Farrell Grimshaw Partnership, 1968–69; Lectr, North Dakota State Univ., 1969; worked for Foster Associates, 1970–73. 3 RIBA awards, Good Housing, 1986; won open competition for redevelt of Grand Buildings, Trafalgar Square, 1986; won competition for redevelt of Winchester Barracks, 1988. *Recreations:* struggling pianist, keen gardener. *Address:* Fitzroy Yard, Fitzroy Road, NW1 8TP. *T:* 071–722 5009.

GIBSON, Rear-Adm. Peter Cecil, CB 1968; *b* 31 May 1913; 2nd *s* of Alexander Horace Cecil Gibson and Phyllis Zeline Cecil Gibson (*née* Baume); *m* 1938, Phyllis Anna Mary Hume, *d* of late Major N. H. Hume, IMS, Brecon; two *s* one *d*. *Educ:* Ealing Priory; RN Engrg Coll., Keyham. RN, 1931; HMS Norfolk, EI, 1936–38; maintenance test pilot, RN Aircraft Yard, Donibristle, 1940–41; Air Engr Officer, RNAS, St Merryn, 1941–42; Staff of RANAS, Indian Ocean, E Africa, 1942–43, Ceylon, 1943–44; Staff Air Engr. Off., British Pacific Fleet, 1945–46; Aircraft Maintenance and Repair Dept, 1946–49; loan service RAN, 1950–52; Trng Off., RNAS, Arbroath, 1952–54; Engr Off., HMS Gambia, 1954–56 and as Fleet Engr. Off, E Indies, 1955–56; Staff Engr. Off., Flag Off. Flying Trng, 1957–60; Dep. Dir Service Conditions, 1960–61; Dir Engr Officers' Appts, 1961–63; Supt RN Aircraft Yard, Fleetlands, 1963–65; Dep. Controller Aircraft (RN), Min. of Aviation, 1966–67, Min. of Technology, 1967–69, retired, 1969. ADC, 1965–66. Comdr 1946; Capt. 1957; Rear-Adm. 1966. Chm. United Services Catholic Assoc., 1966–69. *Recreations:* vintage cars, bridge. *Address:* Pangmere, Hampstead Norreys, Newbury, Berks RG16 0TR. *Club:* Army and Navy.

GIBSON, Hon. Sir Peter (Leslie), Kt 1981; **Hon. Mr Justice Peter Gibson;** Judge of the High Court of Justice, Chancery Division, since 1981; Chairman, Law Commission, since 1990; *b* 10 June 1934; *s* of late Harold Leslie Gibson and Martha Lucy (*née* Diercking); *m* 1968, Katharine Mary Beatrice Hadow; two *s* one *d*. *Educ:* Malvern Coll.; Worcester Coll., Oxford (Scholar). 2nd Lieut RA, 1953–55 (National Service). Called to the Bar, Inner Temple, 1960; Bencher, Lincoln's Inn, 1975. 2nd Jun. Counsel to Inland Revenue (Chancery), 1970–72; Jun. Counsel to the Treasury (Chancery), 1972–81. A Judge of the Employment Appeal Tribunal, 1984–86. *Address:* Royal Courts of Justice, Strand, WC2A 2LL.

GIBSON, Prof. Quentin Howieson, FRS 1969; Professor of Biochemistry and Molecular Biology, Cornell University, Ithaca, NY, 1966–90, now Emeritus; *b* 9 Dec. 1918; *s* of William Howieson Gibson, OBE, DSc; *m* 1951, Audrey Jane, *yr d* of G. H. S. Pinsent, CB, CMG, and Katharine Kentisbeare, *d* of Sir George Radford, MP; one *s* three *d*. *Educ:* Repton. MB, ChB, BAO, Belfast, 1941, MD 1944, PhD 1946, DSc 1951. Demonstrator in Physiology, Belfast, 1941–44; Lecturer in Physiology: Belfast, 1944–46; Sheffield Univ., 1946–55; Professor of Biochem., Sheffield Univ., 1955–63; Prof. of Biophys. Chem., Johnson Research Foundn, University of Pennsylvania, 1963–66. Fellow, Amer. Acad. of Arts and Sciences, 1971; MNAS 1982. *Recreation:* sailing. *Address:* 98 Dodge Road, Ithaca, NY 14850, USA.

GIBSON, Rt. Hon. Sir Ralph (Brian), PC 1985; Kt 1977; **Rt. Hon. Lord Justice Ralph Gibson;** a Lord Justice of Appeal, since 1985; *b* 17 Oct. 1922; 2nd *s* of Roy and Emily Gibson; *m* 1949, Ann Chapman Ruether, Chicago; one *s* two *d*. *Educ:* Charterhouse; Brasenose Coll., Oxford (Hon. Fellow 1986). MA Oxon 1948. Army Service, 1941–45: Lieut, 1st KDG; Captain, TJFF. Called to Bar, Middle Temple, 1948, Bencher 1974; QC 1968. A Recorder of the Crown Court, 1972–77; Judge of the High Court of Justice, Queen's Bench Div., 1977–85. Chm., Law Commn, 1981–85. Bigelow Teaching Fellow, University of Chicago, 1948–49. Member: Council of Legal Educn, 1971–86; Parole Bd, 1979–81; Pres., Central Council of Probation Cttees, 1982–86. Hon. LLD Dalhousie, 1983. *Address:* 8 Ashley Gardens, SW1P 1QD. *T:* 071–828 9670. *Clubs:* Garrick; Emsworth Sailing.

GIBSON, Prof. Robert Dennis, PhD, DSc; FIMA, FAIM; first Vice-Chancellor, Queensland University of Technology, since 1989; *b* 13 April 1942; *m*; one *s* two *d*. *Educ:* Hull Univ. (BSc Hons); Newcastle upon Tyne Univ. (MSc, PhD); DSc CNAA. FIMA 1977; FAIM 1982; Asst Lectr, Maths Dept, Univ. of Newcastle upon Tyne, 1966–67; Scientific Officer, Culham Plasma Lab., UKAEA, 1967–68; Lectr in Maths, Univ. of Newcastle upon Tyne, 1968–69; Sen. Lectr, Maths and Statistics, Teesside Polytechnic, 1969–77; Head, Dept of Maths, Stats and Computing (later Sch. of Maths, Stats and Computing), Newcastle upon Tyne Polytechnic, 1977–82; Queensland Institute of Technology: Dep. Dir then Actg Dir, 1982–83; Dir, 1983–89. Mem., 1988–92, Dep. Chm., 1991–92, Aust. Res. Council. *Publications:* numerous research papers on various aspects of mathematical modelling. *Recreations:* jogging, cricket. *Address:* Queensland University of Technology, GPO Box 2434, Brisbane, Qld 4001, Australia.

GIBSON, Prof. Robert Donald Davidson, PhD; Professor of French, University of Kent at Canterbury, since 1965 (Master of Rutherford College, 1985–90); *b* Hackney, London, 21 Aug. 1927; *o s* of Nicol and Ann Gibson, Leyton, London; *m* 1953, Sheila Elaine, *o d* of Bertie and Ada Goldsworthy, Exeter, Devon; three *s*. *Educ:* Leyton County High Sch. for Boys; King's Coll., London; Magdalene Coll., Cambridge; Ecole Normale Supérieure, Paris. BA (First Class Hons. French) London, 1948; PhD Cantab. 1953. Asst Lecturer, St Salvator's Coll., University of St Andrews, 1954–55; Lecturer, Queen's Coll., Dundee, 1955–58; Lecturer, Aberdeen Univ., 1958–61; Prof., Queen's Univ. of Belfast, 1961–65. *Publications:* The Quest of Alain-Fournier, 1953; Modern French Poets on Poetry, 1961; (ed) Le Bestiaire Inattendu, 1961; Roger Martin du Gard, 1961; La Mésentente Cordiale, 1963; (ed) Brouart et le Désordre, 1964; (ed) Provinciales, 1965; (ed) Le Grand Meaulnes, 1968; The Land Without a Name, 1975; Alain-Fournier and Le Grand Meaulnes, 1986; (ed) Studies in French Fiction, 1988; Annals of Ashdon, 1988; reviews and articles in: French Studies, Modern Language Review, The London Magazine, Times Literary Supplement, Encyclopædia Britannica, Collier's Encyclopædia. *Recreations:* reading, writing, talking. *Address:* 7 Sunnymead, Tyler Hill, Canterbury, Kent CT2 9NW.

GIBSON, Roy; Special Adviser to the Director-General, International Maritime Satellite Organisation, since 1987; Director General, British National Space Centre, 1985–87; *b* 4 July 1924; *s* of Fred and Jessie Gibson; *m* 1st, 1946, Jean Fallowes (marr. diss. 1971); one *s* one *d*; 2nd, 1971, Inga Elgerus. *Educ:* Chorlton Grammar Sch.; Wadham College, Oxford; SOAS. Malayan Civil Service, 1948–58; Health and Safety Br., UKAEA, 1958–66; European Space Research Orgn, 1967–75 (Dir of Admin, 1970–75); Dir Gen., European Space Agency, 1975–80; aerospace consultant, 1980–85. DSC (Kedah, Malaysia), 1953; Das Grosse Silberne Ehrenzeichen mit Stern (Austria), 1977. *Publications:* numerous articles in aerospace technical jls. *Recreations:* music, chess, walking. *Address:* 8 Battersea Bridge Road, SW11 3AG. *T:* 071–585 1302. *Club:* Naval and Military.

GIBSON, Ven. Terence Allen; Archdeacon of Ipswich, since 1987; *b* 23 Oct. 1937; *s* of Fred William Allen and Joan Hazel Gibson. *Educ:* Jesus Coll., Cambridge (MA); Cuddesdon Coll., Oxford. Curate of St Chad, Kirkby, 1963–66; Warden of Centre 63, Kirkby C of E Youth Centre, 1966–75; Rector of Kirkby, Liverpool, 1975–84; RD of

Walton, Liverpool, 1979–84; Archdeacon of Suffolk, 1984–87. *Address*: 99 Valley Road, Ipswich, Suffolk IP1 4NF. *T*: Ipswich (0473) 250333.

GIBSON, Thomas, FRCSE, FRCSGlas, FRSE; Director, Glasgow and West of Scotland Regional Plastic and Maxillofacial Surgery Service, 1970–80; Consultant Plastic Surgeon to Greater Glasgow Health Board (formerly Western Regional Hospital Board), 1947–80; *b* 24 Nov. 1915; *s* of late Thomas Gibson and Mary Munn; *m* 1944, Patricia Muriel McFeat; two *s* two *d*. *Educ*: Paisley Grammar Sch.; Glasgow Univ. (MB, ChB 1938). FRCSE 1941, FRFPSG 1955, FRCSGlas 1962; FRSE 1974. House Surg. and Phys., Western Infirmary, Glasgow, 1939–40; Asst Lectr in Surg., Glasgow Univ., and Extra Dispensary Surg., Western Infirm., Glasgow, 1941–42; full-time appt with MRC, Burns Unit, Glasgow Royal Infirm., 1942–44; RAMC, 1944–47: Lieut, rank of Major 1945; OC No 1 Indian Maxillofacial Unit, 1945–47. Emeritus Prof., Bioengrg Unit, Univ. of Strathclyde, 1985– (Vis. Prof., 1966–85). Royal Coll. of Physicians and Surgeons of Glasgow: Hon. Librarian, 1963–73; Visitor, 1975–76; Pres., 1977–78. Hon. FRACS 1977; Hon. FRCS 1988. Hon. DSc Strathclyde, 1972. Editor, British Jl of Plastic Surgery, 1968–79. *Publications*: Modern Trends in Plastic Surgery: vol. 1, 1964; vol. 2, 1966; The Royal College of Physicians and Surgeons of Glasgow, 1983; contrib. med. and surg. jls. *Recreations*: history, horticulture, handicrafts. *Address*: Eastbrae, 26 Potterhill Avenue, Paisley PA2 8BA. *T*: 041–884 2181.

GIBSON, Wilford Henry, CBE 1980; QPM 1976; Assistant Commissioner (Administration and Operations), Metropolitan Police, 1977–84, retired; *b* 12 Oct. 1924; *s* of late Ernest Gibson and Frances Mary (*née* Kitching); *m* 1949, Betty Ann Bland; two *d*. Served War, Signaller, RAF, 1943–47. Joined Metropolitan Police as Constable, 1947; Inspector 1960; Supt 1965; Comdr 1971; Dep. Asst Comr, A Dept (Operations), 1974. Chm., Met. Police Flying Club and Met. Police Modern Pentathlon Club, 1976–84. OStJ 1977. *Recreations*: riding, boxing, swimming, flying. *Club*: Special Forces.

GIBSON, Major William David; Chairman, W. J. Tatem Ltd, since 1974 (Director, since 1957); *b* 26 Feb. 1925; *s* of late G. C. Gibson, OBE, Landwade Hall, Exning, Newmarket, Suffolk; *m* 1st, 1959, Charlotte Henrietta (*d* 1973), *d* of N. S. Pryor; three *s* one *d*; 2nd, 1975, Jane Marion, *d* of late Col L. L. Hassell, DSO, MC. *Educ*: St Peter's Court; Harrow; Trinity Coll., Cambridge. Commissioned into Welsh Guards, July 1945; retired as Major, 1957. Dir, West of England Ship Owners Mutual Protection & Indemnity Assoc., 1959–86; Chairman: Atlantic Shipping and Trading Co., 1969–77; Internat. Shipowners Investment Co., SA Luxembourg, 1978–83; Waverley Components and Products, 1990–. National Hunt Cttee, Oct. 1959– (Sen. Steward, 1966); Jockey Club, 1966– (Dep. Sen. Steward, 1969–71); Tattersalls Cttee, 1963–69 (Chm., 1967–69). Master, Worshipful Co. of Farriers, 1979. *Recreations*: racing (won 4 Grand Military Gold Cups, 1950–52 and 1956); shooting, sailing. *Address*: Bishopswood Grange, Bishopswood, near Ross-on-Wye, Herefordshire HR9 5QX. *T*: Dean (0594) 60444. *Clubs*: Cavalry and Guards, Royal Thames Yacht; Royal Yacht Squadron.

GIBSON-BARBOZA, Mario, GCMG 1968; Brazilian Ambassador to the Court of St James's, 1982–86; *b* Olinda, Pernambuco, 13 March 1918; *s* of Oscar Bartholomeu Alves Barboza and Evangelina Gibson Barboza; *m* 1975, Julia Blacker Baldassarri Gibson-Barboza. *Educ*: Law School of Recife, Pernambuco (graduated in Law, 1937); Superior War College, 1951. Entered Brazilian Foreign Service, 1940; served: Houston, Washington and Brussels, 1943–54; Minister-Counsellor: Buenos Aires, 1956–59; Brazilian Mission to United Nations, New York, 1959–60; Ambassador: to Vienna, 1962–66; to Asunción, 1967–68; Secretary General for Foreign Affairs, 1968–69; Ambassador to Washington, 1969; Minister of State for External Relations, 1969–74; Ambassador: to Athens, 1974–77; to Rome, 1977–82. Several Grand Crosses of Orders of Brazil and other countries. *Recreations*: riding, reading, theatre. *Address*: c/o Ministry of Foreign Affairs, Palácio do Hamaraty, Esplanada dos Ministérios, 70.170 Brasília, DF, Brazil. *Clubs*: Athenæum, Travellers', White's; Jockey Clube Brasileiro (Rio de Janeiro).

GIBSON-CRAIG-CARMICHAEL, Sir David Peter William, 15th Bt *cr* 1702 (Gibson Carmichael) and 8th Bt *cr* 1831; *b* 21 July 1946; *s* of Sir Archibald Henry William Gibson-Craig-Carmichael, 14th Bt and Rosemary Anita (*d* 1979), *d* of George Duncan Crew, Santiago, Chile; *S* father, 1969; *m* 1973, Patricia, *d* of Marcos Skarnic, Santiago, Chile; one *s* one *d*. *Educ*: Queen's Univ., Canada (BSc, Hons Geology, 1971). *Heir*: *s* Peter William Gibson-Craig-Carmichael, *b* 29 Dec. 1975.

GIBSON-WATT, Baron *cr* 1979 (Life Peer), of the Wye in the District of Radnor; **James David Gibson-Watt,** MC 1943 and 2 Bars; PC 1974; DL; a Forestry Commissioner, 1976–86; Chairman, Timber Growers United Kingdom, 1987–90; *b* 11 Sept. 1918; *er s* of late Major James Miller Gibson-Watt, DL, JP; *m* 1942, Diana, 2nd *d* of Sir Charles Hambro; two *s* two *d* (and one *s* decd). *Educ*: Eton; Trinity Coll (BA). Welsh Guards, 1939–46; N African and Italian campaigns. Contested (C) Brecon and Radnor constituency, 1950 and 1951; MP (C) Hereford, Feb. 1956–Sept. 1974; a Lord Commissioner of the Treasury, 1959–61; Minister of State, Welsh Office, 1970–74. FRAgS; Pres., Royal Welsh Agric. Soc., 1976 (Chm. Council, 1976–). Chm., Council on Tribunals, 1980–86. Mem., Historic Buildings Council, Wales, 1975–79. DL Powys, 1968; JP Rhayader, retd 1989. *Address*: Doldowlod, Llandrindod Wells, Powys. *T*: Newbridge-on-Wye (059789) 208. *Club*: Boodle's.

GICK, Rear-Adm. Philip David, CB 1963; OBE 1946; DSC and Bar, 1942; Chairman, Emsworth Shipyard Group, 1965–90; *b* 22 Feb. 1913; *s* of late Sir William John Gick, CB, CBE; *m* 1938, Aylmer Rowntree; one *s* three *d*. *Educ*: St Lawrence Coll., Ramsgate. Joined RN, 1931; qualified as Pilot, 1936. Capt. 1952; Comd HMS Daring, RNAS, Lossiemouth, HMS Bulwark, 1952–58; Rear-Adm. 1961; Flag Officer, Naval Flying Training, 1961–64, retd. *Recreation*: sailing. *Address*: Furzefield, Bosham Hoe, West Sussex PO18 8ET. *T*: Bosham (0243) 572219. *Clubs*: Royal Yacht Squadron, Royal Ocean Racing; Royal Naval Sailing Association; Bosham Sailing.

GIDDEN, Barry Owen Barton, CMG 1962; *b* Southampton, 4 July 1915; *s* of late Harry William Gidden, MA, PhD. *Educ*: King Edward VI Sch., Southampton; Jesus Coll., Cambridge (Scholar; Class. Tripos Pts 1 and 2; BA). Apptd Asst Principal, HM Office of Works, 1939. Served War of 1939–45: BEF, 1939–40, Major 1943. Principal, Min. of Works, 1946; Private Sec. to Minister of Works, 1946–48; Principal, Colonial Office, 1949, Asst Sec 1951; Counsellor, UK Mission to UN, New York, 1954–58; Establishment Officer, Colonial Office, 1958–65; Asst Sec., DHSS, 1965–75. *Recreation*: golf. *Address*: 15 Chesham Street, SW1X 8ND. *T*: 071–235 4185. *Club*: Walton Heath.

GIDDENS, Prof. Anthony, PhD; Professor of Sociology, in the Faculty of Economics and Politics, since 1985, and Fellow of King's College, since 1969, University of Cambridge; *b* 18 Jan. 1938; *s* of T. G. Giddens; *m* 1963, Jane M. Ellwood. *Educ*: Hull Univ. (BA); LSE (MA); MA 1970, PhD 1974, Cantab. Lectr in Sociology, subseq. Reader, Cambridge Univ., 1969–85. *Publications*: Capitalism and Modern Social Theory, 1971; (ed) Sociology of Suicide, 1972; Politics and Sociology in the Thought of Max Weber, 1972; (ed and trans) Emile Durkheim: Selected Writings, 1972; (ed) Positivism and Sociology, 1974; New Rules of Sociological Method, 1976; Studies in Social and Political Theory, 1976; Central Problems in Social Theory, 1979; Class Structure of the Advanced Societies, 2nd edn 1981; Contemporary Critique of Historical Materialism: vol. 1, Power, Property and State, 1981, vol. 2, Nation, State and Violence, 1985; (jtly) Classes, Power and Conflict, 1982; Profiles and Critiques in Social Theory, 1983; (ed jtly) Social Class and the Division of Labour, 1983; Constitution of Society, 1984; Durkheim, 1985; Sociology: a brief but critical introduction, 1986; Social Theory and Modern Sociology, 1987; (ed jtly) Social Theory Today, 1987; Sociology, 1989; The Consequences of Modernity, 1990. *Address*: King's College, Cambridge.

GIDDINGS, Air Marshal Sir (Kenneth Charles) Michael, KCB 1975; OBE 1953; DFC 1945; AFC 1950 and Bar 1955; Independent Panel Inspector, Department of the Environment, since 1979; *b* 27 Aug. 1920; *s* of Charles Giddings and Grace Giddings (*née* Gregory); *m* 1946, Elizabeth McConnell; two *s* two *d*. *Educ*: Ealing Grammar Sch. Conscripted, RAF, 1940; Comd, 129 Sqdn, 1944; Empire Test Pilots Sch., 1946; Test pilot, RAE, 1947–50; HQ Fighter Command, 1950–52; RAF Staff Coll., 1953; OC, Flying Wing, Waterbeach, 1954–56; CFE, 1956–58; OC, 57 Sqdn, 1958–60; Group Captain Ops, Bomber Command, 1960–62; Supt of Flying, A&AEE, 1962–64; Dir Aircraft Projects, MoD, 1964–66; AOC, Central Reconnaissance Estabt, 1967–68; ACAS (Operational Requirements), 1968–71; Chief of Staff No 18 (M) Group, Strike Command, RAF, 1971–73; Dep. Chief of Defence Staff, Op. Requirements, 1973–76. Dir, Nat. Counties Building Soc., 1982–85. *Recreations*: golf, gardening, music. *Address*: 159 Long Lane, Tilehurst, Reading, Berks. *T*: Reading (0734) 423012.

GIELGUD, Sir (Arthur) John, CH 1977; Kt 1953; Hon. LLD St Andrews 1950; Hon. DLitt Oxon 1953; Hon. DLitt London 1977; Actor; *b* 14 April 1904; *s* of late Frank Gielgud and Kate Terry Lewis; unmarried. *Educ*: Westminster. First appearance on stage at Old Vic, 1921; among parts played are Lewis Dodd in Constant Nymph, Inigo Jollifant in The Good Companions, Richard II in Richard of Bordeaux, Hamlet, and Romeo; Valentine in Love for Love, Ernest Worthing in The Importance of Being Earnest, Macbeth and King Lear. Directed Macbeth, Piccadilly, 1942. Raskolnikoff in Crime and Punishment, Jason in The Medea, New York, 1947. Eustace in The Return of the Prodigal, Globe, 1948; directed The Heiress, Haymarket, 1949; directed and played Thomas Mendip, The Lady's not for Burning, Globe, 1949; Shakespeare Festival, Stratford-on-Avon, 1950; Angelo in Measure for Measure, Cassius in Julius Caesar, Benedick in Much Ado About Nothing, the name part in King Lear; directed Much Ado About Nothing and King Lear; Shakespeare season at Phoenix, 1951–52; Leontes in The Winter's Tale, Phoenix, 1951, directed Much Ado About Nothing and played Benedick, 1952. Season at Lyric, Hammersmith, 1953; directed Richard II and The Way of the World (played Mirabel); played Jaffeir in Venice Preserved; directed A Day by the Sea, and played Julian Anson, Haymarket, Nov. 1953–54; also directed Charley's Aunt, New Theatre, Dec. 1953, and directed The Cherry Orchard, Lyric, May, 1954, and Twelfth Night, Stratford, 1955; played in King Lear and Much Ado About Nothing (also produced Much Ado), for Shakespeare Memorial Theatre Company (London, provinces and continental tour), 1955; directed The Chalk Garden, Haymarket, 1956; produced (with Noel Coward) Nude with Violin, and played Sebastien, Globe, 1956–57; produced The Trojans, Covent Garden, 1957; played Prospero, Stratford, and Drury Lane, 1957; played James Callifer in The Potting Shed, Globe, 1958 and Wolsey in Henry VIII, Old Vic, 1958; directed Variation on A Theme, 1958; produced The Complaisant Lover, Globe, 1959; (Shakespeare's) Ages of Man, Queen's, 1959 (recital, based on Shakespeare anthology of G. Rylands); previous recitals at Edinburgh Fest. and in US, also subseq. in US, at Haymarket, 1960 and tour of Australia and NZ, 1963–64; Gothenburg, Copenhagen, Warsaw, Helsinki, Leningrad, Moscow and Dublin, 1964; produced Much Ado About Nothing, at Cambridge, Mass, Festival, and subseq. in New York, 1959; prod. Five Finger Exercise, Comedy, 1958, NY, 1959; acted in The Last Joke, Phœnix, 1960; prod. Britten's A Midsummer Night's Dream, Royal Opera House, 1961; prod Big Fish Little Fish, New York, 1961; prod Dazzling Prospect, Globe, 1961. Stratford-on-Avon Season, 1961: took part of Othello, also of Gaieff in The Cherry Orchard, Aldwych, 1962; produced The School for Scandal, Haymarket, 1962; prod The School for Scandal, and played Joseph Surface, USA tour, and New York, 1962–63; dir. The Ides of March, and played Julius Caesar, Haymarket, 1963; dir. Hamlet, Canada and USA, 1964; Julian in Tiny Alice, New York, 1965; played Ivanov and directed Ivanov, Phœnix, 1965, United States and Canada, 1966; played Orgon in Tartuffe, Nat. Theatre, 1967; directed Halfway up the Tree, Queen's, 1967; played Oedipus in Oedipus, Nat. Theatre, 1968; produced Don Giovanni, Coliseum, 1968; played Headmaster in 40 Years On, Apollo, 1968; played Sir Gideon in The Battle of Shrivings, Lyric, 1970; Home, Royal Court, 1970, NY 1971 (Evening Standard Best Actor award and Tony award, NY, 1971); dir, All Over, NY, 1971; Caesar and Cleopatra, Chichester Festival, 1971; Veterans, Royal Ct, 1972; dir, Private Lives, Queen's, 1972; dir, The Constant Wife, Albery, 1973; played Prospero, Nat. Theatre, 1974; Bingo, Royal Court, 1974; dir, The Gay Lord Quex, Albery, 1975; No Man's Land, Nat. Theatre, 1975, Toronto, Washington, NY, 1977; Julius Caesar, Volpone, Nat. Theatre, 1977; Half-Life, NT and Duke of York's, 1977; The Best of Friends, Apollo, 1988; *films include*: (GB and US) The Good Companions, 1932; The Secret Agent, 1937; The Prime Minister (Disraeli), 1940; Julius Caesar (Cassius), 1952; Richard III (Duke of Clarence), 1955; The Barretts of Wimpole Street (Mr Moulton Barrett), 1957; St Joan (Warwick), 1957; Becket (Louis VII), 1964; The Loved One, 1965; Chimes at Midnight, 1966; Mister Sebastian, 1967; The Charge of the Light Brigade, 1968; Shoes of the Fisherman, 1968; Oh What a Lovely War!, 1968; Julius Caesar, 1970; Eagle in a Cage, Lost Horizon, 1973; 11 Harrowhouse, 1974; Gold, 1974; Murder on the Orient Express, 1974; Aces High, 1976; Providence, Joseph Andrews, Portrait of a Young Man, Caligula, 1977; The Human Factor, The Elephant Man, 1979; The Conductor, Murder by Decree, Sphinx, Chariots of Fire, The Formula, Arthur (Oscar, 1982), 1980; Lion of the Desert, 1981; Priest of Love, 1982; Wagner, Invitation to the Wedding, Scandalous, The Wicked Lady, 1983; Camille, 1984; The Shooting Party, 1985; Plenty, 1985; Leave All Fair; The Whistle Blower, 1987; Arthur on the Rocks, Getting Things Right, Loser Takes All, 1988; Prospero's Books, 1991. President: Shakespeare Reading Soc., 1958–; RADA, 1977–89 (Hon. Fellow, 1989). Has appeared on television, including The Mayfly and the Frog, 1966; Great Acting, Dorian Gray, 1967; In Good King Charles's Golden Days, 1970; Parson's Pleasure, 1980; Richard Wagner, Brideshead Revisited, 1981; Inside the Third Reich, Neck, The Scarlet and the Black, 1983; presenter of Six Centuries of Verse, 1984; Time After Time, 1985; Marco Polo, Oedipus the King, 1986; War and Remembrance, The Canterville Ghost, 1987; Summer's Lease, 1989. Special award for services to theatre, Laurence Olivier Awards, 1985. Hon. degree Brandeis Univ. Companion, Legion of Honour, 1960. *Publications*: Early Stages, 1938; Stage Directions, 1963; Distinguished Company, 1972; (jtly) An Actor and His Time (autobiog.), 1979; Backward Glances, 1989. *Recreations*: music, painting. *Address*: South Pavilion, Wotton Underwood, Aylesbury, Bucks. *Clubs*: Garrick, Arts; Players' (New York).

GIELGUD, Maina; free-lance ballerina; Artistic Director, Australian Ballet, since 1983; *b* 14 Jan. 1945; *d* of Lewis Gielgud and Elisabeth Grussner. *Educ*: BEPC (French). Ballet du Marquis de Cuevas, 1962–63; Ballet Classique de France, 1965–67; Ballet du XXème Siècle, Maurice Béjart, 1967–72; London Festival Ballet, 1972–77; Royal Ballet, 1977–78;

free-lance, 1978–; rehearsal director, London City Ballet, 1981–82. Hon. AO 1991. *Address:* c/o Australian Ballet, 2 Kavanagh Street, South Melbourne, Vic 3205, Australia; Stirling Court, 3 Marshall Street, W1. *T:* 071–734 6612.

GIFFARD, family name of **Earl of Halsbury.**

GIFFARD, Adam Edward; *b* 3 June 1934; *o s* of 3rd Earl of Halsbury, *qv* (but does not use courtesy title Viscount Tiverton); *m* 1st, 1963, Ellen, *d* of late Brynjolf Hovde; 2nd, 1976, Joanna Elizabeth, *d* of late Frederick Harry Cole; two *d. Address:* 406 James Street, Milford, Pa 18337, USA.

GIFFARD, Sir (Charles) Sydney (Rycroft), KCMG 1984 (CMG 1976); HM Diplomatic Service, retired; *b* 30 Oct. 1926; *s* of Walter Giffard and Minna Giffard (*née* Cotton); *m* 1st, 1951, Wendy Vidal (marr. diss. 1976); one *s* one *d*; 2nd, 1976, Hazel Roberts, OBE. Served in Japan, 1952; Foreign Office, 1957; Berne, 1961; Tokyo, 1964; Counsellor, FCO, 1968; Royal Coll. of Defence Studies, 1971; Counsellor, Tel Aviv, 1972; Minister in Tokyo, 1975–80; Ambassador to Switzerland, 1980–82; Dep. Under-Sec. of State, FCO, 1982–84; Ambassador to Japan, 1984–86. Gov., Repton Sch. Hon. Fellow, Wadham Coll., Oxford Univ., 1991. *Address:* Winkelbury House, Berwick St John, Wilts, near Shaftesbury, Dorset. *Club:* Lansdowne.
See also Dr B. J. Greenhill.

GIFFORD, family name of **Baron Gifford.**

GIFFORD, 6th Baron, *cr* 1824; **Anthony Maurice Gifford;** QC 1982; Barrister at Law, practising since 1966; Attorney-at-Law, Jamaica, since 1990; *b* 1 May 1940; *s* of 5th Baron Gifford and Lady Gifford (*née* Margaret Allen) (*d* 1990), Sydney, NSW; *S* father, 1961; *m* 1st, 1965, Katherine Ann (marr. diss. 1988), *o d* of Dr Mundy; one *s* one *d*; 2nd, 1988, Elean Roslyn, *d* of Bishop David Thomas, Kingston, Jamaica. *Educ:* Winchester Coll. (scholar); King's Coll., Cambridge (scholar; BA 1961). Student at Middle Temple, 1959–62, called to the Bar, 1962. Chairman: Cttee for Freedom in Mozambique, Angola and Guiné, 1968–75; Mozambique Angola Cttee, 1982–90. Chairman: N Kensington Neighbourhood Law Centre, 1974–77 (Hon. Sec., 1970–74); Legal Action Gp, 1978–83; Vice-Chm., Defence and Aid Fund (UK), 1983–. Pres., Cttee for Human Rights, Grenada, 1987–; Vice-Pres., Haldane Soc. of Socialist Lawyers, 1986–. Chairman: Broadwater Farm Inquiry, 1986; Liverpool 8 Inquiry, 1988–89. *Publication:* Where's the Justice?, 1986. *Heir: s* Hon. Thomas Adam Gifford, *b* 1 Dec. 1967. *Address:* 8 King's Bench Walk, Temple, EC4Y 7DU. *T:* 071–353 7851, *Fax:* 071–936 2584.

GIFFORD, Prof. (Charles) Henry, FBA 1983; Winterstoke Professor of English, University of Bristol, 1967–75, Professor of English and Comparative Literature, Jan.-July 1976, retired; *b* 17 June 1913; *s* of Walter Stanley Gifford and Constance Lena Gifford (*née* Henry); *m* 1938, Mary Rosamond van Ingen; one *s* one *d. Educ:* Harrow Sch.; Christ Church, Oxford. BA 1936, MA 1946. War Service, 1940–46, Royal Armoured Corps; Univ. of Bristol: Asst Lectr, 1946; Sen. Lectr, 1955; Prof. of Modern English Literature, 1963. Clark Lectr, Trinity Coll., Cambridge, 1985. Gen. Editor, Cambridge Studies in Russian Literature, 1980–84. *Publications:* The Hero of his Time, 1950; (with Charles Tomlinson) Castilian Ilexes: versions from Antonio Machado, 1963; The Novel in Russia, 1964; Comparative Literature, 1969; Tolstoy: a critical anthology, 1971; Pasternak: a critical study, 1977; Tolstoy, 1982; Poetry in a Divided World (1985 Clark Lectures), 1986; articles and reviews on English and comparative literature. *Address:* 10 Hyland Grove, Bristol BS9 3NR. *T:* Bristol (0272) 502504.

GIFFORD, Michael Brian; Managing Director and Chief Executive, Rank Organisation, since 1983; *b* 9 Jan. 1936; *s* of Kenneth Gifford and Maude Gifford (*née* Palmer); *m* Asa Margareta Lundin; one *s* one *d* (one *s* one *d* by previous marr.). *Educ:* LSE (BSc Econ). Joined Leo Computers (later part of ICL), 1960; Man. Dir, ICL (Pacific), 1973–75; Chief Exec., Cadbury Schweppes Australia, 1975–78; Finance Dir, Cadbury Schweppes plc, 1978–83. *Address:* c/o Rank Organisation plc, 6 Connaught Place, W2 2EZ. *T:* 071–706 1111.

GIGGALL, Rt. Rev. George Kenneth, OBE 1961; Assistant Bishop, Diocese of Blackburn, since 1982; *b* 15 April 1914; *s* of Arthur William and Matilda Hannah Giggall; unmarried. *Educ:* Manchester Central High Sch.; Univ. of Manchester; St Chad's Coll., Univ. of Durham. BA, DipTheol. Deacon, 1939; Priest, 1940. Curate of St Alban's Cheetwood, Dio. Manchester, 1939–41, St Elisabeth's Reddish, 1941–45; Chaplain, RN, 1945; HMS Braganza, 1945; 34th Amphibious Support Regt, RM, 1945–46; Chaplain, Sch. of Combined Ops, 1946–47; HMS: Norfolk, 1947–49; Ocean, 1949–50; Flotilla Comd Mediterranean and HMS Phoenicia, 1950–52; HMS Campania for Operation Hurricane, 1952; RNC Dartmouth, 1952–53; HMS: Centaur, 1953–56; Ceylon, 1956–58; Fisgard, 1958–60; Royal Arthur and Lectr RAF Chaplains' Sch., 1960–63; HMS: Eagle, 1963–65; Drake, 1965–69; QHC, 1967–69; Dean of Gibraltar and Officiating Chaplain, HMS Rooke and Flag Officer, Gibraltar, 1969–73; Bishop of St Helena, 1973–79; Chaplain of San Remo with Bordighera, Italy, and Auxiliary Bishop, dio. of Gibraltar, 1979–81. *Recreation:* music. *Address:* Fosbrooke House, 8 Clifton Drive, Lytham, Lancs FY8 5RQ. *T:* Lytham (0253) 735683. *Clubs:* Commonwealth Trust, Sion College; Exiles (Ascension Island).

GILBART, Andrew James; QC 1991; *b* 13 Feb. 1950; *s* of Albert Thomas Gilbart and Carol Christie Gilbart; *m* 1979, Morag Williamson; one *s* one *d. Educ:* Westminster Sch. (Queen's Scholar); Trinity Hall, Cambridge (MA). Called to the Bar, Middle Temple, 1972; elected to Northern Circuit, 1973. Mem. Cttee, Local Govt and Planning, Bar Assoc., 1988–91. *Publications:* articles in Jl of Planning and Environment Law and Local Govt Chronicle. *Recreations:* history, walking, theatre. *Address:* 40 King Street, Manchester M2 6BA. *T:* 061–832 9082; 4 Breams Buildings, EC4A 1AQ. *T:* 071–353 5835. *Club:* Heaton Chapel Reform (Heaton Moor).

GILBART-DENHAM, Lt-Col Seymour Vivian; Crown Equerry, since 1987; *b* 10 Oct. 1939; *s* of Major Vivian Vandeleur Gilbart-Denham (killed in action, Narvik, 1940), Irish Guards and Diana Mary Beaumont; *m* 1976, Patricia Caroline Brooking; two *d.* Commissioned, Life Guards, 1960; served UK, Germany, Cyprus and Far East; Adjutant, Life Guards, 1965–67; Commanded Household Cavalry Regt, 1986–87. *Recreations:* riding, shooting, fishing, ski-ing. *Address:* The Royal Mews, Buckingham Palace, SW1W 0QH. *T:* 071–930 4832. *Club:* Cavalry and Guards.

GILBERD, Rt. Rev. Bruce Carlyle; *see* Auckland (NZ), Bishop of.

GILBERT; *see* Johnson-Gilbert.

GILBERT, Prof. Geoffrey Alan, FRS 1973; Professor of Biochemistry, University of Birmingham, 1969–85, now Emeritus; *b* 3 Dec. 1917; *s* of A. C. Gilbert and M. M. Gilbert (*née* Cull); *m* 1948, Lilo M. Gilbert (*née* Czigler de Egerszalok); two *s. Educ:* Kingsbury County Sch., Mddx; Emmanuel Coll., Cambridge; Dept of Colloid Science, Cambridge. MA, PhD, ScD (Cantab). Lectr, Chemistry Dept, Univ. of Birmingham, 1943–46. Research Fellow, Medical Sch., Harvard Univ., 1946–47. Univ. of Birmingham: Sen. Lectr, Chemistry Dept, 1947–61, Reader, 1961–69. Chm., British Biophysical Soc., 1974. Mem., Editorial Bd, Jl of Molecular Biol., 1972–87. *Publications:* articles and papers in scientific jls. *Recreations:* photography, gardening, fox-watching. *Address:* 194 Selly Park Road, Birmingham B29 7HY. *T:* 021–472 0755.

GILBERT, Maj.-Gen. Glyn Charles Anglim, CB 1974; MC 1944; Executive Chairman, The Airborne Initiative Holdings Ltd, since 1990; Director: Windward Rum Co. Ltd, since 1987; Fitness for Industry Ltd, since 1980; *b* 15 Aug. 1920; *s* of late C. G. G. Gilbert, OBE, MC, and H. M. Gilbert, MBE; *m* 1943, Heather Mary Jackson; three *s* one *d. Educ:* Eastbourne Coll.; RMC Sandhurst. Commnd 1939; served with 2nd Lincolns, 1940–47, NW Europe and Palestine; Instructor, Sch. of Infantry, 1948–50; 3rd Bn Para. Regt, 1951; Staff Coll., 1952; staff and regimental appts in MoD, Airborne Forces, Royal Lincolns and Para. Regt, 1952–66, Cyprus, Egypt and Malaya; idc 1966; comd Sch. of Infantry, 1967–70; GOC 3rd Div., 1970–72; Comdt, Joint Warfare Estab., 1972–74, retired. *Recreation:* following the sun. *Clubs:* Army and Navy; Royal Bermuda Yacht.

GILBERT, Hugh Campbell; Chairman: Camden and Islington Family Health Service Authority, since 1989; Price & Pierce Group Limited, 1973–87 (Chief Executive Officer, 1969–87); *b* 25 March 1926; *s* of Hugh Gilbert and Nessie Campbell; *m* 1956, Beti Gwenllian, *d* of Prof. Henry Lewis, CBE. *Educ:* John Neilson High Sch.; Univ. of Glasgow (MA 1st Cl. Hons Pol. Econ.). Mil. Service in Scots Gds, then in Argyll and Sutherland Highlanders, Europe and ME, 1944–48; Territorial Service with 5/6 Argyll and Sutherland Highlanders (Captain), 1948–53. Imperial Chemical Industries, 1951–53; PA Management Consultants Ltd, 1953–62; Dir, Blyth, Greene, Jourdain & Co. Ltd, 1962–81; Dir, Tozer, Kemsley & Millbourn (Holdings) Ltd, 1971–83. Hon. Professorial Fellow, UCNW, Bangor, 1975–79. *Recreations:* racing, opera, travel. *Address:* 59 Wynnstay Gardens, W8 6UU. *T:* 071–937 3134. *Clubs:* Caledonian, MCC.

GILBERT, Ian Grant; Clerk/Adviser to Select Committee on European Legislation, House of Commons, 1987–90; Under Secretary, International Relations Division, Department of Health and Social Security, 1979–85; retired; *b* Kikuyu, Kenya, 18 June 1925; *s* of Captain Alexander Grant Gilbert, DCM, indust. missionary, Lossiemouth and Kenya, and Marion Patrick Cruickshank; *m* 1960, Heather Margaret Donald, PhD (biographer of Lord Mount Stephen), *y d* of Rev. Francis Cantlie and Mary Donald, Lumphanan, Aberdeenshire. *Educ:* Fordyce Acad., Banffshire; Royal High Sch. of Edinburgh; Univ. of Edinburgh (MA 1950). Served HM Forces (Captain Indian Artillery), 1943–47. Entered Home Civil Service as Asst Principal and joined Min. of National Insurance, 1950; Private Sec. to Perm. Sec., 1953, and to Parly Sec., 1955; Principal, Min. of Pensions and Nat. Ins., 1956; seconded to HM Treasury, 1962–66; Asst Sec., Min. of Social Security (later DHSS), 1967; Head of War and Civilian Disabled Branches, DHSS, 1974–79. UK Member: Social Security, Health and Social Affairs Cttees, Council of Europe, Strasbourg, 1979–85; EEC Adv. Cttee on Social Security for Migrant Workers, Brussels, 1979–85; UK Delegate, Governing Body, Internat. Soc. Security Assoc., Geneva, 1979–85; Mem., UK Delegn to World Health Assembly, Geneva, 1979–84. Hon. Treasurer, Presbytery of England (Church of Scotland), 1965–77; Session Clerk, Crown Court Ch. of Scotland, Covent Garden, 1975–80. A Ch. of Scotland Mem., The Churches Main Cttee, 1986–. Chm., Caledonian Christian Club, 1984–86. *Recreations:* keeping half-an-acre in good heart, local and natural history, choral singing, France. *Address:* Wellpark, Moorside, Sturminster Newton, Dorset DT10 1HJ. *T:* Marnhull (0258) 820306. *Club:* Commonwealth Trust.
See also C. R. C. Donald.

GILBERT, Prof. John Cannon; Professor of Economics in the University of Sheffield, 1957–73, now Emeritus; Dean of Faculty of Economic and Social Studies, 1959–62; *b* 28 Sept. 1908; *s* of James and Elizabeth Louisa Gilbert; *m* 1938, Elizabeth Hadley Crook; two *s. Educ:* Bancroft's Sch.; The London Sch. of Economics and Political Science, University of London. Student of the Handels-Hochschule, Berlin (Sir Ernest Cassel Travelling Schol.), 1927–28; BCom Hons London, 1929. Asst on teaching staff, LSE, 1929–31; Lecturer in Economics, Sch. of Economics, Dundee, 1931–41. Ministry of Supply, 1941–45. Lecturer in Economics, University of Manchester, 1945–48; Senior Lecturer in Economics, University of Sheffield, 1948–56, Reader, 1956–57. Mem. Editorial Bd Bulletin of Economic Research, 1949–73. *Publications:* A History of Investment Trusts in Dundee, 1873–1938, 1939; Keynes's Impact on Monetary Economics, 1982; articles in Economica, Review of Economic Studies, etc. *Recreations:* walking, hill climbing. *Address:* 81 High Storrs Drive, Ecclesall, Sheffield S11 7LN. *T:* Sheffield (0742) 663544.

GILBERT, John Orman, CMG 1958; retired; *b* London, 21 Oct. 1907; *s* of Rev. T. H. Gilbert, late of Chedgrave Manor, Norfolk; *m* 1935, Winifred Mary Harris, Dublin; two *s* two *d. Educ:* Felsted Sch., Essex; Pembroke Coll., Oxford. Joined Sarawak Civil Service, 1928; various posts, from Cadet, to District Officer in 1940. During War of 1939–45 served in Bengal Sappers and Miners stationed in India and attained rank of Major. Came back to Sarawak with BM Administration, 1946; Resident, 4th Div., Sarawak, 1946–53; British Resident, Brunei, 1953–58; retd 1959. Coronation Medal, 1953. *Recreations:* conservation of wild life, animal welfare. *Address:* PO Box 100, Somerset West, Cape, South Africa.

GILBERT, Rt. Hon. Dr John (William); PC 1978; MP (Lab) Dudley East, since Feb. 1974 (Dudley, 1970–74); *b* April 1927; *m* 1963, Jean Olive Ross Skinner; two *d* of previous marriage. *Educ:* Merchant Taylors' Sch.; St John's Coll., Oxford; New York Univ. (PhD in Internat. Economics, Graduate Sch. of Business Administration). Chartered Accountant, Canada. Contested (Lab): Ludlow, 1966; Dudley, March 1968. Opposition front-bench spokesman on Treasury affairs, 1972–74; Financial Secretary to the Treasury, 1974–75; Minister for Transport, DoE, 1975–76; Minister of State, MoD, 1976–79. Member: Select Cttee on Corporation Tax, 1973; Select Cttee on Defence, 1979–87; Select Cttee on Trade and Industry, 1987–; Chm., PLP Defence Gp, 1981–83; Vice-Chm., Lab. Finance and Industry Group, 1983–. Member: Fabian Soc.; Council, RUSI; RIIA; NCCL; IISS; Council for Arms Control; Amnesty Internat.; GMBATU; WWF. Hon. LLD Wake Forest, N Carolina, 1983. *Address:* House of Commons, SW1. *Club:* Reform.

GILBERT, Air Chief Marshal Sir Joseph (Alfred), KCB 1985 (CB 1983); CBE 1974; Deputy Commander-in-Chief, Allied Forces Central Europe, 1986–89; retired; *b* 15 June 1931; *s* of Ernest and Mildred Gilbert; *m* 1955, Betty, *yr d* of late William and Eva Lishman; two *d. Educ:* William Hulme's Sch., Manchester; Univ. of Leeds (BA Hons, Econ. and Pol Science; Hon. LLD 1989). Commnd into RAF, 1952; Fighter Sqdns, 1953–61; Air Secretary's Dept, 1961–63; RAF Staff Coll., 1964; CO 92 (Lightning) Sqdn, 1965–67; jssc 1968; Sec., Defence Policy Staff, and Asst Dir of Defence Policy, 1968–71; CO, RAF Coltishall, 1971–73; RCDS, 1974; Dir of Forward Policy (RAF), 1975; ACAS (Policy), MoD, 1975–77; AOC 38 Group, 1977–80; ACDS (Policy), 1980–82; Asst Chief of Staff (Policy), SHAPE, 1983–84; Dep. C-in-C, RAF Strike Command, 1984–86. Comr, Commonwealth War Graves Commn, 1991–. Pres., RAFA, 1991–. *Publications:* articles in defence jls. *Recreations:* hockey, tennis, grandchildren, fly-fishing, strategic affairs. *Address:* Brook House, Salisbury Road, Shrewton, Salisbury, Wiltshire SP3 4EQ. *T:* Shrewton (0980) 620627. *Club:* Royal Air Force.

GILBERT, Martin (John), CBE 1990; MA; FRSL; historian; Fellow of Merton College, Oxford, since 1962; Official Biographer of Sir Winston Churchill since 1968; *b* 25 Oct. 1936; *s* of Peter and Miriam Gilbert; *m* 1st, 1963, Helen Constance, *yr d* of late Joseph Robinson, CBE; one *d*; 2nd, Susan, *d* of late Michael Sacher; two *s*. *Educ:* Highgate Sch.; Magdalen Coll., Oxford. Nat. Service (Army), 1955–57; Sen. Research Scholar, St Antony's Coll., Oxford, 1960–62; Vis. Lectr, Budapest Univ., 1961; Res. Asst (sometime Sen. Res. Asst) to Hon. Randolph S. Churchill, 1962–67; Vis. Prof., Univ. of S Carolina, 1965; Recent Hist. Correspt for Sunday Times, 1967; Res. Asst (Brit. Empire) for BBC, 1968; Historical Adviser (Palestine) for Thames Television, 1977–78. Visiting Professor: Tel-Aviv Univ., 1979; Hebrew Univ. of Jerusalem, 1980– (Vis. Lectr 1975); Visiting Lecturer: Univ. of Cape Town (Caplan Centre), 1984; MoD and Acad. of Sciences, Moscow, 1985. Non-Govtl Rep., UN Commn on Human Rights (43rd Session), Geneva, 1987, (44th Session), Geneva, 1988. Script designer and co-author, Genocide (Acad. Award winner, best doc. feature film), 1981; Historical Consultant to Southern Pictures TV series, Winston Churchill: The Wilderness Years, 1980–81; Historical Adviser, BBC TV, for Auschwitz and the Allies, 1981–82; historical consultant, Yalta 1945, for BBC TV, 1982–83; writer and narrator, Churchill, BBC TV, 1989–91. Governor, Hebrew Univ. of Jerusalem, 1978–. Hon. DLitt Westminster Coll., Fulton, 1981. *Publications:* The Appeasers, 1963 (with Richard Gott) (trans. German, Polish, Rumanian); Britain and Germany Between the Wars, 1964; The European Powers, 1900–1945, 1965 (trans. Italian, Spanish); Plough My Own Furrow: The Life of Lord Allen of Hurtwood, 1965; Servant of India: A Study of Imperial Rule 1905–1910, 1966; The Roots of Appeasement, 1966; Recent History Atlas 1860–1960, 1966; Winston Churchill (Clarendon Biogs for young people), 1966; British History Atlas, 1968; American History Atlas, 1968; Jewish History Atlas, 1969, 3rd edn 1985 (trans. Spanish, Dutch, Hebrew, Russian); First World War Atlas, 1970; Winston S. Churchill, vol. iii, 1914–1916, 1971, companion volume (in two parts) 1973; Russian History Atlas, 1972; Sir Horace Rumbold: portrait of a diplomat, 1973; Churchill: a photographic portrait, 1974; The Arab-Israeli Conflict: its history in maps, 1974, 4th edn 1985 (trans. Spanish, Hebrew); Churchill and Zionism (pamphlet), 1974; Winston S. Churchill, vol. iv, 1917–1922, 1975, companion volume (in three parts), 1977; The Jews in Arab Lands: their history in maps, 1975, illustr. edn, 1976 (trans. Hebrew, Arabic, French, German); Winston S. Churchill, vol. v, 1922–1939, 1976, companion volume, part one, The Exchequer Years 1922–1929, 1980, part two, The Wilderness Years 1929–1935, 1981, part three, The Coming of War 1936–1939, 1982; The Jews of Russia: Illustrated History Atlas, 1976 (trans. Spanish); Jerusalem Illustrated History Atlas, 1977 (trans. Hebrew, Spanish); Exile and Return: The Emergence of Jewish Statehood, 1978; Children's Illustrated Bible Atlas, 1979; Final Journey, the Fate of the Jews of Nazi Europe, 1979 (trans. Dutch, Hebrew); Auschwitz and the Allies, 1981 (trans. German, Hebrew); Churchill's Political Philosophy, 1981; The Origin of the 'Iron Curtain' speech, 1981 (pamphlet); Atlas of the Holocaust (Macmillan Atlas of the Holocaust, in USA), 1982 (trans. German, Hebrew); Winston S. Churchill, vol. vi, Finest Hour, 1939–41, 1983 (Wolfson Award, 1983); The Jews of Hope: the plight of Soviet Jewry today, 1984 (trans. Hebrew, Japanese); Jerusalem: rebirth of a city, 1985; The Holocaust: the Jewish tragedy, 1986; Winston S. Churchill, vol vii, Road to Victory, 1986; Shcharansky: hero of our time, 1986 (trans. Dutch, Hebrew); Winston S. Churchill, vol viii, 'Never Despair', 1945–65, 1988; Second World War, 1989 (trans. German, Italian, Portuguese); Churchill, A Life, 1991; Editor: A Century of Conflict: Essays Presented to A. J. P. Taylor, 1966; Churchill, 1967, and Lloyd George, 1968 (Spectrum Books); compiled Jackdaws: Winston Churchill, 1970; The Coming of War in 1939, 1973; contribs historical articles and reviews to jls (incl. Purnell's History of the Twentieth Century, Reader's Digest, Voprosi Historii). *Recreation:* drawing maps. *Address:* Merton College, Oxford. *T:* Oxford (0865) 49651. *Club:* Athenæum.

GILBERT, Michael Francis, CBE 1980; TD 1950; crime writer; *b* 17 July 1912; *s* of Bernard Samuel Gilbert and Berwyn Minna Cuthbert; *m* 1947, Roberta Mary, *d* of Col R. M. W. Marsden; two *s* five *d*. *Educ:* Blundell's Sch.; London University. LLB 1937. Served War of 1939–45, Hon. Artillery Co., 12th Regt RHA, N Africa and Italy (despatches 1943). Joined Trower Still & Keeling, 1947 (Partner, 1952–83). Legal Adviser to Govt of Bahrain, 1960. Member: Arts Council Cttee on Public Lending Right, 1968; Royal Literary Fund, 1969; Council of Soc. of Authors, 1975; (Founder) Crime Writers' Assoc.; Mystery Writers of America, Grand Master, 1987. *Publications: novels:* Close Quarters, 1947; They Never Looked Inside, 1948; The Doors Open, 1949; Smallbone Deceased, 1950; Death has Deep Roots, 1951; Death in Captivity, 1952; Fear to Tread, 1953; Sky High, 1955; Be Shot for Sixpence, 1956; The Tichborne Claimant, 1957; Blood and Judgement, 1958; After the Fine Weather, 1963; The Crack in the Tea Cup, 1965; The Dust and the Heat, 1967; The Etruscan Net, 1969; The Body of a Girl, 1972; The Ninety Second Tiger, 1973; Flash Point, 1974; The Night of the Twelfth, 1976; The Empty House, 1978; Death of a Favourite Girl, 1980; The Final Throw, 1983; The Black Seraphim, 1983; The Long Journey Home, 1985; Trouble, 1987; Paint Gold and Blood, 1989; *short stories:* Game Without Rules, 1967; Stay of Execution, 1971; Petrella at Q, 1977; Mr Calder and Mr Behrens, 1982; Young Petrella, 1988; Anything for a Quiet Life, 1990; *plays:* A Clean Kill; The Bargain; Windfall; The Shot in Question; *edited:* Crime in Good Company, 1959; The Oxford Book of Legal Anecdotes, 1986; The Fraudsters, 1988; has also written radio and TV scripts. *Recreations:* walking, croquet, contract bridge. *Address:* The Old Rectory, Luddesdown, Gravesend, Kent DA13 0XE. *T:* Meopham (0474) 814272. *Club:* Garrick.

GILBERT, Patrick Nigel Geoffrey; General Secretary of the Society for Promoting Christian Knowledge, since 1971; *b* 12 May 1934; adopted *s* of late Geoffrey Gilbert and Evelyn (*née* Miller), Devon. *Educ:* Cranleigh Sch.; Merton Coll., Oxford. OUP, 1964–69; Linguaphone Group (Westinghouse), 1969–71 (Man. Dir in Group, 1970). World Assoc. for Christian Communication: Trustee, 1975–87; European Vice-Chm., 1975–82; representative to EEC, 1975–82, to Conf. of Eur. Churches, 1976–82, to Council of Europe, 1976–82, and to Central Cttee, 1979–84. Member: Bd for Mission and Unity of Gen. Synod, 1971–78 (Mem. Exec., 1971–76); Archbishops' Cttee on RC Relations, 1971–81; Church Inf. Cttee, 1978–81; Church Publishing Cttee, 1980–84; Council, Conf. of British Missionary Socs, 1971–78; Council, Christians Abroad, 1974–79; Exec., Anglican Centre, Rome, 1981–91 (Vice Chm. of Friends, 1984–91); British National Cttee, UNESCO World Bank Congress, 1982. Greater London Arts Association: Mem. Exec., 1968–78; Hon. Life Mem., 1978; Chm., 1980–84 (Dep. Chm., 1979–80); Initiator, 1972 Festivals of London. Art Workers' Guild: Hon. Brother, 1971; Chm. Trustees and Hon. Treas., 1976–86 (Trustee, 1975). Chairman: Standing Conf. of London Arts Councils, 1975–78; Embroiderers' Guild, 1977–78 (Hon. Treas., 1974–77); Concord Multicultural Arts Trust, 1980–89; Harold Buxton Trust, 1983–; Nikaean Club, 1984–; Vice-President: Camden Arts Council, 1974–89 (Chm., 1970–74); Nat. Assoc. of Local Arts Councils, 1980–89 (Founder Chm., 1976–80); Mem., Arts Adv. Cttee, CRE, 1979; Steward, Artists' Gen. Benevolent Instn, 1971–. Rep. of Archbishop of Canterbury to Inter-Church Travel, 1987–. Trustee: Overseas Bishoprics Fund, 1973–; All Saints Trust, 1978– (Chairman: F and GP and Investment Cttees); Schulze Trust, 1980–83; Dancers' Resettlement Fund, 1982–90 (Chm., Finance Cttee); Richards Trust; ACC Res. Fund, 1982–84; Vis. Trustee, Seabury Press, NY, 1978–80; Chm., Dancers' Resettlement Trust, 1987–90. Mem. Executive: GBGSA, 1981–84, 1988–89; Assoc. of Vol. Colls, 1979–87; Mem. Governing Body: SPCK Australia, 1977–; SPCK (USA), 1984–; SPCK NZ, 1989–; Partners for World Mission, 1979–; Governor: Contemp. Dance Trust, 1981–90; All Saints Coll., Tottenham, 1971–78; St Martin's Sch. for Girls, 1971– (Vice Chm., 1978–; Rep. to Tertiary Educn Council, 1983–89); Ellesmere Coll., 1977–87 (Mem. ISCO Exec., 1984–86); St Michael's Sch., Petworth, 1978–88 (rep. to GBGSA); Roehampton Inst., 1978– (rep. to Assoc. of Vol. Colls, 1978–88; Chm., Audit Cttee, 1989–); Pusey House, 1985–; Patron, Pusey House Appeal, 1984–88; Fellow, Corp. of SS Mary and Nicholas (Woodard Schs), 1972– (Mem. Exec., 1981–; Chm., S Div. Res. Cttee, 1972–84; Trustee, Endowment Fund; Dir, Corp. Trustee Co.). Member Development Cttee: SPAB, 1985–87; London Symphony Chorus, 1985–87; Bd Mem., Nat. Youth Dance Co., 1988–; Mem. Council, Publishers Assoc., 1990. Mem. Court, City Univ., 1987–. Dir, Surrey Building Soc., 1988–. Hon. Mem., Assoc. for Develt in the Arts. Freeman, City of London, 1966; Liveryman, Worshipful Co. of Woolmen (Master, 1985–86; Rep. to City and Guilds); Parish Clerk, All Hallows, Bread Street; Member: Worshipful Co. of Parish Clerks; Guild of Freemen. Lord of the Manor of Cantley Netherhall, Norfolk. FRSA 1978; FBIM 1982; FInstD 1982. Hon. DLitt Columbia Pacific, 1982. Order of St Vladimir, 1977. *Publications:* articles in various jls. *Recreations:* walking, reading, travel, enjoying the Arts, golf. *Address:* 3 The Mount Square, NW3 6SU. *T:* 071–794 8807. *Clubs:* Athenæum, City Livery; Walton Heath Golf.

GILBERT, Stuart William, CB 1983; Director, Department for National Savings, 1981–86 (Deputy Secretary); *b* 2 Aug. 1926; *s* of Rodney Stuart Gilbert and Ella Edith (*née* Esgate); *m* 1955, Marjorie Laws Vallance; one *s* one *d*. *Educ:* Maidstone Grammar Sch.; Emmanuel Coll., Cambridge (Open Exhibnr and State Scholar; MA). Served RAF, 1944–47. Asst Principal, Min. of Health, 1949; Asst Private Sec.: to Minister of Housing and Local Govt, 1952; to Parly Sec., 1954; Principal, 1955; Sec., Parker Morris Cttee on Housing Standards, 1958–61, Rapporteur to ECE Housing Cttee, 1959–61; Reporter to ILO Conf. on Workers' Housing, 1960; Asst Sec., Local Govt Finance Div., 1964; Under-Sec., DoE, 1970–80 (for New Towns, 1970, Business Rents, 1973, Construction Industries, 1974, Housing, 1974, Planning Land Use, 1977); Dep. Dir, Dept for Nat. Savings, 1980–81. *Recreations:* sailing, music, woodwork. *Address:* 3 Westmoat Close, Beckenham, Kent BR3 2BX. *T:* 081–650 7213. *Club:* United Oxford & Cambridge University.

GILBERT, Prof. Walter; Carl M. Loeb University Professor, Department of Cellular and Developmental Biology, Harvard University, since 1987; Founder, 1978, and Director, Biogen NV (Chairman and Principal Executive Officer, 1981–84); *b* Boston, 21 March 1932; *s* of Richard V. Gilbert and Emma (*née* Cohen); *m* 1953, Celia Stone; one *s* one *d*. *Educ:* Harvard Coll. (AB *summa cum laude* Chem. and Phys., 1953); Harvard Univ. (AM Phys., 1954); Cambridge Univ. (PhD Maths, 1957). National Science Foundn pre-doctoral Fellow, Harvard Univ. and Cambridge Univ., 1953–57, post-doctoral Fellow in Phys., Harvard, 1957–58; Harvard University: Lectr in Phys., 1958–59; Asst Prof. in Phys., 1959–64; Associate Prof. of Biophys., 1964–68; Prof. of Biochem., 1968–72; Amer. Cancer Soc. Prof. of Molecular Biology, 1972–81; H. H. Timken Prof. of Science, 1986–87. Guggenheim Fellow, Paris, 1968–69. Member: Amer. Acad. of Arts and Sciences, 1968; National Acad. of Sciences, 1976; Amer. Phys. Soc.; Amer. Soc. of Biol Chemists; Foreign Mem., Royal Soc., 1987–. Lectures: V. D. Mattia, Roche Inst. of Molecular Biol., 1976; Smith, Kline and French, Univ. of Calif, Berkeley, 1977. Hon. DSc: Chicago, 1978; Columbia, 1978; Rochester, 1979; Yeshiva, 1981. Many prizes and awards, incl. (jtly) Nobel Prize for Chemistry, 1980. *Publications:* chapters, articles and papers on theoretical physics and molecular biology. *Address:* Biological Laboratories, 16 Divinity Avenue, Cambridge, Mass 02138, USA. *T:* (617) 495–0760; 15 Gray Gardens West, Cambridge, Mass 02138. *T:* (617) 864–8778.

GILBEY, family name of **Baron Vaux of Harrowden.**

GILBEY, Sir (Walter) Derek, 3rd Bt, *cr* 1893; Lieut 2nd Bn Black Watch; *b* 11 March 1913; *s* of Walter Ewart Gilbey and Dorothy Coysgarne Sim; *S* grandfather, 1945; *m* 1948, Elizabeth Mary, *d* of Col Keith Campbell and Marjorie Syfret; one *s* one *d*. *Educ:* Eton. Served War of 1939–45 (prisoner). *Heir:* *s* Walter Gavin Gilbey [*b* 14 April 1949; *m* 1st, 1980, Mary Pacetti, *d* of late William E. E. Pacetti and of Mrs Mary Greer; 2nd, 1985, Mrs Anna Olsson, *d* of Edmund Prosser]. *Address:* Grovelands, Wineham, near Henfield, Sussex BN5 9AW. *T:* Bolney (0444) 881311.

See also Sir C. B. Frederick, Bt.

GILCHRIST, Sir Andrew (Graham), KCMG 1964 (CMG 1956); HM Diplomatic Service, retired; formerly Ambassador and administrator; *b* 19 April 1910; *e s* of late James Graham Gilchrist, Kerse, Lesmahagow; *m* 1946, Freda Grace (*d* 1987), *d* of late Alfred Slack; two *s* one *d*. *Educ:* Edinburgh Acad.; Exeter Coll., Oxford. Diplomatic career, 1933–70, included junior posts in Bangkok, Paris, Marseilles, Rabat, Stuttgart, Singapore, Chicago, also in FO; subseq. Ambassador at Reykjavik, Djakarta and Dublin, retired. Chm., Highlands and Islands Develt Bd, 1970–76. War Service as Major, Force 136 in SE Asia (despatches). *Publications: memoirs:* Bangkok Top Secret, 1970; Cod Wars and How to Lose Them, 1978 (Icelandic edn 1977); *history:* Disaster in Malaya 1941, 1991; *novels:* The Russian Professor, 1984; The Watercress File, 1985; The Ultimate Hostage, 1986; South of Three Pagodas, 1987; Death of an Admiral, 1988; Did Van Gogh Paint His Bed?, 1991. *Address:* Arthur's Crag, Hazelbank, by Lanark ML11 9XL. *T:* Crossford (055586) 263. *Clubs:* Special Forces; New (Edinburgh).

GILCHRIST, (Andrew) Rae, CBE 1961; MD Edinburgh, FRCPE, FRCP; Consulting Physician Royal Infirmary, Edinburgh; *b* 7 July 1899; *o s* of late Rev. Andrew Gilchrist, BA, Edinburgh; *m* 1st, 1931, Emily Faulds (*d* 1967), *yr d* of late W. Work Slater, Edinburgh and Innerleithen, Peeblesshire; one *s* one *d*; 2nd, 1975, Elspeth, *widow* of Dr Arthur Wightman. *Educ:* Belfast, Edinburgh, New York. MB, ChB Edinburgh, 1921; Lauder-Brunton Prizeman, Milner-Fothergill Medallist, McCunn Medical Res. Scholar, Edinburgh Univ., 1924; MD (gold medal) 1933; FRCPE 1929; FRCP 1944. RFA 1917–18. Resident hospital appointments at Addenbrooke's Hosp., Cambridge, Princess Elizabeth Hosp. for Children, London, E1, and at Royal Infirmary, Edinburgh, 1922–24; Resident Asst Physician Rockefeller Hosp. for Medical Research, New York, USA, 1926–27; Asst Physician, 1930; Physician, Royal Infirmary, Edinburgh, 1939–64; Gibson Lecturer RCP Edinburgh, 1944; Lecturer: Canadian Heart Assoc., 1955; Litchfield Lecture, Oxford Univ., 1956; Californian Heart Assoc., 1957; St Cyres Lecturer, National Heart Hosp., London, 1957; Hall Overseas Lecturer, Australia and NZ, 1959; Carey Coombs Memorial Lecture, Bristol Univ., 1960; Gwladys and Olwen Williams Lecture in Medicine, Liverpool Univ., 1961; Orford Lectr, College of Physicians of S Africa, 1962. William Cullen Prize, 1962 (shared). Pres. of the Royal College of Physicians of Edinburgh, 1957–60. Examr in Med. in Univs of Edinburgh, Glasgow, Aberdeen, St Andrews, East Africa (Makerere Coll.), and Baghdad. Mem. Assoc. of Physicians of Gt Brit., of Brit. Cardiac Soc. Hon. Mem. Cardiac Soc. of Australia and NZ. Hon. FRACP 1959; Hon. FRFPSG 1961. *Publications:* numerous contributions on disorders of heart and circulation, in British and American medical journals. *Recreation:* fishing. *Address:* 16 Winton Terrace, Edinburgh EH10 7AP. *T:* 031–445 1119. *Clubs:* Flyfishers'; New (Edinburgh).

GILCHRIST, Archibald; Managing Director, 1971–79, and Chairman, 1978–79, Govan Shipbuilders; *b* 17 Dec. 1929; *m* 1958, Elizabeth Jean Greenlees; two *s* one *d*. *Educ:* Loretto; Pembroke Coll., Cambridge (MA). Barclay Curle & Co. Ltd, Glasgow, 1954–64, various managerial posts; ultimately Dir, Swan Hunter Group; Brown Bros & Co. Ltd, Edinburgh, 1964–72: Dep. Man. Dir, 1964; Man. Dir, 1969; Man. Dir, Vosper Private, Singapore, 1980–86; Dir, Management Search Internat. Ltd, 1986–89; Pt-time Bd Mem., Scottish Legal Aid Bd, 1986–; non-executive Director: F. J. C. Lilley plc, 1987–; RMJM Ltd, 1988–; Glasgow Friendly Soc., 1988–; Caledonian MacBrayne, 1990–. Vice Chm., Scottish National Orchestra, 1989– (Dir, 1987–). Chm. Council, St Leonard's Sch., 1989–; Gov., Glasgow Polytechnic. *Recreations:* golf, shooting, fishing, music. *Address:* Inchmaholm, 35 Barnton Avenue, Edinburgh EH4 6JJ. *Clubs:* New (Edinburgh); Hon. Company of Edinburgh Golfers.

GILCHRIST, Rae; *see* Gilchrist, A. R.

GILDER, Robert Charles, FIA; Directing Actuary, Government Actuary's Department, 1979–83; *b* 22 April 1923; *s* of Charles Henry Gilder and Elsie May (*née* Sayer); *m* 1954, Norah Mary Hallas; two *s*. *Educ:* Brentwood School. Liverpool Victoria Friendly Soc., 1940–41 and 1946–48. Served War, RAF, 1941–46. Government Actuary's Dept, 1948–83; Actuary, 1959; Principal Actuary, 1973. FIA 1951. *Recreations:* cricket, playing the clarinet, hill-walking, golf.

GILES; *see* Giles, Carl Ronald.

GILES, Carl Ronald, OBE 1959; Cartoonist, Daily and Sunday Express, since 1943; *b* 29 Sept. 1916; *m* 1942, Sylvia Joan Clarke. Trained as animated cartoonist; Animator for Alexander Korda, 1935; Cartoonist, Reynolds News, 1937–43. Cartoons extensively reproduced in US and syndicated throughout world. Produced and animated Documentary Films for Min. of Information, also War Correspondent-cartoonist in France, Belgium, Holland and Germany, War of 1939–45. *Publications:* "Giles" Annual, 1945–; various overseas collections. *Recreations:* sailing, workshops. *Address:* Express Newspapers, Ludgate House, 245 Blackfriars Road, SE1 9UX. *Clubs:* Saints & Sinners, Lord's Taverners; British Racing Drivers'.

GILES, Frank Thomas Robertson; Editor, The Sunday Times, 1981–83 (Deputy Editor, 1967–81); *b* 31 July 1919; *s* of late Col F. L. N. Giles, DSO, OBE, and Mrs Giles; *m* 1946, Lady Katharine Pamela Sackville, *o d* of 9th Earl De La Warr and Countess De La Warr; one *s* two *d*. *Educ:* Wellington Coll.; Brasenose Coll., Oxford (Open Scholarship in History; MA 1946). ADC to Governor of Bermuda, 1939–42; Directorate of Mil. Ops, WO, 1942–45; temp. mem. of HM Foreign Service, 1945–46 (Private Sec. to Ernest Bevin; Mem. of Sir Archibald Clark Kerr's mission to Java); joined editorial staff of The Times, 1946; Asst Correspondent, Paris, 1947; Chief Corresp., Rome, 1950–53, Paris, 1953–60; Foreign Editor, Sunday Times, 1961–77; Dir, Times Newspapers Ltd, 1981–85. Lectures: tours, USA, 1975, FRG, 1984; Gritti, Venice, 1985. Mem., Exec. Cttee, GB-USSR Assoc., 1966–. Chm., Painshill Park Trust, 1985–; Mem., Governing Body, British Inst. of Florence, 1986–; Governor: Wellington Coll., 1965–89; Sevenoaks Sch., 1967–. *Publications:* A Prince of Journalists: the life and times of de Blowitz, 1962; Sundry Times (autobiog.), 1986; The Locust Years: the story of the Fourth French Republic 1946–1958, 1991. *Recreations:* going to the opera; collecting, talking about, consuming the vintage wines of Bordeaux and Burgundy. *Address:* 42 Blomfield Road, W9 2PF; Bunns Cottage, Lye Green, Crowborough, East Sussex TN6 1UY. *Clubs:* Brooks's, Beefsteak.

GILES, Prof. Geoffrey Reginald, FRCS; Professor of Surgery, and Head, University of Leeds Department of Surgery, St James's Hospital, Leeds, since 1973; *b* 17 Dec. 1936; *s* of Reginald Samuel Giles and Phyllis May Giles; *m* 1966, Pamela Billie Hoey; three *s*. *Educ:* Bablake Sch., Coventry; Manchester Univ. (MB ChB, MD); FRCS 1964. Postgrad. trng, Manchester Royal Inf., 1962–64; Gen. Inf., Leeds, 1964–68; Fellow: Harvard Med. Sch., Boston, 1968–69; Univ. of Colorado, 1969–71; Sen. Lectr, Univ. of Leeds, 1971–73. *Publication:* Essential Surgical Practice (with Cuschieri and Moosa), 1982, 2nd edn 1986. *Recreation:* game fishing. *Address:* 1 North Park Avenue, Roundhay, Leeds LS8 1DN. *T:* Leeds (0532) 661883. *Club:* East India.

GILES, Rear-Adm. Sir Morgan Charles M.; *see* Morgan-Giles.

GILES, Air Comdt Dame Pauline; *see* Parsons, Air Comdt Dame P.

GILES, Robert Frederick; Senior Clerk, House of Commons, 1979–83; *b* 27 Dec. 1918; *s* of Robert and Edith Giles; *m* 1948, Mabel Florence Gentry; two *d*. *Educ:* Drayton Manor Sch., Hanwell. Min. of Agriculture, 1936–39. Royal Navy, 1939–45: CO, HMS Tango, 1942–44. Various assignments, MAF, from 1945; Regional Controller, Northern Region MAFF, 1963–68; Head, Food Standards/Food Science Div., 1968–74; Under Sec., MAFF, 1975–78; Food Standards and Food Subsidies Gp, 1975; Food Feedingstuffs and Fertilizer Standards Gp, 1977. *Recreations:* walking, theatre. *Address:* 8 The Ridings, Copthill Lane, Kingswood, Surrey KT20 6HJ. *Club:* Civil Service.

GILES, Roy Curtis, MA; Head Master, Highgate School, 1974–89; *b* 6 Dec. 1932; *s* of Herbert Henry Giles and Dorothy Alexandra Potter; *m* 1963, Christine von Alten; two *s* one *d*. *Educ:* Queen Elizabeth's Sch., Barnet; Jesus Coll., Cambridge (Open Scholar). Asst Master, Dean Close Sch., 1956–60; Lektor, Hamburg Univ., 1960–63; Asst Master, Eton Coll., 1963–74, Head of Modern Languages, 1970–74. Educnl Selector, ACCM, 1981–; Mem., House of Bishops' Panel on Marriage Educn, 1983–89. Mem., Council of Management, Vernon Educnl Trust (formerly Davies's Educn Services), 1975–; Governor: The Hall, Hampstead, 1976–89; Channing Sch., 1977–89. *Recreations:* music, theatre. *Address:* Wayfield House, Venlake Lane, Uplyme, Lyme Regis, Dorset DT7 3SA. *T:* Lyme Regis (02974) 3065.

GILL, Sir Anthony Keith, Kt 1991; FEng 1983; FIMechE, FIProdE; Chairman and Chief Executive, Lucas Industries plc, since 1987; *b* 1 April 1930; *s* of Frederick William and Ellen Gill; *m* 1953, Phyllis Cook; one *s* two *d*. *Educ:* High Sch., Colchester; Imperial Coll., London (BScEng Hons). National Service officer, REME, 1954–56. Joined Bryce Berger Ltd, 1956, subseq. Director and Gen. Manager until 1972; Lucas CAV Ltd, 1972, subseq. Director and Gen. Manager until 1978; Divisional Managing Director, Joseph Lucas Ltd, 1978; Jt Gp Man. Dir, 1980–83, Gp Man. Dir, 1984–87 and Dep. Chm., 1986–87, Lucas Industries. Non-exec. Director: Post Office Bd, 1989–; National Power, 1990–. Member: Adv. Council on Science and Technology (formerly Adv. Council for Applied R&D), 1985–; DTI Technology Requirements Bd, 1986–88; Engineering Council, 1988–. Pres., IProdE, 1986–87; Mem., Council, IMechE, 1986–; Vice-Pres., Engineering Employers Fedn, 1987–. Mem. Court, Univ. of Warwick, 1986; Pro-Chancellor, Cranfield Inst of Technology, 1991–. FCGI 1979; Fellow, City of Birmingham Polytechnic, 1989. Hon. DEng Birmingham, 1990. Hon. DSc Cranfield, 1991. *Recreations:* sailing, music. *Address:* Mockley Close, Gentleman's Lane, Ullenhall, near Henley in Arden, Warwickshire. *T:* Tanworth in Arden (05644) 2337.

GILL, Brian; QC (Scot.) 1981; *b* 25 Feb. 1942; *s* of Thomas and Mary Gill, Glasgow; *m* 1969, Catherine Fox; five *s* one *d*. *Educ:* St Aloysius' Coll., Glasgow; Glasgow Univ. (MA 1962, LLB 1964); Edinburgh Univ. (PhD 1975). Asst Lectr, 1964–65, Lectr, 1965–69 and 1972–77, Faculty of Law, Edinburgh Univ.; Advocate, 1967; Advocate Depute, 1977–79; Standing Junior Counsel: Foreign and Commonwealth Office (Scotland), 1974–77; Home Office (Scotland), 1979–81; Scottish Education Dept, 1979–81; Chm., Industrial Tribunals, 1981–88. Called to the Bar, Lincoln's Inn, 1991. Keeper of the Advocates' Library, 1987–; Trustee, Nat. Liby of Scotland, 1987–. Chm., Cttee of Investigation for Scotland (Agricl Marketing), 1985– (Mem., Cttees for GB and for England and Wales); Dep. Chm., Copyright Tribunal, 1989–; Member: Scottish Legal Aid Bd, 1987–90; Scottish Valuation Adv. Council, 1989–. *Publications:* The Law of Agricultural Holdings in Scotland, 1982, 2nd edn 1990; articles in legal jls. *Recreation:* church music. *Address:* 13 Lauder Road, Edinburgh EH9 2EN. *T:* 031–667 1888. *Club:* Western (Glasgow).

GILL, Christopher John Fred, RD 1971; MP (C) Ludlow, since 1987; butcher and farmer; *b* 28 Oct. 1936; *m* 1960, Patricia M. (*née* Greenway); one *s* two *d*. *Educ:* Shrewsbury School. Chm., F. A. Gill Ltd, 1968–. Mem., Agriculture Select Cttee, 1989–. Sec., Cons. Agric. Cttee, 1990–; Vice Chm., Cons. European Affairs Cttee, 1989–; Pres., Midlands W European Cons. Council, 1984–85. Councillor, Wolverhampton BC, 1965–72. *Address:* House of Commons, SW1A 0AA.

GILL, Cyril James, CB 1965; Senior Lecturer in Education, University of Keele, 1968–71, retired (Gulbenkian Lecturer in Education, 1965–68); *b* 29 March 1904; *s* of William Gill, Carnforth, Lancs; *m* 1939, Phyllis Mary, *d* of Joseph Windsor, Ramsey, Isle of Man. *Educ:* Ulverston Grammar Sch.; Liverpool Univ. Sch. Master, Ramsey, IOM and Archbishop Tenison's, London, 1926–42; Head Master, Salford Grammar Sch., 1942–45. HM Inspectorate of Schools, 1945–65; Midland Divisional Inspector, 1954–61; Chief Inspector (Teacher Training), 1961–65. *Publications:* articles on counselling and guidance. *Recreations:* gardening, walking, photography, theatre. *Address:* Grosvenor House, Ballure Road, Ramsey, Isle of Man.

GILL, David; television producer; *b* 9 June 1928; *s* of Cecil and Iona Gill; *m* 1953, Pauline Wadsworth; two *d*. *Educ:* Belmont Abbey, Hereford. Dancer with Sadler's Wells Theatre Ballet, 1948–55; joined film-cutting rooms, Associated-Rediffusion TV, 1955; produced Stations of the Cross (mime), BBC, 1957; Film Editor, This Week, Rediffusion TV, 1957–68 (also documentaries); Technical Advisor and Editor, Dave Clark Special, 1968; directed for Thames Television: This Week, 1969–73; Till I End My Song (documentary), 1970; Destination America (documentary series), 1975; with Kevin Brownlow: co-wrote and produced: Hollywood, 1980; Unknown Chaplin, 1983; Buster Keaton: a hard act to follow, 1987; Harold Lloyd—the Third Genius, 1990; co-produced: Abel Gance's Napoleon (TV version) 1983; British Cinema—Personal View, 1986; Thames Silents/Live Cinema (also TV versions for Channel 4), 1980–. *Recreations:* cinema, theatre, music, planting trees. *Address:* Photoplay Productions, 21 Princess Road, NW1.

GILL, (George) Malcolm, FCIB; Deputy Head, Banking Department, Bank for International Settlements, since 1991; *b* 23 May 1934; *s* of Thomas Woodman Gill and late Alice Muriel Gill (*née* Le Grice); *m* 1966, Monica Kennedy Brooks; one *s* one *d*. *Educ:* Cambridgeshire High Sch.; Sidney Sussex Coll., Cambridge (MA). Entered Bank of England, 1957: seconded to UK Treasury Delegation, Washington DC, 1966–68; Private Sec. to Governor, 1970–72; Asst Chief Cashier, 1975; seconded to HM Treasury, 1977–80; Chief Manager, Banking and Credit Markets, 1980–82; Head of Foreign Exchange Div., 1982–88; Asst Dir, 1987–88; Chief of the Banking Dept and Chief Cashier, 1988–91. *Recreations:* family, music, gardening. *Address:* Bank for International Settlements, Basle, CH 4002, Switzerland.

GILL, Air Vice-Marshal Harry, CB 1979; OBE 1968; Director-General of Supply, Royal Air Force, 1976–79; *b* 30 Oct. 1922; *s* of John William Gill and Lucy Gill, Newark, Notts; *m* 1951, Diana Patricia, *d* of Colin Wood, Glossop; one *d*. *Educ:* Barnby Road Sch.; Newark Technical Coll. Entered RAF, 1941; pilot trng, 1942; commnd 1943; flying duties, 1943–49; transf. to Equipment Br., 1949; Officer Commanding: Supply Sqdns, RAF Spitalgate and RAF North Coates, 1949–52; HQ Staff No 93 Maintenance Unit Explosives and Fuels Supply Ops, 1952–55; Explosives and Fuels Sch., 1955–58; Staff Officer Logistics Div., HQ Allied Forces Northern Europe, 1958–61; Head of Provision Br., Air Min., 1961–64; Chief Equipment Officer, No 25 Maintenance Unit, RAF Hartlebury, 1964–66; Equipment Staff Officer, HQ Air Forces Middle East, 1966–67; Dep. Dir Supply Systems, MoD Air, 1968–70; RCDS, 1971; Comdt, RAF Supply Control Centre, 1972–73; Dir, Supply Management, MoD Air, 1973–76. Internat. rifle and pistol shot; Silver Medallist, King's Prize, Bisley, 1951. *Recreations:* shooting, fishing, tennis, cricket. *Club:* Royal Air Force.

GILL, Maj.-Gen. Ian Gordon, CB 1972; OBE 1959 (MBE 1949); MC 1940, Bar 1945; idc, psc; Colonel, 4/7 Royal Dragoon Guards, 1973–78; *b* Rochester, 9 Nov. 1919; *s* of late Brig. Gordon Harry Gill, CMG, DSO and Mrs Doris Gill, Rochester, Kent; *m* 1963, Elizabeth Vivian Rohr, MD, MRCP (*d* 1990), *o d* of late A. F. Rohr; no *c*. *Educ:* Edinburgh House, Hants; Repton School. Commnd from SRO into 4th/7th Roy. Dragoon Guards, 1938; served with Regt in: BEF, France, 1939–40; BLA, NW Europe, 1944–45 (despatches, 1945); Palestine, 1946–48; Tripolitania, 1951–52; Instructor, Armoured Sch., 1948–50; Staff Coll., Camberley, 1952; Bde Maj., HQ Inf. Bde, 1953–55; comdg 4th/7th RDG, 1957–59; Asst Mil. Sec., HQ, BAOR, 1959–61; Coll. Comdt RMA Sandhurst, 1961–62; Imp. Def. Coll., 1963; Comdr, 7th Armoured Bde, 1964–66; Dep. Mil. Sec. 1, MoD (Army), 1966–68; Head, British Defence Liaison Staff, Dept of Defence, Canberra, 1968–70; Asst Chief of Gen. Staff (Op. Requirements), 1970–72, retired. Hon. Liveryman, Coachmakers' Co., 1974. *Recreations:* equitation, ski-ing, cricket, squash rackets. *Address:* Cheriton House, Thorney, Peterborough PE6 0QD. *Clubs:* Cavalry and Guards, MCC.

GILL, Jack, CB 1984; Chief Executive (formerly Secretary), Export Credits Guarantee Department, 1983–87; Executive Director(part-time), Government Relations, BICC plc, since 1987; *b* 20 Feb. 1930; *s* of Jack and Elizabeth Gill; *m* 1954, Alma Dorothy; three *d*. *Educ:* Bolton Sch. Export Credits Guarantee Department: Clerical Officer, 1946; Principal, 1962; Asst Sec., 1970; Asst Sec., DTI, 1972–75; Export Credits Guarantee Department: Under Sec., 1975–79; Principal Finance Officer, 1978–79; Sec., Monopolies and Mergers Commn, 1979–81; Dep. Sec., and Dir of Industrial Develt Unit, DoI, 1981–83. Mem., BOTB, 1981–87. Consultant: NEI Power Projects Ltd, 1987–90; British Aerospace plc, 1987–89; CBI Council, 1988– (Chm., Public Procurement Contact Gp, 1990–; Mem., Overseas Cttee, 1990–). National Service, REME, 1948–50. *Recreations:* music, chess; occasional crossword setter for The Listener. *Address:* 9 Ridley Road, Warlingham, Surrey CR6 9LR. *T:* Upper Warlingham (088362) 2688.

GILL, (James) Kenneth; President, Saatchi and Saatchi Company PLC, since 1985; *b* 27 Sept. 1920; *s* of late Alfred Charles and Isabel Gill; *m* 1948, Anne Bridgewater; one *s*. *Educ:* Highgate Sch. Served RAC, 24th Lancers and Intelligence Corps, GSO II, 1939–45. Copywriter, S. T. Garland Advertising Service, 1938–39; Chm., Garland-Compton Ltd, 1970–76; Saatchi and Saatchi Company: Chm., 1976–85; Pres. and Dir, 1985–89; retd from Bd, 1989, and re-apptd Pres. FIPA. *Recreations:* the theatre, the cinema, cricket. *Address:* Davenport House, Duntisbourne Abbots, Cirencester, Glos GL7 7JN. *T:*

Miserden (028582) 468; (office) Berkeley Square, W1X 5DH. *Clubs:* Royal Automobile, MCC.

GILL, Kenneth; General Secretary, Manufacturing, Science, Finance, since 1989; Member of General Council of TUC, since 1974; *b* 30 Aug. 1927; *s* of Ernest Frank Gill and Mary Ethel Gill; *m* 1967, Sara Teresa Paterson; two *s* one *d*. *Educ:* Chippenham Secondary School. Engrg apprentice, 1943–48; Draughtsman Designer, Project Engr, Sales Engr in various cos, 1948–62; District Organiser, Liverpool and Ireland TASS, 1962–68; Editor, TASS Union Jl, 1968–72; Dep. Gen. Sec., 1972–74; Gen. Sec. AUEW (TASS), 1974–86, TASS—the Manufacturing Union, 1986–88; Jt Gen. Sec., MSF, 1988–89. Pres., CSEU, 1987–88. Chm., Gen. Council TUC, and Pres. of TUC, 1985–86. Mem., Commn for Racial Equality, 1981–87. *Recreations:* sketching, political caricaturing. *Address:* 164 Ramsden Road, Balham, SW12. *T:* 081–675 1489.

GILL, Rt. Rev. Kenneth Edward; Assistant Bishop of Newcastle (full time), since 1980; *b* 22 May 1932; *s* of Fred and Elsie Gill; *m* 1957, Edna Hammond; one *s* two *d*. *Educ:* Harrogate Grammar School; Hartley Victoria Coll., Manchester. Presbyter in Church of South India, Mysore Diocese, 1958–72; Bishop of Karnataka Central Diocese, Church of South India, 1972–80. *Publications:* Meditations on the Holy Spirit, 1979; Count us Equal, 1990. *Recreation:* gardening. *Address:* 83 Kenton Road, Newcastle upon Tyne NE3 4NL. *T:* 091–285 1502.

GILL, Air Vice-Marshal Leonard William George, DSO 1945; Consultant in personnel planning, since 1973; Chairman, since 1985, and Director, since 1979, Merton Associates (Consultants) Ltd; *b* 31 March 1918; *s* of L. W. Gill, Hornchurch, Essex, and Marguerite Gill; *m* 1st, 1943, Joan Favill Appleyard (marr. diss.); two *s* two *d*; 2nd, Mrs Constance Mary Cull. *Educ:* University Coll. Sch., London. Joined RAF, 1937; served in Far East until 1942; then UK as night fighter pilot; comd No 68 Sqdn for last 6 months of war; subseq. served in various appts incl. comd of Nos 85 and 87 night fighter Sqdns and tour on directing staff at RAF Staff Coll.; Stn Comdr No 1 Flying Trng Sch., Linton-on-Ouse, 1957–60; Dir of Overseas Ops, 1960–62; Nat. Def. Coll. of Canada, 1962–63; Dir of Organisation (Estabs), 1963–66; SASO, RAF Germany, 1966–68; Dir-Gen., Manning (RAF), MoD, 1968–73, retired. Manpower and Planning Advr, P&O Steam Navigation Co., 1973–79. Vice-Pres., RAF Assoc., 1973– (Pres. E Area, 1974–81; Vice-Chm., Central Council, 1984–88). FIPM; FBIM. *Recreations:* shooting, cricket, boats, amateur woodwork. *Address:* 3 Wickham Court, 7 Ashburn Gardens, Kensington, SW7 4DG. *T:* 071–370 2716. *Clubs:* Royal Air Force; Phyllis Court (Henley).

GILL, Malcolm; *see* Gill, G. M.

GILL, Peter, OBE 1980; dramatic author; Associate Director, Royal National Theatre, since 1980; *b* Cardiff, 7 Sept. 1939; *s* of George John Gill and Margaret Mary Browne. *Educ:* St Illtyd's Coll., Cardiff. Associate Dir, Royal Court Theatre, 1970–72; Dir, 1976–80, Associate Dir, 1980, Riverside Studios, Hammersmith; Dir, Royal Nat. Theatre Studio, 1984–90. Productions include: Royal Court: A Collier's Friday Night, 1965; The Local Stigmatic, A Provincial Life, 1966; A Soldier's Fortune, The Daughter-in-law, Crimes of Passion, 1967; The Widowing of Mrs Holroyd, 1968; Life Price, Over Gardens Out, The Sleepers' Den, 1969; The Duchess of Malfi, 1971; Crete & Sergeant Pepper, 1972; The Merry-go-round, 1973; Small Change, The Fool, 1976; Riverside Studios: As You Like It, 1976; Small Change, 1977; The Cherry Orchard (own version), The Changeling, 1978; Measure for Measure, 1979; Julius Caesar, 1980; Scrape off the Black, 1980; Royal National Theatre: A Month in the Country, Don Juan, Scrape off the Black, Much Ado about Nothing, 1981; Danton's Death, Major Barbara, 1982; Kick for Touch, Tales from Hollywood, Antigone (co-dir), 1983; Venice Preserv'd, Fool for Love (transf. Lyric), 1984; The Murderers, As I Lay Dying (also adapted), A Twist of Lemon, In the Blue, Bouncing, Up for None, The Garden of England (co-dir), 1985; Mean Tears, 1987; Mrs Klein, 1988 (transf. Apollo, 1989); Juno and the Paycock, 1989; other London theatres: O'Flaherty VC, Mermaid, 1966; has also produced plays by Shakespeare and modern writers at Stratford-upon-Avon, Nottingham, Edinburgh and in Canada, Germany, Switzerland and USA; Music Theatre and Opera includes: Down By the Green Wood Side (co-dir), Bow Down (co-dir), Queen Elizabeth Hall, 1987; Marriage of Figaro, Opera North, 1987; Television productions include: Grace, 1972; Girl, 1973; A Matter of Taste, Fugitive, 1974; Hitting Town, 1976. *Publications:* plays: The Sleepers' Den, 1965; Over Gardens Out, 1969; Small Change, 1976; Small Change, Kick for Touch, 1985; In the Blue, Mean Tears, 1987. *Address:* c/o Margaret Ramsay, 14a Goodwin's Court, St Martin's Lane, WC2N 4LL.

GILL, Robin Denys; Chairman, Organisation and Executive and Trustee, Royal Anniversary Trust, since 1990; *b* 7 Oct. 1927; *s* of Thomas Henry Gill and Marjorie Mary (*née* Butler); *m* 1st, 1951, Mary Hope Alexander (*d* 1986); three *s*; 2nd, 1991, Denise Spencer Waterhouse. *Educ:* Dulwich Coll.; Brasenose Coll., Oxford (MA). Unilever plc, 1949–54; British Internat. Paper Ltd, 1954–59; Founder and Man. Dir, Border TV Ltd, 1960–64; Man. Dir, ATV Corp. Ltd, 1964–69; Chairman: ITN, 1968–69; 1970 Trust Ltd, 1970–; Ansvar Insce Co. Ltd, 1975–; Standard Ind. Trust Ltd, 1970–81; Director: Reed Paper Gp Ltd, 1970–75; Hewlett Packard Ltd, 1975–; Yarrow Plc, 1979–88; Baring Hambrecht Alpine Ltd, 1986–; SD-Scicon plc, 1988–. Member: Nat. Adv. Bd for Higher Educn; Vis. Cttee, RCA; Cttee, Royal Family Film, 1968–70. *Recreations:* golf, travel, art collecting, gardening. *Address:* 1970 Trust Ltd, 52 Queen Anne Street, W1M 9LA; PO Box 1, East Horsley, Surrey KT24 6RE. *T:* East Horsley (04865) 5290. *Clubs:* Vincent's (Oxford); St George's Hill Golf; Free Foresters Cricket.

GILL, His Honour Stanley Sanderson; a Circuit Judge, 1972–87; *b* Wakefield, 3 Dec. 1923; *s* of Sanderson Henry Briggs Gill, OBE and Dorothy Margaret Gill (*née* Bennett); *m* 1954, Margaret Mary Patricia Grady; one *s* two *d*. *Educ:* Queen Elizabeth Grammar Sch., Wakefield; Magdalene Coll., Cambridge (MA). Served in RAF, 1942–46: 514 and 7 (Pathfinder) Sqdns, Flt Lt 1945. Called to Bar, Middle Temple, 1950; Asst Recorder of Bradford, 1966; Dep. Chm., WR Yorks QS, 1968; County Court Judge, 1971. Mem., County Court Rule Cttee, 1980–84. Chm., Rent Assessment Cttee, 1966–71. *Recreations:* walking, reading. *Address:* Arden Lodge, Thirkleby, Thirsk, North Yorks YO7 2AS.

GILLAM, Patrick John; Deputy Chairman, Standard Chartered PLC, since 1991 (Director, since 1988); Chairman, Booker Tate Ltd, since 1991; *b* 15 April 1933; *s* of late Cyril B. Gillam and of Mary J. Gillam; *m* 1963, Diana Echlin; one *s* one *d*. *Educ:* London School of Economics (BA Hons History). Foreign Office, 1956–57; British Petroleum Co. Ltd, 1957–91; Vice-Pres., BP North America Inc., 1971–74; General Manager, Supply Dept, 1974–78; Dir, BP International Ltd (formerly BP Trading Ltd), 1978–82; Man. Dir, BP, 1981–91; Chairman: BP Shipping Ltd, 1987–88; BP Minerals Internat. Ltd/Selection Trust Ltd, 1982–89; BP Coal Ltd, 1986–88; BP Coal Inc., 1988–90; BP America Inc., 1989–91; BP Nutrition, 1989–91; BP Oil International, 1990–91. Chm., ICC UK, 1989–; Dir, Commercial Union, 1991–. Member: Imperial War Mus. Redevelopment Appeal Exec. Cttee, 1984–; Court of Governors, LSE, 1989–; Trustee, Queen Elizabeth's Foundn for Disabled Develt Trust, 1984–. *Recreation:* gardening. *Address:* Standard Chartered PLC, 1 Aldermanbury Square, EC2V 7SB. *T:* 071–280 7500.

GILLAM, Stanley George, MA, MLitt; Librarian, The London Library, 1956–80; *b* 11 Aug. 1915; *s* of Harry Cosier Gillam, Oxford; *m* 1950, Pauline, *d* of Henry G. Bennett, Oxford; one *s*. *Educ:* Southfield Sch.; Saint Catherine's Coll., Oxford. Bodleian Library, Oxford, 1931–40 and 1946–54. Oxfordshire and Bucks Light Infantry (1st Bucks Bn), 1940–46. Asst Sec. and Sub-Librarian, The London Library, 1954–56. *Publications:* The Building Accounts of the Radcliffe Camera, 1958; The Divinity School and Duke Humfrey's Library at Oxford, 1988; articles in The Bodleian Library Record and other periodicals. *Address:* 18 Forest Side, Kennington, Oxford OX1 5LQ. *T:* Oxford (0865) 730832.

GILLANDERS, Prof. Lewis Alexander; Clinical Professor in Radiology, University of Aberdeen, and Consultant in Charge, Radiology Services (Grampian Health Board), 1964–88, now Professor Emeritus in Radiology; *b* 7 Feb. 1925; *s* of Kenneth John Alexander Gillanders and Nellie May Sherris; *m* 1960, Nora Ellen Wild; one *s* one *d*. *Educ:* Dingwall Academy; Univ. of Glasgow (graduated in medicine, 1947). Commissioned, RAMC, 1948–50; general medical practice, Scottish Highlands, 1950–52; trained in Diagnostic Radiology, Glasgow Royal Infirmary and United Birmingham Hosps, 1953–58; Consultant Radiologist, Aberdeen Teaching Hosps, 1958. Examiner in Radiology for: RCR, 1969–79, and DMRD, 1983–; Faculty of Radiologists, RCSI, 1975–77; Univ. of Nairobi, 1978–80; Univ. of Wales, 1981–83. Member, GMC, 1979–84; Vice-Pres., RCR, 1981–83. *Publications:* chapter in Pye's Surgical Handicraft (1st edn 1884), 19th edn 1969, 20th edn 1977; papers in general medical and radiological literature, students' magazines, etc. *Recreations:* derivations and meanings; golf, do-it-yourself. *Address:* Lyndhurst, 41 Deeview Road South, Cults, Aberdeen AB1 9NA. *Clubs:* Victory Services; Royal Northern & University (Aberdeen).

GILLARD, Francis George, CBE 1961 (OBE 1946); public broadcasting interests in USA, since 1970; *b* 1 Dec. 1908; *s* of late Francis Henry Gillard and of late Emily Jane Gillard, Stockleigh Lodge, Exford; unmarried. *Educ:* Wellington Sch., Som.; St Luke's Coll., Exeter (BSc London). Schoolmaster, 1932–41; Freelance broadcaster, 1936–; joined BBC as Talks Producer, 1941; BBC War Correspondent, 1941. BBC Head of West Regional Programmes, 1945–55; Chief Asst to Dir of Sound Broadcasting with Controller rank, 1955–56; Controller, West Region, BBC, 1956–63; Dir of Sound Broadcasting, 1963–68; Man. Dir, Radio, BBC, 1969–70, retired. Distinguished Fellow, Corp. for Public Broadcasting, Washington, 1970–73. Mem., Council, Educational Foundn for Visual Aids, 1970–87 (Chm., 1977–86). Mem. Finance Cttee, Exeter Univ., 1968–86; Governor, Wellington Sch., Somerset, 1961– (Chm., 1974–80). FRSA 1971. Hon. LLD Exeter, 1987. *Address:* Trevor House, Poole, Wellington, Somerset TA21 9HN. *T:* Wellington (082347) 2890.

GILLES, Prof. Dennis Cyril; Professor of Computing Science, University of Glasgow, since 1966–90; *b* 7 April 1925; *s* of George Cyril Gilles and Gladys Alice Gilles (*née* Batchelor); *m* 1955, Valerie Mary Gilles; two *s* two *d*. *Educ:* Sidcup Gram. Sch.; Imperial Coll., University of London. Demonstrator, Asst Lectr, Imperial Coll., 1945–47; Asst Lectr, University of Liverpool, 1947–49; Mathematician, Scientific Computing Service, 1949–55; Research Asst, University of Manchester, 1955–57; Dir of Computing Lab., University of Glasgow, 1957–66. *Publications:* contribs to Proc. Royal Society and other scientific jls. *Address:* Ardbeg House, Kilmun, Dunoon, Argyll PA23 8SE. *T:* Kilmun (036984) 423.

GILLES, Prof. Chevalier Herbert Michael Joseph, MD; FRCP, FFPHM; Alfred Jones and Warrington Yorke Professor of Tropical Medicine, University of Liverpool, 1972–86, now Emeritus; *b* 10 Sept. 1921; *s* of Joseph and Clementine Gilles; *m* 1955, Wilhelmina Caruana (*d* 1972); three *s* one *d*; *m* 1979, Dr Mejra Kačić-Dimitri. *Educ:* St Edward's Coll., Malta; Royal Univ. of Malta (MD). Rhodes Schol. 1942. MSc Oxon; FMCPH (Nig.), DTM&H. Served War of 1939–45 (1939–45 Star, Africa Star, VM). Mem., Scientific Staff, MRC Lab., Gambia, 1954–58; University of Ibadan: Lectr, Tropical Med., 1958–63; Prof. of Preventive and Social Med., 1963–65; Liverpool University: Sen. Lectr, Tropical Med., 1965–70; Prof. of Tropical Med. (Personal Chair), 1970; Dean, Liverpool Sch. of Tropical Medicine, 1978–83. Vis. Prof., Tropical Medicine, Univ. of Lagos, 1965–68; Royal Society Overseas Vis. Prof., Univ. of Khartoum, Sudan, 1979–80; Hon. Prof. of Tropical Medicine, Zhongshan Med. Coll., Guangzhou, People's Republic of China, 1984; Vis. Prof. of Public Health, Univ. of Malta, 1989–. Consultant Physician in Tropical Medicine, Liverpool AHA(T) and Mersey RHA, 1965–86; Consultant in Malariology to the Army, 1974–86; Consultant in Tropical Medicine to the RAF, 1978–86, to the DHSS, 1980–86. Pres., RSTM&H, 1985–87; Vice President: Internat. Fedn of Tropical Medicine, 1988–92; Liverpool Sch. of Tropical Medicine, 1991–. KStJ 1972. Title of Chevalier awarded for medical work in the tropics. Hon. MD Karolinska Inst., 1979; Hon. DSc Malta, 1984. Darling Foundn Medal and Prize, WHO, 1990. *Publications:* Tropical Medicine for Nurses, 1955, 4th edn 1975; Pathology in the Tropics, 1969, 2nd edn 1976; Management and Treatment of Tropical Diseases, 1971; A Short Textbook of Preventive Medicine for the Tropics, 1973, 3rd edn 1990; Atlas of Tropical Medicine and Parasitology, 1976, 3rd edn 1989; Recent Advances in Tropical Medicine, 1984; Human Antiparasitic Drugs, Pharmacology and Usage, 1985; The Epidemiology and Control of Tropical Diseases, 1987. *Recreations:* swimming, music. *Address:* 3 Conyers Avenue, Birkdale, Southport PR8 4SZ. *T:* Southport (0704) 66664.

GILLESPIE, Prof. Iain Erskine, MD, MSc, FRCS; Professor of Surgery, University of Manchester, since 1970 (Dean of Medical School, 1983–86); *b* 4 Sept. 1931; *s* of John Gillespie and Flora McQuarie; *m* 1957, Mary Muriel McIntyre; one *s* one *d*. *Educ:* Hillhead High Sch., Glasgow; Univ. of Glasgow. MB, ChB, 1953; MD (Hons) 1963; MSc Manchester 1974; FRCSE 1959; FRCS 1963; FRCSGlas 1970. Series of progressive surgical appts in Univs of Glasgow, Sheffield, Glasgow (again), 1953–70. Nat. service, RAMC, 1954–56; MRC grantee, 1956–58; US Postdoctoral Research Fellow, Los Angeles, 1961–62; Titular Prof. of Surgery, Univ. of Glasgow, 1969. Vis. Prof. in USA, Canada, S America, Kenya, S Africa, Australia and New Zealand. Member: Cttee of Surgical Res. Soc. of GB and Ireland, 1975–; Medical Sub-Cttee, UGC, 1975–86; Univs and Polytechnics Grants Cttee, Hong Kong, 1984–89. *Publications:* jt editor and contributor to several surgical and gastroenterological books; numerous articles in various med. jls of GB, USA, Europe. *Recreations:* none. *Address:* 27 Athol Road, Bramhall, Cheshire SK7 1BR. *T:* 061–439 2811.

GILLESPIE, Prof. John Spence; Head of Department of Pharmacology, Glasgow University, since 1968; *b* 5 Sept. 1926; *s* of Matthew Forsyth Gillespie and Myrtle Murie Spence; *m* 1956, Jemima Simpson Ross; four *s* one *d*. *Educ:* Dumbarton Academy; Glasgow Univ. MB ChB (Commendation), PhD. FRCP; FRSE. Hosp. Residency (Surgery), 1949–50; Nat. Service as RMO, 1950–52; hosp. appts, 1952–53; McCunn Res. Schol. in Physiology, Glasgow Univ., 1953–55; Faulds Fellow then Sharpey Schol. in Physiology Dept, University Coll. London, 1955–57; Glasgow University: Lectr in Physiol., 1957–59; Sophie Fricke Res. Fellow, Royal Soc., in Rockefeller Inst., 1959–60; Sen. Lectr in Physiol., 1961–63; Henry Head Res. Fellow, Royal Soc., 1963–68; Vice-Principal, 1983–87, 1988–. *Publications:* articles in Jls of Physiol. and Pharmacol.

Recreations: gardening, painting. *Address:* 5 Boclair Road, Bearsden, Glasgow G61 2AE. *T:* 041–942 0318.

GILLESPIE, Prof. Ronald James, PhD, DSc; FRS 1977; FRSC; FRSC (UK); FCIC; Professor of Chemistry, McMaster University, Hamilton, Ont, since 1960; *b* London, England, 21 Aug. 1924; Canadian citizen; *s* of James A. Gillespie and Miriam G. (*née* Kirk); *m* 1950, Madge Ena Garner; two *d. Educ:* London Univ. (BSc 1945, PhD 1949, DSc 1957). FRSC 1965; FCIC 1960; FRIC; Mem., Amer. Chem. Soc. Asst Lectr, Dept of Chemistry, 1948–50, Lectr, 1950–58, UCL; Commonwealth Fund Fellow, Brown Univ., RI, USA, 1953–54; McMaster University: Associate Prof., Dept of Chem., 1958–60; Prof., 1960–62; Chm., Dept of Chem., 1962–65. Professeur Associé, l'Univ. des Sciences et Techniques de Languedoc, Montpellier, 1972–73; Visiting Professor: Univ. of Geneva, 1976; Univ. of Göttingen, 1978. Member: Chem. Soc. (Nyholm Lectr 1979); Faraday Soc. Hon. LLD: Dalhousie Univ., 1988; Concordia Univ., 1988. Medals: Ramsay, UCL, 1949; Harrison Meml, Chem. Soc., 1954; Canadian Centennial, 1967; Chem. Inst. of Canada, 1977; Silver Jubilee, 1978; Henry Marshall Tory, Royal Soc. of Canada, 1983. Awards: Noranda, Chem. Inst. of Canada, 1966 (for inorganic chem.); Amer. Chem. Soc. N-Eastern Reg., 1971 (in phys. chem.); Manufg Chemists Assoc. Coll. Chem. Teacher, 1972; Amer. Chem. Soc., 1973 (for distinguished service in advancement of inorganic chem.), 1980 (for creative work in fluorine chem.); Chem. Inst. of Canada/Union Carbide, 1976 (for chemical educn); Izaak Walton Killam Meml, Canada Council (for outstanding contrib. to advancement of res. in chemistry), 1987. *Publications:* Molecular Geometry, 1972 (London; German and Russian trans, 1975); (jtly) Chemistry, 1986, 2nd edn, 1989; The VSEPR Model of Molecular Geometry, 1990; papers in Jl Amer. Chem. Soc., Canadian Jl of Chem., and Inorganic Chem. *Recreations:* skiing, sailing. *Address:* Department of Chemistry, McMaster University, Hamilton, Ont L8S 4M1, Canada. *T:* (416) 525–9140, ext. 3304.

GILLESPIE, William Hewitt, MD, FRCP; FRCPsych; Emeritus Physician, Maudsley Hospital (Physician, 1936–70); Hon. Member, British Psychoanalytical Society, 1975; *b* 6 Aug. 1905; *s* of Rev. W. H. Gillespie, Manchuria and Co. Down, and of Isabella B. Gillespie (*née* Grills), Co. Down, N Ireland; *m* 1st, 1932, Dr Helen Turover (*d* 1975); one *s* one *d*; 2nd, 1975, Sadie Mervis. *Educ:* George Watson's Coll.; Universities of Edinburgh and Vienna. University of Edinburgh: 1st pl. Open Bursary Exam., 1924, MB, ChB (hons), 1929, Dip. in Psychiatry, 1931, MD 1934; MRCP 1936; FRCP 1962; McCosh Travelling Scholarship, in Vienna, 1930–31. LCC Mental Hosps Service, 1931–36; Lecturer, Inst. of Psychiatry, 1944–70; Dir, London Clinic of Psychoanalysis, 1944–47. Freud Meml Vis. Prof. of Psychoanalysis, Univ. Coll. London, 1976–77. Trng Sec., Inst. of Psychoanalysis, 1947–50; Chm., Inst of Psychoanalysis, 1954–56; President: British Psychoanalytical Soc., 1950–53 and 1971–72; Internat. Psychoanalytic Assoc., 1957–61. FRSocMed. *Publications:* contrib to: Recent Advances in Psychiatry, 1944; Psychiatrie sociale de l'enfant, 1951; Psychoanalysis and the Occult, 1953; The Sexual Perversions, 1956; The Pathology and Treatment of Sexual Deviation, 1964; Foundations of Child Psychiatry, 1968. Various articles in medical, psychiatric and psychoanalytic jls. *Recreations:* music, reading, walking. *Address:* 4 Eton Villas, NW3 4SX.

GILLETT, Rev. Canon David Keith; Principal, Trinity Theological College, Bristol, since 1988; *b* 25 Jan. 1945; *s* of Norman and Kathleen Gillett; *m* 1988, Valerie Shannon. *Educ:* Leeds Univ. (BA Theol. 1st cl. 1965; MPhil 1968). Curate, St Luke's, Watford, 1968–71; Northern Sec., Pathfinders and Church Youth Fellowship's Assoc., 1971–74; Lectr, St John's Coll., Nottingham, 1974–79; Co-Leader, Christian Renewal Centre for Reconciliation, NI, 1979–82; Vicar of St Hugh's, Luton, 1982–88. Mem., Gen. Synod of C of E, 1985–88, 1990–. Hon. Canon of Bristol Cathedral, 1991–. *Publications:* Learning in the Local Congregation, 1979; The Darkness where God is, 1983; co-author and contributor to various books and reference works. *Recreations:* photography, gardening. *Address:* 16 Ormerod Road, Stoke Bishop, Bristol BS9 1BB. *T:* Bristol (0272) 682646.

GILLETT, Sir Robin (Danvers Penrose), 2nd Bt *cr* 1959; GBE 1976; RD 1965; Underwriting Member of Lloyd's; Lord Mayor of London for 1976–77; *b* 9 Nov. 1925; *o s* of Sir (Sydney) Harold Gillett, 1st Bt, MC, and Audrey Isabel Penrose Wardlaw (*d* 1962); *S* father, 1976; *m* 1950, Elizabeth Marion Grace, *e d* of late John Findlay, JP, Busby, Lanarks; two *s. Educ:* Nautical Coll., Pangbourne. Served Canadian Pacific Steamships, 1943–60; Master Mariner 1951; Staff Comdr 1957; Hon. Comdr RNR 1971. Elder Brother of Trinity House; Fellow and Founder Mem., Nautical Inst. City of London (Ward of Bassishaw): Common Councilman 1965–69; Alderman 1969; Sheriff 1973; one of HM Lieuts for City of London, 1975; Chm. Civil Defence Cttee, 1967–68; Pres., City of London Civil Defence Instructors Assoc., 1967–78; Vice-Pres., City of London Centre, St John Ambulance Assoc.; Pres., Nat. Waterways Transport Assoc., 1979–83; Dep. Commonwealth Pres., Royal Life Saving Soc. Vice-Chm., PLA, 1979–84. Master, Hon. Co. of Master Mariners, 1979–80. Trustee, Nat. Maritime Mus., 1982–. Chm. of Governors, Pangbourne Coll. Chancellor, City Univ., 1976–77. FIAM (Pres., 1980–84; Gold Medal, 1982). Hon. DSc City, 1976. Gentleman Usher of the Purple Rod, Order of the British Empire, 1985–. KStJ 1977 (OStJ 1974). Gold Medal, Administrative Management Soc., USA, 1983. Officer, Order of Leopard, Zaire, 1973; Comdr, Order of Dannebrog, 1974; Order of Johan Sedia Mahkota (Malaysia), 1974; Grand Cross of Municipal Merit (Lima), 1977. *Recreation:* sailing. *Heir: s* Nicholas Danvers Penrose Gillett, BSc, ARCS [*b* 24 Sept. 1955; *m* 1987, Haylie, *er d* of Dennis Brooks]. *Address:* 4 Fairholt Street, Knightsbridge, SW7 1EQ. *T:* 071–589 9860. *Clubs:* City Livery, City Livery Yacht (Admiral), Guildhall, Royal Yacht Squadron, Royal London Yacht (Cdre, 1984–85), Guild of World Traders' Yacht (Admiral).

GILLFORD, Lord; Patrick James Meade; with Ian Greer & Associates, since 1990; *b* 28 Dec. 1960; *s* and *heir* of Earl of Clanwilliam, *qv*; *m* 1989, Serena Emily, *d* of Lt-Col B. J. Lockhart; one *d. Educ:* Eton College. 1 Bn, Coldstream Guards, 1979–83. Exec., Hanson plc, 1983–90, attached Home Office as special advr to Home Sec., 1986–88. Councillor (C) Royal Bor. of Kensington and Chelsea, 1990–. *Recreations:* prison reform and prison sentencing policy, free fall parachuting, Palladian architecture. *Address:* 19 Catherine Place, SW1E 6DX. *T:* 071–630 5651. *Clubs:* Turf; Mill Reef (Antigua, WI).

GILLIAM, Terry; animator, actor, writer; film director, since 1973; *b* Minneapolis, USA, 22 Nov. 1940; *s* of James H. and Beatrice Gilliam; *m* 1973, Maggie Weston; one *s* two *d. Educ:* Occidental Coll., LA, Calif. *Television:* resident cartoonist, We Have Ways of Making You Laugh, 1968; animator: Do Not Adjust Your Set, 1968–69; (also actor and co-writer), Monty Python's Flying Circus, 1969–74 and 1979; The Marty Feldman Comedy Machine, 1971–72; The Do-It-Yourself Film Animation, 1974; *films:* co-writer, actor and animator: And Now For Something Completely Different, 1971; (also co-director) Monty Python and the Holy Grail, 1974; Monty Python's Life of Brian, 1979; Monty Python Live at the Hollywood Bowl, 1982; Monty Python's The Meaning of Life, 1983; (animator, writer) The Miracle of Flight, 1974; (writer, director) Jabberwocky, 1977; (co-writer, producer, director) Time Bandits, 1981; (co-writer, director) Brazil, 1985; (co-writer, director) The Adventures of Baron Münchhausen, 1989. Hon. DFA Occidental Coll., 1987; Hon. Dr RCA, 1989. *Publications:* Animations of Mortality, 1978; contributed to: Monty Python's Big Red Book, 1971; The Brand New Monty Python Book, 1973, Monty Python and the Holy Grail, 1977; Monty Python's Life of Brian, 1979; Time Bandits, 1981; Monty Python's The Meaning of Life, 1983; (jtly) The Adventures of Baron Münchhausen, 1989. *Recreations:* too busy. *Address:* Mayday, c/o Prominent Studios, 68A Delancey Street, NW1. *T:* 071–284 0242.

GILLIAT, Lt-Col Sir Martin (John), GCVO 1981 (KCVO 1962; CVO 1954); MBE 1946; DL; Private Secretary to Queen Elizabeth the Queen Mother since 1956; Vice-Lieutenant of Hertfordshire, 1971–86; *b* 8 Feb. 1913; *s* of late Lieut-Col John Babington Gilliat and Muriel Helen Lycette Gilliat; unmarried. *Educ:* Eton; RMC, Sandhurst. Joined KRRC, 1933. Served War of 1939–45 (despatches, Prisoner of War). Dep. Military Sec. to Viceroy and Governor-Gen. of India, 1947–48; Comptroller to Commissioner-Gen. for UK in South-East Asia, 1948–51; Mil. Sec. to Governor-Gen. of Australia, 1953–55. Hon. Bencher, Middle Temple, 1977. Hon. LLD London, 1977. DL Herts, 1963. *Address:* Appletrees, Welwyn, Herts. *T:* Welwyn (043871) 4675; 31A St James's Palace, SW1. *T:* 071–930 1440. *Clubs:* Travellers', Buck's, Brooks's.

GILLIATT, Penelope Ann Douglass Conner, FRSL; fiction writer for the New Yorker, since 1967; also employed by The Sunday Times and The Observer; freelance fiction writer of books, plays and films; *b* London, 25 March 1932; UK citizen; *d* of late Cyril Conner and Mary Stephanie Douglass; *m* 1st, 1954, Prof. R. W. Gilliatt, MC (marr. diss.; he *d* 1991); 2nd, 1963, John Osborne, *qv* (marr. diss.); one *d. Educ:* Queen's Coll., Harley St, London; Bennington Coll., Vermont. FRSL 1978. Contributor to New Statesman, Spectator, Guardian, Sight and Sound, Encore, Grand Street, Encounter, London Magazine, London Review of Books, etc; film critic, Observer, 1961–65 and 1966–67, theatre critic, 1965–66; film critic, New Yorker, 1967–79 (six months of each yr). Mem., Bd of Adv. Sponsors, Symphony of UN, 1985–. Mem., Labour Party. Property, and Nobody's Business (plays), perf. Amer. Place Theatre, New York, 1980; But When All's Said and Done (play), Actor's Studio, 1981; BBC plays incl. Living on the Box, The Flight Fund, 1978, and In the Unlikely Event of an Emergency, 1979; Beach of Aurora (original libretto, with music by Tom Eastwood), ENO, 1982. Grant for creative achievement in fiction, National Inst. of Arts and Letters, 1972. *Publications: novels:* One by One, 1965; A State of Change, 1967; The Cutting Edge, 1979; Mortal Matters, 1983; A Woman of Singular Occupation, 1988; *short story collections:* What's It Like Out?, 1968 (Come Back If It Doesn't Get Better, NY 1967); Nobody's Business, 1972; Splendid Lives, 1978; Quotations from Other Lives, 1982; They Sleep Without Dreaming, 1985; 22 stories, 1986; Lingo, 1990; selected as contributor to: Penguin Modern Stories, 1970; Best Short Stories of 1987; Best Short Stories of 1988; Best Short Stories of 1989; *non-fiction:* Unholy Fools: film and theatre, 1975; Jean Renoir: essays, conversations, reviews, 1975; Jacques Tati, 1977; Three-Quarter Face: profiles and reflections (with much additional material), 1980; To Wit, 1990; *screenplay:* Sunday Bloody Sunday, 1971 (Oscar nomination for best orig. screenplay; awards for best orig. screenplay, NY Film Critics Circle, Nat. Soc. of Film Critics, USA, and British Soc. of Film Critics), repr. entitled with new essay by author Making Sunday Bloody Sunday, 1986; lengthy essays in Grand Street about Northumberland, Polish films, new British film-makers; profiles: in New Yorker on Jean Renoir, Woody Allen, Jean-Luc Godard, Jacques Tati, Henri Langlois of the French Cinemathèque, Jeanne Moreau, Diane Keaton, Graham Greene, Luis Buñuel, John Cleese, and Jonathan Miller; in Sunday Telegraph Magazine on John Huston; in Observer on Fred Astaire, Fellini, Whoopi Goldberg, Woody Allen, Stanley Kubrick. *Address:* c/o New Yorker Magazine, 25 West 43rd Street, New York, NY 10036, USA; 29 Burnham Court, W2.

GILLIBRAND, Sydney, CBE 1991; FEng 1987; FRAeS; Director, British Aerospace PLC, since 1987; Chairman, Aerospace Companies, British Aerospace PLC, since 1990; *b* 2 June 1934; *s* of Sydney and Maud Gillibrand; *m* 1960, Angela Ellen Williams; three *s* (and one *s* decd). *Educ:* Preston Grammar Sch.; Harris Coll., Preston; College of Aeronautics, Cranfield (MSc). FRAeS 1975. English Electric: apprentice, Preston, 1950; Chief Stress Engr, 1966; Works Man., Preston, 1974; Special Dir, BAC (Preston) Ltd, 1974; Dir of Manufacturing, Mil. Aircraft Div., 1977; British Aerospace Aircraft Group: Div. Prodn Dir, Warton, 1978; Dep. Man. Dir, Warton Div., and Bd Mem., Aircraft Gp, 1981; Div. Man. Dir, Kingston/Brough Div., 1983, Weybridge Div., 1984; Man. Dir, Civil Aircraft Div., BAe, 1986; Chm., British Aerospace (Commercial Aircraft) Ltd, 1988. Pres., SBAC, 1990–91. Silver Medal, RAeS, 1981. *Recreation:* golf. *Address:* British Aerospace PLC, 11 Strand, WC2N 5JT. *T:* 071–930 1020. *Club:* St James's.

GILLICK, Rev. John, SJ; MA Oxon; Spiritual Director, St Peter's National Seminary, Hammanskraal, S Africa, 1986–90, retired; *b* Wallasey, 27 March 1916; 2nd *s* of Laurence Gillick and Catherine Devine. *Educ:* St Francis Xavier's Coll., Liverpool; Heythrop and Campion Hall, Oxford (1st Cl. Hons Mod. History). Asst Master at Mount St Mary's and Beaumont. Two years writing and photography in Italy and Africa. Headmaster, Beaumont Coll., 1964–67; studied psychology at Loyola Univ., Chicago, 1967–68 (MA); Dir, Laboratories for the Training of Religious Superiors in S Africa, 1969; Dir, Fons Vitae (Pastoral Institute for Religious), 1970–84. *Publications:* Teaching the Mass, 1961; Baptism, 1962; followed by Teaching the Mass: African, 1963; Teaching the Sacraments: African, 1964; Teaching Confirmation: African, 1964, etc; *illustrations for:* The Breaking of Bread, 1950; The Pilgrim Years, 1956; Our Faith, 1956; The Holy Mass, 1958; Christ Our Life, 1960. *Address:* 8 The Elms, York Road, Rosebank, 7700, South Africa; c/o 114 Mount Street, W1Y 6AH.

GILLIES, (Maurice) Gordon, TD and Bar 1948; QC (Scotland) 1958; Sheriff Principal of South Strathclyde, Dumfries and Galloway, 1982–88; *b* 17 Oct. 1916; *s* of James Brown Gillies, Advocate in Aberdeen, and Rhoda Ledingham; *m* 1954, Anne Bethea McCall-Smith. *Educ:* Aberdeen Grammar Sch.; Merchiston Castle; Edinburgh Univ. Advocate, 1946; Advocate Depute, 1953–58; Sheriff of Lanarkshire, later S Strathclyde, Dumfries and Galloway, 1958–82. *Recreation:* golf. *Address:* 1 The Warren, Gullane, East Lothian EH31 2BE. *T:* Gullane (0620) 842857. *Clubs:* New (Edinburgh); Hon. Company of Edinburgh Golfers.

GILLILAND, David; *see* Gilliland, J. A. D.

GILLILAND, David Jervois Thetford; practising solicitor and farmer; *b* 14 July 1932; *s* of late Major W. H. Gilliland and of Mrs N. H. Gilliland; *m* 1st, 1958, Patricia, *o d* of late J. S. Wilson and late Mrs Wilson (marr. diss. 1976); two *s* three *d*; 2nd, 1976, Jennifer Johnston, *qv. Educ:* Rockport Prep. Sch.; Wrekin Coll.; Trinity Coll., Dublin. BA 1954, LLB 1955. Qualified as solicitor, 1957, own practice. Mem. ITA, 1965–70; Chm., N Ireland Adv. Cttee of ITA, 1965–70. Mem. Council, Internat. Dendrology Soc., 1966–75; etc. *Recreations:* gardening, sailing, fishing. *Address:* Brook Hall, 65 Culmore Road, Londonderry, Northern Ireland BT48 8JE. *T:* Londonderry (0504) 351297.

GILLILAND, (James Andrew) David; QC 1984; a Recorder, since 1989; *b* 29 Dec. 1937; *s* of James Albin Gilliland and Mary Gilliland (*née* Gray); *m* 1961, Elsie McCully; two *s. Educ:* Campbell College; Queen's University Belfast. LLB (1st Class Hons) 1960. Called to the Bar, Gray's Inn, 1964 (Holt Scholar, Atkin Scholar, Macaskie Scholar); Lectr in Law, Manchester University, 1960–72. *Recreations:* music, opera, stamp collecting, wind surfing, skiing. *Address:* 7 New Square, Lincoln's Inn, WC2A 3QS. *T:* 071–405

1266; 20 North John Street, Liverpool L2 9RL. *T:* 051–236 6757. *Club:* Athenæum (Liverpool).

GILLILAND, Jennifer, (Mrs David Gilliland); *see* Johnston, J.

GILLING, Lancelot Cyril Gilbert, OBE 1985; CBiol, FIBiol; FRAgS; Member, Royal Commission on Environmental Pollution, 1984–89; *b* 7 March 1920; *s* of Gilbert Joseph Gilling and Esther Marianne Gilling (*née* Clapp); *m* 1951, Brenda Copp; two *d*. *Educ:* Shebbear Coll., N Devon; Reading Univ. (BSc Agr). Pres. Union, Reading Univ., 1948–49. Lectr, Dorset Coll. of Agric., 1949–51; Head of Agric. Dept, Writtle Coll. of Agric., Essex, 1951–57; Principal, Askham Bryan Coll. of Agric. & Hortic., 1957–84. Member: Technical Develt Cttee and Educn and Gen. Purposes Cttee, Royal Agricl Soc., 1970–85; Northern Regional Panel, MAFF, 1982–88; Adv. Cttee on Agric. and Vet. Sci., British Council, 1972–86; Chm., York Agricl Soc., 1983– (Pres., 1981–82). Vice-Chm., Sub-Cttee, Yorkshire Museum, 1985–; Chm. and Life Vice-Pres., Yorks Philosophical Soc., 1982–88. Mem. Council and Chm., F and GP Cttee, Yorks Wildlife Trust, 1985–; Chm. York Centre, Nat. Trust, 1988–. Gov., Diocesan Coll. of Ripon and York St John, 1976–. Hon. Mem., CGLI. *Publications:* contribs to Agricultural Progress, Jl of Agricl Educn Assoc. and Jl of Royal Agricl Soc. *Recreations:* tennis, badminton, choral music. *Address:* The Spinney, Brandsby, York YO6 4RQ.

GILLINGHAM, (Francis) John, CBE 1982 (MBE 1944); FRSE 1970; Professor of Neurological Surgery, University of Edinburgh, 1963–80, now Emeritus; at Royal Infirmary of Edinburgh and Western General Hospital, Edinburgh, 1963–80; Consultant Neuro-Surgeon to the Army in Scotland, 1966–80; *b* 15 March 1916; *s* of John H. Gillingham, Upwey, Dorset; *m* 1945, Irene Judy Jude; four *s*. *Educ:* Hardye's Sch., Dorset; St Bartholomew's Hosp. Medical Coll., London. Matthews Duncan Gold Medal, 1939, MRCS, LRCP Oct. 1939; MB, BS (London) Nov. 1939; FRCS 1947; FRCSE 1955; FRCPE 1967; FRCPGlas 1982. Prof. of Surgical Neurol., King Saud Univ., Saudi Arabia, 1983–85, now Emeritus. Advr in Neuro-Surgery, MoD, Kingdom of Saudi Arabia, 1980–83. Hunterian Prof., RCS, 1957; Morison Lectr, RCP of Edinburgh, 1960; Colles Lectr, College of Surgeons of Ireland, 1962; Elsberg Lectr, College of Physicians and Surgeons, NY, 1967; Penfield Lectr, Middle East Med. Assembly, 1970. Hon. Mem., Soc. de Neurochirurgie de Langue Française, 1964; Hon. Mem., Soc. of Neurol. Surgeons (USA), 1965; Hon. Mem., Royal Academy of Medicine of Valencia, 1967; Hon. and Corresp. Mem. of a number of foreign neuro-surgical societies; Hon. Pres., World Fedn of Neurosurgical Socs. President: Medico-Chirurgical Soc. of Edinburgh, 1965–67; European Soc. of Stereostatic and Functional Neurosurgery, 1972–76; RCSE, 1979–82 (Vice-Pres., 1974–77; Mem., Court of Regents, 1990). Hon. MD Thessaloniki, 1973. Jim Clark Foundn Award, 1979; Medal of City of Gdansk, Poland, 1980. *Publications:* Clinical Surgery: Neurological Surgery, 1969; papers on surgical management of cerebral vascular disease, head and spinal injuries, Parkinsonism and the dyskinesias, epilepsy and other neurosurgical subjects. *Recreations:* sailing, travel, photography. *Address:* Easter Park House, Barnton Avenue, Edinburgh EH4 6JR. *T:* 031–336 3528. *Clubs:* New (Edinburgh); Nautico (Javea, Alicante).

GILLINGHAM, Michael John, FSA; Chairman, Advisory Board for Redundant Churches, since 1989 (Member, since 1979); *b* 26 June 1933; *s* of John Morey Gillingham and Marion Gillingham. *Educ:* Yeovil School; Corpus Christi College, Cambridge (MA, LLB). Director, John Sparks Ltd, 1976–. Member: London Diocesan Adv. Cttee for Care of Churches, 1965–; Organs Adv. Cttee, Council for Care of Churches, 1967–; Westminster Abbey Architectural Adv. Panel, 1990–; Chichester Cathedral Fabric Cttee, 1990–; Chm., British Inst. of Organ Studies, 1976–83; Organ Consultant: St Michael, Framlingham, 1968; St James, Clerkenwell, 1978; Peterborough Cathedral, 1980; Chichester Cathedral, 1986; St Andrew, Holborn, 1989; St Matthew, Westminster, 1989; for restoration of organ-case, Gloucester Cathedral, 1971; and other historic organs in London and elsewhere. Hon. RCO 1986. *Publications:* articles on organ-cases, organ history, Chinese art. *Recreation:* looking at buildings and works of art. *Address:* 4 Fournier Street, Spitalfields, E1 6QE. *T:* 071–377 1576. *Club:* Athenæum.

GILLINGHAM, Rev. Canon Peter Llewellyn, LVO 1955; MA 1940; Chaplain to the Queen, 1952–84; Hon. Canon of Chichester Cathedral (Wisborough Prebendary), 1969–77, Canon Emeritus since 1977; *b* 3 May 1914; *s* of late Rev. Canon Frank Hay Gillingham; *m* 1947, Diana, *d* of Lieut-Gen. Sir Alexander Hood; two *s* two *d*. *Educ:* Cheam; Marlborough; Oriel Coll., Oxford. Curate, Tonbridge Parish Church, 1937–40; Curate-in-Charge, St George's Church, Oakdale, Poole, 1940–43. Served War of 1939–45, Chaplain, RNVR, 1943–46; Chaplain, Blundell's Sch., Tiverton, 1946–49; Hon. Chaplain to King George VI, 1949–52; Chaplain to Royal Chapel of All Saints, Windsor Great Park, 1949–55; Vicar of St Mildred's, Addiscombe, 1955; Vicar of St Mary the Virgin, Horsham, 1960–77; Rural Dean of Horsham, 1974–77; Asst Chaplain, Sherborne Girls' Sch., 1977–79, Chaplain and Librarian, 1979–82. *Recreations:* golf, sailing. *Address:* Maplestead Cottage, Leiston Road, Aldeburgh, Suffolk. *T:* Aldeburgh (072845) 2739.

GILLIS, His Honour Bernard Benjamin, QC 1954; MA Cantab; a Circuit Judge (Additional Judge, Central Criminal Court), 1964–80; *m*; one *s*. *Educ:* Downing Coll., Cambridge, Hon. Fellow, 1976. Squadron Leader, RAF, 1940–45. Called to the Bar, Lincoln's Inn, 1927, Bencher 1960, Treasurer 1976; North Eastern Circuit and Central Criminal Court. Commr, Central Criminal Court, 1959; Commissioner of Assize: Lancaster, 1960; Chelmsford, 1961; Bodmin, 1963. Recorder of Bradford, 1958–64. *Address:* 3 Adelaide Crescent, Hove, E Sussex BN3 2JD. *Club:* Royal Air Force.

GILLMAN, Bernard Arthur, (Gerry Gillman); Member, Police Complaints Authority, since 1986; General Secretary, Society of Civil and Public Servants, 1973–85; *b* 14 April 1927; *s* of Elias Gillman and Gladys Gillman; *m* 1951, Catherine Mary Antonia Harvey. *Educ:* Archbishop Tenison's Grammar Sch. Civil Service, 1946–53; Society of Civil Servants, 1953–85. *Address:* 2 Burnham Street, Kingston-upon-Thames, Surrey KT2 6QR. *T:* 081–546 6905. *Club:* MCC.

GILLMORE, Air Vice-Marshal Alan David, CB 1955; CBE 1944; RAF (retired); *b* 17 Oct. 1905; *s* of late Rev. David Sandeman Gillmore and Allis Emily Widmer; *m* 1931, Kathleen Victoria Morris; three *s*. *Educ:* St Dunstan's Sch., Burnham-on-Sea; King's Sch., Ely. RAF Cadet Coll., Cranwell, Lincs, 1923–25; Commission in RAF, 1925; 13 Sqdn, 1925–27; 208 Sqdn (Egypt), 1927–29; Instr, Sch. of Air Pilotage, 1931–33; O i/c Navigation Flight, 1934–35; 202 Flying Boat Sqdn (Malta), 1935–36; HQ no 6 (Aux.) Gp, 1936–39; RN Staff Coll., 1939; Future Ops Planning Staff, 1940–41; Dep. Dir, Overseas Orgn (Air Min.), 1940–41; Instr, RAF Staff Coll., 1942; OC RAF Station Wick, 1943–44; Dir, Maritime Ops (Air Min.), 1944–45; AOC RAF W Africa, 1945–46; Dir of Postings (Air Min.), 1946–47; IDC, 1948; AOC 64 Gp, 1949–51; Commandant RAF Staff Coll., Bracknell, 1951–53; SASO, FEAF, 1953–56; SASO, Home Command, 1956–59; retired 1959. *Address:* Southpen, 17 Naish Road, Burnham-on-Sea, Som. *Club:* Royal Air Force.

See also Sir D. H. Gillmore.

GILLMORE, Sir David (Howe), KCMG 1990 (CMG 1982); HM Diplomatic Service; Permanent Under-Secretary of State and Head of the Diplomatic Service, since 1991; *b* 16 Aug. 1934; *s* of Air Vice-Marshal A. D. Gillmore, *qv*; *m* 1964, Lucile Morin; two *s*. *Educ:* Trent Coll.; King's Coll., Cambridge (MA). Reuters Ltd, 1958–60; Asst to Dir-Gen., Polypapier, SA, Paris, 1960–65; Teacher, ILEA, 1965–69; HM Diplomatic Service, 1970; Foreign and Commonwealth Office, 1970–72; First Sec., Moscow, 1972–75; Counsellor, UK Delegn, Vienna, 1975–78; Head of Defence Dept, FCO, 1979–81; Asst Under Sec. of State, FCO, 1981–83; High Comr in Malaysia, 1983–86; Dep. Under-Sec. of State, FCO, 1986–90; Visiting Fellow: Harvard Univ., 1990–91; WEU Inst., Paris, 1990–91. *Publication: novel* A Way From Exile, 1967. *Recreations:* books, music, exercise. *Address:* Foreign and Commonwealth Office, Downing Street, SW1.

GILLON, Dr Raanan Evelyn Zvi, FRCP; Director, Imperial College Health Service, since 1982; Editor, Journal of Medical Ethics, since 1980; *b* 15 April 1941; *s* of Diana Gillon and late Meir Gillon; *m* 1966, Angela Spear; one *d*. *Educ:* Christ's Hospital; University College London (MB BS 1964); Christ Church, Oxford; Birbeck College London (BA Phil 1st cl. Hons 1979). MRCP 1974, FRCP 1988. Medical journalism, 1964–71 (Ed., Medical Tribune); part-time GP, part-time philosophy student then teacher, 1974–; Dir of Teaching in Medical Ethics, KCL, 1986–89. Vis. Prof. in Med. Ethics, KCL, 1988–91, St Mary's Hosp. Med. Sch. and Imperial Coll., 1989–. Chm., Imperial Coll. Ethics Cttee, 1984–. Mem., BMA, 1964; MRSM 1966. Hon RCM 1986. *Publications:* Philosophical Medical Ethics, 1986; numerous papers on medical ethics. *Recreations:* enjoying the company of wife and daughter; reading moral philosophy and, intermittently, thrillers; playing (own) trumpet, or rather, Uncle Peter's trumpet, kindly lent in 1954; ski-ing, swimming, cooking, winetasting. *Address:* 42 Brynmaer Road, SW11 4EW. *T:* 071–622 1450; (office) 14 Prince's Gardens, SW7 1NA. *T:* 071–584 6301.

GILMARTIN, Hugh, OBE 1981; HM Diplomatic Service, retired; *b* 20 Nov. 1923; *s* of late Edward Gilmartin and Catherine Gilmartin (*née* McFadyen); *m* 1962, Olga, *d* of late Nicholas Alexander Plotnikoff; two *s* one *d*. *Educ:* Holy Cross Academy; Edinburgh Univ. Entered HM Diplomatic Service, 1945; Rome, 1945; Vienna, 1945–47; FO, 1947; UN Special Cttee on the Balkans, 1948; Bahrain, 1949–50; FO, 1951–53; Jakarta, 1953–55; Buenos Aires, 1955–57; Second Secretary, Asuncion, 1957–58; Bahrain, 1959–60; Panama, 1961–63; FO, 1963–65; First Sec. and Head of Chancery, Tegucigalpa, 1965–67; Zürich, 1968–73; First Sec., Office of UK Permanent Representative to the European Communities, Brussels, 1973–75; Asst Head of Training Dept, FO, 1975–79; Basle, 1979–80; Consul-Gen., Brisbane, 1980–83; retired 1983; assigned to Falkland Is Dept, FCO, 1984–85. Governor, Rye St Antony Sch., Oxford. Life Mem., Nat. Trust for Scotland. *Recreations:* walking, swimming, gardening. *Address:* 19 Phillimore Road, Emmer Green, Reading, Berks RG4 8UR. *T:* Reading (0734) 476902. *Clubs:* Civil Service; Royal Commonwealth Society (Queensland).

GILMORE, Brian Terence; Deputy Secretary, Office of the Minister for the Civil Service, Cabinet Office, since 1988; *b* 25 May 1937; *s* of John Henry Gilmore and Edith Alice Gilmore; *m* 1962, Rosalind Edith Jean Fraser (*see* R. E. J. Gilmore). *Educ:* Wolverhampton Grammar Sch.; Christ Church, Oxford (Passmore-Edwards Prize, 1956; BA Lit. Hum.; MA 1961). CRO and Diplomatic Service Admin Office, 1958–65: Private Sec. to Perm. Sec., 1960–61, to Parly Under Sec., 1961–62; Asst Private Sec. to Sec. of State, 1962–64; British Embassy, Washington, 1965–68; Min. of Technology and DTI, 1968–72: Private Sec. to Minister of State, Industry, 1969–70, and to Lord Privy Seal and Leader of the House of Lords, 1971–72; CSD, 1972–81; Under Sec., 1979; Principal, CS Coll., 1979–81; HM Treasury, 1981–88; Principal Estab. Officer and Principal Finance Officer, 1982–84. *Recreations:* reading, music, Greece. *Address:* c/o Cabinet Office (OMCS), Horse Guards Road, SW1P 3AL. *Club:* Athenæum.

GILMORE, Carol Jacqueline; *see* Ellis, C. J.

GILMORE, Rosalind Edith Jean, (Mrs B. T. Gilmore); Chairman (First Commissioner), Building Societies Commission, since 1991; Chief Registrar of Friendly Societies and Industrial Assurance Commissioner, since 1991; *b* 23 March 1937; *o c* of Sir Robert Brown Fraser, OBE, and Betty Fraser; *m* 1962, Brian Terence Gilmore, *qv*. *Educ:* King Alfred Sch.; University Coll. London (BA; Fellow, 1989); Newnham Coll., Cambridge (BA, MA; Associate Fellow, 1986). Asst Principal, HM Treasury, 1960–65; IBRD, 1966–67; Principal, HM Treasury, 1968–73; Prin. Pvte Sec. to Chancellor of Duchy of Lancaster, Cabinet Office, 1974; HM Treasury: Asst Sec., 1978–80; Press Sec. and Hd of Inf., 1980–82; Gen. Man., Corporate Planning, Dunlop Ltd, 1982–83; Dir of Marketing, Nat. Girobank, 1983–86; Directing Fellow, St George's House, Windsor Castle, 1986–89; re-instated, HM Treasury, and seconded to Bldg Socs Commn, 1989; Dep. Chm., Bldg Socs Commn, 1989–91. Director: Mercantile Gp plc, 1987–89; London and Manchester Gp plc, 1988–89; Cons. Man., FI Gp plc, 1987–89. FRSA 1985. *Recreations:* swimming (Half Blue, Cambridge Univ.), music, house in Greece. *Address:* Building Societies Commission, 15–17 Great Marlborough Street, W1X 2AX.

GILMOUR, Dr Alan Breck, CVO 1990; CBE 1984; FRCGP; Director, National Society for the Prevention of Cruelty to Children, 1979–89, retired; *b* 30 Aug. 1928; *er* surv. *s* of late Andrew Gilmour, CMG and Nelle Twigg; *m* 1957, Elizabeth, *d* of late H. and L. Heath; two *d*. *Educ:* Clayesmore Sch.; King's Coll., London; King's Coll. Hosp. (Raymond Gooch Schol.). MB BS, LMSSA 1956; FRCGP 1974 (MRCGP 1965). General medical practitioner, 1958–67; during this period served as Member: Standing Med. Adv. Cttee, Min. of Health; Working Party on General Practice; Educn Cttee, RCGP; BMA Council, and others. British Medical Association Secretariat, 1967–79: Asst Sec., 1967; Under Sec., 1972; Dep. Sec., 1977; appts included: Overseas Sec. and Med. Dir, Commonwealth Med. Adv. Bureau, 1967–72; Med. Dir, Career Service, 1967–76; Sec., Bd of Sci. and Educn, 1972–76 (Commonwealth Med. Assoc. meetings, Singapore/Malaysia, Jamaica, Ghana; Observer, Commonwealth Med. Conf., Mauritius, 1971); Jt Sec., Med. Sci. meetings, Vancouver, Jamaica, Dublin; Dep. Sec., Jt Consultants Cttee, 1976–79. Chairman: Internat. Alliance on Child Abuse and Neglect, 1983–; Michael Sieff Foundn, 1990–; Mem., Health Educn Authority, 1989–; Hon. Treas., Assoc. for Study of Med. Educn, 1975–80; Vice-Pres., Sect. Med. Educn, RSM, 1979–82. Advr, Gracewell Inst., 1990; Trustee: Kidscape, 1991. FInstD. Liveryman, Worshipful Soc. of Apothecaries of London, 1973–. *Publications:* Innocent Victims: the question of child abuse, 1988; various articles on child abuse and on med. educn, careers in medicine, gen. practice; ed or ed jtly, Care of the Elderly, Primary Health Care Teams, Competence to Practise, and other reports. *Recreations:* gardening, homecare, walking, music. *Address:* 106 Crock Lane, Bothenhampton, Bridport, Dorset DT6 4DH. *T:* Bridport (0308) 23116. *Clubs:* Royal Over-Seas League, Royal Society of Medicine.

GILMOUR, Alexander Clement, CVO 1990; Director, London Wall Capital Group, since 1989; *b* 23 Aug. 1931; *s* of Sir John Little Gilmour, 2nd Bt, and of Lady Mary Gilmour; *m* 1954, Barbara M. L. Constance Berry; two *s* one *d*; *m* 1983, Susan Lady Chetwode. *Educ:* Eton. National Service, commn in Black Watch, 1950–52. With Joseph Sebag & Co. (subseq. Carr, Sebag), 1954–82; Director: Safeguard Industrial Investments,

1974–84; Tide (UK) Ltd, 1986–87; Exec. Dir, Equity Finance Trust Ltd, 1984–86. Consultant, Grieveson Grant, 1982. Chm., Nat. Playing Fields Assoc., 1976–88 (Past-Chm. Appeals Cttee, 10 yrs). Dir, Tate Gallery Foundn, 1986–88. Governor, LSE, 1969–. *Recreations:* tennis, skiing, fishing, gardening, golf. *Address:* c/o Drummonds Branch, Royal Bank of Scotland, 49 Charing Cross, SW1A 2DX. *Clubs:* White's; Hon. Company of Edinburgh Golfers.

See also Rt Hon. Sir Ian Gilmour, Bt.

GILMOUR, Colonel Sir Allan (Macdonald), KCVO 1990; OBE 1961; MC 1942, and Bar 1943; Lord-Lieutenant of Sutherland, 1972–91; Member, Highland Regional Council, since 1977; Vice-Chairman, Highland River Purification Board, since 1986; *b* 23 Nov. 1916; *o s* of late Captain Allan Gilmour, of Rosehall, Sutherland, and late Mary H. M. Macdonald, of Viewfield, Portree, Skye; *m* 1941, Jean Wood; three *s* one *d. Educ:* Winchester Coll. Gazetted, The Seaforth Highlanders, Jan. 1939. Served War, in Middle East, France and Germany (despatches, 1945); DSC (USA) 1945. Staff Coll., 1946; Regimental and Staff Service in: Germany, Middle East, UK, Pakistan and Africa, 1946–67, incl. Instructor, Staff Coll., Quetta, on loan to Pakistan Army, 1952–54. Chief of Gen. Staff, Ghana Armed Forces, 1959–62; service in Congo, 1961–62; retired from Army, 1967. Vice-Pres., Highland TA&VRA, 1972–89, Pres., 1989–91. Chairman: East Sutherland Council of Social Service, 1973–77; Highland Health Bd, 1981–83 (Mem., 1974–81). Mem., Highlands and Is Develt Consultative Council, 1975–87. Mem., 1978–88. Chm., 1974–78, Sutherland District Council; Mem., Sutherland CC, 1970–74. DL Sutherland, 1971. *Recreations:* fishing, local government. *Address:* Invernauld, Rosehall, Lairg, Sutherland. *T:* Rosehall (054984) 204.

GILMOUR, Rt. Hon. Sir Ian (Hedworth John Little), 3rd Bt *cr* 1926, of Liberton and Craigmillar; PC 1973; MP (C) Chesham and Amersham, since 1974 (Norfolk Central, Nov. 1962–1974); *b* 8 July 1926; *er s* of Lt-Col Sir John Little Gilmour, 2nd Bt, and Hon. Victoria Laura, OBE, TD (*d* 1991), *d* of late Viscount Chelsea (*e s* of 5th Earl Cadogan); *S* father, 1977; *m* 1951, Lady Caroline Margaret Montagu-Douglas-Scott, *yr d* of 8th Duke of Buccleuch and Queensberry, KT, GCVO, PC; four *s* one *d. Educ:* Eton; Balliol Coll., Oxford. Served with Grenadier Guards, 1944–47; 2nd Lieut 1945. Called to the Bar, Inner Temple, 1952. Editor, The Spectator, 1954–59. Parly Under-Sec. of State, MoD, 1970–71; Minister of State: for Defence Procurement, MoD, 1971–72; for Defence, 1972–74; Sec. of State for Defence, 1974; Lord Privy Seal, 1979–81. Chm., Cons. Res. Dept, 1974–75. *Publications:* The Body Politic, 1969; Inside Right: a study of Conservatism, 1977; Britain Can Work, 1983. *Heir: s* David Robert Gilmour [*b* 14 Nov. 1952; *m* 1975, Sarah Anne, *d* of M. H. G. Bradstock; one *s* three *d*]. *Address:* The Ferry House, Old Isleworth, Mddx. *T:* 081–560 6769. *Clubs:* Pratt's, White's.

See also A. C. Gilmour.

GILMOUR, Col Sir John (Edward), 3rd Bt, *cr* 1897; DSO 1945; TD; JP; Lord-Lieutenant of Fife, 1980–87 (Vice Lord-Lieutenant, 1979–80); Lord High Commissioner, General Assembly of the Church of Scotland, 1982 and 1983; *b* 24 Oct. 1912; *o s* of Col Rt Hon. Sir John Gilmour, 2nd Bt, GCVO, DSO, MP, and Mary Louise (*d* 1919), *e d* of late E. T. Lambert, Telham Court, Battle, Sussex; *S* father, 1940; *m* 1941, Ursula Mabyn, *yr d* of late F. O. Wills; two *s. Educ:* Eton; Trinity Hall, Cambridge. Served War of 1939–45 (DSO). Bt Col 1950; Captain, Royal Company of Archers (Queen's Body Guard for Scotland); Hon. Col, The Highland Yeomanry, RAC, T&AVR, 1971–75. MP (C) East Fife, 1961–79. Chm., Cons. and Unionist Party in Scotland, 1965–67. DL Fife, 1953. *Heir: s* John Gilmour [*b* 15 July 1944; *m* 1967, Valerie, *yr d* of late G. W. Russell, and of Mrs William Wilson; two *s* two *d*]. *Address:* Montrave, Leven, Fife. *TA:* Leven. *T:* Leven (0333) 26159. *Clubs:* Cavalry and Guards; Royal and Ancient Golf (St Andrews).

See also Dame Anne Bryans, Viscount Younger.

GILMOUR, Nigel Benjamin Douglas; QC 1990; a Recorder, since 1990; *b* 21 Nov. 1947; *s* of late Benjamin Waterfall Gilmour and of Barbara Mary Gilmour (now Mrs E. Harborow); *m* 1972, Isobel Anne, *d* of E. Harborow; two *d. Educ:* Tettenhall Coll., Staffordshire; Liverpool Univ. (LLB Hons). Called to the Bar, Inner Temple, 1970; an Asst Recorder, 1984–90. *Recreations:* wine, food. *Address:* Peel House, 5 Harrington Street, Liverpool L2 9QA. *T:* 051–236 4321.

GILROY BEVAN, David; *see* Bevan, A. D. G.

GILSENAN, Prof. Michael Dermot Cole; Khalid bin Abdullah al Saud Professor for the study of the contemporary Arab world, Oxford, since 1984; *b* 6 Feb. 1940; *s* of Michael Eugene Cole Gilsenan and Joyce Russell Horn. *Educ:* Eastbourne Grammar Sch.; Oxford Univ. BA (Oriental Studies), Dip. Anth., MA, DPhil (Soc. Anthropology). Research Fellow, Amer. Univ. in Cairo, 1964–66; Research studentship, St Antony's Coll., Oxford, 1966–67; Research Fellow, Harvard Middle East Center, 1967–68; Asst Prof., Dept of Anthropology, UCLA, 1968–70; Research Lectr, Univ. of Manchester, 1970–73; Associate Fellow, St Antony's Coll., Oxford, 1970–73; Lectr, 1973–78, Reader, 1978–83, Dept of Anthropology, University College London; Mem., Sch. of Social Sci., Inst. for Advanced Study, Princeton, 1979–80. Anthrop. field work, Egypt, 1964–66, Lebanon, 1971–72. Mem. Editl Bds, Past and Present, History and Anthropology, and formerly of Man, and Internat. Jl of Middle Eastern Studies; Series Editor, Society and Culture in the Modern Middle East, 1987–. *Publications:* Saint and Sufi in Modern Egypt, 1973; Recognizing Islam, 1982. *Recreations:* music, theatre, being elsewhere. *Address:* Magdalen College, Oxford. *T:* Oxford (0865) 276000.

GILSON, Rev. Nigel Langley, DFC 1944; Methodist minister, retired; President of the Methodist Conference, 1986–87; *b* 11 April 1922; *s* of Clifford Edric and Cassandra Jeanette Gilson; *m* 1951, Mary Doreen (*née* Brown); four *d. Educ:* Holcombe Methodist Elementary; Midsomer Norton Co. Secondary; St Catherine's Soc., Oxford Univ. (MA Hons); Wesley House and Fitzwilliam House, Cambridge Univ. (BA Hons). Served RAF, 1941–45 (Navigator (Wireless) 107 Sqdn, 1944–45), Flying Officer. Methodist Minister: Tintagel, Cornwall, 1950–52; Newark-upon-Trent, 1952–58; Rhodesia Dist, 1958–67; Chaplain, Hunmanby Hall Sch., Filey, Yorks, 1967–71; Supt Minister of Oxford Methodist Circuit, 1971–75 and 1988–89; Chm., Wolverhampton and Shrewsbury Dist, 1975–88. *Recreations:* gardening, theatre, family, community and multi-cultural activities. *Address:* 30 Spencer Avenue, Yarnton, Kidlington, Oxon OX5 1NG. *T:* Kidlington (08675) 78058.

GIMINGHAM, Prof. Charles Henry, OBE 1990; FRSE 1961; Regius Professor of Botany, University of Aberdeen, 1981–88 (Professor of Botany, since 1969); *b* 28 April 1923; *s* of late Conrad Theodore Gimingham and Muriel Elizabeth (*née* Blake), Harpenden; *m* 1948, Elizabeth Caroline, *o d* of late Rev. J. Wilson Baird, DD, Minister of St Machar's Cathedral, Aberdeen; three *d. Educ:* Gresham's Sch., Holt, Norfolk; Emmanuel Coll., Cambridge (Open scholarship; BA 1944; ScD 1977); PhD Aberdeen 1948. FIBiol 1967. Research Asst, Imperial Coll., Univ. of London, 1944–45; University of Aberdeen: Asst, 1946–48, Lectr, 1948–61, Sen. Lectr, 1961–64, Reader, 1964–69, Dept of Botany. Pres., British Ecological Soc., 1986–87. Vice Chm., NE Regl Bd, NCC for Scot., 1991–92; Member: Countryside Commn for Scotland, 1980–92; Bd of Management, Hill Farming Res. Organisation, 1981–87; Council of Management, Macaulay Inst. for Soil Research, 1983–87; Governing Body, Macaulay Land Use Res. Inst., 1987–90. Mem. Governing Body, Aberdeen Coll. of Educn, 1979–87. *Publications:* Ecology of Heathlands, 1972; An Introduction to Heathland Ecology, 1975; papers, mainly in botanical and ecological jls. *Recreations:* hill walking, photography, foreign travel, history and culture of Japan. *Address:* 4 Gowanbrae Road, Bieldside, Aberdeen AB1 9AQ.

GIMSON, George Stanley, QC (Scotland) 1961; Sheriff Principal of Grampian, Highland and Islands, 1975–82; Chairman: Pensions Appeals Tribunals, Scotland, since 1971 (President, 1971–75); Medical Appeal Tribunals, 1985–91; *b* 1915. *Educ:* High School of Glasgow; Glasgow Univ. Advocate, 1949; Standing Junior Counsel, Department of Agriculture for Scotland and Forestry Commission, 1956–61; Sheriff Principal of Aberdeen, Kincardine and Banff, 1972–74. Mem., Board of Management: Edinburgh Central Hosps, 1960–70 (Chm., 1964–70); Edinburgh Royal Victoria Hosps, 1970–74 (Vice-Chm.); Dir, Scottish Nat. Orchestra Soc. Ltd, 1962–80; Trustee, Nat. Library of Scotland, 1963–76; Chm., RSSPCC, Edinburgh, 1972–76. Hon. LLD Aberdeen, 1981. *Address:* 11 Royal Circus, Edinburgh EH3 6TL. *T:* 031–225 8055. *Clubs:* University Staff (Edinburgh); Royal Northern and University (Aberdeen).

GINGELL, Air Chief Marshal Sir John, GBE 1984 (CBE 1973; MBE 1962); KCB 1978; RAF, retired; Gentleman Usher of the Black Rod, Serjeant-at-Arms, House of Lords, and Secretary to the Lord Great Chamberlain, 1985–92; *b* 3 Feb. 1925; *e s* of late E. J. Gingell; *m* 1949, Prudence, *d* of late Brig. R. F. Johnson; two *s* one *d. Educ:* St Boniface Coll., Plymouth. Entered RAF, 1943; Fleet Air Arm, 1945–46 as Sub-Lt (A) RNVR; returned to RAF, 1951; served with Nos 58 and 542 Sqdns; CFS 1954; psc 1959; jssc 1965; comd No 27 Sqdn, 1963–65; Staff of Chief of Defence Staff, 1966; Dep. Dir Defence Ops Staff (Central Staff), 1966–67; Mil. Asst to Chm. NATO Mil. Cttee, Brussels, 1968–70; AOA, RAF Germany, 1971–72; AOC 23 Group, RAF Trng Comd, 1973–75; Asst Chief of Defence Staff (Policy), 1975–78; Air Member for Personnel, 1978–80; AOC-in-C, RAF Support Comd, 1980–81; Dep. C-in-C, Allied Forces Central Europe, 1981–84. Mem., Commonwealth War Graves Commn, 1986–91. Hon. Bencher, Inner Temple, 1990. *Recreations:* ornithology, walking, music. *Address:* c/o Lloyd's Bank, Shaftesbury, Dorset SP7 8JJ. *Club:* Royal Air Force.

GINGELL, Maj.-Gen. Laurie William Albert, CB 1980; OBE 1966 (MBE 1959); General Secretary, Officers' Pensions Society, 1979–90; *b* 29 Oct. 1925; *s* of late Major William George Gingell, MBE, MM, and of Elsie Grace Gingell; *m* 1949, Nancy Margaret Wadsworth; one *s* one *d. Educ:* Farnborough Grammar Sch.; Oriel Coll., Oxford. Commissioned into Royal Gloucestershire Hussars, 1945; transf. Royal Tank Regt, 1947; psc 1956; jssc 1961; Commanded: 1st Royal Tank Regt, 1966–67; 7th Armoured Bde, 1970–71; DQMG, HQ BAOR, 1973–76; Maj.-Gen. Admin, HQ UKLF, 1976–79. ADC to the Queen, 1974–76. FBIM 1979. *Recreations:* golf, tennis, swimming, reading. *Address:* 54 Station Road, Thames Ditton, Surrey KT7 0NS. *T:* 081–398 4521.

GINGER, Phyllis Ethel, (Mrs Leslie Durbin), RWS 1958 (ARWS 1952); freelance artist since 1940; *b* 19 Oct. 1907; *m* 1940, Leslie Durbin, *qv*; one *s* one *d. Educ:* Tiffin's Girls' Sch., Kingston on Thames. LCC three years' scholarship at Central School of Arts and Crafts, 1937–39. Water colours for Pilgrim Trust Recording Britain Scheme, 1941–42; Royal Academy Exhibitor; Drawings and Lithographs purchased by: Washington State Library, 1941; Victoria and Albert Museum, 1952; London Museum, 1954; South London Art Gallery, 1960. *Publications:* Alexander the Circus Pony, 1941; book jacket designs; book illustrations include: London by Mrs Robert Henrey, 1948; The Virgin of Aldemanbury, by Mrs Robert Henrey, 1960. *Address:* 298 Kew Road, Kew, Richmond, Surrey. *T:* 081–940 2221.

GINSBURG, David; company director; economic, marketing and market research consultant; broadcaster; *b* 18 March 1921; *o s* of late N. Ginsburg; *m* 1954, Louise, *er d* of late S. P. Cassy. *Educ:* University Coll. Sch.; Balliol Coll., Oxford. Chm. OU Democratic Socialist Club, 1941; 2nd Cl, Hons Sch. of Politics, Philosophy and Economics, 1941. Commissioned Oxford and Bucks LI, 1942; Capt. Intelligence duties, 1944–45. Senior Research Officer, Govt Social Survey, 1946–52; Sec. of Research Dept of Labour Party and Sec. of Home Policy Sub-Cttee of National Executive Cttee, 1952–59. MP Dewsbury, 1959–83 (Lab, 1959–81, SDP, 1981–83). Chm., Parly and Scientific Cttee, 1968–71 (Life Mem., 1984); Mem., Select Cttee, Parly Comr for Admin, 1982–83. Contested (SDP) Dewsbury, 1983. FRSM 1986. *Publications:* miscellaneous articles and book reviews in contemporary publications. *Recreations:* walking, swimming, opera. *Address:* 3 Bell Moor, East Heath Road, NW3. *Club:* Reform.

GINSBURY, Norman; playwright; *b* Nov. 1902; *s* of late J. S. and Rachel Cecily Ginsbury; *m* 1945, Dorothy Jennings. *Educ:* Grocers' Co. Sch.; London University (BSc (Hons)). Plays produced: Viceroy Sarah, Arts Theatre, 1934, Whitehall Theatre, 1935; Walk in the Sun, "Q", and Embassy, 1939; Take Back Your Freedom (with late Winifred Holtby), Neighbourhood, 1940; The Firstcomers, Bradford Civic Playhouse, 1944; The First Gentleman (written, 1935), New and Savoy, 1945; Belasco, New York, 1956; The Gambler (from the story of Dostoievsky), Embassy, 1946; The Happy Man, New, 1948; Portrait by Lawrence (with M. Moiseiwitsch), Theatre Royal, Stratford, 1949; School for Rivals, Bath Assembly and Old Vic, Bristol, 1949. Also following adaptations of plays by Henrik Ibsen: Ghosts, Vaudeville, 1937; Enemy of the People, Old Vic, 1939; Peer Gynt, Old Vic Season at New Theatre, 1944; A Doll's House, Winter Garden, 1946; John Gabriel Borkman, Mermaid, 1961. A new version of Strindberg's Dance of Death at Tyrone Guthrie Theatre, Minneapolis; and at Yvonne Arnaud Theatre, Guildford, 1966; for the Mayflower 350th anniv., The Forefathers, Athenaeum Theatre, Plymouth, 1970; The Wisest Fool, Yvonne Arnaud, 1974. *Publications:* Viceroy Sarah, 1934; Take Back Your Freedom (collab.), 1939; The First Gentleman, 1946; and the following versions of plays by Ibsen: Ghosts, 1938; Enemy of the People, 1939; Peer Gynt, 1945; A Doll's House, 1950; John Gabriel Borkman, 1960; Rosmersholm, 1961; Pillars of Society, 1962. The Old Lags' League (from a story by W. Pett Ridge), in The Best One-Act Plays of 1960–61; version of Dance of Death by Strindberg in Plays of the Year, 1966; The Shoemaker And The Devil (from a story by Tchehov), in The Best Short Plays of 1968 (NY); The Safety Match (from a story by Tchehov), in Best Short Plays of the World Theatre 1968–73 (NY). *Address:* c/o Messrs Goodman Derrick & Co., 9–11 Fulwood Place, Gray's Inn, WC1V 6HQ. *T:* 071–404 0606. *Club:* Dramatists'.

GIOLITTI, Dr Antonio; Member, Commission of the European Communities, 1977–85; Senator, Italian Parliament, since 1987; *b* 12 Feb. 1915; *s* of Giuseppe and Maria Giolitti; *m* 1939, Elena d'Amico; one *s* two *d. Educ:* Rome Univ. (Dr Law); Oxford; München. Dep., Italian Parlt, 1946–77; Minister of Budget and Economic Planning, 1964, 1970–72, 1973–74. Member: Italian Communist Party, 1943–57; Italian Socialist Party, 1958–83; Exec., Italian Socialist Party, 1958–83. *Publications:* Riforme e rivoluzione, 1957; Il comunismo in Europa, 1960; Un socialismo possibile, 1967. *Recreations:* music, walking. *Address:* Senato della Repubblica, 00186 Rome, Italy.

GIORDANO, Richard Vincent, Hon. KBE 1989; Chairman, 1985–Jan. 1992, and Chief Executive Officer, 1979–91, The BOC Group; *b* March 1934; *s* of late Vincent Giordano and of Cynthia Giordano; *m* 1956, Barbara Claire Beckett; one *s* two *d. Educ:* Harvard

Coll., Cambridge, Mass, USA (BA); Columbia Univ. Law Sch. (LLB). Shearman & Sterling, 1959; Airco, Inc., 1964–78: Gp Vice Pres., 1967; Gp Pres., Chief Operating Officer and Mem. Bd, 1971; Dir, BOC Internat. Ltd, 1974; Chief Exec. Officer, Airco, Inc., 1978; Gp Man. Dir, BOC, 1979–85. Mem., CEGB, 1982–; part-time Mem. Bd, Georgia Pacific Corp., Atlanta, Ga, 1984–; Bd Mem., Grand Metropolitan plc, 1985–. Hon. Dr of Commercial Science, St John's Univ., 1975. *Recreations:* ocean sailing, tennis. *Address:* c/o The BOC Group plc, Chertsey Road, Windlesham, Surrey GU20 6HJ. *T:* Bagshot (0276) 77222. *Clubs:* The Links, New York Yacht (New York), Edgartown Yacht (Mass); Duquesne (Pittsburgh, Pa).

GIPPSLAND, Bishop of, since 1987; **Rt. Rev. Colin Davies Sheumack;** *b* 9 Feb. 1929; *s* of Joseph Sheumack and Gwladys (*née* Davies); *m* 1951, Ena Beryl Dickson; one *s* three *d*. *Educ:* Tingha Central and Inverell High School; Moore Theological Coll. (ThL 2nd cl. Hons). Deacon 1952, priest 1953, Canberra Goulburn; Rector: Kemeruka, 1954–59; Kyabram, Vic., 1959–67; Archdeacon of Bendigo, 1967–83; Vicar General, 1968–83; Dean of Bathurst, 1983–87. *Recreations:* gardening, fishing. *Address:* Bishopscourt, 51 Raglan Street, Sale, Vic 3850, Australia. *Club:* Royal Automobile of Victoria (Melbourne).

GIRDWOOD, Ronald Haxton, CBE 1984; MD, PhD, FRCP, FRCPE, FRCPI, FRCPath; FRSE 1978; Chairman, Scottish National Blood Transfusion Association, since 1980; President, Royal College of Physicians of Edinburgh, 1982–85; *b* 19 March 1917; *s* of late Thomas Girdwood and Elizabeth Stewart Girdwood (*née* Haxton); *m* 1945, Mary Elizabeth, *d* of late Reginald Williams, Calstock, Cornwall; one *s* one *d*. *Educ:* Daniel Stewart's Coll., Edinburgh; University of Edinburgh; University of Michigan. MB, ChB (Hons) Edinburgh 1939; Ettles Schol., Leslie Gold Medallist, Royal Victoria Hosp.; Tuberculosis Trust Gold Medallist, Wightman, Beaney and Keith Memorial Prize Winner, 1939; MD (Gold Medal for thesis), 1954. Pres. Edinburgh Univ. Church of Scotland Soc., 1938–39. Served RAMC, 1942–46 (mentioned in Orders); Nutrition Research Officer and Officer i/c Med. Div. in India and Burma. Lectr in Medicine, University of Edinburgh, 1946; Rockefeller Research Fellow, University of Michigan, 1948–49; Cons. Phys., Chalmers Hosp., Edinburgh, 1950–51; Sen. Lectr in Med. and Cons. Phys., Royal Infirmary, 1951; Vis. Lectr, Dept of Pharmacology, Yale Univ., 1956; Reader in Med., University of Edinburgh, 1958; Dean of Faculty of Medicine, Edinburgh Univ., 1975–79; Prof. of Therapeutics and Clinical Pharmacology, Univ. of Edinburgh, 1962–82, Emeritus 1982; Consultant Physician, Royal Infirmary of Edinburgh, 1951–82. Sometime External Examiner for Universities of London, Sheffield, St Andrews, Dundee, Dublin, Glasgow and Hong Kong, and for Med. Colls in Singapore, Dhaka and Karachi. Chm., SE Scotland Blood Transfusion Assoc., 1970–; Mem. Council, RCPE, 1966–70, 1978–80, Vice-Pres., 1981–82, Pres. 1982–85; Member: South-Eastern Reg. Hosp. Board (Scotland), 1965–69; Board of Management, Royal Infirmary, Edinburgh, 1958–64; Cttee on Safety of Medicines, 1972–83; Exec., Medico-Pharmaceutical Forum, 1972–74 (Vice-Chm., 1983–85; Chm., 1985–87); Chairman: Scottish Group of Hæmophilia Soc., 1954–60; Non-Professorial Medical Teachers and Research Workers Gp Cttee (Scot.) of BMA, 1956–62; Scottish Gp of Nutrition Soc., 1961–62; Consultative Council, Edinburgh Medical Gp, 1977–82; Pres. Brit. Soc. for Hæmatology, 1963–64; Member: Coun. Brit. Soc. of Gastroenterology, 1964–68; Council of Nutrition Soc., 1957–60 and 1961–64; Pres., Univ. of Edinburgh Graduates' Assoc., 1991 (Vice-Pres., 1989–90). British Council visitor to W African Hosps, 1963, to Middle East, 1977, to India, 1980; Visiting Prof. and WHO Consultant, India, 1965, Pakistan, 1985. Gov., St Columba's Hospice, 1985–. Former Chm., Bd of Management, Scottish Med. Jl and Mem., Editl Bds, Blood, and British Jl of Haematology; Mem. Editl Bd, Brit. Jl of Nutrition, 1960–65. Awarded Freedom of the township of Sirajgunj, Bangladesh, 1984. Hon. FACP 1983; Hon. FRACP 1985. Cullen Prize, 1970, Lilly Lectr, 1979, RCPE; Suniti Panja gold medal, Calcutta Sch. Trop. Med., 1980. *Publications:* about 300, particularly in relation to nutrition, hæmatology, gastroenterology and medical history; (contrib.) Davidson's Principles and Practice of Medicine, all edns 1952–81; (ed with A. N. Smith) Malabsorption, 1969; (ed with S. Alstead) Textbook of Medical Treatment, 12th edn 1971 to 14th edn 1978, (ed with J. Petrie) 15th edn, 1987; (ed) Blood Disorders due to Drugs and Other Agents, 1973; (ed) Clinical Pharmacology, 23rd edn 1976, 25th edn 1984; Travels with a Stethoscope, 1991. *Recreations:* photography, writing. *Address:* 2 Hermitage Drive, Edinburgh EH10 6DD. *T:* (home) 031–447 5137. *Clubs:* East India, Devonshire, Sports and Public Schools; University Staff (Edinburgh).

GIROLAMI, Sir Paul, Kt 1988; FCA; Chairman, Glaxo Holdings, since 1985 (Chief Executive, 1980–86); *b* 25 Jan. 1926; *m* 1952, Christabel Mary Gwynne Lewis; two *s* one *d*. *Educ:* London School of Economics (Hon. Fellow, 1989). Chantrey & Button, Chartered Accountants, 1950–54; Coopers & Lybrand, Chartered Accountants, 1954–65; Glaxo Holdings: Financial Controller, 1965; Finance Director, 1968; Chief Exec., 1980. Director: Inner London Board of National Westminster Bank, 1974–89; Credito Italiano Internat. UK, 1990–. Member: Bd of Dirs, Amer. Chamber of Commerce (UK), 1983–; CBI Council, 1986–; Appeal Cttee, ICA, 1987–; Stock Exchange Listed Cos Adv. Cttee, 1987–. Chm., Senate for Chartered Accountants in Business, 1990–. Mem., Open Univ. Vis. Cttee, 1987–89. Freeman, City of London; Liveryman, Goldsmiths' Co., 1980– (Mem., Ct of Assistants, 1986–). Accademico: Accad. Romana di sci. med. e biologiche, 1990; Accad. Internazionale per l'Unita della Cultura, Rome and St Gallen, 1991. Hon. DSc: Aston, 1990; Trieste, 1991. Grande Ufficiale, Ordine al Merito della Repubblica Italiana, 1987. *Recreations:* reading, golf, music. *Address:* (office) Lansdowne House, Berkeley Square, W1X 6PB.

GIROUARD, Mark, PhD; writer and architectural historian; Slade Professor of Fine Art, University of Oxford, 1975–76; *b* 7 Oct. 1931; *s* of late Richard D. Girouard and Lady Blanche Girouard; *m* 1970, Dorothy N. Dorf; one *d*. *Educ:* Ampleforth; Christ Church, Oxford (MA); Courtauld Inst. of Art (PhD); Bartlett Sch., UCL (BSc, Dip. Arc). Staff of Country Life, 1958–66; studied architecture, Bartlett Sch., UCL, 1966–71; staff of Architectural Review, 1971–75. George Lurcy Vis. Prof., Columbia Univ., NY, 1987. Member: Council, Victorian Soc., 1979– (Founder Mem. 1958; Mem. Cttee, 1958–66); Royal Fine Art Commn, 1972–; Royal Commn on Historical Monuments (England), 1976–81; Historic Buildings Council (England), 1978–84; Commn for Historic Buildings and Monuments, 1984–90 (Mem., Buildings Adv. Cttee, 1984–86; Mem., Historic Areas Adv. Cttee, 1985–89; Mem., Historic Bldgs Cttee, 1988–90); Chm., Spitalfields Historic Buildings Trust, 1977–83. Mem., Adv. Council, Paul Mellon Centre for Studies in British Art, 1990–. Hon. FRIBA, 1980. Hon. DLitt: Leicester, 1982; Buckingham, 1991. *Publications:* Robert Smythson and the Architecture of the Elizabethan Era, 1966, 2nd edn, Robert Smythson and the Elizabethan Country House, 1983; The Victorian Country House, 1971, 2nd edn 1979; Victorian Pubs, 1975, 2nd edn 1984; (jtly) Spirit of the Age, 1975 (based on BBC TV series); Sweetness and Light: the 'Queen Anne' movement 1860–1900, 1977; Life in the English Country House, 1978 (Duff Cooper Meml Prize; W. H. Smith Award, 1979); Historic Houses of Britain, 1979; Alfred Waterhouse and the Natural History Museum, 1981; The Return to Camelot: chivalry and the English gentleman, 1981; Cities and People, 1985; A Country House Companion, 1987; The English Town, 1990; articles in Country Life, Architect. Rev., Listener. *Address:* 35 Colville Road, W11. *Club:* Beefsteak.

GISBOROUGH, 3rd Baron, *cr* 1917; **Thomas Richard John Long Chaloner,** JP; Lord-Lieutenant of Cleveland, since 1981; *b* 1 July 1927; *s* of 2nd Baron and Esther Isabella Madeleine (*d* 1970), *yr d* of late Charles O. Hall, Eddlethorpe; *S* father 1951; *m* 1960, Shane, *e d* of late Sidney Newton, London, and *g d* of Sir Louis Newton, 1st Bt; two *s*. *Educ:* Eton; Royal Agricultural Coll. 16th/5th Lancers, 1948–52; Captain Northumberland Hussars, 1955–61; Lt-Col Green Howards (Territorials), 1967–69. Mem., Rural Develt Commn, 1985–89. CC NR Yorks, 1964–74, Cleveland, 1974–77. Hon. Col, Cleveland County Army Cadet Force, 1981. Pres., British Ski Fedn, 1985–90. DL N Riding of Yorks and Cleveland, 1973; JP Langbaurgh East, 1981–. KStJ 1981. *Recreations:* field sports, ski-ing, bridge, piano. *Heir:* *s* Hon. Thomas Peregrine Long Chaloner, *b* 17 Jan. 1961. *Address:* Gisborough House, Guisborough, Cleveland. *T:* Guisborough (0287) 32002.

GISCARD d'ESTAING, Valéry; Grand Croix de la Légion d'Honneur; Croix de Guerre (1939–45); President of the French Republic, 1974–81; Member, European Parliament, since 1989 (Chairman, Liberal Group); President: Conseil Régional d'Auvergne, since 1986; Union pour la Démocratie Française, since 1988; European Movement International, since 1989; *b* Coblence, 2 Feb. 1926; *s* of late Edmond Giscard d'Estaing and May Bardoux; *m* 1952, Anne-Aymone de Brantes; two *s* two *d*. *Educ:* Lycée Janson-de-Sailly, Paris; Ecole Polytechnique; Ecole Nationale d'Administration. Inspection of Finances: Deputy, 1952; Inspector, 1954; Dep. Dir, Cabinet of Président du Conseil, June-Dec. 1954. Elected Deputy for Puy-de-Dôme, 1956; re-elected for Clermont N and SW, Nov. 1958, Nov.–Dec. 1962, March 1967, June 1968, March 1973, 1984, 1986 and 1988–89; Sec. of State for Finance, 1959; Minister of Finance, Jan.-April 1962; Minister of Finance and Economic Affairs, April-Nov. 1962 and Dec. 1962–Jan. 1966; Minister of Economy and Finance, 1969–74. Pres., Nat. Fedn of Indep. Republicans, 1966–73 (also a Founder); Pres., comm. des finances de l'économie générale et du plan de l'Assemblée nationale, 1967–68; Chm., Foreign Affairs Commn, Nat. Assembly, 1987–89. Mayor of Chamalières, 1967–74. Deleg. to Assembly of UN, 1956, 1957, 1958. Nansen Medal, 1979. *Publications:* Démocratie Française, 1976 (Towards a New Democracy, 1977); 2 Français sur 3, 1984; Le Pouvoir et la Vie (memoirs), 1988. *Address:* 11 rue Bénouville, 75116 Paris, France; (office) 19 rue François Ier, 75008 Paris. *Club:* Polo (Paris).

GISH, Lillian Diana; Actress; *b* 14 Oct. 1899. *Educ:* privately. Began acting in theatre at five years of age and at twelve entered motion pictures. Katrina in Crime and Punishment (with John Gielgud), 1948, Ophelia to John Gielgud's Hamlet, The Curious Savage, 1950, Miss Mabel, 1951 (USA). Acting mainly on television, 1952; in play, The Trip to Bountiful (for the Theatre Guild), 1953–54; The Chalk Garden, 1957; The Family Reunion, 1958; directed, The Beggar's Opera, 1958; All the Way House, 1960–61 (won Drama Critics and Pulitzer prize as best play); A Passage to India, play (Chicago), 1962–63; Too True to be Good (G. B. Shaw's play) (New York), 1963; Romeo and Juliet (Stratford Festival Theatre), 1965; Anya (musical), 1967; I Never Sang for my Father, 1968; Uncle Vanya, NY, 1973; A Musical Jubilee (musical), NY, 1975. Lillian Gish and the Movies: the art of film, 1900–28 (concert programmes), Moscow, Paris, London and USA, 1969–73, QE2 World tour, 1975; lecturing and performing for The Theatre Guild at Sea on the Rotterdam, 1975; Celebration, Metropolitan Opera 100th Gala Benefit (Spectre de la Rose, with Patrick DuPond), 1984. *Early films include:* Birth of a Nation; Intolerance; Souls Triumphant; Hearts of the World; The Great Love; Broken Blossoms; Way Down East; The Orphans of the Storm; The White Sister; Romola; The Wind; *later films include:* The Night of the Hunter, 1954; The Cobweb, 1955; Orders to Kill, 1957; The Unforgiven, 1959; Follow Me Boys, 1966; Warning Shot, 1966; The Comedians, 1967; A Wedding, 1978; Hambone and Hillie, 1984; Sweet Liberty, 1986; The Whales of August, 1987. *Television:* frequent appearances include three plays, 1962; plays, 1963; Arsenic and Old Lace, 1969; Sparrow, CBS, 1978; Love Boat, and Thin Ice, CBS, 1980. Life of Lillian Gish (documentary film by Jeanne Moreau); Hommage à Lillian Gish (ballet by Catherine Berge), France, 1984. Dorothy and Lillian Gish Film Theatre, founded Bowling Green State Univ., Ohio, 1976. Hon. AFD, Rollins Coll., Fla; Hon. HHD, Holyoke Coll.; Hon. Dr of Performing Arts, Bowling Green State Univ., Ohio, 1976. Hon. Oscar, Acad. Motion Picture Arts and Scis, 1971; Life Achievement Award, AFI, 1984; Handel Medallion, NYC, 1973; Medal of Arts and Letters (France), 1983. *Publications:* Lillian Gish: an autobiography, 1968; Lillian Gish, The Movies, Mr Griffith and Me, 1969; Dorothy and Lillian Gish, 1973; An Actor's Life for Me!, 1987. *Recreation:* travel. *Address:* 430 East 57th Street, New York, NY 10022, USA.

GITTINGS, Harold John; Chairman, Hardie-Brown Gittings Hawkins Ltd; Managing Director, Brian Norman Associates Ltd, since 1991; *b* 3 Sept. 1947; *s* of Harold William Gittings and Doris Marjorie Gittings (*née* Whiting); *m* 1988, Andrea (*née* Fisher); two step *c*. *Educ:* Duke of York's Royal Military School, Dover. ACIS. Beecham Group, 1971–73; Peat Marwick Mitchell, Hong Kong, 1973–74; N. M. Rothschild & Sons, 1974–81; Continental Bank, 1981–82; Target Group, 1982–85; Managing Director: Touche Remnant Unit Trust Management, 1985–90; Touche Remnant & Co. 1987–90. *Recreations:* entertaining, travel, collecting, theatre, opera. *Address:* Jacobs Ladder, Froghole, Crockham Hill, Kent TN8 6TD. *T:* Edenbridge (0732) 866267.

GITTINGS, Robert (William Victor), CBE 1970; LittD Cantab, 1970; poet; biographer; playwright; *b* 1 Feb. 1911; *s* of late Surg.-Capt. Fred Claude Bromley Gittings, RN (retd) and late Dora Mary Brayshaw; *m* 1st, 1934, Katherine Edith Cambell (marr. diss.); two *s*; 2nd, 1949, Joan Grenville Manton; one *d*. *Educ:* St Edward's Sch., Oxford; Jesus Coll., Cambridge (Scholar). 1st Cl. Historical Tripos, 1933. Research Student, and Research Fellow, 1933–38, Supervisor in History, 1938–40, Hon. Fellow, 1979, Jesus Coll., Cambridge, Leslie Stephen Lectr, 1980; writer and producer for broadcasting, 1940–63; Professor: Vanderbilt University, Tennessee, 1966; Boston Univ., 1970; Univ. of Washington, 1972, 1974 and 1977 (Danz Lectr); Meiji Univ., Tokyo, 1985. Hon. LittD Leeds, 1981. *Publications: poetry and verse-plays:* The Roman Road, 1932; The Story of Psyche, 1936; Wentworth Place, 1950; The Makers of Violence (Canterbury Festival), 1951; Through a Glass Lightly, 1952; Famous Meeting, 1953; Out of This Wood (sequence of plays), 1955; This Tower My Prison, 1961; Matters of Love and Death, 1968; Conflict at Canterbury, 1970; American Journey, 1972; Collected Poems, 1976; People, Places, Personal, 1985; *biography and criticism:* John Keats: The Living Year, 1954; The Mask of Keats, 1956; Shakespeare's Rival, 1960; (ed) The Living Shakespeare, 1960; (ed with E. Hardy) Some Recollections by Emma Hardy, 1961; (with Jo Manton) The Story of John Keats, 1962; The Keats Inheritance, 1964; (ed) Selected Poems and Letters of John Keats, 1966; John Keats, 1968 (W. H. Smith Literary Award, 1969); John Keats: Selected Letters, 1970; The Odes of Keats, 1970; Young Thomas Hardy, 1975 (Christian Gauss Award, Phi Beta Kappa, 1975); The Older Hardy, 1978 (RSL Heinemann Award, 1979, James Tait Black Meml Prize, 1979); The Nature of Biography, 1978; (with Jo Manton) The Second Mrs Hardy, 1979; (ed with J. Reeves) Selected Poems of Thomas Hardy, 1981; (with Jo Manton) Dorothy Wordsworth, 1985 (Southern Arts Literary Prize, 1987); contrib. to Keats-Shelley Memorial Bulletin, Keats-Shelley Journal, Harvard Library Bulletin, etc. *Recreations:* outdoor pursuits except blood-sports. *Address:* The Stables, East Dean, Chichester, West Sussex. *T:* Singleton (024363) 328.

GITTUS, John Henry, DSc; FEng 1989; Director General, British Nuclear Forum, since 1990; *b* 25 July 1930; *s* of Henry Gittus and Amy Gittus; *m* 1953, Rosemary Ann Geeves;

one *s* two *d*. *Educ:* BSc London 1952; DSc Phys London 1976; DTech Metall Stockholm 1975. CEng, FIMechE, FIS, FIM. British Cast Iron Res. Assoc., 1947–55; Mond Nickel Co., R&D Labs, Birmingham, 1955–60 (develt Nimonic series high temp. super alloys for aircraft gas turbine engines); United Kingdom Atomic Energy Authority, 1960–89: Research Manager, Springfields; Head, Water Reactor fuel develt; Head, Atomic Energy Tech. Br., Harwell; Director: Water Reactor Safety Research; Safety and Reliability Directorate, Culcheth; Communication and Information. Consultant: Argonne Nat. Lab., USA, 1968; Oak Ridge Nat. Lab., 1969. Visiting Professor: Ecole Polytechnique Fédérale, Lausanne, 1976; Univ. de Nancy, 1984; Regents' Prof., UCLA, 1990–91. Editor-in-Chief, Res Mechanica, 1980–91. *Publications:* Uranium, 1962; Creep, Viscoelasticity and Creep-fracture in Solids, 1979; Irradiation Effects in Crystalline Solids, 1979; (with W. Crosbie) Medical Response to Effects of Ionizing Radiation, 1989; numerous articles in learned jls. *Recreations:* old houses, old motor cars, old friends. *Address:* (office) 22 Buckingham Gate, SW1E 6LB. *T:* 071–828 0116. *Clubs:* Royal Society of Medicine, Institute of Directors.

GIULINI, Carlo Maria; conductor; Music Director, Los Angeles Philharmonic Orchestra, 1978–84; *b* 9 May 1914; *m*; three *s*. *Educ:* Accademia Santa Cecilia, Rome. Début as conductor, Rome, 1944; formed Orchestra of Milan Radio, 1950; Principal Conductor, La Scala, Milan, 1953–55; début in Great Britain, conducting Verdi's Falstaff, Edinburgh Festival, 1955; closely associated with Philharmonia Orchestra, 1955–; début at Royal Opera House, Covent Garden, Don Carlos, 1958; Principal Guest Conductor, Chicago Symphony Orch., 1969–78; Music Dir, Vienna Symphony Orch., 1973–76; Music Dir, Los Angeles Philharmonic Orch., 1978–84; conducted new prodn of Falstaff in Los Angeles and at Covent Garden, 1982, after 14 year absence from opera (co-prodn by LA Philharmonic, Covent Garden and Teatro Comunale). Hon. Mem., Gesell. der Musikfreunde, Vienna, 1978; Hon. DHL DePaul Univ., Chicago, 1979. Gold Medal: Bruckner Soc., 1978; International Mahler Society; Una Vita Nella Musica. *Recreation:* sailing. *Address:* c/o Robert Leslie, 121C King's Avenue, SW4.

GIVEN, Edward Ferguson, CMG 1968; CVO 1979; HM Diplomatic Service, retired; *b* 13 April 1919; *s* of James K. Given, West Kilbride, Ayrshire; *m* 1st, 1946, Philida Naomi Bullwinkle; one *s*; 2nd, 1954, Kathleen Margaret Helena Kelly. *Educ:* Sutton County Sch.; University Coll., London. Served RA, 1939–46. Entered HM Foreign Service, 1946; served at Paris, Rangoon, Bahrain, Bordeaux, Office of Political Adviser to C-in-C Far East, Singapore, Moscow, Beirut; Ambassador: United Republic of Cameroon and Republic of Equatorial Guinea, 1972–75; Bahrain, 1975–79, retired, 1979. Dir-Gen., Middle East Assoc., 1979–83. *Recreation:* sailing. *Address:* 10 Clarendon Park, Lymington, Hants SO41 8AX. *Club:* Army and Navy.

GIVENS, Willie Alan; Liberian Ambassador to the Court of St James's, since 1985; *b* 27 Aug. 1938; *s* of Isaac and Frances Givens; *m* 1963, Marion Cooper; one *s* three *d*. *Educ:* Regent Street Polytechnic (journalism); Morgan State University, USA (sociology, anthropology). Ministry of Information, Liberia, 1964–67; Afro-American newspapers, Baltimore, USA, 1968–73; Dir, Culture Center, Cape Mount, Liberia, 1974–76; Press Sec. to President of Liberia, 1977–80; Dep. Minister of State for Public Affairs, Exec. Mansion, 1980–85. Grand Band, Order of Star of Africa (Liberia), 1985; Order of the Republic (Sudan), 1982; Diplomatic Service Merit (Republic of Korea), 1983. *Recreation:* listening to music. *Address:* The Conifers, Traps Lane, New Malden, Surrey KT3 4SG. *T:* 081–942 7997.

GLADSTONE, David Arthur Steuart, CMG 1988; HM Diplomatic Service; High Commissioner, Colombo, 1987–91; *b* 1 April 1935; *s* of Thomas Steuart Gladstone and Muriel Irene Heron Gladstone; *m* 1961, April (*née* Brunner); one *s* one *d*. *Educ:* Eton; Christ Church, Oxford (MA History). National Service, 1954–56; Oxford Univ., 1956–59. Annan, Dexter & Co. (Chartered Accountants), 1959–60; FO, 1960; MECAS, Lebanon, 1960–62; Bahrain, 1962–63; FO, 1963–65; Bonn, 1965–69; FCO, 1969–72; Cairo, 1972–75; British Mil. Govt, Berlin, 1976–79; Head of Western European Dept, FCO, 1979–82; Consul-Gen., Marseilles, 1983–87. *Recreations:* squash, tennis, music, theatre, cinema, dreaming, carpentry, gardening. *Address:* c/o Foreign and Commonwealth Office, King Charles Street, SW1A 2AH.

GLADSTONE, Sir (Erskine) William, 7th Bt *cr* 1846; JP; Lord-Lieutenant of Clwyd, since 1985; *b* 29 Oct. 1925; *s* of Charles Andrew Gladstone, (6th Bt), and Isla Margaret (*d* 1987), *d* of late Sir Walter Erskine Crum; *S* father, 1968; *m* 1962, Rosamund Anne, *yr d* of late Major A. Hambro; two *s* one *d*. *Educ:* Eton; Christ Church, Oxford. Served RNVR, 1943–46. Asst Master at Shrewsbury, 1949–50, and at Eton, 1951–61; Head Master of Lancing Coll., 1961–69. Chief Scout of UK and Overseas Branches, 1972–82; Mem., World Scout Cttee, 1977–83 (Chm., 1979–81). DL Flintshire, 1969, Clwyd, 1974, Vice Lord-Lieut, 1984; Alderman, Flintshire CC, 1970–74. Chm., Rep. Body of Church in Wales 1977–; Chm., Council of Glenalmond Coll. (formerly Trinity Coll., Glenalmond), 1982–86. JP Clwyd 1982. *Publications:* various school textbooks. *Recreations:* reading history, watercolours, shooting, gardening. *Heir:* *s* Charles Angus Gladstone [*b* 11 April 1964; *m* 1988, Caroline, *o d* of Sir Derek Thomas, *qv*; one *s* one *d*]. *Address:* Hawarden Castle, Clwyd CH5 3PB. *T:* Hawarden (0244) 520210; Fasque, Laurencekirk, Kincardineshire AB3 1DJ. *T:* Fettercairn (05614) 341.

GLADWIN, Derek Oliver, CBE 1979 (OBE 1977); JP; Regional Secretary (Southern Region), General and Municipal Workers' Union, 1970–90; Member: Post Office Board (formerly Post Office Corporation), since 1972; British Aerospace, since 1977; *b* 6 June 1930; *s* of Albert Victor Gladwin and Ethel Gladwin (*née* Oliver); *m* 1956, Ruth Ann Pinion; one *s*. *Educ:* Carr Lane Junior Sch., Grimsby; Wintringham Grammar Sch.; Ruskin Coll., Oxford; London Sch. of Economics. British Railways, Grimsby, 1946–52; fishing industry, Grimsby, 1952–56; Regional Officer 1956–63, Nat. Industrial Officer 1963–70, Gen. and Municipal Workers' Union. Chm., Labour Party's Conf. Arrangements Cttee, 1974–90. Member: Exec. Cttee, Industrial Soc.; Council, Ditchley Foundn. Trustee, Duke of Edinburgh's Commonwealth Study Conf. (UK Fund); Chm., Governing Council, Ruskin Coll., Oxford, 1979–. Vis. Fellow, Nuffield Coll., Oxford, 1978–86. JP Surrey, 1969. *Address:* 2 Friars Rise, Ashwood Road, Woking, Surrey. *T:* Guildford (0483) 714591.

GLADWIN, Very Rev. John Warren; Provost of Sheffield Cathedral, since 1988; *b* 30 May 1942; *s* of Thomas Valentine and Muriel Joan Gladwin; *m* 1981, Lydia Elizabeth Adam. *Educ:* Hertford Grammar School; Churchill Coll., Cambridge (BA History and Theology, MA 1969); St John's Coll., Durham (Dip. Theol). Asst Curate, St John the Baptist Parish Church, Kirkheaton, Huddersfield, 1967–71; Tutor, St John's Coll., Durham and Hon. Chaplain to Students, St Nicholas Church, Durham, 1971–77; Director, Shaftesbury Project on Christian Involvement in Society, 1977–82; Secretary, Gen. Synod Board for Social Responsibility, 1982–88; Prebendary, St Paul's Cathedral, 1984–88. Mem., Gen Synod of C of E, 1990–. *Publications:* God's People in God's World, 1979; The Good of the People, 1988. *Recreations:* gardening, travel. *Address:* Provost's Lodge, 22 Hallamgate Road, Sheffield S10 5BS. *T:* Sheffield (0742) 662373.

GLADWYN, 1st Baron *cr* 1960; **Hubert Miles Gladwyn Jebb,** GCMG 1954 (KCMG 1949; CMG 1942); GCVO 1957; CB 1947; Grand Croix de la Légion d'Honneur, 1957; Deputy Leader of Liberal Party in House of Lords, and Liberal Spokesman on foreign affairs and defence, 1965–88; *b* 25 April 1900; *s* of late Sydney Jebb, Firbeck Hall, Yorks; *m* 1929, Cynthia (*d* 1990), *d* of Sir Saxton Noble, 3rd Bart; one *s* two *d*. *Educ:* Eton; Magdalen Coll., Oxon. 1st in History, Oxford, 1922. Entered Diplomatic Service, 1924; served in Tehran, Rome, and Foreign Office; Private Sec. to Parliamentary Under-Sec. of State, 1929–31; Private Sec. to Permanent Under-Sec. of State, 1937–40; appointed to Ministry of Economic Warfare with temp. rank of Asst Under-Sec., Aug. 1940; Acting Counsellor in Foreign Office, 1941; Head of Reconstruction Dept, 1942; Counsellor, 1943, in that capacity attended the Conferences of Quebec, Cairo, Tehran, Dunbarton Oaks, Yalta, San Francisco and Potsdam. Executive Sec. of Preparatory Commission of the United Nations (Aug. 1945) with temp. rank of Minister; Acting Sec.-Gen. of UN, Feb. 1946; Deputy to Foreign Sec. on Conference of Foreign Ministers, March 1946; Assistant Under-Sec. of State and United Nations Adviser, 1946–47; UK rep. on Brussels Treaty Permanent Commission with personal rank of Ambassador, April 1948; Dep. Under-Sec., 1949–50; Permanent Representative of the UK to the United Nations, 1950–54; British Ambassador to France, 1954–60, retired. Mem., European Parlt, 1973–76 (Vice Pres., Political Cttee); contested (L) Suffolk, European Parlt, 1979. Pres., European Movement; former Pres., Atlantic Treaty Assoc.; Chm., Campaign for European Political Community; Mem., Parly Delegns to Council of Europe and WEU Assemblies, 1966–73. Hon. DCL: Oxford; Syracuse, NY 1954; Essex 1974; Hon. Fellow Magdalen Coll. *Publications:* Is Tension Necessary?, 1959; Peaceful Co-existence, 1962; The European Idea, 1966; Half-way to 1984, 1967; De Gaulle's Europe, or, Why the General says No, 1969; Europe after de Gaulle, 1970; The Memoirs of Lord Gladwyn, 1972. *Recreations:* gardening, cooking. *Heir:* *s* Hon. Miles Alvery Gladwyn Jebb [*b* 3 March 1930. *Educ:* Eton and Oxford]. *Address:* Bramfield Hall, Halesworth, Suffolk. *T:* Bramfield (098684) 241; 62 Whitehall Court, SW1A 2EL. *T:* 071–930 3160. *Club:* Garrick.
See also Baron Thomas of Swynnerton.

GLAISYER, Ven. Hugh; Archdeacon of Lewes and Hastings, since 1991; *b* 20 Jan. 1930; *s* of Rev. Canon Hugh Glaisyer and Edith Glaisyer; *m* 1962, Alison Marion Heap; one *s* two *d*. *Educ:* Tonbridge Sch.; Oriel Coll., Oxford (MA 2nd cl. Hon. Mods, 2nd Cl. Theol.); St Stephen's House, Oxford. FO, RAF, 1954. Ordained, Manchester, 1956; Curate: St Augustine's, Tonge Moor, Bolton, 1956–62; Sidcup, 1962–64; Vicar, Christ Church, Milton-next-Gravesend, 1964–81; RD, Gravesend, 1974–81; Vicar, Hove, 1981–91; RD, Hove, 1982–91; Canon of Chichester Cathedral, 1982–91. *Recreations:* squash rackets, Shetland sheepdogs. *Address:* 27 The Avenue, Lewes, East Sussex BN7 1QT. *T:* Lewes (0273) 479530.

GLAMANN, Prof. Kristof, OBE 1985; Hon. FBA 1985; President, Carlsberg Foundation, since 1976 (Director, since 1969); Chairman, Carlsberg Ltd, since 1977 (Director, since 1970); *b* 26 Aug. 1923; *s* of Kai Kristof Glamann, bank manager, and Ebba Henriette Louise (*née* Madsen); *m* 1954, Kirsten Lise (*née* Jantzen), MA, lecturer; two *s*. *Educ:* Odense Katedral-skole; Univ. of Copenhagen (MA Hist. 1948, PhD Econ. Hist., 1958). Univ. of Copenhagen: Research Fellow, 1948–56; Associated Prof., 1956–60; Prof. of History, 1960–80. Visiting Professor: Pennsylvania, 1960; Wisconsin, 1961; LSE 1964; Vis. Overseas Fellow, Churchill Coll., Cambridge, 1971–72; Toho Gakkai, Japan, 1977; Master, 4th May and Hassager Coll., Copenhagen, 1961–81. Chm., Scand. Inst. of Asian Studies, 1967–71; Hon. Pres., Internat. Econ. Hist. Assoc., 1974 (Pres., 1970–74; Vice-Pres., 1968–70). Director: Carlsberg Brewery Ltd, UK, 1977; Fredericia Brewery Ltd, 1975; Royal Copenhagen (Holmegaard) Ltd, 1975; Politiken Foundn, 1990. Chm., Danish State Research Council of Humanities, 1968–70; Mem. Bd, HM Queen Ingrid's Roman Foundn, 1980; Vice-Pres., Scandinavia-Japan Sasakawa Foundn, 1985–; Member: Royal Danish Acad. of Science and Letters, 1969; Royal Danish Hist. Soc., 1961; Swedish Acad., Lund, 1963; Hist. Soc. of Calcutta, 1962; Corresp. FRHistS 1972; Founding Mem., Acad. Europaea, 1988; Fellow, Royal Belgian Acad., 1989. Editor, Scand. Econ. History Review, 1961–70. Hon. LittD Gothenburg, 1974, Festschrift 1983. Comdr, Order of the Dannebrog, 1990 (Kt 1984); Comdr, Northern Star of Sweden, 1984; Order of Orange-Nassau, Netherlands, 1984; Comdr, Falcon of Iceland, 1987; Das Grosse Verdienstkreuz, FRG, 1989; Order of Gorkha Dakshina Bahu, 3rd Cl., Nepal, 1989. *Publications:* History of Tobacco Industry in Denmark 1875–1950, 1950; Dutch-Asiatic Trade 1620–1740, 1958, 2nd edn 1981; (with Astrid Friis) A History of Prices and Wages in Denmark 1660–1800, vol. I, 1958; A History of Brewing in Denmark, 1962; Studies in Mercantilism, 1966, 2nd edn 1984; European Trade 1500–1750, 1971; The Carlsberg Foundation, 1976; Cambridge Econ. Hist. of Europe, vol. V, 1977; J. C. Jacobsen of Carlsberg (biog.), 1990. *Recreations:* painting, walking. *Address:* The Carlsberg Foundation, 35 H. C. Andersens Boulevard, DK-1553 Copenhagen V, Denmark. *T:* 33 14 21 28.

GLAMIS, Lord; Simon Patrick Bowes Lyon; *b* 18 June 1986; *s* and *heir* of Earl of Strathmore and Kinghorne, *qv*.

GLAMORGAN, Earl of; Robert Somerset; *b* 20 Jan. 1989; *s* and *heir* of Marquess of Worcester, *qv*.

GLANDINE, Viscount; Richard James Graham-Toler; *b* 5 March 1967; *s* and *heir* of 6th Earl of Norbury, *qv*.

GLANUSK, 4th Baron, *cr* 1899; **David Russell Bailey;** Bt, *cr* 1852; Lieutenant-Commander RN (retired); *b* 19 Nov. 1917; *o s* of late Hon. Herbert Crawshay Bailey, 4th *s* of 1st Baron Glanusk and late Kathleen Mary, *d* of Sir Shirley Harris Salt, 3rd Bt; *S* cousin 1948; *m* 1941, Lorna Dorothy, *o d* of late Capt. E. C. H. N. Andrews, MBE, RA; one *s* one *d*. *Educ:* Orley Farm Sch., Harrow; Eton. RN, 1935–51. Managing Dir, Wandel & Goltermann (UK) Ltd, 1966–81; Chm., W&G Instruments Ltd, 1981–87. *Heir:* *s* Hon. Christopher Russell Bailey [*b* 18 March 1942; *m* 1974, Frances, *d* of Air Chief Marshal Sir Douglas Lowe, *qv*; one *s* one *d*]. *Address:* Por Fin, La Sort, Pollenca, Mallorca, Spain.

GLANVILLE, Alec William; Assistant Under-Secretary of State, Home Office, 1975–81, retired; *b* 20 Jan. 1921; *y s* of Frank Foster and Alice Glanville; *m* 1941, Lilian Kathleen Hetherton; one *s* one *d*. *Educ:* Portsmouth Northern Secondary Sch.; Portsmouth Municipal Coll. War service, RAMC, 1939–46. Exchequer and Audit Dept, 1939–47; General, Criminal, Police and Probation and After-care Depts, Home Office, 1947–81 (seconded to Cabinet Office, 1956–58); Private Sec. to Permanent Under Sec. of State, 1949–50; Principal Private Sec. to Sec. of State, 1960–63; Sec., Interdepartmental Cttee on Mentally Abnormal Offenders, 1972–75.

GLANVILLE, Brian Lester; author and journalist since 1949; *b* 24 Sept. 1931; *s* of James Arthur Glanville and Florence Glanville (*née* Manches); *m* 1959, Elizabeth Pamela de Boer (*née* Manasse), *d* of Fritz Manasse and Grace Manasse (*née* Howden); two *s* two *d*. *Educ:* Newlands Sch.; Charterhouse. Joined Sunday Times (football correspondent), 1958. *Publications:* The Reluctant Dictator, 1952; Henry Sows the Wind, 1954; Along the Arno, 1956; The Bankrupts, 1958; After Rome, Africa, 1959; A Bad Streak, 1961; Diamond, 1962; The Director's Wife, 1963; The King of Hackney Marshes, 1965; A Second Home, 1965; A Roman Marriage, 1966; The Artist Type, 1967; The Olympian, 1969; A Cry of Crickets, 1970; The Financiers, 1972; The History of the World Cup, 1973; The Thing He Loves, 1973; The Comic, 1974; The Dying of the Light, 1976;

Never Look Back, 1980; (jtly) Underneath The Arches (musical), 1981; A Visit to the Villa (play), 1981; Kissing America, 1985; Love is Not Love, 1985; (ed) The Joy of Football, 1986; The Catacomb, 1988; *juvenile:* Goalkeepers are Different (novel), 1971; Target Man (novel), 1978; The Puffin Book of Football, 1978; The Puffin Book of Tennis, 1981. *Recreation:* playing football. *Address:* 160 Holland Park Avenue, W11. *T:* 071–603 6908. *Club:* Chelsea Casuals.

GLANVILLE BROWN, William; *see* Brown, W. G.

GLANVILLE-JONES, Thomas; *see* Jones, T. G.

GLASBY, (Alfred) Ian; HM Diplomatic Service, retired; Director: Trust Co. of Australia (UK) Ltd, since 1990; Truco (Australia) Europe Ltd, since 1990; *b* 18 Sept. 1931; *s* of Frederick William Glasby and Harriet Maria Glasby; *m* 1970, Herma Fletcher; one *d.* *Educ:* Doncaster Grammar Sch.; London School of Economics and Political Science (BSc). Served HM Forces, 1950–52. Home Office, 1952–68; Second Sec., CO, later FCO, 1968–71; Second, later First Sec. (Commercial and Energy), Washington, 1971–76; Dep. High Comr, Hd of Chancery and Consul, Kampala, 1976; Hd, British Interests Sect., French Embassy, Kampala, 1976–77; First Sec., Hd of Chancery and Consul, Yaoundé, 1977–81, concurrently non-resident Chargé d'Affaires, Central Afr. Empire, Gabon, and Equatorial Guinea; Asst Hd, Consular Dept, FCO, 1981–84; Dep. Consul Gen., Sydney, 1984–88; Ambassador to People's Republic of the Congo, 1988–90. Hon. Chevalier, Ordre de Mérite (Republique Populaire du Congo). *Recreations:* Rugby, cricket, international affairs, reading, gardening. *Address:* High Pitch, Strande Lane, Cookham, Maidenhead, Berks SL6 9DW. *T:* Bourne End (06285) 28054. *Clubs:* Commonwealth Trust; Bristol RUF; Yorkshire CC; Australasian Pioneers, NSW Rugby (Sydney); Lions (Brazzaville).

GLASER, Prof. Donald Arthur; Professor of Physics and of Molecular and Cell Biology, University of California, since 1960; *b* 21 Sept. 1926; *s* of William Joseph and Lena Glaser. *Educ:* Case Institute of Technology (BS 1946); California Inst. of Technology (PhD 1950). University of Michigan: Instr. of Physics, 1949–53; Asst Prof., 1953–55; Associate Prof., 1955–57; Prof. of Physics, 1957–59; University of California, Berkeley: Vis. Prof., 1959–60; Prof. of Physics, 1960–; Miller Res. Biophysicist, 1962–64; Prof. of Molecular Biol., 1964–89; Prof. of Molecular and Cell Bio., 1989–. National Science Foundation Fellow, 1961; Guggenheim Fellow, 1961–62. Member: National Academy of Sciences (USA), 1962; NY Acad. of Science; Fellow Amer. Physical Soc.; FAAAS. Henry Russel Award, 1955; Charles Vernon Boys Prize, 1958; Amer. Phys. Soc. Prize, 1959; Nobel Prize for Physics, 1960. Hon. ScD Case Inst., 1959. *Publications:* chapters in: Topics in the Biology of Aging, 1965; Biology and the Exploration of Mars, 1966; Frontiers of Pattern Recognition, 1972; New Approaches to the Identification of Microorganisms, 1975; contrib. to Yearbook of the Physical Soc., London, 1958, to World Book Encyclopedia; articles in Physical Review, Bulletin of Amer. Phys. Soc., Nuovo Cimento, Handbuch der Physik, Jl Molecular Biol., Jl of Bacteriol., Cell, Applied and Environmental Microbiol., Annual of NY Acad. of Scis, Pattern Recognition and Image Processing, Somatic Cell Genetics, Cell Tissue Kinetics, Computers and Biomed. Res., Proc. Nat. Acad. of Scis (USA), Cold Spring Harbor Symposium Quant. Biol. 1968, Suppl. to Investigative Ophthalmol & Visual Sci., Jl Opt. Soc. of Amer. A, Vision Res., Visual Neurosci., etc. *Address:* 229 Stanley Hall, Department of Molecular and Cell Biology, University of California, Berkeley, Calif 94720, USA; 41 Hill Road, Berkeley, Calif 94708, USA.

GLASGOW, 10th Earl of, *cr* 1703; **Patrick Robin Archibald Boyle;** Lord Boyle, 1699; Viscount of Kelburn, 1703; Baron Fairlie (UK), 1897; television director/producer; *b* 30 July 1939; *s* of 9th Earl of Glasgow, CB, DSC, and of Dorothea, *o d* of Sir Archibald Lyle, 2nd Bt; *S* father, 1984; *m* 1975, Isabel Mary James; one *s* one *d.* *Educ:* Eton; Paris Univ. National Service in Navy; Sub-Lt, RNR, 1959–60. Worked in Associated Rediffusion Television, 1961; worked at various times for Woodfall Film Productions; Asst on Film Productions, 1962–64; Asst Dir in film industry, 1962–67; producer/director of documentary films, Yorkshire TV, 1968–70; freelance film producer, 1971–, making network television documentaries for BBC Yorkshire Television, ATV and Scottish Television. Formed Kelburn Country Centre, May 1977, opening Kelburn estate and gardens in Aryshire to the public. *Recreations:* ski-ing, theatre. *Heir:* *s* Viscount of Kelburn, *qv.* *Address:* Kelburn, Fairlie, Ayrshire. *T:* Fairlie (0475) 568204; (office) South Offices, Kelburn Estate, Fairlie, Aryshire. *T:* Fairlie (0475) 568685.

GLASGOW, Archbishop of, (RC), since 1974; **Most Rev. Thomas J. Winning,** DCL, STL, DD. Formerly parish priest, St Luke, Braidhurst, Motherwell; Auxiliary Bishop of Glasgow, 1971–74; parish priest, Our Holy Redeemer's, Clydebank, 1972–74. Mem., Sacred Congregation for the Doctrine of the Faith, 1978–83. Pres., Bishops' Conf. of Scotland, 1985–. Grand Prior, Scottish Lieutenancy of Equestrian Order of Holy Sepulchre of Jerusalem, 1989–. FEIS 1986. Hon. DD Glasgow, 1983. *Address:* 40 Newlands Road, Glasgow G43 2JD.

GLASGOW, Auxiliary Bishop of, (RC); *see* Renfrew, Rt Rev. C. McD.

GLASGOW, (St Mary's Cathedral), Provost of; *no new appointment at time of going to press.*

GLASGOW, Edwin John; QC 1987; *b* 3 Aug. 1945; *s* of Richard Edwin, (Dick), Glasgow and Diana Geraldine Mary Glasgow (*née* Markby); *m* 1967, Janet Coleman; one *s* one *d.* *Educ:* St Joseph's Coll., Ipswich; University Coll. London (LLB). Called to the Bar, Gray's Inn, 1969. Trustee: London Opera Players, 1985–; Mary Glasgow Language Trust, 1984– (Chm.). *Recreations:* family, friends, France, music. *Address:* 2 Garden Court, Temple, EC4. *T:* 071–353 4741; Copper Hall, Thames Ditton, Surrey; Entrechaux, Vaucluse, France. *Club:* Royal Automobile.

GLASGOW AND GALLOWAY, Bishop of, since 1991; **Rt. Rev. John Mitchell Taylor;** *b* 23 May 1932; *m* 1959, Edna Elizabeth (*née* Maitland); one *s* one *d.* *Educ:* Banff Acad.; Aberdeen Univ. (MA 1954); Edinburgh Theol Coll. Ordained deacon, 1956, priest, 1957; Asst Curate, St Margaret, Aberdeen, 1956–58; Rector: Holy Cross, Glasgow, 1958–64; St Ninian, Glasgow, 1964–73; St John the Evangelist, Dumfries, 1973–91; Chaplain: Crichton Royal Hospital; Dumfries and Galloway Royal Infirmary, 1973–91; Canon, St Mary's Cathedral, 1979–91. *Recreations:* angling, hill walking, badminton, swimming, music, ornithology. *Address:* 25 Quadrant Road, Newlands, Glasgow G43 2QP. *T:* 041–637 5659.

GLASGOW AND GALLOWAY, Dean of; *see* Reid, Very Rev. D. W. J.

GLASHOW, Prof. Sheldon Lee, PhD; Higgins Professor of Physics, Harvard University, since 1979 (Professor of Physics, since 1966); *b* 5 Dec. 1932; *s* of Lewis and Bella Glashow; *m* 1972, Joan (*née* Alexander); three *s* one *d.* *Educ:* Cornell Univ. (AB); Harvard Univ. (AM, PhD). National Science Foundn Fellow, Copenhagen and Geneva, 1958–60; Res. Fellow, Calif Inst. of Technol., 1960–61; Asst Prof., Stanford Univ., 1961–62; Associate Prof., Univ. of Calif at Berkeley, 1962–66. Vis. Professor: CERN, 1968; Marseille, 1971; MIT, 1974 and 1980; Boston Univ., 1983; Univ. Schol., Texas A&M Univ., 1983–. Consultant, Brookhaven Nat. Lab., 1966–; Affiliated Senior Scientist, Univ. of Houston, 1983–. Pres., Sakharov Internat. Cttee, Washington, 1980–. Hon. DSc: Yeshiva, 1978; Aix-Marseille, 1982. Nobel Prize for Physics (jtly), 1979. *Publications:* articles in learned jls. *Recreations:* scuba diving, tennis. *Address:* 30 Prescott Street, Brookline, Mass 02146, USA. *T:* 617–277–5446.

GLASS, Anthony Trevor; QC 1986; a Recorder of the Crown Court, since 1985; *b* 6 June 1940. *Educ:* Royal Masonic School; Lincoln College, Oxford (MA). Called to the Bar, Inner Temple, 1965. *Address:* Queen Elizabeth Building, Temple, EC4. *T:* 071–583 5766.

GLASS, Ven. Edward Brown; Archdeacon of Man, 1964–78, now Emeritus; Rector of Kirk Andreas, Isle of Man, 1964–78; *b* 1 July 1913; *s* of William and Phoebe Harriet Glass; *m* 1940, Frances Katharine Calvert; one *s* two *d.* *Educ:* King William's Coll., IoM; Durham Univ. (MA). Deacon 1937, priest 1938, dio. Manchester; Curate: St Mary's, Wardleworth, Rochdale, 1937; Gorton Parish Church, Manchester, 1937–42; Vicar: St John's, Hopwood, Heywood, Manchester, 1942–51; St Olave's, Ramsey, IoM, 1951–55; Castletown, IoM, 1955–64. Sec., Diocesan Convocation, 1958–64; Proctor for Clergy, Convocation of York, 1959–64; Member, Church Assembly and General Synod, 1959–78; Warden of Diocesan Readers, 1969–78; Chm., Diocesan Advisory Cttee, 1975–78. *Recreations:* gardening, ornithology, touring in Norway. *Address:* The Croft, Coburg Road, Ramsey, Isle of Man. *T:* Ramsey (0624) 812932.

GLASSCOCK, John Lewis, FCIS; aerospace consultant; Director, EH Industries Ltd, since 1989; *b* 12 July 1928; *s* of Edgar Henry and Maude Allison Glasscock; *m* 1959, Anne Doreen Baker; two *s.* *Educ:* Tiffin Sch.; University Coll. London (BA Hons). Served Royal Air Force, 1950–53. Joined Hawker Aircraft Ltd, 1953, Asst Sec., 1956, Commercial Man., 1961; Hawker Siddeley Aviation Ltd: Divl Commercial Man., 1964; Dir and Gen. Man. (Kingston), 1965; Dir and Gen. Man., 1977; British Aerospace Aircraft Group: Admin. Dir, 1978; Commercial Dir, 1979; Man. Dir (Military), 1981; BAe PLC: Dir, 1982–87; Dep. Chief Exec. and Man. Dir, Civil Aircraft Div., 1982–87; Commercial Dir, 1986–87. Mem. Supervisory Bd, Airbus Industrie, 1983–85. Mem. Council, SBAC, 1979–87. *Recreations:* golf, tennis. *Address:* West Meadow, The Wedges, West Chiltington Lane, near Horsham, W Sussex RH13 7TA. *Clubs:* Royal Air Force, Royal Automobile.

GLASSE, Thomas Henry, CMG 1961; MVO 1955; MBE 1946; retired as Counsellor in HM Diplomatic Service, and Head of Protocol Department, Foreign Office (1957–61); *b* 14 July 1898; *s* of late Thomas and Harriette Glasse; *m* 1st, 1935, Elsie May Dyter (*d* 1965); no *c*; 2nd, 1966, Ethel Alice Needham (*d* 1985); 3rd, 1988, Maria Philomena Cover. *Educ:* Latymer Foundation Upper Sch., Hammersmith. Entered Civil Service as a Boy Clerk, 1914. Army Service, 1/10th Bn Mx Regt, 1917–19. Joined the Foreign Office, 1921. Delegate of United Kingdom to Vienna Conference on Diplomatic Relations, 1961. *Recreations:* books, music, garden, travel. *Address:* 72 Lynch Road, Farnham, Surrey GU9 8BT. *T:* Farnham (0252) 716662. *Club:* Travellers'.

GLASSPOLE, Most Hon. Sir Florizel (Augustus), ON 1973; GCMG 1981; GCVO 1983; CD 1970; Governor-General of Jamaica, since 1973; *b* Kingston, Jamaica, 25 Sept. 1909; *s* of late Rev. Theophilus A. Glasspole (Methodist Minister) and Florence (*née* Baxter); *m* 1934, Ina Josephine Kinlocke; one *d.* *Educ:* Central British Elementary Sch.; Wolmer's Sch.; Ruskin Coll., Oxford. British TUC Schol., 1946–47. Accountant (practising), 1932–44. Gen. Sec: Jamaica United Clerks Assoc., 1937–48; Jamaica TUC, 1939–52, resigned; Water Commn and Allied Workers Assoc., 1941–48; Municipal and Parochial Gen. Workers Union, 1945–47; First Gen. Sec., Nat. Workers Union, 1952–55; President: Jamaica Printers & Allied Workers Union, 1942–48; Gen. Hosp. and Allied Workers Union, 1944–47; Mental Hosp. Workers Union, 1944–47; Machado Employees Union, 1945–52; etc. Workers rep. on Govt Bds, etc, 1942–. Mem. Bd of Governors Inst. of Jamaica, 1944–57; Mem., Kingston Sch. Bd, 1944–. Founding Mem., PNP, 1938; MHR (PNP) for Kingston Eastern and Port Royal, 1944; Sec., PNP Parly Gp, 1944–73, resigned; Vice-Pres., People's National Party; Minister of Labour, Jamaica, 1955–57; Leader, House of Representatives, 1957–62, 1972–73; Minister of Educn, 1957–62, 1972–73; A Rep. for Jamaica, on Standing Fedn Cttee, West Indies Federation, 1953–58; Mem. House of Reps Cttee which prepared Independence of Jamaica Constitution, 1961; Mem. Delegn to London which completed Constitution document, 1962. Hon. LLD Univ. of the West Indies, 1982. Order of Andres Bello (1st cl.), Venezuela, 1973; Order of the Liberator, Venezuela, 1978. *Recreations:* gardening, sports, reading. *Address:* Kings House, Hope Road, Kingston 10, Jamaica.

GLAUERT, Audrey Marion, ScD; Head of Electron Microscopy Department, Strangeways Research Laboratory, Cambridge, 1956–89 (Associate Director, 1979–85); Fellow of Clare Hall, Cambridge, since 1966; *b* 21 Dec. 1925; *d* of late Hermann Glauert, FRS and Muriel Glauert (*née* Barker). *Educ:* Perse Sch. for Girls, Cambridge; Bedford Coll., Univ. of London. BSc 1946, MSc 1947, London; MA Cantab 1967, ScD Cantab 1970. Asst Lectr in Physics, Royal Holloway Coll., Univ. of London, 1947–50; Mem. Scientific Staff, Strangeways Res. Lab., Cambridge, Sir Halley Stewart Research Fellow, 1950–89. Chairman: British Joint Cttee for Electron Microscopy, 1968–72; Fifth European Congress on Electron Microscopy, 1972; Pres., Royal Microscopical Soc., 1970–72, Hon. Fellow, 1973. Hon. Member: French Soc. for Electron Microscopy, 1967; Electron Microscopy Soc. of America, 1990. JP Cambridge, 1975–88. Editor: Practical Methods in Electron Microscopy, 1972–; Jl of Microscopy, Royal Microscopial Soc., 1986–88. Dist. Scientist Award for Biol Scis, Electron Microscopy Soc. of America, 1990. *Publications:* Fixation Dehydration and Embedding of Biological Specimens, 1974; (ed) The Control of Tissue Damage, 1988; papers on cell and molecular biology in scientific jls. *Recreations:* sailing, gardening. *Address:* 29 Cow Lane, Fulbourn, Cambridge CB1 5HB. *T:* Cambridge (0223) 880463; Clare Hall, Herschel Road, Cambridge CB3 9AL.

GLAVES-SMITH, Frank William, CB 1975; Deputy Director-General of Fair Trading, 1973–79, retired; *b* 27 Sept. 1919; *m* 1st, 1941, Audrey Glaves (*d* 1989); one *s* one *d*; 2nd, 1990, Ursula Mary Murray. *Educ:* Malet Lambert High Sch., Hull. War Service, 1940–46 (Captain, Royal Signals). Called to Bar, Middle Temple, 1947. Board of Trade, 1947; Princ. Private Sec. to Pres. of Bd of Trade, 1952–57; Asst Secretary: HM Treasury, 1957–60; Cabinet Office, 1960–62; Bd of Trade, 1962–65; Under-Sec., BoT, 1965–69, Dept of Employment and Productivity, 1969–70, DTI, 1970–73; Dep. Sec., 1975. Mem., Export Guarantees Adv. Council, 1971–73. *Recreations:* rock-climbing, fell-walking. *Address:* 8 Grange Park, Keswick, Cumbria CA12 4AY; 14 Priory Road, West Kirby, Wirral L48 7EU.

GLAVIN, William Francis; President, Babson College, Wellesley, Mass, since 1989; *b* 29 March 1932; *m* 1955, Cecily McClatchy; three *s* four *d.* *Educ:* College of the Holy Cross, Worcester, Mass (BS); Wharton Graduate Sch. (MBA). Vice-Pres., Operations, Service Bureau Corp. (subsid. of IBM), 1968–70; Exec. Vice-Pres., Xerox Data Services, 1970; Pres., Xerox Data Systems, 1970–72; Gp Vice-Pres., Xerox Corp., and Pres., Business Development Gp, 1972–74; Rank Xerox Ltd: Man. Dir, 1974–80; Chief Operating Officer, 1974–77; Chief Exec. Officer, 1977–80; Xerox Corp.: Exec. Vice-Pres. Chief

Staff Officer, 1980–82; President: Reprographics and Ops, 1982–83; Business Equipment Gps, 1983–89 (Vice Chm., 1985–89). *Recreations:* golf, music, boating, tennis. *Address:* 56 Whiting Road, Wellesley, Mass 02181, USA.

GLAZE, Michael John Carlisle, (James), CMG 1988; HM Diplomatic Service; Ambassador to Ethiopia, since 1990; *b* 15 Jan. 1935; *s* of late Derek Glaze and of Shirley Gardner (formerly Glaze, *née* Ramsay); *m* 1965, Rosemary Duff; two step-*d*. *Educ:* Repton; St Catharine's Coll., Cambridge (open Exhibitioner, BA 1958); Worcester Coll., Oxford. Colonial Service, Basutoland, 1959–65; HMOCS, Dep. Permanent Sec., Finance, Lesotho, 1966–70; Dept of Trade (ECGD), 1971–73; FCO, 1973–75; Abu Dhabi, 1975–78; Rabat, 1978–80; Consul-Gen., Bordeaux, 1980–84; Ambassador: Republic of Cameroon, 1984–87; Angola, 1987–90. *Recreations:* golf, grand opera, the garden. *Address:* c/o Foreign and Commonwealth Office, SW1. *Club:* Athenæum.

GLAZEBROOK, (Reginald) Mark; writer and art dealer; Director, Albemarle Gallery, London, since 1986; *b* 25 June 1936; *s* of late Reginald Field Glazebrook; *m* 1st, 1965, Elizabeth Lea Claridge (marr. diss. 1969); one *d*; 2nd, 1974, Wanda Barbara O'Neill (*née* Osińska); one *d*. *Educ:* Eton; Pembroke Coll., Cambridge (MA); Slade School of Fine Art. Worked at Arts Council, 1961–64; Lectr at Maidstone Coll. of Art, 1965–67; Art Critic, London Magazine, 1967–68; Dir, Whitechapel Art Gall., 1969–71; Head of Modern English Paintings and Drawings, P. and D. Colnaghi & Co. Ltd, 1973–75; Gallery Director and Art History Lectr, San José State Univ., 1977–79. FRSA 1971. *Publications:* (comp.) Artists and Architecture of Bedford Park 1875–1900 (catalogue), 1967; (comp.) David Hockney: paintings, prints and drawings 1960–1970 (catalogue), 1970; Edward Wadsworth 1889–1949: paintings, prints and drawings (catalogue), 1974; (introduction) John Armstrong 1893–1973 (catalogue), 1975; (introduction) John Tunnard (catalogue), 1976; articles in: Studio International, London Magazine. *Recreations:* travelling, theatre, tennis, swimming. *Address:* 5 Priory Gardens, Bedford Park, W4 1TT. *Clubs:* Beefsteak, Garrick, Groucho, Lansdowne, Ognisko Polski.

GLEDHILL, Anthony John, GC 1967; company executive, since 1988; *b* 10 March 1938; *s* of Harold Victor and Marjorie Edith Gledhill; *m* 1958, Marie Lilian Hughes; one *s* one *d*. *Educ:* Doncaster Technical High Sch., Yorks. Accounts Clerk, Officers' Mess, RAF Bruggen, Germany, 1953–56. Metropolitan Police: Cadet, 1956–57; Police Constable, 1957–75; Detective Sergeant, 1976–87; Investigator, PO Investigation Dept, 1987–88. *Recreations:* football, carpentry. *Address:* 98 Pickhurst Lane, Hayes, Bromley, Kent BR2 7JD. *T:* 081–462 4033. *Club:* No 4 District Metropolitan Police (Hayes, Kent).

GLEDHILL, David Anthony, JP; Chairman: John Swire & Sons (HK), since 1988; Swire Pacific, since 1988; *b* 16 Oct. 1934; *s* of Arnold Grosland Gledhill and Marjorie Yates Johnson; *m* 1968, Kyoko Gledhill. *Educ:* Ellesmere College, Shropshire; Sidney Sussex College, Cambridge. Joined John Swire and Sons (HK), 1958; served Hong Kong, Osaka, Yokohama, Tokyo; China Navigation Co., Hong Kong, 1963–65; Shipping Manager, John Swire & Sons (Japan), 1966–73; Dir, John Swire & Sons (HK), 1973–84, Dep. Chm., 1984–88; Dir, Swire Pacific, 1973–88, Dep. Chm., 1984–88; Chairman: Swire Pacific Offshore Services, 1975–88; Modern Terminals, 1981– (Dir, 1973–81); Director: Hongkong & Shanghai Banking Corp., 1988–; Lee Gardens Internat. Hotels, 1988–; Community Chest of Hong Kong, 1988–; Mass Transit Railway Corp., 1990–; Mem. Bd, IBM World Trade Asia/Pacific Group Bd, 1989–. Chm., Employers' Fedn of Hong Kong, 1989– (Council Mem., 1985–88); Member: Aviation Adv. Bd, 1988–; Council, Hong Kong Gen. Chamber of Commerce, 1988–; Consultative Cttee for Basic Law, 1988–. Mem. Council, Univ. of Hong Kong. JP Hong Kong, 1988. *Recreations:* swimming, sailing, fishing. *Address:* 25 Peak Road, Hong Kong. *T:* 5–8496912. *Clubs:* Hong Kong, Shek O, Hong Kong Country.

GLEESON, Anthony Murray, AO 1986; **Hon. Mr Justice Gleeson;** Chief Justice of New South Wales, since 1988; Lieutenant-Governor of New South Wales, since 1989; *b* 30 Aug. 1938; *s* of Leo John Gleeson and Rachel Alice Gleeson; *m* 1965, Robyn Paterson; one *s* three *d*. *Educ:* St Joseph's Coll., Hunters Hill; Univ. of Sydney (BA, LLB). Called to the NSW Bar, 1963; QC 1974. Tutor in Law, St Paul's Coll., Sydney Univ., 1963–65; Part-time Lectr in Company Law, Sydney Univ., 1965–74. Mem. Council, NSW Bar Assoc., 1979–85 (Pres., 1984 and 1985). Hon. Bencher, Middle Temple, 1989. *Recreations:* tennis, ski-ing. *Address:* c/o Chief Justice's Chambers, Supreme Court, Queen's Square, Sydney, NSW 2000, Australia. *T:* 230 8218. *Club:* Australian (Sydney).

GLEESON, Most Rev. James William, AO 1979; CMG 1958; DD 1957; FACE 1967; Archbishop Emeritus of Adelaide, (RC), since 1985; *b* 24 Dec. 1920; *s* of John Joseph and Margaret Mary Gleeson. *Educ:* St Joseph's Sch., Balaklava, SA; Sacred Heart Coll., Glenelg, SA. Priest, 1945; Inspector of Catholic Schs, 1947–52; Dir of Catholic Education for South Australia, 1952–58; Auxiliary Bishop to the Archbishop of Adelaide and Titular Bishop of Sesta, 1957–64; Coadjutor Archbishop of Adelaide and Titular Archbishop of Aurusuliana, 1964–71; Archbishop of Adelaide, 1971–85. Episcopal Chm., Young Catholic Students Movement of Australia, 1958–65. *Address:* Archbishop's House, 91 West Terrace, Adelaide, SA 5000, Australia. *T:* (08) 231 3551.

GLEISSNER, Dr Heinrich; at Federal Ministry for Foreign Affairs, Vienna, since 1982; *b* Linz, Upper Austria, 12 Dec. 1927; *s* of Heinrich and Maria Gleissner. *Educ:* Univ. of Vienna (Dr jur 1950); Univ. of Innsbruck; Bowdoin Coll., Brunswick, Maine, USA; Coll. of Europe, Bruges. Entered Austrian Foreign Service, 1951; Austrian Embassy, Paris, and Office of Austrian Observer at Council of Europe, Strasbourg, 1952–53; Min. for Foreign Affairs, Vienna, 1953–55; Austrian Embassy, London, 1955–57; sabbatical, Univ. of Vienna, 1957–59; Min. for For. Affairs, 1959–61; Austrian National Bank, 1961; Min. for For. Affairs, 1961–62; Mission to Office of UN, Geneva, 1962–65; Consulate-General, New York, 1965–66, Consul-Gen., 1966–73; Min. for For. Affairs, 1973–75 (Head, Western Dept, 1974–75); Dir, Security Council and Polit. Cttees Div., UN, New York, 1975–79; Austrian Ambassador to the Court of St James's, 1979–81. *Recreation:* music. *Address:* Federal Ministry for Foreign Affairs, Ballhausplatz 2, 1010 Vienna, Austria. *Club:* St Johann's (Wien).

GLEN, Sir Alexander (Richard), KBE 1967 (CBE 1964); DSC 1942 (and Bar, 1945); President, British Air Line Pilots' Association, since 1982; *b* 18 April 1912; *s* of late R. Bartlett Glen, Glasgow; *m* 1947, Baroness Zora de Collaert. *Educ:* Fettes Coll.; Balliol Coll., Oxford. BA, Hons Geography. Travelled on Arctic Expeditions, 1932–36; Leader, Oxford Univ. Arctic Expedition, 1935–36; Banking, New York and London, 1936–39. RNVR, 1939–59, Capt. 1955. Export Council for Europe: Dep. Chm., 1960–64; Chm., 1964–66; Chairman: H. Clarkson & Co., 1965–73; Anglo World Travel, 1978–81; Dep. Chm., British Transport Hotels, 1978–83; Director: BICC, 1964–70; Gleneagles Hotels, 1980–83. Chm., BTA, 1969–77; Member: BNEC, 1966–72; Board of BEA, 1964–70; Nat. Ports Council, 1966–70; Horserace Totalisator Bd, 1976–84. Chm., Adv. Council, V&A Museum, 1978–84; Mem., Historic Buildings Council, 1976–80. Awarded Cuthbert Peek Grant by RGS, 1933; Bruce Medal by RSE, 1938; Andrée Plaque by Royal Swedish Soc. for Anthropology and Geography, 1939; Patron's Gold Medal by RGS, 1940. Polar Medal (clasp Arctic 1935–36), 1942; Norwegian War Cross, 1943; Chevalier (1st Class), Order of St Olav, 1944; Czechoslovak War Cross, 1946. *Publications:* Young Men in the Arctic, 1935; Under the Pole Star, 1937; Footholds Against a Whirlwind (autobiog.), 1975. *Recreations:* travel, ski-ing, sailing. *Address:* The Dower House, Stanton, Broadway, Worcs WR12 7NE. *Clubs:* City of London; Explorers (NY).

GLEN, Archibald; Solicitor; *b* 3 July 1909; *m* 1938, Phyllis Mary; one *s* two *d*. *Educ:* Melville Coll., Edinburgh. Admitted Solicitor, 1932. Town Clerk: Burnley, Lancs, 1940–45; Southend-on-Sea, 1945–71. President: Soc. of City and Borough Clerks of the Peace, 1960; Soc. of Town Clerks, 1963–64; Assoc. of Town Clerks of British Commonwealth, 1963–64, etc. Lay Member, Press Council, 1969–75; Mem., Local Govt Staff Commn for England, 1972–76. Hon. Freeman, Southend-on-Sea, 1971. *Recreations:* golf, swimming. *Address:* Harbour House, 2 Drummochy, Lower Largo, Fife KY8 6BZ. *T:* Lundin Links (0333) 320724.

GLEN HAIG, Mrs Mary Alison, CBE 1977 (MBE 1971); *b* 12 July 1918; *e d* of late Captain William James and Mary (*née* Bannochie); *m* 1943, Andrew Glen Haig (decd). *Educ:* Dame Alice Owen's Girls' School. Mem., Sports Council, 1966–82; Vice Pres., CCPR, 1982– (Chm., 1974–80); Mem., Internat. Olympic Cttee, 1982–; Pres., British Sports Assoc. for the Disabled, 1981–90; Vice Pres., Sports Aid Foundn, 1987–. Hon. Pres., Amateur Fencing Assoc., 1986– (Pres., 1974–86); Pres., Ladies' Amateur Fencing Union, 1964–74. British Ladies' Foil Champion, 1948–50. Olympic Games, 1948, 1952, 1956, 1960; Commonwealth Games Gold Medal, 1950, 1954, Bronze Medal, 1958; Captain, Ladies' Foil Team, 1950–57. Asst Dist Administrator, S Hammersmith Health District, 1975–82. Chm. of Trustees, HRH The Princess Christian Hosp., Windsor, 1981–. *Recreations:* fencing, gardening. *Address:* 66 North End House, Fitzjames Avenue, W14 0RX. *T:* 071–602 2504; 2 Old Cottages, Holyport Street, Holyport, near Maidenhead, Berks. *T:* Maidenhead (0628) 33421. *Club:* Lansdowne.

GLENAMARA, Baron *cr* 1977 (Life Peer), of Glenridding, Cumbria; **Edward Watson Short,** PC 1964; CH 1976; Chairman, Cable and Wireless Ltd, 1976–80; *b* 17 Dec. 1912; *s* of Charles and Mary Short, Warcop, Westmorland; *m* 1941, Jennie, *d* of Thomas Sewell, Newcastle upon Tyne; one *s* one *d*. *Educ:* Bede College, Durham. LLB London. Served War of 1939–45 and became Capt. in DLI. Headmaster of Princess Louise County Secondary School, Blyth, Northumberland, 1947; Leader of Labour Group on Newcastle City Council, 1950; MP (Lab) Newcastle upon Tyne Central, 1951–76; Opposition Whip (Northern Area), 1955–62; Dep. Chief Opposition Whip, 1962–64; Parly Sec. to the Treasury and Govt Chief Whip, 1964–66; Postmaster General, 1966–68; Sec. of State for Educn and Science, 1968–70; Lord Pres. of the Council and Leader, House of Commons, 1974–76. Dep. Leader, Labour Party, 1972–76. Mem. Council, WWF, 1983–. Pres., Finchale Abbey Training Coll. for the Disabled (Durham), 1985–. Chancellor, Polytechnic of Newcastle upon Tyne, 1984–. Hon. FCP, 1965. Hon. DCL Dunelm, 1989; DUniv Open, 1989; Hon. DLitt CNAA, 1990. *Publications:* The Story of The Durham Light Infantry, 1944; The Infantry Instructor, 1946; Education in a Changing World, 1971; Birth to Five, 1974; I Knew My Place, 1983; Whip to Wilson, 1989. *Recreation:* painting. *Address:* 21 Priory Gardens, Corbridge, Northumberland NE45 5HZ. *T:* Corbridge (0434) 632880; Glenridding, Cumbria. *T:* Glenridding (08532) 273.

GLENAPP, Viscount; (Kenneth) Peter (Lyle) Mackay, AIB; Director: Duncan Macneill & Co. Ltd, London, since 1985; Inchcape Family Investments Ltd, since 1985; Inchcape UK Ltd, since 1987; *b* 23 Jan. 1943; *er s* and *heir* of 3rd Earl of Inchcape, *qv*; *m* 1966, Georgina, *d* of S. C. Nisbet and late Mrs G. R. Sutton; one *s* two *d*. *Educ:* Eton. Late Lieut 9/12th Royal Lancers. *Recreations:* shooting, fishing, golf, farming. *Heir:* *s* Hon. Fergus James Kenneth Mackay, *b* 9 July 1979. *Address:* Manor Farm, Clyffe Pypard, near Swindon, Wilts SN4 7PY; 63E Pont Street, SW1. *Clubs:* White's, Oriental, City of London; Royal Sydney (Sydney, NSW).

GLENARTHUR, 4th Baron *cr* 1918; **Simon Mark Arthur;** Bt 1903; DL 1988; *b* 7 Oct. 1944; *s* of 3rd Baron Glenarthur, OBE, and of Margaret, *d* of late Captain H. J. J. Howie; *S* father, 1976; *m* 1969, Susan, *yr d* of Comdr Hubert Wyndham Barry, RN; one *s* one *d*. *Educ:* Eton. Commissioned 10th Royal Hussars (PWO), 1963; ADC to High Comr, Aden, 1964–65; Captain 1970; Major 1973; retired 1975; Royal Hussars (PWO), TA, 1976–80. British Airways Helicopters Captain, 1976–82. A Lord in Waiting (Govt Whip), 1982–83; Parly Under Sec. of State, DHSS, 1983–85, Home Office, 1985–86; Minister of State: Scottish Office, 1986–87; FCO, 1987–89. Dir, Aberdeen and Texas Corporate Finance Ltd, 1977–82; Hanson PLC, 1989–; Consultant, BAe PLC, 1989–. Mem., Queen's Body Guard for Scotland (Royal Co. of Archers), 1985–. MCIT 1979. DL Aberdeenshire, 1988. *Recreations:* field sports, flying, gardening, choral singing, photography. *Heir:* *s* Hon. Edward Alexander Arthur, *b* 9 April 1973. *Address:* House of Lords, SW1A 0PW. *Club:* Cavalry and Guards.

GLENCONNER, 3rd Baron *cr* 1911; **Colin Christopher Paget Tennant;** Bt 1885; Governing Director, Tennants Estate Ltd, since 1967; Chairman, Mustique Co. Ltd, 1969–87; *b* 1 Dec. 1926; *s* of 2nd Baron Glenconner, and Pamela Winefred (*d* 1989), 2nd *d* of Sir Richard Paget, 2nd Bt; *S* father, 1983; *m* 1956, Lady Anne Coke, VO, *e d* of 5th Earl of Leicester, MVO; two *s* twin *d* (and one *s* decd). *Educ:* Eton; New College, Oxford. Director, C. Tennant Sons & Co. Ltd, 1953; Deputy Chairman, 1960–67, resigned 1967. *Heir:* *s* Hon. Charles Edward Pevensey Tennant, *b* 15 Feb. 1957. *Address:* Hill Lodge, Hillsleigh Road, W8. *T:* 071–221 0698.

GLENCROSS, David; Chief Executive, Independent Television Commission, since 1991; *b* 3 March 1936; *s* of John William and Elsie May Glencross; *m* 1965, Elizabeth Louise, *d* of John and Edith Richardson; one *d*. *Educ:* Salford Grammar School; Trinity College, Cambridge. BBC: general trainee, 1958; talks producer, Midlands, 1959; TV Midlands at Six, 1962; Staff Training section, 1964; Senior Producer, External Services, 1966; Asst Head of Programmes, N Region, 1968; Senior Programme Officer, ITA, 1970; Head of Programme Services, IBA, 1976; Dep. Dir, 1977, Dir, 1983–90, Television, IBA. FRTS 1981; FRSA 1985. *Publications:* articles on broadcasting in newspapers and jls. *Recreations:* music, reading, listening to radio, walking. *Address:* Independent Television Commission, 70 Brompton Road, SW3. *T:* 071–584 7011.

GLENDEVON, 1st Baron, *cr* 1964; **John Adrian Hope;** ERD 1988; PC 1959; Director and Deputy Chairman, Ciba-Geigy (UK) Ltd (formerly Geigy (UK) Ltd), 1971–78 (Chairman, 1967–71); Director: ITT (UK) Ltd; Colonial Mutual Life Assurance Society Ltd, 1952–54, 1962–82; British Electric Traction Omnibus Services Ltd, 1947–52, 1962–82; *b* 7 April 1912; *yr* twin *s* of 2nd Marquess of Linlithgow, KG, KT, PC; *m* 1948, Elizabeth Mary, *d* of late (William) Somerset Maugham, CH; two *s*. *Educ:* Eton; Christ Church, Oxford (MA 1936). Served War of 1939–45 (Scots Guards) at Narvik, Salerno and Anzio (despatches twice); psc†. MP (C) Northern Midlothian and Peebles, 1945–50, Pentlands Div. of Edinburgh, 1950–64; (Joint) Parliamentary Under-Sec. of State for Foreign Affairs, Oct. 1954–Nov. 1956; Parliamentary Under-Sec. of State for Commonwealth Relations, Nov. 1956–Jan. 1957; Jt Parly Under-Sec. of State for Scotland, 1957–Oct. 1959; Minister of Works, Oct. 1959–July 1962. Mem., Departmental Cttee to examine operation of Section 2 of Official Secrets Act, 1971. Chairman: Royal Commonwealth Society, 1963–66; Historic Buildings Council for England, 1973–75. Fellow of Eton, 1956–67. FRSA 1962. *Publication:* The Viceroy at Bay, 1971. *Heir:* *s*

Hon. Julian John Somerset Hope, *b* 6 March 1950. *Address:* Mount Lodge, Mount Row, St Peter Port, Guernsey, Channel Islands.

GLENDINING, Rev. Canon Alan, LVO 1979; Chaplain to the Queen, since 1979; Hon. Canon of Norwich Cathedral, since 1977; *b* 17 March 1924; *s* of late Vincent Glendining, MS, FRCS and Freda Alice; *m* 1948, Margaret Locke, *d* of Lt-Col C. M. Hawes, DSO and Frances Cooper Richmond; one *s* one *d* (and one *d* decd). *Educ:* Radley; Westcott House, Cambridge. Newspaper publishing, 1945–58. Deacon, 1960; Priest, 1961. Asst Curate, South Ormsby Group of Parishes, 1960–63; Rector of Raveningham Group of Parishes, 1963–70; Rector, Sandringham Group of Parishes, and Domestic Chaplain to the Queen, 1970–79; Rural Dean of Heacham and Rising, 1972–76; Rector of St Margaret's, Lowestoft, and Team Leader of Lowestoft Group, 1979–85; Vicar of Ranworth with Panxworth with Woodbastwick, Bishop's Chaplain for the Broads and Senior Chaplain for Holidaymakers, 1985–89; RD of Blofield, 1987–89. *Recreation:* writing. *Address:* 7 Bellfosters, Kings Staithe Lane, Kings Lynn, Norfolk.

GLENDINNING, James Garland, OBE 1973; Executive Secretary, Japan Society, since 1985; various company directorships, since 1983; *b* 27 April 1919; *er s* of late George M. Glendinning and Isabella Green; *m* 1st, 1943, Margaret Donald (*d* 1980); one *d*; 2nd, Mrs Anne Ruth Law. *Educ:* Boroughmuir Sch., Edinburgh; Military Coll. of Science. Mil. Service, 1939–46: 2nd Bn London Scottish and REME in UK and NW Europe. HM Inspector of Taxes, 1946–50; various appts with Shell Petroleum Co. Ltd, 1950–58; Dir Anglo Egyptian Oilfields Ltd in Egypt, 1959–61; Gen. Manager in Borneo and East Java for Shell Indonesia, 1961–64; Head of Industrial Studies (Diversification) in Shell Internat. Petroleum Co. Ltd, London, 1964–67; various Shell appts in Japan, 1967–72, incl.: Vice-President: Shell Sekiyu KK; Shell Kosan KK; Dir, various Shell/Showa and Shell/Mitsubishi jt venture cos. Chm., British Chamber of Commerce in Japan, 1970–72; Mem., London Transport Exec., 1972–80; Chairman: London Transport Pension Fund Trustees Ltd, 1974–80; North American Property Unit Trust, 1975–80; Director: Industrial and Commercial Property Unit Trust, 1977–81; The Fine Art Society plc, 1972–89; Man. Dir, Gestam International Realty Ltd, 1981–83. FCIT 1973; FRSA 1977. *Address:* 20 Albion Street, W2 2AS. *Clubs:* Caledonian, Oriental.

GLENDINNING, Hon. Victoria, (Hon. Mrs de Vere White), FRSL; author and journalist, since 1969; *b* 23 April 1937; *d* of Baron Seebohm, TD and Evangeline, *d* of Sir Gerald Hurst, QC; *m* 1st, 1958, Prof. (Oliver) Nigel (Valentine) Glendinning (marr. diss. 1981); four *s*; 2nd, 1982, Terence de Vere White, *qv*. *Educ:* St Mary's Sch., Wantage; Millfield Sch.; Somerville Coll., Oxford (MA Mod. Langs); Southampton Univ. (Dip. in Social Admin). FRSL 1982. Part-time teaching, 1960–69; part-time psychiatric social work, 1970–73; Editorial Asst, TLS, 1974–78. FRSA. *Publications:* A Suppressed Cry, 1969; Elizabeth Bowen: portrait of a writer, 1977; Edith Sitwell: a unicorn among lions, 1981; Vita: a biography of V. Sackville-West, 1983; Rebecca West: a life, 1987; The Grown-Ups (novel), 1989; Hertfordshire, 1989; Trollope, 1992; reviews and articles in newspapers and magazines in Britain, Ireland and USA. *Recreation:* gardening. *Address:* c/o David Higham Associates, 5–8 Lower John Street, Golden Square, W1R 4HA. *Club:* Academy.

GLENDYNE, 3rd Baron, *cr* 1922; **Robert Nivison,** Bt 1914; Chairman, Glenfriars Holdings Ltd, since 1977; *b* 27 Oct. 1926; *o s* of 2nd Baron and late Ivy May Rose; *S* father, 1967; *m* 1953, Elizabeth, *y d* of late Sir Cecil Armitage, CBE; one *s* two *d*. *Educ:* Harrow. Grenadier Guards, 1944–47. *Heir: s* Hon. John Nivison, *b* 18 Aug. 1960. *Address:* Craigeassie, by Forfar, Angus DD8 3SE.

See also Maj.-Gen. P. R. Leuchars, Maj.-Gen. D. J. St M. Tabor.

GLENISTER, Prof. Tony William, CBE (mil.) 1979; TD; Professor Emeritus, University of London (Professor of Anatomy, at Charing Cross Hospital Medical School, 1970–84, at Charing Cross and Westminster Medical School, 1984–89); Dean, Charing Cross and Westminster Medical School, 1984–89; *b* 19 Dec. 1923; *o s* of late Dudley Stuart Glenister and Maria (*née* Leytens); *m* 1948, Monique Marguerite, *o d* of Emile and Marguerite de Wilde; four *s*. *Educ:* Eastbourne Coll.; St Bartholomew's Hosp. Med. Coll. MRCS, LRCP 1947; MB, BS 1948, PhD 1955, DSc 1963, London. House appts, St Bartholomew's Hosp. and St Andrew's Hosp., Dollis Hill, 1947–48; served in RAMC, 1948–50; Lectr and Reader in Anatomy, Charing Cross Hosp. Med. Sch., 1950–57; Internat. Project Embryological Res., Hubrecht Lab., Utrecht, 1954; Prof. of Embryology, Univ. of London, 1967–70; Dean, Charing Cross Hosp. Med. Sch., 1976–84 (Vice-Dean, 1966–69, 1971–76); Hon. Cons. in Clin. Anatomy and Genetics to Charing Cross Gp of Hosps, 1972–89; Brig. late RAMC, TA, retd (TD, TA 1963 and TAVR 1978). Apothecaries' Soc. Lectr in History of Medicine, 1971–89; Arnott Demonstrator, RCS, 1972, 1986; Pres., Anatomical Soc. GB and Ireland, 1979–81 (Sec., 1974–76). ADMS 44 (Home Counties) Div. TA, 1964–67; CO 217 (London) Gen. Hosp. RAMC(V), 1968–72; QHP 1971–73; Hon. Col 220 (1st Home Counties) Field Amb. RAMC(V), 1973–78; TAVR Advr to DGAMS, 1976–79; Hon. Col 217 (London) Gen. Hosp. RAMC, TAVR, 1981–86. Member: Ealing, Hammersmith and Hounslow AHA(T), 1976–82; Hammersmith and Fulham DHA, 1982–83; North West Thames RHA, 1983–88; GMC, 1979–; GDC, 1983–; sometime examiner: Univs of Cambridge, Liverpool, London, St Andrews, Singapore, NUI, Chinese Univ., Hong Kong; RCS; RCSE; RCPGlas. Trustee, Tablet Trust. Master, Soc. of Apothecaries of London, 1991–92; Freeman, City of London. OStJ 1967. *Publications:* (with J. R. W. Ross) Anatomy and Physiology for Nurses, 1965, 3rd edn 1980; (contrib.) A Companion to Medical Studies, ed Passmore, 1963, 2nd edn 1976; (contrib.) Methods in Mammalian Embryology, ed Daniel, 1971; (contrib.) Textbook of Human Anatomy, ed Hamilton, 1976; papers and articles mainly on prenatal development. *Recreations:* the countryside, sketching, history. *Club:* Army and Navy.

GLENN, Sir Archibald; *see* Glenn, Sir J. R. A.

GLENN, Senator John H(erschel), Jr; US Senator from Ohio (Democrat), since 1975; *b* Cambridge, Ohio, 18 July 1921; *s* of John H. and Clara Glenn; *m* 1943, Anna Castor; one *s* one *d*. *Educ:* Muskingum Coll., New Concord, Ohio. Joined US Marine Corps, 1943; Served War (2 DFC's, 10 Air Medals); Pacific Theater, 1944; home-based, Capt., 1945–46; Far East, 1947–49; Major, 1952; served Korea (5 DFC's, Air Medal with 18 clusters), 1953. First non-stop supersonic flight, Los Angeles-New York (DFC), 1957; Lieut-Col, 1959. In Jan. 1964, declared candidacy for US Senate from Ohio, but withdrew owing to an injury; recovered and promoted Col USMC, Oct. 1964; retired from USMC, Dec. 1964. Became one of 7 volunteer Astronauts, man-in-space program, 1959; made 3–orbit flight in Mercury capsule, Friendship 7, 20 Feb. 1962 (boosted by rocket; time 4 hrs 56 mins; distance 81,000 miles; altitude 160 miles; recovered by destroyer off Puerto Rico in Atlantic). Vice-Pres. (corporate develt), Royal Crown Cola Co., 1966–68; Pres., Royal Crown Internat., 1967–69. Holds hon. doctorates, US and foreign. Awarded DSM (Nat. Aeronautics and Space Admin.), Astronaut Wings (Navy), Astronaut Medal (Marine Corps), etc, 1962; Galabert Internat. Astronautical Prize (jointly with Lieut-Col Yuri Gagarin), 1963; also many other awards and citations from various countries and organizations.

GLENN, Sir (Joseph Robert) Archibald, Kt 1966; OBE 1965; BCE; FIChemE, FIE (Aust.); Chairman: Collins Wales Pty Ltd, 1973–84; I. C. Insurance Australia Ltd, 1973–85; *b* 24 May 1911; *s* of late J. R. Glenn, Sale, Vic., Aust.; *m* 1939, Elizabeth M. M. (*d* 1988), *d* of late J. S. Balderstone; one *s* three *d*. *Educ:* Scotch Coll. (Melbourne); University of Melbourne; Harvard (USA). Joined ICI Australia Ltd, 1935; Design and Construction Engr, 1935–44; Explosives Dept, ICI (UK), 1945–46; Chief Engineer, ICI Australia Ltd, 1947–48; Controller, Nobel Group, 1948–50; ICI Australia Ltd: General Manager, 1950–52; Managing Director, 1953–73; Chm., 1963–73; Director: Westpac Banking Corp. (formerly Bank of NSW), 1967–84; ICI, London, 1970–75; Hill Samuel Australia Ltd, 1973–83; Westralian Sands Ltd, 1977–85; Alcoa of Australia Ltd, 1973–86; Tioxide Australia Ltd, 1973–86; Newmont Pty Ltd, 1977–88; Chairman: Fibremakers Ltd, 1963–73; IMI Australia Ltd, 1970–78. Chancellor, La Trobe Univ., 1967–72 (Hon. DUniv 1981); Chairman: Council of Scotch Coll., 1960–81. Ormond Coll. Council, 1976–81; Member: Manufacturing Industry Advisory Council, 1960–77; Industrial Design Council, 1958–70; Australia/Japan Business Co-operation Cttee, 1965–75; Royal Melbourne Hospital Bd of Management, 1960–70; Melbourne Univ. Appointments Bd; Bd of Management, Melbourne Univ. Engrg Sch. Foundn, 1982–88; Council, Inst. of Pacific Affairs, 1976–; Governor, Atlantic Inst. of Internat. Affairs, 1970–88. J. N. Kirby Medal, 1970. *Recreations:* golf, tennis, collecting rare books. *Address:* 1A Woorigoleen Road, Toorak, Vic 3142, Australia. *T:* 827 6367. *Clubs:* Australian, Melbourne, Frankston Golf, Melbourne Univ. Boat (all in Melbourne); Australian (Sydney).

GLENNIE, Angus James Scott; QC 1991; barrister; *b* 3 Dec. 1950; *yr s* of Robert Nigel Forbes Glennie and Barbara Scott (*née* Nicoll); *m* 1981, Patricia Jean Phelan, *er d* of His Honour Judge Phelan, *qv*; three *s* one *d*. *Educ:* Sherborne Sch.; Trinity Hall, Cambridge (MA Hons). Called to the Bar, Lincoln's Inn, 1974. *Recreations:* sailing, real tennis. *Address:* Thamescote, Chiswick Mall, W4 2PR. *T:* 081–747 8241. *Clubs:* Queen's; Petworth House Tennis Court; Itchenor Sailing.

GLENNIE, Evelyn Elizabeth Ann; percussionist; *b* 19 July 1965; *d* of Isobel and Arthur Glennie. *Educ:* Royal Academy of Music (GRSM Hons, LRAM, ARAM; Queen's Commendation Prize). Shell Gold Medal, 1984; studied with Keiko Abe, Japan; Leonardo da Vinci Prize, 1987; début, Wigmore Hall, 1986; soloist in Zürich, Paris, Schwetzingen, Holland, Dublin, Norway, Australia; festivals of Aldeburgh, Bath, Edinburgh, Chichester, Salisbury; percussion and timpani concertos specially written by British composers; TV and radio; numerous recordings and awards. Hon. DMus Aberdeen, 1991. *Publication:* Good Vibrations (autobiog.), 1990. *Recreations:* reading, walking, sport. *Address:* c/o Harrison Parrott, 12 Penzance Place, W11 4PA. *T:* 071–229 9166.

GLENNY, Dr Robert Joseph Ervine, CEng, FIM; Consultant to UK Government, European Economic Community and industry, since 1983; *b* 14 May 1923; *s* of late Robert and Elizabeth Rachel Glenny; *m* 1947, Joan Phillips Reid; one *s* one *d*. *Educ:* Methodist Coll., Belfast; QUB (BSc Chemistry); London Univ. (BSc Metallurgy, PhD). CEng, 1979; FIM 1958. Res. Metallurgist, English Electric Co. Ltd, Stafford, 1943–47; National Gas Turbine Establishment, 1947–70; Materials Dept, 1947–66; Head of Materials Dept, 1966–70; Supt, Div. of Materials Applications, National Physical Lab., 1970–73; Head of Materials Dept, RAE, 1973–79; Group Head of Aerodynamics, Structures and Materials Depts, RAE, 1979–83. *Publications:* research and review papers on materials science and technology, mainly related to gas turbines, in ARC (R&M series) and in Internat. Metallurgical Rev. *Recreations:* reading, gardening, walking. *Address:* 77 Gally Hill Road, Fleet, Hants GU13 0RU. *T:* Fleet (0252) 615877.

GLENTORAN, 2nd Baron, *cr* 1939, of Ballyalloly; **Daniel Stewart Thomas Bingham Dixon,** 4th Bt, *cr* 1903; PC (Northern Ireland) 1953; KBE 1973; Lord-Lieutenant, City of Belfast, 1976–85 (HM Lieutenant, 1950–76); *b* 19 Jan. 1912; *s* of 1st Baron, PC, OBE and Hon. Emily Ina Florence Bingham (*d* 1957), *d* of 5th Baron Clanmorris; *S* father 1950; *m* 1933, Lady Diana Mary Wellesley, (*d* 1984), *d* of 3rd Earl Cowley; two *s* one *d*. *Educ:* Eton; RMC Sandhurst. Reg. Army, Grenadier Guards; served War of 1939–45 (despatches); retired 1946 (with hon. rank of Lieut-Col); psc. MP (U) Bloomfield Division of Belfast, NI Parliament, Oct. 1950–Feb. 1961; Parliamentary Sec., Ministry of Commerce, NI, 1952–53; Minister of Commerce, 1953–61; Minister in Senate, NI, 1961–72, Speaker of Senate, 1964–72. Hon. Col 6th Battalion Royal Ulster Rifles, 1956–61, retd rank of Hon. Col. *Heir: s* Hon. Thomas Robin Valerian Dixon, MBE [*b* 21 April 1935; *m* 1st, 1959, Rona, *d* of Capt. G. C. Colville, Mill House, Bishop's Waltham, Hants; three *s*; 2nd, 1979, Alwyn Mason; 3rd, 1990, Margaret Rainey]. *Address:* Drumadarragh House, Doagh, Co. Antrim, Northern Ireland. *T:* Ballyclare (09603) 40222. *Club:* Ulster (Belfast).

GLENTWORTH, Viscount; Edmund Christopher Pery; HM Diplomatic Service; Second Secretary, Senegal, since 1990; *b* 10 Feb. 1963; *s* and *heir* of 6th Earl of Limerick, *qv*; *m* 1990, Emily Kate, *o d* of Michael Thomas. *Educ:* Eton; New Coll., Oxford (MA); Pushkin Inst., Moscow; City Univ. (Dip. Law). Called to the Bar, Middle Temple, 1987. FCO, 1987–88; Ecole Nationale d'Administration, Paris, 1988–89; attachment to Ministère des Affaires Etrangères, Paris, 1990. *Recreations:* skiing, travelling. *Address:* c/o Foreign and Commonwealth Office, King Charles Street, SW1A 2AH.

GLESTER, John William; Chief Executive, Central Manchester Development Corporation, since 1988; *b* 8 Sept. 1946; *o s* of George Ernest Glester and late Maude Emily Glester; *m* 1970, Ann Gleave Taylor; two *s*. *Educ:* Plaistow Grammar Sch.; Reading Univ. (BA Hons). Joined Civil Service 1968; served DEA, DoE and Merseyside Task Force; Regl Controller, NW, DoE, 1985–88. Director: Manchester Arts Fest.; Salford Phoenix; Manchester Olympic Bid Cttee. *Recreations:* cricket, football (West Ham United in particular), theatre, cooking. *Address:* Central Manchester Development Corporation, 56 Oxford Street, Manchester M1 6EV. *T:* 061–236 1166. *Club:* St James's (Manchester).

GLICK, Ian Bernard; QC 1987; *b* 18 July 1948; *s* of late Dr Louis Glick and of Phyllis Esty Glick; *m* 1986, Roxane Eban; one *s*. *Educ:* Bradford Grammar School; Balliol College, Oxford (MA, BCL). President, Oxford Union Society, 1968. Called to the Bar, Inner Temple, 1970. Junior Counsel to the Crown, 1985–87; Standing Junior Counsel to DTI in Export Credit Cases, 1985–87. *Address:* 1 Essex Court, Temple, EC4.

GLIDEWELL, Rt. Hon. Sir Iain (Derek Laing), Kt 1980; PC 1985; **Rt. Hon. Lord Justice Glidewell;** a Lord Justice of Appeal, since 1985; *b* 8 June 1924; *s* of late Charles Norman and Nora Glidewell; *m* 1950, Hilary, *d* of late Clinton D. Winant; one *s* two *d*. *Educ:* Bromsgrove Sch.; Worcester Coll., Oxford (Hon. Fellow 1986). Served RAFVR, 1942–46. Called to the Bar, Gray's Inn, 1949, Bencher 1977. QC 1969; a Recorder of the Crown Court, 1976–80; Judge of Appeal, Isle of Man, 1979–80; a Judge of the High Court of Justice, Queen's Bench Division, 1980–85; Presiding Judge, NE Circuit, 1982–85. Chm., Judicial Studies Bd, 1989–; Member: Senate of Inns of Court and the Bar, 1976–79; Supreme Court Rule Cttee, 1980–84. Chm., Panels for Examination of Structure Plans: Worcestershire, 1974; W Midlands, 1975; conducted Heathrow Fourth Terminal Inquiry, 1978. Associate, RICS, 1982. *Recreations:* beagling, walking, theatre. *Address:* Royal Courts of Justice, Strand, WC2A 2LL. *Club:* Garrick.

GLIN, Knight of; *see* Fitz-Gerald, D. J. V.

GLOAK, Graeme Frank, CB 1980; Solicitor for the Customs and Excise, 1978–82; *b* 9 Nov. 1921; *s* of late Frank and of Lilian Gloak; *m* 1944, Mary, *d* of Stanley and Jane Thorne; one *s* one *d* (and one *s* decd). *Educ:* Brentwood School. Royal Navy, 1941–46; Solicitor, 1947; Customs and Excise: Legal Asst, 1947; Sen. Legal Asst, 1953; Asst Solicitor, 1967; Principal Asst Solicitor, 1971. Sec., Civil Service Legal Soc., 1954–62. Member: Dairy Produce Quota Tribunal, 1984–85; Agricl Wages Cttee for Essex and Herts, 1984–90 (Vice-Chm., 1987–90); Chm., Agricl Dwelling House Adv. Cttee, Essex and Herts, 1984–. Member: Barking and Havering FPC, 1986–90; Barking and Havering FHSA, 1990–. *Publication:* (with G. Krikorian and R. K. F. Hutchings) Customs and Excise, in Halsbury's Laws of England, 4th edn, 1973. *Recreations:* badminton, walking, watching cricket. *Address:* Northwold, 123 Priests Lane, Shenfield, Essex CM15 8HJ. *T:* Brentwood (0277) 212748. *Clubs:* MCC; Essex County Cricket (Chelmsford).

GLOCK, Sir William (Frederick), Kt 1970; CBE 1964; Controller of Music, BBC, 1959–72; *b* London, 3 May 1908. *Educ:* Christ's Hospital; Caius Coll., Cambridge. Studied pianoforte under Artur Schnabel. Joined The Observer, 1934; chief music critic, 1939–45. Served in RAF, 1941–46. Dir, Summer Sch. of Music, Bryanston, 1948–52, Dartington Hall, 1953–79; Artistic Dir, Bath Fest., 1975–84. Editor of music magazine The Score, 1949–61; adjudicated at Canadian music festivals, 1951; has lectured on music throughout England and Canada. Music Critic, New Statesman, 1958–59. Editor, Eulenburg books on music, 1973–86. Chm., London Orchestral Concerts Bd, 1975–86; Member: Bd of Dirs, Royal Opera House, 1968–73; Arts Council, 1972–75; South Bank Bd, 1986–. Pres., Bath Fest. Soc., 1991. Hon. Mem., Royal Philharmonic Soc., 1971. Hon. DMus Nottingham Univ., 1968; DUniv York, 1972; Hon. DLitt Bath, 1984. Albert Medal, RSA, 1971. *Publication:* Notes in Advance (autobiog.), 1991. *Address:* Vine House, Brightwell cum Sotwell, Wallingford, Oxon OX10 0RT. *T:* Wallingford (0491) 37144.

GLOSSOP, Peter; Principal Baritone, Royal Opera House, Covent Garden, until 1967, now Guest Artist; *b* 6 July 1928; *s* of Cyril and Violet Elizabeth Glossop; *m* 1st, 1955, Joyce Elizabeth Blackham (marr. diss. 1977); no *c*; 2nd, 1977, Michèle Yvonne Amos; two *d*. *Educ:* High Storrs Grammar Sch., Sheffield. Began singing professionally in chorus of Sadler's Wells Opera, 1952, previously a bank clerk; promoted to principal after one season; Covent Garden Opera, 1962–67. Début in Italy, 1964; La Scala, Milan, début, Rigoletto, 1965. Sang Otello and Rigoletto with Metropolitan Opera Company at Newport USA Festival, Aug. 1967; Rigoletto and Nabucco with Mexican National Opera Company, Sept. 1967. Guest Artist (Falstaff, Rigoletto, Tosca) with American National Opera Company, Oct. 1967. Has sung in opera houses of Bologna, Parma Catania, Vienna, 1967–68, and Berlin and Buenos Aires. Is a recording artist. Hon. DMus, Sheffield, 1970. Winner of 1st Prize and Gold Medal in First International Competition for Young Opera Singers, Sofia, Bulgaria, 1961; Gold Medal for finest performance (in Macbeth) of 1968–69 season, Barcelona. *Films:* Pagliacci, Otello. *Recreations:* New Orleans jazz music, golf. *Address:* c/o S. A. Gorlinsky Ltd, 33 Dover Street, W1X 4NJ; End Cottage, Hawkchurch, Axminster, Devon. *Club:* Green Room.

GLOSTER, Elizabeth, (Mrs S. E. Brodie); QC 1989; *b* 5 June 1949; *d* of Peter Gloster and Betty Gloster (*née* Read); *m* 1973, Stanley Eric Brodie, *qv*; one *s* one *d*. *Educ:* Roedean Sch., Brighton; Girton Coll., Cambridge (BA Hons). Called to the Bar, Inner Temple, 1971. Mem., panel of Counsel who appear for DTI in company matters, 1982–89. *Address:* 1 Essex Court, Temple, EC4Y 9AR. *T:* 071–583 2000.

GLOSTER, Prof. John, MD; Hon. Consulting Ophthalmologist, Moorfields Eye Hospital; Emeritus Professor of Experimental Opthalmology, University of London; *b* 23 March 1922; *m* 1947, Margery (*née* Williams); two *s*. *Educ:* Jesus Coll., Cambridge; St Bartholomew's Hosp. MB, BChir 1946; MRCS, LRCP 1946; DOMS 1950; MD Cantab 1953; PhD London 1959. Registrar, Research Dept, Birmingham and Midland Eye Hosp., 1950–54; Mem. Staff, Ophth. Research Unit, MRC, 1954–63; Prof. of Experimental Ophthalmology, Inst. of Ophth., Univ. of London, 1975–82; Dean of the Inst. of Ophthalmology, 1975–80. Mem. Ophth. Soc. UK; Hon. Mem., Assoc. for Eye Res. *Publications:* Tonometry and Tonography, 1966; (jtly) Physiology of the Eye, System of Ophthalmology IV, ed Duke-Elder, 1968; contribs to jls. *Address:* Oversley, 24C Ickenham Road, Ruislip, Middlesex.

GLOUCESTER, Bishop of; *no new appointment at time of going to press.*

GLOUCESTER, Dean of; *see* Jennings, Very Rev. K. N.

GLOUCESTER, Archdeacon of; *see* Wagstaff, Ven. C. J. H.

GLOVER, Anthony Richard Haysom; Chief Executive Officer, City Council of Norwich, 1980–88; *b* 29 May 1934; 2nd *s* of late Arthur Herbert Glover and late Marjorie Florence Glover; *m* 1960, Ann Penelope Scupham, *d* of late John Scupham, OBE; two *s* one *d*. *Educ:* Culford Sch., Bury St Edmunds; Emmanuel Coll., Cambridge (BA). HM Customs and Excise: Asst Principal, 1957; Principal, 1961; on secondment to HM Treasury, 1965–68; Asst Sec., 1969; Asst Sec., HM Treasury, 1972–76; Dep. Controller, HM Stationery Office, 1976–80. MBIM 1978. Mem. Council, UEA Norwich, 1984–88. FRSA 1985. *Recreations:* music, reading, writing, alpine gardening. *Address:* 7 Hillside Road, Thorpe St Andrew, Norwich. *T:* Norwich (0603) 33508. *Club:* Norfolk (Norwich).

GLOVER, Eric; Secretary-General, Chartered Institute of Bankers (formerly Institute of Bankers), since 1982; *b* 28 June 1935; *s* of William and Margaret Glover; *m* 1960, Adele Diane Hilliard; three *s*. *Educ:* Liverpool Institute High Sch.; Oriel Coll., Oxford (MA). Shell International Petroleum (Borneo and Uganda), 1957–63; Institute of Bankers, later Chartered Institute of Bankers, 1963–; Asst Sec., 1964–69; Dir of Studies, 1969–82. Member: Council for Accreditation of Correspondence Colls, 1983–; British Accreditation Council for Indep. Further and Higher Educn, 1985–. *Publications:* articles on banking education. *Recreations:* mainly sport-golf, squash, tennis. *Address:* 12 Manor Park, Tunbridge Wells, Kent TN4 8XP. *T:* Tunbridge Wells (0892) 31221; (business) 071–623 3531. *Club:* Overseas Bankers'.

GLOVER, Gen. Sir James (Malcolm), KCB 1981; MBE 1964; Chairman, IT Security International Ltd, since 1989; Director, British Petroleum plc, since 1987; *b* 25 March 1929; *s* of Maj.-Gen. Malcolm Glover, CB, OBE and Jean Catherine Ogilvy (*née* Will); *m* 1958, Janet Diones De Pree; one *s* one *d*. *Educ:* Wellington College; RMA, Sandhurst. Commissioned, 1949; RHA, 1950–54; Instructor RMA Sandhurst, 1955–56; transferred to Rifle Brigade, 1956; Brigade Major, 48 Gurkha Inf. Bde, 1960–62; Directing Staff, Staff Coll., 1966–68; CO, 3rd Bn Royal Green Jackets, 1970–71; Col General Staff, Min. of Defence, 1972–73; Comdr 19 Airportable Bde, 1974–75; Brigadier General Staff (Intelligence), Min. of Defence, 1977–78; Commander Land Forces N Ireland, 1979–80; Dep. Chief of Defence Staff (Intelligence), 1981–83; Vice Chief of General Staff, and Mem., Army Bd, 1983–85; C-in-C, UKLF, 1985–87. Has served in W Germany, Malaya, Singapore, Hong Kong, Cyprus and N Ireland. Col Comdt, RGJ, 1984–88. *Recreations:* travel, gardening, shooting, mountain walking. *Address:* c/o Lloyds Bank, Cox's & King's Branch, 7 Pall Mall, SW1Y 5NA. *Club:* Boodle's.

GLOVER, Jane Alison, DPhil; conductor; Musical Director, London Choral Society, since 1983; Principal Conductor, Huddersfield Choral Society, since 1989; a Governor, BBC, since 1990; Senior Research Fellow, St Hugh's College, Oxford, since 1982; *b* 13 May 1949; *d* of Robert Finlay Glover, *qv*. *Educ:* Monmouth School for Girls; St Hugh's Coll., Oxford (BA, MA, DPhil). Junior Research Fellow, St Hugh's Coll., 1973–75; Lecturer in Music: St Hugh's Coll., 1976–84; St Anne's Coll., 1976–80; Pembroke Coll., 1979–84; elected to OU Faculty of Music, 1979. Professional conducting début at Wexford Festival, 1975; thereafter, operas and concerts for: BBC; Glyndebourne (Musical Dir, Touring Opera, 1982–85); Royal Op. House, Covent Garden (début, 1988); ENO (début, 1989); Teatro la Fenice, Venice; London Symphony Orch.; London Philharmonic Orch.; Philharmonia Orch.; Royal Philharmonic Orch.; English Chamber Orch.; BBC Welsh Symphony Orch.; Scottish Nat. Orch.; Bournemouth Symphony Orch.; Bournemouth Sinfonietta; and many others in Italy, Holland, Denmark, Canada, Hong Kong, Austria, Yugoslavia, Germany, France, etc.; Artistic Dir, London Mozart Players, 1984–91. Member: BBC Central Music Adv. Cttee, 1981–85; Music Adv. Panel, Arts Council, 1986–87. Television documentaries and series, and presentation for BBC and LWT, esp. Orchestra, 1983, Mozart, 1985. Governor, RAM, 1985–90. Hon. DMus Exeter, 1986; Hon. DLitt Loughborough, 1988; DUniv Open, 1988; Hon. DMus CNAA, 1991. ABSA/Daily Telegraph Arts Award, 1990. *Publications:* Cavalli, 1978; contribs to: The New Monteverdi Companion, 1986; Monteverdi 'Orfeo' handbook, 1986; articles in Music and Letters, Proc. of Royal Musical Assoc., Musical Times, The Listener, TLS, Early Music, Opera, and others. *Recreations:* The Times crossword puzzle, theatre. *Address:* c/o Lies Askonas Ltd, 186 Drury Lane, WC2B 5RY. *T:* 071–405 1808.

GLOVER, John Neville, CMG 1963; *b* 12 July 1913; *s* of John Robert Glover and Sybil Glover (*née* Cureton); *m* 1st, 1940, Margot Burdick; one *s*; 2nd, 1956, June Patricia Bruce Gaskell. *Educ:* Tonbridge Sch. Commissioned 6th Bn Devonshire Regt (TA), 1933; RAF (Gen. Duties Branch), 1934. Served RAF, 1934–46; RAFRO, 1946–59 (retained rank of Group Capt.). Called to Bar, Gray's Inn, 1949. Appointed to Colonial Legal Service, 1951; served: Ghana (Crown Counsel and Senior Crown Counsel), 1951–57; Western Pacific High Commission (Legal Adviser and Attorney-General, British Solomon Islands Protectorate), 1957–63. QC (Western Pacific), 1962. Retired from HM Overseas Civil Service, 1963. Comr to examine Human Rights Laws in the Bahamas, 1964–65. Legal Draftsman in the Bahamas, 1965–66. Law Revision Comr for certain overseas territories, 1967–91. *Recreation:* fishing. *Address:* Clam End, Trebullett, near Launceston, Cornwall PL15 9QQ. *T:* Coad's Green (0566) 82347. *Club:* Royal Air Force.

GLOVER, Prof. Keith; Professor of Engineering, since 1989, and Fellow of Sidney Sussex College, since 1976, University of Cambridge; *b* 23 April 1946; *s* of William Frank Glover and Helen Ruby Glover (*née* Higgs); *m* 1970, Jean Elizabeth Priestley; one *s* one *d*. *Educ:* Dartford Grammar Sch., Kent; Imperial College London (BScEng); MIT (PhD). Development engineer, Marconi Co., 1967–69; Kennedy Meml Fellow, MIT, 1969–71; Asst Prof. of Electrical Engineering, Univ. of S California, 1973–76; Department of Engineering, University of Cambridge: Lectr, 1976–87; Reader in Control Engineering, 1987–89. *Publications:* Robust Controller Design using Normalized Coprime Factor Plant Descriptions (with D. C. McFarlane), 1989; contribs to control and systems jls. *Address:* 41 Gough Way, Cambridge CB3 9LN. *T:* Cambridge (0223) 312197.

GLOVER, Kenneth Frank; Assistant Under-Secretary of State (Statistics), Ministry of Defence, 1974–81, retired; *b* 16 Dec. 1920; *s* of Frank Glover and Mabel Glover; *m* 1951, Iris Clare Holmes. *Educ:* Bideford Grammar Sch.; UC of South West, Exeter; LSE (MScEcon). Joined Statistics Div., MoT, 1946; Statistician, 1950; Statistical adviser to Cttee of Inquiry on Major Ports (Rochdale Cttee), 1961–62; Dir of Econs and Statistics at Nat. Ports Council, 1964–68; Chief Statistician, MoT and DoE, 1968–74. *Publications:* various papers; articles in JRSS, Dock and Harbour Authority. *Recreations:* boating, idleness. *Address:* Riverdown, 11 Platway Lane, Shaldon, Teignmouth, South Devon TQ14 0AR. *T:* Shaldon (0626) 872700.

GLOVER, Myles Howard; Secretary, Conference for Independent Further Education, since 1991; *b* 18 Dec. 1928; *yr s* of Cedric Howard Glover and Winifred Mary (*née* Crewdson); *m* 1969, Wendy Gillian, *er d* of C. M. Coleman; one *s* two *d*. *Educ:* Rugby; Balliol Coll., Oxford (MA). Called to the Bar, Lincoln's Inn, 1954. Clerk, Skinners' Co., 1959–90. Chm., Cttee of Clerks to Twelve Chief Livery Cos of City of London, 1975–81. Hon. Sec., GBA, 1967–91. Member: City & Guilds Art Sch. Cttee, 1960–71; Adv. Cttee, Gresham Coll., 1985–86; Governing Council, St Paul's Cathedral Choir Sch., 1986–; Governing Body, St Leonards-Mayfield Sch., 1988–. Hon. Member: Old Tonbridgian Soc., 1986; Old Skinners' Soc., 1990 (Leopard of the Year Trophy, 1990); Hon. Freeman, Fellmongers' Co., Richmond, N Yorks, 1991. *Recreation:* music. *Address:* Buckhall Farm, Bull Lane, Bethersden, near Ashford, Kent TN26 3HB. *T:* Bethersden (023382) 634. *Club:* Savile.

GLOVER, Maj.-Gen. Peter James, CB 1966; OBE 1948; *b* 16 Jan. 1913; *s* of late G. H. Glover, CBE, Sheephatch House, Tilford, Surrey, and late Mrs G. H. Glover; *m* 1946, Wendy Archer; one *s* two *d*. *Educ:* Uppingham; Cambridge (MA). 2nd Lieut RA, 1934; served War of 1939–45, BEF France and Far East; Lieut-Col 1956; Brig. 1961; Comdt, Sch. of Artillery, Larkhill, 1960–62; Maj.-Gen. 1962; GOC 49 Infantry Division TA and North Midland District, 1962–63; Head of British Defence Supplies Liaison Staff, Delhi, 1963–66; Director, Royal Artillery, 1966–69, retd. Col Comdt, RA, 1970–78. *Address:* Lukesland, Diptford, Totnes, Devon TQ9 7NW.

GLOVER, Robert Finlay, TD 1954; Headmaster, Monmouth School, 1959–76; *b* 28 June 1917; *yr s* of T. R. Glover, Public Orator in University of Cambridge, and Alice, *d* of H. G. Few; *m* 1941, Jean, *d* of late N. G. Muir, Lincoln; one *s* two *d*. *Educ:* The Leys Sch.; Corpus Christi Coll., Oxford. Served in Royal Artillery (TA), 1939–46; Staff Coll., Camberley, 1944; Major, 1944. Asst Master, Ampleforth Coll., 1946–50; Head of Classics Dept, King's Sch., Canterbury, 1950–53; Headmaster, Adams' Grammar Sch., Newport, Salop, 1953–59; Dep. Sec., Headmasters' Conference and Assoc., 1977–82. Fellow, Woodard Corp., 1982–87. *Publications:* Notes on Latin, 1954; (with R. W. Harris) Latin for Historians, 1954. *Recreations:* normal. *Address:* Brockhill Lodge, West Malvern Road, The Wyche, Malvern, Worcs WR14 4EJ. *T:* Malvern (0684) 564247. *Club:* East India, Devonshire, Sports and Public Schools.
See also J. A. Glover.

GLOVER, Stephen Charles Morton; journalist; *b* 13 Jan. 1952; *s* of Rev. Prebendary John Morton Glover and Helen Ruth Glover (*née* Jones); *m* 1982, Celia Elizabeth (*née* Montague); two *s*. *Educ:* Shrewsbury Sch.; Mansfield Coll., Oxford (MA). Daily Telegraph, 1978–85: leader writer and feature writer, 1978–85; parly sketch writer, 1979–81; Independent: Foreign Editor, 1986–89; Editor, The Independent on Sunday, 1990–91. Dir, Newspaper Publishing, 1986–. *Address:* c/o Aitken & Stone, 29 Fernshaw Road, SW10 0TG. *Club:* Beefsteak.

GLOVER, Trevor David; UK Managing Director, The Penguin Group, since 1987; Chairman, Penguin Books, Australia, Ltd, since 1987; *b* 19 April 1940; *s* of Frederick Percy and Eileen Frances Glover; *m* 1967, Carol Mary Roberts; one *s* one *d*. *Educ:* Tiffin Sch., Kingston-upon-Thames; Univ. of Hull (BA Hons English Lang. and Lit.). Newspaper reporter, BC, Canada, 1963; began publishing career as college rep. with McGraw-Hill, Sydney, 1964; Coll. Sales Manager, 1966, later Gen. Manager, Professional and Reference Book Div., McGraw-Hill, UK; joined Penguin UK, 1970; UK Sales Manager, later UK Sales and Marketing Dir; Viking Penguin, NY, 1975–76; Man. Dir, Penguin Australia, 1976–87. Pres., Australian Book Publishers Assoc., 1983–85 and 1986–87. *Recreation:* choral singing. *Clubs:* Groucho, Scribes West.

GLOVER, Hon. Sir Victor (Joseph Patrick), Kt 1989; **Hon. Mr Justice Glover;** Chief Justice, Mauritius, since 1988; *b* 5 Nov. 1932; *s* of Joseph George Harold Glover and Mary Catherine (*née* Reddy); *m* 1960, Marie Cecile Ginette Gauthier; two *s*. *Educ:* Collège du St Esprit; Royal Coll., Mauritius; Jesus Coll., Oxford (BA (Hons) Jurisprudence). Called to the Bar, Middle Temple, 1957. District Magistrate, 1962; Crown Counsel, 1964; Sen. Crown Counsel, 1966; Prin. Crown Counsel, 1970; Parly Counsel, 1972; Puisne Judge, 1976; Sen. Puisne Judge, 1982. Actg Govenor General, July 1988, May 1989, June 1990 and Feb. 1991. Hon. Prof. of Civil Law, Univ. of Mauritius, 1986. *Publications:* Abstract of Decisions of Supreme Court of Mauritius 1966–1981, 1982, Supplement 1982–1986, 1987. *Recreations:* reading, swimming, bridge. *Address:* Supreme Court, Port Louis, Mauritius. *T:* 21905/20578/20275. *Clubs:* Oxford Union Society; Oxford University Boat.

GLOVER, William James, QC 1969; a Recorder of the Crown Court, 1975–91; *b* 8 May 1924; *s* of late H. P. Glover, KC and Martha Glover; *m* 1956, Rosemary D. Long; two *s*. *Educ:* Harrow; Pembroke Coll., Cambridge. Served with Royal West African Frontier Force in West Africa and Burma, 1944–47. Called to Bar, Inner Temple, 1950, Bencher, 1977. Second Junior Counsel to Inland Revenue (Rating Valuation), 1963–69. *Recreation:* golf. *Address:* 1 Mitre Court Buildings, Temple, EC4Y 7BS; Lomea Barn, Stone-cum-Ebony, Kent TN30 7HY.

GLUE, George Thomas; Director-General of Supplies and Transport (Naval), Ministry of Defence, 1973–77; *b* 3 May 1917; *s* of Percy Albert Glue and Alice Harriet Glue (*née* Stoner); *m* 1947, Eileen Marion Hitchcock; one *d*. *Educ:* Portsmouth Southern Secondary School. Admiralty: Asst Naval Store Officer, 1937; Dep. Naval Store Officer, Mediterranean, 1940; Naval Store Officer, Mediterranean, 1943; Asst Dir of Stores, 1955; Suptg Naval Store Officer, Devonport, 1960; Dep. Dir of Stores, 1963; Dir of Stores, 1970; Dir, Supplies and Transport (Naval), 1971. *Recreations:* gardening, bridge. *Address:* 18 Late Broads, Winsley, near Bradford-on-Avon, Wilts BA15 2NW. *T:* Bath (0225) 722717.

GLYN, family name of **Baron Wolverton.**

GLYN, Sir Alan, Kt 1990; ERD; MP (C) Windsor and Maidenhead, since 1974 (Windsor, 1970–74); *b* 26 Sept. 1918; *s* of John Paul Glyn, late Royal Horse Guards (Blues), Barrister-at-Law, Middle Temple, and late Margaret Johnston, Edinburgh; *m* 1962, Lady Rosula Caroline Windsor Clive, OStJ, *y d* of 2nd Earl of Plymouth, PC, GCStJ (*d* 1943), St Fagan's, Cardiff, S Wales; two *d*. *Educ:* Westminster; Caius Coll., Cambridge; St Bartholomew's and St George's Hosps. BA (Hons) Cantab 1939. Qualified medical practitioner, 1948. Served War of 1939–45; Far East, 1942–46; psc 1945; Bde Major, 1946; re-employed Captain (Hon. Major) Royal Horse Guards (ER) until 1967; att. French Foreign Legion, 1960. Called to Bar, Middle Temple, 1955. Co-opted Mem. LCC Education Cttee, 1956–58. MP (C) Clapham Div. of Wandsworth, 1959–64. Member: Chelsea Borough Council, 1959–62; No 1 Divisional Health Cttee (London), 1959–61; Inner London Local Med. Cttee, 1967–; Governing Body, Brit. Postgrad. Med. Fedn, 1967–82; Greater London Cent. Valuation Panel, 1967–; Bd of Governors, Nat. Heart and Chest Hosps Special Health Auth., 1982–90. Former Governor, Henry Thornton and Aristotle Schs; Manager, Macaulay C of E Sch., Richard Atkins, Henry Cavendish, Telfescot, Glenbrook and Boneville Primary Schs in Clapham. One of Earl Marshal's Green Staff Officers at Investiture of HRH Prince of Wales, Caernarvon, 1969. Freeman, Worshipful Soc. of the Art and Mystery of Apothecaries of the City of London, 1961. Supported freedom fighters in Hungary during Hungarian Revolution, 1956; Pro-Hungaria Medal of SMO Malta, 1959. *Publication:* Witness to Viet Nam (the containment of communism in South East Asia), 1968. *Address:* 17 Cadogan Place, Belgrave Square, SW1. *T:* 071–235 2957. *Clubs:* Carlton, Pratt's, Special Services.

GLYN, Sir Anthony (Geoffrey Leo Simon), 2nd Bt, *cr* 1927; author; *b* 13 March 1922; *s* of Sir Edward Davson, 1st Bt, and Margot, OBE (*d* 1966), *er d* of late Clayton Glyn and late Mrs Elinor Glyn; *S* father, Sir Edward Rae Davson, KCMG, 1937; assumed by deed poll, 1957, the surname of Glyn in lieu of his patronymic, and the additional forename of Anthony; *m* 1946, Susan Eleanor, barrister-at-law, 1950, *er d* of Sir Rhys Rhys-Williams, 1st Bt, DSO, QC, and Dame Juliet Rhys-Williams, DBE; one *d* (and one *d* decd). *Educ:* Eton. Jnd Welsh Guards, 1941; served Guards Armoured Div., 1942–45; Staff Captain, 1945. Vermeil Medal, City of Paris, 1985. *Publications:* Romanza, 1953; The Jungle of Eden, 1954; Elinor Glyn, a biography, 1955 (Book Society Non-Fiction Choice); The Ram in the Thicket, 1957 (Dollar Book Club Choice); I Can Take it All, 1959 (Book Society Choice); Kick Turn, 1963; The Terminal, 1965; The Seine, 1966; The Dragon Variation, 1969; The Blood of a Britishman, 1970 (US edn, The British; trans. French, Spanish, Japanese); The Companion Guide to Paris, 1985 (trans. Dutch). *Recreations:* skiing, chess. *Heir:* *b* Christopher Michael Edward Davson, ACA, late Capt. Welsh Guards [*b* 26 May 1927; *m* 1962, Evelyn Mary (marr. diss. 1971), *o d* of late James Wardrop; one *s*; 2nd, 1975, Kate, *d* of Ludovic Foster, Greatham Manor, Pulborough]. *Address:* Marina Baie des Anges, Ducal Apt. U-03, 06270 Villeneuve Loubet, Alpes Maritimes, France. *T:* 93.73.67.52; Friedegg, Westendorf, Tyrol, Austria. *T:* 5334 2263. *Club:* Pratt's.

GLYN, Hilary B.; *b* 12 Jan. 1916; *s* of Maurice Glyn and Hon. Maud Grosvenor; *m* 1938, Caroline Bull; one *s* two *d*. *Educ:* Eton; New Coll., Oxford. DipEconPolSc. Joined Gallaher Ltd, 1937. Served, RASC Supp. Reserve, 1939–46 (A/Major). Director, Gallaher Ltd, 1962; Asst. Man. Dir, 1975; retd, 1976. *Recreations:* shooting, horse trials. *Address:* Castle Hill Cottage, Boothby Graffoe, Lincoln LN5 0LF. *T:* Lincoln (0522) 810885.

GLYN, Sir Richard (Lindsay), 10th Bt *cr* 1759, and 6th Bt *cr* 1800; *b* 3 Aug. 1943; *s* of Sir Richard Hamilton Glyn, 9th and 5th Bt, OBE, TD, and Lyndsay Mary (*d* 1971), *d* of T. H. Baker; *S* father, 1980; *m* 1970, Carolyn Ann Williams (marr. diss. 1979); one *s* one *d*. *Educ:* Eton. Co-Founder, High Lea Sch., 1982; Founder, Gaunts House Centre, 1989. *Recreation:* tennis. *Heir:* *s* Richard Rufus Francis Glyn, *b* 8 Jan. 1971. *Address:* Ashton Farmhouse, Wimborne, Dorset. *T:* Witchampton (0258) 840585.

GLYNN, Prof. Alan Anthony, MD; FRCP, FRCPath; Director, Central Public Health Laboratory, Colindale, London, 1980–88, retired; Visiting Professor of Bacteriology, London School of Hygiene and Tropical Medicine, 1983–88; *b* 29 May 1923; *s* of late Hyman and Charlotte Glynn; *m* 1962, Nicole Benhamou; two *d*. *Educ:* City of London Sch.; University Coll. London (Fellow, 1982) and UCH Med. Sch., London (MB, BS 1946, MD 1959). MRCP 1954, FRCP 1974; MRCPath 1963, FRCPath 1973. House Physician, UCH, 1946; Asst Lectr in Physiol., Sheffield Univ., 1947–49; National Service, RAMC, 1950–51; Registrar, Canadian Red Cross Meml Hosp., Taplow, 1955–57; St Mary's Hospital Medical School: Lectr in Bacteriology, 1958–61; Sen. Lectr, 1961–67; Reader, 1967–71; Prof., 1971–80; Hon. Consultant Bacteriologist, 1961–83; Visiting Prof. of Bacteriology, St. Mary's Hosp., 1980–83. Examr in Pathol., Univs of Edinburgh, 1974–76, 1983–85, Glasgow, 1975–78, and London, 1979–80. Member: DHSS Jt Cttee on Vaccination and Immunization, 1979–85; Adv. Gp, ARC Inst. for Res. in Animal Diseases. Almroth Wright Lectr, Wright-Fleming Inst., 1972; Erasmus Wilson Demonstrator, RCS, 1973. Mem. Editorial Board: Immunology, 1969–79; Parasite Immunity, 1979–87. *Publications:* papers on bacterial infection and immunity in jls. *Recreations:* theatre, walking, carpentry. *Club:* Athenæum.

See also Prof. I. M. Glynn.

GLYNN, Prof. Ian Michael, MD, PhD, FRS 1970; FRCP; Professor of Physiology, University of Cambridge, since 1986; Fellow, Trinity College, since 1955 (Vice-Master, 1980–86); *b* 3 June 1928; 2nd *s* of late Hyman and Charlotte Glynn; *m* 1958, Jenifer Muriel, 2nd *d* of Ellis and Muriel Franklin; one *s* two *d*. *Educ:* City of London Sch.; Trinity Coll., Cambridge; University Coll. Hosp. 1st cl. in Pts I and II of Nat. Sci. Tripos; BA (Cantab) 1949; MB, BChir, 1952; MD 1970; FRCP 1987. House Phys., Central Mddx Hosp., 1952–53; MRC Scholar at Physiol. Lab., Cambridge; PhD 1956. Nat. Service in RAF Med. Br., 1956–57. Cambridge University: Res. Fellow, 1955–59, Staff Fellow and Dir of Med. Studies, 1961–73, Trinity Coll.; Univ. Demonstrator in Physiology, 1958–63; Lecturer, 1963–70; Reader, 1970–75; Prof. Membrane Physiology, 1975–86. Vis. Prof., Yale Univ., 1969. Member: MRC, 1976–80 (Chm., Physiological Systems and Disorders Bd, 1976–78); Council, Royal Soc., 1979–81; AFRC (formerly ARC), 1981–86. Hon. Foreign Mem., Amer. Acad. of Arts and Scis, 1984. Hon. MD Aarhus, 1988. Chm., Editorial Bd, Jl of Physiology, 1968–70. *Publications:* (with J. C. Ellory) The Sodium Pump, 1985; scientific papers dealing with transport of ions across living membranes, mostly in Jl of Physiology. *Address:* Physiological Laboratory, Cambridge. *T:* Cambridge (0223) 333869.

See also Prof. A. A. Glynn.

GOAD, Sir (Edward) Colin (Viner), KCMG 1974; Director, Liberian Services Inc., since 1980; Consultant, Liberian Shipowners' Council, since 1978; *b* 21 Dec. 1914; *s* of Maurice George Viner Goad and Caroline (*née* Masters); *m* 1939, Joan Olive Bradley (*d* 1980); one *s*. *Educ:* Cirencester Grammar Sch.; Gonville and Caius Coll., Cambridge (Scholar, BA). Ministry of Transport: Asst Principal, 1937; Principal, 1942; Asst Sec., 1948; Imperial Defence Coll., 1953; Under-Sec., 1963; Dep. Sec.-Gen., 1963–68, Sec.-Gen., 1968–73, Inter-Govtl Maritime Consultative Orgn. *Address:* The Paddock, Ampney Crucis, Glos. *T:* Cirencester (0285) 851353.

GOBBO, Hon. Sir James (Augustine), Kt 1982; **Hon. Mr Justice Gobbo;** Judge of the Supreme Court of Victoria, Australia, since 1978; *b* 22 March 1931; *s* of Antonio Gobbo and Regina Gobbo (*née* Tosetto); *m* 1957, Shirley Lewis; two *s* three *d*. *Educ:* Xavier Coll., Kew, Victoria; Melbourne Univ. (BA Hons); Magdalen Coll., Oxford Univ. (MA). Called to Bar, Gray's Inn, London, 1956; Barrister and Solicitor, Victoria, Aust., 1956; signed Roll of Counsel, Victorian Bar, 1957; QC 1971. Indep. Lectr in Evidence, Univ. of Melbourne, 1963–68. Comr, Victorian Law Reform Commn, 1985–88. Chairman: Aust. Refugee Council, 1977; Aust. Multicultural Affairs Council, 1987–; Mercy Private Hosp., Melbourne, 1977–87 (Mem. Bd, Mercy Maternity Hosp., 1972–); Caritas Christi Hospice, 1986–; Order of Malta Hospice Home Care, 1986–; Italian Historical Soc. of Vic, 1980–; Member: Council, Order of Australia, 1982–; Exec., Council of Judges, 1986–; Nat. Population Council, 1983–87; Victorian Health Promotion Foundn, 1989–; Newman Coll. Council, 1970–85; Pres., CO-AS-IT, 1979–84, 1986–. Trustee: Victorian Opera Foundn, 1983–; WWF, Australia, 1991–. Vice-Pres., Aust. Assoc. of SMO Malta, 1984–87, Pres., 1987–; Pres., Scout Assoc. of Victoria, 1987–. Commendatore all'Ordine di Merito, Republic of Italy, 1973; Kt Grand Cross SMO Malta, 1982. *Publications:* (ed) Cross on Evidence (Australian edn), 1970–1978; various papers. *Address:* 6 Florence Avenue, Kew, Victoria 3101, Australia. *T:* (03) 817–1669.

GOBLE, John Frederick; Solicitor; Consultant, Herbert Smith, since 1988 (Partner, 1953–88, Senior Partner, 1983–88; Hong Kong office, 1982–83); *b* 1 April 1925; *o s* of late John and Evileen Goble; *m* 1953, Moira Murphy O'Connor; one *s* three *d*. *Educ:* Finchley Catholic GS; Highgate Sch.; Brasenose Coll., Oxford. Sub-Lieut, RNVR, 1944–46. Admitted solicitor, 1951. Crown Agents, 1974–82 (Dep. Chm., 1975–82); Director: British Telecommunications, 1983–; Wren Underwriting Agencies, 1988–. A Dep. Chm., City Panel on Takeovers and Mergers, 1989–. Governor, Highgate Sch., 1976–. Chm., The Friends of Highgate Sch. Soc., 1978–87; Pres., Old Cholmeleian Soc., 1983–84. *Recreations:* music, golf, wine. *Address:* (office) Exchange House, Primrose Street, EC2A 2HS. *T:* 071-374 8000. *Clubs:* Garrick, MCC, Hurlingham; New Zealand Golf (West Byfleet); Hon. Company of Edinburgh Golfers.

GODBER, Geoffrey Chapham, CBE 1961; DL; Chief Executive, West Sussex County Council, 1974–75, retired (Clerk of the Peace and Clerk to the Council, 1966–74); Clerk to the Lieutenancy of West Sussex, 1974–76 (Sussex, 1968–74); *b* 22 Sept. 1912; *s* of late Isaac Godber, Willington Manor, near Bedford; *m* 1937, Norah Enid (*née* Finney); three *s*. *Educ:* Bedford Sch. LLB (London) 1935; Solicitor, 1936. Deputy Clerk of the Peace, Northants, 1938–44; Clerk of the Peace, Clerk of the County Council and Clerk of the Lieutenancy, Salop, 1944–66; Hon. Sec., Soc. of Clerks of the Peace of Counties, 1953–61 (Chm., 1961–64); Chm., Assoc. of County Chief Executives, 1974–75. Member: Probation Adv. and Trg Bd, 1949–55; Child Care Adv. Council, 1953–56; Cttee of Inquiry into Inland Waterways, 1956–58; Redevelopment Adv. Cttee, Inland Waterways, 1959–62; Waterways Sub-Commn, Brit. Transport, 1959–62; Central Adv. Water Cttee, 1961–70; Minister of Health's Long Term Study Group, 1965–69; W Midlands Economic Planning Council, 1965–66; S-E Economic Planning Council, 1969–75; CS Adv. Council, 1971–78; British Waterways Bd, 1975–81; Chichester Harbour Conservancy, 1975–78; Shoreham Port Authority, 1976–82 (Dep. Chm., 1978–82); Chm., 1975–82, Pres., 1988–90, Open Air Museum, Weald and Downland. DL W Sussex 1975. *Recreation:* sailing. *Address:* Pricklows, Singleton, Chichester, West Sussex PO18 0HA. *T:* Singleton (024363) 238. *Club:* Naval and Military.

See also Sir G. E. Godber.

GODBER, Sir George (Edward), GCB 1971 (KCB 1962; CB 1958); Chief Medical Officer, Department of Health and Social Security, Department of Education and Science, and Home Office, 1960–73; *b* 4 Aug. 1908; *s* of late I. Godber, Willington Manor, Bedford; *m* 1935, Norma Hathorne Rainey; two *s* one *d* (and two *s* two *d* decd). *Educ:* Bedford Sch.; New Coll., Oxford (Hon. Fellow, 1973); London Hospital; London Sch. of Hygiene. BA 1930, BM 1933, DM 1939, Oxon; MRCP 1935, FRCP 1947; DPH London 1936. Medical Officer, Min. of Health, 1939; Dep. Chief Medical Officer, Min. of Health, 1950–60. Chm., Health Educn Council, 1977–78 (Mem., 1976–78). QHP, 1953–56. Scholar in Residence, NIH Bethesda, 1975. Vice-Pres., RCN, 1973. Fellow: American Hospital Assoc., and American Public Health Assoc., 1961; British Orthopaedic

Assoc.; Mem. Dietetic Assoc., 1961; Hon. Member: Faculty of Radiologists, 1958; British Pædiatric Assoc.; Royal Pharmaceut. Soc., 1973. FRCOG *ad eundem,* 1966; FRCPsych 1973; FFCM 1974; Hon. FRCS, 1973; Hon. FRCGP, 1973; Hon. FRSM, 1973. Hon. LLD: Manchester, 1964; Hull, 1970; Nottingham, 1973; Hon. DCL: Newcastle 1972; Oxford 1973; Hon. DSc Bath, 1979. Hon. Fellow, London Sch. of Hygiene and Tropical Medicine, 1976. Bisset Hawkins Medal, RCP, 1965; 150th Anniversary Medal, Swedish Med. Soc., 1966; Leon Bernard Foundn Medal, 1972; Ciba Foundn Gold Medal, 1970; Therapeutics Gold Medal, Soc. of Apothecaries, 1973. Lectures: Thomas and Edith Dixon Belfast, 1962; Bartholomew, Rotunda, Dublin, 1963; Woolmer, Bio-Engineering Soc., 1964; Monkton Copeman, Soc. of Apothecaries, 1968; Michael M. Davis, Chicago, 1969; Harold Diehl, Amer. Public Health Assoc., 1969; Rhys Williams, 1969; W. M. Fletcher Shaw, RCOG, 1970; Henry Floyd, Inst. of Orthopaedics, 1970; First Elizabeth Casson Meml, Assoc. of Occ. Therapists, 1973; Cavendish, W London Med.-Chir. Soc., 1973; Heath Clark, London Univ., 1973; Rock Carling, Nuffield Provincial Hosps Trust, 1975; Thom Bequest, RCSE, 1975; Maurice Bloch, Glasgow, 1975; Ira Hiscock, Yale, 1975; John Sullivan, St Louis, 1975; Fordham, Sheffield, 1976; Lloyd Hughes, Liverpool, 1977; Gale Meml, SW England Faculty RCGP, 1978; Gordon, Birmingham, 1979; Samson Gamgee, Birm. Med. Inst., 1979; W. H. Duncan, Liverpool, 1984; W. Pickles, RCGP, 1985; Green Coll., Oxford, 1988. *Publications:* (with Sir L. Parsons and Clayton Fryers) Survey of Hospitals in the Sheffield Region, 1944; The Health Service: past, present and future (Heath Clark Lectures), 1974; Change in Medicine (Rock Carling monograph), 1975; British National Health Service: Conversations, 1977; papers in Lancet, BMJ, Public Health. *Recreation:* golf. *Address:* 21 Almoners' Avenue, Cambridge CB1 4NZ. *T:* Cambridge (0223) 247491.

See also G. C. Godber.

GODDARD, Ann Felicity, QC 1982; a Recorder of the Crown Court, since 1979; *b* 22 Jan. 1936; *o c* of late Graham Elliott Goddard and Margaret Louise Hambrook Goddard (*née* Clark). *Educ:* Grey Coat Hosp., Westminster; Birmingham Univ. (LLB); Newnham Coll., Cambridge (LLM and Dip. in Comparative Legal Studies). Called to the Bar, Gray's Inn, 1960; Bencher, 1991. Mem., Gen. Council of the Bar, 1988–. *Recreation:* travel. *Address:* 3 Temple Gardens, Temple, EC4Y 9AU. *T:* 071–353 3102.

GODDARD, David Rodney, MBE 1985; Director, International Sailing Craft Association, since 1966; *b* 16 March 1927; *s* of Air Marshal Sir Victor Goddard, KCB, CBE, and Mildred Catherine Jane, *d* of Alfred Markham Inglis; *m* 1952, Susan Ashton; two *s* one *d. Educ:* Bryanston School; Wanganui Collegiate Sch., New Zealand; Peterhouse, Cambridge. MA Hons Geography. Joined Royal Marines, 1944, hostilities only commn, 1946, demob. 1948. Whaling, United Whalers, 1949; Schoolmaster, 1950–52. Joined Somerset Light Infantry, 1952; active service, Malaya (mentioned in despatches, 1954); served: Germany, Kenya (King's African Rifles), Bahrein, N Ireland; retired at own request, as Major, 1968, to found and direct Internat. Sailing Craft Assoc. and Exeter Maritime Museum; Dir, Exeter Maritime Mus., 1968–88. *Recreations:* shooting, fishing, sailing, bird watching, photography. *Address:* The Mill, Lympstone, Exmouth, Devon. *T:* Exmouth (0395) 265575.

GODDARD, Lt-Gen. Eric Norman, CB 1947; CIE 1944; CBE 1942 (OBE 1919); MVO 1936; MC; IA, retired; *b* 6 July 1897; 3rd *s* of late Arthur Goddard, Chartered Acct, London; *m* 1939, Elizabeth Lynch, *d* of late Major Lynch Hamilton, and late Frances Prioleau; one *s. Educ:* Dulwich Coll. Commissioned Indian Army, 1915; service in Mesopotamia, Persia and Kurdistan, 1916–19 (despatches twice, OBE, MC); GSO3 AHQ India, 1923–25; 12th Frontier Force Regt, 1928; Staff Coll., Quetta, 1928–29; Bde Major, Nowshera Bde, 1932–34; Chitral relief, 1932 (despatches, bar to MC); Mohmand operations, 1933 (despatches); Bt Major, 1933; GSO2 Eastern Comd, 1934–36; Officer i/c King's Indian Orderly Officers, 1936 (MVO 4th class); Comdt 4th Bn 15 Punjab Regt, 1936; Bt Col 1939 and Col i/c Administration, Burma Army; Brigade Commander, Oct. 1940; Maj.-Gen. i/c Administration Army in Burma, Dec. 1941; served in Burma and on Eastern front, Dec. 1941–Dec. 1944, including Maj.-Gen. i/c Admin 11th Army Group and Allied Land Forces SE Asia, 1943–44 (despatches four times, CIE, CBE); GOC-in-C Southern Comd, India, 1947–48; Subst. Maj.-Gen. 1944; Actg Lieut-Gen. 1947; retired Nov. 1948 with hon. rank of Lieut-Gen. Special appointment CC Germany, 1949–53; Dir of Civil Defence, North-Western Region (Manchester), 1955–63; Pres., East Lancs Br., British Red Cross, 1964–66. *Address:* Kent House, Camden Park, Tunbridge Wells, Kent TN2 5AD. *T:* Tunbridge Wells (0892) 513755.

GODDARD, Harold Keith; QC 1979; barrister-at-law; a Recorder of the Crown Court, since 1978; *b* 9 July 1936; *s* of late Harold Goddard and Edith Goddard, Stockport, Cheshire; *m* 1st, 1963, Susan Elizabeth (marr. diss.), *yr d* of late Ronald Stansfield and of Evelyn Stansfield, Wilmslow, Cheshire; two *s*; 2nd, 1983, Alicja Maria, *d* of late Czeslaw Lazuchiewicz and of Eleonora Lazuchiewicz, Lodz, Poland. *Educ:* Manchester Grammar Sch.; Corpus Christi Coll., Cambridge (Scholar; 1st Cl. Law Tripos 1957; MA, LLM). Bacon Scholar, Gray's Inn; called to the Bar, Gray's Inn, 1959. Practised on Northern Circuit, 1959–. Chm., Disciplinary Appeals Cttee, 1974–80, Mem. Council, 1980–, Mem. Ct of Governors, 1981, UMIST. *Recreation:* golf. *Address:* Deans Court Chambers, Cumberland House, Crown Square, Manchester M3 3HA. *T:* 061–834 4097. *Club:* Wilmslow Golf.

GODDARD, Prof. John Burgess, OBE 1986; Henry Daysh Professor of Regional Development Studies, University of Newcastle upon Tyne, since 1975; *b* 5 Aug. 1943; *s* of Burgess Goddard and Molly Goddard (*née* Bridge); *m* 1966, Janet Patricia (*née* Peddle); one *s* two *d. Educ:* Latymer Upper Sch.; University Coll. London; LSE. BA, PhD. Lectr, LSE, 1968–75; Leverhulme Fellow, Univ. of Lund, 1974; Hon. Dir, Centre for Urban and Regional Develt Studies, Univ. of Newcastle, 1978–. Member: Northern Economic Planning Council, 1976–79; Human Geography Cttee, SSRC, 1976–80; Bd, Port of Tyne Authority, 1990–. Governor, Newcastle upon Tyne Polytechnic, 1989–. Editor, Regional Studies, 1980–85. *Publications:* Office Linkages and Location, 1973; Office Location in Urban and Regional Development, 1975; The Urban and Regional Transformation of Britain, 1983; Technological Change, Industrial Restructuring and Regional Development, 1986; articles in professional jls. *Address:* Woodruff, Long Rigg, Riding Mill, Northumberland NE44 6AL. *T:* Riding Mill (043482) 355.

GODDARD, Peter, PhD; FRS 1989; Reader in Mathematical Physics, since 1989, and Deputy Director, Isaac Newton Institute for Mathematical Sciences, since 1991, University of Cambridge; Fellow, St John's College, Cambridge, since 1975; *b* 3 Sept. 1945; *s* of Herbert Charles Goddard and Rosina Sarah Goddard (*née* Waite); *m* 1968, Helen Barbara Ross; one *s* one *d. Educ:* Emanuel Sch., London; Trinity Coll., Cambridge (BA, MA, PhD). Res. Fellow, Trinity Coll., Cambridge, 1969–73; Vis. Scientist, CERN, Geneva, 1970–72, 1978; Lectr in Applied Maths, Univ. of Durham, 1972–74; Mem., Inst. for Advanced Study, Princeton, NJ, 1974, 1988; Asst Lectr 1975–76, Lectr 1976–89, Univ. of Cambridge; Lectr in Maths 1975–91, Tutor 1980–87, Sen. Tutor 1983–87, St John's Coll., Cambridge. Vis. Prof. of Maths and Physics, Univ. of Virginia, 1983; SERC Vis. Fellow, Imperial Coll., 1987. Mem., Inst. for Theoretical Physics, Univ. of California, Santa Barbara, 1986, 1990. *Publications:* articles on elementary particle physics and mathematical physics in sci. jls. *Address:* 99 Queen Edith's Way, Cambridge CB1 4PL. *T:* Cambridge (0223) 247348.

GODDARD, Roy; independent business consultant, since 1988; Member, Independent Television Commission, since 1990; Chairman, Dyslexia Institute, since 1990; *b* 21 Feb. 1939; *s* of Roy Benjamin Goddard and Emma Annie Coronation (*née* Beckett); *m* 1961, Sally Anne Pain; one *s* one *d. Educ:* Henry Thornton Grammar Sch.; Regent Street Polytechnic. Cummins Engine Co., 1964–68; Partner, Alexander Hughes & Associates, executive search consultants, 1968–70; Founder, Goddard Kay Rogers & Associates, 1970–88. Liveryman, Co. of Glaziers and Painters of Glass. *Recreations:* squash, bad golf, water gardening, reading, eating, debating. *Address:* Newells, Brighton Road, Lower Beeding, West Sussex RH13 6NQ. *T:* Lower Beeding (0403) 891110. *Club:* Royal Automobile.

GODDEN, Charles Henry, CBE 1982; HM Diplomatic Service, retired; Governor (formerly HM Commissioner), Anguilla, 1978–83; *b* 19 Nov. 1922; *s* of late Charles Edward Godden and Catherine Alice Godden (*née* Roe); *m* 1943, Florence Louise Williams; two *d. Educ:* Tweeddale Sch., Carshalton; Morley Coll., Westminster. Served Army, 1941–46. Colonial Office, 1950–66 (seconded British Honduras, 1961–64: Perm. Sec., External Affairs; Dep. Chief Sec.; Clerk of Executive Council); FCO, 1966–: First Sec., 1968; Asst Private Sec. to Sec. of State for Colonies; Private Secretary: to Minister of State, FCO, 1967–70; to Parly Under Sec. of State, 1970; First Sec. (Commercial), Helsinki, 1971–75; First Sec., Belize, 1975–76; Dep. High Comr and Head of Chancery, Kingston, 1976–78. *Recreations:* cricket, walking, reading. *Address:* Stoneleigh, Blackboys, Sussex. *T:* Framfield (082582) 410. *Clubs:* MCC, Commonwealth Trust.

GODDEN, Prof. Malcolm Reginald, PhD; Rawlinson and Bosworth Professor of Anglo-Saxon, and Fellow of Pembroke College, Oxford, since 1991; *b* 9 Oct. 1945. *Educ:* Devizes Grammar Sch.; Barton Peveril Sch., Eastleigh; Pembroke Coll., Cambridge (BA 1966; MA, PhD 1970). Res. Fellow, Pembroke Coll., Cambridge, 1969–72; Asst Prof., Cornell Univ., 1970–71; Lectr in English, Liverpool Univ., 1972–75; Univ. Lectr in English, and Fellow, Exeter Coll., Oxford, 1976–91. Vice-Pres., Internat. Soc. of Anglo-Saxonists, 1989–. Editl Sec., EETS, 1985–; Editor, Anglo-Saxon England, 1989–. *Publications:* (ed) Ælfric's Catholic Homilies, second series, 1979; The Making of Piers Plowman, 1990; The Cambridge Companion to Old English Literature, 1991; contribs to Anglia, English Studies, Anglo-Saxon England, Rev. of English Studies. *Address:* Pembroke College, Oxford OX1 1DW. *T:* Oxford (0865) 276444.

GODDEN, Ven. Max Leon; Archdeacon of Lewes and Hastings, 1975–88 (of Lewes, 1972–75); *b* 25 Nov. 1923; *s* of Richard George Nobel and Lucy Godden; *m* 1945, Anne, *d* of Kenneth and Edith Hucklebridge; four *d. Educ:* Sir Andrew Judd Sch., Tonbridge; Worcester Coll., Oxford (MA 1950). Served RAFVR, 1940–47 (despatches). Deacon, 1952; priest, 1953; Assistant Curate: Cuckfield, 1952–53; Brighton, 1953–57; Vicar of Hangleton, 1957–62; Vicar of Glynde, Firle and Beddingham, 1962–82. *Recreations:* life in a country parish, the garden. *Address:* 14 Oak Close, Chichester, W Sussex PO19 3AJ. *T:* Chichester (0243) 531344.

GODDEN, Rumer, (Margaret Rumer Haynes-Dixon); writer, playwright, poet; *b* 10 Dec. 1907; *d* of late Arthur Leigh Godden, Lydd House, Aldington, Kent, and Katherine Norah Hingley; *m* 1934, Laurence Sinclair Foster (decd), Calcutta; two *d*; *m* 1949, James Haynes Dixon, OBE (*d* 1973). *Educ:* abroad and Moira House, Eastbourne. *Publications: novels:* Chinese Puzzle, 1935; Lady and Unicorn, 1937; Black Narcissus (novel and play), 1938; Gypsy Gypsy, 1940; Breakfast with the Nikolides, 1941; Fugue in Time (novel and play), 1945; The River, 1946 (filmed 1950); Candle for St Jude, 1948; A Breath of Air, 1950; Kingfishers Catch Fire, 1953; An Episode of Sparrows, 1955 (filmed 1957); The Greengage Summer, 1958 (filmed 1961); China Court, 1961; The Battle of the Villa Florita, 1963 (filmed 1964); (with Jon Godden) Two Under the Indian Sun, 1966; In This House of Brede, 1969; The Old Woman Who Lived in a Vinegar Bottle, 1972; (with Jon Godden) Shiva's Pigeons, 1972; The Peacock Spring, 1975; Five for Sorrow, Ten for Joy, 1979; The Dark Horse, 1981; Thursday's Children, 1984; Coromandel Sea Change, 1991; A Kindle of Kittens, 1991; *biography:* Rungli-Rungliot, 1943; Hans Christian Andersen, 1955; The Tale of the Tales, 1971; Gulbadan Begum: portrait of a Rose Princess at the Mughal Court, 1980; *poetry:* In Noah's Ark, 1949; *short stories:* Mooltiki, 1957; Swan and Turtles, 1968; (with Jon Godden) Indian Dust, 1989; *non-fiction:* (comp.) The Raphael Bible, 1970; *autobiography:* A Time to Dance, No Time to Weep, 1987; A House with Four Rooms, 1989; *children's books,* include: The Kitchen Madonna, 1967; The Diddakoi, 1972 (Whitbread Award); The Dragon of Og, 1981; Four Dolls, 1983; Fu-Dog, 1989; published internationally (11 languages). *Address:* Macmillan & Co., 4 Little Essex Street, WC2R 3LF.

GODDEN, Tony Richard Hillier, CB 1975; Secretary, Scottish Development Department, 1980–87, retired; *b* 13 Nov. 1927; *o s* of late Richard Godden and Gladys Eleanor Godden; *m* 1953, Marjorie Florence Snell; one *s* two *d. Educ:* Barnstaple Grammar Sch.; London Sch. of Economics (BSc (Econ.) 1st cl.). Commissioned, RAF Education Branch, 1950. Entered Colonial Office as Asst Principal, 1951; Private Sec. to Parly Under-Sec. of State, 1954–55; Principal, 1956; Cabinet Office, 1957–59; transferred to Scottish Home Dept, 1961; Asst Sec., Scottish Development Dept, 1964; Under-Sec., 1969; Sec., Scottish Economic Planning Dept, 1973–80. Member: Council on Tribunals, 1988–; Ancient Monuments Board for Scotland, 1990–. Sec., Friends of Royal Scottish Acad., 1987–. *Address:* 9 Ross Road, Edinburgh EH16 5QN. *T:* 031–667 6556. *Club:* New (Edinburgh).

GODFREY, Gerald Michael; Hon. Mr Justice Godfrey; a Judge of the High Court of Hong Kong, since 1986; *b* 30 July 1933; *s* of late Sidney Godfrey and late Esther (*née* Lewin); *m* 1960, Anne Sheila, *er d* of David Goldstein; three *s* two *d. Educ:* Lower Sch. of John Lyon, Harrow; King's Coll., London Univ. LLB 1952, LLM 1954. Called to the Bar: Lincoln's Inn, 1954 (Bencher 1978); Bahamas, 1972; Hong Kong, 1974; Kenya, 1978; Singapore, 1978; Malaysia, 1979; Brunei, 1979; National Service as 2nd Lt, RASC, 1955; Temp. Captain, 1956. In practice at the Chancery Bar, 1957–86; QC 1971. Chm., Justice Cttee on Parental Rights and Duties and Custody Suits (Report, 1975); DoT Inspector into Affairs of Saint Piran Ltd (Report, 1981). Member: Senate of Inns of Court and the Bar, 1974–77, 1981–84 (Chm., Law Reform Cttee, 1981–83); Council of Justice, 1976–81. *Publication:* Editor, Business Law Review, 1958. *Recreations:* walking, travel. *Address:* c/o Supreme Court, Hong Kong.

GODFREY, Rt. Rev. Harold William; *see* Uruguay, Bishop of.

GODFREY, Howard Anthony; QC 1991; *b* 17 Aug. 1946; *s* of late Emanuel and of Amy Godfrey; *m* 1972, Barbara Ellinger; two *s. Educ:* William Ellis Sch.; LSE (LLB). Called to the Bar, Middle Temple, 1970; practising on SE Circuit, 1972–; Asst Recorder of Crown Court, 1987–. *Recreations:* wine and food, travel, humour. *Address:* 3 Hare Court, Temple, EC4Y 7BJ. *T:* 071–353 7561, *Fax:* 071–353 7741; The Red House, Swallowfield Road, Arborfield Cross, Berks RG2 9JZ. *T:* Arborfield Cross (0734) 760657.

GODFREY, Louise Sarah, (Mrs Stanley Bland); QC 1991; a Recorder of the Crown Court, since 1989; *b* 17 April 1950; *d* of Philip Godfrey and Pearl (*née* Goodman); *m* 1977, Stanley Leslie Bland; two *d. Educ:* Tadcaster Grammar Sch.; St Hugh's Coll., Oxford (MA Jurisprudence). Called to the Bar, Middle Temple, 1972. *Recreations:* cooking, walking. *Address:* Park Court Chambers, 40 Park Cross Street, Leeds LS1 2QH. *T:* Leeds (0532) 433277.

GODFREY, Dr Malcolm Paul Weston, CBE 1986; JP; Second Secretary, Medical Research Council, 1983–88; Chairman, Public Health Laboratory Service Board, since 1989; *b* 11 Aug. 1926; *s* of late Harry Godfrey and of Rose Godfrey; *m* 1955, Barbara Goldstein; one *s* two *d. Educ:* Hertford Grammar Sch.; King's Coll., London Univ.; KCH Med. Sch. MB, BS (Hons and Univ. Medal) 1950; MRCP 1955, FRCP 1972. Hosp. posts at KCH, Nat. Heart and Brompton Hosps; RAF Med. Br., 1952–54; Fellow in Med. and Asst Physician, Johns Hopkins Hosp., USA, 1957–58; MRC Headquarters Staff, 1960–74: MO, 1960; Sen. MO, 1964; Principal MO, 1970; Sen. Principal MO, 1974; Dean, Royal Postgrad. Med. Sch., 1974–83 (Mem. Council, 1974–83, 1988–; Hon. Fellow, 1985). University of London: Member: Senate, 1980–83; Court, 1981–83; Chm., Jt Med. Adv. Cttee, 1979–82. Mem., Faculty Bd of Clinical Medicine, Univ. of Cambridge, 1988–89. Chm., Brit. Council Med. Adv. Cttee, 1985–; Member: Sci. Adv. Panel CIBA Foundn, 1974–; Ealing, Hammersmith and Hounslow AHA(T), 1975–80; NW Thames RHA, 1980–83, 1985–88; Hammersmith SHA, 1982–83; Sec. of States Adv. Gp on London Health Services, 1980–81; GMC, 1979–81. Lay Mem., Professional Standards Dept, Gen. Council of the Bar. Consultant Advr, WHO Human Reproduction Programme, 1979–; Scientific Advr, Foulkes Foundn, 1983–89. QHP, 1987–90. Member, Council: Charing Cross Hosp. Med. Sch., 1975–80; St Mary's Hosp. Med. Sch., 1983–88; Member: Governing Body, British Postgrad. Med. Fedn, 1974–89; Council of Governors, UMDS of Guy's and St Thomas' Hosps, 1990–. Mem. Court of Assts, Worshipful Soc. of Apothecaries, 1979–89 (Master, 1989–90). JP Wimbledon, 1972 (Chm. of the Bench and of Merton Magistrates' Courts Cttee, 1988– (Dep. Chm., 1987); Chm., Juvenile Panel, 1983–87). FRSA 1989. *Publications:* contrib. med. jls on cardiac and respiratory disorders. *Recreations:* theatre, planning holidays (sometimes taking them), walking. *Address:* 17 Clifton Hill, St John's Wood, NW8 0QE. *T:* 071–624 6335.

GODFREY, Norman Eric; *b* 16 Aug. 1927; *s* of Cecil and Beatrice Godfrey. *Educ:* Northampton Grammar Sch.; London Sch. of Econs (BScEcon). Career mainly in HM Customs but also served in Min. of Transport/DoE, 1968–71, and Price Commn, 1976–79; Comr, HM Customs and Excise, 1979–86. *Recreations:* music, especially opera, theatre, travel, tennis, walking. *Address:* 2 Belsize Avenue, NW3 4AU. *T:* 071–435 6085.

GODFREY, Peter, FCA; Senior Partner, Ernst & Whinney, Chartered Accountants, 1980–86, retired; Chairman, Accounting Standards Committee, 1984–Sept. 1986 (Member, 1983–86); *b* 23 March 1924; *m* 1951, Heather Taplin; two *s* one *d. Educ:* West Kensington Central Sch. Served Army, 1942, until released, rank Captain, 1947. Qual. as an Incorporated Accountant, 1949; joined Whinney Smith & Whinney, 1949; admitted to partnership, 1959; Chm., Ernst & Whinney Internat., 1981–83, 1985–86. Appointed: BoT Inspector into Affairs of Pinnock Finance Co. (GB) Ltd, Aug. 1967; DTI Inspector into Affairs of Rolls-Royce Ltd, April 1971; Mem., ODM Cttee of Inquiry on Crown Agents, April 1975. Institute of Chartered Accountants: Mem., Inflation Accounting Sub-Cttee, 1982–84; Mem., Council, 1984–86. *Recreation:* family. *Address:* 2N Maple Lodge, Lythe Hill Park, Haslemere, Surrey GU27 3TE. *T:* Haslemere (0428) 656729.

GODFREY, Rt. Rev. William; *see* Godfrey, Rt Rev. H. W.

GODLEY, family name of **Baron Kilbracken.**

GODLEY, Prof. Hon. Wynne Alexander Hugh; Professor of Applied Economics, since 1980, University of Cambridge (Director, 1970–85, Acting Director, 1985–87, Department of Applied Economics); Fellow of King's College, Cambridge, since 1970; *b* 2 Sept. 1926; *yr s* of Hugh John, 2nd Baron Kilbracken, CB, KC and Elizabeth Helen Monteith, *d* of Vereker Monteith Hamilton; *m* 1955, Kathleen Eleonora, *d* of Sir Jacob Epstein, KBE; one *d. Educ:* Rugby; New Coll., Oxford; Conservatoire de Musique, Paris. Professional oboist, 1950. Joined Economic Section, HM Treasury, 1956; Dep. Dir, Economic Sect., HM Treasury, 1967–70. Dir, Investing in Success Equities Ltd, 1970–85; a Dir, Royal Opera House, Covent Garden, 1976–87. An Economic Consultant, HM Treasury, 1975; Official Advr, Select Cttee on Public Expenditure, 1971–73. Vis. Prof., Aalborg Univ., 1987–88. *Publications:* (with T. F. Cripps) Local Government Finance and its Reform, 1976; The Planning of Telecommunications in the United Kingdom, 1978; (with K. J. Coutts and W. D. Nordhaus) Pricing in the Trade Cycle, 1978; (with T. F. Cripps) Macroeconomics, 1983; articles, in National Institute Review, Economic Jl, London and Cambridge Economic Bulletin, Cambridge Economic Policy Review, Economica, Jl of Policy Modelling, Manchester School, Nationalokonomisk Tidsskrift, Political Qly, New Statesman and Society. *Address:* Jasmine House, The Green, Cavendish, Suffolk. *T:* Glemsford (0787) 281166.

GODMAN, Norman Anthony, PhD; MP (Lab) Greenock and Port Glasgow, since 1983; *b* 19 April 1938; *m* Patricia. *Educ:* Westbourne Street Boys' Sch., Hessle Road, Hull; Hull Univ. (BA); Heriot-Watt Univ. (PhD 1982). Nat. Service, Royal Mil. Police, 1958–60. Shipwright to trade teacher in Scottish further and higher educn. Mem., Select Cttee on European Legislation, 1989–. Contested (Lab) Aberdeen South, 1979. *Address:* House of Commons, SW1A 0AA.

GODMAN IRVINE, Rt. Hon. Sir Bryant; *see* Irvine, Rt. Hon. Sir B. G.

GODSELL, Stanley Harry; Regional Director (South West), Departments of Environment and Transport, 1978–80; retired; *b* 19 March 1920; *s* of Thomas Harry Godsell and Gladys Godsell; *m* 1946, Rosemary Blackburn (*d* 1990); one *s* (and one *s* decd). *Educ:* Alsop High Sch., Liverpool. Civil Service: PO, 1937–48; Min. of Town and Country Planning, 1948; Asst Sec., Min. of Housing and Local Govt, 1965. *Recreations:* bridge, swimming, photography. *Address:* 6 Pitch and Pay Park, Sneyd Park, Bristol BS9 1NJ. *T:* Bristol (0272) 683791.

GODWIN, Dame (Beatrice) Anne, DBE 1962 (OBE 1952); a Governor of the BBC, 1962–68; a full-time Member of the Industrial Court, 1963–69; *b* 1897. Gen. Sec., Clerical and Administrative Workers' Union, 1956–62. Chm. of the TUC, 1961–62. *Address:* 25 Fullbrooks Avenue, Worcester Park, Surrey KT4 7PE.

GODWIN, William Henry; Fellow in European Community Law, British Institute of International and Comparative Law, since 1990; *b* 29 Nov. 1923; *s* of George Godwin and Dorothy (*née* Purdon); *m* 1961, Lela Milosevic; one *s* one *d. Educ:* Colet Court; Lycée Français de Londres; St John's Coll., Cambridge. Called to the Bar, Middle Temple, 1948. Treasury Solicitor's Office, 1948–90; Under Sec., 1977; UK Agent before Europ. Ct of Justice, 1973–85; Legal Advr to Cabinet Office, European Secretariat, 1982–85. *Address:* 54 Gerard Road, SW13 9QQ.

GOEHR, Prof. Alexander; composer; Professor of Music, and Fellow of Trinity Hall, University of Cambridge, since 1976; *b* 10 Aug. 1932; *s* of Walter and Laelia Goehr. *Educ:* Berkhamsted; Royal Manchester Coll. of Music; Paris Conservatoire. Lectr, Morley Coll., 1955–57; Music Asst, BBC, 1960–67; Winston Churchill Trust Fellowship, 1968; Composer-in-residence, New England Conservatory, Boston, Mass, 1968–69; Associate Professor of Music, Yale University, 1969–70; West Riding Prof. of Music, Leeds Univ., 1971–76. Artistic Dir, Leeds Festival, 1975; Vis. Prof., Peking Conservatoire of Music, 1980. Reith Lectr, BBC, 1987. Mem., Bd of Dirs, Royal Opera House, 1982–. Hon. Vice-Pres., SPNM, 1983–. Hon. Mem., Amer. Acad. and Inst. of Arts and Letters. Hon. FRMCM; Hon. FRAM 1975; Hon. FRNCM 1980; Hon. FRCM 1981. Hon. DMus: Southampton, 1973; Manchester, 1990. *Compositions include:* Fantasia Op. 4; Violin Concerto; Little Symphony; Pastorals; Romanza for 'cello; Symphony in one Movement, Op. 29; Piano Concerto, 1970; Concerto for Eleven, 1972; Metamorphosis/Dance, 1973; Lyric Pieces, 1974; Konzertstück, 1974; Kafka Fragments, 1979; Sinfonia, 1980; Deux Etudes, 1981; Eve Dreams in Paradise, 1989; chamber music; *operas:* Arden must die, 1967; Behold the Sun, 1985; *cantatas:* Sutter's Gold; The Deluge; Triptych (Naboth's Vineyard; Shadowplay; Sonata about Jerusalem); Babylon the Great is Fallen. *Address:* Trinity Hall, Cambridge; University Music School, West Road, Cambridge; c/o Schott & Co Ltd, 48 Great Marlborough Street, W1.

GOFF, family name of **Baron Goff of Chieveley.**

GOFF OF CHIEVELEY, Baron *cr* 1986 (Life Peer), of Chieveley in the Royal County of Berkshire; **Robert Lionel Archibald Goff;** Kt 1975; PC 1982; DCL; FBA 1987; a Lord of Appeal in Ordinary, since 1986; *b* 12 Nov. 1926; *s* of Lt-Col L. T. Goff and Mrs Goff (*née* Denroche-Smith); *m* 1953, Sarah, *er d* of Capt. G. R. Cousins, DSC, RN; one *s* two *d* (and one *s* decd). *Educ:* Eton Coll.; New Coll., Oxford (MA 1953, DCL 1972; Hon. Fellow, 1986). Served in Scots Guards, 1945–48 (commnd 1945). 1st cl hons Jurisprudence, Oxon, 1950. Called to the Bar, Inner Temple, 1951; Bencher, 1975; QC 1967. Fellow and Tutor, Lincoln Coll., Oxford, 1951–55; in practice at the Bar, 1956–75; a Recorder, 1974–75; Judge of the High Ct, QBD, 1975–82; Judge i/c Commercial List, and Chm. Commercial Court Cttee, 1979–81; a Lord Justice of Appeal, 1982–86. Chm., Sub-Cttee E (Law and Instns), H of L Select Cttee on EC, 1986–88. Chairman: Council of Legal Educn, 1976–82 (Vice-Chm., 1972–76; Chm., Bd of Studies, 1970–76); Common Professional Examination Bd, 1976–78; Court, London Univ., 1986–91; Pegasus Scholarship Trust, 1987–. Hon. Prof. of Legal Ethics, Univ. of Birmingham, 1980–81; Lectures: Maccabean, British Acad., 1983; Lionel Cohen Meml, Hebrew Univ. of Jerusalem, 1987. Member: Gen. Council of the Bar, 1971–74; Senate of Inns of Court and Bar, 1974–82 (Chm., Law Reform and Procedure Cttee, 1974–76). Chm., British Inst. of Internat. and Comparative Law, 1986–. President: CIArb, 1986–91; Bentham Club, 1986; Holdsworth Club, 1986–87. Hon. Fellow: Lincoln Coll., Oxford, 1985; New Coll., Oxford, 1986. Hon. DLitt: City, 1977; Reading, 1990; Hon. LLD: Buckingham, 1990; London, 1990. *Publication:* (with Prof. Gareth Jones) The Law of Restitution, 1966. *Address:* House of Lords, Westminster, SW1.

GOFF, Martyn, OBE 1977; Chief Executive, Book Trust (formerly Director of the National Book League), 1970–88, now Consultant; Executive Chairman, Sotherans, since 1988; *b* 7 June 1923; *s* of Jacob and Janey Goff. *Educ:* Clifton College. Served in Royal Air Force, 1941–46. Film business, 1946–48; Bookseller, 1948–70. Has lectured on: music; English fiction; teenager morality; the book trade, 1946–70; fiction reviewer, 1975–88, non-fiction, 1988–, Daily Telegraph. Founder and Chm., Bedford Square Bookbang, 1971. Member: Arts Council Literature Panel, 1970–78; Arts Council Trng Cttee, 1973–78; Greater London Arts Assoc. Literature Panel, 1973–81; British Nat. Bibliography Res. Fund, 1976–88; British Library Adv. Council, 1977–82; PEN Exec. Cttee, 1978–; Exec. Cttee, Gtr London Arts Council, 1982–88; Library and Information Services Council, 1984–86; Bd Mem., British Theatre Assoc., 1983–85; Chairman: Paternosters '73 Library Adv. Council, 1972–74; New Fiction Soc., 1975–88; School Bookshop Assoc., 1977–; Soc. of Bookmen, 1982–84; 1890s Soc., 1990–; Trustee: Cadmean Trust, 1981–; Battersea Arts Centre, 1981–85. FIAL 1958, FRSA 1979. *Publications: fiction:* The Plaster Fabric, 1957; A Season with Mammon, 1958; A Sort of Peace, 1960; The Youngest Director, 1961, new edn 1985; Red on the Door, 1962; The Flint Inheritance, 1965; Indecent Assault, 1967; The Liberation of Rupert Bannister, 1978; Tar and Cement, 1988; *non-fiction:* A Short Guide to Long Play, 1957; A Further Guide to Long Play, 1958; LP Collecting, 1960; Why Conform?, 1968; Victorian and Edwardian Surrey, 1972; Record Choice, 1974; Royal Pavilion, 1976; Organising Book Exhibitions, 1982; Publishing, 1988; Prize Writing, 1989. *Recreations:* travel, collecting paintings and sculptures, music. *Address:* 95 Sisters Avenue, SW11 5SW. *Clubs:* Athenæum, Savile, Groucho.

GOFF, Sir Robert (William Davis-), 4th Bt *cr* 1905; Director, O'Connor & Co., Art Dealers and Property Investment Co., Dublin; *b* 12 Sept. 1955; *s* of Sir Ernest William Davis-Goff, 3rd Bt, and of Alice Cynthia Davis-Goff (*née* Woodhouse); *S* father, 1980; *m* 1978, Nathalie Sheelagh, *d* of Terence Chadwick; three *s* one *d. Educ:* Cheltenham College, Glos. *Recreation:* shooting. *Heir: s* William Nathaniel Davis-Goff, *b* 20 April 1980. *Address:* Seafield, Donabate, Co. Dublin. *Club:* Kildare Street and University (Dublin).

GOGUEN, Prof. Joseph Amadee; Professor of Computing Science, University of Oxford, since 1988; *b* 28 June 1941; *s* of Joseph Amadee Goguen and Helen Stratton; *m* 1st, 1961, Nancy Hammer; one *s* one *d*; 2nd, 1981, Kathleen Morrow; one *d. Educ:* Harvard Univ. (BA); Univ. of California at Berkeley (MA, PhD). Asst Prof., Cttee on Inf. Sciences, Univ. of Chicago, 1968–73; Academic Staff, Naropa Inst., Boulder Colo, 1974–78; Prof., Computer Sci. Dept, UCLA, 1973–79; Man. Dir, Structural Semantics, Palo Alto, 1978–; Sen. Staff Scientist, SRI Internat., Menlo Park, Calif, 1979–88; Mem., Center for Study of Language and Inf., Stanford Univ., 1984–88. IBM Postdoctoral Fellowship, T. J. Watson Res. Center, 1971; Sen. Vis. Fellow, Univ. of Edinburgh, 1976, 1977, 1983. Exceptional Achievement Award, SRI Internat., 1984. *Publications:* (ed) Theory and Practice of Software Technology, 1983; over 100 articles in professional jls. *Address:* Programming Research Group, University of Oxford, 8–11 Keble Road, Oxford OX1 3QD. *T:* Oxford (0865) 272567.

GOH Chok Tong; Prime Minister of Singapore, since 1990; Minister for Defence, since 1985; *b* 20 May 1941; *m* Tan Choo Leng; one *s* one *d* (twins). *Educ:* Raffles Instn; Univ. of Singapore (1st cl Hons Econs); Williams Coll., USA. Joined Admin. Service, Singapore Govt, 1964, Econ. Planning Unit; Min. of Finance; Planning and Projects Manager, Neptune Orient Lines, 1969–73, Man. Dir, 1973–77. MP for Marine Parade, 1976–; Sen. Minister of State for Finance, 1977–79; Minister: for Trade and Industry, 1979–81; for Health and for Trade and Industry, then for Defence and for Health, 1981–85; First Dep. Prime Minister, 1985–90. People's Action Party: Mem., Central Exec. Cttee, 1979–; First Asst Sec. Gen. Dir, Singapore Labour Foundn, 1977, Chm. 1981–; formerly Chairman: NTUC Income, NTUC Fairprice; Bd of Trustees, Singapore Ind. Labour Orgn Multi-Purpose Co-operative Soc. Medal of Honour, NTUC, 1987. *Recreations:* golf, tennis. *Address:* c/o Ministry of Information and the Arts, #36-00 PSA Building, 460 Alexandra Road, Singapore 0511.

GOHEEN, Robert Francis; educator; President Emeritus, and Senior Fellow, Public and International Affairs, since 1981, Princeton University; Director, Mellon Fellowships in Humanities, since 1982; *b* Venguria, India, 15 Aug. 1919; *s* of Dr Robert H. H. Goheen and Anne Ewing; *m* 1941, Margaret M. Skelly; two *s* four *d*. *Educ:* Princeton Univ. AB 1940; PhD 1948. Princeton University: Instructor, Dept of Classics, 1948–50; Asst Prof., 1950–57; Prof., 1957–72; President, 1957–72. Chm., Council on Foundns, 1972–77; US Ambassador to India, 1977–80. Sen. Fellow in Classics, Amer. Academy in Rome, 1952–53; Dir Nat. Woodrow Wilson Fellowship Program, 1953–56. Member: Adv. Commn on Oceans and Internat. Scientific and Environmental Affairs, US State Dept; Adv. Bd, Nat. Foreign Language Center; Adv. Council, Woodrow Wilson Sch., Princeton Univ.; American Philosophical Soc.; American Academy of Arts and Sciences; Phi Beta Kappa; Trustee: Midlantic Nat. Bank; Thomson Newspapers Inc.; American Univ. in Beirut; Carnegie Endowment for Internat. Peace; United Bd of Christian Higher Educn in Asia; Bharatiya Vidya Bhavan (USA). Former Mem. Internat Adv. Bd, Chemical Bank; former Member of Board: Carnegie Foundn for Advancement of Teaching; Rockefeller Foundn; Asia Soc.; Amer. Acad. in Rome; Inst. of Internat. Educn; Equitable Life; Dreyfus Third Century Fund; Reza Shah Kabir Univ., Iran. Hon. degrees: Harvard, Rutgers, Yale, Temple, Brown, Columbia, New York, Madras, Pennsylvania, Hamilton, Middlebury, Saint Mary's (Calif), State of New York, Denver, Notre Dame, N Carolina, Hofstra, Nebraska, Dropsie, Princeton; Tusculum Coll.; Trinity Coll., USA; Coll. of Wooster; Jewish Theological Seminary of America; Ripon Coll.; Rider Coll. *Publications:* The Imagery of Sophocles' Antigone, 1951; The Human Nature of a University, 1969; articles. *Recreations:* books, golf. *Address:* 1 Orchard Circle, Princeton, New Jersey 08540, USA. *T:* 452–3000. *Clubs:* Princeton, University, Century Association (New York); Cosmos (Washington); Nassau (Princeton); Gymkhana, Delhi Golf (Delhi).

GOHEL, Sir Jayvantsinhji (Kayaji), Kt 1989; CBE 1984; Director, Meghraj Group Ltd, including Meghraj Bank Ltd and other subsidiaries, since 1960; *b* 14 Aug. 1915; *s* of Kayaji Kesarisinhji Gohel and Nandakunver Kayaji Gohel; *m* 1941, Sajjankunver; two *s*. *Educ:* schs in India and England; Middle Temple. Barrister at Law, 1941. Judge, Mem. of Administrative Council and Diwan, Morvi princely state, W India, 1942–48; Indian Administrative Services, 1948–60: Dist Collector and Magistrate; Settlements Comr under Min. of Rehabilitation; Perm. Sec. to State Govt of Saurashtra in Educn, Rehabilitation and Communications; Political Adviser with Internat. Commn for Supervision and Control in Indo-China. *Recreation:* working for various charities (Indian and particularly British). *Address:* Meghraj Court, 18 Jockey's Fields, WC1R 4BW. *T:* 071–831 6881. *Club:* Overseas Bankers'.

GOLD, Sir Arthur (Abraham), Kt 1984; CBE 1974; Chairman: Commonwealth Games Council for England, since 1979; British Olympic Association, since 1988; Honorary Secretary, British Amateur Athletic Board, 1965–77 (Life Vice President, 1977); President, Counties Athletic Union, since 1978; *b* 10 Jan. 1917; *s* of late Mark and Leah Gold; *m* 1942, Marion Godfrey, *d* of late N. Godfrey; one *s*. *Educ:* Grocers' Company's Sch. Inst. of Motor Industry Wakefield Gold Medallist, 1945. Internat. high jumper, 1937; Past President: London AC; Middlesex County AAA; Athletics Team Leader Olympic Games: Mexico, 1968; Munich, 1972; Montreal, 1976. Council Mem., 1966–76, Pres., 1976–87, European Athletic Assoc.; Member: Sports Council, 1980–88; Exec. Cttee, CCPR. *Publications:* Ballet Training Exercises for Athletes, 1960; various contribs to technical books on athletics. *Recreations:* walking, talking, reading, weeding. *Address:* 49 Friern Mount Drive, Whetstone, N20 9DJ. *T:* 081–445 2848. *Clubs:* City Livery, MCC; London Athletic.

GOLD, Jack; film director; *b* 28 June 1930; British; *m* 1957, Denyse (*née* Macpherson); two *s* one *d*. *Educ:* London Univ. (BSc (Econs), LLB). Asst Studio Manager, BBC radio, 1954–55; Editor, Film Dept, BBC, 1955–60; Dir, TV and film documentaries and fiction, 1960–. Desmond Davies Award for services to television, BAFTA, 1976. *TV films:* Tonight; Death in the Morning (BAFTA Award, 1964); Modern Millionairess; Famine; Dispute; 90 Days; Dowager in Hot Pants; World of Coppard (BAFTA Award, 1968); Mad Jack (Grand Prix, Monte Carlo, 1971); Stocker's Copper (BAFTA Award, 1972); Arturo Ui; The Lump; Catholics (Peabody Award, 1974); The Naked Civil Servant (Italia Prize, 1976, Internat. Emmy, and Critics Award, 1976); Thank You Comrades; Marya; Charlie Muffin; A Walk in the Forest; Merchant of Venice; Bavarian Night; A Lot of Happiness (Kenneth Macmillan), 1981 (Internat. Emmy Award); Praying Mantis, Macbeth, L'Elegance, 1982; The Red Monarch, 1983; Good and Bad at Games, 1983; Sakharov, 1984 (Assoc. Cable Enterprises Award); Murrow, 1986 (Assoc. Cable Enterprises Award); Me and the Girls, 1985; Escape from Sobibor, 1987 (Golden Globe Award); Stones for Ibarra, 1988; The Tenth Man, 1989; Masterclass, 1989; Ball-trap on the Côte Sauvage, 1989; The Rose and the Jackal, 1990; *cinema:* The Bofors Gun, 1968; The Reckoning, 1969; The National Health, 1973 (Evening News Best Comedy Award); Who?, 1974; Man Friday, 1974; Aces High, 1976 (Evening News Best Film Award); The Medusa Touch, 1977; The Sailor's Return, 1978 (jt winner, Martin Luther King Meml Prize, 1980; Monte Carlo Catholic Award, 1981; Monte Carlo Critics Award, 1981); Little Lord Fauntleroy, 1981 (Christopher Award); The Chain, 1985; Stones for Ibarra, 1988; *theatre:* The Devil's Disciple, Aldwych, 1976; This Story of Yours, Hampstead, 1987; Danger! Memory, Hampstead, 1988. *Recreations:* music, reading. *Address:* 18 Avenue Road, N6 5DW.

GOLD, John (Joseph Manson); Public Relations Consultant, 1979–90, retired; Manager of Public Relations, Hong Kong Mass Transit Railway, 1975–79; *b* 2 Aug. 1925; *m* 1953, Berta Cordeiro; one *d*. *Educ:* Clayesmore Sch., Dorset. Yorkshire Evening News, 1944–47; London Evening News, 1947–52; Australian Associated Press (New York), 1952–55; New York Corresp., London Evening News, 1955–66; Editor, London Evening News, 1967–72; Dir, Harmsworth Publications Ltd, 1967–73. Free-lance writer and lectr, Far East, 1973–75.

GOLD, Sir Joseph, Kt 1980; Senior Consultant, International Monetary Fund, since 1979; *b* 12 July 1912; *m* 1939, Ruth Schechter; one *s* two *d*. *Educ:* Univ. of London (LLB 1935, LLM 1936); Harvard Univ. (SJD). Asst Lectr, University Coll., London, 1937–39; British Mission, Washington, DC, 1942–46; joined IMF, 1946; General Counsel and Dir, Legal Dept, 1960–79. Hon. LLD Southern Methodist Univ., 1985. Silver Medal, Columbia Univ., 1982; Theberge Medal in Internat. Law, Amer. Bar Assoc., 1989. *Publications:* The Fund Agreement in the Courts, vol. I 1962, vol. II 1982, vol. III 1986; The Stand-by Arrangements of the IMF, 1970; Voting and Decisions in the IMF, 1972; Membership and Nonmembership in the IMF, 1974; Los Acuerdos de Derechos de Giro del Fondo Monetario Internacional, 1976; Legal and Institutional Aspects of the International Monetary System, vol I, 1979, vol II, 1984; Aspectos Legales de La Reforma Monetario Internacional, 1979; Exchange Rates in International Law and Organisation, 1988; Legal Effects of Fluctuating Exchange Rates, 1990; numerous pamphlets and articles on internat. and nat. monetary law in many countries. *Recreations:* collecting first editions 20th century English and American poetry, assemblages of found objects, gardening, defence of English language. *Address:* 7020 Braeburn Place, Bethesda, Maryland 20817, USA. *T:* 301–229–3278.

GOLD, Stephen Charles, MA, MD, FRCP; Consulting Physician to: the Skin Department, St George's Hospital; St John's Hospital for Diseases of the Skin; King Edward VII Hospital for Officers; Former Hon. Consultant in Dermatology: to the Army; to Royal Hospital, Chelsea; *b* Bishops Stortford, Herts, 10 Aug. 1915; *yr s* of late Philip Gold, Stansted, Essex, and late Amy Frances, *er d* of James and Mary Perry; *m* 1941, Betty Margaret, *o d* of late Dr T. P. Sheedy, OBE; three *s* one *d*. *Educ:* Radley Coll.; Gonville and Caius Coll., Cambridge; St George's Hosp. (Entrance Exhibnr); Zürich and Philadelphia. BA 1937; MRCS, LRCP 1940; MA, MB, BChir 1941; MRCP 1947; MD 1952; FRCP 1958. Served RAMC, 1941–46. Late Med. First Asst to Out-Patients, St George's Hosp., Senior Registrar, Skin Dept, St George's Hosp., Sen. Registrar, St John's Hosp. for Diseases of the Skin; Lectr in Dermatology, Royal Postgraduate Med. Sch., 1949–69. Sec., Brit. Assoc. of Dermatology, 1965–70 (Pres., 1979). FRSM (late Sec. Dermatological Section, Pres., 1972–73); Fellow St John's Hosp. Dermatological Soc. (Pres., 1965–66).

GOLD, Prof. Thomas, FRS 1964; John L. Wetherill Professor of Astronomy, Cornell University, 1971–86, Professor Emeritus of Astronomy, 1987; *b* 22 May 1920; *s* of Max and Josefine Gold; *m* 1st, 1947, Merle E. Gold (*née* Tuberg); three *d*; 2nd, 1972, Carvel B. Gold (*née* Beyer); one *d*. *Educ:* Zuoz Coll., Switzerland; Trinity Coll., Cambridge (Hon. Fellow, 1986). BA Mechanical Sciences (Cambridge), 1942; MA Mechanical Sciences, Cambridge, 1946; ScD, Cambridge, 1969. Fellow Trinity Coll., Cambridge, 1947–51. British Admiralty, 1942–46; Cavendish Laboratory, Cambridge, 1946–47 and 1949–52; Med. Research Council, Zoological Lab., Cambridge, 1947–49; Sen. Principal Scientific Officer (Chief Asst), Royal Greenwich Observatory, 1952–56; Prof. of Astronomy, 1957–58, Robert Wheeler Willson Prof. of Applied Astronomy, 1958–59, Harvard Univ. Dir, Center for Radio-Physics and Space Research, Cornell Univ., 1959–81. Hon. MA (Harvard), 1957. Member: Amer. Philosophical Soc.; Nat. Acad. of Sciences; Fellow, Amer. Acad. of Arts and Sciences. Gold Medal, RAS, 1985. *Publications:* Power from the Earth, 1987; contribs to learned journals on astronomy, physics, biophysics, geophysics. *Recreations:* ski-ing, travelling. *Address:* 7 Pleasant Grove Lane, Ithaca, NY 14850, USA.

GOLDBERG, Prof. Sir Abraham, Kt 1983; Regius Professor of the Practice of Medicine, University of Glasgow, 1978–89, now Emeritus (Regius Professor of Materia Medica, 1970–78); Consultant Physician, Western Infirmary, Glasgow; *b* 7 Dec. 1923; *s* of late Julius Goldberg and Rachel Goldberg (*née* Varinofsky); *m* 1957, Clarice Cussin; two *s* one *d*. *Educ:* George Heriot's Sch., Edinburgh; Edinburgh University. MB, ChB 1946, MD (Gold Medal for thesis) 1956, Edinburgh; DSc Glasgow 1966; FRCP, FRCPE, FRCPGlas, FRSE. RAMC, 1947–49. Nuffield Research Fellow, UCH Med. Sch., London, 1952–54; Eli Lilly Trav. Fellow in Medicine (MRC) in Dept of Medicine, Univ. of Utah; Lectr in Medicine 1956, Titular Prof. 1967, Univ. of Glasgow. Mem., Grants Cttee, Clinical Res. Bd, MRC, 1971–77, Chm., Grants Cttee I, Clinical Res. Bd, MRC, 1973–77. Mem., Chief Scientist Cttee, SHHD, 1977–83; Chm., Biomed. Res. Cttee, SHHD Chief Scientist Orgn, 1977–83; Chm., Cttee on Safety of Medicines, 1980–86. Mem., Editorial Bd, Jt Formulary Cttee, British Nat. Formulary, 1972–78. Foundn Pres., Faculty of Pharmaceutical Medicine, RCP, 1989–. Editor, Scottish Medical Jl, 1962–63. Lectures: Sydney Watson Smith, RCPE, 1964; Henry Cohen, Hebrew Univ., Jerusalem, 1973; Fitzpatrick, RCP, 1988; Archibald Goodall Meml, RCPSG, 1989. Watson Prize, RCPGlas, 1959; Alexander Fleck Award, Univ. of Glasgow, 1967. *Publications:* (jtly) Diseases of Porphyrin Metabolism, 1962; (ed jtly) Recent Advances in Haematology, 1971; (jtly) Disorders of Porphyrin Metabolism, 1987; papers on clinical and investigative medicine. *Recreations:* walking, swimming, writing. *Address:* 16 Birnam Crescent, Bearsden, Glasgow G61 2AU.

GOLDBERG, David Gerard; QC 1987; *b* 12 Aug. 1947; *s* of late Arthur Goldberg and of Sylvia Goldberg; *m* 1981, Alison Ninette Lunzer; one *s* one *d*. *Educ:* Plymouth Coll.; London School of Economics (LLB, LLM). Called to the Bar, Lincoln's Inn, 1971; practice at Revenue Bar, 1972–. *Publications:* (jtly) Introduction to Company Law, 1971, 3rd edn 1987; (jtly) The Law of Partnership Taxation, 1976, 2nd edn 1979; various articles and notes in legal periodicals mainly concerning taxation and company law. *Recreations:* reading, writing letters, working out, thinking. *Address:* Gray's Inn Chambers, Gray's Inn, WC1R 5JA. *T:* 071–242 2642.

GOLDBERG, Jonathan Jacob; QC 1989; *b* 13 Nov. 1947; *s* of late Rabbi Dr P. Selvin Goldberg and Frimette Yudt; *m* 1980, Alexis Jane, *e d* of George Martin, *qv*; one *s* one *d*. *Educ:* Manchester Grammar Sch.; Trinity Hall, Cambridge (MA, LLB). Called to the Bar, Middle Temple, 1971; admitted to NY State Bar, 1985. Northern Circuit, 1972–73; SE Circuit, 1973–; Asst Recorder, 1987. *Recreations:* music, cinema, wine. *Address:* 5 King's Bench Walk, Temple, EC4Y 7DN. *T:* 071–353 4713.

GOLDBERGER, Marvin Leonard, PhD; Director, Institute for Advanced Study, Princeton, New Jersey, since 1987; *b* 22 Oct. 1922; *s* of Joseph Goldberger and Mildred (*née* Sedwitz); *m* 1945, Mildred Ginsburg; two *s*. *Educ:* Carnegie Inst. of Technology (BS); Univ. of Chicago (PhD). Asst to Associate Prof., Univ. of Chicago, 1950–55; Prof., Univ. of Chicago, 1955–57; Princeton University: Higgins Prof. of Mathematical Physics, 1957–77; Chm., Dept of Physics, 1970–76; Joseph Henry Prof. of Physics, 1977–78; Pres., California Inst. of Technology, 1978–87. Hon. ScD: Carnegie-Mellon, 1979; Notre Dame, Indiana, 1979; Hon. DHL: Hebrew Union Coll., 1980; Univ. of Judaism, 1982; Hon. LLD Occidental Coll., 1980. *Publications:* (jtly) Collision Theory, 1964; professional papers in Physical Rev. *Recreations:* jogging, cooking. *Address:* Institute for Advanced Study, Princeton, NJ 08540, USA. *T:* 609–734–8200.

GOLDBLATT, Simon, QC 1972. Called to the Bar, Gray's Inn, 1953 (Bencher, 1982). *Address:* 2 Garden Court, Temple, EC4Y 9BL.

GOLDBY, Prof. Frank; Professor of Anatomy, London University, St Mary's Hospital Medical School, 1945–70, now Emeritus; *b* Enfield, Middlesex, 25 May 1903; *s* of Frank and Ellen Maud Goldby; *m* 1932, Helen Rosa Tomlin; five *s* one *d*. *Educ:* Mercers' School, Holborn; Gonville and Caius College, Cambridge; King's College Hospital; MRCS, LRCP 1926; MRCP 1928; MD (Cambridge), 1936; FRCP, 1963; Resident appointments King's Coll. Hospital, 1926–28; Asst Clinical Pathologist, King's College Hospital, 1929–30; Senior Demonstrator in Anatomy, University College, London, 1931; Lecturer in charge of Anatomy Dept, Hong Kong, 1932–33; Lecturer in Anatomy, University of Cambridge and Fellow of Queens' College, 1934–37; Prof. of Anatomy, Univ. of Adelaide, 1937–45. *Publications:* papers on Embryology and on the Pathology and Comparative Anatomy of the Nervous System. *Address:* 1 St Mark's Court, Barton Road, Cambridge CB3 9LE.

GOLDEN, Surgeon Rear-Adm. Francis St Clair, OBE 1981; QHP 1990; Surgeon Rear-Admiral, Support Medical Services, since 1990; *b* 5 June 1936; *s* of Harry Golden and Nora Golden (*née* Murphy); *m* 1964, Jennifer; two *s* one *d*. *Educ:* Presentation Coll., Cork; University Coll., Cork (MB BCh, BAO); London Univ. (DAvMed); Leeds Univ. (PhD Physiol). GP, Kingston on Thames, 1961–63; HMS Jaguar, 1963–64; RNAS Culdrose, 1964–67; RN Air Med. Sch., 1967–73; Inst. of Naval Medicine, 1973–85; MoD, 1985–86; Fleet MO, 1986–88; MO i/c Haslar, 1988–90. Hon. FNI, 1982. OStJ. *Publications:* papers in sci. jls and chapters in medical textbooks on immersion, drowning, hypothermia. *Recreations:* golf, Rugby, music, reading, cooking. *Address:* c/o Naval Secretary, Ministry of Defence, Old Admiralty Building, Whitehall, SW1. *Club:* Royal Society of Medicine.

GOLDEN, Grace Lydia, ARCA (London); *b* 2 April 1904; *d* of H. F. Golden. *Educ:* City of London Sch. for Girls. Art Training at Chelsea Art Sch. and Royal College of Art; further studies at Regent Street Polytechnic; Black and White Illustrator, Posters, Panoramas, watercolour artist and wood-engraver; Exhibitor at Royal Academy, 1936, 1937, 1938 and 1940; watercolour, Summer Evening, Embankment Gardens, and oil-painting, Free Speech, purchased by Chantry Trustees; work also purchased by V&A Mus., Imp. War Mus., Mus. of London, and S London Art Gall. Retrospective exhibn, South London Art Gall., 1979. *Publication:* Old Bankside, 1951. *Recreation:* theatre. *Address:* 21 Douglas Waite House, 73–75 Priory Road, NW6 3NJ. *T:* 071–624 3204.

GOLDIE, Peter Lawrence; reading philosophy, University College London, since 1990; *b* 5 Nov. 1946; *s* of Kenneth and Norah Goldie; *m* 1990, Sophie Hamilton; two *s* by previous marriage. *Educ:* Felsted Sch., Essex. Chartered Accountant. Chief Executive: Abaco Investments PLC, 1983–86; British & Commonwealth Hldgs, 1987–89; Dir, Guinness Mahon, 1973–83. *Recreation:* physical and mental exercise.

GOLDING, Dame (Cecilie) Monica, DBE 1958; RRC 1950 (ARRC 1940); *b* 6 Aug. 1902; *o d* of Ben Johnson and Clara (*née* Beames); *m* 1961, Brig. the Rev. Harry Golding, CBE (*d* 1969). *Educ:* Croydon Secondary Sch. Professional training: Royal Surrey County Hospital, Guildford, 1922–25; Louise Margaret Hosp., Aldershot and Queen Victoria's Institute of District Nursing. Joined Army Nursing Services, 1925; India, 1929–34; France, 1939–40; Middle East, 1940–43 and 1948–49; Southern Comd, 1943–44 and 1950–52; WO, 1945–46; India and SE Asia, 1946–48; Far East, 1952–55; Eastern Comd, 1955–56; Matron-in-Chief and Dir of Army Nursing Services, 1956–60, retired (with rank of Brig.), 1960. QHNS 1956–60; Col Commandant, Queen Alexandra's Royal Army Nursing Corps, 1961–66. OStJ 1955. *Recreations:* motoring; amateur bird watching and nature study. *Address:* 9 Sandford Court, 32 Belle Vue Road, Southbourne, Bournemouth, Dorset BH6 3DR. *T:* Bournemouth (0202) 431608.

GOLDING, John; General Secretary, National Communications Union, 1986–88; *b* Birmingham, 9 March 1931; *m* 1958, Thelma Gwillym; one *s*; *m* 1980, Llinos Lewis (*see* Llinos Golding). *Educ:* Chester Grammar Sch.; London Univ.; Keele Univ. BA History, Politics, Economics, 1956. Asst Res. Officer, 1960–64, Education Officer, 1964–69, Political and Parly Officer, 1969–86, Post Office Engineering Union. MP (Lab) Newcastle-under-Lyme, 1969–86; PPS to Minister of State, Min. of Technology, Feb.-June 1970; Opposition Whip, July 1970–74; a Lord Comr, HM Treasury, Feb.-Oct. 1974; Parly Under-Sec. of State, Dept of Employment, 1976–79. Chm., Select Cttee on Employment, 1979–82; Former Mem. Select Cttee on Nationalised Industries. Mem., NEC, Lab. Party, 1978–83; Chm., Lab. Party Home Policy Cttee, 1982–83. Governor: University Coll. Hosp., 1970–74; Ruskin Coll., 1970–. *Publications:* co-author Fabian Pamphlets: Productivity Bargaining; Trade Unions—on to 1980. *Address:* 6 Lancaster Avenue, Newcastle-under-Lyme, Staffs ST5 1DR; 31 Westminster Mansions, Great Smith Street, SW1.

GOLDING, John, PhD; painter; Senior Tutor in the School of Painting, Royal College of Art, 1981–86 (Tutor, 1973); *b* 10 Sept. 1929; *s* of Harold S. Golding and Dorothy Hamer. *Educ:* Ridley Coll. (St Catherine's, Ontario); Univ. of Toronto; Univ. of London. BA; MA; PhD. Lectr, 1962–77, and Reader in History of Art, 1977–81, Courtauld Inst., Univ. of London; Slade Prof. of Fine Art, Cambridge Univ., 1976–77. Trustee, Tate Gallery, 1984–91. Hon. Fellow, RCA, 1987. *Publications:* Cubism 1907–14, 1959, 3rd edn 1988; (with Christopher Green) Leger & Purist Paris, 1970; Duchamp: The Bride Stripped Bare by her Bachelors, Even, 1972; (ed with Roland Penrose) Picasso, 1881–1973, 1973. *Address:* 24 Ashchurch Park Villas, W12. *T:* 081–749 5221.

GOLDING, John Anthony, CVO 1966; Queen's Messenger, 1967–80; *b* 25 July 1920; *s* of George Golding, Plaxtol, Kent; *m* 1950, Patricia May, *d* of Thomas Archibald Bickel; two *s*. *Educ:* Bedford Sch.; King's Coll., Auckland. Served with King's African Rifles and Military Administration, Somalia, 1939–46 (Captain). Entered Colonial Service, 1946; Dep. Provincial Comr, Tanganyika, 1961; Administrator, Turks and Caicos Is, 1965–67. *Publication:* Colonialism: the golden years, 1987. *Recreations:* gardening, fishing.

GOLDING, Hon. Sir John (Simon Rawson), Kt 1986; OJ 1980; CD 1974; OBE 1959; Princess Alice Professor of Orthopaedic Surgery, University of the West Indies, since 1965; *b* 15 April 1921; *s* of Mark Golding and Louise Golding; *m* 1961, Alice Patricia Levy; one *s* one *d*. *Educ:* Marlborough College; Cambridge Univ. MA, MB BChir. FRCS 1948. Middlesex Hosp., 1941–46 and 1948–52; RAMC, 1946–48; Royal Nat. Orthop. Hosp., 1952–53; Univ. of the West Indies, 1953–. ABC Travelling Fellow, Amer., British and Canadian Orthopaedic Assoc., 1956; Hunterian Prof., RCS, 1956; Nuffield Fellow, 1961–62. Hon. LLD Univ. of Toronto, 1984. *Publications:* papers in Jl of Bone and Joint Surgery, West Indian Med. Jl, etc. *Recreations:* sailing, walking, bridge. *Address:* 2A Bamboo Avenue, Kingston 6, Jamaica, WI.

GOLDING, Llinos; MP (Lab) Newcastle-under-Lyme, since July 1986; *b* 21 March 1933; *d* of Rt Hon. Ness Edwards, MP and Elina Victoria Edwards; *m* 1st, 1957, Dr John Roland Lewis; one *s* two *d*; 2nd, 1980, John Golding, *qv*. *Educ:* Caerphilly Girls' Grammar Sch.; Cardiff Royal Infirmary Sch. of Radiography. Mem., Soc. of Radiographers. Worked as a radiographer at various times; Assistant to John Golding, MP, 1972–86. An Opposition Whip, 1987–. Vice Chairman: PLP Cttee on Home Affairs; PLP Cttee on Parly Affairs; All Party Parly Gp on Children; Jt Chm., All Party Parly Gp on Homeless. Match Sec., Lords and Commons Fly Fishing Club. Mem., BBC Adv. Council. Former Mem., Dist Manpower Services Cttee; Mem., N Staffs DHA, 1983–. Sec., Newcastle (Dist) Trades Council, 1976–. *Address:* 6 Lancaster Avenue, Newcastle-under-Lyme, Staffs ST5 1DR. *T:* Newcastle (Staffs) (0782) 636200. *Clubs:* King Street Working Men's (Newcastle-under-Lyme); Halmerend Working Men's (Audley).

GOLDING, Dame Monica; *see* Golding, Dame C. M.

GOLDING, Prof. Raymund Marshall, FNZIC; FRACI; FInstP; Vice-Chancellor, James Cook University of North Queensland, since 1986; *b* 17 June 1935; *s* of Austin E. Golding and Marion H. R. Golding; *m* 1962, Ingeborg Carl; two *d*. *Educ:* Auckland Univ., NZ (BSc 1957, MSc 1958); Cambridge Univ. (PhD 1963). Res. and Sen. Res. Scientist, DSIR, NZ, 1957–68; Prof. of Theoretical and Physical Chemistry, 1968–86, Pro-Vice-Chancellor, 1978–86, Univ. of NSW. Hon. DSc Univ. of NSW, 1986. *Publications:* Applied Wave Mechanics, 1969; contribs to books on chem. subjects; numerous research papers and articles. *Recreations:* music, photography. *Address:* James Cook University of North Queensland, Townsville, Queensland 4811, Australia. *T:* (077) 814442. *Clubs:* North Queensland (Townsville); Australasian Pioneers' (Sydney).

GOLDING, Terence Edward, FCA; Chief Executive: National Exhibition Centre, Birmingham, since 1978; International Convention Centre, Birmingham, since 1990; *b* 7 April 1932; *s* of Sydney Richard Golding and Elsie Golding; *m* 1955, Sheila Jean (*née* Francis); one *s* one *d*. *Educ:* Harrow County Grammar Sch. FCA 1967. Earls Court Ltd (Exhibition Hall Proprietors): Chief Accountant, 1960; Co. Sec., 1965; Financial Dir, 1972; Financial Dir, Olympia Ltd, and Earls Court & Olympia Ltd, 1973; Commercial Dir, Earls Court & Olympia Group of Cos, 1975. Chairman: Exhibition Liaison Cttee, 1979 and 1980; Nat. Assoc. of Exhibn Hallowners, 1988–. Director: British Exhibitions Promotion Council, 1981–83; Birmingham Convention and Visitor Bureau, 1981–; Heart of England Tourist Bd, 1984–; Exec. Cttee, Exhibn Industry Fedn, 1988–; Sport Aid Promotions Ltd, 1986–87. Hon. Mem. Council, Birmingham Chamber of Industry and Commerce, 1990–. *Recreation:* following sport. *Address:* Pinn Cottage, Pinner Hill, Pinner, Mddx. *T:* 081–866 2610.

GOLDING, Sir William (Gerald), Kt 1988; CBE 1966; CLit 1984; FRSL 1955; author; *b* 19 Sept. 1911; *s* of Alec A. and Mildred A. Golding; *m* 1939, Ann, *e d* of late E. W. Brookfield, The Homestead, Bedford Place, Maidstone; one *s* one *d*. *Educ:* Marlborough Grammar Sch.; Brasenose Coll., Oxford. MA Oxon 1961. Hon. Fellow, Brasenose Coll., Oxford, 1966. Hon. DLitt: Sussex, 1970; Kent, 1974; Warwick, 1981; Oxford, 1983; Sorbonne, 1983; Hon. LLD Bristol, 1984. Nobel Prize for Literature, 1983. *Publications:* Lord of the Flies, 1954 (filmed 1963); The Inheritors, 1955; Pincher Martin, 1956; Brass Butterfly (play), 1958; Free Fall, 1959; The Spire, 1964; The Hot Gates (essays), 1965; The Pyramid, 1967; The Scorpion God, 1971; Darkness Visible, 1979 (James Tait Black Memorial Prize, 1980); Rites of Passage, 1980 (Booker McConnell Prize); A Moving Target (essays), 1982; The Paper Men, 1984; An Egyptian Journal (travel), 1985; Close Quarters, 1987; Fire Down Below, 1989. *Recreations:* music, Greek, riding. *Address:* c/o Faber & Faber, 3 Queen Square, WC1N 3AU. *Clubs:* Athenæum, Savile.

GOLDINGAY, Rev. Dr John; Principal, St John's College, Nottingham, since 1988; *b* 20 June 1942; *s* of Edgar Charles and Ada Irene Goldingay; *m* 1967, Ann Elizabeth Wilson; two *s*. *Educ:* King Edward's School, Birmingham; Keble Coll., Oxford (BA); Nottingham University (PhD). Asst Curate, Christ Church, Finchley, 1966; Tutor, St John's Coll., Nottingham, 1970. *Publications:* Songs from a Strange Land, 1978; Approaches to Old Testament Interpretation, 1981; Theological Diversity and the Authority of the Old Testament, 1987; Daniel, 1989; (ed) Signs, Wonders and Healing, 1989. *Recreations:* family, Old Testament, France, Israel, rock music. *Address:* 7 Peache Way, Bramcote, Nottingham NG9 3DX. *T:* Nottingham (0602) 224046/251114.

GOLDMAN, Antony John; Under Secretary, Civil Aviation Policy, Department of Transport; *b* 28 Feb. 1940; *s* of Sir Samuel Goldman, *qv*; *m* 1964, Anne Rosemary Lane; three *s*. *Educ:* Marlborough College; Peterhouse, Cambridge (BA). International Computers Ltd, 1961–73; entered Civil Service, DoE, 1973; Private Sec. to Sec. of State for Transport, 1976–78; Asst Sec., 1977; seconded to HM Treasury, 1981–83; Under Sec., 1984. Non. exec. Dir, Hugh Baird & Sons, 1985–86. *Recreations:* music, sailing.

GOLDMAN, Sir Samuel, KCB 1969 (CB 1964); *b* 10 March 1912; *y s* of late Philip and late Sarah Goldman; *m* 1st, 1933, Pearl Marre (*d* 1941); one *s*; 2nd, 1943, Patricia Rosemary Hodges (*d* 1990). *Educ:* Davenant Foundation Sch.; Raine's Sch.; London Sch. of Economics, London Univ. Inter-Collegiate Scholar. BSc (Econ.), First Class Hons in Economics and Gladstone Memorial Prize, 1931; MSc (Econ.), 1933. Hutchinson Silver Medallist. Moody's Economist Services, 1934–38; Joseph Sebag & Co., 1938–39; Bank of England, 1940–47. Entered Civil Service, 1947, as Statistician in Central Statistical Office; transferred to Treasury, Sept. 1947; Chief Statistician, 1948; Asst Sec., 1952; Under-Sec., 1960–62; Third Sec., 1962–68; Second Perm. Sec., 1968–72. UK Alternate Executive Dir, International Bank, 1961–62. Exec. Dir, 1972–74, Man. Dir, 1974–76, Orion Bank Ltd. Chm., Henry Ansbacher Holdings Ltd and Henry Ansbacher Ltd, 1976–82. Chm., Covent Garden Market Authority, 1976–81. Hon. Fellow LSE. *Publication:* Public Expenditure Management and Control, 1973. *Recreations:* music, gardening. *Address:* 3 Little Tangley, Wonersh, Guildford, Surrey GU5 0PW. *T:* Guildford (0483) 68913. *Club:* Reform.

See also A. J. Goldman.

GOLDREIN, Neville Clive, CBE 1991; Consultant, Deacon Goldrein Green, Solicitors, since 1985; Senior Partner, Goldrein & Co., 1953–85; *b* 28 Aug.; *s* of Saville and Nina Goldrein; *m* 1949, Dr Sonia Sumner, MB, BS Dunelm; one *s* one *d*. *Educ:* Hymers Coll., Hull; Pembroke Coll., Cambridge (MA). Served Army: commnd E Yorks Regt; served East Africa Comd (Captain). Admitted Solicitor of the Supreme Court, 1949. Mem., Crosby Bor. Council, 1957–71; Mayor of Crosby, 1966–67, Dep. Mayor, 1967–68; Mem., Lancs CC, 1965–74; Merseyside County Council: Mem., 1973–86; Dep. Leader, Cons. Gp, 1974–77; Vice-Chm. of Council, 1977–80; Leader, 1980–81; Leader, Cons. Gp, 1981–86. Chm., Crosby Constituency Cons. Assoc., 1986–89. Area Vice-Pres., Sefton, St John Ambulance, 1980–87 (Chm., S Sefton Div., 1975–87); Member: NW Econ. Planning Council, 1966–72; Bd of Deputies of British Jews, 1966–85; Council, Liverpool Univ., 1977–81; Council, Merseyside Chamber of Commerce. Director: Merseyside Economic Develt Co. Ltd, 1981–87; Merseyside Waste Derived Fuels Ltd, 1983–86. Vice-Pres., Crosby Mencap, 1967–; Chm., Crosby Hall Residential Trust Appeal. Governor, Merchant Taylors' Sch., Crosby, 1965–74. *Recreations:* swimming, video photography, music, grandchildren. *Address:* Torreno, St Andrew's Road, Blundellsands, Merseyside L23 7UR. *T:* 051–924 2065; (office) Peel House, 5/7 Harrington Street, Liverpool L2 9XP. *T:* 051–255 0600, *Fax:* 051–255 0463. *Club:* Athenæum (Liverpool).

GOLDRING, John Bernard; QC 1987; a Recorder, since 1987; *b* 9 Nov. 1944; *s* of Joseph and Marianne Goldring; *m* 1970, Wendy Margaret Lancaster Bennett; two *s*. *Educ:* Wyggeston Grammar Sch.; Exeter Univ. (LLB). Called to the Bar, Lincoln's Inn, 1969. Standing Prosecuting Counsel to Inland Revenue, Midland and Oxford Circuit, 1985–87. *Recreations:* gardening, ski-ing. *Address:* c/o 2 Crown Office Row, Temple, EC4Y 7HJ. *T:* 071–353 1365.

GOLDRING, Mary Sheila, OBE 1987; freelance economist; presenter, Answering Back, Channel 4 interviews, since 1989; *Educ:* Our Lady's Priory, Sussex; Lady Margaret Hall, Oxford (PPE). Air and Science correspondent, 1949–74, Business editor, 1966–74, Economist Newspaper; economist and broadcaster, 1974–; Presenter, Analysis, BBC, 1977–87. Mem. Selection Cttee, Harkness Fellowships, 1980–86. Trustee, Science Museum, 1987–. Blue Circle Award for industrial journalism, 1979; Sony Radio Award for best current affairs programme (Analysis: Post-Recession Britain), 1985; Industrial Journalist Award, Industrial Soc., 1985; Outstanding Personal Contribution to Radio, Broadcasting Press Guild, 1986; Harold Wincott Award for Broadcasting, 1991. *Publication:* Economics of Atomic Energy, 1957. *Recreation:* small-scale landscaping. *Address:* 37 Sloane Avenue, SW3.

GOLDS, Anthony Arthur, CMG 1971; LVO 1961; HM Diplomatic Service, retired; Director, British National Committee, International Chamber of Commerce, 1977–83; *b* 31 Oct. 1919; *s* of late Arthur Oswald Golds and Florence Golds (*née* Massey); *m* 1944, Suzanne Macdonald Young; one *s* one *d*. *Educ:* King's Sch., Macclesfield; New Coll., Oxford (Scholar). HM Forces (Royal Armoured Corps), 1939–46; CRO, 1948; 1st Sec., Calcutta and Delhi, 1951–53; Commonwealth Office, 1953–56; Head of Chancery, British Embassy, Ankara, 1957–59; Karachi, 1959–61; Counsellor in Commonwealth

Office and Foreign Office, 1962–65; Head of Joint Malaysia/Indonesia Dept, 1964–65; Counsellor, HM Embassy, Rome, 1965–70; Ambassador to the Republic of Cameroon, the Republic of Gabon and the Republic of Equatorial Guinea, 1970–72; High Comr to Bangladesh, 1972–74; Senior Civilian Instructor, RCDS, 1975–76. *Recreations:* music, cricket, golf, literature. *Address:* 4 Oakfield Gardens, SE19 1HF. *T:* 081–670 7621. *Club:* Dulwich & Sydenham Hill Golf.

GOLDSACK, Alan Raymond; QC 1990; a Recorder, since 1988; *b* 13 June 1947; *s* of Raymond Frederick Goldsack, MBE and Mildred Agnes Goldsack (*née* Jones); *m* 1971, Christine Marion Clarke; three *s* one *d*. *Educ:* Hastings Grammar School; Leicester Univ. (LLB). Called to the Bar, Gray's Inn, 1970. *Recreations:* gardening, walking. *Address:* 12 Paradise Square, Sheffield S1 2DE. *T:* Sheffield (0742) 738951.

GOLDSACK, John Redman, MBE 1971; Minister and UK Permanent Representative to UN Food and Agriculture Organisation, Rome, since 1988; *b* 15 Aug. 1932; 2nd *s* of late Bernard Frank and Dorothy Goldsack; *m* 1962, Madeleine Amelia Rowena, *d* of late Stanley and Grace Kibbler; two *s* one *d*. *Educ:* Sutton Grammar Sch., Surrey; Wye Coll., London Univ. (BScAgric); Queens' Coll., Cambridge (DipAgric); Imperial Coll. of Tropical Agric., Trinidad (DTA). Agricl Officer, HMOCS, Kenya, 1956; Hd of Soil Conservation and Planning Officer, Min. of Lands and Settlement, Kenya, 1963–67; Hd of Land Develt Div., Min. of Agriculture, Kenya, 1967–70; Asst Agric. Advr, ODM, 1970–74; Agriculture Adviser: S African Develt Div., 1974–78; ME Develt Div., 1979–81; E. African Develt Div., 1981–83; Sen. Agric. Advr, Asia Div., ODA, 1983–86; Dep. Chief Natural Resources Advr and Prin. Agriculture Advr, ODA, 1986–88. *Recreations:* cricket, golf, natural history. *Address:* c/o Foreign and Commonwealth Office, King Charles Street, SW1A 2AH. *T:* Rome 4825551. *Clubs:* Farmers', MCC.

GOLDSMITH, Alexander Kinglake, (Alick); Deputy Director-General, Export Group for the Constructional Industries; *b* 16 Jan. 1938; *s* of Maj.-Gen. Robert Frederick Kinglake Goldsmith, *qv*; *m* 1971, Deirdre Stafford; one *s* one *d*. *Educ:* Sherborne; Trinity Coll., Oxford (MA Modern History). National Service, 1956–58 (DCLI and Queen's Own Nigeria Regt). Asst Principal, CRO, 1961; Hindi student, SOAS, 1962; Third Sec., New Delhi, 1963; FCO, 1967; First Sec. (Inf.), Wellington, NZ, 1971; FCO, 1975; Head of Chancery, E Berlin, 1978; FCO, 1980; Hd of Commonwealth Co-ordination Dept, FCO, 1982; seconded to Hong Kong Govt, 1984; Consul-Gen., Hamburg, 1986–90. *Recreations:* walking, swimming. *Address:* c/o Lloyds Bank, Butler Place, SW1H 0PR. *Club:* Royal Automobile.

GOLDSMITH, Edward René David; author; Publisher and Editor, The Ecologist, since 1970; *b* 8 Nov. 1928; *s* of late Frank B. H. Goldsmith, OBE, TD, MP (C) for Stowmarket, Suffolk, 1910–18, and Marcelle (*née* Mouiller); *m* 1st, 1953, Gillian Marion Pretty; one *s* two *d*; 2nd, 1981, Katherine Victoria James; two *s*. *Educ:* Magdalen Coll., Oxford (MA Hons). Adjunct Associate Prof., Univ. of Michigan, 1975; Vis. Prof., Sangamon State Univ., 1984. Contested (Ecology Party): Eye, Feb. 1974; Cornwall and Plymouth, European parly election, 1979. *Publications:* (ed) Can Britain Survive?, 1971; (with R. Allen) A Blueprint for Survival, 1972; The Future of an Affluent Society: the case of Canada (report for Env. Canada) 1976; The Stable Society, 1977; (ed with J. M. Brunetti) La Médecine à la Question, 1981; The Social and Environmental Effects of Large Dams, vol. I (with N. Hildyard), 1984, vol. II (ed with N. Hildyard), 1986; (ed with N. Hildyard) Green Britain or Industrial Wasteland?, 1986; (ed with N. Hildyard) The Earth Report, 1988; The Great U-Turn, 1988; (with N. Hildyard and others) 5,000 Days to Save the Planet, 1990. *Address:* 9 Montague Road, Richmond, Surrey TW10 6QW. *Clubs:* Brooks's; Travellers' (Paris).
See also Sir James Goldsmith.

GOLDSMITH, Sir James (Michael), Kt 1976; Chief Executive, Goldsmith Foundation, since 1991; founder of a number of industrial, commercial and financial enterprises; retired from active business, 1990; *b* 26 Feb. 1933; *s* of Frank Goldsmith, OBE and Marcelle Mouiller; *m* 1st, Maria Isabel Patino (*d* 1954); one *d*; 2nd, Ginette Lery; one *s* one *d*; 3rd, Lady Annabel Vane Tempest Stewart; two *s* one *d*. *Educ:* Eton College. Chevalier, Légion d'Honneur, 1978. *Publications:* Counterculture, vol. I, 1985, vol. II, 1987, vol. III, 1990, vol. IV, 1991; Pour la Révolution Permanente, 1986. *Address:* Casa La Loma, Costa Cuixmala, Jalisco, Mexico. *Club:* Travellers' (Paris).
See also E. R. D. Goldsmith.

GOLDSMITH, John Stuart, CB 1984; Director General Defence Accounts, Ministry of Defence, 1980–84; *b* 2 Nov. 1924; *o s* of R. W. and S. E. Goldsmith; *m* 1948, Brenda; two *s* one *d*. *Educ:* Whitgift Middle Sch.; St Catharine's Coll., Cambridge. Royal Signals, 1943–47 (Captain). War Office, 1948; Principal, 1952; Treasury, 1961–64; Asst Sec., MoD, 1964; RCDS 1971; Asst Under-Sec. of State, MoD, 1973; Chm. Civil Service Selection Bd, 1973. *Recreations:* gardening, jazz, travel. *Address:* Cobthorne House, Church Lane, Rode, Somerset BA3 6PN. *T:* Frome (0373) 830681.

GOLDSMITH, Peter Henry; QC 1987; a Recorder, since 1991; *b* 5 Jan. 1950; *s* of Sydney Elland Goldsmith, solicitor, and Myra Goldsmith; *m* 1974, Joy; three *s* one *d*. *Educ:* Quarry Bank High Sch., Liverpool; Gonville and Caius Coll., Cambridge (Sen. Schol., Tapp Postgrad. Schol., Schuldham Plate, 1968–71; MA); UCL (LLM 1972). Called to the Bar, Gray's Inn (Birkenhead Schol.), 1972; a Jun. Counsel to the Crown, Common Law, 1985–87. *Address:* Fountain Court, Temple, EC4. *T:* 071–583 3335.

GOLDSMITH, Philip; Director (observation of the Earth and its environment), European Space Agency, Paris, since 1985; *b* 16 April 1930; *s* of late Stanley Thomas Goldsmith and Ida Goldsmith (*née* Rawlinson); *m* 1st, 1952, Daphne (*d* 1983), *d* of William Webb; two *s* two *d*; 2nd, 1990, Gail Lorrain, *d* of Jack Eyre Rogers. *Educ:* Almondbury Grammar Sch.; Pembroke Coll., Oxford (MA). Meteorologist with the Meteorological Office, 1947–54, incl. National Service, RAF, 1948–50; Research Scientist, AERE Harwell, 1957–67; Meteorological Office: Asst Director (Cloud Physics Research), 1967–76; Dep. Director (Physical Research), 1976–82; Dir (Res.), 1982–84. President: Royal Meteorological Society, 1980–82; Internat. Commn on Atmospheric Chem. and Global Pollution, 1979–83. *Publications:* articles in scientific jls mainly on atmospheric physics and chemistry and associated environmental matters. *Recreations:* golf, gardening, antiques, old cars. *Address:* 83 Boulevard de Montmorency, Paris 75016, France; Hill House, Broad Lane, Bracknell, Berks RG12 3BY. *Clubs:* East Berks Golf, Woodsome Hall Golf.

GOLDSMITH, Maj.-Gen. Robert Frederick Kinglake, CB 1955; CBE 1952; retired; *b* 21 June 1907; *s* of late Col Harry Dundas Goldsmith, CBE, DSO; *m* 1935, Brenda (*d* 1983), *d* of Frank Bartlett, late Ceylon Civil Service; one *s*. *Educ:* Wellington Coll., Berks. Commnd Duke of Cornwall's LI, 1927; served War of 1939–45, in N Africa, Italy, NW Europe; Dep. Chief of Staff, First Allied Airborne Army, 1944–45; comd 131 Inf. Bde (TA), 1950–51; Chief of Staff, British Troops in Egypt, 1951–54, and of HQ Western Command, 1956–59; GOC Yorks District, 1959–62; Col, Duke of Cornwall's LI, 1958–59; Col Somerset and Cornwall LI, 1960–63. Editor, The Army Quarterly, 1966–73. Comdr, Legion of Merit (US) 1945. *Address:* 4 Paternoster House, Colebrook Street, Winchester, Hants SO23 9LG. *Club:* Army and Navy.
See also A. K. Goldsmith.

GOLDSMITH, Walter Kenneth, FCA; FRSA; CBIM; Chairman, Ansoll Estates Ltd, since 1989; *b* 19 Jan. 1938; *s* of Lionel and Phoebe Goldsmith; *m* 1961, Rosemary Adele, *d* of Joseph and Hannah Salter; two *s* two *d*. *Educ:* Merchant Taylors' School. Admitted Inst. of Chartered Accountants, 1960; Manager, Mann Judd & Co., 1964; joined Black & Decker Ltd, 1966: Dir of Investment, Finance and Administration, Europe, 1967; Gen. Man., 1970; Man. Dir, 1974; Chief Executive and European Dir, 1975; Black & Decker USA, 1976–79: Corporate Vice-Pres. and Pres. Pacific Internat. Operations; Dir Gen., Inst. of Dirs, 1979–84; Korn/Ferry International Ltd: Chm., 1984–86; Chief Exec., 1984–85; Chm., Leisure Develt Ltd, 1984–85; Gp Planning and Marketing Dir, Trusthouse Forte plc, 1985–87; Chairman: Food from Britain, 1987–90; Betterware Consumer Products, 1990–; Trident Ltd, 1990–; Dep. Chm., British Food & Farming Ltd, 1990–; Director: Bestobell PLC, 1980–85; BUPA Medical Centre, 1980–84; Director Publications Ltd, 1983–84; The Lesser Group, 1983–85; Bank Leumi (UK), 1984–; Trusthouse Forte Inc., 1985–87; The Winning Streak Ltd, 1985–; The Watts Gp plc, 1987–; Spong plc, 1987–89; Isys Ltd (Dep. Chm.), 1987–; Pearson Paul Haworth Nolan Ltd, 1989–; Mem. Exec. Cttee, Bank Leumi PLC, 1988–. Underwriting Mem., Lloyd's. Member: English Tourist Board, 1982–84; BTA, 1984–86; Chairman: BOTB for Israel, 1987–; Governing Bd, Marketing Quality Assurance, 1990–. Treas., Leo Baeck Coll., 1987–89. Council Member: Co-operation Ireland, 1985–; RASE, 1988–. Trustee, Israel Diaspora Trust, 1982–; Chm. of Trustees, Stress Foundation, 1984–88. Pres., Inst. of Word Processing, 1983–. Liveryman, Worshipful Co. of Chartered Accountants in England and Wales, 1985. Free Enterprise Award, Aims for Industry, 1984. *Publications:* (with D. Clutterbuck): The Winning Streak, 1984; The Winning Streak Workout Book, 1985; (with Berry Ritchie) The New Elite, 1987. *Recreations:* boating, music, painting, property. *Address:* 11 Halland Way, Northwood, Mddx HA6 2AG. *Club:* Carlton.

GOLDSTEIN, Alfred, CBE 1977; FEng; consulting engineer; Senior Partner, Travers Morgan & Partners, 1972–85; Chairman, Travers Morgan Group, 1985–87; *b* 9 Oct. 1926; *s* of late Sigmund and Regina Goldstein; *m* 1959, Anne Milford, *d* of late Col R. A. M. Tweedy and of Maureen Evans, and step *d* of Hubert Evans; two *s*. *Educ:* Rotherham Grammar Sch.; Imperial Coll., Univ. of London. BSc (Eng); ACGI 1946; DIC. FICE 1959; FIStructE 1959; FIHE 1959; MConsE 1959; FEng 1979; FCIT; FCGI 1984. Partner, R. Travers Morgan & Partners, 1951; responsible for planning, design and supervision of construction of major road and bridge projects and for planning and transport studies, incl. M23, Belfast Transportation Plan, Clifton Bridge, Nottingham, Elizabeth Bridge, Cambridge, Itchen Bridge, Southampton. Transport Consultant to Govt SE Jt Planning Team for SE Regional Plan; in charge London Docklands Redevelopment Study; Cost Benefit Study for 2nd Sydney Airport for Govt of Australia; Mem. Cttee on Review of Railway Finances, 1982; UK full mem., EC Article 83 Cttee (Transport), 1982–; TRRL Visitor on Transport Res. and Safety, 1983–87. Member: Building Research Bd, subseq. Adv. Cttee on Building Research, 1963–66; Civil Engrg EDC on Contracting in Civil Engrg since Banwell, 1965–67; Baroness Sharp's Adv. Cttee on Urban Transport Manpower Study, 1967–69; Commn of Inquiry on Third London Airport, 1968–70; Urban Motorways Cttee, 1969–72; Genesys Bd, 1969–74; Chairman: DoE and Dept of Transport Planning and Tnspt Res. Adv. Council, 1973–79; DoE Environmental Bd, 1975–78; Mem., TRRL Adv. Cttee on Transport, 1974–80; Mem. Bd, Coll. of Estate Management, Reading Univ., 1979–. *Publications:* papers and lectures (inc. Criteria for the Siting of Major Airports, 4th World Airports Conf., 1973; Highways and Community Response, 9th Rees Jeffreys Triennial Lecture, RTPI, 1975; Environment and the Economic Use of Energy, (Plenary Paper, Hong Kong Transport Conf., 1982); Decision-taking under Uncertainty in the Roads Sector, PIARC Sydney, 1983; Investment in Transport (Keynote address, CIT Conf., 1983); Buses: social enterprise and business (main paper, 9th annual conf., Bus and Coach Council, 1983); Public Road Transport: a time for change (Keynote address, 6th Aust. passenger trans. conf., 1985); Private Enterprise and Highways (Nat. Res. Council conf., Baltimore, 1986); The Expert and the Public: local values and national choice (Florida Univ.), 1987; Travel in London: is chaos inevitable? (LRT), 1989). *Recreations:* carpentry, music, bridge. *Address:* 136 Long Acre, WC2E 9AE. *T:* 071–836 5474; Kent Edge, Crockham Hill, Edenbridge, Kent TN8 6TA. *T:* Edenbridge (0732) 866227. *Club:* Athenæum.

GOLDSTEIN, Joan Delano, (Mrs Julius Goldstein); *see* Aiken, J. D.

GOLDSTEIN, Prof. Joseph Leonard; physician, genetics educator; Paul J. Thomas Professor of Medicine, and Chairman, Department of Molecular Genetics, since 1977, Regental Professor, since 1985, University of Texas Health Science Centre at Dallas (Member of Faculty, since 1972); *b* 18 April 1940; *s* of Isadore E. and Fannie A. Goldstein. *Educ:* Washington and Lee University (BS); Univ. of Texas Health Science Center at Dallas (MD). Intern, then Resident in Medicine, Mass Gen. Hosp., Boston, 1966–88; clinical associate, NIH, 1968–70; Postdoctoral Fellow, Univ. of Washington, Seattle, 1970–72. Harvey Soc. Lecture, Rockefeller Univ., 1977. Member: Sci. Rev. Bd, Howard Hughes Med. Inst., 1978–84, Med. Adv. Bd, 1985–; Bd of Dirs, Passano Foundn, 1985–; Sci. Adv. Bd, Welch Foundn, 1986–; Fellow, Salk Inst., 1983–. Member, editorial board: Jl Clin. Investigation, 1977–82; Annual Review of Genetics, 1980–85; Arteriosclerosis, 1981–87; Jl Biol Chemistry, 1981–85; Cell, 1983–; Science, 1985–87. Member: Nat. Acad. of Scis (Lounsbery Award, 1979); Amer. Acad. of Arts and Scis, and other bodies. Hon. DSc: Chicago, 1982; Rensselaer Polytechnic Inst., 1982; Washington and Lee Univ., 1986; Univ. of Paris-Sud, 1988; Univ. of Buenos Aires, 1990. Numerous awards from scientific instns, incl. Pfizer Award in Enzyme Chemistry, Amer. Chem. Soc., 1976; award in biol and med. scis, NY Acad. Scis, 1981; Albert Lasker Award in Basic Science (with Michael Brown), 1985; Nobel Prize (with Michael Brown) for Physiology or Medicine, 1985; US Nat. Medal of Science, 1988. *Publications:* (jtly) The Metabolic Basis of Inherited Diseases, 5th edn 1983; papers on genetics educn and science subjects. *Address:* Department of Molecular Genetics, University of Texas Health Science Center, 5323 Harry Hines Boulevard, Dallas, Texas 75235, USA; 3831 Turtle Creek Boulevard, Apt 22-B, Texas 75219, USA.

GOLDSTEIN, Dr Michael, FRSC; Director, Coventry Polytechnic, since 1987; *b* 1 May 1939; *s* of Sarah and Jacob Goldstein; *m* 1962, Janet Sandra Skevington; one *s*. *Educ:* Hackney Downs Grammar School; Northern Polytechnic, London. BSc, PhD, DSc; CChem. Lectr, sen. lectr, principal lectr, Polytechnic of N London, 1963–73; Head of Dept of Chemistry, 1974–83 and Dean of Faculty of Science, 1979–83, Sheffield City Polytechnic; Dep. Dir, Coventry Lanchester Polytechnic, 1983–87. Mem., cttees and bds, CNAA, 1975–, incl. Chm., CNAA Chem. Bd, 1978–84; Member: RSC Council, 1983–86; other RSC cttees, 1975–. *Publications:* contribs to sci. jls, chapters in review books. *Recreations:* soccer, exercise. *Address:* 26 Fairlands Park, Coventry CV4 7DS. *T:* Coventry (0203) 416818.

GOLDSTEIN, Simon Alfred; His Honour Judge Goldstein; a Circuit Judge, since 1987; *b* 6 June 1935; *s* of Harry and Constance Goldstein; *m* 1973, Zoë Philippa, *yr d* of Basil Gerrard Smith, *qv*. *Educ:* East Ham Grammar Sch.; Fitzwilliam Coll., Cambridge

(BA 1956). Educn Officer, RAF, 1957–60. Called to the Bar, Middle Temple, 1961; Dep. Circuit Judge, 1975; a Recorder, 1980–87. *Recreation:* bridge. *Address:* 1 Albion Close, W2. *Club:* London Duplicate Bridge.

GOLDSTEIN-JACKSON, Kevin Grierson, JP; writer; company director; *b* 2 Nov. 1946; *s* of H. G. and W. M. E. Jackson; *m* 1975, Jenny Mei Leng, *e d* of Ufong Ng, Malaysia; two *d*. *Educ:* Reading Univ. (BA Phil. and Sociol.); Southampton Univ. (MPhil Law). Staff Relations Dept, London Transport (Railways), 1966; Scottish Widows Pension & Life Assurance Soc., 1967; Prog. Organizer, Southern TV, 1970–73; Asst Prod., HK-TVB, Hong Kong, 1973; freelance writer/TV prod., 1973–75; Head of Film, Dhofar Region TV Service, Sultanate of Oman, 1975–76; Founder and Dir, Thames Valley Radio, 1974–77; Asst to Head of Drama, Anglia TV, 1977–81; Founder, TSW-Television South West: Programme Controller and Dir of Progs, 1981–85; Jt Man. Dir, 1981–82; Chief Exec., 1982–85. Writer of TV scripts. Dir of private cos. Gov., Lilliput First Sch., Poole, 1988–. FRSA 1978; FBIM 1982; FInstD 1982; FFA 1988; FRGS 1989. JP Poole, 1990. *Publications:* books incl.: The Right Joke for the Right Occasion, 1973; Experiments with Everyday Objects, 1976; Things to make with Everyday Objects, 1978; Magic with Everyday Objects, 1979; Dictionary of Essential Quotations, 1983; Jokes for Telling, 1986; Share Millions, 1989; contrib. law, sociol, financial and gen. pubns. *Recreations:* writing, TV, films, theatre, travel, music, walking, philosophical and sociological investigation. *Address:* c/o Alcazar, 18 Martello Road, Branksome Park, Poole, Dorset BH13 7DH.

GOLDSTONE, David Israel, CBE 1971; JP; DL; Chairman, Sterling McGregor Ltd Group of Companies; *b* Aug. 1908; *s* of Philip and Bessie Goldstone; *m* 1931, Belle Franks; one *s* two *d*. Manchester Chamber of Commerce and Industry: Pres., 1970–72; Emeritus Dir, 1978; Chm., Pension Bd, 1968; Chm., NW Regions Chambers of Commerce Council, 1970–73; Exec. Mem., Association British Chambers of Commerce Nat. Council, 1970–73; Exec. Mem., British Nat. Council, Internat. Chambers of Commerce; Mem., NW Telecommunications Bd. Vice-Pres., Greater Manchester Youth Assoc.; Founder Trustee and Vice-Pres., Greater Manchester Museum of Science and Industry; Mem. local tribunals, charitable organisations, etc. JP Manchester, 1958; DL Manchester, 1978; High Sheriff of Greater Manchester, 1980–81. Hon. MA Manchester, 1979. *Address:* Dellstar, Elm Road, Didsbury, Manchester M20 0XD. *T:* 061–445 1868.

GOLDSTONE, David Joseph; Chairman since 1990, and Chief Executive since 1970, Regalian Properties Plc; *b* 21 Feb. 1929; *s* of Solomon Goldstone and Rebecca Goldstone (*née* Degotts); *m* 1957, Cynthia (*née* Easton); one *s* two *d*. *Educ:* Dynevor Secondary Sch., Swansea; London School of Economics and Political Science (LLB Hons). Admitted Solicitor (Hons), 1955. Legal practice, 1955–66. Member Council: Football Assoc. of Wales, 1970–72; WNO, 1984–89. Member, Court of Governors: LSE, 1985–; Atlantic Coll., 1987–. *Recreations:* family, reading, farming, sport. *Address:* 44 Grosvenor Hill, W1A 4NR. *T:* 071–493 9613. *Clubs:* Royal Automobile; Bath & Racquets, Riverside Racquet Centre.

GOLDSTONE, Prof. Jeffrey, PhD; FRS 1977; Cecil and Ida Green Professor in Physics, Massachusetts Institute of Technology, since 1983 (Director, Center for Theoretical Physics, 1983–89); *b* 3 Sept. 1933; *s* of Hyman Goldstone and Sophia Goldstone; *m* 1980, Roberta Gordon; one *s*. *Educ:* Manchester Grammar Sch.; Trinity Coll., Cambridge (MA 1956, PhD 1958). Trinity Coll., Cambridge: Entrance Scholar, 1951; Res. Fellow, 1956; Staff Fellow, 1962; Cambridge University: Lectr, 1961; Reader in Math. Physics, 1976; Prof. of Physics, MIT, 1977. Vis. appointments: Institut for Teoretisk Fysik, Copenhagen; CERN, Geneva; Harvard Univ.; MIT; Inst. for Theoretical Physics, Santa Barbara; Stanford Linear Accelerator Center; Lab. de Physique Théorique, L'Ecole Normale Supérieure, Paris; Università di Roma I. Smith's Prize, Cambridge Univ., 1955; Dannie Heineman Prize, Amer. Phys. Soc., 1981; Guthrie Medal, Inst. of Physics, 1983. *Publications:* articles in learned jls. *Address:* Department of Physics, (6–313) Massachusetts Institute of Technology, Cambridge, Mass 02139, USA. *T:* (office) 617–253–6263.

GOLDSTONE, Peter Walter; His Honour Judge Goldstone; a Circuit Judge, since 1978; *b* 1 Nov. 1926; *y s* of late Adolph Lionel Goldstone and Ivy Gwendoline Goldstone; *m* 1955, Patricia (*née* Alexander), JP; one *s* two *d*. *Educ:* Manchester Grammar Sch.; Manchester Univ. Solicitor, 1951. Fleet Air Arm, 1944–47. Partner in private practice with brother Julian S. Goldstone, 1951–71. Manchester City Councillor (L), 1963–66; Chm., Manchester Rent Assessment Panel, 1967–71; Reserve Chm., Manchester Rent Tribunal, 1969–71; Dep. Chm., Inner London QS, Nov. 1971; a Metropolitan Stipendiary Magistrate, 1971–78; a Recorder of the Crown Court, 1972–78. *Recreations:* walking, gardening, reading. *Address:* c/o St Albans Crown Court, Civic Centre, St Albans, Herts. *T:* 081–954 1901. *Club:* MCC.

GOLDSWORTHY, Rt. Rev. (Arthur) Stanley; Parish Priest of Tailem Bend, Meningie, SA; *b* 18 Feb. 1926; *s* of Arthur and Doris Irene Goldsworthy; *m* 1952, Gwen Elizabeth Reeves; one *s* one *d*. *Educ:* Dandenong High School, Vic; St Columb's Theological Coll., Wangaratta. Deacon 1951, priest 1952; Curate of Wodonga, in charge of Bethanga, 1951–52; Priest of Chiltern, 1952; Kensington, Melbourne, 1955; Yarrawonga, Wangaratta, 1959; Shepparton (and Archdeacon), 1972; Parish Priest of Wodonga, and Archdeacon of Diocese of Wangaratta, 1977; Bishop of Bunbury, 1977–83; Parish Priest of St John, Hendra, Brisbane, 1983; an Assisting Bishop to Primate of Australia, 1983. Chaplain to Community of the Sisters of the Church, 1956–77. *Recreations:* music, bush walking. *Address:* PO Box 191, Meningie, SA 5264, Australia. *T:* (085) 75 1020.

GOLDTHORPE, Brian Lees, FCIB; Director, since 1983, and Deputy Chief Executive, since 1989, Midland Bank plc; *b* 11 June 1933; *s* of Gordon and Winifred Mary Goldthorpe; *m* 1957, Mary (Molly) Commins; one *s* one *d*. *Educ:* Wath-on-Dearne Grammar Sch. Midland Bank: joined, 1949; various Br., Reg. and Hd Office posts, 1949–77; Gen. Man. (Operations), 1977–80; Gen. Man., N Div., 1980–81; Sen. Gen. Man. and Chief Exec., Forward Trust Gp, 1981–83; Chief Executive: Gp Risk Management, 1983–86; Corporate Banking, 1986–87; UK Banking Sector, 1987–89. *Recreations:* music, golf. *Address:* Midland Bank, Poultry, EC2P 2BX. *T:* 071–260 8000.

GOLDTHORPE, John Harry, FBA 1984; Official Fellow, Nuffield College, Oxford, since 1969; *b* 27 May 1935; *s* of Harry Goldthorpe and Lilian Eliza Goldthorpe; *m* 1963, Rhiannon Esyllt (*née* Harry); one *s* one *d*. *Educ:* Wath-upon-Dearne Grammar School; University College London (BA Hons 1st Class Mod. Hist.); LSE. MA Cantab; MA Oxon. Asst Lectr, Dept of Sociology, Univ. of Leicester, 1957–60; Fellow of King's College, Cambridge, 1960–69; Asst Lectr and Lectr, Faculty of Economics and Politics, Cambridge, 1962–69. Lectures: Fuller, Univ. of Essex, 1979; Marshall, Univ. of Southampton, 1989. Mem., Academia Europaea, 1988. Hon. FilDr Stockholm Univ., 1990. *Publications:* The Affluent Worker: industrial attitudes and behaviour (with David Lockwood and others), 1968; The Affluent Worker: political attitudes and behaviour (with David Lockwood and others), 1968; The Affluent Worker in the Class Structure (with David Lockwood and others), 1969; The Social Grading of Occupations (with Keith Hope), 1974; The Political Economy of Inflation (with Fred Hirsch), 1978; Social Mobility and Class Structure in Modern Britain, 1980, 2nd edn 1987; Order and Conflict

in Contemporary Capitalism, 1984; Die Analyse Sozialer Ungleichheit (with Hermann Strasser), 1985; (contrib.) John H. Goldthorpe: consensus and controversy (ed Clark, Modgil and Modgil), 1990; papers in American Jl of Sociology, British Jl of Sociology, Sociological Review, Sociology, European Jl of Sociology, Sociologie du Travail. *Recreations:* lawn tennis, bird watching, computer chess. *Address:* 32 Leckford Road, Oxford OX2 6HX. *T:* Oxford (0865) 56602.

GOLDWATER, Barry M(orris); US Senator from Arizona, 1953–64, and 1969–87; *b* Phoenix, Arizona, 1 Jan. 1909; *s* of late Baron Goldwater and Josephine Williams; *m* 1934, Margaret Johnson (*d* 1985); two *s* two *d*. *Educ:* Staunton Mil. Acad., Virginia; University of Arizona. 2nd Lieut, Army Reserve, 1930; transferred to USAAF, 1941; served as ferry-command and fighter pilot instructor, Asia, 1941–45 (Lieut-Col); Chief of Staff, Arizona Nat. Guard, 1945–52 (Col); Maj.-Gen., USAF Reserves. Joined Goldwater's Inc., 1929 (Pres., 1937–53). City Councilman, Phoenix, 1949–52; Republican Candidate for the Presidency of the USA, 1964. Chm., Senate Armed Services Cttee, 1985–; Member: Advisory Cttee on Indian Affairs, Dept of Interior, 1948–50; Commerce, Science and Transportation Cttee; Small Business Cttee; Heard Museum; Museum of Northern Arizona; St Joseph's Hosp.; Vice-Chairman: Amer. Graduate Sch. of Internat. Management; Bd of Regents, Smithsonian Institution; Member: Veterans of Foreign Wars; American Legion; Royal Photographic Society, etc. US Junior Chamber of Commerce Award, 1937; Man of the Year, Phoenix, 1949; Medal of Freedom, 1986. 33° Mason. *Publications:* Arizona Portraits (2 vols), 1940; Journey Down the River of Canyons, 1940; Speeches of Henry Ashurst: The Conscience of a Conservative, 1960; Why Not Victory?, 1962; Where I Stand, 1964; The Face of Arizona, 1964; People and Places, 1967; The Conscience of the Majority, 1970; Delightful Journey, 1970; The Coming Breakpoint, 1976; With No Apologies, 1979. *Address:* PO Box 1601, Scottsdale, Arizona 85252, USA.

GOLIGHER, Prof. John Cedric, ChM, FRCS; Professor and Chairman, Department of Surgery, Leeds University, 1954–77, now Emeritus; Consulting Surgeon, St Mark's Hospital for Diseases of Rectum and Colon, London, since 1954; *b* Londonderry, N Ireland, 13 March 1912; *s* of John Hunter Goligher; *m* 1952, Gwenllian Nancy, *d* of Norman R. Williams, Melbourne, Aust.; one *s* two *d*. *Educ:* Foyle Coll., Londonderry; Edinburgh Univ. MB, ChB 1934; ChM 1948, Edinburgh; FRCS, FRCSE 1938. Junior hosp. appts mainly in Edinburgh area; Res. Surg. Officer, St Mark's Hosp., London; served War 1940–46, RAMC, as Surgical Specialist; then Surgical Registrar, St Mary's Hosp., London; Surg., St Mary's Hosp., and St Mark's Hosp. for Diseases of the Rectum and Colon, 1947–54. Mem. Council, RCS, 1968–80. FRSocMed (Past Pres., Section of Proctology); Fellow, Assoc. Surgeons of Gt Brit. and Ire. (Past Pres.); Mem. Brit. Soc. of Gastroenterology (Past Pres.). Hon. FACS, 1974; Hon. FRCSI, 1977; Hon. FRACS, 1978; Hon. FRSM 1986; Hon. Fellow: Brasilian Coll. of Surgeons; Amer. Surg. Assoc.; Amer. Soc. of Colon and Rectal Surgeons; Soc. for Surgery of the Alimentary Tract. Corresp. Mem., German Surgical Soc.; Hon. Mem., French, Swiss and Austrian Surg. Socs. Many vis. professorships and named lectures in UK, Europe, N and S America, ME, FE and the Antipodes. Hon. MD: Göteborg, 1976; Belfast, 1981; Uruguay, 1983; Hon. DSc Leeds, 1980. Liston Award, RCSE, 1977; Lister Award, RCS, 1981. *Publications:* Surgery of the Anus, Rectum and Colon, 1961, 5th edn 1984; numerous contribs to books and med. journals, dealing mainly with gastric and colorectal surgery. *Recreations:* reading, tennis, music, gastronomy, travel. *Address:* Ladywood, Northgate Lane, Linton, Wetherby, West Yorks LS22 4HP.

GOLLANCZ, Livia Ruth; Chairman, Victor Gollancz Ltd, 1983–89 (Governing Director, Joint Managing Director, 1965–85, Consultant, since 1990); *b* 25 May 1920; *d* of Victor Gollancz and Ruth Lowy. *Educ:* St Paul's Girls' Sch.; Royal Coll. of Music (ARCM, solo horn). Horn player: LSO, 1940–43; Hallé Orch., 1943–45; Scottish Orch., 1945–46; BBC Scottish Orch., 1946–47; Covent Garden, 1947; Sadler's Wells, 1950–53. Joined Victor Gollancz Ltd as editorial asst and typographer, 1953; Dir, 1954. *Publication:* (ed and introd) Victor Gollancz, Reminiscences of Affection, 1968 (posthumous). *Recreations:* singing, hill walking, gardening. *Address:* 14 Henrietta Street, WC2E 8QJ. *Club:* Alpine.

GOLLIN, Prof. Alfred M., DLitt; FRSL; Professor of History, University of California, Santa Barbara, since 1967 (Chairman, Department of History, 1976–77); *b* 6 Feb. 1926; 2nd *s* of Max and Sue Gollin; *m* 1st, 1951, Gurli Sørensen (marr. diss.); two *d*; 2nd, 1975, Valerie Watkins (*née* Kilner). *Educ:* New York City Public Schs; City College of New York; Harvard Univ.; New Coll., Oxford (BA); St Antony's Coll., Oxford (MA); DPhil Oxon 1957; DLitt Oxon 1968. Served US Army, 1943–46; taught history at New Coll., Oxford, 1951–54; official historian for The Observer, 1952–59; Lectr, City Coll. of New York, 1959; Univ. of California, Los Angeles: Acting Asst Prof., 1959–60; Research Associate, 1960–61; Associate Prof., Univ. of California, Santa Barbara, 1966–67. Dir, Study Center of Univ. of California, UK and Ire., 1971–73; Mem., US-UK Educnl Commn, 1971–72. Fellow: J. S. Guggenheim Foundn, 1962, 1964, 1971; Amer. Council of Learned Socs, 1963, 1975; Nat. Endowment for Humanities, 1989; FRHistS 1976; FRSL 1986. *Publications:* The Observer and J. L. Garvin, 1960; Proconsul in Politics: a study of Lord Milner, 1964; From Omdurman to V. E. Day: the Life Span of Sir Winston Churchill, 1964; Balfour's Burden, 1965; Asquith, a New View, in A Century of Conflict, Essays for A. J. P. Taylor, 1966; Balfour, in The Conservative Leadership (ed D. Southgate), 1974; No Longer an Island, 1984; The Impact of Air Power on the British People and their Government 1909–14, 1989; articles and reviews in various jls. *Recreation:* swimming. *Address:* Department of History, University of California, Santa Barbara, Calif 93106, USA. *Clubs:* Reform, National Liberal.

GOLOMBEK, Harry, OBE 1966; Chess Correspondent, The Times, since 1945; writer on chess; *b* London, 1 March 1911; *s* of Barnet and Emma Golombek; unmarried. *Educ:* Wilson's Gram. Sch.; London Univ. Editor British Chess Magazine, 1938, 1939, 1940. Served in RA, 1940–42, Foreign Office, 1942–45. Joint Editor, British Chess Magazine, 1949–67; Chess corresp. for The Observer, 1955–79. British Chess Champion, 1947, 1949, and 1955 (prize-winner 14 times); Jt British Veteran Chess Champion, 1984; 1st prize in 4 international chess tournaments. Recognized as international master by Federation Internationale des Echecs, 1948; Internat. Grandmaster, World Chess Fedn, 1985. Represented Great Britain in 9 Chess Olympiads and capt. Brit. team, Helsinki, 1952, Amsterdam, 1954, Munich, 1958, Leipzig, 1960, Varna, 1962. Pres., Zone 1 World Chess Fedn, 1974–78. *Publications:* 50 Great Games of Modern Chess, 1942; Capablanca's 100 Best Games of Chess, 1947; World Chess Championship, 1948, 1949; Pocket Guide to Chess Openings, 1949; Hastings Tournament, 1948–49, 1949; Southsea Tournament, 1949, 1949; Prague, 1946, 1950, Budapest, 1952, 1952; Reti's Best Games of Chess, 1954; World Chess Championship, 1954, 1954; The Game of Chess (Penguin), 1954; 22nd USSR Chess Championship, 1956; World Chess Championship, 1957, 1957; Modern Opening Chess Strategy, 1959; Fischer *v* Spassky 1972, 1973; A History of Chess, 1976; (with W. Hartston) The Best Games of C. H. O'D. Alexander, 1976; Encyclopedia of Chess, 1977 (new edn 1981 as Penguin Handbook); Beginning Chess, 1981. *Recreations:* music, the Stock Exchange and the theatre. *Address:* Albury, 35 Albion Crescent, Chalfont

St Giles, Bucks HP8 4ET. *T:* Chalfont (02407) 2808. *Clubs:* Athenæum; Surrey County Cricket.

GOLT, Sidney, CB 1964; Consultant; Director: Malmgren Inc. (Washington DC); Malmgren, Golt, Kingston & Co. Ltd; *b* West Hartlepool, 31 March 1910; *s* of late Wolf and Fanny Golt; *m* 1947, Jean, *d* of Ralph Oliver; two *d. Educ:* Portsmouth Grammar Sch.; Christ Church, Oxford. PPE 1931; James Mew Scholar, Oxford, 1934; Statistician, Tin Producers' Assoc., 1936–40; joined Central Price Regulation Cttee, 1941; Asst Sec., Bd of Trade, 1945–60; Sec., Central Price Regulation Cttee, 1945–46; Under-Sec., Bd of Trade, 1960–68, Adviser on Commercial Policy, 1964–68, Deputy Secretary, 1968–70. UK Mem., Preparatory Cttee for European Free Trade Assoc., Geneva, 1960; Leader, UK Delegns to UN Conf. on Trade and Development, New Delhi, 1968, and to Trade and Development Bd, 1965–68; UK Mem., Commonwealth Gp of Experts on Internat. Economic Policy, 1975–77; Advr on Internat. Trade, Internat. Chamber of Commerce, 1978–90. Chm., Linked Life Assurance Gp, 1972–81. *Publications:* Ed., Tin, and Tin World Statistics, 1936–40; (jtly) Towards an Open World Economy, 1972; The GATT Negotiations, 1974, 1978; The New Mercantilism, 1974; The Developing Countries in the GATT System, 1978; (jtly) Western Economies in Transition, 1980; Trade Issues in the Mid 1980's, 1982; The GATT Negotiations 1986–1990, 1988. *Recreations:* travel, looking at pictures, bridge. *Address:* 37 Rowan Road, W6 7DT. *T:* 071–602 1410. *Club:* Reform.

GOMBRICH, Sir Ernst (Hans Josef), OM 1988; Kt 1972; CBE 1966; FBA 1960; FSA 1961; PhD (Vienna); MA Oxon and Cantab; Director of the Warburg Institute and Professor of the History of the Classical Tradition in the University of London, 1959–76, now Emeritus Professor; *b* Vienna, 30 March 1909; *s* of Dr Karl B. Gombrich, Vice-Pres. of Disciplinary Council of Lawyers' Chamber, Vienna, and Prof. Leonie Gombrich (*née* Hock), pianist; *m* 1936, Ilse Heller; one *s. Educ:* Theresianum, Vienna; Vienna Univ. Research Asst, Warburg Inst., 1936–39. Served War of 1939–45 with BBC Monitoring Service. Senior Research Fellow, 1946–48, Lectr, 1948–54, Reader, 1954–56, Special Lectr, 1956–59, Warburg Inst., Univ. of London; Durning-Lawrence Prof. of the History of Art, London Univ., at University Coll., 1956–59; Slade Prof. of Fine Art in the University of Oxford, 1950–53; Visiting Prof. of Fine Art, Harvard Univ., 1959; Slade Prof. of Fine Art, Cambridge Univ., 1961–63; Lethaby Prof., RCA, 1967–68; Andrew D. White Prof.-at-Large, Cornell, 1970–77. A Trustee of the British Museum, 1974–79; Mem., Museums and Galleries Commn (formerly Standing Commn on Museums and Galleries), 1976–82. Hon. Fellow, Jesus Coll., Cambridge, 1963; FRSL 1975; Foreign Hon. Mem., American Academy of Arts and Sciences, 1964; For. Mem., Amer. Philosophical Soc., 1968; Hon. Member: American Acad. and Inst. of Arts and Letters, 1985; Akad. der Wissenschaften zu Göttingen, 1986; Modern Lang. Assoc. of America, 1988; Deutsche Akademie für Sprache und Dichtung, 1988; Austrian Acad. of Scis, 1991; Corresponding Member: Accademia delle Scienze di Torino, 1962; Royal Acad. of Arts and Sciences, Uppsala, 1970; Koninklijke Nederlandse Akademie van Wetenschapen, 1973; Bayerische Akad. der Wissenschaften, 1979; Royal Swedish Acad. of Sciences, 1981; European Acad. of Arts, Scis and Humanities, 1980; Accademia Nazionale dei Lincei, 1983; Royal Belgian Acad. of Science, Letters and Fine Arts, 1989. Hon. FRIBA, 1971; Hon. Fellow: Royal Acad. of Arts, 1982; Bezalel Acad. of Arts and Design, 1983. Hon. DLit: Belfast, 1963; London, 1976; Hon. LLD St Andrews, 1965; Hon. LittD: Leeds, 1965; Cambridge, 1970; Manchester, 1974; Hon. DLitt: Oxford, 1969; Harvard, 1976; New York, 1986; Hon. Dr Lit. Hum.: Chicago, 1975; Pennsylvania, 1977; DU Essex, 1977; Hon. DHL: Brandeis, 1981; Emory, 1991; Hon. Dr RCA, 1984. W. H. Smith Literary Award, 1964; Medal of New York Univ. for Distinguished Visitors, 1970; Erasmus Prize, 1975; Ehrenkreuz für Wissenschaft und Kunst, 1st cl., Austria, 1975; Hegel Prize, 1976; Medal of Collège de France, 1977; Orden Pour le Mérite für Wissenschaften und Künste, 1977; Ehrenzeichen für Wissenschaft und Kunst, Austria 1984; Premio Rosina Viva of Anacapri, 1985; Internat. Balzan Prize, 1985; Kulturpreis der Stadt Wien, 1986; Ludwig Wittgenstein-Preis der Österreichischen Forschungsgemeinschaft, 1988; Britannica Award, Encyclopedia Britannica, 1989; Goethe Medaille, 1989. *Publications:* Weltgeschichte für Kinder, 1936, rev. and enl. edn 1985; (with E. Kris) Caricature, 1940; The Story of Art, 1950, 15th edn 1989; Art and Illusion (The A. W. Mellon Lectures in the Fine Arts, 1956), 1960; Meditations on a Hobby Horse, 1963; Norm and Form, 1966; Aby Warburg, an intellectual biography, 1970; Symbolic Images, 1972; In Search of Cultural History, 1972; (jtly) Art, Perception and Reality, 1973; (ed jtly) Illusion in Nature and Art, 1973; Art History and the Social Sciences (Romanes Lect.), 1975; The Heritage of Apelles, 1976; Means and Ends (W. Neurath Lect.), 1976; The Sense of Order (Wrightsman Lect.), 1979; Ideals and Idols, 1979; The Image and the Eye, 1982; Tributes, 1984; New Light on Old Masters, 1986; Oskar Kokoschka in his Time, 1986; Reflections on the History of Art (ed R. Woodfield), 1987; contributions to learned journals.*Address:* 19 Briardale Gardens, NW3 7PN. *T:* 071–435 6639.

See also R. F. Gombrich.

GOMBRICH, Prof. Richard Francis, DPhil; Boden Professor of Sanskrit, Oxford University, since 1976; Fellow of Balliol College, Oxford, since 1976; Emeritus Fellow of Wolfson, 1977; *b* 17 July 1937; *s* of Sir Ernst Gombrich, *qv*; *m* 1st, 1964, Dorothea Amanda Friedrich (marr. diss. 1984); one *s* one *d*; 2nd, 1985, Sanjukta Gupta. *Educ:* Magdalen Coll., Oxford (MA, DPhil); Harvard Univ. (AM). Univ. Lectr in Sanskrit and Pali, Oxford Univ., 1965–76; Fellow of Wolfson Coll., 1966–76. Stewart Fellow, Princeton Univ., 1986–87. Hon. Sec., Pali Text Soc., 1982–. *Publications:* Precept and Practice: traditional Buddhism in the rural highlands of Ceylon, 1971; (with Margaret Cone) The Perfect Generosity of Prince Vessantara, 1977; On being Sanskritic, 1978; (ed with Heinz Bechert) The World of Buddhism, 1984; Theravada Buddhism: a social history from ancient Benares to modern Colombo, 1988; (with G. Obeyesekere) Buddhism Transformed, 1988; contribs to oriental and anthropological journals. *Recreations:* singing, walking, photography. *Address:* Balliol College, Oxford OX1 3BJ.

GOMERSALL, Stephen John; HM Diplomatic Service; Head of Security Policy Department, Foreign and Commonwealth Office, since 1990; *b* 17 Jan. 1948; *s* of Harry Raymond Gomersall and Helen Gomersall; *m* 1975, Lydia Veronica (*née* Parry); two *s* one *d. Educ:* Forest Sch., Snaresbrook; Queens' Coll., Cambridge (Mod. Langs, MA); Stanford Univ., Calif (MA 1970). Entered HM Diplomatic Service, 1970; Tokyo, 1972–77; Rhodesia Dept, FCO, 1977–79; Private Sec. to Lord Privy Seal, 1979–82; Washington, 1982–85; Econ. Counsellor, Tokyo, 1986–90. *Recreations:* music, composing silly songs. *Address:* c/o Foreign and Commonwealth Office, King Charles Street, SW1A 2AH.

GOMEZ, Jill; singer; *b* Trinidad, of Spanish and English parents. *Educ:* Royal Academy of Music and Guildhall School of Music, London. Operatic début with Glyndebourne Festival Opera, 1969, where she won the John Christie Award and has subseq. sung leading roles, incl. Mélisande, Calisto, Anne Truelove in The Rake's Progress, Helena in A Midsummer Night's Dream; has appeared with The Royal Opera, English Opera Gp, ENO, WNO and Scottish Opera in roles including Pamina, Ilia, Fiordiligi, The Countess in Figaro, Elizabeth in Elegy for Young Lovers, Tytania, Lauretta in Gianni Schicchi, the Governess in The Turn of the Screw, Jenifer in The Midsummer Marriage, Leila in Les Pêcheurs de Perles; with Kent Opera: Tatiana in Eugene Onegin, 1977; Violetta in La Traviata, 1979; Amyntas in Il Re Pastore, 1987; Violetta in La Traviata, 1988; Donna Anna in Don Giovanni, 1989; created the role of Flora in Tippett's The Knot Garden, at Covent Garden, and of the Countess in Thea Musgrave's Voice of Ariadne, Aldeburgh, 1974; created title role in William Alwyn's Miss Julie for radio, 1977; title rôle BBC world première, Prokoviev's Maddalena, 1979; other rôles include Donna Elvira, Cinna in Mozart's Lucio Silla, Cleopatra in Giulio Cesare, Teresa in Benvenuto Cellini, title rôle in Massenet's Thaïs, Desdemona in Otello, at Edinburgh, Wexford, and in Austria, France, Germany and Switzerland. Also recitalist; première of Eighth Book of Madrigals, Monteverdi Fest., Zürich, 1979; concert repertoire includes Rameau, Bach, Handel (Messiah and cantatas), Haydn's Creation and Seasons, Mozart's Requiem and concert arias, Beethoven's Ninth, Berlioz's Nuits d'Eté, Brahms's Requiem, Fauré's Requiem, Ravel's Shéhérazade, Mahler's Second, Fourth and Eighth Symphonies, Strauss's Four Last Songs, Britten's Les Illuminations, Spring Symphony and War Requiem, Tippett's A Child of Our Time, Messiaen's Poèmes pour Mi, Webern op. 13 and 14 songs, and Schubert songs orch. Webern. Commissioned Cantiga—the song of Iñes de Castro (dramatic scena for soprano and orch.) from David Matthews (world première, BBC Prom., 1988). Regular engagements in France, Belgium, Holland, Germany, Scandinavia, Switzerland, Italy, Spain, Israel, America; festival appearances include Aix-en-Provence, Spoleto, Bergen, Versailles, Flanders, Holland, Prague, Edinburgh, Aldeburgh, and BBC Prom. concerts. Recent recordings include three solo recitals (French, Spanish, and songs by Mozart), Ravel's Poèmes de Mallarmé, Handel's Admeto, Acis and Galatea, Elvira in Don Giovanni, Fauré's Pelléas et Mélisande, Handel's Ode on St Cecilia's Day, Rameau's La Danse, Britten's Quatre Chansons Françaises, and Les Illuminations, Canteloube's Songs of the Auvergne, Villa Lobos' Bachianas Brasilieras no 5, Samuel Barber's Knoxville—Summer of 1915, Cabaret Classics (with John Constable), and South of the Border. *Address:* 16 Milton Park, N6 5QA.

GOMM, Richard Culling C.; *see* Carr-Gomm, R. C.

GOMME, Robert Anthony, CB 1990; Under Secretary, Department of the Environment, 1981–90, retired; *b* 19 Nov. 1930; *s* of Harold Kenelm Gomme and Alice Grace (*née* Jacques); *m* 1960, Helen Perris (*née* Moore); one *s* one *d. Educ:* Colfe's Grammar Sch., Lewisham; London School of Economics, Univ. of London (BScEcon 1955). National Service, Korea, with Royal Norfolk Regt, 1951–52; Pirelli Ltd, 1955–66; NEDO, 1966–68; direct entrant Principal, Min. of Public Building and Works, 1968; Asst Sec., DoE, 1972; RCDS 1975; Cabinet Office, 1976–78. *Address:* 14 Vanbrugh Fields, Blackheath, SE3 7TZ. *T:* 081–858 5148.

GOMPERTZ, (Arthur John) Jeremy; QC 1988; *b* 16 Oct. 1937; *s* of late Col Arthur William Bean Gompertz and Muriel Annie Gompertz (*née* Smith). *Educ:* Beaumont Coll.; Trinity Coll., Cambridge (BA). Called to the Bar, Gray's Inn, 1962; in practice, South East Circuit; a Recorder, 1987. *Recreations:* racing, travel, pottering. *Address:* 5 Essex Court, Temple, EC4Y 9AH. *T:* 071–583 2825.

GONZÁLEZ MÁRQUEZ, Felipe; Prime Minister of Spain, since 1982; *b* 5 March 1942; *s* of Felipe González and Juana Márquez; *m* 1969, Carmen Romero Lopez; two *s* one *d. Educ:* Univ. of Seville (Law degree); Univ. of Louvaine. Opened first labour law office, Seville, 1966; Spanish Socialist Party (PSOE), 1964–: Mem., Seville Provincial Cttee, 1965–69; Mem., Nat. Cttee, 1969–70; Mem., Exec. Bd, 1970; First Sec., 1974–79, resigned; re-elected, 1979; now Sec.-Gen. Pres., Council of Ministers, 1982–; Chm., Socialist Parly Group. Grand Cross, Order of Military Merit, 1984. *Publications:* What is Socialism?, 1976; PSOE, 1977. *Address:* Palacio de la Moncloa, Madrid, Spain. *T:* 2668000.

GOOCH, Prof. John, PhD; FRHistS; Professor of History, Lancaster University, since 1988; *b* 25 Aug. 1945; *s* of George Gooch and Doris Evelyn (*née* Mottram); *m* 1967, Catherine Ann Staley; one *s* one *d. Educ:* Brockenhurst County High Sch.; King's Coll., Univ. of London (BA Hons History, class 1, 1966; PhD War Studies 1969). FRHistS 1975. Asst Lectr in History, 1966–67, Asst Lectr in War Studies, 1969, KCL; University of Lancaster: Lectr in History, 1969–81; Sen. Lectr, 1981–84; Reader in History, 1984–88. Sec. of the Navy Sen. Res. Fellow, US Naval War Coll., 1985–86; Vis. Prof. of Military and Naval History, Yale Univ., 1988. Chm. of Council, Army Records Soc., 1983–. Editor, Jl of Strategic Studies, 1978–; Gen. Editor, Internat. Relations of the Great Powers; Member of Editorial Board: European History Qly; Diplomacy and Statecraft; Terrorism and Small Wars. Premio Internazionale di Cultura, Città di Anghiari, 1983; Associate Fellow, Davenport Coll., Yale Univ., 1988. *Publications:* The Plans of War: the general staff and British military strategy *c.* 1900–1916, 1974; Armies in Europe, 1980; The Prospect of War: studies in British defence policy 1847–1942, 1981; Politicians and Defence: studies in the formulation of British defence policy 1847–1970, 1981; Strategy and the Social Sciences, 1981; Military Deception and Strategic Surprise, 1982; Soldati e Borghesi nell' Europa Moderna, 1982; Army, State and Society in Italy 1870–1915, 1989; Decisive Campaigns of the Second World War, 1989; (with Eliot A. Cohen) Military Misfortunes: the anatomy of failure in war, 1990. *Recreations:* Italian food and wine. *Address:* The Coach House, Chapel Lane, Ellel, Lancaster LA2 0PN. *T:* Lancaster (0524) 751525.

GOOCH, Sir Peter; *see* Gooch, Sir T. S.

GOOCH, Sir (Richard) John Sherlock, 12th Bt *cr* 1746; JP; *b* 22 March 1930; *s* of Sir Robert Eric Sherlock Gooch, 11th Bt, KCVO, DSO and Katharine Clervaux (*d* 1974), *d* of late Maj.-Gen. Sir Edward Walter Clervaux Chaytor, KCMG, KCVO, CB; *S* father, 1978. *Educ:* Eton. Captain, The Life Guards; retired, 1963. JP Suffolk, 1970. *Heir: b* Major Timothy Robert Sherlock Gooch, MBE [*b* 7 Dec. 1934; *m* 1963, Susan Barbara Christie, *o d* of late Maj.-Gen. Kenneth Christie Cooper, CB, DSO, OBE; two *d*]. *Address:* Benacre Hall, Beccles, Suffolk. *T:* Lowestoft (0502) 740333.

GOOCH, Sir Trevor Sherlock, (Sir Peter), 5th Bt *cr* 1866, of Clewer Park, Berkshire; *b* 15 June 1915; *s* of Charles Trevor Gooch (*d* 1963; *g s* of Sir Daniel Gooch, 1st Bt), and Hester Stratford (*d* 1957), *d* of late Lt-Col Wright Sherlock; *S* kinsman, 1989; *m* 1st, 1956, Denys Anne (*d* 1976), *o d* of Harold Victor Venables; one *s* four *d*; 2nd, 1978, Jean, *d* of late Joseph Wright. *Educ:* Charterhouse. Flt Lt, RAFVR, 1939–46. *Heir: s* Miles Peter Gooch, *b* 3 Feb. 1963. *Address:* Jardin de la Rocque, Mont de la Rocque, St Aubin, Jersey, CI. *T:* Jersey (0534) 42980. *Club:* Royal Channel Islands Yacht (Jersey).

GOOD, Tan Sri Donal Bernard Waters, CMG 1962; JMN (Malaysia), 1965; PSM (Malaysia), 1970; Commissioner of Law Revision, Malaysia, 1963; *b* 13 April 1907; *er s* of William John and Kathleen Mary Good, Dublin; *m* 1930, Kathryn, *er d* of Frank Lucas Stanley and Helena Kathleen Stanley, Dublin; one *s* one *d. Educ:* The High Sch., and Trinity Coll., Dublin. Scholar and Moderator in Classics, TCD, 1927–29; MA 1932; LLB 1933; Barrister, King's Inns, Dublin (Benchers' Prizeman), 1935; Barrister, Gray's Inn, 1948. Resident Magistrate, Kenya, 1940–45; Malayan Planning Unit, 1945; Crown

Counsel, Malayan Union, 1946–48; Legal Adviser: Negri Sembilan and Malacca, 1948–49; Johore, 1949–50; Legal Draftsman, Sierra Leone, 1951–52; Legal Adviser, Selangor, 1952; Senior Federal Counsel, Federation of Malaya, 1952–55; Actg Solicitor-Gen., 1953 and 1955; Actg Judge of Supreme Court, 1953; Judge of Supreme Court, 1955–59; Judge of the Court of Appeal, Federation of Malaya, 1959–62. Chm. Detainees Review Commn, 1955–60; Pres. Industrial Court, 1956–57; Chm. Detained Persons Advisory Board, 1960. Coronation Medal, 1953. *Address:* 1 Broadbridge Close, SE3 7AD.

GOOD, Sir John K.; *see* Kennedy-Good.

GOOD, Prof. Ronald D'Oyley, ScD; Head of Department of Botany, University of Hull, 1928–59, Professor Emeritus, 1959; *b* 5 March 1896; 2nd *s* of William Ernest and Mary Gray Good; *m* 1927, Patty Gwynneth Griffith (*d* 1975); one *d*. *Educ:* Weymouth Coll.; Downing Coll., Cambridge (Senior Scholar). MA, ScD Cantab. Served European War, 1914–18, 4th Bn Dorset Regt, and 2/5th Bn Lincolnshire Regt (France); Staff of Botany Department, British Museum (Nat. Hist.), 1922–28. *Publications:* Plants and Human Economics, 1933; The Old Roads of Dorset, 1940, 1966; Weyland, 1945; The Geography of the Flowering Plants, 1947, revd new edn, 1974; A Geographical Handbook of the Dorset Flora, 1948; Features of Evolution in the Flowering Plants, 1956, new edn USA, 1974; The Last Villages of Dorset, 1979; The Philosophy of Evolution, 1981; A Concise Flora of Dorset, 1984; contribs to scientific journals. *Address:* Thamesfield Nursing Home, Wargrave Road, Henley-on-Thames, Oxon RG9 2LX.

GOODACRE, Kenneth, TD 1952; DL; Deputy Clerk to GLC, 1964–68; Clerk and Solicitor of Middlesex CC, 1955–65; Clerk of the Peace for Middlesex, 1959–65; *b* 29 Oct. 1910; *s* of Clifford and Florence Goodacre; *m* 1936, Dorothy, *d* of Harold Kendall, Solicitor, Leeds; one *s*. *Educ:* Doncaster Grammar Sch. Admitted Solicitor, 1934; Asst Solicitor: Doncaster Corp., 1934–35; Barrow-in-Furness Corp., 1935–36; Sen. Solicitor, Blackburn Corp., 1936–39; served War of 1939–45, TA with E Lancs Regt and Staff 53 Div. (Major), and 2nd Army (Lieut-Col); released from Army Service, 1945, and granted hon. rank of Major; Dep. Town Clerk: Blackburn, 1945–49, Leicester, 1949–52; Town Clerk, Leicester, 1952–55. Partner, Gillhams, Solicitors, 1968–71; practised under name of K. Goodacre & Co., Solicitors, 1971–89. DL, Greater London (DL Middlesex, 1960–65), 1965. *Address:* 4 Chartfield Avenue, Putney, SW15. *T:* 081–789 0794. *Club:* Hurlingham.

GOODALE, Cecil Paul; *b* 29 Dec. 1918; *s* of Cecil Charles Wemyss Goodale and Annie Goodale; *m* 1st, 1946, Ethel Margaret (*née* Studer); 2nd, 1984, Margaret Beatrice (*née* Cook). *Educ:* East Sheen County Sch. War Office, 1936; Min. of Supply, 1939; Min. of Health, later DHSS, 1947–: Sen. Exec. Officer, 1950; Principal, 1953; Principal Regional Officer, 1962; Asst Sec., 1967; Under-Sec., 1976–78. *Recreations:* music, photography. *Address:* 37 Highfield Drive, Kingsbridge, Devon TQ7 1JR. *T:* Kingsbridge (0548) 853511.

GOODALL, His Honour Anthony Charles, MC 1942; DL; a Circuit Judge (formerly a Judge of County Courts), 1968–86; *b* 23 July 1916; *er s* of late Charles Henry and Mary Helen Goodall, The Manor House, Sutton Veny, Wilts; *m* 1947, Anne Valerie, *yr d* of late John Reginald Chichester and of Audrey Geraldine Chichester, Lurley Manor, Tiverton, Devon; one *s* two *d*. *Educ:* Eton; King's Coll., Cambridge. Called to Bar, Inner Temple, 1939 (Certif. of Hon.). Served War of 1939–45, 1st Royal Dragoons; taken prisoner (twice), 1944. Practised at Bar, 1946–67. Pres., Plymouth Magistrates' Assoc., 1976–84; Mem., County Court Rule Cttee, 1978–83; Jt Pres., Council of HM Circuit Judges, 1986 (Jt Vice-Pres., 1985). DL Devon 1987. *Publications:* (ed jtly) Faraday on Rating; contrib. to Encycl. Court Forms and Precedents. *Address:* Mardon, Moretonhampstead, Devon TQ13 8LX. *T:* Moretonhampstead (0647) 40239.

GOODALL, Sir (Arthur) David (Saunders), GCMG 1991 (KCMG 1987; CMG 1979); HM Diplomatic Service, retired; *b* 9 Oct. 1931; *o c* of late Arthur William and Maisie Josephine Goodall; *m* 1962, Morwenna, *y d* of late Percival George Beck Peecock; two *s* one *d*. *Educ:* Ampleforth; Trinity Coll., Oxford. 1st Cl. Hons Lit. Hum., 1954; MA. Served 1st Bn KOYLI (2nd Lieut), 1955–56. Entered HM Foreign (now Diplomatic) Service, 1956; served at: Nicosia, 1956; FO, 1957–58; Djakarta, 1958–60; Private Sec. to HM Ambassador, Bonn, 1961–63; FO, 1963–68; Head of Chancery, Nairobi, 1968–70; FCO, 1970–73; UK Delegn, MBFR, Vienna, 1973–75; Head of Western European Dept, FCO, 1975–79; Minister, Bonn, 1979–82; Dep. Sec., Cabinet Office, 1982–84; Dep. Under-Sec. of State, FCO, 1984–87; High Comr to India, 1987–91. Chm., Internat. Cttee, Leonard Cheshire Foundn, 1992–; Co-Chm., Anglo-Irish Encounter, 1992–. *Publications:* contribs to: Ampleforth Jl; Tablet; Irish Genealogist; The Past. *Recreation:* painting in watercolours. *Address:* c/o The Leonard Cheshire Foundation International, 26–29 Maunsel Street, SW1P 2QN. *Clubs:* Garrick, United Oxford & Cambridge University.

GOODALL, David William, PhD (London); DSc (Melbourne); ARCS, DIC, FLS; FIBiol; Hon. Fellow, CSIRO Division of Wildlife and Ecology (formerly Division of Wildlife and Rangelands Research), since 1983; *b* 4 April 1914; *s* of Henry William Goodall; *m* 1st, 1940, Audrey Veronica Kirwin (marr. diss. 1949); one *s*; 2nd, 1949, Muriel Grace King (marr. diss. 1974); two *s* one *d*; 3rd, 1976, Ivy Nelms (*née* Palmer). *Educ:* St Paul's Sch.; Imperial Coll. of Science and Technology (BSc). Research under Research Inst. of Plant Physiology, on secondment to Cheshunt and East Malling Research Stns, 1935–46; Plant Physiologist, W African Cacao Research Inst., 1946–48; Sen. Lectr in Botany, University of Melbourne, 1948–52; Reader in Botany, University Coll. of the Gold Coast, 1952–54; Prof. of Agricultural Botany, University of Reading, 1954–56; Dir, CSIRO Tobacco Research Institute, Mareeba, Qld, 1956–61; Senior Principal Research Officer, CSIRO Div. of Mathematical Statistics, Perth, Australia, 1961–67; Hon. Reader in Botany, Univ. of Western Australia, 1965–67; Prof. of Biological Science, Univ. of California Irvine, 1966–68; Dir, US/IBP Desert Biome, 1968–73; Prof. of Systems Ecology, Utah State Univ., 1969–74; Sen. Prin. Res. Scientist, 1974–79, Sen. Res. Fellow, 1979–83, Land Resources Management Div., CSIRO. Hon. Dr in Natural Scis, Trieste Univ., 1990. *Publications:* Chemical Composition of Plants as an Index of their Nutritional Status (with F. G. Gregory), 1947; ed, Evolution of Desert Biota, 1976; editor-in-chief, Ecosystems of the World (series), 1977–; co-editor: Productivity of World Ecosystems, 1975; Simulation Modelling of Environmental Problems, 1977; Arid-land Ecosystems: Structure, Functioning and Management, vol. 1 1979, vol. 2 1981; Mediterranean-type Shrublands, 1981; Hot Deserts, 1985; numerous papers in scientific jls and symposium vols. *Recreations:* acting, reading, walking. *Address:* CSIRO, Locked Bag No 4, PO Midland, WA 6056, Australia.

GOODALL, Rt. Rev. Maurice John, MBE 1974; Bishop of Christchurch, 1984–90; *b* 31 March 1928; *s* of John and Alice Maud Goodall; *m* 1st, 1953, Nathalie Ruth Cummack; two *s* four *d*; 2nd, 1981, Beverley Doreen Moore. *Educ:* Christchurch Technical Coll.; College House, Univ. of NZ (BA 1950); Univ. of Canterbury (LTh 1964); Dip. Social Work (Distinction) 1977; CQSW 1982. Asst Curate, St Albans, Dio. of Christchurch, 1951–54; Vicar of: Waikari, 1954–59; Shirley, 1959–67; Hon. Asst, Christchurch, St John's 1967–69; Chaplain, Kingslea Girls' Training Centre, 1967–69; City Missioner (dio. Christchurch), 1969–76; Nuffield Bursary, 1973; Dir, Community Mental Health Team, 1976–82; Dean of Christchurch Cathedral, 1982–84. *Publications:* (with Colin Clark) Worship for Today, 1967; (contrib.) Christian Responsibility in Society (ed Yule), 1977; contribs to journals. *Recreations:* walking, reading, NZ history. *Address:* Flat 1, 50 Crofton Road, Christchurch 5, New Zealand.

GOODALL, Peter, CBE 1983; TD 1950; Executive Chairman and Chief Executive, 1977–86, and Director, 1970–89, Hepworth Ceramic Holdings PLC; *b* 14 July 1920; *s* of Major Tom Goodall, DSO, MC and Alice (*née* Black); *m* 1948, Sonja Jeanne (*née* Burt); one *s* one *d*. *Educ:* Ashville Coll., Harrogate. Admitted Solicitor, 1948. Served War, Duke of Wellington's Regt and Parachute Regt, 1939–46 (Captain). Practised as Solicitor with family firm, Goodall & Son, and Whitfield Son & Hallam, 1948–67; Dir, Hepworth Iron Co. Ltd, 1967–70; company merged with General Refractories Group Ltd to form Hepworth Ceramic Holdings Ltd, 1970; Man. Dir, 1971–77. Member Council: CBI, 1981–88; British United Industrialists, 1984–89. *Recreations:* shooting, fishing. *Address:* Springfield House, Sicklinghall Road, Wetherby, W Yorks. *T:* Wetherby (0937) 581297.

GOODCHILD, David Hicks, CBE 1973; Partner of Clifford Chance (formerly Clifford-Turner), Solicitors, 1962–90 (resident in Paris); *b* 3 Sept. 1926; *s* of Harold Hicks Goodchild and Agnes Joyce Wharton Goodchild (*née* Mowbray); *m* 1954, Nicole Marie Jeanne (*née* Delamotte); one *s* one *d*. *Educ:* Felsted School. Lieut, Royal Artillery, 1944–48; articled clerk, Longmores, Hertford; qual. Solicitor, 1952; HAC, 1952–56. *Recreations:* golf, cricket. *Address:* 53 Avenue Montaigne, 75008 Paris, France. *T:* 42–25–49–27. *Clubs:* MCC, HAC; Cercle Interallié, Polo (Paris).

GOODCHILD, David Lionel Napier, CMG 1986; a Director, Directorate-General of External Relations, Commission of the European Communities, 1985–86; *b* 20 July 1935; *s* of Hugh N. Goodchild and Beryl C. M. Goodchild. *Educ:* Eton College; King's College, Cambridge (MA). Joined Foreign Office, 1958; served Tehran, NATO (Paris), and FO, 1959–70; Dep. Political Adviser, British Mil. Govt, Berlin, 1970–72; transferred to EEC, Brussels, 1973; Head of Division, 1973, Principal Counsellor then Director, 1979–86. *Address:* Orchard House, Thorpe Morieux, Bury St Edmunds, Suffolk. *T:* Cockfield Green (0284) 828181.

GOODCHILD, Peter Robert Edward; Executive Producer, BBC Films, since 1989; *b* 18 Aug. 1939; *s* of Douglas Richard Geoffrey Goodchild and Lottie May Goodchild; *m* 1968, Penelope Jane Pointon-Dick; two *d*. *Educ:* Aldenham Sch., Elstree; St John's College, Oxford (MA). CChem, FRSC 1979. General trainee, BBC, 1963; BBC TV: Director/Producer, Horizon, 1965–69, Editor, 1969–76; Editor, Special Features, 1977–80; Head, Science Features Dept, 1980–84; Head, Plays Dept, 1984–89. SFTA Mullard Award, 1967, 1968, 1969; BAFTA Awards: best factual series, 1972, 1974; best drama series, 1977–80. *Publication:* J. Robert Oppenheimer: shatterer of worlds, 1980. *Recreations:* tennis, music, painting, environmental action. *Address:* BBC Television Centre, Wood Lane, W12 7RJ. *T:* 081–743 8000. *Club:* Groucho.

GOODCHILD, Rt. Rev. Ronald Cedric Osbourne; an Assistant Bishop, Diocese of Exeter, since 1983; *b* 17 Oct. 1910; *s* of Sydney Osbourne and Dido May Goodchild; *m* 1947, Jean Helen Mary (*née* Ross); one *s* four *d*. *Educ:* St John's School, Leatherhead; Trinity Coll. (Monk Schol.), Cambridge; Bishops' Coll., Cheshunt. 2nd Cl. Hist. Tripos Parts I and II, 1931, Dealtry Exhibn. 1932, 3rd Class Theol. Tripos, 1932, Asst Master, Bickley Hall Sch., Kent, 1932–34; Curate, Ealing Parish Church, 1934–37; Chap. Oakham Sch., 1937–42. Chap. RAFVR, 1942–46 (despatches), Warden St Michael's House, Hamburg, 1946–49; Gen. Sec., SCM in Schools, 1949–53; Rector of St Helen's Bishopgate with St Martin Outwich, 1951–53; Vicar of Horsham, Sussex, 1953–59; Surrogate and Rural Dean of Horsham, 1954–59; Archdeacon of Northampton and Rector of Ecton, 1959–64; Bishop Suffragan of Kensington, 1964–80. Examiner, Religious Knowledge, Southern Univs Jt Bd, 1954–58; Examining Chaplain to Bishop of Peterborough, 1959. Chairman Christian Aid Dept, British Council of Churches, 1964–74. Mem. of General Synod of C of E, 1974–80. *Publication:* Daily Prayer at Oakham School, 1938. *Recreations:* tennis, golf, photography. *Address:* Mead, Welcombe, near Bideford, N Devon EX39 6HH. *Club:* Royal Air Force.

GOODCHILD, Lt-Col Sidney, LVO 1969; DL; retired; Vice-Lieutenant of Caernarvonshire, 1969–74; *b* 4 Jan. 1903; *s* of late Charles Goodchild; *m* 1934, Elizabeth G. P. Everett; two *s* one *d*. *Educ:* Friars Sch.; Staff Coll., Quetta. Commnd Royal Welch Fusiliers, 1923; 14th Punjab Regt, Indian Army, 1930; Staff Captain, 4th Inf. Bde, 1937; DAQMG (Movements), Army HQ India, 1939; AQMG (Movts), Iraq, 1940; comd 7/14 Punjab Regt, 1942; AQMG, Army HQ India, 1945; comd 1st Sikh LI and 5th Bde, 4th Indian Div., 1946; despatches thrice, 1940–44. Chm., NW Wales War Pensioners' Cttee; Pres., Gwynedd Br., SSAFA, 1969–. Alderman, Caernarvonshire CC, 1972–74. DL Caernarvonshire, 1964; DL Gwynedd, 1974. *Address:* Plas Oerddwr, Beddgelert, Gwynedd, N Wales. *T:* Beddgelert (076686) 237.

GOODDEN, Robert Yorke, CBE 1956; RDI 1947; Architect and Designer; Professor, School of Silversmithing and Jewellery, 1948–74, and Pro-Rector, 1967–74, Royal College of Art; *b* 7 May 1909; 2nd *s* of late Lieut-Col R. B. Goodden, OBE and Gwendolen Goodden; *m* 1st, 1936, Kathleen Teresa Burrow; 2nd, 1946, Lesley Macbeth Mitchell; two *s* two *d*. *Educ:* Harrow Sch. Trained AA Sch. of Architecture, 1926–31; AA Diploma 1932; ARIBA 1933; private practice as architect and designer, 1932–39; served RAFVR, 1940–41; RNVR, 1941–45; resumed private practice, 1946. Joint architect and designer: Lion and Unicorn Pavilion, South Bank Exhibition, 1951; Western Sculpture Rooms, Print Room Gall. and Gall. of Oriental Art, British Museum, 1969–71; designer of: domestic pressed glassware for Chance Brothers, 1934–48; Asterisk Wallpapers, 1934; sports section, Britain Can Make It Exhbn, 1946; Coronation hangings for Westminster Abbey, 1953; gold and silver plate in collections: Victoria and Albert Museum, Worshipful Co. of Goldsmiths, Royal Society of Arts, Downing Coll. and Sidney Sussex Coll., Cambridge, Royal Coll. of Art; glass for King's Coll., Cambridge, Grosvenor House, Min. of Works, and others; metal foil mural decorations in SS Canberra, 1961. Consulting Architect to Board of Trade for BIF, Olympia, 1947, Earls Ct, 1949, Olympia, 1950 and 1951. Member: Council of Industrial Design, 1955; National Council for Diplomas in Art and Design, 1961; Adv. Council, V&A Museum, 1977; Chm., Crafts Council, 1977–82. Mem. Council, Essex Univ., 1973. FSIA, 1947; Hon. Fellow, Sheffield Polytechnic, 1971. Hon. DesRCA, 1952; Hon. Dr RCA, 1974; Sen. Fellow, RCA, 1981. SIAD Design Medal, 1972. Master of Faculty, RDI, 1959–61. Liveryman, Worshipful Co. of Goldsmiths, Prime Warden 1976. *Publication:* (with P. Popham) Silversmithing, 1972. *Recreation:* daydreaming. *Address:* 16 Hatfield Buildings, Widcombe Hill, Bath, Avon BA2 6AF.

GOODE, (Penelope) Cary (Anne); Director of National Asthma Campaign (formerly Asthma Research Council), since 1988; *b* 5 Dec. 1947; *d* of Ernest Edgar Spink and Rachel Atcherly Spink; *m* 1987, Richard Nicholas Goode. *Educ:* Westwing Sch. Royal Ascot Enclosure Office, 1971; MoD, 1973; Manager, retail business, 1978; Domestic and Social Sec., RCOG, 1980; Educn Administrator, British Heart Foundn, 1982. *Recreations:* gardening and garden design, vintage cars, dogs. *Address:* 28 Bryanston Square, W1H 7LS. *T:* 071–262 0490.

GOODE, Prof. Royston Miles, OBE 1972; QC 1990; FBA 1988; barrister; Norton Rose Professor of English Law, Oxford University, since 1990; Fellow, St John's College, Oxford, since 1990; *b* 6 April 1933; *s* of Samuel and Bloom Goode; *m* 1964, Catherine Anne Rueff; one *d. Educ:* Highgate School. LLB London, 1954; LLD London, 1976. Admitted Solicitor, 1955. Partner, Victor Mishcon & Co., solicitors, 1966–71, Consultant 1971–88. Called to the Bar, Inner Temple, 1988. Queen Mary College, University of London: Prof. of Law, 1971–73; Head of Dept and Dean of Faculty of Laws, 1976–80; Crowther Prof. of Credit and Commercial Law, 1973–89; Dir and Founder, Centre for Commercial Law Studies, 1980–89. Vis. Prof., Melbourne, 1975; Aust. Commonwealth Vis. Fellow, 1975; Falconbridge Vis. Prof., Osgoode Hall Law Sch., 1987. Chm., Advertising Adv. Cttee, IBA, 1976–80. Member: Cttee on Consumer Credit, 1968–71; Monopolies and Mergers Commn, 1981–86; Departmental Cttee on Arbitration Law, DTI, 1986–; Council of the Banking Ombudsman, 1989–. Member: Council, Justice; Council of Management, British Inst. of Internat. and Comparative Law. Fellow, QMW, 1991. FRSA 1990. *Publications:* Hire-Purchase Law and Practice, 1962, 2nd edn 1970, with Supplement 1975; The Hire-Purchase Act 1964, 1964; (with J. S. Ziegel) Hire-Purchase and Conditional Sale: a Comparative Survey of Commonwealth and American Law, 1965; Introduction to the Consumer Credit Act, 1974; (ed) Consumer Credit Legislation, 1977; Consumer Credit, 1978; Commercial Law, 1982; Legal Problems of Credit and Security, 1982, 2nd edn 1988; Payment Obligations in Commercial and Financial Transactions, 1983; Proprietary Rights and Insolvency in Sales Transactions, 1985, 2nd edn 1989; Principles of Corporate Insolvency Law, 1990; contrib. Halsbury's Laws of England, 4th edn. *Recreations:* chess, reading, walking, browsing in bookshops. *Address:* St John's College, Oxford OX1 3JP; 42 St John Street, Oxford OX1 2LH.

GOODENOUGH, Anthony Michael, CMG 1990; HM Diplomatic Service; High Commissioner to Ghana and Ambassador (non-resident) to Togo, since 1989; *b* 5 July 1941; *s* of late Rear-Adm. Michael Grant Goodenough, CBE, DSO, and of Nancy Waterfield (*née* Slater); *m* 1967, Veronica Mary, *d* of Col Peter Pender-Cudlip, MVO; two *s* one *d. Educ:* Wellington Coll.; New Coll., Oxford. MA 1980. Voluntary Service Overseas, Sarawak, 1963–64; Foreign Office, 1964; Athens, 1967; Private Secretary to Parliamentary Under Secretary, 1971, and Minister of State, FCO, 1972; Paris, 1974; First Sec., FCO, 1977; Counsellor on secondment to Cabinet Office, 1980; Hd of Chancery, Islamabad, 1982; Counsellor, FCO, 1986–89. *Address:* c/o Foreign and Commonwealth Office, SW1A 2AH.

GOODENOUGH, Cecilia Phyllis, MA; STh; DD; *b* 9 Sept. 1905; *d* of late Adm. Sir William Goodenough, GCB, MVO. *Educ:* Rochester Grammar Sch.; Liverpool Coll., Huyton; St Hugh's Coll., Oxford. LCC Care Cttee Sec., 1927–30; Sunday Sch. and Evangelistic work, Diocese of Caledonia, Fort St John, BC, Canada, 1931–36; Head of Talbot Settlement, 14 Bromley Hill, Bromley, Kent, 1937–45; Asst to Diocesan Missioner, Diocese of Southwark, 1954–72. *Address:* 115 Camberwell Grove, Camberwell, SE5 8JH. *T:* 071–701 0093.

GOODENOUGH, Frederick Roger, FCIB; DL; Director: Barclays PLC, 1985–89; *b* 21 Dec. 1927; *s* of Sir William Macnamara Goodenough, 1st Bt, and late Lady (Dorothea Louisa) Goodenough; *m* 1954, Marguerite June Mackintosh; one *s* two *d. Educ:* Eton; Magdalene Coll., Cambridge (MA). MA Oxon; FCIB (FIB 1968). Joined Barclays Bank Ltd, 1950; Local Director: Birmingham, 1958; Reading, 1960; Oxford, 1969–87; Director: Barclays Bank UK Ltd, 1971–87; Barclays Internat. Ltd, 1977–87; Barclays Bank PLC, 1979–89; Adv. Dir, Barclays Bank Thames Valley Region, 1988–89; Mem., London Cttee, Barclays Bank DCO, 1966–71; Barclays Bank Internat. Ltd, 1971–80. Supernumerary Fellow, Wolfson Coll., Oxford, 1989. Sen. Partner, Broadwell Manor Farm, 1968–; Curator, Oxford Univ. Chest, 1974–; Trustee: Nuffield Med. Benefaction, 1968– (Chm., 1987–); Nuffield Dominions Trust, 1968– (Chm., 1987–); Nuffield Orthopaedic Trust, 1978– (Chm., 1981–); Oxford and Dist Hosps Improvement and Develt Fund, 1968– (Chm., 1982–88); Oxford Preservation Trust, 1980–89; Radcliffe Med. Foundn, 1987–. Governor: Shiplake Coll., 1963–74 (Chm., 1966–70); Wellington Coll., 1968–74; London Hse for Overseas Graduates, 1985–. Fellow of Linnean Soc. (Mem. Council, 1968–75, Treasurer, 1970–75); FRSA. High Sheriff, 1987–88, DL 1989, Oxfordshire. *Recreations:* shooting, fishing, photography, ornithology. *Address:* Broadwell Manor, Lechlade, Glos GL7 3QS. *T:* Filkins (036786) 326. *Club:* Brooks's.

GOODENOUGH, Prof. John Bannister; Virginia H. Cockrell Centennial Professor of Engineering, University of Texas at Austin, since 1986; *b* 25 July 1922; *s* of Erwin Ramsdell Goodenough and Helen Lewis Goodenough; *m* 1951, Irene Johnston Wiseman. *Educ:* Yale Univ. (AB, Maths); Univ. of Chicago (MS, PhD, Physics). Meteorologist, US Army Air Force, 1942–48; Research Engr, Westinghouse Corp., 1951–52; Research Physicist (Leader, Electronic Materials Gp), Lincoln Laboratory, MIT, 1952–76; Prof. and Hd of Dept of Inorganic Chemistry, Oxford Univ., 1976–86. Raman Prof., Indian Acad. of Science, 1982–83 (Hon. Mem., 1980–). Member: Nat. Acad., of Engrg, 1976–; Presidential Commn on Superconductivity, 1989–90. Dr *hc*, Bordeaux, 1967. Von Hippel Award, Materials Res. Soc., 1989. Associate Editor: Materials Research Bulletin, 1966–; Jl Solid State Chemistry, 1969–; Structure and Bonding, 1978–; Solid State Ionics, 1980–; Superconductor Science and Technology, 1987–; Jl of Materials Chem., 1990–; Chem. of Materials, 1990–; Co-editor, International Series of Monographs on Chemistry, 1979–86; Exec., Editl Bd, Jl of Applied Electrochem., 1983–88. *Publications:* Magnetism and the Chemical Bond, 1963; Les oxydes des elements de transition, 1973; numerous research papers in learned jls. *Recreations:* walking, travel. *Address:* Center for Materials Science & Engineering, University of Texas at Austin, ETC 5.160, Austin, Texas 78712, USA. *T:* (512) 471–1646.

GOODENOUGH, Sir Richard (Edmund), 2nd Bt *cr* 1943; *b* 9 June 1925; *e s* of Sir William (Macnamara) Goodenough, 1st Bt, and Dorothea (Louisa) (*d* 1987), *er d* of late Ven. and Hon. K. F. Gibbs, DD; *S* father 1951; *m* 1951, Jane, *d* of late H. S. P. McLernon and of Mrs McLernon, Gisborne, NZ; one *s* two *d. Educ:* Eton Coll.; Christ Church, Oxford. Military service, 1943–45, invalided. Christ Church, Oxford, 1945–47. *Heir: s* William McLernon Goodenough [*b* 5 Aug. 1954; *m* 1982, Louise Elizabeth, *d* of Captain Michael Ortmans, MVO, RN and Julia Ortmans; one *d*].

GOODFELLOW, Mark Aubrey; HM Diplomatic Service, retired; Ambassador to Gabon, 1986–90; *b* 7 April 1931; *y s* of Alfred Edward Goodfellow and Lucy Emily (*née* Potter); *m* 1964, Madelyn Susan Scammell; one *s* one *d. Educ:* Preston Manor County Grammar Sch. Served RAF, 1949–51. Joined HM Foreign (subseq. Diplomatic) Service, 1949; FO, 1951–54; British Mil. Govt, Berlin, 1954–56; Second Sec., Khartoum, 1956–59; FO, 1959–63; Second Sec., Yaoundé, 1963–66; Asst Comr, later Trade Comr, Hong Kong, 1966–71; FCO, 1971–74; First Sec., Ankara, 1974–78; Consul, Atlanta, 1978–82; Counsellor: Washington (Hong Kong Commercial Affairs), 1982–84; Lagos (Econ. and Comm.), 1984–86. *Recreations:* travelling, photography, visiting historic sites and buildings, gardening. *Clubs:* Travellers', Civil Service; Hong Kong (Hong Kong); Ikoyi (Lagos).

GOODFELLOW, Mrs Rosalind Erica, JP; Moderator of the General Assembly of the United Reformed Church, 1982–83; *b* 3 April 1927; *d* of late Rev. William Griffith-Jones

and Kathleen (*née* Speakman); *m* 1949, Keith Frank Goodfellow, QC (*d* 1977); two *s* one *d. Educ:* Milton Mount Coll. (now Wentworth Milton Mount); Royal Holloway Coll., London Univ. (BA Hons). Member: British Council of Churches Div. of Community Affairs Bd, 1980–83; Churches' Council for Covenanting, 1981–82; Chm., World Church and Mission Dept, URC, 1983. Chm., Surrey and W Sussex CAB, 1985. JP Surrey (Esher and Walton PSD), 1960. *Recreation:* attending committee meetings. *Address:* Kilverstone House, Gordon Road, Claygate, Surrey. *T:* Esher (0372) 67656.

GOODHART, Hon. Lady; Celia McClare Goodhart; Principal, Queen's College, London, since 1991; *b* 25 July 1939; *d* of 2nd Baron Hemingford and Elizabeth (*née* Clark) (*d* 1979); *m* 1966, Sir William Howard Goodhart, *qv*; one *s* two *d. Educ:* St Michael's, Limpsfield; St Hilda's Coll., Oxford (Hon. Fellow 1989). MA Oxon. HM Civil Service, MAFF, seconded to Treasury, 1960–66; Hist. Tutor, Queen's Coll., London and Westminster Tutors, 1966–81. Contested: (SDP) Kettering, 1983; (SDP Liberal Alliance) Kettering, 1987; Northants (for European Parlt), 1984. Member: SDP Nat. Cttee, 1984–88; Liberal Democrats Fed. Exec. Cttee, 1988–90; Pres., E Midlands Liberal Democrats, 1988–91. Mem., Nat. Gas Consumer Councils, 1978–81 (also Chm., N Thames Gas Consumer Council); Pres., London Marriage Guidance Council, 1991–; Chm., Youth Clubs, UK, 1988–91. Trustee: CPRE, 1987–91; Nuffield Medical Benefaction, 1988–. Governor: Godolphin and Latymer, 1976–86; St Michael's, Limpsfield, 1975–83; Isaac Newton Comprehensive, 1977–81. FRSA 1989. *Recreations:* sociability, shopping. *Address:* 43 Campden Hill Square, W8 7JR. *T:* 071–221 4830; Youlbury House, Boars Hill, Oxford OX1 5HH. *T:* Oxford (0865) 735477. *Clubs:* Reform; Cosmopolitan (New York).

GOODHART, Charles Albert Eric, PhD; FBA 1990; Norman Sosnow Professor of Banking and Finance, London School of Economics and Political Science, since 1985; *b* 23 Oct. 1936; *s* of late Prof. Arthur Goodhart, Hon. KBE, QC, FBA, and Cecily (*née* Carter); *m* 1960, Margaret (Miffy) Ann Smith; one *s* three *d. Educ:* Eton; Trinity Coll., Cambridge (scholar; 1st Cl. Hons Econs Tripos); Harvard Grad. Sch. of Arts and Sciences (PhD 1963). National Service, 1955–57 (2nd Lieut KRRC). Prize Fellowship in Econs, Trinity Coll., Cambridge, 1963; Asst Lectr in Econs, Cambridge Univ., 1963–64; Econ. Adviser, DEA, 1965–67; Lectr in Monetary Econs, LSE, 1967–69; Bank of England: Adviser with particular reference to monetary policy, 1969–80; a Chief Adviser, 1980–85. Mem., Adv. Cttee, Hong Kong Exchange Fund, 1990–. *Publications:* The New York Money Market and the Finance of Trade, 1900–13, 1968; The Business of Banking, 1891–1914, 1972; Money, Information and Uncertainty, 1975, 2nd edn 1989; Monetary Theory and Practice: the UK experience, 1984; The Evolution of Central Banks, 1985, rev. edn 1988; (ed jtly) The Operation and Regulation of Financial Markets, 1987; articles in econ. jls and papers contrib. to econ. books. *Recreations:* keeping sheep, gardening, tennis. *Address:* London School of Economics and Political Science, Houghton Street, WC2A 2AE. *T:* 071–955 7555.
See also Sir P. C. Goodhart, Sir W. H. Goodhart.

GOODHART, Rear-Adm. (Hilary Charles) Nicholas, CB 1972; FRAeS; *b* 28 Sept. 1919; *s* of G. C. Goodhart; *m* 1975, Molly Copsey. *Educ:* RNC Dartmouth; RNEC Keyham. Joined RN, 1933; served in Mediterranean in HM Ships Formidable and Dido, 1941–43; trained as pilot, 1944; served as fighter pilot in Burma Campaign, 1945; trained as test pilot, 1946; served on British Naval Staff, Washington, 1953–55; idc 1965; Rear-Adm. 1970; Mil. Dep. to Head of Defence Sales, MoD, 1970–73, retired. British Gliding Champion, 1962, 1967 and 1971. Holder of UK gliding distance record, 360 miles. Freedom of London, 1945; Mem. Ct of Grocers' Co., 1975, Master, 1981. US Legion of Merit, 1958. *Recreations:* computer programming, bee-keeping. *Address:* Church House, Uffculme, Cullompton, Devon EX15 3AX. *T:* Cullompton (0884) 840215. *Club:* Army and Navy.

GOODHART, Sir Philip (Carter), Kt 1981; MP (C) Beckenham, since March 1957; *b* 3 Nov. 1925; *s* of late Prof. Arthur Goodhart, Hon. KBE, QC, FBA, and Cecily (*née* Carter); *m* 1950, Valerie Winant; three *s* four *d. Educ:* Hotchkiss Sch., USA; Trinity Coll., Cambridge. Served KRRC and Parachute Regt, 1943–47. Editorial staff, Daily Telegraph, 1950–54; Editorial staff, Sunday Times, 1955–57. Contested (C) Consett, Co. Durham, Gen. Election, 1950; Member: LCC Educn Cttee, 1956–57; British Delegation to Council of Europe and WEU, 1961–63; British Delegation to UN Gen. Assembly, 1963; North Atlantic Assembly, 1964–79 and 1983–. Parly Under-Sec. of State, Northern Ireland Office, and Minister responsible for Dept of the Environment (NI), 1979–81; Parly Under Sec. of State, MoD, 1981. Joint Hon. Sec., 1922 Cttee, 1960–79; Mem., Cons. Adv. Cttee on Policy, 1973–79; Chairman: Cons. Parly Defence Cttee, 1972–74 (Vice-Chm., 1974–79); Parly NI Cttee, 1976–79; Parly Select Cttee on Sound Broadcasting, 1983–87. Member: Council, Consumers' Assoc., 1959–68, 1970–79 (Vice-Pres., 1983–); Adv. Council on Public Records, 1970–79; Exec. Cttee, British Council, 1974–79; Council, RUSI, 1973–76. Chairman: Bd of Sulgrave Manor, 1982–; Warship Preservation Trust, 1988–. *Publications:* The Hunt for Kimathi (with Ian Henderson, GM), 1958; In the Shadow of the Sword, 1964; Fifty Ships that Saved the World, 1965; (with Christopher Chataway) War without Weapons, 1968; Referendum, 1970; (with Ursula Branston) The 1922: the history of the 1922 Committee, 1973; Full-Hearted Consent, 1975; various pamphlets incl.: Stand on Your Own Four Feet: a study of work sharing and job splitting, 1982; Jobs Ahead, 1984; Skip Ahead, 1985. *Recreation:* skiing (Chm., Develt Cttee, Nat. Ski Fedn of GB, 1970–71; Chm., Lords and Commons Ski Club, 1971–73). *Address:* 27 Phillimore Gardens, W8. *T:* 071–937 0822; Whitebarn, Boars Hill, Oxford. *T:* Oxford (0865) 735294. *Clubs:* Beefsteak, Carlton, Garrick.
See also C. A. E. Goodhart, Sir W. H. Goodhart.

GOODHART, Sir Robert (Anthony Gordon), 4th Bt *cr* 1911; Medical Practitioner, Beaminster, Dorset; *b* 15 Dec. 1948; *s* of Sir John Gordon Goodhart, 3rd Bt, FRCGP, and of Margaret Mary Eileen, *d* of late Morgan Morgan; *S* father, 1979; *m* 1972, Kathleen Ellen, *d* of late Rev. A. D. MacRae; two *s* two *d. Educ:* Rugby; Guy's Hospital Medical School, London Univ. MB BS (Lond.), MRCS, LRCP, MRCGP, DObstRCOG. Qualification, 1972; Junior Medical Registrar, Guy's Hosp., 1974; GP, Bromley, 1976–80. *Recreation:* cricket. *Heir: s* Martin Andrew Goodhart, *b* 9 Sept. 1974.

GOODHART, Sir William (Howard), Kt 1989; QC 1979; *b* 18 Jan. 1933; *s* of late Prof. A. L. Goodhart, Hon. KBE, QC, FBA and Cecily (*née* Carter); *m* 1966, Hon. Celia McClare Herbert (*see* Hon. Lady Goodhart); one *s* two *d. Educ:* Eton; Trinity Coll., Cambridge (Scholar, MA). Harvard Law Sch. (Commonwealth Fund Fellow, LLM). Nat. Service, 1951–53 (2nd Lt, Oxford and Bucks Light Infantry). Called to Bar, Lincoln's Inn, 1957, Bencher, 1986. Chm., Exec. Cttee, Justice (British Section, Internat. Commn of Jurists), 1988– (Vice-Chm., 1978–88); Member: Council of Legal Educn, 1986–; Conveyancing Standing Cttee, Law Commn, 1987–89. Contested Kensington: (SDP) 1983; (SDP/Alliance) 1987; (Lib Dem) July 1988. Chairman: SDP Council Arrangements Cttee, 1982–88; Lib Dem Conf. Cttee, 1988–; Lib Dem Lawyers Assoc., 1988–; Mem., Lib Dem Policy Cttee, 1988–. Trustee, Campden Charities, 1975–90. *Publications:* (with Prof. Gareth Jones) Specific Performance, 1986; contribs to Halsbury's Laws of England; articles in legal periodicals. *Recreations:* walking, skiing. *Address:* 43 Campden Hill Square,

W8 7JR. *T:* 071–221 4830; Youlbury House, Boars Hill, Oxford OX1 5HH. *T:* Oxford (0865) 735477. *Club:* Brooks's.
See also C. A. E. Goodhart, Sir P. C. Goodhart.

GOODHEW, Rt. Rev. Harry; *see* Goodhew, Rt Rev. R. H.

GOODHEW, Rt. Rev. Richard Henry, (Harry); Bishop of Wollongong, since 1982 (Assistant Bishop, Diocese of Sydney); *b* 19 March 1931; *s* of Baden Powell Richard Goodhew and Christina Delgarno Goodhew (*née* Fraser); *m* 1958, Pamela (*née* Coughlan); two *s* two *d*. *Educ:* Univ. of Wollongong (MA Hons); Moore Theol Coll. (ThL 2nd cl. Hons, Diploma 2nd cl. Hons). Ordained 1958; Curate, St Matthew's, Bondi, NSW, 1958; Curate-in-charge, St Bede's, Beverly Hills, NSW, 1959–63; with Bush Church Aid, Ceduna, SA, 1963–66; Rector: St Paul's, Carlingford, NSW, 1966–71; St Stephen's, Coorparoo, Qld, 1971–76; Rector and Senior Canon, St Michael's Cathedral, Wollongong, 1976–79; Archdeacon of Wollongong and Camden, 1979–82. *Recreations:* jogging, reading, tennis, swimming. *Address:* Anglican Church Centre, 74 Church Street, Wollongong, NSW 2500, Australia. *T:* (042) 28–8487.

GOODHEW, Sir Victor (Henry), Kt 1982; *b* 30 Nov. 1919; *s* of late Rudolph Goodhew, Mannings Heath, Sussex; *m* 1st, 1940, Sylvia Johnson (marr. diss.); one *s* one *d*; 2nd, 1951, Suzanne Gordon-Burge (marr. diss. 1972); 3rd, 1972, Eva Rittinghausen (marr. diss. 1981). *Educ:* King's Coll. Sch. Served War of 1939–45: RAF, 1939–46; comd Airborne Radar Unit, attached 6th Airborne Div.; Sqdn Ldr 1945. Member: Westminster City Council, 1953–59; LCC, 1958–61. Contested (C) Paddington North, 1955; MP (C) St Albans Div., Herts, Oct. 1959–83. PPS to Mr C. I. Orr-Ewing, OBE, MP (when Civil Lord of the Admiralty), May 1962–63; PPS to Hon. Thomas Galbraith, MP (Jt Parly Sec., Min. of Transport), 1963–64; Asst Govt Whip, June-Oct. 1970; a Lord Comr, HM Treasury, 1970–73. Member: Speaker's Panel of Chairmen, 1975–83; Select Cttee, House of Commons Services, 1978–83; House of Commons Commn, 1979–83; Jt Sec. 1922 Cttee, 1979–83; Vice-Chm., Cons. Defence Cttee, 1974–83. Chm., Bd of Management, Inst. of Sports Medicine, 1982– (Mem., 1967–70, 1973–82). *Recreations:* swimming, reading. *Address:* The Coach House, St Leonard's Dale, Winkfield Road, Windsor, Berks SL4 4AQ. *T:* Windsor (0753) 859073. *Clubs:* Buck's, United and Cecil, 1900; Constitutional (Windsor).

GOODING, Anthony James Joseph S.; *see* Simonds-Gooding.

GOODING, Air Vice-Marshal Keith Horace, CB 1966; OBE 1951; *b* 2 Sept. 1913; *s* of Horace Milford Gooding, Romsey, Hants; *m* 1st, 1943, Peggy Eileen (*d* 1962), *d* of Albert William Gatfield, Guildford, Surrey; one *s*; 2nd, 1968, Jean, *d* of Maurice Stanley Underwood, Andover, Hants; two *s* one *d* (of whom one *s* one *d* are twins). *Educ:* King Edward VI Sch., Southampton. Joined RAF 1938; served Aden, Fighter Comd, 1939–45; Germany, 1945–47; NATO, 1953–55; Bomber Comd, 1958–61; AOA Maintenance Comd, 1965–68; Dir-Gen. of Supply (RAF), 1968–71, retired. Dir, Oxley Developments Co. Ltd., 1981–. Chm., Crohn's in Childhood Res. Assoc. (formerly Appeal), 1986–90. *Recreations:* tennis, bridge. *Club:* Royal Air Force.

GOODINGS, Rt. Rev. Allen, Bishop of Quebec, 1977–91; *b* Barrow-in-Furness, Lancs, 7 May 1925; *s* of late Thomas Jackson Goodings and Ada Tate; *m* 1959, Joanne Talbot; one *s* one *d*. *Educ:* Sir George Williams Univ. (BA); McGill Univ. (BD); Diocesan Theological Coll., Montreal (LTh; Hon. DD). Studied engineering and worked for Vickers Armstrongs (Britain) and Canadian Vickers (Montreal); studied in Montreal and ordained into Ministry of Anglican Church of Canada, 1959. Chaplain, Canadian Grenadier Guards, Montreal, 1966–69. Dean of Holy Trinity Cathedral, Quebec, 1969–77. Played Rugby Union (capped for Lancashire, 1947/8, including County Championship). *Recreations:* skiing, tennis, squash, cycling. *Address:* 1-C Castlebrook Lane, Nepean, Ontario KTG 5E4, Canada. *Clubs:* Cercle Universitaire (Quebec); Mess (Royale 22nd Regiment, Quebec); Quebec Garrison (Hon. Mem.).

GOODISON, Sir Alan (Clowes), KCMG 1985 (CMG 1975); CVO 1980; HM Diplomatic Service, retired; Director, The Wates Foundation, since 1988; *b* 20 Nov. 1926; *o s* of late Harold and Winifred Goodison (*née* Ludlam); *m* 1956, Anne Rosemary Fitton; one *s* two *d*. *Educ:* Colfe's Grammar Sch.; Trinity Coll., Cambridge. Scholar, Mod. and Medieval Langs Tripos, first cl.; MA 1951. Army, Lieut, 1947–49. Foreign Office, Third Sec., 1949; Middle East Centre for Arab Studies, 1950; served in Cairo, Tripoli, Khartoum, Lisbon, Amman, and Bonn, with spells in Foreign Office, 1950–68; Counsellor, Kuwait, 1969–71; Head of Trg Dept and Dir, Diplomatic Service Lang. Centre, FCO, 1971–72; Head of S European Dept, FCO, 1973–76; Minister, Rome, 1976–80; Asst Under-Sec. of State, FCO, 1980–83; Ambassador, Dublin, 1983–86. Pres., Beckenham Chorale, 1972–73. Licensed Lay Reader of Anglican Church, 1959–62, 1966–82, 1988–. A Bishop's Selector for ACCM, 1989–; Moderator of Reader Training, Edmonton Episcopal Area, 1990–. Mem. Council: Jerusalem and the East Mission, 1964–65; Anglican Centre, Rome, 1977–80. Grande Ufficiale dell'Ordine al Merito della Repubblica Italiana (Hon.), 1980. *Publications:* articles on devotional subjects and trans. for Encyclopaedia of Islam. *Recreations:* looking at pictures, music, acting, reading. *Address:* 12 Gardnor Mansions, Church Row, NW3 6UR; The Wates Foundation, 1260 London Road, SW16 4EG. *T:* 081–764 5000.

GOODISON, Sir Nicholas (Proctor), Kt 1982; Chairman, TSB Group plc, since 1989; *b* 16 May 1934; *s* of Edmund Harold Goodison and Eileen Mary Carrington Proctor; *m* 1960, Judith Abel Smith; one *s* two *d*. *Educ:* Marlborough Coll.; King's Coll., Cambridge (Scholar; BA Classics 1958, MA; PhD Architecture and History of Art, 1981). H. E. Goodison & Co. (later Quilter Goodison & Co., then Quilter Goodison Co. Ltd), 1958–88: Partner, 1962; Chm., 1975–88. Mem. Council, Stock Exchange, 1968–88; Chairman: Stock Exchange, 1976–86; Internat. Stock Exchange, 1986–88; Pres., Internat. Fedn of Stock Exchanges, 1985–86. Director: Gen. Accident Fire and Life Assce Corp. plc, 1987–; Ottoman Bank, 1988–; British Steel, 1989–. Dep. Chm., Cttee of London and Scottish Clearing Bankers, 1989–91; Vice Chm., Chartered Inst. of Bankers, 1989– (FCIB 1989); Pres., British Bankers' Assoc., 1991–. Member: Council, Industrial Soc., 1976–; Exec. Cttee, Nat. Art-Collections Fund, 1976– (Chm., 1986–); Chm., Courtauld Inst. of Art, 1982–; Director: ENO, 1977– (Vice-Chm., 1980–); City Arts Trust; Burlington Magazine Ltd. Hon. Keeper of Furniture, Fitzwilliam Museum, Cambridge; President: Furniture History Soc., 1990– (Hon. Treas., 1970–90); Antiquarian Horological Soc. Governor, Marlborough Coll. CBIM; FInstD 1989; FSA, FRSA. Hon. Fellow RA. Hon. DLitt City, 1985; Hon. LLD Exeter, 1989. Chevalier, Légion d'Honneur, 1990. *Publications:* English Barometers 1680–1860, 1968, 2nd edn 1977; Ormolu: The Work of Matthew Boulton, 1974; many papers and articles on history of furniture, clocks and barometers. *Recreations:* history of furniture and decorative arts, opera, walking, fishing. *Address:* 25 Milk Street, EC2V 8LU. *Clubs:* Athenæum, Beefsteak, Arts.

GOODISON, Robin Reynolds, CB 1964; consultant; Deputy Chairman, 1972–77, Acting Chairman, Jan.-March 1972, Civil Aviation Authority; *b* 13 Aug. 1912; *s* of Arthur Leathley Goodison; *m* 1936, Betty Lydia, *d* of Comdr L. Robinson, OBE, Royal Navy (retired); three *d*. *Educ:* Finchley Grammar Sch.; University Coll., London Univ. (MA). Joined Ministry of Labour, 1935, transferred to Ministry of Transport, 1936; Principal, 1940; Asst Sec., 1946; Imperial Defence Coll., 1950; Under-Sec., Ministry of Transport and Civil Aviation, 1957, Ministry of Aviation, 1959, Board of Trade, 1966; Second Sec., BoT, 1969–70; Dep. Sec., DTI, 1970–72. Assessor, Heathrow Terminal Inquiry, 1978–79; Specialist Adviser, House of Lords Select Cttee, 1979–80, 1984–85. *Recreation:* sailing. *Address:* 37 Coldharbour Lane, Bushey, Herts WD2 3NU. *T:* 081–950 1911.

GOODLAD, Alastair Robertson; MP (C) Eddisbury, since 1983 (Northwich, Feb. 1974–1983); Deputy Government Chief Whip and Treasurer of HM Household, since 1990; *b* 4 July 1943; *y s* of late Dr John Goodlad and late Isabel (*née* Sinclair); *m* 1968, Cecilia Barbara, 2nd *d* of late Col Richard Hurst and Lady Barbara Hurst; two *s*. *Educ:* Marlborough Coll.; King's Coll., Cambridge (MA, LLB). Contested (C) Crewe Div., 1970. An Asst Govt Whip, 1981–82; a Lord Commissioner of HM Treasury, 1982–84; Parly Under-Sec. of State, Dept of Energy, 1984–87; Comptroller of HM Household, 1989–90. Member: Select Cttee on Agric., 1979–81; Select Cttee on Televising of Proceedings of the House, 1987–89; Jt Hon. Secretary: Cons. Party Trade Cttee, 1978–81 (Jt Vice-Chm., 1979–81); Cons. NI Cttee, 1979–81; Hon. Sec., All Party Heritage Gp, 1979–81; Chm., All Party Parly Cttee for Refugees, 1987–89. Chm., NW Area Cons. Members, 1987–89. *Address:* House of Commons, SW1A 0AA. *Clubs:* Brooks's, Beefsteak.

GOODLAND, Judith Mary; Headmistress, Wycombe Abbey School, since 1989; *b* 26 May 1938; *d* of Rolf Thornton Ferro and Joan (*née* O'Hanlon); *m* 1961, A. T. Goodland (marr. diss.); one *s* two *d*. *Educ:* Howell's Sch., Denbigh; Bristol Univ. (BA Hons); Charlotte Mason Coll., Ambleside (Cert Ed). Oral Examiner in French O level for NUJMB; Head, Modern Languages Dept, Cartmel Priory C of E Comprehensive Sch., 1968–72; Casterton Sch., Kirkby Lonsdale, 1980–83; Headmistress, St George's Sch., Ascot, 1983–88. *Recreations:* fell walking, bridge, golf. *Address:* Wycombe Abbey School, High Wycombe, Bucks HP11 1PE. *T:* High Wycombe (0494) 20381. *Club:* University Women's.

GOODMAN, family name of **Baron Goodman.**

GOODMAN, Baron, *cr* 1965, of the City of Westminster (Life Peer); **Arnold Abraham Goodman,** CH 1972; MA, LLM; Master of University College, Oxford, 1976–86 (Hon. Fellow, 1986); Senior Partner, Goodman Derrick and Co., Solicitors; *b* 21 Aug. 1913; *s* of Joseph and Bertha Goodman; unmarried. *Educ:* University Coll., London (Fellow 1967); Downing Coll., Cambridge (Hon. Fellow, 1968). Enlisted Gunner, RA, TA, Sept. 1939, retd as Major, Nov. 1945. Chairman: British Lion Films, 1965–72; Charter Film Productions, 1973–84. Dir, The Observer Ltd, 1976–81; Chairman: Observer Editl Trust, 1967–76; Newspaper Publishers Assoc., 1970–76; Jewish Chronicle Trust, 1970–. Chairman: Housing Corp., 1973–77; Nat. Building Agency, 1973–78; Mem., IRC, 1969–71. Chairman: Cttee of Inquiry into Charity Law, 1974–76; Motability, 1977–; Council for Charitable Support, 1986–89. Chm., Arts Council of GB, 1965–72; Dep. Chm., British Council, 1976–91 (Mem., 1967–91); President: NBL, 1972–85; Inst. of Jewish Affairs, 1975–. Chairman: Cttee (on behalf of Arts Council) on London Orchestras, 1964, reported 1965; Australian Music Foundn, 1975–; Mem., S Bank Theatre Bd, 1968–82; President: Theatres Adv. Council, 1972–; Theatre Investment Fund, 1985– (Chm., 1976–85); ENO, 1986– (Chm., 1977–86); Theatres Trust, 1987– (Chm., 1976–87); Union of Liberal & Progressive Synagogues, 1988–; Assoc. for Business Sponsorship of the Arts, 1989– (Chm., 1976–89); Dir, Royal Opera House, Covent Garden, 1972–83; Gov., Royal Shakespeare Theatre, 1972–. Gov., Coll. of Law, 1975–84. Life Mem., RPO, 1976. Hon. LLD: London, 1965; Bath, Liverpool, 1976; Hon. DLitt City, 1975; hon. degrees from other univs. *Address:* 9–11 Fulwood Place, Gray's Inn, WC1V 6HQ. *T:* 071–404 0606.

GOODMAN, Dame Barbara, DBE 1989; QSO 1981; JP; *b* 5 Oct. 1932; *d* of late Horace Robinson and Lillie Robinson (*née* Shieff); *m* 1954, Harold Goodman (decd); two *s* one *d*. *Educ:* Parnell Sch.; St Cuthbert's Coll. Mayoress, City of Auckland, 1968–80; founding Trustee, Help Foundn, 1980–85; Chm., Auckland Spastic Soc., 1980–84; Chm., Odyssey House Trust, 1981–; Mem. Exec. Cttee, NZ Fedn of Voluntary Welfare Organisations. Mem., Auckland City Council, 1989–. Mem., NZ Internat. Trade Fair Cttee, 1985–; Chm., Auckland 1990 Trust Board, 1989–. *Publication:* For Flying Kiwis, 1990. *Recreations:* meeting people, travel, reading, cooking, embroidery, gardening. *Address:* 65 St Stephens Avenue, Parnell, Auckland 1001, New Zealand. *T:* (09) 790–650. *Clubs:* Athene, Zonta (Auckland); Auckland Women's Cricket Association.

GOODMAN, Maj.-Gen. David; *see* Goodman, Maj.-Gen. J. D. W.

GOODMAN, Geoffrey George; Editor, British Journalism Review, since 1989; Broadcaster, BBC Current Affairs and IRN, since 1986; *b* 2 July 1921; *s* of Michael Goodman and Edythe (*née* Bowman); *m* 1947, Margit (*née* Freudenbergova); one *s* one *d*. *Educ:* elementary schs, Stockport and Manchester; grammar schs, London; LSE (BScEcon). RAF, 1940–46. Manchester Guardian, 1946–47; Daily Mirror, 1947–48; News Chronicle, 1949–59; Daily Herald, 1959–64; The Sun (IPC), 1964–69; Daily Mirror, 1969–86 (Industrial Editor, 1969–86; Asst Editor, 1976–86). Fellow, Nuffield Coll., Oxford, 1974–76. Head of Govt's Counter-inflation Publicity Unit, 1975–76; Member: Labour Party Cttee on Industrial Democracy, 1966–67; Royal Commn on the Press, 1974–77; TGWU; NUJ. Hon. MA Oxon. Gerald Barry Award for Journalism, Granada TV Press Awards, 1984. *Publications:* General Strike of 1926, 1951; Brother Frank, 1969; The Awkward Warrior, 1979; The Miners' Strike, 1985; contrib. London Inst. of World Affairs, 1948. *Recreations:* pottering, poetry, supporting Tottenham Hotspur FC, and climbing—but not social. *Address:* 64 Flower Lane, Mill Hill, NW7. *Club:* Savile.

GOODMAN, Howard; *see* Goodman, R. H.

GOODMAN, Maj.-Gen. (John) David (Whitlock), CB 1987; Director and defence advisor to ML Holdings plc, since 1989; Consultant, Landair International Defence Services Ltd, since 1987; *b* 20 May 1932; *s* of late Brig. Eric Whitlock Goodman, DSO, MC and Norah Dorothy Goodman (*née* Stacpoole); *m* 1957, Valerie-Ann McDonald; one *s* two *d*. *Educ:* Wellington Coll.; RMA Sandhurst. Commnd RA, 1952; served in UK and Northern Ireland, BAOR, Aden and Hong Kong; Staff Coll. 1962; Battery Comdr, 3rd Regt Royal Horse Artillery, 1966–69; Jt Services Staff Coll., Latimer, 1970; BMRA 2nd Div., 1970–72; Instr, Staff Coll. Camberley and Sudan, 1972–73; CO 26 Field Regt, RA, 1973–76; Comdt, Royal Sch. of Artillery, 1977–79; Royal Coll. of Defence Studies, 1980; Asst Military Secretary, MoD, 1981–82; Dir, Army Air Corps, 1983–87. Hon. Colonel: 26 Field Regt RA, 1985–; 3 Regt, AAC, 1987–; 266 (Glos Volunteer Artillery) Observation Post Batt. RA (Vol.), 1990–. Trustee: Mus. of Army Flying Develt Trust, 1989–; Kelly Holdsworth Trust, 1990–. FBIM 1980. Freeman, GAPAN, 1987. *Recreations:* the countryside, tennis. *Address:* c/o Lloyds Bank, 37 Market Place, Warminster, Wilts BA12 9BD. *Club:* Naval and Military.

GOODMAN, Prof. John Francis Bradshaw, PhD; CIPM; Frank Thomas Professor of Industrial Relations, University of Manchester Institute of Science and Technology, since 1975 (Vice-Principal, 1979–81); *b* 2 Aug. 1940; *s* of Edwin and Amy Goodman; *m* 1967,

Elizabeth Mary Towns; one s one d. *Educ:* Chesterfield Grammar Sch.; London Sch. of Economics (BSc Econ; PhD); MSc Manchester. FIPM. Personnel Officer, Ford Motor Co. Ltd, 1962–64; Lectr in Industrial Econs, Univ. of Nottingham, 1964–69; Industrial Relations Adviser, NBPI, 1969–70; Sen. Lectr in Industrial Relations, Univ. of Manchester, 1970–74; Chm., Manchester Sch. of Management, UMIST, 1977–79, 1987–. Vis. Professor: Univ. of WA, 1981, 1984; McMaster Univ., 1985. Pres., British Univs Industrial Relations Assoc., 1983–86. Mem. Council, ACAS, 1987–. *Publications:* Shop Stewards in British Industry, 1969; Shop Stewards, 1973; Rulemaking and Industrial Peace, 1977; Ideology and Shop-floor Industrial Relations, 1981; Employment Relations in Industrial Society, 1984; Unfair Dismissal Law and Employment Practice, 1985; contribs to British Jl of Industrial Relations, ILR, Industrial Relations Jl, Monthly Labor Rev., Jl of Management Studies, Personnel Management, etc. *Recreations:* fell walking, ornithology, squash, football. *Address:* Lundy Rise, Brookledge Lane, Adlington, Macclesfield, Cheshire SK10 4JX. *T:* Macclesfield (0625) 572480.

GOODMAN, Michael Bradley; **His Honour Judge Goodman;** a Circuit Judge, since 1983; *b* 3 May 1930; *s* of Marcus Gordon Goodman and Eunice Irene May Goodman (*née* Bradley); *m* 1967, Patricia Mary Gorringe; two *d* (one *s* decd). *Educ:* Aldenham; Sidney Sussex Coll., Cambridge (MA). Called to Bar, Middle Temple, 1953; Western Circuit; a Recorder of the Crown Court, 1972–83. Prosecuting Counsel to DHSS, 1975–83; Pres., Wireless Telegraphy Appeals Tribunal, 1977–88; Member: Commn on Deployment and Payment of the Clergy, 1965–67; C of E Legal Adv. Commn, 1973– (Chm., 1986–); General Synod, Church of England, 1977–83; Faculty Jurisdiction Commn, 1980–83; Chancellor: Dio. Guildford, 1968–; Dio. Lincoln, 1970–; Dio. Rochester, 1971–; Lay Chm., Dulwich Deanery Synod, 1970–73; Vicar-Gen., Province of Canterbury, 1977–83. Chairman: William Temple Assoc., 1963–66; Ecclesiastical Judges Assoc., 1987–. Governor: Liddon Hse, London, 1964–; Pusey Hse, Oxford, 1965–88. *Address:* Bromley County Court, College Road, Bromley, Kent.

GOODMAN, Michael Jack, PhD; Social Security Commissioner (formerly National Insurance Commissioner), since 1979; *b* 3 Oct. 1931; *s* of Vivian Roy Goodman and Muriel Olive Goodman; *m* 1958, Susan Kerkham Wherry; two *s* one *d. Educ:* Sudbury Grammar Sch., Suffolk; Corpus Christi Coll., Oxford (MA). PhD Manchester. Solicitor. Lectr, Gibson & Weldon, 1957; solicitor, Lincoln, 1958–60; Lectr, Law Society's Sch., 1961–63; Lectr, then Sen. Lectr in Law, Manchester Univ., 1964–70; Prof. of Law, Durham Univ., 1971–76; Perm. Chm. of Indust. Tribunals, Newcastle upon Tyne, 1976–79. Gen. Editor, Encyclopedia of Health and Safety at Work, 1974–. *Publications:* Industrial Tribunals' Procedure, 1976, 4th edn 1987; Health and Safety at Work: law and practice, 1988; contrib. Mod. Law Rev., and Conveyancer. *Recreations:* amateur radio (licence holder), model railways, The Times crossword. *Address:* Office of the Social Security Commissioners, Harp House, 83 Farringdon Street, EC4A 4DH. *T:* 071–353 5145.

GOODMAN, Rt. Rev. Morse Lamb; *b* Rosedale, Ont, 27 May 1917; *s* of Frederick James Goodman and Mary Mathilda Arkwright; *m* 1943, Patricia May Cunningham; three *s* one *d. Educ:* Trinity Coll., Univ. of Toronto. BA Trin., 1940; LTh Trin., 1942. Deacon, 1942, Priest, 1943, Diocese of Algoma; Asst Curate, St Paul's, Ft William, 1942–43; Incumbent, Murillo, Algoma, 1943–46; Rector, St Thomas, Ft William, 1946–53; Rector, St James, Winnipeg, 1953–60; Dean of Brandon, 1960–65; Rector, Christ Church, Edmonton, 1965–67; Bishop of Calgary, 1968–83. Conductor of Canadian Broadcasting Corporation Programme, Family Worship, 1954–68. Patron, Nat. Prayer Book Soc. Hon. DD: Trinity, 1961; Emmanuel and St Chad's, 1968. Companion, Order of Coventry Cross of Nails, 1974; GCKLJ. Columnist, Country Guide, 1961–. *Publication:* Let's Think It Over (A Christian's Day Book), 1986. *Recreations:* fishing, walking, photography, enology. *Address:* Box 15, Blind Bay, BC V0E 1H0, Canada. *Club:* Ranchman's.

GOODMAN, Perry; Director (Industry and Regions), The Engineering Council, since 1990; *b* 26 Nov. 1932; *s* of Cyril Goodman and Anne (*née* Rosen); *m* 1958, Marcia Ann (*née* Morris); one *s* one *d. Educ:* Haberdashers' Aske's Hampstead Sch.; University Coll., London. BSc, MICeram. 2nd Lieut, Royal Corps of Signals, 1955–57; Jt Head, Chemistry Res. Lab., then Project Leader, Morgan Crucible Co. Ltd, 1957–64; Sen. Scientific Officer, DSIR, 1964–65; Principal Scientific Officer, Process Plant Br., Min. of Technology, 1965–67; 1st Sec. (Scientific), 1968–70, Counsellor (Scientific), 1970–74, British Embassy, Paris; Research Gp, DoI, 1974–79; Hd, Policy and Perspectives Unit, DoI, 1980–81; Department of Trade and Industry: Hd, Design Policy/Technical Adv. Services for Industry, 1981–86; Hd, Electrical Engrg Br., 1986–90. FRSA 1986. *Recreations:* travel, walking, conversation. *Address:* 118 Westbourne Terrace Mews, W2 6QG. *T:* 071–262 0925.

GOODMAN, (Robert) Howard, ARIBA; DipArch (Hons); Partner, MPA Health Planners, since 1988; *b* 29 March 1928; *s* of Robert Barnard Goodman and Phyllis Goodman; *m* 1955; two *s. Educ:* St George Grammar Sch., Bristol; Northern Polytechnic, London. Articled pupil, 1944–47; Arch. Asst to City of Bristol, 1947–49; Asst Architect to SW Regional Hosp. Bd, 1949–54. Design of various hosp. projects in SW England; with various private architects, 1954–60; design of several hosps in UK, Africa and India. MOH (now DoH): Main Grade Arch., 1960; Sen. Grade, 1961; Principal Arch., 1963; Asst Chief Arch., 1966; Chief Arch., 1971–78; Dir of Develt, 1978–85; Dir, Health Bldg, 1986–88. Councillor (Lab) Reigate and Banstead BC, 1989–. Member: Constr. and Housing Res. Adv. Council; Bldg Res. Estab. Adv. Council; Council of Centre on Environment for the Handicapped. Research and develt into health planning, systems building and computer aided design. Hon. FICW, 1984; Hon. FBID, 1985; Hon. FIHopsE, 1988. *Publications:* contribs to: Hospitals Handbook, 1960; Hospital Design, 1963; Hospital Traffic and Supply Problems, 1968; Portfolio for Health, 1971; Technology of the Eighties, 1972; Industrialised Hospital Building, 1972; CAD Systems, 1976; various articles in architectural, medical and general press. *Recreations:* eating, drinking, talking. *Address:* Ion House, 44 Nutley Lane, Reigate, Surrey.

GOODPASTER, Gen. Andrew Jackson; United States Army, retired; US Medal of Freedom, 1984; DSC (US); DSM (Def.) (Oak Leaf Cluster); DSM (Army) (3 Oak Leaf Clusters); DSM (Navy); DSM (Air Force); Silver Star; Legion of Merit (Oak Leaf Cluster); Purple Heart (Oak Leaf Cluster); Superintendent, United States Military Academy, West Point, New York (in grade of Lt-Gen.), 1977–81; *b* 12 Feb. 1915; *s* of Andrew Jackson Goodpaster and Teresa Mary Goodpaster (*née* Mrovka); *m* 1939, Dorothy Anderson Goodpaster (*née* Anderson); two *d. Educ:* McKendree Coll., Lebanon, Ill; US Mil. Academy, 1935–39 (BS); Princeton Univ., 1947–50 (MSE, MA, PhD). 11th Eng. Panama, 1939–42; Ex O, 390th Eng. Gen. Svc Regt, Camp Claiborne, La, 1942–43; Comd and Gen. Staff Sch., Ft Leavenworth, Kansas, Feb.-April 1943; CO, 48th Eng. Combat Bn, II Corps, Fifth Army, 1943–44; Ops Div., Gen. Staff, War Dept (incl. Jt War Plans Cttee, JCS, 1945–46), 1944–47; Student, Civil Eng. Course and Polit. Sc. Grad. Sch., Princeton Univ., 1947–50; Army Mem., Jt Advanced Study Cttee, JCS, 1950–51; Special Asst to Chief of Staff, SHAPE, 1951–54; Dist Eng., San Francisco Dist, Calif, July-Oct. 1954; Def. Liaison Officer and Staff Sec. to President of US, 1954–61; Asst Div. Comdr,

3rd Inf. Div., April-Oct. 1961, and CG, 8th Inf. Div., Oct. 1961–Oct. 1962, USAREUR; Sp. Asst (Policy) to Chm., JCS, Washington, DC, Nov. 1962–Jan. 1964; Asst to Chm., JCS, Washington, DC, Jan. 1964–July 1966; Dir Joint Staff, JCS, Washington, DC, Aug. 1966–Mar. 1967; Dir of Sp. Studies, Office Chief of Staff, USA, Washington, DC, April 1967–July 1967; Senior US Army Mem., Mil. Staff UN, May 1967–July 1968; Comdt, Nat. War Coll., Washington, DC, Aug. 1967–July 1968; Mem. US Delegn for Negotiations with N Vietnam, Paris (addl duty), April 1968–July 1968; Dep. Comdr, US Mil. Assistance Comd, Vietnam, July 1968–April 1969; Supreme Allied Commander Europe, 1969–74; C-in-C, US European Command, 1969–74. Sen. Fellow, Woodrow Wilson Internat. Center for Scholars, Washington DC, 1975–76; Prof. of Govt and Internat. Studies, The Citadel, Charleston, SC, 1976–77. Pres., Inst. for Defence Analyses, Alexandria, Va, 1983–85; Chm., Atlantic Council of the US, 1985–. *Publication:* For the Common Defense, 1977. *Recreations:* golf, fishing, music. *Address:* 409 North Fairfax Street, Alexandria, Va 22314, USA.

GOODRICH, David, CEng, RCNC; Managing Director, since 1985 and Chief Executive, since 1986, British Maritime Technology Ltd; *b* 15 April 1941; *s* of William B. Goodrich and Florence B Goodrich; *m* 1965, Margaret R. Riley; one *s* three *d.* MBA. Shipbuilding management apprentice, 1958–63; shipbuilding designer/estimator, 1963–65; Constructor, RCNC, 1965–77; Manager, Shipbuilding Technology, 1977–79, Man. Dir, 1979–85, BSRA. FRINA (Mem. Council). *Publication:* paper to Royal Soc. *Recreations:* squash, walking, family. *Address:* Whitecroft, Hatton Hill, Windlesham, Surrey.

GOODRICH, Rt. Rev. Philip Harold Ernest; *see* Worcester, Bishop of.

GOODRIDGE, Hon. Noel Herbert Alan; Chief Justice of Court of Appeal and of Newfoundland, since 1986; *b* 18 Dec. 1930; *s* of William Prout Goodridge and Freda Dorothy (*née* Hayward); *m* 1956, Isabelle (*née* Galway); three *s* one *d. Educ:* Bishop Field Coll.; King's Collegiate Sch., Windsor, NS; Bishop's College Sch., Lennoxville, PQ; Dalhousie Univ., Halifax, NS (BA, LLB). Practised law, 1953–75; QC (Newfoundland), 1972; originally with Hunt, Emerson, Stirling and Higgins, later Stirling, Ryan and Goodridge; at time of leaving practice, a sen. partner; Puisne Judge, Trial Div. of Supreme Ct of Newfoundland, 1975; Puisne Judge, Ct Martial Appeal Ct, 1981–. Canadian Bar Association: Mem., 1956–; Mem. Nat. Exec., 1975–76; Pres., Nfld Br., 1973–75. Bencher, Law Soc. of Nfld, 1970–75, Sec., 1973–75; Member: Judicial Council estabd under the Provincial Ct Act, 1974–76; Canadian Judicial Council, 1986–; Canadian Judges Conf., 1976–. Exec. positions with Jun. Ch. of Commerce, 1954–57, and Nfld BoT, 1962–64. Vice-Chm., Gen. Hosp. Corp., 1970–75; Chm., St John's Transportation Commn, 1971–75; Mem., Newfoundland Assoc. for the Help of Retarded Children, 1960–62. Life Mem., Assoc. of Kinsmen Clubs of Canada. *Recreations:* golf, tennis, walking, bridge, skiing. *Address:* Supreme Court of Newfoundland, Court of Appeal, PO Box 937, St John's, Newfoundland A1C 5M3, Canada. *T:* (709) 722–3310.

GOODSMAN, James Melville; Director, Conservative Party in Scotland, since 1990; *b* 6 Feb. 1947; *s* of James K. Goodsman and Euphamia Goodsman, Elgin, Moray; *m* 1990, Victoria, *y d* of late Col Philip Smitherman and of Rosemary Smitherman, CBE. *Educ:* Elgin Academy. Joined Cons. Party organisation, 1966; Agent: to Rt Hon. Betty Harvie Anderson, 1970–74; to Rt Hon. Maurice Macmillan, 1974–80; Conservative Central Office: Dep. Agent, NW Area, 1980–84; Asst Dir (Community Affairs), 1984–90; Head, Community and Legal Affairs, May-Sept. 1990. Hon. Sec., One Nation Forum, 1986–90. *Publications:* contribs to Cons. party and community relations papers. *Recreations:* golf, shooting, church music. *Address:* (office) Suite 1/1, 14 Links Place, Leith, Edinburgh EH6 7EZ. *Club:* Buck's.

GOODSON, Sir Mark (Weston Lassam), 3rd Bt *cr* 1922, of Waddeton Court, Co. Devon; *b* 12 Dec. 1925; *s* of Major Alan Richard Lassam Goodson (*d* 1941) (2nd *s* of 1st Bt) and Clarisse Muriel Weston (*d* 1982), *d* of John Weston Adamson; *S* uncle, 1986; *m* 1949, Barbara Mary Constantine, *d* of Surg.-Capt. Reginald Joseph McAuliffe Andrews, RN; one *s* three *d. Educ:* Radley; Jesus College, Cambridge. **Heir:** *s* Alan Reginald Goodson, *b* 15 May 1960. *Address:* Kilham, Mindrum, Northumberland TD12 4QS. *T:* Mindrum (089085) 217.

GOODSON, Michael John; Assistant Auditor General, National Audit Office, since 1984; *b* 4 Aug. 1937; *s* of late Herbert Edward William Goodson and Doris Maud Goodson; *m* 1958, Susan Elizabeth (*née* Higley); one *s* one *d. Educ:* King Henry VIII Sch., Coventry. Joined Exchequer and Audit Dept, 1955; Asst Auditor, 1955; Auditor, 1965; Private Sec. to Comptroller and Auditor Gen., 1967–70; Sen. Auditor, 1970; Health Service Ombudsman (on secondment), 1973–76; Chief Auditor, Exchequer and Audit Dept, 1976; Dep. Dir of Audit, 1978; Dir of Audit, 1981. *Recreations:* ornithology, model engineering, caravanning. *Address:* 5 Alzey Gardens, Harpenden, Herts AL5 5SZ. *T:* Harpenden (05827) 62744.

GOODSON-WICKES, Dr Charles; MP (C) Wimbledon, since 1987; *b* 7 Nov. 1945; *s* of late Ian Goodson Wickes, FRCP, Consultant Paediatrician and farmer, of Stock Harvard, Essex and of Monica Goodson-Wickes; *m* 1974, Judith Amanda Hopkinson, *d* of late Comdr John Hopkinson, RN, of Sutton Grange, nr Stamford, Lincs; two *s. Educ:* Charterhouse; St Bartholomew's Hosp. (MB BS 1970). Called to the Bar, Inner Temple, 1972. Ho. Physician, Addenbrooke's Hosp., Cambridge, 1972; Surgeon-Capt., The Life Guards, 1973–77 (served BAOR, N Ireland, Cyprus); Silver Stick MO, Hsehold Cavalry, 1977; RARO, 1977–90; re-enlisted as Lt-Col, 1991, for Gulf Campaign (served S Arabia, Iraq, Kuwait, with HQ 7 Armoured Bde). Clin. Asst, St Bart's Hosp., 1977–80; Consulting Phys., BUPA, 1977–86; Occupational Phys., 1980–; Med. advr to Barclays Bank, RTZ, McKinsey, Christie's, British Alcan, Collins, Meat & Livestock Commn etc.; UK Advr, Norwegian Directorate of Health, 1983–, Chm., Appeals Bd, Asbestos Licensing Regulations, 1982–; Member: Med. Adv. Cttee, Industrial Soc., 1981–87; Fitness Adv. Panel, Inst. of Dirs, 1982–84. Contested (C) Islington Central, 1979. Vice-Pres., Islington South and Finsbury Cons. Assoc., 1982–; Sec., 1987–90, Vice-Chm., 1990–, Constitutional Affairs Cttee; Sec., Arts and Heritage Cttee, 1990–; Mem., Jt Cttee, Consolidation of Bills, 1987–. Treas., Dr Ian Goodson Wickes Fund for Handicapped Children, 1979–88; Mem., Public Affairs Cttee, British Field Sports Soc., 1980–. Governor, Highbury Grove Sch., 1977–85. Pte, The Parachute Regt (TA), 1963–65. Founder Chm., Essex Kit Cat Club, 1965. *Publication:* The New Corruption, 1984. *Recreations:* hunting, shooting, real tennis, gardening, travel, history. *Address:* Watergate House, Bulford, Wilts. *T:* Stonehenge(0980) 32344; 37 St James's Place, SW1. *T:* 071-629 0981; (consulting rooms) 8 Devonshire Place, W1. *T:* 071-935 5011. *Clubs:* Boodle's, Pratt's, MCC.

GOODWIN, Prof. Albert, MA; Professor of Modern History in the University of Manchester, 1953–69 (Dean of the Faculty of Arts, 1966–68), now Emeritus Professor; *b* 2 Aug. 1906; 3rd *s* of Albert and Edith Ellen Goodwin; *m* 1st, 1935, Mary Ethelwyn (*d* 1981), *e d* of late Capt. W. Millner, Tettenhall, Staffs; two *s* one *d*; 2nd, 1985, Mrs Barbara Mallows (*d* 1990). *Educ:* King Edward VII School, Sheffield; Jesus Coll., Oxford; Sorbonne. Scholar; Gladstone Memorial Prizeman (Oxford), 1926; 1st Cl. Mod. Hist., 1928; Laming Travelling Fellow, The Queen's Coll., Oxford, 1928–29. Asst Lectr in European History, Univ. of Liverpool, 1929–31; Lectr in Mod. Hist. and Economics,

1931, Fellow and Tutor, Jesus Coll., Oxford, 1933; Junior Dean, Librarian and Dean of Degrees, 1931–39; Univ. Lectr in Mod. French Hist., 1938. Staff Officer (Sqdn Ldr) in RAFVR in Air Ministry War Room, 1940–43; Historical Branch, Air Ministry, 1944–45. Senior Tutor, 1947–48, and Vice-Principal of Jesus Coll., Oxford, 1949–51. Examiner in Final Hon. Sch. of Mod. Hist. (Oxford) 1948–49, Chm., 1950; Senior Univ. Lectr in Revolutionary and Napoleonic Period, 1948–53; Vis. Fellow, All Souls Coll., Oxford, 1969–70. Member: Council of Royal Historical Soc. (Vice-Pres.); Royal Commn on Historical MSS, 1966–81; Governor of John Rylands Library, Manchester. Pres., Sherborne Hist. Soc.; Chm., Sherborne Museum Council, 1981–82. *Publications:* The Abbey of St Edmundsbury, 1931; The Battle of Britain (Air Ministry Pamphlet 156), 1943; The French Revolution, 1953; The European Nobility in the Eighteenth Century (contrib. and ed), 1953; A select list of works on Europe and Europe Overseas, 1715–1815 (co-editor contributor), 1956; The Friends of Liberty: the English democratic movement in the age of the French Revolution, 1979; (ed and contrib.) Vol. VIII New Cambridge Modern History; articles in Eng. Hist. Review, History, Encyclopædia Britannica, etc. *Recreations:* golf, antiques. *Address:* Tyndale Nursing Home, 36 Preston Road, Yeovil, Somerset BA21 3AQ.

GOODWIN, Air Vice-Marshal Edwin Spencer, CB 1944; CBE 1941; AFC. Served European War, 1914–19; Flt Sub-Lieut RNAS, 1916; War of 1939–45 (CBE, CB). Group Capt. 1939; Air Commodore, 1941; Air Vice-Marshal, 1948. Air Officer i/c Administration, HQ Bomber Command, 1945; retired, 1948.

GOODWIN, Dr Eric Thomson, CBE 1975; retired; *b* 30 July 1913; *s* of John Edward Goodwin and Florence Goodwin; *m* 1st, 1940, Isobel Philip (*d* 1976); two *s*; 2nd, 1977, Avis Mary (*née* Thomson). *Educ:* King Edward VI Sch., Stafford; Harrow County Sch.; Peterhouse, Cambridge. BA 1934, Rayleigh Prize 1936, MA 1937, PhD 1938. Asst Lectr, Sheffield Univ., 1937–39; war service: Mathematical Lab., Cambridge, 1939–43; Admty Signal Estabt, Witley, 1943–44; Admty Computing Service, Bath, 1945; Maths Div., Nat. Physical Lab., 1945–71 (Supt 1951–71); Dep. Dir, Nat. Phys. Lab., 1971–74, retd. *Publications:* papers in learned jls on theoretical physics and numerical analysis. *Recreations:* music, reading, the countryside, philately. *Address:* 32 Castle Mount Crescent, Bakewell, Derbyshire DE4 1AT. *T:* Bakewell (0629) 813647.

GOODWIN, Prof. Geoffrey Lawrence, BSc (Econ.); Montague Burton Professor of International Relations in the University of London (tenable at London School of Economics), 1962–78, now Emeritus; *b* 14 June 1916; *s* of Rev. J. H. Goodwin and Mrs E. M. Goodwin; *m* 1951, Janet Audrey (*née* Sewell) (*d* 1986); one *s* two *d*. *Educ:* Marlborough Coll.; RMC, Sandhurst; London Sch. of Economics. Regular Army Officer, 1936–43 (The Suffolk Regt; Army Physical Training Staff; Combined Ops; Major, comdg Indep. Company, Gibraltar). Foreign Office, 1945–48; London Sch. of Economics, 1948–81. Principal, St Catharine's, Windsor Great Park, 1971–72. Comr on Internat. Affairs, World Council of Churches, 1968–76. Mem. Council, 1974–77, Sen. Advr, 1983–84, RIIA; Vis. Mem., Inst. for Advanced Study, Princeton 1959; Vis. Prof., Institut Universitaire des Hautes Etudes Internationales, Geneva, 1962; Vis. Fellow, ANU, Canberra, 1978. Hon. Pres., British Internat. Studies Assoc., 1977–80. FRSA 1975. *Publications:* (ed) The University Teaching of International Relations, 1951; Britain and the United Nations, 1958; (ed) New Dimensions of World Politics, 1975; (ed) A New International Commodity Regime, 1979; (ed) Ethics and Nuclear Deterrence, 1982; articles in International Affairs, International Organization, Political Studies, etc. *Recreations:* painting, sketching, singing. *Address:* Norton Priory, Church Norton, Selsey, Chichester, W Sussex PO20 9DT.

GOODWIN, Prof. John Forrest, MD, FRCP; Professor of Clinical Cardiology, Royal Postgraduate Medical School, London, 1963–84, now Emeritus; Consulting Physician, Hammersmith Hospital, since 1949; Hon. Consulting Cardiologist: St Mary's Hospital, Paddington, since 1982; St George's Hospital, since 1986; *b* 1 Dec. 1918; *s* of late Col William Richard Power Goodwin, DSO, RAMC, and late Myrtle Dale Goodwin (*née* Forrest); *m* 1943, Barbara Cameron Robertson; one *s* one *d*. *Educ:* Cheltenham Coll.; St Mary's Hosp. Medical Sch. (Univ. of London). FRSocMed 1943; MD London 1946; FRCP 1957. Med. Registrar, St Mary's Hosp., 1943–44; Physician, Anglo-Iranian Oil Co., Abadan, 1944–45; Med. 1st Asst, Royal Infirmary, Sheffield, 1946–49; Lectr in Medicine and Cons. Physician, Postgraduate Med. Sch., London, 1949–59; Sen. Lecturer, 1959–63. Visiting Professor: Univ. of California at Los Angeles, 1966; Georgetown Univ. Sch. of Med., Washington, 1973; Mayo Clinic, 1985; Pfizer Vis. Prof., Massachusetts Gen. Hosp., 1987; Lumleian Lectr, RCP, 1980. Mem., Expert Cttee on Cardiovascular Diseases, WHO, 1979. Member: Brit. Cardiac Soc., 1950 (Pres., 1972–76); Med. Res. Soc., 1952; Assoc. of Physicians of Great Britain and Ireland, 1953; Council, Brit. Heart Foundation, 1964; Past Pres., Internat. Soc. and Fedn of Cardiology (Pres., 1977–81); 2nd Vice-Pres., RCP, 1979–80; Vice Pres., Coronary Prevention Gp, 1988– (Chm., 1985–88); Chm., Nat. Forum for the Prevention of Coronary Heart Disease, 1987–. Member: Società Italiana di Cardiologia, 1964; Assoc. of European Pædiatric Cardiologists, 1967; Cardiac Soc. of Australia and NZ, 1974; Venezuelan Soc. of Cardiology, 1969; Burma Medical Assoc., 1987–; Hon. Member: Swiss Cardiol. Soc.; Cardiac Soc., Ecuador; Hellenic Cardiac Soc., 1974; Cardiac Soc. of Mexico, 1977; Fellow: Amer. Coll. of Cardiology, 1967; Council on Clinical Cardiology, Amer. Heart Assoc., 1970; European Soc. of Cardiology, 1988; Hon. FACP 1985. Dr *hc* Lisbon, 1985. Gifted Teacher Award, Amer. Coll. of Cardiol., 1984. SPk 1968. Commander, Order of Icelandic Falcon, 1972. *Publications:* (jt ed. with R. Daley and R. E. Steiner) Clinical Disorders of the Pulmonary Circulation, 1960; (with W. Cleland, L. McDonald, D. Ross) Medical and Surgical Cardiology, 1969; (ed) Heart Muscle Disease, 1985; (ed with G. Baroldi and F. Camerini) Advances in Cardiomyopathies, 1990; (ed with P. Yu) Progress in Cardiology, annually 1973–88; papers on diagnosis and treatment of congenital and acquired heart disease in British and foreign cardiac and other journals. *Recreations:* photography, history, travel. *Address:* 2 Pine Grove, Lake Road, Wimbledon, SW19 7HE. *T:* 081-947 4851. *Clubs:* Athenæum, Royal Society of Medicine.

GOODWIN, Leonard George, CMG 1977; FRCP; FRS 1976; Director, Nuffield Laboratories of Comparative Medicine, Institute of Zoology, The Zoological Society of London, 1964–80; Director of Science, Zoological Society of London, 1966–80; Consultant, Wellcome Trust, since 1984; *b* 11 July 1915; *s* of Harry George and Lois Goodwin; *m* 1940, Marie Evelyn Coates; no *c*. *Educ:* William Ellis Sch., London; University Coll. London (Fellow, 1981); School of Pharmacy, London; University Coll. Hospital. BPharm 1935, BSc 1937, MB, BS 1950, (London). MRCP 1966, FRCP 1972. Demonstrator, Sch. of Pharmacy, London, 1935–39; Head of Wellcome Labs of Tropical Medicine, 1958–63 (Protozoologist, 1939–63). Jt Hon. Sec., Royal Soc. of Tropical Medicine and Hygiene, 1968–74, Pres., 1979–81. Chairman: Trypanosomiasis Panel, ODM, 1974–77; Filariasis Steering Cttee, WHO Special Programme, 1978–82. Hon. Dir, Wellcome Museum for Med. Sci., 1984–85. Hon. FPS, 1977; Hon. DSc Brunel, 1986. Soc. of Apothecaries Gold Medal, 1975; Harrison Meml Medal, 1978; Schofield Medal, Guelph Univ., 1979; Silver Medal, Zoological Soc., 1980. Chm. Editorial Bd, Parasitology, 1980–. *Publications:* (pt author) Biological Standardization, 1950; (contrib.) Biochemistry and Physiology of Protozoa, 1955; (jointly) A New Tropical Hygiene, 1960, 2nd edn 1972; (contrib.) Recent Advances in Pharmacology, 1962; many contribs to scientific jls, mainly on pharmacology and chemotherapy of tropical diseases, especially malaria, trypanosomiasis and helminth infections. *Recreations:* Dabbling in arts and crafts especially pottery (slipware), gardening and passive participation in music and opera. *Address:* Shepperlands Farm, Park Lane, Finchampstead, Berks RG11 4QF. *T:* Eversley (0734) 732153.

GOODWIN, Sir Matthew (Dean), Kt 1989; CBE 1981; CA; Chairman, Hewden Stuart PLC, since 1979; *b* 12 June 1929; *s* of Matthew Dean Goodwin and Mary Gertrude Barrie; *m* Margaret Eileen Colvil; two *d*. *Educ:* Hamilton Acad.; Glasgow Acad. FO, RAF, 1952–54. Raeburn & Verel, Shipowners, 1954–56; Partner, Davidson Downe McGowan, CA, 1956–68; Exec. Dir, Hewden Stuart, 1960–79. Director: Irvine Develt Corp., 1980–90; F/S Assurance, 1980–89; Murray Ventures PLC, 1981–; Easpark Children's Home, 1989–; Chairman: Scotcare Ltd, 1988–; Murray Enterprise plc, 1988–. Mem., Scottish Econ. Council, 1991–. Jt Dep. Chm., Scottish Conservative Party, 1991– (Hon. Treas., 1982–90). *Recreations:* bridge, fishing, shooting, farming. *Address:* 87 Kelvin Court, Anniesland, Glasgow G12 0AH. *T:* 041-221 7331. *Club:* Western (Glasgow).

GOODWIN, Noël; *see* Goodwin, T. N.

GOODWIN, Peter Austin, CBE 1986; Secretary, Public Works Loan Commission, 1979–87; Comptroller General, National Debt Office, 1980–87; Director, National Investment and Loans Office, 1980–87; *b* 12 Feb. 1929; *s* of late Stanley Goodwin and of Louise Goodwin; *m* 1950, Audrey Vera Webb; one *d*. *Educ:* Harrow County School. Served Royal Air Force, 1947–49. Executive Officer, Public Works Loan Commn, 1950; Principal, Civil Aviation Authority, 1973–76; Asst Secretary and Establishment Officer, Public Works Loan Commn, 1976–79. UK Mem., Gp of Experts advising on management of Pension Reserve Fund, Europ. Patent Office, 1986–87. *Recreations:* theatre, opera, ballet, country dancing, model railways. *Address:* 87 Woodmansterne Road, Carshalton Beeches, Surrey SM5 4JW. *T:* 081–643 3530.

GOODWIN, Prof. Richard Murphey; Professor of Economic Science, Siena University, since 1980; *b* 24 Feb. 1913; *s* of William Murphey Goodwin and Mary Florea Goodwin; *m* 1937, Jacqueline Wynmalen; no *c*. *Educ:* Harvard Univ. (AB, PhD); Oxford Univ. (BA, BLitt). Harvard Univ.: Instructor in Econs, 1939–42; Instructor in Physics, 1942–45; Asst Prof. of Econs, 1945–51; Lectr in Econs, 1951–69, Reader in Economics, 1969–80, and Fellow of Peterhouse, 1956–80 (Emeritus Fellow, 1982), Univ. of Cambridge. *Publications:* Elementary Economics from the Higher Standpoint, 1970; Essays in Economic Dynamics, 1982; Essays in Linear Economic Structures, 1983; (with L. F. Punzo) The Dynamics of a Capitalist Economy, 1987; Essays in Nonlinear Economic Dynamics, 1988; Chaotic Economic Dynamics, 1990; contrib. Econ. Jl, Econometrica, Review of Econs and Statistics. *Recreations:* painting, walking. *Address:* Dorvis's, Ashdon, Saffron Walden, Essex CB10 2HP. *T:* Ashdon (079984) 302.

GOODWIN, (Trevor) Noël; freelance critic, writer and broadcaster, specialising in music and dance; *b* 25 Dec. 1927; *s* of Arthur Daniel Goodwin and Blanche Goodwin (*née* Stephens); *m* 1st, 1954, Gladys Marshall Clapham (marr. diss. 1960); 2nd, Anne Myers (*née* Mason); one step *s*. *Educ:* mainly in France. BA (London). Assistant Music Critic: News Chronicle, 1952–54; Manchester Guardian, 1954–55; Music and Dance Critic, Daily Express, 1956–78; Exec. Editor, Music and Musicians, 1963–71; regular reviewer for: The Times, 1978–; Internat. Herald Tribune, 1978–84; Opera News, 1975–90; Ballet News, 1979–86; Dance and Dancers, 1957– (Associate Editor, 1972–); Opera, 1984– (Overseas News Editor, 1985–). Member: Arts Council of GB, 1979–81 (Mem., 1973–81, Chm., 1979–81, Dance Adv. Panel; Mem., 1974–81, Dep. Chm., 1979–81, Music Adv. Panel; Council's rep. on Visiting Arts Unit of GB, 1979–81); Dance Adv. Panel, UK Branch, Calouste Gulbenkian Foundn, 1972–76; Nat. Enquiry into Dance Educn and Trng in Britain, 1975–80; Drama and Dance Adv. Cttee, British Council, 1973–88; HRH The Duke of Kent's UK Cttee for European Music Year 1985, 1982–84 (Chm., sub-cttee for Writers and Critics); Trustee-dir, Internat. Dance Course for Professional Choreographers and Composers, 1975–. Pres., The Critics' Circle, 1977 (Jt Trustee, 1984–). Planned and presented numerous radio programmes of music and records for BBC Home and World Services during past 25 years, and contributed frequently to music and arts programmes on Radios 3 and 4. *Publications:* London Symphony: portrait of an orchestra, 1954; A Ballet for Scotland, 1979; (with Sir Geraint Evans) A Knight at the Opera, 1984; editor, Royal Opera and Royal Ballet Yearbooks, 1978, 1979, 1980; area editor and writer, New Grove Dictionary of Music and Musicians, 1981; (ed) A Portrait of the Royal Ballet, 1988; contribs to: Encyclopaedia Britannica, 15th edn, 1974; Encyclopaedia of Opera, 1976; Britannica Books of the Year, annually 1980–; Cambridge Encyclopaedia of Russia and the Soviet Union, 1982; New Oxford Companion to Music, 1983; Pipers Enzyklopädie des Musiktheaters, 1986. *Recreation:* travel. *Address:* 76 Skeena Hill, SW18 5PN. *T:* 081–788 8794.

GOODWIN, Prof. Trevor Walworth, CBE 1975; FRS 1968; Johnston Professor of Biochemistry, University of Liverpool, 1966–83; *b* 22 June 1916; British; *m* 1944, Kathleen Sarah Hill; three *d*. *Educ:* Birkenhead Inst.; Univ. of Liverpool. Lectr 1944, Sen. Lectr 1949, in Biochemistry, University of Liverpool; Prof. of Biochemistry and Agricultural Biochemistry, UCW, Aberystwyth, 1959. Chairman: British Photobiol. Gp, 1964–66; Phytochemical Soc., 1968–70; MRC Biol Grants Cttee B, 1969–73; Cttee, Biochem. Soc., 1970–73; Wirral Educn Cttee, 1972–83; Brit. Nat. Cttee for Biochem., 1976–82; Royal Soc. Internat. Exchange Cttee (Panel A), 1986–89; Member: Council, Royal Society, 1972, 1974, 1985; UGC, 1974–81; SRC Science Bd, 1975–78; ARC Grants Bd, 1975–82; Wirral Educn Cttee, 1974–84; Lawes Agricl Trust Cttee, 1977–91; Exec. Cttee, FEBS, 1975–83 (Chm., Publication Cttee, 1975–83); Vice-Pres., Comité Internat. de Photobiologie, 1967–69. Mem. Court, Univ. of N Wales, Bangor, 1983–; Royal Soc. Rep., Court, Univ. of Liverpool, 1985–. Gov., Birkenhead Inst., 1976–79; Chm. of Govs, Wirral County Grammar Sch. for Girls, 1980–. Morton Lectr, Biochem. Soc., 1983. Corresp. Mem., Amer. Soc. Plant Physiologists, 1982; Hon. Member: Phytochemical Soc. of Europe, 1983; Biochem Soc., 1985. Diplôme d'honneur, FEBS, 1984. Ciba Medallist, Biochemical Soc., 1970; Prix Roussel, Societé Roussel Uclaf, 1982. *Publications:* Comparative Biochemistry of Carotenoids, 1952, 2nd edn, vol. 1 1980, vol. 2 1983; Recent Advances in Biochemistry, 1960; Biosynthesis of Vitamins, 1964; (ed) Chemistry and Biochemistry of Plant Pigments, 1965, 3rd edn 1988; (with E. I. Mercer) Introduction to Plant Biochemistry, 1972, 2nd edn 1982 (trans. Russian, 1986); History of the Biochemical Society, 1987; numerous articles in Biochem. Jl, Phytochemistry, etc. *Recreation:* gardening. *Address:* Monzar, 9 Woodlands Close, Parkgate, S Wirral L64 6RU. *T:* 051–336 4494.

GOODY, Prof. John Rankine, FBA 1976; William Wyse Professor of Social Anthropology, University of Cambridge, 1973–84; Fellow, St John's College, Cambridge, since 1960; *b* 27 July 1919; *m* 1956, Esther Robinson Newcomb; one *s* four *d*. *Educ:* St Albans Sch.; St John's Coll., Cambridge; Balliol Coll., Oxford. BA 1946, Dip. Anthrop. 1947, PhD 1954, ScD 1969, Cantab; BLitt Oxon 1952. HM Forces, 1939–46. Educnl admin, 1947–49; Cambridge Univ.: Asst Lectr, 1954–59; Lectr, 1959–71; Dir, African Studies Centre, 1966–73; Smuts Reader in Commonwealth Studies, 1972. Foreign Hon. Mem., Amer. Acad. of Arts and Scis, 1980. *Publications*: The Social Organisation of the LoWiili, 1956; (ed) The Developmental Cycle in Domestic Groups, 1958; Death, Property and the Ancestors, 1962; (ed) Succession to High Office, 1966; (with J. A. Braimah) Salaga: the struggle for power, 1967; (ed) Literacy in Traditional Societies, 1968; Comparative Studies in Kinship, 1969; Technology, Tradition and the State in Africa, 1971; The Myth of the Bagre, 1972; (with S. J. Tambiah) Bridewealth and Dowry, 1973; (ed) The Character of Kinship, 1973; (ed) Changing Social Structure in Ghana, 1975; Production and Reproduction, 1977; The Domestication of the Savage Mind, 1977; (with S. W. D. K. Gandah) Une Recitation du Bagré, 1981; Cooking, Cuisine and Class, 1982; The Development of the Family and Marriage in Europe, 1983; The Logic of Writing and the Organization of Society, 1986; The Interface between the Oral and the Written, 1987; The Oriental, the Ancient and the Primitive, 1990; contrib. learned jls. *Address*: St John's College, Cambridge CB2 1TP. *T*: Cambridge (0223) 61621.

GOODY, Most Rev. Launcelot John, KBE 1977; PhD, DD; Former Archbishop of Perth (RC); *b* 5 June 1908; *s* of late Ernest John Goody and of Agnes Goody. *Educ*: Christian Brothers' College, Perth, WA; Urban University, Rome. PhD 1927, DD 1931. Ordained priest at Rome, 1930; Asst Parish Priest, Perth Cathedral, 1932–35, Kalgoorlie, 1935–37; Parish Priest, Toodyay, 1937; Director of Seminary, Guildford, 1940–47; Domestic Prelate to the Pope, 1947; Parish Priest, Bedford Park, 1947–51; Auxiliary Bishop of Perth, 1951; first RC Bishop of Bunbury, 1954–68; Archbishop of Perth, 1968–83. *Address*: St Mary's Cathedral, Perth, WA 6000, Australia. *T*: 3259177.

GOOLD, family name of **Baron Goold**.

GOOLD, Baron *cr* 1987 (Life Peer), of Waterfoot in the District of Eastwood; **James Duncan Goold;** Kt 1983; DL; CA; Director, Mactaggart & Mickel Ltd, since 1965; *b* 28 May 1934; *s* of John Goold and Janet Agnes Kirkland; *m* 1959, Sheena Paton; two *s* one *d*. *Educ*: Belmont House; Glasgow Acad. CA 1958. W. E. C. Reid & Co., Accts, NZ, 1958–60; Price Waterhouse & Co., Accts, Aust., 1960; Sec., Mactaggart & Mickel Ltd, 1961–65. Director: Gibson & Goold Ltd, 1978–; American Trust plc, 1984–; Edinburgh Oil & Gas PLC, 1986–; Biomac Ltd, 1988–. President: Scottish Bldg Contractors Assoc., 1971; Scottish Bldg Employers Fedn, 1977; Chm., CBI Scotland, 1981–83. Scottish Conservative Party: Hon. Treas., 1981–83; Chm., 1983–90; Hon. Pres., Eastwood Cons. Assoc., 1978–. Chm., Royal Scottish Nat. Orch., 1991–. Dir, Strathclyde Graduate Business Sch., 1990–; Dep. Chm. Court, Univ. of Strathclyde. Governor: Belmont House Sch., 1972–84; Glasgow Acad., 1982–89. DL Renfrewshire, 1985. FRSA 1987; Hon. FCIOB 1979; Hon. FFB 1983. *Recreations*: gardening, the open air, golf, tennis. *Address*: Sandyknowe, Waterfoot, Clarkston, Glasgow G76 8RN. *T*: 041–644 2764. *Clubs*: Carlton; The Western, Royal Scottish Automobile (Glasgow); Royal Troon Golf (Troon).

GOOLD, Sir George (Leonard), 7th Bt *cr* 1801; retired engineer; *b* 26 Aug. 1923; *s* of Sir George Ignatius Goold, 6th Bt, and Rhoda Goold; *S* father, 1967; *m* 1945, Joy Cecelia, *d* of William Cutler, Melbourne; one *s* four *d*. *Educ*: Port Pirie, S Australia. *Heir*: *s* George William Goold [*b* 25 March 1950; *m* 1973, Julie Ann, *d* of Leonard Crack; two *s*]. *Address*: 60 Canterbury Road, Victor Harbour, SA 5211, Australia. *T*: (085) 522872.

GOOLD-ADAMS, Richard John Moreton, CBE 1974; MA; Vice-President, SS Great Britain Project, since 1982 (Chairman, 1968–82); *b* Brisbane, Australia, 24 Jan. 1916; *s* of Sir Hamilton Goold-Adams, Governor of Qld, and Elsie Riordon, Montreal; *m* 1939, Deenagh Blennerhassett. *Educ*: Winchester; New Coll., Oxford. Served 1939–46 in Army, Major, in Middle East and Italy. The Economist, latterly as an Asst Editor, 1947–55. Councillor: Internat. Inst. for Strategic Studies, 1958–76 (a Founder and Vice-Chm., 1958–62; Chm., 1963–73; Hon. Mem., 1985); National Inst. of Industrial Psychology, 1956–70; Royal Inst. of Internat. Affairs, 1957–81; Soc. for Nautical Research, 1970–73, 1975–78; Chm., British Atlantic Cttee, 1959–62, Vice-Pres., 1963–83. Governor: Atlantic Inst. in Paris, 1962–71; Academic Council, Wilton Park, 1963–83. Dep. Chm., Guthrie Estates Agency Ltd, 1962–63, resigned; re-elected to board, 1964; merged into The Guthrie Corp., 1965; Dir, 1965–69. Formerly broadcasting and television on current affairs, and lecturing. *Publications*: South Africa To-day and Tomorrow, 1936; Middle East Journey, 1947; The Time of Power: a reappraisal of John Foster Dulles, 1962; The Return of the Great Britain, 1976. *Recreation*: photography. *Address*: c/o National Westminster Bank, 116 Fenchurch Street, EC3M 5AN. *Club*: Travellers'.

GOONERATNE, Tilak Eranga; Ambassador of Sri Lanka to the Commission of the European Communities, and concurrently to Belgium, 1975–78; *b* 27 March 1919; *m* 1948, Pamela J. Rodrigo (*d* 1978); two *d*. *Educ*: BA (London Univ.); Ceylon Law Coll. Advocate, Supreme Ct of Ceylon. Joined Ceylon Civil Service, 1943; Asst Sec., Min. of External Affairs, 1947–51; Govt Agent: Trincomalee, 1951–54; Matara, 1954–56; Registrar Gen., Marriages, Births and Deaths, 1956–58; Dir-Gen. of Broadcasting and Dir of Information, Ceylon, 1958–60; Comr Co-operative Develt, 1960–63; Dir of Economic Affairs, 1963; Dep. Sec. to Treasury, 1963–65; Pres., Colombo Plan Council for Technical Co-operation in S and SE Asia, 1964–65; Ceylon deleg. to UN Gen. Assembly, 1964–65; Dep. Sec.-Gen., Commonwealth Secretariat, London, 1965–70; High Comr in UK, 1970–75. Commonwealth Fund for Technical Co-operation: Chm., Bd of Representatives, 1975–76; Chm., Review Gp of Experts. *Publications*: An Historical Outline of the Development of the Marriage and Divorce Laws of Ceylon; An Historical Outline of the Development of the Marriage and Divorce Laws Applicable to Muslims in Ceylon; Fifty Years of Co-operative Development in Ceylon. *Address*: 17B Warwick Avenue, W9. *T*: 071–286 4675.

GOPAL, Dr Sarvepalli; Professor of Contemporary History, Jawaharlal Nehru University, New Delhi, 1972–83, now Emeritus; Fellow of St Antony's College, Oxford, since 1966; *b* 23 April 1923; *y c* and *o s* of Sir Sarvepalli Radhakrishnan, Hon. OM, Hon. FBA. *Educ*: Mill Hill School; Madras Univ.; Oxford Univ. MA (Madras and Oxon), BL (Madras), DPhil (Oxon), DLitt (Oxon). Lecturer and Reader in History, Andhra Univ., Waltair, 1948–52; Asst Dir, Nat. Archives of India, 1952–54; Dir, Historical Div., Min. of Extl Affairs, New Delhi, 1954–66; Commonwealth Fellow, Trin. Coll., Cambridge, 1963–64; Reader in S Asian History, Oxford Univ., 1966–71. Chm. Nat. Book Trust, India, 1973–76; Member: Indian UGC, 1973–79; UNESCO Exec. Bd, 1976–80; Vis. Prof., Leeds, 1977. Pres., Indian History Congress, 1978. Corresp. FRHistS. Hon. Professor: Tirupati, 1971; Hyderabad, 1990. Hon. DLitt: Andhra Univ., 1975; Tirupati Univ., 1979; Banaras Univ., 1984. Sahitya Akademi award, 1976. *Publications*: The Permanent Settlement in Bengal, 1949; The Viceroyalty of Lord Ripon, 1953; The Viceroyalty of Lord Irwin, 1957; British Policy in India, 1965; Modern India, 1967; Jawaharlal Nehru, vol. 1, 1975, vol. 2, 1979, vol. 3, 1984; Radhakrishnan, 1989; general editor, Selected Works of Jawaharlal Nehru; contribs articles to historical jls. *Recreations*: good food and travel. *Address*: St Antony's College, Oxford OX2 6JF; 97 Radhakrishna Salai, Mylapore, Madras 4, India. *Club*: United Oxford & Cambridge University.

GOPALAN, Coluthur, MD, DSc; FRCP, FRCPE; FRS 1987; President, Nutrition Foundation of India, New Delhi, since 1979; *b* 29 Nov. 1918; *s* of C. Doraiswami Iyengar and Mrs Pattammal; *m* 1940, Seetha Gopalan; one *s* one *d* (and one *s* decd). *Educ*: Univ. of Madras (MD); Univ. of London (PhD, DSc). Fellow, Acad. of Med. Scis, India, 1961; FIASc 1964; FNA 1966. Dir, Nat. Inst. of Nutrition, Hyderabad, 1960–74; Dir-Gen., Indian Council of Med. Res., New Delhi, 1975–79. Hon. DSc. Banares Hindu, 1982. *Publications*: Nutritive Value of Indian Foods, 1966; Nutrition and Health Care, 1984; Use of Growth Charts for Promoting Child Nutrition: a review of global experience, 1985; Combating Undernutrition: basic issues and practical approaches, 1987; Nutrition Problems and Programmes in South East Asia, 1987; over 200 contribs to sci. jls; chapters on specific topics to several books on nutrition in internat. pubns on nutrition. *Recreation*: music. *Address*: Nutrition Foundation of India, B-37, Gulmohar Park, New Delhi 110049, India. *T*: 669254. *Clubs*: India International Centre (New Delhi); Secunderabad.

GORAI, Rt. Rev. Dinesh Chandra; *see* Calcutta, Bishop of.

GORARD, Anthony John; restaurant owner; *b* 15 July 1927; *s* of William James and Rose Mary Gorard; *m* 1954, Barbara Kathleen Hampton; one *s* three *d*. *Educ*: Ealing Grammar School. Chartered Accountant, 1951; Manufacturing Industry, 1952–58; Anglia Television Ltd, 1959–67, Executive Director and Member of Management Cttee; Managing Director, HTV Ltd, 1967–78; Chief Exec., HTV Gp Ltd, 1976–78; Director: Independent Television Publications Ltd, 1967–78; Independent Television News Ltd, 1973–78; Chief Exec., Cardiff Broadcasting Co. Ltd, 1979–81; Consultant, Mitchell Beazley Television, 1982–83; hotel proprietor, 1983–87. Chm., British Regional Television Association, 1970–71. *Recreations*: tennis, rambling. *Address*: The Old Market House, Cerne Abbas, Dorset DT2 7JG. *T*: Cerne Abbas (0300) 341680.

GORAY, Narayan Ganesh; High Commissioner for India in London, 1977–79; *b* 15 June 1907; *s* of Ganesh Govind Gore and Saraswati; *m* 1935, Sumati Kirtani (decd); one *d*. *Educ*: Fergusson Coll., Poona. BA, LLB. Mem., Congress Socialist Party, 1934; (Mem. Nat. Exec., 1934); Jt Sec., Socialist Party, 1948; Gen. Sec., Praja Socialist Party, 1953–65, Chm., 1965–69; Member: Lok Sabha, 1957–62; Rajya Sabha, 1970–76. Mayor of Pune, 1968. Editor, Janata Weekly, 1971–. *Publications include*: History of the United States of America, 1959. *Recreations*: music, painting, writing. *Address*: 1813 Sadashiv Peth, Poona 30, Maharashtra State, India.

GORBACHEV, Mikhail Sergeyevich; Executive President of the Soviet Union, since 1990; President, Presidium of the Supreme Soviet of USSR, 1989–90 (Member, 1985–90; Chairman, 1988–89); Deputy to Supreme Soviet, 1970–90; *b* 2 March 1931; *m* Raisa Gorbacheva; one *d*. *Educ*: Moscow State Univ. (law graduate); Stavropol Agric. Inst. Machine operator, 1946; joined CPSU 1952; First Sec., Stavropol Komsomol City Cttee, 1955–58, later Dep. Head of Propaganda; 2nd, later 1st Sec., Komsomol Territorial Cttee; Party Organizer, Stavropol Territorial Production Bd of Collective and State Farms, 1962–66; Head, Dept of party bodies, CPSU Territorial Cttee, 1962–66; 1st Sec., Stavropol City Party Cttee, 1966–68; 2nd Sec., 1968–70, 1st Sec., 1970–78, Stavropol Territorial CPSU Cttee; Central Committee, Communist Party of Soviet Union: Mem., 1971; Sec., with responsibility for agric., 1978–85; Alternate Mem., 1979–80, then Mem., Political Bureau; Gen. Sec., 1985–91. Deputy to Supreme Soviet, RSFSR, 1979; Chm., Foreign Affairs Commn of the Soviet of the Union, 1984–85. Nobel Peace Prize, 1990. Orders of Lenin, of Red Banner of Labour, Badge of Honour. *Publications*: A Time for Peace, 1985; The Coming Century of Peace, 1986; Speeches and Writings, 1986; Peace has no Alternative, 1986; Moratorium, 1986; Perestroika: new thinking for our country and the world, 1987. *Address*: The Kremlin, Moscow, USSR.

GORDIMER, Nadine; author; *b* 20 Nov. 1923; *d* of Isidore Gordimer; *m* Reinhold Cassirer; one *s* one *d*. *Educ*: Convent Sch.; Witwatersrand Univ. Neil Gunn Fellowship, Scottish Arts Council, 1981. Hon. Member: Amer. Acad. of Art and Literature, 1979; Amer. Acad. of Arts and Sciences, 1980. DLitt *hc* Leuven, Belgium, 1980; DLitt *hc*: City Coll. of NY, 1985; Smith Coll., 1985; Harvard, 1986; Yale, 1986; Columbia, 1987; New Sch. for Social Res., 1987; York, 1987. MLA Award, USA, 1981; Malaparte Prize, Italy, 1985; Nelly Sachs Prize, W Germany, 1985; Bennett Award, USA, 1986. *Publications*: *novels*: The Lying Days, 1953; A World of Strangers, 1958; Occasion for Loving, 1963; The Late Bourgeois World, 1966; A Guest of Honour, 1971 (James Tait Black Meml Prize, 1971); The Conservationist, 1974 (jtly, Booker Prize 1974; Grand Aigle d'Or, France, 1975); Burger's Daughter, 1979; July's People, 1981; A Sport of Nature, 1987; My Son's Story, 1990; *stories*: The Soft Voice of the Serpent, 1953; Six Feet of the Country, 1956; Friday's Footprint, 1960 (W. H. Smith Lit. Award, 1961); Not for Publication, 1965; Livingstone's Companions, 1972; Selected Stories, 1975; Some Monday for Sure, 1976; A Soldier's Embrace, 1980; Something Out There, 1984; Jump, 1991; *non-fiction*: South African Writing Today (jt editor), 1967; The Essential Gesture: writing, politics and places, 1988. *Address*: 7 Frere Road, Parktown West, Johannesburg 2193, South Africa.

GORDINE, Dora, (Hon. Mrs Richard Hare); FRBS; FRSA; sculptor and painter; *b* 1906; *d* of late Mark Gordin, St Petersburg, Russia; *m* 1936, Hon. Richard Hare (*d* 1966). Studied sculpture, Paris. First exhibited in the Salon des Tuileries, Paris, 1932. One-man exhibitions: Leicester Galleries, London, 1928, 1933, 1938, 1945, 1949; Flechtheim Gallery, Berlin, 1929. Commissioned to decorate with bronzes new Town Hall in Singapore, 1930–35; built studio and sculpture gallery in London according to her own designs (1936). Spent a year in America, executing commissions in Hollywood and delivering lectures on art (1947). Also represented by Sculpture in American, Asiatic, African and Australian collections. In England 3 works are in Tate Gallery; other bronzes in: Senate House, London Univ.; RIBA; Westminster Infant Welfare Centre; Maternity Ward in Holloway Prison; Esso Petroleum Refinery, Milford Haven; Royal Marsden Hospital, Surrey; Herron Museum of Art, Indianapolis; schs, institutions and many private collections. *Publications*: articles in Journal of Royal Asiatic Society. *Address*: Dorich House, Kingston Vale, SW15.

GORDON, family name of **Marquess of Aberdeen and Temair** and **Marquess of Huntly.**

GORDON, (Alexander) Esmé, RSA, FRIBA, FRIAS; *b* 12 Sept. 1910; *s* of Alexander Shand Gordon, WS and Elizabeth Catherine (*née* Logan); *m* 1937, Betsy (*d* 1990), *d* of James and Bessie McCurry, Belfast; two *s* one *d*. *Educ*: Edinburgh Acad.; School of Arch., Edinburgh Coll. of Art. RIBA. Owen Jones Schol., 1934. War Service with RE in Europe. RSA 1967 (ARSA 1956); Sec., RSA, 1973–78; Pres., Edinburgh AA, 1955–57; Mem. Scottish Cttee, Arts Council of Gt Brit., 1959–65. *Work in Edinburgh includes*: Third Extension and other work for Heriot-Watt Coll.; Head Office for Scottish Life Assce Co. Ltd; Head Office and Showroom for S of Scotland Elec. Bd; for the High Kirk of St Giles: East End treatment for National Service in Coronation year, War Memorial Chapel, and (in Chapel of Order of Thistle) Memorial to HM King George VI, and other work. Exhibn of watercolours and drawings, Scottish Gall., Edinburgh, 1988. *Publications*: A Short History of St Giles Cathedral, 1954; The Principles of Church Building, Furnishing, Equipment and Decoration, 1963; The Royal Scottish Academy 1826–1976, 1976; The Making of the Royal Scottish Academy, 1988. *Address*: Flat 23, 2 Barnton Avenue West,

Edinburgh EH4 6EB. *T:* 031–339 8073.
See also G. A. E. Gordon.

GORDON, Sir Alexander John, (Sir Alex Gordon), Kt 1988; CBE 1974 (OBE 1967); RIBA; architect; Consultant, Alex Gordon Partnership, since 1983; *b* 25 Feb. 1917; *s* of John Tullis Gordon and Euphemia Baxter Simpson Gordon. *Educ:* Swansea Grammar Sch.; Welsh Sch. of Architecture (Diploma with Special Distinction). ARIBA 1949; FRIBA 1962; FSIAD 1975. Served RE, 1940–46. Partnership with T. Alwyn Lloyd, 1948–60; Sen. Partner, Alex Gordon and Partners, 1960–82. Member: Welsh Arts Council, 1959–73 (Vice-Chm. 1969–73); Central Housing Adv. Cttee, 1959–71; Exec. Bd, BSI, 1971–74 (Chm., Codes of Practice Cttee for Building, 1965–77); UGC Planning, Architecture and Building Studies Sub-Cttee, 1971–74; UGC Technology Sub-Cttee, 1974–79; NAB UGC Review Gp in Architecture, 1983–84; Construction and Housing Res. Adv. Council, 1971–79; ARCUK, 1968–71; Design Council, 1973–77; Council, Architectural Heritage Year (and Welsh Cttee), 1973–76; Royal Fine Art Commn, 1973–91; RCA Visiting Cttee, 1973–82; Council for Sci. and Soc., 1973– (Vice-Chm., 1982–); Bldg Res. Estab. Adv. Council (Chm., 1975–83); Adv. Cttee, York Centre for Continuing Educn, 1975–80; Construction Industry Continuing Professional Develt Gp (Chm. 1981–86); Standing Cttee on Structural Safety, 1976–87; British Council Wales Cttee, 1976–87 (Chm., 1980–87, and Mem. Bd British Council); Pres., Comité de Liaison des Architectes du Marché Commun, 1974–75. Trustee, Civic Trust Board for Wales, 1965–. Pres., Building Centre Trust, 1976–87. Life Mem., Court, UWIST (Mem. Council, 1980–85, Vice-Pres., 1982–85); Vis. Prof., Sch. of Environmental Studies, UCL, 1969, Mem. Bd of Studies, 1970–83, Governor, Centre for Environmental Studies, 1974–77. Vis. Fellow, Clare Hall, Cambridge Univ., 1983. Associate, RICS, 1986. RIBA: Chm., Bd of Educn, 1968–70; Pres., 1971–73; Chm., European Affairs Cttee, 1973–80; Chm., Co-ordinating Cttee for Project Inf., 1979–87. Reg. Dir, Nationwide Bldg Soc., 1972– (Chm., Welsh Bd, 1986–89); Mem., Cardiff Bay Develt Corp., 1987–90. Extraord. Hon. Mem., Bund Deutscher Architekten, 1980; Hon. Mem., Soc. Mexican Architects, 1972; Hon. Corresp. Mem., Fedn of Danish Architects, 1976; Hon. FRAIC; Hon. FAIA, 1974; Hon. FCIBSE 1975; Hon. FISE 1980. Hon. LLD Univ. of Wales, 1972. *Publications:* periodic contribs to professional jls. *Recreations:* skiing, the visual arts. *Address:* River Cottage, Llanblethian, near Cowbridge, S Glam CF7 7JL. *T:* Cowbridge (04463) 3672; 32 Grosvenor Street, W1. *T:* 071–629 7910. *Clubs:* Arts; Cardiff and County.

GORDON, Sir Andrew C. L. D.; *see* Duff Gordon.

GORDON, Rev. Canon (Archibald) Ronald (McDonald); Canon of Christ Church, Oxford, since 1991; *b* 19 March 1927; *s* of late Sir Archibald Gordon, CMG, and late Dorothy Katharine Gordon, Bridge House, Gerrards Cross, Bucks. *Educ:* Rugby Sch.; Balliol Coll., Oxford (Organ Schol., MA 1950); Cuddesdon Theol. Coll. Deacon 1952; Priest 1953; Curate of Stepney, 1952–55; Chaplain, Cuddesdon Coll., 1955–59; Vicar of St Peter, Birmingham, 1959–67; Res. Canon, Birmingham Cathedral, 1967–71; Vicar of University Church of St Mary the Virgin with St Cross and St Peter in the East, Oxford, 1971–75; Bishop of Portsmouth, 1975–84; Bishop to the Forces, 1985–90; Bishop at Lambeth (Hd of Archbp's Staff), 1984–91; an Asst Bishop, Dio. of Southwark, 1985–91. Mem., H of L, 1981–84. Fellow of St Cross Coll., Oxford, 1975; Select Preacher, Univ. of Oxford, 1985. Mem., Church Assembly and General Synod and Proctor in Convocation, 1965–71; Chm., ACCM, 1976–83. *Address:* Christ Church, Oxford OX1 1DP.

GORDON, Aubrey Abraham; a Recorder of the Crown Court, since 1978; *b* 26 July 1925; *s* of Isaac and Fanny Gordon; *m* 1949, Reeva R. Cohen; one *s* twin *d. Educ:* Bede Collegiate Boys' Sch., Sunderland; King's Coll., Durham Univ., Newcastle upon Tyne (LLB 1945). Admitted solicitor, 1947. President: Houghton le Spring Chamber of Trade, 1955; Hetton le Hole Rotary Club, 1967; Sunderland Law Soc., 1976; NE Joel Intract Meml Home, 1990–; Chairman: Houghton Round Table, 1959; Sunderland Victims Support Scheme, 1978–80; Sunderland Guild of Help, 1984–. *Recreations:* local communal and religious interests, photography. *Address:* 1 Acer Court, Sunderland SR2 7EJ. *T:* 091–565 8993.

GORDON, Boyd; fisheries consultant; Fisheries Secretary, Department of Agriculture and Fisheries for Scotland, 1982–86; *b* 18 Sept. 1926; *er s* of David Gordon and Isabella (*née* Leishman); *m* 1951, Elizabeth Mabel (*née* Smith); two *d. Educ:* Musselburgh Grammar School. Following military service with the Royal Scots, joined the Civil Service, initially with Min. of Labour, then Inland Revenue; Department of Agriculture and Fisheries for Scotland: joined, 1953; Principal, Salmon and Freshwater Fisheries Administration and Fisheries R&D, 1962–73; Asst Secretary, Agriculture Economic Policy, EEC Co-ordination and Agriculture Marketing, 1973–82. *Recreations:* family and church affairs, gardening, sport of all kinds, though only golf as participant now, reading, playing and writing Scottish fiddle music. *Address:* 87 Duddingston Road, Edinburgh EH15 1SP. *Club:* Civil Service.

GORDON, Brian William, OBE 1974; HM Diplomatic Service, 1949–81, retired; Commercial Counsellor, Caracas, 1980–81; *b* 24 Oct. 1926; *s* of William and Doris Margaret Gordon; *m* 1951, Sheila Graham Young; two *s* one *d. Educ:* Tynemouth Grammar School. HM Forces (Lieut in IA), 1944–47; joined HM Foreign Service (now Diplomatic Service), 1949; served in: Saigon; Libya; Second Sec. in Ethiopia, 1954–58 and in Peru, 1959–61; HM Consul: Leopoldville, Congo, 1962–64; New York, 1965–67; Puerto Rico, 1967–69; Consul-General, Bilbao, 1969–73; Asst Head, Trade Relations and Export Dept, FCO, 1974–77; Dep. Consul-Gen., Los Angeles, 1977–80. *Recreations:* golf, walking. *Address:* Woodlands, Fourstones, Northumberland NE47 5DL.

GORDON, Sir Charles (Addison Somerville Snowden), KCB 1981 (CB 1970); Clerk of the House of Commons, 1979–83; *b* 25 July 1918; *s* of late C. G. S. Gordon, TD, Liverpool, and Mrs E. A. Gordon, Emberton and Wimbledon; *m* 1943, Janet Margaret Beattie; one *s* one *d. Educ:* Winchester; Balliol Coll., Oxford. Served in Fleet Air Arm throughout War of 1939–45. Apptd Asst Clerk in House of Commons, 1946; Senior Clerk, 1947; Fourth Clerk at the Table, 1962; Principal Clerk of the Table Office, 1967; Second Clerk Assistant, 1974; Clerk Asst, 1976. Sec., Soc. of Clerks-at-the-Table in Commonwealth Parliaments, and co-Editor of its journal, The Table, 1952–62. *Publications:* Parliament as an Export (jointly), 1966; Editor, Erskine May's Parliamentary Practice, 20th edn, 1983 (Asst Editor, 19th edn); contribs to: The Table; The Parliamentarian. *Recreation:* dolce far niente. *Address:* 279 Lonsdale Road, Barnes, SW13 9QB. *T:* 081–748 6735.

GORDON, (Cosmo) Gerald (Maitland); His Honour Judge Gordon; a Circuit Judge, since 1990; *b* 26 March 1945; *s* of John Kenneth Maitland Gordon and Erica Martia Clayton-East; *m* 1973, Vanessa Maria Juliet Maxine Reilly-Morrison; two *s. Educ:* Eton. Called to the Bar, Middle Temple, 1966. Asst Recorder, 1982–86; Recorder, 1986–90. Royal Borough of Kensington and Chelsea: Mem. Council, 1971–90; Chm., Works Cttee, 1978–80; Chm., Town Planning Cttee, 1988; Dep. Leader, 1982–88; Mayor, 1989–90. *Recreations:* planning conservation, cooking, food and wine. *Address:* c/o 36 Essex Street, WC2 3AS. *T:* 071–413 0353.

GORDON, Prof. Cyrus H.; Director, Center for Ebla Research, New York University, since 1982 (Gottesman Professor of Hebrew, 1973–89, now Emeritus Professor of Hebrew and other Near East Languages and Literatures); *b* 29 June 1908; *s* of Dr Benj. L. and Dorothy Cohen Gordon; *m* 1st, 1946, Joan Elizabeth Kendall (*d* 1985); two *s* three *d*; 2nd, 1986, Constance Victoria Wallace. *Educ:* Univ. of Pennsylvania (AB, MA, PhD). Harrison Schol., Univ. of Pennsylvania 1928–29, and Harrison Fellow, 1929–30; US Army Officer on active duty, 1942–46 (Col, US Air Force Reserve, retired). Instructor of Hebrew and Assyrian, University of Penn., 1930–31; Fellow and Epigrapher, American Schs of Oriental Research in Jerusalem and Baghdad, 1931–35; Fellow, Amer. Coun. of Learned Socs, 1932–33; Teaching Fellow, Oriental Seminary, Johns Hopkins Univ., 1935–38; Lecturer in Hebrew and Ancient History, Smith Coll., 1938–39 and 1940–41; Fellow, Amer.-Scandinavian Foundn, 1939; Mem., Institute for Advanced Study, Princeton, NJ, 1939–40 and 1941–42; Professor of Assyriology and Egyptology, Dropsie Coll., 1946–56; Joseph Foster Prof. of Near Eastern Studies, and Chm., Dept of Mediterranean Studies, Brandeis Univ., 1956–73 (Dean of Graduate Sch. and Associate Dean of Faculty, 1957–58). Mem. Managing Cttee, Amer. Sch. of Classical Studies, Athens, 1958–73; Vis. Fellow in Humanities, Univ. of Colorado, March 1967; Vis. Prof., New York Univ., 1970–73; Vis. Prof. in History and Archaeology, Univ. of New Mexico, 1976; Distinguished Vis. Professor: in Humanities, SW Missouri State Univ., 1977–79; in Archaeology, New Mexico State Univ., 1979; Gay Lectr, Simmons Coll., 1970; Visitor's Fellowship, Japan Foundn, 1974; Dal Grauer Meml Lectr, Univ. of British Columbia, 1988; Fellow: Amer. Acad. of Arts and Sciences, 1968–; Explorers Club, 1968–; Amer. Acad. of Jewish Res., 1981–; Japan Soc. for Promotion of Science, 1989; Hon. Fellow, Royal Asiatic Soc., 1975–. Member: Amer. Oriental Soc.; Soc. of Biblical Literature; Archæological Inst. of America; Amer. Historical Assoc.; Amer. Philological Assoc.; Amer. Assoc. of Univ. Professors. Corresp. Mem., Inst. for Antiquity and Christianity, Claremont Graduate Sch. and University Center, 1967–. Trustee: Boston Hebrew Coll., 1965–; Internat. Council for Etruscan Studies, Jerusalem, 1970–; Fenster Gallery of Jewish Art, Tulsa, Oklahoma, 1977–. Hon. Dr of Hebrew Letters, Baltimore Hebrew Coll., 1981; Hon. DHL Hebrew Union Coll., 1985. Alumni Award, Gratz Coll., 1961; Directory of Educational Specialists Award, 1970; elected to Soc. of Scholars, Johns Hopkins Univ., 1990. *Publications:* Nouns in the Nuzi Tablets, 1936; Lands of the Cross and Crescent, 1948; Ugaritic Literature, 1949; Smith College Tablets, 1952; Ugaritic Manual, 1955; Adventures in the Nearest East, 1957; Hammurapi's Code, 1957; World of the Old Testament, 1958 (rev. edn: The Ancient Near East, 1965); Before the Bible, 1962 (rev. edn: The Common Background of Greek and Hebrew Civilizations, 1965); Ugaritic Textbook, 1965, rev. edn 1967; Ugarit and Minoan Crete, 1966; Evidence for the Minoan Language, 1966; Forgotten Scripts: How they were deciphered and their Impact on Contemporary Culture, 1968, rev. edn, Forgotten Scripts: their ongoing discovery and decipherment, 1982; Poetic Legends and Myths from Ugarit, 1977; The Pennsylvania Tradition of Semitics, 1986; (ed and contrib.) Publications of the Center for Ebla Research, vol. I, Eblaitica: essays on the Elba archives and Eblaite Language, 1987, vol. II, 1990; some works translated other languages; numerous articles in learned jls dealing with Near East, Mediterranean, OT and Egypto-Semitic philology; *relevant publications:* Orient and Occident: essays presented to Cyrus H. Gordon on the occasion of his Sixty-Fifth Birthday, 1973; The Bible World: essays in honor of Cyrus H. Gordon, 1980. *Address:* (office) Center for Ebla Research, 51 Washington Square South, New York University, New York, NY 10012, USA. *T:* 212–998–8983; (home) 130 Dean Road, Brookline, Mass 02146. *T:* 617–734–3046.

GORDON, David Sorrell; Group Chief Executive (formerly Group Managing Director), The Economist Newspaper Ltd, since 1981; *b* 11 Sept. 1941; *s* of Sholom and Tania Gordon; *m* 1st, 1963, Enid Albagli (marr. diss. 1969); 2nd, 1974, Maggi McCormick; two *s. Educ:* Clifton College; Balliol College, Oxford (PPE, BA 1963); LSE; Advanced Management Program, Harvard Business Sch. FCA. Articles with Thomson McLintock, 1965–68; The Economist: editorial staff, 1968–78; Production and Develt Dir, 1978–81. Dir, Financial Times, 1983–. Dir, South Bank Bd, 1986–; a Governor, BFI, 1983–; Dir, Target Gp plc, 1988–91. *Publication:* (with Fred Hirsch) Newspaper Money, 1975. *Recreations:* movies, magic lanterns. *Address:* Greenwood, 56 Duke's Avenue, Chiswick, W4 2AF. *T:* 081–994 3126. *Clubs:* Garrick, Groucho; Harvard (New York).

GORDON, Maj.-Gen. Desmond Spencer, CB 1961; CBE 1952; DSO 1943; JP; DL; Commissioner-in-Chief, St John Ambulance Brigade, 1973–78; *b* 25 Dec. 1911; *s* of late Harold Easty Gordon and Gwendoline (*née* Blackett); *m* 1940, Sybil Mary Thompson; one *s* one *d. Educ:* Haileybury Coll.; RMC Sandhurst. Commissioned into Green Howards, 1932; India, 1933–38: Adjutant, Regimental Depot, 1938–40; War of 1939–45 (despatches 1944): Norway with Green Howards, 1940; Bde Major, 69 Inf. Bde, 1941–42; Student Staff Coll., Quetta, 1942; Comd 1/7 Queens, 1943; Comd 151 (Durham) Inf. Bde, 146 Inf. Bde, 131 Lorried Inf Bde, 1944–46; Col. GSHQ BAOR, 1946–49; Student Joint Service Staff Coll., 1949; GSO1 Inf. Directorate, War Office, 1950; Dep. Dir Inf., War Office, 1951–52; Comd 16 Indep. Para. Bde Gp, 1952–55; Asst Comd RMA Sandhurst, 1956–57; Student, Imperial Defence Coll., 1958; DA & QMG HQ I (BR) Corps, 1959; GOC 4th Division, 1959–61; Chief Army Instructor, Imperial Defence Coll., 1962–64; Asst Chief of Defence Staff (G), 1964–66: Col The Green Howards, 1965–74. JP Hants, 1966; DL Hants, 1980. KStJ 1973 (CStJ 1972). Knight Commander, Order of Orange Nassau with swords (Holland), 1947. *Recreations:* fishing, gardening. *Address:* Southfields, Greywell, Basingstoke, Hants RG25 1BZ. *T:* Basingstoke (0256) 702088. *Club:* Army and Navy.

GORDON, Douglas; *see* Gordon, R. D.

GORDON, Rt. Rev. Eric; *see* Gordon, Rt Rev. G. E.

GORDON, Esmé; *see* Gordon, A. E.

GORDON, Rt. Rev. (George) Eric; *b* 29 July 1905; *s* of George Gordon, Dulwich; *m* 1938, Elizabeth St Charaine (*d* 1970), *d* of Lt-Comdr A. J. Parkes, OBE, RN, Squeen, Ballaugh, Isle of Man; one *d*; *m* 1971, Rose Gwynneth Huxley-Jones, FRBS, *d* of Benjamin Holt, Wednesbury, and *widow* of Thomas Bayliss Huxley-Jones, FRBS, Broomfield, Essex. *Educ:* St Olave's Sch., London; St Catharine's Coll., Cambridge (MA); Wycliffe Hall, Oxford. Deacon, Leicester, 1929; Priest, Peterborough for Leicester, 1930; Vice-Principal, Bishop Wilson Coll., Isle of Man, 1931, Principal, and Domestic Chaplain to Bishop of Sodor and Man, 1935; Rector of Kersal, and Examining Chaplain to Bishop of Manchester, 1942; Rector and Rural Dean of Middleton, Manchester, 1945; Proctor in Convocation, 1948; Provost of Chelmsford Cathedral and Rector of Chelmsford, 1951–66; Bishop of Sodor and Man, 1966–74. *Publication:* Eynsham Abbey 1005–1228: a small window into a large room, 1990. *Recreation:* local history. *Address:* Cobden, Queen Street, Eynsham, Oxford OX8 1HH. *T:* Oxford (0865) 881378.

GORDON, Gerald; *see* Gordon, C. G. M.

GORDON, Gerald Henry, QC (Scot.) 1972; LLD; Sheriff of Glasgow and Strathkelvin, since 1978; *b* 17 June 1929; *er s* of Simon Gordon and Rebecca Gordon (*née* Bulbin), Glasgow; *m* 1957, Marjorie Joseph, *yr d* of Isaac and Aimée Joseph (*née* Strump), Glasgow; one *s* two *d. Educ:* Queen's Park Senior Secondary Sch., Glasgow; Univ. of Glasgow (MA

(1st cl. Hons Philosophy with English Literature) 1950; LLB (Distinction) 1953; PhD 1960); LLD Edinburgh 1968. National Service, RASC, 1953–55 (Staff-Sgt, Army Legal Aid, BAOR, 1955). Admitted Scottish Bar 1953; practice at Scottish Bar, 1953, 1956–59; Faulds Fellow, Univ. of Glasgow, 1956–59. Procurator Fiscal Depute, Edinburgh, 1960–65. University of Edinburgh: Sen. Lectr, 1965; Personal Prof. of Criminal Law, 1969–72; Head of Dept of Criminal Law and Criminology, 1965–72; Prof. of Scots Law, 1972–76; Dean of Faculty of Law, 1970–73; Sheriff of S Strathclyde, Dumfries and Galloway at Hamilton, 1976–77. Commonwealth Vis. Fellow and Vis. Res. Fellow, Centre of Criminology, Univ. of Toronto, 1974–75. Temporary Sheriff, 1973–76. Mem., Interdepartmental Cttee on Scottish Criminal Procedure, 1970–77. *Publications:* The Criminal Law of Scotland, 1967, 2nd edn 1978; (ed) Renton and Brown's Criminal Procedure, 4th edn 1972, 5th edn 1983; (ed) Scottish Criminal Case Reports, 1981–; various articles. *Recreations:* Jewish studies, coffee conversation, swimming.

GORDON, Giles Alexander Esme: Literary Agent and Director, Sheil and Associates (formerly Anthony Sheil Associates), since 1973; *b* 23 May 1940; *s* of Alexander Esmé Gordon, *qv*; *m* 1st, 1964, Margaret Anna Eastoe (*d* 1989); two *s* one *d*; 2nd, 1990, Margaret Anne McKernan; one *d*. *Educ:* Edinburgh Academy; (briefly) Edinburgh College of Art. FRSL 1990. Trainee publisher, Oliver & Boyd, Edinburgh, 1959–63; advertising manager, Secker & Warburg, 1963–64; editor, Hutchinson, 1964–66; plays editor, Penguin Books, 1967–68; editl dir, Victor Gollancz, 1968–73. C. Day Lewis Fellow in Writing, KCL, 1974–75. Sec. and Chm., Soc. of Young Publishers; Member: Literature Panel, Arts Council, 1968–72; Cttee of Management, Soc. of Authors; Cttee, Assoc. of Authors' Agents. Lectr, Tufts Univ. in London, 1970–74; Lectr, Hollins Coll. in London, 1983–86. Theatre critic: Spectator; London Daily News; Drama; Editor, Drama. *Publications:* Pictures from an Exhibition, 1970; The Umbrella Man, 1971; About a Marriage, 1972; Girl with Red Hair, 1974; (ed with A. Hamilton) Factions, 1974; (with Margaret Gordon) Walter and the Balloon (for children), 1974; (ed) Beyond the Words, 1975; Farewell, Fond Dreams, 1975; (ed) Prevailing Spirits, 1976; 100 Scenes from Married Life, 1976; (ed with Dulan Barber) Members of the Jury, 1976; (ed jtly) You Always Remember the First Time, 1976; (ed) A Book of Contemporary Nightmares, 1977; Enemies, 1977; The Illusionist, 1978; (ed with Fred Urquhart) Modern Scottish Short Stories, 1978; Ambrose's Vision, 1980; (ed) Shakespeare Stories, 1982; (ed) English Short Stories 1940–1980, 1982; (ed with David Hughes) Best Short Stories (annually), 1986–; (ed) English Short Stories: 1900 to the present, 1988; (ed) The Twentieth Century Short Story in English: a bibliography, 1989. *Recreations:* theatre, opera, walking, travelling, eating, drinking, book collecting. *Address:* c/o Sheil and Associates, 43 Doughty Street, WC1N 2LF. *T:* 071–405 9351. *Club:* Garrick.

GORDON, Hannah Cambell Grant; actress; *b* 9 April 1941; *d* of William Munro Gordon and Hannah Grant Gordon; *m* 1970, Norman Warwick; one *s*. *Educ:* St Denis School for Girls, Edinburgh; Glasgow Univ. (Cert. Dramatic Studies); College of Dramatic Art, Glasgow (Dip. in speech and drama). FRSAMD 1980. Winner, James Bridie Gold Medal, Royal Coll. of Music and Dramatic Art, Glasgow, 1962. *Stage:* Dundee Rep., Glasgow Citizens Theatre, Belgrade Theatre, Coventry, Ipswich, Windsor; Can You Hear me at the Back, Piccadilly, 1979; The Killing Game, Apollo, 1980; The Jeweller's Shop, Westminster, 1982; The Country Girl, Apollo, 1983; Light Up the Sky, Old Vic, 1985; Mary Stuart, Edinburgh Fest., 1987; Shirley Valentine, Duke of York's, 1989; Hidden Laughter, Vaudeville, 1991; *television:* 1st TV appearance, Johnson Over Jordan, 1965; series: Great Expectations, 1969; Middlemarch, 1969; My Wife Next Door, 1972; Upstairs, Downstairs, 1976; Telford's Change, 1979; Goodbye Mr Kent, 1983; Gardener's Calendar, 1986; My Family and Other Animals, 1987; Joint Account, 1989; *films:* Spring and Port Wine, 1970; The Elephant Man, 1979; numerous radio plays. *Recreations:* tennis, gardening, cooking. *Address:* c/o Hutton Management, 200 Fulham Road, SW10. *Club:* St James's.

GORDON, Prof. Ian Alistair, CBE 1971; MA, PhD; Professor of English Language and Literature, University of Wellington, NZ, 1936–74, now Emeritus; *b* Edinburgh, 1908; *e s* of Alexander and Ann Gordon; *m* 1936, Mary Ann McLean Fullarton, Ayr; one *s* three *d*. *Educ:* Royal High Sch., Edinburgh; University of Edinburgh. Bruce of Grangehill Bursar, Sloan Prizeman, Gray Prizeman, Scott Travelling Scholar (Italy), Dickson Travelling Scholar (Germany), Elliot Prizeman in English Literature, Pitt Scholar in Classical and English Literature; MA (Hons Classics) 1930, (Hons English) 1932; PhD 1936. Asst Lecturer in English language and lit., University of Edinburgh, 1932; Sub-Ed., Scot. Nat. Dictionary, 1930–36; Dean: Faculty of Arts, Victoria Univ. Coll., Wellington, 1944–47, 1952, 1957–61; Faculty of Languages, 1965–68; Vice-Chancellor Univ. of New Zealand, 1947–52; Chm., Academic Bd, 1954–61. Visiting Professor: KCL 1954; Univ. of Edinburgh, 1962; Univ. of South Pacific, Fiji, 1972; France and Belgium, 1976; Univ. of Waikato, 1980; Research Associate, UCL, 1969; Vis. Fellow, Edinburgh Univ., 1974–75; Vis. Fellow in Commonwealth Literature, Univ. of Leeds, 1975. Columnist, NZ Listener, 1977–88. Member: Copyright Cttee and Tribunal, 1958; UGC, 1960–70; Chairman: English Language Institute,, 1961–72; NZ Literary Fund, 1951–73; Exec. Council, Assoc. of Univs of Br. Commonwealth, 1949–50. NZ representative at internat. confs: Utrecht, 1948; Bangkok, 1960; Kampala, 1961; Karachi, 1961. Army Educ. Service, 2 NZEF, Hon. Major. Hon. LLD Bristol, 1948; Hon. DLitt NZ, 1961; DUniv Stirling, 1975. *Publications:* John Skelton, Poet Laureate, 1943; New Zealand New Writing, 1943–45; The Teaching of English, a study in secondary education, 1947; English Prose Technique, 1948; Shenstone's Miscellany, 1759–1763, 1952; Katherine Mansfield, 1954; The Movement of English Prose, 1966; John Galt (biog.), 1972; Word (festschrift), 1974; Undiscovered Country, 1974; Katherine Mansfield's Urewera Notebook, 1979; Word Finder, 1979; A Word in Your Ear, 1980; (ed) Collins Concise English Dictionary, NZ edn, 1982; (ed) Collins Compact New Zealand Dictionary, 1985; edited the following works of John Galt: The Entail, 1970; The Provost, 1973; The Member, 1975; The Last of the Lairds, 1976; Short Stories, 1978; part-author: Edinburgh Essays in Scottish Literature, 1933; Essays in Literature, 1934; The University and the Community, 1946; John Galt (bicent. vol.), 1980; Lexicographical and Linguistic Studies, 1988; The Fine Instrument, 1989; articles in research journals and other periodicals. *Address:* 91 Messines Road, Wellington, NZ. *Club:* Aorangi Ski, New Zealand (former Pres.).

GORDON, James Stuart, CBE 1984; Chief Executive, Radio Clyde Holdings, since 1991; Managing Director, Radio Clyde, since 1973; Vice-Chairman, Melody Radio, since 1991 (Director, since 1990); *b* 17 May 1936; *s* of James Gordon and Elsie (*née* Riach); *m* 1971, Margaret Anne Stevenson; two *s* one *d*. *Educ:* St Aloysius' Coll., Glasgow; Glasgow Univ. (MA Hons). Political Editor, STV, 1965–73. Chm., Scottish Exhibn Centre, 1983–89; Member: Scottish Develt Agency, 1981–90; Scottish Adv. Bd, BP, 1990–. Mem., Cttee of Inquiry into Teachers' Pay and Conditions, 1986. Mem. Court, Univ. of Glasgow, 1984–. *Recreations:* walking, genealogy, golf. *Address:* Deil's Craig, Strathblane, Glasgow G63 9ET. *T:* Blanefield (0360) 70604. *Clubs:* Caledonian; New (Edinburgh); Buchanan Castle Golf, Prestwick Golf.

GORDON, Rt. Hon. John Bowie, (Peter), QSO 1989; PC 1978; retired politician; company director (banking, investment, tyres); *b* 24 July 1921; *s* of Dr W. P. P. Gordon, CBE, and Dr Doris Gordon, OBE; *m* 1943, Dorothy Elizabeth (*née* Morton); two *s* one *d*. *Educ:* Stratford Primary Sch.; St Andrew's Coll., Christchurch; Lincoln Coll., Canterbury. Served War, RNZAF, 1941–45 (Flt Lt, pilot; mentioned in despatches, 1943). Farming cadet, 1936–39; road transp. industry, 1945–47; farming on own account, 1947–89; Nuffield Scholarship, farming, 1954; co. dir, 1950–60; MP Clutha, 1960–78; Minister: Transport, Railways and Aviation, 1966–72; Marine and Fisheries, 1969–71; Labour and State Services, 1975–78; retd from politics on med. grounds, 1978. Past Pres., Returned Services, Federated Farmers, and A. & P. Show Assoc. Mem., Nat. Transition Cttee, Local Govt Reform, 1988– (Dep. Chm., 1988–90). Mem. Council, Otago Univ., 1980–89. USA Leadership Award, 1964. *Publication:* Some Aspects of Farming in Britain, 1955. *Recreations:* golf, gardening, cooking. *Address:* Tapanui, Otago, New Zealand. *T:* Tapanui 20–48–397. *Club:* Tapanui Services.

GORDON, John Gunn Drummond, CBE 1964; Director: Grindlays Bank Ltd, 1969–79; Steel Brothers Holdings Ltd, 1974–79; *b* 27 April 1909; *s* of late Rev. J. Drummond Gordon, MA, BD, BSc, and A. S. Gordon; *m* 1947, Mary Livingstone Paterson; two *s* one *d*. *Educ:* Edinburgh Academy. Served War, King's African Rifles, 1940–45. Career: spent 30 years out of 45, overseas, mainly in Eastern Africa, but also in India, with Grindlays Bank Ltd, finishing up as Group Managing Director; retired 1974. Mem., Bd of Crown Agents, 1974–77. *Address:* Threeways, Boneashe Lane, St Mary's Platt, near Sevenoaks, Kent TN15 8NW. *T:* Sevenoaks (0732) 884749. *Club:* Nairobi (Nairobi).

GORDON, John Keith; environmentalist; Deputy and Policy Director, Global Environment Research Centre, Imperial College of Science, Technology and Medicine, London, since 1990; *b* 6 July 1940; *s* of James Gordon and Theodora (*née* Sinker); *m* 1965, Elizabeth Shanks; two *s*. *Educ:* Marlborough Coll.; Cambridge Univ. (1st Cl. Hons History). Henry Fellow, Yale Univ., 1962–63; research in Russian history, LSE, 1963–66; entered FCO, 1966; Budapest, 1968–70; seconded to Civil Service Coll., 1970–72; FCO, 1972–73; UK Mission, Geneva, 1973–74; Head of Chancery and Consul, Yaoundé, 1975–77 (concurrently Chargé d'Affaires, Gabon and Central African Republic); FCO, 1977–80; Cultural Attaché, Moscow, 1980–81; Office of UK Rep. to European Community, Brussels, 1982–83; UK Perm. Deleg. to UNESCO, Paris, 1983–85; Head of Nuclear Energy Dept, FCO, 1986–88; Academic Visitor, Centre for Envmtl Technol., Imperial Coll., London, 1988–90. *Publications:* articles and reports on internat. envmtl issues. *Recreations:* jogging, sailing, reading. *Address:* Global Environment Research Centre, 56 Queen's Gate, SW7 5JR. *T:* 071–225 1818. *Club:* Commonwealth Trust.

GORDON, Sir Keith (Lyndell), Kt 1979; CMG 1971; Chairman, Public Service Board of Appeal, St Lucia, 1978–88, retired; Justice of Appeal, West Indies Associated States Supreme Court, 1967–72, retired; *b* 8 April 1906; 3rd *s* of late George S. E. Gordon, Journalist, and Nancy Gordon; *m* 1947, Ethel King; one *d*. *Educ:* St Mary's Coll., St Lucia, WI; Middle Temple, London. Magistrate, Grenada, 1938; Crown Attorney, Dominica, 1942; Trinidad and Tobago: Magistrate, 1943–46 and 1949–53; Exec. Off., Black Market Board, 1946–48; Puisne Judge, Windward Islands and Leeward Islands, 1954–59; Puisne Judge, British Guiana, 1959–62; Chief Justice, West Cameroon, 1963–67. *Recreation:* gardening. *Address:* Vigie, Castries, St Lucia.

GORDON, Sir Lionel Eldred Peter S.; *see* Smith-Gordon.

GORDON, Mildred; MP (Lab) Bow and Poplar, since 1987; *b* 24 Aug. 1923; *d* of Dora and Judah Fellerman; *m* 1st, 1948, Sam Gordon (*d* 1982); one *s*; 2nd, 1985, Nils Kaare Dahl. *Educ:* Raines Foundation School; Forest Teacher Training College. Teacher, 1945–85. Mem. Exec., London Labour Party, 1983–86; Jt Chm., Greater London Labour Policy Cttee, 1985–86. School Governor. *Publications:* essays and articles on education. *Recreations:* pottery, designing and making costume jewellery. *Address:* 28 Cumbrian Gardens, NW2 1EF. *T:* 081–455 0823.

GORDON, Nadia, (Mrs Charles Gordon); *see* Nerina, N.

GORDON, Pamela Joan; Chief Executive, City of Sheffield Metropolitan District, since 1989; *b* 13 Feb. 1936; *d* of Frederick Edward Bantick and Violet Elizabeth Bantick; *m* 1959, Wallace Henry Gordon (*d* 1980); two *s*. *Educ:* Richmond (Surrey) Grammar School for Girls: St Hilda's Coll., Oxford (MA). Variety of posts with ILEA, GLC and LCC, 1957–81; Greater London Council: Asst Dir Gen., 1981–83; Dep. Dir of Industry and Employment, 1983–85; Chief Exec., London Bor. of Hackney, 1985–89. Hon. Fellow, Inst. of Local Govt Studies, Birmingham Univ., 1990. *Publications:* articles on management, etc, in local govt jls. *Recretions:* opera, eating out, foreign travel. *Address:* Town Hall, Sheffield S1 2HH. *T:* Sheffield (0742) 734000.

GORDON, Patrick W.; *see* Wolrige-Gordon.

GORDON, Rt. Hon. Peter; *see* Gordon, Rt Hon. J. B.

GORDON, Peter Macie, CMG 1964; *b* 4 June 1919; *o s* of late Herbert and Gladys Gordon (*née* Simpson); *m* 1945, Marianne, *er d* of Dr Paul Meerwein, Basle; two *d*. *Educ:* Cotham Sch., Bristol; University Coll., Exeter; Merton Coll., Oxford. Served War, 1940–46; commissioned Argyll and Sutherland Highlanders, 1941; Campaign in North-West Europe, 1944–45 (despatches). Entered Colonial Administrative Service as District Officer, 1946; Senior District Commissioner, 1957; Asst Sec., Ministry of Agriculture, 1958; Under-Sec., 1960; Permanent Sec., Ministry of Agriculture and Animal Husbandry, Kenya, 1961; retired, 1964; Asst Sec., Univ. of Exeter, 1964–70. Supervisor, Zimbabwe-Rhodesia Elections, 1980; Mem., Commonwealth Observer Gp, Uganda Elections, 1980. *Address:* Old Poplars Farm House, Chipping Campden, Glos GL55 6EG.

GORDON, Richard, (Dr Gordon Ostlere), MB BChir (Cantab); FCAnaes; *b* 1921; *m*; two *s* two *d*. Formerly: anaesthetist at St Bartholomew's Hospital, and Oxford University; assistant editor, British Medical Jl; ship's surgeon. Mem., Punch Table. Author of: Anaesthetics for Medical Students; Doctor in the House, and 14 sequels; 29 other novels and non-fiction (adapted for 7 films and 4 plays, radio and TV); screenplay, The Good Dr Bodkin Adams (TV); TV series, A Gentlemen's Club; contribs to Punch.

GORDON, (Robert) Douglas; HM Diplomatic Service; High Commissioner, Guyana, since 1990, and Ambassador (non-resident) to Republic of Suriname, since 1990; *b* 31 July 1936; *s* of Robert Gordon and Helen (*née* MacTaggart); *m* 1st, 1960, Margaret Bruckshaw (marr. diss. 1990); one *s*; 2nd, 1990, Valerie Janet Brownlee, MVO (5th class). *Educ:* Greenock Acad.; Cardiff High Sch. for Boys. FO, 1954. National Service with RM, 1955–57; commnd 2 Lieut Wilts Regt, 1957. FO, 1958; Amman, 1958; MECAS, 1959; Abu Dhabi, 1961; Vienna, 1963; Second Sec. (Commercial), Kuwait, 1966; FCO, 1969; Second, later First Sec., Hd of Chancery and Consul, Doha, 1973; Asst to Dep. Gov., Gibraltar, 1976; FCO, 1979; HM Asst Marshal of the Diplomatic Corps, 1982; First Sec. (Commercial), Washington, 1984; Consul (Commercial), Cleveland, 1986; Ambassador, 1989–90, Consul-General, 1990, Aden. Freeman, City of London, 1984. Order of: Gorkha Dakshina Bahu, 5th Cl. (Nepal), 1980; King Abdul Aziz ibn Saud, 4th Cl. (Saudi Arabia), 1982; Officier, l'Ordre Nat. du Mérite (France), 1984. *Recreations:* golf, tennis, walking.

Address: c/o Foreign and Commonwealth Office, SW1A 2AH. *Clubs:* Royal Over-Seas League; Harewood Downs Golf (Chalfont St Giles).

GORDON, Sir Robert James, 10th Bt *cr* 1706, of Afton and Earlston, Kirkcudbrightshire; farmer since 1958; *b* 17 Aug. 1932; *s* of Sir John Charles Gordon, 9th Bt and of Marion, *d* of late James B. Wright; *S* father, 1982; *m* 1976, Helen Julia Weston Perry. *Educ:* Barker College, Sydney; North Sydney Boys' High School; Wagga Agricultural Coll., Wagga Wagga, NSW (Wagga Dip. of Agric., Hons I and Dux). *Recreations:* tennis, ski-ing, swimming. *Heir:* none. *Address:* Earlstoun, Guyra, NSW 2365, Australia. *T:* (067) 79 1343.

GORDON, Robert Wilson, MC 1944; Deputy Chairman of the Stock Exchange, London, 1965–68; Partner, Pidgeon de Smitt (Stockbrokers), 1978–80; *b* 3 March 1915; *s* of late Malcolm Gordon and late Blanche Fayerweather Gordon; *m* 1st, 1946, Joan Alison (*d* 1965), *d* of late Brig. A. G. Kenchington, CBE, MC; one *d*; 2nd, 1967, Mrs Dianna E. V. Ansell (*née* Tyrwhitt-Drake) (*d* 1980). *Educ:* Harrow. Served War of 1939–45 (despatches); Royal Ulster Rifles, and Parachute Regt; Instructor, Staff Coll., 1943–44. Elected to the Council, Stock Exchange, London, 1956. Chm., Airborne Forces Security Fund, 1974–. *Recreation:* golf. *Address:* 41 Cadogan Square, SW1. *T:* 071–235 4496.

GORDON, Rt. Rev. Ronald; *see* Gordon, Rt Rev. A. R. McD.

GORDON, Prof. Siamon, PhD; Professor of Cellular Pathology, Oxford University, since 1989; Fellow, Exeter College, Oxford, since 1976; *b* 29 April 1938; *s* of Jonah and Liebe Gordon; *m* 1963, Lyndall Getz; two *d*. *Educ:* South African Coll. Sch., Cape Town; Univ. of Cape Town (MB ChB 1961); Rockefeller Univ. (PhD 1971). Res. Asst, Wright-Fleming Inst., St Mary's, London, 1964–65; Rockefeller University, NY: Res. Associate, 1965–71; Asst Prof. of Cellular Immunology, 1971–76; Adjunct Associate Prof., 1976–; Reader in Exptl Pathology, Sir Wm Dunn Sch. of Pathology, Univ. of Oxford, 1976–89, Actg Hd of Dept, 1989–90. Chm., Physiol Scis Bd, 1984–86; Member: Lister Scientific Adv. Cttee, 1987–; General Bd, Univ. of Oxford, 1989–. Special Fellow and Scholar, Leukaemia Soc. of America, 1971–76; Vis. Scientist, Genetics, Oxford Univ., 1974–75. *Publications:* contribs to jls of exptl medicine, immunology, cell biology, neuroscience. *Recreations:* reading biography, medical history. *Address:* Sir William Dunn School of Pathology, South Parks Road, Oxford OX1 3RE. *T:* Oxford (0865) 275534.

GORDON, Sir Sidney, Kt 1972; CBE 1968 (OBE 1965); CA; JP; Chairman, Sir Elly Kadoorie & Sons, Ltd; Deputy Chairman, China Light & Power Co. Ltd; *b* 20 Aug. 1917; *s* of late P. S. Gordon and late Angusina Gordon; *m* 1950, Olive W. F. Eldon, *d* of late T. A. Eldon and late Hannah Eldon; two *d*. *Educ:* Hyndland Sch., Glasgow; Glasgow Univ. Sen. Partner, Lowe Bingham & Matthews, Chartered Accountants, Hong Kong, 1956–70. MLC, 1962–66, MEC, Hong Kong, 1965–80. Chairman: Univ. and Polytechnic Grants Cttee, 1974–76; Standing Commn on Civil Service Salaries and Conditions of Service, 1988–. JP Hong Kong, 1961. Hon. LLD The Chinese University of Hong Kong, 1970. *Recreation:* golf. *Address:* 7 Headland Road, Hong Kong. *T:* 8122577. *Clubs:* Oriental; Hong Kong, Royal Hong Kong Jockey (Hon. Steward), Royal Hong Kong Golf (Pres.), Hong Kong Country, Hong Kong Cricket, Shek O Country, etc.

GORDON, Vera Kate, (Mrs E. W. Gordon); *see* Timms, V. K.

GORDON, Lt-Col William Howat Leslie, CBE 1957 (MBE 1941); MC 1944; Adviser on overseas business to firms, to Ministry of Overseas Development, 1971–75, and to International Finance Corporation; *b* 8 April 1914; *o s* of late Frank Leslie Gordon, ISE, FICE; *m* 1944, Margot Lumb; one *s* three *d*. *Educ:* Rugby; RMA Woolwich. Commnd Royal Signals, 1934; Palestine, Africa, Italy, NW Europe; 1 Armoured, 1 Airborne Divs (despatches); Instructor, Staff Coll., Camberley, 1947–49. Chief Executive, The Uganda Co. Ltd, 1949–60; John Holt & Co. (Liverpool) Ltd and Lonrho Exports Ltd, 1960–71; MLC Uganda, 1952–57; Chm., Rickmansworth Water Co., 1986–88. Chm., St John Council, Bucks, 1974–82; KStJ. *Recreation:* trout fishing. *Address:* Acre End, Chalfont St Giles, Bucks. *T:* Little Chalfont (02404) 2047. *Clubs:* White's, MCC.

GORDON-BROWN, Alexander Douglas, CB 1984; Receiver for the Metropolitan Police District, 1980–87; *b* 5 Dec. 1927; *s* of late Captain and Mrs D. S. Gordon-Brown; *m* 1959, Mary Hilton; three *s*. *Educ:* Bryanston Sch.; New Coll., Oxford. MA; 1st cl. hons PPE. Entered Home Office, 1951; Sec., Franks Cttee on section 2 of Official Secrets Act 1911, 1971; Asst Under-Sec. of State, Home Office, 1972–75, 1978–80; Under Sec., Cabinet Office, 1975–78. Chm., Home Office Wkg Gp on Costs of Crime, 1988. *Recreations:* music, golf, walking.

GORDON-CUMMING, Alexander Roualeyn, CMG 1978; CVO 1969; Director, Invest in Britain Bureau, Department of Industry, 1979–84; *b* 10 Sept. 1924; *s* of late Lt-Comdr R. G. Gordon-Cumming and Mrs M. V. K. Wilkinson; *m* 1st, 1965, Beryl Joyce Macnaughton Dunn (*d* 1973); one *d*; 2nd, 1974, Elizabeth Patricia Blackley (*d* 1983); one *d*. *Educ:* Eton Coll. RAF, 1943; retd with rank of Gp Captain, 1969. Board of Trade, 1969; Dept of Trade and Industry, 1973; seconded HM Diplomatic Service, 1974–78. *Recreations:* gardening, skiing, fell walking, ballet. *Address:* Woodstock, West Way, West Broyle, Chichester, Sussex PO19 3PW. *T:* Chichester (0243) 776413. *Club:* Royal Air Force.

GORDON CUMMING, Sir William Gordon, 6th Bt, *cr* 1804; Royal Scots Greys; *b* 19 June 1928; *s* of Major Sir Alexander Penrose Gordon Cumming, 5th Bt, MC, and of Elizabeth Topham, *d* of J. Topham Richardson, Harps Oak, Merstham; *S* father, 1939; *m* 1953, Elisabeth (marr. diss. 1972), *d* of Maj.-Gen. Sir Robert Hinde, KBE, CB, DSO; one *s* three *d*; *m* 1989, Sheila Bates. *Educ:* Eton; RMC, Sandhurst. Late Royal Scots Greys; retired 1952. *Heir:* *s* Alexander Penrose Gordon Cumming, *b* 15 April 1954. *Address:* Altyre, Forres, Morayshire.

GORDON DAVIES, Rev. John; *see* Davies, Rev. John G.

GORDON-DUFF, Col Thomas Robert, MC 1945; JP; Lord-Lieutenant of Banffshire, 1964–87; Convener of County Council, 1962–70; *b* 1911; *er s* of Lachlan Gordon-Duff (killed in action, 1914); *m* 1946, Jean (*d* 1981), *d* of late Leslie G. Moir, Bicester; one *s*. *Educ:* Eton; RMC, Sandhurst. Entered Army, 2nd Lieut, Rifle Brigade, 1932; served War of 1939–45 (MC); retired, 1947. Lt-Col 5/6 Bn Gordon Highlanders (TA), 1947, retiring as Col. DL 1948, JP 1959, Vice-Lieut 1961, Banffshire. *Address:* Drummuir, Keith, Banffshire. *T:* Drummuir (054281) 300. *Club:* Army and Navy.

GORDON-FINLAYSON, Maj.-Gen. Robert, OBE 1957 (MBE 1945); JP; DL; *b* 28 Oct. 1916; *yr s* of late Gen. Sir Robert Gordon-Finlayson, KCB, CMG, DSO, DL; *m* 1945, Alexandra, *d* of late John Bartholomew, Rowde Court, Rowde, Wilts; two *s*. *Educ:* Winchester Coll.; RMA, Woolwich. 2 Lt RA, 1936; Major, BEF, 1940; Staff Coll., 1941; Middle East, 1942–43; NW Europe, 1944–45; India and Burma, 1945–47; GSO 1 1945; RHA, 1952–53; JSSC, 1953; Bt Lieut-Col, 1955; AA and QMG, 3 Inf. Div., 1955–57; Near East (Suez Ops), 1956; Middle East, 1958; Lieut-Col 1958; Comdr, 26 Field Regt RA, 1958–59; Col 1959; GSO 1, Staff Coll., 1960–62; Brig. CRA, 49 Div. TA, 1962–64; Brig. DQMG, HQ, BAOR, 1964–66. GOC 49 Inf. Div., TA/N Midland Dist, 1966–67; GOC E Midland District, 1967–70; retd, 1970. Hon. Col, 3rd (Volunteer) Bn The Worcestershire and Sherwood Foresters Regt, TAVR, 1971–78; Chm., Notts Co. Army Benevolent Fund, 1970–85; Mem., Notts Co. and E Midlands TAVR Assocs, 1971–85. Branch Patron, Notts Co. Dunkirk Veterans Assoc., 1990–; Pres., Notts Co. Royal British Legion, 1971–79; Vice-President: Notts Co. SSAFA, 1970–; Notts Co. PDSA, 1970–87; Central Notts Scout Assoc., 1971–80. JP 1972, High Sheriff 1974, DL 1974, Notts. *Recreations:* shooting, fishing, ski-ing, gardening, walking. *Address:* South Collingham Manor, near Newark, Notts NG23 7LW. *T:* Newark (0636) 892204; c/o Lloyds Bank, Cox's & King's Branch, 7 Pall Mall, SW1Y 5NA.

GORDON JONES, Air Marshal Sir Edward, KCB 1967 (CB 1960); CBE 1956 (OBE 1945); DSO 1941; DFC 1941; idc; jssc; qs; Air Officer Commanding-in-Chief, Near East Air Force, and Administrator, Sovereign Base Areas, 1966–69; Commander, British Forces Near East, 1967–69; retired 1969; *b* 31 Aug. 1914; *s* of late Lt-Col Dr A. Jones, DSO, MC, MD, DPH; *m* 1938, Margery Thurston Hatfield, BSc; two *s*. Served War of 1939–45 (despatches, DFC, DSO, OBE, Greek DFC). ACOS (Intelligence), Allied Air Forces Central Europe, 1960–61; Air Officer Commanding RAF Germany, 1961–63; Senior RAF Directing Staff, Imperial Defence Coll., 1963–65; AOC, RAF, Malta, and Dep. C-in-C (Air), Allied Forces, Mediterranean, 1965–66. Comdr Order of Orange Nassau. *Recreations:* sport, photography, travel, music. *Address:* 20 Marlborough Court, Grange Road, Cambridge CB3 9BQ. *T:* Cambridge (0223) 63029. *Club:* Royal Air Force.

GORDON-LENNOX, family name of **Duke of Richmond.**

GORDON LENNOX, Maj.-Gen. Bernard Charles, CB 1986; MBE 1968; Regimental Lieutenant-Colonel, Grenadier Guards, since 1989; *b* 19 Sept. 1932; *s* of Lt-Gen. Sir George Gordon Lennox and Nancy Brenda Darell; *qv*; *m* 1958, Sally-Rose Warner; three *s*. *Educ:* Eton; Sandhurst. 2nd Lt, Grenadier Guards, 1953; Hong Kong, 1965; HQ Household Div., 1971; Commanding 1st Bn Grenadier Guards, 1974; Army Directing Staff, RAF Staff College, 1976–77; Command, Task Force H, 1978–79; RCDS, 1980; Dep. Commander and Chief of Staff, SE District, 1981–82; GOC Berlin (British Sector), 1983–85; Sen. Army Mem., RCDS, 1986–88, retd. Dir of Regions, Motor Agents Assoc., 1988–89. *Recreations:* field sports, cricket, squash, music. *Address:* c/o Regimental Headquarters, Grenadier Guards, Wellington Barracks, Birdcage Walk, SW1E 6HQ. *Clubs:* Army and Navy, MCC.

GORDON LENNOX, Lord Nicholas Charles, KCMG 1986 (CMG 1978); KCVO 1989 (LVO 1957); HM Diplomatic Service, retired; a Governor, BBC, since 1990; director of companies; *b* 31 Jan. 1931; *yr s* of 9th Duke of Richmond and Gordon and of Elizabeth Grace, *y d* of late Rev. T. W. Hudson; *m* 1958, Mary, *d* of late Brig. H. N. H. Williamson, DSO, MC; one *s* three *d*. *Educ:* Eton; Worcester Coll., Oxford (Scholar). 2nd Lieut KRRC, 1950–51. Entered HM Foreign Service, 1954; FO, 1954–57; Private Sec. to HM Ambassador to USA, 1957–61; 2nd, later 1st Sec., HM Embassy, Santiago, 1961–63; Private Sec. to Perm. Under-Sec., FO, 1963–66; 1st Sec. and Head of Chancery, HM Embassy, Madrid, 1966–71; seconded to Cabinet Office, 1971–73; Head of News Dept, FCO, 1973–74, Head of N America Dept, 1974–75; Counsellor and Head of Chancery, Paris, 1975–79; Asst Under-Sec. of State, FCO, 1979–84; Ambassador to Spain, 1984–89. Director, 1990–: Foreign and Colonial Investment Trust; Nat West March SA (Spain); Sturze Holdings; Sothebys; Savills (Europe); Commercial Union Vida (Spain). Hon. Col, 4th Bn Royal Green Jackets, TA, 1990–. Grand Cross, Order of Isabel la Católica (Spain), 1986. *Address:* c/o Nexus, 110 Euston Road, NW1 2DQ. *T:* 071–383 7736. *Clubs:* Boodle's, Beefsteak.

GORDON-SMITH, David Gerard; CMG 1971; Director-General in Legal Service, Council of Ministers, European Communities, 1976–87; *b* 6 Oct. 1925; *s* of late Frederic Gordon-Smith, QC, and Elsie Gordon-Smith (*née* Foster); *m* 1952, Angela Kirkpatrick Pile; one *d* (and one *s* decd). *Educ:* Rugby Sch.; Trinity Coll., Oxford. Served in RNVR, 1944–46. BA (Oxford) 1948; called to Bar, Inner Temple, 1949; Legal Asst, Colonial Office, 1950; Sen. Legal Asst, 1954; CRO, 1963–65; Asst Legal Adviser, CO, 1965–66; Legal Counsellor, CO, later FCO, 1966–72; Dep. Legal Advr, FCO, 1973–76. *Address:* Kingscote, Westcott, Surrey RH4 3NX.

GORDON-SMITH, Ralph; President, since 1973 (Chairman, 1951–73), Smiths Industries Ltd (formerly Smith and Sons (England) Ltd); *b* 22 May 1905; *s* of late Sir Allan Gordon-Smith, KBE, DL and Hilda Beatrice Cave; *m* 1932, Beryl Mavis Cundy; no *c*. *Educ:* Bradfield Coll. Joined Smiths Industries, 1927; Dir, 1933. Dir of EMI Ltd, 1951–75. FBHI 1961. *Recreations:* shooting, fishing. *Address:* Brook House, Bosham, West Sussex PO18 8LY. *T:* Bosham 573475; 23 Kingston House East, Princes Gate, SW7. *T:* 071–584 9428. *Club:* Bosham Sailing.

GORE, family name of **Earl of Arran.**

GORE; *see* Ormsby Gore.

GORE, (Francis) St John (Corbet), CBE 1986; FSA; *b* 8 April 1921; *s* of late Francis Gore and Kirsteen Corbet-Singleton; *m* 1st, 1951, Priscilla (marr. diss. 1975), *d* of Cecil Harmsworth King; one *s* one *d*; 2nd, 1981, Lady Mary Strachey, *d* of 3rd Earl of Selborne, PC, CH. *Educ:* Wellington; Courtauld Inst. of Art. Served War, 1940–45, Captain, Royal Northumberland Fusiliers. Employed Sotheby's, 1950–55; National Trust: Adviser on pictures, 1956–86, Hon. Advr, 1986–; Historic Buildings Sec., 1973–81. Mem., Exec. Cttee, Nat. Art Collections Fund, 1964–; Trustee: Wallace Collection, 1975–89; National Gall., 1986–. *Publications:* Catalogue, Worcester Art Museum, Mass (British Pictures), 1974; various exhibn catalogues, incl. RA; contribs to Apollo, Country Life, etc. *Recreation:* sight-seeing. *Address:* 25 Elvaston Place, SW7 5NL; Grove Farm, Stoke-by-Nayland, Suffolk. *Clubs:* Boodle's, Brooks's, Beefsteak.

See also Baron O'Hagan.

GORE, Frederick John Pym, CBE 1987; RA 1972 (ARA 1964); Painter; Head of Painting Department, St Martin's School of Art, WC2, 1951–79, and Vice-Principal, 1961–79; *b* 8 Nov. 1913; *s* of Spencer Frederick Gore and Mary Johanna Kerr. *Educ:* Lancing Coll.; Trinity Coll., Oxford; studied art at Ruskin, Westminster and Slade Schs. Taught at: Westminster Sch. of Art, 1937; Chelsea and Epsom, 1947; St Martin's, 1946–79. Chm., RA exhibitions cttee, 1976–87. Trustee, Imperial War Mus., 1967–84 (Chm., Artistic Records Cttee, 1972–1986). *One-man exhibitions:* Gall. Borghèse, Paris, 1938; Redfern Gall., 1937, 1949, 1950, 1953, 1956, 1962; Mayor Gall., 1958, 1960; Juster Gall., NY, 1963; RA (retrospective), 1989. *Paintings in public collections include:* Contemporary Art Soc., Leicester County Council, GLC, Southampton, Plymouth, Rutherston Collection and New Brunswick. Served War of 1939–45: Mx Regt and RA (SO Camouflage). *Publications:* Abstract Art, 1956; Painting, Some Principles, 1965; Piero della Francesca's 'The Baptism', 1969. *Recreation:* Russian folk dancing. *Address:* Flat 3, 35 Elm Park Gardens, SW10. *T:* 071–352 4940.

GORE, Michael Edward John, CBE 1991; HM Diplomatic Service; High Commissioner to the Bahamas, since 1991; *b* 20 Sept. 1935; *s* of late John Gore and Elsa Gore (*née*

Dillon); *m* 1957, Monica Shellish; three *d*. *Educ:* Xaverian College, Brighton. Reporter, Portsmouth Evening News, 1952–55; Captain, Army Gen. List, 1955–59; Air Ministry, Dep. Comd. Inf. Officer, Cyprus and Aden, 1959–63; CRO, later FCO, 1963; served Jesselton, 1963–66, FCO, 1966–67, Seoul, 1967–71, Montevideo, 1971–74; First Sec., Banjul, 1974–78; FCO, 1978–81; Nairobi, 1981–84; Dep. High Comr, Lilongwe, 1984–87; Ambassador to Liberia, 1988–90. Mem., British Ornithologists' Union; FRPS. *Publications:* The Birds of Korea (with Pyong-Oh Won), 1971; Las Aves del Uruguay (with A. R. M. Gepp), 1978; Birds of the Gambia, 1981, 2nd edn 1991; On Safari in Kenya: a pictorial guide to the national parks and reserves, 1984; papers on birds and conservation; wild-life photographs in books and magazines. *Recreations:* ornithology, wildlife photography, fishing. *Address:* c/o Foreign and Commonwealth Office, SW1A 2AH. *Clubs:* Army and Navy, Royal Automobile.

GORE, Paul Annesley, CMG 1964; CVO 1961; *b* 28 Feb. 1921; *o s* of late Charles Henry Gore, OBE and late Hon. Violet Kathleen (*née* Annesley); *m* 1946, Gillian Mary, *d* of T. E. Allen-Stevens; two *s* (and one *s* decd). *Educ:* Winchester Coll.; Christ Church, Oxford. Military Service, 1941–46: 16/5 Lancers. Colonial Service, 1948–65; Dep. Governor, The Gambia, 1962–65. JP City of Oxford, 1973–74; JP Suffolk, 1977–83. *Address:* 1 Burkitt Road, Woodbridge, Suffolk.

GORE, Sir Richard (Ralph St George), 13th Bt *cr* 1621; *b* 19 Nov. 1954; *s* of Sir (St George) Ralph Gore, 12th Bt, and of Shirley, *d* of Clement Tabor; *S* father, 1973. *Educ:* The King's Sch., Parramatta; Univ. of New England; Queensland Coll. of Art. *Heir: uncle* Nigel Hugh St George Gore [*b* 23 Dec. 1922; *m* 1952, Beth Allison (*d* 1976), *d* of R. W. Hooper; one *d*]. *Address:* 16 Claremont Street, Red Hill, Queensland 4059, Australia.

GORE, St John; *see* Gore, F. St J. C.

GORE-BOOTH, Sir Angus (Josslyn), 8th Bt *cr* 1760 (Ire.), of Artarman, Sligo; *b* 25 June 1920; *s* of Sir Josslyn Augustus Richard Gore-Booth, 6th Bt and Mary Sibell (*d* 1968), *d* of Rev. S. L'Estrange-Malone; *S* brother, 1987; *m* 1948, Hon. Rosemary Myra Vane (marr. diss. 1954), *o d* of 10th Baron Barnard; one *s* one *d*. *Educ:* Radley; Worcester Coll., Oxford. Served War of 1939–45, Captain Irish Guards. *Heir: s* Josslyn Henry Robert Gore-Booth [*b* 5 Oct. 1950; *m* 1980, Jane Mary, *o d* of Rt Hon. Sir Roualeyn Hovell-Thurlow-Cumming-Bruce, *qv*; two *d*]. *Address:* Lissadell, Sligo, Irish Republic. *T:* Sligo (71) 63150.

GORE-BOOTH, Hon. David Alwyn, CMG 1990; HM Diplomatic Service; Assistant Under Secretary of State (Middle East), Foreign and Commonwealth Office, since 1989; *b* 15 May 1943; twin *s* of late Baron Gore-Booth, GCMG, KCVO; *m* 1st, 1964, Jillian Sarah (*née* Valpy) (marr. diss. 1970); one *s*; 2nd, 1977, Mary Elisabeth Janet (*née* Muirhead). *Educ:* Eton Coll.; Christ Church, Oxford (MA Hons). Entered Foreign Office, 1964; Middle East Centre for Arabic Studies, 1964; Third Secretary, Baghdad, 1966; Third, later Second Sec., Lusaka, 1967; FCO, 1969; Second Sec., Tripoli, 1969; FCO, 1971; First Sec., UK Permanent Representation to European Communities, Brussels, 1974; Asst Head of Financial Relations Dept, FCO, 1978; Counsellor, Jedda, 1980; Counsellor and Hd of Chancery, UK Mission to UN, NY, 1983; Hd of Policy Planning Staff, FCO, 1987. *Recreations:* tennis, squash, the island of Hydra (Greece). *Address:* c/o Foreign and Commonwealth Office, SW1A 2AH. *Clubs:* MCC, Hurlingham; Bill's Bar (Hydra).

GORE-LANGTON; *see* Temple-Gore-Langton, family name of Earl Temple of Stowe.

GORELL, 4th Baron *cr* 1909; **Timothy John Radcliffe Barnes;** *b* 2 Aug. 1927; *e s* of 3rd Baron Gorell and Elizabeth Gorell, *d* of Alexander Nelson Radcliffe; *S* father, 1963; *m* 1954, Joan Marion, *y d* of late John Edmund Collins, MC, Sway, Hants; two adopted *d*. *Educ:* Eton Coll.; New Coll., Oxford. Lieut, Rifle Brigade, 1946–48. Barrister, Inner Temple, 1951. Sen. Executive, Royal Dutch/Shell Group, 1959–84. *Heir: b* Hon. Ronald Alexander Henry Barnes [*b* 28 June 1931; *m* 1957, Gillian Picton Hughes-Jones; one *s* one *d*]. *Address:* 4 Roehampton Gate, SW15. *T:* 081–876 5522. *Club:* Roehampton Golf.

GORING, Marius, CBE 1991; FRSL; actor, manager, director; *b* Newport, IoW, 23 May 1912; *s* of Dr Charles Buckman Goring, MD, BSc, criminologist, and Katie Winifred (Macdonald), pianist; *m* 1931, Mary Westwood Steel (marr. diss.); one *d*; *m* 1941, Lucie Mannheim (*d* 1976); *m* 1977, Prudence FitzGerald. *Educ:* Perse Sch., Cambridge; Universities of Frankfurt, Munich, Vienna, and Paris. Studying for stage under Harcourt Williams and at Old Vic dramatic school, 1929–32. First stage appearance in Crossings, ADC, Cambridge, 1925; first professional appearance in Jean Sterling Mackinlay's matinées (Rudolph Steiner Hall), 1927; toured in France and Germany with English Classical Players, 1931; stage managed two seasons at Old Vic and Sadler's Wells, playing Romeo, Macbeth, Epihodov and other rôles, 1932–34. First West End appearance as Hugh Voysey, Shaftesbury, 1934; toured France, Belgium, and Holland with Compagnie des Quinze (acting in French), also Hamlet, Old Vic, Noah, New, Hangman, Duke of York's, Sowers of the Hills, Westminster, 1934–35; Mary Tudor, Playhouse, The Happy Hypocrite, His Majesty's, Girl Unknown, New, Wild Duck, Westminster, 1936; rôles in Witch of Edmonton, Hamlet, Twelfth Night and Henry V at Old Vic, Satyr, Shaftesbury, 1937; The Last Straw, Comedy, Surprise Item, Ambassadors, The White Guard, Phoenix, 1938; in management at Duke of York's, 1939: dir, Nora (A Doll's House); Lady Fanny; first player in Hamlet, Lyceum and Elsinore; Pip in Great Expectations (produced with George Devine and Alec Guinness at Rudolph Steiner, first theatre to re-open after war closure); dir (with G. Devine) The Tempest (also played Ariel), Old Vic. Served in Queen's Royal Regiment, 1940; lent to Foreign Office, 1941–45; supervisor of BBC productions broadcast to Germany under name of Charles Richardson. Toured British zone of Germany, 1947 (in German); Rosmersholm, Too True to be Good, Cherry Orchard, Marriage, at Arts Theatre; Daphne Laureola, Berlin (playing in German), 1949; One Hundred Thousand Pounds, Berlin, 1950; The Madwoman of Chaillot, St James's, 1951; Richard III, Antony and Cleopatra, Taming of the Shrew, King Lear, Stratford-upon-Avon, 1953; Marriage, Wuppertal, 1954; toured France, Holland, Finland, and India with own company of English comedians, 1957–58; Tonight at 8.30 (in German), Berlin Fest., 1960; Measure for Measure, Stratford-upon-Avon, 1962; A Penny for a Song, Aldwych, 1962; Ménage à Trois, Lyric, 1963; The Poker Session, Dublin, and Globe, 1964; The Apple Cart, Cambridge, 1965; The Bells, Derby Playhouse and Midlands tour, 1966–67, and Vaudeville, 1968; The Demonstration, Nottingham, 1969; Sleuth, St Martin's, 1970–73; The Wisest Fool, Guildford and tour, 1975; Habeas Corpus, Liverpool Playhouse, 1976; The Concert, Theatre Royal York, 1977; Habeas Corpus, Lyceum, Edinburgh, 1979; Sleuth, Liverpool Playhouse, 1981; Zaïde, Old Vic, 1982; Lloyd George Knew my Father, nat. tour, 1982; Peer Gynt, Nottingham, 1982; Dame of Sark, nat. tour, 1983; The Winslow Boy, nat. tour, 1984; I Have Been Here Before, nat. tour, 1985; God in Mystery plays in Canterbury Cathedral, 1986; The Applecart, Haymarket, 1986; Beyond Reasonable Doubt, Queen's, 1988; Towards Zero, Churchill Theatre, Bromley and nat. tour, 1989; Sunsets and Glories, Playhouse, Leeds, 1990. Co-founder, London Theatre Studio with Michel St Denis and George Devine. *Films include:* Rembrandt; The Case of the Frightened Lady, 1940; A Matter of Life and Death, 1946; The Red Shoes, 1948; Odette, 1950; So Little Time, 1951; Pandora and the Flying Dutchman, 1952; The Barefoot Contessa, 1955; Ill Met by Moonlight, 1956; The Inspector, 1961; La Fille en Robe bleue, 1980; Loser Takes All, 1988. Broadcaster and writer of radio scripts. *Radio:* first performance, Bulldog Drummond; Hitler in the Shadow of the Swastika (first BBC war programme), 1939; for BBC Third Programme, The Divine Comedy, Browning Monologues, Henry Reed's Leopardi, Streets of Pompeii, Tennyson's Maud, 1959; *Television:* first appearance in Tchekov's The Bear, 1938; exec. producer and played lead in Adventures of the Scarlet Pimpernel (series), 1955; The Expert (series), 1968–70, 1974; Fall of Eagles Hindenburg (series), 1977; Edward and Mrs Simpson (series), 1978; The Old Men at the Zoo (series), 1983; Gnostics (series), 1987; War at Woburn, 1987; autobiographical documentary, 1987. FRSL 1976. Vice-Pres. British Actors' Equity Assoc., 1963–65 and 1975–82. *Recreations:* skating and riding. *Address:* c/o Film Rights Ltd, 483 Southbank House, Black Prince Road, Albert Embankment, SE1 7SJ. *T:* 071–735 8171. *Club:* Garrick.

GORING, Sir William (Burton Nigel), 13th Bt, *cr* 1627; Member of London Stock Exchange since 1963; *b* 21 June 1933; *s* of Major Frederick Yelverton Goring (*d* 1938) (6th *s* of 11th Bt) and Freda Margaret, *o d* of N. V. Ainsworth, 2 Closewalks, Midhurst, Sussex; *S* uncle, Sir Forster Gurney Goring, 12th Bt, 1956; *m* 1960, Hon. Caroline Thellusson, *d* of 8th Baron Rendlesham, *qv*, and of Mrs Patrick Barthropp. *Educ:* Wellington; RMA Sandhurst, Lieut, The Royal Sussex Regt. *Recreation:* bridge. *Heir: kinsman* Richard Harry Goring [*b* 10 Sept. 1949; *m* 1972, Penelope Ann, *d* of J. K. Broadbent; two *s* two *d*]. *Address:* 16 Linver Road, SW6 3RB. *T:* 071–600 4177. *Club:* Hurlingham.

GORLEY PUTT, Samuel; *see* Putt.

GORMAN, John Peter, QC 1974; a Recorder of the Crown Court, since 1972; *b* 29 June 1927; *er s* of James S. Gorman, Edinburgh; *m* 1st, 1955; one *s* three *d*; 2nd, 1979, Patricia (*née* Myatt). *Educ:* Stonyhurst Coll.; Balliol Coll., Oxford (MA). Served with RA, 1945–48. Called to Bar, Inner Temple, 1953, Bencher 1983; Midland and Oxford Circuit. Dep. Chm. 1969, Chm. 1972–79, Agricultural Lands Tribunal (E Midlands); Dep. Chm., Northants QS, 1970–71. *Address:* 2 Dr Johnson's Buildings, Temple, EC4Y 7AY. *Club:* Reform.

GORMAN, John Reginald, CVO 1961; CBE 1974 (MBE 1959); MC 1944; DL; Director, Institute of Directors, Northern Ireland, since 1986; *b* 1 Feb. 1923; *s* of Major J. K. Gorman, MC; *m* 1948, Heather, *d* of George Caruth, solicitor, Ballymena; two *s* two *d*. *Educ:* Rockport, Haileybury and ISC; Portora; Glasgow Univ.; Harvard Business Sch. FCIT, FIPM; MIH. Irish Guards, 1941–46, Normandy, France, Belgium, Holland, Germany (Captain, 1944–46). Royal Ulster Constabulary, 1946–60; Chief of Security, BOAC, 1960–63 (incl. Royal Tour of India, 1961); Personnel Dir and Mem. Bd of Management, BOAC, 1964–69; British Airways: Regional Man., Canada, 1969–75; Regional Man., India, Bangladesh, Sri Lanka, 1975–79; Vice-Chm. and Chief Exec., NI Housing Exec., 1979–85. Dir, NI Airports Bd, 1985–; Mem., NI Bd, Nationwide Building Soc., 1986–. Pres., British Canadian Trade Assoc., 1972–74; Vice-Chm., Federated Appeal of Montreal, 1973–74. Chm., Bd of Airline Representatives, India, 1977–79; Chm., Inst. of Housing (NI), 1984. Bd Mem., Co-operation North, 1987–. DL, 1982, High Sheriff, 1987–88, Co. Down. *Recreations:* gardening, bee keeping, country pursuits. *Address:* The Forge, Jericho Road, Killyleagh, Co. Down. *T:* Killyleagh (0396) 828400. *Clubs:* Cavalry and Guards; Ulster (Belfast); St James (Montreal); Gymkhana (Delhi).

GORMAN, Teresa Ellen; MP (C) Billericay, since 1987; *b* Sept. 1931; *m*. *Educ:* Fulham Co. Sch.; London Univ. (BSc 1st cl. Hons). Founder and manager of own company. Mem., Westminster City Council, 1982–86. Contested (Ind.) Streatham, Oct. 1974. Founder and Chairman: Alliance of Small Firms & Self Employed People Ltd, 1974; Amarant Trust, 1986. Mem., Cons. Women's Nat. Cttee, 1983–. *Publications:* research papers for IEA, Adam Smith Inst., CPS. *Address:* c/o House of Commons, SW1A 0AA.

GORMAN, William Moore, FBA 1978; Emeritus Fellow, Nuffield College, Oxford, since 1990 (Fellow, 1962–67 and 1979–90); *b* 17 June 1923; *s* of late Richard Gorman, Lusaka, Northern Rhodesia, and Sarah Crawford Moore, Kesh, Northern Ireland; *m* 1950, Dorinda Scott. *Educ:* Foyle Coll., Derry; Trinity Coll., Dublin (Hon. Fellow 1990). Asst Lectr, 1949, Lectr, 1951, and Sen. Lectr, 1957, in Econometrics and Social Statistics, University of Birmingham; Prof. of Economics, University of Oxford, 1962–67; Prof. of Economics, London Univ., at LSE, 1967–79. European Chm., 1970–72, Pres. 1972, Econometric Soc. Mem., Academia Europaea, 1990; Hon. Foreign Member: Amer. Acad. of Arts and Scis, 1986; Amer. Economic Assoc., 1987. Hon. DSocSc Birmingham, 1973; Hon. DSc(SocSc) Southampton, 1974; Hon. DEconSc NUI, 1986. *Publications:* articles in various economic journals. *Address:* Nuffield College, Oxford OX1 1NF. *T:* Oxford (0865) 278579; Moorfield, Fountainstown, Myrtleville, Co. Cork, Ireland. *T:* Cork (21) 831174.

GORMANSTON, 17th Viscount *cr* 1478; **Jenico Nicholas Dudley Preston;** Baron Gormanston (Ire.), 1365; Baron Gormanston (UK), 1868; Premier Viscount of Ireland; *b* 19 Nov. 1939; *s* of 16th Viscount and Pamela (who *m* 2nd, 1943, M. B. O'Connor, Irish Guards; he *d* 1961, she *d* 1975), *o d* of late Capt. Dudley Hanly, and Lady Marjorie Heath (by her 1st marriage); *S* father, who was officially presumed killed in action, France, 9 June 1940; *m* 1974, Eva Antoine Landzianowska (*d* 1984); two *s*. *Educ:* Downside. *Heir: s* Hon. Jenico Francis Tara Preston, *b* 30 April 1974. *Address:* 8 Dalmeny House, Thurloe Place, SW7 2RY.

GORMLEY, family name of **Baron Gormley.**

GORMLEY, Baron *cr* 1982 (Life Peer), of Ashton-in-Makerfield in Greater Manchester; **Joseph Gormley,** OBE 1969; President, National Union of Mineworkers, 1971–82; *b* 5 July 1917; *m* 1937, Sarah Ellen Mather; one *s* one *d*. *Educ:* St Oswald's Roman Catholic Sch., Ashton-in-Makerfield. Entered Mining Industry at age of 14 and was employed in practically every underground job in mining. Served as Councillor in Ashton-in-Makerfield. Elected to Nat. Exec. Cttee of Nat. Union of Mineworkers, 1957; Gen. Sec. of North Western Area, 1961, when he relinquished his appt as a JP, owing to other commitments. Mem., Nat. Exec. Cttee, Labour Party, 1963–73; former Chm., Internat. and Organisation Cttee, Labour Party. Member: TUC Gen. Council, 1973–80. Dir, United Racecourses Ltd, 1982–. *Publication:* Battered Cherub (autobiog.), 1982.

GORMLY, Allan Graham, CBE 1991; Group Managing Director, John Brown PLC, since 1983; *b* 18 Dec. 1937; *s* of William Gormly and Christina Swinton Flockhart Arnot; *m* 1962, Vera Margaret Grant; one *s* one *d*. *Educ:* Paisley Grammar School. CA. Peat Marwick Mitchell & Co., 1955–61; Rootes Group, 1961–65; John Brown PLC, 1965–68; Brownlee & Co. Ltd, 1968–70; John Brown PLC, 1970: Finance Director, John Brown Engineering Ltd, 1970–77; Director, Planning and Control, John Brown PLC, 1977–80; Dep. Chairman, John Brown Engineers and Constructors Ltd, 1980–83; Chairman: Roxby Engineering International Ltd, 1980–83; UDI Group Ltd, 1980–83; CJB (Developments) Ltd, 1980–83; Director: Trafalgar House plc, 1986–; BREL Gp Ltd, 1989–; Royal Insurance Hldgs, 1990–. Chm., Overseas Projects Bd, 1988–; Dep. Chm.,

Export Guarantees Adv. Council, 1990–; Member: BOTB, 1988–; Review Body on Top Salaries, 1990–. *Recreation:* golf. *Address:* 56 North Park, Gerrards Cross, Bucks SL9 8JR. *T:* Gerrards Cross (0753) 885079. *Club:* Caledonian.

GORRINGE, Christopher John; Chief Executive, All England Lawn Tennis and Croquet Club, Wimbledon, since 1983; *b* 13 Dec. 1945; *s* of Maurice Sydney William Gorringe and Hilda Joyce Gorringe; *m* 1976, Jennifer Mary Chamberlain; two *d*. *Educ:* Bradfield Coll., Berks; Royal Agricl Coll., Cirencester. ARICS. Asst Land Agent, Iveagh Trustees Ltd (Guinness family), 1968–73; Asst Sec., 1973–79, Sec., 1979–83, All England Lawn Tennis and Croquet Club. *Recreations:* lawn tennis, squash, soccer. *Address:* All England Lawn Tennis Club, Church Road, Wimbledon, SW19 5AE. *T:* 081–946 2244. *Clubs:* East India, Devonshire, Sports and Public Schools; All England Lawn Tennis and Croquet, International Lawn Tennis of GB, Queen's, St George's Hill Lawn Tennis, Jesters.

GORROD, Prof. John William, CChem, FRSC; FRCPath; Professor of Biopharmacy, King's College London, since 1984; Research Professor, Chelsea Department of Pharmacy, since 1990; *b* 11 Oct. 1931; *s* of Ernest Lionel and Carrie Rebecca Gorrod; *m* 1954, Doreen Mary Collins; two *s* one *d*. *Educ:* Brunel Coll. of Advanced Technology; Chelsea Coll. (DCC, PhD, DSc). Biochem. Asst, Inst. of Cancer Res., 1954–64; Res. Fellow, Univ. of Bari, Italy, 1964; Sen. Student, Royal Commn for Exhibn of 1851, 1965–68; University of London: Lectr 1968–80, then Reader 1980–84, in Biopharmacy, Chelsea Coll.; Hd, Chelsea Dept of Pharmacy, King's Coll., 1984–90; Chm., Univ. Bd of Studies in Pharmacy, 1986–88; Hd of Div. of Health Scis, KCL, 1988–89. Dir, Drug Control and Teaching Centre, Sports Council, 1985–. Member: Council, Internat. Soc. for Study of Xenobiotics (Chm., Memship Affairs Cttee); Educn Cttee, Pharmaceutical Soc. of GB, 1986–; Assoc. for Res. in Indoor Air, 1989–; Council, Indoor Air Internat., 1990–; Associates for Res. in Substances of Enjoyment, 1990–; Air Transport Users Cttee, CAA, 1990–. Vis. Prof., Univs of Bologna, Bari, and Kebangsan, Malaysia; Canadian MRC Vis. Prof., Univs of Manitoba and Saskatchewan, 1988. Hon. MPS, 1982; Corresp. Mem., German Pharm. Soc., 1985. Hon. Fellow: Greek Pharmaceutical Soc., 1987; Turkish Assoc. of Pharmacists, 1988. Editorial Board: Xenobiotica; Europ. Jl of Metabolism and Pharmacokinetics; Toxicology Letters; Anti-Cancer Res. *Publications:* Drug Metabolism in Man (jtly), 1978; Biological Oxidation of Nitrogen, 1978; Drug Toxicity, 1979; Testing for Toxicity, 1981; (jtly) Biological Oxidation of Nitrogen in Organic Molecules, 1985; (jtly) Development of Drugs and Modern Medicines, 1986; (jtly) Metabolism of Xenobiotics, 1987; (jtly) Molecular Aspects of Human Disease, 1989; contribs to Xenobiotica, Europ. Jl Drug Metabolism, Jl Pharm. Pharmacol, Mutation Res., Anti-Cancer Res., Jl Nat. Cancer Inst., Drug Metabolism Revs. *Recreations:* trying to understand government policies on tertiary education, travel, books, running (slowly!), badminton. *Address:* Kingsmead, 13 Park Lane, Hayes, Mddx UB4 8AA; The Rest Orchard, Polstead Heath, Suffolk. *Clubs:* Athenæum; Hillingdon Athletic (Mddx).

GORST, John Michael; MP (C) Hendon North, since 1970; *b* 28 June 1928; *s* of late Derek Charles Gorst and Tatiana (*née* Kolotinsky); *m* 1954, Noël Harington Walker; five *s*. *Educ:* Ardingly Coll.; Corpus Christi Coll., Cambridge (MA). Advertising and Public Relations Manager, Pye Ltd, 1953–63; and Trade Union and Public Affairs Consultant, John Gorst & Associates, 1964–. Public relations adviser to: British Lion Films, 1964–65; Fedn of British Film Makers, 1964–67; Film Production Assoc. of GB, 1967–68; BALPA, 1967–69; Guy's Hosp., 1968–74. Founder: Telephone Users' Assoc., 1964–80 (Sec. 1964–70); Local Radio Assoc. 1964 (Sec., 1964–71). Contested (C) Chester-le-Street, 1964; Bodmin, 1966. Sec., Cons. Consumer Protection Cttee, 1973–74; Mem., Employment Select Cttee, 1979–87; Vice-Chm., All Party War Crimes Cttee, 1987–; Chm., Cons. Media Cttee, 1987–90. *Recreations:* gardening, photography and video recording, chess. *Address:* House of Commons, SW1A 0AA. *Club:* Garrick.

GORT, 8th Viscount (Ire.), *cr* 1816; **Colin Leopold Prendergast Vereker,** JP; Baron Kiltarton 1810; company director; *b* 21 June 1916; *s* of Commander Leopold George Prendergast Vereker, RD, RNR (*d* 1937) (*g s* of 4th Viscount) and Helen Marjorie Campbell (*d* 1958); *S* kinsman, 1975; *m* 1946, Bettine Mary Mackenzie, *d* of late Godfrey Greene; two *s* one *d*. *Educ:* Sevenoaks. Trained at Air Service Training, Hamble, in Aeronautical Engineering, etc., 1937–39; served Fleet Air Arm, 1939–45 (despatches). Member of House of Keys, IOM, 1966–71. JP IOM 1962. *Recreations:* golf, fishing, gardening. *Heir:* *er s* Hon. Foley Robert Standish Prendergast Vereker [*b* 24 Oct. 1951; *m* 1979, Julie Denise (marr. diss. 1986), *o d* of D. W. Jones, Ballasalla, IoM]. *Address:* Westwood, The Crofts, Castletown, Isle of Man. *T:* Castletown (0624) 822545.

GORTON, Rt. Hon. Sir John (Grey), PC 1968; GCMG 1977; AC 1988; CH 1971; MA; retired; *b* 1911; *m* 1935, Bettina, *d* of G. Brown, Bangor, Me, USA; two *s* one *d*. *Educ:* Geelong Gram. Sch.; Brasenose Coll., Oxford (MA, Hon. Fellow, 1968). Orchardist. Enlisted RAAF, Nov. 1940; served in UK, Singapore, Darwin, Milne Bay; severely wounded in air ops; discharged with rank of Flt-Lt, Dec. 1944. Councillor, Kerang Shire, 1947–52 (Pres. of Shire); Mem., Lodden Valley Regional Cttee. Senator for State of Victoria, Parlt of Commonwealth of Australia, 1949–68 (Govt Leader in Senate, 1967–68); Minister for Navy, 1958–63; Minister Assisting the Minister for External Affairs, 1960–63 (Actg Minister during periods of absence overseas of Minister); Minister in Charge of CSIRO, 1962–68; Minister for Works and, under Prime Minister, Minister in Charge of Commonwealth Activities in Educn and Research, 1963–66; Minister for Interior, 1963–64; Minister for Works, 1966–67; Minister for Educn and Science, 1966–68; MHR (L) for Higgins, Vic, 1968–75; Prime Minister of Australia, 1968–71; Minister for Defence, and Dep. Leader of Liberal Party, March-Aug. 1971; Mem. Parly Liberal Party Exec., and Liberal Party Spokesman on Environment and Conservation and Urban and Regional Develt, 1973–75; Dep. Chm., Jt Parly Cttee on Prices, 1973–75. Contested Senate election (Ind.), ACT, Dec. 1975. *Address:* Unit 2, 11 Murray Crescent, Griffith, ACT 2603, Australia.

GORTVAI, Dame Rosalinde; *see* Hurley, Dame R.

GOSCHEN, family name of **Viscount Goschen**.

GOSCHEN, 4th Viscount *cr* 1900; **Giles John Harry Goschen;** *b* 16 Nov. 1965; *s* of 3rd Viscount Goschen, KBE, and of Alvin Moyanna Lesley, *yr d* of late Harry England, Durban, Natal; *S* father, 1977. *Address:* Hilton House, Crowthorne, Berks.

GOSCHEN, Sir Edward (Christian), 3rd Bt, *cr* 1916; DSO 1944; Rifle Brigade; *b* 2 Sept. 1913; *er s* of Sir Edward Henry Goschen, 2nd Bt, and Countess Mary, 7th *d* of Count Danneskiold Samsoe, Denmark; *S* father, 1933; *m* 1946, Cynthia, *d* of late Rt Hon. Sir Alexander Cadogan, PC, OM, GCMG, KCB and Lady Theodosia Cadogan; one *s* one *d*. *Educ:* Eton; Trinity Coll., Oxford. Mem., Stock Exchange Council (Dep. Chm., 1968–71). Commonwealth War Graves Comr, 1977–86. *Heir:* *s* Edward Alexander Goschen [*b* 13 March 1949; *m* 1976, Louise Annette, *d* of Lt-Col R. F. L. Chance, MC, and Lady Ava Chance; one *d*]. *Address:* Lower Farm House, Hampstead Norreys, Newbury, Berks RG16 0SG. *T:* Hermitage (0635) 201270.

GOSFORD, 7th Earl of, *cr* 1806; **Charles David Nicholas Alexander John Sparrow Acheson;** Bt (NS) 1628; Baron Gosford 1776; Viscount Gosford 1785; Baron Worlingham (UK) 1835; Baron Acheson (UK) 1847; *b* 13 July 1942; *o s* of 6th Earl of Gosford, OBE, and Francesca Augusta, *er d* of Francesco Cagiati, New York; *S* father, 1966; *m* 1983, Lynnette Redmond. *Educ:* Harrow; Byam Shaw Sch. of drawing and painting; Royal Academy Schs. Chm., Artists Union, 1976–80; Mem. Visual Arts Panel, Greater London Arts Assoc., 1976–77; Council Member, British Copyright Council, 1977–80. Recent one-man shows: Barry Stern Exhibiting Gall., Sydney, Aust., 1983; Von Bertouch Galls, Newcastle, NSW, 1985. *Heir:* *u* Hon. Patrick Bernard Victor Montagu Acheson [*b* 4 Feb. 1915; *m* 1946, Judith, *d* of Mrs F. B. Bate, Virginia, USA; three *s* two *d*]. *Address:* c/o House of Lords, SW1.

GOSKIRK, (William) Ian (Macdonald), CBE 1986; Partner, Coopers & Lybrand Deloitte, since 1990; *b* 2 March 1932; *s* of William Goskirk and Flora Macdonald; *m* 1969, Hope Ann Knaizuk; one *d*. *Educ:* Carlisle Grammar Sch.; Queen's Coll., Oxford (MA). Served REME, 1950–52. Shell Internat. Petroleum, 1956–74; Anschutz Corp., 1974–76; BNOC, 1976–85; Man. Dir, BNOC Trading, 1980–82; Chief Exec., BNOC, 1982–85; Dir, Coopers & Lybrand Associates, 1986–90. *Recreation:* gardening. *Address:* c/o 107 Pall Mall, SW1Y 5ER. *Club:* Athenæum.

GOSLING, Allan Gladstone; Sales Director, PSA Projects, Property Services Agency, Department of the Environment, since 1991 (Operational Director, 1990–91); *b* 4 July 1933; *s* of late Gladstone Gosling and of Elizabeth Gosling (*née* Ward); *m* 1961, Janet Pamela (*née* Gosling); one *s* one *d*. *Educ:* Kirkham Grammar Sch.; Birmingham Sch. of Architecture. DipArch; RIBA 1961; FRIAS 1988 (RIAS 1984). Asst Architect, Lancs County Council, 1950–54; Birmingham Sch. of Architecture, 1954–57; Surman Kelly Surman, Architects, 1957–59; Royal Artillery, 1959–61; Army Works Organisation, 1961–63; Min. of Housing R&D Group, 1963–68; Suptg Architect, Birmingham Regional Office, Min. of Housing, 1968–72; Regional Works Officer, NW Region, PSA, 1972–76; Midland Regional Dir, PSA, 1976–83; Dir, Scottish Services, PSA, 1983–90. *Recreations:* walking, gardening, DIY. *Address:* PSA Projects Office, Five Ways House, Islington Row, Middleway, Birmingham B15 1SL.

GOSLING, Sir Donald, Kt 1976; Joint Chairman, National Car Parks Ltd, since 1950; Chairman, Palmer & Harvey Ltd, since 1967; *b* 2 March 1929; *m* 1959, Elizabeth Shauna (marr. diss. 1988), *d* of Dr Peter Ingram and Lecky Ingram; three *s*. Joined RN, 1944; served Mediterranean, HMS Leander. Mem., Council of Management, White Ensign Assoc. Ltd, 1970– (Chm., 1978–83; Vice Pres., 1983–); Mem., Exec. Cttee, Imperial Soc. of Kts Bachelor, 1977–. Chm., Berkeley Square Ball Trust, 1982–; Trustee: Fleet Air Arm Museum, Yeovilton, 1974– (Chm., Mountbatten Meml Hall Appeals Cttee, 1980); RYA Seamanship Foundn, 1981–; Patron: Submarine Meml Appeal, 1978–; HMS Ark Royal Welfare Trust, 1986–. *Recreations:* swimming, sailing, shooting. *Address:* National Car Parks Ltd, 21 Bryanston Street, Marble Arch, W1A 4NH. *T:* 071–499 7050. *Clubs:* Royal Thames Yacht, Royal London Yacht, Royal Naval Sailing Association, Thames Sailing; Saints and Sinners.

GOSLING, Justin Cyril Bertrand; Principal, St Edmund Hall, Oxford, since 1982; *b* 26 April 1930; *s* of Vincent and Dorothy Gosling; *m* 1958, Margaret Clayton; two *s* two *d*. *Educ:* Ampleforth Coll.; Wadham Coll., Oxford (BPhil, MA). Univ. of Oxford: Fereday Fellow, St John's Coll., 1955–58; Lectr in Philosophy, Pembroke Coll. and Wadham Coll., 1958–60; Fellow in Philosophy, St Edmund Hall, 1960–82; Sen. Proctor, 1977–78. Barclay Acheson Prof., Macalester Coll., Minnesota, 1964; Vis. Res. Fellow, ANU, Canberra, 1970 (Pro-Vice-Chancellor, 1989–90). *Publications:* Pleasure and Desire, 1969; Plato, 1973; (ed) Plato, Philebus, 1975; (with C. C. W. Taylor) The Greeks on Pleasure, 1982; Weakness of the Will, 1990; articles in Mind, Phil Rev. and Proc. Aristotelian Soc. *Recreations:* gardening, intaglio printing, recorder music. *Address:* St Edmund Hall, Oxford OX1 4AR. *T:* Oxford (0865) 279000.

GOSLING, Col Richard Bennett, OBE 1957; TD 1947; DL; *b* 4 Oct. 1914; 2nd *s* of late T. S. Gosling, Dynes Hall, Halstead; *m* 1st, 1950, Marie Terese Ronayne (*d* 1976), Castle Redmond, Co. Cork; one adopted *s* one adopted *d* (one *s* decd); 2nd, 1978, Sybilla Burgers van Oyen, *widow* of Bernard Burgers, 't Kasteel, Nijmegen. *Educ:* Eton; Magdalene Coll., Cambridge (MA). CEng, FIMechE, FIMC. Served with Essex Yeomanry, RHA, 1939–45; CO, 1953–56; Dep. CRA, East Anglian Div., 1956–58. Dir-Gen., British Agricl Export Council, 1971–73. Chairman: Constructors, 1965–68; Hearne & Co., 1971–82. Director: P-E International, 1956–76; Doulton & Co., 1962–72; Revertex Chemicals, 1974–81; Press Mouldings, 1977–. DL 1954, High Sheriff 1982, Essex. French Croix de Guerre, 1944. *Recreation:* country pursuits. *Address:* Canterburys Lodge, Margaretting, Essex. *T:* Ingatestone (0277) 353073. *Clubs:* Naval and Military, MCC; Beefsteak (Chelmsford).

GOSS, Prof. Richard Oliver, PhD; Professor, Department of Maritime Studies, University of Wales Institute of Science and Technology, since 1980; *b* 4 Oct. 1929; *s* of late Leonard Arthur Goss and Hilda Nellie Goss (*née* Casson); *m* Lesley Elizabeth Thurbon (marr. diss. 1983); two *s* one *d*. *Educ:* Christ's Coll., Finchley; HMS Worcester; King's Coll., Cambridge. Master Mariner 1956; BA 1958; MA 1961; PhD 1979. FCIT 1970; MNI (Founder) 1972; FNI 1977. Merchant Navy (apprentice and executive officer), 1947–55; NZ Shipping Co. Ltd, 1958–63; Economic Consultant (Shipping, Shipbuilding and Ports), MoT, 1963–64; Econ. Adviser, BoT (Shipping), 1964–67; Sen. Econ. Adviser (Shipping, Civil Aviation, etc), 1967–74; Econ. Adviser to Cttee of Inquiry into Shipping (Rochdale Cttee), 1967–70; Under-Sec., Depts of Industry and Trade, 1974–80. Nuffield/Leverhulme Travelling Fellow, 1977–78. Governor, Plymouth Polytechnic, 1973–84; Mem. Council: RINA, 1969–; Nautical Inst. (from foundn until 1976); Member: CNAA Nautical Studies Bd, 1971–81; CNAA Transport Bd, 1976–78. Editor and Editor-in-Chief, Maritime Policy and Management, 1985–. *Publications:* Studies in Maritime Economics, 1968; (with C. D. Jones) The Economies of Size in Dry Bulk Carriers, 1971; (with M. C. Mann, et al) The Cost of Ships' Time, 1974; Advances in Maritime Economics, 1977; A Comparative Study of Seaport Management and Administration, 1979; Policies for Canadian Seaports, 1984; Port Authorities in Australia, 1987; Collected Papers, 1990; numerous papers in various jls, transactions and to conferences. *Recreations:* cruising inland waterways, travel. *Address:* 8 Dunraven House, Castle Court, Westgate Street, Cardiff CF1 1DL. *T:* Cardiff (0222) 344338.

GOSS, Very Rev. Thomas Ashworth; Dean of Jersey, Rector of St Helier, and Hon. Canon of Winchester, 1971–85; *b* 27 July 1912; *s* of George Woolnough Goss and Maud M. (*née* Savage); *m* 1946, Frances Violet Patience Frampton; one *s* one *d*. *Educ:* Shardlow Hall; Aldenham Sch.; St Andrews Univ. (MA). Deacon, 1937; Priest, 1938; Curate of Frodingham, 1937–41. Chaplain, RAFVR, 1941–47 (PoW Japan, 1942–45). Vicar of Sutton-le-Marsh, 1947–51; Chaplain, RAF, 1951–67; QHC, 1966–67. Rector of St Saviour, Jersey, 1967–71. Canon Emeritus, Winchester, 1985–. *Recreations:* gardening, theatricals. *Address:* Les Pignons, Mont de la Rosière, St Saviour, Jersey, CI. *Clubs:* Royal Air Force; Victoria, Royal Yacht (Jersey).

GOSSCHALK, Joseph Bernard; His Honour Judge Gosschalk; a Circuit Judge, since 1991; *b* 27 Aug. 1936; *s* of late Lionel Samuel Gosschalk and of Johanna (*née* Lion); *m* 1973, Ruth Sandra Jarvis; two *d*. *Educ:* East Ham Grammar Sch.; Magdalen Coll., Oxford (MA Jurisprudence). Called to the Bar, Gray's Inn, 1961; Asst Recorder, 1983–87; Head of Chambers, Francis Taylor Bldg, Temple, EC4, 1983–91; a Recorder, SE Circuit, 1987–91. *Recreations:* theatre, tennis, foreign travel. *Address:* The Crown Court, Snaresbrook, Hollybush Hill, E11 1QW. *T:* 081–989 6666.

GOSTIN, Larry, DJur; Executive Director, American Society of Law and Medicine, since 1986; Adjunct Associate Professor in Health Law, School of Public Health, Harvard University, since 1988 (Senior Fellow of Health Law, 1985–86; Lecturer, 1986–87); Associate Director, Harvard University/World Health Organization Collaborating Center on Health Legislation, since 1988; *b* 19 Oct. 1949; *s* of Joseph and Sylvia Gostin; *m* 1977, Jean Catherine Allison; two *s. Educ:* State Univ. of New York, Brockport (BA Psychology); Duke Univ. (DJur 1974). Dir of Forensics and Debate, Duke Univ., 1973–74; Fulbright Fellow, Social Res. Unit, Univ. of London, 1974–75; Legal Dir, MIND (Nat. Assoc. for Mental Health), 1975–83; Gen. Sec., NCCL, 1983–85. Legal Counsel in series of cases before Eur. Commn and Eur. Court of Human Rights, 1974–. Vis. Prof., Sch. of Social Policy, McMaster Univ., 1978–79; Vis. Fellow in Law and Psychiatry, Centre for Criminological Res., Oxford Univ., 1982–83. Chm., Advocacy Alliance, 1981–83; Member: National Cttee, UN Internat. Year for Disabled People, 1981; Legal Affairs Cttee, Internat. League of Socs for Mentally Handicapped People, 1980–; Cttee of Experts, Internat. Commn of Jurists to draft UN Human Rights Declarations, 1982–; Adv. Council, Interights, 1984–; AE Trust, 1984–85; WHO Expert Cttee on Guidelines on the Treatment of Drug and Alcohol Dependent Persons, 1985; WHO Steering Cttee, Internat. Ethical Guidelines for Human Population Res.; Nat. Bd of Dirs, Amer. Civil Liberties Union, 1986– (Mem. Exec. Cttee, 1988–). Western European and UK Editor, Internat. Jl of Law and Psychiatry, 1978–81; Exec. Ed., Amer. Jl of Law and Medicine, 1986–; Ed.-in-chief, Jl of Law, Medicine and Health Care, 1986–. Rosemary Delbridge Meml Award for most outstanding contribution to social policy, 1983. *Publications:* A Human Condition: vol. 1, 1975; vol. 2, 1977; A Practical Guide to Mental Health Law, 1983; The Court of Protection, 1983; (ed) Secure Provision: a review of special services for mentally ill and handicapped people in England and Wales, 1985; Mental Health Services: law and practice, 1986; Human Rights in Mental Health: an international report for the World Federation for Mental Health, 1988; Civil Liberties in Conflict, 1988; Surrogate Motherhood: politics and privacy, 1990; AIDS and the Health Care System, 1990; articles in learned jls. *Recreations:* family outings, walking on the mountains and fells of the Lake District. *Address:* American Society of Law and Medicine, 765 Commonwealth Avenue, 16th Floor, Boston, Mass 02215, USA. *T:* 617–2624990; Harvard School of Public Health, Department of Health Policy and Management, 677 Huntington Avenue, Boston, Mass 02115, USA. *T:* 617–7321090.

GOSWELL, Sir Brian (Lawrence), Kt 1991; FSVA; Deputy Senior Partner, Healey & Baker, Surveyors, since 1988; *b* 26 Nov. 1935; *s* of late Albert George Goswell and Florence Emily (*née* Barnett); *m* 1961, Deirdre Gillian Stones; two *s.* FSVA 1968; ACIArb 1980. Mil. service, Oxford and Bucks Light Infantry, 1954–57. Joined Healey & Baker, Surveyors, 1957; Partner, 1968; Managing Partner, 1975. Chm., Roux Restaurants Ltd; Dir, Westminster Scaffolding Gp plc. Mem., Adv. Bd, Sir Alexander Gibb & Partners. Dir, Amer. Chamber of Commerce in London. *Recreations:* cricket, horse-racing, shooting. *Address:* 27 Austin Friars, EC2N 2AA. *T:* 071–628 4361. *Clubs:* Carlton, Turf, City of London, City Livery, MCC.

GOTTLIEB, Bernard, CB 1970; industrial relations consultant; *b* 1913; *s* of late James Gottlieb and Pauline (*née* Littaur); *m* 1955, Sybil N. Epstein; one *s* one *d. Educ:* Haberdashers' Hampstead Sch.; Queen Mary Coll., London Univ. BSc First Class Maths, 1932. Entered Civil Service as an Executive Officer in Customs and Excise, 1932. Air Ministry, 1938; Asst Private Sec., 1941, and Private Sec., 1944, to Permanent Under-Sec. of State (late Sir Arthur Street), Control Office for Germany and Austria, 1945; Asst Sec., 1946. Seconded to National Coal Board, 1946; Min. of Power, 1950; Under-Sec., 1961, Dir of Establishments, 1965–69; Under-Sec., Min. of Posts and Telecommunications, 1969–73; Secretariat, Pay Board, 1973–74, Royal Commn for Distribution of Income and Wealth, 1974–78. Gwilym Gibbon Research Fellow, Nuffield Coll., Oxford, 1952–53. *Address:* 49 Gresham Gardens, NW11 8PA. *T:* 081–455 6172. *Club:* Reform.

GOTTLIEB, Robert Adams; Editor-in-Chief, The New Yorker, since 1987; *b* 29 April 1931; *s* of Charles and Martha Gottlieb; *m* 1st, 1952, Muriel Higgins (marr. diss. 1965); one *s*; 2nd, 1969, Maria Tucci; one *s* one *d. Educ:* Columbia Coll., NY; Cambridge Univ. Simon & Schuster, publishers, 1955–68 (final positions, Editor-in-Chief and Vice-Pres.); Pres. and Editor-in-Chief, Alfred A. Knopf, publishers, 1968–87. *Recreations:* ballet, classic film, shopping.

GOTTMANN, Prof. Jean, FRGS; FBA 1977; Professor of Geography, University of Oxford, 1968–83, now Emeritus; Fellow of Hertford College, Oxford, 1968–83, now Emeritus; *b* 10 Oct. 1915; *s* of Elie Gottmann and Sonia-Fanny Ettinger Gottmann; *m* 1957, Bernice Adelson. *Educ:* Lycée Montaigne; Lycée St Louis; Sorbonne. Research Asst Human Geography, Sorbonne, 1937–40; Mem., Inst. for Advanced Study, Princeton, NJ, several times, 1942–65; Lectr, then Associate Prof. in Geography, Johns Hopkins Univ., Baltimore, 1943–48; Dir of Studies and Research, UN Secretariat, NY, 1946–47; Chargé de Recherches, CNRS, Paris, 1948–51; Lectr, then Prof., Institut d'Etudes Politiques, University of Paris, 1948–56; Research Dir, Twentieth Century Fund, NY, 1956–61; Prof. Ecole des Hautes Etudes, Sorbonne, 1960–84. Pres., World Soc. for Ekistics, 1971–73. Governor, Univ. of Haifa, 1972–. Hon. Member: Amer. Geograph. Soc., 1961; Royal Netherlands Geog. Soc., 1963; Soc. Géographique de Liège, 1977; Società Geografica Italiana, 1981; Ateneo Veneto, 1986; For. Hon. Mem., Amer. Acad. of Arts and Sciences, 1972. Hon. LLD Wisconsin, 1968; Hon. DSc S Illinois, 1969; Hon. LittD Liverpool, 1986. Charles Daly Medal of Amer. Geograph. Soc., 1964; Prix Bonaparte-Wyse, 1962; Prix Sully-Olivier de Serre, Min. of Agriculture, France, 1964; Palmes Académiques, 1968; Victoria Medal, RGS, 1980; Grand Prix, Société de Géographie, Paris, 1984. Hon. Citizen: Yokohama, 1976; Guadalajara, 1978. Chevalier, Légion d'Honneur, 1974. *Publications:* Relations Commerciales de la France, 1942; L'Amérique, 1949 (3rd edn 1960); A Geography of Europe, 1950 (4th edn 1969); La politique des Etats et leur géographie, 1952; Virginia at Mid-century, 1955; Megalopolis, 1961; Essais sur l'Aménagement de l'Espace habité, 1966; The Significance of Territory, 1973; Centre and Periphery, 1980; The Coming of the Transactional City, 1983; La Citta invincibile, 1984; Orbits, 1984; Megalopolis Revisited, 1987; (with R. A. Harper) Since Megalopolis, 1990. *Address:* 19 Belsyre Court, Woodstock Road, Oxford OX2 6HU. *T:* Oxford (0865) 57076. *Club:* United Oxford & Cambridge University.

GOUDIE, Prof. Andrew Shaw; Professor of Geography and Head of Department, University of Oxford, since 1984; *b* 21 Aug. 1945; *s* of William and Mary Goudie; *m* 1987, Heather (*née* Viles); two *d. Educ:* Dean Close Sch., Cheltenham; Trinity Hall, Cambridge. BA, PhD Cantab; MA Oxon. Departmental Demonstrator, Oxford, 1970–76; Univ. Lectr, 1976–84; Fellow of Hertford College, Oxford, 1976–. Hon. Secretary: British Geomorphological Res. Gp. 1977–80 (Chm., 1988–89); RGS, 1981–88; Member: Council, Inst. of British Geographers, 1980–83; British Nat. Cttee for Geography, 1982–87. Dep. Leader: Internat. Karakoram Project, 1980; Kora Project, 1983. Hon. Vice Pres., Geographical Assoc., 1987–. Cuthbert Peek award, RGS, 1975; Geographic Soc. of Chicago Publication award, 1982. *Publications:* Duricrusts of Tropical and Sub-tropical Landscapes, 1973; Environmental Change, 1976, 2nd edn, 1983; The Warm Desert Environment, 1977; The Prehistory and Palaeogeography of the Great Indian Desert, 1978; Desert Geomorphology, 1980; The Human Impact, 1981, 3rd edn 1990; Geomorphological Techniques, 1981, 3rd edn 1990; The Atlas of Swaziland, 1983; Chemical Sediments and Geomorphology, 1983; The Nature of the Environment, 1984; (jtly) Discovering Landscape in England and Wales, 1985; The Encyclopædic Dictionary of Physical Geography, 1985; (jtly) Landshapes, 1989; The Geomorphology of England and Wales, 1990; Techniques for Desert Reclamation, 1990; contribs to learned jls. *Recreations:* bush life, old records, old books. *Address:* Hertford College, Oxford OX1 3BW. *T:* Oxford (0865) 241791. *Clubs:* Geographical; Gilbert (Oxford).

GOUDIE, James; *see* Goudie, T. J. C.

GOUDIE, Rev. John Carrick, CBE 1972; Assistant Minister at St John's United Reformed Church, Northwood, 1985–88, retired; *b* 25 Dec. 1919; *s* of late Rev. John Goudie, MA and late Mrs Janet Goudie, step *s* of late Mrs Evelyn Goudie; unmarried. *Educ:* Glasgow Academy; Glasgow Univ. (MA); Trinity Coll., Glasgow. Served in RN: Hostilities Only Ordinary Seaman and later Lieut RNVR, 1941–45; returned to Trinity Coll., Glasgow to complete studies for the Ministry, 1945; Asst Minister at Crown Court Church of Scotland, London and ordained, 1947–50; Minister, The Union Church, Greenock, 1950–53; entered RN as Chaplain, 1953; Principal Chaplain, Church of Scotland and Free Churches (Naval), 1970–73; on staff of St Columba's Church of Scotland, Pont Street, 1973–77; Minister of Christ Church URC, Wallington, 1977–80; on staff of Royal Scottish Corp., London, 1980–84. QHC 1970–73. *Recreations:* tennis, the theatre. *Address:* 309 Howard House, Dolphin Square, SW1V 3PF. *T:* 071–798 8537. *Club:* Army and Navy.

GOUDIE, (Thomas) James (Cooper), QC 1984; a Recorder, since 1986; *b* 2 June 1942; *s* of late William Cooper Goudie and Mary Isobel Goudie; *m* 1969, Mary Teresa Brick; two *s. Educ:* Dean Close Sch.; London School of Economics (LLB Hons). Solicitor, 1966–70; called to the Bar, Inner Temple, 1970 (Bencher, 1991). Contested (Lab) Brent North, General Elections, Feb. and Oct. 1974; Leader of Brent Council, 1977–78. *Address:* 11 King's Bench Walk, Temple, EC4Y 7EQ. *T:* 071–583 0610.

GOUDIE, Hon. William Henry, MC 1944; Executive Director and Deputy Chairman, Law Reform Commission of Tasmania, 1974–81; *b* 21 Aug. 1916; *s* of Henry and Florence Goudie; *m* 1948, Mourilyan Isobel Munro (*d* 1981); two *s. Educ:* Bristol Grammar School. Solicitor (England), 1938; called to Bar, Gray's Inn, 1952. War service, 1939–45, London Scottish Regt and Som LI; JAG's Dept, 1945–48; Prosecutor, Dep. JA, Officer i/c branches Italy, Greece, Austria; Officer i/c Legal Section War Crimes Gp, SE Europe; Sen. Resident Magistrate, Acting Judge, Kenya, 1948–63; Puisne Judge, Aden, 1963–66; Puisne Judge, Uganda (Contract), 1967–71; Puisne Judge, Fiji (Contract), 1971–73. Editor, Kenya and Aden Law Reports. *Recreations:* golf, swimming. *Address:* 24 Nimala Street, Rosny, Hobart, Tasmania 7018, Australia. *Club:* Commonwealth Trust.

GOUGH, family name of **Viscount Gough.**

GOUGH, 5th Viscount (of Goojerat, of the Punjaub, and Limerick), *cr* 1849; **Shane Hugh Maryon Gough;** Irish Guards, 1961–67; *b* 26 Aug. 1941; *o s* of 4th Viscount Gough and Margaretta Elizabeth (*d* 1977), *o d* of Sir Spencer Maryon-Wilson, 11th Bt; *S* father 1951. *Educ:* Abberley Hall, Worcs; Winchester Coll. Mem. Queen's Bodyguard for Scotland, Royal Company of Archers. *Heir:* none. *Address:* Keppoch Estate Office, Strathpeffer, Ross-shire IV14 9AD. *T:* Strathpeffer (0997) 224; 17 Stanhope Gardens, SW7 5RQ. *Clubs:* Pratt's, White's; MCC.

GOUGH, Brandon; *see* Gough, C. B.

GOUGH, Cecil Ernest Freeman, CMG 1956; Director and Secretary, 1974–78, Assistant Director-General, 1978–80, acting Director-General, 1980–81, British Property Federation; *b* 29 Oct. 1911; *s* of Ernest John Gough; *m* 1938, Gwendolen Lily Miriam Longman; one *s* one *d. Educ:* Southend High Sch.; London Sch. of Economics (School of Economics Scholar in Law, 1932). LLB (Hons) 1934. Asst Examiner Estate Duty Office, Board of Inland Revenue, 1930; Air Ministry, 1938; Principal, 1944; Ministry of Defence, 1947; Asst Sec., 1949; on loan to Foreign Office, as Counsellor, United Kingdom Delegation to NATO, Paris, 1952–56; Chm., NATO Infrastructure Cttee, 1952–53; First Chm., Standing Armaments Cttee Western European Union, 1956; returned Ministry of Defence, 1956; Under-Sec., 1958; Under-Sec. at the Admiralty, 1962–64; Asst Under-Sec. of State, Min. of Defence, 1964–68. Man. Dir, Airwork (Overseas) Ltd, 1968–71; Dir, Airwork Services Ltd and Air Holdings Ltd, 1968–73; Sec., Associated Owners of City Properties, 1975–77. Medal of Freedom (USA), 1946; Coronation Medal, 1953. *Recreations:* cookery, reading, travel. *Address:* 23 Howbridge Road, Witham, Essex CM8 1BY. *T:* Witham (0376) 518969. *Clubs:* Naval and Military, Civil Service.

GOUGH, (Charles) Brandon, FCA; Chairman, Coopers & Lybrand Deloitte (formerly Coopers & Lybrand), Chartered Accountants, since 1983; *b* 8 Oct. 1937; *s* of Charles Richard Gough and Mary Evaline (*née* Goff); *m* 1961, Sarah Smith; one *s* two *d. Educ:* Douai Sch.; Jesus Coll., Cambridge (MA). FCA 1974. Joined Cooper Brothers & Co. (now Coopers & Lybrand Deloitte), 1964, Partner 1968; Mem., Exec. Cttee, Coopers & Lybrand (Internat.), 1982– (Chm., 1985 and 1991–); Chm., Coopers & Lybrand Europe, 1989. Govt Dir, BAe plc, 1987–88; Dir, British Invisibles, 1990–. Mem. Council, Inst. of Chartered Accountants in England and Wales, 1981–84; Chm., CCAB Auditing Practices Cttee, 1981–84 (Mem., 1976–84); Member: Accounting Standards Review (Dearing) Cttee, 1987–88; Financial Reporting Council, 1990–. City University Business School: Chm., City Adv. Panel, 1986–91 (Mem., 1980–91); Mem. Council, 1986–; Chm., Finance Cttee, 1988–; Member: Council of Lloyd's, 1983–86; Cambridge Univ. Careers Service Syndicate, 1983–86; Governing Council, 1984–88, Council, 1988–, Business in the Community; Council for Industry and Higher Educn, 1985–; Management Council, GB–Sasakawa Foundn, 1985–; UK Nat. Cttee, Japan-European Community Assoc., 1989–; CBI Task Force, Vocational Educn and Trng, 1989; CBI Educn & Trng Affairs Cttee, 1990–; Council, Foundn for Educn Business Partnerships, 1990–91; Council, City Univ., 1991–. Chm., Common Purpose Within Our Cities, 1991– (Trustee, 1989–); Trustee, GSMD Foundn, 1990–. CBIM 1985; FRSA 1988. Lloyd's Silver Medal, 1986. *Recreations:* music, gardening. *Address:* Long Barn, Weald, Sevenoaks, Kent TN14 6NH. *T:* Sevenoaks (0732) 463714.

GOUGH, Rt. Rev. Hugh Rowlands, CMG 1965; OBE (mil.) 1945; TD 1950; DD Lambeth; *b* 19 Sept. 1905; *o s* of late Rev. Charles Massey Gough, Rector of St Ebbe's, Oxford; *m* 1929, Hon. Madeline Elizabeth, *d* of 12th Baron Kinnaird, KT, KBE; one *d. Educ:* Weymouth Coll.; Trinity Coll., Cambridge; London Coll. Divinity. BA 1927, MA Cantab 1931. Deacon, 1928; Priest, 1929; Curate of St Mary, Islington, 1928–31; Perpetual Curate of St Paul, Walcot, Bath, 1931–34; Vicar of St James, Carlisle, 1934–39; Chaplain to High Sheriff of Cumberland, 1937; CF (TA), 1937–45; Chaplain to 4th Bn The Border Regt, 1937–39; Vicar of St Matthew, Bayswater 1939–46; Chaplain to 1st Bn London Rifle Bde, 1939–43; served Western Desert and Tunisia (wounded); Senior

Chap. to 1st Armd Div., Tunisia, 1943; DACG 10 Corps, Italy, 1943–45 (despatches); DACG, North Midland Dist, 1945. Hon. Chaplain to the Forces (2nd cl.) 1945. Vicar of Islington, Rural Dean of Islington, 1946–48. Preb. St Paul's Cathedral, 1948; Suffragan Bishop of Barking, 1948–59; Archdeacon of West Ham, 1948–58; Archbishop of Sydney and Primate of Australia, also Metropolitan of New South Wales, 1959–66, retired, 1966. Rector of Freshford, dio. of Bath and Wells, 1967–72; Vicar of Limpley Stoke, 1970–72. Chaplain and Sub-Prelate, Order of St John of Jerusalem, 1959–72. Formerly Member Council: London Coll. of Divinity, Clifton Theol. Coll. (Chm.), Haileybury Coll., Monkton Combe Sch., St Lawrence Coll. (Ramsgate), Chigwell Sch., Stowe Sch., Kingham Hill Trust. Golden Lectr Haberdashers' Co., 1953 and 1955. Pres. Conference, Educational Assoc., 1956. Mem., Essex County Education Cttee, 1949–59; DL Essex, 1952–59. Hon. DD Wycliffe Coll., Toronto; Hon. ThD, Aust. *Address:* Forge House, Over Wallop, Stockbridge, Hants. *T:* Andover (0264) 781315. *Club:* National.

GOUGH, John, CBE 1972; Director of Administration, and Secretary, Confederation of British Industry, 1965–74; *b* 18 June 1910; *o s* of H. E. and M. Gough; *m* 1939, Joan Renee Cooper; one *s* one *d.* *Educ:* Repton Sch.; Keble Coll., Oxford. BA 1st cl. hons History. Senior History Tutor, Stowe Sch., 1933; Fedn of British Industries: Personal Asst to Dir, 1934; Asst Sec., 1940; Sec., 1959; Dir of Administration and Sec., CBI, 1965. *Recreations:* walking, reading, music. *Address:* West Yard, North Bovey, Newton Abbot, Devon TQ13 8RT. *T:* Moretonhampstead (0647) 40395.

GOUGH-CALTHORPE, family name of **Baron Calthorpe.**

GOULD, Bryan Charles; MP (Lab) Dagenham, since 1983; *b* 11 Feb. 1939; *s* of Charles Terence Gould and Elsie May Driller; *m* 1967, Gillian Anne Harrigan; one *s* one *d.* *Educ:* Auckland Univ. (BA, LLM); Balliol Coll., Oxford (MA, BCL). HM Diplomatic Service: FO, 1964–66; HM Embassy, Brussels, 1966–68; Fellow and Tutor in Law, Worcester Coll., Oxford, 1968–74. MP (Lab) Southampton Test, Oct. 1974–1979; an opposition spokesman on trade, 1983–86, on economy and party campaigns, 1986–87, on Trade and Industry, 1987–89, on the environment, 1989– (Mem. of Shadow Cabinet, 1986–). Presenter/Reporter, TV Eye, Thames Television, 1979–83. *Publications:* Monetarism or Prosperity?, 1981; Socialism and Freedom, 1985; A Future for Socialism, 1989. *Recreations:* gardening, food, wine. *Address:* House of Commons, SW1. *T:* 071–219 3423.

GOULD, Cecil Hilton Monk; Keeper and Deputy Director of the National Gallery, 1973–78; *b* 24 May 1918; *s* of late Lieut Commander R. T. Gould and Muriel Hilda Estall. *Educ:* Westminster Sch. Served in Royal Air Force: France, 1940; Middle East, 1941–43; Italy, 1943–44; Normandy, Belgium and Germany, 1944–46. National Gallery: Asst Keeper, 1946; Dep. Keeper, 1962. Vis. Lectr, Melbourne Univ., 1978. FRSA 1968. *Publications:* An Introduction to Italian Renaissance Painting, 1957; Trophy of Conquest, 1965; Leonardo da Vinci, 1975; The Paintings of Correggio, 1976; Bernini in France, 1981; various publications for the National Gallery, including 16th-century Italian Schools catalogue; articles in Encyclopædia Britannica, Chambers's Encyclopedia, Dizionario Biografico degli Italiani, and specialist art journals of Europe and USA. *Recreations:* music, travel. *Address:* Jubilee House, Thorncombe, Dorset. *Club:* Reform.

GOULD, Donald (William), BSc (Physiol.), MRCS, DTM&H; writer and broadcaster on medical and scientific affairs; *b* 26 Jan. 1919; *s* of late Rev. Frank J. Gould; *m* 1st, 1940, Edna Forsyth; three *s* four *d*; 2nd, 1969, Jennifer Goodfellow; one *s* one *d.* *Educ:* Mill Hill Sch.; St Thomas's Hosp. Med. Sch., London. Orthopædic House Surg., Botley's Park Hosp., 1942; Surg. Lieut, RNVR, 1942–46; Med. Off., Hong Kong Govt Med. Dept, 1946–48; Lectr in Physiol., University of Hong Kong, 1948–51, Sen. Lectr, 1951–57; King Edward VII Prof. of Physiol., University of Malaya (Singapore), 1957–60; Lectr in Physiol., St Bartholomew's Hosp. Med. Coll., London, 1960–61, Sen. Lectr, 1961–63; External Examr in Physiol., University of Durham (Newcastle), 1961–63; Dep. Ed., Medical News, 1963–65; Editor: World Medicine, 1965–66; New Scientist, 1966–69; Med. Correspondent, New Statesman, 1966–78. Chm., Med. Journalists' Assoc., 1967–71; Vice-Chm., Assoc. of British Science Writers, 1970–71. *Publications:* The Black & White Medicine Show, 1985; The Medical Mafia, 1987; Nurses, 1988; Examining Doctors, 1991; contributions to: Experimentation with Human Subjects, 1972; Ecology, the Shaping Enquiry, 1972; Better Social Services, 1973; scientific papers in physiological jls; numerous articles on medical politics, ethics and science in lay and professional press. *Recreations:* writing poems nobody will publish, listening, talking, and walking. *Address:* 15 Waterbeach Road, Landbeach, Cambs CB4 4EA. *T:* Cambridge (0223) 861243.

GOULD, Edward John Humphrey, JP; MA; FRGS; Headmaster, Felsted School, since 1983; *b* Lewes, Sussex, 31 Oct. 1943; *s* of Roland and Ruth Gould; *m* 1970, Jennifer Jane, *d* of I. H. Lamb; two *d.* *Educ:* St Edward's Sch., Oxford; St Edmund Hall, Oxford (BA 1966, MA 1970, DipEd 1967). FRGS 1974. Harrow School, 1967–83: Asst Master, 1967–83; Head, Geography Dept, 1974–79; Housemaster, 1979–83. Mem., Indep. Schs Curriculum Cttee, 1985– (Chm., 1990–); Chm., ISIS East, 1989–. JP Essex, 1989. *Recreations:* Rugby (Oxford Blue, 1963–66), swimming (Half Blue, 1965), rowing (rep. GB, 1967), music. *Address:* The Headmaster's House, Felsted School, Dunmow, Essex CM6 3LL. *T:* Great Dunmow (0371) 820258. *Clubs:* East India, Devonshire, Sports and Public Schools; Vincent's (Oxford).

GOULD, Maj.-Gen. John Charles, CB 1975; Paymaster-in-Chief and Inspector of Army Pay Services, 1972–75, retired; *b* 27 April 1915; *s* of late Alfred George Webb and Hilda Gould; *m* 1941, Mollie Bannister; one *s* one *d.* *Educ:* Brighton, Hove and Sussex Grammar School. Surrey and Sussex Yeomanry (TA), 1937; Royal Army Pay Corps, 1941; served: N Africa, Sicily, Italy (despatches), Austria, 1941–46; Egypt, Jordan, Eritrea, 1948–51; Singapore, 1957–59; Dep. Paymaster-in-Chief, 1967–72. *Recreations:* golf, bridge. *Address:* Squirrels Wood, Ringles Cross, near Uckfield, East Sussex TN22 1HB. *T:* Uckfield (0825) 764592. *Clubs:* Lansdowne; Piltdown Golf.

GOULD, Joyce Brenda; Director of Organisation, Labour Party, since 1985; *b* 29 Oct. 1932; *d* of Sydney and Fanny Manson; *m* 1952, Kevin Gould (separated); one *d.* *Educ:* Cowper Street Primary Sch.; Roundhay High Sch. for Girls; Bradford Technical Coll. Dispenser, 1952–65; Asst Regional Organiser, 1969–75, Asst Nat. Agent and Chief Women's Officer, 1975–85, Labour Party. Sec., National Jt Cttee of Working Women's Orgns, 1975–; Vice-Pres., Socialist Internat. Women, 1978–. *Publications:* (ed) Women and Health, 1979; pamphlets on feminism, socialism and sexism, women's right to work, and on violence in society; articles and reports on women's rights and welfare. *Recreations:* relaxing, sport as a spectator, theatre, cinema, reading. *Address:* 5 Foulser Road, SW17.

GOULD, Patricia, CBE 1978; RRC 1972; Matron-in-Chief, Queen Alexandra's Royal Naval Nursing Service, 1976–80; *b* 27 May 1924; *d* of Arthur Wellesley Gould. *Educ:* Marist Convent, Paignton. Lewisham Gen. Hosp., SRN, 1945; Hackney Hosp., CMB Pt I, 1946; entered QARNNS, as Nursing Sister, 1948; accepted for permanent service, 1954; Matron, 1966; Principal Matron, 1970; Principal Matron Naval Hosps, 1975. QHNS 1976–80. OStJ (Comdr Sister), 1977. *Recreations:* gardening, photography. *Address:* 18 Park Road, Denmead, Portsmouth PO7 6NE. *T:* Waterlooville (0705) 255499.

GOULD, Thomas William, VC 1942; Lieutenant RNR retired; *b* 28 Dec. 1914; *s* of late Mrs C. E. Cheeseman and late Reuben Gould (killed in action, 1916); *m* 1941, Phyllis Eileen Eldridge (*d* 1985); one *s.* *Educ:* St James, Dover, Kent. Royal Navy, 1933–37; Submarines, 1937–45 (despatches); invalided Oct. 1945. Business Consultant, 1965–; company director. Pres., Internat. Submarine Assoc. of GB. *Address:* 6 Howland, Orton Goldhay, Peterborough, Cambs PE2 0QY. *T:* Peterborough (0733) 238918.

GOULDEN, (Peter) John, CMG 1989; HM Diplomatic Service; Assistant Under-Secretary of State, Foreign and Commonwealth Office, since 1988; *b* 21 Feb. 1941; *s* of George Herbert Goulden and Doris Goulden; *m* 1962, Diana Margaret Elizabeth Waite; one *s* one *d.* *Educ:* King Edward VII Sch., Sheffield; Queen's Coll., Oxford (BA 1st Cl. Hons History, 1962). FCO, 1962–: Ankara, 1963–67; Manila, 1969–70; Dublin, 1976–79; Head of Personnel Services Dept, 1980–82; Head of News Dept, FCO, 1982–84; Counsellor and Hd of Chancery, Office of the UK Permt Rep. to EEC, Brussels, 1984–87. *Recreations:* early music, bookbinding, tennis, skiing. *Address:* c/o Foreign and Commonwealth Office, King Charles Street, SW1.

GOULDING, Sir (Ernest) Irvine, Kt 1971; Judge of the High Court of Justice, Chancery Division, 1971–85; *b* 1 May 1910; *s* of late Dr Ernest Goulding; *m* 1935, Gladys (*d* 1981), *d* of late Engineer Rear-Adm. Marrack Sennett; one *s* one *d.* *Educ:* Merchant Taylors' Sch., London; St Catharine's Coll., Cambridge, Hon. Fellow, 1971–. Served as Instructor Officer, Royal Navy, 1931–36 and 1939–45. Called to Bar, Inner Temple, 1936; QC 1961; Bencher, Lincoln's Inn, 1966, Treasurer, 1983. Pres., Internat. Law Assoc., British branch, 1972–81, Hon. Pres., 1983–. President: Omar Khayyám Club, 1988–89; Selden Soc., 1988–91. *Address:* Penshurst, Wych Hill Way, Woking, Surrey GU22 0AE. *T:* Woking (0483) 761012. *Club:* Travellers'.
See also M. I. Goulding.

GOULDING, Sir Lingard; *see* Goulding, Sir W. L. W.

GOULDING, Marrack Irvine, CMG 1983; Under Secretary-General, Special Political Affairs, United Nations, New York, since 1986; *b* 2 Sept. 1936; *s* of Sir Irvine Goulding, *qv*; *m* 1961, Susan Rhoda D'Albiac, *d* of Air Marshal Sir John D'Albiac, KCVO, KBE, CB, DSO, and of Lady D'Albiac; two *s* one *d.* *Educ:* St Paul's Sch.; Magdalen Coll., Oxford (1st cl. hons. Lit. Hum. 1959). Joined HM Foreign (later Diplomatic) Service, 1959; MECAS, 1959–61; Kuwait, 1961–64; Foreign Office, 1964–68; Tripoli (Libya), 1968–70; Cairo, 1970–72; Private Sec., Minister of State for Foreign and Commonwealth Affairs, 1972–75; seconded to Cabinet Office (CPRS), 1975–77; Counsellor, Lisbon, 1977–79; Counsellor and Head of Chancery, UK Mission to UN, NY, 1979–83; Ambassador to Angola, and concurrently to São Tomé e Principe, 1983–85. *Recreations:* travel, birdwatching. *Address:* 82 Claverton Street, SW1V 3AX. *T:* 071–834 3046; 40 East 61st Street, Apt 18, New York, NY 10021, USA. *T:* (212) 935 6157. *Club:* Royal Over-Seas League.

GOULDING, Sir (William) Lingard (Walter), 4th Bt *cr* 1904; Headmaster of Headfort School, since 1977; *b* 11 July 1940; *s* of Sir (William) Basil Goulding, 3rd Bt, and of Valerie Hamilton (Senator, Seanad Éireann), *o d* of 1st Viscount Monckton of Brenchley, PC, GCVO, KCMG, MC, QC; *S* father, 1982. *Educ:* Ludgrove; Winchester College; Trinity College, Dublin (BA, HDipEd). Computer studies for Zinc Corporation and Sulphide Corporation, Conzinc Rio Tinto of Australia, 1963–66; Systems Analyst, Goulding Fertilisers Ltd, 1966–67; Manager and European Sales Officer for Rionore, modern Irish jewellery company, 1968–69; Racing Driver, formulae 5000, 3 and 2, 1967–71; Assistant Master: Brook House School, 1970–74; Headfort School (IAPS prep. school), 1974–76. *Recreations:* squash, cricket, running, bicycling, tennis, music, reading, computers. *Heir:* *b* Timothy Adam Goulding, *b* 15 May 1945. *Address:* Headfort School, Kells, Co. Meath. *T:* Navan 40065; Dargle Cottage, Enniskerry, Co. Wicklow. *T:* Dublin 862315.

GOULTY, Alan Fletcher; HM Diplomatic Service; Deputy Head of Mission, British Embassy, Cairo, since 1990; *b* 2 July 1947; *s* of Anthony Edmund Rivers Goulty and Maisie Oliphant Goulty (*née* Stein); *m* 1983, Lillian Craig Harris; one *s* by former marr. *Educ:* Bootham School, York; Corpus Christi College, Oxford (MA 1971). FCO 1968; MECAS, 1969–71; Beirut, 1971–72; Khartoum, 1972–75; FCO, 1975–77; Cabinet Office, 1977–80; Washington, 1981–85; FCO, 1985–90; Counsellor, 1987; Head of Near East and N Africa Dept, 1987–90. Grand Cordon du Wissam Alaouite (Morocco), 1987. *Recreations:* real tennis, lawn tennis, chess, bird-watching. *Address:* Foreign and Commonwealth Office, SW1A 2AH. *Club:* MCC.

GOURLAY, Gen. Sir (Basil) Ian (Spencer), KCB 1973; CVO 1990; OBE 1956 (MBE 1948); MC 1944; Vice President, United World Colleges, since 1990 (Director General, 1975–90); *b* 13 Nov. 1920; *er s* of late Brig. K. I. Gourlay, DSO, OBE, MC; *m* 1948, Natasha Zinovieff; one *s* one *d.* *Educ:* Eastbourne Coll. Commissioned, RM, 1940; HMS Formidable, 1941–44; 43 Commando, 1944–45; 45 Commando, 1946–48; Instructor, RNC Greenwich, 1948–50; Adjt RMFVR, City of London, 1950–52; Instructor, RM Officers' Sch., 1952–54; psc 1954; Bde Major, 3rd Commando Bde, 1955–57 (despatches); OC RM Officers' Trng Wing, Infantry Training Centre RM, 1957–59; 2nd in Comd, 42 Commando, 1959–61; GSO1, HQ Plymouth Gp, 1961–63; CO 42 Commando, 1963–65; Col GS, Dept of CGRM, Min. of Defence, 1965–66; Col 1965; Comdr, 3rd Commando Bde, 1966–68; Maj.-Gen. Royal Marines, Portsmouth, 1968–71; Commandant-General, Royal Marines, 1971–75; Lt-Gen., 1971; Gen., 1973. Admiral, Texas Navy. Vice Patron, RM Museum. *Recreations:* do-it-yourself, watching cricket, playing at golf. *Address:* c/o Lloyds Bank, 15 Blackheath Village, SE3. *Clubs:* Army and Navy, MCC; Royal Navy Cricket (Vice-Pres.).

GOURLAY, Gen. Sir Ian; *see* Gourlay, Gen. Sir B. I. S.

GOURLAY, Dame Janet; *see* Vaughan, Dame Janet.

GOURLAY, Sir Simon (Alexander), Kt 1989; President, National Farmers' Union, 1986–91; *b* 15 July 1934; *s* of David and Helga Gourlay; *m* 1st, 1956, Sally Garman; one *s*; 2nd, 1967, Caroline Mary Clegg; three *s.* *Educ:* Winchester; Royal Agricultural College. National Service, Commission 16th/5th Lancers, 1954–55. Farm manager, Cheshire, 1956–58; started farming on own account at Knighton, 1958; Man. Dir, Maryvale Farm Construction Ltd, 1977–85. *Recreations:* gardening, music, hill walking. *Address:* Hill House Farm, Knighton, Powys LD7 1NA. *T:* Knighton (0547) 528542. *Club:* Farmers'.

GOVAN, Sir Lawrence (Herbert), Kt 1984; Deputy Chairman, Lichfield (NZ) Ltd, since 1979; *b* 13 Oct. 1919; *s* of Herbert Cyril Charles Govan and Janet Armour Govan (*née* Edmiston); *m* 1946, Clara Hiscock; one *s* three *d.* *Educ:* Christchurch Boys' High School. Started in garment industry with Lichfield (NZ) Ltd, 1935, Managing Director, 1950, retired 1979. Pres., NZ Textile and Garment Fedn, 1961–63, Life Mem., 1979. Director: Superannuation Investments Ltd; Lichfield (NZ) Ltd. Pres., Canterbury Med. Res. Foundn. *Recreations:* golf, swimming, horticulture. *Address:* 11 Hamilton Avenue, Christchurch 4, New Zealand. *T:* 3519557. *Club:* Rotary (Christchurch) (Pres. 1963–64).

GOVETT, William John Romaine; *b* 11 Aug. 1937; *s* of John Romaine Govett and Angela Mostyn (*née* Pritchard); *m* 1st, Mary Hays (marr. diss. 1970); two *s* one *d*; 2nd, 1970, Penelope Ann Irwin; one *d*. *Educ:* Sandroyd; Gordonstoun. National Service, commnd Royal Scots Greys, 1956–58. Joined John Govett & Co. Ltd, 1961; Chm., 1974–86; Dep. Chm., 1986–90. Director: Legal & General Gp, 1972–; Govett Oriental Investment Trust, 1972–; Govett Strategic Investment Trust, 1975–; Scottish Eastern Investment Trust, 1977–; Govett Atlantic Investment Trust, 1979–; Union Jack Oil Co., 1981–; LEP Gp, 1983–; Investors in Industry, subseq. 3i, 1984–; Coal Investment Nominees NCB Pension Fund, 1985–; Ranger Oil (UK) Ltd, 1988–; Chm., Hungarian Investment Co. Ltd, 1990–. Trustee: Nat. Arts Collection Fund, 1985–; Tate Gall., 1988–. *Recreations:* modern art, fishing. *Address:* 62 Glebe Place, SW3 5JB; Fosbury Manor, Marlborough, Wiltshire SN8 3JN.

GOW, Gen. Sir (James) Michael, GCB 1983 (KCB 1979); Commandant, Royal College of Defence Studies, 1984–86; *b* 3 June 1924; *s* of late J. C. Gow and Mrs Alastair Sanderson; *m* 1946, Jane Emily Scott, *e d* of late Capt. and Hon. Mrs Mason Scott; one *s* four *d*. *Educ:* Winchester College. Enlisted Scots Guards, 1942; commnd 1943; served NW Europe, 1944–45; Malayan Emergency, 1949; Equerry to HRH the Duke of Gloucester, 1952–53; psc 1954; Bde Major 1955–57; Regimental Adjt Scots Guards, 1957–60; Instructor Army Staff Coll., 1962–64; comd 2nd Bn Scots Guards, Kenya and England, 1964–66; GSO1, HQ London District, 1966–67; comd 4th Guards Bde, 1968–69; idc 1970; BGS (Int) HQ BAOR and ACOS G2 HQ Northag, 1971–73; GOC 4th Div. BAOR, 1973–75; Dir of Army Training, 1975–78; GOC Scotland and Governor of Edinburgh Castle, 1979–80; C-in-C BAOR and Comdr, Northern Army Gp, 1980–83 (awarded die Plakette des deutschen Heeres); ADC Gen. to the Queen, 1981–84. Colonel Commandant: Intelligence Corps, 1973–86; Scottish Division, 1979–80. Brig., Queen's Body Guard for Scotland, Royal Company of Archers. UK Mem., Eurogroup US Tour, 1983. UK Kermit Roosevelt Lectr, USA, 1984. President: Royal British Legion, Scotland, 1986–; Earl Haig Fund, Scotland, 1986–; Chm., Scottish Ex-Service Charitable Orgn, 1989–. Vice-Pres., Royal Patriotic Fund Corp., 1983–88. Vice-President: Queen Victoria Sch., Dunblane, 1979–80; Royal Caledonian Schs, Bushey, 1980–. County Comr, British Scouts W Europe, 1980–83 (Silver Acorn). Freeman: City of London, 1980; State of Kansas, USA, 1984; Freeman and Liveryman, Painters' and Stainers' Co., 1980. Elder of Church of Scotland, Canongate Kirk, 1988. *Publications:* Trooping the Colour: a history of the Sovereign's birthday parade by the Household troops, 1989; Jottings in a General's Notebook, 1989; articles in mil. and hist. jls. *Recreations:* sailing, music, travel, reading. *Address:* 18 Ann Street, Edinburgh EH4 1PJ. *T:* 031–332 4752. *Clubs:* Pratt's; New (Edinburgh).

See also Lt-Col W. H. M. Ross.

GOW, Dame Jane (Elizabeth), DBE 1990; *b* 14 July 1944; *d* of Major Charles Packe (killed in action, July 1944) and Hon. Margaret Lane Fox; *m* 1966, Ian Gow, TD, MP (*d* 1990); two *s*. *Educ:* St Mary's School, Wantage. *Recreations:* music, reading, swimming, tennis. *Address:* The Dog House, Hankham, Pevensey, East Sussex BN24 5AY.

GOW, John Stobie, PhD; CChem, FRSC; FRSE 1978; Secretary-General, Royal Society of Chemistry, since 1986; *b* 12 April 1933; *s* of David Gow and Anne Scott; *m* 1955, Elizabeth Henderson; three *s*. *Educ:* Alloa Acad.; Univ. of St Andrews (BSc, PhD). Res. Chemist, ICI, Billingham, 1958; Prodn Man., Chem. Co. of Malaysia, 1966–68; ICI: Res. Man., Agric. Div., 1968–72; Gen. Man. (Catalysts), Agric. Div., 1972–74; Res. Dir, Organics, 1974–79; Dep. Chm., Organics, 1979–84; Man. Dir, Speciality Chemicals, 1984–86. Assessor, SERC, 1988–. FRSA 1980. *Publications:* papers and patents in Fertilizer Technology and Biotechnology. *Recreations:* choral music, Rugby. *Address:* 19 Longcroft Avenue, Harpenden, Herts AL5 2RD. *T:* Harpenden (05827) 764889.

GOW, Sir Leonard Maxwell H.; *see* Harper Gow.

GOW, Gen. Sir Michael; *see* Gow, Gen. Sir J. M.

GOW, Neil, QC (Scot.) 1970; Sheriff of South Strathclyde, at Ayr, since 1976; *b* 24 April 1932; *s* of Donald Gow, oil merchant, Glasgow; *m* 1959, Joanna, *d* of Comdr S. D. Sutherland, Edinburgh; one *s*. *Educ:* Merchiston Castle Sch., Edinburgh; Glasgow and Edinburgh Univs. MA, LLB. Formerly Captain, Intelligence Corps (BAOR). Carnegie Scholar in History of Scots Law, 1956. Advocate, 1957–76. Standing Counsel to Min. of Social Security (Scot.), 1964–70. Contested (C): Kirkcaldy Burghs, Gen. Elections of 1964 and 1966; Edinburgh East, 1970; Mem. Regional Council, Scottish Conservative Assoc. An Hon. Sheriff of Lanarkshire, 1971. Pres., Auchinleck Boswell Soc. FSA (Scot.). *Publications:* A History of Scottish Statutes, 1959; Jt Editor, An Outline of Estate Duty in Scotland, 1970; A History of Belmont House School, 1979; numerous articles and broadcasts on legal topics and Scottish affairs. *Recreations:* golf, books, antiquities. *Address:* Old Auchenfail Hall, by Mauchline, Ayrshire. *T:* Mauchline (0290) 50822. *Clubs:* Western (Glasgow); Prestwick Golf.

GOW, Dame Wendy; *see* Hiller, Dame Wendy.

GOW, Very Rev. William Connell; Dean of Moray, Ross and Caithness, 1960–77, retired; Canon of St Andrew's Cathedral, Inverness, 1953–77, Hon. Canon, since 1977; Rector of St James', Dingwall, 1940–77; *b* 6 Jan. 1909; *s* of Alexander Gow, Errol, Perthshire; *m* 1938, Edith Mary, *d* of John William Jarvis, Scarborough; two *s*. *Educ:* Edinburgh Theological Coll.; Durham Univ. (LTh). Deacon, 1936; Priest, 1937; Curate St Mary Magdalene's, Dundee, 1936–39. Awarded Frihetsmedalje (by King Haakon), Norway, 1947. *Recreations:* fishing, bridge. *Address:* 14 Mackenzie Place, Maryburgh, Ross-shire IV7 8DY. *T:* Dingwall (0349) 61832.

GOWANS, Sir Gregory; *see* Gowans, Sir U. G.

GOWANS, Sir James (Learmonth), Kt 1982; CBE 1971; FRCP 1975; FRS 1963; Director-General, Human Frontier Science Programme, Strasbourg, since 1989; Secretary, Medical Research Council, 1977–87; *b* 7 May 1924; *s* of John Gowans and Selma Josefina Ljung; *m* 1956, Moyra Leatham; one *s* two *d*. *Educ:* Trinity Sch., Croydon; King's Coll. Hosp. Med. Sch. (MB BS (Hons) 1947; Fellow, 1979); Lincoln Coll., Oxford (BA (1st cl. Hons Physiology) 1948; MA; DPhil 1953; Hon. Fellow, 1984). MRC Exchange Scholar, Pasteur Institute, Paris, 1952–53; Research Fellow, Exeter Coll., Oxford, 1955–60 (Hon. Fellow, 1983–); Fellow, St Catherine's Coll., Oxford, 1961–87 (Hon. Fellow, 1987); Henry Dale Res. Prof. of Royal Society, 1962–77; Hon. Dir, MRC Cellular Immunology Unit, 1963–77; Dir, 1980–86, Sen. Sci. Advr, 1988–, Celltech Ltd. Consultant. WHO Global Prog. on AIDS, 1987–88. Member: MRC, 1965–69; Adv. Bd for Res. Councils, 1977–87. Royal Society: Mem. Council and a Vice-Pres., 1973–75; Assessor to MRC, 1973–75. Mem. Council, St Christopher's Hospice, 1987–. Vis. Prof., NY Univ. Sch. of Med., 1967; Lectures: Harvey, NY, 1968; Dunham, Harvard, 1971; Bayne-Jones, Johns Hopkins, 1973; Harveian Orator, RCP, 1987. Foreign Associate, Nat. Acad. of Scis, USA, 1985. Hon. Member: Amer. Assoc. of Immunologists; Amer. Soc. of Anatomists. Hon. ScD Yale, 1966; Hon. DSc: Chicago, 1971; Birmingham, 1978; Rochester, 1987; Hon. MD Edinburgh, 1979; Hon. DM Southampton, 1987; Hon. LLD Glasgow, 1988. Gairdner Foundn Award, 1968; Paul Ehrlich Award, 1974; Royal Medal, Royal Society, 1976; Feldberg Foundn Award, 1979; Wolf Prize in Medicine, 1980; Medawar Prize, 1990. *Publications:* articles in scientific journals. *Address:* 75 Cumnor Hill, Oxford OX2 9HX. *T:* Oxford (0865) 862304.

GOWANS, James Palmer, JP; DL; Member, Dundee City Council; Lord Provost of Dundee and Lord-Lieutenant of the City of Dundee, 1980–84; *b* 15 Sept. 1930; *s* of Charles Gowans and Sarah Gowans (*née* Palmer); *m* 1950, Davina Barnett; one *s* four *d* (and one *s* decd). *Educ:* Rockwell Secondary School, Dundee. Joined National Cash Register Co., Dundee, 1956; now employed testing electronic modules. Elected to Dundee DC, May 1974. JP 1977; DL Dundee 1984. *Recreations:* golf, motoring. *Address:* 41 Dalmahoy Drive, Dundee DD2 3UT. *T:* Dundee (0382) 84918.

GOWANS, Hon. Sir (Urban) Gregory, Kt 1974; Judge of Supreme Court of Victoria, Australia, 1961–76; *b* 9 Sept. 1904; *s* of late James and Hannah Theresa Gowans; *m* 1937, Mona Ann Freeman; one *s* four *d*. *Educ:* Christian Brothers Coll., Kalgoorlie, WA; Univs of Western Australia and Melbourne. BA (WA) 1924; LLB (Melb.) 1926. Admitted Victorian Bar, 1928; QC 1949; Mem., Overseas Telecommunications Commn (Aust.), 1947–61; Lectr in Industrial Law, Melb. Univ., 1948–56. Constituted Bd of Inquiry into Housing Commn Land Deals, 1977–78. *Publication:* The Victorian Bar: professional conduct practice and etiquette, 1979. *Club:* Melbourne (Melbourne).

GOWAR, Prof. Norman William; Principal, Royal Holloway and Bedford New College, University of London, since 1990; *b* 7 Dec. 1940; *s* of Harold James and Constance Dawson-Gowar; *m* 1st, 1963, Diane May Parker (marr. diss.); one *s* one *d*; 2nd, 1981, Prof. Judith Margaret Greene, *d* of Lord Gordon-Walker, PC, CH. *Educ:* Sir George Monoux Grammar Sch.; City Univ. (BSc, MPhil). FIMA. English Electric Co., 1963; Lectr in Maths, City Univ., 1963; Open University: Lectr and Sen. Lectr, 1969; Prof. of Mathematics, 1983; Dir, Centre for Maths Educn, 1984; Pro-Vice Chancellor, 1977–81; Dep. Vice-Chancellor, 1984; Dir, Open Coll. Vis. Fellow, Keble Coll., Oxford, 1972. Dir, Surrey TEC. Member: Council, CNAA; Council, NCET (Chm., Trng Cttee). Chm. and Dir, Open Univ. Educational Enterprises Ltd. Mem., Educn Cttee, London Math. Soc. FRSA. *Publications:* Mathematics for Technology: a new approach, 1968; Basic Mathematical Structures, vol. 1, 1973, vol. 2, 1974; Fourier Series, 1974; Invitation to Mathematics, 1980; articles and TV series. *Address:* Royal Holloway and Bedford New College, University of London, Egham Hill, Egham, Surrey TW20 0EX.

GOWDA, Prof. Deve Javare, (De-Ja-Gou); Vice-Chancellor, University of Mysore, 1969–76; Senior Fellow, International School of Dravidian Linguistics, Trivandrum, Kerala; *b* Chakkare, Bangalore, 6 July 1918; *s* of Deve Gowda; *m* 1943, Savithramma Javare Gowda; one *s* one *d*. *Educ:* Univ. of Mysore. MA Kannada, 1943. Mysore University: Lectr in Kannada, 1946; Asst Prof. of Kannada and Sec., Univ. Publications, 1955; Controller of Examinations, 1957; Principal, Sahyadri Coll., Shimoga, Mysore Univ., 1960; Prof. of Kannada Studies, 1966. Hon. Dir of Researches, Kuvempu Vidyavardhaka Trust, Mysore. DLit Karnataka, 1975. Soviet Land Award, 1967. *Publications:* (as De-Ja-Gou) numerous books in Kannada; has also edited many works. *Recreations:* writing, gardening. *Address:* Kalanilaya, J. L. Puram, Mysore-12, India. *T:* 21920.

GOWDY, David Clive; Under Secretary, Department of Health and Social Services, Northern Ireland, since 1990; *b* 27 Nov. 1946; *s* of Samuel David Gowdy and Eileen Gowdy (*née* Porter); *m* 1973, Linda Doreen Traub; two *d*. *Educ:* Royal Belfast Academical Instn; Queen's Univ. Belfast (BA, MSc). Min. of Finance, NI, 1970; N Ireland Office, 1976; Exec. Dir, Industrial Develt Bd for NI 1985; Under Sec., Dept of Econ. Develt, NI, 1987. *Recreations:* music, reading, theatre, sport. *Address:* Department of Health and Social Services, Castle Buildings, Stormont, Belfast BT4 3SN.

GOWENLOCK, Prof. Brian Glover, CBE 1986; PhD, DSc; FRSE; FRSC; Professor of Chemistry, 1966–90, Leverhulme Emeritus Fellow, 1990–Sept. 1992, Heriot-Watt University; *b* 9 Feb. 1926; *s* of Harry Hadfield Gowenlock and Hilda (*née* Glover); *m* 1953, Margaret L. Davies; one *s* two *d*. *Educ:* Hulme Grammar Sch., Oldham; Univ. of Manchester (BSc, MSc, PhD). DSc Birmingham. FRIC 1966; FRSE 1969. Asst Lectr in Chemistry 1948, Lectr 1951, University Coll. of Swansea; Lectr 1955, Sen. Lectr 1964, Univ. of Birmingham; Dean, Faculty of Science, Heriot-Watt Univ., 1969–72, 1987–90. Vis. Scientist, National Res. Council, Ottawa, 1963; Erskine Vis. Fellow, Univ. of Canterbury, NZ, 1976. Mem., UGC, 1976–85, Vice-Chm., 1983–85. *Publications:* Experimental Methods in Gas Reactions (with Sir Harry Melville), 1964; First Year at the University (with James C. Blackie), 1964; contribs to scientific jls. *Recreations:* genealogy, foreign travel. *Address:* 49 Lygon Road, Edinburgh EH16 5QA. *T:* 031–667 8506.

GOWER; *see* Leveson Gower.

GOWER, Most Rev. Godfrey Philip, DD; *b* 5 Dec. 1899; *s* of William and Sarah Ann Gower; *m* 1932, Margaret Ethel Tanton; two *s* one *d*. *Educ:* Imperial College, University of London; St John's College, Winnipeg, University of Manitoba. Served RAF, 1918–19. Deacon 1930; Priest 1931; Rector and Rural Dean of Camrose, Alta, 1932–35; Rector of Christ Church, Edmonton, Alta, 1935–41; Exam. Chaplain to Bishop of Edmonton, 1938–41; Canon of All Saints' Cathedral, 1940–44. Chaplain, RCAF, 1941–44. Rector of St Paul's, Vancouver, 1944–51; Bishop of New Westminster, 1951–71; Archbishop of New Westminster, and Metropolitan of British Columbia, 1968–71. Holds Hon. doctorates in Divinity. *Address:* 305–1520 Vidal Street, White Rock, BC V4B 3T7, Canada. *T:* 604–531–7254.

GOWER, Jim; *see* Gower, L. C. B.

GOWER, John Hugh, QC 1967; **His Honour Judge Gower;** a Circuit Judge, since 1972; *b* 6 Nov. 1925; *s* of Henry John Gower, JP and Edith (*née* Brooks); *m* 1960, Shirley Mameena Darbourne; one *s* one *d*. *Educ:* Skinners' Sch., Tunbridge Wells. RASC, 1945–48 (Staff Sgt). Called to Bar, Inner Temple, 1948. Dep. Chm., Kent QS, 1968–71; Resident and Liaison Judge of Crown Courts in E Sussex, 1986–. Mem., Lord Chancellor's Adv. Cttee on Legal Educn and Conduct, 1991–. Pres., Tunbridge Wells Council of Voluntary Service, 1974–88. Hon. Vice-Pres., Kent Council of Voluntary Service, 1971–86. Freeman, City of London (by purchase), 1960. *Recreations:* fishing, foxhunting, gardening. *Address:* The Crown Court, High Street, Lewes, E Sussex.

GOWER, Laurence Cecil Bartlett, (Jim), FBA 1965; Solicitor; Professor Emeritus, Southampton University; *b* 29 Dec. 1913; *s* of Henry Lawrence Gower; *m* 1939, Helen Margaret Shepperson, *d* of George Francis Birch; two *s* one *d*. *Educ:* Lindisfarne Coll.; University Coll., London. LLB 1933; LLM 1934. Admitted Solicitor, 1937. Served War of 1939–45, with RA and RAOC. Sir Ernest Cassel Prof. of Commercial Law in University of London, 1948–62, Visiting Prof., Law Sch. of Harvard Univ., 1954–55; Adviser on Legal Educn in Africa to Brit. Inst. of Internat. and Comparative Law and Adviser to Nigerian Council of Legal Educn, 1962–65; Prof. and Dean of Faculty of Law of Univ. of Lagos, 1962–65; Law Comr, 1965–71; Vice-Chancellor, Univ. of Southampton, 1971–79. Holmes Lectr, Harvard Univ., 1966. Fellow of University Coll.,

London; Comr on Company Law Amendment in Ghana, 1958; Member: Jenkins Cttee on Company Law Amendment, 1959–62; Denning Cttee on Legal Education for Students from Africa, 1960; Ormrod Cttee on Legal Education, 1967–71; Royal Commn on the Press, 1975–77. Trustee, British Museum, 1968–83. For. Hon. Mem., Amer. Acad. of Arts and Scis, 1986; Lee Kuan Yew Distinguished Visitor, Nat. Univ. of Singapore, 1987. Hon. Fellow: LSE, 1970; Portsmouth Polytech., 1981; Hon. LLD: York Univ., Ont; Edinburgh Univ.; Dalhousie Univ.; Warwick Univ.; QUB; Southampton Univ.; Bristol Univ.; London Univ.; Hon. DLitt Hong Kong. Hon. QC 1991. *Publications:* Principles of Modern Company Law, 1954, 4th edn 1979; Independent Africa: The Challenge to the Legal Profession, 1967; Review of Investor Protection, Part 1, 1984, Part 2, 1985; numerous articles in legal periodicals. *Recreation:* travel. *Address:* 26 Willow Road, Hampstead, NW3 1TL. *T:* 071–435 2507. *Club:* Athenæum.

GOWER ISAAC, Anthony John; *see* Isaac.

GOWING, Prof. Margaret Mary, CBE 1981; FRS 1988; FBA 1975; FRHistS; Professor of the History of Science, University of Oxford, and Fellow of Linacre College, 1973–86; *b* 26 April 1921; *d* of Ronald and Mabel Elliott; *m* 1944, Donald J. G. Gowing (*d* 1969); two *s*. *Educ:* Christ's Hospital; London Sch. of Economics (BSc(Econ); Hon. Fellow, 1988). Bd of Trade, 1941–45; Historical Section, Cabinet Office, 1945–59; Historian and Archivist, UK Atomic Energy Authority, 1959–66; Reader in Contemporary History, Univ. of Kent, 1966–72. Member: Cttee on Deptl Records (Grigg Cttee), 1952–54; Adv. Council on Public Records, 1974–82; BBC Archives Adv. Cttee, 1976–79; Public Records Inquiry (Wilson Cttee), 1978–80; Trustee: Nat. Portrait Gall., 1978–; Imperial War Mus., 1986–87. Hon. Dir, Contemporary Scientific Archives Centre, 1973–86. Foundation Mem., Academia Europaea, 1988. Royal Society Wilkins Lectr, 1976; Enid Muir Lectr, Newcastle, 1976; Bernal Lectr, Birkbeck, 1977; Rede Lectr, Cambridge, 1978; Herbert Spencer Lectr, Oxford, 1982; CEGB Lectr, Southampton, 1987. Hon. DLitt: Leeds, 1976; Leicester, 1982; Hon. DSc: Manchester, 1985; Bath, 1987. *Publications:* (with Sir K. Hancock) British War Economy, 1949; (with E. L. Hargreaves) Civil Industry and Trade, 1952; Britain and Atomic Energy, 1964; Dossier Secret des Relations Atomiques, 1965; Independence and Deterrence: vol. I, Policy Making, vol. II, Policy Execution, 1974; Reflections on Atomic Energy History, 1978; (with Lorna Arnold) The Atomic Bomb, 1979; various articles and reviews. *Address:* Linacre College, Oxford.

GOWING, Prof. Noel Frank Collett; Emeritus Professor of Pathology, University of London; Consultant Pathologist and Director of the Department of Histopathology, The Royal Marsden Hospital, SW3, 1957–82; Professor of Tumour Pathology (formerly Senior Lecturer), Institute of Cancer Research: The Royal Cancer Hospital, 1971–82; *b* 3 Jan. 1917; *s* of Edward Charles Gowing and Annie Elizabeth Gowing; *m* 1942, Rela Griffel; one *d*. *Educ:* Ardingly Coll., Sussex; London Univ. MRCS, LRCP 1941; MB, BS, London, 1947; MD London, 1948. Served RAMC (Capt.), 1942–46, 52nd (Lowland) Div. Lectr in Pathology, St George's Hosp. Med. Sch., 1947–52; Sen. Lectr in Pathology and Hon. Cons. Pathologist, St George's Hosp., 1952–57. Vis. Pathologist, St Vincent's Hosp., Worcester, Mass and Vis. Prof. of Pathology, Univ. of Mass, 1979. Sometime Examiner in Pathology to: Univ. of London; RCPath; Univ. of Newcastle-upon-Tyne; Univ. of Malta; Nat. Univ. of Malaysia. Lectures: Kettle Meml, RCPath, 1968; Whittick Meml, Saskatchewan Cancer Soc., 1974; Symeonidis Meml, Thessaloniki Cancer Inst., Greece, 1977. Pres., Assoc. of Clinical Pathologists, 1982–83. FRCPath (Founder Fellow, Coll. of Pathologists, 1964). *Publications:* A Colour Atlas of Tumour Histopathology, 1980; articles on pathology in medical journals. *Recreations:* gardening, astronomy.

GOWLLAND, (George) Mark, LVO 1979; HM Diplomatic Service; Head of Chancery, Rome, since 1990; *b* 24 Feb. 1943; *s* of late Mr G. P. Gowlland and Mrs A. M. Gowlland; *m* 1967, Eleanor Julia Le Mesurier; two *s* one *d*. *Educ:* Tonbridge Sch.; Balliol Coll., Oxford. Entered Foreign Service, 1964; served Warsaw, Accra, Lomé, Kuala Lumpur, Dubai, Algiers; Overseas Inspectorate, FCO, 1986–90. *Address:* c/o Foreign and Commonwealth Office, SW1A 2AH.

GOWON, Gen. Dr Yakubu, PhD; jssc, psc; Head of the Federal Military Government and C-in-C of Armed Forces of the Federal Republic of Nigeria 1966–75; Visiting Professor in Politics and International Relations, University of Jos, Nigeria; *b* Pankshin Div., Plateau State, Nigeria, 19 Oct. 1934; *s* of Yohanna Gowon (an Angas, a Christian evangelist of CMS) and Saraya Gowon; *m* 1969, Victoria Hansatu Zakari; one *s* two *d*. *Educ:* St Bartholomew's Schs (CMS), Wusasa, and Govt Coll., Zaria, Nigeria; Warwick Univ. (BA Hons 1978; PhD). Regular Officer's Special Trng Sch., Teshie, Ghana; Eaton Hall Officer Cadet Sch., Chester, RMA, Sandhurst, Staff Coll., Camberley and Joint Services Staff Coll., Latimer (all in England). Enlisted, 1954; commissioned, 1956; served in Cameroon, 1960; Adjt, 4th Bn Nigerian Army, 1960 (Independence Oct. 1960); UN Peace-Keeping Forces, Congo, Nov. 1960–June 1961 and Jan.-June 1963 (Bde Major). Lt-Col and Adjt-Gen., Nigerian Army, 1963; Comd, 2nd Bn, Nigerian Army, Ikeja, 1966; Chief of Staff, 1966; Head of State and C-in-C after July 1966 coup; Maj.-Gen. 1967. Maintained territorial integrity of his country by fighting, 1967–70, to preserve unity of Nigeria (after failure of peaceful measures) following on Ojukwu rebellion, and declared secession of the Eastern region of Nigeria, July 1967; created 12 equal and autonomous states in Nigeria, 1967; Biafran surrender, 1970. Promoted Gen., 1971. Chm., Base Development (Nigeria) Ltd (formerly Kanawa Industries (Nigeria) Ltd), Kano, Nigeria, 1987–. Chm. Trustees, Commonwealth Human Ecology Foundn, 1986–. Is a Christian; works for internat. peace and security within the framework of OAU and UNO. Hon. LLD Cambridge, 1975; also hon. doctorates from Univs of Ibadan, Lagos, Abu-Zaria, Nigeria at Nsuka, Benin, Ife, and Shaw Univ., USA, 1973. Holds Grand Cross, etc, of several foreign orders. *Publication:* Faith in Unity, 1970. *Recreations:* squash, lawn tennis, pen-drawing, photography, cinephotography. *Address:* c/o Department of Politics, Warwick University, Coventry CV4 7AL; c/o Department of Developmental Studies, University of Jos, Plateau State, Nigeria. *Clubs:* Army and Navy, Les Ambassadeurs.

GOWRIE, 2nd Earl of, *cr* 1945; **Alexander Patrick Greysteil Hore-Ruthven;** PC 1984; Baron Ruthven of Gowrie, 1919; Baron Gowrie, 1935; Viscount Ruthven of Canberra, 1945; Chairman, Sotheby's, since 1987 (Chairman, Sotheby's International, 1985–86); Provost, Royal College of Art, since 1986; *b* 26 Nov. 1939; *er s* of late Capt. Hon. Alexander Hardinge Patrick Hore-Ruthven, Rifle Bde, and Pamela Margaret (as Viscountess Ruthven of Canberra, she *m* 1952, Major Derek Cooper, MC, The Life Guards), 2nd *d* of late Rev. A. H. Fletcher; *S* grandfather, 1955; *m* 1st, 1962, Xandra (marr. diss. 1973), *yr d* of Col R. A. G. Bingley, CVO, DSO, OBE; one *s*; 2nd, 1974, Adelheid Gräfin von der Schulenburg, *y d* of late Fritz-Dietlof, Graf von der Schulenburg. *Educ:* Eton; Balliol Coll., Oxford. Visiting Lectr, State Univ. of New York at Buffalo, 1963–64; Tutor, Harvard Univ., 1965–68; Lectr in English and American Literature, UCL, 1969–72. Fine Art consultant, 1974–79. Chm., The Really Useful Gp, 1985–90. A Conservative Whip, 1971–72; Parly Rep. to UN, 1971; a Lord in Waiting (Govt Whip), 1972–74; Opposition Spokesman on Economic Affairs, 1974–79; Minister of State: Dept of Employment, 1979–81; NI Office, 1981–83 (Dep. to Sec. of State); Privy Council Office (Management and Personnel), 1983–84; Minister for the Arts, 1983–85; Chancellor, Duchy of Lancaster, 1984–85. *Publications:* A Postcard from Don Giovanni, 1972; (jt) The Genius of British Painting, 1975; (jt) The Conservative Opportunity, 1976; Derek Hill: an appreciation, 1987. *Recreation:* book reviewing. *Heir:* *s* Viscount Ruthven of Canberra, *qv*. *Address:* Sotheby's, 35 New Bond Street, W1.

GOY, David John Lister; QC 1991; *b* 11 May 1949; *s* of Rev. Leslie Goy and Joan Goy; *m* 1970, Jennifer Anne Symington; three *s*. *Educ:* Haberdashers' Aske's School, Elstree; King's College London. Called to the Bar, Middle Temple, 1973. *Publication:* VAT on Property, 1989. *Recreations:* marathon running and other sports. *Address:* Gray's Inn Chambers, Gray's Inn, WC1R 5JA. *T:* 071–242 2642.

GOYDER, Daniel George; solicitor; Consultant to Birkett Westhorp Long (formerly Birketts), Ipswich, since 1983 (Partner, 1968–83); *b* 26 Aug. 1938; *s* of George Armin Goyder, *qv*; *m* 1962, Jean Mary Dohoo; two *s* two *d*. *Educ:* Rugby Sch.; Trinity Coll., Cambridge (MA, LLB); Harvard Law Sch. (Harkness Commonwealth Fund Fellow, LLM). Admitted Solicitor, 1962; Asst Solicitor, Messrs Allen & Overy, 1964–67. Pt-time Lectr in Law, Univ. of Essex, 1981–91. Chm., St Edmundsbury and Ipswich Diocesan Bd of Finance, 1977–85; Hon. Lay Canon, St Edmundsbury Cathedral, 1987–. Dep. Chm., Monopolies and Mergers Commn, 1991– (Mem., 1980–). Leverhulme Trust Res. Grant, for research into EEC competition law, 1986. *Publications:* The Antitrust Laws of the USA (with Sir Alan Neale), 3rd edn 1981; EEC Competition Law, 1988. *Recreations:* choral singing, table tennis, sport. *Address:* Manor House, Old London Road, Capel St Mary, Ipswich, Suffolk IP9 2JU. *T:* Ipswich (0473) 310583. *Clubs:* Law Society; Ipswich and Suffolk (Ipswich).

GOYDER, George Armin, CBE 1976; Managing Director, British International Paper Ltd, 1935–71; *b* 22 June 1908; *s* of late William Goyder and Lili Julia Kellersberger, Baden, Switzerland; *m* 1937, Rosemary, 4th *d* of Prof. R. C. Bosanquet, Rock, Northumberland; five *s* three *d*. *Educ:* Mill Hill Sch.; London Sch. of Economics; abroad. Gen. Man., Newsprint Supply Co., 1940–47 (responsible for procurement supply and rationing of newsprint to British Press); The Geographical Magazine, 1935–58. Mem., Gen. Synod of C of E (formerly Church Assembly), 1948–75; Chm., Liberal Party Standing Cttee on Industrial Partnership, 1966. Vice-Pres., Centre for Internat. Briefing, Farnham Castle. Founder Trustee, William Blake Trust; Governor: Mill Hill Sch., 1943–69; Monkton Combe Sch.; Trustee and Hon. Fellow, St Peter's Coll., Oxford; Mem. Council, Wycliffe Hall; Founder Mem. and Sec., British-North American Cttee, 1969. Chm., Suffolk Preservation Soc., 1983–85. *Publications:* The Future of Private Enterprise, 1951, 1954; The Responsible Company, 1961; The People's Church, 1966; The Responsible Worker, 1975; The Just Enterprise, 1987. *Recreations:* music, old books, theology. *Address:* Mansel Hall, Long Melford, Sudbury, Suffolk CO10 9JB. *Club:* Reform.

See also D. G. Goyder.

GRAAFF, Sir de Villiers, 2nd Bt *cr* 1911; MBE 1946; BA Cape, MA, BCL Oxon; Barrister-at-Law, Inner Temple; Advocate of the Supreme Court of S Africa; MP for Hottentots Holland in Union Parliament 1948–58, for Rondebosch, Cape Town, 1958–77; *b* 8 Dec. 1913; *s* of 1st Bt and Eileen (*d* 1950), *d* of Rev. Dr J. P. Van Heerden, Cape Town; *S* father, 1931; *m* 1939, Helena Le Roux, *d* of F. C. M. Voigt, Provincial Sec. of Cape Province; two *s* one *d*. Served War of 1939–45 (prisoner, MBE). Leader, United Party, S Africa, 1956–77; formerly Leader of Official Opposition. Hon. Col, Cape Garrison Artillery, 1980. Hon. LLD Rhodes, 1969; Hon. DLit South Africa, 1989. Decoration for Meritorious Service (RSA), 1979. *Heir:* *s* David de Villiers Graaff [*b* 3 May 1940; *m* Sally Williams; three *s* one *d*]. *Address:* De Grendel, Private Bag, GPO, Capetown, South Africa. *Club:* Civil Service (Cape Town).

GRABHAM, Sir Anthony (Herbert), Kt 1988; FRCS; Chairman, BMA Service; Director, Private Patients Plan, since 1984; *b* 19 July 1930; *s* of John and Lily Grabham; *m* 1960, Eileen Pamela Rudd; two *s* two *d*. *Educ:* St Cuthbert's Grammar School, Newcastle upon Tyne. MB, BS Durham. RSO, Royal Victoria Infirmary, Newcastle upon Tyne; Consultant Surgeon, Kettering and District Gen. Hosp., 1965–. Chairman: Jt Consultants Cttee, 1984–90; Central Cttee for Hosp. Med. Services, BMA, 1975–79; Council, BMA, 1979–84; Member: GMC, 1979–; Council, World Med. Assoc., 1979–84; Hon. Sec. and Treasurer, Commonwealth Med. Assoc., 1982–86 (Vice-Pres., 1980–84). *Recreations:* dropping committees, working parties and porcelain. *Address:* (home) Rothesay House, 56 Headlands, Kettering, Northants. *T:* Kettering (0536) 513299; (business) British Medical Association, Tavistock Square, WC1H 9JP. *T:* 071–387 4499. *Club:* Army and Navy.

GRABINER, Anthony Stephen, QC 1981; a Recorder, since 1990; *b* 21 March 1945; *e s* of late Ralph Grabiner and of Freda Grabiner (*née* Cohen); *m* 1983, Jane, *er d* of Dr Benjamin Portnoy, TD, JP, MD, PhD, FRCP, Hale, Cheshire; two *s*. *Educ:* Central Foundn Boys' Grammar Sch., London, EC2; LSE, Univ. of London (LLB 1st Cl. Hons 1966, LLM with Distinction 1967). Lincoln's Inn: Hardwicke Scholar, 1966; called to the Bar, 1968; Droop Scholar, 1968; Bencher, 1989. Standing Jun. Counsel to Dept of Trade, Export Credits Guarantee Dept, 1976–81; Jun. Counsel to the Crown, 1978–81. Mem., Ct of Govs, LSE, 1990–. *Publications:* (ed jtly) Sutton and Shannon on Contracts, 7th edn 1970; contrib. Banking Documents, to Encyclopedia of Forms and Precedents, 5th edn, 1986. *Recreations:* theatre, swimming, tennis. *Address:* 1 Essex Court, Temple, EC4Y 9AR. *T:* 071–583 2000. *Clubs:* Garrick, Royal Automobile, MCC.

GRACEY, Howard, FIA, FIAA, FPMI; consulting actuary; Partner, R. Watson and Sons, since 1970; *b* 21 Feb. 1935; *s* of late Charles Douglas Gracey and of Margaret Gertrude (*née* Heggie); *m* 1960, Pamela Jean Bradshaw; one *s* two *d*. *Educ:* Birkenhead Sch. FIA 1959; FIAA 1982; FPMI 1977; ASA 1978. National Service, 1960–61 (2nd Lieut). Royal Insurance Co., 1953–69. Church Comr, 1978–; Member: Gen. Synod of CofE, 1970–; CofE Pensions Bd, 1970– (Chm., 1980–); Treasurer, S Amer. Missionary Soc., 1975–; Pres., Pensions Management Inst., 1983–85. *Recreations:* fell-walking, tennis, photography. *Address:* Timbers, 18 Broadwater Rise, Guildford, Surrey GU1 2LA. *Club:* Army and Navy.

GRACEY, John Halliday, CB 1984; Director General (Deputy Secretary), Board of Inland Revenue, 1981–85; Commissioner of Inland Revenue 1973–85; *b* 20 May 1925; *s* of Halliday Gracey and Florence Jane (*née* Cudlipp); *m* 1950, Margaret Procter; three *s*. *Educ:* City of London Sch.; Brasenose Coll., Oxford (MA). Army, 1943–47. Entered Inland Revenue, 1950; HM Treasury, 1970–73. Hon. Treas., NACRO, 1987–. *Recreations:* walking, bee-keeping. *Address:* 3 Woodberry Down, Epping, Essex CM16 6RJ. *T:* Epping (0378) 72167. *Club:* Reform.

See also T. A. Lloyd Davies.

GRADE, family name of **Baron Grade.**

GRADE, Baron *cr* 1976 (Life Peer), of Elstree, Herts; **Lew Grade,** Kt 1969; Chairman, The Grade Co., since 1985; *b* 25 Dec. 1906; *s* of late Isaac Winogradsky and Olga Winogradsky; *m* 1942, Kathleen Sheila Moody; one *s*. *Educ:* Rochelle Street Sch. Joint Managing Dir of Lew and Leslie Grade Ltd, until Sept. 1955; Chm. and Man. Dir, ITC Entertainment Ltd, 1958–82; Chm. and Chief Exec., Associated Communications Corp.

Ltd, 1973–82; Pres., ATV Network Ltd, 1977–82; Chairman: Bentray Investments Ltd, 1979–82; ACC Enterprises Inc., 1973–82; Stoll Moss Theatres Ltd, 1969–82; Chm. and Chief Exec., Embassy Communications Internat. Ltd, 1982–85. Governor, Royal Shakespeare Theatre. Fellow, BAFTA, 1979. KCSS 1979. *Publication:* (autobiog.) Still Dancing, 1987. *Address:* 8 Queen Street Mayfair, W1X 7PH.

See also Baron Delfont.

GRADE, Michael Ian; Chief Executive of Channel Four, since 1988; *b* 8 March 1943; *s* of Leslie Grade and *g s* of Olga Winogradski; *m* 1967, Penelope Jane (*née* Levinson) (marr. diss. 1981); one *s* one *d*; 2nd, 1982, Hon. Sarah Lawson (marr. diss. 1991), *y d* of Baron Burnham, *qv. Educ:* St Dunstan's Coll., London. Daily Mirror: Trainee Journalist, 1960; Sports Columnist, 1964–66; Theatrical Agent, Grade Organisation, 1966; joined London Management and Representation, 1969, Jt Man. Dir until 1973; London Weekend Television: Dep. Controller of Programmes (Entertainment), 1973; Dir of Programmes and Mem. Bd, 1977–81; Pres., Embassy Television, 1981–84; Controller, BBC1, 1984–86; Dir of Programmes, BBC TV, 1986–87. Dir, First Leisure, 1991–. Member: Council, LAMDA, 1981–; Council BAFTA, 1981–82, 1986–88; 300 Group; Milton Cttee; Bd, Open Coll., 1989–; ITN News, 1989–; British Screen Adv. Council; Chm., Wkg Gp, Fear of Crime, 1989; President: TV and Radio Industries Club, 1987–88; Newspaper Press Fund, 1988–89; Director: Cities in Schools, 1991–; Gate Theatre, Dublin, 1990–. Trustee, Healthcare Foundn. Hon. Treas., Stars Organisation for Spastics, 1986–. FRTS 1991. *Recreation:* entertainment. *Address:* Channel Four Television, 60 Charlotte Street, W1P 2AX. *T:* 071–631 4444. *Club:* Royal Thames Yacht.

GRADY, Terence, MBE 1967; HM Diplomatic Service, retired; Ambassador at Libreville, 1980–82; *b* 23 March 1924; *s* of Patrick Grady and Catherine (*née* Fowles); *m* 1960, Jean Fischer; one *s* four *d. Educ:* St Michael's Coll., Leeds. HM Forces, 1942–47; Foreign Office, 1949; HM Embassy: Baghdad, 1950; Paris, 1951; Asst Private Secretary to Secretary of State for Foreign Affairs, 1952–55; HM Legation, Budapest, 1955–58; HM Embassy, Kabul, 1958–60; FO, 1960–63; Vice Consul, Elisabethville, 1963; Consul, Philadelphia, 1964–69; UK High Commission, Sydney, 1969–72; FCO, 1972–75; Head of Chancery, Dakar, 1975–77; Consul, Istanbul, 1977–80. *Recreations:* tennis, walking. *Address:* 2 Camberley Road, Norwich NR4 6SJ. *Club:* Commonwealth Trust.

GRAEF, Roger Arthur; writer, director and producer of films; *b* NYC, 18 April 1936; *m* 1st, 1971, Karen Bergemann (marr. diss. 1983); one *s* one *d*; 2nd, 1986, Susan Mary Richards. *Educ:* Horace Mann Sch., NYC; Putney Sch., Vermont; Harvard Univ. (BA Hons). Directed, USA, 26 plays and operas; also directed CBS drama; Observer/Dir, Actors Studio, NYC, 1958–62; resident in England, 1962–; Director, London: Period of Adjustment (Royal Court); Afternoon Men; has written, produced and directed more than 80 films; *films for television include:* The Life and Times of John Huston, Esq., 1965; (Exec. Producer) 13–part Who Is series, 1966–67 (wrote/dir. films on Pierre Boulez, Jacques Lipchitz, Walter Gropius, Maurice Béjart); Günter Grass' Berlin, 1965; Why Save Florence?, 1968; In the Name of Allah, 1970; The Space between Words, 1971–72; A Law in the Making, 1973; Inside the Brussels HQ, 1975; Is This the Way to Save our Cities?, 1975; Decision series: British Steel, etc., 1976–77, British Communism, 1978 (Royal Television Soc. Award); Pleasure at Her Majesty's, The Secret Policeman's Ball, 1977–78; Inside Europe, 1977–78; Police series, 1980–82 (BAFTA Award); Police: Operation Carter, 1981–82; Nagging Doubt, 1984; The Fifty-Minute Hour, 1984; Maybe Baby, 1985; Comic Relief, 1986; Stress, 1986; Closing Ranks, 1987; The Secret Life of the Soviet Union, 1990; Series Editor, Signals, 1988–89. Dept of Environment: Mem., Develt Control Review (Dobry Cttee), Chm., Study Gp on Public Participation in Planning, and Mem., Cttee on Control of Demolition, 1974–76. Chm., AIP, 1988–89; Member: Council, ICA, 1970–82; Council, BAFTA, 1976–77; Bd, Channel Four, 1980–85; Governor, BFI, 1974–78. Adviser on broadcasting to Brandt Commn, 1979–80; Media Consultant: Collins Publishing, 1983–88; London Transport (Mem. Bd, LTE, 1976–79; co-designer, new London Bus Map). Pres., Signals Internat. Trust, 1990–. *Publications:* Talking Blues, 1989; Bad!, 1991; contrib. Daily Telegraph, The Times, Sunday Telegraph, Observer, Independent on Sunday, Evening Standard, Police Review, The Independent, Guardian, Sunday Times. *Recreations:* tennis, photography. *Address:* 72 Westbourne Park Villas, W2 5EB. *T:* 071–727 7868. *Clubs:* Beefsteak, Groucho.

GRÆME, Maj.-Gen. Ian Rollo, CB 1967; OBE 1955; *b* 23 May 1913; *s* of late Col J. A. Græme, DSO, late RE; *m* 1941, Elizabeth Jean Dyas (*d* 1991); two *d. Educ:* Boxgrove; Stowe; RMA Woolwich. King's Medal and Benson Memorial Prize, RMA, 1933. 2nd Lt RA 1933; pre-war service at regimental duty UK; War Service in Singapore, Java, India, Burma, Siam; psc 1942; Instructor Staff Coll., Quetta, 1944; CO 1st Burma Field Regt, 1945–46; OC, K Battery, RHA, 1949; jssc 1952; GSO1, HQ Northern Army Group, 1953–54; CO 27 Regt RA, 1955–57; Col GS Staff Coll., Camberley, 1957–59; idc 1960; Dep. Mil. Sec., WO, 1961–63; Dep. Dir Personnel Admin, WO, 1963–64; Dir Army Recruiting, 1964–67; Retd 1967. Mem. Royal Yachting Assoc., 1950–; Life Governor, Royal Life Saving Soc., 1956–; Life Mem., British Olympic Assoc., 1958–; Chm., Army Holiday Cttee for ski-ing, 1963–67; Council, Army Ski Assoc., 1958–; Member: Council, Nat. Ski Fedn of GB, 1964–67 (Sec., 1967–78; Life Mem. Fedn); Cttee, Sports Aid Foundn, 1976– (Governor, 1982); Trustee, Sports Aid Trust, 1983–; Vice-President: English Ski Council, 1979–82; British Ski Fedn, 1981–84. Pres., Old Stoic Soc., 1990. Chm., Hampshire Sch. Trust, 1980–. FBIM; MInstD. Gold Medal, Austrian Govt, 1972. *Recreations:* ski-ing, sailing, mountains. *Clubs:* Army and Navy, English-Speaking Union (Life Mem.); Ski Club of Great Britain, Army Ski Association, Alpbach Visitors Ski, Garvock Ski (Pres. 1969–), Kandahar Ski; Royal Artillery Yacht.

GRAESSER, Col Sir Alastair Stewart Durward, Kt 1973; DSO 1945; OBE 1963; MC 1944; TD; DL; President: National Union of Conservative and Unionist Associations, 1984–85 (Chairman, 1974–76; Hon. Vice President, 1976); Wales and Monmouth Conservative and Unionist Council, 1972–77; *b* 17 Nov. 1915; *s* of Norman Hugo Graesser and Annette Stewart Durward; *m* 1939, Diana Aline Elms Neale; one *s* three *d. Educ:* Oundle; Gonville and Caius Coll., Cambridge. Director: Municipal Life Assurance Ltd, 1977–88; Municipal General Assurance Ltd, 1977–88; Managing Trustee, Municipal Mutual Insurance Ltd, 1977–88; Trustee, TSB of Wales and Border Counties, 1970–86; Mem., CBI Regional Council for Wales (Past Chm.). Pres., Wales and Monmouth Conservative Clubs Council, 1972–76. Vice-Chm., Wales and Monmouth TA&VR Assoc.; Hon. Col, 3rd Bn Royal Welch Fusiliers (TA), 1972–80. High Sheriff of Flintshire, 1962; DL 1960, JP 1956–78, Vice Lord-Lieut, 1980–83, Clwyd (formerly Flints). CStJ 1980. *Recreation:* shooting. *Address:* Sweet Briar, Berghill Lane, Babbinswood, Whittington, Oswestry, Salop SY11 4PF. *T:* Oswestry (0691) 662395. *Clubs:* Naval and Military; Hawks (Cambridge); Leander (Henley-on-Thames); Grosvenor (Chester).

GRAFTON, 11th Duke of, *cr* 1675; **Hugh Denis Charles FitzRoy;** KG 1976; DL; Earl of Euston, Viscount Ipswich; Captain Grenadier Guards; *b* 3 April 1919; *e s* of 10th Duke of Grafton, and Lady Doreen Maria Josepha Sydney Buxton (*d* 1923), *d* of 1st Earl Buxton; *S* father, 1970; *m* 1946, Fortune (*see* Duchess of Grafton); two *s* three *d. Educ:* Eton; Magdalene Coll., Cambridge. ADC to the Viceroy of India, 1943–46. Member: Historic Buildings Council for England, 1953–84; Historic Bldgs Adv. Cttee, 1984–; Royal Fine Art Commn, 1971–; Chm., Architectural Heritage Fund; Mem., National Trust Properties Cttee; Pres., SPAB, 1989–; Nat. Pres., Council of British Soc. of Master Glass Painters; Chairman of Trustees: Historic Churches Preservation Trust; Sir John Soane's Museum; Vice-Chm. Trustees, Nat. Portrait Gallery; President: Internat. Students Trust; E Anglian Tourist Bd, 1973–. Patron, Hereford Herd Book Soc. Hon. Air Cdre, No 2623 RAuxAF Regt Sqdn, 1982–. DL Suffolk, 1973. Hon. DCL East Anglia, 1990. *Heir: s* Earl of Euston, *qv. Address:* Euston Hall, Thetford, Norfolk IP24 2QW. *T:* Thetford (0842) 3282. *Club:* Boodle's.

See also C. D. Mackenzie.

GRAFTON, Duchess of; (Ann) Fortune FitzRoy, GCVO 1980 (DCVO 1970; CVO 1965); Mistress of The Robes to The Queen since 1967; *o d* of Captain Eric Smith, MC, LLD, Lower Ashfold, Slaugham; *m* 1946, Duke of Grafton, *qv*; two *s* three *d*. Lady of the Bedchamber to the Queen, 1953–66. SRCN Great Ormond Street, 1945; Mem. Bd of Governors, The Hospital for Sick Children, Great Ormond Street, 1952–66; Patron, Nurses' League. President: W Suffolk Mission to the Deaf; W Suffolk Decorative and Fine Arts Soc.; Vice-President: Suffolk Br., Royal British Legion Women's Section; Trinity Hospice, 1951. Governor: Felixstowe Coll.; Riddlesworth Hall. JP County of London, 1949, W Suffolk, 1972–90. *Address:* Euston Hall, Thetford, Norfolk. *T:* Thetford (0842) 753282.

See also Jeremy F. E. Smith, Sir John L. E. Smith.

GRAFTON, NSW, Bishop of, since 1985; **Rt. Rev. Bruce Allan Schultz;** *b* 24 May 1932; *s* of Percival Ferdinand and Elsie Amelia Schultz; *m* 1962, Janet Margaret Gersbach; two *s* two *d* (and one *s* decd). *Educ:* Culcairn High School; St Columb's Hall and St John's Coll., Morpeth. ThL (ACT) 1960. Sheep and wheat property, Manager–Owner, 1950–57. Theolog. student, 1957–60; deacon 1959, priest 1960, dio. Riverina; Asst Priest, Broken Hill, 1961–63; Priest-in-charge, Ariah Park, Ardlethan and Barellan with Weethalle, 1964–67; Rector: Deniliquin, 1967–73; Gladstone, dio. Rockhampton, 1973–79; Archdeacon and Commissary of Rockhampton, 1975–79; Rector of Grafton and Dean of Christ Church Cathedral, 1979–83; Asst Bishop of Brisbane (Bishop for the Northern Region), 1983–85. Nat. Chm., Anglican Boys' Soc. in Australia, 1987–; Chm., NSW Provincial Commn on Christian Educn, 1989; Bd Mem., Australian Bd of Missions, 1988–. *Recreations:* family, fishing, tennis, water skiing, gardening. *Address:* Bishopsholme, 35 Victoria Street, Grafton, NSW 2460, Australia. *T:* (home) (066) 42 2070, (office) (066) 42 4122. *Club:* Grafton (Grafton).

GRAFTON, Col Martin John, CBE 1976 (OBE 1964, MBE 1944); TD 1958; DL; Director-General, National Federation of Building Trades Employers, 1964–79, retired; *b* 28 June 1919; *o s* of Vincent Charles Grafton and Maud (*née* Brazier); *m* 1948, Jean Margaret, *d* of James Drummond-Smith, OBE, MA, and Edith M. Drummond-Smith, MBE, MA; two *d. Educ:* Bromsgrove Sch. Served War, RE, 1940–46: Normandy and NW Europe, 1944–46 (MBE 1944, Rhine Crossing); served TA RE, 1947–66 (TD 1958, Bar 1963): Lt-Col 1960, Col 1964; comd 101 Fd Engr Regt, 1960–64; Dep. Chief Engr, E Anglian Dist, 1964–66. Joined John Lewis Partnership, 1948: Dir of Bldg, 1954–60; a Man. Dir, 1960–63. Member: Council, CBI, 1964–79; EDC for Building, 1964–75; Nat. Consult. Council for Building and Civil Engrg, 1964–79. Hon. FCIOB 1978; DL Greater London, 1967–83; Freeman, City of London, 1978. *Address:* Urchfont House, Urchfont, Devizes, Wiltshire SN10 4RP. *T:* Devizes (0380) 840404.

GRAFTON, Peter Witheridge, CBE 1972; Senior Partner, G. D. Walford & Partners, Chartered Quantity Surveyors, 1978–82 (Partner 1949–78), retired; *b* 19 May 1916; *s* of James Hawkins Grafton and Ethel Marion (*née* Brannan); *m* 1st, 1939, Joan Bleackley (*d* 1969); two *d* (and one *s* one *d* decd); 2nd, 1971, Margaret Ruth Ward; two *s. Educ:* Westminster City Sch.; Sutton Valence Sch.; Coll. of Estate Management. FRICS, FCIArb. Served War of 1939–45, Queen's Westminster Rifles, Dorsetshire Regt and RE, UK and Far East (Captain). Pres., RICS, 1978–79 (Vice-Pres., 1974–78); Mem. and Past Chm., Quantity Surveyors Council; Mem. Council, Construction Industries Research and Information Assoc., 1963–69; Member: Research Adv. Council to Minister of Housing and Construction, 1967–71; Nat. Cons. Council for Building and Civil Engrg Industries, 1968–76; British Bd of Agrément, 1973–88; Chm., Nat. Jt Consultative Cttee for Building Industry, 1974–75 (Mem., 1970–77). Master, Worshipful Co. of Chartered Surveyors, 1983–84. Trustee, United Westminster Schs; Governor, Sutton Valence Sch., 1971– (Chm., 1976–91); Past Chm., Old Suttonians Assoc. Contested (L) Bromley, 1959. *Publications:* numerous articles on techn. and other professional subjects. *Recreations:* golf (founder and Chm., Public Schs Old Boys Golf Assoc., Co-donor Grafton Morrish Trophy; past Captain of Chartered Surveyors Golfing Soc.); writing. *Address:* Longacre, Hookwood Park, Limpsfield, Oxted, Surrey RH8 0SQ. *T:* Oxted (0883) 6685. *Clubs:* Reform; Rye Golf, Tandridge Golf.

GRAHAM, family name of **Duke of Montrose** and **Baron Graham of Edmonton.**

GRAHAM, Marquis of; James Graham; *b* 6 April 1935; *s* of 7th Duke of Montrose, *qv*; *m* 1970, Catherine Elizabeth MacDonell, *d* of late Captain N. A. T. Young, and of Mrs Young, Ottawa; two *s* one *d. Educ:* Loretto. Brig. Royal Company of Archers (Queen's Body Guard for Scotland), 1986 (Mem., 1965–). Area Pres., Scottish NFU, 1986 (Mem. Council, 1982–86 and 1987–90). OStJ 1978. *Heir: s* Lord Fintrie, *qv. Address:* Auchmar, Drymen, Glasgow. *T:* Drymen (0360) 221.

GRAHAM OF EDMONTON, Baron *cr* 1983 (Life Peer), of Edmonton in Greater London; **Thomas Edward Graham;** Opposition Chief Whip, House of Lords, since 1990; *b* 26 March 1925; *m* 1950, Margaret, *d* of Frederick Golding; two *s. Educ:* elementary sch.; WEA Co-operative College. BA Open Univ., 1976. FBIM. Newcastle-on-Tyne Co-operative Soc., 1939–52; Organiser, British Fedn of Young Co-operators, 1952–53; Educn Sec., Enfield Highway Co-operative Soc., 1953–62; Sec., Co-operative Union Southern Section, 1962–67; Nat. Sec., Co-operative Party, 1967–74. MP (Lab and Co-op) Enfield, Edmonton, Feb. 1974–1983; PPS to Minister of State, Dept of Prices and Consumer Protection, 1974–76; A Lord Comr of HM Treasury, 1976–79; Opposition spokesman on the environment, 1980–83. Contested (Lab) Edmonton, 1983. Mem. and Leader, Enfield Council, 1961–68. *Address:* 17a Queen Annes Grove, Bush Hill Park, Enfield, Mddx EN1 2JR.

GRAHAM, Prof. Alastair, DSc; FRS 1979; Professor of Zoology, University of Reading, to 1972, now Emeritus Professor; *b* 6 Nov. 1906. *Educ:* Edinburgh Univ. (MA, BSc); London Univ. (DSc). Fellow, Zoological Soc., 1939 (Frink Medal, 1976). *Publications:* British Prosobranch Molluscs (jtly), 1962; Other Operculate Gastropod Molluscs, 1971. *Address:* 207 Wokingham Road, Reading, Berks. *T:* Reading (0734) 64154.

GRAHAM, Alastair Carew; FRSA; Head Master, Mill Hill School, 1979–Aug. 1992; *b* 23 July 1932; *s* of Col J. A. Graham and Mrs Graham (*née* Carew-Hunt); *m* 1969, Penelope Rachel Beaumont; two *d. Educ:* Winchester Coll.; Gonville and Caius Coll., Cambridge (1st Cl. Mod. and Med. Langs). Served 1st Bn Argyll and Sutherland Highlanders, 1951–53. Foy, Morgan & Co. (City), 1956–58; Asst Master, Eton, 1958; House Master, 1970–79. *Recreations:* ball games, walking; theatre and opera; music

listening, gardening, youth club. *Address:* (until Aug. 1992) The Grove, Mill Hill, NW7. *T:* 081–959 1006; (from Sept. 1992) Longbourn, Chawton, Alton, Hants.
See also Maj.-Gen. J. D. C. Graham.

GRAHAM, Sir Alexander (Michael), GBE 1990; JP; FCII, FBIBA; FCIS; Deputy Chairman, Frizzell Group Ltd, since 1990 (Director, since 1967); Lord Mayor of London, 1990–91; *b* 27 Sept. 1938; *s* of Dr Walter Graham and Suzanne Graham (*née* Simon); *m* 1964, Carolyn, *d* of Lt-Col Alan Wolryche Stansfeld, MBE; three *d. Educ:* Fyvie Village Sch.; Hall Sch., Hampstead; St Paul's Sch. MBIM. Joined Norman Frizzell & Partners Ltd, 1957, Man. Dir, 1973–90; Underwriting Member of Lloyd's. National Service, 1957–59; commnd Gordon Highlanders; TA 1959–67. Mercers' Co.: Liveryman, 1971–; Mem., Ct of Assistants, 1980; Master, 1983–84; Mem., Ct of Common Council, City of London, 1978; Alderman for Ward of Queenhithe, 1979–; Pres., Queenhithe Ward Club, 1979–. Sheriff, City of London, 1986–87. Governor: Hall Sch., Hampstead, 1975–; St Paul's Sch., 1980–; St Paul's Girls' Sch., 1980–; City of London Boys' Sch., 1983–85; Mem. Council, Gresham Coll., 1983–; Trustee, Morden College, 1988–. Trustee, United Response, 1988–. FRSA. JP City of London, 1979–; HM Lieut, City of London, 1989; KStJ 1990. Order of Wissam Alouite (Morocco), 1987. *Recreations:* wine, genealogy, music, reading, silver, bridge, golf, swimming, tennis, shooting. *Address:* Walden Abbotts, Whitwell, Hitchin, Herts SG4 8AJ. *T:* Whitwell (Herts) (0438) 871223. *Clubs:* Carlton, City Livery; Highland Brigade.
See also Lt-Gen. Sir P. W. Graham.

GRAHAM, Alistair; *see* Graham, J. A.

GRAHAM, Rt. Rev. Andrew Alexander Kenny; *see* Newcastle, Bishop of.

GRAHAM, Andrew Winston Mawdsley; Fellow, and Tutor in Economics, Balliol College, Oxford, since 1969; *b* 20 June 1942; *s* of Winston Mawdsley Graham, *qv*; *m* 1970, Peggotty Fawssett. *Educ:* Charterhouse; St Edmund Hall, Oxford. MA (PPE). Economic Assistant: NEDO, 1964; Dept of Economic Affairs, 1964–66; Asst to Economic Adviser to the Cabinet, 1966–68; Economic Adviser to Prime Minister, 1968–69; Policy Adviser to Prime Minister (on leave of absence from Balliol), 1974–75. Tutor, Oxford Univ. Business Summer Sch., 1971, 1972, 1973 and 1976. Estates Bursar, 1978, Investment Bursar, 1979–83, Vice Master, 1988, Balliol Coll. Vis. Researcher, SE Asian Central Banks Res. and Trng Centre, Malaysia, 1984; Vis. Fellow, Griffith Univ., Brisbane, 1984. Member: Wilson Cttee to Review the Functioning of Financial Institutions, 1977–80; Economics Cttee, SSRC, 1978–80; British Transport Docks Bd, 1979–82; Chm., St James Gp (Economic Forecasting), 1982–84, 1985–. Mem., ILO/Jobs and Skills Prog. for Africa (JASPA) Mission to Ethiopia, 1982; Hd, Queen Elizabeth House/Food Studies Gp team assisting Govt of Republic of Zambia, 1984. Founder Mem. Editorial Bd, Library of Political Economy, 1982–. *Publications:* (ed) Government and Economies in the Postwar Period, 1990; contribs to books on economics and philosophy. *Recreation:* sail-boarding on every possible occasion. *Address:* Balliol College, Oxford OX1 3BJ. *T:* Oxford (0865) 277777.

GRAHAM, Mrs Anne Silvia; Chairman, South Cumbria Health Authority, since 1988; *b* 1 Aug. 1934; *o d* of late Benjamin Arthur Garcia and Constance Rosa (*née* Journeaux); *m* Peter Graham, *qv. Educ:* Francis Holland Sch., SW1; LSE (LLB). Called to the Bar, Inner Temple, 1958; Yarborough-Anderson Scholar, 1959. Joined Min. of Housing and Local Govt, 1960; Dep. Legal Advr, DoE, 1978–86. *Recreations:* gardening, cookery. *Address:* Stony Dale, Field Broughton, Grange over Sands, Cumbria LA11 6HN.

GRAHAM, Antony Richard Malise; management consultant; Director, Clive & Stokes International, since 1985; *b* 15 Oct. 1928; *s* of late Col Patrick Ludovic Graham, MC, and late Barbara Mary Graham (*née* Jury); *m* 1958, Gillian Margaret, *d* of late L. Bradford Cook and of Mrs W. V. Wrigley; two *s* one *d. Educ:* Abberley Hall; Nautical Coll., Pangbourne. Merchant Navy, 1945–55 (Master Mariner). Stewarts and Lloyds Ltd, 1955–60; PE Consulting Group Ltd, management consultants, 1960–72 (Regional Dir, 1970–72); Regional Industrial Dir (Under-Sec.), DTI, 1972–76; Dir, Barrow Hepburn Group Ltd, and Maroquinerie Le Tanneur et Tanneries du Bugey SA, 1976–81; Chm., Paton & Sons (Tillicoultry) Ltd, 1981–82. Contested (C) Leeds East, 1966. *Address:* The Gardens, Nun Appleton Hall, York YO5 7BG.

GRAHAM, Billy; *see* Graham, William F.

GRAHAM, Sir Charles (Spencer Richard), 6th Bt *cr* 1783; Lord-Lieutenant of Cumbria, since 1983; *b* 16 July 1919; *s* of Sir (Frederick) Fergus Graham, 5th Bt, KBE, and of Mary Spencer Revell, CBE (*d* 1985), *d* of late Maj.-Gen. Raymond Reade, CB, CMG; *S* father, 1978; *m* 1944, Isabel Susan Anne, *d* of late Major R. L. Surtees, OBE; two *s* one *d. Educ:* Eton. Served with Scots Guards, 1940–50, NW Europe (despatches) and Malaya. President, Country Landowners' Assoc., 1971–73. Mem., Nat. Water Council, 1973–83. Master, Worshipful Co. of Farmers, 1982–83. High Sheriff 1955, DL 1971, Cumbria (formerly Cumberland). KStJ 1983. *Heir: s* James Fergus Surtees Graham [*b* 29 July 1946; *m* 1975, Serena Jane, *yr d* of Ronald Frank Kershaw; one *s* two *d*]. *Address:* Crofthead, Longtown, Cumbria CA6 5PA. *T:* Longtown (0228) 791231. *Clubs:* Brooks's, Pratt's.

GRAHAM, Dr Christopher Forbes, FRS 1981; Professor of Animal Development, and Professorial Fellow, St Catherine's College, University of Oxford, since 1985; *b* 23 Sept. 1940. *Educ:* Oxford Univ. (BA 1963, DPhil 1966). Formerly Junior Beit Memorial Fellow in Med. Research, Sir William Dunn Sch. of Pathology. Lectr, Zoology Dept, Oxford Univ., 1970–85. Member: Brit. Soc. Cell Biology; Brit. Soc. for Developmental Biology; Soc. for Experimental Biology; Genetical Soc. *Publication:* The Developmental Biology of Plants and Animals, 1976, new edn as Developmental Control in Plants and Animals, 1984. *Address:* Department of Zoology, University of Oxford, South Parks Road, Oxford OX1 3PS.

GRAHAM, Clifford; Director, Institute of Health, King's College London, since 1990 (on secondment from Department of Health); *b* 3 April 1937; *s* of late James Mackenzie and Monica Graham; *m* 1960 (marr. diss. 1990); two *s* one *d. Educ:* Alsop High Sch., Liverpool; London Univ. (LLB). Called to the Bar, Gray's Inn, 1969. Nat. Service, RAF, Aden, 1955–57. Clerical Officer, Admiralty, 1954–59; Exec. Officer, Customs and Excise, 1959–65; Higher Exec. Officer, Min. of Health, 1965–68; Principal, 1969–74, Asst Sec., 1975–82, Under Sec., 1983–, DHSS, later Dept of Health; on sabbatical, Senior Res. Fellow, LSE, researching and reporting to govt on ways of improving the planning management and delivery of the health and social services for the benefit of the consumer, 1985–86. *Publications:* Public Administration and Health Services in England, 1983; contrib. to Oxford Textbook of Public Health, 1984, rev. edn 1989; articles in journals and DHSS reports. *Recreations:* cycling, walking, reading, music. *Address:* Highcroft, Milton Clevedon, Shepton Mallet, Somerset BA4 6NS. *T:* Evercreech (0749) 0308. *Club:* Gray's Inn.

GRAHAM, Colin; Artistic Director: English Music Theatre, since 1975; Aldeburgh Festival, since 1969; Opera Theatre of St Louis, since 1984 (Associate Artistic Director, 1979–84); Director of Productions, English National Opera, 1977–84, Associate Artist,

since 1984; stage director, designer, lighting designer, and author; *b* 22 Sept. 1931; *s* of Frederick Eaton Graham-Bonnalie and Alexandra Diana Vivian Findlay. *Educ:* Northaw Prep. Sch.; Stowe Sch.; RADA (Dip.). Dir of Productions, English Opera Gp, 1963–74; Associate Dir of Prodns, Sadler's Wells Opera/English National Opera, 1967–75. Principal productions for: English Music Theatre; Royal Opera, Covent Garden; Scottish Opera; New Opera Co.; Glyndebourne Opera; BBC TV; Brussels National Opera; St Louis Opera Theatre; Santa Fe Opera; Metropolitan Opera, New York; NYC Opera; dir. world premières: of all Benjamin Britten's operas since 1954; of other contemp. composers. Theatre productions for: Old Vic Co.; Bristol Old Vic; Royal Shakespeare Co. Ordained minister, New Covenant Church, St Louis, Mo, 1987. Hon. DA Webster Univ., 1985. Orpheus award (Germany) for best opera production, 1973 (War and Peace, ENO); Opera America award for production, 1988 (Albert Herring, Banff Fest. Opera). *Publications:* A Penny for a Song (libretto for Richard Rodney Bennett), 1969; The Golden Vanity (libretto for opera by Britten), 1970; King Arthur (libretto for new version of Purcell opera), 1971; The Postman Always Rings Twice (libretto for opera by Stephen Paulus), 1981; Jōruri (libretto for opera by Minoru Miki), 1985; The Woodlanders (libretto for opera by Stephen Paulus), 1984; production scores for Britten's: Curlew River, 1969; The Burning Fiery Furnace, 1971; The Prodigal Son, 1973; contrib. Opera. *Recreations:* motor cycles, movies, weight training. *Address:* PO Box 191910, Saint Louis, Mo 63119, USA.

GRAHAM, David; *see* Graham, S. D.

GRAHAM, Douglas; *see* Graham, M. G. D.

GRAHAM, Duncan Gilmour, CBE 1987; Chairman and Chief Executive, National Curriculum Council, 1988–91; *b* 20 Aug. 1936; *s* of Robert Gilmour Graham and Lilias Turnbull Graham (*née* Watson); *m* 1st, 1962, Margaret Gray Graham (*née* Cairns) (marr diss. 1991); two *s* one *d*; 2nd, 1991, Wendy Margaret Wallace. *Educ:* Hutcheson's, Glasgow; Univ. of Glasgow (MA (Hons) History); Jordanhill Coll. of Education (Teachers' Secondary Cert.). Teacher of History: Whitehill Sec. Sch., Glasgow, 1959–62; Hutcheson's, Glasgow, 1962–65; Lectr in Social Studies, Craigie Coll. of Educn, Ayr, 1965–68; Asst Dir of Educn, Renfrewshire, 1968–70; Sen. Depute Dir of Educn, Renfrewshire, 1970–74, Strathclyde Regl Council, 1974–79; Advr to COSLA and Scottish Teachers' Salaries Cttee, 1974–79; County Educn Officer, Suffolk, 1979–87; Chief Exec., Humberside CC, 1987–88. Advr to ACC, 1982–88; Mem., Burnham Cttee, 1983–87 and of ACAS Indep. Panel, 1986. Sec., Co. Educn Officers Soc., 1985–87; Chm., Assoc. of Educn Officers, 1985–; Project Dir, DES Teacher Appraisal Study, 1985–86; Chm., Nat. Steering Gp on Teacher Appraisal, 1987–90. Member: BBC North Adv. Council, 1988–; Lincs and Humberside Arts Council, 1988–; Council of Nat. Foundn for Econ. Res., 1984, and 1989–90; Mem. Exec. Council, Industrial Soc., 1988–90; Chm., Nat. Mathematics Wkg Gp, 1988. FRSA 1981. *Publications:* Those Having Torches, 1985; In the Light of Torches, 1986; many articles in nat. press and educn and local govt jls. *Recreations:* golf, sailing, the arts, fishing. *Address:* Gilmour Mews, Battlebarrow, Appleby, Cumbria CA16 6XT. *Clubs:* Caledonian; Western Gailes Golf, Clyde Cruising.

GRAHAM, Euan Douglas, CB 1985; Principal Clerk of Private Bills, House of Lords, 1961–84; *b* 29 July 1924; *yr s* of Brig. Lord D. M. Graham, CB, DSO, MC; RA. *Educ:* Eton; Christ Church, Oxford (MA). Served RAF, 1943–47. Joined Parliament Office, House of Lords, 1950; Clerk, Judicial Office, 1950–60; Principal Clerk of Private Bills, Examiner of Petitions for Private Bills, Taxing Officer, 1961–84. *Address:* 122 Beaufort Mansions, Beaufort Street, SW3. *Clubs:* Brooks's, Beefsteak, Pratt's.

GRAHAM, George Boughen, QC 1964; *b* 17 July 1920; *s* of Sydney Boughen and Hannah Graham, Keswick, Cumberland; *m* Mavis, *o d* of late Frederick Worthington, Blackpool. *Educ:* Keswick Sch. Royal Signals, 1940–46. Barrister, Lincoln's Inn, 1950, Bencher, 1972. Chancellor, Diocese of Wakefield, 1959, Dio. of Sheffield, 1971. Member of Lloyd's, 1968. Comdr, Order of Merit (W Germany); Order of Aztec Eagle (Mexico). *Publications:* Covenants, Settlements and Taxation, 1953; Estate Duty Handbook, 1954. *Recreations:* walking and dining. *Address:* Brocklehurst, Keswick, Cumbria. *T:* Keswick (0596) 72042. *Clubs:* Athenæum; Derwent (Keswick).

GRAHAM, George Ronald Gibson, CBE 1986; Partner, Maclay, Murray & Spens, Solicitors, Glasgow and Edinburgh, since 1968; Director, Scottish Widows' Fund and Life Assurance Society, since 1984; *b* 15 Oct. 1939; *o s* of James Gibson Graham, MD, and Elizabeth Waddell; *m* 1965, Mirren Elizabeth Carnegie; three *s. Educ:* Glasgow Academy; Loretto Sch., Musselburgh; Oriel Coll., Oxford (MA); Glasgow Univ. (LLB). Co-ordinator of Diploma in Legal Practice, 1979–83; Clerk to Gen. Council, Glasgow Univ., 1990–. Mem. Council, 1977–89, Pres., 1984–85, Law Soc. of Scotland. *Recreations:* fishing, swimming, walking. *Address:* 44 Kingsborough Gardens, Glasgow G12 9NL. *T:* 041–334 2730. *Clubs:* The Western, Western Baths (Glasgow).

GRAHAM, Gordon; *see* Graham, W. G.

GRAHAM, Gordon, CBE 1980; PPRIBA; consultant architect; Director, Foster Associates Ltd, 1984–89; *b* Carlisle, 4 June 1920; *s* of late Stanley Bouch Graham and Isabel Hetherington; *m* 1946, Enid Pennington; three *d. Educ:* Creighton Sch.; Nottingham Sch. of Architecture. DipArch, RIBA, 1949; RIBA Arthur Cates Prizeman, 1949; travelling schol., S and Central America, 1953. Served Royal Artillery, N Africa, Italy and NW Europe, 1940–46. Sen. Lectr, Nottingham Sch. of Architecture, 1949–61; Sen. Partner, Architects Design Gp, 1958–84. Pres., Nottingham, Derby and Lincoln Soc. of Architects, 1965–66; RIBA: Chm., E Midlands Region, 1967–69; Mem. Council, 1967–73 and 1974; Vice-Pres., 1969–71; Hon. Sec., 1971–72 and 1975–76; Sen. Vice-Pres., 1976; Pres., 1977–79. Mem., Building EDC, 1978–83. Hon. FRAIC 1978. Hon. MA Nottingham, 1979. *Recreations:* Rugby football, architecture. *Club:* Reform.

GRAHAM, Ian James Alastair, FSA; Assistant Curator, Peabody Museum of Archaeology, Harvard University; *b* 12 Nov. 1923; *s* of Captain Lord Alastair Graham, RN, *y s* of 5th Duke of Montrose, and Lady Meriel Olivia Bathurst (*d* 1936), *d* of 7th Earl Bathurst; unmarried. *Educ:* Winchester Coll.; Trinity Coll., Dublin. RNVR (A), 1942–47; TCD 1947–51; Nuffield Foundn Research Scholar at The National Gallery, 1951–54; independent archaeological explorer in Central America from 1959. Occasional photographer of architecture. MacArthur Foundn Prize Fellowship, 1981. *Publications:* Splendours of the East, 1965; Great Houses of the Western World, 1968; Archaeological Explorations in El Peten, Guatemala, 1967; Corpus of Maya Hieroglyphic Inscriptions, 15 parts, 1975–; other reports in learned jls. *Address:* Chantry Farm, Campsey Ash, Suffolk; c/o Peabody Museum, Harvard University, Cambridge, Mass, USA.

GRAHAM, Sir James Bellingham, 11th Bt *cr* 1662; Research Assistant, Cecil Higgins Museum and Art Gallery, Bedford; *b* 8 Oct. 1940; *e s* of Sir Richard Bellingham Graham, 10th Bt, OBE, and of Beatrice, *d* of late Michael Spencer-Smith, DSO, MC; *S* father, 1982; *m* 1986, Halina, *d* of Wiktor and Eleonora Grubert. *Educ:* Eton College; Christ Church, Oxford (MA). *Publications:* Guide to Norton Conyers, 1976; (with Halina Graham) A Guide to the Cecil Higgins Art Gallery, 1987. *Recreations:* reading, visiting historic houses and museums. *Heir: b* William Reginald Graham, *b* 7 July 1942. *Address:*

Norton Conyers, Ripon, N Yorks. *T:* Melmerby (076584) 333; 1 Oberon Court, Shakespeare Road, Bedford MK40 2EB. *T:* Bedford (0234) 67667.

GRAHAM, James Lowery, OBE 1991; Managing Director, Border Television, Carlisle, since 1982, Deputy Chairman, since 1990; *b* 29 Oct. 1932; *s* of William and Elizabeth Graham; *m* 1984, Ann Routledge; two *d* by previous marr. *Educ:* Whitehaven Grammar School. Journalist, North West Evening Mail, Barrow, 1955–62; News Editor, Border Television, 1962–67; Producer, BBC, Leeds, 1967–70; BBC: Regional News Editor, North, 1970–75; Regional Television Manager, North East, 1975–80; Head of Secretariat, Broadcasting House, 1980–82; Sec., Central Music Adv. Council, 1981–82. Jt Sec., Broadcasters' Audience Res. Bd, 1980–82. Dir, Indep. Television Publications, 1982–89. Chm., Independent Television Facilities Centre Ltd, 1987–; Director: Oracle Teletext, 1988–; Radio Borders, 1989–; Radio SW Scotland, 1989– (Chm.). Prix Italia, ITVA rep., 1987–. Member: BAFTA; RTS; European movement; Co-operative Internationale de Recherche et d'Action en Matière de Communication (European Producers). Governor, Newcastle Polytechnic, 1975–80. FRSA 1987. News Film Award, RTS, 1975; Beffroi d'Or, Lille (European regional broadcasting award), 1983; RTS Regl Broadcasting Award, 1989. *Recreations:* hill walking, ski-ing. *Address:* Oak House, Great Corby, Carlisle, Cumbria. *Clubs:* Groucho; Carlisle Ski.

GRAHAM, Sir James (Thompson), Kt 1990; CMG 1986; farmer, since 1946; Director, 1979–89, Chairman, 1982–89, New Zealand Dairy Board, retired; *b* 6 May 1929; *s* of Harold Graham and Florence Cecily Graham; *m* 1955, Ina Isabelle Low; one *s* two *d*. *Educ:* New Plymouth Boys' High Sch. Dir, NZ Co-op Dairy Co., 1974–89 (Chm., 1979–82). *Recreations:* golf, tennis, bowls. *Address:* 245 Oceanbeach Road, Mount Maunganui, New Zealand. *T:* Tauranga NZ 754043.

GRAHAM, John, CB 1976; Fisheries Secretary, Ministry of Agriculture, Fisheries and Food, 1967–76; *b* 17 March 1918; *s* of late John Graham; *m* 1940, Betty Ramage Jarvie; two *s* three *d*. *Educ:* Fettes Coll., Edinburgh; Trinity Coll., Cambridge (Schol.). Classical Tripos, MA Cantab. Entered Post Office as Asst Principal, 1939; Min. of Food, 1940.

GRAHAM, Sir John (Alexander Noble), 4th Bt *cr* 1906, of Larbert; GCMG 1986 (KCMG 1979; CMG 1972); HM Diplomatic Service, retired; Registrar, Order of Saint Michael and Saint George, since 1987; Director, Ditchley Foundation, 1987–July 1992; *b* 15 July 1926; *s* of Sir John Reginald Noble Graham, 3rd Bt, VC, OBE and Rachel Septima (*d* 1984), *d* of Col Sir Alexander Sprot, 1st and last Bt; *S* father, 1980; *m* 1956, Marygold Ellinor Gabrielle Austin (*d* 1991); two *s* one *d*. *Educ:* Eton Coll.; Trinity Coll., Cambridge. Army, 1944–47; Cambridge, 1948–50; HM Foreign Service, 1950; Middle East Centre for Arab Studies, 1951; Third Secretary, Bahrain 1951, Kuwait 1952, Amman 1953; Asst Private Sec. to Sec. of State for Foreign Affairs, 1954–57; First Sec., Belgrade, 1957–60, Benghazi, 1960–61; FO 1961–66; Counsellor and Head of Chancery, Kuwait, 1966–69; Principal Private Sec. to Foreign and Commonwealth Sec., 1969–72; Cllr (later Minister) and Head of Chancery, Washington, 1972–74; Ambassador to Iraq, 1974–77; Dep. Under-Sec. of State, FCO, 1977–79; Ambassador to Iran, 1979–80; Deputy Under-Sec. of State, FCO, 1980–82; Ambassador and UK Permanent Representative to NATO, Brussels, 1982–86. *Heir: s* Andrew John Noble Graham, Major, Argyll and Sutherland Highlanders [*b* 21 Oct. 1956; *m* 1984, Suzi M. B. O'Riordan, *er d* of Rear-Adm. J. P. B. O'Riordan, *qv*; one *s* two *d*]. *Address:* (until July 1992) West Wing, Ditchley Park, Enstone, Oxford OX7 4ER. *Club:* Army and Navy.

GRAHAM, (John) Alistair; Chief Executive, Calderdale & Kirklees Training and Enterprise Council, since 1991; *b* 6 Aug. 1942; *s* of late Robert Graham and of Dorothy Graham; *m* 1968, Dorothy Jean Wallace; one *s* one *d*. *Educ:* Royal Grammar Sch., Newcastle upon Tyne. Clerical Asst, St George's Hosp., Morpeth, 1961; Admin Trainee, Northern Regional Hosp. Bd, 1963; Higher Clerical Officer, Royal Sussex County Hosp., Brighton, 1964; Legal Dept, TGWU, 1965; The Civil and Public Services Association: Asst Sec., 1966; Asst Gen. Sec., 1975; Dep. Gen. Sec., 1976; Gen. Sec., 1982–86; Dir, Industrial Soc., 1986–91. Vis. Fellow, Nuffield Coll., Oxford, 1984–; Vis. Prof., Management Sch., Imperial Coll., London Univ., 1989–91. Chm., BBC S and E Regl Adv. Council, 1987–90; Mem., TUC Gen. Council, 1982–84, 1985–86. Bd Mem., Opera North, 1989–. Assessor, Guildford and Woolwich Inquiry, 1990–. Contested (Lab), Brighton Pavilion, 1966. *Recreations:* music, theatre. *Address:* Parkview House, Woodvale Office Park, Woodvale Road, Brighouse, W Yorks HD6 4AB.

GRAHAM, Maj.-Gen. John David Carew, CB 1978; CBE 1973 (OBE 1966); Secretary to the Administrative Trustees of the Chevening Estate, 1978–86; *b* 18 Jan. 1923; *s* of late Col J. A. Graham, late RE, and Constance Mary Graham (*née* Carew-Hunt); *m* 1956, Rosemary Elaine Adamson; one *s* one *d*. *Educ:* Cheltenham Coll. psc 1955; jssc 1962. Commissioned into Argyll and Sutherland Highlanders, 1942 (despatches, 1945); served with 5th (Scottish) Bn, The Parachute Regt, 1946–49; British Embassy, Prague, 1949–50; HQ Scottish Comd, 1956–58; Mil. Asst to CINCENT, Fontainebleau, 1960–62; comd 1st Bn, The Parachute Regt, 1964–66; Instr at Staff Coll., Camberley, 1967; Regtl Col, The Parachute Regt, 1968–69; Comdr, Sultan's Armed Forces, Oman, 1970–72; Indian Nat. Defence Coll., New Delhi, 1973; Asst Chief of Staff, HQ AFCENT, 1974–76; GOC Wales, 1976–78. Hon. Col, Kent ACF, 1981–88 (Chm. Kent ACF Cttee, 1979–86); Hon. Col, 203 (Welsh) Gen. Hosp., RAMC, TA, 1983–88. OStJ 1978, and Chm., St John Council for Kent, 1978–86; CStJ 1983. Order of Oman, 1972. *Address:* c/o RHQ The Parachute Regiment, Browning Barracks, Aldershot, Hants GU11 2BS.
See also A. C. Graham.

GRAHAM, Sir John (Moodie), 2nd Bt *cr* 1964; Director, Kinnegar Inns Ltd, since 1981; Chairman, John Graham (Dromore) Ltd, 1966–83; *b* 3 April 1938; *s* of Sir Clarence Graham, 1st Bt, MICE, and Margaret Christina Moodie (*d* 1954); *S* father, 1966; *m* 1970, Valerie Rosemary (marr. diss. 1983), *d* of late Frank Gill, Belfast; three *d*. *Educ:* Trinity Coll., Glenalmond; Queen's Univ., Belfast. BSc, Civil Engineering, 1961. Joined family firm of John Graham (Dromore) Ltd, Building and Civil Engineering Contractors, on graduating from University. Director: Electrical Supplies Ltd, 1967–83; Concrete (NI) Ltd, 1967–83; Ulster Quarries Ltd; Graham (Contracts) Ltd, 1971–83; Fieldhouse Plant (NI) Ltd, 1976–83. Chm., Concrete Soc., NI, 1972–74; Senior Vice-Pres., Concrete Soc., 1980; Pres., Northern Ireland Leukaemia Research Fund, 1967. *Recreations:* sailing, squash, photography. *Address:* Lista de Correos, 07819 Jesus, Ibiza, Spain. *T:* (34.71) 31 38 34; Les Bordes d'Arinsal, Andorra. *T:* 37863.

GRAHAM, Sir (John) Patrick, Kt 1969; Judge of the High Court of Justice, Chancery Division, 1969–81; Senior Patent Judge; *b* 26 Nov. 1906; *s* of Alexander Graham and Mary Adeline Cock; *m* 1931, Annie Elizabeth Newport Willson; four *s*. *Educ:* Shrewsbury; Caius Coll., Cambridge. Called to Bar, Middle Temple, 1930; read with Sir Lionel Heald, QC, MP; QC 1953; Treasurer, Middle Temple, 1979. Served War of 1939–45: RAF (VR) and with SHAEF, demobilised, 1945, with rank of Group Capt. Dep.-Chm., Salop Quarter Sessions, 1961–69. Mem., Standing Cttee on Structural Safety, 1975–82. *Publication:* Awards to Inventors, 1946. *Recreations:* golf, tennis, sailing. *Address:* Tall Elms, Radlett, Herts WD7 8JB. *T:* Radlett (0923) 856307.

GRAHAM, John Strathie; Under Secretary (Local Government), Scottish Office Environment Department, since 1991; *b* 27 May 1950; *s* of Sir Norman Graham, *qv*; *m* 1979, Anne Janet Stenhouse; two *s* one *d*. *Educ:* Edinburgh Academy; Corpus Christi College, Oxford (BA Lit Hum). Joined Scottish Office, 1972; Private Sec. to Minister of State, 1975–76; Industrial Develt and Electricity Divs, 1976–82; Private Sec. to Sec. of State, 1983–85; Asst Sec., Planning and Finance Divs, 1985–91. *Recreations:* music, hillwalking. *Address:* Scottish Office, New St Andrew's House, Edinburgh. *T:* 031–244 4722.

GRAHAM, Kathleen Mary, CBE 1958 (MBE 1945); *d* of late Col R. B. Graham, CBE, and Mrs M. G. Graham, London; unmarried. *Educ:* Cheltenham Ladies' Coll.; Univ. of London (Courtauld Inst. of Art). Courtauld Inst., Dept of Technology War-time Laboratory, 1940–41; Political Warfare Executive, 1942–45; entered HM Foreign Service, 1945; served in FO, 1946–49; Consul (Information) at San Francisco, Calif, 1949–53; served in FO, 1953–55; made Counsellor in HM Foreign Service in 1955 and appointed Dep. Consul-Gen. in New York, 1955–59; HM Consul-Gen. at Amsterdam, 1960–63; in FO, 1964–69, retired. Exec. Dir, 1970–73, a Governor, 1973–80, E-SU. *Recreations:* music, history of art. *Address:* 16 Graham Terrace, SW1W 8JH. *T:* 071–730 4611.

GRAHAM, Kenneth, CBE 1987 (OBE 1971); Deputy General Secretary, Trades Union Congress, 1985–87 (Assistant General Secretary, 1977–85); Member: Board, The Open College, since 1987; Board, Remploy Ltd, since 1987; Management Board, Universities' Staff Development and Training Unit, since 1989; Professional Conduct Committee, General Council of the Bar, since 1990; *b* 18 July 1922; *er s* of late Ernest Graham and Ivy Hutchinson, Cleator, Cumbria; *m* 1945, Ann Winifred Muriel Taylor. *Educ:* Workington Techn. Sch.; Leyton Techn. Coll.; Univ. of London (external). Engrg apprentice, 1938–42; Wartime Radar Research Unit, 1942–45; Air Trng Sch., qual. licensed engr, Air Registration Bd, 1947; employed in private industry, Mins of Aircraft Prodn and Supply, BOAC, and RN Scientific Service. Joined AEU, 1938: Mem. Final Appeal Court, Nat. Cttee, Divisional Chm., District Pres., etc, 1947–61; Tutor (part-time) in Trade Union Studies, Univ. of Southampton and WEA, 1958–61; joined TUC Organisation Dept, 1961, Head of TUC Organisation and Industrial Relations Dept, 1966–77. Comr, MSC, 1974–87; Member: Council, Inst. of Manpower Studies, 1975–; Bd, European Foundn for Improvement of Living and Working Conditions, 1976–87; Adv. Cttee, European Social Fund, 1976–87; Council, Templeton Coll. (Oxford Centre for Management Studies), 1984–; NCVQ, 1986–; Interim Adv. Cttee to Sec. of State for Educn and Sci., on Teachers' Pay and Conditions, 1987–89; Employment Appeal Tribunal, 1989–. A Vice-Pres., Golden Jubilee Appeal, Airborne Forces Charities Develt Trust, 1990–. FRSA, 1987. Hon. LLD CNAA, 1986. Special Award of Merit, AEU, 1981; TUC Trades Councils Silver Badge for Merit, 1987; TUC Congress Gold Badge, 1987. *Publication:* contrib. Job Satisfaction: Challenge and Response in Modern Britain, 1976. *Recreations:* music, military history. *Address:* 90 Springfield Drive, Ilford, Essex IG2 6QS. *T:* 081–554 0839.

GRAHAM, (Malcolm Gray) Douglas; Chairman, The Midland News Association Ltd, since 1984 (Deputy Chairman, 1978–84); *b* 18 Feb. 1930; *s* of Malcolm Graham and Annie Jeanette Robinson; *m* 1980, Sara Anne Elwell (*née* Anderson). *Educ:* Shrewsbury Sch. National Service, RM, 1948–50. Newspaper trng, UK and Australia, 1950–53; Dir, Express & Star (Wolverhampton) Ltd, 1957. President: Young Newspapermen's Assoc., 1969; W Midlands Newspaper Soc., 1973–74; Chm., Evening Newspaper Advertising Bureau, 1978–79. *Recreation:* shooting. *Address:* Roughton Manor, Bridgnorth, Shropshire WV15 5HE. *T:* Worfield (07464) 209.

GRAHAM, Martin, QC 1976; **His Honour Judge Graham;** a Circuit Judge, since 1986; *b* 10 Feb. 1929; *m* 1962, Jane Filby; one *d*. *Educ:* Emanuel School; Trinity College, Oxford (Scholar; MA, PPE). Called to Bar, Middle Temple, 1952; a Recorder, 1986. Nat. Service, Officer BAOR, 1953–55. *Recreations:* swimming, tennis. *Address:* 1 Garden Court, Temple, EC4. *Clubs:* Reform, Royal Automobile, Hurlingham.

GRAHAM, Sir Norman (William), Kt 1971; CB 1961; FRSE; Secretary, Scottish Education Department, 1964–73, retired; *b* 11 Oct. 1913; *s* of William and Margaret Graham; *m* 1949, Catherine Mary Strathie; two *s* one *d*. *Educ:* High Sch. of Glasgow; Glasgow Univ. Dept of Health for Scotland, 1936; Private Sec. to Permanent Under-Sec. of State, 1939–40; Ministry of Aircraft Production, 1940; Principal Private Sec. to Minister, 1944–45; Asst Sec., Dept of Health for Scotland, 1945; Under-Sec., Scottish Home and Health Dept, 1956–63. Hon. DLitt Heriot-Watt, 1971; DUniv Stirling, 1974. *Recreations:* golf, gardening. *Address:* 6 The Steading, Chesterhall, Longniddry, East Lothian EH32 0PQ. *T:* Longniddry (0875) 52130. *Club:* New (Edinburgh).
See also J. S. Graham.

GRAHAM, Hon. Sir Patrick; *see* Graham, Hon. Sir J. P.

GRAHAM, Peter, CB 1982; QC 1990; First Parliamentary Counsel since 1991; *b* 7 Jan. 1934; *o s* of late Alderman Douglas Graham, CBE, Huddersfield, and Ena May (*née* Jackson); *m* 1st, Judith Mary Dunbar; two *s*; 2nd, Anne Silvia Garcia (*see* A. S. Graham). *Educ:* St Bees Sch., Cumberland (scholar); St John's Coll., Cambridge (scholar, 1st cl. Law Tripos, MA, LLM, McMahon Law Studentship). Served as pilot in Fleet Air Arm, 1952–55, Lieut, RNR. Called to Bar, Gray's Inn, 1958 (Holker Exhbn; H. C. Richards Prize, Ecclesiastical Law), Lincoln's Inn, 1982; joined Parliamentary Counsel Office, 1959; Parly Counsel, 1972–86; Second Parly Counsel, 1987–91. External Examr (Legislation), Univ. of Edinburgh, 1977–81; with Law Commn, 1979–81. Hon. Legal Adviser, Historic Vehicle Clubs Cttee, 1967–86. *Recreations:* village church organist, gardening, bridge. *Address:* Stony Dale, Field Broughton, Grange over Sands, Cumbria LA11 6HN. *Club:* Sette of Odd Volumes.

GRAHAM, Sir Peter (Alfred), Kt 1987; OBE 1969; FCIB, CBIM; Chairman, Crown Agents for Oversea Governments and Administrations, 1983–90; *b* 25 May 1922; *s* of Alfred Graham and Margaret (*née* Winder); *m* 1953, Luned Mary (*née* Kenealy-Jones); two *s* two *d*. *Educ:* St Joseph's Coll., Beulah Hill. FIB 1975; CBIM 1981. Served War, RNVR: Pilot, FAA. Joined The Chartered Bank of India, Australia and China, 1947; 24 yrs overseas banking career, incl. appts in Japan, India and Hong Kong; i/c The Chartered Bank, Hong Kong, 1962–70; Chm. (1st), Hong Kong Export Credit Insurance Corp., 1965–70; General Manager 1970, Dep. Man. Dir 1975, Gp Man. Dir, 1977–83, Sen. Dep. Chm., 1983–87, Chm., 1987–88, Standard Chartered Bank, London. Director: Standard Chartered Finance Ltd, Sydney (formerly Mutual Acceptance Corp.), 1974–87; First Bank Nigeria, Lagos, 1976–87; Union Bank Inc., Los Angeles, 1979–88; Singapore Land Ltd, 1988–89; Employment Conditions Abroad Ltd, 1988–; Chairman: Standard Chartered Merchant Bank Ltd, 1977–83; Mocatta Commercial Ltd, 1983–87; Mocatta & Goldsmid Ltd, 1983–87; Equatorial Bank, 1989–; Deputy Chairman: Chartered Trust plc, 1983–85; Governing Body, ICC UK, 1985–; Mem., Bd of Banking Supervision, 1986–87; Pres., Inst. of Bankers, 1981–83. City University: Chm., Adv. Cttee, 1981–86, Council, 1986–, Business Sch.; Chm., Council, 1986–. Formerly Chm., Exchange Banks' Assoc., Hong Kong; Mem., Govt cttees connected with trade and industry, Hong Kong.

Hon. DSc City Univ., 1985. *Recreations:* golf, tennis, ski-ing. *Address:* Heron Lea, Hobbs Lane, Beckley, near Rye, Sussex TN31 6TT. *Clubs:* Naval, Royal Automobile; Hong Kong (Hong Kong); Rye Golf.

GRAHAM, Lt.-Gen. Sir Peter Walter, KCB 1991; CBE 1981 (OBE 1978; MBE 1972); GOC Scotland and Governor of Edinburgh Castle, since 1991; *b* 14 March 1937; *s* of Dr Walter Graham and Suzanne Graham (*née* Simon); *m* 1963, Alison Mary, MB ChB, MRCGP, *d* of D. B. Morren, TD; three *s*. *Educ:* Fyvie Village School, Aberdeenshire; Hall Sch., Hampstead; St Paul's Sch.; RMA Sandhurst; ocds (Can), psc (Aust). Commissioned, The Gordon Highlanders, 1956; regtl appts, Dover, BAOR, Scotland, Kenya, 1957–62; HQ Highland Bde, 1962–63; Adjt, 1 Gordons, Kenya, Scotland, Borneo (despatches), 1963–66; Staff Capt., HQ (1 Br) Corps, 1966–67; Aust. Staff Coll., 1968; Co. Comdr, 1 Gordons, BAOR, 1969–70; Bde Maj., 39 Inf. Bde, 1970–72; 1 Gordons, Scotland, Ulster, Singapore, 1972–74; MA to Adjt-Gen., 1974–75; CO, 1 Gordons, Scotland, Ulster, 1976–78; COS, HQ 3rd Armd Div., BAOR, 1978–82; Comdr UDR, 1982–84 (despatches); Nat. Defence Coll., Canada, 1984–85; Dep. Mil. Sec., MoD, 1985–87; GOC Eastern Dist, 1987–89; Comdt, RMA, Sandhurst, 1989–91. Col, The Gordon Highlanders, 1986–. Mem., Royal Company of Archers, Queen's Body Guard for Scotland, 1986. *Publications:* (with Pipe Major B. MacRae) The Gordon Highlanders Pipe Music Collection, Vol. 1, 1983, 3rd edn 1986, Vol. 2, 1985; (contrib.) John Baynes, Soldiers of Scotland, 1988; contrib. to Jl of RUSI. *Recreations:* stalking, hill walking, fishing, shooting, reading, pipe music, gardening under wife's directions. *Address:* Headquarters Scotland (Army), Edinburgh EH1 2YX. *Club:* Caledonian.
See also Sir A. M. Graham.

GRAHAM, Prof. Philip Jeremy; Professor of Child Psychiatry, Institute of Child Health, University of London, since 1975; *b* 3 Sept. 1932; *s* of Jacob Rackham Graham and Pauline Graham; *m* 1960, Nori (*née* Burawoy); two *s* one *d*. *Educ:* Perse Sch., Cambridge; Cambridge Univ. (MA); University Coll. Hosp., London. FRCP 1973; FRCPsych 1972. Consultant Psychiatrist: Maudsley Hosp., London, 1966–68; Hosp. for Sick Children, Great Ormond Street, London, 1968–74; Dean, Inst. of Child Health, London Univ., 1985–90. Pres., European Soc. for Child and Adolescent Psychiatry, 1987–; Chm., Child Policy Rev. Gp, Nat. Children's Bureau, 1987–89. *Publications:* A Neuropsychiatric Study in Childhood (jtly), 1970; (ed) Epidemiological Approaches to Child Psychiatry, 1977; Child Psychiatry: a developmental approach, 1986, 2nd edn 1991; various publications on child and adolescent psychiatry. *Recreations:* reading, play-going, tennis. *Address:* Department of Child Psychiatry, Hospital for Sick Children, Great Ormond Street, WC1N 3JH

GRAHAM, Sir Ralph Stuart, 14th Bt *cr* 1629 (NS), of Esk, Cumberland; *b* 5 Nov. 1950; *s* of Sir Ralph Wolfe Graham, 13th Bt and of Geraldine, *d* of Austin Velour; *S* father, 1988; *m* 1st, 1972, Roxanne (*d* 1978), *d* of Mrs Lovette Gurzan; 2nd, 1979, Deena Vandergrift; one adopted *s*. *Heir:* *b* Robert Bruce Graham [*b* 14 Nov. 1953; *m* 1974, Denise, *d* of T. Juranich; two *s*].

GRAHAM, Robert Martin; Chief Executive, British United Provident Association, 1984–91; *b* 20 Sept. 1930; *s* of Francis P. Graham and Margaret M. Graham (*née* Broderick); *m* 1959, Eileen (*née* Hoey); two *s* two *d*. *Educ:* Dublin; ACII. Hibernian Fire and General Insurance Co. Ltd, 1948–57; Voluntary Health Insurance Board, 1957–82 (to Chief Exec.); Dep. Chief Exec., BUPA 1982. Chm., Board of Management, Meath Hosp., 1972–82; Pres., Internat. Fedn of Voluntary Health Service Funds, 1988–90 (Dep. Pres., 1986–88); Vice-Pres., Assoc. Internationale de la Mutualité, 1990– (Mem. Bd of Govs, 1978–91); Mem., Central Council, Federated Voluntary Hosps, Ireland, 1978–82. *Address:* 20 Hampton Grove, Ewell, Epsom, Surrey KT17 1LA. *T:* 081–393 2837. *Clubs:* Royal Automobile, Rotary Club of London.

GRAHAM, Dr Ronald Cairns; General Manager, Tayside Health Board, since 1985 (Chief Administrative Medical Officer, 1973–85); *b* 8 Oct. 1931; *s* of Thomas Graham and Helen Cairns; *m* 1959, Christine Fraser Osborne; two *s* one *d*. *Educ:* Airdrie Acad.; Glasgow Univ. MB, ChB Glasgow 1956; DipSocMed Edin. 1968; FFCM 1973; FRCPE 1983. West of Scotland; house jobs, gen. practice and geriatric med., 1956–62; Dep. Med. Supt, Edin. Royal Infirmary, 1962–65; Asst Sen. Admin. MO, SE Regional Hosp. Bd, 1965–69; Dep. and then Sen. Admin. MO, Eastern Regional Hosp. Bd, 1969–73. *Recreation:* fishing. *Address:* 34 Dalgleish Road, Dundee DD4 7JT. *T:* Dundee (0382) 455426.

GRAHAM, Sir Samuel Horatio, Kt 1988; CMG 1965; OBE 1962; **Mr Justice Graham;** Chief Justice of Grenada, since 1987; *b* Trinidad, 3 May 1912; *o s* of late Rev. Benjamin Graham and Mrs Graham, Trinidad; *m* 1943, Oris Gloria (*née* Teka); two *s* four *d*. *Educ:* Barbados; External Student, London Univ. BA (London) 1945; LLB (London) 1949. Teacher and journalist until called to Bar, Gray's Inn, 1949. Private practice as Barrister in Grenada, 1949–53; Magistrate, St Lucia, 1953–57; Crown Attorney, St Kitts, 1957–59; Attorney-General, St Kitts, 1960–62; Administrator of St Vincent, 1962–66; Puisne Judge, British Honduras, 1966–69; Pres., Industrial Court of Antigua, 1969–70, Associate Pres., 1981–84; Puisne Judge, Supreme Court of the Commonwealth of the Bahamas, 1973–78. Acted Chief Justice: British Honduras, Feb.-May 1968; Bahamas, Oct. 1977; Temp. Judge, Belize Court of Appeal, 1980. Judicial Mem., Bermuda Constituencies Boundaries Commn, 1979. Chairman: Grenada Develt Bank, 1985–87; Grenada Industrial Develt Corp., 1985–87. Mem., Council of Legal Educn, WI, 1971–. Chairman Inquiries into: Income Tax Reliefs; Coconut Industry, St Lucia, 1955; Legislators' Salaries, St Kitts, 1962. Acted Administrator of St Lucia, St Kitts and Dominica on various occasions. CStJ 1964. *Recreations:* bridge, swimming. *Address:* PO Box 99, St George's, Grenada, West Indies.

GRAHAM, (Stewart) David, QC 1977; Director, Cork Gully, since 1985; *b* 27 Feb. 1934; *s* of late Lewis Graham and of Gertrude Graham; *m* 1959, Corinne Carmona; two *d*. *Educ:* Leeds Grammar Sch.; St Edmund Hall, Oxford (MA, BCL). Called to the Bar, Middle Temple, 1957; Harmsworth Law Scholar, 1958. Member: Council of Justice, 1976–; Insolvency Rules Adv. Cttee, 1984–86; Chm., Law, Parly and Gen. Purposes Cttee, Bd of Deputies of British Jews, 1983–88. Chm. Editorial Bd, Insolvency Intelligence, 1988–. *Publications:* (ed jtly) Williams and Muir Hunter on Bankruptcy, 18th edn 1968, 19th edn 1979; (contrib.) Longman's Insolvency, 1986; (ed) legal textbooks. *Recreations:* biography, music, travel. *Address:* (office) Shelley House, 3 Noble Street, EC2V 7DQ. *T:* 071–606 7700; (home) 133 London Road, Stanmore, Mddx HA7 4PQ. *T:* 081–954 3783.

GRAHAM, Stuart Twentyman, CBE 1981; DFC 1943; FCIS, FCIB; Chairman, Aitken Hume Bank Ltd, since 1985; *b* 26 Aug. 1921; *s* of late Twentyman Graham; *m* 1948, Betty June Cox; one *s*. *Educ:* Kilburn Grammar Sch. Served War, 1940–46: commissioned, RAF, 1942. Entered Midland Bank, 1938; Jt Gen. Manager, 1966–70; Asst Chief Gen. Manager, 1970–74; Chief Gen. Manager, 1974–81; Gp Chief Exec., 1981–82; Dir, 1974–85. Chairman: Northern Bank Ltd, 1982–85; International Commodities Clearing House Ltd, 1982–86; Director: Allied Lyons plc, 1981–; Sheffield Forgemasters Holdings, 1983–85; Aitken Hume International, 1985–; Efamol Hldgs, 1985–. *Recreations:* music, reading. *Club:* Royal Air Force.

GRAHAM, Thomas; MP (Lab) Renfrew West and Inverclyde, since 1987; *b* 1944; *m* Joan Graham; two *s*. Former engineer with Rolls-Royce; manager, solicitors' office. Mem., Strathclyde Reg. Council, 1978–. *Address:* c/o House of Commons, SW1A 0AA; 265 Gilmartin Road, Linwood, Paisley PA3 3SU.

GRAHAM, Walter Gerald Cloete, CBE 1952; retired 1975; *b* 13 May 1906; *s* of late Lance Graham Cloete Graham, of HBM Consular Service in China; *m* 1937, Nellor Alice Lee Swan; one *s*; *m* 1949, Cynthia Anne, *d* of late Sir George Clayton East, Bt; one *s* one *d*. *Educ:* Malvern Coll.; The Queen's Coll., Oxford. Laming Travelling Fellow of Queen's, 1927–29. Entered Consular Service in China, 1928; served in Peking, Nanking, Shanghai, Mukden Chefoo and Tientsin; Consul: Port Said, 1942–44, Chengtu, 1944–45, Urumchi (Chinese Turkestan), 1945–47; Consul-General, Mukden, 1947–49; Chinese Counsellor, Peking, 1949–50; Counsellor, Foreign Office, 1951–52; Minister to Republic of Korea, 1952–54; Ambassador to Libya, 1955–59; Asia Adviser to Defence Intelligence Staff (formerly Jt Intell. Bureau), Min. of Defence, 1959–67; Res. Adviser, FCO Res. Dept, 1967–75. *Recreations:* golf, watching cricket, gardening. *Address:* Knabb's Farmhouse, Fletching, Uckfield, Sussex TN22 3SX. *T:* Newick (082572) 2198.

GRAHAM, Rear-Adm. Wilfred Jackson, CB 1979; *b* 17 June 1925; *s* of William Bryce Graham and Jean Hill Graham (*née* Jackson); *m* 1951, Gillian Mary Finlayson; three *s* one *d*. *Educ:* Rossall Sch., Fleetwood, Lancs. Served War of 1939–45, Royal Navy: Cadet, 1943; specialised in gunnery, 1951; Comdr 1960; Captain 1967; IDC, 1970; Captain, HMS Ark Royal, 1975–76; Flag Officer, Portsmouth, 1976–79, retired. Dir and Sec., RNLI, 1979–87. Mem. Council, Rossall Sch., 1988–. FNI 1987. *Recreations:* sailing, walking. *Address:* Driscolls, Horsebridge Road, Broughton, near Stockbridge, Hants SO20 8BD. *Clubs:* Royal Naval Sailing Association, Royal Yacht Squadron, Royal Lymington Yacht.

GRAHAM, William Franklin, (Billy Graham); Evangelist; *b* Charlotte, NC, 7 Nov. 1918; *s* of late William Franklin Graham and Morrow (*née* Coffey); *m* 1943, Ruth McCue Bell; two *s* three *d*. *Educ:* Florida Bible Institute, Tampa (ThB); Wheaton Coll., Ill (AB). Ordained to Baptist ministry, 1940; first Vice-Pres., Youth for Christ Internat., 1946–48; Pres., Northwestern Coll., Minneapolis, 1947–52; Evangelistic campaigns, 1946–; world-wide weekly broadcast, 1950–; many evangelistic tours of Great Britain, Europe, the Far East, South America, Australia and Russia. Chairman, Board of World Wide Pictures Inc. FRGS. Holds numerous honorary degrees in Divinity, Laws, Literature and the Humanities, from American universities and colleges; also varied awards from organisations, 1954–, inc. Templeton Foundn Prize, 1982; President's Medal of Freedom Award, 1983. *Publications include:* Peace with God, 1954; World Aflame, 1965; Jesus Generation, 1971; Angels—God's Secret Agents, 1975; How to be Born Again, 1977; The Holy Spirit, 1978; Till Armageddon, 1981; Approaching Hoofbeats: the four horsemen of the Apocalypse, 1983; A Biblical Standard for Evangelists, 1984; Unto the Hills, 1986; Facing Death and the Life After, 1987; Answers to Life's Problems, 1988. *Recreations:* swimming, aerobic walking. *Address:* (office) 1300 Harmon Place, Minneapolis, Minnesota 55403, USA. *T:* (612) 338–0500.

GRAHAM, (William) Gordon, MC 1944 (Bar 1945); FRSA; Editor, LOGOS, since 1990; Group Chairman, Butterworth Publishers, 1975–90 (Chief Executive, 1974–87); *b* 17 July 1920; *s* of Thomas Graham and Marion Hutcheson; *m* 1st, 1943, Margaret Milne, Bombay (*d* 1946); one *d*; 2nd, 1948, Friedel Gramm, Zürich; one *d*. *Educ:* Hutchesons' Grammar Sch.; Glasgow Univ. (MA 1940). Commissioned, Queen's Own Cameron Highlanders, 1941; served in India and Burma, 1942–46: Captain 1944, Major 1945; GSO II India Office, 1946. Newspaper correspondent and publishers' representative in India, 1946–55; Internat. Sales Manager, 1956–63, Vice-Pres., 1961, McGraw-Hill Book Co., New York; US citizen, 1963; Man. Dir, McGraw-Hill Publishing Co., UK, 1963–74; Director: W & R Chambers, Edinburgh, 1974–83; International Publishing Corp., 1975–82; Reed Publishing Gp, 1982–90; Chairman: Internat. Electronic Publishing Res. Centre Ltd, 1981–84; Publishers Database Ltd, 1982–84; Bd, R. R. Bowker Co., 1986–90. Chm., Soc. of Bookmen, 1972–75; Publishers Association: Mem. Council, 1972–87; Chm., Electronic Publishing Panel, 1980–83; Vice Pres., 1984–85, 1987–88; Pres., 1985–87. Mem. Board, British Libr., 1980–86. Correspondent, Christian Science Monitor, 1946–56. FRSA 1978. *Publications:* articles in US and British trade press. *Recreations:* ski-ing, writing, fostering transatlantic understanding, landscape gardening. *Address:* White Lodge, Beechwood Drive, Marlow, Bucks SL7 2DH. *T:* Marlow (0628) 483371; Juniper Acres, East Hill, Keene, New York State, USA.

GRAHAM, Winston Mawdsley, OBE 1983; FRSL; *b* Victoria Park, Manchester; *m* 1939, Jean Mary Williamson; one *s* one *d*. Chm., Soc. of Authors, 1967–69. Books trans. into 17 languages. *Publications:* some early novels (designedly) out of print, and: Night Journey, 1941 (rev. edn 1966); The Merciless Ladies, 1944 (rev. edn 1979); The Forgotten Story, 1945 (ITV prodn, 1983); Ross Poldark, 1945; Demelza, 1946; Take My Life, 1947 (filmed 1947); Cordelia, 1949; Night Without Stars, 1950 (filmed 1950); Jeremy Poldark, 1950; Fortune is a Woman, 1953 (filmed 1956); Warleggan, 1953; The Little Walls, 1955; The Sleeping Partner, 1956 (filmed 1958; ITV prodn, 1967); Greek Fire, 1957; The Tumbled House, 1959; Marnie, 1961 (filmed 1963); The Grove of Eagles, 1963 (Book Society Choice); After the Act, 1965; The Walking Stick, 1967 (filmed 1970); Angell, Pearl and Little God, 1970; The Japanese Girl (short stories), 1971; The Spanish Armadas, 1972; The Black Moon, 1973; Woman in the Mirror, 1975; The Four Swans, 1976; The Angry Tide, 1977; The Stranger from the Sea, 1981; The Miller's Dance, 1982; Poldark's Cornwall, 1983; The Loving Cup, 1984; The Green Flash, 1986; Cameo, 1988; The Twisted Sword, 1990. BBC TV Series Poldark (the first four Poldark novels), 1975–76, second series (the next three Poldark novels), 1977; Circumstantial Evidence (play), 1979. *Recreations:* golf, gardening. *Address:* Abbotswood House, Buxted, East Sussex TN22 4PB. *Clubs:* Savile, Beefsteak.
See also A. W. M. Graham.

GRAHAM-BRYCE, Ian James, DPhil; Head of Environmental Affairs Division, Shell Internationale Petroleum Maatschappij BV, since 1986; *b* 20 March 1937; *s* of late Alexander Graham-Bryce, FRCS, and of Dame Isabel Graham-Bryce, *qv*; *m* 1959, Anne Elisabeth Metcalf; one *s* three *d*. *Educ:* William Hulme's Grammar Sch., Manchester; University Coll., Oxford (Exhibnr). BA, MA, BSc, DPhil (Oxon); FRSC, CChem 1981. Research Asst, Univ. of Oxford, 1958–61; Lectr, Dept of Biochemistry and Soil Sci., UCNW, Bangor, 1961–64; Sen. Scientific Officer, Rothamsted Exper. Station, 1964–70; Sen. Res. Officer, ICI Plant Protection Div., Jealott's Hill Res. Station, Bracknell, Berks, 1970–72; Special Lectr in Pesticide Chemistry, Dept of Zoology and Applied Entomology, Imperial Coll. of Science and Technology, 1970–72 (Vis. Prof., 1976–79); Rothamsted Experimental Station: Head, Dept of Insecticides and Fungicides, 1972–79; Dep. Director, 1975–79; Dir, East Malling Res. Stn, Maidstone, Kent, 1979–86 (Trustee, Develt and Endowment Fund, 1986–); Cons. Dir, Commonwealth Bureau of Horticulture and Plantation Crops, 1979–86; Hon. Lectr, Dept of Biology, Univ. of Strathclyde, 1977–80.

Society of Chemical Industry, London: Pres., 1982–84; Mem. Council, 1969–72 and 1974–89; Hon. Sec., Home Affairs, 1977–80; Chm., Pesticides Gp, 1978–80; Sec., Physico-Chemical and Biophysical Panel, 1968–70, Chm., 1973–75; Mem., British Nat. Cttee for Chemistry, 1982–84. Pres., Assoc. of Applied Biologists, 1988 (Vice-Pres., 1985–87). Chm., Agrochemical Planning Gp, IOCD, 1985–88; Mem., Scientific Cttee, Eur. Chemical Industry Ecol. and Toxicol. Centre, 1988–; Vice-Chm., Environmental Res. Wkg Gp, Industrial R&D Adv. Cttee to EC, 1988–; Mem., NERC, 1989–. Governor: Wye Coll., 1979–86, Imperial Coll., 1985–, Univ. of London. Member, Editorial Board: Chemico-Biological Interactions, 1973–77; Pesticide Science, 1978–80; Agriculture, Ecosystems and Environment, 1978–87. *Publications:* Physical Aspects of Pesticide Behaviour, 1980; papers on soil science, plant nutrition and crop protection in sci. jls. *Recreations:* music (espec. opera), fly fishing, windsurfing. *Address:* HSE/3 Shell Internationale Petroleum Maatschappij BV, Postbus 162, 2501 AN Den Haag, Netherlands. *Club:* Athenæum.

GRAHAM-BRYCE, Dame Isabel, DBE 1968; Chairman: Oxford Regional Hospital Board, 1963–72; National Nursing Staff Committee, 1967–75; National Staff Committee, 1969–75; Consultant, British Transport Hotels, 1979–81 (Board Member, 1962–79); Vice-President, Princess Christian College, Manchester, since 1953; *b* 30 April 1902; *d* of late Prof. James Lorrain Smith, FRS; *m* 1934, Alexander Graham-Bryce, FRCS (*d* 1968); two *s. Educ:* St Leonards Sch., St Andrews; Edinburgh Univ. (MA). Investigator, Industrial Fatigue Research Board, 1926–27; HM Inspector of Factories, 1928–34; Centre Organiser, WVS, Manchester, 1938–39; Dir of Organization, Ontario Div., Canadian WVS, 1941–42; Tech. Adviser, American WVS, 1942–43; Res. Fellow Fatigue Lab. Harvard Univ., 1943–44; Nat. Council of Women: Chm., Manchester Br., 1947–50; Vice-Chm., Education Cttee, 1950–51; Mem., Oxford Assoc., 1987–. JP and Mem. Juvenile Court Panel, Manchester City, 1949–55; Vice-Chairman: Assoc. of HMC's, 1953–55; Bd of Visitors, Grendon Prison, 1962–67. Member: Nurses and Midwives Whitley Council, 1953–57; General Nursing Council, 1956–61; Bd of Governors, Eastman Dental Hosp., 1957–63; Maternity and Midwifery Standing Cttee, 1957–72; Public Health Insp., Education Bd, 1958–64; Independent Television Authority, 1960–65 (Chm., General Advisory Council, 1964–65); Bd, ATV Network Ltd, 1968–72; Ancillary Dental Workers Cttee, 1956–68; Experimental Scheme for Dental Auxiliaries, 1958–69. President: Goring and Dist. Day Centre for the Elderly, 1980–89; League of Friends, Radcliffe Infirmary, Oxford, 1988–; Patron, Oxford Br., Motor Neurone Disease Assoc., 1990–. Life Mem., British Fedn Univ. Women. Hon. Mem., Oxford Br., Zouta International. *Publications:* (joint) reports on research into industrial psychological problems. *Address:* 1 Quinton House, 98 Woodstock Road, Oxford OX2 7NE.
See also I. J. Graham-Bryce.

GRAHAM-CAMPBELL, David John, MA Cantab; Liaison Officer to Schools, Aberdeen University, 1972–76; *b* 18 Feb. 1912; *s* of late Sir R. F. Graham-Campbell; *m* 1940, Joan Sybil, *d* of late Major H. F. Maclean; three *s. Educ:* Eton Coll.; Trinity Coll., Cambridge (Exhibitioner). Master, Eton Coll., 1935–64 (Housemaster 1950–64); Warden, Trinity Coll., Glenalmond, 1964–72. Served with 2nd Bn KRRC and on the staff, 1939–45 (Lt-Col). *Publications:* Writing English, 1953; Portrait of Argyll and the Southern Hebrides, 1978; Portrait of Perth, Angus and Fife, 1979; Scotland's Story in her Monuments, 1982. *Address:* 17 Muirton Bank, Perth, Perthshire PH1 5DW.

GRAHAM-DIXON, Anthony Philip, QC 1973; *b* 5 Nov. 1929; *s* of late Leslie Charles Graham-Dixon, QC; *m* 1956, Margaret Suzanne Villar; one *s* one *d. Educ:* Westminster School; Christ Church, Oxford. MA (1st Cl. Hon. Mods, 1st Cl. Lit. Hum.). RNVR, 1953–55, Lieut (SP). Called to the Bar, Inner Temple, 1956, Bencher 1982; Member of Gray's Inn, 1965–. Mem. Council, Charing Cross Hosp. Medical School, 1976–83. Chm., London Concertino Ltd, 1982–. Dep. Chm., PHLS, 1988– (Bd Mem., 1987–). Gov., Bedales Sch., 1988–. Trustee, SPNM, 1988–. *Publication:* (mem. adv. bd) Competition Law in Western Europe and the USA, 1976. *Recreations:* music (especially opera), gardening, tennis. *Address:* 31 Hereford Square, SW7 4NB. *T:* 071–370 1902; Masketts Manor, Nutley, Uckfield, East Sussex. *T:* Nutley (082571) 2719.

GRAHAM HALL, Jean; *see* Hall, J. G.

GRAHAM-HARRISON, Francis Laurence Theodore, CB 1962; Deputy Under-Secretary of State, Home Office, 1963–74; *b* 30 Oct. 1914; *s* of late Sir William Montagu Graham-Harrison, KCB, KC, and Lady Graham-Harrison, *d* of Sir Cyril Graham, 5th and last Bt, CMG; *m* 1941, Carol Mary St John, 3rd *d* of late Sir Francis Stewart, CIE; one *s* three *d. Educ:* Eton; Magdalen Coll., Oxford. Entered Home Office, 1938. Private Secretary to Parliamentary Under-Secretary of State, 1941–43; Asst Private Secretary to Prime Minister, 1946–49; Secretary, Royal Commission on Capital Punishment, 1949–53; Asst Secretary, Home Office, 1953–57; Asst Under-Secretary of State, Home Office, 1957–63. Chm., Nat. Sound Archive Adv. Cttee, British Library, 1984–88; Trustee: Tate Gallery, 1975–82; Nat. Gallery, 1981–82. Gov., Thomas Coram Foundn, 1975–. Chm., Exec. Finance Cttee, Dr Barnardo's, 1978–81. *Address:* 32 Parliament Hill, NW3 2TN. *T:* 071–435 6316.
See also R. M. Graham-Harrison.

GRAHAM-HARRISON, Robert Montagu; UK Alternate Executive Director, World Bank, Washington, since 1989; *b* 16 Feb. 1943; *s* of Francis Laurence Theodore Graham-Harrison, *qv*; *m* 1977, Kathleen Patricia Maher; two *d. Educ:* Eton Coll.; Magdalen Coll., Oxford. VSO India, 1965; GLC, 1966; Min. of Overseas Development (later Overseas Development Administration), 1967; World Bank, Washington, 1971–73; Private Sec. to Minister for Overseas Development, 1978; Asst Sec., ODA, 1979; Hd, British Develt Div. in E Africa, Nairobi, 1982–86; Hd, E Asia Dept, ODA, 1986–89. *Address:* c/o Foreign and Commonwealth Office, SW1.

GRAHAM-MOON, Sir Peter Wilfred Giles; *see* Moon.

GRAHAM-SMITH, Sir Francis; *see* Smith.

GRAHAM-TOLER, family name of the **Earl of Norbury.**

GRAHAME-SMITH, Prof. David Grahame; Professor of Clinical Pharmacology, University of Oxford, since 1972; Hon. Director: Medical Research Council Unit of Clinical Pharmacology, Radcliffe Infirmary, Oxford, since 1972; Smith Kline Beecham Centre of Applied Neuropsychobiology, Oxford University, since 1990; Fellow of Corpus Christi College, Oxford, since 1972; *b* 10 May 1933; *s* of George E. and C. A. Smith; *m* 1957, Kathryn Frances, *d* of Dr F. R. Beetham; two *s. Educ:* Wyggeston Grammar Sch., Leicester; St Mary's Hosp. Medical Sch., Univ. of London. MB, BS (London) 1956; MRCS, LRCP 1956; MRCP 1958; PhD (London) 1966; FRCP 1972. House Phys., Paddington Gen. Hosp., London, 1956; House Surg., Battle Hosp., Reading, 1956–57. Captain, RAMC, 1957–60. Registrar and Sen. Registrar in Medicine, St Mary's Hosp., Paddington, 1960–61; H. A. M. Thompson Research Scholar, RCP, 1961–62; Saltwell Research Scholar, RCP, 1962–65; Wellcome Trust Research Fellow, 1965–66; Hon. Med. Registrar to Med. Unit, St Mary's Hosp., 1961–66; MRC Travelling Fellow, Dept of Endocrinology, Vanderbilt Univ., Nashville, Tennessee, USA, 1966–67; Sen. Lectr in Clinical Pharmacology and Therapeutics, St Mary's Hosp. Med. Sch., Univ. of London, 1967–71; Hon. Cons. Physician, St Mary's Hosp., Paddington, 1967–71. Vis. Prof., Peking Union Medical Coll., Beijing, China, 1985–. Member: Cttee on Safety of Medicines, 1975–86; Jt Cttee on Vaccination and Immunisation, 1987–89; Chairman: Adv. Gp on Hepatitis, 1987–89; Adv. Council on Misuse of Drugs, 1988–. *Publications:* (with J. K. Aronson) Oxford Textbook of Clinical Pharmacology and Drug Therapy, 1984; papers on biochemical, therapeutic and med. matters in scientific jls. *Recreations:* horse riding, jazz. *Address:* University Department and MRC Unit of Clinical Pharmacology, Radcliffe Infirmary, Woodstock Road, Oxford OX2 6HE. *T:* Oxford (0865) 241091.

GRAHAMSTOWN, Bishop of, since 1987; **Rt. Rev. David Hamilton Russell;** *b* 6 Nov. 1938; *s* of James Hamilton Russell and Kathleen Mary Russell; *m* 1980, Dorothea Madden; two *s. Educ:* Diocesan College, Rondebosch; Univ. of Cape Town (BA, PhD); Univ. of Oxford (MA). Assistant Priest, 1965–75; Chaplain to migrant workers, 1975–86; banned and house arrested by SA Government, 1977–82; Suffragan Bishop, Diocese of St John's, 1986. *Address:* 17 Durban Street, Grahamstown, South Africa; PO Box 162, Grahamstown, CP 6140, South Africa. *T:* (home) 0461 22500, (office) 0461 23460.

GRAINGER, Leslie, CBE 1976; BSc; FEng; MInstF; Chairman, Mountain Petroleum PLC, 1984–88; *b* 8 August 1917. Mem. for Science, NCB, 1966–77; Chairman: NCB (Coal Products) Ltd, 1975–78; NCB (IEA Services) Ltd, 1975–79; Man. Dir, Branon PLC, 1981–83; Dir, Cavendish Petroleum Plc, 1982–85 (Chm., 1982–84). *Publication:* Coal Utilisation: Technology, Economics and Policy (with J. G. Gibson), 1981. *Address:* 16 Blackamoor Lane, Maidenhead, Berks SL6 8RD. *T:* Maidenhead (0628) 23923.

GRANADO, Donald Casimir, TC 1970; *b* 4 March 1915; *m* 1959, Anne-Marie Faustin Lombard; one *s* two *d. Educ:* Trinidad. Gen. Sec., Union of Commercial and Industrial Workers, 1951–53; Sec./Treas., Fedn of Trade Unions, 1952–53; Elected MP for Laventille, Trinidad, 1956 and 1961; Minister of: Labour and Social Services, 1956–61; Health and Housing, and Dep. Leader House of Representatives, 1961–63. Ambassador to Venezuela, 1963–64; High Comr to Canada, 1964–69; Ambassador to Argentina and to Brazil, 1965–69; High Comr to London, 1969–71, and Ambassador to France, Germany, Belgium, Switzerland, Italy, Holland, Luxembourg and European Common Market, 1969–71. Led Trinidad and Tobago delegations to: India, Ceylon, Pakistan, 1958; CPA in Nigeria, Israel, Uganda, 1962; UN, 1965; St Lucia, 1966; attended Heads of Commonwealth Govts Conf., Singapore, 1971; rep. Trinidad and Tobago at missions to Grenada, Jamaica, France, and inaugurations of heads of govt of Chile and Brazil. First Gen. Sec., People's National Movement. Formerly: Vice-Chm., West India Cttee, London; Governor, Commonwealth Inst; Vice-Pres., Trinidad & Tobago Contract Bridge League. President: Fidelis Youth Club; National Golf Club; Vice-Pres., Trinidad & Tobago Golf Assoc., Hon. Mem., Potentials Sports Club. National Father of the Year 1981. Speaks, reads and writes French and Spanish. *Recreations:* cricket, soccer, bridge and golf; music (tape-recording), writing. *Address:* 20 Grove Road, Valsayn North, Trinidad, West Indies. *T:* 662–5905.

GRANARD, 9th Earl of, *cr* 1684; **Arthur Patrick Hastings Forbes,** AFC, 1941; Bt 1628; Viscount Granard and Baron Clanehugh, 1675; Baron Granard (UK), 1806; Air Commodore late RAFVR; *b* 10 April 1915; *e s* of 8th Earl of Granard, KP, PC, GCVO, and Beatrice (*d* 1972), OBE, *d* of Ogden Mills, Staatsburg, Dutchess County, USA; *S* father, 1948; *m* 1949, Marie-Madeleine Eugènie (*d* 1990), *y d* of Jean Maurel, Millau, Aveyron, formerly wife of late Prince Humbert de Faucigny Lucinge; two *d. Educ:* Eton; Trinity Coll., Cambridge. Served War of 1939–45 (despatches, AFC). Mem. Jockey Club of France. Commandeur Légion d'Honneur; Croix de Guerre with Palm; Officer Legion of Merit, USA; Croix des Vaillants of Poland; Order of George I of Greece. *Heir: nephew* Peter Arthur Edward Hastings Forbes, [*b* 15 March 1957; *m* Noreen Mitchell; three *s* one *d*]. *Address:* 11 rue Louis de Savoie, 1110 Morges, Switzerland. *Clubs:* White's, Pratt's; Kildare Street and University (Dublin); Royal St George's Yacht, Royal Yacht Squadron.
See also Marquess of Bute.

GRANBY, Marquis of; David Charles Robert Manners; *b* 8 May 1959; *s* and *heir* of 10th Duke of Rutland, *qv*. Dealer in antique weapons. Mem. Civilian cttee, ATC Sqdn, Grantham. Member: CLA Cttee for Leicestershire/Rutland; Successor Cttee, and Regional Cttee (E Midlands Area), HHA; Salmon and Trout Assoc.; Game Conservancy. President: Notts Rifle Assoc.; Ex-Aircrew Assoc., Grantham and Dist Br. Freeman, City of London; Liveryman, Gunsmiths' Co. Governor, RNLI, 1985–. *Recreations:* shooting, fishing. *Address:* The Old Saddlery, Belvoir, Grantham, Lincs NG32 1PD. *T:* Grantham (0476) 870798. *Clubs:* Turf; Annabel's.

GRANDY, Marshal of the Royal Air Force Sir John, GCB 1967 (KCB 1964; CB 1956); GCVO 1988; KBE 1961; DSO 1945; RAF; Constable and Governor of Windsor Castle, 1978–88; *b* Northwood, Middlesex, 8 Feb. 1913; *s* of late Francis Grandy and Nellie Grandy (*née* Lines); *m* 1937, Cecile Elizabeth Florence Rankin, CStJ, *yr d* of Sir Robert Rankin, 1st and last Bt; two *s. Educ:* University College Sch., London. Joined RAF 1931. No 54 (Fighter) Sqdn, 1932–35; 604 (Middx) Sqdn., RAuxAF, 1935–36; Adjt and Flying Instructor, London Univ. Air Sqdn, 1937–39; Comd No 249 (Fighter) Sqdn during Battle of Britain; Staff Duties, HQ Fighter Comd, and Wing Comdr Flying RAF Coltishall, 1941; commanded: RAF Duxford, 1942 (First Typhoon Wing); HQ No 210 Group, No 73 Op Training Unit, and Fighter Conversion Unit at Abu Sueir, 1943–44; No 341 Wing (Dakotas), SE Asia Comd, 1944–45; DSO 1945, despatches 1943 and 1945. SASO No 232 Gp, 1945; *psc* 1946; Dep. Dir Operational Training, Air Min., 1946; Air Attaché, Brussels, 1949; Comd Northern Sector, Fighter Comd, 1950; Air Staff HQ Fighter Comd, 1952–54; Comdt, Central Fighter Estab., 1954–57; *idc* 1957; Comdr, Task Force Grapple (British Nuclear Weapon Test Force), Christmas Is., 1957–58; Assistant CAS (Ops), 1958–61; Commander-in-Chief, RAF, Germany and Comdr, Second Allied TAF, 1961–63; AOC-in-C, Bomber Command, 1963–65; C-in-C, British Forces, Far East, and UK Mil. Adviser to SEATO, 1965–67; Chief of the Air Staff, 1967–71; Governor and C-in-C, Gibraltar, 1973–78. Dir, Brixton Estate Ltd, 1971–73, 1978–83; Trustee, Imperial War Museum, 1971–78 (Chm., 1978–89); Dep. Chm. Council, RAF Benevolent Fund, 1980–; Trustee: Burma Star Assoc., 1979– (Vice-Pres.); Shuttleworth Remembrance Trust, 1978–88 (Chm., Aerodrome Cttee, 1980–88); RAF Church, St Clement Danes, 1971–; Prince Philip Trust Fund, Windsor and Maidenhead, 1982–; past Pres., Officers' Assoc.; Vice-President: Officers' Pension Soc., 1971–; Nat. Assoc. of Boys' Clubs, 1971–; Life Vice-Pres., RNLI, 1988– (Vice-Pres., 1986–88, Mem. Management Cttee, 1971–); Friends of Gibraltar Heritage Soc., 1986–; President: Disablement in the City, 1980–; Berks Br., BLESMA, 1981–; Air League, 1984–87; Mem. Cttee, Royal Humane Soc., 1978–; Patron: King Edward VII League of Hosp. Friends, Windsor, 1979–88; Polish Air Force Assoc. in GB, 1979–. PMN 1967. Hon. Liveryman, Haberdashers' Co., 1968. Freeman, City of London, 1968. KStJ 1974. *Clubs:* White's, Pratt's, Buck's, Royal Air Force; Royal Yacht Squadron (Cowes); Swinley Forest Golf.

GRANGE, Kenneth Henry, CBE 1984; RDI, FCSD; industrial designer; in private practice since 1958; Founder Partner, Pentagram Design, since 1972; *b* 17 July 1929; *s* of

Harry Alfred Grange and Hilda Gladys (*née* Long). *Educ:* London. Technical Illustrator, RE, 1948–50; Design Asst, Arcon Chartered Architects, 1948; Bronek Katz & Vaughn, 1950–51; Gordon Bowyer & Partners, 1951–54; Jack Howe & Partners, 1954–58. Pres., CSD, 1987–88; Master of Faculty, RDI, 1985–87. RDI 1969; FCSD (FSIAD 1959). Hon. Prof., Heriot-Watt, 1987. Hon. Dr RCA, 1985; DUniv Heriot-Watt, 1986. 10 Design Council Awards; Duke of Edinburgh Award for Elegant Design, 1963. *Recreations:* tennis, ski-ing. *Address:* Pentagram, 11 Needham Road, W11 2RP.

GRANGER, Stewart; (James Lablache Stewart); actor (stage and films); *b* London, 6 May 1913; *s* of late Major James Stewart, RE, and Frederica Lablache; *m* 1st, Elspeth March (marr. diss., 1948); two *c*; 2nd, 1950, Jean Simmons, *qv* (marr. diss. 1960); one *c*; 3rd, 1964, Viviane Lecerf (marr. diss. 1969). *Educ:* Epsom Coll. Began training as doctor but decided to become an actor. Studied at Webber-Douglas School of Dramatic Art; played at Little Theatre, Hull, and with Birmingham Repertory Company; appeared at Malvern Festivals, 1936–37; first London appearance as Captain Hamilton in The Sun Never Sets, Drury Lane, 1938; appeared on London stage, 1938–39; joined Old Vic Company, 1939; Dr Fleming in Tony Draws a Horse, Criterion, 1940; George Winthrop in A House in the Square, St Martin's, 1940; toured, 1940; served War of 1939–45, Army, 1940–42 (invalided); toured, 1942; succeeded Owen Nares as Max de Winter in Rebecca, Lyric, 1942; returned to stage as Clive in The Circle, NY, 1989. Began film career in 1938, and has appeared in many films, including: The Man in Grey, The Lamp Still Burns, Fanny by Gaslight, Waterloo Road, Love Story, Madonna of the Seven Moons, Cæsar and Cleopatra, Caravan, The Magic Bow, Captain Boycott, Blanche Fury, Saraband for Dead Lovers, Woman Hater, Adam and Evelyne, King Solomon's Mines, Soldiers Three, Light Touch, Wild North, Scaramouche, Young Bess, Salome, Prisoner of Zenda, All the Brothers were Valiant, Beau Brummell, Footsteps in the Fog, Moonfleet, Green Fire, Bhowani Junction, Last Hunt, The Little Hut, Gun Glory, The Whole Truth, Harry Black and the Tiger, North to Alaska, Sodom and Gomorrah, Swordsman of Siena, The Secret Invasion, The Trygon Factor, Last Safari, The Wild Geese. *Publication:* Sparks Fly Upward (autobiog.), 1981.

GRANT, family name of **Baron Strathspey.**

GRANT, Alec Alan; a Master of the Supreme Court, Queen's Bench Division, since 1982; *b* 27 July 1932; *s* of late Emil Grant, OBE and Elsie Louise (*née* Marks). *Educ:* Highgate Sch.; Merton Coll., Oxford (MA). National Service, RA, 1951–52. Pres., Oxford Union, 1956. Called to the Bar, Middle Temple, 1957; practised at the Bar, 1958–82. Member: Mddx CC, 1961–65; GLC, 1964–67 and 1970–73; Governing Body, SOAS, 1965– (Vice-Chm., 1978–); Court of Governors, Thames Polytechnic, 1972– (Chm., 1982–85). *Recreations:* hill-walking, watching cricket. *Address:* Royal Courts of Justice, Strand, WC2A 2LL. *Clubs:* MCC; Austrian Alpine.

GRANT, Alexander (Marshall), CBE 1965; Artistic Director, National Ballet of Canada, 1976–83; *b* Wellington, New Zealand, 22 Feb. 1925; *s* of Alexander and Eleather Grant. *Educ:* Wellington Coll., NZ. Arrived in London, Feb. 1946, to study with Sadler's Wells School on Scholarship given in New Zealand by Royal Academy of Dancing, London; joined Sadler's Wells Ballet (now Royal Ballet Company), Aug. 1946. Dir, Ballet for All (touring ballet company), 1971–76 (Co-director, 1970–71). Senior Principal, English National Ballet (formerly London Festival Ballet), 1985–; Guest Artist: Royal Ballet, 1985–86; Joffrey Ballet, USA, 1987–88. Frequent judge at internat. ballet competitions, notably Jackson, Mississippi and Moscow. Danced leading rôles in following: Mam'zelle Angot, Clock Symphony, Boutique Fantasque, Donald of the Burthens, Rake's Progress, Job, Three Cornered Hat, Ballabile, Cinderella, Sylvia, Madame Chrysanthème, Façade, Daphnis and Chloé, Coppélia, Petrushka, Ondine, La Fille Mal Gardée, Jabez and the Devil, Perséphone, The Dream, Jazz Calendar, Enigma Variations, Sleeping Beauty (Carabosse), A Month in the Country, La Sylphide, The Nutcracker; *films:* Tales of Beatrix Potter (Peter Rabbit and Pigling Bland); Steps of the Ballet. *Recreations:* gardening, cinema going, cuisine.

GRANT, Alistair; *see* Grant, D. A. A.

GRANT, Alistair; *see* Grant, M. A.

GRANT, Allan Wallace, OBE 1974; MC 1941; TD 1947; President, Ecclesiastical Insurance Office Ltd, 1981–87 (Managing Director, 1971–77; Chairman, 1975–81); retired; *b* 2 Feb. 1911; *s* of late Henry Grant and late Rose Margaret Sheppard; *m* 1st, 1939, Kathleen Rachel Bamford (marr. diss. 1990); one *d*; 2nd, 1990, Mary Wyles. *Educ:* Dulwich Coll. LLB Hons (London). FCII. Eccles. Insurance Office, 1929; Chief Officer, 1952; Dir, 1966. Served War of 1939–45: Major, 2 i/c, 3rd Co. of London Yeomanry (Sharpshooters), N Africa, Sicily, Italy, NW Europe. Pres., Sharpshooters Assoc. Called to Bar, Gray's Inn, 1948. President: Insurance Inst. of London, 1966–67; Chartered Insce Inst., 1970–71; Insce Charities, 1973–74; Insce Orchestral Soc., 1973–74; Chairman: Insce Industry Training Council, 1973–75; Clergy Orphan Corp., 1967–80 (Vice-Pres., 1980); Coll. of All Saints, Tottenham, 1967–76; Chm., Allchurches Trust Ltd, 1975–85; Governor: St Edmund's Sch., Canterbury, 1967–; St Margaret's Sch., Bushey, 1967–; Mem., Policyholders Protection Bd, 1975–81; Treasurer: Historic Churches Preservation Trust, 1977–85; Soc. for Advancing Christian Faith, 1977–87. Master, Coopers' Co., 1984–85; Asst, Insurers' Co., 1979–86. Hon. DCanL Lexington, 1975. *Recreations:* golf, travel. *Address:* 5 Queens Court, Queens Road, Richmond, Surrey TW10 6LA. *T:* 081–940 2626. *Clubs:* City Livery; Richmond Golf (Captain 1977).

GRANT, Andrew Francis Joseph, CB 1971; BSc, CEng, FICE; *b* 25 Feb. 1911; *er s* of Francis Herbert and Clare Grant; *m* 1934, Mary Harrison; two *s* two *d*. *Educ:* St Joseph's Coll., Beulah Hill; King's Coll., London. Asst Civil Engr with Contractors on London Underground Rlys, 1931; Port of London Authority, 1935; entered Civil Engineer-in-Chief's Dept, Admiralty, and posted to Singapore, 1937; Suptg Civil Engr, Durban, 1942; Civil Engr. Adviser, RN Home Air Comd, 1947; Suptg Civil Engr, Malta, 1951; Asst Dir, Navy Works, 1959; Fleet Navy Works Officer, Mediterranean, 1960; Director for Wales, MPBW, 1963; Regional Director, Far East, 1966; Dir, Home Regional Services, DoE, 1968–71. *Recreations:* painting, golf, travel. *Address:* 48 Cecil Road, Norwich, Norfolk NR1 2QN. *T:* Norwich (0603) 622017. *Club:* Civil Service.

GRANT, Andrew Young; Principal, Grant Leisure Group, since 1982; Managing Director, Zoo Operations Ltd, Zoological Society, since 1988; *b* 8 April 1946; *s* of Marshall Grant and Marilyn Greene (*née* Phillips); *m* 1st, 1969, Dietra (marr. diss.); one *d*; 2nd, 1973, Lindy Lange; one *d*. *Educ:* Univ. of Oregon (BSc). Personnel Manager, Universal Studios Tour, Universal City, Calif., 1967–69; Dir of Personnel, Busch Gardens, LA, 1969–71, Ops Dir, 1971–73; Gen. Manager, Squaw Valley Ski Resort, 1973–74; Gen. Manager, Busch Gardens, 1974–76; Dir, Economic Research Associates, LA, 1976–79; Dep. Dir, Zoological Soc., San Diego, 1979–83; Dir, Leeds Castle Enterprises, 1983–88; Dir, Granada Studios Tour, 1987–90. Member: Tourism and Leisure Industries Sector Gp, NEDC; Tourism Soc. *Recreations:* running, fishing, golf, tennis. *Address:* Grant Leisure Group, 12 Adeline Place, WC1B 3AJ. *T:* 071–436 9592.

GRANT, Sir Anthony, Kt 1983; MP (C) Cambridgeshire South-West, since 1983 (Harrow Central, 1964–83); Solicitor and Company Director; *b* May 1925; *m* Sonia Isobel; one *s* one *d*. *Educ:* St Paul's Sch.; Brasenose Coll., Oxford. Admitted a Solicitor, 1952; Liveryman, Worshipful Company of Solicitors; Freeman, City of London; Master, Guild of Freemen, 1979. Army 1943–48, Third Dragoon Guards (Capt.). Opposition Whip, 1966–70; Parly Sec., Board of Trade, June-Oct. 1970; Parliamentary Under-Secretary of State: Trade, DTI, 1970–72; Industrial Develt, DTI, 1972–74; Chm., Cons. back bench Trade Cttee, 1979–83; Mem., Foreign Affairs Select Cttee, 1980–83; a Vice-Chm., Conservative Party Organisation, 1974–76. Member: Council of Europe (Chm., Econ. Cttee, 1980–87); WEU. Pres., Guild of Experienced Motorists. *Recreations:* watching Rugby and cricket, playing golf; Napoleonic history. *Address:* House of Commons, SW1. *Clubs:* Walton Heath Golf, Gog Magog Golf.

GRANT of Monymusk, Sir Archibald, 13th Bt, *cr* 1705; *b* 2 Sept. 1954; *e s* of Captain Sir Francis Cullen Grant, 12th Bt, and of Lady Grant (Jean Margherita, *d* of Captain Humphrey Douglas Tollemache, RN), who *m* 2nd, Baron Tweedsmuir, *qv*; *S* father, 1966; *m* 1982, Barbara Elizabeth, *e d* of A. G. D. Forbes, Drumminnor Castle, Rhynie, Aberdeenshire; two *d*. *Heir:* *b* Francis Tollemache Grant, *b* 18 Dec. 1955. *Address:* House of Monymusk, Aberdeenshire AB3 7HL. *T:* Monymusk (04677) 220.

GRANT, Bernard Alexander Montgomery; MP (Lab) Tottenham, since 1987; *b* 17 Feb. 1944; *s* of Eric and late Lily Grant; *m* (separated); three *s*. *Educ:* St Stanislaus College, Georgetown, Guyana; Tottenham Technical College. Analyst, Demerara Bauxite Co., Guyana, 1961–63; Clerk, British Rail, 1963–65; Telephonist, Internat. Telephones, GPO, 1969–78; Area Officer, NUPE, 1978–83; Develt Worker, Black Trade Unionists Solidarity Movement, 1983–84; Local Govt Officer, London Borough of Newham, 1985–87. Councillor, London Borough of Haringey, 1978 (Council Leader, 1985–87). Chm. and Founder Mem., Parly Black Caucus, 1988; Chm., Campaign Gp of Labour MPs, 1990–; Mem., NEC, Anti-Apartheid Movement. Editor, Black Parliamentarian Magazine, 1990–. *Recreations:* cooking, gardening. *Address:* House of Commons, SW1A 0AA.

GRANT, His Honour Brian; *see* Grant, His Honour H. B.

GRANT, Sir Clifford (Harry), Kt 1977; Chief Stipendiary Magistrate, Western Australia, 1982–90; *b* England, 12 April 1929; *m* 1962, Karen Ann Ferguson. *Educ:* Montclair, NJ, USA; Harrison Coll., Barbados; Liverpool Coll.; Liverpool Univ. (LLB (Hons) 1949). Solicitor, Supreme Court of Judicature, 1951; Comr for Oaths, 1958; in private practice, London; apptd to HM Overseas Judiciary, 1958; Magistrate, Kenya, 1958, Sen. Magistrate, 1962; transf. to Hong Kong, Crown Solicitor, 1963, Principal Magistrate, 1965; transf. to Fiji, Sen. Magistrate, 1967; admitted Barrister and Solicitor, Supreme Court of Fiji, 1969; Chief Magistrate, 1971; Judge of Supreme Court, 1972; Chief Justice of Fiji, 1974–80. Pres., Fiji Court of Appeal, and Chm., Judicial and Legal Services Commn, 1974–80; sole Comr, Royal Commn on Crime, 1975 (report published 1976). Sometime Actg Governor-General, 1973–79. Fiji Independence Medal, 1970. *Publications:* articles for legal jls. *Recreations:* sociobiology, photography, literature, music. *Address:* c/o Under Secretary for Law, PO Box F317, Perth, WA 6001, Australia.

GRANT, David James, CBE 1980; JP; Chairman, Darchem Ltd, since 1963 (Chief Executive, 1959–88); Deputy Chairman, William Baird plc, since 1981; Lord-Lieutenant and Custos Rotulorum of County Durham, since 1988; *b* 18 Jan. 1922; *s* of late Frederick Grant, MC, QC and Grace Winifred Grant (*née* McLaren); *m* 1949, Jean Margaret, *d* of Gp Capt. T. E. H. Birley, OBE; two *s* one *d*. *Educ:* Fettes Coll., Edinburgh; Oriel Coll., Oxford (Open Schol.; MA). Served RAFVR, Bomber Command and overseas 1940–45 (Flight Lieut). Chairman: Teesside Productivity Assoc., 1965–68; Northern Regl Council, CBI, 1973–75; Northern Regl Council, BIM, 1982–87; Member: Northern Econ. Planning Council, 1968–79; NE Industrial Develt Bd, 1975–84. President: N of England TA & VRA, 1990–; N of England Anglo-Japanese Soc., 1990–. Chm., Council, Univ. of Durham, 1985– (Hon. DCL, 1988). Hon. DCL Newcastle upon Tyne, 1989. Co. Durham: DL 1982; High Sheriff, 1985–86; Vice Lord-Lieut, 1987–88; JP Durham, 1988. KStJ 1988. CBIM. *Recreations:* lawn tennis, golf. *Address:* Aden Cottage, Durham DH1 4HJ. *T:* Durham (091) 3867161. *Club:* Naval and Military.

GRANT, His Honour Derek Aldwin, DSO 1944; QC 1962; a Circuit Judge (formerly an Additional Judge of the Central Criminal Court), 1969–84; *b* 22 Jan. 1915; *s* of late Charles Frederick Grant, CSI, ICS; *m* 1954, Phoebe Louise Wavell-Paxton; one *s* three *d*. *Educ:* Winchester Coll.; Oriel Coll., Oxford. Called to Bar 1938. Served in RAF, 1940–46 (King's Commendation, DSO). Master of the Bench, Inner Temple, 1969. Deputy Chairman, East Sussex County Sessions, 1962–71; Recorder of Salisbury, 1962–67, of Portsmouth, 1967–69. *Address:* Carters Lodge, Handcross, West Sussex.

GRANT, Donald Blane, CBE 1989; TD 1964; Partner, KMG Thomson McLintock, CA (formerly Moody Stuart & Robertson, then Thomson McLintock & Co.), 1950–86; *b* 8 Oct. 1921; *s* of Quintin Blane Grant and Euphemia Phyllis Grant; *m* 1944, Lavinia Margaret Ruth Ritchie; three *d*. *Educ:* High Sch. of Dundee. CA 1948. Served War, RA, 1939–46: TA Officer, retd as Major. Director: Dundee & London Investment Trust PLC, 1969–; HAT Group PLC, 1969–86; Don Brothers Buist PLC, 1984–87. Inst. of Chartered Accountants of Scotland: Mem. Council, 1971–76; Vice Pres., 1977–79, Pres., 1979–80. Chairman: Tayside Health Bd, 1984–91; Scottish Legal Aid Bd, 1986–. Hon. LLD Dundee, 1989. *Recreations:* shooting, fishing, golf, bridge, gardening. *Address:* Summerfield, 24 Albany Road, West Ferry, Dundee. *T:* Dundee (0382) 737804. *Clubs:* Institute of Directors; New (Edinburgh); Royal and Ancient Golf (St Andrews); Panmure Golf (Carnoustie); Blairgowrie Golf (Rosemount).

GRANT, Donald David, CB 1985; Director General, Central Office of Information, 1982–85; *b* 1 Aug. 1924; *s* of Donald Herbert Grant and Florence Emily Grant; *m* 1954, Beatrice Mary Varney; two *d*. *Educ:* Wandsworth Sch. Served War, RNVR, Sub-Lt (A), 1942–46. Journalist, Evening Standard, Reuters, 1946–51; Dir, Sidney Barton Ltd, PR Consultants, 1951–61; Chief Information Officer, Min. of Aviation and Technology, 1961–67; Dir, Public Relations, STC Ltd, 1967–70; Director of Information: GLC, 1971–72; DTI, 1972–74; Home Office, 1974–82. Vis. Prof., Graduate Centre for Journalism, City Univ., 1986–90. *Recreation:* sailing. *Address:* 16 Clarence Street, Dartmouth, Devon TQ6 9NW. *T:* Dartmouth (0803) 833095. *Club:* Dartmouth Yacht.

GRANT, Douglas Marr Kelso; Sheriff of South Strathclyde, Dumfries and Galloway (formerly of Ayr and Bute), 1966–88; *b* 5 April 1917; *m* 1952, Audrey Stevenson Law; two *s* two *d*. *Educ:* Rugby; Peterhouse, Cambridge. Entered Colonial Admin. Service, Uganda Protectorate, 1939. Army Service, 1940–46. Called to Bar, Gray's Inn, 1945; Judicial and Legal Dept, Malaya, 1946–57. Admitted to Faculty of Advocates and Scottish Bar, 1959. *Address:* Drumellan House, Maybole, Ayrshire. *T:* Maybole (0655) 82279.

GRANT, Prof. (Duncan) Alistair (Antoine), RBA, RE, ARCA; Professor of Printmaking, 1984–90, Head of Printmaking Department, 1970–90, Royal College of Art; Professor Emeritus, 1990; Chairman, Faculty of Printmaking, British School at Rome, since 1978; *b* London, 3 June 1925; *s* of Duncan and Germaine Grant; *m* 1949,

Phyllis Fricker (*d* 1988); one *d*. *Educ:* Froebel, Whitehill, Glasgow; Birmingham Sch. of Art; Royal Coll. of Art. Joined staff of RCA, 1955. *One Man Shows* at the following galleries: Zwemmer; Piccadilly; AIA; Ashgate; Bear Lane, Oxford; Midland Group, Nottingham; Balclutha; Ware, London; 46, Edinburgh; Editions Alecto; Redfern; Scottish Gall. *Works in the collections of:* V&A Museum; Tate Gallery; Min. of Works; DoE; LCC (later GLC); Arts Council; Carlisle Art Gall.; Ferens Art Gall., Hull; The King of Sweden; Dallas Museum; Dallas Art Gall.; Cincinnati; Boston; Museum of Modern Art, New York; Public Library, NY; Chicago Art Inst.; Lessing J. Rosenwald Collection; Beaverbrook Foundn, Fredericton, NB; Vancouver Art Gall.; Victoria Art Gall; Tel Aviv Museum; Cairo Art Gall.; Nat. Gall. of S Australia; Nat. Museum of Stockholm; IBM; Mobil Oil; Unilever; BP International; BM; Hunterian Mus., Glasgow. *Group Exhibitions* in Bahamas, Canada, Europe, S America, USA and UK. FRSA. Awarded Silver Medal, Internat. Festival of Youth, Moscow, 1957. *Address:* 13 Redcliffe Gardens, SW10 9BG. *T:* 071–352 4312.

GRANT, Edward; Lord Mayor, City of Manchester, May 1972–May 1973; *b* 10 Aug. 1915; *s* of Edward and Ada Grant; *m* 1942, Winifred Mitchell. *Educ:* Moston Lane Sch.; Manchester High Sch. of Commerce. City Councillor, Manchester, 1950–84 (Alderman, 1970–74); Hosp. Administrator, Manchester AHA (T) North Dist (formerly NE Manchester HMC), 1948–75, now retired. *Recreations:* swimming, reading, gardening. *Address:* 14 Rainton Walk, New Moston, Manchester M10 0FR. *T:* 061–681 4758.

GRANT, Brig. Eneas Henry George, CBE 1951; DSO 1944 and Bar, 1945; MC 1936; JP; Hon. DL; retired; *b* 14 Aug. 1901; *s* of late Col H. G. Grant, CB, late Seaforth Highlanders and late Mrs Grant, Balnespick, Inverness-shire; *m* 1926, Lilian Marion (*d* 1978), *d* of late S. O'Neill, Cumberstown House, Co. Westmeath; one *s* (and *er s*, Lieut Seaforth Highlanders, killed in action, Korea, 1951). *Educ:* Wellington Coll., Berks; RMC, Sandhurst. 2nd Lieut Seaforth Highlanders, 1920; Adjt Lovat Scouts, 1928–33; served in Palestine, 1936; War of 1939–45; France 1940; France and Germany, 1944–45. Lieut-Colonel 1942 (Subs. 1947); Colonel 1944 (Subs. 1948); Brigadier 1944 (Subs. 1952); Bde Commander, 1944–49; Comdr Gold Coast District, 1949–52. Col Comdt Gold Coast Regt, 1949–52; Deputy Commander, Northumbrian District, 1952–55; retired 1955. JP Inverness-shire, 1957. DL Inverness-shire, 1958–80. Chairman Inverness-shire TA and Air Force Association, 1961–65. *Recreations:* country pursuits. *Address:* Inverbrough Lodge, Tomatin, Inverness-shire IV13 7XY. *Club:* Highland (Inverness).

GRANT, George; *b* 11 Oct. 1924; *m* 1948, Adeline (*née* Conroy), Morpeth; one *s* four *d*. *Educ:* Netherton Council Sch. and WEA. Member Bedlingtonshire UDC, 1959–70 (Chm. for two years). Member: Labour Party, 1947–; NUM (Chm., 1963–70). MP (Lab) Morpeth, 1970–83; PPS to Minister of Agriculture, 1974–76. *Recreations:* sport, gardening. *Address:* 4 Ringway, Choppington, Northumberland. *Clubs:* Working Men's, in the Bedlington and Ashington area.

GRANT, His Honour (Hubert) Brian; a Circuit Judge of Sussex and Kent (formerly Judge of County Courts), 1965–82; *b* Berlin, 5 Aug. 1917; *m* 1946, Jeanette Mary Carroll; one *s* three *d*. *Educ:* Trinity Coll., Cambridge (Sen. Schol.). 1st cl. hons, Law Tripos, 1939; MA. War service, 1940–44: Commandos, 1942–44. Called to Bar, Gray's Inn, 1945 (Lord Justice Holker Senior Scholar). Mem., Law Reform Cttee, 1970–73. Vice-Chm., Nat. Marriage Guidance Council, 1970–72; Founder Pres., Parenthood, 1979. *Publications:* Marriage, Separation and Divorce, 1946; Family Law, 1970; Conciliation and Divorce, 1981; The Quiet Ear, 1987; The Deaf Advance, 1990. *Address:* Eden Hill, Armathwaite, Carlisle CA4 9PQ. *Club:* Penrith Golf.

GRANT, Ian David, CBE 1988; farming, since 1962; Chairman, Scottish Tourist Board, since 1990 (Board Member, 1988–90); *b* Dundee, 28 July 1943; *s* of late Alan H. B. Grant and of Florence O. Grant; *m* 1968, Eileen May Louisa Yule; three *d*. *Educ:* Strathallan Sch.; East of Scotland College of Agriculture (Dip.). Vice Pres. 1981–84, Pres. 1984–90, National Farmers' Union of Scotland; Mem., Scottish Council, CBI, 1984–90. Director: Clydesdale Bank PLC, 1989–; NFU Mutual Insce Soc. Ltd, 1990–. FRAgS 1988. *Recreations:* travel, swimming, shooting, reading, music. *Address:* Thorn, Blairgowrie PH11 8NP. *T:* Alyth (08283) 2253.

GRANT, Maj.-Gen. Ian Hallam L.; *see* Lyall Grant.

GRANT, (Ian) Nicholas; Chairman, Pearson Grant Associates, since 1990 (Director, since 1989); *b* 24 March 1948; *s* of late Hugo and of Cara Grant; *m* 1977, Rosalind Louise Pipe; one *s* one *d*. *Educ:* Univ. of London (LLB); Univ. of Warwick (MA, Industrial Relns). Confederation of Health Service Employees: Research Officer, 1972–74; Head of Research and Public Relations, 1974–82; Dir of Information, Labour Party, 1982–85; Public Affairs Advr to Robert Maxwell, 1985–89. Member: Council London Borough of Lambeth, 1978–84; Lambeth, Southwark and Lewisham AHA, 1978–82; W Lambeth DHA, 1982–83. Contested (Lab) Reigate, 1979. *Publications:* contrib. to: Economics of Prosperity, ed D. Blake and P. Ormerod, 1980; Political Communications: the general election campaign of 1983, ed I. Crewe and M. Harrop, 1985. *Recreations:* walking, reading, photography. *Address:* 23 Orlando Road, Clapham, SW4 0LD. *T:* 071–720 1091; (office) 071–498 6288. *Club:* Reform.

GRANT, Rt. Rev. James Alexander; Bishop Coadjutor, Diocese of Melbourne, since 1970; Dean of St Paul's Cathedral, Melbourne, since 1985; *b* 30 Aug. 1931; *s* of late V. G. Grant, Geelong; *m* 1983, Rowena Margaret Armstrong. *Educ:* Trinity College, Univ. of Melbourne (BA Hons); Melbourne College of Divinity (BD). Deacon 1959 (Curate, St Peter's, Murrumbeena), Priest 1960; Curate, West Heidelberg 1960, Broadmeadows 1961; Leader Diocesan Task Force, Broadmeadows, 1962; Domestic and Examining Chaplain to Archbishop of Melbourne, 1966; Chairman, Brotherhood of St Laurence, 1971–87 (Director, 1969); Chaplain, Trinity Coll., Univ. of Melbourne, 1970–75, Fellow, 1975–; Pres., Diocesan Mission to Streets and Lanes, 1987–. *Publications:* (with Geoffrey Serle) The Melbourne Scene, 1957; Perspective of a Century-Trinity College, 1872–1972, 1972. *Recreation:* historical research. *Address:* Cathedral Buildings, Flinders Lane, Melbourne, Vic 3000, Australia. *Club:* Melbourne (Melbourne).

GRANT, James Pineo; Executive Director, United Nations Children's Fund (UNICEF), since 1980; *b* 12 May 1922; *s* of John B. and Charlotte Grant; *m*; 1st, 1943, Ethel Henck (decd); three *s*; 2nd, 1989, Ellan Young. *Educ:* Univ. of California, Berkeley (BA); Harvard Univ. (JD). US Army, 1943–45; UN Relief and Rehabilitation Admin, 1946–47; Acting Exec. Sec. to Sino-American Jt Cttee on Rural Reconstruction, 1948–50; Law Associate, Covington and Burling, Washington, DC, 1951–54; Regional Legal Counsel in New Delhi for US aid programs for S Asia, 1954–56; Dir, US aid mission to Ceylon, 1956–58; Dep. to Dir of Internat. Co-operation Admin, 1959–62; Dep. Asst Sec. of State for Near East and S Asian Affairs, 1962–64; Dir, AID program in Turkey, with rank of Minister, 1964–67; Asst Administrator, Agency for Internat. Develt (AID), 1967–69; Pres., Overseas Develt Council, 1969–80. Hon. Prof., Capital Medical Coll. of China, 1983. Hon. LLD: Notre Dame, 1980; Maryville Coll., 1981; Tufts, 1983; Denison, 1983; Hon. DrSci Hacettepe, Ankara, 1980. Rockefeller Public Service Award, 1980; Boyaca Award, Colombia, 1984; Gold Mercury Internat. Award, Internat. Orgn for Co-operation, 1984; Presidential Citation, APHA, 1985. *Publications:* The State of the World's Children Report, annually, 1980–; articles in Foreign Affairs, Foreign Policy, Annals. *Address:* 3 United Nations Plaza, New York, NY 10017, USA. *T:* (212) 326–7035. *Clubs:* Metropolitan, Cosmos (Washington, DC).

GRANT, James Shaw, CBE 1968 (OBE 1956); Member, Highlands and Islands Development Board, 1970–82; *b* 22 May 1910; *s* of William Grant and Johanna Morison Grant, Stornoway; *m* 1951, Catherine Mary Stewart (*d* 1988); no *c*. *Educ:* Nicolson Inst.; Glasgow Univ. Editor, Stornoway Gazette, 1932–63; Mem., Crofters' Commn, 1955–63, Chm., 1963–78. Dir, Grampian Television, 1969–80. Mem. Scottish Adv. Cttee, British Council, 1972. Governor, Pitlochry Festival Theatre, 1954–84, Chairman, 1971–83; Chm., Harris Tweed Assoc. Ltd, 1972–84. Mem. Council, Nat. Trust for Scotland, 1979–84. FRAgS 1973; FRSE 1982. Hon. LLD Aberdeen, 1979. *Publications:* Highland Villages, 1977; Their Children Will See, 1979; The Hub of My Universe, 1983; Surprise Island, 1983; The Gaelic Vikings, 1984; Stornoway and the Lews, 1985; Discovering Lewis and Harris, 1987; Enchanted Island, 1989; several plays. *Recreations:* golf, photography. *Address:* Ardgrianach, Inshes, Inverness. *T:* Inverness (0463) 231476. *Clubs:* Royal Over-Seas League; Highland (Inverness).

GRANT, Rear-Adm. John, CB 1960; DSO 1942; *b* 13 Oct. 1908; *s* of late Maj.-Gen. Sir Philip Grant, KCB, CMG, and Annette, *d* of John Coventry, JP, Burgate Manor, Fordingbridge; *m* 1935, Ruth Hayward Slade; two *s* two *d*. *Educ:* St Anthony's, Eastbourne; RN Colls, Dartmouth and Greenwich. Midshipman, HMS Queen Elizabeth, 1926; Sub-Lieut, HMS Revenge, 1930; Lieut, HMS Kent, China Station, 1932; specialised in anti-submarine warfare, 1933–39; Staff Officer Convoys, Rosyth, 1940; in comd HMS Beverley, 1941–42 (DSO); Trng Comdr, HMS Osprey, 1942, and subseq. in HMS Western Isles; in comd HMS Philante, 1943; Trng Comdr, HMS Osprey, 1944; in comd HMS Opportune, Fame and Crispin, 1945–47; Joint Staff Coll., 1947; Executive Officer, HMS Vernon; Capt. 1949; Dep. Dir Torpedo Anti-Submarine and Mine Warfare Div., Naval Staff, Admiralty, 1949–51; in comd HMS Cleopatra, 1952–53; Imperial Defence Coll., 1954; in comd HMS Vernon, 1955–57; on staff of Chief of Defence Staff, Min. of Defence, 1957–59; Rear-Adm., 1959; Flag Officer Commanding Reserve Fleet (HMS Vanguard), 1959–60; retired list, 1961. Rank Organisation, 1961–65; Director, Conference of the Electronics Industry, 1965–71. *Address:* 9 Rivermead Court, Ranelagh Gardens, SW6 3RT.

See also B. V. M. Strickland.

GRANT, Sir (John) Anthony; *see* Grant, Sir A.

GRANT, John Donald; Consultant, Grant & Fairgrieve, since 1988; *b* 31 Oct. 1926; *s* of Ian and Eleanor Grant; *m* 1951, Helen Bain Fairgrieve Wilson, *d* of late James Wilson and of Clara Wilson; two *s*. *Educ:* various schs; King's Coll., Cambridge (Exhibnr; MA Nat. Sciences). National Service, REME, 1947–49; TA, London Rifle Bde, 1949–56. N Thames Gas Bd, 1949–60; Imperial Chemical Industries: Plastics Div., 1960–71; Head Office, 1971–82; Chief Exec., FIMBRA (formerly NASDIM), 1983–88. Chairman: Strategic Planning Soc., 1989–91; Fedn of Software Systems, 1989–. *Recreations:* opera, music, travel (particularly to islands). *Address:* 6 Bailey Mews, Auckland Road, Cambridge CB5 8DR; also in Westmorland. *Club:* United Oxford & Cambridge University.

GRANT, John Douglas; writer; Head of Communications, Electrical, Electronic, Telecommunication and Plumbing Union, 1984–89; Member, Radio Authority, since 1990; *b* 16 Oct. 1932; *m* 1955, Patricia Julia Ann; two *s* one *d*. *Educ:* Stationers' Company's Sch., Hornsey. Reporter on various provincial newspapers until 1955; Daily Express, 1955–70 (Chief Industrial Correspondent, 1967–70). Contested: (Lab) Beckenham, 1966; (SDP) Islington N, 1983; (SDP/Alliance) Carshalton and Wallington, 1987. MP Islington East, 1970–74, Islington Central, 1974–83 (Lab, 1970–81, SDP, 1981–83). Opposition Front Bench Spokesman for policy on broadcasting and the press, 1973–74, on employment, 1979–81; Parly Sec., CSD, March-Oct. 1974; Parliamentary Under-Secretary of State: ODM, 1974–76; Dept of Employment, 1976–79; SDP employment spokesman, 1981–83; SDP industry spokesman, 1982–83. Chm., Bromley Constituency Labour Party, 1966–70. Chm., Labour and Industrial Correspondents' Group, 1967. *Publications:* Member of Parliament, 1974; articles in national newspapers and periodicals. *Recreations:* tennis, watching soccer. *Address:* Branscombe, Upper Street, Kingsdown, near Deal, Kent CT14 8BJ. *T:* Deal (0304) 363991.

GRANT, John James, CBE 1960; Director, University of Durham Institute of Education, 1963–77; *b* 19 Oct. 1914; *s* of John and Mary Grant; *m* 1945, Jean Graham Stewart; two *s*. *Educ:* Shawlands Academy, Glasgow; Univ. of Glasgow (MA, EdB). Supply teaching, Glasgow, 1939–40. Served War: UK, India, Burma, 1940–46. Mod. Lang. Master, High Sch. of Glasgow, 1946–48; Lectr in Educn, Univ. of Durham, 1948–52; Vice-Principal, Fourah Bay Coll., Sierra Leone, 1953–55, Principal, 1955–60; Principal, St Cuthbert's Soc., Univ. of Durham, 1960–63. Hon. DCL Durham, 1960. *Recreations:* theatre, gardening. *Address:* 1 Marklands, Julian Road, Sneyd Park, Bristol BS9 1JY.

GRANT, Keith Wallace; Dean, Faculty of Design, Kingston Polytechnic, since 1988; *b* 30 June 1934; *s* of Randolph and Sylvia Grant; *m* 1968, Deanne (*née* Bergsma); one *s* one *d*. *Educ:* Trinity Coll., Glenalmond; Clare Coll., Cambridge (MA). Account Exec., W. S. Crawford Ltd, 1958–62; General Manager: Covent Garden Opera Co., later Royal Opera, 1962–73; English Opera Group, 1962–73; Sec., Royal Soc. of Arts, 1973–77; Dir, Design Council, 1977–88. Member: Adv. Council, V&A Mus., 1977–83; PO Stamp Adv. Cttee, 1978–89; Exec. Bd, Internat. Council of Socs of Industrial Design, 1983–87. Chm., English Music Theatre Co., 1979–; Mem., Management Cttee, Park Lane Gp, 1988–; Sec., Peter Pears Award for Singers, 1988–. Governor: Central Sch. of Art and Design, 1974–77; Birmingham Polytechnic, 1981–86; Edinburgh Coll. of Art, 1982–86; Mem., Ct, Brunel Univ., 1985–89. Hon. Prof., Heriot-Watt Univ., 1987. Hon. Fellow, Birmingham Polytechnic, 1988. Hon. FCSD (Hon. FSIAD, 1983). *Address:* c/o Kingston Polytechnic, Knights Park, Kingston upon Thames, KT1 2QJ. *Clubs:* Garrick, Arts.

GRANT, Very Rev. Malcolm Etheridge; Provost and Rector of St Andrew's Cathedral, Inverness, since 1991; Rector of St Paul's, Strathnairn, and Priest in Charge of St Mary's-in-the-Fields, Balloch, since 1991; *b* 6 Aug. 1944; *s* of Donald Etheridge Grant and Nellie Florence May Grant (*née* Tuffey); *m* 1984, Katrina Russell Nuttall (*née* Dunnett); one *s* one *d*. *Educ:* Dunfermline High School; Univ. of Edinburgh (Bruce of Grangehill Bursar, 1962; BSc (Hons Chemistry); BD (Hons New Testament); Divinity Fellowship, 1969); Edinburgh Theological College. Deacon 1969, priest 1970; Assistant Curate: St Mary's Cathedral, Glasgow, 1969; St Wulfram's, Grantham (in charge of Church of the Epiphany, Earlesfield), 1972; Team Vicar of Earlesfield, Grantham, 1972; Priest-in-charge, St Ninian's, Invergordon, 1978; Examining Chaplain to Bishop of Moray, Ross and Caithness, 1979; Provost and Rector, St Mary's Cathedral, Glasgow, 1981. Member, Highland Regional Council Education Cttee, 1979–81. *Address:* 15 Ardross Street, Inverness IV3 5NS. *T:* Inverness (0463) 233535.

GRANT, (Matthew) Alistair; Chief Executive, since 1986, Chairman, since 1988, Argyll Group (Deputy Chairman, 1986–88); Chairman, Agricultural and Food Research Council, since 1990; *b* 6 March 1937; *s* of John and Jessie Grant; *m* 1963, Judith Mary Dent; two *s* one *d*. *Educ:* Woodhouse Grove School, Yorks. 2nd Lieut Royal Signals, 1955–57. Unilever, 1958–63; J. Lyons, 1963–65; Connell May & Steavenson, 1965–68; Dir, Fine Fare, 1968–72; Managing Dir, Oriel Foods, 1973–77; Argyll Group, 1977–. Vis. Prof., Retail, Stirling Univ., 1984–. Chm., Food Policy Cttee, Retail Consortium, 1986–89. Pres., Nat. Grocers' Benevolent Fund, 1987–89. Pres., Advertising Assoc., 1989–. Mem., Listed Companies Adv. Cttee, 1990–. FRSA 1988. *Recreations:* books, paintings, horses, friends. *Address:* 16 Campden Hill Square, Kensington, W8 7JY. *T:* 071–727 7874; The Library House, Tyninghame, E Lothian. *Club:* Caledonian.

GRANT, Michael, CBE 1958 (OBE 1946); MA, LittD (Cambridge); *b* 21 Nov. 1914; *s* of late Col Maurice Harold Grant and Muriel, *d* of C. Jörgensen; *m* 1944, Anne Sophie Beskow, Norrköping, Sweden; two *s*. *Educ:* Harrow Sch.; Trinity Coll., Cambridge. Porson Prizeman, First Chancellor's Classical Medallist, Craven Student; Fellow Trinity Coll., Cambridge, 1938–49. Served War of 1939–45, Army, War Office, 1939–40, Actg Capt.; first British Council Rep. in Turkey, 1940–45; Prof. of Humanity at Edinburgh Univ., 1948–59; first Vice-Chancellor, Univ. of Khartoum, 1956–58; Pres. and Vice-Chancellor of the Queen's Univ. of Belfast, 1959–66; Pres., 1953–56, Medallist, 1962, and Hon. Fellow, 1984, Royal Numismatic Soc.; Huntington Medalist, American Numismatic Soc., 1965. J. H. Gray Lectr, Cambridge, 1955; FSA. Chairman, National Council for the Supply of Teachers Overseas, 1963–66. President: Virgil Soc., 1963–66; Classical Assoc., 1977–78. Chm., Commonwealth Conf. on Teaching of English as 2nd Language at Makerere, Uganda, 1961. Hon. LittD Dublin, 1961; Hon. LLD QUB, 1967. Gold Medal for Educn, Sudan, 1977; Premio Internazionale Le Muse, Florence, 1989. *Publications:* From Imperium to Auctoritas, 1946; Aspects of the Principate of Tiberius, 1950; Roman Anniversary Issues, 1950; Ancient History, 1952; The Six Main Aes Coinages of Augustus, 1953; Roman Imperial Money, 1954; Roman Literature, 1954; translations of Tacitus and Cicero; Roman History from Coins, 1958; The World of Rome, 1960; Myths of the Greeks and Romans, 1962; Birth of Western Civilization (ed), 1964; The Civilizations of Europe, 1965; The Gladiators, 1967; The Climax of Rome, 1968; The Ancient Mediterranean, 1969 (Premio del Mediterraneo, Mazara del Vallo, 1983, for Italian edn); Julius Caesar, 1969; The Ancient Historians, 1970; The Roman Forum, 1970; Nero, 1970; Cities of Vesuvius, 1971; Herod the Great, 1971; Roman Myths, 1971; Cleopatra, 1972; The Jews in the Roman World, 1973; (with J. Hazel) Who's Who in Classical Mythology, 1973 (Premio Latina for Italian edition, 1986); The Army of the Caesars, 1974; The Twelve Caesars, 1975; (ed) Greek Literature, 1976; The Fall of the Roman Empire, 1976; Saint Paul, 1976; Jesus, 1977; History of Rome, 1978; (ed) Latin Literature, 1978; The Etruscans, 1980; Greek and Latin Authors 800 BC-AD 1000, 1980; The Dawn of the Middle Ages, 1981; From Alexander to Cleopatra, 1982; History of Ancient Israel, 1984; The Roman Emperors, 1985; A Guide to the Ancient World, 1986; The Rise of the Greeks, 1987; (ed with R. Kitzinger) Civilization of the Ancient Mediterranean, 1988; The Classical Greeks, 1989; The Visible Past, 1990; Short History of Classical Civilization, 1991. *Address:* Le Pitturacce, Gattaiola, Lucca 55050, Italy. *Club:* Athenæum.

GRANT, Nicholas; *see* Grant, I. N.

GRANT of Dalvey, Sir Patrick Alexander Benedict, 14th Bt *cr* 1688 (NS); Chieftain of Clan Donnachy; (Donnachaidh); Managing Director, Grant's of Dalvey Ltd, since 1988; *b* 5 Feb. 1953; *e s* of Sir Duncan Alexander Grant, 13th Bt, and Joan Penelope (*d* 1991), *o d* of Captain Sir Denzil Cope, 14th Bt; *S* father, 1961; *m* 1981, Dr Carolyn Elizabeth Highet, MB, ChB, DRCOG, MRCGP, *d* of Dr John Highet, Glasgow; two *s*. *Educ:* St Conleth's Coll., Dublin; The Abbey Sch., Fort Angustus; Univ of Glasgow (LLB 1981). FSAScot. Former deer-stalker, inshore fisherman. *Recreations:* professional competing piper, deerstalking, shooting. *Heir: s* Duncan Archibald Ludovic Grant, *b* 19 April 1982. *Address:* Tomintoul House, Flichity, Inverness-shire IV1 2XD. *Club:* New (Edinburgh).

GRANT, Peter James; Chairman, Sun Life Assurance Society plc, since 1983 (Director, since 1973, Vice-Chairman, 1976); *b* 5 Dec. 1929; 2nd *s* of late Lt-Col P. C. H. Grant, Scots Guards, and Mrs Grant (*née* Gooch); *m* 1st, Ann, *d* of late Christopher Pleydell-Bouverie; one *s* one *d*; 2nd, Paula, *d* of late E. J. P. Eugster; one *s* two *d*. *Educ:* Winchester; Magdalen Coll., Oxford. Lieut, Queen's Own Cameron Highlanders. Edward de Stein & Co., 1952, merged with Lazard Brothers & Co. Ltd, 1960; Vice-Chm., 1983–85, Dep. Chm., 1985–88, Lazard Bros & Co.; Dep. Chm., LEP Gp, 1988–. Director: Walter Runciman plc, 1973–90; Standard Industrial Gp, 1966–72; Charrington, Gardner, Lockett & Co. Ltd, 1970–74; London Merchant Securities, 1985–; Scottish Hydro, 1990–; Union des Assurances de Paris International, 1989–; BNP (UK) plc, 1991–. Mem., Industrial Develt Adv. Bd, 1985–. Mem. Council and Chm., Finance Cttee, British Red Cross Soc., 1972–85; Mem., Council and Policy Exec. Cttee, Inst. of Dirs, 1989–. *Recreations:* shooting, golf, gardening. *Address:* Mountgerald, near Dingwall, Ross-shire IV15 9TT. *T:* Dingwall (0349) 62244; 14 Eaton Row, SW1W 0JA. *T:* 071–235 2092. *Clubs:* Boodle's, Caledonian.

GRANT, Prof. Peter John, MA, PhD; MIMechE, FINucE; FInstP; Professor of Nuclear Power, Imperial College of Science, Technology and Medicine, since 1966; Deputy Vice-Chancellor, University of London, 1990–Sept. 1992; *b* London, 2 July 1926; *s* of Herbert James Grant; *m* Audrey, *d* of Joseph Whitham; one *s*. *Educ:* Merchant Taylors' Sch.; Sidney Sussex Coll., Cambridge. BA 1947, MA, PhD 1951. Research in Nuclear Physics at Cavendish Laboratory, 1947–50; Lectr in Natural Philosophy, Univ. of Glasgow, 1950–55; Chief Physicist, Atomic Energy Div., GEC Ltd, 1956–59; Reader in Engineering Science, Imperial Coll. of Science and Technology, 1959–66; Mem. Governing Body, Imperial Coll., 1985–89; London University: Dean of Engrg, 1984–86; Chm. of Academic Council, 1986–89; Mem., Court, 1988–. Mem., Adv. Cttee on Safety of Nuclear Installation, 1983–. Gov., Hampton Sch., 1984–. *Publications:* Elementary Reactor Physics, 1966; Nuclear Science, 1971; papers on radioactivity, nuclear reactions, physics of nuclear reactors. *Address:* 49 Manor Road South, Esher, Surrey.

GRANT, Prof. Peter Raymond, FRS 1987; Class of 1877 Professor of Zoology, Princeton University, since 1989; *b* 26 Oct. 1936; *s* of Frederick Thomas Charles and Mavis Irene Grant (now Reading); *m* 1962, Barbara Rosemary Matchett; two *d*. *Educ:* Whitgift Sch.; Cambridge Univ. (BA Hons); Univ. of British Columbia (PhD). Seessel-Anonymous Postdoctoral Fellow in Biology Dept of Yale Univ., 1964–65; Asst Prof. 1965–68, Associate Prof. 1968–73, Prof. 1973–78, McGill Univ.; Prof., Univ. of Michigan, 1977–85; Prof. of Biology, Princeton Univ., 1985–89. FLS 1986. Hon. PhD Uppsala, 1986. *Publications:* Ecology and Evolution of Darwin's Finches, 1986; (with B. R. Grant) Evolutionary Dynamics of a Natural Population, 1989 (Wildlife Soc. Publication Award, 1991); contribs to Science, Nature, Proc. Royal Society, Proc. Nat. Acad. of Scis (USA), etc. *Recreations:* walking, tennis, music. *Address:* Department of Ecology and Evolutionary Biology, Princeton University, Princeton, NJ 08544-1003, USA. *T:* 609–258–5156.

GRANT-FERRIS, family name of **Baron Harvington.**

GRANT-SUTTIE, Sir (George) Philip; *see* Suttie, Sir G. P. G.

GRANTCHESTER, 2nd Baron *cr* 1953; **Kenneth Bent Suenson-Taylor,** CBE 1985; QC 1971; a Recorder of the Crown Court, 1975–89; Chairman: Value Added Tax Tribunals, 1988–90 (President, 1972–87); Dairy Produce Quota Tribunal, since 1984; Financial Services Tribunal, since 1988; *b* 18 Aug. 1921; *s* of 1st Baron Grantchester, OBE, and of Mara Henriette (Mamie), *d* of late Albert Suenson, Copenhagen; *S* father, 1976; *m* 1947, Betty, *er d* of Sir John Moores, *qv*; three *s* three *d*. *Educ:* Westminster School; Christ's College, Cambridge (MA, LLM). Lieut RA, 1941–45. Called to the Bar, Middle Temple, 1946; admitted *ad eundem* by Lincoln's Inn, 1947. Lecturer in Company Law, Council of Legal Education, 1951–72. Chm., Licensed Dealers' Tribunal, 1976–88; Pres., Aircraft and Shipbuilding Ind. Arbitration Tribunal, 1980–83. Dep. Chm. of Cttees, H of L, 1988–. *Heir: e s* Hon. Christopher John Suenson-Taylor [*b* 8 April 1951; *m* 1972, Jacqueline, *d* of Dr Leo Jaffé; two *s* two *d*]. *Address:* The Gate House, Coombe Wood Road, Kingston Hill, Surrey.

GRANTHAM, Bishop Suffragan of, since 1987; **Rt. Rev. William Ind;** Dean of Stamford, since 1988; *b* 26 March 1942; *s* of William Robert and Florence Emily Ind; *m* 1967, Frances Isobel Bramald; three *s*. *Educ:* Univ. of Leeds (BA); College of the Resurrection, Mirfield. Asst Curate, St Dunstan's, Feltham, 1966–71; Priest in charge, St Joseph the Worker, Northolt, 1971–74; Team Vicar, Basingstoke, 1974–87; Diocesan Director of Ordinands, 1982–87; Hon. Canon of Winchester, 1985–87. *Recreations:* bird watching, cricket watching, orchid finding. *Address:* Fairacre, 243 Barrowby Road, Grantham, Lincs NG31 8NP. *T:* Grantham (0476) 64722.

GRANTHAM, Adm. Sir Guy, GCB 1956 (KCB 1952; CB 1942); CBE 1946; DSO 1941; retired; Governor and Commander-in-Chief of Malta, 1959–62; *b* 9 Jan. 1900; *s* of late C. F. Grantham, The Hall, Skegness, Lincs; *m* 1934, Beryl Marjorie, *d* of late T. C. B. Mackintosh-Walker, Geddes, Nairn; two *d*. Served War of 1939–45 (despatches, twice, DSO, CB, CBE); Chief of Staff to C-in-C, Mediterranean, 1946–48; Naval ADC to the King, 1947–48; Flag Officer (Submarines), 1948–50; Flag Officer, Second-in-Command, Mediterranean Fleet, 1950–51; Vice-Chief of Naval Staff, 1951–54; Comdr-in-Chief, Mediterranean Station, and Allied Forces, Mediterranean, 1954–57; Comdr-in-Chief, Portsmouth, Allied Comdr-in-Chief, Channel and Southern North Sea, 1957–59; First and Principal Naval ADC to the Queen, 1958–59. Retired list, 1959. Hon. Freeman of Haberdashers' Company. Mem., Commonwealth War Graves Commn 1962–70 (Vice-Chm. 1963–70). Governor, Corps of Commissionaires, 1964–. *Address:* Tandem House, 6 High Street, Nayland, Suffolk CO6 4JF. *T:* Nayland (0206) 262511.

GRANTHAM, Roy Aubrey, CBE 1990; National Secretary, APEX Partnership (white collar section of GMB), since 1989; *b* 12 Dec. 1926; *m* 1964; two *d*. *Educ:* King Edward Grammar Sch., Aston, Birmingham. Association of Professional, Executive, Clerical & Computer Staff: Midland area Organiser, 1949; Midland area Sec., 1959; Asst Sec., 1963; Gen. Sec., 1970–89, when APEX merged with GMB. Mem., TUC Gen. Council, 1983–. Exec. Member: Labour Cttee for Europe; Confedn of Shipbuilding and Engineering Unions. Member: Royal Commn on Environmental Pollution, 1976–79; CNAA, 1976–79; IBA, 1984–90; former Mem., MSC, subseq. Training Commn. A Dir, Chrysler UK Ltd, 1977–79, Talbot UK Ltd, 1979–81. Governor, Henley Management Coll., 1979–; Mem., Ditchley Foundn, 1982–. Chm., UK Temperance Alliance, 1989–. *Publication:* Guide to Grading of Clerical and Administrative Work, 1968. *Recreations:* walking, reading, chess. *Address:* 16 Owendale, 359 Grange Road, SE19 3BN.

GRANTLEY, 7th Baron, *cr* 1782; **John Richard Brinsley Norton,** MC 1944; Baron of Markenfield, 1782; a Member of Lloyd's; *b* 30 July 1923; *o s* of 6th Baron and Jean Mary (*d* 1945), *d* of Sir David Alexander Kinloch, CB, MVO, 11th Bt; *S* father 1954; *m* 1955, Lady Deirdre Mary Freda, *e d* of 5th Earl of Listowel, *qv*; two *s*. *Educ:* Eton; New Coll., Oxford. Served War of 1939–45, 1942–45, in Italy as Capt. Grenadier Guards (MC). *Heir: s* Hon. Richard William Brinsley Norton, *b* 30 Jan. 1956. *Address:* 53 Lower Belgrave Street, SW1; Markenfield Hall, Ripon, North Yorks. *Clubs:* White's, Pratt's.

GRANVILLE, family name of **Baron Granville of Eye.**

GRANVILLE, 5th Earl, *cr* 1833; **Granville James Leveson Gower,** MC 1945; Viscount Granville, 1815; Baron Leveson, 1833; Major Coldstream Guards (Supplementary Reserve); Lord-Lieutenant, Islands Area of the Western Isles, since 1983 (Vice Lord-Lieutenant, 1976–83); *b* 6 Dec. 1918; *s* of 4th Earl Granville, KG, KCVO, CB, DSO, and Countess Granville, GCVO; *S* father, 1953; *m* 1958, Doon Aileen, *d* of late Hon. Brinsley Plunket and of Mrs V. Stux-Rybar, Luttrellstown Castle, Co. Dublin; two *s* one *d*. *Educ:* Eton. Served throughout War, 1939–45, Tunisia and Italy (twice wounded, despatches, MC). DL Inverness, 1974. *Heir: s* Lord Leveson, *qv*. *Address:* 49 Lyall Mews, SW1. *T:* 071–235 1026; Callernish, Sollas, North Uist, Outer Hebrides, Inverness-shire. *T:* Bayhead (08765) 213.

GRANVILLE OF EYE, Baron *cr* 1967, of Eye (Life Peer); **Edgar Louis Granville;** *s* of Reginald and Margaret Granville; *b* Reading, 12 Feb. 1899; *m* 1943, Elizabeth *d* of late Rev. W. C. Hunter; one *d*. *Educ:* High Wycombe, London and Australia. Served as officer in AIF, Gallipoli, Egypt and France. Capt. RA, 1939–40. MP (L) Eye Div. of Suffolk, 1929–51; Hon. Sec., Liberal Agricultural Group, House of Commons, 1929–31; Hon. Sec. Foreign Affairs Group, Vice-Pres. National League of Young Liberals; Chm., Young Liberals Manifesto Group; Parliamentary Private Sec. to Sir Herbert Samuel, first National Government, 1931; Parliamentary Private Sec. to Sir John Simon, National Government, 1931–36; Mem. of Inter-Departmental Cttee for the World Economic Conference, 1933. Sits in House of Lords as an Independent. *Recreations:* cricket, football, ski-ing. *Address:* 112 Charlton Lane, Cheltenham, Glos.

GRANVILLE SLACK, George; *see* Slack, G. G.

GRAPPELLI, Stéphane; musician; *b* 26 Jan. 1908; *s* of Prof. Ernest Grappelli and Anna Grappelli (*née* Hanocke); one *d*. Placed in orphanage, 1911; 6 months training in dance with Isadora Duncan, 1914; orphanage to 1918; learnt to play violin together with father; studied for short period at Paris Conservatoire; musical accompanist for silent films, 1923–25; played at social functions, incl. Ambassadeurs Club, 1927–29; joined Grégor and Grégorians, Nice, 1929 (piano and violin, later saxophone and accordion); returned to Paris, 1931; played several instruments at La Croix du Sud, informally with Django Reinhardt, later founding Quintette de Hot Club de France; specialized in jazz improvisations; numerous recordings, 1935–39; spent war years, 1939–45, in London; teamed occasionally with Reinhardt, 1946–53; clubs in London and Paris (incl. Paris Hilton house band, 1967–71); concerts and recordings with fellow musicians, incl. Jean-Luc Ponty, George Shearing, Diz Disley, Oscar Peterson, Baden Powell, Barney Kessel, Earl Hines, Teddy Wilson, Martial Solal, Michel Legrand, Benny Goodman, John Etheridge, Yehudi Menuhin, Yo-Yo Ma, Juillard String Quartet; US début, Newport Jazz Festival, 1969, début Carnegie Hall, 1974. Has homes in Paris and Cannes. Officier, Légion d'honneur; Officier, Ordre Nat. du Mérite; Commandeur des Arts et des Lettres; Médaille de Vermeil, Paris. *Address:* 87 rue de Dunkerque, 75009 Paris, France.

GRASS, Günter Wilhelm; German writer and artist; *b* Danzig, 16 Oct. 1927; *m* 1st 1954, Anna Schwarz; three *s* (inc. twin *s*) one *d*; 2nd, 1979, Ute Grunert. *Educ:* Volksschule and

Gymnasium, Danzig; Düsseldorf Kunstakademie; Hochschule für Bildende Künste. Lecture Tour of US, 1964, and many other foreign tours. Member: Akademie der Künste, Berlin; Deutscher PEN, Zentrum der Bundesrepublik; Verband Deutscher Schriftsteller; Amer. Academy of Arts and Sciences. Prizes: Lyric, Süddeutscher Rundfunk, 1955; Gruppe 47, 1959; Bremen Literary, 1959 (prize money withheld); Literary, Assoc. of German Critics, 1960; Meilleur livre étranger, 1962; Georg-Büchner, 1965; Fontane, Berlin, 1968; Theodor-Heuss, 1969; Internat. Literatur, 1978; Antonio-Feltrinelli, 1982. *Publications: novels:* Die Blechtrommel, 1959 (The Tin Drum, 1962; filmed 1979); Katz und Maus, 1961 (Cat and Mouse, 1963); Hundejahre, 1963 (Dog Years, 1965); Örtlich Betäubt, 1969 (Local Anaesthetic, 1970); Der Butt, 1977 (The Flounder, 1978); Das Treffen in Telgte, 1979 (The Meeting at Telgte, 1981); Kopfgeburten, 1980 (Headbirths, 1982); *poetry:* Die Vorzüge der Windhühner, 1956; Gleisdreieck, 1960; Ausgefragt, 1967; Ach Butt, dein Märchen geht böse aus, 1983; *poetry in translation:* Selected Poems, 1966; Poems of Günter Grass, 1969; In the Egg and other poems, 1978; *drama:* Hochwasser, 1957 (Flood, 1968); Noch zehn Minuten bis Buffalo, 1958 (Only Ten Minutes to Buffalo, 1968); Onkel, Onkel, 1958 (Onkel, Onkel, 1968); Die bösen Köche, 1961 (The Wicked Cooks, 1968); Die Plebejer proben den Aufstand, 1966 (The Plebeians rehearse the Uprising, 1967); Davor, 1969; *prose:* Über das Selbsverständlische, 1968 (Speak Out!, 1969); Aus dem Tagebuch einer Schnecke, 1972 (From the Diary of a Snail, 1974); Dokumente zur politischen Wirkung, 1972; Der Bürger und seine Stimme, 1974; Denkzettel, 1978; Aufsätze zur Literatur, 1980; Zeichnen und Schreiben, Band I, 1982, Band II, 1984; Widerstand lernen, 1984; On Writing and Politics 1967–83, 1985; Die Rättin, 1986 (The Rat, 1987); Zünge Zeigen, 1988 (Show Your Tongue, 1989); Two States – One Nation?, 1990. *Address:* Niedstrasse 13, 1 Berlin 41, Federal Republic of Germany.

GRATTAN, Donald Henry, CBE 1989; Chairman: Adult Continuing Education Development Unit, 1984–91; National Council for Educational Technology (formerly Council for Educational Technology), 1985–91 (Member, 1973–84); *b* St Osyth, Essex, 7 Aug. 1926; *s* of Arthur Henry Grattan and Edith Caroline Saltmarsh; *m* 1950, Valmai Dorothy Morgan; one *s* one *d*. *Educ:* Harrow Boys Grammar Sch.; King's Coll., Univ. of London. BSc 1st Cl. Hons, Mathematics Dip. in Radio-Physics. Jun. Scientific Officer, TRE, Gt Malvern, 1945–46; Mathematics Teacher, Chiswick Grammar Sch., 1946–50; Sen. Master, Downer Grammar Sch., Mddx, 1950–56. BBC: Sch. Television Producer, 1956–60; Asst Head, Sch. Television, 1960–64; Head of Further Educn, Television, 1964–70; Asst Controller, Educnl Broadcasting, 1970–72, Controller, 1972–84. Member: Open Univ. Council, 1972–84 and Univ. Delegacy for Continuing Educn, 1978–84; Vis. Cttee, Open Univ., 1987–; Adv. Council for Adult and Continuing Educn, 1978–83; European Broadcasting Union Working Party on Educn, 1972–84; Venables' Cttee on Continuing Educn, 1976–78. Chm., Adult Literacy Support Services Fund, 1975–80. Mem., Royal TV Soc., 1982–. FRSA 1988. DUniv Open, 1985. Burnham Medal of BIM for services to Management Educn, 1969. *Publications:* Science and the Builder, 1963; Mathematics Miscellany (jt, BBC), 1966; numerous articles. *Recreations:* education (formal and informal), planning and organizing, people. *Address:* Delabole, Gossmore Close, Marlow, Bucks. *T:* Marlow (0628) 473571.

GRATTAN-BELLEW, Sir Henry Charles, 5th Bt, *cr* 1838; *b* 12 May 1933; *s* of Lt-Col Sir Charles Christopher Grattan-Bellew, 4th Bt, MC, KRRC and Maureen Peyton, *niece* and adopted *d* of late Sir Thomas Segrave, Shenfield, Essex; *S* father, 1948; *m* 1st, 1956, Naomi Ellis (marr. diss. 1966); 2nd, 1967, Gillian Hulley (marr. diss. 1973); one *s* one *d*; 3rd, 1978, Elzabé Amy (*née* Body), *widow* of John Westerveld, Pretoria, Tvl, SA. *Educ:* St Gerard's, Bray, Co. Wicklow; Ampleforth Coll., York. Publisher: Horse and Hound, SA, and Sustagen Supersport, 1977. Sports administrator, leading radio and TV commentator, hotelier, thoroughbred breeder and owner. *Heir:* *s* Patrick Charles Grattan-Bellew, *b* 7 Dec. 1971.

GRATTAN-COOPER, Rear Admiral Sidney, CB 1966; OBE 1946; *b* 3 Dec. 1911; *s* of Sidney Cooper; *m* 1940, Felicity Joan Pitt; two *s*. *Educ:* privately. Entered RN 1936; served in war of 1939–45; Chief of Staff Flag Officer (Air) Home, 1957–59; Staff of Supreme Allied Cdr Atlantic (NATO), 1961–63; Dep. Controller (Aircraft) RN, Min. of Aviation, 1964–66; retired 1966. *Recreations:* golf, swimming. *Address:* Hursley, St James, Cape 7951, S Africa. *Club:* Army and Navy.

GRATWICK, John, OBE 1979; Chairman, Empire Stores Group plc (formerly Empire Stores (Bradford)), 1978–90 (Director, 1973–90); *b* 23 April 1918; *s* of Percival John and Kathleen Mary Gratwick; *m* 1944, Ellen Violet Wright; two *s* two *d*. *Educ:* Cranbrook Sch., Kent; Imperial Coll., Univ. of London. Asst Production Manager, Armstrong Siddeley, 1941–45; Director, Urwick, Orr & Partners Ltd, 1959, Man. Dir, 1968, Vice-Chm., 1971. Chm., EDC for the Clothing Industry, 1985–90 (Mem., 1967–85); Member: Monopolies and Mergers Commn, 1969–76; CAA, 1972–74. Chm., Management Consultants Assoc., 1971–72. University of London: Member: Careers Adv. Bd, 1962–78; Senate, 1967–; Court, 1987–; Governor, Cranbrook Sch., Kent, 1972–85; Trustee, Foundn for Business Responsibilities. Liveryman, Worshipful Co. of Glovers. *Recreations:* golf, sailing, photography, philately. *Address:* Silver Howe, Nuns Walk, Virginia Water, Surrey GU25 4RT. *T:* Wentworth (0344) 843121. *Clubs:* Royal Automobile, City Livery; Wentworth (Surrey).

See also Stephen Gratwick.

GRATWICK, Stephen, QC 1968; *b* 19 Aug. 1924; *s* of late Percival John Gratwick, Fawkham, Kent; *m* 1954, Jocelyn Chaplin, Horton Kirby, Kent; four *d*. *Educ:* Charterhouse, Balliol Coll., Oxford. Oxford 1942–44; Signals Research and Develt Estab., 1944–47. BA (Physics) 1946; MA 1950. Called to Bar, Lincoln's Inn, 1949, Bencher, 1976. *Recreations:* tennis, swimming, making and mending things. *Address:* 11 South Square, Gray's Inn, WC1R 5EU.

See also John Gratwick.

GRAVE, Walter Wyatt, CMG 1958; MA (Cambridge); Hon. LLD (Cambridge and McMaster); Hon. Fellow of Fitzwilliam College, Cambridge; *b* 16 Oct. 1901; *o s* of late Walter and Annie Grave; *m* 1932, Kathleen Margaret, *d* of late Stewart Macpherson; two *d*. *Educ:* King Edward VII Sch., King's Lynn; Emmanuel Coll., Cambridge (Scholar); Fellow of Emmanuel Coll., 1926–66, 1972–; Tutor, 1936–40; University Lecturer in Spanish, 1936–40; Registrary of Cambridge Univ., 1943–52; Principal of the University Coll., of the West Indies, Jamaica, 1953–58; Censor of Fitzwilliam House, Cambridge, 1959–66; Master of Fitzwilliam Coll., Cambridge, 1966–71. Temporary Administrative Officer, Ministry of Labour and National Service, 1940–43. *Publication:* Fitzwilliam College Cambridge 1869–1969, 1983. *Address:* 16 Kingsdale Court, Peacocks, Great Shelford, Cambridge CB2 5AT. *T:* Cambridge (0223) 840722.

GRAVES, family name of **Baron Graves.**

GRAVES, 8th Baron, *cr* 1794; **Peter George Wellesley Graves;** Actor; *b* 21 Oct. 1911; *o s* of 7th Baron Graves; *S* father, 1963; *m* 1960, Vanessa Lee. *Educ:* Harrow. First appeared on London stage in 1934, and has subsequently played many leading parts. Mem. Windsor repertory co., 1941. Has appeared in films since 1940. *Recreation:* lawn tennis. *Heir:* *kinsman,* Evelyn Paget Graves [*b* 17 May 1926; *m* 1957, Marjorie Ann, *d* of late Dr Sidney Ernest Holder; two *s* two *d*]. *Address:* c/o Messrs Coutts & Co., 440 Strand, WC2. *Club:* All England Lawn Tennis.

GRAY, family name of **Baron Gray of Contin.**

GRAY, 22nd Lord, *cr* 1445; **Angus Diarmid Ian Campbell-Gray;** *b* 3 July 1931; *s* of Major Hon. Lindsay Stuart Campbell-Gray, Master of Gray, MC (*d* 1945), and Doreen (*d* 1948), *d* of late Cyril Tubbs, Thedden Grange, Alton, Hants; *S* grandmother 1946; *m* 1959, Patricia Margaret (*d* 1987), *o d* of late Capt. Philip Alexander, Kilmorna, Lismore, Co. Waterford; one *s* three *d*. *Heir:* *s* Master of Gray, *qv*. *Address:* Airds Bay House, Taynuilt, Argyll PA35 1JR. *Clubs:* Carlton, MCC.

GRAY, Master of; Hon. Andrew Godfrey Diarmid Stuart Campbell-Gray; *b* 3 Sept. 1964; *s* and *heir* of 22nd Lord Gray, *qv*.

GRAY OF CONTIN, Baron *cr* 1983 (Life Peer), of Contin in the District of Ross and Cromarty; **James, (Hamish), Hector Northey Gray;** PC 1982; DL; parliamentary and business consultant, since 1986; *b* 28 June 1927; *s* of late J. Northey Gray, Inverness, and Mrs E. M. Gray; *m* 1953, Judith Waite Brydon, BSc, Helenburgh; two *s* one *d*. *Educ:* Inverness Royal Academy. Served in Queen's Own Cameron Hldrs, 1945–48. A director of private and family companies, 1950–70. MP (C) Ross and Cromarty, 1970–83; an Asst Govt Whip, 1971–73; a Lord Comr, HM Treasury, 1973–74; an Opposition Whip, 1974–Feb. 1975; Opposition spokesman on Energy, 1975–79; Minister of State: Dept of Energy, 1979–83; Scottish Office, 1983–86; Govt spokesman on Energy, H of L, 1983–86. Contested (C) Ross, Cromarty and Skye, 1983. Member, Inverness Town Council, 1965–70. DL Inverness, Nairn and Lochaber, 1989. *Recreations:* golf, cricket, walking, family life. *Address:* Achneim House, Flichity, Inverness-shire IV1 2XE.

GRAY, Alexander Stuart, FRIBA; Consultant to Watkins, Gray, Woodgate International, 1968–75, retired; *b* 15 July 1905; *s* of Alexander and Mary Gray; *m* 1932, Avis (*d* 1980), *d* of John Radmore, Truro; one *s* two *d*. *Educ:* Mill Hill Sch. Articled to R. S. Balgarnie Wyld, ARIBA; studied at Central Sch. of Arts and Crafts; Royal Academy Schools (Bronze Medal, 1928; Silver Medal and Travelling Studentship, 1932; Gold Medal and Edward Stott Trav. Studentship (Italy), 1933); Brit. Instn Schol., 1929. Lectr on Arch. subjects at Central Sch. of Arts and Crafts, Brixton Sch. of Bldg, and Hammersmith Sch. of Bldg, 1936–39; Lectr on Hosp. Planning at King Edward VII Hosp. Fund Colleges, 1950–. In partnership with W. H. Watkins won architectural comp. for new St George's Hosp., Hyde Park Corner, London (partnership 1939–68); before retirement Architect with partners to: Radcliffe Infirmary, Oxford, United Bristol Hospitals, Royal Free Hospital, Guy's Hospital, London Hospital, Eastman Dental Hospital, St Mary's, Manchester, and other hosps in London and the provinces; also in West Indies, where they were responsible for banks, and commercial buildings as well; hospitals for Comptroller of Development and Welfare in BWI, 1941–46; rebuilding of centre of Georgetown, British Guiana, after the fire of 1945, including new GPO, Telecommunications Building, etc. In Nigeria, University Coll. Hosp., Ibadan, and other works, also in Qatar (Persian Gulf), etc. *Publications:* Edwardian Architecture: a biographical dictionary, 1985; (jtly) Fanlights, 1990; various papers read at confs on Hosp. Planning with special ref. to designing for the tropics, and contrib. Tech. Jls. *Address:* 1 Temple Fortune Hill, NW11 7XL. *T:* 081–458 5741. *Clubs:* Arts, Old Millhillians.

GRAY, Andrew Aitken, MC 1945; Chairman, Wellcome Foundation Ltd, 1971–77; *b* 11 Jan. 1912; *s* of John Gray and Margaret Eckford Gray (*née* Crozier); *m* 1st, 1939, Eileen Mary Haines (*d* 1980); three *s*; 2nd, 1984, Jess, *widow* of C. M. Carr. *Educ:* Wyggeston School, Leicester; Christ Church, Oxford. Served Royal Engineers, 1939–46 (MC, despatches). Unilever Ltd, 1935–52. Dir, Wellcome Foundation Ltd, 1954, Dep. Chm., 1967; Chm. and Man. Dir, Cooper, McDougall & Robertson, 1963–70. Chm., Herts AHA, 1974–77. Comdr, Orden del Mérito Agricola; Comdr, Order of Merit, Italy. *Recreations:* fishing, gardening, theatre. *Address:* Rainhill Spring, Stoney Lane, Bovingdon, Herts. *T:* Hemel Hempstead (0442) 833277. *Club:* East India, Devonshire, Sports and Public Schools.

GRAY, Sir Anthony; *see* Gray, Sir F. A.

GRAY, Anthony James; *b* 12 Feb. 1936; *o s* of Sir James Gray, CBE, MC, FRS; *m* 1963, Lady Lana Mary Gabrielle Baring (*d* 1974), *d* of Earl of Cromer, *qv*; one *s* one *d*; *m* 1980, Mrs Maxine Redmayne, *er d* of Captain and Mrs George Brodrick. *Educ:* Marlborough Coll.; New Coll., Oxford. C. T. Bowring & Co. (Insurance) Ltd, 1959–64; Sen. Investment Analyst, de Zoete & Gorton, 1965–67; Head of Investment Research and Partner, James Capel & Co., 1967–73. Member, London Stock Exchange, 1971–73. Dep. Dir, Industrial Development Unit, Dept of Industry, 1973–75; Special Industrial Advr, DoI, 1975–76; Assoc., PA Management Consultants Ltd, 1977–81; Chief Exec., Cogent (Hldgs), 1982–88. Chm., Bioscot, 1986–88. Member: Foundries EDC (NEDO), 1977–79; Hammersmith and Fulham DHA, 1982–85; Research and Manufacturing Cttee, CBI, 1988–90; Science and Industry Cttee, BAAS, 1989–91. Member Council: Charing Cross Hosp. Med. Sch., 1982–84; ERA Technology Ltd (formerly Electrical Res. Assoc.), 1986–89. Director: Apollo Soc., 1966–73; Nat. Trust Concert Soc., 1966–73; PEC Concerts, 1979–81. *Recreations:* golf, fishing, music. *Address:* 5 Ranelagh Avenue, SW6. *Club:* Garrick.

GRAY, Charles Antony St John, QC 1984; a Recorder, since 1990; *b* 6 July 1942; *s* of late Charles Herbert Gray and Catherine Margaret Gray; *m* 1968, Rosalind Macleod Whinney; one *s* one *d*. *Educ:* Winchester; Trinity College, Oxford (scholar). Called to Bar, Lincoln's Inn, 1966. *Recreations:* skiing, tennis, walking. *Address:* 45 Ladbroke Grove, W11 3AR; Matravers House, Uploders, Dorset. *Club:* Brooks's.

GRAY, Charles Horace, MD (London), DSc, FRCP, FRSC, FRCPath; Emeritus Professor of Chemical Pathology in the University of London (Professor, at King's College Hospital Medical School, 1948–76); Consulting Chemical Pathologist, King's College Hospital District, 1976–81 (Consultant, 1938–76); *b* 30 June 1911; *s* of Charles H. Gray and Ethel Hider, Erith, Kent; *m* 1938, Florence Jessie Widdup, ARCA, *d* of Frank Widdup, JP, Barnoldswick, Yorks; two *s*. *Educ:* Imperial Coll. and University Coll., London (Fellow, UCL, 1979); University Coll. Hospital Medical Sch. Demonstrator in Biochemistry, University Coll., London, 1931–36; Bayliss-Starling Scholar in Physiology and Biochemistry, 1932–33; Visiting Teacher in Biochemistry, Chelsea Polytechnic, 1933–36; Demonstrator and Lecturer in Physiology, University Coll., 1935–36; Graham Scholar in Pathology, UCH Medical Sch., 1936–38; Pathologist in Charge Sector Biochemical Laboratory, Sector 9, Emergency Health Service, 1939–44; Hon. Consultant, Miles Laboratories Ltd, 1953–76. Acting Head, Dept of Chem. Pathol., Hosp. for Sick Children, Gt Ormond St, Jan.-Dec. 1979. Vis. Prof., Div. of Clinical Chem., MRC Clinical Res. Centre, Harrow, 1976–83. Member: Clinical Res. Bd of Med. Res. Council, 1964–68; Arthritis and Rheumatism Council Res. Cttee, 1960–68 (Chm., 1963–66); Chairman: MCB Exams Cttee, 1971–73; Steroid Reference Collection and Radioactive Steroid Synthesis Steering Cttee, MRC, 1973–76; Regional Scientific Cttee, SE Thames RHA, 1974–76 (Mem. Regional Research Cttee, 1974–82). Sec., Soc. for Endocrinology,

1950–53; Chm. Cttee of Management, Jl of Endocrinology Ltd, 1970–74; Member: Cttee of Management, Inst. of Psychiatry, 1966–73; Council and Chm., Specialist Adv. Cttee in Chemical Pathology, RCPath, 1972–75; Assoc. of Clinical Biochemists, 1961– (Pres. 1969–71, Emeritus Mem., 1980–). Mem. Livery, Worshipful Soc. of Apothecaries of London, 1951–. Mem., Editorial Bd, Biochemical Jl, 1955–60. *Publications:* The Bile Pigments, 1953; Clinical Chemical Pathology, 1953, 10th edn (jtly), 1985; The Bile Pigments in Health and Disease, 1961; (ed) Laboratory Handbook of Toxic Agents; (ed jtly) Hormones in Blood, 1961, 3rd edn vols 1–3, 1979, vols 4–5, 1983; (ed jtly) High Pressure Liquid Chromatography in Clinical Chemistry, 1976; contributions to medical and scientific journals. *Recreations:* music and travel. *Address:* Barn Cottage, Linden Road, Leatherhead, Surrey KT22 7JF. *T:* Leatherhead (0372) 372415; 34 Cleaver Square, SE11 4EA. *T:* 071–735 9652. *Clubs:* Athenæum, Royal Over-Seas League.

GRAY, Charles Ireland, JP; Leader of Strathclyde Regional Council, since 1986; *b* 25 Jan. 1929; *s* of Timothy Gray and Janet (*née* Brown); *m* 1952, Catherine Creighton Gray; three *s* two *d*. *Educ:* Coatbridge. Dept of Public Affairs, Scotrail, 1946; Mem. (later Chm.), Lanark DC, 1958–64; Mem., Lanark CC, 1964–75; founder Mem., 1975–, and first Vice-Convener, Strathclyde Regl Council. JP Strathclyde, 1970. *Recreations:* music, reading, politics. *Address:* 9 Moray Place, Chryston G69 9LZ. *T:* 041–779 2962.

GRAY, David, CBE 1977 (OBE 1964); QPM 1960; HM Chief Inspector of Constabulary for Scotland, 1970–79; retired; *b* 18 Nov. 1914; *s* of William Gray and Janet Borland Gray; *m* 1st, 1944, Mary Stewart Scott (*d* 1985); two *d*; 2nd, 1989, Laura Margaret Mackinnon. *Educ:* Preston Grammar Sch. Chief Constable: Greenock, 1955–58; Stirling and Clackmannan, 1958–69. Hon. Sec., Chief Constables' (Scotland) Assoc., 1958–69. English-Speaking Union Thyne Scholar, 1969. *Recreations:* fishing, shooting, golf. *Address:* Kingarth, 42 East Barnton Avenue, Edinburgh EH4 6AQ. *T:* 031–312 6342. *Club:* Bruntsfield (Edinburgh).

GRAY, Dr Denis Everett, CBE 1983 (MBE 1972); JP; Resident Staff Tutor since 1957, and Senior Lecturer, 1967–84, Department of Extramural Studies, University of Birmingham; *b* 25 June 1926; *s* of Charles Norman Gray and Kathleen Alexandra (*née* Roberts); *m* 1949, Barbara Joyce, *d* of Edgar Kesterton. *Educ:* Bablake Sch., Coventry; Univ. of Birmingham (BA); Univ. of London; Univ. of Manchester (PhD). Tutor-organiser, WEA, S Staffs, 1953–57. Chairman: Jt Negotiating Cttees for Justices' Clerks and Justices' Clerks' Assts, 1978–86; Central Council of Magistrates' Courts Cttees, 1980–86 (Dep. Chm., 1978–80); Member: Magistrates' Courts Rule Cttee, 1982–86; Lord Chancellor's Adv. Cttee on Trng of Magistrates, 1974–84. JP Solihull, 1962; Dep. Chm., 1968–71 and 1978–82, Chm., 1971–75, Solihull Magistrates; Chm., Licensing Cttee, 1972–76. *Publication:* Spencer Perceval: the evangelical Prime Minister, 1963. *Recreations:* travel, church architecture, reading. *Address:* 11 Brueton Avenue, Solihull, West Midlands B91 3EN. *T:* 021–705 2935.

GRAY, Prof. Denis John Pereira, OBE 1981; FRCGP; General Medical Practitioner, since 1962; Professor of General Practice, since 1986, Dir of Postgraduate Medical School, since 1987, University of Exeter; *b* 2 Oct. 1935; *s* of late Dr Sydney Joseph Pereira Gray and of Alice Evelyn Gray; *m* 1962, Jill Margaret Hoyte; one *s* three *d*. *Educ:* Exeter Sch.; St John's Coll., Cambridge (MA); St Bartholomew's Hosp. Med. Sch. MB BChir. Sen. Lectr in Charge, Univ. of Exeter, 1973–86. Regional Adviser in Gen. Practice, Univ. of Bristol, 1975–; Consultant Adviser in Gen. Practice to Chief MO, DHSS, 1984–87. Chm. Council, RCGP, 1987–90 (Hon. Editor, Journal, 1972–80, Publications, 1976–). Editor, Medical Annual, 1983–87. Lectures: James Mackenzie, RCGP, 1977; Pfizer, N England Faculty, RCGP, Gale Meml, SW England Faculty, RCGP, 1979; Eli Lilly, Haliburton Hume Meml, Newcastle upon Tyne and Northern Counties Med. Soc., Northcott Meml, Harvard Davis, McConaghey Meml, 1988; Murray Scott Meml, 1990. Gold Medal, Hunterian Soc., 1966, 1969; Sir Charles Hastings Prize, BMA, 1967, 1970; George Abercrombie Award, RCGP, 1978; Foundn Council Award, RCGP, 1980; Sir Harry Platt Prize, Modern Medicine Jl, 1981. *Publications:* Running a Practice (jtly), 1978, 3rd edn 1981; Training for General Practice, 1981; articles in BMJ, Jl RCGP. *Recreation:* reading. *Address:* Alford House, 9 Marlborough Road, Exeter EX2 4TJ. *T:* Exeter (0392) 55235.

GRAY, Rev. Canon Dr Donald Clifford, TD 1970; Canon of Westminster and Rector of St Margaret's, Westminster, since 1987; Chaplain to HM The Queen, since 1982; Chaplain to the Speaker, House of Commons, since 1987; *b* 21 July 1930; *s* of Henry Hackett Gray and Constance Muriel Gray; *m* 1955, Joyce (*née* Jackson); one *s* two *d*. *Educ:* Newton Heath Technical High Sch.; King's Coll., London and Warminster (AKC); Univ. of Liverpool (MPhil); Univ. of Manchester (PhD) FRHistS. Curate, Leigh Parish Church, 1956–60; Vicar: St Peter's, Westleigh, 1960–67; All Saints', Elton Bury, 1967–74; Rector of Liverpool, 1974–87; RD of Liverpool, 1975–81; Canon Diocesan of Liverpool, 1982–87. Proctor-in-Convocation for Manchester, 1964–74; Mem., Gen. Synod, 1980–87. Chm., Soc. for Liturgical Study, 1978–84; President, Societas Liturgica, 1987–89 (Treas. 1981–87); Mem., Liturgical Commn, 1968–86; Chm., Jt Liturgical Gp, 1989– (Mem., 1969–; Sec., 1980–89). Chm., Alcuin Club, 1987–. CF (TA), 1958–67; CF (T&AVR), 1967–77; QHC, 1974–77; Chaplain, Order of St John of Jerusalem, 1990 (Sub Chaplain, 1982). *Publications:* (contrib.) Worship and the Child, 1975; (contrib.) Getting the Liturgy Right, 1982; (contrib.) Liturgy Reshaped, 1982; (ed) Holy Week Services, 1983; Earth and Altar, 1986; (ed) The Word in Season, 1988; (contrib.) Towards Liturgy 2000, 1989; (contrib.) Liturgy for a New Century, 1990; Chaplain to Mr Speaker, 1991. *Recreations:* watching cricket, reading modern poetry. *Address:* 1 Little Cloister, Westminster Abbey, SW1P 3PL. *T:* 071–222 4027. *Club:* Athenæum (Liverpool).

GRAY, Prof. Douglas, FBA 1989; J. R. R. Tolkien Professor of English Literature and Language, University of Oxford, since 1980; *b* 17 Feb. 1930; *s* of Emmerson and Daisy Gray; *m* 1959, Judith Claire Campbell; one *s*. *Educ:* Wellington College, NZ; Victoria Univ. of Wellington (MA 1952); Merton Coll., Oxford (BA 1954, MA 1960). Asst Lecturer, Victoria Univ. of Wellington, 1952–54; Lectr, Pembroke and Lincoln Colls, Oxford, 1956–61; Fellow, Pembroke Coll., 1961–80, now Emeritus; University Lectr in English Language, 1976–80; Professorial Fellow, Lady Margaret Hall, Oxford, 1980–. Mem. Council, EETS, 1981–; Pres., Soc. for Study of Mediæval Langs and Lit., 1982–86. De Carle Lectr, Univ. of Otago, 1989; M. M. Bhattacharya Lectr, Calcutta Univ., 1991. *Publications:* (ed) Spenser, The Faerie Queene, Book 1, 1969; Themes and Images in the Medieval English Religious Lyric, 1972; (ed) A Selection of Religious Lyrics, 1975; (part of) A Chaucer Glossary, 1979; Robert Henryson, 1979; (ed with E. G. Stanley): Middle English Studies presented to Norman Davies, 1983; Five Hundred Years of Words and Sounds for E. J. Dobson, 1983; (ed) The Oxford Book of Late Medieval Verse and Prose, 1985; (ed) J. A. W. Bennett, Middle English Literature, 1986; articles on medieval literature. *Address:* Lady Margaret Hall, Oxford OX2 6QA.

GRAY, Dulcie; *see* Denison, D. W. C.

GRAY, Dr Edward George, FRS 1976; Head of the Laboratory of Ultrastructure, National Institute for Medical Research, Mill Hill, 1977–83; *b* 11 Jan. 1924; *s* of Will and Charlotte Gray; *m* 1953, May Eine Kyllikki Rautiainen; two *s*. *Educ:* University Coll. of Wales, Aberystwyth (BSc, PhD). Anatomy Dept, University Coll., London: Lectr, 1958; Reader, 1962; Prof. (Cytology), 1968–77. *Recreations:* violin playing, water colouring, gardening. *Address:* 58 New Park Road, Newgate Street, Hertford SG13 8RF. *T:* Cuffley (0707) 872891.

GRAY, Sir (Francis) Anthony, KCVO 1981; Secretary and Keeper of the Records of the Duchy of Cornwall, 1972–81; *b* 3 Aug. 1917; *s* of late Major F. C. Gray; *m* 1947, Marcia, *d* of late Major Hugh Wyld; one *s* two *d*. *Educ:* Marlborough; Magdalen Coll., Oxford. Treas., Christ Church, Oxford, 1952–72, Emeritus Student, 1972. Mem., Agricultural Adv. Council, 1963–68; Mem. Council, Royal Coll. of Art, 1967–73. *Recreations:* weeding, washing-up and other manly sports. *Address:* Temple House, Upton Scudamore, Warminster, Wilts. *Club:* Travellers'.

GRAY, Geoffrey Leicester, CMG 1958; OBE 1953; Secretary for Local Government, N Borneo (now Sabah), 1956–61, retired; *b* 26 Aug. 1905; *s* of late Leonard Swainson Gray, Resident Magistrate of Kingston, Jamaica, and of late Marion Scotland, Vale Royal, Kingston, Jamaica; *m* 1932, Penelope Milnes (*d* 1971), MBE 1962, *o c* of late Philip Henry Townsend, OBE and late Gwenyth Gwendoline Roberts. *Educ:* Latymer Upper Sch. Cadet, North Borneo Civil Service, under British North Borneo (Chartered) Co., 1925; after qualifying in Malay and Law, served in various admin. posts, 1925–30; studied Chinese in Canton, 1931; attached Secretariat for Chinese Affairs and Educ. Dept, Hong Kong, 1931; Dist Officer, Jesselton, Supt, Govt Printing Office, and Editor, British North Borneo Herald and Official Gazette, 1932–35; Dist Officer, Kudat, 1935; Under-Sec., 1935–38; Govt Sec. Class 1b and *ex-officio* MLC, 1938–46; Additional Sessions and High Court Judge, 1938–46; interned by Japanese, 1941–45; Class 1a, 1946; accredited to HQ Brit. Mil. Admin (Brit. Borneo) at Labuan, 1946; assimilated into HM Colonial Admin. Service (later HM Overseas Service) on cession of North Borneo to the Crown, 1946; Actg Dep. Chief Sec., 1946; Protector of Labour and Sec. for Chinese Affairs, 1947; Resident, E Coast, in addition, 1947; Mem. Advisory Council, 1947–50; Comr of Immigration and Labour, 1948–51: Official MLC and MEC, 1950–61; Actg Fin. Sec., 1951–52; Dep. Chief Sec., Staff Class, 1952–56; represented North Borneo at Coronation, 1953; Chm., Bd of Educn and Town and Country Planning Bd, 1956–61; Actg Chief Sec. (intermittently), 1952–60; administered Govt, 1958, 1959; acted as High Comr, Brunei, 1959; retd, 1961. Life Associate, N Borneo and UK Branches, CPA, 1961. Commissary for Bp of Jesselton (later Sabah), 1961. Incorporated Mem. of USPG (formerly SPG), 1964– (Mem. Council, and various Cttees and Gps, 1965–83); Cttee Mem., Borneo Mission Assoc., 1961– (Chm. 1961–76). *Clubs:* Commonwealth Trust, Travellers'.

GRAY, George Thomas Alexander; Second Legislative Counsel for Northern Ireland, since 1988; *b* 20 Jan. 1949; *s* of George Gray and Eveline Gray; *m* 1985, Mary Louise Gray; one *s*. *Educ:* Annadale Grammar Sch., Belfast; The Queen's University of Belfast (LLB 1st Cl. Hons). Called to the Bar of N Ireland; Draftsman, Office of the Legislative Counsel, 1971–88. *Recreation:* cricket. *Address:* Office of the Legislative Counsel, Parliament Buildings, Stormont, Belfast BT4 3SW. *T:* Belfast (0232) 63210.

GRAY, Prof. George William, CBE 1991; PhD; FRS 1983; FRSE; CChem, FRSC; Advanced Materials Consultant, Merck (formerly BDH) Ltd, since 1990; Visiting Professor, Southampton, since 1990; *b* 4 Sept. 1926; *s* of John William Gray and Jessie Colville (*née* Hunter); *m* 1953, Marjorie Mary (*née* Canavan); three *d*. *Educ:* Univ. of Glasgow (BSc); Univ. of London (PhD). CChem, FRSC 1972; FRSE 1989. Staff of Chem. Dept, Univ. of Hull, 1946–: Sen. Lectr, 1960; Reader, 1964; Prof. of Organic Chem., 1978; G. F. Grant Prof. of Chem., 1984–90; Hon. Prof., 1990–. Clifford Paterson Prize Lectr, Royal Soc., 1985. Queen's Award for Technol Achievement, 1979; Rank Prize for Optoelectronics, 1980; Leverhulme Medal, Royal Soc., 1987. *Publications:* Molecular Structure and the Properties of Liquid Crystals, 1962; (ed and jtly with P. A. Winsor) Liquid Crystals and Plastic Crystals, 1974; (ed jtly with G. R. Luckhurst) The Molecular Physics of Liquid Crystals, 1979; (with J. W. Goodby) Smectic Liquid Crystals – textures and structures, 1984; (ed) Thermotropic Liquid Crystals, 1987; 300 pubns on liquid crystals in Jl Chem. Soc., Trans Faraday Soc., Phys. Rev., Molecular Cryst. and Liquid Cryst., Jl Chem. Phys., and Proc. IEEE. *Recreations:* gardening, philately. *Address:* R and D Administration, Merck Ltd, West Quay Road, Poole, Dorset BH15 1HX. *T:* Poole (0202) 745520; Juniper House, Furzehill, Wimborne, Dorset BH21 4HD. *T:* Poole (0202) 880164.

GRAY, Gilbert, QC 1971; a Recorder of the Crown Court, since 1972; *b* 25 April 1928; *s* of late Robert Gray, JP, Scarborough, and of Mrs Elizabeth Gray; *m* 1954, Olga Dilys Gray (*née* Thomas), BA, JP; two *s* two *d*. *Educ:* Scarborough Boys' High Sch.; Leeds Univ. (LLB). Pres., Leeds Univ. Union. Called to the Bar, Gray's Inn, 1953; Bencher, 1979. Leader of NE Circuit, 1984–. *Recreation:* sailing. *Address:* Treasurer's House, York; 2 Park Square, Leeds LS1 2NE; 4 Paper Buildings, Temple, EC4Y 7EX; Lingholm Farm, Lebberston, Scarborough.

GRAY, His Eminence Cardinal Gordon Joseph, MA (Hon.) St Andrews; Hon. DD St Andrews, 1967; Retired Archbishop of St Andrews and Edinburgh; *b* 10 August 1910; 2nd *s* of Francis William and Angela Gray. *Educ:* Holy Cross Acad., Edinburgh; St John's Seminary, Wonersh. Assistant-Priest, St Andrews, 1935–41; Parish Priest, Hawick, 1941–47; Rector of Blairs College, Aberdeen (Scottish National Junior Seminary), 1947–51; Archbishop of St Andrews and Edinburgh, 1951–85. Cardinal, 1969. Member: Pontifical Congregation for Evangelization of Peoples; Congregation of the Sacraments; Congregation for Clergy. Hon. FEIS, 1970. DUniv. Heriot–Watt, 1981. *Address:* The Hermitage, Whitehouse Loan, Edinburgh EH9 1BB.

GRAY, Rear-Adm. Gordon Thomas Seccombe, CB 1964; DSC 1940; *b* 20 Dec. 1911; *s* of late Rev. Thomas Seccombe Gray and Edith Gray; *m* 1939, Sonia Moore-Gwyn; one *s* one *d*. *Educ:* Nautical Coll., Pangbourne. Entered RN, 1929; Sub-Lieut and Lieut, Mediterranean Fleet, 1934–36, ashore Arab revolt in Palestine (despatches); 1st Lieut, HMS Stork, 1939, Norwegian campaign (despatches, DSC); Comd HMS Badsworth, 1942–43 (despatches); Comd HMS Lamerton, 1943–45 (despatches). After the War comd destroyers Consort, Contest and St Kitts; JSSC, 1948; Comdr 1949; Directing Staff, RN Staff Coll., Greenwich, 1950; Exec. Officer, cruiser HMS Glasgow, 1951–53; Capt. 1953; Naval Deputy to UK Nat. Military Representative, at SHAPE; Capt. of 5th Frigate Sqdn, and Comd HMS Wakeful and HMS Torquay, 1956–59; Asst Chief of Staff to C-in-C Eastern Atlantic Command, 1959–61; in comd of Naval Air Anti-Submarine Sch. at Portland and Chief Staff Officer to Flag Officer Sea Trng, 1961–62; Senior Naval Instructor, Imperial Defence Coll., 1963–65, retd. *Recreation:* yachting. *Address:* c/o Lloyds Bank, Liphook, Hants GU30 7RE.

GRAY, Hanna Holborn, PhD; President, University of Chicago, since 1978; *b* 25 Oct. 1930; *d* of Hajo and Annemarie Holborn; *m* 1954, Charles Montgomery Gray. *Educ:* Bryn Mawr Coll., Pa (BA); Univ. of Oxford (Fulbright Schol.); Univ. of Harvard (PhD). Instructor, Bryn Mawr Coll., 1953–54; Harvard University: Teaching Fellow, 1955–57, Instr, 1957–59, Asst Prof., 1959–60, Vis. Lectr, 1963–64; Asst Prof., Univ. of Chicago,

1961–64, Associate Prof., 1964–72; Dean and Prof., Northwestern, Evanston, Ill, 1972–74; Provost, and Prof. of History, Yale Univ., 1974–78, Acting Pres., 1977–78. Hon. degrees include: LHD: Brandeis, 1983; Amer. Coll. of Greece, 1986; LLD: Dartmouth Coll., Yale, 1978; Brown, 1979; Rochester, Notre Dame, 1980; Michigan, 1981; Princeton, 1982; Georgetown, 1983; Columbia, 1987; DLitt: Oxford, 1979; Washington, 1985. *Publications:* ed (with Charles M. Gray) Jl Modern History, 1965–70; articles in professional jls. *Address:* (office) 5801 South Ellis Avenue, Chicago, Illinois 60637, USA. *T:* (312) 962–8001. *Clubs:* Commercial, Mid-America, Economic, Fortnightly, Quadrangle, Women's Athletic, University, Chicago (Chicago); University, Cosmopolitan (New York City).

GRAY, Harold James, CMG 1956; retired, 1972; *b* 17 Oct. 1907; 2nd *s* of late John William Gray and of Amelia Frances (*née* Miller); *m* 1928, Katherine Gray (*née* Starling) (*d* 1985); one *d. Educ:* Alleyn's Sch.; Dover County Sch.; Queen Mary Coll., London Univ. (MSc, LLB); Gray's Inn; Harvard University, USA (MPA). MInstP, CPhys; FRSA. Customs and Excise Dept, 1927; Asst Examiner, Patent Office, 1930, Examiner, 1935; Industries and Manufactures Dept, Board of Trade, 1938; Ministry of Supply, 1939; Asst Sec., Min. of Supply, 1942. transf. to Bd of Trade, 1946; Commercial Relations and Exports Dept, Board of Trade, 1950; Under-Sec., 1954; UK Senior Trade Comr and Economic and Commercial Adviser to High Comr in Australia, 1954–58; UK Senior Trade Comr and Economic Adviser to the High Comr in Union of South Africa, 1958–60; Dir, Nat. Assoc. of British Manufacturers, 1961–65; Dir, Legal Affairs, CBI, 1965–72. Commonwealth Fund Fellowship, 1949–50. Chm., NUMAS (Management Services) Ltd. *Publications:* Electricity in the Service of Man, 1949; Economic Survey of Australia, 1955; Dictionary of Physics, 1958; (jtly) New Dictionary of Physics, 1975. *Recreations:* golf, swimming, riding. *Address:* Copper Beeches, 58 Tudor Avenue, Maidstone, Kent ME14 5HJ.

GRAY, Hugh, BSc(Soc), PhD; International Secretary, Theosophical Society; *b* 19 April 1916; *s* of William Marshall Kemp Gray; *m* 1954, Edith Esther (*née* Rudinger); no *c. Educ:* Battersea Grammar Sch.; London Sch. of Economics. Army Service, Intelligence Corps. UNRRA and Internat. Refugee Organisation, 1945–52; Social Worker; Lectr at SOAS, University of London, 1962–66 and 1970–81; Chm., Centre for S Asian Studies, 1980–81; Gen. Sec., Theosophical Soc. in England, 1983–89. MP (Lab) Yarmouth, 1966–70. *Publications:* various articles on Indian politics and philosophy. *Address:* Theosophical Society, Adyar, Madras 600020, India; 22 Bridstow Place, W2 5AE; Castello 1852, Venice.

GRAY, Maj.-Gen. John; *see* Gray, Maj.-Gen. R. J.

GRAY, Rev. Prof. John; Professor of Hebrew, University of Aberdeen, 1961–80, now Professor Emeritus; *b* 9 June 1913; *s* of James Telfer Gray; *m* Janet J. Gibson; five *c. Educ:* Kelso High Sch.; Edinburgh Univ. (MA, BD, PhD). Colonial Chaplain and Chaplain to Palestine Police, 1939–41; Minister of the Church of Scotland, Kilmory, Isle of Arran, 1942–47; Lectr in Semitic Languages and Literatures, Manchester Univ., 1947–53; Lectr in Hebrew and Biblical Criticism, University of Aberdeen, 1953–61. Mem., Soc. for Old Testament Study. Hon. DD St Andrews, 1977. *Publications:* The Krt Text in the Literature of Ras Shamra, 1955 (2nd edn 1964); The Legacy of Canaan, 1957 (2nd edn 1965); Archæology and the Old Testament World, 1962; The Canaanites, 1964; Kings I and II: a Commentary, 1964, 3rd edn 1977; Joshua, Judges and Ruth, 1967, 3rd edn 1986; A History of Jerusalem, 1969; Near Eastern Mythology, 1969, 2nd edn 1982; The Biblical Doctrine of the Reign of God, 1979; contribs to various Bible Dictionaries, memorial volumes and learned journals. *Recreations:* beekeeping, gardening, trout-fishing. *Address:* Tanlaw Cottage, Hendersyde, Kelso, Roxburgh. *T:* Kelso (0573) 24374.

GRAY, Sir John (Archibald Browne), Kt 1973; MA, MB, ScD; FRS 1972; Member, External Scientific Staff, MRC, 1977–83: working at Marine Biological Association Laboratory, Plymouth, since 1977; *b* 30 March 1918; *s* of late Sir Archibald Gray, KCVO, CBE; *m* 1946, Vera Kathleen Mares; one *s* one *d. Educ:* Cheltenham Coll.; Clare Coll., Cambridge (Hon. Fellow, 1976); University Coll. Hospital. BA 1939; MA 1942; MB, BChir 1942; ScD 1962. Service Research for MRC, 1943–45; Surg. Lieut, RNVR, 1945–46; Scientific Staff of MRC at Nat. Inst. for Med. Research, 1946–52; Reader in Physiology, University Coll., London, 1952–58; Prof. of Physiology, University Coll., London, 1959–66; Medical Research Council: Second Sec., 1966–68; Sec., 1968–77; Dep. Chm., 1975–77. QHP 1968–71. FIBiol; FRCP 1974. Hon. DSc Exeter, 1985. *Publications:* papers, mostly on sensory receptors and sensory nervous system, in Jl of Physiology, Procs of Royal Soc. series B, Jl of Marine Biol Assoc., etc. *Recreations:* painting, sailing, tennis. *Address:* Seaways, North Rock, Kingsand, near Plymouth PL10 1NG. *T:* Plymouth (0752) 822745; Marine Biological Association Laboratory, Citadel Hill, Plymouth.

GRAY, John Magnus, CBE 1971 (MBE 1945); ERD 1946; Chairman, Northern Ireland Electricity Service, 1974–80 (Deputy Chairman, 1973–74); *b* 15 Oct. 1915; *o s* of Lewis Campbell Gray, CA and Ingeborg Sanderson Gray (*née* Ross), Glasgow; *m* 1947, Patricia Mary, OBE 1976, *widow* of Major Aubrey D. P. Hodges and *d* of John Norman Eggar and Emma Frances Eggar (*née* Garrett), Epsom and Godalming; one *d. Educ:* Horris Hill, Newbury; Winchester College. Served RA, 1939–46 (Major). Joined Wm Ewart & Son Ltd, Linen Manufrs, Belfast, 1934; Dir 1950; Man. Dir 1958–72. Chairman: Irish Linen Guild, 1958–64; Central Council, Irish Linen Industry, 1968–74 (Mem., 1957; Vice-Chm., 1966–68); Linen Industry Standards Cttee of BSI, 1969–74; Belfast Br., RNLI, 1970–76; Member: Council of Belfast T&AFA, 1948–68; Council of Belfast Chamber of Commerce, 1955–59; Gen. Synod of Church of Ireland, 1955–84; Councils of FBI and CBI, 1956–74, 1979–80; NI Legal Aid Cttee, 1958–59; Export Council for Europe, 1964–70; Northern Ireland Adv. Council for BBC, 1968–72; Design Council, 1974–80; Asst Comr for Commn on Constitution, 1969–73. Captain, Royal Co. Down Golf Club, 1963. *Recreations:* golf, gardening. *Address:* Blairlodge, Dundrum, Newcastle, Co. Down BT33 0NF. *T:* Dundrum (039675) 271. *Club:* Army and Navy.

GRAY, Vice Adm. Sir John (Michael Dudgeon), KBE 1967 (OBE 1950); CB 1964; *b* Dublin, 13 June 1913; British; *m* 1939, Margaret Helen Purvis; one *s* one *d. Educ:* RNC, Dartmouth. HMS Nelson, 1931; Midshipman, HMS Enterprise, 1932–33; Sub-Lieut, HMS Devonshire, 1934; specialised in Gunnery, 1938. Served War of 1939–45; HMS Hermes; HMS Spartan; with US in Anzio; 8th Army in Italy; French Army in France (despatches). HMS Duke of York, 1945, Comdr 1947; Naval Adviser, UK Mission, Japan, 1947–50 (OBE Korean War); HMS Swiftsure, 1950, Capt. 1952; HMS Lynx, 1956; HMS Victorious, 1961; Rear Adm. 1962; Dir-Gen. of Naval Trng, Min. of Def., 1964–65 (Admiralty, 1962–64); Vice Adm. 1965; C-in-C, S Atlantic and S America Station, 1965–67. Sec., Oriental Ceramic Soc., 1974–. *Recreations:* squash, tennis, athletics (represented RN in 220 and 440 yds). *Address:* Flat 5, 55 Elm Park Gardens, SW10 9PA. *T:* 071–352 1757. *Club:* Naval and Military.

GRAY, Prof. John Richard; Professor of African History, University of London, 1972–89, now Emeritus; *b* 7 July 1929; *s* of Captain Alfred William Gray, RN and of Christobel Margaret Gray (*née* Raikes); *m* 1957, Gabriella, *d* of Dr Camillo Cattaneo; one *s* one *d. Educ:* Charterhouse; Downing Coll., Cambridge (Richmond Scholar). BA Cantab 1951; PhD London 1957. Lectr, Univ. of Khartoum, 1959–61; Res. Fellow, Sch. of Oriental and African Studies, London, 1961–63, Reader, 1963–72. Vis. Prof., UCLA, 1967. Editor, Jl African History, 1968–71; Chairman: Africa Centre, Covent Garden, 1967–72; Britain-Zimbabwe Soc., 1981–84. Mem., Pontifical Cttee of Historical Sciences, 1982–. Order of St Silvester, 1966. *Publications:* The Two Nations: aspects of the development of race relations in the Rhodesias and Nyasaland, 1960; A History of the Southern Sudan, 1839–1889, 1961; (with D. Chambers) Materials for West African History in Italian Archives, 1965; (ed, with D. Birmingham) Pre-Colonial African Trade, 1970; (ed) The Cambridge History of Africa, vol. 4, 1975; (ed, with E. Fasholé-Luke and others) Christianity in Independent Africa, 1978; Black Christians and White Missionaries, 1990. *Recreation:* things Italian. *Address:* 39 Rotherwick Road, NW11 7DD. *T:* 081–458 3676.

GRAY, John Walton David, CMG 1986; HM Diplomatic Service; Ambassador and UK Permanent Representative to OECD, Paris, since 1988; *b* Burry Port, Carmarthenshire, 1 Oct. 1936; *s* of Myrddin Gray and Elsie Irene (*née* Jones), Llanelli, Carms; *m* 1957, Anthoula, *e d* of Nicolas Yerasimou, Nicosia, Cyprus; one *s* two *d. Educ:* Blundell's Sch.; Christ's Coll., Cambridge (MA; Scholar and Tancred Student); ME Centre, Oxford; Amer. Univ., Cairo. National Service, 1954–56. Joined Foreign Service, 1962; served: Mecas, 1962; Bahrain Agency, 1964; FO, 1967; Geneva, 1970; Sofia, 1974; Counsellor (Commercial), 1978, Counsellor and Hd of Chancery, 1980, Jedda; Hd of Maritime, Aviation and Environment Dept, FCO, 1982–85; Ambassador to Lebanon, 1985–88. *Recreations:* most spectator sports, amateur dramatics, light history, things Welsh. *Address:* c/o Foreign and Commonwealth Office, SW1A 2AH. *T:* 071–270 3000. *Clubs:* Athenæum, Commonwealth Trust.

GRAY, Rt. Rev. Joseph; *see* Shrewsbury, Bishop of, (RC).

GRAY, Kenneth Walter, PhD; Technical Director, THORN EMI plc, since 1986 (Director of Research, 1984–86); *b* 20 March 1939; *s* of Robert W. Gray and late Ruby M. Gray; *m* 1962, Jill Henderson; two *s* one *d. Educ:* Blue Coat Sch.; Univ. of Wales (BSc, PhD). Research on magnetic resonance, as Nat. Res. Council of Canada post-doctoral Fellow, Univ. of British Columbia, Vancouver, 1963–65; research on semiconductor devices and on radiometry, N American Rockwell Science Center, Thousand Oaks, Calif, 1965–70; research on devices and systems at Royal Signals and Radar Estabt, 1971; Supt Solid State Physics and Devices Div., 1976; Head of Physics Group, 1979; RCDS 1981. Royal Signals and Radar Establishment: CSO, MoD, Dep. Dir (Applied Physics), 1982–84; Under Sec., Dep. Dir (Information Systems), 1984. Exec. Chm., Thorn Software, 1987–89. Visiting Research Fellow: Univ. of Newcastle, 1972–74; Univ. of Leeds, 1976–; Vis. Prof., Univ. of Nottingham, 1986–. *Publications:* over 30 scientific and technical papers in various learned jls. *Recreations:* running, tennis, bridge. *Address:* Broadgates, Manor Road, Penn, Buckinghamshire HP10 8JA.

GRAY, Linda Esther, (Mrs Peter McCrorie); opera singer; *b* 29 May 1948; *d* of James and Esther Gray; *m* 1971, Peter McCrorie; one *d. Educ:* Greenock Academy; Royal Scottish Academy of Music and Drama. Cinzano Scholarship, 1969; Goldsmith Schol., 1970; James Caird Schol., 1971; Kathleen Ferrier Award, 1972; Christie Award, 1972. London Opera Centre, 1969–71; Glyndebourne Festival Opera, 1972–75; Scottish Opera, 1974–79; Welsh Opera, 1980–; English National Opera, 1979–; American début, 1981; Royal Opera House: Sieglinde, 1982; Fidelio, 1983. Records: Tristan und Isolde, 1981; Wagner's Die Feen, 1983. Principal rôles: Isolde, Sieglinde, Kundry (Wagner); Tosca (Puccini); Fidelio (Beethoven). *Recreations:* cooking, swimming. *Address:* 35 Green Lane, New Malden, Surrey KT3 5BX.

GRAY, Margaret Caroline, MA Cantab; Headmistress, Godolphin and Latymer School, 1963–Dec. 1973; *b* 25 June 1913; *d* of Rev. A. Herbert Gray, DD, and Mrs Gray (Mary C. Dods, *d* of Principal Marcus Dods of New Coll., Edinburgh). *Educ:* St Mary's Hall, Brighton; Newnham Coll., Cambridge. Post graduate fellowship to Smith Coll., Mass, USA, 1935–36. Asst History mistress, Westcliff High Sch. for Girls, 1937–38; Head of History Dept, Mary Datchelor Girls' Sch., Camberwell, 1939–52; Headmistress, Skinners' Company's Sch., Stamford Hill, 1952–63. Chm., Nat. Advisory Centre on Careers for Women, 1970–. Governor: Francis Holland Schs, 1974–; Hampton Sch., 1976–; West Heath Sch., Sevenoaks, 1974–; Unicorn Sch., Kew, 1974; Chm. of Trustees, Godolphin and Latymer Bursary Fund, 1976–. *Recreations:* gardening, motoring, walking. *Address:* 15 Fitzwilliam Avenue, Kew, Richmond, Surrey TW9 2DQ. *T:* 081–940 4439.

GRAY, Lt-Gen. Sir Michael Stuart, KCB 1986; OBE 1970; General Officer Commanding, South East District, and Commander Joint Force Headquarters, 1985–88, retired; Defence Industries Adviser, Wardle Storeys, since 1989; *b* Beverley, E Yorkshire, 3 May 1932; *e s* of late Lieut Frank Gray, RNVR, and Joan Gray (*née* Gibson); *m* 1958, Juliette Antonia Noon, Northampton; two *s* one *d. Educ:* Beverley Grammar Sch.; Christ's Hosp., Horsham; RMA, Sandhurst. FBIM; FInstD; FICFM. Enlisted RA, 1950; commissioned E Yorkshire Regt, 1952; served Malaya; transf. to Parachute Regt, 1955; served Cyprus, Suez, Jordan, Greece, Bahrein, Aden, N Ireland; sc Camberley, 1963; commanded 1st Bn Parachute Regt, 1969–71; DS Staff Coll., Camberley, 1971–73; Col GS 1 Div. BAOR, 1973–75; RCDS 1976; last Comdr 16 Para Bde, 1977; Comdr 6 Field Force and COMUKMF, 1977–79; Comdr British Army Staff and Mil. Attaché, Washington, 1979–81, and Head of British Def. Staff and Def. Attaché, Washington, 1981; GOC SW District, and Maj.-Gen., UKMF(L), 1981–83; COS, HQ BAOR, 1984–85. Dep. Col Comdt, Parachute Regt, 1986–90, Col Comdt, 1990–. Consultant, Brittany Ferries (writing Battlefield Tours), 1988. Dir, Airborne Initiative Hldgs Ltd; Chm., (non-exec.) Redmart Promotions Ltd (Praetorian Project). Chm., Airborne Assault Normandy Trust (AAN), to preserve the history of 6 AB Division in Normandy, 1978–; Chairman Trustees: AB Forces Museum, 1986–; Military Aerospace Museums Trust, Aldershot, 1990–; Chm., AB Forces Charities Develt Trust; President: Forces Retirement Assoc., 1987–; Parachute Regt Assoc. (Pres., Portsmouth and York Brs); Trustee, AB Forces Security Fund, 1986–; Vice President: Army Parachute Assoc., 1980–; Normandy Veterans Assoc., Goole Br., 1988–; Area Organiser (NE), King George's Fund for Sailors, 1988–; Mem., Amicable Soc. of Blues, 1989–; Patron, Combined Ex-Service Assoc., Bridlington, 1988–. Freeman, City of London, 1983. *Recreations:* military history, travelling, DIY, photography, painting. *Address:* c/o National Westminster Bank, 60 Market Place, Beverley, North Humberside.

GRAY, Milner Connorton, CBE 1963; RDI 1938; FCSD; AGI; FInstPack; Founder Partner and Senior Consultant, Design Research Unit; Past Master, Faculty of Royal Designers for Industry; Past President, Society of Industrial Artists and Designers (now Chartered Society of Designers); Past Master Art Workers' Guild; *b* 8 Oct. 1899; *s* of late Archibald Campbell Gray and Katherine May Hart, Eynsford, Kent; *m* 1934, Gnade Osborne-Pratt; no *c. Educ:* studied painting and design, London Univ., Goldsmiths' Coll. Sch. of Art. Head of Exhibitions Branch, Ministry of Information, 1940–41, and Adviser on Exhibitions, 1941–44; Senior Partner in Industrial Design Partnership, 1934–40; Principal, Sir John Cass Coll. of Art, 1937–40; on Visiting Staff: Goldsmiths' Coll. Sch. of Art, London Univ., 1930–40; Chelsea Sch. of Art, 1934–37; Royal Coll. of Art, 1940;

Founder Mem., Soc. of Industrial Artists, 1930, Hon. Sec., 1932–40, Pres., 1943–48 and 1968; Member of Council: Design and Industries Assoc., 1935–38; RSA, 1959–65; Artists Gen. Benevolent Instn, 1959– (Vice Pres., 1986); Adviser to BBC "Looking at Things" Schs Broadcasts, 1949–55. Member: Min. of Education Nat. Adv. Cttee on Art Examinations, 1949–52; Nat. Adv. Council on Art Education, 1959–69; Royal Mint Adv. Cttee, 1952–86. Mem. Council, RCA, 1963–67, Mem. Court 1967–, Senior Fellow, 1971. British Pres., Alliance Graphique Internationale, 1963–71. Consultant Designer: BR Bd for BR Corporate Design Prog., 1963–67; (jointly) to Orient Line, SS Oriana, 1957–61; Ilford Ltd, 1946–66; Internat. Distillers and Vintners, 1954–69; Watney Mann Group, 1956–70; British Aluminium Co., 1965–72; ICI, 1966–70; Min. of Technology, 1970–. Governor: Central Sch. of Art and Design, 1944–46; Hornsey Coll. of Art and Design, 1959–65. Hon. Fellow, Soc. of Typographic Designers, 1979. Hon. Des. RCA, 1963, Hon. Dr RCA, 1979; Hon. DA Manchester, 1964. Freeman City of London, 1987. Served in 19th London Regt, and Royal Engineers, attached Camouflage Sch., 1917–19; admitted HAC, 1923. Gold Medal, Soc. of Ind. Artists and Designers, 1955. *Publications:* The Practice of Design (jointly), 1946; Package Design, 1955; (jtly) Lettering for Architects and Designers, 1962; articles, lectures and broadcasts on various aspects of design. *Address:* 8 Holly Mount, Hampstead, NW3 6SG. *T:* 071–435 4238; Felix Hall, Kelvedon, Essex. *Club:* Arts.

GRAY, Monique Sylvaine, (Mrs P. F. Gray); *see* Viner, M. S.

GRAY, Paul Edward, ScD; Chairman of the Corporation, Massachusetts Institute of Technology, since 1990; *b* 7 Feb. 1932; *s* of Kenneth Frank Gray and Florence (*née* Gilleo); *m* 1955, Priscilla Wilson King; one *s* three *d*. *Educ:* Massachusetts Inst. of Technol. (SB 1954, SM 1955, ScD 1960). Served Army, 1955–57 (1st Lieut). Massachusetts Inst. of Technology: Mem., Faculty of Engrg, 1960–71, 1990–; Class of 1922 Prof. of Electrical Engrg, 1968–71; Dean, Sch. of Engrg, 1970–71; Chancellor, 1971–80; Pres., 1980–90; Mem. of Corp., 1971–. Director: Shawmut National Corp., Boston; The New England, Boston; A. D. Little Inc., Cambridge; Boeing Co., Seattle; Eastman Kodak, Rochester. Trustee and Mem. of Corporation: Museum of Science, Boston; Woods Hole Oceanographic Inst.; Trustee: Wheaton Coll., Mass; Kennedy Meml Trust, London; Nat. Action Council for Minorities in Engrg; Whitaker Health Scis Fund, Cambridge, Mass. Fellow, Amer. Acad. of Arts and Sciences; Member: National Acad. of Engrg; Mexican National Acad. of Engrg; AAAS; Fellow, IEEE. *Address:* Massachusetts Institute of Technology, 77 Massachusetts Avenue, Cambridge, Mass 02139, USA; 100 Memorial Drive, Cambridge, Mass 02142.

GRAY, Paul Richard Charles; Under Secretary, Monetary Group, HM Treasury, since 1990; *b* 2 Aug. 1948; *s* of Rev. Sidney Gray and Ina (*née* Maxey); *m* 1972, Lynda Elsie Braby; two *s*. *Educ:* Wyggeston Boys' Sch., Leicester; LSE (BSc Econ 1969). Dept of Econ. Affairs, 1969; HM Treasury, 1969–77; with Booker McConnell Ltd, 1977–79; HM Treasury: Principal, 1979–83; Asst Sec., 1984–87; Econ. Affairs Private Sec. to Prime Minister, 1988–90. *Recreations:* family, walking, lawn-mowing. *Address:* HM Treasury, Parliament Street, SW1P 3AG. *T:* 071–270 3000.

GRAY, Prof. Peter, MA, PhD, ScD (Cantab); FRS 1977; CChem, FRSC; Master of Gonville and Caius College, Cambridge, since 1988; *b* Newport, 25 Aug. 1926; *er s* of late Ivor Hicks Gray and Rose Ethel Gray; *m* 1952, Barbara Joan Hume, PhD, 2nd *d* of J. B. Hume, London; two *s* two *d*. *Educ:* Newport, High Sch.; Gonville and Caius Coll., Cambridge. Major Schol., 1943; Prizeman, 1944, 1945 and 1946, Gonville and Caius Coll.; BA 1st cl hons Nat. Sci. Tripos, 1946; Dunlop Res. Student, 1946; Ramsay Mem. Fellow, 1949–51; PhD 1949; Fellow, Gonville and Caius Coll., 1949–53; ICI Fellow, 1951; ScD 1963. University Demonstrator in Chem. Engrg, University of Cambridge, 1951–55; Physical Chemistry Dept, University of Leeds: Lectr, 1955; Reader, 1959; Prof., 1962; Head of Dept, 1965–88; Chm., Bd of Combined Faculties of Science and Applied Science, 1972–74; Hon. Vis. Prof., 1988–. Visiting Professor: Univ. of BC, 1958–59; Univ. of W Ont., 1969; Univ. of Göttingen, 1979, 1986; Macquarie Univ., 1980; Univ. of Paris, 1986; Visitor, Fire Res. Organisation, 1984–. Mem. Council: Faraday Soc., 1965 (Vice-Pres., 1970; Treasurer, 1973; Pres., 1983–85); Chemical Soc., 1969. Meldola Medal, Royal Inst. Chem., 1956; Marlow Medal, Faraday Soc., 1959; Gold Medal, Combustion Inst., 1978; Award for Combustion, Royal Soc. of Chemistry, 1986; Italgas Prize for Chemistry, 1988. Associate Editor, Royal Society, 1983–. *Publications:* (with S. K. Scott) Chemical Oscillations and Instabilities, 1990; numerous papers on phys. chem. subjects in scientific jls. *Recreation:* hill walking. *Address:* The Master's Lodge, Gonville and Caius College, Cambridge CB2 1TA. *T:* Cambridge (0223) 332404. *Club:* United Oxford & Cambridge University.

GRAY, Peter Francis; Chairman, Exmoor Dual Investment Trust, since 1988; Director: New Zealand Investment Trust, since 1988; Gartmore Value Investments, since 1989; Contra-Cyclical Investment Trust, since 1991; *b* 7 Jan. 1937; *s* of Revd George Francis Selby Gray; *m* 1978, Fiona Bristol; two *s*. *Educ:* Marlborough; Trinity College, Cambridge. MA; FCA. Served Royal Fusiliers, attached 4th Kings African Rifles, Uganda, 1956–58. Coopers & Lybrand, 1967–69; Samuel Montagu & Co., 1970–77; Head of Investment Div., Crown Agents for Oversea Govts & Admins, 1977–83; Man. Dir, Touche Remnant Hldgs Ltd, 1983–87; Dir, TR Industrial & General Trust, 1984–88. Dep. Chm., Assoc. of Investment Trust Cos, 1985–87. Trustee, John Hancock Global Trust, 1985–87. *Address:* 1 Bradbourne Street, SW6 3TF. *Club:* Brooks's.

GRAY, Maj.-Gen. (Reginald) John, CB 1973; Chairman, RAMC Association, 1980–88; *b* 26 Nov. 1916; *s* of late Dr Cyril Gray and Frances Anne Higgins, Higginsbrook, Co. Meath; *m* 1943, Esme, *d* of late G. R. G. Shipp; one *s* one *d*. *Educ:* Rossall Sch.; Coll. of Medicine, Univ. of Durham. MB, BS. Commissioned into RAMC, 1939; served War of 1939–45 in India; later Burma, NW Europe, Egypt, Malta, BAOR. Comd of 9 (Br.) CCS, 1945; Medical Gold Staff Officer, 1953; Asst Dir-Gen., AMS, WO, AMD3, 1954–57; comd of David Bruce Mil. Hosp., Mtarfa, 1957–60; 14 Field Amb., 4 Guards Bde, 1960–63; Brit. Mil. Hosp., Rinteln, 1963–64; The Queen Alexandra Mil. Hosp., Millbank, 1964–67; Asst Dir-Gen., AMS, Min. of Defence AMD1, 1967–69; Dep. Dir-Gen., AMS, 1969–71. QHS 1970–73; DMS, UK Land Forces, 1972–73, retired. Col Comdt, RAMC, 1977–81. Chief MO, British Red Cross Soc., 1974–83; Chm., BMA Armed Forces Cttee, 1981–85. Dir, International Generics Ltd, 1974–83. Mem., Casualty Surgeons Assoc., 1976–; Hon. Mem., St Andrews Ambulance Assoc., 1982; Life Mem., BRCS, 1983; Hon. Mem., Inst. of Civil Defence, 1983. FRSM; FFPHM (FFCM 1972). CStJ 1971 (OStJ 1957). *Recreations:* gardening, brewing, d-i-y slowly. *Address:* 11 Hampton Close, Wimbledon, SW20 0RY. *T:* 081–946 7429.

GRAY, Robert, CBE 1988; JP; DL; building consultant and clerk of works; Lord Provost and Lord-Lieutenant of Glasgow, 1984–88; *b* 3 March 1928; *s* of John Gray and Mary (*née* McManus); *m* 1955, Mary (*née* McCartney); one *d*. *Educ:* St Mungo's Acad., Glasgow. LIOB 1970. Lecturer: Glasgow Coll. of Building, 1964–65; Anniesland Coll., 1965–70; Sen. Lectr, Cardonald Coll., 1970–84. Mem. (Lab) Glasgow Dist Council, 1974–. DL City of Glasgow, 1988. OStJ. Fellow, Glasgow Coll. of Technol., 1987. Hon. LLD Strathclyde, 1987. *Recreations:* walking, reading, music. *Address:* 106 Churchill Drive, Glasgow G11 7EZ. *T:* 041–357 3328. *Clubs:* Royal Scottish Automobile, Art (Glasgow).

GRAY, Robert Michael Ker, QC 1983; QC (NI) 1984; a Recorder, since 1985. *Educ:* Radley (Scholar); Humboldt Gymnasium, Düsseldorf (Exchange Scholar); Balliol College, Oxford (Scholar) (MA 1963); St John's College, Cambridge (LLM (LLB 1967), Russian Tripos 1968). Articled to Sir Anthony Lousada, Messrs Stephenson, Harwood and Tatham; Solicitor, 1962. Called to the Bar, Lincoln's Inn, Gray's Inn, and Inner Temple, 1969, King's Inns, Dublin, 1989; MacMahon Studentship, St John's College, Cambridge, 1969–73. European Office, UN, Geneva, 1962–64; Dept of Slavonic Studies, Cambridge, 1964. Chancellor, dio. of Southwark, 1990–. Mem., Gen. Council of the Bar, 1972–74; Mem., Senate of the Bar, 1974–79, 1980–87 (Chm., Young Barristers, 1978–79). Chm., Harrison Homes (formerly Homes for the Aged Poor), 1980–; Sec., London Friends of St George's Cathedral, Cape Town, 1983–; Mem., Cttee, Nat. Aural Gp, 1988–; Trustee, Holy Cross Centre Trust, 1988–. *Recreations:* walking, swimming. *Clubs:* Garrick, Royal Automobile; Budleigh Salterton; Pangbourne Working Men's; City and Civil Service (Cape Town).

GRAY, Robin; Under Secretary, Department of the Environment, since 1988; Director, Marketing and Planning, PSA Projects, since 1990; *b* 16 April 1944; *s* of Robert George and Jeannie Gray; *m* 1971, Kathleen Rosemary Kuhn; two *d*. *Educ:* Woking County Grammar Sch. for Boys; Birkbeck Coll., London Univ. (BA Hons). UKAEA, 1962–64; HM Treasury, 1964–70; Asst Sec. to Crowther Cttee on Consumer Credit, 1968–70; Min. of Housing and Local Govt, subseq. DoE, 1970–; seconded to Water Resources Bd/Central Water Planning Unit, 1973–75, to W Sussex CC, 1982–83; Sec., London and Metropolitan Govt Staff Commn, 1984–86; PSA, 1986–; Under Sec. and Dir of Civil Accommodation, 1988; Dir, Civil Projects and Head, Projects Business Policy Unit, 1989. *Recreations:* cricket, walking and other outdoor activities, talking. *Address:* PSA Projects, Whitgift Centre, Wellesley Road, Croydon, Surrey CR9 3LY. *T:* 081–760 4578.

GRAY, Robin, (Robert Walker Gray), CB 1977; Deputy Secretary, Department of Trade, 1975–84; retired; part-time consultant on international trade relations; *b* 29 July 1924; *s* of Robert Walker Gray and Dorothy (*née* Lane); *m* 1955, Shirley Matilda (*née* Taylor); two *s* one *d*. *Educ:* John Lyon Sch., Harrow; London Sch. of Economics. BScEcons 1946; Farr Medal in Statistics. Air Warfare Analysis Section of Air Min., 1940–45; BoT, 1947; UK Delegn to OEEC, 1950–51; BoT, 1952–66; Commercial Counsellor, British High Commn, Ottawa, 1966–70; Under-Secretary: DTI, 1971–74; Dept of Prices and Consumer Protection, 1974–75; Dep. Sec., DoI, 1975. Sec. and Governor, INFORM. *Address:* Tansy, Brook Road, Wormley, Godalming, Surrey GU8 5UA. *T:* Wormley (0428) 682486.

GRAY, Hon. Robin (Trevor), BAgrSc; MHA (L) for Lyons, Tasmania, since 1985 (for Wilmot, 1976–85); Premier of Tasmania and Treasurer, 1982–89; Leader of the Opposition, 1981–82 and since 1989; *b* 1 March 1940; *s* of late Rev. W. J. Gray; *m* 1965, Judith, *d* of late A. G. Boyd; two *s* one *d*. *Educ:* Box Hill High Sch.; Dookie Agricl Coll., Melbourne Univ. (Dookie Dip. of Agric.). Teacher, 1961–65 (in UK, 1964); agricl consultant, Colac, Vic, 1965, Launceston, Tas, 1965–76; pt-time Lectr in Agricl Econs, Univ. of Tasmania, 1970–76. Dep. Leader of the Opposition, Tasmania, 1979–81; Minister: for Racing and Gaming, 1982–84; for Energy, 1982–88; for Forests, 1984–86; for State Develt, 1984–89; for Small Business, 1986–89; for Status of Women, 1989; for Antarctic Affairs, 1989; for Science and Technology, 1989. *Recreations:* gardening, golf. *Address:* House of Assembly, Parliament House, Hobart, Tas 7000, Australia; 11 Beech Road, Launceston, Tas 7250, Australia.

GRAY, Roger Ibbotson, QC 1967; a Recorder of the Crown Court, since 1972; *b* 16 June 1921; *o s* of Arthur Gray and Mary Gray (*née* Ibbotson); *m* 1st, 1952, Anne Valerie (marr. diss.), 2nd *d* of late Capt. G. G. P. Hewett, CBE, RN; one *s*; 2nd, 1987, Lynne Jacqueline, *er d* of Eric Towell, FRIAA, RIBA. *Educ:* Wycliffe Coll.; Queen's Coll., Oxford. 1st cl. hons Jurisprudence, Oxon, 1941. Commissioned RA, 1942; served with Ayrshire Yeomanry, 1942–45; Normandy and NW Europe, 1944–45; GSO3 (Mil. Ops), GHQ, India, 1946. Pres. of Oxford Union, 1947. Called to Bar, Gray's Inn, 1947; South-Eastern Circuit. A Legal Assessor: GNC, 1976–83; UKCC, 1983–. Contested (C) Dagenham, 1955. *Publication:* (with Major I. A. Graham Young) A Short History of the Ayrshire Yeomanry (Earl of Carrick's Own) 151st Field Regiment, RA, 1939–46, 1947. *Recreations:* cricket, reading, talk. *Address:* The Old Cottage, 20 Friday Street, Minchinhampton, Glos GL6 9JL; Queen Elizabeth Building, Temple, EC4. *T:* 071–583 7837. *Clubs:* Carlton, Pratt's, MCC.

GRAY, Simon James Holliday; writer; *b* 21 Oct. 1936; *s* of Dr James Davidson Gray and Barbara Cecelia Mary Holliday; *m* 1965, Beryl Mary Kevern; one *s* one *d*. *Educ:* Westminster; Dalhousie Univ.; Trinity Coll., Cambridge (MA). Trinity Coll., Cambridge: Sen. Schol., Research Student and Harper-Wood Trav. Student, 1960; Supervisor in English, 1960–63; Sen. Instructor in English, Univ. of British Columbia, 1963–64; Lectr in English, QMC, London Univ., 1965–85 (Hon. Fellow, 1985). Co-dir, The Common Pursuit, Promenade Theatre, NY, 1986, and dir, Phoenix Theatre, 1988. Screenplay: A Month in the Country, 1987. *Publications: novels:* Colmain, 1963; Simple People, 1965; Little Portia, 1967, repr. 1986; (as Hamish Reade) A Comeback for Stark, 1968; *plays:* Wise Child, 1968; Sleeping Dog, 1968; Dutch Uncle, 1969; The Idiot, 1971; Spoiled, 1971; Butley, 1971; Otherwise Engaged, 1975 (voted Best Play, 1976–77, by NY Drama Critics Circle); Plaintiffs and Defendants, 1975; Two Sundays, 1975; Dog Days, 1976; Molly, 1977; The Rear Column, 1978; Close of Play, 1979; Stage Struck, 1979; Quartermaine's Terms, 1981 (televised 1987); adap. Tartuffe (for Washington, DC; unpublished), 1982; The Common Pursuit, 1984; Plays One, 1986; After Pilkington, 1987 (televised 1987); Melon, 1987; The Holy Terror and Tartuffe, 1990; *non-fiction:* An Unnatural Pursuit and Other Pieces, 1985; How's That for Telling 'Em, Fat Lady?, 1988. *Recreations:* watching cricket and soccer, tennis, swimming. *Address:* c/o Judy Daish Associates, 83 Eastbourne Mews, W2 6LQ.

GRAY, Prof. Thomas Cecil, CBE 1976; KCSG 1982; JP; MD, FRCS, FRCP, FCAnaes; FFARCS; FFARACS (Hon.); FFARCSI (Hon.); Professor of Anæsthesia, The University of Liverpool, 1959–76, now Emeritus; Dean of Postgraduate Medical Studies, 1966–70, of Faculty of Medicine, 1970–76; *b* 11 March 1913; *s* of Thomas and Ethel Gray; *m* 1st, 1937, Marjorie Kathleen (*née* Hely) (*d* 1978); one *s* one *d*; 2nd, 1979, Pamela Mary (*née* Corning); one *s*. *Educ:* Ampleforth Coll.; University of Liverpool. General Practice, 1937–39. Hon. Anaesthetist to various hospitals, 1940–47. Active Service, Royal Army Medical Corps, 1942–44. Demonstrator in Anæsthesia, University of Liverpool, 1942, 1944–46; Reader in Anæsthesia, University of Liverpool, 1947–59; Hon. Cons Anæsthetist: United Liverpool Hosps, Royal Infirmary Branch; Liverpool Thoracic Surgical Centre, Broadgreen Hosp.; Mem. Bd, Faculty of Anæsthetists, RCSEng, 1948–69 (Vice-Dean, 1952–54; Dean, 1964–67). Member Council: RCS, 1964–67; Assoc. of Anæsthetists of Great Brit. and Ire., 1948–67 (Hon. Treas. 1950–56; Pres. 1957–59); ASME, 1972–76; FRSocMed (Mem. Council, 1958–61; Pres. Anæsthetic Section, 1955–56; Mem. Council, Sect. of Med. Educn, 1969–72); Chm. BMA Anæsthetic Group,

1957–62; Mem., Liverpool Regional Hosp. Board, 1968–74 (Chm., Anæsthetic Adv. Cttee, 1948–70; Chm., Med. Adv. Council, 1970–74); Mem., Merseyside RHA, 1974–77; Mem., Bd of Governors, United Liverpool Hosp., 1969–74; Mem. Clinical Res. Bd, Med. Res. Council, 1965–69; Hon. Civilian Consultant in Anæsthetics to the Army at Home, 1964–78 (Guthrie Medal 1977), Emeritus Consultant to the Army, 1979. Hon. Consultant to St John's Ambulance; Member Council, Order of St John for Merseyside; Asst Dir-Gen., St John Ambulance, 1977–82; Vice-Pres., Med. Defence Union, 1954–88 (Treasurer, 1977–82); Chm., Bd of Governors, Linacre Center for Study of Ethics of Health Care, 1973–83. Examiner in FFARCS, 1953–70; FFARCSI 1967–70: Dip. Vet. Anæsth., RCVS, 1968–76. Hon. FRSocMed, 1979; Hon. Member: Sheffield and East Midlands Soc. of Anæsthetists; Yorks Soc. of Anæsthetists; SW Regl Soc. of Anæsthetists; Austrian Soc. of Anæsthetists; Soc. Belge d'Anesthesie et de Reanimation; Argentinian and Brazilian Socs of Anesthesiologists; Australian and Malaysian Socs of Anæsthetists; Assoc. of Veterinary Anæsthetists. Hon. Corresp. Member: Sociedade das Ciencias Medical di Lisboa; W African Assoc. of Surgeons. Clover Lectr and Medallist, RCS, 1953; Lectures: Simpson-Smith Meml, W London Sch. of Med., 1956; Jenny Hartmann Meml, Univ. of Basle, 1958; Eastman, Univ. of Rochester, NY, 1958; Sir James Young Simpson Meml, RCSE, 1967; Torsten Gordh, Swedish Soc. of Anaesthetists, 1978; Kirkpatrick, Faculty of Anaesthetists, RCSI, 1981; John Gillies, Scottish Soc. of Anaesthetists, 1982; Mitchiner Meml, RAMC, 1983; Florence Elliott, Royal Victoria Hosp., Belfast, 1984. Sims Commonwealth Travelling Prof., 1961. JP City of Liverpool, 1966 (retd list). Freeman, City of London, 1984; Liveryman, Soc. of Apothecaries, 1956. OStJ 1979. Medallist, Univ. of Liège, 1947; Henry Hill Hickman Medal, 1972; Hon. Gold Medal, RCS, 1978; Ralph M. Waters medal and award, Illinois Soc. of Anesthesiologists, 1978; Silver Medal, Assoc. of Anaesthetists, 1982. *Publications:* Modern Trends in Anæsthesia (ed jtly), 1958, 3rd edn 1967; (ed jtly) General Anæsthesia, 1959, 4th edn 1980 (Spanish edns, 1974, 1983); (ed jtly) Paediatric Anæsthesia, 1981; many contribs to gen. med. press and specialist jls. *Recreations:* music, golf, amateur dramatics. *Address:* 6 Raven Meols Lane, Formby, Liverpool L37 4DF.

GRAY, Sir William (Hume), 3rd Bt *cr* 1917; Director, Egglestone Estate Co.; *b* 26 July 1955; *s* of William Talbot Gray (*d* 1971) (*er s* of 2nd Bt), and of Rosemarie Hume Gray, *d* of Air Cdre Charles Hume Elliott-Smith; *S* grandfather, 1978; *m* 1984, Catherine Victoria Willoughby, *y d* of late John Naylor and of Mrs Jerram, Wadebridge, Cornwall; one *s* two *d*. *Educ:* Aysgarth School, Bedale, Yorks; Eton College; Polytechnic of Central London BA (Hons) Architecture; DipArch; RIBA. *Recreation:* sport. *Heir:* *s* William John Cresswell Gray, *b* 24 Aug. 1986. *Address:* Eggleston Hall, Barnard Castle, Co. Durham. *T:* Teesdale (0833) 50403.

GRAY, Sir William (Stevenson), Kt 1974; JP; DL; solicitor and notary public; Lord Provost, City of Glasgow and Lord Lieutenant, County of the City of Glasgow, 1972–75; *b* 3 May 1928; *o s* of William Stevenson Gray and Mary Johnstone Dickson; *m* 1958, Mary Rodger; one *s* one *d*. *Educ:* Hillhead High Sch.; Glasgow Univ. Admitted solicitor, 1958; notary public, 1960. Chairman: Scottish Special Housing Assoc., 1966–72; WPHT Scotland Ltd (formerly World of Property Housing Trust Scottish Housing Assoc. Ltd), 1974–; Irvine New Town Develt Corp., 1974–76; Scotland W Industrial Promotion Gp, 1972–75; Scottish Develt Agency, 1975–79; The Oil Club, 1975–; Barrell Selection Ltd, 1987–; Gap Housing Assoc. Ltd, 1988–; Gap Housing Assoc. (Ownership) Ltd, 1988–; Norcity Homes plc, 1988–; Norcity II plc, 1990–; Clan Homes plc, 1988–; Manchester Village Homes plc, 1989–; Norhomes plc, 1989–; Dermalase Ltd, 1989–; First to Sixth Tax Homes Plc (Paragon), 1990–; Home Partners Plus 01 & 02 Plc, 1991–. Member: Exec., Scottish Council (Develt and Industry), 1971–75; Scottish Econ. Council, 1975–83; Lower Clyde Water Bd, 1971–72; Clyde Port Authority, 1972–75; Adv. Council for Energy Conservation, 1974–84; Convention of Royal Burghs, 1971–75; Central Adv. Cttee on JPs, 1975–; Glasgow Adv. Cttee on JPs, 1975–; Third Eye Centre Ltd, Glasgow, 1984– (Chm., 1975–84); Hodgson Martin Ltd Adv. Bd, 1988–. Chairman: Glasgow Independent Hosp. Ltd (Ross Hall Hosp.), 1982–89; Clyde Tourist Assoc., 1972–75; Res. Trust for Inst. of Neurol Scis, 1978–. Member: Nat. Trust for Scotland, 1971–72; Scottish Opera Bd, 1971–72; Scottish Nat. Orch. Soc., 1972–75; Vice-President: Glasgow Citizens' Theatre, 1975– (Mem., Bd of Dirs, 1970–75); Strathclyde Theatre Gp, 1975–86; Charles Rennie Mackintosh Soc., 1974–; Scottish Assoc. for Care and Resettlement of Offenders, 1982–86 (Chm., 1975–82); Governor, Glasgow Sch. of Art, 1961–75; Patron: Scottish Youth Theatre, 1978–; Scottish Pakistani Soc., 1984–. Member: Court, Glasgow Univ., 1972–75; Council, Strathclyde Univ. Business Sch., 1978–. Hon. LLD: Strathclyde, 1974; Glasgow, 1980. Mem., Glasgow Corp., 1958–75 (Chm., Property Management Cttee, 1964–67); Treasurer, City of Glasgow, 1971–72. JP City of Glasgow, 1961–64, Co. of City of Glasgow 1965; DL Co. of City of Glasgow, 1971, City of Glasgow 1976. *Recreations:* sailing, theatre. *Address:* 13 Royal Terrace, Glasgow G3 7NY. *T:* 041–332 8877.

GRAY DEBROS, Winifred Marjorie, (Mrs E. Gray Debros); *see* Fox, W. M.

GRAYDON, Air Chief Marshal Sir Michael (James), KCB 1989; CBE 1984; Air Officer Commanding-in-Chief, RAF Strike Command and Commander-in-Chief, United Kingdom Air Forces, since 1991; *b* 24 Oct. 1938; *s* of James Julian Graydon and Rita Mary Alkan; *m* 1963, Margaret Elizabeth Clark. *Educ:* Wycliffe Coll.; RAF Coll., Cranwell. Qualified Flying Instructor No 1 FTS, Linton-on-Ouse, 1960–62; No 56 Sqn, 1962–64; No 226 OCU, 1965–67 (Queen's Commendation); Flight Comd, No 56 Sqn, 1967–69; RAF Staff Coll., Bracknell, 1970; PSO to Dep. C-in-C Allied Forces Central Region, Brunssum, 1971–73; Operations, Joint Warfare, MoD, 1973–75; NDC, Latimer, 1976; OC No 11 Sqn, Binbrook, 1977–79; MA to CDS, MoD, 1979–81; OC RAF Leuchars, 1981–83; OC RAF Stanley, Falkland Is, 1983; RCDS, 1984; SASO 11 Gp, Bentley Priory, 1985–86; ACOS Policy, SHAPE, 1986–89; AOC-in-C, RAF Support Comd, 1989–91. Gov., Wycliffe Coll., 1986–. *Publications:* contrib. to professional jls. *Recreations:* golf, birdwatching, reading. *Address:* c/o Lloyds Bank, Cox and King's Branch, PO Box 1190, 7 Pall Mall, SW1Y 5NA. *Clubs:* Royal Air Force; Royal & Ancient Golf (St Andrews).

GRAYSON, Prof. Cecil, MA; FBA 1979; Serena Professor of Italian Studies in the University of Oxford, and Fellow of Magdalen College, 1958–87 (Emeritus Fellow, 1987); *b* 5 Feb. 1920; *s* of John M. Grayson and Dora Hartley; *m* 1947, Margaret Jordan; one *s* three *d*. *Educ:* Batley Grammar Sch.; St Edmund Hall, Oxford (Hon. Fellow, 1986). Army service (UK and India), 1940–46 (Major); First Class Hons (Mod. Langs), 1947; Univ. Lectr in Italian, Oxford, 1948; Lectr at St Edmund Hall, 1948; Lectr at New Coll., 1954. Corresp. Fellow, Commissione per i Testi di Lingua, Bologna, 1957; Mem., Accademia Letteraria Ital. dell' Arcadia, 1958; Corresp. Mem., Accademia della Crusca, 1960; Accademia delle Scienze, Bologna, 1964; Accademia dei Lincei, 1967; Istituto Veneto di Scienze, Lettere ed Arti, 1977; Barlow Lecturer, University Coll., London, 1963; Resident Fellow, Newberry Library, Chicago, 1965; Visiting Professor: Yale Univ., 1966; Berkeley, Calif, 1969, 1973; UCLA, 1980, 1984, 1989; Perth, WA, 1973, 1980; Cape Town, 1980, 1983. Pres., Modern Humanities Res. Assoc., 1988. Premio Internazionale Galileo (storia della lingua italiana), 1974; Serena Medal for Italian Studies, British Academy, 1976. Comdr, Order of Merit, Italy, 1975. *Publications:* Early Italian Texts (with Prof. C. Dionisotti), 1949; Opuscoli inediti di L. B. Alberti, 1954; Alberti and the Tempio Malatestiano, 1957; Vincenzo Calmeta, Prose e Lettere edite e inedite, 1959; A Renaissance Controversy: Latin or Italian?, 1960; L. B. Alberti, Opere volgari, I, 1960, II, 1966, III, 1973; L. B. Alberti e la prima grammatica volgare, 1964; Cinque saggi su Dante, 1972; (trans.) The Lives of Savonarola, Machiavelli and Guicciardini by Roberto Ridolfi, 1959, 1963, 1967; (ed) selected works of Guicciardini, 1964; (ed and trans.) L. B. Alberti, De pictura, De statua, 1972; (ed) The World of Dante, 1980; articles in Bibliofilia, Burlington Mag., English Misc., Giorn. Stor. d. Lett. Ital., Ital. Studies, Lettere Italiane, Lingua Nostra, Rassegna d. Lett. Ital., Rinascimento, The Year's Work in Mod. Languages. *Recreation:* music. *Address:* 11 Norham Road, Oxford. *T:* Oxford (0865) 57045.

GRAYSON, Sir Jeremy (Brian Vincent Harrington), 5th Bt *cr* 1922, of Ravenspoint, Co. Angelsey; photographer; *b* 30 Jan. 1933; *s* of Brian Harrington Grayson (*d* 1989), 3rd *s* of 1st Bt and of Sofia Maria (*née* Buchanan); *S* uncle, 1991; *m* 1958, Sara Mary, *d* of C. F. Upton; three *s* three *d* (and one *d* decd). *Educ:* Downside. *Heir:* *s* Simon Jeremy Grayson, *b* 12 July 1959. *Address:* 88 Broomwood Road, SW11 6LA. *T:* 071–223 1949.

GRAYSTON, Rev. Prof. Kenneth, MA, DLitt; Professor of Theology, Bristol University, 1965–79, now Emeritus Professor; Pro-Vice-Chancellor, Bristol University, 1976–79; *b* Sheffield, 8 July 1914; *s* of Ernest Edward and Jessie Grayston; *m* 1942, Elizabeth Alison, *d* of Rev. Walter Mayo and Beatrice Aste, Elsfield, Oxon.; no *c*. *Educ:* Colfe's Grammar Sch., Lewisham; Universities of Oxford and Cambridge; DLitt Bristol 1991. Ordained Methodist Minister, 1942; Ordnance Factory Chaplain, 1942–44; Asst Head of Religious Broadcasting, BBC, 1944–49; Tutor in New Testament Language and Literature, Didsbury Coll., 1949–64; Special Lecturer in Hellenistic Greek, Bristol Univ., 1950–64; Dean, Faculty of Arts, Bristol Univ., 1972–74. Select Preacher to Univ. of Cambridge, 1952, 1962, to Univ. of Oxford, 1971; Sec. Studiorum Novi Testamenti Societas, 1955–65; Chairman: Theolog. Adv. Gp, British Council of Churches, 1969–72; Christian Aid Scholarships Cttee, 1973–78. *Publications:* The Epistles to the Galatians and to the Philippians, 1957; The Letters of Paul to the Philippians and the Thessalonians, 1967; The Johannine Epistles, 1984; Dying, We Live, 1990; The Gospel of John, 1990; (contrib. in): A Theological Word Book of the Bible, 1950; The Teacher's Commentary, 1955; The Interpreter's Dictionary of the Bible, 1962; A New Dictionary of Christian Theology, 1983, etc; contrib. to Expository Times, New Testament Studies, Theology, Epworth Review, etc. *Recreation:* travel. *Address:* 11 Rockleaze Avenue, Bristol BS9 1NG. *T:* Bristol (0272) 683872.

GREATHEAD, Dr David John; Director, International Institute of Biological Control, since 1985; *b* 12 Dec. 1931; *s* of Harold Merriman Greathead and Kathleen May (*née* Collett); *m* 1958, Annette Helen Blankley; one *s* two *d*. *Educ:* Merchant Taylors' Sch., Middx; Imperial Coll., London Univ. (BSc, PhD, DSc). ARCS; CBiol; FIBiol. Anti-Locust Res. Centre, 1953–59; research on desert locust in Ethiopia, Somalia, Kenya, Aden Protectorates, Desert Locust Survey, 1959–61; Commonwealth (later Internat.) Institute of Biological Control: set up and managed East African Station in Uganda, res. on crop pests and weeds, 1962–73; based in UK, 1973–; Asst Dir, 1976–85. *Publications:* A Review of Biological Control in the Ethiopian Region, 1971; A Review of Biological Control in Western and Southern Europe, 1976; (with J. K. Waage) Insect Parasitoids, 1986; numerous publications in learned jls. *Recreations:* natural history, walking, travelling. *Address:* International Institute of Biological Control, Silwood Park, Buckhurst Road, Ascot, Berks SL5 7TA. *T:* Bracknell (0344) 872999; 29 Dale Lodge Road, Sunningdale, Ascot, Berks SL5 0LY.

GREAVES, Jeffrey; HM Diplomatic Service, retired; Consul General, Alexandria, 1978–81; *b* 10 Dec. 1926; *s* of Willie Greaves and Emily Verity; *m* 1949, Joyce Mary Farrer; one *s* one *d*. *Educ:* Pudsey Grammar Sch. Served RN, 1945–48. Joined HM Foreign Service, 1948; FO, 1948; Benghazi, 1951; Vice Consul, Tehran, 1953; ME Centre for Arab Studies, 1955; Second Sec. and Vice Consul, Paris, 1960; Vice Consul, Muscat, 1962; Second Sec. and Consul, Athens, 1965; Second Sec. (Commercial), Cairo, 1968; First Sec. and Consul, Muscat, 1970; First Sec. (Com.), Bangkok, 1972; FCO, 1976. *Address:* 38A Alexandra Road, Pudsey, West Yorks LS28 8BY. *T:* Leeds (0532) 577238.

GREAVES, Prof. Malcolm Watson, MD; FRCP; Dean, Institute of Dermatology, since 1989; Professor of Dermatology, University of London, since 1975; *b* 11 Nov. 1933; *s* of Donald Watson Greaves and Kathleen Evelyn Greaves; *m* 1964, Evelyn Yeo, JP; one *s* one *d*. *Educ:* Epsom College; Charing Cross Med. Sch. MD, PhD London. MRC Clinical Res. Fellow, UCL, 1963–66; Reader in Dermatology, Univ. of Newcastle upon Tyne, 1966–75. Pres., European Soc. for Dermatological Research, 1984. Alvin J. Cox Award for dist. research in psoriasis, 1984. *Publications:* Pharmacology of the Skin, Vol. I, Pharmacology of Skin Systems and Autocoids in Normal and Inflamed Skin, 1989; Vol. II, Methods, Absorption, Metabolism, Toxicity, Drugs and Diseases, 1989. *Recreation:* equestrian activities. *Address:* Dovecote House, Church Street, Guilden Morden, Royston, Herts SG8 0JD. *T:* Royston (0763) 853188. *Club:* Athenæum.

GREAVES, Prof. Melvyn Francis; Director, Leukaemia Research Fund Centre, Institute of Cancer Research, London, since 1984; *b* 12 Sept. 1941; *s* of Edward and Violet Greaves; *m* 1966, Josephine Pank; one *s* one *d*. *Educ:* City of Norwich Grammar Sch.; University Coll. London; Middlesex Hosp. Med. Sch. BSc, PhD London. MRCPath. Vis Scientist, Karolinska Inst., Stockholm, 1968–69; Res. Fellow, Nat. Inst. for Med. Res., London, 1969–72; Res. Scientist, Dept of Zoology, UCL, 1972–76; Hd, Membrane Immunology Dept, Imperial Cancer Res. Fund, 1976–84. Hon. MRCP 1987. Paul Martini Prize (Germany), 1977; Peter Debye Prize (Holland), 1981; King Faisal Internat. Prize for Medicine, 1988. *Publications:* T and B Lymphocytes, 1973; Cellular Recognition, 1975; Atlas of Blood Cells, 1981, 2nd edn 1988; Monoclonal Antibodies to Receptors, 1984; contribs to bio-med. jls. *Recreations:* photography, tennis, natural history. *Address:* 24 Newhouse Park, St Albans, Herts AL1 1UQ. *T:* St Albans (0727) 63713.

GREBENIK, Eugene, CB 1976; MSc (Economics); Managing Editor, Population Studies; Consultant, Office of Population Censuses and Surveys, 1977–84; *b* 20 July 1919; *s* of S. Grebenik; *m* 1946, Virginia, *d* of James D. Barker; two *s* one *d*. *Educ:* abroad; London Sch. of Economics. Statistician, Dept of Economics, Univ. of Bristol, 1939–40; London Sch. of Economics: Asst. 1940–44 and Lecturer, 1944–49, in Statistics (on leave, 1944–46; served in RN, 1944; Temp. Statistical Officer, Admiralty, 1944–45; Secretariat, Royal Commn on Population, 1945–46); Reader in Demography, Univ. of London, 1949–54; Research Sec., Population Investigation Cttee, 1947–54; Prof. of Social Studies, Univ. of Leeds, 1954–69. Principal, Civil Service Coll., 1970–76 and Dep. Sec., Civil Service Dept, 1972–76. Mem., Impact of Rates Cttee, Ministry of Housing, 1963–64. Social Science Research Council: Statistics Cttee, 1966–69; Cttee on Social Science and Government, 1968–72; Population Panel, 1971–73; Member: Cttee on Governance of London Univ., 1970–72; Council, RHBNC (formerly RHC), Univ. of London, 1971–90. Pres., British Soc. for Population Studies, 1979–81. Sec.-Treasurer, Internat. Union for Scientific Study of Population, 1963–73. Hon. Fellow, LSE, 1969; Vis. Fellow, ANU, 1982–83; Hon. Vis. Prof., City Univ., 1986–89. *Publications:* (with H. A. Shannon) The Population of Bristol,

1943; (with D. V. Glass) The Trend and Pattern of Fertility in Great Britain; A Report on the Family Census of 1946, 1954; various articles in statistical and economic journals. *Address:* Little Mead, Tite Hill, Egham, Surrey TW20 0NH. *T:* Egham (0784) 432994.

GREEN, Prof. Albert Edward, FRS 1958; MA, PhD, ScD (Cambridge); Sedleian Professor of Natural Philosophy, University of Oxford, 1968–77, now Emeritus Professor; Supernumerary Fellow, The Queen's College, Oxford, since 1977 (Fellow, 1968–77); *m* 1939, Gwendoline May Rudston. *Educ:* Jesus Coll., Cambridge Univ. (Scholar). PhD 1937; MA 1938; ScD 1943. Fellow, Jesus Coll., Cambridge, 1936–39; Lecturer in Mathematics, Durham Colls, University of Durham, 1939–48; Prof. of Applied Mathematics, University of Newcastle upon Tyne, 1948–68. Hon. DSc: Durham, 1969; NUI, 1977; Hon. LLD Glasgow, 1975. Timoshenko Medal, ASME, 1974; Theodore von Karmen Medal, ASCE, 1983. *Address:* 20 Lakeside, Oxford.

GREEN, Sir Allan (David), KCB 1991; QC 1987; Director of Public Prosecutions and Head of the Crown Prosecution Service, since 1987; *b* 1 March 1935; *s* of late Lionel and of Irene Green; *m* 1967, Eva, *yr d* of Prof. Artur Attman and Elsa Attman, Gothenburg, Sweden; one *s* one *d*. *Educ:* Charterhouse; St Catharine's Coll., Cambridge (Open Exhibnr, MA). Served RN, 1953–55. Called to the Bar, Inner Temple, 1959, Bencher, 1985; Jun. Prosecuting Counsel to the Crown, Central Criminal Court, 1977, Sen. Prosecuting Counsel, 1979, First Senior Prosecuting Counsel, 1985; a Recorder, 1979–87. *Publications:* trans. with wife several Swedish books. *Recreation:* music. *Address:* (office) 4–12 Queen Anne's Gate, SW1H 9AZ. *Clubs:* Athenæum, Brooks's.

GREEN, Andrew Curtis; farmer and horticulturist, since 1960; *b* 28 March 1936; *s* of Christopher Green and Marjorie (*née* Bennett); *m* 1966, Julia Margaret (*née* Davidson); two *s*. *Educ:* Charterhouse; Magdalene Coll., Cambridge. MA (Nat. Scis), Dip. of Agriculture. Commnd RNVR, 1954–56. Farm management, 1960–67; founded Greens of Soham farming and horticultural business, 1967; Dir, Elsoms Spalding Seed Co., 1982–; Chm., Hassy Ltd, 1983–. Mem., AFRC, 1984–88. FLS 1978; Hon. Fellow, Inst. Hort. 1986 (Industrial Mem. Council, 1988–). *Recreations:* sailing, fishing, shooting, ski-ing. *Address:* Kingfishers Bridge, Wicken, Ely, Cambs CB7 5XL. *T:* Ely (0353) 721112. *Clubs:* Army and Navy, Farmers'; Hawks (Cambridge); Royal Thames Yacht.

GREEN, Andrew Fleming, CMG 1991; HM Diplomatic Service; Ambassador to Syria, since 1991; *b* 6 Aug. 1941; *s* of late Gp Captain J. H. Green, RAF, and Beatrice Mary (*née* Bowditch); *m* 1968, C. Jane Churchill; one *s* one *d*. *Educ:* Haileybury and ISC; Magdalene Coll., Cambridge (MA). Served Army, 1962–65; joined HM Diplomatic Service, 1965; Middle East Centre for Arab Studies, 1966–68; Aden, 1968–69; Asst Political Agent, Abu Dhabi, 1970–71; First Secretary, FCO, 1972–74; Private Sec. to Minister of State, FCO, 1975, and to Parliamentary Under Sec. of State, 1976; First Secretary, UK Delegn to OECD, Paris, 1977–79; First Sec., FCO, 1980–81; Counsellor, Washington, 1982–85; Counsellor, Hd of Chancery and Consul Gen., Riyadh, 1985–88; Counsellor, FCO, 1988–90. *Recreations:* tennis, sailing, bridge. *Address:* c/o Foreign and Commonwealth Office, SW1A 2AH.

GREEN, Anthony Eric Sandall, RA 1977 (ARA 1971); Member, London Group, 1964; Artist (Painter); *b* 30 Sept. 1939; *s* of late Frederick Sandall Green and Marie Madeleine (*née* Dupont); *m* 1961, Mary Louise Cozens-Walker; two *d*. *Educ:* Highgate Sch., London; Slade Sch. of Fine Art, University Coll. London (Fellow, UCL, 1991). Henry Tonks Prize for drawing, Slade Sch., 1960; French Govt Schol., Paris, 1960; Gulbenkian Purchase Award, 1963; Harkness Fellowship, in USA, 1967–69. Has exhibited in: London, New York, Haarlem, Rotterdam, Stuttgart, Hanover, Helsingborg, Malmö, Tokyo, Brussels, W Berlin, Chicago and Sydney. Paintings in various public collections, including: Tate Gallery; Metropolitan Mus. of Art, N York; Olinda Museum, Brazil; Baltimore Mus. of Art, USA; Nat. Mus. of Wales; Gulbenkian Foundn; Arts Council of Gt Brit.; British Council; Victoria and Albert Mus.; Contemporary Art Soc.; Frans Hals Mus., Holland; Boymans-van Bevningen Mus., Holland; Ulster Mus., Belfast; Ikeda and Niigata Mus., Setagaya Art Mus., Metropolitan, Tokyo; Hiroshima; Fukuoka. Exhibit of the Year award, RA, 1977. *Publication:* A Green Part of the World, 1984. *Recreations:* travelling, family life. *Address:* 17 Lissenden Mansions, Highgate Road, NW5. *T:* 071–485 1226.

GREEN, Arthur; Senior Partner, Grant Thornton, 1986–88, retired; President, Institute of Chartered Accountants in England and Wales, 1987–88; *b* 15 June 1928; *s* of Arthur Henry and Elizabeth Burns Green; *m* 1952, Sylvia Myatt; one *s* one *d*. *Educ:* Liverpool Collegiate. FCA. Qualified Chartered Accountant, 1950; Partner, Bryce Hanmer & Co., Liverpool, 1954 (merged Thornton Baker; later Grant Thornton); Nat. Managing Partner, Thornton Baker, 1975–84; Chm. and Man. Dir, Grant Thornton International, 1984–85. Vice-Pres., 1985–86, Dep. Pres., 1986–87, ICA. *Recreations:* tennis, walking, theatre, chess, watching soccer. *Address:* Up Yonder, Herbert Road, Salcombe, Devon TQ8 8HP. *T:* Salcombe (054884) 2075.

GREEN, Arthur Edward Chase, MBE (mil.) 1955; TD (and Bar) 1950; DL; FRICS; Chartered Surveyor; Chief Estates Surveyor, Legal and General Assurance Society, 1946–71 (Surveyor, 1934–46); *b* 5 Nov. 1911; *s* of Harry Catling and Sarah Jane Green, Winchmore Hill, London; *m* 1941, Margaret Grace (*d* 1991), *yr d* of John Lancelot and Winifred Churchill, Wallington, Surrey; one *s* one *d* (and one *d* decd). *Educ:* Merchant Taylors' Sch.; Coll. of Estate Management. HAC, 1932–: commnd, 1939; Adjt 11 (HAC) Regt RHA, 1941–42; 8th Army, Western Desert, ME; PoW 1942; despatches, Germany, 1945; Territorial Efficiency Medal and bar; Court of Assistants, HAC, 1946–76, Treasurer, 1966–69, Vice-Pres., 1970–72; Metropolitan Special Constabulary, HAC Div., 1937–39 and 1946–74 (Long Service Medal and bar); Hon. Mem., Transvaal Horse Artillery. Property Adviser, J. H. Schroder Wagg & Co., 1972–82; Dir, Schroder Properties Ltd, 1974–82; Mem., Cttee of Management, Pension Fund Property Unit Trust, 1972–82; Advr on Policy, Post Office Staff Superannuation Fund, until 1977, Dir, Mereacre Ltd, and Mereacre Farms Ltd (PO Staff Superann. Fund), 1977–83; Member: Chancellor of the Exchequer's Property Adv. Panel, 1975–80; Govt Cttee of Inquiry into Agriculture in GB, 1977–79 (Northfield Cttee). Chm., Elecrent Properties Ltd (Electronic Rentals Gp), 1974–83; Director: Marlborough Property Hldgs plc, 1978–86; Studley Farms Ltd, 1980–82. Mem., TA&VR Assocs for City of London, 1970–77, and for Greater London, 1970–81. President: Camden and Islington Corps, St John Ambulance, 1974–75, No 7 Corps, City of London and Hackney, 1976–77, City of London, 1978–. Governor: Bridewell Royal Hosp., 1962–88; City of London Sch., 1976–81; Queenswood Sch., 1966–78; Mem. Court of Assistants and Governor, Corp. of Sons of the Clergy, 1966–86; Vice-Pres., Brunswick Boys' Club Trust, 1978– (Founder-Trustee, 1945–78, elected while POW, Oflag 79). City of London Court of Common Council (Bread Street Ward), 1971–81. Freedom of the City of London, 1939; Liveryman: Merchant Taylors' Co., 1946; Gunmakers' Co. DL Greater London, 1967 (Representative DL for London Borough of Islington, 1967–81). CStJ 1988. *Recreations:* shooting, gardening, travel, photography. *Address:* The Coach House, High Street, Cranleigh, Surrey GU6 8AS. *T:* Cranleigh (0483) 267372. *Clubs:* HAC, Guildhall.

GREEN, Arthur Jackson; Under Secretary, Department of Education for Northern Ireland, 1983–87, retired; *b* 12 Nov. 1928; *s* of F. Harvey Green and Sylvia Green (*née* Marsh), MB; *m* 1957, Rosemary Bradley, MA; two *s*. *Educ:* Friends Sch., Lisburn, Co. Antrim; Leighton Park Sch., Reading; Lincoln Coll., Oxford (BA Mod. Hist.); Haverford Coll., Philadelphia (MA Philosophy). Asst Principal, NICS, 1952; Secretary: Cameron Commn, 1969; Scarman Tribunal, 1969–72; Asst Sec., NI Dept of Finance, 1972–78; Under Sec., NI Office, 1978–79; Dir, NI Court Service (Lord Chancellor's Dept), 1979–82; Fellow, Center for Internat. Affairs, Harvard Univ., 1982–83. First Chm., S Down Conservative Assoc., 1990–91. *Publications:* articles on Anglo-Irish topics. *Address:* 36 St Patrick's Road, Saul, Downpatrick, N Ireland BT30 7JQ. *T:* Downpatrick (0396) 614360. *Club:* Reform.

GREEN, Barry Spencer; QC 1981; a Recorder of the Crown Court, since 1979; *b* 16 March 1932; *s* of Lionel Maurice Green, FRCS and Juliette Green; *m* 1st, 1960, Marilyn Braverman (marr. diss. 1987); two *s*; 2nd, 1988, Muriel Coplan. *Educ:* Westminster Sch.; Christ Church, Oxford (MA, BCL). Called to the Bar, Inner Temple, 1954, Bencher, 1987. Legal Mem., Mental Health Review Tribunal, 1983–; Mem., Criminal Injuries Compensation Bd, 1988–. *Recreation:* tennis. *Address:* 4 Paper Buildings, Temple, EC4Y 7EX. *T:* 071–353 1131. *Clubs:* Garrick, Roehampton.

GREEN, Father Benedict; *see* Green, Rev. H. C.

GREEN, Benny; free-lance writer; *b* 9 Dec. 1927; *s* of David Green and Fanny Trayer; *m* 1962, Antoinette Kanal; three *s* one *d*. *Educ:* Clipstone Street Junior Mixed; subsequently uneducated at St Marylebone Grammar Sch. Mem., West Central Jewish Lads Club (now extinct). Saxophonist, 1947–60 (Most Promising New Jazz Musician, 1953); Jazz Critic, Observer, 1958–77; Literary Critic, Spectator, 1970–80; Film Critic, Punch, 1972–77, TV Critic, 1977–87; frequent radio and TV appearances, 1955–. Artistic Dir, New Shakespeare Co., 1973–; Mem., BBC Archives Cttee, 1976. Book and lyrics, Boots with Strawberry Jam, Nottingham Playhouse, 1968; revised libretto, Showboat, Adelphi Theatre, London, 1972; co-deviser: Cole, Mermaid, 1974; Oh, Mr Porter, Mermaid, 1977; lyrics, Bashville, Open Air Theatre, 1983–84. Sony Radio Award for best popular music series, 1984. *Publications:* The Reluctant Art, 1962; Blame it on my Youth, 1967; 58 Minutes to London, 1969; Drums in my Ears, 1973; I've Lost my little Willie, 1976; Swingtime in Tottenham, 1976; (ed) Cricket Addict's Archive, 1977; Shaw's Champions, 1978; Fred Astaire, 1979; (ed) Wisden Anthology, vol. I 1864–1900, 1979, vol. II 1900–1940, 1980, vol. III 1940–1963, 1982, vol. IV 1963–1982, 1983; P. G. Wodehouse: a literary biography, 1981; Wisden Book of Obituaries, 1986; (ed) The Last Empires, 1986; (ed) The Lord's Companion, 1987; (ed) A Hymn to Him, 1987; A History of Cricket, 1988; Let's Face the Music, 1989; (ed) The Wisden Papers 1888–1946, 1989. *Recreation:* cricket. *Address:* c/o New Shakespeare Company, Regent's Park, NW1; c/o BBC, Broadcasting House, Portland Place, W1.

GREEN, Rev. Bernard; General Secretary, Baptist Union of Great Britain, 1982–May 1991; Moderator of the Free Church Federal Council, 1988–89; *b* 11 Nov. 1925; *s* of George Samuel Green and Laura Annie Agnes (*née* Holliday); *m* 1952, Joan Viccars; two *s* one *d*. *Educ:* Wellingborough Sch.; Bristol Baptist Coll.; Bristol Univ. (BA); Regent's Park Coll., Oxford, and St Catherine's Coll., Oxford (MA); London Univ. BD taken externally. Served War as coal-miner, 1944–47. Ordained as Baptist Minister, 1952; pastorates at: Yardley, Birmingham, 1952–61; Mansfield Road, Nottingham, 1961–76; Horfield, Bristol, 1976–82. Regular broadcaster on BBC Radio Nottingham until 1976 and on BBC Radio Bristol until 1982. *Publication:* (jtly) Patterns and Prayers for Christian Worship, 1991. *Recreations:* reading, music (listening), gardening. *Address:* 6 Alexander Close, Abingdon, Oxon OX14 1XA. *T:* Abingdon (0235) 534886.

GREEN, Rev. Canon Bryan Stuart Westmacott, BD; DD; Canon Emeritus of Birmingham Cathedral since 1970 (Hon. Canon, 1950–70); *b* 14 Jan. 1901; *s* of late Hubert Westmacott Green and late Sarah Kathleen Green (*née* Brockwell); *m* 1926, Winifred Annie Bevan; one *s* one *d*. *Educ:* Merchant Taylors' Sch.; London Univ. BD 1922; Curate, New Malden, 1924–28; Staff of Children's Special Service Mission, 1928–31; Chap., Oxford Pastorate, 1931–34; Vicar of Christ Church, Crouch End, 1934–38; Vicar of Holy Trinity, Brompton, 1938–48; Rector of Birmingham, 1948–70. Conducted evangelistic campaigns: Canada and America, 1936, 1944, and annually, 1947–; Australia and New Zealand, 1951, 1953, 1958, 1974; West Africa, 1953; S Africa, 1953, 1955, 1956, 1957, 1959 and 1960; Ceylon, 1954, 1959. DD Hon. St John's Coll. Winnipeg, 1961; DD Lambeth, 1985. *Publications:* The Practice of Evangelism, 1951; Being and Believing, 1956; Saints Alive, 1959. *Recreation:* golf. *Address:* West Field, Southern Road, Thame, Oxon OX9 2DZ. *T:* Thame (084421) 2026. *Club:* National.

GREEN, Prof. Brynmor Hugh; Sir Cyril Kleinwort Professor of Countryside Management, University of London, Wye College, since 1987; a Countryside Commissioner, since 1984; *b* 14 Jan. 1941; *s* of Albert Walter Green and Margaret Afona Green (*née* Griffiths); *m* 1965, Jean Armstrong; two *s*. *Educ:* Dartford Grammar Sch.; Univ. of Nottingham (BSc 1st Cl. Hons Botany, PhD Plant Ecol.). Lectr in Plant Ecology, Dept of Botany, Univ. of Manchester, 1965–68; Dep. Regl Officer (SE) 1968–69, Regl Officer (SE) 1969–75, Nature Conservancy Council; Lectr and Sen. Lectr, Wye Coll., 1975–87. FRSA. *Publications:* Countryside Conservation: the protection and management of amenity ecosystems, 1981, 2nd edn 1985; (jtly) The Diversion of Land: conservation in a period of farming contraction, 1990; numerous chapters in books, conf. reports, sci. jls. *Recreations:* golf, watercolour sketching, bird-watching. *Address:* 19 Chequers Park, Wye, Ashford, Kent TN25 5BB. *T:* Wye (Kent) (0233) 812575.

GREEN, Charles Frederick; Director, 1982–89, and Deputy Group Chief Executive, 1986–89, National Westminster Bank; *b* 20 Oct. 1930; *m* 1956; two *s* one *d*. *Educ:* Harrow County School. FCIB (FIB 1971); FBIM 1982. Joined National Provincial Bank, 1946, Secretary, 1967–70; Head of Planning, National Westminster Bank, 1970; Manager, Lombard Street, 1972; Managing Dir, Centre-file, 1974; General Manager: Business Develt Div., 1977; Financial Control Div., 1982. Chairman: CBI/ICC Multinational Affairs Panel, 1982–87; Overseas Cttee, CBI, 1987–89; Dir, Business in the Community, 1981–91 (Vice-Chm., 1985–89); Treasurer, PSI, 1984–. Mem., General Synod, 1980–90; Vice-Chm., C of E Bd for Social Responsibility, 1983–; Chm., Industrial and Econ. Affairs Cttee, 1986–; Trustee, Church Urban Fund, 1987–89. Mem., Council for Charitable Support, 1989–; Trustee, Charities Aid Foundn, 1989–. Governor: Westonbirt Sch., 1990–; Monkton Combe Sch., 1990–. Fellow, Cheltenham & Gloucester Coll. of Higher Educn, 1990. Hon. FLCM 1988. *Recreations:* opera, concert music, drama. *Address:* The Old House, Parks Farm, Old Sodbury, Avon BS17 6PX. *Clubs:* Athenæum, National, Langbourn Ward.

GREEN, Christopher Edward Wastie, MA, FCIT; Director, Network SouthEast, British Rail, since 1986; *b* 7 Sept. 1943; *s* of James Wastie Green and Margarita Mensing; *m* 1966, Mitzie Petzold; one *s* one *d*. *Educ:* St Paul's School, London; Oriel College, Oxford. MA Mod. Hist. Management Trainee, British Rail, 1965–67; served Birmingham, Nottingham, Hull, Wimbledon; Passenger Operating Manager, BR HQ, 1979–80; Chief Operating Manager, Scotland, 1980–83; Dep. Gen. Manager, Scotland, 1983–84; Gen. Manager, Scottish Region, BR, 1984–86. Member: Regl Council, CBI, 1986–; Transmark Bd, 1989–. Pres., Railway Study Assoc., 1989–90; Vice Pres., CIT, 1988–. *Recreations:*

music, reading, walking, architecture. *Address:* Network SouthEast, Euston House, Eversholt Street, NW1 1DF.

GREEN, David; *see* Green, G. D.

GREEN, Prof. David Headley, FRS 1991; FAA; Professor of Geology, University of Tasmania, since 1977; *b* 29 Feb. 1936; *s* of Ronald Horace Green and Josephine May Headley; *m* 1959, Helen Mary McIntyre; three *s* three *d*. *Educ:* Univ. of Tasmania (BSc Hons 1957; MSc 1959; DSc 1988); Univ. of Cambridge (PhD 1962). FAA 1974; Fellow, Aust. Inst. of Mining and Metallurgy, 1987. Geologist, Bureau of Mineral Resources, Geology and Geophysics, Canberra, 1957–59; Postgrad. Scholarship, Royal Commn for Exhibn of 1851, 1959–62; Res. Fellow, Res. Sch. of Earth Scis, ANU, 1962–76. Hon. Fellow: Eur. Union of Geoscis, 1985; Geolog. Soc. of America, 1986. Edgeworth David Medal, Royal Soc., NSW, 1968; Stilwell Medal, Geol Soc. of Australia, 1977; Mawson Medal, 1982, Jaeger Medal, 1990, Aust. Acad. of Sci. *Publications:* numerous articles in fields of experimental petrology and geochemistry, in learned jls. *Recreations:* tennis, music. *Address:* Geology Department, University of Tasmania, Box 252C, GPO Hobart, Tas 7001, Australia. *T:* (002) 202477.

GREEN, Prof. Dennis Howard; Schröder Professor of German, University of Cambridge, 1979–89; Fellow of Trinity College, Cambridge, since 1949; *b* 26 June 1922; *s* of Herbert Maurice Green and Agnes Edith Green (*née* Fleming); *m* 1972, Margaret Parry. *Educ:* Latymer Upper Sch., London; Trinity Coll., Cambridge; Univ. of Basle. Univ. of Cambridge, 1940–41 and 1945–47; Univ. of Basle (Dr Phil.), 1947–49; Military service (RAC), 1941–45; Univ. Lecturer in German, St Andrews, 1949–50; Research Fellowship, Trinity Coll., Cambridge (first year held *in absentia*), 1949–52; Univ. Asst Lectr in German, Cambridge, 1950–54; Teaching Fellowship, Trinity Coll., Cambridge, 1952–66; Head of Dept of Other Languages, 1956–79, and Prof. of Modern Languages, Cambridge, 1966–79; Visiting Professor: Cornell Univ., 1965–66; Auckland Univ., 1966; Yale Univ., 1969; ANU, Canberra, 1971; UCLA, 1975; Univ. of Pennsylvania, 1975; Univ. of WA, 1976; Univ. of Freiburg, 1990; Vis. Fellow, Humanities Res. Centre, Canberra, 1978. *Publications:* The Carolingian Lord, 1965; The Millstätter Exodus: a crusading epic, 1966; (with Dr L. P. Johnson) Approaches to Wolfram von Eschenbach, 1978; Irony in the Medieval Romance, 1979; The Art of Recognition in Wolfram's Parzival, 1982; reviews and articles in learned journals. *Recreations:* walking and foreign travel. *Address:* Trinity College, Cambridge; 7 Archway Court, Barton Road, Cambridge CB3 9LW. *T:* Cambridge (0223) 358070.

GREEN, Rev. Canon (Edward) Michael (Bankes); Professor of Evangelism at Regent College, Vancouver, University of British Columbia, since 1987; *b* 20 Aug. 1930; British; *m* 1957, Rosemary Wake (*née* Storr); two *s* two *d*. *Educ:* Clifton Coll.; Oxford and Cambridge Univs. BD Cantab 1966. Exeter Coll., Oxford, 1949–53 (1st cl. Lit. Hum.); Royal Artillery (Lieut, A/Adjt), 1953–55; Queens' Coll., Cambridge, 1955–57 (1st cl. Theol. Tripos Pt III; Carus Greek Testament Prize; Fencing Blue), and Ridley Hall Theol Coll., 1955–57; Curate, Holy Trinity, Eastbourne, 1957–60; Lectr, London Coll. of Divinity, 1960–69; Principal, St John's Coll., Nottingham (until July 1970, London Coll. of Divinity), 1969–75; Canon Theologian of Coventry, 1970–76, Canon Theologian Emeritus, 1978–; Rector of St Aldate's, Oxford, 1975–87 (with Holy Trinity, Oxford, 1975–82 and with St Matthew, 1982–87). Member: Doctrine Commission of the Church, 1968–77; Church Unity Commn, 1974–. Leader of missions, overseas and in UK. *Publications:* Called to Serve, 1964; Choose Freedom, 1965; The Meaning of Salvation, 1965; Man Alive, 1967; Runaway World, 1968; Commentary on 2 Peter and Jude, 1968; Evangelism in the Early Church, 1970; Jesus Spells Freedom, 1972; New Life, New Lifestyle, 1973; I Believe in the Holy Spirit, 1975, new edn 1985; You Must Be Joking, 1976; (ed) The Truth of God Incarnate, 1977; Why Bother With Jesus?, 1979; Evangelism—Now and Then, 1979; What is Christianity?, 1981; I Believe in Satan's Downfall, 1981; The Day Death Died, 1982; To Corinth with Love, 1982; World on the Run, 1983; Freed to Serve, 1983; The Empty Cross of Jesus, 1984; Come Follow Me, 1984; Lift Off to Faith, 1985; Baptism, 1987; Matthew for Today, 1988; Ten Myths about Christianity, 1988; Evangelism Through the Local Church, 1990; Reflections from the Lions Den, 1990; Who is this Jesus?, 1991; contribs to various jls. *Recreations:* family, countryside pursuits, cricket, squash, fly fishing. *Address:* Regent College, 5800 University Boulevard, Vancouver, BC V6T 2E4, Canada. *T:* (604) 224 3245; 3715 West 20th Avenue, Vancouver, BC V6S 1E9, Canada.

GREEN, Sir (Edward) Stephen (Lycett), 4th Bt, *cr* 1886; CBE 1964; JP; Chairman, East Anglian Regional Hospital Board, 1959–74; *b* 18 April 1910; *s* of Sir E. A. Lycett Green, 3rd Bt, and Elizabeth Williams; *S* father, 1941; *m* 1935, Constance Mary, *d* of late Ven. H. S. Radcliffe; one *d*. *Educ:* Eton; Magdalene Coll., Cambridge. Called to Bar, Lincoln's Inn, 1933. Served War of 1939–45 (Major, RA). CC 1946–49, JP 1946, DL 1963–88, High Sheriff 1973, Norfolk; Dep. Chairman Norfolk QS, 1948–71. Chairman: King's Lynn Hospital Management Cttee, 1948–59; Assoc. of Hosp. Management Cttees, 1956–58; Cttee of Inquiry into Recruitment, Training and Promotion of Administrative and Clerical Staff in Hospital Service, 1962–63; Docking RDC, 1950–57. *Recreations:* watching TV, reading. *Heir:* *b* Lt-Col Simon Lycett Green, TD, Yorks Dragoons Yeomanry [*b* 11 July 1912; *m* 1st, 1935, Gladys (marr. diss. 1971; she *d* 1980), *d* of late Arthur Ranicar, JP, Springfield, Wigan; one *d*; 2nd, 1971, Mary, *d* of late George Ramsden]. *Address:* Ken Hill, Snettisham, King's Lynn. *TA:* Snettisham, Norfolk. *T:* Heacham (0485) 70001. *Clubs:* White's, Pratt's; Norfolk (Norwich); Allsorts (Norfolk).

GREEN, Dr Frank Alan, CEng; FIM, FBIM; Senior Associate Consultant, General Technology Systems Ltd, Brentford, since 1984; Senior Consultant, Centre for Consultancy plc, since 1990; Managing Director, Charing Green Associates, Kent, since 1990 (Principal, 1983) ; *b* 29 Oct. 1931; *s* of Frank Green and Winifred Hilda (*née* Payne); *m* 1957, Pauline Eleanor Tayler; one *s* two *d*. *Educ:* Mercers Sch., London; Univ. of London (BScEng, PhD). CEng 1980; FIM 1978; FBIM 1979. UKAEA, 1956–57; various appts, Glacier Metal Co. Ltd (Associated Engrg Gp), 1957–65; Technical Dir, Alta Friccion SA, Mexico City, 1965–68; Manufg Dir, Stewart Warner Corp., 1968–72; Marketing Develt Manager, Calor Gp, 1972–74; Manufg Dir, 1974–77, Man. Dir, 1977–81, British Twin Disc Ltd, Rochester; Industrial Advr (Under-Sec.), DTI, 1981–84. Director: Gen. Technology Systems (Scandinavia), since 1989; Gen. Technology Systems (Portuguesa), since 1991. Dir, Anglo-Mexican Chamber of Commerce, Mexico City, 1966–68. Mem. Council, Inst. of Metals, 1990– (Chm., Initial Formation Cttee, 1988–; Chm., Gen. Educn Cttee, 1986–88). *Publications:* contrib. technical, historical and managerial jls in UK and Mexico. *Recreations:* photography, military history, rough walking, wine. *Address:* Courtwood House, Burleigh Road, Charing, Kent TN27 0JB. *T:* Charing (023371) 3152. *Club:* Old Mercers.

GREEN, Geoffrey Hugh, CB 1977; Deputy Under-Secretary of State (Policy), Procurement Executive, Ministry of Defence, 1975–80; *b* 24 Sept. 1920; *o s* of late Duncan M. and Kate Green, Bristol; *m* 1948, Ruth Hazel Mercy; two *d*. *Educ:* Bristol Grammar Sch.; Worcester Coll., Oxford (Exhibr), 1939–41, 1945–47 (MA). Served with Royal Artillery (Ayrshire Yeomanry): N Africa and Italy, 1942–45 (Captain). Entered Min. of Defence, Oct. 1947; Principal, 1949; Asst Sec., 1960; Asst Under-Sec. of State, 1969; Dep. Under-Sec. of State, 1974. *Recreations:* travel, music, walking. *Address:* 47 Kent Avenue, Ealing, W13 8BE.

GREEN, Major George Hugh, MBE; MC 1945; TD and 3 bars; DL; Vice-Lieutenant of Caithness, 1973–86; retired; *b* 21 Oct. 1911; *s* of George Green, The Breck, John O'Groats; *m* 1936, Isobel Elizabeth Myron (*d* 1987); two *s*. *Educ:* Wick High Sch.; Edinburgh Univ. (MA). Retired as schoolmaster, 1977. Commnd into Seaforth Highlanders, TA, 1935; served War of 1939–45 with 5th Seaforths in 51st (H) Div., N Africa, Sicily and NW Europe; retd from TA, 1963. DL Caithness 1965. *Recreations:* gardening, bee-keeping. *Address:* Tjaldur, Halkirk, Caithness KW12 6XQ. *T:* Halkirk (084783) 639. *Club:* Highland Brigade (Inverness).

GREEN, Gerard Nicholas Valentine; Regional General Manager, South East Thames Regional Health Authority, since 1989; *b* 6 Aug. 1950; *s* of James Arnold Green and Margarathe Ella Green; *m* 1977, Maralyn Ann Ranger; one *s* one *d*. *Educ:* Highgate Sch.; University Coll., London (BA); Univ. of Warwick (MA); Birkbeck Coll., London (MA). AHSM. Nat. admin. trainee, 1974–75; Dep. Hosp. Sec., St George's Hosp., SW17, 1975–77; Asst Sector Administrator, Cane Hill Hosp., Surrey, 1977–79; Sector Administrator, Farnborough Hosp., Kent, 1979–82; Administrator, KCH, 1982–84; Chief Exec. Officer, Tabuk Military Hosp., Saudi Arabia, 1984–87; Dist Gen. Man., Bromley HA, 1987–89. FRSA 1989. *Recreations:* travel, reading. *Address:* 21 Stambourne Way, West Wickham, Kent BR4 9NE. *Club:* Reform.

GREEN, (Gregory) David; Director of Voluntary Service Overseas, since 1990; *b* 2 Dec. 1948; *s* of Thomas Dixon Green and Mary Mabella Green (*née* Walley); *m* 1977, Corinne Butler; three *d*. *Educ:* Leys Sch., Cambridge; Keswick Hall Coll. of Educn, Norwich (Cert Ed); Trinity Hall, Cambridge (BEd). Volunteer, VSO, Pakistan, 1967–68; teaching, Conisborough and Rotherham, 1972–76; Dir, Children's Relief Internat., 1976–79; Save the Children Fund: Staff Develt and Trng Officer, 1979; Dep. Dir of Personnel, 1982; Dir of Personnel, 1983; Dir of Personnel and Admin., 1988–90. Dir and Council Mem., Council for Colony Holidays for School-children, 1970–80. Mem., Laurence Olivier Awards Panel, 1984–85. FRSA. *Publication:* Chorus, 1977. *Recreations:* theatre, music, painting, woodworking. *Address:* 317 Putney Bridge Road, SW15 2PN. *T:* 081–780 2266.

GREEN, Hon. Sir Guy (Stephen Montague), KBE 1982; Chief Justice of Tasmania, since 1973; Lieutenant-Governor of Tasmania, since 1982; Chancellor, University of Tasmania, since 1985; *b* 26 July 1937; *s* of Clement Francis Montague Green and Beryl Margaret Jenour Green; *m* 1963, Rosslyn Mary Marshall; two *s* two *d*. *Educ:* Launceston Church Grammar Sch.; Univ. of Tasmania. Alfred Houston Schol. (Philosophy) 1958; LLB (Hons) 1960. Admitted to Bar of Tasmania, 1960; Partner, Ritchie & Parker Alfred Green & Co. (Launceston), 1963–71; Mem., Faculty of Law, Univ. of Tas, 1974–85. Pres., Tasmanian Bar Assoc., 1968–70 (Vice-Pres., 1966–68); Magistrate 1971–73. Chm., Council of Law Reporting, 1978–85. Dep. Chm., Australian Inst. of Judicial Admin, 1986–88. Chairman: Tasmanian Cttee, Duke of Edinburgh's Award Scheme in Australia, 1975–80; Sir Henry Baker Meml Fellowship Cttee, 1973–; Dir, Winston Churchill Meml Trust, 1975–85 (Dep. Nat. Chm., 1980–85; Chm. Tasmanian Regional Cttee, 1975–80); Mem., Tasmanian Cttee, United World Colls, 1981–. Priory Exec. Officer, Order of St John in Australia, 1984–; Pres., St John Council for Tasmania, 1984–. KStJ 1984. *Address:* Judges' Chambers, Supreme Court, Salamanca Place, Hobart, Tasmania 7000. *Clubs:* Tasmanian, Athenæum (Hobart).

GREEN, Rev. Humphrey Christian, (Father Benedict Green, CR); formerly Principal, College of the Resurrection, Mirfield; *b* 9 Jan. 1924; *s* of late Rev. Canon Frederick Wastie Green and Marjorie Susan Beltt Green (*née* Gosling). *Educ:* Dragon Sch., Oxford; Eton (King's Scholar); Merton Coll., Oxford (Postmaster). BA 1949, MA 1952. Served War, RNVR, 1943–46. Deacon 1951, priest 1952; Asst Curate of Northolt, 1951–56; Lectr in Theology, King's Coll., London, 1956–60. Professed in Community of the Resurrection (taking additional name of Benedict), 1962; Vice-Principal, Coll. of the Resurrection, 1965–75; Principal, 1975–84. Associate Lectr in Dept of Theology and Religious Studies, Univ. of Leeds, 1967–87. *Publications:* The Gospel according to Matthew (New Clarendon Bible), 1975; contrib.: Towards a Church Architecture (ed P. Hammond), 1962; The Anglican Synthesis (ed W. R. F. Browning), 1964; Synoptic Studies (ed C. M. Tuckett), 1984; The Making of Orthodoxy (ed R. Williams), 1989; theological jls. *Recreations:* walking, synoptic criticism. *Address:* House of the Resurrection, Mirfield, W Yorks WF14 0BN. *T:* Mirfield (0924) 494318.

GREEN, John Dennis Fowler; *b* 9 May 1909; *s* of late Capt. Henry and Amy Gertrude Green, Chedworth, Glos; *m* 1946, Diana Judith, JP, *y d* of late Lt-Col H. C. Elwes, DSO, MVO, Colesbourne, Glos. *Educ:* Cheltenham Coll.; Peterhouse, Cambridge. President of the Union. Called to the Bar, Inner Temple, 1933 (entrance schol.); BBC, 1934–62 (Controller, Talks Div., 1956–61); established agricultural broadcasting, 1935. Special Agric. Mission to Aust. and NZ (MAFF), 1945–47; Pres. National Pig Breeders Assoc., 1955–56; Chm., Agricultural Adv. Council, 1963–68; Exec. Mem., Land Settlement Assoc., 1965–80; Trustee, RASE, 1984– (Dep. Pres., 1983–84); Council for the Protection of Rural England: Mem., Nat. Exec., 1967–80; Pres., Glos. Br., 1985– (Chm., 1964–85). Chm., Cirencester and Tewkesbury Conservative Assoc., 1964–78. FRASE 1990. *Publications:* Mr Baldwin: A Study in Post War Conservatism, 1933; articles and broadcasts on historical and agricultural subjects. *Recreations:* livestock breeding, forestry, shooting. *Address:* The Manor, Chedworth, Cheltenham GL54 4AA. *T:* Fossebridge (028572) 233. *Clubs:* Oriental, Naval and Military, Buck's, Farmers'.

GREEN, John Edward, PhD, CEng, FRAeS; Chief Executive, Aircraft Research Association Ltd, since 1988; *b* 26 Aug. 1937; *s* of John Green and Ellen O'Dowd; *m* 1959, Gillian (*née* Jackson); one *s* one *d*. *Educ:* Birkenhead Inst. Grammar Sch.; St John's Coll., Cambridge (Scholar). BA 1959; MA 1963; PhD 1966. Student Apprentice, Bristol Aircraft Ltd, 1956; De Havilland Engine Co., 1959–61; Royal Aircraft Establishment, 1964–81: Head of Transonic/Supersonic Wind Tunnel Div., 1971; Head of Propulsion Div., 1973; Head of Noise Div., 1974; Head of Aerodynamics Dept., 1978–81; Dir, Project Time and Cost Analysis, MoD (PE), 1981–84; Minister–Counsellor Defence Equipment, and Dep. Head of British Defence Staff, Washington, 1984–85; Dep. Dir (Aircraft), RAE, 1985–87. Mem., Internat. Council of the Aeronautical Scis, 1986–. Member Council: RAeS, 1986–; AIRTO, 1988–. *Publications:* contribs to books and learned jls, chiefly on fluid mechanics and aerodynamics. *Recreations:* music, mountain walking. *Address:* Aircraft Research Association Ltd, Manton Lane, Bedford, Beds MK41 7PF. *T:* Bedford (0234) 350681.

GREEN, John Michael, CB 1976; Commissioner, 1971–85, Deputy Chairman, 1973–85, Board of Inland Revenue; Member, North West Surrey Health Authority, since 1989; *b* 5 Dec. 1924; *s* of late George Green and of Faith Green; *m* 1951, Sylvia (*née* Crabb); one *s* one *d*. *Educ:* Merchant Taylors' Sch., Rickmansworth; Jesus Coll., Oxford (MA (Hons)). Served War, Army, RAC, 1943–46. Entered Inland Revenue as Asst Principal, 1948; served in HM Treasury, as Principal, 1956–57; Asst Sec., 1962; Under Sec., Bd of Inland

Revenue, 1971. *Recreation:* gardening. *Address:* 5 Bylands, White Rose Lane, Woking, Surrey GU22 7LA. *T:* Woking (0483) 772599. *Club:* Reform.

GREEN, Julian Hartridge; American and French writer; Member of Académie Française, 1971; *b* Paris, France, 6 Sept. 1900; one *s*. *Educ:* Lycée Janson, Paris; Univ. of Virginia. Member: Acad. de Bavière, 1950; Royal Acad. of Belgium, 1951; Raven club, 1922; Acad. de Mannheim, 1952; Phi Beta Kappa, 1948; Amer. Acad. of Arts and Sciences. Prix Harper, Prix Bookman, Prix de Monaco, 1951; Grand Prix National des Lettres, 1966; Grand Prix, Académie Française, 1970; Grand Prix Littérature de Pologne, 1985; Grand Prix Cavour, 1991. *Publications: fiction:* The Apprentice Psychiatrist, 1920; Le voyageur sur la terre, 1924, new edn 1989; Mont-Cinère, 1926; Adrienne Mesurat, 1927; Les clés de la mort, 1928; Léviathan, 1929; L'autre sommeil, 1930; Epaves, 1932; Le visionnaire, 1934; Minuit, 1936; Varouna, 1940; Si j'étais vous ...., 1947; Moira, 1950; Le malfaiteur, 1956, new enl. edn 1974; Chaque homme dans sa nuit, 1960; L'autre, 1971; La nuit des fantômes, 1976; Le Mauvais Lieu, 1977; Histoires de Vertige, 1984; Les Pays Lointains, 1987; Les Etoiles du Sud, 1989; Merveilles et Démons (trans. of Lord Dunsany's Tales), 1991; *plays:* Sud, 1953; L'ennemi, 1954; L'ombre, 1956; Demain n'existe pas, 1979; L'automate, 1980; *autobiography and journals:* Memories of Happy Days, 1942; Jeunes Années: i, Partir avant le jour, 1963; ii, Mille chemins ouverts, 1964; iii, Terre lointaine, 1966; iv, Jeunesse, 1974; Ce qu'il faut d'amour à l'homme, 1978; Journal: i, Les années faciles, 1928–34, 1938; ii, Derniers beaux jours, 1935–39, 1939; iii, Devant la porte sombre, 1940–43, 1946; iv, L'œil de l'ouragan, 1943–45, 1949; v, Le revenant, 1946–50, 1952; vi, Le miroir intérieur, 1950–54, 1955; vii, Le bel aujourd'hui, 1955–58, 1958; viii, Vers l'invisible, 1958–66, 1967; ix, Ce qui reste de jour, 1967–72, 1972; x, La bouteille à la mer, 1972–76, 1976; xi, La Terre est si belle, 1976–78, 1982; xii, La lumière du monde, 1978–81, 1983; xiii, L'arc-en-ciel, 1981–84, 1988; xiv, L'expatrié, 1984–90, 1990; Dans la gueule du temps (illust. jl), 1979–; Journal du Voyageur (illust. jl), 1985; Œuvres complètes (La Pléïade), vol. I, 1972; vols II and III, 1973; vols IV and V, 1974; Vol. VI, 1990; *history:* Frère François, 1983; *essays:* Pamphlet contre les catholiques de France, 1924; Suite Anglaise, 1925; Liberté Chérie, 1974; Qui sommes-nous?, 1971; Une grande amitié: correspondance avec Jacques Maritain, 1982; Paris, 1983; Le Langage et son double, 1985; L'homme et son ombre, 1991. *Address:* Editions de la Pléïade, 5 rue Sébastien-Bottin, 75007 Paris, France.

GREEN, Sir Kenneth, Kt 1988; MA; Director, Manchester Polytechnic, since 1981; *b* 7 March 1934; *s* of James William and Elsie May Green; *m* 1961, Glenda (*née* Williams); one *d*. *Educ:* Helsby Grammar Sch.; Univ. of Wales, Bangor (BA 1st Cl. Hons); Univ. of London (MA). 2nd Lieut, S Wales Borderers, 1955–57. Management Trainee, Dunlop Rubber Co., 1957–58; Teacher, Liverpool, 1958–60; Lecturer: Widnes Technical Coll., 1961–62; Stockport College of Technology, 1962–64; Sen. Lectr, Bolton College of Education, 1964–68; Head of Educn, City of Birmingham College of Education, 1968–72; Dean of Faculty, Manchester Polytechnic, 1973–81. Member: Council, CNAA, 1985–; UFC, 1989–; Management Bd, Polys and Colls Employers' Forum, 1989–; Bd, Manchester TEC, 1989–; Bd of Govs, Sheffield Poly., 1989–; Governing Body, The Heath Comprehensive Sch., Runcorn, 1988–; Governing Body, Victoria Rd Co. Primary Sch., Runcorn, 1990–. Hon. Mem., Manchester Literary & Philosophical Soc. Hon. MRNCM. *Recreations:* Rugby football, beer tasting. *Address:* 40 Royden Avenue, Runcorn, Cheshire WA7 4SP. *T:* Runcorn (09285) 75201.

GREEN, Prof. Leslie Leonard, CBE 1989; PhD; FInstP; Professor of Experimental Physics, University of Liverpool, 1964–86, now Emeritus, and Hon. Research Fellow; Director, Daresbury Laboratory, 1981–88; *b* 30 March 1925; *s* of Leonard and Victoria Green; *m* 1952, Dr Helen Therese Morgan; one *s* one *d*. *Educ:* Alderman Newton's Sch., Leicester; King's Coll., Cambridge (MA, PhD). FInstP 1966. British Atomic Energy Proj., 1944–46; Univ. of Liverpool: Lectr, 1948–57; Sen. Lectr, 1957–62; Reader, 1962–64; Dean, Faculty of Sciences, 1969–72; Pro-Vice-Chancellor, 1978–81. Mem., SRC Nuclear Physics Bd, 1972–75 and 1979–82. *Publications:* articles on nuclear physics in scientific jls. *Address:* Seafield Cottage, De Grouchy Street, West Kirby, Merseyside L48 5DX.

GREEN, Lucinda Jane, MBE 1978; three-day event rider; *b* 7 Nov. 1953; *d* of late Maj.-Gen. George Erroll Prior-Palmer, CB, DSO, and of Lady Doreen Hersey Winifred Prior-Palmer; *m* 1981, David, *s* of Burrington Green, Brisbane; one *s* one *d*. *Educ:* St Mary's, Wantage; Idbury Manor, Oxon. Member of winning Junior European Team, 1971; Winner, 3 Day Events: Badminton Horse Trials Championships, 1973, 1976, 1977, 1979, 1983, 1984; Burghley, 1977, 1981; Individual European Championships, 1975, 1977; World Championship, 1982; Member: Olympic Team, Montreal, 1976, Los Angeles, 1984; European Championship Team: Luhmühlen, W Germany, 1975 (team Silver Medallist and individual Gold Medallist); Burghley, 1977 (team Gold Medallist), 1985 (team Gold Medallist), 1987 (team Gold Medallist); European Team, 1979, 1983 (team and individual Silver Medallist); Alternative Olympic Team, 1980; World Championship Team: Kentucky, 1978; Luhmühlen, W Germany, 1982 (team and individual Gold Medallist). Co-presenter, Horses, Channel 4, 1987. Editorial Consultant, Eventing, 1989–. *Publications:* Up, Up and Away, 1978; Four Square, 1980; Regal Realm, 1983; Cross-Country Riding, 1986. *Recreations:* driving, ski-ing, scuba diving, travelling abroad. *Address:* The Tree House, Appleshaw, Andover, Hants. *T:* Andover (0264) 773322.

GREEN, Dr Malcolm, FRCP; Consultant Physician, Brompton Hospital, since 1975; Director, British Postgraduate Medical Federation, since 1991; *b* 25 Jan. 1942; *s* of James Bisdee Malcolm Green and Frances Marjorie Lois Green; *m* 1971, Julieta Caroline Preston; two *s* two *d* (and one *d* decd). *Educ:* Charterhouse Sch. (Foundn Scholar); Trinity Coll., Oxford (Exhibnr; BA 1963; BSc 1965; MA, BM, BCh 1967; DM 1978); St Thomas's Hosp. Med. Sch. (Scholar). FRCP 1980 (MRCP 1970). Jun. appts, St Thomas' and Brompton Hosps, 1968–71; Lectr, Dept of Medicine, St Thomas' Hosp., 1971–74; Radcliffe Travelling Fellow, Harvard University Med. Sch., 1971–73; Sen. Registrar, Westminster and Brompton Hosps, 1974–75; Consultant Physician and Physician i/c Chest Dept, St Bartholomew's Hosp. 1975–86; Dean, Nat. Heart and Lung Inst., 1988–90. Chm., Exec. Cttee and Nat. Council, British Lung Foundn, 1984–; Chm. Acad. Steering Gp, BPMF, 1989–90. Mem. Bd of Govs, Nat. Heart and Chest Hosps, 1988–. Trustee, Heart Disease and Diabetes Res. Trust, 1988–. Treasurer, United Hosps Sailing Club, 1977–85. *Publications:* chapters and articles in med, books and jls on gen. medicine, respiratory medicine and respiratory physiology. *Recreations:* sailing, ski-ing. *Address:* 38 Lansdowne Gardens, SW8 2EF. *T:* 071–622 8286. *Clubs:* Royal Thames Yacht; Imperial Poona Yacht (Hon. Sec.); West Mersea Yacht.

GREEN, Prof. Malcolm Leslie Hodder, PhD; FRS 1985; CChem, FRSC; Professor of Inorganic Chemistry, since 1989, and Head of Department, Inorganic Chemistry Laboratory, since 1988, University of Oxford; Fellow of St Catherine's College, Oxford, since 1988; *b* 16 April 1936; *s* of late Leslie Ernest Green, MD and Sheila Ethel (*née* Hodder); *m* 1965, Jennifer Clare Bilham; two *s* one *d*. *Educ:* Denstone Coll.; Acton Technical Coll. (BSc); Imperial Coll. of Science and Technol., London Univ. (DIC, PhD 1958); MA Cantab. CChem, FRSC 1981. Asst Lectr in Inorganic Chem., Univ. of Cambridge, 1960–63; Fellow of Corpus Christi Coll., Cambridge, 1961–63; University of Oxford: Septcentenary Fellow and Tutor in Inorganic Chem., Balliol Coll., 1963–88; Deptl Demonstrator, 1963; Lectr, 1965–88; British Gas Royal Soc. Sen Res. Fellow, 1979–86. A. P. Sloan Vis. Prof., Harvard Univ., 1973; Sherman Fairchild Vis. Scholar, CIT, 1981. Tilden Lectr and Prize, RSC, 1982; Debye Lectr, Cornell Univ., 1985; Sir Edward Frankland Prize Lectr, 1988. Corday–Morgan Medal and Prize in Inorganic Chem., Chemical Soc., 1974; Medal for Transition Metal Chem., Chemical Soc., 1978; Award for Inorganic Chem., Amer. Chemical Soc., 1984; RSC Award for Organometallic Chem., 1986. *Publications:* Organometallic Compounds: Vol. II, The Transition Elements, 1968; (with G. E. Coates, P. Powell and K. Wade) Principles of Organometallic Chemistry, 1968. *Address:* St Catherine's College, Oxford.

GREEN, Malcolm Robert, DPhil; Lecturer, University of Glasgow, since 1967; Chairman, Strathclyde Region Education Committee, since 1982; *b* 4 Jan. 1943; *m* 1971; one *s* two *d*. *Educ:* Wyggeston Boys' School, Leicester; Magdalen College, Oxford. MA, DPhil. Member: Glasgow Corp., 1973–75; Strathclyde Regional Council, 1975–; Chairman: Educn Cttee, Strathclyde Regional Council, 1982–90; Educn Cttee, Convention of Scottish Local Authorities, 1978–90; Management Side, Scottish Jt Negotiating Cttees for Teaching Staff in Sch. and Further Educn, 1977–90; Nat. Cttee for In-Service Training of Teachers, 1977–86; Scottish Cttee for Staff Develt in Educn, 1987–. Commissioner, Manpower Services Commn, 1983–85. *Recreation:* talking politics. *Address:* 46 Victoria Crescent Road, Glasgow G12 9DE. *T:* 041–339 2007.

GREEN, Rt. Rev. Mark, MC 1945; Hon. Assistant, Christ Church, St Leonards-on-Sea, since 1982; an Assistant Bishop, Diocese of Chichester, since 1982; *b* 28 March 1917; *s* of late Rev. Ernest William Green, OBE, and Miranda Mary Green; unmarried. *Educ:* Rossall Sch.; Lincoln Coll., Oxford (MA). Curate, St Catherine's Gloucester, 1940; Royal Army Chaplains' Dept, 1943–46 (despatches, 1945); Dir of Service Ordination Candidates, 1947–48; Vicar of St John, Newland, Hull, 1948–53; Short Service Commn, Royal Army Chaplains' Dept, 1953–56; Vicar of South Bank, Teesside, 1956–58; Rector of Cottingham, Yorks, 1958–64; Vicar of Bishopthorpe and Acaster Malbis, York, 1964–72; Hon. Chaplain to Archbp of York, 1964–72; Rural Dean of Ainsty, 1964–68; Canon and Prebendary of York Minster, 1963–72; Bishop Suffragan of Aston, 1972–82; Chm. of Governing Body, Aston Training Scheme, 1977–83; Provost, Woodard Schs Southern Div., 1982–89. Hon. DSc Aston, 1980. *Publication:* Diary of Doubt and Faith, 1974. *Recreations:* Aston Villa, ballet. *Address:* 13 Archery Court, Archery Road, St Leonards-on-Sea, E Sussex TN38 0HZ. *T:* Hastings (0424) 444649.

GREEN, Dame Mary Georgina, DBE 1968; BA; Head Mistress, Kidbrooke School, SE3, 1954–73; Chairman, BBC London Local Radio Council, 1973–78; Chairman, General Optical Council, 1979–85 (Member, 1977–79); *b* 27 July 1913; *er d* of late Edwin George Green and Rose Margaret Green (*née* Gibbs). *Educ:* Wellingborough High Sch.; Westfield Coll., University of London. Assistant Mistress: Clapham High Sch., 1936–38; Streatham Hill and Clapham High Sch., 1938–40; William Hulme's Sch., Manchester, 1940–45; Head Mistress, Colston's Girls' Sch., Bristol, 1946–53. Member: Central Advisory Council for Education (Eng.), 1956–63; Church of England Board of Education, 1958–65; Council King George's Jubilee Trust, 1963–68; Court of Governors, London Sch. of Economics and Political Science, 1964–83; Royal Commission on Trade Unions and Employers' Assocs, 1965–68; Council, City University, 1969–78; Cttee of Inquiry into Nurses' Pay, 1974; Press Council, 1976–79; Review Body on Doctors' and Dentists' Remuneration, 1976–79. Dep. Chm., E-SU, 1976–82 (Governor, 1974–82); a Governor: BBC, 1968–73; Royal Ballet Sch., 1969–72; Centre for Educnl Develt Overseas, 1970–74; Rachel McMillan Coll. of Educn, 1970–73; Ditchley Foundn, 1978–. Hon. Fellow, Queen Mary and Westfield (formerly Westfield) Coll., 1976. Hon. DSc: City, 1981; Bradford, 1986. Hon. MADO 1985; Hon. FBCO 1985. *Address:* 45 Winn Road, SE12 9EX. *T:* 081–857 1514.

GREEN, Rev. Canon Michael; *see* Green, Rev. Canon E. M. B.

GREEN, Prof. Michael Boris, FRS 1989; Professor of Physics, Queen Mary and Westfield (formerly Queen Mary) College, University of London, since 1985; *b* 22 May 1946; *s* of Absalom and Genia Green. *Educ:* Cambridge Univ. (BA, PhD; Rayleigh Prize 1969). Res. Fellow, Inst. for Advanced Study, Princeton, NJ, 1970–72; Fellowships in Cambridge, 1972–77; SERC Advanced Fellow, Oxford, 1977–79; Lectr, Queen Mary Coll., 1979–85. Vis. Associate, Caltech, Pasadena, for periods during 1981–85; Nuffield Science Fellowship, 1984–86; SERC Sen. Fellowship, 1986–91. Maxwell Medal and Prize, Inst. of Physics, 1987; Hopkins Prize, Cambridge Philosophical Soc., 1987; Dirac Medal, Internat. Centre for Theoretical Physics, Trieste, 1989. *Publications:* Superstring Theory, vols I and II (with J. H. Schwarz and E. Witten), 1987; many contribs to physics and mathematics jls. *Address:* Physics Department, Queen Mary and Westfield College, Mile End Road, E1 4NS. *T:* 071–975 5078.

GREEN, Dr Michael Frederick; Consultant Physician, Department of Geriatric Medicine, Board of Health, Guernsey, since 1984; *b* 29 Aug. 1939; *s* of Frederick and Kathleen Green; *m* 1977, Janet Mary; seven *s* one *d*. *Educ:* Dulwich Coll.; Jesus Coll., Cambridge (MA); St Thomas' Hosp. (MB, BChir). FRCP 1980. Consultant, N Middlesex and St Ann's Hosps, 1969–71; Consultant Physician, Dept of Geriatric Medicine, Royal Free Hospital, 1972–84. Mem., GMC, 1973–79. Medical Adviser, Royal Life Saving Soc., 1970–84. Member various bodies mainly involved with the elderly, including: British Geriatrics Soc.; Age Concern; Cruse (Nat. Assoc. for Widows); London Medical Gp; British Soc. for Research on Ageing. Governor: Queen Elizabeth Schs, Barnet, 1973–79; Christchurch Sch., Hampstead, 1980–83. Mem. Bd, Jl of Medical Ethics, 1980–84; Chm., Editl Bd, Geriatric Medicine, 1983–. *Publications:* Health in Middle Age, 1978; co-author books on medical admin; articles on geriatric medicine, heating, lifesaving, hypothermia, endocrinology, medical records, psychiatry in old age, pressure sores. *Recreations:* family, magic, swimming and lifesaving, writing, lecturing and teaching, gardening, boating. *Address:* Glenview, Les Effards Road, St Sampson's, Guernsey.

GREEN, Michael John; Controller, BBC Radio 4, since 1986; *b* 28 May 1941; *s* of David Green and Kathleen (*née* Swann); *m* 1965, Christine Margaret Constance Gibson; one *s* one *d*. *Educ:* Repton Sch.; Barnsley Grammar Sch.; New Coll., Oxford (BA Modern Langs). Swiss Broadcasting Corp., 1964–65; Sheffield Star, 1965–67; Producer, BBC Radio Sheffield, 1967–70; Documentary Producer, BBC Manchester, 1970–77; Editor, File on Four, 1977; Head of Network Radio, Manchester, 1978–86. Chm., Radio Acad., 1990–. *Recreations:* France, canals, cinema, collecting glass. *Address:* BBC, Broadcasting House, W1A 1AA. *Club:* Rugby.

GREEN, Michael Philip; Chairman, Carlton Communications Plc, since 1983 (Chief Executive, 1983–91); first Chairman, Open College, since 1986; *b* 2 Dec. 1947; *s* of Cyril and Irene Green; *m* 1st, 1972, Hon. Janet Frances (marr. diss. 1989), *d* of Lord Wolfson, *qv*; two *d*; 2nd, 1990, Theresa Buckmaster. *Educ:* Haberdashers' Aske's School. Director and Co-Founder, Tangent Industries, 1968. Founder, Tangent Charitable Trust, 1984; Dir, Central Independent Television, 1991. *Recreations:* reading, bridge, television. *Address:* Carlton Communications Plc, 15 St George Street, W1R 9DE. *T:* 071–499 8050. *Clubs:* Portland, Carlton.

GREEN, Prof. Mino, FIEE; Professor of Electrical Device Science, Electrical Engineering, Imperial College of Science and Technology, since 1983; *b* 10 March 1927; *s* of Alexander and Elizabeth Green; *m* 1951, Diana Mary Allen; one *s* one *d. Educ:* Dulwich Coll.; University Coll., Durham Univ. (BSc, PhD, DSc). Group Leader: Solid State Res., Lincoln Laboratory, MIT, 1951–55; Res., Zenith Radio Corp., USA, 1956–60; Associate Dir, Electrochemistry Lab., Univ. of Pennsylvania, 1960–62; Man. Dir, Zenith Radio Research Corp. (UK) Ltd, 1962–72; Lectr, then Reader, Elec. Engrg Dept, Imperial Coll. of Science and Technology, 1972–83. *Publications:* Solid State Surface Science, vols I, II and III (ed), 1969–73; many pubns (and some patents) on various aspects of semiconductor science. *Recreations:* walking, art appreciation. *Address:* 55 Gerard Road, SW13 9QH. *T:* 081–748 8689. *Club:* Hurlingham.

GREEN, Dr Norman Michael, FRS 1981; Research Staff, Division of Biochemistry, National Institute for Medical Research, since 1964; *b* 6 April 1926; *s* of Ernest Green and Hilda Margaret Carter; *m* 1953, Iro Paulina Moschouti; two *s* one *d. Educ:* Dragon Sch., Oxford; Clifton Coll., Bristol; Magdalen Coll., Oxford (BA; Athletics Blue, Cross Country Blue); UCH Med. Sch., London (PhD). Res. Student, Univ. of Washington, Seattle, 1951–53; Lectr in Biochemistry, Univ. of Sheffield, 1953–55; Res. Fellow and Lectr in Chem. Pathol., St Mary's Hosp. Med. Sch., London, 1956–62; Vis. Scientist, NIH, Maryland, 1962–64. *Publications:* research papers on the structure of proteins and of membranes, in scientific jls. *Recreations:* mountain climbing, pyrotechnics. *Address:* 57 Hale Lane, Mill Hill, NW7 3PS.

GREEN, Sir Owen (Whitley), Kt 1984; Chairman, BTR plc, since 1984 (Managing Director, 1967–86); *b* Stockton-on-Tees, 14 May 1925; *m* Doreen Margaret Spark; one *s* two *d.* FCA 1950. Served RNVR, 1942–46. With Charles Wakeling & Co., accountants, 1947–56; BTR, 1956; Asst Man. Dir, 1966. Dir, The Spectator, 1988–. Trustee, Natural History Mus., 1986–. Businessman of the Year, 1982; BIM Gold Medal, 1984; Founding Societies' Centenary Award, ICA, 1985. *Recreation:* golf. *Address:* (office) Silvertown House, Vincent Square, SW1P 2PL. *T:* 071–834 3848.

GREEN, Pauline; Member (Lab) London North, European Parliament, since 1989; *b* 8 Dec. 1948; *d* of late Bertram Wiltshire and of Lucy Wiltshire; *m* 1971, Paul Adam Green; one *s* one *d. Educ:* John Kelly Secondary Modern Sch. for Girls, Brent; Kilburn Poly.; Open Univ. (BA); London School of Economics (MSc). Sec., 1981, Chair, 1983, Chipping Barnet Labour Party. Contested (Lab) Arkley ward, Barnet Council elecns, 1986. Lobbyist on European Affairs for Co-operative Movement, 1986–89. *Recreations:* music, swimming. *Address:* (office) Gibson House, 800 High Road, Tottenham, N17 0DH. *T:* 081–365 1892.

GREEN, Brig. Percy William Powlett, CBE 1960 (OBE 1956); DSO 1946; *b* 10 Sept. 1912; *er s* of late Brig.-Gen. W. G. K. Green, CB, CMG, DSO, Indian Army; *m* 1943, Phyllis Margery Fitz Gerald May, *d* of late Lieut-Col A. H. May, OBE; one *s* one *d. Educ:* Wellington Coll.; RMC. Commnd Northamptonshire Regt, 1932; Op. NW Frontier, India, 1936–37; BEF 1939–40; Lt-Col Comdg 2nd W Yorks Regt, 1945–46; Burma, 1944–45; Lt-Col Comdg 1 Malay Regt, 1946–47; Comd 4th King's African Rifles, 1954–56; Op. against Mau Mau; Col, Gen. Staff, War Office, 1956–57; Chief of Staff (Brig.) E Africa Comd, 1957–60; DDMI, War Office, 1961–63; Chief of Staff, N Ireland Command, 1963–65; Dep. Comdr, Aldershot District, 1965–67; retired, 1967. ADC to the Queen, 1965–67. Dep. Colonel, Royal Anglian Regt, 1966–76. *Recreations:* field sports. *Address:* Grudds, South Warnborough, Basingstoke, Hants RG25 1RW. *T:* Basingstoke (0256) 862472. *Club:* Army and Navy.

GREEN, Sir Peter (James Frederick), Kt 1982; Chairman, Janson Green Holdings Ltd, 1986–89 (Chairman, Janson Green Ltd, 1966–86); Chairman, Lloyd's, 1980, 1981, 1982, 1983; *b* 28 July 1924; *s* of J. E. Green and M. B. Holford; *m* 1st, 1950, A. P. Ryan (*d* 1985); 2nd, 1986, Jennifer Whitehead. *Educ:* Harrow Sch.; Christ Church, Oxford. Lloyd's: Underwriter, 1947; Mem. Cttee, 1974–77; Dep. Chm., 1979; Gold Medal, 1983. *Recreations:* shooting, fishing, sailing, farming. *Address:* 85 Burton Court, SW3 4SX. *Clubs:* City of London, Royal Ocean Racing, Pratt's; Royal Yacht Squadron (Cowes); Cruising of America (New York).

GREEN, Prof. Peter Morris; author and translator since 1953; Professor of Classics, University of Texas at Austin, since 1972 (James R. Dougherty Jr Centennial Professor of Classics, 1982–84 and since 1985); *b* 22 Dec. 1924; *o c* of late Arthur Green, CBE, MC, LLB, and Olive Slaughter; *m* 1st, 1951, Lalage Isobel Pulvertaft (marr. diss.); two *s* one *d*; 2nd, 1975, Carin Margreta, *y d* of late G. N. Christensen, Saratoga, USA. *Educ:* Charterhouse; Trinity Coll., Cambridge. Served in RAFVR, 1943–47: overseas tour in Burma Comd, 1944–46. 1st Cl. Hons, Pts I and II, Classical Tripos, 1949–50; MA and PhD Cantab 1954; Craven Schol. and Student, 1950; Dir of Studies in Classics, 1951–52; Fiction Critic, London Daily Telegraph, 1953–63; Literary Adviser, The Bodley Head, 1957–58; Cons. Editor, Hodder and Stoughton, 1960–63; Television Critic, The Listener, 1961–63; Film Critic, John o'London's, 1961–63; Mem. Book Soc. Cttee, 1959–63. Former Mem. of selection cttees for literary prizes: Heinemann Award, John Llewellyn Rhys, W. H. Smith £1000 Award for Literature. Translator of numerous works from French and Italian, including books by Simone de Beauvoir, Fosco Maraini, Joseph Kessel. FRSL 1956; Mem. Council, Royal Society of Literature, 1958–63 (resigned on emigration). In 1963 resigned all positions and emigrated to Greece as full-time writer (1963–71). Vis. Prof. of Classics: Univ. of Texas, 1971–72; UCLA, 1976; Mellon Prof. of Humanities, Tulane Univ., 1986; Sen. Fellow for independent study and res., National Endowment for the Humanities, 1983–84. *Publications:* The Expanding Eye, 1953; Achilles His Armour, 1955; Cat in Gloves (pseud. Denis Delaney), 1956; The Sword of Pleasure (W. H. Heinemann Award for Literature), 1957; Kenneth Grahame, 1859–1932: A Study of his Life, Work and Times, 1959; Essays in Antiquity, 1960; Habeas Corpus and other stories, 1962; Look at the Romans, 1963; The Laughter of Aphrodite, 1965; Juvenal: The Sixteen Satires (trans.), 1967; Armada from Athens: The Failure of the Sicilian Expedition, 415–413 BC, 1970; Alexander the Great: a biography, 1970; The Year of Salamis, 480–479 BC, 1971; The Shadow of the Parthenon, 1972; The Parthenon, 1973; A Concise History of Ancient Greece, 1973; Alexander of Macedon 356–323 BC: a historical biography, 1974; Ovid: The Erotic Poems (trans.), 1982; Beyond the Wild Wood: the world of Kenneth Grahame, 1982; Medium and Message Reconsidered: the changing functions of classical translation, 1986; Classical Bearings: interpreting ancient history and culture, 1989; Alexander to Actium: the historical evolution of the Hellenistic Age, 1990. *Recreations:* travel, swimming, spear-fishing, lawn tennis, table-tennis, squash racquets, amateur archæology, avoiding urban life. *Address:* c/o Department of Classics, University of Texas, Waggener Hall 123, Austin, Texas 78712, USA. *T:* (512) 471–5742. *Club:* Savile.

GREEN, Robert James; Under Secretary, Local Government, Department of the Environment, since 1991; *b* 27 Jan. 1937; *er s* of Ronald Percy Green and Doris Rose (*née* Warman); *m* 1960, Jill Marianne Small; one *d* (one *s* decd). *Educ:* Kent College, Canterbury. Executive Officer, Board of Trade, 1957; Asst Principal, 1963, Principal, 1967, Min. of Housing and Local Govt; Secretary, Water Resources Board, 1972–74;

Asst Secretary: Dept of the Environment, 1974; Dept of Transport, 1980; Under Sec., 1982; Regl Dir, Northern Reg., 1982–83, and Yorks and Humberside Reg., 1982–86, Dir, Senior Staff Management, 1986–88, Depts of the Environment and Transport; Dir of Rural Affairs, DoE, 1988–91. Non-exec. Dir, Butterley Bricks Ltd, 1988–90. *Recreation:* theatre, including amateur dramatics. *Address:* c/o Department of the Environment, 2 Marsham Street, SW1.

GREEN, Maj.-Gen. Robert Leslie Stuart; Chairman, Care for the Mentally Handicapped, since 1991 (Executive Governor, 1980); *b* 1 July 1925; *s* of Leslie Stuart Green and Eliza Dorothea Andrew; *m* 1952, Nancy Isobel Collier; two *d. Educ:* Chorlton Sch. 2nd Bn Black Watch, India, 1944–46; 6 Airborne Div., Palestine, 1946; 2 Parachute Bde, UK and Germany, 1946–47; 1st Bn HLI, UK, ME and Cyprus, 1947–56; ptsc 1959; jssc 1962; 1st Bn Royal Highland Fusiliers, UK, Germany and Gibraltar, 1959–69, Comd 1967–69; staff apptmt 1970; Military Dir of Studies, RMCS, 1970–72; Sen. Military Officer, Royal Armament Res. and Develt Estabt, 1973–75; Vice-Pres., Ordnance Bd, 1976–78, Pres., March-June 1978. Col, The Royal Highland Fusiliers, 1979–. Freeman, City of London, 1983. FBIM. *Recreations:* rough shooting, painting, music and sailing. *Address:* Royal Bank of Scotland, 43 Curzon Street, Mayfair, W1. *Club:* Naval and Military.

GREEN, Sam, CBE 1960; Chairman: Dula (ISMA) Ltd, since 1969; Green & Associates Ltd, since 1970; Spear Bros Ltd, since 1970; Vice Chairman, Royal British Legion Poppy Factory, Richmond (Director since 1964); Director, Royal British Legion Industries, since 1967; *b* Oldham, Lancs, 6 Feb. 1907; *s* of Fred Green; *m* 1942, Dr Lilly (*née* Pollak); one *d. Educ:* Manchester Coll. of Technology. Apprentice, Platt Bros, Oldham, 1920–34; Designer and Development Engr, British Northrop Automatic Loom Co., Blackburn, 1934–39 (invented 4–colour loom); Chief Engr, Betts & Co., London, 1939–42; Works Manager, Morphy-Richards Ltd, St Mary Cray, Kent, 1942–44; General Works Manager, Holoplast Ltd, New Hythe, near Maidstone, 1944–47; Industrial Adviser, Industrial and Commercial Finance Corp., London, 1947–52; Managing Dir of Remploy Ltd, 1952–64; Chm. and Man. Dir, Ralli Bros (Industries) Ltd, 1964–69; Chm., Industrial Advisers to the Blind, 1964–74; Director: J. E. Lesser Group Ltd, 1969–74; New Day Holdings Ltd, 1972–74. Chm., Inst. of Patentees and Inventors, 1975 (Vice-Chm., 1961); Vice Pres., Internat. Fed. of Inventors' Assocs, 1984–. FRSA 1962. CEng; FIEE; FIProdE. Gold Medal, World Intellectual Property Orgn, 1984. *Recreations:* reading, gardening, cycling, walking, golf. *Address:* Holly Lodge, 39 Westmoreland Road, Bromley, Kent BR2 0TF. *T:* 081–460 3306. *Clubs:* Reform, Directors', Pickwick (oldest Bicycle Club).

GREEN, Sir Stephen; see Green, Sir E. S. L.

GREEN, Terence Arthur; Director and Deputy Group Chief Executive, National Westminster Bank, 1987–89; *b* 19 May 1934; *m* 1956, Leeta (*née* Beales); two *s* one *d. Educ:* South East Essex County Technical College; Harvard Business School (AMP 1980). ACIB. Joined Westminster Bank, 1950; Dep. Gen. Manager, Internat. Banking Div., Nat. Westminster Bank, 1982; Gen. Manager, Business Development Div., 1985. *Recreations:* golf, cricket.

GREEN, Thomas Charles, CB 1971; Chief Charity Commissioner, 1966–75; *b* 13 Oct. 1915; *s* of late Charles Harold Green and late Hilda Emma Green (*née* Thomas); *m* 1945, Beryl Eva Barber, *widow* of Lieut N. Barber; one *d* (and one step *d*). *Educ:* Eltham Coll.; Oriel Coll., Oxford. Entered Home Office, 1938. Served with RAF, 1940–45. Asst Secretary: Home Office, 1950–64; Charity Commn, 1964–65. UK representative on UN Commn on Narcotic Drugs, 1957–64. Nuffield Travelling Fellowship, 1959–60. *Recreations:* gardening, photography. *Address:* Coombe Bungalow, Coombe Lane, Compton Bishop, Somerset BS26 2HE.

GREEN, Rev. Vivian Hubert Howard, DD, FRHistS; Fellow and Tutor in History, 1951–83, Rector, 1983–87, Hon. Fellow, 1987, Lincoln College, Oxford; *b* 18 Nov. 1915; *s* of Hubert James and Edith Eleanor Playle Green; unmarried. *Educ:* Bradfield Coll., Berks; Trinity Hall, Cambridge (Scholar). Goldsmiths' Exhibnr; 1st Cl. Hist. Tripos, Parts I and II; Lightfoot Schol. in Ecclesiastical Hist.; Thirlwall Medal and Prize, 1941; MA 1941; MA Oxon by incorp., 1951; DD Cambridge, 1958; DD Oxon by incorp., 1958. Gladstone Research Studentship, St Deiniol's Library, Hawarden, 1937–38; Fellow of St Augustine's Coll., Canterbury, 1939–48; Chaplain, Exeter Sch. and St Luke's Training Coll., Exeter, 1940–42; Chaplain and Asst Master, Sherborne Sch., Dorset, 1942–51; Lincoln College, Oxford: Chaplain, 1951–69; Sen. Tutor, 1953–62 and 1974–77; Sub-Rector, 1970–83; acting Rector, 1972–73. Deacon, 1939; Priest, 1940. Select Preacher, Oxford, 1959–60. Vis. Prof. of History, Univ. of S Carolina, 1982. *Publications:* Bishop Reginald Pecock, 1945; The Hanoverians, 1948; From St Augustine to William Temple, 1948; Renaissance and Reformation, 1952; The Later Plantagenets, 1955; Oxford Common Room, 1957; The Young Mr Wesley, 1961; The Swiss Alps, 1961; Martin Luther and the Reformation, 1964; John Wesley, 1964; Religion at Oxford and Cambridge (historical survey), 1964; The Universities, 1969; Medieval Civilization in Western Europe, 1971; A History of Oxford University, 1974; The Commonwealth of Lincoln College 1427–1977, 1979; Love in a Cool Climate: the letters of Mark Pattison and Meta Bradley 1879–1884, 1985; (ed) Memoirs of an Oxford Don: Mark Pattison, 1988; (with William Scoular) A Question of Guilt: the murder of Nancy Eaton, 1988; contributor to: Dictionary of English Church History (ed Ollard, Crosse and Bond); The Oxford Dictionary of the Christian Church (ed Cross); European Writers, The Middle Ages and Renaissance (ed W. T. H. Jackson and G. Stade), vols I and II, 1983; The History of the University of Oxford, vol. V, The Eighteenth Century (ed L. S. Sutherland and L. G. Mitchell), 1986. *Address:* Lincoln College, Oxford OX1 3DR. *T:* Oxford (0865) 279830; Calendars, Burford, Oxford OX8 4LS. *T:* Burford (099382) 3214.

GREEN-PRICE, Sir Robert (John), 5th Bt, *cr* 1874; Assistant Professor of English, Chiba University of Commerce, since 1982; *b* 22 Oct. 1940; *o s* of Sir John Green-Price, 4th Bt, and Irene Marion (*d* 1954), *d* of Major Sir (Ernest) Guy Lloyd, 1st Bt, DSO; *S* father, 1964. *Educ:* Shrewsbury. Army Officer, 1961–69; Captain, RCT, retd. ADC to Governor of Bermuda, 1969–72. Lectr in English, Teikyo Univ., 1975–82. Part-time Lecturer: Keio Univ., 1977–; Waseda Univ., 1986–; Guest Lectr, NHK Radio, 1978–83. *Heir:* uncle Powell Norman Dansey Green-Price [*b* 22 July 1926; *m* 1963, Ann Stella, *d* of late Brig. Harold George Howson, CBE, MC, TD; one *s* one *d*]. *Address:* 4–A Shoto Mansions, 5–4–20 Shinden, Ichikawa-shi, Chiba-ken, Japan 272. *T:* 0472–23–4693; Villa De Avellanos, Poblacion 1 Currimao, Ilocos Norte, Philippines. *T:* 077–792 2913.

GREENALL, family name of **Baron Daresbury.**

GREENAWAY, Alan Pearce, JP; Vice-President, Daniel Greenaway & Sons Ltd, 1978–82 (Joint Managing Director, 1951–78; Vice-Chairman, 1965–76; Chairman, 1976–78); *b* 25 Nov. 1913; *yr s* of Sir Percy Walter Greenaway, 1st Bt, and Lydie Amy (*d* 1962), *er d* of James Burdick; *m* 1948, Patricia Frances (*d* 1982), *yr d* of Ald. Sir Frederick Wells, 1st Bt; one *s* one *d. Educ:* Canford. Served in King's Liverpool Regt during War of 1939–45, reaching rank of Captain. Liveryman: Worshipful Co. of Merchant Taylors; Worshipful Co. of Stationers and Newspaper Makers (Under-Warden 1971–72, Upper

Warden, 1972–73, Master 1973–74). Mem. Court of Common Council for Ward of Bishopsgate, 1952–65; Sheriff for the City of London, 1962–63; JP, Co. London, 1964; Alderman, Lime Street Ward, City of London, 1965–72; Chm. and Treasurer, City of London Sheriffs' Soc., 1979–82. Officer, l'Ordre de la Valeur Camerounaise, 1963; Commandeur, l'Ordre de Leopold Class III, 1963; Commander, Royal Order of the Phoenix, 1964. *Recreations:* golf, fishing, swimming, bowls. *Address:* West Byfleet, Surrey. *Clubs:* City Livery (Vice-Pres. 1971–72, Pres., 1972–73), Royal Automobile, United Wards.

GREENAWAY, Sir Derek (Burdick), 2nd Bt *cr* 1933; CBE 1974; TD; JP; DL; First Life President, Daniel Greenaway & Sons Ltd, 132 Commercial Street, E1, since 1976 (Chairman, 1956–76); *b* 27 May 1910; *er s* of Sir Percy Walter Greenaway, 1st Bt and Lydie Amy (*d* 1962), *er d* of James Burdick; *S* father 1956; *m* 1937, Sheila Beatrice, *d* of late Richard Cyril Lockett, 58 Cadogan Place, SW1; one *s* one *d*. *Educ:* Marlborough. Served in Field Artillery during War of 1939–45; Hon. Col: 44 (HC) Signal Regt (Cinque Ports) TA, 1966; 36th (Eastern) Signal Regt (V), 1967–74. Joint Master, Old Surrey and Burstow Foxhounds, 1958–66. Chm. Sevenoaks Constituency C & U Assoc., 1960–63; Pres. 1963–66; Vice Pres., 1966–. Asst Area Treasurer, SE Area Nat. Union of Cons. Assocs, 1966–69, Area Treasurer, 1969–75, Chm. 1975–79. Master, Stationers' and Newspapermakers Co., 1974–75 (Silver Medal, 1984). JP County of Kent, 1962–; High Sheriff, 1971, DL 1973, Kent. FRSA. Life Mem., Assoc. of Men of Kent and Kentish Men. *Recreations:* hunting, shooting. *Heir: s* John Michael Burdick Greenaway [*b* 9 Aug. 1944; *m* 1982, Susan M., *d* of Henry Birch, Tattenhall, Cheshire; one *s* one *d*. Late Lieut, The Life Guards]. *Address:* Dunmore, Four Elms, Edenbridge, Kent. *T:* Four Elms (073270) 275. *Clubs:* Carlton, City of London, MCC.

See also A. P. Greenaway, H. F. R. Sturge.

GREENAWAY, Frank, MA, PhD; CChem, FRSC, FSA, FMA; Research Fellow, The Science Museum, 1980–91; Reader in the History of Science, Davy-Faraday Research Laboratory of the Royal Institution, 1970–85; *b* 9 July 1917; 3rd *s* of late Henry James Greenaway; *m* 1942, Margaret (Miranda), 2nd *d* of late R. G. Heegaard Warner and *widow* of John Raymond Brumfit; two *s* three *d*. *Educ:* Cardiff High Sch.; Jesus Coll., Oxford (Meyricke Exhibitioner); University Coll. London. MA Oxon, PhD London. Served War of 1939–45, RAOC, as Inspecting Ordnance Officer, 1940–41 (invalided). Science Master: Bournemouth Sch., 1941–42; Epsom Gram. Sch., 1942–43; Research Labs, Kodak Ltd, 1944–49; Asst Keeper, Science Museum, 1949; Dep. Keeper, 1959; Keeper, Dept of Chemistry, 1967–80. Regents' Fellow, Smithsonian Instn, Washington, DC, 1985. Member Council: Brit. Soc. for the Hist. of Science, 1958–68, 1974–78 (Vice-Pres. 1962–65); Museums Assoc., 1961–70, 1973–76 (Hon. Editor, 1965–70); Royal Instn, 1990– (Chm., Cttee of Visitors, 1964–65); Mem. Brit. Nat. Cttee of Internat. Council of Museums, 1956–58, 1962–71, 1977–83; Membre Correspondant de l'Académie Internationale d'Histoire des Sciences, 1963. Member: Council, Soc. for History of Alchemy and Chemistry, 1967– (Sec., 1967–74); History of Medicine Adv. Panel, The Wellcome Trust, 1968–74; Higher Educn Adv. Cttee, The Open Univ., 1970–73; British Nat. Cttee for Hist. of Sci., 1972–81; British Nat. Cttee, ICSU, 1972–77; Council, Internat. Union of the Hist. and Philos. of Science, 1972–81 (Sec., 1972–77); Council of Management, Royal Philharmonic Soc., 1980–84, 1986–89; Pres., Commonwealth Assoc. of Museums, 1979–83. Boerhaave Medal, Leyden Univ., 1968. *Publications:* Science Museums in Developing Countries, 1962; John Dalton and the Atom, 1966; (ed) Lavoisier's Essays Physical and Chemical, 1971; (ed) Science in the Early Roman Empire, 1986; Editor, Royal Institution Archives, 1971–; Official Publications of the Science Museum; Papers on history of chemistry and on museology. *Recreations:* music, travel. *Address:* 135 London Road, Ewell, Epsom, Surrey KT17 2BS. *T:* 081–393 1330. *Club:* Athenæum.

See also C. J. Brumfit.

GREENBAUM, Prof. Sidney; Director of the Survey of English Usage, since 1983, and Visiting Professor, since 1991, University College, London; *b* 31 Dec. 1929; *s* of Lewis and Nelly Greenbaum. *Educ:* Univ. of London (BA Hons and MA Hebrew and Aramaic; Postgrad. Cert. in Educn; BA Hons English; PhD Mod. English Grammar). Teacher at London primary sch., 1954–57; Head of English Dept at London grammar sch., 1957–64; Research asst, Survey of English Usage, UCL, 1965–68; Vis. Asst Prof., English Dept, Univ. of Oregon, 1968–69; Associate Prof., English Dept, Univ. of Wisconsin-Milwaukee, 1969–72; Vis. Prof., English Dept, Hebrew Univ., Jerusalem, 1972–73; Prof., English Dept, Univ. of Wisconsin-Milwaukee, 1972–83; Quain Prof. of English Lang. and Lit., 1983–90, Dean of the Faculty of Arts, 1988–90, UCL; Dean, Faculty of Arts, London University, 1986–88. Hon. DH Wisconsin-Milwaukee, 1989. Editor of series: (with C. Cooper) Written Communication Annual, 1984–; Studies in English Language, 1987–. *Publications:* Studies in English Adverbial Usage, 1969; Verb-Intensifier Collocations in English: an experimental approach, 1970; (with R. Quirk) Elicitation Experiments in English: linguistic studies in use and attitude, 1970; (jtly) A Grammar of Contemporary English, 1972; (with R. Quirk) A University Grammar of English (Amer. edn A Concise Grammar of Contemporary English), 1973; Acceptability in Language, 1977; (jtly) Studies in English Linguistics: for Randolph Quirk, 1980; The English Language Today, 1985; (jtly) A Comprehensive Grammar of the English Language, 1985; (with C. Cooper) Studying Writing: linguistic approaches, 1986; (with J. Whitcut) rev. edn of Gower's Complete Plain Words, 1986; Good English and the Grammarian, 1988; (with J. Whitcut) Longman Guide to English Usage, 1988; A College Grammar of English, 1989; (with R. Quirk) A Student's Grammar of the English Language, 1990; An Introduction to English Grammar, 1991; numerous articles in learned jls. *Address:* Department of English, University College London, Gower Street, WC1E 6BT. *T:* 071–387 7050. *Club:* Reform.

GREENBOROUGH, Sir John Hedley, KBE 1979 (CBE 1975); Chairman, Newarthill, since 1980; Deputy Chairman: Bowater Industries (formerly Bowater Corporation), 1984–87 (Director, since 1979); Lloyds Bank, since 1985 (Director, since 1980); Director, Hogg Robinson Group, since 1980; *b* 7 July 1922; *s* of William Greenborough and Elizabeth Marie Greenborough (*née* Wilson); *m* 1951, Gerta Ebel; one step *s*. *Educ:* Wandsworth School. War service: Pilot, RAF, later Fleet Air Arm, 1942–45; graduated Pensacola; Naval Aviator, USN, 1944. Joined Asiatic Petroleum Co., London, 1939; served with Shell Oil, Calif, 1946–47; Shell Brazil Ltd, 1948–57; Commercial Dir, later Exec. Vice-Pres., Shell Argentina Ltd, Buenos Aires, 1960–66; Area Coordinator, East and Australasia, Shell Internat., London, 1967–68; Man. Dir (Marketing), Shell-Mex and BP Ltd, 1969–71, Man. Dir and Chief Exec., 1971–75; Chm., UK Oil Pipelines Ltd, 1971–77; Dep. Chm., 1976–80, Man. Dir, 1976–78, Shell UK Ltd. Dir, Laporte Industries (Hldgs), 1983–86. President of Confederation of British Industry, 1978–80 (Mem. Council, 1971–). Chairman: UK Oil Ind. Emergency Cttee, 1971–80; UK Petroleum Ind. Adv. Cttee, 1971–77; Member: British Productivity Council, 1969–72; Clean Air Council, 1971–75; Bd of Fellows, BIM, 1973–78 (Chm., 1976–78); NEDC, 1977–80; Vice-Chairman: British Chamber of Commerce in Argentina, 1962–66; British Road Fedn, 1969–75. President: Nat. Soc. for Clean Air, 1973–75; Incorporated Soc. of British Advertisers (ISBA), 1976–78; Inst. of Petroleum, 1976–78; Nat. Council for Voluntary Orgns, 1980–86; Strategic Planning Soc., 1986–. Chm., Review Body for Nursing and Midwifery Staff and Professions Allied to Medicine, 1983–86. Fellow, Inst. Petroleum; CBIM; FCIM (Vice-Pres.). Mem., Management Bd, Adam Smith Inst., 1989–. Governor, Ashridge Management Coll., 1972– (Chm., 1977–); Chm. Governing Council, UMDS of Guy's and St Thomas' Hosps, 1982–89. Liveryman, Co. of Distillers, 1975–. Freeman, City of London. Hon. LLD Birmingham, 1983. *Recreations:* golf, travel, music. *Address:* 30 Burghley House, Oakfield, Somerset Road, Wimbledon Common, SW19 5JB. *Clubs:* Carlton, MCC; Royal and Ancient Golf; Royal Wimbledon Golf.

GREENBURY, Richard; Chairman, since 1991, and Chief Executive, since 1988, Marks & Spencer plc; *b* 31 July 1936; *s* of Richard Oswald Greenbury and Dorothy (*née* Lewis); *m* 1st, 1959, Sian Eames Hughes; two *s* two *d*; 2nd, 1985, Gabrielle Mary McManus. *Educ:* Ealing County Grammar Sch. Joined Marks & Spencer Ltd as Jun. Management Trainee, 1953; Alternate Dir, 1970; Full Dir, 1972; Jt Man. Dir, 1978–86; Chief Operating Officer, 1986–88. Non-exec. Director: British Gas, 1976–87; MB Group (formerly Metal Box), 1985–89. *Recreation:* tennis (Member Mddx County Team for 12 years, has also played for International Tennis Club of GB). *Address:* c/o 57 Baker Street, W1A 1DN. *Club:* International Tennis Club of GB.

GREENE, family name of **Baron Greene of Harrow Weald.**

GREENE OF HARROW WEALD, Baron *cr* 1974 (Life Peer), of Harrow; **Sidney Francis Greene,** Kt 1970; CBE 1966; Director: Trades Union Unit Trust, 1970–80; RTZ Corporation, 1975–80; Times Newspapers Holdings Ltd, 1980–82 (Times Newspapers Ltd, 1975–80); *b* 12 Feb. 1910; *s* of Frank James Greene and Alice (*née* Kerrod); *m* 1936, Masel Elizabeth Carter; three *d*. *Educ:* elementary. Joined Railway Service, 1924; appointed Union Organiser, 1944, Asst Gen. Sec., 1954, Gen. Sec., Nat. Union of Railwaymen, 1957–75. Mem., TUC Gen. Council, 1957–75 (Chm., 1969–70); Chm., TUC Economic Cttee, 1968–75. Member: National Economic Development Council, 1962–75; Advisory Council, ECGD, 1967–70; part-time Member: Southern Electricity Board, 1964–77; Nat. Freight Corp., 1973–77; a Dir, Bank of England, 1970–78. JP London, 1941–65. FCIT. *Recreations:* reading, gardening. *Address:* 26 Kynaston Wood, Boxtree Road, Harrow Weald, Mddx HA3 6UA.

GREENE, Graham Carleton, CBE 1986; publisher; Chairman, Museums and Galleries Commission, since 1991; *b* 10 June 1936; *s* of Sir Hugh Carleton Greene, KCMG, OBE and Helga Mary Connolly; *m* 1957, Judith Margaret (marr. diss.), *d* of Rt Hon. Lord Gordon-Walker, CH, PC; *m* 1976, Sally Georgina Horton, *d* of Sidney Wilfred Eaton; one *s*. *Educ:* Eton; University Coll., Oxford (MA). Merchant Banking, Dublin, New York and London, 1957–58; Secker & Warburg Ltd, 1958–62; Jonathan Cape, 1962–90 (Man. Dir, 1966–88). Director: Chatto, Virago, Bodley Head & Jonathan Cape Ltd, 1969–88 (Chm., 1970–88); Jackdaw Publications Ltd (Chm. 1964–88); Cape Goliard Press Ltd, 1967–88; Guinness Mahon Holdings Ltd, 1968–79; Australasian Publishing Co. Pty Ltd, 1969–88 (Chm., 1978–88); Sprint Productions Ltd, 1971–80; Book Reps (New Zealand) Ltd, 1971–88 (Chm., 1984–88); CVBC Services Ltd (Chm. 1972–88); Guinness Peat Group PLC, 1973–87; Grantham Book Storage Ltd (Chm. 1974–88); Triad Paperbacks Ltd, 1975–88; Chatto, Virago, Bodley Head & Jonathan Cape Australia Pty Ltd (Chm., 1977–88); Greene, King & Sons PLC, 1979–; Statesman & Nation Publishing Co. Ltd, 1980–85 (Chm., 1981–85); Statesman Publishing Co. Ltd, 1980–85 (Chm., 1981–85); Nation Pty Co. Ltd (Chm., 1981–86); New Society Ltd (Chm., 1984–86); Random House Inc., 1987–88; Random House UK Ltd, 1988–90; Chm., British Museum Publications Ltd, 1988–; Merlin Internat. Green Investment Trust plc, 1989–; Henry Sotheran Ltd, 1990–; Ed Victor Ltd, 1991–. Pres., Publishers Assoc., 1977–79 (Mem. Council, 1969–88); Member: Book Develt Council, 1970–79 (Dep. Chm., 1972–73); Internat. Cttee, Internat. Publishers Assoc., 1977–88 (Exec. Cttee, 1981–88); Groupe des Editeurs de Livres de la CEE, (Fedn of European Publishers), 1977–86 (Pres., 1984–86); Arts Council Working Party Sub-Cttee on Public Lending Right, 1970; Paymaster General's Working Party on Public Lending Right, 1970–72; Board, British Council, 1977–88; Chm., Nat. Book League, 1974–76 (Dep. Chm., 1971–74); Mem. Gen. Cttee, Royal Literary Fund, 1975. Trustee: British Museum, 1978–; Open Coll. of the Arts, 1990–; Chm., BM Develt Trust, 1986–; Pres., BM Foundn Inc., 1989–90; Dir, American Friends of BM, 1990–. Chm., GB-China Centre, 1986–. Chevalier de l'Ordre des Arts et des Lettres, France, 1985. *Address:* 11 Lord North Street, Westminster, SW1P 3LA. *T:* 071–799 6808. *Clubs:* Garrick, Groucho.

GREENE, Ian Rawdon; *b* 3 March 1909; *o s* of Rawdon Greene and Marie Louise, Rahan, Bray, County Wicklow, Ireland; *m* 1937, Eileen Theodora Stack; one *d*. *Educ:* Cheltenham Coll.; Trinity Coll., Dublin (BA, LLB). Barrister at Law, Kings Inns, Dublin, 1932; Crown Counsel, Tanganyika, 1935; Resident Magistrate, Zanzibar, 1937. Military Service, Kenya, 1940–41. Sen. Resident Magistrate, Zanzibar, 1950; Actg Asst Judge, Zanzibar, on numerous occasions; Actg Chief Justice, Zanzibar, June 1954, and May-Oct. 1955; Judge-in-charge, Somaliland Protectorate, 1955; Chief Justice, Somaliland Protectorate, 1958–60, retired; Stipendiary Magistrate, North Borneo, 1961–64. Registrar to Dean and Chapter, St Patrick's Cathedral, Dublin, 1973–82. Order of Brilliant Star of Zanzibar (4th Cl.), 1953. *Publications:* Jt Ed., Vols VI and VII, Zanzibar Law Reports. *Recreations:* cricket, golf, bridge, chess. *Address:* Malindi, Kilmacanogue, Co. Wicklow, Ireland. *T:* Dublin (0001) 867322. *Clubs:* English (Zanzibar); Hargeisa (Somaliland).

GREENE, Jenny; Editor, Country Life, since 1986; *b* 9 Feb. 1937; *d* of James Wilson Greene and Mary Emily Greene; *m* 1971, John Gilbert (marr. diss. 1987). *Educ:* Rochelle Sch., Cork; Trinity Coll., Dublin; Univ. of Montpellier, France. Researcher, Campbell-Johnson Ltd, 1963–64; Account-Exec., Central News, 1964–65; Account-Exec., Pemberton Advertising, 1965–66; Publicity Exec., Revlon, 1966–71; Beauty Editor, Woman's Own, 1971–75; Features Writer and Theatre Critic, Manchester Evening News, 1975–77; Asst Editor, Woman's Own, 1977–78; Editor: Homes and Gardens, 1978–86; A La Carte, 1984–85; food columnist, Today, 1985–87. *Publications:* contrib. The Times, The Independent, Daily Mail, BBC. *Recreations:* gardening, cooking. *Address:* Michaelmas House, Church Yard, Kimbolton, Cambs PE18 0HH.

GREENE, Sir (John) Brian M.; *see* Massy-Green.

GREENE, Dame Judith; *see* Anderson, Dame Judith.

GREENER, Anthony Armitage, FCMA; Joint Managing Director, Guinness PLC, since 1989; Managing Director, United Distillers, since 1987; *b* 26 May 1940; *s* of William and Diana Marianne Greener; *m* 1974, Audrey Ogilvie; one *s* one *d*. *Educ:* Marlborough Coll. Marketing Man., Thames Board Mills, 1969; Retail Controller 1972, Dir 1974, Alfred Dunhill Ltd; Man. Dir, Alfred Dunhill Ltd, subseq. Dunhill Holdings plc, 1975; Director: Guinness PLC, 1986–; Louis Vuitton Moet Hennessy, 1989–; Reed International, 1990–. *Recreation:* sailing. *Address:* United Distillers, Landmark House, Hammersmith Bridge Road, W6 9DP; Holly House, Church Street, Chiswick, W4 2PH. *T:* 081–994 3923. *Club:* Royal Ocean Racing (Treasurer, 1980–).

GREENEWALT, Crawford Hallock; *b* Cummington, Mass, 16 Aug. 1902; *s* of Frank Lindsay and Mary Hallock Greenewalt; *m* 1926, Margaretta Lammot du Pont; two *s* one *d. Educ:* William Penn Charter Sch.; Mass. Institute of Technology (BS). With E. I. du Pont de Nemours & Co., Inc., 1922–90; Asst Dir Exptl Station, Central Research Dept, 1939; Dir Chem. Div., Industrial and Biochemicals Dept, 1942; Technical Dir, Explosives Department, 1943; Asst Dir, Development Dept, 1945; Asst Gen. Man. Pigments Dept, 1945–46; Vice-Pres., 1946; Vice-Pres. and Vice-Chm. Exec. Cttee, 1947; Pres., Chm. Exec. Cttee and Mem. Finance Cttee, 1948–88; Chm. Board, 1962–67; Chm. Finance Cttee, 1967–74; Member Board of Directors of various other organisations. Member: Amer. Acad. of Arts and Sciences, National Academy of Sciences, Amer. Philos. Soc. (Pres., 1984–87). Trustee Emeritus: Nat. Geographic Soc.; Carnegie Inst. of Washington. Holds hon. degrees in Science, Engineering and Laws, and has various scientific awards and medals. *Publications:* The Uncommon Man, 1959; Hummingbirds, 1960; Bird Song: acoustics and physiology, 1969. *Recreation:* photography. *Address:* Box 3652, Greenville, Delaware 19807, USA; (office) Du Pont Building, Wilmington, Delaware 19898, USA. *Clubs:* Wilmington, Du Pont Country, Greenville Country (USA).

GREENFIELD, Prof. (Archibald) David (Mant), CBE 1977; FRCP; Foundation Dean of the Medical School, 1966–81 and Professor of Physiology, 1966–82 in the University of Nottingham; now Professor Emeritus; *b* 31 May 1917; *s* of late A. W. M. Greenfield, MA, and Winifred (*née* Peck), Parkstone, Dorset; *m* 1943, Margaret (*née* Duane); one *s* one *d. Educ:* Poole Grammar Sch.; St Mary's Hospital Medical Sch. BSc London, 1st class hons Physiology, 1937; MB, BS, 1940, MSc 1947, DSc 1953, London; FRCP, 1973. Dunville Prof. of Physiology in the Queen's Univ. of Belfast, 1948–64; Prof. of Physiology in the Univ. of London, at St Mary's Hosp. Med. Sch., 1964–67. WHO Visiting Prof., India, 1960; Visiting Prof., Univ. of California, San Francisco Medical Centre, 1962–63. Sometime Examr, Oxford, Cambridge and 21 other Univs, RCS and RCSI; Chm., Special Trustees, Nottingham Univ. Hosps., 1984–90. Member: Physiol. Systems Bd, MRC, 1976–77; UGC, 1977–82 (Chm. Med. and dental Sub-Cttees, Assessor to MRC); UPGC, Hong Kong, 1984–89 (Mem. 1981–89 and Chm. 1985–89, Med. Sub-Cttee); GMC and GMC Educn Cttee, 1979–82; Med. Acad. Adv. Cttee, Chinese Univ., Hong Kong, 1976–80; Foundn Cttee, Sultan Qaboos Univ., Oman, 1981–86; Councils for Postgrad. Med. Educn, for England and Wales, and Scottish Council, 1977–82; DHSS Adv. Cttee on Artificial Limbs, 1971–75; DHSS Med. Manpower and Educn Liaison Cttee, 1974–78; DHSS Academic Forum, 1980–82; Sheffield RHB, 1968–74; Nottingham Univ. HMC, 1969–74; Notts AHA(T), 1974–79. Pres., Sect. of Biomed. Scis, British Assoc. for Advancement of Sci., 1972; Mem., Biochemical and Medical Research Societies. Hon. Mem., Physiological Soc., 1987. Chm., Editorial Bd, Monographs of the Physiological Soc., 1975–79; Member, Editorial Board: Amer. Heart Jl, 1959–66; Clinical Science, 1960–65; Cardiovascular Research, 1966–79; Circulation Res., 1967–73. OStJ 1978. Hon. LLD Nottingham, 1977; Hon DSc QUB, 1978. Order of Sultan Qaboos of Oman, 2nd Class, 1986. *Publications:* papers on control of circulation of the blood, mainly in Lancet, Journal of Physiology, Clinical Science, and Journal of Applied Physiology. *Recreations:* sketching, bird watching, travel. *Address:* 25 Sutton Passeys Crescent, Nottingham NG8 1BX. *T:* Nottingham (0602) 782424.

GREENFIELD, Edward Harry; Chief Music Critic, The Guardian, since 1977; *b* 30 July 1928; *s* of Percy Greenfield and Mabel (*née* Hall). *Educ:* Westcliff High Sch.; Trinity Hall, Univ. of Cambridge (MA). Joined staff of Manchester Guardian, 1953: Record Critic, 1955; Music Critic, 1964; succeeded Sir Neville Cardus as Chief Music Critic, 1977. Broadcaster on music and records for BBC radio, 1957–. Mem., critics' panel, Gramophone, 1960–. Goldener Verdienstzeichen, Salzburg, 1981. *Publications:* Puccini: keeper of the seal, 1958; monographs on Joan Sutherland, 1972, and André Previn, 1973; (with Robert Layton, Ivan March and initially Denis Stevens) Stereo Record Guide, 9 vols, 1960–74; Penguin Stereo Record Guide, 5th edn 1986; (jtly) Penguin Guide to Compact Discs, Cassettes and LPs, 1986, revised as New Penguin Guide to Compact Discs, 1988. *Recreations:* work, living in Spitalfields. *Address:* 16 Folgate Street, E1. *T:* 071–377 7555. *Club:* Critics' Circle.

GREENFIELD, Howard; see Greenfield, R. H.

GREENFIELD, Hon. Julius MacDonald, CMG 1954; Judge of the High Court of Rhodesia, 1968–74; *b* Boksburg, Transvaal, 13 July 1907; *s* of late Rev. C. E. Greenfield; *m* 1935, Florence Margaret Couper; two *s* one *d. Educ:* Milton Sch., Bulawayo; Universities of Capetown and Oxford. BA, LLB Cape; Rhodes Scholar, 1929; BA, BCL Oxon. Called to the Bar at Gray's Inn, 1933. QC 1949; practised at Bar in S Rhodesia, 1933–50; elected MP for Hillside, S Rhodesia, 1948, and appointed Minister of Internal Affairs and Justice, 1950; participated in London Conferences on Federation in Central Africa. MP Federal Parliament, in Umguza Constituency, 1953–63; Minister of Law, Federation of Rhodesia and Nyasaland, 1954–63; Minister for Home Affairs, 1962–63. *Publications:* Instant Crime, 1975; Instant Statute Case Law, 1977; Testimony of a Rhodesian Federal, 1978. *Address:* Flat 40 Berkeley Square, 173 Main Road, Rondebosch, 7700, Cape, South Africa. *Clubs:* Bulawayo, Harare (Zimbabwe).

GREENFIELD, Dr Peter Rex; Senior Principal Medical Officer, Department of Health (formerly of Health and Social Security), 1983–91; *b* 1 Dec. 1931; *s* of late Rex Youhill Greenfield and Elsie Mary Greenfield (*née* Douthwaite); *m* 1954, Faith Stella, *d* of George and Stella Gigg; eight *s* two *d. Educ:* Cheltenham College; Pembroke College, Cambridge (BA 1954; MB, BChir 1957; MA 1985); St George's Hosp. Med. Sch., London. DObst RCOG 1960. 2nd Lieut, R Signals, 1950–51; House appts, St George's Hosp., 1958; Gen. Med. Pract., Robertsbridge, Sussex, 1959–69; MO, Vinehall Sch., Robertsbridge, 1964–69; MO, Battle Hosp., 1964–69; joined DHSS, 1969; Chief Med. Advr (Social Security), with rank of SPMO, 1983–86. Mem., Jt Formulary Cttee, British Nat. Formulary, 1978–82; Chm., Informal Working Gp on Effective Prescribing, 1981–82; Trustee, Chaseley Home for Disabled Ex-Servicemen, Eastbourne, 1983–; Divl Surgeon, Robertsbridge Div., St John Ambulance Brigade, 1965–. QHP 1987–90. Hon. Mem., BPA, 1991. *Publications:* contribs to med. jls on geriatric day care, hypothermia and DHSS Regional Med. Service. *Recreations:* golf, swimming, walking, music, pinball. *Address:* Lorne House, Robertsbridge, East Sussex TN32 5DW. *T:* Robertsbridge (0580) 880209.

GREENFIELD, (Robert) Howard, FCA; CIGasE; CBIM; Project Director, Regional Organisation Review, British Gas plc, 1990, retired; *b* 4 Feb. 1927; *s* of James Oswald Greenfield and Doris Burt Greenfield; *m* 1951, Joyce Hedley Wells; one *s* one *d. Educ:* Rutherford Coll., Newcastle upon Tyne. FCA 1953; CIGasE 1982; CBIM 1986. Northern Gas Board: Chief Accountancy Asst, 1956; Dep. Divl Manager, Tees Area, 1961; Divl Manager, Cumberland Div., 1963; Regional Service Manager, 1968; Northern Gas: Dir of Customer Service, 1974; Dir of Marketing, 1976; Dep. Chm., 1977; Chm., N Eastern Reg., 1982–85; Regl Chm., British Gas, N Western, 1985–89. OStJ 1988. *Recreations:* salmon fishing, photography. *Address:* Manor Top, Chestnut Hill, Keswick, Cumbria CA12 4LT.

GREENGROSS, Sir Alan (David), Kt 1986; DL; Managing Director, Indusmond (Diamond Tools) Ltd; Director, Blazy & Clement Ltd and associated companies; Chairman, Bloomsbury and Islington Health Authority, since 1990; *b* 1929; *m* (*see* Sally Greengross); one *s* three *d. Educ:* University Coll. Sch.; Trinity Coll., Cambridge (Sen.

Schol.; MA). Formerly Member Council, London Borough of Camden (past Alderman). Dep. Traffic Comr, 1968–70. GLC: Member (C), 1977–84; Leader, Planning and Communications Policy, 1979–81; Leader of the Opposition, 1983–84. Dir, Port of London Authority, 1979–83; Mem., London Regl Passenger Cttee, 1988–. Vis Prof., City of London Polytechnic, 1988–. Dir, The Roundhouse Black Arts Centre, 1988–89. Chm., Steering Gp, Inst. for Metropolitan Studies, 1989–. Member, Governing Council: UCS, 1987–; UCL, 1991–. DL Greater London, 1986. *Address:* 9 Dawson Place, W2 4TD. *Club:* Hurlingham.

GREENGROSS, Sally, (Lady Greengross); Director, Age Concern England, since 1987; Vice-President (Europe), International Federation on Ageing, since 1987 (Secretary General, 1982–87); Secretary General, Eurolink Age, since 1989; *b* 29 June 1935; *m* Sir Alan Greengross, *qv*; one *s* three *d. Educ:* Brighton and Hove High Sch.; LSE. Formerly linguist, executive in industry, lectr and researcher; Asst Dir, 1977–82, Dep. Dir, 1982–87, Age Concern England. Jt Chm. Bd, Age Concern Inst. of Gerontology, KCL, 1987–; Co-ordinator, Prog. for Elderly People within Second EEC Prog. to Combat Poverty, 1985–89; Mem., Standing Adv. Cttee on Transport for Disabled and Elderly People, 1986–; Independent Member: UN Network on Ageing, 1983–; WHO Network on Ageing, 1983–. Former Member: Inner London Juvenile Court Panel; Management Bd, Hanover Housing Gp. FRSH. UK Woman of Europe Award, EC, 1990. *Publications:* (ed) Ageing: an adventure in living, 1985; (ed) The Law and Vulnerable Elderly People, 1986; (jtly) Living, Loving and Ageing, 1989; and others on ageing issues and social policy. *Recreations:* countryside, music. *Address:* 9 Dawson Place, W2 4TD. *T:* 071–229 1939. *Clubs:* Reform, Hurlingham.

GREENHALGH, Jack; Vice-Chairman, Cavenham Ltd, 1974–81; retired; *b* 25 July 1926; *s* of Herbert Greenhalgh and Alice May (*née* Clayton); *m* 1951, Kathleen Mary Hammond (*d* 1983); two *s* two *d. Educ:* Manchester Grammar Sch.; Trinity Coll., Cambridge (MA Hons). FBIM. Marketing Dept, Procter & Gamble Ltd, Newcastle upon Tyne, 1950–59; Marketing Dir, Eskimo Foods Ltd, Cleethorpes, 1959–64; Dir of Continental Ops, Compton Advertising Inc., NY, 1964–65; Cavenham Ltd, 1965–81: Man. Dir, 1968–79. *Recreations:* golf, sailing.

GREENHALGH, Prof. Roger Malcolm, FRCS; Professor of Surgery, and Chairman, Department of Surgery, Charing Cross and Westminster Medical School; Hon. Consultant Surgeon, Charing Cross Hospital, since 1976; *b* 6 Feb. 1941; *s* of John Greenhalgh and Phyllis Poynton; *m* 1964, Karin Maria Gross; one *s* one *d. Educ:* Clare Coll., Cambridge; St Thomas' Hosp., London. BA 1963, BChir 1966, MB, MA 1967, MChir 1974, MD 1983 (Cantab); FRCS 1971. Ho. Surg., 1967, Casualty Officer, 1968, St Thomas' Hosp.; Sen. Ho. Officer, Hammersmith Hosp., 1969; Registrar in Surgery, Essex County Hosp., Colchester, 1970–72; Lectr and Sen. Registrar in Surgery, St Bartholomew's Hosp., 1972–76; Sen. Lectr in Surgery, Charing Cross Hosp., 1976–81; Head of Dept of Surgery, 1981, Prof. of Surgery, 1982–, Chm. of Dept of Surgery, 1989–, Charing Cross Hosp. Med. Sch., later Charing Cross and Westminster Med. Sch. Sometime examiner, Univs of Cambridge, London, Bristol, Leicester, UCD, Southampton, Birmingham, Hong Kong. Chm., Liaison Cttee, Bioengrg Centre, Roehampton, London, 1985–; Member: Ind. Scientific Enquiry into Smoking and Health, 1979–; Specialist Adv. Cttee in Gen. Surgery, 1989–. Sec. Gen. and Chm. Exec. Cttee, Assoc. of Internat. Vascular Surgeons, 1982–; Mem. Council, European Soc. for Vascular Surgery, 1987–. Moynihan Fellow of Assoc. of Surgeons, 1974; Hunterian Prof., RCS, 1980. Chm. Editl Bd, European Jl of Vascular Surgery, 1987–. *Publications:* Progress in Stroke Research, 1, 1979; Smoking and Arterial Disease, 1981; Hormones and Vascular Disease, 1981; Femoro-distal bypass, 1981; Extra-Anatomic and Secondary Arterial Reconstruction, 1982; Progress in Stroke Research, 2, 1983; Vascular Surgical Techniques, 1984, 2nd edn 1989; Diagnostic Techniques and Assessment Procedures in Vascular Surgery, 1985; Vascular Surgery: issues in current practice, 1986; Indications in Vascular Surgery, 1988; Limb Salvage and Amputations for Vascular Disease, 1988; The Cause and Management of Aneurysms, 1990; The Maintenance of Arterial Reconstruction, 1991. *Recreations:* tennis, skiing, swimming, music. *Address:* 271 Sheen Lane, East Sheen, SW14 8RN. *T:* 081–878 1110. *Club:* Athenæum.

GREENHAM, Peter George, CBE 1978; RA 1960 (ARA, 1951); PPRBA; RP; NEAC; Keeper of the Royal Academy Schools, 1964–85; *b* 9 Sept. 1909; *s* of George Frederick Greenham, MBE, civil servant; *m* 1964, Jane, *d* of late Dr G. B. Dowling, FRCP, and Mary Elizabeth Kelly; one *s* one *d. Educ:* Dulwich Coll.; Magdalen Coll., Oxford (Hist. Demy, BA); Byam Shaw Sch. of Art. Pres., RBA, to 1982. Paintings in permanent collections: Tate Gall.; Nat. Portrait Gall.; Arts Council; Contemp. Art Soc.; Carlisle Gall.; Plymouth Gall., Gulbenkian Collection. *Publication:* Velasquez, 1969. *Address:* c/o Royal Academy, Piccadilly, W1V 0DS.

GREENHILL, family name of **Barons Greenhill** and **Greenhill of Harrow.**

GREENHILL, 3rd Baron *cr* 1950, of Townhead; **Malcolm Greenhill;** retired from Ministry of Defence; *b* 5 May 1924; *s* of 1st Baron Greenhill, OBE and Ida (*d* 1985), *d* of late Mark Goodman; *S* brother, 1989. *Educ:* Kelvinside Acad., Glasgow; Glasgow Univ. (BSc). CPA. Ministries of Aircraft Production and Supply, 1944–54; UK Scientific Mission, Washington DC, USA, 1950–51; UKAEA, 1954–73; MoD, 1973–89. *Recreation:* gardening. *Address:* 28 Gorselands, Newbury, Berks RG14 6PX. *T:* Newbury (0635) 45651. *Club:* Civil Service.

GREENHILL OF HARROW, Baron *cr* 1974 (Life Peer), of the Royal Borough of Kensington and Chelsea; **Denis Arthur Greenhill,** GCMG 1972 (KCMG 1967; CMG 1960); OBE 1941; HM Government Director, British Petroleum Co. Ltd, 1973–78; Member, Security Commission, 1973–82; *b* 7 Nov. 1913; *s* of James and Susie Greenhill, Loughton; *m* 1941, Angela McCulloch; one *s* (and one *s* decd). *Educ:* Bishop's Stortford Coll.; Christ Church, Oxford (Hon. Student 1977). Served War of 1939–45 (despatches twice): Royal Engineers; in Egypt, N Africa, Italy, India and SE Asia; demobilised with rank of Col. Entered Foreign Service, 1946; served: Sofia, 1947–49; Washington, 1949–52; Foreign Office, 1952–54. Imperial Defence Coll., 1954; UK Delegation to NATO, Paris, 1955–57; Singapore, 1957–59; Counsellor, 1959–62; Minister, 1962–64, Washington DC; Asst Under-Sec. of State, FO, 1964–66; Dep. Under-Sec. of State, FO, 1966–69; Perm. Under-Sec. of State, FCO, and Head of the Diplomatic Service, 1969–73. Director: S. G. Warburg & Co., 1974–87 (Adviser, 1987–); Clerical Medical and General Assce Soc., 1974–86; Wellcome Foundn Ltd, 1974–85; BAT Industries Ltd, 1974–83; Hawker Siddeley Group, 1974–84; Leyland International, 1977–82; Mem., Internat. Adv. Cttee, First Chicago Ltd, 1976–81. A Governor of the BBC, 1973–78. Mem., several H of L Select Cttees on European Communities, 1985–. Governor, BUPA, 1978–84, Dep. Chm., 1979–84. President: Royal Soc. for Asian Affairs, 1976–84; Anglo-Finnish Soc., 1981–84. Chm., KCH Med. Sch. Council, 1977–83; Fellow, King's Coll., London, 1984. Trustee, Rayne Foundn, 1974; Governor, Wellington Coll., 1974–83; Chm. of Governors, SOAS, 1978–85. Grand Cross, Order of the Finnish Lion, 1984. *Address:* 25 Hamilton House, Vicarage Gate, W8. *T:* 071–937 8362. *Club:* Travellers'.

GREENHILL, Dr Basil Jack, CB 1981; CMG 1967; FRHistS; FSA; author; Chairman: SS Great Britain Project, since 1982; Centre for Maritime Historical Studies, University of Exeter, since 1991; Consultant, Conway Maritime Press, since 1990; *b* 26 Feb. 1920; *o c* of B. J. and Edith Greenhill; *m* 1st, 1950, Gillian (*d* 1959), *e d* of Capt. Ralph Tyacke Stratton, MC; one *s*; 2nd, 1961, Ann, *d* of Walter Ernest Giffard; one *s*. *Educ:* Bristol Grammar Sch.; Bristol Univ. (T. H. Green Scholar; PhD 1980). Served War of 1939–45: Lieut RNVR (Air Br.). Diplomatic Service, 1946–66; served: Pakistan; UK Delegn, New York; Tokyo; UK Delegate to Conf. on Law of the Sea, Geneva; British Dep. High Comr in E Pakistan; Ottawa. Dir, Nat. Maritime Mus., Greenwich, 1967–83, Caird Res. Fellow, 1983–86. Member: Ancient Monuments Bd for England, 1972–84; Council, Maritime Trust, 1977–83 (Hon. Vice-Pres., 1984–); Finnish Exhibn 1985 Cttee, 1983–85; Vice Chm. Bd, Trustees of the Royal Armouries, 1984–88; Vice Pres., Soc. for Nautical Res., 1975–; First Pres., Internat. Congress of Maritime Museums, 1975–81 (Hon. Life Mem., 1981); Pres., Devonshire Assoc., 1984; Trustee: Royal Naval Museum, Portsmouth, 1973–83; Mary Rose Trust, 1979–83; RAF Museum, 1987–. Governor, Dulwich Coll., 1974–88; Chairman: Dulwich Picture Gall., 1977–88; Nat. Museums' Directors' Conf., 1980–83; Govt Adv. Cttee on Historic Wreck Sites, 1986–. Principal Advisor: BBC TV series: The Commanding Sea, 1980–82; Trade Winds, 1984–85; BBC Radio series, The British Seafarer, 1980–82. Hon. Fellow, Univ. of Exeter, 1985. Kt Comdr, Order of White Rose, Finland, 1980. *Publications:* The Merchant Schooners, Vol. I, 1951, Vol. II, 1957, rev. edns 1968, 1978, 1988; (ed and prefaced) W. J. Slade's Out of Appledore, 1959, rev. edns 1972, 1974, 1980; Sailing For A Living, 1962; (with Ann Giffard) Westcountrymen in Prince Edward's Isle, 1967, 3rd edn 1990 (Amer. Assoc. Award) (filmed 1975); (with Ann Giffard) The Merchant Sailing Ship: A Photographic History, 1970; (with Ann Giffard) Women under Sail, 1970; Captain Cook, 1970; Boats and Boatmen of Pakistan, 1971; (with Ann Giffard) Travelling by Sea in the Nineteenth Century, 1972; (with Rear-Adm. P. W. Brock) Sail and Steam, 1973; (with W. J. Slade) West Country Coasting Ketches, 1974; A Victorian Maritime Album, 1974; A Quayside Camera, 1975; (with L. Willis) The Coastal Trade: Sailing Craft of British Waters 900–1900, 1975; Archaeology of the Boat, 1976; (with Ann Giffard) Victorian and Edwardian Sailing Ships, 1976, rev. edns 1981, 1982, 1987; (with Ann Giffard) Victorian and Edwardian Ships and Harbours, 1978; (ed and prefaced) Georg Kåhrés The Last Tall Ships, 1978; (with Ann Giffard) Victorian and Edwardian Merchant Steamships, 1979; Schooners, 1980; The Life and Death of the Sailing Ship, 1980; (with Michael Mason) The British Seafarer, 1980; (with Denis Stonham) Seafaring Under Sail, 1981; Karlsson, 1982; The Woodshipbuilders, 1986; The Grain Races, 1986; (with Ann Giffard) The British Assault on Finland 1854–55, 1988; The Evolution of the Wooden Ship, 1988; (ed and prefaced) Edmund Eglinton's The Mary Fletcher, 1990; (with John Hackman) The Herzogin Cecilie, 1991 (trans. Swedish, 1991); numerous articles, reviews and broadcasts. *Recreations:* boating, travel, coarse gardening. *Address:* West Boetheric Farmhouse, St Dominic, Saltash, Cornwall PL12 6SZ. *Clubs:* Arts (Hon. Mem.); Royal Western Yacht (Plymouth); Karachi Yacht (Karachi); Åland Nautical (Mariehamn).
See also Sir C. S. R. Giffard.

GREENING, Rear-Adm. Sir Paul (Woollven), KCVO 1985; Master of HM's Household, since 1986; an Extra Equerry to the Queen, since 1983; *b* 4 June 1928; *s* of late Captain Charles W. Greening, DSO, DSC, RN, and Mrs Molly K. Greening (*née* Flowers); *m* 1951, Monica, *d* of late Mr and Mrs W. E. West, East Farndon, Market Harborough; one *s* one *d*. *Educ:* Mowden Sch., Brighton; Nautical Coll., Pangbourne. Entered RN, 1946; Midshipman, HMS Theseus, 1947–48; Sub-Lt and Lieut, HM Ships Zodiac, Neptune, Rifleman, Asheldham (CO), and Gamecock, 1950–58; Lt-Comdr, HM Ships Messina (CO), Loch Killisport, Urchin, and Collingwood, 1958–63; Comdr 1963; CO HMS Lewiston, and SO 2nd Minesweeping Sqdn, 1963–64; jssc 1964; Naval Plans, MoD (Navy), 1965–67; CO HMS Jaguar, 1967–68; Fleet Plans Officer, Far East Fleet, 1969; Captain 1969; CO HMS Aurora, 1970–71; Captain Naval Drafting, 1971–74; Sen. Officers War Course, 1974; Dir of Officers Appts (Seamen), MoD (Navy), 1974–76; Captain BRNC Dartmouth, 1976–78; Naval Secretary, 1978–80; Flag Officer, Royal Yachts, 1981–85; retired 1985. ADC to the Queen, 1978. Younger Brother of Trinity House, 1984. *Recreations:* cricket, tennis, gardening. *Club:* Army and Navy.

GREENING, Wilfrid Peter, FRCS; Consultant Surgeon to Royal Marsden Hospital, 1952–79; Consulting Surgeon, Charing Cross Hospital since 1975; Lecturer in Surgery to Charing Cross Hospital Medical School; *s* of Rev. W. Greening and M. M. Waller, Saxlingham, Norfolk; *m* 1st, 1939, Hilary Berryman (marr. diss., 1961); one *d*; 2nd, 1962, Susan Ann Clair Huber (marr. diss. 1977); 3rd, 1978, Touba Ghazinoor. *Educ:* St Edmund's Sch., Canterbury; King's Coll.; Charing Cross Hospital Medical Sch. MRCS 1937; LRCP 1937; FRCS 1939. Houseman and Surgical Registrar, Charing Cross Hosp., 1938. Served War of 1939–45 (despatches); Wing Comdr i/c Surgical Div., RAFVR, 1943. Surgical Registrar, Gordon Hospital, 1946; Consultant Surgeon: Woolwich Hospital, 1948; Bromley and District Hospital, 1947–66. *Publications:* contributions to medical literature. *Recreations:* fishing, golf. *Address:* 67 Harley Street, W1. *Club:* Garrick.

GREENLAND, Dennis James, DPhil; FIBiol; Scientific Director, CAB-International, since 1987, and Visiting Professor, University of Reading, since 1988; *b* 13 June 1930; *s* of James John and Lily Florence Greenland; *m* 1955, Edith Mary Johnston; one *s* two *d*. *Educ:* Portsmouth Grammar Sch.; Christ Church, Oxford (MA, DPhil). Lecturer: Univ. of Ghana, 1955–59; Waite Agricl Res. Inst., Adelaide, 1959–63; Reader and Head of Soil Science, Waite Agricl Res. Inst., 1963–70; Professor and Head of Dept of Soil Science, Univ. of Reading, 1970–79; Director of Research, Internat. Inst. of Tropical Agriculture, Nigeria, 1974–76 (on secondment from Univ. of Reading); Dep. Dir Gen., Internat. Rice Res. Inst., Los Baños, Philippines, 1979–87. FIBiol 1974; FWA 1987. Hon. DrAgSci Ghent, 1982. *Publications:* contributions: (jtly) The Soil Under Shifting Cultivation, 1960; (ed jtly) Soil Conservation and Management in the Humid Tropics, 1977; (ed jtly) Chemistry of Soil Constituents, 1978; (ed jtly) Soil Physical Properties and Crop Production in the Tropics, 1979; (ed) Characterisation of Soils in Relation to Their Classification and Management for Crop Production: some examples from the humid tropics, 1981; (ed jtly) The Chemistry of Soil Processes, 1981; numerous scientific articles in learned jls. *Recreations:* golf, bridge, watching cricket. *Address:* CAB-International, Mongewell Park, Wallingford, Oxon OX10 8DE.

GREENOCK, Lord; Charles Alan Andrew Cathcart, ACA; Director, Gardner Mountain and Capel-Cure Agencies Ltd, since 1987; *b* 30 Nov. 1952; *s* and *heir* of 6th Earl Cathcart, *qv*; *m* 1981, Vivien Clare, *o d* of F. D. McInnes Skinner; one *s* one *d*. *Educ:* Eton. Commnd Scots Guards, 1972–75. Whinney Murray, 1976–79; Ernst & Whinney, 1979–83. *Heir:* *s* Hon. Alan George Cathcart, *b* 16 March 1986. *Address:* 18 Smith Terrace, SW3. *Club:* Cavalry and Guards.

GREENOUGH, Beverly, (Mrs P. B. Greenough); *see* Sills, B.

GREENSHIELDS, Robert McLaren; HM Diplomatic Service, retired; Counsellor, Foreign and Commonwealth Office, 1985–88; *b* 27 July 1933; *s* of late Brig. James Greenshields, MC, TD, and of Mrs J. J. Greenshields; *m* 1960, Jean Alison Anderson; one *s* two *d*. *Educ:* Edinburgh Academy; Lincoln Coll., Oxford (MA Hons). National Service, 2nd Lieut Highland Light Infantry, 1952–54. District Officer, Tanganyika, HMOCS, 1958–61; Asst Master and Housemaster, Gordonstoun Sch., 1962–68; HM Diplomatic Service, 1969–88. *Recreations:* ornithology, golf. *Club:* Royal Over-Seas League.

GREENSLADE, Roy; Editor, Daily Mirror, 1990–91; *b* 31 Dec. 1946; *s* of Ernest Frederick William Greenslade and Joan Olive (*née* Stocking); *m* 1985, Noreen Anna Taylor (*née* McElhone); one step *s* one step *d*. *Educ:* Dagenham County High Sch.; Sussex Univ. (BA (Hons) Politics, 1979). Trainee journalist, Barking Advertiser, 1962–66; Sub-Editor: Lancashire Evening Telegraph, 1966–67; Daily Mail, 1967–69; The Sun, 1969–71; researching and writing book, 1973–75; Daily Star, 1979–80; Daily Express, 1980–81; Daily Star, 1981; Asst Editor, The Sun, 1981–87; Man. Editor, Sunday Times, 1987–90. *Publication:* Goodbye to the Working Class, 1975. *Recreations:* squash, tennis. *Address:* Kensington.

GREENSMITH, Edward William, OBE 1972; BScEng; FCGI; Deputy President, Executive Board of the British Standards Institution, 1973–79 (Chairman, 1970–73); *b* 20 April 1909; *m* 1937, Edna Marjorie Miskin (*d* 1971); three *s*; *m* 1972, Margaret Boaden Miles. ICI, Engrg Adviser, 1964–71. Dir (non-executive), Peter Brotherhood Ltd, 1970–78. *Publications:* contribs: Chemistry Ind., 1957, 1959. *Recreations:* walking, gardening. *Address:* Pound Cottage, Graffham, near Petworth, W Sussex GU28 0QA. *T:* Graffham (07986) 374.

GREENSMITH, Edwin Lloydd, CMG 1962; *b* 23 Jan. 1900; *s* of Edwin Greensmith; *m* 1932, Winifred Bryce; two *s* two *d*. *Educ:* Victoria Univ., Wellington, NZ. MCom (Hons), 1930. Accountant; Solicitor. Chief Accountant, Ministry of Works, New Zealand, to 1935; then Treasury (Secretary, 1955–65). Chm., NZ Wool Commn, 1965–72. *Recreation:* gardening. *Address:* Unit 42, Crestwood Village, Titirangi, Auckland, New Zealand. *Club:* Wellington (Wellington NZ).

GREENSPAN, Alan; Chairman, Board of Governors of the Federal Reserve System, since 1987; *b* 6 March 1926; *o s* of Herbert Greenspan and Rose (*née* Goldsmith). *Educ:* New York Univ. (BS 1948; MA 1950; PhD 1977). Vice-Pres., 1954–58, Pres., 1954–74 and 1977–87, Townsend-Greenspan & Co., NY; co-founder, Greenspan O'Neil Associates, NY, 1985–87. Adjunct Prof., Graduate Sch. of Business Management, NY Univ., 1977–87. Director: Trans World Financial Co., 1962–74; Dreyfus Fund, 1970–74; Gen. Cable Corp., 1973–74, 1977–78; Sun Chemical Corp., 1973–74; Gen. Foods Corp., 1977–85; J. P. Morgan & Co., 1977–87; Mobil Corp., 1977–87; ALCOA, 1978–87. Consultant to Council of Economic Advisers, 1970–74, to US Treasury, 1971–74, to Fed. Reserve Board, 1971–74; Chairman: Council of Economic Advisers, 1974–77; Nat. Commn on Social Security Reform, 1981–83; Dir, Council on Foreign Relations; Member: President's Econ. Policy Adv. Board, 1981–87; President's Foreign Intell. Adv. Board, 1983–85. Jefferson Award, 1976; William Butler Meml Award, 1977. *Address:* Federal Reserve System, 20th Street & Constitution Avenue NW, Washington, DC 20551, USA.

GREENSTOCK, Jeremy Quentin, CMG 1991; HM Diplomatic Service; Assistant Under-Secretary of State, Foreign and Commonwealth Office, since 1990; *b* 27 July 1943; *s* of John Wilfrid Greenstock and late Ruth Margaret Logan; *m* 1969, Anne Derryn Ashford Hodges; one *s* two *d*. *Educ:* Harrow Sch.; Worcester Coll., Oxford (MA Lit. Hum.). Asst Master, Eton Coll., 1966–69; entered HM Diplomatic Service, 1969; MECAS, 1970–72; Dubai, 1972–74; Private Sec. to the Ambassador, Washington, 1974–78; FCO, 1978–83 (Planning Staff, Personnel Ops Dept, N East and N African Dept); Counsellor (Commercial), Jedda, 1983–85, Riyadh, 1985–86; Hd of Chancery, Paris, 1987–90. *Recreations:* travel, photography, court games. *Address:* c/o Foreign and Commonwealth Office, Whitehall, SW1A 2AH.

GREENTREE, (William Wayne) Chris, FInstPet; Chief Executive, LASMO PLC, since 1982; *b* 6 April 1935; *s* of J. Murray and Grace M. Greentree; *m* 1956, Patricia Ann Hugo (marr. diss. 1990); four *d* (and one *d* decd); *m* 1990, Hilary J. Wilson. *Educ:* Moose Jaw Technical High Sch., Saskatoon; Univ. of Alberta (BSc Hons, PEng). Joined Shell Canada, 1957: technical and managerial appts, onshore and offshore exploration; Ranger Oil London, 1972–79: Man. Dir, 1976; Mapco Inc. USA: Sen. Vice Pres. Exploration and Production, 1979–82; Chief Exec., LASMO Gp, 1982–. Ordre National du Mérite (Gabon), 1987. *Recreations:* golf, ski-ing. *Address:* LASMO PLC, 100 Liverpool Street, EC2M 2BB. *T:* 071–945 4545. *Clubs:* Highgate Golf; Petroleum (USA).

GREENWAY, family name of **Baron Greenway.**

GREENWAY, 4th Baron *cr* 1927; **Ambrose Charles Drexel Greenway;** Bt 1919; photographer and author; *b* 21 May 1941; *s* of 3rd Baron Greenway and of Cordelia Mary, *d* of late Major Humfrey Campbell Stephen; *S* father, 1975; *m* 1985, Mrs Rosalynne Schenk. *Educ:* Winchester. *Publications:* Soviet Merchant Ships, 1976; Comecon Merchant Ships, 1978; A Century of Cross Channel Passenger Ferries, 1980; A Century of North Sea Passenger Steamers, 1986. *Recreations:* ocean racing and cruising, swimming. *Heir:* *b* Hon. Mervyn Stephen Kelvynge Greenway, *b* 19 Aug. 1942. *Address:* c/o House of Lords, SW1. *Club:* House of Lords Yacht.

GREENWAY, Harry; MP (C) Ealing North, since 1979; *b* 4 Oct. 1934; *s* of John Kenneth Greenway and Violet Adelaide (*née* Bell); *m* 1969, Carol Elizabeth Helena, *e d* of late John Robert Thomas Hooper, barrister at law and Metropolitan Stipendiary Magistrate; one *s* two *d*. *Educ:* Warwick Sch.; College of St Mark and St John, London; Univ. of Caen, Normandy. Assistant Master, Millbank Sch., 1957–60; successively, Head of English Dept, Sen. Housemaster, Sen. Master, Acting Dep. Head, Sir William Collins Sch., 1960–72; Dep. Headmaster, Sedgehill Sch. (Comprehensive for 2,000 plus pupils), 1972–79. Vice-Chm., Greater London Cons. Members, 1981–; Chairman: All Party Adult Educn Cttee, 1979–; All Party Parly Friends of Cycling, 1987–; Mem., Parly Select Cttee on Educn, Science and the Arts, 1979–; Vice-Chairman: Cons. Parly Educn Cttee, 1983– (Sec., 1981); Cons. Parly Sports Cttee, 1986–; Parly Sec., Cons. National Adv. Cttee on Educn, 1981–; Sec., Cons. Parly Arts and Heritage Cttee, 1986–87. Led All Party Parly Delegn to Sri Lanka, 1985, to Gibraltar, 1989. Pres., Cons. Trade Unionist Teachers, 1982–83; Chm., Atlantic Educn Cttee, 1981–85; Member: Educn Cttee, NACRO, 1985–; Council, Open Univ., 1982–; Trustee, St Clare's Coll., Oxford, 1982–. British Horse Soc. Award of Merit, 1980. *Publications:* Adventure in the Saddle, 1971; regular contributor to educnl and equestrian jls. *Recreations:* riding (Asst Instructor, BHS, 1966), ski-ing, choral music, hockey (Vice-Pres., England Schoolboys' Hockey Assoc.; Founder, Lords and Commons Hockey Club), cricket, parliamentary parachutist. *Address:* House of Commons, SW1. *Clubs:* St Stephen's Constitutional, Ski Club of Gt Britain.

GREENWAY, John Robert; MP (C) Ryedale, since 1987; *b* 15 Feb. 1946; *s* of Thomas William and Kathleen Greenway; *m* 1974, Sylvia Ann Gant; two *s* one *d*. *Educ:* Sir John Deane's Grammar School, Northwich; London College of Law. Midland Bank, 1964; Metropolitan Police, 1965–69; Equitable Life Assurance Soc., 1970–71; National Provident Instn, 1971–72; own firm of insurance brokers, J. R. Greenway & Co. Ltd, York, 1972–. Treasurer, Ryedale Cons. Assoc., 1984–86; Mem., North Yorks CC, 1985–87; Vice-Chm., N Yorks Police Authy., 1986–87. PPS to Minister of State, MAFF,

1991–; Mem., Home Affairs Select Cttee, 1987–. Sec., Cons. Backbench Health Cttee, 1988–; Vice-Chairman: Cons. Backbench Agricl Cttee, 1989–; All Party Football Cttee, 1989–. *Recreations:* opera, football (Pres., York City FC), wine, travel, gardening. *Address:* 11 Oak Tree Close, Strensall, York. *T:* York (0904) 490535.

GREENWELL, (Arthur) Jeffrey, CBE 1991; Chief Executive, Northamptonshire County Council, since 1973; *b* 1 Aug. 1931; *s* of late George Greenwell and of Kate Mary Greenwell (*née* Fleming), Durham, *m* 1958, Margaret Rosemary, *d* of late Sidney David Barnard; one *s* two *d. Educ:* Durham Sch.; University Coll., Oxford (MA). FCIS. Solicitor (Hons). Nat. Service, RHA, 1950–51. Articled to Town Clerk, Newcastle upon Tyne, 1955–58; law tutor, Gibson & Weldon, 1958–59; Asst Solicitor, Birmingham Corp., 1959–61; Hants County Council: Asst Solicitor, 1961–64; Asst Clerk, 1964–67; Dep. Clerk of Council, Dep. Clerk of the Peace and Dep. Clerk, Hants River Authy, 1967–73; Clerk of Northants Lieutenancy, 1977–. Hon. Sec., Assoc. of Co. Chief Execs, 1980–84; Hon. Sec., SOLACE, 1984–88 (Pres., 1991–92); President: CIS, 1989; Northants Assoc. of Local Councils. Chm., Home Office Gp on Juvenile Crime, 1987; Dir and Treas., Crime Concern. Vice-Pres., Internat. City Management Assoc., 1990–92. Mem., Peterborough Dio. Synod. Trustee, Central Festival Opera. Gov., Nene Coll. *Recreations:* bridge, travel, local history, going to meetings. *Address:* County Hall, Northampton NN1 1DN. *T:* Northampton (0604) 236050, *Fax:* Northampton (0604) 236223. *Club:* Northampton and County (Northampton).

GREENWELL, Sir Edward (Bernard), 4th Bt *cr* 1906; DL; farmer, since 1975; *b* 10 June 1948; *s* of Sir Peter McClintock Greenwell, 3rd Bt, TD, and of Henrietta (who *m* 1985, Hugh Kenneth Haig), 2nd *d* of late Peter and Lady Alexandra Haig-Thomas; *S* father, 1978; *m* 1974, Sarah Louise Gore-Anley; one *s* three *d. Educ:* Eton; Nottingham University (BSc); Cranfield Institute of Technology (MBA). DL Suffolk, 1988. *Heir: s* Alexander Bernard Peter Greenwell, *b* 11 May 1987. *Address:* Gedgrave Hall, Woodbridge, Suffolk IP12 2BX. *T:* Orford (0394) 450440. *Club:* Turf.

GREENWELL, Jeffrey; *see* Greenwell, A. J.

GREENWOOD, family name of **Viscount Greenwood.**

GREENWOOD, 2nd Viscount, *cr* 1937; **David Henry Hamar Greenwood;** Baron, *cr* 1929; Bt, *cr* 1915; *b* 30 Oct. 1914; *e s* of 1st Viscount Greenwood, PC, KC, LLD, BA, and Margery (*d* 1968), 2nd *d* of Rev. Walter Spencer, BA; *S* father 1948; unmarried. *Educ:* privately and at Bowers Gifford. Agriculture and Farming. *Heir: b* Hon. Michael George Hamar Greenwood, *b* 5 May 1923. *Recreations:* shooting and reading.

GREENWOOD, Allen Harold Claude, CBE 1974; JP; Deputy Chairman, British Aerospace, 1977–83 (Member, Organizing Committee, 1976–77); Chairman, British Aircraft Corporation, 1976 (Deputy Chairman, 1972–75); *b* 4 June 1917; *s* of Lt-Col Thomas Claude Greenwood and Hilda Letitia Greenwood (*née* Knight). *Educ:* Cheltenham Coll. Coll. of Aeronautical Engineering. Pilot's Licence, 1939. Joined Vickers-Armstrongs Ltd, 1940; served RNVR (Fleet Air Arm), 1942–52 (Lt-Cmdr); rejoined Vickers-Armstrongs Ltd, 1946, Dir, 1960; British Aircraft Corp., 1962, Dep. Man. Dir, 1969; Director: British Aircraft Corp. (Holdings), 1972; BAe Australia Ltd, 1977–83; Chm., BAe Inc., 1977–80. Director: SEPECAT SA, 1964; Europlane Ltd, 1974–83; Chairman: Panavia GmbH, 1969–72; Remploy Ltd, 1976–79 (Vice-Chm., 1973). Pres., Assoc. Européenne des Constructeurs de Material Aerospatial, 1974–76; Pres., 1970–72, Dep. Pres., 1981–82, SBAC; Vice-Pres., Engineering Employers' Fedn, 1982–83; Mem., National Def. Industry Council, 1970–72. Pres., Cheltenham Coll. Council, 1980–85; Member: Council, Cranfield Inst. of Technology, 1970–79; Council, CBI, 1970–77; Assoc. of Governing Bodies of Public Schools, 1982–85; Council, St John's Sch., Leatherhead, 1970–85 (Chm., 1979–85). JP Surrey 1962, Hampshire, 1975. Freeman, City of London. Liveryman, Company of Coachmakers, Guild of Air Pilots. General Comr for Income Tax, 1970–74. *Address:* 2 Rookcliff, Park Lane, Milford-on-Sea, Hants SO41 0SD. *T:* Lymington (0590) 642893. *Clubs:* White's, Royal Automobile; Royal Lymington Yacht.

GREENWOOD, David Ernest; Director, Centre for Defence Studies, University of Aberdeen, since 1976; *b* 6 Feb. 1937; *s* of Ernest Greenwood and Doris (*née* Cowsill); *m* 1st, 1960, Helen Ramshaw (marr. diss.); two *s*; 2nd, 1986, Margaret McRobb (*née* Cruickshank). *Educ:* Manchester Grammar Sch.; Liverpool Univ. (BA, MA). Educn Officer, RAF, 1959–66; Economic Advr, MoD, 1966–67; Lectr 1967, Sen. Lectr 1970, Reader 1975, in Higher Defence Studies, Univ. of Aberdeen. Vis. Fellow, IISS, 1974–75; Vis. Prof., Nat. Defense Acad., Yokosuka, 1981–82. Member: FCO Adv. Panel on Arms Control and Disarmament, 1974–; Honeywell Adv. Council, 1981–85; ACOST Study Gp on Defence R&D, 1987–88; Council, Internat. Inst. for Defence Procurement Studies, 1989–. Cons., EEC, 1980–85 and 1987–. Director: BDMI Ltd, 1984–; IIDPS Ltd, 1989–. Member: Editorial Panel, Jl of Strategic Studies, 1977–; Editl Adv. Bd, Defence Economics, 1989–. *Publications:* Budgeting for Defence, 1972; (jtly) British Security Policy and the Atlantic Alliance: prospects for the 1990s, 1987; numerous monographs, res. reports, contribs to symposia, jl and newspaper articles. *Recreations:* cooking, gardening, reading, walking, watching television. *Address:* Lindores, Kinmuck, Inverurie AB51 0LY. *T:* Inverurie (0467) 20561. *Club:* Royal Air Force.

GREENWOOD, Duncan Joseph, PhD, DSc; FRS 1985; CChem, FRSC; FIHort; Head of Soils and Crop Nutrition, AFRC Institute of Horticultural Research (formerly National Vegetable Research Station), Wellesbourne, Warwick, since 1966; Visiting Professor of Plant Sciences, Leeds University, since 1985; Hon. Professor of Agricultural Chemistry, Birmingham University, since 1986; *b* 16 Oct. 1932; *s* of Herbert James Greenwood and Alison Fairgrieve Greenwood. *Educ:* Hutton Grammar Sch., near Preston; Liverpool Univ. (BSc 1954); Aberdeen Univ. (PhD 1957; DSc 1972). CChem, FRSC 1977; FIHort 1986. Res. Fellow, Aberdeen Univ., 1957–59; Res. Leader, National Vegetable Res. Station, 1959–66. Chm., Agriculture Gp, Soc. of Chemical Industry, 1975–77; President: Internat. Cttee of Plant Nutrition, 1978–82; British Soc. of Soil Science, 1991–92. Lectures: Blackman, Univ. of Oxford, 1982; Distinguished Scholars, QUB, 1982; Hannaford, Univ. of Adelaide, 1985; Shell, Univ. of Kent, 1988; Amos, Wye Coll., 1989. Sir Gilbert Morgan Medal, Soc. of Chemical Industry, 1962; Res. Medal, RASE, 1979. *Publications:* over 150 scientific papers on soil science, crop nutrition and fertilizers. *Address:* 23 Shelley Road, Stratford-upon-Avon, Warwicks CV37 7JR. *T:* Stratford-upon-Avon (0789) 204735.

GREENWOOD, James Russell, LVO 1975; HM Diplomatic Service, retired; Professor of Asian Studies, Matsusaka University, Japan, since 1983; *b* 30 April 1924; *s* of late J. Greenwood and L. Greenwood (*née* Moffat), Padiham; *m* 1957, Mary Veronica, *d* of late Dr D. W. Griffith and Dr Grace Griffith, Bures; one *s. Educ:* RGS, Clitheroe; Queen's Coll., Oxford. Army Service, 1943–47. BA, MA (Oxon) 1949; Foreign Office, 1949; subseq. service in Bangkok, 1950–52; Tokyo and Osaka, 1952–54; London, 1955–58; Rangoon, 1958–61; Rome, 1961–63; Bangkok, 1964–68; Counsellor (Information), Tokyo, 1968–73; Consul-General, Osaka, 1973–77. PRO, The APV Company and APV International, 1980–82. Order of Sacred Treasure (3rd cl.) Japan, 1975. *Recreations:* travel, golf, cricket. *Address:* Faculty of Political Science and Economics, Matsusaka University, 1846 Kubo-Cho, Matsusaka, Mie 515, Japan. *Clubs:* United Oxford & Cambridge University, MCC.

GREENWOOD, Jeffrey Michael; Senior Partner, Nabarro Nathanson, since 1987; *b* 21 April 1935; *s* of Arthur Greenwood and Ada Greenwood (*née* Gordon); *m* 1964, Naomi Grahame; three *s* one *d. Educ:* Raine's Foundation Sch.; LSE; Downing Coll., Cambridge (MA, LLM). Admitted solicitor 1960; Partner, Nabarro Nathanson, 1963; Head of Property Dept, 1972–87. Director: Bank Leumi (UK); Jewish Chronicle. Chairman: Jewish Welfare Bd, 1986–90; Jewish Care, 1990; Council Member: Business in the Community; Hampstead Garden Suburb Trust (Law Soc. Appointee, 1984–87). Liveryman, Glovers' Co. *Publications:* articles in learned jls. *Recreations:* running, swimming, ski-ing, literature, travel. *Address:* 50 Stratton Street, W1X 5FL. *T:* 071–493 9933.

GREENWOOD, Dr Jeremy John Denis; Director, British Trust for Ornithology, since 1988; *b* 7 Sept. 1942; *s* of Denis Greenwood and Phyllis Marjorie Greenwood (*née* Leat); *m* 1971, Cynthia Anne Jones; two *d. Educ:* Royal Grammar Sch., Worcester; St Catherine's Coll., Oxford (BA 1964); Univ. of Manchester (PhD 1972). Dundee University: Asst Lectr in Zoology, 1967–70; Lectr in Biol. Scis, 1970–87; Hon. Lectr, 1988–. Vis. Prof. in Animal Ecology, Univ. of Khartoum, 1976. Natural Environment Research Council: Workshop on Grey Seal Population Biol., 1979–84; Special Cttee on Seals, 1986–; Terrestrial Life Scis Cttee, 1988–91; Member: Council, RSPB, 1983–88; Adv. Cttee on Birds, NCC, 1988–; Envtl Res. Cttee, British Agrochem. Assoc., 1988–; Grants Cttee, Internat. Council for Bird Preservation, British Section, 1988–; Council, British Ornith. Union, 1989–; Sci. Adv. Cttee, Wildfowl & Wetlands Trust, 1989–; Pres., Scottish Ornithologists' Club, 1987. Editor, Bird Study, 1984–87; Mem., Editl Bd, Heredity, 1988–. *Publications:* (ed jtly) Joint Biological Expedition to North East Greenland 1974, 1978; papers in learned jls; chapters in books. *Recreations:* birdwatching, walking, gardening. *Address:* National Centre for Ornithology, Thetford, Norfolk IP24 2PU. *T:* Thetford (0842) 750050.

GREENWOOD, John Arnold Charles, OBE 1943; Chief General Manager, Sun Alliance & London Insurance Group, 1971–77; *b* 23 Jan. 1914; *o s* of late Augustus George Greenwood and Adele Ellen O'Neill Arnold; *m* 1940, Dorothy Frederica Pestell; two *d. Educ:* King's College Sch., Wimbledon. FCII; FRES. Joined Sun Insce Office Ltd, 1932; posted India, 1937–47; served War of 1939–45, TA, 36th Sikh Regt and AA&QMG 4th Indian Div. (Lt-Col, OBE, despatches); subseq. various appts; a Gen. Man., Sun Alliance & London, 1965; Dep. Chief Gen. Man., 1969. Morgan Owen Medal, 1939. *Publications:* papers on insurance, entomology. *Recreations:* entomology, writing, gardening. *Address:* Hambledon House, Rogate, Petersfield, Hants GU31 5EE. *T:* Rogate (0730) 821744.

GREENWOOD, Prof. Norman Neill, DSc Melbourne; PhD; ScD Cambridge; FRS 1987; CChem, FRSC; Professor of Inorganic and Structural Chemistry, University of Leeds, 1971–90, now Emeritus; *b* Melbourne, Vic., 19 Jan. 1925; *er s* of Prof. J. Neill Greenwood, DSc and Gladys, *d* of late Moritz and Bertha Uhland; *m* 1951, Kirsten Marie Rydland, Bergen, Norway; three *d. Educ:* University High School, Melbourne; University of Melbourne; Sidney Sussex Coll., Cambridge. Laboratory Cadet, CSIRO Div. of Tribophysics, Melbourne, 1942–44; BSc Melbourne 1945, MSc Melbourne 1948; DSc Melbourne 1966. Masson Memorial Medal, Royal Australian Chem. Institute, 1945. Resident Tutor and Lecturer in Chemistry, Trinity Coll., Melbourne, 1946–48. Exhibn of 1851, Overseas Student, 1948–51; PhD Cambridge 1951; ScD Cambridge 1961. Senior Harwell Research Fellow, 1951–53; Lectr, 1953–60 Senior Lectr, 1960–61, in Inorganic Chemistry, Univ. of Nottingham; Prof. of Inorganic Chemistry, Univ. of Newcastle upon Tyne, 1961–71. Vis. Professor: Univ. of Melbourne, 1966; Univ. of Western Australia, 1969; Univ. of Western Ontario, 1973; Univ. of Copenhagen, 1979; La Trobe Univ., Melbourne, 1985; Toho Univ., Tokyo, 1991–; National Science Foundation Distinguished Vis. Prof., Michigan State Univ., USA, 1967. International Union of Pure and Applied Chemistry: Mem., 1963–83; Vice-Pres., 1975–77, Pres., 1977–81, Inorganic Chemistry Div.; Chm., Internat. Commn on Atomic Weights, 1969–75. Chemical Society: Tilden Lectr, 1966–67; Vice Pres., 1979–80; Pres., Dalton Div., 1979–81; Award in Main Group Chemistry, 1975. Vice-Pres., 1989–90, Pres., 1990–91, BAAS. Lectures: Hofmann, Ges. Deutscher Chemiker, 1983; Liversidge , RSC, 1983; first Egon Wiberg, Munich Univ., 1989; Ludwig Mond, RSC, 1991. Dr *hc* de l'Université de Nancy I, 1977. *Publications:* Principles of Atomic Orbitals, 1964 (rev. edns 1968, 1973, 1980); Ionic Crystals, Lattice Defects, and Nonstoichiometry, 1968; (jointly) Spectroscopic Properties of Inorganic and Organometallic Compounds, vols I-IX, 1968–76; (with W. A. Campbell) Contemporary British Chemists, 1971; (with T. C. Gibb) Mössbauer Spectroscopy, 1971; Periodicity and Atomic Structure, 1971; (with B. P. Straughan and E. J. F. Ross) Index of Vibrational Spectra, vol. I, 1972, (with E. J. F. Ross) vol. II, 1975, vol. III, 1977; The Chemistry of Boron, 1973 (rev. edn 1975); (with A. Earnshaw) Chemistry of the Elements, 1984; numerous original papers and reviews in chemical jls and chapters in scientific monographs. *Recreations:* ski-ing, music. *Address:* School of Chemistry, The University, Leeds LS2 9JT.

GREENWOOD, Peter Bryan; His Honour Judge Greenwood; a Circuit Judge, since 1972. Called to the Bar, Gray's Inn, 1955. Dep. Chm., Essex QS, 1968–71.

GREENWOOD, Peter Humphry, DSc; FRS 1985; FIBiol; Deputy Chief Scientific Officer, Ichthyologist, British Museum (Natural History), 1985–89 (Senior Principal Scientific Officer, 1967–85); *b* 21 April 1927; *s* of Percy Ashworth Greenwood and Joyce May Wilton; *m* 1950; four *d. Educ:* St John's Coll., Johannesburg; Krugersdorp High Sch.; Univ. of Witwatersrand. BSc (Hons), DSc. S African Naval forces, seconded to RN, 1944–46. Colonial Office Fishery Res. Student, 1950–51; Res. Officer, E African Fisheries Res. Orgn, Jinja, Uganda, 1951–58; British Museum (Natural History): Sen. Res. Fellow, 1958–59; Sen., later Principal, Scientific Officer and Curator of Fishes, 1959–67. Res. Associate, Amer. Mus. of Natural Hist., 1965; H. B. Bigelow Vis. Prof. of Ichthyology, Harvard Univ., 1979; Res. Associate, J. L. B. Smith Inst. of Ichthyology, S Africa, 1977. Mem., British subcttee on productivity of freshwaters, Internat. Biol Prog., 1964–75; Chm., Royal Soc./Internat. Biol Prog. subcttee on res. in Lake George, 1967–74. Pres., Linnean Soc. of London, 1976–79. Hon. For. Mem., Amer. Soc. of Ichthyologists and Herpetologists, 1972; For. Mem., Swedish Royal Acad. of Science, 1984. DSc (*hc*) Rhodes Univ., South Africa, 1991. Scientific Medal, Zoological Soc. of London, 1963; Medal for Zoology, Linnean Soc., 1982. *Publications:* Fishes of Uganda, 1958, 2nd edn 1966; The Cichlid Fishes of Lake Victoria: the biology and evolution of a species flock, 1974; (ed) J. R. Norman, A History of Fishes, 1st revd edn 1963, 2nd revd edn 1975; (ed with C. Patterson) Fossil Vertebrates, 1967; (ed with C. Patterson and R. Miles) Interrelationships of Fishes, 1973; The Haplochromine Fishes of the East African Lakes, 1981; numerous papers on taxonomy, anatomy, biology and evolution of fishes. *Recreations:* ballet, art, reading, thinking, model building. *Address:* 20 Cromer Villas Road, SW18 1PN. *T:* 081–874 9588.

GREENWOOD, Ronald, CBE 1981; Manager, England Association Football Team, 1977–82, retired; *b* 11 Nov. 1921; *s* of Sam and Margaret Greenwood; *m* Lucy Joan

Greenwood; one *s* one *d*. *Educ:* Alperton School. Apprenticed signwriter, 1937; joined Chelsea FC, 1940; served RAF, 1940–45; Bradford Park Avenue FC, 1945 (Captain); Brentford FC, 1949 (over 300 matches); rejoined Chelsea FC, 1952 (League Champions, 1954–55); Fulham FC, Feb. 1955; coached Oxford Univ. team, 3 years, Walthamstow Avenue FC, 2 years; Manager, Eastbourne United FC and England Youth team; Asst Manager, Arsenal FC, 1958; Team Manager, England Under-23, 1958–61; Manager and Coach, later Gen. Manager, West Ham United FC, 1961–77 (FA Cup, 1964 and 1975; European Cup Winners' Cup, 1965); a FIFA technical adviser, World Cup series, 1966 and 1970. *Publication:* Yours Sincerely, 1984. *Address:* 8 Kestrel Close, Upper Drive, Hove, Sussex BN3 6NS.

GREER, Prof. David Clive; Professor of Music and Chairman of Music Department, University of Durham, since 1986; *b* 8 May 1937; *s* of William Mackay Greer and Barbara (*née* Avery); *m* 1961, Patricia Margaret Regan; two *s* one *d*. *Educ:* Dulwich Coll.; Queen's Coll., Oxford (MA). Lectr in Music, Birmingham Univ., 1963–72; Hamilton Harty Prof. of Music, QUB, 1972–84; Prof. of Music, Univ. of Newcastle upon Tyne, 1984–86. FRSA 1986. Editor, Jl Royal Musical Assoc, 1977–90. *Publications:* (ed) English Madrigal Verse, 1967; Hamilton Harty: his life and music, 1979, 2nd edn 1980; Hamilton Harty: early memories, 1979; (ed) Collected English Lutenist Partsongs, 2 vols, 1987–89, and other editions of 16th and 17th century music; articles in Music and Letters, Music Review, Musical Times, Shakespeare Qly, Notes & Queries, Lute Soc. Jl. *Recreations:* reading, cinema, walking. *Address:* The Music School, Palace Green, Durham DH1 3RL. *T:* Durham (091) 3742000. *Club:* Athenæum.

GREER, Germaine, PhD; author and lecturer; Founder Director, The Tulsa Centre for the Study of Women's Literature, 1979–82; *b* 29 Jan. 1939. *Educ:* Melbourne Univ. (BA 1959); Sydney Univ. (MA 1962); Cambridge Univ. (PhD 1967). Lecturer in English, Warwick Univ., 1968–73; Prof. of Modern Letters, Univ. of Tulsa, 1980–83; Special Lectr and Unofficial Fellow, Newnham Coll., Cambridge, 1989–. Vis. Prof., Univ. of Tulsa, 1979. Dir, Stump Cross Books, 1988–. *Publications:* The Female Eunuch, 1970; The Obstacle Race, 1979; Sex and Destiny: the politics of human fertility, 1984; (contrib.) Women: a world report, 1985; Shakespeare, 1986; The Madwoman's Underclothes: essays and occasional writings 1968–85, 1986; (ed jtly) Kissing the Rod: an anthology of 17th century women's verse, 1988; Daddy, We Hardly Knew You, 1989 (J. R. Ackerly Prize; Premio Internazionale Mondello); (ed) The Uncollected Verse of Aphra Benn, 1989; contribs: articles to Listener, Spectator, Esquire, Harpers Magazine, Playboy, Private Eye (as Rose Blight). *Address:* c/o Aitken and Stone, 29 Fernshaw Road, SW10 0TG.

GREET, Rev. Dr Kenneth Gerald; Secretary of the Methodist Conference, 1971–84; President of the Methodist Conference, 1980–81; Moderator, Free Church Federal Council, 1982–83; President, World Disarmament Campaign, since 1989 (Co-Chairman, 1983–86; Vice-Pres., 1986–89); *b* 17 Nov. 1918; *e s* of Walter and Renée Greet, Bristol; *m* 1947, Mary Eileen Edbrooke; one *s* two *d*. *Educ:* Cotham Grammar Sch., Bristol; Handsworth Coll., Birmingham. Minister: Cwm and Kingstone Methodist Church, 1940–42; Ogmore Vale Methodist Church, 1942–45; Tonypandy Central Hall, 1947–54; Sec. Dept of Christian Citizenship of Methodist Church, 1954–71; Member: BCC, 1955–84 (Chm. of Exec., 1977–81); World Methodist Council, 1957– (Chm., Exec. Cttee, 1976–81); Chairman: Exec., Temperance Council of Christian Churches, 1961–71; World Christian Temperance Fedn, 1962–72. Rep. to Central Cttee, World Council of Churches, Addis Ababa, 1971, Nairobi, 1975; Beckly Lectr, 1962; Willson Lectr, Kansas City, 1966; Cato Lectr, Sydney, 1975. Hon. DD Ohio, USA. *Publications:* The Mutual Society, 1962; Man and Wife Together, 1962; Large Petitions, 1964; Guide to Loving, 1965; The Debate about Drink, 1969; The Sunday Question, 1970; The Art of Moral Judgement, 1970; When the Spirit Moves, 1975; A Lion from a Thicket, 1978; The Big Sin: Christianity and the arms race, 1983; What Shall I Cry?, 1986. *Recreations:* tennis, photography. *Address:* 89 Broadmark Lane, Rustington, Sussex BN16 2JA. *T:* Rustington (0903) 773326.

GREETHAM, (George) Colin; Headmaster, Bishop's Stortford College, 1971–84; *b* 22 April 1929; *s* of late George Cecil Greetham and of Gertrude Greetham (*née* Heavyside); *m* 1963, Rosemary (*née* Gardner); two *s* one *d*. *Educ:* York Minster Song Sch.; St Peter's Sch., York; (Choral Scholar) King's Coll., Cambridge. BA (Hons) History Tripos Cantab, Class II, Div. I, 1952; Certif. of Educn (Cantab), 1953. Chm., Strathisla and Grange Community Councils, Banffs. *Recreations:* music, choral training, horticulture, bowls. *Address:* Chapelhead Farm, Crossroads, Keith, Banffshire AB5 3LQ.

GREGG, Hubert Robert Harry; actor, composer, lyric writer, author, playwright and director; *b* London, 19 July 1914; *s* of Robert Joseph Gregg and Alice Maud (*née* Bessant); *m* 1st, 1943, Zoe Gail (marr. diss. 1950); one *d*; 2nd, 1956, Pat Kirkwood (marr. diss. 1979); 3rd, 1980, Carmel Lytton; one *s* one *d*. *Educ:* St Dunstan's Coll.; Webber-Douglas Sch. of Singing and Dramatic Art. Served War, 1939–44: private, Lincs Regt, 1939; commnd 60th Rifles, 1940; transf. Intell.; with Polit. Warfare Exec., 1942 (duties included broadcasting in German). *Stage:* 1st London appearance, Julien in Martine, Ambassadors', 1933; Birmingham Rep., 1933–34; Shakespearean roles, Open Air Theatre, Regent's Park and at Old Vic, 1934, 1935; 1st New York appearance, Kit Neilan in French without Tears, 1937 (and London, 1938–39); London appearances include: Pip in The Convict, 1935; roles in classics (Orlando, Henry V, Hamlet), 1935–36; Frederick Hackett in Great Possessions, 1937; Peter Scott-Fowler in After the Dance, 1939; Polly in Men in Shadow, 1942; Michael Caraway in Acacia Avenue, 1944; Earl of Harpenden in While the Sun Shines, 1945, 1946; Tom D'Arcy in Off the Record, 1947; Gabriel Hathaway in Western Wind, 1949; (1st musical), John Blessington-Briggs in Chrysanthemum, 1958; Lionel Toope in Pools Paradise, 1961. *Chichester Festival Theatre:* Alexander MacColgie Gibbs in The Cocktail Party, Antonio in The Tempest, and Announcer in The Skin of our Teeth, 1968; Sir Lucius O'Trigger in The Rivals, Britannus in Caesar and Cleopatra, and Marcellin in Dear Antoine (also London), 1971. *Directed, London:* The Hollow (Agatha Christie's 1st stage success), 1951; re-staged To Dorothy - a Son, 1952 (subseq. toured in play, 1952–53); The Mousetrap (for 7 yrs from 1953); Speaking of Murder, 1958; The Unexpected Guest, 1958; From the French, 1959; Go Back for Murder, 1960; Rule of Three, 1962; re-staged The Secretary Bird, 1969 (subseq. toured in play, 1969–70). 1st solo performance, Leicester, 1970; subseq. performances in Britain and America (subjects include Shakespeare, Shaw, Jerome K. Jerome, the London Theatre, and the 20s, 30s and 40s); solo perf., Words by Elgar, Music by Shaw, Malvern Fest., 1978, Edinburgh Fest., 1979. *Films include:* In Which We Serve; Flying Fortress; Acacia Avenue (USA as The Facts of Love); The Root of all Evil; Vote for Huggett; Once upon a Dream; Robin Hood (Walt Disney); The Maggie (USA as High and Dry); Svengali; Doctor at Sea (also wrote music and lyrics); Simon and Laura; Speaking of Murder; Final Appointment; Room in the House; Stars in Your Eyes (also co-dir. and wrote music and lyrics). *Author of plays:* We Have Company (played in tour, 1953); Cheque Mate (dir. and appeared in); Villa Sleep Four (played in tour, 1965); From the French (written under pseudonym of Jean-Paul Marotte); Who's Been Sleeping . . . ? (also appeared in); The Rumpus (played in tour, 1967); Dear Somebody (perf. Germany as Geliebtes Traumbild, 1984); (screenplay) After the Ball (adapted from own television biog. of Vesta Tilley). *Songs:* Author of over 200, including: I'm going to get lit up; Maybe it's because I'm a Londoner. BBC broadcasts in drama, revue, poetry, etc, 1933–; announcer, BBC Empire Service, 1934–35; radio musical of Three Men in a Boat, 1962 (adapted, wrote music and words, and appeared in); weekly radio progs with accent on nostalgia, 1965– (A Square Deal, I Remember it Well, Now and Then, Thanks for the Memory); Chairman: BBC TV Brains Trust, 1955; Youth Wants to Know, ITV, 1957; 40 week radio series on London theatres, 1974–75; biog. series: I Call it Genius, 1980–81; I Call it Style, 1981–; Hubert Gregg Remembers, ITV solo series, 1982–; 50 Years of Broadcasting, BBC celebration prog. (Hubert Gregg says Maybe It's Because . . .), 1984 (Sony Radio Award, 1985); Hubert Gregg Remembers (series for BBC World Service), 1985–; (wrote book, music and lyrics, and appeared in) Sweet Liza (radio musical play), 1985; (wrote script, music and lyrics for, and presented) My London (radio), 1986; (devised and wrote) Mark Time (television serial), 1988–89. Has dir., lectured and adjudicated at Webber-Douglas Sch., Central Sch. of Speech Trng and RADA. Patron, Cinema Theatre Assoc., 1973–; President: Northern Boys' Book Club, 1975– (succeeded P. G. Wodehouse); Concert Artists Assoc., 1979–80. Freedom of City of London, 1981. Gold Badge of Merit, British Acad. of Composers, Authors and Song Writers, 1982. *Publications:* April Gentleman (novel), 1951; We Have Company (play), 1953; A Day's Loving (novel), 1974; Agatha Christie and all that Mousetrap, 1980; Thanks for the Memory (biographies collected from radio series I Call it Genius and I Call it Style), 1983; Geliebtes Traumbild (play), 1984; music and lyrics. *Recreation:* cinematography. *Address:* 260 King's Drive, Eastbourne, East Sussex BN21 2XD. *T:* Eastbourne (0323) 501946. *Club:* Garrick.

GREGOIRE, His Eminence Cardinal Paul, OC 1979; Archbishop Emeritus of Montreal (Archbishop, 1968–90); *b* Verdun, 24 Oct. 1911. *Educ:* Ecole Supérieure Richard; Séminaire de Ste-Thérèse; Univ. of Montreal. Priest, 1937; became Professor, but continued his studies: PhD, STL, LèsL, MA (Hist.), dip. in pedagogy. Subseq. became Director, Séminaire de Ste-Thérèse; Prof. of Philosophy of Educn at l'Ecole Normale Secondaire and at l'Institut Pédagogique; Chaplain of the Students, Univ. of Montreal, 1950–61; consecrated Bishop, 1961, and became auxiliary to Archbishop of Montreal; Vicar-General and Dir of Office for the Clergy; Apostolic Administrator, Archdiocese of Montreal, Dec. 1967–Apr. 1968. Cardinal, 1988. Pres., Episcopal Commn on Ecumenism (French sector), 1965. Has presided over several Diocesan Commns (notably Commn for study of the material situation of the Clergy), 1965–68. Member: Canadian delegn to Bishop's Synod, Rome, 1971–; Congregation for the Clergy, 1978–83; Congregation for Catholic Educn, 1983–; Pontifical Commn for pastoral care of Migrations and of Tourism, 1988–; Congregation for the Oriental Churches, 1989–. Dr *hc*: Univ. of Montreal, 1969; St Michael's Coll., Winooski, Vt, 1970. *Address:* Archbishop's House, 1071 Cathedral Street, Montreal, Quebec H3B 2V4, Canada.

GREGORIOS, His Eminence The Most Rev. the Archbishop of Thyateira and Great Britain; *see* Theocharus, Archbishop Gregory.

GREGORY, Alan Thomas, CBE 1984; Director, Willis Corroon (formerly Willis Faber) plc, since 1987; *b* 13 Oct. 1925; *s* of Lloyd Thomas Gregory and Florence Abbott; *m* 1st, 1952, Pamela Douglas Scott (*d* 1986); one *s* two *d*; 2nd, 1988, Mrs Marion Newth (*née* Nash), JP. *Educ:* Dulwich Coll.; St John's Coll., Cambridge (Classics). Directed into coal mining, coal face worker, 1944; Min. of Power, 1948; JSSC 1957; Chm., NATO Petroleum Planning Cttee, 1967–70; joined British Petroleum, 1971; Gen. Manager, BP Italiana, 1972–73; Dir, Govt and Public Affairs, 1975–85, and Dir, UK and Ireland Region, 1980–85, British Petroleum Co.; Chm., BP Oil Ltd, 1981–85; Director: BP Chemicals International Ltd, 1981–85; National Home Loans Corp., 1985–91. Governor, Queen Mary Coll., London Univ., 1981–87. President, Inst. of Petroleum, 1982–84. Univ. Comr, 1988–. *Recreations:* books, gardening, theatre. *Address:* Red Oak, 31 Fairmile Avenue, Cobham, Surrey KT11 2JA. *T:* Cobham (0932) 864457. *Club:* Travellers'.

GREGORY, Clifford; Chief Scientific Officer, Department of Health and Social Security, 1979–84, retired; *b* 16 Dec. 1924; *s* of Norman and Grace Gregory; *m* 1948, Wyn Aveyard; one *d* (one *s* decd). *Educ:* Royal Coll. of Science, London Univ. (2nd Cl. Hons Physics; ARCS). Served War, RN, 1943–46. Lectr, Mddx Hosp. Med. Sch., 1949; Sen. Physicist, Mount Vernon Hosp., 1954; Dep. Reg. Physicist, Sheffield, 1960; Sen. Principal Scientific Officer, Min. of Health, 1966; Dep. Chief Scientific Officer, DHSS, 1972. *Publications:* scientific papers in med. and scientific jls. *Recreations:* outdoor pursuits, natural history. *Address:* 53 Roundwood Park, Harpenden, Herts AL5 3AG. *T:* Harpenden (0582) 712047.

GREGORY, Conal Robert; MP (C) York, since 1983; company director, wine consultant and lecturer; *b* 11 March 1947; *s* of Patrick George Murray Gregory and Marjorie Rose Gregory; *m* 1971, Helen Jennifer Craggs; one *s* one *d*. *Educ:* King's College Sch., Wimbledon; Univ. of Sheffield (BA Hons Mod. Hist. and Pol Theory and Instns, 1968). Master of Wine by examination, Vintners' Co., 1979. Manager, Saccone & Speed Vintage Cellar Club, 1971–73; Wine Buyer, Reckitt & Colman, 1973–77; Editor, Internat. Wine and Food Soc's Jl, 1980–83; Dir, Standard Fireworks Ltd, 1987–. Contested Lakenham, Norwich City election, 1976; Norfolk County Councillor, Thorpe Div., 1977–81; Vice-Pres., Norwich Jun. Chamber of Commerce, 1975–76; Mem., E Anglia Tourist Bd, 1979–81. Chairman: Norwich N Cons. Assoc., 1980–82; Norwich CPC, 1978–81; Vice-Chm., Eastern Area CPC, 1980–83; Member: Cons. Eastern Area Agric. Cttee, 1975–79; Norfolk Cons. Eur. Constituency Council, 1981–82; Cons. Provincial Council, Eastern Area, 1978–82; Chm. and Founder, Bow Gp of E Anglia, 1975–82; Nat. Vice-Chm., Bow Gp, 1976–77. Hon. Treas., British/Cyprus CPA Gp, 1987–; Secretary: All Party Parly Tourism Cttee, 1983–; UK-Manx Parly Gp, 1987–; Chm., Cons. Parly Food and Drinks Industries Cttee, 1989– (Vice-Chm., 1985–89); Vice-Chairman: Cons. Parly Tourism Cttee, 1985–; Cons. Parly Transport Cttee, 1987–89 and 1990– (Sec., 1983–87); All Party Parly Hospice Gp, 1990–; Mem., Cttee, British Atlantic Gp of Young Politicians, 1983– (Chm., 1988–89; Pres., 1989–); Pres., York Young Conservatives, 1982–; Vice-President: Nat. Soc. of Cons. and Unionist Agents, Yorks Br., 1983–; York Br., UNA, 1983–. Parly Consultant: The Market Res. Soc., 1984–91; Consort Hotels Ltd, 1984–; Andry Montgomery Ltd, 1983–. Fellow, Industry and Parlt Trust, 1984–87. Private Member's Bill on consumer safety, 1985. Patron, Nat. Trust for Welfare of the Elderly, 1983–; Founder Mem., Wymondham Br., CEMS, 1979; Member: Wymondham Abbey PCC, 1982–83; Humbleyard Deanery Synod, 1982–83; High Steward's Cttee, York Minster Fund, 1983–89; York Archaeol Trust, 1983–; York Georgian Soc., 1982–; York Civic Trust, 1982–. A Friend of York Festival. Governor, Heartsease Sch., Norwich, 1977–83; Mem., Court of Governors: Univ. of Sheffield, 1977–; Univ. of York, 1983–; Univ. of Hull, 1983–. Wine Corresp., Catering Times, 1979–83. *Publications:* (with W. Knock) Beers of Britain, 1975; (with R. A. Adley) A Policy for Tourism?, 1977; A Caterer's Guide to Drinks, 1979; (with M. Shersby and A. McCurley) Food for a Healthy Britain, 1987; contribs to The Times, Wine and Spirit, Travel GBI, Conference Britain, etc. *Address:* House of Commons, SW1A 0AA. *T:* 071–219 4603. *Club:* Acomb and District Conservative (York).

GREGORY, John Peter, JP; CEng, FIMechE; Director, ASL Ltd, 1986–91; *b* 5 June 1925; *s* of Mr and Mrs P. Gregory; *m* 1949, Lilian Mary (*née* Jarvis); one *s* one *d*. *Educ:*

Ernest Bailey Sch., Matlock; Trinity Hall, Cambridge (Scholar, MA). CEng, FIMechE 1970. Served War, RAF Pilot, 1943–47. Joined Cadbury Bros Ltd, 1949, Dir 1962; Vice Chm., Cadbury Ltd, 1969–70, Dir, Cadbury Schweppes, 1971–82 (Chm., Overseas Gp and Internat. Tech. Dir, 1973–80); Director: National Vulcan Engrg Ins. Group Ltd, 1970–79; Amalgamated Power Engrg Ltd, 1973–81; Chm., Data Recording Instruments Ltd, 1982–84. Gen. Comr of Income Tax, 1978–82. Chm. Trustees, Middlemore Homes, 1970–82. Liveryman, Worshipful Co. of Needlemakers. JP Birmingham, 1979. *Recreations:* music, bridge, country pursuits, sailing. *Address:* Moorgreen Hall, Weatheroak, Alvechurch, Worcs. *T:* Wythall (0564) 822303. *Clubs:* Carlton; Royal Fowey Yacht.

GREGORY, Leslie Howard James; former National Officer of EETPU; *b* 18 Jan. 1915; *s* of J. F. and R. E. Gregory; *m* 1949, D. M. Reynolds; one *s* one *d*. *Educ:* Junior Section, Ealing College (formerly Acton Coll.) and state schools. Mem. Exec. Council, ETU, 1938–54; full-time Nat. Officer, 1954–79, retired. Member: CSEU Nat. Sub-Cttees, for Shipbuilding, 1966–79, for Railway Workshops, 1968–78; Craft Training Cttees of Shipbuilding ITB, 1965–77, and Engineering ITB, 1965–68; EDC for Elec. Engrg, 1967–74; EDC for Shipbuilding, 1974–76; Org. Cttee, British Shipbuilders, 1976–77; Bd, British Shipbuilders (part-time), 1977–80. *Address:* 3 Addington Court, Keats Avenue, Milford-on-Sea, Hants SO41 0WN. *T:* Lymington (0590) 645883.

GREGORY, Michael Anthony, OBE 1990; freelance journalist and author; Chief Legal Adviser, Country Landowners' Association, 1977–90; *b* 8 June 1925; *s* of late Wallace James Ignatius Gregory, FRIBA, FRICS, AMIMechE, and Dorothy Gregory; *m* 1951, Patricia Ann, *d* of late Frank Hodges and late Gwendoline Hodges; three *s* four *d* (and one *d* decd). *Educ:* Douai Sch.; University Coll. London (LLB). Served RAF, Air Navigator, 1943–47; called to the Bar, Middle Temple, 1952; practised at Bar, 1952–60; Legal Dept, Country Landowners' Assoc., 1960–. Member: BSI Cttee on Installation of Pipelines in Land, 1965–83; Thames Water Authority (now NRA (Thames)) Reg. Fisheries Adv. Cttee, 1974–; Inland Waterways Amenity Adv. Council, 1982–; Council, John Eastwood Water Protection Trust, 1984–. Hon. Legal Advr, Nat. Anglers' Council, 1968–; Member Council: Salmon and Trout Assoc., 1980–90; Anglers' Co-op. Assoc., 1980–. Founder Mem., Agricl Law Assoc., 1975; Trustee, CLA Charitable Trust, 1980–. Hon. Sec., Soc. of Our Lady of Good Counsel, 1953–58; Mem., Management Cttee, Bourne Trust (formerly Catholic Social Services for Prisoners), 1952– (Chm., 1960–71 and 1974–85; Hon. Sec., 1953–60); Pres., Douai Soc., 1984–86. Chm., Internat. Help for Children, Fleet and Dist Br., 1967–77; Mem. Cttee, 1981–, and Trustee, 1987–, Fedn for Promotion of Horticulture for Disabled People. Papal medal *pro ecclesia et pontifice*, 1988. *Publications:* Organisational Possibilities in Farming, 1968; (with C. Townsend) Joint Enterprises in Farming, 1968, 2nd edn 1973; Angling and the Law, 1967, 2nd edn 1974, supp. 1976; Title, Pipelines, for Encycl. of Forms and Precedents, 1970; (with Richard Seymour) All for Fishing, 1970; contributor to Walmsley's Rural Estate Management, 6th edn, 1978; (with G. R. Williams) Farm Partnerships, 1979; (with Margaret Parrish) Essential Law for Landowners and Farmers, 1980, 3rd edn (with Angela Sydenham), 1990; (with Richard Stratton and G. R. Williams) Share Farming, 1983, 2nd edn 1985; numerous articles, booklets, short stories. *Recreations:* fishing, ball and saloon games, music, playing saxophones. *Address:* 63 Gally Hill Road, Church Crookham, Fleet, Hants GU13 0RU.

GREGORY, Peter Roland; Under Secretary, Transport, Planning and Environment Group, Welsh Office, since 1990; *b* 7 Oct. 1946; *s* of Tom and Ruby Gregory; *m* 1978, Frances Margaret Hogan. *Educ:* Sexeys Grammar Sch., Som.; University College Swansea (BA Hons 1968); Manchester Univ. (PhD 1972). Joined Welsh Office, 1971; Private Sec. to Perm. Sec., 1974–75; Principal, 1976; Asst Sec., 1982. *Recreations:* walking, theatre, music. *Address:* Welsh Office, Cathays Park, Cardiff CF1 3NQ.

GREGORY, Prof. Richard Langton, CBE 1989; DSc; FRSE 1969; Professor of Neuropsychology and Director of Brain and Perception Laboratory, University of Bristol, 1970–88, now Emeritus; *b* 24 July 1923; *s* of C. C. L. Gregory, astronomer, and Patricia (*née* Gibson); *m* 1st, 1953, Margaret Hope Pattison Muir (marr. diss. 1966); one *s* one *d*; 2nd, 1967, Freja Mary Balchin (marr. diss. 1976). *Educ:* King Alfred Sch., Hampstead; Downing Coll., Cambridge, 1947–50. DSc Bristol, 1983. Served in RAF (Signals), 1941–46; Research, MRC Applied Psychology Research Unit, Cambridge, 1950–53; Univ. Demonstrator, then Lecturer, Dept of Psychology, Cambridge, 1953–67; Fellow, Corpus Christi Coll., Cambridge, 1962–67; Professor of Bionics, Dept of Machine Intelligence and Perception, Univ. of Edinburgh, 1967–70 (Chm. of Dept, 1968–70). Visiting Prof.: UCLA, 1963; MIT, 1964; New York Univ., 1966. Founder and Chm. Trustees, The Exploratory Hands-on Science Centre, 1983–. President: Section J, British Assoc. for Advancement of Science, 1975, Section X, 1986, and Section Q, 1989 and 1990; Experimental Psychol. Soc., 1981–82. Member: Royal Soc. Cttee for Public Understanding of Sci., 1986–; BBC Sci. Consultative Gp, 1988–. Royal Instn Christmas Lectr, 1967–68. Manager, Royal Instn, 1971–74. FRSA 1973. DUniv: Open, 1990; Stirling, 1990. CIBA Foundn Research Prize, 1956; Craik Prize for Physiological Psychology, St John's Coll., Cambridge, 1958; Waverley Gold Medal, 1960. Founder Editor, Perception, 1972. *Publications:* Recovery from Early Blindness (with Jean Wallace), 1963; Eye and Brain, 1966, 4th edn 1990; The Intelligent Eye, 1970; Concepts and Mechanisms of Perception, 1974; (ed jtly) Illusion in Nature and Art, 1973; Mind in Science, 1981; Odd Perceptions (essays), 1986; (ed) Oxford Companion to the Mind, 1987; articles in various scientific jls and patents for optical and recording instruments and a hearing aid; radio and television appearances. *Recreations:* punning and pondering. *Address:* 23 Royal York Crescent, Clifton, Bristol BS8 4JX. *Clubs:* Athenæum, Savile.

GREGORY, Roger Michael; Deputy Receiver for the Metropolitan Police, since 1989; *b* 1 June 1939; *s* of Walter James Gregory and Catherine Emma Gregory (*née* Regan); *m* 1961, Johanna Margaret O'Rourke; five *s* two *d*. *Educ:* Gillingham (Kent) Grammar Sch. Joined Metropolitan Police Civil Staff, 1957; Hd of Operations, Police National Computer Unit, 1976; Dep. Dir of Finance, Metropolitan Police, 1981; Dir of Computing, Metropolitan Police, 1983. *Recreations:* cricket, bridge, gentle gardening. *Address:* New Scotland Yard, Broadway, SW1H 0BG.

GREGORY, Roland Charles Leslie; *see* Gregory, Roy.

GREGORY, Ronald, CBE 1980; QPM 1971; DL; Chief Constable of West Yorkshire Metropolitan Police, 1974–83, retired; *b* 23 Oct. 1921; *s* of Charles Henry Gregory and Mary Gregory; *m* 1942, Grace Miller Ellison; two *s*. *Educ:* Harris College. Joined Police Service, Preston, 1941. RAF (Pilot), 1942–44; RN (Pilot), 1944–46. Dep. Chief Constable, Blackpool, 1962–65; Chief Constable, Plymouth, 1965–68; Dep. Chief Constable, Devon and Cornwall, 1968–69; Chief Constable, West Yorkshire Constabulary, 1969–74. DL West Yorks, 1977. *Recreations:* golf, sailing, ski-ing.

GREGORY, Roy, (Roland Charles Leslie Gregory), CBE 1973; QC 1982; *b* 16 Jan. 1916; *s* of Charles James Alfred and Lilian Eugenie Gregory; *m* 1st, 1949, Olive Elizabeth (*d* 1973), *d* of late Andrew Gay; one *s*; 2nd, 1974, Charlotte, *d* of late Lt-Col Peter Goddard, MBE. *Educ:* Strand Sch.; London Univ (LLB Hons). Served in Army, 1941–42. Called to Bar, Gray's Inn, 1950. First entered Civil Service, 1933; Head of Civil Procedure Br., Lord Chancellor's Office, 1966–79, retired; Consultant, 1979–82. Secretary: Austin Jones Cttee on County Court Procedure, 1947–49; Evershed Cttee on Supreme Court Practice and Procedure, 1949–53; County Court Rule Cttee, 1962–79; Matrimonial Causes Rule Cttee, 1967–79; Asst Sec., Supreme Court Rule Cttee, 1968–79; Chm., Working Party on Revision of County Court Rules, 1979–81; Mem., Expert Cttees of Council of Europe, 1978–82. *Publications:* County Court Manual, 1st edn 1946 to 4th edn 1962; editor, County Court Practice, 1950–; contribs to legal publications on civil procedure. *Recreations:* music, travel. *Address:* 36 Howard Avenue, Ewell, Surrey KT17 2QJ. *T:* 081–393 8933; 16 Ratton Garden, Ratton Drive, Eastbourne, E Sussex BN20 9BT. *T:* Eastbourne (0323) 509716.

GREGSON, family name of **Baron Gregson.**

GREGSON, Baron *cr* 1975 (Life Peer), of Stockport in Greater Manchester; **John Gregson,** AMCT, CBIM; DL; Non-Executive Director, Fairey Group plc, since 1989 (formerly Fairey Holdings Ltd); Director, Manchester Industrial Centre Ltd, since 1982; Part-time Member, British Steel plc (formerly British Steel Corporation), since 1976; *b* 29 Jan. 1924. Joined Stockport Base Subsidiary, 1939; Fairey R&D team working on science of nuclear power, 1946; appointed to Board, 1966. Non-executive Dir, Otto-Simon Carves Ltd; Mem., Electra Corporate Ventures Ltd, 1989–. Mem., Hse of Lords Select Cttee on Sci. & Technol., 1980–; Pres., Parly and Scientific Cttee, 1986–89; Chm., Finance and Industry Gp of Labour Party, 1978–; Vice Pres., Assoc. of Metropolitan Authorities, 1984–. Pres., Defence Manufacturers Assoc., 1984–. Mem. Court Univ. of Manchester Inst. of Science and Technology, 1976–. Hon. Fellow, Manchester Polytechnic, 1983; Hon. FIProdE 1982; Hon. FEng 1986; Hon FICE 1987; DUniv Open, 1986; Hon. DSc Aston, 1987; Hon. DTech Brunel, 1989. Pres., Stockport Youth Orch.; Vice-Pres., Fedn of British Police Motor Clubs. DL Greater Manchester, 1979. *Recreations:* mountaineering, skiing. *Address:* Fairey Group plc, Cranford Lane, Heston, Hounslow, Middlesex TW5 9NQ; The Spinney, Cragg Vale, Mytholmroyd, Hebden Bridge, West Yorks HX7 5SR; 407 Hawkins House, Dolphin Square, SW1V 3XL.

GREGSON, Sir Peter (Lewis), KCB 1988; (CB 1983); Permanent Secretary, Department of Trade and Industry, since 1989; *b* 28 June 1936; *s* of late Walter Henry Gregson and of Lillian Margaret Gregson. *Educ:* Nottingham High Sch.; Balliol Coll., Oxford. Classical Hon. Mods, class I; Lit. Hum. class I; BA 1959; MA 1962. Nat Service, 1959–61; 2nd Lieut RAEC, attached to Sherwood Foresters. Board of Trade: Asst Principal, 1961; Private Sec. to Minister of State, 1963–65; Principal, 1965; Resident Observer, CS Selection Bd, 1966; London Business Sch., 1967; Private Sec. to the Prime Minister, 1968–72 (Parly Affairs, 1968–70; Econ. and Home Affairs, 1970–72); Asst Sec., DTI, and Sec., Industrial Development Adv. Bd, 1972–74; Under Sec., DoI, and Sec., NEB, 1975–77; Under Sec., Dept of Trade, 1977–80, Dep. Sec. (Civil Aviation and Shipping), 1980–81; Dep. Sec., Cabinet Office, 1981–85; Perm. Under-Sec. of State, Dept of Energy, 1985–89. Council Mem., Industrial Soc., 1990. CBIM 1988. *Recreations:* gardening, listening to music. *Address:* Department of Trade and Industry, Ashdown House, 123 Victoria Street, SW1E 6RB.

GREGSON, William Derek Hadfield, CBE 1970; DL; company director; Deputy Chairman, British Airports Authority, 1975–85; *b* 27 Jan. 1920; *s* of William Gregson; *m* 1944, Rosalind Helen Reeves; three *s* one *d*. *Educ:* King William's Coll., IoM; Alpine Coll., Villars; Faraday House Engrg College. DFH, CEng, FIEE, CBIM, FIIM. Served with RAF, NW Europe, 1941–45 (Sqdn Ldr); Techn. Sales Man., Ferranti Ltd, Edinburgh, 1946–51, London Man., 1951–59; Asst Gen. Man., Ferranti (Scotland) Ltd, 1959–83; Director: Ferranti EI, New York, 1969–83; Ferranti Hldgs, 1983–85. Director: British Telecom Scotland (formerly Scottish Telecommunications Bd), 1977–85; Anderson Strathclyde plc, 1978–86; Brammer plc, 1983–88; East of Scotland Industrial Investments plc, 1980–; Consultant to ICI, 1984–88. Chm., Scottish Gen. Practitioners Res. Support Unit, 1971–79; Dep. Chm., Scottish Council (Develt and Industry), 1982–88 (Dir, 1974–88); Mem. Council: Electronic Engrg Assoc. 1959–83 (Pres. 1963–64); Soc. of British Aerospace Companies, 1966–83 (Chm. Equipment Gp Cttee 1967); BIM, 1975–80. BEAMA: Chm. Industrial Control and Electronics Bd 1964; Mem. Council, 1970–; Chm., Measurement, Control and Automation Conference Bd, 1973; Dep. Pres., 1982–83; Pres., 1983–85. Member: BIM Adv. Bd for Scotland, 1969–85 (Chm., 1970–75); Electronics EDC, 1965–75; Bd of Livingston New Town, 1968–76; Jt BIM/NEDO Prof. Management Adv. Cttee on Indust. Strategy, 1976–78; Management Assoc. of SE Scotland, 1977– (Chm., 1980–81); Scottish Econ. Planning Council, 1965–71; Machine Tool Expert Cttee, 1969–70; Scottish Design Council, 1974–81; Design Council, 1980–85; CBI (Mem., Scottish Council, 1977–81); Bd, BSI, 1985–87; Edinburgh Chamber of Commerce, 1975–83. Commissioner, Northern Lighthouse Bd, 1975–90 (Chm., 1979). Dir, Scottish Nat. Orch., 1977–85 (Vice-Chm., 1981–84; Chm., 1984–85). DL City of Edinburgh, 1984–. FRSA. *Recreations:* reading, cabinet-making, automation in the home. *Address:* 15 Barnton Avenue, Edinburgh EH4 6AJ. *T:* 031–336 3896. *Clubs:* Royal Air Force; New (Edinburgh).

GREIG, (Henry Louis) Carron, CVO 1973; CBE 1986; Chairman, Horace Clarkson PLC (formerly H. Clarkson (Holdings) plc), since 1976; Director: James Purdey & Sons Ltd, since 1972; Royal Bank of Scotland, since 1985; Charterhouse, since 1990; Gentleman Usher to the Queen, since 1961; *b* 21 Feb. 1925; *s* of late Group Captain Sir Louis Greig, KBE, CVO, DL; *m* 1955, Monica Kathleen, *d* of Hon. J. J. Stourton, *qv*; three *s* one *d*. *Educ:* Eton. Scots Guards, 1943–47, Captain. Joined H. Clarkson & Co. Ltd, 1948; Dir, 1954; Man. Dir, 1962; Chairman: H. Clarkson & Co. Ltd, 1973–85; Baltic Exchange (formerly Baltic Mercantile and Shipping Exchange), 1983–85 (Dir, 1978–85); Dir, Williams & Glyn's Bank, 1983–85. Vice-Chm., Not Forgotten Assoc., 1979–. Dep. Chm., Schoolmistresses and Governesses Benevolent Instn, 1966–. Governor, United World Coll. of the Atlantic, 1985–. *Address:* Brook House, Fleet, Hants GU13 8RF; Binsness, Forres, Moray. *Clubs:* White's; Royal Findhorn Yacht.

GREIG, Prof. James, MSc (London), PhD (Birmingham); William Siemens Professor of Electrical Engineering, University of London, King's College, 1945–70, now Emeritus Professor; *b* 24 April 1903; *s* of James Alexander Greig and Helen Bruce Meldrum, Edinburgh; *m* 1931, Ethel May, *d* of William Archibald, Edinburgh; one *d*. *Educ:* George Watson's Coll. and Heriot-Watt Coll., Edinburgh; University Coll., University of London. Experience in telephone engineering with Bell Telephone Company, Montreal, 1924–26; Mem. research staff, General Electric Company, London, 1928–33; Asst lectr, University Coll., London, 1933–36; Lectr, Univ. of Birmingham, 1936–39; Head of Dept of Electrical Engineering, Northampton Polytechnic, 1939–45. FIEE (Chm. Measurement Section, 1949–50; Mem. Council, 1955–58); Dean of the Faculty of Engineering, Univ. of London, 1958–62, and Mem. Senate, 1958–70; Mem. Court, Univ. of London, 1967–70. MRI; Fellow Heriot-Watt Coll., 1951; FRSE 1956; FKC 1963. Mem., British Assoc. for the Advancement of Science. Chm., Crail Preservation Soc., 1959–74. *Publications:* papers (dealing mainly with subject of electrical and magnetic measurements) to: Jl Inst. Electrical Engineers, The Wireless Engineer, and Engineering. *Address:* Inch of Kinnordy, Kirriemuir, Angus. *T:* Kirriemuir (0575) 72350. *Club:* Athenæum.

GREIG of Eccles, James Dennis, CMG 1967; *b* 1926; *o s* of late Dennis George Greig of Eccles and Florence Aileen Marjoribanks; *m* 1st, 1952, Pamela Marguerite Stock (marr. diss., 1960); one *s* one *d*; 2nd, 1960 (marr. diss., 1967); one *s*; 3rd, 1968, Paula Mary Sterling. *Educ:* Winchester Coll.; Clare Coll., Cambridge; London Sch. of Economics. Military Service (Lieut, The Black Watch, seconded to Nigeria Regt), 1944–47. HMOCS: Administrative Officer, Northern Nigeria, 1949–55; Fedn of Nigeria, 1955–59; Dep. Financial Sec. (Economics), Mauritius, 1960–64; Financial Secretary, Mauritius, 1964–67; retired voluntarily on Mauritius achieving internal self-government, 1967. With Booker Bros. (Liverpool) Ltd, 1967–68; Head of Africa and Middle East Bureau, IPPF, 1968–76; Dir, Population Bureau, ODA, 1976–80; retired. *Recreations:* rough shooting, bowls, gardening, national hunt racing. *Address:* 6 Beverley Close, Barnes, SW13 0EH. *T:* 081–876 5354; The Braw Bothy, Eccles, Kelso, Roxburghshire. *Clubs:* Hurlingham, Annabel's.

GREINER, Hon. Nicholas Frank; MP (L) Ku-ring-gai, since 1980; Premier of New South Wales, since 1988; *b* 27 April 1947; *s* of Nicholas and Clare Greiner; *m* 1970, Kathryn Callaghan; one *s* one *d*. *Educ:* St Ignatius Coll., Riverview; Sydney Univ. (BEc Hons); Harvard Univ. (MBA High Dist.). Asst Vice-Pres., Boise Cascade Corp., USA, 1970–71; NSW Dir and Chief Exec., White River Corp., 1972–80; Chm., Harper & Row (Australasia), 1977–83. Shadow Minister for Urban Affairs, June 1981; Shadow Treasurer, and Shadow Minister for Housing and Co-operatives, Oct. 1981; Leader of State Opposition, 1983; Shadow Treasurer, and Shadow Minister for Ethnic Affairs, 1983; Premier, Treasurer, and Minister for Ethnic and Aboriginal Affairs, NSW Coalition Govt, 1988–. *Recreations:* squash, ski-ing, theatre, opera, spectator sports. *Address:* Premier's Office, State Office Block, Macquarie Street, Sydney, NSW 2000, Australia. *T:* 228 5239.

GRENFELL, family name of **Baron Grenfell.**

GRENFELL, 3rd Baron *cr* 1902; **Julian Pascoe Francis St Leger Grenfell;** Head of External Affairs, European Office, World Bank, since 1990; *b* 23 May 1935; *o s* of 2nd Baron Grenfell, CBE, TD, and of Elizabeth Sarah Polk, *o d* of late Captain Hon. Alfred Shaughnessy, Montreal, Canada; *S* father, 1976; *m* 1st, 1961, Loretta Maria (marr. diss. 1970), *e d* of Alfredo Reali, Florence, Italy; one *d*; 2nd, 1970, Gabrielle Katharina (marr. diss. 1987), *o d* of late Dr Ernst Raab, Berlin, Germany; two *d*; 3rd, 1987, Mrs Elisabeth Porter (*née* Scott), Georgetown, Washington, DC. *Educ:* Eton; King's Coll., Cambridge. BA (Hons), President of the Union, Cambridge, 1959. 2 Lieut, KRRC (60th Rifles), 1954–56; Captain, Queen's Royal Rifles, TA, 1963; Programme Asst, ATV Ltd, 1960–61; frequent appearances and occasional scripts, for ATV religious broadcasting and current affairs series, 1960–64. Film and TV adviser, Encyclopaedia Britannica Ltd, 1961–64. Joined World Bank, Washington, DC, 1965; Chief of Information and Public Affairs for World Bank Group in Europe, 1970; Dep. Dir, European Office of the World Bank, 1973; Special rep. of World Bank to UN, 1974–81; Special Advr, 1983–87, Sen. Advr, 1987–90, World Bank. *Publication:* (novel) Margot, 1984. *Recreations:* walking, diplomatic history. *Heir: cousin* Francis Pascoe John Grenfell [*b* 28 Feb. 1938; *m* 1977, Elizabeth Katharine, *d* of Hugh Kenyon]. *Address:* c/o World Bank, 66 avenue d'Iéna, 75116 Paris, France. *T:* (1) 40693012. *Clubs:* Travellers', Royal Green Jackets.

GRENFELL, Andrée, (Mrs David Milman); Chairman, Kelly Burrell & Jones, since 1988; Non-Executive Director, NAAFI, since 1981; *b* 14 Jan. 1940; *d* of Stephen Grenfell (writer) and Sybil Grenfell; *m* 1972, Roy Warden; two step *s*; *m* 1984, David Milman; two step *s*. *Educ:* privately. Graduate Diploma in Agric., 1989. Man. Dir, Elizabeth Arden Ltd, UK, 1974–76; Pres., Glemby Internat., UK and Europe, 1976–80; Sen. Vice Pres., Glemby Internat., USA, 1976–80. Director: Harvey Nichols Knightsbridge, 1972–74; Peter Robinson Ltd, 1968–72. Mem. Council, Inst. of Dirs, 1976; FBIM 1977. Mem., Cercle des Amis de la Veuve. Business Woman of the Year, FT, 1979. *Recreations:* riding, dressage, swimming, yoga. *Address:* Jacaranda, 24 Cranbrook Road, Rose Bay, Sydney, NSW 2029, Australia. *Fax:* 326 2289.

GRENFELL, Simon Pascoe; a Recorder of the Crown Court, since 1985; *b* 10 July 1942; *s* of Osborne Pascoe Grenfell and Margaret Grenfell; *m* 1974, Ruth De Jersey Harvard; one *s* three *d*. *Educ:* Fettes College; Emmanuel College, Cambridge (MA). Called to the Bar, Gray's Inn, 1965; practice on NE Circuit. *Recreations:* music, sailing, coarse gardening. *Address:* St John's House, Sharow, Ripon, North Yorks HG4 5BN. *T:* Ripon (0765) 5771. *Club:* Ripon.

GRENFELL-BAINES, Prof. Sir George, Kt 1978; OBE 1960; DL; FRIBA; FRTPI; consultant architect-planner; consultant to Building Design Partnership; *b* Preston, 30 April 1908; *s* of Ernest Charles Baines and Sarah Elizabeth (*née* Grenfell); *m* 1st, 1939, Dorothy Hodson (marr. diss. 1952); two *d*; 2nd, 1954, Milena Ruth Fleischmann; one *s* one *d*. *Educ:* Roebuck Street Council Sch.; Harris Coll., Preston; Manchester Univ. (DipTP). RIBA Dist Town Planning, 1963. Commenced architectural practice, 1937; founded: Grenfell Baines Gp, 1940; Building Design Partnership, a multi-disciplinary practice covering all aspects of built environment, 1959 (Partner/Chm.), retired 1974; The Design Teaching Practice, 1974, retired 1979. Prof. and Head of Dept of Architecture, Univ. of Sheffield, 1972–75, Emeritus, 1976. Lectr/Critic, 14 USA and Canadian univs, 1966; initiated own lecture tour USSR, visiting 19 cities, 1971; expert adviser: UNESCO Conf. Bldgs; Higher Educn, Chile, 1968; Conescal, Mexico City, 1973. RIBA: Mem. Council (nationally elected), 1952–70; Vice-Pres., 1967–69; Ext. Examr, 12 Schs of Architecture, 1953–70. Chm. of Cttees on Professional Practice, Town Planning, Gp Practice and Consortia; Architectural Competition Assessor 8 times; competition entrant, several awards: first place in 7 (one internat.); 18 premiums (four internat.). Hon. Fellow: Manchester Polytechnic, 1974; Lancashire Polytechnic, 1985; Hon. Vice-Pres., N Lancs Soc. Architects, 1977. Hon. Fellow, Amer. Inst. of Architects, 1982. Broadcaster, UK and Canada. Hon. DLitt Sheffield, 1981. DL Lancs, 1982. *Publications:* contribs to tech. jls. *Recreations:* brooding: on economics and alternative medicine; walking: on hills and by sea-shore. *Address:* 56 & 60 West Cliff, Preston, Lancs PR1 8HU. *T:* Preston (0772) 52131, 555824.

GRENIER, Rear-Adm. Peter Francis, (Frank), CB 1989; self-employed artist; Defence Advisor, House of Commons Defence Committee; *b* 27 Aug. 1934; *s* of late Dr F. W. H. Grenier and Mrs M. Grenier; *m* 1957, Jane Susan Bradshaw; two *s* one *d* (and one *s* decd). *Educ:* Montpelier School, Paignton; Blundell's School, Tiverton. Entered RN (Special Entry), 1952; Midshipman, Mediterranean Fleet, 1953; commissioned, 1955; joined Submarine service, 1956; 1st command (HMS Ambush), 1965; final command (HMS Liverpool), 1982; Chief of Staff to C-in-C Naval Home Command, 1985–87; FO Submarines, and Comdr Submarine Forces E Atlantic, 1987–89. Vice-Pres., Royal Naval FA, 1988–. Liveryman: Painter-Stainers' Co., 1984; Glass Sellers' Co., 1987. Governor, Blundell's Sch., 1986–. *Recreations:* family, sketching and painting, glass engraving, golf. *Clubs:* Army and Navy; West Wilts Golf.

GRENSIDE, Sir John (Peter), Kt 1983; CBE 1974; Senior Partner, Peat, Marwick, Mitchell & Co., Chartered Accountants, 1977–86; *b* 23 Jan. 1921; *s* of late Harold Cutcliffe Grenside and late Muriel Grenside; *m* 1946, Yvonne Thérèse Grau; one *s* one *d*. *Educ:* Rugby School. ACA 1948, FCA 1960. War Service, Royal Artillery, 1941–46 (Captain). Joined Peat, Marwick, Mitchell & Co., 1948, Partner, 1960, Senior Partner, 1977; Chm., Peat Marwick Internat., 1980–83. Inst. Chartered Accountants: Mem. Council, 1966–83; Chm. of Parliamentary and Law Cttee, 1972–73; Vice-Pres., 1973–74; Dep. Pres., 1974–75; Pres., 1975–76; Chm., Overseas Relations Cttee, 1976–78; UK Rep. on Internat. Accounting Standards Cttee, 1976–80. Jt Vice-Pres., Groupe d'Etudes des Experts Comptables de la CEE, 1972–75; Chm., Review Bd for Govt Contracts, 1983–86; Mem. Panel of Judges for Accountants' Award for Company Accounts, 1973–77. Director: Allied-Lyons plc, 1986–; Nomura Bank Internat. plc, 1987–. Master, Worshipful Co. of Chartered Accountants in England and Wales, 1987–88. *Publications:* various articles for UK and US accountancy jls. *Recreations:* tennis, bridge. *Address:* 51 Cadogan Lane, SW1X 9DT. *T:* 071–235 3372. *Clubs:* Pilgrims, MCC, All England Lawn Tennis, Hurlingham.

GRENVILLE; *see* Freeman-Grenville.

GRENVILLE, Prof. John Ashley Soames; Professor of Modern History, University of Birmingham, since 1969; *b* Berlin, 11 Jan. 1928; *m* 1st, 1960, Betty Anne Rosenberg (*d* 1974), New York; three *s*; 2nd, 1975, Patricia Carnie; one *d* one step *d*. *Educ:* Mistley Place and Orwell Park Prep. Sch.; Cambridge Techn. Sch.; corresp. courses; Birkbeck Coll.; LSE; Yale Univ. BA, PhD London; FRHistS. Postgrad. Schol., London Univ., 1951–53; Asst Lectr, subseq. Lectr, Nottingham Univ., 1953–64; Commonwealth Fund Fellow, 1958–59; Postdoctoral Fellow, Yale Univ., 1960–63; Reader in Modern History, Nottingham Univ., 1964–65; Prof. of Internat. History, Leeds Univ., 1965–69. Vis. Prof., Queen's Coll., NY City Univ., 1964, etc; Guest Professor, Univ. of Hamburg, 1980. Chm., British Univs History Film Consortium, 1968–71; Mem. Council: RHistS, 1971–73; List and Index Soc., 1966–71; Baeck Inst., London, 1981–. Consultant, American and European Bibliographical Centre, Oxford and California and Clio Press, 1960–; Dir of Film for the Historical Assoc., 1975–78; Historical Adviser, World History, ZDF, German Television, 1982–. Editor, Fontana History of War and Society, 1969–78. *Publications:* (with J. G. Fuller) The Coming of the Europeans, 1962; Lord Salisbury and Foreign Policy, 1964 (2nd edn 1970); (with G. B. Young) Politics, Strategy and American Diplomacy: studies in foreign policy 1873–1917, 1966 (2nd edn 1971); Documentary Films (with N. Pronay), The Munich Crisis, 1968; The End of Illusions: from Munich to Dunkirk, 1970; The Major International Treaties 1914–1973: a history and guide, 1974, enlarged edn in 2 vols, 1987; Europe Reshaped 1848–78, 1975; Nazi Germany, 1976; World History of the Twentieth Century I, 1900–1945, 1980; contrib. various learned jls. *Recreation:* listening to music. *Address:* University of Birmingham, PO Box 363, Birmingham B15 2TT. *Club:* Athenæum.

GRENVILLE-GREY, Wilfrid Ernest; International Development Director, Icewalk, 1988–89; *b* 27 May 1930; *s* of late Col Cecil Grenville-Grey, CBE and of Monica Grenville-Grey (*née* Morrison-Bell); *m* 1963, Edith Sibongile Dlamini (marr. diss. 1989), *d* of Rev. Jonathan Dlamini, Johannesburg; two *s* one *d*. *Educ:* Eton; Worcester College, Oxford (scholar; MA); Yale University (Henry Fellow, 1953–54). 2nd Lieut, KRRC, 1949–50. Overseas Civil Service, Nyasaland, 1956–59; Booker McConnell Ltd, 1960–63; Mindolo Ecumenical Foundn, Zambia, 1963–71 (Dir, 1966–71); Sec., Univ. Study Project on Foreign Investments in S Africa, 1971–72; Dir, Centre for Internat. Briefing, Farnham Castle, 1973–77; Internat. Defence and Aid Fund for Southern Africa, London and UN, 1978–83; Sec. for Public Affairs to Archbishop of Canterbury, 1984–87; British Dir, Global Forum of Spiritual and Parly Leaders on Human Survival, 1987–88. *Publications:* All in an African Lifetime, 1969; Sixty Marker Buoys for a Sixtieth Birthday (anthology), 1990. *Recreations:* gardening, apophthegms. *Club:* Travellers'.

GRENYER, Herbert Charles, FRICS; Vice-President, London Rent Assessment Panel, 1973–79; Deputy Chief Valuer, Board of Inland Revenue, 1968–73; *b* 22 Jan. 1913; *s* of Harry John and Daisy Elizabeth Grenyer (*née* De Maid); *m* 1940, Jean Gladwell Francis; one *s* one *d*. *Recreations:* golf, gardening, listening to music. *Address:* Old Rickford, Worplesdon, Surrey. *T:* Worplesdon (0483) 232173.

GRESHAM, Prof. (Geoffrey) Austin, TD 1966; FRCPath; Professor of Morbid Anatomy and Histopathology, Cambridge, since 1973; Fellow and President, Jesus College, Cambridge, since 1964; Home Office Pathologist, since 1968; *b* 1 Nov. 1924; *s* of Thomas Michael and Harriet Anne Gresham; *m* 1950, Gweneth Margery Leigh; three *s* two *d*. *Educ:* Grove Park Sch., Wrexham; Caius Coll., Cambridge (Tancred Student and Schol.; MA; ScD); King's Coll. Hosp., London (Burney Yeo Schol., Todd and Jelf Medallist; MB BChir, MD). Served RAMC, 1950–52, Lt-Col RAMC V, 1961. Demonstrator and Lectr in Pathology, Cambridge, 1953–62; Univ. Morbid Anatomist, 1962–73. Sec., Faculty Bd of Medicine, 1956–61; Consultant Mem., Cambridge Dist Management Team, 1974–84; Chairman: Cambridge Dist Medical Cttee, 1974–84; Medical Staff Leave Cttee, 1974–84; Cambridge Dist Ethical Cttee, 1974–84; Member: European Atherosclerosis Soc., 1959–; British Atherosclerosis Discussion Gp, 1965–. Roy Cameron Meml Lectr, RC Path, 1983. Mem. Bd of Governors, United Cambridge Hosps, 1972–74. Scientific Medal, Univ. of Tokyo, 1985. *Publications:* Introduction to Comparative Pathology, 1962; Biological Aspects of Occlusive Vascular Disease, 1964; Colour Atlas of General Pathology, 1971; Primate Atherosclerosis, 1976; Colour Atlas of Forensic Pathology, 1977; Post Mortem Procedures, 1979; Reversing Atherosclerosis, 1980; Arterial Pollution, 1981; Wounds and Wounding, 1987; contrib. chapters, and papers in many jls, about pathology. *Recreations:* gardening, playing organ, wine, silver, talking. *Address:* 18 Rutherford Road, Cambridge CB2 2HH. *T:* Cambridge (0223) 841326.

GRESWELL, Air Cdre Jeaffreson Herbert, CB 1967; CBE 1962 (OBE 1946); DSO 1944; DFC 1942; RAF, retired; *b* 28 July 1916; *s* of William Territt Greswell; *m* 1939, Gwyneth Alice Hayes; one *s* three *d*. *Educ:* Repton. Joined RAF, 1935, Pilot. Served War of 1939–45, in Coastal Command, Anti-Submarine No. 217 Sqdn, 1937–41; No. 172 Sqdn, 1942; OC No. 179 Sqdn, Gibraltar, 1943–44. Air Liaison Officer, Pacific Fleet, 1946–47; Staff of Joint Anti-Submarine Sch., 1949–52; Staff of Flying Coll., Manby, 1952–54; Planning Staff, Min. of Defence, 1954–57; OC, RAF Station Kinloss, 1957–59; Plans HQ, Coastal Comd, 1959–61; Standing Group Rep. to NATO Council, Paris, 1961–64; Commandant, Royal Observer Corps, 1964–68. Sqdn Ldr 1941; Wing Comdr 1942; Gp Capt. 1955; Air Cdre 1961. *Recreation:* croquet. *Address:* Red Cedars, Oddley Lane, Saunderton, Aylesbury, Bucks HP17 9NQ.

GRETTON, family name of **Baron Gretton.**

GRETTON, 4th Baron *cr* 1944, of Stapleford; **John Lysander Gretton;** *b* 17 April 1975; *s* of 3rd Baron Gretton and of Jennifer Ann, *o d* of Edmund Moore; *S* father, 1989. *Educ:* Shrewsbury. *Heir:* none. *Address:* Somerby House, Somerby, Melton Mowbray, Leics LE14 2PZ. *T:* Somerby (066477) 607.

GRETTON, Vice-Adm. Sir Peter (William), KCB 1963 (CB 1960); DSO 1942; OBE 1941; DSC 1936; MA; *b* 27 Aug. 1912; *s* of Major G. F. Gretton; *m* 1943, D. N. G. Du Vivier; three *s* one *d*. *Educ:* Roper's Preparatory Sch.; RNC, Dartmouth. Prize for Five First Class Certificates as Sub.-Lieut; Comdr 1942; Capt. 1948; Rear-Adm. 1958; Vice-

Adm. 1961. Served War of 1939–45 (despatches, OBE, DSO and two Bars). Senior Naval Mem. of Directing Staff of Imperial Defence Coll., April 1958–60; Flag Officer, Sea Training, 1960–61; a Lord Commissioner of the Admiralty, Dep. Chief of Naval Staff and Fifth Sea Lord, 1962–63, retd. Domestic Bursar, University Coll., Oxford, 1965–71, Senior Research Fellow, 1971–79. Vice-Pres., Royal Humane Soc. (Testimonial of Royal Humane Society, 1940). *Publications:* Convoy Escort Commander, 1964; Maritime Strategy: A Study of British Defence Problems, 1965; Former Naval Person: Churchill and the Navy, 1968; Crisis Convoy, 1974. *Address:* 29 Northmoor Road, Oxford OX2 6UR.

GREVE, Prof. John; Senior Research Fellow, University of York, since 1988; Professor of Social Policy and Administration, University of Leeds, 1974–87; *b* 23 Nov. 1927; *s* of Steffen A. and Ellen C. Greve; *m* (marr. diss. 1986); one *s* one *d*. *Educ:* elementary and secondary Schs in Cardiff; London Sch. of Economics (BSc(Econ)). Various jobs, incl. Merchant Navy, Youth Employment Service, and insurance, 1946–55; student, 1955–58; research work, then Univ. teaching, 1958–. Has worked in Norway at research institutes. Community Programmes Dept, Home Office, 1969–74; Prof. of Social Admin, Univ. of Southampton, 1969–74. Hon. Vis. Prof., Univ. of York, 1987–88. Mem., Royal Commn on Distribution of Income and Wealth, 1974–79; directed GLC Enquiry into Homelessness in London, 1985–86; Mem., Management Cttee E London Housing Assoc., 1988–. *Publications:* The Housing Problem, 1961 (and 1969); London's Homeless, 1964; Private Landlords in England, 1965; (with others) Comparative Social Administration, 1969, 2nd edn 1972; Housing, Planning and Change in Norway, 1970; Voluntary Housing in Scandinavia, 1971; (with others) Homelessness in London, 1971; Low Incomes in Sweden, 1978; (jtly) Sheltered Housing for the Elderly, 1983; Homelessness in Britain, 1990; various articles and papers, mainly on social problems, policies and administration, a few short stories. *Recreations:* walking, painting, listening to music, writing, good company. *Address:* c/o Institute for Research in the Social Sciences, University of York, York YO1 5DD.

GREVILLE, family name of **Earl of Warwick.**

GREVILLE, Brig. Phillip Jamieson, CBE 1972; freelance writer on defence, foreign affairs and Australian history; *b* 12 Sept. 1925; *s* of Col S. J. Greville, OBE and Mrs D. M. Greville; *m* 1948, June Patricia Anne Martin; two *s* one *d* (and one *s* one *d* decd). *Educ:* RMC Duntroon; Sydney Univ. (BEng). 2/8 Field Co., 2nd AIF, New Guinea, 1945; 1 RAR Korea (POW), 1951–53; Senior Instructor SME Casula, 1953–55; CRE, RMC Duntroon, 1955–58; Staff Coll., Camberley and Transportation Trng UK, 1959–61; Dir of Transportation AHQ, 1962–65; GSO1 1st Div., 1966; CE Eastern Comd, 1969–71; Comdr 1st Australian Logistic Support Group, Vietnam, 1971; Actg Comdr 1st Australian Task Force, Vietnam, 1971–72 (CBE); Dir of Transport, 1973–74; Dir Gen., Logistics, 1975–76; Comdr, Fourth Mil. District, 1977–80, retired. Adelaide Advertiser: Defence Writer, 1980–86; Pacific Defence Reporter, 1987–. Dir, Dominant Australia Pty, 1982–86. Nat. Pres., RUSI of Aust., 1983–. FIE(Aust), FCIT. *Publications:* A Short History of Victoria Barracks Paddington, 1969; The Central Organisation for War and its Application to Movements, 1975, Sapper series (RE Officers in Australia); The Army Portion of the National Estate, 1977; Why Australia Should Not Ratify the New Law of War, 1989. *Recreation:* golf. *Address:* 3 River Downs Crescent, River Downs, Qld 4210, Australia. *Clubs:* Adelaide; United Services (Brisbane).

GREWAL, Harnam Singh, CBE 1990; ED 1976; Secretary for the Civil Service, Government Secretariat, Hong Kong, 1987–90; *b* 5 Dec. 1937; *s* of late Joginder Singh Grewal and Ajaib Kaur; *m* 1973, Shiv Pal Kaur Chima; one *s* one *d*. *Educ:* Sir Ellie Kadoorie Sch.; King's Coll., Univ. of Hong Kong (BA Hons 1959; DipEd 1960); Pembroke Coll., Cambridge Univ. (BA 1962; MA 1974). Asst Educn Officer, Hong Kong, 1962; Admin Officer, 1964; Dist Officer, Tai Po, 1970; Dep. Dir of Urban Services, Hong Kong, 1976; Dep. Sec. for CS, 1980; Comr of Customs and Excise, 1984; Sec. for Transport, 1986. Royal Hong Kong Regt (The Volunteers), 1963–84, Major (retd); Hon. Col, 1987–90. *Recreations:* hockey, squash. *Address:* c/o Government Secretariat, Lower Albert Road, Hong Kong. *Club:* Royal Hong Kong Jockey (Hong Kong).

GREY, family name of **Earl Grey,** and of **Baron Grey of Naunton.**

GREY; *see* De Grey.

GREY, 6th Earl, *cr* 1806; **Richard Fleming George Charles Grey;** Bt 1746; Baron Grey, 1801; Viscount Howick, 1806; *b* 5 March 1939; *s* of late Albert Harry George Campbell Grey (Trooper, Canadian Army Tanks, who *d* on active service, 1942) and Vera Helen Louise Harding; *S* cousin, 1963; *m* 1st, 1966, Margaret Ann (marr. diss. 1974), *e d* of Henry Bradford, Ashburton; 2nd, 1974, Stephanie Caroline, *o d* of Donald Gaskell-Brown and formerly wife of Surg.-Comdr Neil Leicester Denham, RN. *Educ:* Hounslow Coll.; Hammersmith Coll. of Bldg (Quantity Surveying). Chm., Academy Beverage Co. Ltd. Pres., Assoc. of Cost and Executive Accountants, 1978. Mem., Liberal Party. *Recreations:* golf, sailing. *Heir:* *b* Philip Kent Grey [*b* 11 May 1940; *m* 1968, Ann Catherine, *y d* of Cecil Applegate, Kingsbridge, Devon; one *s* one *d*]. *Address:* House of Lords, SW1.

GREY OF CODNOR, 5th Baron *cr* 1397 (in abeyance 1496–1989); **Charles Legh Shuldham Cornwall-Legh,** CBE 1977 (OBE 1971); AE 1946; DL; *b* 10 Feb. 1903; *er s* of late Charles Henry George Cornwall Legh, of High Legh Hall, Cheshire, and late Geraldine Maud, *d* of Lt-Col Arthur James Shuldham, Royal Inniskilling Fusiliers; *S* to barony on termination of abeyance, 1989; *m* 1930, Dorothy, *er d* of late J. W. Scott, Seal, Sevenoaks; one *s* two *d*. Served 1939–45 with AAF and RAF. JP Cheshire, 1938–73; High Sheriff, 1939; DL, 1949; CC 1949–77. Chm., Cheshire Police Authority, 1957–74; Chm., New Cheshire CC, 1974–76 (Shadow Chm., 1973); Hon. Alderman, 1977. *Heir:* *s* Hon. Richard Henry Cornwall-Legh [*b* 14 May 1936; *m* 1974, Joanna Storm, *y d* of Sir Kenelm Cayley, 10th Bt; three *s* one *d*]. *Address:* High Legh House, Knutsford, Cheshire WA16 0QR. *T:* Lymm (092575) 2303. *Clubs:* Carlton, MCC.

GREY OF NAUNTON, Baron, *cr* 1968 (Life Peer); **Ralph Francis Alnwick Grey,** GCMG 1964 (KCMG 1959, CMG 1955); GCVO 1973 (KCVO 1956); OBE 1951; Chancellor, University of Ulster, since 1984 (New University of Ulster, 1980–84); Lord Prior of the Order of St John, 1988–91; *b* 15 April 1910; *o s* of late Francis Arthur Grey and Mary Wilkie Grey (*née* Spence); *m* 1944, Esmé, DStJ, *widow* of Pilot Officer Kenneth Kirkcaldie, RAFVR, and *d* of late A. V. Burcher and Florence Burcher, Remuera, Auckland, New Zealand; two *s* one *d*. *Educ:* Wellington Coll., NZ; Auckland Univ. Coll.; Pembroke Coll., Cambridge. LLB (NZ). Barrister and Solicitor of Supreme Court of New Zealand, 1932; Associate to Hon. Mr Justice Smith, 1932–36; Probationer, Colonial Administrative Service, 1936; Administrative Service, Nigeria: Cadet, 1937; Asst Financial Sec., 1949; Administrative Officer, Class I, 1951; Development Sec., 1952; Sec. to Governor-Gen. and Council of Ministers, 1954; Chief Sec. of the Federation, 1955–57; Dep. Gov.-Gen., 1957–59; Gov. and C-in-C, British Guiana, 1959–64; Governor and C-in-C of The Bahamas, 1964–68, and of the Turks and Caicos Islands, 1965–68; Governor of N Ireland, 1968–73. Dep. Chm., Commonwealth Development Corp., 1973–79, Chm. 1979–80. Pres., Chartered Inst. of Secretaries, NI, 1970–; Hon. Life Mem., NI Chamber of Commerce and Industry, 1970; Hon. Pres., Lisburn Chamber of Commerce, 1972–. Mem., Bristol Regional Bd, Lloyds Bank Ltd, 1973–81; Chm., Central Council, Royal Over-Seas League, 1976–81, Pres., 1981–. President: Scout Council, NI, 1968–; Britain–Nigeria Assoc., 1983–89; Overseas Service Pensioners' Assoc., 1983–. Mem. Council, Cheltenham Ladies' College, 1975–87. Hon. Bencher, Inn of Court of N Ireland. Hon. Freeman: City of Belfast, 1972; Lisburn, 1975; Freeman, City of London, 1980. Hon. LLD: QUB, 1971; NUI, 1985; Hon. DLitt NUU, 1980; Hon. DSc Ulster, 1985. GCStJ (Chancellor of the Order, 1987–88); Kt Comdr, Commandery of Ards, 1968–76. Bailiff of Egle, 1975–87. GC Merito Melitense, 1989. *Recreation:* golf. *Address:* Overbrook, Naunton, near Cheltenham, Glos. *T:* Guiting Power (0451) 850263. *Club:* Travellers'.

GREY, Alan Hartley; HM Diplomatic Service, retired; re-employed in Foreign and Commonwealth Office (as Staff Assessor), 1985–90; *b* 26 June 1925; *s* of William Hartley Grey and Gladys Grey; *m* 1950, Joan Robinson (*d* 1985); one *s* one *d*. *Educ:* Bootle Secondary Sch. for Boys. RAF, 1943–48; Foreign Service (Br. B), 1948; Tel Aviv, 1949; Tabriz and Khorramshahr, 1950–52; 3rd Sec., Belgrade, 1952–54; Vice-Consul, Dakar, 1954–57; Second Sec. (Commercial), Helsinki, 1958–61; FO, 1961–64; Second Sec. (Econ.), Paris, 1964–66; FO (later FCO), 1966–70; Consul (Commercial), Lille, 1970–74; FCO, 1974–82; Ambassador at Libreville, 1982–84. *Recreations:* gardening, bamboo pipe making and playing.

GREY, Sir Anthony (Dysart), 7th Bt *cr* 1814; former Inspector, Department of Industrial Affairs, Government of Western Australia; *b* 19 Oct. 1949; *s* of Edward Elton Grey (*d* 1962) (*o s* of 6th Bt) and of Nancy, *d* of late Francis John Meagher, Perth, WA; *S* grandfather, 1974; *m* 1970 (marr. diss.). *Educ:* Guildford Grammar School, WA. *Recreations:* fishing, painting. *Address:* 86 Ringsway Gardens, 38 Rings Park Road, W Perth, WA 6005, Australia.

GREY, Dame Beryl, DBE 1988 (CBE 1973); Prima Ballerina, Sadler's Wells Ballet, now Royal Ballet, 1942–57; Artistic Director, London Festival Ballet, 1968–79; *b* London, 11 June 1927; *d* of late Arthur Ernest Groom; *m* 1950, Dr Sven Gustav Svenson; one *s*. *Educ:* Dame Alice Owens Girls' Sch., London. Professional training: Madeline Sharp Sch., Sadler's Wells Sch. (Schol.), de Vos Sch. Début Sadler's Wells Co., 1941, with Ballerina rôles following same year in Les Sylphides, The Gods Go A'Begging, Le Lac des Cygnes, Act II, Comus. First full-length ballet, Le Lac des Cygnes on 15th birthday, 1942. Has appeared since in leading rôles of many ballets including: Sleeping Beauty, Giselle, Sylvia, Checkmate, Ballet Imperial, Donald of the Burthens, Homage, Birthday Offering, The Lady and the Fool. Film: The Black Swan (3 Dimensional Ballet Film), 1952. Left Royal Ballet, Covent Garden, Spring 1957, to become free-lance ballerina. Regular guest appearances with Royal Ballet at Covent Garden and on European, African, American and Far Eastern Tours. Guest Artist, London's Festival Ballet in London and abroad, 1958–64. First Western ballerina to appear with Bolshoi Ballet: Moscow, Leningrad, Kiev, Tiflis, 1957–58; First Western ballerina to dance with Chinese Ballet Co. in Peking and Shanghai, 1964. Engagements and tours abroad include: Central and S America, Mexico, Rhodesia and S Africa, Canada, NZ, Lebanon, Germany, Norway, Sweden, Denmark, Finland, Belgium, Holland, France, Switzerland, Italy, Portugal, Austria, Czechoslovakia, Poland, Rumania; Producer: Sleeping Beauty, 1967; Swan Lake, 1972, London Fest. Ballet; Giselle, Western Australia Ballet, 1984; Sleeping Beauty, Royal Swedish Co., Stockholm, 1985. Regular television and broadcasts in England and abroad; concert narrator. Dir-Gen., Arts Educational Trust, 1966–68. Pres., Dance Council of Wales, 1981–; Vice-Pres., Royal Acad. of Dancing, 1980– (Exec. Mem., 1982–89); Chm., Imperial Soc. of Teachers of Dancing, 1984–91 (Mem. Council, 1966); Trustee: London City Ballet, 1978–; Adeline Genée Theatre, 1982–90; Royal Ballet Benevolent Fund, 1982–; Dance Teachers Benevolent Fund, 1981–; Vice-President: Keep Fit Assoc., 1968–; British Fedn of Music Festivals, 1985. Governor: Dame Alice Owens Girls' Sch., London, 1960–77; Frances Mary Buss Foundn, 1963–72. FISTD 1960; FRSA 1989. Hon. DMus Leicester, 1970; Hon. DLitt City, 1974; Hon. DEd CNAA, 1989. *Publications:* Red Curtain Up, 1958; Through the Bamboo Curtain, 1965; My Favourite Ballet Stories, 1981. *Relevant publications:* biographical studies (by Gordon Anthony), 1952, (by Pigeon Crowle), 1952; Beryl Grey, Dancers of Today (by Hugh Fisher), 1955; Beryl Grey, a biography (by David Gillard), 1977. *Recreations:* music, painting, reading, swimming. *Address:* Fernhill, Priory Road, Forest Row, Sussex RH18 5JE. *T:* Forest Row (034282) 2539.

GREY, John Egerton, CB 1980; Clerk Assistant and Clerk of Public Bills, House of Lords, 1974–88; *b* 8 Feb. 1929; *s* of late John and Nancy Grey; *m* 1961, Patricia Hanna; two adopted *s*. *Educ:* Dragon Sch., Oxford; Blundell's; Brasenose Coll., Oxford. MA, BCL. Called to Bar, Inner Temple, 1954; practised at Chancery Bar, 1954–59. Clerk in Parliament Office, House of Lords, 1959–88. Adviser, Colchester CAB, 1989–. *Recreations:* gardening, boating. *Address:* 51 St Peters Road, West Mersea, Colchester, Essex CO5 8LL. *T:* West Mersea (0206) 383007. *Clubs:* Arts; West Mersea Yacht.

GREY, Maj.-Gen. John St John, CB 1987; Clerk, Worshipful Company of Pewterers; *b* 6 June 1934; *s* of late Major Donald John Grey, RM and Doris Mary Grey (*née* Beavan); *m* 1958, Elisabeth Ann (*née* Langley); one *s* one *d*. *Educ:* Christ's Hospital. rcds, ndc, psc(M), osc(US). FBIM. Commissioned 2/Lt 1952; Commando service, Malta, Egypt, Cyprus, 1955–58; Support Co. Comdr, 43 Cdo RM, 1962–64; Cruiser HMS Lion as OC RM, 1964–65; Instructor, Army Sch. of Infantry, 1967–69; Rifle Co. Comdr, 41 Cdo RM (incl. 1st emergency tour in W Belfast), 1969–70; with US Marine Corps, 1970–71; Commanded 45 Cdo Gp (incl. tours in N Ireland and Arctic Norway), 1976–78; Mil. Sec. and Col Ops/Plans, MoD, 1979–84; Maj.-Gen. RM Commando Forces, 1984–87; RM COS, 1987–88, retired. Governor, Internat. Inst. of Security. *Recreation:* sailing. *Address:* c/o Lloyds Bank, 4 Regent Street, Teignmouth, S Devon TQ14 8SL. *Clubs:* Army and Navy; Royal Naval Sailing Association (Portsmouth); Royal Marines Sailing.

GREY, Robin Douglas, QC 1979; a Recorder of the Crown Court, since 1979; *b* 23 May 1931; *s* of Dr Francis Temple Grey, MA, MB, and Eglantine Grey; *m* 1972, Berenice Anna Wheatley; one *s* one *d*. *Educ:* Summer Fields Prep. Sch., Oxford; Eastbourne Coll.; London Univ. (LLB Hons). Called to the Bar, Gray's Inn, 1957. Crown Counsel, Colonial Legal Service, Aden, 1959–63 (Actg Registrar Gen. and Actg Attorney Gen. for short periods); practising barrister, 1963–; Dep. Circuit Judge, 1977. Mem., British Acad. of Forensic Sciences. *Recreations:* tennis, golf, fishing. *Address:* Queen Elizabeth Building, Temple, EC4Y 9BS. *T:* 01–583 5766; Dun Cottage, The Marsh, Hungerford, Berks RG17 0SN. *T:* Hungerford (0488) 683578. *Club:* Hurlingham.

GREY, Wilfrid Ernest G.; *see* Grenville-Grey.

GREY EGERTON, Sir (Philip) John (Caledon), 15th Bt, *cr* 1617; *b* 19 Oct. 1920; *er s* of Sir Philip Grey Egerton, 14th Bt; *S* father, 1962; *m* 1st, 1952, Margaret Voase (*d* 1971) (who *m* 1941, Sqdn Ldr Robert A. Ullman, *d* 1943), *er d* of late Rowland Rank; 2nd, 1986, Frances Mary (who *m* 1941 Sqdn Ldr William Dudley Williams, DFC, *d* 1976), *y d* of late Col R. M. Rainey-Robinson. *Educ:* Eton. Served Welsh Guards, 1939–45.

Recreation: fishing. *Heir*: *b* Brian Balguy Le Belward Egerton, *b* 5 Feb. 1925. *Address*: Rylstone, Martinstown, Dorchester, Dorset DT2 9JR. *Club*: Marylebone Cricket (MCC).

GRIBBLE, Rev. Canon Arthur Stanley, MA; Canon Residentiary and Chancellor of Peterborough Cathedral, 1967–79; Canon Emeritus since 1979; *b* 18 Aug. 1904; *er s of* J. B. Gribble; *m* 1938, Edith Anne, *er d of* late Laurence Bailey; one *s. Educ*: Queens' Coll. and Westcott House, Cambridge (Burney Student, Univ. of Cambridge); Univ. of Heidelberg. Curate: St Mary, Windermere, 1930–33, Almondbury, 1933–36; Chaplain Sarum Theological Coll., 1936–38; Rector of Shepton Mallet, 1938–54. Examining Chaplain to Bp of Bath and Wells, 1947–54; Proctor in Convocation, diocese Bath and Wells, 1947–54; Rural Dean of Shepton Mallet, 1949–54; Prebendary of Wiveliscombe in Wells Cathedral, 1949–54; Principal, Queen's Coll., Birmingham, 1954–67; Recognised Lectr, Univ. of Birmingham, 1954–67. Hon. Canon, Birmingham Cathedral, 1954–67. Commissary for the Bishop of Kimberley and Kuruman, 1964–66. Examng Chaplain to Bishop of Peterborough, 1968–84. Visiting Lectr, Graduate Theological Union, Berkeley, USA, 1970. *Recreation*: mountaineering. *Address*: 2 Princes Road, Stamford, Lincs PE9 1QT. *T*: Stamford (0780) 55838.

GRIBBON, Edward John; Under Secretary, Board of Inland Revenue, since 1990; Director, Business Profits Division, since 1991; *b* 10 July 1943; *s of* Henry Derwent Gribbon and late Dorothy Gribbon (*née*Boyd); *m* 1968, Margaret Nanette Flanagan; one *s* two *d. Educ*: Coleraine Academical Instn; Univ. of London (LLB). FCA. Qualified as Chartered Accountant, 1965; joined Inland Revenue as HM Inspector of Taxes, 1966; HM Principal Inspector of Taxes, 1981; Dep. Dir of Operations, Compliance, 1989. *Recreations*: family, photography, local church. *Address*: Board of Inland Revenue, Somerset House, Strand, WC2R 1LB. *T*: 071–438 6774.

GRIBBON, Maj.-Gen. Nigel St George, OBE 1960; Director, Chancellor Insurance Co. Ltd, since 1986; Consultant, Chancellor Group Ltd, since 1987; *b* Feb. 1917; *s of* late Brig. W. H. Gribbon, CMG, CBE; *m* 1943, Rowan Mary MacLeish; two *s* one *d. Educ*: Rugby Sch.; Sandhurst. King's Own, 1937–42; active service, Iraq (Habbaniya), 1941 (wounded), Western Desert, 1942; GSO3 10th Indian Div., 1942; Staff Coll. Quetta, 1943; Bde Major, 1st Parachute Bde, 1946; served Palestine, 1946, Trieste, 1947–48, Malaysia, 1948–50; RAF Staff Coll., 1947; OC 5 King's Own, 1958–60; AMS WO, 1960–62; Comdr 161 Bde, 1963–65; Canadian Nat. Defence Coll., 1965–66; DMC MoD, 1966–67; ACOS NORTHAG, 1967–69; ACOS (Intelligence), SHAPE, 1970–72. Managing Director: Partnerplan Public Affairs Ltd, 1973–75; Sallingbury Ltd, 1977–85 (Chm., 1975–77 and 1984–85); Sallingbury Casey Ltd, 1986–87; Dir, Gatewood Engineers Ltd, 1976–83. Operational Planning Consultant, Venice-Simplon Orient Express, 1980–84. Canada-UK Chamber of Commerce: Mem. Council, 1979–; Chm., Trade Cttee, 1980; Pres., 1981; Chm., Jt Cttee, 1982–. Chm. and Hd of Secretariat, European Channel Tunnel Gp Public Affairs Cttee, 1980–85; Chairman: UK Falkland Islands Trust, 1982–; Forces Financial Services, 1983–85; SHAPE Assoc. (UK Chapter), 1984–. Member: Council, British Atlantic Cttee, 1975– (Mem. Exec. Cttee, 1983–88); Cttee, Amer. European Atlantic Cttee, 1985–; Eur. Atlantic Gp, 1974–87; Council, Mouvement Européen Français (Londres), 1979–87; Council, Wyndham Place Trust, 1979–82; Canadian War Meml Foundn, 1988–. Vice-Pres., King's Own Affairs, 1974–88. Radio commentator and lectr on public affairs. Freeman, City of London; Liveryman, Worshipful Co. of Shipwrights. *Recreations*: sailing, ski-ing, swimming. *Address*: 99 Pump Street, Orford, Woodbridge, Suffolk IP12 2LX. *T*: Orford (0394) 450413. *Clubs*: Army and Navy (Mem., Gen. and Finance Cttees, 1989–), Canada; Little Ship (Rear Commodore Training, 1978–80); Royal Yachting Association; Army Sailing Association.

GRIDLEY, family name of **Baron Gridley.**

GRIDLEY, 2nd Baron, *cr* 1955; **Arnold Hudson Gridley;** *b* 26 May 1906; *er* surv. *s of* 1st Baron Gridley, KBE, Culwood, Lye Green, Chesham, Bucks; *S* father, 1965; *m* 1948, Edna Lesley, *d of* late Richard Wheen of Shanghai, China; one *s* three *d. Educ*: Oundle. Colonial Civil Service, Malaya, 1928–57; interned during Japanese occupation in Changi Gaol, Singapore, 1941–45; returned to duty, 1946; Dep.-Comptroller of Customs and Excise, Malaya, 1956, retired 1957. Mem. Council and Exec. Cttee, Overseas Service Pensioners Assoc., 1961–; Govt Trustee, Far East (POW and Internee) Fund, 1971–; with Parly Delegn to BAOR, 1976; visited and toured Rhodesia during Lancaster House Conf., speaking to local civil servants on the future of their pensions, 1979; special duty in Singapore and Malaya during visit of HRH the Duke of Kent, 1985. Dir, New Homes Bldg Soc., 1963 (incorp. into Britannia Bldg Soc., 1970); Chm., Centralised Audio Systems Ltd, 1971–86, Life Pres., 1987; Chm. and Dir, Family Insurance Advisory Services, 1981–. Mem., Somerset CC Rating Appeals Tribunal, 1970–73; Political Adviser to Peoples' Trust for Endangered Species, 1979–. Chm., Board of Governors, Hall Sch., Bratton Seymour, Som, 1970–76. *Heir*: *s* Hon. Richard David Arnold Gridley [*b* 22 Aug. 1956; *m* 1983, Suzanne Elizabeth Ripper; one *s* one *d*]. *Address*: Coneygore, Stoke Trister, Wincanton, Somerset BA9 9PG. *T*: Wincanton (0963) 32209. *Club*: Royal Over-Seas League.

GRIER, Patrick Arthur, OBE 1963; HM Diplomatic Service, retired; *b* 2 Dec. 1918; *s of* late Very Rev. R. M. Grier, Provost of St Ninian's Cath., Perth, and Mrs E. M. Grier; *m* 1946, Anna Fraembs, *y d of* Hüttendirektor H. Fraembs, Rasselstein, Neuwied, Germany; one *d. Educ*: Lancing; King's Coll., Cambridge (MA 1946). Served War of 1939–45 with RA and Indian Mountain Artillery, NW Frontier of India and Burma (Major). Kreis Resident Officer of Mönchen-Gladbach, 1946–47; Colonial Administrative Service, N Nigeria, 1947, later HMOCS; Clerk to Exec. Council, Kaduna, 1953–55; W African Inter-territorial Secretariat, Accra, 1955–57; Principal Asst Sec. to Governor of N Nigeria, 1957–59; Dep. Sec. to Premier, 1959–63; retired from HMOCS, 1963. CRO, 1963–64; First Sec., Canberra, 1964–66; Head of Chancery, Port of Spain, 1966–69; Dep. UK Permanent Rep. to Council of Europe, Strasbourg, 1969–74; Counsellor and Head of Chancery, Berne, 1974–78. *Recreations*: tennis, ski-ing. *Address*: Buffalo Cottage, Wootton, New Milton, Hants. *T*: New Milton (0425) 618398. *Club*: Commonwealth Trust.

GRIERSON, Sir Michael (John Bewes), 12th Bt *cr* 1685 (NS), of Lag, Dumfriesshire; retired; *b* 24 July 1921; *s of* Lt-Col Alexander George William Grierson, RM retd (*d* 1951) (2nd *s of* 9th Bt) and Violet Ethel (*d* 1980), *d of* Lt-Col Arthur Edward Bewes, CMG; *S* cousin, 1987; *m* 1971, Valerie Anne, *d of* late Russell Wright, Gidea Park, Essex; one *d. Educ*: Warden House School, Deal; St Edmund's School, Canterbury. Served War, RAF, 1941–46; subsequent career in civil engineering and local government, retired, 1986. *Recreations*: gardening, motoring, plane spotting, woodwork, photography. *Heir*: none. *Address*: 40c Palace Road, Streatham Hill, SW2 3NJ.

GRIERSON, Prof. Philip, MA, LittD; FBA 1958; FSA; Fellow, since 1935, Librarian, 1944–69, and President, 1966–76, Gonville and Caius College, Cambridge; Professor of Numismatics, University of Cambridge, 1971–78, now Emeritus; Professor of Numismatics and the History of Coinage, University of Brussels, 1948–81; Hon. Keeper of the Coins, Fitzwilliam Museum, Cambridge, since 1949; Adviser in Byzantine Numismatics to the Dumbarton Oaks Library and Collections, Harvard University, at Washington, USA, since 1955; *b* 15 Nov. 1910; *s of* Philip Henry Grierson and Roberta Ellen Jane Pope. *Educ*: Marlborough Coll.; Gonville and Caius Coll., Cambridge (MA 1936, LittD 1971). University Lectr in History, Cambridge, 1945–59; Reader in Medieval Numismatics, Cambridge, 1959–71. Literary Dir of Royal Historical Society, 1945–55; Ford's Lectr in History, University of Oxford, 1956–57. Pres. Royal Numismatic Society, 1961–66. Corresp. Fellow, Mediaeval Acad. of America, 1972; Corresp. Mem., Koninklijke Vlaamse Acad., 1955; Assoc. Mem., Acad. Royale de Belgique, 1968. Hon. LittD: Ghent, 1958; Leeds, 1978. *Publications*: les Annales de Saint-Pierre de Gand, 1937; Books on Soviet Russia, 1917–42, 1943; Sylloge of Coins of the British Isles, Vol. I (Fitzwilliam Museum: Early British and Anglo-Saxon Coins), 1958; Bibliographie numismatique, 1966, 2nd edn 1979; English Linear Measures: a study in origins, 1973; (with A. R. Bellinger) Catalogue of the Byzantine Coins in the Dumbarton Oaks Collection and in the Whittemore Collection, vols 1, 2, 3, 1966–73; Numismatics, 1975; Monnaies du Moyen Age, 1976; The Origins of Money, 1977; Les monnaies, 1977; Dark Age Numismatics, 1979; Later Medieval Numismatics, 1979; Byzantine Coins, 1982; (with M. Blackburn) Medieval European Coinage, vol. 1 The Early Middle Ages, 1986; The Coins of Medieval Europe, 1991; (with M. Mays) Catalogue of Late Roman Coins in the Dumbarton Oaks Collection and in the Whittemore Collection, 1991; trans. F. L. Ganshof, Feudalism, 1952; editor: C. W. Previté-Orton, The Shorter Cambridge Medieval History, 1952; H. E. Ives, The Venetian Gold Ducat and its Imitations, 1954; Studies in Italian History presented to Miss E. M. Jamison, 1956; (with U. Westermark) O. Mørkholm, Early Hellenistic Coins, 1991; Studies in Numismatic Method, presented to Philip Grierson (Festschrift), 1983. *Recreations*: squash racquets, science fiction. *Address*: Gonville and Caius College, Cambridge CB2 1TA. *T*: Cambridge (0223) 332450.

GRIERSON, Sir Ronald (Hugh), Kt 1990; Vice-Chairman, General Electric Co., since 1983 (Director, since 1968); Director: W. R. Grace & Co., since 1987, and other cos; *b* Nürnberg, Bavaria, 1921; *s of* Mr and Mrs E. J. Griessmann (name changed by Deed Poll in 1943); *m* 1966, (Elizabeth) Heather, Viscountess Bearsted, *er d of* Mr and Mrs G. Firmston-Williams; one *s. Educ*: Realgymnasium, Nürnberg; Lycée Pasteur, Paris; Highgate Sch., London; Balliol Coll., Oxford. Served War 1939–45 (despatches). Staff Mem., The Economist, 1947–48; S. G. Warburg & Co., 1948–68 (Dir, 1958–68 and 1980–86); Dep. Chm. and Man. Dir, IRC, 1966–67; Chm., Orion Bank, 1971–73; Dir-Gen., Industrial and Technological Affairs, EEC, 1973–74. Board Member: BAC, 1970–71; Internat. Computers, 1974–76; Davy Internat., 1969–73; Nat. Bus Co., 1984–86; RJR Nabisco Inc. (formerly R. J. Reynolds), 1977–89; Chrysler Corp., 1983–91. Chm., South Bank Bd, then South Bank Centre, 1985–90. Mem., Bd of Trustees, Phillips Collection, Washington, 1980–. Chm., EORTC Foundation, 1975–; Member: Harvard Coll. Faculty, 1964–65; CNAA, 1978–84; Arts Council of GB, 1984–88; Ernst von Siemens Foundn, 1977–; Bd of Visitors, N Carolina Sch. of the Arts, 1984–90; European Arts Foundn, 1987–88. Hon. Mem., Philharmonia Orch., 1981–. Hon. Dr of Law, Grove City Coll., USA, 1986. Comdr, Order of Merit of the Republic of Italy, 1980. *Address*: General Electric Company, 1 Stanhope Gate, W1A 1EH.

GRIESE, Sister Carol, CHN; Religious Sister since 1970; Member, Crown Appointments Commission, since 1990; *b* 26 Sept. 1945; *d of* Gwendoline and Donald Griese. *Educ*: Merrywood Grammar School, Bristol; King's College London (BA Hons English 1968); Clare Hall, Cambridge (Cert. Theol. 1970). Member, Community of the Holy Name, 1970–; Lay Rep. of Religious in General Synod, 1980–. *Recreations*: reading, walking. *Address*: Convent of the Holy Name, Morley Road, Oakwood, Derby DE2 4QZ. *T*: Derby (0332) 671716; Lee Abbey, Lynton, Devon EX35 6JJ.

GRIEVE, Hon. Lord; William Robertson Grieve, VRD 1958; a Senator of the College of Justice in Scotland, 1972–88; *b* 21 Oct. 1917; *o s of* late William Robertson Grieve (killed in action 1917) and late Mrs Grieve; *m* 1947, Lorna St John (*d* 1989), *y d of* late Engineer Rear-Adm. E. P. St J. Benn, CB; one *s* one *d. Educ*: Glasgow Academy; Sedbergh; Glasgow Univ. MA 1939, LLB 1946 (Glasgow); Pres. Glasgow Univ. Union, 1938–39. John Clark (Mile-end) Scholar, 1939. RNVR: Sub-Lt 1939; Lieut 1942; Lt-Comdr 1950; served with RN, 1939–46. Admitted Mem. of Faculty of Advocates, 1947; QC (Scot.) 1957. Junior Counsel in Scotland to Bd of Inland Revenue, 1952–57. Advocate-Depute (Home), 1962–64; Sheriff-Principal of Renfrew and Argyll, 1964–72; Procurator of the Church of Scotland, 1969–72; a Judge of the Courts of Appeal of Jersey and Guernsey, 1971. Independent Chm., Fish Farming Adv. Cttee, 1989. Chm. of Governors, Fettes Trust, 1978–86. *Recreations*: golf, painting. *Address*: 20 Belgrave Crescent, Edinburgh EH4 3AJ. *T*: 031–332 7500. *Clubs*: New (Edinburgh); Hon. Company of Edinburgh Golfers; West Sussex Golf.

GRIEVE, Percy; *see* Grieve, W. P.

GRIEVE, Prof. Sir Robert, Kt 1969; MA, FRSE, FRTPI, MICE; Professor Emeritus, University of Glasgow; Hon. Professor, Heriot-Watt University, since 1986; *b* 11 Dec. 1910; *s of* Peter Grieve and Catherine Boyle; *m* 1933, Mary Lavinia Broughton Blackburn; two *s* two *d. Educ*: N. Kelvinside Sch., Glasgow; Royal Coll. of Science and Technology (now Univ. of Strathclyde), Glasgow. Trng and qual. as Civil Engr, eventually Planner. Local Govt posts, 1927–44; preparation of Clyde Valley Regional Plan, 1944–46; Civil Service, 1946–54; Chief Planner, Scottish Office, 1960–64. Prof. of Town and Regional Planning, Glasgow Univ., 1964–74; retired from Chair, 1974. Chairman: Highlands and Islands Develt Bd, 1965–70; Highlands and Islands Development Consultative Council, 1978–86; Royal Fine Art Commn for Scotland, 1978–83; President: Scottish Countryside Rangers Assoc.; Saltire Soc., 1991; Hon. President: Scottish Rights of Way Soc.; New Glasgow Soc.; Inverness Civic Trust; Stewartry Mountaineering Club; Scottish Branch, RTPI (Vice-Pres., 1971–73); Friends of Loch Lomond. Former President: Scottish Mountaineering Council; Scottish Mountaineering Club; Former Vice-Pres., Internat. Soc. of Town and Regional Planners. Hon. Vice-Pres., Scottish Youth Hostels Assoc. Gold Medal, RTPI, 1974. Hon. DLitt Heriot-Watt; Hon. LLD Strathclyde, 1984; Dr *hc* Edinburgh, 1985. Hon. FRIAS; Hon. FRSGS 1989. Lord Provost's Award, Glasgow, 1989. *Publications*: part-author and collaborator in several major professional reports and books; many papers and articles in professional and technical jls. *Recreations*: mountains, poetry. *Address*: 5 Rothesay Terrace, Edinburgh EH3 7RY. *Club*: Scottish Arts (Edinburgh).

GRIEVE, William Percival, (W. Percy Grieve), QC 1962; a Recorder, 1972–87 (Recorder of Northampton, 1965–71); *b* 25 March 1915; *o s of* 2nd Lieut W. P. Grieve, the Middlesex Regt (killed in action, Ypres, Feb. 1915), Rockcliffe, Dalbeattie, and Dorothy Marie Hartley (she *m* 2nd, 1925, Dr W. Cunningham, Monkseaton); *m* 1949, Evelyn Raymonde Louise (*d* 1991), *y d of* late Comdt Hubert Mijouain, Paris, and of Liliane, *e d of* late Sir George Roberts, 1st and last Bt; one *s* (and one *s* one *d* decd). *Educ*: privately; Trinity Hall, Cambridge (Exhibitioner, 1933); Lord Kitchener Nat. Memorial Schol., 1934; MA 1940. Called to Bar, Middle Temple, 1938 (Harmsworth Law Schol., 1937); Bencher, 1969; Master Reader, 1985. Joined Midland Circuit, 1939. Called to the Hong Kong Bar, 1960. Commissioned the Middlesex Regt, 1939; Liaison Officer, French Mil. Censorship, Paris, 1939–40; Min. of Information, 1940–41; HQ Fighting France, 1941–43; Staff Capt. and Exec. Officer, SHAEF Mission to Luxembourg, 1944; Major and GSO2 Brit. Mil. Mission to Luxembourg, 1945; DAAG, BAOR, 1946. Asst Recorder of Leicester, 1956–65; Dep. Chm., Co. of Lincoln (Parts of Holland) QS, 1962–71. Mem. Mental Health Review Tribunal, Sheffield Region, 1960–64. Has served on Gen. Council of the Bar. Contested (C) Lincoln By-election, 1962; MP (C) Solihull Div., Warks, 1964–83. Member: House of Commons Select Cttees on Race Relations and Immigration, 1968–70, on Members' Interests, 1979–83; UK Delegn, Council of Europe (Chm., Legal Affairs Cttee) and WEU (Chm. Procedure Cttee), 1969–83; Hon. Vice-Pres., Franco-British Parly Relations Cttee, 1975–83 (Chm., 1970–75); Chm., Luxembourg Soc., 1975; Chm., Parly Anglo Benelux Group, 1979–83; Hon. Associate: Council of Europe, 1989; WEU, 1990. Pres., Fulham Cons. Assoc., 1982–. Member: Council, Officers' Assoc., 1969–88; Council of Justice, 1971–; Council, Franco-British Soc., 1970; Council, Alliance Française, 1974. Officier avec Couronne, Order of Adolphe of Nassau; Chevalier, Order of Couronne de Chêne and Croix de Guerre avec Palmes (Luxembourg), 1945–46; Bronze Star (USA), 1945; Chevalier de la Légion d'Honneur, 1974; Commandeur de l'Ordre de Mérite (Luxembourg), 1976; Officer de l'ordre de la Couronne (Belgium), 1980; Silver Medal, Council of Europe, 1983; Commandeur de l'Ordre de la Couronne de Chêne (Luxembourg), 1990. *Recreations:* swimming, travel, the theatre. *Address:* 1 King's Bench Walk, Temple, EC4Y 7DB. *T:* 071–353 8436; 32 Gunterstone Road, W14 9BU. *T:* 071–603 0376. *Clubs:* Carlton, Hurlingham, Royal Automobile, Special Forces.

GRIEVE, William Robertson; *see* Grieve, Hon. Lord.

GRIEVES, David, CBE 1988; Director, British Steel plc (formerly British Steel Corporation), since 1983; Chairman, British Steel Distribution, since 1989; *b* 10 Jan. 1933; *s* of Joseph and Isabel Grieves; *m* 1960, Evelyn Muriel Attwater; two *s. Educ:* Durham Univ. BSc. PhD. Graduate apprentice, United Steel cos, 1957; Labour Manager, Appleby Frodingham Steel Co., 1962; British Steel Corporation: Manager, Industrial Relations, S Wales Group, 1967; Gen. Man., Stocksbridge and Tinsley Park Works, 1971; Personnel Dir, Special Steels Div., 1973; Dir, Indust. Relations, 1975; Man. Dir, Personnel and Social Policy, 1977; Dep. Chm. BSC Industry plc, 1980. Mem. (non-exec), Post Office, 1990–. Mem., Employment Appeal Tribunal, 1983. *Address:* 4 Oak Way, West Common, Harpenden, Herts AL5 2NT. *T:* Harpenden (0582) 767425.

GRIEVES, John Kerr; Senior Partner, Freshfields, since 1990; *b* 7 Nov. 1935; *s* of Thomas and Nancy Grieves; *m* 1961, Ann Gorrell (*née* Harris); one *s* one *d. Educ:* King's Sch., Worcester; Keble Coll., Oxford (MA Law); Harvard Business Sch. (AMP). Articled clerk and asst solicitor, Pinsent & Co., Birmingham, 1958–61; joined Freshfields, 1963; Partner, 1964–; Deptl Man. Partner, Company Dept, 1974–78; Man. Partner, 1979–85; Head, Corporate Finance Group, 1985–89. *Recreations:* the arts (especially music), running. *Address:* 7 Putney Park Avenue, SW15 5QN. *T:* 081–876 1207. *Clubs:* Athenæum, Roehampton.

GRIEW, Prof. Stephen, PhD; Dean, Atkinson College, York University, Toronto, since 1987; *b* 13 Sept. 1928; *e s* of late Harry and Sylvia Griew, London, England; *m* 1st, 1955, Jane le Geyt Johnson (marr. diss.); one *s* two *d* (and one *s* decd); 2nd, 1977, Eva Margareta Ursula, *d* of late Dr and Fru Johannes Ramberg, Stockholm, Sweden; one *d* and one step *s. Educ:* Univ. of London (BSc, Dip Psych); Univ. of Bristol (PhD). Vocational Officer, Min. of Labour, 1951–55; Univ. of Bristol: Research Worker, 1955–59; Lectr, 1959–63; Kenneth Craik Research Award, St John's Coll., Cambridge, 1960; Prof. of Psychology: Univ. of Otago, Dunedin, NZ, 1964–68 (Dean, Faculty of Science, 1967–68); Univ. of Dundee, 1968–72; Vice-Chancellor, Murdoch Univ., Perth, WA, 1972–77; Chm., Dept of Behavioural Science, Faculty of Medicine, Univ. of Toronto, 1977–80; Pres., 1980–85, University Prof., 1986–87, Athabasca Univ. Consultant, OECD, Paris, 1963–64; Expert, ILO, 1966–67; Mem., Social Commn of Rehabilitation Internat., 1967–75; Consultant, Dept of Employment, 1970–72; Vis. Prof., Univ. of Western Ont., London, Canada, 1970 and 1971; Vis. Fellow, Wolfson Coll., Cambridge, 1985–86. Vice-Pres., Australian Council on the Ageing, 1975–76. FBPsS 1960; Fellow, Gerontological Soc. (USA), 1969. *Publications:* handbooks and monographs on ageing and vocational rehabilitation, and articles in Jl of Gerontology and various psychological jls. *Recreations:* music, travel. *Address:* Atkinson College, York University, 4700 Keele Street, North York, Ont M3J 1P3, Canada.

GRIFFIN, Adm. Sir Anthony (Templer Frederick Griffith), GCB 1975 (KCB 1971; CB 1967); President, Royal Institution of Naval Architects, 1981–84; Chairman, British Shipbuilders, 1977–80 (Chairman-designate, Dec. 1975); *b* Peshawar, 24 Nov. 1920; *s* of late Col F. M. G. Griffin, MC, and B. A. B. Griffin (*née* Down); *m* 1943, Rosemary Ann Hickling; two *s* one *d. Educ:* RN Coll., Dartmouth. Joined RN, 1934; to sea as Midshipman, 1939; War Service in E Indies, Mediterranean, Atlantic, N Russia and Far East; specialised in navigation, 1944; Staff Coll., 1952; Imp. Defence Coll., 1963; comd HMS Ark Royal, 1964–65; Naval Secretary, 1966; Asst Chief of Naval Staff (Warfare), 1966–68; Flag Officer, Second-in-Command, Far East Fleet, 1968–69; Flag Officer, Plymouth, Comdr Central Sub Area, Eastern Atlantic, and Comdr Plymouth Sub Area, Channel, 1969–71; Adm. Supt Devonport, 1970–71; Controller of the Navy, 1971–75. Rear-Adm. of the UK, 1986–88, Vice-Adm., 1988–90. Comdr 1951; Capt. 1956; Rear-Adm. 1966; Vice-Adm. 1968; Adm., 1971. Vice-Pres., Wellington College, 1980–90; Chm., British Maritime League, 1982–87. Hon. FRINA 1984. *Recreation:* sailing. *Address:* Moat Cottage, The Drive, Bosham, West Sussex PO18 8JG. *T:* Bosham (0243) 573373. *Clubs:* Army and Navy, Pratt's.
See also S. C. Finch.

GRIFFIN, Major Sir (Arthur) John (Stewart), KCVO 1990 (CVO 1974; MVO 1967); Press Secretary to HM Queen Elizabeth the Queen Mother, 1956–91; *b* 1924; *s* of Arthur Wilfrid Michael Stewart Griffin and Florence May Griffin; *m* 1962, Henrietta Montagu-Douglas-Scott; two *s. Educ:* Harrow School. Regular Army Officer, The Queen's Bays, later The Queen's Dragoon Guards, 1942–58. *Recreations:* cricket, fishing, shooting. *Address:* Barton's Cottage, Bushy Park, Teddington, Middx TW11 0EA. *Clubs:* Cavalry and Guards, MCC.

GRIFFIN, Sir (Charles) David, Kt 1974; CBE 1972; Chairman: Icle Finance Corporation Ltd, since 1986; Mirvac Funds Ltd, since 1983; *b* 8 July 1915; *s* of Eric Furnival Griffin and Nellie Clarendon Griffin (*née* Devenish-Meares); *m* 1941, Jean Falconer Whyte; two *s. Educ:* Cranbrook Sch., Sydney; Univ. of Sydney (LLB and Golf Blue). 8th Aust. Div. 2nd AIF, 1940–45; POW Changi, Singapore, 1942–45. Associate to Sir Dudley Williams and Mem. Bar NSW, 1946–49; Solicitor, Sydney, 1949–64. Alderman, Sydney City Council, 1962–74, Chm. Finance Cttee, 1969–72; Lord Mayor of Sydney, 1972–73. Hon. Chm., Nabalco Pty Ltd, 1980–. Mem. Council, Royal Agricl Soc.; Mem. Nat. Council, Scout Assoc. of Australia (Life Councillor, NSW Br). *Publications:* The Happiness Box (for children); The Will of the People; sundry speeches and short stories. *Recreations:* golf, fly-fishing. *Address:* Mirvac Trust Building, Suite 409, 185 Elizabeth Street, Sydney, NSW 2000, Australia. *Clubs:* Union (Sydney); Royal Sydney Golf, Pine Valley Golf (NJ, USA).

GRIFFIN, Col Edgar Allen, CMG 1965; OBE (mil.) 1943; ED 1945; Regional Director, Northern Region (Arras, France), Commonwealth War Graves Commission, 1969–72; *b* 18 Jan. 1907; 3rd *s* of Gerald Francis and Isabella Margaret Griffin; *m* 1936, Alethea Mary Byrne; two *s* two *d.* Retired from AMF, 1947; Australian Govt Nominee to Staff of War Graves Commn, 1947; Chief Admin. Officer, Eastern Dist (Cairo), 1947–54; UK Dist (London), 1954–58; Regional Dir, Southern Region (Rome), 1958–69. *Address:* 9 Arley Close, Plas Newton, Chester CH2 1NW.

GRIFFIN, Jasper, FBA 1986; Reader in Classical Literature, Oxford University, since 1990; Fellow and Tutor in Classics, Balliol College, Oxford, since 1963; *b* 29 May 1937; *s* of Frederick William Griffin and Constance Irene Griffin (*née* Cordwell); *m* 1960, Miriam Tamara Dressler; three *d. Educ:* Christ's Hospital; Balliol College, Oxford (1st Cl. Hon. Mods 1958; 1st Cl. Lit. Hum. 1960; Hertford Scholar 1958; Ireland Scholar 1958). Jackson Fellow, Harvard Univ., 1960–61; Dyson Research Fellow, Balliol Coll., Oxford, 1961–63. T. S. Eliot Meml Lectr, Univ. of Kent at Canterbury, 1984. *Publications:* Homer on Life and Death, 1980; Homer, 1980; Snobs, 1982; Latin Poets and Roman Life, 1985; The Mirror of Myth, 1986; (ed with J. Boardman and O. Murray) The Oxford History of the Classical World, 1986; Virgil, 1986; Homer, The Odyssey, 1987. *Address:* Balliol College, Oxford OX1 3BJ. *T:* Oxford (0865) 77782.

GRIFFIN, Sir John; *see* Griffin, Sir A. J. S.

GRIFFIN, Sir John Bowes, Kt 1955; QC 1938; *b* 19 April 1903; *o s* of late Sir Charles Griffin; *m* 1st, Eva Orrell (*d* 1977), 2nd *d* of late John Mellifont Walsh, Wexford; two *d*; 2nd, 1984, Margaret Guthrie (*née* Sinclair) (*d* 1991), *widow* of H. F. Lever. *Educ:* Clongowes; Dublin Univ. (MA, LLD, First Cl. Moderatorship, Gold Medallist); Cambridge. Barrister-at-Law, Inner Temple, 1926. Administrative Officer, Uganda, 1927; Asst District Officer, 1929; Registrar, High Court, 1929; Crown Counsel, 1933; Actg Solicitor-Gen. and Attorney-Gen., various periods; Attorney-Gen., Bahamas, 1936 (Acting Governor and Acting Chief Justice, various periods); Solicitor-Gen., Palestine, 1939, Acting Attorney-Gen., various periods; Attorney-Gen., Hong Kong, 1946; Chief Justice of Uganda, 1952–56. Secretary: East Africa Law Officers Conference, 1933; Commission of Enquiry Admin. of Justice, East Africa, 1933; Chm. Prisons Enquiry, Bahamas, 1936; miscellaneous Bds and Cttees; Chairman: Tel Aviv Municipal Commn of Enquiry, Palestine, 1942; Review Cttees, Detainees (Defence and Emergency Regulations), Palestine, 1940–46. Retired, Dec. 1956; Actg Chief Justice, N Rhodesia, 1957; Chm. Commn of Enquiry Gwenbe Valley Disturbances, N Rhodesia, 1958; Speaker, Legislative Council, Uganda, 1958–62; Speaker, Uganda National Assembly, 1962–63, retd. Chairman: Public Service Commissions, 1963 and Constitutional Council, 1964, N Rhodesia; retd 1965. CStJ 1960. *Publications:* Revised Edn of Laws (Uganda), 1935; (joint) Hong Kong, 1950. *Address:* 1 Marina Court, Tigne Sea Front, Sliema, Malta. *Clubs:* East India; Union (Malta).
See also M. H. M. Reid.

GRIFFIN, Dr John Parry, BSc, PhD, MB, BS; FRCP, FRCPath; Director, Association of the British Pharmaceutical Industry, since 1984; Hon. Consultant, Lister Hospital, Stevenage; *b* 21 May 1938; *o s* of David J. Griffin and Phyllis M. Griffin; *m* 1962, Margaret, *o d* of late Frank Cooper and of Catherine Cooper; one *s* two *d. Educ:* Howardian High Sch., Cardiff; London Hosp. Medical Coll. Lethby and Buxton Prizes, 1958; BSc (1st Cl. Hons) 1959; PhD 1961; George Riddoch Prize in Neurology, 1962; MB, BS 1964; LRCP, MRCS 1964; MRCP 1980, FRCP 1990; FRCPath 1986 (MRCPath 1982). Ho. Phys., London Hosp. Med. Unit, and Ho. Surg., London Hosp. Accident and Orthopaedic Dept, 1964–65; Lectr in Physiology, King's Coll., London, 1965–67; Head of Clinical Research, Riker Laboratories, 1967–71; SMO, Medicines Div., 1971–76; PMO, Medicines Div., and Medical Assessor, Cttee on Safety of Medicines, 1976–77; SPMO and Professional Head of Medicines Div., DHSS, 1977–84; Med. Assessor, Medicines Commn, 1977–84. Mem., Jt Formulary Cttee for British Nat. Formulary, 1978–84; UK Rep., EEC Cttee on Proprietary Med. Products; Chm., Cttee on Prop. Med. Products Working Party on Safety Requirements, 1977–84. FRSM. *Publications:* (jtly) Iatrogenic Diseases, 1972, 3rd edn 1985; (jtly) Manual of Adverse Drug Interactions, 1975, 4th edn 1988; (jtly) Drug Induced Emergencies, 1980; Medicines: research, regulation and risk, 1989; (jtly) International Medicines Regulations, 1989; numerous articles in sci. and med. jls, mainly on aspects of neurophysiology and clinical pharmacology and toxicology. *Recreations:* gardening, local history. *Address:* (office) 12 Whitehall, SW1A 2DY. *Club:* Athenæum.

GRIFFIN, Keith Broadwell, DPhil; Professor of Economics, and Chairman, Department of Economics, University of California, Riverside, since 1988; *b* 6 Nov. 1938; *s* of Marcus Samuel Griffin and Elaine Ann Broadwell; *m* 1956, Dixie Beth Griffin; two *d. Educ:* Williams Coll., Williamstown, Mass (BA; Hon DLitt, 1980); Balliol Coll., Oxford (BPhil, DPhil). Fellow and Tutor in Econs, Magdalen Coll., Oxford, 1965–76, Fellow by special election, 1977–79; Warden, Queen Elizabeth House, Oxford, 1978–79 (Actg Warden, 1973 and 1977–78); Dir, Inst. of Commonwealth Studies, Oxford, 1978–79 (Actg Dir, 1973 and 1977–78); Pres., Magdalen Coll., Oxford, 1979–88. Chief, Rural and Urban Employment Policies Br., ILO, 1975–76; Vis. Prof., Inst. of Econs and Planning, Univ. of Chile, 1962–63 and 1964–65. Consultant: ILO, 1974, 1982; Internat. Bank for Reconstruction and Develt, 1973; UN Res. Inst. for Social Develt, 1971–72; FAO, 1963–64, 1967, 1978; Inter-Amer. Cttee for Alliance for Progress, 1968; US Agency for Internat. Develt, 1966. Res. Adviser, Pakistan Inst. of Develt Econs, 1965, 1970; Sen. Adviser, OECD Develt Centre, Paris, 1986–88; Economic Advr, Govt of Bolivia, 1989–. Member: Council, UN Univ., 1986–; UN Cttee for Develt Planning, 1987–; Chm., UN Res. Inst. for Social Develt, 1988–. Pres., Develt Studies Assoc., 1978–80. *Publications:* (with Ricardo ffrench-Davis) Comercio Internacional y Politicas de Desarrollo Economico, 1967; Underdevelopment in Spanish America, 1969; (with John Enos) Planning Development, 1970; (ed) Financing Development in Latin America, 1971; (ed with Azizur Rahman Khan) Growth and Inequality in Pakistan, 1972; The Political Economy of Agrarian Change, 1974, 2nd edn 1979; (ed with E. A. G. Robinson) The Economic Development of Bangladesh, 1974; Land Concentration and Rural Poverty, 1976, 2nd edn 1981; International Inequality and National Poverty, 1978; (with Ashwani Saith) Growth and Equality in Rural China, 1981; (with Jeffrey James) The Transition to Egalitarian Development, 1981; (ed) Institutional Reform and Economic Development in the Chinese Countryside, 1984; World Hunger and the World Economy, 1987; Alternative Strategies for Economic Development, 1989; (ed with John Knight) Human Development and the International Development Strategy for the 1990s, 1990; (ed) The Economy of Ethiopia, 1992. *Recreation:* travel. *Address:* Department of Economics, University of California, Riverside, California 92521, USA. *Clubs:* Athenæum, United Oxford & Cambridge University.

GRIFFIN, Kenneth James, OBE 1970; a Deputy Chairman, British Shipbuilders, 1977–83; *b* 1 Aug. 1928; *s* of late Albert Griffin and late Catherine (*née* Sullivan); *m* 1951, Doreen Cicely Simon; one *s* one *d* (and one *s* decd). *Educ:* Dynevor Grammar Sch., Swansea; Swansea Technical College. Area Sec., ETU, 1960; Dist Sec., Confedn of Ship Building Engrg Unions, 1961; Sec., Craftsmen Cttee (Steel), 1961; Mem., Welsh Council, 1968; Mem., Crowther Commn on Constitution (Wales), 1969; Joint Sec., No 8 Joint Industrial Council Electrical Supply Industry, 1969; Industrial Adviser, DTI, 1971–72; Co-ordinator of Industrial Advisers, DTI, 1972–74; Special Adviser, Sec. of State for Industry, 1974; part-time Mem., NCB, 1973–82; Chm., Blackwall Engrg, 1983–85;

Member: Suppl. Benefits Commn, 1968–80; Solicitors Disciplinary Tribunal, 1982–. Chm., Castleton Retirement Homes, 1989–; Vice-Chm., UK Housing Trust, 1989–; Exec. Advr, Mobile Training, 1989. *Recreations:* golf, music, reading. *Address:* 214 Cyncoed Road, Cyncoed, Cardiff CF2 6RS. *T:* Cardiff (0222) 752184. *Club:* Reform.

GRIFFIN, Rear-Adm. Michael Harold, CB 1973; antiquarian horologist; *b* 28 Jan. 1921; *s* of late Henry William Griffin and Blanche Celia Griffin (*née* Michael); *m* 1947, Barbara Mary Brewer; two *d.* *Educ:* Plymouth Junior Techn. Coll. CEng, FIMechE, FIMarE. MBHI. Commnd, 1941; HMS Kent, 1942; HM Submarines Trusty, Tactician, Tally Ho, Alderney, 1944–50; Admty, 1950–52; HMS Eagle, 1952–54; staff C-in-C Portsmouth, 1954–57; HM Dockyard, Rosyth, 1957–60; Third Submarine Sqdn, 1960–62; Captain, 1962; HM Dockyard, Chatham, 1963–65; HMS St Vincent, 1966–69; Cdre Supt, Singapore, 1969–71; Dir of Dockyard Production and Support, MoD, 1972–77, retired. Naval Adviser to Vosper Shiprepairers Ltd, 1977–81. *Recreations:* horology, motoring, grandchildren. *Address:* 48 Little Green, Alverstoke, Gosport, Hants. *T:* Gosport (0705) 583348.

GRIFFIN, Paul, MBE 1961; MA Cantab; writer; *b* 2 March 1922; *s* of late John Edwin Herman Griffin; *m* 1946, Felicity Grace, *d* of late Canon Howard Dobson; one *s* one *d.* *Educ:* Framlingham Coll.; St Catharine's Coll., Cambridge. Served War in Gurkhas, India, Burma, Malaya, 1940–46; North-West Frontier, 1941–43; Chindits, 1943–44. Asst Master and Senior English Master, Uppingham Sch., 1949–55; Principal, English Sch. in Cyprus, 1956–60; Headmaster, Aldenham Sch., 1962–74; Principal, Anglo-World Language Centre, Cambridge, 1976–82; Treasurer, Corp. of Sons of the Clergy, 1978–86. *Publications:* collaborated in: How to Become Ridiculously Well-Read in One Evening, 1985; How to Become Absurdly Well-Informed about the Famous and Infamous, 1987; The Dogsbody Papers, 1988; How to Be Tremendously Tuned-in to Opera, 1989; How to Be Well-Versed in Poetry, 1990; Europe or Bust, 1991; poems, humour, articles, broadcasts. *Recreations:* sea angling, literary competitions. *Address:* 1 Strickland Place, Southwold, Suffolk IP18 6HN. *T:* Southwold (0502) 723709. *Club:* Army and Navy.

GRIFFIN, Very Rev. Victor Gilbert Benjamin; Dean of St Patrick's Cathedral, Dublin, 1969–91; *b* 24 May 1924; *s* of Gilbert B. and Violet M. Griffin, Carnew, Co. Wicklow; *m* 1958, Daphne E. Mitchell; two *s.* *Educ:* Kilkenny Coll.; Mountjoy Sch., and Trinity Coll., Dublin. MA, 1st class Hons in Philosophy. Ordained, 1947; Curacy, St Augustine's, Londonderry, 1947–51; Curacy, Christ Church, Londonderry, 1951–57; Rector of Christ Church, Londonderry, 1957–69. Lecturer in Philosophy, Magee Univ. Coll., Londonderry, 1950–69. *Publications:* Trends in Theology, 1870–1970, 1970; Anglican and Irish, 1976; Pluralism and Ecumenism, 1983; contrib. to New Divinity. *Recreations:* music, golf. *Address:* 7 Tyler Road, Limavady, N Ireland. *Club:* Friendly Brothers of St Patrick (Dublin).

GRIFFITH, Rev. (Arthur) Leonard; Lecturer in Homiletics, Wycliffe College, Toronto, 1977–87, retired; *b* 20 March 1920; *s* of Thomas Griffiths and Sarah Jane Taylor; *m* 1947, Anne Merelie Cayford; two *d.* *Educ:* Public and High Schs, Brockville, Ont; McGill Univ., Montreal (BA, McGill, 1942); United Theological Coll., Montreal (BD 1945; Hon. DD 1962); Mansfield Coll., Oxford, England, 1957–58. Ordained in The United Church of Canada, 1945; Minister: United Church, Arden, Ont, 1945–47; Trinity United Church, Grimsby, Ont, 1947–50; Chalmers United Church, Ottawa, Ont, 1950–60; The City Temple, London, 1960–66; Deer Park United Church, Toronto, 1966–75; ordained in Anglican Church 1976; Minister, St Paul's Church, Bloor St, Toronto, 1975–85. Hon. DD Wycliffe Coll., Toronto, 1985. *Publications:* The Roman Letter Today, 1959; God and His People, 1960; Beneath The Cross of Jesus, 1961; What is a Christian?, 1962; Barriers to Christian Belief, 1962; A Pilgrimage to the Holy Land, 1962; The Eternal Legacy, 1963; Pathways to Happiness, 1964; God's Time and Ours, 1964; The Crucial Encounter, 1965; This is Living!, 1966; God in Man's Experience, 1968; Illusions of our Culture, 1969; The Need to Preach, 1971; Hang on to the Lord's Prayer, 1973; We Have This Ministry, 1973; Ephesians: a positive affirmation, 1975; Gospel Characters, 1976; Reactions to God, 1979; Take Hold of the Treasure, 1980; From Sunday to Sunday, 1987. *Recreations:* music, drama, golf, fishing. *Address:* 71 Old Mill Road #105, Etobicoke, Ont M8X 1G9, Canada.

GRIFFITH, (Edward) Michael (Wynne), CBE 1986; Vice Lord-Lieutenant for the County of Clwyd, since 1986; Chairman, Countryside Council for Wales, since 1991; *b* 29 Aug. 1933; *e s* of Major H. W. Griffith, MBE; *m* Jill Grange, *d* of Major D. P. G. Moseley, Dorfold Cottage, Nantwich; two *s* (and one *s* decd). *Educ:* Eton; Royal Agricultural College. Regional Dir, National Westminster Bank Ltd, 1974–; Mem. Welsh Bd, Nationwide Anglia Bldg Soc., 1986–89. High Sheriff of Denbighshire, 1969. Chairman: Clwyd HA, 1980–90; National Trust Cttee for Wales, 1984–91 (Mem., National Trust Exec. and Council, 1989–); Dir, Land Authority Wales, 1989–90. Member: Countryside Commn Cttee for Wales, 1972–78; Min. of Agriculture Regional Panel, 1972–77; ARC, 1973–82; UFC (Wales), 1989–. DL Clwyd, 1985. *Address:* Greenfield, Trefnant, Clwyd. *T:* Trefnant (074574) 633. *Club:* Boodle's.

GRIFFITH, Prof. John Aneurin Grey, LLB London, LLM London; Hon. LLD Edinburgh 1982, York, Toronto, 1982, Manchester 1987; FBA 1977; Barrister-at-law; Chancellor of Manchester University, since 1986; Emeritus Professor of Public Law, University of London; *b* 14 Oct. 1918; *s* of Rev. B. Grey Griffith and Bertha Griffith; *m* 1941, Barbara Eirene Garnet, *d* of W. Garnet Williams; two *s* one *d.* *Educ:* Taunton Sch.; LSE. British and Indian armies, 1940–46. Lectr in Law, UCW, Aberystwyth, 1946–48; Lectr in Law and Reader, LSE, 1948–59, Prof. of English Law, 1959–70, Prof. of Public Law, 1970–84. Vis. Professor of Law: Univ. of California at Berkeley, 1966; York Univ., 1985. Mem., Marlow UDC, 1950–55, and Bucks CC, 1955–61. Editor, Public Law, 1956–81. *Publications:* (with H. Street) A Casebook of Administrative Law, 1964; Central Departments and Local Authorities, 1966; (with H. Street) Principles of Administrative Law, 5th edn, 1973; Parliamentary Scrutiny of Government Bills, 1974; (with T. C. Hartley) Government and Law, 1975, 2nd edn 1981; (ed) From Policy to Administration, 1976; The Politics of the Judiciary, 1977, 4th edn 1991; Public Rights and Private Interests, 1981; (with M. T. Ryle) Parliament, 1989; articles in English, Commonwealth and American jls of law, public administration and politics. *Recreations:* drinking beer and writing bad verse. *Address:* 25 Bedford Row, WC1.

GRIFFITH, Kenneth; actor, writer and documentary film-maker; formed own film company, Breakaway Productions Ltd, 1982; *b* 12 Oct. 1921; *g s* of Ernest and Emily Griffith; three marriages dissolved; three *s* two *d.* *Educ:* council and grammar schs, Tenby, Pembrokeshire, SW Wales. Became a professional actor at Festival Theatre, Cambridge, 1937; films and television; served War, RAF; post war, associated with Tyrone Guthrie at Old Vic; unknown number of films, partic. for Boulting brothers; unknown number of television plays; rarely theatre; made first documentary film at invitation of David Attenborough and Huw Wheldon, 1964; best documentaries include: Life of Cecil Rhodes; Hang Out Your Brightest Colours (life of Michael Collins; suppressed by Lew Grade at behest of IBA); The Public's Right to Know; The Sun's Bright Child (life of Edmund Kean); Black as Hell, Thick as Grass (the 24th Regt in Zulu War); The Most Valuable Englishman Ever (life of Thomas Paine for BBC TV); Clive of India (Channel Four); The Light (life of David Ben Gurion for Channel Four); But I Have Promises to Keep (life of Jawaharlal Nehru for Indian Govt), 1987; The Girl Who Didn't Run (on Zola Budd for BBC TV), 1989. *Publications:* Thank God we kept the Flag Flying, 1974; (with Timothy O'Grady) Curious Journey, 1981 (based on unshown TV documentary); The Discovery of Nehru, 1989. *Recreations:* talking; collecting British Empire military postal history (envelopes, post-cards), also ephemera connected with southern Africa. *Address:* 110 Englefield Road, Islington, N1 3LQ. *T:* 071–226 9013.

GRIFFITH, Rev. Leonard; *see* Griffith, Rev. A. L.

GRIFFITH, Michael; *see* Griffith, E. M. W.

GRIFFITH, Owen Glyn, CBE 1980 (OBE 1969); MVO 1954; HM Diplomatic Service, retired; High Commissioner in Lesotho, 1978–81; *b* 19 Jan. 1922; *s* of late William Glyn Griffith and Gladys Glyn Griffith (*née* Picton Davies); *m* 1949, Rosemary Elizabeth Cecil Earl; two *s.* *Educ:* Oundle Sch.; Trinity Hall, Cambridge. Commnd in Welsh Guards (twice wounded in N Africa), 1941–43; Colonial Service (later HMOCS), Uganda, 1944–63: District Officer, 1944–51; Private Sec. to Governor, 1952–54; Dist Comr, 1954–61; Perm. Sec., Min. of Commerce and Industry, 1961–63; Principal, CRO, 1963; 1st Sec. and Head of Chancery, British Embassy, Khartoum, 1965; 1st Sec. (Commercial), British Embassy, Stockholm, 1969; Dep. British High Comr, Malaŵi, 1973; Inspector, 1976–78. *Recreations:* golf, fishing. *Address:* The Sundial, Marsham Way, Gerrards Cross, Bucks SL9 8AD. *Club:* Denham Golf.

GRIFFITH, Stewart Cathie, CBE 1975; DFC 1944; TD 1954; Secretary, MCC, 1962–74; *b* 16 June 1914; *yr s* of H. L. A. Griffith, Middleton, Sussex; *m* 1939, Barbara Reynolds; one *s* one *d.* *Educ:* Dulwich Coll.; Pembroke Coll., Cambridge (MA). Asst Master, Dulwich Coll., 1937–39. Army, 1939–46. Glider Pilot Regt, Lieut-Col. Sec., Sussex County Cricket Club, 1946–50; Cricket Correspondent, Sunday Times, 1950–52; Asst Sec., MCC, 1952–62; Secretary: Internat. Cricket Conference, 1962–74; Cricket Council, 1969–74; Test and County Cricket Bd, 1969–73; President: Sussex CCC, 1975–77; MCC, 1979–80. *Recreations:* cricket, golf, real tennis, walking. *Address:* 7 Sea Way, Middleton, Sussex PO22 7RZ. *T:* Middleton-on-Sea (0243) 583000. *Clubs:* East India, Devonshire, Sports and Public Schools, MCC; Hawks (Cambridge), etc.

GRIFFITH EDWARDS, James; *see* Edwards, J. G.

GRIFFITHS, family name of **Barons Griffiths** and **Griffiths of Fforestfach.**

GRIFFITHS, Baron *cr* 1985 (Life Peer), of Govilon in the County of Gwent; **William Hugh Griffiths;** Kt 1971; MC 1944; PC 1980; a Lord of Appeal in Ordinary, since 1985; Chairman, Security Commission, since 1985; *b* 26 Sept. 1923; *s* of late Sir Hugh Griffiths, CBE, MS, FRCS; *m* 1949, Evelyn, *d* of Col K. A. Krefting; one *s* three *d.* *Educ:* Charterhouse; St John's Coll., Cambridge (Hon. Fellow, 1985). Commissioned in Welsh Guards, 1942; demobilised after war service, 1946. Cambridge, 1946–48. BA 1948. Called to the Bar, Inner Temple, 1949, Bencher, 1971; QC 1964; Treasurer of the Bar Council, 1968–69. Recorder of Margate, 1962–64, of Cambridge, 1964–70; a Judge of the High Court of Justice, Queen's Bench Division, 1971–80; a Lord Justice of Appeal, 1980–85. A Judge, National Industrial Relations Court, 1973–74. Mem., Adv. Council on Penal Reform, 1967–70; Chm., Tribunal of Inquiry on Ronan Point, 1968; Vice-Chm., Parole Bd, 1976–77; Mem., Chancellor's Law Reform Cttee, 1976–; Pres., Senate of the Inns of Court and the Bar, 1982–84; Chm., Lord Chancellor's Adv. Cttee on Legal Educn and Conduct, 1991–. Hon. Mem., Canadian Bar Assoc., 1981; Hon. Fellow: Amer. Inst. of Judicial Admin, 1985; Amer. Coll. of Trial Lawyers, 1988. Hon. LLD Wales, 1987. *Recreations:* cricket, golf, fishing. *Address:* c/o House of Lords, SW1. *Clubs:* Garrick, MCC (Pres., 1990–91); Hawks (Cambridge); Royal and Ancient (St Andrews); Sunningdale Golf.

GRIFFITHS OF FFORESTFACH, Baron *cr* 1991 (Life Peer), of Fforestfach in the county of West Glamorgan; **Brian Griffiths;** Adviser, Goldman Sachs, since 1991; Director: Thorn-EMI, since 1991; Hermann Miller, since 1991; *b* 27 Dec. 1941; *s* of Ivor Winston Griffiths and Phyllis Mary Griffiths (*née* Morgan); *m* 1965, Rachel Jane Jones; one *s* two *d.* *Educ:* Dynevor Grammar School; London School of Economics, Univ. of London. BSc (Econ), MSc (Econ). Assistant Lecturer in Economics, LSE, 1965–68, Lecturer in Economics, 1968–76; City University: Prof. of Banking and Internat. Finance, 1977–85; Dir, Centre for Banking and Internat. Finance, 1977–82; Dean, Business Sch., 1982–85; Head of Prime Minister's Policy Unit, 1985–90. Vis. Prof., Univ. of Rochester, USA, 1972–73; Prof. of Ethics, Gresham Coll., 1984–87; Dir, Bank of England, 1984–86 (Mem., Panel of Academic Consultants, 1977–86). Chairman: Centre for Policy Studies, 1991–; Sch. Exams and Assessment Council, 1991–; Nat. Curriculum Council, 1991–. *Publications:* Is Revolution Change? (ed and contrib.) 1972; Mexican Monetary Policy and Economic Development, 1972; Invisible Barriers to Invisible Trade, 1975; Inflation: The Price of Prosperity, 1976; (ed with G. E. Wood) Monetary Targets, 1980; The Creation of Wealth, 1984; (ed with G. E. Wood) Monetarism in the United Kingdom, 1984; Morality and the Market Place, 1989. *Recreations:* the family and reading. *Address:* c/o House of Lords, SW1A 0PW. *Club:* Garrick.

GRIFFITHS, Prof. Allen Phillips; Professor of Philosophy, University of Warwick, since 1964; Director, Royal Institute of Philosophy, since 1979; *b* 11 June 1927; *s* of John Phillips Griffiths and Elsie Maud (*née* Jones); *m* 1st, 1948, Margaret Lock (*d* 1974); one *s* one *d*; 2nd, 1984, Vera Clare (marr. diss. 1990). *Educ:* University Coll., Cardiff (BA; Hon. Fellow 1984); University Coll., Oxford (BPhil). Sgt, Intell. Corps, 1945–48 (despatches). Asst Lectr, Univ. of Wales, 1955–57; Lectr, Birkbeck Coll., Univ. of London, 1957–64. Pro-Vice-Chancellor, Univ. of Warwick, 1970–77. Vis. Professor: Swarthmore Coll., Pa, 1963; Univ. of Calif, 1967; Univ. of Wisconsin, 1965 and 1970; Carleton Coll., Minnesota, 1985. Silver Jubilee Medal, 1977. *Publications:* (ed) Knowledge & Belief, 1967; (ed) Of Liberty, 1983; (ed) Philosophy and Literature, 1984; Philosophy and Practice, 1985; (ed) Contemporary French Philosophy, 1988; (ed) Key Themes in Philosophy, 1989; (ed) Wittgenstein Centenary Essays, 1990; (ed) A. J. Ayer Memorial Essays, 1991; articles in learned philosophical jls. *Address:* Department of Philosophy, University of Warwick, Coventry CV4 7AL. *T:* Coventry (0203) 523320. *Club:* Conservative (Kenilworth).

GRIFFITHS, Rt. Rev. Ambrose; *see* Griffiths, Rt. Rev. M. A.

GRIFFITHS, Air Vice-Marshal Arthur, CB 1972; AFC 1964; Director, Trident Safeguards Ltd; *b* 22 Aug. 1922; *s* of late Edward and Elizabeth Griffiths; *m* 1950, Nancy Maud Sumpter; one *d.* *Educ:* Hawarden Grammar School. Joined RAF, 1940; war service with No 26 Fighter Reconnaissance Sqdn; post-war years as Flying Instructor mainly at CFS and Empire Flying Sch.; pfc 1954; comd No 94 Fighter Sqdn Germany, 1955–56; Dirg Staff, RCAF Staff Coll., Toronto, 1956–59; HQ Bomber Comd, 1959–61; comd No 101 Bomber Sqdn, 1962–64; Gp Captain Ops, Bomber Comd, 1964–67; comd RAF Waddington, 1967–69; AOA and later Chief of Staff, Far East Air Force, 1969–71; Head of British Defence Liaison Staff, Canberra, 1972–74; Dir Gen., Security (RAF), 1976–77, and Comdt-Gen. RAF Regt, 1975–77. *Address:* Water Lane House, Marholm Road, Castor, Peterborough PE5 7BJ. *T:* Peterborough (0733) 380742. *Club:* Royal Air Force.

GRIFFITHS, His Honour Bruce (Fletcher); QC 1970; a Circuit Judge, 1972–86; *b* 28 April 1924; *s* of Edward Griffiths and Nancy Olga (*née* Fuell); *m* 1952, Mary Kirkhouse Jenkins, *y d* of late Judge George Kirkhouse Jenkins, QC; two *s* one *d. Educ:* Whitchurch Grammar Sch., Cardiff; King's Coll., London. LLB (Hons) London, 1951 (Jelf Medallist); Cert. Theol. St David's UC, 1988. RAF, 1942–47. Chm., Local Appeals Tribunal (Cardiff), Min. of Social Security, 1964–70; an Asst Recorder of Cardiff, Swansea and Merthyr Tydfil, 1966–71; Vice-Chm., Mental Health Review Tribunal for Wales, 1968–72; Dep. Chm., Glamorgan QS, 1971; Comr of Assize, Royal Cts of Justice, London, 1971; Mem., Parole Bd, 1983–85; Chancellor, Dio. of Monmouth, 1977–; President of Provincial Court, and Mem. Governing Body (Panel of Chairmen), Church in Wales. Chm., Welsh Sculpture Trust; former Mem., Welsh Arts Council, and Chm., Art Cttee; Chm., Contemp. Art Soc. for Wales, 1987– (Purchaser, 1975–76; Vice-Chm., 1977–87). *Address:* 15 Heol Don, Whitchurch, Cardiff CF4 2AR. *T:* Cardiff (0222) 625001; Camp de sa Mar No 4, Es Traves, Port de Soller, Mallorca, Spain. *T:* Mallorca 633008. *Clubs:* Naval and Military; Cardiff and County (Cardiff).

GRIFFITHS, David Howard, OBE 1982; Chairman, Eastern Region, British Gas Corporation, 1981–87; *b* 30 Oct. 1922; *s* of David Griffiths and Margaret (*née* Jones); *m* 1949, Dilys Watford John; two *d. Educ:* Monmouth Sch.; Sidney Sussex Coll., Cambridge (Exhibnr; BA 1941, MA 1946, LLB 1946). Admitted Solicitor of the Supreme Court, 1948. Asst Solicitor, Newport Corp., 1948; Wales Gas Board: Solicitor, 1949; Management Develt Officer, 1965; Dir of Develt, 1967; Wales Gas: Dir of Conversion, 1970; Sec., 1973; Dep. Chm., Eastern Gas, 1977. Vice Pres., Contemporary Arts Soc., Wales, 1977. *Recreations:* reading, golf, music. *Address:* 12 Fallows Green, Harpenden, Herts AL5 4HD. *Club:* Salcombe Yacht.

GRIFFITHS, David Hubert; Director of Establishments, Ministry of Agriculture, Fisheries and Food, since 1990; *b* 24 Dec. 1940; *s* of Hubert Griffiths and Margaret Joan Waldron; *m* Mary Abbott; one *s. Educ:* Kingswood School, Bath; St Catharine's College, Cambridge (MA). Joined Ministry of Agriculture, Fisheries and Food as Asst Principal, 1963; Principal, 1968; Asst Secretary, 1975; Under Secretary, 1982–; Fisheries Sec., 1983–87; Hd, Food, Drink and Marketing Policy Gp, 1987–90. Non-exec. Dir, ICI (Paints Div.), 1985–87. *Recreations:* golf, cooking, music. *Address:* c/o Ministry of Agriculture, Fisheries and Food, Whitehall Place, SW1. *Club:* Richmond Golf.

GRIFFITHS, David John; His Honour Judge David Griffiths; a Circuit Judge, since 1984; *b* 18 Feb. 1931; *m* Anita; three *s* one *d. Educ:* St Dunstan's Coll., Catford, SE6. Admitted to Roll of Solicitors, 1957; apptd Notary Public, 1969; Principal: D. J. Griffiths & Co., Bromley, 1960–84; Harveys, Lewisham, 1970–84. A Recorder, 1980–84. Mem., Scriveners Co., 1983. *Recreations:* riding, music (male voice choir). *Address:* Crosswell Farm, Fosten Green, Biddenden, Kent TN27 8ER.

GRIFFITHS, David Laurence; His Honour Judge Griffiths; a Circuit Judge, since 1989; *b* 3 Aug. 1944; *s* of late Edward Laurence Griffiths and of Mary Middleton Pudge; *m* 1971, Sally Hollis; four *d. Educ:* Christ's Hospital; Jesus College, Oxford (MA). Called to the Bar, Lincoln's Inn, 1967; an Asst Recorder, 1981; Recorder, 1985. *Recreations:* gardening, running, sailing, walking, swimming, squash, watching Rugby and cricket, opera, history. *Address:* Lord Chancellor's Department, Trevelyan House, Great Peter Street, SW1P 2BY. *T:* 071–210 8500.

GRIFFITHS, Ven. David Nigel, FSA; Archdeacon of Berkshire, since 1987; Chaplain to The Queen, since 1977; *b* 29 Oct. 1927; *o s* of late William Cross Griffiths, LDS, and Doris May (*née* Rhodes); *m* 1953, Joan Fillingham; two *s* one *d. Educ:* King Edward's Sch., Bath; Cranbrook; Worcester Coll., Oxford (MA; Gladstone Meml Prize, Arnold Historical Essay Prize); Lincoln Theol Coll. An economist before ordination; Consultant at FAO, Rome, 1952–53. Curate, St Matthew, Northampton, 1958–61; Headquarters Staff, SPCK, 1961–67; Rector of Minster Parishes, Lincoln, 1967–73; Vice-Chancellor and Librarian, Lincoln Cathedral, 1967–73; Rector of Windsor, 1973–87; Rural Dean of Maidenhead, 1977–82 and 1985–87; Hon. Canon of Christ Church, Oxford, 1983–88. Served TARO and RMFVR, 1946–50; Chaplain, RNR, 1963–77 (Reserve Decoration, 1977); OCF: Household Cavalry, 1973–87; 1st Bn Irish Guards, 1977–80. FSA 1973. *Publications:* articles on bibliography and church history. *Recreations:* walking, bibliomania. *Address:* 21 Wilderness Road, Earley, Reading, Berks RG6 2RU. *T:* Reading (0734) 663459; Choristers' Mews, 1A Nettleham Road, Lincoln LN2 1RF. *T:* Lincoln (0522) 512014.

GRIFFITHS, Edward; *b* 7 March 1929; Welsh; *m* 1954, Ella Constance Griffiths; one *s* one *d. Educ:* University Coll. of N Wales, Bangor. Industrial Chemist, 1951. Mem., Flintshire CC, 1964. MP (Lab) Brightside Div. of Sheffield, June 1968–Sept. 1974; contested (Ind Lab) Sheffield Brightside, Oct. 1974. *Recreation:* sport.

GRIFFITHS, Sir Eldon (Wylie), Kt 1985; MA Cantab, MA Yale; MP (C) Bury St Edmunds, since May 1964; *b* 25 May 1925; *s* of Thomas H. W. Griffiths and Edith May; *m*; one *s* one *d. Educ:* Ashton Grammar Sch.; Emmanuel Coll., Cambridge. Fellow, Saybrook Coll., Yale, 1948–49; Correspondent, Time and Life magazines, 1949–55; Foreign Editor, Newsweek, 1956–63; Columnist, Washington Post, 1962–63; Conservative Research Department, 1963–64. Parly Sec., Min. of Housing and Local Govt, June-Oct. 1970; Parly Under-Sec. of State, DoE, and Minister for Sport, 1970–74; opposition spokesman on Europe, 1975–76. Chairman: Anglo-Iranian Parly Gp; Anglo-Polish Parly Gp. Chm., Special Olympics (UK). Consultant/Adviser, Nat. Police Federation, to 1988; Consultant, National Caravan Council; President: Assoc. of Public Health Inspectors, 1969–70; Friends of Gibraltar; World Affairs Council, Orange County, California. Regents' Prof., Univ. of California, Irvine. Hon. Freeman, City of London; Hon. Citizen, Orange County, California. Medal of Honour, Republic of China, Taiwan. *Recreations:* reading, swimming, cricket. *Address:* The Wallow, East Barton, Bury St Edmunds, Suffolk. *Clubs:* Carlton; Dutch Treat (New York).

GRIFFITHS, Sir (Ernest) Roy, Kt 1985; Deputy Chairman, National Health Service Policy Board, since 1989; Adviser to the Government on the National Health Service, since 1986; *b* 8 July 1926; *s* of Ernest and Florence Griffiths; *m* 1952, Winifred Mary Rigby; one *s* two *d. Educ:* Wolstanton Grammar Sch., N Staffs; Keble Coll., Oxford (Open Scholar; MA, BCL; Hon. Fellow 1987); Columbia Business Sch., New York. Solicitor; FCIS 1959; FIGD 1975 (Pres., 1985–87); CBIM 1980; Hon. FCGI (Technology), 1988. Monsanto Cos, 1956–68: Legal Adviser, 1956; Dir, Monsanto Europe, 1964–68; J. Sainsbury plc, 1968–91: Dir, Personnel, 1969; Man. Dir, 1979–88; Dep. Chm., 1975–91. Chm., Management Enquiry, NHS, 1983 (report publd 1983); Mem., Health Services Supervisory Bd, 1983–89; Dep. Chm., NHS Management Bd, 1986–89. Pres., Age Concern England, 1989–. Provost and Chm. of Governors, London Univ. Sch. of Agric., Wye Coll., Kent, 1989–. Hon. DCL Kent, 1990; Hon. LLD Keele, 1991. Author of Community Care: agenda for action (report to Govt), 1988. *Recreations:* cricket, gardening. *Address:* Little Earlylands, Crockham Hill, Edenbridge, Kent TN8 6SN. *T:* Edenbridge (0732) 866362.

GRIFFITHS, Harold Morris; Assistant Secretary, HM Treasury, 1978–86; *b* 17 March 1926; *s* of Rt Hon. James Griffiths, CH; *m* 1st, 1951, Gwyneth Lethby (*d* 1966); three *s* one *d*; 2nd, 1966, Elaine Burge (*née* Walsh); two *s. Educ:* Llanelly Grammar Sch.; London Sch. of Economics. Editorial Staff: Glasgow Herald, 1949–55; Guardian, 1955–67; Information Division, HM Treasury: Deputy Head, 1967–68, Head, 1968–72; Asst Sec., HM Treasury, 1972–75; Counsellor (Economic), Washington, 1975–78. *Address:* 32 Teddington Park, Teddington, Mddx TW11 8DA. *T:* 081–977 2464.

GRIFFITHS, Howard; Assistant Under Secretary of State (Policy), Ministry of Defence, since 1988; *b* 20 Sept. 1938; *s* of Bernard and Olive Griffiths; *m* 1963, Dorothy Foster (*née* Todd); one *s* one *d. Educ:* London School of Economics (BScEcon, MScEcon). Ministry of Defence: Research Officer, 1963–69; Principal, Army Dept, 1970–72; Central Staffs, 1972–76; Asst Secretary, Head of Civilian Faculty, National Defence Coll., 1976–78; Procurement Executive, 1978–80; Deputy and Counsellor (Defence), UK Delegn, Mutual and Balanced Force Reductions (Negotiations), Vienna, 1980–84; Asst Sec., Office of Management and Budget, MoD, 1984–86; Asst Sec. and Head of Defence Arms Control Unit, MoD, 1986–88. *Address:* c/o Ministry of Defence, Whitehall, SW1A 2HB.
See also L. *Griffiths.*

GRIFFITHS, Howard; Editor: Pulse, since 1979; The Practitioner, since 1988; Group Editor, Financial Pulse, since 1987; *b* 6 Aug. 1947; *m* 1977, Lynda Smith; three *d. Educ:* Cowbridge Grammar School; Merton College, Oxford (BA). Feature writer, Pulse, 1973. *Recreations:* family, walking the dog. *Address:* Morgan-Grampian House, Calderwood Street, SE18 6QH. *T:* 081–316 3577.

GRIFFITHS, Islwyn Owen, QC 1973; a Recorder of the Crown Court, 1972–84; *b* 24 Jan. 1924; *m* 1951, Pamela Norah Blizard. *Educ:* Swansea Grammar Sch.; Christ Church, Oxford (MA, BCL). Army (Royal Artillery), 1942–47; TA (RA), 1947–51; TARO, 1951. Called to Bar, Lincoln's Inn, 1953; Dep. Chm., Bucks QS, 1967–71. Comr, 1979–84, Chief Comr, 1981–84, National Insurance, later Social Security, Commn. *Recreation:* sailing. *Address:* Kings Farm House, Wimland Road, Faygate, near Horsham, Sussex RH12 4SS. *Club:* Garrick.

GRIFFITHS, John Calvert, CMG 1983; QC 1972; a Recorder of the Crown Court, since 1972; *b* 16 Jan. 1931; *s* of Oswald Hardy Griffiths and Christina Flora Griffiths; *m* 1958, Jessamy, *er d* of Prof. G. P. Crowden and Jean Crowden; three *d. Educ:* St Peter's Sch., York (scholar); Emmanuel Coll., Cambridge (sen. exhibnr) (BA 1st Cl. Hons 1955; MA 1960). Called to Bar, Middle Temple, 1956 (Bencher, 1983). Attorney-General of Hong Kong, Mem. Exec. and Legislative Councils, and Chm. Hong Kong Law Reform Commn, 1979–83. Member: Exec. Cttee, General Council of the Bar, 1967–71 (Treas., 1987); Senate of Inns of Court and the Bar, 1983– (Mem., Exec. Cttee, 1973–77); Council of Legal Educn, 1983–; Nat. Council of Social Service, 1974–; Greater London CAB Exec. Cttee, 1978–79; (co-opted) Develt and Special Projects Cttee, 1977–79; Court, Hong Kong Univ., 1980–; Exec. Cttee, Prince Philip Cambridge Scholarships, 1980–. Lieutenant, RE, 1949–50 (Nat. Service). *Recreations:* fishing reading, gardening. *Address:* 1 Brick Court, Temple, EC4. *T:* 01–583 0777. *Clubs:* Flyfishers', Hurlingham; Hong Kong, Royal Hong Kong Jockey (Hong Kong).

GRIFFITHS, John Charles, JP; Chairman: Rodhales Ltd, since 1978; Minerva Arts Channel, since 1989; Minerva Vision, since 1989; *b* 19 April 1934; *s* of Sir Percival Griffiths, *qv*; *m* 1st, 1956, Ann Timms (marr. diss.); four *s*; 2nd, 1983, Carole Jane Mellor (marr. diss.); one *d. Educ:* Uppingham; Peterhouse, Cambridge (MA). Dep. General Manager, Press Association, 1968–70; PR adviser, British Gas, 1970–74; Chm., MSG Public Relations, 1974–78; Chm. and founder, The Arts Channel, 1983–89. Chairman: National League of Young Liberals, 1962–64 (Mem., Nat. Exec., 1964–66); Assoc. of Liberals in Small Business and Self Employed, 1980; Pres., Liberal Party, 1982–83. Contested (L): Ludlow, 1964; Wanstead and Woodford, 1966; Bedford, Feb. 1974, Oct. 1974. JP Cardiff, 1960. *Publications:* The Survivors, 1964; Afghanistan, 1967; Modern Iceland, 1969; Three Tomorrows, 1980; The Science of Winning Squash, 1981; Afghanistan: key to a Continent, 1981; The Queen of Spades, 1983; Flashpoint Afghanistan, 1986. *Recreations:* squash, conversation, reading, music. *Address:* Neuaddfach Barn, Llangynidr, Crickhowell, Powys NP8 1LN. *T:* Brecon (0874) 730164. *Club:* Royal Automobile.

GRIFFITHS, John Edward Seaton, CMG 1959; MBE 1934; retired; *b* 27 Sept. 1908; *s* of A. E. Griffiths, MA, Cape Town; *m* 1937, Helen Parker, *d* of C. C. Wiles, MA, Grahamstown, SA; two *s* one *d. Educ:* South African Coll. Sch.; Cape Town Univ.; Selwyn Coll., Cambridge. Colonial Service (later HM Oversea Civil Service), Tanganyika, 1931–59; Asst Comr, East African Office, 1960–63; Director of Studies, Royal Inst. Public Administration, 1963–67; Administrative Training Officer, Govt of Botswana, 1967–73. *Publications:* articles in Tanganyika Notes and Records, Botswana Notes and Records and in Journal of Administration Overseas. *Address:* c/o National Westminster Bank, 249 Banbury Road, Summertown, Oxford. *Clubs:* Commonwealth Trust; Mountain Club of South Africa (Cape Town).

GRIFFITHS, Sir John N.; *see* Norton-Griffiths.

GRIFFITHS, John Pankhurst, RIBA; Director, Building Conservation Trust, since 1979; *b* 27 Sept. 1930; *s* of late William Bramwell Griffiths and Ethel Doris Griffiths (*née* Pankhurst); *m* 1959, Helen Elizabeth (*née* Tasker); two *s* one *d. Educ:* Torquay Grammar School; King George V School, Southport; School of Architecture, Manchester Univ. Dip Arch. Resident architect, Northern Nigeria, for Maxwell Fry, 1956–58; staff architect, Granada Television, 1959; Founder and first Dir, Manchester Building Centre, 1959–65; Head of Tech. Inf., Min. of Public Buildings and Works, later DoE, 1965–77; formed Building Conservation Assoc. (now Building Conservation Trust), 1977. *Publications:* articles in tech. and prof. jls. *Recreations:* designing odd things, examining buildings, cooking on solid fuel Aga. *Address:* The Building Conservation Trust, Apartment 39, Hampton Court Palace, East Molesey, Surrey KT8 9BS. *T:* 081–943 2277.

GRIFFITHS, Prof. John William Roger; Professor of Electronics, Department of Electronic and Electrical Engineering, Loughborough University of Technology, 1967–84, now Emeritus; *b* 27 Nov. 1921; *s* of Samuel William Henry Griffiths and Alice Griffiths; *m* 1945, Pauline Edyth Griffiths (*née* Marston); one *s. Educ:* Waterloo Grammar Sch.; Bristol Univ. BSc 1949, PhD 1958. CEng, FIEE; FIOA. Served War, HM Forces, 1939–46. Scientific Civil Service, 1949–55; Lectr, then Sen. Lectr, Birmingham Univ., 1955–67; Loughborough Univ. of Technology: Head of Dept, 1968–80; Dean of Engineering, 1972–75; Sen. Pro-Vice-Chancellor, 1978–80. Vis. Prof., Inst. of Radio Physics, Calcutta, 1963–65. Mem., Govt Adv. Panel on Satellite TV Standards, 1983. *Publications:* Signal Processing in Underwater Acoustics, 1972; many papers in learned jls. *Recreations:* sport, gardening. *Address:* 80 Rectory Road, Wanlip, Leicestershire LE7 8PL. *T:* Leicester (0533) 676336.

GRIFFITHS, Lawrence; a Recorder of the Crown Court, since 1972; *b* 16 Aug. 1933; *s* of Bernard Griffiths and Olive Emily Griffiths (*née* Stokes); *m* 1959, Josephine Ann (*née* Cook); one *s* two *d. Educ:* Gowerton Grammar Sch.; Christ's Coll., Cambridge (MA).

Called to Bar, Inner Temple, 1957; practised Swansea, 1958–; Mem. Wales and Chester Circuit; Prosecuting Counsel to Inland Revenue for Wales and Chester Circuit, 1969; Standing Counsel to HM Customs and Excise for Wales and Chester Circuit, 1989–. Mem., Mental Health Review Tribunal for Wales, 1970–. *Address:* 26 Hillside Crescent, Uplands, Swansea SA2 0RD. *T:* Swansea (0792) 473513; (chambers) Iscoed Chambers, 86 St Helens Road, Swansea SA1 4BQ. *T:* Swansea (0792) 652988. *Club:* Bristol Channel Yacht (Swansea).

See also H. Griffiths.

GRIFFITHS, Rev. Dr Leslie John; Superintendent Minister, West London Mission, Methodist Church, since 1986; *b* 15 Feb. 1942; *s* of late Sidney and Olwen Griffiths; *m* 1969, Margaret, *d* of Alfred and Kathleen Rhodes; two *s* one *d. Educ:* Llanelli Grammar Sch.; Univ. of Wales (BA); Univ. of Cambridge (MA); Univ. of London (PhD). Junior Res. Fellow, University Coll. of S Wales and Monmouthshire, Cardiff, 1963; Asst Lectr in English, St David's Coll., Lampeter, 1964–67; trained for Methodist Ministry, Wesley Ho., Cambridge, 1967–70; Asst Minister, Wesley Church, Cambridge, 1969–70; Petit Goâve Circuit, Haïti, 1970–71; Port-au-Prince Circuit and Asst Headmaster, Nouveau Collège Bird, 1971–74; Minister, Reading Circuit, 1974–77; Superintendent Minister: Cap Haïtien Circuit, Haïti, 1977–80; Wanstead and Woodford Circuit, 1980–86. Governor: Kingswood Sch., Bath, 1982–90; Central London YMCA, 1987–89; Bd of Christian Aid, 1990–; Chm., Methodist Church's Caribbean and Latin America Adv. Group, 1982–89. *Publication:* A History of Haïtian Methodism, 1991. *Recreations:* fun and fellowship spiced with occasional moments of solitude. *Address:* 18 Beaumont Street, W1N 1FF. *T:* 071–486 9924. *Club:* Graduate Centre (Cambridge).

GRIFFITHS, Rt. Rev. (Michael) Ambrose, OSB; Parish Priest, St. Mary's, Leyland, Preston, since 1984; *b* 4 Dec. 1928; *s* of Henry and Hilda Griffiths. *Educ:* Ampleforth Coll.; Balliol Coll., Oxford (MA, BSc Chemistry). Entered monastery at Ampleforth, 1950; theological studies at S Anselmo, Rome, 1953–56; ordained priest, 1957; Prof. of Theology at Ampleforth, 1963; Sen. Science Master, Ampleforth Coll., 1967; Inspector of Accounts for English Benedictine Congregation, 1971 and 1985–; Procurator (Bursar) at Ampleforth, 1972; Abbot of Ampleforth, 1976–84. Mem. Public School Bursars' Assoc. Cttee, 1975. *Recreation:* walking. *Address:* St Mary's, Leyland, Preston PR5 1PD.

GRIFFITHS, Nigel, JP; MP (Lab) Edinburgh South, since 1987; *b* 20 May 1955; *s* of Lionel and Elizabeth Griffiths; *m* 1979, Sally, *d* of Hugh and Sally McLaughlin. *Educ:* Hawick High Sch.; Edinburgh Univ. (MA 1977); Moray House Coll. of Education. Joined Labour Party, 1970; Pres., EU Labour Club, 1976–77; Sec., Lothian Devolution Campaign, 1978; Rights Adviser to Mental Handicap Pressure Group, 1979–87. City of Edinburgh: District Councillor, 1980–87 (Chm., 1986–87; Chm., Housing Cttee; Chm., Decentralisation Cttee); Member: Edinburgh Festival Council, 1984–87; Edinburgh Health Council, 1982–87; Exec., Edinburgh Council of Social Service, 1984–87; Wester Hailes Sch. Council, 1981. Opposition Whip, 1987–89; Opposition frontbench spokesman on consumer affairs, 1989–. Exec. Mem. and Convenor, Finance Cttee, Scottish Constitutional Convention. Member: War on Want, SEAD, Amnesty Internat., Anti-apartheid, Friends of the Earth, Nat. Trust, Ramblers' Assoc. *Publications:* Guide to Council Housing in Edinburgh, 1981; Council Housing on the Point of Collapse, 1982; Welfare Rights Survey, 1981; Welfare Rights Guide, 1982; A Guide to DHSS Claims and Appeals, 1983; Welfare Rights Advice for Doctors, Health Visitors and Social Workers, 1983; Claiming Attendance Allowance, 1982. *Recreations:* squash, travel, live entertainment, badminton, hill walking and rock climbing, architecture, reading, politics. *Address:* 30 McLaren Road, Edinburgh EH9 2BN. *T:* 031–667 1947; (office) 93 Causewayside, Edinburgh. *T:* 031–662 4520; House of Commons, SW1A 0AA. *T:* 071–219 3442.

GRIFFITHS, Paul Anthony; Music Critic of The Times, since 1982; *b* 24 Nov. 1947; *s* of Fred Griffiths and Jeanne Veronica (*née* George); *m* 1977, Rachel Isabel Reader (*née* Cullen); two *s. Educ:* King Edward's Sch., Birmingham; Lincoln Coll., Oxford (BA, MSc). Area Editor for Grove's Dictionary of Music and Musicians, 6th edn, 1973–76; Asst Music Critic of The Times, 1979–82. *Publications:* A Concise History of Modern Music, 1978; Boulez, 1978; A Guide to Electronic Music, 1979; Modern Music, 1980; Cage, 1981; Igor Stravinsky: The Rake's Progress, 1982; Peter Maxwell Davies, 1982; The String Quartet, 1983; György Ligeti, 1983; Bartók, 1984; Olivier Messiaen, 1985; New Sounds, New Personalities, 1985; The Thames & Hudson Encyclopaedia of 20th-Century Music, 1986; Myself and Marco Polo, 1989; The Lay of Sir Tristram, 1991; The Jewel Box, 1991. *Recreation:* swimming. *Address:* The Old Bakery, Lower Heyford, Oxford OX6 3NJ. *T:* Steeple Aston (0869) 40584.

GRIFFITHS, Sir Percival Joseph, KBE 1963; Kt 1947; CIE 1943; ICS (retired); formerly President, India, Pakistan and Burma Association; Director of various companies; *b* 15 Jan. 1899; *s* of late J. T. Griffiths, Ashford, Middx; *m* 1st, Kathleen Mary (*d* 1979), *d* of late T. R. Wilkes, Kettering; two *s* (and one *s* decd); 2nd, 1985, Marie, *widow* of Sir Hubert Shirley Smith. *Educ:* Peterhouse, Cambridge (MA). BSc London; entered Indian Civil Service, 1922; retired, 1937. Leader, European Group, Indian Central Legislature, 1946; Central Organiser, National War Front, India, and Publicity Adviser to Government of India; Mem. Indian Legislative Assembly, 1937. Hon. Fellow, SOAS, 1971. *Publications:* The British in India, 1947; The British Impact on India, 1952; Modern India, 1957; The Changing Face of Communism, 1961; The Road to Freedom, 1964; History of the Indian Tea Industry, 1967; Empire into Commonwealth, 1969; To Guard My People: the history of the Indian Police, 1971; A Licence to Trade: the History of English Chartered Companies, 1975; A History of the Inchcape Group, 1977; A History of the Joint Steamer Companies, 1979; Vignettes of India, 1986. *Address:* St Christopher, Abbots Drive, Wentworth, Virginia Water, Surrey. *Club:* Oriental.

See also J. C. Griffiths.

GRIFFITHS, Peter Anthony; Chief Executive, Guy's and Lewisham Trust, since 1991; *b* 19 May 1945; *m* 1966, Margaret Harris; two *s. Educ:* Swansea Technical Coll. Regl admin. trainee, Welsh Hosp. Bd, Cardiff Royal Inf., 1963–66; nat. admin. trainee, Birmingham Reg./Nuffield Centre, Leeds, 1966–69; Dep. Hosp. Sec., E Birmingham HMC, 1969–71; Dep. Dist Administrator, Hosp. Sec., Southampton and SW Hampshire Health Dist (Teaching), 1971–76; Dist Administrator, Medway Health Dist, 1976–81; Actg Area Administrator, Kent AHA, 1981–82; Dist Administrator 1982–84, Dist Gen. Man. 1984–88, Lewisham and N Southwark HA; Regl Gen. Manager, SE Thames RHA, 1988–89; Dep. Chief Exec., NHS Management Exec., 1990–91. *Recreation:* golf. *Address:* Longlands, 38 Holmewood Ridge, Langton Green, Tunbridge Wells, Kent TN3 0ED.

GRIFFITHS, Prof. Peter Denham, CBE 1990; MD, FRCPath; Professor of Biochemical Medicine 1968–89, and Dean, Faculty of Medicine and Dentistry, 1985–89, University of Dundee (Vice-Principal, 1979–85); Hon. Consultant Clinical Chemist, Tayside Health Board, 1966–89; *b* 16 June 1927; *s* of Bernard Millar Griffiths and Florence Marion Fletcher; *m* 1949, Joy Burgess; three *s* one *d. Educ:* King Edward VI Sch., Southampton; Guy's Hosp. Med. Sch., Univ. of London (BSc 1st Cl. Hons, MD). LRCP, MRCS; FRCPath 1978. Served RN, 1946–49. Jun. Lectr in Physiol., Guy's Hosp. Med. Sch., 1957–58; Registrar, then Sen. Registrar in Clin. Path., Guy's and Lewisham Hosps,

London, 1958–64; Consultant Pathologist, Harlow Gp of Hosps, Essex, 1964–66; Sen. Lectr in Clin. Chemistry, Univ. of St Andrews and subseq. Univ. of Dundee, 1966–68. Pres., Assoc. of Clin. Biochemists, UK, 1987–89 (Chm. Council, 1973–76); Member: Tayside Health Bd, 1977–85; GMC, 1986–; various cttees of SHHD and DHSS, 1969–. Dir, Drug Development (Scotland), 1982–89. Dir, Dundee Rep. Theatre, 1977–90. FBIM; FRSA. Consulting Editor, Clinica Chimica Acta, 1986– (Mem. Editl Bd, 1976; Jt Editor-in-Chief, 1979–85). *Publications:* contrib. scientific and med. jls (pathology, clin. chemistry, computing). *Recreations:* music, gardening, decorating, walking. *Address:* 52 Albany Road, West Ferry, Dundee DD5 1NW. *T:* Dundee (0382) 76772. *Clubs:* Commonwealth Trust; New (Edinburgh).

GRIFFITHS, Peter Harry Steve; MP (C) Portsmouth North, since 1979; *b* 24 May 1928; *s* of W. L. Griffiths, West Bromwich; *m* 1962, Jeannette Christine (*née* Rubery); one *s* one *d. Educ:* City of Leeds Training Coll. BSc (Econ.) Hons London, 1956; MEd Birmingham, 1963. Headmaster, Hall Green Road Sch., West Bromwich, 1962–64. Senior Lectr in Economic Hist., The Polytechnic, Portsmouth (formerly Portsmouth Coll. of Technology), 1967–79. Fulbright Exchange Prof. of Economics, Pierce Coll., Los Angeles, Calif, 1968–69. Chm., Smethwick Education Cttee; Leader, Conservative Group of Councillors in Smethwick, 1960–64. MP (C) Smethwick, 1964–66; Contested (C) Portsmouth N, Feb. 1974. *Publication:* A Question of Colour?, 1966. *Recreations:* motoring, writing, camping. *Address:* c/o House of Commons, SW1A 0AA. *Clubs:* Sloane; Conservative (Smethwick and Portsmouth).

GRIFFITHS, Peter John; Clerk of the Court, University of London, since 1987; *b* 19 April 1944; *s* of Ronald Hugh Griffiths and Emily Vera (*née* Cockshutt); *m* 1968, Lesley Florence (*née* Palmer); two *d. Educ:* Battersea Grammar Sch.; Univ. of Leicester (BA Classics); McMaster Univ. (MA Classics). University of London: Asst to Principal, 1968–70; Asst Sec. to Cttee of Enquiry into governance of the university, 1970–72; Special Duties Officer, Vice-Chancellor's and Principal's Office, 1972–78; Dep. Head, Legal and Gen. Div., Court Dept, 1978–82; Asst Clerk of the Court, 1982–85; Dep. Clerk of the Court, 1985–87. *Recreation:* choral singing (Pro Musica chorus). *Address:* Senate House, University of London, Malet Street, WC1E 7HU. *T:* 071–636 8000.

GRIFFITHS, Roger Noel Price, MA Cantab; Membership Secretary, The Headmasters' Conference, since 1990 (Deputy Secretary, The Headmasters' Conference and Secondary Heads' Association, 1986–89); *b* 25 Dec. 1931; *er s* of late William Thomas and of Annie Evelyn Griffiths; *m* 1966, Diana, *y d* of late Capt. J. F. B. Brown, RN; three *d. Educ:* Lancing Coll.; King's Coll., Cambridge. Asst Master at Charterhouse, 1956–64; Headmaster, Hurstpierpoint Coll., 1964–86. Governor: Mill Hill Sch., 1987–; Tormead Sch., 1987–; Prebendal Sch., Chichester, 1987–; Worth Sch., 1990–. Mem., Management Cttee, Pallant House Trust, Chichester, 1987–. Asst to Court of Worshipful Co. of Wax Chandlers, 1985, Master, 1990. MA Oxon, by incorporation, 1960. JP Mid Sussex, 1976–86. *Recreations:* music, theatre, bowls. *Address:* Hanbury Cottage, Cocking, near Midhurst, West Sussex GU29 0HF. *T:* Midhurst (0730) 813503. *Clubs:* East India, Devonshire, Sports and Public Schools; Sussex (Sussex).

GRIFFITHS, Sir Roy; *see* Griffiths, Sir (Ernest) Roy.

GRIFFITHS, Trevor, BScEng, CEng, FIMechE, FIEE; registered professional engineer, State of California; Engineer Specialist (retired), Bechtel Power Corporation, Norwalk, California; *b* 17 April 1913; *m* 1939, Evelyn Mary Colborn; one *d. Educ:* Bishop Gore Gram. Sch., Swansea; University Coll., London. Metropolitan Vickers Electrical Co. Ltd, 1934; Air Min., 1938; UKAEA, 1955; Min. of Power, 1960; Min. of Technology, 1969 (Chief Inspector of Nuclear Installations, 1964–71); Dep. Chief Inspector of Nuclear Installations, DTI, 1971–73. *Address:* 12705 SE River Road 512E, Portland, Oregon 97222, USA.

GRIFFITHS, Trevor; playwright; *b* 4 April 1935; *s* of Ernest Griffiths and Anne Connor. *Educ:* Manchester Univ. BA (Hons) Eng. Lang. and Lit. Teaching, 1957–65; Educn Officer, BBC, 1965–72. Writer's Award, BAFTA, 1981. *Publications:* Occupations, 1972, 3rd edn 1980; Sam Sam, 1972; The Party, 1974, 2nd edn 1978; Comedians, 1976, 2nd edn 1979; All Good Men, and Absolute Beginners, 1977; Through the Night, and Such Impossibilities, 1977; Thermidor and Apricots, 1977; (jtly) Deeds, 1978; (trans.) The Cherry Orchard, 1978; Country, 1981; Oi for England, 1982; Sons and Lovers (television version), 1982; Judgement Over the Dead (television screenplays of The Last Place on Earth), 1986; Fatherland (screenplay), and Real Dreams, 1987; Collected Plays for Television, 1988; Piano, 1990. *Address:* c/o Peters, Fraser & Dunlop, 5th Floor, The Chambers, Chelsea Harbour, Lots Road, SW10 0XF.

GRIFFITHS, William Arthur; management consultant; *b* 25 May 1940; *s* of Glyndwr and Alice Rose Griffiths; *m* 1963, Margaret Joan Dodd; two *s* one *d. Educ:* Owen's Sch., London; Queens' Coll., Cambridge; Univ. of Manchester. Probation Officer, Southampton, 1965–71; Home Office, 1971–76; Chief Probation Officer, N Ireland, 1977–84; Dir, NCVO, 1985–86. Member Executive Committee: NI Council for Voluntary Action, 1985; Wales Council for Voluntary Action, 1985; Scottish Council for Community and Voluntary Organisations, 1985; Trustee, Charities Aid Foundn, 1985. Chm. Finance, Westminster CC, 1990–. *Recreation:* literature. *Address:* 86 Bryanston Court, George Street, W1H 7HD.

GRIFFITHS, Winston James; MP (Lab) Bridgend, since 1987; *b* 11 Feb. 1943; *s* of (Rachel) Elizabeth Griffiths and (Evan) George Griffiths; *m* 1966, (Elizabeth) Ceri Griffiths; one *s* one *d. Educ:* State schools in Brecon; University College of South Wales and Monmouthshire, Cardiff. BA, DipEd. Taught in Tanzania, Birmingham, Barry, Cowbridge. MEP (Lab) Wales South, 1979–89; a Vice Pres., 1984–87; formerly Chm., Parliamentarians Global Action for Disarmament, Develt and World Reform (formerly Parliamentarians for World Order); formerly Mem., delegn to S Asia; Hon. Mem., European Parlt, 1989. Member: World Development Movement; Christian Socialist Movement; Amnesty International; Campaign for Nuclear Disarmament; Fabian Society; Anti-Apartheid Movement; VSO; Socialist Educn Assoc., 1986–. Vice Pres., Wales Aid to Poland. Pres., Kenfig Hill and Dist Male Voice Choir, 1986–. Methodist local preacher, 1966–. *Address:* Tŷ Llon, John Street, Y Graig, Cefn Cribwr, Mid Glamorgan CF32 0AB. *T:* Kenfig Hill (0656) 740526.

GRIGG, John (Edward Poynder), FRSL; writer; *b* 15 April 1924; *s* of late 1st Baron Altrincham and Joan Dickson-Poynder; *m* 1958, Patricia, *d* of late H. E. Campbell and of Marion Wheeler; two *s. Educ:* Eton; New Coll., Oxford (Exhibitioner). MA, Modern History; Gladstone Memorial Prize. Grenadier Guards, 1943–45. Editor, National and English Review, 1954–60; Columnist for The Guardian, 1960–70; with The Times, 1986–. Chm., The London Library, 1985–. Pres., Blackheath Soc.; Vice-Chm., Greenwich Festival Trustees. Contested (C) Oldham West, 1951 and 1955. Pres., Greenwich Cons. Assoc., 1979–82. Joined SDP, 1982, SLD, 1988. *Publications:* Two Anglican Essays, 1958; The Young Lloyd George, 1973; Lloyd George: the People's Champion, 1978 (Whitbread Award); 1943: The Victory That Never Was, 1980; Nancy Astor: Portrait of a Pioneer, 1980; Lloyd George: From Peace to War 1912–1916, 1985 (Wolfson Literary Prize);

contribs to other books; articles and reviews. *Address:* 32 Dartmouth Row, SE10. *T:* 081–692 4973. *Clubs:* Garrick, Beefsteak.
See also Sir W. A. Campbell.

GRIGGS, Rt. Rev. Ian Macdonald; *see* Ludlow, Bishop Suffragan of.

GRIGGS, Norman Edward, CBE 1976; Vice-President, The Building Societies Association, since 1981 (Secretary-General, 1963–81); *b* 27 May 1916; *s* of late Archibald Griggs and late Maud Griggs (*née* Hewing); *m* 1947, Livia Lavinia Jandolo; one *s* one step *s. Educ:* Newport Grammar Sch.; London Sch. of Econs and Polit. Science (BScEcon). FCIS. Accountancy Dept, County of London Electric Supply Co. Ltd, 1933–40; service in RE and RAPC, Middle East, 1940–46; Asst Sec., Glass Manufrs' Fedn, 1946–52; Sec., Plastics Inst., 1952–56; Asst Sec., Building Socs Assoc., 1956–61, Dep. Sec. 1961–63; Sec.-Gen., Internat. Union of Building Socs and Savings Assocs, 1972–77; Vice-Pres., Chartered Building Socs Inst., 1981–. *Publication:* Life in the Withered Shell (poetry). *Recreation:* print addict. *Address:* 5 Gledhow Gardens, SW5 0BL. *T:* 071–373 5128.

GRIGSON, Geoffrey Douglas; His Honour Judge Grigson; a Circuit Judge, since 1989; *b* 28 Oct. 1944; *s* of Frederic Walter Grigson and Nora Marion Grigson; *m* 1967, Jay Sibbring; two *s* one *d. Educ:* Denstone Coll.; Selwyn Coll., Cambridge (MA). Called to the Bar, Gray's Inn, 1968; Midland and Oxford Circuit; a Recorder, 1985–89. *Recreation:* reading newspapers. *Address:* Devereux Chambers, Devereux Court, Temple, WC2R 3JJ. *Club:* Achilles.

GRILLER, Sidney Aaron, CBE 1951; Leader of Griller String Quartet since 1928; *b* London, 10 Jan. 1911; *s* of Salter Griller and Hannah (*née* Green); *m* 1932, Elizabeth Honor, *y d* of James Linton, JP, Co. Down, N Ireland; one *s* one *d. Educ:* Royal Academy of Music. Toured British Isles, Holland, Germany, Switzerland, France, Italy, 1928–38; first concert tour in USA, 1939. Served RAF, 1940–45. Lecturer in Music, University of California, 1949; world tours, 1951, 1953. Prof. of Music: Royal Irish Acad. of Music, 1963; Royal Academy of Music, 1964 (Dir of Chamber Music, 1983–86); Associate Sen. Tutor, Menuhin Sch., 1987–. Worshipful Company of Musicians Medal for Chamber Music, 1944; FRAM, 1945. DUniv York, 1981. *Address:* 63 Marloes Road, W8. *T:* 071–937 7067.

GRILLET, Alain R.; *see* Robbe-Grillet.

GRILLS, Michael Geoffrey; a Recorder of the Crown Court, since 1982; a District Judge, since 1991; *b* 23 Feb. 1937; *s* of Frank and Bessie Grills; *m* 1969, Ann Margaret Irene (*née* Pyle); two *d. Educ:* Lancaster Royal Grammar Sch.; Merton Coll., Oxford (MA). Admitted Solicitor, 1961; Partner with Crombie Wilkinson & Robinson, York, 1965; County Court and District Registrar, York and Harrogate District Registries, 1973–90. *Recreations:* music, tennis. *Address:* Cobblestones, Skelton, York YO3 6XX. *T:* York (0904) 470 246.

GRIMA, Andrew Peter; Jeweller by appointment to HM the Queen; Managing Director: H. J. Co. Ltd, since 1951; Andrew Grima Ltd, since 1966; *b* 31 May 1921; *s* of late John Grima and Leopolda Farnese; *m* 1st, 1947, Helène Marianne Haller (marr. diss. 1977); one *s* two *d*; 2nd, 1977, Joanne Jill Maughan-Brown, *d* of late Captain Nigel Maughan-Brown, MC and of Mrs G. Rawdon; one *d. Educ:* St Joseph's Coll., Beulah Hill; Nottingham Univ. Served War of 1939–45, REME, India and Burma, 1942–46 (despatches, 1945); commanded div. workshop. Director and jewellery designer, H. J. Co., 1947–. Exhibitions in numerous cities all over the world; designed and made prestige collection of watches, "About Time", 1970; exhibited at Goldsmiths' Hall. Opened shops in Sydney and New York, 1970; Zürich, 1971; Tokyo, 1973. Has donated annual Andrew Grima award to Sir John Cass Coll. of Art, 1963–. Duke of Edinburgh Prize for Elegant Design, 1966; 11 Diamond Internat. New York Awards, 1963–67. Freeman, City of London, 1964; Liveryman, Worshipful Co. of Goldsmiths, 1968. *Publications:* contribs to: International Diamond Annual, S Africa, 1970; 6 Meister Juweliere unserer Zeit, 1971. *Recreations:* paintings, sculpture, food and wine, campaign to rule out red tape. *Address:* CP 2541, Lugano, CH 6901, Switzerland; Albany, Piccadilly, W1V 9RR.

GRIME, Mark Stephen Eastburn; QC 1987; a Recorder, since 1990; *b* 16 March 1948; *s* of R. T. Grime, ChM, FRCS and M. D. Grime; *m* 1973, Christine Emck; two *d. Educ:* Wrekin College; Trinity College, Oxford (Scholar; MA). Called to the Bar, Middle Temple, 1970; practising Northern Circuit, 1970–; Asst Recorder, 1988–90. Chm., Disciplinary Appeal Tribunal, UMIST, 1980–; Mem. Council, Northern Arbitration Assoc., 1990–. *Recreations:* antiquarian horology, sailing. *Address:* Deans Court Chambers, Cumberland House, Crown Square, Manchester M3 3HA. *T:* 061–834 4097.

GRIMLEY EVANS, Prof. John, FRCP; Professor of Geriatric Medicine, University of Oxford, since 1985; Fellow of Green College, Oxford, since 1985; *b* 17 Sept. 1936; *s* of Harry Walter Grimley Evans and Violet Prenter Walker; *m* 1966, Corinne Jane Cavender; two *s* one *d. Educ:* King Edward's Sch., Birmingham; St John's Coll., Cambridge (Rolleston Scholar; MA, MD); Balliol Coll., Oxford (DM); FFCM. Res. Asst, Nuffield Dept of Clin. Med., Oxford, 1963–65; Vis. Scientist, Sch. of Public Health, Univ. of Michigan, 1966; Res. Fellow, Med. Unit, Wellington Hosp., NZ, 1966–69; Lectr in Epidemiology, LSHTM, 1970–71; Prof. of Medicine (Geriatrics), Univ. of Newcastle upon Tyne, 1973–84. Chm., Specialist Adv. Cttee on Geriatric Medicine, Jt Cttee for Higher Med. Trng, 1979–86; Mem., WHO Expert Panel on Care of Elderly, 1984– (Rapporteur, 1987); Chm., RCP Geriatric Medicine Cttee, 1989–. Chm., Examining Bd, Dip. in Geriatric Medicine, 1985–90. Pro-censor, RCP, 1990–. Editor, Age and Ageing, 1988–. *Publications:* Care of the Elderly, 1977; (jtly) Advanced Geriatric Medicine (series), 1981–; (jtly) Improving the Health of Older People: a world view, 1990; papers on geriatric medicine and epidemiology of chronic disease. *Recreations:* photography, fly-fishing, literature. *Address:* Donnington Farmhouse, Meadow Lane, Iffley, Oxford OX4 4ED. *Club:* Royal Society of Medicine.

GRIMOND, family name of **Baron Grimond.**

GRIMOND, Baron *cr* 1983 (Life Peer), of Firth in the County of Orkney; **Joseph Grimond,** TD; PC 1961; Leader of the Parliamentary Liberal Party, 1956–67, and May–July 1976; Trustee, The Manchester Guardian and Evening News Ltd, 1967–83; Chancellor of University of Kent at Canterbury, 1970–90; *b* 29 July 1913; *s* of Joseph Bowman Grimond and Helen Lydia Richardson; *m* 1938, Hon. Laura Miranda, *d* of late Sir Maurice Bonham Carter, KCB, KCVO, and Baroness Asquith of Yarnbury, DBE; two *s* one *d* (and one *s* decd). *Educ:* Eton; Balliol Coll., Oxford (Brackenbury Scholar; 1st Class Hons (Politics, Philosophy, and Economics); Hon. Fellow 1984). Called to the Bar, Middle Temple (Harmsworth Scholar), 1937. Served War of 1939–45, Fife and Forfar Yeomanry and Staff 53 Div. (Major). Contested Orkney and Shetland (L), 1945; MP (L) Orkney and Shetland, 1950–83. Dir of Personnel, European Office, UNRRA, 1945–47; Sec. of the National Trust for Scotland, 1947–49. Rector: Edinburgh Univ., 1960–63; Aberdeen Univ., 1969–72. Chubb Fellow, Yale; Romanes Lectr, 1980. Hon. LLD: Edinburgh, 1960; Aberdeen, 1972; Birmingham, 1974; Buckingham, 1983; Hon. DCL Kent, 1970; DUniv Stirling, 1984. *Publications:* The Liberal Future, 1959; The Liberal Challenge, 1963; (with B. Neve) The Referendum, 1975; The Common Welfare, 1978; Memoirs, 1979; A Personal Manifesto, 1983; contributor: The Prime Ministers, 1976; My Oxford, 1977; Britain—a view from Westminster, 1986. *Address:* 24 Priory Avenue, W4 1TY.

GRIMSBY, Bishop Suffragan of, since 1979; **Rt. Rev. David Tustin;** *b* 12 Jan. 1935; *s* of John Trevelyan Tustin and Janet Reynolds; *m* 1964, Mary Elizabeth (*née* Glover); one *s* one *d. Educ:* Solihull School; Magdalene Coll., Cambridge (MA Hons); Geneva Univ. (Cert. in Ecumenical Studies); Cuddesdon Coll., Oxford. Philip Usher Memorial Scholar (in Greece), 1957–58; Deacon 1960, priest 1961; Curate of Stafford, 1960–63; Asst Gen. Sec., C of E Council on Foreign Relations and Curate of St Dunstan-in-the-West, Fleet St, 1963–67; Vicar of S Paul's, Wednesbury, 1967–71; Vicar of Tettenhall Regis, 1971–79; RD of Trysull, 1977–79. Canon and Prebendary of Lincoln Cathedral, 1979–. Co-Chm., Anglican/Lutheran Internat. Commn, 1986–; Pres., Anglican/Lutheran Soc., 1987–; Mem., Gen. Synod of C of E, 1990–. *Recreations:* music, family life, languages, travel. *Address:* Bishop's House, Church Lane, Irby-upon-Humber, Grimsby DN37 7JR. *T:* Swallow (0472) 371715.

GRIMSHAW, Maj.-Gen. Ewing Henry Wrigley, CB 1965; CBE 1957 (OBE 1954); DSO 1945; *b* 30 June 1911; *s* of Col E. W. Grimshaw; *m* 1943, Hilda Florence Agnes Allison; two *s* one *d. Educ:* Brighton Coll. Joined Indian Army, 1931. Served War of 1939–45, Western Desert and Burma (despatches twice). Transferred to Royal Inniskilling Fusiliers, 1947; Active Service in Malaya, 1948 and 1950, Kenya, 1954, Suez, 1956 and Cyprus, 1958. GOC 44th Div. (TA) and Home Counties Dist, 1962–65. Col, The Royal Inniskilling Fusiliers, 1966–68; Dep. Col, The Royal Irish Rangers, 1968–73.

GRIMSHAW, Nicholas Thomas; Chairman, Nicholas Grimshaw & Partners Ltd, architects, planners and industrial designers, since 1980; *b* 9 Oct. 1939; *s* of Thomas Cecil Grimshaw and Hannah Joan Dearsley; *m* 1972, Lavinia, *d* of John Russell, *qv*; two *d. Educ:* Wellington College, Edinburgh College of Art; Architectural Assoc. Sch. AA Dip. Hons 1965; RIBA 1967; FCSD (FSIAD 1969); numerous prizes and scholarships. Major projects include: Channel Tunnel terminal, Waterloo; British Pavilion for Expo '92, Seville, Spain; Financial Times Printing Plant; New Satellite and Piers, Heathrow Airport; Research Centre for Rank Xerox; BMW headquarters, Bracknell; Hartspring Business Park; Herman Miller Factory, Bath; Oxford Ice Rink; Gillingham Business Park; J. Sainsbury Superstore, Camden; Head Office and Printing Press for Western Morning News. Assessor for: British Construction Industry Awards; DoE; British Gas; Scottish Develt Agency. Awards and Commendations include: RIBA, 1975, 1978, 1980, 1983, 1986, 1989, 1990; Financial Times (for Industrial Architecture), 1977, 1980; Structural Steel Design. 1969, 1977, 1980, 1989; Civic Trust, 1978, 1982, 1989, 1990; British Construction Industry Awards, 1988, 1989; Royal Fine Art Commn/Sunday Times Building of the Year Award, 1989. *Publications:* Nicholas Grimshaw & Partners: product and process, 1988; articles for RSA Jl. *Recreations:* sailing, tennis. *Address:* 1 Conway Street, Fitzroy Square, W1P 5HA. *T:* 071–631 0869.

GRIMSTON, family name of **Baron Grimston of Westbury** and of **Earl of Verulam.**

GRIMSTON, Viscount; James Walter Grimston; *b* 6 Jan. 1978; *s* and *heir* of Earl of Verulam, *qv*.

GRIMSTON OF WESTBURY, 2nd Baron *cr* 1964; **Robert Walter Sigismund Grimston;** Bt 1952; Director, Gray's Inn (Underwriting Agencies) Ltd, 1965–90 (Chairman, 1970–88); Director, River Clyde Holdings, 1986–88; *b* 14 June 1925; *s* of 1st Baron Grimston of Westbury and Sybil Edith Muriel Rose (*d* 1977), *d* of Sir Sigismund Neumann, 1st Bt; *S* father, 1979; *m* 1949, Hon. June Mary Ponsonby, *d* of 5th Baron de Mauley; two *s* one *d. Educ:* Eton. Served as Lt Scots Guards, 1943–47; NW Europe, 1944–45. Oil Industry, 1948–53; Sales Director, Ditchling Press, 1953–61; Dir, Hinton Hill & Coles Ltd, 1962–83. Freeman, City of London, 1981; Liveryman, Worshipful Co. of Gold and Silver Wyre Drawers, 1981. *Recreations:* tennis, shooting, golf, walking. *Heir:* *s* Hon. Robert John Sylvester Grimston [*b* 30 April 1951; *m* 1984, Emily Margaret, *d* of Major John Shirley; one *d. Educ:* Eton; Reading Univ. (BSc). Chartered Accountant. Commnd The Royal Hussars (PWO), 1970–81, Captain 1976]. *Address:* The Old Rectory, Westwell, near Burford, Oxon. *Clubs:* Boodle's, City of London.

GRIMTHORPE, 4th Baron, *cr* 1886; **Christopher John Beckett,** Bt 1813; OBE 1958; DL; Deputy Commander, Malta and Libya, 1964–67; *b* 16 Sept. 1915; *e s* of 3rd Baron Grimthorpe, TD, and Mary Lady Grimthorpe (*d* 1962); *S* father, 1963; *m* 1954, Lady Elizabeth Lumley, (*see* Lady Grimthorpe); two *s* one *d. Educ:* Eton. 2nd Lieut, 9 Lancers, 1936; Lt-Col, 9 Lancers, 1955–58; AAG, War Office, 1958–61; Brigadier, Royal Armoured Corps, HQ, Western Command, 1961–64. Col, 9/12 Royal Lancers, 1973–77. ADC to the Queen, 1964–67. Director: Standard Broadcasting Corp. of Canada (UK), 1972–86; Thirsk Racecourse Ltd, 1972–; Yorkshire Post Newspapers, 1973–86; Pres., London Metropolitan Region YMCA, 1972–86. Mem., Jockey Club. DL North Yorkshire, 1969. *Recreations:* travel, horse sports. *Heir:* *s* Hon. Edward John Beckett, *b* 20 Nov. 1954. *Address:* 87 Dorset House, Gloucester Place, NW1. *T:* 071–486 4374; Westow Hall, York. *T:* Whitwell-on-the-Hill (065381) 225. *Clubs:* Cavalry and Guards, Portland.

GRIMTHORPE, Lady; Elizabeth Beckett, CVO 1983; Lady of the Bedchamber to HM Queen Elizabeth The Queen Mother, since 1973; *b* 22 July 1925; 2nd *d* of 11th Earl of Scarbrough, KG, GCVO, PC and Katharine Isobel, Countess of Scarbrough, DCVO, K-i-H Gold Medal; *m* 1954, 4th Baron Grimthorpe, *qv*; two *s* one *d. Address:* Westow Hall, York. *T:* Whitwell-on-the-Hill (065381) 225.

GRIMWADE, Sir Andrew (Sheppard), Kt 1980; CBE 1977; Australian industrialist; *b* 26 Nov. 1930; *s* of late Frederick and Gwendolen Grimwade; *m* 1959, Barbara (*d* 1990), *d* of J. B. D. Kater; one *s. Educ:* Melbourne C of E Grammar Sch.; Trinity Coll., Melbourne Univ. (Exhib. Eng.; BSc); Oriel Coll., Oxford (swimming blue; MA). FRACI, FAIM. Vice-Chm., Nat. Mutual Life Assoc., 1988– (Dir, 1970–); Dep. Chm., NZ Ski Fields Ltd; Director: IBM (Aust.); Sony (Aust.) Pty Ltd; Nat. Aust. Bank, 1965–85; Commonwealth Ind. Gases, 1960–90. Mem., first Aust. Govt Trade Mission to China, 1973. Mem., Australian Govt Remuneration Tribunal, 1974–82. Pres., Walter and Eliza Hall Inst. of Med. Research, 1978– (Mem. Bd, 1963–). Chairman: Australian Art Exhibn Corp. (Chinese Exhibn), 1976–77; Australian Govt Official Estabts Trust, 1976–82; Trustee, Victorian Arts Centre, 1980–90; Emeritus Trustee, Nat. Gallery of Vic, 1990– (Trustee, 1964–90; Pres., 1976–90). Member: Council for Order of Australia, 1975–82; Felton Bequests' Cttee, 1973–. *Publication:* Involvement: The Portraits of Clifton Pugh and Mark Strizic, 1969. *Recreations:* skiing, cattle breeding, Australian art. *Address:* PO Box 134, E Melbourne, Vic 3002, Australia. *T:* (03) 822 5990. *Clubs:* Melbourne, Australian (Melbourne).

GRIMWADE, Rev. Canon John Girling; Chaplain to the Queen, 1980–90; permission to officiate, dioceses of Gloucester and Oxford, since 1989; *b* 13 March 1920; *s* of Herbert Alfred and Edith Grimwade; *m* 1951, Adini Anne Carus-Wilson; one *s* one *d. Educ:* Colet Court; St Paul's Sch.; Keble Coll., Oxford; Cuddesdon Coll. MA Oxon. Friends'

Ambulance Unit, 1940–45. Curate of Kingston-upon-Thames, 1950–53; Curate, University Church of St Mary-the-Virgin, Oxford, and Secretary of Oxford Univ. Student Christian Movement, 1953–56; Vicar of St Mark's, Smethwick, 1956–62; Rector of Caversham, 1962–81, and Priest-in-Charge of Mapledurham, 1968–81; Rector of Caversham and Mapledurham, 1981–83; Priest-in-Charge, Stonesfield, Oxford, 1983–89. Chm., House of Clergy, Oxford Diocesan Synod, 1976–82; Agenda Sec., Oxford Dio. Synod, 1983–88; Diocesan Press Officer, Oxford, 1983–89. Hon. Canon of Christ Church, Oxford, 1974–90, Hon. Canon Emeritus, 1990–. *Recreations:* gardening, walking. *Address:* 88 Alexander Drive, Cirencester, Glos GL7 1UJ.

GRINDEA, Miron, OBE 1986 (MBE 1977); Editor, ADAM International Review (Anglo-French literary magazine), since 1941; *b* 31 Jan. 1909; *m* 1936, Carola Rabinovici, concert pianist; one *d. Educ:* Bucharest Univ.; Sorbonne. Literary and music critic, 1928–39; settled in England, Sept. 1939; together with Benjamin Britten, Stephen Spender and Henry Moore founded the International Arts Guild, 1943; war-time work with BBC European Service and Min. of Information; coast to coast lecture tours, USA. Visiting Lecturer: Univs of Paris, Aix-en-Provence, Athens, Karachi, Kyoto, Montreal, Toronto, Rejkiavik, Jerusalem, etc. Hon. DLitt Kent, 1983. Prix de l'Académie Française, 1955; Lundquist Literary Prize, Sweden, 1965. Chevalier de la Légion d'Honneur, 1974; Comdr, Order of Arts and Letters, France, 1985. *Publications:* Malta Calling, 1943; Henry Wood (a symposium), 1944; Jerusalem, a literary chronicle of 3000 years, 1968, 2nd edn, Jerusalem, the Holy City in literature, preface by Graham Greene, 1982; Natalie Clifford Barney, 1963; The London Library (a symposium), 1978; contrib. The Listener, TLS, Figaro, Les Nouvelles Littéraires, New Statesman, The Times, Independent, Guardian, Sunday Times, Observer, Spectator, Books and Bookmen. *Recreations:* Mozart, lazing in the sun. *Address:* 28 Emperor's Gate, SW7. *T:* 071–373 7307.

GRINDON, John Evelyn, CVO 1957; DSO 1945; AFC 1948; Group Captain, RAF retired; *b* 30 Sept. 1917; *s* of Thomas Edward Grindon (killed in action, Ypres, Oct. 1917), and Dora (*née* Eastlake), Corisande, East Pentire, Cornwall. *Educ:* Dulwich College. Flight Cadet at RAF College, Cranwell, 1935–37; served in Advanced Air Striking Force, BEF, France, 1939–40 (No 150 Sqdn) and in No 5 Group Bomber Command (Nos 106, 630 and 617 Sqdns) during War of 1939–45, as Flight and Sqdn Comdr; Chief Instructor, Long Range Transport Force, 1946–49; Commanded The Queen's Flight, 1953–56; V-bomber captain and Station Comdr, 1956–57; retired at own request 1959. Dir/Gen. Manager in printing/publishing, 1961–71; Metropolitan Police, New Scotland Yard, 1976–81. *Recreations:* opera, ocean surf, racing. *Club:* Royal Air Force.

GRINDROD, Helen Marjorie, QC 1982; a Recorder of the Crown Court, since 1981; *b* 28 Feb. 1936; *d* of late Joseph and Marjorie Pritchard; *m* 1958, Robert Michael Grindrod; one *s. Educ:* Liverpool Inst. High Sch. for Girls; St Hilda's Coll., Oxford. MA. Teacher, 1957–59. Called to the Bar, Lincoln's Inn, 1966, Bencher, 1990; Northern Circuit, 1966–. *Address:* 14 Gray's Inn Square, WC1R 5JP; 18 St John Street, Manchester M3 4EA.

GRINDROD, Most Rev. John Basil Rowland, KBE 1983; Archbishop of Brisbane and Metropolitan of Queensland, 1980–89; Primate of Australia, 1982–89; *b* 14 Dec. 1919; *s* of Edward Basil and Dorothy Gladys Grindrod; *m* 1949, Ailsa W. (*d* 1981), *d* of G. Newman; two *d*; *m* 1983, Mrs Dell Cornish, *d* of S. J. Caswell. *Educ:* Repton School; Queen's College, Oxford; Lincoln Theological College. BA 1949; MA 1954. Deacon, 1951; Priest, 1952, Manchester. Curate: St Michael's, Hulme, 1951–54; Bundaberg, Qld, 1954–56; Rector: All Souls, Ancoats, Manchester, 1956–60; Emerald, Qld, 1960–61; St Barnabas, N Rockhampton, Qld, 1961–65; Archdeacon of Rockhampton, Qld, 1960–65; Vicar, Christ Church, S Yarra, Vic, 1965–66; Bishop of Riverina, NSW, 1966–71; Bishop of Rockhampton, 1971–80. Hon. ThD, 1985. *Address:* Box 421, GPO, Brisbane, Qld 4001, Australia.

GRINLING, Jasper Gibbons, CBE 1978; CBIM; Chairman, London Jazz Radio plc, since 1989; *b* 29 Jan. 1924; *s* of late Lt-Col Antony Gibbons Grinling, MBE, MC, and Jean Dorothy Turing Grinling; *m* 1950, Jane Moulsdale; one *s* two *d. Educ:* Harrow (Scholar); King's Coll., Cambridge (Exhibnr, BA). FBIM 1969. Served War, 12th Lancers, 1942–46 (Captain). Joined W. & A. Gilbey Ltd, 1947, Dir 1952; Man. Dir, Gilbeys Ltd, 1964; Man. Dir, International Distillers & Vintners Ltd, 1967; Dir, North British Distillery Co. Ltd, 1968–86; Dir of Corporate Affairs, Grand Metropolitan, 1981–85, Dir of Trade Relations, 1985–86; Chm., The Apple & Pear Develt Council, 1986–89. Pres., EEC Confedn des Industries Agricoles et Alimentaires, 1976–80; Mem. Council, Scotch Whisky Assoc., 1968–86. FRSA. Chevalier, Ordre National du Mérite, France, 1983. *Publication:* The Annual Report, 1986. *Recreations:* gardening, jazz drumming, painting, vineyard proprietor. *Address:* The Old Vicarage, Helions Bumpstead, near Haverhill, Suffolk CB9 7AS. *T:* Steeple Bumpstead (0440) 730316.

GRINSTEAD, Sir Stanley (Gordon), Kt 1986; FCA; CBIM; Chairman and Director, Harmony Leisure Group, since 1989; *b* 17 June 1924; *s* of Ephraim Grinstead and Lucy Grinstead (*née* Taylor); *m* 1955, Joyce Preston; two *d. Educ:* Strodes, Egham. Served Royal Navy, 1943–46 (Pilot, FAA). Franklin, Wild & Co., Chartered Accountants, 1946–56; Hotel York Ltd, 1957; Grand Metropolitan Ltd, 1957–62; Union Properties (London) Ltd, 1958–66; Grand Metropolitan Ltd, 1964–87: Dep. Chm. and Group Man. Dir, 1980–82; Gp Chief Exec., 1982–86; Chm., 1982–87; Chm., Reed Internat., 1988–89 (Dir, 1981–90). Trustee, FAA Museum. Vice-Pres., CGLI, 1986–90. Master, Brewers' Co., 1983–84. *Recreations:* gardening, cricket, racing, breeding of thoroughbred horses. *Clubs:* Army and Navy, MCC; Surrey County Cricket.

GRINT, Edmund Thomas Charles, CBE 1960; *b* 14 Feb. 1904; *e s* of Edmund Albert Grint; *m* 1930, Olive Maria (*d* 1991), *d* of Albert Cheyne Sherras; one *s* two *d. Educ:* London Univ. (Dip. Econs). Joined ICI 1929; Commercial Dir, Nobel Div., 1946; Director: Billingham Div., 1952–61; Alkali Div., 1961–63; Mond Div., 1964. Dep. Chief Labour Officer, 1951; Chief Labour Officer, 1952–63; Gen. Manager Personnel, 1963–65. Chm., Nat. Dock Labour Board, 1966–69; Pres., Midland Iron and Steel Wages Bd, 1971–79. *Recreations:* golf, gardening. *Address:* Old Walls, Seal, Sevenoaks, Kent TN15 0JB. *T:* Sevenoaks (0732) 61364.

GRINYER, Prof. Peter Hugh; Esmée Fairbairn Professor of Economics (Finance and Investment), University of St Andrews, since 1979; *b* 3 March 1935; *s* of Sidney George and Grace Elizabeth Grinyer; *m* 1958, Sylvia Joyce Boraston; two *s. Educ:* Balliol Coll., Oxford (BA, subseq. MA, PPE); LSE (PhD in Applied Economics). Unilever Sen. Managerial Trainee, 1957–59; PA to Man. Dir, E. R. Holloway Ltd, 1959–61; Lectr and Sen. Lectr, Hendon Coll. of Tech., 1961–64; Lectr, 1965–69, Sen. Lectr, 1969–72, City Univ.; Reader, 1972–74, Prof. of Business Strategy, 1974–79, City Univ. Business School; Vice-Principal, 1985–87, Actg Principal, 1986, St Andrews Univ. Chairman: St Andrews Management Inst., 1989; St Andrews Strategic Management Ltd, 1989. Mem., Business and Management Studies Sub-Cttee, UGC, 1979–85. Founding Dir, Glenrothes Enterprise Trust, 1983–86; Director: John Brown PLC, 1984–86; Don and Low (Hldgs) Ltd (formerly Don Bros Buist), 1985–; Ellis and Goldstein (Hldgs) PLC, 1987–88; Chm., McIlroy Coates, 1991–. *Publications:* Corporate Models Today (with J. Wooller), 1975, 2nd edn 1979; (with G. D. Vaughan and S. Birley) From Private to Public, 1977; (with J.-C. Spender) Turnaround: the fall and rise of Newton Chambers, 1979; (with D. G. Mayes and P. McKiernan) Sharpbenders, 1988; over 40 papers in academic jls. *Recreations:* hill walking, golf. *Address:* 60 Buchanan Gardens, St Andrews, Fife KY16 9LX. *Club:* Royal & Ancient Golf (St Andrews).

GRISEWOOD, Harman Joseph Gerard, CBE 1960; Chief Assistant to the Director-General, BBC, 1955–64, retired; *b* 8 Feb. 1906; *e s* of late Lieut-Col Harman Grisewood and Lucille Cardozo; *m* 1940, Clotilde Margaret Bailey; one *d. Educ:* Ampleforth Coll., York; Worcester Coll., Oxford. BBC Repertory Co., 1929–33; Announcer, 1933–36; Asst to Programme Organiser, 1936–39; Asst Dir Programme Planning, 1939–41; Asst Controller, European Div., 1941–45; Actg Controller, European Div., 1945–46; Dir of Talks, 1946–47; Planner, Third Programme, 1947–48; Controller of the Third Programme, BBC, 1948–52; Dir of the Spoken Word, BBC, 1952–55. Member: Younger Cttee on Privacy, 1970–72; Lord Chancellor's Cttee on Defamation, 1971; Res. Officer, Royal Commn on Civil Liberty, 1973–75. Vice-President: European Broadcasting Union, 1953–54; Royal Literary Fund. Chm., The Latin Mass Soc., 1969. King Christian X Freedom Medal, 1946. Mem. Hon. Soc. of Cymmrodorion, 1956. Knight of Grace and Devotion, SMO Malta, 1960. *Publications:* Broadcasting and Society, 1949; The Recess, 1963 (novel); The Last Cab on the Rank, 1964 (novel); David Jones: Welsh National Lecture, 1966; One Thing at a Time (autobiography), 1968; The Painted Kipper, 1970; Stratagem, 1987. *Address:* The Old School House, Castle Hill, Eye, Suffolk IP23 7AP.

GRIST, Ian; MP (C) Cardiff Central, since 1983 (Cardiff North, Feb. 1974–1983); *b* 5 Dec. 1938; *s* of late Basil William Grist, MBE and Leila Helen Grist; *m* 1966, Wendy Anne (*née* White), JP, BSc; two *s. Educ:* Repton Sch.; Jesus Coll., Oxford (Schol.). Plebiscite Officer, Southern Cameroons, 1960–61; Stores Manager, United Africa Co., Nigeria, 1961–63; Wales Information Officer, Conservative Central Office, 1963–74; Conservative Research Dept, 1970–74. Chm., Cons. W African Cttee, 1977–87. Vice-Chm., Assoc. of Conservative Clubs, 1978–82. PPS to Secretary of State for Wales, 1979–81; Parly Under Sec. of State, Welsh Office, 1987–90. Mem., Select Cttee on: Violence in the Family, 1977–79; Welsh Affairs, 1981–83 and 1986–87; Register of Members' Interests, 1983–87. *Recreations:* reading, listening to music, politics. *Address:* House of Commons, SW1A 0AA; 126 Penylan Road, Cardiff CF2 5RD.

GRIST, John Frank; broadcasting consultant; Supervisor of Parliamentary Broadcasting of the House of Commons, since 1989 (Specialist Adviser to the Select Committee on Televising of Proceedings of the House of Commons, 1988–89); Managing Director, Services Sound and Vision Corporation, 1982–88; *b* 10 May 1924; *s* of Austin Grist, OBE, MC, and Ada Mary Grist (*née* Ball); *m* Gilian, *d* of Roger Cranage and Helen Marjorie Rollett; one *s* two *d. Educ:* Ryde Sch., IoW; London Sch. of Economics and Political Science (BSc Econ); Univ. of Chicago. RAF Pilot, 1942–46. BBC External Services, 1951–53; Talks Producer, Programme Organiser, Northern Region; Controller, Nat. Programmes, Nigerian Broadcasting Service, 1953–56; BBC TV Talks and Current Affairs at Lime Grove, 1957–72, producer of political programmes and Editor of Gallery and of Panorama; Hd of Current Affairs Gp, 1967–72; Controller, English Regions BBC, 1972–77; US Rep., BBC, 1978–81; Founder and first Man. Dir, NY World Television Fest., 1978. BP Press Fellow, Wolfson Coll., Cambridge, 1988. Chm., Howard Steele Foundn for Training in Television, Film and Video, 1985–88. Gov., Royal Star and Garter Home, 1986–. FRTS 1986 (Mem. Council, 1984–88). *Address:* 4 Burlington House, Kings Road, Richmond, Surrey TW10 6NW. *T:* 081–940 6351. *Club:* Reform.

GRIST, Prof. Norman Roy, FRCPEd; Professor of Infectious Diseases, University of Glasgow, 1965–83, now Emeritus; *b* 9 March 1918; *s* of Walter Reginald Grist and Florence Goodwin Grist (*née* Nadin); *m* 1943, Mary Stewart McAlister. *Educ:* Shawlands Acad., Glasgow; University of Glasgow. Postgrad. studies at Dept of Bacteriology, University of Liverpool, 1948–49; Virus Reference Lab., Colindale, London, 1951–52; Dept of Epidemiology, University of Michigan, 1956–57. BSc 1939; MB, ChB (Commendation), 1942; Mem. 1950, Fellow 1958, RCP, Edinburgh; Founder Mem., 1963, FRCPath 1967; Mem. 1980, Fellow 1983, RCPGlas. Ho. Phys. Gartloch Hosp., 1942–43; RAMC, GDO 223 Fd Amb. and RMO 2/KSLI, 1943–46; Ho. Surg. Victoria Inf., Glasgow, 1946–47; Res. Phys, Ruchill Hosp., Glasgow, 1947–48; Research Asst, Glasgow Univ. Dept of Infectious Diseases, 1948–52; Lectr in Virus Disease, Glasgow Univ., 1952–62, and Regional Adviser in Virology to Scottish Western Reg. Hosp. Bd, 1960–74; Reader in Viral Epidemiology, Glasgow Univ., 1962–65. Mem., Expert Adv. Panel on Virus Diseases to WHO, 1967–. Hon. Mem., Assoc. of Clin. Pathology, 1989. Bronze Medal, Helsinki Univ., 1973; Orden Civil de Sanidad, cat. Encomienda, Spain, 1974. *Publications:* Diagnostic Methods in Clinical Virology, 1966, 3rd edn, 1979; (with D. Reid and I. W. Pinkerton) Infections in Current Medical Practice, 1986; (with D. O. Ho-Yen, E. Walker and G. R. Williams) Diseases of Infection, 1987; numerous contribs. to British and international med. jls. *Recreations:* gardener's mate, natural history. *Address:* 5A Hyndland Court, 6A Sydenham Road, Glasgow G12 9NR. *T:* 041–339 5242. *Clubs:* Royal Automobile; Royal Scottish Automobile (Glasgow).

GRIST, Maj.-Gen. Robin Digby, OBE 1979; Director Army Air Corps, since 1989; *b* 1940; *s* of Lt-Col and Mrs Digby Grist; *m* 1971, Louise Littlejohn; one *s* two *d. Educ:* Hazlegrove House; Radley Coll.; Royal Military Acad., Sandhurst. Commnd, Gloucestershire Regt, 1960; service in UK and Cyprus, 1961–65; seconded to Army Air Corps, 1965–69; active service, Aden and S Arabia, 1966–67 (despatches); service with 1 Glosters, incl. active service in NI, 1969–70; Army Staff course, 1971–72; Staff Officer, MoD, 1973–74 and 1977–79; service with 1 Glosters, Germany, UK and Belize, 1975–76; CO 1st Bn Gloucestershire Regt, 1979–82; Mil. Dir of Studies, RMCS, 1982–84; Comdr 6 Airmobile Bde, 1985–86; RCDS 1987; Mil. Attaché and Comdr Brit. Army Staff, Washington, USA, 1988–89. Col, The Gloucestershire Regt, 1990–. Gov., Royal Sch., Bath, 1989–. *Publications:* articles in mil. jls, particularly on airmobility. *Recreations:* fishing, gardening. *Club:* Army and Navy.

GROBLER, Richard Victor; Deputy Secretary of Commissions, since 1984; *b* Umtali, S Rhodesia, 27 May 1936; *m* 1961, Julienne Nora de la Cour (*née* Sheath); one *s* three *d. Educ:* Bishop's, Capetown; Univ. of Cape Town (BA). Called to the Bar, Gray's Inn, 1961; joined staff of Clerk of the Court, Central Criminal Court, 1961; Dep. Clerk of the Court, 1970; Dep. Courts Administrator, 1972; Courts Administrator, Inner London Crown Court, 1974; Sec., Lord Chancellor's Adv. Cttee on Justices of the Peace for Inner London and Jt Hon. Sec., Inner London Br. of Magistrates' Assoc., 1974–77; Courts Administrator, Central Criminal Court, and Co-ordinator, Crown Courts Taxations, SE Circuit, 1977–79; Dep. Circuit Administrator, S Eastern Circuit, 1979–83. Liveryman, Worshipful Company of Gold and Silver Wyre Drawers. *Recreations:* gardening, swimming, golf. *Address:* Commissions Office, 26 Old Queen Street, SW1H 9HP. *T:* 071–210 3479.

GROCOTT, Bruce Joseph; MP (Lab) The Wrekin, since 1987; *b* 1 Nov. 1940; *s* of Reginald Grocott and Helen Grocott (*née* Stewart); *m* 1965, Sally Barbara Kay Ridgway; two *s. Educ:* Hemel Hempstead Grammar Sch.; Leicester and Manchester Univs. BA(Pol), MA(Econ). Admin. Officer, LCC, 1963–64; Lectr in Politics, Manchester Univ.,

Birmingham Polytechnic, and N Staffs Polytechnic, 1964–74. Television presenter and producer, 1979–87. Chm., Finance Cttee, Bromsgrove UDC, 1972–74. MP (Lab) Lichfield and Tamworth, Oct. 1974–1979; PPS to: Minister for Local Govt and Planning, 1975–76; Minister of Agriculture, 1976–78; Dep. Shadow Leader, H of C. Contested (Lab): Lichfield and Tamworth, 1979; The Wrekin, 1983. *Recreations:* cricket, snooker, fiction writing, steam railways. *Address:* House of Commons, SW1. *Club:* Trench Labour.

GRONHAUG, Arnold Conrad; *b* 26 March 1921; *s* of James Gronhaug, MBE, and Beatrice May Gronhaug; *m* 1945, Patricia Grace Smith; two *d*. *Educ:* Barry Grammar Sch.; Cardiff Technical Coll. CEng, FIEE; Hon. FCIBSE. Electrical Officer, RNVR, 1941–46. Air Ministry Works Directorate, 1946–63: Area Mech. and Elec. Engr, AMWD Malaya, 1951–52; Air Min. Headquarters, 1952–60; Dep. Chief Engr, AMWD, RAF Germany, 1960–63; Sen. Mech. and Elec. Engr, Portsmouth Area MPBW, 1963–67; Jt Services Staff Coll., 1964–65; Suptg Engr, MPBW, 1967–71; Dir Defence Works (Overseas), MPBW, 1971–73; Dir of Social and Research Services, DoE, 1973–75; Dir of Engrng Services Develt, 1975–76; Dir of Mechanical and Electrical Engineering Services, 1976–81. Member: Engrg Council Nominations Cttee, 1983–; IEE Memship Cttee, 1975–82 (Chm., 1979–82); CIBSE Qualifications Bd, 1981–87; IEE Memship Advr, Surrey, 1984–90. Freeman, City of London, 1979; Liveryman, Engineers Co., 1984. *Recreations:* music, photography, do-it-yourself. *Address:* 6 Pine Hill, Epsom, Surrey KT18 7BG. *T:* Epsom (0372) 721888.

GRONOW, David Gwilym Colin, MSc, PhD; Member, Electricity Council, 1985–90; *b* Leigh-on-Sea, 13 Jan. 1929; *s* of David Morgan Gronow and Harriet Hannah Gronow; *m* 1st, 1953, Joan Andrew Bowen Jones (marr. diss. 1970); one *s* one *d*; 2nd, 1970, Rosemary Freda Iris Keys. *Educ:* North Street Elem. Sch., Leigh-on-Sea; Grammar Sch., Swansea; University Coll. London (MSc, PhD). Institute of Aviation Medicine, RAF Farnborough, Hants: Jun. Technician, 1951–53; Sci. Officer, then Sen. Sci. Officer, 1953–57; Sen. Sci. Officer, UKAEA, Capenhurst, Cheshire, 1957; Second Asst Engr, then Sen. Asst Engr, CEGB, HQ Operations Dept, London, 1957–64; Asst Commercial Officer/Asst Chief Commercial Officer/Chief Commercial Officer, SSEB, Glasgow, 1964–78; Marketing Advr, 1978–80, Commercial Advr, 1980–85, Electricity Council, London. *Recreations:* travel, bird watching, theatre, clarinet. *Address:* 8 Arundel Way, Highcliffe, Christchurch, Dorset BH23 5DX.

GROOM, Maj.-Gen. John Patrick, CB 1984; CBE 1975 (MBE 1963); Director General, Guide Dogs for the Blind Association, 1983–89; *b* Hagley, Worcs, 9 March 1929; *s* of Samuel Douglas Groom and Gertrude Groom (*née* Clinton); *m* 1951, Jane Mary Miskelly; three *d*. *Educ:* King Charles I Sch., Kidderminster; Royal Military Academy, Sandhurst. Enlisted as Sapper, Dec. 1946; commnd into RE, 1949; regimental service, N Africa, Egypt, Singapore, Malaya, UK, 1949–59; sc Camberley, 1960; War Office, 1961–63; regimental service, UK, Aden, 1963–65 (despatches); Directing Staff, Staff Coll., 1965–68; Regimental Comdr, BAOR, 1968–70; MoD, Military Operations, 1970–71; Dep. Sec., Chiefs of Staff Cttee, 1971–73; HQ Near East Land Forces, Cyprus, 1973–75; RCDS 1976; Comdr, Corps of Royal Engineers, BAOR (Brig.), 1976–79; Chief Engineer, HQ BAOR, 1979–82; Head of Army Trng Rev. Team, MoD (Army), 1982–83. Col Comdt, 1983–91, Rep. Col Comdt, 1986, RE. Chairman: GDBA (Trading Co.) Ltd, 1984–89; GDBA Recreational Services Co. Ltd, 1989; Dir, GDBA (Pension Fund Trustee) Ltd, 1985–89; Chm., Internat. Fedn of Guide Dog Schs, 1987–. Governor: Gordon's Sch., Woking, 1982–88; Sandle Manor Sch., Fordingbridge, 1984–88. FBIM 1979; FIPlantE 1976. Liveryman, Worshipful Co. of Plumbers, 1978. Mem., Windsor Constitutional Club, 1985–. *Recreations:* ocean racing, riding, painting, antiques, ornithology, the environment. *Address:* Withybed, All Saints Road, Lymington, Hants SO41 8FB. *Clubs:* Army and Navy, Royal Ocean Racing; Royal Engineer Yacht; Royal Lymington Yacht; British Kiel Yacht (W Germany) (Life Mem.); Kieler Yacht (W Germany) (Hon. Mem.).

GROOTENHUIS, Prof. Peter, FEng 1982, FIMechE; Professor of Mechanical Engineering Science, Imperial College of Science, Technology and Medicine, 1972–89, now Emeritus Professor and Senior Research Fellow; *b* 31 July 1924; *yr s* of Johannes C. Grootenhuis and Anna C. (*née* van den Bergh); *m* 1954, Sara J. Winchester, *o c* of late Major Charles C. Winchester, MC, The Royal Scots (The Royal Regt), and Margaret I. (*née* de Havilland); one *d* one *s*. *Educ:* Nederlands Lyceum, The Hague; City and Guilds College. BSc MechEng 1944, PhD, DIC, DSc London Univ.; FCGI 1976, Mem., Inst. of Acoustics; Fellow, Soc. of Environmental Engineers (Pres., 1964–67). Apprenticeship and Design Office, Bristol Aero Engine Co., 1944–46; Lectr 1949, Reader 1959, Mech. Eng. Dept, Imperial College, research in heat transfer and in dynamics; Dir, Derritron Electronics, 1969–82; Partner, Grootenhuis Allaway Associates, consultants in noise and vibration, 1970–; Associate Mem., Ordnance Board, 1965–70; Mem. Governing Body, Imperial College, 1974–79. *Publications:* technical papers to learned jls, and patents. *Recreations:* sailing, gardening. *Club:* Athenæum.

GROSBERG, Prof. Percy, PhD; CEng, MIMechE, FTI; Research Professor of Textile Engineering, 1961–90, and Head of Department of Textile Industries, 1975–83 and 1987–89, University of Leeds, now Emeritus Professor; Hon. Consultant, Shenkar College of Textile Technology and Fashion, Ramat Gan, Israel; *b* 5 April 1925; *s* of late Rev. and Mrs Gershon Grosberg, Tel-Aviv; *m* 1951, Queenie Fisch; one *s* one *d* (and one *s* decd). *Educ:* Parktown Boys' High Sch., Johannesburg; Univ. of the Witwatersrand; Univ. of Leeds. BScEng, MScEng, PhD Witwatersrand; CEng, MIMechE 1965; FTI 1966 (Hon. FTI 1988). Sen. Res. Officer S African Wool Textile Res. Inst., 1949–55; Univ. of Leeds: ICI Res. Fellow, 1955; Lectr in Textile Engrg, 1955–61. FRSA 1990. Warner Memorial Medal, 1968; Textile Inst. Medal, 1972; Distinguished Service Award, Indian Inst. of Technol., Delhi, 1985. *Publications:* An Introduction to Textile Mechanisms, 1968; Structural Mechanics of Fibres, Yarns and Fabrics, 1969; papers on rheology of fibrous assemblies, mechan. processing of fibres, and other res. topics in Jl of Textile Inst., Textile Res. Jl, and other sci. jls. *Recreations:* music, gardening, travel. *Address:* 2 Sandringham Crescent, Leeds LS17 8DF. *T:* Leeds (0532) 687478.

GROSE, Vice-Adm. Sir Alan, KBE 1989; Flag Officer Plymouth, Naval Base Commander Devonport, Commander Central Sub Area Eastern Atlantic, and Commander Plymouth Sub Area Channel, since 1990; *b* 24 Sept. 1937; *s* of George William Stanley Grose and Ann May Grose (*née* Stanford); *m* 1961, Gillian Ann (*née* Dryden-Dymond); two *s* one *d*. *Educ:* Strodes School; Britannia Royal Naval College, Dartmouth. Served: Mediterranean and S Atlantic, 1957–63; sub-specialised in Navigation, 1964; RAN, 1964–66; Home, W Indies, Med., 1966–72; Comd, HMS Eskimo, 1973–75; Staff of C-in-C, Naval Home Command, 1975–77; MoD, 1977–79; RCDS 1980; Comd, HMS Bristol, 1981–82; RN Presentation Team, 1983–84; Comd, HMS Illustrious, 1984–86; Flag Officer, Sept. 1986; ACDS, Operational Requirements (Sea Systems), MoD, 1986–88; Flag Officer Flotilla Three and Comdr, Anti-Submarine Warfare Striking Force, 1988–90. *Recreations:* tennis, walking, reading. *Address:* c/o Barclays Bank, Plymouth. *Club:* Royal Naval Reserve.

GROSS, John Jacob; writer and editor; theatre critic, Sunday Telegraph, since 1989; *b* 12 March 1935; *s* of late Abraham Gross and Muriel Gross; *m* 1965, Miriam May; one *s* one *d*. *Educ:* City of London Sch.; Wadham Coll., Oxford. Editor, Victor Gollancz Ltd, 1956–58; Asst Lectr, Queen Mary Coll., Univ. of London, 1959–62; Fellow, King's Coll., Cambridge, 1962–65; Literary Editor, New Statesman, 1973; Editor, TLS, 1974–81; editorial consultant, Weidenfeld (Publishers) Ltd, 1982; on staff of New York Times, 1983–88; Dir, Times Newspapers Holdings, 1982. A Trustee, National Portrait Gall., 1977–84. *Publications:* The Rise and Fall of the Man of Letters (1969 Duff Cooper Memorial Prize), 1969; Joyce, 1971; (ed) The Oxford Book of Aphorisms, 1983; (ed) The Oxford Book of Essays, 1991. *Address:* 74 Princess Court, Queensway, W2. *Club:* Beefsteak.

GROSS, Solomon Joseph, CMG 1966; Director, Barnes Court (New Barnet) Ltd, since 1984; *b* 3 Sept. 1920; *s* of late Abraham Gross; *m* 1948, Doris Evelyn (*née* Barker); two *d*. *Educ:* Hackney Downs Sch.; University Coll., London. RAF, Burma, India. Ministry of Supply, 1947; OEEC, Paris, 1948–51; British Embassy, Washington, 1951–53; Board of Trade, 1954–57; British Trade Commr, Pretoria, SA, 1958–62; Principal British Trade Commr, Ghana, 1963–66; British Deputy High Commr, Ghana, 1966–67; Board of Trade, 1967–69; Minister, British Embassy, Pretoria, 1969–73; Chargé d'Affaires at various times in Ghana and S Africa; Under-Sec., Dept of Industry, 1974–80; Dir for Regional Affairs, British Technology Gp, 1983–84. Bd Mem., BSC, later British Steel plc, 1978–90; Dir, Technical Audit Group Ltd, 1986–90. Mem., Overseas Cttee, CBI, 1987–90; Mem., External Relations Cttee and Chm., USA Wkg Pty, UNICE, Brussels, 1987–90. *Recreations:* gardening, history, do-it-yourself. *Address:* 38 Barnes Court, Station Road, New Barnet, Herts EN5 1QY. *T:* 081–449 2710. *Club:* Royal Automobile.

GROSSART, Angus McFarlane McLeod, CBE 1990; Managing Director, Noble Grossart Ltd, Merchant Bankers, Edinburgh, since 1969; Chairman, Scottish Investment Trust PLC, since 1975; director of companies; *b* 6 April 1937; 3rd *s* of William John White Grossart and Mary Hay Gardiner; *m* 1978, Mrs Gay Thomson; one *d*. *Educ:* Glasgow Acad.; Glasgow Univ. (MA 1958, LLB 1960). CA 1962; Mem., Faculty of Advocates, 1963. Practised at Scottish Bar, 1963–69. Major directorships include: American Trust PLC, 1973–; Alexander & Alexander, USA, 1985–; Royal Bank of Scotland plc, 1982–; Scottish Financial Enterprise, 1987–; Hewden Stuart PLC, 1988–; Scottish TV plc, 1989–. British Petroleum Scottish Bd, 1990–; Dep. Chm., Edinburgh Fund Managers PLC, 1991– (Chm., 1983–91). Mem., Scottish Develt Agency, 1974–78. Chm., Bd of Trustees, National Galleries of Scotland, 1988– (Trustee, 1986–); Vice Pres., Scottish Opera, 1986–. Trustee, Scottish Cot Death Trust, 1986–. Formerly: Trustee, Scottish Civic Trust; Dir, Scottish Nat. Orch.; Mem., Scottish Industrial Develt Adv. Bd. Livingstone Captain of Industry Award, 1990. Hon. LLD Glasgow, 1985. Formerly, Scottish Editor, British Tax Encyc., and British Tax Rev. *Recreations:* golfing (runner-up, British Youths' Golf Championship, 1957; Captain, Scottish Youths Internat., 1956 and 1957), the decorative arts, Scottish castle restoration. *Address:* 48 Queen Street, Edinburgh EH2 3NR. *T:* 031–226 7011. *Clubs:* New, Honourable Company of Edinburgh Golfers (Edinburgh); Royal and Ancient (St Andrews).

GROSSCHMID-ZSÖGÖD, Prof. Géza (Benjamin), LLD; Professor, 1955–89, now Professor Emeritus, and Chairman, 1978–89, Division of Economic Sciences, Duquesne University, Pittsburgh, USA, retired; *b* Budapest, Hungary, 29 Oct. 1918; *o s* of late Prof. Lajos de Grosschmid and Jolán, *o d* of Géza de Szitányi; *m* 1946, Leonora Martha Nissler, 2nd *d* of Otto Nissler and Annemarie Dudt; one *d*. *Educ:* Piarist Fathers, Budapest; Royal Hungarian Pázmány Péter Univ., Budapest (LLD 1943). With private industry in Hungary, 1943–44; Royal Hungarian Army, 1944–45; UNRRA, 1946–47; Duquesne University: Asst Prof. of Econs, 1948–52; Associate Prof., 1952–55; Dir, Inst. of African Affairs, 1958–70; Dir, African Language and Area Center, 1960–74; Academic Vice Pres., 1970–75. Ford Foundn Fellow, 1958; Fulbright-Hays Fellow, S Africa, 1965; attended Cambridge Colonial Conf., King's Coll., 1961. Director: World Affairs Council of Pittsburgh, 1974–80; Afuture Fund of Philadelphia, 1976–84. Mem., Bd of Visitors, Coll. of Arts and Sciences, Univ. of Pittsburgh, 1970–86; Governor, Battle of Britain Museum Foundn, 1977–84. Consultore pro lingua hungarica, Collegio Araldico, Rome. Lord of the manors of Brassington and of North Tamerton. Kt of Malta, 1955 (Comdr of Merit, 1956; Kt of Obedience, 1974; Grand Cross of Obedience, 1984); Kt, Sacred Mil. Constantinian Order of St George (Naples), 1959 (Grand Cross of Justice, 1988; Pres., Amer. Assoc., 1978); Kt Comdr of St Gregory, 1968. Order of: Valour, Cameroon, 1967; Zaire, 1970; Equatorial Star, Gabon, 1973; Lion, Senegal, 1977. *Publications:* (jtly) Principles of Economics, 1959; (trans. with P. Colombo) The Spiritual Heritage of the Sovereign Military Order of Malta, 1958; (ed, with S. B. Vardy and L. S. Domonkos) Louis the Great King of Hungary and Poland, 1986; contrib. Encyc. Britannica; articles in learned jls. *Recreations:* walking, golf, heraldry, polo. *Address:* 3115 Ashlyn Street, Pittsburgh, Pa 15204, USA. *T:* (412) 331–7744. *Clubs:* Athenæum, MCC; Royal Forth Yacht (Edinburgh); Duquesne (Pittsburgh); Metropolitan, Army & Navy (Washington); Jockey (Vienna).

GROSVENOR, family name of **Baron Ebury,** and of **Duke of Westminster.**

GROSVENOR, Earl; Hugh Richard Louis Grosvenor; *b* 29 Jan. 1991; *o s* and *heir of* Duke of Westminster, *qv.*

GROTRIAN, Sir Philip Christian Brent, 3rd Bt *cr* 1934; *b* 26 March 1935; *s* of Robert Philip Brent Grotrian (*d* on active service, 1945) (*y s* of 1st Bt) and Elizabeth Mary, *d* of Major Herbert Hardy-Wrigley; *S* uncle, 1984; *m* 1st, 1960, Anne Isabel, *d* of Robert Sieger Whyte, Toronto; one *s*; 2nd, 1979, Sarah Frances, *d* of Reginald Harry Gale, Montreal; one *s* one *d*. *Educ:* Eton; Trinity Coll., Toronto. *Heir: s* Philip Timothy Adam Brent Grotrian, *b* 9 April 1962. *Address:* RR3, Mansfield, Ontario LON 1MO.

GROUES, Henri Antoine, *see* Pierre, Abbé.

GROUND, (Reginald) Patrick, QC 1981; MP (C) Feltham and Heston, since 1983; *b* 9 Aug. 1932; *s* of late Reginald Ground and Ivy Elizabeth Grace (*née* Irving); *m* 1964, Caroline Dugdale; three *s* one *d*. *Educ:* Beckenham and Penge County Grammar Sch.; Lycée Gay Lussac, Limoges, France; Selwyn Coll., Cambridge (Open Exhibnr; MA Mod. Langs, French and Spanish); Magdalen Coll., Oxford (MLitt, Mod. History). Inner Temple Studentship and Foster Boulton Prize, 1958; called to the Bar, Inner Temple, 1960, Bencher, 1987. National Service, RN, 1954–56: Sub-Lt RNVR; served in Mediterranean Fleet and on staff of C-in-C Mediterranean; rep. RN at hockey and lawn tennis; Lt-Comdr RNR. Worked for FO on staff of Wilton Park European Conf. Centre, 1958–60. Councillor, London Bor. of Hammersmith, 1968–71 (Chm., Cttees responsible for health and social services, 1969–71); contested (C), Hounslow, Feltham and Heston, Feb. and Oct. 1974, and 1979. PPS to the Solicitor General, 1987–. Treasurer and Pres., Oxford Univ. Cons. Assoc., 1958; Chm., Fulham Soc., 1975–. *Publications:* articles on housing, security of tenure and the Rent Acts in jls and periodicals. *Recreations:* lawn tennis, sailing, travel. *Address:* 13 Ranelagh Avenue, SW6 3PJ. *T:* 071–736 0131. *Clubs:* Brooks's, Carlton.

GROUNDS, Stanley Paterson, CBE 1968; Charity Commissioner, 1960–69; *b* 25 Oct. 1904; 2nd *s* of late Thomas Grounds and Olivia Henrietta (*née* Anear), Melbourne, Australia; *m* 1932, Freda Mary Gale Ransford; twin *s* and *d*. *Educ:* Melbourne High Sch.;

Queen's Coll., Melbourne Univ. (1st Cl. hons, MA). With Melbourne Herald, 1926–28; British Empire Producers' Organisation, London, 1928–33. Called to Bar, Middle Temple, 1933; at Chancery Bar, 1934–40. Served Royal Air Force, 1940–45 (Squadron Leader). Asst Charity Commissioner, 1946–58; Sec., Charity Commission, 1958–60. *Publications:* contrib. Encyclopædia of Forms and Precedents, Encyclopædia of Court Forms (on Charities), Halsbury's Laws of England, 3rd edn (on Charities). Articles in law jls. *Recreation:* other men's flowers. *Address:* St Helena, 19 Bell Road, Haslemere, Surrey GU27 3DQ. *T:* Haslemere (0428) 651230. *Club:* Army and Navy.

GROVE, Sir Charles Gerald, 5th Bt *cr* 1874; *b* 10 Dec. 1929; *s* of Walter Peel Grove (*d* 1944) (3rd *s* of 2nd Bt) and Elena Rebecca, *d* of late Felipe Crosthwaite; *S* brother, 1974. *Heir:* *b* Harold Thomas Grove, *b* 6 Dec. 1930.

GROVE, Dennis; *see* Grove, W. D.

GROVE, Sir Edmund (Frank), KCVO 1982 (CVO 1974; LVO 1963; MVO 1953); Chief Accountant of the Privy Purse, 1967–82, and Serjeant-at-Arms, 1975–82, retired; *b* 20 July 1920; *s* of Edmund Grove and Sarah Caroline (*née* Hunt); *m* 1945, Grete Elisabet, *d* of Martinus Skou, Denmark; two *d*. Served War, RASC, ME, 1940–46. Entered the Household of King George VI, 1946 and of Queen Elizabeth II, 1952. Chevalier: Order of the Dannebrog, Denmark, 1974; Légion d'Honneur, France, 1976; Officer, Order of the Polar Star, Sweden, 1975. *Recreation:* gardening. *Address:* Chapel Cottage, West Newton, King's Lynn, Norfolk PE31 6AU.

GROVE, Rear-Adm. John Scott, CB 1984; OBE 1964; RN retired, 1985; Defence Consultant, Babcock Energy Ltd, since 1986; Director, Devonport Management Ltd, Devonport Royal Dockyard, since 1987; *b* 7 July 1927; *s* of late William George Grove and Frances Margaret Scott Grove; *m* 1950, Betty Anne (*née* Robinson); one *s* (one *d* decd). *Educ:* Dundee High Sch.; St Andrews Univ. University Coll., 1944–47 (BScEng 1st Cl. Hons). National Service, Royal Engineers, 1947–48; Instructor Br., Royal Navy, 1948–50; Electrical Engrg Br., RN, 1950, qualified in Submarines, 1953; post graduate trng in Nuclear Engrg, Imperial Coll., London, 1958–59; sea service in HMS Forth and HM Submarines Tally-Ho, Turpin, Porpoise, Dreadnought; service in Ship Dept, 1964–67; staff of Flag Officer Submarines, 1967–70; Naval Asst to Controller of the Navy, 1970–73; staff of Flag Officer Submarines, 1975–77; commanded HMS Fisgard, 1977–79; Chief Strategic Systems Exec. (formerly Chief Polaris Exec.), 1980–85; Chief Naval Engr Officer, 1983–85. Comdr 1963; Captain 1970; Rear-Adm. 1980. *Recreation:* walking. *Address:* Maryfield, South Close, Wade Court, Havant, Hants PO9 2TD. *T:* Havant (0705) 475116. *Clubs:* Army and Navy, Commonwealth Trust.

GROVE, Trevor Charles; Editor, Sunday Telegraph, since 1989; *b* 1 Jan. 1945; *s* of Ronald and Lesley Grove; *m* 1975, Valerie Jenkins (*née* Smith); one *s* three *d*. *Educ:* St George's, Buenos Aires; Radley; St Edmund Hall, Oxford. Editorial Staff, Spectator, 1967–70; Leader Writer, then Features Editor, Evening Standard, 1970–78; Asst Editor, Sunday Telegraph, 1978–80; Sen. Asst Editor, Observer, 1980–83; Editor, Observer Magazine, 1983–86; Asst Editor, Daily Telegraph, 1986–89. *Publications:* (co-ed) Singlehanded, 1984; (ed) The Queen Observed, 1986. *Recreations:* family life, tennis, cooking. *Address:* 14 Avenue Road, Highgate, N6 5DW. *T:* 071–538 5000.

GROVE, (William) Dennis; Chairman, North West Water Group, since 1989; *b* 23 July 1927; *s* of late William Grove and Elizabeth Charlotte Grove (*née* Bradley); *m* 1953, Audrey Irma Saxel; one *s* one *d*. *Educ:* Gowerton School; King's College, London (BSc). Joined Dunlop Group, 1951, subseq. Overseas Gen. Manager, to 1970; Chm. and Chief Exec., TPT, 1970–85; Vice-Pres., Sonoco International, 1978–85; Chm., NW Water Authy, 1985–89. *Recreations:* sports bystander, travel, golf. *Address:* Sandringham Court, Wilmslow, Cheshire SK9 1PW. *T:* (office) Warrington (0925) 234000. *Club:* Bramall Park Golf.

GROVE-WHITE, Robin Bernard; Senior Research Fellow in Environmental Research Policy, Lancaster University, since 1989; *b* 17 Feb. 1941; *s* of Charles William Grove-White and Cecile Mary Rabbidge; *m* 1st, 1970, Virginia Harriet Ironside (marr. diss.); one *s*; 2nd, 1979, Helen Elizabeth Smith; two *s* one *d*. *Educ:* Uppingham Sch.; Worcester Coll., Oxford (BA). Freelance writer for TV, radio, press and advertising in UK, Canada and US, 1963–70; McCann-Erickson Ltd, London, 1970; Asst Secretary, 1972–80, Dir, 1981–87, CPRE; Res. Fellow, Centre for Envmtl Technol., Imperial Coll., London, 1987–89. *Publications:* (contrib.) Politics of Physical Resources, 1975; (contrib.) Future Landscapes, 1976; (with Michael Flood) Nuclear Prospects, 1976; contribs to New Scientist, Nature, Times, Vole, etc. *Recreations:* walking, cricket. *Address:* Conder Mill Cottage, Quernmore, Lancaster LA2 9EE. *T:* Lancaster (0524) 382501.

GROVER, Derek James Langlands; Director of Training Strategy and Standards, Employment Department, since 1990; *b* 26 Jan. 1949; *s* of Donald James Grover and late Mary Barbara Grover; *m* 1972, Mary Katherine Morgan; one *s*. *Educ:* Hove County Grammar Sch. for Boys; Clare Coll., Cambridge (Foundn Schol. 1970; BA Eng. Lit. 1971, MA 1975; Grene Prize 1971). Various positions, Dept. of Employment, 1971–78; Cabinet Office, 1978–80; MSC, 1980–87; Head of Personnel, Training Agency, 1987–89; Dir of Youth Training, 1989; Dir of Systems and Strategy, 1989. *Recreations:* music, reading, walking, watching cricket. *Address:* c/o Employment Department, Moorfoot, Sheffield S1 4PQ. *T:* Sheffield (0742) 753275.

GROVES, Sir Charles (Barnard), Kt 1973; CBE 1968 (OBE 1958); FRCM, Hon. RAM, CRNCM; conductor; Associate Conductor, Royal Philharmonic Orchestra, since 1967; Music Director, Leeds Philharmonic Society, since 1988; *b* 10 March 1915; *s* of Frederick Groves and Annie (*née* Whitehead); *m* 1948, Hilary Hermione Barchard; one *s* two *d*. *Educ:* St Paul's Cathedral Choir Sch.; Sutton Valence Sch.; Royal College of Music. Free lance accompanist and organist. Joined BBC, Chorus-Master Music Productions Unit, 1938; Asst Conductor BBC Theatre Orchestra, 1942; Conductor BBC Revue Orchestra, 1943; Conductor BBC Northern Orchestra, 1944–51; Dir of Music, Bournemouth Corporation, and Conductor, Bournemouth Municipal Orchestra, 1951–54; Conductor of Bournemouth Symphony Orchestra, 1954–61; Resident Musical Dir, Welsh National Opera Company, 1961–63; Musical Dir and Resident Conductor, Royal Liverpool Philharmonic Orchestra, 1963–77; Music Dir, ENO, 1978–79; Pres. and Artistic Advr, English Sinfonia, 1984–; Principal Conductor, Guildford Philharmonic Orchestra, 1987–. President: Nat. Youth Orchestra of GB, 1977–; Incorporated Soc. of Musicians, 1982–83; Life Mem., RPO, 1976; Hon. Mem., Royal Philharmonic Soc., 1990. Hon. Fellow: Manchester Poly., 1973; Liverpool Poly., 1987. FRCM 1961; Hon. RAM 1967; Hon. FTCL 1974; Hon. GSM 1974; CRNCM 1983 (Hon. FRNCM 1974). Conductor of the Year Award, 1968, 1978. Freeman, City of London, 1976. Has toured Australia, New Zealand, South Africa, N and S America, Japan and Europe. Hon. DMus Liverpool, 1970; DUniv. Open, 1978; Hon. DLitt Salford, 1980. *Recreation:* English literature. *Address:* 12 Camden Square, NW1 9UY.

GROVES, John Dudley, CB 1981; OBE 1964; Director-General, Central Office of Information, 1979–82; Head of Profession for Government Information Officer Group, 1981–82; *b* 12 Aug. 1922; *y s* of late Walter Groves; *m* 1943, Pamela Joy Holliday; one *s*

two *d*. *Educ:* St Paul's Sch. Reporter, Richmond Herald, 1940–41; Queen's Royal Regt, 1941–42; commnd in 43rd Reconnaissance Regt, 1942; served in NW Europe, 1944–45 (despatches); Observer Officer, Berlin, 1945; Press Association (Press Gallery), 1947–51; Times (Press Gallery and Lobby), 1951–58; Head of Press Sect., Treasury, 1958–62; Dep. Public Relations Adviser to Prime Minister, 1962–64 (Actg Adviser, 1964); Chief Information Officer, DEA, 1964–68; Chief of Public Relations, MoD, 1968–77; Dir of Information, DHSS, 1977–78. Mem., Working Party on Censorship, 1983. *Publication:* (with R. Gill) Club Route, 1945. *Recreations:* walking, painting. *Address:* Mortimers, Manningford Bohune, Pewsey, Wilts SN9 5PG.
See also L. Whistler.

GROVES, Richard Bebb, TD 1966; RD 1979; **His Honour Judge Groves;** a Circuit Judge, since 1985; *b* 4 Oct. 1933; *s* of George Thomas Groves and Margaret Anne (*née* Bebb); *m* 1958, Eileen Patricia (*née* Farley); one *s* one *d*. *Educ:* Bancroft's Sch., Woodford Green, Essex. Admitted Solicitor of the Supreme Court, 1960. Partner, H. J. Smith & Co. and Richard Groves & Co., 1962–85. Dep. Circuit Judge, 1978–80; a Recorder, 1980–85. Nijmegen Medal, Royal Netherlands League for Physical Culture, 1965 and 1966. *Recreations:* Royal Naval Reserve, tennis, philately, walking, reading. *Clubs:* Royal Automobile; Colchester Garrison Officers (Colchester); Chelmsford (Chelmsford).

GROVES, Ronald Edward, CBE 1972; CBIM; Chairman, 1982–87, and Managing Director, 1984–86, Meyer International plc (following merger of International Timber with Montague L. Meyer in 1982); *b* 2 March 1920; *s* of Joseph Rupert and Eva Lilian Groves; *m* 1940, Beryl Doris Lydia Collins; two *s* one *d*. *Educ:* Watford Grammar School. Joined J. Gliksten & Son Ltd; served War of 1939–45, Flt-Lt RAF, subseq. Captain with BOAC; re-joined J. Gliksten & Son Ltd, 1946: Gen. Works Man. 1947; Dir 1954; Jt Man. Dir 1964; Vice-Chm. 1967; Dir, Gliksten (West Africa) Ltd, 1949; Vice-Chm., International Timber Corp. Ltd, 1970 (name of J. Gliksten & Son Ltd changed to International Timber Corp. Ltd, 1970 following merger with Horsley Smith & Jewson Ltd); Chief Exec., 1973, Chm., 1976, Internat. Timber. Dir, Nat. Building Agency, 1978–82; Mem., EDC for Building, 1982–86; President: National Council of Building Material Producers, 1987–90 (Mem., Cttee of Management, 1982–); Timber Trade Fedn of UK, 1969–71; London and District Sawmill Owners Assoc., 1954–56; Timber Res. and Develt Assoc., 1990–; Chm., Nat. Sawmilling Assoc., 1966–67; Mem., London and Regional Affairs Cttee, 1980–, and Mem. Council, 1982–, London Chamber of Commerce and Industry; Mem., London Regl Council, CBI, 1983–87; Dir, Business in the Community, 1984–87. Chairman: Rickmansworth UDC, 1957–58, 1964–65 and 1971–72; W Herts Main Drainage Authority, 1970–74; Three Rivers District Council, 1977–78; Mem., Herts CC, 1964–74. Chairman of Governors: Watford Grammar Sch. for Girls, 1980–; Watford Grammar Sch. for Boys, 1980–. *Recreations:* visiting theatre and opera; local community work. *Address:* 8 Pembroke Road, Moor Park, Northwood, Mddx HA6 2HR. *T:* Northwood (09274) 23187.

GRUENBERG, Prof. Karl Walter; Professor of Pure Mathematics in the University of London, at Queen Mary and Westfield (formerly Queen Mary) College, since 1967; *b* 3 June 1928; *s* of late Paul Gruenberg and Anna Gruenberg; *m* 1973, Margaret Semple; one *s* one *d*. *Educ:* Shaftesbury Grammar Sch.; Kilburn Grammar Sch.; Cambridge Univ. BA 1950, PhD 1954. Asst Lectr, Queen Mary Coll., 1953–55; Commonwealth Fund Fellowship, 1955–57 (at Harvard Univ., 1955–56; at Inst. for Advanced Studies, Princeton, 1956–57). Queen Mary College: Lectr, 1957–61; Reader, 1961–67; Prof., 1967–. Visiting Professor: Univ. of Michigan, 1961–62, 1978; Cornell Univ., 1966–67; Univ. of Illinois, 1972; Australian Nat. Univ., 1979 and 1987. Mem., Maths Cttee, SERC, 1983–86. *Publications:* Cohomological Topics in Group Theory, 1970; Relation Modules of Finite Groups, 1976; Linear Geometry (jtly with A. J. Weir), 2nd edn 1977; articles on algebra in various learned jls. *Address:* Department of Pure Mathematics, Queen Mary and Westfield College (University of London), Mile End Road, E1 4NS. *T:* 081–980 4811.

GRUFFYDD, Prof. (Robert) Geraint, FBA 1991; Director, University of Wales Centre for Advanced Welsh and Celtic Studies, Aberystwyth, since 1985; *b* 9 June 1928; *s* of Moses and Ceridwen Griffith; *m* 1953, Elizabeth Eluned Roberts; two *s* one *d*. *Educ:* University Coll. of N Wales, Bangor (BA); Jesus Coll., Oxford (DPhil). Asst Editor, Geiriadur Prifysgol Cymru, 1953–55; Lectr, Dept of Welsh, UCNW, 1955–70; Prof. of Welsh Language and Literature, UCW, Aberystwyth, 1970–79; Librarian, Nat. Library of Wales, 1980–85. *Publications:* (ed) Meistri'r Canrifoedd, 1973; (ed) Cerddi '73, 1973; (ed) Bardos, 1982; (ed) Cerddi Saunders Lewis, 1986; Dafydd ap Gwilym, 1987; (ed) Y Gair ar Waith, 1988; Llenyddiaeth y Cymry, ii, 1989; articles, etc, on Welsh literary and religious history in various collaborative vols and learned jls. *Recreations:* reading, walking, travel. *Address:* Eirianfa, Caradog Road, Aberystwyth, Dyfed SY23 2JY. *T:* Aberystwyth (0970) 623396.

GRUFFYDD JONES, Daniel; *see* Jones, D. G.

GRUGEON, Sir John (Drury), Kt 1980; DL; Chairman, Tunbridge Wells Health Authority, since 1984; *b* 20 Sept. 1928; *s* of Drury Grugeon and Sophie (*née* Pratt); *m* 1st, 1955, Mary Patricia (*née* Rickards) (marr. diss. 1986); one *s* one *d*; 2nd, 1989, Pauline Lois, *widow* of Dr Roland Phillips. *Educ:* Epsom Grammar Sch.; RMA, Sandhurst. Commissioned, The Buffs, Dec. 1948; served 1st Bn in Middle and Far East and Germany; Regimental Adjt, 1953–55; Adjt 5th Bn, 1956–58; left Army, 1960. Joined Save and Prosper Group, 1960. Kent County Council: Mem., 1967–; Leader, 1973–82; Vice-Chm., 1987–89; Chm., 1989–91; Chairman: Superannuation Fund, 1982–87; Fire and Public Protection Cttee, 1984–87. Chm., Policy Cttee, Assoc. of County Councils, 1978–81 (Chm., Finance Cttee, 1976–79). Dir, Internat. Garden Fest. '84, Liverpool, 1982–83. Member: SE Economic Planning Council, 1971–74; Cons. Council on Local Govt Finance, 1975–82; Medway Ports Authority, 1977–; Dep. Chm., Medway (Chatham) Dock Co., 1983–. DL Kent, 1986. *Recreations:* cricket, shooting, local govt. *Address:* 2 Shrublands Court, Sandrock Road, Tunbridge Wells, Kent TN2 3PS. *T:* Tunbridge Wells (0892) 31936. *Clubs:* Carlton, MCC; Kent County CC.

GRUNDY, David Stanley; Commissioner for Finance and Administration, Forestry Commission, since 1990; *b* 10 April 1943; *s* of Walter Grundy and Anne Grundy (*née* Pomfret); *m* 1965, Elizabeth Jenny Schadla Hall; one *s*. *Educ:* De La Salle Coll., Manchester; Jesus Coll., Cambridge (MA); Jesus Coll., Oxford (MPhil). Asst Principal, MOP, 1967–70; Asst Private Sec. to Minister, Min. of Technology, 1970–71; Principal, DTI, 1971–73; Economic Adviser: FCO, 1976–78; DoE, 1978–79; Chief Economic Advr, Govt of Vanuatu, 1979–81; Chief Economist, Forestry Commn, 1982–90. Mem., Scottish Ornithological Club. *Recreations:* angling, bird watching, gardening, tennis. *Address:* Forestry Commission, 231 Corstorphine Road, Edinburgh EH12 7AT. *T:* 031–334 0303. *Clubs:* Commonwealth Trust; Dean Tennis (Edinburgh).

GRUNDY, (James) Milton; Founder and Chairman of the Warwick Arts Trust, since 1978; *b* 13 June 1926. *Educ:* Sedbergh Sch.; Gonville and Caius Coll., Cambridge (MA). Called to the Bar, Inner Temple, 1954. Founder and Chm., Gemini Trust for the Arts, 1959–66; Founder Mem. and Pres., Internat. Tax Planning Assoc., 1975–; Charter Mem., Peggy Guggenheim Collection, 1980–89; Chm., Internat. Management Trust, 1986–;

Trustee, Nat. Museums and Galls of Merseyside, 1987–. *Publications:* Tax and the Family Company, 1956, 3rd edn 1966; Tax Havens, 1968, 5th edn 1987; Venice, 1971, 4th edn 1985; The World of International Tax Planning, 1984; (with John Briggs) Asset Protection Trusts, 1990. *Recreation:* conversation. *Address:* New House, Shipton-under-Wychwood, Oxon OX7 6DD. *T:* Shipton-under-Wychwood (0993) 830495.

GRUNDY, Stephanie Christine; Assistant Parliamentary Counsel, since 1985; *b* 11 Dec. 1958; *d* of Harry Grundy and June (*née* Hazell). *Educ:* Grange Sch., Oldham; Hertford Coll., Oxford (Schol.; MA, BCL). Called to the Bar, Middle Temple, 1983. Research Asst, Law Commn, 1985; joined Office of the Parliamentary Counsel, 1985; with Law Commn, 1988–90. *Recreations:* running, cycling, racket sports, piano music. *Address:* Office of the Parliamentary Counsel, 36 Whitehall, SW1A 2AY.

GRUNFELD, Prof. Cyril; Professor of Law, London School of Economics, 1966–82; *b* 26 Sept. 1922; *o s* of Samuel and Sarah Grunfeld; *m* 1945, Phyllis Levin; one *s* two *d.* *Educ:* Canton High Sch., Cardiff; Trinity Hall, Cambridge (MA, LLB). Called to Bar, Inner Temple. British Army, 1942–45; Trinity Hall (Studentship), 1946–48; LSE: Asst, 1946–47; Asst Lectr, 1947–49; Lectr, 1949–56; Reader in Law, 1956—66; Pro-Dir, 1973–76; Convener, Law Dept, 1976–79; Dean, Faculty of Law, Univ. of London, 1978–80. Vis. Research Fellow, ANU, 1970–71; Legal Adviser: to Commn on Industrial Relations, 1971–74; to Industrial Soc., 1982–87; to Nat. Assoc. of Port Employers, 1988–89. *Publications:* Modern Trade Union Law, 1966; The Law of Redundancy, 1971, 3rd edn, 1989; contrib. to books and learned jls. *Recreations:* reading, walking. *Address:* c/o London School of Economics and Political Science, Houghton Street, WC2A 2AE.

GRUNFELD, Henry; President, S. G. Warburg Group plc, since 1987 (Chairman, 1969–74, President, 1974–87, S. G. Warburg & Co. Ltd); *b* 1 June 1904; *m* 1931, Berta Lotte Oliven; one *s* one *d.* *Address:* 2 Finsbury Avenue, EC2M 2PA. *T:* 071–606 1066.

GRUNSELL, Prof. Charles Stuart Grant, CBE 1976; PhD; Professor of Veterinary Medicine, University of Bristol, 1957–80, now Emeritus; *b* 6 Jan. 1915; *s* of Stuart and Edith Grunsell; *m* 1939, Marjorie Prunella Wright; one *s* two *d.* *Educ:* Shanghai Public Sch.; Bristol Grammar Sch. Qualified as MRCVS at The Royal (Dick) Veterinary Coll., Edinburgh, 1937; FRCVS 1971. In general practice at Glastonbury, Som., 1939–48. PhD Edinburgh, 1952. Senior Lecturer in Veterinary Hygiene and Preventive Medicine, University of Edinburgh, 1952. Pro-Vice-Chancellor, Univ. of Bristol, 1974–77. Chm., Veterinary Products Cttee, 1970–80. Mem., General Synod of C of E, 1980–85; a Diocesan Reader. Editor, Veterinary Annual. Defence Medal 1946. *Publications:* papers on the Erythron of Ruminants, on Vital Statistics in Veterinary Medicine, on Preventive Medicine, and on veterinary education. *Recreation:* gardening. *Address:* Greenleaves, Mead Lane, Sandford, Bristol BS19 5RG. *T:* Banwell (0934) 822461.

GRYLLS, (William) Michael (John); MP (C) North West Surrey, since 1974 (Chertsey, 1970–74); *b* 21 Feb. 1934; *s* of Brig. W. E. H. Grylls, OBE; *m* 1965, Sarah Smiles Justice, *d* of Captain N. M. Ford and of Lady (Patricia) Fisher, *qv*; one *s* one *d.* *Educ:* RN College, Dartmouth; Univ. of Paris. Lieut, Royal Marines, 1952–55. Mem., St Pancras Borough Council, 1959–62. Contested (C) Fulham, Gen. Elecs, 1964 and 1966; Mem., Select Cttee on Overseas Develt, 1970–78; Chairman: Cons. Trade and Industry Cttee, 1981– (Vice-Chm., Cons. Industry Cttee, 1975–81); Small Business Bureau, 1979–; Parly Spokesman, Inst. of Directors, 1979–. Mem. GLC, 1967–70; Dep. Leader, Inner London Educn Authority, 1969–70; Chm., Further and Higher Educn, 1968–70. *Recreations:* sailing, riding, gardening. *Address:* c/o House of Commons, SW1. *Club:* Royal Yacht Squadron (Cowes).

GRYN, Rabbi Hugo Gabriel; Senior Rabbi, West London Synagogue, since 1964; *b* 25 June 1930; *s* of Bella and Geza Gryn; *m* 1957, Jacqueline Selby; one *s* three *d.* *Educ:* Univs of Cambridge, London and Cincinnati (BA, MA); Hebrew Union Coll., Cincinnati (BHL, MHL, DHL). Ordained rabbi, 1957; Rabbi, Jewish Religious Union, Bombay, 1957–60; Exec. Dir, World Union for Progressive Judaism, 1960–62; Senior Exec., American Jewish Jt Distrib. Cttee, 1962–64; Vice-Pres. and Lectr, Leo Baeck Coll., 1964–. Chairman: European Bd, World Union for Progressive Judaism, 1980–; Standing Cttee for Interfaith Dialogue in Educn, 1972–; Joint Chairman: Interfaith Network (UK), 1987–; London Rainbow Group, 1975–; Pres., Reform Synagogues of GB, 1990–; Mem., numerous educnl and Jewish organisations. Hon. DD Hebrew Union Coll., 1982. *Publications:* Forms of Prayer, 1977; contribs to publications of Standing Conf. on Interfaith Dialogue in Educn, British Jl of Religious Educn, Jl of Central Conf. of Amer. Rabbis, Jewish Chronicle. *Recreations:* swimming, travel, biblical archaeology. *Address:* 33 Seymour Place, W1H 6AT. *T:* 071–723 4404.

GUAZZELLI, Rt. Rev. Victor; Auxiliary Bishop of Westminster (Bishop in East London) (RC), and Titular Bishop of Lindisfarne since 1970; *b* 19 March 1920; *s* of Cesare Guazzelli and Maria (*née* Frepoli). *Educ:* Parochial Schools, Tower Hamlets; English Coll., Lisbon. Priest, 1945. Asst, St Patrick's, Soho Square, 1945–48; Bursar and Prof. at English Coll., Lisbon, 1948–58; Westminster Cathedral: Chaplain, 1958–64; Hon. Canon, 1964; Sub-Administrator, 1964–67; Parish Priest of St Thomas', Fulham, 1967–70; Vicar General of Westminster, 1970. President: Pax Christi; Handicapped Children's Pilgrimage Trust. *Address:* The Lodge, Pope John House, Hale Street, E14 0BT. *T:* 071–987 4663.

GUBBAY, Raymond Jonathan; Managing Director, Raymond Gubbay Ltd, since 1966; *b* 2 April 1946; *s* of David and Ida Gubbay; *m* 1972, Johanna Quirke (marr. diss. 1988); two *d.* *Educ:* University Coll. Sch., Hamstead. Concert promoter, 1966–: regular series of concerts at major London concert halls, including: Royal Festival Hall; Royal Albert Hall; The Barbican (*c* 1,000 concerts, 1982–); has presented many of the world's great artists in concert; also Royal Opera prodn of Turandot, Wembley Arena, 1991. Founder, annual City of London Antiques and Fine Art Fair, Barbican Exhibn Halls, 1987–. Hon. FRAM 1988. *Recreations:* gardening, going to the opera. *Address:* Stamford Lodge, Dury Road, Hadley Green, Herts EN5 5SU. *T:* 081–440 9120.

GUDERLEY, Mrs C.; *see* Hyams, Daisy Deborah.

GUÐMUNDSSON, Guðmundur I., Comdr with Star, Order of the Falcon, 1957; Ambassador of Iceland to Belgium, 1977–79, and concurrently to Luxembourg, NATO and EEC; *b* 17 July 1909; *m* 1942, Rósa Ingólfsdóttir; four *s.* *Educ:* Reykjavík Grammar Sch.; Univ. of Iceland. Grad. in Law 1934. Practised as Solicitor and Barrister from 1934; Barrister to Supreme Court, 1939; Sheriff and Magistrate, 1945–56. Mem. Central Cttee, Social Democratic Party, 1940–65, Vice-Chm. of Party, 1954–65; Member of Althing (Parlt), 1942–65; Minister of Foreign Affairs, 1956–65; Minister of Finance, 1958–59; Chm., Icelandic Delegn to UN Conf. on Law of the Sea, Geneva, 1958 and 1960; Mem. and Chm. of Board of Dirs, Fishery Bank in Reykjavík, 1957–65; Ambassador of Iceland: to UK, 1965–71, and concurrently to the Netherlands, Portugal and Spain; to United States, 1971–73, and concurrently to Argentina, Brazil, Canada, Mexico and Cuba; to Sweden, 1973–77 and concurrently to Finland, Austria and Yugoslavia. Establishment of Republic Medal, 1944. Hon. KBE; Grand Cross, Order of: White Rose (Finland); North Star (Sweden); Orange-Nassau (Netherlands); Chêne (Luxembourg); Southern Cross (Brazil); St Olav (Norway); Phoenix (Greece). *Address:* Solvallagata 8, 101 Reykjavik, Iceland.

GUERITZ, Rear-Adm. Edward Findlay, CB 1971; OBE 1957; DSC 1942, and Bar, 1944; defence consultant, writer and broadcaster; *b* 8 Sept. 1919; *s* of Elton and Valentine Gueritz; *m* 1947, Pamela Amanda Bernhardina Britton, *d* of Commander L. H. Jeans; one *s* one *d.* *Educ:* Cheltenham Coll. Entered Navy, 1937; Midshipman, 1938; served War of 1939–45 (wounded; DSC and Bar): HMS Jersey, 5th Flotilla, 1940–41; Combined Ops (Indian Ocean, Normandy), 1941–44; HMS Saumarez (Corfu Channel incident), 1946; Army Staff Coll., Camberley, 1948; Staff of C-in-C S Atlantic and Junior Naval Liaison Officer to UK High Comr, S Africa, 1954–56; Near East Operations, 1956 (OBE); Dep. Dir, RN Staff Coll., 1959–61; Naval Staff, Admty, 1961–63; idc 1964; Captain of Fleet, Far East Fleet, 1965–66; Dir of Defence Plans (Navy), 1967; Dir, Jt Warfare Staff, MoD, 1968; Admiral-President, Royal Naval Coll., 1968–70 (concurrently first Pres., RN Staff Coll.); Comdt, Jt Warfare Estabt, 1970–72. Lt-Comdr 1949; Comdr 1953; Captain 1959; Rear-Adm. 1969; retd 1973. Dep. Dir and Editor, 1976–79, Dir and Editor-in-Chief, 1979–81, RUSI. Specialist Adviser, House of Commons Select Cttee on Defence, 1975–. Chief Hon. Steward, Westminster Abbey, 1975–85. Pres., Soc. for Nautical Res., 1974–90 (Hon. Vice Pres., 1990); Vice Chairman: Council for Christian Approaches to Defence and Disarmament, 1974–80; Victoria League, 1985–88; Member Council: Marine Soc. (Vice Chm., 1988); Fairbridge-Drake Soc., 1981–90; British Atlantic Cttee, 1977–89; HOST (Hosting for Overseas Students Trust), 1987–90 (founding Governor). Mem., Bd of War Studies, Univ. of London, 1969–85. *Publications:* (jtly) The Third World War, 1978; (ed jtly) Ten Years of Terrorism, 1979; (ed jtly) Will the Wells Run Dry, 1979; (ed jtly) Nuclear Attack: Civil Defence, 1982; editor, RUSI Brassey's Defence Year Book, 1977–78, 1978–79, 1980, 1981. *Recreations:* history, reading. *Address:* 56 The Close, Salisbury, Wilts. *Club:* Army and Navy.

GUERNSEY, Lord; Charles Heneage Finch-Knightley; Vice Lord-Lieutenant for West Midlands, since 1990; *b* 27 March 1947; *s* and *heir* of 11th Earl of Aylesford, *qv*; *m* 1971, Penelope Anstice, *y d* of Kenneth A. G. Crawley; one *s* four *d* (incl. twin *d*). *Educ:* Oundle, Trinity Coll., Cambridge. DL West Midlands, 1986. *Recreations:* shooting, fishing, Real tennis, cricket. *Heir: s* Hon. Heneage James Daniel Finch-Knightley, *b* 29 April 1985. *Address:* Packington Hall, Meriden, Coventry CV7 7HF. *T:* Meriden (0676) 22274.

GUERNSEY, Dean of; *see* Fenwick, Very Rev. J. R.

GUEST, family name of **Viscount Wimborne.**

GUEST; *see* Haden-Guest.

GUEST, Prof. Anthony Gordon, CBE 1989; QC 1987; FCIArb; Barrister-at-Law; Professor of English Law, King's College, University of London, since 1966; *b* 8 Feb. 1930; *o s* of late Gordon Walter Leslie Guest and of Marjorie (*née* Hooper), Maidencombe, Devon; unmarried. *Educ:* Colston's Sch., Bristol; St John's Coll., Oxford (MA). Exhibr and Casberd Schol., Oxford, 1950–54; 1st cl. Final Hon. Sch. of Jurisprudence, 1954. Bacon Schol., Gray's Inn, 1955; Barstow Law Schol., 1955; called to Bar, Gray's Inn, 1956, Bencher, 1978. University Coll., Oxford: Lectr, 1954–55; Fellow and Prælector in Jurisprudence, 1955–65; Dean, 1963–64; Reader in Common Law to Council of Legal Educn (Inns of Court), 1967–80. Travelling Fellowship to S Africa, 1957; Mem., Lord Chancellor's Law Reform Cttee, 1963–84; Mem., Adv. Cttee on establishment of Law Faculty in University of Hong Kong, 1965; UK Deleg. to UN Commn on Internat. Trade Law, NY, Geneva and Vienna, 1968–84 and 1986–87, to UN Conf. on Limitation of Actions, 1974; Mem., Board of Athlone Press, 1968–73; Mem. Governing Body, Rugby Sch., 1968–88. FKC 1982; FCIArb 1984. Served Army and TA, 1948–50 (Lieut RA). *Publications:* (ed) Anson's Principles of the Law of Contract, 21st to 26th edns, 1959–84; Chitty on Contracts: (Asst Editor) 22nd edn, 1961, (Gen. Editor) 23rd to 26th edns, 1968–89; (ed) Oxford Essays in Jurisprudence, 1961; The Law of Hire-Purchase, 1966; (Gen. Editor) Benjamin's Sale of Goods, 1st to 3rd edns, 1974–87; (ed jtly) Encylopedia of Consumer Credit, 1975; (jtly) Introduction to the Law of Credit and Security, 1978; Chalmers' Bills of Exchange, 14th edn, 1991; articles in legal jls. *Address:* 16 Trevor Place, SW7. *T:* 071–584 9260. *Club:* Garrick.

GUEST, Douglas Albert, CVO 1975; MA Cantab and Oxon; MusB Cantab; MusD Cantuar; FRCM, Hon. RAM, FRCO, FRSCM; Organist Emeritus, Westminster Abbey, since 1981; *b* 9 May 1916; 2nd *s* of late Harold Guest, Henley-on-Thames, Oxon; *m* 1941, Peggie Florentia, *d* of late Thomas Falconer, FRIBA, Amberley, Gloucestershire; two *d.* *Educ:* Reading Sch.; Royal College of Music, London; King's Coll., Cambridge. Organ Scholar, King's Coll., Cambridge, 1935–39; John Stewart of Rannoch Scholar in Sacred Music, Cambridge Univ., 1936–39. Served War of 1939–45, Major (Battery Comdr), Royal Artillery (HAC) (despatches 1944). Gazetted Hon. Major, RA, April 1945. Dir of Music, Uppingham Sch., 1945–50; Organist and Master of the Choristers, Salisbury Cathedral, 1950–57; Conductor of Salisbury Musical Soc., 1950–57; Dir of Music St Mary's Sch., Calne, 1950–57; Master of the Choristers and Organist, Worcester Cathedral, 1957–63; Conductor Worcester Festival Chorus and Three Choirs Festival, 1957–63; Organist and Master of the Choristers, Westminster Abbey, 1963–81. Examiner, Associated Bd of Royal Schs of Music, 1948–81; Prof., RCM, 1963–81. First Vice-Pres., National Youth Orchestra of Great Britain, 1984– (Chm. Council, 1953–84); Member Council: RCO, 1966–; Musicians' Benevolent Fund, 1968–. Hon. Mem., Royal Soc. of Musicians, 1963–. *Recreations:* fly fishing, golf. *Address:* The Gables, Minchinhampton, Glos GL6 9JE. *T:* Brimscombe 883191. *Club:* Flyfishers'.

GUEST, Eric Ronald; Metropolitan Magistrate (West London), 1946–68; Barrister-at-Law; *b* 7 June 1904; *s* of late William Guest; *m* 1932, Sybil Blakelock; one *d.* *Educ:* Berkhamsted Sch.; Oriel Coll., Oxford. BA 1925 (1st Class Hons Sch. of Jurisprudence); BCL 1926; called to Bar, 1927; practised in London and on Oxford Circuit. Recorder of Worcester, 1941–46; served as Sqdn Leader with RAFVR, 1940–45.

GUEST, George Howell, CBE 1987; MA, MusB (Cantab); MusD (Lambeth), 1977; FRCO 1942; FRSCM 1973; Hon. RAM 1984; Organist of St John's College, Cambridge, 1951–91 (Fellow, 1956); University Organist, Cambridge University, 1974–91; Special Commissioner, Royal School of Church Music, since 1953; Examiner to Associated Board of Royal Schools of Music, since 1959; *b* 9 Feb. 1924; *s* of late Ernest Joseph Guest and late Gwendolen (*née* Brown); *m* 1959, Nancy Mary, *o d* of late W. P. Talbot; one *s* one *d.* *Educ:* Friars Sch., Bangor; King's Sch., Chester; St John's Coll., Cambridge. Chorister: Bangor Cath., 1933–35; Chester Cath., 1935–39. Served in RAF, 1942–46. Sub-Organist, Chester Cath., 1946–47; Organ Student, St John's Coll., Cambridge, 1947–51; John Stewart of Rannoch Scholar in Sacred Music, 1948; University Asst Lectr in Music, Cambridge, 1953–56, Univ. Lectr, 1956–82; Prof. of Harmony and Counterpoint, RAM, London, 1960–61. Director: Berkshire Boy Choir, USA, 1967, 1970; Arts Theatre, Cambridge, 1977–90. Concerts with St John's Coll. Choir in USA, Canada, Japan, Aust., Brazil, most countries in W Europe; concerts and choral seminars in the Philippines and in S Africa; concerts with Community of Jesus Choir, USA, in Hungary, Yugoslavia and

USSR. Mem. Council: RCO, 1964– (Pres., 1978–80); RSCM, 1983–. Aelod er Anrhydedd, Gorsedd y Beirdd, Eisteddfod Genedlaethol Cymru, 1977; Dir, Côr Cenedlaethol Ieuenctid Cymru, 1984; Artistic Dir, Llandaff Festival, 1985. President: Cathedral Organists' Assoc., 1980–82; IAO, 1987–89. Hon. Fellow, UCNW, 1989. Hon. DMus Wales, 1989. John Edwards Meml Award, Guild for Promotion of Welsh Music, 1986. *Recreation:* the Welsh language. *Address:* 9 Gurney Way, Cambridge. *T:* Cambridge (0223) 354932. *Club:* United Oxford & Cambridge University.

GUEST, Henry Alan, MBE 1990; Chairman, Rhodes Foods Ltd, since 1980; *b* 29 Feb. 1920; *m* 1947, Helen Mary Price; one *s* one *d*. *Educ:* Lindisfarne College. FHCIMA. War Service, 1940–46, France, India, Malaya; Captain RA. Supplies Man., J. Lyons & Co. Ltd, Catering Div., 1955; Rank Organisation, Theatre Div.: Dep. Controller, Catering, 1963; Controller, 1965; Group Catering Adviser, Associated British Foods, 1966; Chief Exec., Civil Service Catering Organisation, 1972–80. Mem. Royal Instn of Great Britain. *Publications:* papers on marketing and organisation in techn. jls and financial press. *Recreation:* swimming. *Address:* 14 Pensford Avenue, Kew, Surrey TW9 4HP.

GUEST, Ivor Forbes, FRAD 1982; Chairman, since 1969, Member, since 1965, Executive Committee of the Royal Academy of Dancing; Solicitor; *b* 14 April 1920; *s* of Cecil Marmaduke Guest and Christian Forbes Guest (*née* Tweedie); *m* 1962, Ann Hutchinson; no *c*. *Educ:* Lancing Coll.; Trinity Coll., Cambridge (MA). Admitted a Solicitor, 1949; Partner, A. F. & R. W. Tweedie, 1951–83, Tweedie & Prideaux, 1983–85. Organised National Book League exhibn of books on ballet, 1957–58; Mem. Cttee, Soc. for Theatre Research, 1955–72; Chm., Exec. Cttee, Soc. for Dance Research, 1982–; Member: Exec. Cttee, British Theatre Museum, 1957–77 (Vice-Chm., 1966–77); Cttee, The Theatre Museum, 1984–89 (Mem., Adv. Council, 1974–83). Editorial Adviser to the Dancing Times, 1963–; Sec., Radcliffe Trust, 1966–; Trustee: Calvert Trust, 1976–; Cecchetti Soc. Trust, 1978–. *Publications:* Napoleon III in England, 1952; The Ballet of the Second Empire, 1953–55; The Romantic Ballet in England, 1954; Fanny Cerrito, 1956; Victorian Ballet Girl, 1957; Adeline Genée, 1958; The Alhambra Ballet, 1959; La Fille mal gardée, 1960; The Dancer's Heritage, 1960; The Empire Ballet, 1962; A Gallery of Romantic Ballet, 1963; The Romantic Ballet in Paris, 1966; Carlotta Zambelli, 1969; Dandies and Dancers, 1969; Two Coppélias, 1970; Fanny Elssler, 1970; The Pas de Quatre, 1970; Le Ballet de l'Opéra de Paris, 1976; The Divine Virginia, 1977; Adeline Genée: a pictorial record, 1978; Lettres d'un Maître de ballet, 1978; contrib. Costume and the 19th Century Dancer, in Designing for the Dancer, 1981; Adventures of a Ballet Historian, 1982; Jules Perrot, 1984; Gautier on Dance, 1986; Gautier on Spanish Dancing, 1987; Dr John Radcliffe and his Trust, 1991. *Address:* 17 Holland Park, W11. *T:* 071–229 3780. *Clubs:* Garrick, MCC.

GUEST, Prof. John Rodney, FRS 1986; Professor of Microbiology, Sheffield University, since 1981; *b* 27 Dec. 1935; *s* of Sidney Ramsey Guest and Dorothy Kathleen Guest (*née* Walker); *m* 1962, Barbara Margaret (*née* Dearsley); one *s* two *d*. *Educ:* Campbell College, Belfast; Leeds Univ. (BSc); Trinity Coll., Oxford Univ. (DPhil). Guinness Fellow, Oxford, 1960–62, 1965; Fulbright Scholar and Research Associate, Stanford, 1963, 1964; Sheffield University: Lectr, Sen. Lectr, Reader in Microbiology, 1965–81. EMBO Fellow, 1977; SERC Special Fellow, 1981–86. *Publications:* contribs to Jl of Gen. Microbiol., Biochem. Jl, European Jl of Biochem. *Recreations:* walking in the Peak District, squash, beekeeping, polyfilling. *Address:* Department of Molecular Biology and Biotechnology, Sheffield University, Western Bank, Sheffield S10 2UH. *T:* Sheffield (0742) 768555.

GUEST, Melville Richard John; HM Diplomatic Service; Counsellor (Political) and Consul General, Stockholm, since 1990; *b* 18 Nov. 1943; *s* of late Ernest Melville Charles Guest and of Katherine Mary Guest; *m* 1970, Beatriz Eugenia, (Jenny), Lopez Colombres de Velasco; four *s*. *Educ:* Rugby Sch.; Magdalen Coll., Oxford (MA Jurisprudence). Entered HM Diplomatic Service, 1966; Third, later Second, Sec., Tokyo, 1967–72; Pvte Sec. to Parly Under-Sec. of State, FCO, 1973–75; First Sec., Paris, 1975–79; FCO, 1979–80; Prés.-Dir Gén., Soc. Française des Industries Lucas, 1980–85; Dir, Thomson-Lucas SA, 1980–85; Bd of Govs, British Sch. of Paris, 1981–85; Director: Franco-British Chamber of Commerce, 1980–85; Channel Tunnel Gp, 1985–86; Counsellor (Commercial), Tokyo, 1986–89. *Recreations:* family, music, ball-games, reading, ski-ing. *Address:* c/o Foreign and Commonwealth Office, SW1A 2AH; 11 Caldervale Road, SW4. *Clubs:* United Oxford & Cambridge University, MCC, Hurlingham.

GUEST, Trevor George; a District Judge (formerly Registrar of the Principal Registry), Family Division of the High Court of Justice, since 1972; Barrister-at-Law; *b* 30 Jan. 1928; *m* 1951, Patricia Mary (*née* Morrison) (*d* 1983); two *d*; *m* 1988, Diane Constance (*née* Platts). *Educ:* Denstone Coll., Uttoxeter, Staffs; Birmingham Univ. (LLB (Hons)). Called to the Bar, Middle Temple, 1953. *Recreations:* dogs, Church affairs. *Address:* The Old Rectory, Purleigh, Essex. *T:* Maldon (0621) 828375.

GUILD, Ivor Reginald, CBE 1985; Partner in Shepherd and Wedderburn, WS, since 1951; *b* 2 April 1924; 2nd *s* of Col Arthur Marjoribanks Guild, DSO, TD, DL, and Phyllis Eliza Cox. *Educ:* Cargilfield; Rugby; New Coll., Oxford (MA); Edinburgh Univ. (LLB). WS 1950. Procurator Fiscal of the Lyon Court, 1960–; Bailie of Holyrood House, 1980–; Registrar, Episcopal Synod of Episc. Church in Scotland, 1967–; Chancellor, dioceses of Edinburgh and St Andrews, 1985–. Chairman: Edinburgh Investment Trust Ltd, 1974– (Dir, 1972–); First Scottish American Trust Co. Ltd, 1973– (Dir, 1964–); Northern American Trust Co. Ltd, 1973– (Dir, 1964–); Director: Fleming Universal Investment Trust, 1977–; Fulcrum Investment Trust, 1986–. Member: Council on Tribunals, 1976–85; Interception of Communications Tribunal, 1985–; Immigration Appeal Adjudicator, 1988–. Chm., Nat. Mus. of Antiquities of Scotland, 1981–85. Editor, Scottish Genealogist, 1959–. *Recreations:* genealogy, golf. *Club:* New (Edinburgh).

GUILDFORD, Bishop of, since 1983; **Rt. Rev. Michael Edgar Adie;** *b* 22 Nov. 1929; *s* of Walter Granville Adie and Kate Emily Adie (*née* Parish); *m* 1957, Anne Devonald Roynon; one *s* three *d*. *Educ:* Westminster School; St John's Coll., Oxford (MA). Assistant Curate, St Luke, Pallion, Sunderland, 1954–57; Resident Chaplain to the Archbishop of Canterbury, 1957–60; Vicar of St Mark, Sheffield, 1960–69; Rural Dean of Hallam, 1966–69; Rector of Louth, 1969–76; Vicar of Morton with Hacconby, 1976–83; Archdeacon of Lincoln, 1977–83. Chm., Gen. Synod Bd of Education and of National Soc., 1989–. *Recreations:* gardening, walking, sneezing. *Address:* Willow Grange, Woking Road, Guildford GU4 7QS. *T:* Guildford (0483) 573922.

GUILDFORD, Dean of; *see* Wedderspoon, Very Rev. A. G.

GUILFORD, 9th Earl of *cr* 1752; **Edward Francis North;** Baron Guilford, 1683; DL; *b* 22 Sept. 1933; *s* of Major Lord North (*d* 1940) and Joan Louise (she *m* 2nd, 1947, Charles Harman Hunt), *er d* of late Sir Merrik Burrell, 7th Bt, CBE; *S* grandfather, 1949; *m* 1956, Osyth Vere Napier, *d* of Cyril Napier Leeston Smith; one *s*. *Educ:* Eton. FRSA 1976. DL Kent 1976. *Heir: s* Lord North, *qv*. *Address:* Waldershare Park, Dover, Kent. *T:* Dover (0304) 820244.

See also Major Hon. Sir Clive Bossom, Bt, Sir Jonathan North, Bt.

GUILFOYLE, Dame Margaret (Georgina Constance), DBE 1980; Senator for Victoria, 1971–87; *b* 15 May 1926; *d* of William and Elizabeth McCartney; *m* 1952, Stanley M. L. Guilfoyle; one *s* two *d*. *Educ:* ANU (LLB 1990). Accountant, 1947–. Minister: for Education, Commonwealth of Australia, 1975; for Social Security, 1975–80; for Finance, 1980–83. FCIS; FASA. *Recreations:* reading, gardening. *Address:* 21 Howard Street, Kew, Vic 3101, Australia. *Club:* Lyceum (Melbourne).

GUILLEMIN, Prof. Roger Charles Louis, MD, PhD; Distinguished Scientist, Whittier Institute for Diabetes and Endocrinology, La Jolla, California, since 1989; Adjunct Professor of Medicine, University of California, San Diego, since 1970; *b* Dijon, France, 11 Jan. 1924 (naturalized US Citizen, 1963); *s* of Raymond Guillemin and Blanche (*née* Rigollot); *m* 1951, Lucienne Jeanne Billard; one *s* five *d*. *Educ:* Univ. of Dijon (BA 1941, BSc 1942); Faculty of Medicine, Lyons (MD 1949); Univ. of Montreal (PhD 1953). Resident Intern, univ. hosps, Dijon, 1949–51; Associate Dir, then Asst Prof., Inst. of Exper. Medicine and Surgery, Univ. of Montreal, 1951–53; Associate Dir, Dept of Exper. Endocrinol., Coll. de France, Paris, 1960–63; Prof. of Physiol., Baylor Coll. of Med., Houston, 1953–70; Adjunct Prof. of Physiol., Baylor Coll. of Med., 1970–; Resident Fellow and Res. Prof., Salk Inst. for Biol Studies, 1970–89. Chm., Labs for Endocrinology, Salk Inst., 1970–89. Member: Nat. Acad. of Sciences, USA; Amer. Acad. Arts and Scis; Amer. Physiol Soc.; Endocrine Soc. (Pres., 1986); Soc. of Exptl Biol. and Medicine; Internat. Brain Res. Orgn; Internat. Soc. Res. Biol Reprodn. Foreign Associate: Acad. des Sciences, France; Acad. Nat. de Médecine, Paris; Hon. Mem., Swedish Soc. of Med. Scis; Foreign Mem., Acad. Royale de Médecine de Belgique. Mem. Club of Rome. Hon. DSc: Rochester, NY, 1976; Chicago, 1977; Manitoba, 1984; Kyung Hee Univ., Seoul, Korea, 1986; Univ. de Paris VII, 1986; Madrid, 1988. Hon. MD: Ulm, 1978; Montreal, 1979; Univ. Libre de Bruxelles, Belgium, 1979; Turin, 1985; Barcelona, 1988; Univ. Claude Bernard, Lyon I, 1989; Hon. LMed Baylor Coll. of Med., 1978. Gairdner Internat. Award, 1974; Lasker Award, USA, 1975; Dickson Prize in Medicine, Univ. of Pittsburgh, 1976; Passano Award in Med. Sci., Passano Foundn, Inc., 1976; Schmitt Medal in Neuroscience, Neurosciences Res. Prog., MIT, 1977; National Medal of Science, USA, 1977; (jtly) Nobel Prize in Physiology or Medicine, 1977; Barren Gold Medal, USA, 1979; Dale Medal (Soc. for Endocrinology), UK, 1980; Ellen Browning Scripps Soc. Medal, Scripps Meml Hosps Foundn, San Diego, 1988. Légion d'Honneur, France, 1974. *Publications:* scientific pubns in learned jls. *Address:* Whittier Institute for Diabetes and Endocrinology, 9894 Genesee Avenue, La Jolla, Calif 92037, USA.

GUILLERY, Prof. Rainer Walter, PhD; FRS 1983; Dr Lee's Professor of Anatomy, and Fellow of Hertford College, University of Oxford, since 1984; *b* 28 Aug. 1929; *s* of Hermann Guillery and Eva (*née* Hackel); *m* 1954, Margot Cunningham Pepper; three *s* one *d*. *Educ:* University Coll. London (BSc, PhD; Fellow, 1987). Asst Lectr, subseq. Reader, Anatomy Dept, UCL, 1953–64; Associate Prof., subseq. Prof., Anatomy Dept, Univ. of Wisconsin, Madison, USA, 1964–77; Prof., Dept of Pharmacol and Physiol Sciences, Univ. of Chicago, 1977–84. Editor-in-chief, European Jl of Neuroscience, 1988–. *Publications:* contrib. Jl of Anat., Jl of Comp. Neurol., Jl of Neuroscience, and Brain Res. *Address:* Department of Human Anatomy, South Parks Road, Oxford OX1 3QX.

GUILLOU, Prof. Pierre John, MD; FRCS; Professor of Surgery, Imperial College of Science, Technology and Medicine, University of London and Director, Academic Surgical Unit, St Mary's Hospital, since 1988; *b* 30 Oct. 1945; *s* of Sarah Anne Guillou (*née* Greenfield) and Yves Guillou; *m* 1974, Elizabeth Anne Sowden; one *s* one *d*. *Educ:* Normanton Grammar Sch.; Univ. of Leeds (BSc; MB ChB 1970; MD 1975). Leeds Gen. Infirmary and St James's Univ. Hosp., 1970–73; S Manchester Univ. Hosp., 1973–74; Surgical Registrar, Leeds Gen. Infirmary, 1974–76; Lectr in Surgery, Univ. of Leeds, 1976–79; MRC Fellow in Immunology, Hôpital Necker, Paris, 1979–80; Sen. Lectr in Surgery, Univ. of Leeds, 1980–88. Vis. Prof., Aust. Surgical Res. Soc., 1989; Crookshank Lectr, Royal Soc. of Radiologists, 1990; Smith Lectr, Univ. of WA, 1991. *Publications:* (ed) Surgical Oncology, 1991; numerous papers on immunology, cell biology and surgery in treatment of cancer. *Recreations:* work, golf, fishing, work. *Address:* Academic Surgical Unit, St Mary's Hospital, W2 1NY. *T:* 071–725 1301. *Club:* Royal Society of Medicine.

GUILLY, Rt. Rev. Richard Lester, SJ; OBE 1945; Parish Priest in Barbados, since 1981; *b* 6 July 1905; *s* of late Richard Guilly. *Educ:* Stonyhurst Coll.; Campion Hall, Oxford (Hons Mod. Hist.; BA, MA); Heythrop Coll. Entered Soc. of Jesus, 1924; Asst Master, Beaumont Coll., 1933–35; ordained 1938. Served War of 1939–45, Chaplain to the Forces: BEF (France), 1939–40; CF 3rd Cl. 1940; Senior RC Chaplain, N Ireland, 1 Corps District, AA Cmd, 2nd Army, 1940–45 (OBE, despatches). Superior of Soc. of Jesus in British Guiana and Barbados, 1946–54; Titular Bishop of Adraa and Vicar Apostolic of British Guiana and Barbados, 1954–56; Bishop of Georgetown, 1956–72; Parish Priest in Barbados, 1972–77; Apostolic Administrator, Archdiocese of Castries, 1977–81. *Publications:* various articles on Church History, Christian Social Doctrine and Church in Guyana. *Address:* Church of Our Lady of Sorrows, Ashton Hall, St Peter, Barbados, WI.

GUINNESS, family name of **Earl of Iveagh** and **Baron Moyne.**

GUINNESS, Sir Alec, Kt 1959; CBE 1955; Hon. DLitt, Hon. DFA; actor; *b* Marylebone, 2 April 1914; *m* 1938, Merula Salaman; one *s*. *Educ:* Pembroke Lodge, Southbourne; Roborough, Eastbourne. On leaving school went into Arks Publicity, Advertising Agents, as copywriter. First professional appearance walking on in Libel at King's Theatre, Hammersmith, 1933; played Hamlet in modern dress, Old Vic, 1938; toured the Continent, 1939. Served War of 1939–45; joined Royal Navy as a rating, 1941; commissioned 1942. Rejoined Old Vic, 1946–47. Fellow, BAFTA, 1989. Hon. DFA Boston Coll., 1962; Hon. DLitt Oxon, 1977. Special Oscar, for contribution to film, 1979; Olivier Award for Services to the Theatre, SWET, 1989. *Films include:* Oliver Twist; Kind Hearts and Coronets; The Bridge on the River Kwai (Oscar for best actor of the year, 1957); Lawrence of Arabia; Star Wars; Little Dorrit; A Handful of Dust. *Plays include:* The Cocktail Party (New York); Dylan (New York) (Antoinette Perry Award); A Voyage Round My Father; Habeas Corpus; The Old Country, 1977; A Walk in the Woods, 1989; *television:* Tinker, Tailor, Soldier, Spy, 1979 (BAFTA Award, 1980); Smiley's People, 1981–82 (BAFTA Award, 1983); Monsignor Quixote, 1985. *Publication:* Blessings in Disguise (autobiog.), 1985. *Address:* c/o McReddie, 91 Regent Street, W1R 7TB. *Clubs:* Athenæum, Garrick.

GUINNESS, Bryan; *see* Moyne, 2nd Baron.

GUINNESS, Hon. Desmond (Walter); writer; President, Irish Georgian Society, since 1958; *b* 8 Sept. 1931; *yr s* of Baron Moyne, *qv*; *m* 1st, 1954, Marie-Gabrielle von Urach (marr. diss. 1981; she *d* 1989); one *s* one *d*; 2nd, Penelope, *d* of Graham and Teresa Cuthbertson. *Educ:* Gordonstoun; Christ Church, Oxford (MA). Founder, 1958, Irish Georgian Society to work for the study of, and protection of, buildings of architectural merit in Ireland, particularly of the Georgian period. Hon. LLD TCD, 1980. *Publications:* Portrait of Dublin, 1967; Irish Houses and Castles, 1971; Mr Jefferson, Architect, 1973; Palladio, 1976; Georgian Dublin, 1980; The White House: an architectural history, 1981;

Newport Preserv'd, 1982. *Clubs:* White's, Chelsea Arts; Kildare Street and University (Dublin).
See also Hon. J. B. Guinness.

GUINNESS, Sir Howard (Christian Sheldon), Kt 1981; VRD 1953; *b* 3 June 1932; *s* of late Edward Douglas Guinness, CBE and Martha Letière (*née* Sheldon); *m* 1958, Evadne Jane Gibbs; two *s* one *d*. *Educ:* King's Mead, Seaford, Sussex; Eton Coll. National Service, RN (midshipman); Lt-Comdr RNR. Union Discount Co. of London Ltd, 1953; Guinness Mahon & Co. Ltd, 1953–55; S. G. Warburg & Co. Ltd, 1955–85 (Exec. Dir, 1970–85). Dir, Harris & Sheldon Gp Ltd, 1960–81; Dir and Dep. Chm., Youghal Carpets (Holdings) Ltd, 1972–80. Chm., N Hampshire Conservative Assoc., 1971–74; Vice-Chm. 1974, Chm. 1975–78, and Treasurer 1978–81, Wessex Area, Cons. Assoc. Mem. Council, English Guernsey Cattle Soc., 1963–72. *Recreations:* skiing, tennis. *Address:* The Manor House, Glanvilles Wootton, Sherborne, Dorset DT9 5QF. *T:* Holnest (096321) 217. *Club:* White's.
See also J. R. S. Guinness.

GUINNESS, James Edward Alexander Rundell, CBE 1986; Director, Guinness Peat Group, 1973–87 (Joint Chairman, 1973–77; Deputy Chairman, 1977–84); Deputy Chairman, Provident Mutual Life Assurance Association, 1983–89; *b* 23 Sept. 1924; *s* of late Sir Arthur Guinness, KCMG and Frances Patience Guinness, MBE (*née* Wright); *m* 1953, Pauline Mander; one *s* four *d*. *Educ:* Eton; Oxford. Served in RNVR, 1943–46. Joined family banking firm of Guinness Mahon & Co., 1946, Partner 1953; Chm., Guinness Mahon Hldgs Ltd, 1968–72. Chm., Public Works Loan Bd, 1979–90 (Comr, 1960–90). *Recreations:* shooting, fishing. *Address:* Coldpiece Farm, Mattingley, Basingstoke RG27 8LQ. *T:* Heckfield (0734) 326292. *Clubs:* Brooks's, Pratt's; Royal Yacht Squadron (Cowes).

GUINNESS, John Ralph Sidney; Second Permanent Secretary, Department of Energy, since 1991; *b* 23 Dec. 1935; *s* of late Edward Douglas Guinness and Martha Letière (*née* Sheldon); *m* 1967, Valerie Susan North; one *s* one *d* (and one *s* decd). *Educ:* Rugby Sch.; Trinity Hall, Cambridge (BA Hons History, MA Hons). Union Discount Co. Ltd, 1960–61; Overseas Develt Inst., 1961–62; joined FO, 1962; Econ. Relations Dept, 1962–63; Third Sec., UK Mission to UN, New York, 1963–64; seconded to UN Secretariat as Special Asst to Dep. Under-Sec. and later Under-Sec. for Econ. and Social Affairs, 1964–66; FCO, 1967–69; First Sec. (Econ.), Brit. High Commn, Ottawa, 1969–72; seconded to Central Policy Rev. Staff, Cabinet Office, 1972–75; Counsellor, 1974; Alternate UK Rep. to Law of the Sea Conf., 1975–77; seconded to CPRS, 1977–79; transferred to Home Civil Service, 1980; Under-Sec., 1980–83, Dep. Sec., 1983–91, Dept of Energy. Governor, Oxford Energy Inst., 1984–. Mem., E Anglia Regl Cttee, NT, 1989–. *Recreation:* iconography. *Address:* c/o Department of Energy, 1 Palace Street, SW1. *T:* 071–238 3129. *Clubs:* Brooks's, Beefsteak.
See also Sir H. C. S. Guinness.

GUINNESS, Hon. Jonathan Bryan; *b* 16 March 1930; *s* and *heir* of Baron Moyne, *qv*, and of Diana (*née* Mitford, now Lady Mosley); *m* 1st, 1951, Ingrid Wyndham (marr. diss. 1962); two *s* one *d*; 2nd, 1964, Suzanne Phillips (*née* Lisney); one *s* one *d*. *Educ:* Eton; Oxford (MA, Mod. Langs). Journalist at Reuters, 1953–56. Merchant Banker: trainee at Erlangers Ltd, 1956–59, and at Philip Hill, 1959–62; Exec. Dir, 1962–64, non-exec. Dir, 1964–91, Leopold Joseph; Dir, Arthur Guinness Son & Co. Ltd, 1961–88. CC Leicestershire, 1970–74; Chairman, Monday Club, 1972–74. *Publications:* (with Catherine Guinness) The House of Mitford, 1984; Shoe: the odyssey of a sixties survivor, 1989. *Address:* Osbaston Hall, Nuneaton, Warwickshire. *Clubs:* Carlton, Beefsteak; Ibstock Working Men's.
See also Hon. D. W. Guinness, Lord Neidpath.

GUINNESS, Sir Kenelm (Ernest Lee), 4th Bt, *cr* 1867; independent engineering consultant; *b* 13 Dec. 1928; *s* of late Kenelm Edward Lee Guinness and Mrs Josephine Lee Guinness; *S* uncle 1954; *m* 1961, Mrs Jane Nevin Dickson; two *s*. *Educ:* Eton Coll.; Massachusetts Institute of Technology, USA. Late Lieut, Royal Horse Guards. With IBRD, Washington, 1954–75. *Heir:* *s* Kenelm Edward Lee Guinness, *b* 30 Jan. 1962. *Address:* (home) Rich Neck, Claiborne, Maryland 21624, USA. *T:* 301 745 5079. *Clubs:* Cavalry and Guards; Household Division Yacht.

GUISE, Sir John (Grant), 7th Bt *cr* 1783; Jockey Club Official since 1968; *b* 15 Dec. 1927; *s* of Sir Anselm William Edward Guise, 6th Bt and Nina Margaret Sophie (*d* 1991), *d* of Sir James Augustus Grant, 1st Bt; *S* father, 1970. *Educ:* Winchester; RMA, Sandhurst. Regular officer, 3rd The King's Own Hussars, 1948–61. *Recreations:* hunting, shooting. *Heir:* *b* Christopher James Guise [*b* 10 July 1930; *m* 1969, Mrs Carole Hoskins Benson, *e d* of Jack Master; one *s* one *d*]. *Address:* Elmore Court, Gloucester. *T:* Gloucester (0452) 720293.

GUJADHUR, Hon. Sir Radhamohun, Kt 1976; CMG 1973; solicitor; Chairman, Consortium Cinematographique Maurice Ltée; Director, Trianon Estates Ltd; Managing Director of Companies; *b* Curepipe Road, Mauritius, 1909; *m*; eight *c*. *Educ:* Church of England Aided Sch., Curepipe; Curepipe De la Salle Sch., Port Louis; Royal Coll., Curepipe; St Xavier Coll., Calcutta. Mem. Municipal Council, 1943–47; Dep. Mayor, Port Louis, 1947; Mem. (nominated) Town Council, Curepipe, 1957–60 (Chm., 1963). MLA, Bon-Accord/Flacq, 1967–82; Dep. Speaker of Legislative Assembly, Mauritius, 1968–69, 1974–82. *Address:* Port Louis, Mauritius. *Club:* Mauritius Turf (Steward, 1970; Chm. 1974).

GULL, Sir Rupert (William Cameron), 5th Bt *cr* 1872, of Brook Street; *b* 14 July 1954; *s* of Sir Michael Swinnerton Cameron Gull, 4th Bt and Yvonne (*d* 1975), *o d* of Dr Albert Oliver Macarius Heslop, Cape Town; *S* father, 1989; *m* 1980, Gillian Lee, *d* of Robert MacFarlaine; two *d*. *Educ:* Diocesan Coll., Cape Town; Cape Town Univ. *Heir:* *great-uncle* John Evelyn Gull, MC [*b* 26 March 1914; *m* 1957, Margaret Colquhoun, *d* of late Capel Berger; one *s*, and one adopted *s* one adopted *d*]. *Address:* Moonrakers, 56 Linersh Wood Close, Bramley, near Guildford, Surrey GU5 0EQ.

GULLIVER, James Gerald; Chairman, James Gulliver Associates Ltd, since 1977; *b* 17 Aug. 1930; *s* of William Frederick and Mary Gulliver; *m* 1st, 1958, Margaret Joan (*née* Cormack) (marr. diss.) three *s* two *d*; 2nd, 1977, Joanne (*née* Sims) (marr. diss.); 3rd, 1985, Marjorie H. Moncrieff. *Educ:* Campbeltown Grammar Sch.; Univ of Glasgow; Georgia Inst. of Technol., USA. Royal Navy (Short Service Commn), 1956–59; Dir, Concrete (Scotland) Ltd, 1960–61; Management Consultant, Urwick, Orr & Partners Ltd, 1961–65; Man. Dir, 1965–72, Chm., 1967–72, Fine Fare (Holdings) Ltd; Dir, Associated British Foods Ltd, 1967–72; Chairman: Argyll Gp PLC (formerly James Gulliver Associates Ltd), 1977–88; Argyll Foods PLC, 1980–88; Amalgamated Distilled Products PLC, 1981–88; Country House Hotels Ltd, 1983–88; Broad Street Gp, 1987–90; Lowndes Queensway, 1988–90; non-executive Chairman: Select Country Hotels, 1986–89; Waverley Cameron, 1987–90; Jackson's of Bourne End, 1988–89; City Gate Estates, 1988–90; Ancasta Marine Hldgs, 1988–. Vis. Prof., Glasgow Univ., 1985–. Mem. Council, Inst. of Directors; Vice-Pres., Marketing Soc. Mem., Prime Minister's Enquiry into Beef Prices, 1973; Member: Scottish Economic Council, 1985–; Governing Council, Scottish Business in the Community, 1983–; Dir, Scottish Investment Trust, 1986–; Chm., Scottish Business Gp, 1988–. Vice-Pres., Manchester United FC, 1984– (Dir, 1979–84). Trustee: Duke of Edinburgh's Award, 1988–; Glasgow Univ. Trust, 1986–. Mem. Council, Buckingham Univ., 1984–. FRSE 1990; FInstD; FRSA; FBIM. Freedom and Livery, Worshipful Co. of Gardeners. DUniv Glasgow, 1989. Guardian Young Businessman of the Year, 1972. *Recreations:* ski-ing, sailing, music, motoring. *Address:* 42 Lowndes Street, SW1X 9HX. *Clubs:* Carlton; Royal Thames Yacht.

GULLY, family name of **Viscount Selby.**

GUMLEY, Frances Jane, (Mrs A. S. Mason), MA; television and radio producer, broadcaster and journalist; *b* 28 Jan. 1955; *o d* of late Franc Stewart Gumley and Helen Teresa (*née* McNicholas); *m* 1988, Andrew Samuel Mason; one *s*. *Educ:* St Augustine's Priory, Ealing; St Benedict's Sch., Ealing (Greek only); Newnham Coll., Cambridge (MA). Parly research, 1974; Braille transcriber, 1975; Catholic Herald: Editorial Assistant and Assistant Literary Editor, Dec. 1975; Literary Editor and Staff Reporter, 1976–79; Editor, 1979–81; RC Asst to Head of Religious Broadcasting, and sen. producer, religious progs, radio, and producer, religious television, 1981–88; Series Editor, Religious Programmes, C4, 1988–89. Mistress of The Keys, Guild of Catholic Writers, 1983–88. *Publications:* (with Brian Redhead): The Good Book, 1987; The Christian Centuries, 1989; The Pillars of Islam, 1990. *Recreations:* deep-sea diving, petit point.

GUMMER, Ellis Norman, CBE 1974 (OBE 1960); Assistant Director-General (Administration), British Council, 1972–75; *b* 18 June 1915; *o s* of late Robert Henry Gummer, engr, and of Mabel Thorpe, Beckenham, Kent; *m* 1949, Dorothy Paton Shepherd; one *s* (and one *s* decd). *Educ:* St Dunstan's Coll.; St Catherine's Society, Oxford. BLitt, MA. Library service: Nottingham Univ., 1939; Queen's Coll., Oxford, 1940–42; served War of 1939–45, Admty, 1942–45; British Council: East Europe Dept, 1945–50; Personnel Dept, 1950–52; Student Welfare Dept, 1952–59; Literature Group, 1959–61; Controller, Arts and Science Div., 1961–66; Controller, Finance Div., 1966–71. *Publication:* Dickens' Works in Germany, 1940. *Recreations:* books, topography, archaeology. *Address:* 9 Campden Street, W8 7EP. *T:* 071–727 4823.

GUMMER, Rt. Hon. John Selwyn, PC 1985; MP (C) Suffolk Coastal, since 1983 (Eye, Suffolk, 1979–83); Minister of Agriculture, Fisheries and Food, since 1989; *b* 26 Nov. 1939; *s* of Canon Selwyn Gummer and Sybille (*née* Mason); *m* 1977, Penelope Jane, *yr d* of John P. Gardner; two *s* two *d*. *Educ:* King's Sch., Rochester; Selwyn Coll., Cambridge (Exhibr). BA Hons History 1961; MA 1971; Chm., Cambridge Univ. Conservative Assoc., 1961; Pres., Cambridge Union, 1962; Chm., Fedn of Conservative Students, 1962. Editor, Business Publications, 1962–64; Editor-in-Chief, Max Parrish & Oldbourne Press, 1964–66; BPC Publishing: Special Asst to Chm., 1967; Publisher, Special Projects, 1967–69; Editorial Coordinator, 1969–70. Mem., ILEA Educn Cttee, 1967–70; Dir, Shandwick Publishing Co., 1966–81; Man. Dir, EP Gp of Cos, 1975–81; Chairman: Selwyn Shandwick Internat., 1976–81, Siemssen Hunter Ltd, 1979–80 (Dir, 1973–80). Contested (C) Greenwich, 1964 and 1966; MP (C) Lewisham W, 1970–Feb. 1974; PPS to Minister of Agriculture, 1972; an additional Vice-Chm., Conservative Party, 1972–74; an Asst Govt Whip, 1981; a Lord Comr of HM Treasury, 1981–83; Parly Under-Sec. of State for Employment, Jan.–Oct. 1983; Minister of State, Dept of Employment, 1983–84; Paymaster-Gen., 1984–85; Chm., Cons. Party, 1983–85; Minister of State: MAFF, 1985–88; DoE, 1988–89. Mem., Gen. Synod of the Church of England, 1979–. *Publications:* (jtly) When the Coloured People Come, 1966; The Permissive Society, 1971; (with L. W. Cowie) The Christian Calendar, 1974; (contrib.) To Church with Enthusiasm, 1969; (contrib.) Faith In Politics, 1987; Christianity and Conservatism, 1990. *Address:* House of Commons, SW1A 0AA.
See also P. S. Gummer.

GUMMER, Peter Selwyn; Chairman and Chief Executive, Shandwick plc, since 1974; *b* 24 Aug. 1942; *s* of Canon Selwyn Gummer and Sybille (*née* Mason); *m* 1982, Lucy Rachel, *er d* of A. Ponsonby Dudley-Hill; one *s* three *d*. *Educ:* King's Sch., Rochester, Kent; Selwyn Coll., Cambridge (BA, MA). Portsmouth and Sunderland Newspaper Gp, 1964–65; Viyella International, 1965–66; Hodgkinson & Partners, 1966–67; Industrial & Commercial Finance Corp., 1967–74; Dir (non-exec.), CIA Group PLC, 1990; Mem. (non-exec.), London Bd, Halifax Building Soc., 1990. Member: NHS Policy Bd, 1991–; Arts Council, 1991. FRSA. *Publications:* various articles and booklets on public relations and marketing. *Recreations:* opera, rugby, cricket. *Clubs:* MCC, Hurlingham.
See also Rt Hon. J. S. Gummer.

GÜMRÜKÇÜOGLU, Rahmi Kamil, Hon. GCVO 1988; Ambassador; Deputy Leader for Foreign Affairs, Democratic Center Party, Turkey, since 1990; *b* 18 May 1927; *m* Elçin; one *s* one *d*. *Educ:* Haydar Pasha Lycée, Istanbul; Faculty of Political Sciences, Ankara Univ. Master's degree in Pol. Economy and Govt, Harvard Univ. Second Secretary, 1952–55, First Sec., 1955, Turkish Embassy, London; Head of Section dealing with Internat. Economic Affairs, Min. of Foreign Affairs, Ankara, 1958–60; Counsellor, Turkish Embassy, Cairo, 1960–63; Dep. Director General, Dept of Internat. Economic Affairs, Ankara, 1963–65; Head of Special Bureau dealing with Economic Co-operation between Turkey and the Soviet Union, 1965–67; Dir Gen., Dept of Internat. Economic Affairs, 1967–71; Turkish Ambassador: to Council of Europe, Strasbourg, 1971–75; to Iran, 1975–78; Sen. Advr to Min. of Foreign Affairs, 1978; Pres., Defence Industry Co-ordination Board, Ankara, 1978–79; Dep. Sec. Gen. for Economic Affairs, Min. of Foreign Affairs, 1979–81; Amb. to UK, 1981–88; Inspector, Min. of Foreign Affairs, 1989–90. *Publications:* various articles and booklets on foreign investment, questions of economic develt, Soviet economic develt, economic integration amongst developing countries. *Address:* Köybasi Caddesi 191, Yeniköy, Istanbul, Turkey.

GUN-MUNRO, Sir Sydney Douglas, GCMG 1979; Kt 1977; MBE 1957; FRCS; Governor-General of St Vincent and the Grenadines, 1979–85, retired (Governor, 1977–79); *b* 29 Nov. 1916; *s* of Barclay Justin Gun-Munro and Marie Josephine Gun-Munro; *m* 1943, Joan Estelle Benjamin; two *s* one *d*. *Educ:* Grenada Boys' Secondary Sch.; King's Coll. Hosp., London (MB, BS Hons 1943); Moorfields Hosp., London (DO 1952). MRCS, LRCP 1943; FRCS 1985. House Surg., EMS Hosp., Horton, 1943; MO, Lewisham Hosp., 1943–46; Dist MO, Grenada, 1946–49; Surg., Gen. Hosp., St Vincent, 1949–71; Dist MO, Bequia, St Vincent, 1972–76. *Recreations:* tennis, boating. *Address:* PO Box 51, Bequia, St Vincent and the Grenadines, West Indies. *T:* St Vincent 83261.

GUNN, (Alan) Richard, CBE 1991; High Commissioner for Eastern Caribbean States in London, since 1987; *b* 19 Jan. 1936; *s* of Alan Leslie Gunn and Violet Gunn; *m* 1962, Flora Beryl (*née* Richardson); one *s* two *d*. *Educ:* Boys' Grammar Sch., St Vincent; Portsmouth College of Architecture; Regent Street Polytechnic, London. Marketing Dir, Hazells Ltd, St Vincent, 1968–74; Chm./Man. Dir, Property Investments Ltd, St Vincent, 1974–87. Director: Vincentian Newspaper Ltd, 1970–; Caribbean Assoc. of Industry and Commerce, 1985–87; Chairman: St Vincent Chamber of Commerce, 1984–85; Nat. Shipping Corp., St Vincent, 1987; Nat. Broadcasting Corp., 1986–87; Sec.-Gen., Caribbean Assoc. of Industry and Commerce/EEC 'Europe-Caribbean Contact II', 1987.

Recreations: yachting, fishing, reading. *Address:* 10 Kensington Court, W8 5DL. *T:* 071-937 9522. *Clubs:* Royal Over-Seas League, Commonwealth Trust; St Vincent Yacht.

GUNN, Mrs Bunty Moffat, OBE 1981; JP; Chairman, Lanarkshire Health Board, since 1981; *b* 4 Sept. 1923; *d* of William M. and Dolina Johnston; *m* 1946, Hugh McVane Houston Gunn; three *s* one *d. Educ:* Grange School for Girls; Grangemouth High School. DSCHE 1980. Councillor: Lanark CC, 1970–73; Strathclyde Regional Council, 1973–82; Chairman, Scottish Council for Health Education, 1974–80; Member, Lanarkshire Health Board, 1973–81. Vice-Pres., Royal British Legion, CS&W Branch, 1978–. JP City of Glasgow 1972. *Recreations:* golf, theatre, music. *Address:* 198 Dukes Road, Burnside, Rutherglen, Glasgow G73 5AA. *T:* 041–647 8258. *Club:* Cathkin Braes Golf (Strathclyde).

GUNN, John Angus Livingston; Head of Heritage and Royal Estate Directorate, Department of the Environment, since 1990; *b* 20 Nov. 1934; *s* of late Alistair L. Gunn, FRCOG, and Mrs Sybil Gunn, JP; *m* 1959, Jane, *d* of Robert Cameron; one *s* one *d. Educ:* Fettes Coll., Edinburgh (Foundationer); Christ Church, Oxford (Scholar). MA Oxford, 1st Cl. Hons in Classical Hon. Mod., 1955, and in final sch. of Psychology, Philosophy and Physiology, 1957; Passmore-Edwards Prizeman, 1956. National Service, commnd in S Wales Borderers (24th Regt), 1957–59. Entered Min. of Transport, 1959; Principal Private Sec. to Ministers of Transport, 1967–68; Asst Sec., MoT, DoE and Civil Service Dept, 1969–75; Under-Sec., DoE, 1976–; Greater London Housing and Planning Directorate, 1976; Water Directorate, 1981; Water Privatisation Directorate, 1987. *Recreation:* gardening. *Address:* Department of the Environment, 2 Marsham Street, SW1P 3EB.

GUNN, Prof. John Charles, MD; FRCPsych; Professor of Forensic Psychiatry, Institute of Psychiatry, since 1978; *b* 6 June 1937; *s* of Albert Charles Gunn and Lily Hilda Edwards; *m* 1959, Celia Willis (marr. diss. 1986, she *d* 1989); one *s* one *d*; *m* 1989, Pamela Taylor. *Educ:* Brighton, Hove and Sussex Grammar Sch.; Reigate Grammar Sch.; Birmingham Univ. (MB ChB 1961; Acad. DPM 1966; MD 1969). MRCPsych 1971, FRCPsych 1980. Queen Elizabeth Hosp., Birmingham, 1961–63; Maudsley Hosp., 1963–67; Institute of Psychiatry: Res. Worker, 1967–69; Lectr, 1969–71; Sen. Lectr, 1971–75; Dir, Special Hosps Res. Unit, 1975–78. H. B. Williams Vis. Prof. to Aust. and NZ, 1985. Chm., Res. Cttee, RCPsych, 1976–80; Advisor, H of C Select Cttees on Violence in Marriage, 1975, on Prison Med. Service, 1986; Mem., Home Sec's Adv. Bd on Restricted Patients, 1982–. WHO Specialist Advisor in Forensic Psychiatry to China, 1987. *Publications:* Epileptics in Prison, 1977; Psychiatric Aspects of Imprisonment, 1978; Current Research in Forensic Psychiatry and Psychology, vols 1–3, 1982–85; Violence in Human Society, 1983; (ed) Criminal Behaviour and Mental Health. *Recreations:* theatre, opera, cinema, photography, walking, living with Pamela. *Address:* Department of Forensic Psychiatry, Institute of Psychiatry, De Crespigny Park, Denmark Hill, SE5 8AF. *T:* 071–701 7063. *Clubs:* Athenæum, Royal Society of Medicine.

GUNN, Prof. Sir John (Currie), Kt 1982; CBE 1976; MA (Glasgow and Cambridge); FRSE, FIMA; FInstP; Cargill Professor of Natural Philosophy, 1949–82 and Head of Department, 1973–82, Dean of Faculties, 1989–91, University of Glasgow; *b* 13 Sept. 1916; *s* of Richard Robertson Gunn and Jane Blair Currie; *m* 1944, Betty Russum (OBE 1984); one *s. Educ:* Glasgow Acad.; Glasgow Univ.; St John's Coll., Cambridge. Engaged in Admiralty scientific service, first at Admiralty Research Laboratory, later at Mine Design Dept, 1939–45; Research Fellow of St John's Coll., Cambridge, 1944; Lecturer in Applied Mathematics: Manchester Univ., 1945–46; University Coll., London, 1946–49. Member: SRC, 1968–72; UGC, 1974–81. Hon. DSc: Heriot-Watt, 1981; Loughborough, 1983; DUniv Open, 1989. *Publications:* papers on mathematical physics in various scientific journals. *Recreations:* golf, music, chess. *Address:* 32 Beaconsfield Road, Glasgow G12 0NY. *T:* 041–357 2001.

GUNN, John Humphrey; Chief Executive, British & Commonwealth Holdings, 1986–87 and 1990 (Chairman, 1987–90); *b* 15 Jan. 1942; *s* of Francis (Bob) Gunn and Doris Gunn; *m* 1965, Renate Sigrid (*née* Boehme); three *d. Educ:* Sir John Deane's Grammar School, Northwich; Univ. of Nottingham (BA Hons 1964). Barclays Bank, 1964–68; Astley & Pearce, 1968–85; Chief Exec., Exco International, 1979–85. Hon. LLD Nottingham, 1989. *Recreations:* golf, ski-ing, mountain walking, classical music, opera. *Address:* Midland and Scottish Resources PLC, 36/37 King Street, EC2. *Club:* MCC.

GUNN, Marion Ballantyne; Head of Water Policy Division, Scottish Office Environment Department, since 1990; *b* 31 Oct. 1947; *d* of Dr Allan Christie Tait and Jean Ballantyne Hay; *m* 1985, Donald Hugh Gunn; one step *s. Educ:* Jordanhill College School; Dumfries Academy; Univ. of Edinburgh (MA Hons 1969); Open Univ. (BA 1975). Management trainee, Lewis's, Bristol, 1969–70; joined Scottish Office, 1970; posts in Scottish Educn Dept and Scottish Develt Dept, 1970–90; Asst Sec., 1984; Head of Roads Policy and Programme Div., 1987. Research Fellow, Univ. of Glasgow, 1983–84. *Recreations:* gardening, Scottish country dancing, squash. *Address:* 32 Warriston Avenue, Edinburgh EH3 5NB. *T:* 031–552 4476.

GUNN, Peter Nicholson; author; *b* 15 Aug. 1914; 2nd *s* of Frank Lindsay Gunn, CBE, and Adèle Margaret (*née* Dunphy); *m* 1953, Diana Maureen James; one *s. Educ:* Melbourne; Trinity Coll., Cambridge (MA). Served War 1939–45: Rifle Bde; POW 1942. Sen. Lectr, RMA, Sandhurst, 1949–54. *Publications:* Naples: a Palimpsest, 1961 (German trans. 1964, Italian trans. 1971); Vernon Lee: a Study, 1964; The Companion Guide to Southern Italy, 1969; My Dearest Augusta: a Biography of Augusta Leigh, Byron's half-sister, 1969; A Concise History of Italy, 1971; (ed) Byron's Prose, 1972; Normandy: Landscape with figures, 1975; Burgundy: Landscape with figures, 1976; The Actons, 1978; Napoleon's Little Pest: The Duchess of Abrantès, 1979; (with R. Beny) Churches of Rome, 1981 (trans. German, Italian and Danish, 1982); Yorkshire Dales: Landscape with figures, 1984; (ed) Lord Byron: Selected Letters and Journals, 1984. *Address:* Trebinshwn Farm House, Llangasty-Talyllyn, Brecon, Powys LD3 7PX. *T:* Bwlch (0874) 730773.

GUNN, Richard; *see* Gunn, A. R.

GUNN, Robert Norman; Chairman, 1985–90, Chief Executive, 1983–87 and Director, 1976–90, The Boots Company PLC; *b* 16 Dec. 1925; *s* of late Donald Macfie Gunn and Margaret (*née* Pallister); *m* 1956, Joan Parry; one *d. Educ:* Royal High Sch., Edinburgh; Worcester Coll., Oxford (MA). Served RAC, 1944–47 (Lieut). Joined Boots, 1951; Merchandise Buyer, 1962–70; Head of Warehousing and Distribn, 1971–73; Dir of Property, 1973–78; Dir, Industrial Div., 1979–83 (Man. Dir 1980–83); Vice-Chm., 1983–85. Director: Foseco plc (formerly Foseco Minsep), 1984–91; East Midlands Electricity, 1990–; Nottingham Building Soc., 1990–. Member: Bd of Management, Assoc. of British Pharmaceutical Industry, 1981–84 (Vice-Pres., 1983–84); Council, CBI, 1985–90; PCFC, 1989–; CBIM 1983; FInstD 1985. *Recreations:* gardening, theatre. *Address:* Tor House, Pinfold Lane, Elston, near Newark, Notts NG23 5PD.

GUNN, Thomson William, (Thom Gunn); poet; Senior Lecturer, English Department, University of California (Berkeley), since 1990; *b* 29 Aug. 1929; *s* of Herbert Smith Gunn, and Ann Charlotte Gunn (*née* Thomson); unmarried. *Educ:* University Coll. Sch., Hampstead; Trinity Coll., Cambridge. British Army (National Service), 1948–50; lived in Paris six months, 1950; Cambridge, 1950–53; lived in Rome, 1953–54; has lived in California since 1954. Lectr, later Associate Prof., English Dept, University of Calif (Berkeley), 1958–66, Vis. Lectr, 1975–90. *Publications:* Poetry from Cambridge, 1953; Fighting Terms, 1954; The Sense of Movement, 1957; My Sad Captains, 1961; Selected Poems (with Ted Hughes), 1962; Five American Poets (ed with Ted Hughes), 1962; Positives (with Ander Gunn), 1966; Touch, 1967; Poems 1950–1966: a selection, 1969; Moly, 1971; Jack Straw's Castle and other poems, 1976; Selected Poems, 1979; The Passages of Joy, 1982; The Occasions of Poetry (ed Clive Wilmer), 1982. *Recreations:* cheap thrills. *Address:* 1216 Cole Street, San Francisco, Calif 94117, USA.

GUNN, Sir William (Archer), AC 1990; KBE 1961; CMG 1955; JP; Australian grazier and company director; Chairman, International Wool Secretariat, 1961–73; *b* Goondiwindi, Qld, 1 Feb. 1914; *s* of late Walter and Doris Isabel Gunn, Goondiwindi; *m* 1939, Mary (Phillipa), *d* of F. B. Haydon, Murrurundi, NSW; one *s* two *d. Educ:* The King's Sch., Parramatta, NSW. Director: Rothmans of Pall Mall (Australia) Ltd; Grazcos Co-op. Ltd; Clausen Steamship Co. (Australia) Pty Ltd; Walter Reid and Co. Ltd; Gunn Rural Management Pty Ltd; Chairman and Managing Director: Moline Pastoral Co. Pty Ltd; Roper Valley Pty Ltd; Coolibah Pty Ltd; Mataranba Pty Ltd; Unibeef Australia Pty Ltd; Gunn Development Pty Ltd; Chairman: Australian Wool Bd, 1963–72; Qld Adv. Bd, Develt Finance Corp., 1962–72; Member: Commonwealth Bank Bd, 1952–59; Qld Bd, Nat. Mutual Life Assoc., 1955–67; Reserve Bank Bd, 1959–; Aust. Meat Bd, 1953–66; Aust. Wool Bureau, 1951–63 (Chm. 1958–63); Aust. Wool Growers Council, 1947–60 (Chm. 1955–58); Graziers Federal Council of Aust., 1950–60 (Pres. 1951–54); Aust. Wool Growers and Graziers Council, 1960–65; Export Develt Council, 1962–65; Australian Wool Corp., 1973; Faculty of Veterinary Science, University of Qld, 1953–; Exec. Council, United Graziers Assoc. of Qld, 1944–69 (Pres., 1951–59; Vice-Pres., 1947–51); Aust. Wool Testing Authority, 1958–63; Council, NFU of Aust., 1951–54; CSIRO State Cttee, 1951–68; Chairman: The Wool Bureau Inc., New York, 1962–69; Trustee: Qld Cancer Fund; Australian Pastoral Research Trust, 1959–71. Coronation Medal, 1953; Golden Fleece Achievement Award (Bd of Dirs of Nat. Assoc. of Wool Manufrs of America), 1962; Award of Golden Ram (Natal Woolgrowers Assoc. of SA), 1973. *Address:* (office) Wool Exchange, 69 Eagle Street, Brisbane, Qld 4000, Australia. *T:* Brisbane 21 4044. *Clubs:* Queensland, Tattersalls, Queensland Turf (Brisbane); Union (Sydney); Australian (Melbourne).

GUNNELL, (William) John; Chairman, Yorkshire Enterprise Ltd (formerly West Yorkshire Enterprise Board), since 1982; *b* 1 Oct. 1933; *s* of late William Henry and Norah Gunnell; *m* 1955, Jean Louise, *d* of late Frank and of Harriet Louise Lacey; three *s* one *d. Educ:* King Edward's Sch., Birmingham; Univ. of Leeds (BSc Hons). Hospital porter, St Bartholomew's, London, 1955–57; Teacher, Leeds Modern Sch., 1959–62; Head of Science, United Nations International Sch., New York, 1962–70; Lectr, Centre for Studies in Science and Mathematics Education, Univ. of Leeds, 1970–88. County Councillor for Hunslet, 1977–86; Leader of Opposition, 1979–81, Leader, 1981–86, W Yorks MCC; Mem. for Hunslet, Leeds MDC, 1986– (Chm., Social Services Cttee, 1990–). Chm., Crown Point Foods, 1988–90. Chairman: Yorks and Humberside Develt Assoc., 1981–; Leeds/Bradford Airport jt cttee, 1981–83; N of England Regional Consortium, 1984–; Member: Audit Commn, 1983–90; Leeds Develt Corp., 1988–; Leeds Eastern AHA, 1990–. Advr to Conseil des Régions d'Europe, subseq. Assembly of Regions of Europe, 1986– (Mem. Bureau, 1985–86). Hon. Pres., RETI, 1985–87. Spokesman for MCCs in their campaign against abolition, 1983–85. Mem., Fabian Soc., 1972–. Director: Opera North, 1982–; Leeds Theatre Trust, 1986–; Belle Isle North Estate Management, 1990–. *Publications:* Selected Experiments in Advanced Level Chemistry, 1975, and other texts (all with E. W. Jenkins); (contrib.) Local Economic Policy, 1990. *Recreations:* music, opera, watching cricket and soccer. *Address:* 6 Arthington View, Hunslet, Leeds LS10 2ND. *T:* Leeds (0532) 770592. *Clubs:* East Hunslet Labour (Leeds); Warwickshire CC; Yorkshire CC.

GUNNING, Prof. Brian Edgar Scourse, FRS 1980; FAA 1979; Professor of Plant Cell Biology, Australian National University, since 1974; *b* 29 Nov. 1934; *s* of William Gunning and Margaret Gunning (*née* Scourse); *m* 1964, Marion Sylvia Forsyth; two *s. Educ:* Methodist Coll., Belfast; Queen's Univ., Belfast (BSc (Hons), MSc, PhD); DSc ANU. Lecturer in Botany, 1957, Reader in Botany, 1965, Queen's Univ., Belfast. *Publications:* Ultrastructure and the Biology of Plant Cells (with Dr M. Steer), 1975; Intercellular Communication in Plants: studies on plasmodesmata (with Dr A. Robards), 1976; contribs to research jls. *Recreations:* hill walking, photography. *Address:* 29 Millen Street, Hughes, ACT 2605, Australia. *T:* (062) 812879.

GUNNING, Sir Charles Theodore, 9th Bt *cr* 1778, of Eltham, Kent; CD 1964; RCN retired; *b* 19 June 1935; *s* of Sir Robert Gunning, 8th Bt and of Helen Nancy, *d* of Vice-Adm. Sir Theodore John Hallett, KBE, CB; *S* father, 1989; *m* 1st, 1969, Sarah (marr. diss. 1982), *d* of Col Patrick Arthur Easton; one *d*; 2nd, 1989, Linda Martin (*née* Kachmar). *Educ:* Canadian Mil. Coll.; RNEC Plymouth; Tech. Univ. of NS. PEng; AMIMechE; AMIMarE. Nat. Canadian Chm., Royal Commonwealth Soc., 1990– (Pres., Ottawa Br.; a Nat. Vice-Chm.). Silver Jubilee Medal, 1977. *Heir: b* John Robert Gunning [*b* 17 Sept. 1944; *m* 1969, Alina Tylicki; two *s* one *d*]. *Address:* 2940 McCarthy Road, Ottawa, Ont K1V 8K6, Canada.

GUNNING, John Edward Maitland, CBE 1960 (OBE 1945); Barrister-at-law; *b* 22 Sept. 1904; *s* of late John Elgee Gunning, Manor House, Moneymore, Co. Derry, and late Edythe, *er d* of T. J. Reeves, London; *m* 1936, Enid Katherine (*d* 1987), *o d* of George Menhinick; two *s. Educ:* Harrow; Magdalene Coll., Cambridge. Called to Bar, Gray's Inn, 1933. Practised South Eastern Circuit, Central Criminal Court, North London Sessions, Herts and Essex Sessions. Joined Judge Advocate General's office, Oct. 1939. War of 1939–45: served BEF, France, 1939–40; N Africa, 1942–43; Italy, 1943–45 (despatches, OBE). Middle East, 1945–50; Deputy Judge Advocate Gen. with rank of Col, CMF, 1945, Middle East, 1946; Deputy Judge Advocate Gen. (Army and RAF): Germany, 1951–53, 1960–63, 1968–70; Far East, 1957–59, 1965–67; Senior Asst Judge Advocate Gen., 1965–70. *Recreations:* bridge, watching cricket, reading. *Clubs:* Travellers', MCC.

GUNSTON, Sir John (Wellesley), 3rd Bt *cr* 1938, of Wickwar, Co. Gloucester; freelance photojournalist; *b* 25 July 1962; *s* of Sir Richard Gunston, 2nd Bt and of Mrs Joan Elizabeth Marie Gunston; *S* father, 1991; *m* 1990, Rosalind, *y d* of Edward Gordon Eliott. *Educ:* Harrow; RMA Sandhurst. BSAP Reserve, Rhodesia, 1979–80 (Operational GSM). Commnd 1st Bn Irish Guards, 1981. Since 1983 has covered wars, revolutions and foreign travel assignments in: Afghanistan, Albania, Brazil, Colombia, Egypt, Eritrea, Israel (West Bank and Gaza), Liberia, South Africa, Sudan, Uganda, Ulster and also in North America, Eastern Europe and South East Asia. FRGS 1988. *Recreation:* present occupation. *Address:* 127 Piccadilly, W1E 6YZ. *T:* 071–499 1261. *Club:* Cavalry and Guards.

GUNTER, John Forsyth; freelance designer; Head of Design, Royal National Theatre, 1989–91; *b* 31 Oct. 1938; *s* of Herbert and Charlotte Gunter; *m* 1969, Micheline

McKnight; two *d*. *Educ:* Bryanston Public Sch.; Central Sch. of Art and Design (Dip. with distinction). Started career in rep. theatre in GB; Resident Designer: English Stage Co., 1965–66 (subseq. designed 28 prodns for co.); Zürich Schauspielhaus, 1970–73 (also designed plays and operas throughout German-speaking theatre); freelance design work for West End, NT, RSC and for Broadway, New York, 1973–; designer of operas: for cos in GB and Germany; Glyndebourne Fest. Op., 1985–; La Scala, Milan, 1988. Head, Theatre Dept, Central Sch. of Art and Design, 1974–82. FRSA 1982. Many awards for design of Guys and Dolls, NT, 1982, incl. SWET Award for Best Design 1982, Drama Magazine Best Design Award 1982, Plays and Players Award for Best Design 1983; Plays and Players and Olivier Awards for Best Design 1984, for design of Wild Honey, NT, 1984. *Recreation:* getting out into the countryside. *Address:* c/o Peter Murphy, Curtis Brown, 162–168 Regent Street, W1R 5TB.

GURDON, family name of **Baron Cranworth.**

GURDON, Prof. John Bertrand, DPhil; FRS 1971; John Humphrey Plummer Professor of Cell Biology, University of Cambridge, since 1983; Fellow of Churchill College, Cambridge, since 1973; Chairman, Wellcome Cancer Research Campaign Institute, Cambridge, since 1991; Fellow of Eton College, since 1978; *b* 2 Oct. 1933; *s* of late W. N. Gurdon, DCM, formerly of Assington, Suffolk, and of late Elsie Marjorie (*née* Byass); *m* 1964, Jean Elizabeth Margaret Curtis; one *s* one *d*. *Educ:* Edgeborough; Eton; Christ Church, Oxford; BA 1956; DPhil 1960. Beit Memorial Fellow, 1958–61; Gosney Research Fellow, Calif. Inst. Technol., 1962; Departmental Demonstrator, Dept of Zool., Oxford, 1963–64; Vis. Research Fellow, Carnegie Instn, Baltimore, 1965; Lectr, Dept of Zoology, Oxford, 1965–72; Research Student, Christ Church, 1962–72; Mem. Staff, MRC Lab. of Molecular Biology, Cambridge, 1972–83 (Hd, Cell Biology Div., 1979–83). Fullerian Prof. of Physiology and Comparative Anatomy, Royal Instn, 1985–. Lectures: Harvey Soc., NY, 1973; Dunham, Harvard, 1974; Croonian, Royal Soc., 1976; Carter-Wallace, Princeton, 1978; Woodhull, Royal Instn, 1980; Florey, Aust., 1988. Hon. Foreign Mem., Amer. Acad. of Arts and Scis, 1978; Foreign Associate: Nat. Acad. of Sciences, USA, 1980; Belgian Royal Acad. of Scis, Letters and Fine Arts, 1984; Foreign Mem., Amer. Philos. Soc., 1983. Hon. Student, Christ Church, Oxford, 1985. Hon. DSc: Chicago, 1978; René Descartes, Paris, 1982; Oxford, 1988. Albert Brachet Prize (Belgian Royal Academy), 1968; Scientific Medal of Zoological Soc., 1968; Feldberg Foundn Award, 1975; Paul Ehrlich Award, 1977; Nessim Habif Prize, Univ. of Geneva, 1979; CIBA Medal, Biochem. Soc., 1980; Comfort Crookshank Award for Cancer Research, 1983; William Bate Hardy Prize, Cambridge Philos. Soc., 1984; Prix Charles Léopold Mayer, Acad. des Scis, France, 1984; Ross Harrison Prize, Internat. Soc. Develt Biol., 1985; Royal Medal, Royal Soc., 1985; Emperor Hirohito Internat. Prize for Biology, Japan Acad., 1987; Wolf Prize in Medicine, Israel, 1989. *Publications:* Control of Gene Expression in Animal Development, 1974; articles in scientific jls, especially on nuclear transplantation. *Recreations:* skiing, tennis, horticulture, Lepidoptera. *Address:* Whittlesford Grove, Whittlesford, Cambridge CB2 4NZ. *Club:* Eagle Ski.

GURNEY, Nicholas Bruce Jonathan; Chief Executive, Wokingham District Council, since 1990; *b* 20 Jan. 1945; *s* of Bruce William George Gurney and Cynthia Joan Watkins Mason (*née* Winn); *m* 1st, 1970, Patricia Wendy Tulip (marr. diss. 1987); two *s* one *d*; 2nd, 1989, Caroline Mary (*née* Bentley). *Educ:* Wimbledon College; Christ's College, Cambridge. BA 1966, MA 1969. Lectr in English, Belize Teachers' Training College, Belize, as part of British Volunteer Programme, 1966–67; MoD 1967; Asst Private Sec., Minister of State for Defence, 1970–72; Civil Service Dept, 1972–74; Private Sec. to Lord Privy Seal and Leader of House of Lords, 1974–77; Civil Service Dept and Management Personnel Office, 1978–83; Grade 3, Cabinet Office, and CS Comr, 1983–88; Dept of Health, 1988–90. *Address:* Council Offices, Shute End, Wokingham, Berks RG11 1WQ.

GURNEY, Oliver Robert, MA, DPhil Oxon; FBA 1959; Shillito Reader in Assyriology, Oxford University, 1945–78; Professor, 1965; Fellow of Magdalen College, 1963–78, now Emeritus; *b* 28 Jan. 1911; *s* of Robert Gurney, DSc, and Sarah Gamzu, MBE, *d* of Walter Garstang, MD, MRCP; *m* 1957, Mrs Diane Hope Grazebrook (*née* Esencourt); no *c*. *Educ:* Eton Coll.; New Coll., Oxford. Served War of 1939–45, in Royal Artillery and Sudan Defence Force. Freeman of City of Norwich. For. Mem., Royal Danish Acad. of Sciences and Letters, 1976. Pres., British Institute of Archaeology at Ankara, 1983–. *Publications:* The Hittites (Penguin), 1952; (with J. J. Finkelstein and P. Hulin) The Sultantepe Tablets, 1957, 1964; (with John Garstang) The Geography of the Hittite Empire, 1959; Ur Excavations, Texts, VII, 1974; Oxford Editions of Cuneiform Texts V (with S. N. Kramer), 1976, XI, 1989; Some Aspects of Hittite Religion (Schweich Lectures, 1976), 1977; The Middle Babylonian Legal and Economic Texts from Ur, 1983; Oxford Editions of Cuneiform Texts XI, 1989; articles in Annals of Archæology and Anthropology (Liverpool), Anatolian Studies, etc. *Recreation:* golf. *Address:* Fir Tree House, 10 Milton Lane, Steventon, Abingdon, Oxon OX13 6SA. *T:* Abingdon (0235) 831212.

GURR, Prof. Michael Ian; Maypole Scientific Services, private nutrition consultancy, since 1990; Visiting Professor: University of Reading, since 1986; Oxford Polytechnic, since 1990; *b* 10 April 1939; *s* of Henry Ormonde Gurr and Hilda Ruth Gurr; *m* 1963, Elizabeth Anne Mayers; two *s* one *d*. *Educ:* Dunstable Grammar Sch.; Univ. of Birmingham (BSc, PhD). Postdoctoral Fellowship, Harvard Univ., 1964–66; Unilever European Fellowship of Biochem. Soc., State Univ. of Utrecht, 1966–67; Res. Scientist, Unilever Res. Lab., Sharnbrook, Bedford, 1967–78; Hd, Department of Nutrition, Nat. Inst. for Res. in Dairying, Shinfield, Reading, 1978–85; Dir, Reading Lab. of AFRC Inst. of Food Res., 1985–86; Nutrition Consultant and Hd of Nutrition Dept, MMB, 1986–90. Chm., Editl Bd, British Jl of Nutrition, 1988–90. *Publications:* Lipid Biochemistry: an introduction (jtly), 1971, 4th edn 1991; Role of Fats in Food and Nutrition, 1984, 2nd edn 1991; numerous original pubns and reviews. *Recreations:* sailing, walking, photography, piano playing. *Address:* Vale View Cottage, Maypole, St Mary's, Isles of Scilly TR21 0NU. *T:* Scillonia (0720) 22224.

GUTFREUND, Prof. Herbert, FRS 1981; Professor of Physical Biochemistry, University of Bristol, 1972–86, now Emeritus; Scientific Member (external), Max-Planck-Institut für medizinische Forschung, Heidelberg, since 1987; *b* 21 Oct. 1921; *s* of late Paul Peter Gutfreund and Clara Angela (*née* Pisko); *m* 1958, Mary Kathelen, *er d* of late Mr and Mrs L. J. Davies, Rugby; two *s* one *d*. *Educ:* Vienna; Univ. of Cambridge (PhD). Research appts at Cambridge Univ., 1947–57; Rockefeller Fellow, Yale Univ., 1951–52; part-time Research Associate, Yale Univ., 1953–58; Principal Scientific Officer, National Inst. for Research in Dairying, Univ. of Reading, 1957–65; Visiting Professor: Univ. of California, 1965; Max Planck Inst., Göttingen, 1966–67; Reader in Biochemistry and Director of Molecular Enzymology Laboratory, Univ. of Bristol, 1967–72. Visiting appointments: Univ. of Leuven, 1972; Univ. of Adelaide, 1979; Univ. of Alberta, 1983. Part-time Scholar in Residence, NIH, Bethesda, 1986–89. *Publications:* An Introduction to the Study of Enzymes, 1966; Enzymes: Physical Principles, 1972; ed, Chemistry of Macromolecules, 1974; ed, Biochemical Evolution, 1981; Biothermodynamics, 1983; papers and reviews on many aspects of physical biochemistry. *Recreations:* mountain walking in Austria, gardening, reading general literature and philosophy of science, listening to music and all other good things in life. *Address:* University of Bristol Medical School, University Walk, Bristol BS8 1TD. *T:* Bristol (0272) 303910; 12a The Avenue, Bristol BS9 1PA. *T:* Bristol (0272) 684453. *Club:* United Oxford & Cambridge University.

GUTFREUND, John Halle; Chairman, President and Chief Executive, Salomon Inc, 1986–91; Chairman and Chief Executive, Salomon Brothers Inc, 1981–91; *b* 14 Sept. 1929; *s* of B. Manuel Gutfreund and Mary Halle Gutfreund; *m* 1st, 1958, Joyce L. Gutfreund; three *s*; 2nd, 1981, Susan K. Gutfreund; one *s*. *Educ:* Oberlin College, Ohio (BA 1951). Served in Army, 1951–53; Salomon Brothers, 1953–91: Exec. Partner, 1966; Managing Partner, 1978; Chief Exec., Chm. and Pres., Phibro-Salomon Inc, 1984. Vice-Chm., NY Stock Exchange, 1985–87. Trustee: Center for Strategic and Internat. Studies; Cttee for Economic Develt; Jt Council on Economic Educn. Chm., Downtown-Lower Manhattan Assoc.; Dir, Montefiore Medical Center Corp.; Treasurer, Bd of Trustees and Chm., Finance Cttee, NY Public Library; Hon. Trustee, Oberlin Coll.; Chm., Wall Street Cttee for Lincoln Center's 1986–87 Corporate Fund Campaign. Hon. DH Oberlin Coll., 1987. *Address:* c/o Salomon Brothers Inc, 7 World Trade Center, New York, NY 10048, USA. *T:* (212) 783–7000.

GUTHRIE, Gen. Sir Charles (Ronald Llewelyn), KCB 1990; LVO 1977; OBE 1980; Commander Northern Army Group and Commander in Chief British Army of the Rhine, since 1992; *b* 17 Nov. 1938; *s* of late Ronald Guthrie and Nina (*née* Llewelyn); *m* 1971, Catherine, *er d* of late Lt Col Claude Worrall, MVO, OBE, Coldstream Guards; two *s*. *Educ:* Harrow; RMA Sandhurst. Commnd Welsh Guards, 1959; served: BAOR, Aden; 22 SAS Regt, 1965–69; psc 1972; MA (GSO2) to CGS, MoD, 1973–74; Brigade Major, Household Div., 1976–77; Comdg 1st Bn Welsh Guards, Berlin and N Ireland, 1977–80; Col GS Military Ops, MoD, 1980–82; Commander: British Forces New Hebrides, 1980; 4th Armoured Brigade, 1982–84; Chief of Staff 1st (BR) Corps, 1984–86; GOC NE Dist and Comdr 2nd Infantry Div., 1986–87; ACGS, MoD, 1987–89; Comdr 1 (BR) Corps, 1989–91. Col Comdt, Intelligence Corps, 1986–. President: Army Saddle Club, 1991–; Army LTA, 1991–. Freeman, City of London, 1988; Liveryman, Painter Stainers' Co., 1989. *Recreations:* tennis, ski-ing, travel. *Address:* c/o Lloyds Bank, Knightsbridge Branch, 79 Brompton Road, SW3 1DD. *Clubs:* White's, Beefsteak.

GUTHRIE, Rev. Donald Angus; Rector, Holy Spirit Episcopal Church, Missoula, Montana, since 1979; *b* 18 Jan. 1931; *s* of Frederick Charles and Alison Guthrie; *m* 1st, 1959, Joyce Adeline Blunsden (*d* 1976); two *s* one *d*; 2nd, 1977, Lesley Josephine Boardman (marr. diss. 1983); 3rd, 1984, Carolyn Wallop Alderson. *Educ:* Marlborough Coll.; Trinity Coll., Oxford (MA). Rector, St John's Church, Selkirk, 1963–69; Vice-Principal, Episcopal Theological Coll., Edinburgh, 1969–74; Priest-in-Charge, Whitburn Parish Church, Tyne and Wear, 1974–76; Provost, St Paul's Cathedral, Dundee, 1976–77; Episcopal Chaplain to Univ. of Montana, 1977–79. *Recreations:* walking, reading. *Address:* 655 West Mountain View Drive, Missoula, Montana 59802, USA.

GUTHRIE, (Garth) Michael; Founder Director, Bright Reasons, since 1990; *b* 30 April 1941; *s* of Harry and Ann Guthrie; *m* 1963, Joyce Fox; one *s* two *d*. *Educ:* Blackpool Catering Coll. (HCIMA). Joined Mecca Leisure, 1961; Man. Dir, 1980; Chm., 1981–90; Chief Exec., 1985–90. *Recreations:* swimming, gardening. *Address:* 36 Battersea Bridge Road, SW11 3AG.

GUTHRIE, Air Vice-Marshal Kenneth MacGregor, CB 1946; CBE 1944; CD 1948; retired; *b* 9 Aug. 1900; *s* of Rev. Donald and Jean Stirton Guthrie; *m* 1926, Catherine Mary Fidler; one *d*. *Educ:* Baltimore, USA; Montreal and Ottawa, Canada. RFC and RAF, 1917–19; RCAMC 1919–20; Canadian Air Board and RCAF since 1920. Asst Director of Military and Air Force Intelligence, General Staff, Ottawa, 1935–38; CO, RCAF Station, Rockcliffe, 1938–39; Senior Air Staff Officer, Eastern Air Command, 1939–41; CO, RCAF Station, Gander, Nfld, 1941; Air Officer i/c Administration, Western Air Command, 1942; Deputy Air Member Air Staff (Plans) AFHQ, Dec. 1942–44; AOC Northwest Air Command, RCAF, 1944–49. Retired, 1949. Legion of Merit (USA), 1946. *Recreations:* hunting, fishing, gardening. *Club:* United Services Institute (Edmonton and Victoria).

GUTHRIE, Sir Malcolm (Connop), 3rd Bt *cr* 1936; *b* 16 Dec. 1942; *s* of Sir Giles Connop McEacharn Guthrie, 2nd Bt, OBE, DSC, and of Rhona, *d* of late Frederic Stileman; *S* father, 1979; *m* 1967, Victoria, *o d* of late Brian Willcock; one *s* one *d*. *Educ:* Millfield. *Heir: s* Giles Malcolm Welcome Guthrie, *b* 16 Oct. 1972. *Address:* Brent Eleigh, Belbroughton, Stourbridge, Worcestershire DY9 0DW.

GUTHRIE, Michael; *see* Guthrie, G. M.

GUTHRIE, Robert Isles Loftus, (Robin); Chief Charity Commissioner for England and Wales, since 1988; *b* 27 June 1937; *s* of late Prof. W. K. C. Guthrie, FBA and of Adele Marion Ogilvy, MA; *m* 1963, Sarah Julia Weltman; two *s* one *d*. *Educ:* Clifton Coll.; Trinity Coll., Cambridge (MA); Liverpool Univ. (CertEd); LSE (MScEcon). Head of Cambridge House (Univ. settlement in S London), 1962–69; teacher, ILEA, 1964–66; Social Develt Officer, Peterborough Develt Corp., 1969–75; Asst Dir, Social Work Service, DHSS, 1975–79; Dir, Joseph Rowntree Meml Trust, 1979–88. Mem., expedns in Anatolia, British Inst. of Archaeol. at Ankara, 1958–62. Member: Arts Council of GB, 1979–81 and 1987–88 (Regional Cttee, 1976–81); Council, Policy Studies Institute, 1979–88; Council, York Univ., 1982–; Chairman: Yorkshire Arts Assoc., 1984–88; Council of Regional Arts Assocs, 1985–88. FRSA. Hon. DLitt Bradford, 1991. *Publications:* (ed) Outlook, 1963; (ed) Outlook Two, 1965; articles, esp. in New Society. *Recreations:* music, mountains, travel, sheep. *Address:* Braeside, Acomb, York YO2 4EZ. *Club:* United Oxford & Cambridge University.

GUTHRIE, Roy David, (Gus), PhD, DSc; CChem, FRSC, FRACI; FAIM; Vice-Chancellor and President, University of Technology, Sydney, since 1988 (President, NSW Institute of Technology, 1986–87); *b* 29 March 1934; *s* of David Ephraim Guthrie and Ethel (*née* Kimmins); *m* 1st, 1956, Ann Hoad (marr. diss. 1981); three *s*; 2nd, 1982, Lyn Fielding. *Educ:* Dorking Grammar Sch.; King's Coll., Univ. of London (BSc, PhD, DSc). Shirley Inst., Manchester, 1958–60; Asst Lectr, then Lectr, Univ. of Leicester, 1960–63; Lectr, then Reader, Univ. of Sussex, 1963–73; Griffith University, Brisbane: Foundation Prof. of Chemistry, 1973–81; Inaugural Chm., School of Science, 1973–78; Pro-Vice-Chancellor, 1980–81; Professor Emeritus, 1982; Sec. Gen., Royal Soc. of Chemistry, 1982–85. Hon. DUniv Griffith, 1981. *Publications:* An Introduction to the Chemistry of Carbohydrates (with J. Honeyman), 2nd edn 1964, 3rd edn 1968, 4th edn 1974; over 130 scientific papers. *Recreations:* theatre, music, antique maps, croquet. *Address:* University of Technology, Sydney, Broadway, NSW 2007, Australia. *T:* 02.218.9101.

GUTTERIDGE, Joyce Ada Cooke, CBE 1962; retired; *b* 10 July 1906; *d* of late Harold Cooke Gutteridge, QC, and late Mary Louisa Gutteridge (*née* Jackson). *Educ:* Roedean Sch.; Somerville Coll., Oxford. Called to the Bar, Middle Temple, Nov. 1938. Served in HM Forces (ATS), War of 1939–45. Foreign Office: Legal Assistant, 1947–50; Asst Legal Adviser, 1950–60; Legal Counsellor, 1960–61; Counsellor (Legal Adviser), UK Mission to the United Nations, 1961–64; Legal Counsellor, FO, 1964–66; re-employed on legal duties, FO, 1966–67. Hon. LLD, Western College for Women, Oxford, Ohio, 1963. *Publications*: The United Nations in a Changing World, 1970; articles in British Year Book of International Law and International and Comparative Law Quarterly. *Address*: 1 Croftgate, Fulbrooke Road, Cambridge CB3 9EG. *Club*: University Women's.

GUY, Geoffrey Colin, CMG 1964; CVO 1966; OBE 1962 (MBE 1957); Governor and Commander in Chief, St Helena and its Dependencies, 1976–81, retired; first elected Speaker of the Legislative Council, St Helena, 1989; *b* 4 Nov. 1921; *s* of late E. Guy, 14 Woodland Park Road, Headingley, Leeds, and of Constance Reed Guy (*née* Taylor); *m* 1946, Joan Elfreda Smith; one *s*. *Educ*: Chatham House Sch., Ramsgate; Brasenose Coll., Oxford. Served RAF, 1941–46: reconnaissance pilot Spitfires and Hurricanes, Middle East and Burma, 1943–45; Special Force 136, 1945 (Flight Lieut). Asst Ed., Courtaulds Works Mag., 1948; management staff, Scribbans-Kemp Ltd, 1948–51; Colonial Administrative Service, Sierra Leone: Cadet, 1951; Asst Sec. Chief Comr Protectorate, 1953–54; District Comr, Tonkolili Dist, 1955; Administrator, Turks and Caicos Islands, and Chm. and Man. Dir, Turks Island Salt Co., 1958–65; Administrator, Dominica, 1965–67, Governor, March-Nov. 1967; Asst Sec., Soil Assoc., 1968; Sec., Forces Help Soc. and Lord Roberts' Workshops, 1970–73; Administrator, Ascension Island, 1973–76. *Recreations*: farming, building houses, swimming. *Address*: Tamarisk Cottage, Kirk Hammerton, York YO5 8DA; Lower Farm Lodge, St Helena, South Atlantic. *Clubs*: Commonwealth Trust, Royal Air Force, Victory Services.

GUY, (Leslie) George; Assistant Secretary, Craft Sector, Amalgamated Union of Engineering Workers/Technical Administrative and Supervisory Section, 1983–84, retired; *b* 1 Sept. 1918; *s* of Albert and Annie Guy; *m* 1940, Audrey Doreen (*née* Symonds); two *d*. *Educ*: secondary modern school. National Union of Sheet Metal Workers: shop steward; Member: Branch and District Cttees; Nat. Executive Cttee; National President, June 1972–74; Asst General Secretary, 1974–77; Gen. Sec., Nat. Union of Sheet Metal Workers, Coppersmiths, Heating and Domestic Engrs, 1977–83, when Union transferred its engagements to AEUW/TASS. Member: General Council, TUC, 1977–83; Exec., CSEU, 1977–84; Engrg Industry Trng Bd, 1979–84; Council, Marine Training Assoc., 1983–. *Recreations*: work and politics.

GUY, Captain Robert Lincoln, LVO 1980; RN; *b* 4 Sept. 1947; *s* of late John Guy and Susan Guy; *m* 1981, Rosemary Ann Walker. *Educ*: Radley Coll. Entered BRNC Dartmouth, 1966; ADC to Governor and Commander-in-Chief, Gibraltar, 1973; commanded: HMS Ashton, 1974; HMS Kedleston, 1975; HMS Sirius, 1984–85. Equerry to the Queen, 1977–80; First Lieut, HMS Antelope, 1981–82. Lieut 1971; Lt-Comdr 1979; Comdr 1983; Captain 1991. *Recreations*: polo, skiing, shooting. *Address*: Stable House, South Warnborough, Basingstoke, Hants. *T*: Basingstoke (0256) 862254. *Clubs*: Army and Navy, White's.

GUY, Gen. Sir Roland (Kelvin), GCB 1987 (KCB 1981); CBE 1978 (MBE 1955); DSO 1972; Governor, Royal Hospital, Chelsea, since 1987; *b* 25 June 1928; *s* of Lt-Col Norman Greenwood Guy and Mrs Edna Guy; *m* 1957, Dierdre, *d* of Brig. P. H. Graves Morris, DSO, MC, and Mrs Auriol Graves-Morris; two *d*. *Educ*: Wellington Coll.; RMA Sandhurst. Commnd KRRC, 1948; 1950–71: Signals Officer, Germany; Adjt Kenya Regt, and 2 KRRC; Weapon Trng Officer 1 KRRC; Staff Coll., Camberley; MoD; Co. Comdr 2 RGJ; DS Staff Coll.; Bn 2 i/c; Mil. Asst to Adjt Gen.; CO 1 RGJ; Col GS HQ Near East Land Forces, 1971; Comd 24 Airportable Bde, 1972; RCDS, 1975; Principal SO to CDS, 1976–78; Chief of Staff, HQ BAOR, 1978–80; Mil. Sec., 1980–83; Adjt Gen., 1984–86; ADC Gen. to the Queen, 1984–87; served in Kenya, Libya, British Guiana, Cyprus, Malaysia, W Germany and Berlin. Col Comdt: 1st Bn Royal Green Jackets, 1981–86 (Rep. Col Comdt, 1985–86); Small Arms School Corps, 1981–87. Chairman: Army Benevolent Fund, 1987–; Royal Cambridge Home for Soldiers' Widows, 1987–; Governor: Wellington Coll., 1987– (Vice Pres., 1990–); Milton Abbey Sch., 1987–. *Recreations*: music, ski-ing, tennis, gardening. *Address*: c/o Grindlays Bank, 13 St James's Square, SW1. *Clubs*: Army and Navy, MCC.

GUYATT, Richard Gerald Talbot, CBE 1969; Rector, Royal College of Art, 1978–81 (Pro-Rector, 1974–78); Professor of Graphic Arts, 1948–78); *b* 8 May 1914; *s* of Thomas Guyatt, sometime HM Consul, Vigo, Spain and Cecil Guyatt; *m* 1941, Elizabeth Mary Corsellis; one step *d*. *Educ*: Charterhouse. Freelance designer: posters for Shell-Mex and BP, 1935. War Service: Regional Camouflage Officer for Scotland, Min. of Home Security. Dir and Chief Designer, Cockade Ltd, 1946–48; Co-designer of Lion and Unicorn Pavilion, Festival of Britain, 1951; Consultant Designer to: Josiah Wedgwood & Sons, 1952–55, 1967–70; Central Electricity Generating Bd, 1964–68; British Sugar Bureau, 1965–68; W. H. Smith, 1970–87. Vis. Prof., Yale Univ., 1955 and 1962. Ceramic Designs for Min. of Works (for British Embassies), King's Coll. Cambridge, Goldsmiths' Co. and Wedgwood commem. mugs for Coronation, 1953, Investiture, 1969 and Royal Silver Wedding, 1973. Designed: silver medal for Royal Mint, Mint Dirs Conf., 1972; 700th Anniv. of Parlt stamp, 1965; Postal Order forms, 1964 for Post Office; Silver Jubilee stamps, 1977; commem. crown piece for 80th birthday of HM Queen Elizabeth The Queen Mother, 1980. Member: Stamp Adv. Cttee, 1963–74; Internat. Jury, Warsaw Poster Biennale, 1968; Bank of England Design Adv. Cttee, 1968–75; Adv. Council, Victoria and Albert Mus., 1978–81. Chm., Guyatt/Jenkins Design Group. Governor, Imperial Coll. of Sci. and Technol., 1979–81. FSIA; Hon. ARCA. *Address*: Forge Cottage, Ham, Marlborough, Wilts SN8 3RB. *T*: Inkpen (04884) 270.

GUZ, Prof. Abraham, MD; FRCP; Professor of Medicine, Charing Cross and Westminster Medical School, University of London, since 1982; *b* 12 Aug. 1929; *s* of Akiwa Guz and Esther Guz; *m* 1957, Nita (*née* Florenz); three *d*. *Educ*: Grocers' Co. Sch.; Charing Cross Hosp. Med. Sch., Univ. of London (MB BS 1952; MD 1967). MRCP 1954, FRCP 1969. Hosp. appts, Charing Cross Hosp., 1952–53; Asst Lectr in Pharmacol., Charing Cross Hosp. Med. Sch., 1953–54; RAMC 1954–56; Hosp. appts, RPMS, Hammersmith Hosp., 1956–57; Research Fellow: Harvard Med. Sch., 1957–59; Cardiovascular Res. Inst., Univ. of California, 1959–61; Lectr in Medicine, 1961, later Sen. Lectr and Reader, Charing Cross Hosp. Med Sch. Pro-Censor and Censor, RCP, 1979–87. *Publications*: Dyspnoea, 1984; articles on mechanisms underlying breathlessness, mechanisms resp. for ventilatory response to exercise, measurement of performance of left ventricle. *Recreations*: family, violin in quartet, Jewish culture study. *Address*: 3 Littleton Road, Harrow, Middx HA1 3SY. *T*: 081–422 2786.

GWANDU, Emir of; Alhaji Haruna, (Muhammadu Basharu), CFR 1965; CMG 1961; CBE 1955; 18th Emir of Gwandu, 1954; Member, North Western State House of Chiefs, and Council of Chiefs; Member, and Chairman, Executive Council, State Self-Development Funds Council; President, former Northern Nigeria House of Chiefs, since 1957 (Deputy President 1956); *b* Batoranke, 1913; *m* 1933; fifteen *c*. *Educ*: Birnin Kebbi Primary Sch.; Katsina Training Coll. Teacher: Katsina Teachers Coll., 1933–35; Sokoto Middle Sch., 1935–37; Gusau Local Authority Sub-Treasurer, 1937–43; Gwandu Local Authority Treasurer, 1943–45; District Head, Kalgo, 1945–54. Member former N Reg. Marketing Board. *Recreations*: hunting, shooting. *Address*: Emir's Palace, PO Box 1, Birnin Kebbi, North Western State, Nigeria.

GWILLIAM, John Albert, MA Cantab; Headmaster of Birkenhead School, 1963–88; *b* 28 Feb. 1923; *s* of Thomas Albert and Adela Audrey Gwilliam; *m* 1949, Pegi Lloyd George; three *s* two *d*. *Educ*: Monmouth Sch.; Trinity Coll., Cambridge. Assistant Master: Trinity Coll., Glenalmond, 1949–52; Bromsgrove Sch., 1952–56; Head of Lower Sch., Dulwich Coll., 1956–63. *Address*: Araulfan, 13 The Close, Llanfairfechan, Gwynedd.

GWILLIAM, Prof. Kenneth Mason; Professor of the Economics of Transport and Logistics, Erasmus University, Rotterdam, since 1989; *b* 27 June 1937; *s* of John and Marjorie Gwilliam; *m* 1987, Sandra Wilson; two *s* by former *m*. *Educ*: Magdalen Coll., Oxford (BA 1st Cl. Hons PPE). Res. Asst, Fisons Ltd, 1960–61; Lecturer: Univ. of Nottingham, 1961–65; Univ. of E Anglia, 1965–67; Prof. of Transport Economics, Univ. of Leeds, 1967–89. Director: Nat. Bus Co., 1978–82; Yorkshire Rider, 1986–88. Editor, Jl of Transport Economics and Policy, 1977–87. *Publications*: Transport and Public Policy, 1964; Economics and Transport Policy, 1975; (jtly) Deregulating the Bus Industry, 1984. *Recreations*: badminton, walking, golf. *Address*: Weavers Home, Old Lane, Low Mill Village, Addingham LS29 0SA; Lauwers 27, TE Zwijndrecht, Netherlands.

GWILLIAM, Robert John; Senior Associate Solicitor, British Telecommunications PLC, since 1990; *b* 6 Jan. 1943; *s* of Benjamin Harold Gwilliam and Dora Gwilliam; *m* 1966, Linda Mary Ellway; two *s*. *Educ*: Lydney Grammar Sch.; Nottingham Univ. (BA Hons Law); Cambridge Univ. (Dip. Criminology); College of Law. Admitted Solicitor, 1969; practised in Local Govt Prosecuting Depts, 1969–83; Chief Prosecuting Solicitor for Hampshire, 1983–86; Chief Crown Prosecutor, Crown Prosecution Service: London South/Surrey Area, 1986; Inner London Area, 1987; London and SE Regl Dir, Grade 3, 1987–89. *Recreations*: listening to all types of music, amateur music making, supporting Rugby, shipping, history. *Address*: Group Legal Services, British Telecommunications PLC, Group Headquarters, 81 Newgate Street, EC1A 7AJ.

GWILT, George David, FFA; General Manager, 1979–84, Managing Director and Actuary, 1984–88, Standard Life Assurance Company; *b* 11 Nov. 1927; *s* of Richard Lloyd Gwilt and Marjory Gwilt (*née* Mair); *m* 1956, Ann Dalton Sylvester; three *s*. *Educ*: Sedbergh Sch.; St John's Coll., Cambridge (MA). FFA 1952; FBCS. Joined Standard Life Assurance Co., 1949: Asst Official, 1956; Asst Actuary, 1957; Statistician, 1962; Mechanisation Manager, 1964; Systems Manager, 1969; Dep. Pensions Manager, 1972; Pensions Actuary, 1973; Asst General Manager and Pensions Manager, 1977; Asst Gen. Man. (Finance), 1978. Dep. Chm., Associated Scottish Life Offices, 1986–88. Special Advr in Scotland, Citicorp, 1989–; Director: Hammerson Property Investment and Develt Corp., 1979–; Scottish Mortgage and Trust, 1983–; European Assets Trust NV, 1979–; Hodgson Martin, 1989–. Trustee, TSB of South of Scotland, 1966–83. Member: Younger Cttee on Privacy, 1970–72; Monopolies and Mergers Commn, 1983–87. Pres., Faculty of Actuaries, 1981–83. Convenor, Scottish Poetry Library Assoc., 1988–. *Recreation*: flute playing. *Address*: 39 Oxgangs Road, Edinburgh EH10 7BE. *T*: 031–445 1266. *Clubs*: Royal Air Force; New (Edinburgh).

GWYN JONES, David; journalist and photographer; Editor, 1987–89, Editorial Consultant, 1989–90, The Geographical Magazine; *b* 6 Dec. 1942. *Educ*: Birkenhead Sch.; Emmanuel Coll., Cambridge (State schol.). Journalist, Western Mail, Cardiff, 1968–71; Dep. Chief Sub-Editor, The Guardian, 1971–78; Asst News Editor, Internat. Edn, Financial Times, 1978–81; News Editor, Chief Sub-Editor, Dep. Man. Editor (News), The Sunday Times, 1981–83; Futures Editor, Thames Television, 1983–85; Editl Consultant, Euromoney, The Builder Gp, 1985–87. FRGS 1987 (Mem., Editl Adv. Cttee, 1988–89); MRIN 1987. *Recreations*: travel, architecture, music, languages, sailing. *Address*: 20 Lower Mall, Hammersmith, W6 9DJ. *T*: 081–741 0859.

GWYNEDD, Viscount; David Richard Owen Lloyd George; *b* 22 Jan. 1951; *s* and heir of 3rd Earl Lloyd George of Dwyfor, *qv*; *m* 1985, Pamela, *o d* of late Alexander Kleyff; two *s*. *Educ*: Eton. *Heir*: *s* Hon. William Alexander Lloyd George, *b* 16 May 1986. *Address*: 43 Cadogan Square, SW1; Brimpton Mill, near Reading, Berks.

GWYNN, Edward Harold, CB 1961; Deputy Under-Secretary of State, Ministry of Defence, 1966–72; retired 1972; *b* 23 Aug. 1912; *y s* of late Dr E. J. Gwynn, Provost of Trinity Coll., Dublin, and late Olive Ponsonby; *m* 1937, Dorothy, *d* of late Geoffrey S. Phillpotts, Foxrock, Co. Dublin; one *s* four *d*. *Educ*: Sedbergh School; TCD. Entered Home Office, 1936; Assistant Secretary, 1947; Assistant Under-Secretary of State, 1956; Principal Finance Officer (Under-Secretary), Ministry of Agriculture, 1961–62; Deputy Under-Secretary of State, Home Office, 1963–66. *Recreations*: gardening, the countryside. *Address*: The Chestnuts, Minchinhampton, Glos GL6 9AR. *T*: Stroud (0453) 832863.

GWYNN-JONES, Peter Llewellyn; Lancaster Herald of Arms, since 1982; *b* 12 March 1940; *s* of late Major Jack Llewellyn Gwynn-Jones, Cape Town, and late Mary Muriel Daphne, *d* of Col Arthur Patrick Bird Harrison, and step *s* of late Lt-Col Gavin David Young, Long Burton, Dorset. *Educ*: Wellington Coll.; Trinity Coll., Cambridge (MA). Assistant to Garter King of Arms, 1970; Bluemantle Pursuivant of Arms, 1973; Secretary, Harleian Society, 1981; House Comptroller of College of Arms, 1982. *Recreations*: tropical forests, wild life conservation, fishing. *Address*: College of Arms, Queen Victoria Street, EC4V 4BT. *T*: 071–248 0911; 79 Harcourt Terrace, SW10. *T*: 071–373 5859.

GWYNNE-EVANS, Sir Francis Loring, 4th Bt *cr* 1913, of Oaklands Park, Awre, Co. Gloucester; *b* 22 Feb. 1914; *s* of Sir Evan Gwynne Gwynne-Evans, 2nd Bt and Ada Jane (*d* 1977), *d* of Walter Scott Andrews, New York; *S* brother, 1985; *m* 1st, 1937, Elisabeth Fforde (marr. diss. 1958), *d* of J. Fforde Tipping; two *s* one *d*; 2nd, 1958, Gloria Marie Reynolds; one *s* three *d* and one adopted *s*. Career as professional singer under name of Francis Loring. *Heir*: *s* David Gwynne Evans-Tipping, *b* 25 Nov. 1943. *Address*: Chantry, Aveton Gifford, near Kingsbridge, S Devon TQ7 4EH.

GWYNNE JONES, family name of **Baron Chalfont.**

GWYTHER, (Arthur) David; Inspector General, Insolvency Service, Department of Trade, 1981–84; *b* 8 Dec. 1924; *s* of late Arthur James Gwyther and of Lily Elizabeth Gwyther; *m* 1949, Agnes, (Nan), Boyd; one *s* two *d*. *Educ*: Sutton High Sch. for Boys, Plymouth. Dept of Trade Insolvency Service: Asst Examiner, 1948; Examiner, 1951; Assistant Official Receiver: Brighton, 1955; Southampton, 1957; Official Receiver, Plymouth, 1959; Inspector of Official Receivers, 1961; Official Receiver, Birmingham, 1965; Dep. Inspector Gen., 1976. *Recreation*: gardening. *Address*: Tarnhow, 65 Abbots Lane, Kenley, Surrey CR2 5JG. *T*: 081–668 6145.

GYLLENHAMMAR, Dr Pehr Gustaf; Executive Chairman, Board of Directors, Volvo, since 1990 (Chairman and Chief Executive Officer, 1983–90); *b* 28 April 1935; *s* of Pehr Gustaf Victor Gyllenhammar and Aina Dagny Kaplan; *m* 1959, Eva Christina, *d* of Gunnar Ludvig Engellau; one *s* three *d*. *Educ*: University of Lund. LLB. Mannheimer & Zetterlöf, solicitors, 1959; Haight, Gardner, Poor & Havens, NY, 1960; Amphion Insurance Co., Gothenburg, 1961–64; Skandia Insurance Co., 1965, Exec. Vice-Pres., 1968, Pres. and Chief Exec. Officer, 1970; AB Volvo, Gothenburg, 1970, Man. Dir and Chief Exec. Officer, 1971; Dir of companies in Sweden, Finland, France, UK and USA. Member: Internat. Adv. Cttee, Chase Manhattan Bank, NA, NY, 1972–; Bd, Cttee of

Common Market Automobile Constructors, 1977–; Bd, Fedn of Swedish Industries, 1979–. Lethaby Prof., Royal Coll. of Art, London, 1977; Mem., Royal Swedish Acad. of Engineering Scis, 1974. Hon. DM Gothenburg Univ., 1981; Hon. DTech Brunel, 1987; Hon. DEng Technical Univ., NS, 1988. Golden Award, City of Gothenburg, 1981. Officer, Royal Order of Vasa, 1973; King's Medal, with Ribbon of Order of Seraphim, 1981; Commander: Order of Lion of Finland, 1977 (Comdr 1st Class 1986); Ordre National du Mérite, France, 1980; St Olav's Order, Norway, 1984; Légion d'honneur, France, 1987; Order of Leopold, Belgium, 1989; Kt Grand Officer, Order of Merit, Italy, 1987. *Publications:* Mot sekelskiftet på måfå (Toward the Turn of the Century, at Random), 1970; Jag tror på Sverige (I Believe in Sweden), 1973; People at Work (US), 1977; En industripolitik för människan (Industrial policy for human beings), 1979. *Recreations:* tennis, sailing, skiing, riding. *Address:* c/o AB Volvo, S405 08, Gothenburg, Sweden.

H

HABAKKUK, Sir John (Hrothgar), Kt 1976; FBA 1965; FRHistS; Fellow, All Souls College, Oxford, 1950–67 and since 1988; Principal of Jesus College, Oxford, 1967–84, Hon. Fellow, 1984; *b* 13 May 1915; *s* of Evan Guest and Anne Habakkuk; *m* 1948, Mary Richards; one *s* three *d*. *Educ:* Barry County Sch.; St John's Coll., Cambridge (scholar and Strathcona student), Hon. Fellow 1971. Historical Tripos: Part I, First Class, 1935; Part II, First Class (with distinction), 1936. Fellow, Pembroke Coll., Cambridge, 1938–50, Hon. Fellow 1973; Director of Studies in History and Librarian, 1946–50; Temporary Civil Servant: Foreign Office, 1940–42, Board of Trade, 1942–46; University Lecturer in Faculty of Economics, Cambridge, 1946–50; Chichele Prof. of Economic History, Oxford, 1950–67; Vice-Chancellor, Oxford Univ., 1973–77, a Pro Vice-Chancellor, 1977–83; Pres, UC Swansea, 1975–84. Visiting Lecturer, Harvard University, 1954–55; Ford Research Professor, University of California, Berkeley, 1962–63; Ford Lecturer, 1984–85. Member: Grigg Cttee on Departmental Records, 1952–54; Advisory Council on Public Records, 1958–70; SSRC, 1967–71; Nat. Libraries Cttee, 1968–69; Royal Comnn on Historic Manuscripts, 1978–90; Admin. Bd, Internat. Assoc. of Univs, 1975–85. Chairman: Cttee of Vice Chancellors and Principals of Univs of UK, 1976–77; Adv. Gp on London Health Servs, 1980–81; Oxfordshire DHA, 1981–84. Pres., RHistS, 1976–80. Foreign Member: Amer. Phil. Soc.; Amer. Acad. of Arts and Sciences. Hon. DLitt: Wales, 1971; Cambridge, 1973; Pennsylvania, 1975; Kent, 1978; Ulster, 1988. *Publications:* American and British Technology in the Nineteenth Century, 1962; Population Growth and Economic Development since 1750, 1971; articles and reviews. *Address:* 28 Cunliffe Close, Oxford. *T:* Oxford (0865) 56583.

HABERFELD, Dame Gwyneth; *see* Jones, Dame Gwyneth.

HABGOOD, Most Rev. and Rt. Hon. John Stapylton; *see* York, Archbishop of.

HACAULT, Most Rev. Antoine; *see* St Boniface, Archbishop of, (RC).

HACKER, Alan Ray, OBE 1988; clarinettist and conductor; *b* 30 Sept. 1938; *s* of Kenneth and Sybil Hacker; *m* 1st, 1959, Anna Maria Sroka; two *d*; 2nd, 1977, Karen Evans; one *s*. *Educ:* Dulwich Coll.; Royal Academy of Music. FRAM. Joined LPO, 1958; Prof., RAM, 1960–76; Lectr, 1976–84, Sen. Lectr in Music, 1984–87, Univ of York. Founded: Pierrot Players (with S. Pruslin and H. Birtwistle), 1965; Matrix, 1971; Music Party for authentic performance of classical music, 1972; Classical Orch., 1977; Guest Cond., Orchestra la Fenice, Venice, 1981–; operatic cond. début, Den Bergtagna, Sweden, 1986, York Fest., 1988; conducted 1st major British prodn of Mozart's La Finta Giardiniera, 1989. First modern "authentic" perfs, 1977–, incl: Mozart's Symphonies 39, 40; Beethoven's Symphonies 2, 3, 7, 9 and Egmont; Haydn's Harmonie and Creation Masses, Symphony 104 and Trumpet Concerto. Revived basset clarinet and restored orig. text, Mozart's concerto and quintet, 1967; revived baroque clarinet (hitherto unplayed), 1975. Premieres of music by Birtwistle, Boulez, Morton Feldman, Goehr, Maxwell Davies, Stockhausen, Blake, Mellers, Salvatore Sciarrino and Judith Weir; cond 5 staged perfs of Bach's St John Passion for European Music Year, 1984. Sir Robert Mayer Lectr, Leeds Univ., 1972–73. Mem. Fires of London, 1970–76; Dir, York Early Music Festival. Many recordings. *Publications:* Scores of Mozart Concerto and Quintet, 1972; 1st edn of reconstructed Mozart Concerto, 1973; Schumann's Soiréestucke, 1985. *Recreation:* cookery. *Address:* 65 The Crossway, Muncastergate, York YO3 9LG.

HACKER, Rt. Rev. George Lanyon; *see* Penrith, Bishop Suffragan of.

HACKETT, Prof. Brian; Professor of Landscape Architecture, University of Newcastle upon Tyne, 1967–77, now Emeritus Professor; *b* 3 Nov. 1911; *s* of Henry and Ida Adeline Mary Hackett; *m* 1st, 1942, Frederica Claire Grundy (*d* 1979); one *s* two *d*; 2nd, 1980, Dr Elizabeth Ratcliff. *Educ:* Grammar Sch., Burton-on-Trent; Birmingham Sch. of Architecture; Sch. of Planning for Regional Development, London. MA Dunelm, PPILA, RIBA, MRTPI. Professional experience, 1930–40; Flt-Lt, RAFVR, 1941–45; Lectr, Sch. of Planning for Regional Develt, London, 1945–47; Univ. of Durham: Lectr in Town and Country Planning, 1947; Lectr in Landscape Architecture, 1948, Sen. Lectr, 1949–59; Vis. Prof. of Landscape Architecture, Univ. of Illinois, 1960–61; Reader in Landscape Arch., Univ. of Newcastle upon Tyne, 1962–66. Member: N England Regl Adv. Cttee, Forestry Commn, 1983–90; Water Space Amenity Commn, 1973–80. Chm., Northumbria Historic Churches Trust, 1987–. Pres., Inst. of Landscape Architects, 1967–68; Hon. Corresp. Mem., Amer. Soc. of Landscape Architects, 1962. European Prize for Nature Conservation and Landscape Develt, 1975. *Publications:* Man, Society and Environment, 1950; (jtly) Landscape Techniques, 1967; Landscape Planning, 1971; Steep Slopes Landscape, 1971; (jtly) Landscape Reclamation, 1971–72; (jtly) Landscape Reclamation Practice, 1977; Planting Design, 1979; Landscape Conservation, 1980; numerous papers in internat. jls. *Recreation:* musical performance. *Address:* 27 Larkspur Terrace, Jesmond, Newcastle upon Tyne NE2 2DT. *T:* 091–281 0747. *Club:* Commonwealth Trust.

HACKETT, Prof. Cecil Arthur, MA Cantab, Docteur de l'Université de Paris; Professor of French, University of Southampton, 1952–70, now Professor Emeritus; *b* 19 Jan. 1908; *s* of Henry Hackett and Alice Setchell; *m* 1942, Mary Hazel Armstrong. *Educ:* King's Norton Grammar Sch., Birmingham; University of Birmingham; Emmanuel Coll., Cambridge (Scholar and Prizeman). Assistant d'Anglais, Lycée Louis-le-Grand, Paris, 1934–36; Lecturer in French and English, Borough Road Coll., Isleworth, 1936–39. Served War of 1939–45: enlisted 1/8th Bn Middlesex Regt, 1939. Education Representative, British Council, Paris, 1945–46; Lecturer in French, University of Glasgow, 1947–52. Hon. DLitt Southampton 1984. Chevalier de la Légion d'Honneur. *Publications:* Le Lyrisme de Rimbaud, 1938; Rimbaud l'Enfant, 1948; An Anthology of Modern French Poetry, 1952, 4th edn 1976; Rimbaud, 1957; Autour de Rimbaud, 1967; (ed and introd) New French Poetry: an anthology, 1973; Rimbaud, a critical introduction, 1981; Rimbaud, Œuvres Poétiques, a critical edition, 1986; contributions to English and French Reviews. *Address:* Shawford Close, Shawford, Winchester, Hants SO21 2BL. *T:* Twyford (0962) 713506.

HACKETT, Dennis William; journalist; publishing and communications consultant; Director, Media Search & Selection Ltd, since 1988; TV critic, The Tablet, since 1984; *b* 5 Feb. 1929; *s* of James Joseph Hackett and Sarah Ellen Hackett (*née* Bedford); *m* 1st, 1953, Agnes Mary Collins; two *s* one *d*; 2nd, 1974, Jacqueline Margaret Totterdell; one *d*. *Educ:* De La Salle College, Sheffield. Served with RN, 1947–49. Sheffield Telegraph, 1945–47 and 1949–54; Daily Herald, 1954; Odhams Press, 1954; Deputy Editor, Illustrated, 1955–58; Daily Express, 1958–60; Daily Mail, 1960; Art Editor, Observer, 1961–62; Deputy Editor, 1962, Editor, 1964–65, Queen; Editor, Nova, 1965–69; Publisher, Twentieth Century Magazine, 1965–72; Editorial Dir, George Newnes Ltd, 1966–69; Dir, IPC Newspapers, 1969–71; Associate Editor, Daily Express, 1973–74; TV critic, The Times, 1981–85; Editorial Consultant, You, The Mail on Sunday magazine, 1982–86; Exec. Editor, 1986–87, Editor-in-chief, 1987, Today; Editor-in-Chief, M, The Observer Magazine, 1987–88. Chm., Design and Art Directors' Assoc., 1967–68. *Publications:* The History of the Future: Bemrose Corporation 1826–1976, 1976; The Big Idea: the story of Ford in Europe, 1978. *Recreations:* reading, walking. *Address:* 4 East Heath Road, NW3 1BN. *Club:* Royal Automobile.

HACKETT, John Charles Thomas, FBIM; Director General, British Insurance and Investment Brokers' Association (formerly British Insurance Brokers' Association), since 1985; *b* 4 Feb. 1939; *s* of Thomas John Hackett and late Doris Hackett; *m* 1958, Patricia Margaret, *d* of Eric Ronald Clifford and Margaret Tubb. *Educ:* Glyn Grammar Sch., Epsom, Surrey; London Univ. (LLB Hons, external). FBIM 1981. Prodn Planning Manager, Rowntree Gp, 1960–64; Prodn Controller, Johnson's Wax, 1964; Commercial Sec., Heating and Ventilating Contractors' Assoc., 1964–70; Sec., Cttee of Assocs of Specialist Engrg Contractors, 1968–79; Dep. Dir, 1970–79, Dir, 1980–84, British Constructional Steelwork Assoc. Member: Council, CBI, 1980–88; CBI Gp of Chief Execs of Major Sector Assocs, 1980–84; Constructional Steelwork EDC, NEDO, 1980–84. MInstD. *Publication:* BCSA Members' Contractual Handbook, 1972, 2nd edn 1979. *Recreations:* music, reading, walking, motoring. *Address:* 15 Downsway Close, Tadworth, Surrey KT20 5DR. *T:* Tadworth (0737) 813024.

HACKETT, John Wilkings, CMG 1989; Director, Financial, Fiscal and Enterprise Affairs, Organisation for Economic Co-operation and Development, Paris, 1979–89; *b* 21 Jan. 1924; *s* of Albert and Bertha Hackett; *m* 1952, Anne-Marie Le Brun. *Educ:* LSE (BSc(Econ) 1950); Institut d'Etudes Politiques, Paris (Diplôme 1952); Univ. of Paris (Dr d'état ès sciences economiques 1957). Served RN, 1942–46. Economic research, 1952–57; OECD, 1958–89. FRSA 1986. *Publications:* Economic Planning in France (with A.-M. Hackett), 1963; L'Economie Britannique—problèmes et perspectives, 1966; (with A.-M. Hackett) The British Economy, 1967; articles on economic subjects in British and French economic jls. *Recreations:* music, painting, reading. *Address:* 48 rue de la Bienfaisance, 75008 Paris, France. *Club:* Cercle de l'Union Interalliée (Paris).

HACKETT, Gen. Sir John Winthrop, GCB 1967 (KCB 1962; CB 1958); CBE 1953 (MBE 1938); DSO 1942 and Bar 1945; MC 1941; DL; BLitt, MA Oxon; FRSL 1982; Principal of King's College, London, 1968–July 1975; *b* 5 Nov. 1910; *s* of late Sir John Winthrop Hackett, KCMG, LLD, Perth, WA; *m* 1942, Margaret, *d* of Joseph Frena, Graz, Austria; one *d* (and two adopted *step d*). *Educ:* Geelong Grammar Sch., Australia; New Coll., Oxford, Hon. Fellow 1972. Regular Army, commissioned 8th KRI Hussars, 1931; Palestine, 1936 (despatches); seconded to Transjordan Frontier Force, 1937–41 (despatches twice); Syria, 1941 (wounded); Sec. Commn of Control Syria and Lebanon; GSO2 9th Army; Western Desert, 1942 (wounded); GSO1 Raiding Forces GHQ, MELF; Comdr 4th Parachute Brigade, 1943; Italy, 1943 (despatches); Arnhem, 1944 (wounded); BGS (1) Austria, 1946–47; Comdr Transjordan Frontier Force, 1947–48; Sen. Army Instr, RNC, Greenwich, 1950; idc 1951; DQMG, BAOR, 1952; Comdr 20th Armoured Bde, 1954; GOC 7th Armoured Div., 1956–58; Comdt, Royal Mil. Coll. of Science, 1958–61; GOC-in-C, Northern Ireland Command, 1961–63; Dep. Chief of Imperial Gen. Staff, 1963–64; Dep. Chief of the Gen. Staff, Ministry of Defence, 1964–66. Comdr-in-Chief, British Army of the Rhine, and Comdr Northern Army Gp in NATO, 1966–68. ADC (Gen.), 1967–68. Col. Commandant, REME, 1961–66; Hon. Colonel: 10th Bn The Parachute Regt, TA, 1965–67; 10th Volunteer Bn, The Parachute Regt, 1967–73; Oxford Univ. Officers Training Corps, 1967–78; Col, Queen's Royal Irish Hussars, 1969–75. Mem., Lord Chancellor's Cttee on Reform of Law of Contempt, 1971–74; Mem., Disciplinary Tribunal, Inns of Court and Bar, 1972–83. Vis. Prof. in Classics, KCL, 1977–. Lectures: Lees Knowles, Cambridge, 1961; Basil Henriques Meml, 1970; Harmon Meml, USAF Acad., 1970; Jubilee, Imperial Coll., 1979. President: UK Classical Assoc., 1971; English Assoc., 1973–. Hon. Liveryman, Worshipful Company of Dyers, 1975; Freeman of City of London, 1976. DL Glos 1982. Hon. LLD: Queen's Univ. Belfast; Perth, WA, 1963; Exeter, 1977; Buckingham, 1987. FKC, 1968; Hon. Fellow St George's Coll., University of Western Australia, 1965. Chesney Gold Medal, RUSI, 1985. *Publications:* I Was a Stranger, 1977; (jtly) The Third World War, 1978; (jtly) The Untold Story, 1982; The Profession of Arms, 1983; (ed) Warfare in the Ancient World, 1989; articles and reviews. *Address:* Coberley Mill, Cheltenham, Glos GL53 9NH. *T:* Coberley (024287) 207. *Clubs:* Cavalry and Guards, Carlton, United Oxford & Cambridge University, White's.

HACKETT, Peter, OBE 1990; PhD; FEng 1983; Principal, Camborne School of Mines, since 1970, first Fellow, 1990; *b* 1 Nov. 1933; *s* of Christopher and Evelyn Hackett; *m* 1958, Esmé Doreen (*née* Lloyd); one *s* one *d*. *Educ:* Mundella Grammar Sch.; Nottingham Univ. (BSc 1st Cl. Hons Mining Engrg; PhD). FIMM. Lecturer, Nottingham Univ.,

1958–70; Vis. Lectr, Univ. of Minnesota, 1969; Vis. Professor, Univ. of California at Berkeley, 1979. Pres., IMM, 1989–90. *Publications:* contribs to learned jls on geotechnical subjects and mining engrg educn. *Recreations:* sailing, vintage vehicles, shooting. *Address:* Camborne School of Mines, Redruth, Cornwall TR15 3SE. *Club:* Royal Cornwall Yacht (Falmouth).

HACKING, family name of **Baron Hacking.**

HACKING, 3rd Baron *cr* 1945, of Chorley; **Douglas David Hacking;** Bt 1938; Solicitor of Supreme Court of England and Wales, since 1977; Partner, Richards Butler; Attorney and Counselor-at-Law of State of New York, since 1975; *b* 17 April 1938; *er s* of 2nd Baron Hacking, and of Daphne Violet, *e d* of late R. L. Finnis; *S* father, 1971; *m* 1982, Dr Tessa M. Hunt, MB, MRCP, FFARCS, *er d* of Roland C. C. Hunt, *qv;* three *s* (two *s* one *d* by former marriage). *Educ:* Aldro School, Shackleford; Charterhouse School; Clare College, Cambridge (BA 1961, MA 1968). Called to the Bar, Middle Temple, Nov. 1963 (Astbury and Harmsworth Scholarships). Served in RN, 1956–58; Ordinary Seaman, 1956; Midshipman, 1957; served in HMS Ark Royal (N Atlantic), 1957; HMS Hardy (Portland) and HMS Brocklesby (Portland and Gibraltar), 1958; transferred RNR as Sub-Lt, 1958, on completion of National Service; transf. List 3 RNR, HMS President, 1961; Lieut 1962; retired RNR, 1964. Barrister-at-Law, 1963–76; in practice, Midland and Oxford Circuits, 1964–75. With Simpson, Thacher and Bartlett, NYC, 1975–76; with Lovell, White and King, 1976–79; with Richards Butler, 1981–. Mem., H of L Select Cttee on the European Community, 1984. Member: Amer. Bar Assoc.; NY State Bar Assoc.; Bar Assoc. of City of New York. Pres., Assoc. of Lancastrians in London, 1971–72. Apprenticed to Merchant Taylors' Co., 1955, admitted to Freedom, 1962; Freedom, City of London, 1962. FCIArb 1979. *Recreations:* running, walking. *Heir: s* Hon. Douglas Francis Hacking, *b* 8 Aug. 1968. *Address:* 21 West Square, SE11 4SN; Richards Butler, Beaufort House, 15 St Botolph Street, EC3A 7EE. *T:* 071–247 6555. *Clubs:* MCC; Century (NY).

HACKING, Anthony Stephen; QC 1983; a Recorder, since 1985; *b* 12 Jan. 1941; *s* of John Kenneth and Joan Horton Hacking, Warwick; *m* 1969, Carin, *d* of Dr Svante and Brita Holmdahl, Gothenburg; one *d* three *s. Educ:* Warwick Sch.; Lincoln Coll., Oxford (MA). Called to the Bar, Inner Temple, 1965. *Address:* 1 King's Bench Walk, Temple, EC4. *T:* 071–583 6266.

HACKLAND, Sarah Ann; *see* Spencer, S. A.

HACKNEY, Archdeacon of; *see* Sharpley, Ven. R. E. D.

HACKNEY, Arthur, RWS 1957 (VPRWS 1974–77); RE 1960; ARCA 1949; artist; Deputy Head of Fine Art Department, West Surrey College of Art and Design (Farnham Centre) (formerly Farnham School of Art), 1979–85, retired; *b* 13 March 1925; *s* of late J. T. Hackney; *m* 1955, Mary Baker, ARCA; two *d. Educ:* Burslem Sch. of Art; Royal Coll. of Art, London. Served in Royal Navy, 1942–46. Travelling scholarship, Royal College of Art, 1949; part-time Painting Instructor, Farnham Sch. of Art, 1949, Lecturer, 1962; Head of Dept: Graphic, 1963–68; Printmaking, 1968–79. Work represented in Public Collections, including Bradford City Art Gallery, Victoria and Albert Museum, Ashmolean Museum, Wellington Art Gallery (NZ), Nottingham Art Gallery, Keighley Art Gallery (Yorks), Wakefield City Art Gallery, Graves Art Gallery, Sheffield, GLC, Preston Art Gallery, City of Stoke-on-Trent Art Gall., Kent Educn Cttee, Staffordshire Educn Cttee. Mem., Fine Art Bd, CNAA, 1975–78. *Address:* Woodhatches, Spoil Lane, Tongham, Farnham, Surrey. *T:* Aldershot (0252) 23919. *Club:* Chelsea Arts.

HACKNEY, Roderick Peter, PPRIBA; Managing Director, Rod Hackney & Associates, since 1972; *b* 3 March 1942; *s* of William Hackney and Rose (*née* Morris); *m* 1964, Christine Thornton; one *s. Educ:* John Bright's Grammar School, Llandudno; Sch. of Architecture, Manchester Univ. (BAArch 1966, MA, PhD). ARIBA, ACIArb, ASAI, FFB; MCIOB 1987. Job Architect, EXPO '67, Montreal, for Monorail Stations; Housing Architect, Libyan Govt, Tripoli, 1967–68; Asst to Arne Jacobsen, Copenhagen, working on Kuwait Central Bank, 1968–71. Established Castward Ltd, building and develt firm, 1983 (Man. Dir, 1983–). Pres., RIBA, 1987–89, Mem. Council, 1978–84 (Vice-Pres., Public Affairs, and Overseas Affairs); Mem. Council, Internat. Union of Architects, 1981–85, First Vice-Pres., 1985–87, Pres., 1988–91. Vis. Prof., Paris, 1984; Special Prof., Nottingham Univ., 1987–. Chm., Times/RIBA Community Enterprise Scheme, 1985–89; Mem. Council, Nat. Historical Bldg Crafts Inst., 1989–; Jury Mem., overseas housing develts; deleg., UK and overseas confs. Chm. of Trustees, Inner City Trust, 1986–; President: Snowdonia Nat. Park Soc., 1987–; N Wales Centre, NT, 1990–. Patron, Llandudno Mus. and Art Gall, 1988–. Hon. FAIA 1988; Hon. FRAIC 1990; Hon. Fellow: United Architects of Philippines, 1988; Fed. de Colegios de Arquitectos, Mexico, 1988; Indian Inst. of Architecture, 1990. Hon. DLitt Keele, 1989. *Television:* Build Yourself a House, 1974; Community Architecture, 1977; BBC Omnibus, 1987. *Publications:* Highfield Hall: a community project, 1982; The Good the Bad and the Ugly, 1990; articles in UK and foreign architectural jls. *Recreations:* outdoor pursuits, walking, Butterfly Society, fossils, travelling, ballooning, looking at buildings, talking at conferences. *Address:* St Peter's House, Windmill Street, Macclesfield, Cheshire SK11 7HS. *T:* Macclesfield (0625) 431792. *Club:* Commonwealth Trust.

HADDINGTON, 13th Earl of, *cr* 1619; **John George Baillie-Hamilton;** Lord Binning, 1613; Lord Binning and Byres, 1619; *b* 21 Dec. 1941; *o s* of 12th Earl of Haddington, KT, MC, TD, and of Sarah, *y d* of G. W. Cook, Montreal; *S* father, 1986; *m* 1st, 1975, Prudence Elizabeth (marr. diss. 1981), *d* of A. Rutherford Hayles; 2nd, 1984, Susan Jane Antonia, 2nd *d* of John Heyworth; one *s* two *d. Educ:* Ampleforth. *Heir: s* Lord Binning, *qv. Address:* Mellerstain, Gordon, Berwickshire; Tyninghame, Dunbar, East Lothian. *Clubs:* Turf, Chelsea Arts; New (Edinburgh).

HADDO, Earl of; Alexander George Gordon; ARICS; Managing Director, Letinvest plc (subsidiary of London & Edinburgh Trust plc), since 1989; *b* 31 March 1955; *s* and *heir* of 6th Marquess of Aberdeen and Temair, *qv; m* 1981, Joanna Clodagh Houldsworth; three *s* one *d. Educ:* Cothill House, Abingdon; Harrow School; Polytechnic of Central London (DipBE). ARICS 1979. With Gardiner and Theobald, Chartered Quantity Surveyors, 1976–82; Speyhawk plc, Property Developers, 1982–86; London & Edinburgh Trust plc, Property Developers, 1986–. *Recreations:* Rugby, golf, cricket, music, theatre. *Heir: s* Viscount Formartine, *qv. Address:* 22 Beauclerc Road, W6 0NS. *T:* 081–748 4849; Estate Office, Haddo House, Aberdeen AB4 0ER. *T:* Tarves (06515) 664. *Clubs:* Arts, MCC; London Scottish Rugby Football; Harrow Wanderers Cricket, Butterflies Cricket.

HADDON-CAVE, Sir (Charles) Philip, KBE 1980; CMG 1973; Director, Kleinwort Benson Group, since 1986; Chairman, Fleming Overseas Investment Trust, since 1988 (Director, since 1986); *b* 6 July 1925; *m* 1948, Elizabeth Alice May Simpson; two *s* one *d. Educ:* Univ. Tasmania; King's Coll., Cambridge. Entered Colonial Administrative Service, 1952: East Africa High Commn, 1952; Kenya, 1953–62; Seychelles, 1961–62; Hong Kong, 1962–85; Financial Secretary, 1971–81, Chief Sec., 1981–85, Hong Kong. *Publication:* (with D. M. Hocking) Air Transport in Australia, 1951. *Address:* The Old Farmhouse, Nethercote Road, Tackley, Oxon OX5 3AW. *Clubs:* Oriental; Hong Kong, Royal Hong Kong Golf.

HADEN, William Demmery, TD, MA; Headmaster, Royal Grammar School, Newcastle upon Tyne, 1960–72, retired; *b* 14 March 1909; *s* of Reverend William Henry and Gertrude Haden, Little Aston; *m* 1939, Elizabeth Marjorie, *d* of R. S. Tewson, Chorley Wood; one *s* two *d. Educ:* Nottingham High Sch.; Wadham Coll., Oxford (2nd Class Lit. Hum.; MA 1934). English Master, Merchant Taylors' Sch., 1938–46; Headmaster, Mercers' Sch., 1946–59. War Service, 1940–45: served as Battery Comdr RA with Fourteenth Army in Burma Campaign (despatches twice); Administrative Commandant, Hmawbi Area, S Burma District, 1945. *Recreations:* games, gardening, listening to music. *Address:* 11 Pensham Hill, Pershore, Worcs WR10 3HA.

HADEN-GUEST, family name of **Baron Haden-Guest.**

HADEN-GUEST, 4th Baron *cr* 1950, of Saling, Essex; **Peter Haden Haden-Guest;** *b* 29 Aug. 1913; *s* of 1st Baron Haden-Guest, MC and Muriel Carmel (*d* 1943), *d* of Colonel Albert Goldsmid, MVO; *S* half-brother, 1987; *m* 1945, Jean, *d* of late Dr Albert George Hindes, NY; two *s* one *d. Educ:* City of London School; New Coll., Oxford (MA). Editorial and theatrical work, 1934–42. Served War of 1939–45, Lieut RCNVR. UN official 1946–72. Took seat in House of Lords as cross-bencher, 1989. *Recreations:* grandchildren, walking, reading, theatre. *Heir: s* Hon. Christopher Haden-Guest [*b* 5 Feb. 1948; *m* 1984, Jamie Lee, *d* of Tony Curtis and Janet Leigh; one *d*]. *Address:* 198 Old Stone Highway, East Hampton, New York 11937, USA; Apt 308, 122 Ocean Park Boulevard, Santa Monica, Calif 90405, USA.

HADFIELD, (Ellis) Charles (Raymond), CMG 1954; *b* 5 Aug. 1909; *s* of Alexander Charles Hadfield, Transvaal Colony Magistracy; *m* 1945, Alice Mary Miller (*d* 1989), *d* of Lt-Col Henry Smyth, DSO; one *s* one *d* (and one *s* decd). *Educ:* Blundell's Sch.; St Edmund Hall, Oxford. Joined Oxford University Press, 1936; Dir of Publications, Central Office of Information, 1946–48; Controller (Overseas), 1948–62. Dir, David and Charles (Publishers) Ltd, 1960–64. Mem., British Waterways Bd, 1962–66. *Publications:* The Young Collector's Handbook (with C. Hamilton Ellis), 1940; Civilian Fire Fighter, 1941; (with Alexander d'Agapayeff) Maps, 1942; (with Frank Eyre) The Fire Service Today, 1944; (with Frank Eyre) English Rivers and Canals, 1945; (with J. E. MacColl) Pilot Guide to Political London, 1945; (with J. E. MacColl) British Local Government, 1948; (as Charles Alexander) The Church's Year, 1950; British Canals, 1950, 7th edn 1984; The Canals of Southern England, 1955; Introducing Canals, 1955; The Canals of South Wales and the Border, 1960; (with John Norris) Waterways to Stratford, 1962; Canals of the World, 1964; Canals and Waterways, 1966; (with Alice Mary Hadfield) The Cotswolds, 1966; The Canals of the East Midlands, 1966; The Canals of the West Midlands, 1966; The Canals of South West England, 1967; Atmospheric Railways, 1967; (with Michael Streat) Holiday Cruising on Inland Waterways, 1968; The Canal Age, 1968; The Canals of South and South East England, 1969; (with Gordon Biddle) The Canals of North West England, 1970; The Canals of Yorkshire and North East England, 1972; Introducing Inland Waterways, 1973; (with Alice Mary Hadfield) Introducing the Cotswolds, 1976; Waterways Sights to See, 1976; Inland Waterways, 1978; (with A. W. Skempton) William Jessop, Engineer, 1979; (with Alice Mary Hadfield) Afloat in America, 1979; World Canals, 1986; Canals: a new look; studies in honour of Charles Hadfield, 1984 (Festschrift ed M. Baldwin and A. Burton). *Recreations:* writing; exploring canals. *Address:* 13 Meadow Way, South Cerney, Cirencester, Glos GL7 6HY. *T:* Cirencester (0285) 860422. *Club:* United Oxford & Cambridge University.

HADFIELD, Esmé Havelock, FRCS; formerly: Consultant Ear, Nose and Throat Surgeon, High Wycombe, Amersham and Chalfont Hospitals; Associate Surgeon (Hon.), Ear, Nose and Throat Department, Radcliffe Infirmary, Oxford; retired; *b* 1921; *o d* of late Geoffrey Hadfield, MD. *Educ:* Clifton High Sch.; St Hugh's Coll., Oxford; Radcliffe Infirmary Oxford. BA (Oxon) 1942; BM, BCh Oxon 1945; FRCS 1951; MA Oxon 1952. House Officer appts, Radcliffe Infirmary, Oxford, 1945; Registrar to ENT Dept, Radcliffe Infirmary, Oxford, 1948; Asst Ohren, Nase, Hals Klinik, Kantonspital, University of Zurich, 1949. First Asst ENT Dept, Radcliffe Infirmary, Oxford, 1950. Mem. Court of Examrs, RCS, 1978–84; External Examr, RCSI, 1986–. Pres., Sect. of Laryngology, RSocMed, 1983–84. British Empire Cancer Campaign Travelling Fellow in Canada, 1953; Hunterian Prof., RCS, 1969–70. Hon. Mem., Assoc. of Surgeons of Pakistan, 1982. *Publications:* articles on ENT surgery in medical journals. *Recreation:* travel. *Address:* 20 Hamilton Road, Oxford OX2 7PZ. *T:* Oxford (0865) 57187.

See also G. J. Hadfield, J. I. H. Hadfield.

HADFIELD, Geoffrey John, CBE 1980; TD 1963; MS, FRCS; Surgeon, Stoke Mandeville Hospital, 1960–88, retired; *b* 19 April 1923; *s* of late Prof. Geoffrey Hadfield, MD, and Eileen D'Arcy Irvine; *m* 1960, Beryl, *d* of late Hubert Sleigh, Manchester; three *d. Educ:* Merchant Taylors' Sch.; St Bartholomew's Hosp., London Univ. MB BS 1947, MS 1954, London; MRCS LRCP 1946, FRCS 1948. Ho. Officer Appts, Demonstr. of Anatomy, Registrar and Sen. Lectr in Surgery, St Bart's Hosp.; Fellow in Surgery, Memorial Hosp., New York; served RAMC, Far East, 1948–50; TAVR, 1950–73; Bt-Col, RAMC RARO, Hon. Col 219 Gen. Hosp., TAVR. Royal College of Surgeons of England: Arris and Gale Lectr, 1954; Hunterian Prof., 1959; Erasmus Wilson Demonstr., 1969; Arnott Demonstr., 1972; Stamford Cade Meml Lectr, 1978; Mem., Council, 1971–83, Vice-Pres., 1982–83; Mem., Court of Examiners, Final FRCS, 1972–78 (Chm., 1977–78); Mem., Ct of Examiners, Primary FRCS, 1982–85. Examiner in Surgery for Univs of Liverpool, Bristol and Leeds, and Vis. Examiner to univs in Middle and Far East. Fellow, Assoc. of Surgs of GB and Ireland, 1955; Senior Member: Brit. Assoc. of Urol Surgs (Mem. Council, 1979–82); Brit. Assoc. of Surg. Oncology (Mem., Nat. Cttee, 1972–75); Brit. Assoc. of Clin. Anatomists (Mem. Council, 1976–80). *Publications:* (with M. Hobsley) Current Surgical Practice, vol. 1, 1976, vol. 2, 1978, vol. 3, 1981, vol. 4, 1986, vol. 5, 1990; (with M. Hobsley and B. C. Morson) Pathology in Surgical Practice, 1985; (jtly) Imaging in Surgical Practice, 1989; articles in jls and chapters in books on diseases of the breast, cancer, urology, trauma, varicose veins and med. educn. *Recreations:* ocean racing and cruising, travel, walking, golf. *Address:* Milverton House, 6 St John's Close, Bishopsteignton, near Teignmouth, Devon TQ14 9RT. *T:* Teignmouth (06267) 79537. *Club:* Teign Corinthian Yacht.

See also E. H. Hadfield, J. I. H. Hadfield.

HADFIELD, James Irvine Havelock, FRCS, FRCSE; Consultant Surgeon (Urologist), Bedford General Hospital, since 1965; *b* 12 July 1930; *s* of Prof. G. Hadfield and S. V. E. Hadfield (*née* Irvine); *m* 1957, Ann Pickernell Milner; one *s* two *d. Educ:* Radley College; Brasenose College, Oxford (MA, BM, BCh 1955, MCh Pt I 1960); St Thomas's Hosp. Med. Sch. FRCS 1960, FRCSE 1960. House Surgeon, St Thomas' Hosp., 1955; Lectr in Anatomy, St Thomas's Hosp. Med. Sch., 1956–57; RSO, Leicester Royal Inf., 1960–62; Surgical Tutor, Oxford Univ., 1962–66; Arris and Gale Lectr, RCS, 1967; Examnr in Surgery, Univ. of Cambridge, 1976–82; Examnr in MRCS, LRCP, 1974–80. *Publications:* articles in surgical jls on Metabolic Response to Trauma, Urology, and Surgical Anatomy of the Veins of the Legs. *Recreations:* watching rowing, shooting, unwilling gardener, trying to catch unwilling salmon in South West Wales. *Address:* Baker's Barn, Stagsden West End, near Bedford MK43 8SZ. *T:* Oakley (02302) 4514. *Clubs:* Leander, London Rowing.

See also E. H. Hadfield, G. J. Hadfield.

HADFIELD, John Charles Heywood; author; Proprietor, The Cupid Press, since 1949; Director, Rainbird Publishing Group, 1965–82; *b* 16 June 1907; 2nd *s* of H. G. Hadfield, Birmingham; *m* 1st, 1931, Phyllis Anna McMullen (*d* 1973); one *s* decd; 2nd, 1975, Joy Westendarp. *Educ:* Bradfield. Editor, J. M. Dent & Sons, Ltd, 1935–42; Books Officer for British Council in the Middle East, 1942–44; Dir of the National Book League, 1944–50; Organiser, Festival of Britain Exhibition of Books, 1951; Editor, The Saturday Book, 1952–73. *Publications:* The Christmas Companion, 1939; Georgian Love Songs, 1949; Restoration Love Songs, 1950; A Book of Beauty, 1952, rev. edn 1976; A Book of Delights, 1954, rev. edn 1977; Elizabethan Love Songs, 1955; A Book of Britain, 1956; A Book of Love, 1958, revd edn 1978; Love on a Branch Line, 1959; A Book of Pleasures, 1960; A Book of Joy, 1962; A Chamber of Horrors, 1965; (ed) The Shell Guide to England, 1970, rev. edn 1981; (ed) Cowardy Custard, 1973; (ed) The Shell Book of English Villages, 1980; (ed) Everyman's Book of English Love Poems, 1980; The Best of The Saturday Book, 1981; Every Picture Tells a Story, 1985; Victorian Delights, 1987; (with Miles Hadfield): The Twelve Days of Christmas, 1961; Gardens of Delight, 1964. *Recreations:* books, pictures, gardens. *Address:* 2 Quay Street, Woodbridge, Suffolk IP12 1BX. *T:* Woodbridge (0394) 7414. *Club:* Savile.

HADFIELD, Ven. John Collingwood; Archdeacon of Caithness, Rector of St John the Evangelist, Wick, and Priest-in-Charge of St Peter and The Holy Rood, Thurso, Caithness, since 1977; *b* 2 June 1912; *s* of Reginald Hadfield and Annie Best Hadfield (*née* Gribbin); *m* 1939, Margretta Mainwaring Lewis Matthews; three *s* three *d*. *Educ:* Manchester Grammar School; Jesus Coll., Cambridge (Exhibnr, BA 1st cl. Hons, Classical Tripos Pt 2 1934, MA 1938); Wells Theological College. Deacon 1935, priest 1936, Manchester; Curate of S Chad, Ladybarn, Manchester, 1935–44 (in charge from 1940); Vicar of S Mark, Bolton-le-Moors, Lancs, 1944–50; Vicar of S Ann, Belfield, Rochdale, Lancs, 1950–62; Surrogate, 1944–62; Proctor in Convocation for Dio. Manchester, 1950–62. Diocese of Argyll and The Isles: Rector of S Paul, Rothesay, Bute, 1962–64; Itinerant Priest, 1964–77; Canon of S John's Cathedral, Oban, 1965–77; Inspector of Schools, 1966–77; Synod Clerk, 1973–77. *Recreation:* music. *Address:* 4 Sir Archibald Road, Thurso, Caithness KW14 8HN. *T:* Thurso (0847) 62047.

HADFIELD, Ronald, QPM 1989; Chief Constable, West Midlands, since 1990; *b* 15 July 1939; *s* of George and Phyllis Marjorie Hadfield; *m* 1961, Anne Phyllisia Worrall; one *s* one *d*. *Educ:* Chadderton Grammar School. Joined Oldham Borough Police Force, 1958; served in Lancashire and Greater Manchester Police Forces; Asst Chief Constable, Derbyshire Constabulary, 1981; Dep. Chief Constable, 1986, Chief Constable, 1987, Nottinghamshire Constabulary. CBIM, 1990. *Recreations:* golf, fishing, Police Athletic Association. *Address:* West Midlands Police, Lloyd House, Colmore Circus, Queensway, Birmingham B4 6NQ.

HADINGHAM, Reginald Edward Hawke, CBE 1988 (OBE 1971); MC 1943 and Bar 1943; TD 1946; Chairman, Sparks, the sportsman's charity, since 1968; Deputy Chairman, Action Research for the Crippled Child, since 1976; *b* 6 Dec. 1915; *s* of Edward Wallace Hadingham and Ethel Irene Penelope Gwynne-Evans; *m* 1940, Lois Pope, *d* of Edward and Nora Pope; two *d*. *Educ:* Rokeby Preparatory, Wimbledon; St Paul's. Joined Slazengers, 1933, European Sales Manager, 1936. Joined TA, 57th Anti-Tank Regt, 1938, commnd into 67th Anti-Tank Regt 1938; served War of 1939–45 with 67th Anti-Tank Regt, RA; commanded 302 Battery, 1942–45 (MC Salerno 1943 and Bar, Garigliano 1943); CO 67 Regt, 1945 until disbanded, Oct. 1945. Returned to Slazengers as Asst Export Manager, Jan. 1946; Export Manager, 1949; Gen. Sales Manager, 1951; Sales Dir, 1952; Man. Dir, 1969; Chm. and Man. Dir, 1973; Chm. (Non-Exec.), 1976–83. All England Lawn Tennis Club: Mem. Cttee, 1976–84; Chm. of Club, and of Cttee of Management, The Championships, Wimbledon, 1984–89; Vice-Pres., 1990–; Pres., Internat. Lawn Tennis Club of GB, 1991–. Vice-Pres., PHAB, 1978–; Twice Pres., Sette of Odd Volumes, Treasurer, 1953–. *Recreations:* lawn tennis and writing verse. *Address:* The Hill Farm House, 118 Wimbledon Hill Road, Wimbledon, SW19 5QU. *T:* 081–946 9611. *Clubs:* Queen's, All England Lawn Tennis, Hurlingham, International Lawn Tennis of GB.

HADLEE, Sir Richard (John), Kt 1990; MBE 1980; New Zealand cricketer, retired; *b* 3 July 1951; *s* of Walter Hadlee; *m* 1973, Karen Ann; two *s*. *Educ:* Christchurch Boys' High Sch. Played for: Canterbury, 1972–89; Nottinghamshire (UK), 1978–87 (made 1000 runs and took 100 wickets in English season, 1984); Tasmania, 1979–80; Test début for NZ, 1973; toured: Australia, 1972–73, 1973–74, 1980–81, 1985–86; England, 1973, 1978, 1983, 1986, 1990; India, 1976, 1988; Pakistan, 1976; Sri Lanka, 1983–84, 1987; West Indies, 1984–85. Holder of world record of 431 Test wickets, 1990 (passed previous record of 373 in 1988). *Publication:* Rhythm and Swing (autobiog.), 1989. *Address:* Box 29186, Christchurch, New Zealand.

HADLEY, David Allen, CB 1991; Deputy Secretary, Cabinet Office, since 1989; *b* 18 Feb. 1936; *s* of Sydney and Gwendoline Hadley; *m* 1965, Veronica Ann Hopkins; one *s*. *Educ:* Wyggeston Grammar Sch., Leicester; Merton Coll., Oxford. MA. Joined MAFF, 1959; Asst Sec., 1971; HM Treas., 1975–78; Under Sec., 1981–87, Dep. Sec., 1987–89, MAFF. *Recreations:* gardening, music. *Address:* c/o Cabinet Office, 70 Whitehall, SW1A 2AS.

HADLEY, Graham Hunter, FRSA; Executive Director, National Power, since 1990; *b* 12 April 1944; *s* of Dr A. L. Hadley and Mrs L.E. Hadley; *m* 1971, Lesley Ann Smith; one *s*. *Educ:* Eltham Coll., London; Jesus Coll., Cambridge (BA Hons Mod. Hist.). Entered Civil Service (Min. of Aviation), 1966; Dept of Energy, 1974; seconded to: Civil Service Commn, 1976–77; British Aerospace, 1980–81; Under-Sec., Dept of Energy, 1983; Sec., CEGB, 1983–90. FRSA 1986. *Recreations:* include cricket, running, golf, theatre, architecture, aviation. *Address:* The Coach House, 14 Genoa Avenue, SW15. *T:* 081–788 2698.

HADLEY, Sir Leonard Albert, Kt 1975; JP; Union Secretary, Wellington, NZ, retired 1984; *b* Wellington, 8 Sept. 1911; *s* of Albert A. Hadley, JP; *m* 1st, 1939, Jean Lyell (*d* 1965), *d* of E. S. Innes; one *s* one *d*; 2nd, 1978, Amelia Townsend. Mem., Nat. Exec., NZ Fedn of Labour, 1946–76; Dir, Reserve Bank of NZ, 1959–85; Mem., Bd of Trustees since formation, 1964–87, Pres., 1976–79, Wellington Trustee Savings Bank. Relieving Mem., Industrial Commn and Industrial Court, 1974 (Arbitration Court, 1960–84); Mem., Waterfront Industry Tribunal, 1981–83. Member: NZ Immigration Adv. Council and Industrial Relations, 1953–75; Periodic Detention Work Centre Adv. Cttee (Juvenile), and Adult Centre, 1962–84 (both since formation); Absolute Liability Enquiry Cttee, 1963–, and Govt Cttees to review Exempted Goods, 1959 and 1962. Rep., NZ Fedn of Labour Delegns to ILO, Geneva, 1949 and 1966; Internat. Confedn of Free Trade Unions Inaugural Conf., 1949; Social Security Conf., Moscow, 1971; SE Asian Trade Union Conf., Tokyo, 1973; OECD Conf., Paris, 1974. Member: Terawhiti Licensing Trust, 1975–80; Witako Regl Prison Adv. Cttee, 1983–88. Life Member: Vogelmorn Tennis Club, 1961; Wellington Working Men's Club and Literary Inst., 1979; NZ Plumbers' Union, 1978; Wellington Clerical Union, 1983. Patron, Vogelmorn Bowling Club, 1982–. Awarded Smith-Mundt Ldr Study Grant in USA, 1953. JP 1967. *Recreations:* reading, music, outdoor bowls, Rugby, tennis, and sport generally. *Address:* (private) 3 Cheesman Street, Brooklyn, Wellington, New Zealand.

HADOW, Sir Gordon, Kt 1956; CMG 1953; OBE 1945; Deputy Governor of the Gold Coast (now Ghana), 1954–57; *b* 23 Sept. 1908; *e s* of late Rev. F. B. Hadow and Una Ethelwyn Durrant; *m* 1946, Marie (*d* 1985), *er d* of late Dr L. H. Moiser; two *s*. *Educ:* Marlborough; Trinity Coll., Oxford. Administrative Service, Gold Coast, 1932; Dep. Financial Sec., Tanganyika, 1946; Under-Sec. Gold Coast, 1948; Sec. for the Civil Service, 1949; Sec. to Governor and to Exec. Council, 1950–54. *Address:* Little Manor, Coat, Martock, Somerset TA12 6AS. *Club:* Athenæum.

HADOW, Sir (Reginald) Michael, KCMG 1971 (CMG 1962); HM Diplomatic Service, retired; *b* 17 Aug. 1915; *s* of Malcolm McGregor Hadow and Constance Mary Lund; *m* 1976, Hon. Mrs Daphne Sieff (*d* 1988). *Educ:* Berkhamsted Sch.; King's Coll., Cambridge. Selected for ICS, 1937; Private Sec. to HM Ambassador, Moscow, 1942; Under-Sec., External Affairs Dept, Delhi, 1946–47; transferred to Foreign Office, 1948; FO, 1948–52; Private Sec. to Minister of State, 1949–52; Head of Chancery, Mexico City, 1952–54; FO, 1955; Head of Levant Dept and promoted Counsellor, 1958; Counsellor, Brit. Embassy, Paris, 1959–62; Head of News Dept, FO, 1962–65; Ambassador to Israel, 1965–69; Ambassador to Argentina, 1969–72. *Recreation:* self-administration. *Address:* Old Farm, Ashford Hill, near Newbury, Berks RG15 8AX.

HAENDEL, Ida, CBE 1991; violinist; *b* Poland, 15 Dec. 1928; Polish parentage. Began to play at age of 3½; amazing gift discovered when she picked up her sister's violin and started to play. Her father, a great connoisseur of music, recognised her unusual talent and abandoned his own career as an artist (painter) to devote himself to his daughter; studied at Warsaw Conservatorium and gained gold medal at age of seven; also studied with such masters as Carl Flesch and Georges Enesco. British début, Queen's Hall, with Sir Henry Wood, playing Brahms' Concerto. Gave concerts for British and US troops and in factories, War of 1939–45; after War, career developed to take in North and South America, USSR and Far East, as well as Europe; has accompanied British orchestras such as London Philharmonic, BBC Symphony and English Chamber on foreign tours including Hong Kong, China, Australia and Mexico. Has performed with conductors such as Beecham, Klemperer, Szell, Barenboim, Mata, Pritchard and Rattle. Sibelius Medal, Finland, 1982. *Publication:* Woman with Violin (autobiog.), 1970. *Address:* c/o Harold Holt, 31 Sinclair Road, W14.

HAFERKAMP, Wilhelm; a Vice-President, Commission of the European Communities, 1970–84; *b* Duisburg, 1 July 1923. *Educ:* Universität zu Köln. German Trade Union Federation: Head of Division for Social Questions, 1950–63, Dep. Chm. 1953, Chm. 1957, N Rhine—Westphalia Area; Mem. Fed. Exec., 1962–67. Socialist Mem., Landtag of North Rhine—Westphalia, 1958–67; Mem., Commn of European Communities, 1967–84, responsible for Energy policy, Euratom Supply Agency and Euratom Safeguards; Vice-Pres., 1970, resp. for internal market and legal harmonisation; 1973, resp. for economic and financial affairs; 1977, resp. for external relations. *Address:* Rodenwaldstrasse 14, 4033 Hösel bei Düsseldorf, Germany.

HAFFNER, Albert Edward, PhD; Chairman, North Eastern Gas Board, 1971–72 (Deputy Chairman, 1966–71); *b* 17 Feb. 1907; 4th *s* of late George Christian and late Caroline Haffner, Holme, near Burnley, Lancs; *m* 1934, Elizabeth Ellen Crossley (*d* 1989), Cheadle Heath, Stockport; one *s* one *d*. *Educ:* Burnley Grammar Sch.; Royal College of Science; Imperial Coll., London; Technische Hochschule, Karlsruhe. BSc (1st Cl. Hons), ARCS, PhD, DIC, London. Burnley Gas Works, 1924–26; Gas Light & Coke Co, 1932–56; Research Chemist and North Thames Gas Bd; Gp Engr, Chief Engineer and later Bd Member, Southern Gas Bd, 1956–66. Past Pres., Instn Gas Engineers (Centenary Pres., 1962–63); Past Vice-Pres., Internat. Gas Union. CEng, MIChemE. *Publications:* Contributor to: Proc. Roy. Soc., Jl Instn Gas Engrs, Instn Chem. Engrs, Inst. of Fuel, New Scientist; papers presented to Canadian Gas Assoc., French Chem. Soc., Japanese Gas Industry and at IGU Confs in USA, USSR and Germany, etc. *Recreations:* photography, travel, gardening, cabinetmaking. *Address:* Burnthwaite, Iwerne Courtney, near Blandford Forum, Dorset DT11 8QL. *T:* Child Okeford (0258) 860749.

HAGARD, Dr Spencer, FFPHM; Chief Executive, Health Education Authority, since 1987; *b* 25 Oct. 1942; *s* of Maurice (Bozzie) Markham (killed in action, 9 June 1944) and Eva Markham (*née* Mearns, subseq. Hagard) and, by adoption, of Noel Hagard; *m* 1968, Michele Dominique, *d* of Stanislas and late Madeleine Aquarone; two *s* one *d*. *Educ:* Varndean Grammar Sch., Brighton; Univ. of St Andrews (MB ChB 1968); Univ. of Glasgow (PhD 1977); MA Cantab 1977. DPH 1972; FFPHM (FFCM 1981). Jun. med. appts, Arbroath, London and Dorking; MO and Med. Supt, Kawolo Hosp., Lugazi, Uganda, 1971–72; MO, Health Dept, Glasgow, 1972–74; Trainee in Community Med., Greater Glasgow Health Bd, 1974–77; Specialist in Comm. Med., Cambs AHA, 1977–82; Dist MO, Cambridge HA, 1982–87. Associate Lectr, Univ. of Cambridge Sch. of Clinical Med., 1977—87. *Publications:* Health, Society and Medicine (with Roy Acheson), 1984; papers in BMJ and other learned jls. *Recreations:* marriage, family, studying human beings, politics, gardening, reading, photography, appreciation of art, music, sporting lost causes (Brighton & Hove Albion, Sussex CCC). *Address:* 396 Milton Road, Cambridge CB4 1SU. *T:* Cambridge (0223) 423970.

HAGART-ALEXANDER, Sir Claud; *see* Alexander.

HAGEN, Victor W. Von; *see* Von Hagen.

HAGERTY, William John Gell; Editor, The People, since 1991; *b* 23 April 1939; *s* of William (Steve) Hagerty and Doris Hagerty (*née* Gell); *m* 1st, 1965, Lynda Beresford (marr. diss. 1990); one *s* one *d* (and one *d* decd); 2nd, 1991, Elizabeth Vercoe. *Educ:* Beal Grammar Sch., Ilford. Local newspapers, East London, 1955–58; RAF Nat. Service, 1958–60; local newspapers, Sunday Citizen, Daily Sketch, 1960–67; Daily Mirror, 1967–81: Asst Editor, Magazine; Features Editor; Showbusiness Editor; Asst Editor, Features; Asst Editor, News/Pictures; Asst Editor, Sunday Mirror and Sunday People, 1981–85; Managing Editor (Features), Today, Editor, Sunday Today, 1986–87; Deputy Editor: Sunday Mirror, 1988–90; Daily Mirror, 1990–91. *Publication:* Flash, Bang, Wallop! (with Kent Gavin), 1978. *Recreations:* musical theatre, film, watching cricket, lunch with Keith Waterhouse. *Address:* The People, Holborn Circus, EC1P 1DQ. *T:* 071–353 0246. *Club:* Royal Automobile.

HAGESTADT, John Valentine; Head, North American Branch, Department of Trade and Industry, since 1987; *b* 11 Oct. 1938; *s* of late Leonard and Constance Hagestadt; *m* 1963, Betty Tebbs; three *d*. *Educ:* Dulwich Coll.; Worcester Coll., Oxford (BA). Asst Principal, Min. of Aviation, 1963; Principal, BoT, 1967; Nuffield Travelling Fellow, 1973–74; Asst Sec., Vehicles Div., Dept of Industry, 1976; Asst Sec., Overseas Trade Div. (Middle East and Latin America), Dept of Trade, 1980; Dir, British Trade Develt Office,

NY 1982; Dir, Invest in Britain Bureau, NY, 1984–87. *Address:* 14 Carlisle Mansions, Carlisle Place, SW1P 1HX. *T:* 071–828 0042.

HAGGARD, William; *see* Clayton, Richard Henry Michael.

HAGGART, Rt. Rev. Alastair Iain Macdonald; *b* 10 Oct. 1915; *s* of Alexander Macdonald Haggart and Jessie Mackay; *m* 1st, 1945, Margaret Agnes Trundle (*d* 1979); two *d*; 2nd, 1983, Mary Elizabeth Scholes, *qv*. *Educ:* Hatfield Coll. (Exhibnr); Durham Univ. (Exhibnr); Edinburgh Theol College. LTh 1941; BA 1942; MA 1945. Deacon, 1941, Priest 1942. Curate: St Mary's Cath., Glasgow, 1941–45; St Mary's, Hendon, 1945–48; Precentor, St Ninian's Cath., Perth, 1948–51; Rector, St Oswald's, King's Park, Glasgow, 1951, and Acting Priest-in-Charge, St Martin's, Glasgow, 1953–58; Synod Clerk of Glasgow Dio. and Canon of St Mary's Cath., Glasgow, 1958–59; Provost, St Paul's Cathedral, Dundee, 1959–71; Principal and Pantonian Prof., Episcopal Theological Coll., Edinburgh, 1971–75; Canon, St Mary's Cathedral, Edinburgh, 1971–75; Bishop of Edinburgh, 1975–85; Primus of the Episcopal Church in Scotland, 1977–85. Exam. Chap. to Bp of Brechin, 1964. Hon. LLD Dundee, 1970. *Recreations:* walking, reading, listening to music, asking questions. *Address:* 19 Eglinton Crescent, Edinburgh EH12 5BY. *T:* 031–337 8948.

HAGGART, Mary Elizabeth; *see* Scholes, M. E.

HAGGERSTON GADSDEN, Sir Peter Drury; *see* Gadsden.

HAGGETT, Prof. Peter; Professor of Urban and Regional Geography, University of Bristol, since 1966, Vice-Chancellor (Acting), 1984–85; *b* 24 Jan. 1933; *s* of Charles and Elizabeth Haggett, Pawlett, Somerset; *m* 1956, Brenda Woodley; two *s* two *d*. *Educ:* Dr Morgan's Sch., Bridgwater; St Catharine's Coll., Cambridge (Exhib. and Scholar; MA 1958; PhD 1970; ScD 1985). Asst Lectr, University Coll. London, 1955; Demonstrator and University Lectr, Cambridge, 1957; Fellow, Fitzwilliam Coll., 1963, Visiting Fellow, 1983; Leverhulme Research Fellow (Brazil), 1959; Canada Council Fellow, 1977; Erskine Fellow (NZ), 1979; Res. Fellow, Res. Sch. of Pacific Studies, ANU, 1983. Visiting Professor: Berkeley; Monash; Pennsylvania State; Toronto; Western Ontario; Wisconsin. Member, SW Economic Planning Council, 1967–72. Governor, Centre for Environmental Studies, 1975–78; Member: Council, RGS, 1972–73, 1977–80; UGC, 1985–89; Nat. Radiological Protection Bd, 1986–. Hon. DSc: York, Canada, 1983; Durham, 1989; Hon LLD Bristol, 1986. Cullum Medal of American Geographical Soc., 1969; Meritorious Contribution Award, Assoc. of American Geographers, 1973; Patron's Medal, RGS, 1986. *Publications:* Locational Analysis in Human Geography, 1965; (ed jtly) Frontiers in Geographical Teaching, 1965; Models in Geography, 1967; (with R. J. Chorley) Network Analysis in Geography, 1969; Progress in Geography, vols 1–9, 1969–77; Regional Forecasting, 1971; Geography: a modern synthesis, 1972, 4th edn, 1983; (with A. D. Cliff and others) Elements of Spatial Structure, 1975; Processes in Physical and Human Geography: Bristol Essays, 1975; Spatial Diffusion, 1981; Spatial Aspects of Epidemics, 1986; Atlas of Disease Distributions, 1988; The Geographer's Art, 1990; research papers. *Recreations:* natural history, cricket. *Address:* 5 Tun Bridge Close, Chew Magna, Somerset. *Club:* United Oxford & Cambridge University.

HAGGETT, Stuart John, MA; Headmaster, Birkenhead School, since 1988; *b* 11 April 1947; *s* of William Francis and Doreen Ada Haggett; *m* 1971, Hilary Joy Hammond; two *d*. *Educ:* Dauntsey's Sch., West Lavington, Wilts; Downing Coll., Cambridge (MA 1972); PGCE London (ext.), 1970. Canford Sch., Wimborne, Dorset, 1970–83: Head of Modern Languages, 1973–83; Housemaster, 1975–83; Second Master, King's Sch., Rochester, 1983–88. *Recreations:* France (travel and culture), sport, theatre, architecture, cooking. *Address:* Birkenhead School, 58 Beresford Road, Birkenhead, Merseyside L43 2JD. *T:* 051–652 4014.

HÄGGLÖF, Gunnar, GCVO (Hon.), 1954; Swedish Diplomat; *b* 15 Dec. 1904; *s* of Richard Hägglöf and Sigrid Ryding, Stockholm, Sweden; *m* Anna, *d* of Count Folchi-Vici, Rome. *Educ:* Upsala Univ., Sweden. Entered Swedish Diplomatic Service, 1926; Minister without Portfolio, 1939. During War of 1939–45, led various Swedish delegns to Berlin, London, and Washington; Envoy to Belgian and Dutch Govts, 1944; Envoy in Moscow, 1946; permanent delegate to UN, 1947; Ambassador to Court of St James's, 1948–67; Ambassador to France, 1967–71. Delegate to Conf. for Constitution, European Council, 1949; delegate to Suez Confs, 1956; Mem. of Menzies Cttee to Cairo, 1956. Hon. DCL Birmingham, 1960. *Publications:* Diplomat, 1972; several books and essays in economics, politics and history. *Recreations:* ski-ing, swimming, reading and writing. *Address:* Vigna Orsini, Bracciano, Rome, Italy.

HAGUE, Prof. Sir Douglas (Chalmers), Kt 1982; CBE 1978; Chairman, Oxford Strategy Network, since 1984; Associate Fellow, Templeton College, Oxford, since 1983; *b* Leeds, 20 Oct. 1926; *s* of Laurence and Marion Hague; *m* 1947, Brenda Elizabeth Fereday (marr. diss. 1986); two *d*; *m* 1986, Janet Mary Leach. *Educ:* Moseley Grammar Sch.; King Edward VI High Sch., Birmingham; University of Birmingham. Assistant Tutor, Faculty of Commerce, Birmingham Univ., 1946; Assistant Lecturer, University College, London, 1947, Lecturer, 1950; Reader in Political Economy in University of London, 1957; Newton Chambers Professor of Economics, University of Sheffield, 1957–63. Visiting Professor of Economics, Duke Univ., USA, 1960–61; Head of Department of Business Studies, University of Sheffield, 1962–63; Professor of Applied Economics, University of Manchester, 1963–65; Prof. of Managerial Economics, Manchester Business Sch., 1965–81, Dep. Dir, 1978–81, Vis. Prof., 1981–; Vis. Prof., Imperial Coll. of Science and Technol., London, 1988–. Chm., Metapraxis Ltd, 1984–90; Director: Economic Models Ltd, 1970–78; The Laird Gp, 1976–79; CRT Gp, 1990–. Rapporteur to International Economic Association, 1953–78, Editor General, 1981–86; Chm., ESRC, 1983–87; Member Working Party of National Advisory Council on Education for Industry and Commerce, 1962–63; Consultant to Secretariat of NEDC, 1962–63; Member: Treasury Working Party on Management Training in the Civil Service, 1965–67; EDC for Paper and Board, 1967–70; (part-time) N Western Gas Board, 1966–72; Working Party, Local Govt Training Bd, 1969–70; Price Commn, 1973–78 (Dep. Chm., 1977); Director: Manchester School of Management and Administration, 1964–65; Centre for Business Research, Manchester, 1964–66. Member Council, Manchester Business School, 1964–81; Chairman, Manchester Industrial Relations Society, 1964–66; President, NW Operational Research Group, 1967–69; British Chm., Carnegie Project on Accountability, 1968–72; Jt Chm., Conf. of Univ. Management Schools, 1971–73; Chm., DoI Working Party, Kirkby Manufacturing and Engineering Co., 1978. Economic adviser to Mrs Thatcher, Gen. Election campaign, 1979; Adviser to PM's Policy Unit, 10 Downing St, 1979–83. Industrial Consultant. Hon. LittD Sheffield, 1987. *Publications:* Costs in Alternative Locations: The Clothing Industry (with P. K. Newman), 1952; (with A. W. Stonier) A Textbook of Economic Theory, 1953, 4th edn 1973; (with A. W. Stonier) The Essentials of Economics, 1955; The Economics of Man-Made Fibres, 1957; (ed) Stability and Progress in the World Economy, 1958; (ed) The Theory of Capital, 1961; (ed) Inflation, 1962; (ed with Sir Roy Harrod) International Trade Theory in a Developing World, 1965; (ed) Price Formation in Various Economies, 1967; Managerial Economics, 1969; (ed with Bruce L. R. Smith) The Dilemma of Accountability in Modern Government, 1970; Pricing in Business, 1971; (with M. E. Beesley) Britain in the Common Market: a new business opportunity, 1973; (with W. E. F. Oakeshott and A. A. Strain) Devaluation and Pricing Decisions: a case study approach, 1974; (with W. J. M. Mackenzie and A. Barker) Public Policy and Private Interests: the institutions of compromise, 1975; (with Geoffrey Wilkinson) The IRC: an experiment in industrial intervention, 1983; (with Peter Hennessy) How Adolf Hitler reformed Whitehall, 1985; (ed) The Management of Science, 1991; Beyond Universities: a new republic of the intellect, 1991; articles in economic, financial and management journals. *Recreations:* church organs, watching Manchester United. *Address:* Templeton College, Oxford OX1 5NY. *T:* Oxford (0865) 735422. *Club:* Athenæum.

HAGUE, William Jefferson; MP (C) Richmond, Yorks, since Feb. 1989; *b* 26 March 1961; *s* of Timothy Nigel Hague and Stella Hague. *Educ:* Wath-upon-Dearne Comprehensive School; Magdalen College, Oxford (MA); Insead (MBA). Pres., Oxford Union, 1981; Pres., Oxford Univ. Cons. Assoc., 1981. Management Consultant, McKinsey & Co., 1983–88. Political Adviser, HM Treasury, 1983. Contested (C) Wentworth, S Yorks, 1987. PPS to Chancellor of the Exchequer, 1990–. *Address:* House of Commons, SW1A 0AA. *T:* 071–219 5867. *Club:* Carlton.

HAHN, Dr Carl Horst; Chairman, Board of Management, Volkswagen AG, Wolfsburg, since 1981; *b* 1 July 1926; *m* 1960, Marisa Traina; three *s* one *d*. Chairman, Supervisory Board: Audi AG; Gerling-Konzern Speziale Kreditversicherungs-AG, Cologne; Deputy Chairman, Supervisory Board, Aktiengesellschaft für Industrie und Verkehrswesen, Frankfurt (Main); Member, Supervisory Board: Gerling-Konzern Allgemeine Versicherungs-AG, Cologne; Gerling Konzern Versicherungs Beteiligung AG; Wilhelm Karmann GmbH, Osnabrück; Deutsche Messe- und Ausstellungs-AG, Hanover; Deutsche BP AG; Erste Allgemeine Versicherungs AG, Vienna; Thyssen AG; Commerzbank AG; Mem., Admin. Council, Deutsche Automobilges. Member: Bd of Dirs, Cttee of Common Market Automobile Constructors; Foreign Trade Adv. Council, Fed. Economics Min.; Internat. Adv. Council, Salk Inst., La Jolla, Calif; Bd of Management, Founders' Adv. Council of German Science; Presidium, Confedn of German Industry (also Vice-Pres.); Assoc. of German Automotive Industry; Bd of Trustees, Volkswagenwerk Foundn. *Address:* Volkswagen AG, Postfach, 3180 Wolfsburg 1, Germany.

HAHN, Prof. Frank Horace, FBA 1975; Professor of Economics, University of Cambridge, since 1972; Fellow of Churchill College, Cambridge, since 1960; *b* 26 April 1925; *s* of Dr Arnold Hahn and Maria Hahn; *m* 1946, Dorothy Salter; no *c*. *Educ:* Bournemouth Grammar School; London School of Economics (Hon. Fellow, 1989). PhD London, MA Cantab. Univ. of Birmingham, 1948–60, Reader in Mathematical Economics, 1958–60; Univ. Lectr in Econs, Cambridge, 1960–67; Prof. of Economics, LSE, 1967–72; Frank W. Taussig Res. Prof., Harvard, 1975–76. Visiting Professor: MIT, 1956–57; Univ. of California, Berkeley, 1959–60; Schumpeter Prof., Vienna Univ. of Econs and Business Admin, 1984. Fellow, Inst. of Advanced Studies in Behavioural Sciences, Stanford, 1966–67. Mem. Council for Scientific Policy, later Adv. Bd of Res. Councils, 1972–75. Fellow, Econometric Soc., 1962; Vice-Pres., 1967–68; Pres., 1968–69; Pres., Royal Economic Soc., 1986–89. Managing Editor, Review of Economic Studies, 1965–68. Foreign Hon. Mem., Amer. Acad. of Arts and Sciences, 1974; Hon. Mem., Amer. Economic Assoc., 1986; For. Associate, US Nat. Acad. Of Scis, 1988. Hon. DSocSci Birmingham, 1981; Hon DLitt East Anglia, 1984; Dr Econ *hc* Strasbourg, 1984; Hon. DSc(Econ) London, 1985. *Publications:* (with K. J. Arrow) General Competitive Analysis, 1971; The Share of Wages in the National Income, 1972; Money and Inflation, 1982; Equilibrium and Macro-Economics, 1984; Money, Growth and Stability, 1985; (ed and contrib.) The Economics of Missing Markets, Information and Games, 1989; articles in learned journals. *Address:* 16 Adams Road, Cambridge CB3 9AD. *T:* Cambridge (0223) 352560; 30 Tavistock Court, Tavistock Square, WC1H 9HE. *T:* 071–387 4293.

HAIG, family name of **Earl Haig.**

HAIG, 2nd Earl, *cr* 1919; **George Alexander Eugene Douglas Haig,** OBE 1966; DL; ARSA 1988; Viscount Dawick, *cr* 1919; Baron Haig and 30th Laird of Bemersyde; is a painter; Member, Queen's Body Guard for Scotland; *b* March 1918; *o s* of 1st Earl and Hon. Dorothy Vivian (*d* 1939) (Author of A Scottish Tour, 1935), *d* of 3rd Lord Vivian; *S* father, 1928; *m* 1st, 1956, Adrienne Thérèse, *d* of Derrick Morley; one *s* two *d*; 2nd, 1981, Donna Geroloma Lopez y Royo di Taurisano. *Educ:* Stowe; Christ Church, Oxford. MA Oxon. 2nd Lieut Royal Scots Greys, 1938; retired on account of disability, 1951, rank of Captain; Hon. Major on disbandment of HG 1958; studied painting Camberwell School of Art; paintings in collections of Arts Council and Scottish Nat. Gallery of Modern Art. War of 1939–45 (prisoner). Member: Royal Fine Art Commission for Scotland, 1958–61; Council and Executive Cttee, Earl Haig Fund, Scotland, 1950–65 and 1966– (Pres., 1980–86); Scottish Arts Council, 1969–75; President, Scottish Craft Centre, 1950–75. Member Council, Commonwealth Ex-Services League; Pres., Officers' Association (Scottish Branch), 1987– (Chm., 1977–87); Vice-President: Scottish National Institution for War Blinded; Royal Blind Asylum and School; President Border Area British Legion, 1955–61; Chairman SE Scotland Disablement Advisory Cttee, 1960–73; Vice-Chairman, British Legion, Scotland, 1960, Chairman, 1962–65, Pres., 1980–86; Chm., Bd of Trustees, Scottish National War Memorial, 1983– (Trustee, 1961–); Trustee, National Gallery of Scotland, 1962–72; Chairman: Berwickshire Civic Soc., 1971–73; Friends of DeMarco Gall., 1968–71. Berwickshire: DL 1953; Vice-Lieutenant, 1967–70; DL Ettrick and Lauderdale (and Roxburghshire), 1977–. KStJ 1977. FRSA 1951. *Heir: s* Viscount Dawick, *qv*. *Address:* Bemersyde, Melrose, Scotland. *T:* St Boswells (0835) 22762. *Clubs:* Cavalry and Guards, Beefsteak; New (Edinburgh).

See also Baron Astor of Hever, Baron Dacre of Glanton.

HAIG, General Alexander Meigs, Jr; Chairman, Worldwide Associates, Inc., since 1984; Chairman, Atlantic and Pacific Advisory Councils, United Technologies, since 1982; *b* 2 Dec. 1924; *m* 1950, Patricia Fox; two *s* one *d*. *Educ:* schs in Pennsylvania; Univ. of Notre Dame; US Mil. Acad., West Point (BS); Univs of Columbia and Georgetown (MA); Ground Gen. Sch., Fort Riley; Armor Sch., Fort Knox; Naval and Army War Colls. 2nd Lieut 1947; Far East and Korea, 1948–51; Europe, 1956–59; Vietnam, 1966–67; CO 3rd Regt, subseq. Dep. Comdt, West Point, 1967–69; Sen. Mil. Adviser to Asst to Pres. for Nat. Security Affairs, 1969–70; Dep. Asst to Pres. for Nat. Security Affairs, 1970–73; Vice-Chief of Staff, US Army, Jan.-July 1973, retd; Chief of White House Staff, 1973–74 when recalled to active duty; Supreme Allied Commander Europe, 1974–79, and Commander-in-Chief, US European Command, 1974–79. President and Chief Operating Officer, United Technologies, 1979–81. Secretary of State, USA, 1981–82. Sen. Fellow, Hudson Inst. for Policy Research, 1982–84. Director: Commodore Internat. Ltd; Leisure Technol. Inc.; Gen. Atomics; Quantum Computer Services; Interneuron Pharmaceuticals, Inc. Member: Presidential Cttee on Strategic Forces, 1983–; Presidential Commn on Chemical Warfare Review, 1985; Bd of Special Advisers, President's Commn on Physical Fitness and Sports, 1984–. Hon. LLD: Niagara; Utah; hon. degrees: Syracuse, Fairfield, Hillsdale Coll., 1981. Awarded numerous US medals, badges and decorations; also Vietnamese orders and Cross of Gallantry; Medal of King Abd el-Aziz (Saudi Arabia). *Publication:* Caveat: realism, Reagan and foreign policy, 1984. *Recreations:* tennis, golf, squash, equitation. *Address:* 1155 15th Street NW (Suite 800), Washington, DC 20005, USA.

HAIG, Ian Maurice, AM 1988; Chief Executive, Monash-ANZ Centre for International Briefing, since 1990; *b* 13 Dec. 1936; *s* of P. K. Haig; *m* 1959, Beverley, *d* of J. A. Dunning, OBE; two *s* one *d*. *Educ:* Pulteney Grammar School, Adelaide; University of Adelaide. Private Sec. to Pres. of Senate, Canberra, 1958–59; Asst Sec., Commonwealth Parly Conf., London, 1960; Public Relations Officer, Shell Co. of Australia, 1962; British Foreign Office School of Middle East Studies, 1963; Asst Trade Comr and Trade Comr, Los Angeles, 1966–68; Trade Comr, Beirut, 1969–73; Ambassador at large, Middle East, 1973; Ambassador to Saudi Arabia, Kuwait and United Arab Emirates, 1974–76; Australian Comr, Hong Kong, 1976–79; Dir of Administration, A.C.I. Ltd, 1979–81; Man. Dir, A.C.I. Fibreglass (Aust.), 1982; Agent Gen. for Victoria in London, 1983–85 and 1988–90; Chm., Immigration Panel, 1987; Dir, Aust. Wheat Bd, 1985–88. *Publications:* Arab Oil Politics, 1978; Oil and Alternative Sources of Energy, 1978; Australia and the Middle East, 1983. *Recreations:* cricket, golf. *Address:* 3 Chastleton Avenue, Toorak, Vic 3142, Australia. *Clubs:* MCC; Melbourne, Australian (Melbourne); Royal Melbourne Golf.

HAIG, Mrs Mary Alison G.; *see* Glen Haig.

HAIGH, Brian Roger; Contracts Consultant and Director of Professional Education and Training, Lion Worldwide (formerly International) Division, Keiser Enterprises Inc., since 1986; *b* 19 Feb. 1931; *s* of Herbert Haigh and Ruth Haigh (*née* Lockwood); *m* 1953, Sheila Carter; one *s* one *d*. *Educ:* Hillhouse Central School, Huddersfield. Min. of Supply, 1949; National Service, RAF, 1949–51. Min. of Supply/Min. of Aviation, 1951–62; NATO Bullpup Production Orgn, 1962–67 (Head of Contracts, Finance and Admin, 1965–67); Min. of Technology, Aviation Supply, Defence (Defence Sales Orgn), 1968–73 (Asst Dir, Sales, 1971–73); Nat. Defence Coll., 1973–74; Ministry of Defence: Asst Dir, Contracts, 1974; Dir of Contracts (Weapons), Dec. 1974; Principal Dir of Navy Contracts, 1978; Under Secretary, 1980; Dir-Gen., Defence Contracts, 1980–86. *Recreations:* family, music, opera, bridge. *Address:* Keiser Enterprises Inc., Moreland House, 80 Goswell Road, EC1B 7DB. *T:* 071–490 1713.

HAIGH, Clement Percy, PhD; CPhys, FInstP; scientific and engineering consultant; *b* 11 Jan. 1920; *m* 1945, Ruby Patricia Hobdey; three *s*. *Educ:* Univ. of Leeds (BSc); King's Coll., London (PhD). Radiochemical Centre, Thorium Ltd, 1943–49; Medical Physicist, Barrow Hosp., Bristol, 1949–56; joined CEGB, 1956: Director, Berkeley Nuclear Laboratories, 1959–73; Dep. Director-General, Design and Construction Div., Gloucester, 1973–78; Dir of Research, BNOC, 1978–81. Dir, South Western Industrial Res., 1981–86. Distinguished Lectr, American Nuclear Soc., San Francisco, 1965; Assessor, Nuclear Safety Adv. Cttee, 1972–76; Member: BBC West Adv. Council, 1972–76; Mechanical Engrg and Machine Tools Requirements Bd, 1973–76; Off-Shore Energy Technology Bd, 1978–81; Board, National Maritime Inst., 1981–82; UK Chm., Joint UK/USSR Working Gp on Problems of Electricity Supply, 1974–78; Chm., Programme Steering Cttee, UK Offshore Steels Res. Project, 1981–87. FRSA. *Publications:* various papers on applied nuclear physics and on nuclear energy. *Recreations:* music; study of magnificent failures in technology. *Address:* Painswick, Old Sneed Park, Bristol, Avon BS9 1RG. *T:* Bristol (0272) 682065. *Clubs:* Savile, Royal Automobile.

HAIGH, Clifford; Editor, The Friend, 1966–73; *b* 5 Feb. 1906; *yr s* of Leonard and Isabel Haigh, Bradford, Yorks; *m* 1st, 1934, Dora Winifred Fowler (*d* 1959); one *s* one *d*; 2nd, 1970, Grace Elizabeth Cross. Editorial Staff: Yorkshire Observer, 1924–27; Birmingham Post, 1928–46; The Times, 1947–61; Assistant Editor, The Friend, 1961–65. *Recreation:* walking. *Address:* 4 Chichester Road, Sandgate, Kent CT20 3BN. *T:* Folkestone (0303) 48212.

HAIGH, Edward; Assistant General Secretary, Transport and General Workers' Union, since 1985; *b* 7 Nov. 1935; *s* of Edward and Sarah Ellen Haigh; *m* 1st, 1958, Patricia (marr. diss. 1982); one *s* two *d*; 2nd, 1982, Margaret; two step *d*. *Educ:* St Patrick's RC Sch., Birstall; St Mary's RC Sch., Batley, W Yorks. Carpet weaver, 1956–69; shop steward, 1960–69; National Union of Dyers, Bleachers and Textile Workers: Dist Organiser, 1969–73; Dist Sec., 1973–77; Nat. Organiser/Negotiator, 1977–79; Asst Gen. Sec., 1979–82; Nat. Sec., Textile Gp, TGWU, 1982–85. Mem., Labour Party NEC, 1982–. JP Batley, W Yorks, 1971–85. *Address:* (office) Transport House, Smith Square, SW1P 3JB. *Recreations:* politics (Labour Party), Rugby League football, cricket. *Club:* Birstall Irish Democratic League (W Yorks).

HAIGH, Maurice Francis; Barrister; a Recorder of the Crown Court, since 1981; a Chairman, Medical Appeal Tribunals, since 1984; *b* 6 Sept. 1929; *s* of William and Ceridwen Francis Haigh. *Educ:* Repton. Asst cameraman in film production; worked for Leslie Laurence Productions Ltd, London, Manchester Film Studios, and finally for Anglo-Scottish Pictures Ltd at London Film Studios, Shepperton, 1946–49; in commerce, 1950–52. Called to the Bar, Gray's Inn, 1955. *Recreations:* reading, cycling, fell and mountain walking. *Address:* Kenworthy's Buildings, 83 Bridge Street, Manchester M3 2RF. *T:* 061–832 4036. *Club:* English-Speaking Union.

HAILEY, Arthur; author; *b* 5 April 1920; *s* of George Wellington Hailey and Elsie Mary Wright; *m* 1st, 1944, Joan Fishwick (marr. diss. 1950); three *s*; 2nd, 1951, Sheila Dunlop; one *s* two *d*. *Educ:* English elem. schs. Pilot, RAF, 1939–47 (Flt-Lt), AE. Emigrated to Canada, 1947; various positions in industry and sales until becoming free-lance writer, 1956. *Publications:* (in 37 languages): Flight Into Danger (with John Castle), 1958; Close-Up (Collected Plays), 1960; The Final Diagnosis, 1959; In High Places, 1962; Hotel, 1965; Airport, 1968; Wheels, 1971; The Moneychangers, 1975; Overload, 1979; Strong Medicine, 1985; The Evening News, 1990. *Films:* Zero Hour, 1956; Time Lock, 1957; The Young Doctors, 1961; Hotel, 1966; Airport, 1970; The Moneychangers, 1976; Wheels, 1978; Strong Medicine, 1986. *Address:* (home) Lyford Cay, PO Box N7776, Nassau, Bahamas; (office) Seaway Authors Ltd, 3400 First Canadian Place, PO Box 130, Toronto, Ont M5X 1A4, Canada. *Club:* Lyford Cay (Bahamas).

HAILSHAM, 2nd Viscount, *cr* 1929, of Hailsham; Baron, *cr* 1928 [disclaimed his peerages for life, 20 Nov. 1963]; *see under* Baron Hailsham of St Marylebone.

HAILSHAM OF SAINT MARYLEBONE, Baron *cr* 1970 (Life Peer), of Herstmonceux; **Quintin McGarel Hogg,** PC 1956; KG 1988; CH 1974; FRS 1973; Editor, Halsbury's Laws of England, 4th edition, since 1972; Chancellor, University of Buckingham, 1983–March 1992; *b* 9 Oct. 1907; *er s* of 1st Viscount Hailsham, PC, KC, and Elizabeth (*d* 1925), *d* of Judge Trimble Brown, Nashville, Tennessee, USA, and *widow* of Hon. A. J. Marjoribanks; *S* father, 1950, as 2nd Viscount Hailsham, but disclaimed his peerages for life, 20 Nov. 1963 (Baron *cr* 1928, Viscount *cr* 1929); *m* 1944, Mary Evelyn (*d* 1978), *d* of late Richard Martin of Ross; two *s* three *d*; *m* 1986, Deirdre Shannon. *Educ:* Eton (Schol., Newcastle Schol.); Christ Church, Oxford (Scholar). First Class Hon. Mods, 1928; First Class Lit. Hum., 1930; Pres., Oxford Union Soc., 1929. Served War of 1939–45: commissioned Rifle Bde Sept. 1939; served Middle East Forces, Western Desert, 1941 (wounded); Egypt, Palestine, Syria, 1942; Temp. Major, 1942. Fellow of All Souls Coll., Oxford, 1931–38, 1961–; Barrister, Lincoln's Inn, 1932; a Bencher of Lincoln's Inn, 1956, Treasurer, 1975; QC 1953. MP (C) Oxford City, 1938–50, St Marylebone, (Dec.) 1963–70; Jt Parly Under-Sec. of State for Air, 1945; First Lord of the Admiralty, 1956–57; Minister of Education, 1957; Dep. Leader of the House of Lords, 1957–60; Leader of the House of Lords, 1960–63; Lord Privy Seal, 1959–60; Lord Pres. of the Council, 1957–59 and 1960–64; Minister for Science and Technology, 1959–64; Minister with special responsibility for: Sport, 1962–64; dealing with unemployment in the North-East, 1963–64; higher education, Dec. 1963–Feb. 1964; Sec. of State for Education and Science, April-Oct. 1964; Lord High Chancellor of GB, 1970–74 and 1979–87. Chm. of the Conservative Party Organization, Sept. 1957–Oct. 1959. Rector of Glasgow Univ., 1959–62. Pres. Classical Assoc., 1960–61. Lectures: John Findley Green Foundation, 1960; Richard Dimbleby, 1976; Hamlyn, 1983; Granada, 1987; Warburton, 1987, F. A. Mann, 1988, Lincoln's Inn. Hon. Student of Christ Church, Oxford, 1962; Hon. Bencher, Inn of Court of NI, 1981; Hon. FICE 1963; Hon. FIEE 1972; Hon. FIStructE 1960. Hon. Freeman, Merchant Taylors' Co., 1971. Hon. DCL: Westminster Coll., Fulton, Missouri, USA, 1960; Newcastle, 1964; Oxon, 1974; Hon. LLD: Cambridge, 1963; Delhi, 1972; St Andrews, 1979; Leeds, 1982; Hon. DLitt Ulster, 1988. *Publications:* The Law of Arbitration, 1935; One Year's Work, 1944; The Law and Employers' Liability, 1944; The Times We Live In, 1944; Making Peace, 1945; The Left was never Right, 1945; The Purpose of Parliament, 1946; Case for Conservatism, 1947; The Law of Monopolies, Restrictive Practices and Resale Price Maintenance, 1956; The Conservative Case, 1959; Interdependence, 1961; Science and Politics, 1963; The Devil's Own Song, 1968; The Door Wherein I Went, 1975; Elective Dictatorship, 1976; The Dilemma of Democracy, 1978; Hamlyn Revisited: the British legal system (Hamlyn Lectures), 1983; A Sparrow's Flight (autobiog.), 1990. *Heir:* (*to disclaimed viscountcy*): *s* Hon. Douglas Martin Hogg, *qv*. *Recreations:* walking, climbing, shooting, etc. *Address:* House of Lords, SW1A 0PW. *Clubs:* Carlton, Alpine, MCC.

See also Hon. M. C. Hogg.

HAIMENDORF, Christoph von F.; *see* Fürer-Haimendorf.

HAIN, Peter Gerald; MP (Lab) Neath, since April 1991; *b* 16 Feb. 1950; *s* of Walter and Adelaine Hain; *m* 1975, Patricia Western; two *s*. *Educ:* Queen Mary College, London (BSc Econ 1st cl. hons); Univ. of Sussex (MPhil). Brought up in S Africa, until family forced to leave in 1966, due to anti-apartheid activity, since when lived in UK. Union of Communication Workers: Asst Research Officer, 1976–87; Head of Research, 1987–91. Chm., Stop the Seventy Tour campaign, 1969–70; Nat. Chm., Young Liberals, 1971–73; Press Officer, Anti-Nazi League, 1977–80. Contested (Lab) Putney, 1983, 1987. *Publications:* Don't Play with Apartheid, 1971; Community Politics, 1976; Mistaken Identity, 1976; (ed) Policing the Police, vol. I, 1978, vol. II, 1980; Neighbourhood Participation, 1980; Crisis and Future of the Left, 1980; Political Trials in Britain, 1984; Political Strikes, 1986; A Putney Plot?, 1987. *Recreations:* soccer, cricket, Rugby player, fan of Chelsea FC and Neath RFC, rock and folk music fan. *Address:* House of Commons, SW1A 0AA. *T:* 071–219 3000; 14 The Parade, Neath SA11 1RA. *T:* Neath (0639) 630152. *Clubs:* Neath Workingmen's; Resolven Rugby, Resolven Royal British Legion Institute.

HAINES, Christopher John Minton; Chief Executive, The Jockey Club, since 1989; *b* 14 April 1939; *m* 1967, Christine Cobbold; two *s* two *d*. *Educ:* Stowe. The Rifle Brigade, 1959–68; sugar trade, 1968–89; Chm., James Budgett & Son. *Recreations:* music, gardening, racing. *Address:* The Jockey Club, 42 Portman Square, W1H 0EN. *Club:* Turf.

HAINES, Joseph Thomas William; Assistant Editor, The Daily Mirror, 1984–90; Group Political Editor, Mirror Group Newspapers, 1984–90; *b* 29 Jan. 1928; *s* of Joseph and Elizabeth Haines; *m* 1955, Irene Betty Lambert; no *c*. *Educ:* Elementary Schools, Rotherhithe, SE16. Parly Correspondent, The Bulletin (Glasgow) 1954–58, Political Correspondent, 1958–60; Political Correspondent: Scottish Daily Mail, 1960–64; The Sun, 1964–68; Dep. Press Sec. to Prime Minister, Jan.-June 1969; Chief Press Sec. to Prime Minister, 1969–70 and 1974–76, and to Leader of the Opposition, 1970–74; Feature Writer, 1977–78, Chief Leader Writer, 1978–90, The Daily Mirror. Director: Mirror Gp Newspapers (1986) Ltd, 1986–; Scottish Daily Record & Sunday Mail Ltd, 1986–. Mem. Tonbridge UDC, 1963–69, 1971–74. Mem., Royal Commn on Legal Services, 1976–79. *Publications:* The Politics of Power, 1977; (co-editor) Malice In Wonderland, 1986; Maxwell, 1988. *Recreations:* heresy and watching football. *Address:* 1 South Frith, London Road, Southborough, Tunbridge Wells, Kent. *T:* Tonbridge (0732) 365919.

HAINING, Thomas Nivison, CMG 1983; HM Diplomatic Service, retired; writer and lecturer on international affairs and Mongolian history; Hon. Research Associate, Department of History, University of Aberdeen, since 1988; *b* 15 March 1927; *m* 1955, Dorothy Patricia Robson; one *s*. *Educ:* Edinburgh Univ.; Göttingen Univ. Foreign Office, 1952; served Vienna, Moscow, Rome and New York; Counsellor, FCO, 1972–79; Ambassador and Consul-Gen. to the Mongolian People's Republic, 1979–82. Hon. Pres., Chinese Studies Gp, Aberdeen Univ, 1989–. FRGS 1980. *Publications:* (contrib.) Mongolia Today, 1989; (trans. and ed) Ratchnevsky, Genghis Khan: his life and legacy, 1991. *Address:* Carseview, 7 The Banks, Brechin, Angus DD9 6JD. *T:* Brechin (03562) 2584. *Clubs:* Royal Automobile; Royal Northern and University (Aberdeen); New (Brechin).

HAINSWORTH, Gordon, MA; Chief Executive, Manchester, since 1988; *b* 4 Nov. 1934; *s* of Harry and Constance Hainsworth; *m* 1962, Diane (*née* Thubron); one *s* one *d*. *Educ:* Leeds Modern Sch.; Trinity Coll., Cambridge (MA). Teaching, Leeds, Birmingham and West Riding, 1958–65; Admin. Assistant, Leeds, 1965–69; Asst Education Officer, Manchester, 1969–74; Under-Secretary (Education), Assoc. of Metropolitan Authorities, 1974–76; Dep. Educn Officer, Manchester, 1976–80; Director of Education, Gateshead, 1980–83; Chief Educn Officer, Manchester, 1983–88. *Recreations:* family, books, golf, bridge, walking. *Address:* 37 Coppleridge Drive, Manchester M8 6PB. *T:* 061–720 7373.

HAINWORTH, Henry Charles, CMG 1961; HM Diplomatic Service, retired; *b* 12 Sept. 1914; *o s* of late Charles S. and Emily G. I. Hainworth; *m* 1944, Mary, *yr d* of late Felix B. and Lilian Ady; two *d*. *Educ:* Blundell's Sch.; Sidney Sussex Coll., Cambridge. Entered HM Consular Service, 1939; HM Embassy, Tokyo, 1940–42; seconded to Ministry of Information (Far Eastern Bureau, New Delhi), 1942–46; HM Embassy, Tokyo, 1946–51; Foreign Office, 1951–53; HM Legation, Bucharest, 1953–55; NATO Defence Coll., Paris, 1956; Political Office, Middle East Forces (Nicosia), 1956; Foreign Office, 1957–61 (Head of Atomic Energy and Disarmament Dept, 1958–61); Counsellor, United Kingdom Delegation to the Brussels Conference, 1961–63; HM Minister and Consul-Gen. at British Embassy, Vienna, 1963–68; Ambassador to Indonesia, 1968–70; Ambassador and Perm. UK Rep. to Disarm. Conf., Geneva, 1971–74. *Publication:* A Collector's Dictionary, 1980. *Recreations:* reading, fishing. *Address:* 23 Rivermead Court, Ranelagh Gardens, SW6 3RU.

HAITINK, Bernard, Hon. KBE 1977; Commander, Order of Orange Nassau, 1988; Music Director, Royal Opera House, Covent Garden, since 1987; *b* Amsterdam, 4 March 1929. *Educ:* Amsterdam Conservatory. Studied conducting under Felix Hupke, but started his career as a violinist with the Netherlands Radio Philharmonic; in 1954 and 1955 attended annual conductors' course (org. by Netherlands Radio Union) under Ferdinand Leitner; became 2nd Conductor with Radio Union at Hilversum with co-responsibility for 4 radio orchs and conducted the Radio Philharmonic in public during the Holland Fest., in The Hague, 1956; conducted the Concertgebouw Orch., Oct. 1956; then followed guest engagements with this and other orchs in the Netherlands and elsewhere. Debut in USA, with Los Angeles Symph. Orch., 1958; 5 week season with Concertgebouw Orch., 1958–59, and toured Britain with it, 1959; apptd (with Eugen Jochum) as the Orchestra's permanent conductor, Sept. 1961; sole artistic dir and permanent conductor of the orch., 1964–88; toured Japan, USSR, USA and Europe; 1974; début at Royal Opera House, Covent Garden, 1977. London Philharmonic Orchestra: Principal Conductor, Artistic Dir, 1967–79, Pres., 1990; toured: Japan, 1969; USA, 1970, 1971, 1976; Berlin, 1972; Holland, Germany, Austria, 1973; USSR, 1975. Musical Dir, Glyndebourne Opera, 1978–88. Hon. RAM 1973; Hon. FRCM 1984. Hon. DMus: Oxford, 1988; Leeds, 1988. Bruckner Medal of Honour, 1970; Gold Medal, Internat. Gustav Mahler Soc., 1971. Chevalier de L'Ordre des Arts et des Lettres, 1972; Officer, Order of the Crown (Belgium), 1977. *Address:* c/o Harold Holt Ltd, 31 Sinclair Road, W14.

HAJNAL, John, FBA 1966; Professor of Statistics, London School of Economics, 1975–86 (Reader, 1966–75); *b* 26 Nov. 1924; *s* of late Kálmán and Eva Hajnal-Kónyi; *m* 1950, Nina Lande; one *s* three *d*. *Educ:* University Coll. Sch., London; Balliol Coll., Oxford. Employed by: Royal Commission on Population, 1944–48; UN, New York, 1948–51; Office of Population Research, Princeton Univ., 1951–53; Manchester Univ., 1953–57; London Sch. of Economics, 1957–. Vis. Fellow Commoner, Trinity Coll., Cambridge, 1974–75; Vis. Prof., Rockefeller Univ., NY, 1981. Mem. Internat. Statistical Institute. *Publications:* The Student Trap, 1972; papers on demography, statistics, mathematics, etc. *Address:* 95 Hodford Road, NW11 8EH. *T:* 081–455 7044.

HALABY, Najeeb Elias; President, Halaby International Corporation; Chairman: Dulles Access Rapid Transit Inc.; National Center for Atmospheric Research Foundation; *b* 19 Nov. 1915; *s* of late Najeeb Elias Halaby and of Laura Wilkins Halaby; *m* 1st, 1946, Doris Carlquist (marr. diss. 1976); one *s* two *d*; 2nd, 1980, Jane Allison Coates. *Educ:* Stanford Univ. (AB); Yale Univ. (LLB); Bonar Law Coll., Ashridge, (Summer) 1939. Called to the Bar: California, 1940; District of Columbia, 1948; NY, 1973. Practised law in Los Angeles, Calif, 1940–42, 1958–61; Air Corps Flight Instructor, 1940; Test pilot for Lockheed Aircraft Corp., 1942–43; Naval aviator, established Navy Test Pilot Sch., 1943; formerly Chief of Intelligence Coordination Div., State Dept; Foreign Affairs Advisor to Sec. of Defense; Chm., NATO Military Production and Supply Board, 1950; Asst Administrator, Mutual Security Economic Cooperation Administration, 1950–51; Asst Sec. of Defense for Internat. Security, 1952–54; Vice-Chm., White House Advisory Group whose report led to formation of Federal Aviation Agency, 1955–56, Administrator of the Agency, 1961–65; Pan American World Airways: Director, 1965–73; Member, Executive Committee of Board, 1965–68; Senior Vice-President, 1965–68, President, 1968–71; Chief Executive, 1969–72; Chairman, 1970–72; Associate of Laurance and Nelson Rockefeller, 1954–57; Past Exec. Vice-Pres. and Dir, Servomechanisms Inc.; Sec.-Treas., Aerospace Corp., 1959–61; Pres., American Technology Corp. Member of Board: Mem. Exec. Cttee, (Founder-Chm., 1971–73), US-Japan Econ. Council; Trustee: Aspen Inst., Aspen, Colo.; Eisenhower Exchange Fellowships, Inc.; Wolf Trap Foundn; Amer. Univ. of Beirut; Governor, Flight Safety Foundn. Fellow, Amer. Inst. of Aeronautics and Astronautics. Hon. LLB: Allegheny Coll., Pa, 1967; Loyola Coll., LA, 1968. Monsanto Safety Award; FAA Exceptional Service Medal; G. L. Cabot Medal, Aero Club of New England, 1964; Gilbert Award, Air Traffic Controllers' Assoc., 1989. *Publication:* Crosswinds (memoir), 1979. *Recreations:* golf, skiing. *Address:* (office) PO Drawer Y, McLean, Va 22101, USA; (residence) 175 Chain Bridge Road, McLean, Va 22101–1907, USA. *Clubs:* F Street, Metropolitan, Chevy Chase (Washington); Bohemian (California); Piping Rock (New York); Tower (Virginia).

HALAS, John, OBE 1972; FCSD; Chairman, Educational Film Centre, since 1960; President: British Federation of Film Societies, since 1980; International Animated Film Association, 1975–85, now Hon. President; *b* 16 April 1912; *s* of Victor and Bertha Halas; *m* 1940, Joy Batchelor; one *s* one *d*. *Educ:* Académie des Beaux-Arts, Paris; Mühely, Budapest. Founded: (with Joy Batchelor) Halas and Batchelor Animation Ltd, 1940; (with Lord Snow, Morris Goldsmith, Joy Batchelor and Roger Manvell) Educational Film Centre, 1960; ASIFA (International Animated Film Assoc.), 1960. Produced 2,000 animated films, 1940–80, incl. first feature-length animated film in GB, Animal Farm; latest productions incl: Autobahn, 1979; First Steps, 1981; Dilemma, 1982 (world's first fully digitized film); Players, 1983; A New Vision: the life and work of Botticelli, 1984; Toulouse-Lautrec, 1985; Leonardo da Vinci, 1985; Masters of Animation series, 1986–87; Light of the World, 1989. Past President, Internat. Council of Graphic Design Assocs. Sen. Fellow, RCA, 1988. Hon. Fellow, BKSTS, 1972. *Publications:* How to Cartoon, 1959; The Technique of Film Animation, 1961; Film and TV Graphics, 1967; Computer Animation, 1974; Visual Scripting, 1977; Film Animation, a Simplified Approach, 1978; Timing for Animation, 1981; Graphics in Motion, 1981; Masters of Animation, 1987. *Recreations:* painting, music. *Address:* 6 Holford Road, Hampstead, NW3 1AD. *T:* 071–435 8674.

HALBERG, Sir Murray (Gordon), Kt 1988; MBE 1961; *b* 7 July 1933; *s* of Raymond Halberg; *m* 1959, Phyllis, *d* of Alex Korff; one *s* one *d*. *Educ:* Avondale College. Started internat. distance running, Commonwealth Games, 1954; Commonwealth Gold Medals, 3 miles, 1958, 1962; Olympic Gold Medal, 5,000 metres, Rome, 1960; world records at 2 miles and 3 miles, 1961, participant in 4 × 1 mile record. Founder, Crippled Children's Sports Aid Foundation. *Address:* 7 Te Aroha Avenue, Oneroa, Auckland, New Zealand. *T:* WH 8470; 14/11 Balfour Street, Parnell, Auckland, New Zealand. *T:* 395 133.

HALE, John Hampton; Director: Pearson plc, since 1983 (Managing Director, 1983–86); Pearson Inc. (USA), since 1983 (Chairman, 1983–86); *b* 8 July 1924; *s* of Dr John Hale and Elsie (Coles) Hale; *m* 2nd, 1980, Nancy Ryrie Birks; one *s* two *d* by former marriage. *Educ:* Eton College (King's Scholar); Magdalene Coll., Cambridge (Mech. Scis Tripos, BA, MA); Harvard Grad. Sch. of Business Admin (Henry Fellow, 1948). RAF and Fleet Air Arm Pilot, 1943–46. Alcan Aluminium Ltd, Montreal, NY and London, 1949–83; Man. Dir, Alcan Booth Industries, 1964–70; Exec. Vice-Pres., Finance, 1970–82, Dir, Alcan Aluminium, 1970–85; Dir, Aluminium Co. of Canada, 1970–85 (Chm., 1979–83). Director: Nippon Light Metal Co., Japan, Indian Aluminium Co. and Alcan Australia, 1970–83; Canadian Adv. Bd, Allendale Mutual Insurance Co., 1977–83; Scovill Inc. (USA), 1978–85; Ritz-Carlton Hotel, Montreal, 1981–83; Concordia Univ. Business Sch., 1981–83; Bank of Montreal, 1985– (Mem., Internat Adv. Council, 1986–89); The Economist Newspaper, 1984–; SSMC Inc. (USA), 1986–89; Chm., Fairey Holdings, 1983–87. Member: Lloyds, 1960–; Exec. Cttee, British-North American Cttee, 1980–90; Council, Industry for Management Educn, 1983–87; Lay Mem., Stock Exchange Council, 1987–. Chairman: Chambly County Protestant Central Sch. Bd, 1957–60; Business Graduates Assoc., 1967–70; Mem., Accounting Research Adv. Bd, Canadian Inst. of Chartered Accountants, 1975–81 (Chm., 1978–81). Director: Mont St Hilaire Nature Conservation Assoc., 1977–83 (Pres., 1980–83); Foundn for Canadian Studies, 1988–; Governor, Stratford Festival, Ontario, 1981–83. CBIM. Mem., Court of Assts, Armourers' & Brasiers' Co., 1985– (Master, 1990). *Recreations:* ski-ing, sailing, fishing, shooting, old Canadian books. *Address:* 71 Eaton Terrace, SW1W 8TN. *T:* 071–730 2929. *Clubs:* Royal Thames Yacht; Mount Royal (Montreal); Toronto.

HALE, Prof. Sir John (Rigby), Kt 1984; FBA 1977; Professor of Italian History, 1981–83, and Professor of Italian, 1985–88, University College London, now Professor Emeritus; Public Orator, University of London, 1981–83; *b* 17 Sept. 1923; *s* of E. R. S. Hale, FRCP, MD, and Hilda Birks; *m* 1st, 1952, Rosalind Williams; one *s* two *d*; 2nd, 1965, Sheila Haynes MacIvor; one *s*. *Educ:* Neville Holt Preparatory Sch.; Eastbourne Coll.; Jesus Coll., Oxford. BA first cl. hons Mod. Hist., 1948; MA (Oxon) 1950; DLitt (Oxon) 1986. Served War, Radio Operator in Merchant Service, 1942–45. Commonwealth Fellow, Johns Hopkins and Harvard Univs, 1948–49; Fellow and Tutor in Modern History, Jesus Coll., Oxford, 1949–64, Hon. Fellow, 1986; Prof. of History, Univ. of Warwick, 1964–69. Editor, Oxford Magazine, 1958–59; Visiting Prof., Cornell Univ., 1959–60; Vis. Fellow, Harvard Centre for Renaissance Studies, I Tatti, 1963; Vis. Prof., Univ. of California, Berkeley, 1969–70; Folger Library Washington, Fellowship, 1970. Fellow, Davis Center, Univ. of Princeton, 1982; Mem., Princeton Inst. for Adv. Study, 1984–85. Chm. of Trustees, Nat. Gallery, 1974–80 (Trustee, 1973–80); Trustee: V&A Museum, 1984–88 (Chm., Theatre Museum Cttee, 1984–87); BM, 1985–; Member: Royal Mint Adv. Cttee, 1979–; Museums and Galleries Commn, 1983– (Chm., Working Party on Museum Professional Trng and Career Structure, report pubd 1987); Royal Commn for Exhibn of 1851, 1983–88. Chairman: British Soc. for Renaissance Studies, 1973–76; Advisory Cttee, Govt Art Collection, 1983–; Pres., British Assoc. of Friends of Museums, 1988–. FSA 1962; FRHistS 1968; FRSA 1974. Socio Straniero: Accademia Arcadia, 1972; Ateneo Veneto, 1987. Academicus ex Classe (Bronze Plaque Award), Academia Medicea, 1980; Commendatore, Ordine al Merito della Repubblica Italiana, 1981; Premio Bolla (services to Venice), 1982; Serena Medal, British Acad., 1986. *Publications:* England and the Italian Renaissance, 1954; The Italian Journal of Samuel Rogers, 1956; Machiavelli and Renaissance Italy, 1961; (trans. and ed) The Literary Works of Machiavelli, 1961; (ed) Certain Discourses Military by Sir John Smythe, 1964; The Evolution of British Historiography, 1964; (co-ed) Europe in the Late Middle Ages, 1965; Renaissance Exploration, 1968; Renaissance Europe 1480–1520, 1971; (ed) Renaissance Venice, 1973; Italian Renaissance Painting, 1977; Renaissance Fortification: art or engineering?, 1978; Florence and the Medici: the pattern of control, 1977; The Travel Journal of Antonio de Beatis, 1979; (ed) A Concise Encyclopaedia of the Italian Renaissance, 1981; Renaissance War Studies, 1983; (with M.E. Mallett) The Military Organisation of a Renaissance State: Venice *c* 1400–1617, 1984; War and Society in Renaissance Europe 1450–1620, 1985 (Edmund Gardner Prize, London Univ., 1983–87); Artists and Warfare in the Renaissance, 1990; contributor: New Cambridge Modern History, vols 1, 2, 3; The History of the King's Works vol. 4; Past and Present; Studi Veneziani, Italian Studies, etc. *Recreation:* Venice. *Address:* 26 Montpelier Row, Twickenham, Mddx TW1 2NQ. *T:* 081–892 9636. *Club:* Beefsteak.

HALE, Kathleen, (Mrs Douglas McClean), OBE 1976; artist; illustrator and author of books for children; *b* 24 May 1898; *d* of Charles Edward Hale and Ethel Alice Aylmer Hughes; *m* 1926, Dr Douglas McClean (*d* 1967); two *s*. *Educ:* Manchester High Sch. for Girls; Manchester Sch. of Art; Art Dept (scholar) of University Coll., Reading; Central Sch. of Art; East Anglian Sch. of Painting and Drawing. Has exhibited paintings at: New English Art Club, Whitechapel Art Gallery, London Group, Grosvenor Galleries, Vermont Gallery, Warwick Public Library Gallery; Gallery Edward Harvane, New Grafton Gallery, Parkin Gallery; metal groups and pictures at: Lefèvre Galleries; Leicester Galleries; Oxford Arts Council, Arts Centre; Mural for South Bank (Festival) Schs Section, 1951; Orlando Ballet for Festival Gardens, 1951; contrib. ballet exhibn and exhibited Orlando Ballet costume and scenery designs, V & A Museum. *Publications:* The Orlando The Marmalade Cat Series, since 1938: Camping Holiday; Trip Abroad; Buys a Farm; Becomes a Doctor; Silver Wedding; Keeps a Dog; A Seaside Holiday; The Frisky Housewife; Evening Out; Home Life; Invisible Pyjamas; The Judge; Zoo; Magic Carpet; Country Peep-Show; Buys a Cottage; and The Three Graces; Goes to the Moon; and the Water Cats; Henrietta, the Faithful Hen, 1946; Puss-in-Boots Peep-Show, 1950; Manda, 1952; Henrietta's Magic Egg, 1973. TV and radio programmes. *Recreation:* painting. *Address:* Tod House, Forest Hill, near Oxford OX9 1EH. *T:* Wheatley (08677) 4552.

HALE, Norman Morgan; Under Secretary, Department of Health (formerly of Health and Social Security), since 1975; *b* 28 June 1933; *s* of late T. N. Hale and Mrs A. E. Hale, Evesham, Worcs; *m* 1965, Sybil Jean (*née* Maton); one *s* one *d*. *Educ:* Prince Henry's Grammar Sch., Evesham; St John's Coll., Oxford (MA). Min. of Pensions and National Insurance, 1955; Asst Sec., Nat. Assistance Bd, 1966; Min. of Social Security, 1966; CSD, 1970–72. *Address:* c/o Department of Health, Alexander Fleming House, Elephant and Castle, SE1 6BY.

HALE, Raymond, IPFA; County Treasurer, Leicestershire County Council, since 1977; *b* 4 July 1936; *s* of Tom Raymond Hale and Mary Jane (*née* Higgin); *m* 1959, Ann Elvidge; one *s*. *Educ:* Baines Grammar Sch., Poulton-le-Fylde. Lancashire CC, 1952–54; served Royal Air Force, 1954–56; Lancashire CC, 1956–61; Nottinghamshire CC, 1961–65; Leicestershire CC, 1965–. *Recreations:* Rugby, cricket, gardening. *Address:* Greenacres, 139 Swithland Lane, Rothley, Leics LE7 7SH. *T:* Leicester (0533) 302230.

HALES, Prof. (Charles) Nicholas, PhD, MD; FRCPath; FRCP; Professor of Clinical Biochemistry, University of Cambridge, since 1977; *b* 25 April 1935; *s* of late Walter Bryan Hales and Phyllis Marjory Hales; *m* 1st, 1959, Janet May Moss; two *s*; 2nd, 1978, Margaret Griffiths; one *d*. *Educ:* King Edward VI Grammar Sch., Stafford; Univ. of Cambridge (BA 1956, MB, BChir, MA 1959, PhD 1964, MD 1971). MRCPath 1971, FRCPath 1980; MRCP 1971, FRCP 1976. House Surgeon, UCH, 1959, House Physician, 1960; Stothert Res. Fellow, Royal Soc., 1963–64; Lectr, Dept of Biochem., Univ. of Cambridge, 1964–70; Clinical Asst, Addenbrooke's Hosp., Cambridge, 1961–68, Hon. Consultant in Clin. Biochem, 1968–70; Prof. of Med. Biochem., Welsh National Sch. of Medicine, Cardiff, and Hon. Consultant in Med. Biochem., University Hosp. of Wales, Cardiff, 1970–77. Consultant in Med. Biochem., South Glam Health Authority (T). Mem., MRC, 1988–90. Lectures: Banting Meml, British Diabetic Assoc., 1991; Croonian, RCP, 1992. Medal, Soc., for Endocrinology, 1981; Foundn Award, Assoc. of Clin. Biochemists, 1991. *Recreations:* music, fishing. *Address:* Department of Clinical Biochemistry, Addenbrooke's Hospital, Hills Road, Cambridge CB2 2QR. *T:* Cambridge (0223) 336787.

HALES, Prof. Frederick David, FEng 1990; FIMechE, FIMA; Professor of Surface Transport, since 1968, and Dean of Engineering, since 1989, Loughborough University of Technology, *b* 19 Dec. 1930; *s* of Christina Frances and Frederick David Hales; *m* 1955, Pamela Hilary Warner; one *s* one *d* (and one *d* decd). *Educ:* Kingswood Grammar Sch.; Bristol Univ. (BSc Hons Maths, PhD). MBCS, Sigma Xi. Asst Chief Aerodynamicist, Bristol Aircraft, 1953–60; Group Research Head, MIRA, 1960–67; Vis. Scientist, Stevens Inst., Hoboken, 1967–68; Loughborough University: Hd of Dept of Transport Technology, 1982–89; Pro-Vice-Chancellor, 1984–85, Sen. Pro-Vice-Chancellor,

1985–87; acting Vice-Chancellor, 1987–88. Mem., Tech. Adv. Council to Ford Motor Co., 1985–; Scientific Visitor to Dept of Transport, 1986–90. *Publications:* papers on dynamics and vehicle control and stability. *Recreations:* sailing, bridge, wine. *Address:* 14 Kenilworth Avenue, Loughborough, Leics LE11 0SL. *T:* Loughborough (0509) 261767. *Clubs:* Rutland Sailing, Clyde Cruising.

HALES, Prof. Nicholas; *see* Hales, Prof. C. N.

HALEY, Prof. Keith Brian, PhD; FIMA, CEng, FIProdE, FOR; Professor of Operational Research since 1968, Head, Centre for Ergonomics and Operational Research, since 1990, and Director, Centre of Applied Gerontology, since 1991, Birmingham University; *b* 17 Nov. 1933; *s* of Arthur Leslie Haley and Gladys Mary Haley; *m* 1960, Diana Elizabeth Mason; one *s*. *Educ:* King Edward VI, Five Ways, Birmingham; Birmingham Univ. (BSc, PhD). FIMA 1970; FOR 1976. OR Scientist, NCB, 1957–59; Birmingham University: Lectr, 1959–63; Sen. Lectr, 1963–68; Head, Dept of Engrg Prodn, 1981–89. Pres., ORS, 1982–83; Vice Pres., IFORS, 1983–86; Editor, Jl of ORS, 1972–80. Governor, Bromsgrove Sch., 1968–. *Publications:* Mathematical Programming for Business and Industry, 1966; Operational Research '75, 1976; Operational Research '78, 1979; Search Theory and Applications, 1980; Applied Operations Research in Fishing, 1981; many articles. *Recreations:* squash, bridge. *Address:* 22 Eymore Close, Selly Oak, Birmingham B29 4LB. *T:* 021–475 3331. *Club:* Royal Over-Seas League.

HALEY, Prof. Kenneth Harold Dobson, FBA 1987; Professor of Modern History, Sheffield University, 1962–82, now Emeritus Professor; *b* 19 April 1920; *s* of Alfred Harold Dobson Haley and Winifred Hetty Haley (*née* Beale); *m* 1948, Iris (*née* Houghton); one *s* two *d*. *Educ:* Huddersfield College; Balliol College, Oxford (MA, BLitt). University of Sheffield: Asst Lectr in Modern History, 1947, later Lectr, Sen. Lectr and Prof.; Dean, Faculty of Arts, 1979–81. Member: Anglo-Netherlands Mixed Cultural Commn, 1976–82; William and Mary Tercentenary Trust, 1985–89. *Publications:* William of Orange and the English Opposition 1672–1674, 1953, repr. 1975; The First Earl of Shaftesbury, 1968; The Dutch in the Seventeenth Century, 1972 (Dutch trans. 1979); Politics in the Reign of Charles II, 1985; An English Diplomat in the Low Countries: Sir William Temple and John de Witt 1665–1672, 1986; The British and the Dutch, 1988; articles in historical jls. *Recreations:* watching cricket, playing chess. *Address:* 15 Haugh Lane, Sheffield S11 9SA. *T:* Sheffield (0742) 361316.

HALFORD, Maj.-Gen. Michael Charles Kirkpatrick, DSO 1946; OBE 1957 (MBE 1944); DL; *b* 28 Oct. 1914; *s* of Lieut-Col M. F. Halford, OBE, and Violet Halford (*née* Kirkpatrick); *m* 1945, Pamela Joy (*née* Wright); three *s*. *Educ:* Wellington Coll.; Trinity Coll., Cambridge. Commissioned Royal Guernsey Militia, 1932; 2nd Lieut York and Lancaster Regt, 1935; served Egypt and Palestine, 1936; France 1940; N Africa, Italy, France and Germany; comd Hallamshire Bn, York and Lancaster Regt, 1945, 1st Bn, 1954; Asst Army Instr, Imperial Defence Coll., 1957; comd 147 Inf. Bde (TA), 1960; GOC 43 (Wessex) Div./District, 1964–67; retd, 1967. Representative Col The York and Lancaster Regt, 1966–79. DL Hants 1975. *Recreations:* fishing, golf. *Club:* Army and Navy.

HALFORD-MacLEOD, Aubrey Seymour, CMG 1958; CVO 1965; HM Diplomatic Service, retired; *b* 15 Dec. 1914; *o s* of late Joseph and Clara Halford; changed name by deed poll from Halford to Halford-MacLeod, 1964; *m* 1939, Giovanna Mary, *o d* of late W. H. Durst; three *s* one *d*. *Educ:* King Edward's Sch., Birmingham; Magdalen Coll., Oxford. Entered HM Diplomatic (subseq. Foreign, now again Diplomatic) Service as Third Sec., 1937; Bagdad, 1939; Second Sec., 1942; transferred to Office of Minister Resident in N Africa, 1943; First Sec., 1943; British mem. of Secretariat of Advisory Council for Italy, 1944; British High Commission in Italy, 1944; Asst Political Adviser to Allied Commission in Italy, Sept. 1944, Political Adviser, 1945; transferred to HM Foreign Office, 1946, Principal Private Sec. to Permanent Under-Sec.; Dep. Exec. Sec. to Preparatory Commission for Council of Europe, May 1949, and promoted Counsellor; Dep. Sec. Gen. of the Council of Europe, 1949–52; Counsellor, HM Embassy, Tokyo, 1953–55; in charge of HM Legation, Seoul, 1954; Counsellor at HM Embassy in Libya, 1955–57; HM Political Agent at Kuwait, 1957–59; HM Consul-Gen., Munich, 1959–65; HM Ambassador to Iceland, 1966–70. Foreign Affairs Adviser, Scottish Council (Develt and Ind.), 1971–78. Dir, Scottish Opera, 1971–78. Pres., Scottish Soc. for Northern Studies, 1973–76. Vice-Pres., Clan MacLeod Soc. of Scotland, 1976–79. *Publication:* (with G. M. Halford) The Kabuki Handbook, 1956. *Recreations:* fishing, shooting, ornithology. *Address:* Mulag House, Ardvourlie, N Harris PA85 3AB. *T:* Harris (0859) 2054.

HALFPENNY, Ven. Brian Norman, CB 1990; Team Rector of Redditch, since 1991; *b* 7 June 1936; *s* of Alfred Ernest Halfpenny and Fanny Doris Halfpenny (*née* Harman); *m* 1961, Hazel Beatrice Cross; three *d*. *Educ:* George Dixon Grammar Sch., Birmingham; St John's Coll., Oxford (BA 1960; MA 1964); Wells Theol Coll. Curate, Melksham, 1962–65; Chaplain, RAF, 1965–91; served RAF Stations Cosford, Wildenrath, Leeming, Hong Kong, Brize Norton, Halton, Akrotiri; RAF Coll., Cranwell, 1982–83; Asst Chaplain-in-Chief, Support Comd, 1983–85, Strike Comd, 1985–88; QHC 1985; Chaplain-in-Chief and Archdeacon, RAF, 1988–91. Canon and Prebendary, Lincoln Cathedral, 1989–. *Recreations:* music, theatre, running. *Address:* St Luke's Rectory, 69 Evesham Road, Redditch B97 4JX. *T:* Redditch (0527) 45521. *Clubs:* Royal Air Force; Oxford Union Society.

HALIFAX, 3rd Earl of, *cr* 1944; **Charles Edward Peter Neil Wood;** Bt 1784; Viscount Halifax, 1866; Baron Irwin, 1925; JP, DL; *b* 14 March 1944; *s* of 2nd Earl of Halifax and Ruth (*d* 1989), *d* of late Captain Rt Hon. Neil James Archibald Primrose, MC, sometime MP; *S* father, 1980; *m* 1976, Camilla, *d* of C. F. J. Younger, *qv*; one *s* one *d*. *Educ:* Eton; Christ Church, Oxford. Contested (C) Dearne Valley, Feb. and Oct. 1974. Director: Hambros Bank, 1978–; Yorkshire Post Newspapers, 1985–. High Steward of York Minster, 1988–. JP Wilton Beacon, 1986, DL Humberside, 1983. *Heir: s* Lord Irwin, *qv*. *Address:* Garrowby, York YO4 1QD. *Clubs:* White's, Pratt's.

HALIFAX (NS), Archbishop of, (RC), since 1967; **Most Rev. James Martin Hayes;** *b* 27 May 1924; *s* of late L. J. Hayes. *Educ:* St Mary's Univ., Halifax; Holy Heart Seminary, Halifax; Angelicum Univ., Rome. Asst, St Mary's Basilica, 1947–54; Chancellor and Sec. of Archdiocese of Halifax, 1957–65; Rector, St Mary's Basilica, 1963–65; Auxil. Bp of Halifax, 1965–66; Apostolic Administrator of Archdiocese of Halifax, 1966–67. Pres., Canadian Conf. of Catholic Bishops, 1987–89. Hon. DLitt St Anne's Coll., Church Point, NS, 1966; Hon. DTh King's Coll., Halifax, NS, 1967; Hon. DHL Mount St Vincent Univ., Halifax, 1985; Hon. LLD: St Mary's Univ., Halifax, 1985; St Thomas Univ., 1989; Hon. DD Atlantic Sch. of Theol., Halifax, 1986. *Address:* 6541 Coburg Road, PO Box 1527, Halifax, Nova Scotia B3J 2Y3, Canada. *T:* 902–429–9388.

HALIFAX, Archdeacon of; *see* Hallatt, Ven. D. M.

HALL, Adam; *see* Trevor, Elleston.

HALL, Rt. Rev. Albert Peter; *see* Woolwich, Bishop Suffragan of.

HALL, Alfred Charles, CBE 1977 (OBE 1966); HM Diplomatic Service, retired; *b* 2 Aug. 1917; *s* of Alfred Hall and Florence Mary Hall; *m* 1945, Clara Georgievna Strunina, Moscow; five *s* one *d*. *Educ:* Oratory Sch.; Polytechnic of Central London; Open Univ. (BA). Served War, RA and Intell. Corps, 1939–43. LCC, 1934–39 and 1946–49; FO, with service in Saudi Arabia, Algeria, Egypt, Iran and USSR, 1943–46; FCO (formerly CRO and CO), with service in Pakistan, India, Nigeria, Canada and Australia, 1949–75; Dep. High Comr in Southern India, 1975–77. Grants Officer, SCF, 1979–82. *Publications:* freelance journalism and technical papers. *Recreations:* music, reading, politics. *Address:* White Cliff, St Margaret's Bay, Kent CT15 6HR. *T:* Dover (0304) 852230. *Club:* Commonwealth Trust.

HALL, Prof. Alfred Rupert, LittD; FBA 1978; Professor of the History of Science and Technology, Imperial College of Science and Technology, University of London, 1963–80; *b* 26 July 1920; *s* of Alfred Dawson Hall and Margaret Ritchie; *m* 1st, 1942, Annie Shore Hughes; two *d*; 2nd, 1959, Marie Boas. *Educ:* Alderman Newton's Boy's Sch., Leicester; Christ's Coll., Cambridge (scholar). LittD Cantab 1975. Served in Royal Corps of Signals, 1940–45. 1st cl. Historical Tripos Part II, 1946; Allen Scholar, 1948; Fellow, Christ's Coll., 1949–59, Steward, 1955–59; Curator, Whipple Science Mus., Cambridge and University Lectr, 1950–59. Medical Research Historian, University of Calif, Los Angeles, 1959–60, Prof. of Philosophy, 1960–61; Prof. of History and Logic of Science, Indiana Univ., 1961–63. Royal Society Lectures: Wilkins, 1973; Leeuwenhoek, 1988. FRHistS. Pres., British Soc. for History of Science, 1966–68; Pres., Internat. Acad. of the History of Science, 1977–81; Wellcome Trust: Chm., Adv. Panel on History of Medicine, 1974–80; Co-ordinator, History of Medicine, 1981–85. Co-editor, A History of Technology, 1951–58. Corresp. Mem., Soc. for the History of Technology, 1970. Silver Medal, RSA, 1974; (jtly) Sarton Medal, History of Science Soc., 1981. *Publications:* Ballistics in the Seventeenth Century, 1952; The Scientific Revolution, 1954; From Galileo to Newton, 1963; The Cambridge Philosophical Society: a history, 1819–1969, 1969; Philosophers at War, 1980; Short History of the Imperial College, 1982; The Revolution in Science 1500–1750, 1983; Henry More: Magic, Religion and Experiment, 1990; with Marie Boas Hall: Unpublished Scientific Papers of Isaac Newton, 1962; Correspondence of Henry Oldenburg, 1965–86; (with Laura Tilling) Correspondence of Isaac Newton, vols 5–7, 1974–77; (ed with Norman Smith) History of Technology, 1976–83; (with B. A. Bembridge) Physic and Philanthropy: a history of the Wellcome Trust, 1986. Contributor to Isis, Annals of Science, etc. *Address:* 14 Ball Lane, Tackley, Oxford OX5 3AG. *T:* Tackley (086983) 257.

HALL, Anthony Stewart, (Tony); Director, Central Council for Education and Training in Social Work, since 1986; *b* 26 Oct. 1945; *s* of Dora Rose Ellen Hall (*née* Rundle) and Albert Hall; *m* 1968, Phoebe Katharine Souster; one *s* one *d*. *Educ:* Gillingham Grammar School; London Sch. of Economics (BScSoc). Research Student, LSE, 1968–71; Lectr in Management and Organisation Studies, Nat. Inst. for Social Work, 1971–73; Lectr in Social Admin, Univ. of Bristol, 1973–78; Dir, Assoc. of British Adoption and Fostering Agencies, 1978–80; Dir and Sec., British Agencies for Adoption and Fostering, 1980–86. *Publications:* A Management Game for the Social Service (with J. Algie), 1974; The Point of Entry: a study of client reception in the social services, 1975; (ed) Access to Birth Records: the impact of S.26 of the Children Act 1975, 1980; (with Phoebe Hall) Part-time Social Work, 1980; (series editor) Child Care Policy and Practice, 1982–86; chapters in books and articles in professional and learned jls. *Recreations:* photography, genealogy, watching sport and old films. *Address:* 115 Babington Road, Streatham, SW16 6AN. *T:* 081–769 1504.

HALL, Anthony William, (Tony); Director, News and Current Affairs, BBC, since 1990; *b* 3 March 1951; *s* of Donald William Hall and Mary Joyce Hall; *m* 1977, Cynthia Lesley Hall (*née* Davis); one *s* one *d*. *Educ:* King Edward's Sch., Birmingham; Birkenhead Sch., Merseyside; Keble Coll., Oxford (Exhibnr; MA). Joined BBC as News trainee, 1973; Producer: World Tonight, 1976; New York (Radio), 1977; Sen. Producer, World at One, 1978; Output Editor, Newsnight, 1980; Sen. Producer, Six O'Clock News, 1984; Asst Editor, Nine O'Clock News, 1985; Editor: News and Election '87, 1987; News and Current Affairs, BBC TV, 1988–90. Liveryman, Painter Stainers' Co., 1989–. *Publications:* King Coal: a history of the miners, 1981; Nuclear Politics, 1984; articles in various periodicals. *Recreations:* reading and writing books, church architecture, opera, walking in Dorset. *Address:* c/o BBC TV Centre, Wood Lane, W12. *T:* 081–743 8000.

HALL, Sir Arnold (Alexander), Kt 1954; FRS 1953; MA; FEng; Chairman, Hawker Siddeley Group plc, 1967–86 (Director, 1955, Vice-Chairman, 1963–67, Managing Director, 1963–81; Executive Chairman, 1967–84); Managing Director, Bristol Siddeley Engines, 1959–63; former Chairman: Hawker Siddeley Diesels Ltd; Hawker Siddeley Electric Ltd; Hawker Siddeley Canada Inc.; Hawker Siddeley Rail Ltd; *b* 23 April 1915. *Educ:* Clare Coll., Cambridge (Rex Moir Prize in Engineering, John Bernard Seely Prize in Aeronautics, Ricardo Prize in Thermodynamics). Res. Fellow in Aeronautics of the Company of Armourers and Brasiers (held at University of Cambridge), 1936–38; Principal Scientific Officer, Royal Aircraft Establishment, Farnborough, Hants, 1938–45; Zaharoff Prof. of Aviation, University of London, and Head of Dept of Aeronautics, Imperial Coll. of Science and Technology, 1945–51; Dir of the Royal Aircraft Establishment, Farnborough, 1951–55. Chm., Fasco Industries Inc., 1980–81. Pres., Royal Aeronautical Society, 1958–59, Hon. Fellow, 1965; Dep. Pres., BEAMA, 1966–67, Pres., 1967–68; Vice-Pres., Engineering Employers' Fedn, 1968–80, 1984–86; President: Locomotive and Allied Manufacturers Assoc. of GB, 1968–69, 1969–70; SBAC, 1972–73. Member: Advisory Council on Scientific Policy, 1962–64; Air Registration Board, 1963–73; Electricity Supply Research Council, 1963–72; Advisory Council on Technology (Min. of Technology), 1964–67; Defence Industries Council, 1969–77; Industrial Develt Adv. Bd, 1973–75; Dep. Chm., Engineering Industries Council, 1975–86. Director: Lloyds Bank, 1966–85; Lloyds Bank UK Management Ltd, 1979–84; Phoenix Assurance, 1969–85; ICI, 1970–85; Onan Corp., 1976–80; Rolls-Royce Ltd, 1983–88; Royal Ordnance, 1984–86. Pro-Chancellor, Warwick Univ., 1965–70; Chancellor, Loughborough Univ. of Technology, 1980–89. Chm. Bd of Trustees, Science Museum, 1983–85. Freeman, City of London, 1988. Fellow, Imperial Coll. of Science and Technology, 1963–; Founder Fellow, Fellowship of Engineering, 1976 (Vice-Pres., 1977); For. Associate, US Nat. Acad. of Engrg, 1976–; Hon. Fellow, Clare Coll., Cambridge, 1966; Hon. ACGI; Hon. FRAeS; Hon. FAIAA; Hon. MIMechE, 1968; Hon. FIEE, 1975; Hon. DTech Loughborough 1976; Hon. DSc: London, 1980; Cambridge, 1986. Gold Medal, RAeS, 1962; Hambro Award (Business Man of the Year), 1975; Gold Medal, BIM, 1981; Albert Medal, RSA, 1983. *Address:* Wakehams, Dorney, near Windsor, Berks SL4 6QD.

HALL, Arthur Herbert; Librarian and Curator, Guildhall Library and Museum, and Director of Guildhall Art Gallery, 1956–66; retired; *b* 30 Aug. 1901; *y s* of Henry and Eliza Jane Hall, Islington, London; *m* 1927, Dorothy Maud (*née* Barton); two *s* one *d*. *Educ:* Mercers' Sch., Holborn, London. Entered Guildhall Library as junior asst, 1918; Dep. Librarian, 1943–56. Hon. Librarian, Clockmakers' and Gardeners' Companies, 1956–66. Served with RAOC, 1942–46. Chm. Council, London and Middlesex

Archæological Soc., 1957–64, Vice-Pres., 1962–; Member: Council of London Topographical Soc., 1960–67; Exec. Cttee, Friends of Nat. Libraries, 1965–69. Hon. Sec., Middlesex Victoria County History Council, 1966–78; Enfield Archaeological Soc. (Hon. Sec., 1966–71); Master, 1974–75, Hon. Clerk, 1965–74, Asst Hon. Clerk, 1975–86, Civic Guild of Old Mercers. Liveryman of the Clockmakers Co.; FLA 1930; FSA 1963.

HALL, Sir Basil (Brodribb), KCB 1977 (CB 1974); MC 1945; TD 1952; Member, European Commission of Human Rights, since 1985; Legal Adviser, Broadcasting Complaints Commission, since 1981; *b* 2 Jan. 1918; *s* of late Alfred Brodribb Hall and of Elsie Hilda Hall, Woking, Surrey; *m* 1955, Jean Stafford Gowland; two *s* one *d. Educ:* Merchant Taylors' Sch. Articled Clerk with Gibson & Weldon, Solicitors, 1935–39; admitted Solicitor, 1942. Served War of 1939–45: Trooper, Inns of Court Regt, 1939; 2nd Lieut, 12th Royal Lancers, 1940; Captain, 27th Lancers, 1941; Major, 27th Lancers, 1942. Legal Asst, Treasury Solicitor's Dept, 1946; Sen. Legal Asst, 1951; Asst Treasury Solicitor, 1958; Principal Asst Solicitor, 1968; Dep. Treasury Solicitor, 1972; HM Procurator Gen. and Treasury Solicitor, 1975–80. Chm., Civil Service Appeal Bd, 1981–84 (Dep. Chm., 1980–81). Mem. Council, Nat. Army Museum, 1981–. *Recreations:* military history, travel. *Address:* Woodlands, 16 Danes Way, Oxshott, Surrey KT22 0LX. *T:* Oxshott (0372) 2032. *Club:* Athenæum.

HALL, Very Rev. Bernard, SJ; Rector, Collegio San Roberto Bellarmino, Rome, 1976–82 and since 1989; *b* 17 Oct. 1921. *Educ:* St Michael's Coll., Leeds; Heythrop Coll., Oxford. LicPhil, STL. Captain RA, 1941–46. Entered Society of Jesus, 1946; ordained priest, 1955; Provincial of the English Province, Society of Jesus, 1970–76; English Asst to Father General, SJ, Rome, 1982–88. *Address:* via del Seminario 120, 00186 Rome, Italy.

HALL, Betty, CBE 1977; Regional Nursing Officer, West Midlands Regional Health Authority, 1974–81; *b* 6 June 1921; *d* of John Hall and Jane (*née* Massey), Eagley, Lancs. *Educ:* Bolton Sch.; Royal Infirm., Edinburgh (RGN); Radcliffe Infirm., Oxford and St Mary's Hosp., Manchester (SCM); Royal Coll. of Nursing (RNT). Nursed tuberculous patients from concentration camps, Rollier Clinic, Leysin, 1948–49; Ward Sister, Salford Royal Hosp., 1949–51; Sister Tutor, Royal Masonic Hosp., London, 1952–54; Principal Tutor, St Luke's Hosp., Bradford, 1954–61 (Mem. Leeds Area Nurse Trng Cttee); King Edward's Hosp. Fund Admin. Staff Coll., 1961–62; Work Study Officer to United Bristol Hosps, 1961–64; Asst Nursing Officer to Birmingham Regional Hosp. Bd, 1964–65, Regional Nursing Officer, 1966–81. Mem., Exec. Cttee, Grange-over-Sands Abbeyfield Soc., 1982–. Hon. Sec., Grange-over-Sands RUKBA. *Recreations:* reading, tapestry making, cricket. *Address:* Chailey, Ash Mount Road, Grange-over-Sands, Cumbria LA11 6BX. *Club:* Naval and Military.

HALL, Dame Catherine (Mary), DBE 1982 (CBE 1967); FRCN; General Secretary, Royal College of Nursing of the United Kingdom, 1957–82; *b* 19 Dec. 1922; *d* of late Robert Hall, OBE and late Florence Irene Hall (*née* Turner). *Educ:* Hunmanby Hall Sch. for Girls, Filey, Yorks. Gen. Infirmary, Leeds: nursing trng, 1941–44 (SRN); Ward Sister, 1945–47; sen. nursing appts, 1949–53; midwifery trng, Leeds and Rotherham, 1948 (SCM); travelling fellowship, US and Canada, 1950–51; student in nursing administration, Royal College of Nursing, 1953–54; Asst Matron, Middlesex Hosp., London, 1954–56. Part-time Member: CIR, 1971–74; British Railways Regional Bd for London and the South East, 1975–77; Mem. GMC, 1979–89; Chm., UK Central Council for Nursing, Midwifery and Health Visiting, 1980–85. Hon. Mem., Florida Nurses Assoc., 1973. FRCN 1976. OStJ 1977. Hon. DLitt City, 1975. *Address:* Barnsfield, Barnsfield Lane, Buckfastleigh, Devon TQ11 0NP. *T:* Buckfastleigh (0364) 42504.

HALL, Christopher Myles; Editor of The Countryman, since 1981; *b* 21 July 1932; *s* of Gilbert and Muriel Hall; *m* 1957, Jennifer Bevan Keech (marr. diss. 1980); one *s* one *d. Educ:* New Coll., Oxford. 2nd cl. Hons PPE. Reporter and Feature-writer, Daily Express, 1955–58; Sub-editor and Leader-writer, Daily Mirror, 1958–61; Feature-writer and Leader-writer, Daily Herald/Sun, 1961–65; Special Asst (Information): to Minister of Overseas Develt, 1965–66; to Minister of Transport, 1966–68; Chief Information Officer, MoT, 1968; Ramblers' Association: Sec., 1969–74; Mem. Exec. Cttee, 1982–84; Vice-Chm., 1984–87; Chm., 1987–90; Pres., 1990–; Chm., Oxfordshire Area, 1984–87; Dir, Council for Protection of Rural England, 1974–80. Pres., The Holiday Fellowship, 1974–77; Vice-Chm., S Reg. Council of Sport and Recreation, 1976–82; Member: DoT Cttee of Inquiry into Operators' Licensing, 1977–79; Common Land Forum, 1984–86; Hon. Sec., Chiltern Soc., 1965–68. *Publications:* How to Run a Pressure Group, 1974; (jtly) The Countryside We Want, 1988; The Countryman's Yesterday, 1989; Scenes from The Countryman; contributions to: Motorways in London, 1969; No Through Road, 1975; The Countryman's Britain, 1976; Book of British Villages, 1980; Sunday Times Book of the Countryside, 1981; Walker's Britain, 1982; Britain on Backroads, 1985; Making Tracks, 1985; (with John Tookey) The Cotswolds, 1990; pamphlets; contrib. to Vole, The Countryman, New Statesman, New Scientist, The Geographical Magazine, Country Living, The Guardian and various jls. *Recreation:* walking in the countryside. *Address:* c/o The Countryman, Sheep Street, Burford, Oxon OX8 4LH.

HALL, David, CBE 1983; QPM 1977; Chief Constable of Humberside Police, 1976–91; *b* 29 Dec. 1930; *s* of Arthur Thomas Hall and Dorothy May Charman; *m* 1952, Molly Patricia Knight; two *s. Educ:* Richmond and East Sheen Grammar School for Boys. Joined Metropolitan Police and rose through ranks from PC to Chief Supt, 1950–68; Staff Officer to Chief Inspector of Constabulary, Col Sir Eric St Johnson, 1968; Asst Chief Constable, 1970, Dep. Chief Constable, 1976, Staffordshire Police. Vice-Pres., Assoc. of Chief Police Officers of England, Wales and NI, 1982–83, Pres. 1983–84. CBIM 1988. Freeman, City of London, 1987. OStJ 1980. *Recreations:* gardening, walking, playing the piano. *Address:* Fairlands, 1 Copper Beech Close, West Leys Park, Kemp Road, Swanland, North Humberside HU14 3LR.

HALL, Prof. David Oakley, PhD; Professor of Biology, King's College London, since 1974; *b* 14 Nov. 1935; *s* of Charles Edward Hall and Ethel Marion Oakley; *m* 1981, Peta Jacqueline Smyth; two *d. Educ:* Kearsney Coll., S Africa (matric. 1952); Univ. of Natal, SA (BSc 1957); Univ. of California, Berkeley (PhD 1962). Fellow, Johns Hopkins Med. Sch., Baltimore, USA, 1963– (Post-doctoral Fellow, 1963–64); Lectr, 1964–68, Reader, 1968–74, KCL. Vis. Sen. Res. Scientist, Princeton Univ., 1990–91. *Publications:* Photosynthesis, 1972, 5th edn 1992; Biomass, 1987; Plants as solar collectors, 1983; numerous articles in jls on photosynthesis, biomass for energy, bioproductivity and biotechnology. *Recreations:* swimming, reading, theatre. *Address:* King's College London, Campden Hill Road, W8 7AH. *T:* 071–333 4317. *Club:* Athenæum.

HALL, Denis C.; *see* Clarke Hall.

HALL, Denis Whitfield, CMG 1962; late Provincial Commissioner, Kenya; *b* 26 Aug. 1913; *s* of late H. R. Hall, Haslemere, Surrey; *m* 1940, Barbara Carman; two *s. Educ:* Dover College; Wadham Coll., Oxford. Dist Officer, Kenya, 1936; Personal Asst to Chief Native Comr, 1948; Senior Dist Comr, 1955; Provincial Comr, Coast Province, 1959. Dep. Chm., Sussex Church Campaign, 1964–73. *Recreations:* sailing, tennis, walking,

motoring. *Address:* Martins, Priory Close, Boxgrove, West Sussex. *Club:* Oxford University Yacht.

HALL, Air Marshal Sir Donald (Percy), KCB 1984 (CB 1981); CBE 1975; AFC 1963; Deputy Chairman, GEC-Marconi, since 1990; *b* 11 Nov. 1930; *s* of William Reckerby Hall and Elsie Hall; *m* 1953, Joyce (*née* Warburton); two *d. Educ:* Hull Grammar Sch. Royal Air Force Coll., 1949; flying appts until 1963; staff and command appointments, 1964–86, including: OC, No 111 Sqdn, Empire Test Pilots Sch., and RAF Akrotiri; AOC No 11 Gp; ACAS (Operational Requirements); AOC No 38 Gp; Dep. Chief, Defence Staff. Chm., Marconi Defence Systems, 1987–89. *Recreations:* flying, walking, swimming. *Address:* c/o Lloyds Bank, Cox's and King's Branch, 6 Pall Mall, SW1. *Club:* Royal Air Force.

HALL, Sir Douglas (Basil), 14th Bt *cr* 1687; KCMG 1959 (CMG 1958); *b* 1 Feb. 1909; *s* of late Capt. Lionel Erskine Hall and late Jane Augusta Hall (*née* Reynolds); *S* brother, Sir Neville Hall, 13th Bt, 1978; *m* 1933, Rachel Marion Gartside-Tippinge (*d* 1990); one *s* two *d* (and one *s* decd). *Educ:* Radley Coll.; Keble Coll., Oxford (MA). Joined Colonial Admin. Service, 1930; posted to N Rhodesia as Cadet; District Officer, 1932; Senior District Officer, 1950; Provincial Commr, 1953; Administrative Sec., 1954; Sec. for Native Affairs to Government of Northern Rhodesia, 1956–59, Acting Chief Sec. for a period during 1958; Governor and C-in-C, Somaliland Protectorate, 1959–60. JP Co. Devon, 1964, Chm., Kingsbridge Petty Sessional Div., 1971–79. *Publications:* various technical articles. *Recreation:* vintage cars. *Heir: s* John Douglas Hoste Hall [*b* 7 Jan. 1945; *m* 1972, Angela Margaret, *d* of George Keys; two *s*]. *Address:* Barnford, Ringmore, near Kingsbridge, Devon. *T:* Bigbury-on-Sea (0548) 810401.

HALL, Duncan; Chief Executive, Teesside Development Corporation, since 1987; *b* 2 Sept. 1947; *s* of Leslie and Joan Elizabeth Hall; *m* 1970, Jane Elizabeth Menzies; two *s* one *d. Educ:* Acklam Hall Grammar Sch. LLB Hons. Articled Clerk and Senior Legal Assistant, Wellingborough UDC, 1970–74; Corby District Council: PA to Chief Exec., 1974–75; Asst Chief Exec., 1975–78; Housing and Property Controller, 1978–79; Chief Exec., 1980–87. CBIM; FRSA. *Recreations:* reading, travel, music, theatre, shooting. *Address:* Teesside Development Corporation, Tees House, Riverside Park, Middlesbrough, Cleveland TS2 1RE. *T:* Middlesbrough (0642) 230636.

HALL, Maj.-Gen. Edward Michael, CB 1970; MBE 1943; DL; *b* 16 July 1915; *s* of late Brig. E. G. Hall, CB, CIE; *m* 1948, Nina Diana (*née* McArthur); three *s. Educ:* Sherborne; RMA; Peterhouse, Cambridge. Commissioned RE, 1935; BA (Cantab) 1937. Served 1939–46, with Royal Bombay Sappers and Miners; Western Desert, India, Burma. CRE, 10th Armd and 3rd Inf. Div., 1957–59; Comd Training Bde, RE, 1962–63; Chief of Staff, Western Command, 1965–66; Military Deputy to Head of Defence Sales, 1966–70. Col Comdt, RE, 1973–76. Comdr and Comr, St John Ambulance, Cornwall, 1971–80. DL Cornwall, 1971, High Sheriff of Cornwall, 1985–86. KStJ 1981. *Recreation:* country pursuits. *Address:* Treworgey Manor, Liskeard, Cornwall.

HALL, Prof. Edward Thomas, CBE 1988; Professor, Research Laboratory for Archaeology and the History of Art, Oxford University, 1975–89, now Emeritus Professor of Archaeological Sciences (Director 1954–89); Fellow of Worcester College, Oxford, 1969–89, now Emeritus; *b* 10 May 1924; *s* of late Lt-Col Walter D'Arcy Hall, MC, and of Ann Madelaine Hall; *m* 1957, Jennifer (Jeffie) Louise de la Harpe; two *s. Educ:* Eton; Oxford Univ. BA 1948, MA 1953, DPhil 1953, Oxon; FPhysS. Dir, GEC plc, 1988–90. Designer and manufacturer of scientific apparatus, Littlemore, Oxford, 1952–. Member: Science Mus. Adv. Council, 1979–84; Ancient Monuments Adv. Cttee, 1984–; Hon. Scientific Cttee, Nat. Gall., 1970– (Chm., 1978–84); Trustee: Nat. Gall., 1977–84; British Museum, 1973–. Pres., Internat. Inst. of Conservation, 1989–; Mem. Court, Goldsmiths' Co., 1976, Prime Warden, 1985–86; Chm., Goldsmiths' Antique Plate Cttee, 1987–. FSA. Hon. FBA 1984. *Publications:* contrib. Archaeometry, various jls concerning science applied to archaeology. *Recreations:* the sea, collecting. *Address:* Beenhams, Littlemore, Oxford OX4 4PY. *T:* Oxford (0865) 777800; 11A Elm Park Lane, SW3 6DD. *T:* 071–352 5847; Lawnfield, Holbeton, Devon PL8 1JL. *T:* Holbeton (075530) 226.

HALL, Ernest, OBE 1986; pianist and composer, since 1954; property developer, since 1971; Chairman, Dean Clough Business, Arts and Education Centre, since 1983; *b* 19 March 1930; *s* of Ernest and Mary Elizabeth Hall; *m* 1st, 1951, June (*née* Annable); two *s* two *d*; *m* 2nd, 1975, Sarah (*née* Wellby); one *s. Educ:* Bolton County Grammar Sch.; Royal Manchester Coll. of Music (ARMCM (teacher and performer) 1950–51; Royal Patron's Fund Prize for Composition, 1951). Textile manufr, 1961–71. Member: PCFC, 1989–; TEC, Calderdale and Kirklees, 1990–. Dep. Chm., Eureka! Children's Museum, 1989–; Member: President's Cttee, Business in the Community, 1988–; Arts Council of GB, 1990–; Chm., Yorks and Humberside Arts Bd, 1991–; Pres., Yorks Business in the Arts, 1990–; Trustee: Tate in the North, 1989–; Yorkshire Sculpture Park, 1989–. Hon. Fellow, Huddersfield Polytechnic, 1989. DUniv York, 1986; Hon. DLitt Bradford, 1990; Hon. DArt Bristol Poly, 1991. Envmt Award, Business and Industry Panel, RSA, 1988; Guildhall Helping Hand, Nat. Fedn of Self-Employed and Small Businesses, 1989; Special Free Enterprise Award, Aims of Industry, 1989. *Recreations:* equestrianism, gardening, art collecting, theatre, languages. *Address:* Dean Clough, Halifax HX3 5AX. *T:* Halifax (0422) 344555.

HALL, Francis Woodall; HM Diplomatic Service, retired 1978; *b* 10 May 1918; *s* of Francis Hall and Florence Adelaide Woodall; *m* 1951, Phyllis Anne Amelia Andrews; one *s* one *d. Educ:* Taunton School. Inland Revenue, 1936–40; Admty (Alexandria, Port Said, Haifa, Freetown), 1940–46; FO, 1946; Bahrain and Baghdad, 1949; Vice-Consul, Malaga, 1950; FO, 1952; 2nd Sec., Cairo, 1955; Consul: Madrid, 1957; Zagreb, 1960; FO 1962; Consul, Stockholm, 1964; Head of Mombasa Office of British High Commn to Kenya, 1969; Consul-Gen., Alexandria, 1971–78; Hon. Consul, Seville, 1979–83. *Recreations:* music, walking. *Address:* 3 Madison Court, 120 Hataitai Road, Hataitai, Wellington, New Zealand.

HALL, Sir (Frederick) John (Frank), 3rd Bt, *cr* 1923; *b* 14 Aug. 1931; *er s* of Sir Frederick Henry Hall, 2nd Bt, and Olwen Irene, *yr d* of late Alderman Frank Collis, Stokeville, Stoke-on-Trent, and Deganwy, Llandudno; *S* father, 1949; *m* 1st, 1956, Felicity Anne (marr. diss. 1960), *d* of late Edward Rivers-Fletcher, Norwich, and of Mrs L. R. Galloway; 2nd, 1961, Patricia Ann Atkinson (marr. diss. 1967); two *d*; re-married, 1967, 1st wife, Felicity Anne Hall; two *d. Heir: b* David Christopher Hall [*b* 30 Dec. 1937; *m* 1962, Irene, *d* of William Duncan, Aberdeen; one *s* one *d*]. *Address:* Carradale, 29 Embercourt Road, Thames Ditton, Surrey KT7 0LH. *T:* 081–398 2801.

HALL, Rear-Adm. Geoffrey Penrose Dickinson, CB 1973; DSC 1943; DL; Hydrographer of the Navy 1971–75; retired; *b* 19 July 1916; *er s* of late Major A. K. D. Hall and late Mrs P. M. Hall; *m* 1945, Mary Ogilvie Carlisle; two *s* one *d. Educ:* Haileybury. Served in American waters, 1935–37 and on Nyon Patrol during Spanish Civil War; joined surveying service, 1938, served in Indian Ocean until 1939 when transf. to minesweeping in Far East; hydrographic duties, home waters, Iceland, W Africa;

navigational and minesweeping duties, Icelandic waters; transf. to Combined Ops, SE Asia; subseq. comd frigate, British Pacific Fleet; from 1947, hydrographic work: with RNZN, 1949–51; subseq. five comds i/c surveys at home and abroad; served ashore and in Atlantic, Indian Ocean, Antarctic waters (Cuthbert Peek Grant, RGS, for work in furtherance of oceanographical exploration); twice Asst Hydrographer; surveyed between S Africa and Iceland, 1965–67; Asst Dir (Naval), Hydrographic Dept, Taunton, 1970. Cadet 1934; Midshipman 1935; Sub-Lt 1938; Lieut 1939; Lt-Comdr 1945; Comdr 1953; Captain 1961; Rear-Adm. 1971. Pres., Hydrographic Soc., 1975. FRGS; FRICS. DL Lincs, 1982. *Publications:* contribs to Nature, Deep Sea Research, Internat. Hydrographic Review, Navy International. *Recreation:* country pursuits. *Address:* Manby House, Manby, Louth, Lincs LN11 8UF. *T:* South Cockerington (0507) 327777. *Clubs:* Naval and Military, Royal Navy; Lincolnshire; Louth (Louth).

HALL, Prof. Geoffrey Ronald, CBE 1985; FEng, CChem, FRSC, SFInstE; Professor, Brighton Polytechnic, since 1986 (Director, 1970–90); *b* 18 May 1928; *er s* of late Thomas Harold Hall, JP, and late Muriel Frances Hall, Douglas, IoM; *m* 1950, Elizabeth Day Sheldon; two *s* one *d*. *Educ:* Douglas High Sch., IoM; Univ. of Manchester (BSc). Research in Nuclear Science and Engineering at AERE, Harwell, 1949–56; sabbatical at Oxford Univ., 1955; Colombo Plan Expert to Indian Atomic Energy Commn, 1956–58; Reader in Nuclear Technology, Imperial Coll., London, 1958–63; Prof. of Nuclear Technology, Imperial Coll., 1963–70. Member: CNAA, 1977–82; Engineering Council, 1981–86 (Vice-Chm., 1984–85); SERC, 1982–86 (Mem., Engrg Bd, SRC, later SERC, 1978–83); NCVQ, 1986–89; Chm., Engrg Working Gp, Nat. Adv. Body for Local Authority Higher Educn, 1982–84. Mem., Educnl Counselling Service, British Council, 1988–91 (Chm., 1989–91). Dir, Macmillan Intek, 1985–89. President: British Nuclear Energy Soc., 1970–71; Inst. of Fuel, 1976–77; Founder Fellow, Fellowship of Engineering, 1976. *Publications:* papers related to nuclear science, fuels and engineering. *Recreations:* travel, caravanning, golf. *Address:* 23 Firsdown Road, Worthing BN13 3BG.

HALL, His Honour George; *see* Hall, H. G.

HALL, Rev. Canon George Rumney; Rector of the Sandringham Group of Parishes, since 1987; Domestic Chaplain, since 1987, Chaplain to The Queen, since 1989; *b* 7 Nov. 1937; *s* of John Hall; *m* 1965, Diana Lesley Brunning; one *s* one *d*. *Educ:* Brasted Place, Kent; Westcott House, Cambridge. Deacon 1962, priest 1963; Assistant Curate: St Philip's, Camberwell, 1962–65; Holy Trinity, Waltham Cross, 1965–67; Rector of Buckenham, Hassingham, Strumpshaw, dio. Norwich, 1967–74; Chaplain: St Andrew's Psychiatric Hosp., Norwich, 1967–72; HM Prison, Norwich, 1972–74; Vicar of Wymondham, 1974–87; RD of Humbleyard, 1986–87; Hon. Canon, Norwich Cathedral, 1987–; RD of Heacham and Rising, 1989–. Founder Mem., Wymondham Branch of Mind Day Centre; Mem. Bd, Cotman Housing Assoc., Norwich. *Recreations:* walking, reading, theatre, music. *Address:* The Rectory, Sandringham, Norfolk PE35 6EH. *T:* Dersingham (0485) 540587.

HALL, His Honour (Harold) George; a Circuit Judge, 1975–91; *b* 20 Sept. 1920; *s* of late Albert Hall and Violet Maud Hall (*née* Etherington); *m* 1950, Patricia Delaney; four *s* one *d*. *Educ:* Archbishop Holgate's Grammar Sch., York. RAF, 1940–46 (Flt-Lt). Called to Bar, Middle Temple, 1958; practised NE Circuit; Dep. Chm., WR Yorks QS, 1970; a Recorder, 1972–75.

HALL, Harold Percival, CMG 1963; MBE 1947; Director of Studies, Royal Institute of Public Administration, 1974–85; *b* 9 Sept. 1913; *s* of late Major George Charles Hall; *m* 1939, Margery Hall, *d* of late Joseph Dickson; three *s* (including twin *s*). *Educ:* Portsmouth Grammar Sch.; Royal Military College, Sandhurst (Prize Cadet; King's India Cadet; Hockey Blue Cricket Cap). Commissioned Indian Army, 1933. Indian Political Service, 1937–47. Private Sec. to Resident, Central India States, 1937; Magistrate and Collector, Meerut, 1938–39. Military Service, 1938–43 (Major). Staff Coll., Quetta, 1941. Asst Political Agent, Loralai, 1943, Nasirabad, 1944; Dir, Food and Civil Supplies, and Dep. Sec., Revenue, Baluchistan, 1945–46; Principal, Colonial Office, 1947; Asst Sec. (Head of Pacific and Indian Ocean Dept), Colonial Office, 1955–62; Sec., Commonwealth Royal Comn on Fedn of Malaya's independence, 1956; Seconded to Office of UK Comr-Gen. for SE Asia, 1962–63; British Dep. High Comr for Eastern Malaysia, Kuching, Sarawak, 1963–64; Asst Sec., Colonial Office, 1965–66; Assistant Under-Secretary of State: Commonwealth Office, 1966–68; MoD, 1968–73. Mem. Governing Body, Sch. of Oriental and African Studies, 1971–74. *Recreation:* gardening. *Address:* Robina, The Chase, Ringwood, Dorset BH24 2AN. *T:* Ringwood (0425) 479880.

HALL, Prof. Henry Edgar, FRS 1982; Professor of Physics, University of Manchester, since 1961; *b* 1928; *s* of John Ainger Hall; *m* 1962, Patricia Anne Broadbent; two *s* one *d*. *Educ:* Latymer Upper Sch., Hammersmith; Emmanuel Coll., Cambridge. BA 1952; PhD 1956. At Royal Society Mond Laboratory, Cambridge, 1952–58; Senior Student, Royal Commission for the Exhibition of 1851, 1955–57; Research Fellow of Emmanuel Coll., 1955–58; Lecturer in Physics, Univ. of Manchester, 1958–61. Simon Memorial Prize (with W. F. Vinen), 1963. Visiting Professor: Univ. of Western Australia, 1964; Univ. of Oregon, 1967–68; Cornell Univ., 1974, 1982–83; Univ. of Tokyo, 1985. *Publications:* Solid State Physics, 1974; papers in scientific journals. *Recreation:* mountain walking. *Address:* The Schuster Laboratory, The University, Manchester M13 9PL.

HALL, Air Vice-Marshal Hubert Desmond, CB 1979; CBE 1972; AFC 1963; RAF retd; Director of Business, Canberra Church of England Girls' Grammar School, Australia, since 1983; *b* 3 June 1925; *s* of Charles William and Violet Victoria Kate Hall; *m* 1951, Mavis Dorothea (*née* Hopkins). *Educ:* Portsmouth Municipal Coll. FBIM. Commissioned RAF, 1945; RAF Coll., Cranwell QFI, 1951–55; Flt Comdr, 9 Sqdn, 1955–56; 232 OCU Gaydon, Sqdn Ldr, Medium Bomber Force; Instructor, Wing Comdr 1962; 3 Group Headquarters (Training), 1963–65; Air Warfare Coll., 1965; commanded No 57 Sqdn (Victors), 1966–68; Gp Captain Nuclear Operations SHAPE HQ, 1968–71; comd RAF Waddington, 1971–73; Overseas Coll. of Defence Studies India, 1974; MoD: Director (Air Cdre) of Establishments, RAF, 1975–77; Air Comdr Malta, 1977–79; Air Vice-Marshal 1979; Defence Advr, Canberra, 1980–82. Queen's Commendation, 1957. Mem. Council, ACT, Aust. Inst. of Management. Mem., St John Council, ACT, 1983–; CStJ 1983. *Recreations:* shooting, gardening, reading. *Address:* 7 Richardson Street, Garran, ACT 2605, Australia; c/o Lloyds Bank, 115 Commercial Road, Portsmouth, Hants PO1 1BY. *Clubs:* Royal Air Force, Commonwealth Trust; Commonwealth (Canberra); Lord's Taverners (ACT).

HALL, Prof. James Snowdon, CBE 1976; Professor of Agriculture, Glasgow University, and Principal, West of Scotland Agricultural College, 1966–80; *b* 28 Jan. 1919; *s* of Thomas Blackburn Hall and Mary Milburn Hall; *m* 1942, Mary Smith; one *s* one *d*. *Educ:* Univ. of Durham (BSc Hons). FRAgS, FIBiol. Asst Technical Adviser, Northumberland War Agric. Exec. Commn, 1941–44; Lectr in Agriculture, Univ. of Newcastle upon Tyne, 1944–54; Principal, Cumbria Coll. of Agriculture and Forestry, 1954–66. *Address:* 26 Earls Way, Doonfoot, Ayr KA7 4HE. *T:* Alloway (0292) 41162. *Club:* Farmers'.

HALL, Her Honour Jean Graham, LLM (London); a Circuit Judge (formerly Deputy Chairman, South-East London Quarter Sessions), 1971–89; *b* 26 March 1917; *d* of Robert Hall and Alison (*née* Graham). *Educ:* Inverkeithing Sch., Fife; St Anne's Coll., Sanderstead; London Sch. of Economics. Gold Medal (Elocution and Dramatic Art), Incorporated London Acad. of Music, 1935; Teacher's Dipl., Guildhall Sch. of Music, 1937; Social Science Cert., London Sch. of Economics, 1937; LLB (Hons), London, 1950. Club Leader and subseq. Sub-Warden, Birmingham Univ. Settlement, 1937–41; Sec., Eighteen Plus (an experiment in youth work), 1941–44; Probation Officer, Hants, subseq. Croydon, 1945–51. Called to Bar, Gray's Inn, 1951. Metropolitan Stipendiary Magistrate, 1965–71. Pres., Gray's Inn Debating Soc., 1953; Hon. Sec., Soc. of Labour Lawyers, 1954–64; Pres., British Soc. of Criminology, 1971–74. Chm. Departmental Cttee on Statutory Maintenance Limits, 1966–68. Contested (Lab) East Surrey, 1955. Pres., Edridge Benevolent Trust, 1984. Hon. LLD Lincoln, USA, 1979. *Publications:* Towards a Family Court, 1971; (jtly) Child Abuse: procedure and evidence in juvenile courts, 1978, 2nd edn 1987. *Recreations:* travel, congenial debate. *Address:* 2 Dr Johnson's Buildings, Temple, EC4. *Club:* University Women's.

HALL, Joan Valerie, CBE 1990; Member, Central Transport Consultative Committee, 1981–86; *b* 31 Aug. 1935; *d* of late Robert Percy Hall and of Winifred Emily Umbers. *Educ:* Queen Margaret's Sch., Escrick, York; Ashridge House of Citizenship. Contested (C) Barnsley, 1964 and 1966. MP (C) Keighley, 1970–Feb. 1974; PPS to Minister of State for Agriculture, Fisheries and Food, 1972–74. Vice-Chm., Greater London Young Conservatives, 1964. Chm., Sudan Studies Soc. of UK, 1989–. Mem. Council, Univ. of Buckingham (formerly University Coll. Buckingham), 1977–. *Address:* Mayfields, Darton Road, Cawthorne, Barnsley, South Yorks S75 4HY. *T:* Barnsley (0226) 790230.

HALL, Sir John; *see* Hall, Sir F. J. F.

HALL, John; *see* Hall, W. J.

HALL, Sir John, Kt 1991; Chairman, Cameron Hall Developments Ltd; *m* Mae; one *s* one *d*. *Educ:* Bedlington Grammar Sch. Mining surveyor. Developed MetroCentre (shopping and leisure complex), Gateshead, 1985. Gordon Grand Fellow, Yale Univ., 1991. Hon. DCL Newcastle upon Tyne, 1988. NE Business Man of the Year, 1987. *Address:* Wynyard Hall, Billingham, Cleveland TS22 5NF.

HALL, John Anthony Sanderson, DFC 1943; QC 1967; FCIArb 1982; *b* 25 Dec. 1921; *s* of late Rt Hon. W. Glenvil Hall, PC, MP, and late Rachel Ida Hall (*née* Sanderson); *m* 1st, Nora Ella Hall (*née* Crowe) (marr. diss. 1974); one *s* two *d*; 2nd, Elizabeth Mary, widow of Alan Riley Maynard. *Educ:* Leighton Park Sch.; Trinity Hall, Cambridge (MA). Served RAF, 1940–46, 85 Squadron and 488 (NZ) Squadron (Squadron Leader; DFC and Bar). Called to Bar, Inner Temple, 1948, Master of the Bench, 1975; Western Circuit; Dep. Chm., Hants Quarter Sessions, 1967; Recorder of Swindon, 1971; a Recorder of the Crown Court, 1972–78. Member: Gen. Council of the Bar, 1964–68, 1970–74; Senate of the Four Inns of Court, 1966–68, 1970–74; Council of Legal Educn, 1970–74. Mem., 1972–79, Chm., 1978–79, UK Deleg. to Consultative Cttee, Bars and Law Socs of EEC; Mem., Foreign Compensation Commn, 1983–. Dir Gen., Internat. Fedn of Producers of Phonograms and Videograms, 1979–81. Governor, St Catherine's Sch., Bramley. *Recreations:* walking, sailing, fishing. *Address:* 2 Dr Johnson's Buildings, Temple, EC4Y 7AY; Swallows, Blewbury, Oxon. *Clubs:* Garrick, Royal Air Force.

HALL, Sir John (Bernard), 3rd Bt *cr* 1919; Managing Director, The Nikko Bank (UK) plc, since 1990; *b* 20 March 1932; *s* of Lieut-Col Sir Douglas Montgomery Bernard Hall, DSO, 2nd Bt, and Ina Nancie Walton, *d* of late Col John Edward Mellor, CB (she *m* 2nd, 1962, Col Peter J. Bradford, DSO, OBE, TD); *S* father, 1962; *m* 1957, Delia Mary, *d* of late Lieut-Col J. A. Innes, DSO; one *s* two *d*. *Educ:* Eton; Trinity Coll., Oxford (MA). FCIB 1976. Lieut, Royal Fusiliers (RARO). J. Henry Schroder Wagg & Co. Ltd, formerly J. Henry Schröder & Co., 1955–73 (Dir, 1967–73); Director: The Antofagasta (Chili) and Bolivia Rly Co. Ltd, 1967–73; Bank of America International, 1974–82; Man. Dir, European Brazilian Bank, subseq. Eurobraz, 1983–89 (Dir, 1976–89); a Vice-Pres., Bank of America NT & SA, 1982–90; Chm., Assoc. of British Consortium Banks, 1985–86. Chm., Anglo-Colombian Soc., 1978–81. FRGS 1988; FRSA 1989. Liveryman, Clothworkers' Co. (Mem., Court of Assts, 1987–). *Recreations:* travel, fishing. *Heir:* *s* David Bernard Hall, *b* 12 May 1961. *Address:* Penrose House, Patmore Heath, Albury, Ware, Herts SG11 2LT. *T:* Albury (0279) 771255. *Clubs:* Boodle's, Lansdowne, Overseas Bankers'.

HALL, Julian; His Honour Judge Julian Hall; a Circuit Judge, since 1986; *b* 13 Jan. 1939; *s* of Dr Stephen Hall, FRCP and late Dr Mary Hall, Boarstall Tower, Bucks; *m* 1st, 1968, M. Rosalind Perry (marr. diss. 1988); one *s* one *d*; 2nd, 1989, Ingrid Cecilia, *er d* of Rev. Canon Ronald Lunt, *qv*. *Educ:* Eton (Scholar); Christ Church, Oxford (Scholar; MA); Trinity Coll., Dublin (LLB). ARCM (flute). Industrial Chemist, Shell Internat. Chemical Co., 1961–63. Called to the Bar, Gray's Inn, 1966; in practice in Common Law Chambers on Northern Circuit, Manchester, 1966–86; Standing Prosecuting Counsel to Inland Revenue, Northern Circuit, 1985–86; a Recorder, 1982–86. *Recreation:* making music, in orchestras, choirs and at home. *Address:* c/o The Crown Court, 27 Guildhall Road, Northampton NN1 1DP. *T:* Northampton (0604) 21083.
See also C. E. Henderson.

HALL, (Laura) Margaret; *see* MacDougall, Laura Margaret.

HALL, Prof. Laurance David, PhD; FRS(Can) 1982; CChem, FRSC, FCIC; Herchel Smith Professor of Medicinal Chemistry, University of Cambridge, since 1984, and Professorial Fellow, Emmanuel College, since 1987; *b* 18 March 1938; *s* of Daniel William Hall and Elsie Ivy Hall; *m* 1962, Winifred Margaret (*née* Golding); two *s* two *d*. *Educ:* Leyton County High Sch.; Bristol Univ. (BSc 1959; PhD 1962); MA Cantab 1990. FCIC 1973; FRSC 1985. Post-doctoral Fellow, Ottawa Univ., 1962–63; Dept of Chemistry, Univ. of British Columbia: Instr II, 1963–64; Asst Prof., 1964–69; Associate Prof., 1969–73; Prof., 1973–84. Alfred P. Sloan Foundn Res. Fellow, 1971–73; Canada Council Killam Res. Fellow, 1982–84. Lederle Prof., RSM, 1984; Vis. Professor: Univ. of NSW, 1967; Univ. of Cape Town, 1974; Northwestern Univ., Evanston, Ill, 1982. Lectures: Van Cleave, Univ. of Saskatchewan, Regina, 1983; Cecil Green, Galveston Univ., Texas, 1983; Brotherton, Leeds Univ., 1985; Philip Morris, Richmond Univ., Va, 1985; Scott, Cambridge Univ., 1986; Larmor, Cambridge Philosophical Soc., 1986; C. B. Purves, McGill Univ., 1987; Eduard Faber Med. Physics, Univ. of Chicago, 1990. Fellow, Cambridge Philosophical Soc. Jacob Bielly Faculty Res. Prize, Univ. of BC, 1974; Tate and Lyle Award for Carbohydrate Chemistry, Chemical Soc., 1974; Merck, Sharpe and Dohme Lecture Award, Chemical Inst. of Canada, 1975; Corday Morgan Medal and Prize, Chemical Soc., 1976; Barringer Award, Spectroscopy Soc. of Canada, 1981; Interdisciplinary Award, RSC, 1988. *Publications:* over 300 research pubns. *Recreations:* sailing, skiing, wine-making, music, travel, research. *Address:* 22 Long Road, Cambridge CB2 2QS. *T:* Cambridge (0223) 211999.

HALL, Sir Laurence Charles B.; *see* Brodie-Hall.

HALL, Margaret Dorothy, OBE 1973; RDI 1974; Head of Design, British Museum, since 1964; *b* 22 Jan. 1936; *d* of Thomas Robson Hall and Millicent (*née* Britton). *Educ:* Bromley County Grammar Sch.; Bromley College of Art; Royal College of Art (DesRCA). Design Assistant: Casson, Condor & Partners, 1960–61; Westwood Piet & Partners, 1961–63; Dennis Lennon & Partners, 1963–64; British Museum, 1964–: exhibitions designed include: Masterpieces of Glass, 1968; Museum of Mankind, 1970; Treasures of Tutankhamun, 1972; Nomad and City, 1976; Captain Cook in the South Seas, 1979. Designer, Manuscripts and Men, National Portrait Gallery, 1969. Chm., Gp of Designers/Interpreters in Museums, 1978–81; Mem. Council, RSA, 1984–89. FCSD (FSIAD 1975–90; MSIAD 1968) (Chm., SIAD Salaried Designers Cttee, 1979–81). Chm., Wynkyn de Worde Soc., 1982. Governor, Ravensbourne College of Art, 1973–78. FRSA 1974; FMA 1983. *Publication:* On Display: a grammar of museum exhibition design, 1987. *Address:* The British Museum, WC1B 3DG. *T:* 071–323 8514. *Club:* Double Crown.

HALL, Michael Kilgour H.; *see* Harrison-Hall.

HALL, Prof. Michael Robert Pritchard, FRCP, FRCPE; Professor of Geriatric Medicine, University of Southampton, 1970–87, now Emeritus; Hon. Consultant Physician, Southampton University Hospitals, 1970–87; *b* 13 May 1922; *s* of Augustus Henry Hall, MC and Elizabeth Jane Lord; *m* 1947, Joan Jardine, (Eileen), *d* of Dr John McCartney; two *d*. *Educ:* Shrewsbury Sch.; Worcester Coll., Oxford (MA, BM, BCh). FRCP 1970; FRCPE 1971. Served War, Indian Army, 1941–46 (Temp. Captain). Consultant Physician, Newcastle-upon-Tyne Gen. Hosp., 1962–70; Hon. Lecturer in Medicine: Univ. of Durham, 1962–63; Univ. of Newcastle upon Tyne, 1963–70. Auckland Savings Bank Vis. Prof., Univ. of Auckland, NZ, 1974; Vis. Lecturer: Dalhousie Univ., NS, 1979; (Tayside Health Bd), Univ. of Dundee, 1981; Examr, Dip. of Geriatric Medicine, RCP, 1985–91. Chairman: British Soc. for Res. on Ageing, 1976–79; Assoc. of Professors of Geriatric Medicine, 1985–86; European Cttee, Sandoz Foundn of Gerontological Research, 1986–90 (Mem., 1990–92); Member: DHSS Cttee for Review of Medicines, 1976–82; Fitness and Health Adv. Gp to Sports Council, 1977–90; Governing Body and Exec. Cttee, Age Concern (England), 1975–77 and 1980–83; Council, Internat. Assoc. of Gerontology, 1981–85; President: Tissue Viability Soc., 1983–84; Bath Res. Inst. for Care of the Elderly, 1987–. Life Vice-Pres., Northumberland Cheshire Home, 1970; Trustee and Governor, British Foundn for Age Res., 1979–; Vice-Chm., Brendoncare Foundn, 1986–; Mem., NEC, Abbeyfield Soc., 1989– (Chm., Extra Care Cttee, 1989–90; Chm., Care and Develt Cttee, 1990–); Trustee, John McCarthy Foundn, 1987–. *Publications:* Medical Care of the Elderly, 1978, 2nd edn 1986; chapters and contribs to various books on aspects of ageing and geriatric medicine; articles and papers in med. jls. *Recreations:* fly-fishing, golf, gardening. *Address:* Peartree Cottage, Emery Down, Lyndhurst, Hants SO43 7FH. *T:* Lyndhurst (0703) 282541. *Club:* MCC.

HALL, Rt. Rev. Peter; *see* Woolwich, Bishop Suffragan of.

HALL, Peter Dalton, CB 1986; Under Secretary, Solicitor's Office, Board of Inland Revenue, 1979–86; *b* 1 Aug. 1924; *s* of Edward and Kathleen Hall; *m* 1952, Stella Iris Breen; four *s* two *d*. *Educ:* Rishworth Sch.; St Catharine's Coll., Cambridge (exhibnr; MA, LLB). Served War of 1939–45, Intelligence Corps; seconded to AIF and served with US Forces in New Guinea and Philippines; GOC Commendation; Major. Called to the Bar, Middle Temple, 1951; entered Inland Revenue Solicitor's Office, 1952. Mem., Bar Council 1967–70; Clerk to City Comrs, 1988–. Parish Councillor, 1967–. *Publications:* contrib.: Simon's Taxes; Foster's Capital Taxes Encyclopaedia. *Recreations:* cricket, gardening, music, conservation. *Address:* Apple Tree Cottage, Woughton-on-the-Green, Bucks MK6 3BE.

HALL, Peter Edward, CMG 1987; HM Diplomatic Service; Ambassador to Yugoslavia, since 1989; *b* 26 July 1938; *s* of Bernard Hall and late Monica Hall (*née* Blackbourn); *m* 1972, Marnie Kay; one *s* one *d*. *Educ:* Portsmouth Grammar Sch.; HM Services (Jt Services Sch. for Linguists); Pembroke Coll., Cambridge (Scholar; 1st Cl. parts I and II, Mediaeval and Modern Langs Tripos). Foreign Office, 1961–63; 3rd Sec., Warsaw, 1963–66; 2nd Sec., New Delhi, 1966–69; FCO (European Integration Dept), 1969–72; 1st Sec., UK Permanent Representation to EEC, 1972–76; Asst Head, Financial Relations Dept, FCO, 1976–77; Counsellor, Caracas, 1977–78; Hd of British Information Services, NY, 1978–83 and Counsellor, British Embassy, Washington, 1981–83; Dir of Res., FCO, 1983–86; Under Sec., Cabinet Office, 1986–88; Vis. Schol., Stanford Univ., 1988–89. *Recreations:* reading (A. Powell, Byron), music (Rolling Stones, Mozart). *Address:* c/o Foreign and Commonwealth Office, King Charles Street, SW1.

HALL, Prof. Peter Geoffrey, FBA 1983; Professor of City and Regional Planning, since 1980, and Director, Institute of Urban and Regional Development, since 1989, University of California, Berkeley; Professor of Geography, University of Reading, 1968–89, now Emeritus; *b* 19 March 1932; *s* of Arthur Vickers Hall and Bertha Hall (*née* Keefe); *m* 1st, 1962, Carla Maria Wartenberg (marr. diss. 1966); 2nd, 1967, Magdalena Mróz; no *c*. *Educ:* Blackpool Grammar Sch.; St Catharine's Coll., Cambridge Univ. (MA, PhD; Hon. Fellow, 1988). Asst Lectr, 1957, Lectr, 1960, Birkbeck Coll., Univ. of London; Reader in Geography with ref. to Regional Planning, London Sch. of Economics and Political Science, 1966; University of Reading: Head, Dept of Geog., 1968–80; Chm., Sch. of Planning Studies, 1971–77 and 1983–86; Dean of Urban and Regional Studies, 1975–78. Member: SE Regional Planning Council, 1966–79; Nature Conservancy, 1968–72; Transport and Road Research Laboratory Adv. Cttee on Transport, 1973–78; Environmental Bd, 1975–79; SSRC, 1975–80 (Chm., Planning Cttee); EEC Expert Gp on New Tendencies of Social and Economic Develt, 1975–77; Standing Adv. Cttee on Trunk Road Assessment, 1978–80; Exec. Cttee, Regional Studies Assoc., 1967– (Hon. Jl Editor, 1967–78); Exec. Cttee, Fabian Soc., 1964–80 (Chm. 1971–72); Governor, Centre for Environmental Studies, 1975–80. Chm., Tawney Soc., 1983–85 (Vice-Chm., 1982–83). FRGS; Hon. RTPI, 1975. Editor, Built Environment, 1977–. *Publications:* The Industries of London, 1962; London 2000, 1963 (reprint, 1969); Labour's New Frontiers, 1964; (ed) Land Values, 1965; The World Cities, 1966, 3rd edn 1984; Containment of Urban England, 1973; Urban and Regional Planning, 1974, 2nd edn 1982; Europe 2000, 1977; Great Planning Disasters, 1980; Growth Centres in the European Urban System, 1980; The Inner City in Context, 1981; Silicon Landscapes, 1985; Can Rail Save the City?, 1985; High Tech America, 1986; Cities of Tomorrow, 1988; London 2001, 1989; The Rise of the Gunbelt, 1991. *Recreations:* writing, reading, talking. *Address:* Institute of Urban and Regional Development, University of California, Berkeley, Calif 94720, USA; 14 Blandford Road, W4 1DU. *Club:* Athenæum.

HALL, Peter George; (part-time) Chairman, Snamprogetti Ltd, since 1988; *b* 10 Dec. 1924; *s* of Charles and Rosina Hall; *m* 1949, Margaret Gladys (*née* Adams); two *s* two *d*. *Educ:* Sandown, IoW, Grammar Sch.; Southampton Univ. (BScEng). FInstPet. Anglo-Iranian Oil Co., 1946–51; Esso Petroleum Co. Ltd: various positions at Fawley Refinery, 1951–63; Manager, Milford Haven Refinery, 1963–66; Employee Relations Manager, 1966–70; Vice-Pres., General Sekiyu Seisei, Tokyo, 1971–74; Asst Gen. Man., Refining, Imperial Oil Ltd, Toronto, 1974–76; Refining Man., Exxon Corp., New York, 1976–77; Director, Esso Petroleum Co. Ltd, London, 1977–78; Vice-Pres., Esso Europe Inc. London, 1979–81; Man. Dir, Esso Petroleum Co., 1982–84; Pres., Esso Norge, 1984–87. *Recreations:* opera, classical music, walking, gardening. *Address:* Oakley, Mill Lawn, Burley, Ringwood, Hants BH24 4HP.

HALL, Sir Peter (Reginald Frederick), Kt 1977; CBE 1963; director of plays, films and operas; own producing company, Peter Hall Co., formed 1988; Director, National Theatre, 1973–88; *b* Bury St Edmunds, Suffolk, 22 Nov. 1930; *s* of late Reginald Edward Arthur Hall and Grace Pamment; *m* 1956, Leslie Caron (marr. diss. 1965); one *s* one *d*; *m* 1965, Jacqueline Taylor (marr. diss. 1981); one *s* one *d*; *m* 1982, Maria Ewing (marr. diss. 1990); one *d*; *m* 1990, Nicola Frei. *Educ:* Perse Sch., Cambridge; St Catharine's Coll., Cambridge (MA Hons; Hon. Fellow, 1964). Dir, Arts Theatre, London, 1955–56 (directed several plays incl. first productions of Waiting for Godot, South, Waltz of the Toreadors); formed own producing company, International Playwrights' Theatre, 1957, and directed their first production, Camino Real; at Sadler's Wells, directed his first opera, The Moon and Sixpence, 1957. First productions at Stratford: Love's Labour's Lost, 1956; Cymbeline, 1957; first prod. on Broadway, The Rope Dancers, Nov. 1957. Plays in London, 1956–58: Summertime, Gigi, Cat on a Hot Tin Roof, Brouhaha, Shadow of Heroes; Madame de . . ., Traveller Without Luggage, A Midsummer Night's Dream and Coriolanus (Stratford), The Wrong Side of the Park, 1959; apptd Dir of Royal Shakespeare Theatre, Jan. 1960, responsible for founding RSC as a permanent ensemble, and its move to Aldwych Theatre, 1960; Man. Dir at Stratford-on-Avon and Aldwych Theatre, London, 1960–68; Co-Dir, RSC, 1968–73; Artistic Dir, Glyndebourne Fest., 1984–90. Plays produced/directed for *Royal Shakespeare Company:* Two Gentlemen of Verona, Twelfth Night, Troilus and Cressida, 1960; Ondine, Becket, Romeo and Juliet, 1961; The Collection, Troilus and Cressida, A Midsummer Night's Dream, 1962; The Wars of the Roses (adaptation of Henry VI Parts 1, 2 and 3, and Richard III), 1963 (televised for BBC, 1965); Sequence of Shakespeare's histories for Shakespeare's 400th anniversary at Stratford: Richard II, Henry IV Parts 1 & 2, Henry V, Henry VI, Edward IV, Richard III, 1964; The Homecoming, Hamlet, 1965; The Government Inspector, Staircase, 1966; The Homecoming (NY), Macbeth, 1967; A Delicate Balance, Silence and Landscape, 1969; The Battle of the Shrivings, 1970; Old Times, 1971 (NY, 1971, Vienna, 1972); All Over, Via Galactica (NY), 1972; plays produced/directed for *National Theatre:* The Tempest, 1974; John Gabriel Borkman, 1975; No Man's Land, Happy Days, Hamlet, 1975; Tamburlaine the Great, 1976; No Man's Land (NY), Volpone, Bedroom Farce, The Country Wife, 1977; The Cherry Orchard, Macbeth, Betrayal, 1978; Amadeus, 1979, NY 1981 (Tony Award for Best Director); Othello, 1980; Family Voices, The Oresteia, 1981, 1986; Importance of Being Earnest, 1982; Other Places, 1982; Jean Seberg, 1983; Animal Farm, Coriolanus, 1984; Martine, Yonadab, 1985; The Petition, 1986; Coming into Land, Antony and Cleopatra, Entertaining Strangers, 1987; The Tempest, Cymbeline, Winter's Tale, 1988; plays produced/directed for *Peter Hall Company:* Orpheus Descending, NY, 1988; Merchant of Venice, 1989; The Wild Duck, Phoenix, 1990; The Homecoming, Comedy, 1991; Twelfth Night, The Rose Tattoo, Playhouse, 1991; Tartuffe. *Films:* Work is a Four Letter Word, 1968; A Midsummer Night's Dream, Three into Two Won't Go, 1969; Perfect Friday, 1971; The Homecoming, 1973; Akenfield, 1974; She's Been Away, 1989; Orpheus Ascending, 1991; The Camomile Lawn, 1991. *Opera:* at Covent Garden: Moses and Aaron, 1965; The Magic Flute, 1966; The Knot Garden, 1970; Eugene Onegin, Tristan and Isolde, 1971; Salome, 1988; Albert Herring, 1989; at Glyndebourne: La Calisto, 1970; Il Ritorno d'Ulisse in Patria, 1972; The Marriage of Figaro, 1973, 1989; Don Giovanni, Così Fan Tutte, 1978, 1984; Fidelio, 1979; A Midsummer Night's Dream, 1981, 1989; Orfeo ed Euridice, 1982; L'Incoronazione di Poppea, 1984, 1986; Carmen, 1985; Albert Herring, 1985, 1986; Simon Boccanegra, 1986; La Traviata, 1987, 1988; Falstaff, 1988; at Metropolitan Opera, NY: Macbeth, 1982; Carmen, 1986; at Bayreuth: The Ring, 1983; at Geneva: Figaro, 1983; at Los Angeles: Salome, 1986; Così Fan Tutte, 1988; at Chicago: Figaro, 1987; Salome, 1988; at Houston: New Year (world première), 1989. *Television:* Presenter, Aquarius (LWT), 1975–77; Carmen, 1985; Oresteia (C4), L'Incoronazione di Poppea, Albert Herring, 1986; La Traviata, 1987; The Marriage of Figaro, 1989. Associate Prof. of Drama, Warwick Univ., 1966–. Mem., Arts Council, 1969–73; Founder Mem., Theatre Dirs' Guild of GB, 1983–. DUniv York, 1966; Hon. DLitt Reading, 1973; Hon. LittD: Liverpool, 1974; Leicester, 1977. Tony Award (NY) for best director, 1966; Hamburg Univ. Shakespeare Prize, 1967; Standard Special Award, 1979; Standard Award Best Director, 1981, 1987; Standard Award for outstanding achievement in Opera, 1981. Chevalier de l'Ordre des Arts et des Lettres, 1965. *Publications:* (with John Barton) The Wars of the Roses, 1970; (with Inga-Stina Ewbank) John Gabriel Borkman, an English version, 1975; Peter Hall's Diaries (ed John Goodwin), 1983; Animal Farm, a stage adaptation, 1986; (with Inga-Stina Ewbank) The Wild Duck, an English adaptation, 1990. *Recreation:* music. *Address:* Peter Hall Company Ltd, Albery Theatre, St Martin's Lane, WC2N 4AH. *Clubs:* Garrick, Royal Automobile.

HALL, Prof. Reginald, CBE 1989; MD; FRCP; Professor of Medicine, University of Wales College of Medicine (formerly Welsh National School of Medicine), 1980–89, Professor Emeritus, 1989; *b* 1 Oct. 1931; *s* of Reginald P. Hall and Maggie W. Hall; *m* 1960, Dr Molly Hill; two *s* three *d*. *Educ:* Univ. of Durham (BSc, MB BS, MD). Harkness Fellow of Commonwealth Fund, Clinical and Research Fellow in Medicine, Harvard, 1960–61; Wellcome Sen. Research Fellow in Clinical Science, 1964–67; Cons. Physician, Royal Victoria Infirmary, Newcastle upon Tyne, 1967–79; Prof. of Medicine, Univ. of Newcastle upon Tyne, 1970–79. *Publications:* Fundamentals of Clinical Endocrinology, 1969, 4th edn 1989; Atlas of Endocrinology, 1980, 2nd edn 1990. *Recreations:* bryology, literature. *Address:* 37 Palace Road, Llandaff, Cardiff CF5 2AG. *T:* Cardiff (0222) 567689.

HALL, Sir Robert de Zouche, KCMG 1953 (CMG 1952); MA; FSA; *b* 27 April 1904; *s* of late Arthur William Hall, Liverpool; *m* 1932, Lorna Dorothy (*née* Markham); one *s* one *d*. *Educ:* Willaston Sch.; Gonville and Caius Coll., Cambridge. MA, 1932. Colonial Administrative Service, Tanganyika, 1926; Provincial Comr, 1947; Senior Provincial Comr, 1950; Mem. for Local Government, Tanganyika, 1950–53. Governor, Comdr-in-Chief, and Vice-Adm., Sierra Leone, 1953–56. Hon. Sec. Vernacular Architecture Group, 1959–72, Pres., 1972–73; Chm. Governing Body, Somerset County Museum, 1961–73; Mem. Gisborne Museum Staff, NZ, 1974–80. *Publication:* (ed) A Bibliography on Vernacular Architecture, 1973. *Address:* 1 Lewis Street, Gisborne, New Zealand.

HALL, Simon Robert Dawson, MA; Warden of Glenalmond College, 1987–91; *b* 24 April 1938; *s* of late Wilfrid Dawson Hall and Elizabeth Helen Hall (*née* Wheeler); *m* 1961, Jennifer Harverson; two *s*. *Educ:* Tonbridge School; University College, Oxford. 2nd Lieut, 7th Royal Tank Regt, 1956–58. Asst Master, Gordonstoun School, 1961–65; Joint Headmaster, Dunrobin School, 1965–68; Haileybury: Asst Master, 1969–79; Senior Modern Languages Master, 1970–76; Housemaster, Lawrence, 1972–79; Second Master, 1976–79; Headmaster, Milton Abbey School, 1979–87. 21st SAS Regt (TA), 1958–61; Intelligence Corps (V), 1968–71. FRSA 1983. *Recreations:* reading, music, motoring, sailing, hill-walking. *Address:* 24 Thorpe Field, Sockbridge, Penrith CA10 2JN.

HALL, Prof. the Rev. Stuart George; Priest-in-Charge, St Michael's, Elie, and St John's, Pittenweem, since 1990; Professor of Ecclesiastical History, King's College, University of

London, 1978–90; *b* 7 June 1928; *s* of George Edward Hall and May Catherine Hall; *m* 1953, Brenda Mary Henderson; two *s* two *d*. *Educ:* University Coll. Sch., Hampstead; New Coll., and Ripon Hall, Oxford (BA 1952, MA 1955, BD 1973). National Service, Army, 1947–48. Deacon 1954, priest 1955; Asst Curate, Newark-on-Trent Parish Church, 1954–58; Tutor, Queen's Coll., Birmingham, 1958–62; Lectr in Theology, Univ. of Nottingham, 1962–73, Sen. Lectr, 1973–78. Editor for early church material, Theologische Realenzyklopädie. *Publications:* Melito of Sardis On Pascha and fragments: (ed) texts and translations, 1979; Doctrine and Practice in the Early Church, 1991; contrib. to Expository Times, Heythrop Jl, Jl of Eccles. History, Jl of Theol Studies, Religious Studies, Studia Evangelica, Studia Patristica, Theology and Theologische Realenzyklopädie. *Recreations:* gardening, choral music. *Address:* 15 High Street, Elie, Leven, Fife KY9 1BY. *T:* Elie (0333) 330216.

HALL, Prof. Stuart McPhail; Professor of Sociology, The Open University, since 1979; *b* 3 Feb. 1932; *s* of Herman and Jessie Hall; *m* 1964, Catherine Mary Barrett; one *s* one *d*. *Educ:* Jamaica Coll.; Merton Coll., Oxford (MA; Rhodes Scholar, 1951). Editor, New Left Review, 1957–61; Lectr, Film and Mass Media Studies, Chelsea Coll., London Univ., 1961–64; Centre for Cultural Studies, Univ. of Birmingham: Res. Fellow, 1964–68; Actg Dir, 1968–72; Dir, 1972–79. A Dir, Polytechnic of E London. Trustee, Photographer's Gall., 1987–. Hon. Fellow, Portsmouth Polytechnic, 1988; Centenary Fellow, Thames Polytechnic, 1990. Hon DLitt Massachusetts Univ., 1989. *Publications:* The Popular Arts, 1964; Resistance Through Rituals, 1974; Policing The Crisis, 1978; Culture, Media, Language, 1980; The Politics of Thatcherism, 1983; State and Society in Contemporary Britain, 1984; Politics and Ideology, 1986; The Hard Road to Renewal, 1988. *Address:* 5 Mowbray Road, Kilburn, NW6.

HALL, Thomas William; Under-Secretary, Department of Transport, 1976–79 and 1981–87; retired; *b* 8 April 1931; *s* of Thomas William and Euphemia Jane Hall; *m* 1961, Anne Rosemary Hellier Davis; two *d*. *Educ:* Hitchin Grammar Sch.; St John's Coll., Oxford (MA); King's Coll., London (MA). Asst Principal, Min. of Supply, 1954; Principal: War Office, Min. of Public Building and Works, Cabinet Office, 1958–68; Asst Sec., Min. of Public Building and Works, later DoE, 1968–76; Under Sec., Depts of Environment and Transport, 1979–81. Member: Road Traffic Law Review, 1985–88; Transport Tribunal, 1990–. *Recreations:* music, literature, gardening, walking. *Address:* 43 Bridge Road, Epsom, Surrey KT17 4AN. *T:* Epsom (0372) 725900.

HALL, Vernon F., CVO 1960; Anæsthetist, King's College Hospital, 1931–69, retired; *b* 25 Aug. 1904; *s* of Cecil S. and M. M. Hall; *m* 1935, C. Marcia Cavell; one *s* two *d*. *Educ:* Haberdashers' Sch.; King's Coll. Hosp., London. MRCS, LRCP, 1927; DA, 1938; FFARCS, 1948. Served War of 1939–45 in Army (Emergency Commission), 1942–46; Consultant Anæsthetist, India Command (Local Brig.), 1945; Dean, King's Coll. Hosp. Medical Sch., 1951–65. FKC 1958; Hon. FFARCS 1975. *Publications:* History of King's College Hospital Dental School, 1973; A Scrapbook of Snowdonia, 1982; chapters on Anaesthesia in Rose & Carless, Surgery, etc. *Recreations:* riding, walking, reading and music. *Address:* 83A Foxgrove Road, Beckenham, Kent BR3 2DA. *T:* 081–650 2212.

HALL, (Wallace) John; Regional Director, DTI East (Cambridge), Department of Trade and Industry, since 1989; *b* 5 Oct. 1934; *s* of Claude Corbett Hall and Dulcie Hall (*née* Brinkworth); *m* 1962, Janet Bowen; three *d*. *Educ:* Crypt Sch., Gloucester; Hertford Grammar Sch.; Downing Coll., Cambridge (MA Classics). National Service, RAF, 1953–55. Pirelli-General Cable Works Ltd, 1958–62; Sales Manager, D. Meredew Ltd, 1962–67; Principal, Min. of Technology, 1967–70; Dept of Trade and Industry, Civil Aviation Policy, 1970–72; Consul (Commercial), São Paulo, Brazil, 1972–76; Asst Secretary, Dept of Trade, Shipping Policy, 1976–79; Counsellor (Economic), Brasilia, 1979–81; Consul-Gen., São Paulo, 1981–83; Assistant Secretary, DTI: Internat. Trade Policy, 1983–85; Overseas Trade (E Africa), 1985–89. *Recreations:* bridge, tennis and other sports, daughters. *Address:* 27 Wilbury Road, Letchworth, Herts.

HALL, William, CBE 1991; DFC 1944, FRICS; Member of the Lands Tribunal for Scotland, since 1971, and for England and Wales, since 1979; *b* 25 July 1919; *s* of Archibald and Helen Hall; *m* 1945, Margaret Semple (*née* Gibson); one *s* three *d*. *Educ:* Paisley Grammar Sch. FRICS 1948. Served War, RAF (pilot) 1939–45 (despatches, 1944). Sen. Partner, R. & W. Hall, Chartered Surveyors, 1949–79. Chm., Scottish Br., RICS, 1971; Member: Valuation Adv. Council, 1970–80; Erskine Hosp. Exec., 1976–. Hon. Sheriff, Paisley, 1974–. *Recreation:* golf. *Address:* Windyridge, Brediland Road, Paisley, Renfrewshire PA2 9HF. *T:* Brediland (050581) 3614. *Club:* Royal Air Force.

HALL, Prof. William Bateman, FEng 1986; Professor of Nuclear Engineering, University of Manchester, 1959–86, now Emeritus; *b* 28 May 1923; *s* of Sidney Bateman Hall and Doris Hall; *m* 1950, Helen Mary Dennis; four *d*. *Educ:* Urmston Grammar Sch.; College of Technology, Manchester. Engineering apprenticeship, 1939–44; Royal Aircraft Establishment, 1944–46; United Kingdom Atomic Energy Authority (formerly Dept of Atomic Energy, Min. of Supply), 1946–59: Technical Engineer, 1946–52; Principal Scientific Officer, 1952–56; Senior Principal Scientific Officer, 1956–58; Dep. Chief Scientific Officer, 1958. Mem., Adv. Cttee on Safety of Nuclear Installations, 1972–83. Pro-Vice-Chancellor, Univ. of Manchester, 1979–82. *Publications:* Reactor Heat Transfer, 1958; papers to scientific and professional institutions. *Recreations:* music, designing and making steam engines. *Address:* High Raise, Eskdale, Holmrook, Cumbria CA19 1UA. *T:* Eskdale (09403) 275.

HALL, Brig. Sir William (Henry), KBE 1979 (CBE 1962); Kt 1968; DSO 1942; ED; Comptroller of Stores, State Electricity Commission of Victoria, 1956–70; Colonel Commandant, RAA Southern Command, since 1967; *b* 5 Jan. 1906; *s* of William Henry Hall, Edinburgh, Scotland; *m* 1930, Irene Mary, *d* of William Hayes; one *s* four *d*. *Educ:* Morgan Acad., Dundee; Melbourne Univ. Joined Staff of State Electricity Commn of Vic, 1924. Enlisted AIF, 1939: Capt. Royal Aust. Artillery, Palestine, Egypt; Syria, Papua, New Guinea, 1941 (Major); Aust. Dir of Armaments at AHQ, 1942 (Lt-Col); Dir of Armament at AHQ, 1945 (Col); CRA 3 Div. Artillery CMF, 1955–59 (Brig.). Director: Royal Humane Society of Vic.; Multiple Sclerosis Soc.; Chairman: War Widows and Widowed Mothers' Trust; RSL War Veterans' Trust; State Pres. Victorian Br., RSL, 1964–74 (now Chm. Trustees); Nat. Pres., Aust. RSL, 1974–78; Aust. Councillor, World Veterans' Foundn; Patron: Aust.-Free China Economic Assoc.; Royal Artillery Assoc. (Vic.); Carry On, Vic.; Vic. Blinded Soldiers Assoc.; Trustee, Victorian Overseas Foundn. Associate Fellow, Aust. Inst. Management; Mem., Inst. of Purchasing and Supply (London). *Recreation:* golf. *Address:* Rosemont, 112 Kooyong Road, Caulfield, Vic. 3162, Australia; Montrose, Flinders, Victoria 3929. *Clubs:* Naval and Military (Melbourne); Victoria Racing; Melbourne Cricket, Peninsula Country Golf, Flinders Golf.

HALL, Willis; writer; *b* 6 April 1929; *s* of Walter and Gladys Hall; *m* 1973, Valerie Shute; one *s* (and three *s* by previous marriages). *Educ:* Cockburn High Sch., Leeds. TV plays include: The Villa Maroc; They Don't all Open Men's Boutiques; Song at Twilight; The Road to 1984; TV series: The Fuzz, 1977; The Danedyke Mystery, 1979; Stan's Last Game, 1983; The Bright Side, 1985; The Return of the Antelope, 1986; The Reluctant Dragon, 1988; (with Keith Waterhouse): The Upper Crusts, 1973; Billy Liar, 1974; Worzel Gummidge, 1979 (adapted as stage musical, 1981). *Publications:* (with Michael Parkinson) The A-Z of Soccer, 1970; Football Report, 1973; Football Classified, 1974; My Sporting Life, Football Final, 1975; *children's books:* The Royal Astrologer, 1960; The Gentle Knight, 1967; The Incredible Kidnapping, 1975; The Summer of the Dinosaur, 1977; The Last Vampire, 1982; The Inflatable Shop, 1984; The Return of the Antelope, 1985; Spooky Rhymes, 1987; The Antelope Company at Large, 1987; Dr Jekyll and Mr Hollins, 1988; Henry Hollins and the Dinosaur, 1988; The Vampire's Holiday, 1991; *plays:* The Long and the Short and the Tall, 1959; A Glimpse of the Sea, 1969; Kidnapped at Christmas, 1975; Walk on, Walk on, 1975; Stag Night, 1976; Christmas Crackers, 1976; A Right Christmas Caper, 1977; (with Keith Waterhouse): Billy Liar, 1960; Celebration, 1961; All Things Bright and Beautiful, 1962; England Our England, 1962; Squat Betty and The Sponge Room, 1963; Say Who You Are, 1965; Whoops-a-Daisy, 1968; Children's Day, 1969; Who's Who, 1972; Saturday, Sunday, Monday (adaptation from de Filippo), 1973; Filumena (adaptation from de Filippo), 1977; *musicals:* (with Keith Waterhouse): The Card, 1973; Budgie, 1989; (with Denis King): Treasure Island, 1985; The Wind in the Willows (adaptation from A. A. Milne), 1985; (with John Cooper) The Water Babies (adaptation from Charles Kingsley), 1987. *Recreation:* magic (Member: Northern Magic Circle; Soc. of Amer. Magicians; Malta Magicians Soc.). *Address:* c/o London Management, 235–241 Regent Street, W1A 2JT. *Clubs:* Garrick, Savage, Lansdowne.

HALL-MATTHEWS, Rt. Rev. Anthony Francis; *see* Carpentaria, Bishop of.

HALL-THOMPSON, Major (Robert) Lloyd, ERD; TD; JP; *b* 9 April 1920; *s* of Lt-Col Rt Hon. S. H. Hall-Thompson, PC (NI), DL, JP, MP; *m* 1948, Alison F. Leitch, MSR; one *s* one *d*. *Educ:* Campbell Coll. Prep. Sch.; Campbell Coll. Royal School. Major, Royal Artillery, 1939–46; TA, 1946–56. Joined Unionist Party, 1938; Vice-Pres., Clifton Unionist Assoc. (Chm. 1954–57); MP (U) Clifton, 1969–73; Mem (U), N Belfast, NI Assembly, 1973–75 (Leader of the House, 1973–74); Chief Whip, NI Executive, 1973–74; Mem. (UPNI) for N Belfast, NI Constitutional Convention, 1975–76. Patron of Friends of the Union, 1986–; Chm., Lagan Valley Cons. Party, NI, 1988–. Director of several companies. Formerly Mem. NI Hosps Authority (Past Vice-Chm. Finance and Gen. Purposes Cttee); Past Vice-Chm., Samaritan Hosp. Management Cttee; Life Governor, Samaritan Hosp.; Pres. and Trustee, North Belfast Working Men's Club, 1954–92; Trustee and Hon. Sec., Belfast Newsboys' Club and W. S. Armour Girls' Club; Vice-Pres., Cliftonville Football and Athletic Club; Founder, Trustee & Pres., Duncairn Friendship Assoc.; Life Mem., (Past Hon. Sec. and Hon. Treas.), Not Forgotten Assoc.; Life Mem., Royal Ulster Agric. Soc.; Chm., Dep. Gov., Freeman and Steward, Down Royal Corp. of Horse Breeders; Founder and Pres., Irish Draught Horse Soc.; Founder and Hon. Sec., Half-Bred Horse Breeders' Soc.; Mem. Cttee, NI Nurses Housing Assoc. *Recreations:* horse riding, hunting, racing, eventing, show jumping, horse breeding; golf, reading. *Address:* Maymount, Ballylesson, Belfast BT8 8JY, Northern Ireland. *T:* Drumbo (0232) 826327. *Club:* Ulster (Belfast).

HALL WILLIAMS; *see* Williams.

HALLADAY, Eric, MA; Principal, St Chad's College, University of Durham, since 1991; *b* 9 July 1930; *s* of Rev. A. R. Halladay and Helena Renton; *m* 1956, Margaret Baister; one *s* two *d*. *Educ:* Durham Sch.; St John's Coll., Cambridge (MA History Tripos Pts I and II, Cl. II Div. I); Ripon Hall, Oxford. National Service, commnd 5th Regt, RHA, 1948–50. Exeter Sch., 1954–60, Sen. History Master, 1956–60; Sen. Lectr in History, RMA, Sandhurst, 1960–64; Grey College, University of Durham: Sen. Tutor, and part-time Lectr in History, 1964–80; Vice-Master, 1967–80; Master, 1980–89; Rector, 1989–91; Rector, St Aidan's Coll., Univ. of Durham, 1990–91. Chm., Northumbrian Univs Military Educn Cttee, 1981–; Mem. Exec. Cttee, Council of Military Educn Cttees of Univs of UK, 1982–87. Mem., TA&VRA, N of England, 1980–; Sec., Durham Br., SSAFA, 1977–89. Chm., Durham Regatta, 1982–88. *Publications:* The Building of Modern Africa (with D. D. Rooney), 1966, 2nd edn 1968; The Emergent Continent: Africa in the Nineteenth Century, 1972; Rowing in England—a Social History, 1990. *Recreations:* gardening, rowing. *Address:* St Chad's College, Durham DH1 3RH; The Coign, Corbridge, Northumberland. *T:* Hexham (0434) 632838. *Club:* Leander (Henley-on-Thames).

HALLAM, Bishop of, (RC), since 1980; **Rt. Rev. Gerald Moverley,** JCD; *b* 9 April 1922; *s* of William Joseph Moverley and Irene Mary Moverley (*née* Dewhirst). *Educ:* St Bede's Grammar Sch., Bradford; Ushaw Coll., Durham; Angelicum Univ., Rome. Priest, 1946; Sec. to Bishop Poskitt, Leeds, 1946–51; Angelicum Univ., 1951–54; Chancellor, Dio. Leeds, 1958–68; Domestic Prelate to HH Pope Paul VI, 1965; apptd Bishop, Dec. 1967; Titular Bishop of Tinisa in Proconsulari and Bishop Auxiliary of Leeds, 1968–80; translated to new diocese of Hallam, established May 1980. *Address:* Quarters, Carsick Hill Way, Sheffield S10 3LT. *T:* Sheffield (0742) 309101.

HALLAM HIPWELL, H.; *see* Vivenot, Baroness Raoul de.

HALLATT, Ven. David Marrison; Archdeacon of Halifax, since 1989; *b* 15 July 1937; *s* of John Vincent Hallatt and Edith Elliott Hallatt; *m* 1967, Margaret Smitton; two *s*. *Educ:* Birkenhead School; Southampton Univ. (BA Hons Geography 1959); St Catherine's Coll., Oxford (BA Theology 1962; MA 1966). Curate, St Andrew's, Maghull, Liverpool, 1963–67; Vicar, All Saints, Totley, dio. Sheffield, 1967–75; Team Rector, St James & Emmanuel, Didsbury, Manchester, 1975–89. *Recreations:* walking, birdwatching, music, crosswords. *Address:* 9 Healey Wood Gardens, Brighouse, West Yorks HD6 3SQ. *T:* Brighouse (0484) 714553.

HALLCHURCH, David Thomas, TD 1965; barrister-at-law; a Recorder of the Crown Court, since 1980; *b* 4 April 1929; *s* of Walter William Hallchurch and Marjorie Pretoria Mary Hallchurch (*née* Cooper); *m* 1st, 1954, Gillian Mary Jagger (marr. diss. 1972); three *s*; 2nd, 1972, Susan Kathryn Mather Brennan; one step *s* one step *d*. *Educ:* Bromsgrove Sch.; Trinity Coll., Oxford (MA Hons). Called to the Bar, Gray's Inn, 1953; Whitehead Travelling Scholarship, Canada and USA, 1953–54; practised as barrister-at-law on Midland and Oxford Circuit, 1954–60 and 1964–. Puisne Judge, Botswana, 1986–88. Major, Staffs Yeomanry (Queen's Own Royal Regiment), TA, 1953–66. Legal Mem., Mental Health Review Tribunal for the West Midlands, 1979–86. *Recreations:* cricket, drawing (cartoons). *Address:* Neachley House, Tong, near Shifnal, Shropshire TF11 8PH. *T:* Albrighton (090722) 3542. *Club:* Vincent's (Oxford).

HALLETT, Cecil Walter; retired as General Secretary, Amalgamated Engineering Union, 1957–64; *b* 10 Dec. 1899; *m* 1923, Edith Nellie Hallett (*d* 1990) (*née* Smith); two *s* two *d*. *Educ:* New City Road Elementary Sch., London. Messenger, Commercial Cable Co., 1913–15; apprentice fitter and turner, Gas Light and Coke Co., Becton, N Woolwich, 1916–18. HM Forces, 10th London Regt, 1918–19; journeyman fitter and turner, various firms, 1923–48; Asst Gen. Sec. AEU, 1948–57. Former Editor, AEU Monthly Jl and The Way. *Address:* St Martin's Home, 15 York Avenue, Chatham, Kent ME5 9EP.

HALLETT, Prof. George Edward Maurice, MDS; Child Dental Health Professor, University of Newcastle upon Tyne (formerly King's College, University of Durham),

1951–77, now Emeritus; Dean, Sutherland Dental School, 1960–77, and Hospital, 1970–77; retired; *b* 30 July 1912; *s* of Edward Henry and Berthe Hallett; *m* 1936, Annetta Eva Grant Napier; three *d*. *Educ:* Birkenhead Institute; Liverpool Univ. (LDS, Gilmour Medal and other prizes). HDD RCSE 1939; FDS RCS 1948; MDS Durham, 1952; DOrth RCS, 1954; FDS RCSE 1960; FFD RCSI 1964. House Surgeon, Liverpool Dental Hosp., 1934–35; School Dental Officer, Doncaster CB, 1935–36, Notts, 1936–40; served War, 1940–46: Army Dental Corps, Major, despatches. University of Durham: Lecturer in Children's Dentistry, 1946, Reader, 1948; Lectr in Orthodontics, 1946. Examiner in Dental subjects, Universities of Dundee, Durham, Edinburgh and Glasgow; RCS of Eng., 1954–77; Consultant, United Teaching Hosps, Newcastle upon Tyne; Head of Dept of Child Dental Health, Dental Hosp., Newcastle upon Tyne, 1948. Mem. Dental Council, RCSE; Past President: Société Française d'Orthopedie Dento-Faciale; European Orthodontic Soc. (also former Editor; Hon. Life Mem.); North of England Odontological Soc.; Brit. Soc. for the study of Orthodontics (Hon. Life Mem.); Newcastle Medico-Legal Soc.; former Mem., Newcastle RHB; former Mem., Newcastle AHA (T). Hon. Life Mem., British Dental Assoc. Past Pres., British Med. Pilots' Assoc. Hon. FDSRCPS Glas 1979. Silver Medal, Ville de Paris, 1980. *Publications:* contribs to scientific and dental jls. *Recreations:* dilettantism in the glyptic arts, flying. *Address:* 63 Runnymede Road, Darras Hall, Ponteland, Newcastle upon Tyne NE20 9HJ. *T:* Ponteland (0661) 22646. *Club:* Newcastle Aero.

HALLETT, Heather Carol; QC 1989; a Recorder, since 1989; *b* 16 Dec. 1949; *d* of Hugh and Doris Hallett; *m* 1974, Nigel Wilkinson; two *s*. *Educ:* St Hugh's Coll., Oxford (MA). Called to the Bar, Inner Temple, 1972. *Recreations:* theatre, music, games. *Address:* 6 Pump Court, Temple, EC4Y 7AR. *T:* 071–353 7242.

HALLETT, Victor George Henry; Social Security (formerly National Insurance) Commissioner, since 1976; *b* 11 Feb. 1921; *s* of Dr Denys Bouhier Imbert Hallett; *m* 1947, Margaret Hamlyn. *Educ:* Westminster; Queen's Coll., Oxford (MA). Served War, 1939–45 (despatches 1946). Called to Bar, Inner Temple, 1949. Mem., Land Registration Rules Cttee, 1971–76; Conveyancing Counsel of the Court, 1971–76. *Publications:* Key and Elphinstone's Conveyancing Precedents (ed jtly), 15th edn, 1952; Prideaux's Precedents in Conveyancing (ed jtly), 25th edn, 1953; Hallett's Conveyancing Precedents, 1965; (with Nicholas Warren) Settlements, Wills and Capital Transfer Tax, 1979. *Address:* Office of the Social Security Commissioners, Harp House, 83/86 Farringdon Street, EC4A 4BL.

HALLEY, Laurence; *see* O'Keeffe, P. L.

HALLGARTEN, Anthony Bernard Richard; QC 1978; a Recorder, since 1990; *b* 16 June 1937; *s* of Fritz and late Friedel Hallgarten; *m* 1962, Katherine Borchard; one *s* three *d*. *Educ:* Merchant Taylors' Sch., Northwood; Downing Coll., Cambridge (BA). Called to the Bar, Middle Temple, 1961 (Barstow Scholar, Inns of Court, 1961); Bencher, 1987. Chm., Bar/Inns' Councils Jt Regulations Cttee, 1990. Chair, Management Cttee, Camden Victim Support, 1989–. *Recreations:* cricket, canals, cycling. *Address:* 3 Essex Court, Temple, EC4Y 9AL. *T:* 071–583 9294. *Clubs:* Garrick, MCC.

HALLIBURTON, Rev. Canon Robert John; Canon Residentiary and Chancellor of St Paul's Cathedral, since 1989; *b* 23 March 1935; *s* of Robert Halliburton and Katherine Margery Halliburton (*née* Robinson); *m* 1968, Jennifer Ormsby Turner; one *s* three *d* (and one *s* decd). *Educ:* Tonbridge Sch.; Selwyn Coll., Cambridge (MA); Keble Coll., Oxford (DPhil); St Stephen's House, Oxford. Curate, St Dunstan and All Saints, Stepney, 1961; Tutor, St Stephen's House, Oxford, 1967; Vice-Principal, St Stephen's House, 1971; Lectr, Lincoln Coll., Oxford, 1973; Principal of Chichester Theol Coll., 1975–82, Canon and Prebend of Chichester Cathedral, 1976–82, Canon Emeritus, 1982–88, Canon and Preb. of Wightring and Theol Lectr, 1988–90; Priest in Charge, All Souls, St Margaret's-on-Thames, 1982–89. Lecturer: Southwark Ordination Course, 1984–89; Missionary Inst., Mill Hill, 1984–89. Select Preacher, Oxford Univ., 1976–77. Consultant, Anglican-Roman Catholic Internat. Commn, 1971–81; Mem., Doctrinal Commn of C of E, 1978–86. Examining Chaplain to Bishop of Kensington, 1983–. *Publications:* The Authority of a Bishop, 1986; Educating Rachel, 1987; contribs to: The Eucharist Today, ed. R. C. D. Jasper, 1974; The Study of Liturgy, ed C. P. M. Jones, 1978; Confession and Absolution, ed G. Rowell and M. Dudley, 1990; reports of C of E Doctrinal Commission, Believing in the Church, 1982, We believe in God, 1987; articles in Studia Patristica, La Revue des Etudes Augustiniennes, Faith and Unity. *Recreations:* music, gardening. *Address:* 1 Amen Court, EC4M 7BU. *T:* 071–248 3314. *Club:* Athenæum.

HALLIDAY, Prof. Fred; Professor of International Relations, London School of Economics and Political Science, since 1985; *b* 22 Feb. 1946; *s* of Arthur Halliday and Rita (*née* Finigan); *m* Dr Maxine Molyneux; one *s*. *Educ:* Univ. of Oxford (BA 1st Cl.); School of Oriental and African Studies (MSc); London School of Economics (PhD 1985). Freelance writer, 1967; Dept. of Internat. Relations, LSE, 1983–. *Publications:* Arabia without Sultans, 1974; Iran: dictatorship and development, 1978; (with Maxine Molyneux) The Ethiopian Revolution, 1981; Threat from the East?, 1982; The Making of the Second Cold War, 1983, 2nd edn 1986; Cold War, Third World, 1989; Revolution and Foreign Policy: the case of South Yemen 1967–1987, 1990. *Recreations:* languages, travel, lunch, Le Monde. *Address:* A136, London School of Economics and Political Science, Houghton Street, WC2A 2AE. *T:* 071–955 7389.

HALLIDAY, Ian Francis, FCA; Finance Director, Lowndes Lambert Group Ltd, 1981–87; *b* 16 Nov. 1927; *s* of Michael and Jean Halliday; *m* 1952, Mary Busfield; one *s* two *d*. *Educ:* Wintringham Grammar Sch., Grimsby; Lincoln Coll., Oxford (MA Mathematics). Armitage & Norton, Chartered Accountants, 1951–69; qual. as Chartered Accountant, 1954; Partner, 1957; Finance Dir, Allied Textile Co. Ltd, 1970–74; on secondment as Dep. Director of Industrial Development Unit, Dept of Industry, 1974–77; Finance Dir, Leslie & Godwin (Holdings) Ltd, internat. insce and re-insce Lloyd's Brokers, 1977–80; Chief Exec., NEB, 1980. Mem., PLA, 1984–. *Recreation:* gardening. *Address:* 40 Finthorpe Lane, Huddersfield HD5 8TU.

HALLIDAY, John Frederick; Deputy Under Secretary of State, Home Office, since 1990; *b* 19 Sept. 1942; *s* of E. Halliday; *m* 1970, Alison Burgess; four *s*. *Educ:* Whitgift School, Croydon; St John's College, Cambridge (MA). Teacher, under VSO, Aitchison College, Lahore, 1964–66; Home Office, 1966; Principal Private Sec. to Home Sec., 1980; Asst Under-Sec. of State, Home Office, 1983–87; Under Sec., DHSS, then Dept of Health, 1987–90, on secondment. *Recreations:* music, squash, theatre.

HALLIDAY, Prof. Michael Alexander Kirkwood; Professor of Linguistics in the University of Sydney, 1976–87, Emeritus Professor since 1988; *b* 13 April 1925; *s* of late Wilfrid J. Halliday and of Winifred Halliday (*née* Kirkwood). *Educ:* Rugby School; University of London. BA London; MA, PhD, Cambridge. Served Army, 1944–47. Asst Lectr in Chinese, Cambridge Univ., 1954–58; Lectr in General Linguistics, Edinburgh Univ., 1958–60; Reader in General Linguistics, Edinburgh Univ., 1960–63; Dir, Communication Res. Centre, UCL, 1963–65; Linguistic Soc. of America Prof., Indiana Univ., 1964; Prof. of General Linguistics, UCL, 1965–71; Fellow, Center for Advanced Study in the Behavioral Sciences, Stanford, Calif., 1972–73; Prof. of Linguistics, Univ. of Illinois, 1973–74; Prof. of Language and Linguistics, Essex Univ., 1974–75. Visiting Professor of Linguistics: Yale, 1967; Brown, 1971; Nairobi, 1972; Lee Kuan Yew Distinguished Visitor, Nat. Univ. of Singapore, 1986. FAHA 1979. Corresp. FBA 1989. Dr *hc* Nancy; Hon. DLitt: Birmingham, 1987; York (Canada), 1988. *Publications:* The Language of the Chinese 'Secret History of the Mongols', 1959; (with A. McIntosh and P. Strevens) The Linguistic Sciences and Language Teaching, 1964; (with A. McIntosh) Patterns of Language, 1966; Intonation and Grammar in British English, 1967; A Course in Spoken English: Intonation, 1970; Explorations in the Functions of Language, 1973; Learning How To Mean, 1975; (with R. Hasan) Cohesion in English, 1976; System and Function in Language, ed G. Kress, 1976; Language as Social Semiotic, 1978; An Introduction to Functional Grammar, 1985; Spoken and Written Language, 1985; articles in Jl of Linguistics, Word, Trans of Philological Soc., etc. *Address:* 5 Laing Avenue, Killara, NSW 2071, Australia.

HALLIDAY, Norman Pryde; QHP; Senior Principal Medical Officer (Under Secretary), Department of Health (formerly of Health and Social Security), since 1977; *b* 28 March 1932; *s* of late James and Jessie Thomson Hunter Halliday; *m* 1953, Eleanor Smith; three *s* one *d*. *Educ:* Woodside, Glasgow; King's Coll., London; King's Coll. Hosp. Med. Sch. SRN 1955; MB, BS, MRCS, LRCP 1964; DCH RCPGlas 1969; MBA Warwick, 1991. Various posts in clinical medicine, incl. Registrar (Paediatrics), KCH, London; SMO, DHSS, 1972. QHP 1990–. *Publications:* articles on medical subjects in professional journals. *Recreations:* photography, sub aqua diving, fashion, DIY, cross-bow shooting. *Address:* 12 Regalfield Close, Guildford, Surrey GU2 6YG. *T:* Worplesdon (0483) 236267.

HALLIDAY, Rt. Rev. Robert Taylor; *see* Brechin, Bishop of.

HALLIDAY, Vice-Adm. Sir Roy (William), KBE 1980; DSC 1944; Director General of Intelligence, Ministry of Defence, 1981–84; *b* 27 June 1923; *m* 1945, Dorothy Joan Meech. *Educ:* William Ellis Sch.; University College Sch. Joined Royal Navy, 1941; served in Fleet Air Arm (fighter pilot) in World War II, in HMS Chaser, HMSs Victorious and Illustrious; test pilot, Boscombe Down, 1947–48; Comdg Officer 813 Sqdn (Wyverns, HMS Eagle), 1954; Army Staff Coll., Camberley; Comdr, 1958; Exec. Officer Coastal Forces Base (HMS Diligence), 1959; Sen. Officer 104th Minesweeping Sqdn, Far East Flt, in comd (HMS Houghton), 1961–62; Naval Asst to Chief of Naval Information, 1962–64; comdr (Air) HMS Albion, 1964–66; Captain, 1966; Dep. Dir Naval Air Warfare, 1966–70; HMS Euryalus in comd and as Captain D3 Far East Fleet and D6 Western Fleet, 1970–71; Commodore, 1971; Cdre Amphibious Warfare, 1971–73; Cdre Intelligence, Defence Intelligence Staff, 1973–75; Comdr British Navy Staff, Washington, Naval Attaché, and UK Nat. Liaison Rep. to SACLANT, 1975–78; Dep. Chief of Defence Staff (Intelligence), 1978–81. ADC to the Queen, 1975. *Recreations:* gardening, walking. *Address:* c/o Barclays Bank, Lyndhurst, Hants. *Club:* Naval.

HALLIDAY, S. F. P.; *see* Halliday, F.

HALLIFAX, Adm. Sir David (John), KCB 1983; KBE 1982; Constable and Governor of Windsor Castle, since 1988; *b* 3 Sept. 1927; *s* of Ronald H. C. Hallifax and Joanne M. Hallifax; *m* 1962, Anne Blakiston Houston; one *s* one *d* (and one *s* decd). *Educ:* Winchester. Joined RN 1945; minesweeping, Gulf of Salonika, 1949–51; CO MTB 5008, 1953; Long TAS Course, 1954; HMS Salerno, Suez, 1956; Staff Coll., Camberley, 1959; CO HMS Agincourt, 1964–65; RCDS 1972; CO HMS Fife, 1973–75; Flag Officer, First Flotilla, 1978–80; Chief of Staff to C-in-C Fleet, 1980–82; Dep. Supreme Allied Comdr, Atlantic, 1982–84; Comdt, RCDS, 1986–87. *Recreations:* sailing, conchology. *Clubs:* Pratt's, Farmers', Royal Yacht Squadron.

HALLINAN, Sir (Adrian) Lincoln, Kt 1971; DL; Barrister-at-law; Stipendiary Magistrate, South Glamorgan (Cardiff), since 1976; a Recorder of the Crown Court, 1972–82; *b* 13 Nov. 1922; *e s* of late Sir Charles Hallinan, CBE and late Theresa Doris Hallinan, JP (*née* Holman); *m* 1955, Mary Parry Evans, *qv*; two *s* two *d*. *Educ:* Downside. Lieut, Rifle Bde, 1942–47; TA, 1950–52 (Captain). Called to Bar, Lincoln's Inn, 1950; Wales and Chester Circuit. A Legal Mem., Mental Health Review Tribunal for Wales, 1966–76; Chm., Med. Appeals Tribunal, 1970–76. Cardiff CC, 1949–74 (serving on several educational and cultural cttees); Alderman, 1961–74; Lord Mayor of Cardiff, 1969–70. Contested (C), Aberdare, 1946, Cardiff West, 1951, 1959. Chm., Cardiff Educn Cttee, 1961–63 and 1965–70; Chm., Governing Body, Cardiff Coll. of Art, and Cardiff Coll. of Music and Drama, 1961–73; First Chm., Nat. Court of Governors, Welsh Coll. of Music and Drama, 1970; Chairman: Commemorative Collectors Soc.; S Wales Gp, Victorian Soc.; Founder and Chm., Cardiff 2000–Cardiff Civic Trust, 1964–73, 1st Pres. 1973; Chm., Cardiff-Nantes Fellowship, 1961–68. Chevalier, Ordre des Palmes Académiques, 1965; Chevalier de la Légion d'Honneur, 1973. OStJ 1969. DL Glamorgan, 1969. *Recreations:* music, the arts.

HALLINAN, Sir Lincoln; *see* Hallinan, Sir A. L.

HALLINAN, Mary Alethea, (Lady Hallinan); *see* Parry Evans, M.A.

HALLIWELL, Brian; Head of Value Added Tax Services, KPMG Peat Marwick McLintock (formerly Peat, Marwick, Mitchell & Co.), since 1989 (VAT Consultant, 1985–89); *b* 17 Dec. 1930; *s* of late Norman and Emma Halliwell; *m* 1957, Agnes Lee. *Educ:* Preston Grammar Sch. DMS 1968. Joined HM Customs and Excise as Clerical Officer, 1947; Principal, 1969; Asst Sec., 1973; Dep. Accountant General, 1976; Accountant and Comptroller Gen., 1980–85. FBIM. *Recreations:* chess, reading, sport. *Address:* 3 Knollcroft, Ulster Avenue, Shoeburyness, Southend-on-Sea SS3 9JY. *T:* Southend-on-Sea (0702) 297570.

HALLIWELL, Prof. Richard Edward Winter; William Dick Professor of Veterinary Clinical Studies, Royal (Dick) School of Veterinary Studies, since 1988, and Dean, Faculty of Veterinary Medicine, since 1990, University of Edinburgh; *b* 16 June 1937; *s* of Arthur Clare Halliwell and Winifred Dorothea Goode; *m* 1963, Jenifer Helen Roper; two *d*. *Educ:* St Edward's Sch., Oxford; Gonville and Caius Coll., Cambridge (MA, VetMB, PhD); MRCVS. Jun. Fellow in Vet. Surgery, Univ. of Bristol, 1961–63; private vet. practice, London, 1963–68; Vis. Fellow in Dermatology, Univ. of Pennsylvania Sch. of Vet. Med., 1968–70; Wellcome Vet. Fellowship Univ. of Cambridge, 1970–73; Asst Prof. of Dermatology, Univ. of Pennsylvania Sch. of Vet. Med., 1973–77; Prof. and Chm., Dept of Med. Scis, Univ. of Florida Coll. of Vet. Med., 1977–88; Prof., Dept of Med. Microbiol., Univ. of Florida Coll. of Med., 1977–88. President: Amer. Acad. of Veterinary Allergy, 1978–80; Amer. Assoc. of Veterinary Immunologists, 1984; Amer. Coll. of Veterinary Dermatology, 1984–86. *Publications:* (with N. T. Gorman) Veterinary Clinical Immunology, 1989; (with C. von Tscharner) Advances in Veterinary Dermatology, 1990; numerous pubns in area of clin. immunology and vet. dermatology. *Recreations:* hill walking, surfing. *Address:* 2A Ainslie Place, Edinburgh EH3 6AR. *T:* 031–225 8765. *Club:* Commonwealth Trust.

HALLOWES, Odette Marie Celine, GC 1946; MBE 1945; Légion d'Honneur, 1950; Vice-President, Women's Transport Services (FANY); Member Royal Society of St

George; housewife; *b* 28 April 1912; *d* of Gaston Brailly, Croix-de-Guerre, Médaille Militaire; *m* 1931, Roy Sansom (decd); three *d*; *m* 1947, late Captain Peter Churchill, DSO; *m* 1956, Geoffrey Macleod Hallowes. *Educ:* The Convent of Ste Therèse, Amiens (France) and privately. Entered Special Forces and landed in France, 1942; worked as British agent until capture by Gestapo, 1943; sentenced to death June 1943; endured imprisonment and torture until 28 April 1945, when left Ravensbrück Concentration Camp (MBE, GC). Member: Military Medallists League (Vice-Pres.); Cttee, Victoria Cross and George Cross Assoc. Pres., 282 (East Ham) Air Cadet Sqdn. Founder Vice-Pres., Women of the Year Luncheon. Hon. Mem., St Dunstan's Ex-Prisoners of War Assoc. *Recreations:* reading, travelling, cooking, trying to learn patience. *Address:* Rosedale, Eriswell Road, Burwood Park, Walton-on-Thames, Surrey. *Clubs:* Naval and Military, FANY, Special Forces.

HALLSWORTH, Prof. Ernest Gordon, DSc, FRSC, FTS; Scientific Consultant and Chairman of Directors, Hallsworth and Associates; *b* 1913; *s* of Ernest and Beatrice Hallsworth, Ashton-under-Lyne, Lancs; *m* 1st, 1943, Elaine Gertrude Seddon (*d* 1970), *d* of R. C. Weatherill, Waverley, NSW; two *s* one *d* and one step *s*; 2nd, 1976, Merrily Ramly; one step *d*. *Educ:* Ashton Grammar Sch., Ashton-under-Lyne, Lancs; Univ. of Leeds. University of Leeds: First Cl. Hons in Agric. Chem., Sir Swire Smith Fellow, 1936; Asst Lectr in Agric. Chem., 1936; PhD 1939; DSc 1964. Lectr in Agric. Chem., Univ. of Sydney, 1940–51; Prof. of Soil Science, Univ. of West Australia, 1960–61; Prof. of Agric. Chem. and Head Dept Agric. Sci., Univ. Nottingham, 1951–64 (Dean, Faculty of Agric. and Hort., 1951–60); Chief of Div. of Soils, CSIRO, 1964–73; Chm., Land Resources Labs, CSIRO, 1973–78; Hon. Professorial Fellow, Science Policy Res. Unit, Sussex Univ., 1979–85. Pres. Lecturers' Assoc., Sydney Univ., 1946–49. Treas., Aust. Assoc. of Scientific Workers, 1943; Member: Science Advisory Panel, Australian Broadcasting Commn, 1949–51; Pasture Improvement Cttee, Australian Dairy Produce Bd (NSW), 1948–51; Chm. Insecticides and Fungicides Cttee, Australian Standards Inst., 1949–51. President: Internat. Soc. of Soil Science, 1964–68; Sect. 13, Aust. and NZ Assoc. for the Advancement of Science, 1976. Mem. Council, Flinders Univ., 1967–79; Chief Scientific Liaison Officer (Aust.), London, 1971. Fellow: Aust. Acad. of Technol Scis and Engrg, 1976–; World Acad. of Art and Science, 1989–; Mem., Académie d'Agriculture de France, 1983–; Hon. Mem., Internat. Soc. of Soil Sci., 1990–. Prescott Medal, Aust. Soc. Soil Science, 1984; Dokuchaev Medal, All-Union Soc. of Soil Sci., 1990. *Publications:* (Ed) Nutrition of the Legumes, 1958; (ed with D. V. Crawford) Experimental Pedology, 1964; (with others) Handbook of Australian Soils, 1968; (with others) Principles of a Balanced Land Use Policy for Australia, 1976; Where Shall We Build Our New Cities?, 1978; Land and Water Resources of Australia, 1979; Socio-economic Effects and Restraints in Tropical Forest Management, 1982; The Anatomy, Physiology and Psychology of Erosion, 1987; contributions to: Aust. Jl Science, Jl Soc. Chem. Indust., Experimental Agric., Jl Agric. Science, Aust. Medical Jl, Jl Soil Science. *Recreations:* talking, pedology. *Address:* 8 Old Belair Road, Mitcham, SA 5062, Australia. *T:* 08–271 6423; 1 Bellevue Cottages, Blackboys, near Uckfield, Sussex. *T:* Framfield (082582) 606. *Club:* Farmers'.

HALLWARD, Bertrand Leslie, MA; *b* 24 May 1901; *er s* of late N. L. Hallward, Indian Educational Service, and Evelyn A. Gurdon; *m* 1926, Catherine Margaret (*d* 1991), 2nd *d* of late Canon A. J. Tait, DD; four *d*. *Educ:* Haileybury Coll. (Scholar); King's Coll., Cambridge (Scholar). Fellow of Peterhouse, 1923–39. Hon. Fellow 1956. Headmaster of Clifton Coll., 1939–48; Vice-Chancellor, Nottingham Univ., 1948–65 (Hallward Library named at Nottingham Univ., 1989). Hon. LLD: Sheffield, 1964; Nottingham, 1965. *Publications:* Chapters II, III, IV, and part of VII (the Second and Third Punic Wars) in Cambridge Ancient History, Vol. VIII, 1930; Editor of the Classical Quarterly, 1935–39. *Address:* Flat 4, Gretton Court, Girton, Cambridge. *T:* Cambridge (0223) 277327.

See also W. O. Chadwick, G. C. H. Spafford.

HALNAN, Patrick John; His Honour Judge Halnan; a Circuit Judge, since 1986; *b* 7 March 1925; *s* of E. T. and A. B. Halnan; *m* 1955, Judith Mary (*née* Humberstone); four *c*. *Educ:* Perse Sch., Cambridge; Trinity Coll., Cambridge (MA). Army, 1943–47; TA, 1951–58. Solicitor. Asst Solicitor, Hants CC, 1954–58; Clerk to the Justices, Cambs, 1958–78; Metropolitan Stipendary Magistrate, 1978–86; a Recorder, 1983–86; SE Circuit. Sec., Justices' Clerks' Soc., 1972–76, Pres., 1978. Chm., Road Traffic Cttee, Magistrates' Assoc., 1981–87. *Publications:* (ed with Prof. R. M. Jackson) Leo Page, Justice of the Peace, 3rd edn 1967; (ed) Wilkinson's Road Traffic Offences, 7th edn 1973 to 14th edn 1989; (with David Latham) Drink/Driving Offences, 1979; Road Traffic, 1981; Drink/Drive: the new law, 1984. *Recreations:* village bridge, holidays abroad, stamp collecting. *Address:* Snaresbrook Crown Court, The Court House, Hollybush Hill, Snaresbrook, E11 1QW. *Club:* United Oxford & Cambridge University.

HALPERN, Prof. Jack, FRS 1974; Louis Block Distinguished Service Professor of Chemistry, University of Chicago, since 1984; *b* Poland, 19 Jan. 1925 (moved to Canada, 1929; USA 1962); *s* of Philip Halpern and Anna Sass; *m* 1949, Helen Peritz; two *d*. *Educ:* McGill Univ., Montreal. BSc 1946, PhD 1949. NRC Postdoc. Fellow, Univ. of Manchester, 1949–50; Prof. of Chem., Univ. of Brit. Columbia, 1950–62 (Nuffield Foundn Travelling Fellow, Cambridge Univ., 1959–60); Prof. of Chem., Univ. of Chicago, 1962–71, Louis Block Prof., 1971–84. Visiting Prof.: Univ. of Minnesota, 1962; Harvard Univ., 1966–67; California Inst. of Techn., 1969; Princeton Univ., 1970–71; Copenhagen Univ., 1978; Firth Vis. Prof., Sheffield, 1982; Sherman Fairchild Dist. Scholar, California Inst. of Technology, 1979; Guest Scholar, Kyoto Univ., 1981; Phi Beta Kappa Vis. Scholar, 1990; R. B. Woodward Vis. Prof., Harvard Univ., 1991; External Sci. Mem., Max Planck Institut für Kohlenforschung, Mulheim, 1983–; Lectureships: 3M, Univ. of Minnesota, 1968; FMC, Princeton Univ., 1969; Du Pont, Univ. of Calif., Berkeley, 1970; Frontier of Chemistry, Case Western Reserve Univ., 1971, 1989; Venable, Univ. of N Carolina, 1973; Ritter Meml, Miami Univ., 1980; University, Univ. of Western Ontario, 1981; F. J. Toole, Univ. of New Brunswick, 1981; Werner, Univ. of Kansas, 1982; Lansdowne, Univ. of Victoria, 1982; Welch, Univ. of Texas, 1983; Kilpatrick, Illinois Inst. of Tech., 1984; Dow, Univ. of Ottawa, 1985; Boomer, Univ. of Alberta, 1985; Bailar, Univ. of Illinois, 1986; Priestley, Penn State Univ., 1987; Taube, Stanford Univ., 1988; Res. Schol., Drew Univ., 1989; Liebig. Univ. of Colorado, 1989. Associate Editor: Jl of Amer. Chem. Soc.; Inorganica Chimica Acta; Mem. Editorial Bds: Accounts of Chemical Research; Jl of Catalysis; Catalysis Reviews; Jl of Coordination Chem.; Inorganic Syntheses; Jl of Molecular Catalysis; Jl of Organometallic Chemistry; Amer. Chem. Soc. Advances in Chemistry series; Gazzetta Chimica Italiana; Organometallics; Catalysis Letters; Reaction Kinetics and Catalysis Letters; Co-editor, OUP International Series of Monographs in Chemistry. Member: Nat. Sci. Foundn Chemistry Adv. Panel, 1967–70; MIT Chemistry Vis. Cttee, 1968–70; Argonne Nat. Lab. Chemistry Vis. Cttee, 1970–73; Amer. Chem. Soc. Petroleum Res. Fund Adv. Bd, 1972–74; NIH Medicinal Chem. Study Sect., 1975–78 (Chm., 1976–78); Princeton Univ. Chem. Adv. Council, 1982–; Encyclopaedia Britannica Univ. Adv. Cttee, 1985–. Mem., Bd of Trustees and Council, Gordon Research Confs, 1968–70; Chm., Gordon Conf. on Inorganic Chem., 1969; Chm., Amer. Chemical Soc. Div. of Inorganic Chem., 1971; Mem., 1985–, Mem., Council, 1990–, Chm., Chem. Sect., Nat. Acad. of Scis (For. Mem., 1984–85). Member: Bd of Dirs, Renaissance Soc., 1984–; Bd of Govs, Smart Gall., Univ. of Chicago, 1988–; Adv. Bd, Court Theatre, Univ. of Chicago, 1989–. Fellow, Amer. Acad. of Arts and Sciences, 1967; Sci. Mem., Max Planck Soc., 1983. Hon. FRSC 1987. Hon. DSc Univ. of British Columbia, 1986. Holds several honours and awards, including: Amer. Chem. Soc. Award in Inorganic Chem., 1968; Chem. Soc. Award, 1976; Humboldt Award, 1977; Kokes Award, Johns Hopkins Univ., 1978; Amer. Chem. Soc. Award for Distinguished Service in the Advancement of Inorganic Chemistry, 1985; Willard Gibbs Medal, 1986; Bailar Medal, Univ. of Illinois, 1986; Hoffman Medal, German Chem. Soc., 1988; Chemical Pioneer Award, Amer. Inst. of Chemists, 1991. *Publications:* Editor (with F. Basolo and J. Bunnett) Collected Accounts of Transition Metal Chemistry, vol. I, 1973, vol. II, 1977; contrib. articles on Catalysis and on Coordination Compounds to Encyclopaedia Britannica; numerous articles to Jl of Amer. Chemical Soc. and other scientific jls. *Recreations:* art, music. *Address:* Department of Chemistry, University of Chicago, 5735 South Ellis Avenue, Chicago, Illinois 60637, USA. *T:* (312) 702–7095. *Clubs:* Quadrangle (Chicago); Chemists (New York).

HALPERN, Sir Ralph (Mark), Kt 1986; Chairman, 1981–90, and Chief Executive, 1978–90, Burton Group plc (Managing Director, 1978); *b* 1938; *m* Joan Halpern, JP; one *d*. *Educ:* St Christopher School, Letchworth. Started career as trainee, Selfridges; joined Burton Group, 1961; co-Founder, Top Shop, 1970. Member: President's Cttee, CBI, 1984; President's Cttee, Business in the Community; Adv. Council, Prince's Youth Business Trust. Chm., British Fashion Council, 1990. FInstD; CBIM. *Club:* Reform.

HALPIN, Most Rev. Charles A.; *see* Regina, Archbishop of, (RC).

HALPIN, Miss Kathleen Mary, CBE 1953 (OBE 1941); Chief Administrator, Regions, WRVS (formerly WVS), 1945–73; *b* 19 Nov. 1903; unmarried. *Educ:* Sydenham High Sch. (GPDST). Organising Sec., Women's Gas Council, 1935, and represented Gas Industry at International Management Congress, Washington, USA, 1938, Sweden, 1947. Appointed Chief of Metropolitan Dept, WVS, 1939; lent to Min. of Health and went to Washington as UK representative on Standing Technical Cttee on Welfare, UNRRA; Comr, Trainer, and Camp Adviser, Girl Guides Assoc., 1924–48; Comdt, BRCS, 1937–39; Mem. Council, London Hostels Assoc., 1941–91; Chm. Women's Gas Fedn, 1945–49, Pres., 1949–60. A Governor of St Bartholomew's Hospital, 1948–74. Chm., Soroptomist (London) Housing Assoc., 1963–89; President Fedn of Soroptomist Clubs of Gt Britain and Ireland, 1959–60; Vice-Pres., Fawcett Soc., 1978– (Chm., 1967–71); Trustee, Women's Service Trust, 1964–89. OStJ. *Recreations:* motoring, reading, theatre. *Address:* 3 Chagford House, Chagford Street, NW1 6EG. *T:* 071–262 6226.

HALSBURY, 3rd Earl of, *cr* 1898; **John Anthony Hardinge Giffard,** FRS 1969; FEng 1976; Baron Halsbury, 1885; Viscount Tiverton, 1898; Chancellor of Brunel University, since 1966; *b* 4 June 1908; *o s* of 2nd Earl and Esmé Stewart (*d* 1973), *d* of late James Stewart Wallace; *S* father, 1943; *m* 1st, 1930, Ismay Catherine, *er d* of late Lord Ninian Crichton-Stuart and Hon. Mrs Archibald Maule Ramsay; one *s*; 2nd, 1936, Elizabeth Adeline Faith (*d* 1983), *o d* of late Major Harry Crewe Godley, DSO, Northamptonshire Regt and of late Mrs Godley, of Claremont Lodge, Cheltenham; two *d*. *Educ:* Eton. BSc (1st Cl. Hons Chem. and Maths) London (External), 1935; FRIC 1947, Hon. FRSC 1983; FInstP 1946; CEng, FIProdE 1956, Hon. FIProdE 1979. Employed by Lever Bros, 1935–42; Brown-Firth Res. Labs, 1942–47; Dir of Res., Decca Record Co., 1947–49; Man. Dir, Nat. Research Development Corporation, 1949–59; Consultant and Director: Joseph Lucas Industries, 1959–74; Distillers Co. Ltd, 1959–78; Head-Wrightson Ltd, 1959–78. External Examiner, OECD, on mission to Japan, 1965. Chairman: Science Museum Advisory Council, 1951–65; Cttee on Decimal Currency, 1961–63; Cttee of Management, Inst. of Cancer Research, Royal Marsden Hosp., 1962–77; Review Body on Doctors' and Dentists' Pay, 1971–74; Deptl Cttee of Enquiry into pay of Nurses, Midwives, Speech Therapists and Professions Supplementary to Medicine, 1974–75; Meteorological Cttee, 1970–82; President: Institution of Production Engineers, 1957–59; Royal Inst. of Philosophy, 1961–90; Parly and Scientific Cttee, 1963–66; Instn of Nuclear Engineers, 1963–65; Nat. Inst. of Industrial Psychol., 1963–75; Machine Tool Industry Res. Assoc., 1964–77; Coll. of Speech Therapists, 1983–87; Nat. Council for Christian Standards in Society, 1986–; Chm., Atlas Computing Lab., 1965–69; Member: Adv. Council to Cttee of Privy Council for Scientific and Industrial Research, 1949–54; SRC, 1965–69; Computer Bd for Univs and Research Councils, 1966–69; Decimal Currency Bd, 1966–71; Nationalised Transport Advisory Council, 1963–67; Standing Commn on Museums and Galleries, 1960–76; MRC, 1973–77; Cttee of Managers, Royal Institution, 1976–79. A Governor: BBC, 1960–62; LSE, 1959–90; UMIST, 1966– (formerly Mem. Council, Manchester Coll. of Sci. and Technol., 1956–65). Hon. FICE 1975; Hon. ARCVS 1984; Hon. FIBiol 1989. Hon. DTech Brunel Univ., 1966; DUniv Essex, 1968. *Heir: s* Adam Edward Giffard, *qv*. *Address:* 4 Campden House, 29 Sheffield Terrace, W8 7NE. *T:* 071–727 3125. *Clubs:* Athenæum, Royal Automobile (a Steward, 1966–).

HALSEY, Prof. Albert Henry; Professor of Social and Administrative Studies, University of Oxford, 1978–90, now Emeritus; Professorial Fellow of Nuffield College, Oxford, 1962–90, now Emeritus; *b* 13 April 1923; *m* 1949, Gertrude Margaret Littler; three *s* two *d*. *Educ:* Kettering Grammar Sch.; London Sch. of Econs. BSc (Econ), PhD London, MA Oxon. RAF, 1942–47; student LSE, 1947–52; Research Worker, Liverpool Univ., 1952–54; Lectr in Sociology, Birmingham Univ., 1954–62; Dir, Dept of Social and Admin. Studies, Oxford Univ., 1962–78. Fellow, Center for Advanced Study of Behavioral Sciences, Palo Alto, Calif, 1956–57; Vis. Prof. of Sociology, Univ. of Chicago, 1959–60. Adviser to Sec. of State for Educn, 1965–68; Chm. of CERI at OECD, Paris, 1968–70. Reith Lectr, 1977. Foreign Associate, Amer. Acad. of Educn.; Foreign Mem., Amer. Acad. of Arts and Scis, 1988. Hon. DSocSc Birmingham, 1987; DUniv Open, 1990. *Publications:* (jtly) Social Class and Educational Opportunity, 1956; (jtly) Technical Change and Industrial Relations, 1956; (with J. E. Floud) The Sociology of Education, Current Sociology VII, 1958; (jtly) Education, Economy and Society, 1961; Ability and Educational Opportunity, 1962; (with G. N. Ostergaard) Power in Co-operatives, 1965; (with Ivor Crewe) Social Survey of the Civil Service, 1969; (with Martin Trow) The British Academics, 1971; (ed) Trends in British Society since 1900, 1972; (ed) Educational Priority, 1972; Traditions of Social Policy, 1976; Heredity and Environment, 1977; Change in British Society, 1978, 3rd edn 1986; (jtly) Origins and Destinations, 1980; (with Norman Dennis) English Ethical Socialism, 1988; numerous articles and reviews. *Address:* 28 Upland Park Road, Oxford. *T:* Oxford (0865) 58625.

HALSEY, Rt. Rev. (Henry) David; Bishop of Carlisle, 1972–89; *b* 27 Jan. 1919; *s* of George Halsey, MBE and Gladys W. Halsey, DSc; *m* 1947, Rachel Margaret Neil Smith; four *d*. *Educ:* King's Coll. Sch., Wimbledon; King's Coll., London (BA); Wells Theol College. Curate, Petersfield, 1942–45; Chaplain, RNVR, 1946–47; Curate, St Andrew, Plymouth, 1947–50; Vicar of: Netheravon, 1950–53; St Stephen, Chatham, 1953–62; Bromley, and Chaplain, Bromley Hosp., 1962–68; Rural Dean of Bromley, 1965–66; Archdeacon of Bromley, 1966–68; Bishop Suffragan of Tonbridge, 1968–72. Entered House of Lords, 1976. *Recreations:* cricket, sailing, reading, gardening, walking. *Address:* Bramblecross, Gully Road, Seaview, Isle of Wight PO34 5BY.

See also D. French.

HALSEY, Rev. John Walter Brooke, 4th Bt *cr* 1920 (but uses designation Brother John Halsey); *b* 26 Dec. 1933; *s* of Sir Thomas Edgar Halsey, 3rd Bt, DSO, and of Jean Margaret Palmer, *d* of late Bertram Willes Dayrell Brooke; *S* father, 1970. *Educ:* Eton; Magdalene College, Cambridge (BA 1957). Deacon, 1961, priest, 1962, Diocese of York; Curate of Stocksbridge, 1961–65; Brother in Community of the Transfiguration, 1965–. *Heir: cousin* Nicholas Guy Halsey, TD [*b* 14 June 1948; *m* 1976, Viola Georgina Juliet, *d* of Maj. George Thorne, MC, DL; one *s*]. *Address:* Community of the Transfiguration, 23 Manse Road, Roslin, Midlothian.

HALSEY, Philip Hugh, CB 1986; LVO 1972; Chairman and Chief Executive, School Examinations and Assessment Council, 1988–91; Deputy Secretary, Department of Education and Science, 1982–88; *b* 9 May 1928; *s* of Sidney Robert Halsey and Edith Mary Halsey; *m* 1956, Hilda Mary Biggerstaff; two *s*. *Educ:* University Coll. London (BSc). Headmaster, Hampstead Sch., 1961; Principal, DES, 1966; Under-Sec., 1977.

HALSTEAD, Sir Ronald, Kt 1985; CBE 1976; Deputy Chairman, British Steel plc (formerly British Steel Corporation), since 1986; *b* 17 May 1927; *s* of Richard and Bessie Harrison Halstead; *m* 1968, Yvonne Cecile de Monchaux (*d* 1978); two *s*. *Educ:* Lancaster Royal Grammar Sch.; Queens' Coll., Cambridge (Hon. Fellow, 1985). MA, FRSC. Research Chemist, H. P. Bulmer & Co, 1948–53; Manufg Manager, Macleans Ltd, 1954–55; Factory Manager, Beecham Products Inc. (USA), 1955–60; Asst Managing Dir, Beecham Research Labs, 1960–62; Vice-Pres. (Marketing), Beecham Products Inc. (USA), 1962–64; Pres., Beecham Research Labs Inc. (USA), 1962–64; Chairman: Food and Drink Div., Beecham Group Ltd, 1964–67; Beecham Products, 1967–84; Man. Dir (Consumer Products) Beecham Gp, 1973–84; Chm. and Chief Exec., Beecham Gp, 1984–85. Dir, Otis Elevator Co. Ltd (UK), 1978–83; Non-Exec. Director: BSC, later British Steel, 1979–; The Burmah Oil PLC, 1983–89; Amer. Cyanamid Co. (USA), 1986–; Davy Corp. plc, 1986–; Gestetner Holdings PLC, 1986–. Mem. Egg Re-organisation Commn, 1967–68; Pres., Incorp. Soc. of Brit. Advertisers, 1971–73; Chairman: British Nutrition Foundn, 1970–73; Knitting Sector Gp (formerly Knitting Sector Working Party), NEDO, 1978–90; Bd for Food Studies, Reading Univ., 1983–86; Garment and Textile Sector Gp, NEDO, 1991–. Vice-Chairman: Proprietary Assoc. of GB, 1968–77; Advertising Assoc., 1973–81; Food and Drink Industries Council, 1973–76; Member: Council and Exec. Cttee, Food Manufrs' Fedn Inc., 1966–85 (Pres., 1974–76); Council, British Nutrition Foundn, 1967–79; Cambridge Univ. Appts Bd, 1969–73; Council, CBI, 1970–86; Council, BIM, 1972–77; Council, Univ. of Buckingham (formerly University Coll. at Buckingham), 1973–; Council, Nat. Coll. of Food Technol., 1977–78 (Chm. Bd, 1978–83); Council, Univ. of Reading, 1978–; AFRC, 1978–84; Council, Trade Policy Res. Centre, 1985–89; Newspaper Panel, Monopolies and Mergers Commn, 1980–; Industrial Develt Adv. Bd, 1984– (Chm., 1985–); Council and Exec. Cttee, Imperial Soc. of Knights Bachelor, 1986–. Dir and Hon. Treas., Centre for Policy Studies, 1984–. Trustee, Inst. of Economic Affairs, 1980–. Governor, Ashridge Management Coll., 1970– (Vice-Chm., 1977–); President: Nat. Advertising Benevolent Soc., 1978–80; Inst. of Packaging, 1981–82 (a Vice-Pres., 1979–81). Fellow, Marketing Soc., 1981; FBIM; FInstM; FIGD; FRSA; FRSC. Hon. Fellow, Inst. of Food Sci. and Technol., 1983–84. Hon. DSc Reading, 1982; Hon. DSc Lancaster, 1987. *Recreations:* sailing, squash racquets, ski-ing. *Address:* 37 Edwardes Square, W8 6HH. *T:* 071–603 9010. *Clubs:* Athenæum, Brooks's, Hurlingham, Carlton, Lansdowne, Royal Thames Yacht.

HAM, David Kenneth R.; *see* Rowe-Ham.

HAM, Prof. James Milton, OC 1980; ScD; FIEEE; President, Canadian Academy of Engineering, 1990–91; President and Professor Emeritus, University of Toronto; *b* 21 Sept. 1920; *s* of James Arthur Ham and Harriet Boomer Gandier; *m* Mary Caroline, *d* of Albert William Augustine; one *s* two *d*. *Educ:* Runnymede Coll. Inst., Toronto, 1936–39; Univ. of Toronto (BASc 1943); MIT (SM, ScD). Served with RCNVR as Elect. Lt, 1944–45. Lectr and Housemaster, Univ. of Toronto, 1945–46; Mass Inst. of Technology: Res. Associate, 1949–51; Res. Fellow in Electronics, 1950; Asst Prof. of Elect. Engrg, 1951–52; University of Toronto: Associate Prof., 1952–59; Prof., 1959–88; Prof. of Science, Technology and Public Policy, 1983–88; Pres., 1978–83; Fellow, New Coll., 1963; Head, Dept of Elect. Engrg, 1964–66; Dean, Fac. of Applied Science and Engrg, 1966–73; Chm., Research Bd, 1974–76; Dean, Sch. of Graduate Studies, 1976–78. Vis. Scientist, Cambridge Univ. and USSR, 1960–61. Dir, Shell Canada, 1981–91. Mem., Nat. Res. Council, 1969–74 (Chm., Associate Cttee on Automatic Control, 1959–65); Governor, Ont. Res. Foundn, 1971–86; Chairman: Cttee on Engrg Educn of World Fed. of Engrg Orgs, 1970; Res. and Technol. Review Bd, Noranda Inc., 1985; Industrial Disease Standards Panel, Ont., 1986–88. Member: Assoc. Prof. Engrs, Ont., 1943–; Internat. Fed. Automatic Control (Exec. Council), 1966–72; Fellow: Engrg Inst. Canada; Canadian Academy of Engrg, 1987. British Assoc. for Advancement of Science Medal, 1943; McNaughton Medal, IEEE, 1977; Centennial Medal, 1967, Engrg Medal, 1974, Gold Medal, 1984, Assoc. Professional Engrs, Ontario; Queens' Jubilee Medal, 1977; Engrg Alumni Medal, 1973; Sir John Kennedy Medal, Engrg Inst. Canada, 1983; Order of Ontario, 1989. Hon. DèsScA Montreal, 1973; Hon. DSc: Queen's, 1974; New Brunswick, 1979; McGill, 1979; McMaster, 1980; Hon. LLD: Manitoba, 1980; Hanyang (Korea), 1981; Hon. DEng: Tech. Univ. of Nova Scotia, 1980; Memorial Univ., 1981; Concordia Univ., 1983; Hon. DSacLet Wycliffe Coll., 1983. *Publications:* Scientific Basis of Electrical Engineering (with G. R. Slemon), 1961; Report of Royal Commission on Health and Safety of Workers in Mines, 1976; papers for scientific jls on automatic control. *Recreations:* sailing, skiing, photography. *Address:* 135 Glencairn Avenue, Toronto, Ontario M4R 1N1, Canada.

HAM, Rear-Adm. John Dudley Nelson, CB 1955; RN retired; *b* 7 Sept. 1902; *s* of Eng. Rear-Adm. John William Ham and Lily Florence Nelson; *m* 1927, Margery Lyne Sandercock (*d* 1990); no *c*. *Educ:* Edinburgh House, Lee-on-Solent; RN Colleges, Osborne and Dartmouth. Junior Service, 1920–37; HMS Ramillies, HMS Ceres; staff of RN Engineering College; Destroyers; Commander, 1937; Engineer Officer, Yangtse, China, 1938–40; served War of 1939–45: Chief Engineer, HMS Danae, 1940–41; Asst Dir Combined Operations Material, 1942; Chief Engineer, HMS Indomitable, 1945; Capt., 1946; Fleet Engineer Officer, Home Fleet, 1949; Staff Air Engineer Officer, 1951; Rear-Admiral, 1953; Dir of Aircraft Maintenance and Repair, 1953–55; Flag Officer Reserve Aircraft, 1955–57, retired. *Recreations:* golf, cabinet-making. *Address:* Green Lane Cottage, Lee-on-Solent, Hants PO13 9JW. *T:* Lee-on-Solent (0705) 550660.

HAMBIDGE, Most Rev. Douglas Walter; *see* New Westminster, Archbishop of.

HAMBLEDEN, 4th Viscount, *cr* 1891; **William Herbert Smith;** *b* 2 April 1930; *e s* of 3rd Viscount and Lady Patricia Herbert (*see* Dowager Viscountess Hambleden); *S* father 1948; *m* 1st, 1955, Donna Maria Carmela Attolico di Adelfia (marr. diss. 1988), *d* of late Count Bernardo Attolico and of Contessa Eleonora Attolico di Adelfia, Via Porta Latina, Rome; five *s*; 2nd, 1988, Mrs Lesley Watson. *Educ:* Eton. *Heir: s* Hon. William Henry Bernard Smith [*b* 18 Nov. 1955; *m* 1983, Sarah Suzanne, *d* of Joseph F. Anlauf and Mrs Suzanne K. Anlauf; two *d*]. *Address:* The Estate Office, Hambleden, Henley-on-Thames, Oxon. *T:* Henley-on-Thames (0491) 571353.

See also Baron Margadale.

HAMBLEDEN, Dowager Viscountess; Patricia, GCVO 1990 (DCVO 1953); Lady of the Bedchamber to HM Queen Elizabeth The Queen Mother, since 1937; *b* 12 Nov. 1904; *d* of 15th Earl of Pembroke, MVO and Lady Beatrice Eleanor Paget, CBE; *m* 1928, William Henry, 3rd Viscount Hambleden (*d* 1948); three *s* two *d*. *Address:* Hill House, Ewelme, Oxford OX9 6HP. *T:* Wallingford (0491) 39242.

HAMBLEN, Derek Ivens Archibald, CB 1978; OBE 1956; *b* 28 Oct. 1917; *s* of Leonard Tom Hamblen and late Ruth Mary Hamblen, *d* of Sir William Frederick Alphonse Archibald; *m* 1950, Pauline Alison, *d* of late Gen. Sir William Morgan, GCB, DSO, MC; one *s* one *d*. *Educ:* St Lawrence Coll., Ramsgate; St John's Coll., Oxford (Casberd Exhibn); Portuguese Essay Prize, 1938; BA Hons (Mod. Langs) 1940, MA 1949. Served War, 1940–46: 1st Army, N Africa, 1942–43; Major, GS, AFHQ, N Africa and Italy, and Adv. Mission to British Mil. HQ, Greece, 1944–45; GSO1, Allied Commn for Austria, 1945–46; Lt-Col, 1946. War Office, later Ministry of Defence, 1946–77: seconded HQ British Troops, Egypt, 1946–47; Asst Sec., Office of UK High Commn in Australia, 1951–55; seconded Foreign Office, 1957–60; Asst Sec., 1964–68; a Special Advr to NATO and SHAPE, 1968–74; Under Sec., 1974–77, retired. Mem. Bd of Governors, St Lawrence Coll., 1977–91 (Vice-Pres., 1991–). FRSA 1987. Medal of Merit, 1st cl. (Czechoslovakia), 1946. *Recreations:* cricket, hockey (represented Oxford v Cambridge, 1940), golf, music, reading. *Address:* c/o Lloyds Bank, East Grinstead, West Sussex. *Clubs:* MCC; Vincent's (Oxford).

HAMBLETON, Kenneth George; Director General, Air 3, Ministry of Defence, since 1990; *b* 15 Jan. 1937; *s* of George William Hambleton and Gertrude Nellie Hambleton (*née* Brighouse); *m* 1959, Glenys Patricia Smith; one *s* one *d*. *Educ:* Chesterfield Grammar Sch.; Queens' Coll., Cambridge (MA). CEng, FIEE. Services Electronics Res. Lab., Baldock, 1958–73; ASWE, Portsdown, 1973–81; a Dep. Dir, ASWE, 1981–82; Dir, Strategic Electronics-Radar, MoD PE, 1982–85; Asst Chief Scientific Advr (Projects and Res.), MoD, 1985–86; Dir Gen., Air Weapons and Electronic Systems, MoD, 1986–90. *Publications:* numerous articles and letters in nat. and internat. physics and electronic jls. *Recreations:* chess, bridge, golf, music—especially jazz. *Address:* c/o Ministry of Defence, Prospect House, 100 New Oxford Street, WC1A 1HE. *Clubs:* does not admit to clubs (or diamonds)—prefers the major suits or no trumps.

HAMBLING, Sir (Herbert) Hugh, 3rd Bt, *cr* 1924; *b* 3 Aug. 1919; *s* of Sir (Herbert) Guy (Musgrave) Hambling, 2nd Bt; *S* father 1966; *m* 1950, Anne Page Oswald (*d* 1990), Spokane, Washington, USA; one *s*; *m* 1991, Helen, *widow* of David Gavin. Educ: Wixenford Preparatory Sch.; Eton Coll. British Airways Ltd, 1937–39. RAF Training and Atlantic Ferry Command, 1939–46. British Overseas Airways: Montreal, 1948; Seattle, 1950; Manager, Sir Guy Hambling & Son, 1956; BOAC Representative, Douglas, Los Angeles, and Boeing Co., Seattle, 1957–75; Royal Brunei Airlines Rep., Boeing Co., Seattle, 1975. *Heir: s* (Herbert) Peter Hugh Hambling [*b* 6 Sept. 1953; *m* 1982, Jan Elizabeth Frederick, *d* of Stanton Willard Frederick, jr, and Mrs Frederick, Seattle, Washington]. *Address:* 1219 Evergreen Point Road, Bellevue, Washington 98004, USA. *T:* 206–454–0905 (USA); Rookery Park, Yoxford, Suffolk, England. *T:* Yoxford (072877) 310.

HAMBRO, Charles Eric Alexander; Chairman: Hambros PLC, since 1983; Guardian Royal Exchange Assurance, since 1988 (Director, since 1968; Deputy Chairman, 1974–88); *b* 24 July 1930; *s* of late Sir Charles Hambro, KBE, MC, and Pamela Cobbold; *m* 1st, 1954, Rose Evelyn (marr. diss. 1976), *d* of Sir Richard Cotterell, 5th Bt, CBE; two *s* one *d*; 2nd, 1976, Cherry Felicity, *d* of Sir John Huggins, GCMG, MC. *Educ:* Eton. Served Coldstream Guards, 1949–51; joined Hambros Bank Ltd, 1952: Man. Dir, 1957; Dep. Chm., 1965; Chm., 1972–83; Director: P&OSN Co., 1987–; Taylor Woodrow, 1962–; General Oriental Investments; Istituto Bancario San Paolo di Torino, 1989. Chm., Royal National Pension Fund for Nurses, 1968. Trustee, British Museum, 1984–. *Recreations:* shooting, cricket. *Address:* Dixton Manor, Gotherington, Cheltenham, Glos GL52 4RB. *T:* Bishops Cleeve (024267) 2011. *Clubs:* White's, MCC.

HAMBRO, Jocelyn Olaf, MC 1944; Chairman: Waverton Property Co. Ltd; J. O. Hambro & Co., since 1986; *b* 7 March 1919; *s* of late Ronald Olaf Hambro and late Winifred Martin-Smith; *m* 1st, 1942, Ann Silvia (*d* 1972), *d* of R. H. Muir; three *s*; 2nd, 1976, Margaret Elisabeth (*d* 1983), *d* of late Frederick Bradshaw McConnel and *widow* of 9th Duke of Roxburghe; 3rd, 1988, Margaret Anne, *d* of Michael Stratton and formerly wife of 7th Earl Fortescue. *Educ:* Eton; Trinity Coll., Cambridge. Coldstream Guards, 1939–45. Joined Hambros Bank Ltd, 1945; Man. Dir, 1947–72; Chm., 1965–72; Chm., Hambros Ltd, 1970–83, Pres. 1983–. Formerly Chairman: The Hambro Trust Ltd; Hambros Investment Trust Ltd; HIT Securities Ltd. Chairman: Phœnix Assurance Co. Ltd, 1978–85; Charter Consolidated, 1982–88 (Dir, 1965–88). Member, Jockey Club. *Recreations:* racing, shooting. *Address:* 101 Eaton Place, SW1. *T:* 071–235 7210; Waverton House, Moreton in Marsh, Glos GL56 9PB. *T:* Blockley (0386) 700700. *Clubs:* Pratt's, White's.

See also R. N. Hambro.

HAMBRO, Rupert Nicholas; Group Managing Director, J. O. Hambro & Co., since 1986; *b* 27 June 1943; *s* of Jocelyn Olaf Hambro, *qv*; *m* 1970, Mary Robinson Boyer; one *s* one *d*. *Educ:* Eton; Aix-en-Provence. Joined Hambros Bank, 1964, Director, 1969, Chm., 1983–86. Director: Anglo American Corporation of South Africa, 1981–; Racecourse Hldgs Trust Ltd, 1985–; Daily Telegraph PLC, 1986–; Sedgwick Group plc, 1987–; Triton Europe plc, 1987–90; Hamleys Ltd, 1988–; Pioneer Concrete Hldgs, 1989–; Tiphook plc, 1990–; Chairman: Wilton's (St James's) Ltd, 1987–; J. O. Hambro Magan & Co. Ltd, 1988–; Mayflower Corp. Plc, 1988–. Chm., Assoc. of International Bond Dealers, 1979–82; Member: SE Econ. Planning Council, 1971–74; Internat. Council, US Information Agency, 1988–. Knight of the Falcon (Iceland), 1986. *Recreations:* racing, shooting. *Address:* 186 Ebury Street, SW1W 8UP. *T:* 071–235 5656; Chalk House, Chalkhouse Green, Kidmore End, Oxon. *T:* Kidmore End (0734) 723544. *Clubs:* White's, Portland; Jupiter Island (Florida).

HAMBURGER, Michael Peter Leopold, MA (Oxon); *b* Berlin, 22 March 1924; *e s* of late Prof. Richard Hamburger and Mrs L. Hamburger (*née* Hamburg); *m* 1951, Anne Ellen File; one *s* two *d*. *Educ:* Westminster Sch.; Christ Church, Oxford. Army Service, 1943–47; Freelance Writer, 1948–52; Asst Lectr in German, UCL, 1952–55; Lectr, then Reader in German, Univ. of Reading, 1955–64. Florence Purington Lectr, Mount Holyoke Coll., Mass, 1966–67; Visiting Professor, State Univ. of NY: at Buffalo, 1969; at Stony Brook, 1971; Vis. Fellow, Center for Humanities, Wesleyan Univ., Conn, 1970; Vis. Prof. Univ. of S Carolina, 1973; Regent's Lectr, Univ. of California, San Diego, 1973; Vis. Prof., Boston Univ., 1975–77; part-time Prof., Univ. of Essex, 1978. Bollingen Foundn Fellow, 1959–61, 1965–66. FRSL 1972–86. Corresp. Mem., Deutsche Akademie für Sprache und Dichtung, Darmstadt, 1973; Akademie der Künste, Berlin; Akad. der Schönen Künste, Munich. Hon. LittD UEA, 1988. Translation Prizes: Deutsche Akademie für Sprache und Dichtung, Darmstadt, 1964; Arts Council, 1969; Arts Prize, Inter

Nationes, Bonn, 1976; Medal, Inst. of Linguists, 1977; Schlegel-Tieck Prize, London, 1978, 1981; Wilhelm-Heinse Prize (medallion), Mainz, 1978; Goethe Medal, 1986; Austrian State Prize for Literary Translation, 1988; European Translation Prize, 1990. *Publications: poetry:* Flowering Cactus, 1950; Poems 1950–1951, 1952; The Dual Site, 1958; Weather and Season, 1963; Feeding the Chickadees, 1968; Penguin Modern Poets (with A. Brownjohn and C. Tomlinson), 1969; Travelling, 1969; Travelling, I-V, 1973; Ownerless Earth, 1973; Travelling VI, 1975; Real Estate, 1977; Moralities, 1977; Variations, 1981; Collected Poems, 1984; Trees, 1988; Selected Poems, 1988; *translations:* Poems of Hölderlin, 1943, rev. edn as Hölderlin: Poems, 1952; C. Baudelaire, Twenty Prose Poems, 1946, repr. 1968 and 1988; L. van Beethoven, Letters, Journals and Conversations, 1951, repr. 1967, 1978; J. C. F. Hölderlin, Selected Verse, 1961, repr. 1986; G. Trakl, Decline, 1952; A. Goes, The Burnt Offering, 1956; (with others) H. von Hofmannsthal, Poems and Verse Plays, 1961; B. Brecht, Tales from the Calendar, 1961; (with C. Middleton) Modern German Poetry 1910–1960, 1962; (with others) H. von Hofmannsthal, Selected Plays and Libretti, 1964; G. Büchner, Lenz, 1966; H. M. Enzensberger, Poems, 1966; (with C. Middleton) G. Grass, Selected Poems, 1966; J. C. F. Hölderlin, Poems and Fragments, 1967, new enlarged edn 1980; (with J. Rothenberg and the author) H. M. Enzensberger, The Poems of Hans Magnus Enzensberger, 1968; H. M. Enzensberger, Poems For People Who Don't Read Poems, 1968; (with C. Middleton), G. Grass, The Poems of Günter Grass, 1969; P. Bichsel, And Really Frau Blum Would Very Much Like To Meet The Milkman, 1968; G. Eich, Journeys, 1968; N. Sachs, Selected Poems, 1968; Peter Bichsel, Stories for Children, 1971; Paul Celan, Selected Poems, 1972, new enlarged edn 1988; (ed) East German Poetry, 1972; Peter Huchel, Selected Poems, 1974; German Poetry 1910–1975, 1977; Helmut Heissenbüttel, Texts, 1977; Franco Fortini, Poems, 1978; An Unofficial Rilke, 1981; Peter Huchel, The Garden of Theophrastus, 1983; Goethe, Poems and Epigrams, 1983; *prose:* Testimonies, selected shorter prose 1950–1987, 1989; *criticism:* Reason and Energy, 1957; From Prophecy to Exorcism, 1965; The Truth of Poetry, 1970, new edn 1982; Hugo von Hofmannsthal, 1973; Art as Second Nature, 1975; A Proliferation of Prophets, 1983; After the Second Flood: essays in modern German Literature, 1986; *autobiography:* A Mug's Game, 1973. *Recreations:* gardening, walking. *Address:* c/o John Johnson Ltd, Clerkenwell House, 45/47 Clerkenwell Green, EC1R 0HT.

See also P. B. Hamlyn.

HAMBURGER, Sir Sidney (Cyril), Kt 1981; CBE 1966; JP; DL; Chairman, North Western Regional Health Authority, 1973–82; *b* 14 July 1914; *s* of Isidore and Hedwig Hamburger; *m* 1940; three *s. Educ:* Salford Grammar Sch. Served in Army, 1940–46, Capt. Salford City Council: Mem., 1946–70; Alderman, 1961–70; Mayor of Salford, 1968–69. Chairman: NE Manchester Hosp. Management Cttee, 1970–74; NW ASH, 1977–; Age Concern, Salford, 1984–; Manchester Cttee for Soviet Jewry, 1984–; Gtr Manchester Area CAB, 1985–; Member: NW Electricity Bd Consultative Council, 1953–59 (Chm. Manchester Cttee, 1963–68); Manchester Regional Hosp. Bd, 1966–74 (Chm. Finance Cttee); Supplementary Benefits Commn, 1967–77; BBC NW Adv. Cttee, 1970–73; Manchester Univ. Court, 1973–84. President: Council, Manchester-Salford Jews, 1962–65; Jt Israel Appeal, Manchester, 1984–; Life-President: Manchester Jewish Homes for the Aged, 1965–; Zionist Central Council of Greater Manchester; Vice-Pres., Friends of Israel Assoc., Manchester; Nat. Pres., Trades Advisory Council, 1984–; Pres., Notability NW, 1989–; Vice-Pres., British Lung Foundn, 1987–. Governor, Ben Gurion Univ., Israel, 1979–. Hon. Fellow, Bar-Ilan Univ., Israel, 1979; Hon. MA Salford, 1979; Hon. LLD Manchester, 1983. Pro Ecclesia, Papal Award, 1982. JP Salford, 1957; DL Greater Manchester, 1981. *Recreation:* football. *Address:* 26 New Hall Road, Salford M7 0JU.

HAMEED, A. C. Shahul; Minister of Higher Education, Science and Technology, Sri Lanka, since 1989; *b* 10 April 1929. Mem., United National Party; Mem. for Harispattuwa, Nat. Parliament, 1960–; former Dep. Chm., Public Accounts Cttee; has been concerned with foreign affairs, public finance and higher education; Minister of Foreign Affairs, 1977–89. Leader of delegns to internat. confs, incl. UN; Chm., Ministerial Conf. of Non-Aligned Countries; Mem., Conf. of UN Cttee on Disarmament. Governor, Univ. of Sri Lanka. *Publications:* In Pursuit of Peace: on non-alignment and regional cooperation, 1983; Owl and the Lotus, 1986; Disarmament—a multilateral approach, 1988; Foreign Policy Perspectives of Sri Lanka, 1988; short stories and poems. *Address:* Ministry of Higher Education, Science and Technology, 18 Ward Place, Colombo 7, Sri Lanka.

HAMER, Hon. Sir Rupert (James), KCMG 1982; ED; LLM (Melb.); FAIM; Premier of Victoria, Australia, and Treasurer, 1972–81; *b* 29 July 1916; *s* of H. R. Hamer; *m* 1944, April F., *d* of N. R. Mackintosh; two *s* two *d. Educ:* Melbourne Grammar and Geelong Grammar Schs; Trinity Coll., Univ. of Melbourne (LLM; Fellow, 1982). Solicitor, admitted 1940. Served War of 1939–45: 5½ years, AIF, Tobruk, Alamein, NG, Normandy. MLA (Lib.) E Yarra, 1958–71, Kew, Vic., 1971–81; Minister for: Immigration, 1962–64; Local Govt, 1964–71; Chief Sec. and Dep. Premier, Victoria, 1971–72; Minister for: the Arts, 1972–79; State Develt, Decentralization and Tourism, 1979–81. Chm., Vic. State Opera; Vice-Chm., Cttee of Management, Werribee Park; Nat. Pres., Save the Children Fund (Australia), 1989–; President: Greenhouse Action, Australia; Vic. Coll. of the Arts; Mem., Melbourne Scots Council; Chieftain, Vic. Pipe Bands Assoc.; Trustee: Yarra Bend Park; Melbourne Cricket Ground. CO, Vic. Scottish Regt, CMF, 1954–58. Hon. LLD Univ. of Melbourne, 1982. *Recreations:* tennis, Australian Rules football, walking, music. *Address:* 39 Monomeath Avenue, Canterbury, Victoria 3126, Australia. *Club:* Naval and Military.

HAMILL, Sir Patrick, Kt 1984; QPM 1979; Chief Constable, Strathclyde Police, 1977–85; *b* 29 April 1930; *s* of Hugh Hamill and Elizabeth McGowan; *m* 1954, Nell Gillespie; four *s* one *d. Educ:* St Patrick's High Sch., Dumbarton; BA. Joined Dunbartonshire Constabulary, 1950; transf. to City of Glasgow Police, 1972; apptd Assistant Chief Constable: Glasgow, 1974; Strathclyde Police, 1975; attended Royal Coll. of Defence Studies Course, 1976. Assoc. of Chief Police Officers (Scotland): Rep. to Interpol, 1977–81; Pres., 1982–83; Hon. Sec., 1983–85. Chm., Management Bd, St Margaret's Hospice, Clydebank, 1986–; Member Board of Governors: Scottish Police Coll., 1977–85; St Aloysius' Coll., Glasgow, 1983–90 (Vice-Chm., 1986–90); St Andrew's Coll. of Educn, Bearsden, 1987–88; Mem., Gen. Convocation, Univ. of Strathclyde, 1984–87. OStJ 1978. *Recreations:* walking, reading history, golf.

HAMILTON, family name of **Duke of Abercorn,** of **Lord Belhaven,** and of **Barons Hamilton of Dalzell** and **HolmPatrick.**

HAMILTON; *see* Baillie-Hamilton, family name of Earl of Haddington.

HAMILTON; *see* Cole-Hamilton.

HAMILTON; *see* Douglas-Hamilton.

HAMILTON, 15th Duke of, *cr* 1643, Scotland, **AND BRANDON,** 12th Duke of, *cr* 1711, Great Britain; **Angus Alan Douglas Douglas-Hamilton;** Premier Peer of Scotland; Hereditary Keeper of Palace of Holyroodhouse; *b* 13 Sept. 1938; *e s* of 14th Duke of Hamilton and Brandon, PC, KT, GCVO, AFC, and of Lady Elizabeth Percy, OBE, DL, *er d* of 8th Duke of Northumberland, KG; *S* father, 1973; *m* 1st, 1972, Sarah (marr. diss. 1987), *d* of Sir Walter Scott, Bt, *qv*; two *s* two *d*; 2nd, 1988, Jillian, *d* of late Noel Robertson, Sydney, Australia. *Educ:* Eton; Balliol Coll., Oxford (MAEngrg). Flt Lieut RAF; invalided, 1967. Flying Instructor, 1965; Sen. Commercial Pilot's Licence, 1967; Test Pilot, Scottish Aviation, 1971–72. Mem. Council, CRC, 1978–. Mem., Queen's Body Guard for Scotland, 1975–. Hon. Mem., Royal Scottish Pipers Soc., 1977; Patron, British Airways Pipe Band, 1977–. Hon. Air Cdre, No 2 (City of Edinburgh) Maritime HQ Unit, RAuxAF, 1982–. KStJ 1975 (Prior, Order of St John in Scotland, 1975–82). *Heir: s* Marquess of Douglas and Clydesdale, *qv. Address:* Lennoxlove, Haddington, E Lothian EH41 4NZ. *T:* Haddington (062082) 3720. *Clubs:* Royal Air Force; New (Edinburgh).

See also Lord James Douglas-Hamilton.

HAMILTON, Marquess of; James Harold Charles Hamilton; *b* 19 Aug. 1969; *s* and *heir* of Duke of Abercorn, *qv*. A Page of Honour to the Queen, 1982–84. *Address:* Barons Court, Omagh, Co. Tyrone BT78 4EZ.

HAMILTON OF DALZELL, 4th Baron *cr* 1886; **James Leslie Hamilton;** *b* 11 Feb. 1938; *s* of 3rd Baron Hamilton of Dalzell, GCVO, MC and of Rosemary Olive, *d* of Maj. Hon. Sir John Coke, KCVO; *S* father, 1990; *m* 1967, Corinna, *yr d* of Sir Pierson Dixon, GCMG, CB; four *s* (incl. twins). *Educ:* Eton. Served Coldstream Guards, 1956–58. Mem., Stock Exchange, 1967–80. Dir, Rowton Hotels plc, 1978–84; Chm., Queen Elizabeth's Foundn for the Disabled, 1989–. *Heir: s* Hon. Gavin Goulburn Hamilton, *b* 8 Oct. 1968. *Address:* Stockton House, Stockton, Norton Shifnal, Salop TF11 9EF; Betchworth House, Betchworth, Surrey RH3 7DJ.

See also Rt Hon. A. G. Hamilton.

HAMILTON, Adrian Walter, QC 1973; a Recorder of the Crown Court, since 1974; *b* 11 March 1923; *er s* of late W. G. M. Hamilton, banker, Fletching, Sussex and of late Mrs S. E. Hamilton; *m* 1966, Jill, *d* of S. R. Brimblecombe, Eastbourne; two *d. Educ:* Highgate Sch.; Balliol Coll., Oxford. BA 1st cl. Jurisprudence 1948, MA 1954. Served with RN, 1942–46: Ord. Seaman, 1942; Sub-Lt RNVR, 1943, Lieut 1946. Balliol Coll., 1946–48: Jenkyns Law Prize; Paton Mem. Student, 1948–49; Cassel Scholar, Lincoln's Inn, 1949; called to Bar, Lincoln's Inn, 1949 (Bencher 1979), Middle Temple and Inner Temple; Mem., Senate of Inns of Court and the Bar, 1976–82, Treas., 1979–82; Mem. Council, Inns of Court, 1987–91. Mem., Council of Legal Educn, 1977–87. Inspector, Peek Foods Ltd, 1977. *Recreations:* family, golf, sailing, gardening. *Address:* 7 King's Bench Walk, Temple, EC4Y 7DS. *T:* 071–583 0404. *Clubs:* Garrick, Roehampton; Piltdown Golf.

HAMILTON, Adrianne Pauline U.; *see* Uziell-Hamilton.

HAMILTON, Rt. Rev. Alexander Kenneth, MA; Hon. Assistant Bishop, Diocese of Bath and Wells, since 1988; *b* 11 May 1915; *s* of Cuthbert Arthur Hamilton and Agnes Maud Hamilton; unmarried. *Educ:* Malvern Coll.; Trinity Hall, Cambridge; Westcott House, Cambridge. MA 1941. Asst Curate of Birstall, Leicester, 1939–41; Asst Curate of Whitworth with Spennymoor, 1941–45. Chaplain, RNVR, 1945–47. Vicar of S Francis, Ashton Gate, Bristol, 1947–58; Vicar of S John the Baptist, Newcastle upon Tyne, 1958–65; Rural Dean of Central Newcastle, 1962–65; Bishop Suffragan of Jarrow, 1965–80. *Publication:* Personal Prayers, 1963. *Recreations:* golf, trout fishing. *Address:* 3 Ash Tree Road, Burnham-on-Sea, Somerset TA8 2LB. *Clubs:* Naval; Burnham and Berrow Golf.

HAMILTON, Alexander Macdonald, CBE 1979; Consultant, McGrigor Donald, Solicitors, Glasgow, since 1990 (Senior Partner, 1977–90); *b* 11 May 1925; *s* of John Archibald Hamilton and Thomasina Macdonald or Hamilton; *m* 1953, Catherine Gray; two *s* one *d. Educ:* Hamilton Acad. (Dux, 1943); Glasgow Univ. (MA 1948, LLB 1951). Solicitor. Served War, RNVR, 1943–46. Dir, Royal Bank of Scotland, 1978– (Vice Chm., 1990–). Law Soc. of Scotland: Mem. Council, 1970–82; Vice-Pres., 1975–76; Pres., 1977–78. Pres., Glasgow Juridical Soc., 1955–56. Vice-Pres. and Chm., Greater Glasgow Scout Council, 1978–85; Cttee Chm., Scottish Council, Scout Assoc., 1986–. Session Clerk, Cambuslang Old Parish Church, 1969–; Vice-Chm., Cambuslang Community Council, 1978–. *Recreations:* golf, sailing. *Address:* 30 Wellshot Drive, Cambuslang, Glasgow G72 8BT. *T:* 041–641 1445. *Clubs:* Royal Scottish Automobile (Glasgow); Royal Northern & Clyde Yacht.

HAMILTON, Rt. Hon. Archibald (Gavin), PC 1991; MP (C) Epsom and Ewell, since April 1978; Minister of State, Ministry of Defence, since 1988; *b* 30 Dec. 1941; *yr s* of 3rd Baron Hamilton of Dalzell, GCVO, MC; *m* 1968, Anne Catharine Napier; three *d. Educ:* Eton Coll. Borough Councillor, Kensington and Chelsea, 1968–71. Contested (C) Dagenham, Feb. and Oct., 1974. PPS to Sec. of State for Energy, 1979–81, to Sec. of State for Transport, 1981–82; an Asst Govt Whip, 1982–84; a Lord Comr of HM Treasury (Govt Whip), 1984–86; Parly Under-Sec. of State for Defence Procurement, MoD, 1986–87; PPS to Prime Minister, 1987–88. *Address:* House of Commons, SW1A 0AA.

HAMILTON, Arthur Campbell; QC (Scot.) 1982; Judge of the Courts of Appeal, Jersey and Guernsey, since 1988; *b* 10 June 1942; *s* of James Whitehead Hamilton and Isobel Walker Hamilton (*née* McConnell); *m* 1970, Christine Ann Croll; one *d. Educ:* The High School of Glasgow; Glasgow Univ.; Worcester Coll., Oxford (BA); Edinburgh Univ. (LLB). Admitted member, Faculty of Advocates, 1968; Standing Junior Counsel: to Scottish Development Dept, 1975–78; to Board of Inland Revenue (Scotland), 1978–82; Advocate Depute, 1982–85. *Recreations:* hill walking, fishing. *Address:* 8 Heriot Row, Edinburgh. *T:* 031–556 4663. *Club:* New (Edinburgh).

HAMILTON, Douglas Owens; Senior Partner, Norton Rose (formerly Norton, Rose, Botterell & Roche), since 1982; *b* 20 April 1931; *s* of Oswald Hamilton and Edith Florence Hamilton; *m* 1962, Judith Mary Wood; three *s. Educ:* John Fisher Sch., Purley, Surrey; Univ. of London (LLB). Admitted Solicitor, 1953; joined Botterell & Roche, 1955, Partner, 1959; Exec. Partner, Norton, Rose, Botterell & Roche, 1976–82. Mem., Court of Benefactors, Oxford Univ.; Hon. Treasurer: British Maritime Charitable Foundn; British Polish Legal Assoc. *Recreations:* tennis, golf, travelling. *Address:* Boarsney, Salehurst, near Robertsbridge, East Sussex TN32 5SR.

HAMILTON, Dundas; *see* Hamilton, J. D.

HAMILTON, Eben William; QC 1981; *b* 12 June 1937; *s* of late Rev. John Edmund Hamilton, MC and Hon. Lilias Maclay; *m* 1st, 1973, Catherine Harvey (marr. diss. 1977); 2nd, 1985, Themy Rusi Bilimoria, *y d* of late Brig. Rusi Bilimoria. *Educ:* Winchester; Trinity Coll., Cambridge. Nat. Service: 4/7 Royal Dragoon Guards, 1955–57; Fife and Forfar Yeomanry/Scottish Horse, TA, 1958–66. Called to the Bar, Inner Temple, 1962, Bencher, 1985. FRSA 1988. *Address:* 1 New Square, Lincoln's Inn, WC2. *T:* 071–405 0884. *Club:* Garrick.

See also Martha Hamilton.

HAMILTON, Sir Edward (Sydney), 7th and 5th Bt, *cr* 1776 and 1819; *b* 14 April 1925; *s* of Sir (Thomas) Sydney (Percival) Hamilton, 6th and 4th Bt, and Bertha Muriel, *d* of James Russell King, Singleton Park, Kendal; *S* father, 1966. *Educ:* Canford Sch. Served Royal Engineers, 1943–47; 1st Royal Sussex Home Guard, 1953–56. *Recreations:* Spiritual matters, music. *Heir:* none. *Address:* The Cottage, East Lavant, near Chichester, West Sussex PO18 0AL. *T:* Chichester (0243) 527414.

HAMILTON, Sheriff Francis Hugh; Sheriff of North Strathclyde, since 1984; *b* 3 Dec. 1927; *s* of late Hugh Hamilton and Mary Catherine (*née* Gallagher); *m* 1968, Angela Haffey; one *d*. *Educ:* Notre Dame Convent, Glasgow; St Aloysius' Coll., Glasgow; Univ. of Glasgow (BL 1948). Nat. Service, 1948–50; commnd RASC. Admitted Solicitor, 1951; Town Clerk's Office, Glasgow, 1952–53; in private practice, 1953–84; Sen. Partner, Hamilton & Co., Solicitors, Glasgow, 1967–84; Temp. Sheriff, 1980; Floating Sheriff, 1984–. Pres., Glasgow Bar Assoc., 1963–64; Mem. Council, Law Soc. of Scotland, 1975–84. *Recreations:* music, playing the piano rather badly and bridge very badly. *Address:* 4 Park Quadrant, Glasgow G3 6BS. *T:* 041–332 2265.

HAMILTON, Prof. George Heard; Director, Sterling and Francine Clark Art Institute, 1966–77, now Emeritus; Professor of Art, Williams College, Williamstown, Massachusetts, 1966–75, now Emeritus; Director of Graduate Studies in Art History, Williams College, 1971–75; *b* 23 June 1910; *s* of Frank A. Hamilton and Georgia Neale Heard; *m* 1945, Polly Wiggin; one *s* one *d*. *Educ:* Yale Univ. BA 1932; MA 1934; PhD 1942. Research Asst, Walters Art Gallery, Baltimore, 1934–36; Mem. Art History Faculty, Yale Univ., 1936–66 (Prof., 1956–66); Robert Sterling Clark Prof. of Art, Williams Coll., 1963–64. Slade Prof. of Fine Art, Cambridge Univ., 1971–72; Kress Prof. in Residence, Nat. Gall of Art, Washington, DC, 1978–79. FRSA 1973; Fellow, Amer. Acad. of Arts and Science, 1979. Hon. LittD Williams Coll., 1977; Wilbur Lucius Cross Medal, Yale Grad. Sch., 1977; Amer. Art Dealers' Assoc. award for excellence in art hist., 1978. *Publications:* (with D. V. Thompson, Jr) De Arte Illuminandi, 1933; Manet and His Critics, 1954; The Art and Architecture of Russia, 1954; Monet's Paintings of Rouen Cathedral, 1960; European Painting and Sculpture, 1880–1940, 1967; (with W. C. Agee) Raymond Duchamp-Villon, 1967; 19th and 20th Century Art: Painting, Sculpture, Architecture, 1970; Articles in Burlington Magazine, Gazette des Beaux-Arts, Art Bulletin, etc. *Recreations:* music, gardening. *Address:* 121 Gale Road, Williamstown, Mass 01267, USA. *T:* (413) 458–8626. *Clubs:* Century Association (New York); Elizabethan (New Haven); Edgartown Yacht (Mass).

HAMILTON, Graeme Montagu, TD; QC 1978; a Recorder of the Crown Court, since 1974; *b* 1 June 1934; *s* of late Leslie Montagu Hamilton and of Joan Lady Burbidge (Joan Elizabeth Burbidge, *née* Moxey); *m* 1978, Mrs Deirdre Lynn. *Educ:* Eton; Magdalene Coll., Cambridge (MA). National Service, 4/7 Royal Dragoon Guards, 1953–55. Called to Bar, Gray's Inn, 1959, Bencher, 1987; Mem., Senate of Inns of Court and Bar, 1975–78. Mem., Criminal Injuries Compensation Bd, 1987–. Gen. Comr of Income Tax, 1989–. TA City of London Yeomanry, Inns of Court and City Yeomanry, 1955–70. *Recreations:* sailing, shooting, gardening. *Address:* 2 Crown Office Row, Temple, EC4Y 7HJ. *Clubs:* Cavalry and Guards, Royal Thames Yacht, Royal Automobile.

HAMILTON, Brig. Hugh Gray Wybrants, CBE 1964 (MBE 1945); DL; Chairman, Forces Help Society and Lord Roberts Workshops, 1976–91; *b* 16 May 1918; *s* of Lt-Col H. W. Hamilton, late 5th Dragoon Guards; *m* 1944, Claire Buxton; two *d*. *Educ:* Wellington Coll., Berks; Peterhouse, Cambridge; Royal Mil. Academy. Commissioned with Royal Engineers, 1938. War Service in BEF, BNAF, BLA, 1939–45. Post War Service in Australia, BAOR, France and UK. Instructor, Army Staff Coll., Camberley, 1954–56; Student, IDC, 1965; retired, 1968. Gen. Manager, Corby Develt Corp., 1968–80. DL Northants, 1977. *Recreations:* riding, sailing, DIY. *Address:* Cherwell House, Hogg End, Chipping Warden, Banbury OX17 1LY. *T:* Chipping Warden (029586) 656.

HAMILTON, Iain Ellis, BMus, FRAM; composer; pianist; Mary Duke Biddle Professor of Music, Duke University, North Carolina, USA, 1962–78 (Chairman of the Department, 1966); *b* Glasgow, 6 June 1922; *s* of James and Catherine Hamilton. *Educ:* Mill Hill; Royal Academy of Music. Engineer (Handley Page Ltd), 1939–46; RAM (Scholar) 1947–51; BMus (London University), 1951. Lecturer at Morley Coll., 1952–58; Lecturer, London Univ., 1956–60. Prizes and awards include: Prize of Royal Philharmonic Society, 1951; Prize of Koussevitsky Foundation (America), 1951; Butterworth Award, 1954; Arnold Bax Gold Medal, 1956; Ralph Vaughan Williams Award, Composers' Guild of GB, 1975. FRAM, 1960. Chm. Composers' Guild, 1958; Chm. ICA Music Cttee, 1958–60. *Works: orchestral works:* Symphonies; Sinfonia for two orchestras (Edinburgh Festival Commission); Concertos, for piano, clarinet, organ and violin; The Bermudas, for baritone, chorus and orchestra (BBC Commission); Symphonic Variations for string orchestra; Overture, Bartholomew Fair; Overture, 1912; Ecossaise; Concerto for jazz trumpet and orchestra (BBC Commn); Scottish Dances; 5 Love Songs for tenor and orchestra; (BBC Commission) Cantos; Jubilee; Arias for small orchestra; Vers Apollinaire, for orch.; Circus (BBC Commn); Epitaph for this World and Time: 3 choruses and 2 organs; Vespers, for chorus, 2 pianos, harp and percussion; Voyage for horn and orchestra; Alastor; Amphion for violin and orchestra; Commedia; Threnos for solo organ; Aubade and Paraphrase for solo organ; Clerk Saunders, a ballet; *chamber works include:* four String Quartets; String Octet; Sonatas for piano, viola, clarinet and flute; Sonata for chamber orchestra; Flute Quartet; Clarinet Quintet; 3 Nocturnes for clarinet and piano; 5 Scenes for trumpet and piano; Sextet; Sonatas and Variants for 10 winds; Dialogues for soprano and 5 instruments; Nocturnes with Cadenzas for solo piano; 4 Border Songs, The Fray of Suport, a Requiem and a Mass for unaccompanied voices; St Mark Passion for 4 soloists, chorus and orchestra; Cleopatra for soprano and orchestra; Sextet for Strings; Prometheus, for soloists, chorus and orch.; La Mort de Phèdre, for mezzo-soprano and orch.; *Opera:* Agamemnon; Royal Hunt of the Sun; Pharsalia; The Catiline Conspiracy; Tamburlaine; Anna Karenina; Dick Whittington; Lancelot; Raleigh's Dream. Music for theatre and films. Hon. DMus Glasgow, 1970. *Publications:* articles for many journals. *Address:* 1 King Street, WC2E 8HN.

HAMILTON, Ian; poet; *b* 24 March 1938; *s* of Robert Tough Hamilton and Daisy McKay; *m* 1st, 1963, Gisela Dietzel; one *s*; 2nd, 1981, Ahdaf Soueif; two *s*. *Educ:* Darlington Grammar Sch.; Keble Coll., Oxford (BA Hons). Editor, Review, 1962–72; Poetry and Fiction Editor, Times Literary Supplement, 1965–73; Lectr in Poetry, Univ. of Hull, 1972–73; Editor, The New Review, 1974–79. Presenter, Bookmark (BBC TV series), 1984–87. E. C. Gregory Award, 1963; Malta Cultural Award, 1974. *Publications:* (ed) The Poetry of War 1939–45, 1965; (ed) Alun Lewis: poetry and prose, 1966; (ed) The Modern Poet, 1968; The Visit (poems), 1970; A Poetry Chronicle, 1973; (ed) Robert Frost: selected poems, 1973; The Little Magazines, 1976; Returning (poems), 1976; Robert Lowell: a biography, 1983; (ed) Yorkshire in Verse, 1984; (ed) The New Review Anthology, 1985; Fifty Poems, 1988; In Search of J. D. Salinger, 1988; (ed) Soho Square, 1989; Writers in Hollywood, 1990. *Address:* 54 Queen's Road, SW19. *T:* 081–946 0291.

HAMILTON, Ian Robertson; QC (Scot.) 1980; *b* Paisley, Scotland, 13 Sept. 1925; *s* of John Harris Hamilton and Martha Robertson; *m* 1974, Jeannette Patricia Mari Stewart, Connel, Argyll; one *s* (one *s* two *d* by former *m*). *Educ:* John Neilson Sch., Paisley; Allan Glens Sch., Glasgow; Glasgow and Edinburgh Univs (BL). Served RAFVR, 1944–48. Called to the Scottish Bar, 1954 and to the Albertan Bar, 1982. Advocate Depute, 1962; Dir of Civil Litigation, Republic of Zambia, 1964–66; Hon. Sheriff of Lanarks, 1967; retd from practice to work for National Trust for Scotland and later to farm in Argyll, 1969; returned to practice, 1974; Sheriff of Glasgow and Strathkelvin, May-Dec. 1984; resigned commn Dec. 1984; returned to practice. Founder, Castle Wynd Printers, Edinburgh, 1955 (published four paper-back vols of Hugh MacDiarmid's poetry, 1955–56). Founder and first Chm., The Whichway Trust, to provide adventure training for young offenders, 1988. Chief Pilot, Scottish Parachute Club, 1979–80. *Publications:* No Stone Unturned, 1952 (also New York); The Tinkers of the World, 1957 (Foyle award-winning play); A Touch of Treason (autobiog.), 1990; To Steal a Stone, 1991; contrib. various jls. *Recreation:* oyster farming. *Address:* Advocates' Library, Parliament House, Edinburgh EH1 1RF.

HAMILTON, James, CBE 1979; *b* 11 March 1918; *s* of George Hamilton and Margaret Carey; *m* 1945, Agnes McGhee; one *s* three *d* (and one *s* decd). *Educ:* St Bridget's, Baillieston; St Mary's, High Whifflet. District Councillor, 6th Lanarks, 1955–58; Lanarks County Council, 1958–64. National Executive Mem., Constructional Engrg Union, 1958–71, Pres., 1968–69; Chm., Trade Union Group, Parly Labour Party, 1969–70. MP (Lab): Bothwell, 1964–83; Motherwell N, 1983–87. Asst Govt Whip, 1969–70; an Opposition Whip, 1970–74; a Lord Comr of the Treasury and Vice-Chamberlain of the Household, 1974–78; Comptroller of HM Household, 1978–79. *Recreations:* tennis, badminton, golf. *Address:* 12 Rosegreen Crescent, North Road, Bellshill, Lanarks.

HAMILTON, Prof. James; Professor of Physics, Nordic Institute for Theoretical Atomic Physics, 1964–85; *b* 29 Jan. 1918; *s* of Joseph Hamilton, Killybegs, Co. Donegal and Jessie Mackay, Keiss, Caithness; *m* 1945, Glen, *d* of Charles Dobbs, London; one *s* one *d* (and one *s* decd). *Educ:* Royal Academical Institution, Belfast; Queen's Univ., Belfast; Institute for Advanced Study, Dublin, 1941–43; Manchester Univ. Scientific Officer (Ops Research), Admiralty, London, and South East Asia Command, 1943–45; ICI Fellow, Manchester Univ., 1945–48; Lectr in Theoretical Physics, Manchester Univ., 1948–49; University Lectr in Mathematics, Cambridge Univ., 1950–60. Fellow of Christ's Coll., Cambridge, 1953–60; Research Associate in Nuclear Physics, Cornell Univ., NY, 1957–58; Prof. of Physics, University Coll., London, 1960–64. Donegall Lectr, TCD, 1969. Dir, Nordita, 1984–85. Foreign Mem., Royal Danish Acad., 1967. Dr *hc* Trondheim, 1982; DrPhil *hc* Lund, 1986. *Publications:* The Theory of Elementary Particles, 1959; (with B. Tromborg) Partial Wave Amplitudes and Resonance Poles, 1972; papers and articles on interaction of radiation with atoms, elementary particle physics, causality, and related topics. *Address:* Nordita, Blegdamsvej 17, DK-2100 Copenhagen Ø, Denmark; 4 Almoners Avenue, Cambridge CB1 4PA. *T:* Cambridge (0223) 244175.

HAMILTON, Sir James (Arnot), KCB 1978 (CB 1972); MBE 1952; FRSE; FEng 1981; Permanent Under-Secretary of State, Department of Education and Science, 1976–83; *b* 2 May 1923; *m* 1947, Christine Mary McKean (marr. diss.); three *s*. *Educ:* University of Edinburgh (BSc). Marine Aircraft Experimental Estab., 1943: Head of Flight Research, 1948; Royal Aircraft Estab., 1952; Head of Projects Div., 1964; Dir, Anglo-French Combat Aircraft, Min. of Aviation, 1965; Dir-Gen. Concorde, Min. of Technology, 1966–70; Deputy Secretary: (Aerospace), DTI, 1971–73; Cabinet Office, 1973–76. Dir, Hawker Siddeley Gp, 1983–; Mem. Adv. Bd, Brown and Root (UK) Ltd, 1983–. Trustee, British Museum (Natural Hist.), 1984–88. President: Assoc. for Science Educn, 1984–85; NFER in England and Wales, 1984–. Vice-Pres., Council, Reading Univ., 1983–; Vice-Chm. Council, UCL, 1985–. DUniv Heriot-Watt, 1983; Hon. LLD CNAA, 1983. *Publications:* papers in Reports and Memoranda series of Aeronautical Research Council, Jl RAeS, and technical press. *Address:* Pentlands, 9 Cedar Road, Farnborough, Hants GU14 7AF. *T:* Farnborough (0252) 543254. *Club:* Athenæum.

HAMILTON, (James) Dundas, CBE 1985; Chairman, Wates City of London Properties plc, since 1984; *b* 11 June 1919; *o s* of late Arthur Douglas Hamilton and Jean Scott Hamilton; *m* 1954, Linda Jean, *d* of late Sinclair Frank Ditcham and Helen Fraser Ditcham; two *d*. *Educ:* Rugby; Clare Coll., Cambridge. Served War, Army (Lt-Col RA), 1939–46. Member, Stock Exchange, 1948, Mem. Council, 1972–78 (Dep. Chm., 1973–76). Partner, 1951–86, Sen. Partner, 1977–85, Fielding, Newson-Smith & Co. Chairman: TSB Commercial Holdings (formerly UDT Holdings), 1985–90 (Dir, 1983–90); United Dominions Trust Ltd, 1985–89; Director: Richard Clay plc, 1971–84 (Vice-Chm., 1981–84); LWT (Holdings) plc, 1981–; Datastream Hldgs Ltd, 1982–86; TSB Gp plc, 1985–90; TSB Investment Management Ltd, 1986–88; Archival Facsimiles Ltd, 1986–89; WIB Publications Ltd, 1987–. Dep. Chm., British Invisible Exports Council, 1976–86; Member: Exec. Cttee, City Communications Centre, 1976–88; City and Industrial Liaison Council, 1987– (Chm., 1970–73). Governor, Pasold Res. Fund, 1976–90 (Chm., 1978–86). Member: Council of Industrial Soc., 1959–78 (Exec. Cttee, 1963–68; Life Mem., 1978); Adv. Bd, RCDS, 1980–87. Contested (C) East Ham North, 1951. FRSA 1988. *Publications:* The Erl King (radio play), 1949; Lorenzo Smiles on Fortune (novel), 1953; Three on a Honeymoon (TV series), 1956; Six Months Grace (play, jointly with Robert Morley), 1957; Stockbroking Today, 1968, 2nd edn 1979; Stockbroking Tomorrow, 1986. *Recreations:* writing, swimming, golf, watching tennis. *Address:* 45 Melbury Court, W8 6NH. *T:* 071–602 3157. *Clubs:* City of London, All England Lawn Tennis and Croquet, Hurlingham; Royal and Ancient Golf (St Andrews); Worplesdon Golf (Life Mem.); Kandahar Ski.

HAMILTON, John; His Honour Judge John Hamilton; a Circuit Judge, since 1987; *b* 27 Jan. 1941; *s* of John Ian Hamilton and of late Mrs Margaret Walker; *m* 1965, Patricia Ann Hamilton (*née* Henman); two *s* one *d*. *Educ:* Durlston Court Prep. Sch., New Milton, Hants; Harrow (schol.); Hertford Coll., Oxford (schol.). MA Jurisp. Oxon. Called to Bar, Gray's Inn, 1965; a Recorder, 1985. KStJ 1982. *Recreations:* jogging, golf, bridge. *Address:* Red Stack, Anstey, near Buntingford, Herts SG9 0BN. *T:* Barkway (0763) 848536.

HAMILTON, Adm. Sir John (Graham), GBE 1966 (KBE 1963; CBE 1958); CB 1960; *b* 12 July 1910; *s* of late Col E. G. Hamilton, CMG, DSO, MC, and Ethel Marie (*née* Frith); *m* 1938, Dorothy Nina Turner, 2nd *d* of late Col J. E. Turner, CMG, DSO; no *c*. *Educ:* RN Coll., Dartmouth. Joined RN 1924; specialised in Gunnery, 1936. Served War of 1939–45: destroyers; on staff of Adm. Cunningham, Mediterranean; Gunnery Officer, HMS Warspite; Admiralty; SE Asia; Comdr, 1943 (despatches). In command, HMS Alacrity, Far East, 1946–48; Capt., 1949; Dep. Dir, Radio Equipment, 1950–51; in command, 5th Destroyer Squadron, 1952–53; Dir of Naval Ordnance, Admiralty, 1954–56; in command HMS Newfoundland, Far East, 1956–58; despatches, 1957; Rear-Adm., 1958; Naval Sec. to First Lord of the Admiralty, 1958–60; Vice-Adm., 1961; Flag Officer: Flotillas, Home Fleet, 1960–62; Naval Air Command, 1962–64; C-in-C Mediterranean, and C-in-C Allied Forces, Mediterranean, 1964–67; Adm. 1965. Dir-Gen., 1968–72, Nat. Pres., 1972–75, Inst. of Marketing. *Recreations:* walking, climbing, photography. *Address:* Chapel Barn, Abbotsbury, Weymouth, Dorset DT3 4LF. *T:* Abbotsbury (0305) 871507.

HAMILTON, Loudon Pearson, CB 1987; Secretary, Scottish Office Agriculture and Fisheries Department, since 1984; *b* 12 Jan. 1932; *s* of Vernon Hamilton and Jean Mair Hood; *m* 1956, Anna Mackinnon Young; two *s*. *Educ:* Hutchesons' Grammar Sch., Glasgow; Glasgow Univ. (MA Hons Hist.). National Service, 2nd Lieut RA, 1953–55. Inspector of Taxes, Inland Revenue, 1956–60; Asst Principal, Dept of Agriculture and Fisheries for Scotland, 1960; Private Sec. to Parly Under-Secretary of State for Scotland, 1963–64; First Secretary, Agriculture, British Embassy, Copenhagen and The Hague, 1966–70; Asst Secretary, Dept of Agriculture and Fisheries for Scotland, 1973–79; Principal Estabt Officer, Scottish Office, 1979–84. Mem., AFRC, 1984–. Chairman: Lothian Marriage Counselling Service, 1983–; Corstorphine Trust, 1990–. *Address:* 5 Belgrave Road, Edinburgh EH12 6NG. *T:* 031–334 5398. *Club:* Commonwealth Trust.

HAMILTON, Sir Malcolm William Bruce S.; *see* Stirling-Hamilton.

HAMILTON, Martha, (Mrs R. R. Steedman),OBE 1988; Headmistress, St Leonards School, St Andrews, 1970–88; *d* of Rev. John Edmund Hamilton and Hon. Lilias Maclay; *m* 1977, Robert Russell Steedman, *qv*. *Educ:* Roedean Sch.; St Andrews Univ. (MA Hons Hist.); Cambridge Univ. (DipEd); Edinburgh Univ. (Dip. Adult Educn). Principal, Paljor Namgyal Girls' High School, Gangtok, Sikkim, 1959–66. Mem., Fife Health Bd, 1991–. Awarded Pema Dorji (for services to education), Sikkim, 1966. *Recreations:* ski-ing, photography. *Address:* Muir of Blebo, Blebo Craigs, by Cupar, Fife KY15 5TZ.
See also E. W. Hamilton.

HAMILTON, Mary Margaret; *see* Kaye, M. M.

HAMILTON, Sir Michael Aubrey, Kt 1983; *b* 5 July 1918; *s* of late Rt Rev. E. K. C. Hamilton, KCVO; *m* 1947, Lavinia, 3rd *d* of late Col Sir Charles Ponsonby, 1st Bt, TD; one *s* three *d*. *Educ:* Radley; Oxford. Served War of 1939–45, with 1st Bn, Coldstream Guards. MP (C): Wellingborough Div. Northants, 1959–64; Salisbury, Feb. 1965–1983; Asst Govt Whip, 1961–62; a Lord Comr of the Treasury, 1962–64; PPS to Sec. of State for Foreign and Commonwealth Affairs, 1982–83. Former Director: Army & Navy Stores; Hops Marketing Board; Royal Exchange Assurance. UK Representative: UN Gen. Assembly, 1970; US Bicentennial Celebrations, 1976. *Address:* Lordington House, Chichester, Sussex PO18 9DX. *T:* Emsworth (0243) 371717.

HAMILTON, (Mostyn) Neil; MP (C) Tatton, since 1983; an Assistant Government Whip, since 1990; *b* 9 March 1949; *s* of Ronald and Norma Hamilton; *m* 1983, (Mary) Christine Holman. *Educ:* Amman Valley Grammar School; University College of Wales, Aberystwyth (BSc Econ, MSc Econ); Corpus Christi College, Cambridge (LLB). Called to the Bar, Middle Temple, 1979. PPS to Minister of State for Transport, 1986–87. Mem., Select Cttee on Treasury and Civil Service, 1987–90; Vice-Chm., Conservative backbench Trade and Industry Cttee, 1984–90 (Sec., 1983); Secretary: Cons. backbench Finance Cttee, 1987–90; UK–ANZAC Parly Gp, 1984–; Chm., All Party Anglo-Togo Parly Gp, 1988–; Vice-Chm., Small Business Bureau, 1985–. Vice-President: League for Introduction of Canine Controls, 1984–; Small Farmers' Assoc., 1985–; Cheshire Agricl Soc., 1986–. *Publications:* UK/US Double Taxation, 1980; The European Community—a Policy for Reform, 1983; (ed) Land Development Encyclopaedia, 1981–; (jtly) No Turning Back, 1985; pamphlets on state industry, schools and the NHS. *Recreations:* gardening, book collecting, the arts, architecture and conservation, country pursuits, silence. *Address:* House of Commons, SW1A 0AA. *T:* 071–219 4157.

HAMILTON, Myer Alan Barry K.; *see* King-Hamilton.

HAMILTON, Neil; *see* Hamilton, M. N.

HAMILTON, Nigel John Mawdesley, QC 1981; *b* 13 Jan. 1938; *s* of Archibald Dearman Hamilton and Joan Worsley Mawdesley; *m* 1963; Leone Morag Elizabeth Gordon; two *s*. *Educ:* St Edward's Sch., Oxford; Queens' Coll., Cambridge. Nat. Service, 2nd Lieut, RE, Survey Dept, 1956–58. Assistant Master: St Edward's Sch., Oxford, 1962–63; King's Sch., Canterbury, 1963–65. Called to the Bar, Inner Temple, 1965, Bencher, 1989. Mem., Gen. Council of the Bar, 1989–. Mem. (C) for Chew Valley, Avon CC, 1989–. *Recreation:* fishing. *Address:* Moonrakers, Compton Martin, Avon BS18 6JP. *T:* West Harptree (0761) 221421. *Club:* Flyfishers'.

HAMILTON, North Edward Frederick D.; *see* Dalrymple Hamilton.

HAMILTON, Sir Patrick George, 2nd Bt, *cr* 1937; MA; President, Possum Controls Ltd; Trustee: Eleanor Hamilton Trust; Sidbury Trust; Erna Simon Trust; *b* 17 Nov. 1908; *o s* of Sir George Clements Hamilton, 1st Bt, and Eleanor (*d* 1958), *d* of late Henry Simon and *sister* of 1st Baron Simon of Wythenshawe; *S* father, 1947; *m* 1941, Winifred Mary Stone (CBE, MA), *o c* of Hammond Jenkins, Maddings, Hadstock, Cambs. *Educ:* Eton; Trinity Coll., Oxford (MA). First Managing Director and later Chairman of Tyresoles Ltd, 1934–53 (Dir, Propeller Production, MAP, 1943–44); Director: Simon Engineering Ltd and other Simon cos, 1937–78; Renold Ltd, 1952–78; Lloyds Bank Ltd, 1953–79; Chm., Expanded Metal Co. Ltd, 1955–78. Chm., Advisory Cttee on Commercial Information Overseas, 1957–59. Dep. Chm., Export Publicity Council, 1960–63. Chm., Transport Users Consultative Cttee, NW Area, 1957–64; Mem., Central Transport Consultative Cttee, 1963–64. Treas., Fedn of Commonwealth Chambers of Commerce, 1962–64. Mem., ITA, 1964–69. Chm., Central Mddx Gp Hosp. Management Cttee, 1964–70. *Recreations:* gardening, travel. *Heir:* none. *Address:* 21 Madingley Road, Cambridge CB3 0EG.

HAMILTON, Richard; painter; *b* 24 Feb. 1922; *s* of Peter and Constance Hamilton; *m* 1947, Terry O'Reilly (*d* 1962); one *s* one *d*. *Educ:* elementary; Royal Academy Schs; Slade Sch. of Art. Jig and Tool draughtsman, 1940–45. Lectr, Fine Art Dept, King's Coll., Univ. of Durham (later Univ. of Newcastle upon Tyne), 1953–66. Devised exhibitions: Growth and Form, 1951; Man, Machine and Motion, 1955. Collaborated on: This is Tomorrow, 1956; 'an Exhibit', 1957; exhibn with D. Roth, ICA New Gall., 1977. One man art exhibitions: Gimpel Fils, 1951; Hanover Gall., 1955, 1964; Robert Fraser Gall., 1966, 1967, 1969; Whitworth Gall, 1972; Nigel Greenwood Inc., 1972; Serpentine Gall., 1975; Stedelijk Mus., Amsterdam, 1976; Waddington Gall., 1980, 1982, 1984; Anthony d'Offay Gall., 1980, 1991; Charles Cowles Gall., NY, 1980; Galérie Maeght, Paris, 1981; Tate Gall., 1983–84; Thorden and Wetterling, Stockholm, 1984; DAAD Gall., Berlin, 1985. Retrospective exhibitions: Tate Gallery, 1970 (also shown in Eindhoven and Bern); Guggenheim Museum, New York, 1973 (also shown in Cincinnati, Munich, Tübingen, Berlin); Musée Grenoble, 1977; Kunsthalle Bielefeld, 1978; other exhibitions abroad include: Kassel, 1967, New York, 1967; Milan, 1968, 1969, 1971, 1972; Hamburg, 1969; Berlin, 1970, 1971, 1973. William and Noma Copley award, 1960; John Moores prize, 1969; Talens Prize International, 1970. *Publication:* Collected Words 1953–1982, 1982. *Address:* c/o Tate Gallery, Millbank, SW1P 4RG.

HAMILTON, Sir Richard Caradoc; *see* Hamilton, Sir Robert C. R. C.

HAMILTON, Richard Graham; His Honour Judge Hamilton; a Circuit Judge, since 1986; Chancellor, Diocese of Liverpool, since 1976; *b* 26 Aug. 1932; *s* of late Henry Augustus Rupert Hamilton and Frances Mary Graham Hamilton; *m* 1960, Patricia Craghill Hamilton (*née* Ashburner); one *s* one *d*. *Educ:* Charterhouse; University Coll., Oxford (MA). Called to Bar, Middle Temple, 1956; a Recorder, 1974–86. Regular broadcasting work for Radio Merseyside, inc. scripts: Van Gogh in England, 1981; Voices from Babylon, 1983; A Longing for Dynamite, 1984; Dark Night, 1988 (winner of first prize for a short religious play, RADIUS); Murder Court productions (dramatised trials), Liverpool: The Maybrick Case, 1989; The Veronica Mutiny, 1990. *Publications:* Foul Bills and Dagger Money, 1979; All Jangle and Riot, 1986; A Good Wigging, 1988. *Recreations:* reading, walking, films. *Club:* Athenæum (Liverpool).

HAMILTON, Sir (Robert Charles) Richard (Caradoc), 9th Bt, *cr* 1647; *b* 8 Sept. 1911; *s* of Sir Robert Caradoc Hamilton, 8th Bt, and Irene Lady Hamilton (*née* Mordaunt) (*d* 1969); *S* father, 1959; *m* 1952, Elizabeth Vidal Barton; one *s* three *d*. *Educ:* Charterhouse; St Peter's Coll., Oxford (MA). Served in the Intelligence Corps, 1940–45. Schoolmaster at Ardingly Coll., Sussex, 1946–60. Owner, Walton Estate, Warwick; Mem., Warwickshire Br., CLA, 1962– (Chm., 1979–83). *Publications:* (trans.) de Luze, A History of the Royal Game of Tennis, 1979; (trans.) Pierre Barcellon, Rules and Principles of Tennis, 1987. *Recreations:* dramatist; Real tennis. *Heir:* *s* Andrew Caradoc Hamilton, *b* 23 Sept. 1953. *Address:* Walton, Warwick CV35 9HX. *T:* Stratford-on-Avon (0789) 840460.

HAMILTON, Robert William, FBA 1960; *b* 26 Nov. 1905; *s* of William Stirling Hamilton and Kathleen Hamilton (*née* Elsmie); *heir-pres.* to Sir Malcolm Stirling-Hamilton, Bt, *qv*; *m* 1935, Eileen Hetty Lowick; three *s* two *d*. *Educ:* Winchester Coll.; Magdalen Coll., Oxford. Chief Insp. of Antiquities, Palestine, 1931–38; Dir of Antiquities, Palestine, 1938–48; Sec.-Librarian, British Sch. of Archæology, Iraq, 1948–49; Senior Lecturer in Near Eastern Archæology, Oxford, 1949–56; Keeper of Dept of Antiquities, 1956–72, Keeper, 1962–72, Ashmolean Museum, Oxford. Fellow Magdalen Coll., Oxford, 1959–72. *Publications:* The Church of the Nativity, Bethlehem, 1947; Structural History of the Aqsa Mosque, 1949; Khirbat al Mafjar, 1959; (with others) Oxford Bible Atlas, 1974; Walid and his Friends: an Umayyad tragedy, 1988. *Address:* The Haskers, Westleton, Suffolk IP17 3AP.

HAMILTON, Prof. William Donald, FRS 1980; Royal Society Research Professor, Department of Zoology, and Fellow of New College, Oxford University, since 1984; *b* 1 Aug. 1936; *s* of Archibald Milne Hamilton and Bettina Matraves Hamilton (*née* Collier); *m* 1967, Christine Ann Friess; three *d*. *Educ:* Tonbridge Sch.; Cambridge Univ. (BA); London Univ. (PhD). Lecturer in Genetics, Imperial Coll., London Univ., 1964–77; Prof. of Evolutionary Biology, Mus. of Zoology and Div. of Biol Scis, Michigan Univ., 1978–84. For. Member, American Acad. of Arts and Sciences, 1978; Mem., Royal Soc. of Scis of Uppsala, 1987. Darwin Medal, Royal Soc., 1988; Linnean Medal for Zoology, Linnean Soc. of London, 1989; Frink Medal for Zoology, Zoological Soc. of London, 1991. *Publications:* contribs to Jl of Theoretical Biology, Science, Nature, Amer. Naturalist. *Address:* Department of Zoology, South Parks Road, Oxford OX1 3PS.

HAMILTON, William Winter; *b* 26 June 1917; *m* (wife died 1968); one *s* one *d*; *m* 1982, Mrs Margaret Cogle. *Educ:* Washington Grammar Sch., Co. Durham; Sheffield Univ. (BA, DipEd). Joined Lab. Party, 1936; contested: W Fife, 1945; S Hams, 1987. MP (Lab): Fife W, 1950–74; Fife Central, 1974–87. Chairman, H of C Estimates Cttee, 1964–70; Vice-Chm., Parly Labour Party, 1966–70; Mem., European Parlt, 1975–79, Vice-Chm., Rules and Procedure Cttee, 1976–79 (Chm., 1975–76). School teacher; Mem. COHSE. Served War of 1939–45, Middle East, Capt. *Publication:* My Queen and I, 1975.

HAMILTON-DALRYMPLE, Sir Hew; *see* Dalrymple.

HAMILTON FRASER, Donald; *see* Fraser.

HAMILTON-JONES, Maj.-Gen. (retd) John, CBE 1977; Vice President, International Marketing, Allied Research Corporation, since 1989; Chairman, Richmond Enterprises Ltd, since 1984; *b* 6 May 1926; *s* of late George and of Lillian Hamilton-Jones; *m* 1952, Penelope Ann Marion Derry; three *d*. *Educ:* Cranbrook Sch.; Edinburgh Univ.; Technical Staff Coll. US Army Guided Missile Grad., 1957. Commnd RA, 1945; Indian Artillery, 1945–47; Regtl Service, Far East/ME, 1947–60; Jt Services Staff Coll., 1966; comd a regt, 1966–69; DS RMCS, 1970–72; MoD Dir, 1975–78 (Brig.). President: Ordnance Bd, 1980–81; Army Advance Class, 1981–83; Vice-Pres., Internat. Marketing, Gen. Defense Corp. of Pennsylvania, 1986–88 (Dir, 1984–86). CEng; FRAeS; FInstD 1987; MIERE; FBIM (MBIM 1979). Commandeur, Assoc. Franco-Britannique, 1979. *Recreations:* rowing, Rugby, squash, music, hi-fi. *Address:* c/o Lloyds Bank, Cox's & King's Branch, PO Box 1190, 7 Pall Mall, SW1Y 5NA.

HAMILTON-RUSSELL, family name of **Viscount Boyne.**

HAMILTON-SMITH, family name of **Baron Colwyn.**

HAMILTON-SPENCER-SMITH, Sir John; *see* Spencer-Smith.

HAMLEY, Donald Alfred, CBE 1985; HM Diplomatic Service, retired; *b* 19 Aug. 1931; *s* of Alfred Hamley and Amy (*née* Brimacombe) *m* 1958, Daphne Griffith; two *d*. *Educ:* Devonport High Sch., Plymouth. Joined HM Foreign (subseq. Diplomatic) Service, 1949; Nat. Service, 1950–52; returned to FO; served in: Kuwait, 1955–57; Libya, 1958–61; FO, 1961–63; Jedda, 1963–65 and 1969–72; Rome, 1965–69; seconded to DTI, 1972–73; Commercial Counsellor, Caracas, 1973–77; seconded to Dept of Trade, 1977–80; Consul-Gen., Jerusalem, 1980–84; retired, 1984. *Address:* 1 Forge Close, Hayes, Bromley BR2 7LP. *T:* 081–462 6696. *Club:* Royal Automobile.

HAMLIN, Prof. Michael John, FICE, FIWEM; FEng 1985; FRSE; Principal and Vice Chancellor of the University of Dundee, since 1987; *b* 11 May 1930; *s* of late Dr Ernest John Hamlin and of Dorothy Janet Hamlin; *m* 1951, Augusta Louise, *d* of late William Thomas Tippins and Rose Louise Tippins; three *s*. *Educ:* St John's Coll., Johannesburg; Dauntsey's Sch.; Bristol Univ. (BSc); Imperial Coll. of Science and Technol., London (DIC). FIWEM (FIWES 1973); FICE 1981; FRSE 1990. Asst Engineer, Lemon & Blizard, Southampton, 1951–53; Engineer: Anglo-American Corp., Johannesburg, 1954–55; Stewart, Sviridov & Oliver, Johannesburg, 1955; Partner, Rowe & Hamlin, Johannesburg, 1956–58; Univ. of Witwatersrand, 1959–60; University of Birmingham, 1961–87: Prof. of Water Engrg, 1970–87; Hd of Dept of Civil Engrg, 1980–87; Pro Vice-Chancellor, 1985–87; Vice-Principal, 1987. Chm., Aquatic and Atmospheric Phys. Scis Grants Cttee, NERC, 1975–79; Member: Severn Trent Water Authority, 1974–79; British National Cttee for Geodesy and Geophysics, 1979–84 (Chm., Hydrology Sub-Cttee, 1979–84); Scottish Econ. Council, 1989–. Pres., Internat. Commn on Water Resource Systems of the Internat. Assoc. of Hydrological Scis (IAHS), 1983–87. Chm., Scottish Centre for Children with Motor Impairment, 1991–. President's Premium, IWES, 1972. Hon. LLD St Andrews, 1989. CBIM 1990. SBStJ 1991. *Publications:* contribs on public health engrg and water resources engrg in learned jls. *Recreations:* walking, gardening. *Address:* 325 Perth Road, Dundee DD2 1LH.

HAMLYN, Prof. David Walter; Professor of Philosophy and Head of Philosophy Department, Birkbeck College, University of London, 1964–88 (Head of Classics

Department, 1981–86); Vice-Master, Birkbeck College, 1983–88, Fellow, 1988; *b* 1 Oct. 1924; *s* of late Hugh Parker Hamlyn and late Gertrude Isabel Hamlyn; *m* 1949, Eileen Carlyle Litt; one *s* one *d*. *Educ:* Plymouth Coll.; Exeter Coll., Oxford. BA (Oxon) 1948, MA 1949 (1st cl. Lit. Hum., 1st cl. Philosophy and Psychology, 1950). War Service, RAC and IAC, Hodson's Horse (Lieutenant), 1943–46. Research Fellow, Corpus Christi Coll., Oxford, 1950–53; Lecturer: Jesus Coll., Oxford, 1953–54; Birkbeck Coll., London, 1954–63, Reader, 1963–64. Pres., Aristotelian Soc., 1977–78. Mem. Council, Royal Inst. of Philosophy, 1968– (Exec., 1971–). Mem., London Univ. Senate, 1981–87 (Mem. several cttees; Chm., Academic Council Standing Sub-cttee in Theology, Arts and Music, 1984–87); Governor: Birkbeck Coll., 1965–69; City Lit., 1982–86 (Vice-Chm., 1985–86); Central London Adult Educn Inst., 1987–90; Chm. Governors, Heythrop Coll., 1971–78, Mem., 1984–, Fellow, 1978. Editor of Mind, 1972–84; Consulting Editor, Jl of Medical Ethics, 1981–90. *Publications:* The Psychology of Perception, 1957 (repr. with additional material, 1969); Sensation and Perception, 1961; Aristotle's *De Anima*, Books II and III, 1968; The Theory of Knowledge, 1970 (USA), 1971 (GB); Experience and the Growth of Understanding, 1978 (Spanish trans., 1981; Korean trans., 1990); Schopenhauer, 1980; Perception, Learning and the Self, 1983; Metaphysics, 1984; History of Western Philosophy, 1987 (Dutch trans., 1988; Portugese trans., 1990); In and Out of the Black Box, 1990; contrib. to several other books and to many philosophical, psychological and classical jls. *Recreations:* playing and listening to music, gardening. *Address:* Briar Patch, Bourton-on-the-Hill, Moreton-in-Marsh, Glos GL56 9AJ. *T:* Blockley (0386) 700346.

HAMLYN, Paul (Bertrand); Founder and Chairman: Octopus Publishing Group (London, New York and Sydney), since 1971 (part of Reed International plc, since 1987); Mandarin Publishers (Hong Kong), since 1971; Chairman: Heinemann Group of Publishers Ltd, since 1985; Octopus Books, since 1971; Hamlyn Publishing Group, since 1986; Co-founder (with David Frost) and Director, Sundial Publications, since 1973; Co-founder (with Doubleday & Co., New York) and Director, Octopus Books International BV (Holland), since 1973; Co-founder (with Sir Terence Conran) and Co-chairman, Conran Octopus, since 1983; *b* 12 Feb. 1926; 2nd *s* of late Prof. Richard Hamburger and Mrs L. Hamburger (*née* Hamburg); *m* 1st, 1952, Eileen Margaret (Bobbie) (marr. diss. 1969), *d* of Col Richard Watson; one *s* one *d*; 2nd, 1970, Mrs Helen Guest. *Educ:* St Christopher's Sch., Letchworth, Herts. Founder of Hamlyn Publishing Gp, which he re-purchased from Reed International, 1986; Formed: Books for Pleasure, 1949; Prints for Pleasure, 1960; Records for Pleasure, Marketing long-playing classical records, and Golden Pleasure Books (jt co. with Golden Press Inc., NY), 1961; Music for Pleasure (with EMI), 1965. Paul Hamlyn Gp acquired by Internat. Publishing Corp, 1964; joined IPC Bd with special responsibility for all Corporation's book publishing activities; Butterworth & Co. acquired 1968; Director, IPC, 1965–70; Chm., IPC Books, controlling Hamlyn Publishing Gp, 1965–70 (formerly Chm., Paul Hamlyn Holdings Ltd, and associated Cos); Jt Man. Dir, News International Ltd, 1970–71; Director: News International, 1971–86; News America, 1980–; Tigerprint, 1980–; TV am, 1981–83; Brimax Books, 1983–; Reed Internat., 1987–. Chm. Trustees, Public Policy Centre, 1985–87. *Address:* (office) Michelin House, 81 Fulham Road, SW3 6RB. *T:* 071–581 9393.

See also M. P. L. Hamburger.

HAMMARSKJÖLD, Knut (Olof Hjalmar Åkesson); Director, since 1948, and Chairman, since 1987, Sydsvenska Dagbladet AB, Newspaper Group, Malmö; Minister Plenipotentiary, since 1966; *b* Geneva, 16 Jan. 1922; Swedish; *m*; four *s*. *Educ:* Stockholm Univ. Entered Swedish Foreign Service, 1946; served in Paris, Vienna, Moscow, Bucharest, Kabul, Sofia, 1947–55; 1st Sec., Foreign Office, 1955–57; Head of Foreign Relations Dept, Royal Bd of Civil Aviation, Stockholm, 1957–59; Dep. Head of Swedish Delegn to OEEC, Paris, 1959–60; Dep. Sec.-Gen., EFTA, Geneva, 1960–66; International Air Transport Association (IATA): Dir Gen., 1966–84; Chm. Exec. Cttee, 1981–84; Internat. Affairs Counsel, 1985–86; Mem., Inst. of Transport, London; Dir, Inst. of Air Transport, Paris, 1974–; Dir.-Gen., 1985–, Chm. and Chief Exec. Officer, 1989–, Atwater Inst. Inf./Communications, Montreal; Mem., Sen. Adv. Cttee, Internat. Aviation Management Training Inst., Montreal; Director: Prisma Transport Consultants Ltd, Geneva/Brussels, 1987–; Blenheim NV, Rotterdam, 1988–; Chm., ABCF Berling, Malmö, 1985–87. Chairman: Ind. Commn for Reform of UNESCO, 1989–; Adv. Cttee, Inst. for Air and Space Law, McGill Univ., Montreal. Hon. Ambassador, UNESCO, 1991. Hon. Fellow, Canadian Aeronautics and Space Inst., Ottawa; Hon. Academician, Mexican Acad. of Internat. Law; Hon. FCIT (London). Edward Warner Award, ICAO, 1983. Comdr (1st cl.), Order of North Star (Sweden); NOR (Sweden); Légion d'Honneur (France); Grand Cross Order of Civil Merit (Spain); Grand Officer, Order of Al-Istiqlal (Jordan); Commander: Order of Lion (Finland); Oranje Nassau (Netherlands); Order of Falcon (1st cl.) (Iceland); Order of Black Star (Benin). *Publications:* articles on political, economic and aviation topics. *Recreations:* music, painting, ski-ing. *Address:* c/o SDS, 19 Krusegatan, Box 145, S-20121 Malmö, Sweden.

HAMMER, James Dominic George, CB 1983; President, International Association of Labour Inspection, since 1984; Chairman, National Steering Committee, European Year of Safety, Health and Hygiene at work 1992; *b* 21 April 1929; *s* of E. A. G. and E. L. G. Hammer; *m* 1955, Margaret Eileen Halse; two *s* one *d*. *Educ:* Dulwich Coll.; Corpus Christi Coll., Cambridge. BA Hons Mod. Langs. Joined HM Factory Inspectorate, 1953; Chief Inspector of Factories, 1975–84; Dep. Dir Gen., HSE, 1985–89. Technical Dir, UK Skills; Chm., Nat. Certification Scheme for In-Service Inspection Bodies. Vice Chm., Camberwell HA. FRSA 1984. *Address:* c/o Health and Safety Executive, Baynards House, 1 Chepstow Place, Westbourne Grove, W2 4TF. *T:* 071–243 6620.

HAMMER, Rev. Canon Raymond Jack, PhD; Visiting Lecturer, University of Warwick, since 1988; Librarian, Worcester Diocesan Library, since 1989; *b* 4 July 1920; *s* of Paul and Lily Hammer; *m* 1949, Vera Winifred (*née* Reed); two *d*. *Educ:* St Peter's Coll., Oxford (MA, Dip.Theol.); Univ. of London (BD, MTh, PhD). Asst Curate, St Mark's, St Helens, 1943–46; Sen. Tutor, St John's Coll., Durham, 1946–49; Lectr in Theol., Univ. of Durham, 1946–49; Prof., Central Theol Coll., Tokyo, 1950–64; Prof. in Doctrine, St Paul's Univ., Tokyo, 1958–64; Chaplain at British Embassy, Tokyo, 1954–64; Hon. Canon, St Michael's Cathedral, Kobe, Japan, 1964–; Lectr, Queen's Coll., Birmingham, and Lectr in Theol., Univ. of Birmingham, 1965–77; Dir, Bible Reading Fellowship, 1977–85. Examining Chaplain to: Bishop of Liverpool, 1965–78; Bishop of Birmingham, 1973–78. Archbishops' Consultant on Relations with Other Faiths, 1978–; Sec. to Archbishops' Consultants, 1983–. Tutor, Open Univ., 1978–85; Extra-Mural Lectr, Univs of London and Birmingham, 1985–. Treasurer, Studiorum Novi Testamenti Societas, 1970–82. *Publications:* Japan's Religious Ferment, 1961 (US 1962), repr. 1985; The Book of Daniel (commentary), 1976; contrib: Theological Word Book of the Bible, 1950; Oxford Dictionary of the Christian Church, 1957, 2nd edn 1975; Concise Dictionary of the Bible, 1966; Concise Dictionary of the Christian World Mission, 1970; Man and his Gods, 1971; Shorter Books of the Apocrypha, 1972; Perspectives on World Religions, 1978; The World's Religions, 1982; World Religions, 1982; consultant editor: The Times Atlas of The Bible, 1987; The Illustrated Reader's Bible, 1990. *Recreations:* travel, literature. *Address:* 22 Midsummer Meadow, Inkberrow, Worcs WR7 4HD. *T:* Inkberrow (0386) 792883. *Clubs:* Athenæum; Sion College.

HAMMERBECK, Brig. Christopher John Anthony, CB 1991; Commander, 4th Armoured Brigade, 1990–92; Deputy Commander, British Forces Hong Kong, from April 1992; *b* 14 March 1943; *s* of Sqn Leader O. R. W. Hammerbeck and A. M. Hammerbeck; *m* 1974, Alison Mary Felica; one *s* two *d*. *Educ:* Mayfield Coll., Sussex. Commnd, 1965; 2nd RTR, 1965–70; Air Adjt, Parachute Sqn, RAC, 1970–72; GSO3 (Ops), HQ 20 Armoured Bde, 1972–74; psc, 1975; DAA&QMG, HQ 12 Mechanised Bde, 1976–78; Sqn Comdr, 4th RTR, 1978–80; DAAG(O), MoD, 1980–82; Directing Staff, Army Staff Coll., 1982–84; CO, 2nd RTR, 1984–87; Col, Tactical Doctrine/Op. Requirement 1 (BR) Corps, 1987–88; RCDS, 1989. MBIM. *Recreations:* sailing, golf, ski-ing, bobsleigh (Vice Chm., Army Bobsleigh Assoc.), reading, travel. *Address:* (until April 1992) HQ 4th Armoured Brigade, BFPO 17. *T:* 49 251 350; (from April 1992) HQ British Forces Hong Kong, BFPO 1. *Club:* Army and Navy.

HAMMERSLEY, Dr John Michael, FRS 1976; Reader in Mathematical Statistics, University of Oxford, and Professorial Fellow, Trinity College, Oxford, 1969–87, now Emeritus Fellow; *b* 21 March 1920; *s* of late Guy Hugh Hammersley and Marguerite (*née* Whitehead); *m* 1951, Shirley Gwendolene (*née* Bakewell); two *s*. *Educ:* Sedbergh Sch.; Emmanuel Coll., Cambridge. MA, ScD (Cantab); MA, DSc (Oxon). War service in Royal Artillery, Major, 1940–45. Graduate Asst, Design and Analysis of Scientific Experiment, Univ. of Oxford, 1948–55; Principal Scientific Officer, AERE, Harwell, 1955–59; Sen. Research Officer, Inst. of Economics and Statistics, Univ. of Oxford, 1959–69; Sen. Research Fellow, Trinity Coll., Oxford, 1961–69. FIMS 1959; FIMA 1964; Fulbright Fellow, 1955; Erskine Fellow, 1978; Rouse Ball lectr, Univ. of Cambridge, 1980. Mem., ISI, 1961. Von Neumann Medal for Applied Maths, Brussels, 1966; IMA Gold Medal, 1984. *Publications:* (with D. C. Handscomb) Monte Carlo Methods, 1964, rev. edn 1966, 5th edn 1984, trans. as Les Méthodes de Monte Carlo, 1967; papers in scientific jls. *Address:* 11 Eynsham Road, Oxford OX2 9BS. *T:* Oxford (0865) 862181.

HAMMERSLEY, Rear-Adm. Peter Gerald, CB 1982; OBE 1965; Director, British Marine Equipment Council, 1985–91; *b* 18 May 1928; *s* of late Robert Stevens Hammersley and of Norah Hammersley (*née* Kirkham); *m* 1959, Audrey Cynthia Henderson Bolton; one *s* one *d*. *Educ:* Denstone Coll.; RNEC Manadon; Imperial Coll., London (DIC). Served RN, 1946–82; Long Engrg Course, RNEC Manadon, 1946–50; HMS Liverpool, 1950–51; Advanced Marine Engrg Course, RNC Greenwich, 1951–53; HMS Ocean, 1953–54; joined Submarine Service, 1954; HMS Alaric, HMS Tiptoe, 1954–58; Nuclear Engrg Course, Imperial Coll., 1958–59; First Marine Engineer Officer, first RN Nuclear Submarine, HMS Dreadnought, 1960–64; DG Ships Staff, 1965–68; Base Engineer Officer, Clyde Submarine Base, 1968–70; Naval Staff, 1970–72; Asst Director, S/M Project Team, DG Ships, 1973–76; CO, HMS Defiance, 1976–78; Captain, RNEC Manadon, 1978–80; CSO (engrg) to C-in-C Fleet, 1980–82. Comdr 1964; Captain 1971; Rear-Adm. 1980; Chief Exec., British Internal Combustion Engine Manufacturers' Assoc., 1982–85. Master, Engineers' Co., 1988–89. *Recreations:* walking, gardening. *Address:* Wistaria Cottage, Linersh Wood, Bramley, near Guildford GU5 0EE. *Club:* Army and Navy.

HAMMERTON, Rolf Eric; His Honour Judge Hammerton; a Circuit Judge, since 1972; *b* 18 June 1926; *s* of Eric Maurice Hammerton and Dora Alice Hammerton (*née* Zander); *m* 1953, Thelma Celestine Hammerton (*née* Appleyard); one *s* three *d*. *Educ:* Brighton, Hove and Sussex Grammar Sch.; Peterhouse, Cambridge (MA, LLB). Philip Teichman Prize, 1952; called to Bar, Inner Temple, 1952. Contributing Editor, Butterworth's County Court Precedents and Pleadings, 1985–. *Recreation:* cooking.

HAMMETT, Sir Clifford (James), Kt 1969; Regional Legal Adviser with British Development Division in the Caribbean, since 1975; *b* 8 June 1917; *s* of late Frederick John and Louisa Maria Hammett; *m* 1946, Olive Beryl Applebee; four *s* one *d*. *Educ:* Woodbridge. Admitted Solicitor, 1939. Indian Army, 1st Punjab Regt, 1940, North Africa, 1941; captured at Singapore, 1942 (despatches); POW on Siam Railway, 1942–45. Magistrate, Nigeria, 1946–52. Called to the Bar, Middle Temple, 1948. Transferred to Fiji, 1952; Senior Magistrate, Fiji, 1954, Puisne Judge, 1955; conjointly Chief Justice, Tonga, 1956–68; Chief Justice, Fiji, 1967–72; Actg Governor Gen. of Fiji, 1971. *Recreation:* gardening. *Address:* c/o Lloyds Bank, 6 Pall Mall, SW1. *Club:* Naval and Military.

HAMMETT, Harold George; British Deputy High Commissioner, Peshawar, 1964–66; *b* 2 Aug. 1906; 2nd *s* of Arthur Henry Hammett; *m* 1st, 1936, Daphne Margaret Vowler; one *s*; 2nd, 1947, Natalie Moira Sherratt; one *s* one *d*. *Educ:* St Olave's; Clare Coll., Cambridge. Malayan Civil Service, 1928–57; retired from post of Resident Commissioner, Malacca, on Malayan Independence, 1957; Commonwealth Office (formerly CRO), 1958–66. *Recreations:* woodwork, gardening. *Address:* Wiltons, 22 East Cliff Road, Dawlish, Devon EX7 0DJ. *T:* Dawlish (0626) 862114.

HAMMICK, Sir Stephen (George), 5th Bt, *cr* 1834; DL; *b* 27 Dec. 1926; *s* of Sir George Hammick, 4th Bt; *S* father, 1964; *m* 1953, Gillian Elizabeth Inchbald; two *s* one *d*. *Educ:* Stowe. Royal Navy as Rating (hostilities only), 1944–48; RAC Coll., Cirencester, 1949–50; MFH Cattistock Hunt, 1961 and 1962. Chm., Dorset CC, 1988– (County Councillor (C), 1958–; Vice-Chm., 1985–88). High Sheriff, Dorset, 1981–82, DL Dorset, 1989. Farmer, with 450 acres. *Recreations:* hunting, fishing, sailing. *Heir:* *s* Paul St Vincent Hammick [*b* 1 Jan. 1955; *m* 1984, Judith Mary, *d* of Ralph Ernest Reynolds]. *Address:* Badgers, Wraxall, Dorchester. *T:* Evershot (0935) 343.

HAMMOND, Anthony Hilgrove; Legal Adviser to Home Office and Northern Ireland Office, and Deputy Under-Secretary of State, Home Office, since 1988; *b* 27 July 1940; *s* of late Colonel Charles William Hilgrove Hammond and Jessie Eugenia Hammond (*née* Francis); *m* 1988, Avril Collinson. *Educ:* Malvern Coll.; Emmanuel Coll., Cambridge (BA, LLB). Admitted Solicitor of Supreme Court, 1965. Articled with LCC, 1962; Solicitor, GLC, 1965–68; Home Office: Legal Assistant, 1968; Sen. Legal Assistant, 1970; Asst Legal Advr, 1974; Principal Asst Legal Advr, Home Office and NI Office, 1980–88. Freeman, City of London, 1991; Liveryman, Glass Sellers' Co., 1991. *Recreations:* bridge, music, opera, walking, birdwatching. *Address:* c/o Legal Adviser's Branch, Home Office, Queen Anne's Gate, SW1H 9AT. *Club:* Athenæum.

HAMMOND, Catherine Elizabeth, CBE 1950; Colonel, WRAC (retired); *b* 22 Dec. 1909; *d* of late Frank Ernest Rauleigh Eddolls and late Elsie Eddolls (*née* Cooper); *m*; one *s* one *d*. *Educ:* Lassington House, Highworth, Wilts; Chesterville Sch., Cirencester, Glos. Joined ATS (TA) (FANY), 1938; Private, 7th Wilts MT Co. 1939; 2nd Subaltern 1940; Capt., 1942; Major, Commanding Devon Bn, 1942; Lieut-Col, Asst Dir ATS Oxford, 1943; Col, Dep. Dir ATS (later WRAC), Eastern Command 1947–50; Hon. Col 54 (East Anglia) Div./Dist WRAC/TA, 1964–67. Chm., WRAC Assoc., 1966–70, Life Vice-Pres., 1971. Chm., Highworth and District Br., RNLI, 1970–; President: Royal British Legion, Highworth (Women's Section), 1977–84; Highworth Amateur Dramatic Soc., 1982–86. Deputy Mayor, Highworth Town Council, 1978, Mayor, 1979–81, 1984–85. SSStJ 1986. *Recreations:* hockey—Army (women), 1947–48; all games; racing. *Address:* Red Down, Highworth, Wilts SN6 7SH. *T:* Swindon (0793) 762331.

HAMMOND, Eric Albert Barratt, OBE 1977; General Secretary, Electrical, Electronic, Telecommunication and Plumbing Union, since 1984; *b* 17 July 1929; *s* of Arthur Edgar Hammond and Gertrude May Hammond; *m* 1953, Brenda Mary Edgeler; two *s*. *Educ:* Corner Brook Public Sch. Shop Steward, 1953–63; Branch Sec., 1958–63, Exec. Councillor, 1963–, EETPU. Borough and Urban District Councillor, 1958–63. Mem., TUC Gen. Council, 1983–88. Member: Electronics EDC, 1967–; Industrial Development Adv. Bd, 1977–87; Adv. Council on Energy Conservation, 1974–77; (part-time) Monopolies and Mergers Commn, 1978–84; Engrg Council, 1984–90; ACARD, 1985–87; NEDC, 1989–; Lord Chancellor's Adv. Cttee on Legal Educn and Conduct, 1991–; Chm., Electronic Components and Technology Sector Gp (formerly Electronic Components Sector Working Party), 1975–. *Recreations:* gardening, photography. *Address:* 9 Dene Holm Road, Northfleet, Kent DA11 8LF. *Club:* Gravesend Rugby.

HAMMOND, James Anthony; His Honour Judge Hammond; a Circuit Judge, since 1986; *b* 25 July 1936; *s* of James Hammond and Phyllis Eileen Hammond; *m* 1963, Sheila Mary Hammond, JP (*née* Stafford); three *d*. *Educ:* Wigan Grammar Sch.; St Catherine's Coll., Oxford (MA). Called to Bar, Lincoln's Inn, 1959; National Service, 1959–61; a Recorder, 1980–86. Councillor: Up Holland UDC, 1962–66; Skelmersdale and Holland UDC, 1970–72. Chairman: NW Branch, Society of Labour Lawyers, 1975–86; W Lancs CAB, 1982–86; Pres., NW Branch, Inst. for Study and Treatment of Delinquency, 1987–. *Recreations:* hockey, walking, sailing. *Clubs:* Wigan Hockey (Vice Pres., 1983–); Orrell Rugby Union Football.

HAMMOND, Dame Joan (Hood), DBE 1974 (CBE 1963; OBE 1953); CMG 1972; Australian operatic, concert, oratorio, and recital singer; *b* 24 May 1912; *d* of late Samuel Hood Hammond and Hilda May Blandford. *Educ:* Presbyterian Ladies Coll., Pymble, Sydney, Australia. Student of violin and singing at Sydney Conservatorium of Music; played with Sydney Philharmonic Orchestra for three years. Sports writer, Daily Telegraph, Sydney. Commenced public appearances (singing) in Sydney, 1929; studied in Europe from 1936; made operatic debut, Vienna, 1939; London debut in Messiah, 1938. World Tours: British Isles, USA, Canada, Australasia, Malaya, India, E and S Africa, Europe, Scandinavia, Russia, etc. Guest Artist: Royal Opera House, Covent Garden; Carl Rosa; Sadler's Wells; Vienna Staatsoper; Bolshoi, Moscow; Marinsky, Leningrad; Riga, Latvia; New York City Centre; Australian Elizabethan Theatre Trust; Netherlands Opera; Barcelona Liceo. Operatic roles: Aida, Madame Butterfly, Tosca, Salome, Otello, Thais, Faust, Don Carlos, Eugene Onegin, Invisible City of Kitej, La Traviata, Il Trovatore, La Bohème, Pique Dame, Manon, Manon Lescaut, La Forza del Destino, Fidelio, Simone Boccanegra, Turandot, Tannhauser, Lohengrin, Damnation of Faust, Martha, Pagliacci, Der Freischutz, Oberon, Magic Flute, Dido and Aeneas; World Premieres: Trojan Women, Wat Tyler, Yerma; British Premiere, Rusalka. HMV Recording artist. Head of Vocal Studies, Victorian College of the Arts. Volunteer Ambulance Driver, London, War of 1939–45. Sir Charles Santley Award, Worshipful Co. of Musicians, 1970. Hon. Life Member: Australian Opera; Victoria State Opera. Hon. MusD Western Australia, 1979. Coronation Medal 1953. *Publication:* A Voice, A Life, 1970. *Recreations:* golf (won first junior Golf Championship of NSW, 1930 and 1931; NSW LGU State Title, 1932, 1934, 1935; runner-up Australian Open Championship, 1933; Mem. first LGU team of Australia to compete against Gt Brit., 1935) (runner-up NSW State Squash Championship, 1934), yachting, swimming, tennis, writing, reading. *Address:* 46 Lansell Road, Toorak, Victoria 3142, Australia. *Clubs:* New Century (London); Royal Sydney Golf; Royal Motor Yacht (Dorset, England).

HAMMOND, (John) Martin; Headmaster, Tonbridge School, since 1990; *b* 15 Nov. 1944; *s* of Thomas Chatterton Hammond and Joan Cruse; *m* 1974, Meredith Jane Shier; one *s* one *d*. *Educ:* Winchester Coll. (Scholar); Balliol Coll., Oxford (Domus Scholar). Oxford University: Hertford Scholar and (1st) de Paravicini Scholar, (2nd) Craven Scholar, 1st Cl. Hons Mods, 1963; Chancellor's Latin Prose Prize, Chancellor's Latin Verse Prize, Ireland Scholar, 1964; Gaisford Greek Prose Prize, Gaisford Greek Verse Prize (jtly), 1965; 2nd Cl. Lit. Hum. 1966. Asst Master, St Paul's Sch., 1966–71; Teacher, Anargyrios Sch., Spetsai, Greece, 1972–73; Asst Master, Harrow Sch., 1973–74; Head of Classics, 1974–80, and Master in College, 1980–84, Eton Coll.; Headmaster, City of London Sch., 1984–90. Mem., General Adv. Council, BBC, 1987–. *Publication:* Homer, The Iliad (trans.), 1987. *Address:* The Headmaster's House, Tonbridge School, Tonbridge, Kent TN9 1JP. *T:* Tonbridge (0732) 365555.

HAMMOND, Michael Harry Frank, CBE 1990; DL; Chief Executive and Town Clerk, Nottingham City Council, 1974–90; *b* 5 June 1933; *s* of late Edward Cecil Hammond and Kate Hammond; *m* 1965, Jenny Campbell; two *s* one *d*. *Educ:* Leatherhead; Law Society Sch. of Law. Admitted solicitor, 1958; Asst Sol. in Town Clerk's office, Nottingham, 1961–63; Prosecuting Sol., 1963–66; Asst Town Clerk, 1966–69; Dep. Town Clerk, Newport, Mon, 1969–71; Dep. Town Clerk, Nottingham, 1971–74. Hon. Secretary: Major City Councils Gp, 1977–88; Notts County Br., Assoc. of District Councils, 1974–88; Chairman: Assoc. of Local Authority Chief Execs, 1984–85; E Midlands Br., Soc. of Local Authority Chief Execs, 1988–90; Pres., Notts Law Soc., 1989–90 (Vice-Pres., 1988–89). Trustee, Hillsborough Disaster Appeal Fund, 1989–. Governor, Nottingham High Sch., 1990–. An Elections Supervisor, Rhodesia/Zimbabwe Independence Elections, 1980. Mem., Magdala Debating Soc. DL Notts, 1990. Rhodesia Medal, 1980; Zimbabwe Independence Medal, 1980. *Recreations:* bowls, gardening, travel. *Address:* 41 Burlington Road, Sherwood, Nottingham NG5 2GR. *T:* Nottingham (0602) 602000. *Clubs:* Nottingham and Notts United Services (Nottingham); Queen Anne Bowling Green.

HAMMOND, Prof. Nicholas Geoffrey Lemprière, CBE 1974; DSO 1944; FBA 1968; DL; Henry Overton Wills Professor of Greek, University of Bristol, 1962–73; a Pro-Vice-Chancellor, 1964–66; *b* 15 Nov. 1907; *s* of late Rev. James Vavasour Hammond, Rector of St Just-in-Roseland, Cornwall, and Dorothy May; *m* 1938, Margaret Campbell, *d* of James W. J. Townley, CBE, MIEE; two *s* three *d*. *Educ:* Fettes Coll. (schol.); Caius Coll., Cambridge (schol.). 1st Cl. Classical Tripos Pts I and II, dist. in Hist., Pt II; Montagu Butler Prize; Sandys Student; Pres. CU Hockey Club; Treas. Union Soc. Fellow Clare Coll., Cambridge, 1930; University Lectr in Classics, 1936; Junior Proctor, 1939; Sen. Tutor, Clare Coll., 1947–54 (Hon. Fellow, 1974); Headmaster, Clifton Coll., 1954–62. Johnson Prof., Wisconsin Univ., 1973–74; Mellon Prof., Reed Coll., Oregon, 1975–76; Brittingham Prof., Wisconsin Univ., 1977; Leverhulme Prof., Univ. of Ioannina, 1978; Benedict Prof., Carleton Coll., Minnesota, 1987; Visiting Professor: Haverford Coll., 1978; Univ. of Auckland, 1980; St Olaf Coll., Minnesota, 1981; Pennsylvania Univ., 1982; Cornell Prof., Swarthmore Coll., Pennsylvania, 1983; Trinity Coll., Hartford, 1984; Adelaide Univ., 1984; Nat. Hellenic Res. Foundn, Athens, 1985; Nat. Humanities Center, N Carolina, 1986; Newcastle Univ., NSW, 1988. Chm., Managing Cttee, British Sch. at Athens, 1972–75. Served War of 1939–45, as Lt-Col, campaigns in Greece, Crete, Syria, and Mem. Allied Mil. Mission, Greece, 1943–44 (despatches twice, DSO). Pres., Hellenic Soc., 1965–68. DL: Bristol, 1965; Cambridge, 1974. Hon. DLett: Wisconsin, 1981; St Olaf Coll., 1982; Carleton Coll., 1988. Steven Runciman Award, Anglo-Hellenic League, 1989. Officer, Order of the Phœnix, Greece, 1946. *Publications:* Memoir of Sir John Edwin Sandys, 1933; History of Greece, 1959, 3rd edn 1986; Epirus, 1967; A History of Macedonia, Vol. 1, Historical Geography and Prehistory, 1972, Vol. 2 (with G. T. Griffith) 550–336 BC, 1974, Vol. 3 (with F. W. Walbank) 336–167 BC, 1988; Studies in Greek History, 1973; The Classical Age of Greece, 1976; Migrations and Invasions in Greece, 1976; Alexander the Great: King Commander and Statesman, 1981, 2nd edn 1989; Venture into Greece: with the guerillas, 1943–44, 1983 (Greek trans., 1986); Three Historians of Alexander the Great, 1983; The Macedonian State, 1989; The Miracle that was Macedonia, 1991; Editor: Clifton Coll. Centenary Essays, 1962; Cambridge Ancient History, 3rd edn, vols I, II, III and IV; Oxford Classical Dictionary, 2nd edn, 1970; Atlas of the Greek and Roman World in Antiquity, 1981; articles and reviews in learned jls. *Address:* 3 Belvoir Terrace, Trumpington Road, Cambridge CB2 2AA. *T:* Cambridge (0223) 357151.

HAMMOND, Prof. Norman David Curle, FSA, FRAS; Archaeology Correspondent, The Times, since 1967; Professor of Archaeology, Boston University, since 1988; *b* 10 July 1944; *o s* of William Hammond and Kathleen Jessie Hammond (*née* Howes); *m* 1972, Jean, *o d* of late A. H. Wilson; one *s* one *d*. *Educ:* Varndean GS; Peterhouse, Cambridge (Trevelyan Schol.; BA 1966; Dip. Classical Archaeol. 1967; MA 1970; PhD 1972; ScD 1987). Centre of Latin American Studies, Cambridge: Res. Fellow, 1967–71; Leverhulme Res. Fellow, 1972–75; Res. Fellow, Fitzwilliam Coll., Cambridge, 1973–75; Sen. Lectr, Univ. of Bradford, 1975–77; Rutgers University: Vis. Prof., 1977–78; Associate Prof., 1978–84; Prof. of Archaeol., 1984–88. Visiting appointments: Univ. of California, Berkeley, 1977; Jilin Univ., Changchun, 1981; Calif. Acad. of Scis, 1984–85; Univ. of Paris, Sorbonne, 1987; Dumbarton Oaks, Washington, 1988; Peabody Mus., Harvard Univ., 1988–; Worcester Coll., Oxford, 1989; Peterhouse, Cambridge, 1991. Curl Lectr, RAI, 1985. Acad. Trustee, Archaeol. Inst. of America, 1990–. Mem. editl bds, archaeol. jls, USA, UK, 1984–; editor, Afghan Studies, 1976–79; Consulting Editor, Liby of Congress, 1977–89; archaeol. consultant, Scientific American, 1979–. Excavations and surveys: Libya and Tunisia, 1964; Afghanistan, 1966; Belize, 1970– (Lubaantun, Nohmul, Cuello); Ecuador, 1972–84. *Publications:* (ed) Mesoamerican Archaeology, 1974; Lubaantun, 1975; (ed) Social Process in Maya Prehistory, 1977; (ed with F. R. Allchin) The Archaeology of Afghanistan, 1978; Ancient Maya Civilisation, 1982, 4th edn 1990; (gen. editor) Archaeology Procs, 44th Congress of Americanists, 1982–84; Nohmul: excavations 1973–83, 1985; Cuello, 1991; contribs to learned jls. *Recreations:* fine wine, intelligent women, good music. *Address:* Wholeway, Harlton, Cambridge CB3 7ET. *T:* Cambridge (0223) 262376; 83 Ivy Street, Apt 32, Brookline, Mass 02146, USA. *T:* (617) 739–9077. *Clubs:* Athenæum; Cosmos (Washington).

HAMMOND, Roy John William; Director, City of Birmingham Polytechnic, 1979–84; *b* 3 Oct. 1928; *s* of John James Hammond and Edith May Hammond; *m* 1949, Audrey Cecilia Dagmar Avello; three *d*; *m* 1990, Dorothy Forder. *Educ:* East Ham Grammar Sch.; University College of the South West, Exeter; Sorbonne, Paris. BA Hons, 1st Cl. French and Latin, London. Royal Air Force Education Branch, 1952–56; Asst Lectr, Blackburn Municipal Technical Coll. and School of Art, 1956–59; Head of Department: Herefordshire Technical Coll., 1960–66; Leeds Polytechnic, 1966–71; Asst Dir, City of Birmingham Polytechnic, 1971–79. *Recreations:* cricket, theatre, music, walking.

HAMMOND-CHAMBERS, (Robert) Alexander; Chairman, Ivory & Sime, 1985–91; *b* 20 Oct. 1942; *s* of late Robert Rupert Hammond-Chambers and of Leonie Elise Noble (*née* Andrews); *m* 1968, Sarah Louisa Madeline (*née* Fanshawe); two *s* one *d*. *Educ:* Wellington College; Magdalene College, Cambridge (Hons Economics). Ivory & Sime: joined 1964; Partner, 1969; Director, 1975, upon incorporation; Dep. Chm., 1982. First Overseas Governor, Nat. Assoc. of Securities Dealers Inc., 1984–87; Dir GBC North America Growth Fund Inc.; Chairman: Covey Advertising Ltd, 1991; Edinburgh Green Belt Trust, 1991; and other cos. Governor, Fettes College. *Recreations:* tennis, sailing, photography, golf. *Address:* Grange Dell, Penicuik, Midlothian EH26 9LE. *T:* Penicuik (0968) 76686. *Club:* New (Edinburgh).

HAMMOND INNES, Ralph, CBE 1978; author and traveller; *b* 15 July 1913; *s* of late William Hammond and Dora Beatrice Innes; *m* 1937, Dorothy Mary Lang (*d* 1989). Staff of Financial News, 1934–40. Served Artillery, 1940–46. Member: various cttees, Soc. of Authors, sailing foundns, Timber Growers' Orgn; Vice President: Assoc. of Sea Training Orgns; World Ship Trust. Hon. DLitt Bristol, 1985. Works regularly translated into numerous languages; many book club and paperback edns throughout the world. *Publications include:* Wreckers Must Breathe, 1940; The Trojan Horse, 1940; Attack Alarm, 1941; Dead and Alive, 1946; The Lonely Skier, 1947; The Killer Mine, 1947; Maddon's Rock, 1948; The Blue Ice, 1948; The White South (Book Society Choice), 1949; The Angry Mountain, 1950; Air Bridge, 1951; Campbell's Kingdom (Book Society Choice), 1952; The Strange Land, 1954; The Mary Deare (chosen by Literary Guild of America, Book Soc. Choice), 1956; The Land God Gave to Cain, 1958; Harvest of Journeys (Book Soc. Choice), 1959; The Doomed Oasis (chosen by Literary Guild of America, Book Soc. Choice), 1960; Atlantic Fury (Book Society Choice), 1962; Scandinavia, 1963; The Strode Venturer, 1965; Sea and Islands (Book Society Choice), 1967; The Conquistadors (Book of the Month and Literary Guild), 1969; Levkas Man, 1971; Golden Soak, 1973; North Star, 1974; The Big Footprints, 1977; The Last Voyage (Cook), 1978; Solomons Seal, 1980; The Black Tide, 1982; High Stand, 1985; Hammond Innes' East Anglia, 1986; Medusa, 1988; Isvik, 1991; *films:* Snowbound, Hell Below Zero, Campbell's Kingdom, The Wreck of the Mary Deare; *TV:* Explorers (Cook), 1975; Golden Soak, 1979; Levkas Man, 1981. *Recreations:* cruising and ocean racing, forestry. *Address:* Ayres End, Kersey, Suffolk IP7 6EB. *T:* Hadleigh (0473) 823294. *Clubs:* Royal Ocean Racing, Royal Cruising; Royal Yacht Squadron.

HAMMOND-STROUD, Derek, OBE 1987; concert and opera baritone; Professor of Singing, Royal Academy of Music, since 1974; *b* 10 Jan. 1926; *s* of Herbert William Stroud and Ethel Louise Elliott. *Educ:* Salvatorian Coll., Harrow, Mddx; Trinity Coll. of Music, London; in Vienna and Munich with Elena Gerhardt and Gerhard Hüsch. Glyndebourne Festival Opera, 1959; Sadler's Wells Opera (later ENO), 1961; Royal Opera, Covent Garden, 1971; Houston Grand Opera, USA, 1975; Netherlands Opera, 1976; Metropolitan Opera, NY, 1977; Teatro Colón, Buenos Aires, 1981; Munich State Opera, 1983. Concerts and Lieder recitals at Edinburgh, Aldeburgh, Munich and Vienna Festivals, and in Spain, Iceland and Denmark. BBC Promenade Concerts, 1968–. Pres., Univ. of London Opera Gp, 1971. Freeman, City of London, 1952; Hon. RAM 1976; Hon. FTCL, 1982. Sir Charles Santley Meml Gift, Worshipful Co. of Musicians, 1988. Recordings include: The Ring (Goodall); Der Rosenkavalier (de Waart). *Recreations:* chess, study of philosophy. *Address:* 18 Sutton Road, Muswell Hill, N10 1HE. *T:* 081–883 2120.

HAMNETT, Thomas Orlando; Chairman, Greater Manchester Council, 1975–1976, Vice-Chairman, 1976; *b* 28 Sept. 1930; *s* of John and Elizabeth Hamnett; *m* 1954, Kathleen Ridgway; one *s* five *d*. *Educ:* Stockport Jun. Techn. Sch. Sheetmetal craftsman, 1946–. Member, Manchester City Council, 1963 until re-organisation (Vice-Chm., Health Cttee, Chm. sub cttee on Staff on Cleansing Cttee, Mem. Policy and Finance Cttees), and 1978– (Member Direct works, Markets, and Personnel Cttees); Mem.

Transportation, Education, and Recreation and Arts Cttees, Greater Manchester Council; Chm., Environmental Services Cttee, City of Manchester, 1982–. *Recreations:* football, cricket, table tennis. *Address:* 199 Chapman Street, Gorton, Manchester M18 8WP. *T:* 061–223 3098. *Club:* Gorton Trades and Labour (Chm.).

HAMPDEN; *see* Hobart-Hampden.

HAMPDEN, 6th Viscount *cr* 1884; **Anthony David Brand,** DL; land agent; *b* 7 May 1937; *s* of 5th Viscount Hampden and of Imogen Alice Rhys, *d* of 7th Baron Dynevor; *S* father, 1975; *m* 1969, Cara Fiona (marr. diss. 1988), *e d* of Claud Proby; two *s* one *d*. *Educ:* Eton. Chairman: Sussex CLA, 1985–88; Governing Body, Emanuel Sch., 1985–. DL E Sussex, 1986. *Publication:* Henry and Eliza, 1980. *Heir: s* Hon. Francis Anthony Brand, *b* 17 Sept. 1970. *Address:* Glynde Place, Glynde, Lewes, Sussex. *Club:* White's.

HAMPSHIRE, Margaret Grace, MA; JP; Principal of Cheltenham Ladies' College, 1964–79; *b* 7 Sept. 1918; *o d* of Dr C. H. Hampshire, CMG, MB, BS, BSc, sometime Sec. of British Pharmacopœia Commission, and Grace Mary Hampshire. *Educ:* Malvern Girls' Coll.; Girton Coll., Cambridge. BA 1941; MA 1945. Entered Civil Service, Board of Trade, 1941. Joined Staff of Courtaulds, 1951. Head of Government Relations Department, 1959–64. Member: Board of Governors, University Coll. Hosp., 1961–64; Marylebone Borough Council, 1962–64; SW Regional Hosp. Board, 1967–70; Midlands Electricity Consultative Council, 1973–80; Vice-Pres., Intensive Care Trust, Cheltenham Hosp., 1985– (Chm., 1982–85). Reader, Painswick and Sheepscombe Parishes, dio. of Gloucester, 1987–. County Sec., Gloucestershire Girl Guides, 1980–85; Governor, Alice Ottley Sch., Worcester, 1979–. JP Cheltenham, 1970. *Recreations:* music, reading, foreign travel. *Address:* Ringwood, 9 The Croft, Painswick, Glos GL6 6QP.

HAMPSHIRE, Prof. Michael John, CBE 1987; CPhys, CEng; Professor of Electronic Information Technology, University of Salford, since 1985; Assistant Managing Director, Salford University Business Services Ltd, since 1989; *b* 13 Oct. 1939; *s* of Jack and Hilda May Hampshire; *m* 1962, Mavis (*née* Oakes); one *d*. *Educ:* Heckmondwike Grammar Sch.; Univ. of Birmingham (BSc Physics, PhD Elec. Engrg). FIEE, FInstP. University of Salford: Lectr, 1964; Sen. Lectr, 1972; Prof. of Solid State Electronics, 1977; Chm., Dept of Electronic and Electrical Engrg, 1981–89. Consultant: Ferranti, 1970–74; Volex Gp, 1977– (Chm., R&D Cttee, 1987–); Thorn EMI Flow Measurement, 1980–88. Founder and Chm., Vertec (Electronics), 1982–. Commendation EPIC Award, 1982; Academic Enterprise Award, 1982; Techmart Technology Transfer Trophy, 1984. Hon. MIED 1982. *Publications:* Electron Physics and Devices, 1969; 80 pubns and patents on solid state electronics and electronic systems, vehicle multiplexing, innovation. *Recreations:* music, golf. *Address:* 3 Brookfield, Upper Hopton, Mirfield, West Yorks WF14 8HL. *T:* Mirfield (0924) 79221.

HAMPSHIRE, Sir Stuart (Newton), Kt 1979; FBA 1960; Professor, Stanford University, since 1985; Warden of Wadham College, Oxford University, 1970–84; *b* 1 Oct. 1914; *s* of G. N. Hampshire and Marie West; *m* 1st, 1961, Renee Ayer (*d* 1980); 2nd, 1985, Nancy Cartwright; two *d*. *Educ:* Repton; Balliol Coll., Oxford. 1st Cl. Lit Hum, Oxford, 1936. Fellow of All Souls Coll., and Lectr in Philosophy, Oxford, 1936–40. Service in Army, 1940–45. Personal Asst to Minister of State, Foreign Office, 1945; Lectr in Philosophy, University Coll., London, 1947–50; Fellow of New Coll., Oxford, 1950–55; Domestic Bursar and Research Fellow, All Souls Coll., 1955–60; Grote Prof. of Philosophy of Mind and Logic, Univ. of London, 1960–63; Prof. of Philosophy, Princeton Univ., 1963–70. Fellow, Amer. Acad. of Arts and Sciences, 1968. Hon. DLitt Glasgow, 1973. *Publications:* Spinoza, 1951; Thought and Action, 1959; Freedom of the Individual, 1965; Modern Writers and other essays, 1969; Freedom of Mind and other essays, 1971; (ed jtly) The Socialist Idea, 1975; Two Theories of Morality, 1977; (ed) Public and Private Morality, 1978; Morality and Conflict, 1983; Innocence and Experience, 1989; articles in philosophical journals. *Address:* 5 Beaumont Road, The Quarry, Headington, Oxford. *T:* Oxford (0865) 750977; 152 Otis Avenue, Calif 94062, USA.

HAMPSHIRE, Susan; actress; *b* 12 May 1942; *d* of George Kenneth Hampshire and June Hampshire; *m* 1st, 1967, Pierre Granier-Deferre (marr. diss. 1974); one *s* (one *d* decd); 2nd, 1981, Eddie Kulukundis, *qv*. *Educ:* Hampshire Sch., Knightsbridge. *Stage:* Expresso Bongo, 1958; 'that girl' in Follow That Girl, 1960; Fairy Tales of New York, 1961; Marion Dangerfield in Ginger Man, 1963; Kate Hardcastle in She Stoops to Conquer, 1966; On Approval, 1966; Mary in The Sleeping Prince, 1968; Nora in A Doll's House, 1972; Katharina in The Taming of the Shrew, 1974; Peter in Peter Pan, 1974; Jeannette in Romeo and Jeannette, 1975; Rosalind in As You Like It, 1975; title rôle in Miss Julie, 1975; Elizabeth in The Circle, 1976; Ann Whitefield in Man and Superman, 1978; Siri Von Essen in Tribades, 1978; Victorine in An Audience Called Edouard, 1978; Irene in The Crucifer of Blood, 1979; Ruth Carson in Night and Day, 1979; Elizabeth in The Revolt, 1980; Stella Drury in House Guest, 1981; Elvira in Blithe Spirit, 1986; Marie Stopes in Married Love, 1988; Countess in A Little Night Music, 1989; Mrs Anna in The King and I, 1990; *TV Serials:* Andromeda (title rôle), Fleur Forsyte in The Forsyte Saga (Emmy Award for Best Actress, 1970), Becky Sharp in Vanity Fair (Emmy Award for Best Actress, 1973), Sarah Churchill, Duchess of Marlborough, in The First Churchills (Emmy Award for Best Actress, 1971), Glencora Palliser in The Pallisers; Lady Melfont in Dick Turpin; Signora Neroni in The Barchester Chronicles; Martha in Leaving, 2 series; Katy in What Katy Did; Going to Pot, 3 series. *Films include:* During One Night, The Three Lives of Thomasina, Night Must Fall, Wonderful Life, Paris in August, The Fighting Prince of Donegal, Monte Carlo or Bust, Rogan, David Copperfield, Living Free, A Time for Loving, Malpertius (E. Poe Prizes du Film Fantastique, Best Actress, 1972), Neither the Sea Nor the Sand, Roses and Green Peppers, Bang. Dir, Conservation Foundn; Mem. Exec. Cttee, Population Concern. Hon. DLitt: City, 1984; St Andrews, 1986. *Publications:* Susan's Story, 1981; The Maternal Instinct, 1984; Lucy Jane at the Ballet, 1989; Lucy Jane on Television, 1989; Trouble Free Gardening, 1989; Every Letter Counts, 1990; Lucy Jane and the Dancing Competition, 1991; Easy Gardening, 1991. *Recreations:* gardening, music, the study of antique furniture. *Address:* c/o Chatto & Linnit Ltd, Prince of Wales Theatre, Coventry Street, W1V 7FE. *T:* 071–930 6677, *Fax:* 071–930 0091.

HAMPSON, Prof. Elwyn Lloyd, MDS, FDSRCS; HDD RCSE; Professor of Restorative Dentistry, University of Sheffield, 1960–81, now Emeritus; Hon. Consultant Dental Surgeon to Sheffield Area Health Authority, since 1981; *b* 31 Jan. 1916; *s* of John and Mary Hampson; *m* 1940, Anne Cottrell; one *s* one *d*. *Educ:* Calday Grange Grammar Sch., W Kirby, Cheshire; Univ. of Liverpool. BDS with 1st Class Hons 1939; HDD RCSE 1944; FDSRCS 1949; MDS 1954; FDSE 1964. House surg., Liverpool Dental Hosp., 1939; Royal Army Dental Corps, 1941–45; Lecturer in Operative Dental Surgery, Edinburgh Dental Sch., 1945–47; Lecturer and later Senior Lecturer in Operative Dental Surgery, Univ. of Sheffield, 1947–60, Dean of Sch. of Clinical Dentistry, 1968–72. Mem., GDC, 1968–73. *Publications:* Hampson's Textbook of Operative Dental Surgery, 1961, 4th edn 1980; many papers in scientific jls. *Recreations:* water colour painting, golf. *Address:* 8 Milborne Close, Chester CH2 1HH.

HAMPSON, Dr Keith; MP (C) Leeds North-West, since 1983 (Ripon, Feb. 1974–1983); *b* 14 Aug. 1943; *s* of Bertie Hampson and Mary Elizabeth Noble; *m* 1st, 1975, Frances Pauline (*d* 1975), *d* of Mr and Mrs Mathieu Donald Einhorn; 2nd, 1979, Susan, *d* of Mr and Mrs John Wilkie Cameron. *Educ:* King James I Grammar Sch., Bishop Auckland, Co. Durham; Univ. of Bristol; Harvard Univ. BA, CertEd, PhD. Personal Asst to Edward Heath, 1966 and 1970 Gen. Elections and in his House of Commons office, 1968; Lectr in American History, Edinburgh Univ., 1968–74. Mem., Gen. Adv. Council, IBA, 1980–88. PPS: to Minister for Local Govt, 1979–83; to Sec. of State for Environment, 1983; to Sec. of State for Defence, 1983–84. Vice Chairman: Cons. Parly Educn Cttee, 1975–79; Cons. Parly Defence Cttee, 1988–89 (Sec., 1984–88); Mem., Select Cttee on Trade and Industry, 1987–. Mem., Educn Adv. Cttee of UK Commn for UNESCO, 1980–84. Vice President: WEA, 1978–; Assoc. of Business Executives, 1979–; Vice-Chm., Youthaid, 1979–83. *Recreations:* DIY, music. *Address:* House of Commons, SW1A 0AA. *T:* 071–219 4463. *Club:* Carlton.

HAMPSON, Prof. Norman, FBA 1980; Professor of History, University of York, 1974–89; *b* 8 April 1922; *s* of Frank Hampson and Elizabeth Jane Fazackerley; *m* 1948, Jacqueline Gardin; two *d*. *Educ:* Manchester Grammar Sch.; University Coll., Oxford (MA); Dr de l'Univ. Paris; DLitt Edinburgh. Service in Royal Navy, 1941–45. Manchester Univ., 1948–67: Lectr and Sen. Lectr; Prof. of Modern History, Univ. of Newcastle, 1967–74. *Publications:* La Marine de l'an II, 1959; A Social History of the French Revolution, 1963; The Enlightenment, 1968; The First European Revolution, 1969; The Life and Opinions of Maximilien Robespierre, 1974; A Concise History of the French Revolution, 1975; Danton, 1978; Will and Circumstance: Montesquieu, Rousseau and the French Revolution, 1983; Prelude to Terror, 1988; Saint-Just, 1991. *Address:* 305 Hull Road, York YO1 3LB. *T:* York (0904) 412661.

HAMPSTEAD, Archdeacon of; *see* Coogan, Ven. R. A. W.

HAMPTON, 6th Baron *cr* 1874; **Richard Humphrey Russell Pakington;** Bt 1846; *b* 25 May 1925; *s* of 5th Baron Hampton, OBE, and Grace Dykes (*d* 1959), 3rd *d* of Rt Hon. Sir Albert Spicer, 1st Bt; *S* father, 1974; *m* 1958, Jane Elizabeth Farquharson, *d* of late T. F. Arnott, OBE, TD, MB, ChB; one *s* two *d*. *Educ:* Eton; Balliol Coll., Oxford. Observer in Fleet Air Arm, RNVR, 1944–47. Varied employment, mainly with advertising agencies, 1949–58; Worcestershire Branch Council for the Protection of Rural England, 1958–71; Tansley Witt & Co., Chartered Accts, Birmingham, 1971–73. *Publication:* (written with his father, Humphrey Pakington) The Pakingtons of Westwood, 1975. *Heir: s* Hon. John Humphrey Arnott Pakington, *b* 24 Dec. 1964. *Address:* Palace Farmhouse, Upton-on-Severn, Worcester WR8 0SN. *T:* Upton-on-Severn (06846) 2512.

HAMPTON, Antony Barmore, TD 1954; DL; President, Record Marples Tools Ltd (formerly Bahco Record Tools), since 1981 (Chairman, 1958–81); President, Engineering Employers Federation, 1980–82; *b* 6 March 1919; *s* of Charles William Hampton and Winifred Elizabeth Hampton; *m* 1948, Helen Patricia Lockwood; five *s*. *Educ:* Rydal Sch.; Christ's Coll., Cambridge, 1938–40 (MA). Indian Army 1941–46 (despatches). C. and J. Hampton Ltd, 1947, until merger with Ridgway, 1972 (Chm. of both, 1958–81); Lloyds Bank Ltd: Chm., Yorkshire Board, 1972–84 (Mem., 1961–85); Director, UK Board, 1972–85. Dir, Black Horse Agencies Ltd, 1983–85; Mem., Engrg Industry Trng Bd, 1979–82; Master Cutler of Hallamshire, 1966–67. Chm., Crucible Theatre Trust, Sheffield, 1970–82. DL S Yorkshire (previously W Riding) 1972. *Recreations:* sailing, fishing. *Address:* Tideway, 20 Wittering Road, Hayling Island, Hants PO11 9SP. *T:* Hayling Island (0705) 464361. *Club:* Little Ship.

HAMPTON, Bryan; Director of Personnel, Department of Energy, since 1989; *b* 4 Dec. 1938; *s* of William Douglas Hampton and Elizabeth Cardwell; *m* 1964, Marilyn Joseph; five *d*. *Educ:* Harrow County Grammar Sch. for Boys. Board of Trade: Exec. Officer, 1957; Asst Private Sec. to Parly Sec., 1961; Private Sec. to Minister of State (Lords), 1963; Asst Principal, 1965; Second Sec., UK Delegn to EFTA/GATT, Geneva, 1966; Principal, DTI, 1969; Asst Sec., Dept of Energy, 1974; Counsellor (Energy), Washington, 1981–86; Head, Br. 1, Atomic Energy Div., Dept of Energy, 1986–89. *Recreations:* music, golf. *Address:* Orchard House, Berks Hill, Chorleywood, Herts WD3 5AG. *T:* Chorleywood (0923) 282311.

HAMPTON, Christopher James, FRSL 1976; playwright; *b* 26 Jan. 1946; *s* of Bernard Patrick Hampton and Dorothy Patience Hampton (*née* Herrington); *m* 1971, Laura Margaret de Holesch; two *d*. *Educ:* Lancing Coll.; New Coll., Oxford (MA). First play: When Did You Last See My Mother?, 1964 (perf. Royal Court Theatre, 1966; transf. Comedy Theatre; prod. at Sheridan Square Playhouse, New York, 1967). Resident Dramatist, Royal Court Theatre, Aug. 1968–70. Mem. Council, RSL, 1984–90. *Plays:* Total Eclipse, Prod. Royal Court, 1968; The Philanthropist, Royal Court and Mayfair, 1970 (Evening Standard Best Comedy Award, 1970; Plays & Players London Theatre Critics Best Play, 1970), Ethel Barrymore Theatre, New York, 1971, Chichester, 1985; Savages, Royal Court, 1973, Comedy, 1973, Mark Taper Forum Theatre, Los Angeles, 1974 (Plays & Players London Theatre Critics Best Play, Jt Winner, 1973; Los Angeles Drama Critics Circle Award for Distinguished Playwriting, 1974); Treats, Royal Court, 1976, Mayfair, 1976; Able's Will, BBC TV, 1977; After Mercer, Nat. Theatre, 1980; The History Man (from Malcolm Bradbury) BBC TV, 1981; Total Eclipse (rev. version) Lyric, Hammersmith, 1981; The Portage to San Cristobal of A. H. (from George Steiner), Mermaid, 1982; Tales from Hollywood, Mark Taper Forum Theatre, Los Angeles, 1982, NT 1983 (Standard Best Comedy Award, 1983); Les Liaisons Dangereuses (from Laclos), RSC, 1985, transf. Ambassadors Th., 1986, NY, 1987 (Plays & Players London Theatre Critics Best Play, Jt Winner, 1985; Time Out Best Production Award, 1986; London Standard Best Play Award, 1986; Laurence Olivier Best Play Award, 1986; NY Drama Critics' Circle Best For. Play Award, 1987); Hotel du Lac (from Anita Brookner), BBC TV, 1986 (BAFTA Best TV Film Award, 1987); White Chameleon, Nat. Theatre, 1991; *translations:* Marya, by Isaac Babel, Royal Court, 1967; Uncle Vanya, by Chekhov, Royal Court, 1970; Hedda Gabler, by Ibsen, Fest. Theatre, Stratford, Ont, 1970, Almeida, Islington, 1984, rev. version, NT, 1989; A Doll's House, by Ibsen, Playhouse Theatre, New York, 1971, Criterion, London, 1973, Vivian Beaumont Theatre, New York, 1975; Don Juan, by Molière, Bristol Old Vic, 1972; Tales from the Vienna Woods, by Horváth, National Theatre, 1977; Don Juan Comes Back from the War, by Horváth, Nat. Theatre, 1978; Ghosts, by Ibsen, Actors' Co., 1978; The Wild Duck, by Ibsen, Nat. Theatre, 1979; The Prague Trial, by Chereau and Mnouchkine, Paris Studio, 1980; Tartuffe, by Molière, RSC, 1983; Faith, Hope and Charity, by Horváth, Lyric, Hammersmith, 1989; *films:* A Doll's House, 1973; Tales From the Vienna Woods, 1979; The Honorary Consul, 1983; The Good Father, 1986 (Prix Italia 1988); Wolf at the Door, 1986; Dangerous Liaisons, 1988 (Academy Award, and Writers Guild of America Award, for best adapted screenplay; Critics' Circle Award for best screenplay, 1989; BAFTA best screenplay award, 1990); *TV serial:* The Ginger Tree (from Oswald Wynd), 1989. *Publications:* When Did You Last See My Mother?, 1967; Total Eclipse, 1969, rev. version, 1981; The Philanthropist, 1970, 2nd edn 1985, The Philanthropist and other plays, 1991; Savages, 1974; Treats, 1976; Able's Will, 1979; Tales from Hollywood, 1983; The Portage to San Cristobal of A. H. (George Steiner), 1983; Les Liaisons Dangereuses, 1985; Dangerous

Liaisons: the film, 1989; The Ginger Tree, 1989; White Chameleon, 1991; *translations:* Isaac Babel, Marya, 1969; Chekhov, Uncle Vanya, 1971; Ibsen, Hedda Gabler, 1972, rev. version 1989; Ibsen, A Doll's House, 1972, 2nd edn 1989; Molière, Don Juan, 1972; Horváth, Tales from the Vienna Woods, 1977; Horváth, Don Juan Comes Back from the War, 1978; Ibsen, The Wild Duck, 1980; Ibsen, Ghosts, 1983; Molière, Tartuffe, 1984, 2nd edn 1991; Horváth, Faith, Hope and Charity, 1989. *Recreations:* travel, cinema. *Address:* 2 Kensington Park Gardens, W11. *Club:* Dramatists'.

HAMPTON, John; a Recorder of the Crown Court, since 1983; *b* 13 Nov. 1926; *e s* of late Thomas Victor Hampton and Alice Maud (*née* Sturgeon), Oulton Broad; *m* 1954, Laura Jessie, *d* of Ronald Mylne Ford and Margaret Jessie Ford (*née* Coghill), Newcastle-under-Lyme; three *d. Educ:* Bradford Grammar School; University College London (LLB). Served Royal Navy, 1945–47. Called to the Bar, Inner Temple, 1952; NE Circuit; Solicitor General and Attorney General; Dep. Circuit Judge, 1975–82. Dep. Chm., Agricultural Land Tribunal, Yorks and Lancs Area, 1980–82, Yorks and Humberside Area, 1982–. *Recreations:* mountaineering, sailing. *Address:* 38 Park Square, Leeds LS1 2PA. *T:* Leeds (0532) 439422. *Club:* Leeds (Leeds).

HAMPTON, Surgeon Rear-Adm. Trevor Richard Walker, CB 1988; FRCPE; Surgeon Rear-Admiral (Operational Medical Services), 1987–89; *b* 6 June 1930; *s* of Violet and Percy Hampton; *m* 1st, 1952, Rosemary (*née* Day); three *d*; 2nd, 1976, Jennifer (*née* Bootle). *Educ:* King Edward VII Grammar School, King's Lynn; Edinburgh University. MB, ChB 1954; MRCPE 1964. Resident House Officer, Edinburgh Royal Infirmary, 1954–55; joined RN as Surgeon Lieut, 1955; served in HM Ships Ganges, Harrier and Victorious, 1955–62; Clinical Asst, Dept of Medicine, Edinburgh Univ., 1964; RN Hosp., Gibraltar, 1965–68; Consultant Physician, RN Hospitals, Plymouth, 1969–74, Haslar, 1975–79; MO i/c, RN Hosp., Gibraltar, 1980–82, RN Hosp., Plymouth, 1982–84; Surgeon Rear-Adm., Support Medical Services, 1984–87. QHP 1983–89. OStJ 1983. *Publications:* contribs to Jl of RN Med. Service. *Recreations:* cricket, amateur theatre, resting. *Address:* c/o Lloyds Bank, Cosham, Hants.

HAMWEE, Baroness *cr* 1991 (Life Peer), of Richmond upon Thames; **Sally Rachel Hamwee;** Partner, Clintons, solicitors; *b* 12 Jan. 1947; *d* of late Alec Hamwee and of Dorothy Hamwee (*née* Saunders). *Educ:* Manchester High Sch. for Girls; Girton Coll., Cambridge (MA). Admitted as solicitor, 1972. Councillor, London Borough of Richmond upon Thames, 1978– (Chm., Planning Cttee, 1983–87; Vice Chm., Policy and Resources Cttee, 1987–); Chair, London Planning Adv. Cttee, 1986–; Chm., Members' Policy Gp, London and SE Regl Planning Conf., 1989–91. Vice Chm., ASLDC (Councillors' and Campaigners' Assoc.), 1988–; Member: Nat. Exec., Liberal Party, 1987–88; Federal Exec., Liberal Democrats, 1989–91. *Address:* 101A Mortlake High Street, SW14 8HQ. *T:* 081–878 1380.

HAMYLTON JONES, Keith, CMG 1979; HM Diplomatic Service, retired; HM Ambassador, to Costa Rica, 1974–79, to Honduras, 1975–78, and to Nicaragua, 1976–79; *b* 12 Oct. 1924; *m* 1953, Eira Morgan; one *d. Educ:* St Paul's Sch.; Balliol Coll., Oxford (Domus Scholar in Classics, 1943); BA 1948; MA 1950. Welsh Guards, 1943; Italy, 1944 (Lieut); S France, 1946 (Staff Captain). HM Foreign Service, 1949; 3rd Sec., Warsaw, 1950; 2nd Sec., Lisbon, 1953; 1st Sec., Manila, 1957; Head of Chancery and HM Consul, Montevideo, 1962; Head of Chancery, Rangoon, 1967; Asst Head of SE Asia Dept, FCO, 1968; Consul-General, Lubumbashi, 1970–72; Counsellor, FCO, 1973–74. Operation Raleigh: Chm. for Devon and Cornwall, 1983–85; led internat. expedn to Costa Rica, Feb.-May 1985. Chairman: Anglo-Costa Rican Soc., 1983–88; Anglo-Central American Soc., 1988–91. *Publication:* (as Peter Myllent) The Ideal World, 1972. *Recreations:* reading, writing, walking. *Address:* Morval House, Morval, near Looe, Cornwall PL13 1PN.

HAN Suyin, (Dr Elizabeth Comber); doctor and author; (*née* Elizabeth Kuanghu Chow); *b* 12 Sept. 1917; *d* of Y. T. Chow (Chinese) and M. Denis (Belgian); *m* 1st, 1938, General P. H. Tang (*d* 1947); one *d*; 2nd, 1952, L. F. Comber (marr. diss. 1968); 3rd, 1971, Vincent Ruthnaswamy. *Educ:* Yenching Univ., Peking, China; Brussels Univ., Brussels, Belgium; London Univ., London, England. Graduated MB, BS, London (Hons) in 1948, a practising doctor until 1964. *Publications: as Han Suyin:* Destination Chungking, 1942; A Many Splendoured Thing, 1952; And the Rain My Drink, 1956; The Mountain Is Young, 1958; Cast but One Shadow and Winter Love, 1962; The Four Faces, 1963; China in the Year 2001, 1967; The Morning Deluge, 1972; Wind in the Tower, 1976; Lhasa, the Open City, 1977; Les Cent Fleurs: La Peinture Chinoise, 1978; La Chine aux Mille Visages, 1980; Chine: Terre Eau et Hommes, 1981; Till Morning Comes, 1982; The Enchantress, 1985; *autobiography:* China: autobiography, history (4 vols): The Crippled Tree, 1965; A Mortal Flower, 1966; Birdless Summer, 1968; My House Has Two Doors, 1980; A Share of Loving, 1987; Han Suyin's China, 1987; Fleur de Soleil, 1988. *Recreations:* botany, riding, swimming, lecturing. *Address:* 37 Montoie, Lausanne 1007, Switzerland.

HANANIYA, Maj.-Gen. Haldu A.; Nigerian Ambassador to Ethiopia, 1984–89; *b* 2 Feb. 1942; *m* Rhoda A. Hananiya; one *s* five *d. Educ:* Boys Secondary School, Gindiri; Nigerian Military Training Centre; Officer Cadet School, UK (commissioned 1963); RSME course, 1963; Plant Engr Officers' Course, 1965–66, Engr Advance Officers' Course, 1971–72, Fort Belvoir, USA. Nigerian Army Engineers: Comdr 1 and 2 Field Engr Sqdns, 1966; Cmdr 1 Field Regt, 1966–70; Comdr 2 Field Engr Regt, 1970–71, 1972–73; Inspector of Engrs, 1974–77; Command and Staff Coll., 1977; Comdr, 1 Inf. Bde, Nigerian Army, 1977–78; Defence Adviser, London, 1979–80; student, Nigerian Inst. for Policy and Strategic Studies, 1979–80; Director of Training, Army HQ, 1981; GOC 2 Mech. Inf. Div., Nigerian Army, 1981–83 (Defence Resources Management Course, 1982); GOC 1 Mech. Inf. Div., 1983–84; High Comr to UK, 1984. *Recreations:* squash, tennis, billiards, snooker. *Address:* c/o Ministry of Defence, Independence Building, Tafawa Balewa Square, Lagos, Nigeria.

HANBURY, Lt-Col Sir Hanmer (Cecil), KCVO 1991 (LVO 1953); MC 1943; JP; HM Lord-Lieutenant of Bedfordshire, 1978–91; *b* 5 Jan. 1916; *yr s* of late Sir Cecil Hanbury, MP, FLS, and late Mrs Hanbury-Forbes, OBE, of Kingston Maurward, Dorchester, Dorset, and La Mortola, Ventimiglia, Italy; *m* 1939, Prunella Kathleen Charlotte, *d* of late Air Cdre T. C. R. Higgins, CB, CMG, DL, JP, Turvey House, Beds; one *s* one *d. Educ:* Eton; RMC, Sandhurst. 2nd Lieut Grenadier Guards, 1936; served 1939–45 with Grenadier Guards, France, Belgium, N Africa, Italy; Capt. 1943; Temp. Major, 1944; Major 1948; Temp. Lt-Col, 1955–57; retired 1958. BRCS, Bedfordshire: Dir, 1959–71; Dep. Pres., 1972–78; Patron, 1978–; Pres., St John's Council for Bedfordshire, 1979–; Chm., Beds T&AVR Cttee, 1970–78, Pres., 1978; Vice-Pres., E Anglia T&AVRA, 1978–80, 1986 (Vice-Chm., 1970–78; Pres., 1980–86). DL 1958, Vice-Lieut, later Vice Lord-Lieut, 1970–78, JP 1959, Beds; High Sheriff, Beds, 1965. KStJ 1980. *Recreations:* shooting and country pursuits. *Address:* Turvey House, Turvey, Beds MK43 8EL. *T:* Turvey (023064) 227. *Clubs:* White's, Army and Navy, Pratt's.

HANBURY, Harold Greville, QC 1960; DCL; Vinerian Professor Emeritus of English Law, Oxford; Hon. Fellow, Lincoln College, Oxford; Hon. Master of the Bench, Inner Temple; *b* 19 June 1898; *s* of late Lt-Col Basil Hanbury and late Hon. Patience Verney; *m* 1927, Anna Margaret (*d* 1980), *d* of late Hannibal Dreyer, Copenhagen, Denmark. *Educ:* Charterhouse; Brasenose Coll., Oxford (Scholar). Vinerian Law Scholar, 1921; Fellow of Lincoln Coll., Oxford 1921–49; Fellow of All Souls Coll., 1949–64, Emeritus Fellow, 1980; Vinerian Prof. of English Law, Oxford, 1949–64. Visiting Prof., Univ. of Ife, 1962–63; Dean of Law Faculty, Univ. of Nigeria, 1964–66. Barrister-at-Law, Inner Temple, 1922; Rhodes Travelling Fellow, 1931–32; Senior Proctor, Oxford Univ., 1933–34 and 1944–45. President: Bentham Club, UCL, 1954–55 (Hon. Mem., 1988); Soc. of Public Teachers of Law, 1958–59. Chairman: Court of Inquiry into Provincial Omnibus Industry, 1954; Board of Inquiry into West Indian Airways, Trinidad, 1958; Tribunal for Industrials, Gibraltar, 1960; Independent Mem. Commns of Inquiry on Retail Distributive Trades, 1946; Minimum Wage Arbitrator in Nigeria, 1955. Hon. Mem., Mark Twain Soc., 1977. *Publications:* Le Système Actuel de l'Equité dans le Système Juridique de l'Angleterre (trans. Robert Kiéfé), 1929; Essays in Equity, 1934, German edn 1977; Modern Equity, 1935 (13th edn *sub nom.* Hanbury and Maudsley, 1989); Traité Pratique des Divorces et des Successions en Droit Anglais (with R. Moureaux), 1939 (2nd edn 1952); English Courts of Law, 1944 (5th edn *sub nom.* Hanbury and Yardley, 1979); Principles of Agency, 1952 (2nd edn, 1960); The Vinerian Chair and Legal Education, 1958; Biafra: a challenge to the conscience of Britain, 1968; Shakespeare as Historian, 1985; articles in legal periodicals. *Recreations:* reading, aelurophily (Vice-Pres. Oxford and District Cat Club), formerly cricket, travelling. *Address:* 14 Dan Pienaar Road, Kloof, Natal, South Africa. *T:* 7644617.

HANBURY, Sir John (Capel), Kt 1974; CBE 1969; Formerly Chairman, Allen and Hanburys Ltd, 1954–73 (Director, 1944); *b* 26 May 1908; *e s* of late Frederick Capel Hanbury; *m* 1st, 1935, Joan Terry Fussell (*d* 1989); two *s* one *d* (and one *s* decd); 2nd, 1990, Rosemary Elizabeth, *widow* of Lt Comdr Paul Coquelle, RN. *Educ:* Downside; Trinity Coll., Cambridge. Mem., Pharmacopoeia Commn, 1948–73; Chm., Central Health Services Council, 1970–76; Pres. Assoc. of Brit. Pharmaceutical Industry, 1950–52; Chm., Assoc. of Brit. Chemical Manufacturers, 1961–63; Pres. Franco-British Pharmaceutical Commn, 1955. Mem., Thames Water Authority, 1974–79. FRSC (FRIC 1947); FPS 1955. Fellow, UCL, 1977. *Recreations:* horticulture, archæology. *Address:* Amwellbury House, Ware, Herts SG12 9RD. *T:* Ware (0920) 462108. *Club:* United Oxford & Cambridge University.

HANBURY-TENISON, Airling Robin, OBE 1981; MA, FLS, FRGS; farmer; President, Survival International (Chairman since 1969); *b* 7 May 1936; *s* of late Major Gerald Evan Farquhar Tenison, Lough Bawn, Co. Monaghan, Ireland, and Ruth, *o* surv. *c* of late John Capel Hanbury, JP, DL, Pontypool Park, Monmouthshire; *m* 1st, 1959, Marika Hopkinson (*d* 1982); one *s* one *d*; 2nd, 1983, Mrs Louella Edwards, *d* of Lt Col G. T. G. Williams, DL, and Mrs Williams, Menkee, St Mabyn, Cornwall; one *s. Educ:* Eton; Magdalen Coll., Oxford (MA). Made first land crossing of South America at its widest point, 1958 (Mrs Patrick Ness Award, RGS, 1961); explored Tassili N'Ajjer, Tibesti and Aïr mountains in Southern Sahara, 1962–66; crossed S America in a small boat from the Orinoco to Buenos Aires, 1964–65; Geographical Magazine Amazonas Expedn, by Hovercraft, 1968; Trans-African Hovercraft Expedn (Dep. Leader), 1969; visited 33 Indian tribes as guest of Brazilian Govt, 1971; Winston Churchill Memorial Fellow, 1971; British Trans Americas Expedn, 1972; explored Outer Islands of Indonesia, 1973; Eastern Sulawesi, 1974; Sabah, Brunei, Sarawak, 1976; RGS Mulu (Sarawak) Expedn (Leader), 1977–78; expedns to Ecuador, Brazil and Venezuela, 1980–81; rode across France, 1984; rode along Great Wall of China, 1986; rode through New Zealand, 1988; rode as pilgrim to Santiago de Compostela, 1989. Comr of Income Tax, 1965–; Mem. of Lloyd's, 1976–. Mem., Invest in Britain (formerly Think British) Campaign, 1987–; Trustee, Ecological Foundn, 1988–; Pres., Cornwall Trust for Nature Conservation, 1988–. Mem. Council, RGS, 1968–70, 1971–76, 1979–82, Vice-Pres., 1982–86; Patron's Medal, RGS, 1979; Krug Award of Excellence, 1980. *Publications:* The Rough and the Smooth, 1969; Report of a Visit to the Indians of Brazil, 1971; A Question of Survival, 1973; A Pattern of Peoples, 1975; Mulu: the rain forest, 1980; Aborigines of the Amazon Rain Forest: the Yanomami, 1982; Worlds Apart (autobiog.), 1984; White Horses Over France, 1985; A Ride along the Great Wall, 1987; Fragile Eden: a ride through New Zealand, 1989; A Canter to St James, 1990; articles in: The Times, Spectator, Blackwood's Magazine, etc; articles and reviews in Geographical Magazine (numerous), Geographical Jl, Ecologist, Expedition, etc. *Recreations:* travelling, riding across countries. *Address:* Maidenwell, Cardinham, Bodmin, Cornwall PL30 4DW. *T:* Cardinham (020882) 224. *Clubs:* Groucho, Geographical; Kildare Street and University (Dublin).

See also R. Hanbury-Tenison.

HANBURY-TENISON, Richard, JP; Lord-Lieutenant of Gwent, since 1979; *b* 3 Jan. 1925; *e s* of late Major G. E. F. Tenison, Lough Bawn, Co. Monaghan, Ireland, and Ruth, *o* surv. *c* of late J. C. Hanbury, JP, DL, Pontypool Park, Monmouthshire; *m* 1955, Euphan Mary, *er d* of late Major A. B. Wardlaw-Ramsay, 21st of Whitehill, Midlothian; three *s* two *d. Educ:* Eton; Magdalen Coll., Oxford. Served Irish Guards, 1943–47 (Captain, wounded). Entered HM Foreign Service, 1949: 1st Sec., Vienna, 1956–58; 1st Sec. (and sometime Chargé d'Affaires), Phnom Penh, 1961–63, and Bucharest, 1966–68; Counsellor, Bonn, 1968–70; Head of Aviation and Telecommunications Dept, FCO, 1970–71; Counsellor, Brussels, 1971–75; retired from Diplomatic Service, 1975. South Wales Regional Dir, Lloyds Bank, 1980–91 (Chm., 1987–91). Mem. Council and Ct, Nat. Museum of Wales, 1980– (Chm., Art Cttee, 1986–). President: Monmouthshire Rural Community Council, 1959–75; Gwent Local Hist. Council; Gwent County Scout Council; Gwent Community Services Council, 1985– (Chm., 1975–85). President: TA&VRA for Wales, 1985–90; S Wales Regl Cttee, TA&VRA, 1990–. Hon. Col, 3rd (V) Bn, The Royal Regt of Wales, 1982–90. DL 1973, High Sheriff 1977, JP 1979, Gwent. KStJ 1990 (CStJ 1980). Award for Forestry and Woodland Management, Timber Growers (UK), 1990. *Recreations:* shooting, fishing, conservation. *Address:* Clytha Park, Abergavenny, Gwent. *T:* Abergavenny (0873) 840300; Lough Bawn, Co. Monaghan. *Clubs:* Boodle's; Kildare Street and University (Dublin).

See also A. R. Hanbury-Tenison.

HANBURY-TRACY, family name of **Baron Sudeley.**

HANCOCK, Christine; General Secretary, Royal College of Nursing, since 1989. *Educ:* London School of Economics (BScEcons). RGN. Formerly: Chief Nursing Officer, Bloomsbury Health Authority; General Manager, Waltham Forest Health Authority. *Address:* Royal College of Nursing, 20 Cavendish Square, W1M 0AB. *T:* 071–409 3333.

HANCOCK, Sir David (John Stowell), KCB 1985; Executive Director, Hambros Bank Ltd, since 1989; Director, Hambros PLC, since 1989; *b* 27 March 1934; *s* of late Alfred George Hancock and Florence Hancock (*née* Barrow); *m* 1966, Sheila Gillian Finlay; one *s* one *d. Educ:* Whitgift Sch.; Balliol Coll., Oxford. Asst Principal, Bd of Trade, 1957; transf. to HM Treasury, 1959; Principal, 1962; Harkness Fellow, 1965–66; Private Sec. to Chancellor of the Exchequer, 1968–70; Asst Sec., 1970; Financial and Economic Counsellor, Office of UK Permanent Rep. to European Communities, 1972–74; Under Sec., 1975–80; Dep. Sec., 1980–82; Dep. Sec., Cabinet Office, 1982–83; Perm. Sec., DES, 1983–89. Dir, European Investment Bank, 1980–82. Chm., British Selection Cttee of

Harkness Fellowships, 1988– (Mem., 1984–); Trustee, St Catharine's Foundn, Cumberland Lodge, 1989–; Governor, Lilian Baylis Sch., Lambeth, 1989–. FRSA 1986; CBIM 1987. *Recreations:* gardening, theatre. *Address:* c/o Hambros Bank Ltd, 41 Tower Hill, EC3N 4HA. *Clubs:* Athenæum, Civil Service.

HANCOCK, Elisabeth Joy; Head, Bromley High School (GPDST), since 1989; *b* 2 Dec. 1947; *d* of Reginald Arthur Lord and Evelyn Maud Mary Lord; *m* 1970, Barry Steuart Hancock; one *d. Educ:* Queen's Coll., Harley Street; Nottingham Univ. (BA Hons); Univ. of Sussex (PGCE). GB East Europe Centre, 1969; Nevill Sch., Hove, 1969–72; Brighton and Hove High Sch. (GPDST), 1972–89, Dep. Hd, 1986–89. FRSA 1988. *Publication:* Teaching History, 1970. *Recreations:* playing tennis, theatre, opera, watching cricket. *Address:* Bromley High School (GPDST), Blackbrook Lane, Bickley, Bromley, Kent BR1 2TW. *T:* 081–468 7981. *Clubs:* Royal Over-Seas League, St James'.

HANCOCK, Geoffrey Francis, CMG 1977; HM Diplomatic Service, retired; Foreign and Commonwealth Office, 1979–82; *b* 20 June 1926; *s* of Lt-Col Sir Cyril Hancock, KCIE, OBE, MC; *m* 1960, Amelia Juana Aragon; one *s* one *d. Educ:* Wellington; Trinity Coll., Oxford. MA 1951. Third Sec., Mexico City, 1953; Second Sec., Montevideo, 1956; Foreign Office, 1958; Madrid, 1958; FO, 1960; MECAS, 1962; First Sec., Baghdad, 1964–67 and 1968–69; FCO, 1969–73; Counsellor, Beirut, 1973–78. Founder, Middle East Consultants, 1983. *Recreations:* music, sailing. *Address:* c/o Lloyds Bank, 6 Pall Mall, SW1Y 5NH. *Clubs:* Athenæum, Royal Air Force.

HANCOCK, Prof. Keith Jackson, AO 1987; Professor of Economics, The Flinders University of South Australia, 1964–87, now Emeritus; Deputy President, Australian Industrial Relations Commission (formerly Australian Conciliation and Arbitration Commission), since 1987; *b* 4 Jan. 1935; *s* of late A. S. Hancock and Mrs R. D. Hancock; three *s* one *d. Educ:* Univ. of Melbourne (BA); Univ. of London (PhD). Tutor in Economic History, Univ. of Melbourne, 1956–57; Lectr in Economics, Univ. of Adelaide, 1959–63; Pro-Vice-Chancellor, 1975–79, Vice-Chancellor, 1980–87, Flinders Univ. of SA. Pres., Acad. of Social Sciences in Australia, 1981–84. FASSA 1968. Hon. Fellow, LSE, 1982. Hon. DLitt Flinders, 1987. *Publications:* (with P. A. Samuelson and R. H. Wallace) Economics (Australian edn), 1969, 2nd edn 1975; articles in Economic Jl, Economica, Amer. Econ. Rev. and other jls. *Recreations:* bridge, sailing, music. *Address:* 6 Maturin Road, Glenelg, SA 5045, Australia. *T:* 08–2948667. *Clubs:* Adelaide (Adelaide); Royal South Australian Yacht Squadron.

HANCOCK, Maj.-Gen. Michael Stephen, CB 1972; MBE 1953; retired 1972; Planning Inspector, Department of the Environment, 1972–87; *b* 19 July 1917; *s* of late Rev. W. H. M. Hancock and late Mrs C. C. Hancock (*née* Sherbrooke); *m* 1941, Constance Geraldine Margaret Ovens, *y d* of late Brig.-Gen. R. M. Ovens, CMG; one *s* one *d. Educ:* Marlborough Coll.; RMA, Woolwich. Commnd into Royal Signals, 1937; Comdr, Corps Royal Signals, 1st British Corps, 1963–66; Sec., Mil. Cttee, NATO, 1967–68; Chief of Staff, FARELF, 1968–70; VQMG, MoD, 1970–72. Col Comdt, Royal Signals, 1970–77. Chm., CCF Assoc., 1972–82, Vice Pres., 1982–; Chm., NE Surrey Dist Scouts, 1979–82, Pres., 1982–. CEng; FIEE. *Recreations:* DIY, chess.

HANCOCK, Michael Thomas; Director, Daytime Club, BBC, since 1987; *b* 9 April 1946; *m* 1967; one *s* one *d. Educ:* well. Member: Portsmouth City Council, 1971–, for Fratton Ward, 1973–; Hampshire County Council, 1973– (Leader of the Opposition, 1977–81). Joined SDP, 1981 (Mem., Nat. Cttee, 1984); contested Portsmouth S (SDP) 1983, (SDP/Alliance) 1987. MP (SDP) Portsmouth S, June 1984–87. Bd of Dirs, Drug Rehabilitation Unit, Alpha Drug Clinic, Alpha House, Droxford, 1971–; Chm., Southern Br., NSPCC, 1989–. Hon. award for contrib. to Anglo-German relations, Homborn, W Germany, 1981. *Publications:* contribs to various jls. *Recreations:* people, living life to the full. *Address:* (office) 196 Fratton Road, Fratton, Portsmouth PO1 5HD. *T:* Portsmouth (0705) 861055; (home) Fareham (0329) 287340. *Clubs:* too many to mention.

HANCOCK, Norman, CB 1976; CEng, FRINA; RCNC; Director of Warship Design, and Project Director, Invincible and Broadsword, Ministry of Defence, 1969–76; *b* 6 March 1916; *o s* of Louis Everard Hancock, Plymouth; *m* 1940, Marie E., *d* of William E. Bow; two *s. Educ:* Plymouth Grammar Sch.; RNC Greenwich. Asst Constructor, AEW, Haslar, 1940; Constructor, Naval Construction Dept, 1944; British Services Observer (Constructor Comdr), Bikini, 1946. HM Dockyard, Singapore, 1949; Frigate design, Naval Construction Dept, 1952; Chief Constructor in charge of R&D, 1954; Prof. of Naval Architecture, RNC, Greenwich, 1957–62; Asst Dir of Naval Construction, in charge of Submarine Design and Construction, 1963–69. Liveryman, Worshipful Co. of Shipwrights; past Mem. Council, RINA. *Recreations:* organ music, cabinet making, travel. *Address:* 41 Cranwells Park, Bath, Avon BA1 2YE. *T:* Bath (0225) 426045.

HANCOCK, P(ercy) E(llis) Thompson, FRCP; Former Hon. Consultant Physician: The Royal Free Hospital; The Royal Marsden Hospital; Potters Bar and District Hospital; National Temperance Hospital; Bishop's Stortford and District Hospital; *b* 4 Feb. 1904; *s* of Frank Hancock; *m* 1932, Dorothy Barnes (*d* 1953); two *d*; *m* 1955, Laurie Newton Sharp. *Educ:* Wellington Coll., Berks; Caius Coll., Cambridge; St Bartholomew's Hospital. MB 1937, BCh 1930, Cantab; FRCP 1944. Formerly: Senior Examiner in Medicine, Univ. of London; Dir of Dept of Clinical Res., Royal Marsden Hosp. and Inst. of Cancer Res. Member: Council, Imperial Cancer Res. Fund; Grand Council, Cancer Research Campaign; Mem. Exec. Cttee, Action on Smoking and Health; Sen. Mem., Assoc. of Physicians, GB and Ireland. Hosp. Visitor, King Edward's Hosp. Fund for London. FRSocMed (Pres., Section of Oncology, 1974–75); Fellow, Assoc. Européene de Médecine Interne d'Ensemble. Corresp. Mem., Società Italiana de Cancerologia. Hon. Member: American Gastroscopic Soc., 1958; Sociedad Chilena de Cancerología; Sociedad Chilena de Hematología; Sociedad Médica de Valparaíso; Medal, Societa Medica Chirurgica di Bologna, 1964. *Publications:* (joint) Cancer in General Practice; The Use of Bone Marrow Transfusion with massive Chemotherapy, 1960; (joint) Treatment of Early Hodgkin's Disease, 1967. *Recreations:* dining and wining. *Address:* 23 Wigmore Place, W1H 9DD. *T:* 071–631 4679.

HANCOCK, Ronald John; business consultant; Director: Insituform Ltd, since 1987; Travelines, since 1991; Permaline, since 1991; *b* 11 Feb. 1934; *s* of George and Elsie Hancock; *m* 1970, Valerie Hancock; two *d. Educ:* Dudley Grammar Sch., Dudley. FCMA. Served HM Forces, 1952–61. Schweppes Ltd, 1962–63; Mullard Ltd, 1963–66; Valor Group, 1966–68; BL Ltd, 1968–85. Chairman: Leyland Vehicles, 1981–85; Leyland Vehicles Exports Ltd, 1981–85; Bus Manufacturers Limited, 1981–85; Bus Manufacturers (Holdings) Ltd, 1981–85; Eastern Coachworks Ltd, 1981–85; Bristol Commercial Vehicles Ltd, 1981–85; Self-Changing Gears Ltd, 1981–85; Bedfordshire Chamber of Training Ltd, 1990–; Director: BL Staff Trustees Ltd, 1981–85; Leyland Nigeria Ltd, 1981–85; BL International Ltd, 1981–85; Land Rover-Leyland International Holdings Ltd (formerly BLIH), 1982–85; Land Rover-Leyland Ltd, 1983–85; Chloride Gp plc, 1985–87; Man. Dir, AWD Ltd, 1987–90. *Recreations:* travel, reading. *Address:* Briar House, Little Shardeloes, Old Amersham, Bucks HP7 0EF.

HANCOCK, Sheila, OBE 1974; actress and director; *d* of late Enrico Hancock and late Ivy Woodward; *m* 1st, 1955, Alexander Ross (*d* 1971); one *d*; 2nd, 1973, John Thaw, *qv*; one *d. Educ:* Dartford County Grammar Sch.; Royal Academy of Dramatic Art. Acted in Repertory, Theatre Workshop, Stratford East, for 8 years. Associate Dir, Cambridge Theatre Co., 1980–82; Artistic Dir, RSC Regional Tour, 1983–84; acted and directed, NT, 1985–86. Dir, The Actors Centre, 1978–. West End starring roles in: Rattle of a Simple Man, 1962; The Anniversary, 1966; A Delicate Balance (RSC), 1969; So What About Love?, 1969; Absurd Person Singular, 1973; Déjà Revue, 1974; The Bed Before Yesterday, 1976; Annie, 1978; Sweeney Todd, 1980; The Winter's Tale, RSC, Stratford 1981, Barbican 1982; Peter Pan, Barbican, 1982–83; The Cherry Orchard, The Duchess of Malfi, National, 1985–86; Greenland, Royal Court, 1988; Prin, Lyric, Hammersmith, 1989, Lyric, Shaftesbury Avenue, 1990. Has starred in several successful revues; appeared on Broadway in Entertaining Mr Sloane. Directed: The Soldier's Fortune, Lyric, Hammersmith, 1981; A Midsummer Night's Dream, RSC, 1983; The Critic, National, 1986. *Films:* The Love Child, 1987; Making Waves, 1987; Hawks, 1988; Buster, 1988; Three Men and a Little Lady, 1990. Many television successes, including her own colour spectacular for BBC2, Jumping the Queue, The Rivals, and several comedy series; wrote and acted in Royal Enclosure, 1990. Awards: Variety Club, London Critics, Whitbread Trophy (for best Actress on Broadway). *Publication:* Ramblings of an Actress, 1987. *Recreations:* reading, music. *Address:* c/o Jeremy Conway Ltd, Eagle House, 109 Jermyn Street, SW1.

HANCOCK, Air Marshal Sir Valston Eldridge, KBE 1962 (CBE 1953; OBE 1942); CB 1958; DFC 1945; retired; grazier; *b* 31 May 1907; *s* of R. J. Hancock, Perth, W Australia; *m* 1932, Joan E. G., *d* of Col A. G. Butler, DSO, VD; two *s* one *d. Educ:* Hale Sch., Perth; RMC, Duntroon; psa; idc. Joined Royal Military College, Duntroon, 1925; transferred RAAF, 1929; Dir of Plans, 1940–41; commanded 71 (Beaufort) Wing, New Guinea, 1945; Commandant RAAF Academy, 1947–49; Deputy Chief of Air Staff, 1951–53; Air Mem. for Personnel, Air Board, 1953–54; Head of Australian Joint Services Staff, UK, 1955–57; Extra Gentleman Usher to the Royal Household, 1955–57; AOC 224 Group, RAF, Malaya, 1957–59; Air Officer Commanding Operational Command, 1959–61; Chief of Air Staff, Royal Australian Air Force, 1961–65. Commissioner-Gen., Australian Exhibit Organization, Expo 1967. Foundation Chm., Australian Defence Assoc., 1975–81, Life Patron, 1982–. Life Mem., Royal Commonwealth Soc. (WA) (Pres., 1976–81). *Recreations:* literature and sport. *Address:* 108a Victoria Avenue, Dalkeith, WA 6009, Australia. *Club:* Weld (Perth).

HAND, Rt. Rev. Geoffrey David, KBE 1984 (CBE 1975); *b* 11 May 1918; *s* of Rev. W. T. Hand. *Educ:* Oriel College, Oxford; Cuddesdon Theological Coll., BA 1941, MA 1946. Deacon, 1942; Priest, 1943. Curate of Heckmondwike, 1942–46; Missioner, Diocese of New Guinea, 1946–50; Priest in charge: Sefoa, 1947–48; Sangara, 1948–50; Archdeacon, North New Guinea, 1950–65; Bishop Coadjutor of New Guinea, 1950–63; Bishop of New Guinea (later Papua New Guinea), 1963–77; Archbishop of Papua New Guinea, 1977–83; Bishop of Port Moresby, 1977–83; Priest-in-charge, East with West Rudham, Houghton next Harpley, Syderstone, Tatterford and Tattersett, dio. Norwich, 1983–85. *Address:* PO Box 49, Gerehu, NCD, Papua New Guinea. *T:* Papua New Guinea 260317.

HAND, Prof. Geoffrey Joseph Philip, DPhil; Barber Professor of Jurisprudence in the University of Birmingham, since 1980; *b* 25 June 1931; *s* of Joseph and Mary Macaulay Hand. *Educ:* Blackrock Coll.; University Coll., Dublin (MA); New Coll., Oxford (DPhil); King's Inns, Dublin. Called to Irish Bar, 1961. Lecturer: Univ. of Edinburgh, 1960; Univ. of Southampton, 1961; University Coll., Dublin, 1965; Professor: University Coll., Dublin, 1972–76; European University Inst., Fiesole, 1976–80; Dean of Faculty of Law, University Coll., Dublin, 1970–75. Chairman, Arts Council of Ireland, 1974–75. *Publications:* English Law in Ireland 1290–1324, 1967; Report of the Irish Boundary Commission 1925, 1969; (with Lord Cross of Chelsea) Radcliffe and Cross's English Legal System, 5th edn 1971, 6th edn 1977; (with J. Georgel, C. Sasse) European Election Systems Handbook, 1979; Towards a Uniform System of Direct Elections, 1981; numerous periodicals. *Recreations:* listening to classical music, playing chess. *Address:* c/o Faculty of Law, University of Birmingham, PO Box 363, Birmingham B15 2TT. *T:* 021–414 6283. *Clubs:* United Oxford & Cambridge University; Royal Irish Yacht (Dun Laoghaire); Kildare Street and University (Dublin).

HAND, John Lester; QC 1988; a Recorder, since 1991; *b* 16 June 1947; *s* of John James and Violet Hand; *m* 1972, Helen Andrea McWatt; 1990, Lynda Ray Ferigno; one *d. Educ:* Huddersfield New College; Univ. of Nottingham (LLB 1969). Called to the Bar, Gray's Inn, 1972; Northern Circuit, 1972. *Recreations:* sailing, travel. *Address:* Crown Square Chambers, 1 Dean's Court, Manchester M3 3HA. *T:* 061–833 9801; 15 Old Square, Lincoln's Inn, WC2A 3UH. *T:* 071–831 0801.

HANDCOCK, family name of **Baron Castlemaine.**

HANDFORD, Ven. (George) Clive; *see* Warwick, Bishop Suffragan of.

HANDLEY, Ven. Anthony Michael; Archdeacon of Norwich, since 1981; *b* 3 June 1936; *s* of Eric Harvey Handley and Janet Handley; *m* 1962, Christine May Adlington; two *s* one *d. Educ:* Spalding Grammar School; Selwyn Coll., Cambridge (MA Hons); Chichester Theological Coll. Asst Curate, Thorpe St Andrew, 1962–66; Anglican Priest on Fairstead Estate, 1966–72; Vicar of Hellesdon, 1972–81; RD of Norwich North, 1979–81. Research Project, The Use of Colour, Shape, and Line Drawings as Experiential Training Resources, 1976. County Scout Chaplain for Norfolk. *Publication:* A Parish Prayer Card, 1980. *Recreations:* climbing mountains, painting, bird watching. *Address:* 40 Heigham Road, Norwich NR2 3AU. *T:* Norwich (0603) 611808.

HANDLEY, Mrs Carol Margaret; Headmistress, Camden School for Girls, 1971–85; *b* 17 Oct. 1929; *d* of Claude Hilary Taylor and Margaret Eleanor Taylor (*née* Peebles); *m* 1952, Eric Walter Handley, *qv. Educ:* St Paul's Girls' Sch.; University Coll., London (BA), Fellow 1977. Asst Classics Mistress: North Foreland Lodge Sch., 1952; Queen's Gate Sch., 1952; Head of Classics Dept, Camden Sch. for Girls, 1956; Deputy Headmistress, Camden Sch. for Girls, 1964. Sen. Mem., Wolfson Coll., Cambridge, 1989–. Member Council: Royal Holloway Coll., 1977–85; Mddx Hosp. Med. Sch., 1980–84; Royal Holloway and Bedford New Coll., 1985–; Mem. Governors and Council, Bedford Coll., 1981–85. *Publications:* articles and book reviews for classical jls. *Recreations:* walking, driving, travel. *Address:* Colt House, High Street, Little Eversden, Cambs.

HANDLEY, Sir David John D.; *see* Davenport-Handley.

HANDLEY, Prof. Eric Walter, CBE 1983; FBA 1969; Regius Professor of Greek, Cambridge University, since 1984; Fellow, Trinity College, Cambridge, since 1984; *b* 12 Nov. 1926; *s* of late Alfred W. Handley and A. Doris Cox; *m* 1952, Carol Margaret Taylor (*see* C. M. Handley). *Educ:* King Edward's Sch., Birmingham; Trinity Coll., Cambridge. Stewart of Rannoch Schol. and Browne Medal, 1945. Asst Lectr in Latin and Greek, University Coll. London, 1946, Lectr, 1949, Reader, 1961, Prof. of Latin and Greek, 1967–68; Prof. and Head of Dept of Greek, UCL, 1968–84, and Dir, Inst. of

Classical Studies, Univ. of London, 1967–84; Hon. Fellow, UCL, 1989; Prof. of Ancient Lit., RA, 1990. Vis. Lectr on the Classics, Harvard, 1966; Vis. Mem., Inst. for Advanced Study, Princeton, 1971; Visiting Professor: Stanford Univ., 1977; Melbourne Univ., 1978; Vis. Senior Fellow, Council of the Humanities, Princeton, 1981. Sec. Council Univ. Classical Depts, 1969–70, Chm., 1975–78. Pres., Classical Assoc., 1984–85; Foreign Sec., British Academy, 1979–88; Member: Comité Scientifique, Fondation Hardt, Geneva, 1978–; Commn des Affaires Internes, Union Académique Internationale, 1984–; Academia Europaea, 1988–. Foreign Mem., Societas Scientiarum Fennica, 1984–. Chm., Gilbert Murray Trust, 1988. Hon. RA 1990. (Jtly) Cromer Greek Prize, 1958. *Publications:* (with John Rea) The Telephus of Euripides, 1957; The Dyskolos of Menander, 1965; (contrib.) Cambridge History of Classical Literature, 1985; (with André Hurst) Relire Ménandre, 1990; Greek literary papyri, papers in class. jls, etc. *Recreations:* boating, hill-walking, travel. *Address:* Trinity College, Cambridge CB2 1TQ. *Club:* United Oxford & Cambridge University.

HANDLEY, Vernon George, FRCM 1972; Principal Guest Conductor, Royal Liverpool Philharmonic Orchestra, since 1989; Associate Conductor, London Philharmonic Orchestra, 1983–86 (Guest Conductor, 1961–83); *b* 11 Nov. 1930; 2nd *s* of Vernon Douglas Handley and Claudia Lilian Handley, Enfield; *m* 1st, 1954, Barbara (marr. diss.), *e d* of Kilner Newman Black and Joan Elfriede Black, Stoke Gabriel, Devon; one *s* one *d* (and one *s* decd); 2nd, 1977, Victoria (marr. diss.), *d* of Vaughan and Nona Parry-Jones, Guildford, Surrey; one *s* one *d*; 3rd, 1987, Catherine, *e d* of Kenneth and Joan Newby, Harrogate, Yorks; one *s*. *Educ:* Enfield Sch.; Balliol Coll., Oxford (BA); Guildhall Sch. of Music. Conductor: Oxford Univ. Musical Club and Union, 1953–54; OUDS, 1953–54; Tonbridge Philharmonic Soc., 1958–61; Hatfield Sch. of Music and Drama, 1959–61; Proteus Choir, 1962–81; Musical Dir and Conductor, Guildford Corp., and Conductor, Guildford Philharmonic Orch. and Choir, 1962–83; Prof. at RCM: for Orchestra and Conducting, 1966–72; for Choral Class, 1969–72. Principal Conductor: Ulster Orch., 1985–89; Malmö SO, 1985–88. Guest Conductor from 1961: Bournemouth Symph. Orch.; Birmingham Symph. Orch.; Royal Philharmonic Orch.; BBC Welsh Orch.; BBC Northern Symph. Orch.; Royal Liverpool Philharmonic Orch.; Ulster Orch.; Scottish Nat. Orch.; Philharmonia Orch.; Strasbourg Philharmonic Orch., 1982–; Helsinki Philharmonic, 1984–; Amsterdam Philharmonic, 1985; Guest Conductor, 1961–83, Principal Guest Conductor, 1983–Sept. 1985, BBC Scottish Symphony Orch.; conducted London Symphony Orch. in internat. series, London, 1971; toured: Germany, 1966, 1980; S Africa, 1974; Holland, 1980; Sweden, 1980, 1981; Germany, Sweden, Holland and France, 1982–83; Australia, 1986; Japan, 1988; Australia, 1989; Artistic Dir, Norwich and Norfolk Triennial Fest., 1985. Regular broadcaster and has made many records. Pres., Nat. Federation of Gramophone Socs, 1984–; Vice-President: Delius Soc., 1983–; Elgar Soc., 1984–; Fellow Goldsmiths' Coll. 1987; Hon. Mem., Royal Philharmonic Soc., 1989. Hon. RCM, 1970; FRCM 1972. Arnold Bax Meml Medal for Conducting, 1962; Conductor of the Year, British Composers' Guild, 1974; Hi-Fi News Audio Award, 1982; BPI Classical Award, 1986, 1988; Gramophone Record of the Year, 1986, 1989. DUniv Surrey, 1980. *Recreations:* bird photography, old-fashioned roses. *Address:* Hen Gerrig, Pen-y-Fan, near Monmouth, Gwent NP5 4RA. *T:* Trelleck (0600) 860318.

HANDLEY-TAYLOR, Geoffrey, FRSL 1950; author; Hon. Home and Overseas Information Correspondent, John Masefield Research and Studies, 1958–90; *b* 25 April 1920; 2nd *s* of Walter Edward Taylor and Nellie Hadwin (*née* Taylor), Horsforth. *Educ:* widely. Served War of 1939–45: Duke of Wellington's Regt and War Office. Literary and ballet lecture tours, UK and overseas, 1946–57. Chairman, British Poetry-Drama Guild, 1948–52; Vice-Pres., Leeds Univ. Tudor Players, 1948–50; Publisher, Leeds University Poetry, 1949; featured in NBC-TV (USA) People series, 1955; Founder, Winifred Holtby Meml Collection, Fisk Univ., Nashville, 1955; Hon. Gen. Sec., Dumas Assoc., 1955–57; Founder, Sir Ralph Perring City of London Collection, Fisk Univ., 1962; Pres., St Paul's Literary Soc., Covent Garden, 1966–68; Chm., General Council, Poetry Society, 1967–68; served on PCC, St Paul's, Covent Garden, 1967–68; Mem. Gen. Council, National Book League, 1968; Dep. Pres., Lancashire Authors' Assoc., 1967–69 (Pres., 1969–72); a Trustee, Gladstone Meml Library, London, 1974–78; Jt Literary Executor, Estate of Vera Brittain, 1979–90. Several Foreign decorations and awards. *Publications:* Mona Inglesby, Ballerina and Choreographer, 1947; Italian Ballet Today, 1949; New Hyperion, 1950; Literary, Debating and Dialect Societies of GB, Ireland and France, 5 pts, 1950–52; A Selected Bibliography of Literature Relating to Nursery Rhyme Reform, 1952; Winifred Holtby Bibliography and Letters, 1955; (with Frank Granville Barker) John Gay and the Ballad Opera, 1956; (with Thomas Rae) The Book of the Private Press, 1958; John Masefield, OM, The Queen's Poet Laureate, 1960; (with Vera Brittain) Selected Letters of Winifred Holtby and Vera Brittain 1920–1935, 1961, 2nd edn 1970; Bibliography of Monaco, 1961, 2nd edn 1968; Bibliography of Iran, 1964, 5th edn 1969; (with Timothy d'Arch Smith) C. Day Lewis, Poet Laureate, 1968; ed, County Authors Today Series, 9 vols, 1971–1973; Pogg (a satire), 1980; (with John Malcolm Dockeray) Vera Brittain, Occasional Papers, 1983–; also contribs to: Encycl. Britannica, Hinrichsen Music Book, 1949–1958; Airs from The Beggar's Opera, arr. Edith Bathurst, 1953; The Beggar's Opera, ed Edward J. Dent, 1954; (foreword to) John Masefield Bibliography, ed Crocker Wight, 1986; Kathleen: the life of Kathleen Ferrier 1912–1953, ed Maurice Leonard, 1988. *Address:* BM Bibliography, WC1N 3XX.

HANDLIN, Prof. Oscar; Carl M. Loeb University Professor, Harvard University, since 1984; Director, Harvard University Library, 1979–84; *b* 29 Sept. 1915; *m* 1st, 1937, Mary Flug; one *s* two *d*; 2nd, 1977, Lilian Bombach. *Educ:* Brooklyn Coll. (AB); Harvard (MA, PhD). Instructor, Brooklyn Coll., 1938–39; Harvard Univ.: Instructor, 1939–44; Asst Prof., 1944–48; Associate Prof., 1948–54; Prof. of History, 1954–65; Charles Warren Prof. of Amer. Hist., and Dir, Charles Warren Center for Studies in Amer. Hist., 1965–72; Carl H. Pforzheimer Univ. Prof., 1972–84; Harmsworth Prof. of Amer. History, Oxford Univ., 1972–73. Dir, Center for Study of History of Liberty in America, 1958–67; Chm., US Bd of Foreign Scholarships, 1965–66 (Vice-Chm. 1962–65). Hon. Fellow, Brandeis Univ., 1965. Hon. LLD Colby Coll., 1962; Hon. LHD: Hebrew Union Coll., 1967; Northern Michigan, 1969; Seton Hall Univ., 1972; Hon. HumD Oakland, 1968; Hon. LittD Brooklyn Coll., 1972; Hon. DHL: Boston Coll., 1975; Lowell, 1980; Cincinnati, 1981; Massachusetts, 1982; Clark Univ., Mass, 1989. *Publications:* Boston's Immigrants, 1790–1865, 1941; (with M. F. Handlin) Commonwealth, 1947; Danger in Discord, 1948; (ed) This Was America, 1949; Uprooted, 1951, 2nd edn 1972; Adventure in Freedom, 1954; American People in the Twentieth Century, 1954 (rev. edn 1963); (ed jtly) Harvard Guide to American History, 1954; Chance or Destiny, 1955; (ed) Readings in American History, 1957; Race and Nationality in American Life, 1957; Al Smith and his America, 1958; (ed) Immigration as a Factor in American History, 1959; John Dewey's Challenge to Education, 1959; (ed) G. M. Capers, Stephen A. Douglas, Defender of the Union, 1959; Newcomers, 1960; (ed jtly) G. Mittleberger, Journey to Pennsylvania, 1960; (ed) American Principles and Issues, 1961; (with M. F. Handlin) The Dimensions of Liberty, 1961; The Americans, 1963; (with J. E. Burchard) The Historian and the City, 1963; Firebell in the Night, 1964; A Continuing Task, 1964; (ed) Children of the Uprooted, 1966; The History of the United States, vol. 1, 1967, vol. 2, 1968; America: a History, 1968; (with M. F. Handlin) The Popular Sources of Political Authority, 1967; The American College and American Culture, 1970; Facing Life: Youth and the Family in American History, 1971; A Pictorial History of Immigration, 1972; (with M. F. Handlin) The Wealth of the American People, 1975; Truth in History, 1979; (with L. Handlin) Abraham Lincoln and the Union, 1980; The Distortion of America, 1981; (with L. Handlin) A Restless People, 1982; (with L. Handlin) Liberty and Power, 1986; (with L. Handlin) Liberty in Expansion, 1989. *Address:* 18 Agassiz Street, Cambridge, Mass 02140, USA. *Clubs:* St Botolph (Boston); Harvard (NY); Faculty (Cambridge, Mass).

HANDS, David Richard Granville; QC 1988; *b* 23 Dec. 1943; *s* of Leonard Frederick Horace Hands and Nancye Wilkes (*née* Kenyon); *m* 1982, Penelope Ann Jervis. *Educ:* Radley. Called to the Bar, Inner Temple, 1965. *Recreations:* gardening, trees, looking after dogs and cats. *Address:* 2 Paper Buildings, Temple, EC4Y 7ET. *T:* 071–353 5835. *Club:* Travellers'.

HANDS, Terence David, (Terry Hands); theatre and opera director; *b* 9 Jan. 1941; *s* of Joseph Ronald Hands and Luise Berthe Kohler; *m* 1st, 1964, Josephine Barstow (marr. diss. 1967); 2nd, 1974, Ludmila Mikael (marr. diss. 1980); one *d*; 3rd, Julia Lintott; one *s*. *Educ:* Woking Grammar Sch.; Birmingham Univ. (BA Hons Eng. Lang. and Lit.); RADA (Hons Dip.). Founder-Artistic Dir, Liverpool Everyman Theatre, 1964–66; Artistic Dir, RSC Theatregoround, 1966–67; Associate Dir, 1967–77, Jt Artistic Dir, 1978–86, chief Exec. and Artistic Dir, 1986–91, RSC; Consultant Dir, Comédie Française, 1975–77. Associate Mem., RADA; Hon. Fellow, Shakespeare Inst. Hon. DLitt Birmingham, 1989. Chevalier des Arts et des Lettres, 1973. *Director* (for Liverpool Everyman Theatre, 1964–66): The Importance of Being Earnest; Look Back in Anger; Richard III; The Four Seasons; Fando and Lis; *Artistic Director* (for RSC Theatregoround): The Proposal, 1966; The Second Shepherds' Play, 1966; The Dumb Waiter, 1967; Under Milk Wood, 1967; *directed for RSC:* The Criminals, 1967; Pleasure and Repentance, 1967; The Latent Heterosexual, 1968; The Merry Wives of Windsor, 1968, Japan tour, 1970; Bartholomew Fair, 1969; Pericles, 1969; Women Beware Women, 1969; Richard III, 1970, 1980; Balcony, 1971, 1987; Man of Mode, 1971; The Merchant of Venice, 1971; Murder in the Cathedral, 1972; Cries from Casement, 1973; Romeo and Juliet, 1973, 1989; The Bewitched, 1974; The Actor, 1974; Henry IV, Parts 1 and 2, 1975; Henry V, 1975, USA and European Tour, 1976; Old World, 1976; Henry VI parts 1, 2 and 3 (SWET Award, Dir of the Year, Plays and Players, Best Production, 1978), Coriolanus, 1977, European tour, 1979; The Changeling, 1978; Twelfth Night, The Children of the Sun, 1979; As You Like It, Richard II, 1980; Troilus and Cressida, 1981; Arden of Faversham, Much Ado About Nothing, 1982 (European tour and Broadway, 1984), Poppy, 1982; Cyrano de Bergerac, 1983 (SWET Best Dir award), Broadway, 1984 (televised, 1984); Red Noses, 1985; Othello, 1985; The Winter's Tale, 1986; Scenes from a Marriage, 1986; Julius Caesar, 1987; Carrie (Stratford and Broadway), 1988; (with John Barton) Coriolanus, 1989; Romeo and Juliet, 1989; Singer, 1989; Love's Labours Lost, 1990; The Seagull, 1990; *directed for Comédie Française:* Richard III, 1972 (Meilleur Spectacle de l'Année award); Pericles, 1974; Twelfth Night, 1976 (Meilleur Spectacle de l'Année award); Le Cid, 1977; Murder in the Cathedral, 1978; *directed for Paris Opéra:* Verdi's Otello, 1976 (televised 1978); *directed for Burg Theatre, Vienna:* Troilus and Cressida, 1977; As You Like It, 1979; *directed for Teatro Stabile di Genova, Italy:* Women Beware Women, 1981; *directed for Royal Opera:* Parsifal, 1979; *recording:* Murder in the Cathedral, 1976. *Publications:* trans. (with Barbara Wright) Genet, The Balcony, 1971; Pleasure and Repentance, 1976; (ed Sally Beauman) Henry V, 1976; contribs to Theatre 72, Playback. *Address:* c/o Royal Shakespeare Theatre, Stratford-upon-Avon, Warwicks CV37 6BB. *T:* Stratford-upon-Avon (0789) 296655.

HANDY, Charles Brian; author; *b* 25 July 1932; *s* of Archdeacon Brian Leslie Handy and Joan Kathleen Herbert Handy (*née* Scott); *m* 1962, Elizabeth Ann Hill; one *s* one *d*. *Educ:* Oriel Coll., Oxford (BA 1956; MA 1966); MIT (SM 1967). Shell Internat. Petroleum Co., 1956–65; Charter Consolidated Ltd, 1965–66; Sloan Sch. of Management, MIT (Internat. Faculty Fellow), 1967–68; London Business School, 1968–: Prof., 1972–77; Vis. Prof., 1977–; St George's House, Windsor Castle, 1977–81. Chm., Royal Soc. for Encouragement of Arts, Manufactures and Commerce, 1987–89. *Publications:* Understanding Organizations, 1976, 3rd edn 1985; Gods of Management, 1978, 2nd edn 1991; Future of Work, 1982; Understanding School as Organizations, 1986; Understanding Voluntary Organizations, 1988; The Age of Unreason, 1989; Inside Organizations, 1990; Waiting for the Mountain to Move, 1991. *Address:* 1 Fairhaven, 73 Putney Hill, SW15 3NT. *T:* 081–788 1610; Old Hall Cottages, Bressingham, Diss, Norfolk IP22 2AG. *T:* Diss (0379) 88546.

HANDY, Dr Nicholas Charles, FRS 1990; Reader in Quantum Chemistry, since 1989, and Fellow of St Catharine's College, since 1965, Cambridge University; *b* 17 June 1941; *s* of Kenneth George Edwards Handy and Ada Mary Handy (*née* Rumming); *m* 1967, Elizabeth Carole Gates; two *s*. *Educ:* Clayesmore Sch., Dorset; St Catharine's College, Cambridge (MA, PhD). Cambridge University: Salters' Fellow, 1967–68; Demonstrator, 1972–77; Lectr, 1977–89; Steward, St Catharine's Coll., 1971–88; Harkness Fellow, Johns Hopkins Univ., 1968–69. Vis. Prof., Berkeley, Bologna, Sydney, Georgia. Lennard-Jones Lectr, RSC, 1983. Mem., Internat. Acad. of Quantum Molecular Science, 1988–. Prize in Theoretical Chem., RSC, 1987. *Publications:* papers in learned jls of chem. phys. *Recreations:* gardening, bridge, philately, travel. *Address:* University Chemical Laboratory, Lensfield Road, Cambridge CB2 1EW. *T:* Cambridge (0223) 336373.

HANFF, Helene; writer and broadcaster; *b* 15 April 1916; *d* of Arthur and Miriam Levy Hanff. *Educ:* none beyond secondary sch. Won a playwriting fellowship from The Theatre Guild, 1939; wrote: unproduced plays through '40s; dramatic TV scripts in '50s; American history books for children in '60s; books in '70s and '80s. Monthly radio broadcasts, Woman's Hour, BBC, 1978–85. *Publications:* Underfoot in Show Business, 1961, repr. 1980; 84 Charing Cross Road, 1970; Duchess of Bloomsbury Street, 1973; Apple of My Eye, 1978; Q's Legacy, 1985. *Recreations:* classical music lover, (Mets) baseball fan; also addicted to Guardian (Weekly) crossword puzzles. *Address:* 305 East 72nd Street, New York, NY 10021, USA. *T:* (212) 879–4952.

HANHAM, Prof. Harold John; Vice-Chancellor, University of Lancaster, since 1985; *b* Auckland, New Zealand, 16 June 1928; *s* of John Newman Hanham and Ellie Malone; *m* 1973, Ruth Soulé Arnon, *d* of Prof. Daniel I. Arnon, Univ. of Calif, Berkeley. *Educ:* Mount Albert Grammar Sch.; Auckland UC (now Univ. of Auckland); Univ. of New Zealand (BA 1948, MA 1950); Selwyn Coll, Cambridge (PhD 1954). FRHistS 1960; FAAAS 1974. Asst Lectr to Sen. Lectr, in Govt, Univ. of Manchester, 1954–63; Prof. and Head of Dept of Politics, Univ. of Edinburgh, 1963–68; Prof. of History, 1968–73 and Fellow of Lowell House, 1970–73, Harvard Univ.; Prof. of History and Political Science, 1972–85 and Dean, Sch. of Humanities and Social Sci., 1973–84, MIT; Hon. Prof. of History, Univ. of Lancaster, 1985–. Mem., ESRC, 1986–. Guggenheim Fellow, 1972–73. Hon. AM Harvard, 1968. John H. Jenkins Prize for Bibliography, Union Coll., 1978. *Publications:* Elections and Party Management, 1969, 2nd edn 1978; The Nineteenth-Century Constitution, 1969; Scottish Nationalism, 1969; Bibliography of British History 1851–1914, 1976. *Recreations:* discovering Canada, squash. *Address:* The Croft, Bailrigg

Lane, Bailrigg, Lancaster LA1 4XP. *T:* Lancaster (0524) 65201. *Clubs:* United Oxford & Cambridge University, Commonwealth Trust; St Botolph (Boston).

HANHAM, Leonard Edward; HM Diplomatic Service, retired; Consul-General, Amsterdam, 1978–80; *b* 23 April 1921; *m* 1945, Joyce Wrenn; two *s* two *d.* Served War, RN, 1939–48. Foreign Office, 1948; Vice-Consul: Rouen, 1949; Basra, 1950; Ponta Delgada, 1952; Foreign Office, 1955; 1st Sec. and Consul: Rangoon, 1957; Tegucigalpa, 1961; Foreign Office, 1963; Consul: Durban, 1965; Medan, 1969; FCO, 1972; Counsellor and Consul-Gen., Lisbon, 1975–78. *Address:* 26 First Avenue, Gillingham, Kent ME7 2LG.

HANHAM, Sir Michael (William), 12th Bt *cr* 1667; DFC 1945; RAFVR; *b* 31 Oct. 1922; *s* of Patrick John Hanham (*d* 1965) and Dulcie (*d* 1979), *yr d* of William George Daffarn and *widow* of Lynn Hartley; *S* kinsman, Sir Henry Phelips Hanham, 11th Bt, 1973; *m* 1954, Margaret Jane, *d* of W/Cdr Harold Thomas, RAF retd, and Joy (*née* MacGeorge); one *s* one *d. Educ:* Winchester. Joined RAF 1942, as Aircrew Cadet; served No 8 (Pathfinder) Gp, Bomber Command, 1944–45; FO 1945. At end of war, retrained as Flying Control Officer; served UK and India, 1945–46; demobilised, 1946. Joined BOAC, 1947, Traffic Branch; qualified as Flight Operations Officer, 1954; served in Africa until 1961; resigned, 1961. Settled at Trillinghurst Farmhouse, Kent and started garden and cottage furniture making business, 1963; moved to Wimborne, 1974; now engaged with upkeep of family house and estate. Governor of Minster and of Dumpton School. *Recreations:* conservation (Vice-Chm. Weald of Kent Preservation Soc., 1972–74 and Wimborne Civic Soc., 1977–); preservation of steam railways; sailing, gardening. *Heir: s* William John Edward Hanham [*b* 4 Sept. 1957; *m* 1982, Elizabeth Anne Keyworth (marr. diss. 1988), *yr d* of Paul Keyworth, Farnham and Mrs Keith Thomas, Petersfield]. *Address:* Deans Court, Wimborne, Dorset. *Club:* Pathfinder.

HANKES-DRIELSMA, Claude Dunbar; *b* 8 March 1949. *Educ:* Grey. With Manufacturers Hanover, 1968–72; Robert Fleming & Co. Ltd, 1972–77, Director 1974–77; Chairman: British Export-Finance Adv. Council, 1981–; Export Finance Co. Ltd, 1982–89; Management Cttee, Price Waterhouse and Partners, 1983–89; Action Resource Centre, 1986– (Mem., 1983–86); Member: Governing Council, 1986–, Pres's Cttee, 1988–91, Business in the Community (Chm., Target Team on Voluntary Sector Initiatives, 1987–90); Nat. Council, Young Enterprise, 1987–; Council for Charitable Support, 1989–. Advr to Bd, (Corange) Boehring/Mannheim, 1988–. Assisted Dr Fritz Leutwiler in his role as independent mediator between South African govt and foreign banks, 1985–86; initiated attempt to secure Thyssen Collection for Britain, 1988. Member: Deanery Synod, 1984–; Sen. Common Room, Corpus Christi Coll., Oxford, 1989–. *Publication:* The Dangers of the Banking System: funding country deficits, 1975. *Recreations:* gardening, walking, ski-ing, reading, ancient art. *Address:* Stanford Place, Faringdon, Oxon SN7 8EX. *T:* Faringdon (0367) 240547, *Fax:* Faringdon (0367) 242853. *Club:* Turf.

HANKEY, family name of **Baron Hankey.**

HANKEY, 2nd Baron *cr* 1939, of The Chart; **Robert Maurice Alers Hankey,** KCMG 1955 (CMG 1947); KCVO 1956; *b* 4 July 1905; *s* of 1st Baron Hankey, PC, GCB, GCMG, GCVO, FRS, and Adeline (*d* 1979), *d* of A. de Smidt; *S* father, 1963; *m* 1st, 1930, Frances Bevyl Stuart-Menteth (*d* 1957); two *s* two *d*; 2nd, 1962, Joanna Riddall Wright, *d* of late Rev. James Johnstone Wright. *Educ:* Rugby Sch.; New Coll., Oxford. Diplomatic Service, 1927; served Berlin, Paris, London, Warsaw, Bucharest, Cairo, Teheran, Madrid, Budapest. HM Ambassador at Stockholm, 1954–60. Permanent UK Delegate to OEEC and OECD, and Chm., Economic Policy Cttee, 1960–65; Vice-Pres., European Inst. of Business Administration, Fontainebleau, 1966–82. Dir, Alliance Bldg Soc., 1970–83. Member: Internat. Council of United World Colleges, 1966–78; Council, Internat. Baccalaureat RMAH Foundn, Geneva, 1967–76. Pres., Anglo-Swedish Soc., 1969–75. Grand Cross of Order of the North Star (Sweden), 1954. *Recreations:* reading, tennis, ski-ing, music. *Heir: er s* Hon. Donald Robin Alers Hankey [*b* 12 June 1938; *m* 1st, 1963, Margaretha, *yr d* of H. Thorndahl, Copenhagen; 2nd, 1974, Eileen Désirée, *yr d* of late Maj.-Gen. Stuart Battye, CB; two *d*]. *Address:* Hethe House, Cowden, Edenbridge, Kent TN8 7DZ. *T:* Cowden (0342) 850538.

See also Sir Jonathan Benn, Hon. H. A. A. Hankey.

HANKEY, Hon. Henry Arthur Alers, CMG 1960; CVO 1959; HM Diplomatic Service, retired; *b* 1 Sept. 1914; *y s* of 1st Baron Hankey, PC, GCB, GCMG, GCVO, FRS; *m* 1941, Vronwy Mary Fisher; three *s* one *d. Educ:* Rugby Sch.; New Coll., Oxford. Entered HM Diplomatic Service, 1937; Third Sec., HM Embassy, Paris, 1939; Second Sec., Madrid, 1942; First Sec., Rome, 1946; Consul, San Francisco, 1950; First Sec., Santiago, 1953; promoted Counsellor and apptd Head of American Dept, Foreign Office, Sept. 1956; Counsellor, HM Embassy, Beirut, 1962–66; Ambassador, Panama, 1966–69; Asst Under-Sec. of State, FCO, 1969–74. Director: Lloyds Bank International, 1975–80; Antofagasta (Chile) & Bolivia Railway Co. Ltd, 1975–82. Sec., British North American Cttee, 1981–85. *Recreations:* ski-ing, tennis, music, painting. *Address:* Hosey Croft, Hosey Hill, Westerham, Kent. *T:* Westerham (0959) 62309. *Club:* United Oxford & Cambridge University.

HANKINS, (Frederick) Geoffrey; Chairman, Fitch Lovell plc, 1983–90 (Chief Executive, 1982–89); Director, Booker plc, since 1990; *b* 9 Dec. 1926; *s* of Frederick Aubrey Hankins and Elizabeth (*née* Stockton); *m* 1951, Iris Esther Perkins; two *d. Educ:* St Dunstan's College. Commissioned Army, 1946–48; J. Sainsbury management trainee, 1949–51, manufacturing management, 1951–55; Production/Gen. Manager, Allied Suppliers, 1955–62; Production Dir, Brains Food Products, 1962–69; Kraft Foods, 1966–69; Gen. Man., Millers, Poole, 1970–72, Man. Dir, 1972–82, Chm., 1975–86; Fitch Lovell: Dir, 1975–90; Chief Exec., 1982; Chm., Manufacturing Div., 1975–84; Chairman: Robirch, 1975–84; Jus Rol, 1976–85; Blue Cap Frozen Food Services, 1975–84; Newforge Foods, 1979–84; Bells Bacon (Evesham), 1980–83; L. Noel, 1982–84; Dir, Salaison Le Vexin, 1980–90. FRSA. Liveryman, Poulters' Co., 1982–. *Recreations:* genealogy, antiques, practical pursuits. *Address:* 51 Elms Avenue, Parkstone, Poole, Dorset BH14 8EE. *T:* Poole (0202) 745874.

HANKINS, Prof. Harold Charles Arthur, PhD; CEng, FIEE; Principal, University of Manchester Institute of Science and Technology, since 1984; *b* 18 Oct. 1930; *s* of Harold Arthur Hankins and Hilda Hankins; *m* 1955, Kathleen Higginbottom; three *s* one *d. Educ:* Crewe Grammar Sch.; Univ. of Manchester Inst. of Science and Technol. (BSc Tech, 1st Cl. Hons Elec. Engrg, 1955; PhD 1971). CEng, FIEE 1975; AMCT 1952. Engrg Apprentice, British Rail, 1947–52; Electronic Engr, subseq. Asst Chief Engr, Metropolitan Vickers Electrical Co. Ltd, 1955–68; Univ. of Manchester Inst. of Science and Technology: Lectr in Elec. Engrg, 1968–71; Sen. Lectr in Elec. Engrg, 1971–74; Prof. of Communication Engrg, and Dir of Med. Engrg Unit, 1974–84; Vice Principal, 1979–81; Dep. Principal, 1981–82; Actg Principal, 1982–84. Non-Exec. Dir, THORN EMI Lighting Ltd, 1979–85. Instn of Electrical Engineers: Mem., NW Centre Cttee, 1969–77, Chm. 1977–78; Chm., M2 Exec. Cttee, 1979–82; Mem., Management and Design Div. Bd, 1980–82. Chm., Chemical Engrg, Instrumentation, Systems Engrg Bd, CNAA, 1975–81; Member: Cttee for Science and Technol., CNAA, 1975–81; Cttee of Vice-Chancellors and Principals, 1984–; Parly Scientific Cttee, 1985–; Bd of Govs, Manchester Polytechnic, 1989– (Hon. Fellow, 1984); Bd of Govs, South Cheshire Coll., 1990–. Reginald Mitchell Gold Medal, 1990. *Publications:* 55 papers in learned jls; 10 patents for research into computer visual display systems. *Recreations:* hill walking, music, choral work. *Address:* Rosebank, Kidd Road, Glossop, Derbyshire SK13 9PN. *T:* Glossop (04574) 3895. *Club:* Athenæum.

HANKS, Patrick Wyndham; Manager, English Dictionaries, Oxford University Press, since 1990; *b* 24 March 1940; *s* of Wyndham George Hanks and Elizabeth Mary (*née* Rudd): *m* 1st, 1961, Helga Gertrud Ingeborg Lietz (marr. diss. 1968); one *s* one *d*; 2nd, 1979, Julie Eyre; two *d. Educ:* Ardingly Coll., Sussex; University Coll., Oxford (BA, MA). Editor, Dictionaries and Reference Books, Hamlyn Group, 1964–70; Man. Dir, Laurence Urdang Associates, 1970–79; Dir, Surnames Res. Project, Univ. of Essex, 1980–83; Project Manager, Cobuild, Univ. of Birmingham, 1983–87; Chief Editor, Collins English Dictionaries, 1987–90. *Publications:* (ed) Hamlyn World Dictionary, 1971; (ed) Collins English Dictionary, 1979, 2nd edn 1986; (with J. Corbett) Business Listening Tasks, 1986; (managing editor) Collins Cobuild English Learners' Dictionary, 1987; (with F. Hodges) Dictionary of Surnames, 1988; (with F. Hodges) Dictionary of First Names, 1990; articles in Computational Linguistics and other jls. *Recreations:* onomastics, hiking, punting. *Address:* Oxford University Press, Walton Street, Oxford OX2 6DP. *T:* Oxford (0865) 56767.

HANLEY, Gerald Anthony; author; *b* 17 Feb. 1916; *s* of Edward Michael Hanly and Bridget Maria Roche. *Publications:* Monsoon Victory, 1946; The Consul at Sunset, 1951; The Year of the Lion, 1953; Drinkers of Darkness, 1955; Without Love (Book Society Choice), 1957; The Journey Homeward (Book Society Choice), 1961; Gilligan's Last Elephant, 1962; See You in Yasukuni, 1969; Warriors and Strangers, 1971; Noble Descents, 1982. *Recreations:* music, languages. *Address:* c/o Gillon Aitken, Aitken & Stone, 29 Fernshaw Road, SW10 0TG.

HANLEY, Howard Granville, CBE 1975; MD, FRCS; Consulting Urologist, King Edward VII's Hospital for Officers, London; Dean, 1968–72, Chairman, 1972–80, President, 1980–88, Institute of Urology, University of London; *b* 27 July 1909; *s* of F. T. Hanley; *m* 1939, Margaret Jeffrey; two *s. Educ:* St Bees Sch., Cumberland. MB 1932; MD 1934; FRCS 1937. Urologist: St Peter's Hosps Gp, 1947–75; Royal Masonic Hosp., London, 1960–77; Urol Consultant to Army, 1951–75; Hon. Consulting Urologist, Royal Hosp., Chelsea, 1951–75. Visiting Prof. of Urology: University of Calif, Los Angeles, 1958; Ohio State Univ., Columbus, 1961; University of Texas Southwestern Medical Sch., 1963; Tulane University, New Orleans, 1967. Royal College of Surgeons: Hunterian Prof., 1955; Dean, Inst. of Basic Med. Scis, 1972–76; Mem. Council, 1969–81; Vice-Pres., 1979–81; Royal Society of Medicine: Pres., Urol Sect., 1969–81; Hon. Librarian. Trustee, St Peter's Research Trust for the Cure of Kidney Disease, 1970–86. Fellow, Assoc. of Surgeons of GB and Ireland; Past Pres. (formerly Sec. and Treasurer), British Assoc. Urological Surgeons; Past Sec., Hunterian Soc.; Past Pres., Chelsea Clinical Soc. Member: Internat. Soc. Urology; German Urol. Soc.; Soc. Française d'Urologie; European Assoc. of Urology. Corresponding Member: Amer. Assoc. Genito-urinary Surgeons; Western Sect. Amer. Urological Assoc. Liveryman, Worshipful Soc. of Apothecaries of London. Hon. FACS; Hon. FRSM 1991. *Publications:* chapters in: British Surgical Practice, 1957; Recent Advances in Urology, 1960; contribs to: A Textbook of Urology, 1960; Modern Trends in Urology, 1960; contribs to jls on surgery and urology. *Recreation:* gardening. *Address:* Brandon House, North End Avenue, NW3 7HP. *T:* 081–458 2035. *Club:* Athenæum.

HANLEY, Jeremy James; MP (C) Richmond and Barnes, since 1983; Parliamentary Under-Secretary of State, Northern Ireland Office, since 1990; chartered accountant, certified accountant, chartered secretary, lecturer and broadcaster; *b* 17 Nov. 1945; *s* of late Jimmy Hanley and of Dinah Sheridan; *m* 1973, Verna, Viscountess Villiers (*née* Stott); two *s* one *d. Educ:* Rugby. FCA 1969; FCCA 1980; FCIS 1980. Peat Marwick Mitchell & Co., 1963–66; Lectr in law, taxation and accountancy, Anderson Thomas Frankel, 1969, Dir 1969; Man. Dir, ATF (Jersey and Ireland), 1970–73; Dep. Chm., The Financial Training Co. Ltd, 1973–90; Sec., Park Place PLC, 1977–83; Chm., Fraser Green Ltd, 1986–90. Parly Advr to ICA, 1986–90. Contested (C) Lambeth Central, April 1978, 1979. PPS to Minister of State, Privy Council Office (Minister for CS and the Arts), 1987–90, to Sec. of State for Envirnt, 1990. Mem., H of C Select Cttee on Home Affairs, 1983–87 (Mem., Subcttee on Race Relns and Immigration, 1983–87); Jt Vice-Chm., Cons. Back-bench Trade and Industry Cttee, 1983–87. Member: British-American Parly Gp; Anglo-French Parly Gp; CPA; IPU; British-Irish Interparly Body, 1990; Vice-Chm., Nat. Anglo-West Indian Cons. Soc., 1982–83; Chm., Cons Candidates Assoc., 1982–83. Mem., Company Law Reform Cttee, Soc. of Cons. Lawyers, 1976–87. Member: Bow Gp, 1974– (Chm., Home Affairs Cttee); European Movt, 1974–; Mensa, 1968–. Freeman, City of London, 1989. *Recreations:* cookery, chess, cricket, languages, theatre, cinema, music, golf. *Address:* House of Commons, SW1A 0AA. *T:* 071–219 4099.

HANLEY, Sir Michael (Bowen), KCB 1974; *b* 24 Feb. 1918; *s* of late Prof. J. A. Hanley, PhD, ARCS; *m* 1957, Hon. Lorna Margaret Dorothy, *d* of late Hon. Claude Hope-Morley. *Educ:* Sedbergh School; Queen's Coll., Oxford (MA). Served War of 1939–45. *Address:* c/o Ministry of Defence, SW1.

HANMER, Sir John (Wyndham Edward), 8th Bt *cr* 1774; JP; DL; *b* 27 Sept. 1928; *s* of Sir (Griffin Wyndham) Edward Hanmer, 7th Bt, and Aileen Mary (*d* 1967), *er d* of Captain J. E. Rogerson; *S* father, 1977; *m* 1954, Audrey Melissa, *d* of Major A. C. J. Congreve; two *s. Educ:* Eton. Captain (retired), The Royal Dragoons. JP Flintshire, 1971; High Sheriff of Clwyd, 1977; DL Clwyd, 1978. *Recreations:* horseracing, shooting. *Heir: s* (Wyndham Richard) Guy Hanmer [*b* 27 Nov. 1955; *m* 1986, Elizabeth A., *yr d* of Neil Taylor; one *s*]. *Address:* The Mere House, Hanmer, Whitchurch, Salop. *T:* Hanmer (094874) 383. *Club:* Army and Navy.

See also Sir James Wilson, Bt.

HANN, Air Vice-Marshal Derek William; art dealer and gallery proprietor; Director-General RAF Personal Services, Ministry of Defence, 1987–89, retired; *b* 22 Aug. 1935; *s* of Claude and Ernestine Hann; *m* 1st, 1958, Jill Symonds (marr. diss. 1987); one *s* one *d*; 2nd, 1987, Sylvia Jean Holder. *Educ:* Dauntsey's Sch., Devizes. Joined RAF, 1954; served in Fighter (65 Sqdn) and Coastal (201 and 203 Sqdns) Commands and at HQ Far East Air Force, 1956–68; MoD, 1969–72 and 1975–77; Comd No 42 Sqdn, RAF St Mawgan, 1972–74; Comd RAF St Mawgan, 1977–79; RCDS 1980; Dir of Operational Requirements 2, MoD, 1981–84; C of S, HQ No 18 Gp, 1984–87. *Recreations:* theatre, music, horology, campanology. *Address:* The Hann Gallery, 2A York Street, Bath BA1 1NG. *T:* Bath (0225) 466904.

HANN, James, CBE 1977; Chairman, Scottish Nuclear, since 1990; *b* 18 Jan. 1933; *s* of Harry Frank and Bessie Gladys Hann; *m* 1958, Jill Margaret Howe; one *s* one *d. Educ:* Peter Symonds Sch., Winchester; IMEDE, Lausanne, Switzerland. FCIM, FInstPet, FInstD. James Hann & Sons, 1950–52; Royal Artillery, 1952–54; United Dairies, 1954–65; IMEDE, 1965–66; Managing Director: Hanson Dairies, Liverpool, 1966–72; Seaforth

Maritime, Aberdeen, 1972–86; Chairman: Bauteil Engineering, Glasgow, 1986–88; Exacta Holdings, Selkirk, 1986–; Associated Fresh Foods, Leeds 1987–89; Strathclyde Inst., Glasgow, 1987–90; Dep. Chm., Scottish Transport Gp, 1987–. Dir, William Baird, 1991–. Comr, Northern Lighthouse Bd, 1990–. Member: Offshore Energy Technology Bd, 1982–85; Offshore Tech. Adv. Gp, 1983–86; Nationalised Industries Chairman's Gp, 1990–. Life Mem., Beaver Club, Montreal, 1981 (for services to Canadian offshore industry). Burgess of Guild, Aberdeen, 1982–. *Recreations:* sailing, reading, music. *Address:* Scottish Nuclear, Minto Building, 6 Inverlair Avenue, Glasgow G44 4AD.

HANNAH, Prof. Leslie; Professor, London School of Economics, since 1982; Director: NRG London Reinsurance Co. Ltd, since 1986; NRG Victory Holdings, (formerly NRG (UK) Holdings), since 1987; *b* 15 June 1947; *s* of Arthur Hannah and Marie (*née* Lancashire); *m* 1984, Nuala Barbara Zahedieh (*née* Hockton), *e d* of Thomas and Deirdre Hockton; one *s* two step *d*. *Educ:* Manchester Grammar Sch.; St John's and Nuffield Colleges, Oxford. MA, PhD, DPhil. Research Fellow, St John's Coll., Oxford, 1969–73; Lectr in economics, Univ. of Essex, 1973–75; Lectr in recent British economic and social history, Univ. of Cambridge, and Fellow and Financial Tutor, Emmanuel Coll., Cambridge, 1976–78; Dir, Business History Unit, LSE, 1978–88. Vis. Prof., Harvard Univ., 1984–85. *Publications:* Rise of the Corporate Economy, 1976, 2nd edn 1983; (ed) Management Strategy and Business Development, 1976; (with J. A. Kay) Concentration in Modern Industry, 1977; Electricity before Nationalisation, 1979; Engineers, Managers and Politicians, 1982; Entrepreneurs and the Social Sciences, 1983; Inventing Retirement, 1986; contribs to jls. *Recreations:* walking, lying on beaches, reading novels. *Address:* London School of Economics, Houghton Street, WC2A 2AE. *T:* 071–955 7110. *Club:* Institute of Directors.

HANNAH, William; His Honour Judge Hannah; a Circuit Judge, since 1988; *b* 31 March 1929; *s* of William Bond Hannah and Elizabeth Alexandra Hannah; *m* 1950, Alma June Marshall; one *s* one *d*. *Educ:* Everton School, Notts. Called to the Bar, Gray's Inn, 1970. RAF 1947–52; Police Officer, 1952–77. *Recreations:* golf, swimming, walking, theatre. *Address:* c/o Newcastle Crown Court, Quayside, Newcastle upon Tyne NE1 3LA. *Club:* South Shields Golf.

HANNAM, John Gordon; MP (C) Exeter, since 1970; *b* 2 Aug. 1929; *s* of Thomas William and Selina Hannam; *m* 1st, 1956, Wendy Macartney; two *d*; 2nd, 1983, Mrs Vanessa Wauchope (*née* Anson). *Educ:* Yeovil Grammar Sch. Studied Agriculture, 1945–46. Served in: Royal Tank Regt (commissioned), 1947–48; Somerset LI (TA), 1949–51. Studied Hotel industry, 1950–52; Managing Dir, Hotels and Restaurant Co., 1952–61; Developed Motels, 1961–70; Chm., British Motels Fedn, 1967–74, Pres. 1974–80; Mem. Council, BTA, 1968–69; Mem. Economic Research Council, 1967–85. PPS to: Minister for Industry, 1972–74; Chief Sec., Treasury, 1974. Secretary: Cons. Parly Trade Cttee, 1971–72; All-Party Disablement Gp, 1974–; 1922 Cttee, 1987–; Mem., Govt Adv. Cttee on Transport for Disabled, 1983–; Chairman: Anglo–Swiss Parly Gp, 1987–; West Country Cons. Cttee, 1973–74, 1979–81; Cons. Party Energy Cttee, 1979–; Arts and Leisure Standing Cttee, Bow Group, 1975–84; Vice-Chairman: Arts and Heritage Cttee, 1974–79; British Cttee of Internat. Rehabilitation, 1979–. Captain: Lords and Commons Tennis Club, 1975–; Lords and Commons Ski Club, 1977–82; Cdre, House of Commons Yacht Club, 1975. Mem., Snowdon Working Party on the Disabled, 1975–76. Vice-President: Disablement Income Gp; Royal Assoc. for Disability and Rehabilitation; Council, Action Research for the Crippled Child; Disabled Motorists Gp; Altzheimer's Disease Soc.; Bd, Nat. Theatre. Member: Glyndebourne Festival Soc.; Council, British Youth Opera, 1989–. Trustee-Dir, Golden Globe Charity Trust, 1989–. Pres., Exeter Chambers of Trade and Commerce. Hon. MA Open, 1986. *Recreations:* music (opera), theatre, sailing (anything), skiing (fast), Cresta tobogganing (foolish), gardening; county tennis and hockey (Somerset tennis champion, 1953). *Address:* House of Commons, SW1A 0AA; Orchard House, Plymtree, near Cullompton, Devon. *Clubs:* Royal Yacht Squadron, All England Lawn Tennis, International Lawn Tennis.

HANNAM, Michael Patrick Vivian, CBE 1980; HM Diplomatic Service, retired; Consul General, Jerusalem, 1976–80; *b* 13 Feb. 1920; *s* of Rev. Wilfrid L. Hannam, BD, and Dorothy (*née* Parker); *m* 1947, Sybil Huggins; one *s* one *d*. *Educ:* Westminster Sch. LMS Railway, 1937–40. Served in Army, 1940–46 (Major, RE). LMS Railway, 1946–50; Malayan Railway, 1950–60. FO, 1960–62; First Sec., British Embassy, Cairo, 1962–65; Principal British Trade Comr, Hong Kong, 1965–69 (and Consul, Macao, 1968–69); Counsellor, Tripoli, 1969–72; Counsellor (Economic and Commercial), Nairobi, 1972–73, Dep. High Commissioner, Nairobi, 1973–76. Mem. Exec. Cttee and Keeper of Written Archive, Palestine Exploration Fund, 1982–. Chm. Governors, Rose Hill Sch., Tunbridge Wells, 1980–85; Chm. Council, British Sch. of Archaeology in Jerusalem, 1983–90. *Recreations:* music, research into 19th century Jerusalem. *Address:* Little Oaklands, Langton Green, Kent TN3 0HP. *T:* Langton (0892) 862163. *Club:* Army and Navy.

HANNAY, Sir David (Hugh Alexander), KCMG 1986 (CMG 1981); HM Diplomatic Service; British Permanent Representative to the United Nations, since 1990; *b* 28 Sept. 1935; *s* of late Julian Hannay; *m* 1961, Gillian Rex; four *s*. *Educ:* Winchester; New Coll., Oxford. Foreign Office, 1959–60; Tehran, 1960–61; 3rd Sec., Kabul, 1961–63; 2nd Sec., FO, 1963–65; 2nd, later 1st Sec., UK Delegn to European Communities, Brussels, 1965–70; 1st Sec., UK Negotiating Team with European Communities, 1970–72; Chef de Cabinet to Sir Christopher Soames, Vice President of EEC, 1973–77; Head of Energy, Science and Space Dept, FCO, 1977–79; Head of Middle East Dept, FCO, 1979; Asst Under-Sec. of State (European Community), FCO, 1979–84; Minister, Washington, 1984–85; Ambassador and UK Permanent Rep. to Eur. Communities, Brussels, 1985–90. *Recreations:* travel, gardening, photography. *Address:* c/o Foreign and Commonwealth Office, SW1A 2AH. *Club:* Travellers'.

HANNAY, Elizabeth Anne Scott, MA; Head Mistress, Godolphin School, Salisbury, 1980–89; *b* 28 Dec. 1942; *d* of Thomas Scott Hannay and Doreen Hewitt Hannay. *Educ:* Heathfield Sch., Ascot; St Hugh's Coll., Oxford (MA). Assistant Mistress: St Mary's Sch., Calne, 1966–70; Moreton Hall Sch., Shropshire, 1970–72; S Michael's, Burton Park, Petworth, 1973–75; Dep. Headmistress, St George's Sch., Ascot, 1975–80. *Address:* Downend Cottage, Tichborne, near Alresford, Hants SO24 0NA.

HANNEN, Rt. Rev. John Edward; *see* Caledonia, Bishop of.

HANNIGAN, Rt. Rev. James; *see* Wrexham, Bishop of, (RC).

HANNIGAN, James Edgar, CB 1981; Deputy Secretary, Department of Transport, 1980–88; *b* 12 March 1928; *s* of late James Henry and of Kathleen Hannigan; *m* 1955, Shirley Jean Bell; two *d*. *Educ:* Eastbourne Grammar Sch.; Sidney Sussex Coll., Cambridge (BA). Civil Service, 1951; Asst Sec., Housing Div., Min. of Housing and Local Govt, 1966–70; Asst Sec., Local Govt Div., DoE, 1970–72. Under Sec. 1972; Regional Dir for West Midlands, DoE, 1972–75; Chm., West Midlands Economic Planning Bd, 1972–75; Dir of Housing 'B', DoE, 1975–78; Dep. Sec., 1978. Mem., Internat. Exec. Cttee, PIARC, 1985–90. Trustee, Clapham Junction Disaster Fund, 1989–90.

HANNON, Rt. Rev. Brian Desmond Anthony; *see* Clogher, Bishop of.

HANON, Bernard; Officier, Ordre National du Mérite, 1980; Chairman and President, Régie Nationale des Usines Renault, 1981–85; *b* 7 Jan. 1932; *s* of Max Hanon and Anne Smulevicz; *m* 1965, Ghislaine de Bragelongne; two *s*. *Educ:* HEC 1955; Columbia Univ. (MBA 1956; PhD 1962). Dir of Marketing, Renault Inc., USA, 1959–63; Asst Prof. of Management Sci., Grad. Sch. of Business, NY Univ., 1963–66; Head, Dept of Economic Studies and Programming, 1966–69, Dir of Corporate Planning and Inf. Systems, 1970–75, Régie Nat. des Usines Renault; Dir, Renault Automotive Ops, 1976; Executive Vice President: i/c Automobile Div., 1976–81; Renault Gp, 1981. *Address:* Hanon Associés, 8 rue du Commandant Schloesing, 75016 Paris, France. *Clubs:* Racing Club de France, Automobile Club de France (Paris); Golf de St Germain.

HANRAHAN, Brian; Foreign Affairs correspondent, BBC Television, since 1989; *b* 22 March 1949; *s* of Thomas Hanrahan and Kathleen McInerney; *m* 1986, Honor Wilson; one *d*. *Educ:* Essex University (BA). BBC, 1971–: Far East correspondent, 1983–85; Moscow correspondent, 1986–89. DU Essex, 1990. *Publication:* (with Robert Fox) I Counted Them All Out and I Counted Them All Back, 1982. *Address:* c/o Foreign News Department, BBC TV Centre, Wood Lane, W12.

HANROTT, Francis George Vivian, CBE 1981; Chief Officer, Technician Education Council, 1973–82; *b* 1 July 1921; *s* of late Howard Granville Hanrott and Phyllis Sarah Hanrott; *m* 1953, Eileen Winifred Appleton; three *d*. *Educ:* Westminster Sch.; King's Coll., Univ. of London (BA Hons). Served War, RN (Air Br.), 1940–45; Lieut (A) RNVR. Asst Master, St Marylebone Grammar Sch., 1948–50; Lectr, E Berks Coll. of Further Educn, 1950–53; Asst Educn Officer, Wilts, 1953–56; Staff Manager, GEC Applied Electronics Labs, 1956–59; Asst Educn Officer, Herts, 1959–66; Registrar and Sec., CNAA, 1966–73. Hon. MA Open Univ., 1977. *Recreations:* music, angling. *Address:* Coombe Down House, Salcombe Road, Malborough, Kingsbridge, Devon TQ7 3BX. *T:* Salcombe (054884) 2721.

HANSENNE, Michel; Director-General, International Labour Office, since 1989; *b* 23 March 1940; *s* of Henri and Charlier Georgette Hansenne; *m* 1978, Mme Gabrielle Vanlandschoot; one *s* one *d*. *Educ:* Liège Univ. (Dr Law 1962; degree in Econs and Finance, 1967). Research work, Univ. of Liège, 1962–72. Mem. Belgian Parliament, 1974–89; Minister: for French Culture, 1979–81; for Employment and Labour, 1981–88; for Civil Service, 1988–89. *Publications:* Emploi, les scénarios du possible, 1985; articles in national and international jls. *Address:* International Labour Office, 1211 Geneva 22, Switzerland. *T:* 22/799.60.20.

HANSFORD, John Edgar, CB 1982; Under-Secretary, Defence Policy and Matériel Group, HM Treasury, 1976–82, retired; *b* 1 May 1922; *s* of Samuel George Hansford, ISO, MBE, and Winifred Louise Hansford; *m* 1947, Evelyn Agnes Whitehorn; one *s*. *Educ:* Whitgift Middle Sch., Croydon. Clerical Officer, Treasury, 1939. Served War of 1939–45: Private, Royal Sussex Regt, 1940; Lieutenant, Royal Fusiliers, 1943; served in: Africa, Mauritius, Ceylon, India, Burma, on secondment to King's African Rifles; demobilised, 1946. Exec. Officer, Treasury, 1946–50; Higher Exec. Officer, Regional Bd for Industry, Leeds, 1950–52; Exchange Control, Treasury, 1952–54; Agricultural Policy, Treasury, 1954–57; Sen. Exec. Officer, and Principal, Defence Div., Treasury, 1957–61; Principal, Social Security Div., Treasury, 1961–66; Public Enterprises Div., 1966–67; Overseas Develt Div., 1967–70; Asst Sec., Defence Policy and Matériel Div., Treasury, 1970–76; Under-Sec. in charge of Gp, 1976. *Recreations:* gardening, motoring.

HANSON, family name of **Baron Hanson.**

HANSON, Baron *cr* 1983 (Life Peer), of Edgerton in the County of West Yorkshire; **James Edward Hanson;** Kt 1976; Chairman: Hanson PLC, since 1965; Hanson Transport Group Ltd, since 1965; *b* 20 Jan. 1922; *s* of late Robert Hanson, CBE and late Louisa Ann (Cis) (*née* Rodgers); *m* 1959, Geraldine (*née* Kaelin); two *s* one *d*. War Service 1939–46, 7th Bn Duke of Wellington's Regt, TA, etc. Trustee, Hanson Fellowship of Surgery, Oxford Univ.; Fellow, Cancer Res. Campaign. Freeman, City of London, 1964; Liveryman, Worshipful Co. of Saddlers, 1965. Hon. LLD Leeds, 1984. FRSA; CBIM. *Address:* 1 Grosvenor Place, SW1X 7JH. *T:* 071–245 1245. *Clubs:* Brooks's; Huddersfield Borough; The Brook (NY); Toronto.

HANSON, Sir Anthony (Leslie Oswald), 4th Bt, *cr* 1887; *b* 27 Nov. 1934; *s* of Sir Gerald Stanhope Hanson, 2nd Bt, and Flora Liebe (*d* 1956), *e d* of late Lieut-Col W. A. R. Blennerhassett; *S* half-brother, 1951; *m* 1964, Denise Jane (Tuppence), *e d* of Richard Rolph; one *d*. *Educ:* Hawtrey's; Gordonstoun, Elgin, Morayshire. Career in Royal Navy until 1955; farming, 1956–67. St Luke's College, Exeter Univ. (BEd Hons 1974). Teacher, 1974–83; took very early retirement due to severe road accident. Conservation Officer, MSC, 1984. Supported by wife, teacher of maladjusted boys, St Luke's, Teignmouth. Member: Light Rescue Section, Devon Emergency Volunteers; Greenpeace; Amnesty International. *Recreations:* riding, talking; looking for a remunerative job. *Address:* Woodland Cottage, Woodland, Ashburton, Devon. *T:* Ashburton (0364) 52711.

HANSON, Dr Bertram Speakman, CMG 1963; DSO 1942; OBE 1941; ED; *b* 6 Jan. 1905; *s* of William Speakman Hanson and Maggie Aitken Hanson; *m* 1932, Mayne, *d* of T. J. Gilpin; three *s* one *d*. *Educ:* St Peter's Coll., Adelaide; University of Adelaide (MB, BS). War Service: Comd 2/8 Aust. Field Amb., 1940–43; ADMS, 9 Aust. Div., 1943–44. Pres., SA Branch of BMA, 1952–53; Pres. College of Radiologists of Australasia, 1961–62 (Gold Medal, 1990); Mem., Radiation Health Cttee of Nat. Health and Med. Research Coun., 1963–67; Hon. Radiotherapist, Royal Adelaide Hospital, 1952–64; Pres., The Australian Cancer Soc., 1964–67 (Gold Medal, 1979); Chairman: Exec. Board, Anti-Cancer Foundation, University of Adelaide, 1955–74; Anti-Cancer Foundation, Universities of South Aust., 1980–86; Mem. Council, International Union Against Cancer, 1962–74. Pres., Nat. Trust of South Aust., 1979–82. FFR (Hon.) 1964; FAMA 1967; FRCR (Hon.) 1975. DUniv Adelaide, 1985. *Publications:* sundry addresses and papers in Med. Jl of Australia. *Recreation:* gardening. *Address:* Private Box, Longwood PO, Longwood, SA 5153, Australia. *Club:* Adelaide.

HANSON, Brian John Taylor; Registrar and Legal Adviser to General Synod of Church of England, since 1975; Joint Principal Registrar, Provinces of Canterbury and York, since 1980; Registrar, Convocation of Canterbury, since 1982; *b* 23 Jan. 1939; *o s* of Benjamin John Hanson and Gwendoline Ada Hanson (*née* Taylor); *m* 1972, Deborah Mary Hazel, *yr d* of Lt-Col R. S. P. Dawson, OBE; two *s* three *d*. *Educ:* Hounslow Coll.; Law Society's Coll. of Law. Solicitor (admitted 1963) and ecclesiastical notary; in private practice, Wilson Houlder & Co., 1963–65; Solicitor with Church Comrs, 1965–; Asst Legal Advr to General Synod, 1970–75. Member: Legal Adv. Commn of General Synod, 1980– (Sec., 1970–86); Gen. Council, Ecclesiastical Law Soc., 1987–. Guardian, Nat. Shrine of Our Lady of Walsingham, 1984–; Fellow, Corp. of SS Mary and Nicholas (Woodard Schools), 1987–; Mem. Council, St Luke's Hosp. for the Clergy, 1985–; Governor, St Michael's Sch., Burton Park, 1987–. Freeman: City of London; Co. of Glaziers and Painters of Glass. *Publications:* (ed) The Canons of the Church of England, 2nd edn 1975, 4th edn 1986; (ed) The Opinions of the Legal Advisory Commission, 6th edn 1985. *Recreations:* the family, gardening, genealogy. *Address:* Dalton's Farm, Bolney, West Sussex RH17 5PG. *T:* Bolney (0444) 881890. *Club:* Commonwealth Trust.

HANSON, Sir (Charles) John, 3rd Bt *cr* 1918; *b* 28 Feb. 1919; *o s* of Major Sir Charles Edwin Bourne Hanson, 2nd Bt, and Violet Sybil (*d* 1966), 3rd *d* of late John B. Johnstone, Coombe Cottage, Kingston Hill, Surrey; *S* father 1958; *m* 1st, 1944, Patricia Helen (marr. diss. 1968), *o c* of late Adm. Sir (Eric James) Patrick Brind, GBE, KCB; one *s* one *d*; 2nd, 1968, Mrs Helen Yorke, *d* of late Charles Ormonde Trew. *Educ:* Eton; Clare Coll., Cambridge. Late Captain, The Duke of Cornwall's Light Infantry; served War of 1939–45. *Heir: s* Charles Rupert Patrick Hanson [*b* 25 June 1945; *m* 1977, Wanda, *d* of Don Arturo Larrain, Santiago, Chile; one *s*]. *Address:* Gunn House, Shelfanger, near Diss, Norfolk. *T:* Diss (0379) 643207. *Clubs:* Army and Navy, MCC.

HANSON, Derrick George; financial adviser; writer, director of companies; Chairman: Moneyguide Ltd, since 1978; A. C. Morrell Employees' Trust, since 1983; Director: Albany Investment Trust plc, since 1980; Toye & Co. plc, since 1981; British Leather Co. Ltd, since 1983; James Beattie PLC, since 1984; Barrister; *b* 9 Feb. 1927; *s* of late John Henry Hanson and of Frances Elsie Hanson; *m* 1st, 1951, Daphne Elizabeth (*née* Marks) (*d* 1974); one *s* two *d*; 2nd, 1974, Hazel Mary (*née* Buckley) (*d* 1984); 3rd, 1986, Patricia (*née* Skillicorn). *Educ:* Waterloo Grammar Sch.; London Univ. (LLB (Hons)); Liverpool Univ. (LLM). Called to Bar, Lincoln's Inn, 1952. Joined Martins Bank Ltd, 1943; Chief Trustee Manager, Martins Bank Ltd, 1963; Dir and Gen. Manager, Martins Bank Trust Co. Ltd, 1968; Dir and Gen. Manager, Barclays Bank Trust Co. Ltd, 1969–76; Chairman: Barclays Unicorn Ltd, 1972–76; Barclays Life Assce Co. Ltd, 1972–76; City of London & European Property Co. Ltd, 1980–86; Key Fund Managers Ltd, 1984–87; Birmingham Midshires Bldg Soc., 1988–90 (Dir, 1982–90); Director: Barclaytrust Property Management Ltd, 1971–76; Barclays Bank plc, Manchester Bd, 1976–77; Sen. Adviser (UK), Manufacturers Hanover Trust Co., 1977–79; Adviser, Phillips Gp, Fine Art Auctioneers, 1977–82. Assessor, Cameron Tribunal, 1962; Dir, Oxford Univ. Business Summer Sch., 1971. Chm., Southport and Formby DHA, 1986–89; Member: NW Industrialists' Council, 1977–83; South Sefton Health Authority, 1979–82; Mersey RHA, 1982–86. Pres., Assoc. of Banking Teachers, 1979–88. Mem. Council, Liverpool Univ., 1980–84; Chm., Christian Arts Trust, 1980–86. Mem., NW Regl Cttee, NT, 1990–. George Rae Prize of Inst. of Bankers; Hon. FCIB 1987. Hon. Fellow, City Univ. *Publications:* Within These Walls: a century of Methodism in Formby, 1974; Service Banking, 1979; Moneyguide: The Handbook of Personal Finance, 1981; Dictionary of Banking and Finance, 1985. *Recreations:* golf, gardening, hill-walking. *Address:* Bridgend, Deepdale Bridge, Patterdale, Cumbria CA11 0NS; Grasshopper House, Freshfield Road, Formby, Merseyside L37 7BJ. *Clubs:* Royal Automobile; Formby Golf (Formby, Lancs).

HANSON, James Donald; Managing Partner, Strategic Affairs and Communications, Arthur Andersen & Co. Worldwide, since 1989; *b* 4 Jan. 1935; *s* of late Mary and Leslie Hanson; *m* 1st, 1959, Patricia Margaret Talent (marr. diss. 1977); two *s*; 2nd, 1978, Anne Barbara Asquith. *Educ:* Heath Grammar School, Halifax. ACA 1956, FCA 1966. Joined Arthur Andersen & Co., Chartered Accountants, 1958; established north west practice, 1966, Managing Partner, North West, 1968–82, Sen. Partner, UK, 1982–89. Member: Internat. Operating Cttee, 1982–; Internat. Board of Partners, 1985–; Manchester Soc. of Chartered Accountants, 1967–81 (Pres., 1979); Council, CBI, 1982–. Mem., Council and Court, Manchester Univ., 1982–. *Recreations:* ski-ing, tennis. *Address:* Arthur Andersen & Co., 1 Surrey Street, WC2R 2PS. *T:* 071–438 3000.

HANSON, Sir John; *see* Hanson, Sir Charles John.

HANSON, John Gilbert, CBE 1979; Deputy Director-General, British Council, since 1988; *b* 16 Nov. 1938; *s* of Gilbert Fretwell Hanson and Gladys Margaret (*née* Kay); *m* 1962, Margaret Clark; three *s*. *Educ:* Manchester Grammar Sch.; Wadham Coll., Oxford (BA Lit. Hum. 1961, MA 1964). Asst Principal, WO, 1961–63; British Council: Madras, India, 1963–66; ME Centre for Arab Studies, Lebanon, 1966–68; Rep., Bahrain, 1968–72; Dep. Controller, Educn and Science Div., 1972–75; Representative, Iran, and Counsellor (Cultural) British Embassy, Tehran, 1975–79; Controller, Finance Div., 1979–82; RCDS, 1983; Head, British Council Div. and Minister (Cultural Affairs), British High Commn, New Delhi, 1984–88. Patron, GAP, 1989–. Member Governing Council: RSAA, 1989–; Soc. for S Asian Studies, 1989–; British Inst. of Persian Studies, 1989–. *Recreations:* books, music, sport, travel. *Address:* c/o The British Council, 10 Spring Gardens, SW1A 2BN. *T:* 071–930 8466. *Clubs:* Athenæum, MCC; Gymkhana (Madras).

HANSON, Neil; Under Secretary, and Controller, Newcastle upon Tyne Central Office, Department of Health and Social Security, 1981–83; *b* 21 March 1923; *s* of late Reginald William Hanson and Lillian Hanson (*née* Benson); *m* 1st, 1950, Eileen Ashworth (*d* 1976); two *s*; 2nd, 1977, Margaret Brown-Smelt. *Educ:* City of Leeds Sch. Served War, 1942–46, N Africa, Sicily, Italy. Jun. Clerk, Leeds Social Welfare Cttee, 1939; Clerical Officer, 1948–50, Exec. Officer, 1950–56, Nat. Assistance Bd; Manager, Suez and Hungarian Refugee Hostels, 1956–59; Higher Exec. Officer, 1959–62, Sen. Exec. Officer, 1963–66, Nat. Assistance Bd; Principal, Min. of Social Security, 1967–73; Sen. Principal, 1973–76, Asst Sec., 1976–80, DHSS. *Recreations:* cricket, music, walking. *Address:* 4 Woodbourne, Park Avenue, Leeds LS8 2JW. *T:* Leeds (0532) 653452.

HANTON, Alastair Kydd, OBE 1986; Chairman, Ethical Investment Research Service; Deputy Managing Director, Girobank (formerly National Girobank, Post Office), 1982–86; *b* 10 Oct. 1926; *er s* of late Peter Hanton and Maude Hanton; *m* 1956, Margaret Mary (*née* Lumsden); two *s* one *d*. *Educ:* Mill Hill Sch.; Pembroke Coll., Cambridge. Commonwealth Develt Corp., 1948–54; ICFC, 1954–57; Unilever, 1957–66; Rio Tinto-Zinc, 1966–68; Post Office, 1968–86. Chm., Envmtl Transport Assoc., 1990–. *Recreation:* forestry. *Address:* 8 Gilkes Crescent, Dulwich Village, SE21 7BS. *T:* 081–693 2618.

HANWORTH, 2nd Viscount, *cr* 1936, of Hanworth; **David Bertram Pollock,** CEng, MIMechE, FIEE, FRPS, FIQA; Baron, *cr* 1926; Bt, *cr* 1922; Lt-Col Royal Engineers, retired; Barrister-at-Law (Inner Temple), 1958; *b* 1 Aug. 1916; *s* of Charles Thomas Anderson Pollock and Alice Joyce Becher; *S* grandfather, 1936; *m* 1940, Isolda Rosamond, *yr d* of Geoffrey Parker, of Cairo; two *s* one *d*. *Educ:* Wellington Coll.; Trinity Coll., Cambridge. (Mechanical Science Tripos, 1939). Joined Social Democratic Party, 1981, Soc & Lib Dem, 1989. *Publications:* Amateur Carbro Colour Prints, 1950; Amateur Dye Transfer Colour Prints, 1956. *Heir: s* Hon. David Stephen Geoffrey Pollock [*b* 16 Feb. 1946; *m* 1968, Elizabeth Liberty, *e d* of Lawrence Vambe; two *d*]. *Address:* Quoin Cottage, Shamley Green, Guildford, Surrey GU5 0UJ.

HAPPOLD, Prof. Edmund, RDI 1983; FEng 1983; Professor of Building Engineering, University of Bath, since 1976; Senior Partner, Buro Happold, consulting engineers, since 1976; *b* 8 Nov. 1930; *s* of late Prof. Frank Charles Happold, PhD, DSc and A. Margaret M. Smith, MA; *m* 1967, Evelyn Claire Matthews; two *s*. *Educ:* Leeds Grammar Sch.; Bootham Sch., York; Leeds Univ. BSc, FICE, FIStructE, FCIOB, FIEHK. Site Engineer, Sir Robert McAlpine & Sons, 1952–54; Engineer, Ove Arup & Partners, 1956–58, Severud Elstad & Kruger, NY, 1958–60; Senior Engineer then Associate, later Exec. Partner, Ove Arup & Partners, 1960–76; assisted Tom Hancock in winning 2nd prize, Houses of Parlt competition, 1972; won jtly with 4 others Centre Pompidou, Plateau Beaubourg competition, 1971; won jtly with 2 others Vauxhall Cross competition, 1982; jtly with 4 others won High Wycombe Cultural Centre Competition, 1987. Chm., Construction Industry Council, 1988–91. Institution of Structural Engineers: Mem. Council, 1974–77, 1979–; Chm., Educn Cttee, 1979–82; Vice-Pres., 1982–86; Pres., 1986–87; Guthrie Brown Medal, 1970; Oscar Faber Medal, 1974, 1977; Henry Adams Award, 1976; Mem., Standing Cttee on Structural Safety, 1976–86; International Association of Bridge and Structural Engineers: Mem., Nat. Council, 1977–; Mem., Internat. Tech. Cttee, 1978–83; Chm., Commn V, 1978–83. Member: Board, Property Services Agency, 1979–81, Adv. Bd, 1981–86; Design Council, 1988–; Building Regulations Adv. Cttee, 1988–. Dep. Master, Faculty RDI. Murray Leslie Medal, CIOB, 1982. Hon. FRIBA 1983; Hon. FCIBSE 1988. Hon. DSc City Univ., 1988. *Publications:* papers in learned journals. *Recreations:* engineering and family activities. *Address:* 4 Widcombe Terrace, Bath, Avon BA2 6AJ. *T:* Bath (0225) 337510; Flat 18, 32 Grosvenor Street, W1X 9FF. *Club:* Athenæum.

HARARE, Diocese; *see* Mashonaland.

HARARE (formerly **SALISBURY), Archbishop of,** (RC), since 1976; **Most Rev. Patrick Chakaipa;** *b* 25 June 1932; *s* of Chakaipa and Chokutaura. *Educ:* Chishawasha Minor and Regional Major Seminary, nr Harare; Kutama Teachers' Coll. Ecclesiastic qualifications in Philosophy and Theology; Teacher Training Cert. Asst priest, Makumbi Mission, 1967–69; Priest-in-Charge, All Souls Mission, Mutoko, 1969–73; Episcopal Vicar, Mutoko-Mrewa Area, 1970–73; Auxiliary Bishop of Salisbury, 1973–76. *Publications:* Karikoga, 1958; Pfumo reRopa, 1961; Rudo Ibofu, 1961; Garandichauya, 1963; Dzasukwa, 1967. *Recreation:* chess. *Address:* PO Box 8060, Causeway, Harare, Zimbabwe. *T:* 792125.

HARARE, Bishop of, since 1981; **Rt. Rev. Ralph Peter Hatendi;** *b* 9 April 1927; *s* of Fabian and Amelia Hatendi; *m* 1954, Jane Mary Chikumbu; two *s* three *d*. *Educ:* St Peter's Coll., Rosettenville, S Africa (LTh); King's Coll. London (DD; AKC). School teacher, 1952–; clergyman, 1957–; Seminary Tutor, 1968–72; Executive Secretary, 1973–75; Distribution Consultant, 1976–78; Suffragan Bishop of Mashonaland, 1979–80. *Publications:* Sex and Society, 1971; Shona Marriage and the Christian Churches, in Christianity South of the Zambezi, 1973. *Recreation:* poultry. *Address:* PO UA7, Harare, Zimbabwe. *T:* 44113. *Club:* Harare (Zimbabwe).

HARBERTON, 10th Viscount *cr* 1791; **Thomas de Vautort Pomeroy;** Baron Harberton 1783; *b* 19 Oct. 1910; *s* of 8th Viscount Harberton, OBE, and Mary Katherine (*d* 1971), *d* of A. W. Leatham; *S* brother, 1980; *m* 1978, Vilma, *widow* of Sir Alfred Butt, 1st Bt. *Educ:* Eton. Joined Welsh Guards, 1932; transferred to RAOC, 1939; served BEF, then in India; retired, 1952. *Heir: b* Hon. Robert William Pomeroy [*b* 29 Feb. 1916; *m* 1953, Winifred Anne, *d* of late Sir Arthur Colegate, MP; two *s*]. *Club:* Cavalry and Guards.

HARBISON, Air Vice-Marshal William, CB 1977; CBE 1965; AFC 1956; RAF, retired; Vice-President, British Aerospace Inc., Washington, DC, since 1979; *b* 11 April 1922; *s* of W. Harbison; *m* 1950, Helen, *d* of late William B. Geneva, Bloomington, Illinois; two *s*. *Educ:* Ballymena Academy, N Ireland. Joined RAF, 1941; 118 Sqdn Fighter Comd, 1943–46; 263, 257 and 64 Sqdns, 1946–48; Exchange Officer with 1st Fighter Group USAF, 1948–50; Central Fighter Estabt, 1950–51; 4th Fighter Group USAF, Korea, 1952; 2nd ATAF Germany: comd No 67 Sqdn, 1952–55; HQ No 2 Group, 1955; psc 1956; Air Min. and All Weather OCU, 1957; comd No 29 All Weather Sqdn Fighter Comd, Acklington and Leuchars, 1958–59; British Defence Staffs, Washington, 1959–62; jssc 1962; comd RAF Leuchars Fighter Comd, 1963–65; ndc 1965–66; Gp Capt. Ops: HQ Fighter Comd, 1967–68; No 11 Group Strike Comd, 1968; Dir of Control (Ops), NATCS, 1968–72; Comdr RAF Staff, and Air Attaché, Washington, 1972–75; AOC 11 Group, RAF, 1975–77. *Recreations:* flying, motoring. *Address:* c/o Lloyds Bank, Cox's & King's Branch, 7 Pall Mall, SW1. *Club:* Royal Air Force.

HARBORD-HAMOND, family name of **Baron Suffield.**

HARBORNE, Peter Gale; HM Diplomatic Service; Counsellor, Foreign and Commonwealth Office, since 1991; *b* 19 June 1945; *s* of Leslie Herbert and Marie Mildred Edith Harborne; *m* 1976, Tessa Elizabeth Henri; two *s*. *Educ:* King Edward's Sch., Birmingham; Birmingham Univ. (BCom). Dept of Health, 1966–72; FCO, 1972–74; 1st Sec., Ottawa, 1974–75; 1st Sec. Commercial, Mexico City, 1975–78; Lloyd's Bank Internat., 1979–81; FCO, 1981–83; Head of Chancery, Helsinki, 1983–87; Dep. Head of Mission, Budapest, 1988–91. *Recreations:* watching cricket, playing bad tennis, music, cross-country ski-ing. *Address:* c/o Foreign and Commonwealth Office, King Charles Street, SW1A 2AH. *Club:* MCC.

HARBOTTLE, Rev. Anthony Hall Harrison, LVO 1979; Rector of East Dean with Friston and Jevington, since 1981; Chaplain to the Queen, since 1968; *b* 3 Sept. 1925; *y s* of Alfred Charles Harbottle, ARIBA, and Ellen Muriel, *o d* of William Popham Harrison; *m* 1955, Gillian Mary, *o d* of Hugh Goodenough; three *s* one *d*. *Educ:* Sherborne Sch.; Christ's Coll., Cambridge (MA); Wycliffe Hall, Oxford. Served War in Royal Marines, 1944–46. Deacon 1952, priest 1953; Asst Curacies: Boxley, 1952–54; St Peter-in-Thanet, 1954–60; Rector of Sandhurst with Newenden, 1960–68; Chaplain of the Royal Chapel, Windsor Great Park, 1968–81. Founder Mem., Kent Trust for Nature Conservation, 1954; Mem., Green Alliance, 1984. County Chaplain, Royal British Legion (Sussex), 1982–. FRES 1971. *Publications:* contribs to entomological jls, on lepidoptera. *Recreations:* butterflies and moths, nature conservancy, entomology, ornithology, philately, coins, Treasury and bank notes, painting, cooking, lobstering. *Address:* East Dean Rectory, Eastbourne, East Sussex BN20 0DL. *T:* East Dean (0323) 423266.

HARBOTTLE, (George) Laurence; Senior Partner, Harbottle & Lewis, Solicitors, since 1956; *b* 11 April 1924; *s* of George Harbottle and Winifred Ellen Benson Harbottle. *Educ:* The Leys Sch., Cambridge; Emmanuel Coll., Cambridge (MA). Solicitor 1952. Served War: commnd RA, 1942; Burma and India; Temp. Captain; Adjt 9th Fd Regt, 1945–47. Theatre Companies: Chairman: Theatre Centre, 1959–88; Prospect, 1966–77; Royal Exchange (69), 1968–83; Cambridge, 1969–; Director: The Watermill, 1970–75; The Bush (Alternative), 1975–77. Arts Council: Mem., 1976–77–78; Mem., Drama Panel, 1974–78; Chairman: Housing the Arts, 1977–78; Trng Cttee, 1977–78; Chairman: Central Sch. of Speech and Drama, 1982– (Vice Chm., 1977–82); ICA, 1986–90 (Dep. Chm., 1977–86). Pres., Theatrical Management Assoc., 1979–85; Vice-Chairman: Music Users Council, 1985–; Theatres Adv. Council, 1986–88; Theatres Nat. Cttee, 1986–. Member: Justice Cttee on Privacy, 1970; Theatres Trust, 1980– (exec. Chm., 1987–). Gov., City Literary Inst., 1990–. *Recreations:* works of art, gardening, tennis. *Address:* Hanover House, 14 Hanover Square, W1R 0BE. *Club:* Savile.

HARBOTTLE, Brig. Michael Neale, OBE 1959; Director, Centre for International Peacebuilding, since 1983; *b* 7 Feb. 1917; *s* of Thomas Benfield Cecil and Kathleen Millicent Harbottle; *m* 1st, 1940, Alison Jean Humfress; one *s* one *d*; 2nd, 1972, Eirwen Helen Simonds. *Educ:* Marlborough Coll.; Royal Military Coll., Sandhurst. Commissioned

Oxfordshire and Buckinghamshire Light Infantry, 1937 (despatches 1944); commanded 1st Royal Green Jackets, 1959–62; Security Commander, Aden, 1962–64; Comd 129 Inf. Bde, TA, 1964–66; Chief of Staff, UN Peacekeeping Force Cyprus, 1966–68; retired, 1968. Vice-Pres., Internat. Peace Academy, 1971–73, Consultant, 1973–; Vis. Sen. Lectr (Peace Studies), Bradford Univ., 1974–79; Vice-Pres., UNA (UK), 1974–; Cons., United World College of Atlantic, 1974–81; Member: Management Cttee, Council for Educn in World Citizenship, 1978–89; Generals (Retd) for Peace and Disarmament, 1981–; Educn Planning Dir, British Council for Aid to Refugees (Vietnamese Sec.), 1979–80; Gen. Sec., World Disarmament Campaign, 1980–82. Cons/Advr, Internat. Inst. for Peaceful Change. *Publications:* The Impartial Soldier, 1970; The Blue Berets, 1971, 2nd edn 1975; (jtly) The Thin Blue Line: International Peacekeeping and its Future, 1974; The Knaves of Diamonds, 1976; (collator) Peacekeeper's Handbook, 1978; (jtly) 10 Questions Answered, 1983; (jtly) Reflections on Security in the Nuclear Age, 1988; contributor to: Unofficial Diplomats, 1977 (USA); The Arab-Israel Conflict, Readings and Documents, 1977 (USA). *Recreations:* cricket, golf, crossword puzzles. *Address:* 9 West Street, Chipping Norton, Oxon OX7 5LH. *T:* Chipping Norton (0608) 642335.

HARCOURT, Prof. Geoffrey Colin, PhD, LittD; FASSA; Fellow and College Lecturer in Economics, since 1982, President, 1988–89 and since 1990, Jesus College, Cambridge; Reader (*ad hominem*) in the History of Economic Theory, Cambridge University, since 1990; *b* 27 June 1931; *s* of Kenneth Kopel Harcourt and Marjorie Rahel (*neé* Gans); *m* 1955, Joan Margaret Bartrop; two *s* two *d*. *Educ:* Malvern Grammar Sch.; Wesley Coll., Melbourne; Queen's Coll., Univ. of Melbourne (BCom (Hons) 1954; MCom 1956); King's Coll., Cambridge. PhD 1960, LittD 1988, Cantab. University of Adelaide: Lectr in Econs, 1958–62; Sen. Lectr, 1963–65; Reader, 1965–67; Prof. of Econs (Personal Chair), 1967–85, Prof. Emeritus 1988; Cambridge University: Lectr in Econs and Politics, 1963–66, 1982–90; Fellow and Dir of Studies in Econs, Trinity Hall, 1964–66. Leverhulme Exchange Fellow, Keio Univ., Tokyo, 1969–70; Vis. Fellow, Clare Hall, Cambridge, 1972–73; Vis. Prof., Scarborough Coll., Univ. of Toronto, 1977, 1980. Howard League for Penal Reform, SA Branch: Sec., 1959–63; Vice-Pres., 1967–74; Pres., 1974–80. Mem., Exec. Cttee, Campaign for Peace in Vietnam, 1967–75 (Chm., 1970–72). Mem., Aust. Labor Party Nat. Cttee of Enquiry, 1978–79. Pres., Econ. Soc. of Aust. and NZ, 1974–77; Mem. Council, Roy. Econ. Soc., 1990–. FASSA 1971 (Exec. Cttee Mem., 1974–77). Lectures: Wellington–Burnham, Tufts Univ., USA, 1975; Edward Shann Meml, Univ. of WA, 1975; Newcastle, in Pol Economy, Univ. of Newcastle, NSW, 1977; Academy, Acad. of Social Scis in Aust., 1978; G. L. Wood Meml, Univ. of Melbourne, 1982; John Curtin Meml, ANU, 1982; Special Lectr in Econs, Manchester Univ., 1983–84; Nobel Conf., Minnesota, USA, 1986. *Publications:* (with P. H. Karmel and R. H. Wallace) Economic Activity, 1967 (trans. Italian, 1969); (ed jtly) Readings in the Concept and Measurement of Income, 1969, 2nd edn 1986; (ed with N. F. Laing) Capital and Growth: Selected Readings, 1971 (trans. Spanish, 1977); Some Cambridge Controversies in the Theory of Capital, 1972 (trans. Italian, 1973, Polish and Spanish, 1975, Japanese 1980); Theoretical Controversy and Social Significance: an evaluation of the Cambridge controversies (Edward Shann Meml Lecture), 1975; (ed) The Microeconomic Foundations of Macroeconomics, 1977; The Social Science Imperialists: selected essays (ed Prue Kerr), 1982; (ed) Keynes and his Contemporaries, 1985; (ed with Jon Cohen) International Monetary Problems and Supply-Side Economics: Essays in Honour of Lorie Tarshis, 1986; Controversies in Political Economy (selected essays, ed O. F. Hamouda), 1986; many articles in learned jls and chapters in edited books. *Recreations:* cricket, Australian rules football, running (not jogging), reading, politics. *Address:* P3, Jesus College, Cambridge CB5 8BL. *T:* Cambridge (0223) 68611; Faculty of Economics and Politics, University of Cambridge, Sidgwick Avenue, Cambridge CB3 9DD. *T:* Cambridge (0223) 335231; 43 New Square, Cambridge CB1 1EZ. *T:* Cambridge (0223) 60833. *Clubs:* Melbourne Cricket, South Australian Cricket Association.

HARCOURT, Geoffrey David, JP; RDI, DesRCA, FCSD; freelance designer, since 1962; Consultant to Artifort, Dutch furniture manufacturer, since 1963; *b* 9 Aug. 1935; *s* of William and Barbara Harcourt; *m* 1965, Jean Mary Vaughan Pryce-Jones; one *s* one *d*. *Educ:* High Wycombe Sch. of Art; Royal Coll. of Art; DesRCA, Silver Medal 1960. FSIAD 1968; RDI 1978. Designer: Latham, Tyler, Jensen, Chicago, 1960–61; Jacob Jensen, Copenhagen, 1961; Andrew Pegram Ltd, London, 1961–62. Vis. Lecturer: High Wycombe Coll. of Art and Design, 1963–74; Leicester Polytechnic, 1982, 1983–; Ext. Assessor for BA Hons degrees, Kingston Polytechnic, 1974–77, Loughborough Coll. of Art and Design, 1978–81, Belfast Polytechnic, 1977–81 and Buckinghamshire Coll. of Higher Educn, 1982–. Chair design for Artifort awarded first prize for creativity, Brussels, 1978; Member: Design Awards Cttee, Design Council, 1979–80; Furniture Design Wkg Party, EDC, 1986–87; Chm., RSA Bursaries Cttee (Furniture Design Section, 1982–86, Ceramics Section, 1989–); approved consultant, Design Council 'Support for Design' initiative. Work exhibited: Steidlijk Mus., Amsterdam, 1967; Prague Mus. of Decorative Arts, 1972; Science Mus., London, 1972; Design Council, London and Glasgow, 1976 and 1981; Eye for Industry Exhibn, V&A, 1987; Nederlands Textielmuseum, 1988; Manchester Prize exhibn, City Art Gall., 1988. FRSA 1979. Freeman, City of London; Liveryman, Worshipful Co. of Furniture Makers. JP E Oxfordshire, 1981. *Recreations:* making things, cooking, golf. *Address:* The Old Vicarage, Benson, Oxfordshire OX10 6SF. *Club:* Goring and Streatley Golf.

HARCOURT-SMITH, Air Chief Marshal Sir David, GBE 1989; KCB 1984; DFC 1957; aviation consultant; Controller Aircraft, Ministry of Defence, Procurement Executive, 1986–89, retired; *b* 14 Oct. 1931; *s* of late Air Vice-Marshal G. Harcourt-Smith, CB, CBE, MVO, and of M. Harcourt-Smith; *m* 1957, Mary (*née* Entwistle); two *s* one *d*. *Educ:* Felsted Sch.; RAF College. Commnd 1952; flying appts with Nos 11, 8 and 54 Squadrons; Staff Coll., 1962; OC No 54 Squadron, 1963–65; PSO to AOC-in-C, Tech. Training Comd, 1965–67; Defence Planning Staff, 1967–68; OC No 6 Squadron, 1969–70; Central Tactics and Trials Organisation, 1970–72; OC RAF Brüggen, 1972–74; Dir of Op. Requirements, 1974–76; RCDS, 1977; Comdt, RAF Coll., Cranwell, 1978–80; Asst Chief of Air Staff (Op. Reqs), 1980–84; AOC-in-C, RAF Support Command, 1984–85. Dir, DESC. Gov., Felsted Sch., 1988–. *Recreations:* walking, golf. *Address:* c/o Barclays Bank, 2/6 High Street, Salisbury SP1 2NP. *Club:* Royal Air Force.

HARDAKER, Rev. Canon Ian Alexander; Clergy Appointments Adviser, since 1985; *b* 14 May 1932; *s* of Joseph Alexander Hardaker and Edna Mary (*née* Theede); *m* 1963, Susan Mary Wade Bottom; two *s* two *d*. *Educ:* Kingston Grammar Sch.; Royal Military Acad., Sandhurst; King's Coll., London (BD, AKC). Commnd East Surrey Regt, 1952. Curate, Beckenham Parish Ch., 1960–65; Vicar of Eynsford and Rector of Lullingstone, 1965–70; Vicar of St Stephen's, Chatham, 1970–85; Rural Dean of Rochester, 1978–85. *Recreations:* walking, photography, family. *Address:* 29 Maidstone Road, Chatham, Kent ME4 6DP. *T:* Medway (0634) 811742. *Club:* Commonwealth Trust.

HARDCASTLE, Alan John, FCA; Chief Accountancy Adviser to HM Treasury and Head of Government Accountancy Service, since 1989; *b* 10 Aug. 1933; *s* of late William and of Catherine Hardcastle; *m* 1st, 1958, Dinah (*née* Beattie) (marr. diss. 1983); two *s*; 2nd, 1983, Ione Marguerite (*née* Cooney); two step *d*. *Educ:* Haileybury Coll. Articled to B. W. Brixey, 1951–56; qualified, 1956; Nat. Service as Sub-Lieut RNVR, 1956–58. Joined Peat, Marwick, Mitchell & Co. (later Peat Marwick McLintock), 1958; Partner 1967; Gen. Partner 1972–88. DoT Inspector into affairs of Saint Piran Ltd (reported 1981). Inst. of Chartered Accountants in England and Wales: Mem. Council, 1974–; Pres., 1983–85; Chairman: London and District Soc. of Chartered Accountants, 1973–74; Consultative Cttee of Accountancy Bodies, 1983–85; Pres., Chartered Accountants Students' Soc. of London, 1976–80. Member: Bd of Banking Supervision, 1986–; Council, Lloyd's, 1987–88. Master, Co. of Chartered Accountants in England and Wales, 1978–79. Mem., Council of Management, The White Ensign Assoc.; Hon. Treas., Berkeley Square Charitable Trust. Speaker and author of papers on accountancy topics. *Recreations:* music, theatre, fishing, the company of family and friends. *Clubs:* Athenæum, City Livery, Naval.

HARDCASTLE, Prof. Jack Donald, MChir (Cantab); FRCP, FRCS; Professor of Surgery, University of Nottingham, since 1970; *b* 3 April 1933; *s* of Albert Hardcastle and Bertha (*née* Ellison); *m* 1965, Rosemary Hay-Shunker; one *s* one *d*. *Educ:* St Bartholomew's Grammar Sch., Newbury; Emmanuel Coll., Cambridge (Senior Scholar 1954; BA, MA; Windsor Postgrad. Schol.); London Hospital (Open Scholarship 1955; MB, BChir, MChir (Distinction)). MRCP 1961; FRCS 1962; FRCP 1984. House Phys./Surg., Resident Accoucheur, London Hosp., 1959–60; Ho. Surg. to Prof. Aird, Hammersmith Postgraduate Hosp., 1961–62; London Hospital: Research Asst, 1962; Lectr in Surgery, 1963; Registrar in Surgery, 1964; Registrar in Surgery, Thoracic Unit, 1965; Sen. Registrar in Surgery, 1965; Sen. Registrar, St Mark's Hosp., London, 1968; Sen. Lectr in Surgery, London Hosp., 1968. Sir Arthur Sims Commonwealth Travelling Prof., RCS, 1985; Mayne Vis. Prof., Univ. of Brisbane, 1987. Mem. Council, RCS, 1987–. *Publications:* Isolated Organ Perfusion (with H. D. Ritchie), 1973; various scientific papers. *Recreation:* field sports. *Address:* Wild Briars, Goverton, Bleasby, Nottingham NG14 7FN. *T:* Newark (0636) 830316.

HARDCASTLE, (Jesse) Leslie, OBE 1974; Controller, British Film Institute (South Bank), 1988–91 (Controller: National Film Theatre, 1968–91; Museum of the Moving Image, 1988–91); *b* 8 Dec. 1926; *s* of Francis Ernest Hardcastle and Dorothy Schofield; *m* 1968, Vivienne Mansel Richards; two *s*. *Educ:* St Joseph's College, Croydon. British Lion Film Productions, 1943–44; Royal Navy, 1944–47. British Film Inst., 1947–91; responsible for admin of London Film Fest., 1968–91; Telekinema Festival of Britain, 1951; Co-ordinator, MOMI, 1981–88. *Recreations:* community work (Pres., The Soho Society), theatre, music, cinema. *Address:* 37c Great Pulteney Street, W1R 3DE.

HARDEN, Donald Benjamin, CBE 1969 (OBE 1956); MA Cantab, MA Oxon, PhD Mich; Hon. FBA; FSA; Director of the London Museum, 1956–70; Acting Director of the Museum of London, 1965–70; *b* Dublin, 8 July 1901; *er s* of late Rt Rev. John Mason Harden, Bishop of Tuam, Killala and Achonry, and Constance Caroline Sparrow; *m* 1st, 1934, Cecil Ursula (*d* 1963), *e d* of late James Adolphus Harriss; one *d*; 2nd, 1965, Dorothy May, *er d* of late Daniel Herbert McDonald. *Educ:* Kilkenny Coll.; Westminster Sch.; Trinity Coll., Cambridge; University of Michigan. Travelled in Italy and Tunisia, 1923–24; Senior Asst, Dept of Humanity, University of Aberdeen, 1924–26; Commonwealth Fund Fellow, University of Michigan, 1926–28; Asst, University of Michigan Archæol. Exped. to Egypt, 1928–29; Asst Keeper, Dept of Antiquities, Ashmolean Museum, Oxford, 1929–45; Keeper, Dept of Antiquities, and Sec., Griffith Institute, 1945–56. Temp. Civil Servant, Ministries of Supply and Production, 1940–45. Vice-Pres. Soc. of Antiquaries of London, 1949–53, 1964–67; President: Council for British Archæology, 1950–54; Oxford Architectural and Historical Soc., 1952–55; Section H, British Assoc., 1955; London and Middlesex Archæol. Soc., 1959–65; Royal Archæol. Inst., 1966–69; Internat. Assoc. for History of Glass, 1968–74; Chm., Directors' Conf. (Nat. Museums), 1968–70; Hon. Sec. Museums Assoc., 1949–54, Chm. Educ. Cttee 1954–59, Pres. 1960; Hon. Editor, Soc. for Medieval Archæology, 1957–73, Pres., 1975–77; Mem. of Council, British School of Archæology in Iraq, 1949–84; Member: Ancient Monuments Board for England, 1959–74; Royal Commission on Historical Monuments (England), 1963–71; Trustee, RAEC Museum, 1966–84. Mem., German Archaeol. Inst. Leverhulme Fellowship for research on ancient glass, 1953. Hon. FBA 1987. Gold Medal, Soc. of Antiquaries, 1977; Hon. Fellow and Rakow Award, Corning Museum of Glass, NY, 1983. *Publications:* Roman Glass from Karanis, 1936; (with E. T. Leeds) The Anglo-Saxon Cemetery at Abingdon, Berks, 1936; (ed) Dark-Age Britain, 1956; The Phoenicians, 1962, rev. edns 1971, 1980; (jtly) Masterpieces of Glass, British Museum, 1968; Catalogue of Greek and Roman Glass in the British Museum, I, 1981; (jtly) Glass of the Caesars (an exhibition of Master Works of Roman Glass shown in Corning, NY, London, Cologne and Rome, 1987–88), 1987; numerous articles on archæology and museums. *Address:* 12 St Andrew's Mansions, Dorset Street, W1H 3FD. *T:* 071–935 5121. *Club:* Athenæum.

HARDEN, Major James Richard Edwards, OBE 1983; DSO; MC; farmer; *b* 12 Dec. 1916; *s* of late Major J. E. Harden, DL, JP, Royal Irish Fusiliers, and L. G. C. Harden; *m* 1948, Ursula Joyce, *y d* of G. M. Strutt, Newhouse, Terling, Chelmsford, Essex; one *s* two *d*. *Educ:* Oriel House, St Asaph; Bedford Sch.; Sandhurst. Commissioned into Royal Tank Regt 1937; retired on agricultural release, 1947; MP (UU) for County Armagh, 1948–54. JP County Armagh, 1956, Cærnarvonshire, later Gwynedd, 1971–82; DL, Co. Armagh, 1946, Cærnarvonshire, later Gwynedd, 1968; High Sheriff, Cærnarvonshire, 1971–72. *Recreations:* shooting, fishing. *Address:* Hendy, Nanhoran, Pwllheli, Gwynedd LL53 8DL. *T:* Botwnnog (075883) 432.

HARDERS, Sir Clarence Waldemar, Kt 1977; OBE 1969; Partner, Freehill, Hollingdale and Page, Canberra, ACT, since 1980; *b* Murtoa, 1 March 1915; *s* of E. W. Harders, Dimboola, Vic; *m* 1947, Gladys, *d* of E. Treasure; one *s* two *d*. *Educ:* Concordia Coll., Unley, S Australia; Adelaide Univ. (LLB). Joined Dept of the Attorney-General, 1947; Dep. Sec., 1965–70; Sec., 1970–79; Legal Adviser, Dept of Foreign Affairs, 1979–80. *Address:* c/o Freehill, Hollingdale and Page, London Court, 13 London Circuit, Canberra City, ACT 2601, Australia; 43 Stonehaven Crescent, Deakin, ACT 2600, Australia. *Clubs:* Commonwealth, National Press, Canberra Bowling (Canberra); Royal Canberra Golf.

HARDIE, Andrew Rutherford; QC (Scot.) 1985; Treasurer, Faculty of Advocates, since 1989; *b* 8 Jan. 1946; *s* of Andrew Rutherford Hardie and Elizabeth Currie Lowe; *m* 1971, Catherine Storrar Elgin; two *s* one *d*. *Educ:* St Mungo's Primary Sch., Alloa; St Modan's High Sch., Stirling; Edinburgh Univ. (MA, LLB Hons). Enrolled Solicitor, 1971; Mem., Faculty of Advocates, 1973; Advocate Depute, 1979–83. *Address:* 27 Hermitage Gardens, Edinburgh EH10 6AZ. *T:* 031–447 2917. *Clubs:* Caledonian, Murrayfield Golf (Edinburgh).

HARDIE, Ven. Archibald George; Archdeacon of West Cumberland and Hon. Canon of Carlisle Cathedral, 1971–79; also Vicar of Haile, 1970–79; *b* 19 Dec. 1908; *s* of late Archbishop Hardie and late Mrs Hardie; *m* 1936, Rosalie Sheelagh Hamilton (*née* Jacob); three *s* one *d*. *Educ:* St Lawrence Coll., Ramsgate; Trinity Coll., Cambridge (MA); Westcott House, Cambridge. Hockey Blue, Cambridge, 1931–32. Curate of All Hallows, Lombard St, EC, and London Sec. of Student Christian Movement, 1934–36; Chaplain,

Repton Sch., 1936–38; Vicar of St Alban, Golders Green, London, NW11, 1938–44; OCF. Rector of Hexham Abbey, 1944–63; Vicar and Rural Dean of Halifax, 1963–71, and Hon. Canon of Wakefield Cathedral. *Recreations:* tilling the soil and chewing the cud. *Address:* Grasslees Cottage, Swindon, Sharperton, Morpeth, Northumberland.

HARDIE, Sir Charles (Edgar Mathewes), Kt 1970; CBE 1963 (OBE 1943); chartered accountant; Partner in Dixon, Wilson and Co., 1934–81, Senior Partner, 1975–81; *b* 10 March 1910; *s* of Dr C. F. and Mrs R. F. Hardie (*née* Moore), Barnet, Herts; *m* 1st, 1937, Dorothy Jean (*née* Hobson) (*d* 1965); one *s* three *d*; 2nd, 1966, Mrs Angela Richli, *widow* of Raymond Paul Richli; 3rd, 1975, Rosemary Margaret Harwood. *Educ:* Aldenham Sch. Qualified as Chartered Accountant, 1932; practised in London, 1934–81. War Service, 1939–45 (Col). Chairman: BOAC, 1969–70 (Dir, 1964–70); Metropolitan Estate & Property Corp., 1964–71; White Fish Authority, 1967–73; Fitch Lovell plc, 1970–77; Director: British American and General Trust plc, 1961–85; British Printing Corp. plc, 1965–82 (Chm., 1969–76); Royal Bank of Canada, 1969–81; Mann Egerton & Co. Ltd, 1959–80; Trusthouse Forte plc, 1970– (Dep. Chm., 1983–); Hill Samuel Group plc, 1970–77. Dep. Chm., NAAFI, 1953–72; Member: BEA Board, 1968–70; Council, Inst. of Directors, 1966–80. Liveryman, Fishmongers' Co., 1968. Legion of Merit, USA, 1944. *Recreation:* bridge. *Address:* Pitt House, 25 New Street, Henley-on-Thames, Oxon RG9 2BP. *T:* Henley-on-Thames (0491) 577944.

See also C. J. M. Hardie.

HARDIE, (Charles) Jeremy (Mawdesley), CBE 1983; Director, John Swire & Sons Ltd, since 1982; *b* 9 June 1938; *s* of Sir Charles Hardie, *qv*; *m* 1st, 1962, Susan Chamberlain (marr. diss. 1976); two *s* two *d*; 2nd, 1978, Xandra, Countess of Gowrie, *d* of late Col R. A. G. Bingley, CVO, DSO, OBE; one *d*. *Educ:* Winchester Coll.; New Coll., Oxford (2nd Cl. Hon. Mods, 1st Cl. Lit. Hum.); Nuffield Coll., Oxford (BPhil Econs). ACA 1965, Peat, Marwick, Mitchell & Co.; Nuffield Coll., Oxford, 1966–67; Jun. Res. Fellow, Trinity Coll., Oxford, 1967–68; Fellow and Tutor in Econs, Keble Coll., Oxford, 1968–75. Partner, Dixon Wilson & Co., 1975–82. Chairman: Nat. Provident Instn, 1980–89 (Dir, 1972–89, Dep. Chm., 1977); Alexander Syndicate Management Ltd, 1982–; Radio Broadland Ltd, 1983–85 (Dir, 1983–90); David Mann Underwriting Agency Ltd, 1983–; Director: Alexanders Discount Co. Ltd, 1978–87 (Dep. Chm., 1981–84; Chm., 1984–86); Amdahl (UK) Ltd, 1983–86; Mercantile House Holdings Ltd, 1984–87; Additional Underwriting Agencies (No 3) Ltd, 1985–90; Alexanders Laing & Cruickshank Gilts Ltd, 1986–87 (Chm., 1986); W. H. Smith Gp, 1988–; Northdoor Hldgs, 1989–. Chm., Centre for Economic Policy Res., 1984–89; Treas., REconS, 1987–; Dep. Chm., NAAFI, 1986– (Dir, 1981–). Member: Monopolies and Mergers Commn, 1976–83 (Dep. Chm., 1980–83); Council, Oxford Centre for Management Studies, 1978–85; Hammersmith Health Authority, 1982–83; Arts Council of GB, 1984–86; Peacock Cttee on Financing of BBC, 1985–86. Contested Norwich South, (SDP) 1983, (SDP/Alliance) 1987. Trustee: Esmée Fairbairn Charitable Trust, 1972–; Butler Trust, 1985–. *Recreations:* sailing, skiing. *Address:* The Old Rectory, Metton, Norwich NR11 8QX. *T:* Cromer (0263) 761765.

HARDIE, Colin Graham; Official Fellow and Tutor in Classics, Magdalen College, Oxford, 1936–73; Public Orator of Oxford University, 1967–73; *b* 16 Feb. 1906; 3rd *s* of William Ross Hardie, Fellow of Balliol Coll. and Prof. of Humanity in Edinburgh Univ., and Isabella Watt Stevenson; *m* 1940, Christian Viola Mary Lucas; two *s*. *Educ:* Edinburgh Acad.; Balliol Coll., Oxford (Warner Exhibitioner and Hon. Scholar); 1st class Classical Moderations, 1926, and Lit Hum BA, 1928; MA, 1931; Craven Scholar, 1925; Ireland Scholar, 1925; Hertford Scholar, 1926; Gaisford Prize for Greek Prose, 1927; Junior Research Fellow of Balliol, 1928–29; Fellow and Classical Tutor, 1930–33; Dir of the British Sch. at Rome, 1933–36. Hon. Prof. of Ancient Lit., RA, 1971–90. *Publications:* Vitae Vergilianae antiquae, 1954; papers on Virgil and Dante. *Recreation:* gardening. *Address:* Rackham Cottage, Greatham, Pulborough, Sussex RH20 2ES. *T:* Pulborough (0789) 873170.

HARDIE, Brig. Donald David Graeme, TD 1968; JP; FPRI; Lord-Lieutenant, Strathclyde Region (Districts of Dumbarton, Clydebank, Bearsden and Milngavie, Strathkelvin, Cumbernauld and Kilsyth), since 1990; Director: Hardie Polymers, since 1976; Hardie Polymers (England), since 1989; Ronaash, since 1988; *b* 23 Jan. 1936; *m* 1961, Rosalind Allan Ker; two *s*. *Educ:* Larchfield, Blairmore and Merchiston Castle Schools. U.T.R. Management Trainee, 1956–59; F. W. Allen & Ker, 1960–61; J. & G. Hardie & Co., 1961–81; Gilbert Plastics, 1973–76. Member: Erskine Hosp. Exec. Cttee; Membership Cttee, Council, PRI. Commissioned 41st Field Regt RA, 1955; Battery Comdr, 277 (Argyll & Sutherland Highlanders) Regt, RA TA, 1966; CO GSV OTC, 1973; TA Colonel: Lowlands, 1976; DES, 1980; Scotland, 1985; ACF Brig. Scotland, 1987; Vice-Chm., RA Council for Scotland; Vice-Pres., ACFA Scotland. JP Dumbarton, 1990. *Recreations:* ski-ing, sailing, shooting, fishing. *Address:* Woodend Lodge, Wardshill, Gartocharn, Dunbartonshire G83 8SB. *T:* Drymen (0360) 60456. *Club:* Royal Northern and Clyde Yacht.

HARDIE, Sir Douglas (Fleming), Kt 1990; CBE 1979; JP; Chairman: Edward Parker & Co. Ltd, since 1960 (Managing Director, 1960–90); Grampian Television Plc, since 1989 (Director, since 1984); Deputy Chairman, Scottish Development Agency, since 1978; *b* 26 May 1923; *s* of late James Dunbar Hardie, JP, and Frances Mary (*née* Fleming); *m* 1945, Dorothy Alice Warner; two *s* one *d*. *Educ:* Arnhall & Seafield House Prep. Schs; Trinity Coll., Glenalmond, Perthshire. Trooper, 58 Trng Regt, RAC, Bovington, 1941; commnd RMA, Sandhurst, 1942; 1st Fife and Forfar Yeomanry, NW Europe, 1942–46 (despatches); demobilised rank of Major. Dir 1964–84, Chm. 1984–85, H. & A. Scott (Holdings) Ltd; Chm., A. G. Scott (Textiles) Ltd, 1985–88; Director: Dayco Rubber (UK) Ltd, 1956–86; Clydesdale Bank, 1981–; Alliance Trust, 1982–; Second Alliance Trust, 1982–. Chm., CBI Scotland, 1976–78; Bd Mem., N of Scotland Hydro Elec. Bd, 1977–83; Mem., Scottish Econ. Council, 1977–91; Dir, Prince's Scottish Youth Business Trust, 1988–. Mem. Council, Winston Churchill Meml Trust, 1985–. Deacon Convener, Nine Incorporated Trades (Dundee), 1951–54. FRSA 1988; CBIM 1990. JP Dundee, 1970. *Recreations:* golf, fishing. *Address:* 6 Norwood Terrace, Dundee DD2 1PB. *T:* Dundee (0382) 69107. *Clubs:* Caledonian; Royal & Ancient Golf (St Andrews); Blairgowrie Golf; Panmure Golf (Barry).

HARDIE, Jeremy; *see* Hardie, C. J. M.

HARDIE, Miles Clayton, OBE 1988; Director General, International Hospital Federation, 1975–87; *b* 27 Feb. 1924; *s* of late Frederick Hardie and Estelle (*née* Clarke); *m* 1st, 1949, Pauline (marr. diss. 1974), *d* of late Sir Wilfrid Le Gros Clark, FRS; two *s*; 2nd, 1974, Melissa (marr. diss. 1984), *d* of late James Witcher, Houston, Texas; 3rd, 1985, Elizabeth, *d* of late Dudley Ash, *widow* of H. Spencer Smith. *Educ:* Charterhouse; Oriel Coll., Oxford (MA). Served War, RAF, 1943–46. Admin. Asst, Hosp. for Sick Children, London, 1949–51; Sec., Victoria Hosp. for Children, 1951–55; Sec., Bahrain Govt Med. Dept, 1956–58; joined staff of King Edward's Hosp. Fund for London, 1958, Dep. Dir, King's Fund Centre, 1963–66, Dir, 1966–75. Hon. Sec., British Hosps Export Council, later British Health-Care Export Council, 1964–67, Mem. Council, 1967–75, 1987–; Mem. Council, Nat. Assoc. of Leagues of Hosp. Friends, 1970–75; Member: Adv. Council, Nat. Corp. Care of Old People, 1973–76; Council of Management, MIND/Nat. Assoc. for Mental Health, 1967–86; Man. Cttee of Spinal Injuries Assoc., 1975–79; Bd of Governors, Volunteer Centre, 1977–80; Council, Appropriate Health Resources and Technologies Action Gp, 1977–89. Adviser to WHO, 1978– (WHO Health for All by the year 2000 Medal, 1987). Hon. Member: Amer. Hosp. Assoc., 1983–; Polish Hosp. Assoc., 1985–. Mem., Ct of Assistants, Salters' Co., 1969–79. *Recreations:* gardening, walking. *Address:* Tallow Cottage, Fishers Lane, Charlbury, Oxon OX7 3RX. *T:* Charlbury (0608) 810088.

HARDING, family name of **Baron Harding of Petherton.**

HARDING OF PETHERTON, 2nd Baron *cr* 1958, of Nether Compton; **John Charles Harding;** farmer, 1968–91; *b* 12 Feb. 1928; *s* of Field Marshal 1st Baron Harding of Petherton, GCB, CBE, DSO, MC, and Mary Gertrude Mabel (*d* 1983), *er d* of late Joseph Wilson Rooke, JP; *S* father, 1989; *m* 1966, Harriet, *d* of Maj.-Gen. James Francis Hare, CB, DSO; two *s* one *d*. *Educ:* Marlborough College; Worcester Coll., Oxford (BA). National Service, 1945–48; 2nd Lieut, 11th Hussars (PAO), 1947; demobilised, 1948; Oxford Univ., 1948–51; Regular Commn, 11th Hussars (PAO), 1953; retired from Army, 1968. *Recreations:* hunting, racing. *Heir: s* Hon. William Allan John Harding, *b* 5 July 1969. *Address:* Barrymore Farm House, Huish Episcopi, Langport, Somerset TA10 9EZ *T:* Langport (0458) 250416. *Club:* Cavalry and Guards.

HARDING, Prof. Anita Elizabeth, MD; FRCP; Professor of Clinical Neurology, Institute of Neurology, University of London, since 1990 (Reader, 1987–90); *b* 17 Sept. 1952; *d* of George Alfred Harding and Jean Luton Harding; *m* 1977, Peter Kynaston Thomas. *Educ:* King Edward VI High Sch. for Girls, Birmingham; Royal Free Hosp. Sch. of Medicine, London (MB, BS 1975); MD London, 1981. LRCP 1975, MRCP 1977, FRCP 1989; MRCS 1975. House Officer and Registrar posts at Radcliffe Infirmary, Oxford, and at Royal Free, Westminster, Middlesex and National Hospitals, London, 1975–82; Lectr and Sen. Lectr in Neurology, RPMS and Inst. of Neurol., London, 1983–87. *Publications:* The Hereditary Ataxias and Related Disorders, 1984; (ed) The Molecular Biology of Neurological Disease, 1988; papers on neurogenetics. *Recreations:* music (eclectic), dining, ski-ing. *Address:* Institute of Neurology, Queen Square, WC1N 3BG. *T:* 071–837 3611.

HARDING, Sir Christopher George Francis, Kt 1991; Chairman, British Nuclear Fuels, since 1986 (Director, since 1984); Managing Director, since 1974, and Vice Chairman, since 1991, Hanson Transport Group; *b* 17 Oct. 1939; *s* of Frank Harding and Phyllis Rachel Pledger (*née* Wise); *m* 1st, 1963, Susan Lilian Berry (marr. diss. 1977); one *s* one *d*; 2nd, 1978, Françoise Marie Baile de Laperrière (marr. diss. 1988). *Educ:* Merchant Taylors' School; Corpus Christi College, Oxford (MA Hons). Imperial Chemical Industries, 1961–69; Hanson PLC, 1969–, Non-Exec. Dir, 1979–. Chm., British Energy Assoc., 1989–. Member: Economic Res. Council, 1988–; Science & Industry Cttee, BAAS, 1989–. Council Member: CBI, 1986–; Business in the Community, 1986–; UK–Japan 2000 GP, 1987–; Prince's Youth Business Trust, 1988–. Rural Enterprise Target Team, 1989–; Council for Industry and Higher Educn, 1990–. Gov., World Energy Forum, 1989–. Dir, North West Business Leadership Team Ltd, 1990–. Member: Adv. Bd, Univ. of Bradford Management Centre, 1981–; Court, UMIST, 1987–. FRSA 1987; CBIM 1988. Freeman, City of London, 1965; Liveryman, Merchant Taylors' Co., 1986. Hon. Fellow, Huddersfield Poly., 1990; Hon. FCGI 1990. *Recreations:* theatre, music, travel, tennis, pocillovy. *Address:* c/o BNFL, 65 Buckingham Gate, SW1E 6AP. *T:* 071–222 9717. *Clubs:* Brooks's; Huddersfield Borough.

HARDING, Prof. Dennis William, MA, DPhil; FRSE; Abercromby Professor of Archaeology, since 1977, and Vice-Principal, since 1988, University of Edinburgh (Dean, Faculty of Arts, 1983–86); *b* 11 April 1940; *s* of Charles Royston Harding and Marjorie Doris Harding. *Educ:* Keble Coll., Oxford (BA, MA, DPhil). Assistant Keeper, Dept of Antiquities, Ashmolean Museum, Oxford, 1965–66; Lecturer in Celtic Archaeology, 1966, Sen. Lectr, 1975–77, Univ. of Durham. Member: Board of Trustees, National Museum of Antiquities of Scotland, 1977–85; Ancient Monuments Board for Scotland, 1979–83. FRSE 1986. *Publications:* The Iron Age in the Upper Thames Basin, 1972; The Iron Age in Lowland Britain, 1974; (with A. J. Challis) Later Prehistory from the Trent to the Tyne, 1975; ed and contrib., Archaeology in the North: Report of the Northern Archaeological Survey, 1976; ed and contrib., Hillforts: later prehistoric earthworks in Britain and Ireland, 1976; Prehistoric Europe, 1978. *Recreation:* private flying. *Address:* Department of Archaeology, 16–20 George Square, Edinburgh EH8 9JZ. *T:* 031–667 1011. *Club:* Athenæum.

HARDING, Denys Wyatt, MA; Emeritus Professor of Psychology, University of London, since 1968; *b* 13 July 1906; *s* of Clement and Harriet Harding; *m* 1930, Jessie Muriel Ward; no *c*. *Educ:* Lowestoft Secondary Sch.; Emmanuel Coll., Cambridge. Investigator and Mem. of research staff, National Institute of Industrial Psychology, 1928–33; Asst (later Lecturer) in Social Psychology, London Sch. of Economics, 1933–38; Senior Lecturer in Psychology, University of Liverpool, 1938–45 (leave of absence for national service, 1941–44); part-time Lecturer in Psychology, University of Manchester, 1940–41 and 1944–45; Prof. of Psychology, Univ. of London, at Bedford Coll., 1945–68. Clark Lectr, Trinity Coll., Cambridge, 1971–72. Hon. Gen. Sec., British Psychological Soc., 1944–48. Mem. of editorial board of Scrutiny, a Quarterly Review, 1933–47. Editor, British Journal of Psychology (Gen. Section) 1948–54. *Publications:* The Impulse to Dominate, 1941; Social Psychology and Individual Values, 1953; Experience into Words: Essays on Poetry, 1963; Words into Rhythm, 1976; ed (with Gordon Bottomley) The Complete Works of Isaac Rosenberg, 1937; translated (with Erik Mesterton) Guest of Reality, by Pär Lagerkvist, 1936; various papers on psychology and literary criticism. *Address:* Ashbocking Old Vicarage, near Ipswich, IP6 9LG. *T:* Helmingham (0473) 890347.

HARDING, Derek William; Executive Secretary, Royal Statistical Society, since 1986; *b* 16 Dec. 1930; *o s* of late William Arthur Harding; *m* 1954, Daphne Sheila, *yr d* of late Reginald Ernest Cooke; one *s* one *d*. *Educ:* Glendale Grammar Sch., London; Univ. of Bristol (BSc). FInstP, CPhys, FIM, CEng. Develt Engr, Pye Ltd, 1954–56; Sen. Physics Master, Thornbury Grammar Sch., Bristol, 1956–60; Sen. Lectr in Physical Science, St Paul's Coll., Cheltenham, 1960–64; Asst Organiser, Nuffield Foundn Science Teaching Project, 1964–67; joined staff of Instn Metallurgists, 1967, Registrar-Sec., 1969–76. Sec.-Gen., British Computer Soc., 1976–86. *Recreation:* off-shore sailing. *Address:* 16 Exeter Road, N14 5JY. *T:* 081–368 1463. *Clubs:* Athenæum, Cruising Association.

HARDING, Sir (George) William, KCMG 1983 (CMG 1977); CVO 1972; HM Diplomatic Service, retired; Director: Lloyds Merchant Bank Holdings, since 1987; Lloyds Bank Plc, since 1988; *b* 18 Jan. 1927; *s* of late Lt Col G. R. Harding, DSO, MBE, and Grace Henley (*née* Darby); *m* 1955, Sheila Margaret Ormond Riddel; four *s*. *Educ:* Aldenham; St John's College, Cambridge. Royal Marines, 1945–48. Entered HM Foreign Service, 1950; served (other than in London) in Singapore, 1951–52; Burma, 1952–55; Paris, 1956–59; Santo Domingo, 1960–63; Mexico City, 1967–70; Paris, 1970–74; Ambassador to Peru, 1977–79; Asst Under-Sec. of State, FCO, 1979–81; Ambassador to

Brazil, 1981–84; Dep. Under-Sec. of State, FCO, 1984–86. Chairman: First Spanish Investment Trust, 1987–; Thai-Euro Fund, 1988–. Chairman: Anglo-Peruvian Soc., 1987–89; Brazilian Chamber of Commerce in Britain, 1988–91. Member, Council: RGS, 1988–; RIIA, 1988–. *Address:* c/o Lloyds Bank, 71 Lombard Street, EC3P 3BS. *Clubs:* Garrick, Beefsteak; Leander.

HARDING, Hugh Alastair, CMG 1958; Under-Secretary, Department of Education and Science, 1967–77; *b* 4 May 1917; 2nd *s* of late Roland Charles Harding, Norton-le-Moors, Staffordshire; *m* 1943, Florence Esnouf; one *s* one *d. Educ:* Rugby; Trinity Coll., Cambridge. Colonial Office, 1939; Asst Sec., 1950; Asst Sec., Treasury, 1961; Under-Sec., Treasury, 1962–64; Minister, UK Delegation to OECD, 1964–67. Served War of 1939–45, Army (Captain RA). *Address:* c/o National Westminster Bank, Town Hall Buildings, Tunstall, Stoke-on-Trent, Staffs.

HARDING, John Philip, PhD; Keeper of Zoology, British Museum (Natural History), 1954–71, retired; *b* 12 Nov. 1911; *s* of Philip William and Eleanor Harding, Rondebosch, Cape Town; *m* 1937, Sidnie Manton, PhD, ScD, FRS (*d* 1979); one *s* one *d. Educ:* Torquay; University Coll., Exeter; University of Cincinnati; King's Coll., Cambridge. Ministry of Agriculture and Fisheries, 1936–37; British Museum (Natural History), 1937–71. Vis. Prof., Westfield Coll., Univ. of London, 1971–77. *Publications:* scientific papers on Crustacea. *Recreations:* photomicrography, mechanical devices, handicap aids. *Address:* 7 Ashcroft Close, Ringmer, Lewes, East Sussex. *T:* Ringmer (0273) 812385.

HARDING, Air Vice-Marshal Peter John, CBE 1985; AFC 1974; Deputy Chief of Staff (Operations), HQ Allied Air Forces Central Europe, since 1991; *b* 1 June 1940; *s* of John Fitz Harding and Marjorie Clare; *m* 1966, Morwenna Jacquiline St John Grey; two *s. Educ:* Solihull School. Joined RAF, 1960; Pilot, 249 Sqn, Cyprus, 1962–65; RAF Coll., 1965–70; Cyprus, 1971–72; Waddington, 1972–74; RNC, 1974; RAF Germany, 1974–76; OC Pilot Buccaneers Sqns, 1977–80; Directing Staff, RAF Staff Coll., 1981; Station Comdr, Honington, 1982–84; RCDS 1985; Dir Nuclear Systems, MoD, 1986–88; Dep. C-in-C, RAF Germany, 1989–91. ADC to the Queen, 1982–84. *Recreations:* cricket, golf, tennis, gardening, family, philately. *Address:* c/o Lloyds Bank, 7 Pall Mall, SW1Y 5NA. *Clubs:* Royal Air Force, Innominate; Royal Cinque Ports (Deal).

HARDING, Air Chief Marshal Sir Peter (Robin), GCB 1988 (KCB 1983; CB 1980); CBIM; FRAeS 1983; Chief of the Air Staff, since 1988; Air ADC to the Queen, since 1988; *b* 2 Dec. 1933; *s* of Peter Harding and Elizabeth Clear; *m* 1955, Sheila Rosemary May; three *s* one *d. Educ:* Chingford High Sch. Joined RAF, 1952; Pilot, 12 Sqdn, 1954–57; QFI and Flt Comdr, RAF Coll., Cranwell, 1957–60; Pilot, 1 Sqdn, RAAF, 1960–62; sc 1963; Air Secretary's Dept, MoD, 1964–66; OC, 18 Sqdn, Gutersloh and Acklington, 1966–69; jssc, Latimer, 1969–70; Defence Policy Staff, MoD, 1970–71; Director, Air Staff, Briefing, MoD, 1971–74; Station Comdr, RAF Brüggen, 1974–76; Dir of Defence Policy, MoD, 1976–78; Asst Chief of Staff (Plans and Policy), SHAPE, 1978–80; AOC No 11 Group, 1981–82; VCAS, 1982–84; VCDS, 1985; AOC-in-C, RAF Strike Comd, and C-in-C, UK Air Forces, 1985–88. ADC to the Queen, 1975. CBIM 1984; FRSA 1988. Liveryman, GAPAN, 1989. Mem. Council, Winston Churchill Meml Trust, 1990–. Gov., Charterhouse Hosp., 1990. Hon. DSc Cranfield, 1990. *Publications:* articles for professional jls, magazines and books. *Recreations:* tennis, pianoforte, bridge, birdwatching, shooting (normally separately). *Address:* c/o Lloyds Bank plc, 6 Pall Mall, SW1. *Clubs:* Royal Air Force, Colonels (Founder Mem.).

HARDING, Peter Thomas; Director General, Petroleum Engineering Division, Department of Energy, 1989–91; *b* 5 Dec. 1930; *s* of late James Alfred Harding and Catherine Frances Harding; *m* 1954, Joyce Holmes; two *s* two *d. Educ:* Ealing Grammar School. Exec. Officer, Min. of Supply, 1949; Principal, Min. of Technology, 1967; Asst Sec., DTI, 1973, Dept of Energy, 1974, Under Sec. (Grade 3), 1989. *Recreations:* music, watching cricket, gardening. *Address:* Pookwell, Ridgway, Pyrford, Woking, Surrey GU22 8PW. *T:* Byfleet (0932) 346766.

HARDING, Roger John, CMG 1986; Director General, Marketing, Ministry of Defence, since 1988; *b* 7 April 1935; *s* of Charles William Harding and Lilian Mabel (*née* Trowbridge); *m* 1960, June Elizabeth Tidy; four *d. Educ:* Price's Sch., Fareham, Hants; Southern Grammar Sch., Portsmouth, Hants. Board of Trade, 1954–74; War Office, then Min. of Defence, 1974–: Head of Defence Secretariat 8, 1979–82; Counsellor, Defence Supply, 1982–86, Minister, Defence Material, 1986–88, Washington. *Recreations:* soccer, cricket, golf, following fortunes of Portsmouth FC. *Club:* St John's Village (Woking).

HARDING, Air Vice-Marshal Ross Philip, CBE 1968; RAF retired; *b* 22 Jan. 1921; *s* of P. J. Harding, Salisbury; *m* 1948, Laurie Joy Gardner; three *s. Educ:* Bishop Wordsworth Sch., Salisbury; St Edmund Hall, Oxford (MA). No 41 Sqdn Fighter Comd and 2 TAF, 1943–45; RAF Staff Coll., Andover, 1951; Air Min. (ACAS Ops), 1952–54; CO No 96 Sqdn, Germany, 1955–58; Directing Staff, RAF Staff Coll., Andover, 1958–60; CO Oxford Univ. Air Sqdn, 1960–62; Dep. Chief, British Mil. Mission, Berlin, 1963–65; CO RAF Valley, 1965–68; Senior Directing Staff (Air), Jt Services Staff Coll., 1968–69; Defence and Air Attaché, Moscow, 1970–72; Dir of Personal Services 1, MoD (Air), 1973; Senior RAF Member, RCDS, 1974–76. Hd of Airwork Services Ltd, Oman, 1976–78. Chm., Civil Service Commn and MoD Selection Bds, 1979–. Specialist Advr to H of C Defence Cttee, 1979–84. *Recreations:* ski-ing, shooting. *Address:* Tally-Ho, 8 Hadrian's Close, Lower Bemerton, Salisbury, Wilts SP2 9NN. *Club:* Royal Air Force.

HARDING, Sir Roy (Pollard), Kt 1985; CBE 1978; education consultant; *b* 3 Jan. 1924; *s* of W. F. N. Harding, BEM and P. E. Harding; *m* 1948, Audrey Beryl Larkin, JP; two *s* one *d. Educ:* Liskeard Grammar Sch.; King's Coll., Univ. of London (BSc; AKC; DPA). FIMA, FZS. Ballistics research, schools and college teaching, to 1950; Educn Admin, Wilts, Bucks, Herts, Leics, to 1960; Dep. Chief Educn Officer, 1960–66, Chief Educn Officer, 1966–84, Bucks. Adviser: County Councils Assoc., 1972–74; Assoc. of County Councils, 1973–84 (incl. Finance, 1978–81, Policy, 1981–84); Council of Local Educn Authorities, 1975–84. Member: Printing and Publishing Ind. Trng Bd, 1970–72; BBC Further Educn Adv. Council, 1970–75; Burnham Cttee, 1972–77; Sec. of State's Vis. Cttee, Cranfield Inst. of Technology, 1976–81; DES/Local Authority Expenditure Steering Gp, Educn, 1976–84; Councils and Educnl Press (Longmans) Editorial Adv. Panel, 1977–86; Teaching of Mathematics in Schools (Cockcroft) Cttee, 1978–82; Educn Management Inf. Exchange, 1981–89; Board, Nat. Adv. Body for Higher Educn, 1982–84; A Level (Higginson) Cttee, 1987–88; AEC Trust, 1989–; CBI Educn Foundn, 1990–; various univ. cttees, incl. Open Univ. Council, 1985–; Chairman: County Educn Officers' Soc., 1978–79 (Sec., 1973–76); Educn Policy Interchange Cttee, 1979–89; Open Univ. INSET Sector Programme Bd, 1983–87; Further Educn Staff Coll. Governing Body, 1986–; Vice-Chm., Secondary Exams Council, 1983–86. President: Soc. of Educn Officers, 1977–78 (Mem. Exec., 1974–79; Chm. Internat. Cttee, 1980–83; Gen. Sec., 1984–89); British Educnl Equipment Assoc., 1980–83; Educn Sect., BAAS, 1986–87; Nat. Inst. Adult Continuing Educn, 1988–; IMA, 1990–91 (Council, 1983–88; Vice-Pres., 1986–88). Chm., EMIS Ltd, 1988–. Centenary Fellow, Thames Polytechnic, 1990. DUniv Open, 1985. Wappenteller, Rheinland/Pfalz, Germany, 1978. Gold Cross of Merit, Polish Govt in Exile, 1984. *Publications:* chapters on educnl matters, miscellaneous contribs to learned jls. *Recreations:* travel, music. *Address:* 27 King Edward Avenue, Aylesbury, Bucks HP21 7JE. *T:* Aylesbury (0296) 23006. *Clubs:* Royal Over-Seas League; Rotary.

HARDING, Wilfrid Gerald, CBE 1978; FRCP, FFCM, DPH; Area Medical Officer, Camden and Islington Area Health Authority (Teaching), 1974–79; Hon. Consultant in Community Medicine, University College Hospital, London, 1971–79; *b* 17 March 1915; *s* of late Dr *hc* Ludwig Ernst Emil Hoffman and Marie Minna Eugenie (*née* Weisbach); *m* 1st, 1938, Britta Charlotta Haraldsdotter, Malmberg (marr. diss. 1970); three *s*; 2nd, 1973, Hilary Maxwell. *Educ:* Französisches Gymnasium, Berlin; Süddeutsches Landerziehungsheim, Schondorf, Bavaria; Woodbrooke Coll., Selly Oak, Birmingham; University Coll. London; University Coll. Hosp. Med. Sch. (interned twice in 1939 and 1940). MRCS, LRCP 1941; DPH London 1949; MRCP 1968; FFCM 1972 (Hon. FFCM 1986); FRCP 1972. Ho. Phys. and Ho. Surg., UCH, 1941–42; Asst MOH, City of Oxford, 1942–43; RAMC, 1943–47, Field Units in NW Europe, 1 Corps Staff and Mil. Govt, Lt-Col (Hygiene Specialist). In charge of health services, Ruhr Dist of Germany, CCG, 1947–48; LSHTM, 1948–49; career posts in London public health service, 1949–64; MOH, London Bor. of Camden, and Principal Sch. MO, ILEA, 1965–74. Hon. Lectr, Dept of Sociol., Bedford Coll., London Univ., 1969–77; Civil Consultant in Community Medicine to RAF, 1974–78. Chm. of Council, Soc. of MOH, 1966–71 (Pres. 1971–72); Chm., Prov. Bd of FCM, Royal Colls of Physicians of UK, 1971–72 (Vice-Pres., 1972–75, Pres., 1975–78). Member: Central Health Services Council and Standing Med. Adv. Cttee, 1966–71 and 1975–78; Standing Mental Health Adv. Cttee, 1966–71; Bd of Studies in Preventive Med. and Public Health, Univ. of London, 1963–79; Council, UCH Med. Sch., 1965–78; Bd of Management, LSHTM, 1968–82; Council for Educn and Trng of Health Visitors, 1965–77; Council, ASH, 1970–73 and 1978–82; Public Health Laboratory Service Bd, 1972–83. Armed Services Med. Adv. Bd, 1975–78; GMC, 1979–84; Vice-Chm., Dartford and Gravesham CHC, 1984–89. Chm., DHSS Working Gp on Primary Health Team, 1978–80 (reported 1981). Hon. Advr, Office of Health Econs, 1977–. Councillor, Sevenoaks DC, 1979–; Chm., Farningham Parish Council, 1983–89. Broadcasts on public health and community medicine. *Publications:* papers on public health and community med. in medical books and jls; Parkes Centenary Meml Lecture (Community, Health and Service), 1976. *Recreations:* watching river birds, music, wine. *Address:* Bridge Cottage, High Street, Farningham, Dartford DA4 0DW. *T:* Farningham (0322) 862733. *Club:* Athenæum.

HARDING, Sir William; *see* Harding, Sir G. W.

HARDINGE, family name of **Viscount Hardinge** and **Baron Hardinge of Penshurst.**

HARDINGE, 6th Viscount *cr* 1846, of Lahore and of King's Newton, Derbyshire; **Charles Henry Nicholas Hardinge;** Manager, Private Banking, for Royal Bank of Canada in London; *b* 25 Aug. 1956; *s* of 5th Viscount Hardinge and of Zoë Anne, *d* of Hon. Hartland de Montarville Molson, OBE, Montreal; *S* father, 1984; *m* 1985, Julie Therese Sillett, *d* of Joan Sillett of Sydney, Australia; two *d* one step *s. Heir: b* Hon. Andrew Hartland Hardinge, *b* 7 Jan. 1960. *Address:* 12 Streathbourne Road, SW17.

HARDINGE OF PENSHURST, 3rd Baron *cr* 1910; **George Edward Charles Hardinge;** *b* 31 Oct. 1921; *o s* of 2nd Baron Hardinge of Penshurst, PC, GCB, GCVO, MC, and Helen Mary Cecil (*d* 1979); *S* father, 1960; *m* 1st, 1944, Janet Christine Goschen (marr. diss. 1962, she *d* 1970), *d* of late Lt-Col F. C. C. Balfour, CIE, CVO, CBE, MC; three *s*; 2nd, 1966, Margaret Trezise; one *s*, and one step-*s*, now adopted. *Educ:* Eton; Royal Naval College, Dartmouth. RN 1940–47; subsequently in publishing; Sen. Editor: Collins; Longmans; Macmillan (London) Ltd, 1968–86 (also dir); Founder and Editor, Winter's Crime series. *Publication:* An Incompleat Angler, 1976. *Recreations:* reading, fishing. *Heir: s* Hon. Julian Alexander Hardinge, *b* 23 Aug. 1945. *Address:* Bracken Hill, 10 Penland Road, Bexhill-on-Sea, East Sussex. *T:* Bexhill (0424) 211866. *Club:* Brooks's.
See also Lt-Col Sir J. F. D. Johnston, Sir J. A. J. Murray.

HARDINGE, Sir Robert Arnold, 7th Bt *cr* 1801; *b* 19 Dec. 1914; *s* of Sir Robert Hardinge, 6th Bt and Emma Vera, *d* of Charles Arnold; *S* father, 1973. *Heir: kinsman* Viscount Hardinge, *qv.*

HARDINGHAM, Sir Robert (Ernest), Kt 1969; CMG 1953; OBE 1947; Chief Executive, Air Registration Board, 1947–68; *b* 16 Dec. 1903; *s* of late Robert Henry Hardingham and Florence Elizabeth Hardingham; *m* 1929, I. Everett; one *s* one *d. Educ:* Farnborough; de Havilland Technical Coll. RAE Farnborough, 1918–21; de Havilland Aircraft Co., 1921–34; Air Min., 1934–37; Air Registration Board, 1937–68. Pres., Soc. of Licenced Aircraft Engineers and Technologists, 1968–72. Liveryman, Guild of Air Pilots and Navigators, 1966. CEng; FRAeS 1949 (Empire and Commonwealth Lecturer, 1952). Wakefield Gold Medal, RAeS, 1965; Silver Medal, Royal Aero Club, 1965. Cavaliere Ordino Merito della Repubblica Italiana. *Publications:* many technical papers. *Recreation:* golf. *Address:* Wortheal House, Southam Lane, Cheltenham GL52 3NY. *T:* Cheltenham (0242) 236765. *Club:* Naval and Military.

HARDMAN, Sir Henry, KCB 1962 (CB 1956); *b* 15 Dec. 1905; *s* of late Harry Hardman and Bertha Hardman; *m* 1937, Helen Diana, *d* of late Robert Carr Bosanquet and Ellen Sophia Bosanquet; one *s* two *d. Educ:* Manchester Central High Sch.; University of Manchester. Lecturer for Workers' Educational Association, 1929–34; Economics Tutor, University of Leeds, 1934–45; joined Ministry of Food, 1940; Deputy Head, British Food Mission to N America, 1946–48; Under-Sec., Ministry of Food, 1948–53; Minister, UK Permanent Delegation, Paris, 1953–54; Dep. Sec., Ministry of Agriculture, Fisheries and Food, 1955–60; Dep. Sec., Ministry of Aviation, 1960; Permanent Sec., 1961–63: Permanent Sec., Ministry of Defence, 1963–64; Permanent Under Sec. of State, Min. of Defence, 1964–66. Mem., Monopolies Commn, 1967–70 (Dep. Chm., 1967–68); Chm., Cttee of enquiry into the Post Office pay dispute, 1971; Consultant to CSD on dispersal of govt work from London, 1971–73 (report published, 1973). Chairman: Covent Garden Mkt Authority, 1967–75; Home-Grown Cereals Authority, 1968–77. Governor and Trustee, Reserve Bank of Rhodesia, 1967–79. Hon. LLD Manchester, 1965. *Address:* 9 Sussex Square, Brighton BN2 1FJ. *T:* Brighton (0273) 688904. *Club:* Reform.

HARDMAN, James Arthur, MBE 1968; HM Diplomatic Service, retired; Member of Secretariat, International Primary Aluminium Institute, since 1988; *b* 12 Sept. 1929; *er s* of late James Sidney Hardman and Rachel Hardman; *m* 1953, Enid Mary Hunter; two *s. Educ:* Manchester Grammar Sch.; Manchester Univ. (BA Hons 1950). FCIS (FCCS 1964). Served in Intelligence Corps, 1951–53; Admiralty, 1953–54. HM Foreign Service, 1954; served: Tehran, 1955; FO, 2nd Sec., 1960; Bonn, 2nd, later 1st, Sec. (Comm.), 1962; Atlanta, Consul, 1967; New York, Consul (Comm.), 1970; FCO, Dep. Dir Diplomatic Service Language Centre, 1972; Consul-Gen., Strasbourg, 1975–79; Consul (Commercial), Düsseldorf, 1979–83; FCO, 1983–85; First Sec. (Commercial), Algiers, 1985–88. *Address:* Gulestan, Apers Avenue, Westfield, Woking, Surrey GU22 9NB. *Club:* Civil Service.

HARDMAN, John Nimrod, FCA; CBIM; Chairman, ASDA Group PLC (formerly ASDA-MFI), 1988–91 (Deputy Chairman, 1986–87; Director, 1984–91); *b* 8 Oct. 1939; *s* of late Harry John Hardman and of Florence Gladys Sybil Anne Hardman (*née* Dolby); *m* 1966, Joan McHugh; one *s* one *d. Educ:* Quarry Bank High Sch., Liverpool; Liverpool

Univ. (BComm Hons). FIGD. Duncan Watson & Short, Chartered Accts, 1962–66; RCA Corp., 1967–69; Finance Dir, Thorn Colour Tubes Ltd, 1969–75; Dir, Europe, Africa and Far East, RCA Corp. Picture Tube Div., 1976–80; Finance Director: Oriel Foods, 1981; ASDA Stores, 1981–84 (Man. Dir, 1984–89). Director: Leeds Develt Corp, 1988–; Yorks Electricity Bd, 1989–. *Recreations:* golf, tennis, shooting, cricket. *Address:* Hillside, Spofforth Hill, Wetherby, Yorks LS22 4SF. *Clubs:* Lord's Taverners'; Liverpool Artists, Royal Liverpool Golf (Liverpool); Pannal Golf (Harrogate).

HARDWICK, Christopher, MD, FRCP; Physician Emeritus, Guy's Hospital, since 1976; *b* 13 Jan. 1911; *s* of Thomas Mold Hardwick and Harriet Taylor; *m* 1938, Joan Dorothy Plummer; two *s. Educ:* Berkhamsted Sch.; Trinity Hall, Cambridge; Middlesex Hospital. MRCS, LRCP 1935; MA (Cambridge) 1937; MD (Cambridge) 1940; FRCP 1947. House Physician, House Surgeon and Med. Registrar, Middlesex Hosp., 1935 and 1938–41; House physician and Registrar, Hosp. for Sick Children, Gt Ormond Street, 1936–38. Wing Comdr, Medical Specialist, RAF Med. Service, 1941–46. Physician, Guy's Hosp., 1946–76. Hon. Vis. Phys., Johns Hopkins Hosp., Baltimore, 1954. Mem. Council, RCP, 1965–68; Mem. Board of Governors, Guy's Hospital, 1967–74. Chm., British Diabetic Assoc., 1974–80. *Publications:* contribs to medical literature. *Recreations:* gardening, reading. *Address:* 8 Sondes Farm, Glebe Road, Dorking, Surrey RH4 3EF.

HARDWICK, Donald, CBE 1980; PhD; Director, Johnson & Firth Brown plc, 1973–89 (Chairman, Steel Division, 1975–85); *b* 1926; *m* 1950, Dorothy Mary Hardwick; two *s. Educ:* Tadcaster Grammar Sch.; Sheffield Univ. (BMet 1st Cl. Hons 1947, Mappin Medal; PhD 1954). FIM. After appointments with English Electric Co., BISRA, and BSA Gp Research Centre, became first C. H. Desch Res. Fellow, Sheffield Univ. Joined Brown Firth Res. Laboratories, 1959; Man. Dir, Firth Brown Ltd, 1974–78; Mem. Bd, Johnson & Firth Brown, on amalgamation with Richard Johnson & Nephew, 1973. Director: Mitchell Somers Gp, 1974–89; Eagle Trust plc, 1987–89. Pres., BISPA, 1977–79. *Recreations:* fell walking, gardening. *Address:* 43 Dore Road, Dore, Sheffield S17 3NA.

HARDWICK, Prof. James Leslie, MSc, PhD, DDS; FDSRCS; Professor of Preventive Dentistry, University of Manchester, 1960–78, now Emeritus; *b* 27 March 1913; *o s* of George Hardwicke and Mary Ann Hardwick; *m* 1954, Eileen Margaret Isobel Gibson; two *s* two *d. Educ:* Rugby Sch.; Birmingham Univ. MDS 1948, PhD 1950, DDS 1984, Birmingham; FDSRCS 1954; MSc 1964. Private and hospital dental practice, 1935–39. Served War of 1939–45, Army Dental Corps. University of Birmingham: Lecturer, 1945–48, Sen. Lecturer in Operative Dental Surgery, 1948–52; Reader in Dental Surgery, 1952–60. *Publications:* editor of and contributor to dental and other scientific journals and textbooks. *Address:* 167 Stanley Road, Cheadle Hulme, Cheshire SK8 6RF. *T:* 061–437 3555.

HARDWICK, Mollie; author; *b* Manchester; *d* of Joseph Greenhalgh and Anne Frances Atkinson; *m* 1961, Michael John Drinkrow Hardwick (*d* 1991); one *s. Educ:* Manchester High Sch. for Girls. Announcer, BBC (Radio) N Region, 1940–45; BBC (Radio) Drama Dept, 1946–62; freelance, 1963–. FRSA 1966. *Publications:* Stories from Dickens, 1968; Emma, Lady Hamilton, 1969; Mrs Dizzy, 1972; Upstairs Downstairs: Sarah's Story, 1973, The Years of Change, 1974, The War to end Wars, 1975, Mrs Bridges' Story, 1975, The World of Upstairs Downstairs, 1976; Alice in Wonderland (play), 1975; Beauty's Daughter, 1976 (Elizabeth Goudge Award for best historical romantic novel of year); The Duchess of Duke Street: The Way Up, 1976, The Golden Years, 1976, The World Keeps Turning, 1977; Charlie is my Darling, 1977; The Atkinson Heritage, 1978; Thomas and Sarah, 1978; Thomas and Sarah: Two for a Spin, 1979; Lovers Meeting, 1979; Sisters in Love, 1979; Dove's Nest, 1980; Willowwood, 1980; Juliet Bravo 1, 1980; Juliet Bravo 2, 1980; Monday's Child, 1981; Calling Juliet Bravo: New Arrivals, 1981; I Remember Love, 1982; The Shakespeare Girl, 1983; By the Sword Divided, 1983; The Merrymaid, 1984; Girl with a Crystal Dove, 1985; Malice Domestic, 1986; Parson's Pleasure, 1987; Uneaseful Death, 1988; Blood Royal, 1988; The Bandersnatch, 1989; Perish in July, 1989; The Dreaming Damozel, 1990; *with Michael Hardwick:* The Jolly Toper, 1961; The Sherlock Holmes Companion, 1962; Sherlock Holmes Investigates, 1963; The Man Who Was Sherlock Holmes, 1964; Four Sherlock Holmes plays, 1964; The Charles Dickens Companion, 1965; The World's Greatest Sea Mysteries, 1967; Writers' Houses: a literary journey in England, 1968; Alfred Deller: A Singularity of Voice, 1968, rev. edn 1980; Charles Dickens As They Saw Him, 1969; The Game's Afoot (Sherlock Holmes Plays), 1969; Plays from Dickens, 1970; Dickens's England, 1970; The Private Life of Sherlock Holmes, 1970; Four More Sherlock Holmes Plays, 1973; The Charles Dickens Encyclopedia, 1973; The Bernard Shaw Companion, 1973; The Charles Dickens Quiz Book, 1974; The Upstairs Downstairs Omnibus, 1975; The Gaslight Boy, 1976; The Hound of the Baskervilles and Other Sherlock Holmes Plays, 1982; numerous plays and scripts for radio and TV; contribs to women's magazines.

HARDWICKE, 10th Earl of, *cr* 1754; **Joseph Philip Sebastian Yorke;** Baron Hardwicke 1733; Viscount Royston 1754; *b* 3 Feb. 1971; *s* of Philip Simon Prospero Rupert Lindley, Viscount Royston (*d* 1973) and Virginia Anne (*d* 1988), *d* of Geoffrey Lyon; *S* grandfather, 1974. *Heir: cousin* Richard Charles John Yorke, *b* 25 July 1916. *Address:* 12 Lansdowne Road, W11.

HARDY; *see* Gathorne-Hardy, family name of Earl of Cranbrook.

HARDY, Alan; Member (C) for Brent North, Greater London Council, 1967–86 (Chairman, Finance and Establishment Committee, 1977–81); *b* 24 March 1932; *s* of late John Robert Hardy and Emily Hardy; *m* 1972, Betty Howe, *d* of late Walter and Hilda Howe. *Educ:* Hookergate Grammar Sch.; Univ. of Manchester; Inst. of Historical Res., Univ. of London (MA). Res. Asst to Sir Lewis Namier, History of Parliament Trust, 1955–56; Res. Officer and Dep. Dir, London Municipal Soc., 1956–63; Mem. British Secretariat, Council of European Municipalities, 1963–64. Lectures on British Monarchy. Member: Local Authorities' Conditions of Service Adv. Bd, 1977–81; Nat. Jt Council for Local Authorities' Services (Manual Workers), 1977–81. Mem. Bd, Harlow Develt Corp., 1968–80. Hon. Life Pres., Brent North Conservative Assoc., 1986. Contested (C) Islington SW, 1966. *Publications:* Queen Victoria Was Amused, 1976; The Kings' Mistresses, 1980. *Recreation:* admiring old things. *Address:* 20 Meadowside, Cambridge Park, Twickenham, Mddx. *T:* 081–892 7968. *Clubs:* Guards' Polo, Exiles.

HARDY, Anna Gwenllian; *see* Somers Cocks, A. G.

HARDY, Prof. Barbara Gladys; Professor of English Literature, Birkbeck College, University of London, 1970–89, now Emeritus; teacher and author; *b* 27 June 1924; *d* of Maurice and Gladys Nathan; *m* Ernest Dawson Hardy (decd); two *d. Educ:* Swansea High Sch. for Girls; University Coll. London. BA, MA. Subsequently on staff of English Dept of Birkbeck Coll., London; Prof. of English, Royal Holloway Coll., Univ. of London, 1965–70. Dir, Yeats Summer School. Mem. Welsh Acad. Pres., Dickens Soc., 1987–88. Hon. Mem., MLA. DUniv. Open, 1981. *Publications:* The Novels of George Eliot, 1959; The Appropriate Form, 1964; (ed) George Eliot: Daniel Deronda, 1967; (ed) Middlemarch: Critical Approaches to the Novel, 1967; The Moral Art of Dickens, 1970; (ed) Critical Essays on George Eliot, 1970; The Exposure of Luxury: radical themes in Thackeray, 1972; (ed) Thomas Hardy: The Trumpet-Major, 1974; Tellers and Listeners: the narrative imagination, 1975; (ed) Thomas Hardy: A Laodicean, 1975; A Reading of Jane Austen, 1975; The Advantage of Lyric, 1977; Particularities: readings in George Eliot, 1982; Forms of Feeling in Victorian Fiction, 1985; Narrators and Novelists: collected essays, vol. 1, 1987. *Address:* c/o Birkbeck College, Malet Street, WC1E 7HX.

HARDY, Rev. Brian Albert; Rector, All Saints, St Andrews, since 1991; *b* 3 July 1931; *s* of Albert Charles Hardy and Edith Maude Sarah Mabe. *Educ:* City Boys' School, Leicester; St John's Coll., Oxford (MA, DipTheol); Westcott House, Cambridge. Curate, Rugeley, Staffs, 1957–62; Chaplain, Downing Coll., Cambridge, 1962–66; Livingston (West Lothian) Ecumenical Team Ministry, 1966–74; Churches' Planning Officer for Telford, Salop, 1974–78; Chaplain, Coates Hall Theological Coll., Edinburgh, 1978–82; Rector, St Columba's by the Castle Episcopal Church, Edinburgh, 1982–91; Episcopalian Chaplain, Royal Infirmary of Edinburgh and Royal Edinburgh Hosp., 1982–86; Dean of the dio. of Edinburgh, 1986–91. *Recreations:* music, especially choral and piano; cycling. *Address:* All Saints Rectory, North Street, St Andrews, Fife KY16 9AZ. *T:* St Andrews (0334) 73193.

HARDY, Rev. Prof. Daniel Wayne; Director, Centre of Theological Inquiry, Princeton, New Jersey, since 1990; *b* 9 Nov. 1930; *s* of John Alexander Hardy and Barbara Wyndham Harrison; *m* 1958, Kate Perrin Enyart; two *s* two *d. Educ:* Phillips Exeter Acad., Exeter, NH; Haverford Coll., Haverford, Penn (BA); Gen. Theological Seminary, NY (STB, STM); St John's Coll., Univ. of Oxford. Deacon 1955, Priest 1956. Asst Minister, Christ Ch., Greenwich, Conn, 1955–59; Vicar, St Barnabas Ch., Greenwich, 1956–59; Instr, Rosemary Hall, Greenwich, 1957–59; Fellow and Tutor, Gen. Theol Seminary, NY, 1959–61; Lectr in Modern Theol Thought, 1965–76, Sen. Lectr, 1976–86, Univ. of Birmingham; Van Mildert Prof. of Divinity, Univ. of Durham, and Residentiary Canon, Durham Cathedral, 1986–90. Moderator, Gen. Ministerial Exam., C of E, 1983–89. Pres., Soc. for the Study of Theology, 1987–88. Editor, Cambridge Studies in Christian Doctrine, 1991–. *Publications:* (with D. F. Ford) Jubilate: theology in praise, 1984; (with D. F. Ford) Praising and Knowing God, 1985; Education for the Church's Ministry, 1986; (contrib.) Schleiermacher and Barth: beyond the impasse, ed R. Streetman, 1987; (contrib.) Keeping the Faith, ed G. Wainwright, 1987; (contrib.) The Modern Theologians, ed D. F. Ford, 1989; (contrib. and ed jtly) On Being the Church, 1989; (contrib. and ed jtly) The Weight of Glory: essays in honour of Peter Baelz, 1991; articles in Theology, Expository Times, Anglican Theol Rev., etc. *Recreations:* tennis, swimming, ski-ing, music, photography. *Address:* 210 Ross Stevenson Circle, Princeton, NJ 08540, USA.

HARDY, David William; Chairman, London Docklands Development Corporation, since 1988 (Deputy Chairman, 1988); Chairman: MGM Assurance, since 1986 (Deputy Chairman and Director, since 1985); Buckingham (formerly Leisuretime) International PLC, since 1988; Europa Minerals, since 1991; *b* 14 July 1930; 3rd *s* of late Brig. John H. Hardy, CBE, MC; *m* 1957, Rosemary, *d* of late Sir Godfrey F. S. Collins, KCIE, CSI, OBE; one *s* one *d. Educ:* Wellington Coll.; Harvard Business School (AMP). Chartered Accountant. Served 2nd RHA, 2/Lt, 1953–54. With Funch Edye Inc., and Imperial Tobacco, USA, 1954–70; HM Govt Co-ordinator of Industrial Advrs, 1970–72; Gp Finance Dir, Tate & Lyle Ltd, 1972–77; Dir, Ocean Transport & Trading PLC, 1977–83; Chairman: Ocean Inchcape, 1980–83; London Park Hotels, 1983–87; Globe Investment Trust, 1983–90 (Dir, 1976–90); Docklands Light Railway, 1984–87; Swan Hunter, 1986–88; 100 Group Chartered Accountants, 1986–88; Deputy Chairman: LRT, 1984–87; Agricultural Mortgage Corp., 1985– (Dir, 1973–); Director: Sturge Holdings PLC, 1985–; Waterford Wedgwood plc (formerly Waterford Glass), 1984–90; Paragon Group, 1985–88; Aberfoyle Holdings, 1986–; Chelsea Harbour Ltd, 1986–90; Electra Kingsway Managers Hldgs Ltd, 1990–; Tootal Gp, 1990–91; CIBA-GEIGY, 1991–. Member: NEDC Cttee for Agriculture, 1970–72; Export Credit Guarantees Adv. Council, 1973–78; Co-opted Council of Inst. of Chartered Accountants, 1974–78; Economic and Fiscal Policy Cttee, CBI, 1981–88; Council, BIM, 1974–78; CBIM 1975. Chm., Engrg Marketing Adv. Cttee, DTI, 1989–90. Mem., Develt Cttee, NACF, 1988–. Mem., St Katherine and Shadwell Trust, 1990–. Hon. British Consul, Norfolk, Va, 1960–62. Member: Co. of Chartered Accountants, 1976; Co. of Shipwrights, 1990. *Address:* 191 Marsh Wall, E14 9TJ. *Clubs:* Brooks's, MCC; Flyfishers', Parlour, HAC.

HARDY, Herbert Charles; Managing Director, Associated Newspapers plc, since 1989 (Director, Associated Newspapers Holdings, since 1986); Chairman, Evening Standard Co. Ltd, since 1989; *b* 13 Dec. 1928; *s* of Charles John Hardy and Margaret Elizabeth (*née* Burniston); *m* 1959, Irene Burrows; one *d. Educ:* RMA, Sandhurst. *Recreations:* golf, horse racing. *Address:* Associated Newspapers plc, Northcliffe House, 2 Derry Street, Kensington, W8 5TT. *T:* 071–938 6000. *Club:* Thirty.

HARDY, Sir James (Gilbert), Kt 1981; OBE 1975; Chairman of Directors: Thomas Hardy & Sons Pty Ltd, since 1981; Houghton Wines Pty Ltd, since 1981; *b* 20 Nov. 1932; *s* of Tom Mayfield Hardy and Eileen C. Hardy; *m* 1956, Anne Christine Jackson (marr. diss. 1991); two *s. Educ:* St Peter's Coll., Adelaide, SA; S Australian Sch. of Mines; S Australian Inst. of Technol. (Dip. in Accountancy). AASA. National Service, 13th Field Artillery Regt, Adelaide, 1951. Elder Smith & Co. Ltd, 1951; J. C. Correll & Co., 1952; Thomas Hardy & Sons Pty Ltd, Winemakers, Adelaide, 1953–: Shipping Clerk, Sales Rep., Sales Supervisor and Lab. Asst, 1953–62; Dir and Manager, Sydney Br., 1962–77; Regional Dir, Eastern Australia, 1977–81. Director: S Australian Film Corp., 1981–87; America's Cup Challenge 1983 Ltd, 1981–85; Advertiser Newspapers Ltd, 1983–88; Dep. Chm., Racing Rules Cttee, Yachting Fedn, 1969–81; Dir of Sailing/Captain, S Australian Challenge for the Defence of America's Cup 1984–87. Vice Pres., Internat. 12 Metre Assoc., 1986–. Treasurer, Liquor Trade Supervisory Council of NSW, 1965–70; Fellow, Catering Inst. of Australia, 1972; Pres., Wine and Brandy Assoc. of NSW, 1980–83. NSW Chm., Aust. National Travel Assoc., 1976; Vice Pres., Royal Blind Soc. of NSW, 1980–88 (Mem. Council, 1967–91); Pres., NSW Aust. Football League and Sydney Football League, 1982–83; Pres., "One and All" Sailing Ship Assoc. of SA Inc., 1981–90; Chm., Adelaide 1998 Commonwealth Games Bid, 1990–; Mem., Bd of Advice, Rothmans Nat. Sport Foundn, 1985–87; Trustee, Rothmans Foundn, 1987–. Chm., Adv. Cttee, Life Educn Centre of SA, 1988–91; Member: Exec. Cttee, Neurosurgical Res. Foundn of SA, 1988–; Adv. Bd, John Curtin Sch. of Medical Res., ANU, Canberra, 1982–87. Dep. Grand Master, United Grand Lodge of NSW, 1977–80. *Recreation:* yachting (skipper or helmsman in America's Cup and Admiral's Cup races). *Address:* Thomas Hardy & Sons Pty Ltd, 104 Bay Street, East Botany, NSW 2019, Australia. *T:* (02) 666–5855, *Fax:* (02) 316–9738. *Clubs:* Royal Ocean Racing; Australian, Tattersalls, Royal Sydney Yacht Squadron (Sydney); Cruising Yacht of Australia (NSW); Brighton and Seacliff Yacht (Cdre, 1957) (SA); Royal Perth Yacht; Southport Yacht (Qld); Fort Worth Boat (Texas, USA); New York Yacht.

HARDY, Maj.-Gen. John Campbell, CB 1985; LVO 1978; Director, British Digestive Foundation, since 1987; *b* 13 Oct. 1933; *s* of late General Sir Campbell Hardy, KCB, CBE, DSO; *m* 1961, Jennifer Mary Kempton; one *s* one *d. Educ:* Sherborne School. Joined Royal Marines, 1952; 45 Commando, 1954; HMS Superb, 1956; Instructor, NCOs'

School, Plymouth, 1957; 42 Commando, 1959; 43 Commando, 1962; Adjt, Jt Service Amphibious Warfare Centre, 1964; Company Comdr, 45 Commando, 1965; sc Bracknell, 1966; Instr, RNC Greenwich, 1967; Extra Equerry to Prince Philip, 1968–69; SO, Dept of CGRM, 1969; Rifle Company Comdr, 41 Commando, 1971; ndc Latimer, 1972; Staff of Chief of Defence Staff, 1973; Staff Officer HQ Commando Forces, 1975; CO RM Poole, 1977; CofS and Asst Defence Attaché, British Defence Staff Washington, 1979; ADC to the Queen, 1981–82; Chief of Staff to Comdt Gen. RM, 1982–84; DCS (Support) to C-in-C Allied Forces N Europe, 1984–87. Col Comdt, RM, 1990–. *Recreations:* sailing, tennis. *Address:* c/o National Westminster Bank plc, 51 The Strand, Walmer, Deal, Kent. *Club:* Army and Navy.

HARDY, Michael James Langley; Director, Directorate-General for Telecommunications, Information Industries and Innovation, Commission of the European Communities, since 1987; *b* 30 Jan. 1933; *s* of James Hardy and Rosina (*née* Langley); *m* 1959, Dr Swana Metger; one *s* two *d*. *Educ:* Beckenham Grammar Sch.; Magdalen Coll., Oxford (Exhibnr; BA 1956; MA 1959); Magdalene Coll., Cambridge (LLB 1957; LLM 1963). Called to the Bar, Gray's Inn, 1957. Asst Lecturer, Law Faculty: Manchester Univ., 1958–59; KCL, 1959–60; Legal Officer, later Sen. Legal Officer, Legal Service, UN, 1960–73; Legal Adviser, Govt of Nepal, 1968–69 (on leave of absence from UN); Commn of the European Communities, 1973–: Legal Adviser, Legal Service, 1973–77; Head of Div., Japan, Australia and NZ, Directorate-General for External Relations, 1978–82; Head of Commn Delegn, New York, 1982–87. *Publications:* Blood Feuds and the Payment of Blood Money in the Middle East, 1963; Modern Diplomatic Law, 1968; articles in legal and political science jls. *Recreations:* walking, talking. *Address:* Castle House, Gidleigh, Devon TQ13 8HR. *T:* Chagford (0647) 433567; 39 rue Père de Deken, 1040 Brussels, Belgium. *T:* Brussels 733 9167.

HARDY, Peter; MP (Lab) Wentworth, since 1983 (Rother Valley, 1970–83); *b* 17 July 1931; *s* of Lawrence Hardy and of Mrs I. Hardy, Wath upon Dearne; *m* 1954, Margaret Anne Brookes; one *s*. *Educ:* Wath upon Dearne Grammar Sch.; Westminster Coll., London; Sheffield Univ. Schoolmaster in S Yorkshire, 1953–70. Member: Wath upon Dearne UDC, 1960–70 (Chm. Council, 1968–69); Governing Body of Wath Grammar Sch. (Chm. of Governors, 1969–70). Pres., Wath upon Dearne Labour Party, 1960–68; contested (Lab): Scarborough and Whitby, 1964; Sheffield, Hallam, 1966. PPS to Sec. of State for the Environment, 1974–76; PPS to Foreign Sec., 1976–79. Mem., UK delegn to Council of Europe, 1976–; Leader, Lab. delegn to Council of Europe and WEU, 1983–; Chm., Cttee on Environment, Council of Europe, 1986–89 (Chm., Sub Cttee on Natural Envmt, 1990–; Vice-Chm., Socialist Gp, 1983–); Chm., PLP Energy Cttee, 1974–. Member: Council, RSPB, 1984–89; Central Exec. Cttee, NSPCC, 1985–; Patron, Yorkshire Wildlife Trust. *Publications:* A Lifetime of Badgers, 1975; various articles on educational and other subjects. *Recreation:* watching wild life, exhibiting dogs. *Address:* 53 Sandygate, Wath upon Dearne, Rotherham, South Yorkshire. *T:* Rotherham (0709) 874590. *Club:* Rawmarsh Trades and Labour.

HARDY, Robert; *see* Hardy, T. S. R.

HARDY, Robert James; His Honour Judge Hardy; a Circuit Judge, since 1979; *b* 12 July 1924; *s* of James Frederick and Ann Hardy; *m* 1951, Maureen Scott; one *s* one *d*. *Educ:* Mostyn House Sch.; Wrekin Coll.; University Coll., London (LLB). Served, 1942–46, Royal Navy, as Pilot, Fleet Air Arm. Called to Bar, 1950; a Recorder of the Crown Court, 1972–79. *Recreation:* sailing. *Address:* Smithy House, Sandlebridge, Little Warford, Cheshire SK9 7TY. *T:* Mobberley (0565) 872535; Betlem, Mallorca.

HARDY, Rt. Rev. Robert Maynard; *see* Lincoln, Bishop of.

HARDY, Sir Rupert (John), 4th Bt, *cr* 1876; Lieutenant-Colonel Life Guards, retired; *b* 24 Oct. 1902; *s* of 3rd Bt and Violet Agnes Evelyn (*d* 1972), *d* of Hon. Sir Edward Chandos Leigh, KCB, KC; *S* father 1953; *m* 1930, Hon. Diana Joan Allsopp, *er d* of 3rd Baron Hindlip; one *s* one *d*. *Educ:* Eton; Trinity Hall, Cambridge. BA 1925. Joined The Life Guards, 1925; Major, 1940; retired, 1948, and rejoined as RARO, 1952; Lieut-Col comdg Household Cavalry Regt, 1952–56; ceased to belong to R of O, Dec. 1956; granted hon. rank of Lieut-Col. *Recreations:* hunting and shooting. *Heir:* *s* Richard Charles Chandos Hardy [*b* 6 Feb. 1945; *m* 1972, Venetia, *d* of Simon Wingfield Digby, *qv*; four *d*]. *Address:* Gullivers Lodge, Guilsborough, Northampton. *Club:* Turf.

HARDY, (Timothy Sydney) Robert, CBE 1981; actor and writer; *b* 29 Oct. 1925; *s* of late Major Henry Harrison Hardy, CBE, and Edith Jocelyn Dugdale; *m* 1st, 1952, Elizabeth (marr. diss.), *d* of late Sir Lionel Fox and Lady Fox; one *s*; 2nd, 1961, Sally (marr. diss. 1986), *d* of Sir Neville Pearson, 2nd Bt, and Dame Gladys Cooper, DBE; two *d*. *Educ:* Rugby Sch.; Magdalen Coll., Oxford (Hons degree, Eng. Lit.). *Stage:* Shakespeare Meml Theatre, 1949–51; London, West End, 1951–53; Old Vic Theatre, 1953–54; USA, 1954 and 1956–58 (plays incl. Hamlet and Henry V); Shakespeare Meml 1959 Centenary Season; Rosmersholm, Comedy, 1960; The Rehearsal, Globe, 1961; A Severed Head, Criterion, 1963; The Constant Couple, New, 1967; I've Seen You Cut Lemons, Fortune, 1969; Habeas Corpus, Lyric, 1974; Dear Liar, Mermaid, 1982; Winnie, Victoria Palace, 1988; *recent films:* The Far Pavilions, 1983; The Shooting Party, 1985; Jenny's War, 1985; Paris by Night, 1988; War and Remembrance, 1988; *television:* David Copperfield; Age of Kings, 1960; Trouble-shooters, 1966–67; Elizabeth R, 1970; Manhunt, 1970; Edward VII, 1973; All Creatures Great and Small, 1978–80, 1983, 1985, 1987–90; Speed King; Fothergill; Winston Churchill—The Wilderness Years, 1981; Paying Guests, 1986; Make and Break, 1986; Churchill in the USA, 1986; Hot Metal, 1987, 1988; Northanger Abbey, 1987; Marcus Welby in Paris (film), 1988. Author of TV documentaries: Picardy Affair, 1962; The Longbow, 1972; Horses in our Blood, 1977; Gordon of Khartoum, 1982. Consultant, Mary Rose Trust, 1979–; Trustee, WWF (UK), 1983–89; Mem., Bd of Trustees of the Royal Armouries, 1984–; Chm., Berkshire, Buckinghamshire and Oxfordshire Naturalists' Trust Appeal, 1984–90. Master, Court of Worshipful Co. of Bowyers, 1988–90. Hon. DLitt Reading, 1990. *Publication:* Longbow, 1976. *Recreations:* archery, horsemanship, bowyery. *Address:* Upper Bolney House, Upper Bolney, near Henley-on-Thames, Oxon RG9 4AQ. *Clubs:* Buck's, Royal Toxophilite, British Longbow.

HARDY-ROBERTS, Brig. Sir Geoffrey (Paul), KCVO 1972; CB 1945; CBE 1944 (OBE 1941); JP; DL; Master of HM's Household, 1967–73; Extra Equerry to the Queen, since 1967; Secretary-Superintendent of Middlesex Hospital, 1946–67; *b* 1907; *s* of A. W. Roberts; *m* 1945, Eldred (*d* 1987), *widow* of Col J. R. Macdonell, DSO. *Educ:* Eton; RMC Sandhurst. Regular Commission, 9th Lancers, 1926–37. Served War of 1939–45 (OBE, CBE, CB). Mem., West Sussex AHA, 1974–82; Dep. Chm., King Edward VII Hospital, Midhurst, 1972–82. JP 1960, DL 1964, West Sussex (formerly Sussex), High Sheriff, 1965, Sussex. Officer, Legion of Merit, 1945. *Address:* The Lodge, Bury Gate House, Pulborough, West Sussex RH20 1HA. *T:* Fittleworth (0798) 831921.

HARDYMAN, Norman Trenchard, CB 1984; Secretary, Universities Funding Council, 1988–90 (University Grants Committee, 1982–89); *b* 5 Jan. 1930; *s* of late Rev. Arnold Victor Hardyman and late Laura Hardyman; *m* 1961, Carol Rebecca Turner; one *s* one *d*. *Educ:* Clifton Coll.; Christ Church, Oxford. Asst Principal, Min. of Educn, 1955; Principal 1960; Private Sec. to Sec. of State for Educn and Science, 1966–68; Asst Sec. 1968–75, Under-Sec., 1975–79, DES; Under-Sec., DHSS, 1979–81. Mem., UGC for Univ. of S Pacific, 1990–. *Recreations:* walking, gardening, reading, photography. *Address:* 16 Rushington Avenue, Maidenhead, Berks SL6 1BZ. *T:* Maidenhead (0628) 24179.

HARE, family name of **Viscount Blakenham** and **Earl of Listowel.**

HARE, Hon. Alan Victor, MC 1942; Deputy Chairman, The Economist, 1985–89; *b* 14 March 1919; 4th *s* of 4th Earl of Listowel and Hon. Freda, *d* of 2nd Baron Derwent; *m* 1945, Jill Pegotty (*née* North); one *s* one *d*. *Educ:* Eton Coll.; New Coll., Oxford (MA). Army, 1939–45. Foreign Office, 1947–61; Industrial and Trade Fairs, 1961–63; Financial Times, 1963–84; Man. Dir, 1971–78, Chm., 1978–84, and Chief Executive, 1975–83, Financial Times Ltd; Director: Pearson Longman Ltd, 1975–83; Economist Newspaper Ltd, 1975–89; Chm., Industrial and Trade Fairs Holdings, 1979–83 (Dir, 1977–83); Dir, English National Opera, 1982–88; Trustee, Reuters plc, 1985–. Pres., Société Civile du Vignoble de Château Latour, 1983–90. Mem., Press Council, 1975–78. Comdr, Order of Merit (FDR), 1985. *Recreations:* walking, opera, swimming. *Address:* Flat 12, 53 Rutland Gate, SW7. *T:* 071–581 2184. *Club:* White's.

See also Viscount Blakenham.

HARE, David, FRSL 1985; playwright; *b* 5 June 1947; *s* of Clifford Theodore Rippon Hare and Agnes Cockburn Hare; *m* 1970, Margaret Matheson (marr. diss. 1980); two *s* one *d*. *Educ:* Lancing Coll.; Jesus Coll., Cambridge (MA Hons). Founded Portable Theatre, 1968; Literary Manager and Resident Dramatist, Royal Court, 1969–71; Resident Dramatist, Nottingham Playhouse, 1973; founded Joint Stock Theatre Group, 1975; US/UK Bicentennial Fellowship, 1977; founded Greenpoint Films, 1982; Associate Dir, Nat. Theatre, 1984–88, 1989–. Author of plays: Slag, Hampstead, 1970, Royal Court, 1971 (Evening Standard Drama Award, 1970); The Great Exhibition, Hampstead, 1972; Knuckle (televised, 1989), Comedy, 1974 (John Llewellyn Rhys Award, 1974); Fanshen, Joint Stock, 1975; The Secret Rapture, NT, 1988 (Drama Award, best play of the year; London Critics Poll, Best Play), NY, 1989 (dir, NY only); Racing Demon, NT, 1990 (Olivier Award, Plays and Players Award, for best play of the year; Critics' Circle Best Play of the Year; Time Out Award, 1990); Murmuring Judges, NT, 1991; *author and director of plays:* Brassneck (with Howard Brenton), Nottingham Playhouse, 1973; Teeth 'n' Smiles, Royal Court, 1975, Wyndhams, 1976; Plenty, NT, 1978, NY, 1983 (NY Critics' Circle Award); A Map of the World, Adelaide Fest., 1982, NT, 1983, NY 1985; (with Howard Brenton) Pravda, NT, 1985 (London Standard Award; Plays and Players Award; City Limits Award); The Bay at Nice, and Wrecked Eggs, NT, 1986; opera libretto, The Knife, NY Shakespeare Fest., 1987 (also directed); *TV plays:* Man Above Men (Play for Today), 1973; Licking Hitler (Play for Today), 1978 (BAFTA award, 1978) (also directed); Dreams of Leaving (Play for Today), 1980 (also directed); Saigon—Year of the Cat (Thames TV), 1983; Heading Home, 1991. *Directed:* The Party, NT, 1974; Weapons of Happiness, NT, 1976; Total Eclipse, Lyric, Hammersmith, 1981; King Lear, NT, 1986. *Films:* wrote and directed: Wetherby, 1985 (Golden Bear award, 1985); Paris by Night, 1988; Strapless, 1989; (screenplay) Plenty, 1985. *Publications:* Slag, 1970; The Great Exhibition, 1972; Knuckle, 1974; Brassneck, 1974; Fanshen, 1976; Teeth 'n' Smiles, 1976; Plenty, 1978; Licking Hitler, 1978; Dreams of Leaving, 1980; A Map of the World, 1982; Saigon, 1983; The History Plays, 1984; Pravda, 1985; Wetherby, 1985; The Asian Plays, 1986; The Bay at Nice and Wrecked Eggs, 1986; The Secret Rapture, 1988; Paris By Night, 1989; Strapless, 1990; Racing Demon, 1990; Writing Lefthanded, 1991; Heading Home, 1991; The Early Plays, 1991; Murmuring Judges, 1991. *Address:* 5 Chepstow Crescent, W11.

HARE, Prof. Frederick Kenneth, CC 1987 (OC 1978); PhD; FRSC 1968; Professor of Geography and Physics, 1969–84, and Director, Institute for Environmental Studies, 1974–79, now University Professor Emeritus in Geography, University of Toronto; Chancellor, Trent University, since 1988; Provost, Trinity College, Toronto, 1979–86; Chairman, Advisory Board on International Programmes, University of Toronto; *b* Wylye, Wilts, 5 Feb. 1919; *s* of Frederick Eli Hare and Irene Smith; *m* 1st, 1941, Suzanne Alice Bates (marr. diss. 1952); one *s*; 2nd, 1953, Helen Neilson Morrill; one *s* one *d*. *Educ:* Windsor Grammar Sch.; King's Coll., University of London (BSc); Univ. of Montreal (PhD). Lectr in Geography, Univ. of Manchester, 1940–41; War service in Air Min., Meteorological Office, 1941–45; McGill University: Asst and Assoc. Prof. of Geography, 1945–52; Prof. of Geography and Meteorology, 1952–64; Chm. of Dept, 1950–62; Dean of Faculty of Arts and Science, 1962–64; Prof. of Geography, Univ. of London (King's Coll.), 1964–66; Master of Birkbeck Coll., Univ. of London, 1966–68; Pres., Univ. of British Columbia, 1968–69. Vis. Centenary Prof., Univ. of Adelaide, 1974. Chm., Adv. Bd on Internat. Programmes, Univ. of Toronto, 1990–. FKC 1967. Sci. Advr, Dept of the Environment, Canada, 1972–74. Mem. Nat. Research Council of Canada, 1962–64; Chm. of Bd, Arctic Inst. of N America, 1963; Mem., NERC, 1965–68; Dir, Resources for the Future, 1968–80; Member: SSRC, Canada, 1974–76; Adv. Council, Electric Power Res. Inst., 1978–80. Chairman: Adv. Cttee on Canadian Demonstration Projects, 1974–75, for 1976 UN Conf. on Human Settlements; Special Prog. Panel on Ecoscis, NATO, 1975; Federal Study Gp on Nuclear Waste Disposal, 1977; Climate Programme Planning Bd, Govt of Canada, 1979–90; Commn on Lead in the Environment, RSC, 1984–86; Section W, AAAS, 1985–86; Comr, Ontario Nuclear Safety Review, 1987–88. President: Canadian Assoc. of Geographers, 1963–64; RMetS, 1967–68 (Vice-Pres., 1968–70); Sigma Xi, 1986–87; Fellow, Amer. Meteorological Soc., 1969; Hon. Fellow, Amer. Geographical Soc., 1963; Hon. Pres., Assoc. of Amer. Geographers, 1964. Hon. Life Mem., Birkbeck Coll., 1969. Hon. LLD: Queen's (Canada) Univ., 1964; Univ. of W Ontario, 1968; Trent Univ., 1979; Memorial Univ., 1985; Toronto, 1987; Hon. DSc: McGill, 1969; York (Canada), 1978; Windsor, 1988; DSc *ad eund.* Adelaide, 1974; Hon. DSLitt Thorneloe Coll., Sudbury (Canada), 1984. Hon. Cert. Graduation, Nat. Defence Coll., Kingston, Canada, 1986. Meritorious Achievement Citation, Assoc. Amer. Geographers, 1961; President's Prize, RMetS (Can.), 1961, 1962; Patterson Medal, Can. Met. Service, 1973; Massey Medal, Royal Can. Geographical Soc., 1974; Patron's Medal, RGS, 1977; Award for Scholarly Distinction, Canadian Assoc. of Geographers, 1979; Univ. of Toronto Alumni Assoc. Faculty Award, 1982; Sir William Dawson Award, RSC, 1987; Cullum Medal, Amer. Geographical Soc., 1987; Internat. Meteorol Orgn Prize, 1988. Order of Ontario, 1989. *Publications:* The Restless Atmosphere, 1953; On University Freedom, 1968; (with M. K. Thomas) Climate Canada, 1974, 2nd edn 1979; numerous articles in Quarterly Jl Royal Meteorological Soc., Geography, and other learned jls. *Recreation:* music. *Address:* 301 Lakeshore Road West, Oakville, Ont L6K 1G2, Canada. *Clubs:* McGill Faculty (Montreal) (Hon. Life Mem.); Toronto Faculty, York (Toronto).

HARE, Kenneth; *see* Hare, F. K.

HARE, Hon. Mrs Richard; *see* Gordine, Dora.

HARE, Rt. Rev. Richard; *see* Hare, Rt Rev. Thomas Richard.

HARE, Prof. Richard Mervyn, FBA 1964; Graduate Research Professor of Philosophy, University of Florida at Gainesville, since 1983; *b* 21 March 1919; *s* of late Charles Francis Aubone Hare and late Louise Kathleen (*née* Simonds); *m* 1947, Catherine, *d* of Sir Harry

Verney, 4th Bt, DSO; one s three d. *Educ:* Rugby (Schol.); Balliol Coll., Oxford (Schol.). Commissioned Royal Artillery, 1940; Lieut, Indian Mountain Artillery, 1941; Prisoner of War, Singapore and Siam, 1942–45. 1st Lit. Hum. 1947. Fellow and Tutor in Philosophy, Balliol Coll., Oxford, 1947–66, Hon. Fellow, 1974; White's Prof. of Moral Philosophy and Fellow of Corpus Christi Coll., Oxford, 1966–83, Hon. Fellow, 1983. Visiting Fellow: Princeton, 1957; ANU, 1966; Center for Advanced Study in Behavioral Sciences, Stanford, 1980; Wilde Lectr in Natural Religion, Oxford, 1963–66; Visiting Professor: Univ. of Michigan, 1968; Univ. of Delaware, 1974. Pres., Aristotelian Soc., 1972–73. Member: Nat. Road Safety Advisory Council, 1966–68; C of E Working Parties on Medical Questions, 1964–75. Hon. Fellow, Inst. of Life Scis, Hastings Center, 1974; For. Hon. Mem., American Acad. of Arts and Sciences, 1975. Hon. PhD Lund, 1991. Tanner Award, 1979. *Publications:* The Language of Morals, 1952; Freedom and Reason, 1963; Essays on Philosophical Method, 1971; Practical Inferences, 1971; Essays on the Moral Concepts, 1972; Applications of Moral Philosophy, 1972; Moral Thinking, 1981; Plato, 1982; Hare and Critics, 1988; Essays in Ethical Theory, 1989; Essays on Political Morality, 1989. *Recreations:* music, gardening. *Address:* Saffron House, Ewelme, near Wallingford, Oxon OX10 6HP.

HARE, Sir Thomas, 5th Bt *cr* 1818; *b* 27 July 1930; *s* of Sir Ralph Leigh Hare, 4th Bt, and Doreen Pleasance Anna (*d* 1985), *d* of late Sir Richard Bagge, DSO; *S* father, 1976; *m* 1961, Lady Rose Amanda Bligh, *d* of 9th Earl of Darnley; two *d. Educ:* Eton; Magdalene College, Cambridge (MA). ARICS. *Heir: cousin* Philip Leigh Hare [*b* 13 Oct. 1922; *m* 1950, Anne Lisle, *d* of Major Geoffrey Nicholson, CBE, MC; one *s* one *d* (twins)]. *Address:* Stow Bardolph, King's Lynn, Norfolk PE34 3HU.

HARE, Rt. Rev. Thomas Richard; *see* Pontefract, Bishop Suffragan of.

HARE DUKE, Rt. Rev. Michael Geoffrey; *see* St Andrews, Dunkeld and Dunblane, Bishop of.

HARES, Phillip Douglas George, CBE 1985; Chairman and Chief Executive, 1986–87, and Board Member for Finance, 1981–86, British Shipbuilders (Deputy Chief Executive, 1983–86); *b* 31 Dec. 1926; *s* of Edgar Sidney George and Edith Winifred Frances Hares; *m* 1955, Violet May Myers; one *s* one *d. Educ:* Richmond and East Sheen Grammar Sch. Involved with management sciences and computing in various commercial, industrial, and consulting organisations, 1952–69, dating from early application of computers in 1952 with J. Lyons & Co. Ltd; Asst Man. Dir (Ops), British Mail Order Corp. Ltd (Great Universal Stores), 1969–77; Man. Dir (Finance), British Shipbuilders, 1978–81, Corporate Man. Dir, 1982–83; Chairman: Falmouth Shiprepair Ltd, 1983–85; Vosper Shiprepairers Ltd, 1983–85; Dir, Iron Trades Insce Gp, 1985–. Member Council: CBI, 1983–87 (Mem., Economic Situation Cttee, 1983–87); Amer. Bureau of Shipping, 1986–87. FRSA 1987. Freeman, City of London, 1983; Liveryman, Worshipful Co. of Shipwrights, 1984–. *Recreations:* reading, music, genealogy. *Address:* Honeywood, Lower Sea Lane, Charmouth, Dorset DT6 6LR. *T:* Charmouth (0297) 60042.

HAREWOOD, 7th Earl of, *cr* 1812; **George Henry Hubert Lascelles,** KBE 1986; Baron Harewood, 1796; Viscount Lascelles, 1812; President, British Board of Film Classification, since 1985; *b* 7 Feb. 1923; *er s* of 6th Earl of Harewood, KG, GCVO, DSO, and HRH Princess Mary (Princess Royal; who *d* 28 March 1965); *S* father, 1947; *m* 1st, 1949, Maria Donata (marr. diss. 1967; she *m* 1973, Rt Hon. (John) Jeremy Thorpe), *d* of late Erwin Stein; three *s;* 2nd, 1967, Patricia Elizabeth, *d* of Charles Tuckwell, Australia; one *s* and one step *s. Educ:* Eton; King's Coll., Cambridge (MA; Hon. Fellow, 1984). Served War of 1939–45, Capt. Grenadier Guards (wounded and prisoner, 1944, released May 1945); ADC to Earl of Athlone, 1945–46, Canada. Editor of magazine "Opera" 1950–53; Royal Opera House, Covent Garden: a Dir, 1951–53; on staff, 1953–60; a Dir, 1969–72; Chm. Bd, ENO (formerly Sadler's Wells Opera), 1986– (Man. Dir, 1972–85); Artistic Director: Edinburgh Internat. Festival, 1961–65; Leeds Festival, 1958–74; Adelaide Festival 1988; Artistic Advr, New Philharmonia Orch., London, 1966–76; Man. Dir, English Nat. Opera North, 1978–81. Governor of BBC, 1985–87. Chm., Music Advisory Cttee of British Council, 1956–66; Chancellor of the Univ. of York, 1963–67; Member: Arts Council, 1966–72; Gen. Adv. Council of BBC, 1969–77. President: English Football Assoc., 1963–72; Leeds United Football Club. Hon. RAM, 1983; Hon. LLD: Leeds, 1959; Aberdeen, 1966; Hon. DMus Hull, 1962; DUniv York, 1982. Janáček Medal, 1978. *Publications:* (ed) Kobbé's Complete Opera Book, 1953, 3rd edn 1987; The Tongs and the Bones (autobiog.), 1981; Kobbé's Illustrated Opera Book, 1989. *Heir: s* Viscount Lascelles, *qv. Address:* Harewood House, Leeds LS17 9LG.
See also Barry Tuckwell.

HARFORD, Sir James (Dundas), KBE 1956; CMG 1943; *b* Great Yarmouth, 7 Jan. 1899; *s* of late Rev. Dundas Harford, MA; *m* 1st, 1932, Countess Thelma, *d* of Count Albert Metaxa; one *s;* 2nd, 1937, Lilias Madeline, *d* of Major Archibald Campbell; two *d. Educ:* Repton; Balliol Coll., Oxford (Hon. Scholar, MA). Served European War, France and Belgium, 1917–19; Asst Master, Eton Coll., 1922–25; Administrative Service, Nigeria, 1926; District administration, Bornu Province, 1926–29; Asst Sec., Nigerian Secretariat, 1930–34 and Clerk to Exec. and Legislative Councils; seconded to Colonial Office, 1934–36; Administrator of Antigua and Federal Sec. of the Leeward Islands, 1936–40; Administrator, St Kitts-Nevis, 1940–47; administered Government of Leeward Islands, on various occasions; seconded to Colonial Office, 1947–48; administered Government of Mauritius, on various occasions; Colonial Sec., Mauritius, 1948–53; Governor and Commander-in-Chief of St Helena, 1954–58. Conference Organiser, Commonwealth Institute, 1959–64. *Address:* Links Cottage, Rother Road, Seaford, East Sussex BN25 4HT.

HARFORD, Sir (John) Timothy, 3rd Bt *cr* 1934; Chairman, Kwik Save Group plc, since 1990; Deputy Chairman: Wolseley Group plc (formerly Wolseley-Hughes Group plc), since 1983; Wesleyan & General Assurance Society, since 1987 (Vice-Chairman, 1985–87); Wagon Industrial Holdings, since 1991; *b* 6 July 1932; *s* of Sir George Arthur Harford, 2nd Bt and Anstice Marion, *d* of Sir Alfred Tritton, 2nd Bt; *S* father, 1967; *m* 1962, Carolyn Jane Mullens; two *s* one *d. Educ:* Harrow Sch.; Oxford Univ.; Harvard Business Sch. (Philip Hill Higginson Erlangers Ltd, 1960–63; Director: Birmingham Industrial Trust Ltd, 1963–67; Singer & Friedlander Ltd 1970–88 (Local Dir, 1967–69). *Recreations:* wine and food, travel. *Heir: s* Mark John Harford, *b* 6 Aug. 1964. *Address:* South House, South Littleton, Evesham, Worcs WR11 5TJ. *T:* Evesham (0386) 830478. *Club:* Boodle's.

HARGREAVES, Andrew Raikes; MP (C) Birmingham, Hall Green, since 1987; *b* 15 May 1955; *m* 1978, Fiona Susan, *o d* of G. W. Dottridge; two *s. Educ:* Eton; St Edmund Hall, Oxford (MA Hons). Auctioneer and valuer, Christies, 1977–81; Hill Samuel & Co. Ltd, 1981–83; Asst Dir, Sanwa Internat. Ltd, 1983–85; Asst Dir J. Henry Schroder Wagg & Co. Ltd, 1985–87. Contested (C) Blyth Valley, 1983. *Address:* House of Commons, SW1A 0AA. *Club:* Boodle's.

HARGREAVES, Prof. David Harold, PhD; Professor of Education, and Fellow of Wolfson College, University of Cambridge, since 1988; *b* 31 Aug. 1939; *s* of Clifford and Marion Hargreaves. *Educ:* Bolton School; Christ's College, Cambridge. MA, PhD. Asst Master, Hull Grammar Sch., 1961–64; Research Associate, Dept. of Sociology and Social Anthropology, Univ. of Manchester, 1964–65; Lectr, Senior Lectr then Reader, Dept. of Education, Univ. of Manchester, 1965–79; Reader in Education and Fellow of Jesus College, Oxford, 1979–84; Chief Inspector, ILEA, 1984–88. University of Cambridge: Member: Gen. Bd of the Faculties, 1989–; Local Exams Syndicate, 1990–; Bd of Grad. Studies, 1990–; Chairman: Council, Sch. of Humanities and Soc. Scis, 1990–; Cttee on the Training and Develt of Univ. Teachers, 1990–; Needs Cttee, 1991–. Member: Educn Res. Bd, SSRC, 1979–82; Educn Adv. Council, Royal Opera House, Covent Garden, 1985–90; Educn Adv. Council, IBA, 1988–90; ESRC, 1991–. Chm., Eastern Arts Bd, 1991–. FRSA 1984. *Publications:* Social Relations in a Secondary School, 1967; Interpersonal Relations and Education, 1972; (jtly) Deviance in Classrooms, 1975; The Challenge for the Comprehensive School, 1982; (jtly) Planning for School Development, 1990; (jtly) The Empowered School, 1991. *Recreations:* opera, British watercolours. *Address:* Department of Education, 17 Trumpington Street, Cambridge CB2 1QA. *Club:* Athenæum.

HARGREAVES, Ian Richard; Deputy Editor, The Financial Times, since 1990; *b* 18 June 1951; *s* of Ronald and Edna Hargreaves; *m* 1972, Elizabeth Anne Crago; one *s* one *d. Educ:* Burnley Grammar Sch.; Altrincham Grammar Sch.; Queens' Coll., Cambridge (MA). Community worker, Kaleidescope Project, 1972–73; Reporter, Keighley News, 1973–74; Journalist, Bradford Telegraph & Argus, 1974–76; Financial Times, 1976–87: Industrial Corresp.; Transport Corresp.; New York Corresp.; Social Affairs Ed.; Resources Ed.; Features Ed.; Man. Ed., 1987–88, Controller, 1988–89, Dir, 1989–90, News and Current Affairs, BBC. *Recreations:* football, fell-walking, tennis. *Address:* 2 Admirals Court, 30 Horsely Down Lane, Tower Bridge, SE1 2LN. *T:* 071–403 1693.

HARGREAVES, Prof. John Desmond; Professor of History, University of Aberdeen, 1962–85; *b* 25 Jan. 1924; *s* of Arthur Swire Hargreaves and Margaret Hilda (*née* Duckworth); *m* 1950, Sheila Elizabeth (*née* Wilks); one *s* two *d. Educ:* Skipton Grammar Sch.; Bootham; Manchester Univ. War service, 1943–46. Asst Princ., War Office, 1948; Lectr in History: Manchester Univ., 1948–52; Fourah Bay Coll., Sierra Leone, 1952–54; Aberdeen Univ., 1954–62. Vis. Prof., Union Coll. Schenectady, New York, 1960–61; Univ. of Ibadan, 1970–71. Mem., Kidd Cttee on Sheriff Court Records, 1966. Pres., African Studies Assoc. (UK), 1972–73. Hon. DLitt Sierra Leone, 1984. *Publications:* Life of Sir Samuel Lewis, 1958; Prelude to the Partition of West Africa, 1963; West Africa: the Former French States, 1967; France and West Africa, 1969; West Africa Partitioned: Vol. I, The Loaded Pause, 1974, Vol. II, The Elephants and the Grass, 1985; The End of Colonial Rule in West Africa, 1979; Aberdeenshire to Africa, 1981; Decolonization in Africa, 1988; (ed) Aberdeen University 1945–81, 1989; many articles and chapters in jls and collaborative volumes. *Recreations:* hill-walking, theatre, lawn tennis. *Address:* Balcluain, Raemoir Road, Banchory, Kincardine AB3 3UJ. *T:* Banchory (03302) 2655.

HARGREAVES, (Joseph) Kenneth; MP (C) Hyndburn, since 1983; *b* 1 March 1939; *s* of James and Mary Hargreaves. *Educ:* St Mary's Coll., Blackburn; Manchester Coll. of Commerce. ACIS. Standard Cost/Wages Clerk, NCB, 1957–61; Audit Asst, Treasurer's Dept, Lancs CC, 1961–63; Office Manager, Shopfitters (Lancashire) Ltd, Oswaldtwistle, 1963–83. ACIS, 1962; FFA, 1989. Fellow, Inst. of Financial Accountants. *Recreations:* Gilbert and Sullivan, classical music, travel. *Address:* 31 Park Lane, Oswaldtwistle, Accrington, Lancs. *T:* Accrington (0254) 396184; (office) 071–219 5138.

HARGREAVES, Maj.-Gen. William Herbert, CB 1965; OBE 1945; FRCP; *b* 5 Aug. 1908; *s* of Arthur William Hargreaves; *m* 1946, Pamela Mary Westray; one *s* one *d. Educ:* Merchant Taylors' Sch.; St Bartholomew's Hospital. FRCP 1950; FRCPE 1965. Served War of 1939–45. Medical Liaison Officer to Surgeon-Gen., US Army, Washington, DC, 1946–48; Prof. of Medicine, Univ. of Baghdad, 1951–59; Physician to late King Faisal II of Iraq, 1951–58; Hon. Consulting Physician, Iraqi Army, 1953–59; Consulting Physician to the Army, 1960–65; retd 1965. Lectr in Tropical Medicine, Middlesex Hosp. Med. Sch., 1960–65, and London Hosp. Med. Sch., 1963–65; Hon. Consulting Physician, Royal Hosp., Chelsea, 1961–65; Chief Med. Advr, Shell Internat. Petroleum Co. Ltd, 1965–72. Examiner: RCP, 1964–66; Soc. Apothecaries, 1966–73. Mem. of Council, Royal Society of Medicine, 1966–69, Vice-Pres., Library (Scientific Research) Section, 1967–69. Counsellor, Royal Soc. of Tropical Med. and Hygiene, 1961–65; Member: Hosp. Cttee, St John's Ophthalmic Hosp., Jerusalem, 1968–71; Finance Cttee, RCP. OStJ 1965. Iraq Coronation Medal, 1953. *Publications:* The Practice of Tropical Medicine (with R. J. G. Morrison), 1965; chapters in: Textbook of Medicine (Conybeare), 16th edn 1975; Modern Trends in Gastro-Enterology (Avery Jones), 1951; Medicine in the Tropics (Woodruff), 1974; numerous articles in med. jls. *Recreations:* art and music. *Address:* 6/3 Gladswood Gardens, Double Bay, NSW 2028, Australia.

HARGROVES, Brig. Sir (Robert) Louis, Kt 1987; CBE 1965; DL; *b* 10 Dec. 1917; *s* of William Robert and Mabel Mary Hargroves; *m* 1940, Eileen Elizabeth Anderson; four *d. Educ:* St John's College, Southsea. Commissioned South Staffordshire Regt, 1938; served War of 1939–45; CO 1 Staffords, 1959–61; GSO1, RMA Sandhurst, 1962–63; Brig. 1964; comd Aden Bde, 1964–66; MoD, 1966–69; N Command, 1969–72; retired, 1972. Col. Staffordshire Regt, 1971–77. DL Staffs 1974. *Recreations:* field sports. *Address:* Hyde Cottage, Temple Guiting, Cheltenham, Glos GL54 5RT. *T:* Guiting Power (0451) 850242.

HARINGTON, Gen. Sir Charles (Henry Pepys), GCB 1969 (KCB 1964; CB 1961); CBE 1957 (OBE 1953); DSO 1944; MC 1940; ADC (General) to the Queen, 1969–71; *b* 5 May 1910; *s* of Lt-Col H. H. Harington and Dorothy Pepys; *m* 1942, Victoire Marion Williams-Freeman; one *s* two *d. Educ:* Malvern; Sandhurst. Commissioned into 22nd (Cheshire) Regt, 1930. Served War of 1939–45: France and Belgium, 2nd Bn Cheshire Regt, 1939–40; CO, 1st Bn Manchester Regt and GSO1, 53 (Welch) Div., NW Europe, 1944–45. DS Staff Coll., 1946; GSO1 Mil. Mission Greece, 1948; CO 1st Bn The Parachute Regt, 1949; Mil. Asst to CIGS, 1951; SHAPE, 1953; Comdr 49 Inf. Bde in Kenya, 1955; idc 1957; Comdt Sch. of Infantry, 1958; GOC 3rd Div., 1959; Comdt, Staff Coll., Camberley, 1961; C-in-C Middle East, 1963; DCGS, 1966; Chief of Personnel and Logistics, to the three Services, 1968–71, retired; Col The Cheshire Regt, 1962–68. Col Comdt, Small Arms Sch. Corps, 1964–70; Col Comdt, The Prince of Wales Div., 1968–71. President: Combined Cadet Force Assoc., 1971–80; Milocarian (Tri-Service) Athletic Club. Chm. Governors, Royal Star and Garter Home, 1972–80. Comr, Duke of York's Royal Military Sch., 1971–89. Knight Officer with swords, Order of Orange Nassau (Netherlands), 1945. *Clubs:* Army and Navy, Hurlingham (Pres.).

HARINGTON, (Edward Henry) Vernon; *b* 13 Sept. 1907; *er s* of late His Honour Edward Harington; *m* 1st, 1937, Mary Elizabeth (marr. diss. 1949), *d* of late Louis Egerton; one *d* (and one *d* decd); 2nd, 1950, Mary Johanna Jean, JP, *d* of late Lt-Col R. G. S. Cox, MC; two *d. Educ:* Eton. Called to Bar, Inner Temple, 1930. Private Sec. to Lord Chancellor and Dep. Serjeant-at-Arms, House of Lords, 1934–40; served with HM Forces, 1940–45 (Major, Coldstream Guards); WO, 1944–45; Austrian Control Commn, Legal Div., 1945; Asst Sec. to Lord Chancellor for Commns of the Peace, 1945; Dep. Judge

Advocate, 1946; Asst Judge Advocate Gen., 1954–73. Dep. Chm., Herefordshire QS, 1969–71; a Recorder of the Crown Court, 1972–75. Chm., Hereford, Worcester, Warwicks and W Midlands Regional Agricl Wages Cttee, 1976–82. Councillor, Malvern Hill DC, 1979–87. JP Herefordshire, 1969–71. *Recreations:* shooting, fishing. *Address:* Woodlands House, Whitbourne, Worcester WR6 5RZ. *T:* Knightwick (0886) 21437.

HARINGTON, Kenneth Douglas Evelyn Herbert; Metropolitan Magistrate, 1967–84; *b* 30 Sept. 1911; *yr s* of late His Honour Edward Harington; *m* 1st, 1939, Lady Cecilia Bowes-Lyon (*d* 1947), *er d* of 15th Earl of Strathmore; 2nd, 1950, Maureen Helen McCalmont, *d* of Brig.-Gen. Sir Robert McCalmont, KCVO, CBE, DSO; two *s. Educ:* Stowe. War of 1939–45: Served NW Europe (Major, Coldstream Guards). Hon. Attaché, British Legation, Stockholm, 1930–32; Barrister, Inner Temple, 1952; Acting Deputy Chm., Inner London and NE London Quarter Sessions, 1966–67. *Recreations:* shooting, fishing. *Address:* Orchard End, Upper Oddington, Moreton-in-Marsh, Glos. *T:* Cotswold (0451) 30988.

HARINGTON, Sir Nicholas (John), 14th Bt *cr* 1611; Legal Adviser, Export Credits Guarantee Department, since 1988; *b* 14 May 1942; *s* of His Honour John Charles Dundas Harington, QC (*d* 1980) (*yr s* of 12th Bt) and Lavender Cecilia Harington (*d* 1982), *d* of late Major E. W. Denny, Garboldisham Manor, Diss; *S* uncle, 1981. *Educ:* Eton; Christ Church, Oxford (MA Jurisprudence). Called to the Bar, 1969. Employed in Persian Gulf, 1971–72. Joined Civil Service, 1972. *Recreations:* numerous. *Heir: b* David Richard Harington [*b* 27 June 1944; *m* 1983, Deborah (*née* Catesby); two *s*]. *Address:* The Ring o'Bells, Whitbourne, Worcester WR6 5RT. *T:* Knightwick (0886) 21819.

HARINGTON, Vernon; *see* Harington, E. H. V.

HARKIN, Brendan; Chairman, Industry Matters (Northern Ireland) Ltd, since 1987; *b* 21 April 1920; *s* of Francis and Catherine Harkin; *m* 1949, Maureen Gee; one *s* two *d. Educ:* St Mary's Christian Brothers' Primary and Grammar Schs, Belfast. Apprentice Electrician, 1936. Asst Sec. 1953, Gen. Sec. 1955–76, NI Civil Service Assoc. (which after amalgamations became Public Service Alliance, 1971). Chm. and Chief Exec., Labour Relations Agency, 1976–85. Chm., Strathearn Audio Ltd, 1974–76; Deputy Chairman: NI Finance Corp., 1972–76; NI Development Agency, 1976. Mem., EEC Economic and Social Cttee, 1973–76. Chm., Industry Year. Pres., Irish Congress of Trade Unions, 1976. Member: Council, NUU, now Univ. of Ulster, 1982–; Council, Co-operation North, 1984–. Pres., NI Hospice, 1985–. MUniv Open, 1986. *Publications:* contrib. on industrial relations. *Recreations:* theatre, music, reading. *Address:* 113 Somerton Road, Belfast 15, Northern Ireland. *T:* 774979.

HARKINS, Gerard Francis Robert; His Honour Judge Harkins; a Circuit Judge, since 1986; *b* 13 July 1936; *o s* of Francis Murphy Harkins and Katherine Harkins (*née* Hunt). *Educ:* Mount St Mary's College, Spinkhill, near Sheffield; King's College in University of Durham (now Univ. of Newcastle upon Tyne). LDS Dunelm 1961. Dental surgeon in general practice, Yorks, 1961–70; called to the Bar, Middle Temple, 1969; practised NE Circuit, 1970–86. Pres., Mount Assoc., 1991–92. Governor, Mount St Mary's, 1990–. *Address:* c/o The Law Courts, Quayside, Newcastle upon Tyne NE1 2LA. *Club:* Lansdowne.

HARKNESS, Lt-Col Hon. Douglas Scott, OC 1978; GM 1943; ED 1944; PC (Canada) 1957; Minister of National Defence, Canada, 1960–63; *b* 29 March 1903; *s* of William Keefer and Janet Douglas Harkness (*née* Scott); *m* 1932, Frances Elisabeth, *d* of James Blair McMillan, Charlottetown and Calgary; one *s. Educ:* Central Collegiate, Calgary; University of Alberta (BA). Served overseas in War (Italy and NW Europe), 1940–45; Major and Lt-Col, Royal Canadian Artillery; with Reserve Army, CO 41st Anti-Tank Regt (SP), Royal Canadian Artillery. MP (Calgary E) gen. elecs, 1945, 1949; Re-elected: (Calgary N) gen. elecs, 1953, 1957, 1958, 1962, 1963, 1965, (Calgary Centre) 1968, retired 1972; Min. for Northern Affairs and Nat. Resources and Actg Minister of Agric., June 1957; Minister of Agric., Aug. 1957; relinquished portfolios of Northern Affairs and Nat. Resources, Aug. 1957, of Agriculture, Oct. 1960. Mem. Alta Military Institute. Hon. LLD Calgary, 1975. *Address:* 716 Imperial Way SW, Calgary, Alta T2S 1N7, Canada. *T:* Calgary (403) 243–0825. *Clubs:* Ranchmen's, Calgary Petroleum (Calgary).

HARKNESS, Jack; *see* Harkness, J. L.

HARKNESS, Rev. James, OBE 1978; QHC 1982; Chaplain General to the Forces, since 1987; *b* 20 Oct. 1935; *s* of James and Jane Harkness; *m* 1960, Elizabeth Anne Tolmie; one *s* one *d. Educ:* Univ. of Edinburgh (MA). Asst Minister, North Morningside Parish Church, Edinburgh, 1959–61; joined RAChD, 1961: Chaplain: 1 KOSB, 1961–65; 1 Queen's Own Highlanders, 1965–69; Singapore, 1969–70; Dep. Warden, RAChD Centre, 1970–74; Senior Chaplain: N Ireland, 1974–75; 4th Div., 1975–78; Asst Chaplain Gen., Scotland, 1980–81; Senior Chaplain: 1st British Corps, 1981–82; BAOR, 1982–84; Dep. Chaplain Gen. to the Forces, 1985–86. OStJ 1988. *Recreations:* general pursuits. *Address:* MoD Chaplains (Army), Bagshot Park, Bagshot, Surrey GU19 5PL. *T:* Bagshot (0276) 71717. *Club:* New (Edinburgh) (Hon. Mem.).

HARKNESS, Rear-Adm. James Percy Knowles, CB 1971; *b* 28 Nov. 1916; *s* of Captain P. Y. Harkness, West Yorkshire Regt, and Gladys Dundas Harkness (*née* Knowles); *m* 1949, Joan, *d* of late Vice-Adm. N. A. Sulivan, CVO; two *d.* Dir-Gen., Naval Manpower, 1970; retired 1972. *Recreation:* sailing.

HARKNESS, John Leigh, (Jack), OBE 1986; Director, R. Harkness & Co. Ltd, since 1960; *b* 29 June 1918; *s* of Verney Leigh Harkness and Olivia Amy Harkness (*née* Austin); *m* 1947, Betty Catherine Moore; two *s* one *d. Educ:* Whitgift School. Army service, 1940–46: Hertfordshire Regt; Sherwood Foresters; 2nd Punjab Regt; mentioned in despatches, Burma; released with hon. rank of Major. Apprentice nurseryman, Donard Nursery, 1934–37; rose grower, R. Harkness & Co., Hitchin, 1937–77; rose breeder, Harkness New Roses, 1962–. Roses bred include: Escapade, 1967; Elizabeth Harkness, 1969; Alexander, Southampton, 1972; Compassion, 1973; Yesterday, 1974; Margaret Merril, 1977; Anna Ford, Anne Harkness, 1980; Princess Michael of Kent, 1981; Mountbatten, 1982; Paul Shirville, 1983; Amber Queen, 1984; Armada, City of London, 1988; Jacqueline du Pré, Savoy Hotel, 1989. Sec., British Assoc. of Rose Breeders, 1973–85. Gold Medal Rose Nord, 1978; DHM, 1980; Rose Growers Assoc. Medal, 1987; Australian Rose Award, 1988. Editor, Royal National Rose Society, 1978–83. *Publications:* Growing Roses, 1967; Roses, 1978; The World's Favourite Roses, 1979; How to Grow Roses, 1980; The Rose Directory, 1982; The Makers of Heavenly Roses, 1985; Rose Classes, 1989. *Recreations:* writing, bird watching, wine. *Address:* 1 Bank Alley, Southwold, Suffolk IP18 6JD. *T:* Southwold (0502) 722030.

HARLAND, Bryce; *see* Harland, W. B.

HARLAND, Rt. Rev. Ian; *see* Carlisle, Bishop of.

HARLAND, Air Marshal Sir Reginald (Edward Wynyard), KBE 1974; CB 1972; AE 1945; engineering and management consultant; *b* 30 May 1920; *s* of Charles Cecil Harland and Ida Maud (*née* Bellhouse); *m* 1942, Doreen Rosalind, *d* of late W. H. C.

Romanis; two *s* two *d.* (and one *s* decd). *Educ:* Summer Fields, Oxford; Stowe; Trinity Coll., Cambridge (MA). Served War of 1939–45: RAE Farnborough, 1941–42; N Africa, Italy and S France, 1942–45. Techn. trng, techn. plans and manning depts, Air Min., 1946–49; pilot trng, 1949–50; Chief Engrg Instructor, RAF Coll., Cranwell, 1950–52; Guided Weapon trng, RMCS Shrivenham, 1952–53; Thunderbird Project Officer: RAE Farnborough, 1953–55; Min. of Supply, 1955–56; psa 1957; Ballistic Missile Liaison Officer, (BJSM) Los Angeles, 1958–60; CO, Central Servicing Develt Estab., Swanton Morley, 1960–62; STSO, HQ No 3 (Bomber) Gp, Mildenhall, 1962–64; AO i/c Engrg, HQ Far East Air Force, Singapore, 1964–66; Harrier Project Dir, HQ Min. of Technology, 1967–68; idc 1969; AOC No 24 Group, RAF, 1970–72; AO Engineering, Air Support Command, 1972; AOC-in-C, RAF Support Command, 1973–77. Technical Dir, W. S. Atkins & Partners, 1977–82; Consultant to Short Brothers Ltd, 1983–88. Member Council: BIM, 1973–78, 1980–86, 1987–90; Pres., Soc. Environmental Engrs, 1974–78; Vice-Chm., CEI, 1983–84. Contested Bury St Edmunds, (SDP) 1983, (SDP/Alliance) 1987. Sen. Academic Fellow, Leicester Poly., 1989. CEng 1966; FIMechE 1967; FIEE 1964; FRAeS 1967; CBIM (FBIM 1974; Verulam Medal, 1991). *Publications:* occasional articles in engrg jls. *Recreations:* better management, better government. *Address:* 49 Crown Street, Bury St Edmunds, Suffolk IP33 1QX. *T:* Bury St Edmunds (0284) 763078. *Club:* Royal Air Force.

HARLAND, (William) Bryce; High Commissioner for New Zealand in the United Kingdom 1985–91; *b* 11 Dec. 1931; *s* of Edward Dugard Harland and Annie McDonald Harland (*née* Gordon); *m* 1st, 1957, Rosemary Anne Gordon (marr. diss. 1977); two *s* (and one *s* decd); 2nd, 1979, Margaret Anne Blackburn; one *s. Educ:* Victoria Univ., Wellington, NZ (MA Hons); Fletcher School of Law and Diplomacy, Boston, Mass, USA (AM). Joined NZ Dept of External Affairs, 1953; diplomatic postings: Singapore, 1956; Bangkok, 1957; NY, 1959; Wellington, 1962; Washington, 1965; Wellington, 1969; First NZ Ambassador to China, 1973–75; Ministry of Foreign Affairs, Wellington: Head of African and European Divs, 1976–77; Asst Sec., 1977–82; Perm. Rep. of NZ to the UN, NY, 1982–85 (Chm., Economic and Financial Cttee, Gen. Assembly, 1984). Vis. Fellow, All Souls Coll., Oxford, 1991. KStJ 1985. Hon. Freeman, City of London, 1987. *Recreations:* reading history, walking. *Address:* 15 Selwyn Avenue, Richmond TW9 2HB. *Clubs:* Brooks's, East India, Royal Automobile.

HARLE, James Coffin, DPhil, DLitt; Keeper, Department of Eastern Art, Ashmolean Museum, Oxford, 1967–87; Student of Christ Church, Oxford, 1970–87, now Emeritus; *b* 5 April 1920; *s* of James Wyly Harle and Elfrieda Frances (*née* Baumann); *m* 1st, 1949, Jacqueline Thérèse Ruch (marr. diss. 1966, she *d* 1968); 2nd, 1967, Mrs Carola Sybil Mary Fleming (*d* 1971); 3rd, 1973, Lady (Betty) Hulbert. *Educ:* St George's Sch., Newport, RI; Princeton Univ. (BA 1942, Phi Beta Kappa); Oxford Univ. (BA 1st cl. Sanskrit and Pali, 1956; DPhil 1959; DLitt 1989). Served War, 1942–46, USNR (Aviation Br.), retd as Lieut; DFC (US). Asst to Dean of the College, Princeton, 1947; Part-time instructor in English, Princeton, 1948–49; Fulbright Lectr, Philippines, 1953–54; Ashmolean Museum: Asst Keeper, 1960; Sen. Asst Keeper, 1962. Pres., Soc. for S Asian Studies (British Acad.), 1990–. *Publications:* Tower Gateways in South India, 1963; Gupta Sculpture, 1974; The Art and Architecture of the Indian Subcontinent, 1986; articles in periodicals on Indian Art. *Address:* Hawkswell, 34 Portland Road, Oxford OX2 7EY. *T:* Oxford (0865) 515236. *Club:* Princeton (New York).

HARLE, John Crofton, FGSM; saxophonist, composer, arranger, conductor; *b* 20 Sept. 1956; *s* of Jack Harle and Joyce Harle (*née* Crofton); *m* 1985, Julia Jane Eisner; two *s. Educ:* Newcastle Royal Grammar Sch.; Royal Coll. of Music (Foundn Schol.); ARCM (Hons)); private study in Paris, 1981–82. FGSM 1990. Leader of Myrha Saxophone Quartet, 1977–82; formed duo with pianist John Lenehan, 1979; saxophone soloist, 1980–, with major internat. orchs, incl. LSO, English Chamber Orch., Basel Chamber Orch., San Diego Symphony Orch; Principal Saxophone, London Sinfonietta, 1987–; Prof. of Saxophone, GSMD, 1988–. Formed: Berliner Band, 1983; John Harle Band, 1988. Compositions for several ensembles, 1983–, incl. London Brass and LSO. Frequent soloist on TV and feature films; regular broadcaster on BBC Radio; featured in One Man and his Sax, BBC2 TV, 1988. Has made many recordings. Major works written for him by Dominic Muldowney, Ned Rorem, Richard Rodney Bennett and Luciano Berio. Dannreuther Concerto Prize, Royal Coll. of Music, 1980; GLAA Young Musician, 1979, 1980. Gen. Ed., Universal Saxophone Edn, 1985–. *Publication:* John Harle's Saxophone Album, 1986. *Recreations:* family life, cooking, becoming a nicer person. *Address:* c/o Horowitz Music Management, Grosvenor Gardens House, 35–37 Grosvenor Gardens, SW1W 0BS. *T:* 071–233 5181; 081–464 5151.

HARLECH, 6th Baron *cr* 1876; **Francis David Ormsby Gore;** *b* 13 March 1954; *s* of 5th Baron Harlech, KCMG, PC, and Sylvia (*d* 1967), *d* of Hugh Lloyd Thomas, CMG, CVO; *S* father, 1985; *m* 1986, Amanda Jane, *d* of Alan T. Grieve; one *s* one *d. Educ:* Worth. *Heir: s* Hon. Jasset David Cody Ormsby Gore, *b* 1 July 1986. *Address:* The Mount, Racecourse Road, Oswestry, Shropshire SY10 7PH.

HARLECH, Pamela, Lady; journalist and producer; *b* 18 Dec. 1934; *d* of Ralph Frederick Colin and Georgia Talmey; *m* 1969, 5th Baron Harlech, PC, KCMG (*d* 1985); one *d. Educ:* Smith Coll., Northampton, Mass; Finch Coll. (BA). London Editor, (American) Vogue, 1964–69; Food Editor, (British) Vogue, 1971–82; freelance journalist, 1972–; prodn work for special events, 1986–87; Commissioning Editor, Thames and Hudson, Publishers, 1987–89. Chairman: Women's Playhouse Trust, 1984–; V & A Enterprises, 1987–; English Nat. Ballet, 1990–; Council, British Amer. Arts Assoc., 1990–; Member: Welsh Arts Council, 1981–85; Arts Council of GB, 1986–90; South Bank Bd, 1986–; Council, Managing Bd, Cruisaid, 1987–; Council, Assoc. of Business Sponsorship for the Arts, 1988– (Chm., Judging Panel for Awards, 1989–90). Trustee, V&A Mus., 1986–. *Publications:* Feast without Fuss, 1976; Pamela Harlech's Complete Guide to Cooking, Entertainment and Household Management, 1981; Vogue Book of Menus, 1985. *Recreations:* music, cooking, laughing. *Address:* English National Ballet, 39 Jay Mews, SW7. *T:* 071–581 1245.

HARLEY, Maj.-Gen. Alexander George Hamilton, CB 1991; OBE 1981; Assistant Chief of Defence Staff (Overseas), since 1990; *b* 3 May 1941; *s* of Lt-Col William Hamilton Coughtrie Harley, 1st Punjab Regt and later Royal Indian Engineers, and Eleanor Blanche (*née* Jarvis); *m* 1967, Christina Valentine, *d* of Edmund Noel Butler-Cole and Kathleen Mary (*née* Thompson); two *s. Educ:* Caterham Sch.; RMA Sandhurst. Commissioned RA 1962; served 7 Para Regt RHA, Instructor, Junior Leaders Regt RA, Staff Captain MoD, and Adjutant, 36 Air Def. Regt RA, 1963–72; Canadian Staff Coll., 1972–73; Mil. Asst, MoD, 1974–75; Battery Comdr, 1975–78 (despatches); Directing Staff, Staff Coll., 1978–79; CO 19 Field Regt RA, 1979–82; Col Defence Staff, MoD, 1983–85; Comdr 33 Armd Brigade, 1985–87; Asst Chief of Staff (Ops), Northern Army Group, 1988–90. Hon. Regtl Col, 19 Field Regt RA. Pres., Army Hockey. *Recreations:* golf, fishing, hockey, clocks. *Address:* Assistant Chief of Defence Staff (Overseas), Main Building, Whitehall, SW1A 2HB. *Club:* Commonwealth Trust.

HARMAN, Harriet; MP (Lab) Peckham, since Oct. 1982; *b* 30 July 1950; *d* of John Bishop Harman, *qv* and Anna Charlotte Harman; *m* 1982, Jack Dromey; two *s* one *d.*

Educ: St Paul's Girls' Sch.; York Univ. Brent Community Law Centre, 1975–78; Legal Officer, NCCL, 1978–82. *Publications:* Sex Discrimination in Schools, 1977; Justice Deserted: the subversion of the jury, 1979. *Address:* House of Commons, SW1A 0AA.

HARMAN, Gen. Sir Jack (Wentworth), GCB 1978 (KCB 1974); OBE 1962; MC 1943; Deputy Supreme Allied Commander, Europe, 1978–81, retired; *b* 20 July 1920; *s* of late Lt-Gen. Sir Wentworth Harman, KCB, DSO, and late Dorothy Harman; *m* 1947, Gwladys May Murphy (*widow* of Lt-Col R. J. Murphy), *d* of Sir Idwal Lloyd; one *d* and two step *d. Educ:* Wellington Coll.; RMC Sandhurst. Commissioned into The Queen's Bays, 1940, Bt Lt-Col, 1958; Commanding Officer, 1st The Queen's Dragoon Guards, 1960–62; commanded 11 Infantry Bde, 1965–66; attended IDC, 1967; BGS, HQ Army Strategic Command, 1968–69; GOC, 1st Div., 1970–72; Commandant, RMA, Sandhurst, 1972–73; GOC 1 (British) Corps, 1974–76; Adjutant-General, 1976–78. ADC Gen. to the Queen, 1977–80. Col, 1st The Queen's Dragoon Guards, 1975–80; Col Comdt, RAC, 1977–80. Dir, Wilsons Hogg Robinson (formerly Wilsons (Insurance Brokers)), 1982–88. Vice-Chairman: Nat. Army Museum, 1980–87; AA, 1986–89 (Mem. Cttee, 1981–85). *Address:* Sandhills House, Dinton, near Salisbury, Wilts SP3 5ER. *T:* Teffont (0722) 716288. *Club:* Cavalry and Guards.

HARMAN, Hon. Sir Jeremiah (LeRoy), Kt 1982; **Hon. Mr Justice Harman;** a Judge of the High Court of Justice, Chancery Division, since 1982; *b* 13 April 1930; *er s* of late Rt Hon. Sir Charles Eustace Harman; *m* 1960, Erica Jane (marr diss. 1986), *e d* of late Hon. Sir Maurice Richard Bridgeman, KBE; two *s* one *d*; *m* 1987, Katharine Frances Goddard, *d* of late Rt Hon. Sir Eric Sachs and *widow* of George Pulay. *Educ:* Horris Hill Sch.; Eton Coll. Served Coldstream Guards and Parachute Regt, 1948–51; Parachute Regt (TA), 1951–55. Called to the Bar, Lincoln's Inn, 1954, Bencher, 1977; QC 1968; called to Hong Kong Bar, 1978, Singapore Bar, 1980; Mem., Bar Council, 1963–67. Dir, Dunford & Elliott Ltd, 1972–79. *Recreations:* fishing, stalking, watching birds. *Address:* Royal Courts of Justice, The Strand, WC2A 2LL.

HARMAN, John Bishop, FRCS, FRCP; Honorary Consulting Physician, since 1972; *b* 10 Aug. 1907; *s* of late Nathaniel Bishop Harman and of Katharine (*née* Chamberlain); *m* 1946, Anna Charlotte Malcolm Spicer; four *d. Educ:* Oundle; St John's Coll., Cambridge (Scholar); St Thomas's Hospital (Scholar). Fearnsides Scholar, Cantab, 1932; 1st Cl. Nat. Sci. Tripos Pt I, 2nd Cl. Pt II, Cantab; MA 1933; MD 1937; FRCS 1932; FRCP 1942. Physician: St Thomas' Hospital, 1938–72; Royal Marsden Hospital, 1947–72. Pres., Medical Defence Union, 1976–81; 2nd Vice Pres., RCP, 1981–82. Late Lt-Col RAMC (despatches). *Publications:* contribs to medical literature. *Recreation:* horticulture. *Address:* 108 Harley Street, W1. *T:* 071–935 7822.

See also H. Harman.

HARMAN, Robert Donald, QC 1974; a Recorder of the Crown Court, since 1972; a Judge of the Courts of Appeal of Jersey and Guernsey, since 1986; *b* 26 Sept. 1928; *o s* of late Herbert Donald Harman, MC; *m* 1st, 1960, Sarah Elizabeth (*d* 1965), *o d* of late G. C. Cleverly; two *s*; 2nd, 1968, Rosamond Geraldine, JP, 2nd *d* of late Cmdr G. T. A. Scott, RN; two *d. Educ:* privately; St Paul's Sch.; Magdalen Coll., Oxford. Called to Bar, Gray's Inn, 1954, Bencher, 1984; South-Eastern Circuit; a Junior Prosecuting Counsel to the Crown at Central Criminal Court, 1967–72; a Senior Treasury Counsel, 1972–74. Mem., Senate of the Inns of Court and the Bar, 1985–87. Jt Hon. Sec., Barristers' Benevolent Assoc. Appeal Steward, BBB of C. Liveryman, Goldsmiths' Co. *Address:* 2 Harcourt Buildings, Temple, EC4. *T:* 071–353 2112; 17 Pelham Crescent, SW7 2NR. *T:* 071–584 4304. *Clubs:* Garrick, Beefsteak, Pratt's; Swinley Forest Golf.

HARMAR-NICHOLLS, family name of **Baron Harmar-Nicholls.**

HARMAR-NICHOLLS, Baron *cr* 1974 (Life Peer), of Peterborough, Cambs; **Harmar Harmar-Nicholls,** JP; Bt 1960; Member (C) Greater Manchester South, European Parliament, 1979–84; *b* 1 Nov. 1912; 3rd *s* of Charles E. C. Nicholls and Sarah Anne Nicholls, Walsall; *m* 1940, Dorothy Elsie, *e d* of James Edwards, Tipton; two *d. Educ:* Dorsett Road Sch., Darlaston; Queen Mary's Gram. Sch., Walsall. Mem. Middle Temple Inn of Court. Chairman: Nicholls and Hennessy (Hotels) Ltd; Malvern Festival Theatre Trust Ltd; Radio Luxembourg (London) Ltd, 1983– (Dir, 1963–); Dir, J. & H. Nicholls & Co., Paints, etc, 1945–. Mem. of Syndicate at Lloyd's. Mem. Darlaston UDC at age of 26 (Chm., 1949–50); County Magistrate, 1946. Vice-Chm. W Midland Fedn, Junior Imperial League, 1937; contested (C): Nelson and Colne, 1945; Preston by-election, 1946; MP (C) Peterborough Div. of Northants, 1950–Sept. 1974; PPS to Asst Postmaster-Gen., 1951–April 1955; Parly Sec., Min. of Agriculture, Fisheries and Food, April 1955–Jan. 1957; Parliamentary Sec., Min. of Works, 1957–60; Mem. Conservative Housing Cttee; Sec. of Parly Road Safety Cttee (Conservative); Jt Sec. All party Parly Group Empire Migration; Mem. Govt Overseas Settlement Board on migration to Commonwealth. War of 1939–45: volunteered as sapper, commnd Royal Engineers; served India and Burma. *Recreations:* gardening, reading, walking, theatre. *Address:* Abbeylands, Weston, Stafford. *T:* Weston (0889) 252. *Clubs:* St Stephen's Constitutional; (Pres.) Unionist, City and Counties (Peterborough); Conservative (Darlaston); Unionist (Walsall).

HARMER, Sir Frederic (Evelyn), Kt 1968; CMG 1945; *b* 3 Nov. 1905; *yr s* of late Sir Sidney Frederic Harmer, KBE, FRS; *m* 1st, 1931, Barbara Susan (*d* 1972), *er d* of late Major J. A. C. Hamilton, JP, Fyne Court, Bridgwater, Som.; one *s* two *d* (and one *d* decd); 2nd, 1973, Daphne Shelton Agar. *Educ:* Eton (KS); King's Coll., Cambridge (Scholar). Wrangler, Maths Tripos Part II, 1926; Class 1, Div. 1, Econs Tripos Part II 1927; BA 1927; MA 1934. Entered Treasury, Sept. 1939; Temp. Asst Sec., 1943–45; served in Washington, March-June 1944 and again in Sept.-Dec. 1945 for Anglo-American economic and financial negotiations; resigned Dec. 1945 and joined New Zealand Shipping Co. (Chm., 1953–65). Dep. Chm., P&OSN Co., 1957–70. Chairman: Cttee of European Shipowners, 1965–68; Internat. Chamber of Shipping, 1968–71; HM Govt Dir, British Petroleum Co. Ltd, 1953–70. Hon. Fellow, LSE, 1970. *Recreations:* sailing, golf. *Address:* Tiggins Field, Kelsale, Saxmundham, Suffolk. *T:* Saxmundham (0728) 3156.

HARMER, Michael Hedley, MA, MB Cantab, FRCS; Consulting Surgeon, Royal Marsden Hospital and Paddington Green Children's Hospital (St Mary's Hospital); *b* 6 July 1912; *y s* of late Douglas Harmer, MC, FRCS, and May (*née* Hedley); *m* 1939, Bridget Jean, *d* of late James Higgs-Walker, MA, and of Muriel Jessie, *e d* of Rev. Harold Smith; one *s* one *d. Educ:* Marlborough; King's Coll., Cambridge; St Bartholomew's Hosp., London. Surgical Specialist, RAFVR, 1943–46. Bellman Snark Club, Cambridge, 1934–. Freeman of Norwich by Patrimony, 1935. *Publications:* A Handbook of Surgery, 1951; Aids to Surgery, 1962; (Jt Editor) Rose and Carless's Manual of Surgery, 19th edn, 1959; The Forgotten Hospital, 1982; Look Back in Happiness, 1991; papers on the surgery and classification of malignant disease. *Recreations:* music, the country. *Address:* Perrot Wood, Graffham, Petworth, Sussex GU28 0NZ. *T:* Graffham (07986) 307.

HARMSWORTH, family name of **Viscount Rothermere** and **Baron Harmsworth.**

HARMSWORTH, 3rd Baron, *cr* 1939, of Egham; **Thomas Harold Raymond Harmsworth;** publisher; *b* 20 July 1939; *s* of Hon. Eric Beauchamp Northcliffe Harmsworth (*d* 1988) and Hélène Marie (*d* 1962), *d* of Col Jules Raymond Dehove; *S* uncle, 1990; *m* 1971, Patricia Palmer, *d* of late M. P. Horsley; two *s* three *d. Educ:* Eton; Christ Church, Oxford (MA). Nat. Service, Royal Horse Guards (The Blues), 1957–59 (2nd Lieut). Stockbroker, 1962–74; DHSS, 1974–88. Chm., Dr Johnson's House Trust. *Recreations:* sundry, including music. *Address:* The Old Rectory, Stoke Abbott, Beaminster, Dorset DT8 3JT. *T:* Broadwindsor (0308) 68139.

HARMSWORTH, Sir Hildebrand Harold, 3rd Bt *cr* 1922; *b* 5 June 1931; *s* of Sir Hildebrand Alfred Beresford Harmsworth, 2nd Bt, and Elen, *d* of Nicolaj Billenstein, Randers, Denmark; *S* father, 1977; *m* 1960, Gillian Andrea, *o d* of William John Lewis; one *s* two *d. Educ:* Harrow; Trinity College, Dublin. *Heir: s* Hildebrand Esmond Miles Harmsworth, *b* 1 Sept. 1964. *Address:* Ewlyn Villa, 42 Leckhampton Road, Cheltenham.

HARMSWORTH, St John Bernard Vyvyan; a Metropolitan Magistrate, 1961–85; *b* 28 Nov. 1912; *e s* of Vyvyan George Harmsworth and Constance Gwendolen Mary Catt; *m* 1937, Jane Penelope (*d* 1984), *er d* of Basil Tanfield Berridge Boothby; three *d. Educ:* Harrow; New Coll., Oxford. Called to the Bar, Middle Temple, 1937. Served in RNVR, Lieut-Comdr, Oct. 1939–Feb. 1946. *Recreations:* fly fishing, tennis. *Clubs:* Boodle's, Pratt's, Beefsteak.

HARNDEN, Arthur Baker, CB 1969; BSc, CEng, FIEE, FBIM; Chairman, Appeals Tribunals, Supplementary Benefits Commission, 1970–82; *b* 6 Jan. 1909; *s* of Cecil Henry Harnden and Susan (*née* Baker); *m* 1st, 1935, Maisie Elizabeth Annie (*d* 1970), *d* of A. H. Winterburn, LRIBA; one *s*; 2nd, 1971, Jean Kathleen, *d* of H. F. Wheeler and *widow* of Eric J. Dedman; one step *s. Educ:* various state schools. Exec. Engr, GPO, 1933; Royal Corps of Signals, 1939–45; Lt-Col GSO1, WO, 1942; DCSO Antwerp, 1944, Hamburg 1945. Dir, London Telecommunications Region, GPO, 1962; Senior Dir, Operations, PO (Telecommunications), 1967–69. Principal, Comrie House Sch., Finchley, 1971–72. *Recreations:* painting and potting. *Address:* Comrie, Park Street, Fairford, Glos GL7 4JL. *T:* Cirencester (0285) 712805.

HARNDEN, Prof. David Gilbert, PhD, FRSE 1982, FIBiol, FRCPath; Director, Paterson Institute for Cancer Research (formerly Paterson Laboratories), Christie Hospital and Holt Radium Institute, Manchester, since 1983; *b* 22 June 1932; *s* of William Alfred Harnden and Anne McKenzie Wilson; *m* 1955, Thora Margaret Seatter; three *s. Educ:* George Heriot's School, Edinburgh; University of Edinburgh. BSc. Lectr, Univ. of Edinburgh, 1956–57; Sci. Mem., Radiobiology Unit, MRC, Harwell, 1957–59; Sci. Mem., Clinical and Population Cytogenetics Unit, MRC, Edinburgh, 1959–69; Prof. of Cancer Studies, Univ. of Birmingham, 1969–83; Hon. Prof. of Experimental Oncology, Univ. of Manchester, 1983–. Chairman: Educn Cttee, Cancer Res. Campaign, 1987–; NW Regl Adv. Cttee on Oncology Services, 1991–. Dir, Christie Hosp. (NHS) Trust, 1991–. Hon. MRCP 1987. Chm., Editorial Bd, British Jl of Cancer, 1983–. *Publications:* papers on cancer research and human genetics in learned jls. *Recreation:* sketching people and places. *Address:* Paterson Institute for Cancer Research, Christie Hospital and Holt Radium Institute, Wilmslow Road, Manchester M20 9BX. *T:* 061–434 8725.

HARNIMAN, John Phillip, OBE 1984; Assistant Controller, Personnel Division, British Council, since 1988; *b* 7 May 1939; *s* of William Thomas Harniman and Maud Kate Florence (*née* Dyrenfurth); *m* 1961, Avryl (*née* Hartley); one *s* one *d. Educ:* Leyton County High School; Culham College, Oxon (DipEd); London University (BA Hons); Université de la Sorbonne. William Morris School, Walthamstow, 1960–62; Ecole Normale Supérieure de Saint-Cloud, 1962–67; British Council: Algeria, 1967–70; Specialist Careers Officer, Personnel, 1970–73; Head, Overseas Careers, Personnel, 1973–76; Representative, Singapore, 1976–81; Cultural Attaché, Romania, 1981–84; Rep. and Cultural Counsellor, Belgium and Luxembourg, 1984–87. *Recreations:* reading, listening to music, letter-writing, cats. *Address:* Riverway, Mill Lane, Cookham-on-Thames, Berks; 68 Church Street, Lavenham, Suffolk. *Club:* Anglo-Belgian.

HARPER, Alfred Alexander, MA, MD; Professor of Physiology, University of Newcastle upon Tyne, 1963–72; *b* 19 June 1907; *er s* of James and Elizabeth Harper. *Educ:* Aberdeen Grammar Sch.; Aberdeen Univ. Lecturer in Physiology, University of Leeds, 1935–36; Demonstrator in Physiology, St Thomas's Hosp., London, 1936–39; Lectr, later Reader, in Human Physiology, Univ. of Manchester, 1939–49; Prof. of Physiology, Univ. of Durham, 1949–63. *Publications:* papers in Jl of Physiology mostly on physiology of digestion. *Address:* Wellburn House, Benwell Lane, Newcastle upon Tyne NE15 6LX. *T:* Tyneside 091–274 8178.

HARPER, Prof. Denis Rawnsley, CBE 1975; BArch, PhD, MSc Tech, FRIBA, MRTPI, PPIOB; building consultant; Professor of Building at the University of Manchester Institute of Science and Technology, 1957–74, now Emeritus; *b* 27 May 1907; *s* of James William Harper, Harrogate; *m* 1st, 1934, Joan Mary Coggin (*d* 1968); one *s* one *d*; 2nd, 1971, Dora Phylis Oxenham (widow). *Educ:* Harrogate Grammar Sch.; Univ. of Liverpool Sch. of Architecture. Asst Architect in Hosp. practice in London, 1930–38; RIBA Saxon Snell Prizeman, 1939; Lectr in Sch. of Architecture, University of Cape Town, 1939–49. In private practice (with Prof. Thornton White), in Cape Town, as architect and town planner, 1940–50; Associate Architect in BBC TV Centre, 1950–52; Chief Architect to Corby New Town, Northants, 1952–57. Hanson Fellow, The Master Builder Fedn of South Africa, 1972. Cttee Mem., CNAA. Mem., Summerland Fire Commn, 1973–74. *Publications:* Building: process and product, 1978; various contribs to technical jls. *Recreations:* gardening, boating. *Address:* 2 Glenfield Drive, Great Doddington, Wellingborough, Northants NN9 7TE. *T:* Wellingborough (0933) 223841.

HARPER, Donald John; Aerospace Systems and Defence Procurement consultant; *b* 6 Aug. 1923; *s* of Harry Tonkin and Caroline Irene Harper; *m* 1947, Joyce Beryl Kite-Powell; two *d. Educ:* Purley County Grammar Sch. for Boys; Queen Mary Coll., London. 1st cl. BSc (Eng) 1943; CEng, FRAeS. Joined Aero Dept, RAE Farnborough, 1943; Scientific Officer, Spinning Tunnel, 1947–49; High Speed and Transonic Tunnel, 1950–59; Sen. Scientific Officer; Principal Scientific Officer, 1955; Dep. Head of Tunnel, 1958–59; Space Dept RAE, Satellite Launching Vehicles, 1960–62; Senior Principal Scientific Officer, MoD, Central Staff, 1963–65; Head of Assessment Div., Weapons Dept RAE, 1966–68; Dir of Project Time and Cost Analysis, MoD (PE), 1968–71; Dir-Gen., Performance and Cost Analysis, MoD (PE), 1972–77; Dir-Gen. Research C, MoD (PE), 1978–83, and Chief Scientist, RAF, 1980–83. Mem. Council, RAeS, 1990–. *Publications:* contrib. Aeronautical Res. Council reports and memoranda and techn. press. *Recreations:* music, especially choral singing; gardening; home improvement. *Address:* Beech Cottage, Beech Gardens, Woking, Surrey GU21 4QT. *T:* Woking (0483) 760541.

HARPER, Heather (Mary), (Mrs E. J. Benarroch), CBE 1965; soprano; Professor of Singing and Consultant, Royal College of Music, since 1985; Director of Singing Studies, Britten-Pears School, Aldeburgh, since 1986; *b* 8 May 1930; *d* of late Hugh Harper, Belfast; *m* 1973, Eduardo J. Benarroch. *Educ:* Trinity Coll. of Music, London. Has sung many principal roles incl. Arabella, Ariadne, Marschallin, Chrysothemis, Elsa and Kaiserin, at Covent Garden, Glyndebourne, Sadler's Wells, Bayreuth, Teatro Colon (Buenos Aires), Edinburgh Fest., La Scala, NY Met, San Francisco, Deutsche Oper (Berlin), Frankfurt, Netherlands Opera, Canadian Opera Co., Toronto, and sang at every Promenade Concert season 1957–90; created the soprano role in Benjamin Britten's War Requiem in Coventry Cathedral in 1962; soloist at opening concerts: Maltings, Snape, 1967; Queen Elizabeth Hall, 1967. Toured USA, 1965, and USSR, 1967, with BBC SO; has toured USA annually, 1967–, and appeared regularly at European music fests; toured: Japan and S Korea as Principal Soloist Soprano with Royal Opera Co., 1979; Australia and Hong Kong with BBC Symph. Orch., 1982; has also sung in Asia, Middle East, Australia and S America; Principal Soloist Soprano with Royal Opera House Co., visit to Los Angeles Olympic Games, 1984; Principal Soloist with BBC Philharmonic Orch's first South American tour, 1989. Has made many recordings, incl. works of Britten, Beethoven, Berg, Mahler, Mozart, Strauss and Verdi; broadcasts frequently throughout the world, and appears frequently on TV; Masterclasses for advanced students and young professionals, Britten-Pears Sch.; retired from operatic stage, 1984, from concert stage, 1991. Member: BBC Music Panel, 1989; RSA Music Panel, 1989. FTCL; FRCM 1988; Hon. RAM, 1972. Hon. DMus, Queen's Univ., Belfast, 1966. Edison Award, 1971; Grammy Nomination, 1973; Grammy Award, 1979, 1984, Best vocal performance for Ravel's Scheherezade; Grand Prix du Disque, 1979. *Recreations:* gardening, painting, cooking. *Address:* c/o 20 Milverton Road, NW6 7AS.

HARPER, James Norman; barrister; a Recorder of the Crown Court, 1980–84; *b* 30 Dec. 1932; *s* of late His Honour Judge Norman Harper and Iris Irene Harper; *m* 1956, Blanka Miroslava Eva Sigmund; one *s* one *d. Educ:* Marlborough Coll.; Magdalen Coll., Oxford (BA Hons). Called to the Bar, Gray's Inn, 1957. Pres., Northumberland County Hockey Assoc., 1982–. *Recreations:* cricket, hockey, painting. *Address:* 33 Broad Chare, Newcastle upon Tyne NE1 3DQ. *T:* Tyneside 091–232 0541. *Club:* MCC.

HARPER, Prof. John Lander, CBE 1989; DPhil; FRS 1978; Head, Unit of Plant Population Biology, School of Plant Biology, Bangor, since 1982; *b* 27 May 1925; *s* of John Hindley Harper and Harriett Mary (*née* Archer); *m* 1954, Borgny Lerø; one *s* two *d. Educ:* Lawrence Sheriff Sch., Rugby; Magdalen Coll., Oxford (BA, MA, DPhil). Demonstr, Dept of Agriculture, Univ. of Oxford, 1951, Lectr 1953; Rockefeller Foundn Fellow, Univ. of Calif, 1960–61; Prof. of Agricultural Botany, 1960, Prof. of Botany, 1977–82 and Head of Sch. of Plant Biology, 1967–82, University Coll. of North Wales, Bangor; now Emeritus Professor. Member: AFRC, until 1990; Jt Nature Conservation Cttee, 1991–. For. Assoc., US Nat. Acad. of Sciences, 1984. Hon. DSc Sussex, 1984. *Publications:* Biology of Weeds, 1960; Population Biology of Plants, 1977; (with M. Begon and C. Townsend) Ecology: organisms, populations and communities, 1985; papers in Jl of Ecol., New Phytologist, Annals of Applied Biol., Evolution, and Proc. Royal Soc. *Recreation:* gardening. *Address:* Cae Groes, Glan y Coed Park, Dwygyfylchi, near Penmaenmawr, N Wales. *T:* Penmaenmawr (0492) 622362. *Club:* Farmers'.

HARPER, John Mansfield; Special Advisor to the Board, NEC Business Systems (Europe) Ltd, 1985–87, NEC (UK), since 1987; Director, International Information Exchange Ltd, since 1990; *b* 17 July 1930; *s* of late T. J. Harper and May (*née* Charlton); *m* 1956, Berenice Honorine, *d* of Harold Haydon; one *s* one *d. Educ:* Merchant Taylors' Sch.; St John's Coll., Oxford. 2nd Lieut Royal Corps of Signals, 1948–49. Asst Principal, Post Office, 1953; Private Sec. to Dir-Gen., 1956–58; Principal, 1958–66; Asst Sec., Reorganization Dept, 1966–69; Dir, North-Eastern Telecommunications Region, 1969–71; Dir, Purchasing and Supply, 1972–75; Sen. Dir, Planning and Provisioning, 1975–77; Asst Man. Dir, Telecommunications, 1978–79; Dep. Man. Dir, British Telecommunications (Post Office), 1979–81; Man. Dir, Inland Division, BT, 1981–83, retired. Chm., Infrastructure Policy Gp, Electronic Engrg Assoc., 1989–. Comp IEE; CBIM. *Publications:* Telecommunications and Computing: the uncompleted revolution, 1986; Telecommunications Policy and Management, 1989; The Third Way: telecommunications and the environment, 1990. *Recreations:* music, gardening, electronics. *Address:* 11 Lullington Close, Seaford, E Sussex. *Club:* National Liberal.

HARPER, Prof. John Martin, FRCO (CHM); Professor of Music, University College of North Wales, Bangor, since 1991; *b* 11 July 1947; *s* of Geoffrey Martin and Kathleen Harper; *m* 1970, Cynthia Margaret Dean (separated); three *s. Educ:* King's Coll. Sch., Cambridge (Chorister); Clifton Coll., Bristol (Music Scholar); Selwyn Coll., Cambridge (Organ Scholar; MA); Birmingham Univ. (PhD); MA Oxon. Music Tutor, West Bromwich Residential Arts Centre, 1970–71; Dir, Edington Music Fest., 1971–78; Dir of Music, St Chad's Cathedral, Birmingham, 1972–78; Lectr in Music, Birmingham Univ., 1974–75, 1976–81; Asst Dir of Music, King Edward's Sch., Birmingham, 1975–76; Fellow, Organist, Informator Choristarum and Tutor in Music, Magdalen Coll., and Univ. Lectr in Music, Oxford, 1981–90. Adviser: Panel of Monastic Musicians, 1976–; OUP (Church Music), 1989–. Recordings, 1974–, incl The English Anthem (5 vols), with Magdalen Coll. Choir. Benemerenti Papal award, 1978. *Publications:* choral compositions, 1974–; (ed) Orlando Gibbons: consort music, 1982; contribs to: New Grove Dictionary of Music and Musicians, 1980; Frescobaldi Studies, 1987; The Forms and Orders of Western Liturgy, 1991; articles and reviews in music jls and papers. *Recreations:* walking, church architecture. *Address:* Department of Music, University College of North Wales, Bangor, Gwynedd LL57 2DG. *T:* Bangor (0248) 351151.

HARPER, Prof. (John) Ross, CBE 1986; Senior Partner, Ross Harper & Murphy, Solicitors, since 1961; Professor of Law, Strathclyde University, since 1986; *b* 20 March 1935; *s* of late Rev. Thomas Harper, BD, STM, PhD and Margaret Simpson Harper (later Clarkson); *m* 1963, Ursula Helga Renate Gathman; two *s* one *d. Educ:* Hutchesons' Boys' Grammar School; Glasgow Univ. (MA, LLB), Pres., Students Rep. Council, 1955. President: Scottish Union of Students, 1956–58; Internat. Students' Conf., 1958. Asst Solicitor, McGettigan & Co., Glasgow, 1959; founded Ross Harper & Murphy, 1961, as two Partner firm (now 29 Partners), specialised in Criminal Law, later developing into Estate Agency and Commercial Law. Temp. Sheriff, 1979–89. Pres., Law Soc. of Scotland, 1988–89 (Vice-Pres., 1987–88). Pres., Glasgow Bar Assoc., 1975–78; Chairman, Criminal Law Div., 1983–87, Gen. Practice Section, 1988–, Internat. Bar Assoc. Chm., Finance Cttee, Greater Glasgow Health Board, 1984–87. Contested (C): Hamilton, 1970; W Renfrewshire, Feb. and Oct. 1974. Founder Chm., Soc. of Scottish Cons. Lawyers, 1982–86; Pres., Scottish Cons. & Unionist Assoc., 1989 (Hon. Sec., 1986–89). *Publications:* A Practitioner's Guide to Criminal Procedure, 1981; My Client, My Lord, 1981; A Practitioner's Guide to the Criminal Courts, 1985; Glasgow Rape Case, 1985; Fingertip Criminal Law, 1986; Rates Re-Valuation: the great myth, 1986; Devolution, 1988. *Recreations:* bridge, angling, shooting. *Address:* 97 Springkell Avenue, Pollokshields, Glasgow G41 4EM. *T:* 041–427 3223. *Clubs:* Western, Royal Scottish Automobile (Glasgow).

HARPER, William Ronald; Deputy Chairman, Thames Water Utilities Ltd, since 1989; *b* 5 June 1944; *s* of William and Dorothy Harper; *m* 1969, Susan Penelope (*née* Rider); two *s* two *d. Educ:* Barton Peveril Grammar Sch., Eastleigh, Hants. IPFA 1965. Hampshire CC, 1960–64; Eastbourne CBC, 1964–68; Chartered Inst. of Public Finance and Accountancy, 1968–70; Greenwich London BC, 1970–74; Thames Water Authority:

joined 1974; Dir of Finance, 1982; Dir of Corporate Strategy, 1984; Man. Dir, 1986; Bd Mem., Thames Water PLC, 1989. Chm., Foundn for Water Res., 1989–. Mem. Council, Water Services Assoc., 1990–. *Address:* Nugent House, Vastern Road, Reading, Berks RG1 8DB. *T:* Reading (0734) 593536.

HARPER GOW, Sir (Leonard) Maxwell, Kt 1985; MBE 1944; CBIM; Director, 1952–87, Chairman, 1964–81, Vice-Chairman, 1981–87, Christian Salvesen PLC; *b* 13 June 1918; *s* of late Leonard Harper Gow and Eleanor Amalie (*née* Salvesen); *m* 1944, Lillan Margaret Kiaer; two *s* one *d. Educ:* Cargilfield; Rugby; Corpus Christi Coll., Cambridge Univ. (BA). CBIM (FBIM 1976). Served War, 1939–46: Major RA 1st Commando Bde. 3 seasons with Antarctic Whaling Fleet, 1946–47, 1948–49 and 1952–53. Director: Scottish Widows' Fund and Life Assurance Soc., 1964–85 (Chm., 1972–75); Royal Bank of Scotland plc, 1965–87; Royal Bank of Scotland Group plc, 1978–87; DFM Holdings Ltd, 1985–89 (Chm., 1985–89); Radio Forth Ltd, 1973–89 (Chm., 1977–87). Member Council: Inst. of Directors, 1983–88; Scottish Council of Develt and Industry, 1972– (Vice Pres., 1985–88; elected Founder Fellow, 1987). Member, Queen's Body Guard for Scotland, the Royal Co. of Archers. Liveryman, Royal Co. of Shipwrights. Hon. Consul for Norway in Edinburgh/Leith, 1949–88. Comdr, Order of St Olav, Norway. *Recreations:* hill farming, fishing. *Address:* Eventyr, Lyars Road, Longniddry, East Lothian EH32 0PT. *T:* Longniddry (0875) 52142. *Club:* New (Edinburgh).

HARPHAM, Sir William, KBE 1966 (OBE 1948); CMG 1953; HM Diplomatic Service, retired; Director, Great Britain-East Europe Centre, 1967–80; *b* 3 Dec. 1906; *o s* of W. Harpham and N. Harpham (*née* Stout); *m* 1943, Isabelle Marie Sophie Droz; one *s* one *d. Educ:* Wintringham Secondary Sch., Grimsby; Christ's Coll., Cambridge. Entered Dept of Overseas Trade, 1929; transferred to Embassy, Brussels, 1931, Rome, 1934; Private Sec. to Parliamentary Sec. for Overseas Trade, 1936; seconded to League of Nations, 1937; reverted to Dept of Overseas Trade, 1939; served: Cairo, 1940–44; Beirut, 1944–47; appointed Counsellor (Commercial) at Berne, 1947; Head of Gen. Dept, Foreign Office, 1950–53; Dep. to UK Delegate to OEEC, 1953–56; Minister, British Embassy, Tokyo, 1956–59; Minister (Economic), Paris, 1959–63; Ambassador to Bulgaria, 1964–66; retd 1967. Order of Madara Horseman, Bulgaria, 1969; Order of Stara Planina, Bulgaria, 1976. *Address:* 9 Kings Keep, Putney Hill, SW15 6RA. *T:* 081–788 1383. *Club:* Royal Automobile.

HARPLEY, Sydney Charles, RA 1981 (ARA 1974); sculptor since 1956; *b* 19 April 1927; *s* of Sydney Frederick Harpley, electrical engr and cabinet maker, and Rose Isabel Harpley, milliner; *m* 1956, Sally Holliday (marr. diss. 1968), illustrator; two *s* one *d. Educ:* Royal Coll. of Art. ARCA 1956. Realist sculptor, portraits and figure; commnd Smuts Memorial, Cape Town, 1963; sculpture in collections of Nat. Gallery, NZ; Nat. Gallery, Cape Town; Paul Mellon, USA; Anton Rupert, SA; Princess Grace of Monaco; Fleur Cowles Meyer, London; S. & D. Josefowitz, Geneva; Lady Verulam; Lord Jersey; Portraits: Edward Heath for Constitutional Club, 1973; Lee Kwan Yew, Singapore, 1983. Visitors' Choice Prize, RA Summer Exhibition, 1978, 1979. *Recreations:* chess, music. *Address:* Belline House, Piltown, Co. Kilkenny, Ireland.

HARRER, Prof. Heinrich; author and explorer; (awarded title of Professor by President of Austrian Republic, 1964); *b* Hüttenberg, 6 July 1912; *m;* one *s; m* 1953, Margaretha Truxa (marr. diss. 1958); *m* 1962, Katharina Haarhaus. *Educ:* University of Graz, Austria (graduated in Geography, 1938). First ascent, Eiger North Wall, 1938; Himalayan Expedition, 1939; interned in India, 1939–44; Tibet, 1944–51; Himalayan Expedition, 1951; expeditions: to the Andes, 1953; to Alaska, 1954; to Ruwenzori (Mountains of the Moon), Africa, 1957; to West New Guinea, 1961–62; to Nepal, 1965; to Xingu Red Indians in Mato Grosso, Brazil; to Bush Negroes of Surinam (Surinam Expedn with King Leopold of Belgium), 1966; to the Sudan, 1970; to North Borneo (Sabah) (with King Leopold of Belgium), 1971; N-S crossing of Borneo, 1972; Valley of Flowers (Alaknanda), 1974; Andaman Islands, 1975; Zangkar-Ladakh, 1976. 35 short films on expeditions; Prize for best documentary book, Donanland, 1982; 70th birthday Orders from Germany, Austria, Carinthia, Styria, 1982; Golden medal, Humboldt Soc., 1985. Hon. Citizen, Hüttenberg, 1983. Austrian National Amateur Golf Champion, 1958; Austrian National Seniors Golf Champion, 1970. Hon. Pres., Austrian Golf Association, 1964 (Pres., 1949–64). *Publications:* Seven Years in Tibet, 1953 (Great Britain, and numerous other countries); Meine Tibet-Bilder, 1953 (Germany); The White Spider, History of the North Face of the Eiger, 1958; Tibet is My Country: Biography of Thubten Jigme Norbu, *e b* of Dalai Lama, 1960 (Eng.); I Come from the Stone Age, 1964 (London); The Last 500, 1975; The Last Caravan, 1976; Return to Tibet, 1984; Meine Forschungsreisen, 1986; Das Buch vom Eiger, 1988; Borneo, 1988; Bhutan, 1989. *Address:* Neudorf 577, 9493–Mauren, Liechtenstein. *Clubs:* Explorers' (New York) (Hon. Mem.), Royal and Ancient (St Andrews); PEN (Liechtenstein).

HARRHY, Eiddwen Mair; soprano; *b* 14 April 1949; *d* of David and Emily Harrhy; *m* Greg Strange, journalist and broadcaster. *Educ:* St Winefride's Convent, Swansea; Royal Manchester College of Music (Gold Medal Opera Prize); Paris (Miriam Licette Prize). Welsh Nat. Opera Chorus, 1970–71; Glyndebourne Festival Opera Chorus, 1971–73; début at Royal Opera House, Covent Garden, Wagner Ring Cycle, 1974; début, ENO, 1975; performances: Welsh Nat. Opera; La Scala Milan; Teatro Colon Buenos Aires; ENO; Glyndebourne; Opera North; Scottish Opera; UK and overseas orchestras; BBC promenade concerts; Australia, NZ, Hong Kong, S America, Europe, Scandinavia, USA; numerous recordings. *Recreations:* chamber music, ski-ing, watching Welsh rugby, enjoying Radios 3 and 4. *Address:* c/o Helen Sykes Artists' Management, 79 Bickenhall Mansions, Bickenhall Street, W1H 2LD. *T:* 071–224 3881.

HARRIES, Rt. Rev. Richard Douglas; *see* Oxford, Bishop of.

HARRINGTON, 11th Earl of, *cr* 1742; **William Henry Leicester Stanhope;** Viscount Stanhope of Mahon and Baron Stanhope of Elvaston, Co. Derby, 1717; Baron Harrington, 1729; Viscount Petersham, 1742; late Captain 15th/19th Hussars; *b* 24 Aug. 1922; *o s* of 10th Earl and Margaret Trelawney (Susan) (*d* 1952), *d* of Major H. H. D. Seaton; *S* father, 1929; *m* 1st, 1942, Eileen (from whom he obtained a divorce, 1946), *o d* of late Sir John Grey, Enville Hall, Stourbridge; one *s* one *d* (and one *d* decd); 2nd, 1947, Anne Theodora (from whom he obtained a divorce, 1962), *o d* of late Major Richard Arenbourg Blennerhassett Chute; one *s* two *d;* 3rd, 1964, Priscilla Margaret, *d* of Hon. A. E. Cubitt and Mrs Ronald Dawnay; one *s* one *d. Educ:* Eton; RMC, Sandhurst. Served War of 1939–45, demobilised 1946. Owns about 700 acres. Became Irish Citizen, 1965. *Heir: s* Viscount Petersham, *qv. Address:* Greenmount Stud, Patrickswell, Co. Limerick, Eire.
See also Baron Ashcombe.

HARRINGTON, Dr Albert Blair, CB 1979; Head of Civil Service Department Medical Advisory Service, 1976–79; *b* 26 April 1914; *s* of late Albert Timothy Harrington and Lily Harrington; *m* 1939, Valerie White; one *d. Educ:* Brisbane Grammar Sch., Qld; Aberdeen Univ. MB, ChB 1938, MD 1944. House Phys., Woodend Hosp., Aberdeen, 1938–39; service in RAMC (Field Amb., Blood Transfusion Phys., Neurologist) 1940–45; MO (Head Injuries) and Dep. Supt, Stoke Mandeville Hosp., 1946–48; Med.

Supt, Dunston Hill Hosp., Gateshead, 1948–50; SMO (Pensions), Cleveleys, 1950–53; Med. Supt, Queen Mary's Hosp., Roehampton, 1954–56; SMO, Dept of Health (Hosp. Bldg and later Regional Liaison Duties), 1956–68; PMO (Hosp. Bldg), 1968–73; SPMO (Under-Sec.), DHSS, 1973–76. Chm., CS Med. Appts Bds, 1979–86. FFCM (Foundn Fellow) 1972. *Publications:* articles on Sjögren's Disease, paralytic poliomyelitis, and hospital planning, medical care and the work of the Medical Advisory Service. *Recreations:* gardening, country life; formerly tennis. *Address:* 59 Lauderdale Drive, Petersham, Richmond, Surrey TW10 7BS. *T:* 081–940 1345. *Club:* Athenæum.

HARRINGTON, Illtyd, JP; DL; *b* 14 July 1931; *s* of Timothy Harrington and Sarah (*née* Burchell); unmarried. *Educ:* St Illtyd's RC Sch., Dowlais; Merthyr County Sch.; Trinity Coll., Caermarthen. Member: Paddington Borough Council, 1959–64; Westminster City Council, 1964–68 and 1971–78, Leader, Lab. Gp, 1972–74; GLC, 1964–67 and for Brent S, 1973–86: Alderman, 1970–73; Chairman, Policy and Resources Cttee, 1973–77, Special Cttee, 1985–86; Dep. Leader, 1973–77, 1981–84; Dep. Leader of the Opposition, 1977–81; Chm. of the Council, 1984–85. Special Advr to Chm. and Leader of ILEA, 1988–90. JP Willesden 1968. First Chairman, Inland Waterways Amenity Adv. Council, 1968–71; Chm., London Canals Consultative Cttee, 1965–67, 1981–; Vice Pres., IWA, 1990–; Member: British Waterways Bd, 1974–82; BTA, 1976–80. Member: Bd, Theatre Royal, Stratford E, 1978–; Bd, Wiltons Music Hall, 1979–; Nat. Theatre Bd, 1975–77; Bd, National Youth Theatre, 1976–; Globe Theatre Trust, 1986–; Chm., Half Moon Theatre, 1978–90; Director: Soho Poly Theatre, 1981–; The Young Vic, 1981–. President: Grand Union Canal Soc., 1974–; Islington Boat Club, 1985–; SE Region, IWA, 1986–; Immunity (Legal aid facility for AIDS victims), 1986–; Chairman: Kilburn Skills, 1977–; Battersea Park Peace Pagoda, 1984–; Limehouse Basin Users Gp, 1986–; Vice Pres., Coventry Canal Soc., 1970–. Patron, Westminster Cathedral Appeal, 1977–. Gov., London Marathon, 1980–91. Trustee: Kew Bridge Pumping Mus., 1976–; Chiswick Family Rescue, 1978–; Queen's Jubilee Walkway, 1986–; Arthur Koestler Awards for Prisoners, 1987–; CARE, 1987–; Dominica Overseas Student Fund, 1987–; Mem., Montgomery Coral Trust, 1988–; Managing Trustee, Mutual Municipal Insurance Co., 1985–. Governor, Brunel Univ., 1981–87. DL Greater London, 1986. *Recreations:* a slave to local government; laughing, singing and incredulity. *Address:* 16 Lea House, Salisbury Street, NW8 8BJ. *T:* 071–402 6356.

HARRIS, family name of **Barons Harris, Harris of Greenwich, Harris of High Cross** and of **Earl of Malmesbury.**

HARRIS, 6th Baron *cr* 1815, of Seringapatam and Mysore, and of Belmont, Kent; **George Robert John Harris;** Captain RA, retired; *b* 17 April 1920; *s* of 5th Baron Harris, CBE, MC, and Dorothy Mary (*d* 1981), *d* of Rev. W. J. Crookes; *S* father, 1984. *Educ:* Eton; Christ Church, Oxford. *Heir: cousin* Derek Marshall Harris [*b* 23 July 1916; *m* 1938, Laura Cecilia, *e d* of late Major Edmund Thomas William McCausland, Gurkha Rifles; one *s* one *d*]. *Address:* Huntingfield, Eastling, near Faversham, Kent.

HARRIS OF GREENWICH, Baron *cr* 1974 (Life Peer), of Greenwich; **John Henry Harris;** director of companies; *b* Harrow, Middlesex, 5 April 1930; *s* of late Alfred George and May Harris; *m* 1st, 1952, Patricia Margaret Alstrom (marr. diss. 1982); one *s* one *d*; 2nd, 1983, Angela Smith. *Educ:* Pinner County Grammar Sch., Middlesex. Journalist on newspapers in Bournemouth, Leicester, Glasgow and London. National Service with Directorate of Army Legal Services, WO. Personal assistant to Rt Hon. Hugh Gaitskell when Leader of the Opposition, 1959–62; Director of Publicity, Labour Party, 1962–64; Special Assistant: to Foreign Secretary, 1964–65; to Rt Hon. Roy Jenkins as Home Secretary, 1965–Nov. 1967, and as Chancellor, Nov. 1967–1970. Staff of Economist newspaper, 1970–74. Minister of State, Home Office, 1974–79. Spokesman on home affairs, Soc & Lib Dem, House of Lords, 1988–. Mem., H of L Select Cttee on Murder and Life Imprisonment, 1988–89. Chm., Parole Bd for England and Wales, 1979–82; Pres., Nat. Assoc. of Senior Probation Officers, 1983–; Trustee, Police Foundn (Chm., Exec. Cttee), 1980–. Eisenhower Exchange Fellow from UK, 1972. Mem. Council, Harlow, Essex, 1957–63, Chm. Council 1960–61, Leader of Labour Gp, 1961–63. Mem. Exec. Cttee, Britain in Europe, referendum campaign, 1975 (Jt Chm., Publicity Cttee). *Address:* House of Lords, SW1. *Clubs:* Reform, MCC.

HARRIS OF HIGH CROSS, Baron *cr* 1979 (Life Peer), of Tottenham in Greater London; **Ralph Harris;** Founder President, Institute of Economic Affairs, since 1990 (General Director, 1957–87, Chairman, 1987–89); *b* 10 Dec. 1924; *m* 1949, Jose Pauline Jeffery; one *s* one *d* (and one *s* decd). *Educ:* Tottenham Grammar Sch.; Queens' Coll., Cambridge (Exhibr, Foundn Schol.). 1st Cl. Hons Econs, MA Cantab. Lectr in Polit. Economy, St Andrews Univ., 1949–56. Contested (C): Kirkcaldy, 1951; Edinburgh Central, 1955. Leader-writer, Glasgow Herald, 1956. Trustee, Wincott Foundn; Trustee and Hon. Treasurer, Ross McWhirter Foundn. Chairman: Council, FARM Africa, 1988–; Bruges Gp, 1989–; FOREST, 1989–; Jt Chm., Internat. Centre for Res. into Market Transformation, Moscow. Mem. Council, Univ. of Buckingham; Dir, (Independent National) Times Newspapers Hldgs Ltd, 1988–. Free Enterprise Award, 1976. Hon. DSc Buckingham, 1984. *Publications:* Politics without Prejudice, a biography of R. A. Butler, 1956; Hire Purchase in a Free Society, 1958, 3rd edn 1961; (with Arthur Seldon) Advertising in a Free Society, 1959; Advertising in Action, 1962; Advertising and the Public, 1962; (with A. P. Herbert) Libraries: Free for All?, 1962; Choice in Welfare, 1963; Essays in Rebirth of Britain, 1964; Choice in Welfare, 1965; Right Turn, 1970; Choice in Welfare, 1970; Down with the Poor, 1971; (with Brendan Sewill) British Economic Policy 1970–74, 1975; Crisis '75, 1975; Catch '76, 1976; Freedom of Choice: consumers or conscripts, 1976; (with Arthur Seldon) Pricing or Taxing, 1976; Not from Benevolence, 1977; (ed, with Arthur Seldon) The Coming Confrontation, 1978; (with Arthur Seldon) Over-ruled on Welfare, 1979; End of Government, 1980; Challenge of a Radical Reactionary, 1981; No, Minister!, 1985; What Price Democracy?, 1985; The Enemies of Progress, 1986; (with Arthur Seldon) Welfare Without the State, 1987; Beyond the Welfare State, 1988; columnist in Truth, Statist, etc. *Recreations:* conjuring and devising spells against over-government. *Address:* 4 Walmar Close, Beech Hill, Hadley Wood, Barnet, Herts EN4 0LA. *Clubs:* Political Economy, Mont Pelerin Society.

HARRIS, Prof. Adrian Llewellyn, FRCP; Imperial Cancer Research Fund Professor of Clinical Oncology, Oxford University, since 1988; *b* 10 Aug. 1950; *s* of Luke and Julia Harris; *m* 1975, Margaret Susan Denman; one *s* one *d*. *Educ:* Univ. of Liverpool (BSc Hons Biochem. 1970; MB ChB Hons 1973); DPhil Oxon 1978. MRCP 1975, FRCP 1985. Hosp. appts, Liverpool, 1973–74; Clinical Scientist, MRC Clinical Pharmacology Unit, Radcliffe Infirmary, Oxford and Nuffield Dept of Medicine, 1975–78; Registrar in Academic Unit, Royal Free Hosp., 1978–80; Lectr and Sen. Registrar, Inst. for Cancer Res., Royal Marsden Hosp., 1980–82; Vis. Researcher, Imp. Cancer Res. Fund Mutagenesis Lab., London, 1982–83; Prof. of Clinical Oncology, Newcastle upon Tyne Univ., 1983–88. *Publications:* papers on growth factors in cancer, mechanisms by which cancers become resistant to treatment, hormone and drug treatment of cancer. *Recreations:* swimming, modern dance, science fiction. *Address:* Imperial Cancer Research Fund Clinical Oncology Unit, Churchill Hospital, Headington, Oxford OX3 7LJ. *T:* Oxford (0865) 64841.

HARRIS, Prof. Sir Alan (James), Kt 1980; CBE 1968; BScEng, FEng, FICE, FIStructE, MConsE; Senior Partner, Harris & Sutherland, Consulting Engineers, 1955–81, consultant since 1981; Professor of Concrete Structures, Imperial College, London, 1973–81, now Emeritus; *b* 8 July 1916; *s* of Walter Herbert Harris and Ethel Roach, Plymouth; *m* 1948, Marie Thérèse, *d* of Prof. Paul Delcourt, Paris; two *s*. *Educ:* Owen's Sch., Islington; Northampton Polytechnic (London Univ.). Local Government engineer, 1933–40; served Royal Engineers (Mulberry, Rhine Bridges) (despatches), 1940–46; with Eugène Freyssinet in Paris studying prestressing, 1946–49; Director, Prestressed Concrete Co. Ltd, 1949–55; in private practice, 1955–81. Member: Council, Agrément Board, 1968–81; Engrg Council, 1981–84; part-time Board Mem., Property Services Agency, 1974–78; Pres., Hydraulics Research Station, 1989– (Chm., 1982–89). President, Instn of Structural Engineers, 1978–79. Trustee, Imperial War Museum, 1983–90. Hon. DSc: City, 1982; Aston, 1982; Exeter, 1984. Croix de Guerre (France) 1945; Ordre du Mérite (France) 1975. *Publications:* numerous papers in learned jls. *Recreation:* sailing. *Address:* 128 Ashley Gardens, Thirleby Road, SW1P 1HL. *T:* 071–834 6924.

HARRIS, Anne Macintosh, (Mrs H. J. L. Harris), CBE 1985; National Chairman, National Federation of Women's Institutes, 1981–85; *b* 17 April 1925; *d* of Montague Macintosh Williams and Marguerite Anne Williams (*née* Barrington); *m* 1950, Henry John Leshley Harris; one *s* three *d*. *Educ:* Battle Abbey Sch.; Swanley Horticultural Coll. and Wye Coll. (Swanley Dip. in Horticulture, 1946). Owned and ran nursery/market garden and shop, 1946–53. Mem., WI, 1947–; Mem., NFWI Exec. Cttee, 1973–85 (Vice-Chm., 1979–81); Chm., NFWI Markets Sub-Cttee, 1972–79; WI representative: on Women's National Commn, 1982–85; on Advertising Adv. Cttee, IBA, 1984–87. Mem. Council Nat. Trust, 1981–85. Trustee, Help the Aged, 1985–. Chm., Tunbridge Wells East District Local Assoc. Girl Guides, 1963–79; Vice-Chm., Brenchley PCC, 1978–82. FRSA 1986. *Recreations:* gardening, walking, reading, music. *Club:* Agricola Club and Swanley Guild (Wye).

HARRIS, Anthony David, LVO 1979; HM Diplomatic Service; Head of Information Department, Foreign and Commonwealth Office, since 1990; *b* 13 Oct. 1941; *s* of Reginald William Harris and Kathleen Mary Harris (*née* Daw); *m* 1st, 1970, Patricia Ann Over (marr. diss. 1988); one *s*; 2nd, 1988, Sophie Kisling; two *s*. *Educ:* Plymouth College; Exeter College, Oxford (BA, 2nd cl. Hons Lit. Hum.). Third Sec., Commonwealth Relations Office, 1964; Middle East Centre for Arab Studies, Lebanon, 1965; Third, later Second Sec., and Vice-Consul, Jedda, 1967; Second Sec. (Inf.), Khartoum, 1969; First Sec., FCO, 1972; First Sec., Head of Chancery and Consul, Abu Dhabi, 1975; First Sec., UK Mission to UN, Geneva, 1979; Counsellor, FCO, 1982; seconded to MoD as Regl Marketing Dir 1 (Arabian Peninsula and Pakistan), 1983; Dep. Head of Mission, Cairo, 1986. *Recreations:* shooting (HM the Queen's Prize, Bisley, 1964; British team to Canada, 1974), skiing, climbing, diving. *Address:* 13A Elm Bank Mansions, The Terrace, Barnes, SW13 0NS. *T:* 081–876 0081. *Clubs:* Reform; North London Rifle, Commonwealth Rifle (Bisley).

HARRIS, Anthony Geoffrey S.; *see* Stoughton-Harris.

HARRIS, Prof. Anthony Leonard, CGeol; FRSE, FGS; Professor of Geology and Head of Department of Earth Sciences, University of Liverpool, since 1987; *b* 11 May 1935; *s* of Thomas Haydn Harris and Dora Harris (*née* Wilkinson); *m* 1959, Noreen Jones; one *s* one *d*. *Educ:* Cardiff High Sch.; University College of Wales, Aberystwyth (BSc, PhD). Geologist and Principal Geologist, British Geol. Survey, 1959–71; Lectr, then Sen. Lectr, Univ. of Liverpool, 1971–87. Pres., Geolog. Soc., 1990–92. Major John Coke Medal, Geolog. Soc., 1985; C. T. Clough Meml Medal, Geolog. Soc. of Edinburgh, 1989. *Publications:* (ed and contrib.) Caledonides of the British Isles, 1979; The Caledonian-Appalachian Orogen, 1988; papers in learned jls. *Recreations:* music, ornithology. *Address:* Department of Earth Sciences, University of Liverpool, PO Box 147, Liverpool L69 3BX; 12 Aigburth Hall Road, Liverpool L91 9DQ.

HARRIS, Sir Anthony (Travers Kyrle), 2nd Bt *cr* 1953; retired; *b* 18 March 1918; *s* of Marshal of the RAF Sir Arthur Travers Harris, 1st Bt, GCB, OBE, AFC, and Barbara Kyrle, *d* of Lt-Col E. W. K. Money, 85th KSLI; *S* father, 1984. *Educ:* Oundle. Served European War, 1939–45 with Queen Victoria's Rifles and Wiltshire Regt; Auxiliary Units, 1941; ADC to GOC-in-C Eastern Command, 1944. Reader for MGM, 1951–52; subsequently work with antiques and objets d'art. *Recreations:* music, horology. *Heir:* none. *Address:* 33 Cheyne Court, Flood Street, SW3 5TR.

See also R.J. Harris.

HARRIS, Rt. Rev. Augustine; *see* Middlesbrough, Bishop of, (RC).

HARRIS, Basil Vivian, CEng, MIEE; Chief Engineer, Communications Division, Foreign and Commonwealth Office, 1979–81, retired; *b* 11 July 1921; *s* of late Henry William and Sarah May Harris; *m* 1943, Myra Winifred Mildred Newport. *Educ:* Watford Grammar School. GPO Engineering Dept (Research), 1939; served RAF, 1943–46; GPO Engineering Dept (Radio Branch), 1946; Diplomatic Wireless Service, FCO, 1963; Dep. Chief Engineer, Communications Division, FCO, 1971. *Publications:* contribs to technical jls on communications. *Recreations:* golf, photography, travel. *Address:* 13 Decoy Drive, Eastbourne, Sussex BN22 0AB. *T:* Eastbourne (0323) 505819. *Club:* Royal Eastbourne Golf.

HARRIS, Ven. Brian; *see* Harris, Ven. R. B.

HARRIS, Brian Nicholas, FRICS; Chairman of Partnership, Richard Ellis, Chartered Surveyors and International Property Consultants, since 1984 (Partner, since 1961); *b* 12 Dec. 1931; *s* of Claude Harris and Dorothy (*née* Harris); *m* 1961, Rosalyn Marion Caines; two *d*. *Educ:* King Alfred's Sch., Wantage; College of Estate Management. Chartered Surveyor. Chm., City of London Br. of RICS, 1984–85; Member of Council: London Chamber of Commerce, 1985– (Dep. Chm., 1990–); Australian British Chamber of Commerce (UK), 1986– (Dep. Chm., 1990). Gov., Woldingham Sch., 1986–. FRSA 1987. Liveryman, 1975, Mem., Ct of Assistants, 1990, Co. of Glaziers and Painters of Glass. *Recreations:* flyfishing, gardening, golf. *Address:* Grants Paddock, Grants Lane, Limpsfield, Surrey RH8 0RQ. *T:* Oxted (0883) 723215. *Clubs:* Carlton, City of London, Flyfishers'.

HARRIS, Brian Thomas, OBE 1983; QC 1982; Director, Professional Conduct Department, Institute of Chartered Accountants in England and Wales, since 1985; *b* 14 Aug. 1932; *s* of Thomas and Eleanor Harris; *m* 1957, Janet Rosina Harris (*née* Hodgson); one *s* one *d*. *Educ:* Henry Thornton Grammar Sch.; King's Coll., Univ. of London. LLB (Hons). Called to the Bar, Gray's Inn, 1960; joined London Magistrates' Courts, 1963; Clerk to the Justices, Poole, 1967–85. Member: Juvenile Courts Committee, Magistrates' Assoc., 1973–85; NACRO Juvenile Crime Adv. Cttee, 1982–85; former member: CCETSW working party on legal trng of social workers (report, 1974); NACRO cttee on diversion (Zander report, 1975); HO/DHSS working party on operation of Children and Young Persons' Act 1969 (report, 1978); ABAFA working party on care proceedings (report, 1979). Pres., Justices' Clerks Soc., 1981–82. Editor, Justice of the Peace Review, 1982–85 (Legal Editor, 1973; Jt Editor, 1978). *Publications:* Criminal Jurisdiction of

Magistrates, 1969, 11th edn 1988; Warrants of Search and Entry, 1973; The Courts, the Press and the Public, 1976; The Rehabilitation of Offenders Act 1974, 1976, 2nd edn 1988; New Law of Family Proceedings in Magistrates' Courts, 1979; (ed jtly) Clarke Hall and Morrison on Children, 1985; (ed) entry on Magistrates in Halsbury's Laws of England, 4th edn 1979. *Recreation:* the contemplation of verse. *Address:* Church Barn, High Street, Yardley Hastings, Northants NN7 1ER. *T:* Yardley Hastings (060129) 387.

HARRIS, Cecil Rhodes, FCIS, FSCA; Deputy Chairman, Trade Indemnity PLC, since 1986; Chief Executive, Commercial Union Assurance Company Ltd, 1982–85; *b* 4 May 1923; *s* of Frederick William Harris and Dorothy Violet Plum; *m* 1946, Gwenyth Evans; one *s* two *d. Educ:* private schools. FCIS 1950; FSCA 1951. Joined Employers Liability Assurance, 1949, Asst Sec., 1961–64, Overseas Manager, Northern & Employers, 1965–68; Commercial Union Assurance Co. Ltd: Asst Gen. Man., 1969–73; Dep. Gen. Man., 1974; Dir and Sec., 1975–78; Exec. Dir, 1979; Dep. Chief Gen. Man., 1980–82. *Recreations:* tennis, study of the Scriptures. *Address:* Ashley, 35a Plough Lane, Purley, Surrey CR8 3QJ. *T:* 081–668 2820.

HARRIS, Charles; *see* Harris, G. C. W.

HARRIS, Sir Charles Herbert S.; *see* Stuart-Harris.

HARRIS, Colin Grendon, CMG 1964; HM Diplomatic Service, retired; *b* 25 Oct. 1912; *m* 1941, Adelaide Zamoiska (decd); *m* 1947, Monique Jacqueline Marcuse-Baudoux; four *s* two *d. Educ:* Rossall Sch.; Pembroke Coll., Cambridge. Entered Foreign (subseq. Diplomatic) Service, 1935; served San Francisco, Antwerp, Elisabethville, Leopoldville, Lisbon, Montevideo, Rio de Janeiro, Vienna, Tokyo, Oslo, retired 1969. *Address:* 263 Avenue Defré, Brussels, Belgium.

HARRIS, David; Director, Commission of the European Communities, Directorate for Social and Demographic Statistics, 1973–87; *b* 28 Dec. 1922; *s* of David and Margaret Jane Harris; *m* 1946, Mildred Alice Watson; two *d. Educ:* Bootle Grammar Sch.; LSE (BScEcon). FSS. Statistician, BoT, 1960; Statistician 1966 and Chief Statistician 1968, HM Treasury; Chief Statistician, Central Statistical Office, Cabinet Office, 1969. *Recreations:* tennis, swimming, economics. *Address:* 401 Ikisco Court, Kallipateras Street, Limassol, Cyprus.

HARRIS, David Anthony; MP (C) St Ives, since 1983; *b* 1 Nov. 1937; *s* of late E. C. Harris and Betty Harris; *m* 1962, Diana Joan Hansford; one *s* one *d. Educ:* Mount Radford Sch., Exeter. Jun. Reporter, Express and Echo, Exeter, 1954–58. Nat. Service, commnd Devonshire and Dorset Regt, 1958; Staff Captain (Public Relns) GHQ, MELF, 1959. Reporter, Western Morning News, 1960–61; joined Daily Telegraph, Westminster Staff, 1961; Political Correspondent, Daily Telegraph, 1976–79; MEP (C) Cornwall and Plymouth, 1979–84. Chm., Parly Lobby Journalists, 1977–78. Mem. (C) Bromley, and Bromley, Ravensbourne, GLC, 1968–77; Chm. Thamesmead Cttee, 1971–73. Contested (C), Mitcham and Morden, Feb. 1974. PPS to Minister of State for Foreign and Commonwealth Affairs, 1987–88, to Sec. of State for Foreign and Commonwealth Affairs, 1988–89, to Dep. Prime Minister and Leader of Commons, 1989–90. Member: Select Cttee on Agriculture, 1983–87; Select Cttee on Broadcasting, 1988–. *Recreations:* gardening, walking the dog. *Address:* House of Commons, SW1A 0AA. *Club:* Farmers'.

HARRIS, David Michael; QC 1989; a Recorder, since 1988; *b* 7 Feb. 1943; *s* of Maurice and Doris Harris; *m* 1970, Emma Lucia Calma; two *s* one *d. Educ:* Liverpool Institute High School for Boys; Lincoln Coll., Oxford (BA 1964; MA 1967); Cambridge Univ. (PhD 1969). Asst Lectr in Law, Manchester Univ., 1967–69. Called to the Bar, Middle Temple, 1969; Asst Recorder, 1984–88. *Publications:* (ed jtly) Winfield and Jolowicz on Tort, 9th edn, 1971; (ed jtly) Supplement to Bingham's Modern Cases on Negligence, 3rd edn, 1985. *Recreations:* the Arts, travel, sport. *Address:* Peel House (Third Floor), 5–7 Harrington Street, Liverpool L2 9XN. *T:* 051–236 0718.

HARRIS, Prof. David Russell, FSA; Professor of Human Environment, since 1979, and Director, since 1989, Institute of Archaeology, University College London; *b* 14 Dec. 1930; *s* of Dr Herbert Melville Harris and Norah Mary Harris; *m* 1957, Helen Margaret Wilson; four *d. Educ:* St Christopher Sch., Letchworth; Oxford Univ. (MA, BLitt); Univ. of California, Berkeley (PhD). Nat. Service, RAF, 1949–50. Teaching Asst and Instructor, Univ. of California, 1956–58; Lectr, QMC, London, 1958–64; Lectr and Reader, UCL, 1964–79. Member: Mus. of London Archaeol. Cttee, 1984–; English Heritage Sci. and Conservation Panel, 1985–; Chm., Sci.-based Archaeol. Cttee, SERC, 1989–. Pres., Prehistoric Soc., 1990–. *Publications:* Plants, Animals and Man in the Outer Leeward Islands, 1965; (with B. W. Hodder) Africa in Transition, 1967; Human Ecology in Savanna Environments, 1980; (with G. C. Hillman) Foraging and Farming, 1989; Settling Down and Breaking Ground: rethinking the neolithic revolution, 1990. *Recreations:* hill walking, archaeological-ecological travel. *Address:* Institute of Archaeology, University College London, 31–34 Gordon Square, WC1H 0PY. *T:* 071–380 7483. *Club:* Athenæum.

HARRIS, Dame Diana R.; *see* Reader Harris.

HARRIS, Rev. Donald Bertram; Vicar of St Paul's, Knightsbridge, 1955–78; *b* 4 Aug. 1904; unmarried. *Educ:* King's Coll. Choir Sch., Cambridge; Haileybury Coll.; King's Coll., Cambridge; Cuddesdon Coll., Oxford. Chorister, King's Coll. Choir, 1915–19; Choral Scholar, King's Coll., Cambridge, 1923–26; BA 1925; MA 1929; Ordained Deacon, 1927; Priest, 1928; Curate of Chesterfield Parish Church, 1927–31; St Mary the Less, Cambridge, 1931–36. Chaplain of King's Coll., Cambridge, 1932–33; Examg Chaplain to Bishop of Wakefield, 1932–36; Rector of Great Greenford, Middx, 1936–45; Archdeacon of Bedford 1946–55, and Rector of St Mary's Bedford, 1945–55, Life Governor, Haileybury and Imperial Service Coll., 1946–. Pres., Assoc. for Promoting Retreats, 1968–71. *Address:* 105 Marsham Court, Marsham Street, SW1P 4LA. *T:* 071–828 1132. *Club:* Royal Thames Yacht.

HARRIS, Dr Edmund Leslie, CB 1981; FRCP, FRCPE, FFPHM, FFPM; Director of Medical Services, Disablement Services Authority, 1988–91, retired; *b* 11 April 1928; *s* of late M. H. and S. Harris; *m* 1959, Robina Semple (*née* Potter). *Educ:* Univ. of Witwatersrand. MB, BCh 1952; MRCPE 1959, FRCPE 1971, MRCP 1959, FRCP 1975; MFCM 1978; FFPHM (FFCM 1980); FFPM 1989. Gen. practice, Benoni, S Africa, 1954; various NHS posts, 1955–61; Medical Dir, pharmaceutical industry, 1962–68; SMO, DHSS, 1969–72; PMO, Cttee on Safety of Medicines and Medicines Commn, 1973; SPMO, Under-Sec., and Head of Medicines Div., DHSS, 1974–77; Dep. Chief Med. Officer, Dept of Health (formerly DHSS), 1977–89. Examiner for Dip. Pharm. Med., Royal Colls of Physicians, 1976–84. Chairman: Assoc. of Med. Advisers in Pharmaceutical Industry, 1966; Adv. Cttee on Nat. Blood Transfusion Service, 1980–89; Expert Gp on Viral Haemorrhagic Fevers, 1984–89; Adv. Cttee, NHS Drugs, 1985–89. Member: Nat. Biol. Bd, 1975–77; Bd, Public Health Lab. Service, 1977–; Central Blood Products Authority, 1982–85; Adviser to WHO, 1970–90. Rep. Governor, Imperial Cancer Res. Fund, 1977–89. Mem., Court of Govs and Bd of Management, LSHTM, 1986–89. *Publications:* various, mainly on aspects of clinical pharmacology and control of medicines. *Recreations:* walking, photography. *Address:* 5 Ashcroft Court, 10 Oaklands Road, Bromley, Kent BR1 3TX. *T:* 081–460 3665.

HARRIS, Frank; *see* Harris, W. F.

HARRIS, Prof. Frank, MD; FRCP, FRCPE; Dean, Faculty of Medicine and Professor of Paediatrics, University of Leicester, since 1990; Hon. Consultant Paediatrician, Leicester Royal Infirmary, since 1990; *b* 6 Oct. 1934; *s* of David and Miriam Harris; *m* 1963, Brenda van Embden; two *s. Educ:* Univ. of Cape Town (MB ChB 1957; MMed (Paed), MD). Groote Schuur and Red Cross War Memorial Children's Hosp., Cape Town; CSIR Res. Fellow, Dept of Medicine, Univ. of Cape Town; Lectr and Sen. Lectr in Child Health, Univ. of Sheffield, 1965–74; University of Liverpool: Prof. of Child Health and Dir, Inst. of Child Health, 1974–89; Pro-Vice-Chancellor, 1981–84; Dean, Faculty of Medicine, 1985–89; Hon. Cons. Paediatrician to Royal Liverpool Children's Hosps at Myrtle Street and Alderhey. Member: Liverpool AHA and DHA, 1977–84; Mersey RHA, 1983–89; Trent RHA, 1990–; Cttee on Review of Medicines, 1981–; Cttee on Safety of Medicines, 1990–; GMC, 1990–. Examr for RCP and Univs, UK and overseas. *Publications:* Paediatric Fluid Therapy, 1973; chapters in med. books; contribs to med. jls. *Recreations:* golf, reading, travel. *Address:* School of Medicine, University of Leicester, PO Box 138, Leicester LE1 9HN. *T:* Leicester (0533) 522962.

HARRIS, (Geoffrey) Charles (Wesson); QC 1989; a Recorder, since 1990; *b* 17 Jan. 1945; *s* of G. Hardy Harris and late M. J. P. Harris (*née* Wesson); *m* 1970, Carol Ann Alston; two *s* one *d. Educ:* Repton; Univ. of Birmingham (LLB). Called to the Bar, Inner Temple, 1967. Practice on Midland and Oxford Circuit and in London. Contested (C) Penistone, Yorks, Oct. 1974. *Publications:* contrib. to Halsbury's Laws of England, 4th edn 1976, and other legal publications; magazine articles on stalking and ballooning. *Recreations:* history, architecture, fireworks, shooting, stalking, ski-ing. *Address:* 1 Harcourt Buildings, Temple, EC4. *T:* 01–353 0375; Westcote Barton Manor, Oxfordshire. *Club:* Carlton.

HARRIS, Geoffrey (Herbert); Member, Transport Users' Consultative Committee for London, 1961–77 (Chairman, 1972–77, Deputy Chairman, 1971–72); Chairman, London Transport Passengers' Committee, 1972–74; *b* 31 Jan. 1914; *s* of late W. Leonard Harris and late Sybil M. Harris; *m* 1945, Eve J. Orton; two *d. Educ:* Colchester Royal Grammar School. FCIS. Commercial Union Gp of Cos, 1932–37; Shell Gp of Cos, 1937–73; Manager Office Administration, London, 1963–73. Royal Artillery, 1937–45. *Recreations:* music, architecture, travel. *Address:* Fyfield Cottage, West Street, Marlow, Bucks SL7 2BU. *T:* Marlow (0628) 472550. *Club:* Phyllis Court (Henley-on-Thames).

HARRIS, Prof. Harry, FRCP; FRS 1966; Harnwell Professor of Human Genetics, University of Pennsylvania, 1976–90, now Emeritus; *b* 30 Sept. 1919; *m* 1948, Muriel Hargest; one *s. Educ:* Manchester Gram. Sch.; Trinity Coll., Cambridge. (MA, MD); FRCP 1973. Research Asst, Galton Laboratory, Dept of Eugenics, Biometry, and Genetics UC, London, 1947–50; Leverhulme Scholar, RCP, 1947–48; Lund Research Fellow, Diabetic Assoc., 1949; Lectr, Dept of Biochem., UC, London, 1950–53; Sen. Lectr, 1953–58, Reader in Biochem. Genetics, 1958–60, Dept of Biochem., The London Hosp. Med. Coll.; Prof. of Biochem., University of London, at King's Coll., 1960–65; Galton Prof. of Human Genetics, London Univ. at UCL, 1965–76. Hon. Lectr, 1950–55, Hon. Research Associate, 1955–60, Dept of Eugenics, Biometry, and Genetics, UCL; Hon. Dir, MRC Human Biochem. Genetics Res. Unit, 1962–76; Hon. Consulting Geneticist, UCH, 1966–76. Joint Editor: Annals of Human Genetics, 1965–79; Advances in Human Genetics, 1970–. Nat. Research Coun. of Canada and Nuffield Foundation Vis. Lectr, British Columbia and McGill, 1967; Fogarty Scholar, Nat. Insts of Health, USA, 1972; Rock Carling Fellowship, Nuffield Provincial Hosps Trust, 1974. Lectures: Thomas Young, St George's Hosp. Med. Sch., 1966; De Frees, University Penna, 1966; Walter R. Bloor, Univ. Rochester, 1967; Langdon Brown, RCP, 1968; Sir William Jackson Pope, RSA, 1968; Darwin, Inst. Biol., 1969; Leonard Parsons, Birmingham Univ., 1969; Sidney Ringer, UCH Med. Sch., 1970; T. H. Huxley, Birmingham Univ., 1971; George Frederic Still, British Paediatric Assoc., 1971; L. S. Penrose Meml, Genetical Soc., 1973; Bicentennial, Coll. of Physicians of Pa, 1976; Noble Wiley Jones, Univ. of Oregon, 1978; Rhodes, Emory Univ., 1978; Thomas S. Hall, Washington Univ., St Louis, 1979; Harvey, Harvey Soc., NY, 1981; Karl Beyer, Wisconsin, 1983. For. Associate, Nat. Acad. of Scis, USA, 1976. Hon. Dr Univ. René Descartes, Paris, 1976. William Allan Meml Award, Amer. Soc. of Human Genetics, 1968. *Publications:* An Introduction to Human Biochemical Genetics (Eugenics Laboratory Memoir Series), 1953; Human Biochemical Genetics, 1959; The Principles of Human Biochemical Genetics, 1970, 3rd edn 1980; Prenatal Diagnosis and Selective Abortion, 1975; (with D. A. Hopkinson) Handbook of Enzyme Electrophoresis in Human Genetics, 1976. *Address:* Dunwoody Village CH30, 3500 West Chester Pike, Newtown Square, Pa 19073, USA. *T:* (215) 353–7096.

See also J. T. Harris.

HARRIS, Prof. Henry, FRCP; FRCPath; FRS 1968; Regius Professor of Medicine, University of Oxford, 1979–Sept. 1992; Head of the Sir William Dunn School of Pathology, 1963–Sept. 1992; Hon. Director, Cancer Research Campaign, Cell Biology Unit, since 1963; Fellow of Lincoln College, 1963–79, Hon. Fellow 1980; Student of Christ Church; *b* 28 Jan. 1925; *s* of late Sam and late Ann Harris; *m* 1950, Alexandra Fanny Brodsky; one *s* two *d. Educ:* Sydney Boys' High Sch. and University of Sydney, Australia; Lincoln Coll., Oxford. Public Exhibnr, University of Sydney, 1942; BA Mod. Langs, 1944; MB BS 1950; Travelling Schol. of Austr. Nat. Univ. at Univ. of Oxford, 1952; MA; DPhil (Oxon.), 1954, DM 1979. Dir of Research, Brit. Empire Cancer Campaign, at Sir William Dunn Sch. of Pathology, Oxford, 1954–59; Visiting Scientist, Nat. Institutes of Health, USA, 1959–60; Head of Dept of Cell Biology, John Innes Inst., 1960–63; Prof. of Pathology, Univ. of Oxford, 1963–79. Vis. Prof., Vanderbilt Univ., 1968; Walker-Ames Prof., University of Washington, 1968; Foreign Prof., Collège de France, 1974. Member: ARC, 1968–78 (Chm., Animals Res. Bd, 1976–78); Council, European Molecular Biology Organization, 1974–76; Council, Royal Society, 1971–72; Scientific Adv. Cttee, CRC, 1961–85; Non-Exec. Mem., Oxford RHA, 1990–. Governor, European Cell Biology Organization, 1973–75. Lectures: Almroth Wright, 1968; Harvey, Harvey Soc. NY, 1969; Dunham, Harvard, 1969; Jenner Meml, 1970; Croonian, Royal Soc., 1971; Nat. Insts of Health, USA, 1971; Foundation, RCPath, 1973; Woodhull, Royal Instn, 1975; Rotherham, Lincoln Coll., Oxford, 1979; Herbert Spencer, Oxford Univ., 1979; Opening Plenary, Internat. Congress of Cell Biology, 1980; First Distinguished, in Experimental Pathology, Pittsburgh Univ., 1982; Louis Gross Meml, NY, 1983; Claude Bernard, Acad. des Sciences, Paris, 1984; Jean Brachet Meml, Vancouver, 1990; Kettle, RCPath, 1991. Foreign Hon. Mem., Amer. Acad. Arts and Sciences; Foreign Mem., Max-Planck Soc.; Hon. Member: Amer. Assoc. of Pathologists; German Soc. of Cell Biology; Corresp. Member: Amer. Assoc. for Cancer Res.; Aust. Acad. of Science. Foreign Correspondent, Waterford Striped Bass Derby Assoc.; Hon. Fellow, Cambridge Philosophical Soc. Hon. FRCPath Aust. Hon. DSc Edinburgh, 1976; Hon. MD: Geneva, 1982; Sydney, 1983. Feldberg Foundn Award, Ivison Macadam Meml Prize, RCSE; Prix de la Fondation Isabelle Decazes de Noüe for cancer research; Madonnina Prize for medical scis (City of Milan), 1979; Royal Medal, Royal Soc., 1980;

Osler Medal, RCP, 1984; Katherine Berkan Judd Award, Sloan-Kettering Inst., NY, 1991. *Publications:* Nucleus and Cytoplasm, 1968, 3rd edn, 1974; Cell Fusion, 1970; La Fusion cellulaire, 1974; The Balance of Improbabilities, 1987; papers on cellular physiology and biochemistry, in scientific books and jls. *Recreation:* history. *Address:* (until Sept. 1992) Sir William Dunn School of Pathology, South Parks Road, Oxford OX1 3RE. *T:* Oxford (0865) 275501.

HARRIS, Hugh Christopher Emlyn, FIPM; Associate Director, Bank of England, since 1988; *b* 25 March 1936; *s* of Thomas Emlyn Harris and Martha Anne (*née* Davies); *m* 1968, Pamela Susan Woollard; one *s* one *d. Educ:* The Leys Sch., Cambridge; Trinity Coll., Cambridge (BA 1959; MA). ACIB 1963; FIPM 1990. Bank of England, 1959–: Chief of Corporate Services, 1984–88. Director: BE Services Ltd, 1984–; BE Museum Ltd, 1989–; BE Property Holdings Ltd, 1989–; Securities Management Trust Ltd, 1987–; Solefield School Educational Trust Ltd, Sevenoaks, 1986–. Member: Governing Council, Business in the Community, 1986–; Windsor Fellowship Adv. Council, 1988–. FRSA. *Recreations:* tennis, watching Rugby, theatre, opera. *Address:* Bank of England, Threadneedle Street, EC2R 8AH. *T:* 071–601 3131.

HARRIS, Lt-Gen. Sir Ian (Cecil), KBE 1967 (CBE 1958); CB 1962; DSO 1945; Member of Family Partnership and Manager, Ballykisteen Stud, Tipperary, and Owner, Victor Stud, Golden, Cashel, Tipperary; Chairman: Irish Bloodstock Breeders Association, since 1977; Irish Bloodstock Breeders Federation, since 1978; *b* 7 July 1910; *y s* of late J. W. A. Harris, Victor Stud, Golden, Tipperary; *m* 1945, Anne-Marie Desmotreux; two *s. Educ:* Portora Royal Sch., Enniskillen, Northern Ireland; RMC, Sandhurst. 2nd Lt Royal Ulster Rifles, 1930; served War of 1939–45, NW Frontier of India, 1939 (despatches); comd 2nd Bn Royal Ulster Rifles, 1943–45; GSO1, 25 Ind. Div. and 7 Div. in Burma and Malaya, 1945–46 (despatches), India and Pakistan, 1946–47; AQMG Scottish Comd, 1949–51; comd 6th Bn Royal Ulster Rifles (TA), 1951–52; Chief of Staff, Northern Ireland, 1952–54; Comdr 1 Federal Infantry Bde, Malaya, 1954–57 (despatches); Dep. Dir of Staff Duties (A), WO, 1957–60; GOC Singapore Base District, 1960–62; Chief of Staff, Contingencies Planning, Supreme HQ, Allied Powers, Europe, 1963–66; GOC-in-C, then GOC, N Ireland, 1966–69. Colonel: Royal Ulster Rifles, 1962–68; Royal Irish Rangers, 1968–72. Pres., Irish Thoroughbreeders' Assoc. *Recreations:* riding and tennis. *Address:* Acraboy House, Monard, Co. Tipperary. *T:* Tipperary 51564. *Club:* Army and Navy.

HARRIS, Air Cdre Irene Joyce, (Joy), CB 1984; RRC 1976; SRN, SCM; Director, Nursing Services (RAF), and Matron-in-Chief, Princess Mary's Royal Air Force Nursing Service, 1981–84; *b* 26 Sept. 1926; *d* of late Robert John Harris and Annie Martha Harris (*née* Breed). *Educ:* Southgate County Sch.; Charing Cross Hosp.; The London Hosp.; Queen Mary's Maternity Home, Hampstead. SRN 1947, SCM 1950. Joined Princess Mary's RAF Nursing Service, 1950; gen. nursing and midwifery duties in UK, Singapore, Germany and Cyprus; Dep. Matron, 1970; Sen. Matron, 1975; Principal Matron, 1978; Dep. Dir, Nursing Services (RAF), 1981. QHNS 1981–84. *Recreations:* travel, ornithology, music, archaeology, gardening. *Address:* 51 Station Road, Haddenham, Ely, Cambs CB6 3XD. *Club:* Royal Air Force.

HARRIS, Sir Jack Wolfred Ashford, 2nd Bt, *cr* 1932; Chairman, Bing Harris & Co. Ltd, Wellington, NZ, 1935–78 (Director until 1982), retired; *b* 23 July 1906; *er s* of Rt Hon. Sir Percy Harris, 1st Bt, PC, and Frieda Bloxam (*d* 1962); *S* father 1952; *m* 1933, Patricia, *o d* of A. P. Penman, Wahroonga, Sydney, NSW; two *s* one *d. Educ:* Shrewsbury Sch.; Trinity Hall, Cambridge. BA (Cantab) History; then one year's study in Europe. Joined family business in New Zealand, 1929, and became director shortly afterwards. Past Pres. Wellington Chamber of Commerce. Served during War of 1939–45, for three years in NZ Home Forces. *Recreations:* gardening, fishing, swimming. *Heir: s* Christopher John Ashford Harris [*b* 26 Aug. 1934; *m* 1957, Anna, *d* of F. de Malmanche, Auckland, NZ; one *s* two *d*]. *Address:* Te Rama, Waikanae, near Wellington, NZ. *Club:* Wellington (Wellington).

HARRIS, John Charles; solicitor; Management and Legal Consultant, John Harris Consultancy; Public Sector Adviser/Associate Consultant: PA Consulting Group, 1986–91; Daniels Bates Partnership, since 1991; Administrator, English Camerata, since 1988; *b* 25 April 1936; *s* of Sir Charles Joseph William Harris, KBE; *m* 1961, Alison Beryl Sturley; one *s* one *d. Educ:* Dulwich College; Clare College, Cambridge. MA, LLM. 2nd Lieut, Intelligence Corps, 1954–56. UKAEA (seconded to OECD), 1959–63; articled to Town Clerk, Poole, 1963–66; Asst Sol., then Senior Asst Sol., Poole BC, 1966–67; Asst Sol., then Principal Asst to Chief Exec. and Town Clerk, 1967–71, Dep. Town Clerk, 1972–73, County Borough of Bournemouth; County Sec., 1973–84, Chief Exec. and County Clerk, 1983–86, S Yorks CC; Dir, S Yorks Passenger Transport Exec., 1984–86; Sec. to Yorkshire and Humberside County Councils Assoc., 1984–86; Advr and Dir, S Yorks Residuary Body, 1985–86; Clerk to Lord Lieutenant of S Yorks, 1984–86. Adviser to AMA Police and Fire Cttee, 1976–86; Member: Home Office Tripartite Working Party on Police Act 1964, 1983–86; Rampton SHA Cttee, 1989–; Arts Council Touring Bd, 1989–; Pontefract HA, 1990–; Bd, Northern Counties Housing Assoc., 1990–. Chm., Soc. of County Secretaries, 1983–84; Mem. Exec. Council, Solace, 1984–86; Mem., Law Society. Hon. PR Officer, S Yorks and Humberside Region, Riding for Disabled Assoc. (Mem., Publications Cttee, 1987–90); Trustee: S Yorks Charity Inf. Service, 1977–87; Founder Mem./Sec., Barnsley Rockley Rotary Club, 1976–79; Vice-Chm. and Sec., Friends of Opera North, 1979–86; Member: Council/Co., Opera North, 1980–; Guild of Freemen, City of London, 1967; Justice; European Movement. DL S Yorks, 1986. FRSA 1984. *Publications:* correspondent on public affairs. *Recreations:* being with family and friends; competitive trail riding; riding Welsh cobs; opera, foreign travel. *Address:* Long Lane Close, High Ackworth, Pontefract, Yorks WF7 7EY. *Club:* Leeds (Leeds).

HARRIS, Dr John Edwin, MBE 1981; FEng 1987; FRS 1988; independent consultant on materials, and freelance writer and lecturer, since 1990; *b* 2 June 1932; *s* of late John Frederick Harris and Emily Margaret (*née* Prosser); *m* 1956, Ann Foote; two *s* two *d. Educ:* Larkfield Grammar Sch., Chepstow; Dept of Metallurgy, Univ. of Birmingham (BSc 1953, PhD 1956, DSc 1973). FIM 1974. Joined Associated Electrical Industries, 1956; CEGB, 1959–89; seconded to Sheffield Univ., 1959–61; Berkeley Nuclear Labs, 1961–89, Sect. Head, 1966–89; Univ. Liaison Manager, Nuclear Electric plc, 1989–90. Member: Metal Science Cttee, Metals Soc., 1974; Bd, British Nuclear Energy Soc., 1974–88; Watt Cttee Wkg Party on Atmospheric Attack on Inorganic Materials, 1987; Home Office Wkg Party on Adjudications in HM Prisons, 1974; Chm., Leyhill Prison Bd of Visitors, 1973–74. Mem., Assoc. of British Science Writers. Public Lectr, Tate Gall., 1984; Molecule Club Lectr, 1985 and 1987. FRSA 1989. Internat. Metallographic Soc. Award, 1976; Esso Gold Medal, Royal Soc., 1979; Interdisciplinary Award, RSC, 1987. *Publications:* (ed) Physical Metallurgy of Reactor Fuel Elements, 1975; Vacancies '76, 1977; scientific papers on nuclear metallurgy, deformation and corrosion; articles in New Scientist and The Guardian. *Recreations:* writing popular science articles, studying decay of buildings. *Address:* Church Farm House, 28 Hopton Road, Upper Cam, Dursley, Glos GL11 5PB. *T:* Dursley (0453) 543165. *Club:* Cam Bowling (non-playing member).

HARRIS, John Frederick, OBE 1986; FSA; Curator, British Architectural Library's Drawing Collection and Heinz Gallery, 1960–86; Consultant to Collection, Canadian Centre for Architecture, 1986–88 (Member Advisory Board, since 1983); *b* 13 Aug. 1931; *s* of Frederick Harris and Maud (*née* Sellwood); *m* 1960, Eileen Spiegel, New York; one *s* one *d. Educ:* Cowley C of E School. Itinerant before 1956; Library of Royal Inst. of Architects, 1956. Mem., Mr Paul Mellon's Adv. Bd, 1966–78; Trustee, Amer. Mus. in Britain, 1974–88; Chm., Colnaghi & Co., 1982–. President: Internat. Confedn on Architectural Museums, 1981–84 (Chm., 1979–81; Hon. Life Pres., 1984); Marylebone Soc., 1978–80; Thirties Soc., 1986– (Mem. Cttee, 1979–); Member: Council, Drawing Soc. of America, 1962–68; Council, Victorian Soc., 1974–; Nat. Council, Internat. Council of Monuments and Sites, 1976–83; Soc. of Dilettanti, 1977–; Mem. Committee: Soc. of Architectural Historians of GB, 1958–66; Georgian Gp, 1970–74, 1986–89; Save Britain's Heritage, 1970–; Stowe Landscape, 1980– (Patron, Stowe Gardens Buildings Trust, 1986–); Bldg Museum Proj., 1980–86; Garden History, 1980–84; Jl of Garden History, 1980–89. Member: Adv. Council, Drawings Center, NY, 1983–89; Management Cttee, Courtauld Inst. of Art, 1983–87; Somerset House Building Cttee, 1986–89; Council, Royal Archaeol. Inst., 1984–86; Adv. Cttees, Historic Bldgs and Monuments Commn, 1984–88; Ashton Meml Steering Gp, 1984–86; GLC Historic Buildings Panel, 1984–86; Ambrose Congreve Award, 1980–82; Ashmole Archive Cttee, 1985–87; Adv. Bd, Irish Architectural Archive, 1988–; Appeal Cttee, Painshill Park Trust, 1988–89; Spencer House Restoration Cttee, 1986–. Andrew W. Mellon Lectr in Fine Arts, Nat. Gall., Washington, 1981; Slade Prof. of Fine Art, Univ. of Oxford, 1982–83. Exhibitions Organizer: The King's Arcadia, 1973; The Destruction of the Country House (with Marcus Binney), 1974; The Garden, 1979; Dir, British Country House Exhibn, Nat. Gall., Washington, 1982–83; many exhibns in Heinz Gall.; travelling exhibns and catalogues: Italian Architectural Drawings, 1966; Sir Christopher Wren, 1970; Designs of the British Country House, 1985. FSA 1968; FRSA 1975; Hon. FRIBA 1972; Hon. MA Oxon, 1982; Hon. Brother Art Workers' Guild, 1972. Editor, Studies in Architecture, 1976–. *Publications:* English Decorative Ironwork, 1960; Regency Furniture Designs, 1961; ed, The Prideaux Collection of Topographical Drawings, 1963; (jtly) Lincolnshire, 1964; contrib. The Making of Stamford, 1965; (jtly) Illustrated Glossary of Architecture, 1966, 2nd edn 1969; (jtly) Buckingham Palace, 1968; Georgian Country Houses, 1968; contrib., Concerning Architecture, 1968; Sir William Chambers, Knight of the Polar Star, 1970 (Hitchcock Medallion 1971); ed, The Rise and Progress of the Present State of Planting, 1970; ed (jtly) The Country Seat, 1970; Catalogue of British Drawings for Architecture, Decoration, Sculpture and Landscape Gardening in American Collections, 1971; A Country House Index, 1971, 2nd edn 1979; Catalogue of the Drawings Collection RIBA: Inigo Jones and John Webb, 1972; contrib., Guide to Vitruvius Britannicus, 1972; (jtly) The King's Arcadia: Inigo Jones and The Stuart Court, 1973; Catalogue of the Drawings Collection RIBA: Colin Campbell, 1973; Headfort House and Robert Adam, 1973; (jtly) The Destruction of the Country House, 1974; Gardens of Delight, The Art of Thomas Robins, 1976; Gardens of Delight, The Rococo English Landscape of Thomas Robins, 1978; (jtly) Catalogue of Drawings by Inigo Jones, John Webb and Isaac de Caus in Worcester College, Oxford, 1979; A Garden Alphabet, 1979; ed, The Garden Show, 1979; The Artist and the Country House, 1979 (Sir Banister Fletcher prize, 1979), 2nd edn 1986; contrib., Village England, 1980; (contrib.) Lost Houses of Scotland, 1980; The English Garden 1530–1840: a contemporary view, 1981; contrib., John Claudius Loudon and the Early Nineteenth Century in Great Britain, Washington, 1980; (jtly) Interiors, 1981; The Palladians, 1981; Die Hauser der Lords und Gentlemen, 1982; William Talman, Maverick Architect, 1982; contrib., Gibraltar: an architectural appreciation, 1982; Architectural Drawings in the Cooper Hewitt Museum, New York, 1982; (contrib.) Vanishing Houses of England, 1982; (contrib.) Macmillan Encyclopedia of Architecture, 1982; (contrib.) Great Drawings from the Collection of Royal Institute of British Architects, 1983; (jtly) Britannia Illustrata Knyff & Kip, 1984; The Design of the British Country House, 1985; (jtly) Inigo Jones—Complete Architectural Drawings, 1989; (contrib.) In Honor of Paul Mellon, Collector and Benefactor, 1986; (contrib.) Canadian Centre for Architecture Building and Gardens, 1989; (contrib.) The Fashioning and Functioning of the British Country House, 1989; articles in Country Life, Arch. Rev., Arch. Hist., and other jls. *Recreations:* grand hotels, history of World War I and flinting. *Club:* Travellers'.

HARRIS, John Frederick, CEng, FIEE; Chairman, East Midlands Electricity plc (formerly East Midlands Electricity Board), since 1982; *b* 9 Dec. 1938; *s* of Jack Harris and Lily Harris; *m* 1960, Diana Joyce Brown; one *s* two *d. Educ:* Central Grammar School, Birmingham. Technical posts, Midlands Electricity, 1955–70; managerial posts, Southern Electricity, 1970–78; Chief Engineer, NW Electricity Board, 1978–79, Dep. Chm., 1979–82. Pres., Nottingham VSO, 1984–. CBIM. *Recreation:* golf. *Address:* 57 Sheepwalk Lane, Ravenshead, Nottingham NG15 9FD. *Club:* Commonwealth Trust.

HARRIS, Air Vice-Marshal John Hulme, CB 1991; CBE 1982; Chief of Staff, HQ No 18 Group (RAF Strike Command) and Maritime Air Eastern Atlantic and Channel, since 1991; *b* 3 June 1938; *s* of late George W. H. Harris and of Dorothy Harris (*née* Hulme); *m* 1962, Williamina (*née* Murray); two *s. Educ:* English Sch., Cairo; King Edward VII Sch., King's Lynn. No. 224 Sqn, RAF, 1960–62; RAF Leeming, Flying Instructor, 1963–67; Exchange Officer, US Navy Air Test and Evaluation Sqn, Florida, 1968–70; Central Tactics and Trials Organisation, 1970–73; OC No 201 Sqn, 1973–75; Nat. Defence Coll., 1975–76; OPCON Project Team, Northwood, 1976–78; SASO, RAF Pitreavie Castle, 1979; OC RAF Kinloss, 1979–81; Internat. Mil. Staff, Brussels, 1982–83; RCDS, 1984; Dir Training (Flying), RAF, 1985–87; Comdt Gen., RAF Regiment and Dir. Gen. of Security (RAF), 1987–89; ACDS (Logistics), 1990–91. ADC to the Queen, 1979–81. *Recreations:* fly fishing for salmon, trout and navigators, gardening, travel. *Address:* c/o Lloyds Bank, Cox's and King's Branch, 7 Pall Mall, SW1Y 5NA. *Club:* Royal Air Force.

HARRIS, John Percival, DSC 1945; QC 1974; **His Honour Judge Harris;** a Circuit Judge, since 1980; *b* 16 Feb. 1925; *o s* of late Thomas Percival Harris and Nora May Harris; *m* 1959, Janet Valerie Douglas; one *s* two *d. Educ:* Wells Cathedral Sch.; Pembroke Coll., Cambridge. BA 1947. Served in RN, 1943–46: Midshipman, RNVR, 1944, Sub-Lt 1945. Called to Bar, Middle Temple, 1949, Bencher 1970. A Recorder of the Crown Court, 1972–80; Dep. Sen. Judge, Sovereign Base Areas, Cyprus, 1983–. *Recreations:* golf, reading, Victorian pictures. *Address:* Tudor Court, Fairmile Park Road, Cobham, Surrey KT11 2PP. *T:* Cobham (0932) 864756; Westminster County Court, 82 St Martin's Lane, WC2N 4AG. *T:* 071–240 1405. *Clubs:* Royal St George's Golf (Sandwich); Woking Golf, Rye Golf.

HARRIS, John Robert, FRIBA; architect; Founder and Senior Partner, John R. Harris Architects, London, since 1949 (also Founder and Senior Partner of associated firms in Brunei, Oman, Qatar, Dubai and Hong Kong); Partner, Courbe Duboz et Harris, Paris, since 1978; *b* 5 June 1919; *s* of late Major Alfred Harris, CBE, DSO and Rosa Alfreda Alderson; *m* 1950, Gillian, *d* of Col C. W. D. Rowe, CB, MBE, TD, DL, JP; one *s* one *d. Educ:* Harrow Sch.; Architectural Assoc. Sch. of Architecture (AA Dipl. Hons). FRIBA 1949; HKIA 1982; Membre de l'Ordre des Architectes Français, 1978. Served War, TA and Active Service, 1939–45 (TEM 1945); Lieut RE, Hong Kong, 1940–41; POW of Japanese, 1941–45; Mem., British Army Aid Gp, China, 1943–45; Hong Kong Resistance, 1942–45. Projects won in internat. competition: State Hosp., Qatar, 1953; New Dubai Hosp., 1976; Corniche Develt and Traffic Intersection, Dubai, 1978; HQ for Min. of Social Affairs and Labour, Oman, 1979; Tuen Mun Hosp., Hong Kong, 1981 (internat. assessment); Ruler's Office develt, Dubai, 1985. Architects and planners for Zhuhai New Town, Economic Zone, People's Republic of China, 1984. Major works in UK include: hospitals: Royal Northern, London, 1973; Ealing, 1976; RAF Upper Heyford, 1982; RAF Bentwaters, 1982; Stoke Mandeville, 1983; Wellesley House and St Peter's Court school re-develt, 1975; apartments, Hyde Park, 1983; dept stores in Barnstaple, Basildon, Cwmbran, Eltham, Harlow, Hammersmith, Sutton Coldfield and Worthing; Redevelt, Dorchester Hotel, 1989; Develt, Gloucester Road Station site. Major works overseas include: Internat. Trade Centre, Dubai, 1982; British Embassy, Chancery Offices and Ambassador's Residence, Abu Dhabi, 1982; shopping centres, Oman, 1978 and 1984; National Bank of Dubai HQ Bldg, 1968; Grindlay's Bank, Muscat, 1969; British Bank of the ME, Salalah, Oman, 1983; Sulaibikhat Hosp., Kuwait, 1968; University Teaching Hosp., Maiduguri, Nigeria, 1982; Caritas Hosp., Hong Kong, 1983; Rashid Hosp., Dubai, 1983; Women's Hosp., Doha, 1984; Shell Recreation Centre, Brunei, 1984; dept stores in Antwerp, Brussels, Lille, Paris and Strasbourg, 1973–83. FRSA 1982. Silver Jubilee Medal, 1977. *Publications:* (jtly) John R. Harris Architects, 1984; contrib. to books and architectural and technical jls. *Recreations:* architecture, sailing, travel. *Address:* 24 Devonshire Place, W1N 2BX. *T:* 071–935 9353. *Clubs:* Athenæum, Royal Thames Yacht.

See also R. M. Harris.

HARRIS, (Jonathan) Toby; Director, Association of Community Health Councils for England and Wales, since 1987; Leader, Haringey Borough Council, since 1987; *b* 11 Oct. 1953; *s* of Prof. Harry Harris, *qv*; *m* 1979, Ann Sarah Herbert; two *s*. *Educ:* Haberdashers' Aske's Sch., Elstree; Trinity Coll., Cambridge (BA Hons NatScis and Econ). Chair, Cambridge Univ. Labour Club, 1973; Pres., Cambridge Union Soc., 1974. Economics Div., Bank of England, 1975–79; Electricity Consumers' Council, 1979–86, Dep. Dir, 1983. Mem., Haringey BC, 1978– (Chair, Social Services Cttee, 1982–87); Deputy Chair: AMA, 1990– (Chair, Social Services Cttee, 1986–); Assoc. of London Authorities, 1990– (Chair, Social Services Cttee, 1984–88); Chair, LBTC-Training for Care, 1986–. Nat. Chair, Young Fabian Gp, 1976–77; Chair, Hornsey Labour Party, 1978, 1979, 1980. Dep. Chair, Nat. Fuel Poverty Forum, 1981–86; Mem., London Drug Policy Forum, 1990–. Gov., Nat. Inst. for Social Work, 1986–. *Publications:* (with Nick Butler and Neil Kinnock) Why Vote Labour?, 1979; contrib. Economics of Prosperity, 1980; (ed with Jonathan Bradshaw) Energy and Social Policy, 1983. *Recreations:* reading, walking. *Address:* c/o Association of Community Health Councils for England and Wales, 30 Drayton Park, N5 1PB; 4 Beatrice Road, N4 4PD. *T:* 071–272 3548.

HARRIS, Air Cdre Joy; *see* Harris, I. J.

HARRIS, Dr Keith Murray, CBiol, FIBiol, FRES; Director, International (formerly Commonwealth) Institute of Entomology, since 1985; *b* 26 Nov. 1932; *s* of Clifford Murray Harris and Doris (*née* Cottam); *m* 1957, Elizabeth Harrison; one *s* one *d*. *Educ:* Lewis Sch., Pengam; Univ. of Wales, Aberystwyth (BSc, DSc); Selwyn Coll., Cambridge (DipAgricSci); Imperial Coll. of Tropical Agric., Trinidad (DipTA). FRES 1960; FIBiol 1985. Entomologist, then Sen. Entomologist, Federal Dept of Agricl Res., Nigeria, 1955–62; Sen. Res. Fellow, BM (Natural History), 1962–66; Entomologist and Sen. Scientist, RHS, Wisley, 1966–74; Principal Taxonomist, Commonwealth Inst. of Entomology, 1974–85. *Publications:* (jtly) Collins Guide to the Pests, Diseases and Disorders of Garden Plants, 1981; scientific research papers and articles on pests of cultivated plants, esp. pests of African cereal crops, and on taxonomy and biol. of gall midges. *Recreations:* walking, cycling in wild places, gardening. *Address:* (office) 56 Queen's Gate, SW7 5JR. *T:* 071–584 0067.

HARRIS, Leonard John; Under Secretary, HM Treasury, since 1987; *b* 4 July 1941; *s* of Leonard and May Harris; *m* 1st, 1965, Jill Christine Tompkins (marr. diss.); one *s* two *d*; 2nd, 1986, Jennifer Dilys Biddiscombe (*née* Barker). *Educ:* Westminster City Sch.; St John's Coll., Cambridge. BA 1964 (Eng. Lit.), MA 1967. HM Customs and Excise: Asst Principal, 1964; Private Sec. to Chairman, 1966–68; Principal, 1969; CS Selection Bd, 1970; HM Customs and Excise, 1971; Cabinet Office, 1971–74; First Sec., UK Rep. to EEC, 1974–76, Counsellor, 1976–77; Asst Sec., HM Customs and Excise, 1977–80, Cabinet Office, 1980–83; Under Sec., 1983; Comr of Customs and Excise, 1983–87; Under Sec., MPO, 1987. *Recreations:* cooking, music, naturism. *Address:* c/o HM Treasury, SW1. *Clubs:* Oxford Naturist (Oxford) (Chm.).

HARRIS, Brigadier Lewis John, CBE 1961 (OBE 1949; MBE 1943); consultant, surveys and mapping; *b* 19 Dec. 1910; *e s* of David Rees Harris and Cecilia Harris; *m* 1975, Thelma Opal, *d* of James Marshall Carr and Zettie Lou Witt, and *widow* of Lt-Col A. L. Nowicki, US Corps of Engineers. *Educ:* Christ Coll., Brecon; RMA, Woolwich; Pembroke Coll., Cambridge (Exhibitioner), Mech. Sci. Tripos, MA. Commissioned RE 1930; Triangulation of Jamaica, 1937–39; served War of 1939–45: British Expeditionary Force, 1939–40 (despatches); First Army in North Africa, 1942–43, AFHQ and American Seventh Army, Italy, 1944; Land Forces SE Asia, India, Burma and Malaya, 1944–46; Chief Instructor, Sch. of Mil. Survey, 1946–49; War Office, Geog. Section GS, 1949–52; Ordnance Survey, 1952–53; Dir, Survey GHQ, Middle East, and GHQ, E Africa, 1953–55; Land Survey Adviser, Allied Forces, Mediterranean, 1954–55; Ordnance Survey of Great Britain, 1955–61; Brig. 1956; Dir, Map Production and Publication, 1956–59; Dir, Field Surveys, 1959–61; Dir of Mil. Survey, MoD and Chief of Geographical Section Gen. Staff, 1961–65. Consultant, Federal Surveys and Mapping, Canada, 1967–85. Hon. Col 135 Survey Engineer Regt, TA, 1965–67. Chm., Nat. Cttee for Cartography, Royal Society, 1961–67. Hon. Foreign Sec., Royal Geographical Soc., 1964–67; Vice-Pres., Internat. Cartographic Assoc., 1958–61. Hon. Vice-Pres., Army Rugby Union. FRAS, FRGS, FRICS. *Publications:* various papers on cartography in learned jls. *Recreations:* music, outdoor sports, travelling. *Address:* 12410 Hound Ears Point, Fox Den, PO Box 22129, Knoxville, Tenn 37933, USA. *Clubs:* Naval and Military, MCC; Hawks (Cambridge); Royal Ottawa Golf; IZ, FF, BB.

HARRIS, Lyndon Goodwin, RI 1958; RSW 1952; RWA 1947; artist in oil, water-colour, stained glass, and etching; *b* 25 July 1928; *s* of late S. E. Harris, ACIS and late Mary Elsie Harris. *Educ:* Halesowen Grammar Sch. Studied Art at: Birmingham Coll. of Art; Slade Sch. of Fine Art, 1946–50; University of London Inst. of Education, 1950–51; Courtauld Inst.; Central Sch. of Art and Crafts, London. Leverhulme Schol., Pilkington Schol., Slade Schol., and Slade Anatomy Prizeman; Dip. Fine Art (London) 1949; Courtauld Certificate, 1950; ATD 1951. *Works exhibited:* Paris Salon (Gold Medal, Oil Painting; Honourable Mention, Etching); RA (first exhibited at age of 13), RSA, RI, RSW, NEAC, RBA, RGI, RWA, and principal provincial galleries. *Works in permanent collections:* Ministry of Works; University Coll., London; Birmingham and Midland Inst.; City of Worcester; (stained glass) Gorsty Hill Methodist Church, Halesowen. *Recreation:* music (organ and pianoforte).

HARRIS, Margaret Frances, OBE 1975; Co-Director of Theatre Design Course (formerly at Riverside, of the English National Opera and Sadler's Wells Design Course); *b* 28 May 1904; *d* of William Birkbeck Harris and Kathleen Marion Carey. *Educ:* Downe House. In partnership with Elizabeth Montgomery and late Sophie Devine as firm of Motley, 1931–. Has designed many productions in London and New York of drama, opera and ballet: first notable production, Richard of Bordeaux, for John Gielgud, 1932; recently, sets and costumes for: Prokofiev's War and Peace, Coliseum, 1972; (with Elizabeth Montgomery) Unknown Soldier and His Wife, New London, 1973; A Family and a Fortune, 1975; Tosca, English Nat. Opera, 1976; Paul Bunyan, English Music Theatre, 1976; The Consul, Coliseum, 1978. *Publications:* Designing and Making Costume, by Motley, 1965; Theatre Props, by Motley, 1976. *Address:* 36 Rocks Lane, Barnes, SW13 0PB. *T:* 081–878 3705.

HARRIS, Mark; Assistant Treasury Solicitor, Department of Education and Science, since 1988; *b* 23 Feb. 1943; *s* of late Solomon Harris and Eva (*née* Lazarus); *m* 1972, Sharon Frances Colin; one *d*. *Educ:* Central Foundation Boys' Grammar Sch., London; London School of Economics and Political Science, London Univ. (LLB Hons). Solicitor of the Supreme Court, 1967. Entered Solicitor's Office, Dept of Employment, as Legal Asst, 1968; Sen. Legal Asst, 1973; Asst Solicitor, 1978; Legal Advr, 1987–88. . *Recreations:* travel, walking, short-story writing, painting. *Address:* c/o Elizabeth House, York Road, SE1. *T:* 071–934 9762.

HARRIS, Prof. Martin Best; Vice-Chancellor, Essex University, since 1987; *b* 28 June 1944; *s* of William Best Harris and Betty Evelyn (*née* Martin); *m* 1966, Barbara Mary (*née* Daniels); two *s*. *Educ:* Devonport High Sch. for Boys, Plymouth; Queens' Coll., Cambridge (BA, MA); Sch. of Oriental and African Studies, London (PhD). Lecturer in French Linguistics, Univ. of Leicester, 1967; University of Salford: Sen. Lectr in Fr. Ling., 1974; Prof. of Romance Ling., 1976–87; Dean of Social Sciences and Arts, 1978–81; Pro-Vice-Chancellor, 1981–87. Member: Internat. Cttee for Historical Linguistics, 1979–86; UGC, 1984–87; Chairman: NI Sub Cttee, UFC (formerly UGC), 1985–; Nat. Curriculum Wkg Gp for Modern Foreign Langs, 1989–. Mem. Council, Philological Soc., 1979–86, 1988–. Chm. of Govs, Centre for Inf. on Lang. Teaching, 1990–; Vice Chm. of Governors, Parrs Wood High Sch., 1982–86; Gov., Colchester Sixth Form Coll., 1988–; Member Governing Body: Anglia Higher Educn Coll., 1989–; SOAS, London Univ., 1990–. Mem. Editorial Board: Journal Linguistics, 1982–91; Diachronica, 1983–; French Studies, 1987–; Jt Gen. Editor, Longman Linguistics Library, 1982–. *Publications:* (ed) Romance Syntax: synchronic and diachronic perspectives, 1976; The Evolution of French Syntax: a comparative approach, 1978; (ed with N. Vincent) Studies in the Romance Verb, 1982; (ed with P. Ramat) Historical Development of Auxiliaries, 1987; (ed with N. Vincent) The Romance Languages, 1988; about 35 articles in appropriate jls and collections. *Recreations:* gardening, travel, wine. *Address:* University of Essex, Wivenhoe Park, Colchester CO4 3SQ. *T:* Colchester (0206) 872000.

HARRIS, Martin Richard; Director: National Westminster Bank PLC, since 1977; NatWest Investment Bank Ltd (formerly County Bank Ltd), since 1977; De La Rue Co. plc, since 1981; *b* 30 Aug. 1922; *m* 1952, Diana Moira (*née* Gandar Dower) JP, Mayor of Merton, 1985–86; four *s*. *Educ:* Wellington Coll. FCA. Captain, RE, ME and Italy, 1941–46. Joined Price Waterhouse & Co., 1946, Partner, 1956–74; Dir Gen., Panel on Take-Overs and Mergers, 1974–77; Director: Reckitt and Colman, 1977–82 (Dep. Chm., 1979–82); Inmos International, 1980–84; Equity & Law Life Assce Soc., 1981–87 (Dep. Chm., 1983–87); Westland plc, 1981–85; TR Industrial & General Trust plc, 1983–86; Chm. and Dir, Nineteen Twenty-Eight Investment Trust plc, 1984–86. Inst. of Chartered Accountants in England and Wales: Mem. Council, 1971–79; Chm., Parly and Law Cttee, 1973–74; Chm., Prof. Standards Cttee, 1977–79; Mem., Accountants Internat. Study Gp, 1972–74. Mem., DTI's Company Law Consultative Gp, 1972–74. Member: Court, Drapers' Co., 1978– (Master, 1987); Court, Co. of Chartered Accountants, 1977– (Master, 1983). Mem. Council, RCM, 1985– (Chm. Development Fund, 1984–); Governor, QMC, London Univ., 1979–89; Chm. Council, Queen Mary & Westfield Coll., London Univ., 1989–. FRCM 1988. US Silver Star 1945. *Recreations:* music and opera, philately, antique furniture and china, keeping busy. *Address:* 29 Belvedere Grove, Wimbledon, SW19 7RQ. *T:* 081–946 0951. *Clubs:* Carlton, MCC.

HARRIS, Maurice Kingston, CB 1976; formerly Secretary, Northern Ireland Ministry of Home Affairs, Jan. 1973, seconded to Northern Ireland Office, 1974–76; *b* 5 Oct. 1916; *s* of Albert Kingston Harris and Annie Rebecca Harris; *m* 1948, Margaret, *d* of Roderick Fraser and Gertrude McGregor; one *s* three *d*. *Educ:* The Perse Sch.; London Univ. 1st cl. Hons Mod. Langs, 1939. Served in Indian Army, 8th Punjab Regt, 1942–46. Colonial Office, 1946–47. Entered Northern Ireland Civil Service, 1947, and served in various Ministries; retired 1976. *Recreations:* music, walking. *Address:* 27 Strangford Avenue, Belfast BT9 6PG. *T:* Belfast (0232) 681409.

HARRIS, Rear-Adm. Michael George Temple; Assistant Chief of the Defence Staff (NATO/UK), since 1989; *b* 5 July 1941; *s* of Cdr Antony John Temple Harris, OBE, RN and Doris Drake Harris; *m* 1970, Katrina Chichester; three *d*. *Educ:* Pangbourne Coll.; RNC, Dartmouth. FRGS 1978; FNI 1988. Qualified Submarines, 1963, TAS 1968; commanded HM Submarines: Osiris, 1970–72; Sovereign, 1975–77 (N Pole, 1976); 3rd Submarine Sqn, 1982–85; commanded HM Ships: Cardiff, 1980–82 (Falkland Is, 1982); Ark Royal, 1987–89. Exchange service with USN, 3rd Fleet Staff, 1972–75. Younger Brother of Trinity House, 1989–. Freeman, City of London, 1990; Liveryman, Shipwrights' Co., 1991–. *Recreations:* fishing, bell-ringing, reading, pelagic bird-watching. *Address:* c/o Naval Secretary, Old Admiralty Building, Spring Gardens, SW1A 2BE. *Club:* Naval and Military.

HARRIS, Nigel John; National Secretary, Foundry Section, and Member, Executive Council, Amalgamated Engineering Union, since 1980; *b* 20 March 1943; *s* of Frederick and Irene Harris; *m* 1964, Cynthia; two *s*. *Educ:* C of E Sch., Dawley, Shropshire; Pool Hill Sec. Modern. Worked at Kemberton Colliery to 1962; ironfounding, John Maddocks & Co., 1963–65; Union representative, Glynwed Foundries, 1965–80; full time Officer, 1980, rep. foundry workers for AEW and on health and safety matters. Member: Exec. Cttee, CSEU, 1985–; NEC, Lab. Party, 1991–. Former Editor, The Foundry Worker. Mem., Royal British Legion. *Recreations:* swimming, driving. *Address:* 18 Merlin Avenue, Knutsford, Cheshire WA16 8HJ. *T:* Knutsford (0565) 652094.

HARRIS, Patricia Ann, (Mrs J. N. K. Harris); Central President, The Mothers' Union, since 1989 (Vice-President, 1986–88); *b* 29 May 1939; *m* 1963, Rev. James Nigel Kingsley Harris, BA; one *s* one *d*. *Educ:* Trinity Coll., Carmarthen. Teaching Dip. Teacher, 1959–63; pt-time special needs teacher, 1963–88; vol. teacher, Gloucester Prison, 1978–85. Member: Glos Dio. Synod, 1980–; C of E General Synod, 1985–. Mothers' Union: Young Wives Leader, 1963–65; Enrolling Mem., 1967–76; Presiding Mem., 1969–74; Diocesan Social Concern Chm., 1974–80; Pres., Glos dio., 1980–85. *Recreations:* swimming, watching Rugby, cooking, craft work. *Address:* The Vicarage, Elm Road, Stonehouse, Glos GL10 2NP. *T:* Stonehouse (045382) 2332.

HARRIS, Rt. Rev. Patrick Burnet; *see* Southwell, Bishop of.

HARRIS, Prof. Peter Charles, MD, PhD, FRCP; Editor, Cardioscience; Simon Marks Professor of Cardiology, University of London, 1966–88, now Emeritus; Consultant Physician, National Heart and Chest Hospitals; *b* 26 May 1923; *s* of late David Jonathan Valentine and Nellie Dean Harris; *m* 1st, 1952, Felicity Margaret Hartridge (marr. diss. 1982); two *d*; 2nd, 1989, Frances Monkarsh. *Educ:* St Olave's Grammar Sch.; Univ. of London. MB, BS (London) 1946; MRCP 1950; MD (Univ. medal) 1951; PhD 1955; FRCP 1965. House appts at King's Coll. Hospital, and elsewhere, 1946–55. Nuffield Fellow, Columbia Univ., New York, 1955–57; Lectr, Sen. Lectr and Reader in Medicine, Univ. of Birmingham, 1957–66; Dir, Inst. of Cardiology, Univ. of London, 1966–73. Pres., Internat. Soc. for Heart Research, 1981–83. Hon. FACC, 1976. *Publications:* The Human Pulmonary Circulation (with D. Heath), 1962, 3rd edn 1986; articles to jls, etc, on cardio-pulmonary physiology and biochemistry. *Recreation:* chamber music. *Address:* 42 Great Percy Street, WC1. *T:* 071–278 2911; Cannaregio 3698A, Venice, Italy. *T:* 041–5289001.

HARRIS, Group Captain Peter Langridge, CBE 1988; AE 1961, Clasp 1971; CEng, FIEE; DL; ADC to the Queen, 1984–88; Inspector, Royal Auxiliary Air Force, 1983–88; *b* 6 Sept. 1929; *s* of Arthur Langridge Harris and Doris Mabel (*née* Offen); *m* 1955, (Yvonne) Patricia Stone; two *d*. *Educ:* St Edward's Sch., Oxford; Univ. of Birmingham (BSc). CEng, FIEE 1976; MBIM 1969. Served: RAF, 1947–49; RAFVR, 1949–60; RAuxAF, 1960–78 and 1982–88; commanded 1 (Co. Hertford) Maritime HQ Unit, 1973–77; Air Force Mem., 1978–, Vice-Chm. (Air), 1988–, TA&VRA for Greater London; Gp Captain 1983. Elliott Bros (London) Ltd, 1952–55; Decca Navigator Co. Ltd, 1955–59; GEC plc, 1959–89; retired. Chm., Hatfield Dist IEE, 1979–80. DL Greater London, 1986. *Recreation:* travel. *Address:* 10 Dolphin Court, St Helens Parade, Southsea, Hants PO4 0QL. *T:* Portsmouth (0705) 817602; 29 Davenham Avenue, Northwood, Mddx HA6 3HW. *T:* Northwood (09274) 24291. *Club:* Royal Air Force.

HARRIS, Peter Michael; Circuit Administrator, Northern Circuit, Lord Chancellor's Department, since 1986; *b* 13 April 1937; *s* of Benjamin Warren Harris and Ethel Evelyn Harris (*née* Mabbutt); *m* 1963, Bridget Burke; one *s* two *d*. *Educ:* Cirencester Grammar School; Britannia Royal Naval College, Dartmouth. Cadet, RN, 1953; Lieut Comdr 1967; retired from RN 1972. Called to the Bar, Gray's Inn, 1971; Lord Chancellor's Department: Legal Asst, 1974; Sen. Legal Asst, 1977; Asst Sol., 1980; Dep. Circuit Administrator, Midland and Oxford Circuit, 1980; Head of Property and Family Law Div., 1982; Head of Civil Courts Div., 1985; Under Sec., 1986. Asst Editor, County Court Practice, 1985–. *Recreations:* reading, walking, swimming, gardening. *Address:* 6 Headlands Road, Bramhall, Stockport SK7 3AN. *T:* 061–439 9565.

HARRIS, Philip; Principal, Monopolies and Mergers Commission, 1977–85, retired; *b* Manchester, 15 Dec. 1915; *er s* of S. D. Harris and Sarah Chazan; *m* 1939, Sarah Henriques Valentine; three *d*. *Educ:* Manchester Grammar Sch.; Trinity Hall, Cambridge (Open Scholarship, BA 1st Cl (with dist.), Historical Tripos, MA 1970). Asst Principal, Board of Trade, 1938–40. Served War, 1940–45; Anti-Aircraft Command and Western Europe; 2nd Lieut RA, 1941; Lieut, 2/8th Lancs Fusiliers, 1944; Capt., 6th Royal Welch Fusiliers, 1945. Principal, Board of Trade, 1946; Asst Sec., Board of Trade, 1948–64; Asst Registrar, Office of the Registrar of Restrictive Trading Agreements, 1964–66, Principal Asst Registrar, 1966–73; Principal Asst Registrar, Fair Trading Div. I, DTI, 1973; Dir, Restrictive Trade Practices Div., Office of Fair Trading, 1973–76. Nuffield Travelling Fellowship, 1956–57 (study of Indian Industrial Development). UK Mem., EEC Adv. Cttee on Cartels and Monopolies, 1973–76. Leader, UK Delgn to Internat. Cotton Advisory Cttee, 1960, 1963. *Publications:* various articles on monopolies and restrictive trade practices policy. *Recreation:* history. *Address:* 23 Court House Gardens, Finchley, N3 1PU. *T:* 081–346 3138.

HARRIS, Sir Philip (Charles), Kt 1985; Chairman: Harris Ventures Ltd, since 1988; Carpetright of London, since 1988; C. W. Harris Properties, since 1988; Blouse House Ltd, since 1989; *b* 15 Sept. 1942; *s* of Charles William Harris and Ruth Ellen (*née* Ward); *m* 1960, Pauline Norma (*née* Chumley); three *s* one *d*. *Educ:* Streatham Grammar School. Chm., 1964–88, Chief Exec., 1987–88, Harris Queensway Plc. Dir, Harveys Hldgs, 1986–; non-executive Director: Great Universal Stores, 1986–; Fisons Plc, 1986–. Chm., Young Entrepreneurs Fund, 1985–. Mem., British Show Jumping Assoc., 1974. Chm., Guy's and Lewisham NHS Trust, 1991–; Member: Council of Governors, Utd Med. and Dental Schs of Guy's and St Thomas's Hosps, 1984–; Court of Patrons, RCOG, 1984–; Chm., Generation Trust, 1984–; Governor, Nat. Hosp. for Nervous Diseases, 1985–. Hon. Fellow, Oriel Coll., Oxford, 1989. Hambro Business Man of the Year, 1983. *Recreations:* football, cricket, show jumping, tennis. *Address:* Harris Ventures Ltd, Central Court, 1b Knoll Rise, Orpington, Kent BR6 0JA.

HARRIS, Phillip, FRCSE, FRCPE, FRCS(Glas); FRS(Ed); Consultant Neurosurgeon, Department of Surgical Neurology, Royal Infirmary and Western General Hospital, Edinburgh, and Spinal Unit, Edenhall Hospital, Musselburgh, since 1955; Senior Lecturer, Department of Neurological Surgery, Edinburgh University, since 1975; Member, MRC Brain Metabolism Unit, University of Edinburgh, since 1952; Chairman: Professional and Linguistic Assessments Board, General Medical Council; Committee of Management, School of Occupational Therapy, Edinburgh; Member, Advisory Council, Society of British Neurological Surgeons; *b* Edinburgh, 28 March 1922; *s* of late Simon Harris, Edinburgh; *m* 1949, Sheelagh Shèna (*née* Coutts); one *s* one *d*. *Educ:* Royal High Sch., Edinburgh; Edinburgh Univ.; Sch. of Med. of Royal Colls, Edinburgh. Medallist in Anatomy, Physiol., Physics, Materia Medica and Therapeutics, Med., Midwifery and Gynaec., and Surgery. LRCP and LRCSEd, LRFP and SG 1944; FRCSE 1948; MRCPE 1954; FRCPE 1959; FRCS(Glas) 1964 (*ad eundem*). Sydney Watson-Smith Lectr, RCPE, 1967; Honeyman-Gillespie Lectr, Edinburgh Univ., 1968; Visiting Prof.: Columbus, Ohio; Cincinnati, Ohio; Phoenix, Arizona; UCLA; Montreal Neurological Inst., Montreal; Chicago; Rangoon; Bangkok; Buenos Aires; La Paz. Guest Chief and Vis. Lectr in Univs in Canada, USA, Japan, Israel, Denmark, Peru, Hong Kong, Uruguay. Member: Amer. Assoc. of Neurolog. Surgeons; Burmese Med. Assoc.; Hong Kong Surg. Soc.; Middle East Neurosurg. Soc.; Brazilian Coll. Surgeons. Chm., Epilepsy Soc. of Edinburgh and SE Reg.; Trustee and Mem. Exec., Scottish Trust for the Physically Disabled Ltd. Pres., Royal High Sch. FP Club, Edinburgh. Captain RAMC, 1945–48. *Publications:* Spinal Injuries, RCSE, 1965; (ed jtly) Epilepsy, 1971; (ed jtly) Head Injuries, 1971; chapters in books on neurological surgery; over 60 papers in scientific jls on various neurosurgical topics. *Recreations:* sport, music, travel. *Address:* 4/5 Fettes Rise, Edinburgh EH4 1QH. *T:* 031–552 8900. *Clubs:* New (Edinburgh); Royal Scottish Automobile (Glasgow); University Staff (Edinburgh).

HARRIS, Ven. (Reginald) Brian; Archdeacon of Manchester, since 1980; a Residentiary Canon of Manchester Cathedral, since 1980, Sub-Dean since 1986; *b* 14 Aug. 1934; *s* of Reginald and Ruby Harris; *m* 1959, Anne Patricia Hughes; one *s* one *d*. *Educ:* Eltham College; Christ's College Cambridge (MA); Ridley Hall, Cambridge. Curate of Wednesbury, 1959–61; Curate of Uttoxeter, 1961–64; Vicar of St Peter, Bury, 1964–70; Vicar of Walmsley, Bolton, 1970–80; RD of Walmsley, 1970–80. *Recreations:* walking, painting, music. *Address:* 4 Victoria Avenue, Eccles, Manchester M30 9HA. *T:* 061–707 6444.

HARRIS, Richard Reader; *b* 4 June 1913; *s* of Richard Reader Harris; *m* 1940, Pamela Rosemary Merrick Stephens; three *d*. *Educ:* St Lawrence Coll., Ramsgate. Called to the Bar, 1941. Fire Service, 1939–45. MP (C) Heston and Isleworth, 1950–70. *Recreations:* squash, tennis.

HARRIS, Richard Travis; Director, Burton Group plc, since 1984; *b* 15 April 1919; 2nd *s* of Douglas Harris and Emmeline Harris (*née* Travis); *m* 1st, 1941, June Constance Rundle (marr. diss. 1953); two *d*; 2nd, 1953, Margaret Sophia Nye (*née* Aron); one *s* one *d*. *Educ:* Charterhouse; RMA Woolwich. Served War of 1939–45, France, Western Desert, Tunisia, Italy (despatches twice); BAOR, 1945–46; Sudan Defence Force Signal Regt, 1947–50 (CO, 1948–50); retired from Royal Signals, 1950, Lt-Col. Man. Dir, Rediffusion (Nigeria) Ltd and Gen. Manager, Rediffusion in Africa, 1951–54; Dep. Gen. Manager, Associated-Rediffusion Ltd, 1954–57; Man. Dir, Coates & Co. (Plymouth) Ltd, 1957–64 (Dir, 1957–68); Man. Dir, 1964–78, Chm., 1970–78, Dollond & Aitchison Ltd; Chm., Dollond & Aitchison Group Ltd (formerly TWW Enterprises Ltd), 1970–78 (Dir, 1968–85); Director: Gallaher Ltd, 1970–87 (Dep. Chm., 1978–84); Dollond International Ltd, 1973–83; Filotechnica Salmoiraghi SpA, 1974–83; Istituto Ottico Vigano SpA, 1974–83; Saunders Valve Co. Ltd, 1978–84; Mono Pumps Ltd, 1978–84; Formatura Iniezione Polimeri SpA, 1978–84; Tobacco Kiosks Ltd, 1978–84; Gallaher Pensions Ltd, 1975–84. Chairman: Fedn of Optical Corporate Bodies, 1970–82; Fedn of Ophthalmic & Dispensing Opticians, 1985–87; Vice-Pres., Inst. of Dirs, 1985–89 (Chm. Council, 1982–85); Mem. Exec. Cttee, Wider Share Ownership Council, 1987–; Mem. Council, Univ. of Birmingham, 1978–, Life Mem., Court, 1981. Governor, Royal Shakespeare Theatre, 1980–; Master, Coachmakers and Coach Harness Makers, 1963–64. *Recreations:* fishing, theatre. *Address:* 21 Lucy's Mill, Stratford-upon-Avon, Warwickshire CV37 6DE. *T:* Stratford-upon-Avon (0789) 266016. *Club:* Athenæum.

HARRIS, Robert; actor since 1922; *b* 28 March 1900; *s* of Alfred H. Harris and Suzanne Amelie (*née* Anstie). *Educ:* Sherborne; New Coll., Oxford. Has appeared in Shakespearean rôles with the Old Vic-Sadler's Wells Company and at Stratford-on-Avon, and in the West End (Hamlet, Oberon, Prospero, Angelo, Henry IV, King John, Shylock and Dr Faustus). Other parts include: St Bernard, in The Marvellous History of St Bernard; Charles Tritton, in The Wind and The Rain; Eugene Marchbanks, in Candida (NY); Orin Mannon, in Mourning Becomes Electra; Thomas More, in A Man for all Seasons (USA); Pope Pius XII in The Deputy (NY); 40 Years On (Canada); J. Robert Oppenheimer, Fortune Theatre; films include: How he lied to her Husband; Decline and Fall; Morta in Roma; Ransom; Love Among the Ruins. Television and radio plays incl.: Old Jolyon in The Forsyte Saga; Prof. Gay in C. P. Snow's Strangers and Brothers (serials); Archdeacon Grantly in The Barchester Chronicles; The Mysterious Death of Charles Bravo; Edward and Mrs Simpson (TV serial); Duke of Burgundy in Henry V. *Recreation:* travel. *Clubs:* Garrick, Chelsea Arts.

HARRIS, Robert Dennis; writer and broadcaster; Political Columnist, Sunday Times, since 1989; *b* 7 March 1957; *s* of Dennis Harris and Audrey (*née* Hardy); *m* 1988, Gillian Hornby; one *d*. *Educ:* King Edward VII Sch., Melton Mowbray; Selwyn Coll., Cambridge (BA Hons English). Chm., Cambridge Fabian Soc., 1977; Pres., Cambridge Union, 1978. Joined BBC TV Current Affairs Dept, 1978; Researcher and Film Dir, Tonight, Nationwide and Panorama, 1978–81; Reporter, Newsnight, 1981–85, Panorama, 1985–87; Political Editor, Observer, 1987–89; Political Reporter, This Week, Thames TV, 1988–89. *Publications:* (with Jeremy Paxman) A Higher Form of Killing: the history of gas and germ warfare, 1982; Gotcha! the media, the government and the Falklands crisis, 1983; The Making of Neil Kinnock, 1984; Selling Hitler: the story of the Hitler diaries, 1986 (televised, 1991); Good and Faithful Servant: the unauthorized biography of Bernard Ingham, 1990; Fatherland (novel), 1992. *Recreations:* reading history, walking, fishing, listening to music. *Address:* 31 St Lawrence Terrace, W10 5SR. *T:* 081–960 1410.

HARRIS, Robin (David Ronald), CBE 1988; Assistant to Rt. Hon. Margaret Thatcher, since 1990; *b* 22 June 1952; *s* of Ronald Desmond Harris and Isabella Jamieson Harris. *Educ:* Canford Sch.; Exeter Coll., Oxford (Stapeldon Schol., MA History, DPhil). Desk Officer, Conservative Res. Dept, 1978–81; Special Adviser: to Financial Sec. to the Treasury, 1981–83; to Home Secretary, 1983–85; Dir, Conservative Res. Dept, 1985–89; Mem., Prime Minister's Policy Unit, 1989–90. *Recreations:* reading, travel. *Club:* United Oxford & Cambridge University.

HARRIS, Sir Ronald (Montague Joseph), KCVO 1960 (MVO 1943); CB 1956; First Church Estates Commissioner, 1969–82; Chairman, Central Board of Finance of Church of England, 1978–82; *b* 6 May 1913; *o s* of late Rev. J. Montague Harris and Edith Annesley Harris (*née* Malcolmson); *m* 1st, 1939, Margaret Julia Wharton (*d* 1955); one *s* three *d*; 2nd, 1957, Marjorie (*d* 1986), *widow* of Julian Tryon, and *e d* of late Sir Harry Verney, 4th Bt, DSO, and late Lady Rachel Verney; one step *d* (one step *s* decd). *Educ:* Harrow; Trinity Coll., Oxford. India Office and Burma Office, 1936–38; Private Sec. to Sec. of Cabinet, 1939–43; India Office and Burma Office, 1944–47; Imperial Defence Coll., 1948; HM Treasury, 1949–52; Cabinet Office, 1952–55; Second Crown Estate Commissioner, 1955–60; Third Sec., HM Treasury, 1960–64; Sec. to Church Commissioners, 1964–68. Director: Yorks Insurance Co., 1966–69; Yorkshire General Life Assurance Co., 1969–84; General Accident Fire and Life Assurance Corp. Ltd, 1970–84. Chairman: Benenden Sch. Council, 1971–77; Friends of Yehudi Menuhin Sch., 1972–89 (Pres., 1989–), Governor, 1976– (Vice-Chm., 1984–89, Chm., 1989–90). *Publication:* Memory—Soft The Air, 1987. *Address:* Slyfield Farm House, Stoke D'Abernon, Cobham, Surrey KT11 3QE. *Club:* Boodle's.

HARRIS, Rosemary Jeanne; author; *b* 1923; *yr d* of Marshal of the RAF Sir Arthur Harris, 1st Bt, GCB, OBE, AFC, LLD, and of Barbara Kyrle Money. *Educ:* privately; Thorneloe Sch., Weymouth; St Martin's, Central and Chelsea Schs of Art. Red Cross Nursing Auxiliary, London, Westminster Div., from 1941. Student, 1945–48; picture restorer, 1949; student at Courtauld Inst. (Dept of Technology), 1950; Reader, MGM, 1951–52; subseq. full-time writer. Reviewer of children's books for The Times, 1970–73. Television plays: Peronik, 1976; The Unknown Enchantment, 1981. *Publications:* The Summer-House, 1956; Voyage to Cythera, 1958; Venus with Sparrows, 1961; All My Enemies, 1967; The Nice Girl's Story, 1968; A Wicked Pack of Cards, 1969; The Double Snare, 1975; Three Candles for the Dark, 1976; *for children:* The Moon in the Cloud, 1968 (Carnegie Medal); The Shadow on the Sun, 1970; The Seal-Singing, 1971; The Child in the Bamboo Grove, 1971; The Bright and Morning Star, 1972; The King's White Elephant, 1973; The Lotus and the Grail, 1974; The Flying Ship, 1974; The Little Dog of Fo, 1976; I Want to be a Fish, 1977; A Quest for Orion, 1978; Beauty and the Beast, 1979; Greenfinger House, 1979; Tower of the Stars, 1980; The Enchanted Horse, 1981; Janni's Stork, 1982; Zed, 1982; (adapted) Heidi, by Johanna Spyri, 1983; Summers of the Wild Rose, 1987; (ed) Poetry Anthology: Love and the Merry-Go-Round, 1988; Colm of the Islands, 1989; Ticket to Freedom, 1991. *Recreations:* music, theatre, gardening.

Address: c/o A P Watt, 20 John Street, WC1N 2DR.
See also Sir A. T. K. Harris, Bt.

HARRIS, Rosina Mary; Consultant, Taylor Joynson Garrett, since 1989; Partner, Joynson-Hicks, Solicitors, 1954–89 (Senior Partner, 1977–86); *b* 30 May 1921; *d* of late Alfred Harris, CBE, DSO, and Rosa Alfreda Harris. *Educ:* St Swithun's Sch., Winchester; Oxford Univ. (BA 1946, MA; BCL). Joined American Ambulance of Gt Britain, 1940. Member, Whitford Committee (a Cttee set up under the Chairmanship of Hon. Mr Justice Whitford to enquire into and report as to copyright law), 1973. The Queen's Silver Jubilee Medal, 1977. *Recreations:* theatre, riding. *Address:* 23 Devonshire Place, W1N 1PD. *T:* (office) 071–836 8456.
See also J. R. Harris.

HARRIS, Prof. Roy, MA, DPhil, PhD; FRSA; Professor of General Linguistics, University of Oxford, 1978–88, now Emeritus; Fellow of Worcester College, Oxford, 1978–88; *b* 24 Feb. 1931; *s* of Harry and Emmie J. Harris; *m* 1955, Rita Doreen Shulman; one *d.* *Educ:* Queen Elizabeth's Hospital, Bristol; St Edmund Hall, Oxford (MA, DPhil; Hon. Fellow 1987); SOAS, London (PhD). Lecteur, Ecole Normale Supérieure, Paris, 1956–57; Asst Lectr, 1957–58, Lectr, 1958–60, Univ. of Leicester; Exeter Coll., Oxford, 1960–76; Keble Coll., Oxford, 1960–67; Magdalen Coll., Oxford, 1960–76; New Coll., Oxford, 1960–67; Faculty of Medieval and Modern Languages, Oxford, 1961–76; Fellow and Tutor in Romance Philology, Keble Coll., Oxford, 1967–76; Prof. of the Romance Langs, Oxford Univ., and Fellow of Trinity Coll., 1976–77; Prof. of English Language, Univ. of Hong Kong, 1988–91. Visiting Professor: Jawaharlal Nehru Univ., New Delhi, 1986; State Univ. of NY, 1987. Council Member, Philological Soc., 1978–82. Editor, Language & Communication, 1980–. Scott Moncrieff prize, Translators' Assoc. (Soc. of Authors), 1984. *Publications:* Synonymy and Linguistic Analysis, 1973; Communication and Language, 1978; The Language-Makers, 1980; The Language Myth, 1981; (trans.) F. de Saussure: Course in General Linguistics, 1983; (ed) Approaches to Language, 1983; (ed) Developmental Mechanisms of Language, 1985; The Origin of Writing, 1986; Reading Saussure, 1987; Language, Saussure and Wittgenstein, 1988; (ed) Linguistic Thought in England 1914–1945, 1988; (with T. J. Taylor) Landmarks in Linguistic Thought: the Western tradition from Socrates to Saussure, 1989; contribs to Analysis, Behavioral and Brain Sciences, Encounter, French Studies, History and Philosophy of Logic, International Jl of Moral and Social Studies, Jl of Linguistics, Language Sciences, Linguistics, Medium Ævum, Mind, Revue de linguistique romane, Semiotica, Studies in Eighteenth-Century Culture, Theoria, TLS, Zeitschrift für romanische Philologie. *Recreations:* cricket, modern art and design. *Address:* 2 Paddox Close, Oxford OX2 7LR. *T:* Oxford (0865) 54256.

HARRIS, (Theodore) Wilson; *b* 24 March 1921; *m* 1st, 1945, Cecily Carew; 2nd, 1959, Margaret Whitaker (*née* Burns). *Educ:* Queen's Coll., Georgetown, British Guiana. Studied land surveying, British Guiana, 1939, and subseq. qualified to practise; led many survey parties (mapping and geomorphological research) in the interior; Senior Surveyor, Projects, for Govt of British Guiana, 1955–58. Came to live in London, 1959. Writer in Residence, Univ. of West Indies and Univ. of Toronto, 1970; Commonwealth Fellow, Leeds Univ., 1971; Vis. Prof., Univ. of Texas at Austin, 1972; Guggenheim Fellow, 1973; Henfield Fellow, UEA, 1974; Southern Arts Writer's Fellowship, 1976; Guest Lectr, Univ. of Mysore, 1978; Vis. Lectr, Yale Univ., 1979; Writer in Residence: Univ. of Newcastle, Australia, 1979; Univ. of Qld, Australia, 1986; Vis. Prof., Univ. of Texas at Austin, 1981–82; Regents' Lectr, Univ. of California, 1983. Hon. DLit Univ. of West Indies, 1984; Hon. DLitt Kent at Canterbury, 1988. Guyana Prize for Fiction, 1985–87. *Publications:* Eternity to Season (poems, privately printed), 1954; Palace of the Peacock, 1960; The Far Journey of Oudin, 1961; The Whole Armour, 1962; The Secret Ladder, 1963; Heartland, 1964; The Eye of the Scarecrow, 1965; The Waiting Room, 1967; Tradition, the Writer and Society: Critical Essays, 1967; Tumatumari, 1968; Ascent to Omai, 1970; The Sleepers of Roraima (a Carib Trilogy), 1970; The Age of the Rainmakers, 1971; Black Marsden, 1972; Companions of the Day and Night, 1975; Da Silva da Silva's Cultivated Wilderness (filmed, 1987), and Genesis of the Clowns, 1977; The Tree of the Sun, 1978; Explorations (essays), 1981; The Angel at the Gate, 1982; The Womb of Space: the cross-cultural imagination, 1983; Carnival, 1985; The Infinite Rehearsal, 1987; The Four Banks of the River of Space, 1990. *Address:* c/o Faber and Faber, 3 Queen Square, WC1N 3AU.

HARRIS, Thomas George; HM Diplomatic Service; Head of East Africa Department, Foreign and Commonwealth Office, since 1991; *b* 6 Feb. 1945; *s* of Kenneth James Harris and Dorothy Harris; *m* 1967, Mei-Ling Hwang; three *s.* *Educ:* Haberdashers' Aske's School; Gonville and Caius College, Cambridge. MA. Board of Trade, 1966–69; British Embassy, Tokyo, 1969–71; Asst Private Sec. to Minister for Aerospace, 1971–72; Dept. of Trade, 1972–76; Cabinet Office, 1976–78; Principal Private Sec. to Sec. of State for Trade and Industry, 1978–79; Asst Sec., Dept of Trade, 1979–83; Counsellor (Commercial), British Embassy, Washington, 1983–88; Head of Chancery, Lagos, 1988–90; Dep. High Comr, Nigeria, 1990–91. *Address:* c/o Foreign and Commonwealth Office, King Charles Street, SW1A 2AH.

HARRIS, Toby; *see* Harris, J. T.

HARRIS, Hon. Walter Edward, PC (Canada), QC (Canada); DCL; *b* 14 Jan. 1904; *s* of Melvin Harris and Helen (*née* Carruthers); *m* 1933, Grace Elma Morrison; one *s* two *d.* *Educ:* Osgoode Hall, Toronto. Served War of 1939–45. First elected to House of Commons, Canada, 1940 (re-elected 1945, 1949, 1953), MP (Canada) until 1957. Parliamentary Asst to Sec of State for External Affairs, 1947; Parly Asst to Prime Minister, 1948; Minister of Citizenship and Immigration, 1950; of Finance, 1954–57. Mem. of the firm of Harris, Willis, Barristers, Markdale. *Address:* Markdale, Ontario, Canada.

HARRIS, (Walter) Frank; retired 1982; *b* 19 May 1920; *m* Esther Blanche Hill; two *s* two *d.* *Educ:* King Edward's Sch., Birmingham; University of Nottingham. Served Royal Air Force, 1939–46. University, 1946–49. Ford Motor Company, 1950–65; Principal City Officer and Town Clerk, Newcastle upon Tyne, 1965–69. Comptroller and Dir, Admin, Massey-Ferguson (UK), 1969–71; Finance Dir, Dunlop SA Ltd, 1972–79; Business Planning Exec., Dunlop Ltd (UK Tyre Gp), 1979–81. *Recreations:* astrophysics (undergraduate at Univ. of S Africa and graduate student at Open Univ.), fell walking, DIY, gardening. *Address:* Acomb High House, Northumberland NE46 4PH. *T:* Hexham (0434) 602844.

HARRIS, William Barclay, QC 1961; *b* 25 Nov. 1911; *s* of W. Cecil Harris, Moatlands, E Grinstead, Sussex; *m* 1937, Elizabeth, 2nd *d* of Capt. Sir Clive Milnes-Coates, 2nd Bt, and of Lady Celia Milnes-Coates, JP; one *s* two *d.* *Educ:* Harrow; Trinity Coll., Cambridge (MA). Served 1940–45: with Coldstream Guards, N Africa, Italy, Germany (despatches), Major. Barrister, Inner Temple, 1937. Chm., Rowton Hotels, 1965–83. A Church Commissioner, 1966–82 (Chm., Redundant Churches Cttee, 1972–82; Mem., Bd of Governors, 1972–82). Pres., Georgian Group, 1990– (Chm., 1985–90). Liveryman, Worshipful Co. of Merchant Taylors. *Address:* Moatlands, East Grinstead, West Sussex. *T:* Sharpthorne 810228; 29 Barkston Gardens, SW5. *T:* 071–373 8793. *Clubs:* Athenæum, MCC, Brooks's.

HARRIS, Sir William (Gordon), KBE 1969; CB 1963; MA (Cantab); FEng; FICE; Director-General, Highways, Ministry of Transport, later Department of the Environment, 1965–73; *b* 10 June 1912; *s* of late Capt. James Whyte Harris, Royal Naval Reserve, and Margaret Roberta Buchanan Forsyth; *m* 1938, Margaret Emily Harvie (*d* 1991); three *s* one *d.* *Educ:* Liverpool Coll.; Sidney Sussex Coll., Cambridge. Mechanical Sciences Tripos and BA 1932, MA 1937. London Midland & Scottish Railway, 1932–35; Sudan Irrigation Dept, 1935–37; Joined Civil Engineer in Chief's Dept, Admiralty, 1937; Asst Civil Engineer in Chief, 1950; Deputy Civil Engineer in Chief, 1955; Civil Engineer in Chief, 1959; Dir-Gen., Navy Works, 1960–63; Dir-Gen. of Works, MPBW, 1963–65. Partner, Peter Fraenkel & Partners, 1973–78; Chm., B & CE Holiday Management Co. & Benefit Trust Co., 1978–87. Dir, British Sch. of Osteopathy, 1982– (Chm., 1990–). Chief British Delegate to: Perm. Internat. Assoc. of Navigation Congresses, 1969–June 1985 (Vice-Pres., 1976–79); Perm. Internat. Assoc. of Road Congresses, 1970–73; Mem., Dover Harbour Bd, 1959–82 (Dep. Chm., 1975–79; Chm., 1980–82); Chm., Construction Industry Manpower Bd, 1976–79. Commonwealth Fund (of New York) Fellowship, 1950–51. A Vice-Pres., Instn Civil Engineers, 1971–74, Pres. 1974–75. FEng 1977. Mem., Smeatonian Soc. of Civil Engineers, 1966– (Pres., 1984). Hon. DSc City, 1977. Hon. Seabee, US Navy, 1961. Decoration for Distinguished Civilian Service to US Army, 1985. *Recreations:* gardening, ten grand-children, walking dog. *Address:* 3 Rofant Road, Northwood, Mddx HA6 3BD. *T:* Northwood (09274) 25899.

HARRIS, Wilson; *see* Harris, T. W.

HARRISON; *see* Graham-Harrison.

HARRISON, (Alastair) Brian (Clarke); DL; farmer; *b* 3 Oct. 1921; *s* of late Brig. E. F. Harrison, Melbourne; *m* 1952, Elizabeth Hood Hardie, Oaklands, NSW, Aust.; one *s* one *d.* *Educ:* Geelong Grammar Sch.; Trinity Coll., Cambridge. Capt. AIF. MP (C) Maldon, Essex, 1955–Feb. 1974; Parliamentary Private Secretary to: Min. of State, Colonial Office, 1955–56; Sec. of State for War, 1956–58; Min. of Agriculture, Fisheries and Food, 1958–60. Mem. Victoria Promotion Cttee (London); Mem. One Nation Gp which published The Responsible Society, and One Europe; toured USA on E-SU Ford Foundation Fellowship, 1959; Commonwealth Parliamentary Assoc. Delegations: Kenya and Horn of Africa, 1960; Gilbert and Ellice Islands, New Hebrides and British Solomon Islands Protectorate. Chm., Standing Conf. of Eastern Sport and Physical Recreation, 1974–. Organizer (with Univ. of WA), expedns to Nepal studying human physiol., 1979–87. High Sheriff, 1979, DL 1980, Essex. *Publications:* (jtly) The cumulative effect of High Altitude on Motor Performance: a comparison between caucasian visitors and native highlanders, 1985; (jtly) Entrainment of respiratory frequency to exercise rhythm during hypoxia, 1987. *Recreations:* photography, gardening. *Address:* Green Farm House, Copford, Colchester, Essex CO6 1DA; Mundethana, Kojonup, WA 6395, Australia. *Clubs:* Pratt's; Melbourne (Melbourne); Weld (Perth).

HARRISON, Albert Norman, CB 1966; CVO 1955; OBE 1946; RCNC; Hon. Vice-President RINA; *b* 12 July 1901; *s* of William Arthur and Sarah Jane Harrison, Portsmouth, Hants; *m* 1941, Queenie Perpetua Parker, Luton, Beds; one *d.* *Educ:* Portsmouth; Royal Naval Coll., Greenwich. Asst Constructor, Royal Corps of Naval Constructors, 1926; Constructor, 1937; Principal Ship Overseer. Vickers-Armstrong, Barrow-in-Furness, 1936–39; Staff of RA (D), Home Fleet, 1940–41; Naval Constructor-in-Chief, Royal Canadian Navy, 1942–48; Chief Constructor, Admiralty, 1948–51; Asst Dir of Naval Construction, Admiralty, 1951–61; Dir of Naval Construction, Min. of Defence (N) (formerly Admiralty), 1961–66. *Address:* Whiteoaks, 126 Bloomfield Road, Bath, Avon BA2 2AS. *T:* Bath (0225) 429145. *Club:* Bath and County (Bath).

HARRISON, Brian; *see* Harrison, A. B. C.

HARRISON, Prof. Bryan Desmond, CBE 1990; PhD; FRS 1987; FRSE; Professor of Plant Virology, University of Dundee, since 1991; *b* 16 June 1931; *s* of John William and Norah Harrison; *m* 1968, Elizabeth Ann Latham-Warde; two *s* one *d.* *Educ:* Whitgift Sch., Croydon; Reading Univ. (BSc Hons Agric. Bot. 1952); London Univ. (PhD 1955). FRSE 1979. Postgraduate student, ARC, 1952; Scottish Hort. Res. Inst., Dundee, 1954; Rothamsted Exp. Station, 1957; Head, Virology Section, 1966, Dep. Dir, 1979, Scottish Hort. Res. Inst.; Head, Virology Dept, Scottish Crop Res. Inst., 1981–91. Visiting Professor: Japan Soc. for Promotion of Science, 1970; Organization of American States, Venezuela, 1973; Hon. Prof., Univ. of St Andrews, 1986; Vis. Hon. Prof., Univ. of Dundee, 1988. Pres., Assoc. of Applied Biologists, 1980–81. *Publications:* Plant Virology: the principles (with A. J. Gibbs), 1976 (trans Russian and Chinese); research papers and reviews on plant viruses and virus diseases. *Recreations:* growing garden crops, foreign travel. *Address:* Scottish Crop Research Institute, Invergowrie, Dundee DD2 5DA. *T:* Dundee (0382) 562731.

HARRISON, Prof. Charles Victor; retired; Professor of Pathology, University of Ife, Nigeria, 1972–75; *b* Newport, Mon, 1907; *s* of Charles Henry Harrison, LDS, and Violet Harrison (*née* Witchell); *m* 1937, Olga Beatrice Cochrane; one *s* one *d.* *Educ:* Dean Close Sch., Cheltenham; University Coll., Cardiff; University Coll. Hosp., London. MB, BCh, BSc (Wales), 1929; MB, BS (London), 1929; MD (London), 1937; FRCPath 1965; FRCP 1967. Demonstrator in Pathology, Welsh National School of Medicine, 1930; Asst Morbid Anatomist, British Postgraduate Medical Sch., 1935; Senior Lecturer, Liverpool Univ., 1939; Reader in Morbid Anatomy, Postgraduate Medical Sch. of London, 1946; Prof., Royal Postgrad. Med. Sch., Univ. of London, 1955–72. Hon. DSc Wales, 1972. Willie Seager Gold Medal in Pathology, 1927. *Publications:* (ed) Recent Advances in Pathology, 1973; various scientific papers in Jl of Pathology and Bacteriology, British Heart Journal, Jl Clin. Pathology, etc. *Recreations:* carpentry and gardening. *Address:* 8 Wattleton Road, Beaconsfield, Bucks HP9 1TS. *T:* Beaconsfield (0494) 672046.

HARRISON, Claude William, RP 1961; Artist; portrait painter and painter of conversation pieces, imaginative landscapes and murals, etc; *b* Leyland, Lancs, 31 March 1922; *s* of Harold Harrison and Florence Mildred Ireton; *m* 1947, Audrey Johnson; one *s.* *Educ:* Hutton Grammar Sch., Lancs. Served in RAF, 1942–46. Royal Coll. of Art, 1947–49; Studio in Ambleside, 1949–52. Exhibited since 1950 at: RA; RSA; Royal Society Portrait Painters; New English Art Club, etc. *Publication:* The Portrait Painter's handbook, 1968. *Recreation:* painting. *Address:* Barrow Wife, Cartmel Fell, near Grange over Sands, Cumbria. *T:* Newby Bridge (05395) 31323.

HARRISON, Sir Colin; *see* Harrison, Sir R. C.

HARRISON, David, CBE 1990; ScD; FEng 1987; Vice-Chancellor, University of Exeter, since 1984; Fellow of Selwyn College, Cambridge, since 1957; Chairman, Committee of Vice-Chancellors and Principals, since 1991; *b* 3 May 1930; *s* of late Harold David Harrison and of Lavinia Wilson; *m* 1962, Sheila Rachel Debes; one *s* one *d* (and one *s* decd). *Educ:* Bede Sch., Sunderland; Clacton County High Sch.; Selwyn Coll., Cambridge (1st Cl. Pts I and II Natural Sciences Tripos, BA 1953, PhD 1956, MA 1957, ScD 1979). CEng; FRSC (FRIC 1961), FIChemE 1968. 2nd Lieut, REME, 1949. Research student, Dept of Physical Chemistry, Cambridge, 1953–56; Univ. Asst Lectr in Chem. Engrg, 1956–61; Univ. Lectr, 1961–79; Sen. Tutor, Selwyn Coll., Cambridge, 1967–79; Vice-

Chancellor, Univ. of Keele, 1979–84. Visiting Professor of Chemical Engineering: Univ. of Delaware, USA, 1967; Univ. of Sydney, 1976. Member, Council of the Senate, Univ. of Cambridge, 1967–75; Chm. of Faculty Bd of Educn, 1976–78; Member Council: Lancing Coll., 1970–82; Haileybury, 1974–84; St Edward's, Oxford, 1977–89; Bolton Girls' Sch., 1981–84; Shrewsbury Sch., 1983– (Chm., 1989–); Taunton Sch., 1986–89; Fellow, Woodard Corporation of Schools, 1972–; Chairman: Bd of Trustees, Homerton Coll., Cambridge, 1979–; UCCA, 1984–91; Voluntary Sector Consultative Council, 1984–88; Southern Univs Jt Bd, 1986–88; Church and Associated Colls Adv. Cttee, PCFC, 1988–91; Bd of Management, Northcott Theatre, 1984–. Pres., IChemE, 1991–92 (Vice-Pres., 1989–91). Mem., Marshall Aid Commemoration Commn, 1982–89. FRSA 1985. Hon. Editor, Trans Instn of Chemical Engrs, 1972–78. *Publications:* (with J. F. Davidson) Fluidised Particles, 1963; (also with J. F. Davidson) Fluidization, 1971, rev. edn (with J. F. Davidson and R. Clift) 1985; numerous articles in scientific and technological jls. *Recreations:* music, tennis, hill walking, good food. *Address:* Northcote House, The Queen's Drive, Exeter EX4 4QJ. *T:* Exeter (0392) 263000. *Clubs:* Athenæum; Federation House (Stoke-on-Trent).

HARRISON, Denis Byrne; Town Clerk and Chief Executive Officer, Sheffield, 1966–74; *b* 11 July 1917; *y s* of late Arthur and Priscilla Harrison; *m* 1956, Alice Marion Vickers (*d* 1989), *e d* of late Hedley Vickers. *Educ:* Birkenhead Sch.; Liverpool Univ. (LLM). Articled to late E. W. Tame, OBE (Town Clerk of Birkenhead). Admitted Solicitor, 1939; Asst Solicitor to Birkenhead Corp., 1939. Legal Associate Mem. RTPI, 1949. Served War, 1939–46: 75th Shropshire Yeo. (Medium Regt) RA, Combined Ops Bombardment Unit; Staff Captain at HQ of OC, Cyprus. First Asst Solicitor, Wolverhampton Co. Borough, 1946–49; Dep. Town Clerk of Co. Boroughs: Warrington, 1949–57; Bolton, 1957–63; Sheffield, 1963–66; Local Comr for Admin in England, 1974–81, and Vice-Chm., Commn for Local Admin, 1975–81. Mem., Advisory Council on Noise, 1970–79. Mem. Council, 1975–82, Pro-Chancellor, 1980–82, Univ. of Sheffield. JP City of London, 1976–86. *Recreations:* reading, walking. *Address:* 2 Leicester Close, Henley-on-Thames, Oxon RG9 2LD. *T:* Henley-on-Thames (0491) 572782.

HARRISON, (Desmond) Roger (Wingate); Deputy Chairman, Capital Radio (Director, since 1975); *b* 9 April 1933; *s* of late Maj.-Gen. Desmond Harrison, CB, DSO and of Kathleen Harrison (*née* Hazley); *m* 1965, Victoria Lee-Barber, MVO, *d* of Rear-Adm. John Lee-Barber, *qv*; four *d* (and one *s* decd). *Educ:* Rugby School; Worcester College, Oxford (MA); Harvard Univ. Business Sch. Writing freelance, principally for The Times, 1951–57; joined staff of The Times, 1957–67; The Observer: joined 1967; Dir, 1970–; Jt Managing Dir, 1977–84; Chief Exec., 1984–87. Dir, The Oak Foundn, 1987–89. Chm., Greater Manchester Cablevision, 1990–; Director: LWT and LWT (Holdings), 1976–; Duke of York's Theatre, 1979–; Sableknight, 1981–. Mem. Council, NPA, 1967–87. Chm., Toynbee Hall, 1990–. Governor, Sadler's Wells, 1984–. *Recreations:* theatre, country pursuits, tennis. *Address:* 35 Argyll Road, W8 7DA. *Clubs:* Cavalry and Guards, Flyfishers', Queen's.

HARRISON, Sir Donald (Frederick Norris), Kt 1990; MD, MS, PhD; FRCS; Professor of Laryngology and Otology (University of London), since 1963, and Dean, since 1989, Institute of Laryngology and Otology, Gray's Inn Road, WC1; Surgeon, Royal National Throat, Nose and Ear Hospital; Civilian Consultant on ENT to RN; *b* 9 March 1925; *s* of Frederick William Rees Harrison, OBE, JP, and Florence, *d* of Robert Norris, Portsmouth, Hants; *m* 1949, Audrey, *o d* of Percival Clubb, Penarth, Glam.; two *d*. *Educ:* Newport High Sch., Mon.; Guy's Hosp. MD (London) 1960; MS (London) 1959; PhD (London) 1983; FRCS 1955. Ho. Surg., Guy's Hosp. and Royal Gwent Hospital, Newport; Surg. Registrar, Shrewsbury Eye and Ear Hosp.; Senior Registrar, Throat and Ear Dept, Guy's Hosp.; University Reader in Laryngology, Inst. of Laryngol. and Otol. Hunterian Prof., RCS, 1962; Eramus Wilson Demonstrator, RCS, 1971. Lectures: Chevalier Jackson, 1964; Yearsley, 1972; Wilde, 1972; Litchfield, 1973; Semon, 1974; Colles, RCSI, 1977; Jobson Horne, BMA, 1979; Conacher, Toronto, 1978; Harris, USA, 1984; Putney, USA, 1985; Baker, USA, 1986; Bryce, Toronto, 1987; McBride, Edinburgh, 1987; Douglas J. Guthrie, Edinburgh, 1988; Bob Owen (first), Cardiff, 1988; Ogura, USA, 1990. Wellcome Prof., S Africa, 1988. W. J. Harrison Prize, RSM, 1978; Medal of Paris, 1988; Gold medal, Internat. Fedn of Oto Rhino Laryngological Socs, 1985; Gold Medal, NY Eye & Ear Alumni Assoc., 1988; Gold Medal, Joshi Meml Lecture, Indian ENT Soc., 1990. Mem. of Court of Examiners, RCS; Examr, NUI; External Examr, Univs of Melbourne, Southampton, Sydney, Manchester, Liverpool, Glasgow, Hong Kong, Belfast and Cambridge; Scientific Fellow, Royal Zoological Soc. of London; FRSM (Pres., Sect. of Laryngology, 1984, former Vice-Pres.); Mem. Council, Sect. of Oncology); Mem. BMA; Mem. Council: Brit. Assoc. of Otolaryngologists; Brit. Assoc. of Head and Neck Oncologists (Pres.); Hon. Sec., RSM, 1987–; Former Chairman: Special Adv. Cttee on Human Communication; Bd Postgrad. Med. Studies, London Univ.; Chm., Centennial Conf., Laryngeal Cancer, 1974; Asst Sec., Collegium Oto-Rhino-Laryngologium; Hon. Sec., RSM; Member: Anatomical Soc. of Great Britain; Cttee of Management, Institute of Cancer Research; Internat. Cttee for Cancer of Larynx; Chm., NE Thames Region Postgrad. Cttee. Editorial Board: Acta Otolaryngologica; Practica Oto-Rhino-Laryngologica; Annals of Oto-Rhino-Laryngology; Excerpta Medica (Sect. II); Otolaryngological Digest. Hon. FRCSE 1981; Hon. Fellow: Acad. ENT, America, 1976; Triol. Soc., USA, 1977; Amer. Laryngol Assoc., 1979; Hon. FRACS, 1977; Hon. FCSSA, 1988; Hon. FACS, 1990; Hon. FRSM 1991. Hon. Member: NZ ENT Soc.; Jamaican ENT Soc.; Polish ENT Soc.; Egyptian ENT Soc.; Otolaryngological Soc., Australia; Yugoslavian ENT Soc.; Spanish ENT Soc.; For. Mem., Internat. Broncho-œsophagological Soc.; Corresp. Member: Amer. Head and Neck Soc.; Soc. Française d'Otorhinolaryngologie; Otolaryngological Soc., Denmark; Amer. Acad. of Facial Plastic Reconstr. Surgery; Pacific Coast Oto-Ophthalmological Soc.; Amer. Laryngological Soc.; Yeoman, Soc. of Apothecaries. *Publications:* (ed jtly) Scientific Basis of Otolaryngology, 1976; articles on familial hæmorrhagic telangiectases, meatal oseomata, cancer chemotherapy, head and neck surgery in learned jls; chapters in Text Books on Ent. and Gen. Surgery. *Recreations:* heraldry, radio control models. *Address:* Institute of Laryngology and Otology, Gray's Inn Road, WC1. *T:* 071–837 8855; Springfield, Fisher's Farm, Horley, Surrey. *T:* Horley (0293) 4307.

HARRISON, Douglas Creese, DSc London, PhD Cantab; CChem; Professor of Biochemistry, Queen's University, Belfast, 1935–67, now Professor Emeritus; *b* 29 April, 1901; *s* of Lovell and Lillian E. Harrison, MBE, JP; *m* 1926, Sylva Thurlow, MA, PhD, Philadelphia, USA; one *s*. *Educ:* Highgate Sch.; King's Coll., London; Emmanuel Coll., Cambridge. MRSC. Keddey Fletcher-Warr Research Studentship, 1925–28; Lecturer at Sheffield Univ., 1926–35. Hon. DSc Belfast, 1987. *Publications:* various papers in the Biochemical Journal, Proc. Royal Society, Lancet, etc. *Address:* 4 Broomhill Park Central, Belfast BT9 5JD. *T:* Belfast (0232) 665685.

HARRISON, Edward Peter Graham, (Ted); broadcaster and writer; *b* 14 April 1948; *s* of Rev. Peter Harrison and Joan Harrison; *m* 1968, Helen Grace Waters; one *s* one *d*. *Educ:* Grenville Coll., Bideford, Devon; University of Kent at Canterbury. Graduate trainee, Kent Messenger, 1968–72; Reporter: Morgan-Grampian Magazines, 1972; Southern Television, 1970–73; BBC World Service, Radio 4 You and Yours, 1972–80; BBC Radio 4 Sunday, 1972–; BBC TV Scotland Current Account, 1981–83; Presenter and Reporter, BBC Radio Scotland News and Current Affairs, 1980–85; Reporter: BBC Radio 4 World Tonight, 1981–83; BBC Radio 4 World at One and PM, 1983–87; Presenter: Radio 4 Opinions, 1986–87; Radio 4 Sunday, 1986–88 and Soundings, 1985–88; ITV series The Human Factor, 1986–; Channel 4 series on Lambeth Conf., 1988; BBC Religious Affairs Corresp., 1988–89. Contested (L) gen. elections: Bexley, 1970; Maidstone, Feb. 1974. London exhibition of caricatures, 1977; exhibition of watercolours, Oxford, Canterbury, 1981. *Publications:* Modern Elizabethans, 1977; (jtly) McIndoe's Army, 1978; Marks of the Cross, 1981; Commissioner Catherine, 1983; Much Beloved Daughter, 1984; The Durham Phenomenon, 1985; Living with kidney failure, 1990. *Recreations:* drawing caricatures, painting in watercolour. *Address:* 28 The Quay, Conyer, Sittingbourne, Kent ME9 9HR. *T:* Sittingbourne (0795) 521752.

HARRISON, Sir Ernest (Thomas), Kt 1981; OBE 1972; FCA; Chairman and Chief Executive, Racal Electronics Plc, since 1966; Chairman, Racal Telecom Plc, since 1988; *b* 11 May 1926; *s* of Ernest Horace Harrison and Gertrude Rebecca Gibbons Harrison; *m* 1960, Phyllis Brenda Knight (Janie); three *s* two *d*. *Educ:* Trinity Grammar Sch., Wood Green, London. Qualified as Chartered Accountant, 1950; served Articles with Harker Holloway & Co.; joined Racal Electronics as Secretary and Chief Accountant, when company commenced manufacturing, 1951; Director, 1958, Dep. Man. Dir, 1961. Active in National Savings movement, 1964–76, for which services awarded OBE. Mem., Jockey Club, 1990–. Mem., RSA. Liveryman, Scriveners' Co. CompIERE 1975; CBIM 1976; CompIEE 1978. Hon. FCGI 1990. Hon. DSc: Cranfield, 1981; City, 1982; DUniv: Surrey, 1981; Edinburgh, 1983. Businessman of the Year, 1981; Founding Society's Centenary Award, ICA, 1990. *Recreations:* horse racing (owner and breeder), gardening, wild life, sport, espec. soccer. *Address:* Racal Electronics Plc, Western Road, Bracknell, Berkshire RG12 1RG.

HARRISON, Sir Francis Alexander Lyle, (Sir Frank Harrison), Kt 1974; MBE 1943; QC (NI); DL; President, Lands Tribunal for Northern Ireland, 1964–83; District Electoral Areas Commissioner, 1984; *b* 19 March 1910; *s* of Rev. Alexander Lyle Harrison and Mary Luise (*née* Henderson), Rostrevor, Co. Down; *m* 1940, Norah Patricia (*née* Rea); two *d*. *Educ:* Campbell Coll., Belfast; Trinity Coll., Dublin. BA (Moderator in Legal Sci.), LLB (Hons). Called to Bar of NI, 1937. Served War: commissioned Gen. List, Oct. 1939; ADC to GOC, NI, 1939–40; Major, Dep. Asst Adjt-Gen., HQ, NI, 1941–45 (MBE). Apptd to determine Industrial Assurance disputes in NI, 1946–62; Counsel to Attorney-Gen., NI, 1946–48; KC 1948. Legal Adviser to Min. of Home Affairs, 1949–64; Sen. Crown Prosecutor, Co. Fermanagh, 1948–54; subseq. for Counties Tyrone, Londonderry and Antrim, 1954–64; Chm., Mental Health Review Tribunal, 1948–64; Counsel to the Speakers of House of Commons and Senate of NI, 1953–64; Mem. Statute Law Cttee, NI, 1953–64; Chm., Advisory Cttee under Civil Authorities Special Powers Acts (NI), 1957–62; Bencher, Inn of Court of NI, 1961; Chm., Shaftesbury Sq. Hosp. Management Cttee, 1964–73; Founder Mem., NI Assoc. of Mental Health, 1959. Boundary Comr under Local Govt (Boundaries) Act (NI), 1971 and 1982–84. DL Co. Down, 1973. *Publications:* Report of Working Party on Drug Dependence, 1968; Recommendations as to Local Government Boundaries and Wards in Northern Ireland, 1972, 1984; Recommendations as to District Electoral Areas in Northern Ireland, 1985. *Recreations:* hybridisation of narcissi, country pursuits, social service. *Address:* Ballydorn Hill, Killinchy, Newtownards, Co. Down, Northern Ireland. *T:* Killinchy (0238) 541 250.

HARRISON, Francis Anthony Kitchener; *b* 28 Aug. 1914; *s* of late Fred Harrison, JP, and Mrs M. M. Harrison (*née* Mitchell); *m* 1955, Sheila Noëlle, *d* of late Lt-Col N. D. Stevenson and of Lady Nye; three *s* one *d*. *Educ:* Winchester; New Coll., Oxford. Asst Principal, India Office, Nov. 1937; 1st Sec., UK High Commn, New Delhi, 1949–51; Commonwealth Relations Office, 1951–56; Asst Sec., 1954; Dep. High Comr for the UK at Peshawar, 1956–59; Asst Sec., CRO, 1959–61; British Dep. High Comr, New Zealand, 1961–64; Asst Sec., Cabinet Office, 1965–67; Asst Dir, Civil Service Selection Bd, 1967–79. *Recreations:* golf, gardening. *Address:* Lea Farm, Bramley, near Guildford, Surrey. *T:* Guildford (0483) 893138.

HARRISON, Sir Frank; *see* Harrison, Sir Francis A. L.

HARRISON, Fred Brian, CBE 1982; FCA; *b* 6 March 1927; *s* of Fred Harrison and Annie Harrison; *m* 1950, Margaret Owen; two *s*. *Educ:* Burnley Grammar Sch. FCA 1960. East Midlands Div., National Coal Board: Divnl Internal Auditor, 1953–55; Financial Accountant, No 3 Area, 1955–57, Cost Accountant, 1957–62; Chief Accountant, No 1 Area, 1962–67; Chief Accountant, N Derbyshire Area, NCB, 1967–68; Finance Dir, Coal Products Div., NCB, 1968–71, Dep. Man. Dir, 1971–73; Dep. Chief Exec., NCB (Coal Products) Ltd, 1973–76, Chm., 1978–83. Mem., British Coal (formerly NCB), 1976–85. Chm., British Investment Trust, 1978–85. *Recreations:* music, theatre. *Address:* Hillcrest, King Harry Lane, St Albans, Herts AL3 4AT. *T:* St Albans (0727) 46938.

HARRISON, George Anthony; DL; solicitor; Clerk to the Lieutenancy of Greater Manchester, since 1986; Chairman and Director, Central Station Properties Ltd, 1976–88; Director of various companies; *b* 20 Aug. 1930; *s* of John and Agnes Catherine Harrison; *m* 1957, Jane Parry; two *s* one *d*. *Educ:* Roundhay Sch., Leeds; Trinity Coll., Cambridge (MA, LLB). Asst Solicitor, Wolverhampton, 1955–58; ICI, 1958–59; Dep. Town Clerk, Wallasey and Bolton, 1962–65; Town Clerk and Clerk of the Peace, Bolton, 1965–69; Dir-Gen., Greater Manchester Transport Exec., 1969–76; Chief Exec., Greater Manchester Council, 1976–86. DL Manchester, 1978. *Recreations:* music, sailing. *Address:* 16 Park View, Sharples, Bolton. *T:* Bolton (0204) 56996.

HARRISON, George Bagshawe, MA Cantab; PhD London; Emeritus Professor of English, University of Michigan, 1964 (Professor, 1949–64); *b* 14 July 1894; *s* of late Walter Harrison, Brighton; *m* 1919, Dorothy Agnes (*d* 1986), *o d* of late Rev. Thomas Barker; one *d* (three *s* decd). *Educ:* Brighton Coll.; Queens' Coll., Cambridge (Classical Exhibitioner); 1st Class English Tripos, 1920. Commnd to 5th Bn The Queen's Royal Regt, and served in India and Mesopotamia, 1914–19; Staff Capt. 42nd Indian Infantry Brigade (despatches); War of 1939–45, RASC and Intelligence Corps, 1940–43. Asst Master, Felsted Sch., 1920–22; Senior Lecturer in English, St Paul's Training Coll., Cheltenham, 1922–24; Asst Lecturer in English Literature, King's Coll., University of London, 1924–27; Lecturer, 1927–29; Frederic Ives Carpenter Visiting Prof. of English, University of Chicago, 1929; Reader in English Literature, University of London, 1929–43; Head of English Dept and Prof. of English, Queen's Univ., Kingston, Ont., Canada, 1943–49; lectured at Sorbonne, 1933, in Holland, 1940; Alexander Lecturer, University of Toronto, Canada, 1947. Mem., Internat. Commn on English in the Liturgy. Hon. LittD Villanova, 1960, Holy Cross, 1961; Marquette, 1963; Hon. LLD Assumption, 1962. KSG 1981. Campion Award for long and eminent service in cause of Christian literature, 1970. *Publications:* Shakespeare: the Man and his Stage (with E. A. G. Lamborn), 1923; Shakespeare's Fellows, 1923; John Bunyan: a Study in Personality, 1928; England in Shakespeare's Day; An Elizabethan Journal, 1591–94, 1928; A Second Elizabethan Journal 1595–98, 1931; A Last Elizabethan Journal, 1599–1603, 1933; Shakespeare at Work, 1933; The Life and Death of Robert Devereux, Earl of Essex, 1937; The Day before Yesterday (a Journal of 1936), 1938; Elizabethan Plays and Players, 1940; A Jacobean Journal, 1603–1606, 1941; A Second Jacobean Journal, 1607–1610, 1950; Shakespeare's Tragedies, 1951; Profession of English, 1962; The Fires of Arcadia, 1965; (with John McCabe) Proclaiming the Word : a handbook for church speaking, 1976; One Man in His Time: memoirs of G. B. Harrison 1894–1984, 1985, etc.; Editor: The Bodley Head Quartos, 1922–26; The New Readers' Shakespeare (with F. H. Pritchard); The Pilgrim's Progress and Mr Badman; The Church Book of Bunyan Meeting, 1928; Breton's Melancholike Humours, 1929; The Trial of the Lancaster Witches, 1612, 1929; The Earl of Northumberland's Advice to his son; translated and edited The Journal of De Maisse (with R. A. Jones), 1931; A Companion to Shakespeare Studies (with Harley Granville-Barker), 1934; The Letters of Queen Elizabeth, 1935; The Penguin Shakespeares, 1937–59; Shakespeare—the compleat works, 1968; Contributor to The Road to Damascus, 1949; etc. *Address*: 36A Manson Street, Palmerston North, New Zealand. *T*: 75–895.

HARRISON, (George) Michael (Antony), CBE 1980; education systems consultant; Chief Education Officer, City of Sheffield, 1967–85; Chairman, British Thornton Harrison Ltd, since 1985; *b* 7 April 1925; *s* of George and Kathleen Harrison; *m* 1951, Pauline (*née* Roberts); two *s* one *d*. *Educ*: Manchester Grammar Sch.; Brasenose Coll., Oxford. MA (LitHum); DipEd. Military service, Lieut, Parachute Regt, 1947. Asst Master, Bedford Modern Sch., 1951–53; Admin. Asst, W Riding CC, Education Dept, 1953–55; Asst Educn Officer, Cumberland CC Educn Dept, 1955–64; Dep. Educn Officer, Sheffield, 1965–67. Advr, Educn Programmes, MSC, later Training Agency, 1985–89. Hon. Research Fellow, Leeds Univ., 1985–89. Member various cttees, incl.: Taylor Cttee of Enquiry on Govt in Schools, 1975–77; UK Nat. Commn for Unesco Educn Adv. Cttee, 1977–83; Yorkshire and Humberside Econ. Planning Council, 1978–79; Technician Educn Council, 1979–83; Engineering Council, 1982–87; Board, Nat. Adv. Body on Local Authority Higher Educn, 1981–83. Pres., Soc. of Educn Officers, 1976; Vice-Pres., Standing Conf. on Schools' Science and Technology, 1980– (Chm. 1975–79). Hon. LLD Sheffield, 1988. *Recreations*: sailing, gardening, music. *Address*: Audrey Cottage, 83 Union Road, Sheffield S11 9EH. *T*: Sheffield (0742) 553783.

HARRISON, Maj.-Gen. Ian Stewart, CB 1970; Captain of Deal Castle, since 1980; *b* 25 May 1919; *s* of Leslie George Harrison and Evelyn Simpson Christie; *m* 1942, Winifred Raikes Stavert; one *s* one *d*. *Educ*: St Albans Sch. Commissioned, Royal Marines, 1937; service at sea, in Norway, Middle East, Sicily, BAOR, 1939–45; Staff Coll., Camberley (student), 1948; HQ 3rd Commando Bde, 1949–51 (despatches); Staff of Comdt-Gen., RM, 1951–52; Staff Coll., Camberley (Directing Staff), 1953–55; Commandant, RM Signal Sch., 1956–58; Joint Services Staff Coll. (Student), 1958; CO 40 Commando, RM, 1959–61; Dir, Royal Marines Reserves, 1962; Staff of Comdt-Gen., RM, 1963–64; Joint Warfare Estabt, 1965–67; British Defence Staff, Washington, DC, 1967–68; Chief of Staff to Comdt-Gen., RM, 1968–70, retired. ADC to HM the Queen, 1967–68. Representative Col Comdt, Royal Marines, 1981–82. Dir-Gen. British Food Export Council, 1970–77; Dir, British Consultants Bureau, 1977–87. Chm., Chichester Festivities, 1979–89. *Recreations*: sailing, real tennis, golf. *Address*: Manor Cottage, Runcton, Chichester, W Sussex PO20 6PU. *T*: Chichester (0243) 785480. *Clubs*: Army and Navy, St Stephen's Constitutional; Royal Yacht Squadron, Royal Naval Sailing Association, Royal Marines Sailing (Commodore, 1968–70), Itchenor Sailing; Royal St George's Golf.

HARRISON, Jessel Anidjah; President, Slimma Group Holdings Ltd, retired 1989; *b* 28 May 1923; *s* of Samuel Harrison and Esta (*née* Romain); *m* 1st, 1943, Irene (*née* Olsberg) (marr. diss. 1956); one *s* one *d*; 2nd, 1961, Doreen Leigh. *Educ*: Vernon House Preparatory Sch.; Brondesbury Coll.; Macauley Coll., Cuckfield, Sussex. Chairman: Slimma Ltd, 1964; Slimma (Wales) Ltd, 1971; Emu Wool Industries, later Slimma Gp Hldgs, 1973; Dir, Tootals Clothing Div., 1977–89. Member: European Trade Cttee, 1975–; Clothing Industry Productivity Resources Agency, 1978–85; British Overseas Trade Adv. Council, 1978–85. Vice Pres., Clothing Export Council of Great Britain, 1977 (Chm., 1973); Chm., British Overseas Trade Group for Israel, 1978–83, Vice-Pres., 1987–. Pres., Clothing Institute, 1978. *Recreations*: golf, walking. *Address*: 113 Abbotsbury Road, W14 8EP. *T*: 071–603 7468. *Club*: Royal Automobile.

HARRISON, Surgeon Vice-Adm. Sir John (Albert Bews), KBE 1982; FRCP, FRCR; Medical Director General (Naval), 1980–83; *b* 20 May 1921; *s* of late Albert William Harrison and Lilian Eda Bews, Dover, Kent; *m* 1943, Jane (*née* Harris) (*d* 1988); two *s*. RN 1947–83: served: RM Infirmary, Deal, 1948; HMS Sparrow, Amer. WI stn, 1949; RN Hosp., Plymouth, 1951; HMS Ganges, 1952; Admiralty Med. Bd and St Bartholomew's Hosp., 1953; RN Hosps, Hong Kong, 1955, Chatham, 1958, Haslar, 1959; St Bart's and Middlesex Hosps, 1961; RN Hosps Malta, 1962, Haslar, 1964–75; Adviser in Radiol., 1967–79; Dep. Med. Dir Gen. and Dir Med. Personnel and Logistics, 1975–77; Dean of Naval Medicine and Surgeon Rear-Adm., Inst. of Naval Medicine, 1977–80. Mem., Council for Med. Postgrad. Educn of Eng. and Wales, 1977–79. Pres., Section of Radiology, RSM, 1984–85. Fellow: RSM; MedSocLond (Pres. 1985–86). CStJ 1983. QHP 1976–83. *Publications*: Hyperbaric Osteonecrosis et al, 1975; articles in med. press on sarcoidosis, tomography, middle ear disease, and dysbaric osteonecrosis. *Recreations*: fishing, cricket, countryman. *Address*: Alexandra Cottage, Swanmore, Hampshire SO3 2PB. *Club*: MCC.

HARRISON, John Audley, CB 1976; a Director, Ministry of Defence, 1969–76; *b* 13 May 1917; *s* of John Samuel Harrison and Florence Rose (*née* Samways); *m* 1940, Dorothea Pearl (*née* West); two *s* one *d*. *Educ*: Caterham Sch., Surrey. Prudential Assce Co. Ltd, 1935–39. London Rifle Bde (TA), 1939–40; York and Lancaster Regt (emergency commn), 1940–46. Attached War Office (later MoD), 1946–76, retd, May 1976. *Recreations*: golf, bridge. *Address*: 43 Hovedene, 95 Cromwell Road, Hove, Sussex BN3 3EH. *T*: Brighton (0273) 770491. *Club*: Dyke Golf (Brighton).

HARRISON, John Clive, LVO 1971; HM Diplomatic Service; Deputy High Commissioner, Islamabad, since 1989; *b* 12 July 1937; *s* of Sir Geoffrey Harrison, GCMG, KCVO; *m* 1967, Jennifer Heather Burston; one *s* two *d*. *Educ*: Winchester Coll.; Jesus Coll., Oxford. BA. Entered Foreign Office, 1960; Rangoon, 1961; Vientiane, 1964; FO, 1964; Second, later First, Sec. (Information), Addis Ababa, 1967; Ankara, 1971; seconded to Cabinet Office, 1973; First Sec., FCO, 1976; First Sec., Head of Chancery and Consul, Luxembourg, 1978; Counsellor and Head of Chancery, Lagos, 1981–84; Counsellor, attached to Protocol Dept, FCO, 1984; Hd of Consular Dept, FCO, 1985–89. *Recreations*: gardening, tennis, golf, family holidays. *Address*: c/o Foreign and Commonwealth Office, King Charles Street, SW1A 2AH. *Club*: Mannings Heath Golf (Sussex).

HARRISON, Prof. John Fletcher Clews, PhD; Emeritus Professor of History, University of Sussex, since 1985 (Professor of History, 1970–82; Hon. Professor of History, 1982–85); Hon. Professor of History, Warwick University, since 1987; *b* 28 Feb. 1921; *s* of William Harrison and Mary (*née* Fletcher); *m* 1945, Margaret Ruth Marsh; one *s* one *d*. *Educ*: City

Boys' Sch., Leicester; Selwyn Coll., Cambridge (Schol. and Prizeman; Goldsmiths' Open Exhibnr in History, BA 1st Cl. Hons 1942, MA 1946); PhD Leeds. Served Army, 1941–45 (overseas 1942–45): commnd, Royal Leics Regt and seconded to KAR, 1942; Captain and Adjt, 17th Bn, KAR, 1943–44; Staff Captain, GSOIII, E Africa Comd, 1944–45. Lectr, Dept of Adult Educn and Extra-Mural Studies, Univ. of Leeds, 1947–58; Dep. Dir, Extra-Mural Studies and Dep. Head of Dept, Univ. of Leeds, 1958–61; Prof. of History, Univ. of Wisconsin, USA, 1961–70. Research and teaching (Fulbright Award), Univ. of Wisconsin, 1957–58; Faculty Res. Fellow, SSRC, USA, 1963–64; Vis. Professorial Res. Fellow, ANU, 1968–69 and 1977; Res. Fellow, Harvard Univ., 1972–73; Social Sci. Res. Fellow, Nuffield Foundn, 1975; Vice-Chancellor's Cttee Visitor, NZ, 1977; Herbert F. Johnson Res. Prof., Univ. of Wisconsin, 1977–78. Vice-Pres., Soc. for Study of Labour History, 1984– (Sec., 1960–61; Chm., 1974–81); Mem., Adv. and Editorial Bds, Victorian Studies, 1963–. Hon. Mem., Phi Beta Kappa, Wisconsin, 1978. *Publications*: A History of the Working Men's College 1854–1954, 1954; Social Reform in Victorian Leeds: The Work of James Hole 1820–1895, 1954; Learning and Living 1790–1960: A Study in the History of the English Adult Education Movement, 1961, Toronto 1961; ed, Society and Politics in England 1780–1960, NY 1965; ed, Utopianism and Education: Robert Owen and the Owenites, NY 1968; Quest for the New Moral World: Robert Owen and the Owenites in Britain and America, 1969, NY 1969 (Walter D. Love Meml Prize, USA, 1969); The Early Victorians 1832–1851, 1971, NY 1971; The Birth and Growth of Industrial England 1714–1867, 1973; ed, Eminently Victorian, BBC 1974; (with Dorothy Thompson) Bibliography of the Chartist Movement 1837–1976, 1978; The Second Coming: Popular Millenarianism 1780–1850, 1979, NJ 1979; The Common People, 1984; Late Victorian Britain 1875–1901, 1990; articles and reviews in Victorian Studies, TLS and usual academic history jls. *Recreations*: walking, gardening, book collecting. *Address*: 13 Woodlands, Barrowfield Drive, Hove, Sussex BN3 6TJ. *T*: Brighton (0273) 554145.

HARRISON, John H.; see Heslop-Harrison.

HARRISON, Hon. Sir (John) Richard, Kt 1980; ED; company director; sheep farmer, since 1946; *b* 23 May 1921; *s* of William Harrison and Jean (*née* Bell); *m* 1948, Margaret Kelly; three *s* one *d*. *Educ*: Wanganui Collegiate Sch.; Canterbury University Coll. (BA). CO, Hawke's Bay Regt, 1956–59. MP (Nat) for Hawke's Bay, 1963–84; Govt Whip, 1970–71; Opposition Whip, 1974–75; Chm. of Cttees, 1972, 1976–77; Speaker, House of Representatives, 1978–84. Pres., Commonwealth Parly Assoc., 1978–79. Pres., Nat. Soc. on Alcoholism and Drug Dependence, 1986–89. *Recreations*: gardening, Rotary. *Address*: Springfield, Takapau, New Zealand. *Club*: Hastings.

HARRISON, Kathleen, (Mrs J. H. Back); leading character actress, stage and films; *b* Blackburn, Lancs, 23 Feb. 1892; *d* of Arthur Harrison, MICE, Civil Engineer, and Alice Maud Harrison (*née* Parker); *m* 1916, John Henry Back, Western Telegraph Co. (*d* 1960); one *s* one *d* (and one *s* decd). *Educ*: St Saviour's and St Olave's Grammar Sch.; Clapham High Sch. RADA, 1915–16 (Du Maurier Bronze Medal). *Notable West End plays include*: The Cage, Savoy, 1927; Badger's Green, Prince of Wales Theatre, 1930; Night Must Fall, Duchess, 1935; The Corn is Green, Duchess, 1938; Flare Path, Apollo, 1942; The Winslow Boy, Lyric, 1946; The Silver Box (revival), Lyric, Hammersmith, 1951; Waters of the Moon, Theatre Royal, Haymarket, 1951; All for Mary, Duke of York's, 1954; Nude with Violin, Globe, 1956; toured N Africa and Italy with Emlyn William's ENSA Co., 1944; Chichester Festival Theatre Co., 1962; *Films include*: Our Boys, 1915; The Man from Toronto, 1932; The Ghoul, 1933; Night Must Fall, 1937; Bank Holiday, 1938; A Girl Must Live, 1939; In Which We Serve, 1942; Holiday Camp, 1947; The Huggett series, from 1948; Oliver Twist, 1948; The Winslow Boy, 1948; Scrooge, 1951; The Pickwick Papers, 1952; Turn the Key Softly, 1953; All for Mary, 1956; Alive and Kicking, 1958. *TV includes*: title role in Mrs Thursday series, 1966; Martin Chuzzlewit and Our Mutual Friend serials. *Address*: c/o T. Plunket Greene, 4 Ovington Gardens, SW3. *T*: 071–584 0688.

HARRISON, Kenneth Cecil, OBE 1980 (MBE mil. 1946); FLA; City Librarian, Westminster, 1961–80, retired; Consultant Librarian, Ranfurly Library Service, 1983–90; *b* 29 April 1915; *s* of Thomas and Annie Harrison; *m* 1941, Doris Taylor; two *s*. *Educ*: Grammar Sch., Hyde. Asst, Hyde Public Library, 1931–37; Branch Librarian, Coulsdon and Purley Public Libraries, 1937–39; Borough Librarian: Hyde, 1939–47; Hove (also Curator), 1947–50; Eastbourne, 1950–58; Hendon, 1958–61. HM Forces, 1940–46; Commnd RMC Sandhurst, 1942; served with E Yorks Regt in Middle East, Sicily and NW Europe (wounded, 1944; Major 1944–46). President: Library Assoc., 1973; Commonwealth Library Assoc., 1972–75, Exec. Sec., 1980–83; Vice-President: Internat. Assoc. Metropolitan Libraries; Westminster Arts Council (Hon. Sec. 1965–80). Member: IFLA Public Libraries Cttee, 1969–81; Central Music Library Council, 1961–80; Library Assoc. Council, 1953–79; MCC Arts and Library Cttee, 1973–89; Chm. Jt Organising Cttee for Nat. Library Week, 1964–69. British Council: Cultural Exchange Scholar to Romania, 1971; Mem., Library Adv. Panel, 1974–80; Consultant to Sri Lanka, 1974, to India, 1981. UNESCO Consultant to the Seychelles and Mauritius, 1977–78; Commonwealth Relations Trust Consultant to Ghana, Sierra Leone and The Gambia, 1979; Library Consultant, Bermuda, 1983. Commonwealth Foundn Scholar, E and Central Africa, 1975. C. C. Williamson Meml Lectr, Nashville, Tenn, 1969. Governor, Westminster College, 1962–80. Editor, The Library World, 1961–71. Knight, First Class, Order of the Lion (Finland), 1976. *Publications*: First Steps in Librarianship, 1950, 5th edn 1980; Libraries in Scandinavia, 1961, 2nd edn 1969; The Library and the Community, 1963, 3rd edn 1977; Public Libraries Today, 1963; Facts at your Fingertips, 1964, 2nd edn 1966; British Public Library Buildings (with S. G. Berriman), 1966; Libraries in Britain, 1968; Public Relations for Librarians, 1973, 2nd edn 1982; (ed) Prospects for British Librarianship, 1976; Public Library Policy, 1981; Public Library Buildings 1975–83, 1987; International Librarianship, 1989; Library Buildings 1984–89, 1990; contribs to many British and foreign jls and encyclopædias. *Recreations*: reading, writing, travel, wine, cricket, crosswords, zoo visiting. *Address*: 5 Tavistock, Devonshire Place, Eastbourne, E Sussex BN21 4AG. *T*: Eastbourne (0323) 26747. *Clubs*: Commonwealth Trust, MCC; Surrey CC, Sussex CC.

HARRISON, Lyndon Henry Arthur; Member (Lab) Cheshire West, European Parliament, since 1989; *b* 28 Sept. 1947; *s* of Charles William Harrison and late Edith (*née* Johnson); *m* 1980, Hilary Anne Plank; one *s* one *d*. *Educ*: Oxford Sch.; Univ. of Warwick (BA Hons 1970); Univ. of Sussex (MA 1971); Univ. of Keele (MA 1978). Part time Lectr, N Staffs Polytechnic, 1973–75; Research Officer, Students' Union, UMIST, 1975–78; Union Manager, NE Wales Inst. of Higher Educn, Wrexham, 1978–89. Cheshire County Councillor, 1981–90 (Chairman: Libraries and Countryside Cttee, 1982, 1984–89; Further Educn, 1984–89; Tourism, 1985–89). Dep. Chm., NW Tourist Bd, 1987–89. Vice Chm., ACC, 1990. *Recreations*: chess, the arts, sport. *Address*: 2 Stanley Street, Chester CH1 2LR. *T*: Chester (0244) 320623.

HARRISON, Michael; see Harrison, G. M. A.

HARRISON, Dr Michael; JP; Regional Director of Public Health and Regional Medical Officer, West Midlands Regional Health Authority, since 1988; *b* 1 March 1939; *s* of

Frank Harrison and Ruby Wilhelmina (née Proctor); *m* 1962, Ann Haiser; two *d. Educ:* Leamington Coll.; Univ. of London (St Mary's Hosp.) (MB BS, BA). LRCP, MRCS, DPH, FFPHM, LHSM, FRSH. Hosp. med. appts, 1964–66; health MO appts, 1966–70; Birmingham RHB, 1971–74; specialist in community medicine, W Midlands RHA, 1974–76; Area MO, Sandwell AHA, 1976–83; Dist MO, 1983–88, Dist Gen. Manager, 1985–88, Sandwell HA; Sen. Clinical Lectr, Univ. of Birmingham, 1988. Cons. Advr, WHO, 1989. FBIM. SBStJ. JP Birmingham, 1980. *Recreations:* sailing, photography, industrial archaeology. *Address:* 6 Moor Green Lane, Moseley, Birmingham B13 8ND. *T:* 021–449 1739. *Club:* Royal Society of Medicine.

HARRISON, Michael Guy Vicat, QC 1983; a Recorder, since 1989; *b* 28 Sept. 1939; *s* of Hugh Francis Guy Harrison and Elizabeth Alban Harrison (née Jones); *m* 1966, Judith (née Gist); one *s* one *d. Educ:* Charterhouse; Trinity Hall, Cambridge (MA). Called to the Bar, Gray's Inn, 1965. *Recreations:* tennis, sailing. *Address:* 2 Harcourt Buildings, Temple, EC4. *T:* 071–353 8415.

HARRISON, Michael Jackson; Director, Wolverhampton Polytechnic (formerly The Polytechnic, Wolverhampton), since 1985; *b* 18 Dec. 1941; *s* of Jackson Harrison and Norah (née Lees); *m* 1974, Marie Ghislaine Félix. *Educ:* Guildford Tech. Coll.; Univ. of Leicester (BA, MA). Lecturer in Sociology: Enfield Coll. of Technol., 1966–67; Univ. of Leeds, 1967–68; Sen. Lectr, Enfield Coll. of Technol., 1968–72; Principal Lectr, Sheffield City Polytechnic, 1972–76; Head of Dept, Hull Coll. of Higher Educn, 1976–81; Asst Dir, 1982–84, Dep. Dir, 1985, The Polytechnic, Wolverhampton. Vis. Lectr, Univ. of Oregon, 1971. FBIM 1983. *Publications:* (jtly) A Sociology of Industrialisation, 1978; contribs to learned jls. *Recreations:* weight training, cinema, travelling, music. *Address:* 34 Mount Road, Penn, Wolverhampton WV4 5SW. *T:* Wolverhampton (0902) 338807.

HARRISON, Sir Michael James Harwood, 2nd Bt *cr* 1961, of Bugbrooke; Director of private companies; Chairman, L. P. H. Pitman Ltd (Lloyd's Brokers), since 1987; *b* 28 March 1936; *s* of Sir (James) Harwood Harrison, 1st Bt, TD, MP (C) Eye, Suffolk 1951–79, and of Peggy Alberta Mary, *d* of late Lt-Col V. D. Stenhouse, TD; *S* father, 1980; *m* 1967, Rosamund Louise, *d* of Edward Clive; two *s* two *d. Educ:* Rugby. Served with 17th/21st Lancers, 1955–56. Member of Lloyd's. Mem. Council, Sail Training Assoc.; Vice-Pres., Assoc. of Combined Youth Clubs. Patron and Lord of the Manor, Bugbrooke, Northampton, 1980–. Master, Mercers' Co., 1986–87; Freeman of the City of London. *Recreations:* sailing, ski-ing, riding (horse and bicycle), Daily Telegraph crossword. *Heir:* *s* Edwin Michael Harwood Harrison, *b* 29 May 1981. *Address:* 35 Paulton's Square, SW3. *T:* 071–352 1760. *Clubs:* Boodle's, MCC, Ski Club of GB; Royal Harwich Yacht.

HARRISON, Mrs Molly, MBE 1967; Curator, Geffrye Museum, 1941–69; *b* Stevenage, 1909; *d* of late Ethel and late Ernest Charles Hodgett; *m* 1940, Gordon Frederick Harrison; three *d. Educ:* Friends Sch., Saffron Walden; Convent in Belgium; Sorbonne. Teaching in various Schs, 1934–39; Asst to Curator, Geffrye Museum, 1939–41. FMA 1952; Member: Council Museums Assoc., 1953–56; Council of Industrial Design, 1958–61; Cttee of Management, Society of Authors, 1967. Lectr on varied educational topics. FRSA 1968. Editor, Local Search Series, 1969–77. *Publications:* Museum Adventure, 1950; Picture Source Books for Social History, 1951, 1953, 1955, 1957, 1958, 1960 and 1966; Furniture 1953; Learning out of School, 1954; Food, 1954; Homes, 1960; Children in History, 1958, 1959, 1960, 1961; Your Book of Furniture, 1960; Shops and Shopping, 1963; How They Lived, 1963; Changing Museums, 1967; Hairstyles and Hairdressing, 1968; The English Home, 1969; People and Furniture, 1971; The Kitchen in History, 1972; Homes, 1973; Museums and Galleries, 1973; On Location: Museums, 1974; People and Shopping, 1975; Home Inventions, 1975; Homes in Britain, 1975; Markets and Shops, 1979; Growing Up in Victorian Times, 1980; Homes in History, 1983; The Story of Travelling (4 vols), 1983, 1984; numerous articles and reviews. *Recreations:* writing, gardening. *Address:* New Place, High Street, Whitchurch-on-Thames, Oxon RG8 7ET. *T:* Pangbourne (0734) 843736.

HARRISON, Patrick Kennard, CBE 1982; Director, Building Museum Project, since 1990 (Project Secretary, 1988–89); *b* 8 July 1928; *e s* of late Richard Harrison and Sheila Griffin; *m* 1955, Mary Wilson, *y d* of late Captain G. C. C. Damant, CBE, RN; one *d. Educ:* Lord Williams's Sch., Thame; Downing Coll., Cambridge (Exhbnr). Asst Principal, Dept of Health for Scotland, 1953; Private Sec. to Deptl Sec. and to Parly Secs, Scottish Office, 1958–60; Principal, Scottish Develt Dept and Regional Develt Div., Scottish Office, 1960–68; Sec., RIBA, 1968–87. Hon. Mem., Amer. Inst. of Architects, 1978. Hon. FRIAS, 1987; Hon. FRIBA, 1988. *Publication:* (ed) Civilising the City: quality or chaos in historic towns, 1991. *Address:* 63 Princess Road, NW1 8JS. *T:* 071–722 8508; Upper Stewarton, Eddleston, Peebles. *Clubs:* Reform; New (Edinburgh).

HARRISON, Hon. Sir Richard; *see* Harrison, Hon. Sir J. R.

HARRISON, Prof. Sir Richard (John), Kt 1984; MD, DSc; FRS 1973; Professor of Anatomy, Cambridge University, 1968–82, now Emeritus; Fellow of Downing College, Cambridge, 1968–82, Hon. Fellow, 1982; *b* 8 Oct. 1920; *er s* of late Geoffrey Arthur Harrison, MD, and Theodora Beatrice Mary West; *m* 1st, 1943, Joanna Gillies (marr. diss. 1967); two *s* one *d*; 2nd, 1967, Barbara Fuller (*d* 1988); 3rd, 1990, Gianetta Drake, *d* of late Capt. C. K. Lloyd, CB, RN retd and Phyllis Lloyd. *Educ:* Oundle; Gonville and Caius Coll., Cambridge (Scholar); St Bartholomew's Hosp. Medical Coll. LRCP, MRCS, 1944. House Surgeon, St Bartholomew's Hosp., 1944. MB, BChir, 1944; MA 1946; MD Cantab 1954. Demonstrator in Anatomy, St Bartholomew's Hosp. Medical Coll., 1944; Lectr in Anatomy, Glasgow Univ., 1946, DSc Glasgow 1948; Sen. Lectr, 1947, and Reader in Anatomy, 1950, Charing Cross Hosp. Medical Sch. (Symington Prize for research in Anatomy); Reader in charge of Anatomy Dept, London Hosp. Medical Coll., 1951–54; Prof. of Anatomy, University of London, at London Hosp. Medical Coll., 1954–68; Fullerian Prof. of Physiology, Royal Institution, 1961–67. Wooldridge Lectr, BVA, 1983. Chairman: Farm Animal Welfare Adv. Cttee, MAFF, 1974–79; Farm Animal Welfare Council, 1979–88. President: European Assoc. for Aquatic Mammals, 1974–76; Anat. Soc. of GB and Ireland, 1978–79. XIIth Internat. Congress of Anatomists, London, 1985; Internat. Fedn of Assocs of Anatomists, 1985–87. A Trustee, British Museum (Natural History), 1978–88 (Chm. Trustees, 1984–88); Member Council: Royal Soc., 1981–82; Zool. Soc., 1974–78, 1980–83; Nat. Trust, 1984–85; Internat. Monachus Cttee, Ministère de l'Environnement, Paris, 1987–90. Hon. Member: American Assoc. of Anatomists; Società Italiana Anatomia. *Publications:* Man the Peculiar Animal, 1958; (with J. E. King) Marine Mammals, 1965, 2nd edn 1979; Reproduction and Man, 1967; (with W. Montagna) Man, 2nd edn 1972; Functional Anatomy of Marine Mammals, vol. I, 1972, vol. II, 1974, vol. III, 1977; (with S. H. Ridgway) Handbook of Marine Mammals, vols I and II, 1981, vol. III, 1985, vol. IV, 1989; (with M. M. Bryden): Research on Dolphins, 1986; Whales, Dolphins and Porpoises, 1988; numerous papers on embryology, comparative and human anatomy. *Recreations:* marine biology, painting. *Address:* 7 Aylesford Way, Stapleford, Cambridge CB2 5DP. *T:* Cambridge (0223) 843287. *Club:* Garrick.

HARRISON, Prof. Richard Martin; Professor of Archaeology of the Roman Empire and Fellow, All Souls College, University of Oxford, since 1985; *b* 16 May 1935; *s* of George Lawrance Harrison and Doris Waring (née Ward); *m* 1959, Elizabeth Anne Harkness Browne; one *s* three *d. Educ:* Sherborne Sch.; Lincoln Coll., Oxford (BA Greats 1958, MA 1961). Scholar 1959, and Fellow 1960, Brit. Inst. of Archaeol., Ankara; Rivoira Scholar, Brit. Sch. at Rome, 1960; Controller of Antiquities, Provincial Govt of Cyrenaica, 1960–61; Lectr in Class. Archaeol., Bryn Mawr Coll., 1961–62; Glanville Res. Student, Lincoln Coll., Oxford, 1962–64; Newcastle upon Tyne University: Lectr in Roman and Romano-British History and Archaeol., 1964–68; Prof. of Roman Hist. and Archaeol., 1968–72; Prof. of Archaeology, 1972–85. Vis. Fellow, Dumbarton Oaks, 1969. Surveys and excavations: Istanbul, 1964–75, Lycia, 1959–63, 1976–85, Phrygia, 1987–. Society of Antiquaries: Fellow, 1965; Vice-Pres., 1984–88; Frend Medal, 1987. Jerome Lectures (Ann Arbor and Rome), 1990. Corresp. Mem., German Archaeol. Inst., 1973. *Publications:* Excavations at Saraçhane in Istanbul, 1986; A Temple for Byzantium, 1989; articles on Roman and Byzantine archaeol. in Anatolian Studies, Dumbarton Oaks Papers, Jl of Roman Studies. *Recreation:* hill-walking in Northumberland and Turkey. *Address:* Institute of Archaeology, 36 Beaumont Street, Oxford OX1 2PG; All Souls College, Oxford OX1 4AL.

HARRISON, Sir (Robert) Colin, 4th Bt, *cr* 1922; *b* 25 May 1938; *s* of Sir John Fowler Harrison, 2nd Bt, and Kathleen, *yr d* of late Robert Livingston, The Gables, Eaglescliffe, Co. Durham; *S* brother, 1955; *m* 1963, Maureen, *er d* of E. Leonard Chiverton, Garth Corner, Kirkbymoorside, York; one *s* two *d. Educ:* St Peter's Coll., Radley; St John's Coll., Cambridge. Commissioned with Fifth Royal Northumberland Fusiliers (National Service), 1957–59. Chm., Young Master Printers Nat. Cttee, 1972–73. *Heir:* *s* John Wyndham Fowler Harrison, *b* 14 Dec. 1972. *Address:* Stearsby Hall, Stearsby, York YO6 4SA. *T:* Brandsby (03475) 226.

HARRISON, Robert Michael; QC 1987; a Recorder, since 1985; *b* 3 Nov. 1945; *s* of Robert William and Bertha Harrison; *m* 1974, Jennifer Armstrong; one *s. Educ:* Heckmondwike Grammar School; Hull Univ. (LLB). Called to the Bar, Gray's Inn, 1969. *Recreations:* history, music, walking, swimming. *Address:* 22 Park Drive, Mirfield, West Yorks. *T:* Mirfield (0924) 492863.

HARRISON, Roger; *see* Harrison, D. R. W.

HARRISON, Ted; *see* Harrison, E. P. G.

HARRISON, Terence, DL; FEng 1988; FIMechE; FIMarE; Director, Rolls-Royce PLC, since 1989; Executive Chairman, Northern Engineering Industries, since 1986; *b* 7 April 1933; *s* of late Roland Harrison and of Doris (née Wardle); *m* 1956, June (née Forster); two *s. Educ:* A. J. Dawson Grammar Sch., Co. Durham; West Hartlepool and Sunderland Tech. Colls. BSc(Eng) Durham. CEng 1964; FIMechE 1984; FIMarE 1973. Marine engrg apprenticeship, Richardson's Westgarth, Hartlepool, 1949–53; commnd REME, service in Nigeria, 1955–57; Clarke Chapman, Gateshead (Marine Division): Res. Engr, 1957; Chief Mechanical Engr, 1967; Man. Dir, 1969; Man. Dir, Clarke Chapman Ltd, Gateshead, 1976; Northern Engineering Industries plc: Dir, 1977; Man. Dir, UK Ops, 1980–83; Chief Exec., 1983–86. Director: Barclays Bank (Regl Bd), 1986; Northumbria Water Authority, 1988. Member: ACOST, 1987; Engrg Council, 1990–. Pres., BEAMA, 1989–90. Pres., NEC Inst., 1988. DL Tyne and Wear, 1989. *Publications:* technical papers to mechanical, marine and mining societies. *Recreations:* golf, fell walking. *Address:* South Lodge, Hepscott, Morpeth, Northumberland NE61 6LH. *T:* Morpeth (0670) 519228; (office) Northern Engineering Industries plc, NEI House, Regent Centre, Newcastle upon Tyne NE3 3SB. *T:* 091–284 3191.

HARRISON, Theophilus George, OBE 1971; JP; Member, Greater Manchester Council, 1973–77 (Chairman, 1973–1974 and 1974–1975, Deputy Chairman, 1975–76); General Secretary, National Association of Powerloom Overlookers, 1947–76, now Life Member; Member Executive, General Union of Associations of Loom Overlookers, 1947–76, now Life Member (President, 1964–66); *b* 30 Jan. 1907; *s* of Alfred and Emma Harrison; *m* 1935, Clarissa Plevin; one *s* one *d*. Swinton and Pendlebury Borough Council: Mem., 1941–56; Alderman, 1956–74; Mayor, 1954–55; Chairman: Housing Cttee; Highways and Lighting Cttee; Mem., Div. Planning Cttee; Lancs CC: Mem. Educn Cttee, 1946–74 (Vice-Chm. 1951–53, Chm. 1953–74); Chm., Road Safety Cttee; Vice-Chairman: Public Health and Housing Cttee; Greater Manchester Transport Cons. Cttee; Pres., Lancs Non-County Boroughs Assoc., 1960–62; Chairman: Swinton and Pendlebury Youth Employment Cttee; Youth Adv. Cttee and Youth Centres; Mem., Div. Exec., Educn Cttee; Member: Gen. Council, Lancs and Merseyside Ind. Develt Corp.; N Counties Textile Trades Fedn Central Board; Life Member: Salford Trades Council (formerly Mem., Swinton and Pendlebury Trades Council); Swinton Labour Club. Member: Manchester Reg. Hosp. Bd, 1961–74; Mental Health Review Tribunals, 1961–70; W Manchester HMC, 1957–74 (Chm. 1963–74); Wrightington HMC, 1957–74; Salford Community Health Council, 1973–83 (former Vice-Chm. and Chm., Develt Cttee); Assoc. of Community Health Councils, 1973–83 (former Vice-Chm., NW Region). Hon. Vice-Pres., Greater Manchester Council for Voluntary Service. Past Chm. or Mem. many other Co. or local organizations and cttees. Former Pres., SE Lancs and Cheshire Accident Prevention Fedn; Dir, RoSPA; Freeman of Swinton and Pendlebury, 1973 (now Salford BC). JP 1949. *Recreations:* reading, Rugby League football (spectator); much of his political and public activities. *Address:* 271 Rivington Crescent, Bolton Road, Pendlebury, Swinton, Manchester M27 2TQ. *T:* 061–794 1112.

HARRISON, Tony, FRSL; poet; *b* 30 April 1937; *s* of Harry Ashton Harrison and Florrie (née Wilkinson-Horner); *m* 1st, 1960, Rosemarie Crossfield (née Dietzsch); one *s* one *d*; 2nd, 1984, Teresa Stratas. *Educ:* Cross Flatts County Primary Sch.; Leeds Grammar Sch.; Univ. of Leeds (BA, Dip.Linguistics). Lecturer in English: Ahmadu Bello Univ., Zaria, N Nigeria, 1962–66; Charles Univ., Prague, 1966–67; Northern Arts Fellow in Poetry, Univs of Newcastle and Durham, 1967–68 and 1976–77; UNESCO Fellow in Poetry, Cuba, Brazil, Senegal, Gambia, 1969; Gregynog Arts Fellow, Univ. of Wales, 1973–74; Resident Dramatist, National Th., 1977–79; UK/US Bi-Centennial Fellow, New York, 1979–80. Pres., Classical Assoc., 1987–88. FRSL 1984. *Publications:* Earthworks, 1964; Aikin Mata, 1966; Newcastle is Peru, 1969; The Loiners (Geoffrey Faber Meml Prize), 1970; The Misanthrope, 1973; Phaedra Britannica, 1975; Palladas: poems, 1975; The Passion, 1977; Bow Down, 1977; From The School of Eloquence and other poems, 1978; The Bartered Bride, 1978; Continuous, 1981; A Kumquat for John Keats, 1981; US Martial, 1981; The Oresteia, 1981; Selected Poems, 1984, expanded edn 1987; The Mysteries, 1985; Dramatic Verse 1973–85, 1985; v., 1985; The Fire-Gap, 1985; Theatre Works 1973–85, 1986; The Trackers of Oxyrhynchus, 1990; v. and other poems, 1990. *Address:* c/o Peters, Fraser & Dunlop, 5th Floor, The Chambers, Chelsea Harbour, Lots Road, SW10 0XF.

HARRISON, Rt. Hon. Walter, PC 1977; JP; public affairs consultant, since 1987; *b* 2 Jan. 1921; *s* of Henry and Ada Harrison; *m* 1948, Enid Mary (née Coleman); one *s* one *d*. *Educ:* Dewsbury Technical and Art Coll. Served RAF, 1940–45. Electrical Inspector and Electrical Foreman, Electricity Supply Industry, 1937–64; Welfare Personnel Officer,

Civil and Engrg Industry, 1945–48. MP (Lab) Wakefield, 1964–87. Asst Govt Whip, 1966–68; a Lord Comr of the Treasury, 1968–70; Dep. Chief Opposition Whip, 1970–74 and 1979–83; Treasurer of HM Household and Dep. Chief Govt Whip, 1974–79. West Riding CC, 1958–64; Alderman, Castleford Borough Council, 1959–66 (Councillor, 1952–59); JP West Riding Yorks, 1962. *Address:* 1 Milnthorpe Drive, Sandal, Wakefield WF2 7HU. *T:* Wakefield (0924) 255550.

HARRISON-CHURCH, Prof. Ronald James; Professor of Geography, University of London, at London School of Economics, 1964–77; *b* 26 July 1915; *s* of late James Walter Church and late Jessie May Church; *m* 1944, Dorothy Violet, *d* of late Robert Colchester Harrison and late Rose Harrison; one *s* one *d. Educ:* Westminster City Sch.; Universities of London and Paris. BSc (Econ) 1936, PhD 1943, London. LSE: Asst Lectr, 1944–47; Lectr, 1947–58; Reader, 1958–64. Consultant to UN Economic Commn for Africa on large scale irrigation schemes, 1962. Geographical Dir, Trans-African Hovercraft Expedition, 1969. Visiting Professor: University of Wisconsin, 1956; Indiana Univ., 1965; Tel Aviv and Haifa Univs, 1972–73. Has lectured in many other univs in Brazil, US, Canada, West Africa, Belgium, France, Germany, Poland and Sweden. Member: French Embassy Scholarships Cttee, 1946–68; British Cttee, Coll. of Europe, 1951–72; Cttee for Staff Fulbright Awards, US-UK Educnl Commn, 1958–61 and 1972–75; Cttee, British Fulbright Schols Assoc., 1981–83; Africa Field Cttee, Oxfam, 1974–80. Chm., Firbank Housing Soc., 1977–83. Vice-Pres., Royal Afr. Soc. 1977– (Mem. Council, 1973–; Mem., Speakers and Publics Cttee, 1972–85). Hon. Mem., Société Géographique de Liège, 1977. Back Award, RGS, 1957; Regl Conf. IGU Award, 1978. *Publications:* Modern Colonization, 1951; West Africa, 1957, 8th edn, 1980; Environment and Policies in West Africa, 1963, 2nd edn 1976; Looking at France, 1970, rev. repr. 1976, French edn 1969, US edn 1970, Spanish edn 1973; (jtly) Africa and the Islands, 1964, 4th edn, 1979; (jtly) An Advanced Geography of Northern and Western Europe, 1967, 3rd edn 1980; contribs to Geograph. Jl, W Africa, etc. *Recreations:* lecturing on cruises, private travel. *Address:* 40 Handside Lane, Welwyn Garden City, Herts AL8 6SJ. *T:* Welwyn Garden (0707) 323293.

HARRISON-HALL, Michael Kilgour; DL; **His Honour Judge Harrison-Hall;** a Circuit Judge, since 1972; *b* 20 Dec. 1925; *s* of late Arthur Harrison-Hall, Oxford; *m* 1951, Jessie Margaret, *d* of late Rev. Arthur William Brown, Collingbourne Ducis, Wilts; two *s* two *d. Educ:* Rugby; Trinity College, Oxford. Called to Bar, Inner Temple, 1949. Dep. Chm., Warwickshire QS, 1968–71; a Recorder of the Crown Court, 1972. DL Warwicks, 1985. *Address:* Ivy House, Church Street, Barford, Warwick CV35 8EN. *T:* Barford (0926) 624272. *Clubs:* United Oxford & Cambridge University; Leander.

HARRISS, Gerald Leslie, DPhil; FBA 1986; Fellow and Tutor, Magdalen College, Oxford, since 1967; Reader in Modern History, Oxford University, since 1990; *b* 22 May 1925; *s* of Walter and Mabel Harriss; *m* 1959, Margaret Anne Sidaway; two *s* three *d. Educ:* Chigwell Sch.; Magdalen Coll., Oxford (BA 1st Cl. History, MA, DPhil). Service in RNVR, 1944–46. Research Fellow, Durham Univ., 1953–55; Asst Lectr, Manchester Univ., 1955–56; Lectr 1956, Sen. Lectr 1965, Reader 1965–67, Durham Univ. *Publications:* King, Parliament and Public Finance in Medieval England, 1975; (ed) Henry V: the practice of kingship, 1985; Cardinal Beaufort, 1988; numerous articles on late medieval English history. *Address:* Dean Court House, 89 Eynsham Road, Botley, Oxford OX2 9BY.

HARROD, Dominick Roy; Economics Editor, BBC Radio, since 1979; *b* 21 Aug. 1940; *s* of Sir Roy Forbes Harrod, FBA and Wilhelmine Harrod (*née* Cresswell); *m* 1974, Christina Hobhouse; one *s. Educ:* Westminster School; Christ Church, Oxford (MA Modern Greats). Journalist and broadcaster; Sunday Telegraph, 1962–66; Daily Telegraph: Washington corresp., 1966–69; Economics corresp., 1969–71; BBC Economics corresp., 1971–78; Dir of Information, Dunlop Ltd, 1979. *Publications:* The Politics of Economics, 1978; Making Sense of the Economy, 1983. *Recreations:* reading, sailing. *Address:* 4 Duke's Avenue, W4 2AE. *Clubs:* Garrick, Beefsteak.

HARROD, Maj.-Gen. Lionel Alexander Digby, OBE 1969; Inspector of Recruiting (Army), 1979–90; Secretary, League of Remembrance, since 1990; *b* 7 Sept. 1924; *s* of Frank Henry Harrod, CBE, and Charlotte Beatrice Emmeline (*née* David); *m* 1952, Anne Priscilla Stormont Gibbs; one *s* two *d. Educ:* Bromsgrove Sch. Grenadier Guards, 1944–63; Bde Major, 19 Bde, 1956–58; WO staff, 1959–60; CO 1 Welch, 1966–69; Brit. Def. Staff, Washington, 1969–70; Military Attaché, Baghdad, 1971; Staff HQ UKLF, 1972–73; Chief, Brit. Mission to Gp of Soviet Forces, Germany, 1974–76; ACOS (Intelligence), SHAPE, 1976–79, retired. Col, Royal Regt of Wales, 1977–82. Vice Chm., N Dorset Conservative Assoc., 1985–90; Cttee, Military Commentators Circle; Member: British Atlantic Cttee; Peace Through NATO; European Atlantic Gp; Pilgrims. *Recreations:* sport, country life. *Address:* The Grange, Marnhull, Dorset DT10 1PS. *T:* Marnhull (0258) 820256. *Clubs:* Army and Navy, MCC, Pratt's.

HARROLD, Roy Mealham; farmer, since 1947; *b* 13 Aug. 1928; *s* of John Frederick Harrold and Ellen Selena Harrold (*née* Mealham); *m* 1968, Barbara Mary, *yr d* of William and Florence Andrews; one *s* one *d. Educ:* Stoke Holy Cross Primary Sch.; Bracondale Sch., Norwich. County Chm., Norfolk Fedn of Young Farmers' Clubs, 1956–57; Mem., Nat. Council of Young Farmers, 1957–60; Mem. Council, Royal Norfolk Agric. Assoc., 1972–75, 1980–83, 1987–89; Mem., Press Council, 1976–83. Lay Chm., Norwich East Deanery Synod, 1970–79; Mem., Norwich Dio. Synod, 1970–; Mem., Norwich Dio. Bd of Patronage, 1970–82; Norwich Dio. Bd of Finance, 1983–; Church Warden, St Peter Mancroft, Norwich, 1978–82, 1988–. *Recreations:* music, opera, ballet. *Address:* Salamanca Farm, Stoke Holy Cross, Norwich NR14 8QJ. *T:* Framingham Earl (05086) 2322.

HARROP, Sir Peter (John), KCB 1984 (CB 1980); Chairman, National Bus Company, 1988–91 (Member of Board, 1987–91); Second Permanent Secretary, Department of the Environment, 1981–86; *b* 18 March 1926; *s* of late Gilbert Harrop, OBE; *m* 1975, Margaret Joan, *d* of E. U. E. Elliott-Binns, CB; two *s. Educ:* King Edward VII Sch., Lytham, Lancs; Peterhouse, Cambridge. MA (Hist. Tripos). Served RNVR, 1945–47 (Sub-Lt). Min. of Town and Country Planning, 1949; Min. of Housing and Local Govt, 1951; Dept of the Environment, 1970 (Chm., Yorks and Humberside Economic Planning Bd, and Regional Dir, 1971–73); Under Sec., HM Treasury, 1973–76; Deputy Secretary: DoE, 1977–79, 1980–81; Cabinet Office, 1979–80. Non-exec. Dir, Thames Water plc, 1989– (Mem., Thames Water Authority, 1986–89). Chm., UK Cttee, European Year of the Environment, 1987–88. Non-exec. Dir, National Home Loans Holdings (formerly Corp.) plc, 1987–92; Managing Trustee, Municipal Mutual Insurance Ltd, 1988–. Hon. Trustee, British Mus., 1987–. *Recreations:* golf, sailing. *Address:* 19 Berwyn Road, Richmond, Surrey TW10 5BP. *Clubs:* United Oxford & Cambridge University, Roehampton; Ski Club of Great Britain; Island Cruising (Salcombe).

HARROWBY, 7th Earl of, *cr* 1809; **Dudley Danvers Granville Coutts Ryder,** TD; Baron Harrowby, 1776; Viscount Sandon, 1809; Chairman, The Private Bank & Trust Company, since 1989; *b* 20 Dec. 1922; *er s* of 6th Earl of Harrowby and Lady Helena Blanche Coventry (*d* 1974), *e d* of late Viscount Deerhurst; *S* father, 1987; *m* 1949, Jeannette Rosalthé, *yr d* of late Captain Peter Johnston-Saint; one *s* one *d. Educ:* Eton. Lt-Col RA; OC 254 (City of London) Field Regt, RA (TA), 1962–64. Served War of 1939–45: 59 Inf. Div., 5 Para. Bde, in NW Europe (wounded); India and Java (political offr), 56 Armoured Div., 1941–45. Man. Dir, 1949–89, Dep. Chm., 1970–89, Coutts & Co.; Director: Dinorwic Slate Quarries Co., 1951–69; United Kingdom Provident Institution, 1955–86 (Dep. Chm., 1956–64); National Provincial Bank, 1964–69; National Westminster Bank Plc, 1968–87 (Dep. Chm., 1971–87); Olympia Group, 1968–73 (Chm., 1971–73); Sheepbridge Engrg Ltd, 1977–79; Saudi Internat. Bank, 1980–82, 1985–87; Powell Duffryn Trustees Ltd, 1981–86; Orion Pacific Ltd, 1980–81; Orion Pension Trustee Co. Ltd, 1980–81; Chairman: International Westminster Bank Plc, 1977–87; Powell Duffryn Gp, 1981–86 (Dir, 1976–86); National Westminster Unit Trust Managers, 1979–83; Orion Bank Ltd, 1979–81; Bentley Engineering Co. Ltd, 1983–86; NatWest Investment Bank, 1986–87; Dowty Group, 1986–91 (Dir, 1986–91). Chm., Nat. Biol Standards Bd, 1973–88. Mem. Kensington Borough Council, 1950–65 (Chm., Gen. Purposes Cttee, 1957–59), Kensington and Chelsea BC, 1965–71 (Chm., Finance Cttee, 1968–71); Mem. Exec. Cttee, London area Cons. Assoc., 1949–50; Hon. Treasurer, S Kensington Cons. Assoc., 1953–56; Pres., Wolverhampton SW Cons. Assoc., 1959–68. Pres., Historical and Civic Soc. Hon. Treasurer: Family Welfare Assoc., 1951–65; Central Council for the Care of Cripples, 1953–60. General Commissioner for Income Tax, 1954–71; Member: Lord Chancellor's Adv. Investment Cttees, for Court of Protection, 1965–77, for Public Trustee, 1974–77; Inst. Internat. d'Etudes Bancaires, 1977–87; Trilateral Commn, 1980–. Manager, Fulham and Kensington Hosp. Group, 1953–56; Member: Cttee of Management, Inst. of Psychiatry, 1953–73 (Chm. 1965–73); Board of Governors, Bethlem Royal and Maudsley (Postgraduate Teaching) Hosps, 1955–73 (Chm. 1965–73); Dep. Chm., London Postgraduate Cttee, Teaching Hosps Assoc., 1968–69; Trustee, Psychiatry Research Trust, 1982–; Mem. Bd of Govs, Univ. of Keele, 1956–68. Pres., Staffordshire Soc., 1957–59 (Hon. Treas., 1947–51). Dep. Pres., Staffs Army Cadet League. Mem., Ct of Assts, Goldsmiths Co., 1972–77. Governor, Atlantic Inst. for Internat. Affairs. MRIIA; CBIM; Hon. FRCPsych 1983–88. *Heir: s* Viscount Sandon, *qv. Address:* 5 Tregunter Road, SW10 9LS. *T:* 01–373 9276; Sandon Hall, Stafford ST18 0BY. *T:* Sandon (08897) 338; Burnt Norton, Chipping Campden, Glos GL55 6PR. *T:* Evesham (0386) 840358.

HARSCH, Joseph Close, CBE (Hon.) 1965; writer; *b* Toledo, Ohio, 25 May 1905; *s* of Paul Arthur Harsch and Leila Katherine Close; *m* 1932, Anne Elizabeth Wood; three *s. Educ:* Williams Coll., Williamstown, Mass (MA); Corpus Christi Coll., Cambridge (MA). Joined staff Christian Science Monitor, 1929; Washington corresp., then foreign corresp.; Asst Dir, Intergovt Cttee, London, 1939; Monitor Corresp. in Berlin, 1940, SW Pacific area, 1941 and 1942. Began radio broadcasting, 1943; Senior European Correspondent, NBC, 1957–65; Diplomatic Correspondent, NBC, 1965–67; Commentator, American Broadcasting Co., 1967–71; Chief Editorial Writer, Christian Science Monitor, 1971–74. Edward Weintal award for writing on foreign affairs, 1979. *Publications:* Pattern of Conquest, 1941; The Curtain Isn't Iron, 1950. *Address:* PO Box 457, Jamestown, RI 02835, USA. *Clubs:* Garrick; Metropolitan, Cosmos (Washington, DC); Century (New York); St Botolph (Boston).

HARSTON, Julian John Robert Clive; HM Diplomatic Service; Counsellor, UK Mission, Geneva, since 1991; *b* 20 Oct. 1942; *s* of Col Clive Harston and Kathleen Harston; *m* 1966, Karen Howard Oake (*née* Longfield); one *s. Educ:* King's Sch., Canterbury; Univ. of London (BSc). British Tourist Authority, 1965–70; FCO, 1970; Consul, Hanoi, 1973; 1st Secretary: Blantyre, 1975; Lisbon, 1982; Counsellor, Harare, 1984–88; FCO, 1988–91. *Recreations:* photography, travel. *Address:* c/o Foreign and Commonwealth Office, SW1. *T:* (home) Godalming (0483) 417393. *Clubs:* East India, Devonshire, Sports and Public Schools; Gremio Literario (Lisbon); Harare (Zimbabwe).

HART, family name of **Baroness Hart of South Lanark.**

HART OF SOUTH LANARK, Baroness *cr* 1988 (Life Peer), of Lanark in the county of Larnark; **Judith Constance Mary Hart,** DBE 1979; PC 1967; *d* of late Harry Ridehalgh and Lily Ridehalgh; *m* 1946, Anthony Bernard Hart, *qv*; two *s. Educ:* Clitheroe Royal Grammar Sch.; London School of Economics, London University (BA Hons 1945). Contested (Lab) Bournemouth West, 1951, and South Aberdeen, 1955. MP (Lab): Lanark Div. of Lanarkshire, 1959–83; Clydesdale, 1983–87. Jt Parly Under-Sec. of State for Scotland, 1964–66; Minister of State, Commonwealth Office, 1966–67; Minister of Social Security, 1967–68; Paymaster-General (in the Cabinet), 1968–69; Minister of Overseas Devel, 1969–70, 1974–75; Minister for Overseas Devel, 1977–79; front bench opposition spokesman on overseas aid, 1979–80. Govt Co-Chm., Women's Nat. Commn, 1969–70. Labour Party: Mem., Nat. Executive, 1969–83; Vice-Chm., 1980–81, Chm., 1981–82. Vice Chm., UNA, 1989– (Chm., Econ. and Social Affairs Cttee, 1985–); Vice-President: World Disarmament Campaign, 1987–; World University Service, 1987–. Hon. Fellow, Inst. of Development Studies, Sussex Univ., 1985. *Publication:* Aid and Liberation, 1973. *Recreations:* theatre, gardening, spending time with her family. *Address:* 3 Ennerdale Road, Kew Gardens, Richmond-upon-Thames, Surrey TW9 3PG.

HART, Alan; Chairman, Eurosport, BBC, since 1989; *b* 17 April 1935; *s* of Reginald Thomas Hart and Lillian Hart; *m* 1961, Celia Mary Vine; two *s* one *d. Educ:* Pinnerwood Primary Sch.; University College Sch., Hampstead. Reporter: Willesden Chronicle and Kilburn Times, 1952–58; Newcastle Evening Chronicle, 1958; London Evening News, 1958–59; Editorial Asst, BBC Sportsview, 1959–61; Television Sports Producer, BBC Manchester, 1962–64; Asst Editor, Sportsview, 1964–65; Editor, Sportsview, 1965–68; Editor, Grandstand, 1968–77; Head of Sport, BBC Television, 1977–81; Controller, BBC1 Television, 1981–84; Special Asst to Dir Gen., BBC, 1985; Controller, Internat. Relations, BBC, 1986–91. FRTS 1983. *Recreations:* sport, music, walking. *Address:* BBC White City, 201 Wood Lane, W12 7TS. *T:* 081–752 5448.

HART, Alan Edward; Chief Executive, Equal Opportunities Commission, 1985–89; *b* 28 July 1935; *m* 1961, Ann Derbyshire; one *s* one *d. Educ:* Varndean County Grammar Sch., Brighton; Lincoln Coll., Univ. of Oxford (MA). Solicitor. Dep. Town Clerk, City of Salford, 1970–73; Dir of Admin, 1973–75, Chief Exec., 1975–85, Wigan MBC.

HART, Alexander Hendry, QC (Canada) 1969; Agent General for British Columbia in the United Kingdom and Europe, 1981–87; *b* Regina, Sask., 17 July 1916; *s* of Alexander Hart and Mary (*née* Davidson); *m* 1948, Janet MacMillan Mackay; three *s* one *d. Educ:* Dalhousie Law School (LLB). Served War, Royal Canadian Artillery, 1939–45; retired with rank of Major. Read law with McInnis, Mcquarrie and Cooper; called to Bar of Nova Scotia, 1947. Vice-Pres., Marketing, 1967–71; Sen. Vice-Pres., Canadian Nat. Rlwys, 1971–81. Dep. Internat. Pres., Pacific Basin Economic Council, 1980–81; Pres., Canada-UK Chamber of Commerce, 1983; Past Pres., Vancouver Board of Trade; Past Chm., Western Transportation Adv. Council; Past Mem., University Council of British Columbia; Past Pres., Canada Japan Soc. of Vancouver. *Recreation:* golf. *Address:* 1515 Dorcas Point Road, Nanoose Bay, British Columbia, Canada. *Clubs:* Royal & Ancient Golf (St Andrews); Vancouver, Men's Canadian, Shaughnessy Golf and Country (Vancouver); Pine Valley (Clementon, NJ).

HART, Anelay Colton Wright; Partner in Appleby, Hope & Matthews, since 1963; *b* 6 March 1934; *s* of Anelay Thomas Bayston Hart and Phyllis Marian Hart; *m* 1979, Margaret Gardner (*née* Dewing). *Educ:* Stamford Sch.; King's Coll., London (LLB). Solicitor. Advisory Director, World Society for the Protection of Animals, 1982–; RSPCA: Mem. Council, 1969–; Hon. Treasurer, 1974–81; Chm. of Council, 1981–83, 1985–86, 1988–90; Vice-Chm. Council, 1983–84, 1986–88; Queen Victoria Silver Medal, 1984. President, Rotary Club of South Bank and Eston, 1972–73. *Recreations:* walking, gardening. *Address:* Village Farm, Moulton, Richmond, N Yorks DL10 6QQ. *T:* (office) Eston Grange (0642) 440444. *Club:* Royal Over-Seas League.

HART, Anthony; *see* Hart, T. A. A.

HART, Anthony Bernard, PhD; Co-Chairman, World Disarmament Campaign, since 1986; Executive Member, Scientists Against Nuclear Arms, since 1981; Head of Chemistry Division, Research Division of Central Electricity Generating Board, 1976–82; *b* 7 July 1917; *s* of late Oliver and Jessie Hart; *m* 1946, Judith Ridehalgh (*see* Baroness Hart of South Lanark); two *s*. *Educ:* Enfield Grammar Sch.; Queen Mary Coll., London. BSc, PhD; CEng, CChem, FRSC, MInstE. RN Cordite Factories, 1940–46; RN Scientific Service, 1946–50; Lectr in Physical Chem., Royal Coll. of Sci. and Technol., Glasgow (now Strathclyde Univ.), 1950–60; Res. Div., CEGB, 1960–82. Exec. Mem., later Chm., Glasgow Trades Council, 1952–60; Nat. Exec. Mem., AUT, 1954–59. Mem., Barnes BC, 1962–64; Mem. and Leader of Opposition, Richmond upon Thames Council, 1964–68 and 1971–74; Chm., Richmond upon Thames Local Govt Cttee, 1968–77; Mem. for Hornsey, GLC, 1981–86 (Chm., F & GP Cttee, 1981–82, Dep. Chief Whip, 1983–86). *Publications:* (with G. J. Womack) Fuel Cells, 1967; (with A. J. B. Cutler) Deposition and Corrosion in Gas Turbines, 1973; contribs to scientific jls. *Recreation:* campaigning for peace and socialism. *Address:* 3 Ennerdale Road, Kew, Richmond, Surrey TW9 3PG. *T:* 081–948 1989.

HART, Anthony John, DSC 1945; JP; Chairman, Cunningham Hart & Co. Ltd, 1985–87 (Senior Partner, 1972–85), retired; *b* 27 Dec. 1923; *s* of Cecil Victor Hart and Kate Winifred Hart (*née* Boncey); *m* 1947, E. Penelope Morris; one *s* one *d*. *Educ:* King's College Sch., Wimbledon; Dauntsey's Sch. ACII, FCILA. RN 1942–46 (Ordinary Seaman to Lieut). Joined Hart & Co., 1946, Partner 1952, Senior Partner 1969; on merger name changed to Cunningham Hart & Co. Mem. Council, CILA, 1964, Pres., 1970–71. Chm., Medic Alert Foundn in UK, 1971–83; Governor, Dauntsey's Sch.; Mem. Council, Mansfield House University Settlement, 1975–90. Liveryman, 1960, Master, 1976–77, Broderers' Co.; Liveryman, 1979, Mem. Court, 1986, Insurers' Co. Alderman, Ward of Cheap, City of London, 1977–84. FRSA. JP City of London, 1977 (Vice-Chm. of Bench, 1991–). *Recreation:* golf. *Address:* 7 Dickens Close, Petersham, Surrey TW10 7AU. *T:* 081–948 0587. *Clubs:* City Livery, Richmond Golf.

HART, Anthony Ronald; QC (NI) 1983; **His Honour Judge Hart;** a County Court Judge, Northern Ireland, since 1985; Chancellor, Diocese of Clogher, Church of Ireland, since 1990; *b* 30 April 1946; *s* of Basil and Hazel Hart; *m* 1971, Mary Morehan; two *s* two *d*. *Educ:* Portora Royal Sch., Enniskillen; Trinity Coll., Dublin (BA Mod.); Queen's Univ., Belfast. Called to the Bar of NI, 1969; called to the Bar, Gray's Inn, 1975. Jun. Crown Counsel for Co. Londonderry, 1973–75 and for Co. Down, 1975–79; Asst Boundary Comr, 1980–81; part-time Chm. of Industrial Tribunals, 1980–83; Dep. County Court Judge, 1983–85; Recorder of Londonderry, 1985–90. Member: Council of Legal Educn (NI), 1977–83; Review Cttee on Professional Legal Educn in NI, 1984–85; Standing Adv. Commn on Human Rights, 1984–85. *Publications:* (Consultant Ed) Valentine on Criminal Procedure in Northern Ireland, 1989; (contrib.) Brehons, Serjeants and Attorneys: studies in the history of the Irish legal profession, 1990. *Recreations:* rowing, gardening, reading. *Address:* c/o Northern Ireland Court Service, Windsor House, Bedford Street, Belfast BT2 7LT. *Club:* Leander (Henley-on-Thames).

HART, David Michael, OBE 1988; General Secretary, National Association of Head Teachers, since 1978; *b* 27 Aug. 1940; *s* of Edwin Henry Hart and Freda Muriel Hart; *m* 1963, Mary Chalmers; two *s*. *Educ:* Hurstpierpoint Coll., Sussex. Solicitor 1963, Herbert Ruse Prizeman. Editor, Heads' Legal Guide, 1984. Hon. FCollP 1986; FRSA 1990. *Recreations:* golf, tennis, bridge. *Address:* Barn Cottage, Fairmile Lane, Cobham, Surrey. *T:* Cobham (0932) 62884. *Clubs:* Commonwealth Trust, Wig and Pen, MCC.

HART, Donald; QC 1978; **His Honour Judge Donald Hart;** a Circuit Judge, since 1989; President, Mental Health Review Tribunals (restricted patients), since 1983; *b* 6 Jan. 1933; *s* of Frank and Frances Hart; *m* 1st, 1958, Glenys Thomas (marr. diss. 1990); two *s* two *d*; 2nd, 1990, Joan Turton. *Educ:* Altrincham Grammar Sch.; Magdalen Coll., Oxford. MA. Macaskie Scholar, Arden and Atkin Prize, Lee Essay Prize (Gray's Inn), 1956. Called to the Bar, Gray's Inn, 1956; Northern Circuit, 1956–; a Recorder, 1978–89. Member: Family Law Bar Assoc., 1979; Internat. Acad. of Matrimonial Lawyers, 1986–89. *Recreations:* garden, travel, opera, cuisine. *Address:* 217 Knutsford Road, Grappenhall, Cheshire WA4 2TX. *T:* Warrington (0925) 860291; Queen Elizabeth II Law Courts, Derby Square, Liverpool L2 1XA. *T:* 051–473 7373. *Club:* United Oxford & Cambridge University.

HART, Dr (Everard) Peter, CChem, FRSC; Rector, Sunderland Polytechnic, 1981–90; *b* 16 Sept. 1925; *s* of Robert Daniel Hart and Margaret Stokes; *m* Enid Mary Scott; three *s* one *d*. *Educ:* Wyggeston Grammar Sch., Leicester; Loughborough Coll.; London Univ. (BSc, PhD). Asst Lectr, Lectr and Sen. Lectr, Nottingham and Dist Technical Coll., 1951–57; Sunderland Technical College, later Sunderland Polytechnic: Head of Dept of Chemistry and Biology, 1958–69; Vice-Principal, 1963–69; Dep. Rector, 1969–80. Member: Cttee for Sci. and Technol., CNAA, 1974–77; Gen. Council, Northern Arts, 1982–90. Royal Institute of Chemistry: Mem. Council, 1963–65, 1970–73; Vice-Pres., 1973–75. FRSA 1985. *Recreations:* music, opera, theatre, travel. *Address:* Redesdale, The Oval, North End, Durham City. *T:* Durham (091) 3848305. *Club:* National Liberal.

HART, F(rancis) Dudley, FRCP; Physician, and Physician-in-charge Rheumatism Unit, Westminster Hospital, SW1, 1946–74; Consulting Physician: Hospital of St John and St Elizabeth, London; Westminster Hospital; lately Consulting Rheumatologist, The Star and Garter Home for Disabled Sailors, Soldiers and Airmen, Richmond; lately Hon. Consulting Physician (Civilian) to the Army; *b* 4 Oct. 1909; *s* of Canon C. Dudley Hart and Kate Evelyn Bowden; *m* 1944, Mary Josephine, *d* of late Luke Tully, Carrigaline, Co. Cork; one *s* two *d*. *Educ:* Grosvenor Sch., Nottingham; Edinburgh Univ. MB, ChB Edinburgh 1933, MD 1939; MRCP 1937, FRCP 1949. House physician and clinical asst, Brompton Hosp., 1937; Med. Registrar, Royal Northern Hosp., 1935–37; Med. Registrar, Westminster Hosp., 1939–42; Med. Specialist and Officer i/c Med. Div., RAMC, 1942–46. Mem., Cttee on Review of Medicines, 1975–82. Ex-Pres. Heberden Soc.; Member: BMA; Med. Soc. of London. Arris and Gale Lectr, RCS, 1955; Ellman Lectr, RCP, 1969; Stanley Davidson Lectr, Univ. of Aberdeen, 1970; Bradshaw Lectr, RCP, 1975; Alexander Brown Meml Lectr, Univ. of Ibadan, Nigeria, 1979; Bernadine Becker Lectr, NY, 1984. Exec. Mem. and Vice-Chm., Arthritis and Rheumatism Council (formerly Empire Rheumatism Council); Hon. FRSM. Hon. Member: British Soc. for Rheumatology; Ligue Française contre le Rheumatisme; La Societa di Rheumatologia Italia; American Rheumatism Association; Australian Rheumatism Association. *Publications:* (co-author) Drugs: actions, uses and dosage, 1963; (ed) French's Differential Diagnosis, 10th edn, 1973, 12th edn, 1985; (ed) The Treatment of Chronic Pain, 1974; Joint Disease: all the arthropathies, 1975, 4th edn 1987; (ed) Drug Treatment of the Rheumatic Diseases, 1978, 3rd edn 1987; (ed) Clinical Rheumatology Illustrated, 1987; (ed) Diagnostic Features of Disease, 1987; Colour Atlas of Rheumatology, 1987; contributions to: Pye's Surgical Handicraft, 1939–72; Cortisone and ACTH, 1953; Miller's Modern Medical Treatment, 1962; Copeman's Textbook of the Rheumatic Diseases (ed J. T. Scott), 3rd edn 1964, 5th edn 1978; Encyclopedia of General Practice, 1964; Chambers's Encyclopædia, 1964; Drug Treatment, 1976; Butterworth's Medical Dictionary (all rheumatological sections), 1978; Overcoming Arthritis, 1981; Practical Problems in Rheumatology, 1983; articles and broadcasts on general medicine and rheumatism. *Recreations:* multi-track recording, travelling. *Address:* 24 Harmont House, 20 Harley Street, W1N 1AN. *T:* 071–935 4252; (private) 19 Ranulf Road, Hampstead, NW2. *T:* 071–794 2525.

HART, Sir Francis Edmund T.; *see* Turton-Hart.

HART, (Frank) Donald; *see* Hart, Donald.

HART, Frank Thomas, BA; JP; *b* London, 9 Nov. 1911; *s* of late Samuel Black and Ada Frances Laura Hart; *m* 1938, Eveline Brenda Deakin, Leek, Staffs; three *s*. *Educ:* Gravesend and Sheerness Junior Technical Schs. DPA (London); Diploma of Economics (London); BA Open, 1982. Asst Sec., Buchanan Hospital, St Leonards-on-Sea, 1931–34; Sec., 1934–42; Sec., Central London Eye Hospital, 1942–44; Sec.-Superintendent, Princess Louise Hospital, 1944–48; Superintendent, Royal Infirmary, Sheffield, 1948–52; House Governor and Sec. to the Bd, Charing Cross Hospital, 1952–73; Hospital Manager, Zambia Medical Aid Soc., 1973–75. Mem. Tribunal set up by President of Zambia to hear applications for release from political detainees. Pres., League of Friends, Charing Cross Hosp., 1985–; Past Pres., Assoc. of Hosp. Secretaries; Past Pres. of the Hospital Officers' Club. JP: Co. Mddx, 1955–65; Co. Surrey, 1965–77, East Sussex, 1978–81. Freeman, City of London, 1959; Mem., Worshipful Soc. of Apothecaries. *Publications:* (jointly) A Study of Hospital Administration, 1948; Roots of Service (A History of Charing Cross Hospital), 1985. *Recreations:* all games, walking, reading. *Address:* 124 Marine Court, St Leonards on Sea, East Sussex TN38 0DY.

HART, George Vaughan; Consultant, Law Reform Division, Department of Justice, Dublin, since 1972; *b* 9 Sept. 1911; *e s* of George Vaughan Hart and Maude (*née* Curran); *m* 1949, Norah Marie, *d* of Major D. L. J. Babington; one *s* one *d*. *Educ:* Rossall; Corpus Christi Coll., Oxford. Called to Bar, Middle Temple, 1937. Served Royal Irish Fusiliers, 1940–45. Entered Home Office as Legal Asst, 1946; Principal Asst Legal Advr, 1967–72. Sec., Criminal Law Revision Cttee, 1959–72. *Recreations:* walking, bird-watching. *Address:* 1 Mount Salus, Knocknacree Road, Dalkey, Co. Dublin. *T:* Dublin 850420. *Clubs:* Athenæum; Kildare Street and University (Dublin).

HART, Graham Allan, CB 1987; Secretary, Home and Health Department, Scottish Office since 1990; *b* 13 March 1940; *s* of Frederick and Winifred Hart; *m* 1964, Margaret Aline Powell; two *s*. *Educ:* Brentwood Sch.; Pembroke Coll., Oxford. Assistant Principal, 1962, Principal, 1967, Ministry of Health; Asst Registrar, General Medical Council, 1969–71; Principal Private Sec. to Secretary of State for Social Services, 1972–74; Asst Sec., 1974, Under Sec., 1979, DHSS; Under Sec., Central Policy Review Staff, 1982–83; Dep. Sec., DHSS, then DoH, 1984–89. *Address:* St Andrew's House, Edinburgh EH1 3DE.

HART, Guy William Pulbrook, OBE 1985; HM Diplomatic Service, retired; High Commissioner to Seychelles, 1989–91; *b* 24 Dec. 1931; *s* of late Ernest Guy Hart and Muriel Hart (*née* Walkington); *m* 1954, Elizabeth Marjorie (*née* Bennett); one *s* two *d*. *Educ:* Cranleigh School. Commissioned, Intelligence Corps, 1951–60. British Cellophane Ltd, 1960–62; CRO, 1962; Consular Officer, Kuala Lumpur, 1963–67; Hungarian Language Course, 1967; Second Sec. (Inf.), Budapest, 1968–71; News Dept, FCO, 1971–74; Second Sec. (Econ.), later First Sec. (Inf.), British Mil. Govt, Berlin, 1974–78; First Sec. (Comm.), Port of Spain, 1978–82, Budapest, 1982–85; Asst Head, Inf. Dept, FCO, 1986; Ambassador to the Mongolian People's Republic, 1987–89. *Recreations:* Alpine sports, shooting, painting. *Club:* Austrian Alpine.

HART, Prof. Herbert Lionel Adolphus; QC 1984; FBA 1962; Principal, Brasenose College, Oxford, 1973–78, Hon. Fellow 1978; Delegate of the Oxford University Press, 1960–74; *b* 18 July 1907; 3rd *s* of Simeon Hart and Rose (*née* Samson); *m* 1941, Jenifer, 3rd *d* of Sir John Fischer Williams, CBE, KC; three *s* one *d*. *Educ:* Cheltenham Coll.; Bradford Grammar Sch.; New Coll., Oxford (Hon. Fellow 1968). Open Classical Scholar, New Coll., Oxford, 1926; First Class Lit. Hum., 1929. Practised at the Chancery Bar, 1932–40. Served War of 1939–45, in War Office, 1940–45. Fellow and Tutor in Philosophy, New Coll., Oxford, 1945; University Lecturer in Philosophy, Oxford, 1948; Prof. of Jurisprudence, Oxford, 1952–68; Fellow, University Coll., Oxford, 1952–68, Res. Fellow 1969–73, Hon. Fellow, 1973; Sen. Res. Fellow, Nuffield Foundn, 1969–73. Visiting Professor: Harvard Univ., 1956–57; Univ. of California, LA, 1961–62. Mem., Monopolies Commn, 1967–73. Pres., Aristotelian Soc., 1959–60; Vice-Pres., British Acad., 1976–77. Hon. Master of the Bench, Middle Temple, 1963. For. Mem., Amer. Acad. of Arts and Sciences, 1966. Hon. Dr of Law: Stockholm, 1960; Hebrew Univ. of Jerusalem, 1985; Hon. LLD: Glasgow, 1966; Chicago, 1966; Cambridge, 1978; Harvard, 1980; Edinburgh, 1980; Georgetown, 1982; Hon. DLitt: Kent, 1969; Hull, 1979; Bradford, 1980; Hon. Dr, Nat. Autonomous Univ. of Mexico, 1979; Hon. PhD Tel Aviv, 1983. Fellow, Accademia delle Scienze, Turin, 1964; Commonwealth Prestige Fellow (Govt of NZ), 1971. *Publications:* (with A. M. Honoré) Causation in the Law, 1959, 2nd edn 1984; The Concept of Law, 1961; Law Liberty and Morality, 1963; The Morality of the Criminal Law, 1965; Punishment and Responsibility, 1968; (ed, with J. H. Burns) Jeremy Bentham: An Introduction to the Principles of Morals and Legislation, 1970; (ed) Jeremy Bentham: Of Laws in General, 1970; (ed jtly) Jeremy Bentham: A Comment on the Commentaries and A Fragment on Government, 1977; Essays on Bentham: jurisprudence and political theory, 1982; Essays in Jurisprudence and Philosophy, 1983; articles in philosophical and legal journals. *Address:* University College, Oxford; 11 Manor Place, Oxford OX1 3UP. *T:* Oxford (0865) 242402.

HART, Michael, CBE 1990; MA; FRSA; Education Consultant, European Commission, since 1990; *b* 1 May 1928; *yr s* of late Dr F. C. Hardt; *m* 1956, Lida Dabney Adams, PhD (Wisconsin Univ.). *Educ:* Collège Français, Berlin; Landerziehungsheim Schondorf; Keble Coll., Oxford (Exhib.). 1st Cl. Hons History, 1951. Administrative Asst, UNRRA, 1945–47; Asst Master and Head of History, Sherborne Sch., 1951–56; Head of History, 1956–61, and Housemaster of School House, 1961–67, Shrewsbury Sch.; Headmaster of Mill Hill Sch., 1967–74; HM Inspector of Schs, DES, 1974–76; Headmaster, European Sch., Mol, Belgium, 1976–80; Headmaster, European Sch., Luxembourg, 1980–89; Dir, European Classes, Alden Biesen, Belgium, 1989–. Commandeur de l'Ordre de Mérite (Luxembourg), 1989. *Publications:* The EEC and Secondary Education in the UK, 1974; contrib. to Reader's Digest World Atlas and Atlas of British Isles. *Recreations:* travel, climbing. *Address:* 21 Avenue du Forum, 1020 Brussels, Belgium.

HART, Prof. Michael, FRS 1982; CPhys, FInstP; Professor of Physics, University of Manchester, since 1984; *b* 4 Nov. 1938; *s* of Reuben Harold Victor Hart and Phyllis Mary (*née* White); *m* 1963, Susan Margaret (*née* Powell); three *d. Educ:* Cotham Grammar Sch., Bristol; Bristol Univ. (BSc, PhD, DSc). FInstP 1971. Research Associate: Dept of Materials Science and Engrg, Cornell Univ., 1963–65; Dept of Physics, Bristol Univ., 1965–67; Lectr in Physics, 1967–72, Reader in Physics, 1972–76, Bristol Univ.; Sen. Resident Res. Associate of Nat. Research Council, Nat. Aeronautics and Space Admin Electronics Research Center, Boston, Mass, 1969–70; Special Advisor, Central Policy Review Staff, Cabinet Office, 1975–77; Wheatstone Prof. of Physics and Head of Physics Dept, KCL, 1976–84; Science Pogramme Co-ordinator (part-time, on secondment), Daresbury Lab., SERC, 1985–88. Amer. Crystallographic Assoc.'s Bertram Eugene Warren Award for Diffraction Physics (jtly with Dr U. Bonse), 1970; Charles Vernon Boys Prize of Inst. of Physics, 1971. *Publications:* numerous contribs to learned jls on x-ray optics, defects in crystals and synchrotron radiation. *Recreations:* weaving, flying kites. *Address:* 54 Manor Park South, Knutsford, Cheshire WA16 8AN. *T:* Knutsford (0565) 632893. *Club:* Athenæum.

HART, Michael Christopher Campbell; QC 1987; *b* 7 May 1948; *s* of Raymond David Campbell Hart and Penelope Mary Hart (*née* Ellis); *m* 1972, Melanie Jane Sandiford; two *d. Educ:* Winchester College; Magdalen College, Oxford (MA, BCL). Called to the Bar, Gray's Inn, 1970. Fellow, All Souls College, Oxford, 1970–77, 1979–86. *Address:* 2 New Square, Lincoln's Inn, WC2A 3RU. *T:* 071-242 6201.

HART, Prof. Oliver Simon D'Arcy, PhD; Professor of Economics, Massachusetts Institute of Technology, since 1985; *b* 9 Oct. 1948; *s* of Philip Montagu D'Arcy Hart, *qv* and Ruth Hart; *m* 1974, Rita Goldberg (who retains maiden name); two *s. Educ:* University Coll. Sch.; Univ. of Cambridge (BA 1969); Univ. of Warwick (MA 1972); Princeton Univ. (PhD 1974). Lectr in Econs, Univ. of Essex, 1974–75; Asst Lectr in Econs, subseq. Lectr, Univ. of Cambridge, 1975–81; Fellow of Churchill Coll., Cambridge, 1975–81; Prof. of Economics, LSE, 1982–85; Prog. Dir, Centre for Economic Policy Res., 1983–84. Fellow: Econometric Soc., 1979 (Mem. Council, 1982–); Amer. Acad. of Arts and Scis, 1988. Editor, Review of Economic Studies, 1979–83. *Publications:* articles on economic theory in Econometrica, Rev. of Econ. Studies, Jl of Pol Economy. *Recreations:* playing and watching tennis. *Address:* Department of Economics, Massachusetts Institute of Technology, Cambridge, Mass 02139, USA.

HART, Peter; *see* Hart, E. P.

HART, P(hilip) M(ontagu) D'Arcy, CBE 1956; MA, MD (Cambridge), FRCP; Medical Research Council grant holder, National Institute for Medical Research, since 1965 (Director, Tuberculosis Research Unit, Medical Research Council, 1948–65); *b* 25 June 1900; *s* of late Henry D'Arcy Hart and late Hon. Ethel Montagu; *m* 1941, Ruth, *d* of late Herbert Meyer and late Grete Meyer-Larsen; one *s. Educ:* Clifton Coll.; Gonville and Caius Coll., Cambridge; University Coll. Hospital. Dorothy Temple Cross Fellowship to USA, 1934–35; Consultant Physician, UCH, 1934–37; Mem. Scientific Staff, MRC, 1937–48; Mem. Expert Cttee on Tuberculosis, WHO, 1947–64. Goldsmith Entrance Exhibnr, Filliter Exhibnr, Magrath Scholarship, Tuke Medals, UCH Medical Sch., 1922–25; Horton Smith MD Prize, Cambridge, 1930; Royal College of Physicians: Milroy Lecture, 1937; Mitchell Lecture, 1946; Weber-Parkes Prize, 1951; Marc Daniels Lecture, 1967; Stewart Prize, BMA, 1964. *Publications:* scientific papers on respiratory disease, epidemiology and cell biology. *Address:* National Institute for Medical Research, Mill Hill, NW7. *T:* 081–959 3666; 37 Belsize Court, NW3 5QN. *Club:* Athenæum.
See also O. S. D'A. Hart.

HART, Captain Raymond, CBE 1963; DSO 1945; DSC 1941, Bar 1943; Royal Navy; *b* 24 June 1913; *o s* of late H. H. Hart, Bassett, Southampton; *m* 1945, Margaret Evanson, *o d* of Capt. S. B. Duffin, Danesfort, Belfast; two *s* one *d. Educ:* Oakmount Preparatory Sch.; King Edward VI Sch. Joined Merchant Navy, 1929; Joined Royal Navy, 1937; HMS Hasty, 2nd Destroyer Flotilla, 1939–42; in command: HMS Vidette, 1942–44 (despatches); HMS Havelock, 1944; Sen. Officer, 21st Escort Gp, 1944–45; served in HMS Vanguard during Royal Tour of S Africa, 1947. RN Staff Course, 1949–52; in command, HMS Relentless, 1952–53; Joint Services Staff Course, 1953–54; Staff C-in-C Allied Forces Mediterranean, as Liaison Officer to C-in-C Allied Forces Southern Europe, HQ Naples, Italy, 1954–56; in command, HMS Undine, and Capt. 6th Frigate Sqdn, 1957–58; Cdre Naval Drafting, 1960–62; retd from RN, 1963. Nautical Advr, British & Commonwealth Shipping Co., 1963–72; Fleet Manager, Cayzer, Irvine & Co. Ltd, 1972–76; Director: Union-Castle Mail Steamship Co. Ltd; Clan Line Steamers Ltd, 1964–76; Cayzer, Irvine & Co. Ltd, 1966–76; British & Commonwealth Shipping Co. Ltd, 1966–76. Mem. Council, Missions to Seamen; Vice President: Seamen's Hosp. Soc., 1983; Marine Soc., 1989. FRIN; FNI. Officer Order of Merit of Republic of Italy, 1958. *Recreations:* swimming, golf, gardening. *Address:* Three Firs Cottage, Bramshott Chase, Hindhead, Surrey GU26 6DG.

HART, (Thomas) Anthony (Alfred), MA; Headmaster, Cranleigh School, since 1984; *b* 4 March 1940; *er s* of Rev. Arthur Reginald Hart and Florence Ivy Hart; *m* 1971, Daintre Margaret Withiel (*née* Thomas); one *s* one *d. Educ:* City of Bath Sch.; New Coll., Oxford (2nd Cl. Hons PPE; MA); Pres., Oxford Union, 1963. Served with VSO, Mzuzu Secondary Sch., Nyasaland, 1959–60. Asst Principal and Principal, Min. of Transport, 1964–69; seconded to Govt of Malaŵi as Transport Adviser, 1969–70; Principal, DoE and CSD, 1970–73; Head, Voluntary Services Unit, Home Office, 1973–75; Asst Sec., CSD and HM Treasury, 1975–84. *Recreations:* reading, travel, listening to music, dining out. *Address:* The Headmaster's House, Cranleigh School, Cranleigh, Surrey GU6 8QQ. *T:* Cranleigh (0483) 276377. *Club:* Travellers'.

HART, Thomas Mure, CMG 1957; *b* 1 March 1909; *s* of late Maxwell M. Hart and of Elizabeth Watson, Aiknut, West Kilbride; *m* 1936, Eileen Stewart Lawson; one *s* one *d. Educ:* Strathallan; Glasgow Univ.; Brasenose Coll., Oxford. Colonial Administrative Service, 1933; seconded Colonial Office, 1933–36; Malayan Civil Service, 1936; Dir of Commerce and Industry, Singapore, 1953; Financial Sec., Singapore, 1954; retired, 1959. Bursar, Loretto Sch., Musselburgh, 1959–69. *Recreation:* golf. *Address:* 44 Frogston Road West, Edinburgh EH10 7AJ. *T:* 031–445 2152. *Club:* Honourable Company of Edinburgh Golfers.

HART, Maj.-Gen. Trevor Stuart, CB 1982; MRCS, LRCP; FFCM; Hospital and Medical Director, National Guard King Khalid Hospital, Jeddah, 1983–84; *b* 19 Feb. 1926; *s* of R. J. Hart and C. G. Hart (*née* Blyfield); *m* 1954, P. G. Lloyd; two *s* one *d. Educ:* Dulwich Coll.; Guy's Hosp. MB, BS; FFCM; DPH, DTM&H. DDMS HQ 1 (BR) Corps, 1975–78; DMS: UKLF, 1978–81; BAOR, 1981–83. Col Comdt, RAMC, 1984–90. Mem., Wessex RHA, 1984–88. OStJ 1973. *Recreations:* gardening, growing orchids (more leaves than blooms). *Address:* c/o Barclays Bank, 72 Cheapside, EC2.

HART, Rt. Rev. Mgr William Andrew; *b* Dumbarton, 9 Sept. 1904; *s* of Daniel Hart and Margaret Gallagher. *Educ:* St Mungo's Academy, Glasgow; St Mary's Coll., Blairs, Aberdeen; Royal Scots Coll. and Pontifical Univ., Valladolid, Spain. Asst Priest, St Mary's, Hamilton, 1929–33; St John's, Glasgow, 1933–39; Army Chaplain, 1939–45; Asst Priest, St Michael's, Glasgow, 1945–48; Vice-Rector, Royal Scots Coll., Valladolid, 1948–49; Parish Priest, St Nicholas', Glasgow, 1949–51, St Saviour's, Glasgow, 1951–55; Bishop of Dunkeld, 1955–81.

HART-DAVIS, Sir Rupert (Charles), Kt 1967; author, editor and former publisher; Director of Rupert Hart-Davis, Ltd, Publishers, 1946–68; Vice-President, Committee of the London Library, since 1971 (Chairman 1957–69); *b* 28 Aug. 1907; *o s* of Richard Vaughan Hart-Davis and Sybil Mary Cooper, *er sister* of 1st Viscount Norwich; *m* 1st, 1929, Peggy Ashcroft (later Dame Peggy Ashcroft) (marr. diss.; she *d* 1991); 2nd, 1933, Catherine Comfort Borden-Turner (marr. diss.), *d* of Mary Borden and George Douglas Turner; two *s* one *d*; 3rd, 1964, Winifred Ruth (*d* 1967), *d* of C. H. Ware, Bromyard, and *widow* of Oliver Simon; 4th, 1968, June (*née* Clifford), *widow* of David Williams. *Educ:* Eton; Balliol Coll., Oxford. Student at Old Vic, 1927–28; Actor at Lyric Theatre, Hammersmith, 1928–29; office boy at William Heinemann Ltd, 1929–31; Manager of Book Soc., 1932; Dir of Jonathan Cape Ltd, 1933–40. Served in Coldstream Guards, 1940–45. Founded Rupert Hart-Davis Ltd, 1946. Hon. DLitt: Reading, 1964; Durham, 1981. *Publications:* Hugh Walpole: a biography, 1952; The Arms of Time: a memoir, 1979; The Power of Chance: a table of memory, 1991; *edited:* The Essential Neville Cardus, 1949; E. V. Lucas: Cricket all his Life, 1950; George Moore: Letters to Lady Cunard, 1957; The Letters of Oscar Wilde, 1962; Max Beerbohm: Letters to Reggie Turner, 1964; Max Beerbohm: More Theatres, 1969; Max Beerbohm: Last Theatres, 1970; Max Beerbohm: A Peep into the Past, 1972; A Catalogue of the Caricatures of Max Beerbohm, 1972; The Autobiography of Arthur Ransome, 1976; William Plomer: Electric Delights, 1978; The Lyttelton Hart-Davis Letters, vol. I, 1978, vol. II, 1979, vol. III, 1981, vol. IV, 1982, vol. V, 1983, vol. VI, 1984; Selected Letters of Oscar Wilde, 1979; Two Men of Letters, 1979; Siegfried Sassoon Diaries: 1920–1922, 1981, 1915–1918, 1983, 1923–25, 1985; The War Poems of Siegfried Sassoon, 1983; A Beggar in Purple: commonplace book, 1983; More Letters of Oscar Wilde, 1985; Siegfried Sassoon: Letters to Max Beerbohm, 1986; Letters of Max Beerbohm 1892–1956, 1989. *Recreations:* reading, book-collecting, watching cricket. *Address:* The Old Rectory, Marske-in-Swaledale, Richmond, N Yorks DL11 7NA.
See also Baron Silsoe.

HART DYKE, Captain David, CBE 1990; LVO 1980; RN; Aide-de-camp to the Queen, since 1988; Clerk to Worshipful Company of Skinners, since 1990; *b* 3 Oct. 1938; *s* of Comdr Rev. Eric Hart Dyke and Mary Hart Dyke; *m* 1967, Diana Margaret, *d* of Sir William Luce, GBE, KCMG; two *d. Educ:* St Lawrence College, Ramsgate; BRNC Dartmouth. RN 1958; served Far East and Middle East; navigation specialist; Exec. Officer, HMS Hampshire, 1974–76; Staff, RN Staff Coll., 1976–78; Comdr, HM Yacht Britannia, 1978–80; Captain HMS Coventry; action in Falklands, 1982; ACOS to C-in-C Fleet, 1982–84; Asst Naval Attaché, Washington, 1985–87; Dir, Naval Recruiting, 1987–89. *Publications:* articles on Falklands campaign for professional jls, incl. Naval Review. *Recreations:* painting, music, reading, military history. *Address:* Hambledon House, Hambledon, Hants PO7 6RU. *T:* Hambledon (070132) 380. *Club:* Naval and Military.

HART DYKE, Sir David (William), 10th Bt *cr* 1677, of Horeham, Sussex; journalist; *b* 5 Jan. 1955; *s* of Sir Derek William Hart Dyke, 9th Bt and Dorothy Moses; *S* father, 1987. *Educ:* Ryerson Polytechnical Institute (BA). *Recreations:* portage camping, ice hockey, reading. *Heir: uncle* (Oliver) Guy Hart Dyke [*b* 9 Feb. 1928; *m* 1974, Sarah Alexander, *d* of late Rev. Eric Hart Dyke; one *s* one *d*]. *Address:* 28 King Street West, Apt 14B, Stoney Creek, Ontario L8G 1H4, Canada.

HART-LEVERTON, Colin Allen; QC 1979; a Recorder of the Crown Court, since 1979; *b* 10 May 1936; *s* of Monty Hart-Leverton and Betty (*née* Simmonds). *Educ:* Stowe; self-taught thereafter. Mem., Inst. of Taxation, 1957 (youngest to have ever qualified); called to the Bar, Middle Temple, 1957 (youngest to have ever qual.). Contested (L): Bristol West, 1959 (youngest cand.); Walthamstow West, 1964. Prosecuting Counsel, Central Criminal Court, 1974–79; Dep. Circuit Judge, 1975; Attorney-at-Law, Turks and Caicos Islands, Caribbean, 1976. Occasional television and radio broadcasts. *Recreations:* table-tennis, jazz. *Address:* 10 King's Bench Walk, EC4Y 7EB. *T:* 071–353 2501.

HARTE, Julia Kathleen; *see* McKenzie, J. K.

HARTE, Dr Michael John; Assistant Under Secretary of State (Resources), Ministry of Defence, since 1990; *b* 15 Aug. 1936; *s* of Harold Edward Harte and Marjorie Irene Harte; *m* 1st, 1962, Diana Hayes (marr. diss. 1971); 2nd, 1975, Mary Claire Preston; four step *d. Educ:* Charterhouse; Trinity Coll., Cambridge (BA); University Coll., London (PhD; Dip. in Biochem. Engrg). Sen. Scientific Officer, Micro-biol Res. Estab., MoD, 1963; Principal, MoD, 1967; Private Sec. to Minister of State for Def., 1972; Asst Sec., Central Policy Rev. Staff, 1973; Asst Sec., MoD, 1975–77; Counsellor, Budget and Infrastructure, UK Delegn to NATO, 1977–81; Chm., NATO Civil and Mil. Budget Cttees, 1981–83; Asst Sec., MoD, 1983–85; Assistant Under Secretary of State: (Dockyard Planning Team), MoD, 1985–87; (Personnel) (Air), MoD, 1987–90. Non-exec. Dir, GlaxoChem., 1988–91. *Recreation:* growing and cooking vegetables. *Address:* Greenman Farm, Wadhurst, E Sussex TN5 6LE. *T:* Wadhurst (089288) 3292.

HARTHAN, John Plant, MA, FLA; Keeper of the Library, Victoria and Albert Museum, 1962–76; *b* 15 April 1916; *y s* of late Dr George Ezra Harthan, Evesham, Worcs, and Winifred May Slater. *Educ:* Bryanston; Jesus Coll., Cambridge; University Coll., London. Asst-Librarian, Southampton Univ., 1940–43; Royal Society of Medicine Library, 1943–44; Asst Under-Librarian, Cambridge Univ. Library, 1944–48; Asst-Keeper of the Library, Victoria and Albert Museum, 1948. FLA 1939. *Publications:* Bookbindings in the Victoria and Albert Museum, 1950, 3rd edn 1985; co-editor, F.D. Klingender, Animals in Art and Thought, 1971; Books of Hours, 1977, 3rd edn 1988; The History of the Illustrated Book, 1981; Introduction to Illuminated Manuscripts, 1983. *Recreations:* history of religion, royalty, music, botany, writing. *Address:* Ludshott Manor, Bramshott, Hants GU30 7RD.

HARTILL, Edward Theodore, FRICS; City Surveyor, Corporation of London, since 1985; *b* 23 Jan. 1943; *s* of Clement Augustus Hartill and late Florence Margarita Hartill; *m* 1975, Gillian Ruth (*née* Todd); two *s*, and two *s* from previous marr. *Educ:* Priory Sch. for Boys, Shrewsbury; Coll. of Estate Management, London Univ. BSc (Estate Management); FRICS 1978. Joined Messrs Burd and Evans, Land Agents, Shrewsbury, 1963; Estates Dept, Legal and Gen. Assce Soc., 1964–73; Property Investment Dept, Guardian Royal Exchange Assce Gp, 1973–85. Vis. Lectr in Law of Town Planning and Compulsory Purchase, Hammersmith and W London Coll. of Advanced Business Studies, 1968–78. Royal Institution of Chartered Surveyors: Mem., City Br. Cttee, 1986–; Mem., Gen. Practice Divl Council, 1989–; Mem., Gen. Council, 1990– (Jun. Vice Chm., 1990–91). Member: Nat. Exec. Cttee, Local Authority Valuers Assoc., 1988–; British Schs Exploring Soc. Liveryman, Worshipful Co. of Chartered Surveyors, 1985–. *Publications:* occasional lectures and articles on professional topics. *Recreations:* travel, hill walking, cinema, family. *Address:* 215 Sheen Lane, East Sheen, SW14 8LE. *T:* 081–878 4494.

See also R. J. Hartill.

HARTILL, Rosemary Jane; broadcaster and writer; Religious Affairs Correspondent, BBC, 1982–88; *b* 11 Aug. 1949; *d* of Clement Augustus Hartill and late Florence Margarita Ford. *Educ:* Wellington Girls' High Sch., Salop; Bristol Univ. (BA (Hons) English). Editor: Tom Stacey (Publishing) Ltd, 1970–73; David and Charles Ltd, 1973–75; Sen. Non-Fiction Editor, Hamish Hamilton Children's Books Ltd, 1975–76; freelance journalist and broadcaster, 1976–82; freelance book and ballet reviewer, TES, 1976–80; Religious Affairs Reporter, BBC, 1979–82; Reporter: BBC Everyman Prog., 1987; ITV Human Factor series, 1989–91; Presenter, BBC Woman's Hour (NE edns), 1989–90. *Publications:* (ed) Emily Brontë: poems, 1973; Wild Animals, 1978; In Perspective, 1988; Writers Revealed, 1989. *Recreations:* theatre, films, wildlife, hill-walking, ballet, being in Northumberland. *Address:* The Old Post Office, 24 Eglingham Village, Alnwick, Northumberland NE66 2TX. *T:* Powburn (066578) 543.

See also E. T. Hartill.

HARTINGTON, Marquess of; Peregrine Andrew Morny Cavendish; *b* 27 April 1944; *s* of 11th Duke of Devonshire, *qv*; *m* 1967, Amanda Carmen, *d* of late Comdr E. G. Heywood-Lonsdale, RN, and of Mrs Heywood-Lonsdale; one *s* two *d*. *Educ:* Eton; Exeter Coll., Oxford. Sen. Steward, Jockey Club, 1989–. *Heir:* *s* Earl of Burlington, *qv*. *Address:* Beamsley Hall, Skipton, N Yorks BD23 6HD.

HARTLAND-SWANN, Julian Dana Nimmo; HM Diplomatic Service; Ambassador to Burma, since 1990; *b* 18 Feb. 1936; *s* of late Prof. J. J. Hartland-Swann and of Mrs Kenlis Hartland-Swann (*née* Taylour); *m* 1960, Ann Deirdre Green; one *s* one *d*. *Educ:* Stowe; Lincoln Coll., Oxford (History). HM Forces, 1955–57. Entered HM Diplomatic Service, 1960; 3rd Sec., Brit. Embassy, Bangkok, 1961–65; 2nd, later 1st Sec., FO, 1965–68; 1st Sec., Berlin, 1968–71; 1st Sec. and Head of Chancery, Vienna, 1971–74; FCO, 1975–77; Counsellor, 1977; Ambassador to Mongolian People's Republic, 1977–79; Counsellor and Head of Chancery, Brussels, 1979–83; Head of SE Asian Dept, FCO, 1983–85; Consul Gen., Frankfurt, 1986–90. *Recreations:* French food, sailing, restoring ruins. *Address:* c/o Foreign and Commonwealth Office, SW1A 2AH.

HARTLEY, Arthur Coulton, CIE 1946; OBE 1943; ICS (retired); *b* 24 March 1906; *s* of late John Aspinall Hartley and Jennie Hartley; *m* 1943, Mrs Cecilie Leslie; one *s*. *Educ:* Cowley Grammar Sch.; Manchester Univ.; Balliol Coll., Oxford. Entered Indian Civil Service, 1929; Asst Magistrate, Comilla, Bengal, 1929–30; Subdivisional Magistrate, Sirajganj, Bengal, 1930–32; Asst Settlement Officer, Rangpur, Bengal, 1932–34; Settlement Officer, Rangpur, Bengal, 1934–37; Asst Sec. to Governor of Bengal, 1938–40; District Magistrate, Howrah, Bengal, 1940–43; Controller of Rationing, Calcutta, Bengal, 1943–45; Dir-Gen. of Food, Bengal, India, 1945–47. *Publication:* Report on Survey and Settlement Operations of Rangpur, 1938. *Recreations:* hill walking, painting. *Address:* 12 Grange Road, Lewes, E Sussex BN7 1TR.

HARTLEY, Brian Joseph, CMG 1950; OBE 1945 (MBE 1934); *b* 1907; *s* of late John Joseph Hartley, Tring, Herts; *m* 1951, Doreen Mary, *d* of Col R. G. Sanders; three *s* one *d*. *Educ:* Loughborough; Midland Agricultural Coll.; Wadham Coll., Oxford; Imperial Coll. of Tropical Agriculture, Trinidad. Entered Colonial Service; Agricultural Officer, Tanganyika, 1929; Aden Protectorate: Agricultural Officer, 1938; Asst Comdt, Govt Guards Auxiliaries (Camel Corps, Subeihi), 1940; Agricultural Adviser, 1944; Dir of Agriculture, 1946–54; retd 1954; Chief, FAO(UN), mission in Iraq, 1955; Mem., Tanganyika Agricultural Corporation, 1956–62; Trustee, Tanganyika Nat. Parks, 1957–64; Mem., Ngorongoro Conservation Authority Advisory Board, 1963–64. UN (Special Fund) Consultant Team Leader, Kafue Basin Survey, N Rhodesia, 1960; Team Leader, Livestock Develt Survey, Somalia, 1966; Chief Livestock Adviser, FAO, Somalia, 1967–70; Project Manager, UNSF Survey of Northern Rangelands Project, Somalia, 1970–72; Consultant, FAO-IBRD Project, Anatolia, Turkey, 1972–73; Consultant, ODA, Wadi Rima and Montane Plains, Yemen Arab Republic, 1975; Consultant, 1973–76, Technical Manager, 1976–79, World Bank Nomadic Rangelands Project, Ethiopia; Consultant: Oxfam Karamoja Relief Prog. in Uganda, 1980; Oxfam E Africa, 1981–85; Oxfam Red Sea Province, Relief Project, Sudan, Jan./Feb. 1988. Estabd Tanganyika Camel Co., 1987. Consultant: Food and Agricl Res. Management; Africa Camel Project, Oman, 1989. *Publications:* Camels in the Horn of Africa, 1979; (contrib.) The Camelid, 1985; Scientific report, Camelus dromedarius in N Tanzania, 1987 (following the introduction of camels to Tanzania by the author). *Address:* Box 337, Malindi, Kenya.

HARTLEY, Prof. Brian Selby, PhD; FRS 1971; Professor of Biochemistry, Imperial College, University of London, since 1974 and Director, Centre for Biotechnology, since 1982; *b* 16 April 1926; *s* of Norman and Hilda Hartley; *m* 1949, Kathleen Maude Vaughan; three *s* one *d*. *Educ:* Queens' Coll., Cambridge; Univ. of Leeds. BA 1947, MA 1952, Cantab; PhD 1952, Leeds. ICI Fellow, Univ. of Cambridge, 1952; Helen Hay Whitney Fellow, Univ. of Washington, Seattle, USA, 1958; Fellow and Lectr in Biochemistry, Trinity Coll., Cambridge, 1964; Scientific Staff, MRC Laboratory of Molecular Biology, 1961–74. Mem. Council: EMBO (European Centre for Molecular Biology), 1978–84; Royal Soc., 1982–84. Hon. Mem., Amer. Soc. of Biological Chemists, 1977. British Drug Houses Medal for Analytical Biochemistry, 1969. *Publications:* papers and articles in scientific jls and books. *Recreations:* fishing, gardening. *Address:* Imperial College of Science and Technology, SW7 2AZ.

HARTLEY, Air Marshal Sir Christopher (Harold), KCB 1963 (CB 1961); CBE 1957 (OBE 1949); DFC 1945; AFC 1944; BA Oxon; *b* 31 Jan. 1913; *s* of late Brig.-Gen. Sir Harold Hartley, GCVO, CH, CBE, MC, FRS; *m* 1st, 1937, Anne Sitwell (marr. diss., 1943); 2nd, 1944, Margaret Watson; two *s*. *Educ:* Eton; Balliol Coll., Oxford (Williams Exhibnr); King's Coll., Cambridge. Zoologist on Oxford Univ. expeditions: to Sarawak, 1932; Spitsbergen, 1933; Greenland, 1937. Asst Master at Eton Coll., 1937–39. Joined RAFVR, 1938. Served War of 1939–45: 604 Sqdn, 256 Sqdn, Fighter Interception Unit, Central Fighter Establishment. Permanent Commission, 1945; AOC 12 Group, Fighter Command, 1959; ACAS (Operational Requirements), Air Min., 1961; DCAS, 1963–66; Controller of Aircraft, Min. of Aviation and Min. of Technology, 1966–70, retired. Dep. Chm., British Hovercraft Corporation, 1979– (Chm., 1974–78); Dir, Westland Aircraft Ltd, 1971–83. *Recreation:* fishing. *Address:* c/o Barclays Bank, PO Box 36, Bank Plain, Norwich NR2 4SP. *Club:* Travellers'.

HARTLEY, David Fielding, PhD; FBCS; Director, University Computing Service, University of Cambridge, since 1970; Fellow of Clare College, Cambridge, since 1987; *b* 14 Sept. 1937; *s* of late Robert M. Hartley and late Sheila E. Hartley, LRAM; *m* 1960, Joanna Mary, *d* of Stanley and Constance Bolton; one *s* two *d*. *Educ:* Rydal Sch.; Clare Coll., Cambridge (MA, PhD). Mathematical Laboratory, Univ. of Cambridge: Sen. Asst in Research, 1964–65; Asst Dir of Research, 1966–67; Univ. Lectr, 1967–70; Jun. Research Fellow, Churchill Coll., Cambridge, 1964–67; Fellow, Darwin Coll., Cambridge, 1969–86. British Computer Society: Mem. Council, 1970–73, 1977–80, 1985–90; Vice Pres. (Technical), 1985–87, (External Relns), 1987–90. Chm., Inter-University Cttee on Computing, 1972–74; Mem., Computer Board for Univs and Research Councils, 1979–83; Mem. Council of Management, Numerical Algorithms Gp Ltd, 1979– (Chm., 1986–); adviser to Prime Minister, Information Technology Adv. Panel, 1981–86; DTI Hon. Adviser in Information Technology (on sabbatical leave), 1983; Mem. various Govt, Res. Council and Industry cttees and consultancies. Mem., BBC Science Consultative Gp, 1984–87. Dir, CADCentre Ltd, 1983–. Governor, Rydal Sch., 1982–88. Medal of Merits, Nicholas Copernicus Univ., Poland, 1984. *Publications:* papers in scientific jls on operating systems, programming languages, computing service management. *Address:* 26 Girton Road, Cambridge CB3 0LL. *T:* Cambridge (0223) 276975.

HARTLEY, Sir Frank, Kt 1977; CBE 1970; PhD London, CChem, FRPharmS, FRSC; Vice-Chancellor, University of London, 1976–78; Dean of the School of Pharmacy, University of London, 1962–76; *b* 5 Jan. 1911; *s* of late Robinson King Hartley and Mary Hartley (*née* Holt); *m* 1937, Lydia May England; two *s*. *Educ:* Municipal Secondary (later Grammar) Sch., Nelson, Lancs; Sch. of Pharmacy (Fellow, 1977), University Coll. (Fellow, 1972), and Birkbeck Coll. (Fellow, 1970), University of London. Jacob Bell Schol., 1930, Silver Medallist in Pharmaceutics, Pharmaceut. Chem. and Pharmacognosy, 1932. Pharmaceutical Chemist, 1932, Demonstrator and Lectr, 1932–40, at Sch. of Pharmacy; 1st cl. hons BSc (Chem.), University of London, 1936, and PhD, 1941; Chief Chemist, Organon Laboratories Ltd, 1940–43; Sec., Therapeutic Research Corp., 1943–46; Sec., Gen. Penicillin Cttee (Min. of Supply), 1943–46; Dir of Research and Sci. Services, The British Drug Houses, Ltd, 1946–62; Chm. Brit. Pharmaceut. Conf., 1957, and of Sci. Adv. Cttee of Pharmaceut. Soc. of Great Britain, 1964–66; Mem. Council, 1955–58, 1961–64, Vice-Pres., 1958–60, 1964–65, 1967–69, Pres., 1965–67, of Royal Institute of Chemistry; Hon. Treasurer, 1956–61, Chm. 1964–68 of Chem. Council; Mem. 1953–80, Vice-Chm. 1963–68, Chm. 1970–80, of British Pharmacopoeia Commn (Mem., Nomenclature Cttee, 1946–), and a UK Deleg., 1964–80, to European Pharmacopoeia Commn; Mem., 1970–84, Vice-Chm., 1977–84, Medicines Commn; Member: Poisons Bd (Home Office), 1958–66; Cttee on Safety of Drugs (Min. of Health), 1963–70; Cttee on Prevention of Microbiol Contamination of Medicinal Products, 1972–73; Nat. Biological Standards Bd, 1975–83; Cttee of Enquiry on Contaminated Infusion Fluids, 1972; NW Thames RHA Univ. Liaison Cttee, 1984–89; Chairman: Bd of Studies in Pharmacy, Univ. of London, 1964–68; Pharmacy Bd, CNAA, 1965–77; Collegiate Council, 1969–73; Panel on Grading of Chief Pharmacists in Teaching Hosps, 1972–74, Qualified Person Adv. Cttee, DHSS, 1979; Comrs for Lambeth, Southwark and Lewisham Health Area, 1979–80; Pharmacy Working Gp, Nat. Adv. Bd for Higher Educn, Local Authorities, 1982–84; Health Care Sci. Adv. Cttee, Council of Science and Technol. Insts, 1982–86; Working Gp on Cardiothoracic Surgery Options, 1986–87; Member: Academic Council, 1969–73; British Council for Prevention of Blindness, 1975– (Chm., 1988–). Co-opted Mem. Senate, 1968–76, 1978–88, ex officio Mem., 1976–78, Senate Mem. of Court, 1970–76, 1978–88, ex officio Mem., 1976–78, Dep. Vice-Chancellor, 1973–76, University of London; Member Council: St Thomas's Hosp. Medical Sch., University of London, 1968–80; Royal Free Hosp. Med. Sch., 1970–88; Mem., Consultative Bd of Regents, Univ. of Qatar, 1978–; Member Bd of Governors: Royal Free Hosp. Gp, 1970–74; Kingston Polytechnic, 1970–75; British Postgrad. Med. Fedn, London Univ., 1972–89; Royal Postgrad. Med. Sch., 1972– (Vice-Chm., 1989–); Inst. of Basic Med. Sci, 1973–86, subseq. Hunterian Inst., RCS, 1986–. Chm., Consortium of Charing Cross and Westminster Med. Schs, London Univ., 1981–84. Lectures: Sir William Pope Meml, RSA, 1962; Wilkinson, Inst. of Dental Surg., 1978; Astor, Middlesex Hosp. Med. Sch., 1980; Bernal, Birkbeck Coll., 1982; Association, Hosp. Physicists Assoc., 1986. Hon. FRCP 1979; Hon. FRCS 1980 (Mem. Finance Bd, RCS, 1985–); Hon. FRSC 1981; Hon. Fellow: Hosp. Physicists Assoc., 1986; Imperial Coll. of Science, Technol. and Medicine, 1990. Liveryman, Worshipful Soc. of Apothecaries of London, 1958. Freeman, City of London, 1959. Hon. DSc Warwick, 1978; Hon. LLD: Strathclyde, 1980; London, 1987. Charter Gold Medal, Pharm. Soc. of GB, 1974. *Publications:* papers on chem. and pharmaceut. research in Quarterly Jl of Pharmacy, Jl of Pharmacy and Pharmacology and Jl of Chem. Soc. Reviews and articles in sci. and tech. jls. *Recreations:* reading, watching sport. *Address:* 24 Old School Close, St Mary's Mead, Merton Park, SW19 3HY. *T:* 081–542 7198. *Club:* Athenæum.

See also F. R. Hartley.

HARTLEY, Prof. Frank Robinson, CChem, FRSC; Vice-Chancellor, Cranfield Institute of Technology, since 1989; Director: CIT (Holdings) Ltd, since 1989; Cranfield Ventures Ltd; *b* 29 Jan. 1942; *s* of Sir Frank Hartley, *qv*; *m* 1964, Valerie Peel; three *d*. *Educ:* King's College Sch., Wimbledon (Sambrooke Schol.); Magdalen Coll., Oxford (Demy; BA, MA, DPhil, DSc). Post-doctoral Fellow, Commonwealth Scientific and Industrial Research Organisation, Div. of Protein Chemistry, Melbourne, Aust., 1966–69; Imperial Chemical Industries Research Fellow and Tutor in Physical Chemistry, University Coll. London, 1969–70; Lectr in Inorganic Chemistry, Univ. of Southampton, 1970–75; Professor of Chemistry and Head of Dept of Chemistry and Metallurgy, 1975–82, Acting Dean, 1982–84, Principal and Dean, 1984–89, RMCS, Shrivenham. Chm., Cranfield IT Inst., 1989–90 (Dir, 1986–89); Non-Executive Director: T & N, 1989–; Eastern Regl Adv. Bd, National Westminster Bank, 1990–. Sen. Travelling Fellow, ACU, 1986. Special Advr to Prime Minister on defence systems, 1988–. Gov., Welbeck Coll., 1984–89; Mem. Court, Bath Univ., 1982–89. Mem., Oxford Union. FRSA. Editor-in-Chief, Brassey's New Battlefield Weapons Systems and Technology series, 1988–. *Publications:* The Chemistry of Platinum and Palladium (Applied Science), 1973; Elements of Organometallic Chemistry (Chemical Soc.), 1974, Japanese edn 1981, Chinese edn 1989; (with C. Burgess and R. M. Alcock) Solution Equilibria, 1980, Russian edn 1983; (with S. Patai) The Chemistry of the Metal—Carbon Bond, vol. 1 1983, vol. 2 1984, vol. 3 1985, vol. 4 1987, vol. 5 1989; Supported Metal Complexes, 1985, Russian edn 1987; The Chemistry of Organophosphorus Compounds, vol. 1, 1990; papers in inorganic, coordination and organometallic chemistry in major English, Amer. and Aust. chemical jls. *Recreations:* Rugby refereeing, golf, swimming, squash, gardening, cliff walking, reading. *Address:* Cayley Lodge, Cranfield Institute of Technology, Wharley End, Cranfield, Bedford MK43 0SX. *Clubs:* Institute of Directors; Shrivenham.

HARTLEY, His Honour Gilbert Hillard; a Circuit Judge (formerly Judge of County Courts), 1967–82; *b* 11 Aug. 1917; *s* of late Percy Neave Hartley and late Nellie Bond (*née* Hillard); *m* 1948, Jeanne, *d* of late C. W. Gall, Leeds; one *s* two *d*. *Educ:* Ashville, Harrogate; Exeter Coll. Oxford. Called to Bar, Middle Temple, 1939. Served with Army, 1940–46. Recorder of Rotherham, 1965–67; Dep. Chm., WR of Yorkshire QS, 1965–71. *Address:* Nidd Rise, Main Street, Moor Monkton, York YO5 8JA.

HARTLEY, Ven. Peter Harold Trahair; Archdeacon of Suffolk, 1970–75, now Archdeacon Emeritus; *b* 11 July 1909; *m* 1938, Ursula Mary Trahair; two *d*. *Educ:* Leys School; University of London (BSc 1935); Queen's College, Oxford (MA 1948); Cuddesdon Theological College. Deacon 1953, Priest 1954, Diocese of St Edmundsbury; Curate of Dennington and Badingham, 1953–55; Rector of Badingham, 1955, with Bruisyard, 1960, and Cransford, 1974; Priest-in-Charge, Badingham with Bruisyard and Dennington, 1976–85. Rural Dean of Loes, 1967–70. *Publications:* papers in zoological journals. *Recreations:* natural history, naval and military history. *Address:* 26 Double Street, Framlingham, Woodbridge, Suffolk IP13 9BN. *T:* Framlingham (0728) 723604.

HARTLEY, Richard Leslie Clifford, QC 1976; *b* 31 May 1932; *s* of late Arthur Clifford Hartley, CBE and late Nina Hartley. *Educ:* Marlborough Coll.; Sidney Sussex Coll., Cambridge (MA). Called to the Bar, Gray's Inn, 1956, Bencher, 1986. *Recreations:* golf, tennis. *Address:* 15 Chesham Street, SW1. *T:* 071–235 2420. *Clubs:* Garrick, MCC; Woking Golf, Rye Golf, St Enodoc Golf.

HARTLING, Poul; Grand Cross of Dannebrog; United Nations High Commissioner for Refugees, 1978–85; Member of Folketing, Denmark, 1957–60 and 1964–78; *b* 14 Aug. 1914; *s* of Mads Hartling and Mathilde (*née* Nielsen); *m* 1940, Elsebeth Kirkemann; three *s* one *d*. *Educ:* Univ. of Copenhagen (Master of Divinity 1939). Curate, Frederiksberg Church, 1941–45; Chaplain, St Luke Foundn, 1945–50; Principal, Zahle's Teachers' Trng Coll., 1950–68. Chm., Liberal Party Parly Group, 1965–68; Mem., Nordic Council, 1964–68 (Pres., 1966–68); Minister of Foreign Affairs, 1968–71; Prime Minister, 1973–75; Chm., Liberal Party, 1964–78. Secretary: Christian Academic Soc., 1934–35; Christian Movement of Sen. Secondary Students, 1939–43. Dr *hc* Valparaiso Univ., Indiana, 1981. Grand-Croix: l'Ordre de la Couronne, Belgique; l'Ordre de Mennlik II, Ethiopie; Grosskreuz des Verdienstordens der Bundesrep, Deutschland; Royal Order of St Olav, Norway; Falcon of Iceland; Merit of Luxembourg; Yugoslovenske Zvezde. *Publications:* Sursum Corda, 1942; Growth of church idea in the missionary field, 1945; (ed) Church, School, Culture, 1963; The Danish Church, 1964 (2nd edn 1967); From 17 Years in Danish Politics, 1974; Autobiography vol. I, 1980, vol. II, 1981, vol. III, 1983, vol. IV, 1985; Erik Eriksen (biog.), 1990. *Recreation:* music. *Address:* Emilievej 6 E, DK 2920 Charlottenlund, Denmark.

HARTMAN, (Gladys) Marea, CBE 1978 (MBE 1967); *b* 1920. Competed as a runner for Spartan Athletic Club and Surrey County; team manager, British athletics team at Olympic and European Games and English athletics team at Commonwealth Games, 1956–78; Head of Delegn, World Championships, European Championships, English Internat. athletics teams and Commonwealth Games teams, 1978–. Mem., Women's Commn of Internat. Amateur Athletic Fedn, 1958– (Chm., 1968–81); Hon. Treasurer, British Amateur Athletic Bd, 1972–84 (Life Vice-Pres., 1980; Chm., 1989–); Hon. Sec., Women's AAA, 1960– (Hon. Treasurer, 1950–60; Life Vice-Pres., 1970; Vice-Chm., 1981–); Hon. Treasurer, CCPR, 1984– (Dep. Chm., 1981–83); Hon. Life Mem., IAAF, 1987. FIPM. *Recreations:* music, reading, theatre. *Address:* c/o Women's Amateur Athletic Association, Francis House, Francis Street, SW1P 1DE. *T:* 071–828 4731, *Telex:* 8956058, *Fax:* 071–630 8820.

HARTNACK, Paul Richard Samuel; Comptroller General and Chief Executive, The Patent Office, since 1990: *b* 17 Nov. 1942; *s* of Carl Samuel and Maud Godden Hartnack; *m* 1966, Marion Quirk; two *s*. *Educ:* Hastings Grammar Sch. Clerical and Exec. posts, BoT, 1961–67; Asst Sec., Cttee of Enquiry into Civil Air Transport, 1967–68; Second Sec., British Embassy, Paris, 1969–71; Exec. posts, DTI, 1972–78; Asst Sec., NEB, 1978–80; Sec., Brit. Technology Gp, 1981–85; Asst Sec., Finance and Resource Management Div., DTI, 1985–89. *Recreation:* gardening. *Address:* The Patent Office, Cardiff Road, Newport, Gwent NP9 1RH. *T:* Newport (Gwent) (0633) 814502.

HARTOG, Harold Samuel Arnold; Knight, Order of the Netherlands Lion; KBE (Hon.) 1970; Advisory Director, Unilever NV, 1971–75; *b* Nijmegen, Holland, 21 Dec. 1910; *m* 1963, Ingeborg Luise Krahn. *Educ:* Wiedemann Coll., Geneva. Joined Unilever, 1931. After service with Dutch forces during War of 1939–45 he joined management of Unilever interests in France, and subseq. took charge of Unilever cos in the Netherlands; elected to Bds of Unilever, 1948; Mem. Rotterdam Group Management and responsible for Unilever activities in Germany, Austria and Belgium, 1952–60; subseq. Mem. Cttee for Unilever's overseas interests, in London; became, there, one of the two world co-ordinators of Unilever's foods interests, 1962; Chm., Unilever NV, 1966–71. *Recreations:* history of art; collecting Chinese pottery and porcelain. *Address:* Kösterbergstrasse 40B, D-2000 Hamburg (Blankensee), Germany. *Clubs:* Dutch; Ubersee (Hamburg); Golf (Falkenstein).

HARTOPP, Sir John Edmund Cradock-, 9th Bt, *cr* 1796; TD; *b* 8 April 1912; *s* of late Francis Gerald Cradock-Hartopp, Barbrook, Chatsworth, Bakewell, Derbyshire (kinsman of 8th Bt) and Elizabeth Ada Mary (*née* Stuart); *S* kinsman, Sir George Francis Fleetwood Cradock-Hartopp, 1949; *m* 1953, Prudence, 2nd *d* of Sir Frederick Leith-Ross, GCMG, KCB; three *d*. *Educ:* Summer Fields, Oxford; Uppingham Sch. Travelled in United States of America before joining at age of 18, Staff of Research Laboratories, Messrs Thos Firth & John Brown Ltd, Steel Makers, Sheffield, 1930; travelled in India and the Far East, 1948–49; Dir, Firth Brown Tools Ltd, 1961–76. War of 1939–45 (despatches twice); joined TA and served with Royal Engineers in UK; Norway, 1940; North Africa (1st Army), 1943; Italy, 1943–45; released, 1945, with rank of Major. Mem. Council: Machine Tool Research Assoc., 1965–70; Machine Tool Trades Assoc., 1970–73. *Recreations:* golf (semi-finalist English Golf Champ., 1935; first reserve, Eng. *v* France, 1935); cricket, tennis, motoring. *Heir: cousin* Lt-Comdr Kenneth Alston Cradock-Hartopp, MBE, DSC, RN [*b* 26 Feb. 1918; *m* 1942, Gwendolyn Amy Lilian Upton; one *d*]. *Address:* The Cottage, 27 Wool Road, Wimbledon Common, SW20. *Clubs:* East India, MCC; Royal and Ancient (St Andrews).

HARTWELL, Baron, *cr* 1968 (Life Peer), of Peterborough Court in the City of London; **(William) Michael Berry,** MBE 1944; TD; Chairman and Editor-in-Chief: The Daily Telegraph, 1954–87; Sunday Telegraph, 1961–87; *b* 18 May 1911; 2nd *s* of 1st Viscount Camrose and Mary Agnes, *e d* of late Thomas Corns, London; *m* 1936, Lady Pamela Margaret Elizabeth Smith (*d* 1982), *yr d* of 1st Earl of Birkenhead, PC, GCSI, KC; two *s* two *d*. *Educ:* Eton (Captain of Oppidans; Editor of Chronicle); Christ Church, Oxford (MA). 2nd Lieut 11th (City of London Yeo.) Light AA Bde, RA (TA), 1938; served War of 1939–45; Capt. and Major, 1940; Lieut-Col 1944 (despatches twice, MBE). Editor, Sunday Mail, Glasgow, 1934–35; Managing Editor, Financial Times, 1937–39; Chm. Amalgamated Press Ltd, 1954–59. Dir, and subseq. Dep. Chm., LWT, 1968–81. Trustee, Reuters, 1962–89. *Publication:* Party Choice, 1948. *Address:* 18 Cowley Street, Westminster, SW1. *T:* 071–222 4673; Oving House, Whitchurch, near Aylesbury, Bucks. *T:* Aylesbury (0296) 641307. *Clubs:* White's, Beefsteak; Royal Yacht Squadron.
See also Viscount Camrose.

HARTWELL, Benjamin James, OBE 1959; Clerk to Southport Borough Justices, 1943–73; *b* Southport, 24 June 1908; *s* of late Joseph Hartwell, Bucks, and late Margaret Ann Hartwell; *m* 1937, Mary (*née* Binns) (*d* 1986), Southport; one *s* one *d*. *Educ:* Kirkcudbright Acad.; King George V Sch., Southport; London Univ. (LLM). Admitted a Solicitor of the Supreme Court, 1936; Hon. Sec. Justices' Clerks' Soc., 1947–59; Pres. Lancs and Cheshire Dist of Boys' Brigade, 1950–63; Chm. Council, Congregational Union of England and Wales, 1952–58; Chm. Congregational Union of England and Wales 1959–60. Member: Central Cttee, World Council of Churches, 1954–61; Home Secretary's Advisory Council on the Treatment of Offenders, 1955–63. *Address:* Willow Cottage, New Road, Pamber Green, near Basingstoke, Hants RG26 6AG.

HARTWELL, Sir Brodrick William Charles Elwin, 5th Bt, *cr* 1805; *b* 7 Aug. 1909; *s* of Sir Brodrick Cecil Denham Arkwright Hartwell, 4th Bt, and Joan Amy (*d* 1962), *o d* of Robert Milne Jeffrey, Esquimault, Vancouver; *S* father, 1948; *m* 1st, 1937, Marie Josephine, *d* of late S. P. Mullins (marriage dissolved 1950); one *s*; 2nd, 1951, Mary Maude, MBE, *d* of J. W. Church, Bedford; one *d* decd. *Educ:* Bedford Sch. Sometime Pilot Officer RAF. Served War of 1939–45; Capt. Leics Regt, 1943. *Heir: s* Francis Antony Charles Peter Hartwell [*b* 1 June 1940; *m* 1968, Barbara Phyllis Rae, *d* of H. Rae Green; one *s*]. *Address:* Little Dale, 50 High Street, Lavendon, Olney, Bucks.

HARTWELL, Eric, CBE 1983; Vice-Chairman, Trusthouse Forte plc, since 1972 (Chief Executive, 1979–82, Joint Chief Executive, 1982–83); *b* 10 Aug. 1915; *m* 1st, 1937, Gladys Rose Bennett (marr. diss.); one *s* one *d*; 2nd, 1952, Dorothy Maud Mowbray; one *s* one *d*. *Educ:* Mall Sch., Twickenham; Worthing High School. FHCIMA; CBIM. Electrical industry, 1932–37; Dir, Fortes & Co. Ltd, 1938; HM Forces, 1940–45; Jt Man. Dir, Forte Holdings Ltd, 1962; Dep. Man. Dir, Trust Houses Forte Ltd, 1970; Dep. Chief Exec., Trust Houses Forte Ltd, 1972–75, Jt Chief Exec., 1975–78. Chm., BHRCA, 1981–85. Mem. Nat. Council, CBI, 1971–86 (Chm., Finance Sub-Cttee, 1981–86). Mem. Council, Thames Heritage Trust Ltd, 1981– (Vice-Chm., 1983–87); Mem. Cttee, Nuffield Hosp., Enfield, 1984–87; Dir, LV Catering Educn Trust Ltd, 1965–87. Liveryman, Upholders' Co., 1952–. FRSA 1984. *Recreations:* yachting, painting, photography, golf. *Address:* Tall Trees, 129 Totteridge Lane, N20 8NS. *T:* 081–445 2321. *Clubs:* National Sporting, River Emergency Service Association, Inner Magic Circle; Thames Motor Yacht; South Herts Golf.

HARTY, Bernard Peter; Chamberlain, City of London Corporation, since 1983; *b* 1 May 1943; *s* of William Harty and Eileen Nora (*née* Canavan); *m* 1965, Glenys Elaine Simpson; one *d*. *Educ:* Ullathorne Grammar Sch., Coventry. CIPFA 1966; MBCS 1983. Accountant, Coventry CBC, 1961–69; Forward Budget Planning Officer, Derbyshire CC, 1969–72; Chief Accountant, Bradford CBC, 1972–74; Chief Finance Officer, Bradford MDC, 1973–76; County Treasurer, Oxfordshire CC, 1976–83. Mem. Nat. Cttee, Information Technol. Year 1982 (IT82); Chm., IT82 Local Govt Cttee, 1982. Chm., Foundn for IT in Local Govt, 1988–. Gov., Oxford Poly. Higher Educn Corp., 1989–. Freeman, City of London, 1983; Liveryman, Worshipful Co. of Tallow Chandlers, 1984; Founder Mem., Co. of Information Technologists, 1987–. *Publications:* papers in professional jls. *Recreations:* theatre, music, National Trust, cricket. *Address:* Chamber of London, PO Box 270, Guildhall, EC2P 2EJ. *T:* 071–606 3030.

HARTY, Most Rev. Michael; *see* Killaloe, Bishop of, (RC).

HARUNA, Alhaji; *see* Gwandu, Emir of.

HARVEY, family name of **Barons Harvey of Prestbury** and **Harvey of Tasburgh.**

HARVEY OF PRESTBURY, Baron *cr* 1971 (Life Peer), of Prestbury in the County Palatine of Chester; **Arthur Vere Harvey,** Kt 1957; CBE 1942; FRAeS; *b* 31 Jan. 1906; *e s* of A. W. Harvey, Kessingland, Suffolk; *m* 1st, 1940, Jacqueline Anne (marr. diss., 1954), *o d* of W. H. Dunnett; two *s*; 2nd, 1955, Mrs Hilary Charmian Williams (marr. diss. 1977); 3rd, 1978, Mrs Carol Cassar Torreggiani; three adopted *d*. *Educ:* Framlingham Coll. Royal Air Force 1925–30, qualified as flying instructor; Dir of Far East Aviation Co. Ltd and Far East Flying Training Sch. Ltd, Hong-Kong, 1930–35; Adviser to Southern Chinese Air Forces with hon. rank of Maj.-Gen., 1932–35; Sqdn Leader AAF, 1937, and founded 615 County of Surrey Squadron and commanded the Squadron in France, 1939–40 (despatches twice); Group Captain 1942; Air Commodore 1944. Dep. Chm., Handley-Page Ltd, 1951–57; Chm., Ciba-Geigy (UK) Ltd, 1957–74. MP (C) Macclesfield Div. of Cheshire, 1945–71; Chairman Cons. Members' 1922 Cttee, 1966–70. Vice-Pres. British Air Line Pilots' Assoc., 1965. FRAeS. Hon. Freeman: Macclesfield, 1969; Congleton, 1970. Hon. DSc Salford, 1972. Comdr, Order of Oranje Nassau, 1969. *Recreations:* private flying (4th King's Cup Race, 1937), sailing. *Address:* Rocklands, Les Vardes, St Peter Port, Guernsey, CI. *Clubs:* Buck's, Royal Air Force; Royal Yacht Squadron (Cowes).

HARVEY OF TASBURGH, 2nd Baron, *cr* 1954, of Tasburgh, Norfolk; **Peter Charles Oliver Harvey;** Bt 1868; FCA; *b* 28 Jan. 1921; *er s* of 1st Baron Harvey of Tasburgh, GCMG, GCVO, CB, and Maud Annora (*d* 1970), *d* of late Arthur Watkin Williams-Wynn; *S* father, 1968; *m* 1957, Penelope Anne, *d* of Lt-Col Sir William Makins, 3rd Bt; two *d*. *Educ:* Eton; Trinity College, Cambridge. Served 1941–46 with Royal Artillery, Tunisia, Italy. Bank of England, 1948–56; Binder Hamlyn & Co., 1956–61; Lloyds Bank International Ltd (formerly Bank of London and South America), 1961–75; English Transcontinental Ltd, 1975–78; Brown, Shipley & Co., 1978–81. *Recreations:* sailing, music. *Heir: nephew* Charles John Giuseppe Harvey, *b* 4 Feb. 1951. *Address:* Crownick Woods, Restronguet, Mylor, Falmouth, Cornwall TR11 5ST. *Clubs:* Brooks's; Royal Cornwall Yacht, Royal Fowey Yacht.

HARVEY, Alan Frederick Ronald, OBE 1970; HM Diplomatic Service, retired; *b* 15 Dec. 1919; *s* of Edward Frederick and Alice Sophia Harvey; *m* 1946, Joan Barbara (*née* Tuckey); one *s*. *Educ:* Tottenham Grammar Sch. Air Ministry, 1936–40 (Civil Service appt). Served War, RAF, 1940–46. Air Min., 1946–49; Foreign Office, 1949–52 (on transfer to Diplomatic Service); HM Vice-Consul, Turin, 1953–55; Second Sec.: Rome, 1956; Tokyo, 1957–59; HM Consul (Information): Chicago, 1959–62; FO, 1963–65; First Sec. (Commercial): Belgrade, 1965–67; Tokyo, 1967–72; Commercial Counsellor: Milan, 1973–74; Rome, 1975–76; Consul-General in Perth, 1976–78. *Recreations:* tennis, golf. *Address:* The Mews, Leigh Court, Forton, near Chard, Somerset TA20 4HW. *Clubs:* Commonwealth Trust, Civil Service; Windwhistle Golf, Squash and Country (Cricket St Thomas).

HARVEY, Rev. Canon Anthony Ernest, DD; Canon of Westminster since 1982, Librarian since 1983, and Sub-Dean since 1987; *b* 1 May 1930; *s* of Cyril Harvey, QC, and Nina (*née* Darley); *m* 1957, Julian Elizabeth McMaster; four *d*. *Educ:* Dragon Sch., Oxford; Eton Coll.; Worcester Coll., Oxford (BA, MA, DD 1983); Westcott House, Cambridge. Curate, Christ Church, Chelsea, 1958; Research Student, Christ Church, Oxford, 1962; Warden, St Augustine's Coll., Canterbury, 1969; Univ. Lectr in Theology and Fellow of Wolfson Coll., Oxford, 1976; Chaplain, The Queen's Coll., 1977. Examining Chaplain to Archbishop of Canterbury, 1975; Six Preacher, Canterbury Cathedral, 1977; Bampton Lectr, 1980. Member: Gen. Synod Doctrine Commn, 1977–86; Archbishop's Commn on Urban Priority Areas, 1983–85. *Publications:* Companion to the New Testament (New English Bible), 1970, 2nd edn 1980; Priest or President?, 1975; Jesus on Trial, 1976; Something Overheard, 1977; (ed) God Incarnate: story and belief, 1981; Jesus and the Constraints of History, 1982; Believing and Belonging, 1984; (ed) Alternative Approaches to New Testament Study, 1985; (ed) Theology in the City, 1989; Strenuous Commands, 1990; articles in classical and theological jls. *Recreations:* music, walking. *Address:* 3 Little Cloister, Westminster Abbey, SW1. *T:* 071–222 4174.

HARVEY, Anthony Peter; Director, Natural History Museum Development Trust, since 1990; Head of Marketing and Development, British Museum (Natural History), since 1988; *b* 21 May 1940; *s* of Frederick William Henry Harvey and late Fanny Evelyn Harvey (*née* Dixon); *m* 1963, Margaret Hayward; three *s* one *d*. *Educ:* Hertford Grammar

Sch. MIInfS. Dept of Oriental Printed Books, British Museum, 1958–60; British Museum (Natural History): Dept of Palaeontology, 1960–75; Librarian, 1963–75; Head, Dept of Library Services, 1981–88; Co-ordinator of Planning and Development, 1985–88. Chm., Geology. Inf. Gp, 1975–78, Liby Cttee, 1981–84, Geolog. Soc.; Member: Printing Hist. Soc., 1965–; Garden Hist. Soc., 1988–; Soc. for Hist. of Natural Hist., 1963– (Treas., 1964–); RGS (Mem. Liby Cttee, 1985–). Freeman, City of London, 1985; Mem., Guild of Freemen, City of London, 1986–; Liveryman, Co. of Marketors, 1991. *Publications:* (ed) Secrets of the Earth, 1967; (ed) Directory of Scientific Directories, 1969, 4th edn 1986; Prehistoric Man, 1972; Guide to World Science, vol. 1, 1974; (ed) Encyclopedia of Prehistoric Life, 1979; European sources of scientific and technical information, 1981, 7th edn 1986; numerous contribs to learned jls, ref. works and periodicals. *Recreations:* music, books, gardens and gardening, the countryside. *Address:* Ragstones, Broad Oak, Heathfield, East Sussex TN21 8UD. *T:* Heathfield (0435) 862012.

HARVEY, Arthur Douglas; Assistant Under-Secretary of State, Ministry of Defence, 1969–76; *b* 16 July 1916; *o s* of late William Arthur Harvey and Edith Alice; *m* 1940, Doris Irene Lodge; one *s* (and one *s* decd). *Educ:* Westcliff High Sch.; St Catharine's Coll., Cambridge. Wrangler, Maths Tripos, 1938. Entered War Office, 1938; served in Army, 1940–45; Princ. 1945; Registrar, Royal Military College of Science, 1951–54; Asst Sec. 1954; Under-Sec. 1969. *Address:* 36b Lovelace Road, Long Ditton, Surrey. *T:* 081–399 0587.

HARVEY, Barbara Fitzgerald, FSA 1964; FBA 1982; Fellow of Somerville College, Oxford, since 1956; Reader (*ad hominem*) in Medieval History, Oxford University, since 1990; *b* 21 Jan. 1928; *d* of Richard Henry Harvey and Anne Fitzgerald (*née* Julian). *Educ:* Teignmouth Grammar Sch.; Bishop Blackall Sch., Exeter; Somerville Coll., Oxford (Schol.). First Cl. Final Honour Sch. of Modern History, Oxford, 1949; Bryce Student, Oxford Univ., 1950–51; BLitt Oxon 1953. Assistant, Dept of Scottish History, Edinburgh Univ., 1951–52; Asst Lectr, subseq. Lectr, Queen Mary Coll., London Univ., 1952–55; Tutor, Somerville Coll., Oxford, 1955–; Vice-Principal, 1976–79, 1981–83. Assessor, Oxford Univ., 1968–69. Ford's Lectr, Oxford, 1989. Mem., Royal Commn on Historical MSS, 1991–; A Vice-Pres., RHistS, 1986–. Gen. Editor, Oxford Medieval Texts, 1987–. *Publications:* Documents Illustrating the Rule of Walter de Wenlok, Abbot of Westminster 1283–1307, 1965; Westminster Abbey and its Estates in the Middle Ages, 1977; (ed, with L. C. Hector) The Westminster Chronicle 1381–94, 1982; contribs to Economic History Rev., Trans Royal Historical Soc., Bulletin of Inst. of Historical Research, etc. *Address:* Somerville College, Oxford OX2 6HD. *T:* Oxford (0865) 270600.

HARVEY, Benjamin Hyde, OBE 1968; FCA; IPFA; DPA; General Manager, Harlow Development Corporation, 1955–73; *b* 29 Sept. 1908; *s* of Benjamin Harvey and Elizabeth (*née* Hyde); *m* 1938, Heather Frances Broome; one *d*. *Educ:* Stationers' Company's Sch. Local Govt, 1924–40; Treas., Borough of Leyton, 1940–47; Comptroller, Harlow Develt Corp., 1947–55. Hon. LLD Newfoundland, 1985. *Publication:* (jtly) Harlow: the story of a new town, 1980. *Recreations:* books, sport. *Address:* Brick House, Broxted, Essex CM6 2BU. *T:* Bishops Stortford (0279) 850233.

HARVEY, Prof. Brian Wilberforce; Professor of Property Law, since 1973, and Pro-Vice-Chancellor, since 1986, University of Birmingham; *b* 17 March 1936; *s* of Gerald and Noelle Harvey. *Educ:* Clifton Coll., Bristol; St John's Coll., Cambridge (Choral Schol., MA, LLM). Solicitor, 1961. Lectr, Birmingham Univ., 1962–63; Sen. Lectr, Nigerian Law Sch., 1965–67; Lectr, Sen. Lectr and Prof. of Law, QUB, 1967–73; Univ. of Birmingham: Dir, Legal Studies, 1973–76; Dean, Faculty of Law, 1982–85. Vis. Prof., Univ. of Singapore, 1985–86. Chairman: Gtr Birmingham Social Security Appeal Tribunals, 1982–; Medical Appeals Tribunals, 1985–. Member: Statute Law Cttee (NI), 1972–73; Cttee on Legal Educn (NI), 1972–73; Adviser, Council of Legal Educn, NI, 1976–79. Mem., British Hallmarking Council, 1989–. *Publications:* Law of Probate Wills and Succession in Nigeria, 1968; (jtly) Survey of Northern Ireland Land Law, 1970; Settlements of Land, 1973; (ed) Vocational Legal Training in UK and Commonwealth, 1975; (ed) The Lawyer and Justice, 1978; The Law of Consumer Protection and Fair Trading, 1978, 3rd edn 1987; (jtly) Consumer and Trading Law Cases and Materials, 1985; (jtly) Law and Practice of Auctions, 1985; (jtly) The Law and Practice of Marketing Goods and Services, 1990. *Recreations:* performing and listening to music. *Address:* c/o Faculty of Law, The University, Birmingham B15 2TT.
See also J. D. Harvey.

HARVEY, Bryan Hugh, CBE 1978; Adviser, Ministry of Defence, since 1985; Chairman, Advisory Committee on Major Hazards, 1975–83; *b* 17 Oct. 1914; *y s* of late Oliver Harvey and Ellen Harvey (*née* Munn); *m* 1st, 1941, Margaret (*d* 1986), 2nd *d* of late E. G. Palmer; one *d*; 2nd, 1989, Christiane, *widow* of Maj. John Walton. *Educ:* KES Birmingham; Bristol Grammar Sch.; Corpus Christi Coll., Oxford; Harvard Univ. BA 1936; MA 1945; MSc 1953 (Industrial Hygiene). RAFVR, 1943–45. Printing industry until 1938, when joined Inspectorate of Factories; Dep. Chief Inspector, 1965; Chief Inspector, 1971–74; Dep. Dir Gen. (Dep. Sec.), Health and Safety Exec., 1975–76. Advr to Employment Cttee, H of C, 1980–83. Rockefeller Foundn Fellow, 1952–53; Hon. Lectr, Dept of Occupational Health, Univ. of Manchester, 1954–59; Vis. Prof., Univ. of Aston in Birmingham, 1972–79; External Examiner, Loughborough Univ. of Technology, 1984–89. Hon. Mem., British Occupational Hygiene Soc. (Pres. 1976–77). FSA 1964; Hon. Fellow, Instn of Occupational Safety and Health. *Publications:* (with R. Murray) Industrial Health Technology, 1958; (ed) Handbook of Occupational Hygiene, 1980; many articles in jls on industrial safety and hygiene, and industrial archaeology. *Recreations:* industrial archaeology, Georgian architecture, steam engines. *Address:* 2 Surley Row, Caversham, Reading, Berks RG4 8LY. *T:* Reading (0734) 479453. *Clubs:* Army and Navy; Leander.

HARVEY, Charles Richard Musgrave; (3rd Bt *cr* 1933, but does not use the title); *b* 7 April 1937; *s* of Sir Richard Musgrave Harvey, 2nd Bt, and Frances Estelle (*d* 1986), *er d* of late Lindsay Crompton Lawford, Montreal; *S* father, 1978; *m* 1967, Celia Vivien, *d* of late George Henry Hodson; one *s* one *d*. *Educ:* Marlborough; Pembroke Coll., Cambridge (BA 1960, MA 1964). Fellow, Institute of Development Studies, Sussex. *Heir:* *s* Paul Richard Harvey, *b* 1971.

HARVEY, Colin Stanley, MBE 1964; TD 1962; DL; a Recorder of the Crown Court, Western Circuit, since 1975; a Solicitor of the Supreme Court; *b* 22 Oct. 1924; *s* of Harold Stanley and Lilian May Harvey; *m* 1949, Marion Elizabeth (*née* Walker); one *s* one *d*. *Educ:* Bristol Grammar Sch.; University Coll., Oxford (BA). Served 1939–45 war in Queen's Regt and RA, India, Burma, Malaya, Java. In private practice as a solicitor. Bt Lt-Col TAVR, 1973. DL Avon, 1977. *Recreations:* TAVR, riding, beagling. *Address:* 12 Southfield Road, Westbury-on-Trym, Bristol BS9 3BH. *T:* Bristol (0272) 620404. *Clubs:* Commonwealth Trust; Clifton (Bristol); Royal Western Yacht (Plymouth).

HARVEY, Prof. David; Halford Mackinder Professor of Geography, and Fellow of St Peter's College, University of Oxford, since 1987; *b* 31 Oct. 1935; *s* of Frederick and Doris Harvey. *Educ:* St John's Coll., Cambridge (BA (Hons), MA, PhD). Lectr, Univ. of Bristol, 1961–69; Prof. of Geography, Johns Hopkins Univ., Baltimore, Md, 1969–86.

Guggenheim Meml Fellow, 1976–77. Outstanding Contributor Award, Assoc. of Amer. Geographers, 1980; Gill Meml Award, RGS, 1982; Anders Retzius Gold Medal, Swedish Soc. for Anthropology and Geography, 1989. *Publications:* Explanation in Geography, 1969, 4th edn 1978; Social Justice and the City, 1973, 3rd edn 1989; The Limits to Capital, 1982, 2nd edn 1984; The Urbanisation of Capital, 1985; Consciousness and the Urban Experience, 1985; The Urban Experience, 1989; The Condition of Postmodernity, 1989. *Address:* St Peter's College, Oxford. *T:* Oxford (0865) 271930.

HARVEY, John Edgar; Director, Burmah Oil Trading Ltd and subsidiary companies in Burmah Oil Group, 1974–80; *b* 24 April 1920; *s* of John Watt Harvey and Charlotte Elizabeth Harvey; *m* 1945, Mary Joyce Lane, BA, JP; one *s*. *Educ:* Xaverian Coll., Bruges, Belgium; Lyme Regis Grammar Sch. Radio Officer, in the Merchant Navy, 1939–45. Contested (C): St Pancras North, 1950; Walthamstow East, 1951; Mem. Nat. Exec. Cttee., Conservative Party, 1950–55; Chm., Woodford Conservative Assoc., 1954–56. MP (C) Walthamstow East, 1955–66. Pres., Wanstead & Woodford Conservative Assoc., 1986–. Mem., NSPCC Central Executive Cttee, 1963–68. Governor, Forest Sch., 1966–78. Verderer of Epping Forest, 1970–. Past Master, Guild of Freemen of City of London. *Recreations:* various in moderation. *Address:* 43 Traps Hill, Loughton, Essex IG10 1TB. *T:* 081–508 8753. *Clubs:* Carlton, City of London, City Livery.

HARVEY, Prof. Jonathan Dean; composer; Professor of Music, University of Sussex, since 1980; *b* 3 May 1939; *s* of Gerald and Noelle Harvey; *m* 1960, Rosaleen Marie Barry; one *s* one *d*. *Educ:* St Michael's Coll., Tenbury; Repton; St John's Coll., Cambridge (MA, DMus); Glasgow Univ. (PhD). Lectr, Southampton Univ., 1964–77; Reader, Sussex Univ., 1977–80. Harkness Fellow, Princeton Univ., 1969–70. Works performed at many festivals and international centres. Mem., Academia Europaea, 1989. Hon. DMus Southampton, 1990. *Publications:* The Music of Stockhausen, 1975; compositions: Persephone Dream, for orch., 1972; Inner Light (trilogy), for performers and tape, 1973–77; Smiling Immortal, for chamber orch., 1977; String Quartet, 1977; Magnificat and Nunc Dimittis, for choir and organ, 1978; Album, for wind quintet, 1978; Hymn, for choir and orch., 1979; Be(com)ing, for clarinet and piano, 1979; Concelebration, instrumental, 1979, rev. 1981; Mortuos Plango, Vivos Voco, for tape, 1980; Passion and Resurrection, church opera, 1981; Resurrection, for double chorus and organ, 1981; Whom Ye Adore, for orch., 1981; Bhakti, for 15 insts and tape, 1982; Easter Orisons, for chamber orch., 1983; The Path of Devotion, for choir and orch., 1983; Nachtlied, for soprano, piano and tape, 1984; Gong-Ring, for ensemble with electronics, 1984; Song Offerings, for soprano and players, 1985; Madonna of Winter and Spring, for orch., synthesizers and electronics, 1986; Lightness and Weight, for tuba and orch., 1986; Forms of Emptiness, for choir, 1986; Tendril, for ensemble, 1987; Timepieces, for orch., 1987; From Silence for soprano and players with electronics, 1988; Valley of Aosta for 13 players, 1988; String Quartet No 2, 1989; Ritual Melodies for tape, 1990; Cello Concerto, 1990; Serenade for wind, 1991. *Recreations:* tennis, walking, meditation. *Address:* c/o Faber Music, 3 Queen Square, WC1N 3AU. *T:* 071–278 7436.
See also B. W. Harvey.

HARVEY, Kenneth George, CEng, FIEE; Chairman, NORWEB plc (formerly North Western Electricity Board), since 1989; *b* 22 July 1940; *s* of George Harvey and Nellie Harvey (*née* Gilmore); *m* 1963, Wendy Youldon (*d* 1982); one *s* one *d*; *m* 1990, Anne Model. *Educ:* Urmston Grammar Sch., Manchester; City Univ. (BSc, 1st Cl. Hons Elec. Eng). Student Apprentice, Westinghouse, 1958–63; Southern and London Electricity Boards, 1963–81; London Electricity Board: Engineering Dir, 1981–84; Dep. Chm., 1984–89. *Recreations:* sport, gardening, DIY. *Address:* c/o NORWEB, Talbot Road, Manchester M16 0HQ. *T:* 061–873 8000.

HARVEY, Prof. Leonard Patrick; Cervantes Professor of Spanish, King's College, University of London, 1973–84, now Professor Emeritus; *b* 25 Feb. 1929; *s* of Francis Thomas Harvey and Eva Harvey; *m* 1954, June Rawcliffe; two *s*. *Educ:* Alleyn's Sch., Dulwich; Magdalen Coll., Oxford. 1st cl. hons BA Mod. Langs 1952; 2nd cl. Oriental Studies 1954; MA 1956; DPhil 1958. Lectr in Spanish, Univ. of Oxford, 1957–58; Univ. of Southampton, 1958–60; Queen Mary Coll., Univ. of London: Lectr, 1960–63; Reader and Head of Dept, 1963; Prof. of Spanish, 1967–73; Dean of Faculty of Arts, 1970–73; Dean of Faculty of Arts, KCL, 1979–81. Vis. Prof., Univ. of Victoria, BC, 1966. Mem. UGC, 1979–83. Chm., Educn Cttee, Hispanic and Luso-Brazilian Council, 1984–87. *Publications:* Islamic Spain 1250–1500, 1990; articles in Al-Andalus, Bulletin of Hispanic Studies, Nueva Revista de Filología Española, Al-Masāq, Al-Qantara, etc. *Address:* Tree Tops, Yester Park, Chislehurst BR7 5DQ. *T:* 081–467 3565.

HARVEY, Mary Frances Clare, (Mrs D. R. Feaver), MA; Headmistress, St Mary's Hall, Brighton, 1981–88; *b* 24 Aug. 1927; *d* of Rev. Oliver Douglas Harvey, West Malling, Kent; *m* 1988, Rt Rev. Douglas Russell Feaver, *qv*. *Educ:* St Mary's Sch., Colchester; St Hugh's Coll., Oxford (BA, Final Honour Sch. of Mod. Hist., 1950; Diploma in Educn, 1951; MA 1954). History Mistress, St Albans High Sch., 1951; Head of History Dept, Portsmouth High Sch., GPDST, 1956; Headmistress: Sch. of St Clare, Penzance, 1962–69; Badminton Sch., Westbury on Trym, Bristol, 1969–81. Governor, Bristol Cathedral Sch., 1978–81. *Recreations:* music, travel, reading, needlework. *Address:* 6 Mill Lane, Bruton, Somerset BA10 0AT.

HARVEY, Michael Llewellyn Tucker, QC 1982; a Recorder, since 1986; *b* 22 May 1943; *s* of Rev. Victor Llewellyn Tucker Harvey and Pauline Harvey (*née* Wybrow); *m* 1972, Denise Madeleine Neary; one *s* one *d*. *Educ:* St John's Sch., Leatherhead; Christ's Coll., Cambridge (BA Hons Law, LLB, MA). Called to the Bar, Gray's Inn, 1966 (Uthwatt Schol. 1965, James Mould Schol. 1966). *Publication:* joint contributor of title 'Damages' in Halsbury's Laws of England, 4th edn 1975. *Recreations:* shooting, golf. *Address:* 2 Crown Office Row, Temple, EC4Y 7HJ. *T:* 071–353 9337. *Clubs:* Athenæum; Hawks (Cambridge).

HARVEY, Neil; Head of Division 2 (formerly of Directorate B and Director of Business Statistics Office), Central Statistical Office, since 1989; *b* 10 Feb. 1938; *s* of Edward Felters and Lucy Felters (*née* Graves; she *m* 2nd, Frederick Harvey); *m* 1963, Clare Elizabeth Joscelyne; two *s*. *Educ:* Eton House Sch., Essex; LSE. BSc(Econ). Economist/Statistician, Kuwait Oil Co., 1959–62; Statistician, Midland Bank Economics Dept, 1962–65; Asst Statistician/Statistician, DEA, 1965–69; Statistician, HM Treasury, 1969–73; Chief Statistician, Inland Revenue, 1973–77; Controller, Statistical Office, HM Customs and Excise, 1977–84; Under Sec., Statistics Div. 1, DTI, 1984–89. *Recreation:* reading.

HARVEY, Prof. Paul Dean Adshead, FSA, FRHistS; Emeritus Professor, University of Durham, since 1985; *b* 7 May 1930; *s* of John Dean Monroe Harvey and Gwendolen Mabel Darlington (*née* Adshead); *m* 1968, Yvonne Crossman. *Educ:* Bishop Feild Coll., St John's, Newfoundland; Warwick Sch.; St John's Coll., Oxford (BA 1953; MA; DPhil 1960); FRHistS 1961, FSA 1963. Asst Archivist, Warwick County Record Office, 1954–56; Asst Keeper, Dept of Manuscripts, British Museum, 1957–66; Lectr, 1966–70, Sen. Lectr, 1970–78, Dept of History, Univ. of Southampton; Prof. of Mediaeval Hist., Univ. of Durham, 1978–85. Mem., Adv. Council on Public Records, 1984–89. Vice-Pres., Surtees Soc., 1978–. Hon. Fellow, Portsmouth Polytechnic, 1987. Jt Gen. Editor,

Southampton Records Series, 1966–78; Gen. Editor, Portsmouth Record Series, 1969–. *Publications:* The printed maps of Warwickshire 1576–1900 (with H. Thorpe), 1959; A Medieval Oxfordshire Village: Cuxham 1240–1400, 1965; (ed with W. Albert) Portsmouth and Sheet Turnpike Commissioners' minute book 1711–1754, 1973; Manorial records of Cuxham, Oxfordshire, circa 1200–1359, 1976; The history of topographical maps: symbols, pictures and surveys, 1980; (ed) The peasant land market in medieval England, 1984; Manorial records, 1984; (ed with R. A. Skelton) Local maps and plans from medieval England, 1986; contribs to: The Victoria History of the County of Oxford, vol. 10, 1972; History of Cartography, vol. 1, 1987; articles in learned jls and periodicals. *Recreations:* British topography and topographical writings. *Address:* Lyndhurst, Farnley Hey Road, Durham DH1 4EA. *T:* Durham (091) 3869396.

HARVEY, Peter, CB 1980; Assistant to Speaker's Counsel, House of Commons, since 1986; *b* 23 April 1922; *o s* of Rev. George Leonard Hunton Harvey and Helen Mary (*née* Williams); *m* 1950, Mary Vivienne, *d* of John Osborne Goss and Elsie Lilian (*née* Bishop); one *s* one *d*. *Educ:* King Edward VI High Sch., Birmingham; St John's Coll., Oxford (MA, BCL). RAF, 1942–45. Called to the Bar, Lincoln's Inn, 1948. Entered the Home Office as a Legal Assistant, 1948; Principal Asst Legal Advr, 1971–77; Legal Advr, DES, 1977–83; Consultant, Legal Advr's Br., Home Office, 1983–86. *Publications:* contributor to Halsbury's Laws of England (3rd and 4th edns). *Recreations:* history, and walking. *Address:* Mannamead, Old Avenue, Weybridge, Surrey KT13 0PS. *T:* Weybridge (0932) 845133.

HARVEY, Rt. Rev. Philip James Benedict, OBE 1973; retired Auxiliary Bishop of Westminster (RC) (Bishop in North London, 1977–91); Titular Bishop of Bahanna; *b* 6 March 1915; *s* of William Nathaniel and Elizabeth Harvey. *Educ:* Cardinal Vaughan Sch., Kensington; St Edmund's Coll., Ware, Herts. Ordained Priest, Westminster, 1939; Assistant Priest: Cricklewood, 1929–45; Kentish Town, 1945–46; Fulham, 1946–53; Asst Administrator, Crusade of Rescue, 1953–63, Administrator 1963–77. *Address:* 205 Nelson Road, Whitton, Middlesex TW2 7BB. *T:* 081–893 3027.

HARVEY, Robert Lambart; Columnist and Leader Writer, Daily Telegraph; *b* 21 Aug. 1953; *s* of Hon. John and Elena Harvey; *m* 1981, Jane Roper; one *s*. *Educ:* Eton; Christ Church, Oxford (BA 1974, MA 1978). Staff Correspondent, The Economist, 1974–81, Asst Editor, 1981–83. MP (C) SW Clwyd, 1983–87. Mem., House of Commons Select Cttee on Foreign Affairs, 1984–87. *Publication:* Portugal: birth of a democracy, 1978. *Recreations:* the arts, films, music, swimming, walking. *Address:* The Daily Telegraph, Peterborough Court At South Quay, 181 Marsh Wall, E14 9SR. *Clubs:* Brooks's, Travellers', Lansdowne.

HARVEY, Major Thomas Cockayne, CVO 1951; DSO 1945; ERD 1990; Extra Gentleman Usher to the Queen, since 1952 (to King George VI, 1951–52); *b* 22 Aug. 1918; *s* of late Col John Harvey, DSO; *m* 1940, Lady Katharine Mary Coke (Woman of the Bedchamber to Queen Elizabeth the Queen Mother, 1961–63), *yr d* of 3rd Earl of Leicester; one *s* two *d*. *Educ:* Radley; Balliol Coll., Oxford. Joined Scots Guards SRO, 1938. Served Norway, 1940, Italy, 1944; Private Sec. to the Queen, 1946–51. *Recreations:* golf, shooting, *Address:* Warham House, Warham, Wells, Norfolk NR23 1NG. *T:* Fakenham (0328) 710457. *Clubs:* White's, Beefsteak.

HARVEY-JAMIESON, Lt-Col Harvey Morro, OBE 1969; TD; DL; WS; Member, Queen's Body Guard for Scotland (Royal Company of Archers), since 1934; *b* 9 Dec. 1908; *s* of late Major A. H. Morro Jamieson, OBE, RGA, Advocate, Edinburgh, and Isobel, *d* of late Maj.-Gen. Sir Robert Murdoch Smith, KCMG; *m* 1936, Frances, *o c* of late Col. J. Y. H. Ridout, DSO; three *s*; assumed additional surname of Harvey, with authority of Lord Lyon King of Arms, 1958. *Educ:* Merchiston Castle Preparatory Sch.; Edinburgh Acad.; RMC Sandhurst (Prize Cadetship); Edinburgh Univ. (BL). Commissioned 1st Bn KOSB, 1928; Capt. RARO 1938; Major, 1939, to raise 291 HAA Battery RA (TA). Served War of 1939–45, Belgium, Holland and Germany, RA and Staff, Lieut-Col, 1942; Comd 3rd Edinburgh HG Bn, 1954–57. France and Germany Star, General Service and Home Defence Medals; Jubilee Medals 1935 and 1977; Coronation Medals, 1937 and 1953. Secretary and Legal Adviser, Co. of Merchants of City of Edinburgh, 1946–71; former Mem., Cttee on Conveyancing Legislation and Practice (apptd by Sec. of State for Scotland, 1964). Mem. Council, Cockburn Assoc. (Edinburgh Civic Trust), 1958–78; Hon. Manager, Edinburgh and Borders Trustee Savings Bank, 1957–78. Chairman, Scottish Committee: HMC; Assocs of Governing Bodies of Boys' and Girls' Public Schs, 1966–71. DL, County of the City of Edinburgh, 1968–84. *Publications:* The Historic Month of June, 1953; contrib. to Juridical Review, Scots Law Times and Yachting Monthly. *Address:* 20 Dean Terrace, Edinburgh EH4 1NL. *T:* 031–332 4589. *Clubs:* Royal Forth Yacht (Granton); Army Sailing Association.

HARVEY-JONES, Sir John (Henry), Kt 1985; MBE 1952; Chairman: Parallax Enterprises, since 1987; Imperial Chemical Industries PLC, 1982–87; business executive; *b* 16 April 1924; *s* of Mervyn Harvey-Jones, OBE, and Eileen Harvey-Jones; *m* 1947, Mary Evelyn Atcheson, *er d* of F. F. Bignell and Mrs E. Atcheson; one *d*. *Educ:* Tormore Sch., Deal, Kent; RNC, Dartmouth, Devon. RN, 1937–56: specialised in submarines; qual. as Russian interpreter, 1946, and subseq. as German interpreter; appts in Naval Intell. (MBE); resigned, 1956, Lt-Comdr. Joined ICI as Work Study Officer, Wilton, 1956; commercial appts at Wilton and Heavy Organic Chemicals Div. until apptd Techno-Commercial Dir, 1967; Dep. Chm., HOC Div., 1968; Chm., ICI Petrochemicals Div., 1970–73; Main Bd, ICI, 1973, Dep. Chm., 1978–82. Chairman: Phillips-Imperial Petroleum, 1973–75; Burns Anderson, 1987–90 (non-exec. Dir, 1987–); The Economist, 1989– (Dir, 1987–); Trendroute Ltd, 1988–; Didacticus Video Productions Ltd, 1989–; Deputy Chairman: Grand Metropolitan PLC, 1987– (Dir, 1983–); GPA Ltd, 1989– (Dir, 1987–); Director: ICI Americas Inc., 1975–76; Fiber Industries Inc., 1975–78; Carrington Viyella Ltd, 1981–82 (non-exec. Dir, 1974–79); non-exec. Dir, Reed International PLC, 1975–84; non-exec. Chm. Bd Cttee, Business Internat., 1988–. Chm., Wider Share Ownership Council, 1988–; Vice-Chairman: PSI, 1980–85; BIM, 1980–85 (FBIM); Pres., CBI, 1984–86 (Mem., President's Cttee, 1982–87); Vice-President: CEFIC, 1982–84; Indust. Participation Assoc., 1983–; Hon. Vice-Pres., Inst. of Marketing, 1982–89. Member: Tees and Hartlepool Port Authy, 1970–73; NE Develt Bd, 1971–73; Welsh Develt Internat., 1989; Cttee for Chem. Industry, NEDO, 1980–82; Council, Chem. Industries Assoc. Ltd, 1980–82; Court, British Shippers' Council, 1982–87; Youth Enterprise Scheme, 1984–86; Foundn Bd, Internat. Management Inst., Geneva, 1984–87; Internat. Council, Eur. Inst. of Business Admin, 1984–87; Adv. Council, Prince's Youth Business Trust, 1986–; Hon. Mem., Econ. Res. Council, 1984–; Hon. Consultant, RUSI, 1987–. Sen. Indust. Fellow, Leicester Polytechnic, 1990. Chancellor, Bradford Univ., 1986–; Chm. Council, St James's and the Abbey Sch., Malvern, 1987–; Member: Council, British Malaysian Soc., 1983–87; Ct of Govs, Kidney Res. Unit for Wales Foundn, 1989–90; Vice Chm., Great Ormond St Redevelt Appeal, 1986–89; Pres., Book Trust Appeal Fund, 1987–; Vice-Pres., Newnham Coll. Appeal, 1987; Hon. President: Univ. of Bradford MBA Alumni Assoc., 1989; Friends of Brecon Jazz, 1989–. Chm. Council, Wildfowl Trust, 1987–; Vice-President: Hearing & Speech Trust, 1985–; Heaton Woods Trust, 1986–; Fellow, Smallpeice Trust, 1988–; Trustee: Police Foundn, 1983–91 (Chm. Trustees, 1984–88); Science Mus., 1983–87; Conf. Bd, 1984–86. Patron: Halton Chem. Industry Mus. Appeal, 1986; Cambridge Univ. Young Entrepreneurs Soc., 1987–; MSC Nat. Trng Awards, 1987; Steer Orgn, 1988–; Nat. Canine Defence League, 1990–; Vice-Patron, British Polio Fellowship, 1988–. Hon. FRSC 1985; Hon. FIChemE 1985, Hon. Mem. CGLI, 1988; FRSA 1979. Hon. LLD: Manchester, 1985; Liverpool, 1986; London, 1987; Cambridge, 1987; DUniv Surrey, 1985; Hon. DSc: Bradford, 1986; Leicester, 1986; Keele, 1989; Exeter, 1989; Hon. DCL Newcastle, 1988; Hon. DBA Internat. Management Centre, 1990. Gold Medal, BIM, 1985; Centenary Medal, SCI, 1986; J. O. Hambro British Businessman of the Year, 1986; Award of Excellence in Communication, Internat. Assoc. of Business Communicators, 1987; Radar Man of the Year, 1987; CGIA in Technol. (*hc*), 1987. Troubleshooter, BBC TV series, 1990. Mem., Adv. Editl Bd, New European, 1987–. *Publications:* Making it Happen: reflections on leadership, 1987; Troubleshooter, 1990; Getting it Together, 1991. *Recreations:* ocean sailing, swimming, the countryside, cooking, contemporary literature. *Address:* c/o Parallax Enterprises Ltd, PO Box 18, Ross-on-Wye, Herefordshire HR9 7TL. *T:* Upton Bishop (098985) 430. *Clubs:* Athenæum, Groucho.

HARVIE-WATT, Sir James, 2nd Bt *cr* 1945, of Bathgate, Co. Lothian; FCA; company director; *b* 25 Aug. 1940; *s* of Sir George Harvie-Watt, 1st Bt, QC, TD and of Bettie, *o d* of late Paymaster-Capt. Archibald Taylor, OBE, RN; *S* father, 1989; *m* 1966, Roseline, *d* of late Baron Louis de Chollet, Fribourg, Switzerland, and Frances Tate, Royal Oak, Maryland, USA; one *s* one *d*. *Educ:* Eton; Christ Church, Oxford (MA). FCA 1975 (ACA 1965). Lieut London Scottish (TA), 1959–67. With Coopers & Lybrand, 1962–70; Executive, British Electric Traction Co. Ltd, and Director of subsid. companies, 1970–78; Man. Dir, Wembley Stadium Ltd, 1973–78; Chm., Cannons Sports & Leisure Ltd, 1990–; Director: Lake & Elliot Industries Ltd, 1988–, and other cos. Mem. Executive Cttee, London Tourist Board, 1977–80; Member: Sports Council, 1980–88 (Vice-Chm., 1985–88; Mem. Sports Council enquiries into: Financing of Athletics in UK, 1983; Karate, 1986); Indoor Tennis Initiative Bd, 1986–89. Chm., Crystal Palace Nat. Sports Centre, 1984–88; Dir, National Centres Bd, 1987–88. Member Management Cttee: Nat. Coaching Foundn, 1984–88; Holme Pierrepont Nat. Water Sports Centre, 1985–88. Mem. Council, NPFA, 1985–90. FRSA 1978. OStJ 1964, and Mem. London Council of the Order, 1975–84. *Heir: s* Mark Louis Harvie-Watt, *b* 19 Aug. 1969. *Recreations:* shooting, tennis, reading, philately, photography. *Address:* 15 Somerset Square, Addison Road, W14 8EE. *T:* 071–602 6944. *Clubs:* White's, Pratt's, Queen's (Vice-Chm., 1987–90; Chm., 1990–); Sunningdale.

HARVINGTON, Baron *cr* 1974 (Life Peer), of Nantwich; **Robert Grant Grant-Ferris,** PC 1971; Kt 1969; AE; *b* 30 Dec. 1907; *s* of late Robert Francis Ferris, MB, ChB; *m* 1930, Florence, *d* of Major W. Brennan De Vine, MC; one *s* one *d*. *Educ:* Douai Sch., Woolhampton; Called to Bar, Inner Temple, 1937; joined RAuxAF, 1933, 605 (County of Warwick) Fighter Sqdn; Flight Comdr 1939–40; Wing Comdr, 1941; Air Efficiency Award, 1942. MP (C) North St Pancras, 1937–45; MP (C) Nantwich, Cheshire, 1955–Feb. 1974; PPS to Minister of Town and Country Planning (Rt Hon. W. S. Morrison, KC, MP), 1944–45; Temp. Chm. House of Commons and Chairman of Cttees, 1962–70; Chm. of Ways and Means and the Dep. Speaker, House of Commons, 1970–74. Contested Wigan, 1935, North St Pancras, 1945, Central Wandsworth, 1950, 1951. Chm., Bd of Management, Hosp. of St John and St Elizabeth, 1963–70. Pres. Southdown Sheep Soc. of England, 1950–52, 1959–60, 1973; Pres. Nat. Sheep Breeders' Assoc., 1956–58; a Vice-Pres. Smithfield Club, 1964, Pres. 1970. Mem., Broderers' Co., 1987–. Mem. Council, Imperial Soc. of Knights Bachelor, 1973–. Knight Grand Cross of Magistral Grace, with Riband, 1985, the Sovereign and Military Order of Malta; holds Grand Cross of Merit with Star of same Order, 1953; Comdr, Order of Leopold II (Belgium), 1964. *Recreations:* formerly hunting, golf, yachting (sometime Hon. Admiral, House of Commons Yacht Club). *Address:* 6 Batisse de la Mielle, St Aubin, Jersey, Channel Islands. *T:* Jersey (0534) 32326. *Clubs:* Carlton, MCC, Royal Thames Yacht; Royal Yacht Squadron (Cowes); Royal and Ancient Golf (St Andrews).

See also Sir T. G. R. Brinckman, Bt.

HARWOOD, John Warwick; Chief Executive, Oxfordshire County Council, since 1989; Clerk, Lieutenancy for Oxfordshire, since 1989; *b* 10 Dec. 1946; *s* of D. G. and Mrs W. G. Harwood; *m* 1967, Diana Thomas; one *s* one *d*. *Educ:* Univ. of Kent at Canterbury (BA Hons); Univ. of London (MA). Admin. Officer, GLC, 1968–73; Private Sec. to Leader of ILEA, 1973–77; Head of Chief Exec.'s Office, London Bor. of Hammersmith and Fulham, 1977–79; Asst Chief Exec., London Bor. of Hammersmith and Fulham, 1979–82; Chief Exec., London Bor. of Lewisham, 1982–89; Hon. Clerk, S London Consortium, 1983–89. Dir, Heart of England TEC, 1990–. Chair, Local Authorities Race Relations Information Exchange, 1990–. *Recreations:* walking, cooking. *Address:* County Hall, Oxford OX1 1ND. *T:* Oxford (0865) 815330.

HARWOOD, Ronald, FRSL; writer; *b* 9 Nov. 1934; *s* of late Isaac Horwitz and late Isobel Pepper; *m* 1959, Natasha Riehle; one *s* two *d*. *Educ:* Sea Point Boys' High Sch., Cape Town; RADA. FRSL 1974. Actor, 1953–60. Artistic Dir, Cheltenham Festival of Literature, 1975; Presenter: Kaleidoscope, BBC, 1973; Read All About It, BBC TV, 1978–79. Chm., Writers Guild of GB, 1969; Mem., Lit. Panel, Arts Council of GB, 1973–78. Visitor in Theatre, Balliol Coll., Oxford, 1986. Mem. Cttee, English PEN, 1987– (Pres., 1989–). TV plays incl.: The Barber of Stamford Hill, 1960; (with Casper Wrede) Private Potter, 1961; The Guests, 1972; Breakthrough at Reykjavik, 1987; Countdown to War, 1989; adapted several of Roald Dahl's Tales of the Unexpected for TV, 1979–80; TV series, All the World's a Stage, 1984; screenplays incl.: A High Wind in Jamaica, 1965; One Day in the Life of Ivan Denisovich, 1971; Evita Perón, 1981; The Dresser, 1983; Mandela, 1987. *Publications: novels:* All the Same Shadows, 1961; The Guilt Merchants, 1963; The Girl in Melanie Klein, 1969; Articles of Faith, 1973; The Genoa Ferry, 1976; Cesar and Augusta, 1978; *short stories:* One. Interior. Day:—adventures in the film trade, 1978; (co-ed) New Stories 3, 1978; *biography:* Sir Donald Wolfit, CBE—his life and work in the unfashionable theatre, 1971; (ed) The Ages of Gielgud, 1984; (ed) Dear Alec: Guinness at seventy-five, 1989; *essays:* (ed) A Night at the Theatre, 1983; *plays:* Country Matters, 1969; The Ordeal of Gilbert Pinfold (from Evelyn Waugh), 1977; A Family, 1978; The Dresser, 1980 (New Standard Drama Award; Drama Critics Award); After the Lions, 1982; Tramway Road, 1984; The Deliberate Death of a Polish Priest, 1985; Interpreters, 1985; J. J. Farr, 1987; Ivanov (from Chekhov), 1989; Another Time, 1989; *musical libretto:* The Good Companions, 1974; *historical:* All the World's a Stage, 1983. *Recreations:* tennis, cricket. *Address:* c/o Judy Daish Associates, 83 Eastbourne Mews, W2 6LQ. *T:* 071–262 1101. *Clubs:* Garrick, MCC; Vanderbilt Racquet.

HASELDEN, Prof. Geoffrey Gordon; Brotherton Professor of Chemical Engineering, University of Leeds, 1960–86, now Emeritus; *b* 4 Aug. 1924; *s* of George A. Haselden and Rose E. (*née* Pleasants); *m* 1945, Eileen Doris Francis; three *d*. *Educ:* Sir Walter St John's Sch.; Imperial Coll. of Science and Technology. BScChemEng London 1944; FCGI; PhD (Eng) Chem Eng London, 1947; DScEng London, 1962; DIC; CEng; FIMechE; FIChemE; MInstR. Mem. Gas Research Bd, 1946–48; Lectr in Low Temperature Technology, Chemical Engrg Dept, 1948–57, Senior Lectr in Chemical

Engrg, 1957–60, Imperial Coll. Chm., British Cryogenics Council, 1967–71. President: Commn A3, Internat. Inst. of Refrigeration, 1971–79; Inst. of Refrigeration, 1981–84; Vice-Pres., IChemE, 1984–85. Gen. Editor, Internat. Jl of Refrigeration, 1978–88. *Publications:* Cyrogenic Fundamentals, 1971; research papers in Trans Inst. Chem. Eng., etc. *Recreation:* Methodist lay preacher. *Address:* 12 High Ash Drive, Wigton Lane, Leeds LS17 8RA. *T:* Leeds (0532) 687047; The University, Leeds. *T:* Leeds (0532) 332402.

HASELDINE, (Charles) Norman; public relations consultant; *b* 25 March 1922; *s* of Charles Edward Haseldine and Lily White; *m* 1946, Georgette Elise Michelle Bernard; four *s*. *Educ:* Nether Edge Grammar Sch., Sheffield. Education Officer, Doncaster Co-operative Soc., 1947–57; PRO, Sheffield & Ecclesall Co-op. Soc., 1957–70. MP (Lab and Co-op) Bradford West, 1966–70; PPS to Minister of Power, 1968–69; PPS to Pres. Bd of Trade, 1969–70; Mem. Select Cttee on Nationalised Inds. *Recreation:* classical music. *Address:* 115 Psalter Lane, Sheffield S11 8YR. *T:* Sheffield (0742) 585974.

HASELER, Dr Stephen Michael Alan; author; Professor of Government, City of London Polytechnic, since 1986; *b* 9 Jan. 1942; *m* 1967, Roberta Alexander. *Educ:* London School of Economics. BSc(Econ), PhD. Contested (Lab): Saffron Walden, 1966; Maldon, 1970. Chm., Labour Political Studies Centre, 1973–78. Mem. GLC, 1973–77, Chm. General Purposes Cttee, 1973–75. Founder Mem., SDP, 1981. Visiting Professor: Georgetown Univ., Washington DC, 1978; Johns Hopkins Univ., 1984; Maryland Univ., 1984–. Founder and Co-Chm., Radical Soc., 1988. MInstD 1987. *Publications:* The Gaitskellites, 1969; Social-Democracy—Beyond Revisionism, 1971; The Death of British Democracy, 1976; Eurocommunism: implications for East and West, 1978; The Tragedy of Labour, 1980; Anti-Americanism, 1985; Battle for Britain: Thatcher and the New Liberals, 1989. *Recreation:* cricket. *Address:* 2 Thackeray House, Ansdell Street, W8. *T:* 071–937 3976.

HASELGROVE, Dennis Cliff, CB 1963; MA; FSA; Under Secretary, Department of the Environment, 1970–75; *b* 18 Aug. 1914; *s* of late H. Cliff Haselgrove, LLB, Chingford; *m* 1941, Evelyn Hope Johnston, MA, *d* of late R. Johnston, Edinburgh; one *s*. *Educ:* Uppingham Sch.; King's Coll., Cambridge. 1st Class, Classical Tripos, Parts I and II. Entered Ministry of Transport, Oct. 1937; Private Sec. to Permanent Sec., and Asst Priv. Sec. to Minister, 1941. Served in Intelligence Corps and 10th Baluch Regt, IA, 1941–45. Min. of Transport: Asst Sec., 1948; Under-Sec., 1957–70. Govt Delegate to: ILO Asian Maritime Conf., 1953; Internat. Conf. on Oil Pollution of the Sea, 1954, 1962; Internat. Lab. Conf. (Maritime Session), 1958; Internat. Conf. on Safety of Life at Sea, 1960. Imperial Defence Coll., 1955. *Recreations:* archæology, travel, philately. *Address:* 10 Church Gate, SW6 3LD. *T:* 071–736 5213.

HASELHURST, Alan Gordon Barraclough; MP (C) Saffron Walden, since July 1977; *b* 23 June 1937; *s* of late John Haselhurst and Alyse (*née* Barraclough); *m* 1977, Angela (*née* Bailey); two *s* one *d*. *Educ:* King Edward VI Sch., Birmingham; Cheltenham Coll.; Oriel Coll., Oxford. Pres., Oxford Univ. Conservative Assoc., 1958; Sec., Treas. and Librarian, Oxford Union Soc., 1959–60; Nat. Chm., Young Conservatives, 1966–68. MP (C) Middleton and Prestwich, 1970–Feb. 1974. PPS to Sec. of State for Educn, 1979–82. Chm., Rights of Way Review Cttee, 1983–. Chairman: Manchester Youth and Community Service, 1974–77; Commonwealth Youth Exchange Council, 1978–81; Chm. Trustees, Community Projects Foundn, 1986–. *Recreations:* gardening, theatre, music. *Address:* House of Commons, SW1A 0AA. *Club:* MCC.

HASHMI, Dr Farrukh Siyar, OBE 1974; FRCPsych; Consultant Psychiatrist, All Saints' Hospital, Birmingham, since 1969; Psychotherapist, HM Prison, Stafford, since 1973; *b* Gujrat, Pakistan, 12 Sept. 1927; *s* of Dr Ziaullah Qureshi and Majida Qureshi; *m* 1972, Shahnaz; one *s* two *d*. *Educ:* King Edward Med. Coll., Lahore (Punjab Univ.). MB, BS; MRCPsych; DPM; FRCPsych 1979. Mayo Hosp. and King Edward Med. Coll., Lahore, March-Sept. 1953; New End Hosp., Hampstead, 1954; Children's Hosp., Birkenhead, 1954–55; Sen. House Officer, Brook Gen. Hosp., Woolwich, 1955–56; Snowdon Road Hosp., Bristol, 1956; Asst MOH, Co. Berwicks, 1957; Scholar, Volkart Foundn, Switzerland, 1958–60; psychiatric medicine: Registrar, Uffculme Clinic and All Saints Hosp., Birmingham, 1960–63, Sen. Registrar, 1966–69; Research Fellow, Dept of Psychiatry, Birmingham Univ., 1963–66. Chairman: Psychiatric Div., West Birmingham Health Dist., 1977–83, and 1988–; Woodbourne Clinic Hosp. Management Team, 1989; Member: Race Relations Bd, W Midlands Conciliation Cttee, 1968–81; Community Relations Working Party, NAYC, 1968–81; Home Secretary's Adv. Cttee on Race, 1976–81 (formerly Mem., HO Adv. Cttee on Race Relations Research); CRE, 1980–86; Working Party on Community and Race Relations Trng, HO Police Trng Council, 1982–83; Wkg Gp on Ethnic Minorities, W Midlands RHA, 1982–; Mental Health Services Cttee, RHA, 1976–; Council, Mind (NAMH), 1976–81; UK Cttee, World Fedn for Mental Health, 1978–81; Health and Welfare Adv. Panel, NCCI, 1966–81; Cttee of Inquiry into Educn of Children from Ethnic Minority Gps (Swann Cttee), 1982–85; Warley Area Social Services Sub-Cttee, 1973–81; Central DHA, Birmingham, 1982–90; BBC Regl Adv. Council, 1970–77; GMC, 1979–84 (GMC Mem., Tribunal on Misuse of Drugs, 1983–84); Parole Board, 1981–85; Alternate Mem., Economic Social Cttee, EEC, 1985; Advisory Consultant, C of E Bd for Social Responsibility, 1984–87. President: Pakistan Med. Soc., UK, 1974–76; Overseas Doctors Assoc., UK, 1975–79; Founder and Chm., Iqbal Acad., Coventry Cathedral, 1972–86. Member Editorial Board: Medicos, 1977–81; New Community, 1980–. Involved in clinical trials and psycho-pharmacological studies, *eg* assessing effects of drugs in anxiety states and neurotic illness, incl. antidepressants. *Publications:* Pakistan Family in Britain, 1965; Mores, Migration and Mental Illness, 1966; Psychology of Racial Prejudice, 1966; Community Psychiatric Problems among Birmingham Immigrants, 1968; In a Strange Land, 1970; Measuring Psychological Disturbance in Asian Immigrants to Britain, 1977. *Recreations:* writing, reading, music. *Address:* Shahnaz, 5 Woodbourne Road, Edgbaston, Birmingham B15 3QJ. *T:* 021–455 0011. *Clubs:* Oriental; Rotary International, Edgbaston Priory (Birmingham).

HASKARD, Sir Cosmo (Dugal Patrick Thomas), KCMG 1965 (CMG 1960); MBE 1945; *b* 25 Nov. 1916; *o c* of late Brig.-Gen. J. McD. Haskard, CMG, DSO; *m* 1957, Phillada, *o c* of late Sir Robert Stanley, KBE, CMG; one *s*. *Educ:* Cheltenham; RMC Sandhurst; Pembroke Coll., Cambridge (MA). Served War of 1939–45 (MBE); 2nd Lieut, TA (Gen. List), 1938; emergency Commn, Royal Irish Fusiliers, 1939; seconded KAR, 1941; served 2nd Bn, E Africa, Ceylon, Burma; Major 1944. Apptd Colonial Service cadet, Tanganyika, 1940, but due to war service did not take up duties until 1946 in which yr transf. to Nyasaland; Dist Comr, 1948; served on Nyasaland-Mozambique Boundary Commn, 1951–52; Provincial Commissioner, 1955; acting Secretary for African Affairs, 1957–58; Sec. successively for Labour and Social Development, for Local Government, and for Natural Resources, 1961–64; Governor and C-in-C, Falkland Islands, and High Comr for the British Antarctic Territory, 1964–70. Trustee, Beit Trust, 1976–. *Address:* Tragariff, Bantry, Co. Cork, Ireland.

HASKELL, (Donald) Keith, CMG 1991; CVO 1979; HM Diplomatic Service; Ambassador to Peru, since 1990; *b* 9 May 1939; *s* of Donald Eric Haskell and Beatrice Mary Haskell (*née* Blair); *m* 1966, Maria Luisa Soeiro Tito de Morais; two *s* two *d* (and one *s* one *d* decd). *Educ:* Portsmouth Grammar Sch.; St Catharine's Coll., Cambridge (BA 1961, MA 1964). Joined HM Foreign Service, 1961; served in: London, Lebanon, Iraq, Libya; HM Consul, Benghazi, 1969–70; First Sec., Tripoli, 1970–72; Foreign and Commonwealth Office, 1972–75; Chargé d'Affaires and Consul-Gen., Santiago, 1975–78; Counsellor and Consul-Gen., Dubai, 1978–81; Hd, Nuclear Energy Dept, FCO, 1981–83; Hd, Middle East Dept, FCO, 1983–84; Hd of Chancery, Bonn, 1985–88; on secondment as an advr to industry, 1988–89. Foundation Medal, Soka Univ. of Japan, 1975. *Recreations:* rifle shooting (captained Cambridge Univ. Rifle Assoc., 1960–61; represented England and GB in shooting competitions on various occasions), squash, tennis, wine and food. *Address:* c/o Foreign and Commonwealth Office, SW1A 2AL. *Club:* Hawks (Cambridge).

HASKELL, Francis James Herbert, FBA 1971; Professor of Art History, Oxford University and Fellow of Trinity College, Oxford, since October 1967; *b* 7 April 1928; *s* of late Arnold Haskell, CBE, and Vera Saitzoff; *m* 1965, Larissa Salmina. *Educ:* Eton Coll.; King's Coll., Cambridge. Junior Library Clerk, House of Commons, 1953–54; Fellow of King's Coll., Cambridge, 1954–67, Hon. Fellow, 1987; Librarian of Fine Arts Faculty, Cambridge Univ., 1962–67. Mem., British Sch. at Rome, 1971–74. A Trustee, Wallace Collection, 1976–. Mem. Exec. Cttee, Nat. Art Collections Fund, 1976–. Foreign Hon. Mem., Amer. Acad. of Arts and Scis, 1979; Corresp. Mem., Accad. Pontaniana, Naples, 1982; Foreign Mem., Ateneo Veneto, 1986. Serena medal for Italian studies, British Acad., 1985. *Publications:* trans., Venturi, Roots of Revolution, 1960; Patrons and Painters: a study of the relations between Art and Society in the Age of the Baroque, 1963, 2nd edn 1980 (trans. Italian and Spanish); Géricault (The Masters), 1966; An Italian Patron of French Neo-Classic Art, 1972; (ed jtly) The Artist and Writer in France, 1975; Rediscoveries in Art, 1976, 2nd edn 1980 (trans. Italian and French) (Mitchell Prize for Art History, 1977; Prix de l'Essai Vasari, 1987); L'arte e il linguaggio delta politica (Florence), 1977; (with Nicholas Penny) Taste and the Antique, 1981, 2nd edn 1982 (trans. Italian and French); Past and Present in Art and Taste: selected essays, 1987 (trans. Italian and French); Painful Birth of the Art Book, 1988; articles in Burlington Mag., Jl Warburg Inst., etc; reviews in New Statesman, NY Review of Books, etc. *Recreation:* foreign travel. *Address:* 7 Walton Street, Oxford; Trinity College, Oxford OX1 2HG; 35 Beaumont Street, Oxford.

HASKELL, Keith; *see* Haskell, D. K.

HASKELL, Peter Thomas, CMG 1975; PhD, FRES, FIBiol; Director, Cleppa Park Field Research Station, University of Wales College of Cardiff (formerly University College, Cardiff), 1984–91; *b* 21 Feb. 1923; *s* of late Herbert James and Mary Anne Haskell; *m* 1st, 1946; one *s*; 2nd, 1979, Aileen Kirkley. *Educ:* Portsmouth Grammar Sch.; Imperial Coll., London. BSc, ARCS, PhD. Asst Lectr, Zoology Dept, Imperial Coll., London, 1951–53; Lectr, 1953–55; Sen. Sci. Officer, Anti-Locust Research Centre, Colonial Office, 1955–57; Principal Sci. Officer, 1957–59; Dep. Dir, 1959–62; Dir, Anti-Locust Research Centre, ODM, 1962–71; Dir, Centre for Overseas Pest Res. and Chief Advr on Pest Control, ODA, 1971–83. Consultant: FAO, UN, 1962–; UNDP, 1970–; WHO, 1973–; OECD, 1975–; UNEP, 1976–; Agricl and Vet. Adv. Cttee, British Council, 1976–90; Plants and Soils Res. Cttee, AFRC, later Plants and Envnt Res. Cttee, 1988–91; UNDP/FAO Special Adv. Cttee on Desert Locust, 1990–. Vice-Pres., Inst. of Biology, 1982. Professorial Res. Fellow, University Coll., Cardiff, 1971–83. Mem., Bd of Governors, Internat. Centre for Insect Physiology and Ecology, Kenya, 1972– (Vice-Chm., 1978; Chm., 1979–). Vis. Prof., Univ. of Newcastle, 1977. Thamisk Lectr, Royal Swedish Acad. of Scis, 1979. Van Den Brande Internat. Prize, 1982. Chief Editor, Tropical Pest Management, 1985–; Mem., Editorial Bd, Review of Applied Entomol., 1988–. *Publications:* Insect Sounds, 1962; The Language of Insects, 1962; Pesticide Application: principles and practice, 1985; many papers and articles in scientific and literary jls. *Recreations:* gardening, reading. *Address:* 7 The Tudors, Melrose Avenue, Cardiff CF3 7BA.

HASKINS, Sam, (Samuel Joseph); photographic designer; *b* 11 Nov. 1926; *s* of Benjamin G. Haskins and Anna E. Oelofse; *m* 1952, Alida Elzabé van Heerden; two *s*. *Educ:* Helpmekaar Sch.; Witwatersrand Technical Coll.; Bolt Court Sch. of Photography. Freelance work: Johannesburg, 1953–68; London, 1968–. One-man Exhibitions: Johannesburg, 1953, 1960; Tokyo, 1970, 1973, 1976, 1981, 1985, 1987–88, 1990; London, 1972, 1976, 1978, 1980, 1987; Paris, 1973; Amsterdam, 1974; NY, 1981; San Francisco, 1982; Toronto, 1982; Bologna, 1982; Auckland, 1991; Sydney, 1991; Hong Kong, 1991; Taipei, 1991; Singapore, 1991. *Publications:* Five Girls, 1962; Cowboy Kate and other stories, 1964 (Prix Nadar, France, 1964); November Girl, 1966; African Image, 1967 (Silver Award, Internat. Art Book Contest, 1969); Haskins Posters, 1972 (Gold Medal, New York Art Directors Club, 1974); Photo-Graphics, 1980 (Kodak Book Award); portfolios in most major internat. photographic magazines. *Recreations:* sculpting, books, music. *Address:* 9A Calonne Road, SW19 5HH. *T:* 081–946 9660.

HASLAM, family name of **Baron Haslam.**

HASLAM, Baron *cr* 1990 (Life Peer), of Bolton in the County of Greater Manchester; **Robert Haslam,** Kt 1985; CEng, FInstME; Chairman: Bechtel Ltd, since 1989; Wasserstein Perella & Co. International Ltd, since 1991; a Director, Bank of England, since 1985; *b* 4 Feb. 1923; *s* of Percy and Mary Haslam; *m* 1947, Joyce Quin; two *s*. *Educ:* Bolton Sch.; Birmingham Univ. (BSc Coal Mining, 1st Cl.). Joined Manchester Collieries Ltd, 1944; National Coal Board, Jan. 1947; Mining Engr, Oct. 1947, Personnel Director, 1960, ICI Nobel Division; Director, 1963, Dep. Chm., 1966, ICI Plastics Div.; Dep. Chm., 1969, Chm., 1971, ICI Fibres Div.; Director, ICI Ltd, 1974; Chairman: ICI Americas Inc., 1978–81; Dep. Chm., ICI plc, 1980–83; Chairman: British Steel Corporation, 1983–86; Tate & Lyle plc, 1983–86 (non-exec. Dep. Chm., 1982; Dir, 1978–86); British Coal, 1986–90 (Non-exec. Dep. Chm., 1985–86; Dep. Chm., 1986); Director: Fibre Industries, Inc., 1971–75; Imperial Metal Industries, 1975–77; AECI Ltd, 1978–79; Carrington Viyella, 1982–83; Cable and Wireless, 1982–83; Adv. Dir, Unilever, 1986–. Chairman: Man-Made Fibres Producers Cttee, 1972–74; Nationalized Industries Chairmen's Group, 1985–86 (Mem., 1983–90); Member: BOTB, 1981–85 (Chm., N America Adv. Gp, 1982–85); NEDC, 1985–89. Pres., IMinE, 1989–90. Chairman: Council, Manchester Business Sch., 1985–90; Governors, Bolton Sch., 1990–. Freeman, City of London, 1985. Hon. FIMinE 1987. Hon. DTech Brunel, 1987; Hon. DEng Birmingham, 1987. *Recreations:* golf, travel. *Address:* c/o House of Lords, SW1A 0PW. *Clubs:* Brooks's; Wentworth.

HASLAM, Hon. Sir Alec (Leslie), Kt 1974; Judge of the Supreme Court of New Zealand, 1957–76, Senior Puisne Judge, 1973–76; *b* 10 Feb. 1904; *s* of Charles Nelson Haslam and Adeline Elsie Haslam; *m* 1933, Kathleen Valerie Tennent (*d* 1985); two *s* two *d*. *Educ:* Waitaki Boys' High Sch.; Canterbury UC; Oriel Coll., Oxford. Rhodes Scholar 1927; 1st cl. hons LLM NZ; DPhil, BCL Oxon. Served with 10th Reinf. 2 NZEF, ME and Italy, 1943–46. Barrister and Solicitor, 1925; in private practice, 1936–57. Lectr in Law, Canterbury Univ., 1936–50 (except while overseas). Chm. Council of Legal Educn, 1962–75 (Mem. 1952); Mem., Rhodes Scholarship Selection Cttee, 1936–74; NZ Sec. to Rhodes Scholarships, 1961–74; Mem., Scholarships (Univ. Grants) Cttee, 1962–80; Pres., Canterbury District Law Soc., 1952–53; Vice-Pres., NZ Law Soc., 1954–57; Mem.,

Waimairi County Council, 1950–56; Mem., NZ Univ. Senate, 1956–61. Sen. Teaching Fellow, Univ. of Canterbury, 1977–81. Hon. LLD Canterbury, 1973. *Publication:* Law Relating to Trade Combinations, 1931. *Recreations:* reading; formerly athletics (rep. Canterbury Univ. and Oriel Coll.) and rowing (rep. Oriel Coll.). *Address:* 22 Brackendale Place, Burnside, Christchurch 4, NZ. *T:* 588–589.

HASLAM, Rear Adm. Sir David William, KBE 1984 (OBE 1964); CB 1979; President, Directing Committee, International Hydrographic Bureau, Monaco, since 1987; *b* 26 June 1923; *s* of Gerald Haigh Haslam and Gladys Haslam (*née* Finley). *Educ:* Ashe Prep. Sch., Etwall; Bromsgrove Sch., Worcs. FRGS, FRIN, FRICS, FNI. Special Entry Cadet, RN, 1941; HMS Birmingham, HMAS Quickmatch, HMS Resolution (in Indian Ocean), 1942–43; specialised in hydrographic surveying, 1944; HMS White Bear (surveying in Burma and Malaya), 1944–46; comd Survey Motor Launch 325, 1947; RAN, 1947–49; HMS Scott, 1949–51; HMS Dalrymple, 1951–53; i/c RN Survey Trng Unit, Chatham, 1953–56; HMS Vidal, 1956–57; comd, HMS Dalrymple, 1958; comd, HMS Dampier, 1958–60; Admty, 1960–62; comd, HMS Owen, 1962–64; Exec. Officer, RN Barracks, Chatham, 1964–65; Hydrographer, RAN, 1965–67; comd, HMS Hecla, 1968–70; Asst Hydrographer, MoD, 1970–72; comd, HMS Hydra, 1972–73; Asst Dir (Naval) to Hydrographer, 1974–75; sowc 1975; Hydrographer of the Navy, 1975–85. Acting Conservator, River Mersey, 1985–87; Advr on Port Appts, Dept of Transport, 1986–87. Underwriting Mem., Lloyd's, 1986–. Pres., Hydrographic Soc., 1977–79. Governor, Bromsgrove Sch., 1977–. President: English Schs Basketball Assoc., 1973–; Derbyshire CCC, 1991–. Liveryman, Chartered Surveyors' Co., 1983. FRSA. *Address:* Palais Saint James, 5 Avenue Princesse Alice, Monte Carlo, MC 98000, Monaco. *T:* Monaco 93 50. 59 21.

HASLAM, Geoffrey; *see* Haslam, W. G.

HASLAM, Rev. John Gordon; a Chariman of Industrial Tribunals, since 1976 (part-time, 1976–81, full-time, since 1981); non-stipendiary Church of England priest; a Chaplain to the Queen, since 1989; *b* 15 July 1932; *s* of Ernest Henry Haslam and Constance Mabel (*née* Moore); *m* 1st, 1957, Margaret Anne Couse (*d* 1985); two *s* one *d*; 2nd, 1987, Marian Kidson Clarke. *Educ:* King Edward's Sch., Birmingham; Birmingham Univ. (LLB); Queen's Coll., Birmingham. National Service, RA, 1956–58 (2nd Lieut). Solicitor's Articled Clerk, Johnson & Co., Birmingham, 1953–56; Asst Solicitor, 1958–62, Partner, 1962–75, Pinsent & Co., Solicitors, Birmingham. Ordained deacon and priest, Birmingham dio., 1977; Hon. Curate: St Michael's, Bartley Green, Birmingham, 1977–79; St Mary's, Moseley, Birmingham, 1980–; Hon. Hosp. Chaplain, 1980–88; temp. service as priest in many Birmingham parishes, 1983–. *Recreations:* gardening, steam railways, fell walking. *Address:* 34 Amesbury Road, Moseley, Birmingham B13 8LE. *T:* 021–449 3394.

HASLAM, (William) Geoffrey, OBE 1985; DFC 1944; Director, Prudential Corporation PLC, 1980–87 (Deputy Chairman, 1980–84); *b* 11 Oct. 1914; *yr s* of late William John Haslam and late Hilda Irene Haslam; *m* 1941, Valda Patricia Adamson; two *s* one *d*. *Educ:* New Coll. and Ashville Coll., Harrogate. War Service with RAF, No 25 Sqdn (night fighters), 1940–46. Joined Prudential Assurance Co. Ltd, 1933: Dep. Gen. Manager, 1963; Gen. Manager, 1969; Chief Gen. Manager, 1974–78; Chief Exec., 1979; Dep. Chm., 1980–84. Chairman: Industrial Life Offices Assoc., 1972–74; British Insurance Assoc., 1977–78. Chm., St Teresa's Hospital, Wimbledon, 1983–87; Vice Pres., NABC, 1983–. *Recreation:* golf. *Address:* 6 Ashbourne Road, W5 3ED. *T:* 081–997 8164. *Clubs:* Royal Air Force, MCC.

HASLEGRAVE, Herbert Leslie, WhSch (Sen.), MA Cantab, PhD London, MSc (Eng), CEng, FIMechE, FIEE, FIProdE; FBIM; Vice-Chancellor, Loughborough University of Technology, 1966–67; *b* 16 May 1902; *s* of late George Herbert Haslegrave and Annie (*née* Tottey), Wakefield; *m* 1938, Agnes Mary, *er d* of Leo Sweeney, Bradford; one *d*. *Educ:* Wakefield Gram. Sch.; Bradford Technical Coll.; Trinity Hall Cambridge (Scholar). Rex Moir Prizeman, John Bernard Seeley Prizeman, Ricardo Prizeman, 1928; 1st Cl. Mechanical Sciences Tripos, 1928. English Electric Co. Ltd: Engineering Apprentice, 1918–23; Asst Designer, Stafford, 1928–30; Lecturer: Wolverhampton and Staffs Technical Coll., 1931; Bradford Technical Coll., 1931–35; Head of Continuative Education Dept, Loughborough Coll., 1935–38; Principal: St Helens Municipal Technical Coll., 1938–43; Barnsley Mining and Technical Coll., 1943–46; Leicester Coll. of Technology, 1947–53; Loughborough Coll. of Technology, 1953–66. Bernard Price Lectr, SA Inst. of Electrical Engrs, 1971. Member of: Productivity Team on Training of Supervisors, visiting USA, 1951; Delegation on Education and Training of Engineers visiting USSR, 1956; Council, IMechE, 1965–66; Council, IEE, 1956–58. Chairman: Council, Assoc. of Technical Institutions, 1963–64; Cttee on Technician Courses and Examinations, 1967–69; Pres., Whitworth Soc., 1972–73. FRSA. Hon. FIMGTechE. Hon. DTech Loughborough Univ. of Technology. *Publications:* various on engineering, education and management in proceedings of professional engineering bodies and educational press; chapter in Management, Labour and Community. *Recreations:* motoring, swimming, music. *Address:* 1 Woodland View, Southwell, Nottinghamshire NG25 0BT. *T:* Southwell (0636) 814018.

HASLEGRAVE, Neville Crompton; Town Clerk, 1965–74, and Chief Executive Officer, 1969–74, Leeds; Solicitor; *b* 2 Aug. 1914; *o s* of late Joe Haslegrave, Clerk of Council, and late Olive May Haslegrave; *m* 1943, Vera May, *o d* of late Waldemar Julius Pedersen, MBE, and Eva Pedersen; two *d*. *Educ:* Exeter Cathedral Choristers School; Leeds Univ. Asst Examr, Estate Duty Office, Bd of Inland Revenue, 1940–44; Asst Solicitor, Co. Borough of Leeds, 1944–46. Chief Prosecuting Solicitor, Leeds, 1946–51; Principal Asst Solicitor, Leeds, 1951–60; Dep. Town Clerk, Leeds, 1960–65. Pres., Leeds Law Soc., 1972–73. Mem., IBA Adv. Council, 1969–73. *Recreations:* cricket, music, walking. *Address:* 37 West Court, Roundhay, Leeds LS8 2JP. *Club:* Headingley Taverners'.

HASLEWOOD, Prof. Geoffrey Arthur Dering; Professor of Biochemistry at Guy's Hospital Medical School, University of London, 1949–77, now Emeritus; *b* 9 July 1910; *s* of N. A. F. Haslewood, Architect, and Florence (*née* Hughes); *m* 1943, B. W. Leeburn (*d* 1949); two *d*; *m* 1953, E. S. Blakiston, Geelong, Vic, Australia. *Educ:* St Marylebone Grammar Sch.; University Coll., London. MSc 1932, PhD 1935, DSc 1946. FRSC (FRIC 1946). Research on polycyclic aromatic hydrocarbons, etc, at Royal Cancer Hosp. (Free), 1933–35; Asst in Pathological Chemistry at British Postgraduate Med. Sch., 1935–39; Reader in Biochemistry at Guy's Hosp. Med. Sch., 1939–49. Mem., Zaire River Expedition, 1974–75. Hon. Mem., Japanese Biochem. Soc., 1969. *Publications:* Bile Salts, 1967; The Biological Importance of Bile Salts, 1978; various articles and original memoirs in scientific literature, mainly on steroids in relation to evolution. *Recreation:* conservation, especially of amphibians and reptiles. *Address:* 28 Old Fort Road, Shoreham-by-Sea, Sussex BN43 5RJ. *T:* Brighton (0273) 453622.

HASLIP, Joan; author; *b* 27 Feb. 1912; *yr d* of late George Ernest Haslip, MD, original planner of the Health Service. *Educ:* privately in London and on the continent. Grew up in Florence. Sub-editor, London Mercury, 1929–39, contributed verse, reviews, etc; travelled extensively Europe, USA, Middle East; Editor, European Service, BBC, 1941–45 (Italian Section); lectured for British Council, Italy and Middle East; broadcast and contributed articles to BBC and various publications and newspapers. FRSL 1958. *Publications:* (several translated); Out of Focus (novel), 1931; Grandfather Steps (novel), 1932 (USA 1933); Lady Hester Stanhope, 1934; Parnell, 1936 (USA 1937); Portrait of Pamela, 1940; Lucrezia Borgia, 1953 (USA 1954); The Sultan, Life of Abdul Hamid, 1958, repr. 1973; The Lonely Empress, a life of Elizabeth of Austria, 1965 (trans. into ten languages); Imperial Adventurer, 1971 (Book of Month choice, USA, 1972); Catherine the Great, 1976; The Emperor and the Actress, 1982; Marie Antoinette, 1987. *Recreations:* travelling and conversation. *Address:* 8 Via Piana, Bellosguardo, Florence, Italy.

HASLUCK, Rt. Hon. Sir Paul (Meernaa Caedwalla), KG 1979; GCMG 1969; GCVO 1970; PC 1966; Governor-General of Australia, 1969–74; *b* 1 April 1905; *s* of E. M. C. Hasluck and Patience (*née* Wooler); *m* 1932, Alexandra Margaret Martin Darker, AD 1978, DStJ 1971; one *s* (and one *s* decd). *Educ:* University of Western Australia (MA). Journalist until 1938. Lectr in History, University of Western Australia, 1939–40; Australian Diplomatic Service, 1941–47; Head of Australian Mission to United Nations, 1946–47; Representative on Security Council, Atomic Energy Commn, General Assembly, etc. Research Reader in History, University of Western Australia, 1948. Official War Historian. Mem. (L) House of Representatives, 1949–69; Minister for Territories in successive Menzies Governments, 1951–63; Minister for Defence, 1963–64; Minister for External Affairs, 1964–69. Fellow, Aust. Acad. of Social Scis. Hon. Fellow, Aust. Acad. of Humanities; Hon. FRAIA; Hon. FRAHS. KStJ 1969. *Publications:* Black Australians, 1942; Workshop of Security, 1946; The Government and the People (Australian Official War History), vol. 1, 1951, vol. 2, 1970; Collected Verse, 1970; An Open Go, 1971; The Office of the Governor-General (Queale Meml Lecture), 1973, rev. edn, 1979; The Poet in Australia, 1975; A Time for Building: Australian administration in Papua New Guinea, 1976; Mucking About (autobiog.), 1977; Sir Robert Menzies (Mannix Lecture), 1980; Diplomatic Witness, 1980; Dark Cottage (verse), 1984; Shades of Darkness: Aboriginal affairs 1925–65, 1988; The Ministerial Role in Australian Government, 1989; Crude Impieties (verse), 1991. *Recreation:* book collecting (Australiana). *Address:* 2 Adams Road, Dalkeith, WA 6009, Australia. *Clubs:* Weld (Perth); Claremont Football.

HASSALL, Prof. Cedric Herbert, FRS 1985; CChem; Hon. Visiting Professor: University of Warwick, since 1985; University College, Cardiff, since 1985; Imperial College, London, since 1989; *b* 6 Dec. 1919; *s* of late H. Hassall, Auckland, NZ; *m* 1st, 1946, H. E. Cotti (marr. diss. 1982); one *d* (and one *s* decd); 2nd, 1984, J. A. Mitchelmore. *Educ:* Auckland Grammar Sch., NZ; Auckland Univ. (MSc); Univ. of Cambridge (PhD, ScD). Lectr, Univ. of Otago, NZ, 1943–45; Sen. studentship, Royal Commn for 1851, Cambridge, 1946–48; Foundn Prof. of Chem., Univ. of WI, 1948–56; Carnegie and Rockefeller Fellowships in USA, 1950, 1956; Head, Dept of Chemistry, Univ. Coll., of Swansea, UCW, 1957–71; Dir of Research, Roche Products Ltd, 1971–84. Comr, Royal Univ. of Malta, 1964–71; Planning Adviser: Univ. of Jordan, 1965–71; Univ. of Aleppo, 1965; Abdul Aziz Univ., Jedda, 1966, 1968. Vis. Professor: Univ. of Kuwait, 1969, 1979; Aligarh Univ., India (Royal Soc.), 1969–70; Univ. of Liverpool, 1971–79. Pres., Chem. Section of British Assoc., 1987; Member: various cttees of Royal Soc. Chem., 1959– (Pres., Perkin Div., 1985–87); Council, British Technol. Gp, 1986–; various Govt cttees relating to sci. affairs; Co-ordinator, Molecular Recognition Initiative, SERC, 1987–90; ODA Advr on science, technology and educn in India, China and Indonesia, 1989–. Chm., Steering Cttee, Oxford Centre for Molecular Scis, 1988–; Hon. Fellow, UC of Swansea, 1986; Hon. DSc West Indies, 1975. *Publications:* papers on aspects of organic chemistry, largely in Jl of Chemical Soc. *Recreation:* travel. *Address:* 2 Chestnut Close, Westoning, Beds MK45 5LR. *T:* Flitwick (0525) 712909.

HASSALL, Tom Grafton, FSA 1971; MIFA; Secretary, Royal Commission on Historical Monuments of England, since 1986; Fellow, St Cross College, Oxford, since 1974; *b* 3 Dec. 1943; *s* of William Owen Hassall, *qv*; *m* 1967, Angela Rosaleen Goldsmith; three *s*. *Educ:* Dragon Sch., Oxford; Lord Williams's Grammar Sch., Thame; Corpus Christi Coll., Oxford (BA History). Assistant local editor, Victoria County History of Oxford, 1966–67; Director, Oxford Archaeological Excavation Cttee, 1967–73; Dir, Oxfordshire (now Oxford) Archaeological Unit, 1973–85; Associate Staff Tutor, Oxford Univ. Dept for External Studies, 1978–85. Trustee, Oxford Preservation Trust, 1973–; Chairman: Standing Conf. of Archaeol Unit Managers, 1980–83; British Archaeological Awards, 1983–88; President: Council for British Archaeology, 1983–86; Oxfordshire Architectural and Historical Soc., 1984–; Mem., Ancient Monuments Adv. Cttee, Historic Buildings and Monuments Commn, 1984–. Crew mem., Athenian Trireme, 1987. *Publications:* Oxford: the city beneath your feet, 1972; specialist articles on archaeology. *Recreations:* gardening, Norfolk Cottage. *Address:* The Manor House, Wheatley, Oxford OX9 1XX. *T:* Wheatley (08677) 4428.

HASSALL, William Owen; Librarian to Earl of Leicester, Holkham, 1937–83; Bodleian Library, Oxford, 1938–80 (Senior Assistant Librarian); *b* 4 Aug. 1912; *s* of Lt-Col Owen Hassall and Bessie Florence Hassall (*née* Cory); *m* 1936, Averil Grafton Beaves; three *s* one *d*. *Educ:* Twyford Sch., Hants; Wellington Coll., Berks; (Classical scholar) Corpus Christi Coll., Oxford. Hon. Mods, 1st cl. Modern History, 1936, DPhil 1941. Lent by RA to Min. Economic Warfare, 1942–46. Formerly: External Examnr in History, Univs of Bristol, Durham, Leicester and Oxford Insts of Educn (Trng Colls); Hon. Editorial Sec., British Records Assoc.; Mem. Council, Special Libraries and Information Bureaux. Hon. Sec., Oxfordshire Record Soc., 1947–76. FSA 1942; FRHistS. *Publications:* A Cartulary of St Mary Clerkenwell, 1949; A Catalogue of the Library of Sir Edward Coke, 1950; The Holkham Bible Picture Book, 1954; Wheatley Records, 956–1956, 1956; They saw it happen: an anthology of eye-witnesses' accounts for events in British history, 55BC-AD1485, 1957; Who's Who in History, vol. I, British Isles, 55BC-1485, 1960; (with A. G. Hassall) The Douce Apocalypse, 1961; How they Lived: an anthology of original accounts written before 1485, 1962; Index of Names in Oxfordshire Charters, 1966; History Through Surnames, 1967; The Holkham Library Illuminations and Illustrations in the Manuscript Library of the Earl of Leicester (printed for presentation to the Members of the Roxburghe Club), 1970; (with A. G. Hassall) Treasures from the Bodleian, 1975; contrib. to various learned publications; work on Holkham records, 1250–1600. *Recreation:* grandchildren. *Address:* Manor House, Wheatley, Oxford OX9 1XX. *T:* Wheatley (08677) 2333.

See also T. G. Hassall.

HASSAN, Sayed Abdullah El; Order of Sudanese Republic; Golden Order of Regional Government; Ambassador of Democratic Republic of the Sudan to the Court of St James's, 1971–72 and 1983–85; *b* 1925; *m* Madame Khadiga Diglal; four *s* one *d*. Diploma in Arts and Public Administration. District Officer, Min. of Interior and Min. of Local Govt, 1949–56; Consul Gen., Uganda and Kenya, 1956–58; Head of Political Section, Min. of Foreign Affairs, 1958–60; Ambassador to Ghana, 1960–64; Dir Gen., Min. of Information, 1964–65; Ambassador to France, 1965–67, to Ethiopia, 1967–69; Under Sec., Ministry of Foreign Affairs, 1969–70; Ambassador to Soviet Union, 1970–71; Mem., Political Bureau, Sudanese Socialist Union, 1972–77; Minister of Rural Develt, 1972–73; Minister of Interior, 1973–75; Sec. Gen. to the Presidency, 1975–76; Minister for Cabinet Affairs, 1976–77; Mem., Nat. Assembly (3rd) and Chm., Foreign Relations Cttee, 1979–80;

Governor designate, Eastern Region, March-Nov. 1980; Ambassador to Tunisia and Perm. Rep. to Arab League, 1982–83. Sec. Gen., Nat. Council for Friendship, Solidarity and Peace, 1973–; Mem., Sudan delegations to UN, OAU, UNHCR and numerous assemblies, conferences and visits. Holds numerous foreign decorations. *Address:* c/o Foreign Office, Khartoum, Sudan.

HASSAN, Hon. Sir Joshua (Abraham), GBE 1988 (CBE 1957); KCMG 1986; Kt 1963; LVO 1954; QC (Gibraltar) 1961; JP; Chief Minister of Gibraltar, 1964–69, and 1972–87; *b* 1915; *s* of late Abraham M. Hassan, Gibraltar; *m* 1945, Daniela (marr. diss. 1969), *d* of late José Salazar; two *d*; *m* 1969, Marcelle, *d* of late Joseph Bensimon; two *d*. *Educ:* Line Wall Coll., Gibraltar. Called to Bar, Middle Temple, 1939; Hon. Bencher, 1983. HM Deputy Coroner, Gibraltar, 1941–64; Mayor of Gibraltar, 1945–50 and 1953–69; Mem. Executive Council, Chief Mem. Legislative Council, Gibraltar, 1950–64; Leader of the Opposition, Gibraltar House of Assembly, 1969–72. Chairman: Cttee of Management, Gibraltar Museum, 1952–65; Gibraltar Govt Lottery Cttee, 1955–70; Central Planning Commn, 1947–70. Hon. LLD Hull Univ., 1985. *Address:* 11/18 Europa Road, Gibraltar. *T:* 77295. *Clubs:* United Oxford & Cambridge University; Royal Gibraltar Yacht.

HASSAN, Mamoun Hamid; independent producer/director; *b* Jedda, 12 Dec. 1937; *s* of late Dr Hamid Hassan and of Fatma Hassan (*née* Sadat); *m* 1966, Moya Jacqueline Gillespie, MA Oxon; two *s*. Formerly script writer, editor and director; Head of Production Board, British Film Inst., 1971–74; Head of Films Branch, UNRWA, Lebanon, 1974–76; Bd Mem., 1978–84, Man. Dir, 1979–84, Nat. Film Finance Corp. Member: Cinematograph Films Council, 1977–78; Scottish Film Production Fund, 1983–87; Advr, European Script Fund, 1989–; Sen. Consultant for UNESCO, Harare, Zimbabwe, 1991–; Governor, Nat. Film and Television Sch., 1983–. Films produced include: No Surrender, 1985. Producer and presenter, Movie Masterclass, C4 series, 1988, 2nd series, 1990. *Address:* High Ridge, 9 High Street, Deddington, Oxford OX5 4SJ.

HASSELL, Prof. Michael Patrick, FRS 1987; Professor of Insect Ecology, Department of Biology, Imperial College of Science, Technology and Medicine, since 1979; Director, Silwood Park, since 1988; *b* 2 Aug. 1942; *s* of Albert Marmaduke Hassell and Gertrude Hassell (*née* Loeser); *m* 1st, 1966, Glynis Mary Everett (marr. diss. 1981); two *s*; 2nd, 1982, Victoria Anne Taylor; one *s* one *d*. *Educ:* Whitgift School; Clare College, Cambridge (BA 1964, MA); Oriel College, Oxford (DPhil 1967); DSc Oxford 1980. NERC Research Fellow, Hope Dept of Entomology, Oxford, 1968–70; Imperial College, London: Lectr, 1970–75, Reader, 1975–79, Dept of Zoology and Applied Entomology; Dep. Head of Dept of Pure and Applied Biology, 1984–. Vis. Lectr, Univ. of California, Berkeley, 1967–68; Storer Life Sciences Lectr, Univ. of California, Davis, 1985. Scientific Medal, Zoological Soc., 1981. *Publications:* Insect Population Ecology (with G. C. Varley and G. R. Gradwell), 1973; The Dynamics of Competition and Predation, 1975; The Dynamics of Arthropod Predator-Prey Systems, 1978; research papers and review articles on dynamics of animal populations, esp. insects. *Recreations:* natural history, hill walking, croquet. *Address:* Silwood Lodge, Silwood Park, Ascot, Berks SL5 7PZ.

HASSETT, Gen. Sir Francis (George), AC 1975; KBE 1976 (CBE 1966; OBE 1945); CB 1970; DSO 1951; LVO 1954; Chief of the Defence Force Staff, 1975–77, retired; *b* 11 April 1918; *s* of John Francis Hassett, Sydney, Australia; *m* 1946, Margaret Hallie Roberts, *d* of Dr Edwin Spencer Roberts, Toowoomba, Qld; one *s* two *d* (and one *s* decd). *Educ:* RMC, Duntroon, Australia. Graduated RMC, 1938. Served War of 1939–45, Middle East and South West Pacific Area (Lt-Col; wounded; despatches twice); CO 3 Bn Royal Australian Regt, Korea, 1951–52; Marshal for ACT Royal Tour, 1954; Comd 28 Commonwealth Bde, 1961–62; idc, 1963; DCGS, 1964–65; Head of Aust. Jt Services Staff, Australia House, 1966–67; GOC Northern Comd, Australia, 1968–70; Chm., Army Rev. Cttee, 1969–70; Vice Chief of Gen. Staff, Australia, 1971–73; CGS, Australia, 1973–75. Extra Gentleman Usher to the Queen, 1966–68. *Recreations:* gardening, writing. *Address:* 42 Mugga Way, Red Hill, Canberra, ACT 2603, Australia. *Club:* Commonwealth.

HASSETT, Maj.-Gen. Ronald Douglas Patrick, CB 1978; CBE 1975; Director, Orient: New Zealand Trading Co. Ltd, 1979; *b* 27 May 1923; *s* of Edmond Hassett and Elinor Douglas; *m* 1953, Lilian Ivy Gilmore; two *s* one *d*. *Educ:* St Patrick's Coll., Wellington; RMC Duntroon. psc, G, rcds. 2nd NZ Expeditionary Force, Italy, 1944–46; NZ Army Liaison Staff, London, 1948–50; served Korea, NZ and Malaya, 1952–62; NZ Instructor, Australian Staff Coll., 1963–65; Dir of Equipment, NZ Army, 1966–67; DQMG, 1967–69; Comdr NZ Inf. Brigade Group, 1969; DCGS, 1970; RCDS, 1971; ACDS (Policy), 1972–74; Dep. Chief of Defence Staff, 1974–76; Chief of General Staff, NZ Army, 1976–78. *Recreations:* gardening, golf.

HASTERT, Roger Joseph Leon; Grand Cross, Order of Adolphe de Nassau, Luxembourg; Hon. CMG 1972; Dr-en-Droit; Hon. Maréchal de la Cour, Luxembourg, since 1986; *b* Luxembourg City, 10 July 1929; *m* Eléonore Heijmerink; one *s* one *d*. Barrister-at-law, Luxembourg, 1956–59; joined Diplomatic Service, 1959 (Political Affairs); First Sec. and Consul Gen., Brussels, 1963–69; Dir of Protocol and Juridical Affairs, Min. of Foreign Affairs; Pres., Commn Internationale de la Moselle; and Mem., Commn de Contrôle des Comptes des Communautés Européennes, 1969–73; Ambassador to The Netherlands, 1973–1978; Ambassador to UK and Perm. Rep. to Council of WEU, 1978–85, concurrently Ambassador to Ireland and Iceland. *Address:* 44 rue de Mersch, L–8181 Kopstal, Luxembourg.

HASTIE, Robert Cameron, CBE 1983; RD 1968 (Bar 1978); JP; DL; Chairman: Bernard Hastie & Co. Ltd, UK and Australia, since 1973; *b* Swansea, 24 May 1933; *s* of B. H. C. Hastie and M. H. Hastie; *m* 1961, Mary Griffiths; two *s* one *d*. *Educ:* Bromsgrove School. Joined RN, National Service, 1951; Midshipman 1953; qual. RNR Ocean comd, 1963; progressive ranks to Captain RNR, 1974, in comd HMS Cambria, 1974–77; Captain Sea Trng RNR, 1977–79; Aide-de-Camp to the Queen, 1977; Commodore RNR 1979. Pres., Swansea Unit Sea Cadet Corps, 1982–. Chm., Mumbles Lifeboat Station Cttee, 1987–. Chm., W Wales TEC, 1990–. Member: Inst. of Directors, 1960–; W Wales Cttee, CBI, 1982–. Vice-Chm., TA & VRA, Wales, 1984–. DL West Glamorgan, 1974; JP 1989; High Sheriff of W Glamorgan County, 1977–78. *Recreations:* sailing, shooting, skiing, tennis. *Address:* Upper Hareslade Farm, Bishopston, Swansea SA3 3BU. *T:* Bishopston (044128) 2957; (day) Swansea (0792) 651541. *Clubs:* Naval; Cardiff and County (Cardiff); Royal Naval Sailing Association (Portsmouth); Bristol Channel Yacht (Swansea); Royal Sydney Yacht Squadron (Sydney, Aust.).

HASTIE-SMITH, Richard Maybury, CB 1984; FIPM 1986; Deputy Under-Secretary of State, Ministry of Defence, since 1981; *b* 13 Oct. 1931; *s* of Engr-Comdr D. Hastie-Smith and H. I. Hastie-Smith; *m* 1956, Bridget Noel Cox; one *s* two *d*. *Educ:* Cranleigh Sch. (Schol.); Magdalene Coll., Cambridge (Schol.; MA). HM Forces, commnd Queen's Royal Regt, 1950–51. Entered Administrative Class, Home CS, War Office, 1955; Private Sec. to Permanent Under-Sec., 1957; Asst Private Sec. to Sec. of State, 1958; Principal, 1960; Asst Private Sec. to Sec. of State for Defence, 1965; Private Sec. to Minister of Defence (Equipment), 1968; Asst Sec., 1969; RCDS, 1974; Under-Sec., MoD, 1975, Cabinet Office, 1979–81. Chm., Magdalene Coll. Assoc., 1983–. Governor: Cranleigh Sch., 1963–; St Catherine's Sch., Bramley, 1972–. *Address:* 18 York Avenue, East Sheen, SW14. *T:* 081–876 4597. *Club:* Army and Navy.

HASTILOW, Michael Alexander; Director, Glynwed Ltd, 1969–81; *b* 21 Sept. 1923; *s* of late Cyril Alexander Frederick Hastilow, CBE, MSc, BCom, FRIC, and Doreen Madge, MA; *m* 1953, Sheila Mary Tipper (*née* Barker); one *s* two *d*. *Educ:* Mill Hill Sch.; Birmingham Univ. (Pres., Guild of Undergrads; BSc Civil Engrg, BCom). Served in Fleet Air Arm, RNVR, 1944–46. Commercial Manager, J. H. Lavender & Co. Ltd, 1948–54; Birmid Industries Ltd, 1954–57: Asst Gen. Man., Birmidal Developments Ltd, 1956–57; Commercial Man., Birmetals Ltd, 1957; Commercial and Gen. Sales Man., Bilston Foundries Ltd, 1957–63; Dir, Cotswold Buildings Ltd, 1963–64; Glynwed Ltd, 1964–81: Dir, The Wednesbury Tube Co. Ltd, 1966–81 (Man. Dir, 1968–74; Chm., 1973–76); dir or chm. of various Glynwed divs and subsids. British Non-Ferrous Metals Federation: Mem. Council, 1973–81; Vice Pres., 1975–79; Pres., 1979–80; Chm., Tube Gp, 1975–77. National Home Improvement Council: Mem. Council, 1975–84; Mem. Bd, 1975–84; Vice Chm., 1979–80; Chm., 1980–81. Member: Commn for New Towns, 1978–86; Construction Exports Adv. Bd, 1975–78; Exec. Cttee, 1973–84, and Council, 1974–84, Nat. Council for Bldg Material Producers; EDC for Building, 1980–82. Hon. Treasurer, Midlands Club Cricket Conf., 1969–81, Pres., 1981–82. *Recreations:* cricket, railways. *Address:* The Mount, 3 Kendal End Road, Rednal, Birmingham B45 8PX. *T:* 021–445 2007. *Clubs:* MCC, Old Millhillians.

HASTINGS; *see* Abney-Hastings, family name of Countess of Loudoun.

HASTINGS, 22nd Baron, *cr* 1290; **Edward Delaval Henry Astley,** Bt 1660; *b* 14 April 1912; *s* of 21st Baron and Lady Marguerite Nevill (*d* 1975), *d* of 3rd Marquess of Abergavenny; *S* father 1956; *m* 1954, Catherine Rosaline Ratcliffe Coats, 2nd *d* of late Capt. H. V. Hinton; two *s* one *d*. *Educ:* Eton and abroad. Supplementary Reserve, Coldstream Guards, 1934; served War of 1939–45, Major 1945; farming in Southern Rhodesia, 1951–57. Mem. of Parliamentary delegation to the West Indies, 1958; a Lord in Waiting, 1961–62; Jt Parly Sec., Min. of Housing and Local Govt, 1962–64. Chairman: British-Italian Soc., 1957–62 (Pres., 1972–); Italian People's Flood Appeal, 1966–67; Governor: Brit. Inst. of Florence, 1959–; Royal Ballet, 1971–; Chairman: Royal Ballet Benevolent Fund, 1966–84; Dance Teachers Benevolent Fund, 1982–; Pres., British Epilepsy Assoc., 1965–. Grand Officer, Order of Merit (Italy), 1968. *Recreations:* riding, ballet, foreign travel. *Heir:* *s* Hon. Delaval Thomas Harold Astley [*b* 25 April 1960; *m* 1987, Veronica, *er d* of Richard Smart]. *Address:* Seaton Delaval Hall, Whitley Bay, Northumberland. *T:* 091–237 0786. *Clubs:* Brooks's, Army and Navy; Northern Counties (Newcastle); Norfolk (Norwich).

HASTINGS, Rev. Prof. Adrian Christopher; Professor of Theology, University of Leeds, since 1985; *b* 23 June 1929; *s* of William George Warren Hastings and Mary Hazel Hastings (*née* Daunais); *m* 1979, Elizabeth Ann Spence. *Educ:* Worcester Coll., Oxford (MA); Christ's Coll., Cambridge (PGCE); Urban Univ., Rome (DTheol). Ordained 1955; Diocesan Priest, Masaka, Uganda, 1958–66; Editor, Post-Vatican II, Tanzania, 1966–68; Mindolo Ecumenical Foundn, Zambia, 1968–70; Res. Officer, SOAS, 1973–76; Fellow, St Edmund's House, Cambridge, 1974–76; Lectr and Reader in Religious Studies, Univ. of Aberdeen, 1976– 82; Prof. of Religious Studies, Univ. of Zimbabwe, 1982–85. Editor, Jl of Religion in Africa, 1985–. *Publications:* Prophet and Witness in Jerusalem, 1958; (ed) The Church and the Nations, 1959; One and Apostolic, 1963; Church and Mission in Modern Africa, 1967; A Concise Guide to the Documents of the Second Vatican Council, 2 vols, 1968–69; Mission and Ministry, 1971; Christian Marriage in Africa, 1973; Wiriyamu, 1974; The Faces of God, 1975; African Christianity, 1976; (ed) Bishops and Writers, 1977; In Filial Disobedience, 1978; A History of African Christianity 1950–1975, 1979; In the Hurricane, 1986; A History of English Christianity 1920–1985, 1986; African Catholicism, 1989; The Theology of a Protestant Catholic, 1990; Robert Runcie, 1991; (ed) Modern Catholicism, 1991; Church and State: the English Experience, 1991. *Recreations:* walking, visiting historic buildings, cutting hedges. *Address:* Department of Theology and Religious Studies, The University, Leeds LS2 9JT. *T:* Leeds (0532) 333641; 3 Hollin Hill House, 219 Oakwood Lane, Leeds LS8 2PE. *T:* Leeds (0532) 400154.

HASTINGS, Alfred James; Registrar of Members' Interests, House of Commons, since 1987; *b* 10 Feb. 1938; *s* of William Hastings and Letitia (*née* Loveridge); *m* 1972, Susan Edge; three *s*. *Educ:* Leamington College; New College, Oxford (MA). A Clerk of the House of Commons, 1960–. *Recreations:* music, high fidelity sound reproduction. *Address:* Committee Office, House of Commons, SW1.

HASTINGS, Max Macdonald; author, journalist and broadcaster; Editor, The Daily Telegraph, since 1986; Director, since 1989, Editor-in-Chief, since 1990, The Daily Telegraph plc; *b* 28 Dec. 1945; *s* of Macdonald Hastings and Anne Scott-James, *qv*; *m* 1972, Patricia Mary Edmondson; two *s* one *d*. *Educ:* Charterhouse (Scholar); University Coll., Oxford (Exhibnr). Served TA Parachute Regt, 1963. Researcher, BBC TV Great War series, 1963–64; Reporter, Evening Standard, 1965–67; Fellow, US World Press Inst., 1967–68; Roving Correspondent, Evening Standard, 1968–70; Reporter, BBC TV Current Affairs, 1970–73; freelance journalist and broadcaster, 1973–; Editor, Evening Standard Londoner's Diary, 1976–77; Columnist, Daily Express, 1981–83; contributor, Sunday Times, 1985–86. As War Correspondent, covered Middle East, Indochina, Angola, India-Pakistan, Cyprus, Rhodesia and S Atlantic. Mem., Press Complaints Commn, 1991–. TV documentaries for BBC and Central TV, 1970–: Ping-Pong in Peking, 1971; The War about Peace, 1983; Alarums and Exercursions, 1984; Cold Comfort Farm, 1985; The War in Korea (series), 1988; We Are All Green Now, 1990. Trustee: Game Conservancy, 1987–; Liddell Hart Archive, KCL, 1988–. FRHistS 1988. Journalist of the Year, British Press Awards, 1982 (cited 1973 and 1980); What The Papers Say, Granada TV: Reporter of the Year, 1982; Editor of the Year, 1988. *Publications:* America 1968: the fire this time, 1968; Ulster 1969: the struggle for civil rights in Northern Ireland, 1970; Montrose: the King's champion, 1977; Yoni: the hero of Entebbe, 1979; Bomber Command, 1979 (Somerset Maugham Prize for Non-Fiction, 1980); (with Len Deighton) The Battle of Britain, 1980; Das Reich, 1981; (with Simon Jenkins) The Battle for The Falklands, 1983 (Yorkshire Post Book of the Year Award); Overlord: D-Day and the battle for Normandy, 1984, 2nd edn 1989 (Yorkshire Post Book of the Year Award); Victory in Europe, 1985; (ed) Oxford Book of Military Anecdotes, 1985; The Korean War, 1987 (NCR Prize shortlist); Outside Days, 1989; contrib. DNB, Country Life, Shooting Times. *Recreations:* shooting, fishing. *Address:* Guilsborough Lodge, Guilsborough, Northants; (office) The Daily Telegraph, South Quay Plaza, E14. *T:* 071–538 5000. *Clubs:* Brooks's, Beefsteak.

HASTINGS, Michael; playwright; *b* 2 Sept. 1938; *s* of Max Emmanuel Gerald and Marie Katherine Hastings; *m* 1975, Victoria Hardie; two *s*; one *d* by previous *m*. *Educ:* various South London schools. Bespoke tailoring apprenticeship, London, 1953–56. FRGS. *Plays:* Don't Destroy Me, 1956; Yes and After, 1957; The World's Baby, 1962; Lee Harvey Oswald: 'a far mean streak of indepence brought on by negleck', 1966; The Cutting of the Cloth (unperformed autobiographical play), 1969; The Silence of Saint-Just, 1971; For the West (Uganda), 1977; Gloo Joo, 1978; Full Frontal, 1979; Carnival War a Go Hot, 1980; Midnite at the Starlite, 1980; Molière's The Miser (adaptation), 1982; Tom and Viv, 1984; The Emperor (adapted with Jonathan Miller), 1987; A Dream of People, 1990; Roberto Cossa's La Nona (adaptation), 1991; *for film and television:* For the West (Congo), 1963; Blue as his Eyes the Tin Helmet He Wore, 1966; The Search for the Nile, 1972; The Nightcomers, 1972; Auntie Kathleen's Old Clothes, 1977; Murder Rap, 1980; Midnight at the Starlight, 1980; Michael Hastings in Brixton, 1980; Stars of the Roller State Disco, 1984; The Emperor (dir. by Jonathan Miller), 1988. *Publications: plays include:* Don't Destroy Me, 1956; Yes and After, 1959; Three Plays, 1965; Lee Harvey Oswald: 'a far mean streak of indepence brought on by negleck', 1968; Three Plays, 1978; Carnival War/Midnite at the Starlite, 1979; Tom and Viv, 1985; Three Political Plays, 1990; *novels:* The Game, 1957; The Frauds, 1960; Tussy is Me, 1968; The Nightcomers, 1971; And in the Forest the Indians, 1975; *poems:* Love me Lambeth, 1959; *stories:* Bart's Mornings and other Tales of Modern Brazil, 1975; *criticism:* Rupert Brooke, The Handsomest Young Man in England, 1967; Sir Richard Burton: a biography, 1978. *Address:* 2 Helix Gardens, Brixton Hill, SW2.

HASTINGS, Sir Stephen (Lewis Edmonstone), Kt 1983; MC 1944; Partner and Manager, Milton Park Stud; *b* 4 May 1921; *s* of late Lewis Aloysius MacDonald Hastings, MC, and of Edith Meriel Edmonstone; *m* 1st, 1948, Harriet Mary Elisabeth (marr. diss. 1971), *d* of Col Julian Latham Tomlin, CBE, DSO; one *s* one *d*; 2nd, 1975, Hon. Elisabeth Anne Lady Naylor-Leyland, *yr d* of late Viscount FitzAlan of Derwent and of Countess Fitzwilliam. *Educ:* Eton; RMC, Sandhurst. Gazetted Ensign, Scots Guards, 1939; served 2nd Bn, Western Desert, 1941–43 (despatches); SAS Regt, 1943. Joined Foreign Office, 1948. British Legation, Helsinki, 1950–52; British Embassy, Paris, 1953–58; First Sec., Political Office, Middle East Forces, 1959–60. MP (C) Mid-Bedfordshire, Nov. 1960–1983. Chm., BMSS Ltd, 1978–; Dir, Fitzwilliam Estates Co., 1980–. Chm., British Field Sports Soc., 1982–88; Mem. Council, Thoroughbred Breeders Assoc. Jt Master, Fitzwilliam Hounds. *Publication:* The Murder of TSR2, 1966. *Recreations:* fieldsports, skiing, painting. *Address:* Milton, Peterborough PE6 7AA; 12A Ennismore Gardens, SW7. *Clubs:* White's, Pratt's, Buck's.

See also Sir P. V. Naylor-Leyland, Bt.

HASTINGS BASS, family name of **Earl of Huntingdon**.

HASWELL, (Anthony) James (Darley), OBE 1985; Insurance Ombudsman, 1981–89; Chairman, Appeals Tribunals, Financial Intermediaries, Managers and Brokers Regulatory Association, 1989; Director, Housing Standards Company Ltd, since 1989; *b* 4 Aug. 1922; *s* of Brig. Chetwynd Henry Haswell, CIE, and Dorothy Edith (*née* Berry); *m* 1957, Angela Mary (*née* Murphy); three *s* one *d*. *Educ:* Winchester Coll.; St John's Coll., Cambridge (MA). Solicitor of the Supreme Court. Admitted Solicitor, 1949; RAC Legal Dept, 1949; private practice, London and Cornwall, 1950–51; commnd, Army Legal Services Staff List (Captain), 1952; Temp. Major 1956; Lt-Col 1967; retired from Army Legal Corps, 1981. *Publications:* Insurance Ombudsman Bureau annual reports for years 1981–88; miscellaneous articles in industry jls. *Recreations:* chamber music, theatre, painting, woodwork, Insurance Orchestra (Chm. and playing member). *Address:* 31 Chipstead Street, SW6 3SR. *T:* 071–736 1163.

HASZELDINE, Dr Robert Neville, ScD; FRS 1968; CChem, FRSC; scientific consultant; Professor of Chemistry, 1957–82, Head of Department of Chemistry, 1957–76, and Principal, 1976–82, University of Manchester Institute of Science and Technology (Faculty of Technology, The University of Manchester); *b* Manchester, 3 May 1925; *s* of late Walter Haszeldine and late Hilda Haszeldine (*née* Webster); *m* 1954, Pauline Elvina Goodwin (*d* 1987); two *s* two *d*. *Educ:* Stockport Grammar Sch.; University of Birmingham (John Watt Meml Schol., 1942; PhD 1947; DSc 1955); Sidney Sussex Coll., Cambridge (MA, PhD 1949); Queens' Coll., Cambridge (ScD 1957). University of Cambridge: Asst in Research in Organic Chemistry, 1949; University Demonstrator in Organic and Inorganic Chemistry, 1951; Asst Dir of Research, 1956; Fellow and Dir of Studies, Queens' Coll., 1954–57, Hon. Fellow, 1976. Mem. various Govt Cttees, 1957–. Tilden Lectr, 1968; Vis. Lectr at universities and laboratories in the USA, Russia, Switzerland, Austria, Germany, Japan, China, Israel, S America and France. Chm., Langdales Soc., 1987–; Lord of the Manor of Langdale, 1988. Meldola Medal, 1953; Corday-Morgan Medal and Prize, 1960. *Publications:* numerous scientific publications in chemical jls. *Recreations:* mountaineering, gardening, natural history, good food, wine, wilderness travel. *Address:* Copt Howe, Chapel Stile, Great Langdale, Cumbria LA22 9JR. *T:* Langdale (09667) 685.

HATCH, family name of **Baron Hatch of Lusby.**

HATCH OF LUSBY, Baron *cr* 1978 (Life Peer), of Oldfield in the County of W Yorks; **John Charles Hatch;** author, lecturer, broadcaster; *b* 1 Nov. 1917; *s* of John James Hatch and Mary White. *Educ:* Keighley Boys' Grammar School; Sidney Sussex Coll., Cambridge (BA). Tutor, Nat. Council of Labour Colls, 1942–44; Nat. Organiser, Independent Labour Party, 1944–48; Lectr, Glasgow Univ., 1948–53; Sec., Commonwealth Dept, Labour Party, 1954–61; Dir, Extra-Mural Dept, Univ. of Sierra Leone, 1961–62; Director: African Studies Programme, Houston, Texas, 1964–70; Inst. of Human Relations, Zambia Univ., 1980–82. Commonwealth Correspondent, New Statesman, 1950–70. Hon. Fellow, School of Peace Studies, Univ. of Bradford, 1976. Hon. DLitt, Univ. of St Thomas, Houston, 1981. *Publications:* The Dilemma of South Africa, 1953; New from Africa, 1956; Everyman's Africa, 1959; Africa Today and Tomorrow, 1960; A History of Post-War Africa, 1964; The History of Britain in Africa, 1966; Africa: The Re-Birth of Self-Rule, 1968; Tanzania, 1969; Nigeria, 1971; Africa Emergent, 1974; Two African Statesmen, 1976. *Recreations:* cricket, music. *Address:* House of Lords, Westminster, SW1A 0PW. *T:* 071–219 5353. *Clubs:* Commonwealth Trust, MCC.

HATCH, David Edwin; Managing Director, Network Radio BBC (formerly BBC Radio), since 1987; Vice-Chairman, BBC Enterprises, since 1987; *b* 7 May 1939; *s* of Rev. Raymond Harold Hatch and Winifred Edith May (*née* Brookes); *m* 1964, Ann Elizabeth Martin; two *s* one *d*. *Educ:* St John's Sch., Leatherhead; Queens' Coll., Cambridge (MA, DipEd). Actor, Cambridge Circus, 1963; BBC: I'm Sorry I'll Read That Again, 1964; Producer, Light Entertainment Radio, 1964, Executive Producer, 1972; Network Editor Radio, Manchester, 1974; Head of Light Entertainment Radio, 1978; Controller: Radio Two, 1980–83; Radio 4, 1983–86; Dir of Programmes, Radio, 1986–87. Dir, The Listener, 1988–90. Vice-Chairman: Sound and Vision Corp., 1991– (Mem., Bd of Management Services, 1981–90); EBU Radio Prog. Cttee, 1987–; Pres., TRIC, 1990. FRSA. *Recreations:* winemaking, laughing, family. *Address:* The Windmill, Ray's Hill, Cholesbury, near Chesham, Bucks HP5 2UJ. *T:* Cholesbury (024029) 542. *Clubs:* Rugby, Lord's Taverners'.

HATCH, Dr Marshall Davidson, AM 1981; FRS 1980; FAA 1975; Chief Research Scientist, Division of Plant Industry, CSIRO, Canberra, since 1970; *b* 24 Dec. 1932; *s* of Lloyd Davidson Hatch and Alice Endesby Hatch (*née* Dalziel); divorced; two *s*. *Educ:* Newington Coll., Sydney; Univ. of Sydney (BSc, PhD). FAA 1975. Res. Scientist, Div. of Food Res., CSIRO, 1955–59; Post Doctoral Res. Fellow, Univ. of Calif., Davis, 1959–61; Res. Scientist, Colonial Sugar Refining Co. Ltd, Brisbane, 1961–66 and 1968–69 (Reader in Plant Biochemistry, Univ. of Queensland, Brisbane, 1967). Foreign Associate, Nat. Acad. of Sciences, USA, 1990. Rank Prize, 1981. *Publications:* 150 papers, reviews and chaps in scientific jls and text books in field of photosynthesis and other areas of plant biochemistry. *Recreations:* skiing, running. *Address:* (office) Division of Plant Industry, CSIRO, PO Box 1600, Canberra City, ACT 2601, Australia. *T:* 062 465264.

HATCHARD, Frederick Henry; Stipendiary Magistrate for Metropolitan County of West Midlands (Birmingham), 1981–91, retired; *b* 22 April 1923; *s* of Francis and May Hatchard; *m* 1955, Patricia Egerton; two *s*. *Educ:* Yardley Grammar Sch., Birmingham. Justices Clerk: Sutton Coldfield and Coleshill, 1963–67; Walsall, 1967–81. *Recreations:* walking, gardening. *Address:* 3(B) Manor Road, Streetly, Sutton Coldfield B74 3NQ.

HATENDI, Rt. Rev. Ralph Peter; *see* Harare, Bishop of.

HATFIELD, Rt. Rev. Leonard Fraser; Bishop of Nova Scotia, 1980–84, retired; *b* 1 Oct. 1919; *s* of Otto Albert Hatfield and Ada Hatfield (*née* Tower). *Educ:* Port Greville and Amherst High School; King's and Dalhousie Univ., Halifax (BA 1940, MA 1943, Sociology). Deacon 1942, priest 1943; Priest Assistant, All Saints Cathedral, Halifax, NS, 1942–46; Rector of Antigonish, NS, 1946–51; Asst. Sec., Council for Social Service of Anglican Church of Canada, 1951–54; Gen. Sec., 1955–61; Rector: Christ Church, Dartmouth, NS, 1961–71; St John's, Truro, NS, 1971–76. Canon of All Saints Cathedral, Halifax, 1969; Bishop Suffragan, Dio. NS, 1976. Has served: Dio. Council, NS Synod; Corpn of Anglican Dio. Centre; Dean and Chapter, All Saints Cathedral; Bd of Governors, King's Coll.; Program Cttee and Unit of Public Social Responsibility, Gen. Synod; Council of Churches on Justice and Corrections; Anglican Cons. Council, and various cttees of WCC; Organizing Sec., Primate's World Relief and Develt Fund; founding mem., Vanier Inst. of the Family, Ottawa; convened Primate's Task Force on Ordination of Women to the Priesthood; rep. Anglican Church of Canada at Internat. Bishops' Seminar, Anglican Centre in Rome, 1980. Hon. DD: Univ. of King's Coll., Halifax, NS, 1956; Atlantic Sch. of Theology, Halifax, NS, 1985. *Publications:* He Cares, 1958; Simon Gibbons (First Eskimo Priest), 1987; Sammy the Prince, 1990. *Recreations:* fishing, gardening, travelling, and playing bridge. *Address:* Port Greville, Site 31, Box O, RR#3, Parrsboro, Nova Scotia B0M 1S0, Canada.

HATFULL, Alan Frederick; Counsellor (Labour), Bonn, 1981–87; *b* 12 June 1927; *s* of Frederick George Hatfull and Florence May Hatfull (*née* Dickinson); *m* 1951, Terttu Kaarina Wahlroos; one *s* one *d*. *Educ:* St Olave's and St Saviour's Grammar School; London School of Economics. BSc (Econ) 1951. Assistant Principal, Min. of Labour, 1951, Principal 1957, Assistant Sec., 1965; Director, Commn on Industrial Relations, 1970–73; Counsellor (Labour), Paris, 1977–81. *Address:* 75 Darwin Court, Gloucester Avenue, NW1 7BQ.

HATHERTON, 8th Baron *cr* 1835; **Edward Charles Littleton;** *b* 24 May 1950; *s* of Mervyn Cecil Littleton (*d* 1970) (*g s* of 3rd Baron) and of Margaret Ann, *d* of Frank Sheehy; *S* cousin, 1985; *m* 1974, Hilda Maria, *d* of Rodolfo Robert; one *s* two *d*. *Heir:* *s* Hon. Thomas Edward Littleton, *b* 7 March 1977. *Address:* PO Box 3358, San José, Costa Rica.

HATTERSLEY, Edith Mary, (Molly Hattersley); educational consultant, since 1990; Visiting Fellow, Institute of Education, University of London (Management Development Centre), since 1990; *b* 5 Feb. 1931; *d* of Michael and Sally Loughran; *m* 1956, Rt Hon. Roy Sydney George Hattersley, *qv*. *Educ:* Consett Grammar Sch.; University College of Hull. BA Hons English (London), CertEd (Hull). Assistant Mistress at schools in Surrey and Yorkshire, 1953–61; Sen. Mistress, Myers Grove Sch., Sheffield, 1961–64; Dep. Headmistress, Kidbrooke Sch., SE3, 1965–69; Headmistress, Hurlingham Sch., SW6, 1969–74; Headmistress, Creighton Sch., N10, 1974–82; Dep. Dir of Educn, ILEA, 1983–90. Advr on educnl matters to Trustees of BM, 1978–86. Chairman of Cttee, Assoc. of Head Mistresses, 1975–77; Pres., Secondary Heads Assoc., 1980–81. Mem. Ct of Governors, LSE, 1970–. FRSA 1982. *Recreation:* reading.

HATTERSLEY, Rt. Hon. Roy Sydney George, PC 1975; BSc (Econ.); MP (Lab) Sparkbrook Division of Birmingham since 1964; Deputy Leader of the Labour Party, since 1983; *b* 28 Dec. 1932; *s* of Frederick Roy Hattersley, Sheffield; *m* 1956, Molly Hattersley, *qv*. *Educ:* Sheffield City Grammar Sch.; Univ. of Hull. Journalist and Health Service Executive, 1956–64; Mem. Sheffield City Council, 1957–65 (Chm. Housing Cttee and Public Works Cttee). PPS to Minister of Pensions and National Insurance, 1964–67; Jt Parly Sec., DEP (formerly Min. of Labour), 1967–69; Minister of Defence for Administration, 1969–70; Labour Party spokesman: on Defence, 1972; on Educn and Sci., 1972–74; Minister of State, FCO, 1974–76; Sec. of State for Prices and Consumer Protection, 1976–79; principal opposition spokesman on environment, 1979–80, on home affairs, 1980–83, on Treasury and economic affairs, 1983–87, on home affairs, 1987–. Visiting Fellow: Inst. of Politics, Univ. of Harvard, 1971, 1972; Nuffield Coll., Oxford, 1984–. Dir, Campaign for a European Political Community 1966–67. Columnist: Punch; The Guardian; The Listener, 1979–82; Columnist of the Year, Granada, 1982. *Publications:* Nelson, 1974; Goodbye to Yorkshire (essays), 1976; Politics Apart, 1982; Press Gang, 1983; A Yorkshire Boyhood, 1983; Choose Freedom: the future for Democratic Socialism, 1987; Economic Priorities for a Labour Government, 1987; The Maker's Mark (novel), 1990; In That Quiet Earth, 1991. *Address:* House of Commons, SW1A 0AA. *Club:* Reform.

HATTO, Prof. Arthur Thomas, MA; FBA 1991; Head of the Department of German, Queen Mary College, University of London, 1938–77; *b* 11 Feb. 1910; *s* of Thomas Hatto, LLB and Alice Walters; *m* 1935, Margot Feibelmann; one *d*. *Educ:* Dulwich Coll.; King's Coll., London (Fellow, 1971); University Coll., London. BA (London) 1931; MA (with Distinction), 1934. Lektor für Englisch, University of Berne, 1932–34; Asst Lectr in German, KCL, 1934–38; Queen Mary Coll., University of London, 1938 (Head of Dept of German). Temp. Sen. Asst, Foreign Office, 1939–45; Part-time Lectr in German, University Coll., London, 1944–45; returned to Queen Mary Coll., 1945; Reader in German Language and Literature, 1946, Prof. of German Language and Literature, 1953, University of London. Governor: SOAS, Univ. of London, 1960 (Foundn Day Lecture, 1970; Hon. Fellow, 1981); QMC, Univ. of London, 1968–70. Chairman: London Seminar on Epic; Cttee 'A' (Theol. and Arts), Central Research Fund, Univ. of London, 1969. Fellow: Royal Anthropological Institute; Royal Asiatic Society (lecture: Plot and character in Kirghiz epic poetry of the mid 19th cent., 1976); Leverhulme Emeritus Fellow (heroic poetry in Central Asia and Siberia), 1977–. Lectr, Rheinisch-Westfälische Akad. der Wissenschaften, Düsseldorf, 1990. Corresp. Mem., Finno-Ugrian Soc., 1978; Associate Mem., Seminar für Sprach-und Kulturwissenschaft Zentralasiens, Univ. of Bonn, 1984. *Publications:* (with R. J. Taylor) The Songs of Neidhart von Reuental, 1958; Gottfried von Strassburg, Tristan (trans. entire for first time) with Tristran of Thomas (newly trans.) with an Introduction, 1960; The Niblungenlied: a new translation, with Introduction and Notes, 1964; editor of Eos, an enquiry by fifty scholars into the theme of the alba in world literature, 1965; (ed for first time with translation and commentary) The Memorial Feast for Kökötöy-khan: a Kirghiz epic poem, 1977; Essays on Medieval

German and Other Poetry, 1980; Parzival, Wolfram von Eschenbach, a new translation, 1980; gen. editor, Traditions of Heroic and Epic Poetry, vol. I 1980, vol. II 1989; (re-ed with trans. and commentary) The Manas of Wilhelm Radloff, 1990; articles in learned periodicals. *Recreations:* reading, gardening, walking.

HATTON; *see* Finch Hatton, family name of Earl of Winchilsea.

HATTY, Hon. Sir Cyril (James), Kt 1963; Minister of Finance, Bophuthatswana, 1979–82; *b* 22 Dec. 1908; *o s* of James Hatty and Edith (*née* Russen); *m* 1937, Doris Evelyn, *o d* of James Lane Stewart and Mable Grace Stewart; two *s*. *Educ:* Westminster City Sch. Deputy Dir, O and M Division, UK Treasury, until Jan. 1947; emigrated to S Africa, in industry, Feb. 1947; moved to Bulawayo, Southern Rhodesia, in industry, Jan. 1948. MP for Bulawayo North, Sept. 1950–Dec. 1962; Minister of Treasury, Jan. 1954–Sept. 1962, also Minister of Mines, Feb. 1956–Dec. 1962. FCIS; Fellow, Inst. of Chartered Management Accountants; FBIM. *Publications:* Digest of SR Company Law, 1952; There's Peace in Baobabwe, 1989. *Recreations:* painting, music. *Address:* Merton Park, Norton, Zimbabwe. *Clubs:* Harare, New (Harare, Zimbabwe).

HAUGHEY, Charles James, Teachta Dala (TD) (FF) for Dublin North Central; Taoiseach (Prime Minister of Ireland), 1979–81, March–Dec. 1982 and since 1987; *b* 16 Sept. 1925; *s* of Seán Haughey and late Sarah Ann (*née* McWilliams); *m* 1951, Maureen Lemass; three *s* one *d*. *Educ:* Scoil Mhuire, Marino, Dublin; St Joseph's Christian Brothers' Sch., Fairview, Dublin; University College Dublin (BCom); King's Inns, Dublin. Called to Irish Bar, 1949. Member, Dublin Corporation, 1953–55; Member (FF) Dail Eireann for a Dublin constituency, 1957–, now representing Dublin North Central; Parliamentary Secretary to Minister for Justice, 1960–61; Minister: for Justice, 1961–64; for Agriculture, 1964–66; for Finance, 1966–70; Chairman, Jt Cttee on the Secondary Legislation of the European Communities, 1973–77; Minister for Health and Social Welfare, 1977–79; Leader of the Opposition, 1982–87. President: Fianna Fail Party, 1979–; European Council, Jan.–June 1990. Hon. Fellow, RHA. Hon. doctorates: Dublin City Univ.; UC Dublin; Univ. of Clermont-Ferrand; Univ. of Notre Dame, USA. *Recreations:* music, art, sailing, riding, swimming. *Address:* Abbeville, Kinsaley, Co. Dublin, Ireland. *T:* (01) 450111. *Clubs:* St Stephen's Green, Ward Union Hunt (Dublin).

HAUGHTON, Surgeon Rear-Adm. John Marsden, LVO 1964; FFARCS; retired, 1982; *b* 27 Oct. 1924; *s* of Col Samuel George Steele Haughton, CIE, OBE, IMS, and Marjory Winifred Haughton (*née* Porter); *m* 1956, Lucy Elizabeth Lee, Tackley, Oxon; three *s* one *d*. *Educ:* Winchester Coll.; St Thomas' Hosp., 1942–48 (MRCS, LRCP, DA). Joined Royal Navy, 1949; 45 Commando RM, Malaya, 1950; Anaesthetic Specialist, RN Hosp., Plymouth, 1952; HMS Superb, 1954; RN Hosps, Haslar, 1956, Chatham, 1958; Sen. Anaesthetist, RN Hosp., Malta, 1959; PMO, Royal Yacht Britannia, 1962; Consultant Anaesthetist, RN Hospital: Haslar, 1964; Malta, 1968; Haslar, 1970; Comd MO and MO in charge RN Hosp., Malta, 1975; MO in charge RN Hosp., Plymouth, 1978; Surg. Rear-Adm. (Naval Hosps), Haslar, 1980–82. QHP 1978–82. *Recreations:* fishing, gardening, walking.

HAUPTMAN, Prof. Herbert Aaron, PhD; President, Medical Foundation of Buffalo, Inc., since 1986; *b* 14 Feb. 1917; *s* of Israel Hauptman and Leah Hauptman (*née* Rosenfeld); *m* Edith Citrynell; two *d*. *Educ:* City Coll., NY (BS 1937); Columbia Univ. (MA 1939); Univ. of Maryland (PhD 1955). Census Bureau, 1940–42; Electronics Instructor, USAF, 1942–43, 1946–47; Aerology Officer, USNR, 1943–46; Naval Research Laboratory: Physicist-Mathematician, 1947–70; Rep. of Univ. of Maryland Math. Dept, 1956–70, and part-time Prof., Univ. of Maryland; Head, Mathematical Physics Br., 1965–67; Acting Supt, Math. and Inf. Scis. Div., 1967–68; Head, Applied Math. Br., Math. Div., 1968–69; Head, Math. Staff, Optical Scis Div., 1969–70; Medical Foundation of Buffalo: Head, Math. Biophysics Lab., 1970–72; Dep. Res. Dir, 1972; Exec. Vice-Pres., and Res. Dir, 1972–85; Res. Prof. of Biophysical Scis, State Univ. of NY at Buffalo, 1970–. Mem., US scientific instns. Holder of numerous honours and awards; Hon. DSc: Maryland, 1985; City Coll. of NY, 1986; D'Youville Coll., 1989; Bar-Ilan Univ., Israel, and Columbia Univ., NY, 1990. Hon. Dr Chem., Univ. of Parma, 1989. Nobel Prize in Chemistry (with Jerome Karle), 1985. *Publications:* Solution of the Phase Problem (with J. Karle), 1953; Crystal Structure Determination, 1972; (ed) Direct Methods in Crystallography (procs 1976 Intercongress Symposium), 1978; numerous articles on crystallography in learned jls. *Recreations:* stained glass art, swimming, hiking. *Address:* Medical Foundation of Buffalo, 73 High Street, Buffalo, NY 14203–1196, USA. *Clubs:* Cosmos (Washington); Saturn (Buffalo).

HAUSER, Frank Ivor, CBE 1968; free-lance director; *b* 1 Aug. 1922; *s* of late Abraham and of Sarah Hauser; unmarried. *Educ:* Cardiff High Sch.; Christ Church, Oxford. Oxford, 1941–42; RA, 1942–45; Oxford, 1946–48. BBC Drama Producer, 1948–51; Director: Salisbury Arts Theatre, 1952–53; Midland Theatre Co., 1945–55. Formed Meadow Players Ltd, which re-opened the Oxford Playhouse, 1956, Dir of Productions, 1956–73; took Oxford Playhouse Co. on tour of India, Pakistan and Ceylon, 1959–60. Produced at Sadler's Wells Opera: La Traviata, 1961; Iolanthe, 1962; Orfeo, 1965; produced: at Oxford Playhouse: Antony and Cleopatra, 1965; Phèdre, 1966; The Promise, 1966; The Silent Woman, 1968; Pippa Passes, 1968; Uncle Vanya, 1969; Curtain Up, 1969; The Merchant of Venice, 1973; also: Il Matrimonio Segreto, Glyndebourne, 1965; A Heritage and its History, Phoenix, 1965; The Promise, Fortune, 1967; Volpone, Garrick, 1967; The Magic Flute, Sadler's Wells, 1967; Kean, Globe, 1971; The Wolf, Apollo, 1973; Cinderella, Casino, 1974; On Approval, Haymarket, 1975; All for Love, Old Vic, 1977; The Importance of Being Earnest, Old Vic, 1980; Captain Brassbound's Conversion, Haymarket, 1982; An Enemy of the People, NY, 1985; Thursday's Ladies, Apollo, 1987; Candida, Arts, 1988. *Recreation:* piano. *Address:* 5 Stirling Mansions, Canfield Gardens, NW6. *T:* 071–624 4690.

HAVARD, John David Jayne, CBE 1989; MD; Secretary, British Medical Association, 1980–89; Hon. Secretary, Commonwealth Medical Association, since 1986; *b* 5 May 1924; *s* of late Dr Arthur William Havard and Ursula Jayne Vernon Humphrey; *m* 1st, 1950, Margaret Lucy Lumsden Collis (marr. diss. 1982); two *s* one *d*; 2nd, 1982, Audrey Anne Boutwood, FRCOG, *d* of Rear Adm. L. A. Boutwood, CB, OBE. *Educ:* Malvern Coll.; Jesus Coll., Cambridge (MA, MD, LLM); Middlesex Hosp. Med. Sch. MRCP 1988. Called to the Bar, Middle Temple, 1953. Professorial Med. Unit, Middlesex Hosp., 1950; National Service, RAF, 1950–52; general practice, Lowestoft, 1952–58 (Sec., E Suffolk LMC, 1956–58). British Medical Assoc.: Asst Sec., 1958–64; Under-Sec., 1964–76; Dep. Sec., 1976–79. Short-term Cons., Council of Europe, 1964–67, OECD 1964–69, WHO 1967–, on Road Accident Prevention. Dep. Chm., Staff Side, Gen. Whitley Council for the Health Services, 1975–89; Sec., Managerial, Professional and Staffs Liaison Gp, 1978–89; Member: various Govt Working Parties on Coroners' Rules, Visual Standards for Driving, Licensing of Professional Drivers, etc. Chm., Internat. Driver Behaviour Res. Assoc., 1971–. Pres., British Acad. of Forensic Scis, 1984–85. Mem., GMC, 1989– (Mem., Professional Conduct and Standards Cttee, 1989–). Lectr, Green Coll., Oxford, 1989. Governor, Malvern Coll., 1984. Gold Medal, Inter-Scandinavian Union for Non-Alcoholic Traffic, 1962; Stevens Lectr and Gold Medallist, 1989; Widmark Award, Internat. Cttee on Alcohol, Drugs and Traffic Safety, 1989; BMA Gold Medal for Dist. Merit, 1990. Pres., CUAC, 1945–46; Captain United Hosps AC, 1946–47; London Univ. Record for 100 yards, 1947. Member, Editorial Board: Blutalkohol, 1968–; Forensic Science Rev. 1989–. *Publications:* Detection of Secret Homicide (Cambridge Studies in Criminology), 1960; Research on Effects of Alcohol and Drugs on Driving Behaviour (OECD), 1968; chapters in textbooks on legal medicine, research advances on alcohol and drugs, etc; many articles in med., legal and sci. periodical lit.; several WHO reports. *Recreations:* Bach Choir, history, English countryside. *Address:* 1 Wilton Square, N1 3DL. *T:* 071–359 2802. *Clubs:* United Oxford & Cambridge University; Achilles.

HAVARD-WILLIAMS, Peter; educational and library management consultant; Professor of Library and Information Studies and Head of Department, University of Botswana, since 1988; *b* 1922; *s* of Graham Havard-Williams and Elizabeth (*née* James); *m* 1st, 1964, Rosine (*d* 1973), *d* of late Paul Cousin, Croix de Guerre; two *d*; 2nd, 1976, Eileen Elizabeth, *d* of Oliver Cumming; one *d*. *Educ:* Bishop Gore Grammar Sch., Swansea; University Coll. of Swansea (Smith's Charity Scholar; MA Wales); Oxford Univ.; PhD Loughborough Univ. FRSA, FBIM, Associate and FLAI, FIInfSc. Sub-Librarian, Univ. of Liverpool, 1951–56; Libr. and Keeper of Hocken Collection, Univ. of Otago, 1956–60; Fellow, Knox Coll., Dunedin, 1958–60; Dep. Libr., Univ. of Leeds, 1960–61; Libr., QUB, 1961–71 (Dir, Sch. of Lib. and Inf. Studies, 1964–70); Dean and Prof., Lib. Sch., Ottawa Univ., 1971–72; Loughborough University: Foundation Prof. and Head of Dept of Library and Information Studies, 1972–87, now Prof. Emeritus; Dean of Educn and Humanities, 1976–79; Warden, Royce Hall, 1978–87; Project Head, Centre for Library and Information Management, 1979–87; Public Orator, 1980–87; Mem. Court, 1978–. Consultant, Council of Europe, 1986–87. Library Association: Vice-Pres., 1970–82; Chm. Council, 1970–71 and 1974–75; Chm. Exec. Cttee, 1976–78; Chm., Cons. Cttee on Nat. Library Co-ordination 1978–80; Chm., Bd of Assessors, 1981; Chm., NI Br., 1963 (when first all-Ireland lib. conf. held at Portrush). President: Internat. Colloquium on Univ. Lib. Bldgs, Lausanne, 1971; Internat. Seminar on Children's Lit., Loughborough, 1976; Vice-Pres., Internat. Fedn of Lib. Assocs, 1970–77. Chm., Botswana Nat. Liby Bd, 1988–; Member: Adv. Cttee on Public Lib. Service, NI, 1965; Lib. Adv. Council, 1976–78; Hon. Soc. of Cymmrodorion, 1970–; Ct of Governors, UWIST, 1979–88. Lib. bldg consultant, UK and abroad, 1961–; Cons. and Mem. Brit. Delegn, Unesco Inter-govtl Conf. on Nat. Inf. Systems, Paris, 1974; Consultant to Unesco, EEC, Council of Europe, British Council and foreign govts and instns, 1974–. Ext. Examr, London, Sheffield, Strathclyde, NUI, CNAA, Kenyatta Univ. and Univs of Ibadan, WI, Zambia; Lectr, European Inst. of Inf. Management, 1983. Hon. Librarian and Organist, Cathedral of Holy Cross, Gaborone, 1988–. Editor, IFLA Communications and Publications, 1971–78; Editorial Consultant, Internat. Library Review, 1969–89; Consultant Editor: Library Progress Internat., 1981–; Library Waves, 1986–, etc. Hon. FLA 1986. Hon. Dr Confucian Univ., Seoul, 1982. *Publications:* (ed) Marsden and the New Zealand Mission, 1961; Planning Information Manpower, 1974; Departmental Profile, 1981; Development of Public Library Services in Sierra Leone, 1984; articles in Jl of Documentation, Libri, Internat. Lib. Rev., Unesco Bull. for Libs, Eng. Studies, Essays in Crit., and Monthly Mus. Record, etc. *Recreations:* collecting Bloomsbury first editions, bears (esp. Winnie the Pooh), music, idling. *Address:* University of Botswana, PB 0022, Gaborone, Botswana. *T:* 267–356963. *Clubs:* Athenæum, Commonwealth Trust; Gaborone.

HAVEL, Václav; President of Czech and Slovak Federal Republic, since 1989; writer; *b* Prague, 5 Oct. 1936; *s* of Václav M. Havel and Božena Havel (*née* Vavrečková); *m* 1964, Olga Šplíchalová. *Educ:* Faculty of Economy, 1955–57 (unfinished); Drama Dept, Acad. of Arts, Prague, 1966. Chemical Lab. Technician, 1951–55; in Czechoslovak army, 1957–59; stagehand, ABC Theatre, Prague, 1959–60; Theatre on the Balustrade, Prague: stagehand, 1960–61; Asst to Artistic Dir, 1961–63; Literary Manager, 1963–68; Resident Playwright, 1968; Editl Bd, Tvář, 1965; freelance work, 1969–74; labourer, Trutnov Brewery, N Bohemia, 1974; freelance work, 1975–89; Co-Founder, Charter '77 (human rights movement), 1977, and one of its first three spokesmen; Co-Founder, Cttee for Defence of Unjustly Persecuted (VONS), 1978; under house arrest, 1978–79; imprisoned, Oct. 1979–March 1983; Editl Bd and regular contributor, Lidové noviny, 1987–89; imprisoned, Jan.–May 1989; Co-Founder, Civic Forum, 1989. Chm., Young Writers, Czechoslovak Writers Assoc., 1965; Member: Czechoslovak Helsinki Cttee, 1989; Czech Pen Club, 1989. Holds hon. degrees from many institutions. Awards received include: Austrian State Prize for European Literature, 1969; Erasmus Prize, 1986; Olof Palme Prize, 1989; Simon Bolivar Prize, UNESCO, 1990. *Publications: plays:* The Garden Party, 1963; The Memorandum, 1965; The Increased Difficulty of Concentration, 1968; The Beggar's Opera, 1972; Audience, 1975; Private View, 1975; The Mountain Hotel, 1976; Protest, 1979; The Mistake, 1983; Largo Desolato, 1984; Temptation, 1985; Redevelopment (US as Slum Clearance), 1987; *others:* (contrib.) The Power of the Powerless, 1986; Letters to Olga, 1988; Disturbing the Peace, 1990; Open Letters: prose 1965–1989, 1991. *Address:* Kancelář prezidenta republiky, 11908 Prague-Hrad, Czechoslovakia; Rašínovo nábřeží 78, 12000 Prague 2, Czechoslovakia.

HAVELOCK, Sir Wilfrid (Bowen), Kt 1963; *b* 14 April 1912; *s* of late Rev. E. W. Havelock and Helen (*née* Bowen); *m* 1st, 1938, Mrs M. E. Pershouse (*née* Vincent) (marr. diss. 1967); one *s*; 2nd, 1972, Mrs Patricia Mumford, *widow* of Major Philip S. Mumford. *Educ:* Imperial Service Coll., Windsor, Berks. Elected to Kenya Legislative Council, 1948; Chairman, European Elected Members, 1952; Mem., Kenya Executive Council, 1952; Minister for Local Government, Kenya, 1954; Minister for Agriculture, Kenya, 1962–63. Dep. Chm., Agricl Finance Corp., Kenya, 1964–84; Member: Nat. Irrigation Bd, 1974–79; Hotels and Restaurant Authority, 1975–81. Dir, Baobab Farm Ltd, 1980–. Chm., Kenya Assoc. of Hotelkeepers and Caterers, 1974, 1975, 1976. *Address:* PO Box 30181, Nairobi, Kenya. *T:* Nairobi 732142. *Clubs:* Commonwealth Trust; Mombasa, Muthaiga Country, Nairobi, Mount Kenya Safari (Kenya).

HAVELOCK-ALLAN, Sir Anthony James Allan, 4th Bt *cr* 1858; film producer; *b* 28 Feb. 1904; *s* of Allan (2nd *s* of Sir Henry Havelock-Allan, 1st Bt, VC, GCB, MP), and Annie Julia, *d* of Sir William Chaytor, 3rd Bt; *S* brother, 1975; *m* 1st, 1939, Valerie Louise Hobson, *qv* (marr. diss. 1952), *d* of late Comdr Robert Gordon Hobson, RN; one *s* (and one *s* decd); 2nd, 1979, Maria Theresa Consuela (Sara) Ruiz de Villafranca, *d* of late Don Carlos Ruiz de Villafranca (formerly Ambassador to Chile and to Brazil), and Doña Julia Ruiz de Villafranca y Osuña, Villafranca, prov. Madrid. *Educ:* Charterhouse; Switzerland. Artists and Recording Manager, Brunswick Gramophone Co., London and Vox AG, Berlin, 1924–29; entered films as Casting Dir and Producer's Asst, 1933; produced quota films for Paramount; produced for Pinebrook Ltd and Two Cities Films, 1938–40; Assoc. Producer to Noel Coward, 1941; with David Lean and Ronald Neame, formed Cineguild, 1942; Producer, Assoc. Producer or in charge of production for Cineguild, 1942–47; formed Constellation Films, independent co. producing for Rank Org. and British Lion, 1949; Mem. Cinematographic Films Council and Nat. Film Production Council, 1948–51; Mem. Home Office Cttee on Employment of Children in Entertainment; Chm. British Film Academy, 1952; formed with Lord Brabourne and

Major Daniel Angel British Home Entertainment to introduce Pay TV, 1958; Chm. Council of Soc. of Film and Television Arts (now BAFTA), 1962, 1963; Mem. Nat. Film Archive Cttee; a Gov. British Film Inst. and Mem. Institute's Production Cttee, 1958–65; Mem. US Academy of Motion Pictures Arts and Sciences, 1970. Films include: This Man is News, This Man in Paris, Lambeth Walk, Unpublished Story, From the Four Corners (documentary prod and dir), Brief Encounter (shared Academy script nomination), Great Expectations (shared Academy script nomination), Take my Life, Blanche Fury, Shadow of the Eagle, Never Take No for an Answer, Interrupted Journey, Young Lovers (dir Anthony Asquith), Orders to Kill (dir Anthony Asquith), Meet Me Tonight, The Quare Fellow, An Evening with the Royal Ballet (directed two ballets); (for television): National Theatre's Uncle Vanya, Olivier's Othello, Zeffirelli's Romeo and Juliet, David Lean's Ryan's Daughter. *Heir: s* (Anthony) Mark David Havelock-Allan [*b* 4 April 1951; *m* 1st, 1976, Lucy Clare, *d* of late Alexander Plantagenet Mitchell-Innes; 2nd, 1986, Alison Lee Caroline, *d* of late Leslie Francis Foster]. *Address:* c/o Lloyds Bank, Berkeley Square, W1.

HAVERS, family name of **Baron Havers.**

HAVERS, Baron *cr* 1987 (Life Peer), of St Edmundsbury in the County of Suffolk; **Robert Michael Oldfield Havers;** Kt 1972; PC 1977; Lord High Chancellor of Great Britain, 1987; *b* 10 March 1923; 2nd *s* of Sir Cecil Havers, QC, and late Enid Snelling; *m* 1949, Carol Elizabeth, *d* of Stuart Lay, London; two *s*. *Educ:* Westminster Sch.; Corpus Christi Coll., Cambridge (Hon. Fellow, 1988). Lieut RNVR, 1941–46. Called to Bar, Inner Temple, 1948; Master of the Bench, 1971; QC 1964; QC (NI) 1973. Recorder: of Dover, 1962–68; of Norwich, 1968–71; a Recorder, 1972; Chm., West Suffolk QS, 1965–71 (Dep. Chairman 1961–65). Chancellor of Dioceses of St Edmundsbury and Ipswich, 1965–73, of Ely, 1969–73. MP (C) Wimbledon, 1970–87; Solicitor-General, 1972–74; Shadow Attorney-General and Legal Adviser to Shadow Cabinet, 1974–79; Attorney General, 1979–87; Mem. Privileges Cttee, 1978–87. Chairman: RHM Outhwaite, Lloyds Underwriters, 1988–; Solicitors Law Stationery Soc., 1988–. Chm., Lakenheath Anglo-American Community Relations Cttee, 1966–71. Chm., Playhouse Theatre, 1988–. *Publications:* (jtly) The Poisoned Life of Mrs Maybrick, 1977; (jtly) The Royal Baccarat Scandal, 1977, new edn, 1988; (jtly) Tragedy in Three Voices: the Rattenbury murder, 1980. *Recreations:* writing, photography, reading. *Address:* House of Lords, SW1A 0PW. *Clubs:* Garrick, Pratt's, Beefsteak.

See also Hon. Dame A. E. O. Butler-Sloss.

HAVERY, Richard Orbell, QC 1980; a Recorder of the Crown Court, since 1986 (an Assistant Recorder, 1982–86); *b* 7 Feb. 1934; *s* of Joseph Horton Havery and late Constance Eleanor (*née* Orbell). *Educ:* St Paul's; Magdalen Coll., Oxford (MA 1961). Called to the Bar, Middle Temple, 1962, Bencher, 1989. *Publication:* (with D. A. McI. Kemp and M. S. Kemp) The Quantum of Damages: personal injury claims, 3rd edn, 1967. *Recreations:* music, croquet, steam locomotives. *Address:* 4 Raymond Buildings, Gray's Inn, WC1R 5BP. *T:* 071–405 7211. *Clubs:* Garrick, Hurlingham.

HAVILAND, Denis William Garstin Latimer, CB 1957; MA; CBIM; FIIM; FRSA; idc; Director, Organised Office Designs Ltd, since 1972; *b* 15 Aug. 1910; *s* of late William Alexander Haviland and of Edyth Louise Latimer. *Educ:* Rugby Sch., St John's Coll., Cambridge (MA, exam. of AMInstT). LMS Rly, 1934–39. Army, RE (Col), 1940–46. Prin., Control Office for Germany and Austria, 1946; Asst Sec., 1947; transf. FO (GS), 1947; seconded to IDC, 1950; transf. Min. of Supply, 1951; Under Sec., 1953; Dep. Sec., 1959; trans. Min. of Aviation, 1959, Deputy Sec., 1959–64. Chm., Preparatory Commn European Launcher Develt Organisation, 1962–64. Jt Man. Dir and Dep. Chm., 1964, Chm. and Man. Dir, 1965–69, Staveley Industries Ltd; Dir, Short Bros Ltd, 1964–81; Chm., Technology and Innovation Exchange, 1981–82; consultant. Mem. Council, BIM, 1967–83 (Vice-Chm., 1973–74; Chm., Professional Standards Cttee, 1975–82). Member: Management Studies Bd, CNAA, 1974–79; Business and Management Cttee and Academic Cttee, CNAA, 1979–83; Ct, Cranfield Inst. of Technology, 1970–83. Chairman: Confedn of Healing Organisations, 1981–90; Holistic Cancer Council, 1984–86. Liveryman, Coachmakers' Co. Verulam Gold Medal, BIM, 1984. *Address:* 113 Hampstead Way, NW11. *T:* 081–455 2638. *Club:* Naval and Military.

HAVILLAND; *see* de Havilland.

HAWAII, Bishop of, (Episcopal Church in the USA); *see* Browning, Rt Rev. E. L.

HAWARDEN, 9th Viscount (Ire.), *cr* 1793; **Robert Connan Wyndham Leslie Maude;** Bt 1705; Baron de Montalt 1785; *b* 23 May 1961; *s* of 8th Viscount and of Susannah Caroline Hyde, *d* of late Maj. Charles Phillips Gardner; *S* father, 1991. *Educ:* St Edmund's Sch., Canterbury; RAC Cirencester. *Heir: b* Hon. Thomas Patrick Cornwallis Maude, *b* 1 Oct. 1964.

HAWKE, family name of **Baron Hawke.**

HAWKE, 10th Baron, *cr* 1776, of Towton; **Julian Stanhope Theodore Hawke;** *b* 19 Oct. 1904; *s* of 8th Baron Hawke and Frances Alice (*d* 1959), *d* of Col J. R. Wilmer, Survey of India; *S* brother, 1985; *m* 1st, 1933, Griselda (marr. diss. 1946; she *d* 1984), *d* of late Capt. Edmund W. Bury; two *d*; 2nd, 1947, Georgette Margaret, *d* of George S. Davidson; one *s* three *d*. *Educ:* Eton; King's College, Cambridge (BA). With Glazebrook Steel & Co. Ltd, 1926–69, Director 1933–69. Served War of 1939–45 with AAF; Wing Comdr, W Africa. A Commissioner of Taxes, Manchester, for about 25 years until 1974 (for some years Head of Manchester Central Section). *Recreations:* golf (½ Blue Cambridge), shooting. *Heir: s* Hon. Edward George Hawke, ARICS, *b* 25 Jan. 1950. *Address:* The Old Mill House, Cuddington, Northwich, Cheshire. *T:* Northwich (0606) 882248. *Club:* Royal Liverpool Golf.

HAWKE, Hon. Robert James Lee, AC 1979; MP (Lab) Wills, Melbourne, since 1980; Prime Minister of Australia, since 1983; *b* 9 Dec. 1929; *m* 1956, Hazel Masterson; one *s* two *d* (and one *s* decd). *Educ:* Univ. of Western Australia (LLB, BA(Econ)); Oxford Univ. (BLitt; Hon. Fellow, University Coll., 1984). Research Officer and Advocate for Aust. Council of Trade Unions, 1958–69. Pres., ACTU, 1970–80. Australian Labor Party: Mem., Nat. Exec., 1971–; Pres., 1973–78; Leader, 1983–. Leader of the Opposition, Feb.–March 1983. Member: Governing Body of Internat. Labour Office, 1972–80; Board, Reserve Bank of Australia, 1973–80; Aust. Population and Immigration Council, 1976–80; Aust. Manufacturing Council, 1977–80. Hon. DLitt W Australia, 1984; Hon. Dr Nanjing, 1986; Hon. DPhil Hebrew Univ. of Jerusalem, 1987; Hon. LLD Univ. of NSW, 1987. *Recreations:* tennis, cricket, reading, golf, horse racing, snooker. *Address:* Parliament House, Canberra, ACT 2600, Australia.

HAWKEN, Lewis Dudley, CB 1983; a Deputy Chairman of the Board of Customs and Excise, 1980–87; *b* 23 Aug. 1931; *s* of late Richard and Doris May Evelyn Hawken; *m* 1954, Bridget Mary Gamble (*d* 1989); two *s* one *d*. *Educ:* Harrow County Sch. for Boys; Lincoln Coll., Oxford (MA). Comr of Customs and Excise, 1975. *Recreations:* collecting Victorian books, tennis. *Address:* 19 Eastcote Road, Ruislip, Mddx HA4 8BE. *T:* Ruislip (0895) 32405. *Clubs:* United Oxford & Cambridge University, MCC.

HAWKER, Albert Henry, CMG 1964; OBE 1960; *b* 31 Oct. 1911; *s* of late H. J. Hawker, Cheltenham and late Mrs G. A. Hawker, Exeter; *m* 1944, Margaret Janet Olivia (*d* 1980), *d* of late T. J. C. Acton (ICS) and Mrs M de C. Acton, BEM, Golden Furlong, Brackley, Northants; two *s*. *Educ:* Pate's Sch., Cheltenham. Served War of 1939–45: Bde Major 12th Bde, 1941–43; Staff Coll., Camberley, 1943–44; Lieut-Col Mil. Asst to CGS in India, 1944–46. RARO; Lieut-Col The Gordon Highlanders, 1946–61. Barclays Bank Ltd, Birmingham and Oxford Local Districts, 1929–39. Joined HM Overseas Civil Service, 1946; served in: Palestine, 1946–48; N Rhodesia, 1948–52; Zanzibar, 1952–64 (Development Sec., Admin. Sec., Perm. Sec. in Min. of Finance, Prime Minister's Office, Vice-President's Office and President's Office); retd, 1964. Director: Thomson Regional Newspapers Ltd, 1965–69; The Times Ltd and The Sunday Times Ltd, 1968–69; The Thomson Organization, 1969–76. Gold Cross, Royal Order of George I of Greece, 1948; Brilliant Star of Zanzibar, 1957. *Recreations:* sailing (Cdre, Zanzibar Sailing Club, 1955 and 1961), gardening, photography. *Address:* Bowling Green Farm, Cottered, near Buntingford, Herts SG9 9PT. *T:* Cottered (076381) 234. *Clubs:* Commonwealth Trust, Royal Yachting Association.

HAWKER, Rt. Rev. Dennis Gascoyne; *b* 8 Feb. 1921; *o s* of late Robert Stephen and Amelia Caroline Hawker; *m* 1944, Margaret Hamilton, *d* of late Robert and Daisy Henderson; one *s* one *d*. *Educ:* Addey and Stanhope Grammar Sch.; Queens' Coll., Cambridge (MA); Cuddesdon Theological Coll., Oxford. Lloyds Bank, 1939–40. Served War, Commissioned Officer, Royal Marines, 1940–46 (War Substantive Major). Deacon, 1950; Priest, 1951; Asst Curate, St Mary and St Eanswythe, Folkestone, 1950–55; Vicar, St Mark, South Norwood, 1955–60; St Hugh's Missioner, Dio. Lincoln, 1960–65; Vicar, St Mary and St James, Gt Grimsby, 1965–72; Bishop Suffragan of Grantham, 1972–87. Canon and Prebendary of Clifton, in Lincoln Cath., 1964–87; Proctor in Convocation, 1964–74. Hon. Chaplain, RNR, 1979–. *Address:* Pickwick Cottage, Hall Close, Heacham, Kings Lynn, Norfolk PE31 7JT. *T:* Heacham (0485) 70450. *Club:* Army and Navy.

HAWKES, (Charles Francis) Christopher, FBA, FSA; Professor of European Archaeology in the University of Oxford, and Fellow of Keble College, 1946–72, Professor Emeritus, since 1972; Hon. Fellow of Keble College, since 1972; Secretary, Committee of Research Laboratory for Archæology and History of Art, 1955–72; *b* 5 June 1905; *o s* of late Charles Pascoe Hawkes; *m* 1st, 1933, Jacquetta (from whom he obtained a divorce 1953) (*see* Jacquetta Hawkes), *yr d* of late Sir Frederick Gowland Hopkins, OM; one *s*; 2nd, 1959, Sonia Elizabeth, *o d* of late Albert Andrew Chadwick. *Educ:* Winchester Coll. (Scholar); New Coll. Oxford (Scholar). 1st in Classical Hon. Mods 1926, in Final Lit. Hum. 1928; BA 1928; MA 1931; entered British Museum, Dept. of British and Medieval Antiquities, 1928; Asst Keeper 1st Class, 1938; in charge of Prehistoric and Romano-British Antiquities, 1946. Principal in Ministry of Aircraft Production, 1940–45. Retired from British Museum, 1946. I/c Inst. of Archæology, Oxford, 1961–67, 1968–72. FBA, 1948; FSA 1932; Fellow of Royal Archæological Institute, Hon. Sec. 1930–35, and Hon. Editor of Archæological Journal, 1944–50; Pres., Prehistoric Soc., 1950–54; a National Sec. for Great Britain, 1931–48, Mem. of Permanent Council, 1948–71, and Mem. Cttee of Honour, 1971–, International Union of Prehistoric and Protohistoric Sciences; Hon. Sec. of Colchester Excavation Cttee and in joint charge of its excavations, 1930–61; in charge of, or associated with various excavations, 1925–64, on Roman and prehistoric sites, especially for the Hants Field Club, and near Oxford; conducted archæological expedns in N Portugal, 1958–59. Vis. Lectr, Univ. of Manchester, 1947–49; Lectures: Dalrymple, Univ. of Glasgow, 1948; George Grant McCurdy, Harvard Univ., 1953; Davies, Belfast, 1974; Myres Meml, Oxford, 1975; British Acad., and Accad. Naz. Lincei, Rome, 1975; Mortimer Wheeler, 1975; travelled in Europe as Leverhulme Research Fellow, 1955–58, and as Leverhulme Emeritus Fellow, 1972–73; Guest Academician, Budapest, 1971; Guest Prof., Univ. of Munich, 1974; a Visitor, Ashmolean Museum, 1961–67. President: Section H., Brit. Assoc., 1957; Hants Field Club, 1960–63; Member: Council for British Archæology 1944–72 (Pres., 1961–64; Group 9 Convener, 1964–67); Ancient Monuments Board for England, 1954–69. Mem., German Archaeological Inst.; Corresp. Mem., RIA; Swiss Soc. for Prehistory; Patronal Mem., Univ. of Barcelona Inst. of Archaeology and Prehistory. Editor of Inventaria Archæologica for Great Britain, 1954–76. Hon. Dr Rennes, 1971; Hon. DLitt NUI, 1972. Various British Acad. awards, 1963–; Gold Medal, Soc. of Antiquaries, 1981. *Publications:* St Catharine's Hill, Winchester (with J. N. L. Myres and C. G. Stevens), 1931; Archæology in England and Wales, 1914–31 (with T. D. Kendrick), 1932; Winchester College: An Essay in Description and Appreciation, 1933; The Prehistoric Foundations of Europe, 1940, 1974; Prehistoric Britain (with Jacquetta Hawkes), 1943, 1947, 1957; Camulodunum: The Excavations at Colchester, 1930–39 (with M. R. Hull), 1947; (contrib. and ed with Sonia Hawkes) Archaeology into History, vol I, 1973; (contrib. and ed with P. M. Duval) Celtic Art in Ancient Europe, 1976; (ed. and co-author with late M. R. Hull) Corpus of Ancient Brooches in Britain, vol. I, 1987; articles in encyclopædias, collaborative books, congress proceedings, and many archæological journals; received complimentary vol. by British and foreign colleagues, 1971; *relevant publication:* Hawkeseye: the early life of Christopher Hawkes, by Diana Bonakis Webster, 1991. *Recreations:* archæology, travelling, music. *Address:* Keble College, Oxford; 19 Walton Street, Oxford OX1 2HQ.

HAWKES, David, MA, DPhil; Research Fellow, All Souls College, Oxford, 1973–83, now Emeritus; *b* 6 July 1923; *s* of Ewart Hawkes and Dorothy May Hawkes (*née* Davis); *m* 1950, Sylvia Jean Perkins; one *s* three *d*. *Educ:* Bancroft's Sch. Open Scholarship in Classics, Christ Church, Oxford, 1941; Chinese Hons Sch., Oxford, 1945–47; Research Student, National Peking Univ., 1948–51. Formerly University Lecturer in Chinese, Oxford; Prof. of Chinese, Oxford Univ., 1959–71. *Publications:* Ch'u Tz'ŭ, Songs of the South, 1959, rev. edn as The Songs of the South: an Ancient Chinese Anthology of Poems by Qu Yuan and Other Poets, 1985; A Little Primer of Tu Fu, 1967; The Story of the Stone, vol. 1, 1973, vol. 2, 1977, vol. 3, 1980; Classical, Modern and Humane: essays in Chinese Literature (ed J. Minford and Siu-kit Wong), 1989.

HAWKES, Jacquetta, OBE 1952; author and archaeologist; *b* 1910; *yr d* of Sir Frederick Gowland Hopkins, OM and Jessie Anne Stephens; *m* 1st, 1933, Christopher Hawkes (*see* Prof. C. F. C. Hawkes) (marr. diss. 1953); one *s*; 2nd, 1953, J. B. Priestley, OM (*d* 1984). *Educ:* Perse Sch.; Newnham Coll., Cambridge. MA. Associate, Newnham Coll., 1951. Research and excavation in Great Britain, Eire, France and Palestine, 1931–40; FSA, 1940. Asst Principal, Post-War Reconstruction Secretariat, 1941–43; Ministry of Education, becoming established Principal and Sec. of UK National Commn for UNESCO, 1943–49; retired from Civil Service to write, 1949. John Danz Vis. Prof., Univ. of Washington, 1971. Vice-Pres. Council for Brit. Archæology, 1949–52; Governor, Brit. Film Inst., 1950–55. Archæological adviser, Festival of Britain, 1949–51. Mem., UNESCO Culture Advisory Cttee, 1966–79. Pres., Warwicks, CPRE, 1989–. Life Trustee, Shakespeare Birthplace Trust, 1985. Hon. DLitt Warwick, 1986. *Publications:* Archæology of Jersey, 1939; Prehistoric Britain (with Christopher Hawkes), 1944; Early Britain, 1945; Symbols and Speculations (poems), 1948; A Land, 1951 (£100 Kemsley Award); Guide to Prehistoric and Roman Monuments in England and Wales, 1951; Dragon's Mouth, (play) (with J. B. Priestley); Fables, 1953; Man on Earth, 1954; Journey Down a Rainbow (with

J. B. Priestley), 1955; Providence Island, 1959; Man and the Sun, 1962; Unesco History of Mankind, Vol. I, Part 1, 1963; The World of the Past, 1963; King of the Two Lands, 1966; The Dawn of the Gods, 1968; The First Great Civilizations, 1973; (ed) Atlas of Ancient Archaeology, 1975; The Atlas of Early Man, 1976; A Quest of Love, 1980; Mortimer Wheeler: Adventurer in Archaeology, 1982; Shell Guide to British Archaeology, 1986; contrib. learned jls and national periodicals. *Recreation:* natural history. *Address:* Littlecote, Leysbourne, Chipping Campden, Glos GL55 6HL.

HAWKES, Prof. John Gregory; Mason Professor of Botany, University of Birmingham, 1967–82, now Emeritus; *b* 27 June 1915; *s* of C. W. and G. M. Hawkes; *m* 1941, Ellen Barbara Leather; two *s* two *d*. *Educ:* Univ. of Cambridge. BA, MA, PhD, ScD. Botanist, Potato Res. Station of Commonwealth Agricultural Bureaux, 1939–48, 1951–52; Dir of Potato Research Project, Min. of Ag., Colombia, S America, 1948–51; Lectr and Sen. Lectr in Taxonomic Botany, 1952–61; Prof. of Taxonomic Botany (Personal Chair), 1961–67. Linnean Soc. Gold Medal, 1984. *Publications:* The Potatoes of Argentina, Brazil, Paraguay, and Uruguay (with J. P. Hjerting), 1969; A Computer-Mapped Flora (with D. A. Cadbury and R. C. Readett), 1971; (with O. H. Frankel) Crop Genetic Resources for Today and Tomorrow, 1975; Conservation and Agriculture, 1978; (with R. N. Lester and A. D. Skelding) The Biology and Taxonomy of the Solanaceae, 1979; The Diversity of Crop Plants, 1983; (with J. P. Hjesting) The Potatoes of Bolivia, 1989; The Potato: evolution, biodiversity and genetic resources, 1990; contribs to various botanical and plant breeding jls. *Recreations:* walking, gardening, travel, art, archaeology. *Address:* 66 Lordswood Road, Birmingham B17 9BY. *T:* 021–427 2944. *Club:* Athenæum.

HAWKES, Michael John; Deputy Chairman, Kleinwort, Benson Group plc, 1988–90; *b* 7 May 1929; *s* of Wilfred Arthur Hawkes and Anne Maria Hawkes; *m* 1st, 1957, Gillian Mary Watts; two *s* two *d*; 2nd, 1973, Elizabeth Anne Gurton. *Educ:* Bedford School; New College, Oxford (Exhibnr; MA); Gray's Inn. Kleinwort Sons & Co. Ltd, 1954; Kleinwort, Benson Ltd: Director, 1967; Vice Chm., 1974; Dep. Chm., 1982; Chm., 1983–87; Director, Kleinwort, Benson, Lonsdale plc, 1974–88; Chairman: Sharps Pixley Ltd, 1971–89; Kleinwort Benson Investment Trust, 1984–89. Mem., Management Bd, W Berks Housing Assoc., 1988–. Gov., The Willink Sch., 1988–. *Recreations:* walking, swimming, gardening. *Address:* Brookfield House, Burghfield Common, Berks RG7 3BD. *T:* Burghfield Common (0734) 832912; White Bays, Daymer Lane, Trebetherick, N Cornwall PL27 6SF. *T:* Trebetherick (0208) 862280. *Club:* Leander (Henley on Thames).

HAWKES, Raymond; Deputy Director, Naval Ship Production, 1977–78, retired; *b* 28 April 1920; *s* of Ernest Hawkes; *m* 1951, Joyce Barbara King; one *s* one *d*. *Educ:* RNC Greenwich. 1st cl. Naval Architecture, RCNC; CEng; FRINA. Ship design, Bath, 1942–45 and 1954–56; aircraft carrier research at RAE Farnborough, 1945–49; hydrodynamic research at A.E.W. (Admiralty Experiment Works) Haslar, 1949–54; Principal Admty Overseer, Birkenhead, 1956–58; ship prodn, Bath, 1958–62; Chief Cons. Design, assault ships, survey fleet, small ships and auxiliaries, 1962–69; Senior Officers War Course 1966; Asst Dir Warship Design and Project Man. for Through Deck Cruiser, 1969–72; Dep. Dir, Warship Design, 1972–77. *Recreation:* golf. *Address:* Wood Meadow, Beechwood Road, Combe Down, Bath BA2 5JS. *T:* Combe Down (0225) 832885.

HAWKESBURY, Viscount; Luke Marmaduke Peter Savile Foljambe; *b* 25 March 1972; *s* and *heir* of 5th Earl of Liverpool, *qv*. *Educ:* Ampleforth. *Recreations:* golf, field sports, sailing, sub-aqua. *Address:* Barham Court, Exton, Oakham, Rutland LE15 8AP. *Club:* Bembridge Sailing.

HAWKESWORTH, John Stanley; film and television producer and dramatist; *b* 7 Dec. 1920; *s* of Lt-Gen. Sir John Hawkesworth, KBE, CB, DSO, and Lady (Helen Jane) Hawkesworth; *m* 1943, Hyacinthe Gregson-Ellis; one *s*. *Educ:* Rugby Sch.; Oxford Univ. (BA war degree). Joined Grenadier Guards, 1940; commnd 1941; demobilised 1946 (Captain). Entered film industry as Designer: The Third Man, The Man Who Never Was, The Prisoner, Father Brown; became Producer/Dramatist, Tiger Bay; TV creations include: Upstairs, Downstairs; The Duchess of Duke Street; Danger UXB; The Flame Trees of Thika; The Tale of Beatrix Potter; By the Sword Divided; Oscar; Sherlock Holmes, The Return of Sherlock Holmes and the Sign of Four; Campion; Chelworth. One man show (paintings), The Studio, Glebe Place, London, 1989; exhibn, film designs, Austin/Desmond Fine Art, London, 1991. Many television awards, incl. Peabody Award, Univ. of Georgia, 1977. *Publications:* Upstairs, Downstairs, 1972; In My Lady's Chamber, 1973. *Recreations:* tennis, hunting, gardening. *Address:* Fishponds House, Knossington, Oakham, Rutland LE15 8LX. *T:* Somerby (066477) 339; Flat 2, 24 Cottesmore Gardens, W8. *T:* 071–937 4869.

HAWKESWORTH, (Thomas) Simon (Ashwell); QC 1982; a Recorder of the Crown Court, since 1982; *b* 15 Nov. 1943; *s* of late Charles Peter Elmhirst Hawkesworth and of Felicity Hawkesworth; *m* 1st, 1970, Jennifer Lewis (marr. diss. 1989); two *s*; 2nd, 1990, Dr May Bamber, MD, MRCP. *Educ:* Rugby Sch.; The Queen's Coll., Oxford. MA. Called to the Bar, Gray's Inn, 1967, Bencher 1990; Head of Chambers at 17 Blake Street, York; Asst Recorder, 1980–82. *Address:* Tanner Beck House, Staveley, Knaresborough, North Yorks HG5 9LD. *T:* Harrogate (0423) 340604.

HAWKEY, Rt. Rev. Ernest Eric; *b* 1 June 1909; *s* of Richard and Beatrice Hawkey; *m* 1943, Patricia Spark. *Educ:* Trinity Grammar Sch., Sydney, NSW. Deacon, 1933; Priest, 1936. Curate: St Alban's, Ultimo, 1933–34; St Paul, Burwood, 1934–40; Priest-in-charge, Kandos, 1940–46, Rector, 1946–47; Aust. Bd of Missions: Actg Organising Sec., 1947–50; Organising Sec., 1950–68; Canon Residentiary, Brisbane, 1962–68; Bishop of Carpentaria, 1968–74. *Recreations:* music, gardening. *Address:* 2/12 Wellington Street, Clayfield, Queensland 4011, Australia. *T:* 262–2108.

HAWKING, Prof. Stephen William, CH 1989; CBE 1982; FRS 1974; Fellow of Gonville and Caius College, Cambridge; Lucasian Professor of Mathematics, Cambridge University, since 1979; *b* 8 Jan. 1942; *s* of Dr F. and Mrs E. I. Hawking; *m* 1965, Jane Wilde; two *s* one *d*. *Educ:* St Albans Sch.; University Coll., Oxford (BA), Hon. Fellow 1977; Trinity Hall, Cambridge (PhD), Hon. Fellow 1984. Research Fellow, Gonville and Caius Coll., 1965–69; Fellow for distinction in science, 1969–; Mem. Inst. of Theoretical Astronomy, Cambridge, 1968–72; Research Asst, Inst. of Astronomy, Cambridge, 1972–73; Cambridge University: Research Asst, Dept of Applied Maths and Theoretical Physics, 1973–75; Reader in Gravitational Physics, 1975–77, Professor, 1977–79. Fairchild Distinguished Schol., Calif Inst. of Technol., 1974–75. Mem., Pontifical Acad. of Scis, 1986–; Foreign Member: Amer. Acad. of Arts and Scis, 1984; Amer. Philosophical Soc., 1985. Hon. Mem., RAS (Can), 1985. Hon. DSc: Oxon, 1978; Newcastle, Leeds, 1987; Cambridge, 1989; hon. degrees: Chicago, 1981; Leicester, New York, Notre Dame, Princeton, 1982. (Jtly) Eddington Medal, RAS, 1975; Pius XI Gold Medal, Pontifical Acad. of Scis, 1975; Dannie Heinemann Prize for Math. Phys., Amer. Phys. Soc. and Amer. Inst. of Physics, 1976; William Hopkins Prize, Cambridge Philosoph. Soc., 1976; Maxwell Medal, Inst. of Physics, 1976; Hughes Medal, Royal Soc., 1976; Albert Einstein Award, 1978; Albert Einstein Medal, Albert Einstein Soc., Berne, 1979; Franklin Medal,

Franklin Inst., USA, 1981; Gold Medal, RAS, 1985; Paul Dirac Medal and Prize, Inst. of Physics, 1987; (jtly) Wolf Foundn Prize for Physics, 1988; Britannica Award, 1989. *Publications:* (with G. F. R. Ellis) The Large Scale Structure of Space-Time, 1973; (ed W. W. Israel) General Relativity: an Einstein centenary survey, 1979; (ed with M. Roček) Superspace and Supergravity, 1981; (ed jtly) The Very Early Universe, 1983; (with W. Israel) 300 Years of Gravitation, 1987; A Brief History of Time, 1988. *Address:* Department of Applied Mathematics and Theoretical Physics, Silver Street, Cambridge CB3 9EW. *T:* Cambridge (0223) 337843.

HAWKINS, Prof. Anthony Donald, PhD; FRSE; Director of Fisheries Research, Scottish Office Agriculture and Fisheries Department, since 1987; Hon. Research Professor, Aberdeen University, since 1987; *b* 25 March 1942; *s* of Kenneth St David Hawkins and Marjorie Lillian Hawkins; *m* 1966, Susan Mary Fulker; one *s*. *Educ:* Poole Grammar Sch.; Bristol Univ. (BSc 1st Cl. Hons Zoology, 1963; PhD 1968). Dept of Agriculture and Fisheries for Scotland: Scientific Officer, Marine Lab., Aberdeen, 1965, Chief Scientific Officer, 1987. Consultant to FAO, Peru, 1975; Hon. Lectr, Univ. of St Andrews, 1983. FRSE 1988. A. B. Wood Medal and Prize, Inst. of Acoustics, 1978. *Publications:* (ed and contrib.) Sound Reception in Fish, 1976; (ed and contrib.) Aquarium Systems, 1981; pubns on marine science, fish physiology and salmon biology. *Recreations:* angling, riding, whippet breeding. *Address:* Kincraig, Blairs, by Aberdeen AB1 5YT. *T:* Aberdeen (0224) 868984.

HAWKINS, Sir Arthur (Ernest), Kt 1976; BSc (Eng); CEng, FIMechE, FIEE, FInstE; Chairman 1972–77, Member, 1970–77, Central Electricity Generating Board; *b* 10 June 1913; *s* of Rev. H. R. and Louisa Hawkins; *m* 1939, Laura Judith Tallent Draper; one *s* two *d*. *Educ:* The Grammar Sch., Gt Yarmouth; City of Norwich Technical Coll. Served (prior to nationalisation) with Gt Yarmouth Electricity Dept, Central Electricity Bd and Islington Electricity Dept (Dep. Engr and Gen. Manager); Croydon Dist Manager of SE Elec. Bd, 1948; joined Brit. Electricity Authority as Chief Asst Engr in System Operation Br., 1951; Personal Engrg Asst to Chief Engr, 1954. With the CEGB since its formation in 1957, at first as System Planning Engr and then as Chief Ops Engr, 1959–64; Midlands Regional Dir, 1964–70. Mem., Nuclear Power Adv. Bd, 1973–. Chm., F International Ltd, 1978–79. CBIM. *Publications:* contrib. Jl of Management Studies; various papers to technical instns. *Recreations:* walking, swimming. *Address:* 61 Rowan Road, W6 7DT. *Club:* Hurlingham.

HAWKINS, Catherine Eileen; Regional General Manager, South Western Regional Health Authority, since 1984; *b* 16 Jan. 1939; *d* of Stanley Richard Hawkins and Mary-Kate Hawkins. *Educ:* La Retraite High Sch., Clifton. SRN, CMB (Pt 1), HVCert, DN London, Queen's Inst. of Nursing Cert, IRCert. General nursing, student, 1956–59; Staff Nursing, Charing Cross Hosp., SRN, 1960–61; Pt 1 midwifery, St Thomas' Hosp., 1961; Health Visitor Student, LCC, RCN, 1961–62; LCC Health Visitor, 1962–63; Bristol CC HV, 1963–64; Project Leader, Bahrain Public Health Service, 1964–66; Field Work Teacher, HV, 1966–68; Health Centre Administrator, 1968–71; Administrator, Res. Div., Health Educn Council, 1971–72; Sen. Nursing Officer, Community Services, 1972–74; Area Nurse Service Capital Planning, Avon AHA, 1974–79; Dist Nursing Officer, Bristol and Weston DHA, 1979–82; Chief Nursing Officer, Southmead DHA, 1982–84; Regional Nursing Officer, SW RHA, 1984. *Recreations:* travel, badminton. *Address:* Thornhill Cottage, Meadow Road, Cockington, Torquay TQ2 6PR.

HAWKINS, Christopher James; MP (C) High Peak, since 1983; *b* 26 Nov. 1937; *s* of Alec Desmond Hawkins and Christina Barbara; *m* Susan Ann Hawkins; two *d*. *Educ:* Bristol Grammar Sch.; Bristol Univ. BA (Hons) Economics. Joined Courtaulds Ltd, Head Office Economics Dept, 1959; seconded to UK aid financed industrial and economic survey of Northern Nigeria, 1960; similar mission to Tunisia to work on 5 year plan, 1961; Research Div. Economist, Courtaulds Ltd, 1961–66, Building Develt Manager, 1965–66; Lectr in Economics, 1966, Sen. Lectr, 1973–83, Univ. of Southampton. *Publications:* Capital Investment Appraisal, 1971; Theory of the Firm, 1973; The British Economy: what will our children think?, 1982; Britain's Economic Future: an immediate programme for revival, 1983; articles in Jl of Industrial Economics, Amer. Economic Review. *Recreations:* reading, music, sailing. *Address:* House of Commons, SW1A 0AA.

HAWKINS, Air Vice-Marshal David Richard, MBE 1975; FITD; Commandant-General, Royal Air Force Regiment and Director-General, Royal Air Force Security, since 1991; *b* 5 April 1937; 2nd *s* of Gp Capt. Charles Richard John Hawkins, OBE, AFC and Norah (née Terry); *m* 1st, 1965, Wendy Elizabeth Harris (marr. diss. 1981); one *s* one *d*.; 2nd, 1982, Elaine Kay, *d* of Dr Henry and Mrs Fay Nelson, Dallas, Texas. *Educ:* Worth; Downside Sch.; RMA Sandhurst. Commnd RAF Regt, 1959; Flt Comdr Cyprus and Singapore, 1960–62; ADC to CAS, Air Chief Marshal Sir Charles Elworthy, 1963–65; jun. RAF Regt instructor, RAF Coll., Cranwell, 1965–68; 2nd i/c 63 Sqdn, Singapore, 1968–69; Sqdn Ldr, 1969; Jt Thai/US Mil. R&D Centre as airfield defence specialist, Bangkok, 1969–71; CO, 37 Sqdn, UK, NI and Belize, 1971–74; CO, Queen's Colour Sqdn of RAF, 1974–76; Wing Comdr, on staff of Comdt-Gen., RAF Regt, MoD, 1976–79; Chief, Survivability Br., HQ AAFCE, 1979–82; Sen. Comd RAF Regt Officer, HQ Strike Comd/HQ UK Air, 1982–86; Gp Capt., 1982; CO, RAF Catterick, RAF Regt Depot, 1986–88; NATO Defence Coll., Rome, 1988–89; Dir, RAF Personal Services 1, MoD, 1989–90; Air Cdre, 1989; Dir, RAF Regt, MoD, 1990–91. Parachute Wings: UK, 1969; Thai Army (Master), 1970; Thai Police (Master), 1970; US Army (1st class), 1971. FBIM. *Recreations:* golf, ski-ing, walking, shooting, acting as unpaid groom to wife's horse. *Address:* c/o Barclays Bank, 2 High Street, Cobham, Surrey KT11 3DZ. *Club:* Royal Air Force.

HAWKINS, Desmond, OBE 1963; BBC Controller, South and West, 1967–69; *b* 1908; *m* Barbara Hawkins (née Skidmore); two *s* two *d*. Novelist, critic and broadcaster, 1935–45; Literary Editor of New English Weekly and Purpose Quarterly; Fiction Chronicler of The Criterion; Features Producer, BBC West Region, 1946; Head of Programmes, 1955; founded BBC Natural History Unit, 1957. FRSL 1977. Hon. LLD Bristol, 1974. Silver Medal, RSPB, 1959; Imperial Tobacco Radio Award for best dramatisation, 1976 and 1978. *Publications:* Poetry and Prose of John Donne, 1938; Hawk among the Sparrows, 1939; Stories, Essays and Poems of D. H. Lawrence, 1939; Lighter than Day, 1940; War Report, 1946 rev. edn (as BBC War Report), 1985; Sedgemoor and Avalon, 1954; The BBC Naturalist, 1957; Hardy the Novelist, 1965; Wild Life in the New Forest, 1972; Avalon and Sedgemoor, 1973; Hardy, Novelist and Poet, 1976; preface to Richard Jefferies' Wild Life in a Southern County, 1978; Cranborne Chase, 1980; Concerning Agnes, 1982; Hardy's Wessex, 1983; (ed and introd) Wake Smart's Chronicle of Cranborne, 1983; The Tess Opera, 1984; (introd.) Thomas Hardy's Collected Short Stories, 1988; When I Was (autobiog.), 1989; Hardy at Home, 1989; Thomas Hardy: his life and landscape, 1990; Wessex: an anthology, 1991. *Address:* 2 Stanton Close, Blandford Forum, Dorset DT11 7RT. *T:* Blandford (0258) 454954. *Clubs:* BBC, Royal Over-Seas League.

HAWKINS, Air Vice-Marshal Desmond Ernest, CB 1971; CBE 1967; DFC and Bar, 1942; *b* 27 Dec. 1919; *s* of Ernest and Lilian Hawkins; *m* 1947, Joan Audrey (née Munro);

one *s*, and one step *s*. *Educ:* Bancroft Sch. Commissioned in RAF, 1938. Served War of 1939–45: Coastal Command and Far East, commanding 36, 230 and 240 Sqdns, 1940–46 (despatches). Commanded RAF Pembroke Dock, 1946–47 (despatches). Staff appts, 1947–50; RAF Staff Coll., 1950; Staff appts, 1951–55; commanded 38 Sqdn, OC Flg, RAF Luqa, 1955–57; jssc, 1957; Staff appts, 1958–61; SASO 19 Gp, 1961–63; commanded RAF Tengah, 1963–66; idc 1967; commanded RAF Lyneham, 1968; SASO, HQ, RAF Strike Command, 1969–71; Dir-Gen., Personal Services (RAF), MoD, 1971–74; Dep. Man. Dir, Services Kinema Corp., 1974–80. *Recreations:* sailing, fishing. *Address:* c/o Barclays Bank, Lymington, Hants. *Clubs:* Royal Air Force, Cruising Association, Royal Cruising; Royal Lymington Yacht.

HAWKINS, Prof. Eric William, CBE 1973; Director, Language Teaching Centre, University of York, 1965–79, now Professor Emeritus; *b* 8 Jan. 1915; *s* of James Edward Hawkins and Agnes Thompson (*née* Clarie); *m* 1938, Ellen Marie Thygesen, Copenhagen; one *s* one *d*. *Educ:* Liverpool Inst. High Sch.; Trinity Hall, Cambridge (Open Exhibn). MA, CertEd, FIL. War Service, 1st Bn The Loyal Regt, 1940–46 (despatches 1945); wounded N Africa, 1943; Major 1945. Asst Master, Liverpool Coll., 1946–49; Headmaster: Oldershaw Grammar Sch., Wallasey, 1949–53; Calday Grange Grammar Sch., Ches, 1953–65. Member: Central Adv. Council for Educn (England) (Plowden Cttee), 1963–66; Rampton Cttee (educn of ethnic minorities), 1979–81. Hon. Prof., University Coll. of Wales, Aberystwyth, 1979–. Gold Medal, Inst. Linguists, 1971. Comdr, Ordre des Palmes Académiques (France), 1986. *Publications:* (ed) Modern Languages in the Grammar School, 1961; (ed) New Patterns in Sixth Form Modern Language Studies, 1970; A Time for Growing, 1971; Le français pour tout le monde, vols 1–5, 1974–79; Modern Languages in the Curriculum, 1981; Awareness of Language: an Introduction, 1984; (ed) Intensive Language Teaching and Learning, 1988. *Recreations:* walking, cello.

See also M. R. Jackson.

HAWKINS, Frank Ernest; Chairman, 1959–73, and Managing Director, 1956–73, International Stores Ltd, Mitre Square, EC3; *b* 12 Aug. 1904; 2nd *s* of late George William and Sophie Hawkins; *m* 1933, Muriel, *d* of late Joseph and Isabella Sinclair; two *s* one *d*. *Educ:* Leyton County High Sch. Joined staff of International Stores Ltd as boy clerk, 1919; apptd: Asst Sec., 1934; Sec., 1935; Director, 1949; Managing Dir, 1956; Vice-Chm., 1958; Chairman, 1959.

HAWKINS, Sir Humphry (Villiers) Cæsar, 7th Bt, *cr* 1778; MB, ChB; Medical Practitioner; *b* 10 Aug. 1923; *s* of Sir Villiers Geoffry Caesar Hawkins, 6th Bt and Blanche Hawkins, *d* of A. E. Hampden-Smithers; *S* father 1955; *m* 1952, Anita, *d* of C. H. Funkey, Johannesburg; two *s* three *d*. *Educ:* Hilton Coll.; University of Witwatersrand. Served War of 1939–45 with 6th SA Armoured Div. *Heir:* *s* Howard Cæsar Hawkins, *b* 17 Nov. 1956. *Club:* Johannesburg Country.

HAWKINS, Sir Paul (Lancelot), Kt 1982; TD 1945; FRICS; *b* 7 Aug. 1912; *s* of L. G. Hawkins and of Mrs Hawkins (*née* Peile); *m* 1st, 1937, E. Joan Snow (*d* 1984); two *s* one *d*; 2nd, 1985, Tina Daniels. *Educ:* Cheltenham Coll. Joined Family Firm, 1930; Chartered Surveyor, 1933. Served in TA, Royal Norfolk Regt, 1933–45; POW Germany, 1940–45. MP (C) SW Norfolk, 1964–87. An Asst Govt Whip, 1970–71; a Lord Comr of the Treasury, 1971–73; Vice-Chamberlain of HM Household, 1973–74. Mem., H of C (Services) Select Cttee, 1976–87. Mem., Delegn to Council of Europe and WEU, 1976–87; Chm., Agricl Cttee, Council of Europe, 1985–87. Consultant to Barry Hawkins, FRICS; Dir (non-exec.), Gorham Bateson (Agriculture) Seed Specialists. CC Norfolk, 1949–70, Alderman, 1968–70. *Recreations:* walking, gardening, travel. *Address:* Stables, Downham Market, Norfolk.

HAWKINS, Richard Graeme; QC 1984; **His Honour Judge Hawkins;** a Circuit Judge, since 1989; *b* 23 Feb 1941; *s* of late Denis William Hawkins and Norah Mary (*née* Beckingsale); *m* 1969, Anne Elizabeth, *d* of Dr and Mrs Glyn Edwards, The Boltons, Bournemouth; one *s* one *d*. *Educ:* Hendon County Sch.; University College London (LLB Hons 1962). Called to the Bar, Gray's Inn, 1963. A Recorder, 1985–89. Mem., Hon. Soc. of Gray's Inn, 1959–. *Recreation:* sailing. *Address:* Inner London Sessions House, Newington Causeway, SE1 6AZ. *T:* 071–407 7111. *Club:* Royal Thames Yacht.

HAWKINS, Rt. Rev. Richard Stephen; *see* Plymouth, Bishop Suffragan of.

HAWKSLEY, John Callis, CBE 1946; PhD, MD, FRCP; formerly Physician, University College Hospital and St Peter's, St Paul's and St Philip's Hospitals, London; *b* 30 Nov. 1903; *s* of late Joseph Hawksley, Great Yarmouth; *m* 1933, Margaret (*d* 1985), *er d* of late Engineer Vice-Adm. Sir Reginald Skelton, KCB, CBE, DSO; two *s* two *d*. *Educ:* Dulwich Coll.; University Coll., London; University Coll. Hospital. Appts on resident staff, University Coll. Hosp., 1926–28; ship's surg., BISN Co., 1929; research appts, Birmingham Children's Hosp., 1930–32; Sebag-Montefiore Research Fellow, Hospital for Sick Children, Gt Ormond Street, 1933–34; Bilton Pollard Travelling Fellowship, University Coll. Hosp., 1935, devoted to work at Bispebjerg Hosp., Copenhagen; Asst Physician, University Coll. Hosp., 1936–39; Physician to University Coll. Hosp., 1940; retd, 1969. Temp. commission RAMC 1939; served with rank of Lieut-Col in MEF, 1941–44 (despatches); Consulting Physician, local Brig., with South East Asia Command, 1945. Fellow of University Coll., London, 1946; Dean of University Coll. Hosp. Med. Sch., 1949–54; Senior Vice-Pres., RCP, 1966. *Publications:* contributions to various medical journals. *Recreations:* mountaineering, music. *Address:* Pencombe Hall, Pencombe, near Bromyard, Herefordshire.

HAWKSLEY, (Philip) Warren; Director, Edderton Hall, since 1989; *b* 10 March 1943; *s* of late Bradshaw Warren Hawksley and Monica Augusta Hawksley. *Educ:* Denstone Coll., Uttoxeter. Employed by Lloyd's Bank after leaving school. Member: Salop County Council, 1970–81; West Mercia Police Authority, 1977–81. Contested (C) The Wrekin, 1987; Prospective Parly Cand. (C) Halesowen and Stourbridge, 1990–. MP (C) The Wrekin, 1979–87. Former Mem., Select Cttee on Employment; former Jt Sec., Cons. Back-bench Cttee for New Town and Urban Affairs. *Recreations:* badminton, reading, travel, beagling. *Address:* Edderton Hall, Forden, near Welshpool, Powys.

HAWKSWORTH, Prof. David Leslie, DSc; FIBiol, FLS; Director, International Mycological Institute, Kew, since 1983; *b* Sheffield, 5 June 1946; *e s* of Leslie Hawksworth and Freda Mary (*née* Dolamore); *m* 1968, Madeleine Una Ford; one *s* one *d*. *Educ:* Herbert Strutt Grammar Sch., Belper; Univ. of Leicester (BSc 1967; PhD 1970; DSc 1980). FIBiol 1982; FLS 1969. Mycologist, Commonwealth Mycological Inst., Kew, 1969–81; sci. asst to Exec. Dir, CAB, 1981–83. Visiting Professor: Univ. of Riyadh, 1978; Univ. of Reading, 1984–; Univ. of Assiut, 1985; Univ. of Kent 1990–. President: British Lichen Soc., 1986–87; Eur. Congress of Mycologists, 1989; Br. Mycol Soc., 1990; Internat. Mycol Assoc., 1990–; Vice-Pres., Linnean Soc., 1985–88; Treasurer and Editor-in-Chief, Systematics Assoc., 1972–86; Sec.-Gen., Internat. Mycol Assoc., 1977–90; Chairman: Internat Commn on Taxonomy of Fungi, 1982–; Ruislip-Northwood Woods Adv. Working Party, 1979–82; Chief Rapp., CAB Internat. Review Confs, 1985, 1990. Hon. Mem., Soc. Lichenologica Italiana, 1989. First Bicent. Medal, Linnean Soc., 1978. Editor: The Lichenologist, 1970–90; Systema Ascomycetum, 1986–. *Publications:* (jtly) Dictionary of the Fungi, 6th edn 1971, 7th edn 1983; (ed jtly) Air Pollution and Lichens, 1973; Mycologist's Handbook, 1974; (ed) The Changing Flora and Fauna of Britain, 1974; (jtly) Lichens as Pollution Monitors, 1976; (ed jtly) Lichenology: progress and problems, 1976; (jtly) Lichenology in the British Isles 1568–1975, 1977; (jtly) Key Works to the Fauna and Flora of the British Isles and Northwestern Europe, 4th edn 1978, 5th edn 1988; (ed) Advancing Agricultural Production in Africa, 1984; (jtly) The Lichen-Forming Fungi, 1984; (jtly) The British Ascomycotina, 1985; (ed jtly) Coevolution and Systematics, 1986; (ed jtly) Coevolution of Fungi with Plants and Animals, 1988; (ed jtly) Living Resources for Biotechnology, 1988; (ed) Prospects in Systematics, 1988; (jtly) International Mycological Directory, 1990; (ed) Frontiers in Mycology, 1991; (ed) Improving the Stability of Names, 1991; (ed) The Biodiversity of Microorganisms and Invertebrates: their role in sustainable agriculture, 1991; (jtly) Lichen Flora of Great Britain and Ireland, 1992; numerous papers on fungi and lichens. *Recreations:* lichenology, natural history, museums, walking, swimming. *Address:* International Mycological Institute, Ferry Lane, Kew, Surrey TW9 3AF.

HAWLEY, Sir Donald (Frederick), KCMG 1978 (CMG 1970); MBE 1955; HM Diplomatic Service, retired; British High Commissioner in Malaysia, 1977–81; Barrister-at-law; consultant in Middle Eastern and South East Asian affairs; *b* 22 May 1921; *s* of late Mr and Mrs F. G. Hawley, Little Gaddesden, Herts; *m* 1964, Ruth Morwenna Graham Howes, *d* of late Rev. P. G. Howes and of Mrs Howes, Charmouth, Dorset; one *s* three *d*. *Educ:* Radley; New Coll., Oxford (MA). Served in HM Forces, 1941. Sudan Political Service, 1944; joined Sudan Judiciary, 1947. Called to Bar, Inner Temple, 1951. Chief Registrar, Sudan Judiciary, and Registrar-Gen. of Marriages, 1951; resigned from Sudan Service, 1955; joined HM Foreign Service, 1955; FO, 1956: Political Agent, Trucial States, in Dubai, 1958; Head of Chancery, British Embassy, Cairo, 1962; Counsellor and Head of Chancery, British High Commission, Lagos, 1965; Vis. Fellow, Dept of Geography, Durham Univ., 1967; Counsellor (Commercial), Baghdad, 1968; HM Consul-General, Muscat, 1971; HM Ambassador to Oman, 1971–75; Asst Under Sec. of State, FCO, 1975–77. Mem., London Adv. Cttee, Hongkong and Shanghai Banking Corp.; Chairman: Ewbank Preece Gp, 1982–86, Special Advr, 1986–; Centre for British Teachers, 1987–. Pres. Council, Reading Univ., 1987–; Vice-Pres., Anglo-Omani Soc., 1981–; Chairman: British Malaysian Soc., 1983–; Confedn of British and SE Asia Socs., 1988–. *Publications:* Handbook for Registrars of Marriage and Ministers of Religion, 1963 (Sudan Govt pubn); Courtesies in the Trucial States, 1965; The Trucial States, 1971; Oman and its Renaissance, 1977; Courtesies in the Gulf Area, 1978; Manners and Correct Form in the Middle East, 1984. *Recreations:* tennis, travel, gardening; Hon. Sec., Sudan Football Assoc., 1952–55. *Address:* Little Cheverell House, near Devizes, Wilts. *T:* Devizes (0380) 813322. *Clubs:* Travellers', Beefsteak.

HAWLEY, Henry Nicholas, (8th Bt *cr* 1795). *S* father, 1988, but does not use the title and his name is not on the Official Roll of Baronets.

HAWORTH, Rev. Betsy Ellen; Non-Stipendiary Minister, St Paul, Astley Bridge, Bolton, Diocese of Manchester, since 1989; *b* 23 July 1924; *d* of Ambrose and Annie Kenyon; *m* 1953, Rev. Fred Haworth (*d* 1981); one *s* two *d*. *Educ:* William Temple Coll. IDC (C of E). Licensed as lay worker, dio. Manchester, 1952, dio. Blackburn, 1965; elected Mem., Church Assembly, 1965–70, Gen. Synod, 1970–75, 1975–80, 1980–85, Ex-officio Mem., 1985–88. Advr for Women's Ministry, dio. Manchester, 1971–81. Third Church Estates Comr, 1981–88. Deaconess 1980; ordained Deacon, 1989. Examining Chaplain to Bishop of Manchester, 1981–. *Address:* 14 Sharples Hall Fold, Sharples, Bolton, Lancs BL1 7EH.

HAWORTH, John Liegh W.; *see* Walker-Haworth.

HAWORTH, Lionel, OBE 1958; FRS 1971; RDI; FEng; Senior Partner, Lionel Haworth and Associates; *b* 4 Aug. 1912; *s* of John Bertram Haworth and Anna Sophia Ackerman; *m* 1956, Joan Irene Bradbury; one *s* one *d*. *Educ:* Rondebosch Boys' High Sch.; Univ. of Cape Town. Cape Town Corp's Gold Medal and schol. tenable abroad. BSc (Eng); FIMechE; FRAeS. Graduate Apprentice, Associated Equipment Co., 1934; Rolls-Royce Ltd, Derby: Designer, 1936; Asst Chief Designer, 1944; Dep. Chief Designer, 1951; Chief Designer (Civil Engines), 1954; Chief Engr (Prop. Turbines), 1962; Bristol Siddeley Engines Ltd: Chief Design Consultant, 1963; Chief Designer, 1964; Dir of Design, Aero Div., 1965, Dir of Design, Aero Div., Rolls-Royce Ltd, 1968–77. Brit. Gold Medal for Aeronautics, 1971; RDI 1976; Founder Fellow, Fellowship of Engineering, 1976. *Recreation:* sailing. *Address:* 10 Hazelwood Road, Sneyd Park, Bristol BS9 1PX. *T:* Bristol (0272) 683032.

HAWORTH, Sir Philip, 3rd Bt *cr* 1911, of Dunham Massey, Co. Chester; farmer; *b* 17 Jan. 1927; *s* of Sir Arthur Geoffrey Haworth, 2nd Bt, and Emily Dorothea, (Dorothy) (*d* 1980), *er d* of H. E. Gaddum; *S* father, 1987; *m* 1951, Joan Helen, *d* of late S. P. Clark, Ipswich; four *s* one *d*. *Educ:* Dauntsey's; Reading Univ. BSc (Agric.) 1948. *Recreations:* music, art, ornithology. *Heir:* *s* Christopher Haworth, *b* 6 Nov. 1951. *Address:* Free Green Farm, Over Peover, Knutsford, Cheshire WA16 9QX. *Club:* Farmers'.

HAWTHORN, Ven. Christopher John; Archdeacon of Cleveland, since 1991; *b* 29 April 1936; *s* of Rev. John Christopher Hawthorn and Susan Mary Hawthorn; *m* 1964, Elizabeth Margaret Lowe; three *s* one *d*. *Educ:* Marlborough Coll.; Queens' Coll., Cambridge (MA Hons); Ripon Hall, Oxford. Deacon 1962, priest 1963; Asst Curate, Sutton-in-Holderness, 1962–66; Vicar: St Nicholas, Hull, 1966–72; Christ Church, Coatham, 1972–79; St Martin's-on-the-Hill, Scarborough, 1979–91; Proctor in Convocation, 1987–90; Canon of York, 1987–. *Recreations:* gardening, fell walking, sport. *Address:* Park House, Rosehill, Great Ayton, Middlesbrough TS9 6BH. *T:* Middlesbrough (0642) 723221.

HAWTHORNE, James Burns, CBE 1982; media consultant; Director, James Hawthorne Associates Ltd, since 1987; *b* 27 March 1930; *s* of Thomas Hawthorne and Florence Hawthorne (*née* Burns); *m* 1958, Patricia King; one *s* two *d*. *Educ:* Queen's Univ., Belfast (BA); Stranmillis Coll. of Educn. Master at Sullivan Upper Sch., Holywood, 1951–60; joined Educn Dept, BBC, 1960; Schools Producer in charge, N Ireland, 1967; Chief Asst, N Ireland, 1969–70; seconded to Hong Kong Govt, as Controller Television, 1970; Dir of Broadcasting, Hong Kong, 1972–77 (resigned from BBC staff, 1976, *ie* seconded status ended; rejoined BBC, Jan. 1978); Controller, BBC NI, 1978–87. Member: NI Council for Educn Develt, 1980–85; Fair Employment Agency, 1981–; Accreditation Panel, Hong Kong Acad. for the Performing Arts, 1988. Chairman: Ulster History Circle, 1987–89; NI Health Promotion Unit, 1988–; Cultural Traditions Gp, 1989–90; NI Community Relations Council, 1990–. JP Hong Kong, 1972–77. Queen's Univ. New Ireland Soc. award for community relations work, 1967; Winston Churchill Fellowship, 1968; FRTS 1988 (Cyril Bennett Award, 1986). Hon. LLD QUB, 1988. *Publications:* (ed) Two Centuries of Irish History, 1966, repr. 1967, 1969, rev. edn 1974; Reporting Violence: lessons from Northern Ireland, 1981. *Recreations:* angling, music. *Address:* 5 Tarawood, Cultra, Holywood, Co. Down, Northern Ireland BT18 0HS. *Club:* BBC.

HAWTHORNE, Nigel Barnard, CBE 1987; self-employed actor and writer; b Coventry, 5 April 1929; s of Charles Barnard Hawthorne and Agnes Rosemary (née Rice). Educ: Christian Brothers' Coll., Cape Town, S Africa. Entered theatre professionally, 1950; returned to England, 1951, where he has worked ever since, with the exception of a small number of engagements abroad. Stage: Otherwise Engaged, 1976; Privates on Parade, 1978 (Best Supporting Actor, SWET and Clarence Derwent awards); Peer Gynt, and Tartuffe, with RSC, 1983–84 (Tartuffe televised 1985); Across from the Garden of Allah, 1986; Jacobowski and the Colonel, NT, 1986; The Magistrate, NT, 1986; Hapgood, Aldwych, 1988; Shadowlands, Queen's, 1989, Broadway, 1990–91; television: Marie Curie, 1977; Destiny, 1978; Edward and Mrs Simpson, 1978; The Knowledge, 1979; Yes Minister (series), annually 1980–83, 1985–86, Yes, Prime Minister (series), 1986, 1987 (Broadcasting Press Guild Award, 1980; BAFTA Best Light Entertainment Performance, 1981, 1982, 1986, 1987); The Critic, 1982; The Barchester Chronicles, 1982; Mapp and Lucia, 1984–86; The Miser, 1988; The Shawl, 1989; Relatively Speaking, 1989; films: Firefox, 1981; Gandhi, 1981; Golda, 1981; John Paul II, 1983; The House, 1984; Turtle Diary, 1984; The Chain. 1985. Hon. MA Sheffield, 1987. Recreations: swimming, gardening, painting.

HAWTHORNE, Prof. Sir William (Rede), Kt 1970; CBE 1959; MA; ScD; FRS 1955; FEng; FIMechE; Master of Churchill College, Cambridge, 1968–83; Hopkinson and ICI Professor of Applied Thermodynamics, University of Cambridge, 1951–80; Head of Department of Engineering, 1968–73; b 22 May 1913; s of William Hawthorne, MInstCE, and Elizabeth C. Hawthorne; m 1939, Barbara Runkle, Cambridge, Massachusetts, USA; one s two d. Educ: Westminster Sch.; Trinity Coll., Cambridge; Massachusetts Institute of Technology, USA. Development Engineer, Babcock & Wilcox Ltd, 1937–39; Scientific Officer, Royal Aircraft Establishment, 1940–44; seconded to Sir Frank Whittle, 1940–41; British Air Commission, Washington, 1944; Dep. Dir Engine Research, Min. of Supply, 1945; Massachusetts Institute of Technology: Associate Prof. of Mechanical Engineering, 1946; George Westinghouse Prof. of Mechanical Engineering, 1948–51; Jerome C. Hunsaker Prof. of Aeronautical Engineering, 1955–56; Vis. Inst. Prof., 1962–63; Mem. Corporation, 1969–74. Chairman: Home Office Scientific Adv. Council, 1967–76; Defence Scientific Adv. Council, 1969–71; Adv. Council for Energy Conservation, 1974–79; Member: Energy Commn, 1977–79; Standing Commn on Energy and the Environment, 1978–81. Director: Dracone Developments Ltd, 1958–87; Cummins Engine Co. Inc., 1974–86. Governor, Westminster Sch., 1956–76. A Vice-Pres., Royal Soc., 1969–70 and 1979–81; Mem. Council, 1968–70, 1979–81 (Royal Medal, 1982). Foreign Associate: US Nat. Acad. of Sciences, 1965; US Nat. Acad. of Engrg, 1976. Fellow, Imperial Coll., London Univ., 1983. Hon. FAIAA; Hon. FRAeS; Hon. FRSE 1983. Hon. DEng: Sheffield, 1976; Liverpool 1982; Hon. DSc: Salford, 1980; Strathclyde, 1981; Bath, 1981; Oxon, 1982; Sussex, 1984. Medal of Freedom (US), 1947. Publications: papers in mechanical and aeronautical journals. Address: Churchill College, Cambridge. Club: Athenæum.

See also J. O'Beirne Ranelagh.

HAWTIN, Brian Richard; Assistant Under Secretary of State, material/naval, Ministry of Defence, since 1989; b 31 May 1946; s of Dick Hawtin and Jean (née Middleton); m 1969, Anthea Fry; two d. Educ: Portsmouth Grammar Sch.; Christ Church, Oxford (MA). MoD 1967; Asst Private Sec. to Permt Under Sec. of State, 1970; on loan to FCO as First Sec., UK Delegn to NATO, Brussels, 1978–80; Asst Sec., 1981; RCDS 1987; Private Sec. to Sec. of State for Defence, 1987–89. Recreations: walking, ceramics. Address: c/o Ministry of Defence, Main Building, Whitehall, SW1.

HAWTIN, Ven. David Christopher; Archdeacon of Newark, since 1992; b 7 June 1943; m. Educ: King Edward VII Sch., Lytham St Annes; Keble Coll., Oxford (BA 1965; MA 1970); Cuddesdon Coll., Oxford. Ordained deacon, 1967, priest 1968; Curate: St Thomas, Pennywell, Sunderland, 1967–71; St Peter's, Stockton, 1971–74; Priest in charge, St Andrew's, Leam Lane, Gateshead, 1974–79; Rector, Washington, 1979–88; Diocesan Ecumenical Officer, Durham, 1988–91. Mem., Gen. Synod, 1983– (Mem., Bd for Mission and Unity, 1986–91); Mem., BCC, 1987–90. Address: c/o Dunham House, Westgate, Southwell, Notts NG25 0JL. T: Southwell (0636) 814331.

HAWTIN, Michael Victor; Director, Resource Management Group, and Principal Establishment and Finance Officer, Export Credits Guarantee Department, since 1988; b 7 Sept. 1942; s of Guy and Constance Hawtin; m 1966, Judith Mary Eeley; one s one d. Educ: Bournemouth Sch.; St John's Coll., Cambridge (MA); Univ. of Calif, Berkeley (MA). Asst Principal, 1964–69, Principal, 1969–77, HM Treasury; seconded to Barclays Bank, 1969–71; Asst Sec., HM Treasury, 1977–83, Under Sec. (Principal Finance Officer), PSA, 1983–86; Under Sec., HM Treasury, 1986–88. Recreations: music, travel. Address: Export Credits Guarantee Department, 2 Exchange Tower, Harbour Exchange Square, E14 9GS. T: 071–512 7008. Club: Overseas Bankers'.

HAWTREY, John Havilland Procter, CBE 1958; FICE; b 16 Feb. 1905; e s of late Edmond Charles Hawtrey and late Helen Mary Hawtrey (née Durand); m 1947, Kathleen Mary, d of late Captain M. T. Daniel, RN, Henley-on-Thames; one s one d. Educ: Eton; City and Guilds Engineering Coll., London (BSc 1927). Asst Engineer, later Dist Engineer, Burma Railways, 1927–47. Served War of 1939–45: with RE, 1940–46; Major 1942, in India and Burma, 1942–46 (despatches). Entered office of Crown Agents for Oversea Govts and Administrations, 1948: Chief Civil Engineer, 1956; Crown Agent and Engineer-in-Chief, 1965; retired, 1969. Address: 76 Makins Road, Henley-on-Thames, Oxon RG9 1PR. T: Henley-on-Thames (0491) 574896.

HAXBY, Donald Leslie, CBE 1988; principal of veterinary practice, Southwell, since 1979; b 4 Aug. 1928; s of Leslie Norman Haxby and Ruth Blount; m 1953, Barbara Mary Smith (marr. diss. 1986); one s two d. Educ: Queen Elizabeth Grammar Sch., Barnet; Royal Veterinary Coll., London. MRCVS 1953. Army Service, Queen's Royal Regt, RAEC, Sudan Defence Force, 1946–48 (Warrant Officer I). Practice in Leics and Shropshire, 1953–55; research, Boots Pure Drug Co., 1955–57 (clinical pathologist); gen. practice, Southwell, 1957–. Lecturer: Animal Husbandry, Nottingham Coll. of Agriculture, 1969–; Poultry Production and Public Health, London and Glasgow Univs, 1978–; External Examiner: Vet. Medicine, Glasgow Univ., 1980–85; Animal Husbandry, Bristol Univ., 1987–. Official Vet. Surgeon, Newark DC, 1979–; Consultant to: W. & J. B. Eastwood, 1972–78; R. B. N. and Imperial Foods, 1978–82; Hillsdown Holdings, 1982–; Smith Kline Animal Health, 1982–; Cyanamid GB, 1982–85; Duphar-Philips, 1982–; I. M. C. & Cambridge-Naremco Products, USA, 1985–. Mem., Parly and Sci. Cttee, H of C, 1979–86; Sci. Advr to Agric. Select Cttee, H of C, 1989. Mem. Council, 1983–84, Hon. Lectr, 1984–, Royal Vet. Coll.; President: E Midlands Vet. Assoc. (and Treasurer), 1973–; BVA, 1977–78; RCVS, 1983–84; Mem., Animal Health and Tech. Cttee, British Poultry Fedn, 1974–; Chm., World Vet. Poultry Assoc., 1985–89. Mem., Farm Animal Welfare Council, 1981–; Trustee and Treasurer, Gordon Meml Trust, 1982–; Governor, Houghton Poultry Res. Station, 1983–. Recreations: work, reading, golf, gardening. Address: Wait & Haxby, Candant House, Main Street, Upton, Newark, Notts NG23 5ST. T: Southwell (0636) 812339. Clubs: Reform, Farmers', Savile.

HAY, family name of Earls of Erroll and Kinnoull, and of Marquis of Tweeddale.

HAY, Lord; Harry Thomas William Hay; b 8 Aug. 1984; s and heir of Earl of Erroll, qv.

HAY, Prof. Allan Stuart, PhD; FRS 1981; Professor of Polymer Chemistry, McGill University, Montreal, since 1987; b 23 July 1929; s of Stuart Lumsden and Verna Emila Hay; m 1956, Janet Mary Keck; two s two d. Educ: Univ. of Alberta (BSc Hon, MSc); Univ. of Illinois (PhD). General Electric Research and Development Center, Schenectady, NY: Research Associate, 1955; Manager, Chemical Laboratory, 1968; Research and Develt Manager, Chemical Labs, 1980–87. Adjunct Professor, Polymer Science and Engineering Dept, Univ. of Massachusetts, 1975. Hon. DSc Alberta, 1987. Soc. of Plastics Engrs Internat. award in Plastics Science and Engineering, 1975; Achievement award, Industrial Res. Inst., 1984. Publications: numerous papers and contribs to learned jls. Recreations: philately, reading, swimming. Address: 5015 Glencairn Avenue, Montreal, Quebec H3W 2B3, Canada.

HAY, Sir Arthur Thomas Erroll, 10th Bt of Park, cr 1663; ISO 1974; DiplArch; ARIBA 1935; retired Civil Servant; b 13 April 1909; o s of 9th Bt and Lizabel Annie (d 1957), o d of late Lachlan Mackinnon Macdonald, Skeabost, Isle of Skye; S father, 1923; m 1st, 1935, Hertha Louise (who was granted a divorce, 1942), d of late Herr Ludwig Stölzle, Nagelberg, Austria, and of H. E. Frau Vaugoin, Vienna; one s; 2nd, 1942, Rosemarie Evelyn Anne, d of late Vice-Adm. Aubrey Lambert and of Mrs Lambert. Educ: Fettes Coll., Edinburgh. Student of architecture, University of Liverpool, 1927–31; Diploma in Architecture, Architectural Assoc., July 1934. Served War of 1939–45; 2nd Lieut RE 1943; Lieut 1944; service in Normandy, Belgium, Holland and Germany in 21 Army Group. Heir: s John Erroll Audley Hay, b 3 Dec. 1935. Address: c/o Lloyds Bank, Castle Street, Farnham, Surrey.

HAY, Sir David (Osborne), Kt 1979; CBE 1962; DSO 1945; retired public servant; b 29 Nov. 1916; 2nd s of late H. A. Hay, Barwon Heads, Victoria; m 1944, Alison Marion Parker Adams; two s. Educ: Geelong Grammar Sch.; Brasenose Coll., Oxford; Melbourne Univ. Joined Commonwealth Public Service, 1939. Australian Imperial Force, 1940–46: Major, 2nd Sixth Infantry Bn; served in Western Desert, Greece, New Guinea. Rejoined External Affairs Dept, 1947; Imp. Def. Coll., 1954; Minister (later Ambassador) to Thailand, 1955–57; High Comr in Canada, 1961–64; Ambassador to UN, New York, 1964–65; First Asst Secretary, External Affairs, 1966; Administrator of Papua and New Guinea, 1967–70; Sec., Dept of External Territories, Canberra, 1970–73; Defence Force Ombudsman, 1974–76; Sec., Dept of Aboriginal Affairs, 1977–79. Publications: The Delivery of Services financed by the Department of Aboriginal Affairs, 1976; Nothing Over Us: the story of the 2nd Sixth Australian Infantry Battalion, 1985. Address: Boomanoomana Homestead, via Mulwala, NSW 2647, Australia. Clubs: Australian, Melbourne (Melbourne).

HAY, Sir David (Russell), Kt 1991; CBE 1981; FRCP; FRACP; (first) Medical Director, National Heart Foundation of New Zealand, since 1977; Cardiologist, Canterbury Hospital (formerly North Canterbury Hospital) Board, 1964–89; Hon. Consulting Physician, Canterbury Area Health Board, since 1990; b 8 Dec. 1927; twin s of Sir James Lawrence Hay, OBE, and Lady (Davidina Mertel) Hay; m 1958, Dr Jocelyn Valerie Bell; two d. Educ: St Andrew's Coll., Christchurch; Otago Univ. (MB, ChB; MD). FRACP 1965; FRCP 1971. Resident appts, Christchurch, Royal South Hants, Hammersmith, Brompton and National Heart Hosps, 1951–55; Sen. Registrar, Dunedin and Christchurch Hosps, 1956–59; Physician, N Canterbury Hosp. Bd, 1959–64; Head of Dept of Cardiology, 1969–78; Chm. of Medical Services and Hd of Dept of Medicine, 1978–84. Chm., Christchurch Hosps Med. Staff Assoc., 1983–85 (Dep. Chm., 1982–83); Clin. Lectr, Christchurch Clinical Sch., Univ. of Otago, 1973–80; Clin. Reader, 1980–88; Foundn Councillor, Nat. Heart Foundn of NZ, 1968– (Mem. Scientific Cttee, 1968–; Sec., 1974–77); Vice-Pres., RACP, 1988–92 (Councillor, 1964–66, 1987–88; Examiner, 1974–75; Censor, 1975–79); Mem. Specialist Adv. Cttee on Cardiology, 1980–90; Chm., Central Specialists Cttee of BMA, 1967–68; Pres., Canterbury Div. of BMA, 1972. Chm., NZ Region of Cardiac Soc. of Australia and NZ, and Councillor, 1977–81. Member: Resuscitation Cttee of Nat. Cttee on Emergency Care, 1979–87; Health Promotion Forum of NZ, 1984–; NZ Govt Adv. Cttee on Prevention of Cardiovascular Disease, 1985–86; NZ Govt Adv. Cttee on Smoking and Health, 1974–88; WHO Expert Adv. Panel on Smoking and Health, 1977–; Hypertension Task Force, 1988–89. Speaker: World Conf. on Smoking and Health, Stockholm, 1979; Internat. Soc. and Fedn of Cardiology Workshop, Jakarta, 1982; Internat. Congress on Preventive Cardiology, Washington, 1989; World Congress of Cardiology, Manila, 1990. Trustee: J. L. Hay Charitable Trust; W. H. Nicholls Charitable Trust; Edna and Winifred White-Parsons Charitable Trust. Commemoration Medal, NZ, 1990. Publications: (ed) Coronary Heart Disease: prevention and control in NZ, 1983; editor of technical report series of National Heart Foundn and author of numerous NHF pubns; over eighty sci. papers in various med. jls, mostly on smoking and health and preventive cardiology. Recreations: golf, tennis. Address: 20 Greers Road, Christchurch 4, New Zealand. T: 3585–482. Club: Christchurch Golf.

See also Sir Hamish Hay, Dame M. L. Salas.

HAY, Prof. Denys, MA; FBA 1970; FRSE 1977; Emeritus Professor of Medieval History, University of Edinburgh; b 29 Aug. 1915; s of Rev. W. K. Hay and Janet Waugh; m 1937, Sarah Gwyneth, d of S. E. Morley; one s two d. Educ: Royal Grammar Sch., Newcastle upon Tyne; Balliol Coll., Oxford. 1st Cl. hons, Modern History, 1937; senior demy, Magdalen Coll., 1937. Temporary Lecturer, Glasgow Univ., 1938; Bryce Studentship, Oxford Univ., 1939; Asst Lecturer, University Coll., Southampton, 1939; RASC 1940–42; War Historian (Civil Depts), 1942–45; Lecturer, 1945, Professor of Medieval History, 1954–80, Emeritus Professor 1980, Edinburgh Univ., Vice-Principal, 1971–75. Literary Dir, RHistS, 1955–58 (Hon. Life Vice-Pres., 1981–); Lectures: Italian, British Acad., 1959; Wiles, QUB, 1960; Birkbeck, Trinity Coll., Cambridge, 1971–72; David Murray, Glasgow Univ., 1983; Visiting Professor: Cornell Univ., 1963; Univ. of Virginia, 1980; Prof. of History, European Univ. Inst., Badia Fiesolana, 1980–82; Senior Fellow, Newberry Library, Chicago, 1966; Trustee, Nat. Library of Scotland, 1966–88; President: Historical Association, 1967–70; Ecclesiastical Hist. Soc., 1980–81; Mem., Reviewing Cttee on Export of Works of Art, 1976–80. Editor, English Historical Review, 1958–65. Hon. For. Mem., Amer. Acad. of Arts and Scis, 1974. Hon. DLitt Newcastle, 1970; Hon. Dr Tours Univ., 1982. Comdr, Order of Merit, Italy, 1980. Publications: Anglica Historia of P. Vergil, 1950; Polydore Vergil, 1952; From Roman Empire to Renaissance Europe, 1953 (The Medieval Centuries, 1964); ed. R. K. Hannay's Letters of James V, 1954; Europe: the emergence of an idea, 1957, new edn 1968; (ed) New Cambridge Modern History, Vol. I: The Renaissance, 1493–1520, 1957, new edn 1976; Italian Renaissance in its Historical Background, 1961, new edn 1976; Design and Development of Weapons (History of Second World War) (with M. M. Postan and J. D. Scott), 1964; Europe in the 14th and 15th Centuries, 1966, new edn 1989; (ed with W. K. Smith) Aeneas Sylvius Piccolomini, De Gestis Concilii Basiliensis, 1967; (ed) The Age of the Renaissance, 1967; Annalists and Historians, 1977; Italian Church in the 15th

Century, 1977; Renaissance Essays, 1987; (with John Law) Italy in the Age of the Renaissance, 1989; articles in historical journals. *Address:* 5/11 Oswald Road, Edinburgh EH9 2HE. *T:* 031–667 2886. *Club:* United Oxford & Cambridge University.
See also Richard Hay.

HAY, Frances Mary, (Mrs Roy Hay); *see* Perry, F. M.

HAY, Rt. Rev. Mgr George Adam; Parish Priest, Sacred Heart and St Teresa, Paignton, since 1984; *b* 14 Nov. 1930; *s* of late Sir William Rupert Hay, KCMG, KCIE, CSI, and late Sybil Ethel, *d* of Sir Stewart Abram. *Educ:* Ampleforth College, York; New Coll., Oxford (BA History, MA); Venerable English Coll., Rome (STL). National Service as Midshipman RNVR, 1949–50; student, Oxford, 1950–53; Venerable English Coll., Rome, 1953–60. Ordained priest at Rome, 1959; Curate, Sacred Heart Church, Exeter, and part-time RC Chaplain to students at Exeter Univ., 1960; Chaplain to students at Exeter Univ. and Priest-in-charge, Crediton, 1966–78; Rector, Venerable English Coll., Rome, 1978–84; Parish Priest, St John the Baptist, Dartmouth, 1984. *Recreations:* fly fishing, squash, mountain walking. *Address:* 24 Cecil Road, Paignton, Devon TQ3 2SH. *T:* Paignton (0803) 557518.

HAY, Sir Hamish (Grenfell), Kt 1982; Mayor of Christchurch, New Zealand, 1974–89; Director: Canterbury Development Corporation, since 1983; Mutual Funds Ltd, since 1983; Christchurch International Airport Ltd, since 1988; *b* 8 Dec. 1927; twin *s* of Sir James Lawrence Hay, OBE, and Lady (Davidina) Hay; *m* 1955, Judith Leicester Gill (QSO 1987); one *s* four *d*. *Educ:* St Andrew's Coll., Christchurch; Univ. of Canterbury, NZ (BCom). FCA(NZ). Councillor, Christchurch City Council, 1959–74. Member: Victory Park Bd, 1974–89; Lyttelton Harbour Bd, 1983–89. Chairman: Christchurch Town Hall Board of Management, 1968–89; Canterbury Museum Trust Bd, 1981–84; Canterbury United Council, 1983–86; President: Christchurch Aged People's Welfare Council, 1974–89; Christchurch Civic Music Council, 1974–89; Christchurch Symphony Orchestra, 1982–88; Chm., Christchurch Arts Festival, 1965–74; past Mem., Queen Elizabeth II Arts Council. Chm., New Zealand Soc. of Accountants (Canterbury Br.), 1958; Dep. Man. Dir, Haywrights Ltd, 1962–74. Mem. Council, Univ. of Canterbury, 1974–89; Chm. of Governors, McLean Inst., 1974–89; Governor, St Andrew's Coll., 1986–. Vice-Pres., Municipal Assoc. of NZ, 1974–88. Trustee, Canterbury Savings Bank, 1962–88 (Pres., 1974–75); Dir, Trustbank Canterbury Ltd, 1988–. Mem., Charles Upham Trust, 1986–; Trustee, Trust Bank Canterbury Community Trust, 1988–. Silver Jubilee Medal, 1977; Commemoration Medal, NZ, 1990; Order of the Rising Sun (with Gold Rays), Japan, 1990. *Publication:* Hay Days (autobiog.), 1989. *Recreations:* gardening, listening to good music. *Address:* 70 Heaton Street, Merivale, Christchurch 5, New Zealand. *T:* 3557–244. *Clubs:* Christchurch, Christchurch Rotary (New Zealand).
See also Sir D. R. Hay, Dame M. L. Salas.

HAY, Sir James B. D.; *see* Dalrymple-Hay.

HAY, John Albert; Managing Director, Walport Group, 1968–84; *b* 24 Nov. 1919; *er s* of Alderman J. E. Hay; *m* 1st, 1947, Beryl Joan (marr. diss. 1973), *o d* of Comdr H. C. Found, RN (retired); one *s* one *d*; 2nd, 1974, Janet May, *y d* of A. C. Spruce. *Educ:* Brighton, Hove and Sussex Grammar Sch. Solicitor admitted May 1945. Chairman: Brighton and Hove Young Conservatives, 1945–47; Sussex Federation of Young Conservatives, 1945–47; Young Conservative and Unionist Central Cttee, 1947–49; Conservative Party Housing and Local Govt Cttee, 1956–59; formerly Dir London Municipal Soc.; formerly Vice-Pres. Urban District Councils Assoc.; Hon. Sec. UK Council of the European Movement, 1965–66; Mem. of Exec. Cttee, Nat. Union of Conservative and Unionist Assoc., 1947–49 and 1950–51. Served War of 1939–45, in RNVR; temp. Sub-Lieut, RNVR, 1940–44; temp. Lieut, RNVR, 1944; invalided 1944. Member: British Delegn, Congress of Europe, 1948, and 1973; UK Delegns, Council of Europe and Western European Union, 1956–59. MP (C) Henley, Oxon, 1950–Feb. 1974; PPS to Pres. of BoT, 1951–56; Parly Sec., MoT, 1959–63; Civil Lord of the Admiralty, 1963–64; Parly Under-Sec. of State for Defence for the Royal Navy, April-Oct. 1964. Chm., British Section, Council of European Municipalities, 1971–76, Vice-Chm., 1976–77, Pres., 1977–81, Vice-Pres., 1981–87. *Recreations:* gardening, music, lapidary, historical study. *Address:* 1134 Hillside, West Vancouver, BC V7S 2G4, Canada. *T:* (604) 925 1623.

HAY, Prof. John Duncan, MA, MD, FRCP; Professor of Child Health, University of Liverpool, 1957–74, now Professor Emeritus; *b* 6 Feb. 1909; *s* of late Prof. John Hay; *m* 1936, Jannett Ceridwen Evans; one *s* two *d*. *Educ:* Liverpool Coll.; Sidney Sussex Coll., Cambridge; Liverpool Univ. MB, ChB, 1st Cl. Hons, Liverpool, 1933; MA 1934, MB 1935, Cambridge; MD Liverpool, 1936; DCH London, MRCP 1939; FRCP 1951. Holt Fellowship in Pathology, Liverpool, 1935; Cons. Pædiatrician to: Royal Liverpool Children's Hospital, 1939–74; Royal Liverpool Babies' Hospital, 1939–61; Birkenhead Children's Hosp., 1937–54; Liverpool Maternity Hosp. 1946–74; Lancashire County Hosp., Whiston, 1942–51; Liverpool Open-Air Hospital, Leasowe, and Mill Road Maternity Hosp., 1947–74; Alder Hey Children's Hosp., 1957–74; Liverpool Education Cttee, 1951–72. Demonstrator in Pathology, University of Liverpool, 1935 and 1938; Asst Lectr in Clinical Pædiatrics, University of Liverpool, 1948–57. Brit. Paediatric Association: Treasurer, 1964–71; Pres., 1972–73; Hon. Mem., 1973–; President: Liverpool Med. Instn, 1972–73; Liverpool Paediatric Club, 1975–; Hon. Mem. Assoc. European Paediatric Cardiologists, 1975–. RAMC (Major and Lieut-Col), 1942–46. *Publications:* contribs to Archives of Disease in Childhood, British Heart Journal, BMJ, Lancet, Practitioner, Brit. Encyclopædia of Medical Practice, Medical Progress, 1957, Cardiovascular Diseases in Childhood. *Recreations:* music, fell walking. *Address:* Fairfield, Cedarway, Gayton, Merseyside L60 3RH. *T:* 051–342 2607.

HAY, Richard; Special Adviser, European Commission, since 1991; *b* 4 May 1942; *s* of Prof. Denys Hay, *qv; m* 1969, Miriam Marguerite Alvin England; two *s*. *Educ:* George Watson's Coll., Edinburgh; Edinburgh Univ.; Balliol Coll., Oxford (BA Hons, Mod. Hist.). Assistant Principal, HM Treasury, 1963–68; Secretary, West Midlands Economic Planning Council, 1966–67; Private Sec. to Financial Sec., Treasury, 1967–68; Principal, Treasury, 1968–73; European Commission: Member, Cabinet of Sir Christopher (now Lord) Soames, Vice-Pres., 1973–75; Dep. Chef de Cabinet, 1975–77; Chef de Cabinet to Mr Christopher Tugendhat, Member, 1977–79; Dir, Economic Structures and Community Interventions, Directorate-Gen. for Economic and Financial Affairs, 1979–81; Dep. Dir-Gen., 1981–86, Dir-Gen., 1986–91, Directorate-General for Personnel and Admin, EC. *Address:* c/o European Commission, 200 rue de la Loi, 1049 Brussels, Belgium. *T:* (02) 235 1111. *Club:* United Oxford & Cambridge University.

HAY, Maj.-Gen. Robert Arthur, CB 1970; MBE 1946; Australian Army Officer, retired 1977; *b* 9 April 1920; *s* of Eric Alexander Hay and Vera Eileen Hay (*née* Whitehead); *m* 1944, Endrée Patricia Hay (*née* McGovern); two *s* one *d*. *Educ:* Brighton Grammar Sch., Melbourne, Victoria; RMC Duntroon, ACT (graduated Dec. 1939); Australian Staff Coll., 1944; USA Staff Coll., Fort Leavenworth, 1944. Lt-Col, 1945; Col, 1955; Col GS HQ Eastern Comd; Military Attaché, Washington, DC, 1956; Dir Administrative Planning, AHQ, 1959; Defence Representative, Singapore and Malaya, 1962; Brig., 1964;

IDC London, 1965; Dir Military Ops and Plans, AHQ, 1966; Maj.-Gen., 1967; Dep. Chief of the General Staff, AHQ; Comdr, Australian Forces, Vietnam, 1969; Comdr, First Australian Div., 1970; Chief, Mil. Planning Office, SEATO, 1971–73; Comdt, Royal Military Coll., Duntroon, 1973–77. Sec., Australian Council of Professions, 1978–86; Exec. Officer, Australian Centre for Publications acquired for Develt, 1982–87. Pres., Veterans Tennis Assoc. of Australia, 1981–. *Recreations:* tennis, golf. *Address:* Unit 6, Kingston Tower, 9 Jardine Street, Kingston, ACT 2604, Australia. *Clubs:* Melbourne Cricket; Commonwealth, Royal Canberra Golf (Canberra); Tanglin (Singapore).

HAY, Robert Colquhoun, CBE 1988; WS; Sheriff Principal of North Strathclyde, since 1989; *b* 22 Sept. 1933; *s* of late J. B. Hay, dental surgeon, Stirling and Mrs J. Y. Hay; *m* 1958, Olive Black; two *s* two *d*. *Educ:* Univ. of Edinburgh (MA, LLB). Legal practice, 1957–63, 1968–76; Depute Procurator Fiscal, Edinburgh, 1963–68; Temp. Sheriff, 1984–89; Chm. 1976–81, Pres., 1981–89, Industrial Tribunals for Scotland. Mem., Sheriff Court Rules Council, 1989–. Comr, Northern Lighthouse Bd, 1989– (Vice-Chm., 1991–March 1992). *Publication:* contrib. Laws of Scotland: Stair Memorial Encyclopedia, 1988. *Recreations:* hillwalking, sailing. *Address:* Sheriff Principal's Chambers, Sheriff Court House, Paisley PA3 2HW. *T:* 041–887 5291. *Clubs:* Western (Glasgow); Royal Northern and Clyde Yacht (Rhu).

HAY, Robin William Patrick Hamilton; Recorder, since 1985; barrister; *b* 1 Nov. 1939; *s* of William R. Hay and Dora Hay; *m* 1969, Lady Olga Maitland, *d* of Earl of Lauderdale, *qv;* two *s* one *d*. *Educ:* Eltham; Selwyn Coll., Cambridge (MA, LLB). Called to the Bar, Inner Temple, 1964. Chm., Young Musicians Symphony Orchestra, 1990–. *Recreations:* church tasting, gastronomy, choral singing. *Address:* 21 Cloudesley Street, N1.

HAY, Sir Ronald Frederick Hamilton, 12th Bt *cr* 1703, of Alderston; *b* 1941; *s* of Sir Ronald Nelson Hay, 11th Bt and of Rita, *d* of John Munyard; *S* father, 1988; *m* 1978, Kathleen, *d* of John Thake; two *s* one *d*. *Heir: s* Alexander James Hay, *b* 1979. *Address:* Aspendale, Vic 3195, Australia.

HAY DAVISON, Ian Frederic; *see* Davison, I. F. H.

HAYBALL, Frederick Ronald, CMG 1969; *b* 23 April 1914; *s* of late Frederick Reuben Hayball and late Rebecca Hayball; *m* 1938, Lavinia Violet Palmer; one *s* one *d*. *Educ:* Alleyn's Sch., Dulwich. Accountant, Myers, Gondouin & Co. Ltd, 1932–39. Flying Officer, RAF, 1939–45. Foreign and Commonwealth Office, 1945–69 (Counsellor, retired); Asst Sec., Longman Gp Ltd, 1969–81. *Recreations:* cricket, angling, motoring, bowls. *Address:* 50 Theydon Park Road, Theydon Bois, Essex CM16 7LP. *T:* Theydon Bois (037881) 2195.

HAYCRAFT, Anna Margaret; writer; *b* 9 Sept. 1932; *d* of John and Alexandra Lindholm; *m* 1956, Colin Haycraft, *qv;* four *s* one *d* (and one *s* one *d* decd). *Educ:* Bangor County Grammar School for Girls; Liverpool School of Art. *Publications: as Anna Haycraft:* Natural Baby Food, 1977; (with Caroline Blackwood) Darling, You Shouldn't Have Gone to So Much Trouble, 1980; *as Alice Thomas Ellis:* The Sin Eater, 1977; The Birds of the Air, 1980; The Twenty-Seventh Kingdom, 1982; The Other Side of the Fire, 1983; Unexplained Laughter, 1985; (with Tom Pitt-Aikens) Secrets of Strangers, 1986; Home Life, 1986; More Home Life, 1987; The Clothes in the Wardrobe, 1987, The Skeleton in the Cupboard, 1988, The Fly in the Ointment, 1989, trilogy; Home Life Three, 1988; (with Tom Pitt-Aikens) The Loss of the Good Authority, 1989; (ed) Wales: an anthology, 1989; Home Life Four, 1989; A Welsh Childhood (autobiog.), 1990; The Inn at the Edge of the World, 1990. *Address:* 22 Gloucester Crescent, NW1 7DY. *T:* 071–485 7408.

HAYCRAFT, Colin Berry; Chairman, Gerald Duckworth & Co. Ltd, publishers, since 1971; *b* 12 Jan. 1929; *yr s* of Major W. C. S. Haycraft, MC and Bar, 5/8 Punjab Regt (killed 1929), and late Olive Lillian Esmée (*née* King); *m* 1956, Anna Margaret Lindholm (*see* A. M. Haycraft); four *s* one *d* (and one *s* one *d* decd). *Educ:* Wellington Coll. (schol.); The Queen's Coll., Oxford (Open Schol. in Classics; 1st Cl. Classical Mods, 1st Cl. Lit.Hum., MA; Hon. Fellow, 1990). Nat. service (army), 1947–49. Personal Asst to Chm., Cecil H. King, Daily Mirror Newspapers Ltd; Dir, Weidenfeld & Nicolson Ltd and Weidenfeld (Publishers) Ltd (original editor and subseq. Man. Dir, World University Library Ltd); joined Duckworth, 1968. Public Schs Rackets Champion (singles and pairs), 1946; Oxford blue for Squash Rackets (4 years, Captain OUSRC, Eng. internat.), Lawn Tennis (Devon Co. player) and Rackets. *Address:* 22 Gloucester Crescent, NW1 7DY. *Clubs:* Beefsteak; Vincent's (Oxford); Jesters; Queen's.
See also J. S. Haycraft.

HAYCRAFT, John Stacpoole, CBE 1982; Director General, International House (formerly English International (International House)), 1975–90 (Consultant, 1990–91); *b* 11 Dec. 1926; *s* of late Major W. C. S. Haycraft and Olive Haycraft; *m* 1953, Brita Elisabeth Langenfelt; two *s* one *d*. *Educ:* Wellington Coll.; Jesus Coll., Oxford (Open Exhibnr; MA). E-SU Fellowship. Yale Univ., 1951–52. Founder and Dir, Academia Britanica, Córdoba, 1953; Founder and Principal: International Language Centre, London, 1960; International Teacher Trng Inst., 1963; Founder and Director: International House, London, 1964; International House, Rome, 1967–68; Dir, International House, Paris, 1971–72; Founder, English Teaching Theatre, 1970. Mem., English Teaching Adv. Cttee, British Council, 1974–80. *Publications:* Babel in Spain, 1958, 2nd edn 1958; Getting on in English, 1964, 7th edn 1982 (trans. 9 langs); Babel in London, 1965; George and Elvira, 1970; Choosing Your English, 1972, 8th edn 1982; Action, 1977; Introduction to English Language Teaching, 1978; Think, Then Speak, 1984; Italian Labyrinth, 1985; In Search of the French Revolution, 1989; contrib. Guardian, Independent, The Times, Observer (Spanish correspondent, 1958–59), Modern English Teacher, etc. *Recreations:* tennis, swimming, chess, cinema, theatre, history, travel. *Address:* 79 Lee Road, SE3. *T:* 081–852 5495. *Club:* Canning.
See also C. B. Haycraft.

HAYDAR, Dr Loutof Allah; Syrian Ambassador to the People's Republic of China, since 1990; *b* 22 March 1940; *s* of Haydar and Mary; *m* 1968, Hayat Hassan; one *s* three *d*. *Educ:* Damascus Univ. (BA English Literature 1964); Moscow State Univ. (PhD 1976). Joined Foreign Office, 1965; served at Syrian Embassy: London, 1965–67; Bonn, 1967–68; Moscow, 1970–75; served with Syrian Delegation to UN, New York, 1978–82. *Publication:* The Ancient History of Palestine and the Middle East (PhD Thesis), 1976. *Address:* Syrian Embassy, No 6 San Li Tun Dong Si Jie, Beijing, China.

HAYDAY, Anthony Victor; HM Diplomatic Service, retired; Ambassador to Madagascar, 1987–90; *b* 1 June 1930; *s* of Charles Leslie Victor Hayday and Catherine (*née* McCarthy); *m* 1966, Anne Heather Moffat; one *s* one *d*. *Educ:* Beckenham and Penge Grammar School. Royal Air Force, 1949–50; HM Foreign (later Diplomatic) Service, 1950; Brazzaville, 1953; British Information Services, New York, 1955; FO, 1958; Vice Consul, Houston, 1961; 2nd Secretary, Algiers, 1962; FO (later FCO), 1966; 1st Secretary, New Delhi, 1969; Head of Chancery, Freetown, 1973; on secondment to Commonwealth Secretariat, 1976–80; Dep. High Comr, Calcutta, 1981–85; Consul-Gen., Cleveland,

1985–87. *Recreations:* birdwatching, athletics. *Address:* Meadow Cottage, Swillbrook, Minety, Malmesbury, Wilts SN16 9QA. *Clubs:* Blackheath Harriers, Mensa; Bengal (Calcutta).

HAYDEN, Hon. William George, AC; Governor-General of Australia, since 1989; *b* Brisbane, 23 Jan. 1933; *s* of G. Hayden, Oakland, Calif, USA; *m* 1960, Dallas, *d* of W. Broadfoot; one *s* two *d*. *Educ:* Brisbane State High Sch. BEcon, Univ. of Qld. Public Service, Qld, 1950–52; Police Constable in Queensland, 1953–61. MHR (Lab) for Oxley, Qld, 1961–88. Parly Spokesman on Health and Welfare, 1969–72; Minister for Social Security, Australian Commonwealth Govt, 1972–75; Federal Treasurer, June-Nov. 1975; Leader of Australian Labor Party and the Opposition, 1977–83; spokesman on defence, 1976–83 and on economic management, 1977–83; Minister for Foreign Affairs, 1983–88, and for Trade, 1987–88. Chancellor, Order of Australia; Prior, Order of St John in Australia. Hon. Dr Griffith Univ.; Hon. LLD Univ. of Qld. Gwangha Medal, Order of Diplomatic Merit, Korea. *Recreations:* reading, music, golf, horse riding, fly-fishing, cross-country skiing, bushwalking. *Address:* Government House, Canberra, ACT, Australia; (home) PO Box 33, Ipswich, Queensland 4305, Australia.

HAYDEN, William Joseph, CBE 1976; Chairman and Chief Executive, Jaguar plc, since 1990; *b* 19 Jan. 1929; *s* of George Hayden and Mary Ann Hayden (*née* Overhead); *m* 1954, Mavis Ballard; two *s* two *d*. *Educ:* Romford Tech. College. Served Army, 1947–49. Ford Motor Co.: Briggs Motor Bodies, Dagenham, 1950–57; financial staff, Dagenham, 1957–63; Div. Controller, Ford Chassis, Transmission and Engine Div., Dagenham, 1963–67; Gen. Ops Manager, Transmission, Chassis and Truck Mfg Ops, 1967–71; Vice-President: Truck Mfg Ops, 1971; Power Train Ops, 1972; Mfg Ford of Europe, Inc., 1974–90. *Recreations:* golf, gardening, soccer. *Address:* Jaguar plc, Browns Lane, Allesley, Coventry, CV5 9DR. *Club:* Thorndon Park Golf.

HAYDON, Francis Edmund Walter; HM Diplomatic Service, retired; *b* 23 Dec. 1928; *s* of late Surgeon Captain Walter T. Haydon, RN and Maria Christina Haydon (*née* Delahoyde); *m* 1959, Isabel Dorothy Kitchin; two *s* two *d*. *Educ:* Downside School; Magdalen College, Oxford. BA (1st cl. Modern History) 1949. Asst London correspondent, Agence France-Presse, 1951–52; Asst diplomatic correspondent, Reuters, 1952–55; joined Foreign Office, 1955; Second Sec., Benghazi, 1959; Beirut, 1962; First Sec., Blantyre, 1969; Ankara, 1978; Counsellor, FCO, 1981–87. *Recreations:* lawn tennis, cricket, enjoying the countryside. *Address:* Le Picachon, La Rue des Bouillons, Trinity, Jersey. *T:* Jersey (0534) 63155.

HAYDON, Sir Walter Robert, (Sir Robin Haydon), KCMG 1980 (CMG 1970); HM Diplomatic Service, retired; *b* 29 May 1920; *s* of Walter Haydon and Evelyn Louise Thom; *m* 1943, Joan Elizabeth Tewson (*d* 1988); one *d* (and one *s* one *d* decd). *Educ:* Dover Grammar Sch. Served in Army in France, India and Burma, 1939–46. Entered Foreign Service, 1946; served at London, Berne, Turin, Sofia, Bangkok, London, Khartoum, UK Mission to UN (New York), Washington; FO spokesman and Head of News Dept, FCO, 1967–71; High Comr, Malaŵi, 1971–73; Chief Press Sec., 10 Downing Street, 1973–74; High Comr, Malta, 1974–76; Ambassador to Republic of Ireland, 1976–80. Dir of Gp Public Affairs, Imperial Gp, 1981–84; Dir, Imperial Tobacco Ltd, 1984–87. Member: Reviewing Cttee on Export of Works of Art, 1984–87; Tobacco Adv. Council, 1984–. Governor: E-SU, 1980–86, 1987–; Dover Grammar Sch., 1982–89. *Recreations:* walking, swimming, tennis. *Address:* c/o Lloyds Bank, Cox's & King's Branch, 7 Pall Mall, SW1Y 5NA. *Clubs:* Travellers', Special Forces.

HAYE, Colvyn Hugh, CBE 1983; Commissioner for Hong Kong, 1984–87; *b* 7 Dec. 1925; 3rd *s* of Colvyn Hugh Haye and Avis Rose Kelly; *m* 1949, Gloria Mary Stansbury; two *d*. *Educ:* Sherwood Coll.; Univ. of Melbourne (BA, Teachers' Cert.); Christchurch Coll., Oxford (Overseas Service Trng Course). Served War, RNVR, Midshipman and Sub-Lt, 1944–46. Victorian State Educn Service, 1947–52; joined Colonial Service, now HMOCS, Hong Kong Government: Educn Officer, 1953; Sen. Educn Officer, 1962; Asst Dir and Head of Educnl Television Service, 1969; Dep. Dir, 1975; Dir of Educn and Official Mem., Legislative Council, 1980; Sec., Administrative Service and Comr, London Office, 1984. Jardine Educn Foundn Visitor, Univs of Oxford and Cambridge, 1990–. Mem., Exec. Cttee and Council, Overseas Service Pensioners' Assoc., 1988–. JP Hong Kong, 1971–87. *Recreations:* reading, writing, talking, walking. *Address:* Wymering, Sheet Common, near Petersfield, Hants GU31 5AT. *T:* Petersfield (0730) 68480. *Clubs:* Hong Kong, Tripehounds, Toastmasters (Hong Kong).

HAYEK, Friedrich August (von), CH 1984; FBA 1944; Dr Jur, DrScPol, Vienna; DSc (Econ.) London; *b* Vienna, 8 May 1899; *s* of late August von Hayek, Prof. of Botany at University of Vienna; certificate of naturalisation, 1938; *m* 1st, Hella von Fritsch (*d* 1960); one *s* one *d*; 2nd, Helene Bitterlich. *Educ:* University of Vienna. Austrian Civil Service, 1921–26; Dir, Austrian Institute for Economic Research, 1927–31; Lecturer in Economics, University of Vienna, 1929–31; Tooke Prof. of Economic Science and Statistics in University of London, 1931–50; Prof. of Social and Moral Science, University of Chicago, 1950–62; Prof. of Economics, Univ. of Freiburg i B, 1962–69. Chm., Adam Smith Inst. Hon. Fellow: LSE; Austrian Acad. of Scis; American Economic Assoc.; Hoover Inst. on War, Revolution and Peace; Argentine Acad. of Economic Sci.; Academia Sinica. Dr jur *hc* Rikkyo Univ., Tokyo, 1964; Dr jur *hc* Univ. of Salzburg, 1974; Dr Lit. Hum. *hc* Univ. of Dallas, 1975; Hon. Dr Soc. Sci., Marroquin Univ., Guatemala, 1977; Hon. Dr: Santa Maria Univ., Valparaiso, 1977; Univ. of Buenos Aires, 1977; Univ. of Giessen, 1982. Nobel Prize in Economic Science (jtly), 1974. Austrian Distinction for Science and Art, 1975; Mem., Orden pour le Mérite für Wissenschaften und Künste, Fed. Rep. of Germany, 1977; Medal of Merit, Baden-Württemberg, 1981; Ring of Honour, City of Vienna, 1983; Gold Medal, City of Paris, 1984; Grosse Goldene Ehrenzeichen mit dem Stern für Verdienste (Austria), 1990. *Publications:* Prices and Production, 1931; Monetary Theory and the Trade Cycle, 1933 (German edition, 1929); Monetary Nationalism and International Stability, 1937; Profits, Interest, and Investment, 1939; The Pure Theory of Capital, 1941; The Road to Serfdom, 1944; Individualism and Economic Order, 1948; John Stuart Mill and Harriet Taylor, 1950; The Counter-revolution of Science, 1952; The Sensory Order, 1952; The Political Ideal of the Rule of Law, 1955; The Constitution of Liberty, 1960; Studies in Philosophy, Politics and Economics, 1967; Freiburger Studien, 1969; Law, Legislation & Liberty, vol. I: Rules and Order, 1973, Vol II: The Mirage of Social Justice, 1976, Vol. III: The Political Order of a Free People, 1979; De-Nationalisation of Money, 1976; New Studies in Philosophy, Politics, Economics and the History of Ideas, 1978; The Fatal Conceit, 1988; edited: Beiträge zur Geldtheorie, 1933; Collectivist Economic Planning, 1935; Capitalism and the Historians, 1954; and the works of H. H. Gossen, 1927; F. Wieser, 1929; C. Menger, 1933–36; and H. Thornton, 1939; articles in economic journal, Economica, and other English and foreign journals. *Address:* Urachstrasse 27, D-7800 Freiburg i. Brg, West Germany. *Club:* Reform (London).

HAYES, Brian, QPM 1985; HM Inspector of Constabulary for South East England, since 1991; *b* 25 Jan. 1940; 2nd *s* of James and Jessie Hayes; *m* 1960, Priscilla Rose Bishop; one *s* three *d*. *Educ:* Plaistow County Grammar Sch.; Sheffield Univ. (BA Hons 1st Cl. Mod. Langs). Metropolitan Police, 1959–77; seconded Northern Ireland, 1971–72; Police

Adviser, Mexico, 1975 and 1976, Colombia, 1977; British Police representative, EEC, 1976–77; Asst Chief Constable, Surrey Constabulary, 1977–81; Dep. Chief Constable, Wiltshire Constabulary, 1981–82; Chief Constable, Surrey Constabulary, 1982–91. Vice-Pres., ACPO, 1990–91. Chm., Police Athletic Assoc., 1989– (Nat. Sec., 1984–88); Pres., Union Sportive des Polices d'Europe, 1990–. OStJ 1987. Police Long Service and Good Conduct Medal, 1981. *Recreations:* martial arts, running, sailing, golf. *Address:* White Rose Court, Oriental Road, Woking, Surrey GU22 7LG. *T:* Woking (0483) 729337, *Fax:* 0483 756812.

HAYES, Sir Brian (David), GCB 1988 (KCB 1980; CB 1976); Permanent Secretary, Department of Trade and Industry, 1985–89, retired (Joint Permanent Secretary, 1983–85); *b* 5 May 1929; *s* of late Charles and Flora Hayes, Bramerton, Norfolk; *m* 1958, Audrey Jenkins; one *s* one *d*. *Educ:* Norwich Sch.; Corpus Christi Coll., Cambridge. BA (Hist.) 1952, PhD (Cambridge) 1956. RASC, 1947–49. Joined Min. of Agriculture, Fisheries and Food, 1956; Asst Private Sec. to the Minister, 1958; Asst Sec., 1967; Under-Sec., Milk and Poultry Gp, 1970–73; Dep. Sec., 1973–78; Permanent Sec., 1979–83. Director: Guardian Royal Exchange, 1989–; Tate & Lyle, 1989–; Adv. Dir, Unilever plc, 1990–. *Recreations:* reading, watching cricket.

HAYES, Sir Claude (James), KCMG 1974 (CMG 1969); MA, MLitt; Chairman, Crown Agents for Oversea Governments and Administrations, 1968–74; *b* 23 March 1912; *er s* of late J. B. F. Hayes, West Hoathly, Sussex; *m* 1940, Joan McCarthy (*d* 1984), *yr d* of Edward McCarthy Fitt, Civil Engineer; two *s* one *d*. *Educ:* Ardingly Coll.; St Edmund Hall, Oxford (Scholar); Sorbonne; New Coll., Oxford (Sen. Scholar). Heath Harrison Travelling Scholarship; Zaharoff Travelling Fellowship; Paget Toynbee Prize; MA, MLitt. Asst Dir of Examinations, Civil Service Commn, 1938. Captain RASC 1st Inf. Div. BEF, 1939; Major 1940, Combined Ops; Lieut-Col, 1942–45 (N Africa, Sicily, Italy, NW Europe). Dep. Dir of Examinations, Civil Service Commn, 1945; Dir and Comr, 1949, also Sec., 1955; Nuffield Foundn Fellowship, 1953–54, toured Commonwealth studying public service recruitment and management. Asst Sec., HM Treasury, 1957; British Govt Mem., Cttee on Dissolution of Central African Fedn, 1963; Under-Sec., HM Treasury, 1964–65; Prin. Finance Officer, Min. of Overseas Development, 1965–68. *Recreations:* music; unaided gardening; antique furniture; 18th century bourgeois chattels; getting value for money from shops. *Address:* Prinkham, Chiddingstone Hoath, Kent. *T:* Cowden (0342) 850335.

HAYES, Colin Graham Frederick, MA; RA 1970 (ARA 1963); painter; *b* 17 Nov. 1919; *s* of Gerald Hayes and Winifred (*née* Yule); *m* 1949, Jean Westbrook Law (*d* 1988); three *d*. *Educ:* Westminster Sch.; Christ Church, Oxford. Served Royal Engineers, 1940–45 (Middle East) (Capt.). Ruskin Sch. of Drawing, 1946–47. Tutor, Sen. Tutor and Reader, Royal College of Art, 1949–84; Hon. ARCA, 1960; Fellow, RCA, 1960–84 (Hon. Fellow, 1984). Work in Collections: Arts Council; British Council; Carlisle Museum, etc. *Publications include:* Renoir, 1961; Stanley Spencer, 1963; Rembrandt, 1969; many articles on painting in jls. *Address:* 26 Cleveland Avenue, W4. *T:* 081–994 8762.

HAYES, Helen, (Mrs Charles MacArthur); actress; *b* Washington, DC 10 Oct. 1900; *d* of Francis Van Arnum Brown and Catherine Estelle Hayes; *m* 1928, Charles MacArthur (*d* 1956); one *s* one *d*. *Educ:* Sacred Heart Academy, Washington, DC. As actress has appeared in USA in stage plays, among others: Pollyanna, Dear Brutus, Clarence, Bab, Coquette, The Good Fairy, To the Ladies, Young Blood, Mary of Scotland, Victoria Regina, Ladies and Gentlemen, Twelfth Night, Harriet, Happy Birthday; The Wisteria Trees, 1950; Mrs McThing, 1952. First appearance in England in The Glass Menagerie, 1948. Is also radio actress. Has appeared in films: Farewell to Arms, The Sin of Madelon Claudet, Arrowsmith, The Son-Daughter, My Son John, Anastasia, Airport (Best Supporting Actress Award, 1971), Candleshoe, etc. Awarded gold statuette by Motion Picture Academy of Arts and Sciences, 1932, as outstanding actress, based on performance in the Sin of Madelon Claudet; Hon. degrees: Smith Coll., Hamilton Coll., Columbia Univ., Princeton Univ., St Mary's Coll. Medal of Freedom, 1986. *Publications:* A Gift of Joy, 1965; On Reflection, 1968; (with Anita Loos) Twice Over Lightly, 1971; (with Marion Glasserow Gladney) Our Best Years, 1984; (with Katherine Hatch) My Life in Three Acts, 1990; *relevant publication:* Front Page Marriage: Helen Hayes and Charles MacArthur, by Jhan Robbins, 1982. *Address:* Nyack, New York, NY 10960, USA. *Clubs:* Cosmopolitan, River, etc.

HAYES, Most Rev. James Martin; *see* Halifax (NS), Archbishop of, (RC).

HAYES, Jeremy Joseph James; MP (C) Harlow, since 1983; barrister; *b* 20 April 1953; *s* of Peter and Daye Hayes; *m* 1979, Alison Gail Mansfield; one *s* one *d*. *Educ:* Oratory Sch.; Chelmer Inst. LLB London. Called to the Bar, Middle Temple, 1977. Proposer, Parents Aid (No 2) Bill; Sponsor: Video Recordings Bill; Children and Young Persons (Protection from Tobacco) Bill. Member: Select Cttee on Social Services, 1987–90; Select Cttee on Health, 1990–; All Party Parly Gp on Human Rights; All Party Parly Gp on Race Relations; Jt Sec., Cons. Backbench Health Cttee. Vice-Pres., Epping Forest YCs. Member: FRAME; Amnesty Internat. Hon. Dir, State Legislative Leaders Foundn, USA. Gov., Oratory Sch. Freeman, City of London; Liveryman, Fletchers' Co.; Freeman, Co. of Watermen and Lightermen. *Recreations:* playing biffing games with my son, practising the violin with my daughter, and slumping in front of the TV with my wife. *Address:* Chestnut Cottage, Royston Road, Wendens Ambo, Saffron Walden, Essex CB11 4JX. *T:* Saffron Walden (0799) 40457. *Clubs:* Carlton; Essex.

HAYES, Vice-Admiral Sir John (Osler Chattock), KCB 1967 (CB 1964); OBE 1945; Lord-Lieutenant of Ross and Cromarty, Skye and Lochalsh, 1977–88; *b* 9 May 1913; *er s* of late Major L. C. Hayes, RAMC and Mrs Hayes; *m* 1939, Hon. Rosalind Mary Finlay, *o d* of 2nd and last Viscount Finlay of Nairn; two *s* one *d*. *Educ:* RN Coll., Dartmouth. Entered RN, 1927. Served War of 1939–45; Atlantic, HMS Repulse, Singapore, Russian Convoys, Malta. The Naval Sec., 1962–64; Flag Officer: Flotillas, Home Fleet, 1964–66; Scotland and NI, 1966–68; retd. Comdr 1948; Capt. 1953; Rear-Adm. 1962; Vice-Adm. 1965. Chm., Cromarty Firth Port Authority, 1974–77. Mem., Queen's Body Guard for Scotland (Royal Company of Archers), 1969. Pres., Scottish Council, King George's Fund for Sailors, 1968–78. King Gustav V of Sweden Jubilee Medal, 1948. *Recreations:* walking, music, writing. *Address:* Wemyss House, Nigg, by Tain, Ross and Cromarty. *T:* Nigg (086285) 212.

HAYES, John Philip, CB 1984; Assistant Under-Secretary of State (Economics), Foreign and Commonwealth Office, 1975–84, retired; *b* 1924; *s* of late Harry Hayes and late Mrs G. E. Hayes (*née* Hallsworth); *m* 1956, Susan Elizabeth, *d* of Sir Percivale Liesching, GCMG, KCB, KCVO; one *s* one *d*. *Educ:* Cranleigh Sch.; Corpus Christi Coll., Oxford. RAFVR, 1943–46. Barnett Memorial Fellowship, 1948–49; Political and Economic Planning, 1950–53; OEEC, 1953–58; Internat. Bank for Reconstruction and Develt, 1958–64; Head, Economic Develt Div., OECD, 1964–67; Dir, World Economy Div., Economic Planning Staff, ODM, 1967–69; Dep. Dir Gen. of Economic Planning, ODM, later ODA, 1969–71; Dir, Econ. Program Dept, later Econ. Analysis and Projections Dept, IBRD, 1971–73; Dir, Trade and Finance Div., Commonwealth Secretariat, 1973–75. Sen.

Fellow, Trade Policy Res. Centre, 1984–89. *Recreations:* music, travel. *Address:* 51 Enfield Road, Brentford, Mddx TW8 9PA. *T:* 081–568 7590.

HAYES, John Trevor, CBE 1986; MA Oxon, PhD London; FSA; Director of the National Portrait Gallery, London, since 1974; *b* 21 Jan. 1929; *er s* of late Leslie Thomas Hayes and late Gwendoline (*née* Griffiths), London. *Educ:* Ardingly; Keble Coll. Oxford (Open Exhibr; Hon. Fellow, 1984); Courtauld Inst. of Art, London; Inst. of Fine Arts, New York. Asst Keeper, London Museum, 1954–70, Dir, 1970–74; Commonwealth Fund Fellow, 1958–59 (NY Univ.); Vis. Prof. in History of Art, Yale Univ., 1969. Chm., Walpole Soc., 1981–. *Publications:* London: a pictorial history, 1969; The Drawings of Thomas Gainsborough, 1970; Catalogue of Oil Paintings in the London Museum, 1970; Gainsborough as Printmaker, 1971; Rowlandson: Watercolours and Drawings, 1972; Gainsborough: Paintings and Drawings, 1975; The Art of Graham Sutherland, 1980; The Landscape Paintings of Thomas Gainsborough, 1982; The Art of Thomas Rowlandson, 1990; Catalogue of the British Paintings in the National Gallery of Art, Washington, 1991; various London Museum and Nat. Portrait Gall. pubns; numerous articles in The Burlington Magazine, Apollo and other jls. *Recreations:* music, walking, gardening, travel. *Address:* c/o The National Portrait Gallery, St Martin's Place, WC2H 0HE. *T:* 071–930 1552. *Clubs:* Beefsteak, Garrick, Arts.

HAYES, John William; Secretary General, Law Society, since 1987; *b* 10 Feb. 1945; *s* of late Dick Hayes and of Bridget Isobel Hayes; *m* 1970, Jennifer Hayes (*née* Harvey); two *s* one *d*. *Educ:* Nottingham High Sch.; Morecambe Grammar Sch.; Victoria Univ. of Manchester (LLB). Solicitor. Articled Thomas Foord, 1966–69; Worthing Borough Council, 1966–69; Nottingham County Borough Council, 1969–71; Somerset CC, 1971–74; Asst, Dep. Clerk and Dep. Chief Exec., Notts CC, 1974–80; Clerk and Chief Exec., Warwicks CC, 1980–86. Chm., Local Govt Gp, Law Soc., 1981–82; Sec., Warwicks Probation Cttee, 1983–86; Clerk to Warwicks Magistrates' Courts' Cttee, 1983–86; Clerk to Lord Lieut of Warwicks, 1980–86. Chm., Coventry Dio. Church Urban Fund, 1989–91; Member: Council, Warwick Univ., 1980–90; Bishop of Coventry's Board of Social Responsibility, 1981–86; Inner Cities' Task Force, 1985–86. Gov., Kingsley School, 1986–. *Recreations:* cooking, cricket, music, idleness. *Address:* Law Society, 113 Chancery Lane, WC2A 1LP. *T:* 071-242 1222. *Clubs:* Athenæum, YMCA.

HAYES, Walter, CBE 1980; Director, Aston Martin Lagonda Ltd; Vice Chairman, Ford of Europe Inc., 1984–89; Vice President, Ford Motor Company, 1977–89; *b* 12 April 1924; *s* of Walter and Hilda Hayes; *m* 1949, Elizabeth (*née* Holland); two *s* one *d*. *Educ:* Hampton Grammar Sch.; Royal Air Force. Editor, Sunday Dispatch, 1956; Associate Editor, Daily Mail, 1959; Director, Ford of Britain, 1965; Vice-Pres., Ford of Europe Incorporated, 1968; Director: Ford Motor Co. Ltd; Ford Werke A.G.; Ford Advanced Vehicles Ltd, 1963–70. Vice-Pres., Public Affairs, Ford Motor Co. in the United States, 1980–84. Mem., Redundant Churches Fund, 1991–. *Publications:* Angelica: a story for children, 1968; The Afternoon Cat and Other Poems, 1976; Henry: a memoir of Henry Ford II, 1990. *Recreations:* old books, cricket. *Address:* Battlecrease Hall, Russell Road, Shepperton TW17 8JW. *Clubs:* MCC, Brooks's, Arts.

HAYES, Prof. William, FRS 1964; FRSE 1968; FAA 1976; Professor and Head of the Department of Genetics, Research School of Biological Sciences, Australian National University, 1974–78, now Emeritus; *b* 18 Jan. 1913; *s* of William Hayes and Miriam (*née* Harris), Co. Dublin, Ireland; *m* 1941, Honora Lee; one *s*. *Educ:* College of St Columba, Rathfarnham, Co. Dublin; Dublin Univ. BA (1st Cl. Mods. Nat. Sci.) Dublin, 1936; MB, BCh, Dublin, 1937; FRCPI 1945; ScD, Dublin, 1949. Served in India as Major, RAMC, Specialist in Pathology, 1942–46. Lectr in Bacteriology, Trinity Coll., Dublin, 1947–50; Sen. Lectr in Bacteriology, Postgraduate Medical Sch. of London, 1950–57, later Hon. Senior Lectr; Dir, MRC Molecular Genetics Unit, 1957–68, Hon. Dir 1968–73; Prof. of Molecular Genetics, Univ. of Edinburgh, 1968–73; Sherman Fairchild Dist. Scholar, Div. of Biology, California Inst. of Technology, 1979–80; Vis. Fellow, Botany Dept, ANU, 1980–86; retired 1987. Hon. Mem., Société Française de Microbiologie, 1988. Hon. Fellow, RPMS, 1985; Hon. DSc: Leicester, 1966; NUI, 1973; Kent, 1973; Hon. LLD Dublin, 1970. *Publication:* The Genetics of Bacteria and their Viruses, 1964. *Recreations:* painting, reading or doing nothing. *Address:* 634/40 Pennant Hills Road, Normanhurst, NSW 2076, Australia.

HAYES, Dr William; President, St John's College, University of Oxford, since 1987; Senior Research Fellow, Clarendon Laboratory, Oxford University, since 1987; Pro-Vice-Chancellor, University of Oxford, since 1990; *b* 12 Nov. 1930; *s* of Robert Hayes and Eileen Tobin; *m* 1962, Joan Ferriss; two *s* one *d*. *Educ:* University Coll., Dublin (MSc, PhD); Oxford Univ. (MA, DPhil). St John's College, Oxford: 1851 Overseas Schol., 1955–57; Official Fellow and Tutor, 1960–87; Principal Bursar, 1977–87; University Lectr, Oxford Univ., 1962–87; Dir and Head of Clarendon Lab., Oxford, 1985–87. Mem., Gen. Bd of the Faculties, 1985–88, Mem., Hebdomadal Council, 1989–, Oxford Univ. Temporary research appointments at: Argonne Nat. Lab., 1957–58; Purdue Univ., 1963–64; RCA Labs, Princeton, 1968; Univ. of Illinois, 1971; Bell Labs, 1974. Mem., Physics Cttee, SERC, 1982–85. Hon. DSc NUI, 1988. *Publications:* (ed) Crystals with the Fluorite Structure, 1974; (with R. Loudon) Scattering of Light by Crystals, 1978; (with A. M. Stoneham) Defects and Defect Processes in non-metallic Solids, 1985; contribs to Procs of Royal Soc., Jl of Physics, Physical Rev., etc. *Recreations:* walking, reading, listening to music. *Address:* St John's College, Oxford OX1 3JP. *T:* Oxford (0865) 277419.

HAYHOE, Rt. Hon. Sir Bernard John, (Sir Barney Hayhoe), Kt 1987; PC 1985; CEng, FIMechE; MP (C) Brentford and Isleworth, since 1974 (Heston and Isleworth, 1970–74); *b* 8 Aug. 1925; *s* of late Frank Stanley and Catherine Hayhoe; *m* 1962, Anne Gascoigne Thornton, *o d* of Bernard William and Hilda Thornton; two *s* one *d*. *Educ:* State schools; Borough Polytechnic. Tool Room Apprentice, 1941–44; Armaments Design Dept, Ministry of Supply, 1944–54; Inspectorate of Armaments, 1954–63; Conservative Research Dept, 1965–70. PPS to Lord President and Leader of House of Commons, 1972–74; an additional Opposition Spokesman on Employment, 1974–79; Parly Under Sec. of State for Defence for the Army, 1979–81; Minister of State: CSD, 1981; HM Treasury, 1981–85; (Minister for Health) DHSS, 1985–86. Member: Select Cttee on Race Relations and Immigration, 1971–73; Select Cttee on Defence, 1987–; H of C Commn, 1987–; Public Accounts Commn, 1987; Hon. Sec., 1970–71, Vice-Chm., 1974, Cons. Parly Employment Cttee; Jt Hon. Sec., 1970–73, Vice-Chm., 1973–76, Cons. Gp for Europe; Vice-Chm., Cons. Party Internat. Office, 1973–79. Mem., Trilateral Commn, 1977–79. Chm., Hansard Soc., 1990–. Governor, Birkbeck Coll., 1976–79. *Address:* 20 Wool Road, SW20 0HW. *T:* 081–947 0037.
See also F. G. J. Hayhoe.

HAYHOE, Prof. Frank George James, MD, FRCP, FRCPath; Leukaemia Research Fund Professor of Haematological Medicine, University of Cambridge, 1968–88; Fellow, Darwin College, Cambridge, since 1964, Vice-Master, 1964–74; *b* 25 Oct. 1920; *s* of late Frank Stanley and Catherine Hayhoe; *m* 1945, Jacqueline Marie Marguerite (*née* Dierkx); two *s*. *Educ:* Selhurst Grammar Sch.; Trinity Hall, Cambridge; St Thomas's Hospital Medical Sch. BA Cantab 1942; MRCS, LRCP 1944; MB, BChir Cantab 1945; MRCP 1949; MA Cantab 1949; MD Cantab 1951; FRCP 1965; FRCPath 1971. Captain RAMC, 1945–47. Registrar, St Thomas' Hosp., 1947–49. Elmore Research Student, Cambridge Univ., 1949–51; Royal Soc. Exchange Res. Schol., USSR, 1962–63; Lectr in Medicine, Cambridge Univ., 1951–68; Mem. Council of Senate, 1967–71. Member: Bd of Governors, United Cambridge Hospitals, 1971–74; Cambs AHA, 1974–75; GMC, 1982–88. Lectures: Langdon Brown, RCP, 1971; Cudlip Meml, Ann Arbor, 1967; vis. lectr at med. schs in N and S America, Europe, Middle East, Africa, India. G. F. Götz Foundn Prize, Zürich Univ., 1974; Suniti Rana Panja Gold Medal, Calcutta Sch. of Trop. Med., 1979. *Publications:* (ed) Lectures in Haematology, 1960; Leukaemia: Research and Clinical Practice, 1960; (jtly) Cytology and Cytochemistry of Acute Leukaemia, 1964; (ed) Current Research in Leukaemia, 1965; (with R. J. Flemans) An Atlas of Haematological Cytology, 1969, 3rd edn 1991; (with J. C. Cawley) Ultrastructure of Haemic Cells, 1973; (jtly) Leukaemia, Lymphomas and Allied Disorders, 1976; (jtly) Hairy Cell Leukaemia, 1980; (with D. Quaglino) Haematological Cytochemistry, 1980, 2nd edn 1988; (ed with D. Quaglino) The Cytobiology of Leukaemias and Lymphomas, 1985; contribs to med. and scientific jls, on haematological topics, especially leukaemia. *Address:* 20 Queen Edith's Way, Cambridge. *T:* Cambridge (0223) 248381.
See also Sir B. J. Hayhoe.

HAYMAN, Mrs Helene (Valerie); Non-executive Member, Bloomsbury and Islington Health Authority, since 1990; *b* 26 March 1949; *d* of Maurice Middleweek and Maude Middleweek; *m* 1974, Martin Hayman; four *s*. *Educ:* Wolverhampton Girls' High Sch.; Newnham Coll., Cambridge (MA). Pres., Cambridge Union, 1969. Worked with Shelter, Nat. Campaign for the Homeless, 1969; Camden Council Social Services Dept, 1971; Dep. Dir, Nat. Council for One Parent Families, 1974. Vice-Chm., Bloomsbury HA, 1988–90 (Mem., 1985–90). Contested (Lab) Wolverhampton SW, Feb. 1974; MP (Lab) Welwyn and Hatfield, Oct. 1974–1979. Member: RCOG Ethics Cttee, 1982–; UCL/UCH Cttee on Ethics of Clinical Investigation, 1987– (Vice-Chm., 1990–).

HAYMAN, John David Woodburn; His Honour Judge Hayman; a Circuit Judge, since 1976; *b* 24 Aug. 1918; *m*; two *s* four *d*. *Educ:* King Edward VII Sch., Johannesburg; St John's Coll., Cambridge (MA, LLM). Served with S African Forces, 1940–42. Called to the Bar, Middle Temple, 1945. Sometime Lecturer in Law: University Coll. of Wales, Aberystwyth; Leeds Univ.; Cambridge Univ.

HAYMAN, Sir Peter (Telford), KCMG 1971 (CMG 1963); CVO 1965; MBE 1945; HM Diplomatic Service, retired; *b* 14 June 1914; *s* of C. H. T. Hayman, The Manor House, Brackley, Northants; *m* 1942, Rosemary Eardley Blomefield; one *s* one *d*. *Educ:* Stowe; Worcester Coll., Oxford. Asst Principal: Home Office, 1937–39; Min. of Home Security, 1939–41; Asst Priv. Sec. to Home Sec. (Rt Hon. Herbert Morrison, MP), 1941–42; Principal, Home Office, 1942. Served War, 1942–45, Rifle Bde, Major. Principal, Home Office, 1945–49; transf. to Min. of Defence as Personal Asst to Chief Staff Officer to the Minister, 1949–52; Asst Sec, Min. of Defence, 1950; UK Delegation to NATO, 1952–54; transf. to FO, 1954; Counsellor, Belgrade, 1955–58; seconded for temp. duty with Governor of Malta, 1958; Couns., Baghdad, 1959–61; Dir-Gen. of British Information Services, New York, 1961–64; Minister and Dep. Comdt, Brit. Milit. Govt in Berlin, 1964–66; Asst Under-Sec., FO, 1966–69; Dep. Under-Secretary of State, FCO, 1969–70; High Comr in Canada, 1970–74. *Publication:* Soult, Napoleon's Maligned Marshal, 1990. *Recreations:* fishing, travel. *Address:* Uxmore House, Checkendon, Oxon RG8 0TY. *T:* Checkendon (0491) 680 658. *Club:* MCC.

HAYMAN, Prof. Walter Kurt, MA; ScD (Cambridge); FRS 1956; FIC; Professor of Pure Mathematics, University of York, since 1985; *b* 6 Jan. 1926; *s* of late Franz Samuel Haymann and Ruth Therese (*née* Hensel); *m* 1947, Margaret Riley Crann, MA Cantab, *d* of Thomas Crann, New Earswick, York; three *d*. *Educ:* Gordonstoun Sch.; St John's Coll., Cambridge. Lecturer at King's Coll., Newcastle upon Tyne, 1947, and Fellow of St John's Coll., Cambridge, 1947–50; Lecturer, 1947, and Reader, 1953–56, Exeter; Prof. of Pure Maths, 1956–85, and Dean of RCS, 1978–81, Imperial Coll., London (FIC 1989). 1st Smiths prize, 1948, shared Adams Prize, 1949, Junior Berwick Prize, 1955; Senior Berwick Prize, 1964. Visiting Lecturer at Brown Univ., USA, 1949–50, at Stanford Univ., USA (summer) 1950 and 1955, and to the American Mathematical Soc., 1961. Co-founder with Mrs Hayman of British Mathematical Olympiad; Vice-Pres., London Mathematical Soc., 1982–84. Foreign Member: Finnish Acad. of Science and Letters; Accademia Nazionale dei Lincei, Rome; Corresp. Mem., Bavarian Acad. of Science. Hon. DSc: Exeter, 1981; Birmingham, 1985. *Publications:* Multivalent Functions (Cambridge, 1958) Meromorphic Functions (Oxford, 1964); Research Problems in Function Theory (London, 1967); Subharmonic Functions, vol I, 1976, vol. II, 1989; papers in various mathematical journals. *Recreations:* music, travel. *Address:* University of York, Heslington, York YO1 5DD. *T:* York (0904) 433076.

HAYMAN, Rev. Canon William Samuel; Chaplain to The Queen's Household, 1961–73; *b* 3 June 1903; *s* of late Rev. William Henry Hayman, Rector of Leckford, and late Louise Charlotte Hayman; *m* 1930, Rosemary Prideaux Metcalfe; one *s* one *d*. *Educ:* Merchant Taylors' Sch.; St John's Coll., Oxford (MA). Deacon, 1926; Priest, 1927; Curate: St Matthew, Brixton, 1926–32; Wimbledon (in charge of St Mark), 1932–34; Vicar of Finstall, Worcs, 1934–38; Rector of Cheam, 1938–72. Hon. Canon of Southwark, 1952–60, Canon Emeritus, 1972. Rural Dean of Beddington, 1955–60; Archdeacon of Lewisham, 1960–72. Scouts Silver Acorn, 1971. *Recreations:* fly-fishing, photography, music. *Address:* 8 Black Jack Mews, Cirencester, Glos GL7 2AA. *T:* Cirencester (0285) 655024.

HAYMAN-JOYCE, Maj.-Gen. Robert John, CBE 1989 (OBE 1979); Director General Land Fighting Systems (formerly Fighting Vehicles and Engineer Equipment), Ministry of Defence (Procurement Executive), since 1989; *b* 16 Oct. 1940; *s* of Major T. F. Hayman-Joyce and B. C. Bruford; *m* 1968, Diana Livingstone-Bussell; two *s*. *Educ:* Radley Coll.; Magdalene Coll., Cambridge (MA). Commnd 11th Hussars (PAO), 1963; CO Royal Hussars (PWO), 1980–82; Comdr RAC, 1 (BR) Corps, 1983–85; Dir, UK Tank Programme, 1988. *Recreations:* ski-ing, horses, sailing. *Address:* c/o Barclays Bank, 5 High Street, Andover, Hants SP1D 1LN. *Clubs:* Cavalry and Guards; Leander (Henley-on-Thames).

HAYNES, David Francis, (Frank); JP; MP (Lab) Ashfield, since 1979; *b* London, March 1926; *m*; one *s* two *d*. *Educ:* secondary schs in London. Fireman, Southern Railway; then coalminer. Member: Notts CC, 1965–81; Mansfield DC; Chm., Central Notts Community Health Council. Mem., NUM. *Address:* House of Commons, SW1; 27 Lawns Road, Annesley Woodhouse, Kirkby in Ashfield, Notts.

HAYNES, Denys Eyre Lankester; Keeper of Greek and Roman Antiquities, British Museum, 1956–76; *b* 15 Feb. 1913; 2nd *s* of late Rev. Hugh Lankester Haynes and late Emmeline Marianne Chaldecott; *m* 1951, Sybille Edith Overhoff. *Educ:* Marlborough; Trinity Coll., Cambridge. Scholar, British School at Rome, 1936; Asst Keeper: Victoria and Albert Museum, 1937; British Museum, 1939–54 (released for war service, 1939–45); Dep. Keeper, British Museum, 1954. Geddes-Harrower Prof. of Greek Art and Archaeology, Univ. of Aberdeen, 1972–73. Chm., Soc. for Libyan Studies, 1974. Corr.

Mem., German Archæological Inst., 1953; Ordinary Mem., 1957. Visitor, Ashmolean Museum, 1979–87. Lectures: Burlington, 1976; Brown and Hayley, Univ. of Puget Sound, 1977. *Publications:* Porta Argentariorum, 1939; Ancient Tripolitania, 1946; Antiquities of Tripolitania, 1956; The Parthenon Frieze, 1958; The Portland Vase, 1964; Fifty Masterpieces of Classical Art, 1970; The Arundel Marbles, 1975; Greek Art and the Idea of Freedom, 1981. *Address:* Flat 17, Murray Court, 80 Banbury Road, Oxford OX2 6LQ.

HAYNES, Edwin William George, CB 1971; *b* 10 Dec. 1911; *s* of Frederick William George Haynes and Lilian May Haynes (*née* Armstrong); *m* 1942, Dorothy Kathleen Coombs; one *s* one *d*. *Educ:* Regent Street Polytechnic Secondary Sch.; University of London (BA, LLM). Barrister-at-law, Lincoln's Inn, 1946. Estate Duty Office, Inland Revenue, 1930–39; Air Min., 1939; Min. of Aircraft Production, 1940; Min. of Supply, 1946; Min. of Aviation, 1959; Under-Sec., 1964; Under-Sec., DTI (formerly Min. of Technology), 1968–71. Chief Exec. Officer, later Sec., Covent Garden Market Authority, 1971–81. *Address:* 92 Malmains Way, Beckenham, Kent. *T:* 081-650 0224. *Club:* Civil Service.

HAYNES, Ernest Anthony, (Tony), CIGasE; Chairman, Yewbridge Electronics, since 1988; Regional Chairman, British Gas plc, East Midlands, 1983–87; *b* 8 May 1922; *s* of Joseph Ernest Haynes and Ethel Rose (*née* Toomer); *m* 1946, Sheila Theresa (*née* Blane); two *s* two *d*. *Educ:* King Edward Sixth Grammar Sch., Totnes, S Devon. Joined gas industry with Torquay and Paignton Gas Co., following demobilisation from Royal Hampshire Regt; appts with: West Midlands and Northern Gas Boards; Gas Council; Eastern; Dep. Chm., North Eastern, 1977–78; Dep. Chm., North Thames Gas, 1979–82. Vice-Pres., Internat. Colloquium about Gas Marketing, 1983–84. Silver Medal, IGasE, for paper, Energy Conservation—a marketing opportunity. *Recreations:* golf, flyfishing.

HAYNES, Frank; *see* Haynes, D. F.

HAYNES, Very Rev. Peter; Dean of Hereford since 1982; Vicar, St John Baptist, Hereford, since 1983; *b* 24 April 1925; *s* of Francis Harold Stanley Haynes and Winifred Annie Haynes; *m* 1952, Ruth, *d* of late Dr Charles Edward Stainthorpe, MRCS, LRCP, Brunton Park, Newcastle upon Tyne; two *s*. *Educ:* St Brendan's Coll., Clifton; Selwyn Coll., Cambridge (MA); Cuddesdon Theol Coll., Oxford. Staff of Barclays Bank, 1941–43; RAF, 1943–47. Deacon 1952, Priest 1953. Asst Curate, Stokesley, 1952–54; Hessle, 1954–58; Vicar, St John's Drypool, Hull, 1958–63; Bishop's Chaplain for Youth and Asst Dir of Religious Educn, Dio. Bath and Wells, 1963–70; Vicar of Glastonbury, 1970–74 (with Godney from 1972); Archdeacon of Wells, Canon Residentiary and Prebendary of Huish and Brent in Wells Cathedral, 1974–82. Proctor in Convocation, 1976–82. Mem., Dioceses Commn, 1978–86. *Recreations:* sailing, model engineering. *Address:* The Deanery, Hereford HR1 2NG. *T:* Hereford (0432) 59880.

HAYNES-DIXON, Margaret Rumer; *see* Godden, Rumer.

HAYR, Air Marshal Sir Kenneth (William), KCB 1988 (CB 1982); KBE 1991 (CBE 1976); AFC 1963 and Bar 1972; Deputy Chief of Defence Staff (Commitments), Ministry of Defence, since 1989; *b* 13 April 1935; *s* of Kenneth James and Jean Templeton Hayr; *m* 1961, Joyce Gardner (*d* 1987); three *s*. *Educ:* Auckland Grammar Sch.; RAF Coll. Cranwell. Served Hunter and Lightning Sqns, 1957–64; Central Fighter Estabt/Fighter Comd Trials Unit, 1964–67; Phantom OCU Sqn Comdr, 1968–69; OC 1(F) Sqn (Harriers), 1970–71; RAF Staff Coll., 1972; OC RAF Binbrook (Lightnings), 1973–76; Inspector of Flight Safety (RAF), 1976–79; RCDS 1980; Asst Chief of Air Staff (Ops), 1980–82; AOC No 11 Group, RAF, 1982–85; Comdr British Forces Cyprus and Administrator Sovereign Base Areas, 1985–88; COS UK Air Forces and Dep. C-in-C, Strike Comd, 1988–89. Freeman, City of London, 1984. *Recreations:* flying, wind surfing, hang gliding, parachuting, ski-ing, tennis. *Address:* c/o Lloyds Bank, Cox's & King's Branch, 7 Pall Mall, SW1Y 5NA. *Club:* Royal Air Force.

HAYTER, 3rd Baron *cr* 1927 of Chislehurst, Kent; **George Charles Hayter Chubb,** KCVO 1977; CBE 1976; Bt 1900; a Deputy Chairman, House of Lords, since 1981; Managing Director, 1941–71, Chairman, 1957–81, Chubb & Son's Lock & Safe Co. Ltd; *b* 25 April 1911; *e s* of 2nd Baron Hayter and Mary (*d* 1948), *d* of J. F. Haworth; *S* father, 1967; *m* 1940, Elizabeth Anne Rumbold, MBE 1975; three *s* one *d*. *Educ:* Leys Sch., Cambridge; Trinity Coll., Cambridge (MA). Chairman: Royal Society of Arts, 1965–66; Management Cttee, King Edward's Hospital Fund for London, 1965–82; Executives Assoc. of GB, 1960; Duke of Edinburgh's Countryside in 1970 Cttee. President: Canada-United Kingdom Chamber of Commerce, 1966–67; Royal Warrant Holders Association, 1967; Business Equipment Trades Association, 1954–55. Mem., CoID, 1964–71; Chairman: EDC International Freight Movement, 1972–79; British Security Industry Assoc., 1973–77. Worshipful Company of Weavers': Liveryman, 1934–; Upper Bailiff, 1961–62. *Publication:* Security offered by Locks and Safes (Lecture, RSA), 1962. *Heir: s* Hon. (George) William (Michael) Chubb [*b* 9 Oct. 1943; *m* 1983, Waltraud, *yr d* of J. Flackl, Sydney, Australia; one *s*]. *Address:* Ashtead House, Ashtead, Surrey KT21 1LU. *T:* Ashtead (0372) 273476.

HAYTER, Dianne; Chief Executive, European Parliamentary Labour Party, since 1990; *b* 7 Sept. 1949; *d* of late Alec Hayter and late Nancy Hayter. *Educ:* Trevelyan Coll., Durham Univ. (BA Hons Sociology and Social Admin). Research Assistant: General and Municipal Workers Union, 1970–72; European Trade Union Confedn (ETUC), Brussels, 1973; Research Officer, Trade Union Adv. Cttee to OECD (TUAC-OECD), Paris, 1973–74; Fabian Society: Asst Gen. Sec., 1974–76; Gen. Sec., 1976–82; Mem. Exec. Cttee, 1986–. Journalist, A Week in Politics, Channel Four, 1982–84; Dir, Alcohol Concern, 1984–90. Mem., Royal Commn on Criminal Procedure, 1978–80. Member: Exec. Cttee, London Labour Party, 1977–83; Nat. Constitution Cttee, Labour Party, 1987–. Member: Labour Party; 300 Group; Soc. of Labour Lawyers; Socialist Health Assoc.; GMBTU; Justice. JP Inner London, 1976–90. *Publications:* The Labour Party: crisis and prospects (Fabian Soc.), 1977; (contrib.) Labour in the Eighties, 1980. *Recreations:* reading, politics. *Address:* European Parliamentary Labour Party, 2 Queen Anne's Gate, SW1H 9AA. *T:* 071-222 1719.

HAYTER, Paul David Grenville; Reading Clerk and Principal Finance Officer, House of Lords, since 1991; *b* 4 Nov. 1942; *s* of Rev. Canon Michael George Hayter and Katherine Patricia Hayter (*née* Schofield); *m* 1973, Hon. Deborah Gervaise, *d* of Baron Maude of Stratford-upon-Avon, *qv*; two *s* one *d*. *Educ:* Eton (King's Scholar); Christ Church, Oxford (MA). Clerk, Parlt Office, House of Lords, 1964; seconded as Private Sec. to Leader of House and Chief Whip, House of Lords, 1974–77; Clerk of Cttees, 1977; Principal Clerk of Cttees, 1985–90. Sec., Assoc. of Lord-Lieutenants, 1977–. *Recreations:* music, gardening, botanising, archery, painting. *Address:* Williamscot, Banbury, Oxon.

HAYTER, Sir William Goodenough, KCMG 1953 (CMG 1948); Warden of New College, Oxford, 1958–76, Hon. Fellow, 1976; *b* 1 Aug. 1906; *s* of late Sir William Goodenough Hayter, KBE; *m* 1938, Iris Marie, *d* of late Lieut-Col C. H. Grey (formerly Hoare), DSO; one *d*. *Educ:* Winchester; New Coll., Oxford. Entered HM Diplomatic Service, 1930; served Foreign Office, 1930; Vienna, 1931; Moscow, 1934; Foreign Office, 1937; China, 1938; Washington, 1941; Foreign Office, 1944 (Asst Under-Sec. of State, 1948); HM Minister, Paris, 1949; Ambassador to USSR, 1953–57; Deputy Under-Sec. of State, Foreign Office, 1957–58. Fellow of Winchester Coll., 1958–76. Trustee, British Museum, 1960–70. Hon. DL Bristol, 1976; Grosses Goldenes Ehrenzeichen mit dem Stern für Verdienste (Austria), 1967. *Publications:* The Diplomacy of the Great Powers, 1961; The Kremlin and the Embassy, 1966; Russia and the World, 1970; William of Wykeham, Patron of the Arts, 1970; A Double Life (autobiog.), 1974; Spooner, 1977. *Address:* Bassetts House, Stanton St John, Oxford OX9 1EX. *T:* Stanton St John (086735) 598.

HAYTHORNE, John; *see* Parsons, Sir R. E. C. F.

HAYTHORNE, Dame Naomi Christine; *see* James, Dame N. C.

HAYWARD, Sir Anthony (William Byrd), Kt 1978; company director; *b* 29 June 1927; *s* of Eric and Barbara Hayward; *m* 1955, Jenifer Susan McCay; two *s* two *d*. *Educ:* Stowe Sch., Buckingham; Christ Church, Oxford. Served RNVR, 1945–48. With family business in Calcutta, 1948–57; Shaw Wallace & Co. Ltd, India, 1957–78; Man. Dir, Guthrie Berhad, Singapore, 1978–81; Pres. and Chief Exec. Officer, Private Investment Co. for Asia (PICA) SA, 1982–84. Pres., Associated Chambers of Commerce and Industry of India, 1977–78. FRSA. *Recreations:* shooting, fishing, golf, photography. *Address:* Dane Street House, Chilham, near Canterbury, Kent CT4 8ER. *T:* Canterbury (0227) 730221. *Clubs:* Boodle's, Oriental; Rye Golf.
See also Ven. J. D. R. Hayward.

HAYWARD, Brian Robin, FCIT; Chairman, Mark IV Management Ltd; *b* 11 Jan. 1937; *s* of Henry Albert and Jesse Agness Hayward; *m* 1954, Kathleen Mary Scott; three *s*. *Educ:* Woodlands, Gillingham, Kent. CBIM; MInstM. Depot Manager, Pickfords, 1963–66; Transport Manager, Hotpoint, 1966–69; Director and General Manager, Carryfast Ltd, 1969–72; Supplies Director, British Domestic Appliances, 1972–75; Managing Director, Southern BRSL, 1975–76; Gp Man. Dir, National Carriers Ltd, 1976–83 (Founder mem., Nat. Freight Consortium Bd, 1982); Chm., Fashion Flow Ltd, 1976–83. *Recreation:* golf. *Address:* 34 Audley Gate, Peterborough. *T:* Peterborough (0733) 263711. *Club:* Royal Automobile.

HAYWARD, Ven. Derek; *see* Hayward, Ven. J. D. R.

HAYWARD, Maj.-Gen. George Victor, BSc; CEng, FICE, FIMechE; *b* 21 June 1918; *e s* of late G. H. Hayward; *m* 1953, Gay Benson, *d* of late H. B. Goulding, MB, BCh, FRCSI; one *s* one *d*. *Educ:* Blundells; Birmingham Univ. (BSc). War of 1939–45: commissioned, 1940; transf. to REME, 1942; GSO1 REME Training Centre, 1958; Comdr, REME 2nd Div., 1960; Asst Mil. Sec., War Office, 1962; Col, RARDE, Fort Halstead, 1963; CO, 38 Central Workshop, 1965; Dep. Comdt, Technical Group, REME, 1966; Comdt, REME Training Centre, 1969; Comdt, Technical Gp, REME, 1971–73; Planning Inspector, DoE, 1973–88. Col Comdt, REME, 1973–78. *Recreations:* sailing, ski-ing, shooting. *Address:* Chart Cottage, Chartwell, Westerham, Kent TN16 1PT. *T:* Edenbridge (0732) 866253. *Club:* Army and Navy.

HAYWARD, Gerald William; HM Diplomatic Service, retired; Cabinet Office (part-time), since 1984; *b* 18 Nov. 1927; *s* of late Frederick William Hayward and Annie Louise (*née* Glasscock); *m* 1956, Patricia Rhonwen (*née* Foster Hall); one *s* three *d*. *Educ:* Tottenham Grammar School; London and Hong Kong Univs. HM Forces, 1946–57. Joined HM Foreign (subseq. HM Diplomatic) Service, 1957; Kuala Lumpur, 1958–60; Bangkok, 1960–62; Hong Kong, 1962–64; FO, 1964–67; Copenhagen, 1967–71; FCO, 1971–76; Kuala Lumpur, 1976–79; FCO, 1980–82. *Recreation:* golf. *Address:* White Mill End, 5 Granville Road, Sevenoaks, Kent TN13 1ES. *T:* Sevenoaks (0732) 451227.

HAYWARD, Sir Jack (Arnold), Kt 1986; OBE 1968; Chairman, Grand Bahama Development Co. Ltd and Freeport Commercial and Industrial Ltd, since 1976; *b* Wolverhampton, 14 June 1923; *s* of late Sir Charles Hayward, CBE and Hilda, *d* of John and Alexandra Arnold; *m* 1948, Jean Mary Forder; two *s* one *d*. *Educ:* Northaw Prep Sch.; Stowe Sch., Buckingham. Joined RAF, 1941; flying training in Florida, USA; active service as officer pilot in SE Asia Comd, demobilised as Flt-Lt, 1946. Joined Rotary Hoes Ltd, 1947; served S Africa branch until 1950. Founded USA operations Firth Cleveland Gp of Companies, 1951; joined Grand Bahama Port Authority Ltd, Freeport, Grand Bahama Island, 1956. President: Lundy Field Soc.; Wolverhampton Wanderers FC; Vice-Pres., SS Great Britain project; Hon. Life Vice-Pres., Maritime Trust, 1971. Paul Harris Fellow (Rotary), 1983. Hon. LLD Exeter, 1971. William Booth Award, Salvation Army, 1987. *Recreations:* promoting British endeavours, mainly in sport; watching cricket; amateur dramatics; preserving the British landscape, keeping all things bright, beautiful and British. *Address:* Seashell Lane (PO Box F-99), Freeport, Grand Bahama Island, Bahamas. *T:* Freeport (809) 352–5165. *Clubs:* MCC, Pratt's, Royal Air Force, Royal Automobile.

HAYWARD, Prof. Jack Ernest Shalom, FBA 1990; Professor of Politics, University of Hull, since 1973; *b* 18 Aug. 1931; *s* of Menahem and Stella Hayward; *m* 1965, Margaret Joy Glenn; one *s* one *d*. *Educ:* LSE (BSc Econ 1952; PhD 1958). Asst Lectr and Lectr, Univ. of Sheffield, 1959–63; Lectr and Sen. Lectr, Univ. of Keele, 1963–73. Sen. Res. Fellow, Nuffield Coll., Oxford, 1968–69; Vis. Prof., Univ. of Paris III, 1979–80; Elie Halévy Vis. Prof., Inst. d'Etudes Politiques, Paris, 1990–91. Political Studies Association: Chm., 1975–77; Pres., 1979–81; Vice-Pres., 1981–. Editor, Political Studies, 1987–. Chevalier de l'Ordre National de Mérite, 1980. *Publications:* Private Interests and Public Policy, 1966; The One and Indivisible French Republic, 1973; The State and the Market Economy, 1986; After the French Revolution, 1991. *Recreations:* music, reading, walking. *Address:* Hurstwood, Church Lane, Kirk Ella, Hull HU10 7TA. *T:* Hull (0482) 655027. *Club:* Commonwealth Trust.

HAYWARD, Ven. (John) Derek (Risdon); Vicar of Isleworth, since 1964; General Secretary, Diocese of London, since 1975; Archdeacon of Middlesex, 1974–75, now Archdeacon Emeritus; *b* 13 Dec. 1923; *s* of late Eric Hayward and of Barbara Olive Hayward; *m* 1965, Teresa Jane Kaye; one *s* one *d*. *Educ:* Stowe; Trinity Coll., Cambridge (BA 1956, MA 1964). Served War of 1939–45, Lieut 27th Lancers, Middle East and Italy, 1943–45 (twice wounded). Man. Dir, Hayward Waldie & Co., Calcutta (and associated cos), 1946–53. Trinity Coll., Cambridge, 1953–56, Westcott House, Cambridge, 1956–57. Asst Curate, St Mary's Bramall Lane, Sheffield, 1957–58; Vicar, St Silas, Sheffield, 1959–63. Mem., General Synod, 1975–90. Dir, SCM Press, 1985–; Trustee, Church Urban Fund, 1987–. Bronze Star (US) 1945. *Recreations:* riding, skiing, sailing (when opportunity offers). *Address:* 61 Church Street, Isleworth, Mddx TW7 6BE. *T:* 081-560 6662.
See also Sir Anthony Hayward.

HAYWARD, Sir Richard (Arthur), Kt 1969; CBE 1966; *b* 14 March 1910; *m* 1936, Ethel Wheatcroft; one *s* one *d*. *Educ:* Catford Central Sch. Post Office: Boy Messenger; Counter Clerk; Union of Post Office Workers: Assistant Secretary, 1947; Deputy General Secretary, 1951. Secretary General, Civil Service National Whitley Council (Staff Side),

1955–66; Chm., Supplementary Benefits Commn, 1966–69; Member, Post Office Board, 1969–71; Chairman: NHS Staff Commn, 1972–75; New Towns Staff Commn, 1976–77; Member: Civil Service Security Appeals Panel, 1967–82; Home Office Adv. Panel on Security (Immigration Act 1972), 1972–81; Parole Board, England and Wales, 1975–79; Solicitors' Disciplinary Tribunal, 1975–82. UK Rep., Meeting of Experts on Conditions of Work and Service of Public Servants, ILO, 1963; overseas visits, inc. Israel, Mauritius, Canada, to advise on Trade Unionism in Public Services. Life Vice-President: Civil Service Sports Council, 1973 (Chm., 1968–73); Assoc. of Kent Cricket Clubs, 1984 (Pres., 1970–84); President: Civil Service Cricket Assoc., 1967–; Civil Service Assoc. Football, 1974–; Hon. Life Mem., Nat. Assoc. of Young Cricketers, 1975. Governor, Guy's Hosp., 1949–72. Freedom, City of London, 1980. *Recreations:* topography of Southwark, watching sport. *Address:* Lower Cowley, Parracombe, Barnstaple, N Devon EX31 4PQ. *T:* Parracombe (05983) 373. *Clubs:* MCC, Civil Service.

HAYWARD, Robert Antony, OBE 1991; MP (C) Kingswood, since 1983; *b* 11 March 1949; *s* of Ralph and Mary Hayward. *Educ:* Abingdon Sch.; Maidenhead Grammar Sch.; University Coll. of Rhodesia; BSc Econ Hons London (external). Personnel Officer, Esso Petroleum, 1971–75; Personnel Manager: Coca Cola Bottlers (S & N) Ltd, 1975–79; GEC Large Machines, 1979–82. PPS to Minister for Corporate and Consumer Affairs, 1985–87, to Minister for Industry, 1986–87, to Sec. of State for Transport, 1987–. Mem., Commons Select Cttee on Energy, 1983–85. *Recreations:* Rugby referee; psephology. *Address:* 2 Bracey Drive, Downend, Bristol BS16 2UG.

HAYWARD, Ronald George, CBE 1970; General Secretary of the Labour Party, 1972–82; *b* 27 June 1917; *s* of F. Hayward, small-holder, Oxon; *m* 1943, Phyllis Olive (*née* Allen); three *d. Educ:* Bloxham C of E Sch.; RAF Technical Schools, Halton, Cosford, Locking. Apprenticed Cabinet-maker, 1933–36. NCO, RAF: Technical Training Instructor, 1940–45. Labour Party: Secretary-Agent: Banbury Constituency, 1945–47; Rochester and Chatham Constituency, 1947–50; Asst Regional Organiser, 1950–59; Regional Organiser, 1959–69; National Agent, 1969–72. *Address:* Haylens, 1 Sea View Avenue, Birchington, Kent.

HAYWARD ELLEN, Patricia Mae; *see* Lavers, P. M.

HAYWARD SMITH, Rodger; QC 1988; a Recorder, since 1986; *b* 25 Feb. 1943; *s* of Frederick Ernest Smith and Heather Hayward (*née* Rodgers); *m* 1975, Gillian Sheila (*née* Johnson); one *s* one *d. Educ:* Brentwood Sch.; St Edmund Hall, Oxford (MA). Called to the Bar, Gray's Inn, 1967. An Asst Recorder, 1981–86. *Address:* 1 King's Bench Walk, Temple, EC4Y 7DB.

HAYWOOD, Sir Harold, KCVO 1988; OBE 1974; DL; Chairman, BBC/IBA Central Appeals Advisory Committee, since 1989; Chairman, YMCA, since 1989; *b* 30 Sept. 1923; *s* of Harold Haywood and Lilian (*née* Barrett); *m* 1944, Amy (*née* Richardson); three *s. Educ:* Guild Central Sch., Burton-on-Trent; Westhill Coll. of Educn, Selly Oak, Birmingham (Certificate of Educn, 1948). Organiser, St John's Clubland, Sheffield, 1948–51; Tutor, Westhill Coll. of Educn, 1951–53; Regional Organiser, Methodist Youth Dept, 1954–55; Dir of Education and Trng, 1955–66; Dir of Youth Work, 1966–74, NAYC; Gen. Sec., Educnl Interchange Council, 1974–77; Dir, Royal Jubilee and Prince's Trusts, 1977–88. Chm., Assoc. of Charitable Foundns, 1989–; Trustee, Charities Aid Foundn, 1988– (Chm., Grants Council, 1989–). DL Greater London, 1983. FRSA. *Recreations:* the garden, books, cinema, theatre. *Address:* 41 Blenheim Road, North Harrow, Mddx HA2 7AQ. *T:* 081–863 1723. *Clubs:* Athenæum, Civil Service, Penn.

HAYWOOD, Thomas Charles Stanley, OBE 1962; JP; Lieutenant of Leicestershire, 1974–84 (Lord Lieutenant of Rutland, 1963–74); *b* 10 March 1911; *s* of late Charles B. Haywood, Woodhatch, Reigate, Surrey; *m* 1937, Anne, *d* of J. B. A. Kessler, London; two *s* one *d. Educ:* Winchester; Magdalene Coll., Cambridge. Served 1939–42 with Leics Yeomanry, Capt. 1940, Hon. Col, 1970–77. Chm. Trustees, Oakham Sch., 1964–81. DL 1962, JP 1957, High Sheriff 1952, County of Rutland. *Address:* Gunthorpe, Oakham, Rutland LE15 8BE. *T:* Manton (057285) 203.

HAZELL, Bertie, CBE 1962 (MBE 1946); Chairman, Special Programme Board, North Yorkshire, Manpower Services Commission, 1978–83; *b* 18 April 1907; *s* of John and Elizabeth Hazell; *m* 1936, Dora A. Barham; one *d. Educ:* various elementary schs in Norfolk. Agricultural worker, 1921; apptd Sec. and Agent to E Norfolk Divisional Labour Party, Sept. 1933; District Organiser, Nat. Union of Agricl Workers, 1937–64, Pres., 1966–78; Mem. W Riding of Yorks, War Agricultural Executive Cttee, 1939 (Chm. several of its Cttees, throughout war period). Contested (Lab) Barkston Ash Parliamentary Division, 1945 and 1950 Gen. Elections; MP (Lab) North Norfolk, 1964–70. Chairman: E and W Ridings Regional Bd for Industry, 1954–64; N Yorks AHA, 1974–82; York DHA, 1981–84; Vice-Chm., Agricultural, Horticultural and Forestry Trng Bd, 1972–74; Member: E Riding Co. Agricultural Exec. Cttee, 1946–64; Agricultural Wages Board, 1946–78; Leeds Regional Hosp. Board, 1948–74 (Chm. Works and Buildings Cttee); Potato Marketing Bd, 1970–79. Magistrate, City of York, 1950–; Chairman: York and District Employment Cttee, 1963–74; N Yorks District Manpower Cttee, 1975–80; Vice-Chm., Leeds Regional Hosp. Bd, 1967–74. Mem. Council, Univ. of E Anglia. MUniv York, 1984. *Recreation:* gardening. *Address:* 42 Fellbrook Avenue, Beckfield Lane, Acomb, York. *T:* York (0904) 798443.

HAZELL, Ven. Frederick Roy; Archdeacon of Croydon, since 1978; *b* 12 Aug. 1930; *s* of John Murdoch and Ruth Hazell; *m* 1956, Gwendoline Edna Armstrong (*née* Vare), *widow* of Major J. W. D. Armstrong; one step-*s. Educ:* Hutton Grammar School, near Preston; Fitzwilliam Coll., Cambridge (MA); Cuddesdon Coll., Oxford. HM Forces, 1948–50. Asst Master, Kingham Hill School, 1953–54; Asst Curate, Ilkeston Parish Church, 1956–59; Priest-in-Charge, All Saints', Marlpool, 1959–62; First Vicar of Marlpool, 1962–63; Chaplain, Univ. of the West Indies, 1963–66; Asst Priest, St Martin-in-the-Fields, 1966–68; Vicar of Holy Saviour, Croydon, 1968–84; Rural Dean of Croydon, 1972–78. Hon. Canon of Canterbury, 1973–84. *Recreations:* music, history. *Address:* St Matthew's House, 100 George Street, Croydon CR0 1PE. *T:* 081–681 5496.

HAZELL, Quinton, CBE 1978 (MBE 1961); DL; Director: Foreign and Colonial Investment Trust, since 1978; Hawker-Siddeley Group, since 1979; *b* 14 Dec. 1920; *s* of late Thomas Arthur Hazell and Ada Kathleen Hazell; *m* 1942, Morwenna Parry-Jones; one *s. Educ:* Manchester Grammar School. FIMI 1964. Management Trainee, Braid Bros Ltd, Colwyn Bay, 1936–39; Royal Artillery, 1939–46; formed Quinton Hazell Ltd, 1946; Chm., 1946–73; Chairman: Edward Jones (Contractors) Ltd, 1973–74; Supra Group plc, 1973–82 (Pres., 1983–85); Humberside Electronic Controls, 1987–89; Aerospace Engineering PLC, 1987–90 (Dir, 1986–90). Chm., W Midlands Econ. Planning Council, 1971–77. Mem., Welsh Adv. Cttee for Civil Aviation, 1961–67; Director: Wales Gas Bd, 1961–65; Winterbottom Energy Trust, 1978–82; Phoenix Assurance Co. plc, 1968–85; Banro Industries plc, 1985–89; British Law Executor and Trustee Co., 1986–87; Wagon Industries plc, 1989–; Non-Exec. Chm., F&C Enterprise Trust plc, 1981–86; Dep. Chm., Warwickshire Private Hosp., Leamington Spa, 1981–; Governor, Lord Leycester Hosp., Warwick, 1971–. Member Council: UC Bangor, 1966–68; Univ. of Birmingham. Freeman, City of London, 1960; Liveryman, Coachmakers' and Coach Harness Makers' Co., 1960. DL Warwicks, 1982. *Recreations:* antiques, horology, water ski-ing. *Address:* Wootton Paddox, Leek Wootton, Warwick CV35 7QX. *T:* Kenilworth (0926) 50704.

HAZELL, Robert John Davidge; Director, Nuffield Foundation, since 1989; *b* 30 April 1948; *s* of Peter Hazell and Elizabeth Complin Fowler; *m* 1981, Alison Sophia Mordaunt Richards; two *s. Educ:* Eton (King's Schol.); Wadham Coll., Oxford (Minor Schol.; BA Hons). Called to the Bar, Middle Temple, 1973; Barrister, 1973–75. Home Office, 1975–89, working in Immigration Dept, Policy Planning Unit, Gaming Bd, Race Relns, Broadcasting, Police and Prison Depts; CS travelling fellowship to investigate freedom of inf. in Australia, Canada, NZ, 1986–87. Haldane Medal, RIPA, 1978. *Publications:* Conspiracy and Civil Liberties, 1974; (ed) The Bar on Trial, 1978; articles in legal and govt jls. *Recreations:* bird-watching, badgers, opera, canoeing. *Address:* 94 Constantine Road, NW3 2LS. *T:* 071–267 4881.

HÁZI, Dr Vencel; Hungarian Ambassador to United States of America, 1983–89; *b* 3 Sept. 1925; *m* 1952, Judit Zell; one *d. Educ:* Technical Univ. and Univ. of Economics, Budapest. Entered Diplomatic Service, 1950; served in Min. of Foreign Affairs, Budapest, 1950; Press Attaché, Hungarian Legation, London, 1951–53; Counsellor, Legation, Stockholm, 1957–58; Ambassador: to Iraq, and to Afghanistan, 1958–61; to Greece, and to Cyprus, 1962–64; Head of Western Dept, Min. of For. Affairs, Budapest, 1964–68; Dep. For. Minister, Budapest, 1968–70, 1976–83; Ambassador to Court of St James's, 1970–76. Golden Grade of Order of Merit for Labour, 1962, and of Medal of Merit of Hungarian People's Republic, 1953; Grand Cordon of Order of Omayoum, 1st Class, Iran. *Recreations:* reading, music, swimming, chess. *Address:* c/o Ministry of Foreign Affairs, 1027 Budapest, Bem rkp 47, Hungary. *Club:* Opera Fans (Budapest).

HAZLERIGG, family name of **Baron Hazlerigg.**

HAZLERIGG, 2nd Baron, *cr* 1945, of Noseley; **Arthur Grey Hazlerigg,** Bt, *cr* 1622; MC 1945; TD 1948; DL, JP; *b* 24 Feb. 1910; *e s* of 1st Baron and Dorothy Rachel (*d* 1972), *e d* of John Henry Buxton, Easneye, Ware, Herts; *S* father 1949; *m* 1945, Patricia (*d* 1972), *e d* of late John Pullar, High Seat, Fields Hill, Kloof, Natal, SA; one *s* two *d. Educ:* Eton; Trinity Coll., Cambridge. BA 1932. FRICS 1946. Served War of 1939–45, Leics Yeomanry (MC); Major, 1941; served in Italy. DL Leics 1946; JP 1946. *Recreation:* golf. *Heir: s* Hon. Arthur Grey Hazlerigg [*b* 5 May 1951; *m* 1986, Laura, *e d* of Sir William Dugdale, Bt, *qv*; one *s* twin *d*]. *Address:* Noseley Hall, Leicester LE7 9EH. *Clubs:* Army and Navy, MCC.

HAZLEWOOD, Prof. Arthur Dennis; Research Professor in Commonwealth Studies, Oxford University, 1986–88, now Emeritus; Professorial Fellow, Pembroke College, Oxford, 1979–88, now Emeritus; *b* 24 April 1921; *s* of Harry Arthur Sinclair Hazlewood and Miriam Esther Maltby; *m* 1954, Tamara Oszpicyn; one *d. Educ:* Finchley County Sch.; LSE (BSc Econ 1948); The Queen's Coll., Oxford (BPhil 1950; MA 1954). Post Office engineer, 1938–48 (RAF radar stations, 1940–44); Oxford University, 1950–: Tutor to Colonial Service courses, 1950–56; research staff, Inst. of Economics and Statistics, 1956–79; tutorial fellow, Pembroke Coll., 1961–79; Warden, Queen Elizabeth House, Dir, Inst. of Commonwealth Studies, 1979–86. Adviser, Nyasaland Govt on Central African Fedn, 1962; Dir, Common Market Secretariat, President's Office, Kenya, 1965–66; Dir, Trade and Finance Div., Commonwealth Secretariat and Special Adviser, Commonwealth Fund for Technical Co-operation, 1975–76. *Publications:* (jtly) Nyasaland: the economics of federation, 1960; The Economy of Africa, 1961; (jtly) An Econometric Model of the UK, 1961; Rail and Road in East Africa, 1964; (ed) African Integration and Disintegration, 1967; Economic Integration: the East African experience, 1975; (jtly) Aid and Inequality in Kenya, 1976; The Economy of Kenya, 1979; (jtly) Irrigation Economics in Poor Countries, 1982; Education, Work, and Pay in East Africa, 1989; articles in jls and symposia. *Address:* 14 Fyfield Road, Oxford OX2 6QE. *T:* Oxford (0865) 59119.

HAZLEWOOD, Air Vice-Marshal Frederick Samuel, CB 1970; CBE 1967 (OBE 1960); AFC 1951 (Bar to AFC, 1954); retired; *b* 13 May 1921; *s* of Samuel Henry and Lilian Hazlewood; *m* 1943, Isabelle Mary (*née* Hunt); one *s. Educ:* Kimbolton Sch. Served War of 1939–45: joined RAF, 1939; ops with Bomber Command, 1941; MEAF and UK Coastal Command, 1940–45. Lancaster Units, 1948–53; Comdg Officer, No 90 Valiant Sqdn, 1958–61; HQ, Bomber Comd, 1961–63; HQ, RAF, Germany, 1963–64; OC RAF Lyneham, 1965–67; HQ, RAF, Germany, 1968–69; AOC and Commandant, Central Flying School, 1970–72; AOC 38 Gp, RAF, 1972–74; Comdt, Jt Warfare Estab., 1974–76. *Recreations:* golf, tennis, rough shooting. *Club:* Royal Air Force.

HAZLEWOOD, Rt. Rev. John; *see* Ballarat, Bishop of.

HEAD, family name of **Viscount Head.**

HEAD, 2nd Viscount *cr* 1960, of Throope; **Richard Antony Head;** *b* 27 Feb. 1937; *s* of 1st Viscount Head, GCMG, CBE, MC, PC, and Dorothea, Viscountess Head (*d* 1987), *d* of 9th Earl of Shaftesbury, KP, GCVO, CBE, PC; *S* father, 1983; *m* 1974, Alicia Brigid, *er d* of Julian Salmond; two *s* one *d. Educ:* Eton; RMA Sandhurst. The Life Guards, 1957–66 (Captain), retd. Trainer of racehorses, 1968–83. *Recreations:* hunting, sailing, golf. *Heir: s* Hon. Henry Julian Head, *b* 30 March 1980. *Address:* Throope Manor, Bishopstone, Salisbury, Wilts SP5 4BA. *T:* Coombe Bissett (072277) 318. *Clubs:* White's, Cavalry and Guards.

HEAD, Adrian Herbert; His Honour Judge Head; a Circuit Judge since 1972; *b* 4 Dec. 1923; *s* of late Judge Head and late Mrs Geraldine Head (*née* Pipon); *m* 1947, Ann Pamela, *d* of late John Stanning and late Mrs A. C. Lewin, of Leyland and Njoro, Kenya; three *s. Educ:* RNC Dartmouth (invalided, polio); privately; Magdalen Coll., Oxford (MA). Arden Scholar, Gray's Inn, 1947. Called to Bar, Gray's Inn, 1947 (subseq. ad eundem Inner Temple). Chm., Agricultural Land Tribunals (SE Region), 1971; Dep. Chm., Middlesex QS, 1971. Dir, later Chm., Norfolk Lavender Ltd, 1953–71. Memorial Lectr, RSL, 1948. Licensed Lay Reader, C of E, 1962. Co-founder and subseq. Sen. Trustee, Norfolk Family Conciliation Service, 1983–; Pres., W Norfolk and Fenland, Marriage Guidance Council, now Relate, 1984–. Hon. DCL East Anglia, 1987. *Publications:* (contrib.) Oxford Poetry 1942–1943, 1943; The Seven Words and The Civilian, 1946; contrib. Essays by Divers Hands, 1953; Safety Afloat (trans. from Dutch of W. Zantvoort), 1965; Consumer Credit Act Supplement to McCleary's County Court Precedents, 1979; Poems in Praise, 1982, 2nd edn 1987; (devised and general ed., 1985–87, consulting ed., 1987–, and contrib.) Butterworths County Court Precedents and Pleadings, 1985, thereafter frequent supplements. *Recreations:* painting, sailing, writing, trees. *Address:* Overy Staithe, Kings Lynn, Norfolk PE31 8TG. *T:* Fakenham (0328) 738312; 5 Raymond Buildings, Gray's Inn, WC1R 5BP. *T:* 071–405 7146. *Clubs:* Jersey Soc.; Norfolk (Norwich); Royal Naval Sailing Association, Guild of World Traders Yacht St Katharine-by-the-Tower.

HEAD, Alan Kenneth, PhD, DSc; FAA 1971; FRS 1988; Hon. Research Fellow, Commonwealth Scientific and Industrial Research Organization, Australia (Chief Research

Scientist, 1969); *b* 10 Aug. 1925; *s* of Rowland Henry John Head and Elsie May (*née* Burrell); *m* 1951, Gwenneth Nancy Barlow. *Educ:* Ballarat Grammar Sch.; Scotch Coll.; Univ. of Melbourne (BA, BSc, DSc); Univ. of Bristol (PhD). Research Scientist: CSIR Div. of Aeronautics, 1947–50; Aeronautical Res. Labs, 1953–57; CSIRO Division: of Tribo Physics, 1957–81; of Chemical Physics, 1981–86; of Materials Science, 1987. Visiting Professor: Brown Univ., 1961–62; Univ. of Florida, 1971; Christensen Fellow, 1986, Vis. Fellow, 1990–, St Catherine's Coll., Oxford. *Publications:* Computed Electron Micrographs and Defect Identification, 1973, Chinese edn 1979; numerous contribs to sci. jls. *Address:* 10 Ellesmore Court, Kew, Vic 3101, Australia.

HEAD, Audrey May; Member, Monopolies and Mergers Commission, 1986–89; Director, 1973–85, Managing Director, 1976–85, Hill Samuel Unit Trust Managers Ltd; *b* 21 Jan. 1924; *d* of Eric Burton Head and Kathleen Irene Head. *Educ:* St Catherine's Sch., Bramley, Surrey. Chartered Auctioneers' and Estate Agents' Institute, 1949–58; Hill Samuel Group, 1958–86, a Manager, 1968; Director: Hill Samuel Investment Management, 1974–86; Hill Samuel Life Assurance, 1983–86; Trade Union Unit Trust Managers Ltd, 1986–89. Chm., Unit Trust Assoc., 1983–85. Non-exec. Mem., Royal Surrey and St Luke's NHS Trust, 1991–. Chm., Governing Body, St Catherine's Sch., Bramley, Surrey, 1988– (Gov. 1979–); Gov., Cranleigh Sch., Surrey, 1988–. Nominated as Business Woman of the Year, 1976. Silver Jubilee Medal, 1977. *Recreations:* golf, gardening. *Address:* West Chantry, 4 Clifford Manor Road, Guildford, Surrey GU4 8AG. *T:* Guildford (0483) 61047. *Club:* Sloane.

HEAD, Dennis Alec, CBE 1979; CEng, FRAeS; Divisional Director (Northern Ireland), STC, since 1986; *b* 8 Nov. 1925; *s* of late Alec Head and Florence Head; *m* 1966, Julia Rosser-Owen, BA; one *s*. *Educ:* Whitgift Sch.; Peterhouse, Cambridge (Mech. Sciences Tripos, MA); Royal Naval Engrg Coll., Manadon. Served FAA, RN, 1943–47: Sub-Lt (A) RNVR, 1945; Air Engr Officer. Rolls-Royce Ltd: grad. apprentice, 1949; Manager, Design Services, Aero Engine Div., 1962, Dir of Personnel and Admin, 1967; Dir and Gen. Man., subseq. Man. Dir, Derby Engine Div., 1973; Man. Dir Aero Div., 1976; Man. Dir Operations, 1980–82; Member Board: Rolls-Royce Ltd, 1973–82; Rolls-Royce Turbomeca, 1973–82 (Chm., 1981–82); Turbo-Union, 1979–82; Chm., Rolls-Royce & Associates, 1981–82; Mem. Bd and Dir Operations, Short Brothers, 1982–86. Member: Reg. Adv. Council for Further Educn, 1968–73; Engrg Employers' Fedn Policy Cttee, 1978–82. *Recreations:* photography, history, music. *Address:* Bodmins, 48D High Street, Marshfield, Wilts.

HEAD, Major Sir Francis (David Somerville), 5th Bt, *cr* 1838; late Queen's Own Cameron Highlanders; *b* 17 Oct. 1916; *s* of 4th Bt and Grace Margaret (*d* 1967), *d* of late David Robertson; *S* father, 1924; *m* 1st, 1950, Susan Patricia (marr. diss. 1965), *o d* of A. D. Ramsay, OBE; one *s* one *d*; 2nd, 1967, Penelope, *d* of late Wilfred Alexander. *Educ:* Eton; Peterhouse, Cambridge, BA 1937. Served War of 1939–45 (wounded and prisoner); retired 1951. *Heir:* *s* Richard Douglas Somerville Head [*b* 16 Jan. 1951. *Educ:* Eton; Magdalene Coll., Cambridge]. *Address:* 63 Chantry View Road, Guildford, Surrey GU1 3XU. *Club:* Naval and Military.

HEAD, Michael Edward, CVO 1991; Assistant Under Secretary of State and Head of Broadcasting and Miscellaneous Department, Home Office, since 1991; *b* 17 March 1936; *s* of Alexander Edward Head and Wilhelmina Head; *m* 1963, Wendy Elizabeth, *d* of R. J. Davies; two *s* two *d*. *Educ:* Leeds, Kingston, and Woking Grammar Schools; University College London (BA; Pollard Prize for History); Univ. of Michigan (MA). 2nd Lieut, Royal Artillery (Nat. Service), 1958–60. Home Office, 1960; Private Sec. to Parly Under Secs of State, 1964–66; Sec., Deptl Cttee on Liquor Licensing (Erroll), 1971–72; Asst Sec., 1974–84: Probation and After Care Dept; Community Programmes and Equal Opportunities Dept; Criminal Dept; Asst Under Sec. of State, General Dept, 1984, Criminal Justice and Constitutional Dept (Registrar of the Baronetage), 1986. *Recreations:* theatre, reading. *Address:* Byways, The Ridge, Woking, Surrey GU22 7EE. *T:* Woking (0483) 772929. *Clubs:* Reform; Rotary (Woking Dist).

HEAD, Mildred Eileen, OBE 1971; owner, director and partner in several furniture and drapery shops, 1950–83; *b* 13 June 1911; *d* of Philip Strudwick Head and Katie Head. *Educ:* Sudbury Girls' Secondary Sch.; Chelsea Coll. of Physical Educn (Dipl.). MCSP. Teacher, Lectr and Organiser of Physical Educn, 1933–50. Pres., Nat. Fedn of Business and Professional Women of Gt Britain and N Ireland, 1966–69; Pres., Nat. Chamber of Trade, 1977–79 (Chm. Bd of Management, 1971–77). Mayor of Borough of Sudbury, 1970–71; Member: Price Commn, 1973–77; Nat. Economic Cttee for Distributive Trades, 1974–84; Retail Consortium, 1971–83; Davignon/Narjes Cttee for Commerce and Distribution (EEC), 1979–86; Discip. Cttee of Assoc. of Certified Accountants, 1980–83; Assessor, Auld Cttee of Inquiry into Shops Hours, 1984–85. Comr of Inland Revenue, 1959–86. Pres., Internat. Fedn of Business and Professional Women, 1977–80 (First Vice-Pres., 1974–77). Chm., Management Cttee, Quay Theatre, Sudbury, 1982–. *Recreations:* theatre, gardening, bridge. *Address:* Rosebank, Ingrams Well Road, Sudbury, Suffolk CO10 6RT. *T:* Sudbury (0787) 72185.

HEAD, Philip John, FRICS; Chief Executive, Welsh Development Agency, since 1991; *b* 24 Nov. 1951; *s* of Dennis George Head and Marjorie Head; *m* 1974, Barbara Fox; two *s*. *Educ:* Surbiton Grammar Sch.; Univ. of Reading (BSc Hons Estate Management). FRICS 1985. Estates Surveyor, 1973–77, Sen. Commercial Surveyor, 1977–78, Milton Keynes Develt Corp.; Welsh Development Agency, 1978–: Develt and Funding Manager, 1981–83; Dep. Commercial Dir, 1983–84; Commercial Dir, 1984–87; Exec. Dir, Property and Regional Services, 1987–91. A Dir, Inst. of Welsh Affairs, 1991–; Mem., CBI Council for Wales, 1991–. *Recreations:* Llantrisant Round Table, swimming, gardening, family. *Address:* c/o Welsh Development Agency, Pearl House, Greyfriars, Cardiff CF1 3XX. *T:* Cardiff (0222) 222666.

HEADFORT, 6th Marquis of, *cr* 1800; **Thomas Geoffrey Charles Michael Taylour,** FRICS; Bt 1704; Baron Headfort, 1760; Viscount Headfort, 1762; Earl of Bective, 1766; Baron Kenlis (UK), 1831; *b* 20 Jan. 1932; *o s* of 5th Marquis and Elsie Florence (*d* 1972), *d* of J. Partridge Tucker, Sydney, NSW, and *widow* of Sir Rupert Clarke, 2nd Bt of Rupertswood; *S* father, 1960; *m* 1st, 1958, Hon. Elizabeth Nall-Cain (from whom he obtained a divorce, 1969), *d* of 2nd Baron Brocket; one *s* two *d*; 2nd, 1972, Virginia, *d* of late Mr Justice Nable, Manila. *Educ:* Stowe; Christ's Coll., Cambridge (MA; Cert. of Proficiency in Rural Estate Management). 2nd Lieut Life Guards, 1950; acting Pilot Officer, RAFVR, 1952. Dir, Bective Electrical Co. Ltd, 1953; Sales Manager and Chief Pilot, Lancashire Aircraft Co. Ltd, 1959. Freeman, Guild of Air Pilots and Air Navigators, 1958. Piloted Prospector aircraft around Africa, 1960, etc. FRICS; FCIArb; Mem., Irish Auctioneers and Valuers Inst. Council, Royal Agricultural Society of England, 1961. Inspector, Royal Hong Kong Police, 1977. Commercial Pilot's Licence, 1967. Underwriting Mem. of Lloyds. *Heir:* *s* Earl of Bective, *qv*. *Address:* 1425 Figueroa Street, Paco, Manila, Philippines. *T:* Manila 59–38–29; telex 64792 HDFT PN; Affix Ltd, Rooms 1603–4, New Victory House, 93–103 Wing Lok Street, Hong Kong. *T:* Hong Kong 545 2977; *Fax:* 854 1229; telex 75204 AFFIX HX. *Clubs:* Cavalry and Guards, Lansdowne, Little Ship, Lloyds Yacht, House of Lords Yacht, Kildare Street and University (Dublin); Ellan Vannin (Isle of Man); Manila, Manila Polo, Manila Yacht, Columbian (Philippines); Hong Kong, Foreign Correspondents, Aberdeen Boat (Hong Kong).

HEADLEY, 7th Baron *cr* 1797; **Charles Rowland Allanson-Winn;** Bt 1660 and 1776; retired; *b* 19 May 1902; *s* of 5th Baron Headley and Teresa (*d* 1919), *y d* of late W. H. Johnson; *S* brother, 1969; *m* 1927, Hilda May Wells-Thorpe (*d* 1989); three *d* (one *s* decd). *Educ:* Bedford School. *Recreations:* golf, fishing. *Heir:* *b* Hon. Owain Gwynedd Allanson-Winn [*b* 15 Feb. 1906; *m* 1938, Ruth, *d* of late Cecil Orpin]. *Address:* Dreys, 7 Silverwood, West Chiltington, Pulborough, W Sussex RH20 2NG. *T:* West Chiltington (07983) 3083.

HEADLY, Derek, CMG 1957; lately Malayan Civil Service; Midlands Secretary, Independent Schools Careers Organisation, 1966–77; *b* 1908; *s* of L. C. Headly, The House-on-the-Hill, Woodhouse Eaves, Leics; *m* 1946, Joyce Catherine (marr. diss. 1975), *d* of C. F. Freeman; one *s* one *d*. *Educ:* Repton Sch.; Corpus Christi Coll., Cambridge (BA). Military Service, 1944–46, Lieut-Col, Special Ops Exec., Force 136 (despatches), and British Mil. Admin. Malayan CS, 1931; served Trengganu, Muar, Pekan etc.; seconded to Palestine Mandate, 1938–44; Resident N Borneo, 1949–53; British Adviser, Kelantan, 1953–57. Dir, Vipan & Headly Ltd, 1957–66. Mem. Melton and Belvoir RDC, 1958–67. Officer (Brother) Order of St John. *Publication:* From Learning to Earning (Independent Schools Careers Organisation Careers Guide), 1977. *Recreations:* hill walking, gardening. *Address:* Rooftree Cottage, Hoby, Melton Mowbray, Leics. *T:* Melton Mowbray (0664) 434214. *Club:* Special Forces.

HEAF, Peter Julius Denison, MD; FRCP; Chairman, Medical Sickness Annuity and Life Insurance Society Ltd, since 1988; *b* 1922; *s* of late Prof. F. R. G. Heaf, CMG; *m* 1947, Rosemary Cartledge; two *s* two *d*. *Educ:* Stamford Sch., Lincs; University Coll., London, Fellow 1973. MB, BS 1946; MD London 1952; MRCP 1954; FRCP 1965. House Physician and Surg., also RMO, University Coll. Hosp., and Capt. RAMC, 1946–51; Research Asst, Brompton Hosp., 1953–54; Sen. Registrar, St Thomas' Hosp., 1955–58; Consultant Physician, UCH, 1958–86, retired. *Publications:* papers on chest disease and pulmonary physiology, in Lancet, etc. *Recreations:* painting, gardening. *Address:* Ferrybrook House, Chalmore Gardens, Wallingford, Oxon OX10 9EP. *T:* Wallingford (0491) 39176.

HEAL, Anthony Standerwick; Head of the Business, Heal & Son Holdings plc, 1981–84; *b* 23 Feb. 1907; *s* of Sir Ambrose Heal and Lady Edith Florence Digby Heal; *m* 1941, Theodora Caldwell (*née* Griffin); two *s*. *Educ:* Leighton Park Sch., Reading. Joined Heal & Son Ltd 1929; Dir 1936; Chm., Heal & Son, later Heal & Son Hldgs, Ltd, 1952–81. Chm. Council, London and S Eastern Furniture Manufrs Assoc., 1947–48; Master, Furniture Makers Guild (now Worshipful Co. of Furniture Makers), 1959–60; Mem. Council of Industrial Design, 1959–67; Mem. Council, City and Guilds of London Inst., 1969–81, Chm., Licentiateship Cttee, 1976–79; Pres., Design and Industries Assoc., 1965; Chm. Indep. Stores Assoc., 1970–72. Hon. FCSD (Hon. FSIA 1974); Hon. FCGI 1981. RSA Bi-Centenary Medal, 1964. Order of White Rose of Finland, 1970; Chevalier (First Class) Order of Dannebrog, 1974. *Recreations:* vintage cars and steam engines. *Address:* Baylins Farm, Knotty Green, Beaconsfield, Bucks HP9 2TN. *Clubs:* Vintage Sports Car, National Traction Engine.

See also O. S. Heal.

HEAL, Oliver Standerwick; Chairman, Heal Textil GmbH, since 1984; *b* 18 April 1949; *s* of Anthony Standerwick Heal, *qv*. *Educ:* Leighton Park Sch., Reading. Joined Heal's, 1970; Dir, Heal & Son Ltd, 1974–83, Chm., 1977–83; Chm., Heal & Son Holdings PLC, 1981–83 (Dir, 1975–83); Dir, Staples & Co. Ltd, 1981–84. *Recreation:* vintage cars. *Address:* Reinsburgstrasse 171, D7000 Stuttgart 1, Germany. *Clubs:* Winnowing; Vintage Sports Car (Newbury).

HEAL, Sylvia Lloyd; JP; MP (Lab) Mid Staffordshire, since March 1990; *b* 20 July 1942; *d* of John Lloyd Fox and Ruby Fox; *m* 1965, Keith Heal; one *s* one *d*. *Educ:* Elfed Secondary Modern School, Buckley, N Wales; Coleg Harlech; University College Swansea (BSc Econ 1968). Medical Records Clerk, Chester Royal Infirmary, 1957–63; social worker, health service and Dept of Employment, 1968–70 and 1980–90. Mem., Select Cttee on Educn, Sci. and Arts. Mem., Exec. Council, SSAFA. JP Surrey, 1973. *Recreations:* walking, theatre, listening to male voice choirs. *Address:* House of Commons, SW1A 0AA. *T:* 071–219 5895.

HEALD, Mervyn; QC 1970; a Social Security Commissioner, since 1988; *b* 12 April 1930; *s* of Rt Hon. Sir Lionel Heald, QC, and of Daphne Constance, CBE 1976, *d* of late Montague Price; *m* 1954, Clarissa Bowen; one *s* three *d*. *Educ:* Eton College; Magdalene College, Cambridge. Called to the Bar, Middle Temple, 1954; Bencher, 1978. A Recorder, 1985–88. *Recreations:* country pursuits. *Address:* Headfoldswood, Loxwood, Sussex. *T:* Loxwood (0403) 752248.

HEALD, Thomas Routledge; His Honour Judge Heald; a Circuit Judge (formerly County Court Judge), since 1970; *b* 19 Aug. 1923; *s* of late John Arthur Heald and Nora Marion Heald; *m* 1950, Jean, *d* of James Campbell Henderson; two *s* two *d*. *Educ:* Merchant Taylors' Sch.; St John's Coll., Oxford. Fish Schol., St John's Coll., Oxford, 1941; Lieut, RAC, 1943–45; BA (Jurisprudence) 1947; MA 1949. Called to Bar, Middle Temple, 1948; Midland Circuit; Prosecuting Counsel to Inland Revenue (Midland Circuit), 1965–70; Deputy Chairman, QS: Lindsey, 1965–71; Notts, 1969–71; Notts designated Family Judge, 1991–. Council of HM Circuit Judges: Asst Sec., 1980–83; Sec., 1984–85; Vice-Pres., 1986–87; Pres., 1988–89; Member: Matrimonial Rules Cttee, 1980–83; President's Cttee on Adoption, 1983–88; President's Family Cttee, 1984–. Mem., Senate of Inns of Court, 1984–86. Mem. Council, Nottingham Univ., 1974– (Chm., Physical Recreation Adv. Cttee, 1979–85; Chm., Law Adv. Cttee, 1976–84; Chm., Estates and Buildings Cttee, 1985–89); Chm., Law Adv. Cttee, Trent Polytechnic, 1979–84. *Recreations:* golf, local history, family history. *Address:* Rebbur House, Nicker Hill, Keyworth, Nottingham NG12 5ED. *T:* Plumtree (06077) 2676. *Clubs:* United Services (Nottingham); Notts Golf, Woking Golf.

HEALEY, Sir Charles Edward C.; *see* Chadwyck-Healey.

HEALEY, Rt. Hon. Denis Winston, CH 1979; MBE 1945; PC 1964; MP (Lab) South East Leeds, Feb. 1952–55, Leeds East since 1955; Deputy Leader of the Labour Party, 1980–83; *b* 30 Aug. 1917; *s* of late William Healey, Keighley, Yorks; *m* 1945, Edna May Edmunds (*see* E. M. Healey); one *s* two *d*. *Educ:* Bradford Grammar Sch.; Balliol Coll., Oxford (Hon. Fellow, 1979). First Cl. Hons Mods 1938; Jenkyns Exhib. 1939; Harmsworth Sen. Schol., First Cl. Lit. Hum., BA 1940; MA 1945. War of 1939–45; entered Army, 1940; served N Africa, Italy. Major RE 1944 (despatches). Contested (Lab) Pudsey and Otley Div., 1945; Sec., International Dept, Labour Party, 1945–52. Shadow Cabinet, 1959–64, 1970–74, 1979–87; Secretary of State for Defence, 1964–70; Chancellor of the Exchequer, 1974–79; opposition spokesman on Foreign and Commonwealth Affairs, 1980–87. Mem. Brit. Delegn to Commonwealth Relations Conf., Canada, 1949; British Delegate to: Consultative Assembly, Council of Europe, 1952–54; Inter Parly Union Conf., Washington, 1953; Western European Union and

Council of Europe, 1953–55. Chm., IMF Interim Cttee, 1977–79. Mem. Exec. Fabian Soc., 1954–61. Mem., Labour Party Nat. Exec. Cttee, 1970–75. Councillor: RIIA, 1948–60; Inst. of Strategic Studies, 1958–61. Hon. Fellow, Leeds Polytechnic, 1987. Hon. DLitt Bradford, 1983. Grand Cross of Order of Merit, Germany, 1979. *Publications*: The Curtain Falls, 1951; New Fabian Essays, 1952; Neutralism, 1955; Fabian International Essays, 1956; A Neutral Belt in Europe, 1958; NATO and American Security, 1959; The Race Against the H Bomb, 1960; Labour Britain and the World, 1963; Healey's Eye, 1980; Labour and a World Society, 1985; Beyond Nuclear Deterrence, 1986; The Time of My Life (autobiog.), 1989; When Shrimps Learn to Whistle (essays), 1990. *Recreations*: travel, photography, music, painting. *Address*: House of Commons, SW1A 0AA. *T*: 071–219 4060.

HEALEY, Deryck John; FRSA 1978; FCSD; artist, sculptor; *b* 30 Jan. 1937; *s* of Leonard Melvon Healey and Irene Isabella Healey (*née* Ferguson); *m* 1962, Mary Elizabeth Pitt Booth (decd); two *s*. *Educ*: Northlands High Sch., Natal, SA (Victoria League Empire Scholar; DipAD, SA, 1955; Golden Jubilee Cert. of Merit, 1957); Manchester Polytechnic (DipAd 1958, Textile Design Prize, 1957, 1958; Design Travel Bursary, 1958; Royal Manch. Inst. Cert. of Merit, 1958; Calico Printers' Assoc. Fellow, 1961–62). Design Man., Good Hope Textiles, SA, 1959–66; Chairman: Deryck Healey Associates, London, 1966–85; Deryck Healey International, 1969–85; Dreamshire, 1985–87; Design Man., WPM London (Wallpaper mfrs), 1966–68; ICI Design Studio Manager, Asst to Elsbeth Juda, 1968–80; Consultant, D. H. I. Interiors Ltd, 1983–85; Design Consultant, Wedgwood, 1984–88. Chm., CNAA Textile and Fashion Bd, 1971–81; Member: CNAA Art and Design Cttee, 1971–81; Design Council Textile Design Selection Cttee, 1978–87; Craft Council Bd, 1983–85 (Textile Panel, 1980; Finance and Gen. Purposes Cttee, 1983–85; Chairman: Textile Develt Group, 1982–84; Projects and Organisations Cttee, 1983–85). RSA: Annual Sponsor, D. Healey Fashion and Colour Bursaries, 1978–85; Mem. Bursary Bd, 1982–88. Patron, New Art Tate Gall., 1983–. Member: Contemp. Art Soc., 1982–; ICA, 1970–; Chelsea Arts Club, 1982–88; Friend of RA, 1980–. SIAD: Mem., British Design Export Gp, 1980; Chm., Textile and Fashion Gp, 1966–67. External Examiner, Textile and Fashion courses: CNAA BA and MA; Liverpool, BA, 1978–80; Manchester, MA, 1976–79; Kingston, BA, 1978–80; St Martin's, BA, 1978–80; Glasgow, BA, 1979–82; RCA, Textiles, 1980; Adviser and External Examiner, Middx Polytechnic, BA, 1982–86; External Examiner: London Coll. of Furniture, BTEC, 1985–86; BA Fashion, St Martin's Sch. of Art, 1985–87. One-man exhibitions: Salama-Caro Gall., London, 1990; Frankfurt Internat. Art Fair, 1990; Venice, 1990; Internat. Art Fairs, Cologne and Chicago, 1990. FCSD (FSIAD 1964). CoID Design Award, 1964; Queen's Award to Industry for Export, 1974; RSA Bicentenary Medal, 1981; Textile Institute Design Medal, 1982. *Publications*: Colour, 1980 (Mem. Editorial Bd and contrib.); Living with Colour, 1982; The New Art of Flower Design, 1986. *Recreations*: drawing, painting, photography, sculpture, gardening, Deryck Healey Trust for the encouragement of Art, Design and Craft graduates. *Address*: 95 Whitelands House, Cheltenham Terrace, SW3 4RA. *Clubs*: various.

HEALEY, Edna May; writer; *b* 14 June 1918; *d* of Rose and Edward Edmunds; *m* 1945, Right Hon. Denis Healey, *qv*: one *s* two *d*. *Educ*: Bell's Grammar School, Coleford, Glos; St Hugh's College, Oxford (BA, Dip Ed). Taught English and History, Keighley Girls' Grammar School, 1940–44; freelance lecturer, England and America; television writer and presenter; radio writer and broadcaster. *Publications*: Lady Unknown: life of Angela Burdett-Coutts, 1978; Wives of Fame, 1986. *Recreations*: gardening, listening to music. *Address*: Pingles Place, Alfriston, East Sussex.

HEALY, Prof. John Francis, MA, PhD; Professor of Classics, London University, 1966–90, now Professor Emeritus; Chairman of Department, Royal Holloway and Bedford New College, 1985–88 (Head of Department, Royal Holloway College, 1966–85); *b* 27 Aug. 1926; *s* of late John Healy and Iris Maud (*née* Cutland); *m* 1st, 1957, Carol Ann McEvoy; one *s*; 2nd, 1985, Barbara Edith Henshall. *Educ*: Trinity Coll., Cambridge (Open Exhbn in Classics 1943; Classical Prelim. Cl. 1 1944; Classical Tripos: 1st Cl. Pt I 1949, 1st Cl. Pt II 1950 (dist. Cl. Archaeol.); Sen. Schol. 1950; BA 1950, MA 1952, PhD 1955). War service, 1944–48; Captain, Intelligence Corps, 1946–48. Walston student, Brit. Sch. of Archaeol., Athens, 1950; G. C. Winter Warr Schol., Cambridge, 1951; Manchester University: Asst Lectr in Classics, 1953–56; Lectr in Classics and Class. Archaeol., 1956–61; London University: Reader in Greek, Bedford Coll., 1961–66; Chm., Bd of Studies in Classics, 1979–81; Dean of Faculty of Arts, Royal Holloway Coll., 1978–81. Chm. Finance Cttee, Inst. of Classical Studies, London, 1967–88. FRNS 1950; FRSA 1971; MRI 1979. *Publications*: contrib. (A. Rowe) Cyrenaican Expeditions of the University of Manchester, 1955–57; Mining and Metallurgy in the Greek and Roman World, 1978; Sylloge Nummorum Graecorum, vol. VII, The Raby and Güterbock collections in Manchester University Museum, 1986; Pliny the Elder, Natural History, 1991; articles and reviews in Jl of Hellenic St., Numismatic Chron., Nature, Amer. Num. Soc.'s Mus. Notes, Jl of Metals, Class. Rev., Gnomon. *Recreations*: travel, music, creative gardening. *Club*: Cambridge Union Society.

HEALY, Maurice Eugene; Director, National Consumer Council, since 1987; *b* 27 Nov. 1933; *s* of late Thomas Healy and Emily Healy (*née* O'Mahoney); *m* 1958, Jose Barbara Speller Dewdney; two *d* (and one *d* decd). *Educ*: Downside School; Peterhouse, Cambridge (BA Classics). Nat. service, Royal Artillery, 1954–56. BoT, 1956–60; Consumers' Assoc., working on Which?, 1960–76; Head of Editl Dept and Editor of Which?, 1973–76; Nat. Consumer Council, 1977–. Mem. Council, Bureau Européen des Unions de Consommateurs, 1977–; Assessor to Auld Cttee on reform of shop hours, 1984. Chm. of Governors, Highgate Wood School, 1983–86. FRSA. *Publications*: contribs to Which? and Nat. Consumer Council and other jls and conf. papers. *Recreations*: jazz, Irish music, gardening. *Address*: 15 Onslow Gardens, Muswell Hill, N10 3JT. *T*: 081–883 8955. *Clubs*: Ronnie Scott's, Burmese Cat.

HEALY, Tim T.; *see* Traverse-Healy.

HEANEY, Henry Joseph, MA, FLA; University Librarian and Keeper of the Hunterian Books and Manuscripts, Glasgow, since 1978; *b* 2 Jan. 1935; *s* of late Michael Heaney and Sarah (*née* Fox); *m* 1976, Mary Elizabeth Moloney. *Educ*: Abbey Grammar Sch., Newry; Queen's Univ. of Belfast (MA). FLA 1967. Asst Librarian, QUB, 1959–62; Libr., Magee University Coll., Londonderry, 1962–67; Dep. Libr., New Univ. of Ulster, 1967–69; Asst Sec., Standing Conf. of National and Univ. Libraries, 1969–72; Librarian: QUB, 1972–74; University Coll., Dublin, 1975–78. Member: Adv. Cttee on Public Lib. Service, NI, 1965; Standing Cttee, Univ. Libraries Sect. IFLA, 1985–91; British Liby Bd, 1989–; Chm., NI Branch, Lib. Assoc., 1966, 1973; Pres., Scottish Liby Assoc., 1990. Trustee: Nat. Lib. of Scotland, 1980–91; Nat. Manuscripts Conservation Trust, 1990–. *Publications*: (ed) IFLA Annual, 1971; (ed) World Guide to Abbreviations of Organisations, 8th edn, 1988, 9th edn 1991. *Address*: Glasgow University Library, Glasgow G12 8QE. *T*: 041–330 5633.

HEANEY, Leonard Martin, CMG 1959; Overseas Civil Service, retired; *b* 28 Nov. 1906; *s* of Alexander John and Lilian Heaney; *m* 1947, Kathleen Edith Mary Chapman; no *c*. *Educ*: Bristol Grammar Sch.; Oriel Coll., Oxford. Joined Colonial Service on leaving Oxford, 1929; served in Tanganyika, retiring as a Senior Provincial Commissioner, 1959. Military service with East African Forces in Abyssinia, Madagascar, Ceylon, Burma, 1940–45. *Recreations*: reading and golf. *Address*: Flat No 9, Salcombe Court, Salcombe Hill Road, Sidmouth, Devon EX10 8JR.

HEANEY, Seamus Justin; Member of Irish Academy of Letters; Professor of Poetry, Oxford University, since 1989; Boylston Professor of Rhetoric and Oratory at Harvard University (formerly Visiting Professor), since 1985; *b* 13 April 1939; *s* of Patrick and Margaret Heaney; *m* 1965, Marie Devlin; two *s* one *d*. *Educ*: St Columb's College, Derry; Queen's University, Belfast. BA first cl. 1961. Teacher, St Thomas's Secondary Sch., Belfast, 1962–63; Lectr, St Joseph's Coll. of Educn, Belfast, 1963–66; Lectr, Queen's Univ., Belfast, 1966–72; free-lance writer, 1972–75; Lectr, Carysfort Coll., 1975–81. Bennett Award, 1982. *Publications*: Eleven Poems, 1965; Death of a Naturalist, 1966 (Somerset Maugham Award, 1967; Cholmondeley Award, 1968); Door into the Dark, 1969; Wintering Out, 1972; North, 1975 (W. H. Smith Award; Duff Cooper Prize); Field Work, 1979; Preoccupations: Selected Prose, 1968–1978, 1980; Selected Poems, 1965–1975, 1980; (ed with Ted Hughes) The Rattle Bag, 1982; Sweeney Astray, 1984; Station Island, 1984; The Haw Lantern, 1987 (Whitbread Award, 1987); The Government of the Tongue, 1988; New Selected Poems 1966–1987, 1990; Seeing Things, 1991. *Address*: c/o Faber & Faber, 3 Queen Square, WC1N 3RU.

HEANLEY, Charles Laurence, TD 1950; FRCS; Consulting Surgeon; Member of Lloyd's; *b* 28 Feb. 1907; *e s* of Dr C. M. Heanley; *m* 1935; three *s*. *Educ*: Epsom Coll.; Downing Coll., Cambridge (Exhib., Schol.); London Hosp. BA Cambridge (Nat. Sci. Tripos) 1929, MA 1934; MRCS, LRCP 1932; MB, BCh Cambridge 1934; FRCS 1933; MRCP 1935. London Hosp., 1929; Surg. First Asst, 1936. Served War of 1939–45; France, Surgical Specialist, 17th Gen. Hosp., 1939–40; Surgeon Specialist, RAMC Park Prewitt Plastic Unit, 1941–42; India, OC No 3 British Maxillo-Facial Surgical Unit and Lieut-Col OC Surgical Div., 1942–45; Surg. in charge of Dept of Plastic Surg., London Hosp., 1946–64. Cons. Surg. Worthing Hosp., Bethnal Green Hosp., and Plastic Unit Queen Victoria Hosp., East Grinstead, 1945; Plastic Surg. London Hosp.; Hon. Cons. Plastic Surg. Royal National and Golden Square Hosps, 1969. *Publications*: varied medical articles. *Recreations*: swimming, archæology. *Address*: Vainona, St George, Woodmancote, Henfield, West Sussex BN5 9ST. *T*: Brighton (0273) 492947.

HEAP, Sir Desmond, Kt 1970; LLM, Hon. LLD, PPRTPI; solicitor; *b* 17 Sept. 1907; *o s* of William Heap, Architect, Burnley, Lancs, and Minnie Heap; *m* 1945, Adelene Mai, *o d* of Frederick Lacey, Harrogate, and Mrs F. N. Hornby; one *s* two *d*. *Educ*: The Grammar Sch., Burnley; Victoria University of Manchester. LLB Hons 1929; LLM 1936; Hon. LLD 1973; admitted Solicitor, 1933; Hons Final Law Examination. Prosecuting Solicitor, 1935–38 and Chief Asst Solicitor for City of Leeds, 1938–40; Dep. Town Clerk of Leeds, 1940–47; Lecturer in the Law of Town and Country Planning and Housing, Leeds Sch. of Architecture, 1935–47; Comptroller and City Solicitor to the Corporation of London, 1947–73. Consultant: Hammond Suddards; Sugden & Spencer. Pres., Law Soc., 1972–73 (Mem. Council, 1954–78, Chm. Law Reform Cttee, 1955–60, and Chm., Town Planning Cttee, 1964–70). Legal Mem., RTPI (formerly TPI), 1935–, Mem. of Council, 1947–77, Pres., 1955–56; Assoc. Mem. Royal Institute of Chartered Surveyors, 1953–, Mem. of Council, 1957–84; Mem. of Colonial Office Housing and Town Planning Adv. Panel, 1953–65; Mem. of Editorial Board of Journal of Planning and Environment Law, 1948–; Mem., Council on Tribunals, 1971–77; Vice-Pres., Statute Law Soc., 1982–. Dep. Pres., City of London Branch, British Red Cross Soc., 1956–76. Chm. of Governors, Hurstpierpoint Coll., 1975–82. Senior Past Master, Worshipful Company of Solicitors (Hon. Associate, 1987); Liveryman of Worshipful Company of Carpenters. Hon. Mem., Court of Worshipful Co. of Chartered Surveyors. FRSA (Mem. Council, 1974–78). Hon. Member: Amer. Bar Foundn, 1971–; Hawaii Chapter, Phi Beta Kappa; Hon. Fellow, Inc. Soc. of Valuers and Auctioneers, 1979–. Gold Medal, RTPI, 1983; Gold Medal, Lincoln Inst. of Land Policy, Cambridge, Mass, 1983. *Publications*: Planning Law for Town and Country, 1938; Planning and the Law of Interim Development, 1944; The Town and Country Planning Act, 1944, 1945; An Outline of Planning Law, 1943 to 1945, 1945; The New Towns Act, 1946, 1947; Introducing the Town and Country Planning Act, 1947, 1947; Encyclopædia of Planning, Compulsory Purchase and Compensation, Vol. 1, 1949; An Outline of Planning Law, 1949, 9th edn 1987; Heap on the Town and Country Planning Act, 1954, 1955; Encyclopædia of Planning Law and Practice, 4 vols, 1960; Introducing the Land Commission Act 1967, 1967; Encyclopædia of Betterment Levy, 1967; The New Town Planning Procedures, 1969; How to Control Land Development, 1974, 2nd edn 1981; The Land and the Development; or, the Turmoil and the Torment (Hamlyn Lectures), 1975; Lectures on tape: The Community Land Act, 1975; articles in legal jls. *Recreations*: swimming, pedal biking, stage and theatre. *Address*: Hammond Suddards, 10 Piccadilly, Bradford BD1 3LR. *T*: Bradford (0274) 734700; Josephs Well, Hanover Walk, Leeds LS3 1AB. *T*: Leeds (0532) 450845; Sugden & Spencer, Arndale House, Charles Street, Bradford BD1 1ER. *T*: Bradford (0274) 732271. *Clubs*: Athenæum, City Livery, Guildhall.

HEAP, Dr John Arnfield, CMG 1991; Head, Polar Regions Section, South Atlantic and Antarctic Department, Foreign and Commonwealth Office, since 1975; Administrator, British Antarctic Territory, since 1989; *b* 5 Feb. 1932; *s* of late David and Ann Heap; *m* 1960, Margaret Grace Gillespie (*née* Spicer); one *s* two *d*. *Educ*: Leighton Park Sch.; Edinburgh Univ. (MA 1955); Clare Coll., Cambridge (PhD 1962). Falkland Islands Dependencies Survey, 1955–62; Res. Fellow, Dept of Geology, 1962–63, Great Lakes Res. Div., 1963–64, Univ. of Michigan; Polar Regions Section, FCO, 1964–. Mem., UK Delegns to Antarctic Treaty Consultative Meetings, 1966–. Editor, Handbook of the Antarctic Treaty System, 1977–. *Publication*: Sea Ice in the Antarctic, 1963. *Address*: The Old House, 25 High Street, Harston, Cambridge CB2 5PX. *T*: Cambridge (0223) 870288; Acharonich, Ulva Ferry, Isle of Mull. *T*: Ulva Ferry (06885) 219.

HEAP, Peter William, CMG 1987; HM Diplomatic Service; British Senior Trade Commissioner, Hong Kong, since 1989; *b* 13 April 1935; *s* of Roger and Dora Heap; *m* 1st, Helen Wilmerding; two *s* two *d*; 2nd, Dorrit Breitenstein; 3rd, 1986, Ann Johnson; one step *s* one step *d*. *Educ*: Bristol Cathedral Sch.; Merton Coll., Oxford. 2nd Lt Glos Regt and RWAFF, 1954–56. CRO, 1959; Third Sec., Dublin, 1960; Third and Second Sec., Ottawa, 1960; First Sec., Colombo, 1963–66; seconded to MoD, 1966–68; FO, 1968–71; Dep. Dir-Gen., British Information Services, New York, 1971–76; Counsellor (Political and Economic), 1976–78, Counsellor (Commercial), 1978–80, Caracas; Head of Energy, Science and Space Dept, FCO, 1980–83; High Comr to the Bahamas, 1983–86; Minister and Dep. High Comr, Lagos, 1986–89. *Address*: c/o Foreign and Commonwealth Office, King Charles Street, SW1A 2AL; 6 Carlisle Mansions, Carlisle Place, SW1.

HEAP, Prof. Robert Brian, FRS 1989; CChem, FRSC; FIBiol; Director, AFRC Institute of Animal Physiology and Genetics Research, Babraham, Cambridge, since 1989; *b* 27 Feb. 1935; *s* of late Bertram Heap and Eva Mary Heap (*née* Melling); *m* 1961, Marion Patricia Grant; two *s* one *d*. *Educ*: New Mills Grammar Sch.; Univ. of Nottingham (Chm. Students' Union, Sch. of Agric., 1958; BSc, PhD); King's Coll., Cambridge (MA, ScD).

Univ. Demonstrator, Cambridge, 1960; Lalor Res. Fellow, ARC Babraham, Cambridge, 1963; Staff Mem., AFRC Babraham, 1964–: Hd, Dept of Physiology, 1976; Hd, Cambridge Res. Station, 1986. Vis. Prof., Univ. of Nairobi, 1974; Vis. Res. Fellow, Murdoch Univ., 1976; Special Prof., Univ. of Nottingham, 1988; Vis. Prof., Univ. of Guelph, 1990. Scientific Advr, Merck, Sharp and Dohme, 1990–. Member Committee: Soc. for Study of Fertility, 1967–72 (Treas. 1968–71); Jls of Reproduction and Fertility Ltd (Associate Ed., 1964–72; Council of Management, 1965–73, 1986–; Exec., 1988–); Bibliography of Reproduction, 1967–70; Soc. and Jl of Endocrinology, 1980–84 (Sci. Ed., 1977–82); Placenta (Associate Ed., 1980–); Oxford Reviews of Reproductive Biology, 1981–. Consultant: WHO, Geneva, 1975–82; China, 1981–85. Chairman: Ciba Foundn Symposium, 1978; Harden Conf., 1984. Hammond Lecture, Soc. for Study of Fertility, 1986. Research Medallist, RASE, 1976; Inventor's Award, AFRC, 1980. Publications: sci. papers on reproductive biology, endocrinology, growth and lactation, in various biol and med. jls. Recreations: music, walking, travel. Address: Lincoln House, 8 Fendon Road, Cambridge CB1 4RT.

HEARD, Peter Graham, CB 1987; FRICS; IRRV; Deputy Chief Valuer, Valuation Office, Board of Inland Revenue, 1983–89; b 22 Dec. 1929; s of late Sidney Horwood Heard and Doris Winifred Heard, MBE; m 1953, Ethne Jean Thomas; two d. Educ: Exmouth Grammar School. Articled to W. W. Needham, 1946; joined Valuation Office, 1950; served in Exeter, Kidderminster, Dudley, Leeds; District Valuer, Croydon, 1971; Superintending Valuer, Chief Valuer's Office, 1973; Asst Sec., Bd of Inland Revenue, 1975; Superintending Valuer, Midlands, 1977; Asst Chief Valuer, 1978. Recreations: cricket, golf, countryside, walking the dog, theatre. Address: Romany Cottage, High Street, Lindfield, Sussex. T: Lindfield (0444) 482095. Clubs: MCC, Civil Service.

HEARN, Barry Maurice William, FCA; Chairman, Matchroom Ltd, since 1982; b 19 June 1948; s of George Sydney and Barbara Winifred Hearn; m 1970, Susan Clark; one s one d. Educ: Buckhurst Hill Grammar School. Publication: The Business, 1990. Recreations: cricket, marathons, fishing, snooker. Address: Matchroom Ltd, 10 Western Road, Romford, Essex RM1 3JT. T: Romford (0708) 730480.

HEARN, David Anthony; General Secretary, Broadcasting Entertainment and Cinematograph Technicians' Union, since 1991 (General Secretary, 1984–90, Joint General Secretary, 1984–87, Broadcasting and Entertainment Trades Alliance); b 4 March 1929; s of James Wilfrid Laurier Hearn and Clara (née Barlow); m 1952, Anne Beveridge; two s. Educ: Trinity Coll., Oxford (MA). Asst to Gen. Sec., Assoc. of Broadcasting Staff, 1955; subseq. Asst Gen. Sec., then Dep. Gen. Sec.; Gen. Sec., Assoc. of Broadcasting and Allied Staffs, 1972–84. Chm., Film and Electronic Media Cttee, Fedn of Entertainment Unions, 1991–; Mem., British Screen Adv. Council; Gen. Sec., W European Sect., Internat. Fedn of Audio Visual Unions, 1984–. Sen. Res. Fellow, Nuffield Coll., Oxford, 1970–71. Address: 4 Stocks Tree Close, Yarnton, Oxford OX5 1LU. T: Kidlington (08675) 4613.

HEARN, Donald Peter; Secretary, since 1989, Finance Director, since 1986, Royal Horticultural Society; b 2 Nov. 1947; s of Peter James Hearn and Anita Margaret Hearn; m 1973, Rachel Mary Arnold; two d. Educ: Clifton College; Selwyn College, Cambridge (MA). FCA. Ernst & Whinney, 1969–79; Group Financial Controller, Saga Holidays, 1979–83; Chief Financial Officer, Lee Valley Water Co., 1983–86. Gen. Comr for Taxes, 1990–. Governor, Woldingham Sch., 1990–. Recreations: gardening, running. Address: Royal Horticultural Society, Vincent Square, SW1P 2PE. T: 071-834 4333.

HEARN, Rear-Adm. Frank Wright, CB 1977; Assistant Chief of Personnel and Logistics, Ministry of Defence, 1974–77; b 1 Oct. 1919; s of John Henry Hearn, Civil Servant, and Elsie Gertrude Hearn; m 1st, 1947, Ann Cynthia Keeble (d 1964); two d; 2nd, 1965, Ann Christina June St Clair Miller. Educ: Abbotsholme Sch., Derbyshire. Joined RN, 1937; HMS Hood, 1937–39. Served War of 1939–45 in various HM Ships in Atlantic, Mediterranean and East Indies. Staff of CinC, Home Fleet, 1951–53; Sec. to Flag Officer, Submarines, 1954–56; after service in USA became Sec. to Dir of Naval Intell., 1958–60, when joined HMS Tiger as Supply Officer; Fleet Supply Officer, Western Fleet, 1962–64; subseq. service in Plans Div, MoD (Navy) and CSO (Admin.) to Flag Officer, Submarines; IDC 1969; commanded HMS Centurion in rank of Cdre, 1970–73; Chm., Review of Officer Structure Cttee, 1973–74. Recreations: golf, tennis, gardening, wine-making. Address: Hurstbrook Cottage, Hollybank Lane, Emsworth, Hants PO10 7UE. T: Emsworth (0243) 372149.

HEARN, Rt. Rev. George Arthur; see Rockhampton, Bishop of.

HEARN, Prof. John Patrick; Director, Wisconsin Regional Primate Research Center and Professor in Physiology, Medical School, University of Wisconsin-Madison, since 1989; b Limbdi, India, 24 Feb. 1943; s of Lt-Col Hugh Patrick Hearn, Barrister, and Cynthia Ellen (née Nicholson); m 1967, Margaret Ruth Patricia McNair; four s one d. Educ: Crusaders' Sch., Headley, Hants; St Mary's Sch., Nairobi, Kenya; University Coll., Dublin (BSc, MSc); ANU, Canberra (PhD). Sen. Demonstrator in Zool., University Coll., Dublin, 1966–67; Lectr in Zool., 1967–69, and Dean of Science, 1968–69, Strathmore Coll., Nairobi; Res. Scholar, ANU, 1969–72; Staff Mem., MRC Reproductive Biology Unit, Edinburgh, 1972–79; Hon. Fellow, Univ. of Edinburgh, 1974–79; Consultant Scientist, WHO Special Prog. of Res. in Human Reproduction, Geneva, 1978–79; Zoological Society of London: Dir, Wellcome Labs of Comparative Physiology, 1979–80; Dir of Science and Dir, Inst. of Zool., 1980–87; Hon. Research Fellow, 1987–; Dep. Sec., AFRC, 1987–90; Dir, MRC/AFRC Comparative Physiology Res. Gp, 1983–89. Vis. Prof. in Biology (formerly in Zoology), UCL, 1979–; Vis. Prof., New England Primate Res. Center, Harvard Univ. Med. Sch., 1989–91. Pres., Internat. Primatological Soc., 1984–88. Scientific Medal, Zool Soc. London, 1983; Osman Hill Medal, Primate Soc. of GB, 1986. Publications: (ed with H. Rothe and H. Wolters) The Biology and Behaviour of Marmosets, 1978; (ed) Immunological Aspects of Reproduction and Fertility Control, 1980; (ed) Reproduction in New World Primates, 1982; (ed) Advances in Animal Conservation, 1985; (ed) Reproduction and Disease in Captive and Wild Animals, 1988; papers on develtl and reproductive physiol. in scientific jls. Recreations: music, travel, wildlife, squash, running, swimming. Address: Wisconsin Regional Primate Research Center, 1223 Capitol Court, Madison, Wisconsin 53715–1299, USA. T: (608) 263 3500, Fax: 263 3041. Club: Athenæum.

HEARNE, Graham James, CBE 1990; Chief Executive, Enterprise Oil plc, since 1984; b 23 Nov. 1937; s of Frank Hearne and Emily (née Shakespeare); m 1961, Carol Jean (née Brown); one s two d (and one d decd). Educ: George Dixon Grammar Sch., Birmingham. Admitted solicitor, 1959: Pinsent & Co., Solicitors, 1959–63; Fried, Frank, Harris, Shriver & Jacobson, Attorneys, NYC, 1963–66; Herbert Smith & Co., Solicitors, 1966–67; IRC, 1967–70; N. M. Rothschild & Sons Ltd, 1970–77; Finance Dir, Courtaulds Ltd, 1977–81; Chief Exec., Tricentrol, 1981–83; Gp Man. Dir, Carless, Capel and Leonard, 1983–84. Non-exec. Director: N. M. Rothschild & Sons Ltd, 1973–; Northern Foods, Ltd, 1976–82; BPB Industries, 1982–; Reckitt & Colman, 1990–; part-time Member: British National Oil Corp., 1975–78; Dover Harbour Bd, 1976–78. Chm., Brindex (Assoc. of British Indep. Oil Exploration Cos), 1986–88; Mem. Council, UK Offshore Operators Assoc.

Ltd, 1985–. Trustee: Philharmonia Orch. Trust, 1982–; Chichester Fest. Theatre Trust, 1988–. Address: 8 Church Row, NW3 6UT. T: 071–794 4987. Clubs: Reform, MCC.

HEARNE, Peter Ambrose; FEng 1984; President (US Operations), GEC Marconi, since 1990; b 14 Nov. 1927; e s of late Arthur Ambrose Hearne, MD, and Helen Mackay Hearne; m 1952, Georgina Gordon Guthrie; three s. Educ: Sherborne Sch., Dorset; Loughborough Coll. of Technol. (DLC); Cranfield Inst. of Technol. (MSc); MIT. Design Engr, Saunders Roe, 1946–47; Ops Develt Engr, BOAC, 1949–54; Helicopter Proj. Engr, BEA, 1954–58; Marketing Manager, British Oxygen, 1958–59; Divl Man., Guided Weapons, Elliott Flt Automation, 1959; Asst Gen. Man., 1960; Dir and Gen. Man., 1965–70; Dir and Gen. Manager, 1970–87, Marconi (later GEC) Avionics; Asst Man. Dir, GEC Marconi, 1987–90. Vis. Prof., Cranfield Inst. of Technol., 1981–82. Chm., Cranfield Soc., 1965–67, Pres., 1981–88; Pres., Royal Aeronautical Society, 1980–81 (Vice-Pres., 1976–79). John Curtis Sword, Aviation Week, 1982; Diamond C badge, 1988. Publications: papers in Jl of RAeS and NATO Agard series. Recreations: flying with and without engines, sailing, model railways. Address: 108 Quay Street, Alexandria, Va 22314, USA; Les Lys, Tallard, France. Clubs: Surrey and Hants Gliding; Southwold Sailing; Aero Alpin (Gap).

HEARST, Stephen, CBE 1980; FRSA; independent television producer, since 1986; b Vienna, Austria, 6 Oct. 1919; m 1948, Lisbeth Edith Neumann; one s one d. Educ: Vienna Univ.; Reading Univ. (Dip. Hort.); Brasenose Coll., Oxford (MA). Free lance writer, 1949–52; joined BBC as producer trainee, 1952; Documentary television: script writer, 1953–55; writer producer, 1955–65; Exec. Producer, Arts Programmes Television, 1965–67; Head of Arts Features, Television, 1967–71; Controller, Radio 3, 1972–78; Controller, Future Policy Gp, 1978–82; Special Adviser to Dir-Gen., BBC, 1982–86. Vis. Fellow, Inst. for Advanced Studies, Edinburgh Univ., 1988. FRSA 1980. Publications: Two Thousand Million Poor, 1965; Artistic Heritage and its Treatment by Television, 1982; contrib. to The Third Age of Broadcasting (ed Wenham), 1982. Recreations: gardening, swimming, reading, listening to music. Address: c/o British Academy of Film and Television Arts, 195 Piccadilly, W1.

HEARST, William Randolph, Jun.; journalist; Editor-in-Chief, The Hearst Newspapers, and Chairman of the Executive Committee, The Hearst Corporation; b NYC, 27 Jan. 1908; s of William Randolph Hearst and Millicent Veronica (née Willson); m 1st, 1928, Alma Walker (marr. diss., 1932); 2nd, 1933, Lorelle McCarver (marr. diss., 1948); 3rd, 1948, Austine McDonnell (d 1991); two s. Educ: Collegiate Sch.; St John's Manlius Mil. Acad., Syracuse; Berkeley High Sch., Berkeley, Calif.; Hitchcock Mil. Acad., San Rafael, Calif; University of Calif. Began career with New York American, NYC, as a reporter, 1928; publisher, 1936–37; publisher, NY Journal-American, 1937–56; The American Weekly, 1945–56; War Correspondent, 1943–45. Mem. Bd, USO, NY; Permanent Charter Mem., For. Correspondents Club of Japan, 1945–. Address: (office) 959 Eighth Avenue, New York, NY 10019, USA. Clubs: Overseas Press, Madison Square Garden, Knickerbocker (New York City); Waccabuc (N Salem, NY); Pacific Union (San Francisco); London Press; Alaska Press; Tokyo Press.

HEARTH, John Dennis Miles, CBE 1983; Chief Executive, Royal Agricultural Society of England, 1972–89; b 8 April 1929; s of late Cyril Howard Hearth, MC, and Dr Pauline Kathleen Hearth, MB, BSc; m 1959, Pamela Anne (née Bryant); two s (one d decd). Educ: The King's Sch., Canterbury; Brasenose Coll., Oxford (MA). Called to the Bar, Gray's Inn, 1962. Administrative Officer, HM Overseas Civil Service, 1953–61; Editor, Fairplay Shipping Journal, Fairplay Publications Ltd, 1961–66; Cunard Steam-Ship Co. Ltd, 1966–71 (various appts and Main Board Joint Ventures Director, 1969–71). Mem., Gen. Adv. Council, BBC, 1990–; Chairman: Rural and Agricl Affairs Cttee, BBC, 1990–; Rural Enterprise Unit, RASE, 1988–; Management Cttee, Nat. Fedn of Young Farmers' Clubs, 1989–. Pres., Nat. Pig Breeders' Assoc., 1990–91. Mem. Council, Conservation Foundn, 1987–; Trustee, Rural Housing Trust (formerly NAC Rural Trust), 1987–; English Villages Housing Assoc., 1990–. Governor, RAC, Cirencester, 1975–; Mem., 1985–, Treasurer, 1989–, Warwick Univ. Council. CBIM 1980. Recreations: travel, history, theatre, golf. Address: Bayard's, Fenny Compton, near Leamington Spa, Warwicks CV33 0XY. T: Fenny Compton (029577) 370. Clubs: Farmers', Anglo-Belgian.

HEASLIP, Rear-Adm. Richard George, CB 1987; Director-General, English-Speaking Union, 1987–90; b 30 April 1932; s of Eric Arthur Heaslip and Vera Margaret (née Bailey); m 1959, Lorna Jean Grayston, Halifax, NS, Canada; three s one d (incl. twin s and d). Educ: Royal Naval Coll., Dartmouth. CO HMS Sea Devil, 1961–62; Exec. Officer, HMS Dreadnought (1st British nuclear submarine), 1965–66; CO HMS Conqueror (nuclear submarine), 1971–72; CO Second Submarine Sqdn, 1975–77; Staff, SACLANT, 1980–82; Staff, CDS, 1982–84; Dep. Asst COS (Ops), Staff of SACEUR, 1984; Flag Officer Submarines, and Comdr Submarine Forces Eastern Atlantic, 1984–87. ADC 1984–85. Member: European Atlantic Gp Cttee, 1988–89; Bureau, Standing Conf. of Atlantic Orgns, 1988–89. Chm., RN Football Assoc., 1976–84. Recreations: walking, music, gardening. Address: South Winds, Wallis Road, Waterlooville, Hants PO7 7RX. T: Portsmouth (0705) 241679.

HEATH, Prof. Bernard Oliver, OBE 1980; CEng, FRAeS; Professor of Aeronautical Engineering (British Aerospace Integrated Chair), Salford University, 1983–89; b 8 March 1925; s of Bernard Ernest Heath and Ethel May Heath; m 1948, Ethel Riley; one s. Educ: Derby Sch.; Bemrose Sch., Derby; University Coll. of Nottingham (BSc Univ. of London 1944); Imperial Coll. of Science and Technology (DIC 1945). CEng 1966; FRAeS 1978; HMIED 1975. English Electric Co.: Stressman (loading and stressing of Canberra), 1945; Aerodynamicist, Lightning, 1948; Aerostructures Gp Leader, 1951; Chief Proj. Engr, 1957; Asst Chief Engr, Canberra and TSR2, 1959; British Aircraft Corporation: TSR2 Proj. Manager (Develt), 1963; Special Dir, 1965; Leader, Jaguar Technical Team, 1965; Proj. Manager, AFVG, 1966; Panavia: Dir, Systems Engrg (Warton), 1969–81; Dir, MRCA, 1970; Dir of Engrg, 1974; British Aerospace: Technical Dir, Warton Div., 1978–81; Divisional Dir of Advanced Engrg, 1981–84. Chm., SBAC Technical Bd, 1980–82. RAeS Silver Medal (for outstanding work over many yrs on design and develt of mil. aircraft), 1977; (jtly) Internat. Council of Aeronautical Sciences Von Karman Award (for successful internat. co-operation on Tornado), 1982. Publications: papers to Internat. Council of Aeronautical Sciences Congresses; contrib. RAeS Jl, Flight, The Times, R & D Mgt and Aircraft Engrg. Recreation: history of transport. Address: c/o Company Secretary, British Aerospace, Warton Aerdrome, Preston, Lancs PR4 1AX.

HEATH, Edward Peter, OBE 1946; b 6 June 1914; a Deputy Chairman, Inchcape & Co. Ltd, 1976–79; m 1953, Eleanor Christian Peck; one s three d. Educ: St Lawrence Coll., Ramsgate. Joined Borneo Co. Ltd, 1934; interned in Thailand, 1941–45. Gen. Manager, Borneo Co. Ltd, 1953–63; a Man. Dir, 1963–67; a Man. Dir, Inchcape & Co. Ltd, 1967–75. Director: Mann Egerton & Co. Ltd, 1973–79; Dodwell & Co. Ltd, 1974–79; Inchcape Far East Ltd, 1972–79; Chairman: Toyota GB and Pride & Clark, 1978–79; Anglo-Thai Corp. Ltd, 1978–79; Dep. Chm., Bewac Motor Corp., 1970–79. Consultant, Matheson & Co. Ltd, 1980–83; Director: Matheson Motor Hldgs, 1981–83; Lancaster Gp Hldgs, 1981–83. Dep. Chairman: Hong Kong Assoc., 1975–79; Anglo Thai Soc.,

1975–85. Order of White Elephant (5th Cl.) (Thailand); Officer, Order of Orange Nassau (Netherlands). *Recreations:* hunting, gardening, motoring. *Address:* Cooks Place, Albury, Guildford, Surrey GU5 9BJ. *T:* Shere (048641) 2698.

HEATH, Rt. Hon. Edward Richard George, PC 1955; MBE 1946; MP (C) Old Bexley and Sidcup, since 1983 (Bexley, 1950–74; Bexley, Sidcup, 1974–83); Member, Public Review Board, Arthur Andersen & Co., since 1978; *b* Broadstairs, Kent, 9 July 1916; *s* of late William George and Edith Anne Heath. *Educ:* Chatham House Sch., Ramsgate; Balliol Coll., Oxford (Scholar; Hon. Fellow, 1969). Scholar, Gray's Inn, 1938 (Hon. Bencher, 1972). Pres. Oxford Univ. Conservative Assoc., 1937; Chm. Federation of Univ. Conservative Assocs, 1938; Pres. Oxford Union, 1939; Oxford Union debating tour of American Univs, 1939–40; Pres. Federation of University Conservative and Unionist Associations, 1959–77, Hon. Life Patron, 1977. Served War of 1939–45 (despatches, MBE); in Army, 1940–46, in France, Belgium, Holland and Germany; gunner in RA, 1940; Major 1945. Lieut-Col comdg 2nd Regt HAC, TA, April 1947–Aug. 1951; Master Gunner within the Tower of London, 1951–54. Administrative Civil Service, 1946–47 resigning to become prospective candidate for Bexley. Asst Conservative Whip, Feb. 1951; Lord Commissioner of the Treasury, Nov. 1951, and Joint Deputy Govt Chief Whip, 1952, and Dep. Govt Chief Whip, 1953–55; Parliamentary Sec. to the Treasury, and Government Chief Whip, Dec. 1955–Oct. 1959; Minister of Labour, Oct. 1959–July 1960; Lord Privy Seal, with Foreign Office responsibilities, 1960–63; Sec. of State for Industry, Trade, Regional Development and Pres. of the Board of Trade, Oct. 1963–Oct. 1964; Leader of the Opposition, 1965–70; Prime Minister and First Lord of the Treasury, 1970–74; Leader of the Opposition, 1974–75. Chm., Commonwealth Parly Assoc., 1970–74. Mem., Indep. Commn on Internat. Development Issues, 1977–79. Mem. Council, Royal College of Music, 1961–70; Chm., London Symphony Orchestra Trust, 1963–70; Vice-Pres., Bach Choir, 1970–; Pres., European Community Youth Orchestra, 1977–80; Hon. Mem., LSO, 1974–. Smith-Mundt Fellowship, USA, 1953; Vis. Fellow, Nuffield Coll., Oxford, 1962–70, Hon. Fellow, 1970; Chubb Fellow, Yale, 1975; Montgomery Fellow, Dartmouth Coll., 1980. Lectures: Cyril Foster Meml, Oxford, 1965; Godkin, Harvard, 1966; Montagu Burton, Leeds, 1976; Edge, Princeton, 1976; Romanes, Oxford, 1976; Ishizaka, Japan, 1979; Felix Neubergh, Gothenburg, 1979, 10th STC Communication, London, 1980, Noel Buxton, Univ. of Essex, 1980; Alastair Buchan Meml, London, 1980; Hoover, Univ. of Strathclyde, 1980; Stanton Griffis Disting., Cornell Univ., 1981; Edwin Stevens, RSM, 1981; William Temple, York, 1981; City of London, Chartered Insce Inst., 1982; John Findley Green, Westminster Coll., Missouri, 1982; Mizuno, Tokyo, 1982; ITT European, Brussels, 1982; Bruce Meml, Keele Univ., 1982; Gaitskell, Univ. of Nottingham, 1983; Trinity Univ., San Antonio, 1983; lect. to mark opening Michael Fowler Centre, Wellington, NZ, 1983; Bridge Meml, Guildhall, 1984; David R. Calhoun Jr Meml, Washington Univ., St Louis, 1984; Corbishley Meml, RSA, 1984; John Rogers Meml, Llandudno, 1985; George Woodcock, Univ. of Leicester, 1985; RIIA, 1985; John F. Kennedy Meml, Oxford, 1986; Edward Boyle Meml, RSA, 1988. Liveryman, Goldsmiths' Co., 1966; Hon. Freeman, Musicians' Co., 1973. Hon. FRCM; Hon. FRCO; Hon. Fellow, Royal Canadian Coll. of Organists. Hon. DCL: Oxon, 1971; Kent, 1985; Hon. DTech Bradford, 1971; Hon. LLD Westminster Coll., Salt Lake City, 1975; Dr *hc* Univ. of Paris, Sorbonne, 1976; Hon. Dr of Public Admin, Wesleyan Coll., Macon, Ga, 1981; Hon. DL, Westminster Coll., Fulton, Missouri, 1982. Charlemagne Prize, 1963; Estes J. Kefauver Prize 1971; Stresseman Gold Medal, 1971; Freiherr Von Stein Foundn Prize, 1972; Gold Medal of City of Paris, 1978; World Humanity Award, 1980; Gold Medal, European Parlt, 1981. Winner, Sydney to Hobart Ocean Race, 1969; Captain: Britain's Admiral's Cup Team, 1971, 1979; Britain's Sardinia Cup Team, 1980. *Publications:* (joint) One Nation—a Tory approach to social problems, 1950; Old World, New Horizons (Godkin Lectures), 1970; Sailing: a course of my life, 1975; Music: a joy for life, 1976; Travels: people and places in my life, 1977; Carols: the joy of Christmas, 1977. *Recreations:* sailing, music. *Address:* House of Commons, SW1. *Clubs:* Buck's, Carlton, St Stephen's Constitutional (Jt Pres., 1979–88); Royal Yacht Squadron.

HEATH, Henry Wylde Edwards, CMG 1963; QPM; Commissioner of Police, Hong Kong, 1959–67, retired; *b* 18 March 1912; *s* of late Dr W. G. Heath and late Mrs L. B. Heath; *m* Joan Mildred Crichett; two *s* one *d*. *Educ:* Dean Close Sch.; HMS Conway. Probationer Sub-Inspector of Police, Leeward Islands, 1931; Asst Supt, Hong Kong, 1934; Superintendent, 1944; Asst Commissioner, 1950. Colonial Police Medal, 1953; QPM, 1957. *Recreations:* golf, ski-ing. *Address:* Quintynes Cottage, 4 Firle Drive, Seaford, Sussex BN25 2HT. *Clubs:* Seaford Golf; Kandahar Ski.

HEATH, Prof. John Baldwin; management consultant; Chairman, EXE Ltd, since 1982; *b* 25 Sept. 1924; *s* of late Thomas Arthur Heath and late Dorothy Meallin; *m* 1953, Wendy Julia Betts; two *s* one *d*. *Educ:* Merchant Taylors' Sch.; St Andrews Univ.; Cambridge Univ. RNVR, 1942–46. Spicers Ltd, 1946–50; Lecturer in Economics, Univ. of Manchester, 1956–64; Rockefeller Foundation Fellowship, 1961–62; Dir, Economic Research Unit, Bd of Trade, 1964–67; Dir, Economic Services Div., BoT, 1967–70; Prof. of Economics, London Business Sch., 1970–86; Dir, London Sloan Fellowship Programme, 1983–86. Member: Mechanical Engrg EDC, 1971–76; British Airports Authy, 1980–86; Economic Adviser, CAA, 1972–78. *Publications:* Public Enterprise at the Crossroads, 1990; articles in many learned jls on competition and monopoly, productivity, cost-benefit analysis. *Recreations:* music, walking. *Address:* 27 Chalcot Square, NW1 8YA. *T:* 071–722 4301.

HEATH, John Moore, CMG 1976; HM Diplomatic Service, retired; *b* 9 May 1922; *s* of late Philip George and Olga Heath; *m* 1952, Patricia Mary Bibby; one *s* one *d*. *Educ:* Shrewsbury Sch.; Merton Coll., Oxford (MA). Served War of 1939–45, France, Belgium and Germany: commnd Inns of Court Regt, 1942; Capt. GSO3 11th Armoured Div., 1944–45 (despatches). Merton Coll., 1940–42, 1946–47. Entered Foreign Service, 1950; 2nd Sec., Comr-Gen.'s Office, Singapore, 1950–52; 1st Sec. (Commercial), Jedda, 1952–56; 1st Sec., FO, 1956–58; Nat. Def. Coll., Kingston, Ont., 1958–59; Head of Chancery and HM Consul, Brit. Embassy, Mexico City, 1959–62; Head of Chancery, Brit. Embassy, Kabul, Afghanistan, 1963–65; Counsellor and Head of Establishment and Organisation Dept, FCO (formerly DSAO), 1966–69; Counsellor (Commercial), Brit. Embassy, Bonn, 1969–74; Overseas Trade Advr, Assoc. of British Chambers of Commerce, on secondment, 1974; Consul-Gen., Chicago, 1975–79; Ambassador to Chile, 1980–82. Dir Gen., Canning House (Hispanic and Luso-Brazilian Council), 1982–87. Orden al Merito por Servicios Distinguidos, Peru, 1984. *Recreations:* walking, travel. *Address:* 6 Cavendish Crescent, Bath, Avon BA1 2UG. *Club:* Naval and Military.

HEATH, Sir Mark, KCVO 1980; CMG 1980; Minister, then Ambassador, to the Holy See, 1980–85; *b* 22 May 1927; *m* 1954, Margaret Alice Bragg; two *s* one *d*. *Educ:* Marlborough; Queens' Coll., Cambridge. RNVR, 1945–48. HM Foreign (subseq. Diplomatic) Service, 1950–85; served in Indonesia, Denmark, Bulgaria, Canada, France; with Hong Kong Government, 1985–88. Chm., Friends of Anglican Centre, Rome, 1984–90. Mem., Adv. Council, CARE, 1986–. *Address:* St Lawrence, Lansdown Road, Bath, Avon BA1 5TD. *Clubs:* Athenæum, Nikaean.

HEATH, Air Marshal Sir Maurice (Lionel), KBE 1962 (OBE 1946); CB 1957; CVO 1978; DL; Gentleman Usher to the Queen, 1966–79, Extra Gentleman Usher to the Queen since 1979; *b* 12 Aug. 1909; *s* of Lionel Heath, Artist and Principal of the Mayo Sch. of Arts, Lahore, India; *m* 1st, 1938, Kathleen Mary (*d* 1988), *d* of Boaler Gibson, Bourne, Lincs; one *s* one *d*; 2nd, 1989, Lisa, *widow* of Col J. M. B. Cooke, MC. *Educ:* Sutton Valence Sch.; Cranwell. Commissioned RAF, 1929; service with Nos 16 and 28 Squadrons; Specialist Armament duties, 1933–42; Chief Instructor, No 1 Air Armament Sch., 1942; Station Commander, Metheringham, No 5 Group, Bomber Comd, 1944 (despatches). Dep. to Dir-Gen. of Armament, Air Min., 1946–48; CO Central Gunnery Sch., 1948–49; Sen. Air Liaison Officer, Wellington, NZ, 1950–52; CO Bomber Comd Bombing Sch., 1952–53; idc, 1954; Dir of Plans, Air Min., 1955; Deputy Air Secretary, Air Ministry, 1955–57; Commander, British Forces, Arabian Peninsula, 1957–59; Commandant, RAF Staff Coll., 1959–61; Chief of Staff, HQ Allied Air Forces Central Europe, 1962–65, retd. Dir, Boyd and Boyd, Estate Agents, 1971–76; Private Agent, Henderson Financial Management, 1980–89. Chief Hon. Steward, Westminster Abbey, 1965–74. Appeal Dir, Voluntary Res. Trust, King's Coll. Hosp. and Med. Sch., 1977–79, Appeal Consultant, 1979–84; Pres., Storrington Br., RAFA, 1966–84, Life Vice Pres., 1984–. DL West Sussex, 1977. *Recreations:* sailing, golf and travel. *Address:* Heronscroft, Rambledown Lane, West Chiltington, Pulborough, Sussex RH20 2NW. *Club:* Royal Air Force.

HEATH, Michael John; freelance cartoonist, since 1956; Cartoons Editor, The Spectator, since 1989; *b* 13 Oct. 1935; *s* of George Heath and Alice (Queenie) Stewert Morrison Bremner; *m* 1959, Hanne Sternkopf; two *d*. *Educ:* no education to speak of (Devon, Hampstead and Brighton); Brighton Art Coll. Trained as animator, Rank Screen Services, 1955; started placing cartoons in Melody Maker, 1955; contributed to: Lilliput; Tatler; John Bull; Man about Town; Men Only; Honey; Punch, 1958–89; Spectator, 1958–; Private Eye, 1964– (strips include The Gays, The Regulars, Great Bores of Today, Baby); Sunday Times, 1967–; London Standard, 1976–86; Mail on Sunday, 1985–; The Independent, 1986–; London Daily News, 1987. Pocket Cartoonist of the Year, Cartoonist Club of GB, 1977; Glen Grant Cartoonist of the Year, 1978; What the Papers Say Cartoonist of the Year, 1982. *Publications:* Private Eye Cartoon Library, 1973, 2nd edn 1975; The Punch Cartoons of Michael Heath, 1976; Book of Bores, No 1, 1976, No 2, Star Bores, 1979, No 3, Bores Three, 1983; Love All, 1982; Best of Heath (foreword by Malcolm Muggeridge), 1984; Welcome to America, 1985. *Recreations:* listening to Charlie Parker and Thelonious Monk, walking. *Address:* 1 Bassett Chambers, 27 Bedfordbury, Covent Garden, WC2H 9AU. *T:* 071–397 0087. *Clubs:* Punch Table, Wig and Pen, Scribes.

HEATH, Maj.-Gen. Michael Stuart, CBE 1991; CEng, FIEE; Director General, Electrical and Mechanical Engineering, Ministry of Defence, since 1991; *b* 7 Sept. 1940; *s* of Bernard Stuart Heath and Blanche Dorothy Ellen Heath (*née* Fairey); *m* 1965, Frances Wood; one *s* one *d*. *Educ:* St Albans Sch.; Welbeck Coll.; Royal Military Coll. of Science (BSc Eng 2nd cl. Hons London). Commissioned REME, 1961; served Malaya, BAOR, Edinburgh, to 1971; RMCS and Staff Coll., 1972–73; Armour Sch., Bovington, 1974–75; Comd 7 Field Workshop, BAOR, 1976–77; Nat. Defence Coll., 1978; Berlin Field Force, 1978–80; Comd Maint., HQ 2 Armd Div., BAOR, 1981–82; MoD, 1982–85; RCDS, 1986; Dir, Support Planning (Army), MoD, 1987–89; Comd Maint., HQ BAOR, 1990–91. FBIM. *Recreations:* walking, music, photography, restoring antique furniture. *Address:* c/o Barclays Bank, 167 High Street, Bromley, Kent BR1 1NL. *Clubs:* Army and Navy, Commonwealth Trust.

HEATH, Oscar Victor Sayer, FRS 1960; DSc (London); Professor of Horticulture, University of Reading, 1958–69, now Emeritus; *b* 26 July 1903; *s* of late Sir (Henry) Frank Heath, GBE, KCB, and Frances Elaine (*née* Sayer); *m* 1930, Sarah Margery, (*d* 1984), *d* of Stephen Bumstead, Guestling, Hastings; two *s* one *d*. *Educ:* Imperial Coll., London (Forbes Medallist), Fellow, 1973. Asst Demonstrator in Botany, Imperial Coll., 1925–26; Empire Cotton Growing Corp. Sen. Studentship, Imperial Coll. of Tropical Agriculture, Trinidad, 1926–27; Plant Physiologist, Empire Cotton Growing Corp., Cotton Experiment Station, Barberton, S Africa, 1927–36; Research Student, Imperial Coll., London, 1936–39; Leverhulme Research Fellow, 1937–39; Research Asst, 1939–40, and Mem. of Staff, Research Inst. of Plant Physiology of Imperial Coll., Rothamsted, 1940–46, London, 1946–58; Sen. Principal Scientific Officer, 1948–58; Special Lectr in Plant Physiology, Imperial Coll., 1945–58; Dir, ARC Unit of Flower Crop Physiology, 1962–70; Mem. ARC, 1965–70; Leverhulme Emeritus Res. Fellow, 1970–72. *Publications:* chapters on physiology of leaf stomata in Encyclopædia of Plant Physiology (ed Ruhland) 1959, in Plant Physiology: a Treatise (ed Steward), 1959, and (with T. A. Mansfield) in Physiology of Plant Growth (ed Wilkins), 1969; The Physiological Aspects of Photosynthesis, 1969 (trans. German, 1972, Russian, 1972); Investigation by Experiment, 1970 (trans. Spanish, 1977, Portuguese, 1981); Stomata, 1975, 2nd edn 1981; papers in scientific jls. *Address:* 10 St Peter's Grove, W6 9AZ. *T:* 081–748 0471.

HEATH-STUBBS, John (Francis Alexander), OBE 1989; poet; Lecturer in English Literature, College of St Mark and St John, Chelsea, 1963–73; *b* 9 July 1918; *s* of Francis Heath Stubbs and Edith Louise Sara (*née* Marr). *Educ:* Bembridge School; Worcester Coll. for the Blind, and privately; Queen's Coll., Oxford. English Master, Hall Sch., Hampstead, 1944–45; Editorial Asst, Hutchinson's, 1945–46; Gregory Fellow in Poetry, Leeds Univ., 1952–55; Vis. Prof. of English: University of Alexandria, 1955–58; University of Michigan, 1960–61. FRSL 1953. Queen's Gold Medal for Poetry, 1973; Oscar Williams/Jean Durwood Award, 1977; Cholmondeley Award, 1989; Commonwealth Poetry Prize, 1989; Howard Sargeant Award, 1989. *Publications: verse:* Wounded Thammuz, 1942; Beauty and the Beast, 1943; The Divided Ways, 1946; The Swarming of the Bees, 1950; A Charm against the Toothache, 1954; The Triumph of the Muse, 1958; The Blue Fly in his Head, 1962; Selected Poems, 1965; Satires and Epigrams, 1968; Artorius, 1973; A Parliament of Birds, 1975; The Watchman's Flute, 1978; Mouse, the Bird and the Sausage, 1978; Birds Reconvened, 1980; Buzz Buzz, 1981; Naming the Beasts, 1982; The Immolation of Aleph, 1985; Cats' Parnassus, 1987; Time Pieces, 1988; Collected Poems, 1988; A Partridge in a Pear Tree, 1988; A Ninefold of Charms, 1989; Selected Poems, 1990; *drama:* Helen in Egypt, 1958; *criticism:* The Darkling Plain, 1950; Charles Williams, 1955; The Pastoral, 1969; The Ode, 1969; The Verse Satire, 1969; *translations:* (with Peter Avery) Hafiz of Shiraz, 1952; (with Iris Origo) Leopardi, Selected Prose and Poetry, 1966; (with Carol A. Whiteside) The Poems of Anyte, 1974; (with Peter Avery) The Rubaiyat of Omar Khayyam, 1979; *edited:* Selected Poems of Jonathan Swift, 1948; Selected Poems of P. B. Shelley, 1948; Selected Poems of Tennyson, 1948; Selected Poems of Alexander Pope, 1964; (with David Wright) The Forsaken Garden, 1950; Images of Tomorrow, 1953; (with David Wright) Faber Book of Twentieth Century Verse, 1953; (with Martin Green) Homage to George Barker on his Sixtieth Birthday, 1973; Selected Poems of Thomas Gray, 1983; (with Phillips Salman) Poems of Science, 1984. *Recreation:* taxonomy. *Address:* 22 Artesian Road, W2 5AR. *T:* 071–229 6367.

HEATHCOAT-AMORY, David Philip, FCA; MP (C) Wells, since 1983; Parliamentary Under Secretary of State, Department of Energy, since 1990; *b* 21 March

1949; *s* of Roderick and Sonia Heathcoat-Amory; *m* 1978, Linda Adams; two *s* one *d*. *Educ:* Eton Coll.; Oxford Univ. (MA PPE). Qual. as Chartered Accountant with Price Waterhouse & Co., 1974; FCA 1980. Worked in industry, becoming Asst Finance Dir of British Technology Gp, until 1983 when resigned to fight Gen. Election. PPS to the Financial Sec. to the Treasury, 1985–87, to the Home Secretary, 1987–88; an Asst Govt Whip, 1988–89; a Lord Comr of HM Treasury, 1989; Parly Under Sec. of State, DoE, 1989–90. *Recreations:* fishing, shooting, music, growing trees. *Address:* 12 Lower Addison Gardens, W14 8BQ. *T:* 071–603 3083. *Clubs:* Avalon (Glastonbury); Shepton Mallet Conservative; Wells Conservative.

HEATHCOAT AMORY, Sir Ian, 6th Bt *cr* 1874; JP; DL; *b* 3 Feb. 1942; *s* of Sir William Heathcoat Amory, 5th Bt, DSO, and of Margaret Isabel Dorothy Evelyn, *yr d* of Sir Arthur Havelock James Doyle, 4th Bt; *S* father, 1982; *m* 1972, Frances Louise, *d* of J. F. B. Pomeroy; four *s*. *Educ:* Eton. Chairman: Lowman Manufacturing Co. Ltd, 1976–; DevonAir Radio Ltd, 1983–90; Dir, Watts Blake Bearne & Co. PLC, 1984–88. Mem., Devon CC, 1973–85. JP, DL Devon. *Heir: s* William Francis Heathcoat Amory, *b* 19 July 1975. *Address:* Calverleigh Court, Tiverton, Devon EX16 8BB.

HEATHCOTE, Dr Frederic Roger; Principal Establishment and Finance Officer, Department of Energy, since 1991; *b* 19 March 1944; *s* of Frederic William Trevor Heathcote and Kathleen Annie Heathcote; *m* 1st, 1970, Geraldine Nixon (marr. diss. 1986); 2nd, 1986, Mary Campbell Syme Dickson; one *s* one step *d*. *Educ:* Bromsgrove Sch.; Birmingham Univ. (BSc (Hons) Physics, PhD). Res. Associate, Birmingham Univ., 1969–70; joined CS as Asst Principal, Min. of Technology (later DTI), 1970; Private Secretary to: Secretary (Industrial Develt), 1973; Permanent Under Sec. of State, Dept of Energy, 1974; Department of Energy: Principal, 1974; Asst Sec., 1978; Dir of Resource Management (Grade 4), 1988; Under Sec., Coal Div., 1989–91. Non-Exec. Dir, Trafalgar House Property Ltd, 1988–. *Recreations:* reading, gardening, painting. *Address:* c/o Department of Energy, 1 Palace Street, SW1E 5HE. *T:* 071–238 3069.

HEATHCOTE, Brig. Sir Gilbert (Simon), 9th Bt *cr* 1733; CBE 1964 (MBE 1941); *b* 21 Sept. 1913; *s* of Col R. E. M. Heathcote, DSO (*d* 1970), Manton Hall, Rutland and Millicent Heathcote (*d* 1977), *d* of William Walton, Horsley Priory, Nailsworth, Glos; *S* to baronetcy of 3rd Earl of Ancaster, KCVO, 1983; *m* lst, 1939, Patricia Margaret (*née* Leslie) (marr. diss. 1984); one *s* one *d*; 2nd, 1984, Ann, *widow* of Brig. J. F. C. Mellor, DSO, OBE. *Educ:* Eton; RMA Woolwich. Commnd RA, 1933, War Service in Europe, 1939–44; Comdr RA, 1960–62; Chief of Staff, Middle East Comd, 1962–64; retd. Vice-Pres., Royal Star and Garter Home, Richmond, 1990–. *Recreations:* sailing, ski-ing, travel. *Heir: s* Mark Simon Robert Heathcote, OBE [*b* 1 March 1941; *m* 1975, Susan, *d* of late Lt-Col George Ashley; two *s*]. *Address:* The Coach House, Tillington, near Petworth, Sussex. *Clubs:* Garrick, Army and Navy; Royal Yacht Squadron.

HEATHCOTE, Sir Michael Perryman, 11th Bt, *cr* 1733; *b* 7 Aug. 1927; *s* of Leonard Vyvyan Heathcote, 10th Bt, and Joyce Kathleen Heathcote (*d* 1967); *S* father, 1963; *m* 1956, Victoria Wilford, *e d* of Comdr J. E. R. Wilford, RN, Retd; two *s* one *d*. *Educ:* Winchester Coll.; Clare Coll., Cambridge. Started farming in England, 1951, in Scotland, 1961. Is in remainder to Earldom of Macclesfield. *Recreations:* fishing, shooting and farming. *Heir: s* Timothy Gilbert Heathcote, *b* 25 May 1957. *Address:* Warborne Farm, Boldre, Lymington, Hants SO41 5QD. *T:* Lymington (0590) 673478.

HEATHCOTE-DRUMMOND-WILLOUGHBY, family name of **Baroness Willoughby de Eresby.**

HEATHCOTE-SMITH, Clifford Bertram Bruce, CBE 1963; HM Diplomatic Service, 1936–72; acting Senior Clerk, Department of Clerk of House of Commons, 1973–77; *b* 2 Sept. 1912; *s* of late Sir Clifford E. Heathcote-Smith, KBE, CMG; *m* 1940, Thelma Joyce Engström; two *s*. *Educ:* Malvern; Pembroke Coll., Cambridge. Entered Consular Service, 1936; served in China, 1937–44; Foreign Office, 1944–47; Political Adviser, Hong-Kong, 1947–50, Montevideo, 1951–56; Commercial Counsellor: Ankara, 1956–60; Copenhagen, 1960–64; Washington, 1964–65; Dep. High Comr, Madras, 1965–68; a Diplomatic Service Inspector, 1969–72. *Address:* Lampool Lodge, Maresfield, East Sussex. *T:* Nutley (082571) 2849.

HEATHER, Stanley Frank, CBE 1980; Comptroller and City Solicitor, City of London Corporation, 1974–80; Attorney and General Counsel, City of London (Arizona) Corporation, 1974–81; *b* 8 Jan. 1917; *s* of Charles and Jessie Heather; *m* 1946, Janet Roxburgh Adams (*d* 1989), Perth; one *s* one *d*. *Educ:* Downhills Sch.; London Univ. Commnd Reconnaissance Corps, RAC, 1941; India/Burma Campaign, 1942–45. Admitted Solicitor, 1959. Asst Solicitor, City of London, 1963; Dep. Comptroller and City Solicitor, 1968. FRSA 1981. *Recreations:* golf, fishing. *Address:* 71 Rosehill, Billingshurst, W Sussex RH14 9QQ. *T:* Billingshurst (0403) 783981. *Clubs:* City Livery, Guildhall; Ifield Golf and Country (W Sussex).

HEATLY, Sir Peter, Kt 1990; CBE 1971; DL; Director, Peter Heatly & Co. Ltd, since 1958; Chairman, Commonwealth Games Federation, 1982–90; *b* 9 June 1924; *s* of Robert Heatly and Margaret Ann Heatly; *m* 1st, 1948, Jean Robertha Hermiston (*d* 1979); two *s* two *d*; 2nd, 1984, Mae Calder Cochrane. *Educ:* Leith Academy; Edinburgh Univ. (BSc). CEng, FICE. Chm., Scottish Sports Council, 1975–87. DL City of Edinburgh, 1984–. *Recreations:* swimming, golf, gardening. *Address:* Lanrig, Balerno, Edinburgh EH14 7AJ. *T:* 031–449 3998. *Club:* New (Edinburgh).

HEATON, David; Assistant Under Secretary of State, Home Office, 1976–83; *b* 22 Sept. 1923; *s* of late Dr T. B. Heaton, OBE, MD; *m* 1961, Joan, *d* of Group Captain E. J. Lainé, CBE, DFC; two *s* one *d*. *Educ:* Rugby Sch. Served RNVR, 1942–46. Ghana, 1948–58; Cabinet Office, 1961–69; Home Office, 1969–83. *Address:* 53 Murray Road, SW19 4PF. *T:* 081–947 0375.

HEATON, Rev. Eric William; Dean of Christ Church, Oxford, 1979–91; Pro-Vice-Chancellor, Oxford University, since 1984; *b* 15 Oct. 1920; *s* of late Robert William Heaton and late Ella Mabel Heaton (*née* Brear); *m* 1951, Rachel Mary, *d* of late Rev. Charles Harold Dodd, CH, FBA; two *s* two *d*. *Educ:* Ermysted's, Skipton; (Exhibnr) Christ's Coll., Cambridge (MA). English Tripos, Part I; Theological Tripos, Part I (First Class). Deacon, 1944; Priest, 1945; Curate of St Oswald's, Durham, 1944–45; Staff Sec., Student Christian Movement in University of Durham, 1944–45; Chaplain, Gonville and Caius Coll., Cambridge, 1945–46; Dean and Fellow, 1946–53; Tutor, 1951–53; Bishop of Derby's Chaplain in University of Cambridge, 1946–53; Canon Residentiary, 1953–60, and Chancellor, 1956–60, Salisbury Cathedral; Tutor in Theology, Official Fellow and Chaplain, 1960–74, Senior Tutor, 1967–73, St John's College, Oxford; Dean of Durham, 1974–79. Chm. Council, Headington Sch., Oxford, 1968–74; Chm. Governors, High Sch., Durham, 1975–79. Moderator, Gen. Ordination Exam., 1971–81. Examining Chaplain to: Archbishop of York, 1951–56; Bishop of Portsmouth, 1947–74; Bishop of Salisbury, 1949–64; Bishop of Norwich, 1960–71; Bishop of Wakefield, 1961–74; Bishop of Rochester, 1962–74. Select Preacher: Cambridge University, 1948, 1958; Oxford Univ., 1958–59, 1967, 1971. Hon. Lectr, Univ. of Durham, 1975–79. Hon. Fellow, Champlain Coll., Univ. of Trent, Ont, Canada, 1973–; Hon. Fellow: St John's Coll., Oxford, 1979; Christ's Coll., Cambridge, 1983. DD Lambeth, 1991. Cavaliere Ufficiale, Order of Merit (Italy), 1991. *Publications:* His Servants the Prophets, 1949 (revised and enlarged Pelican edn, The Old Testament Prophets, 1958, 2nd rev. edn, 1977); The Book of Daniel, 1956; Everyday Life in Old Testament Times, 1956; Commentary on the Sunday Lessons, 1959; The Hebrew Kingdoms, 1968; Solomon's New Men, 1974; articles in Jl of Theological Studies, Expository Times, etc. *Address:* Christ Church, Oxford OX1 1DP. *T:* Oxford (0865) 276161.

HEATON, Ralph Neville, CB 1951; *b* 4 June 1912; *s* of late Ernest Heaton; *m* 1939, Cecily Margaret Alabaster; three *s* one *d*. *Educ:* Westminster; Christ Church, Oxford. Formerly Deputy Secretary various Govt Depts, including Education, Transport, and Economic Affairs. Commonwealth Fund Fellow, 1951–52. *Address:* 38 Manor Park Avenue, Princes Risborough, Bucks HP17 9AS.

HEATON, Sir Yvo (Robert) Henniker-, 4th Bt *cr* 1912; *b* 24 April 1954; *s* of Sir (John Victor) Peregrine Henniker-Heaton, 3rd Bt, and of Margaret Patricia, *d* of late Lieut Percy Wright, Canadian Mounted Rifles; *S* father, 1971; *m* 1978, Freda, *d* of B. Jones; one *s* one *d*. Mem., North West Leics DC. Chm., Kegworth Cons. Assoc., 1988–92. *Publication:* Corporate Computer Insurance, 1990. *Heir: s* Alastair (John) Henniker-Heaton, *b* 4 May 1990. *Address:* 34 High Street, Kegworth, Derby DE7 2DA.

HEATON-WARD, Dr William Alan, FRCPsych; Lord Chancellor's Medical Visitor, 1978–89; *b* 19 Dec. 1919; *s* of Ralph Heaton-Ward, MA, and Mabel Orton; *m* 1945, Christine Edith Fraser; two *d*. *Educ:* Sefton Park Jun. Sch.; Queen Elizabeth's Hosp., Bristol; Univ. of Bristol Med. Sch. MB, ChB, 1944; DPM 1948; FRCPsych 1971. Jun. Clerk, Messrs W. D. & H. O. Wills, 1936–38; House Phys., Bristol Royal Inf., 1944–45; MO, Littlemore Mental Hosp., 1945–46; served RNVR, 1946–48: Surg. Lt-Comdr; Neuropsychiatrist, Nore Comd; Sen. Registrar, St James Hosp., Portsmouth, 1948–50; Dep. Med. Supt, Hortham Brentry Gp, 1950–54; Stoke Park Hosp. Group: Consultant Psych., 1954–78, Hon. Consultant, 1978–; Med. Supt, 1954–61; Cons. Psych. i/c, 1963–74; Clinical Teacher in Mental Health, Univ. of Bristol, 1954–78; Cons. Psych., Glos Royal Hosp., 1962–67. Mem., SW Mental Health Review Tribunal, 1985–. Hon. Cons. Adviser: NAMH, 1966–73; CARE, 1970–78; British Council Vis. Lectr, Portugal, 1971. Royal Coll. of Psychiatrists: Vice Pres., 1976–78; Blake Marsh Lectr, 1976; Burden Res. Gold Medal and Prize Winner, 1978. Pres., Brit. Soc. for Study of Mental Subnormality, 1978–79; Vice-Pres., Fortune Centre of Riding Therapy, 1980–; Mem. Council, Inst. of Mental Subnormality, 1972–76; Hon. Mem., Amer. Assoc. of Physician Analysts, 1976–. Mem., Adv. Council, Radio Bristol, 1985–88. *Publications:* Notes on Mental Deficiency (jtly), 1952, 3rd edn 1955; Mental Subnormality, 1960, 5th edn, (jtly) as Mental Handicap, 1984; Left Behind, 1977; papers on all aspects of care and treatment of mentally handicapped people and on gen. psychiatric topics; book revs. *Recreations:* following all forms of outdoor sport, gardening, seeking the sun, philately, asking Why? *Address:* Flat 2, 38 Apsley Road, Clifton, Bristol BS8 2SS. *T:* Bristol (0272) 738971. *Clubs:* Savages (Bristol); Bristol Football.

HEAVENER, Rt. Rev. Robert William; Bishop of Clogher, 1973–80, retired; *b* 28 Feb. 1906; *s* of Joseph and Maria Heavener; *m* 1936, Ada Marjorie, *d* of Rev. Chancellor Thomas Dagg; one *s* one *d*. *Educ:* Trinity Coll., Dublin (MA). Ordained, 1929; Curate, Clones; Diocesan Curate, 1930; Curate-in-charge, Lack, 1933–38; Rector, Derryvullen N, 1938–46; Rector, Monaghan, 1946–73; Rural Dean, 1946. Examining Chaplain and Canon of Clogher, 1951–62; Canon of St Patrick's Cathedral, Dublin, 1962–68; Archdeacon of Clogher, 1968–73. OCF, 1938–43; Member of Staff of Command Welfare Officer, NI District, 1938–43. *Publications:* Co. Fermanagh, 1940 (a short topographical and historical account of NI); Diskos, 1970 (a collection of material for Adult Education); (as Robert Cielou) Spare My Tortured People, 1983 (an attempt to understand the Ulster situation today). *Recreations:* tennis, rare book collecting. *Address:* 12 Church Avenue, Newtownabbey, Co. Antrim BT57 0PJ. *T:* Belfast (0232) 863242. *Club:* Friendly Brother House (Dublin).

HEBBLETHWAITE, Rev. Canon Brian Leslie; Fellow and Dean of Chapel, Queens' College, Cambridge, since 1969, and University Lecturer in Divinity, since 1977; *b* 3 Jan. 1939; *s* of Alderman Cyril Hebblethwaite and Sarah Anne Hebblethwaite; *m* 1991, Emma Sîan, *d* of John Ivor Disley, *qv*. *Educ:* Clifton Coll.; Magdelen Coll., Oxford (BA LitHum 1961; MA 1967); Magdelene Coll., Cambridge (BA Theol 1963; MA 1968; BD 1984); Westcott House, Cambridge; Univ. of Heidelberg. Curate, All Saints', Elton, Bury, 1965–68; Bye-Fellow and Chaplain, Queens' Coll., Cambridge, 1968; Univ. Asst Lectr in Divinity, Cambridge, 1973–77; Examng Chaplain to Bishop of Manchester, 1977–; Canon Theologian, Leicester Cathedral, 1982–. Pres., Soc. for Study of Theology, 1989–91. Editor for Ethics, Theologische Realenzyklopädie, 1980–. *Publications:* Evil, Suffering and Religion, 1976; The Problems of Theology, 1980; (ed jtly) Christianity and Other Religions, 1980; The Adequacy of Christian Ethics, 1981; (ed jtly) The Philosophical Frontiers of Christian Theology, 1982; The Christian Hope, 1984; Preaching Through the Christian Year 10, 1985; The Incarnation, 1987; The Ocean of Truth, 1988; (ed jtly) Divine Action, 1990. *Recreations:* fell-walking, opera, cathedral and church architecture, books. *Address:* Queens' College, Cambridge CB3 9ET. *T:* Cambridge (0223) 335511.

HEBBLETHWAITE, Peter; Vatican Affairs Writer for The National Catholic Reporter (USA), since 1979; *b* 30 Sept. 1930; *s* of Charles and Elsie Ann Hebblethwaite; *m* 1974, Margaret I. M. Speaight; two *s* one *d*. *Educ:* Xaverian Coll., Manchester; Campion Hall, Oxford; Heythrop Coll., Oxon. MA (1st Cl.) Oxford; LTh. Editor, The Month, a Jesuit review of Church and world affairs, 1965–73; Asst Editor, Frontier, 1974–76; Lectr in French, Wadham Coll., Oxford, 1976–79; thence to Rome as free-lance and Vatican Affairs Writer, for National Catholic Reporter, 1979–. *Publications:* Georges Bernanos, 1965; The Council Fathers and Atheism, 1966; Theology of the Church, 1968; The Runaway Church, 1975; Christian-Marxist Dialogue and Beyond, 1977; The Year of Three Popes, 1978; The New Inquisition?, 1981; The Papal Year, 1981; Introducing John Paul II, the Populist Pope, 1982; John XXIII, Pope of the Council, 1984; Synod Extraordinary, 1986; In the Vatican, 1986; contribs to TLS, Guardian, Tablet etc. *Recreations:* singing songs, Lieder and chansons. *Address:* 45 Marston Street, Oxford OX4 1JU. *T:* Oxford (0865) 723771.

HEBDITCH, Maxwell Graham; Director, Museum of London, since 1977 (Deputy Director, 1974–77); *b* 22 Aug. 1937; *s* of late Harold Hebditch, motor engr, Yeovil, and Lily (*née* Bartle); *m* 1963, Felicity Davies; two *s* one *d*. *Educ:* Yeovil Sch.; Magdalene Coll., Cambridge. MA, FSA, FMA. Field Archaeologist, Leicester Museums, 1961–64; Asst Curator in Archaeology, later Curator in Agricultural and Social History, City Museum, Bristol, 1965–71; Dir, Guildhall Mus., London, 1971–74. Chm., UK Nat. Cttee, ICOM, 1981–87; Pres., Museums Assoc., 1990–July 1992 (Vice-Pres., 1988–90). *Publications:* contribs to archaeological and museological jls and books. *Recreation:* archaeology. *Address:* Museum of London, London Wall, EC2Y 5HN. *T:* 01–600 3699.

HEBER-PERCY, Algernon Eustace Hugh; Vice Lord-Lieutenant for Shropshire, since 1990; *b* 2 Jan. 1944; *s* of Brig. A. G. W. Heber-Percy, DSO and Daphne Wilma Kenyon (*née* Parker Bowles); *m* 1966, Hon. Margaret Jane Lever, *y d* of 3rd Viscount Leverhulme, *qv*; one *s* three *d. Educ:* Harrow; Mons OTC. Lieut Grenadier Guards, 1962–66. Farmer and landowner. Chm., Mercia Regional Cttee, Nat. Trust, 1990–; Trustee, Nat. Gardens Scheme, 1990–; Mem., Historic Houses Gardens Cttee, 1980–; Pres., Shropshire and Mid Wales Hospice, 1988–; Mem., Walker Trust Cttee, 1990–; Chm., Pines and Lyneal Trusts for Disabled, 1980–. DL Shropshire, 1986; High Sheriff of Shropshire, 1987. *Recreations:* gardening, country sports. *Address:* Hodnet Hall, Hodnet, Market Drayton, Shropshire TF9 3NN. *T:* Hodnet (063084) 202. *Club:* Cavalry and Guards.

HECTOR, Gordon Matthews, CMG 1966; CBE 1961 (OBE 1955); Secretary to the Assembly Council, General Assembly of the Church of Scotland, 1980–85; *b* 9 June 1918; *m* 1954, Mary Forrest, MB, ChB, *o d* of late Robert Gray, Fraserburgh, Aberdeenshire; one *s* two *d. Educ:* Edinburgh Academy; Lincoln Coll., Oxford. Military Service with East Africa Forces, 1940–45. Apptd Dist Officer, Kenya, 1946; Asst Sec., 1950; Sec. to Road Authority, 1951; Sec. to Govt of Seychelles, 1952; Acting Governor, 1953; Dep. Resident Comr and Govt Sec., Basutoland, 1956; Chief Sec., Basutoland, 1964; Deputy British Government Representative, Lesotho (lately Basutoland), 1965. Sec., Basutoland Constitutional Commn, 1957–58. Clerk to the Univ. Court, Aberdeen, 1967–76; Dep. Sec. and Establishment Officer, Aberdeen Univ., 1976–80. Fellow of the Commonwealth Fund, 1939. Chm., Council of Victoria League in Scotland, 1983–88; Vice-Pres., St Andrew Soc., 1983–. Chm., Great N of Scotland Rly Assoc., 1989–. Mem., West End Community Council, 1983–89 (Chm., 1986–89). Mem. Bd of Governors, Oakbank D List Sch., 1969–90. Burgess of Guild, Aberdeen City. *Recreations:* railways ancient and modern, grandchildren. *Address:* 4 Montgomery Court, 110 Hepburn Gardens, St Andrews, Fife KY16 9LT. *Clubs:* Royal Over-Seas League; Vincent's (Oxford).

HEDDY, Brian Huleatt; HM Diplomatic Service, retired; Regional Co-ordinator and Resettlement Officer, British Refugee Council, 1979–82; *b* 8 June 1916; *o s* of late Dr William Reginald Huleatt Heddy, Barrister-at-Law, and Ruby Norton-Taylor; *m* 1st, 1940, Barbara Ellen Williams (*d* 1965); two *s* one *d*; 2nd, 1966, Ruth Mackarness (*née* Hogan) (*d* 1967); (one step *s* two step *d*); 3rd, 1969, Horatia Clare Kennedy. *Educ:* St Paul's Sch.; Pembroke Coll., Oxford. Commissioned in 75th (Highland) Field Regt, Royal Artillery, Nov. 1939; served in France 1940; WA, 1943; War Office and France, 1944–45; Mem. of Gray's Inn. Entered Foreign Service, 1945. Appointed to Brussels, 1946; Denver, 1948; Foreign Office, 1952; Tel Aviv, 1953; UK Delegation to ECSC, Luxembourg, 1955; Foreign Office, 1959; promoted Counsellor, 1963; Consul-Gen. at Lourenço Marques, 1963–65; Head of Nationality and Consular Dept, Commonwealth Office, 1966–67; Head of Migration and Visa Dept, FCO, 1968–71; Consul-Gen. in Durban, 1971–76. *Recreations:* travel, reading. *Address:* Wynyards, Winsham, near Chard, Somerset TA20 4JG. *T:* Winsham (0460) 30260. *Clubs:* East India, Devonshire, Sports and Public Schools, MCC.

HEDGECOE, Prof. John, Dr RCA; FCSD; Professor of Photography, Royal College of Art, London; Pro Rector, since 1981, Acting Rector, 1983–84; *b* 24 March 1937; *s* of William Hedgecoe and Kathleen Don; *m* 1960, Julia Mardon; two *s* one *d. Educ:* Gulval Village Sch., Cornwall; Guildford Sch. of Art. Staff Photographer, Queen Magazine, 1957–72; Freelance: Sunday Times and Observer, 1960–70; most internat. magazines, 1958–; Portrait, HM the Queen, for British and Australian postage stamps, 1966; photographed The Arts Multi-Projection, British Exhibn, Expo Japan Show, 1970. Started Photography Sch. at RCA, 1965: Head of Dept and Reader in Photography, 1965–74; Fellow, 1973; awarded Chair of Photography, 1975; started Audio/Visual Dept, 1980; started Holography Unit, 1982; Managing Trustee, RCA, 1983. Vis. Prof., Norwegian Nat. Television Sch., Oslo, 1985. Man. Dir, Lion & Unicorn Press Ltd, 1986; Director: John Hedgecoe Ltd, 1965–; Perennial Pictures Ltd, 1980. Mem. Photographic Bd, CNAA, 1976–78; Gov., W Surrey Coll. of Art (and Mem. Acad. Adv. Bd), 1975–; Acad. Gov., Richmond Coll., London; Trustee, The Minories Victor Batte-Lay Trust, 1985–88. Has illustrated numerous books, 1958–; has contributed to numerous radio broadcasts. Television: Tonight, Aust. TV, 1967; Folio, Anglia, 1980; 8 progs on Photography, Channel Four, 1983, repeated 1984; Winners, Channel Four, 1984; Light and Form, US Cable TV, 1985. Exhibitions: London, Sydney, Toronto, Edinburgh, Venice, Prague; Collections: V&A Museum; Art Gall. of Ontario; Nat. Portrait Gall., London; Citibank, London; Henry Moore Foundn; Museum of Modern Art, NY; Leeds City Art Gall. FRSA. Laureate and Medal for contribution to photography, Govt of Czechoslovakia, 1989. *Publications:* Henry Moore, 1968 (prize best art book, world-wide, 1969); (jtly) Kevin Crossley-Holland book of Norfolk Poems, 1970; Sculptures of Picasso, 1970; (jtly) Photography, Material and Methods, 1971–74 edns; Henry Moore, Energy in Space, 1973; The Book of Photography, 1976; Handbook of Photographic Techniques, 1977, 2nd edn 1982; The Art of Colour Photography, 1978 (Kodak Photobuchpreis Stuttgart 1979; Grand Prix Technique de la Photographie, Musée Français de la Photographie, Paris 1980); Possessions, 1978; The Pocket Book of Photography, 1979; Introductory Photography Course, 1979; Master Classes in Photography: Children and Child Portraiture, 1980; (illus.) Poems of Thomas Hardy, 1981; (illus.) Poems of Robert Burns, 1981; The Book of Advanced Photography, 1982; What a Picture!, 1983; The Photographer's Work Book, 1983; Aesthetics of Nude Photography, 1984; The Workbook of Photo Techniques, 1984; The Workbook of Darkroom Techniques, 1984; Pocket Book of Travel and Holiday Photography, 1986; Henry Moore: his ideas, inspirations and life as an artist, 1986; The Three Dimensional Pop-up Photography Book, 1986; (with A. L. Rowse) Shakespeare's Land, 1986; Photographer's Manual of Creative Ideas, 1986; (with A. L. Rowse) Rowse's Cornwall, 1987; Practical Portrait Photography, 1987; Practical Book of Landscape Photography, 1988; Hedgecoe on Video, 1988; Hedgecoe on Photography, 1988; Complete Photography Guide, 1990. *Recreations:* sculpture, building, gardening. *Address:* c/o Royal College of Art, Kensington Gore, SW7 2EU. *T:* 01-584 5020. *Club:* Arts.

HEDGELAND, Air Vice-Marshal Philip Michael Sweatman, CB 1978; OBE 1957 (MBE 1948); CEng, FIEE; *b* 24 Nov. 1922; *s* of Philip and Margaret Hedgeland, Maidstone, Kent; *m* 1946, Jean Riddle Brinkworth, *d* of Leonard and Anne Brinkworth, Darlington, Co. Durham; two *s. Educ:* Maidstone Grammar Sch.; City and Guilds Coll., Imperial Coll. of Science and Technology, London. BSc(Eng), ACGI (Siemens Medallist). Served War: commnd into Technical Br., RAF, 1942; Radar Officer, Pathfinder Force and at TRE, Malvern. Radar Develt Officer, Central Bomber Estabt, 1945–48; Radio Introd. Unit Project Officer for V-Bomber Navigation and Bombing System, 1952–57; Wing Comdr Radio (Air) at HQ Bomber Comd, 1957–60; jssc 1960; Air Ministry Technical Planning, 1961–62; aws 1963; Dir of Signals (Far East), Singapore, 1963–65; commanded RAF Stanbridge (Central Communications Centre), 1966–67; SASO, HQ Signals Comd/90 Gp, 1968–69; IDC, 1970; MoD Procurement Exec., Project Dir for Airborne Radar, 1971–74; Vice-Pres., Ordnance Bd, 1975–77, Pres., 1977–78. FCGI 1977. Pres., Pathfinder Assoc., 1985–87. *Recreations:* audio engineering, horticulture, amateur radio. *Club:* Royal Air Force.

HEDGER, Eric Frank, CB 1979; OBE 1960; Director General of Defence Contracts, Under Secretary, Ministry of Defence, 1969–80; *b* 15 Sept. 1919; *s* of late Albert Frank Hedger and Ellen Agnes Hedger (*née* Laffey); *m* 1945, Joan Kathleen Bernas; two *s* one *d. Educ:* St Luke's, Southsea. War Service, 1939–46 (despatches 1945): Adjutant, 10 Air Formation Signals; Adjutant, then 2nd i/c, 7 Indian Air Formation Signals. Secretary, Admiralty Awards Council, 1946–49; Admin. Staff Coll., 1958; Dir of Navy Contracts, 1968. Mem. of Council and Bd of Management, Inst. of Purchasing and Supply, 1974–75. Advr, Defence Manufacturers Assoc., 1983–88. FInstPS. *Recreations:* music, reading, gardening. *Address:* Helere House, Ridgeway Mead, Sidmouth, Devon EX10 9DT. *T:* Sidmouth (0395) 577741.

HEDGER, John Clive; Under Secretary and Head of Schools Branch 1, Department of Education and Science, since 1988; *b* 17 Dec. 1942; *s* of late Leslie John Keith Hedger and of Iris Hedger (*née* Friedlos); *m* 1966, Jean Ann Felstead; two *s* one *d. Educ:* Quirister Sch., Winchester; Victoria Coll., Jersey; Univ. of Sussex (BA 1965; MA 1966). Dept of Educn and Science, 1966; Asst Private Sec., 1970; Sec., Cttee of Enquiry on Educn of Handicapped, 1974–76. *Recreations:* coarse acting, walking, coarse sailing, growing things. *Address:* c/o Department of Education and Science, Sanctuary Buildings, Great Smith Street, SW1; Poultons, Cookham, Berks SL6 9HW. *T:* Bourne End (06285) 23911. *Club:* Odney (Cookham).

HEDGES, Anthony (John); Reader in Composition, University of Hull, since 1978; *b* 5 March 1931; *s* of late S. G. Hedges; *m* 1957, Delia Joy Marsden; two *s* two *d. Educ:* Bicester Grammar Sch.; Keble Coll., Oxford. MA, BMus, LRAM. National Service as solo pianist and arranger Royal Signals Band, 1955–57. Teacher and Lecturer, Royal Scottish Academy of Music, 1957–63. During this period became a regular contributor to Scotsman, Glasgow Herald, Guardian, Musical Times, etc. Lecturer in Music, Univ. of Hull, 1963, Sen. Lectr, 1968. The Composers' Guild of Great Britain: Chm., Northern Br., 1966–67; Mem. Exec. Cttee of Guild, 1969–73, 1977–81, 1982–87; Chm. of Guild, 1972, Jt Chm., 1973. Member: Council, Central Music Library, Westminster, 1970; Council, Soc. for Promotion of New Music, 1974–81; Music Bd, CNAA, 1974–77; Music Panel, Yorks Arts Assoc., 1974–75, Lincs and Humberside Arts Assoc., 1975–78; Founder-conductor, The Humberside Sinfonia, 1978–81. Wrote regularly for Yorkshire Post, 1963–78, and contributed to many jls, incl. Composer, Current Musicology, etc, and also broadcast on musical subjects. *Publications include: (works): orchestral:* Comedy Overture, 1962 (rev. 1967); Overture, October '62, 1962 (rev. 1968); Sinfonia Semplice, 1963; Expressions for Orchestra, 1964; Prelude, Romance and Rondo, strings, 1965; Concertante Music, 1965; Four Miniature Dances, 1967; A Holiday Overture, 1968; Variations on a theme of Rameau, 1969; Kingston Sketches, 1969; An Ayrshire Serenade, 1969; Four Diversions, strings, 1971; Celebrations, 1973; Symphony, 1972–73; Festival Dances, 1976; Overture, Heigham Sound, 1978; Four Breton Sketches, 1980; Sinfonia Concertante, 1980; Scenes from the Humber, 1981; A Cleveland Overture, 1984; Concertino for Horn and String Orchestra, 1987; *choral:* Gloria, unaccompanied, 1965; Epithalamium, chorus and orch. (Spencer), 1969; To Music, chorus and orch. (various texts), 1972; Psalm 104, 1973; A Manchester Mass, chorus, orch. and brass band, 1974; A Humberside Cantata, 1976; Songs of David, 1978; The Temple of Solomon, 1979; I Sing the Birth: canticles for Christmas, 1985; I'll make me a world, 1990; *chamber music:* Five Preludes, piano, 1959; Four Pieces, piano, 1966; Rondo Concertante, violin, clarinet, horn, violoncello, 1967; Sonata for violin and harpsichord, 1967; Three Songs of Love, soprano, piano (from Song of Songs), 1968; String Quartet, 1970; Rhapsody, violin, piano, 1971, revd 1988; piano sonata, 1974; Song Cycle, 1977; Piano Trio, 1977; Fantasy for Violin and Piano, 1981; Sonatinas for Flute, Viola, Cello, 1982; Wind Quintet, 1984; Flute Trios, 1985, 1989; Fantasy Sonata for bassoon and piano, 1986; Clarinet Quintet, 1987; Flute Sonata, 1988; Five Aphorisms, piano, 1990; In such a night, string quartet, 1990; Bassoon Quintet, 1991; *opera:* Shadows in the Sun (lib. Jim Hawkins), 1976; *musical:* Minotaur (lib. Jim Hawkins), 1978; *miscellaneous:* many anthems, partsongs, albums of music for children; music for television, film and stage. *Recreations:* family life, reading, walking. *Address:* Malt Shovel Cottage, 76 Walkergate, Beverley, HU17 9ER. *T:* Beverley (0482) 860580.

HEDLEY, Prof. Anthony Johnson, MD; FRCPE, FRCPGlas, FRCP, FFPHM; Professor of Community Medicine, University of Hong Kong, since 1988; *b* 8 April 1941; *s* of Thomas Johnson Hedley and Winifred Duncan; *m* 1967, Elizabeth-Anne Walsh. *Educ:* Rydal Sch.; Aberdeen Univ. (MB, ChB 1965; MD 1972); Edinburgh Univ. (Dip. Soc. Med. 1973). MRCP 1973; FRCPE 1981; FRCPGlas, 1985; FRCP 1987; FFPHM (FFCM 1981; MFCM 1975). Lectr in Community Medicine, Univ. of Aberdeen, 1974–76; Sen. Lectr in Community Health, Univ. of Nottingham, 1976–83; Prof.-Designate in Community Medicine, 1983–84, Henry Mechan Prof. of Public Health, 1984–88, Univ. of Glasgow. Med. Adviser (Thailand), ODA, 1977–. Hon. MD Khon Kaen Univ., 1983. *Publications:* papers and chapters on endocrine disease, surveillance of chronic disease and on med. educn. *Recreations:* long-distance running, photography, rifle shooting. *Address:* 39 Foxhill Road, Burton Joyce, Nottinghamshire. *T:* Burton Joyce (060231) 2558; Flat B6, Block 2, Tam Towers, 25 Sha Wan Drive, Victoria Road, Pok fu Lam, Hong Kong. *T:* (852) 8194708, *Fax:* (852) 8559528. *Clubs:* Rydal Veterans (Colwyn Bay); Freelancers (Nottingham).

HEDLEY, Prof. Ronald; Director, Trent Polytechnic, Nottingham, 1970–80, Emeritus Professor, 1980; *b* 12 Sept. 1917; *s* of Francis Hedley, Hebburn, Co. Durham; *m* 1942; one *s* one *d. Educ:* Jarrow Grammar Sch.; Durham Univ. (MA, DipEd); Ecole Normale d'Instituteurs, Evreux. Various appts in teaching and educational administration, 1947–64; Dep. Dir of Education, Nottingham, 1964–70. Chm., Regional Acad. Bd, Regional Adv. Council for Further Educn in E Midlands, 1972–76; Member: Central Council for Educn and Trng in Social Work, 1971–77; Nat. Adv. Council for Educn for Ind. and Commerce, 1973–77; Central Council for Educn and Trng of Health Visitors, 1972–77; Cttee for Arts and Social Studies, CNAA, 1974–76; Personal Social Services Council, 1974–78; Cttee on Recreation Management Training, 1977–80; Local Govt Trng Bd, 1978–81; Adv. Cttee for Supply and Educn of Teachers, 1980–81, Chm., Local Cttee for Teacher Educn, King Alfred's Coll., Winchester, 1986–89. FRSA 1970. Hon. Fellow, Trent Polytechnic, 1980. Hon. Senator, Fachhochschule, Karlsruhe, Germany, 1980. Hon. LlD Nottingham, 1981. *Address:* Evergreen, Haydn Close, Kings Worthy, Hants SO23 7RD. *T:* Winchester (0962) 884142.

HEDLEY, Ronald Henderson, CB 1986; DSc, PhD; FIBiol; Director, British Museum (Natural History), 1976–88; *b* 2 Nov. 1928; *s* of Henry Armstrong Hedley and Margaret Hopper; *m* 1957, Valmai Mary Griffith, New Zealand; one *s. Educ:* Durham Johnston Sch.; King's Coll., Univ. of Durham. Commissioned in Royal Regt of Artillery, 1953–55. Sen. Scientific Officer, British Museum (Natural History), 1955–61; New Zealand Nat. Research Fellow, 1960–61; Principal Scientific Officer, 1961–64; Dep. Keeper of Zoology, 1964–71; Dep. Dir, 1971–76. Vis. Lectr in Microbiology, Univ. of Surrey, 1968–75. Mem. Council, Fresh Water Biological Assoc., 1972–76; Trustee, Percy Sladen Meml Fund, 1972–77; Pres., British Section, Soc. of Protozoology, 1975–78; Member Council: Marine Biolog. Assoc., 1976–79, 1981–; Zoological Soc., London, 1981–85 (Hon. Sec., 1977–80; Vice-Pres., 1980–85); Mem., Internat. Trust for Zoological Nomenclature, 1977–. Member: Council, Royal Albert Hall, 1982–88; National Trust, 1985–88. FRSA. *Publications:* (ed with C. G. Adams) Foraminifera, vols 1–3, 1974, 1976, 1978; (with C.

G. Ogden) Atlas of Testate Amoebae, 1980; technical papers, mainly on biology, cytology and systematics of protozoa, 1956–. *Recreations:* horology, horticulture, humour. *Clubs:* Lansdowne, Civil Service.

HEDLEY-MILLER, Dame Mary (Elizabeth), DCVO 1989; CB 1983; Ceremonial Officer, Cabinet Office, 1983–88; *b* 5 Sept. 1923; *d* of late J. W. Ashe; *m* 1950, Roger Latham Hedley-Miller; one *s* two *d. Educ:* Queen's Sch., Chester; St Hugh's Coll., Oxford (MA). Joined HM Treasury, 1945; served in UK Treasury Delegn, Washington DC, 1947–49; Under-Sec., HM Treasury, 1973–83. Alternate Dir, Monetary Cttee, EEC, and Alternate Exec. Dir, European Investment Bank, 1977–83. *Recreations:* family, including family music; reading. *Address:* 108 Higher Drive, Purley, Surrey CR8 2HL. *T:* 081–660 1837. *Club:* United Oxford & Cambridge University.

HEENAN, Maurice, CMG 1966; QC (Hong Kong) 1962; The General Counsel, United Nations Relief and Works Agency for Palestine Refugees in the Near East, 1973–77; *b* NZ, 8 Oct. 1912; 2nd *s* of late David Heenan and of Anne Frame; *m* 1951, Claire, 2nd *d* of late Emil Ciho and Iren Rothbauer, Trenčín, Bratislava, Czechoslovakia; two *d. Educ:* Canterbury Coll., University of New Zealand. Law Professional, LLB, Barrister and Solicitor of Supreme Court of New Zealand, Practised law in NZ, 1937–40. War of 1939–45; Major, 2nd NZEF; active service Western Desert, Libya, Cyrenaica and Italy, 1940–45 (despatches). Crown Counsel, Palestine, 1946–48. Solicitor-Gen., Hong Kong, 1961; HM's Attorney-Gen., Hong Kong, and *ex officio* MEC and MLC, Hong Kong, 1961–66; Dep.-Dir, Gen. Legal Div., Office of Legal Affairs, Offices of the Sec.-Gen., UN, NY, 1966–73. *Recreations:* Rugby football, tennis, squash, ski-ing, golf. *Address:* Plane Trees, West Road, New Canaan, Conn 06840, USA. *Clubs:* Hong Kong; Country (New Canaan).

HEEPS, William, CBE 1990; Chairman, Thomson Regional Newspapers Ltd, since 1984 (Chief Executive, 1984–90); Director: The Thomson Corp. (formerly International Thomson plc, and International Thomson Organisation plc), since 1984; Thomson Television, since 1984; *b* 4 Dec. 1929; *er s* of late William Headrick Heeps and Margaret Munro Heeps; *m* 1st, 1956, Anne Robertson Paton (*d* 1974); two *d*; 2nd, 1983, Jennifer Rosemary Bartlett; one step *d. Educ:* Graeme High School, Falkirk. Journalist, Falkirk Mail, Linlithgowshire Jl and Gazette, Daily Record, Evening News and Dispatch, Edinburgh; Editor, Evening Gazette, Middlesbrough, 1966–68; Managing Director: Celtic Newspapers, 1968–71; North Eastern Evening Gazette, Middlesbrough, 1972–75; Evening Post-Echo, Hemel Hempstead, 1976–78; Thomson Magazines, 1978–80; Thomson Data, 1980–82; Editorial Dir, Thomson Regional Newspapers, 1982, Man. Dir and Editor-in-Chief, 1983. Director: The Scotsman Publications; Aberdeen Jls; Chester Chronicle & Associated Newspapers; North Eastern Evening Gazette; Celtic Newspapers; Belfast Telegraph Newspapers; Thomson International Press Consultancy; Thames Valley Newspapers; Thomson Free Newspapers; Barwell Gurney Advertising; Garethward; WP Publications; Vantagecrest. Pres., Newspaper Soc., 1988–89 (Mem. Council, 1984–). Trustee, Thomson Foundn, 1986–. Hon. Vice-Pres., Boys' Bde, 1990. Chm., Royal Caledonian Schools, 1986–. Elder, Church of Scotland. CBIM 1988. *Recreations:* golf, badminton. *Address:* The Old Vicarage, Pipers Hill, Great Gaddesden, Herts HP1 3BY. *T:* Hemel Hempstead (0442) 253524. *Club:* Caledonian.

HEES, Hon. George H., PC (Canada) 1957; OC (Can.) 1989; Ambassador-at-Large, Canada; *b* Toronto, 17 June 1910; *s* of Harris Lincoln Hees, Toronto, and Mabel Good, New York; *m* 1934, Mabel, *d* of late Hon. E. A. Dunlop; three *d. Educ:* Trinity Coll. Sch., Port Hope, Ont; RMC, Kingston, Ont; University of Toronto; Cambridge Univ. Formerly Dir, George H. Hees & Son & Co. Served War of 1939–45: Royal Canadian Artillery, 1941–44; 3rd Anti-Tank Regt, Royal Canadian Artillery; Bde Major, 5th Infantry Bde, Holland (wounded); retd as Major. Contested (Prog. C) Spadina Riding, 1945; MP (Prog. C): Toronto–Broadview, May 1950–1963; Prince Edward—Hastings Riding, subseq. Northumberland, Ont, Nov. 1965–88; Minister of Transport, Canada, 1957–60; Minister of Trade and Commerce, 1960–63; Minister of Veterans Affairs, 1984–88. Pres., Montreal and Canadian Stock Exchanges, 1964–65. Executive with George H. Hees Son & Co., Toronto; Dir, Expo 67. Hon. LLD Waterloo UC (now Sir Wilfrid Laurier Univ.), 1961; Hon. DMilSc Royal Mil. Coll., Kingston, Ont, 1988. *Recreations:* reading, ski-ing, swimming, golf, tennis, riding, bridge; formerly boxing. *Address:* 7 Coltrin Place, Ottawa, Ontario K1M 0A5, Canada. *Clubs:* Toronto Golf, Toronto Badminton and Racquet, Osler Bluff Ski (Toronto); Royal Ottawa Golf.

HEGARTY, Most Rev. Séamus; *see* Raphoe, Bishop of, (RC).

HEGGS, Geoffrey Ellis; Chairman of Industrial Tribunals, since 1977, Regional Chairman, London North, since 1990; a Recorder of the Crown Court, since 1983; *b* 23 Oct. 1928; *s* of George Heggs, MBE and Winifred Grace Heggs; *m* 1953, Renée Fanny Madeleine Calderan (*see* R. F. M. Heggs); two *s* one *d. Educ:* Elizabeth Coll., Guernsey; LLB London. Admitted Solicitor, 1952. Rotary Foundn Fellow, Yale Univ., 1953–54; LLM Yale; Asst Sec., Law Soc., 1956–58; practised as solicitor in London, 1958–77. Member: Law Society; City of London Solicitors' Company. *Recreations:* military history, music, painting. *Address:* 19/21 Woburn Place, WC1H 0LU. *T:* 071–239 9265.

HEGGS, Renée Fanny Madeleine; a Social Security Commissioner, since 1981; Legal Member, Mental Health Review Tribunal, since 1985; *b* 29 Nov. 1929; *d* of E. and G. Calderan; *m* 1953, Geoffrey Ellis Heggs, *qv*; two *s* one *d. Educ:* Notting Hill and Ealing High Sch., GPDST; London Univ. (LLB 1952). Admitted Solicitor, 1955; practising Solicitor, 1955–81. Chm., Nat. Insce Local Tribunal, 1976–81; pt-time Chm. of Industrial Tribunals, 1978–81; Pres., Appeal Tribunal under London Building Acts, 1979–81. *Recreations:* music, travelling. *Address:* (office) Harp House, 83 Farringdon Street, EC4A 4DH. *T:* 071-353 5145.

HEGINBOTHAM, Christopher John; Fellow in Health Services Management, King's Fund College, London, since 1989; *b* 25 March 1948; *s* of Joseph William and Marjorie Heginbotham; *m* 1988, Barbara Joyce, *d* of Charles and Lois-Ella Gill, Cincinnati, Ohio. *Educ:* Univ. of Birmingham (BSc Hons); Univ. of Essex (MSc); MA Wales. Area Manager, Circle Thirty Three Housing Trust, 1977–80; Assistant Borough Housing Officer, London Borough of Haringey, 1980–82; Nat. Dir, MIND (Nat. Assoc. for Mental Health), 1982–88. Member: Hampstead DHA, 1981–87; Waltham Forest DHA, 1989–; Nat. Adv. Council on Employment of Disabled People, 1983–; Bd, World Fedn for Mental Health, 1985–89 (rep., UN Commn on Human Rights, 1985–); Bd, Internat. Acad. of Law and Mental Health, 1987–89. Vis. Res. Fellow, Univ. of Glasgow Inst. of Law and Ethics in Medicine, 1987–91. *Publications:* Housing Projects for Mentally Handicapped People, 1981; Promoting Residential Services for Mentally Handicapped People, 1982; Webs and Mazes: approaches to community care, 1984; The Rights of Mentally Ill People, 1987; Mental Health and Human Rights, 1990; Return to Community, 1990; (with T. Campbell) Mental Illness Discrimination, 1990. *Recreations:* writing, painting. *Address:* King's Fund College, 2 Palace Court, W2. *T:* 071–727 0581.

HEGINBOTHAM, Prof. Wilfred Brooks, OBE 1978; FEng 1985; Director General, Production Engineering Research Association of Great Britain (PERA), Melton Mowbray, 1979–84; *b* 9 April 1924; *s* of Fred and Alice Heginbotham; *m* 1957, Marjorie Pixton; three *d. Educ:* Manchester Univ. (UMIST). BScTech 1949; MScTech 1950; PhD (Manchester) 1956; DSc (Manchester) 1979. FIProdE; MIMechE; FRSA. Started in industry as wood pattern maker; part-time courses to HNC, 1938–46; Walter Preston Schol., Manchester Coll. of Tech., 1946; joined staff, 1951; Lectr in Production Engineering subjects, UMIST, 1951–58; industrial experience for 10 years; Nottingham University: Sen. Lectr, 1958; started first BSc course in Prod. Engrg in UK, 1961; Head of Dept of Prod. Engrg and Prod. Management, 1961–63; Cripps Prof., 1963–79; Dean, Faculty of Applied Science, 1967–71; Special Prof. of Prodn Engrg, 1983–86; Prof. Emeritus, 1990. Hon. Prof., Dept of Engrg, Univ. of Warwick, 1984–89; Vis. Prof., Univ. of RI, USA, 1987; Vis. Sen. Res. Fellow, Dept of Mech. Engrg, Univ. of Birmingham, 1989–. Developed group to study Automatic Assembly Systems and Industrial Robot devices, including computer vision and tactile sense, and co-operated with industry in development of advanced automation equipment. Chm. Org. Cttee for establishment of Brit. Robot Assoc., 1977, Chm. of Council, 1977–80, Pres., 1980–84. Editor-in-Chief: The Industrial Robot; Assembly Automation; Advanced Manufacturing Technology Journal. Hon. DTech Scis Eindhoven, 1981; Hon. DSc Aston, 1983. Engelberger Award, Robot Inst. of America, 1983. *Publications:* Programmable Assembly, 1984; (ed with D. T. Pham) Robot Grippers, 1986; contribs to Encyc. Brit. on Robot Devices and to prof. pubns on metal cutting, automated assembly, industrial robots, artificial intelligence and production processes. *Recreations:* gliding, model aircraft construction and operation (radio controlled). *Address:* Bardsley Brow, 14 Middleton Crescent, Beeston, Notts NG9 2TH. *T:* Nottingham (0602) 257796.

HEGLAND, David Leroy, DFC 1944; Director: Kemtron Ltd; Galena; Massey-Ferguson Holdings (Australia) Ltd; Carlton and United Breweries Holdings Ltd; Plessey Pacific Pty Ltd; cattle grazier; *b* 12 June 1919; *s* of Lee and Jennie Hegland; *m* 1944, Dagmar Cooke; two *s* one *d. Educ:* Whitman Coll., Washington, USA (BA). Served War, 1942–45; USN aircraft pilot in Pacific Ocean areas; Lt Comdr USNR, 1945. Managing Director: GM International, Copenhagen, 1956–58; GM South African, Port Elizabeth, 1958–61; GM Holden's Pty Ltd, Melbourne, 1962–65; Chm. and Man. Dir, Vauxhall Motors Ltd, Luton, 1966–70; Dir, General Motors Ltd, London, 1966–70; Chm., GKN Australia Ltd, and Dir, Ajax GKN Holdings Pty Ltd, and Guest, Keen & Nettlefolds (Overseas) Ltd, 1972–80. Member: Albury-Wodonga Develt Corp., 1980–81; Industry Forum, Aust. Acad. of Science, 1972–; Aust. Inst. of Dirs; Delta Sigma Rho. FIMI. Richard Kirby medal for production engrg, 1964. *Recreations:* flying, tennis, riding. *Clubs:* Royal & Ancient Golf (St Andrews); Melbourne, Victoria Racing (Melbourne); Albury (Albury, NSW).

HEILBRON, Hilary Nora Burstein; QC 1987; *b* 2 Jan. 1949; *d* of Dr Nathaniel Burstein and Dame Rose Heilbron, *qv. Educ:* Huyton College; Lady Margaret Hall, Oxford (MA). Called to the Bar, Gray's Inn, 1971. *Address:* Brick Court Chambers, 15/19 Devereux Court, WC2R 3JJ. *T:* 071–583 0777.

HEILBRON, Dame Rose, DBE 1974; a Judge of the High Court of Justice, Family Division, 1974–88; *b* 19 Aug. 1914; *d* of late Max and Nellie Heilbron; *m* 1945, Dr Nathaniel Burstein; one *d. Educ:* Belvedere Sch., GPDST; Liverpool University, LLB 1st Class Hons, 1935; Lord Justice Holker Scholar, Gray's Inn, 1936; LLM 1937. Called to Bar, Gray's Inn, 1939, Bencher, 1968, Treasurer, 1985; joined Northern Circuit, Leader, 1973–74, Presiding Judge, 1979–82; QC 1949; Recorder of Burnley, 1956–71, a Recorder, and Hon. Recorder of Burnley, 1972–74. Mem., Bar Council, 1973–74. Chm., Home Sec's Adv. Gp on Law of Rape, 1975–. Hon. Fellow: Lady Margaret Hall, Oxford, 1976; UMIST, 1986; Hon. LLD: Liverpool, 1975; Warwick, 1978; Manchester, 1980; CNAA, 1988. Hon. Col, WRAC(TA).

See also H. N. B. Heilbron.

HEIM, Most Rev. Bruno Bernard, PhD, JCD; Apostolic Pro-Nuncio to the Court of St James's, 1982–85 (Apostolic Delegate, 1973–82); *b* Olten, Switzerland, 5 March 1911; *s* of Bernard and Elisabeth Heim-Studer. *Educ:* Olten, Engelberg and Schwyz; St Thomas of Aquino Univ.; Gregorian Univ.; Univ. of Fribourg; Papal Acad. of Diplomacy. Priest 1938; Vicar in Basle and Arbon, 1938–42; Chief Chaplain for Italian and Polish Internees in Switzerland, 1943–45; Sec., Papal Nunciature in Paris; Auditor at Nunciature in Vienna; Counsellor and Chargé d'affaires at Nunciature in Germany; titular Archbp of Xanthos, 1961; Apostolic Delegate to Scandinavia, 1961–69; Apost. Pro-Nuncio (Ambassador): to Finland, 1966–69; to Egypt, 1969–73; President of Caritas Egypt, 1969–73. Lauréat, French Acad.; Corresp. Mem., Real Academia de la Historia, Madrid, 1950; Mem. Council, Internat. Heraldic Acad.; Patron, Cambridge Univ. Heraldic and Genealogical Soc. Grand Cross: Order of Malta, 1950; Teutonic Order, 1961; Order of Finnish Lion, 1969; Order of St Maurice and Lazarus, 1973; (1st Class) Order of the Republic, Egypt, 1975; Bailiff Grand Cross and Grand Prior, Constantinian Order of St George; Sub-Prelate, Order of St John; Comdr, Order of Isabel la Catolica; Gr. Officer Order of Holy Sepulchre; Orders of Merit: Germany, Italy, Austria; Officier Légion d'honneur, etc. *Publications:* Die Freundschaft nach Thomas von Aquin, 1934; Wappenbrauch und Wappenrecht in der Kirche, 1947; Coutumes et droit héraldiques de l'Eglise, 1949; L'oeuvre héraldique de Paul Boesch, 1973; Heraldry in the Catholic Church, 1978, rev. and enlarged edn 1981; Armorial Liber Amicorum, 1981; contrib. Adler, Zeitschrift f. Heraldik und Genealogie, Heraldisk Tidskrift. *Recreations:* heraldry, heraldic painting, cooking, gardening. *Address:* Zehnderweg 31, CH–4600 Olten, Switzerland.

HEIM, Paul Emil, CMG 1988; a Chairman: Financial Services Tribunal, since 1988; Value Added Tax Tribunal, since 1989; President, FIMBRA Appeal Tribunals, since 1990; Visiting Professor, Leicester University, since 1988; *b* 23 May 1932; *s* of George Heim and Hedy Heim (*née* Herz); *m* 1962, Elizabeth, *er d* of late Lt-Col G. M. Allen, MBE; one *s* two *d. Educ:* Prince of Wales School, Nairobi; King's Coll., Univ. of Durham (LLB). Called to the Bar, Lincoln's Inn, 1955, Bencher, 1986. Dep. Registrar, Supreme Court of Kenya, then Sen. Dep. Registrar, Magistrate and Acting Registrar (HMOCS), 1954–65; admitted Advocate, Supreme Court, 1959; Administrator, European Court of Human Rights, Strasbourg, 1965, European Commn of Human Rights, Strasbourg, 1966; Principal Administrator, Political Directorate, Council of Europe, 1967, Dep. Head, Private Office, 1969; Head of Div., then Dir, European Parlt, 1973–81; Registrar, European Court of Justice, 1982–88; Pres., Heads of Admin of EC Instns, 1986–88; Special Advr, European Court of Justice, 1988–89. *Address:* Wearne Wych, Langport, Somerset TA10 9AA.

HEINE, Prof. Volker, FRS 1974; Professor of Theoretical Physics, University of Cambridge, since 1976; Fellow of Clare College, Cambridge, since 1960; *b* 19 Sept. 1930; *m* 1955, M. Daphne Hines; one *s* two *d. Educ:* Otago Univ. (MSc, DipHons); Cambridge Univ. (PhD). FInstP. Demonstrator, Cambridge Univ., 1958–63, Lectr 1963–70; Reader in Theoretical Physics, 1970–76. Vis. Prof., Univ. of Chicago, 1965–66; Vis. Scientist, Bell Labs, USA, 1970–71. For. Mem., Max-Planck Inst., Stuttgart, 1980–. Fellow, Amer. Phys. Soc., 1987. *Publications:* Group Theory in Quantum Mechanics, 1960; (jtly) Solid

State Physics Vol. 24, 1970, Vol. 35, 1980; articles in Proc. Royal Soc., Jl Physics, Physical Review, etc. *Address:* Cavendish Laboratory, Madingley Road, Cambridge CB3 0HE.

HEISBOURG, François; Director, International Institute for Strategic Studies, since 1987; *b* 24 June 1949; *s* of Georges Heisbourg, *qv*; *m* 1989, Elyette, *d* of Georges Levy. Educ: Landon School, Bethesda, Maryland; Collège Stanislas, Paris; Inst. d'Etudes Politiques, Paris; Ecole Nationale d'Administration, Paris. French Foreign Ministry: Asst to Head of Economics Dept, 1978; Mem., Policy Planning Staff, 1979; 1st Sec., French Mission to UN, NY, 1979–81; Diplomatic Adviser to Minister of Defence, 1981–84. Vice-Pres., Thomson SA, Paris, 1984–87. Numerous foreign orders. *Publications:* Emiliano Zapata et la Révolution mexicaine, 1978; (with P. Boniface) La Puce, les Hommes et la Bombe, 1986; (contrib.) The Conventional Defence of Europe, 1986; (contrib.) Conventional Arms Control and East-West Security, 1989; (ed) The Changing Strategic Landscape, 1989; (ed) The Strategic Implications of Change in the Soviet Union, 1990; contribs to internat. jls. *Recreations:* hiking, old atlas collecting. *Address:* International Institute for Strategic Studies, 23 Tavistock Street, WC2E 7NQ. *T:* 071-379 7676. *Club:* Travellers' (Paris).

HEISBOURG, Georges; Ambassador of Luxembourg, retired; *b* 19 April 1918; *s* of Nicolas Heisbourg and Berthe (*née* Ernsterhoff); *m* 1945, Hélène Pinet; two *s* one *d*. *Educ:* Athénée, Luxembourg; Univs of Grenoble, Innsbruck and Paris. Head of Govt Press and Information Office, Luxembourg, 1944–45; Attaché 1945–48, Sec. 1948–51, of Legation, London; Head of Internat. Organisations Section, Dir of Political Affairs, Min. of For. Affairs, Luxembourg, 1951–58; Luxembourg Ambassador to USA, Canada and Mexico, 1958–64; Perm. Rep. to UN, 1958–61; Luxembourg Ambassador: to Netherlands, 1964–67; to France, 1967–70; Perm. Rep. to OECD, 1967–70; Sec. Gen., WEU, 1971–74; Ambassador to USSR, Finland, Poland and Outer Mongolia, 1974–77; Perm. Rep. to Council of Europe, 1978–79; Ambassador to Fed. Rep. of Germany and to Denmark, 1979–83. Médaille de l'Ordre de la Résistance, Grand Officer, Nat. Order of Crown of Oak, 1980 (Chevalier, 1958), Comdr, Order of Adolphe de Nassau, 1963, and Grand Officer, Order of Merit, 1976, Luxembourg; also holds decorations from Austria, Belgium, France, Germany, Italy, Mexico, and the Netherlands. *Publication:* Le Gouvernement Luxembourgeois en exil 1940, Vol. I, 1986, Vol. II, 1987, Vol. III, 1989. *Recreation:* swimming. *Address:* J.-P. Brasseur 32, 1258–Luxembourg.

See also F. Heisbourg.

HEISER, Sir Terence Michael, KCB 1987 (CB 1984); Permanent Secretary, Department of the Environment, since 1985; *b* 24 May 1932; *s* of David and Daisy Heiser; *m* 1957, Kathleen Mary Waddle; one *s* two *d*. *Educ:* Grafton Road Primary Sch., Dagenham; London Evacuee Sch., Sunninghill, Berks; Windsor County Boy's Sch., Berks; Birkbeck Coll., Univ. of London; BA (Hons English). Served in RAF, 1950–52; joined Civil Service 1949, served with Colonial Office, Min. of Works, Min. of Housing and Local Govt; Principal Private Sec. to Sec. of State for the Environment, 1975–76; Under Secretary: Housing Directorate, 1976–79; Local Govt Finance Directorate, 1979–81; Dep. Sec., DoE, 1981–85. Governor and Fellow, Birkbeck Coll., London, 1990–. Freeman, City of London, 1990. Hon. Fellow, Birkbeck Coll., London, 1988. Hon. DLitt Bradford, 1988. *Recreations:* reading, walking, talking. *Clubs:* Reform, Garrick.

HEISKELL, Andrew; Chairman Emeritus, New York Public Library (Chairman, 1981); Chairman of the Board, 1960–80, and Chief Executive Officer, 1969–80, Time Inc., retired; *b* Naples, 13 Sept. 1915; *s* of Morgan Heiskell and Ann Heiskell (*née* Hubbard); *m* 1937, Cornelia Scott (marr. diss.); one *s* one *d*; *m* 1950, Madeleine Carroll (marr. diss.); *m* 1965, Marian, *d* of Arthur Hays Sulzberger, and *widow* of Orvil E. Dryfoos. *Educ:* Switzerland; France; University of Paris. Science teacher, Ecole du Montcel, Paris, 1935. Life Magazine: Science and Medicine Editor, 1937–39; Asst Gen. Manager, 1939–42; Gen. Manager, 1942–46; Publisher, 1946–60; Vice-Pres., Time, Inc., 1949–60. Chm., President's Cttee on Arts and Humanities, 1982–90; Vice-Chm., Vivian Beaumont Theater; Director: Internat. Executive Service Corps; Enterprise Foundn, People for the American Way. Chm., Bryant Park Restoration Corp.; Vice Chm., Hon. Chm., and Hon. Trustee, Brookings Instn; Trustee, Inst. of Internat. Educn. Mem. Bd of Visitors, Graduate Sch. and University Center, City Univ. of New York; Chm., Exec. Cttee, Amer. Acad. in Rome. Fellow, Harvard Coll., 1979–89. Gold Medal Award of Merit, Wharton Sch. Alumni Soc., Univ. of Pennsylvania, 1968; John W. Gardner Leadership Award. Hon. LLD: Shaw Univ., 1968; Lake Erie Coll., 1969; Hofstra Univ., 1972; Hobart and William Smith Colls, 1973; Harvard, 1989; Hon. DLitt Lafayette Coll., 1969. *Address:* Time and Life Building, Rockefeller Center, New York, NY 10020; 870 United Nations Plaza, New York, NY 10017; Darien, Conn, USA.

HELAISSI, Sheikh Abdulrahman Al-; Hon. GCVO; retired; Saudi Arabian Ambassador to the Court of St James's, 1966–76; *b* 24 July 1922. *Educ:* Universities of Cairo and London. Secretary to Embassy, London, 1947–54; Under-Sec., Min. of Agriculture, 1954–57; Head of Delegn to FAO, 1955–61; Ambassador to Sudan, 1957–60; Representative to UN, and to various confs concerned with health and agriculture; Delegate to Conf. of Non-aligned Nations, Belgrade, 1961; Ambassador: Italy and Austria, 1961–66; UK and Denmark (concurrently), 1966–76. Versed in Islamic Religious Law. *Publication:* The Rehabilitation of the Bedouins, 1959. *Address:* PO Box No 8062, Riyadh-11482, Saudi Arabia.

HELE, Desmond George K.; *see* King-Hele.

HELE, Sir Ivor (Henry Thomas), Kt 1983; CBE 1969 (OBE 1954); artist; *b* 13 June 1912; *s* of Arthur Hele and Ethel May Hele; *m* 1957, May E. Weatherly. *Educ:* Prince Alfred Coll., Adelaide. Studied art in Paris, Munich and Italy, 1929–32. Enlisted AIF, 1940; War Artist: ME and New Guinea, 1941–46; Korea, 1952. Work represented in: National War Meml, Canberra; King's Hall, Parlt House, Canberra; various national galls. Archibald Prize, 1951, 1953, 1954, 1955 and 1957. *Relevant publications:* The Art of Ivor Hele, by Vernon Branson, 1966; Ivor Hele: the soldier's artist, by Gavin Fry, 1984. *Recreations:* swimming, gardening. *Address:* Box 35, Aldinga, SA 5173, Australia.

HELE, James Warwick, CBE 1986; High Master of St Paul's School 1973–86; *b* 24 July 1926; *s* of John Warwick Hele, Carlisle; *m* 1948, Audrey Whalley; four *d*. *Educ:* Sedbergh Sch.; Hertford Coll., Oxford; Trinity Hall, Cambridge (Schol., MA). 1st cl. hons History Tripos 1951. 5th Royal Inniskilling Dragoon Guards, 1946–48. Asst Master, Kings College Sch., Wimbledon, 1951–55; Rugby School: Asst Master, 1955–73; Housemaster, Kilbracken, 1965–73; 2nd Master, 1970–73. Chairman: Headmasters' Conference, 1982 (Chm., Acad. Cttee, 1979–81); Indep. Schs Adv. Cttee, 1983–88; Member: Secondary Exams Council, 1986–88; Exec. Cttee, GBA, 1988–. Mem., Dorset FHSA, 1990–. Trustee, Brathay Hall, 1977–. Chm. of Govs, Sherborne Sch., 1990–. *Recreations:* Rugby football (Oxford Univ. XV 1944), hill walking. *Address:* Hillside, Hawkesdene Lane, Shaftesbury, Dorset. *T:* Shaftesbury (0747) 54205. *Club:* East India, Devonshire, Sports and Public Schools.

HELLABY, Sir (Frederick Reed) Alan, Kt 1981; Managing Director, 1963–83, and Chairman, 1983–85, R. & W. Hellaby Ltd; Chairman, P & O New Zealand, since 1986; *b* 21 Dec. 1926; *s* of Frederick Allan Hellaby and Mavis Reed; *m* 1954, Mary Dawn Trotter; three *s* one *d*. *Educ:* King's Coll., Auckland; Auckland Univ. Joined R. & W. Hellaby Ltd, 1948, Dir, 1960–87, Dep. Chm., 1969–87. Chairman: NZ Steel Ltd, 1974–86 (Dir, 1964–86); NZ Insurance Co., 1979–81 (Dir, 1966); NZI Corp. (formed from merger of NZ Insurance and S British Insurance Gp), 1981–87 (Dir, 1981–89); NZ Steel Develt Co. Ltd, 1981–86; Director: Rheem NZ Ltd, 1979–88; IBM (NZ) Ltd, 1981–; Alcan NZ Ltd, 1985–88; P&O Australia, 1986–; NZ Guardians Trust, 1987–; Alcan Australia Ltd, 1988–; NZI Bank Ltd, 1989–; former Director: NZ Steel Mining; Pacific Steel Ltd. Mem., Commn of Inquiry into Meat Industry, 1973. Chm., NZ Export Year Cttee, 1978–79. President: Auckland Chamber of Commerce, 1985–87; NZ Chamber of Commerce, 1987–. Chm. Bd of Governors, King's Coll.; Chm. and Trustee, NZ Police Centennial Trust, 1986; Former Trustee: Massey Univ. Agricl Res. Foundn (also Patron); NZ Red Cross Foundn. Hon. DSc Massey, 1982. *Recreation:* weekend farming. *Address:* 519 Remuera Road, Auckland, New Zealand. *T:* 5247423. *Clubs:* Northern, Royal NZ Yacht Squadron, Auckland Golf (all Auckland).

HELLIER, Maj. Gen. Eric Jim, CBE 1977 (OBE 1970, MBE 1967); Regional Manager, International Military Services, since 1982; *b* 23 July 1927; *s* of Harry and Elizabeth Hellier; *m* 1952, Margaret Elizabeth Leadeham; one *s* one *d* (and one *s* decd). *Educ:* Hugh Saxons Sch.; Cardiff Univ. Served, 1945–66: Navigating Officer, RNVR; regtl duty, Royal Signals; Staff Coll. and Jt Services Staff Coll; GSO2 WO; DAA&QMG 39 Inf. Bde; CO, 24 Signals Regt, 1967–69; GSO1 Plans (Operational Requirements) MoD, 1970; Col A/Q HQ 4 Div, 1971–72; Comd Bde Royal Signals and Catterick Garrison, 1973–74; RCDS, 1975; Brig A/Q HQ 1(BR), Corps, 1976–79; Maj. Gen. Admin, UKLF, 1979–81. Col Comdt, 1981–87, Rep. Col Comdt, 1983, Royal Corps of Signals. Chairman: Gen. Purposes Cttee, Regular Forces Employment Assoc., 1983–; Royal Signals Instn, 1984–89. *Recreations:* squash, ski-ing, sailing. *Address:* Wayside, West Hatch, Taunton TA3 5RJ. *T:* Taunton (0823) 480099. *Clubs:* Army and Navy, Lansdowne.

HELLINGA, Dr Lotte, FBA 1990; a Deputy Keeper, Humanities and Social Sciences, British Library, since 1986; *b* 9 Sept. 1932; *d* of Arie Querido and Catharina Geertruida Querido (*née* Nagtegaal); *m* Wytze Hellinga (*d* 1985); one *s*. *Educ:* Univ. of Amsterdam. Lectr, then Sen. Lectr, Univ. of Amsterdam, 1967–76; Asst Keeper, British Liby, 1976–86. Gutenberg Preis, Mainz, 1989. *Publications:* The Fifteenth Century Printing Types of the Low Countries, 1966; Caxton in Focus, 1982; numerous articles in learned jls. *Address:* 40A Canonbury Square, N1 2AW. *T:* 071–359 2083.

HELLYER, Arthur George Lee, MBE 1967; FLS; Gardening Correspondent to the Financial Times; Editor of Amateur Gardening, 1946–67; Editor of Gardening Illustrated, 1947–56; *b* 16 Dec. 1902; *s* of Arthur Lee Hellyer and Maggie Parlett; *m* 1933, Grace Charlotte Bolt (*d* 1977); two *s* one *d*. *Educ:* Dulwich Coll. Farming in Jersey, 1918–21; Nursery work in England, 1921–29; Asst Editor of Commercial Horticulture, 1929; Asst Editor of Amateur Gardening, 1929–46. Associate of Hon. of Royal Horticultural Society; Victoria Medal of Honour in Horticulture. *Publications:* Your New Garden, 1937; Your Garden Week by Week, 1938; Amateur Gardening Pocket Guide, 1941, 4th rev. edn 1971; The Amateur Gardener, 1948, 4th rev. edn 1972; Encyclopaedia of Plant Portraits, 1953; Encyclopaedia of Garden Work and Terms, 1954; Flowers in Colour, 1955; English Gardens Open to the Public, 1956; Amateur Gardening Popular Encyclopaedia of Flowering Plants, 1957; Garden Plants in Colour, 1958; Garden Pests and Diseases, 1966; Starting with Roses, 1966; Shrubs in Colour, 1966, rev. edn as The Collingridge Book of Ornamental Garden Shrubs, 1981; Find Out About Gardening, 1967; Gardens to Visit in Britain, 1970; Your Lawn, 1970; Carter's Book for Gardeners, 1970; All Colour Gardening Book, 1972; All Colour Book of Indoor and Greenhouse Plants, 1973; Picture Dictionary of Popular Flowering Plants, 1973; Bulbs Indoors, 1976; The Collingridge Encyclopaedia of Gardening, 1976; Shell Guide to Gardens, 1977; Gardens of Genius, 1980; The Dobies Book of Greenhouses, 1981; Gardening Through the Year, 1981; Garden Shrubs, 1982; Climbing and Wall Plants, 1988. *Recreations:* gardening, photography, travelling. *Address:* Orchard Cottage, Rowfant, near Crawley, West Sussex RH10 4NJ. *T:* Copthorne (0342) 714838.

HELLYER, Hon. Paul Theodore, PC (Canada) 1957; FRSA 1973; Syndicated Columnist, Toronto Sun, 1974–84; *b* Waterford, Ont, Canada, 6 Aug. 1923; *s* of A. S. Hellyer and Lulla M. Anderson; *m* 1945, Ellen Jean, *d* of Henry Ralph, Toronto, Ont; two *s* one *d*. *Educ:* Waterford High Sch., Ont; Curtiss-Wright Techn. Inst. of Aeronautics, Glendale, Calif; University of Toronto (BA). Fleet Aircraft Mfg Co., Fort Erie, Ont. Wartime service, RCAF and Cdn Army. Propr Mari-Jane Fashions, Toronto, 1945–56; Treas., Curran Hall Ltd, Toronto, 1950 (Pres., 1951–62). Elected to House of Commons, 1949; re-elected, 1953; Parly Asst to Hon. Ralph Campney, Minister of Nat. Defence, 1956; Associate Minister of Nat. Defence, 1957; defeated in gen. elections of June 1957 and March 1958; re-elected to House of Commons in by-election Dec. 1958 and again re-elected June 1962, April 1963, Nov. 1965, June 1968, and Oct. 1972; defeated gen. election July 1974; Minister of National Defence, 1963–67; Minister of Transport, 1967–69, and Minister i/c Housing, 1968–69; resigned 1969 on question of principle relating to housing. Chm., Federal Task Force on Housing and Urban Develt, 1968. Served as a Parly Rep. to NATO under both L and C administrations. Joined Parly Press Gallery, Oct. 1974. Distinguished visitor, York Univ., 1969–70. Founder and Leader, Action Canada, 1971; joined Progressive Cons. Party, 1972; Candidate for leadership of Progressive Cons. Party, Feb. 1976; re-joined Liberal Party, Nov. 1982. *Publications:* Agenda: a Plan for Action, 1971; Exit Inflation, 1981; Jobs for All—Capitalism on Trial, 1984; Canada at the Crossroads, 1990; Damn the Torpedoes, 1990. *Recreations:* philately, music. *Address:* Suite 506, 65 Harbour Square, Toronto, Ont M5J 2L4, Canada. *Club:* Ontario.

HELMORE, Roy Lionel, CBE 1980; Principal, Cambridgeshire College of Arts and Technology, 1977–86; Fellow of Hughes Hall, Cambridge, since 1982; *b* 8 June 1926; *s* of Lionel Helmore and Ellen Helmore (*née* Gibbins); *m* 1969, Margaret Lilian Martin. *Educ:* Montrose Academy; Edinburgh Univ. (BScEng); MA (Cantab). FIEE, FBIM. Crompton Parkinson Ltd, 1947–49; Asst Lectr, Peterborough Techn. Coll., 1949–53; Lectr, subseq. Sen. Lectr, Shrewsbury Techn. Coll., 1953–57; Head of Electrical Engrg and Science, Exeter Techn. Coll., 1957–61; Principal, St Albans Coll. of Further Education, 1961–77. Association of Principals of Colleges: Hon. Sec., 1968–71; Pres., 1972–73; Hon. Treasurer, 1983–86; Chm., of Council, Assoc. of Colls of Further and Higher Educn, 1987–88. Member: BBC Further Educn Adv. Council, 1967–73; Air Transport and Travel ITB, 1967–73; Technician Educn Council, 1973–79 (Vice-Chm.); Manpower Services Commn, 1974–82; RAF Trng and Educn Adv. Cttee, 1976–79; Chm., Trng and Further Educn Cons. Gp, 1977–82. JP St Albans, 1964–78. *Publication:* CCAT—a brief history, 1989. *Recreations:* gardening, watercolours, opera. *Address:* 5 Beck Road, Saffron Walden, Essex CB11 4EH. *T:* Saffron Walden (0799) 23981.

HELMSING, Most Rev. Charles H.; Former Bishop (RC) of Kansas City-St Joseph (Bishop, 1962–77, retired); *b* 23 March 1908; *s* of George Helmsing and Louise Helmsing (*née* Boschert). *Educ:* St Michael's Parochial Sch.; St Louis Preparatory Seminary; Kenrick Seminary. Sec. to Archbishop of St Louis, 1946–49; Auxiliary Bishop to Archbishop of

St Louis, and Titular Bishop of Axum, 1949; first Bishop, Diocese of Springfield-Cape Girardeau, Mo, 1956–62. Member: Secretariat of Christian Unity, 1963–76; US Bishops Cttee for Ecumenical Affairs, 1964–76; Preparatory Cttee for Dialogue between Anglican Communion and Roman Catholic Church, 1966–67 (Chm., Roman Catholic Members); Chm., Special Cttee for Dialogue with Episcopal Church, US, 1964–76. Hon. Doctorates: Letters: Avila Coll. 1962; Humanities, Rockhurst Coll., 1963. Law: St Benedict's Coll. 1966. Order of Condor, Bolivia, 1966. *Address:* Cathedral House, 416 West 12th, Kansas City, Missouri 64105, USA.

HELY, Air Commodore Arthur Hubert McMath, CB 1962; OBE 1945; Air Commodore Operations, HQ Maintenance Command, 1961–64, retired; *b* 16 Feb. 1909; *s* of Hamilton McMath Hely, OBE, RD and Lubie Thrine Hely (*née* Jörgensen); *m* 1935, Laura Mary Sullivan, 6th *d* of Serjeant A. M. Sullivan, QC; two *s* two *d*. *Educ:* Truro Sch.; Mt Albert GS, Auckland, NZ; Auckland University. Joined Royal Air Force, 1934; Staff Coll., 1942; HQ SACSEA, 1944, 1945; Joint Chiefs of Staff, Australia, 1946–48; Joint Services Staff Coll., 1948; Group Capt. 1950; HQ Fighter Command, 1953–56; HQ Far East Air Force, 1956, 1958; ADC to HM the Queen, 1957–59; Air Ministry (acting Air Commodore), 1958; Air Commodore, 1959. *Recreations:* golf, painting. *Address:* 5 Brewer's Yard, Storrington, West Sussex. *Club:* West Sussex Golf.

HELY-HUTCHINSON, family name of **Earl of Donoughmore.**

HEMANS, Simon Nicholas Peter, CVO 1983; HM Diplomatic Service; Assistant Under-Secretary of State, Central and Southern Africa Department, Foreign and Commonwealth Office, since 1990; *b* 19 Sept. 1940; *s* of Brig. P. R. Hemans, CBE, and Mrs M. E. Hemans (*née* Melsome); *m* 1970, Ursula Martha Naef; three *s* one *d*. *Educ:* Sherborne; London School of Economics (BScEcon). Joined Foreign Office, 1964; British Embassy, Moscow, 1966–68; FO, 1968–69; Dep. Commissioner, Anguilla, March-Oct. 1969; FO, 1969–71; UK Mission to UN, New York, 1971–75; British Embassy, Budapest, 1975–79; FO, 1979–81; Dep. High Comr, Nairobi, 1981–84; Head of Chancery, Moscow, 1985–87; Head of Soviet Dept, FCO, 1987–90. *Recreation:* travel. *Address:* c/o Foreign and Commonwealth Office, SW1.

HEMINGFORD, 3rd Baron; *see* Herbert, D. N.

HEMINGWAY, Albert, MSc, MB, ChB; Emeritus Professor, University of Leeds (Professor of Physiology, 1936–67); *b* 27 July 1902; *s* of Herbert Hemingway, Leeds; *m* 1930, Margaret Alice Cooper; one *d*. *Educ:* University of Leeds. Demonstrator in Physiology, King's Coll., London, 1925; Senior Asst in Physiology, University Coll., London, 1926; Lecturer in Experimental Physiology, Welsh National Sch. of Medicine, 1927. Vis. Prof., Makerere University Coll., Uganda, 1968. Examiner in Physiology, Universities of St Andrews, Birmingham, Bristol, Cambridge, Durham, Glasgow, Liverpool, London, Manchester, Wales and RCS. Mem. various cttees of MRC on work and exercise physiology; Mem. Cttee, Physiological Soc. (Editor, Jl Physiology); Pres., Section I, British Assoc., 1959. *Publications:* original papers on the physiology of the circulation, exercise and the kidney in scientific and medical journals. *Recreation:* travel. *Address:* 4 Helmsley Drive, Leeds LS16 5HY. *T:* Leeds (0532) 785720.

HEMINGWAY, Peter, FCA; Director and Chief General Manager, Leeds Permanent Building Society, 1982–87; *b* 19 Jan. 1926; *s* of William Edward and Florence Hemingway; *m* 1952, June Maureen, *d* of Maurice and Lilian A. Senior. *Educ:* Leeds College of Commerce. With John Gordon, Walton & Co., Chartered Accountants, Leeds, 1941–62, Partner 1959–62; Director, Provincial Registrars Ltd, 1955–62; joined Leeds Permanent Bldg Soc. as Secretary, 1962. Local Dir (Leeds), Royal Insurance (UK) Ltd, 1983–; Dir, Homeowners Friendly Soc., 1983–86. Hon. Sec. 1970–82, Vice-Chm. 1982–84, Chm. 1984–86, Yorkshire and North Western Assoc. of Building Societies; Vice Pres., Northern Assoc. of Building Socs, 1988–; Mem. Council: Building Societies Assoc., 1981–87; Chartered Building Societies Inst., 1982–87. *Recreations:* travel, motor racing, music, gardening. *Address:* Old Barn Cottage, Kearby, near Wetherby, Yorks LS22 4BU. *T:* Harewood (0532) 886380.

HEMLOW, Prof. Joyce; Professor Emerita, McGill University, Montreal, Canada; author; *b* 30 July 1906; *d* of William Hemlow and Rosalinda (*née* Redmond), Liscomb, NS. *Educ:* Queen's Univ., Kingston, Ont (MA; Hon. LLD 1967); Harvard Univ., Cambridge, Mass (AM, PhD). Preceding a univ. career, period of teaching in Nova Scotia, Canada; lecturer in English Language and Literature at McGill Univ.; Prof. of English Language and Literature, McGill Univ., 1955, Greenshields Professor 1965. FRSC 1960. Guggenheim Fellow, 1951–52, 1960–62 and 1966. Member, Phi Beta Kappa, The Johnsonians, and of other literary and professional organizations. Hon. LLD Dalhousie, 1972. James Tait Black Memorial Book Prize, 1958; Brit. Academy Award (Crawshay Prize), 1960. *Publications:* The History of Fanny Burney, 1958 (GB); (ed with others) The Journals and Letters of Fanny Burney (Madame d'Arblay), vols i-xii, 1972–84; (ed) Fanny Burney: selected letters and journals, 1986; articles in learned jls on Fanny Burney's novels and unpublished plays. *Address:* (home) Liscomb, Nova Scotia, Canada; 1521 Le Marchant Street, Apt 3-G, Halifax, NS B3H 3R2, Canada. *Club:* English-Speaking Union (Canadian Branch).

HEMMING, Air Commodore Idris George Selvin, CB 1968; CBE 1959 (OBE 1954); retired; *b* 11 Dec. 1911; *s* of late George Hemming, Liverpool; *m* 1939, Phyllis, *d* of Francis Payne, Drogheda, Eire; two *s*. *Educ:* Chalford, Glos.; Wallasey, Cheshire. Joined RAF, 1928; served War of 1939–45, UK, India and Burma; Gp Capt. 1957; Air Cdre 1962; Dir of Equipment (Pol.) (RAF), MoD, 1962–66; Dir of Equipment (1) (RAF), MoD, Harrogate, 1966–68. *Recreations:* cricket, golf. *Address:* Ash House, St Chloe Green, Amberley, near Stroud, Glos GL5 5AP. *T:* Amberley (0453) 873581. *Club:* Royal Air Force.

HEMMING, John Henry, DLitt; Joint Chairman: Hemming Publishing Ltd (formerly Municipal Journal Ltd), since 1976 (Director, since 1962; Deputy Chairman, 1967–76); Municipal Group Ltd (formerly Municipal Publications Ltd), since 1976; Director and Secretary, Royal Geographical Society, since 1975; *b* 5 Jan. 1935; *s* of late Henry Harold Hemming, OBE, MC, and of Alice Louisa Weaver, OBE; *m* 1979, Sukie, *d* of late M. J. Babington Smith, CBE; one *s* one *d*. *Educ:* Eton College; McGill University; Oxford University (DLitt 1981). Chairman: Brintex Ltd, 1979– (Man. Dir, 1963–70, Dep. Chm. 1976–78); Newman Books, 1979–. Member, Iriri River Expedition, Brazil, 1961; Leader, Maracá Rainforest Project, Brazil, 1987–88. Member Council: Lepra; Anglo-Brazilian Soc.; Inst. of Latin American Studies. Corres. Mem., Academia Nacional de la Historia, Venezuela. Sponsor, Survival International; Trustee: L. S. B. Leakey Trust; Gilchrist Educnl Trust; Greencard Trust; Chm., Empire and Commonwealth Mus. Trust. Hon. DLitt Warwick, 1989; DUniv. Stirling, 1991. Mungo Park Medal, RSGS, 1988; Founder's Medal, RGS, 1990; Washburn Medal, Boston Mus. of Sci., 1990. Orden de Mérito (Peru). *Publications:* The Conquest of the Incas, 1970 (Robert Pitman Literary Prize, 1970, Christopher Award, NY, 1971); (jt) Tribes of the Amazon Basin in Brazil, 1972; Red Gold: The Conquest of the Brazilian Indians, 1978; The Search for El Dorado, 1978; Machu Picchu, 1981; Monuments of the Incas, 1982; The New Incas, 1983; (ed) Change in the Amazon Basin (2 vols), 1985; Amazon Frontier: the defeat of the Brazilian Indians, 1987; Maracá, 1988; Roraima: Brazil's northernmost frontier, 1990. *Recreations:* writing, travel. *Address:* 10 Edwardes Square, W8 6HE. *T:* 071–602 6697. *Clubs:* Boodle's, Beefsteak, Geographical (Mem. Council).

See also L. A. Service.

HEMMINGS, David Leslie Edward; actor, director and producer; engaged in entertainment industry since 1949; *b* 18 Nov. 1941; *m* 1st, 1960, Genista Ouvry; one *d*; 2nd, 1969, Gayle Hunnicutt (marr. diss. 1975); one *s*; 3rd, 1976, Prudence J. de Casembroot; two *s*. *Educ:* Glyn Coll., Epsom, Surrey. The Turn of the Screw, English Opera Group, 1954; Five Clues to Fortune, 1957; Saint Joan, 1957; The Heart Within, 1957; Men of Tomorrow, 1958; In the Wake of a Stranger, 1958; No Trees in the Street, 1959; Some People, 1962; Play it Cool, 1962; Live it Up, 1963; Two Left Feet, 1963; The System, 1964; Be my Guest, 1965; Eye of the Devil, 1966; Blow Up, 1966; Camelot, 1967; Barbarella, 1967; Only When I Larf, 1968; The Charge of the Light Brigade, 1968; The Long Day's Dying, 1968; The Best House in London, 1968; Alfred the Great, 1969; Fragment of Fear, 1970; The Walking Stick, 1970; Unman, Wittering & Zigo, 1971; The Love Machine, 1971; Voices, 1973; Don't Worry Momma, 1973; Juggernaut, 1974; Quilp, 1974; Profundo Rosso, 1975; Islands in the Stream, 1975; The Squeeze, 1976; Jeeves (musical), Her Majesty's, 1975; Power Play, 1978; Thirst, 1979; Beyond Reasonable Doubt, 1980; Jekyll and Hyde, 1980; Harlequin, 1980. BBC TV, Scott Fitzgerald, 1975; ITV, The Rime of the Ancient Mariner, 1978; ITV, Charlie Muffin, 1979. Directed: Running Scared, 1972; The 14, 1973 (Silver Bear Award, Berlin Film Festival, 1973); Disappearance, 1977; Power Play, 1977; Just a Gigolo, 1978; David Bowie Stage, 1979; Murder By Decree, 1979; Survivor, 1979; Race to the Yankee Zephyr, 1980; also in Australia, NZ etc. Produced: Strange Behaviour, 1981; Turkey Shoot, 1981. Director: International Home Video FGH Pty Ltd (Melbourne); Film and General Holdings Inc. (California). *Recreation:* painting. *Address:* c/o Michael Whitehall Ltd, 125 Gloucester Road, SW7. *Clubs:* Turf, Chelsea Arts, Magic Circle.

HEMP, Prof. William Spooner, MA, FRAeS; Stewarts and Lloyds Professor of Structural Engineering, Oxford University, 1965–83; Emeritus Fellow of Keble College, Oxford, since 1984 (Professorial Fellow, 1965–83); *b* 21 March 1916; *s* of late Rev. William James Hemp and Daisy Lilian Hemp; *m* 1938, Dilys Ruth Davies; one *s*. *Educ:* Paston Grammar Sch., North Walsham; Jesus Coll., Cambridge (Scholar, MA). Aeronautical Engineer, Bristol Aeroplane Co., 1938–46. Coll. of Aeronautics: Senior Lecturer, 1946–50; Prof. of Aircraft Structures and Aeroelasticity, 1950–65; Head of Dept of Aircraft Design, 1951–65; Dep. Principal, 1957–65. Mem. of various cttees of Aeronautical Research Council since 1948. Visiting Prof., Stanford Univ., Calif, 1960–61. *Publications:* Optimum Structures, 1973; research papers in the Theory of Structures, Solid Mechanics and Applied Mathematics. *Recreations:* mountain walking, music. *Address:* Duffryn House, Church Lane, Horton-cum-Studley, Oxford OX9 1AW.

HEMPHILL, 5th Baron *cr* 1906, of Rathkenny and Cashel; **Peter Patrick Fitzroy Martyn Martyn-Hemphill;** *b* 5 Sept. 1928; *o s* of 4th Baron Hemphill and Emily, *d* of F. Irving Sears, Webster, Mass; *S* father 1957; *m* 1952, Olivia Anne, *er d* of Major Robert Francis Ruttledge, MC, Cloonee, Ballinrobe, County Mayo; one *s* two *d*; assumed surname of Martyn in addition to Hemphill, 1959. *Educ:* Downside; Brasenose Coll., Oxford (MA). Sen. Steward, Irish Turf Club, 1985–88; Steward, Irish Nat. Hunt Steeplechase Cttee, 1973–76 and 1978–81. *Heir:* *s* Hon. Charles Andrew Martyn Martyn-Hemphill [*b* 8 Oct. 1954; *m* 1985, Sarah J. F., *e d* of Richard Lumley; one *s* two *d*]. *Address:* Raford, Kittulla, Co. Galway, Eire. *Clubs:* White's; Royal Irish Automobile (Dublin); County (Galway); Royal Irish Yacht, Irish Cruising.

HEMSLEY, Thomas Jeffrey; free-lance opera and concert singer; Professor: Guildhall School of Music and Drama, since 1987; Trinity College of Music, since 1988; *b* 12 April 1927; *s* of Sydney William Hemsley and Kathleen Annie Hemsley (*née* Deacon); *m* 1960, Hon. Gwenllian Ellen James, *d* of 4th Baron Northbourne; three *s*. *Educ:* Ashby de la Zouch Grammar Sch.; Brasenose Coll., Oxford (MA). Vicar Choral, St Paul's Cathedral, 1950–51; Prin. Baritone, Stadttheater, Aachen, 1953–56; Deutsche Oper am Rhein, 1957–63; Opernhaus, Zurich, 1963–67; Glyndebourne, Bayreuth, Edinburgh Festivals, etc. Vis. Prof., RCM, 1986; Guest Prof., Royal Danish Acad. of Music, 1990–91. Hon. RAM 1974; Hon. FTCL 1988. *Address:* 10 Denewood Road, N6 4AJ. *T:* 081–348 3397. *Club:* Garrick.

HENAO, Rev. Sir Ravu, Kt 1982; OBE 1975; Executive Secretary, Bible Society of Papua New Guinea, 1980–87; retired; *b* 27 March 1927; *s* of Boga Henao and Gaba Asi; *m* 1944, Lahui Peri; four *s* five *d*. *Educ:* Port Moresby (completed standard 5); Lawes Theol Coll., Fife Bay, Milne Bay Province. Primary sch. teacher, various schs in Central Dist, 1944–66 (pastor as well as teacher, 1946); Chm. (full-time), Papua Ekalesia (national church related to London Missionary Soc.), 1967; Bishop of United Church for Papua Mainland Region, 1968–80. Hon. DTech PNG Univ. of Technology, 1987. *Publications:* (with Raymond Perry) Let's Discuss These Things, 1966; (with Alan Dunstan) Paul's Letter to the Galatians, 1974. *Recreations:* fishing, hunting, gardening. *Address:* c/o PO Box 18, Port Moresby, Papua New Guinea. *T:* 21–7893.

HENBEST, Harold Bernard; *see* Herbert, H. B.

HENDER, John Derrik, CBE 1986; DL; public sector consultant; Chief Executive, West Midlands Metropolitan County Council, 1973–86; *b* 15 Nov. 1926; *s* of late Jessie Peter and late Jennie Hender; *m* 1949, Kathleen Nora Brown; one *d*. *Educ:* Great Yarmouth Grammar School. IPFA, FCA, FBIM. Deputy Borough Treasurer: Newcastle-under-Lyme, 1957–61; Wolverhampton County Borough, 1961–64; City Treas. 1965–69, Chief Exec. and Town Clerk 1969–73, Coventry County Borough. DL West Midlands, 1975. *Publications:* numerous articles relating to various aspects of local govt and related matters. *Recreation:* gardening. *Address:* Chaseleigh, Cringleford Chase, Cringleford, Norwich NR4 7RS.

HENDERSON, family name of **Barons Faringdon** and **Henderson of Brompton.**

HENDERSON OF BROMPTON, Baron *cr* 1984 (Life Peer), of Brompton in the Royal Borough of Kensington and Chelsea and of Brough in the County of Cumbria; **Peter Gordon Henderson,** KCB 1975; Clerk of the Parliaments, 1974–83; *b* 16 Sept. 1922; *m* 1950, Susan Mary Dartford; two *s* two *d*. *Educ:* Stowe Sch.; Magdalen Coll., Oxford (Demy). Served War, Scots Guards, 1942–44. Clerk, House of Lords, 1954–60; seconded to HM Treasury as Sec. to Leader and Chief Whip, House of Lords, 1960–63; Reading Clerk and Clerk of Public Bills, 1964–74; Clerk Asst, 1974. Mem., Cttee on Preparation of Legislation, 1973–74. Member: Rayner Foundn, 1988–; Intermediate Treatment Fund, 1988–; Chairman: John Hunt Award Trust, 1989–; Action on Youth Crime, 1989–. Governor: Godolphin and Latymer Sch., 1983–; Lake District Art Gall. and Museum Trust, 1984–. *Address:* 16 Pelham Street, SW7 2NG; Helbeck Cottage, Brough, Kirkby Stephen, Cumbria CA17 4DD.

HENDERSON, Barry; *see* Henderson, J. S. B.

HENDERSON, Bernard Vere, CBE 1987; Chairman, Anglian Water, since 1981; *b* 8 July 1928; *s* of Percy Cecil and Ruth Elizabeth Henderson; *m* 1952, Valerie Jane Cairns; two *s* one *d. Educ:* Ampleforth Coll.; Harvard Business Sch. Served Army, RE, 1946–48. P. C. Henderson Group, 1949–80 (Man. Dir, 1958–80). Chm., Water Services Assoc., 1990–91. *Recreations:* countryside, narrow boat cruising. *Address:* Anglian Water Plc, Ambury Road, Huntingdon, Cambridgeshire PE18 6NZ. *T:* Huntingdon (0480) 433433.

HENDERSON, Charles Edward, FIA; Head of the Office of Arts and Libraries, since 1989; *b* 19 Sept. 1939; *s* of late David Henderson and of Giorgiana Leggatt Henderson; *m* 1966, Rachel Hilary Hall, *d* of Dr Stephen Hall, FRCP and late Dr Mary Hall, Boarstall Tower, Bucks; one *s* one *d. Educ:* Charterhouse; Pembroke Coll., Cambridge (MA). FIA 1965. Actuarial Trainee, subseq. Asst Investment Sec., Equity & Law Life Assurance Soc., 1960–70; ECGD, 1971–73; DTI, 1973–74; Dept of Energy, 1974–88: Asst Sec., 1975; Under Sec., 1982; Atomic Energy Div., 1982; Oil Div., 1985; Prin. Estabt and Finance Officer, 1986–88. Dir, Aluminium Corp. Ltd, 1981–84. *Recreations:* making and listening to music, mountaineering, golf. *Address:* 33 Fairfax Road, Bedford Park, W4 1EN. *T:* 081–994 1345.

See also Julian Hall.

HENDERSON, Rt. Rev. Charles Joseph; Auxiliary Bishop in Southwark, (RC), since 1972; Titular Bishop of Tricala, since 1972; Area Bishop with responsibility for South East Metropolitan London, since 1980; *b* 14 April 1924; *s* of Charles Stuart Henderson and Hanora Henderson (*née* Walsh). *Educ:* Mount Sion Sch., Waterford; St John's Seminary, Waterford. Priest, 1948; Curate, St Stephen's, Welling, Kent, 1948–55; English Martyrs, Streatham, SW16, 1955–58; Chancellor, RC Diocese of Southwark, 1958–70; Vicar General, RC Diocese of Arundel and Brighton, 1965–66; Episcopal Vicar for Religious, Southwark, 1968–73; Vicar General, RC Archdiocese of Southwark, 1969; Parish Priest, St Mary's, Blackheath, 1969–82; Canon of Cathedral Chapter, 1972; Provost of Cathedral Chapter, 1973. Member: Ecumenical Commn for England and Wales, 1976–; Nat. Catholic Commn for Racial Justice, 1978–81; English Anglican/RC Cttee, 1982–, Co. Chm. 1983–; Methodist/RC Nat. Ecumenical Cttee, 1983 and Co. Chm. 1984–; Chm., RC Cttee for Dialogue with Other Faiths, 1984–; RC Consultant-Observer, BCC, 1982–86; Mem., Pontifical Council for Inter-religious Dialogue, 1990–. Papal Chamberlain, 1960; Prelate of Papal Household, 1965. Freeman, City of Waterford, 1973. Kt Comdr with Star of Equestrian Order of Holy Sepulchre, Jerusalem, 1973. *Recreation:* special interest in sport. *Address:* Park House, 6A Cresswell Park, Blackheath, SE3 9RD. *T:* 081–318 1094.

HENDERSON, David; see Henderson, P. D.

HENDERSON, Sir Denys (Hartley), Kt 1989; Chairman, Imperial Chemical Industries PLC, since 1987; *b* 11 Oct. 1932; *s* of John Hartley Henderson and Nellie Henderson (*née* Gordon); *m* 1957, Doreen Mathewson Glashan, *o d* of Robert and Mary Glashan; two *d. Educ:* Aberdeen Grammar School; Univ. of Aberdeen (MA, LLB). Solicitor; Mem., Law Soc. of Scotland. Joined ICI as lawyer in Secretary's Dept, London, 1957; commercial appts at Agricl Div. and Nobel Div.; Dir, Fertiliser Sales and Marketing, Agricl Div., 1972; Corporate Gen. Manager, Commercial, 1974; Chm., ICI Paints Div., 1977; ICI Main Bd Dir, 1980; Dep. Chm., 1986–87. Non-Exec. Director: Dalgety plc, 1981–87; Barclays Bank, 1983–; Barclays, 1985–; Barclays International, 1985–87; RTZ Corp., 1990–. Chm., Stock Exchange Listed Companies Adv. Cttee, 1987–; Mem., NY Stock Exchange Listed Co. Adv. Cttee, 1988–90. Trustee, Natural Hist. Mus., 1989–. Member: BBC's Consultative Group on Industrial and Business Affairs, 1984–86; CEFIC Presidential Adv. Gp, 1987; CBI President's Cttee, 1987–; Advertising Assoc. President's Cttee, 1988–; Opportunity Japan Campaign Cttee, 1988–; Japan Fest. 1991 Council, 1989–; Industry and Commerce Gp, SCF, 1988–; Adv. Council, Prince's Youth Business Trust, 1986–; Appeal Council, Winston Churchill Meml Trust, 1988–; Council, British Malaysian Soc., 1987–. Pres., Soc. of Business Economists, 1990–. Patron, Assoc. Internationale des Etudiants en Sciences Economiques et Commerciales, 1989–. Mem. Court of Governors, Henley—the Management Coll., 1986– (Chm., 1989–). Hon. Vice-Pres., Chartered Inst. of Marketing, 1989–; CBIM 1981; FInstM 1987; FRSA 1987. Hon. FCGI 1990. DUniv Brunel, 1987; Hon. LLD: Aberdeen, 1987; Nottingham, 1990; Manchester, 1991; Hon. DSc Cranfield Inst. of Technol., 1989. *Recreations:* family life, swimming, reading, travel, minimal gardening, unskilled but enjoyable golf. *Address:* ICI Group Headquarters, 9 Millbank, SW1P 3JF. *T:* 071-834 4444. *Club:* Royal Automobile.

HENDERSON, Derek, FDSRCS; Senior Consultant Oral and Maxillo-facial Surgeon, St Thomas' Hospital, since 1975; Consultant, St George's Hospital, 1975–86; Hon. Consultant, Charing Cross Hospital, since 1977; Recognised Teacher, University of London, since 1977; Hon. Civilian Consultant in Oral Surgery: Royal Navy, since 1971; Army, since 1981; *b* 9 April 1935; *s* of Robert Henderson and Dorothy Edith Henderson; *m* 1961, Jennifer Jill Anderson; one *s* one *d. Educ:* Dulwich Coll.; London Univ. (BDS Hons 1956, MB, BS Hons 1963). FDSRCS (Eng) 1960 (LDS 1956); MRCS, LRCP 1963. Dental and med. trng, KCH, London, 1952–56 and 1959–63 (Prizeman); house surg. appts, KCH and Royal Dental Hosp., 1956–59; King's Coll. Hospital: Lectr in Dental Materials, 1958–65; ENT House Officer, and Casualty Off., 1964; Registrar in Oral Surg., Queen Mary's Hosp., Roehampton, and Westminster Hosp., 1965; Sen. Registrar in Oral Surg., United Cardiff Hosps, 1965–67; Consultant Oral Surgeon to Eastern Reg. Hosp. Bd, Scotland, and Dundee Dental Hosp., 1967–69 (Hon. Sen. Lectr, Univ. of Dundee); Consultant i/c Reg. Maxillo-facial Service to Glasgow and West of Scotland, based on Canniesburn Plastic and Oral Surg. Unit, Glasgow, 1969–75 (Hon. Clinical Teacher, Glasgow Univ.); Consultant, Royal Dental Hosp., 1975–85. Hon. Civilian Consultant, Queen Elizabeth Mil. Hosp., Woolwich (formerly Queen Alexandra Mil. Hosp., Millbank), 1976–81; Hon. Sen. Lectr in Oral Surg., Royal Dental Sch., London, 1977–85. Vis. Prof. and Lectr, Brazil, Argentina, Chile, USA, Spain, Venezuela, Australia, Holland, Saudi Arabia, Uruguay, SA. Royal College of Surgeons: Hunterian Prof., 1975–76; Mem. Council, 1984–86; Kelsey Fry Adviser in Postgraduate Educnl Trng, 1975–80, Mem. Bd, 1978–86, Mem. Exec. Cttee, 1983–86, and Vice-Dean, 1984–85, Faculty of Dental Surgery (also Examr, FDSRCS). Member: Central Cttee for Hospital Dental Services, 1978–85 (Mem. Exec. Cttee, 1980–85); Central Cttee for Univ. Dental Teachers and Research Workers, 1978–81; Negotiating Subcttee, CCHMS, 1980–85; European Assoc. for Maxillo-Facial Surg.; BMA; BDA; Craniofacial Soc. (Mem. Council, 1973–77); Oral Surgery Club GB. Fellow: BAOMS (Mem. Council, 1974–76, 1977–80, 1984–86); Internat. Assoc. of Oral Surgeons. Hon. Mem., Amer. Assoc. of Oral Surgeons in Europe; Hon. Associate Life Mem., Soc. of Maxillo-facial and Oral Surgeons of SA; Hon. Pres., Inst. of Maxillo-Facial Technol., 1977–78. *Publications:* An Atlas and Textbook of Orthognathic Surgery, 1985 (Astra Prize, Soc. of Authors, 1986); contribs on general oral surgery to British Jl of Oral Surgery and British Dental Jl, and especially on surgery of facial and jaw deformity to Brit. Jl of Oral Surg. and Brit. Jl of Plastic Surg. *Recreation:* fly fishing. *Address:* Mallington, Headley Road, Leatherhead, Surrey KT22 8PU. *T:* Leatherhead (0372) 378513; 107 Harley Street, W1N 1DG. *T:* 071–935 6906. *Clubs:* Savage, East India; Royal Navy Medical; Piscatorial Soc.

HENDERSON, Dr Derek Scott; Principal and Vice-Chancellor, Rhodes University, Grahamstown, South Africa, since 1975; *b* 28 Oct. 1929; *s* of late Ian Scott and Kathleen Elizabeth Henderson (*née* White); *m* 1958, Thelma Muriel, *d* of W. E. B. Mullins; two *d. Educ:* St John's Coll., Johannesburg; Rhodes University Coll. (BSc); Oxford Univ. (MA); Cambridge Univ. (MA); Harvard Univ. (PhD). Exec. Trainee, Anglo American Corp. of S Africa, 1953–56; Engr, Advanced Systems Develt, IBM Corp., Poughkeepsie, NY, 1960–62; Univ. of the Witwatersrand: Dir of Computer Centre, 1964–69; Prof. of Computer Science, 1967–75; Dean of Science Faculty, 1974–75. Chm., J. L. B. Smith Inst. of Ichthyology, 1976–; Mem. Council, CSIR, 1982–87; Mem., Scientific Adv. Council, 1988–; Mem. Bd, SABC, 1990–; Vice-Chm., Leather Res. Inst., 1976–; Mem. Council, 1820 Foundn (Vice-Chm., 1976–89); Pres., SA Council of Automation and Computation, 1974. Chairman: Hillbrow Br., Progressive Party, 1964–65; Johannesburg Br., Kolbe Assoc. of Catholic Graduates, 1964; Mem. Council, St Andrew's Coll., 1986–; Trustee, SA Foundn, 1976–; Patron, All Saints Coll., Bisho, 1986–. Dir, Sabinet, 1983–88. Fellow, Computer Soc. of SA, 1974. *Recreation:* golf. *Address:* Rhodes University, PO Box 94, Grahamstown, 6140, S Africa. *T:* 0461–22023. *Club:* Port Elizabeth (Port Elizabeth, S Africa).

HENDERSON, Douglas John; MP (Lab) Newcastle upon Tyne North, since 1987; *b* 9 June 1949; *s* of John and Joy Henderson; *m* 1974, Janet Margaret Graham; one *s. Educ:* Waid Academy, Anstruther, Fife; Central Coll., Glasgow (Scottish Nat. Council Cert.); Univ. of Strathclyde (BA). Apprentice, Rolls Royce, 1966–68; Clerk, British Rail, 1969; Research Officer, GMWU, 1973–75; Regional Organiser, GMWU, then GMB, 1975–87. Mem. Exec., Scottish Council, Labour Party, 1979–87 (Chm., 1984–85). Opposition spokesman on trade and industry, 1988–. Sec., GMB Parly Gp, 1987–. *Recreations:* athletics, mountaineering. *T:* 091–267 2427. *Clubs:* Elswick Harriers, Lemington Labour, Newburn Memorial, Dinnington, Union Jack (Newcastle).

HENDERSON, Douglas Mackay, CBE 1985; FRSE 1966; FLS; Administrator, Inverewe, National Trust for Scotland, since 1987; HM Botanist in Scotland, since 1987; *b* 30 Aug. 1927; *s* of Captain Frank Henderson and Adine C. Mackay; *m* 1952, Julia Margaret Brown; one *s* two *d. Educ:* Blairgowrie High Sch.; Edinburgh Univ. (BSc). Scientific Officer, Dept of Agriculture and Fisheries for Scotland, 1948–51. Royal Botanic Garden, Edinburgh, 1951–87; Regius Keeper, 1970–87. Hon. Prof., Edinburgh Univ., 1983–. Sec., Internat. Assoc. of Botanical Gardens, 1969–81. Curator of Library and Museum, Royal Soc. of Edinburgh, 1978–87. VMH, 1985. *Publications:* British Rust Fungi (with M. Wilson), 1966; many papers on taxonomy of cryptogams. *Recreations:* music, hill walking, cooking, painting, sailing. *Address:* Inverewe House, Poolewe, W Ross IV22 2LQ. *T:* Poolewe (044586) 200; 38E Cramond Vale, Edinburgh EH4 6RB. *T:* 031–312 8432.

HENDERSON, Ven. Edward Chance, BD, ALCD; Archdeacon of Pontefract, 1968–81, now Archdeacon Emeritus; *b* 15 Oct. 1916; *s* of William Edward and Mary Anne Henderson; *m* 1942, Vera Massie Pattison; two *s* three *d. Educ:* Heaton Grammar Sch.; London University. Asst Curate, St Stephen, Newcastle upon Tyne, 1939–42; Organising Sec., CPAS, 1942–45; Vicar of St Mary of Bethany, Leeds, 1945–51; Priest i/c: Armley Hall, Leeds, 1948–51; St John, New Wortley, Leeds, 1949–51; Vicar of: All Souls, Halifax, 1951–59; Dewsbury, 1959–68; Darrington with Wentbridge, 1968–75. Examining Chaplain to Bishop of Wakefield, 1972–81. *Address:* 12 Park Lane, Balne, Goole, North Humberside DN14 0EP. *T:* Goole (0405) 85284.

HENDERSON, Edward Firth, CMG 1972; HM Diplomatic Service, retired; *b* 12 Dec. 1917; *m* 1960, Jocelyn (*née* Nenk), MBE; two *d. Educ:* Clifton Coll.; BNC, Oxford. Served War of 1939–45 in Army (despatches); served in Arab Legion, 1945–47. With Petroleum Concessions Ltd, in Arabian Gulf, 1948–56; Foreign Service, 1956; served in Middle East posts and in Foreign Office; Political Agent, Qatar, 1969–71; and Ambassador there 1971–74. Lectr and Res. Schol., Sch. of Advanced Internat. Studies, Johns Hopkins Univ., 1976, 1977 and 1979; Lectr, Univs of Texas, NY and Princeton, 1979; Hon. Fellow, LSE, 1980–81. Research specialist, Centre for Documentation and Res., Presidential Court, Abu Dhabi, 1976–81; Dir, Council for the Advancement of Arab-British Understanding, 1981–82; Chm., Amer. Educal Trust, Washington, DC, 1982–83. Returned to Abu Dhabi as res. specialist, 1984. *Publication:* This Strange Eventful History: memoirs of earlier days in the UAE and Oman, 1988. *Address:* 2 The Gallery, Northwick Park, Blockley, Moreton-in-Marsh GL56 9RJ. *Clubs:* Travellers', Special Forces.

HENDERSON, Prof. George David Smith, FSA; Professor of Medieval Art, Cambridge, since 1986; Fellow of Downing College, Cambridge, since 1974; *b* 7 May 1931; *yr s* of late Very Rev. Prof. George David Henderson, DLitt, DTh, DD and Jenny Holmes McCulloch Henderson (*née* Smith); *m* 1957, Isabel Bisset Murray; one *s* one *d. Educ:* Aberdeen Grammar Sch.; Univ. of Aberdeen (MA 1953); Courtauld Inst., Univ. of London (BA 1956); Trinity Coll., Cambridge (MA, PhD 1961). Research Fellow, Barber Inst. of Art, Univ. of Birmingham, 1959–60; Graham Robertson Research Fellow, Downing Coll., Cambridge, 1960–63; University of Manchester: Asst Lectr in History of Art, 1962–64; Lectr, 1964–66; University of Edinburgh: Lectr in Fine Arts, 1966–71; Reader in Fine Arts, 1971–73; University of Cambridge: Lectr in History of Art, 1974–79; Head of Dept, 1974–88; Reader in Medieval Art, 1979–86; a Syndic, Fitzwilliam Museum, 1974–. Mem., Ely Cathedral Fabric Adv. Cttee, 1990–. *Publications:* Gothic, 1967; Chartres, 1968; Early Medieval, 1972; (ed with Giles Robertson) Studies in Memory of David Talbot Rice, 1975; Bede and the Visual Arts (Jarrow Lect.), 1980; Losses and Lacunae in Early Insular Art (Garmonsway Lect.), 1982; Studies in English Bible Illustration, 1985; From Durrow to Kells, 1987; articles in UK and Amer. jls. *Recreations:* listening to Wagner, porphyrology, looking for agates. *Address:* Downing College, Cambridge. *T:* Cambridge (0223) 334800. *Club:* United Oxford & Cambridge University.

HENDERSON, Rt. Rev. George Kennedy Buchanan; see Argyll and the Isles, Bishop of.

HENDERSON, Prof. George Patrick, FRSE 1980; Professor of Philosophy in the University of Dundee (formerly Queen's College, Dundee), 1959–80, Dean, Faculty of Arts and Social Sciences, 1973–76; *b* 22 April 1915; *e s* of Rev. George Aitchison Henderson, MA, and Violet Margaret Mackenzie; *m* 1939, Hester Lowry Douglas McWilliam, BSc (*d* 1978), *d* of Rev. John Morell McWilliam, BA. *Educ:* Elgin Academy; St Andrews Univ. (Harkness Scholar); Balliol Coll., Oxford. 1st Class Hons in Philosophy, University of St Andrews, 1936; Miller Prize and Ramsay Scholarship; MA 1936; Ferguson Scholarship in Philosophy, 1936; 2nd Class Lit Hum, University of Oxford, 1938; BA 1938. Asst in Logic and Metaphysics, University of St Andrews, 1938; Shaw Fellow in Mental Philosophy, University of Edinburgh, 1938. MA Oxon, 1943. Army Service, 1940–46; Royal Artillery (commissioned 1940, Adjutant 1942–43) and Gen. Staff (GSO 3 1945); served in UK, Italy and Greece. Lecturer in Logic and Metaphysics, University of St Andrews, 1945; Senior Lecturer, 1953. Corresp. Member: Acad. of Athens, 1973; Ionian Acad., 1975. Editor of the Philosophical Quarterly, 1962–72. *Publications:* The Revival of Greek Thought, 1620–1830, 1970; The Ionian Academy (in Greek trans.), 1980; E. P. Papanoutsos, 1983; The Ionian Academy, 1988; numerous articles and reviews in learned jls. *Recreations:* modern Greek studies, gardening. *Address:* The Pendicle, Waterside Road, Invergowrie, Dundee DD2 5DQ.

HENDERSON, Ian Dalton, ERD 1960 (1st clasp 1966, 2nd clasp 1972); FRCS; Consultant Surgeon, Tunbridge Wells District, 1956–82, now Honorary Consultant Surgeon; *b* 4 Nov. 1918; *s* of Stewart Dalton Henderson and Grace Aird (*née* Masterson); *m* 1951, Rosa Hertz, MB, BS, MRCOG; two *d. Educ:* Fettes Coll., Edinburgh; Guy's Hosp., Univ. of London (MB, BS 1943). LMSSA 1943; FRCS 1949. Served War, RAMC, 1943–46: served India; Major, 1945–46. Lectr in Anatomy and Surg. Registrar, Guy's Hosp., 1947–50; Sen. Surg. Registrar, Royal Postgrad. Med. Sch. of London, 1952–56. Hon. Surgeon to the Queen, 1971–73. Member: Kent AHA, 1973–82; Société Internat. de Chirurgie, 1972–. FRSM 1947–. Served TA and AER, subseq. T&AVR, 1948–79; former Hon. Col and OC 308 Gen. Hosp., T&AVR. Silver Jubilee Medal, 1978. *Recreations:* archaeology, skiing, golf, photography. *Address:* 5 Thornbury Court, Chepstow Villas, W11 2RE. *T:* 071–221 3822.

HENDERSON, James Ewart, CVO 1988; MA, DSc; Chairman, Mastiff Electronic Systems Ltd, since 1985 (Managing Director, 1982–90); *b* 29 May 1923; *s* of late Rev. James Ewart Henderson, MA, BD and Agnes Mary (*née* Crawford); *m* 1st, 1949, Alice Joan Hewlitt; one *d*; 2nd, 1966, Nancy Maude Dominy; two *s. Educ:* private sch.; Glasgow Univ.; Edinburgh Univ. Research on air rockets and guns, MAP, 1943–44; hon. commn in RAFVR, 1944–46; operational assessment of air attacks in Belgium, Holland and Germany, 2TAF, 1944–45; exper. research on fighter and bomber capability, and on the use of radar and radio aids: RAF APC Germany, 1945–46, Fighter Comd, 1946–49 and CFE, 1949–52; research on weapons effects and capability: Air Min., 1952–54, AWRE 1955, Air Min., 1955–58; Asst Scientific Adviser (Ops), Air Min., 1958–63; Dep. Chief Scientist (RAF), MoD, 1963–69; Chief Scientist (RAF) and Mem., Air Force Bd, 1969–73. Aviation Consultant, Hawker Siddeley Aviation Ltd, 1973–77; Financial Consultant, Charles Stapleton & Co. Ltd, 1973–78; freelance Operational Res. and Management Consultant, 1975–78; Scientific Advr, BAe, 1978–82; Director: Lewis Security Systems Ltd, 1976–77; Mastiff Security Systems Ltd, 1977–82; Pres. and Chief Exec., Mastiff Systems US Inc., 1982–88; Chm., TIB Netherlands, 1982–86. Pres., Air League, 1987– (Mem. Council, 1979–80; Chm., 1981–87); Chm., Air League Educational Trust, 1983–87. FInstD 1978. *Publications:* technical papers on operational capability of aircraft and weapons; UK manual on Blast Effects of Nuclear Weapons. *Recreations:* sailing, golf, opera, photography. *Address:* Mastiff Electronic Systems Ltd, Little Mead, Cranleigh, Surrey GU6 8ND. *Clubs:* Naval and Military; Royal Scottish Automobile (Glasgow); Moor Park Golf; New Zealand Golf; Royal Western Yacht.

HENDERSON, (James Stewart) Barry; Director, Industry and Public Policy, British Paper and Board Industry Federation, since 1990; *b* 29 April 1936; *s* of James Henderson, CBE and Jane Stewart McLaren; *m* 1961, Janet Helen Sprot Todd; two *s. Educ:* Lathallan Sch.; Stowe Sch. MBCS. Nat. Service, Scots Guards, 1954–56; electronics and computer industries, 1957–65; Scottish Conservative Central Office, 1966–70; computer industry, 1971–74; management consultant, 1975–86; paper industry, 1987–90. Contested (C): E Edinburgh, 1966; E Dunbartonshire, 1970; Fife NE, 1987. MP (C): East Dunbartonshire, Feb.-Sept. 1974; E Fife, 1979–83; Fife NE, 1983–87. PPS to Economic Sec. to HM Treasury, 1984–87. Member: Select Cttee on Scottish Affairs, 1979–87; H of C Chairmen's Panel, 1981–83; Chm., Scottish Cons. Back Bench Cttee, 1983–84; Vice-Chm., PITCOM, 1986–87. Trustee, St Andrews Links Trust, 1979–87. Comr, Gen. Assembly of Church of Scotland, 1986. MInstD. *Address:* 15 Kennington Park Place, SE11 4AS. *T:* 071–735 6024.

HENDERSON, Sir James Thyne, KBE 1959; CMG 1952; *b* 18 Jan. 1901; *s* of late Sir Thomas Henderson; *m* 1930, Karen Margrethe Hansen; one *s* four *d. Educ:* Warriston, Moffat; Sedbergh Sch.; Queen's Coll., Oxford. Entered Diplomatic Service, 1925, apptd to FO; transf. to Tehran, 1927; Athens, 1929; Helsinki, 1932, where acted as Chargé d'Affaires in 1932, 1933, 1934 and 1935; Foreign Office, 1935. First Sec., 1936; attached to Representative of Finland at the Coronation of King George VI, 1937; Tokyo, 1938; Santiago, 1941; Foreign Office, 1944; Stockholm, 1946, Chargé d'Affaires there in 1946 and 1947; Counsellor, 1947; Consul-Gen., Houston, 1949; HM Minister to Iceland, 1953–56; HM Ambassador to Bolivia, 1956–60, retired. *Recreation:* gardening. *Address:* 43/14 Gillespie Crescent, Edinburgh EH10 4HY. *T:* 031–229 8191.

HENDERSON, Dame Joan; *see* Kelleher, Dame Joan.

HENDERSON, Sir (John) Nicholas, GCMG 1977 (KCMG 1972; CMG 1965); KCVO 1991; HM Diplomatic Service, retired; re-appointed, Ambassador to Washington, 1979–82; author and company director; *b* 1 April 1919; *s* of Prof. Sir Hubert Henderson; *m* 1951, Mary Barber (*née* Cawadias) (OBE 1988); one *d. Educ:* Stowe Sch.; Hertford Coll., Oxford (Hon. Fellow 1975). Mem. HM Diplomatic Service. Served Minister of State's Office, Cairo, 1942–43; Asst Private Sec. to the Foreign Sec., 1944–47; HM Embassy, Washington, 1947–49; Athens, 1949–50; Permanent Under Secretary's Dept, FO, 1950–53; HM Embassy, Vienna, 1953–56; Santiago, 1956–59; Northern Dept, FO, 1959–62; Permanent Under Secretary's Dept, 1962–63; Head of Northern Dept, Foreign Office, 1963; Private Sec. to the Sec. of State for Foreign Affairs, 1963–65; Minister in Madrid, 1965–69; Ambassador to Poland, 1969–72, to Federal Republic of Germany, 1972–75, to France, 1975–79. Lord Warden of the Stannaries, Keeper of the Privy Seal of the Duke of Cornwall, and Mem. of Prince's Council, 1985–90. Mem., BBC General Adv. Council, 1983–87; Chm., Channel Tunnel Gp, 1985–86; Director: Foreign & Colonial Investment Trust, 1982–; M&G Reinsurance, 1982–; Hambros, 1983–; Tarmac, 1983–; F&C Eurotrust, 1984–; Eurotunnel, 1986–88; Supervisory Bd, Fuel-Tech NV, 1987–; Sotheby's, 1989–. Trustee, Nat. Gallery, 1985–89. Pres., Hertford Soc., 1984–89. Romanes Lectr, 1986. Hon. DCL Oxford, 1987. *Publications:* Prince Eugen of Savoy (biography), 1964; The Birth of Nato, 1982; The Private Office, 1984; Channels and Tunnels, 1987; various stories and articles in Penguin New Writing, Horizon, Apollo, Country Life, The Economist and History Today. *Recreations:* tennis, gardening. *Address:* 6 Fairholt Street, SW7 1EG. *T:* 071–589 4291; School House, Combe, near Newbury, Berks. *T:* Inkpen (04884) 330. *Clubs:* Brooks's, Garrick, Beefsteak, Pratt's.
See also Earl of Drogheda.

HENDERSON, John Ronald, CVO 1985; OBE 1985 (MBE 1945); Lord-Lieutenant of Berkshire, since 1989; Chairman, Henderson Administration (Group), 1983–90; *b* 6 May 1920; *s* of Major R. H. W. Henderson and Mrs Marjorie Henderson (*née* Garrard); *m* 1st, 1949, Sarah Katherine Beckwith-Smith (*d* 1972); two *s* one *d*; 2nd, 1976, Catherine Christian; one step *s* two step *d. Educ:* Eton; Cambridge Univ. Served War: ADC to Field Marshal Montgomery, 1942–46; retd Major, 12th Royal Lancers, 1946. Trustee, Winston Churchill Meml Trust, 1985–. Vice Lord-Lieutenant, Berks, 1979–89. KStJ 1989. *Recreations:* racing, shooting, golf, tennis. *Address:* West Woodhay House, Newbury, Berks. *T:* Inkpen (04884) 271. *Club:* White's.

HENDERSON, John Stuart Wilmot; Under Secretary, Ministry of Defence, and Director General of Ordnance Factories, Finance, Procurement and Administration, retired 1976; *b* 31 March 1919; *s* of Bruce Wilmot Henderson and Sarah (*née* Marchant); *m* 1st, 1941, Elsie Kathleen (*née* Rose) (*d* 1981); one *s* three *d*; 2nd, 1984, Yvonne Crawley (*née* Smith), *widow* of Victor James Crawley. *Educ:* Wade Deacon Grammar Sch., Widnes. Exec. Officer, Royal Ordnance Factories, 1938–39; served War of 1939–45: Royal Fusiliers, 1939–43; Intell. Corps, 1944–47; various appts in Ministries of Supply, Aviation, Technology and Defence, 1947–76. *Recreations:* gardening, enjoying music. *Address:* Tregaron, Llantrissent, near Usk, Gwent NP5 1LG. *T:* Usk (02913) 2297.

HENDERSON, Leslie Edwin, CBE 1982; Director of Contracts, Property Services Agency, 1978–82, retired; *b* 16 Dec. 1922; *s* of Thomas Edwin and Mabel Mary Henderson; *m* 1946, Marjorie (*née* Austin); two *s. Educ:* Ealing County Sch., London. Entered Civil Service (BoT) as Clerical Officer, 1939; Min. of Shipping, 1939; served in RAF, 1941–46; Min. of War Transport, 1946; subsequently in: Min. of Transport and Civil Aviation, MoT, DoE; Head of Contracts, Highways, Dept of Transport, 1968–78. *Recreations:* gardening, do-it-yourself. *Address:* 61 Greenacres Avenue, Ickenham, Mddx UB10 8HH. *T:* Ruislip (0895) 672536.

HENDERSON, Michael John Glidden; Chairman, Cookson Group plc, 1990; *b* 19 Aug. 1938; *s* of William Glidden Henderson and Aileen Judith Henderson (*née* Malloy); *m* 1965, Stephanie Maria Henderson; four *s. Educ:* St Benedict's Sch., Ealing. Took articles with William Dyson Jones & Co., 1956; qual. as chartered accountant, 1961; Whinney Smith & Whinney & Co., 1963; Goodlass Wall & Lead Industries, later Cookson Group plc, 1965; Cookson Group: Dir, 1975; Man. Dir, 1979; Gp Man. Dir, 1984; Chief Exec., 1987–90; Dir, Guinness Mahon & Co. *Recreations:* tennis, cricket, watching all sports.

HENDERSON, Sir Nicholas; *see* Henderson, Sir J. N.

HENDERSON, Admiral Sir Nigel Stuart, GBE 1968 (OBE 1944); KCB 1962 (CB 1959); DL; *b* 1 Aug. 1909; *s* of late Lt-Col Selby Herriott Henderson, IMS; *m* 1939, Catherine Mary Maitland, *d* of Lt-Col C. A. S. Maitland of Dundrennan; one *s* two *d. Educ:* Cheltenham Coll. Entered RN, 1927; served War of 1939–45 in HM Ships and as Fleet Gunnery Officer, Mediterranean; Comdr 1942; Capt. 1948; Naval Attaché, Rome, 1949–51; in comd HMS Protector, 1951; in comd RN Air Station, Bramcote, 1952; Imperial Defence Coll., 1954; in command HMS Kenya, 1955; Rear-Admiral, 1957; Vice-Naval Dep. and Naval Dep. to Supreme Allied Comdr, Europe, 1957–Dec. 1959; Vice-Adm. 1960; Dir-Gen. of Training, Admiralty, 1960–62; C-in-C Plymouth, 1962–65; Adm. 1963; Head of British Defence Staffs, Washington, British Mem., Standing Gp, and UK Rep., Mil. Cttee, NATO, 1965–68; Chm., Mil. Cttee, NATO, 1968–71; retired 1971. Rear-Admiral of the United Kingdom, 1973–76; Vice-Admiral of the United Kingdom, and Lieutenant of the Admiralty, 1976–79. Pres., Royal British Legion, Scotland, 1974–80. DL Stewartry of Kirkcudbright, 1973. *Recreations:* sketching, golf, bird-watching. *Address:* Hensol, Mossdale, Castle Douglas, Kirkcudbrightshire DG7 2NE. *T:* Laurieston (06445) 207.

HENDERSON, (Patrick) David; Head of Economics and Statistics Department, Organization for Economic Co-operation and Development, 1984–April 1992; *b* 10 April 1927; *s* of late David Thomson Henderson and late Eleanor Henderson; *m* 1960, Marcella Kodicek; one *s* one *d. Educ.* Ellesmere Coll., Shropshire; Corpus Christi Coll., Oxford. Fellow and Tutor in Economics, Lincoln Coll., Oxford, 1948–65; Univ. Lectr in Economics, Oxford, 1950–65; Commonwealth Fund Fellow (Harvard), 1952–53; Junior Proctor, Oxford Univ., 1955–56; Economic Adviser, HM Treasury, 1957–58; Chief Economist, Min. of Aviation, 1965–67; Adviser Harvard Development Advisory Service (Athens and Kuala Lumpur), 1967–68; Vis. Lectr, World Bank, 1968–69; Economist, World Bank, 1969–75, Dir of Economics Dept 1971–72; Prof. of Political Economy, UCL, 1975–83. Mem., Commn on Environmental Pollution, 1977–80; Special Adviser, Sec. of State for Wales, 1978–79; Member: Nat. Ports Council, 1979–81; Bd, Commonwealth Develt Corp., 1980–83. Reith Lectr, BBC, 1985; Copland Meml Address, 1989. *Publications:* India: the energy sector, 1975; Innocence and Design: the influence of economic ideas on policy, 1986; (jointly) Nyasaland: The Economics of Federation, 1960; ed and contrib.: Economic Growth in Britain, 1965; contrib: The British Economy in the 1950's, 1962; Public Enterprise, 1968; Public Economics, 1969; Unfashionable Economics, 1970; The World Bank, Multilateral Aid and the 1970's, 1973; The Economic Development of Yugoslavia, 1975; Contemporary Problems of Economic Policy, 1983; Protectionism and Growth, 1985; Economic Policies for the 1990s, 1991; articles in economic and other jls. *Address:* c/o OECD, 2 rue André Pascal, 75775 Paris, Cedex 16, France.

HENDERSON, Prof. Paul, DPhil; Keeper of Mineralogy, Natural History Museum, since 1989; *b* 7 Nov. 1940; *s* of Thomas William Henderson and Dorothy Violet (*née* Marriner); *m* 1966, Elizabeth Kathryn Ankerson; one *s* one *d. Educ:* King's Coll. Sch., Wimbledon; Univ. of London (BSc 1963); Univ. of Oxford (DPhil 1966). FGS 1990; CGeol 1990. Asst Lectr in Chemistry, Glasgow Univ., 1967–68; Lectr in Geochem., Chelsea Coll., Univ. of London, 1968–76; Department of Mineralogy, British Museum (Natural History): PSO, 1977; Grade 6, 1984; Dep. Keeper, 1987. Visiting Professor: Univ. of Bern, Switzerland, 1989; UCL, 1990–; Vis. Res. Fellow, Univ. of Alberta, Canada, 1976; Hon. Research Fellow: Chelsea Coll., Univ. of London, 1979–85; RHBNC, Univ. of London, 1985–86. Pres., Mineralogical Soc., 1989–91 (Mem. Council, 1974–76 and 1986–89); Member Council: Eur. Assoc. for Geochem., 1986–; Internat. Mineralog. Assoc., 1989–. Fourmarier Medal, Belgian Geol Soc., 1989. *Publications:* Inorganic Geochemistry, 1982; (ed) Rare Earth Element Geochemistry, 1984; contribs to jls on geochem. and mineral chem. *Recreations:* music, Paris, wine, Gothic architecture. *Address:* Department of Mineralogy, Natural History Museum, Cromwell Road, SW7 5BD. *T:* 071–938 9226.

HENDERSON, Dr Richard, FRS 1983; Member of Scientific Staff, Medical Research Council Laboratory of Molecular Biology, Cambridge, since 1973; Fellow of Darwin College, Cambridge, since 1981; *b* 19 July 1945; *s* of John and Grace Henderson; *m* 1969, Penelope FitzGerald; one *s* one *d* (and one *d* decd). *Educ:* Hawick High Sch.; Boroughmuir Secondary Sch.; Edinburgh Univ. (BSc); Cambridge Univ. (PhD). Helen Hay Whitney Fellow, Yale, 1970–73. William Bate Hardy Prize, Cambridge Phil Soc., 1978; Ernst Ruska Prize for Electron Microscopy, Ernst Ruska Foundn, 1981. *Publications:* research pubns and reviews in scientific jls. *Recreations:* canoeing, wine-tasting. *Address:* MRC Laboratory of Molecular Biology, Hills Road, Cambridge CB2 2QH. *T:* Cambridge (0223) 248011.

HENDERSON, Major Richard Yates, TD 1966; JP; Lord-Lieutenant of Ayrshire and Arran, since 1991; *b* 7 July 1931; *s* of late John Wishart Henderson and Dorothy (*née* Yates); *m* 1957, Frances Elizabeth Chrystal; two *s* one *d* (and one *s* decd). *Educ:* Rugby; Hertford Coll., Oxford (BA); Glasgow Univ. (LLB). Served Royal Scots Greys, 1950–52; Ayrshire Yeomanry TA, 1953–69. Partner, Mitchells Robertson, Solicitors, Glasgow, 1958–90; Trustee, TSB, Glasgow, 1966–74; Dir, West of Scotland TSB, 1974–83. Mem., Royal Company of Archers, Queen's Body Guard for Scotland. DL Ayrshire, 1970–90. *Recreations:* shooting, tennis, golf. *Address:* Blairston, by Ayr KA7 4EF. *T:* Alloway (0292) 41601. *Club:* Western (Glasgow).

HENDERSON, Robert Alistair; Chairman: Kleinwort, Benson, Lonsdale plc, 1978–88; Kleinwort Development Fund PLC (formerly Cross Investment Trust Ltd), 1969–91; Merchants Trust PLC, since 1985; Deputy Chairman, Cadbury Schweppes plc, since 1983 (Director, since 1977); *b* 4 Nov. 1917; *s* of Robert Evelyn Henderson and Beatrice Janet Elsie Henderson; *m* 1947, Bridget Elizabeth, *d* of late Col J. G. Lowther, CBE, DSO, MC, TD, and Hon. Lilah White, *er d* of 3rd Baron Annaly; two *s* one *d*. *Educ:* Eton; Magdalene Coll., Cambridge. Hons degree in History. Served War: 60th Rifles, 1940–45, Captain. Jessel Toynbee & Co. Ltd, 1945–48; Borneo Co. Ltd, 1948–51; Robert Benson, Lonsdale & Co. Ltd, 1951 (Dir, 1957); Dir, Kleinwort, Benson Ltd, 1961 (on merger of Robert Benson, Lonsdale & Co. Ltd with Kleinwort Sons & Co.; Vice-Chm., 1970–71, Dep. Chm., 1971–75, Chm., 1975–83). Dir, Equitable Life Assurance Soc., 1958–81; Dir, 1981–89, Dep. Chm., 1985–89, British Airways; Chm., MT Oil & Gas, 1985–87. *Recreations:* gardening, shooting, fishing. *Address:* 7 Royal Avenue, Chelsea, SW3 4QE; North Ecchinswell Farm, Ecchinswell, near Newbury, Berks RG15 8UJ. *T:* Headley (063523) 244. *Clubs:* White's, Brooks's.

HENDERSON, Robert Brumwell, CBE 1979; Director, Ulster Television, since 1991 (Managing Director, 1959–83, Deputy Chairman, 1977–83; Chairman, 1983–90); *b* 28 July 1929; *s* of late Comdr Oscar Henderson, CVO, CBE, DSO, RN, and of Mrs Henderson; *m*; two *d*; *m* 1970, Patricia Ann Davison. *Educ:* Brackenber House Sch., Belfast; Bradfield Coll., Berks; Trinity Coll., Dublin. BA (Hons) 1951, MA 1959. Journalism: London, Liverpool, Glasgow and Belfast, 1951–59. Director: ITN, 1964–68; Independent Television Publications, 1969–86; Chm., Publicity Assoc. of NI, 1959–60; Vice-Chm., Co-operation North, 1984–; Dep. Chm., Powerscreen Internat. PLC; President: Radio Industries Club of NI, 1963–70, 1972–80; NI Chamber of Commerce and Industry, 1980–81; NI Br., Inst. of Marketing 1984–; NI Br., Chartered Inst. of Marketing, 1984–; Assoc. of Ulster Drama Festivals, 1984–; Member: Exec. Council, Cinema and Television Benevolent Fund, 1980–84; Council for Continuing Educn, 1975–85; NI Council for Educnl Develt, 1980–; Cttee to Review Higher Educn in NI, 1964; various cttees of Trinity Coll. Dublin, Univ. of Ulster; Senate, Queen's Univ. of Belfast, 1980–; Council, Inst. of Dirs, 1981– (Chm., NI Br., 1973–79); Governor, Ulster Polytechnic, 1979–84. FRTS 1977 (Mem. Council, 1981–84, Chm., 1982–84, Vice Pres., 1986–). Hon. DLitt Ulster, 1982. *Publications:* Midnight Oil, 1961; A Television First, 1977; Amusing, 1984. *Recreations:* reading, theatre and cinema, golf. *Address:* 8 Crabtree Road, Ballynahinch, Co. Down BT24 8RH. *Clubs:* Naval and Military; Royal County Down Golf; Malone Golf.

HENDERSON, Robert Ewart, QC (Scot.) 1982; *b* 29 March 1937; *s* of William Ewart Henderson and Agnes Ker Henderson; *m* 1st, 1958, Olga Sunter; two *s* two *d*; 2nd, 1982, Carol Black. *Educ:* Larchfield Sch., Helensburgh; Morrison's Acad., Crieff; Glasgow Univ. (BL 1962). Admitted to Faculty of Advocates, 1963. National Service, 2nd Lieut RA, 1956–58. Hon. Sheriff-Substitute, Stirling, Dunbarton and Clackmannan, 1968; Standing Jun. Counsel in Scotland, DTI, 1970–74, Dept of Trade, 1974–77; Temp. Sheriff, 1978. Pres., Glasgow Univ. Law Soc., 1961–62; Chairman: NHS Appeal Tribunal, 1972; Medical Appeal Tribunal (Scotland), 1985–; War Pensions Appeal Tribunal, 1986–. Contested (C) Inverness-shire, Feb. and Oct. 1974. *Recreations:* golf, sailing. *Address:* The Old Schoolhouse, Gullane, East Lothian EH31 2AF. *T:* Gullane (0620) 842012. *Clubs:* New (Edinburgh); Hon. Company of Edinburgh Golfers (Muirfield); Royal St George's Golf (Sandwich).

HENDERSON, Roger Anthony, QC 1980; a Recorder of the Crown Court, since 1983; *b* 21 April 1943; *s* of late Dr Peter Wallace Henderson and of Dr Stella Dolores Henderson; *m* 1968, Catherine Margaret Williams; three *d* (and one *d* decd). *Educ:* Radley Coll.; St Catharine's Coll., Cambridge (Scholar; 1st Cl. Hons degree in Law, MA; Adderley Prize for Law, 1964). Inner Temple: Duke of Edinburgh Award, 1962; Major Scholarship, 1964; called to the Bar, 1964; Bencher, 1985. Counsel to King's Cross Inquiry, 1988. Mem., Bar Council, 1988–; Chm., Public Affairs Cttee of Bar, 1989–90. Member: Exec. Council, British Acad. of Forensic Sciences, 1977–90 (Pres., 1986–87); Council of Legal Educn, 1983–90. Gov., London Hosp. Med. Coll., 1989–; Chm., Special Cttee, St Peter's Hosps, 1989–. *Recreations:* fly-fishing, gardening, shooting. *Address:* 2 Harcourt Buildings, Temple, EC4Y 9DB. *T:* 071–583 9020; 9 Brunswick Gardens, W8 4AS; Holbury Mill, Lockerley, Romsey, Hants. *T:* Lockerley (0794) 40583; Upper Round Road, St John's Parish, Nevis, West Indies.

HENDERSON, Roy (Galbraith), CBE 1970; FRAM; retired baritone and Teacher of Singing (private); Professor of Singing, RAM, London, 1940–74; *b* Edinburgh, 4 July 1899; *er s* of late Rev. Dr Alex. Roy Henderson, formerly Principal of Paton Coll., Nottingham; *m* 1926, Bertha Collin Smyth (*d* 1985); one *s* two *d*. *Educ:* Nottingham High Sch.; Royal Academy of Music, London (Worshipful Company of Musicians Medal). Debut as baritone singer, Queen's Hall, London, 1925; has sung at all leading Festivals in England, Internat. Festival for contemporary music, Amsterdam, 1933; recitals at first two Edinburgh Festivals, 1947 and 1948; principal parts in all Glyndebourne Opera festivals, 1934–40, associated chiefly with works of Delius, Elgar and Vaughan Williams, and sang many first performances of contemp. music. Retired from concert platform, 1952, to devote his whole time to teaching (among his pupils was late Kathleen Ferrier). Conductor, Huddersfield Glee and Madrigal Soc., 1932–39; Founder and Conductor, Nottingham Oriana Choir, 1937–52. Conductor of Bournemouth Municipal Choir, 1942–53. Adjudicator at International Concours, Geneva, 1952, and Triennially, 1956–65. Mem. of the Jury of the International Muziekstad s'Hertogenbosch, Holland, 1955–62, 1965, and Barcelona, 1965. Master classes in singing: Royal Conservatory of Music, Toronto, 1956; Toonkunst Conservatorium, Rotterdam, 1957, 1958; s'Hertogenbosch, 1967. Awarded the Sir Charles Santley memorial by Worshipful Company of Musicians for distinguished services to the art of singing, 1958. *Publications:* contributed to: Kathleen Ferrier, ed Neville Cardus, 1954; Opera Annual, 1958; The Voice, ed Sir Keith Falkner, 1983. *Recreations:* fishing, gardening and cricket. *Address:* 90 Burbage Road, SE24 9HE. *T:* 071–274 9004.

HENDERSON, William Crichton; Advocate; Sheriff of Tayside, Central and Fife (formerly Stirling, Dunbarton and Clackmannan) at Stirling, since 1972 (also at Alloa, 1972–81); *b* 10 June 1931; *s* of late William Henderson, headmaster, and late Helen Philp Henderson (*née* Crichton); *m* 1962, Norma Sheila Hope Henderson (*née* Grant) (marr. diss. 1985); two *d*. *Educ:* George Watson's Boys' Coll., Edinburgh; Edinburgh Univ. MA Edinburgh 1952, LLB Edinburgh 1954. Admitted Solicitor, 1954; Diploma in Administrative Law and Practice, Edinburgh, 1955; called to Scottish Bar, 1957; practised as Advocate, 1957–68; Sheriff of Renfrew and Argyll at Paisley, 1968–72. Pres., Sheriffs' Assoc., 1985–88 (formerly Sec. and Vice-Pres.). Chm., Supreme Court Legal Aid Cttee, 1967–68. Assoc. Mem., Commonwealth Magistrates' and Judges' Assoc. *Recreations:* gardening, travel. *Address:* 7 Magdala Crescent, Edinburgh EH12 5BE. *Clubs:* New, University Staff (Edinburgh).

HENDERSON, Sir William (MacGregor), Kt 1976; FRS 1976; FRSE 1977; President, Zoological Society of London, 1984–89; *b* 17 July 1913; *s* of late William Simpson Henderson and late Catherine Alice Marcus Berry; *m* 1941, Alys Beryl Goodridge; four *s*. *Educ:* George Watson's Coll., Edinburgh; Royal (Dick) Veterinary Coll., Edinburgh (MRCVS); Univ. of Edinburgh (BSc, DSc). Assistant, Dept of Medicine, Royal (Dick) Veterinary Coll., Edinburgh, 1936–38; Member Scientific Staff, Animal Virus Research Inst., Pirbright, 1939–56, Dep. Dir, 1955–56; Director, Pan American Foot-and-Mouth Disease Center, Rio de Janeiro, 1957–65; Head, Dept of Microbiology, ARC Inst. for Research on Animal Diseases, Compton, 1966–67, Director, 1967–72; Sec., ARC, 1972–78. Visiting Prof., Univ. of Reading, 1970–72. Chm., Genetic Manipulation Adv. Gp, 1979–81. Mem., Science Council, 1980–82, Bd Mem., 1982–84, Celltech Ltd; Chm., Woodstock Breeding Services, 1988–89. Pres., Royal Assoc. of British Dairy Farmers, 1985–87. Corresp. Member: Argentine Assoc. of Microbiology, 1959; Argentine Soc. of Veterinary Medicine, 1965; Foreign Mem., Argentine National Acad. of Agronomy and Veterinary Science, 1980; Hon. Mem. Brasilian Soc. of Veterinary Medicine, 1965; FRCVS, by election, 1973; FIBiol; Hon. Fellow, RASE, 1979. Hon. DVMS Edinburgh, 1974; Hon. DVSc Liverpool, 1977; Hon. DSc Bristol, 1985; DUniv Stirling, 1989. Orden de Mayo, Argentina, 1962. Dalrymple-Champneys Award, 1974; Massey-Ferguson National Award, 1980; Underwood-Prescott Award, 1981. *Publications:* Quantitative Study of Foot-and-Mouth Disease Virus, 1949; Man's Use of Animals, 1981; British Agricultural Research and the Agricultural Research Council, 1981; contribs to scientific jls principally on foot-and-mouth disease. *Recreation:* gardening. *Address:* Yarnton Cottage, Streatley, Berks RG8 9HY. *Clubs:* Athenæum; New (Edinburgh).

HENDERSON, William Ross, CBE 1988; TD 1972, clasps 1978, 1984; Conservative Central Office Agent, Western Area, since 1989; *b* 15 Sept. 1936; *s* of Major William Ross Henderson and Jean Elizabeth Doxford Henderson; *m* 1969, Valerie Helen Thomas; one *s* one *d*. *Educ:* Argyle House School, Sunderland. Agent and Secretary, Newcastle upon Tyne West Cons. Assoc., 1961–68; Dep. Central Office Agent, Greater London Area, 1968–76; Cons. Party Training Officer, 1976–80; Central Office Agent, East of England Area, 1980–84; Dir, Scottish Cons. and Unionist Central Office, 1984–87. Cross of Merit, Gold Class, Poland, 1972. *Recreations:* gardening, reading. *Address:* Applegarth, Priesthill, Kentisbeare, Cullompton, Devon EX15 2BG. *Clubs:* St Stephen's Constitutional; Caledonian (Edinburgh).

HENDERSON-STEWART, Sir David (James), 2nd Bt *cr* 1957; *b* 3 July 1941; *s* of Sir James Henderson-Stewart, 1st Bt, MP, and of Anna Margaret (*née* Greenwell); *S* father, 1961; *m* 1972, Anne, *d* of Count Serge de Pahlen; three *s* one *d*. *Educ:* Eton Coll.; Trinity Coll., Oxford. *Heir:* *s* David Henderson-Stewart, *b* 2 Feb. 1973. *Address:* 90 Oxford Gardens, W10. *T:* 01–960 1278.

HENDRICKSE, Prof. Ralph George, MD; FRCP, FRCPE; Professor and Head of Department of Tropical Paediatrics, 1974–91, and Dean, 1988–91, Liverpool School of Tropical Medicine; *b* 5 Nov. 1926; *s* of William George Hendrickse and Johana Theresa Hendrickse (*née* Dennis); m 1948, Begum Johanara Abdurahman; one *s* four *d*. *Educ:* Livingstone High Sch.; Univ. of Cape Town (MD). FMCPaed (Hon. Foundn Fellow). Res. MO, McCord Zulu Hosp., Durban, 1949–54, incl. secondment to Willis F. Pierce Meml Hosp., S Rhodesia, as MO i/c, 1951; postgrad. studies, Glasgow and Edinburgh, 1955; Sen. Registrar, UCH, Ibadan, Nigeria, 1955–57; Sen. Lectr, Univ. of Ibadan, 1957–62, and Hon. Consultant Paediatrician, UCH, 1957–69; Prof. and Head of Paediatrics, Univ. of Ibadan, 1962–69. Dir, Inst. of Child Health, 1964–69; Sen. Lectr, Liverpool Univ. Sch. of Trop. Med., 1969–74. Hon. Vis. Prof., Santo Tomas Univ., Philippines. Hon. Mem., Philippines Paed. Soc. Founder and Editor-in-Chief, Annals of Tropical Paediatrics, 1981–. Frederick Murgatroyd Prize, RCP, 1970. *Publications:* Paediatrics in the Tropics: current review, 1981; (ed and contrib.) Paediatrics in the Tropics, 1991; papers in learned jls. *Recreations:* photography, sketching, theatre, swimming, travel. *Address:* Beresford House, 25 Riverbank Road, Heswall, Wirral, Merseyside L60 4SQ. *T:* 051–342 5510.

HENDRIE, Dr Gerald Mills; Professor of Music, The Open University, 1969–90; *b* 28 Oct. 1935; *s* of James Harold Hendrie and Florence Mary MacPherson; *m* 1st, 1962, Dinah Florence Barsham (*d* 1985); two *s*; 2nd, 1986, Dr Lynette Anne Maddern, MB, BS. *Educ:* Framlingham Coll., Suffolk; Royal Coll. of Music; Selwyn Coll., Cambridge (MA, MusB, PhD). FRCO, ARCM. Director of Music, Homerton Coll., Cambridge, 1962–63; Lectr in the History of Music, Univ. of Manchester, 1963–67; Prof. and Chm., Dept of Music, Univ. of Victoria, BC, Canada, 1967–69; Reader in Music, subseq. Prof., The Open Univ., 1969–90; Dir of Studies in Music, St John's Coll., Cambridge, 1981–84, Supervisor, 1977–84. Vis. Fellow in Music, Univ. of WA, 1985. *Publications:* Musica Britannica XX, Orlando Gibbons: Keyboard Music, 1962, 2nd rev. edn, 1967; G. F. Handel: Anthems für Cannons, 3 vols, 1985, 1987, 1991; articles for Die Musik in Geschichte und Gegenwart; musical compositions include: Five Bagatelles for piano, 1980; Four Excursions for piano, 1983; Three Pieces for flute and piano, 1985; Specula Petro for organ, 1988; Quintet for Brass, 1988; Choral: Hommage à César Franck for organ, 1990; Prelude and Fugue: Le Tombeau de Marcel Dupré for organ, 1991; Toccata and Fugue, Le Tombeau de Marcel Dupré for organ, 1991; choral music. *Recreations:* windsurfing, walking, gardening, needlepoint. *Address:* The Garth, 17 The Avenue, Dallington, Northampton NN5 7AJ. *T:* Northampton (0604) 587267.

HENDRY, Prof. Arnold William; Professor of Civil Engineering, University of Edinburgh, 1964–88, now Emeritus; *b* 10 Sept. 1921; *s* of late Dr George Hendry, MB, ChB, Buckie, Scotland; *m* 1st, 1946, Sheila Mary Cameron Roberts (*d* 1966), Glasgow; one *s* one *d* (and one *s* decd); 2nd, 1968, Elizabeth Lois Alice Inglis, Edinburgh. *Educ:* Buckie High Sch.; Aberdeen Univ. Civil engineer with Sir William Arrol & Co. Ltd, Bridge builders and Engineers, Glasgow, 1941–43; Asst in Engineering, University of Aberdeen, 1943–46; Lecturer in Civil Engineering, 1946–49; Reader in Civil Engineering, Univ. of London, King's Coll., 1949–51; Prof. of Civil Engrg and Dean of Fac. of Engrg, Univ. of Khartoum, 1951–57; Prof. of Building Science, University of Liverpool, 1957–63. *Publications:* An Introduction to Photo-Elastic Analysis, 1948; (with L. G. Jaeger) The Analysis of Grid Frameworks, 1958; The Elements of Experimental Stress Analysis, 1964, 2nd edn 1977; Structural Brickwork, 1981; An Introduction to the Design of Load Bearing Brickwork, 1981; Structural Masonry, 1990; (ed) Reinforced and Prestressed Masonry, 1991; about 100 papers and articles in professional and technical jls. *Address:* c/o Department of Civil Engineering and Building Science, School of Engineering, The King's Buildings, Edinburgh EH9 3JL; 146/6 Whitehouse Loan, Edinburgh EH9 2AN.

HENDRY, Prof. David Forbes, PhD; FBA 1987; Professor of Economics, University of Oxford, since 1982; Fellow, Nuffield College, Oxford, since 1982; *b* 6 March 1944; *s* of Robert Ernest Hendry and Catherine Helen (*née* Mackenzie); *m* 1966, Evelyn Rosemary (*née* Vass); one *d*. *Educ:* Aberdeen Univ. (MA 1st Cl. Hons); LSE (MSc Distinction, PhD). Fellow, Econometric Soc., 1975. Lectr, LSE, 1969, Reader, 1973, Prof. of Econometrics, 1977. Vis. Professor: Yale Univ., 1975; Univ. of Calif, Berkeley, 1976; Catholic Univ. of Louvain, 1980; Univ. of Calif, San Diego, 1981, 1989–90; Vis. Research Prof., Duke Univ., 1987–. Hon. LLD Aberdeen, 1987. Guy Medal in Bronze, Royal Statistical Soc., 1986. Editor: Rev. of Econ. Studies, 1971–75; Econ. Jl, 1976–80; Oxford Bulletin of Economics and Statistics, 1983–. *Publications:* (ed with K. F. Wallis) Econometrics and

Quantitative Economics, 1984; PC-GIVE, 1989; papers in econometrics, statistics and economics jls. *Recreations:* squash, cricket. *Address:* Nuffield College, Oxford OX1 1NF; 26 Northmoor Road, Oxford OX2 6UR. *T:* Oxford (0865) 515588.

HENDY, John Giles; QC 1987; *b* 11 April 1948; *s* of Jack and Mary Hendy; *m*; one *d*. *Educ:* Ealing Technical College (LLB); Queen's Univ., Belfast (DipLL, LLM). Called to the Bar, Gray's Inn, 1972; Dir, Newham Rights Centre, 1973–76; Lectr, Middlesex Polytechnic, 1976–77; Barrister, 1977–. Chm., Inst. of Employment Rights, 1989–. *Address:* 15 Old Square, Lincoln's Inn, WC2A 3UH. *T:* 071–831 0801.

HENES, John Derek; Director, International Transport, Department of Transport, since 1989; *b* 8 June 1937; *s* of Frederick William Kingaby Henes and Joan Elizabeth Henes (*née* Colbourne); *m* 1981, Virginia Elizabeth Evans; one *s* one *d*. *Educ:* Christ's Hospital; Gonville and Caius College, Cambridge (MA). Ministry of Aviation, 1963 (mostly on defence procurement); Dept of Trade, 1971; Private Sec. to Christopher Chataway, 1973–74, to Lord Beswick, 1974–75; Asst Sec., 1975; Dept. of Transport, 1983–. *Recreations:* reading, music. *Address:* Department of Transport, 2 Marsham Street, SW1P 3EB.

HENHAM, John Alfred; His Honour Judge Henham; a Circuit Judge, since 1983; *b* 8 Sept. 1924; *s* of Alfred and Daisy Henham; *m* 1946, Suzanne Jeanne Octavie Ghislaine Pinchart (*d* 1972); two *s*. Stipendiary Magistrate for S Yorks, 1975–82; a Recorder of the Crown Court, 1979–82. *Address:* Crown Court, Castle Street, Sheffield S3 8LW.

HENIG, Prof. Stanley; Professor of European Politics, since 1982 and Dean of Faculty of Social Studies, since 1985, Lancashire (formerly Preston) Polytechnic; *b* 7 July 1939; *s* of Sir Mark Henig and Grace (*née* Cohen); *m* 1966, Ruth Beatrice Munzer; two *s*. *Educ:* Wyggeston Grammar Sch.; Corpus Christi Coll., Oxford. BA 1st Cl. Hons, 1961; MA 1965 Oxon. Teaching Asst, Dept of Politics, Univ. of Minnesota, 1961; Research Student, Nuffield Coll., 1962; Lecturer in Politics, Lancaster Univ., 1964–66. MP (Lab) Lancaster, 1966–70; Lectr in Politics, Warwick Univ., 1970–71; Lectr, Civil Service Coll., 1972–75. Governor, British Inst. of Recorded Sound, 1975–80. Secretary: Historic Masters Ltd, 1983–; Historic Singers Trust, 1985–. Chm., Court, RNCM, 1986–89. Asst Editor, Jl of Common Market Studies, 1964–72, Editor, 1973–76. *Publications:* (ed) European Political Parties, 1969; External Relations of the European Community, 1971; (ed) Political Parties in the European Community, 1979; Power and Decision in Europe, 1980. *Recreation:* collector of old gramophone records. *Address:* 10 Yealand Drive, Lancaster LA1 4EW. *T:* Lancaster (0524) 69624.

HENLEY, 8th Baron (Ire.), *cr* 1799; **Oliver Michael Robert Eden;** Baron Northington (UK) 1885; Parliamentary Under-Secretary of State, Department of Social Security, since 1989; *b* 22 Nov. 1953; *er s* of 7th Baron Henley and of Nancy Mary, *d* of Stanley Walton, Gilsland, Cumbria; *S* father, 1977; *m* 1984, Caroline Patricia, *d* of A. G. Sharp, Mackney, Oxon; one *s* one *d*. *Educ:* Clifton; Durham Univ. (BA 1975). Called to the Bar, Middle Temple, 1977. A Lord in Waiting (Govt Whip), 1989. Mem., Cumbria CC, 1986–89. Chm., Penrith and the Border Conservative Assoc., 1987–89. Pres., Cumbria Assoc. of Local Councils, 1981–89. Pres., Cumbria Trust for Nature Conservation, 1988–89. *Heir:* *s* Hon. John Michael Oliver Eden, *b* 30 June 1988. *Address:* Scaleby Castle, Carlisle, Cumbria CA6 4LN. *Clubs:* Brooks's; Pratt's.

HENLEY, Sir Douglas (Owen), KCB 1973 (CB 1970); Comptroller and Auditor General, 1976–81; *b* 5 April 1919; *m* 1942, June Muriel Ibbetson; four *d*. *Educ:* Beckenham County Sch.; London Sch. of Economics (Hon. Fellow, 1974). BSc (Econ.), 1939; Gerstenberg Studentship and Leverhulme Res. Studentship (not taken up). Served Army, 1939–46; Queen's Own Royal West Kent Regt and HQ 12th Inf. Bde (despatches twice, 1945). Treasury, 1946; Treas. rep. (Financial Counsellor) in Tokyo and Singapore, 1956–59; Asst Under-Sec. of State, DEA, 1964–69, Dep. Under-Sec. of State, 1969; Second Permanent Sec., HM Treasury, 1972–76. Mem. Council, GPDST, 1982–. Hon. LLD Bath, 1981. *Address:* Walwood House, Park Road, Banstead, Surrey SM7 3ER. *T:* Burgh Heath (0737) 352626.

HENLEY, Rear-Adm. Sir Joseph (Charles Cameron), KCVO 1963; CB 1962; *b* 24 April 1909; *e s* of Vice-Adm. J. C. W. Henley, CB; *m* 1934, Daphne Ruth (marr. diss. 1965), *d* of late A. A. H. Wykeham, of Pitt Place, Brighstone, IW; one *s* three *d*; *m* 1966, Patricia Sharp, MBE 1952, *d* of late Roy Eastman, Alberta, Canada. *Educ:* Sherborne. Joined Royal Navy, 1927. Served War of 1939–45, in HMS Birmingham and King George V. Capt., 1951, in command HMS Defender, 1954–55; Naval Attaché; Washington (as Commodore), 1956–57; Dir, Royal Naval Staff Coll., 1958; Chief of Staff, Mediterranean Station, 1959–61, as Commodore; Rear-Adm. 1960; Flag Officer, Royal Yachts and Extra Naval Equerry to the Queen, 1962–65; retd 1965. *Address:* 11a Hopewood Gardens, Darling Point, Sydney, NSW 2027, Australia. *T:* 321068. *Clubs:* Royal Yacht Squadron; Royal Sydney Golf.

HENLEY, Ven. Michael Harry George, CB 1991; QHC 1989; Chaplain of the Fleet, since 1989; *b* 16 Jan. 1938; *s* of Eric Edward Henley and Evelyn Agnes Henley (*née* Lilly); *m* 1965, Rachel Jean (*née* Allen); two *d*. *Educ:* St Marylebone Grammar Sch.; St John's Hall, London (LTh). Curate, St Marylebone Parish Ch., 1961–64; Chaplain: RN, 1964–68; St Andrews Univ., 1968–72; Royal Hosp. Sch., 1972–74; RN, 1974–. Hon. Canon, Holy Trinity Cathedral, Gibraltar, 1989–. *Recreations:* golf, fishing. *Address:* Ministry of Defence, Lacon House, Theobalds Road, WC1X 8RY; Afton House, St Andrews, Fife KY16 9JW. *Clubs:* Army and Navy; Leander (Henley); Royal and Ancient Golf (St Andrews).

HENN, Charles Herbert; Assistant Under Secretary of State, Ministry of Defence, 1979–88; *b* 11 July 1931; *s* of Herbert George Henn and Ellen Anne Henn; *m* 1955, Ann Turner; one *s* one *d*. *Educ:* King's Coll. Sch., Wimbledon; Queen's Coll., Oxford (BA). National Service, REME, 1952–54 (2/Lieut). Scientific Officer, WO, 1954; Sen. Scientific Officer, 1957; Principal, 1964; Private Sec. to Minister of State for Defence, 1969; Asst Sec., 1972. *Recreations:* walking, running, listening to music.

HENNELL, Rev. Canon Michael Murray; Residentiary Canon, Manchester Cathedral, 1970–84, Canon Emeritus, since 1984; *b* 11 Sept. 1918; *s* of Charles Murray and Jessie Hennell; *m* 1950, Peggy Glendinning; four *s*. *Educ:* Bishops Stortford Coll. (Prep.); Royal Masonic Sch.; St Edmund Hall and Wycliffe Hall, Oxford. MA Oxon and, by incorporation, MA Cantab. Asst Curate: St Stephen's With St Bartholomew's, Islington, N1, 1942–44; All Saints, Queensbury, Middx, 1944–48; Tutor, Ridley Hall, Cambridge, 1948–51. St Aidan's Coll., Birkenhead: Sen. Tutor, 1951; Vice-Principal, 1952–59; Principal, 1959–63; Principal, Ridley Hall, Cambridge, 1964–70. Examining Chaplain to the Bishops of: Chelmsford, 1964–70; Liverpool, 1964–75; Manchester, 1965–85; Derby, 1970–85. Commissary to the Bishop on the Niger, 1975–84. *Publications:* John Venn and the Clapham Sect, 1958; Sons of the Prophets, 1979; ed and contrib., Charles Simeon, 1759–1836, 1959; The Deans and Canons of Manchester Cathedral 1840–1948, 1989; contribs to: The Anglican Synthesis, 1964; Popular Belief and Practice, 1972; A Dictionary of Christian Spirituality, 1983; The Study of Spirituality, 1986. *Address:* 53 Cleveley Road, Meols, Wirral, Merseyside L47 8XN.

HENNESSY, family name of **Baron Windlesham.**

HENNESSY, Christopher; journalist; Chairman, Associated Catholic Newspapers (1912) Ltd, 1970–79; Trustee, The Universe, 1979–87 (Editor, 1954–72); *b* 29 Dec. 1909; *e s* of Daniel and Anne Hennessy; *m* 1942, Kathleen Margaret Cadley, Liverpool. *Educ:* St Edward's Coll., Liverpool. Served War of 1939–45 as Commissioned Officer in British and Indian Armies; commanded a Territorial Army Unit in the North-West, 1950–55. KCSG 1975. *Recreation:* travel. *Address:* Flat 49, The Metropole, The Leas, Folkestone, Kent CT20 2LU.

HENNESSY, Sir James (Patrick Ivan), KBE 1982 (OBE 1968; MBE 1959); CMG 1975; HM Diplomatic Service, retired; *b* 26 Sept. 1923; *s* of late Richard George Hennessy, DSO, MC; *m* 1947, Patricia, *o d* of late Wing Comdr F. H. Unwin, OBE; five *d* (one *s* decd). *Educ:* Bedford Sch.; King's Coll., Newcastle; Sidney Sussex Coll., Cambridge; LSE. Served RA, 1942–44; seconded IA, 1944–46, Adjt and Battery Comdr, 6th Indian Field Regt. Apptd to HM Overseas Service, Basutoland, District Officer, 1948; Judicial Comr, 1953; Dist Comr, 1954–56; Jt Sec., Constitutional Commn, 1957–59; Supervisor of Elections, 1959; Sec. to Exec. Council, 1960; seconded to Office of High Comr, Cape Town/Pretoria, 1961–63; Perm. Sec. for local govt, 1964; MLC, 1965; Sec. for External Affairs, Defence and Internal Security, 1967; Prime Minister's Office, 1968. Retired, later apptd to HM Diplomatic Service; FO, 1968–70; Chargé d'Affaires, Montevideo, 1971–72; High Comr to Uganda and Ambassador (non-resident), Rwanda, 1973–76; Consul-Gen., Cape Town, 1977–80; Governor and C-in-C, Belize, 1980–81; HM Chief Inspector of Prisons for England and Wales, 1982–87. Mem., Parole Bd, 1988–. Trustee, Butter Trust, 1989–. *Clubs:* Naval and Military, Commonwealth Trust.

HENNESSY, Sir John Wyndham P.; *see* Pope-Hennessy.

HENNESSY, Brig. Mary Brigid Teresa, (Rita), CBE 1988 (MBE 1967); RRC 1982; Matron-in-Chief, Queen Alexandra's Royal Army Nursing Corps, 1985–89 and Director of Defence Nursing Service, 1986–89; *b* 27 Jan. 1933; *d* of late Bartholomew and Nora Agnes Hennessy. *Educ:* Convent of Mercy, Ennis, Co. Clare; Whittington Hosp., Highgate, London; Victoria Maternity Hosp., Barnet. SRN; SCM. Joined QARANC, 1959; service in Britain, Singapore, Malaya, Germany; various hosp. appts, 1959–74; seconded to office of Chargé d'affaires, Peking, 1965–67; Dep. Matron, Hongkong, 1976; Lt-Col 1979; Col 1982; Brig., Matron-in-Chief and Dir of Army Nursing Services, 1985. QHNS 1985–89. *Recreations:* music, theatre, gardening. *Address:* 28 Wulwyn Court, Edgcumbe Park, Crowthorne, Berks. *T:* Crowthorne (0344) 771030.

HENNESSY, Peter John; journalist and broadcaster; Visiting Professor of Government, Strathclyde University, since 1989; adviser, Institute of Contemporary British History (Co-Founder and Co-Director, 1986–89); *b* 28 March 1947; *s* of William Gerald and Edith Hennessy; *m* 1969, Enid Mary Candler; two *d*. *Educ:* Marling Sch., Stroud; St John's Coll., Cambridge (BA 1969), PhD Cantab 1990; LSE; Harvard, 1971–72 (Kennedy Meml Scholar). Reporter, THES, 1972–74, The Times, 1974–76; Lobby corresp., Financial Times, 1976; Whitehall corresp., The Times, 1976–82; journalist, The Economist, 1982; home leader writer and columnist, The Times, 1982–84; columnist: New Statesman, 1986–87; The Independent, 1987–; Director, 1989–. Vis. Lectr, Dept of Politics, Univ. of Strathclyde, 1983–84 (Hon. Res. Fellow, 1985–89); Visiting Fellow: Policy Studies Inst., 1986– (Sen. Fellow, 1984–85); Univ. Depts of Politics, Reading 1988–, Nottingham 1989–; RIPA, 1989–; Hon. Res. Fellow, Dept of Politics and Sociology, Birkbeck Coll., London, 1990–. Vice-Pres., Politics Assoc., 1985–. Trustee, Attlee Foundn, 1985–. Presenter: Under Fire, Granada TV, 1985–87; BBC Radio 4 Analysis programme, 1986–; numerous other radio and TV productions. *Publications:* (with Keith Jeffery) States of Emergency, 1983; (with Michael Cockerell and David Walker) Sources Close to the Prime Minister, 1984; What the Papers Never Said, 1985; Cabinet, 1986; (ed with Anthony Seldon) Ruling Performance, 1987; Whitehall, 1989; (with Caroline Anstey) From Clogs to Clogs?—Britain's relative economic decline since 1851, 1991. *Recreations:* reading, listening to music, running. *Address:* c/o Institute of Contemporary British History, 34 Tavistock Square, WC1H 9EZ. *T:* 071–387 2331. *Club:* Attlee Memorial Runners.

HENNIKER, 8th Baron *cr* 1800; **John Patrick Edward Chandos Henniker-Major,** KCMG 1965 (CMG 1956); CVO 1960; MC 1945; Bt 1765; Baron Hartismere (UK) 1866; DL; Director, Wates Foundation, 1972–78; *b* 19 Feb. 1916; *s* of 7th Baron Henniker, and Molly (*d* 1953), *d* of Sir Robert Burnet, KCVO; *S* father, 1980; *m* 1946, Margaret Osla Benning (*d* 1974); two *s* one *d*; *m* 1976, Julia Marshall Poland (*née* Mason). *Educ:* Stowe; Trinity Coll., Cambridge. HM Foreign Service, 1938; served 1940–45, Army (Major, The Rifle Brigade). HM Embassy Belgrade, 1945–46; Asst Private Secretary to Secretary of State for Foreign Affairs, 1946–48; Foreign Office, 1948–50; HM Embassy, Buenos Aires, 1950–52; Foreign Office, 1952–60 (Counsellor and Head of Personnel Dept, 1953); HM Ambassador to Jordan, 1960–62; to Denmark, 1962–66; Civil Service Commission, 1966–67; Asst Under-Secretary of State, FO, 1967–68. Dir-Gen., British Council, 1968–72. Lay Mem., Mental Health Review Tribunal (Broadmoor), 1975–81; Member: Parole Bd, 1979–83; Council and Finance Bd, Univ. of E Anglia, Norwich, 1979–86; Council, Toynbee Hall, 1978–, Dep. Chm., 1982–86. Chairman: Suffolk Community Alcohol Services, 1983–90; Suffolk Rural Housing Assoc., 1984–; President: Suffolk Community Council, 1988–; Suffolk Agricl Assoc., 1989; Rainer Foundn, 1985–90 (Chm., Intermediate Treatment Fund, 1985–90); Vice-Pres., Suffolk Trust for Nature Conservation, 1985–. Trustee: City Parochial Foundn, 1973–90; London Festival Ballet, 1975–85. Governor: Cripplegate Foundn, 1979–90; Stowe Sch., 1982–90. Hon. (Lay) Canon of St Edmundsbury Cathedral, 1986–. DL Suffolk, 1988. Hon. DCL UEA, 1989. *Recreations:* gardening, ornithology. *Heir:* *s* Hon. Mark Ian Philip Chandos Henniker-Major [*b* 29 Sept. 1947; *m* 1973, Lesley Antoinette Masterton-Smith, *d* of Wing Comdr G. W. Foskett; two *s* three *d*]. *Address:* Red House, Thornham Magna, Eye, Suffolk. *Club:* Special Forces.

HENNIKER, Brig. Sir Mark Chandos Auberon, 8th Bt, *cr* 1813; CBE 1953 (OBE 1944); DSO 1944; MC 1933; DL; retired, 1958; *b* 23 Jan. 1906; *s* of late F. C. Henniker, ICS, and of Ada Russell (*née* Howell); *S* cousin (Lieut-Col Sir Robert Henniker, 7th Bt, MC) 1958; *m* 1945, Kathleen Denys (*née* Anderson); one *s* one *d*. *Educ:* Marlborough Coll.; Royal Military Academy, Woolwich; King's Coll., Cambridge. Royal Engineers, 1926; served India, 1928–34 (MC); Aldershot, 1937–39; BEF, 1939–40; North Africa, 1943; Sicily, 1943 (wounded); Italy, 1943 (OBE); NW Europe, 1944–45 (immediate award of DSO, Oct. 1944); India, 1946–47; Malaya, 1952–55 (CBE); Port Said, 1956 (despatches). Hon. Col, Parachute Engineer Regt (TA), 1959–68; Hon. Col, REME (TA), 1964–68. DL Gwent (formerly County of Mon), 1963. *Publications:* Memoirs of a Junior Officer, 1951; Red Shadow over Malaya, 1955; Life in the Army Today, 1957; An Image of War, 1987. *Recreations:* appropriate to age and rank. *Heir:* *s* Adrian Chandos Henniker [*b* 18 Oct. 1946; *m* 1971, Ann, *d* of Stuart Britton; twin *d*]. *Address:* c/o Lloyds Bank, Cox's & King's Branch, 6 Pall Mall, SW1. *Club:* Athenæum.

HENNIKER HEATON, Sir Yvo Robert; *see* Heaton.

HENNIKER-MAJOR, family name of **Baron Henniker.**

HENNINGS, Richard Owen, CMG 1957; retired as Deputy Chief Secretary, Kenya (1960–63); *b* 8 Sept. 1911; *s* of W. G. Hennings; *m* 1939, Constance Patricia Milton Sexton; one *d*. *Educ:* Cheltenham; New Coll., Oxford. Newdigate Prize Poem, 1932. District Officer, Kenya, 1935; Political Officer, Ethiopia, 1941; Secretary for Agriculture, Kenya, 1953; Permanent Secretary, Ministry of Agriculture, Animal Husbandry and Water Resources, Kenya, 1956. Nominated Member of Kenya Legislative Council, 1960, and of East African Central Legislative Assembly, 1960. Hon. Editor, Ski Notes and Queries, 1964–71; Editor, Ski Survey, 1972–73. *Publications:* Arnold in Africa, 1941; African Morning, 1951; articles in The Geographical Magazine, Journal of African Administration, Corona, British Ski Year Book, Ski Notes and Queries. *Recreations:* ski-ing, tennis, gardening, reefing. *Address:* July Farm House, Great Chesterford, Saffron Walden, Essex. *Clubs:* Ski Club of Great Britain; Nairobi (Nairobi).

HENREY, Mrs Robert; authoress; *b* Paris, 13 Aug. 1906; maiden name Madeleine Gal; *m* 1928, Robert Selby Henrey (*d* 1982), *o s* of Rev. Thomas Selby Henrey, Vicar of Old Brentford, Mddx, and Euphemia, *d* of Sir Coutts and Lady Lindsay of Balcarres; one *s*. *Educ:* Protestant Girls' Sch., Clichy; Convent of The Holy Family, Tooting, SW. *Publications:* autobiographical sequence in the following chronological order: The Little Madeleine, 1951, New York, 1953; An Exile in Soho, 1952; Julia, 1971; A Girl at Twenty, 1974; Madeleine Grown Up, 1952, New York 1953; Green Leaves, 1976; Madeleine Young Wife, New York 1954, London 1960; London under Fire 1940–45, 1969; A Month in Paris, 1954; Milou's Daughter, 1955, New York 1956; Her April Days, 1963; Wednesday at Four, 1964; Winter Wild, 1966; She Who Pays, 1969; The Golden Visit, 1979 (read in the above order these volumes make one consecutive narrative); *other books:* A Farm in Normandy, 1941; A Village in Piccadilly, 1943; The Incredible City, 1944; The Foolish Decade, 1945; The King of Brentford, 1946; The Siege of London, 1946; The Return to the Farm, 1947; London (with illustrations by Phyllis Ginger RWS) 1948, New York, 1949; A Film Star in Belgrave Square, 1948; A Journey to Vienna, 1950; Matilda and the Chickens, 1950; Paloma, 1951, New York, 1955; A Farm in Normandy and the Return, 1952; Madeleine's Journal, 1953; This Feminine World, 1956; A Daughter for a Fortnight, 1957; The Virgin of Aldermanbury (illustrations by Phyllis Ginger), 1958; Mistress of Myself, 1959; The Dream Makers, 1961; Spring in a Soho Street, 1962. *Recreations:* most feminine occupations: sewing, knitting, ironing, gardening. *Address:* c/o J. M. Dent & Sons, Aldine House, 33 Welbeck Street, W1M 8LX; Ferme Robert Henrey, 14640 Villers-sur-Mer, Calvados, France. *T:* Calvados (31) 87 03 88.

HENRI, Adrian Maurice; President, Liverpool Academy of Arts, 1972–81; *b* Birkenhead, 10 April 1932; *s* of Arthur Maurice Henri and Emma Johnson; *m* 1959, Joyce Wilson (*d* 1987). *Educ:* St Asaph Grammar Sch., N Wales; Dept of Fine Art, King's Coll., Newcastle upon Tyne, 1951–55. Hons BA Fine Art (Dunelm) 1955; DLitt Liverpool, 1990. Worked for ten seasons in Rhyl fairground, later as a scenic-artist and secondary school teacher; taught at Manchester then Liverpool Colls of Art, 1961–67. Led the poetry/rock group, Liverpool Scene, 1967–70; since then, freelance poet/painter/singer/songwriter/lecturer. Tour of USA, 1973; Bicentennial Poetry Tour of USA, 1976; exchange tour of Canada, 1980. Pres., Merseyside Arts Assoc., 1978–80; Writer-in-Residence: Tattenhall Centre, Cheshire, 1980–82; Liverpool Univ., 1989. *Exhibitions:* include: Biennale della Giovane Pintura, Milan, 1968; Pen as Pencil, Brussels, 1973; John Moores Liverpool Exhibns, 1962, 1965, 1967, 1974, 1978, 1980, 1989; Peter Moores Project, Real Life, Liverpool, 1977; Art and the Sea, 1980–81; Hedgerow mural, 1980, Summer Terrace mural, 1983. Royal Liverpool Hosp. John Moores Liverpool £2000 prize, 1972. *Major One-Man Shows:* ICA, London, 1968; ArtNet, London, 1975; Williamson Art Gall., Birkenhead, 1975; Retrospective 1960–76, Wolverhampton City Art Gall., 1976; Demarco Gall., Edinburgh, 1978; Touring Retrospective, The Art of Adrian Henri, South Hill Park and elsewhere, 1986–87; Hanover Gall., Liverpool, 1987; Library Centre, Skelmersdale, 1989; Poetry Soc., 1990. Various recordings. *Publications:* Tonight at Noon, 1968; City, 1969 (out of print); Autobiography, 1971; (with Nell Dunn) I Want (novel), 1972; World of Art Series: Environments and Happenings, 1974; The Best of Henri, 1975; City Hedges 1970–76, 1977; From The Loveless Motel, poems 1976–79, 1980; Penny Arcade, poems 1978–82, 1983; Collected Poems, 1986; Wish You Were Here (poems), 1990; *for children:* Eric, the Punk Cat, 1982; The Phantom Lollipop-Lady (poems), 1986; Eric and Frankie in Las Vegas, 1987; Rhinestone Rhino (poems), 1989; The Postman's Palace, 1990; *for teenagers:* Box (poems), 1990; *anthologies:* The Oxford Book of Twentieth Century Verse, 1973; The Liverpool Scene (ed Edward Lucie-Smith), 1967; Penguin Modern Poets No 10: The Mersey Sound, 1967, rev. and enlarged edn, 1974, rev. edn, 1983; British Poetry since 1945 (ed Edward Lucie-Smith: Penguin), 1970; New Volume, 1983; *plays:* I Wonder, a Guillaume Apollinaire Show (with Mike Kustow), 1968; (with Nell Dunn) I Want, 1983; The Wakefield Mysteries, 1988; (jtly) Fears and Miseries of the Third Term, 1989; *TV plays:* Yesterday's Girl, 1973; The Husband, the Wife and the Stranger, 1986. *Recreations:* watching Liverpool FC; visiting Shropshire and Normandy; old movies; SF, Gothic and crime novels. *Address:* 21 Mount Street, Liverpool L1 9HD. *T:* 051–709 6682; (literary agent) Deborah Rogers Ltd, 20 Powis Mews, W11. *Clubs:* Chelsea Arts; Private Chauffeurs' (Liverpool).

HENRIQUES, Richard Henry Quixano; QC 1986; barrister; a Recorder of the Crown Court, since 1983; *b* 27 Oct. 1943; *s* of Cecil Quixano Henriques and late Doreen Mary Henriques; *m* Joan Hilary, (Toni), (*née* Senior); one *s* and one step *s*. *Educ:* Bradfield Coll., Berks; Worcester Coll., Oxford (BA). Called to the Bar, Inner Temple, 1967. Mem., Northern Circuit. Council Mem., Rossall Sch. *Recreations:* bridge, golf. *Address:* Ilex House, Woodhouse Road, Thornton-Cleveleys, Lancs FY5 5LQ. *T:* Cleveleys (0253) 826199. *Clubs:* The Manchester (Manchester); North Shore Golf (Blackpool).

HENRISON, Dame (Anne) Rosina (Elizabeth), DBE 1984; *b* 7 Dec. 1902; *d* of Amelina Marie (*née* Malepa) and Julius Marie; *m* 1st, 1931, Charles Duval; three *s* one *d*; 2nd, 1943, Edward Henrison. *Educ:* Loreto Convent, Port Louis. Hon. Citizen, Town of Bangui, Central Africa, 1975; Ordre de Mérite, Centre Africaine; Mother Gold Medal. *Recreations:* reading, travelling. *Address:* Melville, Grandgaube, Mauritius. *T:* 039–518. *Club:* Port Louis Tennis (Mauritius).

HENRY, David; Senior Director, Postal Services, 1978–82, retired; *b* 19 April 1925; *s* of Thomas Glanffrwd Henry and Hylda Frances Henry. *Educ:* Midhurst Grammar Sch.; St John's Coll., Cambridge (MA Hons). Assistant Postal Controller, 1950; Head Postmaster, Norwich, 1961; Postal Controller, 1966; Controller Operations, 1968; Director, Midlands Postal Region, 1969; Chairman, Midlands Postal Board, 1974; Dir, London Postal Region, 1977. *Recreations:* Rugby football, cricket.

HENRY, Sir Denis (Aynsley), Kt 1975; OBE 1962; QC Grenada 1968; barrister-at-law; Senior Partner, Henry, Henry & Bristol, St George's, Grenada, WI; *b* 3 Feb. 1917; *s* of Ferdinand H. Henry and Agatha May Henry; *m* 1966, Kathleen Carol (*née* Sheppard); two *s* three *d*. *Educ:* Grenada Boys' Secondary Sch.; King's Coll., London (LLB Hons). Called to Bar, Inner Temple (Certif. of Honour), 1939. In practice at Bar, Grenada, 1939–. Served three terms as nominated MLC, Grenada, 1952–65; Sen. nominated Mem. Exec. Council, 1956–65; Senator in First Parlt of Associated State of Grenada, 1966–67. Mem. Council, Univ. of West Indies, 1956–68. Pres. and Dir, Windward Islands Banana Growers Assoc., 1957–75; Pres., Commonwealth Banana Exporters Assoc., 1973–75; Chairman: Grenada Banana Co-operative Soc., 1953–75; Grenada Cocoa Assoc., 1973–75. Vice-Pres., Commonwealth Caribbean Society for the Blind, 1972–75; Mem. Exec., West India Cttee, London, 1972–75. *Recreations:* golf, swimming, tennis. *Clubs:* Commonwealth Trust; Grenada Golf, Richmond Hill Tennis (Grenada).

HENRY, Hon. Sir Denis (Robert Maurice); Kt 1986; **Hon. Mr Justice Henry;** a Judge of the High Court of Justice, Queen's Bench Division, since 1986; *b* 19 April 1931; *o s* of late Brig. Maurice Henry and of Mary Catherine (*née* Irving); *m* 1963, Linda Gabriel Arthur; one *s* one *d* (and one *d* decd). *Educ:* Shrewsbury; Balliol Coll., Oxford (MA). 2nd Lieut, KORR, 1950–51. Called to the Bar, Inner Temple, 1955, Bencher, 1985; QC 1977; a Recorder, 1979–86. Part-time Tutor, New Coll., Oxford, 1985–. *Recreation:* golf. *Address:* Royal Courts of Justice, Strand, WC2.

HENRY, Sir James Holmes, 2nd Bt, *cr* 1922; CMG 1960; MC 1944; TD 1950; QC (Tanganyika) 1953, (Cyprus) 1957; Chairman, Foreign Compensation Commission, 1977–83 (Commissioner, 1960–77); *b* 22 Sept. 1911; *er s* of Rt Hon. Sir Denis Stanislaus Henry, 1st Baronet, Cahore, Draperstown, Co. Londonderry, 1st Lord Chief Justice of Northern Ireland, and Violet (*d* 1966), 3rd *d* of late Rt Hon. Hugh Holmes, Court of Appeal, Ireland; *S* father, 1925; *m* 1st, 1941 (marriage terminated by divorce and rescript of Holy Office in Rome); 2nd, 1949, Christina Hilary, *widow* of Lieut-Commander Christopher H. Wells, RN, and *e d* of late Sir Hugh Holmes, KBE, CMG, MC, QC (formerly Mixed Courts, Egypt); three *d*. *Educ:* Mount St Mary's Coll., Chesterfield; Downside Sch.; University College, London. BA (Hons) Classics (1st Class), University Scholarships. Called to Bar, Inner Temple, 1934; practised, London, 1934–39. Served War of 1939–45, London Irish Rifles (wounded). Crown Counsel, Tanganyika, 1946; Legal Draftsman, 1949; jt comr, Revised Edn of Laws of Tanganyika (1947–49), 1950; Solicitor-General, 1952; Attorney-General, Cyprus, 1956–60. *Heir: nephew* Patrick Denis Henry, *b* 20 Dec. 1957. *Address:* Kandy Lodge, 18 Ormond Avenue, Hampton on Thames, Mddx TW12 2RU. *Clubs:* Travellers', Commonwealth Trust.

HENRY, John Philip; Regional Director, Yorkshire and Humberside Regional Office, Departments of the Environment and Transport, since 1990; *b* 8 Oct. 1946; *s* of late L. Henry, MD, FRCS and P. M. Henry, MB, ChB. *Educ:* Cheltenham Coll.; Queen's Coll., Oxford (MA). Psychologist, Road Research Lab., 1968; Admin Trainee, DoE, 1972; Principal, 1976; Private Sec., Minister for Housing and Construction, 1981–83; Asst Sec., 1983–89. *Address:* City House, Leeds LS1 4JD; 4 William Henry Street, Saltaire, Shipley, West Yorks BD18 4PP. *T:* Bradford (0274) 589478.

HENRY, Thomas Cradock, FDS, RCS; MRCS; LRCP; retired; Hon. Consultant Oral Surgeon, Hospital for Sick Children, Great Ormond Street; Consultant Maxillo-Facial Surgeon, Royal Surrey County Hospital; Consultant Oral Surgeon, Italian Hospital, London; *b* 30 Dec. 1910; *s* of late Thomas Henry and Rose Emily Bowdler, Moorgate, Park Retford; *m* 1939, Claire Mary, 7th *c* of late R. A. Caraman, The Grange, Elstree; two *s*. *Educ:* King Edward VI Grammar Sch., Retford; King's Coll., University of London; Middlesex and Royal Dental Hospital; Saunders Scholar; qualified as Doctor, 1935. Formerly: House Physician, House Surgeon and Resident Anæsthetist St James's Hosp., London; House Surgeon, St Bartholomew's Hosp.; Squadron Leader and Surgical Specialist, RAFVR, 1939–46; Surgical Registrar, Plastic and Jaw Injuries Centre, East Grinstead, 1941–42; Surgeon in charge of Maxillo-Facial and Burns Unit, RAF Hosp., Cosford, 1942–46; Hunterian Prof., RCS, 1944–45. FRSocMed; Founder Fellow and Pres., British Assoc. of Oral Surgeons; Member: British Assoc. of Plastic Surgeons (Mem. Council); BMA. *Publications:* Fracture of the Facial Bones (chapter in Fractures and Dislocations in General Practice, 1949); Labial Segment Surgery (chapter in Archer's Oral Surgery, 1971); Melanotic Ameloblastoma (in Trans 3rd ICOS); numerous contrib. to leading medical and dental journals, including BMJ and Jl of Bone and Joint Surgery. *Recreations:* shooting and fishing. *Address:* Redwing Cottage, Bridge Road, Cranleigh, Surrey GU6 7HH. *T:* Cranleigh (0483) 277730.

HENRY, Hon. Sir Trevor (Ernest), Kt 1970; Judge, Fiji Court of Appeal, 1974–85; *b* 9 May 1902; *s* of John Henry and Edith Anna (*née* Eaton); *m* 1930, Audrey Kate Sheriff; one *s* one *d*. *Educ:* Rotorua District High Sch.; Univ. of New Zealand (Auckland). LLB 1925, LLM Hons 1926, NZ. Solicitor of Supreme Court of NZ, 1923, Barrister, 1925. Judge of the Supreme Court of NZ, 1955–77. *Recreation:* fishing. *Address:* Arbour Vale, Old North Road, Waimauki RD2, Auckland, New Zealand. *Club:* Northern (Auckland).

HENRY, Wendy Ann; Editor, The People, 1989; *d* of Bernard and Elsa Henry; *m* 1980, Tim Miles; one *d*. *Educ:* Queen Mary School, Lytham. Reporter, Daily Mail, Manchester, 1975, News of the World, 1976; Features Editor, Woman Magazine, 1979; Asst Editor, The Sun, 1981; Editor: Sunday Magazine, 1986; The News of the World, 1987–88; Dep. Editor, The Sun, 1988. Mem., Weight Watchers. *Recreation:* sleeping.

HENRY, William Robert, CBE 1979; Chairman: Coats Patons Ltd, 1975–81; Scottish Amicable Life Assurance Society, 1981–84; *b* 30 April 1915; *s* of William Henry and Sarah (*née* Lindsay); *m* 1947, Esther Macfayden; two *s* one *d*. *Educ:* Govan High Sch.; London Univ. Entered Company's service, 1934; Head of Financial Dept, 1953; Asst Accountant, 1957; Dir, J. & P. Coats Ltd (Parent Co.), 1966; Dep. Chm., Coats Patons Ltd, 1970. FBIM 1976. *Recreations:* golf, gardening. *Address:* Hawkstone Lodge, Ascog, Isle of Bute, Scotland.

HENSCHEL, Ruth Mary; *see* Ashton, R. M.

HENSHALL, Rt. Rev. Michael; *see* Warrington, Bishop Suffragan of.

HENSHAW, Frank Charles, FRICS; General Manager, Milton Keynes Development Corporation, since 1980; *b* 28 Aug. 1930; *s* of Frank and Edith Annie Henshaw; *m* 1966, Patricia Jane McDonald; one *s* one *d*. *Educ:* Towcester Grammar Sch.; Coll. of Estate Management. FRICS 1959; FBIM 1984. Nat. service, RAF, 1948–50. Quantity Surveyor: Northants CC, 1947–53; Coventry City Council, 1953–63; Prin. Quantity Surveyor, Midlands Housing Consortium, 1963–65; Chief Quantity Surveyor: Runcorn Develt Corp., 1965–70; Sheffield City Council, 1970–71; Milton Keynes Development Corporation: Chief Quantity Surveyor, 1971–74; Exec. Dir, 1974–78; Dep. Gen. Manager, 1978–80. Chm., Milton Keynes Housing Assoc., 1985–88; Dep. Chm., Central Milton Keynes Shopping Man. Co., 1978–89. Dir, Milton Keynes and N Bucks TEC, 1990–. OON 1989. *Recreations:* golf, travel. *Address:* Milton Keynes Development Corporation, Saxon Court, 502 Avebury Boulevard, Central Milton Keynes MK9 3HS. *T:* Milton Keynes (0908) 692692. *Club:* Woburn Golf and Country.

HENSLEY, John; *b* 28 Feb. 1910; *s* of late Edward Hutton and Marion Hensley; *m* 1st, 1940, Dorothy Betty (*d* 1969), *d* of Percy George and Dorothy Coppard; one *s*; 2nd, 1971, Elizabeth, *widow* of Charles Cross and *d* of Harold and Jessie Coppard. *Educ:* Malvern; Trinity Coll., Cambridge (Chancellor's Classical Medal, MA). Entered Min. of

Agriculture and Fisheries, 1933; Priv. Sec. to Chancellor of Duchy of Lancaster and Minister of Food, 1939; Priv. Sec. to Minister of Agriculture and Fisheries, 1945; Asst Sec., 1946; Under Sec., 1957. Member: Agricultural Research Council, 1957–59; Council, Nat. Inst. of Agricultural Botany, 1970–73; Sec., Cttee of Inquiry into Veterinary Profession, 1971–75; retired 1975. *Recreations:* theatre, opera, genealogy, gardening. *Address:* 109 Markfield, Courtwood Lane, Croydon CR0 9HP. *T:* 081–657 6319.

HENSON, Marguerite Ann, (Mrs Nicky Henson); *see* Porter, M. A.

HENSON, Nicholas Victor Leslie, (Nicky); actor; *b* 12 May 1945; *s* of Leslie Henson and Billie Collins; *m* 1st, 1968, Una Stubbs (marr. diss.); two *s*; 2nd, 1986, Marguerite Porter, *qv*; one *s*. *Educ:* St Bede's, Eastbourne; Charterhouse. Formerly popular song writer; Founder Mem., Young Vic; first stage appearance, 1962; *London stage:* All Square, Camelot, Passion Flower Hotel, Canterbury Tales, Ride Across Lake Constance, Hamlet, Midsummer Night's Dream, Cinderella, Mardi Gras, Rookery Nook, Noises Off, The Relapse, Sufficient Carbohydrate, Journey's End; The Three Sisters, Royal Court, 1990; *Young Vic:* Scapino, Waiting for Godot, She Stoops to Conquer, Taming of the Shrew, Measure for Measure, Soldier's Tale, Oedipus, Romeo and Juliet, The Maids, Look Back in Anger, Rosencrantz and Guildenstern are Dead, Charley's Aunt; *National Theatre:* Cherry Orchard, Macbeth, The Woman, The Double Dealer, A Fair Quarrel, Browning Version, Provok'd Wife, Elephant Man, Mandragola; *Royal Shakespeare Co.:* Man and Superman, Merry Wives of Windsor, As You Like It; *television series:* Life of Balzac, 1976; Seagull Island, 1981; Happy Apple, 1983; Thin Air, 1988; The Green Man, 1990; 25 films. *Recreation:* music. *Address:* c/o Richard Stone, 25 Whitehall, SW1A 2BS. *T:* 071–839 6421.

HENSON, Ronald Alfred, MD, FRCP; Physician and Neurologist, 1949–81, Chairman, Section of Neurological Sciences, 1968–81, The London Hospital; Physician, National Hospitals for Nervous Diseases, Maida Vale Hospital, 1952–81; *b* 4 Oct. 1915; *s* of late Alfred and Nellie Henson, Chippenham, Wilts; *m* 1941, Frances, *d* of A. Francis and Jessie Sims, Bath; three *d*. *Educ:*King Edward VI Sch., Bath; London Hospital Medical Coll.; Univ. of London (Dip. Hist. Music). Major, RAMC, 1940–46. Mem., Archbishops' Commission on Divine Healing, 1953–57. Dir of Studies, Institute of Neurology, University of London, 1955–64, Chm. Academic Bd, 1974–77; Dir, Cancer Res. Campaign Neuropathological Res. Unit, London Hosp. Med. Coll., 1967–71, Chm., London Hosp. Med. Council, 1974–77. Examiner: RCP, 1965–68, 1969–75; Univ. of London, 1971–74; Langdon-Brown Lectr, RCP, 1977; Fest. lectr, Univ. of Bergen, 1981; Vis. lectr at med. schs and neurological socs in N America, Europe, India, Thailand, Australia, NZ, 1959–86. Member: Med. Appeals Tribunal, 1980–87; Attendance Allowance Bd, 1980–86. Hon. Consulting Neurologist, Royal Soc. Musicians, GB, 1966–81; formerly Mem. Board of Governors: The London Hosp.; Nat. Hosps for Nervous Diseases. Chairman: Advance in Medicine, 1976–83; Scientific Adv. Panel, Action Research, 1983 (Mem., 1977; Vice-Chm., 1981); President: Neurological Section, RSM, 1976–77 (Sec., 1956–58; Vice-Pres. 1974); Assoc. of British Neurologists, 1976–77 (Sec., 1964–68). Commonwealth Fellow 1964. Special Trustee, The London Hosp., 1974–82. Member: Assoc. of Physicians of Great Britain and Ireland; British Neuropathological Soc.; Hon. Corresponding Mem. Amer. Neurological Assoc., 1966; Hon. Member: Canadian Neurological Soc., 1971; Belgian Neurological Soc., 1976; Assoc. of British Neurologists, 1983. Chm., London Bach Soc., 1977–85; Arts Council of GB: Mem., 1981–85; Vice-Chm., Regional Adv. Cttee, 1982–86; Chm., Study Gp on Opera Provision Outside London, 1985. Chm., Cheltenham Internat. Music Fest., 1990– (Vice-Chm., 1983–90); Chm., Glos Arts Cttee, 1984–89; Member: Exec. Cttee, Southern Arts, 1982–86; Management Cttee, 1983–86, Music Panel, 1986–88, SW Arts (Chm., Music Sub-Panel, 1986–88). Mem. Bd of Governors, King Edward's Sch., Bath, 1983–89. Dep. Editor, Brain, 1974–81. *Publications:* Music and the Brain (ed jtly), 1977; Cancer and the Nervous System (jtly), 1982; various contributions to the neurological literature. *Address:* The Nab, Church Road, Newnham-on-Severn, Glos GL14 1AY. *Club:* Athenæum.

HENZE, Hans Werner; composer; Professor of Composition, Royal Academy of Music, 1987; *b* 1 July 1926; *s* of Franz Gebhard Henze and Margarete Geldmacher. *Educ:* Bünde i/W; Bielefeld i/W; Braunschweig. Studying music in Heidelberg, 1945; First Work performed (Chamber Concerto), at Darmstadt-Kranichstein, 1946; Musical Dir, Municipal Theatre, Constance, 1948; Artistic Dir of Ballet, Hessian States Theatre, Wiesbaden, 1950; Prof. of Composition, Acad. Mozarteum, Salzburg, 1961. Definite departure for Italy, living first in Forio d'Ischia, then Naples, then Castelgandolfo as a composer; Artistic Director: Internat. Art Workshop, Montepulciano, Tuscany, 1976–80, Munich, 1989–; Philharmonic Acad., Rome, 1981–; Munich Biennale, 1988; Prof. of Composition, Hochschule für Musik, Cologne, 1980–91; Composer-in-Residence, Berlin Philharmonic Orchestra, 1991–. Frequent international conducting tours. Member: German Acad. of Arts, Berlin; Philharmonic Acad., Rome. Hon. Member: Deutsche Oper, Berlin, 1982; AAIL, 1982. Hon. DMus Edinburgh, 1970. Robert Schumann Prize, 1952; Prix d'Italia, 1953; Nordrhein-Westphalien Award, 1955; Berlin Prize of Artists, 1958; Great Prize for Artists, Hanover, 1962; Louis Spohr Prize, Brunswick, 1977; Bach Prize, Hamburg, 1983; Siemens Prize, 1990. *Publications:* a book of Essays; 6 symphonies; 10 full length operas, 3 one-act operas, 1 children's opera; 6 normal ballets and 5 chamber ballets; chamber music; choral works; concerti for violin, viola, violoncello, double bass, oboe, clarinet and harp; various symphonic works; song cycle; music theatre works incl. El Cimarrón, La Cubana, Natascha Ungeheuer, and El Rey de Harlem. *Address:* B. Schott's Söhne, 6500 Mainz, Weihergarten 1–5, West Germany.

HEPBURN, Audrey; actress; *b* Brussels, 4 May 1929; *d* of J. A. Hepburn; *m* 1st, 1954, Mel Ferrer (marr. diss. 1968); one *s*; 2nd, 1969, Dr Andrea Dotti; one *s*. Studied ballet in Amsterdam and in Marie Rambert's ballet sch. First stage part in musical production, High Button Shoes; first film appearance in Laughter in Paradise. Played leading rôles in Gigi (play), New York, 1951 (tour of America, Oct. 1952–May 1953); Ondine (play by Jean Giraudoux), 1954. Special Ambassador for UNICEF, 1988–. Commander, Order of Arts and Letters (France), 1987. *Films:* One Wild Oat; The Lavender Hill Mob; The Young Wives' Tale; The Secret People; Nous Irons à Monte Carlo; Roman Holiday, 1952; Sabrina Fair, 1954; War and Peace, 1956; Funny Face, 1957; Love in the Afternoon, 1957; The Nun's Story, 1958, also Green Mansions; The Unforgiven, 1960; Breakfast at Tiffany's, 1961; Paris When it Sizzles, 1962; Charade, 1962; My Fair Lady, 1964; How to Make a Million, 1966; Two for the Road, 1967; Wait Until Dark, 1968; Robin Hood and Maid Marion, 1975; Bloodline, 1979; They All Laughed, 1980; Always, 1990.

HEPBURN, John William; Under Secretary, Ministry of Agriculture, Fisheries and Food, since 1982; *b* 8 Sept. 1938; *s* of late Dugald S. Hepburn and of Margarita R. Hepburn; *m* 1972, Isla Marchbank; one *s*. *Educ:* Hutchesons' Grammar Sch.; Glasgow Univ. (MA); Brasenose Coll., Oxford. Assistant Principal, 1961, Principal, 1966, MAFF; First Secretary, UK Delegn to European Communities, Brussels, 1969–71; Private Sec. to Minister of Agriculture, Fisheries and Food, 1971–73; Asst Sec., MAFF, 1973–81. *Recreation:* golf. *Address:* c/o Ministry of Agriculture, Fisheries and Food, SW1.

HEPBURN, Katharine; actress; *b* 9 Nov. 1909; *d* of late Dr Thomas N. Hepburn and Katharine Houghton; *m* Ludlow Ogden Smith (marr. diss.). *Educ:* Hartford; Bryn Mawr College. First professional appearance on stage, Baltimore, 1928, in Czarina; first New York appearance, 1928, in Night Hostess (under name Katherine Burns), The Millionairess, New Theatre, London, 1952. Entered films, 1932; notable films: A Bill of Divorcement; Morning Glory; Little Women; The Little Minister; Mary of Scotland; Quality Street; Stage Door; The Philadelphia Story; Keeper of the Flame; Dragon Seed; Woman of the Year; Under-current; Without Love; Sea of Grass; Song of Love; State of the Union; Adam's Rib; The African Queen; Pat and Mike; Summer Madness; The Iron Petticoat; The Rainmaker; His Other Woman; Suddenly, Last Summer; Long Day's Journey into Night; Guess Who's Coming to Dinner; The Madwoman of Chaillot; The Lion in Winter; The Trojan Women; A Delicate Balance; Rooster Cogburn; On Golden Pond. *Stage:* Warrior's Husband; The Philadelphia Story; Without Love; As You Like It; Taming of the Shrew; Merchant of Venice; Measure for Measure, Australia, 1955; Coco, 1970; A Matter of Gravity, NY, 1976, tour, 1977; The West Side Waltz, NY, 1981. Academy Awards for performances in Morning Glory, Guess Who's Coming to Dinner, The Lion in Winter, On Golden Pond. *Publications:* The Making of The African Queen, 1987; Me: stories of my life, 1991.

HEPBURN, Surg. Rear-Adm. Nicol Sinclair, CB 1971; CBE 1968; *b* 2 Feb. 1913; *s* of late John Primrose and Susan Hepburn, Edinburgh; *m* 1939, Dorothy Blackwood (*d* 1989); two *s*. *Educ:* Broughton; Edinburgh Univ. MB, ChB 1935; DPH London, 1948; DIH London, 1952. Barrister-at-law, Gray's Inn, 1956. Joined RN, 1935; served during war in Atlantic and Pacific Stations; SMO, HM Dockyard: Plymouth, 1952; Portsmouth, 1955; Naval Medical Officer of Health: Portsmouth, 1959; Malta, 1962; Surg. Cdre and Dep. Med. Dir-Gen., 1966; Surg. Rear-Adm. 1969; MO i/c, RN Hosp., Haslar, 1969–72; retd. MO, DHSS, 1972–80. FRSM; FFCM 1973. *Address:* Mallows, 10 Chilbolton Avenue, Winchester, Hants SO22 5HD.

HEPBURN, Sir Ninian B. A. J. B.; *see* Buchan-Hepburn.

HEPBURN, Prof. Ronald William; Professor of Moral Philosophy, University of Edinburgh, since 1975 (Professor of Philosophy, 1964–75); *b* 16 March 1927; *s* of late W. G. Hepburn, Aberdeen; *m* 1953, Agnes Forbes Anderson; two *s* one *d*. *Educ:* Aberdeen Grammar Sch.; University of Aberdeen. MA 1951, PhD 1955 (Aberdeen). National service in Army, 1944–48. Asst, 1952–55, Lecturer, 1955–60, Dept of Moral Philosophy, University of Aberdeen; Visiting Associate Prof., New York University, 1959–60; Prof. of Philosophy, University of Nottingham, 1960–64. Stanton Lecturer in the Philosophy of Religion, Cambridge, 1965–68. *Publications:* (jointly) Metaphysical beliefs, 1957; Christianity and Paradox, 1958; Wonder and Other Essays: eight studies in aesthetics and neighbouring fields, 1984; contrib. to learned journals; broadcasts. *Recreations:* music, hill-walking. *Address:* Department of Philosophy, University of Edinburgh, David Hume Tower, George Square, Edinburgh EH8 9JX.

HEPBURNE-SCOTT, family name of **Lord Polwarth.**

HEPHER, Michael Leslie; Group Managing Director, British Telecommunications, since 1991; *b* 17 Jan. 1944; *s* of Leslie and Edna Hepher; *m* 1971, Janice Morton; one *s* two *d*. *Educ:* Kingston Grammar School. FIA; Associate, Soc. of Actuaries; FLIA. Provident Life Assoc., UK, 1961–67; Commercial Life Assurance, Canada, 1967–70; Maritime Life Assurance Co., Canada, 1970–79; Chm. and Man. Dir, Abbey Life Group, UK, subseq. Lloyds Abbey Life, 1980–91. Dir, Lloyds Bank, 1989–. *Recreation:* reading. *Address:* Valverde, Granville Road, St George's Hill, Weybridge, Surrey KT13 0QJ. *T:* Weybridge (0932) 858810.

HEPPELL, (Thomas) Strachan, CB 1986; Deputy Secretary, Department of Health (formerly of Health and Social Security), since 1983; *b* 15 Aug. 1935; *s* of late Leslie Thomas Davidson Heppell and Doris Abbey Heppell (*née* Potts); *m* 1963, Felicity Ann Rice; two *s*. *Educ:* Acklam Hall Grammar Sch., Middlesbrough; The Queen's Coll., Oxford. National Assistance Board, Ministry of Social Security/DHSS: Asst Principal, 1958; Principal, 1963–73 (seconded to Cabinet Office, 1967–69); Asst Director of Social Welfare, Hong Kong, 1971–73; Asst Sec., DHSS, 1973–78 (Social Security Adviser, Hong Kong Govt, 1977); Under Sec., DHSS, 1979–83. *Publications:* contribs to social administration jls. *Recreations:* gardening, travelling. *Address:* Department of Health, Richmond House, 79 Whitehall, SW1A 2NS.

HEPPER, Anthony Evelyn, CEng, FIMechE; CBIM; Chairman, Hyde Sails Ltd, since 1984; *b* 16 Jan. 1923; *s* of Lieut-Col J. E. Hepper; *m* 1970, Jonquil Francisca Kinloch-Jones. *Educ:* Wellington Coll., Berks. Royal Engrs, 1942–47 (retd as Hon. Major); Courtaulds Ltd, 1947–53; Cape Asbestos Co. Ltd 1953–57; Thomas Tilling Ltd, 1957–68 (Dir from 1963 until secondment), seconded as Industrial Adviser, DEA, 1966–67, and Mem., SIB, 1967; Chairman: Upper Clyde Shipbuilders Ltd, 1968–71; Henry Sykes Ltd, 1972–81; Richardsons Westgarth plc, 1982–85; Director: Cape plc, 1968–; Cardinal Investment Trust plc, 1982–84; General Investors Trustees plc, 1982–84; F. & Pacific Investment Trust PLC, 1984–87; Lamont & Partners, 1986–90. *Recreation:* golf. *Address:* 70 Eaton Place, SW1X 8AT. *T:* 071–235 7518. *Club:* Boodle's.

HEPPLE, Prof. Bob Alexander; Professor of English Law, since 1982, Dean of the Faculty of Laws and Head of the Department of Laws, since 1989, University College, London; a part-time Chairman of Industrial Tribunals (England and Wales), 1975–77 and since 1982 (full-time, 1977–82); *b* 11 Aug. 1934; *s* of late Alexander Hepple and of Josephine Zwarenstein; *m* 1960, Shirley Goldsmith; one *s* one *d*. *Educ:* Univ. of Witwatersrand (BA 1954, LLB *cum laude* 1957); Univ. of Cambridge (LLB 1966, MA 1968). Attorney, S Africa, 1958; Lectr in Law, Univ. of Witwatersrand, 1959–62; Advocate, S Africa, 1962–63. Left S Africa after detention without trial for anti-apartheid activities, 1963. Called to Bar, Gray's Inn, 1966; Lectr in Law, Nottingham Univ., 1966–68; Fellow of Clare Coll., Cambridge and Univ. Lectr in Law, 1968–76; Prof. of Comparative Social and Labour Law, Univ. of Kent, 1976–77 (Hon. Prof., 1978–83). Mem., Judicial Studies Bd (Tribunals Cttee), 1988–. Mem., CRE, 1986–90. *Publications:* various books and articles on labour law, race relations, law of tort, etc; Founding Editor, Industrial Law Jl, 1972–77; Gen. Ed (jtly) Encyclopedia of Labour Relations Law, 1972–90; Chief Editor, International Encyclopedia of Comparative Law, Vol. XV, Labour Law, 1979–. *Address:* Faculty of Laws, University College, 4–8 Endsleigh Gardens, WC1H 0EG.

HEPPLE, (Robert) Norman, RA 1961 (ARA 1954); RP 1948; NEAC 1950; *b* 18 May 1908; *s* of Robert Watkin Hepple and Ethel Louise Wardale; *m* 1948, Jillian Constance Marigold Pratt; one *s* one *d*. *Educ:* Goldsmiths' Coll.; Royal Acad. Schools. Figure subject and portrait painter. Pres., Royal Soc. of Portrait Painters, 1979–83. *Address:* (studio) 16 Cresswell Place, South Kensington, SW10; (home) 10 Sheen Common Drive, Richmond, Surrey TW10 5BN. *T:* 081–878 4452.

HEPPLESTON, Prof. Alfred Gordon; Professor of Pathology, University of Newcastle upon Tyne (formerly Durham), 1960–77, now Emeritus Professor; *b* 29 Aug. 1915; *s* of Alfred Heppleston, Headmaster, and Edith (*née* Clough); *m* 1942, Eleanor Rix Tebbutt;

two *s*. *Educ:* Manchester Grammar Sch. Chief Asst, Professorial Medical Unit, University of Manchester; Asst Lecturer in Pathology, Welsh Nat. Sch. of Medicine, Univ. of Wales, 1944–47; Dorothy Temple Cross Research Fellow, Univ. of Pennsylvania, 1947–48; Sen. Lectr in Pathology, Univ. of Wales, 1948–60. *Publications:* on pathological topics, largely in reference to pulmonary disorders. *Recreations:* ornithology, cricket and music. *Address:* Bridgeford Gate, Bellingham, Hexham, Northumberland NE48 2HU. *T:* Bellingham (0434) 220431.

HEPPLEWHITE, Rosalind Mary Joy, (Ros); National Director, MIND (National Association of Mental Health), since 1989; *b* 20 Dec. 1952; *d* of Anne and Anthony Phillips; *m* 1971, Julian Hepplewhite; one *s* one *d*. *Educ:* University College London (BA Hons). Asst House Governor, 1980–83, and Hosp. Sec., 1983–84, Bethlem Royal and Maudsley Hosps; Unit Administrator (Mental Health), Hammersmith and Fulham HA, 1984–85; Unit Gen. Manager (Mental Health and Mental Handicap), 1985–88, Dir, Corporate Develt, 1988–89, Brighton HA. *Recreation:* music. *Address:* National Association for Mental Health, 22 Harley Street, W1N 2ED. *T:* 071–637 0741.

HEPTINSTALL, Leslie George; HM Diplomatic Service, retired; *b* 20 Aug. 1919; *s* of late Victor George Heptinstall and of Maud Maunder; *m* 1949, Marion Nicholls (*d* 1986); one *d*. *Educ:* Thames Valley County Sch.; London Univ. (BSc Econ.). Served War of 1939–45: Capt., Royal Artillery; Middle East, Mediterranean, North-West Europe. Asst Principal, Colonial Office, 1948; Principal, 1951; seconded to West African Inter-Territorial Secretariat, Accra, 1955; Acting Chief Sec., 1958; Acting Administrator, W African Research Office, 1959; Principal, CRO, 1961; First Sec. on Staff of Brit. High Comr, Wellington, NZ, 1962–64; Brit. Dep. High Comr, Lahore, 1964–65; Head of South Asia Dept, ODM, 1966–68; Dep. Senior Trade Comr, Montreal, 1968–70; Internat. Coffee Orgn, 1971–73. *Recreations:* sailing, golf and tennis. *Address:* 63 Richmond Way, Great Bookham, Surrey KT22 9NY. *T:* Bookham (0372) 458457.

HEPWORTH, Rear-Adm. David, CB 1976; retired from RN, 1976; *b* 6 June 1923; *s* of Alfred Ernest Hepworth and Minnie Louisa Catherine Bennet Tanner (*née* Bowden); *m* 1st, 1946, Brenda June Case (marr. diss. 1974); one *s* one *d*; 2nd, 1975, Eileen Mary Macgillivray (*née* Robson). *Educ:* Banbury Grammar School. Boy Telegraphist, RN, 1939; HMS Ganges, 1939–40; served in Atlantic, Mediterranean and E Indies Fleets; commnd 1944; submarines and midget submarines, 1945–50; Home, Australian and Far East Stns, 1951–58; Sen. Officer Submarines Londonderry, 1959–61; CO HMS Ashanti, 1961–64; jssc 1964; Dep. Dir Undersea Warfare, MoD, 1964–66; idc 1967; CO HMS Ajax and Captain (D) 2nd Far East Destroyer Sqdn, 1968–69; Dir RN Tactical Sch. and Maritime Tactical Sch., 1969–71; Dir Naval Warfare, MoD, 1971–73; Staff of Vice-Chief of Naval Staff, 1973–76. Lt-Comdr 1952; Comdr 1958; Captain 1964; Rear-Adm. 1974. Naval Advr to Internat. Military Services Ltd, 1977–83. *Recreations:* home and garden. *Address:* Darville House, Lower Heyford, Oxon OX5 3PD. *T:* Steeple Aston (0869) 47460.

HEPWORTH, Noel Peers, OBE 1980; Director, Chartered Institute of Public Finance and Accountancy, since 1980; *b* 22 Dec. 1934; *m* 1963, Jean Margaret Aldcroft; one *s* three *d*. *Educ:* Crewe County Grammar Sch.; London Univ. IPFA 1958; DPA 1963. Nat. Service, RAF, 1953–55. NW Gas Bd, 1951–58; Asst City Treasurer, Manchester, 1965–72; Dir of Finance, Croydon, 1972–80. Financial Advr to London Boroughs Assoc. and AMA, 1972–80; Mem., London Treasurers' Adv. Body, 1972–80; Member: Dept of Envt Property Adv. Group, 1980–88; Audit Commn, 1983–91. Pres., Internat. Consortium on Governmental Financial Management, 1987–. Chm., FEE Public Sector Cttee, 1988–. FRSA 1985. *Publications:* Finance of Local Government, 1970, 7th edn 1984, Japanese edn 1983; Housing Rents, Costs and Subsidies, 1978, 2nd edn 1981; contribs to technical and financial jls, local govt press and nat. and internat press. *Recreations:* gardening, walking. *Address:* Chartered Institute of Public Finance and Accountancy, 2–3 Robert Street, WC2N 6BH. *T:* 071–895 8823.

HERAT, (James Edward) Harold, MP (United National Party) Puttalam, Sri Lanka, since 1989; Minister of Foreign Affairs, since 1990; State Minister of Finance, since 1989; *b* 10 Nov. 1930; *s* of Dr Albert Edward Herat and Enid Evangeline Henrietta Dagmar Herat; *m* 1965, Gwendoline; one *s* two *d*. *Educ:* Maris Stella Coll., Negombo; St Joseph's Coll., Colombo. Attorney-at-Law. MP (UNP) Nattandiya, NW Province, 1977; Minister of Coconut Industries, 1978, and concurrently Dep. Minister, Janatha Estates Develt, 1980. Mem., Court of Univ. of Sri Lanka, 1980, 1981, 1982. JP and Unofficial Magistrate, 1968. *Recreations:* tennis, riding, swimming. *Address:* 12B Stanmore Crescent, Colombo 7, Sri Lanka. *T:* 452540, 508691; Mudukatuwa Estate, Marawila, Sri Lanka. *Clubs:* Sri Lanka Tennis Association (Vice-Patron), Marawila Sports (Patron).

HERBECQ, Sir John (Edward), KCB 1977; a Church Commissioner, since 1982; *b* 29 May 1922; *s* of late Joseph Edward and Rosina Elizabeth Herbecq; *m* 1947, Pamela Filby; one *d*. *Educ:* High Sch. for Boys, Chichester. Clerical Officer, Colonial Office, 1939; Asst Principal, Treasury, 1950; Private Sec. to Chm., UK Atomic Energy Authority, 1960–62; Asst Sec., Treasury, 1964; Asst Sec., 1968, Under Sec., 1970, Dep. Sec., 1973, Second Permanent Sec., 1975–81, CSD. Dep. Chm., Review Body for Nursing Staff, Midwives, Health Visitors and Professions Allied to Medicine, 1986–91 (Mem., 1983–91); Chm., Malaŵi Civil Service Review Commn, 1984–85. Member: C of E Pensions Bd, 1985–89; Chichester Diocesan Bd of Finance, 1983– (Chm., 1989–). *Recreations:* Scottish country dancing (ISTD Supreme Award with Hons), walking, watching cricket. *Address:* Maryland, Ledgers Meadow, Cuckfield, Haywards Heath, West Sussex RH17 5EW. *T:* Haywards Heath (0444) 413387.

HERBERT, family name of **Earls of Carnarvon, Pembroke,** and **Powis,** and **Baron Hemingford.**

HERBERT, Lord; William Alexander Sidney Herbert; *b* 18 May 1978; *s* and *heir* of Earl of Pembroke and Montgomery, *qv*.

HERBERT, Alfred James; British Council Representative, Portugal, 1980–84, retired; *b* 16 Oct. 1924; *s* of Allen Corbyn Herbert and Betty Herbert; *m* 1st, 1958, Helga Elberling (*d* 1981); two *s*; 2nd, 1982, Dr Wanda Wolska. *Educ:* Royal Masonic Schs; University Coll. London (BA 1950, MA 1952). Guest Prof. of English Lit., Univs of Yokohama and Tokyo, 1958–60; Lectr, English Dept, Birmingham Univ., 1960–62; joined British Council, 1962: Sierra Leone, 1962–65; Brazil, 1965–68; Representative: Somalia, 1968–70; Pakistan, 1974–77; Poland, 1977–80. *Publications:* Modern English Novelists, (Japan), 1960; Structure of Technical English, 1965. *Recreations:* travelling, reading. *Address:* Quinta do Val do Riso, São Simão, Azeitão, 2900 Setubal, Portugal.

HERBERT, Brian Douglas; Director of Performance Review, East Anglian Regional Health Authority, since 1989; *b* 29 May 1930; *s* of Stanley and Kathleen Herbert; *m* 1st, 1952, Linda (marr. diss.); two *s* one *d*; 2nd, 1973, Lila; one *d*. *Educ:* Ipswich School. IPFA. Local Govt Finance, 1946–63; Health Service: Asst Treasurer, NW Metropolitan RHB, 1963; Group Treasurer, SW Middlesex HMC, 1967; Area Treasurer, Ealing, Hammersmith and Hounslow AHA(T), 1973; Regional Treasurer, 1981, Dir of Finance and Administration, 1985, E Anglian RHA. *Address:* 3 Dane Drive, Cambridge CB3 9LP. *T:* Cambridge (0223) 355823.

HERBERT, Ven. Christopher William; Archdeacon of Dorking, since 1990; *b* 7 Jan. 1944; *s* of Walter Meredith Herbert (who *m* 1950, Dorothy Margaret Curnock) and late Hilda Lucy (*née* Dibbin); *m* 1968, Janet Elizabeth Turner; two *s*. *Educ:* Monmouth School; St David's Coll., Lampeter (BA); Univ. of Bristol (PGCE); Wells Theol Coll. Asst Curate, Tupsley, Hereford, 1967–71; Asst Master, Bishop's Sch., Hereford, 1967–71; Adv in Religious Educn, 1971–76, Dir of Educn, 1976–81, Dio. of Hereford; Vicar, St Thomas on the Bourne, Farnham, Surrey, 1981–90; Dir, Post-ordination Training, Dio. of Guildford, 1984–90; Hon. Canon of Guildford, 1984–. *Publications:* The New Creation, 1971; A Place to Dream, 1976; St Paul's: A Place to Dream, 1981; The Edge of Wonder, 1981; Listening to Children, 1983; On the Road, 1984; Be Thou My Vision, 1985; This Most Amazing Day, 1986; The Question of Jesus, 1987; Alive to God, 1987; Ways into Prayer, 1987; Help in your Bereavement, 1988. *Recreations:* walking, cycling, reading, gardening, writing unpublished novels. *Address:* Littlecroft, Heathside Road, Woking, Surrey GU22 7EZ. *T:* Woking (0483) 772713.

HERBERT, (Dennis) Nicholas; (3rd Baron Hemingford, *cr* 1943, of Watford); Editorial Director, Westminster Press, since 1974; *b* 25 July 1934; *s* of 2nd Baron Hemingford and Elizabeth McClare (*d* 1979), *d* of Col J. M. Clark, Haltwhistle, Northumberland; *S* father, 1982; remains known professionally as Nicholas Herbert; *m* 1958, Jennifer Mary Toresen Bailey, *d* of F. W. Bailey, Harrogate; one *s* three *d*. *Educ:* Oundle Sch.; Clare Coll., Cambridge (MA). Reuters Ltd, 1956–61; The Times: Asst Washington Corresp., 1961–65; Middle East Corresp., 1965–68; Dep. Features Editor, 1968–70; Editor, Cambridge Evening News, 1970–74. Vice-Pres., Guild of British Newspaper Editors, 1979, Pres., 1980–81. Sec., Assoc. of British Editors, 1985–. Chm., East Anglia Regl Cttee, Nat. Trust, 1990–. Trustee, Bell Educnl Trust, 1985–. *Heir:* *s* Hon. Christopher Dennis Charles Herbert, *b* 4 July 1973. *Address:* Old Rectory, Hemingford Abbots, Huntingdon PE18 9AH. *T:* St Ives (Hunts) (0480) 66234. *Clubs:* Commonwealth Trust, City Livery.
See also Hon. Lady Goodhart.

HERBERT, Frederick William; Emeritus Fellow in Industrial Relations, International Management Centre, Buckingham, since 1985; Chairman, NALGO Insurance Association Ltd, since 1981; *b* London, 18 Dec. 1922; *s* of late William Herbert and Alice Herbert; *m* 1948, Nina Oesterman; two *d*. *Educ:* Ealing Boys' Grammar Sch. Served RAFVR, 1942–46. Local Govt Finance, Mddx CC, 1939–65; Greater London Council: Local Govt Finance, 1965–72; Personnel Management, Estabt Officer, 1972–77; Asst Dir of Personnel, 1977–80; Head of Industrial Relations, 1980–82; Controller of Personnel, 1982–84. Parly Correspondent, Eurotunnel (UK), 1986–87. FRSA 1986. *Recreations:* cricket, music (classical and jazz), theatre, Antient Society of Cogers (debating). *Address:* 20 Priory Hill, Wembley, Mddx HA0 2QF. *T:* 081–904 8634. *Clubs:* Royal Over-Seas League, MCC.

HERBERT, Prof. Harold Bernard; consultant, holistic learning; *b* 10 March 1924; *s* of late A. Bernard Henbest and Edith Winifred Henbest (*née* Herbert); *m* 1948, Rosalind Eve Skone James; two *s* one *d*. *Educ:* Barking Abbey Sch.; Imperial Coll. of Science, London. Beit Research Fellow, 1947–48; Lectr, University of Manchester, 1948–56; Research Fellow, Harvard Univ., 1953–54; Vis. Prof., UCLA, 1954; Reader, KCL, 1956–57; Prof of Organic Chemistry, QUB, 1958–73. Founder, The Learning Soc., 1988. *Publications:* Organic Chemistry (with M. F. Grundon), 1968; contribs to Jl of Chemical Soc. *Address:* 5 Witley Court, Coram Street, WC1N 1HD. *T:* 071–278 0888.

HERBERT, Jocelyn, Hon. ARCA 1964; RDI 1971; *b* 22 Feb. 1917; *d* of Sir Alan Patrick Herbert, CH, and Gwendolen (*née* Quilter); *m* 1937, Anthony Lousada (marr. diss. 1960); one *s* three *d*. *Educ:* St Paul's Girls' Sch.; Paris and Vienna; London Theatre Studio; Slade School of Art. Started painting at André L'Hote's Sch., Paris, 1932–33; studied drawing and painting with Leon Underwood, 1934; trained as theatre designer with Michel St Denis and George Devine, London Th. Studio, 1936–37; joined staff of English Stage Co., Royal Court Th., 1956; became freelance designer, 1958, centred largely on Royal Court. Hon. FRA, 1991. *Plays designed*, 1957–: Royal Court Theatre: Ionesco: The Chairs, The Lesson, Exit the King; W. B. Yeats: Purgatory; Ann Jellico: Sport of My Mad Mother; Samuel Beckett: Krapp's Last Tape, Happy Days, Not I, Footfalls, That Time; Arnold Wesker: Roots, The Kitchen, I'm Talking about Jerusalem, Chips with Everything, The Merchant; Arden: Serjeant Musgrave's Dance; Christopher Logue: Trials by Logue, Antigone, The Trial of Cob and Leach; Middleton: The Changeling; Shakespeare: Richard III, Midsummer Night's Dream, Julius Caesar; John Osborne: Luther, A Patriot for Me, Inadmissible Evidence; Barry Reckford: Skyvers; W. Solvonka: The Lion and the Jewel; O'Neil and Seabrook: Life Price; Donald Howarth: Three Months Gone; David Storey: Home, The Changing Room, Cromwell, Life Class, Early Days; Christopher Hampton: Savages, The Portage to San Cristobal of A. H.; Joe Orton: What the Butler Saw; David Hare: Teeth 'n' Smiles; Mustapha Matura: Rum and Coca Cola; RSC: Richard III; Ibsen's Ghosts; Phoenix: Brecht's Baal; National Theatre: Othello; Brecht's Mother Courage and Life of Galileo; A Woman Killed with Kindness; Adrian Mitchell's Tyger; David Storey's Early Days; Aeschylus' The Oresteia; Queen's Theatre: The Seagull; Brecht's Joan of the Stockyard; The Trackers of Oxyrhynchus; Round House: Hamlet; Albery Theatre: Pygmalion; Aldwych: Saratoga; (New York) Wesker's The Merchant; Haymarket: Heartbreak House; Lyric, Hammersmith: The Devil and the Good Lord; Lyric, Shaftesbury Ave: Gigi. *Opera*, 1967, and 1975–: Sadler's Wells: Gluck's Orpheus and Euridice; Paris Opera: Verdi's The Force of Destiny, 1975; Metropolitan, NY: Alban Berg's Lulu, 1977; Mozart's The Abduction, 1979; Brecht and Weil's Rise and Fall of the City of Mahagonny, 1979; Coliseum: Birtwistle's The Mask of Orpheus, 1986. *Films:* Tony Richardson: (colour cons. and costumes) Tom Jones, 1961, (prodn designer) Hamlet, 1969, Ned Kelly, 1970, Hotel New Hampshire, 1983; Karel Reiss: (prodn designer) Isadora, 1968; Lindsay Anderson: (prodn designer) If . . ., 1969, O Lucky Man!, 1972; Whales of August, 1987. *Recreations:* the country, painting. *Address:* 45 Pottery Lane, W11. *T:* 071–727 1104.

HERBERT, Nicholas; *see* Herbert, D. N.

HERBERT, Adm. Sir Peter (Geoffrey Marshall), KCB 1983; OBE 1969; Chairman of Council, Soldiers', Sailors', and Airmen's Families Association, since 1985; Non-Executive Director: Radamec Group plc, since 1985; Milerule Ltd, since 1987; consultant; *b* 28 Feb. 1929; *s* of A. G. S. Herbert and P. K. M. Herbert; *m* 1953, Ann Maureen (*née* McKeown); one *s* one *d*. *Educ:* Dunchurch Hall; RN Coll., Dartmouth. Specialised in submarines, 1949; served in submarines, 1950–68: Comd HM Submarines Scythian, Porpoise and Excalibur, 1956–60; Submarine Staff, 1960–62; Comd nuclear submarine, HMS Valiant, 1963–68; Comd HMS Venus, 1964; Dep. Dir, Naval Equipment, 1969; Comd 10th (Polaris) Submarine Squadron, 1970–72; COS to Flag Officer Submarines, 1972–74; Comd HMS Blake, 1974–75; Dep. Chief, Polaris Exec., 1976–78; Flag Officer Carriers and Amphibious Ships, 1978–79; Dir Gen., Naval Manpower and Training, 1980–81; Flag Officer Submarines and Comdr Submarines Eastern Atlantic, 1981–83; VCDS (Personnel and Logistics), 1983–84. Chm., N-Trust, 1985–. Pres., Glos Br., King George's Fund for Sailors. Gov., Cheam School, 1987–. CBIM, MINucE. *Recreations:*

woodwork, gardening, golf, swimming. *Address:* Dolphin Square, SW1. *T:* 071–798 8330. *Club:* Army and Navy.

HERBERT, Prof. Robert Louis, PhD; Professor, Department of Art, Mount Holyoke College, Mass., since 1990; *b* 21 April 1929; *s* of John Newman Herbert and Rosalia Harr Herbert; *m* 1953, Eugenia Randall Warren; one *s* two *d*. *Educ:* Wesleyan Univ., Middletown, Conn (BA 1951); Yale Univ. (MA 1954, PhD 1957). Fulbright Scholar, Paris, 1951–52; Faculty, Yale Univ., 1956–90: Associate Prof., 1963; Prof., 1966; Departmental Chm., 1965–68; Robert Lehman Prof. of Hist. of Art, 1974–90. Guggenheim Fellow, 1971–72; Slade Prof. of Fine Art, Oxford, 1978. Organizer of exhibitions: Barbizon Revisited, Boston Museum of Fine Arts and others, 1962–63; Neo-Impressionism, Solomon R. Guggenheim Mus., 1968; J. F. Millet, Musées Nationaux, Paris, and Arts Council, London, 1975–76; Léger's Le Grand Déjeuner, Minneapolis Inst. of Arts and Detroit Inst. of Arts, 1980; Seurat, Museés Nationaux, Paris and Metropolitan Mus., NY, 1991. Fellow, Amer. Acad. of Arts and Sciences, 1978. Chevalier, 1976, Officier, 1990, Ordre des Arts et des Lettres. *Publications:* Barbizon Revisited, 1962–63; Seurat's Drawings, 1963; The Art Criticism of John Ruskin, 1964; Modern Artists on Art, 1964; Neo-Impressionism, 1968; David, Voltaire, 'Brutus' and the French Revolution, 1972; J. F. Millet, 1975; (ed jtly) Société Anonyme and Dreier Bequest at Yale University: a catalogue raisonné, 1984; Impressionism: art, leisure and Parisian society, 1988; articles in learned jls. *Address:* Department of Art, Mount Holyoke College, South Hadley, Mass 01075, USA.

HERBERT, Robin Arthur Elidyr, DL; JP; Chairman: Leopold Joseph Holdings PLC, since 1978; Union Discount Company of London, since 1990 (Director, since 1989); Director, National Westminster Bank (Chairman, Western Advisory Board); President and Chairman of Council, Royal Horticultural Society, since 1984 (Member of Council, 1971–74 and since 1979); *b* 5 March 1934; *s* of late Sir John Arthur Herbert, GCIE and Lady Mary Herbert; *m* 1st, 1960, Margaret Griswold Lewis (marr. diss. 1988); two *s* two *d*; 2nd, 1988, Philippa Harriet King. *Educ:* Eton; Christ Church, Oxford (MA); Harvard Business School (MBA). ARICS. 2nd Lieut Royal Horse Guards, 1953–54; Captain Royal Monmouthshire RE, 1962–68. Chm., Lands Improvement Gp Ltd, 1991–; Director: Agricl Mortgage Corp., 1985–; Marks & Spencer, 1986–; Consolidated Gold Fields, 1986–89 (Dep. Chm., 1988–89). Financial Advisor: Water Superannuation Fund, 1986–89; Nat. Rivers Authy, 1989–. Dep. Chm., Countryside Commn, 1971–80; Member: Council, National Trust, 1969–87 (Mem., Exec. Cttee, 1969–84; Chm. Cttee for Wales, 1969–84); Nat. Water Council, 1980–83; Welsh Develt Agency, 1980–86. Trustee, Royal Botanic Gardens, Kew, 1987–. DL 1968, JP 1964, High Sheriff 1972, Monmouthshire. *Recreations:* dendrology, walking. *Address:* Llanover, Abergavenny, Gwent NP7 9EF. *T:* Nantyderry (0873) 880232. *Clubs:* Brooks's, Pratt's.

HERBERT, Walter William, (Wally Herbert); *b* 24 Oct. 1934; *s* of Captain W. W. J. Herbert and Helen (*née* Manton); *m* 1969, Marie, *d* of Prof. C. A. McGaughey; two *d*. Trained as surveyor in RE; Egypt, 1953–54, demob. 1955; travelled in Middle East, 1955; Surveyor with Falkland Is Dependencies Survey; Hope Bay, Antarctica, 1955–58; travelled in S America, 1958–59; Mem. expedn to Lapland and Spitzbergen, 1960; travelled in Greenland, 1960; Surveyor, NZ Antarctic Expedn, 1960–62; leader Southern Party; mapped 26,000 sq. miles of Queen Maud Range and descended Amundsen's route to Pole on 50th anniv.; led expedn to NW Greenland, 1966–67; dog-sledged 1,400 miles Greenland to Canada in trng for trans-Arctic crossing; led British Trans-Arctic Expedn, 1968–69, which made 3,800–mile first surface crossing of Arctic Ocean from Alaska via North Pole to Spitzbergen; led Ultima Thule expedn (filming Eskimos, Thule District), 1971–73; led expedn to Lapland, 1975; led expedn to Greenland, 1978–82 (attempting first circumnavigation by dog sledge and skin boat); led filming expedn to NW Greenland, Ellesmere Island and North Pole, 1987. Hon. Mem., British Schools Exploring Soc.; Jt Hon. Pres., World Expeditionary Assoc. FRGS. Polar Medal 1962, and clasp 1969; Livingstone Gold Medal, RSGS, 1969; Founder's Gold Medal, RGS, 1970; City of Paris Medal, 1983; French Geog. Soc. Medal, 1983; Explorers' Medal, Explorers' Club, 1985; Finn Ronne Award, 1985. *Publications:* A World of Men, 1968; Across the Top of the World, 1969; (contrib.) World Atlas of Mountaineering, 1969; The Last Great Journey on Earth, 1971; Polar Deserts, 1971; Eskimos, 1976 (Jugendbuchpreis, 1977); North Pole, 1978; (contrib.) Expeditions the Expert's Way, 1977; (contrib.) Bell House Book, 1978; Hunters of the Polar North, 1982; The Noose of Laurels, 1989. *Recreation:* painting. *Address:* c/o Royal Geographical Society, SW7. *Clubs:* Lansdowne; Explorers (NY).

HERBERT, William Penry Millwarden; Member, Cardiff City Council, since 1970; Lord Mayor of Cardiff, 1988–89; *b* 31 March 1921; *s* of William John Herbert and Esabella Marinda Francis; *m* 1945, Ellen Vera McCarthy; two *d* (one *s* decd). *Educ:* Argoed Elementary Sch., Blackwood, Monmouthshire. Cert. of Professional Competence, Transport, 1977. Miner, 1934–37; Railwayman, 1937–45. Served RE, 1945–47. 1947–78: Guest Keen Iron and Steel Works; Guest Keen and Baldwins British Steel Corp.; Plant Supervisor, Traffic Foreman, Transport Manager. *Recreations:* dancing, gardening, reading, travel. *Address:* 27 Wellwood, Llanedeyrn, Cardiff, South Glamorgan CF3 7JP. *Club:* City Social (Cathays, Cardiff).

HERBERT-JONES, Hugh (Hugo) Jarrett, CMG 1973; OBE 1963; HM Diplomatic Service, retired; company director; *b* 11 March 1922; *s* of late Dora Herbert-Jones (*née* Rowlands), and Captain Herbert-Jones; *m* 1954, Margaret, *d* of Rev. J. P. Veall; one *s* two *d*. *Educ:* Bryanston; Worcester Coll., Oxford. History Scholar. Commnd Welsh Guards, 1941; served NW Europe and Middle East; wounded 1944; demobilised 1946 (Major). Entered Foreign (later Diplomatic) Service, 1947; served: Hamburg, 1947; Berlin, 1949; Hong Kong, 1951; Phnom Penh, 1955; Saigon, 1956; Nairobi, 1959; Pretoria/Cape Town, 1963; FCO, 1966; Paris, 1973; FCO, 1975–79; Internat. Affairs Dir, CBI, 1979–87. Chm., Aldeburgh Soc., 1988–. *Recreations:* sailing, golf, shooting, music, spectator sports. *Address:* Prior's Hill, Aldeburgh, Suffolk IP15 5ET. *T:* Aldeburgh (0728) 453335; 408 Nelson House, Dolphin Square, SW1V 3NZ. *T:* 071–821 1183. *Clubs:* Garrick, MCC; London Welsh Rugby Football; Aldeburgh Golf; Aldeburgh Yacht.

HERBISON, Dame Jean (Marjory), DBE 1985; CMG 1976; Associate Director, Christchurch Polytechnic, New Zealand, 1975–84, retired; *b* 29 April 1923; *d* of William Herbison and Sarah Jane Herbison (*née* McKendry). *Educ:* Univ. of Canterbury (BA); Auckland Teachers' Coll. (Dip Teaching); Univ. of Northern Iowa (MA); Inst. of Education, Univ. of London. AIE 1974. Teaching, Avonside Girls' High School, Christchurch, 1952–59; Dean, 1960–68, Vice-Principal, 1968–74, Christchurch Teachers' Coll.; Assoc. Dir, Christchurch Polytechnic, 1975–84; Mem. Council, 1970–84, Chancellor, 1979–84, Univ. of Canterbury. Chairperson, NZ Council for Educnl Research, 1986–88 (Mem., 1977–88); Member: UGC, 1985–90; Ministerial Cttee of Inquiry into Curriculum, Assessment and Qualifications in the Senior Secondary Sch., 1985–87; Commonwealth Council for Educnl Admin, 1970– (Vice-Pres., 1982–86); NZ Vice-Chancellors' Cttee, Univ. Review Panel, 1987. Fellow: Commonwealth Council for Educnl Admin., 1986; NZ Educnl Admin. Soc., 1990; Hon. Fellow: NZ Educnl Inst.; NZ Inst. of Management. Hon. DLitt Canterbury, 1987. Queen's Silver Jubilee Medal, 1977. *Recreations:* gardening, walking, reading. *Address:* 2/172 Soleares Avenue, Christchurch 8, New Zealand. *T:* Christchurch 849–086.

HERBISON, Rt. Hon. Margaret McCrorie, PC 1964; Lord High Commissioner to the General Assembly of the Church of Scotland, 1970–71; *b* 11 March 1907. *Educ:* Dykehead Public Sch., Shotts; Bellshill Acad.; Glasgow Univ. Teacher of English and History in Glasgow Schs; MP (Lab) North Lanark, 1945–70; Jt Parly Under-Sec. of State, Scottish Office, 1950–51; Minister of Pensions and National Insurance, Oct. 1964–Aug. 1966, of Social Security, 1966–67. Chm., Select Cttee on Overseas Aid, 1969–. Member National Executive Cttee, Labour Party; Chm. Labour Party, 1957. Mem., Royal Commn on Standards of Conduct in Public Life, 1974–. Scotswoman of the Year, 1970. Hon. LLD Glasgow, 1970. *Recreations:* reading, gardening. *Address:* 8 Mornay Way, Shotts, Lanarkshire ML7 4EG. *T:* Shotts (0501) 21944.

HERCUS, Hon. Dame (Margaret) Ann, DCMG 1988; international consultant, since 1991; *b* 24 Feb. 1942; *d* of Horace Sayers and Mary (*née* Ryan); *m* John Hercus; two *s*. *Educ:* Victoria Univ. of Wellington; Univs. of Auckland (BA) and Canterbury (LLB). Lawyer and Staff Training Officer, Beath & Co., Christchurch, 1969–70; Mem., Price Tribunal and Trade Practices Commn, 1973–75; Dep. Chm., Commerce Commn, 1975–78; Chm., Consumer Rights Campaign, 1975; MP (Lab) Lyttleton, 1978–87; in opposition, 1978–84; Minister of Social Welfare, Police and Women's Affairs, 1984–87; Ambassador to UN, 1988–90. *Address:* 8 Park Terrace, Christchurch 1, New Zealand.

HERD, Frederick Charles; Assistant Under-Secretary of State (Civilian Management, General), Ministry of Defence, 1970–75; *b* 27 April 1915. *Educ:* Strode's Sch., Egham; Sidney Sussex Coll., Cambridge. Asst Principal, Admiralty, 1937; Principal, 1941; Asst. Sec., 1950; Asst Under-Sec. of State, 1964. *Recreations:* music, lawn tennis, bridge. *Address:* 11 Bloemfontein Avenue, W12.

HERDMAN, (John) Mark (Ambrose), CBE 1990; LVO 1979; HM Diplomatic Service; Governor of the British Virgin Islands, 1986–91; retired April 1992; *b* 26 April 1932; *s* of Comdr Claudius Alexander Herdman, DL, RN, and of late Joan Dalrymple Herdman (*née* Tennant); *m* 1963, Elizabeth Anne Dillon; one *s* two *d*. *Educ:* St Edward's Sch., Oxford; Trinity Coll., Dublin (BA, MA); Queen's Coll., Oxford (postgrad.). HMOCS, Kenya, 1954–64; joined HM Diplomatic Service, 1964; Second, later First Sec., CRO, 1964–65; ODM, 1965; MECAS, 1965–66; Amman, 1966–68; FCO, 1969–71; Lusaka, 1971–74; Hd of Chancery, Jedda, 1974–76; FCO, 1976–78; Lilongwe, 1978–81; FCO, 1981–83; Dep. Governor, Bermuda, 1983–86. *Recreations:* fishing, golf, philately. *Address:* c/o Foreign and Commonwealth Office, SW1A 2AH. *Clubs:* Commonwealth Trust, Ebury Court.

HERDON, Christopher de Lancy, OBE 1971; HM Diplomatic Service, retired; contributor to The Tablet, since 1983, editorial assistant, since 1986; *b* 24 May 1928; *s* of Wilfrid Herdon and Clotilde (*née* Parsons); *m* 1953, Virginia Grace; two *s* two *d* (and one *s* decd). *Educ:* Ampleforth; Magdalen Coll., Oxford. Foreign Office, 1951; Vienna, 1953; 2nd Sec., Baghdad, 1957; Beirut, 1961; 1st Sec., Amman, 1962; FO, 1965; Aden, 1967; FCO, 1970; Counsellor: Rome, 1973; FCO, 1977; retired 1983. Clerk to Lurgashall Parish Council, 1988–. RC Observer, BCC, 1984–90; Mem., Assembly of Council of Churches for Britain and Ireland, 1990–. *Recreations:* painting, music, sailing, long-distance walking. *Address:* Moses Farm, Lurgashall, Petworth, W Sussex GU28 9EP. *T:* North Chapel 323. *Clubs:* Reform; Thorney Island Sailing.

HEREFORD, 18th Viscount *cr* 1550; **Robert Milo Leicester Devereux;** Bt 1611; Premier Viscount of England; *b* 4 Nov. 1932; *o s* of Hon. Robert Godfrey de Bohun Devereux (*d* 1934) and Audrey Maureen Leslie, DStJ 1963 (*d* 1978) (she *m* 2nd 1961, 7th Earl of Lisburne, who *d* 1965), *y d* of late James Meakin, Westwood Manor, Staffs and of late Countess Sondes; *S* grandfather, 1952; *m* 1969, Susan Mary (marr. diss. 1982), *o c* of Major Maurice Godley, Ide Hill, Sevenoaks, Kent, and of Mrs Glen Godley, Ascott, Shipston-on-Stour, Warwicks; two *s*. *Educ:* Eton. Served Royal Horse Guards (The Blues), 1960–63. Member: Royal Philharmonic Soc.; Royal Philharmonic Orchestra Assoc. OStJ. *Heir:* *s* Hon. Charles Robin de Bohun Devereux, *b* 11 Aug. 1975. *Address:* The Lyford Cay Club, PO Box N7776, Nassau, Bahamas.

HEREFORD, Bishop of, since 1990; **Rt. Rev. John Keith Oliver;** *b* 14 April 1935; *s* of Walter Keith and Ivy Oliver; *m* 1961, Meriel Moore; two *s* one *d*. *Educ:* Westminster School; Gonville and Caius Coll., Cambridge (MA, MLitt); Westcott House. Asst Curate, Hilborough Group of Parishes, Norfolk, 1964–68; Chaplain and Asst Master, Eton College, 1968–72; Team Rector: South Molton Group of Parishes, Devon, 1973–82; Parish of Central Exeter, 1982–85; Archdeacon of Sherborne, 1985–90. *Publications:* The Church and Social Order, 1968; contribs to Theology, Crucible. *Recreations:* railways, music, architecture, fencing. *Address:* Bishop's House, The Palace, Hereford HR4 9BN.

HEREFORD, Dean of; *see* Haynes, Very Rev. Peter.

HEREFORD, Archdeacon of; *see* Moss, Ven. L. G.

HEREN, Louis Philip, FRSL; journalist and author; *b* 6 Feb. 1919; *s* of William Heren and Beatrice (*née* Keller); *m* 1948, Patricia Cecilia O'Regan (*d* 1975); one *s* three *d*. *Educ:* St George's Sch., London. FRSL 1974. Army, 1939–46. Foreign Corresp. of The Times, 1947–70; India, 1947–48; Israel and Middle East, 1948–50; Southeast Asian Corresp., 1951–53; Germany, 1955–60; Chief Washington Corresp. and American Editor, 1960–70; Co-Dep. Editor (Foreign), 1970–73; Dep. Editor and Foreign Editor, 1973–78; Dep. Editor, 1978–81; Associate Editor, and Dir, Times Newspapers Hldgs Ltd, 1981. War Correspondent: Kashmir, 1947; Israel-Arab war, 1948; Korean war, 1950. Hannan Swaffer Award for Internat. Reporting, 1967; John F. Kennedy Memorial Award, 1968. *Publications:* New American Commonwealth, 1968; No Hail, No Farewell, 1970; Growing Up Poor in London, 1973; The Story of America, 1976; Growing Up on The Times, 1978; Alas, Alas for England, 1981; The Power of the Press?, 1985; Memories of Times Past, 1988. *Address:* Fleet House, Vale of Health, NW3 1AZ. *T:* 071–435 0902. *Club:* Garrick.

HERFORD, Geoffrey Vernon Brooke, CBE 1956 (OBE 1946); MSc; FIBiol; Director of Pest Infestation Research, Agricultural Research Council, 1940–68, retired; *b* 1905; *s* of late Henry J. R. Herford, Hampstead; *m* 1933, Evelyn Cicely (*d* 1969), *d* of W. G. Lambert. *Educ:* Gresham's School, Holt; Magdalen College, Oxford (BA); Minnesota University (MSc). *Address:* Rose Cottage, Wells Road, Eastcombe, Stroud, Glos.

HERFT, Rt. Rev. Roger Adrian; *see* Waikato, Bishop of.

HERIOT, Alexander John, MS, FRCS, FDS; Senior Surgeon, King's College Hospital, 1969–79; Postgraduate Regional Dean, South East Thames Regional Health Authority, 1973–79; *b* 28 May 1914; *s* of Robert Heriot; *m* 1940, Dr Christine Stacey (*d* 1958); two *s*; *m* 1959, Dr Cynthia Heymeson; one *s* one *d*. Major RAMC. *Address:* 47 Upper Tooting Park, SW17 7SN. *T:* 081–673 3734.

HERITAGE, John Langdon, CB 1991; Head of Judicial Appointments, Lord Chancellor's Department, since 1989; *b* 31 Dec. 1931; *s* of Frank and Elizabeth Heritage; *m* 1956, Elizabeth Faulkner, *d* of Charles and Ethel Robertson; two *s* one *d*. *Educ:* Berkhamsted Sch., Exeter Coll., Oxford (MA). Called to the Bar, Middle Temple, 1956. National Service, Royal Hampshire Regt and Royal W African Frontier Force. Legal Asst, Treasury Solicitor's Office, 1957, Sen. Legal Asst 1964; Asst Solicitor, Lord Chancellor's Dept, 1973; Sec., Royal Commn on Legal Services, 1976–79; Under Sec., 1983; Circuit Administrator, South Eastern Circuit, 1983–88. *Publications:* articles in legal jls. *Recreation:* making things. *Address:* Lord Chancellor's Department, House of Lords, SW1A 0PW. *T:* 071–219 5554. *Club:* United Oxford & Cambridge University.

HERITAGE, Robert, CBE 1980; RDI, DesRCA, FCSD; Professor, School of Furniture Design, Royal College of Art, 1974–85; *b* 2 Nov. 1927; *m* Dorothy; two *s* one *d*. *Educ:* Royal College of Art, RCA, 1950; freelance designer, 1961. RDI 1963. *Recreations:* tennis, fishing. *Address:* 12 Jay Mews, Kensington Gore, SW7 2EP. *Club:* Chelsea Arts.

HERITAGE, Rev. Canon Thomas Charles; Canon Residentiary of Portsmouth Cathedral, 1964–76, now Canon Emeritus; *b* 3 March 1908; *s* of Thomas and Sarah Ellen Heritage; *m* 1934, Frances Warrington (*d* 1979); twin *d*. *Educ:* The King's Sch., Chester; St Edmund Hall, Oxford. BA 1929; MA 1944; Diploma in Education (Oxford), 1930; ATCL 1931. Deacon, 1934; Priest, 1938. Curate of Christ Church, Chesterfield and Asst Master, Chesterfield Grammar Sch., 1934–38; Asst Master, Portsmouth Grammar Sch., 1938–64; Curate of St Mark, Portsmouth, 1938–40, St Christopher, Bournemouth, 1940–44; Chaplain of Portsmouth Cathedral, 1945–64. Hon. Canon, 1958–64. Examining Chaplain to the Bishop of Portsmouth, 1965–74. Warden, Portsmouth Diocesan Readers' Assoc., 1966–76. *Publications:* A New Testament Lectionary for Schools, 1943; The Early Christians in Britain (with B. E. Dodd), 1966. *Recreations:* music, the theatre, reading, travel. *Address:* 117 The Close, Salisbury, Wilts SP1 2EY. *T:* Salisbury (0722) 329104.

HERLIE, Eileen; actress; *b* 8 March 1920; *d* of Patrick Herlihy (Irish) and Isobel Cowden (Scottish); *m* 1st, 1942, Philip Barrett; 2nd, 1951, Witold Kuncewicz. *Educ:* Shawlands Academy, Glasgow. Varied repertoire with own company, 1942–44; Old Vic, Liverpool, 1944–45; Lyric Theatre, Hammersmith, 1945–46; Andromache in Trojan Women, Alcestis in Thracian Horses, Queen in Eagle has Two Heads, 1946–47; Gertrude in Hamlet (film), 1948; Medea, 1949; Angel with the Trumpet (film), 1949; Paula in The Second Mrs Tanqueray, Haymarket, 1950–51; Helen D'Oyly Carte in Gilbert and Sullivan (film), 1952; Mother in Isn't Life Wonderful? (film), 1952; John Gielgud Season, 1953: Mrs Marwood in The Way of the World; Belvidera in Venice Preserv'd; Irene in Sense of Guilt, 1953; Mrs Molloy in The Matchmaker, 1954; She Didn't Say No! (film), 1958; acted in George Dillon (New York), 1958; Take Me Along (New York), 1959; All America (New York), 1963; The Queen in Hamlet (New York), 1964; Halfway up the Tree, 1967; Emperor Henry IV, NY, 1973; Crown Matrimonial, 1973; The Seagull (film). *Recreations:* riding, reading, music.

HERMAN, Josef, OBE 1980; RA 1990; painter; *b* 3 Jan. 1911; *m* 1955, Eleanor Ettlinger; one *s* (one *d* decd). *Educ:* Warsaw. First exhibition, Warsaw, 1932; left for Belgium, 1938; arrived in Britain, June 1940; lived in: Glasgow, 1940–43; Ystradgynlais (mining village, Wales), 1944–53. Exhibitions include: Glasgow, 1942; Edinburgh, 1942; London, 1943; Roland, Browse and Delbanco Gallery, 1946–; British Council; Arts Council; (retrospective) Whitechapel Art Gallery, 1956; (retrospective) Camden Arts Centre, 1980; contrib. to British Mining exhbn, Science Museum, 1983. Work in permanent collections: Arts Council; British Council; British Museum; National Museum, Cardiff; Contemporary Art Society; National Museum Bezalel, Jerusalem; National Gallery, Johannesburg; Tate Gallery, London; Victoria and Albert Museum, London; National Gallery, Melbourne; National Gallery, Ottawa; National Gallery, Wellington, etc. Gold Medal, Royal National Eisteddfod, Llanelly, 1962; Contemporary Art Society prize, 1952 and 1953; prize, John Moore Exhibition, 1956; Trust House Award, 1962. *Publication:* Related Twilights (autobiog.), 1975. *Address:* 120 Edith Road, W14.

HERMANN, Alexander Henry Baxter; HM Diplomatic Service, retired; *b* 28 Dec. 1917; *m* Rita Rosalind Fernandes. Joined Foreign Service, 1939; served 1942–55; Peking, Ahwaz, Chengtu, Chungking, Shanghai, Quito, Panama, Tamsui; Foreign Office, 1956; Commercial Counsellor and Consul-General, Rangoon, 1957–61; HM Consul-General at Marseilles, also to Monaco, 1961–65; Diplomatic Service Inspector, 1965–66; Counsellor, Hong Kong Affairs, Washington, 1967–70, 1974–77; Consul-General, Osaka, 1971–73. *Address:* Old Place, Aldwick, Sussex.

HERMER, Julius; solicitor; Partner with Grossman, Hermer & Seligman; Lord Mayor of Cardiff, 1987–88; *b* 18 Nov. 1933; *s* of Saul and Cissie Hermer; *m* 1960, Gloria Cohen; three *s* one *d*. *Educ:* St Illtyd's Coll., Cardiff; Peterhouse, Cambridge (BA, MA). Partner, 1959–, Grossman & Hermer, later Crowley, Grossman & Hermer, later Grossman, Hermer & McCarthy. Member: Cardiff City Council, 1964–88 (Chm., Planning Cttee, 1980–84, 1986–87; Dep. Lord Mayor of Cardiff, 1979–80); S Glam CC, 1974– (Vice-Chm. of Council and Dep. Leader of Cons. Party, 1977–78). Dep. Chm., Cardiff W Cons. Assoc., 1985. *Recreations:* sport, wine, food, travel. *Address:* 28 Palace Road, Llandaff, Cardiff. *T:* Cardiff (0222) 566198.

HERMON, Sir John (Charles), Kt 1982; OBE 1975; QPM 1988; Chief Constable, Royal Ulster Constabulary, 1980–89; *b* 23 Nov. 1928; *s* of late William Rowan Hermon and Agnes Hermon; *m* 1954, Jean Webb (*d* 1986); one *s* one *d*; *m* 1988, Sylvia Paisley, LLB; one *s*. *Educ:* Larne Grammar Sch. Accountancy training and business, 1946–50; joined RUC, 1950. CStJ 1984. *Recreations:* boating, reading, walking. *Club:* Royal Ulster Yacht (Bangor, Co. Down).

HERMON, Peter Michael Robert; Head of Information Systems, CL-Alexanders Laing and Cruickshank Holdings Ltd, 1989–90; *b* 13 Nov. 1928; British; *m* 1954, Norma Stuart Brealey; two *s* two *d*. *Educ:* Nottingham High Sch.; St John's and Merton Colls, Oxford. 1st cl. hons Maths Oxon. Leo Computers Ltd, 1955–59; Manager, Management and Computer Divs, Dunlop Co., 1959–65; Information Handling Dir, BOAC, 1965–68; Management Services Dir, BOAC, and Mem. Bd of Management, 1968–72; Mem. of Board, BOAC, 1972; British Airways: Gp Management Services Dir, 1972–78; Board Mem., 1978–83; Management Services Dir, 1978–82; Man. Dir, European Services Div., 1982–83. Man. Dir, Tandem Computers Ltd, 1983–84; Dir, Tandem UK, 1983–85; Head of Systems and Communications, Lloyd's of London, 1984–86; Informations Systems Dir, Harris Queensway, 1986–88. Mem. Bd of Dirs, Internat. Aeradio Ltd, 1966–83, Chm., 1982–83; Chm., Internat. Aeradio (Caribbean) Ltd, 1967–83; Mem. Bd, SITA, 1972–83, Chm., 1981–83. *Publication:* Hill Walking in Wales, 1991. *Recreations:* hill walking, music, cats. *Address:* White Flints, Quentin Way, Wentworth, Virginia Water, Surrey.

HERMON-HODGE, family name of **Baron Wyfold.**

HERMON-TAYLOR, Prof. John, FRCS; Professor of Surgery, St George's Hospital Medical School, since 1976; *b* 16 Oct. 1936; *s* of Hermon Taylor, *qv*; *m* 1971, Eleanor Ann Pheteplace, of Davenport, Iowa; one *s* one *d*. *Educ:* Harrow Sch. (Shepherd-Churchill Open Major Entrance Schol.); St John's Coll., Cambridge (travelling schol., 1955; BA 1957, MB BChir 1960, MChir 1968); London Hosp. Med Coll. (Open Entrance Schol., 1957, prizes in Med., Path., and Obst.). FRCS 1963 (Hallett Prize, 1962). Training in surgery, 1962–68; MRC Travelling Fellow to Mayo Clinic, USA, 1968–69; Senior Lectr, 1970, Reader in Surgery, 1971–76, London Hosp. Med. Coll. Hon. Consultant in Gen. Surgery to RN, 1989–. Mem. Council, Assoc. of Surgeons of GB and Ireland, 1981–84; Dir, James IV Assoc. of Surgeons, 1983–86; Mem., Clinical Panel, Wellcome Trust, 1985–88; Home Office Assessor, Animals Scientific Procedures Act 1986. Director: Chermont Ltd; BioScience Internat. Inc. Mem., numerous professional bodies, UK and overseas. Innovator of the Year award, Times Newspaper/Barclays Bank, 1988. *Publications:* scientific papers on purification and biochem. of enteropeptidase, diseases of pancreas, peptide chem., enzymeactivation in gastric disorders, on causation and specific treatment of Crohn's disease, mycobacterial genetics, epidemiology of breast cancer, biolog. res. on common solid tumours. *Recreations:* sailing, shooting, growing soft fruit and vegetables. *Address:* 11 Parkside Avenue, Wimbledon, SW19 5ES. *T:* 081–767 7631. *Club:* Royal Thames Yacht.

HERN, Major William Richard, (Dick), CVO 1980; racehorse trainer; *b* Holford, Somerset, 20 Jan. 1921. Served War of 1939–45, North Irish Horse. Asst Trainer to Major M. B. Pope, MC, 1952–57; licence to train under Jockey Club rules, 1957–; leading trainer, 1962, 1972, 1980, 1983. Races won include: Derby, 1979, 1980, 1989 (Troy, Henbit, Nashwan); 2,000 Guineas, 1971, 1989 (Brigadier Gerard, Nashwan); 1,000 Guineas, 1974 (Highclere); St Leger, 1962, 1965, 1974, 1977, 1981, 1983 (Hethersett, Provoke, Bustino, Dunfermline, Cut Above, Sun Princess); Epsom Oaks, 1977, 1980, 1983 (Dunfermline, Bireme, Sun Princess); King George VI and Queen Elizabeth Diamond Stakes, 1972, 1979, 1980, 1985, 1989 (Brigadier Gerard, Troy, Ela-Mana-Mou, Petoski, Nashwan); Champion Stakes, 1971, 1972 (Brigadier Gerard); Eclipse Stakes, 1972, 1980, 1989 (Brigadier Gerard, Ela-Mana-Mou, Nashwan); Coronation Cup, 1974, 1975 (Buoy, Bustino). Leading Trainer, Flat Seasons, 1962, 1972, 1980, 1983. *Address:* Kingwood House Stables, Lambourn, Newbury, Berks RG16 7RS. *T:* (office) Lambourn (0488) 73300; (home) East Ilsley (063528) 251.

HERNIMAN, Ven. Ronald George; Archdeacon of Barnstaple 1970–88; *b* 18 April 1923; *s* of George Egerton and Rose Herniman; *m* 1949, Grace Jordan-Jones; one *s* two *d*. *Educ:* Geneva; Bideford, Devon. Served RAF, 1941–46. Birkbeck Coll., London Univ., 1948–51 (BA); Oak Hill Theological Coll., 1951–53; Tutor, Oak Hill Coll., 1953–54; Asst Curate, Christ Church, Cockfosters, 1954–56; Dir of Philosophical Studies, Oak Hill, 1956–61; Rector of Exe Valley Group of Churches (Washfield, Stoodleigh, Withleigh, Calverleigh Oakford, Morebath, Rackenford, Loxbeare and Templeton), 1961–72; Rector of Shirwell with Loxhore, 1972–82. *Recreations:* sailing; making and mending things. *Address:* Castleland House, Oakfordbridge, Tiverton, Devon EX16 9JA.

HERON, Sir Conrad (Frederick), KCB 1974 (CB 1969); OBE 1953; Permanent Secretary, Department of Employment, 1973–76; *b* 21 Feb. 1916; *s* of Richard Foster Heron and Ida Fredrika Heron; *m* 1948, Envye Linnéa Gustafsson; two *d*. *Educ:* South Shields High Sch.; Trinity Hall, Cambridge. Entered Ministry of Labour, 1938; Principal Private Secretary to Minister of Labour, 1953–56; Under-Secretary, Industrial Relations Dept, 1963–64 and 1965–68, Overseas Dept, 1964–65; Dep. Under-Sec. of State, Dept of Employment, 1968–71; Dep. Chm., Commn on Industrial Relations, 1971–72; Second Permanent Sec., Dept of Employment, 1973. *Address:* Old Orchards, West Lydford, Somerton, Somerset TA11 7DG. *T:* Wheathill (096324) 387.

HERON, Patrick, CBE 1977; painter; *b* 30 Jan. 1920; *e s* of late T. M. and Eulalie Heron; *m* 1945, Delia Reiss (*d* 1979); two *d*. *Educ:* St Ives, Cornwall; Welwyn Garden City; St Georges, Harpenden; Slade School. Art criticism in: New English Weekly, 1945–47; New Statesman and Nation, 1947–50 (Art Critic); London correspondent, Arts (NY), 1955–58. John Power Lectr, Sydney Univ., 1973; Doty Prof., Univ. of Texas at Austin, 1978. Trustee, Tate Gall., 1980–87. One-man exhibitions: Redfern Gallery, London, 1947, 1948, 1950, 1951, 1954, 1956 and 1958; Waddington Galleries, London, 1959, 1960, 1963, 1964, 1965, 1967, 1968, 1970 (canvases), 1970 (prints), 1973, 1975, 1977, 1979, 1983, 1987; Bertha Schaefer Gallery, NY, 1960, 1962 and 1965; Galerie Charles Lienhard, Zürich, 1963; Traverse Theatre Gallery, Edinburgh, 1965; São Paulo Bienal VIII, 1965 (Silver Medal) (exhibn toured S Amer., 1966); Harrogate Festival, 1970; Rudy Komon Gall., Sydney, 1970; Waddington Fine Arts, Montreal, 1970; Whitechapel Gallery, 1972; Bonython Art Gall., Sydney, 1973; Rutland Gall., London, 1975; Galerie le Balcon des Arts, Paris, 1977; Retrospective exhibitions: Wakefield City Art Gallery, Leeds, Hull, Nottingham, 1952; Richard Demarco Gallery, Edinburgh, 1967; Kunstnernes Hus, Oslo, 1967; Museum of Modern Art, Oxford, 1968; Univ. of Texas at Austin Art Mus., 1978 (69 works); Oriel Gallery, Cardiff, 1979; Barbican Art Gall., 1985. Twelve paintings shown at São Paulo Bienal II, Brazil, 1953–54. Carnegie International, Pittsburgh, 1961; British Art Today, San Francisco, Dallas, Santa Barbara, 1962–63; Painting and Sculpture of a Decade, 1954–64, Tate Gallery, 1964; British Painting and Sculpture, 1960–70, National Gallery of Art, Washington DC; British Painting 1952–1977, RA, 1977; Color en la Pintura Británica (tour of S Amer.), 1977–78. Exhibited in group and British Council exhibitions in many countries; works owned by: Tate Gallery; Arts Council; British Council; V&A Museum; British Museum; Gulbenkian Foundation; Leeds City Art Gallery; Stuyvesant Foundation; National Portrait Gallery; Broadcasting House; Wakefield City Art Gallery; Manchester City Art Gallery; Contemporary Art Society; Oldham Art Gallery; CEMA, N Ireland; Abbot Hall Art Gallery, Kendal; The Art Gallery, Aberdeen; National Gallery of Wales, Cardiff; Art Gall. of Ont., Toronto; Scottish Nat. Portrait Gall., Scottish Nat. Gall. of Modern Art; Univ. of Galway; Eliot Coll., Univ. of Kent; Montreal Museum of Fine Art; Vancouver Art Gallery; Toledo Museum of Art, Ohio; Smith College Museum of Art, Mass; Brooklyn Museum, NY; Albright-Knox Art Gallery, Buffalo, NY; Univ. of Michigan Museum of Art; Univ. of Texas at Austin Art Museum; Museum of Art, Carnegie Inst., Pittsburgh; Yale Center for British Art, New Haven, Conn; Stuyvesant Foundn, Holland; Boymans Museum, Rotterdam; Musée d'Art Contemporain, Montreal; Western Australian Art Gallery, Perth; Art Gall. of NSW, Sydney; Pembroke, Merton and Nuffield Colleges, Oxford; Bristol City Art Gall.; Exeter Art Gallery; Exeter Univ. (Cornwall House); Plymouth City Art Gallery; Power Collection, Sydney; London Art Gall., London, Ont.; Hatton Art Gall., Newcastle Univ.; Southampton Art Gall.; Norwich Art Gall; also represented in Fitzwilliam Museum, Cambridge, and in municipal collections at Glasgow, Reading and Sheffield. Hon. FRIBA 1991. Hon. DLitt: Exeter, 1982; Kent, 1986; Hon. Dr RCA, 1987. Awarded Grand Prize by international jury, John Moores' 2nd Liverpool Exhibition, 1959. *Publications:* Vlaminck: Paintings, 1900–1945, 1947; The Changing Forms of Art, 1955; Ivon Hitchens, 1955; Braque, 1958; The Shape of Colour, 1973; Paintings by Patrick Heron 1965–1977, 1978; The Colour of Colour, 1978; Patrick Heron, 1988; contrib. The Guardian, Studio International, etc. *Address:* Eagles Nest, Zennor, near St Ives, Cornwall. *T:* Penzance (0736) 796921; 12 Editha Mansions, Edith Grove, SW10. *T:* 071–352 1787.

HERON, Raymond, CBE 1984; retired; Deputy Director, Propellants, Explosives and Rocket Motor Establishment, Ministry of Defence (Procurement Executive), 1977–84; *b*

10 April 1924; *s* of Lewis and Doris Heron; *m* 1948, Elizabeth MacGathan; one *s* one *d*. *Educ*: Heath Grammar Sch., Halifax; Queen's Coll., Oxford (BA Physics). Shell Refining and Marketing Co., 1944–47; RN, Instructor Branch, 1947–52; Rocket Propulsion Estabt, Min. of Supply (later Min. of Technology), 1952–67; Cabinet Office, 1967; Asst Dir, Min. of Technology, 1967–73; Dep. Dir, Explosives Research and Development Estabt, MoD, 1973; Special Asst to Sec. (Procurement Exec.), MoD, 1973–74; Head of Rocket Motor Exec. and Dep. Dir/2, Rocket Propulsion Estabt, MoD (PE), 1974–76. *Publications*: articles in scientific and technical jls. *Recreations*: music, hill walking, golf. *Address*: 9 Grange Gardens, Wendover, Aylesbury, Bucks HP22 6HB. *T*: Wendover (0296) 622921. *Club*: Ashridge Golf.

HERON, Robert, CVO 1988; MA; Director, Duke of Edinburgh's Award Scheme, 1978–87; *b* 12 Oct. 1927; *s* of James Riddick Heron and Sophie Leathem; *m* 1953, Patricia Mary Pennell; two *s* one *d*. *Educ*: King Edward's Sch., Birmingham; St Catharine's Coll., Cambridge. Housemaster: Strathallan, Perthshire, 1952–59; Christ Coll., Brecon, 1959–62; Headmaster, King James I Sch., IOW, 1962–66. Head of Educational Broadcasting, ATV Network Ltd, 1966–69, responsible for production of TV programme series in the scis, langs, soc. documentary, leisure interests, music, drama; Deleg., EBU study gps on educnl broadcasting, 1967–69; Programme Dir, The Electronic Video Recording Partnership (CBS Inc. USA/ICI/Ciba-Geigy UK), 1970–77; Managing Dir, EVR Ltd, 1974–77, and of EVR Enterprises Ltd, 1975–77. Freeman, City of London, 1981. Formerly 6/7th Bn, The Black Watch (RHR) TA. FRGS 1988. *Recreations*: shooting, hill walking, sport. *Address*: The Oast, Ingleden Park, Tenterden, Kent. *Clubs*: Rugby; Island Sailing (Cowes); Hawks (Cambridge); Achilles.

HERON-MAXWELL, Sir Nigel (Mellor), 10th Bt *cr* 1683; *b* 30 Jan. 1944; *s* of Sir Patrick Ivor Heron-Maxwell, 9th Bt and of D. Geraldine E., *yr d* of late Claud Paget Mellor; *S* father, 1982; *m* 1972, Mary Elizabeth Angela, *o d* of late W. Ewing, Co. Donegal; one *s* one *d*. *Educ*: Milton Abbey. *Heir*: *s* David Mellor Heron-Maxwell, *b* 22 May 1975. *Address*: 105 Codicote Road, Welwyn, Herts AL6 9TY.

HERRIDGE, Geoffrey Howard, CMG 1962; Chairman, Iraq Petroleum Co. Ltd and Associated Companies, 1965–70, retired (Managing Director, 1957–63; Deputy Chairman, 1963–65); *b* 22 Feb. 1904; 3rd *s* of late Edward Herridge, Eckington, Worcestershire; *m* 1935, Dorothy Elvira Tod; two *s* two *d*. *Educ*: Crypt Sch., Gloucester; St John's Coll., Cambridge. Joined Turkish Petroleum Co. Ltd (later Iraq Petroleum Co. Ltd), Iraq, 1926; served in Iraq, Jordan, Palestine, 1926–47; General Manager in the Middle East, Iraq Petroleum Co. and Associated Companies, 1947–51; Executive Director, 1953–57; Member of London Cttee, Ottoman Bank, 1964–79. Chairman, Petroleum Industry Training Board, 1967–70. *Address*: Flint, Sidlesham Common, Chichester, West Sussex PO20 7PY. *Club*: Oriental.

HERRIES OF TERREGLES, Lady (14th in line, of the Lordship *cr* 1490); **Anne Elizabeth Fitzalan-Howard;** *b* 12 June 1938; *e d* of 16th Duke of Norfolk, EM, KG, PC, GCVO, GBE, TD, and of Lavinia Duchess of Norfolk, *qv*; *S* to lordship upon death of father, 1975; *m* 1985, Colin Cowdrey, *qv*. Racehorse trainer. *Recreations*: riding, golf, breeding spaniels. *Heir*: *sister* Lady Mary Katharine Mumford, CVO 1982 [*b* 14 Aug. 1940; *m* 1986, Gp Capt Anthony Mumford]. *Address*: Angmering Park, Littlehampton, West Sussex BN16 4EX. *T*: Patching (090674) 421.

HERRIES, Sir Michael Alexander Robert Young-, Kt 1975; OBE 1968; MC 1945; Chairman, The Royal Bank of Scotland Group plc (formerly National and Commercial Banking Group Ltd), 1978–91 (Director since 1976); Director, The Royal Bank of Scotland plc, since 1972 (Vice-Chairman, 1974–75; Deputy Chairman, 1975–76; Chairman, 1976–90); Chairman, Scottish Mortgage and Trust PLC, since 1984 (Director, since 1975); Lord-Lieutenant, Dumfries and Galloway Region (District of Stewartry), since 1989; *b* 28 Feb. 1923; *s* of Lt-Col William Dobree Young-Herries and Ruth Mary (*née* Thrupp); *m* 1949, Elizabeth Hilary Russell (*née* Smith); two *s* one *d*. *Educ*: Eton; Trinity Coll., Cambridge (MA). Served KOSB, 1942–47; Temp. Captain, Actg Maj., Europe and ME; Adjt 5th (Dumfries and Galloway) Battalion and 1st Battalion TARO, 1949. Joined Jardine Matheson & Co. Ltd, 1948; served in Hong Kong, Japan and Singapore; Director, 1959; Managing Director, 1962; Chm. and Man. Dir, 1963–70; Chairman: Jardine Japan Investment Trust Ltd, 1972–76; Crossfriars Trust Ltd, 1972–76; Dep. Chm., Williams & Glyn's Bank, 1978–85; Advr, Jardine Matheson (Hldgs), 1988– (Dir, 1959–88); Director: Matheson & Co. Ltd (Chm., 1971–75); Scottish Widows' Fund and Life Assce Soc., 1974– (Chm., 1981–84, Dep. Chm., 1979–81 and 1984–85); Banco de Santander SA, 1989–. Formerly Mem., Exec. Legislative Council, Hong Kong; Chm., Hong Kong Univ. and Polytechnics Grant Cttee, 1965–73. Former Mem. Council, London Chamber of Commerce and Industry, Hon. Mem., 1980–; Chairman: Scottish Trust for the Physically Disabled, 1981–83; Scottish Disability Foundn, 1982–; Mem. Council, Missions to Seamen. Mem., Royal Company of Archers (Queen's Body Guard for Scotland), 1973–. DL Dumfries and Galloway, 1983. Hon. LLD: Chinese Univ. of Hong Kong, 1973; Univ. of Hong Kong, 1974. Hon. DLitt Heriot-Watt, 1984. *Recreations*: shooting, walking, swimming, tennis. *Address*: (office) The Royal Bank of Scotland plc, 42 St Andrew Square, Edinburgh EH2 2YE. *T*: 031–556 8555; Spottes, Castle Douglas, Stewartry of Kirkcudbright. *T*: Haugh of Urr (055666) 202; 30 Heriot Row, Edinburgh. *T*: 031–226 2711; Flat 14, Lochmore House, Cundy Street, SW1W 9JX. *T*: 071–730 1119. *Clubs*: Caledonian, Farmers', City of London; New (Edinburgh).

HERRING, Cyril Alfred; Chairman and Managing Director, Southern Airways Ltd, since 1978; *b* Dulwich, 17 Jan. 1915; *s* of Alfred James Herring and Minnie Herring (*née* Padfield); *m* 1939, Helen (*née* Warnes); three *s*. *Educ*: Alleyn's Sch.; London School of Economics. BSc(Econ); FCMA; JDipMA; IPFA; FCIT. Chief Accountant, Straight Corporation Ltd, 1936–46; joined BEA, 1946; Chief Accountant, 1951–57; Personnel Director, 1957–65; Financial Director, 1965–71; Executive Board Member, 1971–74; Mem., British Airways Bd, 1972–78; Chief Executive, British Airways Regional Div., 1972–74; Finance Dir, 1975–78; Chm. and Man. Dir, British Air Services Ltd, 1969–76; Chairman: Northeast Airlines Ltd, 1969–76; Cambrian Airways Ltd, 1973–76; London Rail Adv. Cttee, 1976–80; CIPFA Public Corporations Finance Group, 1976–78. Member Council: Chartered Inst. of Transport, 1971–74; Inst. of Cost and Management Accountants, 1967–77 (Vice-Pres., 1971–73, Pres., 1973–74); CBI, 1975–78 (Mem. Financial Policy Cttee, 1975–78, Finance and General Purposes Cttee, 1977–78). Freeman, City of London; Liveryman, Guild of Air Pilots and Air Navigators. *Recreations*: flying, motoring, boating. *Address*: Cuddenbeake, St Germans, Cornwall PL12 5LY. *Clubs*: Reform, Royal Aero.

HERRINGTON, Air Vice-Marshal Walter John, CB 1982; RAF retd; aviation and security consultant; *b* 18 May 1928; *s* of Major H. Herrington, MBE, MM and Daisy Restal Gardiner; *m* 1958, Joyce Maureen Cherryman; two *s*. *Educ*: Peter Symonds, Winchester; Woking Grammar Sch.; RAF Coll., Cranwell. FBIM. Commnd RAF, 1949, Pilot; 1950–69: Long Range Transp. Sqdns; ADC to C-in-C Bomber Comd; Reconnaissance Sqdns; RAF Staff Coll.; Exchange Officer, USAF Acad., Colo; Comd 100 Sqdn; Jt Services Staff Coll.; Air Sec.'s Dept; Stn Comdr RAF Honnington, 1969–71; Ops

Dept, MoD, 1971–73; RCDS (student) 1974; Defence Attaché, Paris, 1975–77. Hon. ADC to the Queen, 1971–74; Senior RAF Mem., Directing Staff, RCDS, 1978–80; Dir of Service Intelligence, 1980–82. Aviation Advr, Internat. Mil. Services, 1982–89. Mem., European Security Study, 1982–83. *Publications*: text books for courses on air power for USAF Academy. *Recreations*: reading, international affairs, sport. *Address*: c/o Lloyds Bank, Obelisk Way, Camberley, Surrey. *Club*: Royal Air Force.

HERRIOT, James; *see* Wight, J. A.

HERROD, Donald, QC 1972; **His Honour Judge Herrod;** a Circuit Judge, since 1978; *b* 7 Aug. 1930; *o s* of Wilfred and Phyllis Herrod, Doncaster; *m* 1959, Kathleen Elaine Merrington, MB, ChB; two *d*. *Educ*: grammar schs, Doncaster and Leeds. Called to Bar, 1956. A Recorder of the Crown Court, 1972–78. Member: Parole Bd, 1978–81; Judicial Studies Bd, 1982–86. *Recreation*: golf. *Address*: The Crown Court, 1 Oxford Row, Leeds LS1 3BE.

HERRON, Very Rev. Andrew; Clerk to the Presbytery of Glasgow, 1959–81; Editor, Church of Scotland Year Book, since 1961; *b* 29 Sept. 1909; *s* of John Todd Herron and Mary Skinner Hunter; *m* 1935, Joanna Fraser Neill; four *d*. *Educ*: Glasgow Univ. (MA, BD, LLB). ATCL 1930. Minister: at Linwood, 1936–40, at Houston and Killellan, 1940–59; Clerk to the Presbytery of Paisley, 1953–59; Moderator of General Assembly of Church of Scotland, 1971–72. Convener: Dept of Publicity and Publications, 1959–68; Gen. Admin Cttee; Business Cttee, Gen. Assembly, 1972–76, 1978; Gen. Trustee, Church of Scotland. Barclay Trust Lectr, 1989. Hon. DD: St Andrews, 1975; Glasgow, 1989. Hon. LLD Strathclyde, 1983. *Publications*: Record Apart, 1974; Guide to the General Assembly of the Church of Scotland, 1976; Guide to Congregational Affairs, 1978; Guide to Presbytery, 1983; Kirk by Divine Right (Baird lectures), 1985; A Guide to the Ministry, 1987; A Guide to Ministerial Income, 1987; Minority Report, 1990. *Address*: 36 Darnley Road, Glasgow G41 4NE. *T*: 041–423 6422. *Club*: Caledonian (Edinburgh).

HERRON, Henry, CBE 1975; Procurator-Fiscal, Glasgow, 1965–76, retired; Deputy Chairman of Traffic Commissioners and Licensing Authority for Scottish Traffic Area, 1978–81; *b* 6 May 1911; *s* of William and Jessie Herron; *m* 1942, Dr Christina Aitkenhead Crawford; one *s* two *d*. *Educ*: Hamilton Academy; Glasgow Univ. (MA, LLB). Solicitor. Depute Procurator-Fiscal, Glasgow, 1946; Procurator-Fiscal, Banff, 1946–51; Asst Procurator-Fiscal, Glasgow, 1951–55; Procurator-Fiscal, Paisley, 1955–65. *Recreations*: gardening, jurisprudence, criminology. *Address*: 51 Craw Road, Paisley PA2 6AE. *T*: 041–889 3091.

HERRON, Ronald James, ARIBA; FCSD; architect; Director, Imagination Ltd, since 1989; *b* 12 Aug. 1930; *s* of James and Louisa Herron; *m* 1952, Patricia Ginn; two *s*. *Educ*: Brixton Sch. of Building; Regent Street Poly. Architect with GLC, 1954–61; Founder, with Peter Cook, Dennis Crompton, Mike Webb and David Greene, Archigram Gp, 1960; Dep. Architect, Taylor Woodrow Construction, 1961–65; Associate, Halpern & Partners, 1965–67; Consultant Architect to Colin St John Wilson, Cambridge, 1967; in private practice, London, 1968; Dir of Urban Design, William Pereira & Partners, LA, 1969–70; Partner, Archigram Architects, 1970–75; in private practice, 1975–77; Partner: Pentagram Design, 1977–80; Derek Walker Associates, 1981–82; Principal, Ron Herron Associates, 1982–85; Partner, Herron Associates, 1985–89; Herron Associates merged with Imagination Ltd to become Herron Associates at Imagination, 1989. Tutor: AA Sch., 1965–; N London Poly. Sch. of Architecture, 1968; Vis. Prof., USC, LA, 1968–69; Artist-in-Residence: Univ. of Wisconsin, 1972; USC, LA, 1976, 1977, 1979; Southern Calif. Inst. for Architecture, LA, 1982; Vis. Prof., Thames Poly. Sch. of Architecture, 1991–; Ext. Examnr and Mem., RIBA Visiting Bd, 1987. Principal designs and projects include: South Bank Develt (QEH and Hayward Gall.), 1961–63; master plan for new town for Ford Motor Co., Dearborn, Mich, air terminal at LA Internat. Airport for Pan American Airlines, 1969; entertainment facility for Monte Carlo (Archigram winning design, internat. competition), 1970; play centre, Calverton End, Milton Keynes, 1975; develt of central area, Heathrow Airport, 1976; D. O. M. Office Headquarters, Cologne (competition with Peter Cook and Christine Hawley), 1980; Wonderworld theme park, Corby, Northants, 1981; travelling exhibn, design and construction of The Human Story, with Richard Leakey, Commonwealth Inst., 1985; R&D Labs for Imperial Tobacco, urban design project for Hamburg docks, by invitation of Hamburg City Council, 1985; mobile exhibn structure for BT, proposals for remodelling Thorn House, London, 1987; German Headquarters for L'Oréal, Karlsruhe (competition special award), 1988; proposals for a European cultural centre, Belgium, 1989; Far Eastern Internat. airport terminal, British Airports Services, 1990; conf. facility at Waddesdon Manor for Lord Rothschild, 1990; Canada Water underground stn for London Underground Ltd, 1991; Exhibitions: Architectural Assoc., London, 1980; Berlin, 1981; Heinz Gall., London, 1989. Member: Architecture Club; Architectural Assoc. FRSA. (Jtly) Building of the Year Award, Sunday Times/Royal Fine Art Commn, 1990; Eternit Nat. Award for Architecture, 1990; Critics' Choice, BBC Design Awards, 1990. *Publications*: (ed jtly) Archigram, 1973; contrib. Pentagram Papers, 1977; articles in professional jls incl. Living Arts, Architectural Design. *Recreations*: cricket, soccer, movies. *Address*: Herron Associates at Imagination, 25 Store Street, South Crescent, WC1E 7BL. *T*: 071–323 3300.

HERSCHBACH, Prof. Dudley Robert; Baird Professor of Science, Harvard University, since 1976; *b* 18 June 1932; *s* of Robert D. Herschbach and Dorothy E. Herschbach; *m* 1964, Georgene L. Botyos; two *d*. *Educ*: Campbell High School; Stanford Univ. (BS Math 1954, MS Chem 1955); Harvard Univ. (AM Physics 1956, PhD Chem Phys 1958). Junior Fellow, Soc. of Fellows, Harvard, 1957–59; Asst Prof., 1959–61, Associate Prof., 1961–63, Univ. of California, Berkeley; Prof. of Chemistry, Harvard Univ., 1963–76. Hon. DSc Univ. of Toronto, 1977. (Jtly) Nobel Prize for Chemistry, 1986. *Publications*: over 250 research papers, chiefly on quantum mechanics, chemical kinetics, reaction dynamics, molecular spectroscopy, collision theory, in Jl of Chemical Physics. *Recreations*: hiking, canoeing, chess, poetry, viola. *Address*: 116 Conant Road, Lincoln, Mass 01773, USA. *T*: (home) (617) 259–1386; (office) (617) 495–3218.

HERSCHELL, family name of **Baron Herschell.**

HERSCHELL, 3rd Baron, *cr* 1886; **Rognvald Richard Farrer Herschell;** late Captain Coldstream Guards; *b* 13 Sept. 1923; *o s* of 2nd Baron and Vera (*d* 1961), *d* of Sir Arthur Nicolson, 10th Bt, of that Ilk and Lasswade; *S* father, 1929; *m* 1948, Lady Heather, *d* of 8th Earl of Dartmouth, CVO, DSO; one *d*. *Educ*: Eton. Page of Honour to the King, 1935–40. *Heir*: none. *Address*: Westfield House, Ardington, Wantage, Oxon. *T*: Abingdon (0235) 833224.

HERSEY, David Kenneth; lighting designer; founder Chairman, DHA Lighting, since 1972; *b* 30 Nov. 1939; *s* of Ella Morgan Decker and C. Kenneth Hersey; *m* Demetra Maraslis; one *s* two *d*. *Educ*: Oberlin Coll., Ohio. Left NY for London, 1968; lighting designer for theatre, opera and ballet cos, incl. Royal Opera House, ENO, Glyndebourne, Ballet Rambert, London Contemporary Dance, Scottish Ballet; lighting consultant to Nat. Theatre, 1974–84; many productions for RSC. Chm., Assoc. of Lighting Designers, 1984–86. *Designs include*: Evita, 1978 (Tony award, 1980); Nicholas Nickleby, 1980;

Cats, 1981 (Tony and Drama Desk awards, 1983); Song and Dance, 1982; Guys and Dolls, 1982; Starlight Express, 1984; Les Misérables, 1985 (Tony award, 1987); Porgy and Bess, 1986; Chess, 1986; Miss Saigon, 1989. *Recreation:* sailing. *Address:* 29 Rotherwick Road, Hampstead Garden Suburb, NW11 7DG.

HERSEY, John; writer; *b* 17 June 1914; *s* of Roscoe M. and Grace B. Hersey; *m* 1st, 1940, Frances Ann Cannon (marr. diss. 1958); three *s* one *d;* 2nd, 1958, Barbara Day Kaufman; one *d. Educ:* Yale Univ.; Clare Coll., Cambridge. Secretary to Sinclair Lewis, 1937; Editor Time, 1937–42; War and Foreign Correspondent, Time, Life, New Yorker, 1942–46. Mem. Council, Authors' League of America, 1946–70 (Vice-Pres., 1948–55, Pres., 1975–80). Fellow, Berkeley Coll., Yale Univ., 1950–65; Master, Pierson Coll., Yale Univ., 1965–70, Fellow, 1965–. Writer in Residence, Amer. Acad. in Rome, 1970–71. Lectr, Yale Univ., 1971–75, Vis. Prof., 1975–76, Adjunct Prof., 1976–84, now Emeritus; Lectr, Salzburg Seminars in Amer. Studies, 1975; Vis. Prof., MIT, 1975. Chm., Connecticut Cttee for the Gifted, 1954–57; Member: Amer. Acad. Arts and Letters, 1953 (Sec., 1962–76; Chancellor, 1981–84); Nat. Inst. Arts and Letters, 1950; Amer. Acad. of Arts and Scis, 1978; Council, Authors' Guild, 1946– (Chm., Contract Cttee, 1963–87); Yale Univ. Council cttees on the Humanities, 1951–56, and on Yale Coll., 1959–69 (Chm., 1964–69) and 1981–; Vis. Cttee, Harvard Grad. Sch. of Educn, 1960–65; Vis. Cttee, Loeb Drama Center, 1980–85; Nat. Citizens' Commn for the Public Schs, 1954–56; Bd of Trustees, Putney Sch., 1953–56; Trustee: Nat. Citizens' Council for the Public Schs, 1956–58; Nat. Cttee for the Support of the Public Schs, 1962–68. Delegate: to White House Conf. on Educn, 1955; to PEN Congress, Tokyo, 1958. Comr, Nat. Commn on New Technological Uses of Copyrighted Works, 1975–78. Hon. Fellow, Clare Coll., Cambridge, 1967. Hon. MA Yale Univ., 1947; Hon. LLD: Washington and Jefferson Coll., 1946; Univ. of New Haven, 1975; Hon. LHD: New Sch. for Social Research, 1950; Syracuse Univ., 1983; Hon. DHL Dropsie Coll., 1950; Hon. LittD: Wesleyan Univ., 1957; Bridgeport Univ., 1959; Clarkson Coll. of Technology, 1972; Yale Univ., 1984; Monmouth Coll., 1985; William and Mary Coll., 1987; Albertus Magnus Coll., 1988. Pulitzer Prize for Fiction, 1945; Sidney Hillman Foundn Award, 1951; Howland Medal, Yale Univ., 1952. *Publications:* Men on Bataan, 1942; Into the Valley, 1943; A Bell for Adano, 1944; Hiroshima, 1946; The Wall, 1950; The Marmot Drive, 1953; A Single Pebble, 1956; The War Lover, 1959; The Child Buyer, 1960; Here to Stay, 1962; White Lotus, 1965; Too Far to Walk, 1966; Under the Eye of the Storm, 1967; The Algiers Motel Incident, 1968; The Conspiracy, 1972; The Writer's Craft, 1974; My Petition for More Space, 1974; The President, 1975; The Walnut Door, 1977; Aspects of the Presidency, 1980; The Call, 1985; Blues, 1987; Life Sketches, 1989; Fling and Other Stories, 1990; Antonietta, 1991.

HERSHEY, Dr Alfred Day; Director, Genetics Research Unit, Carnegie Institution of Washington, 1962–74, retired; *b* 4 Dec. 1908; *s* of Robert D. Hershey and Alma (*née* Wilbur); *m* 1945, Harriet Davidson; one *s. Educ:* Michigan State Coll. (now Univ.). BS 1930; PhD 1934. Asst Bacteriologist, Washington Univ. Sch. of Medicine, St Louis Missouri, 1934–36; Instructor, 1936–38; Asst Prof., 1938–42; Assoc. Prof., 1942–50; Staff Mem., Dept of Genetics (now Genetics Research Unit), Carnegie Instn of Washington, 1950–. Albert Lasker Award, Amer. Public Health Assoc., 1958; Kimber Genetics Award, Nat. Acad. Sci., US, 1965. Hon. DSc, Chicago, 1967; Hon. Dr Med. Science, Michigan State, 1970. Nobel Prize for Physiology or Medicine (jtly), 1969. *Publications:* numerous articles in scientific jls or books. *Address:* RD Box 1640, Moores Hill Road, Syosset, NY 11791, USA. *T:* 516 692 6855.

HERTFORD, 8th Marquess of, *cr* 1793; **Hugh Edward Conway Seymour;** Baron Conway of Ragley, 1703; Baron Conway of Killultagh, 1712; Earl of Hertford, Viscount Beauchamp, 1750; Earl of Yarmouth, 1793; DL Warwick, 1959; formerly Lieutenant Grenadier Guards; *b* 29 March 1930; *s* of late Brig.-General Lord Henry Charles Seymour, DSO (2nd *s* of 6th Marquess) and Lady Helen Frances Grosvenor (*d* 1970), *d* of 1st Duke of Westminster; *S* uncle, 1940; *m* 1956, Comtesse Louise de Caraman Chimay, *o d* of late Lt-Col Prince Alphonse de Chimay, TD; one *s* three *d. Educ:* Eton. Chm., Hertford Public Relations Ltd, 1962–73. Chief interests are estate management (Diploma, Royal Agricultural Coll., Cirencester, 1956) and opening Ragley to the public. *Heir: s* Earl of Yarmouth, *qv. Address:* Ragley Hall, Alcester, Warwickshire B49 5NJ. *T:* Alcester (0789) 762455/762090/762845. *Clubs:* White's, Pratt's, Turf.

HERTFORD, Bishop Suffragan of, since 1990; **Rt. Rev. Robin Jonathan Norman Smith;** *b* 14 Aug. 1936; *s* of Richard Norman and Blanche Spurling Smith; *m* 1961, Hon. Lois Jean, *d* of Baron Pearson, CBE, PC; three *s* one *d. Educ:* Bedford Sch.; Worcester Coll., Oxford (MA); Ridley Hall, Cambridge. RAF Regiment Commission, 1955–57. Curate, St Margaret's, Barking, 1962–67; Chaplain, Lee Abbey, 1967–72; Vicar, Chesham St Mary, 1972–80; Rector, Great Chesham, 1980–90. Hon. Canon, Christ Church, Oxford, 1988–90. *Recreations:* gardening, walking. *Address:* Hertford House, Abbey Mill Lane, St Albans AL3 4HE.

HERTFORDSHIRE, Bishop in, (RC); *see* O'Brien, Rt Rev. J. J.

HERVEY, family name of **Marquess of Bristol.**

HERVEY, Rear Adm. John Bethell, CB 1982; OBE 1970; independent naval consultant; *b* 14 May 1928; *s* of late Captain Maurice William Bethell Hervey, RN, and Mrs Joan Hervey (*née* Hanbury); *m* 1950, (Audrey) Elizabeth Mote; two *s* one *d. Educ:* Marlborough Coll., Wilts. Joined RN, 1946; specialised in submarines, 1950, nuclear submarines, 1968; command appointments: HMS Miner VI, 1956; HMS Aeneas, 1956–57; HMS Ambush, 1959–62; HMS Oracle, 1962–64; Sixth Submarine Div., 1964–66; HMS Cavalier, 1966–67; HMS Warspite, 1968–69; Second Submarine Sqdn, 1973–75; HMS Kent, 1975–76; staff appointments: Course Officer, Royal Naval Petty Officers Leadership Sch., 1957–59; Submarine Staff Officer to Canadian Maritime Comdr, Halifax, NS, 1964–66; Ops Officer to Flag Officer Submarines, 1970–71; Def. Op. Requirements Staff, 1971–73; Dep. Chief of Allied Staff to C-in-C Channel and C-in-C Eastern Atlantic (as Cdre), 1976–80; Comdr British Navy Staff, and British Naval Attaché, Washington, and UK Nat. Liaison Rep. to SACLANT, 1980–82, retired. Comdr 1964, Captain 1970, Rear Adm. 1980. Marketing Vice-Pres., Western Hemisphere, MEL, 1982–86. FBIM 1983. *Recreations:* walking, talking, reading. *Address:* c/o National Westminster Bank, 26 Haymarket, SW1Y 4ER. *Clubs:* Army and Navy, Royal Navy of 1765 and 1785, Anchorites (Pres., 1988).

HERVEY-BATHURST, Sir F.; *see* Bathurst.

HERWARTH von BITTENFELD, Hans Heinrich; Grand Cross (2nd Class), Order of Merit, Federal Republic of Germany, 1963; Hon. GCVO 1958; State Secretary, retired; *b* Berlin, 14 July 1904; *s* of Hans Richard Herwarth von Bittenfeld and Ilse Herwarth von Bittenfeld (*née* von Tiedemann); *m* 1935, Elisabeth Freiin von Redwitz; one *d. Educ:* Universities of Berlin, Breslau and Munich (Law and Nat. Econ.). Entered Auswärtiges Amt, Berlin, 1927; Attaché, Paris, 1930; Second Secretary and Personal Secretary to Ambassador, Moscow, 1931–39. Military Service, 1939–45. Oberregierungsrat, Regierungsdirektor, Bavarian State Chancellery, 1945–49; Ministerialdirigent and Chief of Protocol, Federal Government, 1950, Minister Plenipotentiary, 1952; German Ambassador to Court of St James's, 1955–61; State Secretary and Chief of German Federal Presidential Office, 1961–65; German Ambassador to Republic of Italy, 1965–69; Pres., Commn for Reform of German Diplomatic Service, 1969–71. Chm., Supervisory Council, Unilever, Germany, 1969–77. Chm., Venice Cttee, German Unesco Commn; Pres., Internat. Adv. Cttee for Venice. Pres., Goethe Institut, Munich, 1971–77. Cavaliere di San Marco, 1989; Hon. Citizen, Augsburg Univ., 1985. *Publications:* Against Two Evils: memoirs of a diplomat-soldier during the Third Reich, 1981 (German edn, Zwischen Hitler und Stalin, 1982); Von Adenauer zu Brandt, 1990. *Recreation:* antiques. *Address:* Schloss, 8643 Küps, Germany. *T:* 09264 7174.

HERZBERG, Charles Francis; consultant; Director, Northern Investors Co. Ltd, 1984–89; *b* 26 Jan. 1924; *s* of Dr Franz Moritz Herzberg and Mrs Marie Louise Palache; *m* 1956, Ann Linette Hoare; one *s* two *d. Educ:* Fettes Coll., Edinburgh; Sidney Sussex Coll., Cambridge (MA). CEng, FIMechE, MIGasE. Alfred Herbert Ltd, 1947–51; Chief Engr and Dir, Hornflowa Ltd, Maryport, 1951–55; Chief Engr, Commercial Plastics Gp of Cos, and Dir, Commercial Plastics Engrg Co. at Wallsend on Tyne, North Shields, and Cramlington, Northumberland, 1955–66; Corporate Planning Dir, Appliance Div., United Gas Industries, and Works Dir, Robinson Willey Ltd, Liverpool, 1966–70; Man. Dir and Chief Exec., Churchill Gear Machines Ltd, Blaydon on Tyne, 1970–72; Regional Industrial Director, Dept of Industry, N Region, 1972–75; Dir of Corporate Develt, Clarke Chapman Ltd, 1975–77; Gp Industrial Planning Adviser, 1977–84, Dir Industrial Planning, 1984–88, Northern Engineering Industries plc. Pres., Tyne & Wear Chamber of Commerce and Industry, 1989– (Vice-Pres., 1986–89). Gov., Newcastle upon Tyne Poly., 1986–; Chm., Newcastle upon Tyne Polytechnic Products Ltd, 1988–. *Recreation:* shooting. *Address:* 3 Furzefield Road, Gosforth, Newcastle upon Tyne NE3 4EA. *T:* 091–285 5202. *Club:* East India, Devonshire, Sports and Public Schools.

HERZBERG, Gerhard, CC (Canada), 1968; FRS 1951; FRSC 1939; Director, Division of Pure Physics, National Research Council of Canada, 1949–69, now Distinguished Research Scientist, National Research Council of Canada; *b* Hamburg, Germany, 25 Dec. 1904; *s* of late Albin Herzberg and Ella Herzberg; *m* 1929, Luise Herzberg, *née* Oettinger (*d* 1971); one *s* one *d; m* 1972, Monika Herzberg, *née* Tenthoff. *Educ:* Inst. of Technology, Darmstadt, Germany; Univ. of Göttingen, Germany; Univ. of Bristol, England. Lecturer, Darmstadt Inst. of Technology, 1930; Research Professor, Univ. of Saskatchewan, 1935; Prof. of Spectroscopy, Yerkes Observatory, Univ. of Chicago, 1945; Principal Research Officer, National Research Council of Canada, 1948. University Medal, Univ. of Liège, Belgium, 1950; President, RSC, 1966 (Henry Marshall Tory Medal, 1953). Joy Kissen Mookerjee Gold Medal of Indian Association for Cultivation of Science, 1954 (awarded 1957). Gold Medal of Canadian Association Phys., 1957; Bakerian Lecture, Royal Society, 1960; Faraday Lecture and Medal, Chem. Soc., 1970; Nobel Prize for Chemistry, 1971; Royal Medal, Royal Soc., 1971. Hon. Fellow: Indian Academy of Science, 1954; Indian Physical Society, 1957; Chemical Society of London, 1968. Hon. Member: Hungarian Academy of Sciences, 1964; Optical Society of America, 1968; Royal Irish Acad., 1970; Japan Acad., 1976; Chem. Soc. of Japan, 1978; Hon. Foreign Member American Academy Arts and Sciences, 1965; Foreign Associate, National Academy of Sciences, US, 1968; Foreign Mem. (Physics), Royal Swedish Acad. of Sciences, 1981. President, Canadian Association of Physicists, 1956; Vice-Pres., International Union of Pure and Applied Physics, 1957–63. Holds numerous hon. degrees, including Hon. ScD Cantab, 1972. *Publications:* Atomic Spectra and Atomic Structure, 1st edition (USA) 1937, 2nd edition (USA) 1944; Molecular Spectra and Molecular Structure: I, Spectra of Diatomic Molecules, 1st edition (USA), 1939, 2nd edition (USA), 1950; II, Infra-red and Raman Spectra of Polyatomic Molecules (USA), 1945; III, Electronic Spectra and Electronic Structure of Polyatomic Molecules (USA), 1966; IV, (with K. P. Huber) Constants of Diatomic Molecules (USA), 1979; The Spectra and Structures of Simple Free Radicals: an introduction to Molecular Spectroscopy (USA), 1971; original research on atomic and molecular spectra published in various scientific journals. *Address:* National Research Council, Ottawa, Ontario K1A 0R6, Canada. *T:* 99–00917; 190 Lakeway Drive, Rockcliffe Park, Ottawa, Ontario K1L 5B3, Canada. *T:* 746–4126.

HERZIG, Christopher, CBE 1988; Director, External Relations, International Atomic Energy Agency, Vienna, 1981–87; *b* 24 Oct. 1926; *s* of late L. A. Herzig and late Mrs Elizabeth Herzig (*née* Hallas); *m* 1952, Rachel Katharine Buxton; four *s* one *d. Educ:* Christ's Hosp.; Selwyn Coll., Cambridge (MA). Asst Principal, Min. of Fuel and Power, 1951–56; Principal, Min. of Supply, 1956–58; Min. of Aviation, 1959–61; Private Sec. to Lord President of the Council, 1961–64; Private Sec. to Minister of Technology, 1964–66; Asst Sec., Min. of Technology, 1966–70; Dept of Trade and Industry, 1970–71, Under-Sec., DTI, 1972–73; Under Sec., Dept of Energy, 1974–81. UK Governor, IAEA, 1972–78. *Address:* 13a The Causeway, Horsham, West Sussex RH12 1HE. *T:* Horsham (0403) 65239.

HERZOG, Chaim, Hon. KBE 1970; President of Israel, since 1983; *b* Ireland, 17 Sept. 1918; *s* of Rabbi Isaac Halevy Herzog, first Chief Rabbi of Israel and formerly of Ireland, and Sarah Herzog (*née* Hillman); *m* 1947, Aura (*née* Ambache); three *s* one *d. Educ:* Univ. of London (LLB). Called to the Bar, Lincoln's Inn, 1942 (Hon. Bencher, 1987); Advocate, Israel Bar. Immigrated to Palestine, 1935; Army service: Jerusalem, 1936–38; British Army, war of 1939–45; RMC; served 2nd Army, NW Europe; Israel Defence Forces: Defence Attaché, USA, 1950–54; Dir of Mil. Intell., 1948–50 and 1959–62; Comdr, Jerusalem Brigade, 1954–57; Chief of Staff, Southern Comd, 1957–59; retired 1962 (Maj.-Gen.); 1st Mil. Governor, W Bank and Jerusalem, 1967. Ambassador and Perm. Rep. to UN, 1975–78; Mem. Tenth Knesset, 1981–83. Director, 1962–83: Israel Aircraft Industries; Industrial Development Bank of Israel; Israel Discount Bank; Man. Dir, G. U. S. Industries, 1962–72; Senior Partner, Herzog, Fox and Neeman, 1972–83. President: Variety Club of Israel, 1967–72; ORT Israel, 1968–83; World ORT Union, 1980–83. Hon. Fellow, UCL, 1986. Hon. degrees from home and overseas univs. *Publications:* Israel's Finest Hour, 1967; Days of Awe, 1973; (ed) Judaism, Law and Ethics, 1974; The War of Atonement, 1975; Who Stands Accused?, 1978; (with Mordechai Gichon) Battles of the Bible, 1978; The Arab-Israeli Wars, 1982; Heroes of Israel, 1990. *Recreations:* sailing, flying light aircraft, golf. *Address:* Office of the President, Jerusalem, Israel.

HESELTINE, Rt. Hon. Michael (Ray Dibdin); PC 1979; MP (C) Henley, since 1974 (Tavistock, 1966–74); Secretary of State for the Environment, since 1990; *b* 21 March 1933; *s* of late Col R. D. Heseltine, Swansea, Glamorgan; *m* 1962, Anne Harding Williams; one *s* two *d. Educ:* Shrewsbury Sch.; Pembroke Coll., Oxford (BA PPE; Hon. Fellow 1986). Pres. Oxford Union, 1954. National Service (commissioned), Welsh Guards, 1959. Contested (C): Gower, 1959; Coventry North, 1964. Director of Bow Publications, 1961–65; Chm., Haymarket Press, 1966–70. Vice-Chm., Cons. Parly Transport Cttee, 1968; Opposition Spokesman on Transport, 1969; Parly Sec., Min. of Transport, June-Oct. 1970; Parly Under-Sec. of State, DoE, 1970–72; Minister for Aerospace and Shipping, DTI, 1972–74; Opposition Spokesman on: Industry, 1974–76; Environment, 1976–79; Sec. of State for the Environment, 1979–83, for Defence, 1983–86. Pres., Assoc. of Conservative Clubs, 1978; Vice-Pres., 1978, Pres., 1982–84,

Nat. Young Conservatives. Mem. Council, Zoological Soc. of London, 1987–. *Publications:* Reviving the Inner Cities, 1983; Where There's a Will, 1987; The Challenge of Europe, 1989. *Address:* c/o House of Commons, SW1A 0AA. *Club:* Carlton.

HESELTINE, Rt. Hon. Sir William (Frederick Payne), GCB 1990 (KCB 1986; CB 1978); GCVO 1988 (KCVO 1982; CVO 1969; MVO 1961); AC 1988; QSO 1990; PC 1986; Private Secretary to the Queen and Keeper of the Queen's Archives, 1986–90, retired; *b* E Fremantle, W Australia, 17 July 1930; *s* of late H. W. Heseltine; *m* 1st, Ann Elizabeth (*d* 1957), *d* of late L. F. Turner, Melbourne; 2nd, Audrey Margaret, *d* of late S. Nolan, Sydney; one *s* one *d*. *Educ:* Christ Church Grammar Sch., Claremont, WA; University of Western Australia (1st class hons, History). Prime Minister's dept, Canberra, 1951–62; Private Secretary to Prime Minister, 1955–59; Asst Information Officer to The Queen, 1960–61; Acting Official Secretary to Governor-General of Australia, 1962; Asst Federal Director of Liberal Party of Australia, 1962–64; attached to Household of Princess Marina for visit to Australia, 1964; attached to Melbourne Age, 1964; Asst Press Secretary to the Queen, 1965–67, Press Secretary, 1968–72; Assistant Private Secretary to the Queen, 1972–77, Dep. Private Secretary, 1977–86. *Club:* Boodle's.

HESKETH, 3rd Baron, *cr* 1935, of Hesketh; **Thomas Alexander Fermor-Hesketh,** Bt 1761; Captain of the Gentlemen at Arms (Government Chief Whip in the House of Lords), since 1991; *b* 28 Oct. 1950; *s* of 2nd Baron and Christian Mary, OBE 1984, *o d* of Sir John McEwen, 1st Bt of Marchmont, DL, JP; *S* father 1955; *m* 1977, Hon. Claire, *e d* of 3rd Baron Manton, *qv*; one *s* two *d*. *Educ:* Ampleforth. A Lord in Waiting (Govt Whip), 1986–89; Parly Under-Sec. of State, DoE, 1989–90; Minister of State, DTI, 1990–91. Hon. FSE. *Heir: s* Hon. Frederick Hatton Fermor-Hesketh, *b* 13 Oct. 1988. *Address:* Easton Neston, Towcester, Northamptonshire NN12 7HS. *T:* Towcester (0327) 50445. *Clubs:* White's, Turf.

HESLAM, (Mary) Noelle, (Mrs David Heslam); *see* Walsh, M. N.

HESLOP, Philip Linnell; QC 1985; *b* 24 April 1948; *s* of late Richard Norman Heslop and of Ina Winifred Heslop, Merstham, Surrey. *Educ:* Haileybury; Christ's Coll., Cambridge (schol.; BA Hons (Law Tripos) 1970; LLM 1971). Called to the Bar, Lincoln's Inn, 1970 (Hardwicke Schol.); Jt Jun. Counsel (Chancery), DTI, 1979–85. Dep. Chm., Membership Tribunal, IMRO, 1988–; DTI Inspector, Consolidated Goldfields PLC, 1988–. Chm., CU Cons. Assoc., 1969; Pres., Cambridge Union Soc., 1971; Chm., Coningsby Club, 1976; contested (C) Lambeth Vauxhall, 1979. *Publication:* (ed jtly) Crew on Meetings, 1975. *Recreations:* travel, sailing, ski-ing, history. *Address:* 4 Stone Buildings, Lincoln's Inn, WC2A 3XT. *T:* 071–242 5524.

HESLOP-HARRISON, Prof. John, MSc, PhD, DSc; FRS 1970; FRSE, MRIA, FRSA, FLS; Royal Society Research Professor, University College of Wales, Aberystwyth, 1977–85; *b* 10 Feb. 1920; *s* of late Prof. J. W. Heslop-Harrison, FRS; *m* 1950, Yolande Massey; one *s*. *Educ:* Grammar School, Chester-le-Street, King's Coll. (University of Durham), Newcastle upon Tyne. MSc (Dunelm), PhD (Belfast), DSc (Dunelm). Army service, 1941–45. Lecturer in Agricultural Botany, King's Coll., Univ. of Durham, 1945–46; Lecturer in Botany: Queen's Univ., Belfast, 1946–50; UCL, 1950–53; Reader in Taxonomy, UCL, 1953–54; Prof. of Botany, Queen's Univ., Belfast, 1954–60; Mason Prof. of Botany, Univ. of Birmingham, 1960–67; Prof. of Botany, Inst. of Plant Develt, Univ. of Wisconsin, 1967–71; Dir, Royal Botanic Gardens, Kew, 1971–76. Visiting Professor: (Brittingham) Univ. of Wisconsin, 1965; US Dept of Agriculture Institute of Forest Genetics, Rhinelander, Wis, 1968; Univ. of Massachusetts, Amherst, Mass, 1976–77, 1978–79; Lectures: Sigma Xi, Geneva, NY, 1969; William Wright Smith, Edinburgh, 1972; George Bidder, Soc. Exptl Biol., Leeds, 1973; Ghosh, Univ. of Calcutta, 1973; Kennedy Orton Meml, UCW, Bangor, 1974; Croonian, Royal Society, 1974; Amos Meml, E Malling, 1975; Holden, Univ. of Nottingham, 1976; Bewley, Glasshouse Crops Res. Inst., 1978; Hooker, Linnean Soc., 1979; Bateson, John Innes Inst., 1979; Waller Meml, Univ. of Ohio, 1980; Blackman, Univ. of Oxford, 1980. Mem., ARC, 1977–82; Vice-President: Botanical Soc. of British Isles, 1972; Linnean Soc., 1973; President: Inst. of Biology, 1974–75; Sect. K, British Assoc. for Advancement of Science, 1974. Editor, Annals of Botany, 1961–67. Corresp. Mem., Royal Netherlands Botanical Soc., 1968; For. Fellow, Indian Nat. Sci. Acad., 1974; For. Associate, National Acad. of Sciences, USA, 1983; Mem., German Acad. of Science, 1975; For. Mem., American Botanical Soc., 1976; For. Hon. Mem., Amer. Acad. Arts and Scis., 1982; For. Mem., Acad. Royale de Belgique (Sci. Div.), 1985. Hon. DSc: Belfast, 1971; Bath, 1982; Edinburgh, 1984; Hull, 1986. Trail-Crisp Award, Linnean Soc., 1967; Univ. of Liège Medal, 1967; Erdtman Internat. Medal for Palynology, 1971; Cooke Award, Amer. Acad. of Allergy, 1974; Darwin Medal, Royal Soc., 1983; Keith Medal, RSE, 1984; Navashin Medal, Komarov Inst., USSR Acad., 1991. *Publications:* papers and monographs on botanical subjects in various British and foreign journals. *Recreations:* hill walking, photography and painting. *Address:* The Pleasaunce, 137 Bargates, Leominster, Herefordshire HR6 8QS. *T:* Leominster (0568) 611566; Institute of Grassland and Environmental Research, Plas Gogerddan, near Aberystwyth SY23 3EB.

HESS, Ellen Elizabeth, NDH; Administrator, Studley College Trust, 1970–80; Principal, Studley College, Warwickshire, 1956–69; *b* 28 Dec. 1908; *d* of Charles Michael Joseph Hess and Fanny Thompson Hess (*née* Alder). *Educ:* Grammar School for Girls, Dalston; Royal Botanic Society, Regents Park. Lecturer in Horticulture, Swanley Horticultural College for Women, 1934–39; Agricultural Secretary, National Federation of Women's Institutes, 1939–46; Ellen Eddy Shaw Fellowship, Brooklyn Botanic Gardens, New York, USA, 1946–47; School of Horticulture, Ambler, Pa., USA, 1947–48; HM Inspector of Schools (Agriculture and Further Education), 1948–56. Veitch Meml Medal, RHS, 1967. *Recreations:* travel, photography, walking. *Address:* The Croft, 54 Torton Hill Road, Arundel, West Sussex BN18 9HH.

HESSAYON, Dr David Gerald; gardening author; Chairman, since 1972, Managing Director, since 1964, Pan Britannica Industries Ltd; Chairman: Turbair Ltd, since 1972; Expert Publications Ltd, since 1988; Director, Tennants Consolidated Ltd, since 1982; *b* 13 Feb. 1928; *s* of Jack and Lena Hessayon; *m* 1951, Joan Parker Gray; two *d*. *Educ:* Salford Grammar Sch.; Leeds Univ. (BSc 1950); Manchester Univ. (PhD 1954). FRMS 1960; FRES 1960; FRSA 1970; FIBiol 1971; FBIM 1972; FIHort 1986. Res. Fellow, UC of Gold Coast, 1953; entered Pan Britannica Industries Ltd, 1955; Technical Manager, 1955; Technical Dir, 1960; Man. Dir, 1964. Chm., British Agrochemicals Assoc., 1980–81. Vice-Patron, Royal Nat. Rose Soc., 1987–. Mem., Guild of Freemen, City of London, 1977–; Liveryman, Gardeners' Co., 1985. Hon. DSc Manchester, 1990. *Publications:* Be Your Own Gardening Expert, 1959, revd edn 1977; Be Your Own House Plant Expert, 1960, revd edn 1980; Potato Growers Handbook, 1961; Silage Makers Handbook, 1961; Be Your Own Lawn Expert, 1962, revd edn 1979; Be Your Own Rose Expert, 1964, revd edn 1977; (with J. P. Hessayon) The Garden Book of Europe, 1973; Vegetable Plotter, 1976; Be Your Own House Plant Spotter, 1977; Be Your Own Vegetable Doctor, 1978; Be Your Own Garden Doctor, 1978; The House Plant Expert, 1980; The Rose Expert, 1981; The Lawn Expert, 1982; The Cereal Disease Expert, 1982; The Tree and Shrub Expert, 1983; The Armchair Book of the Garden,

1983; The Flower Expert, 1984; The Vegetable Expert, 1985; The Indoor Plant Spotter, 1985; The Garden Expert, 1986; The Gold Plated House Plant Expert, 1987; The Home Expert, 1987; Vegetable Jotter, 1989; Rose Jotter, 1989; House Plant Jotter, 1989; The Fruit Expert, 1990; Be Your Own Greenhouse Expert, 1990; The Bio Friendly Gardening Guide, 1990. *Recreations:* American folk music, cartophily, thinking about the book I should be writing. *Address:* Hilgay, Mill Lane, Broxbourne, Herts EN10 7AX.

HESSE, Mary Brenda, MA, MSc, PhD; FBA 1971; Professor of Philosophy of Science, University of Cambridge, 1975–85; Fellow of Wolfson College (formerly University College), Cambridge, since 1965; *b* 15 Oct. 1924; *d* of Ethelbert Thomas Hesse and Brenda Nellie Hesse (*née* Pelling). *Educ:* Imperial Coll., London; University Coll., London. MSc, PhD (London); DIC; MA (Cantab). Lecturer: in Mathematics, Univ. of Leeds, 1951–55; in Hist. and Philosophy of Science, UCL, 1955–59; in Philosophy of Science, Univ. of Cambridge, 1960–68; Reader in Philosophy of Sci., Cambridge Univ., 1968–75; Vice-Pres., Wolfson Coll., 1976–80. Member: Council, British Acad., 1979–82; UGC, 1980–85. Visiting Prof.: Yale Univ., 1961; Univ. of Minnesota, 1966; Univ. of Chicago, 1968. Stanton Lectr, Cambridge, 1977–80; Joint Gifford Lectr, Edinburgh, 1983. Hon. DSc: Hull, 1984; Guelph, Ontario, 1987. Editor, Brit. Jl for the Philosophy of Science, 1965–69. *Publications:* Science and the Human Imagination, 1954; Forces and Fields, 1961; Models and Analogies in Science, 1963; The Structure of Scientific Inference, 1974; Revolutions and Reconstructions in the Philosophy of Science, 1980; (jtly) The Construction of Reality, 1987; articles in jls of philosophy and of the history and the philosophy of science. *Recreations:* walking, local archaeology. *Address:* Department of History and Philosophy of Science, Free School Lane, Cambridge CB2 3RH. *Club:* Commonwealth Trust.

HESTER, Rev. Canon John Frear; Canon Residentiary and Precentor of Chichester Cathedral, since 1985; Chaplain to HM the Queen, since 1984; *b* 21 Jan. 1927; *s* of William and Frances Mary Hester; *m* 1959, Elizabeth Margaret, *d* of Sir Eric Riches, MC, MS, FRCS; three *s*. *Educ:* West Hartlepool Grammar School; St Edmund Hall, Oxford (MA); Cuddesdon Coll., Oxford. Captain RAEC, 1949–50. Personal Asst to Bishop of Gibraltar, 1950; Deacon, 1952; Priest, 1953; Assistant Curate: St George's, Southall, 1952–55; Holy Redeemer, Clerkenwell, 1955–58; Sec., Actors' Church Union, 1958–63; Chaplain, Soc. of the Sisters of Bethany, Lloyd Sq., 1959–62; Dep. Minor Canon of St Paul's Cathedral, 1962–75; Rector of Soho, 1963–75; Priest-in-charge of St Paul's, Covent Garden, 1969–75; Senior Chaplain, Actors' Church Union, 1970–75; Chaplain to Lord Mayor of Westminster, 1970–71; in residence at St George's Coll. and the Ecumenical Inst., Tantur, Jerusalem, 1973; Chm., Covent Garden Conservation Area Adv. Ctee, 1971–75; Vicar of Brighton, 1975–85; Canon and Prebendary of Chichester Cathedral, 1976–85; RD of Brighton, 1976–85. Chm., Chichester Diocesan Overseas Council, 1985–. Editor, Christian Drama, 1957–59. Lectr and preacher, US, 1961–; Leader of Pilgrimages to the Holy Land, 1962–. Mem., Worshipful Co. of Parish Clerks, 1970–86; Chaplain, Brighton and Hove Albion FC, 1979–. Vice-Pres., 1979– and Hon. Chaplain, 1975–79 and 1988–, Royal Theatrical Fund (formerly Royal Gen. Theatrical Fund Assoc.); Chm. of Trustees, Chichester Centre of Arts, 1989–; Chm., Chichester Arts Liaison Gp, 1990–; Hon. Mem., British Actors' Equity Assoc. *Publication:* Soho Is My Parish, 1970. *Recreations:* sitting down; pulling legs; watching soccer and other drama; Middle Eastern studies. *Address:* The Residentiary, Canon Lane, Chichester PO19 1PX. *T:* Chichester (0243) 782961.

HESTER, Prof. Ronald Ernest, DSc,. PhD; CChem, FRSC; Professor of Chemistry, University of York, since 1983; *b* 8 March 1936; *s* of Ernest and Rhoda Hester; *m* 1958, Bridget Ann Maddin; two *s* two *d*. *Educ:* Royal Grammar Sch., High Wycombe; London Univ. (BSc / DSc 1979); Cornell Univ. (PhD 1962). CChem 1975; FRSC 1971. Res. Fellow, Cambridge Univ., 1962–63; Asst Prof., Cornell Univ., 1963–65; University of York: Lectr, 1965–71; Sen. Lectr, 1971–76; Reader, 1976–83. Science and Engineering Research Council: Chm., Chemistry Cttee, 1988–90; Mem., Science Bd, 1988–90; Mem., Council, 1990–. Chm., Envmt Group, RSC, 1982–85. *Publications:* (jtly) Inorganic Chemistry, 1965; (ed with R. J. H. Clark) Advances in Infrared and Raman Spectroscopy, 12 vols, 1975–85; (ed with R. J. H. Clark) Advances in Spectroscopy, 7 vols, 1986–90; 200 research papers. *Recreations:* tennis, squash, golf, ski-ing, travel. *Address:* Department of Chemistry, University of York, York YO1 5DD. *T:* York (0904) 432557.

HESTON, Charlton; actor (films, stage and television), USA; *b* Evanston, Ill, 4 Oct. 1924; *s* of Russell Whitford Carter and Lilla Carter (*née* Charlton); *m* 1944, Lydia Marie Clarke (actress), Two Rivers, Wisconsin; one *s* one *d*. *Educ:* New Trier High Sch., Ill; Sch. of Speech, Northwestern Univ., 1941–43. Served War of 1939–45, with 11th Army Air Forces in the Aleutians. Co-Dir (with wife), also both acting, Thomas Wolfe Memorial Theatre, Asheville, NC (plays: the State of the Union, The Glass Menagerie, etc.). In Antony and Cleopatra, Martin Beck Theatre, New York, 1947; also acting on Broadway, 1949 and 1950, etc.; London stage début (also dir.), The Caine Mutiny Court Martial, Queen's, 1985; A Man for All Seasons, Savoy, 1987, tour 1988. *Films:* (1950–) include: Dark City, Ruby Gentry, The Greatest Show on Earth, Arrowhead, Bad For Each Other, The Savage, Pony Express, The President's Lady, Secret of the Incas, The Naked Jungle, The Far Horizons, The Private War of Major Benson, The Ten Commandments (Moses), The Big Country, Ben Hur (Acad. Award for best actor, 1959), The Wreck of the Mary Deare, El Cid, 55 Days at Peking, The Greatest Story Ever Told, Major Dundee, The Agony and the Ecstacy, Khartoum, Will Penny, Planet of the Apes, Soylent Green, The Three Musketeers, Earthquake, Airport 1975, The Four Musketeers, The Last Hard Men, Battle of Midway, Two-Minute Warning, Gray Lady Down, Crossed Swords, The Mountain Men, The Awakening, Mother Lode, Music Box. TV appearances, esp. in Shakespeare. Mem., Screen Actors' Guild (Pres., 1966–69); Mem., Nat. Council on the Arts, 1967–; Chm., Amer. Film Inst., 1961–; Chm., Center Theatre Group, LA, 1963; Chm. on the Arts for Presidential Task Force on the Arts and Humanities, 1981–. Is interested in Shakespearian roles. Hon. Dr: Jacksonville Univ., Fla; Abilene Christian Univ., Texas. Academy Award, 1978; Jean Hersholt Humanitarian Award, 1978. *Publications:* (ed Hollis Alpert) The Actor's Life: Journals 1956–1976, 1979; Beijing Diary, 1990. *Address:* c/o ICM, 388–396 Oxford Street, W1 9HE. *Club:* All England Lawn Tennis.

HETHERINGTON, Alastair; *see* Hetherington, H. A.

HETHERINGTON, (Arthur) Carleton, CBE 1971 (MBE 1945); Secretary of Association of County Councils, 1974–80; *b* 13 Feb. 1916; *s* of late Arthur Stanley and Mary Venters Hetherington, Silloth, Cumberland; *m* 1941, Xenia, *d* of late Nicholas Gubsky, Barnes; three *s*. *Educ:* St Bees Sch. Admitted Solicitor 1938. Asst Solicitor: Peterborough, 1938–39; Stafford, 1939. Served Royal Artillery, 1939–46 (Hon. Lt-Col); Temp. Lt-Col 1944–46. Dep. Clerk of the Peace and Dep. Clerk of County Council: of Cumberland, 1946–52; of Cheshire, 1952–59; Clerk of the Peace and Clerk of County Council of Cheshire, 1959–64. Sec., County Councils Assoc., 1964–74. Mem., Departmental Cttee on Jury Service, 1963–64; Sec., Local Authorities Management Services and Computer Cttee, 1965–80. *Recreations:* music, golf, family. *Address:* 33 Campden Hill Court, W8 7HS. *Club:* Royal Automobile.

HETHERINGTON, Sir Arthur (Ford), Kt 1974; DSC 1944; FEng 1976; Chairman, British Gas Corporation, 1973–76 (Member 1961, Deputy Chairman 1967–72, Chairman 1972, Gas Council); *b* 12 July 1911; *s* of late Sir Roger Hetherington and Lady Hetherington; *m* 1937, Margaret Lacey; one *s* one *d*. *Educ:* Highgate Sch.; Trinity Coll., Cambridge (BA). Joined staff of Gas Light & Coke Company, 1935. Served War, RNVR, 1941–45. North Thames Gas Board, 1945–55; joined staff of Southern Gas Board, 1955; Deputy Chairman, 1956; Chairman 1961–64; Chairman, E Midlands Gas Board, 1964–66. Hon. FIGasE. Hon. DSc London, 1974. *Address:* 32 Connaught Square, W2 2HL. *T:* 071–723 3128. *Club:* Athenæum.

HETHERINGTON, Carleton; *see* Hetherington, A. C.

HETHERINGTON, Rear-Adm. Derick Henry Fellowes, CB 1961; DSC 1941 (2 Bars 1944, 1945); MA (Oxon), 1963; Domestic Bursar and Fellow of Merton College, Oxford, 1963–76; Emeritus Fellow, 1976; *b* 27 June 1911; *s* of Commander H. R. Hetherington, RD, Royal Naval Reserve, and Hilda Fellowes; *m* 1942, Josephine Mary, *d* of Captain Sir Leonard Vavasour, 4th Bt, RN; one *s* three *d* (and one *s* decd). *Educ:* St Neot's, Eversley, Hants; RNC Dartmouth. Cadet, HMS Barham, 1928–29; Midshipman-Comdr (HMS Effingham, Leander, Anthony, Wildfire, Kimberley, Windsor, Lookout, Royal Arthur, Cheviot), 1929–50; Captain 1950; Chief of Staff, Canal Zone, Egypt, 1950–52; Senior British Naval Officer, Ceylon, 1953–55; Captain (D) 4th Destroyer Squadron, 1956–57; Director of Naval Training, Admiralty, 1958–59; Flag Officer, Malta, 1959–61; retired 1961. Croix de Guerre (France) 1945. *Address:* Gatehouse Cottage, Pyrton, Oxford OX9 5AN. *T:* Watlington (049161) 2338.

HETHERINGTON, (Hector) Alastair; journalist; Research Professor in Media Studies, Stirling University, 1982–87, now Emeritus; former Editor of The Guardian; *b* Llanishen, Glamorganshire, 31 Oct. 1919; *yr s* of late Sir Hector Hetherington and Lady Hetherington; *m* 1st, 1957, Miranda (marr. diss. 1978), *d* of Professor R. A. C. Oliver, *qv*; two *s* two *d*; 2nd, 1979, Sheila Janet Cameron, *widow* of Hamish Cameron; one step *s* two step *d*. *Educ:* Gresham's Sch., Holt; Corpus Christi Coll., Oxford (Hon. Fellow, 1971). Royal Armoured Corps, 1940–46. Editorial staff, The Glasgow Herald, 1946–50; joined Manchester Guardian, 1950, Asst Editor and Foreign Editor, 1953–56, Editor, 1956–75; Director: Guardian and Manchester Evening News Ltd, 1956–75; Guardian Newspapers Ltd, 1967–75; Controller, BBC Scotland, 1975–78; Manager, BBC Highland, 1979–80. Member, Royal Commission on the Police, 1960–62. Vis. Fellow, Nuffield Coll., Oxford, 1973–79. Trustee, Scott Trust, 1970–89 (Chm., 1984–89). Dr *hc* Univ. of Lille 3, 1989. Journalist of the Year, Nat. Press awards, 1970. *Publications:* Guardian Years, 1981; News, Newspapers and Television, 1985; News in the Regions, 1989; Highlands and Islands: a generation of progress, 1990. *Recreations:* hill walking, golf. *Address:* 38 Chalton Road, Bridge of Allan, Stirling FK9 4EF. *T:* Stirling (0786) 832168; Tigh na-Fraoich, High Corrie, Isle of Arran KA27 8JB. *T:* Brodick (0770) 81652. *Clubs:* Athenæum, Caledonian.

HETHERINGTON, Sir Thomas Chalmers, (Tony), KCB 1979; CBE 1970; TD; QC 1978; Director of Public Prosecutions, 1977–87; Head of the Crown Prosecution Service, 1986–87; *b* 18 Sept. 1926; *er s* of William and Alice Hetherington; *m* 1953, June Margaret Ann Catliff; four *d*. *Educ:* Rugby Sch.; Christ Church, Oxford. Served in Royal Artillery, Middle East, 1945–48; Territorial Army, 1948–67. Called to Bar, Inner Temple, 1952; Bencher, 1978. Legal Dept, Min. of Pensions and Nat. Insce, 1953; Law Officers' Dept, 1962, Legal Sec., 1966–75; Dep. Treasury Solicitor, 1975–77. Jt Head, War Crimes Inquiry, 1988–89. Pres., Old Rugbeians Soc., 1988–90. *Publication:* Prosecution and the Public Interest, 1989. *Address:* Rosemount, Mount Pleasant Road, Lingfield, Surrey RH7 6BH. *Club:* Garrick.

HETZEL, Phyllis Bertha Mabel, (Mrs R. D. Hetzel, jr); President, Lucy Cavendish College, Cambridge, 1979–84; *b* 10 June 1918; *d* of Stanley Ernest and Bertha Myson; *m* 1st, 1941, John Henry Lewis James (*d* 1962); one *d*; 2nd, 1974, Baron Bowden (marr. diss. 1983, he *d* 1989); 3rd, 1985, Ralph Dorn Hetzel. *Educ:* Wimbledon High Sch.; Newnham Coll., Cambridge (MA). Commonwealth (now Harkness) Fellow, 1957–58. BoT, 1941; Principal 1947; Asst Sec., 1960; DEA, 1964–69; Min. of Technology, 1969–70; Dept of Trade and Industry, 1970–75; Asst Under-Sec. of State 1972; Regional Dir, NW Region, DTI, subseq. DoI, 1972–75. Member: Monopolies and Mergers Commn, 1975–78; Local Govt Boundary Commn for England, 1977–81; W Midlands Cttee, National Trust, 1976–81. Chm., Manchester, Marriage Guidance Council, 1976–79. Member: Court, Manchester Univ., 1976–83; Court and Council, UMIST, 1978–80; Council of Senate, Cambridge Univ., 1983–84; Bd, American Friends of Cambridge University Inc., 1985–. Vice-Pres., Oxford and Cambridge Club of Los Angeles, 1986–. *Publications:* The Concept of Growth Centres, 1968; Gardens through the Ages, 1971; Regional Policy in Action, 1980; contrib. Public Administration, Cambridge Review, Encycl. Britannica. *Recreations:* landscape architecture, conservation, writing, piano, family. *Address:* 4411 Gloria Avenue, Encino, Calif 91436, USA. *T:* 818 990 5224; Lucy Cavendish College, Cambridge CB3 0BU; 18 Trafalgar Road, Cambridge CB4 1EU.

HEUSTON, Prof. Robert Francis Vere, DCL Oxon 1970; MRIA 1978; Regius Professor of Laws, Trinity College, Dublin, 1970–83; *b* Dublin, 17 Nov. 1923; *e s* of late Vere Douglas Heuston and late Dorothy Helen Coulter; *m* 1962, Bridget Nancy (*née* Bolland), *widow* of Neville Ward-Perkins; four step *c*. *Educ:* St Columba's Coll.; Trinity Coll., Dublin; St John's Coll., Cambridge. Barrister, King's Inns, 1947 (Hon. Bencher, 1983), Gray's Inn, 1951 (Hon. Bencher, 1988); Hon. Member, Western Circuit, 1966. Fellow, Pembroke Coll., Oxford, 1947–65 (Hon. Fellow, 1982), Dean, 1951–57, Pro-Proctor, 1953; Professor of Law, Univ. of Southampton, 1965–70. Arthur Goodhart Prof. of Legal Sci., and Fellow, Jesus Coll., Cambridge, 1986–87. Member, Law Reform Cttee (England), 1968–70, (Ireland), 1975–81. Visiting Professor: Univ. of Melbourne, 1956; Univ. of British Columbia, 1960, 1985; ANU, 1977; Gresham Professor in Law, 1964–70. Corresponding FBA, 1988. *Publications:* (ed) Salmond and Heuston on Torts, 11th edn 1953, to 19th edn 1987; Essays in Constitutional Law, 2nd edn 1964; Lives of the Lord Chancellors, vol. I, 1885–1940, 1964, vol. II, 1940–70, 1987; various in learned periodicals. *Address:* Kentstown House, Brownstown, Navan, Co. Meath, Ireland. *T:* Drogheda 25195. *Clubs:* Beefsteak, United Oxford & Cambridge University; Royal Irish Yacht.

HEWARD, Air Chief Marshal Sir Anthony Wilkinson, KCB 1972 (CB 1968); OBE 1952; DFC and bar; AFC; Air Member for Supply and Organisation, Ministry of Defence, 1973–76; *b* 1 July 1918; *s* of late Col E. J. Heward; *m* 1944, Clare Myfanwy Wainwright, *d* of late Maj.-Gen. C. B. Wainwright, CB; one *s* one *d*. Gp Captain RAF, 1957; IDC 1962; Air Cdre 1963; Dir of Operations (Bomber and Reconnaissance) MoD (RAF), 1963; Air Vice-Marshal 1966; Dep. Comdr, RAF Germany, 1966–69; AOA, HQ RAF Air Support Command, 1969–70; Air Marshal 1970; Chief of Staff, RAF Strike Command, 1970–72; AOC, No 18 (Maritime) Group, 1972–73; Air Chief Marshal, 1974. County Councillor, Wilts, 1981–89. *Address:* Home Close, Donhead St Mary, near Shaftesbury, Dorset. *Clubs:* Royal Air Force, Flyfishers'.

HEWARD, Edmund Rawlings, CB 1984; Chief Master of the Supreme Court (Chancery Division), 1980–85 (Master, 1959–79); *b* 19 Aug. 1912; *s* of late Rev. Thomas Brown Heward and Kathleen Amy Rachel Rawlings; *m* 1945, Constance Mary Sandiford, *d* of late George Bertram Crossley, OBE. *Educ:* Repton; Trinity Coll., Cambridge. Admitted a solicitor, 1937. Enlisted Royal Artillery as a Gunner, 1940; released as Major, DAAG, 1946. Partner in Rose, Johnson and Hicks, 9 Suffolk St, SW1, 1946. LLM 1960. *Publications:* Guide to Chancery Practice, 1962 (5th edn 1979); Matthew Hale, 1972; (ed) Part 2, Tristram and Coote's Probate Practice, 24th edn, 1973, 26th edn, 1983; (ed) Judgments and Orders in Halsbury's Laws of England, 4th edn; Lord Mansfield, 1979, paperback 1985; Chancery Practice, 1983, 2nd edn 1990; Chancery Orders, 1986; Lord Denning—A Biography, 1990; Masters in Ordinary, 1991. *Address:* 36a Dartmouth Row, Greenwich, SE10 8AW. *T:* 081–692 3525. *Clubs:* United Oxford & Cambridge University, Travellers'.

HEWER, Thomas Frederick, MD (Bristol); FRCP, FLS; Professor of Pathology, 1938–68, and Pro-Vice-Chancellor, 1966–68, University of Bristol; Professor Emeritus, 1968; *b* 12 April 1903; *s* of William Frederick Hewer and Kathleen Braddon Standerwick; *m* 1941, Anne Hiatt Baker, OBE 1977, MA; two *s* two *d*. *Educ:* Bristol Gram. Sch.; University of Bristol. Commonwealth Fund Fellow and Asst Pathologist, Johns Hopkins Univ., USA, 1927–29; Bacteriologist Sudan Government, 1930–35; Sen. Lectr in Pathology, University of Liverpool, 1935–38. Botanical explorer, FAO/UN, 1975–80; consultant, WHO, investigating causation of cancer among Turkoman, NE Iran, making botanical exploration of desert E of Caspian Sea, 1976–77. Mem. Council and Chm. Animal Cttee, Bristol Zoo, 1953–83. Vice-Pres., Bristol Br., E-SU, 1967– (Chm., 1942–67). *Publications:* articles in medical and horticultural journals. *Recreations:* gardening and travel. *Address:* Vine House, Henbury, Bristol BS10 7AD. *T:* Bristol (0272) 503573. *Club:* English-Speaking Union.

HEWES, Robin Anthony Charles; Head, Regulatory Services Group, Lloyd's of London, since 1988; *b* 15 April 1945; *s* of Leslie Augustus Hewes and late Lily Violet Hewes (*née* Norfolk); *m* 1967, Christine Diane Stonebridge; one *s* two *d*. *Educ:* Colchester Royal Grammar School; Bristol Univ. (LLB Hons 1966). Inspector of Taxes, 1966; Department of Industry, 1974; Cabinet Office (Management and Personnel Office), 1985–87; Dir, Enterprise and Deregulation Unit, DTI, 1987–88. Non-exec. Dir, Comforto-Vickers (formerly Vickers Business Equipment Div.), 1984–88. *Recreation:* swimming. *Address:* 38 Plovers Mead, Wyatts Green, Brentwood, Essex CM15 0PS. *T:* Brentwood (0277) 822891.

HEWETSON, Sir Christopher (Raynor), Kt 1984; TD 1967; DL; Partner, Lace Mawer (formerly Laces), Solicitors, Liverpool, since 1961; President, Law Society, 1983–84; *b* 26 Dec. 1929; *s* of Harry Raynor Hewetson and Emma Hewetson; *m* 1962, Alison May Downie, *d* of late Prof. A. W. Downie, FRCP, FRS; two *s* one *d*. *Educ:* Sedbergh Sch.; Peterhouse, Cambridge (MA). National Service, 2nd Lieut 4th RHA, 1951–53; Territorial Service, 1953–68: Lt-Col commanding 359 Medium Regt, RA, TA, 1965–68. Qualified as solicitor, 1956. Mem. Council, Law Society, 1966–87; Vice-Pres., 1982–83; President, Liverpool Law Society, 1976. Gov., Coll. of Law, 1969– (Chm., 1977–82). DL Merseyside, 1986. *Recreations:* golf, walking. *Address:* 24c Westcliffe Road, Birkdale, Southport, Merseyside PR8 2BU. *T:* Southport (0704) 67179. *Clubs:* Army and Navy; Athenæum (Liverpool); Royal Birkdale Golf (Southport).

HEWETSON, Gen. Sir Reginald (Hackett), GCB 1966 (KCB 1962; CB 1958); CBE 1945 (OBE 1943); DSO 1944; Adjutant-General, Ministry of Defence (Army), 1964–67; retired; *b* Shortlands, Kent, 4 Aug. 1908; *s* of late J. Hewetson, ICS, and E. M. M. Hackett-Wilkins; *m* 1935, Patricia Mable, *y d* of late F. H. Burkitt, CIE; one *s* one *d*. *Educ:* Repton; RMA, Woolwich. Regular Commission in RA, 1928; Service in India (including Active Service, 1930–32), 1929–35; RA depot and home stations, 1935–39; psc 1939; Staff Capt. RA 4 Div., 1938; Adjt 30 Fd Regt and Capt. 1939; France, Oct. 1939–Jan. 1940; 2nd war course at Staff Coll., Camberley, Jan.-April 1940; Brigade Major RA 43 (Wessex) Div. May-Sept. 1940. Temp. Major; various GSO2 appts incl. instructor Senior Officers Sch., 1940–42; GSO1 (Lieut-Col) HQ L of C North Africa, Sept.-Nov. 1942; 78 Div. (in North Africa), 1942–43 (OBE); Lieut-Col Comdg Fd Regt in 56 (London) Div. in Italy, 1943–44 (DSO); BGS HQ 10 Corps, 1944–45; BGS, British Troops, Austria, 1945–47; Student, IDC, 1949; Dep. Dir Staff Duties, WO, 1950–52; CRA 2nd Infantry Div., BAOR, 1953–55; GOC 11th Armoured Div., March 1956; GOC, 4th Infantry Div. 1956–58; Commandant, Staff Coll., Camberley, 1958–61; Commander, British Forces, Hong Kong, Dec. 1961–March 1963; GOC-in-C, Far East Land Forces, 1963–64. Col Comdt, RA, 1962–73; Col Comdt, APTC, 1966–70; ADC (Gen.), 1966–67. Chm., Exec. Cttee, Army Benevolent Fund, 1968–76. Governor and Mem. Administrative Bd, Corps of Commissionaires, 1964–84 (Pres., 1980–84); retd. *Recreations:* cricket (Army and Kent 2nd XI MCC, IZ), hockey (Norfolk and RA), golf. *Address:* North Manor House, Uckfield, East Sussex TN22 1EH. *Club:* MCC.

HEWETT, Sir Peter (John Smithson), 6th Bt *cr* 1813, of Nether Seale, Leicestershire, MM 1956; *b* 27 June 1931; *s* of Sir John George Hewett, 5th Bt, MC and Yuilleen Maude (*d* 1980), *d* of late Samuel Frederick Smithson; *S* father, 1990; *m* 1958, Jennifer Ann Cooper, *o c* of late Emrys Thomas Jones, OBE; two *s* one *d*. *Educ:* Bradfield Coll.; Jesus Coll., Cambridge (BA). Called to Bar, Gray's Inn, 1954; now a practising Advocate in Kenya. *Heir:* *s* Richard Mark John Hewett, *b* 15 Nov. 1958. *Address:* PO Box 15669, Nairobi, Kenya.

HEWETT, Major Richard William; Vice President and Director, International Operations, Reader's Digest Association Inc., 1986–88; *b* 22 Oct. 1923; *s* of late Brig. W. G. Hewett, OBE, MC, and Louise S. Hewett (*née* Wolfe); *m* 1954, Rosemary Cridland; two *d*. *Educ:* Wellington Coll., Berks. Enlisted RA, 1941; commnd RA, 1943; regular commn 1944: served Normandy, India, UK, Malaya; regtl duty, flying duties Air OP, Instr, OCTU, Mons, 1954; sc 1955; Staff and regtl duties, Germany, 1956–59; Mil. Mission, USA, 1959–61. Joined Reader's Digest Assoc. Ltd, 1962; Dir 1976; Man. Dir, 1981–84; Chm. and Man. Dir, 1984–86. *Recreations:* tennis, fishing, travelling.

HEWISH, Prof. Antony, MA, PhD; FRS 1968; Professor of Radioastronomy, University of Cambridge, 1971–89, now Emeritus (Reader, 1969–71); Fellow of Churchill College since 1962; *b* 11 May 1924; *s* of late Ernest William Hewish and Frances Grace Lanyon Pinch; *m* 1950, Marjorie Elizabeth Catherine Richards; one *s* one *d*. *Educ:* King's Coll., Taunton; Gonville and Caius Coll., Cambridge (Hon. Fellow, 1976). BA (Cantab.) 1948, MA 1950, PhD 1952; Hamilton Prize, Isaac Newton Student, 1952. RAE Farnborough, 1943–46; Research Fellow, Gonville and Caius Coll., 1952–54; Asst Dir of Research, 1954–62; Fellow, Gonville and Caius Coll., 1955–62; Lectr in Physics, Univ. of Cambridge, 1962–69. Dir, Mullard Radio Astronomy Observatory, Cambridge, 1982–87. Visiting Prof. in Astronomy, Yale, 1963; Prof. of the Royal Instn, 1977; Vikram Sarabhai Prof., Physical Res. Lab., Ahmedabad, India, 1988. Lectures: Karl Schwarzschild, Bonn, 1971; Halley, Oxford, 1979; Krishnan Meml, New Delhi, 1989. Hon. DSc: Leicester, 1976; Exeter, 1977; Manchester, 1989; Santa Maria, Brazil, 1989. Foreign Hon. Mem., Amer. Acad. of Arts and Sciences; Foreign Fellow, Indian Nat. Sci. Acad., 1982; Hon. Fellow, Instn of Electronics and Telecommunication Engrs, India, 1985. Eddington Medal, Royal Astronomical Soc., 1969; Charles Vernon Boys Prize, Inst. of Physics and Physical

Soc., 1970; Dellinger Gold Medal, Internat. Union of Radio Science, 1972; Michelson Medal, Franklin Inst., 1973; Hopkins Prize, Cambridge Phil Soc., 1973; Holweck Medal and Prize, Soc. Française de Physique, 1974; Nobel Prize for Physics (jtly), 1974; Hughes Medal, Royal Soc., 1977. *Publications:* Papers in Proc. Royal Society, Phys. Soc., Mon. Not. Royal Astr. Soc., etc. *Recreations:* music, gardening, sailing. *Address:* Pryor's Cottage, Kingston, Cambridge CB3 7NQ. *T:* Cambridge (0223) 262657.

HEWITT, family name of **Viscount Lifford.**

HEWITT, Cecil Rolph; *see* Rolph, C. H.

HEWITT, Sir (Cyrus) Lenox (Simson), Kt 1971; OBE 1963; company chairman and director; Director, Ansett Transport Industries Ltd, since 1982; *b* 7 May 1917; *s* of Cyrus Lenox Hewitt and Ella Louise Hewitt; *m* 1943, Alison Hope (*née* Tillyard); one *s* two *d* (and one *d* decd). *Educ:* Scotch Coll., Melbourne; Melbourne Univ. (BCom). FASA, FCIS, CPA. Broken Hill Proprietary Co. Ltd, 1933–46; Asst Sec., Commonwealth Prices Br., Canberra, 1939–46; Economist, Dept of Post War Reconstruction, 1946–49; Official Sec. and Actg Dep. High Comr, London, 1950–53; Commonwealth Treasury: Asst Sec., 1953–55; 1st Asst Sec., 1955–62; Dep. Sec., 1962–66; Chm., Australian Univs Commn, 1967; Secretary to: Prime Minister's Dept, 1968–71; Dept of the Environment, Aborigines and the Arts, 1971–72; Dept of Minerals and Energy, 1972–75. Lectr, Econs and Cost Accountancy, Canberra UC, 1940–49, 1954. Acting Chairman: Pipeline Authority, 1973–75; Petroleum and Minerals Authority, 1974–75; Chairman: Qantas Airways Ltd, 1975–80 (Dir, 1973–80); Qantas Wentworth Hldgs Ltd, 1975–80; QH Tours Ltd, 1975–80 (Dir, 1974–80); Petroleum and Minerals Co. of Aust. Pty Ltd, 1975–; Austmark Internat. Ltd, 1983–88; Northern Mining Corp. NL, 1984–85; State Rail Authority of NSW, 1985–88; Director: East/Aust. Pipeline Corp. Ltd, 1974–75; Mary Kathleen Uranium Ltd, 1975–80; Aust. Industry Develt Corp., 1975; Santos Ltd, 1981–82; Pontello Constructions Ltd, 1980–82; Aberfoyle Ltd, 1981–89; Endeavour Resources Ltd, 1982–86; Short Brothers (Australia) Ltd, 1981–; Airship Industries PLC, 1984–; Qintex Australia Ltd, 1985–90; British Midland Airways (Australia) Pty Ltd, 1985–; Universal Telecasters Securities Ltd, 1986–90; Mirage Management Ltd, 1986–91; Qintex Ltd, 1987–90; Qintex America Ltd, 1987–90; Fortis Pacific Aviation Ltd, 1987–. Dep. Chm., Aust. Atomic Energy Commn, 1972–77; Chairman: Exec. Cttee, IATA, 1976–77 (Mem., 1975–80); Orient Airlines Assoc., 1977; State Rail Authority of NSW, 1985–88; Mem., Judicial Commn of NSW, 1986–89. *Recreations:* tennis, farming. *Address:* 9 Torres Street, Red Hill, Canberra, ACT 2603, Australia. *T:* 952446; (office) 3, 70 Pitt Street, Sydney, NSW 2000, Australia. *T:* 231 3233. *Clubs:* Brooks's; Melbourne (Melbourne); Union (Sydney).

See also P. H. Hewitt.

HEWITT, Eric John, PhD, DSc; FRS 1982; Head of Biochemistry Group in Plant Sciences Division, Long Ashton Research Station, and Reader in Plant Physiology, University of Bristol, 1967–84, retired; *b* London, 27 Feb. 1919; *s* of Harry Edward Hewitt, OBE, MD, DPH, and Blanche (*née* Du Roveray); *m* 1943, Hannah Eluned (*née* Williams); one *s. Educ:* Whitgift Sch., S Croydon; King's Coll., Univ. of London, 1936–40 (BSc 1st Cl., AKC; DipEd); PhD, DSc Bristol; FIBiol. Asst Chemist/Chemist, MoS, 1940–42; Long Ashton Research Station: ARC Res. Grant Research Asst, 1942–45; Sen. Plant Physiologist, 1945–84; seconded to ARC Unit of Plant Nutrition (Micronutrients), 1952–59; SPSO (merit promotion), 1967. *Publications:* Sand and Water Culture Methods Used in the Study of Plant Nutrition, 1952, 2nd edn 1966; (with T. A. Smith) Plant Mineral Nutrition, 1975; (ed, with C. V. Cutting): (sympos.) Nitrogen Metabolism in Plants, 1968; (sympos.) Nitrogen Assimilation of Plants, 1979; approx. 150 research contribs to jls. *Recreations:* squash, gardening, fell walking, TV and records. *Address:* Langdales, 63 Ridgeway Road, Long Ashton, Bristol BS18 9EZ. *T:* Long Ashton (0275) 392274.

HEWITT, Francis Anthony; Deputy Chief Executive, Industrial Development Board for Northern Ireland, since 1988; *b* 1 July 1943; *s* of Joseph and Mary Hewitt; *m* 1968, Carol Burch; two *d. Educ:* Queen's Univ., Belfast (BScEcon). NI Min. of Agriculture, 1961–63; HM Customs and Excise, 1963–72; NI Min. of Commerce Rep. in W Germany, 1973–78; NI Dept of Commerce, 1978–82; HM Consulate-Gen., LA, 1982–84; Exec. Dir, Marketing, Industrial Develt Bd for NI, 1984–88. *Recreations:* music, walking.

HEWITT, Gavin Wallace; HM Diplomatic Service; Counsellor, Head of Chancery and Deputy Permanent Representative, UK Mission to the United Nations, Geneva, since 1987; *b* 19 Oct. 1944; *s* of George Burrill and Elisabeth Murray Hewitt; *m* 1973, Heather Mary Clayton; two *s* two *d. Educ:* George Watson's Boys' Coll., Edinburgh; Edinburgh Univ. (MA). Min. of Transport, 1967–70; on secondment from MoT as Third, later Second, Sec. to UK Delegn, EEC, Brussels, 1970–72; FCO, 1972–73; First Sec., British High Commn, Canberra, 1973–78; FCO, 1978–81; First Sec. and Head of Chancery, HM Embassy, Belgrade, 1981–84; Mem., Jt FCO/BBC Review Gp, BBC External Services, 1984; Counsellor on loan to Home Civil Service, 1984–87. Vice Chm., Bd of Geneva English Sch., 1990– (Mem., 1989–). *Recreations:* music, squash, tinkering. *Address:* c/o Foreign and Commonwealth Office, SW1A 2AH.

HEWITT, Prof. Geoffrey Frederick, FRS 1989; FEng 1984; Professor of Chemical Engineering, Imperial College of Science, Technology and Medicine, since 1985; *b* 3 Jan. 1934; *s* of Frederick and Elaine Hewitt; *m* 1956, Shirley Foulds; two *d. Educ:* Boteler Grammar School, Warrington; UMIST (BScTech, PhD). FIChemE, FRSC, FIMechE, CEng, CChem. Scientist, Group Leader, Div. Head, Harwell Lab., specialising in heat transfer and fluid flow in multiphase systems, 1957–90. Pres., IChemE, 1989–90. Hon. DSc Louvain, 1988. *Publications:* (with N. S. Hall Taylor) Annular Two Phase Flow, 1970; (co-author) Two Phase Flow, 1973; Measurement of Two Phase Flow Parameters, 1978; (with J. G. Collier) Introduction to Nuclear Power, 1986; contribs to books, numerous papers. *Recreations:* bridge, music. *Address:* Department of Chemical Engineering and Chemical Technology, Imperial College of Science, Technology and Medicine, Prince Consort Road, SW7 2BY. *T:* 071–589 5111.

HEWITT, Rev. Canon George Henry Gordon; Residentiary Canon, Chelmsford Cathedral, 1964–78, Canon Emeritus since 1978; *b* 30 May 1912; *s* of Rev. G. H. Hewitt; *m* 1942, Joan Ellen Howden; two *s* one *d. Educ:* Trent Coll.; Brasenose, Oxford; Wycliffe Hall, Oxford. Asst Curate, St Clement, Leeds, 1936–39; Chaplain, Ridley Hall, Cambridge, 1939–41; Asst Curate, Leeds Parish Church, 1941–43; Religious Book Editor, Lutterworth Press, 1943–52; Diocesan Education Sec., Sheffield, 1952–58; Residentiary Canon, Sheffield Cathedral, 1953–58; Vicar of St Andrew, Oxford, 1958–64. Chaplain to the Queen, 1969–82. *Publications:* Let the People Read, 1949; The Problems of Success: a history of the Church Missionary Society, 1910–1942, vol. I, 1971, vol. II, 1977. *Address:* 8 Rainsford Avenue, Chelmsford, Essex CM1 2PJ.

HEWITT, His Honour Harold; a Circuit Judge, 1980–90; *b* 14 March 1917; *s* of George Trueman Hewitt and Bertha Lilian Hewitt; *m* 1946, Doris Mary Smith; two *s. Educ:* King James I Grammar Sch., Bishop Auckland. Admitted solicitor (Hons), 1938; HM Coroner, S Durham, 1948–80; a Recorder of the Crown Court, 1974–80. Chm. (part-time), Industrial Tribunal, 1975–80. Member Council, Law Society, 1976–80. *Recreations:* gardening, French literature, bird-watching. *Address:* Longmeadows, Etherley, Bishop Auckland, Co. Durham. *T:* Bishop Auckland (0388) 832386. *Clubs:* Carlton, Lansdowne.

HEWITT, Harold; solicitor; consultant since 1973; *b* 1 Jan. 1908; *m* 1949, Jeannette Myers; one *d. Educ:* Bede Collegiate Sch., Sunderland; Armstrong Coll., Univ. of Durham. Solicitor, admitted 1930. Legal Adviser, High Commissioner for Austria, Allied Commission, 1946–49. Member, Law Society; Past Pres., Bexley and Dartford Law Soc. *Recreation:* social welfare work. *Address:* 121 Dorset House, Gloucester Place, NW1 5AQ.

HEWITT, Harry Ronald, FEng; Chairman, Johnson Matthey PLC, 1983–84; retired; *b* 12 April 1920; *s* of Charles William Hewitt and Florence Hewitt; *m* 1954, Rosemary Olive, *d* of Walter George Hiscock and Olive Mary Hiscock; two *s* one *d. Educ:* City of Leeds High Sch,; Leeds Coll. of Technol. (BSc London 1941). FEng 1982; MIChemE 1949; MRSC 1944; CBIM 1983 (MBIM 1947). Jun. Chemist, Joseph Watson & Sons, soap manufrs, Leeds, 1936–41; Chemist, Royal Ordnance Factories (explosive manuf.), 1941–45; Control Officer, Chemical Br., Control Commn, Germany, 1945–47; Works Manager, Consolidated Zinc Corp., Avonmouth and Widnes, 1947–58; Johnson Matthey: Gen. Man., 1958–62; Exec. Dir, 1962–76; Gp Man. Dir, 1976–83. Freeman, City of London, 1979; Liveryman, Worshipful Co. of Clockmakers, 1979. FRSA. *Recreations:* golf, tennis, skiing, music. *Address:* 6 Loom Lane, Radlett, Herts WD7 8AD. *T:* Radlett (0923) 5243.

HEWITT, Sir Lenox; *see* Hewitt, Sir C. L. S.

HEWITT, Michael Earling; Director of Central Banking Studies, Bank of England, since 1990; *b* 28 March 1936; *s* of late Herbert Erland Hewitt and Dorothy Amelia Hewitt; *m* 1961, Elizabeth Mary Hughes Batchelor; one *s* one *d. Educ:* Christ's Hospital; Merton College, Oxford (Chancellor's Prize for Latin Prose, 1958; MA (Modern Hist.)); BSc Econ London. Entered Bank of England, 1961; Economic Adviser, Govt of Bermuda, 1970–74; Financial Forecaster, 1976–78; Adviser, Financial Instns, 1981–83; Head of Financial Supervision, Gen. Div., 1984–87; Head of Finance and Industry Area, 1987–88; Senior Advr, Finance and Industry, 1988–90. Chm., OECD Gp of Experts on Securities Markets, 1988–90. *Recreations:* chess, wine, travel. *Address:* Bank of England, Threadneedle Street, EC2R 8AH. *T:* 071–601 4444.

HEWITT, Sir Nicholas Charles Joseph, 3rd Bt *cr* 1921; *b* 12 Nov. 1947; *s* of Sir Joseph Hewitt, 2nd Bt and of Marguerite, *yr d* of Charles Burgess; *S* father, 1973; *m* 1969, Pamela Margaret, *o d* of Geoffrey J. M. Hunt, TD; two *s* one *d. Heir: s* Charles Edward James Hewitt, *b* 15 Nov. 1970. *Address:* Colswayn House, Huttons Ambo, Yorks YO6 7HJ. *T:* Malton (0653) 696557.

HEWITT, Patricia Hope; Deputy Director, Institute for Public Policy Research, since 1989 (Senior Research Fellow, 1989); *b* 2 Dec. 1948; *d* of Sir (Cyrus) Lenox (Simson) Hewitt, *qv*, and Alison Hope Hewitt; *m* 1981, William Birtles; one *s* one *d. Educ:* C of E Girls' Grammar Sch., Canberra; Australian Nat. Univ.; Newnham Coll., Cambridge. BA, AMusA (piano). Public Relations Officer, Age Concern (Nat. Old People's Welfare Council), 1971–73; Women's Rights Officer, Nat. Council for Civil Liberties, 1973–74, Gen. Secretary 1974–83; Press and Broadcasting Sec., 1983–88, Policy Co-ordinator, 1988–89, to Leader of Opposition. Trustee: Cobden Trust, 1974–83; Areopagitica Trust, 1981–84; Member: Sec. of State's Adv. Cttee on Employment of Women, 1977–84; Unofficial Cttee of Enquiry into Southall, 23 April 1979; National Labour Women's Cttee, 1979–83; Labour Party Enquiry into Security Services, 1980–81; Council, Campaign for Freedom of Information, 1983–89; Bd, Internat. League for Human Rights, 1984–; Exec. Cttee, Fabian Soc., 1988–; Co-Chm., Human Rights Network, 1979–81. Contested (Lab) Leicester East, 1983. Mem., Editorial Adv. Panel, New Socialist, 1980–90. Associate, Newnham Coll., Cambridge, 1984–. *Publications:* Your Rights (Age Concern), 1973, 14th edn 1986; Rights for Women (NCCL), 1975; Civil Liberties, the NCCL Guide (co-ed 3rd edn), 1977; The Privacy Report (NCCL), 1977; Your Rights at Work (NCCL), 1978, 2nd edn 1981; The Abuse of Power, 1981; (jtly) Your Second Baby, 1990. *Recreations:* reading, theatre, music, politics, gardening. *Address:* 21 Rochester Square, NW1 9SA. *T:* 071–267 2567.

HEWITT, Penelope Ann; Stipendiary Magistrate, Leeds, since 1990; *b* 4 May 1932; *d* of late William Mottershead, JP, MB ChB and Eileen Mottershead; *m* 1954, Peter Nisbet Hewitt; one *s* two *d. Educ:* Howell's Sch., Denbigh; BA Open Univ., 1975. Called to the Bar, Gray's Inn, 1978; in practice, Liverpool, 1978–90; Mem., Northern Circuit. Lay Chm., Bolton Deanery Synod, 1984–90. JP Bolton, 1968–90. *Recreations:* music, reading, choral singing, opera, embroidery. *Address:* Leeds Magistrates' Court, Town Hall, Leeds LS1 1NY. *T:* Leeds (0532) 459653. *Club:* Leeds (Leeds).

HEWITT, Peter McGregor, OBE 1967; Regional Director, East Midlands, Departments of the Environment and Transport, 1984–89; *b* 6 Oct. 1929; *e s* of late Douglas McGregor Hewitt and of Audrey Vera Hewitt; *m* 1962, Joyce Marie Gavin; three *d. Educ:* De Aston Sch., Market Rasen, Lincs; Keble Coll., Oxford (MA). National Service (Army), 1947–49. HM Overseas Civil Service, 1952–64: served in Malaya and N Borneo; HM Diplomatic Service, 1964–71: served in FO, Shanghai and Canberra; Home Civil Service: Principal, 1971–77; Asst Sec., 1977–83; Grade 4, 1984. *Recreations:* cricket, music, gardening. *Address:* 14 Dovedale Road, West Bridgford, Nottingham NG2 6JA. *Club:* Commonwealth Trust.

HEWITT, Richard Thornton, OBE 1945; retired; Executive Director, Royal Society of Medicine, 1952–82; Vice-President, The Royal Society of Medicine Foundation, Inc., New York, 1969–89; *b* 1917; *yr s* of late Harold and Elsie Muriel Hewitt, Bramhall, Cheshire. *Educ:* King's Sch., Macclesfield; Magdalen Coll., Oxford (Exhibitioner). Served War, Lt-Col, infantry and special forces, 1939–46. Asst Registrary, Cambridge Univ., 1946. Incorporated MA, Magdalene Coll., Cambridge, 1946. Sec., Oxford Univ. Medical Sch., 1947–52. FKC 1985. Hon. Mem., Honourable Soc. of Middle Temple, 1978; Hon. Fellow: Swedish Med. Soc., 1968; RSocMed, 1985; Chelsea Coll., 1985. Liveryman, Worshipful Society of Apothecaries of London, 1954. Freeman of the City of London, 1954. *Recreations:* gentle golf and gardening, listening to music, contemplating the nature of time. *Address:* The White House, Iffley, Oxford OX4 4EG. *T:* Oxford (0865) 779263. *Clubs:* MCC, Royal Automobile; Frewen (Oxford); Royal and Ancient (St Andrews).

HEWLETT-DAVIES, Mrs Janet Mary; journalist; public affairs consultant; *b* 13 May 1938; *d* of Frederick Charles and Margaret Ellen Hewlett; *m* 1964, Barry Davies. *Educ:* King Edward VI High School for Girls, Birmingham. Journalist, West Midlands 1956–59; BBC, 1959–65; Films Division, Central Office of Information, 1966–67; Press Officer: Prime Minister's Office, 1967–72; HM Customs and Excise, 1972–73; Principal Information Officer, Dept of Trade and Industry, 1973–74; Dep. Press Secretary to Prime Minister, 1974–76; Head of Information, Dept of Transport, 1976–79; Director of Information: DoE, 1979–82; DHSS, 1982–86; Dir of Public Affairs, Pergamon, BPCC and Mirror Gp of Cos, 1986–87. Vice-Chm., WHO Working Gp on Information and Health, 1983. FRSA 1985. *Recreations:* cooking, theatre, needlework, Radio 4. *Address:* 44 Sussex Square, Brighton BN2 1GE. *T:* Brighton (0273) 693792. *Club:* Reform.

HEWSON, John Robert, PhD; MP (L) Wentworth, New South Wales, since 1987; Leader of the Opposition, Australia, since 1990; *b* 28 Oct. 1946; *m* Carolyn Somerville; two *s* one *d*. *Educ:* Univ. of Sydney (BEc); Univ. of Saskatchewan (MA 1969); Johns Hopkins Univ. (MA, PhD 1971). Lecturer: Towson State Coll., 1972–73; Monash Univ., 1975; Res. Economist, Reserve Bank of Australia, 1976; Economic Advr to Fed. Treas., 1976–77; University of New South Wales: Prof. of Econs, 1978–87; Head, Sch. of Econs, 1983–86; Dir, Japanese Econs Management Studies Centre, 1984–87. Shadow Minister for Finance, 1988–89; Shadow Treas., 1989–90. *Publications:* Liquidity Creation and Distribution in the Eurocurrency Market, 1975; (jtly) The Eurocurrency Markets and their Implications, 1975; Offshore Banking in Australia, 1981. *Address:* Parliament House, Canberra, ACT 2600, Australia.

HEXHAM AND NEWCASTLE, Bishop of, (RC), since 1974; **Rt. Rev. Hugh Lindsay;** *b* 20 June 1927; *s* of William Stanley Lindsay and Mary Ann Lindsay (*née* Warren). *Educ:* St Cuthbert's Grammar Sch., Newcastle upon Tyne; Ushaw Coll., Durham. Priest 1953. Asst Priest; St Lawrence's, Newcastle upon Tyne, 1953; St Matthew's, Ponteland, 1954; Asst Diocesan Sec., 1953–59; Diocesan Sec., 1959–69; Chaplain, St Vincent's Home, West Denton, 1959–69; Auxiliary Bishop of Hexham and Newcastle and Titular Bishop of Chester-le-Street, 1969–74. *Recreation:* walking. *Address:* Bishop's House, East Denton Hall, 800 West Road, Newcastle upon Tyne NE5 2BJ.

HEXHAM AND NEWCASTLE, Auxiliary Bishop of, (RC); *see* Swindlehurst, Rt Rev. O. F.

HEY, Air Vice-Marshal Ernest, CB 1967; CBE 1963 (OBE 1954); CEng; Air Member for Technical Services, Department of Air, Canberra, 1960–72, retired; *b* Plymouth, Devon, 29 Nov. 1912; *s* of Ernest Hey, Terrigal, NSW; *m* 1936, Lorna, *d* of Sqdn Ldr A. Bennett, Melbourne; one *s* one *d*. *Educ:* Sydney Technical High Sch.; Sydney University. RAAF cadet, 1934; served War of 1939–45; Dir Technical Services, 1947–54; AOC Maintenance Comd, 1956–57; Imp. Defence Coll., 1957; Liaison Air Materiel Comd, USAF, 1958–59. *Recreations:* painting, lawn bowls.

HEY, James Stanley, MBE 1945; DSc; FRS 1978; retired; Research Scientist at Royal Radar Establishment, 1952–69; Chief Scientific Officer, 1966–69; *b* 3 May 1909; *s* of William Rennie Hey and Barbara Elizabeth Hey (*née* Matthews); *m* 1934, Edna Heywood. *Educ:* Rydal Sch.; Manchester Univ. BSc (Physics), 1930; MSc (X-ray Crystallography), 1931; DSc (Radio Astronomy and Radar Research), 1950. Army Operational Research Group, 1940–52 (Head of Estab., 1949–52). Hon. DSc: Birmingham, 1975; Kent, 1977. Eddington Medal, RAS, 1959. *Publications:* The Radio Universe, 1971, rev. 3rd edn 1983; The Evolution of Radio Astronomy, 1973; research papers in scientific jls (RAS, Royal Society, Phys Soc., Philosophical Magazine, Nature, etc) including pioneering papers in radio astronomy. *Address:* 4 Shortlands Close, Willingdon, Eastbourne, East Sussex BN22 0JE.

HEY, Prof. John Denis; Professor of Economics and Statistics, University of York, since 1984; *b* 26 Sept. 1944; *s* of George Brian Hey and Elizabeth Hamilton Hey (*née* Burns); *m* 1968, Margaret Robertson Bissett; one *s* two *d*. *Educ:* Manchester Grammar Sch.; Cambridge Univ. (MA); Edinburgh Univ. (MSc). Econometrician, Hoare & Co., 1968–69; Lectr in Economics, Univ. of Durham, 1969–73, Univ. of St Andrews, 1974–75; Lectr in Social and Economic Statistics, Univ. of York, 1975–81, Sen. Lectr, 1981–84. Co-Dir, Centre for Experimental Economics, Univ. of York, 1986–. Economic Consultant, Wise Speke & Co., 1972–87. Editor: Bulletin of Economic Research, 1984–86; Economic Journal, 1986–. *Publications:* Statistics in Economics, 1974; Uncertainty in Microeconomics, 1979; Britain in Context, 1979; Economics in Disequilibrium, 1981; Data in Doubt, 1983; (ed jtly) Surveys in the Economics of Uncertainty, 1987; (ed) Current Issues in Microeconomics, 1989; (ed jtly) A Century of Economics, 1990; Experiments in Economics, 1991; articles in academic economics jls. *Recreations:* squash, walking, eating. *Address:* Department of Economics and Related Studies, University of York, Heslington, York YO1 5DD. *T:* York (0904) 433786.

HEYERDAHL, Thor; author and anthropologist, since 1938; *b* Larvik, Norway 6 Oct. 1914; *s* of Thor Heyerdahl and Alison Heyerdahl (*née* Lyng); *m* 1st, 1936, Liv Coucheron Torp (*d* 1969); two *s*; 2nd, 1949, Yvonne Dedekam-Simonsen; three *d*. *Educ:* University of Oslo, 1933–36. Researches in the Marquesas Islands (Pacific), 1937–38; Researches among Coast Indians of Brit. Columbia, 1939–40. Active service Free Norwegian Army-Air Force parachute unit, 1942–45. Organised and led Kon-Tiki expedition, 1947. Continued research in USA and Europe, with authorship, 1948–. Organised and led Norwegian Archæological Expedition to the Galapagos Islands, 1952; experiments revealing tacking principles of balsa raft in Ecuador, 1953; field research, Bolivia, Peru, Colombia, 1954. Organised and led Norwegian Archæological Expedition to Easter Island and the East Pacific, 1955–56. Continued research, 1957–59. Made crossing from Safi, Morocco, to W Indies in papyrus boat, Ra II, 1970; sailed from Qurna, Iraq, to Djibouti in reed boat, Tigris, 1977–78; organised and led two archaeol expedns to Maldive Islands, 1982–84; leader, organiser jt Norwegian/Chilean archaeol expedn, Easter Island, 1986–88; organiser Kon-Tiki Mus.—Museo Brüning archaeol project. Tucume, Peru, 1988–. Participation in: Internat. Congress of Americanists, 1952–; Pacific Science Congresses, 1961–, all with lectures subseq. publ. in Proc. Congress. Vice-Pres., World Assoc. of World Federalists, 1966–; Trustee, Internat. Bd, World Wildlife Fund, 1977–; Internat. Patron, United World Colls, 1980. Mem., Royal Norwegian Acad. of Science, 1958; Fellow: New York Acad. of Sciences, 1960; Amer. Anthropological Assoc., 1966. Hon. Prof., Inst. Politecnico Nacional, Mexico, 1972. Hon. Dir, Explorers' Club, NY, 1982. Hon. Mem. Geog. Soc.: Peru, 1953; Norway, 1953; Brazil, 1954; USSR, 1964. Hon. Doctor: Oslo, 1961; USSR Acad. of Scis, 1980. Retzius Medal, Swedish Soc. for Anthropology and Geography, 1950; Mungo Park Medal, Royal Scottish Geographical Society, 1951; Prix Bonaparte-Wyse from Société de Géographie, Paris, 1951; Elish Kent Kane Gold Medal, Geog. Soc. of Philadelphia, 1952; Vega Medal, Swedish Soc. of Anthropology and Geography, 1962; Lomonosov Medal, Moscow Univ., 1962; Royal Gold Medal, Royal Geog. Society, London, 1964; Officer of El Orden por Méritos Distinguidos, Peru, 1953; Gold Medal City of Lima; Gr.-Officer, Order Al Merito della Repubblica Italiana, Italy, 1965; Comdr, Knights of Malta, 1970; Comdr with Star, Order of St Olav, Norway, 1970; Order of Merit, Egypt, 1971; Grand Officer, Royal Alaouites Order, Morocco, 1971; Hon. Citizen, Larvik, Norway, 1971; Kiril i Metodi Order, Bulgaria, 1972; Internat. Pahlavi Environment Prize, UN, 1978; Order of Golden Ark, Netherlands, 1980; Bradford Washburn Award, Boston Mus. of Science, USA, 1982. *Films:* The Kon-Tiki Expedition (Oscar award for camera achievement, Nat. Acad. Motion Picture Arts and Scis, 1951); Galapagos Expedition; Aku-Aku, The Secret of Easter Island; The Ra Expeditions; The Tigris Expedition; The Maldive Mystery. *Publications:* Paa Jakt efter Paradiset, 1938; The Kon-Tiki Expedition, 1948; American Indians in the Pacific: the theory behind the Kon-Tiki expedition, 1952; (with A. Skjolsvold) Archæological Evidence of Pre-Spanish Visits to the Galapagos Islands, 1956; Aku-Aku: The Secrets of Easter Island, 1957; Co-editor (with E. N. Ferdon, Jr) Reports of the Norwegian Achæological Expedition to Easter Island and the East Pacific, Vol. I: The Archæology of Easter Island, 1961, vol. II: Miscellaneous Papers, 1965; Navel of the World (Chapter XIV) in Vanished Civilizations, 1963; Indianer und Alt-Asiaten im Pazifik: Das Abenteuer einer Theorie, 1965 (Vienna); Sea Routes to Polynesia, 1968; The Ra Expeditions, 1970; Chapters in Quest for America, 1971; Fatu-Hiva Back to Nature, 1974; Art of Easter Island, 1975; Zwischen den Kontinenten, 1975; Early Man and the Ocean, 1978; The Tigris Expedition, 1980; The Maldive Mystery, 1986; Easter Island: the mystery solved, 1989; contrib. National Geographical Magazine, Royal Geographical Journal, The Geographical Magazine, Archiv für Völkerkunde, Ymer, Swedish Geogr. Year-book, South-western Journal of Anthropology, Russian Academy of Sciences Yearbook, American Antiquity, Antiquity (Cambridge); works trans. into numerous languages; *relevant publication:* Senor Kon-Tiki, by Arnold Jacoby, 1965; The Kon-Tiki Man, by Christopher Ralling, 1990. *Recreations:* outdoor life, travelling. *Address:* Kon-Tiki Museum, Oslo, Norway.

HEYGATE, Sir George Lloyd, 5th Bt *cr* 1831; *S* father, 1976. *Heir: b* Richard John Gage Heygate.

HEYHOE, David Charles Ross; Assistant Under Secretary of State (Fleet Support), Ministry of Defence, since 1991; *b* 29 June 1938; *s* of late Cecil Ross Heyhoe and Clara Beatrice (*née* Woodard Knight); *m* 1972, Pauline Susan (*née* Morgan); one *s* one *d*. *Educ:* Beckenham and Penge Grammar Sch.; Worcester Coll., Oxford (Schol.; MA LitHum). Served HM Forces, RAEC, 1957–59. Asst Principal, War Office, 1963; Asst Private Sec. to Minister (Army), 1966; Principal, MoD, 1967; Asst Sec., 1975; Res. Associate, Inst. for Strategic Studies, 1975–76; Private Sec. to Leader of H of C, 1981–84; Asst Under Sec. of State, 1986, Dir Gen. of Management Audit, 1986–91, MoD. *Recreations:* books, sports, antiques. *Address:* c/o Ministry of Defence, SW1. *Clubs:* Roehampton, Rosslyn Park FC.

HEYHOE FLINT, Rachael, MBE 1972; public relations consultant; journalist, broadcaster, public speaker, sportswoman; *b* 11 June 1939; *d* of Geoffrey Heyhoe and Roma (*née* Crocker); *m* 1971, Derrick Flint, BSc; one *s* and one step *s* two step *d*. *Educ:* Wolverhampton High Sch. for Girls; Dartford Coll. of Physical Educn (Dip. in Phys. Educn). Head of Phys. Education: Wolverhampton Municipal Grammar Sch., 1960–62; Northicote Sch., 1962–64; US Field Hockey Assoc. Coach, 1964 and 1965; Journalist, Wolverhampton Express & Star, 1965–72; Sports Editor, Wolverhampton Chronicle, 1969–71; first woman Sports Reporter, ITV, 1972; Daily Telegraph Sports Writer, 1967–; Vice-Chm., 1981–86, and Public Relations Officer, 1982–86, Women's Cricket Assoc.; Marketing and Promotions Consultant: National Mutual Life Assurance Soc., Hitchin, Herts, 1983–; La Manga Country Club, Southern Spain, 1983–; PR Consultant, Patshull Park Hotel, 1988–. Mem., Sportswriters Assoc., 1967. England Hockey rep., 1964 (goalkeeper); Mem., England Women's Cricket team, 1960–83, Captain, 1966–77. Hit first 6 in Women's Test Cricket 1963 (England *v* Australia, Oval); scored highest test score by England player in this country and 3rd highest in world, 1976 (179 runs for England *v* Australia, Oval). Best After Dinner Speakers Award, Guild of Professional Toastmasters, 1972. *Publications:* Just for Kicks, (Guide to hockey goalkeeping), 1966; Women's Hockey, 1975; (with Netta Rheinberg) Fair Play, The Story of Women's Cricket, 1976; (autobiog.) "Heyhoe!", 1978. *Recreations:* golf, cricket; former county squash player (Staffs). *Address:* Danescroft, Wergs Road, Tettenhall, Wolverhampton, West Midlands. *T:* Wolverhampton (0902) 752103. *Clubs:* Lord's Taverners; Wolverhampton Lawn Tennis & Squash; Patshull Park Golf; South Staffs Golf; La Manga (Spain).

HEYMAN, Allan, QC 1969; *b* 27 Feb. 1921; *e s* of late Erik Heyman and Rita Heyman (*née* Meyer); *m* 1958, Anne Marie (*née* Castenschiold); one *d*. *Educ:* Stenhus Kostskole, Denmark; Univ. of Copenhagen. Master of Law (Univ. of Copenhagen), 1947. Called to Bar, Middle Temple, 1951, Bencher, 1975, Treasurer, 1992. Pres., Internat. Lawn Tennis Fedn, 1971–74, Hon. Life Vice-Pres., 1979. Kt of Dannebrog (Denmark). *Recreations:* shooting, stalking, reading, music. *Address:* 1 New Square, Lincoln's Inn, WC2; Marshland House, Iken, Woodbridge, Suffolk IP12 2HA. *Clubs:* Naval and Military, Shikar; All England Lawn Tennis and Croquet.

HEYMAN, Sir Horace (William), Kt 1976; CEng, FIEE; Chairman, English Industrial Estates Corporation, 1970–77; Hotelplan International AG: Member, Supervisory Board, Zurich, 1955–84; Director: UK Group, 1965–86; Ingham Travel, 1965–77; *b* 13 March 1912; *m* 1st, 1939; one *s* one *d*; 2nd, 1966, Dorothy Forster Atkinson. *Educ:* Ackworth Sch.; Technische Hochschule, Darmstadt; Birmingham Univ. BSc hons, electrical engrg, 1936. Electricars Ltd, 1936–40; Metropolitan Vickers Ltd, Sheffield, 1940–45; Smith's Electric Vehicles Ltd and Subsids, 1945–64 (Man. Dir, 1949–64); Co-Founder, Sevcon Engineering Ltd, 1960; Vice-Pres., Battronic Corp., Philadelphia, 1960–64. Export Marketing Adviser for Northern Region, BoT, 1969–70; Consultant: DoI Invest in Britain Bureau, 1977–79; Elmwood Sensors Ltd, 1977–86; Thermal Quarz Schmelz GmbH, 1983–86; Chm., Newcastle Polytechnic Products Ltd, 1983–86. Newcastle Polytechnic: Governor, 1974–86; Vice-Chm., 1983–86; Hon. Fellow, 1985. Mem. Council, Soc. of Motor Manufrs and Traders, 1949–64 (Man. Cttee, 1952–64); Chm., Electric Vehicle Assoc. of Gt Britain, 1953–55. Witness at US Senate hearings on air and water pollution, 1967. Chairman: N Region Energy Conservation Group, 1973–77; NEDO Working Party on House Bldg Performance, 1976–79. Pres., Northumbria Tourist Bd, 1983–86. FIEE 1952; FRSA 1969. *Address:* 20 Whitburn Hall, Whitburn, Sunderland SR6 7JQ.

HEYMAN, Prof. Jacques, MA, PhD; FICE; FSA; FEng; Professor of Engineering, since 1971, and Head of Department of Engineering, since 1983, University of Cambridge; Fellow of Peterhouse, 1949–51, and since 1955; *b* 8 March 1925; *m* 1958, Eva Orlans (*d* 1982); three *d*. *Educ:* Whitgift Sch.; Peterhouse, Cambridge. Senior Bursar, Peterhouse, 1962–64; University Demonstrator, Engineering Dept, Cambridge Univ., 1951, University Lectr, 1954, Reader, 1968. Vis. Professor: Brown Univ., USA, 1957–58; Harvard Univ., 1966. Consultant Engineer: Ely Cathedral, 1972–; St Albans Cathedral, 1978–; Lichfield Cathedral, Worcester Cathedral, 1986–; Gloucester Cathedral, Lincoln Cathedral, 1989–. Member: Architectural Adv. Panel, Westminster Abbey, 1973–; Cathedrals Fabric Commn (formerly Cathedrals Adv. Commn) for England, 1981–; Council, ICE, 1960–63 and 1975–78; Smeatonian Soc. of Civil Engrs, 1982–. Hon. DSc Sussex, 1975. James Watt Medal, 1973. *Publications:* The Steel Skeleton, vol. 2 (with Lord Baker, M. R. Horne), 1956; Plastic Design of Portal Frames, 1957; Beams and Framed Structures, 1964, 2nd edn 1974; Plastic Design of Frames, vol. 1, 1969 (paperback 1980), vol. 2, 1971; Coulomb's Memoir on Statics, 1972; Equilibrium of Shell Structures, 1977; Elements of Stress Analysis, 1982; The Masonry Arch, 1982; articles on plastic design, masonry construction and general structural theory. *Address:* Engineering Laboratory, Trumpington Street, Cambridge CB2 1PZ. *T:* Cambridge (0223) 332617.

HEYMANN, Prof. Franz Ferdinand, PhD; CPhys, FInstP; Quain Professor of Physics, and Head of Department of Physics and Astronomy, University College, University of London, 1975–87, now Professor Emeritus; *b* 17 Aug. 1924; *s* of Paul Gerhard Heymann and Magdalena Petronella Heymann; *m* 1950, Marie Powell. *Educ:* Univ. of Cape Town (BScEng with Distinction, 1944); Univ. of London (PhD 1953). FInstP 1966. Engr, Cape Town, 1944–45; Jun. Lectr in Engrg, Univ. of Cape Town, 1945–47; Special Trainee,

Metropolitan Vickers, Manchester, 1947–50; University Coll. London: Asst Lectr in Physics, 1950–52; Lectr, 1952–60; Reader, 1960–66; Prof. of Physics, 1966–75; Fellow, 1987. *Publications:* scientific papers on res. done mainly in fields of particle accelerators and elementary particle physics. *Recreations:* music, gemmology, gardening. *Address:* Sunnybank, Gayle, Hawes, N Yorks DL8 3RS.

HEYTESBURY, 6th Baron *cr* 1828; **Francis William Holmes à Court;** Bt 1795; *b* 8 Nov. 1931; *s* of 5th Baron Heytesbury and Beryl (*d* 1968), *y d* of late A. E. B. Crawford, LLD, DCL, Aston Clinton House, Bucks; *S* father, 1971; *m* 1962, Alison, *e d* of Michael Graham Balfour, CBE; one *s* one *d*. *Educ:* Bryanston; Pembroke College, Cambridge (BA 1954). *Heir: s* Hon. James William Holmes à Court, *b* 30 July 1967.

HEYWARD, Rt. Rev. Oliver Spencer; Bishop of Bendigo, 1975–91; *b* Launceston, Tasmania, 16 March 1926; *s* of Harold and Vera Heyward; *m* 1952, Peggy Butcher; four *s*. *Educ:* Church Gram. Sch., Launceston; Univ. of Tasmania (BA Hons 1949); Oriel Coll., Univ. of Oxford (BA 1953, MA 1956); Cuddesdon Coll., Oxford. RAAF, 1944–46. Rhodes Scholar, 1949. Deacon 1953, priest 1954, dio. Chichester; Asst Curate, St Peter's, Brighton, 1953–56; Rector of Sorell, Tasmania, 1956–60; Rector of Richmond, Tasmania, 1960–62; Precentor, St David's Cathedral, Hobart, 1962–63; Warden, Christ Coll., Univ. of Tasmania, 1963–74. Pres., Bendigo Coll. of Advanced Educn, 1976–86; Comr, Victorian Post-Secondary Educn Commn, 1982–. *Recreation:* gardening. *Address:* 7 Waltham Street, Richmond, Vic 3121, Australia.

HEYWOOD, Francis Melville, MA; Warden of Lord Mayor Treloar College, 1952–69, retired 1969; *b* 1 Oct. 1908; 4th *s* of late Rt Rev. B. O. F. Heywood, DD; *m* 1937, Dorothea Kathleen (*d* 1983), *e d* of late Sir Basil Mayhew, KBE; one *s* two *d* (and one *s* decd). *Educ:* Haileybury Coll. (Scholar); Gonville and Caius Coll. Cambridge (Scholar), 1st Class Hons, Classical Tripos, Part I, 1929; Part II, 1931; Rugby Football blue, 1928. Asst Master, Haileybury Coll., 1931–35; Fellow, Asst Tutor and Praelector, Trinity Hall, Cambridge, 1935–39; Master of Marlborough Coll., 1939–52. *Publication:* A Load of New Rubbish, 1985. *Recreations:* walking, writing. *Address:* 30 The Bayle, Folkestone, Kent CT20 1SQ.

HEYWOOD, Geoffrey, MBE (mil.) 1945; JP; Consulting Actuary; *b* 7 April 1916; *s* of Edgar Heywood and Annie (*née* Dawson), Blackpool; *m* 1941, Joan Corinna Lumley; one *s* one *d*. *Educ:* Arnold Sch., Blackpool; Open Univ. (BA). Served War, 1940–46: Royal Artillery, N Africa, Italy, Greece; commissioned, 1941, Major, 1944; despatches, 1945. Refuge Assce Co. Ltd, 1933–40; Duncan C. Fraser & Co. (Consulting Actuaries), 1946–86 (Sen. Partner, 1952–86). Pres., Manchester Actuarial Soc., 1951–53; Chm., Assoc. of Consulting Actuaries, 1959–62; Chm., Internat. Assoc. of Consulting Actuaries, 1968–72; Pres., Inst. of Actuaries, 1972–74 (Vice-Pres., 1964–67). Mem. Page Cttee to Review National Savings. Dep. Chm., Mersey Docks & Harbour Co., 1975–85; Mem., Nat. Bus Co., 1978–85. Chm., Merseyside Cable Vision, 1982–90; Director: Barclays Bank Trust Co., 1967–86; Liverpool Bd Barclays Bank, 1972–86; Barclays Unicorn Gp, 1977–85; Universities Superannuation Scheme, 1974–86. Corresp. Mem., Assoc. des Actuaires Suisses, 1973. FFA 1939; FIA 1946; FRAS 1982; FRSA 1986. Founder Master, Actuaries Co., 1979; Liveryman, Clockmakers' Co. JP Liverpool 1962. *Publications:* contribs to Jl Inst. Actuaries. *Recreations:* golf, antiquarian horology. *Address:* Drayton, Croft Drive East, Caldy, Wirral, Merseyside L48 1LS. *T:* 051–625 6707. *Clubs:* Army and Navy, Royal Automobile.

HEYWOOD, Sir Oliver Kerr, 5th Bt, *cr* 1838; *b* 30 June 1920; *s* of late Maj.-Gen. C. P. Heywood, CB, CMG, DSO (2nd *s* of 3rd Bt) and late Margaret Vere, *d* of late Arthur Herbert Kerr; *S* uncle 1946; *m* 1947, Denise Wymondham, 2nd *d* of late Jocelyn William Godefroi, MVO; three *s*. *Educ:* Eton; Trinity Coll. Cambridge (BA). Served in Coldstream Guards, 1940–46 (despatches). Profession: artist. *Heir: s* Peter Heywood [*b* 10 Dec. 1947; *m* 1970, Jacqueline Anne, *d* of Sir Robert Hunt, *qv*; two *d*]. *Address:* Rose Cottage, Elcombe, Stroud, Glos GL6 7LA.

HEYWOOD, Prof. Vernon Hilton; Director, Botanic Gardens Conservation Secretariat, since 1987, Chief Scientist (Plant Conservation) and Director of Plant Science, since 1988, International Union for the Conservation of Nature and Natural Resources; Emeritus Professor, University of Reading, since 1988; *b* 24 Dec. 1927; *s* of Vernon William and Marjorie Elizabeth Heywood; *m* 1st, 1952, María de la Concepción Salcedo Manrique; four *s*; 2nd, 1980, Christine Anne Brighton. *Educ:* George Heriot's Sch., Edinburgh; Edinburgh Univ. (BSc, DSc); Pembroke Coll., Cambridge (PhD). Lecturer 1955–60, Sen. Lectr 1960–63, Reader 1963–64, Professor 1964–68, Dept of Botany, Univ. of Liverpool; University of Reading: Prof. of Botany and Hd of Dept of Botany, 1968–88; Dean, Faculty of Science, 1978–81. Hon. Prof., Botanical Inst., Nanjing, 1989–. Storer Lecturer, Univ. of California, Davis, 1990. Chm., European Plants Specialist Gp, Species Survival Commn of IUCN, 1984–87. Trustee, Royal Botanic Gardens, Kew, 1983–87. Corresponding Mem., Botanical Soc. of Amer., 1987–. Councillor of Honour, Consejo Superior de Investigaciones Científicas, Spain, 1970. Linnean Medal, Linnean Soc. of London, 1987; Hutchinson Medal, Chicago Hortl Soc., 1989. Order of the Silver Dog (Gran Canaria), 1989. *Publications:* Principles of Angiosperm Taxonomy (with P. H. Davis), 1963, 2nd edn 1965; Plant Taxonomy, 1967, 2nd edn 1976; Flowering Plants of the World, 1978, 2nd edn 1985; (jtly) Our Green and Living World, 1984; Las Plantas con Flores, 1985; (jtly) Botanic Gardens and the World Conservation Strategy, 1987; The Botanic Gardens Conservation Strategy, 1989; (jtly) International Directory of Botanic Gardens V, 1990; nearly 200 papers in sci. jls. *Recreations:* cooking, travel, music, writing. *Address:* White Mead, 22 Wiltshire Road, Wokingham RG11 1TP. *T:* Wokingham (0734) 780185.

HEYWOOD-LONSDALE, Lt-Col Robert Henry, MBE 1952; MC 1945; Vice Lord-Lieutenant for Oxfordshire, since 1989; *b* 18 Dec. 1919; *s* of Col John Pemberton Heywood-Lonsdale, DSO, OBE, TD and Hon. Mrs Helen Annesley; *m* 1952, Hon. Jean Helen Rollo, *d* of 12th Lord Rollo; one *s* three *d*. *Educ:* Eton. Grenadier Guards, 1938–56; Royal Wilts Yeo., 1961–67. Farmer. High Sheriff, Wilts, 1975; DL Wilts, 1972, Oxon, 1983. *Recreation:* country pursuits. *Address:* Mount Farm, Churchill, Oxon OX7 6NP. *T:* Kingham (0608) 658316. *Clubs:* Pratt's, Boodle's.

HEYWORTH, Peter Lawrence Frederick; Music Critic of The Observer, 1955–87; *b* 3 June 1921; *er s* of Lawrence Ormerod Heyworth and Ellie Stern. *Educ:* Charterhouse; Balliol Coll., Oxford. HM Forces, 1940–46; Balliol, 1947–50; University of Göttingen, 1950. Music critic of Times Educational Supplement, 1952–56; Record reviewer for New Statesman, 1956–58; Guest of the Ford Foundation in Berlin, 1964–65. Critic of the Year, British Press Awards, 1980, commendation 1979. *Publications:* (ed) Berlioz, Romantic and Classic: selected writings by Ernest Newman, 1972; (ed) Conversations with Klemperer, 1973; Otto Klemperer: his life and times, Vol. 1 1885–1933, 1983. *Address:* 32 Bryanston Square, W1H 7LS. *T:* 071–262 8906; Yew Tree Cottage, Hinton St Mary, Sturminster Newton, Dorset. *T:* Sturminster Newton (0258) 72203.

HEZLET, Vice-Admiral Sir Arthur Richard, KBE 1964; CB 1961; DSO 1944 (Bar 1945); DSC 1941; *b* 7 April 1914; *s* of late Maj.-Gen. R. K. Hezlet, CB, CBE, DSO; *m* 1948, Anne Joan Patricia, *e d* of late G. W. N. Clark, Carnabane, Upperlands, Co. Derry; two adopted *d*. *Educ:* RN College, Dartmouth. Comd HM Submarines: H44, Ursula, Trident, Thrasher and Trenchant, 1941–45; comd HMS Scorpion, 1949–50; Chief Staff Officer to Flag Officer (Submarines), 1953–54; Capt. (D), 6th Destroyer Squadron 1955–56; Dir, RN Staff Coll., Greenwich, 1956–57; comd HMS Newfoundland, 1958–59; Rear-Adm. 1959; Flag Officer (Submarines), 1959–61; Flag Officer, Scotland, 1961–62; Vice-Adm. 1962; Flag Officer, Scotland and Northern Ireland, 1963–64; retired 1964. Legion of Merit (Degree of Commander) (US), 1945. *Publications:* The Submarine and Sea Power, 1967; Aircraft and Sea Power, 1970; The 'B' Specials, 1972; Electron and Sea Power, 1975. *Address:* Bovagh House, Mullaghinch Road, Aghadowey, Co. Londonderry, N Ireland. *T:* Aghadowey (0265) 868206. *Clubs:* Army and Navy, Royal Ocean Racing.

HIBBARD, Prof. Bryan Montague, MD, PhD; FRCOG; Professor of Obstetrics and Gynaecology, University of Wales College of Medicine (formerly Welsh National School of Medicine), 1973–91; Consultant Obstetrician and Gynaecologist, University Hospital of Wales; *b* 24 April 1926; *s* of Montague Reginald and Muriel Irene Hibbard; *m* 1955, Elizabeth Donald Grassie. *Educ:* Queen Elizabeth's Sch., Barnet; St Bartholomew's Hosp. Med. Coll., London (MD); PhD (Liverpool). MRCS. Formerly: Sen. Lectr, Liverpool Univ.; Consultant Obstetrician and Gynaecologist, Liverpool RHB. Chairman, Joint Standing Committee: Obstetric Anaesthesia, 1988–; RCOG/RCM, 1988–; Member: Cttee on Safety of Medicines, 1979–83; Maternity Services Adv. Cttee, 1981–85; Council, RCOG, 1982–88, 1989–; S Glam HA, 1983–88; Medicines Commn, 1986–89. Pres., Welsh Obst. and Gynaecol Soc., 1985–86. *Publications:* Principles of Obstetrics, 1988; The Obstetric Forceps, 1988; numerous contribs to world medical literature. *Recreations:* collecting 18th century drinking glasses, fell walking, coarse gardening. *Address:* The Clock House, Cathedral Close, Llandaff, Cardiff CF5 2ED. *T:* Cardiff (0222) 566636.

HIBBERT; *see* Holland-Hibbert, family name of Viscount Knutsford.

HIBBERT, Rev. Barrie Edward; Minister, Bloomsbury Central Baptist Church, London, since 1987; *b* 9 June 1935; *s* of Joseph and Eva Hibbert, Gisborne, NZ; *m* 1957, Ellen Judith Eade; one *s* two *d*. *Educ:* Victoria Univ. of Wellington, NZ (BA); Melbourne Coll. of Divinity, Vic, Australia (LTh); NZ Baptist Theol Coll. Minister: Baptist churches in Gore, Tawa and Dunedin, NZ, 1962–79; Flinders St Baptist Church, Adelaide, SA, 1979–87. *Address:* 11 Mornington Crescent, NW1 7RH. *T:* 071–388 9278.

HIBBERT, Christopher, MC 1945; author; *b* 5 March 1924; *s* of late Canon H. V. Hibbert; *m* 1948, Susan Piggford; two *s* one *d*. *Educ:* Radley; Oriel Coll., Oxford (MA). Served in Italy, 1944–45; Capt., London Irish Rifles. Partner in firm of land agents, auctioneers and surveyors, 1948–59. Fellow, Chartered Auctioneers' and Estate Agents' Inst., 1948–59. Pres., Johnson Soc., 1980. FRSL, FRGS. Heinemann Award for Literature, 1962; McColvin Medal, LA, 1989. *Publications:* The Road to Tyburn, 1957; King Mob, 1958; Wolfe at Quebec, 1959; The Destruction of Lord Raglan, 1961; Corunna, 1961; Benito Mussolini, 1962; The Battle of Arnhem, 1962; The Roots of Evil, 1963; The Court at Windsor, 1964; Agincourt, 1964; (ed) The Wheatley Diary, 1964; Garibaldi and His Enemies, 1965; The Making of Charles Dickens, 1967; (ed) Waterloo: Napoleon's Last Campaign, 1967; (ed) An American in Regency England: The Journal of Louis Simond, 1968; Charles I, 1968; The Grand Tour, 1969; London: Biography of a City, 1969; The Search for King Arthur, 1970; (ed) The Recollections of Rifleman Harris, 1970; Anzio: the bid for Rome, 1970; The Dragon Wakes: China and the West, 1793–1911, 1970; The Personal History of Samuel Johnson, 1971; (ed) Twilight of Princes, 1971; George IV, Prince of Wales, 1762–1811, 1972; George IV, Regent and King, 1812–1830, 1973; The Rise and Fall of the House of Medici, 1974; (ed) A Soldier of the Seventy-First, 1975; Edward VII: a portrait, 1976; The Great Mutiny: India 1857, 1978; Disraeli and His World, 1978; The Court of St James's, 1979; (ed) Boswell's Life of Johnson, 1979; The French Revolution, 1981; (ed) Greville's England, 1981; Africa Explored: Europeans in the Dark Continent, 1769–1889, 1982; (ed with Ben Weinreb) The London Encyclopaedia, 1983; Queen Victoria in Her Letters and Journals, 1984; Rome, Biography of a City, 1985; Cities and Civilizations, 1986; The English: A Social History 1066–1945, 1987; A Guide to Royal London, 1987; The Grand Tour, 1987; London's Churches, 1988; (ed) The Encyclopaedia of Oxford, 1988; Venice: biography of a city, 1988; Redcoats and Rebels: the war for America 1770–1781, 1990; The Virgin Queen: a portrait of Elizabeth I, 1990; (ed) Captain Gronow: his reminiscences of Regency and Victorian Life 1810–60, 1991. *Recreations:* gardening, travel, cooking. *Address:* 6 Albion Place, West Street, Henley-on-Thames, Oxon RG9 2DT. *Clubs:* Garrick, Army and Navy.

HIBBERT, Eleanor; author; *b* London. *Educ:* privately. *Publications:* as *Jean Plaidy:* Together They Ride, 1945; Beyond The Blue Mountains, 1947; Murder Most Royal (and as The King's Pleasure, USA), 1949; The Goldsmith's Wife, 1950; Madame Serpent, 1951; Daughter of Satan, 1952; The Italian Woman, 1952; Sixth Wife, 1953, new edn 1969; Queen Jezebel, 1953; St Thomas's Eve, 1954; The Spanish Bridegroom, 1954; Gay Lord Robert, 1955; The Royal Road to Fotheringay, 1955, new edn 1968; The Wandering Prince, 1956; A Health Unto His Majesty, 1956; Here Lies Our Sovereign Lord, 1956; Flaunting Extravagant Queen, 1956, new edn 1960; Triptych of Poisoners, 1958, new edn 1970; Madonna of the Seven Hills, 1958; Light on Lucrezia, 1958; Louis the Wellbeloved, 1959; The Road to Compiegne, 1959; The Rise of the Spanish Inquisition, 1959; The Growth of the Spanish Inquisition, 1960; Castile For Isabella, 1960; Spain for the Sovereigns, 1960; The End of the Spanish Inquisition, 1961; Daughters of Spain, 1961; Katherine, The Virgin Widow, 1961; Meg Roper, Daughter of Sir Thomas More (for children), 1961; The Young Elizabeth (for children), 1961; The Shadow of the Pomegranate, 1962; The King's Secret Matter, 1962; The Young Mary, Queen of Scots, 1962; The Captive Queen of Scots, 1963; Mary, Queen of France, 1964; The Murder in the Tower, 1964; The Thistle and the Rose, 1965; The Three Crowns, 1965; Evergreen Gallant, 1965; The Haunted Sisters, 1966; The Queen's Favourites, 1966; The Princess of Celle, 1967; Queen in Waiting, 1967; The Spanish Inquisition, its Rise, Growth and End (3 vols in one), 1967; Caroline The Queen, 1968; Katharine of Aragon (3 vols in one), 1968; The Prince and the Quakeress, 1968; The Third George, 1969; Catherine de Medici (3 vols in one), 1969; Perdita's Prince, 1969; Sweet Lass of Richmond Hill, 1970; The Regent's Daughter, 1971; Goddess of the Green Room, 1971; Victoria in the Wings, 1972; Charles II (3 vols in one), 1972; The Captive of Kensington Palace, 1972; The Queen and Lord M, 1973; The Queen's Husband, 1973; The Widow of Windsor, 1974; The Bastard King, 1974; The Lion of Justice, 1975; The Passionate Enemies, 1976; The Plantagenet Prelude, 1976; The Revolt of the Eaglets, 1977; The Heart of the Lion, 1977; The Prince of Darkness, 1978; The Battle of the Queens, 1978; The Queen from Provence, 1979; Edward Longshanks, 1979; The Follies of the King, 1980; The Vow on the Heron, 1980; Passage to Pontefract, 1981; Star of Lancaster, 1981; Epitaph for Three Women, 1981; Red Rose of Anjou, 1982; The Sun in Splendour, 1982; Uneasy Lies the Head, 1982; Myself My Enemy, 1983; Queen of this Realm, 1984; Victoria Victorious, 1985; The Lady in the Tower, 1986; The Courts of Love, 1987; In the Shadow of the Crown, 1988; The Queen's Secret, 1989; The Reluctant Queen, 1990; The Pleasures of Love,

1991; *as Eleanor Burford:* Daughter of Anna, 1941; Passionate Witness, 1941; Married Love, 1942; When All The World Was Young, 1943; So The Dreams Depart, 1944; Not In Our Stars, 1945; Dear Chance, 1947; Alexa, 1948; The House At Cupid's Cross, 1949; Believe The Heart, 1950; Love Child, 1950; Saint Or Sinner?, 1951; Dear Delusion, 1952; Bright Tomorrow, 1952; When We Are Married, 1953; Leave Me My Love, 1953; Castles in Spain, 1954; Hearts Afire, 1954; When Other Hearts, 1955; Two Loves In Her Life, 1955; Married in Haste, 1956; Begin To Live, 1956; To Meet A Stranger, 1957; Pride of the Morning, 1958; Blaze of Noon, 1958; Dawn Chorus, 1959; Red Sky At Night, 1959; Night of Stars, 1960; Now That April's Gone, 1961; Who's Calling?, 1962; *as Ellalice Tate:* Defenders of The Faith, 1956 (under name of Jean Plaidy, 1970); Scarlet Cloak, 1957 (2nd edn, under name of Jean Plaidy, 1969); Queen of Diamonds, 1958; Madame Du Barry, 1959; This Was A Man, 1961; *as Elbur Ford:* The Flesh and The Devil, 1950; Poison in Pimlico, 1950; Bed Disturbed, 1952; Such Bitter Business, 1953 (as Evil in the House, USA 1954); *as Kathleen Kellow:* Danse Macabre, 1952; Rooms At Mrs Oliver's, 1953; Lilith, 1954 (2nd edn, under name of Jean Plaidy, 1967); It Began in Vauxhall Gardens, 1955 (2nd edn under name of Jean Plaidy, 1968); Call of the Blood, 1956; Rochester-The Mad Earl, 1957; Milady Charlotte, 1959; The World's A Stage, 1960; *as Victoria Holt:* Mistress of Mellyn, 1961; Kirkland Revels, 1962; The Bride of Pendorric, 1963; The Legend of the Seventh Virgin, 1965; Menfreya, 1966; The King of the Castle, 1967; The Queen's Confession, 1968; The Shivering Sands, 1969; The Secret Woman, 1971; The Shadow of the Lynx, 1972; On the Night of the Seventh Moon, 1973; The Curse of the Kings, 1973; The House of a Thousand Lanterns, 1974; Lord of the Far Island, 1975; The Pride of the Peacock, 1976; My Enemy the Queen, 1978; The Spring of the Tiger, 1979; The Mask of the Enchantress, 1980; The Judas Kiss, 1981; The Demon Lover, 1982; The Time of the Hunter's Moon, 1983; The Landower Legacy, 1984; The Road to Paradise Island, 1985; Secret for a Nightingale, 1986; The Silk Vendetta, 1987; The India Fan, 1988; The Captive, 1989; Snare of Serpents, 1990; Daughter of Deceit, 1991; *as Philippa Carr:* The Miracle at St Bruno's, 1972; Lion Triumphant, 1974; The Witch from the Sea, 1975; Saraband for Two Sisters, 1976; Lament for a Lost Lover, 1977; The Love Child, 1978; The Song of the Siren, 1979; The Drop of the Dice, 1980; The Adulteress, 1981; Zipporah's Daughter, 1983; Voices in a Haunted Room, 1984; Return of the Gypsy, 1985; Midsummer's Eve, 1986; The Pool at St Branok, 1987; The Changeling, 1989; The Black Swan, 1990; A Time for Silence, 1991. *Address:* c/o Robert Hale Ltd, 45/47 Clerkenwell Green, EC1.

HIBBERT, Sir Jack; KCB 1990; Director, Central Statistical Office, and Head of Government Statistical Service, 1985–Feb. 1992; *b* 14 Feb. 1932; *s* of late William Collier Hibbert and Ivy Annie (*née* Wigglesworth); *m* 1957, Joan Clarkson; two *s* one *d*. *Educ:* Leeds Grammar Sch.; London Sch. of Economics (BScEcon). Served Royal Air Force, 1950–52. Exchequer and Audit Dept, 1952–60; Central Statistical Office, 1960–65; LSE, 1965–66; CSO, 1966; Chief Statistician, 1970; Asst Dir, 1977; OECD and EUROSTAT Consultant 1981; Under Sec., DTI, 1982–85. *Publications:* Measuring the Effects of Inflation on Income, Saving and Wealth (OECD), 1983; articles in Economic Trends, Rev. of Income and Wealth. *Recreations:* bridge, walking. *Address:* c/o Central Statistical Office, Great George Street, SW1P 3AQ. *Club:* Reform.

HIBBERT, Sir Reginald (Alfred), GCMG 1982 (KCMG 1979; CMG 1966); HM Diplomatic Service, retired; *b* 21 Feb. 1922; *s* of Alfred Hibbert, Sawbridgeworth, Herts; *m* 1949, Ann Alun Pugh, *d* of late Sir Alun Pugh; two *s* one *d*. *Educ:* Queen Elizabeth's Sch., Barnet; Worcester Coll., Oxford (Hon. Fellow, 1991). Served with SOE and 4th Hussars in Albania and Italy, 1943–45. Entered Foreign Service, 1946; served in Bucharest, Vienna, Guatemala, Ankara, Brussels; Chargé d'Affaires, Ulan Bator, 1964–66; Research Fellow, Leeds Univ., 1966–67; Political Adviser's Office, Singapore, 1967–69; Political Adviser to C-in-C Far East, 1970–71; Minister, Bonn, 1972–75; Asst Under-Sec. of State, FCO, 1975–76; Dep. Under-Sec. of State, FCO, 1976–79; Ambassador to France, 1979–82; Dir, Ditchley Foundn, 1982–87. Vis. Fellow, Nuffield Coll., Oxford, 1984–88; Hon. Res. Fellow, UC, Swansea, 1988–. *Publication:* The Albanian National Liberation Struggle: the bitter victory, 1991. *Address:* Frondeg, Pennal, Machynlleth, Powys SY20 9JX. *T:* Pennal (0654) 791220. *Club:* Reform.

HICHENS, Antony Peverell, RD 1969; Chairman: Caradon plc; Y. J. Lovell (Holdings) plc; *b* 10 Sept. 1936; *s* of late Lt-Comdr R. P. Hichens, DSO (and Bar), DSC (and 2 Bars), RNVR, and Catherine Gilbert Enys; *m* 1963, Sczerina Neomi Hobday; one *d*. *Educ:* Stowe; Magdalen Coll., Oxford (MA Law); Univ. of Pennsylvania, Wharton Sch. (MBA). Midshipman, RNVR, 1954–56. Called to Bar, Inner Temple, 1960. Rio Tinto-Zinc Corp., 1960–72; Financial Dir, Redland, 1972–81; Man. Dir and Chief Financial Officer, Consolidated Gold Fields, 1981–89. *Recreations:* travel, wine, shooting. *Address:* Slape Manor, Netherbury, near Bridport, Dorset DT6 5HL. *T:* Netherbury (0308) 88232. *Clubs:* Naval and Military, City of London.

HICK, Prof. John Harwood; Danforth Professor since 1979, and Director of Blaisdell Programs in World Religions and Cultures since 1983, Claremont Graduate School, California; *b* 20 Jan. 1922; *s* of Mark Day Hick and Mary Aileen (Hirst); *m* 1953, (Joan) Hazel, *d* of F. G. Bowers, CB, CBE, and Frances Bowers; three *s* one *d*. *Educ:* Bootham Sch., York; Edinburgh Univ. (MA 1948 (1st cl. hons Philos); DLitt 1974); Oriel Coll., Oxford (Campbell-Fraser schol.; DPhil 1950); Westminster Coll., Cambridge. Friends' Ambulance Unit, 1942–45. Ordained, Presb. C of E, 1953; Minister, Belford Presb. Church, Northumberland, 1953–56; Asst Prof. of Philosophy, Cornell Univ., 1956–59; Stuart Prof. of Christian Philosophy, Princeton Theolog. Seminary, 1959–64; S. A. Cook Bye-Fellow, Gonville and Caius Coll., Cambridge, 1963–64; PhD by incorporation; Lectr in Divinity, Cambridge Univ., 1964–67; H. G. Wood Prof. of Theology, Univ. of Birmingham, 1967–82. Guggenheim Fellow, 1963–64, and 1985–86; Leverhulme Res. Fellow, 1976; Scholar-in-residence, Rockefeller Foundn Research Center, Bellagio, Italy, 1986. Lectures: Mead-Swing, Oberlin Coll., USA, 1962–63; Mary Farnum Brown, Haverford Coll., USA 1964–65; James W. Richard, Univ. of Virginia, 1969; Distinguished Vis., Univ. of Oregon, 1969; Arthur Stanley Eddington Meml, 1972; Stanton, Cambridge Univ., 1974–77; Teape, Delhi and Madras, 1975; Ingersoll, Harvard, 1977; Hope, Stirling, 1977; Younghusband, London, 1977; Mackintosh, East Anglia, 1978; Riddell, Newcastle, 1978–79; Berkeley, TCD, 1979; Greenhoe, Louisville Pres. Sem., 1979; Potter, Washington State Univ., 1980; Montefiore, London, 1980; Brooks, Univ. of S California, 1982; Mars and Shaffer, Northwestern Univ., 1983; Niebuhr, Elmhurst Coll., 1986; Gifford, Edinburgh, 1986–87; Kegley, Calif State Univ.: Bakersfield, 1988; Suarez, Spring Hill Coll., 1988; Gates, Grimmell Coll., 1989; Birks, McGill Univ., 1989; Fritz Marti, Univ. of Southern Illinois, 1989; Brooke Anderson, Brown Univ., 1990; Eliot, Reed Coll., 1990; Resler, Ohio State Univ., 1991. Visiting Professor: Banares Hindu Univ., 1971; Visva Bharati Univ., 1971; Punjabi Univ., Patiala, 1971; Goa Univ., 1990; Visiting Fellow: British Acad. Overseas, 1974 and 1990; Univ. of Ceylon, 1974. Hulsean Preacher, Cambridge Univ., 1969; Select Preacher, Oxford Univ., 1970. Chairman: Religious and Cultural Panel, Birmingham Community Relations Cttee, 1969–74; Coordinating Working Party, Statutory Conf. for Revision of Agreed Syllabus of Religious Educn, Birmingham, 1971–74; Birmingham Inter-Faiths Council, 1975; President: Soc. for the Study of Theology, 1975–76; All Faiths for One Race, 1980–85 (Chm., 1972–73, 1978–80); Member: Amer. Soc. for the Study of Religion, 1983–; Amer. Philosophical Assoc., 1980–; Amer. Acad. of Religion, 1980–. Mem. Council, Selly Oak Colls, 1967–80; Governor, Queen's Coll., Birmingham, 1972–80. Member Editorial Board: The Encyclopedia of Philosophy; Religious Studies; Jl of Religion; Studies in Religion; Modern Theology. Hon. Teol. Dr Uppsala, 1977. *Publications:* Faith and Knowledge, 1957, 2nd edn 1966; Philosophy of Religion, 1963, 4th edn 1990 (Spanish, Portuguese, Chinese, Japanese, Korean, Finnish and Swedish edns); (ed) Faith and the Philosophers, 1963; (ed) The Existence of God, 1963; (ed) Classical and Contemporary Readings in the Philosophy of Religion, 1963, 3rd edn 1990; Evil and the God of Love, 1966, 2nd edn 1977; (ed) The Many-Faced Argument, 1967; Christianity at the Centre, 1968, 2nd edn as The Centre of Christianity, 1977 (trans. Dutch, Korean and Chinese); Arguments for the Existence of God, 1971; Biology and the Soul, 1972; God and the Universe of Faiths, 1973; (ed) Truth and Dialogue, 1974; Death and Eternal Life, 1976 (trans. Dutch); (ed) The Myth of God Incarnate, 1977 (trans. German and Arabic); God has Many Names, 1980 (trans. German, Japanese); (ed with Brian Hebblethwaite) Christianity and Other Religions, 1980; The Second Christianity, 1983 (trans. Japanese); (with Michael Goulder) Why Believe in God?, 1983; Problems of Religious Pluralism, 1985 (trans. Japanese); (ed with Hasan Askari) The Experience of Religious Diversity, 1985; An Interpretation of Religion, 1989; (ed with Edmund Meltzer) Three Faiths—One God, 1989; (ed with Lamont Hempel) Gandhi's Significance for Today, 1989. *Address:* Department of Religion, Claremont Graduate School, Claremont, Calif 91711, USA; 144 Oak Tree Lane, Selly Oak, Birmingham B29 6HU.

HICKEY, Sir Justin, Kt 1979; Chairman and Managing Director, Bartinon Securities Ltd (formerly Accident Insurance Mutual Ltd), since 1968; Chairman, Queensland Science & Technology Ltd, since 1984; *b* 5 April 1925; *s* of Hon. Simon Hickey, Speaker, New South Wales Parliament, and Hilda Ellen Hickey (*née* Dacey); *m* 1964, Barbara Standish Thayer; one *s* four *d*. *Educ:* De La Salle College, Sydney. Chairman: Australian Family Trust, 1965; Thayer Foundation (US), 1972; Director: SciRad Ltd, 1986–; SciRad Fund Ltd, 1986–; Biocom Internat. Ltd (Bermuda), 1987–; Chemical Fuels Corp. (Atlanta, Ga), 1987–. Mem., Lloyd's of London, 1979. FRSA 1978. JP 1950. *Recreations:* yachting, art collection. *Address:* Bartinon, 20 Marseille Court, Sorrento, Qld 4217, Australia.

HICKLIN, Denis Raymond, OBE 1969; Partner, Middle Greadow Dairy Farm, Lanlivery, Cornwall, since 1986; *b* 15 April 1918; *s* of Joseph Herbert and Florence May Hicklin; *m* 1949, Joyce Grisdale Smith; two *s*. *Educ:* Merchant Taylors' Sch. Served War, 1939–46, RA (Major). John Dickinson, 1936–48; St Anne's Board Mill Co. Ltd, 1948–78 (Chm. and Man. Dir, 1966–78). Pt-time Mem., Forestry Commn, 1978–81. *Recreations:* gardening, golf. *Address:* 1 Bumpers Batch, Midford Road, Bath BA2 5SQ. *T:* Bath (0225) 833123.

HICKLING, Rev. Canon Colin John Anderson; Vicar of All Saints, Arksey, Sheffield, since 1986; Hon. Lecturer in Biblical Studies, University of Sheffield, since 1986; Canon Theologian, Leicester Cathedral, since 1983; *b* 10 July 1931; *s* of late Charles Frederick Hickling, CMG, ScD, and late Marjorie Ellerington, *d* of late Henry Blamey. *Educ:* Taunton Sch.; Epsom Coll.; King's Coll., Cambridge; Chichester Theol Coll. BA 1953, MA 1957. Deacon 1957, Priest 1958. Asst Curate, St Luke's, Pallion, Sunderland, 1957–61; Asst Tutor, Chichester Theol Coll., 1961–65; Asst Priest Vicar, Chichester Cath., 1964–65; Asst Lectr in New Testament Studies, King's Coll., Univ. of London, 1965–68, Lectr, 1968–84; Dep. Minor Canon, St Paul's Cath., 1969–78; Dep. Priest in Ordinary to the Queen, 1971–74; Priest in Ordinary to the Queen, 1974–84; Subwarden of King's Coll. Hall, 1969–78; Warden of King's Coll. Hostel, 1978–81; Tutor in Biblical Studies, Queen's Coll., Birmingham, 1984–85; E. W. Benson Fellow, Lincoln Theol Coll., 1985–86. Mem., Liturgical Commn, 1981–86. Boyle Lectr, 1973–76; Select Preacher: Univ. of Cambridge, 1979; Univ. of Oxford, 1983. *Publications:* contributed to: Church without Walls, 1968; Catholic Anglicans Today, 1968; Bible Bibliography 1967–73, 1974; (also ed jtly) What About the New Testament?, 1975; St Paul: Teacher and Traveller, 1975; L'Evangile de Jean, 1977; Les Actes des Apôtres, 1979; The Ministry of the Word, 1979; This is the Word of the Lord, 1980; Studia Biblica 1978, Vol. III, 1980; Logia: the sayings of Jesus, 1982; Studia Evangelica, Vol. VII, 1982; A Dictionary of Biblical Interpretation, 1990; The Bible in Three Dimensions, 1990; reviews and articles. *Recreation:* music. *Address:* All Saints Vicarage, Station Road, Arksey, by Doncaster, S Yorks DN5 0SP. *T:* Doncaster (0302) 874445.

HICKLING, Reginald Hugh, CMG 1968; PhD (London); QC (Gibraltar) 1970; *b* 2 Aug. 1920; *er s* of late Frederick Hugh Hickling and Elsie May Hickling, Malvern, Worcs; *m* 1945, Beryl Iris (*née* Dennett); two *s* one *d* (and one *s* decd). *Educ:* Buxton Coll.; Nottingham Univ. RNVR, 1941–46. Dep. Solicitor, Evening Standard, London, 1946–50; Asst Attorney-Gen., Sarawak, 1950–55; Legal Adviser, Johore, 1956; Legal Draftsman, Malaya, 1957; Parly Draftsman, Malaya, 1959; Comr of Law Revision, Malaya, 1961; Commonwealth Office, 1964; Legal Adviser to High Comr, Aden and Protectorate of S Arabia, 1964–67; Maritime Law Adviser: Thailand, 1968–69; Malaysia, 1969; Sri Lanka, 1970; Yemen Arab Republic, 1984, 1986; Attorney-General, Gibraltar, 1970–72. Lectr in SE Asian Law, SOAS, 1976–78, 1981–82; Visiting Professor, Faculty of Law: Univ. of Singapore, 1974–76 and 1978–80; Univ. of Malaya, 1983–84, 1986–88; Nat. Univ. of Malaysia, 1988–91. Consumer Law Advr, Fiji, 1990. Hon. JMN (Malaya), 1960. *Publications:* The Furious Evangelist, 1950; The English Flotilla, 1954 (US as Falconer's Voyage, 1956); Sarawak and Its Government, 1955; Festival of Hungry Ghosts, 1957; An Introduction to the Federal Constitution, 1960; Lieutenant Okino, 1968; A Prince of Borneo, 1985; The Ghost of Orchard Road and other stories, 1985; Malaysian Law, 1987. *Recreation:* not watching TV. *Address:* 1 Highfield Road, Malvern, Worcs. *T:* Malvern (0684) 573477.

HICKMAN, Sir Glenn; *see* Hickman, Sir R. G.

HICKMAN, John Kyrle, CMG 1977; HM Diplomatic Service, retired; Director: Anaconda (South America) Inc., since 1988; Chartered Express Distribution Service plc, since 1990; *b* 3 July 1927; *s* of late J. B. Hickman and Joan Hickman; *m* 1956, Jennifer Love; two *s* one *d*. *Educ:* Tonbridge; Trinity Hall, Cambridge. Served in RA, 45th Field Regt, Commonwealth Bde, 1948–50. Asst Principal, WO, 1950; Principal, 1955; transf. to CRO, 1958; UK High Commn, Wellington, 1959–62; HM Diplomatic Service, 1965; British Embassy, Madrid, 1966; Counsellor and HM Consul-General, Bilbao, 1967; Dep. High Comr, Singapore, 1969–71; Head of SW Pacific Dept, FCO, 1971–74; Counsellor, Dublin, 1974–77; Ambassador to Ecuador, 1977–81, to Chile, 1982–87. Alternate Chm., Belize Independence Conf., 1981. *Publications:* The Enchanted Islands: the Galápagos Discovered, 1985; occasional historical articles. *Recreations:* history, golf. *Address:* 48A Fitzgeorge Avenue, W14. *T:* 071-602 5624. *Clubs:* Garrick; Los Leones Golf (Santiago).

HICKMAN, Michael Ranulf; His Honour Judge Hickman; a Circuit Judge, since 1974; *b* 2 Oct. 1922; *s* of John Owen Hickman and Nancy Viola Hickman (*née* Barlow); *m* 1943, Diana Richardson; one *s* one *d*. *Educ:* Wellington; Trinity Hall, Cambridge. 2nd cl. Hons in Law. Served War, RAFVR, 1940–46. Cambridge Univ., 1946–48; called to Bar, Middle Temple, 1949. Actg Dep. Chm., Hertfordshire QS, 1965–72; a Recorder of

Crown Court, 1972–74. *Recreations:* shooting, fishing, gun dog training. *Address:* The Acorn, Bovingdon, Herts HP3 0NA. *T:* Hemel Hempstead (0442) 832226.

HICKMAN, Sir (Richard) Glenn, 4th Bt *cr* 1903; *b* 12 April 1949; *s* of Sir Alfred Howard Whitby Hickman, 3rd Bt, and of Margaret D., *o d* of Leonard Kempson; *S* father, 1979; *m* 1981, Heather Mary Elizabeth, *er d* of late Dr James Moffett, Swindon, and late Dr Gwendoline Moffett; two *s* one *d. Educ:* Eton. *Heir: s* Charles Patrick Alfred Hickman, *b* 5 May 1983. *Address:* Leaper Cottage, Letchmore Heath, Herts WD2 8ES. *Club:* Turf.

HICKMET, Richard Saladin; barrister-at-law; *b* 1 Dec. 1947; *s* of Ferid and Elizabeth Hickmet; *m* 1973, Susan (*née* Ludwig); three *d. Educ:* Millfield Sch.; Sorbonne; Hull Univ. (BA). Dir, private hotel group, 1972–74. Called to the Bar, Inner Temple, 1974. Mem., Wandsworth Borough Council, 1978–83 (Chm., Leisure and Amenities Cttee, 1980–83; privatised street cleansing, refuse collection, parks maintenance). Contested (C): Glanford and Scunthorpe, 1987; Eastbourne, Oct. 1990. MP (C) Glanford and Scunthorpe, 1983–87. *Recreations:* squash, hunting. *Address:* 3 Dr Johnson's Buildings, Temple, EC4. *T:* 071–353 8778.

HICKOX, Richard Sidney, FRCO(CHM); conductor; Music Director: City of London Sinfonia, since 1971; Richard Hickox Singers, since 1971; London Symphony Chorus, since 1976; Bradford Festival Choral Society, since 1978; Associate Conductor, London Symphony Orchestra, since 1985; *b* Stokenchurch, Bucks, 5 March 1948; *m* 1976, Frances Ina Sheldon-Williams; one *s. Educ:* in organ, piano and composition, Royal Acad. of Music (LRAM); Organ Scholar, Queens' Coll., Cambridge (MA). Début as professional conductor, St John's Smith Square, 1971; Organist and Master of the Music, St Margaret's, Westminster, 1972–82; Prom début, 1973. Artistic Director: Wooburn Fest., 1967–; St Endellion Fest., 1974–; Christ Church Spitalfields Fest., 1978–; Truro Fest., 1981–; Chester Summer Fest., 1989–; Principal Guest Conductor: Dutch Radio Orch., 1980–84; Northern Sinfonia, 1990– (Artistic Dir, 1982–90); Associate Conductor, San Diego Symphony Orch., 1983–84; also regularly conducts Philharmonia, RPO, Bournemouth Symphony Orch. and Sinfonietta, Royal Liverpool Phil. Orch., BBC Symphony, Concert, Scottish and Welsh Orchs, BBC Singers, Hallé Orch.; San Francisco Symphony Orch.; Detroit Symphony Orch.; Houston Symphony Orch.; National Symphony Orch., Washington; Rotterdam Philharmonic; Oslo Philharmonic; Turku Philharmonia; Salzburg Mozarteum; Suisse Romande; Stockholm Philharmonic. Conducted: ENO, 1979; Opera North, 1982, 1986; Scottish Opera, 1985, 1987; Royal Opera, 1985; has appeared at many music festivals incl. Proms, Flanders, Bath and Cheltenham. Co-founder, Opera Stage, 1985. Many recordings of choral and orchestral music. *Address:* 35 Ellington Street, N7 8PN. *T:* 071–607 8984.

HICKS; *see* Joynson-Hicks.

HICKS, Dr Colin Peter, CChm, FRSC; Head of Research and Technology Policy Division, Department of Trade and Industry, since 1990; *b* 1 May 1946; *s* of George Stephen Frederick Hicks and Irene Maud (*née* Hargrave); *m* 1967, Elizabeth Joan Payne; two *d. Educ:* Rutlish Grammar Sch., Merton; Univ. of Bristol (BSc, PhD). Lectr in Chemistry, Univ. of W Indies, Jamaica, 1970–73; ICI Res. Fellow, Univ. of Exeter, 1973–75; DTI, 1975–; NPL, 1975–80; Laboratory of Govt Chemist, 1984–87; Sec., Ind. Develt Adv. Bd, 1988–90. *Address:* Research and Technology Policy Division, Department of Trade and Industry, 151 Buckingham Palace Road, SW1W 9SS

HICKS, Gp Captain David; *see* Hicks, Gp Captain H. D.

HICKS, David (Nightingale); interior decorator, designer, author and garden designer; Director, David Hicks Ltd, since 1960; *b* 25 March 1929; 3rd surv. *s* of late Herbert Hicks (stockbroker and twice past Master Salter's Company) and late Mrs Hicks; *m* 1960, Lady Pamela Carmen Louise Mountbatten, *yr d* of Admiral of the Fleet Earl Mountbatten of Burma, KG, GCB, OM, GCSI, GCIE, GCVO, DSO, PC, FRS; one *s* two *d. Educ:* Charterhouse; Central School of Arts and Crafts, London. Interiors for: Helena Rubinstein; QE2; HRH the Prince of Wales; Govt of NSW; British Steel Corp.; Aeroflot Offices; Marquess of Londonderry; Library in British Embassy, Washington, and Royal Yacht for HM King Fahd. Associate offices in: Karachi, Paris, Athens, Tokyo, Sydney. Designer of fabrics, carpets, furniture, etc. Master, Salters' Co., 1977–78. FRSA. CoID (now Design Council) design award, 1970. *Publications:* David Hicks on Decoration, 1966; David Hicks on Living—with taste, 1968; David Hicks on Bathrooms, 1970; David Hicks on Decoration—with fabrics, 1971; David Hicks on Decoration—5, 1972; David Hicks Book of Flower Arranging, 1976; David Hicks Living with Design, 1979; David Hicks Garden Design, 1982; David Hicks Style and Design, 1988. *Recreations:* shooting, gardening, preservation. *Address:* Albany, Piccadilly, W1. *T:* (office) 081–994 9222.

HICKS, Group Captain (Harry) David, MBE 1967; Director General, English-Speaking Union, since 1990; *b* 13 July 1923; *s* of Walter Hicks and Clara Ann (*née* Jagger); *m* 1948, Jane Irene Mary Tibbs; one *s* one *d. Educ:* Grange Grammar Sch., Bradford; London Univ. (BA Hons 1947); Nottingham Univ. (PGCE 1948). Served War, 1942–45, as Pilot, 149 Sqdn, Bomber Comd. Schoolmaster, Surbiton Grammar Sch., 1948–49; Royal Air Force: Educn Br., 1950–54; Admin. Br., 1954–76, finally as Dep. Dir, Recruiting; English-Speaking Union: Dir of Educn, 1976–85; Dep. Dir General, 1985–90. *Recreations:* golf, tennis, playing piano. *Address:* Highgrove, 24 Clifton Road, Chesham Bois, Bucks HP6 5PU. *T:* Chesham (0494) 727239. *Clubs:* Royal Air Force, English-Speaking Union.

HICKS, John Charles; QC 1980; **His Honour Judge Hicks;** a Circuit Judge, since 1988; *b* 4 March 1928; *s* of late Charles Hicks and late Marjorie Jane Hicks; *m* 1957, Elizabeth Mary, *o d* of late Rev. J. B. Jennings; one *d* (one *s* decd). *Educ:* King Edward VI Grammar Schs, Chelmsford and Totnes; London Univ. LLM 1954. Served RA (National Service), 1946–48. Admitted solicitor, 1952; called to the Bar, Middle Temple, 1966; a Recorder, 1978–88. Legal Dept, Thomas Tilling Ltd, 1953–54; Partner in Messrs Burchells, solicitors, 1955–65; Methodist Missionary Soc., Caribbean, 1965–66. Jl Sec., Methodist Conf., 1989–. *Publications:* (ed jtly) The Constitution and Discipline of the Methodist Church in the Caribbean and the Americas, 1967, with annual supplements to 1987; (ed) The Constitutional Practice and Discipline of the Methodist Church, 6th edn 1974, 7th edn 1988, with annual supplements, 1974–; articles in Mod. Law Rev., Cambridge Law Jl, and Epworth Rev. *Recreations:* squash rackets, music, theatre, opera, the Methodist Constitution. *Address:* Flat 3, 17 Montagu Square, W1H 1RD. *T:* 071–935 6008.

HICKS, Sir John (Richard), Kt 1964; FBA 1942; Fellow of All Souls College, since 1952; *b* 1904; *s* of late Edward Hicks, Leamington Spa; *m* 1935, Ursula K. Webb (*d* 1985). *Educ:* Clifton Coll.; Balliol Coll., Oxford. Lectr, London Sch. of Economics, 1926–35; Fellow of Gonville and Caius Coll., Cambridge, 1935–38, Hon. Fellow, 1971; Prof. of Political Economy, University of Manchester, 1938–46; Official Fellow of Nuffield Coll., Oxford, 1946–52; Drummond Prof. of Political Economy, University of Oxford, 1952–65; Member: Revenue Allocation Commn, Nigeria, 1950; Royal Commn on the Taxation of Profits and Income, 1951. Hon. Fellow, LSE, 1969. (Jtly) Nobel Memorial Prize for Economics, 1972. *Publications:* The Theory of Wages, 1932 (revised edn, 1963); Value

and Capital, 1939; The Taxation of War Wealth (with U. K. Hicks and L. Rostas), 1941; The Social Framework, 1942 (4th edn, 1971); Standards of Local Expenditure (with U. K. Hicks), 1943; The Problem of Valuation for Rating (with U. K. Hicks and C. E. V. Leser), 1944; The Incidence of Local Rates in Great Britain (with U. K. Hicks), 1945; The Problem of Budgeting Reform, 1948; A Contribution to the Theory of the Trade Cycle, 1950; (with U. K. Hicks) Report on Finance and Taxation in Jamaica, 1955; A Revision of Demand Theory, 1956; Essays in World Economics, 1960; Capital and Growth, 1965; Critical Essays in Monetary Theory, 1967; A Theory of Economic History, 1969; Capital and Time, 1973; The Crisis in Keynesian Economics, 1974; Economic Perspectives, 1977; Causality in Economics, 1979; Collected Papers, 3 vols, 1981–83; A Market Theory of Money, 1989. *Address:* Porch House, Blockley, Glos.

HICKS, Maureen Patricia; MP (C) Wolverhampton North East, since 1987; *b* 23 Feb. 1948; *d* of Ron and Nora Cutler; *m* 1973, Keith Hicks; one *s* one *d. Educ:* Ashley Secondary School; Brockenhurst Grammar School; Furzedown College of Education. Teacher's Cert. Secondary Teacher, Drama and English, 1969–70; Marks & Spencer Management, 1970–74; Asst Area Educn Officer, 1974–76; Dir, Motor Museum, 1976–82. Mem., Stratford DC, 1979–84. PPS to Minister of State and Parly Under-Sec. of State, FCO, 1991–; Sec. H of C Tourism Cttee, 1987–. *Recreations:* amateur dramatics, music, golf, travel. *Address:* House of Commons, SW1A 0AA. *Club:* Royal Over-Seas League.

HICKS, Maj.-Gen. Michael; *see* Hicks, Maj.-Gen. W. M. E.

HICKS, Robert; MP (C) Cornwall South-East, since 1983 (Bodmin, 1970–Feb. 1974 and Oct. 1974–1983); *b* 18 Jan. 1938; *s* of W. H. Hicks; *m* 1962, Maria Elizabeth Ann Gwyther (marr. diss. 1988); two *d. Educ:* Queen Elizabeth Grammar Sch., Crediton; University Coll., London; Univ. of Exeter. Taught at St Austell Grammar Sch., 1961–64; Lecturer in Regional Geography, Weston-super-Mare Technical Coll., 1964–70. An Asst Govt Whip, 1973–74; Mem., Select Cttee of House of Commons, European Legislation, 1973, 1976–; Vice-Chm., Cons. Parly European Affairs Cttee, 1979–81; Chm., Cons. Parly Agric. Cttee, 1988–90 (Vice-Chm., 1972–73 (Chm., Horticultural Sub-Cttee), and 1974–82); Chairman: Westcountry Gp of Cons. MPs, 1976–77; UK Gp, Parly Assoc. for Euro-Arab Co-operation, 1982–; Treasurer, Cons. Party ME Council, 1980–; Parly Adviser to British Hotels, Restaurants and Caterers Assoc., 1974–, to Milk Marketing Bd, 1985–. *Recreations:* cricket, gardening, golf. *Address:* 7 Carew Wharf, Marine Drive, Torpoint, Cornwall. *Club:* MCC.

HICKS, Robin Edgcumbe; Chief Executive, Royal Agricultural Society of England, since 1989; *b* 6 Dec. 1942; *s* of Ronald Eric Edgcumbe Hicks and Fredrica Hicks; *m* 1970, Sue (*née* Dalton); one *s* one *d. Educ:* Bancrofts' Sch.; Seale Hayne Coll. (NDA; Dip. Farm Management); Univ. of Reading (DipAgric Extension). Farm worker, 1961–63; Agricl Advr, MAFF, 1967–69; Producer/Presenter, BBC Farming Today, 1969–71; Churchill Fellow, 1973; various production posts, radio and television, 1973–77; Hd of Marketing and Develt, RASE, 1977–79; Hd of Network Radio, BBC South and West, 1979–88. Mem., Bristol and Weston HA, 1986–88; Vice-Chm., Radio Acad., 1986–88; Trustee: St George's Music Trust, 1981–88; Rural Housing Trust, 1990–; Member: Exec. Cttee, SW Arts, 1981–85; SW Concerts Bd, 1981–88; Trustee, Head Injury Recovery Trust, 1986–. Freeman, City of London, 1977; Liveryman, Drapers' Co, 1981. *Recreations:* family, photography, canal boating, gardening, theatre. *Address:* 9 Clarendon Crescent, Royal Leamington Spa, Warwickshire CV32 5NR. *Clubs:* Farmers', Anglo-Belgian.

HICKS, Thomas; *see* Steele, Tommy.

HICKS, Maj.-Gen. (William) Michael (Ellis), CB 1982; OBE 1967; Secretary, Royal College of Defence Studies, since 1983; *b* 2 June 1928; *s* of late Group Captain William Charles Hicks, AFC, and Nellie Kilbourne (*née* Kay); *m* 1950, Jean Hilary Duncan; three *s. Educ:* Eton Coll.; RMA Sandhurst. Commnd 2 Lieut Coldstream Guards, 1948; served, 1948–67: regtl service, UK, Tripoli and Canal Zone; Instr, Sch. of Inf. (Captain); Staff Coll. (Major); GSO2 (Ops) HQ 4 Div.; regtl service, BAOR, UK and Kenya; JSSC; GSO (DS) Staff Coll.; GSO1 MO1, MoD, 1967–70 (Lt-Col); CO 1st Bn Coldstream Guards, 1970–72; RCDS, 1973 (Col); comd 4th Guards Armoured Bde, 1974–76 (Brig.); BGS Trng HQ UKLF, 1977–79; BGS (Author) attached to DMO, MoD, 1979; GOC NW Dist, 1980–83, retd. *Recreations:* golf, gardening. *Address:* c/o Lloyds Bank, Cox's & King's, PO Box 1190, 7 Pall Mall, SW1Y 5NA.

HICKS BEACH, family name of **Earl St Aldwyn.**

HIDAYATULLAH, Mohammed, OBE 1946; Vice-President of India, 1979–84 (Acting President, 1969 and 1982); *b* 17 Dec. 1905; *y s* of Khan Bahadur Hafiz M. Wilayatullah, ISO; *m* 1948, Pushpa Shah, *d* of A. N. Shah, ICS; one *s* (one *d* decd). *Educ:* Govt High Sch., Raipur; Morris Coll., Nagpur (Phillips Schol.; BA; Malak Gold Medal); Trinity Coll., Cambridge (MA; Pres., Indian Majlis, 1928); Lincoln's Inn; Bencher 1968. Nagpur High Court: Advocate, 1930–46; Govt Pleader, 1942–43; Advocate General, CP & Berar, 1943–46; Puisne Judge, 1946–54; Chief Justice, 1954–56; Chief Justice, Madhya Pradesh High Court, 1956–58; Puisne Judge, Supreme Court of India, 1958–68, Chief Justice, 1968–70. Dean, Faculty of Law, Nagpur Univ., 1950–54; Mem., Faculty of Law, Sagar, Vikram and Aligarh Univs; President: Indian Law Inst., 1968–70; Internat. Law Assoc. (Indian Br.), 1968–70; Indian Soc. of Internat. Law, 1968–70; Member: Internat. Inst. of Space Law, Paris; British Inst. of Internat. and Comparative Law, 1982–; Exec. Coun., World Assembly of Judges; Advr, Council for World Peace through Law; rep. India at Internat. Confs at Bangkok, Helsinki, Durham, Geneva, Port of Spain, Belgrade, Venice, Canberra, Melbourne, Washington, New York, Tunis, The Hague, Tokyo and Stockholm; Vice Pres., Heritage Fund, Lincoln's Inn, 1986–. Chancellor: Muslim Nat. Univ., New Delhi, 1968–86; Delhi Univ., 1979–85; Punjab Univ., 1979–85; Hyderabad Central Univ., 1986–. Assoc. Mem., Royal Acad. of Morocco. Pres., Indian Red Cross Soc., 1982–; Member: World Assoc. for Orphans and Abandoned Children, Geneva; Internat. Council of Former Scouts and Guides (awarded Silver Elephant, 1948); Chief Scout, All India Boy Scouts Assoc. (awarded Bronze Medal for Gallantry, 1969). Patron-in-Chief: Schizophrenic Foundn for Res., India; India Islamic Cultural Centre; Patron, Hungar Project, India. Kt of Mark Twain, 1985. Fellow, Indian Law Inst., 1986. Hon. LLD: Univ. of Philippines, 1970; Ravishankar Univ., 1970; Rajasthan Univ., 1976; Benares Hindu Univ.; Berhampore Univ.; Kashmir Univ., 1983; Punjab Univ.; Nagpur Univ., 1985; Agra Univ., 1987; Hyderabad Central Univ., 1991; Hon. DLitt: Bhopal Univ.; Kakatiya Univ.; Hon. DCL Delhi Univ. Medallion and plaque of Merit, Philconsa, Manila; Order of Jugoslav Flag with Sash, 1972; Shromani Award, 1986; Grand Cross (1st class) for Arts and Literature, Austrian People, 1989; Lokshree Award, India, 1989; Singhui Award, Benares Hindu Univ., 1991; Royal Insignia, Acad. of Morocco. *Publications:* Democracy in India and the Judicial Process, 1966; The South-West Africa Case, 1967; Judicial Methods, 1969; A Judge's Miscellany, vol. 1 1972, second series 1979, third series 1983, fourth series, 1985; USA and India, 1977; 5th and 6th Schedules to Constitution of India 1979; My Own Boswell (memoirs), 1980; (ed) Mulla's Mohamedan Law, 16th, 17th and 18th edns; Taqrir-o Tabir (Urdu), Right to Property and the Indian Constitution, The Indian Constitution (ed, 3 vols); Miscellanea, 1988; numerous monographs and articles.

Recreations: golf, bridge. *Address:* A-10 Rockside, 112 Walkeshwar Road, Bombay 6, India. *T:* 8129798. *Clubs:* Delhi Gymkhana (New Delhi); Willingdon (Bombay).

HIDDEN, Hon. Sir Anthony Brian, Kt 1989; **Hon. Mr Justice Hidden;** a Judge of the High Court of Justice, Queen's Bench Division, since 1989; *b* 7 March 1936; *s* of late James Evelyn Harold Hidden, GM and Gladys Bessie (*née* Brooks); *m* 1982, Mary Elise Torriano Pritchard, *d* of R. C. Pritchard of Barton Abbotts, Tetbury, Glos; three *s* one *d*. *Educ:* Reigate Grammar Sch.; Emmanuel Coll., Cambridge (BA Hons 1957, MA 1960). 2nd Lieut, 1st Royal Tank Regt, Far East Land Forces, Hong Kong, 1958–59. Called to the Bar, Inner Temple, 1961, Bencher, 1985; Mem., Hon. Soc. of Inner Temple, 1956–, and of Lincoln's Inn (*ad eundem*), 1973–. QC 1976; a Recorder, 1977–89; Leader, SE Circuit, 1986–89. *Recreations:* reading, playing bad golf. *Address:* Royal Courts of Justice, Strand, WC2.

HIDE, Prof. Raymond, CBE 1990; FRS 1971; Director of Robert Hooke Institute, and Visiting Professor of Physics, Oxford University, since 1990; Fellow, Jesus College, Oxford, since 1983; *b* 17 May 1929; *s* of late Stephen Hide and of Rose Edna Hide (*née* Cartlidge; now Mrs Thomas Leonard); *m* 1958, (Phyllis) Ann Licence; one *s* two *d*. *Educ:* Percy Jackson Grammar Sch., near Doncaster; Manchester Univ.; Caius Coll., Cambridge. BSc 1st cl. hons Physics Manchester, 1950; PhD 1953, ScD 1969, Cantab. Res. Assoc. in Astrophysics, Univ. of Chicago, 1953–54; Sen. Res. Fellow, AERE Harwell, 1954–57; Lectr in Physics, Univ. of Durham (King's Coll., Newcastle), 1957–61; Prof. of Geophysics and Physics, MIT, 1961–67; Hd of Geophysical Fluid Dynamics Lab., and CSO, Met. Office, 1967–90. Short-term vis. appts at Princeton Inst. for Advanced Study, 1954 and at MIT and UCLA, 1960; Visiting Professor: UCL, 1967–84; Reading Univ., 1976–91; Leeds Univ., 1986–91; Gresham Prof. of Astronomy, 1985–90; Adrian Fellow, Univ. of Leicester, 1980–83. Hon. Res. Fellow, Inst. of Oceanographic Scis Deacon Lab., 1990–. Member Council: RAS, 1969–72 and 1983–86 (Pres., 1983–85); Royal Meteorological Soc., 1969–72 and 1974–77 (Pres., 1974–76; Hon. Mem., 1989); NERC, 1972–75; Eur. Geophysical Soc., 1981–85 (Pres., 1982–84, Hon. Mem., 1988); Royal Soc., 1988–90. Lectures: Symons Meml, RMetS, 1970; R. A. Fisher Meml, 1977; Halley, Oxford, 1980; Jeffreys, RAS, 1981; Union, Internat. Union of Geodesy and Geophysics, Hamburg, 1983; Scott, Cambridge, 1984; Thompson, Toronto, 1984; Lindsay, NASA, 1988. Fellow: Amer. Acad. of Arts and Sciences, 1964; Academia Europaea, 1988. Hon. DSc Leicester, 1985. Charles Chree Medal, Inst. Physics, 1975; Holweck Medal, Soc. Franç. de Physique, 1982; Gold Medal, RAS, 1989. *Publications:* papers in scientific jls. *Address:* Robert Hooke Institute, Old Observatory, Clarendon Laboratory, Parks Road, Oxford OX1 3PU. *T:* Oxford (0865) 272084.

HIELSCHER, Sir Leo (Arthur), Kt 1987; Under Treasurer of Queensland (Civil Service Head of Treasury Department of Queensland Government), 1974–88; Chairman, Queensland Treasury Corporation; *b* 1 Oct. 1926; *s* of Leslie Charles Hielscher and Elizabeth Jane Petersen; *m* 1948, Mary Ellen Pelgrave; one *s* one *d* (and one *s* decd). *Educ:* Brisbane State High Sch.; Univ. of Queensland (BComm, AAUQ). AASA, FAIM. Queensland Public Service, 1942; RAAF, 1945–47; Asst Under Sec. (Budget), Qld Treasury, 1964, Dep. Under Treasurer, 1969–74. Eisenhower Exchange Fellow, 1973. Director: Qld Provincial Newspapers; Crusader; Chairman: Gladstone Special Steel Corp.; Autsafe Pty. Chm., Finance Cttee, Griffith Univ. Council. Chm., Brisbane Cricket Ground. Mem., Lyric Opera, Qld. *Recreations:* golf, fishing, boating, theatre. *Address:* 16 Auckland Street, Wishart, Brisbane, Qld 4122, Australia. *T:* (home) 07 343 3071; (business) 07 224 45760. *Clubs:* Brisbane, Gailes Golf, Tattersalls (Brisbane).

HIGGINBOTTOM, Donald Noble; HM Diplomatic Service, retired; Counsellor, Foreign and Commonwealth Office, 1976–79; *b* 19 Dec. 1925; *s* of late Harold Higginbottom and Dorothy (*née* Needham); *m* 1950, Sarah Godwin. *Educ:* Calday Grange Grammar Sch., Cheshire; King's Coll., Cambridge (1st Cl. Hons Hist.); Yale Univ., USA (MA Hist.). Lectr in Humanities, Univ. of Chicago, 1951. Entered Foreign Office, 1953; Buenos Aires, 1955; Peking, 1958; Saigon, 1960; Phnom Penh, 1962; Singapore, 1964; Bangkok, 1971; Buenos Aires, 1974. *Recreations:* electronic clocks, power boating. *Address:* Apartado 54, Benicarló, Castellón, Spain. *Clubs:* Athenæum; Yacht Club Olivos (Buenos Aires).

HIGGINS; *see* Longuet-Higgins.

HIGGINS, Alec Wilfred, MBE 1944; MC 1940; TD 1945; Deputy Chairman of Lloyd's, 1975, 1976, 1980 and 1981; Chairman: Higgins, Brasier & Co. Ltd (formerly Higgins & Doble Ltd), 1962–88; M. J. Marchant Underwriting Ltd, 1982–88; *b* 1 Nov. 1914; *s* of late Frederick Gladstone Higgins and Beatrice Louisa Scriven; *m* 1939, Denise May Philcox; two *s* one *d*. *Educ:* Merton Court Sch., Sidcup; Sutton Valence Sch. Joined Woods & Maslen Ltd, 1937, Chm., 1963–80. Underwriting Mem. of Lloyd's, 1948 (Mem. Cttee, 1967–73, 1975–77, 1980–83); Mem. Cttee, Lloyd's Insce Brokers Assoc., 1960–63 and 1965–68 (Dep. Chm. 1965, Chm. 1966); Mem., Gen. Cttee, Lloyd's Register of Shipping, 1978–81; Chm., Insce Section, London Chamber of Commerce, 1963–64; Vice-Pres., Insce Inst. of London, 1967; Member: Council, Chartered Insce Inst., 1972–80; Insce Industry Trng Council, 1969; Export Guarantee Adv. Council, 1977–83 (Dep. Chm., 1982–83). Mem., Court of Assistants, Insurers' Co., 1980, Master 1984. Councillor, Chislehurst and Sidcup UDC, 1962–65 (Vice-Chm. of Council, 1964); Alderman, London Borough of Bexley, 1968–78; JP Bexley, 1967–84; DL Greater London, 1973, Representative DL, Havering, 1978–89. *Recreation:* swimming. *Address:* Farthings, Beaulieu Road, Cooden, E Sussex TN39 3AD. *T:* Cooden (04243) 2659. *Clubs:* City of London, Royal Automobile.

HIGGINS, Andrew James, PhD; MRCVS; Director, Animal Health Trust, Newmarket, since 1988; *b* 7 Dec. 1948; *s* of late Edward James Higgins and of Gabrielle Joy, *d* of late Sir John Kelland; *m* 1981, Nicola, *d* of late Peter Eliot and of Jenifer Eliot; one *s* two *d*. *Educ:* St Michael's Coll., Leeds; Royal Veterinary Coll., Univ. of London (BVetMed 1973; PhD 1985); Centre for Tropical Med., Univ. of Edinburgh (MSc 1977). Commnd RAVC 1973. Vet. Officer to Sultan of Oman, 1975–76; Vet. Advr, ME and N Africa, Wellcome Foundn, 1977–82; Cons., FAO 1981–. Member: Council, Soc. for Protection of Animals in N Africa, 1985– (Vice-Chm., 1986–89); Conservation and Welfare Cttee, Zoological Soc. of London, 1987–; Council, Brit. Equine Vet. Assoc., 1983– (Hon. Sec., 1984–88). Hon. Vet. Advr to Jockey Club, 1988–; Hon. Scientific Advr, FEI, 1990–. Editor, British Vet. Jl, 1991– (Dep. Ed., 1990–91); Mem., Adv. Bd, Equine Vet. Jl, 1985–. Univ. of London Laurel, 1971; Ciba-Geigy Prize for Res. in Animal Health, 1985; Equine Veterinary Jl Open Award and medal, 1986; Centenary Prize, Central Vet. Soc., 1986; George Flemming Prize, British Vet. Jl, 1987. *Publications:* (contrib.) An Anatomy of Veterinary Europe, 1972; (ed and contrib.) The Camel in Health and Disease, 1986; papers in sci. and gen. pubns and communications to learned socs. *Recreations:* ski-ing, riding, opera, camels. *Address:* Animal Health Trust, PO Box 5, Newmarket, Suffolk CB8 7DW. *T:* Newmarket (0638) 661111. *Club:* Buck's.

HIGGINS, Sir Christopher (Thomas), Kt 1977; Chairman, Peterborough Development Corporation, 1968–81; *b* 14 Jan. 1914; *s* of late Thomas Higgins and Florence Maud Higgins; *m* 1936, Constance Joan Beck; one *s* one *d*. *Educ:* West Kensington Central Sch.; London Univ. Executive with Granada Group Ltd, 1939–68. Served War of 1939–45: with RA, 1940–46. Member: Acton Borough Council, 1945–65; GLC, 1964–67; Hemel Hempstead Develt Corp., 1947–52; Bracknell Develt Corp., 1965–68. Chm., North Thames Gas Consumers' Council, 1969–79. *Recreations:* reading, gardening, walking; watching most sports. *Address:* 2 North Lodge, Bicester House, Kings End, Bicester, Oxon OX6 7HZ.

HIGGINS, Hon. Sir Eoin; *see* Higgins, Hon. Sir J. P. B.

HIGGINS, Frank, FCIT 1979; *b* 30 Aug. 1927; *s* of Wilfred and Hilda Higgins; *m* 1948, Betty Pulford; one *s* one *d*; *m* 1985, Margaret Roberts. *Educ:* Hanley High Sch., Stoke-on-Trent; St Paul's Coll., Cheltenham. Teacher: Stoke-on-Trent, 1946; Notts, 1948–58; Organising Sec., Youth Gp, 1958–60; Teacher, Nottingham, Derby, 1960–73; Mem. Nat. Bus Co., 1974–79. Contested (Lab) Harborough 1966, Grantham 1970. Mem., Nottingham City Council, 1971–74, 1979–87 (Chm. Transportation Cttee, 1972–74, 1979–81); Lord Mayor of Nottingham, 1986–87; Mem., Notts CC, 1973–77 and 1981–89 (Chm. Environment Cttee, 1973–77; Chm. Resources Cttee, 1981–86; Chm., Police Cttee, 1987–89); Chm., E Midlands Airport Jt Cttee, 1986–87. Chm., Central Transport Consultative Cttee, 1977–80. Chairman: Bridge Housing Assoc., 1987–; Notts Building Preservation Trust, 1988–. *Recreations:* travelling, talking. *Address:* 8 River View, The Embankment, Nottingham NG2 2GF. *T:* Nottingham (0602) 863135.

HIGGINS, Jack; *see* Patterson, Harry.

HIGGINS, John Andrew; Assistant Auditor General, National Audit Office, since 1989; *b* 19 Feb. 1940; *s* of George Henry and Mildred Maud Higgins; *m* 1965, Susan Jennifer Mathis; one *s*. *Educ:* Hendon County Sch.; Hastings Grammar Sch. ARCO. Exchequer and Audit Department: Asst Auditor, 1958; Auditor, 1968; Sen. Auditor, 1971; Chief Auditor, 1977; Dep. Dir, 1981; Office of Auditor Gen. of Canada, 1983–84; Dir, Nat. Audit Office, 1984. Hon. Mem., CIPFA, 1984–. Mem., Crawley and Horsham Dist Organists' Assoc., 1989–. *Recreations:* classical organ playing, golf, bridge, gardening, supporting Crystal Palace. *Address:* Zaria, 65 Milton Mount Avenue, Pound Hill, Crawley, Sussex RH10 3DP. *T:* Crawley (0293) 883869. *Club:* Ifield Golf and Country.

HIGGINS, Prof. John Christopher, CEng, FIEE; CBIM; Director of Management Centre, University of Bradford, and Professor of Management Sciences, 1972–89, Hon. Professor, since 1989; *b* 9 July 1932; *s* of Sidney James Higgins and Margaret Eileen Higgins (*née* Dealtrey); *m* 1960, Margaret Edna Howells; three *s*. *Educ:* Gonville and Caius Coll., Cambridge (MA); Univ. of London (BSc, MSc); PhD Bradford. Short service commission, RAF, 1953–56; 1956–70: Electronics Industry; Dept of Chief Scientist (RAF) in MoD; management consultancy; Director of Economic Planning and Research for IPC Newspapers Ltd. Member: Final Selection Bd for Civil Service Commn, 1976–; Defence Scientific Adv. Council's Assessments Bd, 1976–83 (Chm. of its Cttee on Operational Analysis, 1980–83); UGC Sub-Cttee on Management and Business Studies, 1979–85; Yorks, Humberside and Midlands Industrial Develt Bd, 1988–; Chm., Social Sciences Res. Council's Accountancy Steering Cttee and Member of its Management and Industrial Relns Cttee, 1976–80. Vis. Fellow, Wolfson Coll., Cambridge, 1985; Vis. Prof., Open Business School, 1991–. *Publications:* Information Systems for Planning and Control: concepts and cases, 1976, new edn as Computer-Based Planning Systems, 1985; Strategic and Operational Planning Systems: Principles and Practice, 1980; numerous papers and articles on corporate planning, information systems and management educn. *Recreations:* violin/viola (ex National Youth Orchestra of Great Britain), cricket, fell-walking. *Address:* Woodfield, 36 Station Road, Baildon, West Yorkshire BD17 5NW. *T:* Bradford (0274) 592836.

HIGGINS, Hon. Sir John Patrick Basil, (Sir Eoin), Kt 1988; **Hon. Mr Justice Higgins;** a Judge of the High Court of Northern Ireland, since 1984; Deputy Chairman, Boundary Commission for Northern Ireland, since 1989; *b* 14 June 1927; *e s* of late John A. and Mary Philomena Higgins, Magherafelt; *m* 1960, Bridget, *e d* of late Dr Matthew F. O'Neill, Hollingwood, Chesterfield; two *s* three *d*. *Educ:* St. Columb's Coll., Derry; Queen's Univ., Belfast (LLB). Called to Bar of N Ireland, 1948, Bencher, 1969–71 and 1983–; QC (N Ire.) 1967; County Court Judge, 1971–84: Armagh and Fermanagh, 1976–79; S Antrim, 1979–82; Recorder of Belfast, 1982–84. Chairman: Mental Health Review Tribunal for NI, 1963–71; Legal Aid Adv. Cttee (NI), 1975–82; Council of HM County Court Judges, 1978–84; Member: County Court Rules Cttee (NI), 1973–82 (Chm., 1982–84); Statute Law Cttee of NI, 1975–; Lowry Cttee on Registration of Title in NI, 1958–67; Jones Cttee on County Courts and Magistrates' Courts in NI, 1972–73; Gardiner Cttee on measures to deal with terrorism in NI, 1974. Chm., Voluntary Service, Belfast, 1975–85. Member: Community Peace Conf., 1969; Bd of Management, St Joseph's Coll. of Educn, Belfast, 1969–85; Bd of Governors, Dominican Coll., Portstewart, 1974–84. *Address:* The Royal Courts of Justice (Ulster), Belfast, Northern Ireland.

HIGGINS, Very Rev. Michael John; Dean of Ely, since 1991; *b* 31 Dec. 1935; *s* of Claud John and Elsie Higgins; *m* 1976, Beryl Margaret; one *d*. *Educ:* Whitchurch Grammar Sch., Cardiff; Univ. of Birmingham (LLB 1957); Gonville and Caius Coll., Cambridge (LLB 1959, PhD 1962); Harvard Univ.; Ridley Hall, Cambridge. Lectr in English Law, Univ. of Birmingham, 1961–63. Ordained, 1965; Curate, Ormskirk Parish Church, dio. of Liverpool, 1965–68; Selection Sec., ACCM, 1968–74; Vicar, Frome and Priest-in-charge of Woodlands, dio. of Bath and Wells, 1974–80; Rector of Preston, and Leader of Preston Town Centre Team Ministry, dio. of Blackburn, 1980–91. *Publication:* The Vicar's House, 1988. *Recreations:* music, walking, travel. *Address:* The Deanery, Ely, Cambridgeshire CB7 4DN. *T:* (0353) 667735.

HIGGINS, Prof. Peter Matthew, OBE 1987; Bernard Sunley Professor and Chairman of Department of General Practice, United Medical Schools of Guy's and St Thomas' Hospitals (formerly Guy's Hospital Medical School), University of London, 1974–88, now Emeritus Professor; *b* 18 June 1923; *s* of Peter Joseph Higgins and Margaret Higgins; *m* 1952, Jean Margaret Lindsay Currie; three *s* one *d*. *Educ:* St Ignatius' Coll., London; UCH, London. MB, BS; FRCP, FRCGP. House Phys., Medical Unit, UCH, 1947; RAMC, 1948–49; House Phys., UCH, St Pancras, 1950; Resident MO, UCH, 1951–52; Asst Med. Registrar, UCH, 1953; Gen. Practice, Rugeley, Staffs, 1954–66, and Castle Vale, Birmingham, 1966–68; Sen. Lectr, Guy's Hosp. Med. Sch., 1968–74. Vice-Chm., SE Thames RHA, 1976–. Chm., Kent FHSA, 1990–. Mem., National Council Family Service Units, 1985–; Chm. Management Cttee, Thamesmead Family Service Unit, 1985–. *Publications:* articles in Lancet, BMJ, Jl RCGP. *Recreations:* squash, swimming, sailing. *Address:* Wallings, Heathfield Lane, Chislehurst, Kent. *T:* 081–467 2756.

HIGGINS, Reynold Alleyne, LittD; FBA 1972; FSA; *b* Weybridge, 26 Nov. 1916; *er s* of late Charles Alleyne Higgins and late Marjorie Edith (*née* Taylor); *m* 1947, Patricia Mary, *d* of J. C. Williams; three *s* two *d*. *Educ:* Sherborne Sch.; Pembroke Coll., Cambridge (Scholar). First Cl., Classical Tripos pts I and II, 1937, 1938; MA, 1960; LittD, 1963. Served War: Queen Victoria's Rifles, KRRC, 1939–46 (Captain, PoW). Asst Keeper, Dept of Greek and Roman Antiquities, British Museum, 1947, Dep. Keeper, 1965–77, Acting Keeper, 1976. Visiting Fellow, British School of Archaeology at Athens, 1969,

Chm., Managing Cttee, 1975–79; Norton Lectr, Archaeol Inst. of America, 1982–83. Corr. Mem., German Archaeological Inst. *Publications:* Catalogue of Terracottas in British Museum, vols I and II, 1954, 1959; Greek and Roman Jewellery, 1961, 2nd edn 1980; Greek Terracotta Figures, 1963; Jewellery from Classical Lands, 1965; Greek Terracottas, 1967; Minoan and Mycenaean Art, 1967, 2nd edn 1981; The Greek Bronze Age, 1970; The Archaeology of Minoan Crete, 1973; The Aegina Treasure, 1979; Tanagra and the Figurines, 1986; also articles and reviews in British and foreign periodicals. *Recreation:* travel. *Address:* Hillside Cottage, Dunsfold, near Godalming, Surrey GU8 4PB. *T:* Dunsfold (048649) 400.

HIGGINS, Prof. Rosalyn, JSD; QC 1986; Professor of International Law at the London School of Economics, University of London, since 1981; *b* 2 June 1937; *d* of Lewis Cohen and Fay Inberg; *m* 1961, Rt Hon. Terence Langley Higgins, *qv*; one *s* one *d*. *Educ:* Burlington Grammar Sch., London; Girton Coll., Cambridge (Scholar; BA 1958, 1st Cl. Law Qualifying 1, 1st Cl. Tripos Pt II; 1st Cl. LLB 1959); Yale Law Sch., (JSD 1962). UK Intern, Office of Legal Affairs, UN, 1958; Commonwealth Fund Fellow, 1959; Vis. Fellow, Brookings Instn, Washington, DC, 1960; Jun. Fellow in Internat. Studies, LSE, 1961–63; Staff Specialist in Internat. Law, RIIA, 1963–74; Vis. Fellow, LSE, 1974–78; Prof. of Internat. Law, Univ. of Kent at Canterbury, 1978–81. Vis. Prof. of Internat. Law: Stanford Univ., 1975; Yale Univ., 1977. Bencher, Inner Temple, 1989. Mem., UN Cttee on Human Rights, 1985–. Hague Lectures on Internat. Law, 1982. Vice Pres., Amer. Soc. of Internat. Law, 1972–74 (Certif. of Merit, 1971). Associé de l'Institut de Droit International. Dr *hc* Univ. of Paris XI, 1980. Membre de l'Ordre des Palmes Académiques (France). *Publications:* The Development of International Law through the Political Organs of the United Nations, 1963; Conflict of Interests: international law in a divided world, 1965; The Administration of the United Kingdom Foreign Policy through the United Nations, 1966; (ed with James Fawcett) Law in Movement—essays in memory of John McMahon, 1974; UN Peacekeeping: documents and commentary: Vol. I, Middle East, 1969; Vol. II, Asia, 1971; Vol. III, Africa, 1980; Vol. IV, Europe, 1981; articles for law jls and jls of internat. relations. *Recreations:* golf, cooking, eating. *Address:* London School of Economics, Houghton Street, WC2A 2AE; 4 Essex Court, Temple, EC4Y 9AJ. *T:* 071–583 9191.

HIGGINS, Rt. Hon. Terence (Langley); PC 1979; MP (C) Worthing since 1964; *b* 18 Jan. 1928; *s* of late Reginald and Rose Higgins, Dulwich; *m* 1961, Prof. Rosalyn Higgins, *qv*; one *s* one *d*. *Educ:* Alleyn's Sch., Dulwich; Gonville and Caius Coll., Cambridge. Brit. Olympic Team (athletics) 1948, 1952; BA (Hons) 1958. MA 1963; Pres. Cambridge Union Soc., 1958. NZ Shipping Co., 1948–55; Lectr in Economic Principles, Dept of Economics, Yale Univ., 1958–59; Economist with Unilever, 1959–64. Dir, Lex Service Group, 1980–. Sec., Cons. Parly Finance Cttee, 1965–66; Opposition Spokesman on Treasury and Economic Affairs, 1966–70; Minister of State, Treasury, 1970–72; Financial Sec. to Treasury, 1972–74; Opposition Spokesman: on Treasury and Econ. Affairs, 1974; for Trade, 1974–76; Chairman: Cons. Parly Cttees, on Sport, 1979–81, Transport, 1979–; Select Cttee on Procedure, 1980–83; Select Cttee on Treasury and CS, 1983– (Mem., 1980–); House of Commons Liaison Cttee, 1984–; Member: Public Accounts Commn, 1984–; Exec. Cttee, 1922 Cttee, 1980–. Member: Council, RIIA, 1979–85; Council, IAM, 1979–. Governor: NIESR, 1989–; Dulwich Coll., 1980–. Special Fellow, PSI, 1986; (Mem. Council, 1989–); Trustee, Industry and Parlt Trust, 1985–; Hon. Mem., Keynes College, Univ. of Kent, 1976–. *Address:* c/o House of Commons, SW1A 0AA. *Clubs:* Yale; Hawks (Cambridge); Royal Blackheath Golf, Worthing Golf.

HIGGINS, Wilfred Frank; *see* Higgins, Frank.

HIGGINS, Rear-Adm. William Alleyne, CB 1985; CBE 1980; government servant; *b* 18 May 1928; *s* of Comdr H. G. Higgins, DSO, RN, and Mrs L. A. Higgins; *m* 1963, Wiltraud Hiebaum; two *s* one *d*. *Educ:* Wellington College. Joined Royal Navy, 1945; Commander 1965; Captain 1973; Commodore, HMS Drake, 1980–82; Flag Officer Medway and Port Adm. Chatham, 1982–83; Dir. Gen. Naval Personal Services, 1983–86; Chief Naval Supply and Secretariat Officer, 1983–86. *Recreations:* skiing, rock climbing and mountaineering. *Club:* Royal Naval and Royal Marines Mountaineering.

HIGGINSON, Dr Gordon Robert; Vice-Chancellor, University of Southampton, since 1985; *b* 8 Nov. 1929; *s* of Frederick John and Letitia Higginson; *m* 1954, Marjorie Forbes Rannie; three *s* two *d*. *Educ:* Leeds Univ. BSc, PhD. FICE; FIMechE. Scientific Officer, then Sen. Scientific Officer, Min. of Supply, 1953–56; Lectr, Leeds Univ., 1956–62; Associate Prof., RMCS, Shrivenham, 1962–65; Durham University: Prof. of Engrg, 1965–85; Dean of Faculty of Science, 1972–75. Dir (non-exec.), Rolls-Royce, 1988–. Member: Engineering Council, 1986–; SERC, 1989– (Chm., Engrg Bd, 1989–). IMechE James Clayton Fund Prize, 1963 and 1979; Gold Medal, Brit. Soc. of Rheology, 1969. *Publications:* Elastohydrodynamic Lubrication (with D. Dowson), 1966, 2nd edn 1977; Foundations of Engineering Mechanics, 1974; papers on mechanics in various jls. *Address:* The University, Southampton SO9 5NH. *T:* Southampton (0703) 592801.

HIGGS, Air Vice-Marshal Barry, CBE 1981; Director General, Fertiliser Manufacturers Association, since 1987; *b* 22 Aug. 1934; *s* of late Percy Harold Higgs and of Ethel Eliza Higgs; *m* 1957, Sylvia May Wilks; two *s*. *Educ:* Finchley County Secondary Grammar Sch. Served with Nos 207, 115, 138, 49 and 51 Sqdns, 1955–70; sc 1968; Forward Policy (RAF), 1971–73; ndc 1974; Comd No 39 (PR) Sqdn, 1975–77; Asst Dir Defence Policy, 1978–79; Comd RAF Finningley, 1979–81; RCDS 1982; Dep. Dir of Intelligence, 1983–85; ACDS (Overseas), 1985–87. *Recreations:* cruising, bridge, gardening, the outdoors, theatre. *Address:* 33 Parsonage Street, Cambridge CB5 8DN. *T:* Cambridge (0223) 69062. *Clubs:* Royal Air Force, Farmers'.

HIGGS, Brian James, QC 1974; a Recorder of the Crown Court, since 1974; Barrister-at-Law; *b* 24 Feb. 1930; *s* of James Percival Higgs and Kathleen Anne Higgs; *m* 1st, 1953, Jean Cameron DuMerton; two *s* three *d*; 2nd, 1980, Vivienne Mary Johnson; one *s*. *Educ:* Wrekin Coll.; London Univ. Served RA, 1948–50 (2nd Lieut). Called to Bar, Gray's Inn, 1955, Bencher, 1986; Mem., Hon. Soc. of Inner Temple (*ad eundem*), 1987. Contested (C) Romford, 1966. *Recreations:* gardening, golf, wine, chess, bridge. *Address:* Butt Hatch House, Dunmow Road, Fyfield, Essex CM5 0NT. *T:* Fyfield (0277) 899509; 9 King's Bench Walk, Temple, EC4Y 7DX. *T:* 071–353 5638. *Club:* Thorndon Park Golf.

HIGGS, Rt. Rev. Hubert Laurence, MA Cantab; *b* 23 Nov. 1911; *s* of Frank William and Mary Ann Higgs; *m* 1936, Elizabeth Clare (*née* Rogers); one *s* one *d*. *Educ:* University Coll. Sch.; Christ's Coll., Cambridge; Ridley Hall, Cambridge. Curate: Holy Trinity, Richmond, 1935; St Luke's, Redcliffe Square, London, 1936–38; St John's, Boscombe (and Jt Sec. Winchester Youth Council), 1938–39. Vicar, Holy Trinity, Aldershot, 1939–45; Editorial Sec., Church Missionary Soc., 1945–52; Vicar, St John's, Woking, 1952–57 (Rural Dean, 1957); Archdeacon of Bradford and Canon Residentiary of Bradford Cathedral, 1957–65; Bishop Suffragan of Hull, 1965–76; RD of Hull, 1972–76; retired 1976. *Recreations:* history, music-listening, gardening. *Address:* The Farmstead, Chediston, Halesworth, Suffolk IP19 0AS. *T:* Halesworth (09867) 2621.

HIGGS, Sir (John) Michael (Clifford), Kt 1969; DL; solicitor, retired; *b* 30 May 1912; *s* of late Alderman A. W. Higgs, Cranford House, Stourton, Staffs; *m* 1st, 1936, Diana Louise Jerrams (*d* 1950); two *d*; 2nd, 1952, Rachel Mary Jones, OBE; one *s* one *d*. *Educ:* St Cuthberts, Malvern; Shrewsbury. LLB (Birmingham), 1932. Admitted solicitor, 1934. Served War of 1939–45 with 73 HAA Regt RA (TA), 1939–42; JAG Staff, 1942–46; demobilised, 1946, with rank of Lieut-Col. Mem. of Staffs County Council, 1946–49; MP (C) Bromsgrove Div. of Worcs, 1950–55; Member: Worcs CC, 1953–73 (Chm. 1959–73; Alderman, 1963); Hereford and Worcester CC, 1973–85 (Chm., 1973–77); West Midlands Economic Planning Council, 1965–79; Chm., W Midlands Planning Authorities' Conf., 1969–73. DL Worcs 1968, Hereford and Worcester, 1974. *Address:* Pixham Cottage, Callow End, Worcester WR2 4TH. *T:* Worcester (0905) 830645.

HIGGS, Sir Michael; *see* Higgs, Sir J. M. C.

HIGGS, Prof. Peter Ware, PhD; FRS 1983; FRSE; Professor of Theoretical Physics, University of Edinburgh, since 1980; *b* 29 May 1929; *s* of Thomas Ware Higgs and Gertrude Maud (*née* Coghill); *m* 1963, Jo Ann, *d* of Jo C. and Meryl Williamson, Urbana, Ill; two *s*. *Educ:* Cotham Grammar Sch., Bristol; King's Coll., Univ. of London (BSc, MSc; PhD 1954). FRSE 1974. Royal Commn for Exhibn of 1851 Sen. Student, KCL, 1953–54 and Univ. of Edinburgh, 1954–55; Sen. Res. Fellow, Univ. of Edinburgh, 1955–56; ICI Res. Fellow, UCL, 1956–57 and Imperial Coll., 1957–58; Lectr in Maths, UCL, 1958–60; Lectr in Mathematical Physics, 1960–70, and Reader in Math. Physics, 1970–80, Univ. of Edinburgh. Hughes Medal, Royal Soc., 1981; Rutherford Medal, Inst. of Physics, 1984. *Publications:* papers on molecular vibrations and spectra, classical and quantum field theories, and on spontaneous breaking of gauge symmetries in theories of elementary particles. *Recreations:* walking, swimming, listening to music. *Address:* 2 Darnaway Street, Edinburgh EH3 6BG. *T:* 031–225 7060.

HIGHAM, Geoffrey Arthur; Chairman, Rugby Group PLC, since 1986 (Director, since 1979); Director and Trustee, Building Centre Group, since 1982 (Chairman, 1984–88); *b* 17 April 1927; *s* of Arthur and Elsie Higham; *m* 1951, Audrey Hill; one *s* and *d*. *Educ:* King William Coll., IOM; St Catharine's Coll., Cambridge (MA MechScis). CBIM 1975. Served RE, 1945–48. Metal Box Co., 1950–64; Montague Burton, 1964–65; Cape Industries, 1965–85: Man. Dir, 1971–80; Chm., 1980–85; Industrial Dir, Charter Consolidated, 1980–87; Director: Pirelli General, 1987–; Travers Morgan, 1988–; Try Gp, 1989–. Chm., BIM Foundn, 1981–83; Vice Chm., Council, BIM, 1984–88; Mem. Council, 1978–88, Chm., 1980–82, UK S Africa Trade Assoc. Trustee, Mansfield Coll., Oxford, 1988–. FRSA 1989. *Recreations:* music, cricket, gardening. *Address:* 32 East St Helen Street, Abingdon, Oxfordshire OX14 5EB. *T:* Abingdon (0235) 529815. *Clubs:* Army and Navy, Middlesex CC.

HIGHAM, John Drew, CMG 1956; *b* 28 Nov. 1914; *s* of Richard and Margaret Higham, Pendleton, Lancs; *m* 1st, 1936, Mary Constance Bromage (*d* 1974); three *d*; 2nd, 1976, Katharine Byard Pailing, FRTPI. *Educ:* Manchester Grammar Sch.; Gonville and Caius Coll., Cambridge (Scholar). Asst Principal, Admiralty, 1936; Asst Private Sec. to First Lord, 1939; Private Sec. to Parliamentary Sec. and Parliamentary Clerk, 1940; Principal, Admiralty, 1941; transferred to Colonial Office, 1946; Asst Sec. Colonial Office, 1948; seconded to Singapore as Under Sec., 1953, and as Dir of Personnel, 1955–57 (acted on various occasions as Chief Sec.); Asst Sec., Min. of Housing and Local Govt, 1965; Head of Development Control Div., DoE, 1970–74. Vice-Chm., Bredon Parish Council, 1985–87. Chevalier 1st Cl. Order of St Olaf (Norway), 1948. *Recreations:* history of art, gardening. *Address:* Avonside, Bredon, Tewkesbury, Glos GL20 7EG. *T:* Bredon (0684) 72468. *Club:* National Liberal.

HIGHAM, Norman, OBE 1984; Librarian, University of Bristol, 1966–89; *b* 14 June 1924; *s* of John Henry Higham, MM, and Edith Fanny (*née* Hubbard); *m* 1954, Jean Elizabeth, *d* of Frederick William and Isabel Traylen; one *s* one *d*. *Educ:* Firth Park Grammar Sch., Sheffield; Univ. of Sheffield (BA 1st Cl. Hons English, Philos., Spanish); MA Leeds 1961. ALA 1956. Served RNVR, 1942–46 (Lieut Coastal Forces). Assistant Librarian: Univ. of Sheffield, 1953–57; Univ. of Leeds, 1957–62; Librarian, Loughborough Coll. of Advanced Technology, 1962–63; Dep. Librarian, Univ. of Leeds, 1963–66. Mem. Council, Standing Conf. on Nat. and Univ. Libraries, 1972–75 and 1979–86 (Chm., 1976–79); Pres., LA, 1983 (Mem. Council, 1975–86, Chm., 1978–81 and 1985–87); Member: UGC Steering Gp on Liby Res., 1977–83; Brit. Liby Bd, 1986–89 (Adv. Council, 1976–79, and 1990–); Liby and Inf. Services Council (England), 1977–83; Sci. Inf. Cttee, Royal Soc., 1982–; Standing Cttee on Libraries, CVCP, 1982–89; Nat. Cttee on Regl Liby Co-operation, 1985–89; Chm., Liby and Inf. Co-operation Council, 1989–. Mem. Council and Trustee, Oxfam, 1973–79 and 1980–86. Hon. DLitt Bristol, 1989. *Publications:* A Very Scientific Gentleman: the major works of Henry Clifton Sorby, 1963; Computer Needs for University Library Operations, 1973; The Library in the University: observations on a service, 1980; articles and reviews in librarianship and history of science. *Recreations:* literature and the arts, music, golf. *Address:* 30 York Gardens, Clifton, Bristol BS8 4LN. *T:* Bristol (0272) 736264.

HIGHAM, Rear-Adm. Philip Roger Canning, CB 1972; *b* 9 June 1920; *s* of Edward Higham, Stoke Bishop, Bristol; *m* 1942, Pamela Bracton Edwards, *er d* of Gerald Edwards, Southport, Lancs; two *s*. *Educ:* RNC Dartmouth. Cadet, 1937; Midshipman, 1938; Sub-Lt 1940; Lieut 1942; qual. Gunnery Officer, 1944; Second Gunnery Off., HMS Vanguard, Royal Tour of S Africa, 1947; psc 1948; Exper. Dept, HMS Excellent, 1951–52; Comdr, Devonport Gunnery Sch., 1953; Trials Comdr, RAE Aberporth, 1954–55; jssc 1956; Exper. Comdr, HMS Excellent, 1957–59; Admty (DTWP), 1960–61; Naval Attaché, Middle East, 1962–64; idc 1965; Dep. Chief Polaris Exec., 1966–68; Cdre i/c Hong Kong, 1968–70; Asst Chief of Naval Staff (Op. Requirements), 1970–72; retired list 1973; Dir, HMS Belfast Trust, 1973–78; Keeper, HMS Belfast, Imperial War Mus., 1978–83. Trustee, Portsmouth Naval Base Property Trust, 1985–. *Recreations:* gardening, fishing. *Address:* Apple Tree Farm, Prinsted, Emsworth, Hants PO10 8HS. *T:* Emsworth (0243) 372195. *Club:* Naval and Military.

HIGHET, Helen Clark; *see* MacInnes, H. C.

HIGHSMITH, Patricia; writer since 1942; *b* 19 Jan. 1921; *o c* of Jay Bernard Plangman and Mary Coates (of German and English-Scots descent respectively); name changed to Highsmith on mother's 2nd marriage; unmarried. *Educ:* Barnard Coll., Columbia Univ., New York. For a year after univ. had a mediocre writing job; after that free-lance until publication of first novel. Lived in Europe and America alternately from 1951, and now has been some years in Switzerland. Prix Littéraire (Deauville), 1987. Officier, l'Ordre des Arts et des Lettres (France), 1990. *Publications: novels:* Strangers on a Train, 1950; The Blunderer, 1955; The Talented Mr Ripley, 1956; Deep Water, 1957; A Game for the Living, 1958; This Sweet Sickness, 1960 (filmed 1979); The Cry of the Owl, 1962; The Two Faces of January, 1964; The Glass Cell, 1965; A Suspension of Mercy, 1965; Those Who Walk Away, 1967; The Tremor of Forgery, 1969; Ripley Under Ground, 1971; A Dog's Ransom, 1972; Ripley's Game, 1974 (filmed as The American Friend, 1978); Edith's Diary, 1977; The Boy Who Followed Ripley, 1980; People Who Knock on the Door, 1983; Found in the Street, 1986; Carol, 1990 (published as The Price of Salt, 1953, under pseudonym Claire Morgan); Ripley under Water, 1991; *short stories:* The Animal-Lover's Book of Beastly Murder, 1975; Little Tales of Misogyny, 1977; Slowly, Slowly in the Wind, 1979; The Black House, 1981; Mermaids on the Golf Course, 1985; Plotting and Writing Suspense Fiction, 1966, 2nd edn, 1983; Tales of Natural and Unnatural Catastrophes, 1987. *Recreations:* drawing, some painting, carpentering, snail-watching, travelling by train. *Club:* Detection.

HIGMAN, Prof. Graham, MA, DPhil; FRS 1958; Waynflete Professor of Pure Mathematics, Oxford University, and Fellow of Magdalen College, Oxford, 1960–84, now Professor Emeritus; *b* 1917; 2nd *s* of Rev. Joseph Higman; *m* 1941, Ivah May Treleaven (*d* 1981); five *s* one *d*. *Educ:* Sutton Secondary Sch., Plymouth; Balliol Coll., Oxford (Hon. Fellow 1984). Meteorological Office, 1940–46; Lecturer, University of Manchester, 1946–55; Reader in Mathematics at Oxford Univ., 1955–60; Senior Research Fellow, Balliol Coll., Oxford, 1958–60. George A. Miller Vis. Prof., Univ. of Illinois, 1984–86. Hon. DSc Exeter, 1979. De Morgan Medal, London Mathematical Soc., 1974; Sylvester Medal, Royal Soc., 1979. *Publications:* papers in Proc. London Math. Soc., and other technical jls. *Address:* 64 Sandfield Road, Oxford.

HIGNETT, John Mulock, FCA; Finance Director, Glaxo Holdings plc, since 1988; *b* 9 March 1934; *s* of Reginald and Marjorie Hignett; *m* 1961, Marijke Inge de Boer; one *s* one *d*. *Educ:* Harrow Sch.; Magdalene Coll., Cambridge (MA). Kemp Chatteris & Co., 1958–61; Deloitte & Co., 1961–63; joined Lazard Brothers & Co. Ltd, 1963; Manager, Issues Dept, 1971; Dir, 1972; Head of Corporate Finance Div., 1980; Man. Dir, 1984–88. Director-General: Panel on Take-Overs and Mergers, 1981–83; Council for the Securities Industry, 1983. *Address:* Glaxo Holdings plc, Lansdowne House, Berkeley Square W1X 6BP. *Clubs:* MCC; Hawks (Cambridge).

HIGNETT, Peter George; Regional Veterinary Officer, People's Dispensary for Sick Animals, 1982–90, retired; *b* 3 June 1925; *s* of Harry Sutton Hignett and Annie Hignett; *m* 1948, Patricia Bishop (marr. diss. 1988); two *s* one *d*. *Educ:* Pontesbury C of E Sch.; King Edward VI Sch., Birmingham; Univ. of Liverpool (MRCVS). General practice, 1947–49; Wellcome Veterinary Res. Station, 1949–54; Reader in Veterinary Reproduction, Univ. of Glasgow, 1954–76; Gen. Man., Hampshire Cattle Breeders' Soc., 1976–82. Mem. Council, RCVS, 1972–, Pres., 1981–82; President: Soc. for Study of Animal Breeding, 1966–68; Southern Counties Veterinary Soc., 1983–84; Secretary: Associated AI Centres, 1977–82; Edgar Meml Trust, 1977–82; Member: Trehane Cttee, 1979–82; Scientific Adv. Cttee, Animal Health Trust, 1983–85. Gov., Berks Coll. of Agric., 1990–. *Publications:* scientific papers on fertility in domestic animals. *Recreations:* gardening, sailing, music. *Address:* 70 Stonerock Cottages, Chilgrove, Chichester, W Sussex PO18 9NA. *T:* East Marden (024359) 330. *Club:* Farmers'.

HIGSON, Gordon Robert; consultant on medical technology; Chairman, Medical Technology Consultants Europe, since 1989; *b* 10 June 1932; *s* of Robert and Agnes Higson; *m* 1955, Eileen Mary Warrington; two *s* one *d*. *Educ:* Thornleigh Coll., Bolton; Manchester Univ. (BSc 1954). FInstP 1968; FIEE 1978. Fairey Aviation Co., 1954–59; NCB Mining Res. Estabt, 1959–68; Department of Health and Social Security: Scientific and Tech. Services Br., 1969; Dir of Scientific and Tech. Services, 1980–84; Controller of Supply, 1984–85; Dir, Supplies Technology Div., 1986–88; Sec. Gen., Internat. Assoc. of Med. Prosthesis Manufacturers, 1988–90. Mayneord Lectr, BIR, 1986. *Publications:* papers in scientific and tech. jls. *Recreations:* walking, theatre. *Address:* 31 Firfield Road, Addlestone, Surrey KT15 1QU. *T:* Weybridge (0932) 846677.

HIGTON, Dennis John, CEng, FIMechE, FRAeS; company director and consultant; *b* 15 July 1921; *s* of John William and Lillian Harriett Higton; *m* 1945, Joy Merrifield Pickett; one *s* one *d*. *Educ:* Guildford Technical Sch.; RAE Farnborough Technical Sch. Mid-Wessex Water Co., 1937. RAE Engineering Apprentice, 1938–42; RAE Aerodynamics Dept (Aero Flight), 1942–52; learned to fly at No 1 EFTS RAF Panshangar, 1946; A&AEE Boscombe Down, Head of Naval Test and Supt of Performance, 1953–66; British Defence Staff, Washington DC, USA, 1966–70; MoD(PE) Anglo-French Helicopter Production, 1970–72; Director Aircraft Production, 1972–75; Under-Sec. and Dir-Gen. of Mil. Aircraft Projects, MoD, 1976–79, of Aircraft 4, 1979–80, of Aircraft 3, 1980–81; Hd, Engrg Profession, Air Systems Controllerate, MoD, 1976–81. Chm., Technology Div., CS Commn, 1984–89. Mem., Fleet Air Arm Officers Assoc., 1960–. Chm., S Wilts and Salisbury Br., NSPCC, 1982–. Mem., Exec. Cttee, Salisbury Gp of Artists, 1987–. *Publications:* research and memoranda papers mainly on aerodynamic flight testing. *Recreations:* beekeeping, skiing, sailing, gardening, walking on Salisbury Plain, shooting, art student at Southampton. *Address:* Jasmine Cottage, Rollestone Road, Shrewton, Salisbury, Wiltshire SP3 4HG. *T:* Shrewton (0980) 620276.

HILALY, Agha, HQA, SPk; Pakistan Foreign Service; *b* 20 May 1911; *s* of late Agha Abdulla; *m* 1938, Malek Taj Begum, *d* of Mirza Kazim, Bangalore; three *s*. *Educ:* Presidency Coll., Madras (MA); King's Coll., Cambridge (MA). Entered former ICS (Bengal cadre), 1936; Under-Sec., Govt of Bengal, 1939–41; Govt of India, 1941–47; entered Pakistan Foreign Service at time of Partition; Jt Sec., Min. of Foreign Affairs, 1951; Imp. Def. Coll., 1955; Ambassador to Sweden, Norway, Denmark and Finland, 1956; Delegate to UN Gen. Assembly, 1958; Ambassador to USSR and Czechoslovakia, 1959; High Commissioner in India and Ambassador to Nepal, 1961; High Commissioner for Pakistan in the UK and Ambassador to Ireland, 1963–66; Ambassador for Pakistan to the United States, 1966–71, also accredited to Mexico, Venezuela and Jamaica. Rep. for Pakistan to UN Human Rights Commn, 1981–84; Mem., UN Cttee on Missing Persons, Geneva, 1980–90. Member Central Bd of Directors: State Bank of Pakistan, 1973–; Federal Bank of Co-operatives (Islamabad), 1973–. Chm. Bd of Govs, Pakistan Inst. of Strategic Studies, 1972–78. Hilal-i-Quaid-i-Azam, Pakistan; Star of Pakistan; Grand Cross, Order of the North Star, Sweden; Grand Cross, Prabol Gurkha Dakshana Bahu (Nepal). *Recreations:* colour photography, shooting. *Address:* 22B Circular Street, Phase 2, Defence Housing Society, Karachi, Pakistan. *Clubs:* Travellers'; International (Washington); Sind (Karachi).

HILARY, David Henry Jephson, CB 1991; Receiver for the Metropolitan Police District, since 1987; *b* 3 May 1932; *s* of late Robert and Nita Hilary; *m* 1957, Phœbe Leonora, *d* of John J. Buchanan and Phoebe (*née* Messel); two *s* two *d*. *Educ:* Tonbridge Sch.; King's Coll., Cambridge (Sandys Student 1954, Craven Student 1955; MA). Royal Artillery, 1953–54. Home Office, 1956–87; Cabinet Office, 1967–69 and 1981–83; Asst Under Sec. of State, Home Office, 1975–87. *Recreations:* cricket, bridge, family pursuits. *Address:* 17 Victoria Square, SW1. *Clubs:* Royal Automobile, MCC.

HILD, Maj.-Gen. John Henry, MBE 1969; CEng, FIEE; FBIM; Director: Siemens (UK) plc, since 1984; Siemens Plessey Electronic Systems Ltd, since 1989; consultant, since 1984; *b* 28 March 1931; *m* 1954, Janet Macdonald Brown; one *s* one *d*. *Educ:* Blackfriars, Laxton; Sandhurst. Joined Army, 1949; commissioned, 1952; Korea, 1952–53; sc 1961; MoD, DAQMG, 1962–64; Borneo, 1965; Hong Kong, 1966–67; 1 (BR) Corps, DAQMG, 1968–69; CO 18 Sig. Regt, 1969–71; DS, Staff Coll., 1972–73; Comd 1 Sig. Gp, 1974–76; Comdt, Sch. of Sigs, 1976–78; RCDS 1979; HQ BAOR, DQMG and CSO, 1980–84. Col Comdt, RCS, 1984–90. Dir, RCS Assoc. Trustee Ltd, 1989–. Mem., Caravan Club Council, 1985–. *Recreations:* entertaining friends, travel, sport. *Address:* c/o Lloyds Bank, 1c Church Street, Weybridge, Surrey KT13 8DA. *Club:* Army and Navy.

HILDER, Rowland, OBE 1986; RI 1938; painter; *b* Greatneck, Long Island, USA, 28 June 1905, British parents; *m* 1929, Edith Blenkiron; one *s* one *d*. *Educ:* Goldsmiths' Coll. Sch. of Art, London. Exhibited, Hayward Gall., 1983. PRI 1964–74. *Publications:* Illustrated editions of: Moby Dick, 1926; Treasure Island, 1929; Precious Bane, 1930; The Bible for To-day, 1940; The Shell Guide to Flowers of the Countryside (with Edith Hilder), 1955; (jointly) Sketching and Painting Indoors, 1957; Starting with Watercolour, 1966, expanded repr., 1988; Painting Landscapes in Watercolour, 1983 (USA, as Expressing Land, Sea and Sky in Watercolour, 1982); *relevant publications:* Rowland Hilder: painter and illustrator, by John Lewis, 1978; Rowland Hilder's England, by Denis Thomas, 1986; Rowland Hilder Country, ed by Denis Thomas, 1987; Rowland Hilder Sketching Country, ed by Denis Thomas, 1991. *Address:* 7 Kidbrooke Grove, Blackheath, SE3 0PG. *T:* 081–858 3072.

HILDRETH, Maj.-Gen. Sir (Harold) John (Crossley), KBE 1964 (CBE 1952; OBE 1945); *b* 12 June 1908; *s* of late Lt-Col H. C. Hildreth, DSO, OBE, FRCS, and late Mrs Hildreth; *m*; two *s* three *d*; *m* 1950, Mary (*d* 1988), *d* of late G. Wroe. *Educ:* Wellington Coll., Berks; RMA, Woolwich. 2nd Lieut, RA, 1928; transferred to RAOC, 1935, as Captain; Major 1944; Lieut-Col 1948; Col 1952; Brig. 1958; Maj.-Gen. 1961. War Office: Col 1942–44; Brig. 1944–47; Inspector of Establishments, 1947–50; Controller of Army Statistics, 1950–51; Comdr RAOC, Ammunition Org., 1951–53; Comdr, Bicester, 1953–57; DOS, BAOR, 1957–60; Inspector, RAOC, War Office, 1960–61; Dir of Ordnance Service, War Office, 1961–64; retired, Dec. 1964. Man. Dir, Army Kinema Corp., 1965–70, Services Kinema Corp., 1970–75. Chm. Greater London Br., SS&AFA, 1977–81. Col Commandant, RAOC, 1963–70. Legion of Merit (degree of Officer), USA. *Recreations:* shooting, sailing. *Address:* 56 The Cottages, North Street, Emsworth, Hants PO10 7PJ. *T:* Emsworth (0243) 373466. *Club:* Emsworth Sailing.

HILDRETH, (Henry) Jan (Hamilton Crossley); independent consultant; Director, Minster Trust Ltd, since 1979; Chairman: Sea Catch PLC, since 1987; Scallop Kings PLC, since 1987; non-executive Director: Dexta Estates PLC; Diveships PLC; Grampian Assured PLC, and other companies; *b* 1 Dec. 1932; *s* of Maj.-Gen. Sir (Harold) John (Crossley) Hildreth, KBE, and late Mrs Joan Elise Hallett (*née* Hamilton); *m* 1958, Wendy Moira Marjorie, *d* of late Arthur Harold Clough, CMG, OBE; two *s* one *d*. *Educ:* Wellington Coll.; The Queen's Coll., Oxford. National Service in RA, BAOR, 1952–53; 44 Parachute Bde (TA), 1953–58. Oxford, Hon. Mods (Nat. Sci.), BA (PPE) 1956, MA. Baltic Exchange, 1956; Royal Dutch Shell Group, 1957: served Philippines (marketing) and London (finance); Kleinwort, Benson Ltd, 1963; NEDO, 1965; Member of Economic Development Cttees for the Clothing, the Hosiery and Knitwear, and the Wool Textile industries; Mem., London Transport Bd, subseq. LTE, 1968–72: main responsibilities Finance, Marketing, Corp. Plan, Data Processing, and Estates; Asst Chief Exec., John Laing & Son Ltd, 1972–74; Dir-Gen., Inst. of Directors, 1975–78. Chm., Carroll Securities Ltd, 1986–91. Member: Cttee, GBA, 1978–86; Council, ISIS, 1979–82; Exec. Cttee, Industrial Soc., 1973–84; Council, British Exec. Service Overseas, 1975–; Council, Spastic Soc., 1980–83, 1985–; Revue Body for Nursing and Midwifery Staff and Professions Allied to Medicine, 1989–; Dir, Contact A Family, 1980–89. Constituency Chm., 1986–89, Pres., 1989–, Wimbledon Cons. Assoc. Governor: Wellington Coll., 1974–; Eagle House Sch., 1986–. FCIT. FRSA. *Recreations:* cross-country, mountain and road running, photography, water mills, and others. *Address:* 50 Ridgway Place, Wimbledon, SW19 4SW. *Clubs:* Athenæum; Vincent's (Oxford); Thames Hare and Hounds.

HILDREW, Bryan, CBE 1977; FEng 1976; Managing Director, Lloyds Register of Shipping, 1977–85; *b* 19 March 1920; *s* of Alexander William Hildrew and Sarah Jane (*née* Clark); *m* 1950, Megan Kathleen Lewis; two *s* one *d*. *Educ:* Bede Collegiate Sch., Sunderland; Technical Coll., Sunderland; City and Guilds, Imperial Coll., London (MSc, DIC). FIMechE, FIMarE. Engineer Officer, RN, 1941–46. Lloyds Register of Shipping: Research Surveyor, 1948–67 (Admiralty Nuclear Submarine Project, 1956–61); Chief Engineer Surveyor, 1967–70; Technical Dir, 1970–77. Chm., Abbeyfield, Orpington, 1985–. President: IMechE, 1980–81; IMarE, 1983–85; Chm., CEI, 1981–82. FCGI 1990. Hon. DEng Newcastle, 1987. *Recreations:* orienteering, walking. *Address:* 8 Westholme, Orpington, Kent. *T:* Orpington (0689) 25451.

HILDYARD, Sir David (Henry Thoroton), KCMG 1975 (CMG 1966); DFC 1943; HM Diplomatic Service, retired; *b* 4 May 1916; *s* of late His Honour G. M. T. Hildyard, QC, and Sybil, *d* of H. W. Hamilton Hoare; *m* 1947, Millicent (*née* Baron), *widow* of Wing Commander R. M. Longmore, OBE; one *s* one *d*. *Educ:* Eton; Christ Church, Oxford. Served with RAF, 1940–46. Entered HM Foreign (subseq. Diplomatic) Service, 1948; Montevideo, 1950; Madrid, 1953; FO, 1957; Counsellor, Mexico City, 1960–65; Head of Economic Relations Dept, FO, 1965–68; Minister and Alternate UK Rep. to UN, 1968–70; Ambassador to Chile, 1970–73; Ambassador and Permanent UK Rep. to UN and other International Organisations, Geneva, 1973–76; Head, UK Delegn to CSCE, 1974–75. Dir, Lombard Odier Internat. Portfolio Management, 1980–. *Address:* 97 Onslow Square, SW7 3LU. *Clubs:* Reform, Hurlingham.

HILEY, Sir Thomas (Alfred), KBE 1966; Chartered Accountant, Australia, since 1932; *b* 25 Nov. 1905; *s* of William Hiley and Maria (*née* Savage); *m* 1929, Marjory Joyce (*née* Jarrott) (*d* 1972); two *s*. *Educ:* Brisbane Grammar Sch.; University of Qld. State Public Service, 1921; Public Accountancy, 1923; in practice (Public Accountant), 1925. Qld Parliament, 1944; Dep. Leader of Opposition, 1950; Treasurer of Qld and Minister for Housing, 1957; Treasurer, 1963; Deputy Premier, 1965; retired from Parliament, 1966. Pres., Inst. of Chartered Accts in Aust., 1946–47. Hon. MCom, University of Qld, 1960. *Recreations:* shooting, fishing, cricket. *Address:* Illawong, 39 The Esplanade, Tewantin, Qld 4565, Australia. *T:* (071) 497–175. *Club:* Queensland (Brisbane).

HILL, family name of **Marquess of Downshire** and **Baron Sandys.**

HILL; *see* Clegg-Hill, family name of Viscount Hill.

HILL; *see* Erskine-Hill.

HILL, 8th Viscount *cr* 1842; **Antony Rowland Clegg-Hill;** Bt 1726–27; Baron Hill 1814; *b* 19 March 1931; *s* of 7th Viscount Hill and Elisabeth Flora (*d* 1967), *d* of Brig.-Gen. George Nowell Thomas Smyth-Osbourne, CB, CMG, DSO; *S* father, 1974; *m* 1st, 1963, Juanita Phyllis (marr. diss. 1976), *d* of John W. Pertwee, Salfords, Surrey; 2nd, 1989, Elizabeth Harriett, *d* of Ronald L. Offer, Salisbury, Wilts. *Educ:* Kelly Coll.; RMA, Sandhurst. Formerly Captain, RA. Freeman of Shrewsbury, 1957. *Heir: cousin* Peter David Raymond Charles Clegg-Hill [*b* 17 Oct. 1945; *m* 1973, Sharon Ruth Deane, Kaikohe, NZ; two *s* five *d*]. *Address:* House of Lords, SW1A 0PW.

HILL, Prof. Alan Geoffrey, MA; Professor of English Language and Literature in the University of London at Royal Holloway and Bedford New College (formerly Royal Holloway College), since 1981; *b* 12 Dec. 1931; *yr s* of Thomas Murton Hill and Alice Marion Hill (*née* Nunn); *m* 1960, Margaret Vincent Rutherford, MA; three *d*. *Educ:*

Dulwich Coll.; St Andrews Univ. (MA 1st Cl. Hons English Lang. and Lit.); Merton Coll., Oxford (BLitt). Asst Lectr/Lectr in English, Exeter Univ., 1958–62; Lectr in English, St Andrews Univ., 1962–68; Sen. Lectr in English, Dundee Univ., 1968–80. Vis. Professor of English, Univ. of Saskatchewan, 1973–74; Ext. Examr in English, Univ. of Buckingham, 1986–90. Crowsley Lectr, Charles Lamb Soc., 1981; Warton Lectr, British Acad., 1986. Founded Centre for Study of Victorian Art, RHC, 1981. Trustee, Dove Cottage Trust, 1969–; General Editor, The Letters of William and Dorothy Wordsworth, 1979–. *Publications:* The Letters of William and Dorothy Wordsworth, vol. III, The Middle Years, Part 2, 1812–1820, 2nd edn (rev. and ed with Mary Moorman), 1970; vol. IV, The Later Years, Part 1, 1821–1828, 2nd edn (rev. and ed), 1978; vol. V, The Later Years, Part 2, 1829–1834, 2nd edn (rev. and ed), 1979; vol. VI, The Later Years, Part 3, 1835–1839, 2nd edn (rev. and ed), 1982; vol. VII, The Later Years, Part 4, 1840–1853, 2nd edn (rev. and ed), 1988; (ed) Selected Letters of Dorothy Wordsworth, 1981; (ed) Selected Letters of William Wordsworth, 1984; (ed) John Henry Newman, Loss and Gain, 1986; Wordsworth's Grand Design, 1987; (ed with Ian Ker) Newman After A Hundred Years, 1990; articles and reviews in lit. and theological jls. *Recreations:* music, fine arts, ecclesiology. *Address:* 1a Northcroft Road, Englefield Green, Surrey TW20 0DP. *T:* Egham (0784) 431659. *Club:* Savile.

HILL, Alan John Wills, CBE 1972; publishing consultant; consultant to the Heinemann Group of Publishers, 1979–84 and since 1986; *b* 12 Aug. 1912; *s* of William Wills Hill and May Frances Hill; *m* 1939, Enid Adela Malin; two *s* one *d. Educ:* Wyggeston Sch., Leicester; Jesus Coll., Cambridge (Schol.). RAF, 1940–45: Specialist Armament Officer (Sqdn Ldr). Publishing Asst, Wm Heinemann Ltd, 1936–40; Dir, 1955; Man. Dir, 1959–61; Chm. and Man. Dir, Heinemann Educational Books Ltd, 1961–79; Man. Dir, Heinemann Group of Publishers Ltd, 1973–79; Chairman: Heinemann Educnl Books (Nigeria), 1969–83; Heinemann companies in Australia, Canada, Caribbean, E Africa, Hong Kong, Malaysia, NZ, Singapore and USA, 1964–79; World's Work Ltd, 1973–79; Hill MacGibbon Ltd, 1984–85; Man. Dir, Heinemann Computers in Education Ltd, 1981–84; Consultant to William Collins, 1985–86. Chm., Soc. of Bookmen, 1965–68; Chm., Educational Publishers' Council, 1969–71; Vice-Chm., Educn Technol. Project, 1985–88; Member: Council, Publishers' Assoc., 1972–79; Exec. Cttee, National Book League, 1973–79; British Council Books Adv. Panel, 1973–83; CNAA (Business Studies Panel), 1975–82; UNESCO Cttee on Copyright in third world countries; Cttee, Friends of the Lake District, 1979–. Chm. of Trustees, Ceres Trust, 1988–; Trustee, Maryport Heritage Trust, 1990–. Mem., Council, Prehistoric Soc., 1987– (PRO, 1988–). Governor, Nuffield-King's Curriculum Trust, 1979–; Mem. Council, Chelsea Coll., London Univ., 1978–85 (Vice-Chm., 1981–85); Mem. Council, King's Coll. London, 1985–89 (Hon. Fellow, 1985). Pres., Keswick Amateur Athletic Club, 1977–. Closely involved with Commonwealth literature and educn. *Publications:* (with R. W. Finn) And So Was England Born, 1939; History in Action, 1962; In Pursuit of Publishing (autobiog.), 1988; articles in jls. *Recreations:* swimming, mountain-walking, gardening. *Address:* 56 Northway, NW11 6PA. *T:* 081–455 8388; New House, Rosthwaite, Borrowdale, Cumbria. *Clubs:* Athenæum, Garrick, Royal Air Force, PEN.

HILL, Alastair Malcolm; QC 1982; a Recorder of the Crown Court, since 1982; *b* 12 May 1936; *s* of Prof. Sir Ian George Wilson Hill, CBE, LLD, FRCP, FRSE and Lady (Audrey) Hill; *m* 1969, Elizabeth Maria Innes; one *s* one *d. Educ:* Trinity Coll., Glenalmond; Keble Coll., Oxford (Stevenson-Chatterton Schol.; BA Hons Jurisp. 1959). Nat. Service, RHA, 1954–56. Called to the Bar, Gray's Inn, 1961; South Eastern Circuit. *Recreations:* collecting prints and watercolours, opera, fly-fishing. *Address:* New Court, Temple, EC4Y 9BE. *T:* 071–583 6166.

HILL, Allen; *see* Hill, H. A. O.

HILL, Antony James de Villiers; Headmaster, Melbourne Church of England Grammar School, since 1988; *b* 1 Aug. 1940; *s* of James Kenneth Hill and Hon. Yvonne Aletta Hill, *d* of 2nd Baron de Villiers; *m* 1974, Gunilla Els-Charlotte Emilie (Elsa) Nilsson; one *d. Educ:* Sydney Grammar School; Sydney Univ. (BA Hons); Boston Univ. (MEd). Law Clerk, 1962–64; Antarctic Expedition, 1964–65; Master, Canberra Grammar Sch., 1965–66; Instructor, Himalayan Mountaineering Inst., Darjeeling, 1967–68; Master, Sydney C of E Grammar Sch., 1967–72, 1977; Mem. Faculty: Phillips Acad., Andover, Mass, 1972–74; Boston Univ., 1974–76; Senior Master, King's Sch., Parramatta, 1977–81; Headmaster, Christ Church Grammar Sch., WA, 1982–87. *Recreations:* running, climbing, sailing, theatre, music, reading. *Address:* Melbourne Church of England Grammar School, Domain Road, South Yarra, Vic 3141, Australia. *T:* 03–867–7622. *Club:* Weld (Perth, WA).

HILL, Sir Arthur (Alfred), Kt 1989, CBE 1980; Chairman, Walsall District Health Authority, since 1982; *b* 14 May 1920; *s* of Arthur James Hill and Phoebe Mary Hill (*née* Prees); *m* 1947, Alma M. E. Bate, CBE; one *s* two *d. Educ:* Langley High Sch.; Halesowen Technical Coll. Served RAFVR, 1939–45. Joint Company Director: Arthur Brook Cars Ltd, 1948–68; Abro Finance Ltd, 1950–65; Cradley Heath Motor Co. Ltd, 1956–65. Chm., CPC, 1969–72, Treas., 1973–76, Chm., 1976–79, Pres., 1985–88, W Midlands Area Cons. Council; Mem., Cons. Nat. Union, 1966–80; Chairman: Kidderminster Cons. Assoc., 1964–67; Walsall S Cons. Assoc., 1981–84. Mem., Rowley Regis BC, 1948–57. Chm., Bd of Govs, Rowley Regis Grammar Sch., 1961–64. *Recreations:* travelling, golf. *Address:* Lichfield, 1 Mellish Road, Walsall, West Midlands WS4 2DQ. *T:* Walsall (0922) 34949; Esplanado de Cervantes 16, Apt 5, Piso 3, Denia, Spain. *Clubs:* Royal Over-Seas League; Calderfields Golf (Aldridge).

HILL, (Arthur) Derek; artist, writer, and organiser of exhibitions; *b* Bassett, Hampshire, 6 Dec. 1916; *s* of A. J. L. Hill and Grace Lilian Mercer. *Educ:* Marlborough Coll. Has designed sets and dresses for Covent Garden and Sadler's Wells. *One-man exhibitions:* Nicholson Gall., London, 1943; Leicester Galls, London, 1947, 1950, 1953 and 1956. *Organised exhibitions:* 1934 onwards: Dégas Exhibn for Edinburgh Fest. and Tate Gall., London, 1952; Landseer exhibn (with John Woodward) at Royal Academy, 1961, etc. Represented in exhibns, Europe and USA, 1957–; exhibns in New York, 1966 and 1969; retrospective exhibitions: Whitechapel Gall., London, 1961; Arts Council of NI, Belfast, 1970; Municipal Gall., Dublin, 1971; portraits, Marlborough Fine Arts, London, 1978; King's Lynn Fest., 1986. *Pictures owned by:* Tate Gall.; Nat. Gall. of Canada; Arts Council; Fogg Museum, Harvard; Nat. Portrait Gall. of Denmark; Liechtenstein Gall., Vaduz; National Gall. of Ireland and Municipal Gall. of Dublin; Ulster Mus., Belfast; Walker Gall., Liverpool; City Art Galleries of: Southampton, Birmingham, Bradford, Coventry, Carlisle, Sheffield, etc. FRGS. DLit TCD, 1990. *Publications:* Islamic Architecture and Its Decoration (with Prof. Oleg Grabar), 1965; Islamic Architecture in North Africa (with L. Golvin), 1976; articles in Illustrated London News, Apollo, Burlington Magazine, etc.; *relevant publication:* Derek Hill: an appreciation, by the Earl of Gowrie, 1987. *Recreations:* gardening, travelling.

HILL, Brian, CBE 1990; DL; Chief Executive and Clerk, Lancashire County Council, 1977–90; *b* 16 Oct. 1930; *m* 1954, Barbara (*née* Hickson); one *d. Educ:* Wigan Grammar Sch.; Univ. of Manchester (LLB). Solicitor. Asst Solicitor, Manchester Corp., 1953–56; Lancashire County Council: Sen. Solicitor appts, finally Second Dep. Clerk of CC, 1956–74; Dep. Clerk, 1974–76. Clerk of Lancs Lieutenancy, 1977–90; County Electoral Returning Officer, 1977–. Secretary: Lancs Adv. Cttee, 1977–90; Lord Chancellor's Adv. Cttee on Gen. Comrs of Income Tax, 1977–; Lancs Probation and After Care Cttee, 1977–; Adviser to ACC on policy matters, 1987–; Co. Sec., Lancashire County Enterprises Ltd (formerly Lancashire Enterprises), 1982–90, Mem., MSC Area Manpower Bd, 1983–86. Mem., Council on Tribunals, 1990–. Chairman: Local Govt Legal Soc., 1970–71; Soc. of County Secs, 1976–77; NW Br., SOLACE, 1985; Assoc. of County Chief Execs, 1989–90 (Sen. Vice-Chm., 1988–89). Mem., Lancs Community Council, 1990–. Vice-Pres., Lancs Youth Clubs Assoc., 1977–; Clerk to Court, 1977–89, Mem. of Council, 1990–, RNCM, Manchester (Hon. RNCM 1979); Member: Court, Univ. of Lancaster, 1977–; Council, Lancs Poly., 1990–. Sec., Lancs Cttee, Royal Jubilee and Prince's Trusts, 1985–; Chm., S Pennine Pack Horse Trails Trust, 1990–. Mem., Bd, 1989–, Dep. Chm., 1990–, Hallé Concerts Soc. Mem., Rossall Sch. Council, 1990–. DL Lancs, 1977. FRSA 1983; CBIM 1987. Hon. Fellow, Lancs Poly., 1990. *Recreation:* music. *Address:* The Cottage, Bruna Hill, Garstang, near Preston, Lancs PR3 1QB. *Club:* Royal Over-Seas League.

HILL, Sir Brian (John), Kt 1989; FRICS; FCIOB; Chairman and Chief Executive, 1983–89, Executive Chairman, 1989–91, non-executive Director, since 1991, Higgs and Hill plc; *b* 19 Dec. 1932; *s* of Doris Winifred Hill and Gerald Aubrey Hill, OBE; *m* 1959, Janet J. Newman; two *s* one *d. Educ:* Stowe School; Emmanuel College, Cambridge. BA (Land Economy); MA. Managing Director, Higgs and Hill Building Ltd, 1966–86, Group Managing Dir, 1972–83. Dir, Evonbrook Properties, 1991–. Pres., London Region, Nat. Fedn of Building Trades Employers, 1981–82; Chairman: Vauxhall Coll. of Building and Further Educn, 1976–86; Nat. Contractors Group, 1983–84; Dir, Building Centre, 1977–85; Pres., Chartered Inst. of Building, 1987–88. Property Services Agency: Mem. Adv. Bd, 1981–86; Mem. Bd, 1986–88. Mem. Cttee, Lazard Property Unit Trust, 1982–. Governor: Great Ormond Street Hosp. for Sick Children, 1985–; Aberdour Sch. Hon. FIStructE. *Recreations:* travelling, tennis, gardening. *Address:* Barrow House, The Warren, Kingswood, Surrey. *T:* Mogador (0737) 832424. *Club:* Royal Automobile.

HILL, Christopher; *see* Hill, J. E. C.

HILL, Rev. Canon Christopher John; a Canon Residentiary, since 1989 and Precentor, since 1990 of St Paul's; a Chaplain to the Queen, since 1987; *b* 10 Oct. 1945; *s* of Leonard and Frances V. Hill; *m* 1976, Hilary Ann Whitehouse; three *s* one *d. Educ:* Sebright Sch., Worcs; King's Coll., London (BD Hons; Relton Prize for Theology, 1967; MTh 1968; AKC 1967). Deacon 1969, priest 1970. Asst Curate, Dio. of Lichfield: St Michael's, Tividale, 1969–73; St Nicholas, Codsall, 1973–74; Asst Chaplain to Archbp of Canterbury for Foreign Relations, 1974–81; Archbp's Sec. for Ecumenical Affairs, 1982–89; Hon. Canon of Canterbury Cathedral, 1982–89. Anglican Secretary: Anglican-RC Internat. Commn (I), 1974–81, Internat. Commn (II), 1983–90 (Mem., 1990–); Anglican-Lutheran Eur. Commn, 1981–82; C of E—German Churches Commn, 1987–90; C of E—Nordic-Baltic Churches Commn, 1989–. Guestmaster, Nikaean Club, 1982–89. Co-Chm., London Soc. of Jews and Christians, 1991–. *Publications:* miscellaneous ecumenical articles. *Recreations:* Radio 3, mountain walking, detective stories, Italian food, unaffordable wine. *Address:* 3 Amen Court, EC4M 7BU. *T:* 071–236 4532. *Club:* Athenæum.

HILL, Rev. Canon Colin Arnold Clifford; Vicar of Croydon and Chaplain to Archbishop Whitgift Foundation, since 1973; Chaplain to the Queen, since 1990; *b* 13 Feb. 1929; *s* of William and May Hill; *m* 1st, 1957, Shirley (*d* 1961); one *s*; 2nd, 1971, Irene Chamberlain; one step *s. Educ:* Reading Sch.; Bristol Univ.; Ripon Hall Theol Coll., Oxford. Ordained deacon, Sheffield Cathedral, 1957, priest, 1958; Rotherham Parish Church; Vicar of Brightside, 1960; Rector of Easthampstead, Bracknell, 1964; Chaplain, RAF Staff Coll., 1968. Hon. Canon, Canterbury, 1975, Canon Emeritus, 1984; Hon. Canon, Southwark, 1984; Proctor in Convocation and General Synod, Dio. Oxford, 1970–73, Dios of Canterbury and Southwark, 1980–84. Religious Advr, London Borough of Croydon; Chm., Croydon Industrial Mission, 1975. Chm., Croydon Crime Prevention Initiative, 1989; Mem., Police Consultative Cttee, 1985. *Recreations:* walking, reading. *Address:* Croydon Vicarage, 22 Bramley Hill, Croydon CR2 6LT. *T:* (home) 081–688 1387; (parish office) 081–688 8104. *Clubs:* Sion, City Livery, Naval.

HILL, Prof. David Keynes, ScD; FRS 1972; Professor of Biophysics, Royal Postgraduate Medical School, University of London, 1975–82; *b* 23 July 1915; *s* of late Prof. Archibald Vivian Hill, CH, OBE, ScD, FRS, and Margaret Neville, *d* of late Dr J. N. Keynes; *m* 1949, Stella Mary Humphrey; four *d. Educ:* Highgate Sch.; Trinity Coll., Cambridge. ScD Cantab 1965. Fellow, Trinity Coll., Cambridge, 1940–48; Physiologist on staff of Marine Biological Assoc., Plymouth, 1948–49; Sen. Lectr, 1949–62, Reader in Biophysics, 1962–75, Vice-Dean, 1969–74, Royal Postgrad. Med. Sch., London Univ. Physiological Society: Editor of Journal, 1969–76; Chm., Bd of Monographs, 1979–81. *Publications:* Scientific papers in Jl Physiology. *Recreations:* woodworking, photography. *Address:* Ivy Cottage, Winksley, Ripon, N Yorks HG4 3NR. *T:* Kirkby Malzeard (0765) 658562.
See also Polly Hill.

HILL, David Neil, MA, FRCO; Organist and Master of Music, Winchester Cathedral, since 1988; *b* 13 May 1957; *s* of James Brian Greatrex Hill and Jean Hill; *m* 1979, Hilary Llystyn Jones; one *s* one *d. Educ:* Chetham's School of Music, Manchester; St John's College, Cambridge (organ student; toured Aust. 1977, USA and Canada, 1978, Japan, 1979; MA). Sub-Organist, Durham Cathedral, 1980–82; Organist and Master of Music, Westminster Cathedral, 1982–88. Conductor: Alexandra Choir, 1979–87; Waynflete Singers, Winchester, 1988–; Associate Chorus Master, Philharmonia, 1987–. Mem. Council, RCO, 1984–. Recordings with Westminster Cathedral Choir (Gramophone award, 1985); concerts abroad; toured Aust. as organist, 1984; USA tour with Cathedral Choir, 1985; toured Aust., Philippines and USA, 1988; toured Aust., NZ and Germany, 1989. *Recreations:* wine, beer, cricket, reading, snooker, walking. *Address:* 10 The Close, Winchester, Hants. *T:* Winchester (0962) 854392, *Fax:* Winchester (0962) 856003.

HILL, Derek; *see* Hill, A. D.

HILL, Prof. Dorothy, CBE 1971; FRS 1965; FAA 1956; Research Professor of Geology, University of Queensland, 1959–72, now Emeritus Professor; President, Professorial Board, 1971–72, Member of Senate, 1976–77; *b* 10 Sept. 1907; *d* of R. S. Hill, Brisbane; unmarried. *Educ:* Brisbane Girls' Grammar Sch.; Univs of Queensland and Cambridge. BSc (Qld) 1928, 1st Cl. Hons in Geol. and Univ. Gold Medal. Foundn Trav. Fellowship of Univ. of Queensland held at Newnham Coll., Cambridge, 1930–32; PhD Cantab 1932; Old Students' Res. Fellowship, Newnham Coll., Cambridge, 1932–35; Sen. Studentship (Exhibn of 1851) held at Cambridge, 1935–37; Coun. for Sci. and Indust. Res. Fellowship, held at Univ. of Queensland, 1937–42; DSc (Qld) 1942. WRANS, Second Off., 1942–45 (RAN Ops Staff). Univ. of Queensland: Lectr in Geol., 1946–56, Reader, 1956–59. Hon. Editor, Geol. Soc. of Aust., 1958–64; Mem. Council, Australian Acad. of Science, 1968–70, Pres. 1970; Pres., Geol Soc. of Aust., 1973–75. Lyell Medal, Geol. Soc. of London, 1964; Clarke Medal, Royal Society of NSW, 1966; Mueller Medal, ANZAAS, 1967; Foreign and Commonwealth Mem. Geol. Soc. London, 1967; Hon.

Fellow, Geol Soc. of America, 1971. Hon. LLD Queensland, 1974. W. R. Browne Medal, Geol. Soc. of Australia, 1980; ANZAAS Medal, 1983. *Publications:* numerous, in geology and palæontology jls on fossil corals, archæocyatha, brachiopods, reef sediments and Australian geology and stratigraphy. *Recreations:* travel, reading. *Address:* 66 Sisley Street, St Lucia, Brisbane, Qld 4067, Australia.

HILL, Col (Edward) Roderick, DSO 1944; JP; Lord-Lieutenant of Gwent, 1974–79 (HM Lieutenant for Monmouthshire, 1965–74); Patron, Chepstow Race Course Co. Ltd (Director, 1958–83; Chairman, 1964–81); *b* 1904; *s* of late Capt. Roderick Tickell Hill; *m* 1934, Rachel (*d* 1983), *e d* of Ellis Hicks Beach, Witcombe Park, Glos; one *s* one *d*. *Educ:* Winchester; Magdalen Coll., Oxford. Gazetted to Coldstream Guards, 1926; served War of 1939–45, with regt (despatches, DSO); commanded 5th Bn and 1st Bn Coldstream Guards and Guards Training Bn; comd Regt, 1949–52. JP Co. Monmouth; High Sheriff of Monmouthshire, 1956; DL Monmouthshire, 1957; Vice-Lieut, 1963–65. Chm. of the Curre Hunt, 1959–65. Chm. of Governors, Monmouth Sch. and Monmouth Sch. for Girls, 1961–66; Chm. Chepstow RDC, 1962–63. Hon. Col, 104 Light AD Regt RA(V), 1967–69. Freeman and Liveryman, Haberdashers Co., 1969. Pres., Royal Welsh Agric. Soc., 1970–71. Pres., TA&VRA for Wales and Monmouthshire, 1971–74. Officer, Order of Orange-Nassau (with swords), 1946. KStJ 1972. *Publication:* (with the Earl of Rosse) The Story of the Guards Armoured Division, 1941–1945, 1956. *Address:* Manor Farm Cottage, Stanford in the Vale, Faringdon, Oxfordshire SN7 8NN. *Club:* Cavalry and Guards.

See also Baron Raglan.

HILL, (Eliot) Michael; QC 1979; a Recorder of the Crown Court, since 1977; *b* 22 May 1935; *s* of Cecil Charles Hill and Rebecca Betty Hill; *m* 1965, Kathleen Irene (*née* Hordern); one *s* two *d*. *Educ:* Bancroft's Sch., Essex; Brasenose Coll., Oxford (MA). Called to the Bar, Gray's Inn, 1958, Bencher, 1986; Member: Senate of the Inns of Court and the Bar, 1976–79 and 1982–86; Bar Council, 1986–87 and 1989–90. South-Eastern Circuit. Prosecuting Counsel to Crown, Inner London Sessions, 1969–74; Jun. Pros. Counsel to Crown, Central Criminal Court, 1974–77; a Sen. Pros. Counsel to Crown, 1977–79. Chm., Criminal Bar Assoc., 1982–86 (Sec., 1973–75; Vice-Chm., 1979–82); Member: Council of Legal Educn, 1977–86; Criminal Law Revision Cttee, 1983–; Exec. Cttee, Soc. for Reform of Criminal Law, 1988–. *Recreations:* family, friends, riding, fishing and just living. *Address:* (chambers) 36 Essex Street, WC2A 3AS. *T:* 071–413 0353.

HILL, Dame Elizabeth (Mary), DBE 1976; Emeritus Professor of Slavonic Studies, Cambridge; *b* 24 Oct. 1900; *m* 1984, Stojan J. Veljković. *Educ:* University and King's Colls, London Univ. BA London 1924, PhD London 1928; MA Cantab 1937. War of 1939–45: Slavonic specialist, Min. of Information. University Lecturer in Slavonic, 1936–48; Prof. of Slavonic Studies, Univ. of Cambridge, 1948–68; Andrew Mellon Prof. of Slavic Languages and Literatures, Pittsburgh Univ., 1968–70. Fellow of University Coll., London; Fellow, Girton Coll., Cambridge; Hon. Fellow, SSEES, Univ. of London, 1990. Hon. LittD East Anglia, 1978. *Address:* 10 Croft Gardens, Cambridge.

HILL, Air Cdre Dame Felicity (Barbara), DBE 1966 (OBE 1954); Director of the Women's Royal Air Force, 1966–69; *b* 12 Dec. 1915; *d* of late Edwin Frederick Hill and late Mrs Frances Ada Barbara Hill (*née* Cocke). *Educ:* St Margaret's Sch., Folkestone. Joined WAAF, 1939; commnd, 1940; served in: UK, 1939–46; Germany, 1946–47; Far East Air Force, 1949–51; other appts included Inspector of WRAF, 1956–59; OC, RAF Hawkinge, 1959–60; OC, RAF Spitalgate, 1960–62; Dep. Dir, 1962–65. Hon. ADC to the Queen, 1966–69. *Address:* Worcester Cottage, Mews Lane, Winchester, Hants. *Club:* Royal Air Force.

HILL, Prof. Geoffrey (William), FRSL; University Professor, Boston University, since 1988; *b* 18 June 1932; *s* of late William George Hill and late Hilda Beatrice Hill (*née* Hands); *m* 1st, 1956, Nancy Whittaker (marr. diss.); three *s* one *d*; 2nd, 1987, Alice Goodman; one *d*. *Educ:* County High Sch., Bromsgrove; Keble Coll., Oxford (BA 1953, MA 1959; Hon. Fellow, 1981). Mem., academic staff, Univ. of Leeds, 1954–80 (Prof. of Eng. Lit., 1976–80); Univ. Lectr in English and Fellow of Emmanuel College, Cambridge, 1981–88. Churchill Fellow, Dept of English, Univ. of Bristol, 1980. Clark Lectr, Trinity Coll., Cambridge, 1986. FRSL 1972. English version of Ibsen's Brand produced at National Theatre, London, 1978. Hon. Fellow, Emmanuel Coll., Cambridge, 1990. Whitbread Award, 1971; RSL Award (W. H. Heinemann Bequest), 1971; Loines Award, Amer. Acad. and Inst. of Arts and Letters, 1983; Ingram Merrill Foundn Award in Literature, 1985. Hon. DLitt Leeds, 1988. *Publications: poetry:* For the Unfallen, 1959 (Gregory Award, 1961); King Log, 1968 (Hawthornden Prize, 1969; Geoffrey Faber Meml Prize, 1970); Mercian Hymns, 1971 (Alice Hunt Bartlett Award, 1971); Somewhere is Such a Kingdom: Poems 1952–1971, 1975; Tenebrae, 1978 (Duff Cooper Meml Prize, 1979); The Mystery of the Charity of Charles Péguy, 1983; Collected Poems, 1985; *poetic drama:* Henrik Ibsen, Brand: a version for the English Stage, 1978; *criticism:* The Lords of Limit: essays on literature and ideas, 1984; The Enemy's Country, 1991.

HILL, George Geoffrey David, CMG 1971; late Assistant Secretary, Department of the Environment (Head of International Transport Division, Ministry of Transport, 1964); *b* 15 Aug. 1911; *o s* of late William George Hill, JP; *m* 1935, Elisabeth Wilhelmina (*née* Leuwer) (*d* 1988); one *d*. *Educ:* Manchester Grammar Sch.; Gonville and Caius Coll., Cambridge (BA (Hons)). Entered Ministry of Transport as Asst Principal, 1934; Principal, 1941; Asst Sec., 1954; retired 1972. *Recreations:* bridge, languages. *Address:* 125 Ember Lane, Esher, Surrey. *T:* 081–398 1851.

HILL, George Raymond, FCA, FCIT; FHCIMA; Director: Regal Hotel Group plc (non-exec. Chairman), since 1989; Chester International Hotel PLC, since 1987; Ashford International Hotel PLC, since 1987; *b* 25 Sept. 1925; *s* of George Mark and Jill Hill; *m* 1948, Sophie (*née* Gilbert); two *d*. *Educ:* St Dunstan's Coll., London. Royal Marines, 1943–46 (Lieut). Distillers Co. Ltd (Industrial Group), 1952–66; BP Chemicals Ltd, 1967–69; British Transport Hotels Ltd: Chief Exec., 1970–76; Chm., 1974–76; Dir, Bass PLC, 1976–84 (Mem. Exec. Cttee); Chm., Bass UK Ltd, 1978–80; Chairman: Howard Machinery PLC (later H. M. Holdings PLC), 1984–85; Sims Catering Butchers plc, 1985–87; Dir, Prince of Wales Hotels PLC, 1985–86. Member Boards: British Railways (Scottish), and British Rail Hovercraft Ltd, 1972–76; British Tourist Auth., 1981–89 (Chm., Marketing Cttee, 1985–89); Chairman: Liquor Licensing Working Party, 1985–; Channel Tunnel Nat. Tourism Working Pty, 1986–89. Member: Hotel and Catering Industry Trng Bd, 1973–80; Civil Service Final Selection Bd, 1973–80; Cttee of Inquiry on Motorway Service Areas, 1978; BHRCA (Bd Chm., 1979–80; Nat. Council Chm., 1985–86); Pres., Licensed Victuallers Schs, 1982–83. FRSA 1980. *Recreations:* music, theatre, works of art, country life. *Address:* 23 Sheffield Terrace, W8 7NQ. *T:* 071–727 3986; The Paddocks, Chedworth, Glos. *Club:* Royal Automobile.

HILL, Gladys, MA, MD; FRCS, FRCOG; retired as Obstetrician and Gynæcologist, Royal Free Hospital (1940–59); *b* 28 Sept. 1894; *d* of late Arthur Griffiths Hill and Caroline Sutton Hill. *Educ:* Cheltenham Ladies' Coll.; Somerville Coll., Oxford; Royal Free Hosp. Med. Sch. MA Oxon, MD, BS London, FRCS 1936; FRCOG 1943. *Publications:* contribs to medical journals. *Recreations:* architecture, amateur dramatics, reading. *Address:* The Captain's Cottage, Bishops Lydeard, near Taunton, Som TA4 3LH. *T:* Bishops Lydeard (0823) 432533.

HILL, Graham Starforth; Resident Partner, Milan office, Frere Cholmeley, solicitors, since 1990; Consultant: to Monaco office, Frere, Cholmeley, solicitors, since 1984; to Rodyk and Davidson, solicitors, Singapore, since 1985; *b* 22 June 1927; *s* of late Harold Victor John Hill and Helen Dora (*née* Starforth); *m* 1952, Margaret Elise Ambler (marr. diss.); one *s* one *d*. *Educ:* Dragon Sch., Oxford; Winchester Coll.; St John's Coll., Oxford (MA Hons). Called to the Bar, Grays Inn, 1951; admitted solicitor, 1961; also admitted solicitor Malaysia, Singapore and Hong Kong; Notary Public and Comr for Oaths, Singapore. Flying Officer, RAF, 1948–50. Crown Counsel, Colonial Legal Service, Singapore, 1953–56; Partner, subseq. Sen. Partner, Rodyk and Davidson, Advocates and Solicitors, Singapore, 1957–76. Chm., Guinness Mahon & Co. Ltd, 1979–83 (Dir, 1977–79); non-exec. Dir, Phelan, Lewis and Peat Ltd, 1984–86. Mem., Malayan Bd of Income Tax, 1957–60. Formerly (all Singapore): Hon. Legal Adviser to High Commn; Law Reform Comr; dir of numerous cos; Member: Univ. Faculty of Law; Constitutional Commn; Council, Law Soc. (Pres., 1970–74, Hon. Mem. 1978); Courts Martial Mil. Ct of Appeal; Council, Internat. Bar Assoc.; Discip. Cttee and Appeal Cttee, ICA, 1980–86. Trustee: Southwark Cathedral Develt Trust Fund, 1980–85; Royal Opera House Trust, 1982–85. FRSA. Cavaliere dell'Ordine della Stella della Solidarieta, and Commendatore dell'Ordine al Merito, Italy. *Publications:* co-editor, The Laws of Singapore, revised edition 1970; report of Constitutional Commission of Singapore. *Recreations:* music, Italy. *Address:* Casa Claudia, Piccolo Pevero, 07020 Porto Cervo, Sardegna, Italy. *T:* 0789 92157; 10 St Thomas Street, Winchester, Hants SO23 9HE. *T:* Winchester (0962) 54146. *Clubs:* Garrick; Costa Smeralda Yacht (Italy).

See also I. S. Hill.

HILL, Harry, OBE 1986; FCCA, FCIS, FTII, CBIM; Director, Beecham Group, 1979–86; Vice-Chairman, Beecham Products, 1984–86; *b* 22 May 1924; *s* of James and Charlotte Hill; *m* 1944, Vera Brydon; two *d*. War service, 1942–45: flying duties, Fleet Air Arm; Lieut RNVR. John Marshall & Co., Newcastle upon Tyne, 1945–50: Professional accounting and auditing; articled clerk, subseq. managing clerk and partner; General Motors Ltd, London, 1950–69: sen. financial appts; Group Gen. Comptroller, 1966–69; Parkinson-Cowan Ltd, London, 1969–71; Dir of Finance and Admin; Beecham Products, Brentford, Mddx: Financial Dir, 1972–76; Admin Dir, 1976–77; Vice-Chm., Food and Drink Div., 1977–80; Chm., Internat. Div., 1977–84; Chm., Proprietaries Div., 1981–86. FCCA 1964 (ACCA 1949); FCIS 1970; FTII 1976; CBIM 1983. Pres., Assoc. of Certified Accountants, 1975–76; Mem., Price Commn, 1977–79; Chm., Apple and Pear Develt Council, 1983–86. *Recreations:* gardening, reading, motoring. *Address:* 77 Howards Thicket, Gerrards Cross, Bucks SL9 7NU. *T:* Gerrards Cross (0753) 883550.

HILL, Rt. Rev. Henry Gordon; on staff of Primate of Canada, episcopal liaison with non-Chalcedonian orthodox church; Co-Chairman, Anglican-Orthodox Joint Doctrinal Commission, since 1980; *b* 14 Dec. 1921; *s* of Henry Knox Hill and Kathleen Elizabeth (*née* Cunningham); unmarried. *Educ:* Queen's Univ., Kingston, Ont. (BA 1945); Trinity Coll., Toronto (LTh 1948); St John's Coll., Cambridge (MA 1952). Deacon, Dio. Ont., 1948; Priest (Bp of Ely for Ontario), 1949; Curate, Belleville, Ont., 1950; Rector of Adolphustown, Ont., 1951; Chaplain, St John's Coll., Cambridge, Eng., 1952; Curate, Wisbech, Cambs, 1955; Rector, St Thomas, Reddendale, Ont., 1957; Asst Prof., Canterbury Coll., Assumption Univ., Windsor, 1962–68; (Vice-Principal, 1965–68); Associate Prof. of History, Univ. of Windsor, Ont., 1968–74; Bishop of Ontario, 1975–81; Asst Bishop of Montreal, 1981–83. Warden, Sisters of St John the Divine, 1976; Vice-Pres., Fellowship of St Alban and St Sergius, 1980. Episcopal Consultant for the Eastern and Oriental Orthodox Churches, Lambeth Conf., 1988. Hon. DD: Trinity Coll., Toronto, 1976; Montreal Dio. Theol Coll., 1976; Hon. LLD Univ. of Windsor, 1976; Hon. Dr, Theological Inst., Bucharest, 1977. KLJ 1980. Patriarchal Cross of Romanian Orthodox Church, 1969. *Publications:* Contemplation and Ecumenism (Monastic Studies No 15), 1984; Light Out of the East: chapters on the life and worship of the ancient orthodox churches, 1988; Engolpion, HH Ignatius Zakka Ivas, Syrian Orthodox Patriarch of Damascus, 1988; articles in Cdn Jl of Theology, Sobornost, Jl Fellowship of St Alban and St Sergius. *Recreations:* walking, reading. *Address:* St John's Convent, 1 Botham Road, Willowdale, Ontario M2N 2JS, Canada.

HILL, Dr (Hugh) Allen (Oliver), FRS 1990; CChem, FRSC; University Reader in Bioinorganic Chemistry, Oxford, since 1990; Fellow and Praelector, The Queen's College, Oxford, since 1965; *b* 23 May 1937; *s* of Hugh Rankin Stewart Hill and Elizabeth Hill (*née* Burns); *m* 1967, Boglárka Anna Pinter; two *s* one *d*. *Educ:* Royal Belfast Academical Institution; QUB (BSc 1959; PhD 1962); Univ. of Oxford (MA 1964; DSc 1986). Research Fellowships, 1962–65; Oxford University: Deptl Demonstrator, 1965–67, Lectr, 1967–90, in Inorganic Chemistry; Sen. Proctor, 1976–77. Vis. appts, Harvard, Univ. of Sydney, Univ. of California, 1970–82. Co-editor-in-chief, Jl of Inorganic Biochemistry. Interdisciplinary Award, RSC, 1987; Chemistry and Electrochemistry of Transition Metals Award, RSC, 1990. *Publications:* Physical Methods in Advanced Inorganic Chemistry (with P. Day), 1968; papers in professional jls. *Recreations:* gardening, music. *Address:* The Queen's College, Oxford OX1 4AW. *T:* Oxford (0865) 279177.

HILL, Ian Macdonald, MS, FRCS; Consulting Cardiothoracic Surgeon, St Bartholomew's Hospital, since 1984 (Consultant Cardio-thoracic Surgeon, 1950–84); Hon. Consultant Thoracic Surgeon, SE Thames Regional Health Authority, since 1984 (Consultant Thoracic Surgeon, 1950–84); *b* 8 June 1919; British; *m* 1944, Agnes Mary Paice; three *s* one *d*. *Educ:* Stationers' Company Sch.; St Bartholomew's Hosp. Medical Coll. Undergrad. schols and medals, 1937–41; MB, BS (Hons) London, 1942; MRCS, LRCP 1942; FRCS 1944; MS London 1945. Demonstrator of Anatomy, St Bartholomew's, 1943; Surgical Chief Asst, St Bart's Hosp., 1944; RAF Medical Branch, 1946; Wing Comdr i/c Surg. Div. No 1 RAF Gen. Hosp., 1947; Senior Registrar, Thoracic Surg. Unit, Guy's Hosp., 1948; Surgical Chief Asst, Brompton Hosp. and Inst. of Diseases of the Chest, 1950. Sub-Dean, St Bart's Hosp. Med. Coll., 1964–73. FRSocMed. Member: Soc. of Apothecaries; Soc. of Thoracic Surgeons; Thoracic and Cardiac Socs. Governor, St Bartholomew's Hosp. Med. Coll., 1985–. Freeman of City of London. *Publications:* articles in professional jls, mainly relating to lung and cardiac surgery, 1942–61. *Recreations:* old cars, furniture, keyboard instruments; gardening and house care. *Address:* Bracken Wood, Church Lane, Fernham, Faringdon, Oxon SN7 7PB. *T:* Uffington (036782) 475.

HILL, (Ian) Starforth, QC 1969; **His Honour Judge Starforth Hill;** a Circuit Judge, since 1974; *b* 30 Sept. 1921; *s* of late Harold Victor John Hill; *m* 1st, 1950, Bridget Mary Footner; one *s* two *d*; 2nd, 1982, Greta Grimshaw; 3rd, 1986, Wendy Elizabeth Stavert. *Educ:* Shrewsbury Sch.; Brasenose Coll., Oxford (MA). 11th Sikh Regt, Indian Army, 1940–45, India, Africa, Italy (despatches). Called to Bar, Gray's Inn, 1949; Dep. Chm., Isle of Wight QS, 1968–71; Western Circuit; a Recorder of the Crown Court, 1972–74. Mem., Parole Bd, 1983–84. *Address:* 2 Crown Office Row, Temple, EC4. *T:* 071–583 8155; Tulls Hill, Preston Candover, Hants RG25 2EW. *T:* Preston Candover (025687) 309. *Club:* Hampshire (Winchester).

See also G. S. Hill.

HILL, Ivan Conrad, CBE 1960; Chairman, Industrial Coal Consumers Council, since 1965; *b* 22 Jan. 1906; *s* of Wilfred Lawson Hill and Annie Jane (*née* England); *m* 1st, 1931, Alexandrina Ewart (marr. diss. 1962); four *d*; 2nd, 1963, Sheila Houghton. *Educ:* Oakham Sch.; St John's Coll., Cambridge. Exhibitioner and Open Scholar of St John's Coll. 1st cl. Hons Law Tripos Cantab 1928. Apptd Jt Man. Dir, Kelsall & Kemp Ltd, 1933. Chm. Wool Industries Research Assoc., 1950–53; Mem. Monopolies and Restrictive Practices Commn, and Monopolies Commn, 1951–63; Chairman: British Rayon Research Assoc., 1956–61; Samuel Courtauld & Co. Ltd, 1962–66; Illingworth Morris & Co. Ltd, 1976–80; Convoy Woollen Co. Ltd, 1984–. Liveryman, Weavers' Company, 1938–. *Recreations:* travel, architecture, sport. *Address:* Crystal Spring, Duchy Road, Harrogate, N Yorks.

HILL, Brig. James; *see* Hill, Brig. S. J. L.

HILL, James; *see* Hill, S. J. A.

HILL, Sir James Frederick, 4th Bt *cr* 1917; Chairman, Sir James Hill & Sons Ltd; Director: Yorkshire Building Society; British Rail (Eastern Region); Airedale Health Authority; *b* 5 Dec. 1943; *s* of Sir James Hill, 3rd Bt and of Marjory, *d* of late Frank Croft; *S* father, 1976; *m* 1966, Sandra Elizabeth, *o d* of J. C. Ingram; one *s* three *d*. Chm., British Wool Fedn, 1987–90. *Heir: s* James Laurence Ingram Hill, *b* 22 Sept. 1973. *Address:* Roseville, Moor Lane, Menston, Ilkley, West Yorks LS29 6AP. *T:* Menston (0943) 874624. *Clubs:* Royal Automobile; Bradford (Yorks); Ilkley Golf.

HILL, James William Thomas, (Jimmy); Chairman: Jimmy Hill Ltd, since 1972; Fulham Football Club (1987) Ltd, since 1987; Soccer analyst to the BBC, since 1973; *m* 1st, 1950, Gloria Mary (marr. diss. 1961); two *s* one *d*; 2nd, 1962, Heather Christine (marr. diss. 1982); one *s* one *d*; 3rd, 1991, Bryony Ruth Jarvis. *Educ:* Henry Thornton School, Clapham. Player, Brentford FC, 1949–52, Fulham FC, 1952–61; Gen. Manager, Coventry City FC, 1961–67, Managing Director, 1975–83, Chm., 1980–83. London Weekend Television: Head of Sport, 1967–72; Controller of Press, Promotion and Publicity, 1971–72; Deputy Controller, Programmes, 1972–73. Mem., Sports Council, 1971–76. Hon. Chm., The Professional Footballers Assoc., 1957–61. *Publications:* Striking for Soccer, 1961; Improve your Soccer, 1964; Football Crazy, 1985. *Recreations:* golf, riding, tennis, soccer, bridge. *Address:* c/o BBC Television, Kensington House, Richmond Way, W14 0AX. *Clubs:* Royal Automobile, The Sportsman, Queen's, All England Lawn Tennis and Croquet; The Berkshire, Addington Golf.

HILL, Jimmy; *see* Hill, James William Thomas.

HILL, John; Hon. Senior Research Fellow, Institute of Local Government Studies, Birmingham University, since 1984; *b* 28 April 1922; *s* of William Hallett Hill and Emily Hill (*née* Massey); *m* 1952, Hilda Mary Barratt; one *s*. *Educ:* Merchant Taylors' Sch., Crosby; Liverpool Univ. (BCom); Inst. of Public Finance and Accountancy, 1954. City Treasurer of Liverpool, 1974–82. Mem., Merseyside Residuary Body, 1985–88. *Recreation:* music. *Address:* 325 Northway, Lydiate, Merseyside L31 0BW. *T:* 051–526 3699.

HILL, John Cameron, TD 1959; FRICS; Part-time Member, Lands Tribunal, since 1987; *b* 8 April 1927; *s* of Raymond Cameron Hill and Margaret (*née* Chadwick); *m* 1954, Jane Edna Austin; one *s* one *d*. *Educ:* Trinity Coll., Oxford; College of Estate Management, London Univ. (BSc EstMan). Hillier Parker May & Rowden, 1953–88, Partner, 1962–88. Served TA (Major), 1949–73; Metropolitan Special Constabulary (Comdt), 1973–86. *Publication:* (jtly) Valuations: Principles into Practice, 1980, 3rd edn 1988. *Recreations:* shooting, DIY. *Address:* Hastoe House, Hastoe, Tring, Herts HP23 6LU. *T:* Tring (044282) 2084. *Clubs:* Army and Navy, Honourable Artillery Company.

HILL, John Edward Bernard; farming in Suffolk since 1946; *b* 13 Nov. 1912; *o s* of late Capt. Robert William Hill, Cambs Regt, and Marjorie Jane Lloyd-Jones, *d* of Edward Scott Miller; *m* 1944, Edith Luard, *widow* of Comdr R. A. E. Luard, RNVR, and 5th *d* of late John Maxwell, Cove, Dunbartonshire; one adopted *d*. *Educ:* Charterhouse; Merton Coll., Oxford (MA). Various journeys; Middle East, Far East, India, USA, 1935–37; Far East, 1956–57; USA, 1958. Called to Bar, Inner Temple (Certificate of Honour), 1938. RA (TA), 1939; Air Observation Post Pilot, 1942; War Office, 1942; 651 (Air OP) RAF, Tunisia, 1942; wounded, 1943; invalided out, 1945. MP (C) South Norfolk, Jan. 1955–Feb. 1974; Mem. Parliamentary delegns: W Germany and Berlin, 1959; Ghana, 1965; IPU Conf., Teheran, 1966; CPA Conf., Uganda, 1967; Bulgaria, 1970; Council of Europe and WEU, 1970–72; Mem., European Parlt, 1973–74; Chm., Cons. Educn Cttee, 1971–73; Member: Select Cttee on Agriculture, 1967–69; Select Cttee on Procedure, 1970–71; Asst Govt Whip, 1959–60; a Lord Comr of the Treasury, 1960–64. Mem. East Suffolk and Norfolk River Board, 1952–62. Mem. Exec. Cttee, CLA, 1957–59, 1977–82. Member: Governing Body, Charterhouse Sch., 1958–90; Langley Sch., Norfolk, 1962–77; Governing Body, Sutton's Hosp., Charterhouse, 1966–; GBA Cttee, 1966–79, 1980–83; Council, Univ. of East Anglia, 1975–82. *Recreations:* association football (Blue; Sec., OUAFC 1934); shooting, concerts, picture galleries. *Address:* Watermill Farm, Wenhaston, Halesworth, Suffolk IP19 9BY. *T:* Blythburgh (050270) 207. *Club:* Garrick.

HILL, Prof. (John Edward) Christopher, FBA 1966; DLitt; Master of Balliol College, Oxford, 1965–78; *b* 6 Feb. 1912; *m* 1st, 1944, Inez Waugh; (one *d* decd); 2nd, 1956, Bridget Irene Sutton; one *s* one *d* (and one *d* decd). *Educ:* St Peter's Sch., York; Balliol Coll., Oxford. BA 1931, DLitt 1965. Fellow of All Souls Coll., Oxford, 1934; Asst Lectr, University Coll., Cardiff, 1936; Fellow and Tutor in Modern History, Balliol Coll., Oxford, 1938. Private in Field Security Police, commissioned Oxford and Bucks Light Inf., 1940, Major; seconded to Foreign Office, 1943. Returned to Balliol, 1945; University Lectr in 16th- and 17th-century history, 1959; Ford's Lectr, 1962. Vis. Prof., Open Univ., 1978–80. Hon. Fellow, Lancs Polytechnic, 1988. Hon. DLitt: Hull, 1966; E Anglia, 1968; Glasgow, 1976; Exeter, 1979; Wales, 1979; Hon. LittD Sheffield, 1967; Hon. LLD Bristol, 1976; DUniv York, 1978; Hon. Dr Sorbonne Nouvelle, 1979; DUniv Open, 1982. Foreign Hon. Member: Amer. Acad. of Sciences, 1973; Hungarian Acad. of Sciences, 1982; Acad. of Sciences, GDR, 1988. *Publications:* The English Revolution 1640, 1940; (under name K. E. Holme) Two Commonwealths, 1945; Lenin and the Russian Revolution, 1947; The Good Old Cause (ed jointly with E. Dell), 1949; Economic Problems of the Church, 1956; Puritanism and Revolution, 1958; Oliver Cromwell, 1958; The Century of Revolution, 1961; Society and Puritanism in Pre-Revolutionary England, 1964; Intellectual Origins of the English Revolution, 1965; Reformation to Industrial Revolution, 1967; God's Englishman, 1970; Antichrist in 17th Century England, 1971; The World Turned Upside Down, 1972; ed, G. Winstanley, The Law of Freedom and other writings, 1973; Change and Continuity in Seventeenth Century England, 1975; Milton and the English Revolution, 1978 (Heinemann award; Milton Soc. of America award); Some Intellectual Consequences of the English Revolution, 1980; (with B. Reay and W. M. Lamont) The World of the Muggletonians, 1983; The Experience of Defeat: Milton and some contemporaries, 1984; Collected Essays Vol. I: Writing and Revolution in 17th Century England, 1985, Vol. II: Religion and Politics in 17th Century England, 1986, Vol. III: People and Ideas in 17th Century England, 1986; A Turbulent, Seditious, and Factious People: John Bunyan and his Church, 1988 (W. H. Smith Literary Award, 1989); A Nation of Change and Novelty: radical politics, religion and literature in 17th century England, 1990; articles in learned journals, etc. *Address:* Woodway House, Sibford Ferris, Banbury, Oxon OX15 5RA.

HILL, John Lawrence; Chairman, Britannia Building Society, since 1990; Chief Executive, Loss Prevention Council, since 1986; *b* 21 July 1934; *s* of late Sidney Hill and of Hilda Wardle Hill; *m* 1960, Elizabeth Godfrey; one *s* three *d*. *Educ:* Abbotsholme Sch.; Sidney Sussex Coll., Cambridge (MA). CEng, MIMechE, FIRM. National Service, Royal Corps of Signals, 1953–55. Royal Dutch Shell Group, 1959–67; PA Consulting Group, 1967–86; Director: Britannia Building Soc., 1984–; Britannia Life, 1989–. Director: Loss Prevention Certification Bd, 1986–; Nat. Approval Council for Security Systems, 1990–. Governor, Inst. of Risk Management, 1987–. *Recreations:* golf, music, opera. *Address:* Warwick Lodge, Warwicks Bench, Guildford, Surrey GU1 3TG. *T:* Guildford (0483) 66413. *Clubs:* Royal & Ancient Golf, Worplesdon Golf.

HILL, Sir John McGregor, Kt 1969; BSc, PhD; FRS 1981; FEng 1982; FInstP; FInstE; Chairman: Rea Brothers Group, since 1987; British Nuclear Fuels PLC, 1971–83; Amersham International PLC, 1975–88; Aurora Holdings PLC, 1984–88; *b* 21 Feb. 1921; *s* of late John Campbell Hill and Margaret Elizabeth Park; *m* 1947, Nora Eileen Hellett; two *s* one *d*. *Educ:* King's Coll., London; St John's Coll., Cambridge. Flt Lieut, RAF, 1941. Cavendish Laboratory, Cambridge, 1946; Lecturer, London Univ., 1948. Joined UKAEA, 1950, Mem. for Production, 1964–67, Chm., 1967–81. Member: Advisory Council on Technology, 1968–70; Nuclear Power Adv. Bd, 1973–81; Energy Commn, 1977–79. Pres., British Nuclear Forum, 1984–. Hon. FIChemE 1977; Hon. FIEE 1981; Foreign Associate, US Nat. Acad. of Engineering, 1976. Hon. DSc Bradford, 1981. Melchett Medal, Inst. of Energy, 1974; Sylvanus Thompson Medal, Inst. of Radiology, 1978. *Recreation:* golf. *Address:* Dominic House, Sudbrook Lane, Richmond, Surrey TW10 7AT. *T:* 081–940 7221. *Club:* East India.

HILL, Sir John (Maxwell), Kt 1974; CBE 1969; DFC 1945; QPM; Chief Inspector of Constabulary, Home Office, 1972–75; *b* 25 March 1914; *s* of late L. S. M. Hill, Civil Servant, Plymouth; *m* 1939, Marjorie Louisa, *d* of late John Oliver Reynolds, Aylesbury, Bucks; one *s* one *d*. *Educ:* Plymouth Coll. Metropolitan Police Coll., Hendon, 1938–39; joined Metropolitan Police, 1933. Served with RAF, 1942–45. Dep. Comdr, New Scotland Yard, 1959; Metropolitan Police: Comdr, No 3 District, 1963, Comdr, No 1 District, 1964; HM Inspector of Constabulary, 1965; Asst Comr (Administration and Operations), 1966–68; Asst Comr (Personnel and Training), 1968–71; Dep. Comr, 1971–72. *Recreations:* walking, golf. *Address:* 4 The Kingsway, Epsom, Surrey KT17 1LT. *Clubs:* Royal Automobile, Royal Air Force.

HILL, Rear-Adm. John Richard; Under-Treasurer, Middle Temple, since 1984; *b* 25 March 1929; *s* of Stanley Hill and May Hill (*née* Henshaw); *m* 1956, Patricia Anne Sales; one *s* two *d*. *Educ:* Royal Naval College, Dartmouth. China Station as midshipman, 1946–47; Sub-Lieut's Courses, 1948–49; Lieut, HM Ships: Gambia, 1950; Chevron, 1950–52; Tintagel Castle, 1952–54; Dryad (Navigation Specialist), 1954; Cardigan Bay, 1954–56; Albion, 1956–58; Roebuck, 1958–59; Lt-Comdr, Pembroke Dock, 1959–60; HMS Duchess, 1960–62; Comdr, MoD, 1963–65 and 1967–69; IDC 1965–67; HMS Dryad, 1969–71; Captain, MoD, 1973–75; Defence and Naval Attaché, The Hague, 1975–77; Cdre, MoD, 1977–80; Rear-Adm. 1981; Flag Officer, Admiralty Interview Bd, 1981–83. Sec., Council of Inns of Court, 1987–; Member: Bd of War Studies, London Univ., 1986–; Council, Foundn for Internat. Security, 1987–. Defence Fellow, University of London King's College, 1972. Editor, The Naval Review, 1983–. *Publications:* The Royal Navy Today and Tomorrow, 1981; Anti-Submarine Warfare, 1984; British Sea Power in the 1980s, 1985; Maritime Strategy for Medium Powers, 1986; Air Defence at Sea, 1988; Arms Control at Sea, 1988; articles in Survival, Navy International, Brassey's Annual, NATO's 15 Nations, Naval Review, Naval Forces. *Recreation:* amateur theatre. *Address:* Cornhill House, The Hangers, Bishop's Waltham, Southampton SO3 1EF. *Club:* Commonwealth Trust.

HILL, Len; *see* Hill, R. K. L.

HILL, Leslie Francis; Chairman and Chief Executive, Central Independent Television plc and subsidiaries, since 1991 (Managing Director, 1987–91); Director, ITN, since 1987; *b* 2 Sept. 1936; *s* of late Elizabeth May and Francis Alfred Hill; *m* 1972, Christine Susan (*née* Bush); two *s*. *Educ:* Cotham Grammar School. FCA. Qualified as Chartered Accountant; with Ware, Ward (now Ernst & Young), 1952–62, Peat, Marwick, Mitchell, 1962–65; IPC Group, 1965–70, finally Finance Director, Music for Pleasure, continuing as such with EMI Group to 1971; EMI Group: Exec. Dir, 1972–73; Man. Dir, EMI NZ, 1973–74; Asst Dir, Group Music, 1975–76; Man. Dir, EMI Records (UK), 1976–78, EMI Music, Europe, 1979–80; Director, 1980–84, Jt Man. Dir, 1984–86, HAT Group plc. Dir, ITVA, 1987–. *Recreations:* listening to music, reading, playing and watching cricket. *Address:* Central Independent Television plc, Central House, Broad Street, Birmingham B1 2JP. *T:* 021–643 9898.

HILL, Martyn Geoffrey; tenor singer; *b* 14 Sept. 1944; *s* of Norman S. L. Hill and Gwendoline A. M. Hill (*née* Andrews); *m* 1974, Marleen M. J. B. (*née* De Maesschalck); three *s* one *d*. *Educ:* Sir Joseph Williamson's Mathematical School, Rochester, Kent; King's College, Cambridge; Royal College of Music (ARCM); vocal studies with Audrey Langford. Concert, oratorio, recital and operatic appearances throughout the world with major orchestras, conductors and choirs; numerous radio, TV and gramophone recordings.

HILL, Michael; *see* Hill, E. M.

HILL, Michael William, President, Fédération Internationale d'Information et de Documentation, since 1985; *b* 1928; *o s* of late Geoffrey William Hill, Ross on Wye and Torquay; *m* 1st, 1957, Elma Jack Forrest (*d* 1967); one *s* one *d*; 2nd, 1969, Barbara Joy Youngman. *Educ:* Nottingham High Sch.; Lincoln Coll., Oxford (BSc, MA). MRIC 1953; CChem; FIInfSc 1982. Research Chemist, Laporte Chemicals Ltd, 1953–56; Morgan Crucible Group: Laboratory Head, 1956; Asst Process Control Manager, 1958; Group Technical Editor, 1963. Asst Keeper, British Museum, 1964. Dep. Librarian, Patent Office Library, 1965; Keeper, Nat. Ref. Library of Science and Invention, 1968–73; British Library: Dir, Science Ref. Library, 1973–86; Associate Dir, Sci. Technology and Industry, 1986–88. Member: Exec. Cttee, Nat. Central Library, 1971–74; EEC/CIDST Working Parties on Patent documentation, 1973–80, and on Information for Industry, 1976–80; Board, UK Chemical Inf. Service, 1974–77; Adv. Cttee for Scottish Science Reference Library, 1983–; Chairman: Circle of State Librarians, 1977–79; Council, Aslib, 1979–81; Vice Pres., IATUL, 1976–81. Series Editor (with D. J. Foskett), Guides to Information Sources. *Publications:* Patent Documentation (with Wittmann and Schiffels), 1979; Michael Hill on Science, Technology and Information (ed by P. Ward), 1988; papers on librarianship, documentation and information science in jls and conf. proceedings. *Address:* 137 Burdon Lane, Cheam, Surrey SM2 7DB. *T:* 081–642 2418. *Club:* United Oxford & Cambridge University.

HILL, Norman A.; *see* Ashton Hill.

HILL, Dr Polly; Fellow, Clare Hall, Cambridge, since 1965; *b* 10 June 1914; *d* of Prof. A. V. Hill, CH, OBE, FRS, and Margaret, *d* of Dr J. N. Keynes and F. A. Keynes; *m* 1953, Kenneth Humphreys (marr. diss. 1961; he *d* 1985); one *d*. *Educ:* Newnham Coll., Cambridge. PhD Cantab 1967. Editorial Asst, REconS, 1936–38; research, Fabian Soc., 1938–39; temp. civil servant, 1940–51; editorial staff, West Africa (weekly), 1951–53; Res. Fellow, then Sen. Res. Fellow, Econs Dept, followed by Inst. of African Studies, Univ. of Ghana, 1954–65; financed by Center for Research on Econ. Develt, Univ. of Mich, Ann Arbor, mainly working in Cambridge and northern Nigeria, 1965–70, and by SSRC, mainly working in northern Nigeria, 1970–72; Smuts Reader in Commonwealth Studies, Cambridge Univ., 1973–79; fieldwork in villages in Karnataka, S India, 1977–78, and (as Leverhulme Emeritus Fellow) in Kerala, S India, 1981–82. *Publications:* The Unemployment Services, 1940; The Gold Coast Cocoa Farmer, 1956; The Migrant Cocoa-Farmers of Southern Ghana, 1963, 3rd edn 1977; Rural Capitalism in West Africa, 1970, 2nd edn 1976; Rural Hausa, 1972; Population, Prosperity and Poverty: rural Kano, 1900 and 1970, 1977 (Amaury Talbot prize for African anthropology, 1977); Dry Grain Farming Families, 1982; Development Economics on Trial, 1986; (ed with R. Keynes) Lydia and Maynard: letters between Lydia Lopokova and J. M. Keynes, 1989; articles on rural W Africa and India in learned jls; monographs and chapters in books. *Address:* The Stilts, Hemingford Abbots, Huntingdon, Cambs PE18 9AR. *T:* St Ives (Huntingdon) (0480) 63296.
See also D. K. Hill.

HILL, Sir Richard (George Rowley), 10th Bt *cr* 1779, of Brook Hall, Londonderry; MBE (mil.) 1974; retired; *b* 18 Dec. 1925; *s* of Sir George Alfred Rowley Hill, 9th Bt, and of Rose Ethel Kathleen, MBE, *d* of late William Spratt; *S* father, 1985; *m* 1st, 1954, Angela Mary (*d* 1974), *d* of late Lt-Col Stanley Herbert Gallon, TD, Berwick-upon-Tweed; 2nd, 1975, Zoreen Joy MacPherson (marr. diss. 1986), *d* of late Norman Warburton Tippett, Kirkland, Berwick-upon-Tweed, and *widow* of Lieut Andrew David Wilson Marshall, KOSB; two *d*; 3rd, 1986, Elizabeth Margaret (*née* Tarbitt) (marr. diss. 1988), *widow* of Laurence Sage, RNVR/FAA. *Recreations:* swimming, riding, reading. *Heir:* half-*b* John Rowley Hill, *b* 1940. *Address:* c/o Barclays Bank, 28 High Street, Great Missenden, Bucks.

HILL, Vice-Adm. Sir Robert (Charles Finch), KBE 1991; FIMechE, FIMarE; Deputy Controller of the Navy and Chief Abovewater Systems Executive, since 1989; *b* 1 May 1937; *s* of Frances Margaret Hill (*née* Lumsden) and Ronald Finch Hill; *m* 1971, Deborah Mary (*née* Windle); one *s* one *d*. *Educ:* Nautical Coll., Pangbourne; RNEC Manadon. BSc(Eng), CEng. HMS Thermopylae, 1964–65; HMS Repulse, 1967–71; MoD (PE), 1971–74; RNEC Manadon, 1975–77; HMS Cleopatra, 1977–78; Nuclear Power Manager, Chatham, 1979–80; MoD (PE), 1980–84; RCDS 1985; HMS Raleigh in Comd, 1986–87; CSO (Engrg) to C-in-C Fleet, 1987–89. *Recreations:* rhythm guitar, sailing. *Club:* Royal Over-Seas League.

HILL, Robert Williamson, (Robin), CEng, FIGasE; Regional Chairman, British Gas, North Western, since 1990; *b* 8 Dec. 1936; *s* of William Hill and Mary Duncanson (*née* Williamson); *m* 1961, Janette Margaret (*née* Bald); one *s* two *d*. *Educ:* Dumbarton Acad.; Strathclyde Univ. (BSc 1st Cl. Hons). CEng, FIGasE 1958. Scottish Gas Board: various appts, 1958–70; Area Service Manager, subseq. Regional Service Manager, 1970–73; British Gas Corporation: Service Ops Manager, 1973–75; Asst Service Dir, 1975–76; Service Dir, 1977–82; Regl Chm., Scotland, 1982–89. Pres., Assoc. for Sci. Educn, Scotland, 1985–86. Pres., IGasE, 1989–90 (Vice-Pres., 1987–89). Mem. Court, Heriot-Watt Univ., 1987–. Hon. Mem., CGLI, 1981. Liveryman, Engineers' Co., 1984–. *Recreation:* golf. *Address:* 11 Vale Road, Pownall Park, Wilmslow, Cheshire SK9 5QA. *T:* Wilmslow (0625) 533131.

HILL, Roderick; *see* Hill, Colonel E. R.

HILL, Rodney, FRS 1961; PhD; ScD; Professor of Mechanics of Solids, University of Cambridge, 1972–79 (Reader, 1969–72); Fellow, Gonville and Caius College, since 1972; *b* 11 June 1921; *o s* of Harold Harrison Hill, Leeds; *m* 1946, Jeanne Kathlyn, *yr d* of C. P. Wickens, Gidea Park; one *d*. *Educ:* Leeds Grammar Sch.; Pembroke Coll., Cambridge. MA, PhD, ScD Cambridge. Armament Research Dept, 1943–46; Cavendish Laboratory, Cambridge, 1946–48; British Iron and Steel Research Assoc., 1948–50; University of Bristol: Research Fellow, 1950–53, Reader, 1953; Univ. of Nottingham: Prof. of Applied Mathematics, 1953–62; Professorial Research Fellow, 1962–63; Berkeley Bye-Fellow, Gonville and Caius Coll., Cambridge, 1963–69. Hon. DSc: Manchester, 1976; Bath, 1978. Von Karman Medal, ASCE, 1978; Gold Medal and Internat. Modesto Panetti Prize, Accademia delle Scienze di Torino, 1988. Editor, Jl of Mechanics and Physics of Solids, 1952–68. *Publications:* Mathematical Theory of Plasticity, 1950; Principles of Dynamics, 1964. *Address:* Department of Applied Mathematics and Theoretical Physics, Silver Street, Cambridge CB3 9EW.

HILL, Roy Kenneth Leonard, (Len), CBE 1983; JP; Chairman, South West Water Authority, 1977–87; *b* 28 May 1924; *m* 1944, Barbara May Kendall. Mem., ASLEF; Plymouth City Councillor, 1961–68, 1970–74 (formerly Dep. Lord Mayor); County Councillor, Devon, 1974 (formerly Leader of Labour Gp). Chm., Water Authorities Assoc., 1983–86. Mem., SW Econ. Planning Council. Chm. Council, Coll. of St Mark and St John, Plymouth; Governor, Plymouth Polytechnic; Mem. Bd of Visitors, Dartmoor Prison. JP Plymouth, 1968. *Address:* 5 Revell Park Road, Plympton, Plymouth PL7 4EH. *T:* Plymouth (0752) 339125.

HILL, (Stanley) James (Allen); MP (C) Southampton Test, 1970–Oct. 1974, and since 1979; company director; *b* 21 Dec. 1926; *s* of James and Florence Cynthia Hill; *m* 1958, Ruby Susan Evelyn Ralph, CBE; two *s* three *d*. *Educ:* Regents Park Sch., Southampton; Southampton Univ.; North Wales Naval Training Coll. Former Pilot. Mem., Southampton City Council, 1966–70, 1976–79, Chm. of Housing, 1967–70, 1976–79; Mem. Cttee, Southampton Conservative and Ratepayers Fedn. Mem., Speaker's Panel of Chairmen, 1990–. Secretary: Cons. Parly Cttee on Housing and Construction, 1971–73; Cons. Industry Cttee, 1979–81; Mem., Select Cttee on European Legislation, 1979–84; Chm., Cons. Cttee on Housing Improvement, 1985–. Vice Chm., All Party Anglo-Sri Lanka Gp; Sec., All Party Anglo-Singapore Gp. Mem., British Delegn to European Parlt, Strasbourg, and Chm., Regional Policy and Transport Cttee, 1973–75; Member: Hon. Cttee for Europe Day, Council of Europe, 1973–75; Scientific, Technol and Aerospace Cttee, Western European Defence, 1979–89; Political and Legal Affairs Cttee, Council of Europe, 1984–89; Govt Whip to Council of Europe and WEU, 1980–89. Pres., Motor Schools Assoc., 1980–85; Mem. Council, IAM, 1982–89. *Recreations:* private aviation, farming. *Address:* Gunsfield Lodge, Melchet Park, Plaitford, near Romsey, Hants. *Clubs:* Carlton, St Stephen's Constitutional.

HILL, Brig. (Stanley) James (Ledger), DSO 1942, and Bars, 1944, 1945; MC 1940; Vice-Chairman, Powell Duffryn Ltd, 1970–76 (Director, 1961–76); Chairman, Pauls & Whites Ltd, 1973–76 (Director, since 1970); Director: Lloyds Bank, 1972–79; Lloyds Bank UK Management Committee Ltd, 1979–81; *b* 14 March 1911; *s* of late Maj.-Gen. Walter Pitts Hendy Hill, CB, CMG, DSO, West Amesbury House, Wilts; *m* 1st, 1937, Denys, *d* of late E. Hubert Gunter-Jones, MC, JP, Gloucester House, Ledbury; one *d*; 2nd, 1986, Joan Patricia Haywood. *Educ:* Marlborough; RMC Sandhurst. 2nd Bn, Royal Fusiliers, 1931–35; 2nd Bn, RF, BEF, 1939; DAAG, GHQ, BEF, 1940; comd 1st Bn, Parachute Regt, N Africa landing, 1942; comd 3rd Parachute Bde, 1943–45; took part in Normandy and Rhine crossing (wounded thrice); comdr 4th Parachute Bde (TA), 1947–48. Apptd to Bd of Associated Coal & Wharf Cos Ltd, 1948; Pres., Powell Duffryn Group of Cos in Canada, 1952–58. Legion of Honour (France), 1942; Silver Star (USA), 1945; King Haakon VII Liberty Cross (Norway), 1945. *Recreation:* birdwatching. *Address:* Hidden House, Guilden Road, Chichester PO19 4LA. *T:* Chichester (0243) 789083. *Clubs:* Army and Navy; Island Sailing (IoW).

HILL, Starforth; *see* Hill, Ian S.

HILL, Susan Elizabeth, (Mrs Stanley Wells); novelist and playwright; *b* 5 Feb. 1942; *d* of late R. H. and Doris Hill; *m* 1975, Prof. Stanley W. Wells, *qv*; two *d* (and one *d* decd). *Educ:* grammar schs in Scarborough and Coventry; King's Coll., Univ. of London. BA Hons English 1963; Fellow, 1978. FRSL 1972. Literary critic, various jls, 1963–; numerous plays for BBC, 1970–; Presenter, Bookshelf, Radio 4, 1986–87. *Publications:* The Enclosure, 1961; Do me a Favour, 1963; Gentleman and Ladies, 1969; A Change for the Better, 1969; I'm the King of the Castle, 1970; The Albatross, 1971; Strange Meeting, 1971; The Bird of Night, 1972; A Bit of Singing and Dancing, 1973; In the Springtime of the Year, 1974; The Cold Country and Other Plays for Radio, 1975; (ed) The Distracted Preacher and other stories by Thomas Hardy, 1979; The Magic Apple Tree, 1982; The Woman in Black: a ghost story, 1983 (adapted for stage, 1989); (ed) Ghost Stories, 1983; (ed) People, an anthology, 1983; Through the Kitchen Window, 1984; Through the Garden Gate, 1986; The Lighting of the Lamps, 1987; Lanterns Across the Snow, 1987; Shakespeare Country, 1987; The Spirit of the Cotswolds, 1988; Family (autobiog.), 1989; Air and Angels, 1991; *for children:* One Night at a Time, 1984; Mother's Magic, 1986; Can it be True?, 1988; Susie's Shoes, 1989; Stories from Codling Village, 1990; I've Forgotten Edward, 1990; I Won't Go There Again, 1990; (ed) The Walker Book of Ghost Stories, 1990; Pirate Poll, 1991; *play:* The Ramshackle Company, 1981. *Recreations:* walking in the English countryside, friends, reading, broadcasting. *Address:* Midsummer Cottage, Church Lane, Beckley, Oxon OX3 9UT.

HILL, Prof. William George, FRS 1985; FRSE 1979; Professor of Animal Genetics, University of Edinburgh, since 1983, and Head, Institute of Cell, Animal and Population Biology, since 1990; *b* 7 Aug. 1940; *s* of late William Hill and Margaret Paterson Hill (*née* Hamilton); *m* 1971, Christine Rosemary Austin; one *s* two *d*. *Educ:* St Albans School; Wye Coll., Univ. of London (BSc 1961); Univ. of California, Davis (MS 1963); Iowa State Univ.; Univ. of Edinburgh (PhD 1965; DSc 1976). Asst Lectr, 1965–67, Lectr, 1967–74, Reader, 1974–83, in Genetics, Univ. of Edinburgh. Visiting Professor/Research Associate: Univ. of Minnesota, 1966; Iowa State Univ., 1967–78; N Carolina State Univ., 1979, 1985. Consultant Geneticist: Cotswold Pig Develt Co., 1965–; British Friesian Cattle Soc., 1978–88; Holstein Friesian Soc., 1988–. Chm., Org Cttee, 4th World Congress, Genetics Applied to Livestock Prodn, 1990. Member: Scientific Study Group, Meat and Livestock Commn, 1969–72; Cattle Res. Consultative Cttee, 1985–86; AFRC Animals Res. Grant Bd, 1986–; Dir's Adv. Gp, AFRC Animal Breeding Res. Orgn, 1983–86; Inst. Animal Physiology and Genetics Res., 1986–. *Publications:* (ed) Benchmark Papers in Quantitative Genetics, 1984; (ed) Evolution and Animal Breeding, 1989; numerous papers on quantitative and population genetics, biometrics and animal breeding, in sci. jls. *Recreations:* farming, bridge. *Address:* 4 Gordon Terrace, Edinburgh EH16 5QH. *T:* 031–667 3680.. *Club:* Farmers'.

HILL, William Sephton; Development Director, International Duty Free Confederation, Brussels, since 1989; *b* 24 July 1926; *s* of late William Thomas and Annie May Hill; *m* 1954, Jean, *d* of Philip Wedgwood; one *d*. *Educ:* Cowley Sch., St. Helens, Merseyside. BA, LLB Cantab. Served RAF, 1944–48, Japanese interpreter. Called to the Bar, Gray's Inn, 1951; practised Northern Circuit, 1951–54. Joined Solicitor's Office, HM Customs and Excise, 1954; Principal Asst Solicitor, 1980–85; Eur. Affairs Advr, BAT, 1985–89. *Recreations:* golf (ex-captain and ex-champion, Civil Service Golfing Society), bridge, listening to and playing piano. *Address:* 31 Hill Rise, Rickmansworth, Herts WD3 2NY. *T:* Rickmansworth (0923) 774756, 897004. *Club:* Moor Park Golf (Herts).

HILL-NORTON, family name of **Baron Hill-Norton.**

HILL-NORTON, Baron *cr* 1979 (Life Peer), of South Nutfield, Surrey; **Admiral of the Fleet Peter John Hill-Norton,** GCB 1970 (KCB 1967; CB 1964); Chairman, Military Committee of NATO, 1974–77; *b* 8 Feb. 1915; *s* of Capt. M. J. Norton and Mrs M. B. Norton; *m* 1936, Margaret Eileen Linstow; one *s* one *d*. *Educ:* RNC Dartmouth. Went to sea, 1932; commnd, 1936; specialised in Gunnery, 1939; War of 1939–45: Arctic Convoys; NW Approaches; Admiralty Naval Staff. Comdr 1948; Capt. 1952; Naval Attaché, Argentine, Uruguay, Paraguay, 1953–55; comd HMS Decoy, 1956–57; comd HMS Ark Royal, 1959–61; Asst Chief of Naval Staff, 1962–64; Flag Officer, Second-in-Command, Far East Fleet, 1964–66; Dep. Chief of the Defence Staff (Personnel and Logistics), 1966; Second Sea Lord and Chief of Naval Personnel, Jan.-Aug. 1967; Vice-Chief of Naval Staff, 1967–68; C-in-C Far East, 1969–70; Chief of the Naval Staff and First Sea Lord, 1970–71; Chief of the Defence Staff, 1971–73. President: Sea Cadets Assoc., 1977–84; Defence Manufacturers' Assoc., 1980–84; British Maritime League, 1982–85; Vice-Pres., RUSI, 1977–90. Liveryman, Shipwrights' Co., 1973, Mem. Court, 1979; Freeman, City of London, 1973. *Publications:* No Soft Options, 1978; Sea Power, 1982. *Recreations:* gardening, shooting. *Address:* Cass Cottage, Hyde, Fordingbridge, Hants. *Clubs:* Army and Navy; Royal Navy of 1765.
See also Vice-Adm. Hon. Sir N. J. Hill-Norton.

HILL-NORTON, Vice-Adm. Hon. Sir Nicholas John, KCB 1991; Flag Officer Flotilla Three and Commander, Anti-Submarine Warfare Striking Force, since 1990; *b* 13 July 1939; *s* of Admiral of the Fleet Baron Hill-Norton, *qv*; *m* 1966, Ann Jennifer, *d* of Vice-Adm. D. H. Mason, *qv*; two *s* one *d*. *Educ:* Marlborough Coll.; RNC, Dartmouth; US Naval War Coll., Newport, RI. Royal Navy, 1957–; Flag Officer, Gibraltar, 1987–90. *Recreations:* country sports, family pursuits.

HILL-SMITH, His Honour Derek Edward, VRD 1958; a Circuit Judge, 1972–87; *b* 21 Oct. 1922; *s* of Charles Hill-Smith and Ivy (*née* Downs); *m* 1950, Marjorie Joanna, *d* of His Honour Montague Berryman, QC; one *s* one *d*. *Educ:* Sherborne; Trinity Coll., Oxford (MA). RNVR, 1942–46; Lt-Comdr RNR. Trinity Coll., Oxford, 1941–42 and 1946–47 (MA, Classics and Modern Greats); BEA, 1947–48; business, 1948–50; teaching, 1950–54; called to Bar, Inner Temple, 1954; Dep. Chm., Kent QS, 1970; Recorder, 1972. Chm., Mental Health Review Tribunals, 1987–. *Publications:* contrib. Law Guardian. *Recreations:* the theatre, food and wine, collecting and restoring Old Masters and New Mistresses, the study of mediaeval church frescoes in Cyprus and Asia Minor. *Address:* c/o National Westminster Bank, North Street, Bishop's Stortford, Herts. *Clubs:* Garrick; Bar Yacht.

HILL-TREVOR, family name of **Baron Trevor.**

HILL-WOOD, Sir David (Basil), 3rd Bt *cr* 1921; Director, Guinness Mahon & Co. Ltd (Bankers), since 1977; *b* 12 Nov. 1926; *s* of Sir Basil Samuel Hill Hill-Wood, 2nd Bt, and Hon. Joan Louisa Brand, *e d* of 3rd Viscount Hampden; *S* father, 1954; *m* 1970, Jennifer, 2nd *d* of late Peter McKenzie Strang, Adelaide; two *s* one *d*. *Educ:* Eton. Served in Army (Grenadier Guards), 1945–48. Morgan Grenfell & Co. Ltd, 1948–55; Myers & Co., Stockbrokers, 1955–71, Sen. Partner, 1971–74; Dir, Capel-Cure Myers Ltd, 1974–77. Aust. Rep., FA Council, 1978–. High Sheriff Berks, 1982. *Recreations:* soccer, farming, forestry. *Heir: s* Samuel Thomas Hill-Wood, *b* 24 Aug. 1971. *Address:* Dacre Farm, Farley Hill, Reading, Berks. *T:* Eversley (0734) 733185; 58 Cathcart Road, SW10. *T:* 071–352 0389. *Clubs:* White's; Melbourne (Australia).

HILLABY, John; writer, naturalist and traveller; *b* 24 July 1917; *er s* of late Albert Ewart Hillaby, Pontefract, and Mabel Colyer; *m* 1940, Eleanor Riley, Leeds (marr. diss.); two *d*; *m* 1966, Thelma Gordon (*d* 1972), child analyst, London and Montreal; *m* 1981, Kathleen Burton, Easingwold, Yorks. *Educ:* Leeds; Woodhouse Grove, Yorkshire. Served War, RA, 1939–44. Local journalism up to 1939; magazine contributor and broadcaster, 1944–; Zoological Corresp., Manchester Guardian, 1949; European science writer, New York Times, 1951–; biological consultant, New Scientist, 1953–. Formerly a dir, Universities Fedn for Animal Welfare; Founder Pres., Backpackers Club. Has travelled on foot through parts of boreal Canada, Appalachian Trail, USA, Congo, traversed Ituri Forest and Mountains of the Moon (Ruwenzori), Sudan, Tanzania; three months foot safari with camels to Lake Rudolf, Kenya, and walked from Lands End to John o'Groats, from The Hague to Nice via the Alps, from Provence to Tuscany, from Lake District to London, and from Athens to Mt Olympus via the Pindos mountains. Woodward Lectr, Yale, 1973. Radio and TV series include: Men of the North, Expedition South, Alpine Venture, Hillaby Walks, Globetrotter, etc. FZS (scientific). *Publications:* Within The Streams, 1949; Nature and Man, 1960; Journey to the Jade Sea, 1964; Journey through Britain, 1968; Journey through Europe, 1972; Journey through Love, 1976; Journey Home, 1983; John Hillaby's Yorkshire: the moors and dales, 1986; John Hillaby's London, 1987; Journey to the Gods, 1991. *Recreations:* talking, reading, music, walking; observing peculiarities of man, beast, fowl and flora. *Club:* Savage.

HILLARD, His Honour Richard Arthur Loraine, MBE 1946; a Circuit Judge (formerly a County Court Judge), 1956–72; *b* 1906; *e s* of Frederick Arthur Hillard, Puriton Manor, Bridgwater, Som; *m* 1st, 1936, Nancy Alford (*d* 1964), *d* of Dr Alford Andrews, Cambridge; one *s* one *d*; 2nd, 1969, Monica Constance, *er d* of John Healey Carus, Darwen, and *widow* of Paul Hillard; one step *s* one step *d*. *Educ:* Worcester Royal Grammar Sch.; Christ Church, Oxford. Barrister, Gray's Inn, 1931; South-Eastern circuit. Served, 1940–45: Military Dept, Judge Advocate General's Office, 1941–45, Lt-Col 1945. Asst Reader and Lecturer, Council of Legal Education, 1945–55. Chm. Agricultural Land Tribunal, South Eastern Province, 1955. *Recreation:* gardening. *Address:* Oakchurch House, Staunton-on-Wye, Hereford HR4 7NE. *T:* Moccas (09817) 345. *Club:* United Oxford & Cambridge University.

HILLARY, Sir Edmund, ONZ; KBE 1953; author; lecturer; mountaineer; *b* 20 July 1919; *s* of Percival Augustus Hillary and Gertrude Hillary (*née* Clark); *m* 1st, 1953, Louise Rose (*d* 1975); one *s* one *d* (and one *d* decd); 2nd, 1989, June Mulgrew. *Educ:* Auckland Grammar Sch., Auckland, New Zealand. Apiarist, 1936–43. RNZAF, navigator on Catalina flying boats in Pacific Area, 1944–45. Apiarist (in partnership with brother W. F. Hillary), 1951–70. Himalayan Expeditions: NZ Gawhal Expedition, 1951; British Everest Reconnaissance, 1951; British Cho Oyu Expedition, 1952; Everest Expedition, 1953; with Sherpa Tenzing reached summit of Mount Everest, May 1953 (KBE). Leader of NZ Alpine Club Expedition to Barun Valley, East of Everest, 1954. Appointed, 1955, leader of New Zealand Transantarctic Expedition; completed overland journey to South Pole, Jan. 1958. Expeditions in Everest region, 1960–61, 1963, 1964, 1965; built first hosp. for Sherpas in Everest Area, with public subscription and NZ doctor, 1966; led expedition to Antarctic for geological and mountaineering purposes incl. first ascent of Mt Herschel, 1967; expedition to E Nepal (explored Himalayan rivers with two jet boats; first ascent of 180 miles of Sun Kosi river from Indian border to Katmandu), 1968; jet boat expedition up the Ganges, 1977. Consultant to Sears Roebuck & Co., Chicago, on camping and outdoor equipment. Hon. LLD: Univ. of Victoria, BC, Canada, 1969; Victoria Univ., Wellington, NZ, 1970. Hubbard Medal (US), 1954; Star of Nepal 1st Class; US Gold Cullum Geographical Medal, 1954; Founder's Gold Medal, Royal Geographical Society, 1958; Polar Medal, 1958. *Publications:* High Adventure; East of Everest, 1956 (with George Lowe); The Crossing of Antarctica, 1958 (with Sir Vivian Fuchs); No Latitude for Error, 1961; High in the Thin Cold Air, 1963 (with Desmond Doig); School House in the Clouds, 1965; Nothing Venture, Nothing Win (autobiog.), 1975; From the Ocean to the Sky: jet boating up the Ganges, 1979; (with Peter Hillary) Two Generations, 1983. *Recreations:* mountaineering, ski-ing, camping. *Address:* 278a Remuera Road, Auckland, SE2, New Zealand. *Clubs:* New Zealand Alpine (Hon. Mem.; Pres. 1965–67); Explorers (New York) (Hon. Pres); Hon. Mem. of many other NZ and US clubs.

HILLER, Dame Wendy, DBE 1975 (OBE 1971); actress; *d* of Frank Watkin and Marie Hiller, Bramhall, Cheshire; *m* 1937, Ronald Gow; one *s* one *d*. *Educ:* Winceby House, Bexhill. Manchester Repertory Theatre; Sir Barry Jackson's tour of Evensong; Sally Hardcastle in Love on the Dole, London and New York; leading parts in Saint Joan and Pygmalion at Malvern Festival, 1936. *Plays include:* Twelfth Night (war factory tour); Cradle Song (Apollo); The First Gentleman (Savoy); Tess of the d'Urbervilles (Piccadilly); The Heiress (Biltmore, NY, and Haymarket, London); Ann Veronica (Piccadilly); Waters of the Moon (Haymarket), 1951–53; The Night of the Ball (New), 1955; Old Vic Season, 1955–56; Moon for the Misbegotten (NY), 1957; Flowering Cherry (Haymarket), 1958; Toys in the Attic (Piccadilly), 1960; Aspern Papers (NY), 1962; The Wings of the Dove (Lyric), 1963; The Sacred Flame (Duke of York's), 1967; When We Dead Awaken (Edinburgh Festival), 1968; The Battle of Shrivings (Lyric), 1970; Crown Matrimonial (Haymarket), 1972; John Gabriel Borkman (National), 1975; Lies! (Albery), 1975; Waters of the Moon (Chichester), 1977, (Haymarket) 1978; The Old Jest, 1980; The Importance of Being Earnest (Watford), 1981, (Royalty), 1987; The Aspern Papers (Haymarket), 1984; Driving Miss Daisy (Apollo), 1988. *Films:* Pygmalion; Major Barbara; I Know Where I'm Going; Outcast of the Islands; Separate Tables (Academy Award); Sons and Lovers; Toys in the Attic; A Man for All Seasons; David Copperfield; Murder on the Orient Express; The Elephant Man; The Lonely Passion of Judith Hearne, etc. *TV:* When We Dead Awaken, 1968; Peer Gynt, 1972; Clochemerle, 1973; Last Wishes, 1978; Richard II, 1979; Miss Morison's Ghosts, 1981; The Kingfisher, Witness for the Prosecution, Attracta, 1982; The Comedy of Errors, 1983; Death of the Heart, 1985; Darley's Folly, All Passion Spent, The Importance of Being Earnest, 1986; Ending Up, 1989. Hon. LLD Manchester, 1984. *Address:* c/o ICM, 388/396 Oxford Street, W1N 9HE.

HILLERY, Dr Patrick John; Uachtarán na hÉireann (President of Ireland), 1976–90; *b* Miltown Malbay, Co. Clare, 2 May 1923; *s* of Dr Michael Joseph Hillery and Ellen (*née* McMahon); *m* 1955, Dr Mary Beatrice Finnegan; one *s* one *d*. *Educ:* Miltown Malbay National Sch.; Rockwell Coll.; University Coll., Dublin. BSc; MB BCh, BAO, DPH. Mem. Health Council, 1955–57; MO, Miltown Malbay, 1957–59; Coroner for West Clare, 1958–59; TD (Mem. Dáil Eireann), Clare, 1951–73; Minister: for Educn, 1959–65; for Industry and Commerce, 1965–66; for Labour, 1966–69; of Foreign Affairs, 1969–72 (negotiated Ireland's accession to European Communities); Comr for Social Affairs and a Vice-Pres., Commn of the European Communities, 1973–76. MRIA 1963. Hon. FRCSI 1977; Hon. FFDRCSI 1977; Hon. FRCPI 1978; Hon. FRCGP 1982; Hon. FFCM RCSI, 1986; Hon. Fellow: Pharmaceutical Soc. of Ireland, 1984; All-India Inst. of Medical Sciences, 1978. Hon. LLD: NUI, 1962; Univ. of Dublin, 1977; Univ. of Melbourne, 1985; Hon. DPh Pontifical Univ. of Maynooth, 1988. Robert Schuman Gold Medal (France), 1986. Grand Cross and Grand Cordon, Order of Merit (Italy), 1986; Grand Cross of the Netherlands Lion, 1986; Grand Cross of the Legion of Honour (France), 1988; Collar of the Pian Order, 1989. *Address:* Grasmere, Greenfield Road, Sutton, Dublin 13, Ireland.

HILLHOUSE, Sir (Robert) Russell, KCB 1991; Permanent Under-Secretary of State, Scottish Office, since 1988; *b* 23 April 1938; *s* of Robert Hillhouse and Jean Russell; *m* 1966, Alison Janet Fraser; two *d*. *Educ:* Hutchesons' Grammar Sch., Glasgow; Glasgow Univ. (MA). Scottish Education Dept, 1962; HM Treasury, 1971; Asst Secretary, Scottish Office, 1974; Scottish Home and Health Dept, 1977; Under Sec. (Principal Finance Officer), Scottish Office, 1980; Under Sec., 1985–87, Sec., 1987–88, Scottish Educn Dept. CBIM 1990. *Recreation:* making music. *Address:* c/o Scottish Office, St Andrew's House, Edinburgh EH1 3DG. *T:* 031–556 8400. *Clubs:* Commonwealth Trust; New (Edinburgh).

HILLIER, Bevis; Editor, Sotheby's Preview, since 1990; *b* 28 March 1940; *s* of J. R. Hillier, *qv*. *Educ:* Reigate Grammar Sch.; Magdalen Coll., Oxford (demy). Gladstone Memorial Prize, 1961. Editorial staff, The Times, 1963–68 (trainee, Home News Reporter, Sale Room Correspondent); Editor, British Museum Society Bulletin, 1968–70; Antiques Correspondent, 1970–84, Dep. Literary Editor, 1981–84, The Times; Guest Curator, Minneapolis Inst. of Arts, USA, 1971; Editor, The Connoisseur, 1973–76; Associate Editor, Los Angeles Times, 1984–88. Commendatore, Order of Merit (Italy), 1976. FRSA 1967. *Publications:* Master Potters of the Industrial Revolution: The Turners of Lane End, 1965; Pottery and Porcelain 1700–1914, 1968; Art Deco of the 1920s and 1930s, 1968; Posters, 1969; Cartoons and Caricatures, 1970; The World of Art Deco, 1971; 100 Years of Posters, 1972; introduction to A Boy at the Hogarth Press by Richard Kennedy, 1972; Austerity/Binge, 1975; (ed with Mary Banham) A Tonic to the Nation: The Festival of Britain 1951, 1976; The New Antiques, 1977; Greetings from Christmas Past, 1982; The Style of the Century 1900–1980, 1983; John Betjeman: a life in pictures, 1984; Young Betjeman, 1988; contributor to The Connoisseur, Apollo, Trans English Ceramic Circle, Proc. Wedgwood Soc., etc. *Recreations:* piano, collecting. *Address:* c/o A. P. Watt, 20 John Street, WC1N 2DL. *Clubs:* Beefsteak, Garrick.

HILLIER, Jack Ronald; freelance writer and expert on Japanese art, since 1950; *b* 29 Aug. 1912; *s* of Charles Hillier and Minnie Hillier (*née* Davies); *m* 1938, Mary Louise Palmer; one *s* one *d*. *Educ:* Fulham Central School. Sotheby Consultant on oriental pictorial art, 1953–67. Uchiyama Susumu Award, Tokyo, 1982, 1988. *Publications:* Old Surrey Water Mills, 1951; Japanese Masters of the Colour Print, 1953; Hokusai Paintings, Drawings and Woodcuts, 1955; The Japanese Print: a new approach, 1957, 4th edn 1975; Utamaro: colour prints and paintings, 1961, 2nd edn 1979; Japanese Drawings: from the 17th to the end of the 19th century, 1965, 3rd edn 1975; Hokusai Drawings, 1966; Catalogue of Japanese Paintings and Prints in Collection of Richard P. Gale, 1970; The Harari Collection of Japanese Paintings and Drawings, 1970–73; Suzuki Harunobu, 1970; The Uninhibited Brush: Japanese art in the Shijō style, 1974; Japanese Prints and Drawings from the Vever Collection, 1976; The Art of Hokusai in Book Illustration, 1980; The Art of the Japanese Book, 1987; The Japanese Picture-book: a selection from the Ravicz Collection, 1991; Japanese and Chinese Prints in the Amstutz Collection, 1991. *Recreations:* wood engraving, water colour painting, classical music (esp. lieder), the English countryside. *Address:* 30 Clarence Road, Meadvale, Surrey RH1 6NG. *T:* Redhill (0737) 241123.

See also Bevis Hillier.

HILLIER, Malcolm Dudley; designer and author; *b* 1 Aug. 1936. *Educ:* St Paul's School; Guildhall School of Music (LGSM). Advertising career, Colman Prentis and Varley; later Dir of Television, S. H. Benson, 1958–74; started garden design co. (with Colin Hilton), and opened flower shop, specialising in dried flowers, 1974; writer since 1985. *Publications:* Complete Book of Dried Flowers, 1986; Malcolm Hillier's Guide to Arranging Dried Flowers, 1987; Flowers, 1988. *Recreations:* poetry, pottery. *Address:* 101 Cheyne Walk, SW10 0DQ. *T:* 071–352 9031. *Club:* PEN.

HILLIER, Prof. Paul Douglas; singer; Professor of Music, University of California, Davis, since 1990; *b* 9 Feb. 1949; *s* of Douglas and Felicity Hillier; *m* 1977, Lena-Liis Kiesel; one *d*. *Educ:* Guildhall School of Music and Drama, London (AGSM). Vicar-Choral, St Paul's Cathedral, 1974–76; Musical Dir, Hilliard Ensemble, 1974–89; Conductor: Western Wind Chamber Choir, 1985–; Klemetti Inst. Chamber Choir, Finland, 1989–; Dir, Theatre of Voices, 1989–. Edison Prize (Holland), 1989. *Publications:* 300 Years of English Partsongs, 1983; Romantic English Partsongs, 1986; The Catch Book, 1987. *Recreations:* reading, spending time in the countryside. *Address:* Music Department, University of California, Davis, Calif 95616, USA.

HILLIER, William Edward, FIEE; Director, Application of Computers and Manufacturing Engineering Directorate, Science and Engineering Research Council, since 1985; *b* 11 April 1936; *s* of William Edward and Ivy Hillier; *m* 1958, Barbara Mary Thorpe; one *s* one *d*. *Educ:* Acton Grammar School; Open Univ. (BA). Missile Electronics Engineer, De Havilland Propellers, 1958–60; Semiconductor Test Equipment Design and Production Manager, 1960–64, Semiconductor Production Manager, 1965–70, Texas Instruments; Computer Aided Engineering Services Manager, up to Tech. Dir, CAD, Racal Redac, 1970–85 (Dep. Man. Dir, 1982–85). FBIM. *Publications:* articles in professional papers. *Recreation:* railway preservation (company secretary to standard gauge railway operating company, Gloucestershire Warwickshire Steam Railway plc). *Address:* 19 Simon de Montfort Drive, Evesham, Worcs WR11 4NR. *T:* Evesham (0386) 443449.

HILLIER-FRY, (William) Norman, CMG 1982; HM Diplomatic Service, retired; High Commissioner in Uganda, 1980–83; *b* 12 Aug. 1923; *o s* of William Henry and Emily Hillier Fry; *m* 1948, Elizabeth Adèle Misbah; two *s* two *d*. *Educ:* Colfe's Grammar School, Lewisham; St Edmund Hall, Oxford (BA 1946). Served Army, 1942–45; commissioned, Loyal Regt, 1942. HM Foreign Service, 1946; served: Iran, 1947–52; Strasbourg (Delegation to Council of Europe), 1955–56; Turkey, 1956–59; Czechoslovakia, 1961–63; Counsellor, UK Disarmament Delegn, Geneva, 1968–71; Hd of ME Dept, ODA, 1971–74; Consul-Gen., Hamburg, 1974–79; Ambassador to Afghanistan, 1979–80. *Recreations:* music, theatre. *Address:* 127 Coombe Lane West, Kingston-upon-Thames, Surrey KT2 7HF.

HILLIS, Arthur Henry Macnamara, CMG 1961; Comptroller General, National Debt Office, 1961–68; *b* 29 Dec. 1905; *s* of late John David Hillis, FRCS, Dublin; *m* 1936, Mary Francis (*d* 1990); no *c*. *Educ:* Trinity Coll., Dublin. Called to Bar, Inner Temple, 1931. HM Treasury, 1941; Harkness Fund Fellow, USA, 1950–51; Minister (Treasury Adviser), UK Permanent Mission to United Nations, 1958–61; Under-Sec., Treasury, 1961. Mem., Internat. CS Commn (UN), 1974–81. *Address:* 2 Hare Court, Temple, EC4Y 7BH. *T:* 071–353 3443. *Club:* Athenæum.

HILLMAN, Ellis Simon; Principal Lecturer in Environmental Studies, Polytechnic of East London (formerly North East London Polytechnic), since 1972 (Head of International Office, 1981–84); *b* 17 Nov. 1928; *s* of David and Annie Hillman; *m* 1967, Louise; one *s*. *Educ:* University Coll. Sch.; Chelsea Coll. of Science and Technol. (BSc). Served RAF, 1947–49. Scientific Technical Officer: Soil Mechanics Ltd; NCB Field Investigation Group; Architectural Assoc.; Organiser of Conference NELP/British Telecom on Rewiring Britain—Technical Challenge of Cable TV; Chm., London Subterranean Survey Assoc., 1968–. Elected to LCC, 1958; GLC Cllr, 1964–81; Councillor (Lab), Colindale, 1986–. Chairman: GLC Arts and Recreation Cttee, 1973–77; AMA Arts and Recreation Cttee, 1974–78; Further and Higher Educn Sub-Cttee, ILEA, 1977–81 (Bldgs Section, 1970–73); London Br. ACFHE, 1987–88 (Vice Chm., 1986–87); Vice-Chm., ILEA, 1980–81. Member: Lee Conservancy Catchment Bd, 1966–67; Lee Valley Reg. Park Authority, 1973–81; Sports Council, 1975–81; TWA, 1975–78; Water Space Amenity Commn, 1977–80; Inland Waterways Amenity Adv. Council, 1977–80; ARCUK Bd of Educn, 1973–82, 1986–. Member: Exec. Cttee, Field Studies Council, 1962–70; Exec. Cttee, Greater London Arts Assoc., 1973–77, 1982–86; Adv. Bd, NFT, 1973–78; Council, Science Fiction Foundn, 1986–; Sen. Vice-Pres., Hackney Soc., 1987– (Vice-Pres., 1984–87). Invited Mem., Green Alliance, 1984–. Founder and Hon. Pres., Lewis Carroll Soc., 1969–. Governor: Imperial Coll. of Science and Technol., later Imperial Coll. of Science, Technol. and Medicine, 1969–, and Queen Mary Coll., 1973–82, Univ. of London; Coombe Lodge Staff Further Educn Coll., 1978–82; London Festival Ballet, 1973–77; Hendon Coll., 1986–; Founding Gov., Museum of London, 1973– (Mem., Archaeol. Cttee, 1982–); Chm. Governors, Hackney Coll., 1974–82, 1985–. Chm., Colson Trust and Mem. Editl Bd, Colson News: Two Way Numbers, 1984–. Guest Editor, The Built Environment (one edn), 1984. FRSA 1979. *Publications:* Essays in Local Government Enterprise, 1964–67; (ed) Towards a Wider Use, 1976; Novellae on the Scroll of Esther, 1982; (ed) Space for the Living or Space for the Dead, 1977; (jtly) London Under London, 1985; contrib. Underground Services; Architects Jl, Arch. Design, Municipal Rev., Municipal Jl and Structural Survey and the Environmentalist. *Recreations:* walking, gardening, allotment cultivation, classical music, reading, writing poetry. *Address:* 29 Haslemere Avenue, NW4 2PU. *T:* 081–202 7792.

HILLMAN, Prof. John Richard, PhD; CBiol; FRSE; FLS, FBIM; Director, Scottish Crop Research Institute, since 1986; *b* 21 July 1944; *s* of Robert Hillman and Emily Irene (*née* Barrett); *m* 1967, Sandra Kathleen Palmer; two *s*. *Educ:* Chislehurst and Sidcup Grammar Sch. for Boys; University Coll. of Wales, Aberystwyth (BSc; PhD 1968). FRSE, FIBiol, CBiol, 1985; FLS 1982; FBIM 1987. Univ. of Nottingham: Asst Lectr in Physiology and Environmental Studies, 1968; Lectr, 1969; Univ. of Glasgow: Lectr in Botany, 1971; Sen. Lectr, 1977; Reader, 1980; Prof. of Botany, 1982. Vis. Professor: Univ. of Dundee, 1986–; Univ. of Strathclyde, 1986–; Univ. of Edinburgh, 1988–. *Publications:* (ed) Isolation of Plant Growth Substances, 1978; (ed with A. Crozier) The Biosynthesis and Metabolism of Plant Hormones, 1984; (ed with C. T. Brett) Biochemistry of Plant Cell Walls, 1985; papers in Nature, Planta, Jl of Experimental Botany, Physiologia Plantarum, Annals of Botany. *Recreations:* landscaping, building renovations, horology, reading. *Address:* Scottish Crop Research Institute, Invergowrie, Dundee DD2 5DA. *T:* Dundee (0382) 562731. *Club:* Farmers'.

HILLS, Andrew Worth; Managing Director, Sites and Personnel, AEA Technology, since 1991; *b* 1 Sept. 1949; *s* of Roland Frederick Hills and Margaret Eunice (*née* Johnson); *m* 1974, Frances Mary Ralston; three *s*. *Educ:* Abingdon Sch.; Corpus Christi Coll., Cambridge (BA 1971; MA 1975). United Kingdom Atomic Energy Authority, 1971–: Gen. Sec., AEE Winfrith, 1981–84; Principal Finance and Programmes Officer, 1984–86; Authority Personnel Officer, 1986–89; Exec. Dir, Finance and Personnel, 1989–91. *Recreations:* church-crawling, music, reading. *Address:* AEA Technology, 11 Charles II Street, SW1Y 4QP; Lavenham, Beech Road, Haslemere, Surrey GU27 2BX. *T:* Haslemere (0428) 642425.

HILLS, Air Vice-Marshal David Graeme Muspratt, CB 1985; OBE 1965; Director, Medical Policy and Plans, Ministry of Defence, 1983–85; *b* 28 Feb. 1925; *s* of late Arthur Ernest Hills and Muriel Steinman Hills (*née* Fisher); *m* 1960, Hilary Enid Mary, *d* of Rev. Raymond Morgan Jones and Mary Jones (*née* Ritson); two *s* one *d*. *Educ:* Salisbury Cathedral School; Epsom College; Middlesex Hosp. Medical School. MB BS 1949; MFCM, DPH, AFOM. Commissioned RAF Med. Branch, 1950; served UK, Korea (Casualty Evacuation and MO to 77 Sqn, RAAF), A&AEE, RAF Stanmore Park, RAF Tengah and MoD, 1951–68; OC RAF Hosp., Muharraq Bahrain, 1968–70; SMO RAF Cranwell, 1970–72; Dep. Dir Medical Personnel, RAF, 1972–75; PMO RAF Germany, 1975–78; Dep. Dir Gen., RAF Medical Services, 1979–83. QHS, 1980–85. CStJ. *Recreations:* music, painting, gardening, golf. *Club:* Royal Air Force.

HILLS, David Henry; Director-General of Intelligence, Ministry of Defence, since 1988; *b* 9 July 1933; *s* of Henry Stanford Hills and Marjorie Vera Lily Hills; *m* 1957, Jean Helen Nichols; one *s* two *d*. *Educ:* Varndean Sch., Brighton; Univ. of Nottingham (BA Econs). Served Army Intell. Corps, 1954–56. Entered MoD, 1956; other appointments include: NBPI, 1967–70; National Indust. Relations Court, 1971–73; Dir of Marketing, Defence Sales Orgn, MoD, 1979–82; Dir of Economic and Logistic Intell., MoD, 1982–88. *Recreation:* gardening. *Address:* Ministry of Defence, Main Building, Whitehall, SW1A 2HB. *T:* 071–218 3156. *Club:* Commonwealth Trust.

HILLS, Air Vice-Marshal Eric Donald, CB 1973; CBE 1968 (MBE 1941); SASO Maintenance Command, 1971–73, retired; *b* 26 Jan. 1917; *s* of late Henry James Hills; *m* 1945, Pamela Mary (*d* 1989), *d* of late Col A. P. Sandeman, Cape Town; one *s* one *d*; *m* 1991, Lady Cynthia Way. *Educ:* Maidstone Grammar Sch. Joined RAF 1939; Group Captain 1962; Dir of Equipment 3 (RAF), 1968–69; Air Cdre 1969; Dir of Equipment (Policy) (RAF), MoD, 1969–71; Air Vice-Marshal 1971. *Recreations:* gardening, sport as spectator. *Address:* c/o National Westminster Bank, Stone, Staffs. *Club:* Royal Air Force.

HILLS, Sir Graham (John), Kt 1988; PhD, DSc; FRSE, CChem, FRSC; Principal and Vice-Chancellor of the University of Strathclyde, 1980–91; Scottish Governor of the BBC, since 1989; *b* 9 April 1926; *s* of Albert Victor Hills and Marjorie Hills (*née* Harper); *m* 1st, 1950, Brenda Stubbington (*d* 1974); one *s* three *d*; 2nd, 1980, Mary Jane McNaughton. *Educ:* Birkbeck Coll., London Univ. (BSc 1946, PhD 1950, DSc 1962; Hon. Fellow 1984). Lecturer in Physical Chemistry, Imperial College, 1949–62; Professor of Physical Chemistry, Univ. of Southampton, 1962–80; Visiting Professor: Univ. of Western Ontario, 1968; Case Western Reserve Univ., 1969; Univ. of Buenos Aires, 1977. President: Internat. Soc. of Electrochemistry, 1983–85; Soc. of Chemical Industry, 1991–. Member: ACOST, 1987–; Council, RSC, 1983–86; Council, CNAA, 1988–; Design Council, 1989–90; Scottish Enterprise, 1991–. Non-Executive Director: Scottish Post Office Bd, 1986–; Scottish Develt Agency, 1988–90; Glasgow Action, 1986–90; Britoil, 1988–90. Hon. ScD Technical Univ. of Łodz, Poland, 1984; Hon. DSc Southampton, 1984; Hon. LLD: Glasgow, 1985; Waterloo, Canada, 1991. Hon. Medal, Univ. of Pavia, 1988. Commander: Polish Order of Merit, 1984; Royal Norwegian Order of Merit, 1986. *Publications:* Reference Electrodes, 1961; Polarography, 1964; contrib. Faraday Transactions, on physical chemistry, espec. electrochemistry. *Recreations:* country life, European political history, rocking the boat. *Address:* Sunnyside of Threepwood, Laigh Threepwood, Beith, Ayrshire KA15 2JW. *T:* Beith (05055) 3479. *Clubs:* Athenæum, Caledonian.

HILLS, Prof. Richard Edwin; Professor of Radio Astronomy, Cambridge, since 1990; *b* 30 Sept. 1945; *s* of Ronald Hills and Betty Dorothy Hills (*née* Davies); *m* 1973, Beverley Bevis; two *s*. *Educ:* Bedford Sch.; Queen's Coll., Cambridge (BA Physics); Univ. of California, Berkeley (PhD Astronomy). Research Scientist, Max Planck Inst. for Radio Astronomy, Bonn, 1972–74; Research Associate, 1974–84, Asst Dir of Research, 1984–90, Cavendish Lab., Cambridge; Project Scientist, James Clerk Maxwell Telescope, 1975–87. FRAS. Jackson-Gwilt Medal, RAS, 1989; MacRobert Award, Fellowship of Engineers, 1990. *Publications:* contribs to professional jls. *Recreations:* travel, DIY, music. *Address:* Cavendish Laboratory, Madingley Road, Cambridge CB3 0HE. *T:* Cambridge (0223) 337300.

HILLSBOROUGH, Earl of; Arthur Francis Nicholas Wills Hill; Finance Director, Scheduling Technology Group Ltd, since 1989 (Finance Controller, 1988–89); *b* 4 Feb. 1959; *s* and *heir* of Marquess of Downshire, *qv*; *m* 1990, Janey, *d* of Gerald Bunting; one *d*. *Educ:* Eton College; Royal Agricultural Coll., Cirencester; Central London Polytechnic. ACA 1985. Touche Ross & Co., 1981–87. *Recreations:* sheep farming, sport. *Heir:* *b* Lord Anthony Ian Hill, *b* 20 Oct. 1961.

HILSUM, Prof. Cyril, CBE 1990; PhD; FRS 1979; FEng 1978; FInstP, FIEE; Director of Research, GEC plc, since 1985 (Chief Scientist, General Electric Co. Research Laboratories, 1983–85); *b* 17 May 1925; *s* of Benjamin and Ada Hilsum; *m* 1947, Betty Cooper (*d* 1987); two *d*. *Educ:* Raines Sch., London; University Coll., London (BSc, PhD). FIEE 1967; FIEEE 1984; FInstP 1960. Joined Royal Naval Scientific Service, 1945; Admiralty Res. Lab., 1947–50, and Services Electronics Res. Lab., 1950–64, working first on infra-red res., then on semiconductors; Royal Signals and Radar Estab., 1964–83, working first on compound semiconductors, later on flat panel electronic displays; CSO, 1974–83. Vis. Prof. in Physics, UCL, 1988–. Mem., SERC, 1984–88. Pres., Inst. of Physics, 1988–90. Foreign Associate, US National Acad. of Engrg, 1983. Max Born Medal and Prize, Inst. of Physics, 1987; Faraday Medal, IEE, 1988. *Publications:* Semiconducting III-V Compounds, 1961; over 100 scientific and technical papers. *Recreations:* ballroom dancing, tennis. *Address:* GEC Research Laboratories, East Lane, Wembley, Mddx HA9 7PP.

HILTON OF EGGARDON, Baroness *cr* 1991 (Life Peer), of Eggardon in the County of Dorset; **Jennifer Hilton,** QPM 1989; *b* 12 Jan. 1936; *d* of John Robert Hilton, *qv*. *Educ:* Bedales Sch.; Manchester Univ. (BA Hons Psychology 1970; MA (Research) 1971); London Univ. (Dip. Criminology 1972; Dip. History of Art 1982). Joined Metropolitan Police, 1956; Univ. Scholarship, 1967; Police Staff Coll. (Directing Staff), 1973–74; Met. Police Management Services Dept, 1975–76; Supt then Chief Supt, Heathrow Airport, Battersea, Chiswick, 1977–83; New Scotland Yard (Traffic, Courts, Obscene Publications, Planning, Neighbourhood Policing), 1983–87; Comdr, 1984; Head of Training, Metropolitan Police, 1988–90. *Publications:* The Gentle Arm of the Law, 1967, 2nd edn 1973; (with Sonya Hunt) Individual Development and Social Experience, 1975, 2nd edn 1981; articles in Police Jl, Police Review, etc. *Recreations:* gardening, history, art, travel. *Address:* House of Lords, SW1A 0PW.

HILTON, (Alan) John Howard; QC 1990; a Recorder, since 1986; *b* 21 Aug. 1942; *s* of Alan Howard Hilton and Barbara Mary Campbell Hilton; *m* 1st, 1968, Jasmina Laila Hamzavi; 2nd, 1978, Nicola Mary Bayley, *qv*; one *s*. *Educ:* Haileybury and Imperial Service Coll.; Manchester Univ. (LLB Hons). Called to the Bar, Middle Temple, 1964. *Recreations:* opera, cooking, magic, 19th century paintings of ladies, enjoying adjournments. *Address:* Queen Elizabeth Building, Temple, EC4Y 9BS. *T:* 071–583 5766.

HILTON, Anthony Victor; Managing Director, Evening Standard, since 1989; *b* 26 Aug. 1946; *s* of Raymond Walwork Hilton and Miriam Eileen Norah Hilton (*née* Kydd); *m* 1st, 1969, Patricia Moore; one *s*; 2nd, 1989, Cynthia June Miles; two *s* one *d*. *Educ:* Univ. of Aberdeen (MA Hons Econs 1968). Financial columnist: Guardian, 1968; Observer, 1969; Daily Mail, 1971; Sunday Express, 1972; Editor, Accountancy Age, 1974–79; NY corresp., Sunday Times, 1979–82; City Editor: The Times, 1982–83; Evening Standard, 1984–89; Dir, Associated Newspapers, 1989. *Publications:* How to communicate financial information to employees, 1979; City within a state: a portrait of the City of London, 1987. *Recreations:* canal cruising, cycling, bonfires. *Address:* 12 Wellington Square, Chelsea SW3 4NJ. *T:* 071–730 3880. *Club:* Lansdowne.

HILTON, Brian James George; Director, Citizen's Charter Unit, Cabinet Office, since 1991; *b* 21 April 1940; *s* of Percival William Hilton and Gladys Hilton (*née* Haylett); *m* 1965, Mary Margaret Kirkpatrick; one *s* two *d*. *Educ:* St Marylebone Grammar Sch., London. Export Credits Guarantee Dept, 1958–68; Board of Trade, 1968–71; Foreign and Commonwealth Office, 1971–74: First Secretary to UK Delegn to OECD, Paris; Asst Sec., Dept of Industry, 1976–84; RCDS 1981; Hd, Financial Services Div., DTI, 1984–87; Hd, Central Unit (Under Sec.), DTI, 1987–89; Dep. Sec., MAFF, 1989–91. Foundation Governor, Hampden Gurney Primary Sch., London W1, 1976–. *Recreations:* cricket, rugby, music, gardening. *Address:* Cabinet Office, Citizen's Charter Unit, Government Offices, Great George Street, SW1P 3AL.

HILTON, John Howard; *see* Hilton, A. J. H.

HILTON, Rear-Adm. John Millard Thomas, FIMechE, FIEE; consulting engineer; *b* 24 Dec. 1934; *s* of late Edward Thomas Hilton and of Margaret Norah Attrill (*née* Millard); *m* 1st, 1958, Patricia Anne Kirby (marr. diss. 1979); one *s* one *d*; 2nd, 1985, Cynthia Mary Caroline Seddon-Brown (*née* Hargreave); one step *d*. *Educ:* Wyggeston Grammar Sch. for Boys, Leicester; County High Sch., Clacton; RNC Dartmouth; RNEC Manadon; RNC Greenwich; City Univ. (MSc 1968); Imperial Coll. of Science and Technology (DIC 1973). Joined RN 1951; served HM Ships Devonshire, Enard Bay, Theseus, Glory, Eagle (Suez operation, 1956); Birmingham, Mohawk, Collingwood; Norfolk, 1968–70; C-in-C Fleet's Engineering Staff, 1970–72; HMS Tamar, Hong Kong, 1973–76; Dir, Naval Engineering, RNEC, 1976–77; Special Study, 1978; Captain Surface Weapon Acceptance, ASWE, 1979–80; MoD Bath, 1980; Dep. Chief Naval Signal Officer, MoD, London, 1980–83; Project Dir, ARE Portsdown, 1984–87; Vice-Pres. (Navy), Ordnance Bd, 1987–88; Pres., Ordnance Bd, 1988–90. ADC to the Queen, 1985–88. Liveryman, Scientific Instrument Makers' Co., 1989–. *Publications:* professional papers. *Recreations:* gardening, personal computing, photography, biblical theology, family life. *Address*: Pennyfold, Church Road, Steep, near Petersfield, Hants GU32 2DF. *Club*: Royal Navy and Royal Albert Yacht (Portsmouth).

HILTON, John Robert, CMG 1965; HM Diplomatic Service (appointed to Foreign Service, 1943), retired 1969; *b* 5 Jan. 1908; *s* of Oscar Hilton, MD, and Louisa Holdsworth Hilton; *m* 1933, Margaret Frances Stephens; one *s* three *d*. *Educ*: Marlborough Coll.; Corpus Christi Coll., Oxford (MA); Bartlett Sch. of Architecture; University Coll., London (Diploma). ARIBA. Dir of Antiquities, Cyprus, 1934–36; Architect to E. S. & A. Robinson Ltd and private practice, 1936–41. Capt. RE, 1941–43. Foreign Service, 1943; transferred to Istanbul, 1944; 2nd Sec., Athens, 1945; Foreign Office, 1947; 1st Sec., Istanbul, 1956; Foreign Office, 1960. Mem. Council, National Schizophrenia Fellowship, 1977–81, 1983– (Pres., 1985–91). FRSA. *Publications*: articles in Architectural Review and other jls, Mind and Analysis; Memoir on Louis MacNeice (as appendix to his autobiography, The Strings are False), 1965. *Recreations*: philosophy, walking. *Address*: Hope Cottage, Nash Hill, Lacock, Wilts SN15 2QL. *T*: Lacock (024973) 369.

See also Baroness Hilton of Eggardon.

HILTON, Nicola Mary; *see* Bayley, N. M.

HILTON, Col Peter, MC 1942 and Bars 1943 and 1944; JP; Lord-Lieutenant and Custos Rotulorum of Derbyshire, since 1978; Managing Director and Company Secretary, 1949–86, Consultant, since 1986, James Smith (Scotland Nurseries) Ltd; *b* 30 June 1919; *er s* of late Maj.-Gen. Richard Hilton, DSO, MC, DFC (and Bar), and Phyllis Martha (*née* Woodin); *m* 1942, Winifred, *d* of late Ernest Smith, Man. Dir Scotland Nurseries, Tansley; one *s* (and one *s* decd). *Educ*: Malvern Coll.; RMA Woolwich; psc. Commnd RA, 1939; BEF, 1939–40, 1st Div. Dunkirk; Western Desert, 1942–43, 7th Armd Div. Alamein (RHA Jacket 1942); Italy, 1943–44, 5th American Army, Adjt 3rd Regt RHA; Normandy, 1944, OC J Bty RHA (wounded Falaise Gap); Greece, 1946–49 (despatches 1948); Instructor Royal Hellenic Staff Coll.; Col RA 1949, retd; RARO; recalled Korean Emergency, 1950; TA Commn, 1951; CO 528 W Notts Regt, RA (TA), 1951–54; ACF Commn, 1962; Comdt Derbyshire ACF, 1962–66, Hon. Col 1972–77. Nat. Pres., Normandy Veterans Assoc.; President: TA & VRA, E Midlands, 1987; 8th Army Veterans; Dunkirk 1940 Veterans; St John Council; SSAFA; FHS; Boys' Brigade; Vice-Pres., Derbys Boys Clubs. President: S Derbys Br., ARC; Derbys Rural Community Council. Trustee: Derby New Theatre; Sherwood Foresters Museum; Crich Meml Trust; Patron, Derby County Show. Shows at Ashover, Ashbourne and Bakewell; Sheepdog Trials at Longshaw and Dovedale; Pres., Belper Musical Theatre; Vice-Pres., British Heart Foundn, Derbys. JP, High Sheriff 1970–71, DL 1972, Derbys; Mem. Wirksworth Div. Derbys CC, 1967–77. KStJ 1979. Greek Order of Minerva, 1949. *Recreations*: ex-Service interests, local activities, horticulture. *Address*: Alton Manor, Idridgehay, Derbs DE4 4JH. *T*: (home) Matlock (0629) 822435, (office) Matlock (0629) 580580.

HILTON, Prof. Peter John, MA, DPhil Oxon, PhD Cantab; Distinguished Professor of Mathematics, State University of New York at Binghamton, since 1982; *b* 7 April 1923; *s* of late Dr Mortimer Hilton and Mrs Elizabeth Hilton; *m* 1949, Margaret (*née* Mostyn); two *s*. *Educ*: St Paul's Sch.; Queen's Coll., Oxford. Asst Lectr, Manchester Univ., 1948–51, Lectr, 1951–52; Lectr, Cambridge Univ., 1952–55; Senior Lecturer, Manchester Univ., 1956–58; Mason Prof. of Pure Mathematics, University of Birmingham, 1958–62; Prof. of Mathematics, Cornell Univ., 1962–71, Washington Univ., 1971–73; Beaumont Univ. Prof., Case Western Reserve Univ., 1972–82. Visiting Professor: Cornell Univ., USA, 1958–59; Eidgenössische Techn. Hochschule, Zürich, 1966–67, 1981–82, 1988–89; Courant Inst., NY Univ., 1967–68; Univ. Aut. de Barcelona, 1989. Mathematician-in-residence, Battelle Research Center, Seattle, 1970–82. Chairman: US Commn on Mathematical Instruction, 1971–74; NRC Cttee on Applied Maths Trng, 1977–; First Vice-Pres., Math. Assoc. of Amer., 1978–80. Corresp. Mem., Brazilian Acad. of Scis, 1979; Hon. Mem. Belgian Mathematical Soc., 1955. Hon. DHum N Michigan, 1977; Hon. DSc: Meml Univ. of Newfoundland, 1983; Univ. Aut. de Barcelona, 1989. Silver Medal, Univ. of Helsinki, 1975; Centenary Medal, John Carroll Univ., 1985. *Publications*: Introduction to Homotopy Theory, 1953; Differential Calculus, 1958; Homology Theory (with S. Wylie), 1960; Partial Derivatives, 1960; Homotopy Theory and Duality, 1965; (with H. B. Griffiths) Classical Mathematics, 1970; General Cohomology Theory and K-Theory, 1971; (with U. Stammbach) Course in Homological Algebra, 1971; (with Y.-C. Wu) Course in Modern Algebra, 1974; (with G. Mislin and J. Roitberg) Localization of Nilpotent Groups and Spaces, 1975; (with J. Pedersen) Fear No More, 1983; Nilpotente Gruppen und Nilpotente Räume, 1984; (with J. Pedersen) Build Your Own Polyhedra, 1987; numerous research articles on algebraic topology, homological algebra and category theory in British and foreign mathematical journals. *Recreations*: travel, sport, reading, theatre, chess, bridge, broadcasting. *Address*: Department of Mathematical Sciences, State University of New York, Binghamton, NY 13902–6000, USA.

HILTON, Prof. Rodney Howard, FBA 1977; Professor of Medieval Social History, University of Birmingham, 1963–82, now Emeritus; *b* 1916; *s* of John James Hilton and Anne Hilton. *Educ*: Manchester Grammar Sch.; Balliol Coll. and Merton Coll., Oxford (BA, DPhil). Army, 1940–46; Lectr and Reader in Medieval History, 1946–63, Dir, Inst. for Advanced Res. in the Humanities, 1984–87, Univ. of Birmingham. *Publications*: The Economic Development of Some Leicestershire Estates in the 14th and 15th Centuries, 1947; (with H. Fagan) The English Rising of 1381, 1950; (ed) Ministers' Accounts of the Warwickshire Estates of the Duke of Clarence, 1952; (ed) The Stoneleigh Leger Book, 1960; A Medieval Society, 1966, rev. edn 1983; The Decline of Serfdom in Medieval England, 1969, rev. edn 1983; Bondmen Made Free, 1973; The English Peasantry in the Later Middle Ages, 1975; (ed) Peasants, Knights and Heretics, 1976; (ed) The Transition from Feudalism to Capitalism, 1976; (ed with T. H. Aston) The English Rising of 1381, 1984; Class Conflict and the Crisis of Feudalism, 1985; articles and reviews in Past and Present, English Historical Review, Economic History Review, etc. *Address*: School of History, University of Birmingham, Birmingham B15 2TT. *T*: 021–414 5736.

HILTON, William (Samuel); Director General, Federation of Master Builders, 1987 (National Director, 1970–87); Managing Director: Trade Press (FMB) Ltd, since 1972; National Register of Warranted Builders Ltd, since 1980; *b* 21 March 1926; *m* 1948, Agnes Aitken Orr; three *s*. *Educ*: Kyleshill, Saltcoats; Ardrossan Academy. Railway Fireman until 1949; Labour Party Agent to late Lord Kirkwood, 1949–52; Research and Education Officer for Building Trade Operatives, 1952–66. MP (Lab and Co-op) Bethnal Green, 1966–Feb. 1974. Director: Trade Debt Recovery Services Ltd, 1986; Construction Industry Services Ltd, 1986. Member: Agrément Bd for Building Industry, 1965–66; EDC for Building Industry, 1964–66; Construction ITB, 1985–; Employers' Sec., Building and Allied Trades Jt Industrial Council, 1979–. Editor, Builders Standard, 1954–66. *Publications*: Building by Direct Labour, 1954; Foes to Tyranny, 1964; Industrial Relations in Construction, 1968; The Plug Dropper, 1986. *Address*: Federation of Master Builders, 33 John Street, WC1N 2BB.

HIME, Martin, CBE 1987; HM Diplomatic Service; Assessor, Foreign and Commonwealth Office, since 1988; *b* 18 Feb. 1928; *s* of Percy Joseph Hime and Esther Greta (*née* Howe); *m* 1st, 1960, Henrietta Fehling (marr. diss.); one *s* three *d*; 2nd, 1971, Janina Christine

Majcher; one *d*. *Educ*: King's Coll. Sch., Wimbledon; Trinity Hall, Cambridge (MA). Served RA, 1946–48. Called to the Bar, Inner Temple, 1951; Marks and Spencer Ltd, 1952–58; joined HM Diplomatic Service, 1960; served in Tokyo, Kobe, Frankfurt and Buenos Aires, 1960–69; 2nd Sec., FCO, 1970–72; Consul, Johannesburg, 1972–74; 1st Sec. (Econ.), Pretoria, 1974–76; Asst Head, S Pacific Dept, FCO, 1976–79; Dep. High Comr in Bangladesh, 1979–82; Consul-General: Cleveland, Ohio, 1982–85; Houston, Texas, 1985–88. *Recreations*: golf, lawn tennis, books, table games. *Address*: c/o Foreign and Commonwealth Office, SW1A 2AH. *Clubs*: All England Lawn Tennis; Hawks (Cambridge); Royal Wimbledon Golf.

HIMSWORTH, Sir Harold (Percival), KCB 1952; MD; FRS 1955; FRCP; Secretary, Medical Research Council, 1949–68, retired (Member and Deputy Chairman, 1967–68); *b* 19 May 1905; *s* of late Arnold Himsworth, Huddersfield, Yorks; *m* 1932, Charlotte (*d* 1988), *yr d* of William Gray, Walmer, Kent; two *s*. *Educ*: King James' Grammar Sch., Almondbury, Yorks; University Coll. and University Coll. Hosp., London. Asst, Medical Unit, University Coll. Hosp., 1930; Beit Memorial Research Fellow, 1932–35; William Julius Mickle Fellow, University of London, 1935; Fellow of University Coll., London, 1936; Deputy Dir, Medical Unit, University Coll. Hospital, 1936; Goulstonian Lecturer, 1939; Oliver-Sharpey Lectr, 1949, RCP; Prof. of Medicine, Univ. of London and Dir of the Medical Unit, University Coll. Hospital, London, 1939–49; Mem. of Medical Research Council, 1948–49; Sydney Ringer Lecturer, 1949; Lowell Lecturer, Boston, Mass., 1947; Harveian Orator, Royal College of Physicians, 1962. Pres., Sect. of Experimental Medicine, Royal Society of Medicine, 1946–47. Chm., Bd of Management, London Sch. of Hygiene and Tropical Med., 1969–76. Prime Warden, Goldsmiths Co., 1975. Docteur *hc* Toulouse, 1950; Hon. LLD: Glasgow, 1953; London, 1956; Wales, 1959; Hon. DSc: Manchester, 1956; Leeds, 1968; Univ. of WI, 1968; Hon. ScD, Cambridge, 1964. New York Univ. Medallist, 1958; Conway Evans Prize, RCP, 1968. Member: Norwegian Med. Soc., 1954; Royal Soc. of Arts and Sciences, Göteborg, Sweden, 1957; Hon. Member: Med. Soc. of Sweden, 1949; Amer. Assoc. of Physicians, 1950; For. Mem., Amer. Philosoph. Soc., 1972; For. Hon. Member: Amer. Acad. of Arts and Sciences, 1957; Belgian Royal Acad. of Medicine, 1958. Hon. FRCR 1958; Hon. FRCPE 1960; Hon. FRSM 1961; Hon. FRCS 1965; Hon. FRCPath 1969; Hon. Fellow LSHTM, 1979; Hon. FRSTM, 1981. *Publications*: The Development and Organisation of Scientific Knowledge, 1970; Scientific Knowledge and Philosophic Thought, 1986; medical and scientific papers. *Recreation*: fishing. *Address*: 13 Hamilton Terrace, NW8. *T*: 071–286 6996. *Club*: Athenæum.

See also R. L. Himsworth.

HIMSWORTH, Prof. Richard Lawrence, MD; FRCP; Regius Professor of Medicine, University of Aberdeen, since 1985; *b* 14 June 1937; *s* of Sir Harold Himsworth, *qv*; *m* 1966, Sara Margaret Tattersall; two *s* one *d*. *Educ*: Westminster Sch.; Trinity Coll., Cambridge (MD 1971); University Coll. Hosp. Med. Sch. FRCP 1977; FRCPE 1988; FRCPGlas 1990. Lectr in Medicine, UCH Med. Sch., 1967–71; MRC Travelling Fellow, New York, 1969–70; MRC Scientific Staff, Clinical Res. Centre, 1971–85: Asst Dir, 1978–82; Head, Endocrinology Res. Gp, 1979–85; Consultant Physician, Northwick Park Hosp., 1972–85. Mem., NW Thames RHA, 1982–85. *Publications*: scientific and medical papers. *Recreation*: painting. *Address*: Mains of Kebbaty, Midmar, Aberdeenshire AB51 7QL. *T*: Sauchen (03303) 430. *Club*: Royal Northern and University (Aberdeen).

HINCHCLIFFE, Peter Robert Mossom, CMG 1988; CVO 1979; HM Diplomatic Service; High Commissioner to Zambia, since 1990; *b* 9 April 1937; *s* of Herbert Peter and Jeannie Hinchcliffe; *m* 1965, Archbold Harriet Siddall; three *d*. *Educ*: Elm Park, Killylea, Co. Armagh, Prep. Sch.; Radley Coll.; Trinity Coll., Dublin (BA (Hons), MA). Military service, short service commission, W Yorks Regt, 1955–57; TCD, Dublin Univ., 1957–61; HMOCS: West Aden Protectorate, South Arabian Fedn, 1961–67; Admin. Asst, Birmingham Univ., 1968–69; FCO: 1st Sec., Near Eastern Dept, 1969–70; 1st Sec., UK Mission to UN, 1971–74; 1st Sec. and Head of Chancery, Kuwait, 1974–76; Asst Head of Science and Technology and Central and Southern African Depts, FCO, 1976–78; Dep. High Comr, Dar es Salaam, 1978–81; Consul-Gen., Dubai, 1981–85; Hd of Information Dept, FCO, 1985–87; Ambassador to Kuwait, 1987–90. *Recreations*: golf, tennis, philately. *Address*: c/o Foreign and Commonwealth Office, SW1A 2AH. *Clubs*: East India, Devonshire, Sports and Public Schools; North Middlesex Golf; Royal Co. Down Golf (Newcastle, Co. Down).

HINCHINGBROOKE, Viscount; *see* Montagu, J. E. H.

HINCHLIFF, Rev. Canon Peter Bingham, MA, DD Oxon, PhD Rhodes; Fellow and Tutor, Balliol College, Oxford, since 1972 (Chaplain, 1972–87); *b* 25 Feb. 1929; *e s* of Rev. Canon Samuel Bingham Hinchliff and Brenda Hinchliff; *m* 1955, Constance, *d* of E. L. Whitehead, Uitenhage, S Africa; three *s* one *d*. *Educ*: St Andrew's Coll., Grahamstown, S Africa; Rhodes Univ., Grahamstown; Trinity Coll., Oxford. Deacon, 1952; Priest, 1953, in Anglican Church in S Africa; Asst in Parish of Uitenhage, 1952–55. Subwarden, St Paul's Theological Coll., Grahamstown, 1955–59; Lectr in Comparative Religion, Rhodes Univ., 1957–59; Prof. of Ecclesiastical History, Rhodes Univ., 1960–69; Canon and Chancellor, Grahamstown Cathedral, 1964–69; Sec., Missionary and Ecumenical Council of the General Synod (formerly the Church Assembly), 1969–72; Examng Chaplain to Bishop of Newcastle, 1973, to Bishop of Oxford, 1974–. Public Orator, Rhodes Univ., 1965; Hulsean Lectr, Cambridge Univ., 1975–76; Bampton Lectr, Oxford Univ., 1982. Provincial Hon. Canon, Cape Town Cathedral, 1959–; Hon. Canon, Grahamstown Cathedral, 1969–; Canon Theologian, Coventry Cathedral, 1972–. Mem., Gen. Synod, 1988–90. Pres., Oxford Soc. of Historical Theol., 1978–79. *Publications*: The South African Liturgy, 1959; The Anglican Church in South Africa, 1963; John William Colenso, 1964; The One-Sided Reciprocity, 1966; A Calendar of Cape Missionary Correspondence, 1967; The Church in South Africa, 1968; The Journal of John Ayliff, 1970; Cyprian of Carthage, 1974; (with D. Young) The Human Potential, 1981; Holiness and Politics, 1982; Benjamin Jowett and the Christian Religion, 1987; contributor to: Jl of Ecclesiastical History; Studia Liturgica, etc. *Recreations*: crossword puzzles, odd jobbery. *Address*: Balliol College, Oxford.

HINCHLIFF, Stephen, CBE 1976; Chairman and Managing Director, Dexion Group, since 1976; *b* 11 July 1926; *s* of Gordon Henry and Winifred Hinchliff; *m* 1987, Anne Fiona Maudsley; one *d* and one *s* one *d* from a previous marriage. *Educ*: Almondbury Grammar Sch., Huddersfield; Boulevard Nautical Coll., Hull; Huddersfield Coll. of Technology; Cranfield Inst. of Technology (MSc). FIMechE, FIProdE. Production Engr, Dowty Auto Units Ltd, 1953–54: Dowty Seals Ltd: Chief Prodn Engr, 1953–54; Works Manager, 1954–56; Dir, 1956–76; Dep. Man. Dir, 1966–67; Man. Dir, 1967–76; Dep. Chm., Dowty Gp Ltd, 1973–76; Man. Dir, Dowty Gp Industrial Div., 1973–76. CBIM; FRSA. *Recreations*: squash, badminton, tennis. *Address*: Bowmore Farm, Hawridge Common, near Chesham, Bucks HP5 2UH. *T*: Cholesbury (024029) 237.

HINCHLIFFE, David Martin; MP (Lab) Wakefield, since 1987; *b* 14 Oct. 1948; *s* of late Robert Victor Hinchliffe and Muriel Hinchliffe; *m* 1982, Julia (*née* North); one *s* one *d*. *Educ*: Lawefield Lane Primary Sch., Wakefield; Cathedral C of E Secondary Modern

Sch., Wakefield; Leeds Polytechnic (Cert. in Social Work); Bradford Univ. (MA Social Work and Community Work); Huddersfield Polytechnic (Cert Ed). Social Work with Leeds Social Services, 1968–79; Social Work Tutor, Kirklees Metropolitan Borough Council, 1980–87. *Recreation:* Rugby League—supporter of Wakefield Trinity RLFC. *Address:* 21 King Street, Wakefield, W Yorks WF1 2SR. *T:* Wakefield (0924) 290134. *Club:* Wakefield Labour.

HIND, Rt. Rev. John William; *see* Horsham, Bishop Suffragan of.

HIND, Kenneth, ERD 1955; Senior Director, Employment and Industrial Relations, Post Office, 1973–80; *b* 14 March 1920; *er s* of late Harry and Edith Hind; *m* 1942, Dorothy Walton; one *s*. *Educ:* Central Sec. Sch., Sheffield; Queens' Coll., Cambridge (Munro Schol.). Army, 1940–48: Major, REME. General Post Office: Asst Principal, 1948; Principal, 1950; Asst Sec., 1960; Dir, Radio and Broadcasting, 1967; Central Services, 1969; Senior Dir, 1971. *Recreations:* cricket, gardening. *Address:* 18 Brocklehurst Avenue, Sheffield S8 8JG. *T:* Sheffield (0742) 745577.

HIND, Kenneth Harvard; MP (C) West Lancashire, since 1983; barrister; *b* 15 Sept. 1949; *s* of George Edward and Brenda Hind; *m* 1977, Patricia Anne (*née* Millar); one *s* one *d*. *Educ:* Woodhouse Grove Sch., Bradford; Leeds Univ. (LLB 1971); Inns of Court Sch. of Law. Pres., Leeds Univ. Union, 1971–72. Called to the Bar, Gray's Inn, 1973; practised North Eastern circuit, 1973–83. PPS to Minister of State: for Defence Procurement, 1986–87; for Employment, 1987–89; for Northern Ireland, 1989–90; PPS to Sec. of State for Northern Ireland, 1990–. Member: Liverpool Univ. Senate, 1983–; Soc. of Conservative Lawyers, 1983–; Justice, Internat. Commn of Jurists, 1983–; Hon. Mem., Anglo Hellenic Assoc., 1983–. Hon. Vice-President: Merseyside Chamber of Commerce, 1983–; Central and West Lancs Chamber of Industry and Commerce, 1983–. Dir, Doctus, 1990–; Chm., De Keyser Europe. MInstD. *Recreations:* music, sailing Enterprise, cricket; Hon. Vice-Pres. Headingley RUFC. *Address:* Ben Lane Farmhouse, Intake Lane, Bickerstaffe, near Ormskirk, Lancs; 54 Red Post Hill, Dulwich, SE24 9JQ. *Clubs:* Farmers (Ormskirk); Ormskirk Conservative.

HINDE, Prof. Robert Aubrey, CBE 1988; FRS 1974; Master of St John's College, Cambridge, since 1989 (Fellow, 1958–89); *b* 26 Oct. 1923; *s* of late Dr and Mrs E. B. Hinde, Norwich; *m* 1st, 1948, Hester Cecily (marr. diss. 1971), *d* of late C. R. V. Coutts; two *s* two *d*; 2nd, 1971, Joan Gladys, *d* of F. J. Stevenson; two *d*. *Educ:* Oundle Sch.; St John's Coll., Cambridge; Balliol Coll., Oxford (Hon. Fellow, 1986). Served Coastal Comd, RAF, Flt-Lt, 1941–45. Research Asst, Edward Grey Inst., Univ. of Oxford, 1948–50; Curator, Ornithological Field Station (now sub-Dept of Animal Behaviour), Madingley, Cambridge, 1950–65; St John's Coll., Cambridge: Research Fellow, 1951–54; Steward, 1956–58; Tutor, 1958–63; Royal Soc. Res. Prof., Cambridge Univ., 1963–89. Hon. Dir, MRC Unit on Develt and Integration of Behaviour, 1970–. Hitchcock Prof., Univ. of California, 1979; Green Vis. Scholar, Univ. of Texas, 1983. Mem. Council, Royal Soc., 1985–87. Croonian Lect., Royal Soc., 1990. Mem., Academia Europaea, 1990. Hon. Member: Assoc. for the Study of Animal Behaviour, 1987; Deutsche Ornithologische Ges., 1988; For. Hon. Mem., Amer. Acad. of Arts and Sciences, 1974; For. Associate, Nat. Acad. of Scis, USA, 1978; Hon. Fellow, Amer. Ornithologists' Union, 1977; Hon FBPsS 1981; Hon. FRCPsych 1988; Hon. FTCD, 1990. Hon. ScD: Univ. Libre, Brussels, 1974; Univ. of Paris (Nanterre), 1979; Stirling Univ., 1991. Scientific Medal, Zoological Soc., 1961; Leonard Cammer Medal in Psychiatry, Columbia Coll., NY, 1980; Osman Hill Award, Primate Soc. of GB, 1980; Albert Einstein Award for Psychiatry, Albert Einstein Coll. of Medicine, NY, 1987; Huxley Medal, RAI, 1990; Distinguished Scientists Award, Soc. for Res. in Child Develt, 1991. *Publications:* Animal Behaviour: a synthesis of Ethology and Comparative Psychology, 1966; (ed) Bird Vocalizations: their relations to current problems in biology and psychology, 1969; (ed jtly) Short Term Changes in Neural Activity and Behaviour, 1970; (ed) Non-Verbal Communication, 1972; (ed jtly) Constraints on Learning, 1973; Biological Bases of Human Social Behaviour, 1974; (ed jtly) Growing Points in Ethology, 1976; Towards Understanding Relationships, 1979; Ethology: its nature and relations with other sciences, 1982; (jtly) Defended to Death, 1982; (ed and contrib.) Primate Social Relationships: an integrated approach, 1983; (ed jtly) Social Relationships and Cognitive Development, 1985; Individuals, Relationships and Culture, 1987; (ed jtly) Relationships within Families, 1988; (ed jtly) Aggression and War, 1989; (ed jtly) Education for Peace, 1989; (ed and contrib) The Institution of War, 1991; (ed jtly) Co-operation and Prosocial Behaviour, 1991; sundry papers in biological and psychological journals. *Address:* The Master's Lodge, St John's College, Cambridge. *T:* Cambridge (0223) 338635.

HINDE, Thomas; *see* Chitty, Sir Thomas Willes.

HINDLEY, Prof. Colin Boothman; Director of Centre for Study of Human Development since 1967, and Professor of Child Development, 1972–84, now Professor Emeritus, Institute of Education, London; *b* Bolton, 1923; *m* 1945; two *s*. *Educ:* Bolton Sch.; Manchester Univ.; University Coll., London. MB, ChB Manchester 1946; BSc London 1949 (1st cl. Psychol.). Asst Med. Officer, Hope Hosp., Salford; Res. Psychologist and subseq. Sen. Lectr, London Univ. Inst. of Educn, 1949–72; Head of Adolescent Development Dip. Course, 1968–72. Psychol. Adviser, Internat. Children's Centre Growth Studies, Paris, 1954–; Editor, Jl of Child Psychol. and Psychiat., 1959–69; Mem. Council, Brit. Psychol. Soc., 1970–73; Mem. Cttee, Internat. Soc. for Study Behavioural Develt, 1969–75; Mem. Assoc. Child Psychol. and Psychiat. (Chm. 1967–68). FBPsS. *Publications:* Conceptual and Methodological Issues in the Study of Child Development, 1980; chapters in Child Development: International Method of Study, ed Falkner, 1960; Learning Theory and Personality Development, in Psychosomatic Aspects of Paediatrics, ed Mackeith and Sandler, 1961; The Place of Longitudinal Methods in the Study of Development, in Determinants of Behavioural Development, ed Mönks, Hartup and de Wit, 1972; (jt ed. and contrib.) Development in Adolescence, 1983; contribs to jls. *Recreations:* jazz, literature, gardening, walking, travel, cinema. *Address:* Department of Child Development and Primary Education, Institute of Education, Bedford Way, WC1H 0AL. *T:* 071–636 1500.

HINDLEY, Michael John; Member (Lab) Lancashire East, European Parliament, since 1984; *b* 11 April 1947; *s* of John and Edna Hindley; *m* 1980, Ewa Agnieszka (*née* Leszczyc-Grabianka); one *d*. *Educ:* Clitheroe Royal Grammar School; London University (BA Hons); Lancaster University (MA); Free University of West Berlin. Labour Councillor, Hyndburn District Council, 1979–84 (Leader, 1981–84); contested (Lab) Blackpool North, 1983. *Recreations:* swimming, walking, reading, music, travel. *Address:* 27 Commercial Road, Great Harwood, Lancs BB6 7HX. *T:* Great Harwood (0254) 887017.

HINDLEY-SMITH, David Dury, CBE 1972; Registrar, General Dental Council (formerly Dental Board of the UK), 1947–81; *b* 20 Feb. 1916; *e s* of late James Dury Hindley-Smith; *m* 1947, Dorothy Westwood Legge (*d* 1987), *e d* of Arthur Collins and Mary Fielding; two *d*. *Educ:* Uppingham; King's Coll., Cambridge (MA); Paris and Vienna. Passed examination for Diplomatic Service, 1939. War Service: Artists' Rifles, 1939; commissioned Royal Fus., 1940; liaison officer to Gén. Leclerc, 1942, to Gén. de Gaulle's first administration, 1944; Acting Col. Mem., W Suffolk HA, 1982–86; Chm., Mental Health Cttee, W Suffolk HA, 1982–86. Mem. Council, Royal Dental Hosp., London Sch. of Dental Surgery, 1976–84 (Chm., 1981–84). Vice-Chm., Surrey Assoc. of Youth Clubs, 1950–70 (Vice-Pres., 1970–); Executive Chm., Nat. Assoc. of Youth Clubs, 1970–74 (Vice-Pres., 1974–); Chm., Sembal Trust, 1972–81; Vice-Pres., Suffolk Assoc. of Youth, 1984– (Chm., 1982–84). Hon. Mem., BDA, 1975; Hon. FDSRCSE 1977; Hon. FDSRCS, 1980. Cecil Peace Prize, 1938. *Recreations:* gardening, cooking. *Address:* The Ark House, Whepstead, Bury St Edmunds, Suffolk IP29 4UB. *T:* Horringer (0284) 735351. *Club:* Royal Society of Medicine.

HINDLIP, 5th Baron *cr* 1886; **Henry Richard Allsopp;** Bt 1880; *b* 1 July 1912; 2nd *s* of 3rd Baron Hindlip and Agatha (*d* 1962), 2nd *d* of late John C. Thynne; *S* brother, 4th Baron, 1966; *m* 1939, Cecily Valentine Jane, *o d* of late Lt-Col Malcolm Borwick, DSO, Hazelbech Hill, Northampton; two *s* one *d*. *Educ:* Eton; RMC Sandhurst. 2nd Lieut, Coldstream Guards, 1932; Major, 1941; retired, 1948. Served War of 1939–45; NW Europe, 1944. JP 1957, DL 1956, Wilts. Bronze Star Medal, USA, 1945. *Recreations:* travel, shooting. *Heir:* *s* Hon. Charles Henry Allsopp, *qv*. *Address:* Tytherton House, East Tytherton, Chippenham, Wilts. *T:* Kelloways (024974) 207. *Club:* Turf.

See also Sir R. J. Hardy, Bt.

HINDMARSH, Frederick Bell; Under-Secretary, Department of Health and Social Security, 1973–79, retired; *b* 31 Jan. 1919; *yr s* of Frederick Hindmarsh and Margaret May Hindmarsh; *m* 1947, Mary Torrance Coubrough; one *d*. *Educ:* County Grammar Sch., Acton. Clerical Officer, Min. of Health, 1936; Exec. Officer, 1937. Served war, Army, 1939–46. Min. of Pensions and Nat. Insurance and Min. of Social Security: Higher Exec. Officer, 1946; Sen. Exec. Officer, 1947; Chief Exec. Officer, 1951; Sen. Chief Exec. Officer, 1959; Prin. Exec. Officer, 1964; Asst Sec., DHSS, 1969. *Recreation:* music.

HINDMARSH, Irene, JP, MA; Principal, St Aidan's College, University of Durham, 1970–88; Second Pro-Vice-Chancellor, University of Durham, 1982–85; *b* 22 Oct. 1923; *d* of Albert Hindmarsh and Elizabeth (*née* White). *Educ:* Heaton High Sch.; Lady Margaret Hall, Oxford (MA Hons French); King's Coll., Univ. of Durham (PGCE). Taught at St Paul's Girls' Sch., London, 1947–49, Rutherford High Sch., Newcastle upon Tyne, 1949–59; Interchange Teacher, Lycée de Jeunes Filles, Dax, Landes, France, 1954–55; Lectr in Educn and French, King's Coll., Durham, 1959–64; Headmistress, Birkenhead High Sch., GPDST, 1964–70. Vis. Prof., New York State Univ., Syracuse, Cornell, Harvard, 1962; Delegate of Internat. Fedn of Univ. Women to UNO, NY, to Commns on Human Rights and Status of Women, 1962; Vis. Professor: Fu-Dan Univ., Shanghai, 1979, and again, 1980; SW China Teachers' Univ., Beibei, Sichuan, and Fu-Dan Univ., Shanghai, 1986. Delegate/Translator to internat. confs of FIPESO, 1963–70; Chairman: Internat. Cttee of Headmistresses' Assoc., 1966–70; Internat. Panel of Joint Four, 1967–70. Editor, Internat. Bull. of AHM, 1966–70. JP Birkenhead 1966, Durham 1974. FRSA 1989. *Publications:* various articles on educnl topics in AGM papers of Assoc. of Head Mistresses; contribs to prelim. papers of FIPESO meetings; seminar papers to symposia on lit. topics, Sèvres, under auspices of Council of Europe; contrib. re St Aidan's to Durham History from the Air. *Recreations:* travel, music, theatre, films, art, architecture, quality of life. *Address:* 8 Dickens Wynd, Merryoaks, Elvet Moor, Durham DH1 3QR. *T:* Durham (091) 3861881.

HINDSON, William Stanley, CMG 1962; BScEng, MIM, FIMechE; engineering and metallurgical consultant since 1974; *b* 11 Jan. 1920; *s* of late W. A. L. Hindson, Darlington; *m* 1944, Mary Sturdy (*d* 1961); one *s* one *d*; *m* 1965, Catherine Leikine, Paris, France; one *s*. *Educ:* Darlington Grammar Sch.; Coatham Sch., Redcar. With Dorman Long (Steel) Ltd, Middlesbrough, 1937–55; Metallurgical Equipment Export Co. Ltd and Indian Steelworks Construction Co. Ltd, 1956–62; Wellman Engineering Corp. Ltd, 1963–69; Cementation Co. Ltd, 1970–71; Humphreys & Glasgow, 1971–74. Mem., Inst. of Directors. *Recreations:* chess, philately. *Address:* 36 Eresby House, Rutland Gate, SW7. *T:* 071–589 3194.

HINE, Air Chief Marshal Sir Patrick (Bardon), GCB 1989 (KCB 1983); GBE 1991; Air Officer Commanding-in-Chief, RAF Strike Command and Commander-in-Chief, United Kingdom Air Forces, 1988–91; *b* 14 July 1932; parents decd; *m* 1956, Jill Adèle (*née* Gardner); three *s*. *Educ:* Peter Symonds Sch., Winchester. Served with Nos 1, 93 and 111 Sqns, 1952–60; Mem., Black Arrows aerobatic team, 1957–59; commanded: No 92 Sqn, 1962–64; No 17 Sqn, 1970–71; RAF Wildenrath, 1974–75; Dir, Public Relations (RAF), 1975–77; RCDS 1978; SASO, HQ RAF, Germany, 1979; ACAS (Policy), 1979–83; C-in-C RAF Germany and Comdr, Second Allied Tactical Air Force, 1983–85; VCDS, 1985–87; Air Mem. for Supply and Orgn, 1987–88. Air ADC to the Queen, 1989–91. Queen's Commendation for Valuable Service in the Air, 1960. CBIM; FRAeS. Winner, Carris Trophy, Hants, IoW and Channel Islands Golf Championship, and Brabazon Trophy, 1949; English Schoolboy Golf Internat., 1948–49; Inter-Services Golf, 1952–57. *Recreations:* golf, ski-ing, caravanning, photography. *Clubs:* Royal Air Force; Brockenhurst Manor Golf, Denham Golf.

HINES, Barry Melvin, FRSL; writer; *b* 30 June 1939; *s* of Richard and Annie Hines; *m* (marr. diss.); one *s* one *d*. *Educ:* Ecclesfield Grammar Sch.; Loughborough Coll. of Educn (Teaching Cert.). FRSL 1977. Teacher of Physical Educn, London, 1960–62 and S Yorks, 1962–72; Yorkshire Arts Fellow in Creative Writing, Sheffield Univ., 1972–74; E Midlands Arts Fellow in Creative Writing, Matlock Coll. of Higher Educn, 1975–77; Sheffield City Polytechnic: Arts Council Fellow in Creative Writing, 1982–84; Hon. Fellow in Creative Writing, 1984; Hon. Fellow, 1985. *Television scripts:* Billy's Last Stand, 1971; Speech Day, 1973; Two Men from Derby, 1976; The Price of Coal (2 films), 1977; The Gamekeeper, 1979; A Question of Leadership, 1981; Threads, 1984; Shooting Stars, 1990; *screenplays:* Kes, 1970; Looks and Smiles, 1981. *Publications:* (fiction): The Blinder, 1966; A Kestrel for a Knave, 1968; First Signs, 1972; The Gamekeeper, 1975; The Price of Coal, 1979; Looks and Smiles, 1981; Unfinished Business, 1983. *Recreations:* walking, supporting Sheffield United Football Club. *Address:* c/o Lemon and Durbridge Ltd, 24 Pottery Lane, Holland Park, W11 4LZ. *T:* 071–229 9216. *Club:* Hoyland Common Workingmen's (near Barnsley).

HINES, Sir Colin (Joseph), Kt 1976; OBE 1973; President: NSW Returned Services League Clubs Association, 1971–90; NSW Branch, Returned Services League of Australia, 1971–90; Vice-President of the National Executive, Returned Services League of Australia, 1971–90 (Deputy National President, 1974–87); *b* 16 Feb. 1919; *s* of J. Hines and Mrs Hines, Lyndhurst, NSW; *m* 1942, Jean Elsie, *d* of A. Wilson, Mandurama, NSW; two *s*. *Educ:* All Saints' Coll., Bathurst, NSW. Farmer and grazier. Army, 1937–45. Hon. Officer, Returned Services League of Aust., 1946–. State Comr, Aust. Forces Overseas Fund, 1971–; Trustee, Anzac Meml Trust, 1971–. Pres., War Veterans Homes, Narrabeen, 1976– (Chm., 1971–76); Chm., Clubs Mutual Services Ltd, 1972–. *Recreations:* rifle shooting, golf. *Address:* The Meadows, Lyndhurst, NSW 2741, Australia. *T:* (063) 675151. *Club:* Imperial Services (Sydney, NSW).

HINGSTON, Lt-Col Walter George, OBE 1964; psc; FRGS; *b* Radcliffe on Trent, Notts, 15 Feb. 1905; *s* of late Charles Hingston, DL and late Mildred (*née* Pleydell Bouverie), Cotgrave, Nottingham; *m* 1939, Elizabeth Margaret, *d* of late Brig. Sir Clinton

Lewis, OBE, and late Lilian Eyre (*née* Wace); two *d*. *Educ:* Harrow; RMC Sandhurst; and Staff Coll. 2nd Lieut, KOYLI, 1925; Nigeria Regt, RWAFF, 1931–36; 1st Punjab Regt, Indian Army, 1936. Served War of 1939–45: 4th Indian Div., North Africa, Eritrea (despatches); Dep. Dir Public Relations, GHQ India, 1942; Chief Information Officer to C-in-C, Ceylon, 1943; retired (invalided), 1945. Chief Information Officer, Dept of Scientific and Industrial Research, 1945–63; Editor, the Geographical Magazine, 1963–68. Mem., Marlborough and Ramsbury RDC, 1970–74. *Publications:* The Tiger Strikes, 1942; The Tiger Kills (with G. R. Stevens), 1944; Never Give Up, 1948. *Recreation:* fishing. *Address:* The Old Vicarage, Ramsbury, Marlborough, Wilts SN8 2QH. *Club:* Army and Navy.

HINKLEY, Prof. David Victor, PhD; Professor of Statistical Science, Oxford University, since 1989; Fellow, St Anne's College, Oxford, since 1989; *b* 10 Sept. 1944; *s* of Eric Samson Hinkley and Edna Gertrude (*née* Alger); *m* 1970, Elizabeth Ann Blake; one *s* one *d*. *Educ:* Birmingham Univ. (BSc 1965); Imperial Coll., London (PhD 1969). MA Oxon 1990. Asst Lectr in Maths, Imperial Coll., London, 1967–69; Asst Prof. in Stats, Stanford Univ., 1969–71; Lectr in Maths, Imperial Coll., 1971–73; Associate Prof. and Prof. in Stats, Univ. of Minnesota, 1973–80; Prof. in Maths, Univ. of Texas, 1980–91. Editor: Annals of Statistics, 1980–82; Biometrika, 1991–. *Publications:* Theoretical Statistics, 1973; Problems and Solutions in Theoretical Statistics, 1977; Statistical Theory and Modelling, 1990; articles in statistical and scientific jls. *Recreations:* philately, football, botanical observation. *Address:* Department of Statistics, 1 South Parks Road, Oxford OX1 3TG. *T:* Oxford (0865) 272860.

HINSLEY, Prof. Sir (Francis) Harry, Kt 1985; OBE 1946; FBA 1981; Master of St John's College, Cambridge, 1979–89 (Fellow, 1944–79; President, 1975–79); *b* 26 Nov. 1918; *s* of Thomas Henry and Emma Hinsley; *m* 1946, Hilary Brett, *d* of H. F. B. and Helena Brett-Smith, Oxford; two *s* one *d*. *Educ:* Queen Mary's Grammar Sch., Walsall; St John's Coll., Cambridge. HM Foreign Office, war service, 1939–46. University of Cambridge: Research Fellow, St John's Coll., 1944–50, Tutor, 1956–63; University Lectr in History, 1949–65; Reader in the History of International Relations, 1965–69; Prof., History of Internat. Relations, 1969–83; Vice-Chancellor, 1981–83; Chm., Faculty Bd of History, 1970–72; Lees-Knowles Lectr on Military Science, Trinity Coll., 1970–71. Lectures: Cecil Green, Univ. of BC, 1976; Sir Douglas Robb, Univ. of Auckland, and Yencken Meml, ANU, 1980; Martin Wight Meml, Univ. of Sussex, 1981; Lindsay Meml, Univ. of Keele, 1985; Chancellor's, Univ. of Witwatersrand, 1985; Earl Grey Meml, Univ. of Newcastle-upon-Tyne, 1985; Chettiar Meml, Univ. of Madras, 1988; Harmon Meml, USAF Acad., Colorado, 1988. UK Rep., Provisional Academic Cttee for European Univ. Inst., 1973–75. Trustee, BM, 1984–89. Hon. Fellow: TCD, 1981; Darwin Coll., Cambridge, 1987. Hon. DLitt Witwatersrand, 1985. Hon. D Mil. Sci. Royal Roads Mil. Coll., Canada, 1987. Editor, The Historical Jl, 1960–71. *Publications:* Command of the Sea, 1950; Hitler's Strategy, 1951; (ed) New Cambridge Modern History, Vol. XI, 1962; Power and the Pursuit of Peace, 1963; Sovereignty, 1966, 2nd edn 1986; Nationalism and the International System, 1973; (ed) British Foreign Policy under Sir Edward Grey, 1977; (jtly) British Intelligence in the Second World War, vol. 1, 1979, vol. 2, 1981, vol. 3 (Pt 1), 1984, (Pt 2), 1988, vol. 4, 1990. *Address:* St John's College, Cambridge CB2 1TP. *T:* Cambridge (0223) 338600.

HINTON, Prof. Denys James, FRIBA; Chairman, Redditch New Town Development Corporation, 1978–85; *b* 12 April 1921; *s* of James and Nell Hinton; *m* 1971, Lynette Payne (*née* Pattinson); one *d*. *Educ:* Reading Sch.; Architectural Assoc. (MSc; AADip.). FRIBA. Asst, Wells Coates, 1950–52; Birmingham Sch. of Architecture: Lectr, 1952–57; Sen. Lectr, 1957–64; Dir, 1964–72; Prof. of Architecture, Univ. of Aston, 1966–81, now Emeritus. Sen. Partner, Hinton Brown Langstone, Architects, Warwick, 1960–86. Chm., Architects Registration Council of UK, 1983–86; Vice-Pres. (formerly Vice-Chm.), Exec. Cttee, Internat. New Towns Assoc., 1980–85. *Publications:* Performance Characteristics of the Athenian Bouleterion, RIBA Athens Bursary, 1962; Great Interiors: High Victorian Period, 1967; contrib. RIBA and Architects Jl, papers on architectural education, Inst. Bulletin (worship and religious architecture), Univ. of Birmingham. *Recreations:* travel, moving house, water colours. *Address:* 45 Park Hill, Moseley, Birmingham B13 8DR. *T:* 021–449 9909.

HINTON, Michael Herbert, JP; FCA; FICM; FRSA; FFA; ACIArb; *b* 10 Nov. 1934; *s* of late Walter Leonard Hinton and of Freda Millicent Lillian Hinton; *m* 1st, 1955, Sarah Sunderland (marr. diss. 1982); one *s* two *d*; 2nd, 1984, Jane Margaret Manley, *d* of Arthur Crichton Howell. *Educ:* Ardingly Coll. Liveryman: Farmers' Co., 1964 (Master, 1981–82); Wheelwrights' Co.; Arbitrators' Co.; Mem. Court of Common Council, 1970–71, Alderman, 1971–79, Ward of Billingsgate; Clerk to Wheelwrights' Co., 1965–71; Sheriff, City of London, 1977–78. JP City of London, 1971. *Recreations:* cricket, Association football, theatre, travel. *Address:* 9E Brechin Place, SW7 4QB. *T:* 071–373 7486. *Clubs:* Farmers, MCC, City Livery (Pres., 1976–77).

HINTON, Nicholas John, CBE 1985; Director-General, Save the Children Fund, since 1985; *b* 15 March 1942; *s* of late Rev. Canon Hinton and Mrs J. P. Hinton; *m* 1971, Deborah Mary Vivian; one *d*. *Educ:* Marlborough Coll., Wiltshire; Selwyn Coll., Cambridge (MA). Asst Dir, Northorpe Hall Trust, 1965–68; Nat. Assoc. for Care and Resettlement of Offenders, 1968–77, Dir, 1973–77; Dir, NCVO (formerly Nat. Council of Social Service), 1977–84. Member: Central Council for Educn and Trng in Social Work, 1974–79; Stonham Housing Assoc., 1976–79; Cttee of Inquiry into UK Prison Services, 1978–79; Exec Cttees, Councils of Social Service, NI, Scotland and Wales, 1977–84; Council, VSO, 1981–; Exec. Cttee, Business in the Community, 1982–88; Parole System Review, 1987–88; Council, Industrial Soc., 1987–; Council, RSA, 1988–; Trustee: Charities Aid Foundn, 1977–84. Dir, Edington Music Festival, 1965–70. Contested (SDP-Liberal Alliance) Somerton and Frome, 1983. FRSA 1981. *Recreation:* music. *Address:* Mary Datchelor House, 17 Grove Lane, SE5 8RD. *T:* 071–703 5400.

HIPKIN, John; Head of English, Meridian School, Royston, Herts, since 1977; *b* 9 April 1935; *s* of Jack Hipkin and Elsie Hipkin; *m* 1963, Bronwyn Vaughan Dewey (marr. diss. 1985); four *s* one *d*; one *d*. *Educ:* Surbiton Grammar Sch. for Boys; LSE (BScEcon). Asst Teacher, 1957–65; Research Officer: King's Coll., Cambridge, 1965–68; Univ. of East Anglia, 1968–71; Sec., Schools Council Working Party on Whole Curriculum, 1973–74; Dir, Adv. Centre for Educn, 1974–77. *Publications:* (jtly) New Wine in Old Bottles, 1967; The Massacre of Peterloo (a play), 1968, 2nd edn 1974; (ed jtly) Education for the Seventies, 1970. *Recreations:* theatre, photography, history, medieval music. *Address:* 15 Oxford Road, Cambridge CB4 3PH. *T:* Cambridge (0223) 321407.

HIPPISLEY-COX, Peter Denzil John; solicitor and parliamentary agent; Senior Partner, Dyson, Bell, Martin & Co. (formerly Dyson, Bell & Co.), London, since 1976; Partner, Bircham & Co., since 1989; *b* 22 May 1921; *s* of late Col Sir Geoffrey Hippisley Cox, CBE, and Lady Hippisley Cox; *m* 1st, 1948, Olga Kay (marr. diss. 1956); one *d*; 2nd, 1956, Frieda Marion Wood; two *d*. *Educ:* Stowe; Trinity Coll., Cambridge (MA). Served War, RAF (Signals), 1941–46 (Flt Lieut). Admitted a solicitor, 1949. Dir, Equity & Law Life Assurance Soc., 1965–87 (Dep. Chm. 1973; Chm., 1977–85). Member: Council, Law Soc., 1956–81; Court, Drapers' Co., 1972– (Master, 1983–84, Renter Warden, 1987–88). Governor, Bancroft's Sch., 1975–. *Recreation:* music. *Address:* 48D Whistlers Avenue, SW11 3TS. *T:* 071–585 2142. *Club:* Carlton.

HIPWELL, Hermine H.; *see* Vivenot, Baroness R. de.

HIRAHARA, Tsuyoshi; Ambassador of Japan to the Court of St James's, 1982–85; *b* 25 Oct. 1920; *m* Kiyo Nishi; two *d*. *Educ:* Faculty of Law, Tokyo Univ. Dep. Dir-Gen. for Gen. Affairs, Economic Affairs Bureau, Min. of For. Affairs, 1962; Consul-Gen., Milan, 1964; Minister, Brussels, 1966; Dep. Dir-Gen., 1969, Dir-Gen., 1970, Economic Affairs Bureau, Min. of For. Affairs; Ambassador to: Morocco, 1972; OECD, Paris, 1975–80. Commander: Legion of Honour (France); Ordre de la Couronne (Belgium); Grand Officer: Ordre de Leopold II (Belgium); Order of Ouissam Alaouit Cherifiam (Morocco). *Recreation:* golf. *Address:* c/o Ministry of Foreign Affairs, Kasumigaseki, Chiyoda-ku, Tokyo, Japan.

HIRD, Thora, (Mrs James Scott), OBE 1983; actress; *b* 28 May 1911; *d* of James Henry Hird and Mary Jane Mayor; *m* 1937, James Scott; one *d*. *Educ:* The Misses Nelson's Prep. Sch., Morecambe, Lancs. Royalty Theatre Repertory Co., Morecambe; first appeared in West End of London, 1940–42: No Medals, Vaudeville; The Queen Came By, Duke of York's; Tobacco Road, Playhouse; The Trouble-Makers, Strand; The Same Sky, Duke of York's; The Love Match, Palace. Film contract, Ealing Studios, 1940; many *films include:* Blacksheep of Whitehall; They Came in Khaki; A Kind of Loving; Once a Jolly Swagman; Maytime in Mayfair. *TV series:* Meet the Wife; The First Lady; In Loving Memory; Hallelujah!; Last of the Summer Wine; Flesh and Blood; Praise Be! (Sunday); many plays, incl. Cream Cracker under the Settee. *Publications:* Scene and Hird (autobiog.), 1976; Praise Be!, 1990; Praise Be!, 1991. *Recreations:* reading, gardening, travelling. *Address:* c/o Felix de Wolfe, Manfield House, 376–378 Strand, WC2R 0LR. *T:* 071–723 5561.

HIRSCH, Prof. Sir Peter (Bernhard), Kt 1975; MA, PhD; FRS 1963; Isaac Wolfson Professor of Metallurgy in the University of Oxford, 1966–Sept. 1992; Fellow, St Edmund Hall, Oxford, since 1966; *b* 16 Jan. 1925; *s* of Ismar Hirsch and Regina Meyerson; *m* 1959, Mabel Anne Kellar (*née* Stephens), *widow* of James Noel Kellar; one step *s* one step *d*. *Educ:* Sloane Sch., Chelsea; St Catharine's Coll., Cambridge (Hon. Fellow, 1982). BA 1946; MA 1950; PhD 1951. Reader in Physics in Univ. of Cambridge, 1964–66; Fellow, Christ's Coll., Cambridge, 1960–66, Hon. Fellow, 1978. Has been engaged on researches with electron microscope on imperfections in crystalline structure of metals and on relation between structural defects and mechanical properties. Chairman: Metallurgy and Materials Cttee (and Mem., Eng. Bd), SRC, 1970–73; UKAEA, 1982–84 (pt-time Mem., 1982–91); Member: Elec. Supply Res. Council, 1969–82; Tech. Adv. Cttee, Advent, 1982–89; Tech. Adv. Bd, Monsanto Electronic Materials, 1985–88. Chm., Isis Innovation Ltd; Dir, Cogent Ltd, 1985–89. FIC 1988. Hon. Fellow: RMS, 1977; Japan Soc. of Electron Microscopy, 1979. Hon. DSc: Newcastle, 1979; City, 1979; Northwestern, 1982; Hon. ScD East Anglia, 1983; Hon. DEng Liverpool, 1991. Rosenhain Medal, Inst. of Metals, 1961; C. V. Boys Prize, Inst. of Physics and Physical Soc., 1962; Clamer Medal, Franklin Inst., 1970; Wihuri Internat. Prize, Helsinki, 1971; Royal Soc. Hughes Medal, 1973; Metals Soc. Platinum Medal, 1976; Royal Medal, Royal Soc., 1977; Arthur Von Hippel Award, Materials Res. Soc., 1983; (jtly) Wolf Prize in Physics, Wolf Foundn, 1983–84; Dist. Scientist Award, Electron Microscopy Soc. of America, 1986; Holweck Prize, Inst. of Physics and French Physical Soc., 1988; Gold Medal, Japan Inst. of Metals, 1989. *Publications:* Electron Microscopy of Thin Crystals (with others), 1965; (ed) The Physics of Metals, vol. 2, Defects, 1975; numerous contribs to learned jls. *Recreation:* walking. *Address:* (until Sept. 1992) Department of Materials, Parks Road, Oxford OX1 3PH. *T:* Oxford (0865) 273737; 104A Lonsdale Road, Oxford OX2 7ET.

HIRSCH, Prof. Steven Richard, FRCP; FRCPsych; Professor of Psychiatry, Charing Cross and Westminster Medical School, since 1975; *b* 12 March 1937; *m* Theresa Hirsch; one *s* three *d*. *Educ:* Amherst Coll., Mass (BA Hons); Johns Hopkins Univ. (MD); London Univ. (MPhil). Res. worker, MRC Social Psychiatry, 1971–73; Hon. Sen. Registrar, Maudsley Hosp., 1971–73; Lectr in Psychiatry, Inst. of Psychiatry, Univ. of London, 1972–73; Sen. Lectr and Hon. Cons., Depts of Psychiatry, Westminster Hosp. and Queen Mary's Hosp., 1973–75. *Publications:* (ed with M. Shepherd) Themes and Variations in European Psychiatry: an anthology, 1974; (with J. Leff) Abnormalities in parents of schizophrenics: review of the literature and an investigation of communication defects and deviances, (monograph) 1975; (ed with R. Farmer) The Suicide Syndrome, 1980; (ed with P. B. Bradley) The Psychopharmacology and Treatment of Schizophrenia, 1986; Psychiatric Beds and Resources: factors influencing bed use and service planning (report of a working party, RCPsych), 1988; (ed with J. Harris) Consent and the Incompetent Patient: ethics, law and medicine, 1988. *Address:* Department of Psychiatry, Charing Cross and Westminster Medical School, St Dunstan's Road, W6 8RP. *T:* 081–846 7390.

HIRSHFIELD, family name of **Baron Hirshfield.**

HIRSHFIELD, Baron *cr* 1967, of Holborn in Greater London (Life Peer); **Desmond Barel Hirshfield;** chartered accountant, as Lord Hirshfield, Chartered Accountants; Chairman, Horwath & Horwath (UK) Ltd, 1967–86; International President, Horwath & Horwath International, 1984–86 (President, 1977–84); Founder and Director, Foundation on Automation and Human Development, 1962–87; *b* 17 May 1913; *s* of late Leopold Hirshfield and Lily Hirshfield (*née* Blackford); *m* 1951, Bronia Eisen. *Educ:* City of London Sch. Chartered Accountant, 1939; Founder and Chm., Trades Union Unit Trust Managers Ltd, 1961–83; Chm., MLH Consultants, 1981–83. Mem., Cttee on Consumer Credit, 1968–71; Dep. Chm., Northampton New Town Develt Corp., 1968–76; Member: Central Adv. Water Cttee, 1969–70; Top Salaries Review Body, 1975–84; Admin. Trustee, Chevening Estate, 1970–81; Pres., Brit. Assoc. of Hotel Accountants, 1969–83; Treasurer: UK Cttee of UNICEF, 1969–83 and 1986–88; Nat. Council for the Unmarried Mother and her Child, 1970–71. President: Norwood Charitable Trust, 1960–83; Norwood Foundn, 1977–83. Gov., LSE, 1975–. Capt., British Team, World Maccabi Games, Prague, 1934. *Publications:* pamphlets and reports on The Accounts of Charitable Institutions; Avoidance and Evasion of Income Tax; Scheme for Pay as You Earn; Investment of Trade Union Funds; Organisations and Methods Reviews; articles in periodicals and newspapers. *Recreations:* travel, painting, caricaturing. *Address:* House of Lords, SW1.

HIRST, Hon. Sir David (Cozens-Hardy), Kt 1982; **Hon. Mr Justice Hirst;** a Judge of the High Court, Queen's Bench Division, since 1982; *b* 31 July 1925; *er s* of late Thomas William Hirst and Margaret Joy Hirst, Aylsham, Norfolk; *m* 1951, Pamela Elizabeth Molesworth Bevan, *d* of Col T. P. M. Bevan, MC; three *s* two *d*. *Educ:* Eton (Fellow, 1976); Trinity Coll., Cambridge. MA. Served 1943–47; RA and Intelligence Corps, Capt. 1946. Barrister, Inner Temple, 1951, Bencher, 1974; QC 1965; Vice-Chm. of the Bar, 1977–78, Chm., 1978–79. Member: Lord Chancellor's Law Reform Cttee; Council on Tribunals, 1966–80; Cttee to review Defamation Act, 1952, 1971–74; Hon. Life Mem., Amer. Bar Assoc. *Recreations:* shooting, lawn tennis, theatre and opera, growing vegetables.

Address: Royal Courts of Justice, Strand, WC2A 2LL. *Clubs:* Boodle's, MCC.
See also J. W. Hirst.

HIRST, David Michael Geoffrey, FBA 1983; Professor of the History of Art, University of London at the Courtauld Institute, since 1991 (Reader, 1980–91); *b* 5 Sept. 1933; *s* of Walter Hirst; *m* 1st, 1960, Sara Vitali (marr. diss. 1970); one *s*; 2nd, 1972, Jane Martineau. (marr. diss. 1984); 3rd, 1984, Diane Zervas. *Educ:* Stowe Sch.; New Coll., Oxford; Courtauld Inst. of Art. Lectr, Courtauld Inst., 1962–80. Fellow at Villa I Tatti, 1969–70; Mem., Inst. for Advanced Study, Princeton, 1975. Mem., Pontifical Commn for Restoration of Sistine Ceiling, 1987–90. Arranged exhibn, Michelangelo Draftsman, Nat. Gall., Washington, 1988, Louvre, Paris, 1989. *Publications:* Sebastiano del Piombo, 1981; Michelangelo and his Drawings, 1988; Michelangelo Draftsman, Milan, 1988 (French edn 1989); many contribs to British and continental periodicals. *Address:* 3 Queensdale Place, W11.

HIRST, Prof. John Malcolm, DSC 1945; PhD; FRS 1970; FIBiol; Consultant on plant pathology and international agriculture; Director, Long Ashton Research Station, and Professor of Agricultural and Horticultural Science, Bristol University, 1975–84, now Professor Emeritus; *b* 20 April 1921; *s* of Maurice Herbert Hirst and Olive Mary (*née* Pank); *m* 1957, Barbara Mary Stokes; two *d*. *Educ:* Solihull Sch.; Reading University (BSc Hons Agric. Bot., 1950); PhD London 1955. Royal Navy (Coastal Forces), 1941–46. Rothamsted Exper. Stn, Harpenden, 1950–75, Hd of Plant Pathology Dept, 1967–75. Vice-Chm. Tech. Adv. Cttee, Consultative Gp, Internat. Agricl Research, 1981–82; Chm., Scientific Adv. Bd, Twyford Plant Labs. Pres., British Aerobiology Fedn, 1991–. Jakob Eriksson Gold Medal (Internat. Botanical Congress), 1959; Research Medal, RASE, 1970. *Publications:* papers in scientific jls mainly in Trans British Mycological Soc., Annals of Applied Biology, Jl of General Microbiology. *Address:* The Cottage, Butcombe, Bristol BS18 6XQ. *T:* Lulsgate (0275) 472880. *Club:* Farmers'.

HIRST, Jonathan William; QC 1990; *b* 2 July 1953; *s* of Sir David (Cozens-Hardy) Hirst, *qv*; *m* 1974, Fiona Christine Mary Hirst (*née* Tyser). *Educ:* Eton Coll.; Trinity Coll., Cambridge (MA). Called to the Bar, Inner Temple, 1975. Mem., Gen. Council of the Bar, 1987–. Gov., Taverham Hall Sch., Norfolk, 1991–. *Recreations:* shooting, gardening, other country pursuits. *Address:* Brickcourt Chambers, 15/19 Devereux Court, Temple, WC2R 3JJ. *T:* 071–583 0777. *Club:* Boodle's.

HIRST, Michael William, LLB, CA; company director; business consultant; Founder, Michael Hirst Associates; President, Scottish Conservative & Unionist Association, since 1989; *b* 2 Jan. 1946; *s* of late John Melville Hirst and of Christina Binning Torrance or Hirst; *m* 1972, Naomi Ferguson Wilson; one *s* two *d*. *Educ:* Glasgow Acad., Glasgow; Univ. of Glasgow (LLB). CA 1970. Exchange Student, Univ. of Iceland, 1967; Partner, Peat, Marwick Mitchell & Co., 1978–83; Consultant, Peat Marwick UK, 1983–. Pres., Glasgow Univ. Conservative Club, 1967; National Vice-Chm., Scottish Young Conservatives, 1971–73; Chm., Scottish Conservative Candidates Assoc., 1978–81; Vice-Chairman: Pty Organisation Cttee, 1985; Conservative Party in Scotland, 1987–89. Contested: Central Dunbartonshire, Feb. and Oct. 1974; E Dunbartonshire, 1979; Strathkelvin and Bearsden, 1987. MP (C) Strathkelvin and Bearsden, 1983–87. PPS to Parly Under-Secs of State, DoE, 1985–87. Mem., Select Cttee on Scottish Affairs, 1983–87. Mem., Exec. Council, British Diabetic Assoc., 1989–. Chm., Park Sch. Educnl Trust, 1988–. Gov., The Queen's Coll., Glasgow, 1989– (Chm., Finance Cttee, 1989–). *Recreations:* golf, walking, ski-ing. *Address:* Enderley, Baldernock Road, Milngavie, Glasgow G62 8DU. *T:* 041–956 1213; 712 Howard House, Dolphin Square, SW1V 3LX. *T:* 071–798 8021. *Clubs:* Carlton; The Western (Glasgow).

HIRST, Prof. Paul Heywood; Professor of Education, University of Cambridge, 1971–88, and Fellow of Wolfson College (formerly University College), Cambridge, since 1971; *b* 10 Nov. 1927; *s* of late Herbert and Winifred Hirst, Birkby, Huddersfield. *Educ:* Huddersfield Coll.; Trinity Coll., Cambridge. BA 1948, MA 1952, Certif. Educn 1952, Cantab; DipEd 1955, London; MA Oxon (by incorporation), Christ Church, Oxford, 1955. Asst Master, William Hulme's Grammar Sch., Manchester, 1948–50; Maths Master, Eastbourne Coll., 1950–55; Lectr and Tutor, Univ. of Oxford Dept of Educn, 1955–59; Lectr in Philosophy of Educn, Univ. of London Inst. of Educn, 1959–65; Prof. of Educn, King's Coll., Univ. of London, 1965–71. Visiting Professor: Univ. of British Columbia, 1964, 1967; Univ. of Malawi, 1969; Univ. of Puerto Rico, 1984; Univ. of Sydney, 1989; Univ. of Alberta, 1989; Inst. of Educn, Univ. of London, 1991. De Carle Lectr, Univ. of Otago, 1976; Fink Lectr, Univ. of Melbourne, 1976. Vice-Pres., Philosophy of Educn Soc. of GB; Member: UGC Educn Sub-Cttee, 1971–80; Educn Cttee, 1972–82, Academic Policy Cttee, 1981–87, Chm., Research Cttee, 1988–, CNAA; Swann Cttee of Inquiry into Educn of Children from Ethnic Minorities, 1981–85. Chm., Univs Council for Educn of Teachers, 1985–88. *Publications:* (with R. S. Peters) The Logic of Education, 1970; (ed with R. F. Dearden and R. S. Peters) Education and the Development of Reason, 1971; Knowledge and the Curriculum, 1974; Moral Education in a Secular Society, 1974; (ed) Educational Theory and its Foundation Disciplines, 1984; (with V. J. Furlong) Initial Teacher Training and the Role of the School, 1988; papers in: Philosophical Analysis and Education (ed R. D. Archambault), 1965; The Study of Education (ed J. W. Tibble), 1965; The Concept of Education (ed R. S. Peters), 1966; Religious Education in a Pluralistic Society (ed M. C. Felderhof), 1985; Education, Value and Mind (ed D. E. Cooper), 1986; Partnership in Initial Teacher Training (ed M. Booth *et al*); also in Brit. Jl Educnl Studies, Jl Curriculum Studies, Jl of Philosophy of Educn. *Recreation:* music, especially opera. *Address:* Flat 3, 6 Royal Crescent, Brighton BN2 1AL. *T:* Brighton (0273) 684118. *Club:* Athenæum.

HIRST, Prof. Rodney Julian, MA; Professor of Logic and Rhetoric, University of Glasgow, 1961–81; *b* 28 July 1920; *s* of Rev. William Hirst and Elsie Hirst; *m* 1st, 1942, Jessica (*d* 1978), *y d* of Charles Alfred Podmore; two *d*; 2nd, 1985, Mary, *widow* of John Patrick. *Educ:* Leeds Grammar Sch.; Magdalen Coll., Oxford. Demy, 1938–47; 1st Cl. Hons Classical Mods, 1940. War Service, 1940–45, mainly as REME Officer (Radar) at home and in Italy. First Class Hons Lit. Hum., Dec. 1947. Lectr in Logic and Metaphysics, St Andrews Univ., 1948; Glasgow University: Lectr, 1949, and Sen. Lectr, 1959, in Logic; Dean of Arts, 1971–73; Senate Assessor on Univ. Court, 1973–78; Vice-Principal, 1976–79. *Publications:* Problems of Perception, 1959; (co-author) Human Senses and Perception, 1964; Perception and the External World, 1965; Philosophy: an outline for the intending student, 1968; contribs to Encyclopedia of Philosophy and philosophical journals. *Address:* 55 Montgomerie Street, Eaglesham, Glasgow G76 0AU. *T:* Eaglesham (03553) 3386.

HISCOCKS, Prof. Charles Richard, MA, DPhil; Professor of International Relations, University of Sussex, 1964–72, now Emeritus; *b* 1 June 1907; *y s* of F. W. Hiscocks; unmarried. *Educ:* Highgate Sch.; St Edmund Hall, Oxford; Berlin University. Asst Master, Trinity Coll. Sch., Port Hope, Ont, 1929–32; Bradfield Coll., 1936–39; Marlborough Coll., 1939–40. Served with Royal Marines, 1940–45, Lieut-Col; seconded to army for mil. govt duties in Germany, 1945; Brit. Council Rep. in Austria, 1946–49, S India, 1949–50; Prof. of Polit. Sci. and Internat. Relations, Univ. of Manitoba, 1950–64. UK Mem., UN Sub-Commn for Prevention of Discrimination and Protection of Minorities, 1953–62; Mem., South Atlantic Council, 1985–. Pres., Winnipeg Art Gall., 1959–60. Vis. Fellow, Princeton Univ., 1970–71; Fellow, Adlai Stevenson Inst. of Internat. Affairs, Chicago, 1971–72. Vice-Pres., UNA 1977–. *Publications:* The Rebirth of Austria, 1953; Democracy in Western Germany, 1957; Poland: Bridge for the Abyss?, 1963; Germany Revived, 1966; The Security Council: a study in adolescence, 1973. *Recreations:* music, art, gardening. *Address:* Dickers, Hunworth, Melton Constable, Norfolk. *T:* Holt (0263) 2503. *Club:* Garrick.

HISLOP, George Steedman, CBE 1976; PhD; FEng, FIMechE; FRSE; Director: Caledonian Airmotive, since 1978; *b* 11 Feb. 1914; *s* of George Alexander Hislop and Marthesa Maria Hay; *m* 1942, Joan Daphne, *d* of William Beer and Gwendoline Fincken; two *s* one *d*. *Educ:* Clydebank High Sch.; Royal Technical Coll., Glasgow (ARTC); Cambridge Univ. (PhD). BScEng London. CEng, FIMechE 1949; FRAeS 1955; Fellowship of Engrg, 1976; FRSE 1976; FRSA 1959. A&AEE, RAF Boscombe Down, 1939–45; RAE, Farnborough, 1945–46; BEA, 1947–53; Chief Engr/Dir, Fairey Aviation Ltd, 1953–60; Westland Aircraft Ltd, 1960: Technical Dir (Develt), 1962–66; Dep. Man. Dir, 1966–68; Man. Dir, 1968–72; Vice-Chm., 1972–76. Chm., CEI, 1979–80 (Vice-Chm., 1978–79); Mem., Airworthiness Requirements Bd, CAA, 1976–83 (Chm., 1982–83). Vis. Prof., Univ. of Strathclyde, 1978–84. Mem. Council, RAeS, 1960–83 (Pres., 1973–74; Hon. FRAeS, 1983); Gov., Inveresk Res. Foundn, 1980–90. Hon. DSc Strathclyde, 1976. *Publications:* contrib. R & M series and RAeS Jl. *Recreations:* hill walking, photography, bird watching. *Address:* Hadley, St John's Hill, Old Coulsdon, Surrey CR5 1HD. *T:* 081–660 1008. *Clubs:* Royal Air Force, MCC.

HISLOP, Ian David; Editor, Private Eye, since 1986; writer; *b* 13 July 1960; *s* of late David Atholl Hislop and of Helen Hislop; *m* 1988, Victoria Hamson; one *d*. *Educ:* Ardingly College; Magdalen College, Oxford (BA Hons Eng. Lang. and Lit.; Underhill Exhibn; Violet Vaughan Morgan Scholarship). Joined Private Eye, 1981, Dep. Editor, 1985–86. Columnist, The Listener, 1985–89; book reviewer, broadcaster, current affairs, arts, entertainment. *Television:* scriptwriter, Spitting Image, 1984–89; (with Nicholas Newman) The Stone Age, 1989; Brief Encounter, 1990. *Publications:* (ed) Secret Diary of a Lord Gnome, 1985; (ed) Gnome of the Rose, 1987; (with Nicholas Newman) Battle for Britain, 1987; (ed) Satiric Verses, 1989; contribs to newspapers and magazines. *Address:* c/o Private Eye, 6 Carlisle Street, W1V 5RG. *T:* 071–437 4017.

HISS, Alger; Commercial printing since 1959 (manufacturing, 1957–59); *b* 11 Nov. 1904; *s* of Charles Alger Hiss and Mary L. Hughes; *m* 1929, Priscilla Fansler Hobson; one *s*. *Educ:* Johns Hopkins Univ. (AB 1926, Hon. LLD 1947); Harvard Univ. (LLB 1929). Sec. and law clerk to Supreme Court Justice Holmes, 1929–30; law practice, 1930–33; asst to gen. counsel and asst gen. counsel, Agricultural Adjustment Admin., 1933–35; legal asst, special Senate cttee investigating munitions industry, 1934–35; special attorney, US Dept of Justice, 1935–36; asst to Asst Sec. of State, 1936; asst to Adviser on Political Relations, 1939; special asst to Dir, Office of Far Eastern Affairs, 1944; special asst to Dir, Office of Special Political Affairs, May 1944; Dep. Dir, Nov. 1944, Dir, 1945; accompanied Pres. Roosevelt and Sec. of State Stettinius to Malta and Yalta Conferences, Feb. 1945; exec. sec., Dumbarton Oaks Conversations, Aug.-Oct. 1944; sec.-gen., United Nations Conference on International Organization, San Francisco, 1945; Principal Adviser to US Delegation, Gen. Assembly of United Nations, London, 1946; elected Pres. and Trustee of Carnegie Endowment for Internat. Peace, Dec. 1946 (Pres. until 1949). Mem., Massachusetts Bar. Mem., Alpha Delta Phi, Phi Beta Kappa. *Publications:* The Myth of Yalta, 1955; In the Court of Public Opinion, 1957, new edn 1972; Holmes-Laski Letters (abridged edn), 1963. *Recreations:* tennis, swimming, ornithology.

HITCH, Brian, CMG 1985; CVO 1980; HM Diplomatic Service, retired; Director, Diploma in European Studies, and Fellow of Rewley House, University of Oxford, since 1991; *b* 2 June 1932; *m* 1954, Margaret Kathleen Wooller; two *d*. *Educ:* Wisbech Grammar Sch. (FRCO, LRAM); Magdalene Coll., Cambridge. Joined FO, 1955; 3rd/2nd Sec., Tokyo, 1955–61; FO, 1961–62; 2nd/1st Sec., Havana, 1962–64; 1st Sec., Athens, 1965–68; 1st Sec. and Head of Chancery, Tokyo, 1968–72; Asst Head, Southern European Dept, FCO, 1972–73; Dep. Head, later Head, Marine and Transport Dept, FCO, 1973–75; Counsellor, Bonn, 1975–77 and Algiers, 1977–80; Consul-Gen., Munich, 1980–84; Minister, Tokyo, 1984–87; High Comr to Malta, 1988–91. *Recreation:* music. *Address:* Rewley House, 1 Wellington Square, Oxford OX1 2JA. *T:* Oxford (0865) 270360. *Club:* United Oxford & Cambridge University.

HITCHCOCK, Dr Anthony John Michael; Visiting Researcher, Program for Advanced Technology on the Highway (PATH), University of California at Berkeley, since 1990; *b* 26 June 1929; *s* of Dr Ronald W. Hitchcock and Hilda (*née* Gould); *m* 1953, Audrey Ellen Ashworth (*d* 1990); one *s* two *d*. *Educ:* Bedales; Manchester Grammar Sch.; Trinity Coll., Cambridge; Univ. of Chicago. PhD, BA; MInstP; MCIT. Asst, Univ. of Chicago, 1951–52; AEA, 1953–67; Department of Transport: Head of Traffic Dept, 1967–71, Head of Transport Ops Dept, 1971–75, TRRL; Head, Res. Policy (Transport) Div., DoE/DoT, 1975–78; Head of Safety and Transportation Dept, TRRL, 1978–89. Vis. Prof., Transport Studies, Cranfield Inst. of Technology, 1978–81. *Publications:* Nuclear Reactor Control, 1960; research reports and articles in learned jls. *Recreation:* bridge. *Address:* 166 Caldecott Lane (#314), Oakland, Calif 94618, USA. *T:* (510) 548–1991, *Fax:* (510) 231–9565.

HITCHCOCK, Prof. Edward Robert, ChM, FRCS; FRCSE; Professor of Neurosurgery, University of Birmingham, since 1978; *b* 10 Feb. 1929; *s* of Edwin Robert and Martha Hitchcock; *m* 1953, Jillian Trenowath; three *s* one *d*. *Educ:* Lichfield Grammar Sch.; Univ. of Birmingham (MB ChB; ChM 1952). FRCS 1959; FRCSE, *ad eundem*, 1971. Leader, Univ. of Birmingham Spitzbergen Expedn, 1951. Lecturer in Anatomy, Univ. of Birmingham, 1953; Captain, RAMC, 1954–56, MO, 2nd Bn Scots Guards; Registrar: Dept of Traumatic Surgery, General Hosp., Birmingham, 1956; Professorial Surgical Unit, University College Hosp., London, 1957–59; Fellow in Clinical Research, MRC, 1960; 1961–65: Ho. Surg./Registrar/Sen. Registrar, Dept of Neurological Surgery, Radcliffe Inf., Oxford, and Dept of Neurosurgery, Manchester Royal Inf.; Research Fellow, Univ. of Oxford; Sen. Lectr and Reader, Dept of Surgical Neurology, Univ. of Edinburgh, 1966–78. Examiner, FRCS, 1971–, RCSE, Surgical Neurology, 1977–90. Pres., Europ Soc. of Functional and Stereotactic Surg., 1986–90 (Mem., Exec. Cttee, 1975–86); Member: Soc. of British Neurol Surgeons, 1966– (Council, 1988–); Bd, World Soc. Stereo and Functional Neurosurgery, 1981–; Internat. Assoc. for Study of Pain, 1975–. Chm., BSI cttee on neurosurgical implants, 1989. Hon. Specialist in Neurosurgery, Brazilian Neurosurg. Soc., 1980–; Hon. Mem., Soc. de Neurocirurgia de Levante, 1983; Corresp. Member: Amer. Assoc. of Neurol Surgeons, 1975; Scandinavian Neurosurg. Soc., 1972; Amer. Physiological Soc., 1988. Ed., Advances in Stereotactic and Functional Neurosurgery, 1969–. *Publications:* Initial Management of Head Injuries (Folia Traumatologica), 1971; Management of the Unconscious Patient, 1971; papers on pain, neuroprosthetics, stereotactic surgery and tumours, in various jls. *Recreations:* history, capology, fishing. *Address:* Cubbold House, Ombersley, near Droitwich, Worcs WR9 0HJ. *T:* Worcester (0905) 620606.

HITCHEN, Brian, CBE 1990; Editor, The Daily Star, since 1987; *b* 8 July 1936; *s* of Fred and Alice Hitchen, Lancs; *m* 1962, Ellen Josephine O'Hanlon, Kildare, Eire; one *s* one *d*. *Educ:* Hegginbottom Sch., Ashton-under-Lyne, Lancs, and elsewhere. Served Army, WO, Whitehall, 1954–56. Copy Boy, Daily Despatch, 1951; Gen. Reporter, Bury Times, 1952–54; Reporter, Manchester Evening News, 1957; Reporter, 1958–63, Foreign Correspondent, Paris Bureau, 1963–64, Daily Mirror; For. Corresp., Mirror US Bureaux, New York and Washington, 1964–72; Dep. News Editor, Daily Mirror, 1972; News Editor, Daily Express, 1973–76; Asst Editor, National Enquirer, USA, 1976, European Bureau Chief, 1977; Asst Editor, Now! magazine, 1978–80; London Editor, The Daily Star, 1981–86; Dep. Editor, Sunday Express, 1986–87. Director: Airspeed Internat. Corp., 1973–; Express Newspapers, 1988–; Independent Star, Eire, 1988–. Mem., Press Complaints Commn, 1991–. *Recreations:* sailing, game fishing, shooting. *Address:* The Daily Star, Ludgate House, 245 Blackfriars Road, SE1 9UX. *Clubs:* Variety of Great Britain; Sussex Yacht.

HITCHEN, John David; a Recorder of the Crown Court, since 1978; *b* 18 July 1935; *s* of late Harold Samuel and Frances Mary Hitchen; *m* 1966, Pamela Ann Cellan-Jones. *Educ:* Woodhouse Grove Sch., nr Bradford; Pembroke Coll., Oxford (BA(Hons)). Called to Bar, Lincoln's Inn, 1961. *Recreations:* music, reading. *Address:* 39 Rutland Drive, Harrogate, Yorks. *T:* Harrogate (0423) 66236.

HITCHENS, Rear Adm. Gilbert Archibald Ford, CB 1988; Director General Ship Refitting, Ministry of Defence, 1985–87, retired; *b* 11 April 1932; *m* 1960, Patricia Hamilton; one *s* one *d*. BA (Open Univ.). Joined Royal Navy, 1950; Commander, 1968; Guided Weapons Staff Officer, Min. of Technology, 1968–70; Exec. Officer, RNEC, 1970–72; Senior Officer while building and Weapon Engineer Officer, HMS Sheffield, 1973–75; MoD (Navy), 1975–77; Naval Attaché, Tokyo and Seoul, 1977–79; Asst Dir, Manpower Requirements, MoD (Navy), 1979–80; Dir, Officers' Appts (Eng.), 1980–82; Captain, HMS Defiance, 1982–84; CSO Engrg to C-in-C Fleet, 1984–85. Mem., Plymouth DHA, 1989–90. Admiralty Gov., Royal Naval Benevolent Trust, 1989–. *Recreation:* any activity in the high hills.

HITCHIN, Prof. Aylwin Drakeford, CBE 1970; Boyd Professor of Dental Surgery, Director of Dental Studies, University of Dundee (formerly University of St Andrews), 1947–77, Professor Emeritus, 1978 and Dean of Dundee Dental Hospital, 1947–73; Dental Consultant, Dundee Royal Infirmary, 1947–77; Civil Consultant Dental Surgeon to Royal Navy, 1957–77; *b* 31 Dec. 1907; *s* of Alfred Leonard Hitchin, FRPS, and Ruth Drakeford; *m* 1942, Alice Stella Michie; one *s* one *d*. *Educ:* Rutherford College, Newcastle upon Tyne; Durham University Coll. of Medicine. LDS (Dunelm) 1931, BDS 1932, MDS 1935; DDSc 1957; FDSRCS Edinburgh 1951; FFDRCS Ire 1964; FDSRCPS Glasgow 1967. Asst Hon. Dental Surgeon and Demonstrator of Dental Surgery, Newcastle upon Tyne Dental Hosp., 1932–36; Private Dental Practice, Newcastle upon Tyne, 1932–46 (except for 6 yrs with AD Corps during War of 1939–45); Dental Surgical Specialist, Scottish Command, 1943–45, with rank of Major. Chairman: Dental Educn Advisory Council, 1951–52; Dental Hosp. Assoc., 1959–60; Chm., Dental Cttee, Scot. Post-Grad. Med. Council, 1969–79; Member: Dental Cttee of MRC, 1966–72; Advisory Cttee on Medical Research (Scotland), 1967–71; Dental Adv. Cttee, Scottish Health Services Council, 1952–57, 1968–74; Convener, Dental Council, RCSE, 1971–74; Jt Cttee on Higher Training in Dentistry, 1969–74; East Scotland Regional Hosp. Bd, 1948–52; Dental Sub Cttee, UGC, 1969–73; Nominated Mem., Gen. Dent. Council, 1956–74; External Examiner Dental Subjects, Universities, Durham, Edinburgh, Queen's, Belfast, Dublin, Manchester, Liverpool, Birmingham, Leeds, Newcastle, Bristol, Wales, RCS in Ireland; Examiner, LDS, FDSRCS Edinburgh, FFDRCS Ire, and FDSRCPS Glasgow. William Guy Meml Lectr, RCSE, 1972; Founders and Benefactors Lectr, Univ. of Newcastle upon Tyne Dental Sch., 1973. President: Oral Surgery Club, 1956–57; Christian Dental Fellowship, 1966–69; Brit. Soc. Dental Radiology, 1961–63; Royal Odonto-Chir. Soc. of Scotland, 1969–70; Pres., Inter-Varsity Fellowship, 1966–67; Foundation Fellow of the British Assoc. of Oral Surgeons; Hon. Mem., Swedish Dental Soc. Dr Odont (*hc*) Lund, 1977; Hon. FDSRCPS Glasgow, 1979. *Publications:* contribs to dental periodical literature. *Address:* Coniston, Prieston Road, Bridge of Weir, Renfrewshire PA11 3AJ. *T:* Bridge of Weir (0505) 614936.

HITCHIN, Prof. Nigel James, DPhil; FRS 1991; Professor of Mathematics, University of Warwick, since 1990; *b* 2 Aug. 1946; *s* of Eric Wilfred Hitchin and Bessie (*née* Blood); *m* 1973, Nedda Vejarano Bernal; one *s* one *d*. *Educ:* Ecclesbourne Sch., Duffield; Jesus Coll., Oxford (BA 1968); Wolfson Coll., Oxford (MA, DPhil 1972). Res. Asst, Inst. for Advanced Study, Princeton, 1971–73; Instructor, Courant Inst., New York Univ., 1973–74; SRC Res. Asst, 1974–77, SRC Advanced Res. Fellow, 1977–79, Oxford Univ.; Fellow and Tutor in Maths, St Catherine's Coll., Oxford, 1979–90. Vis. Prof., SUNY, Stony Brook, 1983. London Mathematical Society: Jun. Whitehead Prize, 1981; Sen. Berwick Prize, 1990. *Publications:* Monopoles, Minimal Surfaces and Algebraic Curves, 1987; (with M. F. Atiyah) The Geometry and Dynamics of Magnetic Monopoles, 1988; articles in learned jls. *Address:* 48 Cumnor Hill, Oxford OX2 9HB. *T:* Oxford (0865) 864683.

HITCHING, Alan Norman; His Honour Judge Hitching; a Circuit Judge, since 1987; *b* 5 Jan. 1941; *s* of late Norman Henry Samuel Hitching and of Grace Ellen Hitching; *m* 1967, Hilda Muriel (*née* King); one *d* two *s*. *Educ:* Forest Sch., Snaresbrook; Christ Church, Oxford (BA 1962; Radcliffe Exhibnr and Dixon Scholar, 1962; BCL 1963; MA). Harmsworth Entrance Scholar, Middle Temple, 1960; Astbury Scholar and Safford Prize, Middle Temple, 1964; called to the Bar, Middle Temple, 1964; Standing Counsel, Inland Revenue, SE Circuit, 1972–87; a Recorder, 1985–87. Cropwood Fellow, Inst. of Criminology, Cambridge, 1990. Vice-Chm., John Grooms Assoc. for the Disabled, 1978–81 and 1989–91 (Chm., 1981–89). Licensed Reader, Dio. of Chelmsford, 1987–. *Address:* 9 Monkhams Drive, Woodford Green, Essex IG8 0LG. *T:* 081–504 4260.

HITCHINGS, Dr George Herbert; Scientist Emeritus and Consultant, Burroughs Wellcome Co., since 1975; Director, since 1971, The Burroughs Wellcome Fund (President, 1971–90); *b* 18 April 1905; *m* 1st, 1933, Beverly Reimer (*d* 1985); one *s* one *d*; 2nd, 1989, Joyce Shaver. *Educ:* Univ. of Washington (BS *cum laude* Chem 1927; MS 1928); PhD Biochem Harvard 1933. Teaching Fellow, Univ. of Washington, 1926–28; Harvard University: Teaching Fellow, 1928–34; Instructor and Tutor, 1932–36; Res. Fellow, 1934–36; Associate, 1936–39; Sen. Instructor, Western Reserve Univ., 1939–42; Burroughs Wellcome Co.: Biochemist, 1942–46; Chief Biochemist, 1946–55; Associate Res. Dir, 1955–63; Res. Dir (Chemotherapy Div.), 1963–67; Vice-Pres. in charge of Res., 1967–75; Dir, 1968–77. Prof. of Pharmacology, Brown Univ., 1968–80; Adjunct Prof. of Pharmacology and Adjunct Prof. of Experimental Medicine, Duke Univ., 1970–85; Staff, Dept of Medicine, Roger Williams Gen. Hosp., Brown Univ., 1970–80; Adjunct Prof. of Pharmacology, Univ. of N Carolina at Chapel Hill, 1972–85; Vis. Prof. of Clinical Pharmacology, Chuang-Ang Univ., Seoul, 1974–77; Vis. Lectr, Pakistan, Iran, Japan, India, Republic of S Africa. Mem., US and internat scientific bodies, incl. Royal Soc., RSocMed, RSC. Hon. degrees from US and UK Univs. Numerous medals and awards; (jtly) Nobel Prize in Physiology or Medicine, 1988; Albert Schweitzer Internat. Prize for Medicine, 1989. Member, Editorial Boards: Research Communications in Chemical Pathology and Pharmacology, 1969–; Molecular Pharmacology, 1967–; Biochemical Pharmacology, 1967–; Life Sciences, 1978. *Publications:* contribs to learned jls on chemotherapy, antimetabolites, organic chemistry of heterocycles, nucleic acids, antitumor, antimalarial and antibacterial drugs. *Address:* Carolina Meadows, Whippoorwill Lane, Apt 1–102, Chapel Hill, NC 27514, USA. *T:* (home) (919) 933–5023, (office) (919) 248–4162.

HIVES, family name of **Baron Hives.**

HIVES, 2nd Baron, *cr* 1950, of Duffield; **John Warwick Hives,** CBE 1989; *b* 26 Nov. 1913; *s* of 1st Baron Hives and of Gertrude Ethel (*d* 1961), *d* of John Warwick; *S* father, 1965; *m* 1st, 1937, Olwen Protheroe Llewellin (*d* 1972); no *c*; 2nd, 1972, Gladys Mary Seals. *Educ:* Manor School, Mickleover, Derby. *Recreation:* shooting. *Heir: nephew* Matthew Peter Hives, *b* 25 May 1971. *Address:* Langdale House, Sutton-on-the-Hill, Derby DE6 5JA. *Club:* Farmers'.

HNATYSHYN, Rt. Hon. Ramon John, CC 1990; CMM 1990; CD 1990; PC (Can.) 1979; QC (Can.) 1988; Governor General and Commander-in-Chief of Canada, since 1990; *b* 16 March 1934; *s* of John Hnatyshyn and Helen Constance Hnatyshyn (*née* Pitts); *m* 1960, Karen Gerda Nygaard Andreasen; two *s*. *Educ:* Victoria Public Sch.; Nutana Collegiate Inst., Univ. of Saskatchewan (BA 1954; LLB 1956). RCAF, 1956–58 (trng 1951–56; 23 Wing Auxiliary). Called to the Bar of Saskatchewan, 1957, QC 1973; practised to 1990; Private Sec. and Exec. Asst to Senate Leader of Govt, 1958–60; Lectr in Law, Univ. of Saskatchewan, 1966–74; MP (PC Party) Saskatoon-Biggar, 1974, Saskatoon West, 1979, 1980, 1984 elections; Minister of State: for Science and Technology, 1979; of Energy, Mines and Resources, 1979–80; Govt House Leader, 1984–86; Minister responsible for Regulatory Affairs, 1986; Minister of Justice and Attorney General of Canada, 1986–88. *Address:* Government House, 1 Sussex Drive, Ottawa, Ontario K1A 0A1, Canada.

HO, Eric Peter, CBE 1981; Chairman, Public Service Commission, Hong Kong, 1987–91, retired; *b* 30 Dec. 1927; *s* of Sai-Ki Ho and Doris (*née* Lo); *m* 1956, Grace Irene, *d* of Mr and Mrs A. V. Young; two *s* one *d*. *Educ:* Univ. of Hong Kong (BA 1950). Inspector of Taxes (under training), London, 1950–53; Hong Kong Civil Service, 1954–87: Sec. for Social Services, 1977–83; Sec. for Trade and Industry, 1983–87. RCDS, London, 1976. *Recreations:* swimming, lawn tennis. *Address:* 26 Greenways Drive, Sunningdale, Berks.

HOAD, Air Vice-Marshal Norman Edward, CVO 1972; CBE 1969; AFC 1951 and Bar, 1956; artist; *b* 28 July 1923; *s* of Hubert Ronald Hoad and Florence Marie (*née* Johnson); two *s*. *Educ:* Brighton. Joined RAF, 1941, pilot trng, S Rhodesia; Lancaster pilot until shot down and taken prisoner in Germany, 1944; various flying and instructional duties, 1945–51; Sqdn Ldr 1951; OC No 192 Sqdn, 1953–55; psc 1956; Wing Comdr, HQ 2 ATAF, 1957–59; pfc 1960; OC No 216 Sqdn, 1960–62; jssc 1963; Gp Capt., MoD, 1963–65; idc 1966; Stn Comdr: RAF Lyneham, 1967, RAF Abingdon, 1968; Defence and Air Attaché, British Embassy, Paris, 1969–72; Dir, Defence Policy (A), 1972–74; Chief of Staff, 46 Gp, RAF Strike Comd, April-Oct. 1974; AOC No 46 Group, and Comdr, UK Jt Airborne Task Force, 1974–75; Senior RAF Mem., RCDS, 1976–78. Director, Air League, 1978–82. Founder Mem., Guild of Aviation Artists; Chm., Soc. of Equestrian Artists. MBIM 1970. *Address:* Little Meadow, Stowupland, Stowmarket, Suffolk IP14 5DF. *T:* Stowmarket (0449) 612006. *Club:* Royal Air Force.

HOAR, Rev. Ronald William Cecil; Chairman, Manchester and Stockport Methodist District, since 1979; President of the Methodist Conference, June 1991–92; *b* 31 Oct. 1931; *s* of Cecil Herbert William and Lilian Augusta Hoar; *m* 1956, Peggy Jean (*née* Stubbington); three *s* two *d*. *Educ:* Shedfield Church of England Primary Sch., Hants; Prices Sch., Fareham, Hants; Richmond Coll., Univ. of London (BD). Methodist Minister: Wells, Somerset, 1955–58; Bermondsey, London, 1958–62; Westminster and Chelsea, 1962–67; Bristol Mission, 1967–76; Great Yarmouth and Gorleston, 1976–79. *Publications:* Methodism in Chelsea to 1963, 1963; A Good Ideal: a history of the Bristol Methodist Mission, 1973; Advertising the Gospel, 1991. *Recreations:* DIY, watching sport, oil painting, gardening. *Address:* 15 Woodlands Road, Handforth, Wilmslow, Cheshire SK9 3AW. *T:* Wilmslow (0625) 523480.

HOARE, Prof. Charles Antony Richard, FRS 1982; Professor of Computation, Oxford University, since 1977; Fellow of Wolfson College, since 1977; *b* 11 Jan. 1934; *s* of Henry S. M. Hoare and Marjorie F. Hoare; *m* 1962, Jill Pym; one *s* one *d* (and one *s* decd). *Educ:* King's Sch., Canterbury; Merton Coll., Oxford (MA, Cert. Stats). Computer Div., Elliott Brothers, London, Ltd, 1959–68: successively Programmer, Chief Engr, Tech. Man., Chief Scientist; National Computer Centre, 1968; Prof. of Computer Science, QUB, 1968–77; Dir, Oxford Univ. Computing Lab., 1982–87. Dist. FBCS 1978; For. Mem., Accademia Nazionale dei Lincei, 1988. Hon. DSc: Southern California, 1979; Warwick, 1985; Pennsylvania, 1986; Belfast, 1987; York, 1989. A. M. Turing Award, Assoc. Comp. Mach., 1980; Harry Goode Meml Award, Amer. Fedn of Inf. Processing Socs, 1981; Faraday Medal, IEE, 1985. *Publications:* Structured Programming (with O.-J. Dahl and E. W. Dijkstra), 1972; Communicating Sequential Processes, 1985; Essays in Computing Science, 1988; articles in Computer Jl, Commun. ACM, and Acta Informatica. *Recreations:* walking, swimming, reading, listening to music. *Address:* 8–11 Keble Road, Oxford OX1 3QD. *T:* Oxford (0865) 273841.

HOARE, John Michael; independent consultant, health services management, since 1990; *b* 23 Oct. 1932; *s* of Leslie Frank Hoare and Gladys Hoare; *m* 1963, Brita Hjalte; one *s* one *d*. *Educ:* Raynes Park; Christ's Coll., Cambridge (BA). Asst Sec., United Bristol Hosps, 1961; House Governor, St Stephen's Hosp., 1963; Asst Clerk, St Thomas' Hosp., 1965; Administrator, Northwick Park Hosp., 1967; Wessex Regional Health Authority: Administrator, 1974–84; Gen. Man., 1984–89; Quality Advr, 1989–90. Mem., Defence Medical Services Inquiry, 1971–73. *Recreations:* reading, walking, music, squash. *Address:* 24 Clausentum Road, Winchester, Hants SO23 9QE. *T:* Winchester (0962) 54192.

HOARE, Hon. Marcus Bertram, CMG 1965; Justice of Supreme Court of Queensland, 1966–80; *b* 3 March 1910; *s* of John George and Emma Hoare; *m* 1936, Eileen Parker; four *s*. *Educ:* Brisbane Grammar Sch. Solicitor, 1933; Barrister-at-Law, 1944; QC (Australia) 1960. *Address:* 97 Chelmer Street West, Chelmer, Brisbane, Qld 4068, Australia. *T:* 379–4181. *Club:* Johnsonian (Brisbane).

HOARE, Sir Peter Richard David, 8th Bt *cr* 1786; *b* 22 March 1932; *s* of Sir Peter William Hoare, 7th Bt, and of Laura Ray, *o d* of Sir John Esplen, 1st Bt, KBE; *S* father, 1973; *m* 1st, 1961, Jane (marr. diss. 1967), *o d* of late Daniel Orme; 2nd, 1978, Katrin Alexa, Lady Hodson (marr. diss. 1982), *o d* of late Edwin Bernstiel; 3rd, 1983, Angela Francesca de la Sierra, *d* of late Fidel Fernando Ayarza. *Educ:* Eton. *Recreations:* travelling, shooting, skiing. *Heir: b* David John Hoare [*b* 8 Oct. 1935; *m* 1st, 1965, Mary Vanessa (marr. diss. 1978), *y d* of Peter Gordon Cardew; one *s*; 2nd, 1984, Virginia Victoria Graham Labes, *d* of Michael Menzies]. *Address:* c/o Crèdit Andorrà, Avenida Princep Benlloch 25, Andorra la Vella, Principality of Andorra. *Club:* Royal Automobile.

HOARE, Rev. Dr Rupert William Noel; Principal of Westcott House, Cambridge, since 1981; *b* 3 March 1940; *s* of Julian Hoare and Edith Hoare (*née* Temple); *m* 1965, Gesine (*née* Pflüger); three *s* one *d*. *Educ:* Rugby School; Trinity Coll., Oxford (BA 1961, MA 1967); Westcott House and Fitzwilliam House, Cambridge (BA 1964); Birmingham Univ. (PhD 1973). Deacon 1964, priest 1965, Dio. Manchester; Curate of St Mary, Oldham, 1964–67; Lecturer, Queen's Theological Coll., Birmingham, 1968–72; Rector, Parish of the Resurrection, Manchester, 1972–78; Residentiary Canon, Birmingham Cathedral, 1978–81. Canon Theologian of Coventry Cathedral, 1970–75. *Publications:* (trans. jtly) Bultmann's St John, 1971; (contrib.) Queen's Sermons, 1973, Queen's Essays, 1980; The Trial of Faith, 1988; articles in Theology. *Recreations:* hill walking, sailing, gardening, listening to music. *Address:* Westcott House, Jesus Lane, Cambridge CB5 8BP.

HOARE, Sir Timothy Edward Charles, 8th Bt *cr* 1784; Director: Career Plan Ltd, since 1970; New Metals and Chemicals Ltd, since 1968; *b* 11 Nov. 1934; *s* of Sir Edward O'Bryen Hoare, 7th Bt and of Nina Mary, *d* of late Charles Nugent Hope-Wallace, MBE; *S* father, 1969; *m* 1969, Felicity Anne, *o d* of Peter Boddington; one *s* twin *d*. *Educ:* Radley College; Worcester College, Oxford (MA Modern Hist.); Birkbeck Coll., London (MA Manpower Studies). FLS 1980. Dir, World Vision of Britain. Member: Gen. Synod of Church of England, 1970–; Crown Appointments Commn, 1987–. *Heir: s* Charles James Hoare, *b* 15 March 1971. *Address:* 10 Belitha Villas, N1 1PD. *Club:* MCC.

HOBAN, Brian Michael Stanislaus; Head Master of Harrow, 1971–81; a part-time Chairman, sundry Civil Service Selection Boards, since 1984; *b* 7 Oct. 1921; 2nd *s* of late Capt. R. A. Hoban; *m* 1947, Jasmine, 2nd *d* of J. C. Holmes, MC, Charterhouse, Godalming; one *s* one *d* (and one *d* decd). *Educ:* Charterhouse (Scholar); University Coll., Oxford (Sch.). 2nd Cl. Hon. Mods, 1947; 2nd Cl. Lit. Hum., 1949; BA 1949, MA 1957. Served War of 1939–45: Capt., Westminster Dragoons; NW Europe, 1944–45 (despatches); demobilised, Nov. 1945. Capt. Northants Yeomanry, TA, 1950–56. Asst Master: Uppingham Sch., 1949–52; Shrewsbury Sch., 1952–59; Headmaster, St Edmund's Sch., Canterbury, 1960–64; Head Master, Bradfield Coll., 1964–71. Hon. Associate Mem., HMC, 1981– (Hon. Treasurer, 1975–80). Sometime Mem., Central Adv. Bd, RAF Coll., Cranwell; Governor: Wellington Coll., 1981–; St Edmund's Sch., Canterbury, 1975–; St Margaret's Sch., Bushey, 1975–. JP Berks, 1967–71. *Publication:* (with Donald Swann) Jesu Parvule, 1965. *Recreations:* music, golf, walking, gardening. *Address:* Upcot, Wantage Road, Streatley, Berks RG8 9LD. *T:* Goring-on-Thames (0491) 873419. *Clubs:* East India, Devonshire, Sports and Public Schools; Vincent's (Oxford).

HOBAN, Russell Conwell, FRSL 1988; full-time writer, since 1967 (with some interruptions); *b* 4 Feb. 1925; *s* of Abram Hoban and Jenny Dimmerman; *m* 1st, 1944, Lillian Aberman (marr. diss. 1975); one *s* three *d*; 2nd, 1975, Gundula Ahl; three *s*. *Educ:* Lansdale High Sch.; Philadelphia Museum Sch. of Industrial Art. Served US Army, 1943–45: 339th Inf., 85th Div., Italy (Bronze Star Medal, 1945). Various jobs, 1945–56; free-lance illustration, 1956–65; copywriter with Doyle, Dane, Bernbach, New York, 1965–67; resident in London, 1969–. Drama: (television), Come and Find Me, 1980; The Carrier Frequency, 1984. *Publications: children's books:* What Does It Do and How Does It Work?, 1959; The Atomic Submarine, 1960; Bedtime for Frances, 1960; Herman the Loser, 1961; The Song in My Drum, 1962; London Men and English Men, 1963; Some Snow Said Hello, 1963; A Baby Sister for Frances, 1964; Nothing To Do, 1964; Bread and Jam for Frances, 1964; The Sorely Trying Day, 1964; Tom and the Two Handles, 1965; The Story of Hester Mouse, 1965; What Happened When Jack and Daisy Tried To Fool the Tooth Fairies, 1965; Goodnight, 1966; Henry and the Monstrous Din, 1966; Charlie the Tramp, 1966; The Little Brute Family, 1966; Save My Place, 1967; The Mouse and His Child, 1967; The Pedalling Man and Other Poems, 1968; The Stone Doll of Sister Brute, 1968; A Birthday for Frances, 1968; Ugly Bird, 1969; Best Friends for Frances, 1969; Harvey's Hideout, 1969; The Mole Family's Christmas, 1969; A Bargain for Frances, 1970; Emmet Otter's Jug-Band Christmas, 1971; Egg Thoughts and Other Frances Songs, 1972; The Sea-Thing Child, 1972; Letitia Rabbit's String Song, 1973; How Tom Beat Captain Najork and His Hired Sportsmen, 1974 (Whitbread Literary Award); Ten What?, 1974; Dinner at Alberta's, 1975; Crocodile and Pierrot, 1975; A Near Thing for Captain Najork, 1975; The Twenty-Elephant Restaurant, 1977; Arthur's New Power, 1978; The Dancing Tigers, 1979; La Corona and Other Tin Tales, 1979; Ace Dragon Ltd, 1980; Flat Cat, 1980; The Serpent Tower, 1981; The Great Fruit Gum Robbery, 1981; They Came from Aargh!, 1981; The Flight of Bembel Rudzuk, 1982; The Battle of Zormla, 1982; Jim Frog, 1983; Big John Turkle, 1983; Charlie Meadows, 1984; Lavinia Bat, 1984; The Rain Door, 1986; The Marzipan Pig, 1986; Ponders, 1988; Monsters, 1989; Jim Hedgehog's Supernatural Christmas, 1989; Jim Hedgehog and the Lonesome Tower, 1990; *novels:* The Lion of Boaz-Jachin and Jachin-Boaz, 1973; Kleinzeit, 1974; Turtle Diary, 1975 (filmed, 1985); Riddley Walker, 1980 (John W. Campbell Meml Award, 1981, Best Internat. Fiction, Aust. Sci. Fiction Achievement Award, 1983; adapted for stage, 1986); Pilgermann, 1983; The Medusa Frequency, 1987; *verse:* contribs to Six of the Best (ed A. Harvey), 1989; stories and essays in Fiction Magazine and Granta. *Recreations:* stones, short wave listening. *Address:* David Higham Associates Ltd, 5–8 Lower John Street, Golden Square, W1R 4HA. *T:* 071–437 7888.

HOBART, Sir John Vere, 4th Bt *cr* 1914, of Langdown, Co. Southampton; *b* 9 April 1945; *s* of Lt-Comdr Sir Robert Hampden Hobart, 3rd Bt, RN and Sylvia (*d* 1965), *d* of Harry Argo; *heir-pres.* to Earl of Buckinghamshire, *qv*; *S* father, 1988; *m* 1980, Kate, *o d* of late George Henry Iddles; two *s*. *Heir: s* George Hampden Hobart, *b* 10 June 1982. *Address:* 63 Queens Road, Cowes, Isle of Wight.

HOBART-HAMPDEN, family name of **Earl of Buckinghamshire.**

HOBBS, Herbert Harry, CB 1956; CVO 1972; Director, Ancient Monuments and Historic Buildings, 1970–72, retired; *b* 7 Nov. 1912; *s* of late Bertie Hobbs and Agnes Dora (*née* Clarke); *m* 1937, Joan Hazel Timmins (*d* 1979); two *s* one *d*. *Educ:* Bedford Sch.; Corpus Christi Coll., Oxford. Entered War Office, 1935; Comptroller of Lands and Claims, 1956–60; Asst Under-Sec. of State (Works), War Office, 1960–63; Under-Sec., MPBW, later DoE, 1963–72. Medal of Freedom with bronze palm (USA), 1946. *Recreations:* music, gardening. *Address:* 9 Hemp Garden, Minehead, Som TA24 5JG. *T:* Minehead (0643) 705350.

HOBBS, John Charles; Chief Insurance Officer, Department of Health and Social Security, 1971–76; *b* 28 May 1917; British; *m* 1961, Doris Gronow. *Educ:* Portsmouth Southern Grammar Sch.; Portsmouth Coll. of Technology. 1st cl. hons BSc, 1936; 1st cl. hons BSc (Spec.) Maths, 1944. FIS 1950. Asst Principal, 1946; Principal, 1947; Asst Sec., 1957.

HOBBS, Ven. Keith; Archdeacon of Chichester, 1981–91; Canon Residentiary of Chichester Cathedral, 1981–91; *b* 3 March 1925; *s* of late Percival Frank and Gwennyth Mary Hobbs; *m* 1950, Mary, *d* of late Louis Lingg and Mary Elizabeth Ruderman; one *s* (and one *s* one *d* decd). *Educ:* St Olave's Grammar School; Exeter Coll., Oxford (MA); Wells Theological Coll. Instr Branch, RN, 1946; retired (Lt Comdr), 1956. Curate, Clewer St Stephen, 1958–60; Soho, 1960–62; St Stephen, S Kensington, 1962–78; Lectr and Co-ordinator of Counselling, Borough Road Coll., 1964–77; Actg Gen. Secretary, Church Union, 1977–78; Chaplain to Bishop of Chichester, 1978–81. *Address:* 2 The Chantry, Canon Lane, Chichester, W Sussex PO19 1PX. *T:* Chichester (0243) 784260.

HOBBS, Prof. Kenneth Edward Frederick, ChM, FRCS; Professor of Surgery, Royal Free Hospital School of Medicine, University of London, and Consultant Surgeon, Royal Free Hospital, since 1973; *b* 28 Dec. 1936; *s* of late Thomas Edward Ernest Hobbs and Gladys May Hobbs (*née* Neave). *Educ:* West Suffolk County Grammar Sch., Bury St Edmunds; Guy's Hosp. Med. Sch., Univ. of London (MB BS 1960). ChM Bristol 1970; FRCS 1964. Lectr in Surgery, Univ. of Bristol, 1966–70; Surgical Res. Fellow, Harvard Univ., 1968–69; Sen. Lectr in Surgery, Univ. of Bristol, 1970–73; University of London: Vice-Dean, Faculty of Medicine, 1986–90; Mem. Senate, 1985–; Chm., Acad. Adv. Bd in Medicine, 1986–90; Dep. Chm., Acad. Council Standing Sub-Cttee in Medicine, 1986–90. Mem., Systems Bd, MRC, 1982–86; Chm., Grants Cttee A, MRC, 1984–86; Mem., Med. Sub-Cttee, UGC, 1986–89. Scientific Advr, Mason Med. Res. Foundn, 1988–. Vis. Prof., Univs in China, Ethiopia, S Africa, Europe, USA, West Indies. Secretary: Patey Soc., 1979–82; 1942 Club, 1985–88; Trustee and Bd Mem., Stanley Thomas Johnson Foundn, Berne, 1976–. *Publications:* chapters on aspects of liver surgery in textbooks; contribs to professional jls. *Recreations:* gourmet dining, the countryside. *Address:* The Rookery, New Buckenham, Norfolk NR16 2AE. *T:* East Harling (0953) 860558. *Club:* Athenæum.

HOBBS, Maj.-Gen. Michael Frederick, CBE 1982 (OBE 1979, MBE 1975); Director, Duke of Edinburgh's Award Scheme, since 1988; *b* 28 Feb. 1937; *s* of late Brig. Godfrey Pennington Hobbs and Elizabeth Constance Mary Hobbs; *m* 1967, Tessa Mary Churchill; one *s* two *d*. *Educ:* Eton College. Served Grenadier Guards, 1956–80; Directing Staff, Staff Coll., 1974–77; MoD, 1980–82; Commander 39 Inf. Bde, 1982–84; Dir of PR (Army), 1984–85; Commander, 4th Armoured Div., 1985–87; retired. *Recreations:* field sports, horticulture. *Address:* (office) 5 Prince of Wales Terrace, W8 5PG. *T:* 071–937 5205. *Clubs:* Cavalry and Guards, MCC.

HOBDAY, Sir Gordon (Ivan), Kt 1979; Lord Lieutenant and Keeper of the Rolls for Nottinghamshire, 1983–91; Chancellor, Nottingham University since 1979 (President of the Council, 1973–82); *b* 1 Feb. 1916; *e s* of late Alexander Thomas Hobday and Frances Cassandra (*née* Meads); *m* 1940, Margaret Jean Joule; one *d*. *Educ:* Long Eaton Grammar Sch.; UC Nottingham. BSc, PhD London; FRSC. Joined Boots Co., 1939; Dir of Research, 1952–68; Man. Dir, 1970–72; Chm., 1973–81; Chm., Central Independent Television, 1981–85; Dir, Lloyds Bank, 1981–86. A Dep. Chm., Price Commn, 1977–78. Pres., Portland Trng Coll. for the Disabled, 1990–. DL Notts, 1981. KStJ 1983. Hon. LLD Nottingham, 1977. *Recreations:* handicrafts, gardening. *Address:* University of Nottingham, University Park, Nottingham NG7 2RD. *T:* Nottingham (0602) 484848.

HOBDEN, Dennis Harry; *b* 21 Jan. 1920; *s* of Charles Hobden and Agnes Hobden (*née* Smith); *m* 1st, 1950, Kathleen Mary Hobden (*née* Holman) (marr. diss. 1970); two *s* two *d*; 2nd, 1977, Sheila Hobden, JP (*née* Tugwell). *Educ:* elementary sch. Entered GPO, 1934; retired 1982. Served as Air Crew, RAF, 1941–46 (Flt Lieut). MP (Lab) Kemptown Div. of Brighton, 1964–70. Mem., Brighton Town Council, 1956–91; Mayor of Brighton, 1979–80; Mem., E Sussex CC, 1973–85; Chairman: Brighton Race Ground Lessees, 1987–91; Brighton Borough Licensing Cttee. *Recreations:* politics, gardening, music, reading, Spiritualism. *Address:* Sea Hawk, 40 McWilliam Road, Woodingdean, Brighton, East Sussex BN2 6BE.

HOBDEN, Reginald Herbert, DFC 1944; HM Diplomatic Service, retired; *b* 9 Nov. 1919; *s* of William Richard and Ada Emily Hobden; *m* 1945, Gwendoline Ilma Vowles; two *s* one *d*. *Educ:* Sir William Borlase's Sch., Marlow. Apptd Colonial Office, Dec. 1936. Served War of 1939–45 (despatches, DFC): RAFVR, Sept. 1940–Jan. 1946 (Sqdn Ldr). Returned to Colonial Office, 1946; seconded to Dept of Technical Co-operation, 1961; First Sec., UK Commn, Malta, 1962–64; HM Diplomatic Service, Nov. 1964: CRO until April 1968; Head of British Interests Section, Canadian High Commn, Dar es Salaam, April 1968; British Acting High Comr, Dar es Salaam, July-Oct. 1968, and Counsellor, Dar es Salaam, Oct. 1968–69; Counsellor (Economic and Commercial), Islamabad, 1970–75; Inst. of Develt Studies, Sussex Univ., 1975; High Comr, Lesotho, 1976–78. Clerk in Clerk's Dept, House of Commons, 1978–84. *Recreations:* chess, bridge. *Address:* 14 Belmont Close, Uxbridge, Mddx UB8 1RF. *T:* Uxbridge (0895) 34754.

HOBHOUSE, Sir Charles John Spinney, 7th Bt *cr* 1812, of Broughton-Gifford, Bradford-on-Avon and of Monkton Farleigh, Wiltshire; *b* 27 Oct. 1962; *s* of Sir Charles Chisholm Hobhouse, 6th Bt, TD and of Elspeth Jean, *yr d* of late Thomas George Spinney; *S* father, 1991. *Heir: uncle* John Spencer Hobhouse [*b* 15 Nov. 1910; *m* 1940, Mary, *yr d* of late Llewelyn Robert, MD].

HOBHOUSE, Hermione; *see* Hobhouse, M. H.

HOBHOUSE, (Mary) Hermione, MBE 1981; FSA; writer and conservationist; Editor, Survey of London, since 1983; *d* of late Sir Arthur Lawrence Hobhouse and Konradin, *d* of Rt Hon. Frederick Huth Jackson; *m* 1958, Henry Trevenen Davidson Graham (marr. diss. 1988); one *s* one *d*. *Educ:* Ladies' Coll., Cheltenham; Lady Margaret Hall, Oxford (Hons Mod. Hist.). Researcher/Writer, Associated-Rediffusion TV and Granada TV, 1957–65; Tutor in Architectural History, Architectural Assoc. Sch., London, 1973–78; Sec., Victorian Soc., 1977–82. Member: Royal Commn for Exhibn of 1851, 1983–; Council, Nat. Trust, 1983–; Council, Soc. of Antiquaries, 1984–87. *Publications:* Thomas Cubitt: Master Builder, 1971 (Hitchcock Medal, 1972); Lost London, 1971; History of Regent Street, 1975; Oxford and Cambridge, 1980; Prince Albert: his life and work, 1983; contrib. Architectural Jl, Architectural Review. *Recreations:* gardening, looking at buildings of all periods. *Address:* 61 St Dunstan's Road, W6. *T:* 081–741 2575. *Club:* Reform.

HOBHOUSE, Penelope, (Mrs John Malins); gardener, garden writer and garden consultant, since 1976; *b* 20 Nov. 1929; *d* of late Captain J. J. L.-C. Chichester-Clark, DSO and Bar, MP and Marion Chichester-Clark (later Mrs C. E. Brackenbury); *m* 1st, 1952, Paul Hobhouse (marr. diss. 1982); two *s* one *d*; 2nd, 1983, Prof. John Malins. *Educ:* Girton Coll., Cambridge (BA Hons Econs, 1951). National Trust tenant of Tintinhull House garden, 1980–. *Publications:* The Country Gardener, 1976, revd edn 1989; The Smaller Garden, 1981; Gertrude Jekyll on Gardening, 1983; Colour in your Garden, 1985; The National Trust: A Book of Gardening, 1986; Private Gardens of England, 1986; Garden Style, 1988; Painted Gardens, 1988; Borders, 1989; The Gardens of Europe, 1990. *Recreations:* reading Trollope and Henry James, Italy. *Address:* Tintinhull House, Yeovil, Som BA22 8PZ. *T:* Yeovil (0935) 822509.

See also Sir R. Chichester-Clark, Baron Moyola.

HOBKIRK, Michael Dalgliesh; *b* 9 Dec. 1924; *s* of Roy and Phyllis Hobkirk; *m* 1952, Lucy Preble; two *d*. *Educ:* Marlborough Coll.; Wadham Coll., Oxford. BA (Social Studies), MA 1949. Served War of 1939–45: Army (RAC, RAEC, Captain), 1943–47. Civil Service: War Office, 1949–63; MoD, 1963–70; Directing Staff, Nat. Defence Coll., 1970–74; Brookings Instn, Washington, DC, USA, 1974–75; Lord Chancellor's Dept, 1975–80 (Principal Establishment and Finance Officer, 1977–80); Asst Under-Sec. of State, MoD, 1980–82. Sen. Fellow, Nat. Defense Univ., Washington, DC, USA, 1982–83.

Publication: contrib. to The Management of Defence (ed L. Martin), 1976; The Politics of Defence Budgeting, 1984. *Address:* 48 Woodside Avenue, Beaconsfield, Bucks HP9 1JH. *Club:* United Oxford & Cambridge University.

HOBLER, Air Vice-Marshal John Forde, CB 1958; CBE 1943; *b* Rockhampton, Qld, Australia, 26 Sept. 1907; *s* of late L. E. Hobler, Rockhampton; *m* 1939, Dorothy Evelyn Diana Haines, Wilsford, Wilts; two *s* one *d*. *Educ:* Rockhampton, Qld. Served whole of War of 1939–45 in Bomber Command; commanded RAF Lossiemouth; Palestine, 1945; Staff Coll., 1946–48; Air Ministry, 1948–50; Comd Habbaniya, Iraq, 1950–52; HQ Flying Trg Comd, 1952–54; Air Ministry, 1954–56; AO i/c Administration, Middle East Air Force, 1956–58; Air Officer Commanding No 25 Gp, 1958–61; Air Officer i/c Administration, Far East Air Force, 1961–63, retd. Mem., RAF Escaping Soc.; Founder Mem., Central Queensland Aero Club, 1929–. FRGS. *Address:* Unit P8, The Domain Country Club, 74 Wardoo Street, Ashmore, Qld 4214, Australia. *Club:* United Services (Brisbane).

HOBLEY, Brian; Director, Hobley Archaeological Consultancy Services Ltd, since 1989; Chief Urban Archaeologist, City of London, 1973–89; *b* 25 June 1930; *s* of William Hobley and Harriet (*née* Hobson); *m* 1953, Laurie Parkes; one *s* one *d*. *Educ:* Univ. of Leicester. BA Hons Leicester 1965; FSA 1969; AMA 1970. Field Officer, Coventry Corp., 1965; Keeper, Dept Field Archaeology, Coventry Museum, 1970. Lectr, Birmingham Univ. Extra-mural Dept, 1965–74. Chm. Standing Cttee, Arch. Unit Managers, 1986–89; Jt Sec., British Archaeologists and Developers Liaison Gp, 1986–89. MBIM 1978; MIFA 1982. *Publications:* (ed jtly) Waterfront Archaeology in Britain and Northern Europe, 1981; Roman Urban Defences in the West, 1983; Roman Urban Topography in Britain and the Western Empire, 1985; Roman and Saxon London: a reappraisal, 1986; British Archaeologists and Developers Code of Practice, 1986; The Rebirth of Towns in the West AD 700–1050, 1988; reports in learned jls incl. Proc. 7th, 8th, 9th and 12th Internat. Congresses of Roman Frontier Studies, Tel Aviv, Univ. Israel and Bucharest Univ., Rumania on excavations and reconstructions at The Lunt Roman fort, Baginton near Coventry. *Recreations:* classical music, chess. *Address:* 21 St Martin's Road, Coventry CV3 6ET. *T:* Coventry (0203) 411068, *Fax:* (0203) 692180.

HOBLEY, John William Dixon, CMG 1976; QC (Hong Kong); Principal Legal Adviser, Wigan Borough Council, 1988; *b* 11 June 1929; *s* of John Wilson Hobley and Ethel Anne Hobley; *m* 1953, Dorothy Cockhill; one *s* one *d*. *Educ:* University Sch., Southport, Merseyside; Univ. of Liverpool (LLB). Called to the Bar, Gray's Inn, 1950; Northern Circuit, 1950–53; Hong Kong: Crown Counsel, 1953–62; Sen. Crown Counsel, 1962–65; Principal Crown Counsel, 1965–72; Attorney-Gen., Bermuda, 1972; Solicitor-Gen., 1973, Attorney-Gen., 1973–79, Hong Kong. *Recreations:* music, bridge.

HOBMAN, David Burton, CBE 1983; Director, Age Concern England (National Old People's Welfare Council), 1970–87; *b* 8 June 1927; *s* of J. B. and D. L. Hobman; *m* 1954, Erica Irwin; one *s* one *d*. *Educ:* University College Sch.; Blundell's. Community work, Forest of Dean, 1954–56; British Council for Aid to Refugees, 1957; Nat. Council of Social Service, 1958–67; Visiting Lectr in Social Admin, Nat. Inst. for Social Work, 1967; Dir, Social Work Adv. Service, 1968–70. Vis. Prof., Sch. of Social Work, McGill Univ., Montreal, 1977. Member: BBC/ITA Appeals Adv. Council, 1965–69; Steering Cttee, Enquiry into Homelessness, Nat. Asstce Bd, 1967–68; Adv. Council, Nat. Corp. for Care of Old People, 1970–74; Metrication Bd, 1974–80; Lord Goodman's Cttee Reviewing Law of Charity, 1975–76; Chairman: Social Welfare Commn Conf. of Bishops, 1968–71; Family Housing Assoc., 1969–70; Oftel Adv. Cttee for Disabled and Elderly Persons, 1984–; Home Concern Housing Assoc., 1985–87; Jt Chm., Age Concern Inst. of Gerontology, KCL, 1986–87; Consultant, UN Div. of Social Affairs, 1968–69; Observer, White House Congress on Ageing, 1971–; Pres., Internat. Fedn on Ageing, 1977–80, 1983–87 (Vice-Pres., 1974–77); Member: Personal Social Services Council, 1978–80; Exec. Cttee, Nat. Council of Voluntary Orgns, 1981–83; Anchor Housing, 1984–86; Exec. Sec., Charities Effectiveness Review Trust, 1987–. Producer, Getting On (television programme), 1987–88. Special Advr, British delegn to World Assembly on Ageing, 1982. Mem. Adv. Bd, Saga Magazine, 1985–; Dir, Cinetel Ltd. Governor: Cardinal Newman Comp. Sch., Hove, 1971–76 (Chm); Volunteer Centre, 1975–79; Conciliator, Sheltered Housing ACAS, 1990–. KSG. *Publications:* A Guide to Voluntary Service, 1964, 2nd edn 1967; Who Cares, 1971; The Social Challenge of Ageing, 1978; The Impact of Ageing, 1981; The Coming of Age, 1989; Planning Your Retirement, 1990; numerous papers, broadcasts. *Recreations:* caravanning, travel, grandchildren. *Address:* Robinswood, George's Lane, Storrington, Pulborough, W Sussex. *T:* Storrington (0903) 742987. *Club:* Reform.

HOBSBAWM, Prof. Eric John Ernest, FBA 1976; Emeritus Professor of Economic and Social History, University of London, since 1982; *b* 9 June 1917; *s* of Leopold Percy Hobsbawm and Nelly Grün; *m* 1962, Marlene Schwarz; one *s* one *d*. *Educ:* Vienna; Berlin; St Marylebone Grammar Sch.; Univ. of Cambridge (BA, PhD). Lectr, Birkbeck Coll., 1947; Fellow, King's Coll., Cambridge, 1949–55, Hon. Fellow, 1973; Reader, Birkbeck Coll., 1959, Prof., 1970–82. Hon. DPhil Univ. of Stockholm, 1970; Hon. Dr Hum. Let.: Univ. of Chicago, 1976; New Sch. of Social Res., 1982; Bard Coll., 1986; Hon. LittD: UEA, 1982; York Univ., Canada, 1986; *Dhc* Univ. of Pisa, 1987. Foreign Hon. Mem., American Academy of Arts and Sciences, 1971; Hon. Mem., Hungarian Acad. of Sciences, 1979. *Publications:* Labour's Turning Point, 1948; Primitive Rebels, 1959; (*pseud.* F. Newton) The Jazz Scene, 1959; The Age of Revolution, 1962; Labouring Men, 1964; (ed) Karl Marx, Precapitalist Formations, 1964; Industry and Empire, 1968; (with G. Rudé) Captain Swing, 1969; Bandits, 1969; Revolutionaries, 1973; The Age of Capital, 1975; (with T. Ranger) The Invention of Tradition, 1983; Worlds of Labour, 1984; The Age of Empire, 1987; Politics for a Rational Left, 1989; Nations and Nationalism since 1780, 1990; Echoes of the Marseillaise, 1990; contribs to jls. *Recreation:* travel. *Address:* Birkbeck College, Malet Street, WC1. *T:* 071–580 6622.

HOBSLEY, Prof. Michael, TD 1969; PhD; FRCS; Head of Department of Surgery, University College and Middlesex School of Medicine, University College London, since 1988; David Patey Professor of Surgery, University of London, since 1986 (Professor of Surgery, since 1984); *b* 18 Jan. 1929; *s* of Henry Hobsley and Sarah Lily Blanchfield; *m* 1953, Jane Fairlie Cambell; one *s* three *d*. *Educ:* La Martinière Coll., Calcutta; Sidney Sussex Coll., Cambridge (MA, MB, MChir); Middlesex Hosp. Med. Sch. PhD London, 1961; DSc London, 1989. FRCS 1958. Training posts in RAMC and at Middlesex, Whittington and Chace Farm Hosps, 1951–68; Comyns Berkeley Fellow, Gonville and Caius Coll., Cambridge and Mddx Hosp. Med. Sch., 1965–66; posts at Mddx Hosp. and Med. Sch., 1968–88: Hon. Consultant Surgeon, 1969; Reader in Surgical Science, 1970–75; Prof. of Surg. Science, 1975–83; Dir, Dept of Surgical Studies, 1983–88. Howard C. Naffziger Surg. Res. Fellow, Univ. of Calif, 1966; Windermere Foundn Travelling Prof. of Surgery, 1984; Glaxo Visitor, Univ. of Witwatersrand, 1985; Vis. Professor: Univ. of Calif, 1980; Univ. of Khartoum, 1976; McMaster Univ., 1982; Monash Univ., 1984. Non-exec. Mem., Enfield HA, 1990–. Royal College of Surgeons: Hunterian Prof., 1962–63; Penrose May Tutor, 1973–78; Sir Gordon Taylor Lectr, 1980; Examr, 1968–. Examiner: Univ. of London, 1978–; Univ. of Nigeria, 1977–; Univ. of

the WI, 1978–; Univ. of Bristol, 1986–88; Univ. of Cambridge, 1986–; St Mary's Hosp. Med. Sch., 1989–. Hon. Fellow: Assoc. of Surgeons of India, 1983; Amer. Surgical Assoc., 1989. FRSM 1960. *Publications:* Pathways in Surgical Management, 1979, 2nd edn 1986; Disorders of the Digestive System, 1982; Colour Atlas of Parotidectomy, 1983; articles in BMJ, Lancet, British Jl of Surgery, Gut, Klinische Wochenschrift. *Recreation:* cricket. *Address:* Fieldside, Barnet Lane, Totteridge, N20 8AS. *T:* 081–445 6507. *Clubs:* Athenæum, MCC.

HOBSON, Anthony Robert Alwyn; bibliographical historian; *b* 5 Sept. 1921; *s* of Geoffrey Dudley Hobson, MVO and Gertrude Adelaide, *d* of Rev. Thomas Vaughan, Rector of Rhuddlan, Flintshire; *m* 1959, Elena Pauline Tanya (*d* 1988), *d* of Igor Vinogradoff; one *s* two *d*. *Educ:* Eton Coll. (Oppidan Scholar); New Coll., Oxford (MA). Served Scots Guards, 1941–46, Captain; Italy, 1943–46 (mentioned in despatches). Joined Sotheby & Co., 1947: Dir, 1949–71, Associate, 1971–77. Sandars Reader in Bibliography, Univ. of Cambridge, 1974–75; Franklin Jasper Walls Lectr, Pierpont Morgan Library, NY, 1979; Vis. Fellow, All Souls Coll., Oxford, 1982–83; Rosenbach Fellow, Univ. of Philadelphia, 1990; Lyell Reader in Bibliography, Univ. of Oxford, 1990–91. President: Bibliographical Soc., 1977–79; Association internationale de Bibliophilie, 1985–; Hon. Pres., Edinburgh Bibliographical Soc., 1971–; Trustee: Eton Coll. Collections Trust, 1977–; Lambeth Palace Library, 1984–90. Hon. Fellow, Pierpont Morgan Library, 1983; For. Associate, Ateneo Veneto, 1987–. Cavaliere Ufficiale, Al Merito della Repubblica Italiana, 1979. *Publications:* French and Italian Collectors and their Bindings, 1953; Great Libraries, 1970; Apollo and Pegasus, 1975; Humanists and Bookbinders, 1989; contrib. The Library, TLS, etc. *Recreations:* travel, opera, visiting libraries founded before 1800. *Address:* The Glebe House, Whitsbury, Fordingbridge, Hants. *T:* Rockbourne (07253) 221. *Clubs:* Brooks's, Beefsteak, Roxburghe; Grolier (New York).

HOBSON, David Constable, CBE 1991; Chartered Accountant; Partner, Coopers & Lybrand, 1953–84, Senior Partner, 1975–83; *b* 1 Nov. 1922; *s* of late Charles Kenneth and Eileen Isabel Hobson; *m* 1961, Elizabeth Anne Drury; one *s* one *d*. *Educ:* Marlborough Coll.; Christ's Coll., Cambridge (Scholar). MA. ACA 1950; FCA 1958. Served War, REME, 1942–47 (Captain). Joined Cooper Brothers & Co. (now Coopers & Lybrand), 1947; Mem., Exec. Cttee, Coopers & Lybrand (International), 1973–83 (Chm., 1975–76, 1978–79, 1981–82). Chm., Cambrian & General Securities, 1986–89; Director: The Laird Gp, 1985–; Fleming High Income Investment Trust, 1989–. Inspector (for Dept of Trade), London & County Securities Group Ltd, 1974; Advr, Prime Minister's Policy Unit, 1983–86. Member: Accounting Standards Cttee, 1970–82; City Capital Markets Cttee, 1980–84; Nat. Biological Standards Bd, 1983–88; Building Socs Commn, 1986–; Board Mem. (repr. UK and Ireland), Internat. Accounting Standards Cttee, 1980–85. Hon. Treasurer, Lister Inst., 1986–. Member of Council: Marlborough Coll., 1967– (Chm., 1987–); Francis Holland Schools, 1975–. *Recreations:* travel, gardening, reading, occasional golf. *Address:* Magnolia, Chiswick Mall, W4 2PR. *T:* 081–994 7511. *Club:* Reform.

HOBSON, Sir Harold, Kt 1977; CBE 1971; Special Writer, The Sunday Times, since 1976 (Drama Critic, 1947–76); contributor to: Times Literary Supplement; Drama; London Drama Critic, The Christian Science Monitor, 1935–74; *b* Thorpe Hesley, near Rotherham, 4 Aug. 1904; *o s* of late Jacob and Minnie Hobson; *m* 1st, 1935, Gladys Bessie (Elizabeth) (*d* 1979), *e d* of late James Johns; one *d*; 2nd, 1981, Nancy Penhale. *Educ:* privately; Oriel Coll., Oxford (Hon. Fellow, 1974). Asst Literary Editor, The Sunday Times, 1942–48; TV Critic, The Listener, 1947–51; for many years took part in BBC Radio programme The Critics. Mem., National Theatre Bd, 1976–79. Hon. DLitt Sheffield, 1977. Chevalier of the Legion of Honour, 1959. Knight of Mark Twain, 1976. *Publications:* The First Three Years of the War, 1942; The Devil in Woodford Wells (novel), 1946; Theatre, 1948; Theatre II, 1950; Verdict at Midnight, 1952; The Theatre Now, 1953; The French Theatre of Today, 1953; (ed) The International Theatre Annual, 1956, 1957, 1958, 1959, 1960; Ralph Richardson, 1958; (with P. Knightly and L. Russell) The Pearl of Days: an intimate memoir of The Sunday Times, 1972; The French Theatre since 1830, 1978; Indirect Journey (autobiog.), 1978; Theatre in Britain: a personal view, 1984. *Recreations:* reading the New Yorker, watching cricket, Stock Exchange. *Address:* Westhampnett Private Nursing Home, Westhampnett, Chichester, W Sussex. *Club:* La Casserole (Paris).

HOBSON, John; Under Secretary, Department of the Environment, since 1986; *b* 30 March 1946; *s* of late John Leslie Hobson and of Beatrice Edith Hobson; *m* 1970, Jeanne Gerrish; one *s* one *d*. *Educ:* Northampton Grammar Sch.; Manchester Grammar Sch.; King's Coll., Cambridge (MA Mathematics). Joined Min. of Transport, 1967; Asst Private Sec. to Sec. of State for the Environment, 1970–72; Private Sec. to Head of CS, 1974–78; Assistant Secretary: Dept of Transport, 1979–80; DoE, 1980–86. *Address:* Department of the Environment, 2 Marsham Street, SW1P 3EB.

HOBSON, Lawrence John, CMG 1965; OBE 1960; with Arab-British Chamber of Commerce, since 1977; *b* 4 May 1921; *er s* of late John Sinton Hobson and Marion Adelaide Crawford; *m* 1946, Patricia Fiona Rosemary Beggs (*née* Green); one step *s* (one *s* decd). *Educ:* Taunton Sch.; St Catharine's Coll., Cambridge. BA 1946, MA 1950. Served War, 1941–42. ADC and Private Sec. to Gov., Aden, 1942; Political Officer, 1944; Asst Chief Sec., 1956; Aden govt Student Liaison Officer, UK, 1960–62; Political Adviser to High Comr, Aden, 1963–66; retired from HMOCS, 1966. With BP Ltd, 1966–77. Mem., Newbury DC, 1973–. *Address:* Saffron House, Stanford Dingley, near Reading, Berks. *T:* Bradfield (0734) 536.

HOBSON, Valerie Babette Louise, (Mrs Profumo); film and stage actress; *b* Larne, Ireland; *d* of Comdr R. G. Hobson, RN, and Violette Hamilton-Willoughby; *m* 1st, 1939, Sir Anthony James Allan Havelock-Allan, Bt (marr. diss. 1952), *qv*; one *s* (and one *s* decd); 2nd, 1954, John Dennis Profumo, *qv*; one *s*. *Educ:* St Augustine's Priory, London; Royal Academy of Dramatic Art. Was trained from early age to become ballet dancer; first stage appearance at Drury Lane in Ball at the Savoy, aged 15. The King and I, Drury Lane, 1953. First film, Badgers Green; went to Hollywood and appeared in Werewolf of London, Bride of Frankenstein, The Mystery of Edwin Drood, etc; at 18 returned to England. Films include: The Drum, This Man is News, This Man in Paris, The Spy in Black, Q Planes, Silent Battle, Contraband, Unpublished Story, Atlantic Ferry, The Adventures of Tartu, The Years Between, Great Expectations, Blanche Fury, The Small Voice, Kind Hearts and Coronets, Train of Events, Interrupted Journey, The Rocking Horse Winner, The Card, Who Goes There?, Meet Me Tonight, The Voice of Merrill, Background, Knave of Hearts. *Recreations:* listening to music, writing, reading, painting.

HOCHHAUSER, Victor; impresario; *b* 27 March 1923; *m* 1949, Lilian Hochhauser (*née* Shields); three *s* one *d*. *Educ:* City of London Coll. Impresario for: David Oistrakh; Sviatoslav Richter; Mstislav Rostropovich; Gilels, Kogan; Margot Fonteyn; Natalia Makarova; Nureyev Festival; Bolshoi Ballet season at Covent Garden, 1963, 1969; Leningrad State Kirov Ballet, Covent Garden, 1961, 1966; concerts, Royal Albert Hall, Barbican and Royal Festival Hall; Peking Opera and other Chinese companies, 1972–; co-presenter, Aida, Earls Court, 1988, Birmingham Arena, 1991. *Recreations:* reading, swimming, sleeping. *Address:* 4 Oak Hill Way, NW3 7LR. *T:* 071–794 0987.

HOCKADAY, Sir Arthur (Patrick), KCB 1978 (CB 1975); CMG 1969; Secretary and Director-General, Commonwealth War Graves Commission, 1982–89; *b* 17 March 1926; *s* of late William Ronald Hockaday and Marian Camilla Hockaday, *d* of Rev. A. C. Evans; *m* 1955, Peggy, *d* of late H. W. Prince. *Educ:* Merchant Taylors' Sch.; St John's Coll., Oxford. BA (1st cl. Lit. Hum.) 1949, MA 1952. Apptd to Home Civil Service, 1949; Admty, 1949–62; Private Sec. to successive Ministers of Defence and Defence Secretaries, 1962–65; NATO Internat. Staff, 1965–69 (Asst Sec. Gen. for Defence Planning and Policy, 1967–69); Asst Under-Sec. of State, MoD, 1969–72; Under-Sec., Cabinet Office, 1972–73; Dep. Under-Sec. of State, MoD, 1973–76; 2nd Permanent Under-Sec. of State, MoD, 1976–82. Chm., British Group, Council on Christian Approaches to Defence and Disarmament, 1989–. Chm., Gallipoli Meml Lecture Trust, 1990–. *Publications:* (contrib.) Ethics and Nuclear Deterrence, 1982; The Strategic Defence Initiative, 1985; (contrib.) Ethics and European Security, 1986; (contrib.) Ethics and International Relations, 1986; (contrib.) Just Deterrence, 1990; occasional articles and reviews. *Recreation:* fell-walking. *Address:* 11 Hitherwood Court, Hitherwood Drive, SE19 1UX. *T:* 081–670 7940. *Clubs:* Naval and Military, Civil Service.

HOCKÉ, Jean-Pierre; international consultant; United Nations High Commissioner for Refugees, 1986–89; *b* 31 March 1938; *s* of Charles and Marie Rose Hocké; *m* 1961, Michèle Marie Weber; two *s*. *Educ:* Univ. of Lausanne (grad. Econ. and Business Admin). With commercial firms in Switzerland and Nigeria, 1961–67; joined Internat. Cttee of Red Cross, 1968: Hd of Operations Dept, 1973; Mem., Directorate, 1981. Member: Jean Monnet Foundn, Lausanne; Arche de la Fraternité, Paris; Vice-Chm., CASIN (internat. negotiations inst.), Geneva; Chm., Bd, InterAssist, Bern. Hon. Dr Lausanne, 1987. *Address:* 11 rue Général Dufour, 1211 Geneva 11, Switzerland. *T:* (022) 781.04.56.

HOCKENHULL, Arthur James Weston, OBE 1966; HM Diplomatic Service, retired; *b* 8 Aug. 1915; *s* of late Frederick Weston Hockenhull and late Jessie Gibson Kaye Hockenhull (*née* Mitchell); *m* 1955, Rachel Ann Kimber; two *d*. *Educ:* Clifton Coll.; Exeter Coll., Oxford. HM Overseas Civil Service; various appts in Far East, Cyprus and British Guiana, 1936–57. Interned by Japanese, in Singapore, 1942–45; First Sec., UK Commn, Singapore, 1958–63; Counsellor, British High Commn, Malaysia, 1964–68; HM Consul-Gen., Houston, 1969–74. *Recreations:* golf, gardening, swimming. *Club:* United Oxford & Cambridge University.

HOCKER, Dr Alexander; Grosses Verdienstkreuz mit Stern des Verdienstordens der Bundesrepublik Deutschland, 1973; Director-General, European Space Research Organisation (ESRO), 1971–74; *m* 1940, Liselotte Schulze; five *s* one *d*. *Educ:* Univs of Innsbruck, Hamburg and Leipzig. Asst, Law Faculty, Leipzig Univ.; County Court Judge; Officer, Advanced Scientific Study Div., Min. of Educn, Hannover, 1947–49; Dep. of Sec.-Gen. of German Res. Assoc. (Deutsche Forschungsgemeinschaft), 1949–56; Ministerialrat and Ministerialdirigent (responsible for res., trng and sci. exchanges), Fed. Min. for Atomic Energy, 1956–61; Mem. Directorate, Nuclear Res. Centre (Kernforschungsanlage) Jülich, 1961–69; Sci. Adviser to Foundn Volkswagenwerk, 1969–71. German Deleg. to CERN, Geneva, 1952–61 (Chm. of Finance Cttee, 1960–61); Chm. of Legal, Admin. and Financial Working Gp of COPERS, 1961–63; Chm. of Council, ESRO, 1965–67 (Vice-Chm. 1964); Member: German Commn for Space Res., 1964–71; Kuratorium Max-Planck-Institut für Physik und Astrophysik, 1968–71; Max-Plank-Institut für Plasmaphysik, 1971–80, Hon. Member 1980–. *Publication:* (jtly) Taschenbuch für Atomfragen, 1968. *Address:* Bad Godesberg, Augustastrasse 63, 5300 Bonn 2, Germany. *T:* (0228) 363961.

HOCKING, Frederick Denison Maurice; formerly Cornwall County Pathologist; Consulting Biologist and Toxicologist, Devon River Board; late Consulting Pathologist, South-Western Regional Hospital Board; Acting Director Public Health Laboratory Service, Cornwall, and other hospitals in Cornwall; late Chemical Pathologist, Biochemist, and Assistant Pathologist, Westminster Hospital; Lecturer in General and Clinical Pathology, Westminster Hospital Medical School, University of London; *b* 28 Feb. 1899; *o s* of late Rev. Almund Trevosso Hocking and Gertrude Vernon Mary, *o d* of J. Parkinson; *m* 1st, 1927, Amy Gladys (*d* 1956), *y d* of A. T. Coucher; two *d*; 2nd, 1957, Kathleen, *e d* of Dr G. P. O'Donnell. *Educ:* High Sch., Leytonstone; City and Guilds of London Coll., Finsbury; Middlesex Hospital Medical Sch. RN Experimental and Anti-gas Station, 1917–18; Asst Laboratory Dir to the Clinical Research Assoc. MB, BS, BSc, MSc London, MRCS, LRCP, CChem, FRSC, FCS, FRMS; FRSA, MIBiol, FRSH. Associate of the City and Guilds of London Tech. Coll., Finsbury; Member: Pathological Soc. of Great Britain and Ireland; Association of Clinical Pathologists (Councillor, 1944–46); Society of Public Analysts; Medico-Legal Society; Brit. Assoc. in Forensic Medicine; former Mem. Court, Univ. of Exeter (representing Royal Institute of Chemistry); Pres. South-Western Branch, British Medical Association, 1946; Chm. South-Western Branch, RIC, 1955–57; Mem. Council, RIC, 1959–62, 1965–68. Mem. Brit. Acad. of Forensic Sciences; Mem. Soc. for Forensic Science. *Publications:* The Employment of Uranium in the Treatment of Malignant New Growths, British Empire Cancer Campaign International Conference, London, 1928; Disseminated Sclerosis (with Sir James Purves-Stewart), 1930; Seaside Accidents, 1958; Delayed Death due to Suicidal Hanging, 1961; Hanging and Manual Strangulation, 1966; Christmas Eve Crime in Falmouth (Murder in the West Country), 1975; The Porthole Murder: Gay Gibson (Facets of Crime), 1975; numerous scientific papers in medical journals, etc. *Recreations:* hotels, good food, wine, conversation. *Address:* Strathaven, Carlyon Bay, Cornwall. *Clubs:* National Liberal (Associate Mem.), English-Speaking Union.

HOCKING, Philip Norman; *b* 27 Oct. 1925; *s* of late Fred Hocking, FIOB; *m* 1950, Joan Mable, *d* of Horace Ernest Jackson, CBE, Birmingham; three *d*. *Educ:* King Henry VIII Sch., Coventry; Birmingham Sch. of Architecture. Dir, F. Hocking & Sons Ltd. Mem. Coventry City Council, 1955–60. Prominent Mem. Young Con. Movement. MP (C) Coventry South, 1959–64; PPS to Minister of State, FO, 1963–64. Contested Coventry S, 1964 and 1966. Chm., Conservative Back Benchers' Housing and Local Govt Cttee, 1962–64. *Recreations:* gardening and sailing.

HOCKLEY, Sir Anthony Heritage F.; *see* Farrar-Hockley.

HOCKLEY, Rev. Canon Raymond Alan; Canon Residentiary, Precentor, Succentor Canonicorum and Chamberlain of York Minster, since 1976; *b* 18 Sept. 1929; 2nd *s* of late Henry Hockley and Doris (*née* Stonehouse); unmarried. *Educ:* Firth Park School, Sheffield; Royal Academy of Music, London; Westcott House, Cambridge. MA, LRAM. Macfarren Schol., Royal Acad. of Music, 1951–54; Charles Lucas Medal, William Corder Prize, Cuthbert Nunn Prize, etc; Theodore Holland Award, 1955. Clements Memorial Prize for Chamber Music by a British subject, 1954. Curate of St Augustine's, Sheffield, 1958–61; Priest-in-charge of Holy Trinity, Wicker, with St Michael and All Angels, Neepsend, 1961–63; Chaplain of Westcott House, Cambridge, 1963–68; Fellow, Chaplain and Dir of Studies in Music, Emmanuel Coll., Cambridge, 1968–76. Works performed include: Songs for Tenor, Soprano; String Quartet; Divertimento for piano duet; Cantata for Easter and the Ascension; Symphony; My Enemies pictured within, a Bitter-Suite for Orchestra; various anthems and motets; incidental music for plays. Other works include: two more Symphonies, A Woman's Last Word for three sopranos; Oratorio on the Destruction and Salvation of the World; Six Suites for piano. *Publications:* Six Songs of Faith; New Songs for the Church; Divertimento; Intercessions at Holy Communion; contribs to theological and musical jls. *Recreations:* cooking, talking, unfinished work. *Address:* 2 Minster Court, York YO1 2JJ. *T:* York (0904) 624965. *Club:* Yorkshire (York).

HOCKMAN, Stephen Alexander; QC 1990; *b* 4 Jan. 1947; *s* of Nathaniel and Trude Hockman; *m* 1972, Hilary Moira Mandleberg; two *s*. *Educ:* Eltham Coll.; Jesus Coll., Cambridge (MA). Called to the Bar, Middle Temple, 1970. *Recreations:* philosophy, politics, the arts. *Address:* 6 Pump Court, Temple, EC4Y 7AR. *T:* 071–353 7242. *Club:* Royal Automobile.

HOCKNEY, David, RA 1991 (ARA 1985); artist; *b* Bradford, 9 July 1937; *s* of Kenneth and Laura Hockney. *Educ:* Bradford Grammar Sch.; Bradford Sch. of Art; Royal Coll. of Art. Lecturer: Maidstone Coll. of Art, 1962; Univ. of Iowa, 1964; Univ. of Colorado, 1965; Univ. of California, Los Angeles, 1966, Berkeley, 1967. One-man shows: Kasmin Ltd, London, 1963, 1965, 1966, 1968, 1969, 1970, 1972; Alan Gallery, New York, 1964–67; Museum of Modern Art, NY, 1964–68; Stedlijk Museum, Amsterdam, 1966; Whitworth Gallery, Manchester, 1969; Louvre, Paris, 1974; Galerie Claude Bernard, Paris, 1975 and 1985; Nicholas Wilder, LA, 1976; Galerie Neundorf, Hamburg, 1977; Warehouse Gall., 1979; Knoedler Gall., 1979, 1981, 1982, 1983, 1984, 1986 and 1988; André Emmerich Gall., 1979, 1980, annually 1982–; Tate, 1986, 1988; Hayward Gall., 1983 and 1985; L. A. Louver, LA, 1986 and 1989, etc; touring show of drawings and prints: Munich, Madrid, Lisbon, Teheran, 1977; USA and Canada, 1978; Tate, 1980. Retrospective Exhibitions: Whitechapel Art Gall., 1970; LA County Museum of Art, Metropolitan Mus. of Art, Tate Gall., 1988–89. Exhibn of photographs, Hayward Gall., 1983. 1st Prize, John Moores Exhibn, Liverpool, 1967. Designer: The Rake's Progress, Glyndebourne, 1975, La Scala, 1979; The Magic Flute, Glyndebourne, 1978; L'Enfant et les sortilèges and Nightingale, Double Bill, and Varii Capricci, Covent Garden, 1983; Tristan und Isolde, LA, 1987; designing costumes and sets for the Metropolitan Opera House, NY, 1980. Films: A Bigger Splash, 1975; A Day on the Grand Canal with the Emperor of China or surface is illusion but so is depth, 1987. Shakespeare Prize, Hamburg Foundn, 1983; First Prize, Internat. Center of Photography, NY, 1985; Silver Progress Medal, RPS, 1988. *Publications:* (ed and illustrated) 14 Poems of C. P. Cavafy, 1967; (illustrated) Six Fairy Tales of the Brothers Grimm, 1969; 72 Drawings by David Hockney, 1971; David Hockney by David Hockney, 1976; The Blue Guitar, 1977; David Hockney: Travels with Pen, Pencil and Ink: selected prints and drawings 1962–77, 1978; Paper Pools, 1980; (with Stephen Spender) China Diary, 1982; Hockney Paints the Stage, 1983; David Hockney: Cameraworks, 1984 (Kodak Photography Book Award); David Hockney: A Retrospective, 1988; Hockney on Photography (conversations with Paul Joyce), 1988. *Address:* c/o 7506 Santa Monica Boulevard, Los Angeles, Calif. 90046, USA; Tradhart Ltd, 19B Buckingham Avenue, Slough, Berks SL1 4QB.

HODDER, Prof. Bramwell William, PhD; Professor of Geography, School of Oriental and African Studies, University of London, 1970–83, now Emeritus; *b* 25 Nov. 1923; *s* of George Albert Hodder and Emily Griggs, Eastbourne; *m* 1971, Elizabeth (*née* Scruton); three *s* two *d* by previous marriages. *Educ:* Oldershaw, Wallasey; Oriel Coll., Oxford (MA, BLitt); PhD London. Served War, 1942–47, commissioned in Infantry (Cameronians), Lieut. Lecturer, Univ. of Malaya, Singapore, 1952–56; Lectr/Sen. Lectr, Univ. of Ibadan, Nigeria, 1956–63; Lectr, Univ of Glasgow, 1963–64; Lectr/Reader, Queen Mary Coll., Univ. of London, 1964–70. Chm., Commonwealth Geog. Bureau, 1968–72; Hon. Dir, 1981–82, Mem. Exec. Council, 1981–84, Internat. African Inst. Joint Hon. Pres., World Expeditionary Assoc., 1972–. *Publications:* Man in Malaya, 1959; Economic Development in the Tropics, 1968, 3rd edn 1980; (jtly) Markets in West Africa, 1969; (jtly) Africa in Transition, 1967; (jtly) Economic Geography, 1974; Africa Today, 1979; articles in various learned jls. *Recreations:* music, hill walking. *Address:* Maris House, Trumpington, Cambridge CB2 2LB. *T:* Cambridge (0223) 841306.

HODDER-WILLIAMS, Paul, OBE 1945; TD; publisher; Consultant, Hodder & Stoughton Ltd, since 1975; *b* 29 Jan. 1910; *s* of late Frank Garfield Hodder Williams, sometime Dean of Manchester, and late Sarah Myfanwy (*née* Nicholson); *m* 1936, Felicity (*d* 1986), 2nd *d* of late C. M. Blagden, DD, sometime Bishop of Peterborough; two *s* two *d*. *Educ:* Rugby; Gonville and Caius Coll., Cambridge (MA). Joined Hodder & Stoughton Ltd, 1931; Dir, 1936, Chm., 1961–75. Served with HAC (Major, 1942), 99th (London Welsh) HAA Regt RA (Lt-Col Comdg, 1942–45). *Recreation:* gardening. *Address:* Court House, Exford, Minehead, Somerset TA24 7LY. *T:* Exford (064383) 268.

HODDINOTT, Prof. Alun, CBE 1983; DMus; Hon. RAM; FRNCM; Professor of Music, University College, Cardiff, 1967–87, now Emeritus (Fellow, 1983); *b* 11 Aug. 1929; *s* of Thomas Ivor Hoddinott and Gertrude Jones; *m* 1953, Beti Rhiannon Huws; one *s*. *Educ:* University Coll. of S Wales and Mon. Lecturer: Cardiff Coll. of Music and Drama, 1951–59; University Coll. of S Wales and Mon, 1959–65; Reader, University of Wales, 1965–67. Member: BBC Music Central Adv. Cttee, 1971–78; Welsh Arts Council, 1968–74; Member Council: Welsh Nat. Opera, 1972–75; Composers' Guild of GB, 1972–; Nat. Youth Orchestra, 1972–. Chm., Welsh Music Archive, 1977–78, 1983–87. Artistic Dir, 1967–89, Pres., 1990–, Cardiff Music Festival. Governor, Welsh Nat. Theatre, 1968–74. Walford Davies Prize, 1954; Arnold Bax Medal, 1957; John Edwards Meml Award, 1967; Hopkins Medal, St David's Soc., NY, 1980. FRNCM 1981; Fellow, Welsh Coll. of Music and Drama, 1991. *Publications: opera:* The Beach of Falesá, 1974; The Magician, 1975; What the Old Man does is always right, 1975; The Rajah's Diamond, 1979; The Trumpet Major, 1981; *choral:* Rebecca, 1961; oratorio, Job, 1962; Medieval Songs, 1962; Danegeld, 1964; Four Welsh Songs, 1964; Cantata: Dives and Lazarus, 1965; An Apple Tree and a Pig, 1968; Ballad, Black Bart, 1968; Out of the Deep, 1972; The Tree of Life, 1971; Four Welsh Songs, 1971; The Silver Swimmer, 1973; Sinfonia Fidei, 1977; Dulcia Iuventutis, 1978; Voyagers, 1978; Hymnus ante Somnum, 1979; Te Deum, 1982; Charge of the Light Brigade, 1983; In Parasceve Domini, 1983; King of Glory, 1984; Bells of Paradise, 1984; Jubilate, 1985; Lady and Unicorn, 1985; In Gravescentem Aetatem, 1985; Ballad of Green Broom, 1985; Christ is Risen, 1986; Sing a New Song, 1986; Flower Songs, 1986; In Praise of Music, 1986; The Legend of St Julian, 1987; Lines from Marlowe's Dr Faustus, 1988; Emynau Pantycelyn, 1990; Advent Carols, 1990; *vocal:* Roman Dream, 1968; Ancestor Worship, 1972; Ynys Mon, 1975; A Contemplation upon Flowers, 1976; Six Welsh Songs, 1982; The Silver Hound, 1986; Songs of Exile (tenor and orch.), 1989; *orchestral:* Symphonies 1955, 1962, 1968, 1969, 1973, 1984; Nocturne, 1952; Welsh Dances I, 1958, II 1969; Folk Song Suite, 1962; Variations, 1963; Night Music, 1966; Sinfonietta I, 1968, II, 1969, III, 1970, IV, 1971; Fioriture, 1968; Investiture Dances, 1969; Divertimento, 1969; the sun, the great luminary of the universe, 1970; the hawk is set free, 1972; Welsh Airs and Dances for Symphonic Band, 1975; Landscapes, 1975; French Suite, 1977; Passaggio, 1977; Nightpiece, 1977; Lanterne des Morts, 1981; Five Studies, 1983; Four Scenes, 1983; Quodlibet, 1984; Hommage à Chopin, 1985; Welsh Dances–3rd Suite, 1985; Scena, 1986; Fanfare with Variants; Concerto for Orchestra; Star Children, 1989; Symphony for Organ and Orchestra, 1989; *concertos:* Clarinet I, 1951, II, 1987; Oboe, 1954; Harp, 1958; Viola, 1958; Piano I, 1950, II, 1960, III, 1966; Violin, 1961; Organ, 1967; Horn, 1969; Nocturnes and Cadenzas (cello), 1969; Ritornelli (trombone), 1974; The Heaventree of Stars, for violin and orchestra, 1980; Doubles (oboe); Scenes and Interludes (trumpet), 1985; Violin, Cello, Piano (Triple Concerto); Divisions (horn); Noctis Equi ('cello and orch.), 1989; *chamber:* Septet, 1956; Sextet, 1960; Variations for Septet, 1962; Wind Quartet, 1963; String Quartet, 1965; Nocturnes and Cadenzas for Clarinet, Violin and Cello, 1968; Divertimento for 8 instruments, 1968; Piano Trio, 1970; Piano Quintet, 1972; Scena for String Quartet, 1979; Ritornell for Brass Quintet, 1979; Ritornelli for four double basses, 1981; String Quartet no 2, 1984; Masks for oboe, bassoon, piano, 1985; Piano Trio no 2, 1985; Divertimenti for flute, bassoon, double-bass and percussion, 1985; Sonata for Four Clarinets; String Quartet no 3, 1988; *instrumental:* sonatas for: piano, 1959, 1962, 1965, 1966, 1968, 1972, 1984, 1986, 1989 (two); harp, 1964; clarinet and piano, 1967; violin and piano, 1969, 1970, 1971, 1976; cello and piano, 1970, 1977; horn and piano, 1971; organ, 1979; two pianos, 1986; sonatinas for: clavichord, 1963; 2 pianos, 1978; guitar, 1978; Suite for Harp, 1967; Fantasy for Harp, 1970; Italian Suite for Recorder and Guitar, 1977; Nocturnes and Cadenzas for Solo Cello, 1983; Bagatelles for Oboe and Harp, 1983; Passacaglia and Fugue for Organ, 1986; Little Suite (trumpet and piano), 1988. *Address:* Maesawelon, Mill Road, Lisvane, Cardiff CF4 5UG.

HODDINOTT, Rear-Adm. Anthony Paul, OBE 1979; Naval Attaché and Commander British Naval Staff, Washington, since 1990; National Military Representative to Saclant, since 1990; *b* 28 Jan. 1942; *s* of Comdr Peter Hoddinott, RN and Marjorie Hoddinott (*née* Kent); *m* 1965, Ellen Ruby Burton (Rue); one *s* two *d. Educ:* St Michael's, Otford; Bloxham; BRNC Dartmouth. Served HM Ships Chawton, Trump, Dreadnought, Repulse, Porpoise; in Comd, HMS Andrew, 1973–75; Staff of Comdr Third Fleet, USN, 1975–76; in Comd, HMS Revenge, 1976–79; Comdr, Submarine Tactics and Weapons Gp, 1979–81; in Comd, HMS Glasgow, 1981–83 (South Atlantic, 1982); Asst Dir, Naval Warfare, 1983–85; NATO Defence Coll., Rome, 1985; Dep. UK Mil. Rep. to NATO, Brussels, 1986–88; COS (Submarines), 1988–90. *Recreations:* theatre, golf, swimming, kitchen bridge. *Address:* HMS Saker, BFPO 2; c/o Lloyds Bank, 2 Spithead, Dartmouth, Devon TQ6 9PU.

HODGART, Prof. Matthew John Caldwell; Professor of English, Concordia University, Montreal, 1970–76; *b* 1 Sept. 1916; *s* of late Matthew Hodgart (Major RE), MC, and Katherine Barbour Caldwell (*née* Gardner); *m* 1st, 1940, Betty Joyce Henstridge (*d* 1948); one *s* one *d*; 2nd, 1949, Margaret Patricia Elliott; one adopted *d. Educ:* Rugby Sch. (Scholar); Pembroke Coll., Cambridge (Scholar; BA 1938, MA 1945). Jebb Studentship, Cambridge, 1938–39. Served War, 1939–45: Argyll and Sutherland Highlanders and in Intelligence (mentioned in despatches). Cambridge University: Asst Lectr in English, 1945–49; Lectr in English, and Fellow of Pembroke Coll., 1949–64; Prof. of English, Sussex Univ., 1964–70. Vis. Professor: Cornell Univ., 1961–62 and 1969; Univ. of Calif, Los Angeles, 1977–78; Stanford Univ., 1979; La Trobe Univ., Australia, 1979–80; Hinckley Prof., Johns Hopkins Univ., 1982. Chevalier de la Légion d'honneur, and Croix de guerre, 1945. *Publications:* The Ballads, 1950; (with Prof. M. Worthington) Song in the Work of James Joyce, 1959; Samuel Johnson, 1962; (ed) Horace Walpole, Memoirs, 1963; (ed) Faber Book of Ballads, 1965; Satire, 1969 (trans. various languages); A New Voyage (fiction), 1969; James Joyce, Student Guide, 1978; contrib. Rev. of English Studies, and TLS. *Recreations:* travel, music, computers. *Address:* 13 Montpelier Villas, Brighton BN1 3DG. *T:* Brighton (0273) 26993.

HODGE, Alexander Mitchell, GC 1940; VRD; DL; Captain RNVR, retired; WS; Member of firm of Cowan & Stewart, WS, Edinburgh, 1946–84; Director, Standard Life Assurance Co., 1965–87 (Chairman, 1977–82); *b* 23 June 1916; *y s* of James Mackenzie Hodge, Blairgowrie, Perthshire; *m* 1944, Pauline Hester Winsome, *o d* of William John Hill, Bristol; one *s* two *d. Educ:* Fettes Coll.; Edinburgh Univ. (MA 1936, LLB 1938). Joined RNVR, 1938; served with Royal Navy, 1939–45 (despatches, GC). Comdr RNVR, 1949, Capt. RNVR, 1953; CO of the Forth Div. RNVR, 1953–57. Chm., Edinburgh Dist Sea Cadet Cttee, 1959–63; Chm., Lady Haig's Poppy Factory, 1961–67; Mem. Council, Earl Haig Fund (Scotland), 1963–67; Chm., Livingston New Town Licensing Planning Cttee, 1963–69; Dir, Edinburgh Western Gen. Hosp. Assoc. of Friends, 1962– (Chm., 1962–68); Trustee and Mem. Cttee of Management: Royal Victoria Hosp. Tuberculosis Trust, 1964–87 (Pres., 1970–87); Royal Edinburgh Inst. for Sailors, Soldiers and Airmen, 1964–71; Chm. General Comrs of Income Tax, Edinburgh South Div., 1967–85; Pres., Edinburgh Chamber of Commerce, 1968–70; Chm., The Cruden Foundn, 1983– (Dir, 1969–72, 1973–). Governor, Fettes Coll., 1970–75; Mem. Court, Heriot-Watt Univ., 1982–88. DL Edinburgh, 1972. *Address:* Springbank, Barnton, Edinburgh EH4 6DJ. *T:* 031–339 3054. *Clubs:* Royal Automobile; New (Edinburgh).

HODGE, David, CBE 1980; JP; DL; Lord Provost of Glasgow, and Lord Lieutenant of County of City of Glasgow, 1977–80; *b* 30 Sept. 1909; *s* of David Hodge and Sarah (*née* Crilly); *m* 1950, Mary Forbes Hodge (*née* Taylor); four *d. Educ:* St Mungo's Acad., Glasgow. Served War, RAF, 1940–46: air crew, Coastal Comd. On staff of Scottish Gas Bd, 1934–50; Prudential Assurance Co. Ltd, 1950–74, retd. Chm., Ruchill Ward and Maryhill Constituency for 20 yrs. Elected to Glasgow Corp., 1971; Magistrate, Corp. of Glasgow, 1972–74; Vice-Chm., Transport Cttee. Mem., City of Glasgow Dist Council, 1974: Chm., Licensing Court, Licensing Cttee, and Justices Cttee; Sec. of Admin; Council Rep., Convention of Scottish Local Authorities, 1974–77. JP, 1975, DL 1980, Glasgow. Hon. LLD Strathclyde, 1980. OStJ 1978. *Recreations:* interested in all sports (former professional footballer; winner of tennis championships; former swimming and badminton coach); theatre, ballet, music. *Address:* 59 Hillend Road, Glasgow G22 6NY. *T:* 041–336 8727. *Clubs:* Royal Automobile, Royal Air Forces Association; Art, Pres, Marist Centenary (Glasgow).

HODGE, James William; HM Diplomatic Service; Counsellor, Foreign and Commonwealth Office, since 1990; *b* 24 Dec. 1943; *s* of William Hodge and late Catherine Hodge (*née* Carden); *m* 1970, Frances Margaret, *d* of Michael Coyne and Teresa Coyne (*née* Walsh); three *d. Educ:* Holy Cross Academy, Edinburgh; Univ. of Edinburgh (MA(Hons) English Lang. and Lit.). Commonwealth Office, 1966; Third Secretary, Tokyo, 1967; Second Secretary (Information), Tokyo, 1970; FCO, 1972; First Sec. (Development, later Chancery), Lagos, 1975; FCO, 1978; First Sec. (Economic), 1981, Counsellor (Commercial), 1982, Tokyo; Counsellor, Copenhagen, 1986. *Recreations:* books, music, Scandinavian studies, tennis. *Address:* c/o Foreign and Commonwealth Office, SW1A 2AH. *Clubs:* MCC, Travellers'.

HODGE, John Dennis; President, J. D. Hodge & Co., International Management and Aerospace Consultants, since 1987; *b* 10 Feb. 1929; *s* of John Charles Henry Hodge and Emily M. Corbett Hodge; *m* 1952, Audrey Cox; two *s* two *d. Educ:* Northampton Engineering Coll., University of London (now The City Univ.). Vickers-Armstrong Ltd, Weybridge, England (Aerodynamics Dept), 1950–52; Head, Air Loads Section, Avro Aircraft Ltd, Toronto, Canada, 1952–59; Tech. Asst to Chief, Ops Div., Space Task Group, NASA, Langley Field, Va, USA, 1959; Chief, Flight Control Br., Space Task Group, NASA, 1961; Asst Chief of Flight Control, 1962, Chief, Flight Control Div., Flight Ops Directorate, NASA, MSC, 1963–68; Manager, Advanced Missions Program, NASA, Manned Spacecraft Centre, 1968–70; Dir, Transport Systems Concepts, Transport Systems Center, 1970; Vice-Pres., R&D, The Ontario Transportation Develt Corp., 1974–76; Department of Transportation, Washington, 1976–82; Chief, R&D Plans and Programs Analysis Div., 1976–77; Actg Dir, Office of Policy, Plans and Admin, 1977–79; Associate Administrator, for Policy, Plans and Program Management, Res. and Special programs Admin, 1979–82; Dir, Space Station Task Force, NASA, Washington, 1982–84; Dep. Associate Administrator for Space Station, NASA, Washington, 1984–85, Actg Associate Administrator, 1985–86. Hon. ScD, The City Univ., London, Eng., 1966; NASA Medal for Exceptional Service, 1967 and 1969; Dept of Transportation Meritorious Achievement Award, 1974; Special Achievement Award, 1979; Presidential Rank Award of Meritorious Executive, NASA, 1985. *Publications:* contribs to NASA publications and various aerospace jls. *Recreation:* reading. *Address:* 1105 Challendon Road, Great Falls, Va 22066, USA.

HODGE, Sir John Rowland, 2nd Bt *cr* 1921; MBE 1940; FRHS; company director; *b* 1 May 1913; *s* of Sir Rowland Hodge, 1st Bt, and Mabel (*d* 1923), *d* of William Edward Thorpe; *S* father, 1950; *m* 1936, Peggy Ann (marr. diss. 1939), *o d* of Sydney Raymond Kent; *m* 1939, Joan (marr. diss. 1961), *o d* of late Sydney Foster Wilson; three *d*; *m* 1967, Vivien Jill, *d* of A. S. Knightley; one *s* one *d. Educ:* Wrekin Coll.; Switzerland. Served War of 1939–45, RNVR; Lt-Comdr, RNVR, 1938; formerly Oxford and Bucks Light Infantry. Mem. Inst. of Directors. Dist Grand Master, Dist Grand Lodge of Freemasons, Malta, 1976–86. Freeman, City of Newcastle upon Tyne. *Heir: s* Andrew Rowland Hodge, *b* 3 Dec. 1968. *Address:* 16 Sutherland Drive, Gunton Park, Lowestoft NR32 4LP. *T:* Lowestoft (0502) 68943. *Clubs:* British Racing Drivers, Naval; Valletta Yacht, Royal Yachting Association, Cruising Association.

HODGE, Sir Julian Stephen Alfred, Kt 1970; Merchant banker; Chairman: Avana Group Ltd, 1973–81; Carlyle Trust (Jersey) Ltd, since 1977; St Aubins Investment Co. Ltd, since 1986; Founder and Chairman, Bank of Wales, 1971–85; Chairman, Bank of Wales (Jersey) Ltd, 1974–87; Director, Bank of Wales (IoM) Ltd, 1974–85; *b* 15 Oct. 1904; *s* of late Alfred and Jane Hodge; *m* 1951, Moira (*née* Thomas); two *s* one *d. Educ:* Cardiff Technical Coll. Certified Accountant, 1930. Fellow, Inst. of Taxation, 1941–. Founded Hodge & Co., Accountants and Auditors; Man. Dir, 1963–75, Exec. Chm., 1975–78, Hodge Group Ltd; former Chairman: Julian S. Hodge & Co. Ltd; Gwent Enterprises Ltd; Hodge Finance Ltd; Hodge Life Assurance Co. Ltd; Carlyle Trust Ltd, 1962–85; Dir, Standard Chartered Bank, 1973–75. Founder and Chairman: The Jane Hodge Foundation, 1962; Sir Julian Hodge Charitable Trust, 1964; Chairman: Aberfan Disaster Fund Industrial Project Sub-Cttee; Member: Welsh Economic Council, 1965–68; Welsh Council, 1968–79; Council, Univ. of Wales Inst. of Science and Technology (Treasurer, 1968–76; Pres., 1981–85); Foundation Fund Cttee, Univ. of Surrey; Duke of Edinburgh Conf., 1974; Prince of Wales Cttee. Pres., S Glamorgan Dist, St John Ambulance Bde; Trustee, Welsh Sports Trust. Former Governor, All Hallows (Cranmore Hall) Sch. Trust Ltd. FTII 1941. FRSA. Hon. LLD Univ. of Wales, 1971. KStJ 1977 (CStJ 1972); KSG 1978. *Publication:* Paradox of Financial Preservation, 1959. *Recreations:* golf, walking, reading, gardening. *Address:* Clos des Seux, Mont du Coin, St Aubin, St Brelade, Jersey, CI. *Clubs:* Victoria (St Helier, Jersey); La Moye Golf (Jersey).

HODGE, Patricia; actress; *b* 29 Sept. 1946; *d* of Eric and Marion Hodge; *m* 1976, Peter Owen; one *s. Educ:* Wintringham Girls' Grammar Sch., Grimsby; St Helen's Sch., Northwood, Mddx; Maria Grey Coll., Twickenham; London Acad. of Music and Dramatic Art. Theatre début, No-one Was Saved, Traverse, Edinburgh, 1971; *West End* theatre includes: Popkiss, Globe, 1972; Two Gentlemen of Verona (musical), 1973; Pippin, Her Majesty's, 1973; Hair, Queen's, 1974; The Mitford Girls, Globe, 1981 (transf. from Chichester); Benefactors, Vaudeville, 1984; Noël and Gertie, Comedy, 1989–90; *other appearances* include: The Beggar's Opera, Nottingham Playhouse, 1975; Pal Joey, and Look Back In Anger, Oxford Playhouse, 1976; Then and Now, Hampstead, 1979; As You Like It, Chichester Fest., 1983; Lady in the Dark, Edinburgh Fest., 1988; *television plays and films* include: The Girls of Slender Means, 1975; The Naked Civil Servant, 1975; Hay Fever, 1984; The Death of the Heart, 1985; Hotel du Lac, 1986; Heat of the Day, 1988; The Shell Seekers, 1989; The Secret Life of Ian Fleming, 1989; *television series and serials* include: Rumpole of the Bailey, 7 series, 1978–90; Edward and Mrs Simpson, 1978; Holding the Fort, 3 series, 1979–82; The Other 'Arf, 1979–80, 1981; Nanny, 1980; Jemima Shore Investigates, 1982; The Life and Loves of a She-Devil, 1986; Rich Tea and Sympathy, 1991; *films* include: Betrayal, 1983. *Address:* c/o Michael Anderson, ICM Ltd, 388–396 Oxford Street, W1N 9HE. *T:* 071–629 8080.

HODGES, C(yril) Walter; free-lance writer, book illustrator, theatrical historian and designer; *b* 18 March 1909; *s* of Cyril James and Margaret Mary Hodges; *m* 1936, Greta (*née* Becker); two *s. Educ:* Dulwich Coll.; Goldsmiths' Coll. Sch. of Art. Commenced as stage designer, 1929, then illustrator for advertising, magazines (esp. Radio Times) and children's books; began writing, 1937; served with Army, 1940–46 (despatches); has designed stage productions (Mermaid Theatre, 1951, 1964), permanent Elizabethan stage, St George's Theatre, 1976; exhibns (Lloyds, UK Provident Instn; retrospective of theatre designs, Folger Shakespeare Library, Washington, 1988); mural decorations painted for Chartered Insce Inst., UK Provident Instn; Art Dir, Encyclopædia Britannica Films, 1959–61; reconstruction drawings for model of excavated Elizabethan Rose Theatre, Museum of London, 1989–91. Judith E. Wilson Lectr in Poetry and Drama, Cambridge, 1974; Co-ordinator, Symposium for the Reconstruction of Globe Playhouse, 1979, Adjunct Prof. of Theatre, 1980–83, Wayne State University, USA; Vis. Scholar, Univ. of Maryland, 1983. Hon. DLitt Sussex, 1979. Kate Greenaway Medal for illustration, 1965; Hons List, Hans Christian Andersen Internat. Award, 1966. *Publications:* Columbus Sails, 1939; The Flying House, 1947; Shakespeare and the Players, 1948; The Globe Restored, 1953 (rev. edn 1968); The Namesake, 1964; Shakespeare's Theatre, 1964; The Norman Conquest, 1966; Magna Carta, 1966; The Marsh King, 1967; The Spanish Armada, 1967; The Overland Launch, 1969; The English Civil War, 1972; Shakespeare's Second Globe, 1973; Playhouse Tales, 1974; The Emperor's Elephant, 1975; Plain Lane Christmas, 1978; The Battlement Garden, 1979; (ed) The Third Globe, 1981; contributor: Shakespeare Survey; Theatre Notebook; (illus.) The New Cambridge Shakespeare, 1984–. *Recreations:* music (listening), letters (writing), museums (visiting). *Address:* 36 Southover High Street, Lewes, East Sussex BN7 1HX. *T:* Lewes (0273) 6530.

HODGES, Elaine Mary, OBE 1975; HM Diplomatic Service; Counsellor, Foreign and Commonwealth Office, 1981–83; retired; *b* 12 Nov. 1928; *d* of late Lancelot James Hodges and of Edith Mary (*née* Crossland). *Educ:* Nottingham High School for Girls; St Anne's Coll., Oxford (BA Hons, MA). Joined Foreign Office, 1952; served in: Germany, 1952–53; Switzerland, 1955–56; Warsaw, 1959; New Delhi, 1963–64; Paris, 1967–69; Brussels, 1974–79. *Recreations:* gardening, antiques, travel. *Address:* 46 Westbridge Road, SW11 3PW. *T:* 071–228 3771.

HODGES, Gerald; Director of Finance, City of Bradford Metropolitan Council, 1974–85; *b* 14 June 1925; *s* of Alfred John Hodges and Gertrude Alice Hodges; *m* 1950, Betty Maire (*née* Brading); one *s* (and one *s* decd). *Educ:* King's Sch., Peterborough. IPFA.

Accountancy Asst, Bexley Borough Council, 1941–48, and Eton RDC, 1948–49; Sen. Accountancy Asst, Newcastle upon Tyne, 1949–53; Chief Accountant, Hemel Hempstead, 1953–56; Dep. Treas., Crawley UDC, 1956–70; Treas., Ilkley UDC, 1970–74. Pres., Soc. of Metropolitan Treasurers, 1984–85. Hon. Treasurer: Yorkshire Arts, 1973–86; Univ. of Bradford, 1986–; Chm., Bradford Flower Fund Homes; Trustee, Bradford Disaster Appeal, 1985. *Publications:* occasional articles in professional jls. *Recreations:* travelling, ornithology, reading. *Address:* 23 Victoria Avenue, Ilkley, West Yorks LS29 9BW. *T:* Ilkley (0943) 607346.

HODGES, Joseph Thomas Charles, FCA, FCIS; Director: Mark Loveday Underwriting Agencies Ltd, since 1984; Cater Allen Members' Agency Ltd, since 1987; *b* 25 July 1932; *s* of Joseph Henry Hodges and Hilda Ellen Susan (*née* Hermitage); *m* 1962, Joan Swan; two *s* one *d*. *Educ:* East Ham Grammar Sch. ACIS 1955, FCIS 1980; ACA 1960, FCA 1971. National Service, RAF, 1950–52. Accounts Dept, Corp. of Lloyd's, 1949–50 and 1953–55; articled to Gerard van de Linde & Son, Chartered Accountants, 1955–60; Corporation of Lloyd's: Audit Dept, 1960–66, Manager of Audit Dept, 1966–74; Head of Advisory and Legislation, 1974–80; Dep. Sec. Gen., 1980; Sec. Gen., 1980–84. *Recreations:* watching West Ham United, caravanning. *Address:* 246 Halfway Street, Sidcup, Kent DA15 8DW. *T:* 081–850 3927.

HODGES, Lew; Finance Director, Arts Council of Great Britain, since 1989; *b* 29 Feb. 1956. *Educ:* University Coll. London (BA (Hons) Classics); MBA London Business Sch., 1990. Chartered Accountant 1981. Subsidy Officer, then Asst Dir of Finance, Arts Council, 1981–87; Head of Finance, CNAA, 1987–89. *Address:* Arts Council of Great Britain, 14 Great Peter Street, SW1P 3NQ.

HODGES, Air Chief Marshal Sir Lewis (Macdonald), KCB 1968 (CB 1963); CBE 1958; DSO 1944 and Bar 1945; DFC 1942 and Bar 1943; *b* 1 March 1918; *s* of late Arthur Macdonald Hodges and Gladys Mildred Hodges; *m* 1950, Elisabeth Mary, *e d* of late G. H. Blackett, MC; two *s*. *Educ:* St Paul's Sch.; RAF Coll., Cranwell. Bomber Command, 1938–44; SE Asia (India, Burma, Ceylon), 1944–45; Palestine, 1945–47; Air Ministry and Min. of Defence, 1948–52; Bomber Command, 1952–59; Asst Comdt, RAF Coll., Cranwell, 1959–61; AO i/c Admin., Middle East Comd, Aden, 1961–63; Imperial Def. Coll., 1963; SHAPE, 1964–65; Ministry of Defence, Asst Chief of Air Staff (Ops), 1965–68; AOC-in-C, RAF Air Support Comd, 1968–70; Air Mem. for Personnel, MoD, 1970–73; Dep. C-in-C, Allied Forces Central Europe, 1973–76, retired. Air ADC to the Queen, 1973–76. Dir, Pilkington Bros Ltd (Optical Div.), 1979–83; Governor, BUPA Med. Foundn Ltd, 1987–; Chm. of Governors, Duke of Kent School, 1979–86; Chm., RAF Benevolent Fund Educn Cttee, 1979–86; Pres., RAF Escaping Soc., 1979–; Pres., Royal Air Forces Assoc., 1981–84. Grand Officier, Légion d'Honneur (France), 1988 (Commandeur, 1950); Croix de Guerre (France), 1944. *Recreations:* gardening, shooting, bee-keeping. *Address:* c/o Lloyds Bank, High Street, Tonbridge, Kent. *Clubs:* Royal Air Force, Special Forces.

HODGES, Mark Willie; Head of the Office of Arts and Libraries, 1982–84; *b* 23 Oct. 1923; *s* of William H. and Eva Hodges; *m* 1948, Glenna Marion (*née* Peacock); one *s* one *d*. *Educ:* Cowbridge Grammar Sch.; Jesus Coll., Oxford (MA 1948). Served War, RN, 1942–45. Lectr, Univ. of Sheffield, 1950–54; DSIR, 1954–56; Asst Scientific Attaché, Washington, 1956–61; Office of Minister for Science, 1961–64; Sec., Royal Commn on Med. Educn, 1965–68; Asst Sec., DES, 1968–79 (Arts and Libraries Br., 1977–79); Office of Arts and Libraries, 1979–84, Under Sec., 1982, Dep. Sec., 1983. Member: South Bank Theatre Bd, 1982– (Chm., 1984–); Council, Royal Albert Hall, 1983–; Council and Management Cttee, Eastern Arts Assoc., 1986–89. *Recreations:* woodwork, computer programming, listening to music. *Address:* The Corner Cottage, Church Way, Little Stukeley, Cambs PE17 5BQ. *T:* Huntingdon (0480) 459266. *Clubs:* Athenæum, United Oxford & Cambridge University.

HODGES, Dr Richard Andrew, FSA 1984; Senior Lecturer in Archaeology and Prehistory, Sheffield University, since 1986; Director, British School at Rome (on secondment), since 1988; *b* 29 Sept. 1952; *s* of Roy Clarence Hodges and Joan (*née* Hartnell); *m* 1976, Deborah Peters; one *s* one *d*. *Educ:* City of Bath Boys' Sch.; Univ. of Southampton (BA, PhD). Lectr in Prehistory and Archaeology, Sheffield Univ., 1976–86. Leverhulme Res. Fellow, British Sch. at Rome, 1980; Visiting Professor: in Medieval Studies, SUNY-Birmingham, 1983; in Medieval Archaeology, Siena Univ., 1984–87; in Archaeology, Copenhagen Univ., 1987–88. Director: Roystone Grange landscape project, Derbyshire, 1978–88; San Vincenzo excavations, S Italy, 1980–86; co-dir, Sheffield-Siena archaeological project, Montarrenti, Tuscany, 1982–87. *Publications:* Walks in the Cotswolds, 1976; The Hamwih Pottery, 1981; (with G. Barker) Archaeology and Italian Society, 1981; Dark Age Economics, 1982, 2nd edn 1989; (with P. Davey) Ceramics and trade, 1983; (with D. Whitehouse) Mohammed, Charlemagne and the origins of Europe, 1983; (with John Mitchell) San Vincenzo al Volturno, 1985; Primitive and Peasant Markets, 1988; (with B. Hobley) Rebirth of the town in the West, 1988; The Anglo-Saxon Achievement, 1989; Wall to Wall History, 1991. *Recreations:* hill walking, music, watching cricket. *Address:* British School at Rome, Via Antonio Gramsci 61, 00197 Roma, Italy. *T:* (06) 8870294, 3214388; Heath Bank, Main Street, Great Longstone, Derbyshire DE4 1TA.

HODGETTS, Robert Bartley; Clerk to Worshipful Company of Glaziers, 1979–85; *b* 10 Nov. 1918; *s* of late Captain Bartley Hodgetts, MN and Florence Hodgetts (*née* Stagg); *m* 1st, 1945, A. K. Jeffreys; one *d*; 2nd, 1949, Frances Grace, *d* of late A. J. Pepper, Worcester; two *d*. *Educ:* Merchant Taylors' Sch., Crosby; St John's Coll., Cambridge (Scholar, MA). Served RNVR (A), 1940–45. Asst Principal, Min. of Nat. Insce, 1947; Principal 1951; Asst Sec. 1964; Under-Sec., DHSS, 1973–78. *Recreations:* watching cricket and Rugby football. *Address:* 9 Purley Bury Close, Purley, Surrey. *T:* 081–668 2827.

HODGINS, Ven. Michael Minden; Archdeacon of Hackney, 1951–71; Secretary of London Diocesan Fund, 1946–74; *b* 26 Aug. 1912; *yr s* of late Major R. Hodgins, Indian Army, and Margaret Hodgins (*née* Wilson); unmarried. *Educ:* Wellington; Cuddesdon Theological Coll. Deacon, 1939; Priest, 1940; Curate, S Barnabas, Northolt Park, 1939; Asst Secretary, London Diocesan Fund, 1943. MA Lambeth 1960. *Address:* 5 Up, The Quadrangle, Morden College, Blackheath, SE3 0PW. *T:* 081–858 4762.

HODGKIN, Sir Alan (Lloyd), OM 1973; KBE 1972; FRS 1948; MA, ScD Cantab; Master of Trinity College, Cambridge, 1978–84 (Fellow, 1936–78 and since 1984); Chancellor, University of Leicester, 1971–84; *b* 5 Feb. 1914; *s* of G. L. Hodgkin and M. F. Wilson; *m* 1944, Marion de Kay, *d* of late F. P. Rous; one *s* three *d*. *Educ:* Gresham's Sch., Holt; Trinity Coll., Cambridge. Scientific Officer working on Radar for Air Ministry and Min. of Aircraft Production, 1939–45. Lecturer and then Asst Dir of Research at Cambridge, 1945–52; Foulerton Research Prof., Royal Soc., 1952–69; John Humphrey Plummer Prof. of Biophysics, Univ. of Cambridge, 1970–81. Baly Medal, RCP, 1955; Royal Medal of Royal Society, 1958; Nobel Prize for Medicine (jointly), 1963; Copley Medal of Royal Society, 1965. Pres., Royal Society, 1970–75; Pres., Marine Biological Assoc., 1966–76. Foreign Member: Royal Danish Acad. of Sciences, 1964; Amer. Acad. of Arts and Sciences, 1962; Amer. Philosophical Soc.; Royal Swedish Acad. of Sciences; Member: Physiological Soc.; Leopoldina Acad., 1964; Hon. Mem., Royal Irish Acad., 1974; Hon. For. Mem., USSR Acad. of Scis, 1976. Fellow, Imperial Coll. London, 1972; Hon. FRSE, 1974; Hon. Fellow: Indian National Science Acad., 1972; Girton Coll., Cambridge, 1979; Pharmaceutical Soc.; For. Assoc., Nat. Acad. of Scis, USA, 1974. Hon. MD: Berne 1956, Louvain 1958; Hon. DSc: Sheffield 1963, Newcastle upon Tyne 1965, E Anglia 1966, Manchester 1971, Leicester 1971, London 1971, Newfoundland 1973, Wales 1973, Rockefeller Univ., 1974, Bristol 1976; Oxford, 1977; Hon. LLD: Aberdeen 1973; Salamanca, 1984; Pisa, 1987. Lord Crook Medal, 1983; Helmerich Prize, Retina Res. Foundn, USA, 1988. *Publications:* scientific papers dealing with the nature of nervous conduction, muscle and vision, Jl Physiology, etc. *Recreations:* travel, ornithology and fishing. *Address:* Physiological Laboratory, Downing Street, Cambridge CB2 3EG; 18 Panton Street, Cambridge CB2 1HP. *T:* Cambridge (0223) 352707.

See also J. A. Hodgkin.

HODGKIN, Prof. Dorothy Mary Crowfoot, OM 1965; FRS 1947; Emeritus Professor, University of Oxford; Hon. Fellow: Somerville College, Oxford; Linacre College, Oxford; Girton College, Cambridge; Newnham College, Cambridge; Fellow, Wolfson College, Oxford, 1977–82; Chancellor, Bristol University, 1970–88; *b* 1910; *d* of late J. W. Crowfoot, CBE; *m* 1937, Thomas Lionel Hodgkin (*d* 1982); two *s* one *d*. *Educ:* Sir John Leman Sch., Beccles; Somerville Coll., Oxford. Fellow, Somerville Coll., 1936–77, Royal Soc. Wolfson Research Prof., 1960–77, Oxford Univ. Pres., BAAS, 1977–78. Fellow: Australian Academy of Science, 1968; Akad. Leopoldina, 1968; Hon. Mem., Royal Instn, 1988; Foreign Member: Royal Netherlands Academy of Science and Letters, 1956; Amer. Acad. of Arts and Sciences, Boston, 1958, and other learned bodies. Hon. Foreign Member: US Nat. Acad. of Scis, 1971; USSR Acad. of Scis, 1976; Bavarian Acad., 1980. Hon. DSc Leeds, Manchester and others; Hon. ScD Cambridge; LLD Bristol; DUniv Zagreb and York; Hon. Dr Medicine and Surgery Modena; Hon. DL Dalhousie; Hon. DSc Oxford. First Freedom of Beccles, 1965. Royal Medallist of the Royal Society, 1956; Nobel Prize for Chemistry, 1964; Copley Medal, Royal Soc., 1976; Mikhail Lomonosov Gold Medal, Soviet Acad. of Science, 1982; Mem., Ehrenzeichens für Kunst and Wissenschaft, Austria, 1983; Dimitrov Prize, 1984. *Publications:* various, on the X-ray crystallographic analysis of structure of molecules, including penicillin, vitamin B_{12} and insulin. *Recreations:* archæology, children. *Address:* Crab Mill, Ilmington, Shipston-on-Stour, Warwicks. *T:* Ilmington (060882) 233.

HODGKIN, Howard, CBE 1977; painter; *b* 6 Aug. 1932; *m* 1955, Julia Lane; two *s*. *Educ:* Camberwell Sch. of Art; Bath Academy of Art. Taught at Charterhouse Sch., 1954–56; taught at Bath Academy of Art, 1956–66; occasional tutor, Slade Sch. of Art and Chelsea Sch. of Art. Vis. Fellow in Creative Art, Brasenose Coll. Oxford, 1976–77. A Trustee: Tate Gall., 1970–76; National Gall., 1978–85. Mem., Exec. Cttee, Nat. Art Collections Fund, 1988. One-man exhibitions include: Arthur Tooth & Sons, London, 1961, 1962, 1964, 1967; Kasmin Gallery, 1969, 1971, 1976; Arnolfini Gall., Bristol, 1970, 1975; Dartington Hall, 1970; Galerie Müller, Cologne, 1971; Kornblee Gall., NY, 1973; Museum of Modern Art, Oxford, 1976, 1977; Serpentine Gall., London and provincial tour, Waddington Gall., 1976; André Emmerich Gall., Zürich and NY, 1977; Third Sydney Biennale, Art Gall. of NSW, 1979; Waddington Galls, 1972, 1980, 1988; Knoedler Gall. NY, 1981, 1982, 1984, 1988, 1990; Bernard Jacobson NY, 1980, 1981, LA, 1981, London, 1982; Tate Gall., 1982, 1985; Bath Fest., 1984; Phillips Collection, Washington DC, 1984; XLI Venice Biennale, 1984; Yale Centre for British Art, New Haven, 1985; Kestner-Gesellschaft, Hanover, 1985; Whitechapel Art Gall., 1985; Michael Werner Gall., Cologne, 1990; Nantes, Barcelona, Edinburgh and Dublin tour, 1990–91. Group Exhibitions include: The Human Clay, Hayward Gall., 1976; British Painting 1952–1977, RA, 1977; A New Spirit in Painting, RA, 1981; Hard Won Image, Tate Gall., 1984; An International Survey of Recent Paintings and Sculpture, Mus. of Mod. Art, 1984; NY, Carnegie International, Mus. of Art, Carnegie Inst., 1985–86; and in exhibns in: Australia, Austria, Belgium, Canada, Denmark, France, Germany, GB, Holland, India, Italy, Japan, Malta, Norway, Sweden, Switzerland, USA. Designs for: Pulcinella, Ballet Rambert, 1987; Piano, Royal Ballet, 1989. Works in public collections: Arts Council of GB; British Council, London; Contemp. Arts Soc.; Kettering Art Gall.; Peter Stuyvesant Foundn; São Paulo Museum; Oldham Art Gall.; Tate; V&A Museum; Swindon Central Lib.; Bristol City Art Gall.; Walker Art Center, Minneapolis; Nat. Gall. of S Aust., Adelaide; Fogg Art Museum, Cambridge, Mass; BM; Louisiana Museum, Denmark; Museum of Modern Art, Edinburgh; Southampton Art Gall.; Museum of Modern Art, NY; Mus. of Art, Carnegie Inst.; Whitworth Art Gall., Manchester; City of Manchester Art Galls; Govt Picture Coll., London. Hon. Fellow, Brasenose Coll., Oxford, 1988. Hon. DLitt London, 1985. 2nd Prize, John Moore's Exhibn, 1976 and 1980; Turner Prize, 1985. *Address:* 32 Coptic Street, WC1A 1NP. *T:* 071–580 7970.

HODGKIN, Jonathan Alan, PhD; FRS 1990; Staff Scientist, Medical Research Council Laboratory of Molecular Biology, since 1977; *b* 24 Aug. 1949; *s* of Sir Alan Hodgkin, *qv*. *Educ:* Bryanston Sch., Dorset; Merton Coll., Oxford (BA); Darwin Coll., Cambridge (PhD). SRC Res. Fellowship, 1974–76. Vis. Prof., Univ. of Wisconsin, 1990. Mem., EMBO, 1989–. *Publications:* contribs to scientific jls. *Recreations:* archaeology, cooking, cinema. *Address:* 7 Little Saint Mary's Lane, Cambridge CB2 1RR. *T:* Cambridge (0223) 313360.

HODGKINS, David John; Director, Safety and General Policy (formerly Safety Policy and Information Services Division, then Safety Policy), since 1984, Member of Executive, since 1988, Health and Safety Executive; *b* 13 March 1934; *s* of Rev. Harold Hodgkins and of late Elsie Hodgkins; *m* 1963, Sheila Lacey; two *s*. *Educ:* Buxton Coll.; Peterhouse, Cambridge. BA 1956, MA 1960. Entered Min. of Labour as Asst Principal, 1956; Principal: Min. of Lab., 1961–65; Treasury, 1965–68; Manpower and Productivity Services, Dept of Employment, 1968–70; Assistant Secretary: Prices and Incomes Div., Dept of Employment, 1970–72; Industrial Relns Div., 1973–76; Under Secretary, Overseas and Manpower Divisions, Dept of Employment, 1977–84. *Address:* Four Winds, Batchelors Way, Amersham, Bucks HP7 9AJ. *T:* Amersham (0494) 725207. *Club:* Commonwealth Trust.

HODGKINSON, Rev. Canon Arthur Edward; Retired Priest-in-Charge of St Ebba's, Eyemouth, Diocese of Edinburgh, 1982–86; *b* 29 Oct. 1913; *s* of Arthur and Rose Hodgkinson. *Educ:* Glasgow High School; Edinburgh Theol College. LTh Durham 1942. Deacon 1939; Priest 1940. Curate, St George's, Maryhill, Glasgow, 1939–43; Choir Chaplain, 1943, and Precentor of St Ninian's Cath., Perth, 1944–47; Curate-in-Charge, St Finnian's, Lochgelly, 1947–52, and Rector, 1952–54; Rector, Holy Trinity, Motherwell, 1954–65; Provost of St Andrew's Cathedral, Aberdeen, 1965–78; Area Sec., Dioceses of Monmouth, Llandaff, Swansea and Brecon, and St Davids, USPG, 1978–82. Commissary to Bp of St John's, 1961–78; Mem., Anglican Consultative Council, 1971–77; Canon of St Mary's Cath., Glasgow, 1963–65. Hon. Canon of Christ Church Cathedral, Connecticut, 1965–78; Hon. Canon of Aberdeen, 1981. *Recreations:* motoring, travel. *Address:* 36 Forbes Road, Edinburgh EH10 4ED.

HODGKINSON, Sir Derek; *see* Hodgkinson, Sir W. D.

HODGKINSON, Terence William Ivan, CBE 1958; Trustee, The Burlington Magazine, since 1986 (Editor, 1978–81; Member, Editorial Board, 1978–86); *b* 7 Oct. 1913; *s* of late Ivan Tattersall Hodgkinson, Wells, Som, and of late Kathryn Van Vleck Townsend, New York (who *m* 2nd, 1929, Sir Gilbert Upcott, KCB); unmarried. *Educ:* Oundle Sch.; Magdalen Coll., Oxford. Served War of 1939–45 Major, Gen. Staff 1943. Joined staff of Victoria and Albert Museum (Dept of Architecture and Sculpture) 1946; Asst to the Dir, 1948–62; Secretary to the Advisory Council, 1951–67; Keeper, Dept of Architecture and Sculpture, 1967–74; Dir, Wallace Collection, 1974–78. Member: Exec. Cttee, Nat. Art Collections Fund, 1975–88; Museums and Galleries Commn, 1981–88 (Vice-Chm., 1987–88). *Publications:* (part author) Catalogue of Sculpture in the Frick Collection, New York, 1970; Catalogue of Sculpture at Waddesdon Manor, 1970; articles in Burlington Magazine, Bulletin and Yearbook of the Victoria and Albert Museum and for Walpole Society. *Recreation:* music. *Address:* 9 The Grove, N6 6JU.

HODGKINSON, Air Chief Marshal Sir (William) Derek, KCB 1971 (CB 1969); CBE 1960; DFC 1941; AFC 1942; *b* 27 Dec. 1917; *s* of late Ernest Nicholls Hodgkinson; *m* 1939, Nancy Heather Goodwin; one *s* one *d*. *Educ:* Repton. Joined RAF 1936; served war of 1939–45, POW Germany, 1942–45; OC 210 and 240 (GR) Sqns; DS Aust. Jt Anti-Sub. Sch. and JSSC, 1946–58; Gp Captain, 1958; OC RAF St Mawgan, 1958–61; Staff of CDS, and ADC to the Queen, 1959–63; Air Cdre, 1963; IDC, 1964; Comdt RAF Staff Coll., Andover, 1965; Air Vice-Marshal, 1966; ACAS, Operational Requirements, 1966–69; SASO, RAF Training Command, 1969; Air Marshal, 1970; AOC-in-C, Near East Air Force, Commander British Forces Near East, and Administrator, Sovereign Base Areas, Cyprus, 1970–73; Air Secretary, 1973–76; Air Chief Marshal, 1974; retired 1976. Report on RAF Officer Career Structure, 1969. Pres., Regular Forces Employment Assoc., 1982–86 (Vice-Chm., 1977–80; Chm., 1980–82). *Recreations:* fishing, cricket. *Clubs:* Royal Air Force, MCC.

HODGSON, Adam Robin; Chief Executive, Hampshire County Council, since 1985; *b* 20 March 1937; *s* of Thomas Edward Highton Hodgson, CB; *m* 1962, Elizabeth Maureen Linda Bovenizer; one *s* two *d*. *Educ:* William Ellis Sch., London; Worcester Coll., Oxford (MA). Admitted Solicitor, 1964. Asst Solicitor, LCC and GLC, 1964–66; Sen. Asst Solicitor, Oxfordshire CC, 1966–71; Asst Clerk, Northamptonshire CC, 1972–74; Dep. County Sec., E Sussex CC, 1974–77; Dep. Chief Exec. and Clerk, Essex CC, 1977–85. *Recreations:* music, drama, geology. *Address:* The Castle, Winchester SO23 8UJ. *T:* Winchester (0962) 847373.

HODGSON, Alfreda Rose, (Mrs Paul Blissett); concert singer; *b* 7 June 1940; *d* of Alfred and Rose Hodgson; *m* 1963, Paul Blissett; two *d*. *Educ:* Northern School of Music (GNSM; Hon. Fellow 1972); LRAM. Won Kathleen Ferrier Memorial Scholarship, 1964; first professional concert with Royal Liverpool Philharmonic Orchestra, 1964; since then has sung with all major orchestras in Britain, also throughout Europe, USA, Canada, Mexico, and elsewhere; Covent Garden début, 1983–84 season (Le Rossignol, and L'Enfant et les Sortilèges). Hon. FRNCM 1990. Sir Charles Santley Meml Gift, Worshipful Co. of Musicians, 1985. *Address:* 16 St Mary's Road, Prestwich, Manchester M25 5AP. *T:* 061–773 1541.

HODGSON, Arthur Brian, CMG 1962; Consultant, League of Red Cross Societies, since 1982; *b* 24 Aug. 1916; *s* of late Major Arthur H. F. Hodgson, Westfields, Iffley, Oxford, and Isabel, *d* of late W. H. Kidston, Rosebank, Edinburgh; *m* 1945, Anne Patricia Halse, *d* of late Lt-Col E. M. Ley, DSO, KRRC; two *s* two *d*. *Educ:* Edinburgh Academy; Eton Coll.; Oriel Coll., Oxford; Trinity Coll., Cambridge. Colonial Civil Service, Tanganyika Administration, 1939–62, retiring as Principal Sec. and Dir of Establishments. British Red Cross Society: Sec., 1964; Dep. Dir-Gen., 1966–70; Dir-Gen., 1970–75; Counsellor, 1975–81. Steward, Henley Royal Regatta. *Recreations:* rowing, rifle shooting, gardening, messing about in boats. *Address:* Chandlers, Furners Green, near Uckfield, Sussex TN22 3RH. *T:* Danehill (0825) 790310. *Clubs:* Naval; Leander.

HODGSON, Hon. Sir Derek; *see* Hodgson, Hon. Sir W. D. T.

HODGSON, George Charles Day, CMG 1961; MBE 1950; lately an Administrative Officer, Nyasaland; retired from HMOCS, Nov. 1964; Secretary, Old Diocesans' Union, Diocesan College, Rondebosch, Cape, South Africa, 1964–86; *b* 21 Sept. 1913; *s* of late P. J. Hodgson and of A. E. Joubert; *m* 1st, 1940, Edna Orde (*d* 1977), *d* of late G. H. Rushmere; one *s*; 2nd, 1978, Cecile Paston Dewar (*née* Foster). *Educ:* Diocesan Coll., Rondebosch, Capetown, S Africa; Rhodes Univ., Grahamstown, S Africa; Cambridge Univ. Joined Colonial Administrative Service as Cadet, 1939. Military Service, 1940–42; Lieut, 1st Bn King's African Rifles. Returned to duty as Distr. Officer, Nyasaland, 1943; seconded for special famine relief duties in Nyasaland, 1949–50; Provincial Commissioner, 1952; Adviser on Race Affairs to Govt of Federation of Rhodesia and Nyasaland, 1958–59; Nyasaland Govt Liaison Officer to Monckton Commn, 1960; Permanent Sec., Ministry of Natural Resources and Surveys, Nyasaland, 1961–62; Permanent Sec., Ministry of Transport and Communications, Nyasaland, 1963–64. *Recreations:* Rugby football, cricket, golf. *Address:* 308 Grosvenor Square, College Road, Rondebosch, Cape, 7700, South Africa. *Clubs:* Royal Cape Golf, Western Province Cricket (Cape Town).

HODGSON, Gordon Hewett; Master of the Supreme Court, Queen's Bench Division, since 1983; *b* 21 Jan. 1929; *s* of late John Lawrence Hodgson and Alice Joan Hodgson (*née* Wickham); *m* 1958, Pauline Audrey Gray; two *s*. *Educ:* Oundle School; University College London. LLB (Hons). National Service, RAEC, 1947–49; called to the Bar, Middle Temple, 1953; private practice, South Eastern Circuit, 1954–83; Asst Boundary Commissioner, 1976; Asst Recorder, 1979. Mem. Cttee, Bentham Club, 1987– (Chm., 1990–). *Recreations:* sailing, enjoying Tuscany. *Address:* Royal Courts of Justice, Strand WC2A 2LL. *T:* 071–936 6031. *Clubs:* East India; Royal Corinthian Yacht, Bar Yacht.

HODGSON, Howard Osmond Paul; *b* 22 Feb. 1950; *s* of late Osmond Paul Charles Hodgson and of Sheila Mary (*née* Ward; now Mrs Baker); *m* 1972, Marianne Denise Yvonne, *d* of Samuel Katibien, Aix-en-Provence, France; two *s* one *d* (and one *s* decd). *Educ:* Aiglon Coll., Villars, Switzerland. DipFD 1970; MBIFD; Affiliated MRSH, 1970. Asst Man., Hodgson & Sons Ltd, 1969–71; life assce exec., 1971–75; acquired: Hodgson & Sons Ltd, 1975 (floated USM, 1986); Ingalls from House of Fraser, 1987; launched Dignity in Destiny Ltd, 1989; merger with Pompes Funèbres Générales, France, Kenyon Securities and Hodgson Hldgs plc to form PFG Hodgson Kenyon Internat. plc, 1989; launched: Bereavement Support Service, 1990; PHKI Nat. Training Sch., 1990; retd, 1991, to pursue career in broadcasting and writing. How Euro Are You, BBC2, 1991. Hon. Vice Pres., Royal Soc. of St George. USM Entrepreneur of the Year, 1987. *Recreations:* cricket, yachting, ski-ing, history. *Club:* RMYC.

HODGSON, James, CBE 1984; Vice-Chairman, British Telecom, 1983–85; Chairman, Printing Equipment Economic Development Committee, 1986–88; *b* 14 Oct. 1925; *s* of late Frederick and Lucy Hodgson; *m* Brenda Dawn (*née* Giles). *Educ:* Exeter Sch.; St John's Coll., Cambridge. Entered GPO, 1950; Private Sec. to Asst PMG, 1952–55 and to Dir Gen. GPO, 1955–56; seconded to Cabinet Office, 1961–63; Head of Telephone Operating Div. of GPO Headquarters, 1965–67; Dir, later Sen. Dir, PO Internat. Telecommunications, 1969–81; Man. Dir, British Telecom Internat., 1981–83. Dir (non-exec.), Cable and Wireless Ltd, 1970–78. FRSA 1984. *Recreations:* travel, archaeology. *Address:* 2 Park Place, Bath BA1 2TY.

HODGSON, John Bury; Special Commissioner of Income Tax, 1970–78; *b* 17 March 1912; *s* of Charles Hodgson and Dorothy Hope Hodgson; *m* 1948, Helen Sibyl Uvedale Beaumont. *Educ:* Derbyshire Grammar Sch.; Manchester Univ. Solicitor, 1942; Asst Solicitor of Inland Revenue, 1956–70. *Publications:* (contrib.) Halsbury's Laws of England; (Consulting Editor) Sergeant on Stamp Duties. *Recreations:* sailing, beekeeping. *Address:* Five Thorns Cottage, Brockenhurst, Hants. *T:* Lymington (0590) 22653. *Clubs:* various yacht.

HODGSON, Ven. John Derek; Archdeacon of Auckland and Canon Residentiary of Durham Cathedral, since 1983; *b* 15 Nov. 1931; *s* of Frederick and Hilda Hodgson; *m* 1956, Greta Wilson; two *s* one *d*. *Educ:* King James School, Bishop Auckland; St John's Coll., Durham (BA Hons History); Cranmer Hall, Durham (Dip. Theology). Short service commission, DLI, 1954–57. Deacon 1959, priest 1960; Curate: Stranton, Hartlepool, 1959–62; St Andrew's, Roker, 1962–64; Vicar: Stillington, 1964–66; Consett, 1966–75; Rector of Gateshead, 1975–83; RD of Gateshead, 1976–83; Hon. Canon of Durham, 1978–83. *Recreations:* walking, music, theatre, country houses. *Address:* 15 The College, Durham DH1 3EQ. *T:* Durham (091) 3847534.

HODGSON, Sir Maurice (Arthur Eric), Kt 1979; Chairman, British Home Stores plc, 1982–87, and Chief Executive, 1982–85; *b* 21 Oct. 1919; *s* of late Walter Hodgson and of Amy Hodgson (*née* Walker); *m* 1945, Norma Fawcett; one *s* one *d*. *Educ:* Bradford Grammar Sch.; Merton Coll., Oxford (Hon. Fellow, 1979). MA, BSc; FEng, FIChemE; CChem, FRSC. Joined ICI Ltd Fertilizer & Synthetic Products Gp, 1942; seconded to ICI (New York) Ltd, 1955–58; Head of ICI Ltd Technical Dept, 1958; Develt Dir, ICI Ltd Heavy Organic Chemicals Div., 1960, Dep. Chm., 1964; Gen. Man., Company Planning, ICI Ltd, 1966; Commercial Dir and Planning Dir, ICI Ltd, 1970; Dep. Chm., ICI Ltd, 1972–78, Chm., 1978–82; Director: Carrington Viyella Ltd, 1970–74; Imperial Chemicals Insce Ltd, 1970–78 (Chm. 1972); Dunlop Holdings plc, 1982–84 (Chm. 1984); Storehouse, 1985–89; Member: Internat. Adv. Bd, AMAX Inc., 1982–85; European Adv. Council, Air Products and Chemicals Inc., 1982–84; Council, Lloyd's of London, 1987–. Chm., Civil Justice Review Adv. Cttee, 1985–88; Member: Court, British Shippers' Council, 1978–82; Council, CBI, 1978–82; Internat. Council, Salk Inst., 1978–; Court, Univ. of Bradford, 1979–. Vis. Fellow, Sch. of Business and Organizational Studies, Univ. of Lancaster, 1970–. Governor, London Grad. Sch. of Business Studies, 1978–87. Hon. DUniv Heriot-Watt, 1979; Hon. DTech Bradford, 1979; Hon. DSc Loughborough, 1981; Hon. FUMIST, 1979. Messel Medal, Soc. of Chemical Industry, 1980; George E. Davis Medal, IChemE, 1982. *Recreations:* horse-racing, swimming, fishing. *Address:* Suite 75/76, Kent House, 87 Regent Street, W1R 7HF. *T:* 071–734 7777.

HODGSON, Patricia Anne, (Mrs George Donaldson); Head of Policy and Planning Unit, BBC, since 1987; *b* 19 Jan. 1947; *d* of Harold Hodgson and Pat Smith; *m* 1979, George Donaldson; one *s*. *Educ:* Brentwood High Sch.; Newnham Coll., Cambridge (MA); LRAM (Drama) 1968. Conservative Res. Dept, Desk Officer for public sector industries, 1968–70; freelance journalism and broadcasting in UK and USA during seventies; Chm., Bow Gp, 1975–76; Editor, Crossbow, 1976–80. Joined BBC as producer for Open Univ., specialising in history and philosophy, 1970; most of prodn career in educn, with spells in current affairs on Today and Tonight. BBC Secretariat, 1982–83, Dep. Sec., 1983–85, The Sec., 1985–87. Director: BARB, 1987–; BBC Subscription Ltd, 1990–. Mem., (C) Haringey BC, 1974–77. Member: London Electricity Consultative Council, 1981–83; London Arts Bd, 1991–. FRSA. *Television series* include: English Urban History, 1978; Conflict in Modern Europe, 1980; Rome in the Age of Augustus, 1981. *Publications:* contribs to The Spectator, Daily Telegraph and Guardian. *Recreation:* quietness. *Address:* Broadcasting House, Portland Place, W1A 0AA. *T:* 071–580 4468. *Club:* Reform.

HODGSON, Prof. Phyllis; Professor of English Language and Mediæval Literature, Bedford College, University of London, 1955–72, retired; *b* 27 June 1909; *d* of late Herbert Henry Hodgson, MA, BSc, PhD, FRIC. *Educ:* Bolling Grammar Sch. for Girls, Bradford; Bedford Coll., University of London (BA); (Sen. Schol.) Lady Margaret Hall, Oxford (BLitt, DPhil). Tutor of St Mary's Coll., Durham Univ., 1936–38; Jex-Blake Fellow, Girton Coll., Cambridge (MA), 1938–40; Lecturer in English Language (Part-time), Queen Mary Coll., University of London, and Lecturer in English, Homerton Coll., Cambridge, 1940–42; Lecturer in English Language and Mediæval Literature, Bedford Coll., University of London, 1942–49; Reader in English Language in the University of London, 1949–55; External examiner for Reading Univ., 1955–57, 1961–63. Mem. Council of Early English Text Soc., 1959–79; Chm., Bd of Studies in English, 1964–66. Sir Israel Gollancz Prize, British Academy, 1971. *Publications:* The Cloud of Unknowing (EETS), 1944, 1958; Deonise Hid Divinite (EETS), 1955, 1958, 1973; The Franklin's Tale, 1960; The Orcherd of Syon and the English Mystical Tradition (Proc. Brit. Acad. 1964), 1965; The Orcherd of Syon (EETS), 1966; Three 14th Century English Mystics, 1967; The General Prologue to the Canterbury Tales, 1969; The Cloud of Unknowing and Related Treatises (Analecta Cartusiana), 1982; articles in Review of English Studies, Modern Language Review, Contemporary Review, etc. *Recreations:* music, walking, travel.

HODGSON, Robin Granville; Group Chief Executive, Granville Holdings plc (formerly Managing Director, Granville & Co. Ltd), since 1979 (Director, since 1972); Director, Johnson Bros & Co. Ltd, Walsall, since 1970; *b* 25 April 1942; *s* of late Henry Edward and of Natalie Beatrice Hodgson; *m* 1982, Fiona Ferelith, *o d* of K. S. Allom, Dorking, Surrey; two *s* one *d* (and one twin *s* decd). *Educ:* Shrewsbury Sch.; Oxford Univ. (BA Hons 1964); Wharton Sch. of Finance, Univ. of Pennsylvania (MBA 1969). Investment Banker, New York and Montreal, 1964–67; Industry in Birmingham, England, 1969–72; Dir, Community Hospitals plc, 1982–85. Mem., W Midlands Industrial Develt Bd, 1989–. Contested (C) Walsall North, Feb. and Oct. 1974; MP (C) Walsall North, Nov. 1976–1979. Chm., Birmingham Bow Gp, 1972–73; National Union of Conservative Associations: Member: Central Council, 1979–; Exec. Cttee, 1988–; Gen. Purposes Cttee, 1990–; Asst Treas., 1985–88, Treas., 1988–91, Chm., 1991–, W Midlands Area. Member: Council for the Securities Industry, 1980–85; Securities and Investments Board, 1985–89; Chm., Nat. Assoc. of Security Dealers and Investment Managers, 1979–85. Trustee, Friends of Shrewsbury Sch.; Associate, St. George's House, Windsor. Liveryman, Goldsmiths' Co., 1983. *Publication:* Britain's Home Defence Gamble, 1978. *Recreations:* squash, theatre. *Address:* 15 Scarsdale Villas, W8 6PT. *T:* 071–937 2964; Astley Abbotts, Bridgnorth, Salop. *T:* Bridgnorth (07462) 3122.

HODGSON, Stanley Ernest, CBE 1974 (OBE 1966); retired; Education Adviser, British High Commission, New Delhi, 1971–77; *b* 11 July 1918; *s* of Harold Frederick Hodgson, MPS, and Winifred Caroline (*née* Gale); *m* 1945, Joan Beryl (*née* Ballard); two *d*. *Educ:* Brentwood Grammar Sch.; London Univ. Teacher's Certif., London, 1941; BA Hons Russian, London, 1949. RA, 1941–46. British Council: India, 1949–54; Uganda, 1956–60;

Reg. Rep., South India, 1965–68; Controller Estabts, 1969–71. Dir, Fest. of India in Britain 1982. *Recreations:* reading, gardening, walking. *Address:* Clarendon, Netherfield Road, Battle, East Sussex TN33 0HJ. *T:* Battle (04246) 2631. *Club:* Commonwealth Trust.

HODGSON, Col Terence Harold Henry, DSO 1945; MC 1944; TD 1953; FSVA; FRSH; Vice Lord Lieutenant of Cumbria, 1983–91; *b* 10 Dec. 1916; *s* of late Michael C. L. Hodgson, Grange-over-Sands; *m* 1st, 1942, Joan Winsome Servant (marr. diss. 1969; she *d* 1974); 2nd, 1972, Doreen Jacqueline Pollit Brünzel (*d* 1985); three *s* three *d*; 3rd, 1985, Elizabeth Robinson. *Educ:* Kendal Grammar Sch. FSVA 1953; FRSH 1954. Served War with Border Regt, Ceylon, India and Burma; Comdr, 4th Bn Border Regt, TA, 1953–56; Dep. Comdr, 126 Inf. Bde, 1956–59; Col TA, 1959; Hon. Colonel: King's Own Royal Border Regt, 1976–82; Cumbria Cadet Force, 1977–86. Dir, Cartmel Steeplechasers Ltd, 1959–; Local Dir, Royal Insurance, 1960–. Chairman: Governors, Kirkbie Kendal Sch., 1970–86; Kendal Almshouse Charities, 1975–86; Cumbria Appeal Cttee, Army Benevolent Fund, 1987–. Past Pres., Cumberland and Westmorland Rugby Union. DL Westmorland, 1958. *Recreations:* Rugby football, horse racing. *Address:* School House, Winster, Windermere, Cumbria LA23 3PU. *T:* Windermere (09662) 5439. *Club:* Army and Navy.

HODGSON, Ven. Thomas Richard Burnham; Archdeacon of West Cumberland, 1979–91, now Archdeacon Emeritus; *b* 17 Aug. 1926; *s* of Richard Shillito Hodgson and Marion Thomasina Bertram Marshall; *m* 1952, Margaret Esther, *o d* of Evan and Caroline Margaret Makinson; one *s* one *d*. *Educ:* Harden House Prep. Sch.; Heversham Grammar School; London Coll. of Divinity, Univ. of London. BD, ALCD. Deacon 1952, priest 1953, dio. Carlisle; Curate of Crosthwaite, Keswick, 1952–55; Curate of Stanwix, Carlisle, 1955–59; Vicar of St Nicholas', Whitehaven, 1959–65; Rector of Aikton, 1965–67; Vicar of Raughtonhead with Gaitsgill, 1967–73; Hon. Canon of Carlisle, 1973–91; Vicar of: Grange-over-Sands, 1973–79; Mosser, 1979–83. Mem., General Synod of C of E, 1983–91. Domestic Chaplain to Bishop of Carlisle, 1967–73, Hon. Chaplain 1973–79; Director of Ordination Candidates, 1970–74; RD of Windermere, 1976–79; Surrogate, 1962–91. FRMetS 1988–91. *Recreations:* listening to music, watching drama, geology, meteorological observing. *Address:* 58 Greenacres, Wetheral, Carlisle CA4 8LD. *T:* Carlisle (0228) 61159.

HODGSON, Hon. Sir (Walter) Derek (Thornley), Kt 1977; **Hon. Mr Justice Hodgson;** a Judge of the High Court of Justice, Queen's Bench Division, since 1977; *b* 24 May 1917; *s* of late Walter Hodgson, Whitefield, Manchester; *m* 1951, Raymonde Valda (*née* de Villiers) (*d* 1965); no *c*. *Educ:* Malvern Coll.; Trinity Hall, Cambridge. Scholar, Trinity Hall; Harmsworth Scholar, Middle Temple; 1st Cl. Law Tripos, Part II, 1938; 1st Cl. LLB, 1939. Served throughout War 1939–46, Royal Artillery; Burma 1942–45; released with rank of Captain, 1946. Called to Bar, Middle Temple, 1946 (Master of the Bench, 1967); QC 1961. Member: Senate of Inns of Court, 1966–69; Gen. Council of the Bar, 1965–69. Judge of the Salford Hundred Court of Record, 1965–71; a Law Comr, 1971–77; a Recorder of the Crown Court, 1972–77. Member: Lord Chancellor's Cttees on: Legal Educn, 1968–71; Contempt of Court, 1971–74; Butler Cttee on Mentally Abnormal Offenders, 1973–75; Parole Board, 1981–83 (Vice-Chm., 1982–83). Chm., Howard League Wkg Pty on Forfeiture (report published as The Profits of Crime and their Recovery, 1984). *Recreation:* travel. *Address:* Royal Courts of Justice, Strand, WC2. *Clubs:* United Oxford & Cambridge University; Tennis and Racquets (Manchester); Hawks (Cambridge).

HODGSON, William Donald John; Broadcasting Consultant; *b* 25 March 1923; *s* of James Samuel Hodgson and Caroline Maud Albrecht; *m* 1946, Betty Joyce Brown; two *s* six *d*. *Educ:* Beckenham Grammar School. Served Beds and Herts Regt, 1940–42; pilot, RAF and Fleet Air Arm, 1942–46. Documentary and feature film editor (with Jean Renoir on The River, Calcutta), 1946–50; Organiser, Festival of Britain Youth Programme, 1950–51; Asst Sec., Central Bureau for Educational Visits and Exchanges, 1951–54; Asst Gen. Man., Press Assoc., 1954–60; Gen. Man., ITN, 1960–82; Dir of Develt, ITN, 1982–86 (Dir, 1972–86). Dir, UPITN Corp., 1967–73. Executive Producer: Battle for the Falklands, 1982; Theft of a Thoroughbred, 1983; Victory in Europe, 1985; writer and producer, Welcome to the Caley (Royal Caledonian Schs), 1987. *Recreations:* grandchildcare, private flying, cricket, swimming. *Address:* 38 Lakeside, Wickham Road, Beckenham, Kent BR3 2LX. *T:* 081–650 8959.

HODIN, Prof. Josef Paul, LLD; author, art historian, art critic; *b* 17 Aug. 1905; *s* of Eduard D. Hodin and Rosa (*née* Klug); *m* 1945, Doris Pamela Simms; one *s* one *d*. *Educ:* Kleinseitner Realschule and Neustädter Realgymnasium, Prague; Charles Univ., Prague; London Univ.; Art Academies of Dresden and Berlin. Press Attaché to Norwegian Govt in London, 1944–45; Dir of Studies and Librarian, Inst. of Contemporary Arts, London, 1949–54; Hon. Mem. Editorial Council of The Journal of Aesthetics and Art Criticism, Cleveland, 1955–; Mem. Exec. Cttee British Soc. of Aesthetics; Pres., British Section, AICA; Editor: Prisme des Arts, Paris, 1956–57; Quadrum, Brussels, 1956–66. 1st internat. prize for art criticism, Biennale, Venice, 1954. Hon. PhD Uppsala, 1969; Hon. Prof. Vienna, 1975. DSM 1st cl. Czechoslovakia, 1947; St Olav Medal, Norway, 1958; Comdr, Order of Merit, Italy, 1966; Grand Cross, Order of Merit, Austria, 1968; Order of Merit, 1st cl., Germany, 1969; Silver Cross of Merit, Austria, 1972; Comdr, Order of Merit, Germany, 1986. *Publications:* Monographs on Sven Erixson (Stockholm), 1940; Ernst Josephson (Stockholm), 1942, Edvard Munch (Stockholm), 1948, (Frankfurt a/M), 1951; Isaac Grünewald (Stockholm), 1949; Art and Criticism (Stockholm), 1944; J. A. Comenius and Our Time (Stockholm), 1944; The Dilemma of Being Modern (London), 1956, (New York), 1959; Henry Moore (Amsterdam, Hamburg), 1956, (London, New York), 1958, (Buenos Aires), 1963; Ben Nicholson (London), 1957; Barbara Hepworth (Neuchatel, London, New York), 1961; Lynn Chadwick (Amsterdam, Hamburg, London, New York), 1961; Bekenntnis zu Kokoschka (Mainz), 1963; Edvard Munch (Mainz), 1963; Oskar Kokoschka: A Biography (London, New York), 1966; Walter Kern (Neuchatel, London), 1966; Ruszkowski (London), 1967; Bernard Leach (London), 1967; Oskar Kokoschka: Sein Leben Seine Zeit (Mainz), 1968; Kafka und Goethe (Hamburg), 1968; Giacomo Manzù (Rome), 1969; Die Brühlsche Terrasse, Ein Künstlerroman, 1970; Emilio Greco, Life and Work (London, New York), 1971; Edvard Munch (London, New York, Oslo), 1972; Modern Art and the Modern Mind (London, Cleveland), 1972; Alfred Manessier (London, NY, Paris), 1972; Bernard Stern (London), 1972; Ludwig Meidner (Darmstadt), 1973; Hilde Goldschmidt (Hamburg), 1974; Paul Berger-Bergner, Leben und Werk (Hamburg), 1974; Die Leute von Elverdingen (Hamburg), 1974; Kokoschka und Hellas (Vienna), 1977; John Milne (London), 1977; Else Meidner, 1979; Elisabeth Frink, 1983; Douglas Portway, 1983; Franz Luby (Vienna), 1983; Dieses Mütterchen hat Krallen, Die Geschichte einer Prager Jugend (Hamburg), 1985; Verlorene Existenzen, Erzählungen (Hamburg), 1986; Friedrich Karl Gotsch (Hamburg), 1987; Manzù Pittore (Bergamo, London, Hamburg), 1988; Jan Brazda (London, Stockholm), 1989; contribs on literary and art subjects to internat. periodicals. *Address:* 12 Eton Avenue, NW3 3EH. *T:* 071–794 3609. *Clubs:* Athenæum, Arts.

HODKIN, Rev. Canon Hedley; Residentiary Canon, Manchester Cathedral, 1957–70, Canon Emeritus, since 1970; Sub-Dean, 1966–70; *b* 3 Jan. 1902; *s* of Walter and Elizabeth Hodkin; *m* 1932, Mary M., *d* of Dr J. A. Findlay; one *s* one *d*. *Educ:* University of Sheffield; Christ's Coll. and Westcott House, Cambridge. Curate of: Morpeth, 1935–38; St George's, Newcastle, 1938–40; Vicar of: St Luke's, Newcastle, 1940–47; Holy Trinity, Millhouses, Sheffield, 1947–57. Examining Chaplain: to Bishop of Newcastle, 1939–47; to Bishop of Sheffield, 1951–57; to Bishop of Manchester, 1957. Hon. Canon of Sheffield, 1955–57. Select Preacher, Cambridge, 1968. *Recreation:* music. *Address:* Dulverton Hall, St Martin's Square, Scarborough YO11 2DQ. *T:* Scarborough (0723) 360364.

HODKINSON, Prof. Henry Malcolm, DM; FRCP; Barlow Professor of Geriatric Medicine, University College London, 1985–91, now Emeritus; *b* 28 April 1931; *s* of Charles and Olive Hodkinson; *m* 1st, (marr. diss.); four *d*; *m* 2nd, 1986, Judith Marie Bryant, *qv*. *Educ:* Manchester Grammar Sch.; Brasenose Coll., Oxford (DM 1975); Middlesex Hospital. FRCP 1974. Consultant Physician in Geriatrics to: Enfield and Tottenham Gps of Hosps, 1962–70; Northwick Park Hosp., 1970–78 (also Mem., Scientific Staff of Clin. Res. Centre); Sen. Lectr in Geriatric Medicine, 1978–79, Prof. of Geriatric Medicine, 1979–84, RPMS. Gov., Research into Ageing. *Publications:* An Outline of Geriatrics, 1975, 2nd edn 1981 (trans. Spanish, Dutch, German, Italian and Japanese); Common Symptoms of Disease in the Elderly, 1976, 2nd edn 1980 (trans. Turkish); Biochemical Diagnosis of the Elderly, 1977; (ed) Clinical Biochemistry of the Elderly, 1984; approx. 100 papers in learned jls, 1961–. *Recreations:* English glass and ceramics. *Address:* 8 Chiswick Square, Burlington Lane, Chiswick, W4 2QG. *T:* 081–747 0239.

HODKINSON, Judith Marie, (Mrs H. M. Hodkinson); *see* Bryant, J. M.

HODSON, Denys Fraser, CBE 1981; Director, Arts and Recreation, Thamesdown Borough Council, since 1974; *b* 23 May 1928; *s* of Rev. Harold Victor Hodson, MC and Marguerite Edmée Ritchie; *m* 1954, Julie Compton Goodwin; one *s* one *d*. *Educ:* Marlborough Coll.; Trinity Coll., Oxford (MA). After a career in commerce and industry, apptd first Controller of Arts and Recreation, Swindon Bor. Council, 1970. Chairman: Southern Arts Assoc., 1974–80 and 1985–87; Council, Regional Arts Assocs, 1975–80; Chief Leisure Officers' Assoc., 1974 and 1982–84; Vice-Chm., Arts Council of GB, 1989– (Mem., 1987–); a Director: Oxford Playhouse Co., 1974–86; Oxford Stage Co., 1988–89; a Governor: BFI, 1976–87; Wyvern Arts Trust, 1984–. *Publications:* (contrib.) Arts Centres, 1981; (contrib.) The Future of Leisure Services, 1988; conf. papers and articles. *Recreations:* bird-watching, fishing, the arts. *Address:* Manor Farm House, Fairford, Glos GL7 4AR. *T:* Cirencester (0285) 712462.

HODSON, Prof. Frank, BSc London 1949; PhD Reading 1951; Professor of Geology in the University of Southampton, 1958–81, now Emeritus; *b* 23 Nov. 1921; *s* of late Matthew and Gertrude Hodson; *m* 1945, Ada Heyworth; three *d*. *Educ:* Burnley Grammar Sch.; Reading Univ.; London Univ. (external student). Demonstrator, Reading Univ., 1947–49; Lecturer, Reading Univ., 1949–58. Dean, Faculty of Science, 1972–74, and 1976–77, Public Orator, 1970–73, Univ. of Southampton. Murchison Fund, Geol. Soc., 1962; Founder Mem. and first Hon. Sec., Palaeontol. Assoc., 1957. Pres. Sect. C (geology), British Assoc. for Adv. of Science, 1975. Hon. Mem. Geol. Soc. de Belg. *Publications:* geological papers in publications of learned societies. *Recreation:* book collecting. *Address:* Department of Geology, The University, Southampton SO9 5NH.

HODSON, Henry Vincent; Consultant Editor, The Annual Register (of world events), since 1988 (Editor, 1973–88); *b* 12 May 1906; *er s* of late Prof. T. C. Hodson; *m* 1933, Margaret Elizabeth Honey, Sydney; four *s*. *Educ:* Gresham's Sch.; Balliol Coll., Oxford. Fellow of All Souls Coll., Oxford, 1928–35; Staff of Economic Advisory Council, 1930–31; Asst Editor of the Round Table, 1931, Editor, 1934–39; Director, Empire Div., Ministry of Information, 1939–41; Reforms Commissioner, Govt of India, 1941–42; Principal Asst Sec., and later head of Non-Munitions Div., Min. of Production, 1942–45; Asst Editor, Sunday Times, 1946–50, Editor, 1950–61; Provost of Ditchley, 1961–71. Sole Partner, Hodson Consultants, 1971–. Consultant Editor, The International Foundation Directory, 1974–89. Past Master, Mercers' Co. *Publications:* Economics of a Changing World, 1933; (part) The Empire in the World, 1937; Slump and Recovery, 1929–37, 1938; The British Commonwealth and the Future, 1939; Twentieth Century Empire, 1948; Problems in Anglo-American Relations, 1963; The Great Divide: Britain-India-Pakistan, 1969 (reissued 1985); The Diseconomics of Growth, 1972; many articles in reviews, etc. *Address:* Flat 1, 105 Lexham Gardens, W8 6JN. *T:* 071–373 2859.

HODSON, John; Chief Executive, Singer & Friedlander Holdings, since 1990; *b* 19 May 1946; *s* of Arthur and Olga Hodson; *m* 1971, Christina McLeod; one *s* two *d*. *Educ:* Worcester Coll., Oxford (PPE). Joined Singer & Friedlander, 1969: Asst Dir, 1974–83; Dir, 1983–; Head of Investment Dept, 1985–90; Dir, Singer & Friedlander Gp PLC, 1987–. *Recreations:* tennis, family. *Address:* 21 New Street, EC2M 4HR. *T:* 071–623 3000.

HODSON, Sir Michael (Robin Adderley), 6th Bt *cr* 1789; Captain, Scots Guards, retired; *b* 5 March 1932; *s* of Major Sir Edmond Adair Hodson, 5th Bt, DSO, and Anne Elizabeth Adderley (*d* 1984), *yr d* of Lt-Col Hartopp Francis Charles Adderley Cradock, Hill House, Sherborne St John; *S* father, 1972; *m* 1st, 1963, Katrin Alexa (marr. diss. 1978), *d* of late Erwin Bernstiel, Dinas Powis, Glamorgan; three *d*; 2nd, 1978, Catherine, *d* of late John Henry Seymour, Wimpole St, W1. *Educ:* Eton. *Heir:* *b* Patrick Richard Hodson [*b* 27 Nov. 1934; *m* 1961, June, *o d* of H. M. Shepherd-Cross; three *s*]. *Address:* The White House, Awbridge, Romsey, Hants.

HODSON, Thomas David Tattersall; His Honour Judge Hodson; a Circuit Judge, since 1987; *b* 24 Sept. 1942; *s* of late Thomas Norman Hodson and Elsie Nuttall Hodson; *m* 1969, Patricia Ann Vint; two *s* one *d*. *Educ:* Sedbergh Sch.; Manchester Univ. (LLB). Leader Writer, Yorkshire Post, 1964–65; called to the Bar, Inner Temple 1966; in practice on Northern Circuit, 1967–87; Junior, 1969; a Recorder, 1983–87. *Recreations:* music, genealogy, fell-walking. *Address:* c/o Manchester Crown Court, Crown Square, Manchester M3 3FL. *T:* 061–832 8393. *Club:* Lancashire CC.

HOEKMAN, Johan Bernard; Knight, Order of Netherlands Lion; Officer, Order of Orange Nassau; Netherlands Ambassador to the Court of St James's, since 1990, and concurrently to Iceland; *b* 11 Sept. 1931; *m* 1957, Jeanne Van Gelder; three *s* one *d*. *Educ:* Univ. of Groningen (degree in Social Geography). Foreign Service, 1961; served Baghdad, Washington, Jeddah; Counsellor, Cairo, 1972–74; Deputy, later Head, Dept for Financial Economic Develt Co-operation, Min. of Foreign Affairs, 1974–80; Ambassador, Dakar, 1980–81, Paramaribo, 1981–84; Dir-Gen. for Internat. Co-operation, 1984–88; Ambassador, Paramaribo, 1988–90. Holds foreign decorations. *Address:* 8 Palace Green, W8 4QA; 38 Hyde Park Gate, SW7 5DP. *T:* 071–584 5040. *Club:* Dutch.

HOEY, Catharine Letitia; MP (Lab) Vauxhall, since June 1989; *b* 21 June 1946; *d* of Thomas Henry and Letitia Jane Hoey. *Educ:* Lylehill Primary Sch.; Belfast Royal Acad.; Ulster Coll. of Physical Educn (Dip. in PE); City of London Coll. (BSc Econs). Lectr, Southwark Coll., 1972–76; Sen. Lectr, Kingsway Coll., 1976–85; Educnl Advr, London Football Clubs, 1985–89. *Recreations:* watching soccer, keeping fit. *Address:* House of Commons, SW1A 0AA. *T:* 071–219 3000. *Club:* Barbican Health and Fitness Centre.

HOFF, Harry Summerfield; *see* Cooper, William.

HOFFBRAND, Prof. (Allan) Victor, DM; FRCP, FRCPath; Professor of Haematology and Honorary Consultant, Royal Free Hospital School of Medicine, since 1974; *b* 14 Oct. 1935; *s* of late Philip Hoffbrand and of Minnie (*née* Freedman); *m* 1963, Irene Jill Mellows; two *s* one *d*. *Educ:* Bradford Grammar Sch.; Queen's Coll., Oxford (BA 1956; MA 1960; BM BCh 1959; DM 1972); Royal London Hospital; DSc London 1987. FRCP 1976; FRCPath 1980; Hon. FRCPE 1986. Jun. hosp. posts, Royal London Hosp., 1960–62; Res. and Registrar posts, RPMS, 1962–66; Lectr, St Bartholomew's Hosp., 1966–67; MRC Fellow, New England Med. Centre, Boston, 1967–68; Sen. Lectr, RPMS, 1968–74. Visiting Professor: Sanaa, Yemen, 1986; Armed Forces Inst. Path., Rawalpindi, 1988; Royal Melbourne Hosp., 1991. Lectures: Los Braun Meml, Johannesburg, 1978; Sir Stanley Davidson, Edinburgh, 1983; G. Izak Meml, Jerusalem, 1984; K. J. R. Wightman, Toronto, 1988. Member: Systems Bd, MRC, 1986–89; Council, RCPath, 1987–90; Council, Royal Free Sch. of Med., 1991–. Adviser Brit. Nat. Formulary; Medical Adviser: UK Thalassaemia Soc.; Helen Manuel Gaucher Foundn. Member: Amer. Soc. Haematology; Brit. Soc. Haematology; Internat. Soc. Haematology. Member, Editorial Board: Brit. Jl Haematology (Chm.); Clinical Haematology; Blood Reviews; Leukaemia Res.; Leukaemia and Lymphoma; Haematologica. *Publications:* (ed with S. M. Lewis) Postgraduate Haematology, 1972, 3rd edn 1989; (ed) Recent Advances in Haematology, 1977, 5th edn 1988; (with J. E. Pettit): Essential Haematology, 1980, 2nd edn 1984; Blood Diseases Illustrated, 1987; Sandoz Atlas of Clinical Haematology, 1988; papers on megaloblastic anaemia, iron chelation, leukaemia and related disorders. *Recreations:* music, antiques, squash, chess, bridge. *Address:* Department of Haematology, Royal Free Hospital, NW3 2QG. *T:* 071–794 0500.

HOFFENBERG, Sir Raymond, (Bill), KBE 1984; President, Wolfson College, Oxford, since 1985; *b* 6 March 1923; *er s* of Benjamin and Dora Hoffenberg; *m* 1949; two *s*. *Educ:* Grey High Sch., Port Elizabeth; Univ. of Cape Town. MB, ChB 1948, MD, PhD; MA Oxon. FRCP 1971; FRCPE, FRCPI; Hon. FRACP 1984; Hon. FACP 1985; Hon. FRCP(C) 1986; Hon. FFOM 1990; Hon. FFPM 1990; Hon. FRCPsych 1991. Wartime Service with S African Armed Forces, N Africa and Italy. Sen. Lectr, Dept of Medicine, Univ. of Cape Town, 1955–67; Carnegie Corp. of NY Trav. Fellow, 1957–58; banned by S African Govt, 1967; emigrated to UK, 1968. Sen. Scientist, MRC (UK), 1968–72; William Withering Prof. of Medicine, Univ. of Birmingham, 1972–85. Member: West Midlands RHA, 1976–83; MRC, 1978–82. Member: Central and Exec. Cttee, Internat. Soc. for Endocrinology, 1976–88; Royal Soc. Med., Endocr. Sect. (Pres., 1978–80); Med. Res. Soc. (Chm., 1978–83); Assoc. of Physicians (Pres., 1985–86); Amer. Assoc. of Physicians; Academia Europaea, 1990; Chm. Council, British Heart Foundn, 1987–; President: Mental Health Foundn, 1989–; Med. Campaign against Nuclear War, 1989–. Member, Editorial Board of several journals. Hon. Mem., Acad. of Medicine of Malaysia, 1989. Royal College of Physicians: Oliver-Sharpey Lectr, 1973; Senior Censor, 1981–82; Pres., 1983–89. Freeman, City of London, 1983. Hon. DSc: Leicester, 1985; City, 1985; Hon. MD Bristol, 1989. *Publications:* Clinical Freedom, 1987 (Rock Carling Fellowship, Nuffield Provincial Hospitals Trust); papers on endocrinology and metabolism. *Recreations:* (largely nostalgic) reading, walking, gardening, golf, tennis. *Address:* Wolfson College, Oxford OX2 6UD. *T:* Oxford (0865) 274102.

HOFFMAN, Dustin Lee; actor; *b* 8 Aug. 1937; *s* of Harry Hoffman and Lillian Hoffman; *m* 1st, 1969, Anne Byrne (marr. diss. 1980); two *d*; 2nd, 1980, Lisa Gottsegen; two *s* one *d*. *Educ:* Santa Monica City Coll.; Pasadena Playhouse. Stage début in Sarah Lawrence Coll. prodn, Yes is For a Very Young Man; Broadway début, A Cook for Mr General, 1961; appeared in: Harry, and Noon and Night, Amer. Place Theatre, NY, 1964–65; Journey of the Fifth Horse, and Star Wagon, 1965; Fragments, Berkshire Theatre Festival, Stockbridge, Mass, 1966; Eh?, 1966–67; Jimmy Shine, Broadway, 1968–69; Death of a Salesman, Broadway, 1984; London début, Merchant of Venice, Phoenix, 1989. Dir, All Over Town, Broadway, 1974. Films: The Graduate, 1967; Midnight Cowboy, 1969; John and Mary, 1969; Little Big Man, 1971; Who Is Harry Kellerman and Why Is He Saying Those Terrible Things About Me?, 1971; Straw Dogs, 1972; Alfredo, Alfredo, 1972; Papillon, 1973; Lenny, 1974; All The President's Men, 1975; Marathon Man, 1976; Straight Time, 1978; Agatha, 1979; Kramer vs Kramer, 1979 (Academy Award); Tootsie, 1983; Death of a Salesman, 1985 (Emmy Award); Ishtar, 1987; Rain Man, 1989 (Academy Award; Golden Globe Award); Family Business, 1990; Billy Bathgale, 1991. Record: Death of a Salesman. Obie Award as best off-Broadway actor, 1965–66, for Journey of the Fifth Horse; Drama Desk, Theatre World, and Vernon Rice Awards for Eh?, 1966; Oscar Award nominee for The Graduate, Midnight Cowboy, and Lenny. *Address:* Punch Productions, 75 Rockefeller Plaza, Suite 1104, New York, NY 10019, USA.

HOFFMAN, Michael Richard, FEng; Chief Executive, Thames Water plc (formerly Thames Water Authority), since 1989; *b* 31 Oct. 1939; *s* of Sydney William Hoffman and Ethel Margaret Hoffman (*née* Hill); *m* 1st, 1963, Margaret Edith Tregaskes (marr. diss. 1978); one *d*; 2nd, 1982, Helen Judith Peters. *Educ:* Hitchin Grammar Sch.; Univ. of Bristol (BScEng Hons). Eur Ing; FIMechE, FIProdE. Rolls Royce, 1961; AE Ltd, 1973; Perkins Engines Group: Managing Director, 1976; Chairman, 1977; Massey Ferguson Ltd: Vice President, 1980; President, Farm Machinery Div., 1981; Chief Exec. and Man. Dir, Babcock Internat., 1983–87; Deputy Chairman: Airship Industries, 1988–90 (Chief Exec., 1987–88); Cosworth Engrg Ltd, 1988–. Pres., IProdE, 1987–88 (Vice Pres., 1985–87); Vice-Pres., EEF, 1985–87. Chm., UK S African Trade Assoc., 1987; Member: Technology Requirements Bd, 1985–88; Monopolies and Mergers Commn, 1988–; BOTB, 1986–89; Engrg Council, 1991–. Mem. Council, Brunel Univ., 1984–. Freeman, City of London, 1984; Liveryman, Engineers' Co., 1984–. *Recreations:* Real tennis, shooting, sailing. *Address:* 43 De Vere Gardens, W8 5AW. *T:* 071–581 4612; 4 St Mark's Mews, Leamington Spa, Warwicks CV32 6EJ. *T:* Leamington Spa (0926) 429643. *Clubs:* Reform, Royal Automobile, MCC.

HOFFMAN, Paul Maxim Laurence; His Honour Judge Hoffman; a Circuit Judge, since 1991; *b* 29 July 1942; *s* of Gerard and Laura Hoffman; *m* 1989, Elaine; two step *c*, and three *s* by previous marriage. *Educ:* Roundhay Boys' Sch., Leeds; Sheffield Univ. (LLB Hons 1962). Called to the Bar, Lincoln's Inn, 1964. Standing Counsel to Inland Revenue, NE Circuit, 1985–91; a Recorder, NE Circuit, 1985–91. *Recreations:* concert going, rambling.

HOFFMAN, Rev. Canon Stanley Harold, MA; Chaplain in Ordinary to the Queen, 1976–87; Hon. Canon of Rochester Cathedral, 1965–80, now Emeritus; *b* 17 Aug. 1917; *s* of Charles and Ellen Hoffman, Denham, Bucks; *m* 1943, Mary Mifanwy Patricia, *d* of late Canon Creed Meredith, Chaplain to the Queen, and of Mrs R. Creed Meredith, Windsor; one *s* one *d*. *Educ:* The Royal Grammar Sch., High Wycombe, Bucks; St Edmund Hall, Oxford (BA 1939, MA 1943); Lincoln Theol Coll., 1940–41. Deacon, 1941; Priest, 1942; Curate: Windsor Parish Ch., 1941–44; All Saints, Weston, Bath, 1944–47; Chertsey (in charge of All SS), 1947–50; Vicar of Shottermill, Haslemere, Sy, 1951–64; Diocesan Director of Education, Rochester, 1965–80; Warden of Readers, 1974–80. Proctor in Convocation, Church Assembly, 1969–70; Exam. Chaplain to Bp of Rochester, 1973–80. Member: Kent Educn Cttee, 1965–80; Bromley Educn Cttee, 1967–80; Kent Council of Religious Educn, 1965–80; Archbps' Commn on Christian Initiation, 1970. Vice-Chm., Christ Church Coll., Canterbury, 1973–80. Hon. MA Kent, 1982. *Publications:* (pt-author): A Handbook of Thematic Material, 1968; Christians in Kent, 1972; Teaching the Parables, 1974; contrib. various pubns on Preaching and Religious Educn; numerous Dio. study papers. *Recreations:* music, walking (in love with Cornwall). *Address:* Cedarwood, Holly Close, Grayshott Road, Headley Down, Bordon, Hants. *T:* Headley Down (0428) 713128.

HOFFMANN, Hon. Sir Leonard Hubert, Kt 1985; **Hon. Mr Justice Hoffmann;** a Judge of the High Court of Justice, Chancery Division, since 1985; *b* 8 May 1934; *s* of B. W. and G. Hoffmann; *m* 1957, Gillian Lorna Sterner; two *d*. *Educ:* South African College Sch., Cape Town; Univ. of Cape Town (BA); The Queen's Coll., Oxford (Rhodes Scholar; MA, BCL, Vinerian Law Scholar). Advocate of Supreme Court of S Africa, 1958–60. Called to the Bar, Gray's Inn, 1964, Bencher, 1984; QC 1977; a Judge, Courts of Appeal of Jersey and Guernsey, 1980–85. Stowell Civil Law Fellow, University Coll., Oxford, 1961–73. Member: Royal Commn on Gambling, 1976–78; Council of Legal Educn, 1983– (Chm., 1989–). Dir, ENO, 1985–. *Publication:* The South African Law of Evidence, 1963. *Address:* Surrey Lodge, 23 Keats Grove, NW3 2RS.

HOFFMANN, Prof. Roald; John A. Newman Professor of Physical Science, Cornell University, since 1974; *b* 18 July 1937; *s* of Hillel Safran and Clara (*née* Rosen, who *m* 2nd, Paul Hoffmann); *m* 1960, Eva Börjesson; one *s* one *d*. *Educ:* Columbia Univ. (BA); Harvard Univ. (MA, PhD). Junior Fellow, Society of Fellows, Harvard Univ., 1962–65; Associate Professor, to Professor, Cornell Univ., 1965–74. Member: Nat. Acad. of Sciences; Amer. Acad. of Arts and Sciences. Foreign Member: Royal Soc., 1984; Indian Nat. Acad. of Sciences; Royal Swedish Acad. of Sciences; USSR Acad. of Sciences; Finnish Acad. of Sciences. Hon. DTech Royal Inst. of Technology, Stockholm, 1977; Hon. DSc: Yale, 1980; Hartford, 1982; Columbia, 1982; City Univ. of NY, 1983; Puerto Rico, 1983; La Plata, 1984; Uruguay, 1984; State Univ. of NY at Binghamton, 1985; Colgate, 1985. Nobel Prize for Chemistry, 1981. *Publications:* The Conservation of Orbital Symmetry, 1970; The Metamict State (poetry), 1987; Solids and Surfaces, 1988; Gaps and Verges (poetry), 1990; many scientific articles. *Address:* Department of Chemistry, Cornell University, Ithaca, NY 14853, USA.

HOFFMEISTER, Maj.-Gen. Bertram Meryl, OC 1982; CB 1945; CBE 1944; DSO 1943; ED; *b* 15 May 1907; *s* of Flora Elizabeth Rodway and Louis George Hoffmeister; *m* 1935, Donalda Strauss; one *s* one *d*. *Educ:* Public Schs, Vancouver. Previous to war of 1939–45 employed by H. R. MacMillan Export Co. Ltd, Vancouver, BC. 1st Lieut Seaforth Highlanders of Canada, 1927; Capt. 1934; Major 1939 and given command of a rifle Co. Served with Seaforth Highlanders in England as Co. Comdr, 1939–40; returned to Canada, 1942, to attend Canadian Junior War Staff Course; given Command of Seaforth Highlanders of Canada and commanded this Bn in assault on Sicily in July 1943 (DSO); Brig. Oct. 1943 and assumed command 2 Canadian Infantry Brigade (Bar to DSO battle of Ortona); Maj.-Gen. and commanded 5 Cdn Armoured Div. March 1944; operations on Hitler Line, May-June 1944 (2nd Bar to DSO, CBE); in NW Europe until conclusion of hostilities (CB). GOC Canadian Army Pacific Force, 1945. Gen. Manager, Canadian White Pine Co. Ltd, and MacMillan Industries Ltd (Plywood Div.), 1945–47; H. R. MacMillan Export Co. Ltd; Gen. Mgr Prod., 1947–49 and Vice-Pres. Prod., 1949; Pres., 1949–51; MacMillan & Bloedel Ltd; Pres. 1951–56; Chm. Bd, 1956–57. Agent-Gen. for British Columbia, 1958–61. Pres., Council of the Forest Industries of BC, Vancouver, 1961–71. Chm., Nature Trust of BC (formerly Nat. Second Century Fund of BC, 1971–). *Recreations:* rugby, rowing, shooting, skiing. *Address:* 3040 Procter Avenue, West Vancouver, BC V7V 1G1, Canada. *Clubs:* Vancouver, Capilano Golf and Country, Vancouver Rowing (Vancouver).

HOFMEYR, Murray Bernard; Member, Executive Committee, Anglo American Corporation of South Africa Limited, since 1972; Chairman, Johannesburg Consolidated Investment Co. Ltd, since 1987; *b* 9 Dec. 1925; *s* of William and Margareta Hofmeyr; *m* 1953, Johanna Hendrika Hofmeyr (*née* Verdurmen); two *s* two *d*. *Educ:* BA (Rhodes), MA (Oxon). Joined Anglo American Corp., 1962; in Zambia, 1965–72; in England, 1972–80; Man. Dir, 1972–76, Chm. and Man. Dir, 1976–80, Charter Consolidated Ltd. *Recreations:* golf, tennis; Captain Oxford Univ. Cricket, 1951; played Rugby for England, 1950. *Address:* 54 Melville Road, Illovo, Johannesburg, South Africa.

HOGAN, Air Vice-Marshal Henry Algernon Vickers, CB 1955; DFC 1940; retired; *b* 25 Oct. 1909; *s* of late Lt-Col Edward M. A. Hogan, IA; *m* 1939, Margaret Venetia, *d* of late Vice-Adm. W. Tomkinson, CB, MVO; one *s* one *d*. *Educ:* Malvern Coll.; RAF Coll., Cranwell. Commissioned 1930. Served in Fighter Sqdns and Fleet Air Arm; Instructor CFS, 1936–37; Mem. RAF Long Distance Flight (Vickers Wellesleys) to Australia, 1938; commanded No 501 Sqdn throughout Battle of Britain; USA, 1941–43 (Arnold Scheme and RAF Delegation Washington); Asst Comdt, Empire CFS, 1944; commanded No 19 Flying Training Sch., RAF Coll., Cranwell, 1945; Staff Coll., 1946; Air Ministry, 1947–48; SPSO, MEAF, 1949–50; commanded RAF, Wattisham 1951; Air Cdre 1953; Sector Comdr, Northern Sector, 1952–53; AOC No 81 Group, 1954; Air Vice-Marshal, 1956; AOC No 83 Group, 2nd ATAF, Germany, 1955–58; SASO, Flying Training Command, 1958–62. Led RAF Mission to Ghana, 1960, and Joint Services Mission to Ghana, 1961. Regional Dir, Civil Defence (Midland), 1964–68. USA Legion of Merit (Officer), 1945. *Recreation:* country pursuits. *Address:* Sugar Hill, Bickley, near Tenbury Wells, Worcs WR15 8LU. *T:* Newnham Bridge (058479) 432. *Club:* Royal Air Force.

HOGAN, Michael Henry; Member, Gaming Board for Great Britain, since 1986 (Secretary, 1980–86); *b* 31 May 1927; *s* of James Joseph Hogan and Edith Mary Hogan; *m* 1st, 1953, Nina Spillane (*d* 1974); one *s* three *d*; 2nd, 1980, Mollie Burtwell. *Educ:* Ushaw Coll.; LSE. Certif. Social Sci., Certif. Mental Health. Asst Warden, St Vincent's Probation Hostel, 1949–50; London Probation Service, 1953–61; Home Office Inspectorate, 1961–80, Chief Probation Inspector, 1972–80. *Recreation:* golf. *Address:* Yew Tree Cottage, The Street, Capel, Surrey RH5 5LD. *T:* Dorking (0306) 711523.

HOGARTH, (Arthur) Paul, OBE 1989; RA 1984 (ARA 1974); RDI 1979; FRSA 1984; painter, illustrator and draughtsman; *b* Kendal, Cumbria, 4 Oct. 1917; *s* of Arthur Hogarth and Janet Bownass; *m* 1963, one *s*. *Educ:* St Agnes Sch., Manchester; Coll. of Art, Manchester; St Martin's Sch. of Art, London. Travels in: Poland and Czechoslovakia, 1953; USSR and China, 1954; Rhodesia and S Africa, 1956; Ireland, with Brendan Behan, 1959; USA, 1961–79. Senior tutor of Drawing: Cambridge Sch. of Art, 1959–61; RCA, 1964–71; Associate Prof., Philadelphia Coll. of Art, 1968–69; Vis. Lectr, RCA, 1971–. Hon. Pres., Assoc. of Illustrators, 1982. Exhibitions: one-man, Leicester Gall., London, 1955; Agnews, London, 1957; Amer. Embassy, London, 1964; retrospectives, Time-Life Bldg, London, 1968; World of Paul Hogarth, Arts Council, RCA Gall., 1970; Travels through the Seventies, Kyle Gall., London; The Other Hogarth, Northern Arts Council, 1985–86; Cold War Reports: drawings 1947–67, Norfolk Inst. of Art & Design, Eastern Arts Council, 1989–90. Dr RCA, 1971. *Publications:* Defiant People, 1953; Looking at

China, 1956; People Like Us, 1958; (illus.) Brendan Behan's Island, 1962; Creative Pencil Drawing, 1964 (6th edn 1979); (illus.) Brendan Behan's New York, 1964; (with Robert Graves) Majorca Observed, 1965; (with M. Muggeridge) London à la Mode, 1966; Artist as Reporter, 1967, revised and enlarged edn, 1986; (with A. Jacob) Russian Journey, 1969; Drawing People, 1971; Artists on Horseback, 1972; Drawing Architecture, 1973; Paul Hogarth's American Album, 1974; Creative Ink Drawing, 1974 (5th edn 1979); Walking Tours of Old Philadelphia, 1976; Walking Tours of Old Boston, 1978; (with Stephen Spender) America Observed, 1979; Arthur Boyd Houghton, 1982; (with Graham Greene) Graham Greene Country, 1986; (with Laurence Durrell) The Mediterranean Shore, 1988; contrib. Graphis, Arts Rev., Design, Sports Illus., D. Tel. Mag., Illus. London News. *Recreation:* sailing. *Address:* c/o Tessa Sayle, 11 Jubilee Place, SW3 3TE. *T:* 071–352 4311. *Club:* Reform.

HOGARTH, James, CB 1973; Under-Secretary, Scottish Home and Health Department, 1963–74, retired; *b* 14 Aug. 1914; *s* of George Hogarth; *m* 1940, Katherine Mary Cameron; two *s* one *d.* *Educ:* George Watson's, Edinburgh; Edinburgh Univ.; Sorbonne, Paris. Joined Dept of Health for Scotland as Asst Principal, 1938; Principal, 1944; Asst Sec., 1948; Under-Sec., 1963. *Publications:* Payment of the General Practitioner, 1963; translations from French, German, Russian, etc. *Recreation:* travel. *Address:* 6A Crawfurd Road, Edinburgh EH16 5PQ. *T:* 031–667 3878.

HOGARTH, Paul; *see* Hogarth, A. P.

HOGBEN, Ven. Peter Graham; Archdeacon of Dorking, 1982–90, now Archdeacon Emeritus; *b* 5 July 1925; *s* of Harold Henry and Winifred Minnie Hogben; *m* 1948, Audree Sayers; two *s.* *Educ:* Harvey Grammar School, Folkestone; Bishops' College, Cheshunt. Served Royal Engineers, 1943–47 (three years in Far East). Office Manager for two firms of Agricultural Auctioneers in Kent and Herts, 1948–59; theological college, 1960–61; ordained, 1961; Asst Curate of Hale, 1961–64; Vicar of Westborough, Guildford, 1964–71; Chaplain to WRAC, 1964–71; Vicar of Ewell, 1971–82; Editor, Guildford Diocesan Leaflet, 1978–82; Hon. Canon of Guildford, 1979–90, Canon Emeritus, 1990. RD of Epsom, 1980–82. *Recreations:* walking, gardening and photography. *Address:* 3 School Road, Rowledge, Farnham, Surrey GU10 4EJ. *T:* Frensham (025125) 3533.

HOGG, family name of **Hailsham Viscountcy** and of **Baron Hailsham of Saint Marylebone.**

HOGG, Sir Arthur (Ramsay), 7th Bt *cr* 1846; MBE (mil.) 1945; retired; *b* 24 Oct. 1896; *s* of Ernest Charles Hogg (*d* 1907) (*g s* of 1st Bt) and Lucy (*d* 1924), *d* of late William Felton Peel; *S* cousin, Sir Kenneth Weir Hogg, 6th Bt, OBE, 1985; *m* 1924, Mary Aileen Hester Lee (*d* 1980), *d* of late P. H. Lee Evans; three *s* one *d.* *Educ:* Sherborne; Christ Church, Oxford (BA 1921; MA 1929). Served European War, 1914–18 (twice wounded), Captain Royal West Kent Regt; War of 1939–45 (MBE), Major, General List. *Heir: s* Michael David Hogg [*b* 19 Aug. 1925; *m* 1956, Elizabeth Anne Thérèse, *d* of Lt-Col Sir Terence Falkiner, 8th Bt; three *s*]. *Address:* 27 Elgin Road, Bournemouth BH3 7DH.

HOGG, Sir Christopher (Anthony), Kt 1985; Chairman: Courtaulds PLC, since 1980; Courtaulds Textiles PLC, since 1990; Reuters Holdings PLC, since 1985 (Dir, since 1984); *b* 2 Aug. 1936; *s* of Anthony Wentworth Hogg and Monica Mary (*née* Gladwell); *m* 1961, Anne Patricia (*née* Cathie); two *d.* *Educ:* Marlborough Coll.; Trinity Coll., Oxford (MA; Hon. Fellow 1982); Harvard Univ. (MBA). National Service, Parachute Regt, 1955–57. Harkness Fellow, 1960–62; IMEDE, Lausanne, 1962–63; Hill, Samuel Ltd, 1963–66; IRC, 1966–68; Courtaulds PLC, 1968–. Member: Indust. Develt Adv. Bd, 1976–81; Cttee of Award for Harkness Fellowships, 1980–86; Internat. Council, J. P. Morgan, 1988–. Trustee, Ford Foundn, 1987–. Hon. FCSD 1987. Hon. DSc: Cranfield Inst. of Technol., 1986; Aston, 1988. BIM Gold Medal, 1986; Centenary Medal, Soc. of Chemical Industry, 1989. *Publication:* Masers and Lasers, 1963. *Recreations:* theatre, reading, walking. *Address:* 18 Hanover Square, W1A 2BB. *T:* 071–629 9080.

HOGG, Douglas Martin; QC 1990; MP (C) Grantham, since 1979; Minister of State, Foreign and Commonwealth Office, since 1990; *b* 5 Feb. 1945; *er s* of Baron Hailsham of Saint Marylebone, *qv*; *m* 1968, Sarah Boyd-Carpenter (*see* S. E. M. Hogg); one *s* one *d.* *Educ:* Eton (Oppidan Schol.); Christ Church, Oxford (Schol.; Pres., Oxford Union). Called to the Bar, Lincoln's Inn, 1968 (Kennedy Law Schol.). Mem., Agric. Select Cttees, 1979–82; PPS to Chief Sec., HM Treasury, 1982–83; an Asst Govt Whip, 1983–84; Parly Under-Sec. of State, Home Office, 1986–89; Minister of State (Minister for Industry and Enterprise), DTI, 1989–90. *Address:* House of Commons, SW1.

HOGG, Sir Edward William L.; *see* Lindsay-Hogg.

HOGG, Gilbert Charles; Director of Regulatory Operations, British Gas plc, since 1990; *b* 11 Feb. 1933; *s* of Charles and Ivy Ellen Hogg; *m* 1st, Jeanne Whiteside; one *s* one *d*; 2nd, 1979, Angela Christina Wallace. *Educ:* Victoria University Coll., Wellington, NZ (LLB 1956). Called to the New Zealand Bar and admitted Solicitor, 1957; admitted Solicitor, GB, 1971. Served RNZAC (TF), 1955–62 (Lieut). Partner, Phillips, Shayle-George and Co., Solicitors, Wellington, 1960–66; Sen. Crown Counsel, Hong Kong, 1966–70; Editor, Business Law Summary, 1970–72; Divl Legal Adviser, BSC, 1974–79; British Gas Corporation, subseq. British Gas: Dir of Legal Services, 1979–84; Sec., 1984–90. Dir, Port Greenwich Ltd, 1990. Mem. Council, Energy Section, Internat. Bar Assoc., 1990. *Publication:* A Smell of Fraud (novel), 1974. *Address:* Rivermill House, 152 Grosvenor Road, SW1V 3JL. *T:* 071–821 1444. *Club:* Royal Automobile.

HOGG, Vice-Adm. Sir Ian (Leslie Trower), KCB 1968 (CB 1964); DSC 1941, Bar to DSC 1944; *b* 30 May 1911; 3rd *s* of Col John M. T. Hogg, IA, and Elma (*née* Brand); *m* 1945, Mary G. J., *e d* of Col and Mrs Marsden; two *s.* *Educ:* Cheltenham Coll. Entered Royal Navy, 1929; specialised in Navigation, 1937; HMS Cardiff, 1939; HMS Penelope, 1940; HMAS Napier, 1941–43; HMS Mauritius, 1944–45; Master of the Fleet, 1946–47; British Admiralty Delegation, Washington, DC, 1948–49; HMS Sluys, in comd, 1950–51; Staff of C-in-C Med., 1952–53; Captain RN, Dec. 1953; Brit. Joint Staff, Washington, DC, 1955–57; idc 1958; Staff of Chief of Defence Staff, 1959–60; Cdre, Cyprus, 1961–62; Dir, Chief of Defence Staff's Commonwealth Exercise, 1962–63; Rear-Adm. 1963; Flag Officer, Medway, and Admiral Superintendent, HM Dockyard, Chatham, 1963–66; Vice-Adm. 1966; Defence Services Sec., 1966–67; Vice-Chief of the Defence Staff, 1967–70, retired. Comptroller, Royal Soc. of St George, 1971–74; Dir, Richard Unwin Internat. Ltd, 1975–86. FRSA 1971. *Address:* 21 Chapel Side, Titchfield, Hants PO14 4AP. *T:* Titchfield (0329) 47515. *Club:* Naval.

HOGG, Sir John (Nicholson), Kt 1963; TD 1946; Deputy Chairman: Williams & Glyn's Bank Ltd, 1970–83; Gallaher Ltd, 1964–78; Chairman, Banque Française de Crédit International Ltd, 1972–83; *b* 4 Oct. 1912; *o s* of late Sir Malcolm Hogg and of Lorna Beaman; *m* 1948, Barbara Mary Elisabeth, *yr d* of Capt. Arden Franklyn, Shedfield, Southampton and *widow* of Viscount Garmoyle (*d* of wounds, 1942); one *s* one *d.* *Educ:* Eton; Balliol Coll., Oxford. Joined Glyn, Mills and Co., 1934. Served War of 1939–45, with KRRC in Greece, Crete, Western Desert, Tunisia, NW Europe. Rejoined Glyn, Mills and Co. 1945, a Man. Dir., 1950–70, Dep. Chm. 1963–68, Chm. 1968–70; Director: Royal Bank of Scotland Gp Ltd, 1969–82; Prudential Corp. Ltd, 1964–85. Fellow of Eton Coll., 1951–70. Mem. of Commonwealth War Graves Commission, 1958–64; A Trustee Imperial War Graves Endowment Fund, 1965–87. Sheriff County of London, 1960; Chm., Export Credits Guarantee Department's Adv. Council, 1962–67. Chm., Abu Dhabi Investment Bd, 1967–75. Hon. Treasurer, Inst. of Child Health, 1974–87 (Hon. Fellow 1987). *Recreations:* cricket, tennis, fishing. *Address:* The Red House, Shedfield, Southampton SO3 2HN. *T:* Wickham (0329) 832121. *Club:* Brooks's.

HOGG, Hon. Mary Claire, (Hon. Mrs Koops); QC 1989; a Recorder, since 1990; *b* 15 Jan. 1947; *d* of Rt Hon. Baron Hailsham of St Marylebone, *qv*; *m* 1987, Eric Koops; one *d.* *Educ:* St Paul's Girls' Sch. Called to the Bar, Lincoln's Inn, 1968; Asst Recorder, 1986–90. Mem. Council, Children's Soc., 1990–; Trustee, Harrison Homes, 1986–. Governor, Polytechnic of Central London, 1983–. Freeman, City of London, 1981. *Address:* 1 Mitre Court Buildings, Temple, EC4Y 7BS.

HOGG, Norman; MP (Lab) Cumbernauld and Kilsyth, since 1983 (Dunbartonshire East, 1979–83); *b* 12 March 1938; *s* of late Norman Hogg, CBE, LLD, DL, JP, and of Mary Wilson; *m* 1964, Elizabeth McCall Christie. *Educ:* Causewayend Sch., Aberdeen; Ruthrieston Secondary Sch., Aberdeen. Local Government Officer, Aberdeen Town Council, 1953–67; District Officer, National and Local Govt Officers Assoc., 1967–79. Select Cttee on Scottish Affairs, 1979–82; Scottish Labour Whip, 1982–83; Chm., Scottish Parly Lab Gp, 1981–82; Dep. Chief Opposition Whip, 1983–87; Scottish Affairs spokesman, 1987–88; Mem., Chairman's Panel, 1988–; Public Accounts Cttee, 1991–. *Recreation:* music. *Address:* House of Commons, SW1A 0AA. *T:* 071–219 5095.

HOGG, Rear-Adm. Peter Beauchamp, CB 1980; Head of British Defence Liaison Staff and Defence Adviser, Canberra, 1977–80, retired; *b* 9 Nov. 1924; *s* of Beauchamp and Sybil Hogg; *m* 1951, Gabriel Argentine Alington; two *s* two *d.* *Educ:* Connaught House, Weymouth; Bradfield Coll., Berks; Royal Naval Engineering Coll., Keyham. Lieut, HMS Sirius, 1947–49; Advanced Engrg Course, RNC Greenwich, 1949–51; HMS Swiftsure and HMS Pincher, 1951–53; Lt Comdr, Loan Service with Royal Canadian Navy, 1953–56; Staff of RN Engrg Coll., Manadon, 1956–58; Comdr (Trng Comdr), HMS Sultan, 1959–62; Marine Engr Officer, HMS Hampshire, 1962–64; JSSC, Latimer, 1964; Ship Dept, Bath, 1965–67; Captain, Ship Dept, Bath, 1968–69; CO, HMS Tyne, 1970–71; RCDS, 1972; CO, HMS Caledonia, 1973–74; Dir of Naval Recruiting, 1974–76. Sec., Sixth Centenary Appeal, and Bursar i/c building works, Winchester Coll., 1980–88. *Address:* Common Hill Farm, Fownhope, Hereford HR1 4PZ.

HOGG, Rear-Adm. Robin Ivor Trower, CB 1988; FNI, FBIM; consultant and adviser; Managing Director, Raidfleet Ltd, since 1988; Chief Executive Officer, Colebrand Ltd, since 1988; *b* 25 Sept. 1932; *s* of Dudley and Nancy Hogg; *m* 1st, 1958, Susan Bridget Beryl Grantham; two *s* two *d*; 2nd, 1970, Angela Sarah Patricia Kirwan. *Educ:* The New Beacon, Sevenoaks; Bedford School. Directorate of Naval Plans, 1974–76; RCDS 1977; Captain RN Presentation Team, 1978–79; Captain First Frigate Sqdn, 1980–82; Director Naval Operational Requirements, 1982–84; Flag Officer, First Flotilla, 1984–86; COS to C-in-C Fleet, 1986–87, retd. *Recreation:* private life. *Address:* c/o Coutts & Co., Chandos Branch, 440 Strand, WC2R 0QS. *T:* 071–379 6262.

HOGG, Sarah Elizabeth Mary; Head of Prime Minister's Policy Unit, since 1990; *b* 14 May 1946; *d* of Baron Boyd-Carpenter, *qv*; *m* 1968, Douglas Martin Hogg, *qv*; one *s* one *d.* *Educ:* St Mary's Convent, Ascot; Lady Margaret Hall, Oxford University. 1st Cl. Hons PPE. Staff writer, Economist, 1967, Literary Editor, 1970, Economics Editor, 1977; Economics Editor, Sunday Times, 1981; Presenter, Channel 4 News, 1982–83; Econs Editor, and Dep. Exec. Editor, Finance and Industry, The Times, 1984–86; Asst Editor, and Business and City Editor, The Independent, 1986–89; Econs Editor, Daily Telegraph and Sunday Telegraph, 1989–90. Director: London Broadcasting Co., 1982–90; Royal Nat. Theatre, 1988–91; Governor: Centre for Economic Policy Research, 1985–; IDS, 1987. Hon. MA Open Univ., 1987. Wincott Foundation Financial Journalist of the Year, 1985. *Address:* c/o 10 Downing Street, SW1A 2AA.
See also Hon. T. P. J. Boyd-Carpenter.

HOGGART, Richard, LittD; Warden, Goldsmiths' College, University of London, 1976–84; *b* 24 Sept. 1918; 2nd *s* of Tom Longfellow Hoggart and Adeline Emma Hoggart; *m* 1942, Mary Holt France; two *s* one *d.* *Educ:* elementary and secondary schs, Leeds; Leeds Univ. (MA, LittD 1978). Served 1940–46, RA; demobilised as Staff Capt. Staff Tutor and Sen. Staff Tutor, University Coll. of Hull and University of Hull, 1946–59; Sen. Lectr in English, University of Leicester, 1959–62; Prof. of English, Birmingham Univ., 1962–73, and Dir, Centre for Contemporary Cultural Studies, 1964–73; an Asst Dir-Gen., Unesco, 1970–75. Vis. Fellow, Inst. of Development Studies, Univ. of Sussex, 1975. Visiting Prof., University of Rochester (NY), USA, 1956–57; Reith Lectr, 1971. Member: Albemarle Cttee on Youth Services, 1958–60; (Pilkington) Cttee on Broadcasting, 1960–62; Arts Council, 1976–81 (Chm., Drama Panel, 1977–80; Vice-Chm., 1980–82); Statesman and Nation Publishing Co. Ltd, 1977–81 (Chm., 1978–81); Chairman: Adv. Council for Adult and Continuing Educn, 1977–83; European Museum of the Year Award, 1977–; Broadcasting Research Unit, 1981–91. Governor, Royal Shakespeare Theatre, 1962–88. Pres., British Assoc. of Former UN Civil Servants, 1979–86. Hon. Professor: UEA, 1984; Univ. of Surrey, 1985; Hon. Fellow: Sheffield Polytechnic, 1983; Goldsmiths' Coll., 1987; DUniv: Open, 1973; Surrey, 1981; Hon DèsL: Univ. of Bordeaux, 1975; Paris, 1987; Hon. LLD: CNAA, 1982; York (Toronto), 1988; Hon. LittD: East Anglia, 1986; Leicester, 1988; Hull, 1988. *Publications:* Auden, 1951; The Uses of Literacy, 1957; W. H. Auden, 1957; W. H. Auden—A Selection, 1961; chap. in Conviction, 1958; chapter in Pelican Guide to English Literature, 1961; Teaching Literature, 1963; chapter in Of Books and Humankind, 1964; The Critical Moment, 1964; How and Why Do We Learn, 1965; The World in 1984, 1965; Essays by Divers Hands XXXIII; Guide to the Social Sciences, 1966; Technology and Society, 1966; Essays on Reform, 1967; Your Sunday Paper (ed), 1967; Speaking to Each Other: vol. I, About Society; vol. II, About Literature, 1970; Only Connect (Reith Lectures), 1972; An Idea and Its Servants, 1978; (ed with Janet Morgan) The Future of Broadcasting, 1982; An English Temper, 1982; Writers on Writing, 1986; (jtly) The British Council and The Arts, 1986; (with Douglas Johnson) An Idea of Europe, 1987; A Local Habitation (autobiog.), 1988; (ed) Liberty and Legislation, 1989; A Sort of Clowning: life and times 1940–59 (autobiog.), 1990; numerous introductions, articles, pamphlets and reviews. *Recreation:* pottering about the house and garden. *Address:* Mortonsfield, Beavers Hill, Farnham, Surrey.
See also S. D. Hoggart.

HOGGART, Simon David; Reporter, The Observer, since 1981; *b* 26 May 1946; *s* of Richard Hoggart, *qv*; *m* 1983, Alyson Clare Corner; one *s* one *d.* *Educ:* Hymer's College, Hull; Wyggeston Grammar Sch., Leicester; King's College, Cambridge. MA. Reporter, The Guardian, 1968–71, N Ireland corresp., 1971–73, political corresp., 1973–81; feature writer, The Observer, 1981–85; political columnist, Punch, 1979–85; US correspondent, The Observer, 1985–89. *Publications:* The Pact (with Alistair Michie), 1978; Michael

Foot: a portrait (with David Leigh), 1981; On the House, 1981; Back on the House, 1982; House of Ill Fame, 1985; (ed) House of Cards, 1988; America: a user's guide, 1990. *Recreations:* reading, writing. *Address:* The Observer, Queenstown Road, SW8 4NN. *T:* 071–627 0700.

HOGGE, Maj.-Gen. (Arthur) Michael (Lancelot), CB 1979; *b* 4 Aug. 1925; *s* of late Lt-Col A. H. F. Hogge, Punjab Regt, Indian Army, and Mrs K. M. Hogge; *m* 1952, Gunilla Jeane Earley; two *s. Educ:* Wellington Coll.; Brasenose Coll., Oxford (war-time course). Commissioned, Oct. 1945; 6th Airborne Armoured Recce Regt and 3rd Hussars, Palestine, 1945–48; regimental appts, 3rd Hussars, BAOR, 1948–58; Queen's Own Hussars, BAOR, and Staff appts, 1958–65; comd Queen's Own Hussars, UK and Aden, 1965–67; Col GS, Staff Coll., 1969–71; Royal Coll. of Defence Studies, 1972; Dir of Operational Requirements, MoD, 1973–74, rank of Brig.; Dir Gen. Fighting Vehicles and Engineer Equipment, 1974–77; Dep. Master-General of the Ordnance, 1977–80; Gen. Man., Regular Forces Employment Assoc., 1981–87. *Recreations:* sailing, horticulture.

HOGGETT, Anthony John Christopher, PhD; QC 1986; a Recorder, since 1988; *b* 20 Aug. 1940; *s* of late Christopher Hoggett and of Annie Marie Hoggett; *m* 1968, Brenda Marjorie Hale (*see* B. M. Hoggett); one *d. Educ:* Leeds Grammar Sch.; Hymers Coll., Hull; Clare Coll., Cambridge (MA, LLB); PhD Manchester. Asst Juridique, Inst. of Comparative Law, Paris, 1962–63; Lectr in Law, Univ. of Manchester, 1963–69; called to Bar, Gray's Inn, 1969, Head of Chambers, 1985; Asst Recorder, 1982. Res. Fellow, Univ. of Michigan, 1965–66. Mem., Civil Service Final Selection Bd for Planning Inspectors, 1987–. *Publications:* articles in Criminal Law Rev., Mod. Law Rev. and others. *Recreations:* swimming, music, walking. *Address:* Flat 29, Chepstow House, Chepstow Street, Manchester M1 5JF. *T:* 061–236 7973.

HOGGETT, Prof. Brenda Marjorie; QC 1989; Law Commissioner, since 1984; Visiting Professor, King's College, London, since 1990; a Recorder, since 1989; *b* 31 Jan. 1945; *d* of Cecil Frederick Hale and Marjorie Hale (*née* Godfrey); *m* 1968, Anthony John Christopher Hoggett, *qv*; one *d. Educ:* Richmond High School for Girls, Yorks; Girton College, Cambridge. MA. Called to the Bar, Gray's Inn, 1969; University of Manchester: Asst Lectr in Law, 1966; Lectr, 1968; Sen. Lectr, 1976; Reader, 1981; Prof., 1986–89. Barrister, Northern Circuit, 1969–72; Legal Mem., Mental Health Review Tribunal for NW Region, 1979–80; Member: Council on Tribunals, 1980–84; Civil and Family Cttee, Judicial Studies Bd, 1990–; Human Fertilisation and Embryology Authy, 1990–. Chm., Nat. Family Conciliation Council, 1989–; Man. Trustee, Nuffield Foundn, 1987–; Governor, Centre for Policy on Ageing, 1990–. Editor, Jl of Social Welfare Law, 1978–84. Hon. LLD Sheffield, 1989. *Publications:* Mental Health Law, 1976, 3rd edn 1990; Parents and Children, 1977, 3rd edn 1987; (with D. S. Pearl) The Family Law and Society: Cases and Materials, 1983, 2nd edn 1987; (with S. Atkins) Women and the Law, 1984; contribs to legal periodicals and other texts. *Recreations:* domesticity and drama. *Address:* Law Commission, Conquest House, 37/38 John Street, WC1N 2BQ. *T:* 071–242 0861.

HOGWOOD, Christopher Jarvis Haley, CBE 1989; harpsichordist, conductor, musicologist, writer, editor and broadcaster; Founder and Director, Academy of Ancient Music, since 1973; *b* 10 Sept. 1941; *s* of Haley Evelyn Hogwood and Marion Constance Higgott. *Educ:* Pembroke Coll., Cambridge (MA); Charles Univ., Prague. Keyboard and orchestral recordings. Editor of books and music. Artistic Director: King's Lynn Festival, 1976–80; Handel and Haydn Soc., Boston, USA, 1986–; Dir of Music, St Paul Chamber Orchestra, USA, 1987–. Hon. Prof. of Music, Keele Univ., 1986–90; Hon. Fellow, Jesus Coll., Cambridge, 1989–. FRSA 1982. Freeman, Co. of Musicians, 1989. Walter Willson Cobbett Medal, Co. of Musicians, 1986. *Publications:* Music at Court (Folio Society), 1977; The Trio Sonata, 1979; Haydn's Visits to England (Folio Society), 1980; (ed with R. Luckett) Music in Eighteenth-Century England, 1983; Handel, 1984. *Address:* 10 Brookside, Cambridge. *T:* Cambridge (0223) 63975.

HOHLER, Henry Arthur Frederick, CMG 1954; HM Diplomatic Service, retired; Ambassador to Switzerland 1967–70; *b* 4 Feb. 1911; *e s* of late Lt-Col Arthur Preston Hohler, DSO; *m* 1st, 1932, Mona Valentine (*d* 1944), *d* of late Lieut-Col Arthur Murray Pirie, DSO; two *s*; 2nd, 1945, Eveline Susan, *d* of late Lieut-Col Hon. Neville Albert Hood, CMG, DSO; two *d. Educ:* Eton; Sandhurst. 2nd Lieut Grenadier Guards, 1931. 3rd Sec. in Foreign Office, 1934; Budapest, 1936; 2nd Sec., 1939; Foreign Office, 1941; 1st Sec., 1945; Berne, 1945; Helsinki, 1948; Moscow, 1949; Counsellor, 1950; Head of Northern Dept, Foreign Office, 1951; Minister in Rome, 1956–60; Ambassador in Saigon, 1960–63; Minister in Paris, 1963–65; Asst Under-Sec., Foreign Office, 1966–67. Liveryman, Grocers' Company. *Address:* RR4, Box 1650, Gloucester, Va 23061, USA. *Clubs:* Boodle's; Metropolitan (Washington).

HOLBOROW, Eric John, MD, FRCP, FRCPath; Emeritus Professor of Immunopathology and Honorary Consultant Immunologist, London Hospital Medical College, E1, retired 1983; *b* 30 March 1918; *s* of Albert Edward Ratcliffe Holborow and Marian Crutchley; *m* 1943, Cicely Mary Foister; two *s* one *d. Educ:* Epsom Coll.; Clare Coll., Cambridge; St Bart's Hosp. MA, MD (Cantab). Served War of 1939–45, Major, RAMC. Consultant Bacteriologist, Canadian Hosp., Taplow, 1953; Mem. Scientific Staff, MRC Rheumatism Unit, Taplow, 1957; Director, 1975; Head, MRC Group, Bone and Joint Res. Group, London Hosp. Med. Coll., 1976–83. Visiting Prof., Royal Free Hosp. Med. Sch., 1975. Bradshaw Lectr, RCP, 1982. Chm., Smith Kline Foundn, 1987–89 (Trustee, 1977–89). Editor, Jl Immunol. Methods, 1971–85. *Publications:* Autoimmunity and Disease (with L. E. Glynn), 1965; An ABC of Modern Immunology, 1968, 2nd edn 1973; (with W. G. Reeves) Immunology in Medicine, 1977, 2nd edn 1983; (with A. Maroudas) Studies in Joint Disease, vol. 1, 1981, vol. 2, 1983; books and papers on immunology. *Recreations:* glebe terriers, ecclesiastical records.

HOLBOROW, Prof. Leslie Charles, MA; Vice-Chancellor, Victoria University of Wellington, since 1985; *b* 28 Jan. 1941; *s* of George and Ivah Vivienne Holborrow; *m* 1965, Patricia Lynette Walsh; one *s* two *d. Educ:* Henderson High Sch.; Auckland Grammar Sch.; Univ. of Auckland (MA 1st Cl. Hons Philosophy); Oxford Univ. (BPhil). Jun. Lectr, Auckland Univ., 1963; Commonwealth schol. at Merton Coll., Coll., Oxford, 1963–65; Lectr, then Sen. Lectr, Univ. of Dundee (until 1967 Queen's Coll., Univ. of St Andrews), 1965–74, Mem. Court, 1972–74; University of Queensland, Brisbane: Prof. of Philosophy, 1974–85; Pres., Academic Bd, 1980–81; Pro-Vice-Chancellor (Humanities), 1983–85. Pres., Qld Br., Ausdt. Inst. of Internat. Affairs, 1984–85; Nat. Pres., NZ Inst. of Internat. Affairs, 1987–90; Member: NZ Cttee for Pacific Economic Co-operation, 1986–; Bd, NZ Inst. of Econ. Res., 1986–. Chair, NZ Vice-Chancellors' Cttee, 1990; Council, ACU, 1990–91. Member: Musica Viva Nat. Bd, 1984–85; Bd of Management, Music Fedn of NZ, 1987–90. Trustee, NZ String Quartet, 1990–. *Publications:* various articles in philosophical and legal jls. *Recreations:* tramping, listening to music. *Address:* 11 Kinross Street, Wellington, New Zealand. *Clubs:* Wellington, Victoria University Staff (Wellington).

HOLBROOK, David Kenneth, MA; author; *b* 9 Jan. 1923; *o s* of late Kenneth Redvers and late Elsie Eleanor Holbrook; *m* 1949, Margot Davies-Jones; two *s* two *d. Educ:* City of Norwich Sch.; Downing Coll., Cambridge (Exhibr). Intell., mines and explosives officer, ER Yorks Yeo., Armd Corps, 1942–45. Asst Editor, Our Time, 1948; Asst Editor, Bureau of Current Affairs, 1949; Tutor organiser, WEA, 1952–53; Tutor, Bassingbourn Village Coll., Cambs, 1954–61; Fellow, King's Coll., Cambridge, 1961–65; Sen. Leverhulme Res. Fellow, 1965; College Lectr in English, Jesus Coll., Cambridge, 1968–70; Compton Poetry Lectr, Hull Univ., 1969 (resigned); Writer in Residence, Dartington Hall, 1970–73 (grant from Elmgrant Trust); Downing Coll., Cambridge: Asst Dir, English Studies, 1973–75; Fellow and Dir of English Studies, 1981–88, Emeritus Fellow, 1988; Leverhulme Emeritus Res. Fellow, 1988–90. Hooker Distinguished Vis. Prof., McMaster Univ., Ontario, 1984. Arts Council Writers Grants, 1970, 1976, 1979. Pres., Forum for the Advancement of Educnl Therapy, 1988–. Mem. Editorial Bd, New Universities Qly, 1976–86. *Publications: poetry:* Imaginings, 1961; Against the Cruel Frost, 1963; Object Relations, 1967; Old World, New World, 1969; Moments in Italy, 1976; Chance of a Lifetime, 1978; Selected Poems, 1980; *fiction:* Lights in the Sky Country, 1963; Flesh Wounds, 1966; A Play of Passion, 1978; Nothing Larger than Life, 1987; Worlds Apart, 1988; A Little Athens, 1990; Jennifer, 1991; The Gold in Father's Heart, 1991; Even If They Fail, 1991; *on education:* English for Maturity, 1961; English for the Rejected, 1964; The Secret Places, 1964; The Exploring Word, 1967; Children's Writing, 1967; English in Australia Now, 1972; Education, Nihilism and Survival, 1977; English for Meaning, 1980; Education and Philosophical Anthropology, 1987; Further Studies in Philosophical Anthropology, 1988; *literary criticism:* Llareggub Revisited, 1962; The Quest for Love, 1965; The Masks of Hate, 1972; Dylan Thomas: the code of night, 1972; Sylvia Plath: poetry and existence, 1976; Lost Bearings in English Poetry, 1977; The Novel and Authenticity, 1987; Images of Woman in Literature, 1989; The Skeleton in the Wardrobe: the fantasies of C. S. Lewis, 1991; Edith Wharton and the Unsatisfactory Man, 1991; Charles Dickens and Woman, 1991; Where D. H. Lawrence was Wrong about Woman, 1991; Wuthering Heights: far beyond realism, 1992; Creativity and Popular Culture, 1992; *music criticism:* Gustav Mahler and the Courage to Be, 1975; *general:* Children's Games, 1957; Human Hope and the Death Instinct, 1971; Sex and Dehumanization, 1972; The Pseudo-revolution, 1972; (ed) The Case Against Pornography, 1972; Evolution and the Humanities, 1987; (ed) What is it to be Human?: report on a philosophy conference, 1990; *anthologies:* edited: Iron, Honey, Gold, 1961; People and Diamonds, 1962; Thieves and Angels, 1963; Visions of Life, 1964; (with Elizabeth Poston) The Cambridge Hymnal, 1967; Plucking the Rushes, 1968; (with Christine Mackenzie) The Honey of Man, 1975; *opera libretti:* (with Wilfrid Mellers) The Borderline, 1958; (with John Joubert) The Quarry, 1967. *Recreations:* painting, cooking, gardening. *Address:* Denmore Lodge, Brunswick Gardens, Cambridge CB5 8DQ. *T:* Cambridge (0223) 315081.

HOLCROFT, Sir Peter (George Culcheth), 3rd Bt *cr* 1921; JP; *b* 29 April 1931; *s* of Sir Reginald Culcheth Holcroft, 2nd Bt, TD, and Mary Frances (*d* 1963), *yr d* of late William Swire, CBE; *S* father, 1978; *m* 1956, Rosemary Rachel (marr. diss. 1987), *yr d* of late G. N. Deas; three *s* one *d. Educ:* Eton. High Sheriff of Shropshire, 1969; JP 1976. *Recreation:* the countryside. *Heir: s* Charles Antony Culcheth Holcroft [*b* 22 Oct. 1959; *m* 1986, Mrs Elizabeth Carter, *y d* of John Raper, Powys; one *d*]. *Address:* Berrington House, Berrington, Shrewsbury.

HOLDEN, Anthony Ivan; author and journalist; *b* 22 May 1947; *s* of late John Holden and Margaret Lois Holden (*née* Sharpe); *m* 1st, 1971, Amanda Juliet (marr. diss. 1988), *d* of Sir Brian Warren, *qv*, and Dame Josephine Barnes, *qv*; three *s*; 2nd, 1990, Cynthia Blake, *d* of Mrs George Blake, Brookline, Mass. *Educ:* Tre-Arddur House Sch., Anglesey; Oundle Sch.; Merton Coll., Oxford (MA Hons Eng. Lang. and Lit.; Editor, Isis). Trainee reporter, Thomson Regional Newspapers, Evening Echo, Hemel Hempstead, 1970–73; home and foreign corresp., Sunday Times, 1973–77; columnist (Atticus), Sunday Times, 1977–79; Washington corresp. and chief US corresp., Observer, 1979–81; columnist, Punch, 1979–81; Features Editor and Asst Editor, The Times, 1981–82; freelance journalist, 1982–85 and 1986–; Exec. Editor, Today, 1985–86. Broadcaster, radio and TV. Young Journalist of 1972; commended for work in NI, News Reporter of the Year, British Press Awards, 1976; Columnist of the Year, British Press Awards, 1977. Opera translations (with Amanda Holden): Don Giovanni, 1985; La Bohème, 1986; The Barber of Seville, 1987. *Publications:* (trans. and ed) Aeschylus' Agamemnon, 1969; (contrib.) The Greek Anthology, 1973; (trans. and ed) Greek Pastoral Poetry, 1974; The St Albans Poisoner, 1974; Charles, Prince of Wales, 1979; Their Royal Highnesses, 1981; Of Presidents, Prime Ministers and Princes, 1984; The Queen Mother, 1985, 2nd edn 1990; Don Giovanni, 1987; Olivier, 1988; Charles, 1988; Big Deal, 1990; A Princely Marriage, 1991. *Recreations:* poker, Arsenal FC, Lancashire CC. *Address:* c/o A. P. Watt, 20 John Street, WC1N 2DL. *T:* 071–405 6774. *Clubs:* Barracuda, Victoria Casino.

HOLDEN, Basil Munroe; Rector, Glasgow Academy, 1959–75, retired; *b* 10 Nov. 1913; *m* 1951, Jean Watters; two *s* two *d. Educ:* Queen Elizabeth's Grammar Sch., Blackburn; King's Coll., Cambridge (Foundation Scholar). BA 1935, Maths Tripos (Wrangler), MA 1939. Mathematical Master, Highgate Sch., 1937. Instructor Lieut RN, 1940. Head of Mathematical Dept, Oundle Sch., 1947; Housemaster, Oundle Sch., 1956. *Address:* Orchard House, Blennerhasset, Carlisle, Cumbria CA5 3QX. *T:* Kirkbride (0697) 320735.

HOLDEN, Sir David (Charles Beresford), KBE 1972; CB 1963; ERD 1954; *b* 26 July 1915; *s* of Oswald Addenbrooke Holden and Ella Mary Beresford; *m* 1948, Elizabeth Jean Odling; one *s* one *d. Educ:* Rossall Sch.; King's Coll., Cambridge. Northern Ireland Civil Service, 1937–76; Permanent Sec., Dept of Finance, NI, and Head of NI Civil Service, 1970–76; Dir, Ulster Office, 1976–77. Royal Artillery, 1939–46. *Address:* Falcons, Wilsford Cum Lake, Amesbury, Salisbury SP4 7BL. *T:* Amesbury (0980) 622493.

HOLDEN, Derek; His Honour Judge Holden; a Circuit Judge, since 1984; *b* 7 July 1935; *s* of Frederic Holden and Audrey Holden (*née* Hayes); *m* 1961, Dorien Elizabeth Holden (*née* Bell); two *s. Educ:* Cromwell House, Staines Grammar Sch. Served Army; Lieut East Surrey Regt, 1953–56. Qualified as Solicitor, 1966; Derek Holden & Co., Staines, Egham, Camberley, Feltham and Ashford, 1966–84; Consultant, Batt Holden & Co., 1966–84. Partner: Dorien Property & Investment Co., 1970–84; Leisure Hire, 1974–79; Black Lake Securities, 1979–84; Dorien Leasing, 1979–84; a Recorder, 1980–84. President: Social Security Appeal Tribunals and Medical Appeal Tribunals, 1990–; Vaccine Damage Tribunals; Chm., Tribunals Cttee, Judicial Studies Bd, 1990–. Mem., Royal Yachting Assoc., 1975– (Dept of Trade Yachtmaster, Instr and Ocean certs). Principal, Chandor Sch. of Sailing, Lymington, 1978–85. President: Staines Amateur Regatta, 1980–; Staines Boat Club, 1984–. *Recreations:* sailing, ski-ing, photography. *Address:* Clements House, Gresham Street, EC2V 7DN. *T:* 071–606 2106. *Clubs:* Law Society; Western (Glasgow); Ski Club of Great Britain; Leander, Remenham (Henley); Burway Rowing (Laleham); Eton Excelsior Rowing (Windsor); Staines Boat; Royal Solent Yacht (Yarmouth, IoW); Queen Mary Sailing (Ashford); Westerly Association; Sonata Association.

HOLDEN, Sir Edward, 6th Bt, *cr* 1893; Consultant Anæsthetist, Darlington & Northallerton Group Hospitals, 1957–74; *b* 8 Oct. 1916; *s* of Sir Isaac Holden Holden, 5th Bt, and Alice Edna Byrom (*d* 1971); *S* father, 1962; *m* 1942, Frances Joan, *e d* of John

Spark, JP, Ludlow, Stockton-on-Tees; two adopted *s. Educ:* Leys Sch. and Christ's Coll., Cambridge (MA); St Thomas's Hosp. MRCS; LRCP 1942; DA Eng., 1946; FFA, RCS, 1958. Formerly Vis. Anæsth., Cumb. Infirm., Carlisle; Cons. Anæsth. W Cumb. Hospital Group. Mem. Council, Harlow Car Gardens. *Recreations:* fishing and gardening. *Heir: b* Paul Holden [*b* 3 March 1923; *m* 1950, Vivien Mary Oldham; one *s* two *d*]. *Address:* Moorstones, Osmotherley, Northallerton, N Yorks DL6 3BG. *Club:* Farmers'.

HOLDEN, Sir John David, 4th Bt *cr* 1919; *b* 16 Dec. 1967; *s* of David George Holden (*d* 1971) (*e s* of 3rd Bt), and of Nancy, *d* of H. W. D. Marwood, Foulrice, Whenby, Brandsby, Yorks; *S* grandfather, 1976; *m* 1987, Suzanne Cummings; one *d. Heir: uncle* Brian Peter John Holden [*b* 12 April 1944; *m* 1984, Bernadette Anne Lopez, *d* of George Gerard O'Malley].

HOLDEN, Maj.-Gen. John Reid, CB 1965; CBE 1960 (OBE 1953); DSO 1941; *b* 8 Jan. 1913; *s* of late John Holden, MA, Edinburgh; *m* 1939, Rosemarie Florence (*d* 1980), *d* of late William Henry de Vere Pennefather, Carlow; one *d. Educ:* Hamilton Academy; Glasgow Univ.; RMC, Sandhurst. 2nd Lieut Royal Tank Corps, 1937; Adjutant, 7th Royal Tank Regt, 1940–41 (despatches, DSO); Bde Major, 32nd Army Tank Bde, 1942; POW, 1942–45. GSO1, GHQ, Far ELF, Singapore, 1951–52 (OBE); CO 3rd Royal Tank Regt, BAOR, 1954–57; AAG, War Office, 1958. Comdr, 7th Armoured Bde Group, BAOR, 1958–61 (CBE). Royal Naval War Coll., 1961. Chief of Mission, British Comdrs-in-Chief Mission to the Soviet Forces in Germany, 1961–63; GOC 43 (Wessex) Div. Dist, 1963–65; Dir, RAC, 1965–68, retired 1968. Col Comdt, RTR, 1965–68. Hon. Col, The Queen's Own Lowland Yeomanry, RAC, T&AVR, 1972–75. *Recreations:* books, birds. *Address:* c/o Royal Bank of Scotland, Kirkland House, Whitehall, SW1A 2EB.

HOLDEN, Patrick Brian, MA, FCIS; Chairman: Steak Away Foods Ltd, since 1982; Holden Homes (Southern) Ltd, since 1984; *b* 16 June 1937; *s* of Reginald John and Winifred Isabel Holden; *m* 1972, Jennifer Ruth (*née* Meddings), MB, BS. *Educ:* Allhallows Sch. (Major Schol.); St Catharine's Coll., Cambridge (BA Hons Law 1960, MA 1963). FCIS 1965. Served Royal Hampshire Regt, 1955–57 regular commn), seconded 1 Ghana Regt, RWAFF. Fine Fare Group: Sec., 1960–69; Legal and Property Dir, 1965–69; Pye of Cambridge Gp, 1969–74; Dir, Pye Telecom. Ltd, 1972–74; Dir and Sec., Oriel Foods Gp, 1975–81; Gp Sec., Fisons plc, 1981–83. Sec., New Town Assoc., 1974–75. FBIM. *Recreations:* bridge, walking. *Address:* The Old School House, Lower Green, Tewin, Herts AL6 0LD. *T:* Tewin (043871) 7573. *Club:* Naval and Military.

HOLDEN-BROWN, Sir Derrick, Kt 1979; Chairman, Allied-Lyons PLC, 1982–91 (Chief Executive, 1982–88); Director, Allied Breweries, 1967–91 (Chairman, 1982–86); *b* 14 Feb. 1923; *s* of Harold Walter and Beatrice Florence (*née* Walker); *m* 1950, Patricia Mary Ross Mackenzie; one *s* one *d. Educ:* Westcliff. Mem., Inst of Chartered Accountants of Scotland. Served War, Royal Navy, 1941–46, Lt RNVR, Coastal Forces. Chartered Accountant, 1948; Hiram Walker & Sons, Distillers, 1949; Managing Director: Cairnes Ltd, Brewers, Eire, 1954; Grants of St James's Ltd, 1960; Dir, Ind Coope Ltd, 1962; Chm., Victoria Wine Co., 1964; Finance Dir, 1972, Vice-Chm., 1975–82, Allied Breweries; Director: Sun Alliance & London Insurance plc, 1977– (Vice Chm., 1983, Dep. Chm., 1985–92); Midland Bank, 1984–88. Chm., FDIC, 1984–85 (Dep. Chm. 1974–76). President: Food and Drink Fedn, 1985–86; Food Manufacturers' Fedn Inc., 1985. Chairman: Brewers' Soc., 1978–80 (Master, Brewers' Co., 1987–88); White Ensign Assoc., 1987–90; Portsmouth Naval Heritage Trust, 1989–. *Recreations:* sailing, offshore cruising. *Address:* Copse House, Milford-on-Sea, Lymington, Hants. *T:* Lymington (0590) 642247. *Clubs:* Boodle's; Royal Yacht Squadron; Royal Lymington Yacht; Royal Canadian Yacht.

HOLDER, Sir (John) Henry, 4th Bt *cr* 1898, of Pitmaston, Moseley, Worcs; Production Director and Head Brewer, Elgood & Sons Ltd, North Brink Brewery, Wisbech, since 1975; *b* 12 March 1928; *s* of Sir John Eric Duncan Holder, 3rd Bt and of Evelyn Josephine, *er d* of late William Blain; *S* father, 1986; *m* 1960, Catharine Harrison, *yr d* of late Leonard Baker; twin *s* one *d. Educ:* Eton Coll.; Birmingham Univ. (Dip. Malting and Brewing); Dip. in Safety Management, British Safety Council. Diploma Mem., Inst. of Brewing. National Service, RAC; commnd 5th Royal Tank Regt, 1947. Shift Brewer, Mitchells & Butlers Ltd, 1951–53; Brewer, Reffels Bexley Brewery Ltd, 1953–56; Asst Manager, Unique Slide Rule Co., 1956–62; Brewer, Rhymney Brewery Co. Ltd, 1962–75. *Recreations:* sailing, computing. *Heir: er* twin *s* Nigel John Charles Holder, *b* 6 May 1962. *Address:* 47 St Paul's Road North, Walton Highway, Wisbech, Cambs PE14 7DN. *T:* Wisbech (0945) 583493. *Club:* Ouse Amateur Sailing (King's Lynn).

HOLDER, Air Marshal Sir Paul (Davie), KBE 1965; CB 1964; DSO 1942; DFC 1941; *b* 2 Sept. 1911; *s* of Hugh John and Frances Rhoda Holder; *m* 1940, Mary Elizabeth Kidd; two *s. Educ:* Bristol Univ.; University of Illinois, USA. MSc Bristol, 1933; Robert Blair Fellow, 1934; PhD Bristol, 1935. Commissioned RAF, 1936; Flt Comdr 84 Sqdn, Iraq 1938–39; Stn Admin. Officer, Habbiniya, Iraq, 1940–41; OC 218 Sqdn Bomber Comd, 1941–42 (1st thousand bomber raid, Cologne); SASO Force 686, Ankara, Turkey, 1943; Group Capt. Plans, MEAF; formed Marshal Tito's first Hurricane Fighter Sqdn, Benina, Libya, 1944; DS RAF Staff Coll., 1945; CO RAF Broadwell, Transport Comd, 1946; Vice-Pres., RAF Selection Bd, 1947–48; Student, Admin. Staff Coll., Henley-on-Thames, 1947; Chief Instr, RAF Officer Cadet Training Sch., 1948–49; CO, RAF, Shallufa, Egypt, 1950–51; CO, RAF, Kabrit, Egypt, 1952; Dep. Dir, Air Staff Policy, Air Min., 1953–55; Student, Imperial Defence Coll., 1956; AOC, Singapore, 1957; AOC, Hong Kong, 1958–59; ACAS (Trng), Air Min., 1960–62; AOC No 25 Gp, RAF Flying Trng Comd, 1963–64; AOC-in-C, RAF Coastal Comd, NATO Comdr Maritime Air, Channel Comd, and Comdr Maritime Air, Eastern Atlantic Area, 1965–68, retired 1968. FRAeS 1966. *Recreations:* gardening, bridge. *Address:* Innisfree, Bramshott Chase, Hindhead, Surrey GU26 6DG. *T:* Hindhead (0428) 604579. *Club:* Royal Air Force.

HOLDERNESS, Baron *cr* 1979 (Life Peer), of Bishop Wilton in the County of Humberside; **Richard Frederick Wood;** PC 1959; DL; Chairman, Disablement Services Authority, 1987–91; *b* 5 Oct. 1920; 3rd *s* of 1st Earl of Halifax, KG, PC, OM, GCSI, GCMG, GCIE, TD; *m* 1947, Diana, *d* of late Col E. O. Kellett, DSO, MP, and Hon. Mrs W. J. McGowan; one *s* one *d. Educ:* Eton; New College, Oxford. Hon. Attaché, British Embassy, Rome, 1940; served War of 1939–45 as Lieutenant, KRRC, 1941–43; retired, wounded, 1943; toured US Army hospitals, 1943–45; New College, Oxford, 1945–47. MP (C) Bridlington, Yorkshire, 1950–79; Parliamentary Private Secretary: to Minister of Pensions, 1951–53; to Minister of State, Board of Trade, 1953–54; to Minister of Agriculture and Fisheries, 1954–55; Joint Parliamentary Secretary: Ministry of Pensions and National Insurance, 1955–58; Ministry of Labour, 1958–59; Minister of Power, October 1959–63, of Pensions and National Insurance, Oct. 1963–64; Minister of Overseas Develt, ODM, June-Oct. 1970, FCO, 1970–74. Dir, Hargreaves Group Ltd, 1974–86; Regional Dir, Yorkshire and Humberside regional board, Lloyds Bank, 1981–90. Mem., Hansard Soc. Commn on Electoral Reform, 1975–76. Pres., Queen Elizabeth's Foundn for the Disabled, 1983–. DL E Riding Yorks, 1967. Hon. LLD: Sheffield Univ., 1962; Leeds, 1978; Hull, 1982. Hon. Colonel: Queen's Royal Rifles, 1962; 4th (Volunteer) Bn Royal Green Jackets, 1967–89. *Address:* Flat Top House, Bishop Wilton, York YO4 1RY. *T:* Bishop Wilton (07596) 266; 65 Les Collines de Guerrevieille, 83120 Ste Maxime, France. *See also Sir E. N. Brooksbank, Bt.*

HOLDERNESS, Sir Richard William, 3rd Bt, *cr* 1920; Partner, Whiteheads, Estate Agents and Surveyors, 1967–86; retired; *b* 30 Nov. 1927; *s* of Sir Ernest William Elsmie Holderness, 2nd Bt, CBE, and Emily Carlton (*d* 1950), *y d* of late Frederick McQuade, Sydney, NSW; *S* father, 1968; *m* 1953, Pamela, *d* of late Eric Chapman, CBE; two *s* one *d. Educ:* Dauntsey's Sch.; Corpus Christi Coll., Oxford. ARICS 1976. *Recreations:* golf, gardening, travel. *Heir: s* Martin William Holderness, CA [*b* 24 May 1957; *m* 1984, Elizabeth, BSc, DipHV, *d* of Dr William and Dr Maureen Thornton, Belfast; one *s. Educ:* Bradfield Coll., Berks]. *Address:* Bramfold Court, Nutbourne, near Pulborough, West Sussex. *Clubs:* East India; West Sussex Golf.

HOLDGATE, Martin Wyatt, CB 1979; PhD; FIBiol; Director General, Internatonal Union for Conservation of Nature and Natural Resources, since 1988; *b* 14 Jan. 1931; *s* of late Francis Wyatt Holdgate, MA, JP, and Lois Marjorie (*née* Bebbington); *m* 1963, Elizabeth Mary (*née* Dickason), *widow* of Dr H. H. Weil; two *s. Educ:* Arnold Sch., Blackpool; Queens' Coll., Cambridge. BA Cantab 1952; MA 1956; PhD 1955; FIBiol 1967. Senior Scientist, Gough Is Scientific Survey, 1955–56; Lecturer in Zoology, Manchester Univ., 1956–57; Lecturer in Zoology, Durham Colleges, 1957–60; Leader, Royal Society Expedition to Southern Chile, 1958–59; Asst Director of Research, Scott Polar Research Institute, Cambridge, 1960–63; Senior Biologist, British Antarctic Survey, 1963–66; Sec., Working Gp on Biology, Scientific Cttee on Antarctic Res., 1964–68; Dep. Dir (Research), The Nature Conservancy, 1966–70; Director: Central Unit on Environmental Pollution, DoE, 1970–74; Inst. of Terrestrial Ecology, NERC, 1974–76; Dir-Gen. of Res., Depts of the Environment and of Transport, 1976–79, Chief Scientist and Dep. Sec., 1979–85; Dep. Sec., Environment Protection and Chief Scientist, DoE, and Chief Scientific Advr, Dept of Transport, 1985–88. Hon. Professorial Fellow, UC Cardiff, 1976–83. Member: NERC, 1976–87; SERC (formerly SRC), 1976–86; ABRC, 1976–88; Chm., Review of Scientific Civil Service, 1980. Chm., British Schools Exploring Society, 1967–78; Vice-Pres., Young Explorer's Trust, 1981– (Chm., 1972, 1979–81); Dir, World Resources Inst., Washington, DC, 1985–; Pres., Governing Council, UN Environment Prog., 1983–84; Chm., Commonwealth Expert Gp on Climate Change, 1988–89. Bruce Medal, RSE, 1964; UNEP Silver Medal, 1983; UNEP Global 500, 1988. *Publications:* A History of Appleby, 1956, 2nd edn 1970; Mountains in the Sea, The Story of the Gough Island Expedition, 1958; (ed jtly) Antarctic Biology, 1964; (ed) Antarctic Ecology, 1970; (with N. M. Wace) Man and Nature in the Tristan da Cunha Islands, 1976; A Perspective of Environmental Pollution, 1979; (ed jtly) The World Environment 1972–82, 1982; numerous papers in biological journals and works on Antarctic. *Address:* International Union for Conservation of Nature and Natural Resources, Avenue du Mont-Blanc, CH-1196, Gland, Switzerland. *Club:* Athenæum.

HOLDING, John Francis; HM Diplomatic Service; Consul-General, Auckland, since 1990; *b* 12 August 1936; *s* of late Francis George Holding, CA, Inland Revenue, and Gwendoline Elizabeth Holding (*née* Jenkins); *m* 1970, Pamela Margaret Straker-Nesbit (marr. diss. 1984); two *d. Educ:* Colwyn Bay Grammar Sch.; LSE (externally). Mil. service, 1955–57; Min. of Housing and Local Govt, 1957; CRO (later FCO), 1964; served Karachi, Islamabad and Kinshasa; First Sec., 1973; Canberra, 1973–78; Dep. High Comr, Banjul, The Gambia, 1978–80; Grenada and Barbados, 1984–87; Dep. High Comr, Dhaka, 1987–90. *Recreations:* tennis, sailing, walking, pianoforte, philately. *Address:* c/o Foreign and Commonwealth Office, SW1A 2AH.

HOLDING, Malcolm Alexander; HM Diplomatic Service, retired; Consul-General, Naples, 1986–90; *b* 11 May 1932; *s* of Adam Anderson Holding and Mary Lillian (*née* Golding); *m* 1955, Pamela Eve Hampshire; two *d. Educ:* King Henry VIII Sch., Coventry. Foreign Office, 1949–51; HM Forces, 1951–53; FO, 1953–55; Middle East Centre for Arab Studies, 1956–57; Third Secretary (Commercial), Tunis, 1957–60; Second Sec. (Commercial), Khartoum, 1960–64; Second, later First Sec. (Commercial), Cairo, 1964–68; Consul, Bari, 1969; FCO, 1970–73; First Sec., British Dep. High Commission, Madras, 1973–75; FCO, 1976–78; Canadian National Defence Coll., Kingston, Ontario, 1978–79; Counsellor (Commercial), Rome, 1979–81; Consul-Gen., Edmonton, 1981–85. Commendatore, Order of Merit of the Republic of Italy, 1980. *Recreations:* sailing, skiing. *Address:* Theatre Cottage, Powderham, Exeter EX6 8JJ.

HOLDSWORTH, His Honour Albert Edward; QC 1969; a Circuit Judge, 1972–82; *b* 1909; *e s* of Albert Edward and Catherine Sarah Holdsworth; *m* 1st, 1941, Barbara Frances (*d* 1968), *e d* of Ernest Henry and Beatrice Maud Reeves; one *s*; 2nd, 1970, Brianne Evelyn Frances, *d* of Arthur James and Evelyn Lock; two *s. Educ:* Sir George Monoux Sch., Walthamstow; Gonville and Caius Coll., Cambridge (Exhibitioner). Pres., Cambridge Union, 1932; Economics and Politics tripos; MA. Formerly journalist: Financial News, 1932–33; Special Correspondent, World Economic Conf., 1933; Yorkshire Post, 1933–46, Polit. Correspondent, later London Editor. Broadcasts for BBC on current affairs topics, 1935–56. Called to Bar, Middle Temple, 1936. Conservative Candidate Ipswich, 1951; moved resolution in favour of UK entry into European Common Market, Conservative Conf., Llandudno, 1962. Dep.-Chm., SW Metropolitan Mental Health Tribunal, 1962–65. *Publication:* Forward Together, 1983. *Address:* 2 Middle Temple Lane, Temple, EC4Y 9AA. *T:* 071–353 7926; Sutton Gate, Sutton, Pulborough, West Sussex RH20 1PN. *T:* Sutton (West Sussex) (07987) 230. *Club:* Reform.

HOLDSWORTH, Lt-Comdr (Arthur) John (Arundell), CVO 1980; OBE 1962; an Extra Gentleman Usher to the Queen, since 1985 (Gentleman Usher, 1967–85); Vice Lord-Lieutenant for Devon, 1982–90; *b* 31 March 1915; *s* of Captain F. J. C. Holdsworth, JP, DL, Totnes, and M. W. Holdsworth (*née* Arundell); *m* 1940, Barbara Lucy Ussher, *d* of Col and Mrs W. M. Acton; one *s* one *d. Educ:* Stanmore Park Prep. Sch.; Royal Naval Coll., Dartmouth. Entered RN, 1928; served War at sea (despatches); Asst Naval Attaché Warsaw, 1947–49; BJSM Washington, 1950–51; Naval Staff, Germany, 1954–56; Flag Lieut to Bd of Admiralty, 1956–65; retired 1965. Steward, Newton Abbot Race Course, 1967–85; Dep. Pres., Devon Br., BRCS, 1971–85 (Patron, 1985–); Chm., Silver Jubilee Trust Council, Devon, 1978–85. DL 1973, High Sheriff, 1976–77, Devon. *Address:* Holbeam Mill, Ogwell, Newton Abbot, Devon TQ12 6LX. *T:* Newton Abbot (0626) 65547.

HOLDSWORTH, Sir (George) Trevor, Kt 1982; Chairman: National Power, since 1990; Allied Colloids Group PLC, since 1983; Director, Prudential Corporation, since 1986 (Joint Deputy Chairman, since 1988); *b* 29 May 1927; *s* of late William Albert Holdsworth and Winifred Holdsworth (*née* Bottomley); *m* 1951, Patricia June Ridler; three *s. Educ:* Hanson Grammar Sch., Bradford; Keighley Grammar Sch. FCA 1950. Rawlinson Greaves & Mitchell, Bradford, 1944–51; Bowater Paper Corp., 1952–63 (financial and admin. appts; Dir and Controller of UK paper-making subsids); joined Guest, Keen & Nettlefolds (later GKN plc), 1963; Dep. Chief Accountant, 1963–64; Gp Chief Accountant, 1965–67; General Man. Dir, GKN Screws & Fasteners Ltd, 1968–70; Dir, 1970–88; Gp Controller, 1970–72; Gp Exec. Vice Chm., Corporate Controls and

Services, 1973–74; Dep. Chm., 1974–77; Man. Dir and Dep. Chm., 1977–80; Chm., 1980–88. Chm., British Satellite Broadcasting, 1987–90; Director: Equity Capital for Industry, 1976–84; THORN EMI, 1977–87; Midland Bank plc, 1979–88. Confederation of British Industry: Mem. Council, 1974–; Mem., Econ. and Financial Policy Cttee, 1978–80; Mem., Steering Gp on Unemployment, 1982; Mem., Special Programmes Unit, 1982; Chm., Tax Reform Working Party, 1984–86; Dep. Pres., 1987–88; Pres., 1988–90. Chm., Review Body on Doctors' and Dentists' Remuneration, 1990–; Dep. Chm., Financial Reporting Council, 1990–; Member: AMF Inc. Europ. Adv. Council, 1982–85; Business in the Community, 1984–; British Institute of Management: Mem. Council, 1974–84; Vice-Chm., 1978; Mem., Bd of Fellows, 1979; Chm., 1980–82; a Vice-Pres., 1982–; Gold Medal, 1987. Vice Pres., Engineering Employers' Fedn, 1980–; Jt Dep. Chm., Adv. Bd, Inst. of Occupational Health, 1980; Duke of Edinburgh's Award: Mem., Internat. Panel, 1980 (Chm., 1987); Internat. Trustee, 1987; UK Trustee, 1988; Member: Exec. Cttee, SMMT, 1980–83; Engineering Industries Council, 1980– (Chm., 1985); Court of British Shippers' Council, 1981–89; British-North American Cttee, 1981–85; Council, RIIA, 1983–; Internat. Council of INSEAD, 1985; Eur. Adv. Cttee, New York Stock Exchange, 1985; Council, Royal Opera House Trust (Trustee, 1981–84); Council, Winston Churchill Meml Trust, 1985–; Hon. Pres., Council of Mechanical and Metal Trade Assocs, 1987. Dir, UK–Japan 2000 Gp. 1987. Trustee: Anglo-German Foundn for the Study of Industrial Society, 1980–; Brighton Fest. Trust, 1980–90 (Chm. 1982–87); Philharmonia Trust, 1982–; Thrombosis Res. Trust, 1989–. Governor, Ashridge Management Coll., 1978. Vice-Pres., Ironbridge Gorge Museum Develt Trust, 1981–. Internat. Counsellor, Conference Bd, 1984. CIEx 1987. FRSA 1988. Freeman, City of London, 1977; Liveryman, Worshipful Co. of Chartered Accountants in England and Wales, 1978. Hon. DTech Loughborough, 1981; Hon. DSc: Aston, 1982; Sussex, 1988; Hon. DEng Bradford, 1983; Hon. DBA Internat. Management Centre, Buckingham, 1986. Chartered Accountants Founding Socs' Centenary Award, 1983; Hon. CGIA 1989. *Recreations:* music, theatre. *Address:* National Power plc, Senator House, 85 Queen Victoria Street, EC4. *Club:* Athenæum.

HOLDSWORTH, Lt-Comdr John; *see* Holdsworth, Lt-Comdr A. J. A.

HOLDSWORTH, Sir Trevor; *see* Holdsworth, Sir G. T.

HOLE, Rev. Canon Derek Norman; Vicar of St James the Greater, Leicester, since 1973; Chaplain to HM the Queen, since 1985; *b* 5 Dec. 1933; *s* of Frank Edwin Hole and Ella Evelyn Hole (*née* Thomas). *Educ:* Public Central Sch., Plymouth; Lincoln Theological College. Deacon, 1960; Priest, 1961; Asst Curate, St Mary Magdalen, Knighton, 1960–62; Domestic Chaplain to Archbishop of Cape Town, 1962–64; Asst Curate, St Nicholas, Kenilworth, 1964–67; Rector, St Mary the Virgin, Burton Latimer, 1967–73; Hon. Canon, Leicester Cathedral, 1983–. Rural Dean, Christianity South, Leicester, 1983–; Chm., House of Clergy, 1986–; Vice-Pres., Diocesan Synod and Mem., Bishop's Council, 1986–. Chaplain to: Lord Mayor of Leicester, 1976–77; High Sheriffs of Leics, 1980–85 and 1987; Leicester High Sch., 1984–. Mem., Leicester Charity Orgn Soc. 1983–; Trustee, Leicester Church Charities, 1983–; Pres., Leicester Rotary Club, 1987–88. Mem., Victorian Soc., 1986–. Governor, Alderman Newton's Sch., Leicester, 1976–82. *Recreations:* music, walking, reading biographies and Victorian history. *Address:* St James the Greater Vicarage, 216 London Road, Leicester LE2 1NE. *T:* Leicester (0533) 542111. *Club:* Leicestershire (Leicester).

HOLFORD, Surgeon Rear-Adm. John Morley, CB 1965; OBE 1954; Senior Principal Medical Officer, Department of Health and Social Security, 1973–74, retired; *b* 10 Jan. 1909; *o s* of late Rev. W. J. Holford and Amy Finnemore Lello; *m* 1935, Monica Peregrine (*d* 1986), *d* of late Preb. P. S. G. Propert; two *s*. *Educ:* Kingswood, Bath; Trinity Hall, Cambridge. MA, MB, Cantab; FRCP; joined RN 1935. War service in HMS Nelson, 1940–42; RN Hosp. Plymouth, 1942–44; consultant in Medicine to RN, 1954–66; Surgeon Capt., 1957; Surgeon Rear-Adm. 1963; Medical Officer in Charge, RN Hosp. Haslar, 1963–66. Retired, 1966. MO, Min. of Health, 1966, SMO, 1967, SPMO, 1973. Gilbert Blanc Medal, 1956; F. E. Williams Prize in Geriatric Medicine, RCP, 1972. CStJ 1964. *Publications:* Articles in medical journals. *Recreations:* chess (jt champion of South Africa, 1946), bridge. *Address:* c/o Lloyds Bank, 84 Park Lane, W1. *Club:* Army and Navy.

HOLGATE, Hon. Harold Norman, MHA; Minister for Tourism, Sport and Recreation, since 1989, for Roads and Transport, since 1990, for Parks, Wildlife and Heritage, since 1991, Government of Tasmania; *b* 5 Dec. 1933; *s* of late H. W. Holgate; *m* 1963, Rosalind, *d* of E. C. Wesley; two *s* two *d*. *Educ:* Maitland (NSW) High Sch.; Univ. of Tasmania (BA). Journalist: Sydney Morning Herald, 1952–55; Melbourne Herald, 1955–62; Political Journalist, Dep. Chief of Staff, Launceston Examiner, 1963–66; Public Relns Manager, Tasmanian Directorate of Industrial Development, 1966–70; Exec. Producer, ABC TV Public Affairs Programme, This Day Tonight, Hobart, 1970–73; Press Sec. to Dep. Prime Minister and Minister for Defence, Govt of Australia, Mr Lance Barnard, 1973–74; MHA (Lab) for Bass, Tasmania, 1974–; Speaker of House of Assembly, 1975–76; Minister (Govt of Tasmania): for Housing and Construction and Minister assisting the Dep. Premier, 1976–77; for Education, Recreation and the Arts and for Racing and Gaming, 1977–79; for Education, Recreation and the Arts, and for Police and Emergency Services, 1979–80; for Education, for Police and Emergency Services, for Racing and Gaming, 1980–81; for Police and Emergency Services, for Local Govt, for the Environment, for Water Resources, for Racing and Gaming, 1981; Premier of Tasmania, Treasurer and Minister for Racing and Gaming, 1981–82; Dep. Leader of the Opposition, Tasmanian House of Assembly, 1982–86; Chm., Tasmanian Parly Labor Party, 1986–89. *Recreations:* horse racing, music, reading, swimming. *Address:* 3 Jacques Road, Hillwood, Tasmania 7252, Australia. *T:* (003) 94 8208.

HOLGATE, Dr Sidney, CBE 1981; Master of Grey College, University of Durham, 1959–80; Member, Academic Advisory Committee, Open University, 1969–81 (Vice-Chairman, 1972–75; Chairman, 1975–77); *b* Hucknall, Notts, 9 Sept. 1918; *e s* of late Henry and Annie Elizabeth Holgate; *m* 1942, Isabel Armorey; no *c*. *Educ:* Henry Mellish Sch., Nottingham; Durham Univ. Open Scholar, Hatfield Coll., Durham, 1937; Univ. Mathematical Scholarship, 1940; BA (1st Cl. Hons Mathematics) 1940; MA 1943; PhD 1945. Asst Master, Nottingham High Sch., 1941–42; Lecturer in Mathematics, University of Durham, 1942–46; Sec. of the Durham Colls, 1946–59; Pro-Vice-Chancellor, Univ. of Durham, 1964–69. Member: Schools Council Gen. Studies Cttee, 1967–70; Chm., BBC Radio Durham Council, 1968–72; Vice-Chm., BBC Radio Newcastle Council, 1972–74. Hon. DUniv. Open, 1980. *Publications:* mathematical papers in Proc. Camb. Phil. Soc. and Proc. Royal Soc. *Recreations:* cricket and other sports, railways, bridge. *Address:* 6 Howlcroft Villas, Neville's Cross, Durham DH1 4DU.

HOLGATE, Surgeon Rear-Adm. (D) William, CB 1962; OBE 1951; Chief Dental Officer, Ministry of Health, 1961–71, and Ministry of Education and Science, 1963–71; *b* 6 July 1906; *s* of Anthony and Jane Holgate; *m* 1933, Inga Ommanney Davis; one *s* one *d*. *Educ:* Scarborough Coll.; Guy's Hospital. LDS, RCS Eng., 1927; FDS, RCS Eng., 1963. Royal Navy, 1928–61; Director of Dental Services, 1960. *Address:* Upalong, The Highway, Luccombe, Shanklin, Isle of Wight. *Club:* Savage.

HOLLAMBY, Edward Ernest, OBE 1970; FRIBA, FRTPI, FCSD; Chief Architect and Planner to London Docklands Development Corporation, 1981–85, retired; architectural consultant; *b* 8 Jan. 1921; *s* of late Edward Thomas Hollamby and Ethel May (*née* Kingdom); *m* 1941, Dori Isabel Parker; one *s* two *d*. *Educ:* School of Arts and Crafts, Hammersmith; University Coll. London. DipTP London. Served RM Engrs, 1941–46. Architect, Miners' Welfare Commn, 1947–49; Sen. Architect, LCC, 1949–62; Borough Architect, Lambeth, 1963–65, Bor. Architect and Town Planning Officer, 1965–69, Dir of Architecture, Planning and Develt, 1969–81. Works, 1957–, incl.: Christopher Wren and N Hammersmith Sec. Schs; Brandon Estate, Southwark; Housing at Elephant and Castle; study for Erith Township, Kent (prototype study for Thamesmead); pioneered rehabil. old houses, LCC Brixton Town Centre Develt Plan; housing schemes, Lambeth, 1965–, incl.: Lambeth Towers; Central Hill, Norwood; Stockwell; Brixton; Clapham; Tulse Hill and Vauxhall; also conservation and historic bldgs restoration, parks and open spaces, sheltered housing, old people's homes, health centres, doctors' gp practices, community centres, commercial and civic offices. Area rehabil. and renewal schemes, Clapham Manor and Kennington; Norwood Libr. and Nettlefold Hall; schs for mentally retarded, Clapham and Kennington; rehabil. centre for disabled, Clapham; recreation centre, Brixton; study, Civic Centre, Brixton; holiday hotel for severely disabled, Netley, near Southampton; Girls' Secure Unit, Croydon, 1978; scheme for village development, Shirley Oaks, Croydon, 1979; Isle of Dogs Urban Design Guide, 1982; develt strategies for Limehouse, Surrey and Greenland Docks, Bermondsey and Wapping, 1982–83; refurbishment of exterior and landscape, St George's in the East, 1983; Royal Docks Develt Strategy, 1984; overall layout, Western Dock, Wapping; Chm., Design Gp, Docklands Light Railway, 1982–84. Assessor, numerous architectural competitions and award schemes. Has lectured on architecture and environmental planning; numerous radio and TV appearances. RIBA: Mem. Council, 1961–70, Hon. Treas., 1967–70. Member: Historic Buildings Council, 1972–82; London Adv. Cttee, English Heritage, 1986–90; Founder Member: William Morris Soc.; Bexley Civic Soc. Hon. ALI; FRSA. Numerous design and Civic Trust awards. *Publications:* Docklands Heritage: conservation and regeneration in Docklands, 1987; Red House: the home of William Morris, 1991; contrib. architectural and town planning jls. *Recreations:* travel, classical music, opera, gardening. *Address:* Red House, Red House Lane, Upton, Bexleyheath, Kent DA6 8JF. *T:* 081–303 8808. *Club:* Arts.

HOLLAND, Rt. Rev. Alfred Charles; *see* Newcastle, NSW, Bishop of.

HOLLAND, Anthony; *see* Holland, J. A.

HOLLAND, Arthur David, CB 1973; TD 1947; Chief Highway Engineer, Department of the Environment, 1970–74; *b* 1 Nov. 1913; *o s* of Col. Arthur Leslie Holland, MC, TD, and Dora Helena Hassé; *m* 1938, Jean Moyra Spowart; two *s*. *Educ:* Malvern Coll.; University of Bristol (BSc(Eng)Hons). Asst Engineer, Great Western Railway Co, 1935–36; N Devon CC, 1936–37; Min. of Transport: Manchester, 1937–38; London, 1938–39. Served War: with RE, 1939–46; in Air Defence Gt Britain, 1939–42; with Middle East Forces, 1942–46, finally as Lt-Col RE (now Hon. Lt-Col), Sen. Staff Officer to Chief Engineer, Italy. Min. of Transport, Nottingham, 1946–47; Bridge Section, London, 1947–61; Divl Road Engr, E Midland Div., Nottingham, 1961–63; Asst Chief Engr (Bridges), 1963–65; Dep. Chief Engr, HQ London, 1965–70. FICE, FIStructE, FInstHE; Pres., Smeatonian Soc. of Civil Engrs, 1991. *Publications:* contribs to Proc. Instn of Civil Engineers and Instn of Highway Engineers. *Address:* Pine Tree Cottage, Pembroke Road, Woking, Surrey GU22 7DS. *T:* Woking (04862) 762403.

HOLLAND, Brian Arthur; Solicitor to the Post Office, since 1981; *b* 14 June 1935; *s* of George Leigh Holland and Hilda Holland, MBE; *m* 1964, Sally Edwards; one *s* one *d*. *Educ:* Manchester Grammar Sch.; Manchester Univ. (LLB Hons). Admitted Solicitor, 1961. Joined Solicitor's Dept, GPO, 1961; Solicitor's Office, Post Office: Head of Civil Litigation Div., 1977–79; Dir, Litigation and Prosecution Dept, 1979–81. *Publication:* (contrib.) Halsbury's Laws of England, 4th edn, vol. 36. *Recreations:* photography, studying railways, sketching, gardening. *Address:* 23 Grasmere Road, Purley, Surrey CR8 1DY. *T:* 081–660 0479.

HOLLAND, Christopher John, QC 1978; barrister-at-law; *b* 1 June 1937; *er s* of late Frank and Winifred Mary Holland; *m* 1967, Jill Iona Holland; one *s* one *d*. *Educ:* Leeds Grammar Sch.; Emmanuel Coll., Cambridge (MA, LLB). National Service (acting L/Cpl), 3rd Royal Tank Regt, 1956–58. Called to the Bar, Inner Temple, 1963, Bencher, 1985; commenced practice on North Eastern Circuit. Vice Chm., Cttee of Inquiry into Outbreak of Legionnaires' Disease at Stafford, 1985. Chm., Lower Washburn Parish Council, 1975–. *Address:* Pearl Chambers, 22 East Parade, Leeds LS1 5BU. *T:* Leeds (0532) 452702; 6 Pump Court, Temple, EC4Y 7AR. *Club:* United Oxford & Cambridge University.

HOLLAND, Sir Clifton Vaughan, (Sir John), AC 1988; Kt 1973; BCE; FTS, FIE(Aust), FAIM, FAIB; Chairman, John Holland Holdings Limited, 1963–86; *b* Melbourne, 21 June 1914; *s* of Thomas and Mabel Ruth Elizabeth Holland; *m* 1942, Emily Joan Atkinson; three *s* one *d*. *Educ:* Flinders State Sch.; Frankston High Sch.; Queen's Coll., Univ. of Melbourne (BCE); Monash Univ. (Hon. DEng 1978). Junior Engineer, BP, 1936–39. Served War of 1939–45, RAE and 'Z' Special Force, Middle East, SW Pacific (Lt-Col). Construction Engr, BP Aust. 1946–49; Founder, John Holland (Constructions) Pty Ltd, 1949, Man. Dir 1949–73, Chm., 1949–86; Chm., Process Plant Constructions Pty Ltd, 1949–82; Director: T & G Life Soc., 1972–82; Aust. and NZ Banking Gp, 1976–81. Foundn Pres., Australian Fedn of Civil Contractors (Life Mem., 1971); Chm., Nat. Construction Industry Conf. Organising Cttee, 1982; Mem., Construction Industry Res. Bd, 1982. Chm., Econ. Consultative Adv. Gp to the Treasurer, 1975–81; Mem., Rhodes Scholar Selection Cttee, 1970–73; Mem. Bd, Royal Melbourne Hosp., 1963–79; Nat. Chm., Outward Bound, 1973–74, Chm. Victorian Div., 1964–77; Councillor, Inst. of Public Affairs, 1980; Mem., Churchill Fellowship Selection Cttee, 1968–82; Director: Winston Churchill Meml Trust, 1976–82 (Chm., Vic. Br., 1977–82); Child Accident Prevention Foundn of Australia, 1979–81; Chairman: La Trobe Centenary Commemoration Council, 1975–76; Matthew Flinders Bi-Centenary Council, 1973–75; History Adv. Council of Victoria, 1975–85; Loch Ard Centenary Commemoration Cttee, 1976–78; Citizens' Council, 150th Anniversary Celebrations, Victoria, 1979–82; Victorian Cttee for Anzac Awards, 1982–; Nat. Chm., Queen's Silver Jubilee Trust for Young Australians, 1981–87 (Vic. Chm., 1977–80); Mem., Centenary Test Co-ordinating Cttee, 1976–77. Dep. Chm., Melbourne Univ. Engineering Sch. Centenary Foundn and Appeal Cttee, 1982–90. Director: Corps of Commissionaires (Victoria) Ltd, 1978–; Australian Bicentenary Celebrations, 1980–82 (Vic. Chm., 1980–82). Pres., Stroke Res. Foundn, 1983–90. Construction projects include: Jindabyne pumping station; Westgate Bridge; Tasman Bridge restoration. Foundation Fellow, Australian Acad. of Technological Scis. Peter Nicoll Russell Meml Medal, 1974; Kernot Meml Medal, Univ. of Melbourne, 1976; Consulting Engineers Advancement Soc. Medal, 1983. *Recreations:* golf, music, gardening, cricket. *Address:* Bunkers, 29 George Road, Flinders, Vic 3929, Australia.

Clubs: Australian, Naval and Military (Melbourne); Royal Melbourne Golf, Frankston Golf, Flinders Golf.

HOLLAND, David Cuthbert Lyall, CB 1975; Librarian of the House of Commons, 1967–76; *b* 23 March 1915; *yr s* of Michael Holland, MC, and Marion Holland (*née* Broadwood); *m* 1949, Rosemary Griffiths, *y d* of David Ll. Griffiths, OBE; two *s* one *d. Educ:* Eton; Trinity Coll., Cambridge (MA). War service, Army, 1939–46; PoW. Appointed House of Commons Library, 1946. Chm., Study of Parlt Gp, 1973–74. *Publications:* book reviews, etc. *Recreation:* book collecting. *Address:* The Barn, Milton Street, Polegate, East Sussex. *T:* Alfriston (0323) 870379. *Club:* Athenæum.

HOLLAND, David George, CMG 1975; Executive Director, The Group of Thirty, since 1986; *b* 31 May 1925; *s* of late Francis George Holland and Mabel Ellen Holland; *m* 1954, Marian Elizabeth Rowles; two *s* one *d. Educ:* Taunton Sch.; Wadham Coll., Oxford. Inst. of Economics and Statistics, Oxford, 1949–63; Internat. Bank for Reconstruction and Development, Washington, DC, 1963–65; Min. of Overseas Development, 1965–67; Chief Economic Adviser, FCO, 1967–75; Dep. Chief, Economic Intelligence and Overseas Depts, Bank of England, 1975–80; Chief Adviser, Bank of England, 1980–85. *Address:* 20 Woodside Avenue, N6.

HOLLAND, Rt. Rev. Edward; *see* Gibraltar in Europe, Bishop Suffragan of.

HOLLAND, Edward Richard Charles, OBE 1983 (MBE 1969); HM Diplomatic Service, retired; *b* 26 March 1925; *s* of Cecil Francis Richard Holland and Joyce Mary (*née* Pyne); *m* 1952, Dorothy Olive Branthwaite; two *s. Educ:* Launceston Coll. Served RAF, 1943–48. Joined FO, 1948; served in Batavia, Bangkok, Oslo, Prague and Helsinki, 1949–57; Consul, Saigon, 1957; FO, 1959; Cape Town, 1962; First Sec., Monrovia, 1964; Consul: Stuttgart, 1969; Düsseldorf, 1971; FCO, 1972; First Sec., Islamabad, 1977; Consul-Gen., Alexandria, 1981–82. *Recreations:* gardening, walking, reading, painting. *Address:* 1 Prospect Cottages, Boughton Aluph, Ashford, Kent TN25 4JA. *T:* Ashford (0233) 628539. *Club:* Civil Service.

HOLLAND, Einion; *see* Holland, R. E.

HOLLAND, Frank Robert Dacre; Chairman, C. E. Heath & Co. PLC, 1973–84, Non-Executive Director, 1984–86; *b* 24 March 1924; *s* of Ernest Albert Holland and Kathleen Annie (*née* Page); *m* 1948, Margaret Lindsay Aird; one *d. Educ:* Whitgift Sch., Croydon. Joined C. E. Heath & Co. Ltd, 1941; entered Army, 1942; Sandhurst, 1943; commissioned 4th Queen's Own Hussars, 1944; served, Italy, 1944–45, Austria and Germany, 1945–47; returned to C. E. Heath & Co. Ltd, 1947; Joint Managing Director, North American Operation, 1965; Director, C. E. Heath & Co. Ltd, 1965, Dep. Chm., 1969. Liveryman: Glass-Sellers' Co., 1976–; Insurers' Co., 1980– (Master, 1985–86). *Recreations:* travel, gardening. *Address:* Moatside, 68 Ashley Road, Walton-on-Thames, Surrey KT12 1HR. *T:* Walton-on-Thames (0932) 227591. *Clubs:* Oriental, Cavalry and Guards.

HOLLAND, Sir Geoffrey, KCB 1989 (CB 1984); Permanent Secretary, Employment Department Group (formerly Department of Employment), since 1988; *b* 9 May 1938; *s* of late Frank Holland, CBE and of Elsie Freda Holland; *m* 1964, Carol Ann Challen. *Educ:* Merchant Taylors' Sch., Northwood; St John's Coll., Oxford (BA 1st cl. Hons; MA). 2nd Lieut, RTR, 1956–58. Entered Min. of Labour, 1961, Asst Private Sec., 1964–65; Principal Private Sec. to Sec. of State for Employment, 1971–72; Manpower Services Commission: Asst Sec., Hd of Planning, 1973; Dir of Special Progs, 1977; Dep. Sec., 1981; Dir, 1981; Second Perm Sec., 1986. Consultant, Industrial Cttee, C of E Bd of Social Responsibility, 1985–. CBIM 1987. Hon. Fellow: Polytechnic of Wales, 1986; Inst. of Training Develt, 1986. Liveryman, Merchant Taylors' Co., 1967– (Jun. Renter Warden, 1990–91). *Publications:* Young People and Work, 1977; many articles on manpower, educn, training, management etc in professional jls. *Recreations:* journeying, opera, exercising the dog. *Address:* Caxton House, Tothill Street, SW1H 9NF. *Club:* East India, Devonshire, Sports and Public Schools.

HOLLAND, Sir Guy (Hope), 3rd Bt *cr* 1917; farmer; art dealer; *b* 19 July 1918; *s* of Sir Reginald Sothern Holland, 1st Bt and Stretta Aimée Holland (*née* Price) (*d* 1949); *S* brother, 1981; *m* 1945, Joan Marianne Street, *d* of late Captain Herbert Edmund Street, XXth Hussars, and of Lady Tottenham; two *d. Educ:* privately and Christ Church, Oxford. Served War of 1939–45 (wounded); Captain, Royal Scots Greys; ADC to Gen. Sir Andrew Thorne, 1944. *Heir:* none. *Address:* Sheepbridge Barn, Eastleach, Cirencester, Gloucestershire GL7 3PS. *T:* Southrop (036785) 296. *Clubs:* Boodle's, Pratt's.

HOLLAND, Sir John; *see* Holland, Sir C. V.

HOLLAND, (John) Anthony; Partner, Foot & Bowden, solicitors, Plymouth, since 1964; *b* 9 Nov. 1938; *s* of John and Dorothy Rita Holland; *m* 1963, Kathleen Margaret Anderson; three *s. Educ:* Ratcliffe Coll., Leics; Nottingham Univ. (LLB). Admitted Solicitor of Supreme Court, 1962; notary public. Joined Foot & Bowden, 1964. Chairman: Young Solicitors Gp, Law Soc., 1972; Social Security Appeals Tribunal, 1974–; South Western Regl Adv. Council, BBC, 1984–87; Member: Council, Law Soc., 1976– (Vice-Pres., 1989–90; Pres., 1990–91); Marre Cttee on future of the Legal Profession, 1986–88. President: Plymouth Law Soc., 1986; Cornwall Law Soc., 1988. Gov., Plymouth Coll., 1976–. Jt Adv. Editor, Mines and Quarries Section, Butterworth's Encyclopædia of Forms and Precedents. *Publications:* (jtly) Principles of Registered Land Conveyancing, 1966; (jtly) Landlord and Tenant, 1968. *Recreations:* opera, literature, journalism, broadcasting. *Address:* 46 Thornhill Way, Mannamead, Plymouth PL3 5NP. *T:* Plymouth (0752) 220529; 66 Andrewes House, Barbican, EC2Y 8AY. *T:* 071–638 5044. *Club:* Royal Western Yacht (Plymouth).

HOLLAND, John Lewis; Managing Director, Herts & Essex Newspapers, since 1990; *b* 23 May 1937; *s* of George James Holland and Esther Holland; *m* 1958, Maureen Ann Adams; one *s* one *d. Educ:* Nottingham Technical Grammar Sch. Trainee Reporter, Nottingham Evening News, subseq. Jun. Reporter, Mansfield Br. Office, 1953–55; Sports Reporter, Mansfield Reporter Co., 1955–56; Sports Reporter, subseq. Sports Editor, Aldershot News Group, 1956–59; News Editor, West Bridgford & Clifton Standard, Nottingham, 1959–61; Chief Sports Sub Editor, Bristol Evening Post, and Editor, Sports Green 'Un (sports edn), 1961–64; Editor, West Bridgford & Clifton Standard, Nottingham, and Partner, Botting & Turner Sports Agency, Nottingham, 1964–66; Birmingham Evening Mail: Dep. Sports Editor, 1966–71; Editor, Special Projects Unit (Colour Prodn Dept), 1971–75; Editor, 1975–79, and Gen. Man., 1979–81, Sandwell Evening Mail; Marketing/Promotions Gen. Man., Birmingham Post & Mail, 1981–82; Editor, The Birmingham Post, 1982–86. Director: Birmingham Post & Mail Circulation and Promotions, 1986–88; Birmingham Post & Mail Publications and Promotions, 1988–90; Birmingham Convention and Visitor Bureau, 1982–. Pres., Chartered Inst. of Marketing, 1989–90. *Recreations:* journalism, most sports (more recently watching soccer and playing squash), keeping horses, gardening, keep fit. *Address:* The Maltings, Maltings Lane, Royston, Herts. *Club:* Press (Birmingham).

HOLLAND, Sir Kenneth (Lawrence), Kt 1981; CBE 1971; QFSM 1974; Chairman, Loss Prevention Certification Board Ltd, since 1984; Consultant, Fire Safety Engineering, since 1981; Chairman, Firelaw Ltd, since 1988; Director, Gent Ltd, since 1981; *b* 20 Sept. 1918; *s* of Percy Lawrence and Edith Holland; *m* 1941, Pauline Keith (*née* Mansfield); two *s* one *d. Educ:* Whitcliffe Mount Grammar Sch., Cleckheaton, Yorks. Entered Fire Service, Lancashire, 1937; Divisional Officer: Suffolk and Ipswich, 1948; Worcestershire, 1952; Dep. Chief Fire Officer, Lancashire, 1955; Chief Fire Officer: Bristol, 1960; West Riding of Yorkshire, 1967; HM Chief Inspector of Fire Services, 1972–80. President: Commonwealth Overseas Fire Services Assoc., 1983–90; Assoc. of Structural Fire Protection Contractors and Manufacturers, 1986–90; Nat. Assoc. for Safety in the Home, 1988–90; Trustee: Fire Services Res. Trng Trust, 1983–; Ivy Owen Award Trust, 1989–; Chairman: ISO Technical Cttee TC/21 Fire Equipment, 1983–91; Multi-technics Council, BSI, 1984–90; Visitor, Fire Res. Station, 1984–90; Vice President: Fire Brigade Soc., 1969; Fire Services Nat. Benevolent Fund, 1973–. FIFireE. Hon. Treasurer, Poole Arts Fedn, 1985–88. OStJ 1964. Defence Medal; Fire Brigade Long Service and Good Conduct Medal. *Recreations:* sports, gardening, the Arts. *Club:* St John House.

HOLLAND, Kevin John William C.; *see* Crossley-Holland.

HOLLAND, Norman James Abbott, FIElecIE; consultant, since 1991; Group Standards Manager, Philips UK, 1983–90; *b* 16 Dec. 1927; *s* of James George Holland and May Stuart Holland; *m* 1951, Barbara Byatt; one *s* one *d. Educ:* Sir Walter St John's Grammar Sch.; Regent Street Polytechnic. Chm., Incorp. Engrg and Engrg Technicians Adv. Cttee, Engrg Council, 1985–91; UK Delegate: IEC Council, 1987–; European CLC Gen. Assembly, 1987–; Member: IEC Finance Cttee, 1985–91; Engrg Council, 1985–91; Bd, Electronic Engrg Assoc., 1985– (Chm., Standards Policy Gp); NACCB, 1987–. *Recreation:* golf. *Address:* Pinehaven, 94 Hiltingbury Road, Chandler's Ford, Hants SO5 1NZ. *Club:* Bramshaw Golf.

HOLLAND, Sir Philip (Welsby), Kt 1983; retired; *b* 14 March 1917; *s* of late John Holland, Middlewich, Cheshire; *m* 1943, Josephine Alma Hudson; one *s. Educ:* Sir John Deane's Grammar Sch., Northwich. Enlisted RAF 1936; commissioned 1943. Factory Manager, Jantzen Knitting Mills, 1946–47; Management Research, 1948–49; Manufacturers' Agent in Engineering and Refractories Products, 1949–60. Contested (C) Yardley Div. of Birmingham, Gen. Election, 1955; MP (C): Acton, 1959–64; Carlton, 1966–83; Gedling, 1983–87. PPS: to Minister of Pensions and Nat. Insurance, 1961–62; to Chief Sec. to Treasury and Paymaster-Gen., 1962–64; to Minister of Aviation Supply, 1970; to Minister for Aerospace, 1971; to Minister for Trade, 1972. Pres., Cons. Trade Union Nat. Adv. Cttee, 1972–74. Personnel Manager, The Ultra Electronics Group of Companies, 1964–66; Personnel Consultant to Standard Telephones and Cables Ltd, 1969–81. Chm., Cttee of Selection, H of C, 1979–84; Standing Cttee Chm., 1983–87. Councillor, Royal Borough of Kensington, 1955–59. Rector's Warden, St Margaret's Church, Westminister, 1990–. *Publications:* The Quango Explosion (jtly), 1978; Quango, Quango, Quango, 1979; Costing the Quango, 1979; The Quango Death List, 1980; The Governance of Quangos, 1981; Quelling the Quango, 1982; (jtly) A–Z Guide to Parliament, 1988; Lobby Fodder?, 1988. *Recreations:* travel, writing. *Address:* 53 Pymers Mead, West Dulwich, SE21 8NH.

HOLLAND, (Robert) Einion, FIA; Chairman: Pearl Assurance PLC, 1983–89; Pearl Group PLC, 1985–89 (Director, since 1985); *b* 23 April 1927; *s* of late Robert Ellis Holland and Bene Holland; *m* 1955, Eryl Haf Roberts (*d* 1988); one *s* two *d. Educ:* University Coll. of N Wales, Bangor (BSc). FIA 1957. Joined Pearl Assurance Co. Ltd, 1953: Dir, 1973; Chief Gen. Manager, 1977–83. Chm., Industrial Life Offices Assoc., 1976–78; Director: Aviation & General Insurance Co. Ltd, 1972–89 (Chm. 1976–78, 1984–85); British Rail Property Board, 1987–90; Community Reinsurance Corp. Ltd, 1973–89 (Chm., 1973–76); Crawley Warren Group, 1987–; Pearl American Corp., 1972–84. Member: Welsh Develt Agency, 1976–86; CS Pay Research Unit Bd, 1980–81; Council, Univ. of Wales, 1990–. *Recreations:* golf and Welsh literature. *Address:* 55 Corkscrew Hill, West Wickham, Kent BR4 9BA. *T:* 081–777 1861.

HOLLAND, Stuart (Kingsley); Professor of Economics, and Director, European Cultural Research Centre, European University Institute, Florence, since 1989; *b* 25 March 1940; *y s* of Frederick Holland and late May Holland, London; *m* 1976, Jenny Lennard; two *c. Educ:* state primary schs; Christ's Hosp.; Univ. of Missouri (Exchange Scholar); Balliol Coll., Oxford (Domus Scholar; 1st Cl. Hons Mod. History); St Antony's Coll., Oxford (Sen. Scholar; DPhil Econs). Econ. Asst, Cabinet Office, 1966–67; Personal Asst to Prime Minister, 1967–68; Res. Fellow, Centre for Contemp. European Studies, Univ. of Sussex, 1968–71, Assoc. Fellow and Lectr, 1971–79. Vis. Scholar, Brookings Instn, Washington, DC, 1970. Adviser to Commons Expenditure Cttee, 1971–72; Special Adviser to Minister of Overseas Develt, 1974–75. MP (Lab) Vauxhall, 1979–89; Opposition frontbench spokesman on overseas develt and co-operation, 1983–87, on treasury and economic affairs, 1987–89. Res. Specialist, RIIA, 1972–74; Associate, Inst. of Develt Studies, 1974–. Consultant: Econ. and Social Affairs Cttee, Council of Europe, 1973; Open Univ., 1973. Rapporteur, Trades Union Adv. Cttee, OECD, 1977. Chm., Public Enterprise Gp, 1973–75. Member: Council, Inst. for Workers' Control, 1974–; Expert Cttee on Inflation, EEC Commn, 1975–76; UN Univ. Working Party on Socio-Cultural Factors in Develt, Tokyo, 1977. Lubbock Lectr, Oxford Univ., 1975; Tom Mann Meml Lectr, Australia, 1977. Mem., Labour Party, 1962–; Mem. sub-cttees (inc. Finance and Econ. Policy, Indust. Policy, EEC, Economic Planning, Defence, Development Cooperation, Public Sector), Nat. Exec. Cttee, Labour Party, 1972–89; Executive Member: Labour Coordinating Cttee, 1978–81; European Nuclear Disarmament Campaign, 1980–83; Mem., Economic Cttee, Socialist International, 1984–. Dir, Bertrand Russell Foundn, 1990–. Hon. MRTPI 1980. *Publications:* (jtly) Sovereignty and Multinational Corporations, 1971; (ed) The State as Entrepreneur, 1972; Strategy for Socialism, 1975; The Socialist Challenge, 1975; The Regional Problem, 1976; Capital versus the Regions, 1976; (ed) Beyond Capitalist Planning, 1978; Uncommon Market, 1980; (ed) Out of Crisis, 1983; (with Donald Anderson) Kissinger's Kingdom, 1984; (with James Firebrace) Never Kneel Down, 1984; The Market Economy, 1987; The Global Economy, 1987; contrib. symposia; articles in specialist jls and national and internat. press. *Recreation:* singing in the bath. *Address:* European University Institute, Via dei Roccettini 5, 50016 San Domenico di Fiesole, Florence, Italy. *T:* (055) 5092 532/537, *Fax:* (055) 587197.

HOLLAND, Rt. Rev. Thomas, DSC 1944; DD (Gregorian); retired Bishop of Salford; *b* 11 June 1908; *s* of John Holland and Mary (*née* Fletcher). *Educ:* Upholland; Valladolid; Rome. PhD Valladolid, 1929; DD Gregorian, Rome 1936. Taught theology: Spain, 1936–41; Lisbon, 1941–43. Chaplain, RN, 1943–46; Port Chaplain, Bombay, 1946–48; CMS, 1948–56; Secretary to Apostolic Delegate, 1956–60; Coadjutor Bp of Portsmouth, 1960–64; Bishop of Salford, 1964–83; Apostolic Administrator, 1983–84. Privy Chamberlain to the Pope, 1958. Member of Vatican Secretariat for Promoting Christian Unity, 1961–73, for Unbelievers, 1965–73; Mem., Vatican Synod, 1974. Hon. DLitt Salford, 1980. *Publications:* Great Cross, 1958; For Better and For Worse (autobiog.), 1989. *Address:* Nazareth House, Scholes Lane, Prestwich, Manchester M25 8AP.

HOLLAND, Prof. Walter Werner, MD; FRCP, FRCPE, FRCGP, FFPHM; Professor of Public Health Medicine, since 1991, and Hon. Director, since 1968, Social Medicine and Health Service Research Unit, United Medical and Dental Schools of Guy's and St Thomas' Hospitals (formerly St Thomas's Hospital Medical School); *b* 5 March 1929; *s* of Henry Holland and Hertha Zentner; *m* 1964, Fiona Margaret Auchinleck Love; three *s*. *Educ:* St Thomas's Hosp. Med. Sch., London (BSc Hons 1951; MB, BS Hons 1954; MD 1964). FFCM 1972; FRCP 1973; FRCGP 1982; FRCPE 1990. House Officer, St Thomas' Hosp., 1954–56; MRC Clin. Res. Fellow, London Sch. of Hygiene, 1959–61; Lectr, Johns Hopkins Univ., Md, USA, 1961–62; St Thomas's Hospital Medical School, later United Medical and Dental Schools of Guy's and St Thomas' Hospitals: Sen. Lectr, Dept of Medicine, 1962–64; Reader and Chm., Dept of Clin. Epidemiol. and Social Medicine, 1965–68; Prof. of Clin. Epidemiol., 1968–91. Fogarty Scholar-in-Residence, NIH, Bethesda, Md, 1984–85; Sawyer Scholar-in-Residence, Case Western Reserve Med. Sch., Cleveland, Ohio, 1985. President: Internat. Epidemiol Assoc., 1987–90; Faculty of Public Health (formerly Community) Medicine, RCP, 1989–92. Life Mem., Soc. of Scholars, Johns Hopkins Univ., 1970; Hon. Mem., Amer. Epidemiol Soc., 1985. Dr *hc*: Univ. of Bordeaux, 1981; Free Univ. of Berlin, 1990. *Publications:* Data Handling in Epidemiology, 1970; Air Pollution and Respiratory Disease, 1972; Epidemiology and Health, 1977; Health Care and Epidemiology, 1978; Measurement of Levels of Health, 1979; Evaluation of Health Care, 1983; Chronic Obstructive Bronchopathies, 1983; Oxford Textbook of Public Health, 1984, 2nd edn 1991; (with Susie Stewart) Screening in Health Care, 1990; pubns on health services res., epidemiol methods and on respiratory disease. *Recreations:* reading, walking. *Address:* Department of Public Health Medicine, St Thomas's Hospital UMDS, SE1 7EH. *T:* 071–922 8100. *Club:* Athenæum.

HOLLAND-HIBBERT, family name of **Viscount Knutsford.**

HOLLAND-MARTIN, Robert George, (Robin); Director, Henderson Administration Group plc, since 1983; *b* 6 July 1939; *y s* of late Cyril Holland-Martin and of Rosa, *d* of Sir Gerald Chadwyck-Healey, 2nd Bt, CBE; *m* 1976, Dominique, 2nd *d* of Maurice Fromaget; two *d*. *Educ:* Eton. Cazenove & Co., 1960–74 (partner, 1968–74); Finance Director, Paterson Products Ltd, 1976–86; Consultant, Newmarket Venture Capital plc (formerly Newmarket Co.), 1982–. Hon. Dep. Treasurer, Cons. and Unionist Party, 1979–82. Member of Council: Metropolitan Hospital-Sunday Fund, 1963– (Chm. of Council, 1977–); Homoeopathic Trust, 1970–90 (Vice Chm., 1975–90). Victoria & Albert Museum: Mem. Adv. Council, 1972–83; Mem. Cttee, Associates of V&A, 1976–85 (Chm., 1981–85); Dep. Chm., Trustees, 1983–85. Mem., Visiting Cttee for Royal Coll. of Art, 1982– (Chm., 1984–). Trustee, Blackie Foundn Trust, 1971– (Chm., 1987–). *Address:* 18 Tite Street, SW3 4HZ. *T:* 071–352 7871. *Clubs:* White's, Royal Automobile.

HOLLAND-MARTIN, Rosamund Mary, (Lady Holland-Martin), DBE 1983 (OBE 1947); DL; Member, Central Executive Committee, National Society for the Prevention of Cruelty to Children, since 1947 (Chairman of the Society, 1969–87); *b* 26 June 1914; *d* of Charles Harry St John Hornby and Cicely Rachel Emily Barclay; *m* 1951, Adm. Sir Deric Holland-Martin, GCB, DSO, DSC (*d* 1977), Lord Lieutenant of Hereford and Worcester; one *s* one *d*. *Educ:* privately. WVS Administrator, South East, 1946–51; Vice-Chm., WRVS, 1978–81; Pres., Friends of Worcester Cathedral, 1978–; Pres., Worcester Sea Cadets, 1978–; Mem. Council, Malvern College, 1979–90. DL Hereford and Worcester, 1983. *Recreations:* needlework, photography, collecting things. *Address:* Bells Castle, Kemerton, Tewkesbury, Glos GL20 7JW. *T:* Overbury (038689) 333.

HOLLENDEN, 3rd Baron *cr* 1912; **Gordon Hope Hope-Morley;** I. & R. Morley Ltd, 1933–67, retired as Chairman; *b* 8 Jan. 1914; *s* of Hon. Claude Hope-Morley (*d* 1968) (*yr s* of 1st Baron) and Lady Dorothy Edith Isabel (*d* 1972), *d* of 7th Earl of Buckinghamshire; *S* uncle, 1977; *m* 1945, Sonja Sundt, Norway; three *s*. *Educ:* Eton. War medals of 1939–45; King Haakon of Norway Liberation medal. *Heir: s* Hon. Ian Hampden Hope-Morley [*b* 23 Oct. 1946; *m* 1st, 1972, Beatrice Saulnier (marr. diss. 1985); one *s* one *d*; 2nd, 1988, Caroline Ash; one *s*]. *Address:* Hall Place, Leigh, Tonbridge, Kent. *T:* Hildenborough (0732) 832255. *Clubs:* Brooks's, Beefsteak.

See also Sir Michael Hanley.

HOLLENWEGER, Prof. Walter Jacob; Professor of Mission, University of Birmingham, 1971–89; *b* 1 June 1927; *s* of Walter Otto and Anna Hollenweger-Spörri; *m* 1951, Erica Busslinger. *Educ:* Univs. of Zürich and Basel. Dr theol Zürich 1966 (and degrees leading up to it). Stock Exchange, Zürich, and several banking appts, until 1948. Pastor, 1949–57; ordained, Swiss Reformed Church, 1961. Study Dir, Ev. Acad., Zürich, 1964–65; Research Asst, Univ. of Zürich, 1961–64; Exec. Sec., World Council of Churches, Geneva, 1965–71; regular guest prof. in Switzerland, Germany and USA. *Publications:* Handbuch der Pfingstbewegung, 10 vols, 1965/66; (ed) The Church for Others, 1967 (also German, Spanish and Portuguese edns); (ed) Die Pfingstkirchen, 1971; Kirche, Benzin und Bohnensuppe, 1971; The Pentecostals, 1972 (also German and Spanish edns); Pentecost between Black and White, 1975 (also German and Dutch edns); Glaube, Geist und Geister, 1975; (ed) Studies in the Intercultural History of Christianity, 70 vols, 1975–; Evangelism Today, 1976 (also German edn); (with Th. Ahrens) Volkschristentum und Volksreligion in Pazifik, 1977; Interkulturelle Theologie, vol. I, 1979, vol. II, 1982, vol. III, 1988 (abridged French edn); Erfahrungen in Ephesus, 1979; Wie Grenzen zu Brücken werden, 1980; Besuch bei Lukas, 1981; Conflict in Corinth—Memoirs of an Old Man, 1982 (also German, Italian, Indonesian and French edns); Jüngermesse/Gomer: Das Gesicht des Unsichtbaren, 1983; Zwingli zwischen Krieg und Frieden, 1983; Das Fest der Verlorenen, 1984; Der Handelsreisende Gottes, 1985; Das Wagnis des Glaubens, 1986; Weihnachtsoratorium, 1986; Mirjam, Mutter, and Michal: Die Frauen meines Mannes (zwei Monodramen), 1987; Bonhoeffer Requiem, 1989; Hiob, 1990; Ostertanz der Frauen/Veni Creator Spiritus, 1990; Kommet her zu mir/Die zehn Aussätzigen, 1990; Christsein in einer multikulturellen Gesellschaft, 1990; Das Friedensmahl, 1991. *Address:* CH-3704 Krattigen, Switzerland. *T:* 033 54 43 02.

HOLLEY, Prof. Robert W., PhD; Resident Fellow, The Salk Institute, since 1968; *b* 28 Jan. 1922; *s* of Charles and Viola Holley, Urbana, Ill, USA; *m* 1945, Ann Dworkin; one *s*. *Educ:* Univ. of Illinois (AB); Cornell Univ. (PhD); Washington State Coll. Research Biochemist, Cornell Univ. Med. Coll., 1944–46; Instructor, State Coll. of Wash., 1947–48; Assistant Prof. and Associate Prof. of Organic Chemistry, NY State Agricultural Experimental Station, Cornell Univ., 1948–57; Research Chemist, US Plant, Soil and Nut. Lab., ARS, USDA, 1957–64; Prof. of Biochem. and Molecular Biol., Biol. Div., Cornell Univ., 1964–69. Various awards for research, 1965–. Hon. DSc Illinois, 1970. Nobel Prize in Physiology or Medicine, 1968. *Publications:* many contribs to: Jl Amer. Chem. Soc., Science, Jl Biol. Chem., Arch. Biochem., Nature, Proc. Nat. Acad. Sci., etc. *Recreations:* sculpture; family enjoys walks along ocean and trips to mountains. *Address:* The Salk Institute, PO Box 85800, San Diego, California 92186–5800, USA. *T:* 453–4100 (ext. 341).

HOLLEY, Rear Adm. Ronald Victor, CB 1987; CEng; FRAeS; Technical Director, Shell Aircraft, since 1987; *b* 13 July 1931; *s* of late Mr and Mrs V. E. Holley; *m* 1954, Sister Dorothy Brierley, QARNNS; two *s* twin *d*. *Educ:* Rondebosch, S Africa; RNEC Manadon; RAFC Henlow (post graduate). MIMechE, MIEE; FRAeS 1988. Served HM Ships Implacable, Finisterre, Euryalus, Victorious, Eagle (899 Sqdn); NATO Defence Coll., Rome, 1968; Naval Plans, 1969–71; Aircraft Dept, 1971–73; Air Engr Officer, HMS Seahawk, 1973–75; Naval Asst to Controller of the Navy, 1975–77; RCDS, 1978; Seaman Officer Develt Study, 1979; Dir, Helicopter Projects, Procurement Exec., 1979–82; RNEC in command, 1982–84; Sen. Naval Mem., Directing Staff, RCDS, 1984–85; Dir Gen. Aircraft (Navy), 1985–87. Sec., European Helicopter Operators Cttee, 1988–. President: RN Volunteer Bands, 1983–87; RN Amateur Fencing Assoc., 1986–87 (Chm., 1983–86). Henson and Stringfellow Lectr, RAeS, 1987. *Publications:* contribs to Naval Jls, and Seaford House Papers, 1978. *Recreations:* playing the bassoon; dinghy sailing, rowing. *Address:* 55 Larksfield, Englefield Green TW20 0RB.

HOLLEY, (William) Stephen, CBE 1979; General Manager, Washington Development Corporation, 1965–80; *b* 26 March 1920; *m* 1947, Dinah Mary Harper; three *s*. *Educ:* King William's Coll. Student Accountant, 1937–39. War service, RA (TA), 1939–45 (Major). Colonial Service, and Overseas Civil Service, 1945–64; Mem. Legislature and State Sec., Head of Civil Service, Sabah, Malaysia, 1964. Hon. ADK (Malaysia). DL Tyne and Wear, 1975–81. *Publications:* Washington—Quicker by Quango, 1983; Entente Cordiale, 1990; contribs to Sarawak Museum Jl and press articles on New Town Development. *Recreations:* golf, writing, gardening, theatre. *Address:* Forge Cottage, The Green, Abthorpe, Northants NN12 8QP. *Club:* Commonwealth Trust.

HOLLICK, family name of **Baron Hollick.**

HOLLICK, Baron *cr* 1991 (Life Peer), of Notting Hill in the Royal Borough of Kensington and Chelsea; **Clive Richard Hollick;** Chief Executive, MAI PLC (formerly Mills & Allen International PLC), since 1974; *b* 20 May 1945; *s* of Leslie George Hollick and Olive Mary (*née* Scruton); *m* 1977, Susan Mary (*née* Woodford); three *d*. *Educ:* Taunton's Sch., Southampton; Univ. of Nottingham (BA Hons). Joined Hambros Bank Ltd, 1968, Dir, 1973; Chairman: Shepperton Studios Ltd, 1976–84; Garban Ltd (USA), 1983–; Director: Logica plc, 1987–; Avenir Havas Media SA, 1989; Satellite Information Systems Ltd, 1990–. Member: Nat. Bus Co. Ltd, 1984–; Adv. Cttee, Dept of Applied Econs, Univ. of Cambridge, 1989–. Trustee, Inst. for Public Policy Res., 1988–. *Recreations:* reading, theatre, cinema, tennis, countryside. *Club:* Royal Automobile.

HOLLIDAY, Sir Frederick (George Thomas), Kt 1990; CBE 1975; FRSE; Independent Chairman, Joint Nature Conservation Committee, 1991; *b* 22 Sept. 1935; *s* of Alfred C. and Margaret Holliday; *m* 1957, Philippa Mary Davidson; one *s* one *d*. *Educ:* Bromsgrove County High Sch.; Sheffield Univ. BSc 1st cl. hons Zool. 1956; FIBiol 1970, FRSE 1971. Fisheries Research Trng Grant (Develt Commn) at Marine Lab., Aberdeen, 1956–58; Sci. Officer, Marine Lab., Aberdeen, 1958–61; Lectr in Zoology, Univ. of Aberdeen, 1961–66; Prof. of Biology, 1967–75, Dep. Principal, 1972, Acting Principal, 1973–75, Univ. of Stirling; Prof. of Zoology, Univ. of Aberdeen, 1975–79; Vice-Chancellor and Warden, Univ. of Durham, 1980–90. Member: Scottish Cttee, Nature Conservancy, 1969; Council, Scottish Field Studies Assoc., 1970–78 (Pres., 1981–); Council, Scottish Marine Biol Assoc., 1967–85 (Pres., 1979–85); Scottish Wildlife Trust (Vice-Pres.); Council, Freshwater Biol Assoc., 1969–72; NERC Oceanography and Fisheries Research Grants Cttee, 1971; Council, NERC, 1973–79; Nature Conservancy Council, 1975–80 (Dep. Chm., 1976–77, Chm., 1977–80); Scottish Economic Council, 1975–80; Council, Marine Biol Assoc. UK, 1975–78; Oil Develt Council for Scotland, 1976–78; Standing Commn on Energy and the Environment, 1978–; Adv. Cttee, Leverhulme Trust Res. Awards, 1978– (Chm., 1989–); PCFC, 1989–; Chm., Independent Review of Disposal of Radioactive Waste at Sea, 1984. Dir, Shell UK, 1980–; Chm., Investors' Cttee, Northern Venture Partnership Fund; Dep. Chm., Northern Regional Bd, Lloyd's Bank, 1989–91 (Mem., 1985–91; Chm., 1986–89); Member: Bd, Northern Investors Ltd, 1984–90; BRB, 1990– (Chm., BR (Eastern), 1986–90). Trustee, Nat. Heritage Meml Fund, 1980–91; Vice-Pres., Civic Trust for NE. Member: Bd of Governors, Rowett Res. Inst., 1976–84; Scottish Civic Trust, 1984–87. DUniv Stirling, 1984; Hon. DSc Sheffield, 1987. DL Durham, 1985–90. *Publications:* (ed and contrib.) Wildlife of Scotland, 1979; numerous on fish biology and wildlife conservation in Adv. Mar. Biol., Fish Physiology, Oceanography and Marine Biology, etc. *Recreations:* walking, gardening. *Club:* Commonwealth Trust.

HOLLIDAY, Leslie John, FCIOB, CBIM; Chairman and Chief Executive, John Laing plc, 1982–85 (Director, 1978); Chairman, John Laing Construction Ltd, since 1980 (Director, 1966); *b* 9 Jan. 1921; *s* of John and Elsie Holliday; *m* 1943, Kathleen Joan Marjorie Stacey; two *s*. *Educ:* St John's, Whitby. FCIOB 1969; CBIM 1982. Denaby & Cadby Colliery, 1937–40; served Merchant Navy, 1940–45; joined John Laing & Son Ltd, 1947, Dir 1977; Chairman: Laing Homes Ltd, 1978–81; Super Homes Ltd, 1979–81; Laing Management Contracting Ltd, 1980–81; John Laing Internat. Ltd, 1981–82; Director: Declan Kelly Holdings, 1985–89; RM Douglas Holdings, 1986–89; Admiral Homes Ltd, 1989–; Redrow Gp, 1989–. Mem., EDC for Bldg, 1979–82. *Recreations:* yachting, golf. *Address:* The White House, Frithsden Copse, Berkhamsted, Herts. *Clubs:* Porters Park Golf, Berkhamsted Golf.

HOLLIDAY, Dr Robin, FRS 1976; Chief Research Scientist, Commonwealth Scientific and Industrial Research Organisation (Australia), since 1988; *b* 6 Nov. 1932; *s* of Clifford and Eunice Holliday; *m* 1st, 1957, Diana Collet (*née* Parsons) (marr. diss. 1983); one *s* three *d*; 2nd, 1986, Lily Irene (*née* Huschtscha). *Educ:* Hitchin Grammar Sch.; Univ. of Cambridge (BA, PhD). Member, Scientific Staff: Dept of Genetics, John Innes Inst., Bayfordbury, Herts, 1958–65; Division of Microbiology, Nat. Inst. for Med. Research, 1965–70; Head, Div. of Genetics, Nat. Inst. for Med. Research, 1970–88. Lord Cohen Medal, 1987. *Publications:* The Science of Human Progress, 1981; Genes, Proteins and Cellular Aging, 1986; over 160 scientific papers on genetic recombination, repair, gene expression and cellular ageing. *Recreations:* travel, sculpture. *Address:* CSIRO Laboratory for Molecular Biology, PO Box 184, North Ryde, Sydney, NSW 2113, Australia. *T:* (02) 886 4888, *Fax:* (02) 888 9271; 44 Barons Crescent, Hunter's Hill, NSW 2110, Australia. *T:* (02) 816 4840.

HOLLIGER, Heinz; oboist and composer; *b* Langenthal, Switzerland, 1939; *m* Ursula Holliger, harpist. *Educ:* Berne Conservatoire; Paris; Basle; studied with Cassagnaud, Veress, Pierlot and Boulez. Played with Basle Orch., 1959–63; Prof. of oboe, Freiburg Music Acad., 1965–. Appeared at all major European music festivals. Has inspired compositions by Berio, Penderecki, Stockhausen, Henze, Martin and others. Compositions include: Der magische Tänzer, Trio, Dona nobis pacem, Pneuma, Psalm, Cardiophonie, Kreis, Siebengesang, H for wind quintet, string quartet Atembogen, Jahreszeiten, Come and Go. Has won many international prizes, incl. Geneva Competition first prize, 1959, and Munich Competition first prize, 1961. *Address:* c/o Ingpen & Williams Ltd, 14 Kensington Court, W8 5DN.

HOLLINGS, Hon. Sir (Alfred) Kenneth, Kt 1971; MC 1944; **Hon. Mr Justice Hollings;** Judge of the High Court of Justice, Family Division (formerly Probate, Divorce and Admiralty Division), since 1971; *b* 12 June 1918; *s* of Alfred Holdsworth

Hollings and Rachel Elizabeth Hollings; *m* 1949, Harriet Evelyn Isabella, *d* of W. J. C. Fishbourne, OBE, Brussels; one *s* one *d*. *Educ:* Leys Sch., Cambridge; Clare Coll., Cambridge. Law Qualifying and Law Tripos, Cambridge, 1936–39; MA. Served RA (Shropshire Yeomanry), 1939–46. Called to Bar, Middle Temple, 1947 (Harmsworth Schol.); Master of the Bench, 1971. Practised Northern Circuit; QC 1966; Recorder of Bolton, 1968; Judge of County Courts, Circuit 5 (E Lancs), 1968–71; Presiding Judge, Northern Circuit, 1975–78. *Recreations:* walking, swimming, music. *Address:* Royal Courts of Justice, Strand, WC2A 2LL. *Clubs:* Garrick, Hurlingham; Tennis and Racquets (Manchester).

HOLLINGS, Rev. Michael Richard, MC 1943; Parish Priest, St Mary of the Angels, Bayswater, since 1978; Dean of North Kensington, since 1980; *b* 30 Dec. 1921; *s* of Lieut-Commander Richard Eustace Hollings, RN, and Agnes Mary (*née* Hamilton-Dalrymple). *Educ:* Beaumont Coll.; St Catherine's Society, Oxford (MA). St Catherine's, 1939; Sandhurst, 1941. Served War of 1939–45 (despatches): commnd Coldstream Guards, 1941; served N Africa, Italy, Palestine, 1942–45; Major. Trained at Beda Coll., Rome, 1946–50. Ordained Rome, 1950; Asst Priest, St Patrick's, Soho Square, W1, 1950–54; Chaplain, Westminster Cathedral, 1954–58; Asst Chaplain, London Univ., 1958–59; Chaplain to Roman Catholics at Oxford Univ., 1959–70; Parish Priest, St Anselm's, Southall, Middx, 1970–78. Religious Adviser: ATV, 1958–59; Rediffusion, 1959–68; Thames Television, 1968; Advr, Prison Christian Fellowship, 1983–. Member: Nat. Catholic Radio and TV Commn, 1968; Westminster Diocesan Schools Commn, 1970–; Southall Chamber of Commerce, 1971–78; Oxford and Cambridge Catholic Educn Bd, 1971–78; Executive, Council of Christians and Jews, 1971–79, 1984–; Lay Mem., Press Council, 1969–75; Nat. Conf. of Priests Standing Cttee, 1974–76; Rampton Cttee, 1979–81; Swann Cttee, 1981–84; Exec., Ealing Community Relations Council, 1973–76; Exec., Notting Hill Social Council, 1980–; Chm., N Kensington Action Group, 1980–81. Mem. Bd, Christian Aid, 1984–87. Chaplain: to Sovereign Military Order of Malta, 1957; to Nat. Council of Lay Apostolate, 1970–74; to Catholic Inst. of Internat. Relations, 1971–80. Gov., St Charles Catholic Sixth Form Coll., 1990–. *Publications:* Hey, You!, 1955; Purple Times, 1957; Chaplaincraft, 1963; The One Who Listens, 1971; The Pastoral Care of Homosexuals, 1971; It's Me, O Lord, 1972; Day by Day, 1972; The Shade of His Hand, 1973; Restoring the Streets, 1974; I Will Be There, 1975; You Must Be Joking, Lord, 1975; The Catholic Prayer Book, 1976; Alive to Death, 1976; Living Priesthood, 1977; His People's Way of Talking, 1978; As Was His Custom, 1979; St Thérèse of Lisieux, 1981; Hearts not Garments, 1982; Chaplet of Mary, 1982; Path to Contemplation, 1983; Go In Peace, 1984; Christ Died at Notting Hill, 1985; Athirst for God, 1985; Prayers before and after Bereavement, 1986; By Love Alone, 1986; Prayers for the Depressed, 1986; You Are Not Alone, 1988; Dying to Live, 1990; Thoughts of Peace, 1991; contrib. Tablet, Clergy Review, Life of the Spirit, The Universe. *Recreations:* reading, walking, people. *Address:* St Mary of the Angels, Moorhouse Road, Bayswater, W2 5DJ. *T:* 071–229 0487.

HOLLINGSWORTH, Dorothy Frances, OBE 1958; *b* 10 May 1916; *d* of Arthur Hollingsworth and Dorothy Hollingsworth (*née* Coldwell). *Educ:* Newcastle upon Tyne Church High Sch.; Univ. of Durham (BSc 1937); Royal Infirmary, Edinburgh, Sch. of Dietetics (Dip. in Dietetics); FRIC 1956; State Registered Dietitian (SRD), 1963; FIBiol 1968. Hosp. Dietitian, Royal Northern Hosp., London, N7, 1939–41; Govt Service, 1941–70: mainly at Min. of Food until its merger with Min. of Agric. and Fisheries, 1955, to form present Min. of Agric., Fisheries and Food. Principal Scientific Officer and Head of a Scientific Br., 1949–70; Dir-Gen., British Nutrition Foundn, 1970–77. Chairman: British Dietetic Assoc., 1947–49; Internat. Cttee of Dietetic Assocs; 3rd Internat. Cong. Dietetics, 1961; Nutrition Panel, Food Gp, Soc. Chem. Ind., 1966–69 (Mem. Food Gp Cttee, 1969–72); Member: Nat. Food Survey Cttee, 1951–85; Dietetics Bd, Council for Professions Supp. to Med., 1962–74; Cttee on Med. Aspects of Food Policy, 1970–79; Physiological Systems and Disorders Bd, MRC, 1974–77; Environmental Medicine Res. Policy Cttee, MRC, 1975–76; Council, Inst. Food Sci. and Technol., 1970–89; Council, Nutrition Soc., 1974–77; (Dep. Chm.) Adv. Cttee on Protein, ODA, FCO, 1970–73; Jt ARC/MRC Cttee on Food and Nutrition Res., 1970–74; Royal Soc. British Nat. Cttee for Nutritional Scis, 1970–89; IBA Med. Adv. Panel, 1970–; Univ. of Reading Delegacy for Nat. Inst. for Res. in Dairying, 1973–85. Sec. Gen., Internat. Union of Nutritional Scis, 1978–85. Fellow, 1968, Vice-Pres., 1978–80, Inst. of Biology; Fellow, 1965, Vice-Pres., 1976–80, Hon. Fellow, 1985, Inst. of Food Science and Technology; Fellow, British Dietetic Assoc., 1979. *Publications:* The Englishman's Food, by J. C. Drummond and Anne Wilbraham (rev. and prod. 2nd edn), 1958; Hutchison's Food and the Principles of Nutrition (rev. and ed 12th edn with H. M. Sinclair), 1969; Nutritional Problems in a Changing World (ed, with Margaret Russell), 1973; (ed with E. Morse) People and Food Tomorrow, 1976; many papers in scientific jls. *Recreations:* talking with intelligent and humorous friends; appreciation of music, theatre and countryside; gardening. *Address:* 2 The Close, Petts Wood, Orpington, Kent BR5 1JA. *T:* Orpington (0689) 823168. *Clubs:* University Women's, Arts Theatre.

HOLLINGSWORTH, Michael Charles; Chief Executive, Venture Broadcasting Ltd, since 1989; Director: New Era Television, since 1988; Studio West, since 1988; Television Production and Management, since 1985; Walshys Group, since 1990; *b* 22 Feb. 1946; *s* of Albert George Hollingsworth and Gwendoline Marjorie Hollingsworth; *m* 1st, 1968, Patricia Margaret Jefferson Winn (marr. diss. 1987); one *d*; 2nd, 1989, Anne Margaret Diamond; two *s*. (and one *s* decd). *Educ:* Carlisle Grammar Sch. Programme Editor, Anglia Television, 1964–67; Producer, BBC Local Radio, 1967–74; Northern Editor, Today, Radio Four, 1974–75; Editor, News and Current Affairs: Southern Television Ltd, 1975–79; ATV Network/Central, 1979–82; Sen. Producer, Current Affairs, BBC TV, 1982–84; Dir of Programmes, TV-am Ltd, 1984–86; Man. Dir, Music Box Ltd, 1986–89. Consultant on television matters to indep. television cos. *Recreations:* DIY (house renovation), gardening, polo. *Address:* 111 Albert Street, NW1 7NB. *T:* 071–267 8737. *Clubs:* Royal Automobile; Guards' Polo (Windsor).

HOLLINGWORTH, Clare, OBE 1984; Far Eastern Correspondent in Hong Kong for Sunday Telegraph, since 1981; Visiting Scholar, Centre of Asian Studies, University of Hong Kong, since 1981; *b* 10 Oct. 1911; *d* of John Albert Hollingworth and Daisy Gertrude Hollingworth; *m* 1st, 1936, Vyvyan Derring Vandeleur Robinson (marr. diss. 1951); 2nd, 1952, Geoffrey Spencer Hoare (*d* 1966). *Educ:* Girls' Collegiate Sch., Leicester; Grammar Sch., Ashby de la Zouch, Leics; Sch. of Slavonic Studies, Univ. of London. On staff, League of Nations Union, 1935–38; worked in Poland for Lord Mayor's Fund for Refugees from Czechoslovakia, 1939; Correspondent in Poland for Daily Telegraph: first to report outbreak of war from Katawice; remained in Balkans as Germans took over; moved to Turkey and then Cairo, 1941–50, covering Desert Campaigns, troubles in Persia and Iraq, Civil War in Greece and events in Palestine; covered trouble spots from Paris for Manchester Guardian, 1950–63, incl. Algerian War, Egypt, Aden and Vietnam (Journalist of the Year Award and Hannan Swaffer Award, 1963); Guardian Defence Correspondent, 1963–67; Daily Telegraph: foreign trouble shooter, 1967–73, covering war in Vietnam; Correspondent in China, 1973–76; Defence Correspondent, 1976–81. *Publications:* Poland's Three Weeks War, 1940; There's a German Just Behind Me, 1945; The Arabs and the West, 1951; Mao and the Men Against Him, 1984; Front Line, 1990. *Recreations:* visiting second-hand furniture and bookshops, collecting modern pictures and Chinese porcelain, music. *Address:* 19 Dorset Square, NW1 6QB. *T:* 071–262 6923; 302 Ridley House, 2 Upper Albert Road, Hong Kong. *T:* 868 1838. *Clubs:* Cercle de l'Union Interalliée (Paris); Foreign Correspondents (Hong Kong and Tokyo).

HOLLINGWORTH, John Harold; Director, Thaxted Festival Foundation, since 1987; Governor, Cambridge Symphony Orchestra Trust, since 1982 (Director and General Manager, 1979–82); *b* 11 July 1930; *s* of Harold Hollingworth, Birmingham; *m* 1969, Susan Barbara (marr. diss. 1985), *d* of late J. H. Walters, Ramsey, IoM. *Educ:* Chigwell House Sch.; King Edward's Sch., Edgbaston. MP (C) All Saints Division of Birmingham, 1959–64. Chm., Edgbaston Div. Conservative Assoc., 1967–72; Vice-Chm., Birmingham Conservative Assoc., 1959–61, 1972–78 (Vice-Pres. 1960–66). Vice-Chm., Elmdon Trust Ltd; dir of other cos. Mem., Cttee of ISSTIP. *Publications:* contributions to political journals. *Recreations:* cricket, tennis. *Address:* 5 South Green, Widdington, Saffron Walden, Essex CB11 3SE. *T:* Saffron Walden (0799) 40369. *Club:* Lansdowne.

HOLLINGWORTH, Most Rev. Peter John; *see* Brisbane, Archbishop of.

HOLLINS, Rear-Adm. Hubert Walter Elphinstone, CB 1974; marine consultant; *b* 8 June 1923; *s* of Lt-Col W. T. Hollins; *m* 1963, Jillian Mary McAlpin; one *s* one *d*. *Educ:* Stubbington House; Britannia RNC Dartmouth. Cadet RN, 1937; Comdr 1957; Captain 1963; Rear-Adm. 1972; comd HM Ships Petard, Dundas, Caesar and Antrim; Flag Officer, Gibraltar, 1972–74; Admiral Commanding Reserves, 1974–77; Gen. Man., ME Navigation Aids Service, Bahrain, 1977–84. Younger Brother of Trinity House; Mem., Trinity House Lighthouse Bd. Commodore, Bahrain Yacht Club, 1981–83. Master Mariner. Mem., RNVR Yacht Club. Trustee, Royal Merchant Navy Sch., Bearwood; Patron, Newbury Sea Cadet Corps, 1986–. MNI, FBIM. *Recreation:* fishing. *Address:* Waunllan, Llandyfriog, Newcastle Emlyn, Dyfed SA38 9HB. *T:* Newcastle Emlyn (0239) 710456.

HOLLIS, family name of **Baroness Hollis of Heigham.**

HOLLIS OF HEIGHAM, Baroness *cr* 1990 (Life Peer), of Heigham in the City of Norwich; **Patricia Lesley Hollis,** DPhil; Senior Lecturer, Modern History, University of East Anglia, since 1967; *b* 24 May 1941; *d* of (Harry) Lesley (George) Wells and Queenie Rosalyn Wells; *m* 1965, (James) Martin Hollis, *qv*; two *s*. *Educ:* Plympton Grammar Sch.; Cambridge Univ. (MA); Univ. of California; Columbia Univ., NY; Nuffield Coll., Oxford (DPhil). Harkness Fellow, 1962–64; Nuffield Scholar, 1964–67. Dean, School of English and American Studies, UEA, 1988–90. Councillor: Norwich City Council, 1968–91 (Leader, 1983–88); Norfolk CC, 1981–85. Member: Regional Econ. Planning Council, 1975–79; RHA, 1979–83; BBC Regional Adv. Cttee, 1979–83. Vice-President: ADC, 1990–; AMA, 1990–. Dir, Radio Broadland, 1983–. Nat. Comr, English Heritage, 1988–91; Mem. Press Council, 1989–90. Contested (Lab) Gt Yarmouth, Feb. and Oct. 1974, 1979. FRHistS. *Publications:* The Pauper Press, 1970; Class and Conflict, 1815–50, 1973; Pressure from Without, 1974; Women in Public 1850–1900, 1979; (with Dr B. H. Harrison) Robert Lowery, Radical and Chartist, 1979; Ladies Elect: Women in English Local Government 1865–1914, 1987. *Recreations:* boating, singing, domesticity. *Address:* House of Lords, SW1A 0PW. *T:* 071–219 3000. *Club:* United Oxford & Cambridge University.

HOLLIS, Hon. Sir Anthony Barnard, Kt 1982; **Hon. Mr Justice Hollis;** a Judge of the High Court of Justice, Family Division, since 1982; *b* 11 May 1927; *er s* of late Henry Lewis Hollis and of Gladys Florence Hollis (*née* Barnard); *m* 1956, Pauline Mary (*née* Skuce); one step *d*. *Educ:* Tonbridge Sch.; St Peter's Hall, Oxford. Called to Bar, Gray's Inn, 1951 (Bencher, 1979); QC 1969; a Recorder of the Crown Court, 1976–82. Chm., Family Law Bar Assoc., 1974–76. *Recreation:* golf. *Address:* Royal Courts of Justice, Strand, WC2. *Clubs:* Woking Golf; Royal St George's Golf (Sandwich).

HOLLIS, Rt. Rev. Crispian; *see* Portsmouth, Bishop of, (RC).

HOLLIS, Daniel Ayrton, VRD; QC 1968; a Recorder of the Crown Court, since 1972; *b* 30 April 1925; *s* of Norman Hollis; *m* 1st, 1950, Gillian Mary Turner (marr. diss., 1961), *d* of J. W. Cecil Turner, Cambridge; one *s* one *d*; 2nd, 1963, Stella Hydleman, *d* of Mark M. Gergel; one *s*. *Educ:* Geelong Grammar Sch., Australia; Brasenose Coll., Oxford. Served N Atlantic and Mediterranean, 1943–46. Lieut-Commander, RNVR. Called to Bar, Middle Temple, 1949; Bencher, 1975. Standing Counsel to Inland Revenue at Central Criminal Court and London Sessions, 1965–68; Dep. Chm., Kent QS, 1970–71. Home Office Adv. Bd on Restricted Patients, 1986. *Recreation:* travel. *Address:* Queen Elizabeth Building, Temple, EC4Y 9BS.

HOLLIS, Ven. Gerald; Archdeacon of Birmingham, 1974–84; *b* 16 May 1919; *s* of Canon Walter Hollis and Enid (*née* Inchbold); *m* 1946, Doreen Emmet Stancliffe; one *s* three *d*. *Educ:* St Edward's Sch., Oxford; Christ Church, Oxford (MA); Wells Theological College. RNVR, 1940–45. Curate: All Saints, Stepney, E1, 1947–50; i/c St Luke's, Rossington, 1950–55; Rector, Armthorpe, 1955–60; Vicar of Rotherham and Rural Dean, 1960–74. Hon. Canon, Birmingham Cathedral, 1984–. Mem. Gen. Synod, C of E, 1975–84. *Publication:* Rugger: do it this way, 1946. *Recreation:* gardening. *Address:* 68 Britford Lane, Salisbury, Wilts SP2 8AH. *T:* Salisbury (0722) 338154. *Club:* Vincent's (Oxford).

HOLLIS, Prof. James Martin, FBA 1990; Professor of Philosophy, University of East Anglia, since 1982; *b* 14 March 1938; *s* of Hugh Marcus Noel Hollis and Ruth Margaret Hollis; *m* 1965, Patricia Lesley Wells (*see* Baroness Hollis of Heigham); two *s*. *Educ:* Winchester Coll.; New Coll., Oxford (BA 1961; MA 1964). Harkness Commonwealth Fund Fellow, Berkeley and Harvard, 1961; FCO, 1964; Extraordinary Lectr, New Coll., Oxford, 1964; Lectr, Balliol Coll., Oxford, 1965; University of East Anglia: Lectr, 1967; Sen. Lectr, 1972. Dist. Vis. and Lectr, Univs of British Columbia, 1980; Kingston, 1982, Bayreuth, 1988. Pres., Aristotelian Soc., 1986. Mem. Council, Univ. of Bayreuth, 1989–; Gov., Eaton (CNS) Sch., 1972–75. JP Norwich, 1972–82. Editor, Ratio, 1980–87. *Publications:* The Light of Reason, 1971; (with E. J. Nell) Rational Economic Man, 1975; Models of Man, 1977; (with F. Hahn) Philosophy and Economic Theory, 1979; (with S. Lukes) Rationality and Relativism, 1982; Invitation to Philosophy, 1985; The Cunning of Reason, 1988; (with S. Smith) Explaining and Understanding International Relations, 1990. *Recreation:* puzzles. *Address:* School of Economic and Social Studies, University of East Anglia, Norwich NR4 7TJ. *T:* Norwich (0603) 56161.

HOLLIS, Posy; *see* Simmonds, P.

HOLLIS, Rt. Rev. Reginald; Assistant Bishop of the Diocese of Central Florida and Episcopal Director of the Anglican Fellowship of Prayer, since 1990; *b* 18 July 1932; *s* of Jesse Farndon Hollis and Edith Ellen Lee; *m* 1957, Marcia Henderson Crombie; two *s* one *d*. *Educ:* Selwyn Coll., Cambridge; McGill Univ., Montreal. Chaplain and Lectr, Montreal Dio. Theol Coll., 1956–60; Chaplain to Anglican Students, McGill Univ.; Asst Rector, St Matthias' Church, Westmount, PQ, 1960–63; Rector, St Barnabas' Church, Pierrefonds,

PQ, 1963–70; Rector, Christ Church, Beaconsfield, PQ, 1971–74; Dir of Parish and Dio. Services, Dio. Montreal, 1974–75; Bishop of Montreal, 1975; Metropolitan of the Ecclesiastical Province of Canada and Archbishop of Montreal, 1989–90. Hon. DD 1975. *Publication:* Abiding in Christ, 1987. *Address:* PO Box 31, Orlando, Fla 32802, USA.

HOLLIS, Rt. Rev. (Roger Francis) Crispian; *see* Portsmouth, Bishop of, (RC).

HOLLMAN, Arthur, MD; FRCP; FLS; Consultant Cardiologist, University College Hospital, London, 1962–87, now Consulting Cardiologist; Consultant Cardiologist, Hospital for Sick Children, London, 1978–88, now Consulting Cardiologist; Hon. Senior Lecturer, University College and Middlesex School of Medicine, since 1962; *b* 7 Dec. 1923; *s* of W. J. and I. R. Hollman; *m* 1949, Catharine Elizabeth Large; four *d. Educ:* Tiffin Boys' Sch., Kingston upon Thames; University Coll. London (Fellow, 1978); UCH Med. Sch. (MD). FRCP 1967. FLS 1983. Jun. hosp. appts, London, Banbury and Taplow, 1946–57; Bilton Pollard Fellow of UCH Med. Sch. at Children's Meml Hosp., Montreal, 1951–52; Clinical Asst, National Heart Hosp., 1954–56; Sen. Registrar and Asst Lectr, Royal Postgraduate Med. Sch., 1957–62; Hon. Consultant Cardiologist, Kingston Hosp., 1964–87. Advisor in Cardiology: to Mauritius Govt, 1966–86; to Republic of Seychelles, 1974–. Councillor, RCP, 1976–79. Member: Cttee of Management, Chelsea Physic Garden, 1971–; Council, British Heart Foundn, 1975–80; British Cardiac Soc. (Mem. Council, Asst Sec., and Sec., 1971–76); Assoc. of Physicians of GB and Ireland. Pres., Osler Club, 1983–84. *Publications:* articles on cardiology, the history of cardiology and the use of plants in medical practice. *Recreations:* gardening, especially medicinal plants; medical history. *Address:* Seabank, Chick Hill, Pett, Hastings, East Sussex TN35 4EQ. *T:* Hastings (0424) 813228. *Club:* Athenæum.

HOLLOM, Sir Jasper (Quintus), KBE 1975; Chairman: Eagle Star Holdings PLC, 1985–87; Eagle Star Insurance Co. Ltd, 1985–87; *b* 16 Dec. 1917; *s* of Arthur and Kate Louisa Hollom; *m* 1954, Patricia Elizabeth Mary Ellis. *Educ:* King's Sch., Bruton. Entered Bank of England, 1936; appointed Deputy Chief Cashier, 1956; Chief Cashier, 1962–66; Director, 1966–70, 1980–84; Deputy Governor, 1970–80. Chairman: Eagle Star Holdings PLC, 1985–87; Eagle Star Insurance Co. Ltd, 1985–87; Director: BAT Industries plc, 1980–87; Portals Hldgs plc, 1980–88. Chairman: Panel on Take-overs and Mergers, 1980–87; Council for the Securities Industry, 1985–86; Commonwealth Develt Finance Co. Ltd, 1980–86; Pres., Council of Foreign Bondholders, 1983–89. *Address:* High Wood, Selborne, Alton, Hants GU34 3LA. *T:* Selborne (042050) 317.

HOLLOWAY, Hon. Sir Barry (Blyth), KBE 1984 (CBE 1974); *b* 26 Sept. 1934; *s* of Archibald and Betty Holloway; *m* 1974, Ikini Aikel; three *s* four *d. Educ:* Launceston Church Grammar Sch., Tasmania; Sch. of Pacific Administration, Sydney, 1957; Univ. of Papua New Guinea. Dip., Pacific Admin. District Officer in Papua New Guinea, 1953–64. Elected to first PNG Parliament, 1964; Foundn Mem., Pangu Pati, 1966; MP Eastern Highlands Province, Member of various parliamentary cttees, incl. Public Accounts; Speaker of Parliament, 1972–77; Finance Minister, 1977–80; Minister for Educn, 1982–85. Chairman of Constituent Assembly responsible for the formation of Constitution of the Independent State of Papua New Guinea, 1974–75. Director of various companies. *Recreations:* reading, agriculture. *Address:* PO Box 6361, Boroko, Papua New Guinea. *T:* Port Moresby 272338. *Club:* Papua (Port Moresby).

HOLLOWAY, David Richard; Literary Editor of The Daily Telegraph, 1968–88 (Deputy Literary Editor, 1960–68); *b* 3 June 1924; *s* of W. E. Holloway and Margaret Boyd (*née* Schleselman); *m* 1952, Sylvia Eileen, (Sally), Gray; two *s* one *d. Educ:* Westminster; Birkbeck Coll., London; Magdalen Coll., Oxford. Served War, RAF, 1942–46 (navigator). Reporter: Middlesex County Times, 1940–41; Daily Sketch, 1941–42; Daily Mirror, 1949; News Chronicle: Reporter and Leader Writer, 1950–53; Asst Lit. Editor and novel reviewer, 1953–58; Book Page Editor, 1958–60. Chairman: Soc. of Bookmen, 1968–71; Booker Prize Judges, 1970; Registrar, Royal Literary Fund, 1982–. *Publications:* John Galsworthy, 1968; Lewis and Clark and the Crossing of America, 1971; Derby Day, 1975; Playing the Empire, 1979; (ed) Telegraph Year, 1–3, 1977–79; (with Michael Geare) Nothing So Became Them . . ., 1986; contrib. Folio Magazine and book trade jls. *Recreation:* listening. *Address:* 95 Lonsdale Road, SW13 9DA. *T:* 081–748 3711. *Club:* Reform.

HOLLOWAY, Derrick Robert Le Blond; Registrar of the Family Division, Principal Registry, 1966–83; retired; *b* 29 May 1917; *s* of Robert Fabyan Le Blond and Mary Beatrice Holloway; *m* 1942, Muriel Victoria Bower; one *s. Educ:* Brentwood; Univ. of London (LLB (Hons)). Principal Probate Registry, 1937. Served War of 1939–45: DCLI, RASC, Claims Commn. Sec., Cttee on Law of Intestate Succession, 1951; Sec., Cttee on Ancient Probate Records, 1953; Asst Sec., Royal Commn on Marriage and Divorce, 1952–56; Acting Registrar, Probate, Divorce and Admiralty Div., 1965. Gp Chm. (Amersham), Civil Service Retirement Fellowship, 1985; Chm., S Bucks Br., CS Retirement Fellowship, 1990. *Publications:* (ed jtly) Latey on Divorce (14th edn), 1952; Editor: Proving a Will (2nd edn), 1952; Obtaining Letters of Administration, 1954; Divorce Forms and Precedents, 1959; Probate Handbook (now Holloway's Probate Handbook), 1961, 7th edn 1984, (Consultant Editor) 8th edn 1987; Phillips' Probate Practice (6th edn), 1963; contrib. to Butterworths' Costs (4th edn), 1971; Acting in Person: how to obtain an undefended divorce, 1977. *Recreations:* marriage, gardening, foreign travel, music, photography. *Address:* 1 Chiltern Manor Park, Great Missenden, Bucks.

HOLLOWAY, Frank, FCA; Managing Director, Supplies and Transport, 1980–83 and Board Member, 1978–83, British Steel Corporation; *b* 20 Oct. 1924; *s* of Frank and Elizabeth Holloway; *m* 1949, Elizabeth Beattie; three *d. Educ:* Burnage High Sch., Manchester. Served War, Royal Navy, 1943–46. Various senior finance appts in The United Steel Companies Ltd and later in British Steel Corp., 1949–72. Managing Director: Supplies and Production Control, 1973–76, Finance and Supplies, 1976–80, British Steel Corp. *Recreations:* cricket, collecting books.

HOLLOWAY, Prof. John, MA, DPhil, DLitt, LittD; Professor of Modern English, Cambridge, 1972–82 (Reader, 1966–72); Fellow of Queens' College, 1955–82, Life Fellow, 1982; *b* 1 Aug. 1920; *s* of George Holloway and Evelyn Astbury; *m* 1946, Audrey Gooding; one *s* one *d; m* 1978, Joan Black. *Educ:* County Sch., Beckenham, Kent; New Coll., Oxford (Open History Scholar). 1st class Modern Greats, 1941; DPhil Oxon 1947; DLitt Aberdeen 1954; LittD Cambridge, 1969. Served War of 1939–45, commnd RA, 1942; subsequently seconded to Intelligence. Temporary Lecturer in Philosophy, New Coll., 1945; Fellow of All Souls Coll., 1946–60; John Locke Scholar, 1947; University Lecturer in English: Aberdeen, 1949–54; Cambridge, 1954–66; Sec., 1954–56, Librarian, 1964–66, Chm., 1970, 1971, English Faculty. FRSL 1956. Lecture Tours: Ceylon, India, Pakistan, 1958; Middle East, 1965; France, 1970; Tunisia, 1972; Hong Kong, NZ, Fiji, 1984; Kyoto, 1986; India, 1988; California, 1989; Visiting appointments: Byron Professor, University of Athens, 1961–63; Alexander White Professor, Chicago, 1965; Hinkley Prof., Johns Hopkins Univ., 1972; Virginia Lectr, Charlottesville, 1979; Berg Prof., New York Univ., 1987. *Publications:* Language and Intelligence, 1951; The Victorian Sage, 1953; (ed) Poems of the Mid-Century, 1957; The Charted Mirror (Essays), 1960; (ed) Selections from Shelley, 1960; Shakespeare's Tragedies, 1961; The Colours of Clarity (essays), 1964; The Lion Hunt, 1964; Widening Horizons in English Verse, 1966; Blake, The Lyric Poetry, 1968; The Establishment of English, 1972; (ed with J. Black) Later English Broadside Ballads, vol. I, 1975, vol. II, 1979; The Proud Knowledge, 1977; Narrative and Structure, 1979; The Slumber of Apollo, 1983; (ed) The Oxford Book of Local Verses, 1987; contributions to journals; *verse:* The Minute, 1956; The Fugue, 1960; The Landfallers, 1962; Wood and Windfall, 1965; New Poems, 1970; Planet of Winds, 1977. *Recreation:* enjoyment. *Address:* Queens' College, Cambridge CB3 9ET.

HOLLOWAY, Reginald Eric, CMG 1984; HM Diplomatic Service; Consul-General, Los Angeles, since 1989; *b* 22 June 1932; *s* of late Ernest and Beatrice Holloway; *m* 1958, Anne Penelope, *d* of late Walter Robert and Doris Lilian Pawley; one *d. Educ:* St Luke's, Brighton. Apprentice reporter, 1947–53; served RAF, 1953–55; journalist in Britain and E Africa, 1955–61; Press Officer, Tanganyika Govt, 1961–63; Dir, British Inf. Service, Guyana, 1964–67; Inf. Dept, FCO, 1967–69 (Anguilla, 1969); 2nd, later 1st Sec., Chancery in Malta, 1970–72; E African Dept, FCO, 1972–74; Consul and Head of Chancery, Kathmandu, 1974–77 (Chargé d'Affaires *ai*, 1975 and 1976); Asst Head, S Asian Dept, FCO, 1977–79; Counsellor, 1979; Inspector, 1979–81; Consul-Gen., Toronto, 1981–85; Sen. British Trade Comr, Hong Kong, 1985–89, and Consul-Gen. (non-resident), Macao, 1986–89. *Recreations:* woodworking, old wirelesses, old cameras. *Address:* c/o Foreign and Commonwealth Office, SW1A 2AH.

HOLLOWAY, Rt. Rev. Richard Frederick; *see* Edinburgh, Bishop of.

HOLLOWAY, Dr Robin Greville; composer; Fellow of Gonville and Caius College, Cambridge, since 1969, and Lecturer in Music, University of Cambridge, since 1975; *b* 19 Oct. 1943; *s* of Robert Charles Holloway and Pamela Mary Jacob. *Educ:* St Paul's Cathedral Choir Sch.; King's Coll. Sch., Wimbledon; King's Coll., Cambridge (MA 1968; PhD 1972; MusD 1976); New Coll., Oxford. *Compositions* include: Garden Music, 1962; First Concerto for Orchestra, 1966–69; Scenes from Schumann, 1969–70; Evening with Angels, 1972; Domination of Black, 1973–74; Sea Surface full of Clouds, 1974–75; Clarissa, 1976 (premièred ENO, 1990); Romanza, 1976; The Rivers of Hell, 1977; Second Concerto for Orchestra, 1978–79; Serenade in C, 1979; Aria, 1980; Brand, 1981; Women in War, 1982; Second Idyll, 1983; Seascape and Harvest, 1984; Viola Concerto, 1984; Serenade in E flat, 1984; Ballad for harp and orch., 1985; Inquietus, 1986; Double Concerto for clarinet and saxophone, 1988; The Spacious Firmament, 1989; Violin Concerto, 1990. *Publications:* Wagner and Debussy, 1978; numerous articles and reviews. *Recreation:* playing on two pianos. *Address:* Gonville and Caius College, Cambridge CB2 1TA. *T:* Cambridge (0223) 335424.

HOLLOWAY, Maj.-Gen. Robin Hugh Ferguson, CB 1976; CBE 1974; Referee, Small Claims Tribunal: Lower Hutt, since 1982; Wellington, since 1985; *b* Hawera, 22 May 1922; *s* of late Hugh Ferguson Holloway and Phyllis Myrtle Holloway; *m* 1947, Margaret Jewell, *d* of E. G. Monk, Temple Cloud, Somerset; one *s* two *d. Educ:* Hawera Technical High Sch.; RMC, Duntroon, Australia. Commnd NZ Staff Corps, 1942; served in 2nd NZEF, Solomon Is, Italy and Japan, 1943–47; qual. Air Observation Post Pilot, 1948–49; Staff Coll., Camberley, 1952; Jt Services Staff Coll., Latimer, 1958; Dir of Mil. Intelligence, 1959–61; Dep. Adjt Gen., 1962–63; Head, NZ Defence Liaison Staff, Singapore and Malaysia, 1964–65; ACDS, 1967–68; IDC, 1969; Comdr Northern Mil. Dist, and Comdr 1st Inf. Bde Gp, 1970; DCGS, 1971–73; CGS, 1973–76; R of O, March 1977. Dir of Civil Defence, NZ, 1977–83. Pres., Scout Assoc. of NZ, 1979–89; Dep. Chief Scout, 1979–89. *Recreations:* gardening, walking. *Address:* 435 Te Moana Road, Waikanae, New Zealand. *T:* Waikanae 34089. *Club:* Wellington (NZ).

HOLM, Sir Carl Henry, (Sir Charles Holm), Kt 1987; OBE 1975; land developer, dairy farmer, cane farmer; *b* 1 Aug. 1915; *s* of Frederick Otto Holm and Johanna Jamieson (formerly Stickens); *m* 1st, 1938, Myrtle Phyllis Murtha (*d* 1987); one *s*; 2nd, 1988, Joyce Elaine Blackbeard (*née* Shell). *Educ:* Baralaba State Sch.; Ipswich Boys' Sch.; Pimpana State Sch.; Coomera State Sch. Sgt, Volunteer Defence Corp., 1942–45. Albert Shire Council: Councillor, 1967–82; Mem., Town Planning Cttee, 1975–82; Chm., Works Cttee, 1975–82; National Party of Australia: Senior Vice-Pres., Qld, 1972–; Federal Sen. Vice-Pres., 1975–; Chm., Evaluation Cttee; Past Chm., Tranport Cttee; Past Chm., Conservation Cttee. Queensland Dairymen's Organisation: Mem., 1946–; Chm., SE District Council, 1961–; Mem., State Council, 1972–; Mem., State Milk Exec., 1967–; Chm., United Milk Producers Co-operative Assoc., 1972–; Pres., Metrop. Milk Producers Co-operative Assoc., 1976–79, Dir, 1979–. *Recreation:* riding horses. *Address:* Kingsholme, Ormeau, Qld 4208, Australia. *T:* 075 466 237 and 075 466 388. *Club:* National (Southport, Qld) (Foundn Mem. and Chm., 1973–).

HOLM, Ian, CBE 1989; actor, since 1954; *b* 12 Sept. 1931; *s* of Dr James Harvey Cuthbert and Jean Wilson Cuthbert; *m* 1955, Lynn Mary Shaw (marr. diss. 1965); two *d*; and one *s* one *d*; *m* 1982, Sophie Baker (marr. diss. 1986); one *s. Educ:* Chigwell Grammar Sch., Essex. Trained RADA, 1950–53 (interrupted by Nat. Service); joined Shakespeare Memorial Theatre, 1954, left after 1955; Worthing Rep., 1956; tour, Olivier's Titus Andronicus, 1957; re-joined Stratford, 1958: roles include: Puck; Ariel; Gremio; Lorenzo; Prince Hal; Henry V; Duke of Gloucester; Richard III; The Fool in Lear; Lennie in The Homecoming (also on Broadway, 1966) (Evening Standard Actor of the Year, 1965); left RSC, 1967. Major film appearances include: Young Winston, The Fixer, Oh! What a Lovely War, The Bofors Gun, Alien, All Quiet on the Western Front, Chariots of Fire (Best Supporting Actor: Cannes, 1981; BAFTA, 1982); Return of the Soldier; Greystoke; Brazil; Laughterhouse; Dance With a Stranger; Wetherby; Dreamchild; Another Woman; Hamlet. TV series include: J. M. Barrie in trilogy The Lost Boys (RTS Best Actor Award, 1979); We, the Accused, 1980; The Bell, 1981; Game, Set and Match, 1988; other TV appearances include: Lech Walesa in Strike, 1981; Goebbels in Inside the Third Reich, 1982; Mr and Mrs Edgehill, 1985; The Browning Version, 1986. *Recreations:* tennis, walking, general outdoor activities. *Address:* c/o Julian Belfrage Associates, 68 St James's Street, SW1A 1LE.

HOLMAN, (Edward) James; QC 1991; *b* 21 Aug. 1947; *o s* of Dr Edward Theodore Holman and Mary Megan Holman, MBE (*née* Morris), Manaccan, Cornwall; *m* 1979, Fiona Elisabeth, *er d* of Dr Ronald Cathcart Roxburgh, FRCP; two *s* one *d. Educ:* Dauntsey's; Exeter College, Oxford (BA Jurisp., MA). Called to the Bar, Middle Temple, 1971; Western Circuit; in practice, 1971–; Standing Counsel to HM Treasury (Queen's Proctor), 1980–91; a Legal Assessor, UK Central Council for Nursing, Midwifery and Health Visiting, 1983–; Asst Recorder, 1989–. Mem., Family Proceedings Rules Cttee, 1991–. Sec., Family Law Bar Assoc., 1988–; Mem., Council, RYA, 1980–83, 1984–87, 1988–91. *Recreations:* sailing, ski-ing, music. *Address:* Queen Elizabeth Building, Temple, EC4Y 9BS. *T:* 071–583 7837; 58 Grove Park, Camberwell, SE5 8LG. *T:* 071–274 0340. *Clubs:* Royal Ocean Racing (Mem. Cttee, 1984–87); Royal Yacht Squadron.

HOLMAN, Norman Frederick; *b* 22 Feb. 1914; *s* of late Walter John and Violet Holman, Taunton; *m* 1940, Louisa Young; one *s* two *d. Educ:* Huish's, Taunton. Entered Post Office as Exec. Officer, 1932; Higher Exec. Officer, 1942. Served in Royal Corps of

Signals, 1942–46. Sen. Exec. Officer, 1950; Asst Accountant-Gen., 1953; Dep. Dir, 1956; Dir of Postal Finance, 1967; Dir of Central Finance and Accounts, PO, 1971–74. *Recreations:* bowls, bridge, The Observer crossword. *Address:* Crosswinds, 32 Richmond Road, Exmouth, Devon EX8 2NA. *T:* Exmouth (0395) 275298.

HOLMBERG, Eric Robert Reginald; Deputy Chief Scientist (Army), Ministry of Defence, 1972–77; *b* 24 Aug. 1917; *s* of Robert and May Holmberg; *m* 1940, Wanda Erna Reich; one *s* one *d*. *Educ:* Sandown (Isle of Wight) Grammar Sch.; St John's Coll., Cambridge (MA); Imperial Coll., London (PhD). Joined Mine Design Department, Admiralty, 1940; Admiralty Gunnery Establishment, 1945; Operational Research Department, Admiralty, 1950; appointed Chief Supt Army Operational Research Group, 1956; Dir, Army Operational Science and Res., subseq. Asst Chief Scientist (Army), MoD, 1961–72. *Publications:* The Trouble with Relativity, 1986; papers in Proc. Royal Astronomical Society. *Address:* 29 Westmoreland Road, Barnes, SW13 9RZ. *T:* 081–748 2568.

HOLME, family name of Baron Holme of Cheltenham.

HOLME OF CHELTENHAM, Baron *cr* 1990 (Life Peer), of Cheltenham in the County of Gloucestershire; **Richard Gordon Holme**, CBE 1983; Chairman, Threadneedle Publishing Group, since 1988; Chairman, Constitutional Reform Centre, since 1985; *b* 27 May 1936; *s* of J. R. Holme and E. M. Holme (*née* Eggleton); *m* 1958, Kathleen Mary Powell; two *s* two *d*. *Educ:* Royal Masonic Sch.; St John's Coll., Oxford; Harvard Business Sch. (PMD). Commnd 10th Gurkha Rifles, Malaya, 1954–56. Vice-Chm., Liberal Party Exec., 1966–67; Pres., Liberal Party, 1980–81; contested: East Grinstead (L) 1964 and by-election, 1965; Braintree (L) Oct. 1974; Cheltenham (L) 1983, (L/Alliance) 1987. Dir, Campaign for Electoral Reform, 1976–85; Sec., Parly Democracy Trust, 1977–; Hon. Treasurer, Green Alliance, 1978–90. Chairman: Dod's Publishing and Research, 1988–; Black Box Publishing, 1988–; Director: AVI Hldgs Ltd, 1987–; City and Corporate Counsel Ltd, 1987–; European Strategy Counsel, 1988–; Political Quarterly, 1988–. Vis. Prof. in Business Administration, Middlesex Polytechnic, 1990–. Associate Mem., Nuffield Coll., 1985–89; Exec. Mem., Campaign for Oxford, 1990–. Vice-Chm., Hansard Soc. for Parly Govt, 1991–. *Publications:* No Dole for the Young, 1975; A Democracy Which Works, 1978; The People's Kingdom, 1987; (ed jtly) 1688–1988, Time for a New Constitution, 1988. *Address:* House of Lords, SW1A 0PW. *Club:* Brooks's, Reform.

HOLME, Maj.-Gen. Michael Walter, CBE 1966; MC 1945; *b* 9 May 1918; *s* of Thomas Walter Holme and Ruth Sangster Holme (*née* Rivington); *m* 1948, Sarah Christian Van Der Gucht; one *s* two *d*. *Educ:* Winchester College. Directing Staff, Staff Coll., Camberley, 1952–55; Comdr 1st Bn 3rd East Anglian Regt, 1960–62; Comdr Land Forces Persian Gulf, 1963–66; Chief of Staff, Western Comd, 1966–67; Divisional Brig., The Queen's Div., 1968–69; GOC Near East Land Forces, 1969–72, retired; Dep. Col, The Royal Anglian Regiment, 1970–77. *Recreations:* various. *Address:* c/o C. Hoare & Co., 37 Fleet Street, EC4. *Club:* Army and Navy.

HOLMER, Paul Cecil Henry, CMG 1973; HM Diplomatic Service, retired; Ambassador to Romania, 1979–83; *b* 19 Oct. 1923; *s* of late Bernard Cecil and Mimi Claudine Holmer; *m* 1946, Irene Nora, *e d* of late Orlando Lenox Beater, DFC; two *s* two *d*. *Educ:* King's Sch., Canterbury; Balliol Coll., Oxford. Served in RA, 1942–46. Entered Civil Service, 1947; Colonial Office, 1947–49; transferred to HM Foreign Service, 1949; FO, 1949–51; Singapore, 1951–55; FO, 1955–56; served on Civil Service Selection Bd, 1956; FO, 1956–58; Moscow, 1958–59; Berlin, 1960–64; FO, 1964–66; Counsellor, 1966; Dep. High Comr, Singapore, 1966–69; Head of Security Dept, FCO, 1969–72; Ambassador, Ivory Coast, Upper Volta and Niger, 1972–75; Minister and UK Dep. Perm. Rep. to NATO, 1976–79. Dir, African Develt Fund, 1973–75. *Address:* Wincott House, Whichford, Shipston-on-Stour, Warwickshire CV36 5PG. *Club:* Commonwealth Trust.

HOLMES, Anthony, CBE 1982; Head of Passport Department, Home Office (formerly Chief Passport Officer, Foreign and Commonwealth Office), 1980–88, retired; *b* 4 Sept. 1931; *s* of Herbert and Jessie Holmes; *m* 1954, Sheila Frances Povall. *Educ:* Calday Grange Grammar School. Joined HM Customs and Excise, 1949; served HM Forces, 1950–52; Passport Office, 1955; Dep. Chief Passport Officer, 1977. *Recreations:* golf, sailing. *Address:* Hilbre, Mill Road, West Chiltington, Pulborough, West Sussex RH20 2PZ. *Clubs:* Cowdray Park Golf (Midhurst); West Sussex Golf (Pulborough).

HOLMES, Barry Trevor; HM Diplomatic Service; Consul-General, Atlanta, since 1985; *b* 23 Sept. 1933; *s* of Edwin Holmes and Marion (*née* Jones); *m* 1956, Dorothy Pitchforth (marr. diss. 1989); three *d*. *Educ:* Bishopshalt Grammar School. Entered HM Foreign Service, 1950; Wages Clerk, 1950–53; Foreign Office, 1955–58; Quito, 1958–62; FO, 1962–65; Vancouver, 1965–68; First Secretary, FCO, 1968–72; Nairobi, 1972–75; FCO, 1975–80; Commercial Counsellor, Helsinki, 1980–85. National Service: Captain, Royal Artillery, Egypt, 1953–55. *Recreations:* chess, lay-preaching when anyone will listen. *Address:* c/o Foreign and Commonwealth Office, SW1A 2AH.

HOLMES, Prof. Brian, PhD, FCP; Professor of Education, since 1981, College of Preceptors (Dean, 1980–89); Editor, Education Today, since 1980; *b* 25 April 1920; *s* of Albert and Gertrude Maud Holmes; *m* 1st, 1945, Mary I. Refoy; two *s*; 2nd, 1971, Margaret Hon-Yin Wong; one *d*. *Educ:* Salt High School, Shipley; University College London (BSc Phys 1941); PhD Univ. of London Inst. of Educn 1962. RAFVR Radar Officer, 1941–45; schoolmaster, St Clement Dane's and King's College School, Wimbledon, 1946–51; Lectr in Educn, Univ. of Durham, 1951–53; Univ. of London Institute of Education: Asst Editor, 1953; Lectr, 1959; Senior Lectr, 1963; Reader, 1964; Professor of Comparative Educn, 1975–85, now Emeritus; Head of Dept of Comparative Educn, 1977–85; Pro-Director, 1983–85; Dean, Faculty of Educn, Univ. of London, 1982–85. Vis. Prof., univs in USA, incl. Univ. of Chicago, 1958–59; Res. Consultant, Univ. of Kyushu, Japan, 1960; Consultant: Unesco; Internat. Bureau of Educn; OECD; foreign govts; professional visits to USSR, 1960–87; Vis. Examr, univs in UK, Australia, India and Singapore. Fellow, Japan Soc. for Promotion of Science, 1987. Pres., Inst. of Educn Soc., 1985–88. *Publications:* Problems in Education, 1965; (ed) Educational Policy and the Mission Schools, 1967; (ed) Diversity and Unity in Education, 1980; International Guide to Educational Systems, 1979; Comparative Education: some considerations of method, 1981; (ed) Equality and Freedom in Education, 1985; (with Martin McLean) Curricula in Comparative Perspective, 1988; (ed jtly) Theories and Methods in Comparative Education, 1988; contribs to Internat. Review of Educn, Comparative Educn Review, Compare, Prospects, foreign periodicals. *Recreation:* antique British clocks. *Address:* 110 Sumatra Road, NW6 1PG. *Club:* Commonwealth Trust.

HOLMES, David, CB 1985; Deputy Secretary, Department of Transport, since 1982; *b* 6 March 1935; *s* of late George A. Holmes and Annie Holmes; *m* 1963, Ann Chillingworth; one *s* two *d*. *Educ:* Doncaster Grammar Sch.; Christ Church, Oxford (MA). Asst Principal, Min. of Transport and Civil Aviation, 1957; Private Sec. to Jt Parly Sec., 1961–63; HM Treasury, 1965–68; Principal Private Sec. to Minister of Transport, 1968–70; Asst Sec., 1970, Under Sec., 1976, Principal Finance Officer, 1982–88, Dept of Transport. *Recreation:* music. *Club:* United Oxford & Cambridge University.

HOLMES, David Vivian; Member, Broadcasting Complaints Commission, since 1987; *b* 12 Oct. 1926; *s* of Vivian and Kathleen Holmes; *m* 1st, 1957, Rhoda Ann, *d* of late Col N. J. Gai; two *d*; 2nd, 1979, Linda Ruth Alexander, *d* of late G. L. Kirk and of Mrs M. M. Kirk. *Educ:* Ipswich Sch.; Allhallows Sch. Served KRRC, 1944–47. Entered journalism, 1948; Evening Standard, 1951–56; Reporter, BBC News, 1956–61; BBC political reporter, 1961–72; Asst Head, BBC Radio Talks and Documentary Programmes; launched Kaleidoscope arts programme, 1973; Presenter, Westminster, BBC2, intermittently, 1969–79; Political Editor, BBC, 1975–80; Chief Asst to Dir-Gen., BBC, 1980–83; Sec. of the BBC, 1983–85. Chm., Parly Lobby Journalists, 1976–77. Member: Council, Hansard Soc., 1981–83; MoD Censorship Study Gp, 1983; Adv. Cttee, W Yorks Media in Politics Gp, Leeds Univ., 1985–90; Exec. Cttee, Suffolk Historic Churches Trust, 1989–90. *Recreations:* music, garden design. *Address:* 5 Salters Lane, Walpole, Halesworth, Suffolk IP19 9BA. *T:* Bramfield (098684) 412. *Club:* Farmers'.

HOLMES, Sir Frank (Wakefield), Kt 1975; JP; company director; consultant; Emeritus Professor, since 1985, Visiting Fellow, since 1986, and Chairman, since 1989, Institute of Policy Studies, Victoria University of Wellington; *b* 8 Sept. 1924; *s* of James Francis Wakefield and Marie Esme Babette Holmes; *m* 1947, Nola Ruth Ross; two *s*. *Educ:* Waitaki Boys' Jun. High Sch. (Dux 1936); King's High Sch. (Dux 1941); Otago Univ.; Auckland University Coll. (Sen. Schol. 1948); Victoria University Coll. MA (1st Cl. Hons) 1949. Flying Officer, Royal NZ Air Force, 1942–45 (despatches). Economic Div., Prime Minister's and External Affairs Depts 1949–52; Lectr to Prof., Victoria Univ. of Wellington, 1952–67; Macarthy Prof. of Economics, 1959–67; Dean, Faculty of Commerce, 1961–63; Economics Manager, Tasman Pulp & Paper Co Ltd, 1967–70; Victoria Univ. of Wellington: Prof. of Money and Finance, 1970–77; Vis. Prof. and Convener, Master of Public Policy Programme, 1982–85; Emeritus Prof., 1985. Adviser, Royal Commn on Monetary, Banking and Credit Systems, 1955; Consultant, Bank of New Zealand, 1956–58 and 1964–67; Chm., Monetary and Economic Council, 1961–64 and 1970–72; Jt Sec., Cttee on Universities, 1959; Mem., NZ Council Educnl Research, 1965–77 (Chm. 1970–74); Chairman: Adv. Council on Educnl Planning and Steering Cttee, Educnl Develt Conf., 1973–74; NZ Govt Task Force on Economic and Social Planning, 1976; NZ Planning Council, 1977–82; Dep. Chm., Inst. of Policy Studies, 1984–89. President: NZ Assoc. of Economists, 1961–63; Economic Section, ANZAAS, 1967, Education Section, 1979; Central Council, Economic Soc. of Australia and NZ, 1967–68. Chairman: South Pacific Merchant Finance Ltd, 1985–89 (Dir, 1984–89); Hugo Consulting Group Ltd, 1989– (Exec. Dir., 1986–); State Insurance Ltd, 1990–; Norwich Holdings Ltd, 1990–; Director: National Bank of NZ Ltd, 1982–; Norwich Union Life Insce Soc. 1983–. Mem., Internat. Organising Cttee, Pacific Trade and Develt Confs, 1982–. FNZIM 1986. Life Mem., VUW Students' Assoc., 1967. JP 1960. FRSA. *Publications:* Money, Finance and the Economy, 1972; Government in the New Zealand Economy, 1977, 2nd edn 1980; Closer Economic Relations with Australia, 1986; Partners in the Pacific, 1988; (ed) Stepping Stones to Freer Trade, 1989; (jtly) Meeting the East Asia Challenge, 1989; Meeting the European Challenge, 1991; pamphlets and articles on econs, finance, educn and internat. affairs. *Recreations:* touring, walking, swimming, music. *Address:* 61 Cheviot Road, Lowry Bay, Wellington, New Zealand. *T:* Wellington 684–719. *Club:* Wellington (Wellington).

HOLMES, Prof. Geoffrey Shorter, DLitt; FBA 1983; FRHistS; Professor of History, University of Lancaster, 1973–83, now Emeritus; *b* 17 July 1928; *s* of Horace and Daisy Lavinia Holmes; *m* 1955, Ella Jean Waddell Scott; one *s* one *d*. *Educ:* Woodhouse Grammar Sch., Sheffield; Pembroke Coll., Oxford (BA 1948; MA, BLitt 1952; DLitt 1978). FRHistS 1968. Served Army, RASC, 1948–50 (Mil. Adviser's Staff, New Delhi, 1949–50). Personnel Dept, Hadfield's Ltd, Sheffield, 1951–52; Asst Lectr, Lectr and Sen. Lectr, Univ. of Glasgow, 1952–69; Reader in History, Univ. of Lancaster, 1969–72. Vis. Fellow, All Souls Coll., Oxford, 1977–78. Raleigh Lectr, British Acad., 1979; James Ford Special Lectr, Oxford, 1981. Vice-Pres., RHistS, 1985– (Mem. Council, 1980–84). *Publications:* British Politics in the Age of Anne, 1967, rev. edn 1987; (with W. A. Speck) The Divided Society, 1967; (ed and jtly) Britain after the Glorious Revolution, 1969; The Trial of Doctor Sacheverell, 1973; The Electorate and the National Will in the First Age of Party, 1976; Augustan England: Professions, State and Society 1680–1730, 1982; (ed with Clyve Jones) The London Diaries of William Nicolson, Bishop of Carlisle, 1702–1718, 1985; Politics, Religion and Society in England 1679–1742, 1986; (contrib.) Stuart England, ed Blair Worden, 1986; articles and reviews in learned jls. *Recreations:* music, gardening, cricket. *Address:* Tatham Lodge, Burton-in-Lonsdale, Carnforth, Lancs LA6 3LF. *T:* Bentham (05242) 61730.

HOLMES, Prof. George Arthur, PhD; FBA 1985; Chichele Professor of Medieval History, University of Oxford, and Fellow of All Souls College, since 1989; *b* 22 April 1927; *s* of late John Holmes and Margaret Holmes, Aberystwyth; *m* 1953, Evelyn Anne, *d* of late Dr John Klein and Audrey Klein; one *s* two *d* (and one *s* decd). *Educ:* Ardwyn County Sch., Aberystwyth; UC, Aberystwyth; St John's Coll., Cambridge (MA, PhD). Fellow, St John's Coll., Cambridge, 1951–54; Tutor, St Catherine's Society, Oxford, 1954–62; Fellow and Tutor, St Catherine's Coll., Oxford, 1962–89 (Vice-Master, 1969–71; Emeritus Fellow, 1990). Mem., Inst. for Advanced Study, Princeton, 1967–68. Chm., Victoria County Hist. Cttee, Inst. of Hist. Res., 1979–89. Jt Editor, English Historical Review, 1974–81; Delegate, Oxford Univ. Press, 1982–. *Publications:* The Estates of the Higher Nobility in Fourteenth-Century England, 1957; The Later Middle Ages, 1962; The Florentine Enlightenment 1400–1450, 1969; Europe: hierarchy and revolt 1320–1450, 1975; The Good Parliament, 1975; Dante, 1980; Florence, Rome and the Origins of the Renaissance, 1986; (ed) The Oxford Illustrated History of Medieval Europe, 1988; The First Age of the Western City 1300–1500, 1990; articles in learned jls. *Address:* Highmoor House, Bampton, Oxon. *T:* Bampton Castle (0993) 850408.

HOLMES, George Dennis, CB 1979; FRSE; Director-General and Deputy Chairman, Forestry Commission, 1977–86, retired; *b* 9 Nov. 1926; *s* of James Henry Holmes and Florence Holmes (*née* Jones); *m* 1953, Sheila Rosemary Woodger; three *d*. *Educ:* John Bright's Sch., Llandudno; Univ. of Wales (BSc (Hons)); FRSE 1982; FICFor. Post-grad Research, Univ. of Wales, 1947; appointed Forestry Commission, 1948; Asst Silviculturist, Research Div., 1948; Asst Conservator, N Wales, 1962; Dir of Research, 1968; Comr for Harvesting and Marketing, 1973. Member: E Scotland Bd, Bank of Scotland, 1987–; Scottish Legal Aid Bd, 1989–. Hon. Prof., Univ. of Aberdeen, 1984. Chm., Scottish Council for Spastics, 1986–. Hon. DSc Wales, 1985. *Publications:* contribs to Forestry Commission pubns and to Brit. and Internat. forestry jls. *Recreations:* sailing, golf, fishing. *Address:* (office) 22 Corstorphine Eoad, Edinburgh EH12 6HP. *T:* 031–337 9876.

HOLMES, Dr John Ernest Raymond; Director, Quality and Performance, United Kingdom Atomic Energy Authority, 1989–90; *b* Birmingham, 13 Aug. 1925; *s* of late Dr John K. Holmes and of Ellen R. Holmes; *m* 1949, Patricia Clitheroe; one *s* one *d*. *Educ:* King Edward's School, Birmingham; University of Birmingham (BSc, PhD). Asst Lectr in Physics, Manchester Univ., 1949–52; Research Scientist, AERE Harwell, 1952–59;

Atomic Energy Establishment, Winfrith: Research Scientist, 1959–66; Chief Physicist, 1966–73; Dep. Dir, 1973–86; Dir, 1986–89. *Publications:* technical papers on nuclear power. *Address:* The Mount, Durlston Road, Swanage, Dorset BH19 2HX. *T:* Swanage (0929) 423330.

HOLMES, John Wentworth, MBE 1983; Chief Agent, Liberal Party, and Deputy Head, Party HQ, 1974–86; *b* 14 Jan. 1925; *s* of Arthur and Annie Holmes; *m* 1969, Sonia Pratt; four *d. Educ:* Caverswall Church School. Foxwell Colliery Co., 1941–47, NCB 1947–51; Labour Agent, Rugby and Meriden, 1951–62; Liberal Agent, Leicester, 1963–65; Regional Sec., Liberal Party, Home Counties Region, 1965–74. Member: National Exec., Liberal Party, 1986–88; Council, Liberal Party, 1986–88. Mem., North Staffs District and Midland Area Council, NUM, 1947–50; formerly Mem., Warwickshire CC; Dir, Rugby Co-operative Soc. Ltd and its subsidiary interests, 1952–70 (Pres. and Chm., Bd of Dirs, 1964–70). *Recreations:* gardening, cooking. *Address:* Crossways, Parsonage Lane, Icklesham, Winchelsea, Sussex TN36 4BL. *T:* Hastings (0424) 814415.

HOLMES, Prof. Kenneth Charles, PhD; FRS 1981; Director of the Department of Biophysics, Max-Planck-Institute for Medical Research, Heidelberg, since 1968; Professor of Biophysics, Heidelberg University, since 1972; *b* 19 Nov. 1934; *m* 1957, Mary Scruby; one *s* three *d. Educ:* St John's Coll., Cambridge (MA 1959); London Univ. (PhD 1959). Res. Associate, Childrens' Hosp., Boston, USA, 1960–61; Mem., Scientific Staff, MRC Lab. of Molecular Biology, Cambridge, 1962–68. Mem., European Molecular Biol. Organisation. Scientific mem., Max Planck Gesellschaft, 1972–; Corresp. Mem., Soc. Royale des Scis, Liège. *Publications:* (with D. Blow) The Use of X-ray Diffraction in the Study of Protein and Nucleic Acid Structure, 1965; papers on virus structure and molecular mechanism of muscular contraction. *Recreations:* rowing, singing. *Address:* Biophysics Department, Max-Planck-Institute for Medical Research, Jahnstrasse 29, 6900 Heidelberg 1, Germany. *T:* Heidelberg 4861.

HOLMES, Brig. Kenneth Soar, CB 1963; CBE 1954; Managing Director, Posts, Postal Headquarters, 1971–72 (Senior Director, 1970–71); *b* 1912; *s* of W. J. Holmes, Ellesmere, Chaddesden Park Road, Derby; *m* 1936, Anne, *d* of C. A. Chapman, Leicester; one *s. Educ:* Bemrose Sch., Derby, and at Derby Technical Coll. Entered Post Office as Asst Traffic Superintendent (Telephones), 1930; Asst Surveyor, 1936; Principal, 1947; Asst Secretary, 1950. Served War of 1939–45 as Officer Commanding 43rd Division Postal Unit, then with 21st Army Group and 2nd Army Headquarters, and as Asst Director of Army Postal Services, British Army of the Rhine. Director of: Army Postal Services, War Office, 1950–59; Mechanisation and Buildings, GPO, 1956–60; Postal Services, GPO, 1960–65; London Postal Region, 1965–70. Chairman Executive Cttee of Universal Postal Union, 1960–64. *Publication:* Operation Overlord: a postal history, 1984. *Address:* 1 Wanderdown Road, Ovingdean, Brighton BN2 7BT. *T:* Brighton (0273) 307847.

HOLMES, Sir Maurice (Andrew), Kt 1969; Barrister-at-Law; *b* 28 July 1911; *o s* of Rev. A. T. Holmes and Ellen Holmes; *m* 1935, Joyce Esther, *d* of late E. C. Hicks, JP, CC; no *c. Educ:* Felsted Sch., Essex. Served with RASC, 1941–45 (Major, despatches). Called to Bar, Gray's Inn, 1948; Practised at Bar, 1950–55. Director, 1955–60, Chairman, 1960–65, The Tilling Association Ltd; Chairman, London Transport Board, 1965–69. Circuit Administrator, South Eastern Circuit, 1970–74. *Recreations:* golf, music. *Address:* The Limes, Felsted, near Dunmow, Essex. *T:* Great Dunmow (0371) 820352. *Club:* Forty.

HOLMES, Maurice Colston, OBE 1985; Director, Safety, British Railways Board, since 1989; *b* 15 Feb. 1935; *s* of Charles Edward Holmes and Ellen Catherine Mary Holmes (*née* Colston); *m* 1985, Margaret Joan Wiscombe. *Educ:* Presentation Coll., Reading. AMIRSE. British Rail: Divl Man., Liverpool Street, 1976–79; Chief Operating Man., 1979–80, Dep. Gen. Man., 1980–82, Southern Region; Dir of Operations, BRB, 1982–88. Major, RE, Engrg and Transport Staff Corps (TA), 1986–. *Recreations:* travel, transport, gardens. *Address:* British Railways Board, Macmillan House, Paddington Station, W2 1FT. *T:* 071–922 4268.

HOLMES, Prof. Patrick, PhD; Professor of Hydraulics, Imperial College of Science, Technology and Medicine, since 1983; Dean, City and Guilds College, 1988–91; *b* 23 Feb. 1939; *s* of Norman Holmes and Irene (*née* Shelbourne); *m* 1963, Olive (*née* Towning); one *s* one *d. Educ:* University Coll. of Swansea, Univ. of Wales (BSc 1960, PhD 1963). CEng, MICE. Res. Engr, Harbour and Deep Ocean Engrg, US Navy Civil Engrg Lab., Port Hueneme, Calif, 1963–65; Lectr, Dept of Civil Engrg, Univ. of Liverpool, 1966–72, Sen. Lectr, 1972–74, Prof. of Maritime Civil Engrg, 1974–83. Chm., Environment Cttee, SERC, 1981–85. *Publications:* (ed) Handbook of Hydraulic Engineering (English edn), by Lencastre, 1987; articles on ocean and coastal engineering, wave motion, wave loading, coastal erosion and accretion, and harbour and breakwater design, in Proc. ICE and Proc. Amer. Soc. of Civil Engrs. *Recreations:* hockey, sailing, walking, choral music. *Address:* Department of Civil Engineering, Imperial College of Science, Technology and Medicine, SW7 2AZ; West Winds, The Green, Steeple Morden, near Royston, Herts SG8 0ND. *T:* Steeple Morden (0763) 852582.

HOLMES, Sir Peter (Fenwick), Kt 1988; MC 1952; Managing Director, Royal Dutch/Shell Group, since 1982; Chairman, Shell Transport and Trading Co., since 1985; *b* 27 Sept. 1932; *s* of Gerald Hugh Holmes and Caroline Elizabeth Holmes; *m* 1955, Judith Millicent (*née* Walker); three *d. Educ:* Trinity Coll., Cambridge (MA). Various posts in Royal Dutch/Shell Group, 1956–, including: Gen. Man., Shell Markets, ME, 1965–68; Chief Rep., Libya, 1970–72; Man. Dir, Shell-BP, Nigeria, 1977–81; Pres., Shell Internat. Trading, 1981–83. Trustee, WWF–UK, 1989–. FRGS. *Publications:* Mountains and a Monastery, 1958; Nigeria, Giant of Africa, 1985; Turkey, A Timeless Bridge, 1988. *Recreations:* mountaineering, ski-ing, travel to remote areas, photography, 19th century travel books, golf. *Address:* c/o Shell Centre, SE1 7NA. *T:* 071–934 5611. *Clubs:* Athenæum, Alpine, Himalayan, Climbers, Kandahar; Sunningdale.

HOLMES, Peter Sloan; Under Secretary, Department of Education for Northern Ireland, since 1987; *b* 8 Dec. 1942; *s* of George H. G. and Anne S. Holmes; *m* 1966, Patricia McMahon; two *s. Educ:* Rossall Sch.; Magdalen Coll., Oxford (BA English Lang. and Lit.). Teacher, Eastbourne Coll., 1965–68; Head of English, Grosvenor High Sch., Belfast, 1968–71; Lectr, then Sen. Lectr, Stranmillis Coll. of Educn, Belfast, 1971–75; Department of Education for Northern Ireland: Inspector, 1975–83 (Sen. Inspector, 1980; Staff Inspector, 1982); Asst Sec., 1983–87. *Recreations:* singing, sailing, walking. *Address:* (office) Rathgael House, Bangor, Co. Down. *T:* 466311. *Club:* United Oxford & Cambridge University.

HOLMES, Richard Gordon Heath, FRSL; writer; *b* 5 Nov. 1945; *s* of Dennis Patrick Holmes and Pamela Mavis Holmes (*née* Gordon). *Educ:* Downside Sch.; Churchill Coll., Cambridge (BA). FRSL 1975. Reviewer and historical features writer for The Times, 1967–. Mem. Cttee, Royal Literary Fund. Ernest Jones Meml Lecture, British Inst. of Psycho-Analysis, 1990. *Publications:* Thomas Chatterton: the case re-opened, 1970; One for Sorrow (poems), 1970; Shelley: the pursuit, 1974 (Somerset Maugham Award, 1977); Gautier: my fantoms (trans.), 1976; Inside the Tower (radio drama documentary), 1977; (ed) Shelley on Love, 1980; Coleridge, 1982; (with Peter Jay) Nerval: the chimeras, 1985; Footsteps: adventures of a romantic biographer, 1985; (ed) Mary Wollstonecraft and William Godwin, 1987; (ed with Robert Hampson) Kipling: something of myself, 1987; De Feministe en de Filosoof, 1988; Coleridge: early visions (Whitbread Book of the Year Prize), 1989. *Recreations:* sailing, hill-walking, rooftop gardening, stargazing. *Address:* c/o Hodder & Stoughton, 47 Bedford Square, WC1B 3DP.

HOLMES, Robin Edmond Kendall; Circuit Administrator, Midland and Oxford Circuit, since 1986; *b* 14 July 1938; *s* of Roy Frederick George Holmes; *m* 1964, Karin Kutter; two *s. Educ:* Wolverhampton Grammar Sch.; Clare Coll., Cambridge (BA); Birmingham Univ. (LLM). Articles, Wolverhampton CBC, 1961–64; admitted solicitor, 1964; Min. of Housing and Local Govt, subseq. DoE, 1965–73 and 1976–82; Colonial Secretariat, Hong Kong, 1973–75; Lord Chancellor's Dept, 1982–; Grade 3, 1983–. *Recreation:* travelling. *Address:* 2 Newton Street, Birmingham B4 7LU. *T:* 021–200 1234.

HOLMES, Prof. William; Professor of Agriculture, Wye College, University of London, 1955–87, Professor Emeritus, since 1985; *b* Kilbarchan, Renfrewshire, 16 Aug. 1922; *s* of William John Holmes, Bank Manager; *m* 1949, Jean Ishbel Campbell, BSc; two *d. Educ:* John Neilson Sch., Paisley; Glasgow Univ.; West of Scotland Agricultural Coll. BSc (Agric), NDD, 1942; NDA (Hons), 1943; PhD Glasgow, 1947; DSc London, 1966. FIBiol 1974. Asst Executive Officer, S Ayrshire AEC, 1943–44; Hannah Dairy Research Inst.: Asst in Animal Husbandry, 1944–47; Head of Department of Dairy and Grassland Husbandry, 1947–55. Member, Cttee on Milk Composition in the UK, 1958–60; Governor, Grassland Research Inst., 1960–75; Pres., British Grassland Soc., 1968–69 (1st recipient, British Grassland Soc. Award, 1979); Pres., British Soc. of Animal Production, 1969–70; Member technical cttees of ARC, JCO MAFF, MMB and Meat and Livestock Commn, 1960–. Correspondent Étranger, Acad. d'Agric. de France, 1984. *Publications:* (ed) Grass, its production and utilization, 1980, 2nd edn 1989; (ed) Grassland Beef Production, 1984; papers in technical agricultural journals. *Recreations:* gardening, beekeeping, travel. *Address:* Amage, Wye, Kent. *T:* Wye (0233) 812372.

HOLMES, Prof. William Neil; Professor of Physiology, University of California, since 1964; *b* 2 June 1927; *s* of William Holmes and Minnie Holmes (*née* Lloyd); *m* 1955, Betty M. Brown, Boston, Mass; two *s* two *d. Educ:* Adams Grammar Sch., Newport, Salop; Liverpool Univ. (BSc, MSc, PhD, DSc); Harvard Univ., Cambridge, Mass. National Service, 2nd Bn RWF, 1946–48. Visiting Scholar in Biology, Harvard Univ., 1953–55; Post-grad. Research Schol., Liverpool Univ., 1955–56; ICI Fellow, Glasgow Univ., 1956–57; Asst Prof. of Zoology, 1957–63, Associate Prof. of Zoology, 1963–64, Univ. of British Columbia, Canada; John Simon Guggenheim Foundn Fellow, 1961–62; Visiting Professor of Zoology: Univ. of Hull, 1970; Univ. of Hong Kong, 1973, 1982–83 and 1987. Scientific Fellow, Zoological Soc. of London, 1967; External examiner: for undergraduate degrees, Univ. of Hong Kong, 1976–79, 1985–88; for higher degrees, Univs of Hong Kong and Hull, 1976–; Consultant to: Amer. Petroleum Inst., Washington, DC (environmental conservation), 1972–74; US Nat. Sci. Foundn (Regulatory Biology Prog.), 1980–83; US Bureau of Land Management (petroleum toxicity in seabirds), 1982–. Mem. Editorial Bd, American Journal of Physiology, 1967–70. Member: Endocrine Soc., US, 1957–; Soc. for Endocrinology, UK, 1955–; Amer. Physiological Soc., 1960–; Zoological Soc. of London, 1964–. *Publications:* numerous articles and reviews in Endocrinology, Jl of Endocrinology, Gen. and Comp. Endocrinology, Cell and Tissue Res., Archives of Environmental Contamination and Toxicology, Environmental Res., Jl of Experimental Biology. *Recreations:* travel, old maps and prints, carpentry and building. *Address:* 117 East Junipero Street, Santa Barbara, California 93105, USA. *T:* (805) 6827256. *Club:* Tennis (Santa Barbara).

HOLMES à COURT, family name of **Baron Heytesbury.**

HOLMES SELLORS, Patrick John; *see* Sellors.

HOLMPATRICK, 4th Baron *cr* 1897; **Hans James David Hamilton;** *b* 15 March 1955; *s* of 3rd Baron Holmpatrick and of Anne Loys Roche, *o d* of Commander J. E. P. Brass, RN (retd); *S* father, 1991; *m* 1984, Mrs G. du Feu, *e d* of K. J. Harding. *Heir: b* Hon. Ion Henry James Hamilton, *b* 12 June 1956.

HOLROYD, Air Marshal Sir Frank (Martyn), KBE 1989; CB 1985; Chief Engineer, 1988–91, and Chief of Logistics Support, 1989–91, Royal Air Force; *b* 30 Aug. 1935; *s* of George L. Holroyd and Winifred H. Holroyd (*née* Ford); *m* 1958, Veronica Christine, *d* of Arthur Booth; two *s* one *d. Educ:* Southend-on-Sea Grammar Sch.; Cranfield College of Technology (MSc). CEng, FIEE; FRAeS. Joined RAF, 1956; Fighter Comd units, 1957–60; Blind Landing Development RAE Bedford, 1960–63; Cranfield Coll. of Tech., 1963–65; HQ Fighter Comd, 1965–67; Far East, 1967–69; Wing Comdr, MoD, 1970–72; RAF Brize Norton, 1972–74; Gp Captain Commandant No 1 Radio School, 1974–76; SO Eng. HQ 38 Gp, 1976–77; Air Cdre Director Aircraft Engrg, MoD, 1977–80; RCDS 1981; Dir Weapons and Support Engrg, MoD, 1982, Air Vice-Marshal 1982; DG Strategic Electronics Systems, MoD (Procurement Exec.), 1982–86; AO Engrg, Strike Comd, 1986–88. Mem., Engrg Council, 1990–. Pres.-elect, RAeS. Member: Court, 1988–, and Council, 1990–, Inst. of Technology, Cranfield; Adv. Council, RMCS, Shrivenham, 1988–; BBC Engrg Adv. Bd, 1984–90. CBIM. *Recreations:* variety of sports, gardening, maintaining 14th century house. *Address:* c/o Ministry of Defence, Neville House, Page Street, SW1P 4LS. *Club:* Royal Air Force.

HOLROYD, John Hepworth; First Civil Service Commissioner and Deputy Secretary, Cabinet Office, since 1989; *b* 10 April 1935; *s* of Harry Holroyd and Annie Dodgshun Holroyd; *m* 1963, Judith Mary Hudson; one *s* one *d. Educ:* Kingswood Sch., Bath; Worcester Coll., Oxford (Open Schol.; BA(Hist.); MA 1987). Joined MAFF, 1959; Asst Private Sec. to Minister, 1961–63; Principal, Forestry Commn and MAFF, 1963–69; Asst. Sec., 1969–78; Under Secretary, 1978; Resident Chm., Civil Service Selection Bd, 1978–80; Dir of Establishments, MAFF, 1981–85; Under Sec., European Secretariat, Cabinet Office, 1985–89. UK Mem., Bd of Admin, European Inst. of Public Admin., 1989–. Treas. to Governors, Kingswood Sch., 1985–. Lay Reader, St Albans Abbey; Methodist Local Preacher. *Recreations:* music, carpentry, bee-keeping, travel. *Address:* 9 Beech Place, St Albans, Herts AL3 5LQ.

See also W. A. H. Holroyd.

HOLROYD, Margaret, (Mrs Michael Holroyd); *see* Drabble, M.

HOLROYD, Michael (de Courcy Fraser), CBE 1989; author; *b* London, 27 Aug. 1935; *s* of Basil Holroyd and Ulla (*née* Hall); *m* 1982, Margaret Drabble, *qv. Educ:* Eton Coll.; Maidenhead Public Library. Vis. Fellow, Pennsylvania State Univ., 1979. Chm., Soc. of Authors, 1973–74; Chm., Nat. Book League, 1976–78; Pres., English PEN, 1985–88. Chm., Strachey Trust, 1990–. Member: BBC Archives Adv. Cttee, 1976–79; Vice-Chm., Arts Council Literature Panel, 1982–83. FRSL 1968 (Mem. Council, 1977–87); FRHistS; FRSA. *Publications:* Hugh Kingsmill: a critical biography, 1964 (rev. edn 1971); Lytton Strachey, 2 vols, 1967, 1968, rev. edn 1971; A Dog's Life: a novel, 1969; (ed) The Best of Hugh Kingsmill, 1970; (ed) Lytton Strachey By Himself, 1971; Unreceived Opinions, 1973; Augustus John (2 vols), 1974, 1975; (with M. Easton) The Art of Augustus John,

1974; (ed) The Genius of Shaw, 1979; (ed with Paul Levy) The Shorter Strachey, 1980; (ed with Robert Skidelsky) William Gerhardie's God's Fifth Column, 1981; (ed) Essays by Divers Hands, vol. XLII, 1982; Bernard Shaw: Vol. I, The Search for Love 1856–1898, 1988; Vol. II, The Pursuit of Power 1898–1918, 1989; Vol. III, The Lure of Fantasy 1918–1950, 1991; various radio and television scripts. *Recreations:* listening to stories, watching people dance, avoiding tame animals, being polite, music, siestas. *Address:* c/o A. P. Watt Ltd, 20 John Street, WC1N 2DL.

HOLROYD, William Arthur Hepworth, FHSM; District General Manager, Durham Health Authority, since 1985; *b* 15 Sept. 1938; *s* of late Rev. Harry Holroyd and Annie Dodgshun Holroyd; *m* 1967, Hilary Gower; three *s*. *Educ:* Kingswood Sch., Bath; Trinity Hall, Cambridge (MA History); Manchester Univ. (DSA). Hospital Secretary: Crewe Memorial Hosp., 1963–65; Wycombe General Hosp., 1965–67; secondment to Dept of Health, 1967–69; Dep. Gp Sec., Blackpool and Fylde HMC, 1969–72; Regional Manpower Officer, Leeds RHB, 1972–74; District Administrator, York Health Dist, 1974–82; Regional Administrator, Yorkshire RHA, 1982–85. Member: National Staff Cttee for Admin. and Clerical Staff in NHS, 1973–82; General Nursing Council for England and Wales, 1978–83; English Nat. Board for Nursing, Midwifery and Health Visiting, 1980–87; NHS Trng Authority, 1988–91. Director, Methodist Chapel Aid Assoc. Ltd, 1978–. *Publication:* (ed) Hospital Traffic and Supply Problems, 1968. *Recreations:* walking, music, visiting the Shetland Isles. *Address:* 3 Dunelm Court, South Street, Durham DH1 4QX. *T:* Durham (091) 3844765.

See also J. H. Holroyd.

HOLROYDE, Geoffrey Vernon; Director, GEC Management College, Dunchurch, since 1989; Director of Coventry Cathedral Chapter House Choir, since 1982; *b* 18 Sept. 1928; *s* of late Harold Vincent Holroyde and Kathleen Olive (*née* Glover); *m* 1960, Elizabeth Mary, *d* of Rev. E. O. Connell; two *s* two *d*. *Educ:* Wrekin Coll.; Birmingham Univ.; BSc. ARCO. Royal Navy, 1949–54 and 1956–61; School-master, Welbeck Coll., 1954–56; English Electric, becoming Principal of Staff Coll., Dunchurch, 1961–70; British Leyland, Head Office Training Staff, 1970–71; Head, Sidney Stringer Sch. and Community Coll., Coventry, 1971–75; Dir, Coventry Lanchester Polytechnic, 1975–87; Higher Educn Adviser to Training Commn, 1987–88. Chairman: Industrial Links Adv. Gp to Cttee of Dirs of Polytechnics, 1980–87; National Forum for the Performing Arts in Higher Educn, 1987–91; Develt Training Steering Gp, 1983–88; Mem., W Midlands RHA, 1986– (Chm., Non Clinical Res. Cttee; Vice-Chm., AIDS Task Force); Mem., RSA Educn Industry Forum, 1986–90. Dir of Music, St Mary's Church, Warwick, 1962–72. Governor, 1978–, Trustee, 1979–, Chm., Governing Body, 1984–89, Brathay Hall Trust; Hon. Life Mem., Royal Sch. of Church Music, 1970. Chm. Trustees, St Mary's Hall, Warwick, 1984–90; Governor: Mid Warwicks Coll. of Further Educn, 1976–87; Kings School, Worcester, 1983–88. *Publications:* Managing People, 1968; Delegations, 1968; Communications, 1969; Organs of St Mary's Church, Warwick, 1969. *Recreations:* music (organ and choir), canals, sailing, outdoor pursuits. *Address:* 38 Coten End, Warwick CV34 4NP. *T:* Warwick (0926) 492329.

HOLT, Arthur Frederick; Chairman, Holt Hosiery Co. Ltd, Bolton, 1971–73; *b* 8 Aug. 1914; *m* 1939, Kathleen Mary, MBE, *d* of A. C. Openshaw, Turton, nr Bolton; one *s* one *d*. *Educ:* Mill Hill Sch.; Manchester Univ. Army Territorial Officer (5th Loyals), 1939–45; taken prisoner, Singapore, 1942–45; despatches twice, 1946. MP (L) Bolton West, 1951–64; Liberal Chief Whip, 1962–63. Pres., Liberal Party, Sept. 1974–Sept. 1975. *Recreation:* golf. *Address:* Trees, High Wray, Ambleside, Cumbria LA22 0JQ. *T:* Ambleside (05394) 32258.

HOLT, Christopher Robert Vesey, CVO 1976; VRD 1952; Member of London Stock Exchange, 1938–82; *b* 17 Oct. 1915; *s* of late Vice-Adm. R. V. Holt, CB, DSO, MVO, and Evelyn Constance Holt; *m* 1945, Margaret Jane Venetia, *d* of late Sir Michael Albert James Malcolm, 10th Bt; one *s* one *d*. *Educ:* Eton. Partner, James Capel & Co., Stockbrokers, 1938, Sen. Partner, 1968–70, Chm. (on firm becoming a company), 1970–75, Dir, 1975–76. Served RNVR, War of 1939–45, mostly in destroyers; retd with rank of Lieut-Comdr, 1957. *Recreations:* painting, wildlife. *Address:* Westbury Manor, West Meon, Petersfield, Hants GU32 1ND. *Clubs:* Boodle's, Lansdowne.

HOLT, Constance, CBE 1975; Area Nursing Officer, Manchester Area Health Authority (Teaching), 1973–77; *b* 5 Jan. 1924; *d* of Ernest Biddulph and of Ada Biddulph (*née* Robley); *m* 1975, Robert Lord Holt, OBE, FRCS. *Educ:* Whalley Range High Sch. for Girls, Manchester; Manchester Royal Infirmary (SRN); Queen Charlotte's Hosp., London; St Mary's Hosp., Manchester (SCM); Royal Coll. of Nursing, London Univ. (Sister Tutor Dipl.); Univ. of Washington (Florence Nightingale Schol., Fulbright Award). Nursing Officer, Min. of Health, 1959–65; Chief Nursing Officer: United Oxford Hosps, 1965–69; United Manchester Hosps, 1969–73. Pres., Assoc. of Nurse Administrators (formerly Assoc. of Hosp. Matrons), 1972–. Reader licensed by Bishop of Sodor and Man. Hon. Lectr, Dept of Nursing, Univ. of Manchester, 1972. Hon. MA Manchester, 1980. *Publications:* articles in British and internat. nursing press. *Recreations:* reading, gardening, music. *Address:* Seabank, Marine Terrace, Port St Mary, Isle of Man.

HOLT, Jack; *see* Holt, John Lapworth.

HOLT, Sir James (Clarke), Kt 1990; FBA 1978; Professor of Medieval History, 1978–88, and Master of Fitzwilliam College, 1981–88, Cambridge University; *b* 26 April 1922; *s* of late Herbert and Eunice Holt; *m* 1950, Alice Catherine Elizabeth Suley; one *s*. *Educ:* Bradford Grammar Sch.; Queen's Coll., Oxford (Hastings Schol.). MA 1947; 1st cl. Modern Hist.; DPhil 1952. Served with RA, 1942–45 (Captain). Harmsworth Sen. Schol., Merton Coll., Oxford, 1947; Univ. of Nottingham: Asst Lectr, 1949; Lectr, 1951; Sen. Lectr, 1961; Prof. of Medieval History, 1962; Reading University: Prof. of History, 1966–78; Dean, Faculty of Letters and Soc. Scis, 1972–76; Professorial Fellow, Emanuel Coll., Cambridge, 1978–81 (Hon. Fellow, 1985). Vis. Prof., Univ. of Calif, Santa Barbara, 1977; Vis. Hinkley Prof., Johns Hopkins Univ., 1983; Vis. JSPS Fellow, Japan, 1986. Raleigh Lectr, British Acad., 1975. Mem., Adv. Council on Public Records, 1974–81. Pres., Royal Historical Soc., 1980–84; Vice-Pres., British Academy, 1987–89. Corres. Fellow, Medieval Acad. of America, 1983. Hon DLitt Reading, 1984. Comdr, Order of Civil Merit (Spain), 1988. *Publications:* The Northerners: a study in the reign of King John, 1961; Praestita Roll 14–18 John, 1964; Magna Carta, 1965; The Making of Magna Carta, 1966; Magna Carta and the Idea of Liberty, 1972; The University of Reading: the first fifty years, 1977; Robin Hood, 1982, 2nd edn 1989; (ed with J. Gillingham) War and Government in the Middle Ages, 1984; Magna Carta and Medieval Government, 1985; (with R. Mortimer) Acta of Henry II and Richard I, 1986; (ed) Domesday Studies, 1987; papers in English Historical Review, Past and Present, Economic History Review, Trans Royal Hist. Soc. *Recreations:* mountaineering, cricket, fly-fishing. *Address:* 5 Holben Close, Barton, Cambs. *T:* Cambridge (0223) 263074. *Clubs:* United Oxford & Cambridge University, National Liberal, MCC; Wayfarers' (Liverpool).

HOLT, (James) Richard; MP (C) Langbaurgh, since 1983; personnel consultant, since 1981; *b* 2 Aug. 1931; *m* 1959, Mary June Leathers; one *s* one *d*. *Educ:* Wembley County Grammar Sch. FIPM. Served RN, 1949–54. Actor, 1954–57. Personnel trainee, Gen. Motors, 1957–63; various personnel appointments with: Smiths Industries, 1963–65; Rolls Royce, 1965–66; William Hill Orgn, 1966–72; E. Gomme Ltd, 1972–78; Bowater Furniture, 1978–81. Member: Brent BC, 1964–74; High Wycombe BC, 1976–83; Bucks CC, 1981–83. Mem., Thames Water Authy, 1981–83. Contested (C) Brent South, Feb. 1974. FBIM. *Address:* Whitecroft, Newton-under-Roseberry, neat Great Ayton, Cleveland; 51 High Street, Marske on Sea, Redcar, Cleveland.

HOLT, Sir John Anthony L.; *see* Langford-Holt.

HOLT, Rear-Adm. John Bayley, CB 1969; DL; Director: Premmit Associates Ltd; Premmit Engineering Services Ltd; Elint Engineering Ltd; *b* 1 June 1912; *s* of Arthur Ogden Holt and Gertrude (*née* Bayley); *m* 1940, Olga Esme Creake; three *d*. *Educ:* William Hulme Grammar Sch., Manchester; Manchester Univ. BScTech (hons) 1933. FIEE. Electrical Engineer with various cos and electric power undertakings, 1933–41. Joined RN; engaged on degaussing and minesweeping research and development, later on radar and electrical engineering, for Fleet Air Arm, 1941–48; served in HMS Cumberland on Gunnery Trials, Naval Air Stations, HQ and Staff appointments; comd HMS Ariel, 1961–63; subsequently Director of Naval Officer Appointments (Engineer Officers), and Dir-Gen. Aircraft (Naval), 1967–70, Ministry of Defence. Former Naval ADC to HM The Queen. Commander 1948; Captain 1958; Rear-Admiral 1967. Vice Pres., Surrey Br., SSAFA. DL Surrey, 1981. *Recreations:* sailing, gardening, sacred music. *Address:* Rowley Cottage, Thursley, Godalming, Surrey GU8 6QW. *T:* Elstead (0252) 702140. *Club:* Naval and Military.

HOLT, John Lapworth, (Jack Holt), OBE 1979; Founder and Director of Jack Holt Ltd and Holt group of companies, designers and suppliers of small boats and their fittings (Managing Director, 1946–76); *b* 18 April 1912; *s* of Herbert Holt and Annie (*née* Dawson); *m* 1936, Iris Eileen Thornton; one *s* one *d*. *Educ:* St Peter's Sch., London; Shoreditch Techn. Inst. (Schol.). Joiner, boat builder and designer, 1929–46; formed Jack Holt Ltd, 1946; designed: first British post-war sailing dinghy class, Merlin; first British factory-made do-it-yourself boat building kit to construct Internat. Cadet, for Yachting World magazine; International Enterprise, National Solo and Hornet, Heron, Rambler, Diamond, Lazy E, GP14, Vagabond, International Mirror Dinghy, Mirror 16, and Pacer; Pandamaran, for World Wildlife Fund. Techn. Adviser to Royal Yachting Assoc. dinghy cttee, 1950–. Jt winner (with Beecher Moore) of 12ft Nat. Championship, 1946 and Merlin Championships, 1946, 1947 and 1949; Merlin Silver Tiller series winner, 1954–56; won Solo Dutch Nat. Championships, 1962. Yachtsman's Award for service to yachting, RYA, 1977. *Recreation:* small boat sailing. *Address:* 17 Elmstead Park Road, West Wittering, West Sussex PO20 8NQ. *T:* Birdham (0243) 3559. *Clubs:* Ranelagh Sailing, Wraysbury Lake Sailing, Chichester Yacht, Aldenham Sailing, Carrum Yacht, Black Rock Sailing.

HOLT, John Michael, MD, FRCP; Consultant Physician, John Radcliffe Hospital, Oxford; Fellow of Linacre College, Oxford, since 1968; *b* 8 March 1935; *s* of late Frank Holt, BSc and of Constance Holt; *m* 1959, Sheila Margaret Morton; one *s* three *d*. *Educ:* St Peter's Sch., York; Univ. of St Andrews. MA Oxon; MD St Andrews; MSc Queen's Univ. Ont. Registrar and Lectr, Nuffield Dept of Medicine, Radcliffe Infirmary, Oxford, 1964–66, Cons. Physician 1968; Chm., Medical Staff, Oxford Hosps, 1982–84. University of Oxford: Med. Tutor, 1967–73; Dir of Clinical Studies, 1971–76; Mem., Gen. Bd of Faculties, 1987–. Examiner in Medicine: Univ. of Oxford; Hong Kong; London; Glasgow; RCP. Member: Assoc. of Physicians; Soc. of Apothecaries; Cttee on Safety of Medicines, 1979–86; Oxford RHA, 1984–88. Editor, Qly Jl of Medicine, 1975–. *Publications:* papers on disorders of blood and various med. topics in BMJ, Lancet, etc. *Recreation:* sailing. *Address:* Old Whitehill, Tackley, Oxon OX5 3AB. *T:* Tackley (086983) 241. *Clubs:* United Oxford & Cambridge University; Royal Cornwall Yacht (Falmouth).

HOLT, Prof. John Riley, FRS 1964; Professor of Experimental Physics, University of Liverpool, 1966–83, now Emeritus; *b* 15 Feb. 1918; *er s* of Frederick Holt and Annie (*née* Riley); *m* 1949, Joan Silvester Thomas; two *s*. *Educ:* Runcorn Secondary Sch.; University of Liverpool. PhD 1941. British Atomic Energy Project, Liverpool and Cambridge, 1940–45. University of Liverpool: Lecturer, 1945–53, Senior Lecturer, 1953–56, Reader, 1956–66. *Publications:* papers in scientific journals on nuclear physics and particle physics. *Recreation:* gardening. *Address:* Rydalmere, Stanley Avenue, Higher Bebington, Wirral L63 5QE. *T:* 051–608 2041.

HOLT, Mary; Her Honour Judge Holt; a Circuit Judge, since 1977; *d* of Henry James Holt, solicitor, and of Sarah Holt (*née* Chapman); unmarried. *Educ:* Park Sch., Preston; Girton Coll., Cambridge (MA, LLB, 1st cl. Hons). Called to the Bar, Gray's Inn, 1949 (Atkin Scholar). Practised on Northern circuit. Former Vice-Chm., Preston North Conservative Assoc.; Member: Nat. Exec. Council, 1969–72; Woman's Nat. Advisory Cttee, 1969–70; representative, Central Council, 1969–71. MP (C) Preston N, 1970–Feb. 1974. Contested (C) Preston N, Feb. and Oct. 1974. Dep. Pres., Lancs Br., BRCS, 1976–. Freedom of Cities of Dallas and Denton, Texas, 1987. Badge of Honour, BRCS, 1989. *Publication:* 2nd edn, Benas and Essenhigh's Precedents of Pleadings, 1956. *Recreation:* walking. *Address:* The Sessions House, Preston, Lancs. *Club:* Commonwealth Trust.

HOLT, Prof. Peter Malcolm, FBA 1975; FSA; Professor of History of the Near and Middle East, University of London, 1975–82, now Professor Emeritus; *b* 28 Nov. 1918; *s* of Rev. Peter and Elizabeth Holt; *m* 1953, Nancy Bury (*née* Mawle); one *s* one *d*. *Educ:* Lord Williams's Grammar Sch., Thame; University Coll., Oxford (Schol.) (MA, DLitt). Sudan Civil Service: Min. of Education, 1941–53; Govt Archivist, 1954–55. School of Oriental and African Studies, London, 1955–82; Prof. of Arab History, 1964–75. FRHistS 1973; FSA 1980. Hon. Fellow, SOAS, 1985. Gold Medal of Science, Letters and Arts, Repub. of Sudan, 1980. *Publications:* The Mahdist State in the Sudan, 1958, 2nd edn 1970; A Modern History of the Sudan, 1961, 2nd edn 1963; (co-ed with Bernard Lewis) Historians of the Middle East, 1962; Egypt and the Fertile Crescent, 1966; (ed) Political and Social Change in Modern Egypt, 1968; (co-ed with Ann K. S. Lambton and Bernard Lewis) The Cambridge History of Islam, 1970; Studies in the History of the Near East, 1973; (ed) The Eastern Mediterranean Lands in the period of the Crusades, 1977; (with M. W. Daly) A History of the Sudan from the Coming of Islam to the Present Day, 4th edn 1988; The Memoirs of a Syrian Prince, 1983; The Age of the Crusades, 1986; trans. P. Thorau, The Lion of Egypt, 1992; articles in: Encyclopaedia of Islam, Bulletin of SOAS, Sudan Notes and Records, Der Islam, English Historical Rev., etc. *Address:* Dryden Spinney, Kirtlington, Oxford OX5 3HG. *T:* Bletchington (0869) 50477. *Club:* United Oxford & Cambridge University.

HOLT, Richard; *see* Holt, J. R.

HOLT, Richard Anthony Appleby; Chairman, 1959–78, Managing Director, 1978–80, Hutchinson Ltd; Chairman: Hutchinson Publishing Group, 1965–80; Hutchinson Printing Trust, 1957–80; *b* 11 March 1920; *s* of Frederick Appleby Holt and Rae Vera Franz (*née* Hutchinson); *m* 1945, Daphne Vivien Pegram; three *s* two *d*. *Educ:* Harrow Sch.; King's Coll., Cambridge. Served War of 1939–45, commissioned 60th Rifles, 1941;

demobilised, 1946 (Major). Admitted Solicitor, 1949. Dir, Constable & Co., 1968–90. *Recreation:* lawn tennis. *Address:* 55 Queen's Gate Mews, SW7 5QN. *T:* 071–589 8469. *Clubs:* All England Lawn Tennis & Croquet (Vice-Pres., 1982–), MCC.

HOLT, Victoria; *see* Hibbert, Eleanor.

HOLTBY, Very Rev. Robert Tinsley, FSA; Dean of Chichester, 1977–89, Dean Emeritus, 1989; *b* 25 Feb. 1921; *o s* of William and Elsie Holtby, Thornton-le-Dale, Yorkshire; *m* 1947, Mary, *er d* of late Rt Rev. Eric Graham; one *s* two *d. Educ:* York Minster Choir Sch.; Scarborough Coll. and High School. St Edmund Hall, Oxford, 1939; MA (2nd Class Mod. Hist.), 1946; BD 1957. Choral Scholar, King's Coll., Cambridge, 1944; MA (2nd Class Theol.), 1952. Cuddesdon Theological Coll. and Westcott House, Cambridge, 1943–46. FSA 1990. Deacon, 1946; Priest, 1947. Curate of Pocklington, Yorks, 1946–48. Chaplain to the Forces, 1948–52: 14/20th King's Hussars, Catterick; Singapore; Priest-in-charge, Johore Bahru. Hon. CF, 1952–; Acting Chaplain, King's Coll., Cambridge, 1952; Chaplain and Asst Master, Malvern Coll., 1952–54; Chaplain and Assistant Master, St Edward's Sch., Oxford, 1954–59; Canon Residentiary of Carlisle and Diocesan Dir of Educn, 1959–67, Canon Emeritus, 1967–; Gen. Sec., Nat. Soc. for Promoting Religious Education, 1967–77; Sec., Schs Cttee, 1967–74, Gen. Sec., 1974–77, Church of England Bd of Educn. Vis. Fellow, W Sussex Inst. of Higher Educn, 1990–. Select Preacher: Cambridge, 1984; Oxford, 1989. Chm., Cumberland Council of Social Service, 1962–67. Chaplain to High Sheriff of Cumberland, 1964, 1966. *Publications:* Daniel Waterland, A Study in 18th Century Orthodoxy, 1966; Carlisle Cathedral Library and Records, 1966; Eric Graham, 1888–1964, 1967; Carlisle Cathedral, 1969; Chichester Cathedral, 1980; Robert Wright Stopford, 1988; Bishop William Otter, 1989; Eric Milner-White, 1990. *Recreations:* music, walking, history. *Address:* 4 Hutton Hall, Huttons Ambo, York YO6 7HW. *T:* Malton (0653) 696366. *Club:* United Oxford & Cambridge University.

HOLTHAM, Mrs Carmen Gloria, JP; Advice/Information Officer, 1980–88, and Legal Executive, 1985–88, Earls Court Centre, Royal Borough of Kensington and Chelsea; *b* Kingston, Jamaica, 13 July 1922; *née* Bradshaw. *Educ:* Adventist Girls Sch.; Kingston Technical Coll., Kingston, Jamaica; London Univ. (Extra-Mural Course, Dip. Sociol.); NW London Polytech. (Cert. Office Management); SW London Polytech. (Cert. in Counselling); NE London Polytech. (Post Grad. Dip. Inf. and Advice Studies). Govt of Jamaica, 1942–57; United Jewish Appeal, NY, USA, 1958; Resident, England, 1959–; HM Factory Inspectorate, 1959; ILEA, 1959–64; Inst. of Med. Social Workers, 1964–66; Social Services Dept, London Borough of Camden, 1966; Willesden Citizens' Advice Bureau, London Bor. of Brent, 1967–70; Organiser, Thurrock Citizens' Advice Bureau, Grays, Essex, 1971–79. Member: ILEA Sch. Care Cttee, 1963–67; Brent Community Relns Council, 1968–70; Brent Youth Service, 1969–70; British Caribbean Assoc., 1969–; Magistrates Assoc., 1969–; Grays Probation and After-Care Service, 1971–80; Thurrock Social Services for Elderly, 1971–80; Supplementary Benefits Commn, 1976–78. Mem., Bd of Governors, Treetops Sch., Grays, 1975–77. JP Mddx (Highgate Magistrates' Court), 1969–71, Essex (Grays Magistrates' Court), 1972–. *Recreations:* reading, the theatre, ceramics. *Address:* 52 Davall House, Grays, Essex. *T:* Grays Thurrock (0375) 70838. *Club:* Friends International.

HOLTON, Michael; Assistant Secretary, Ministry of Defence, 1976–87, retired; *b* 30 Sept. 1927; 3rd *s* of late George Arnold Holton and Ethel (*née* Fountain); *m* 1st, 1951, Daphne Bache (marr. diss. 1987); one *s* two *d*; 2nd, 1987, Joan Catherine Thurman (*née* Hickman), Huddersfield. *Educ:* Finchley County Grammar Sch.; London Sch. of Economics. National Service, RAF, 1946–48; Min. of Food, 1948–54; Air Ministry, 1955–61; MoD, 1961–68; Sec., Countryside Commn for Scotland, 1968–70; Sec., Carnegie UK Trust, 1971–75. Sec., European Conservation Year Cttee for Scotland, 1970; Mem. Council, 1976–, Hon. Sec., 1988–, RSNC; Member: YHA, 1946–; Consultative Cttee, Family Fund, 1973–75; Bd, Cairngorm Chairlift Co., 1973–; Museums Assoc., 1976–; Inverliever Lodge Trust, 1979–90. Hon. Sec., RAF Mountaineering Assoc., 1952–54; Hon. Sec., British Mountaineering Council, 1954–59. *Publication:* Training Handbook for RAF Mountain Rescue Teams, 1953. *Address:* 4 Ludlow Way, Hampstead Garden Suburb, N2 0LA. *T:* 081–444 8582. *Clubs:* Athenæum, Alpine; Himalayan (Bombay).

HOLWELL, Peter, FCA; Principal, University of London, since 1985; *b* 28 March 1936; *s* of Frank Holwell and Helen (*née* Howe); *m* 1959, Jean Patricia Ashman; one *s* one *d. Educ:* Palmers Endowed Sch., Grays, Essex; Hendon Grammar Sch.; London Sch. of Econs and Pol Science (BSc Econ). FCA 1972; MBCS 1974; FZS 1988. Articled Clerk, 1958–61, Management Consultant, 1961–64, Arthur Andersen and Co.; University of London: Head of Computing, Sch. Exams Bd, 1964–67; Head of University Computing and O & M Unit, 1967–77; Sec. for Accounting and Admin. Computing, 1977–82; Clerk of the Court, 1982–85; Dir, School Exams Council, 1988–. Chm., UCCA Computing Gp, 1977–82. Director: Zoo Operations Ltd, 1988–; London E Anglian Gp Ltd, 1990–. Trustee, Samuel Courtauld (formerly Home House) Trust, 1985–. *Recreations:* walking, music, horology. *Address:* University of London, Malet Street, WC1E 7HU. *T:* 071–636 8000. *Club:* Athenæum.

HOLZACH, Dr Robert; Hon. Chairman, Union Bank of Switzerland, since 1988; *b* 28 Sept. 1922. *Educ:* Univ. of Zürich (Dr of Law). Union Bank of Switzerland: trainee, Geneva, London, 1951–52; Vice-Pres., 1956; Senior Vice-Pres., Head of Commercial Div., Head Office, 1962; Mem., Exec. Board, 1966; Exec. Vice-Pres., 1968; President, 1976; Chm. of Board, 1980–88. *Publication:* Herausforderungen, 1988. *Address:* Union Bank of Switzerland, PO Box, 8021 Zurich, Switzerland. *T:* 01/234 11 11.

HOMAN, Maj.-Gen. John Vincent, CB 1980; CEng, FIMechE; Facilities Manager, Marconi Space Systems, Portsmouth, 1982–91; *b* 30 June 1927; *s* of Charles Frederic William Burton Homan and Dorothy Maud Homan; *m* 1953, Ann Bartlett; one *s* two *d. Educ:* Haileybury; RMA Sandhurst; RMCS Shrivenham. BSc (Eng). Commnd, REME, 1948; Lt-Col 1967; Comdr REME 2nd Div., 1968–70; Col 1970; MoD 1970–72; CO 27 Comd Workshop REME, 1972–74; Brig. 1974; Dep. Dir, Electrical and Mechanical Engineering, 1st British Corps, 1974–76; Dir of Equipment Management, MoD, 1976–77; Dir Gen., Electrical and Mechanical Engrg, MoD, 1978–79; Maj.-Gen. 1978; Sen. Army Mem., RCDS, 1980–82. Col Comdt, REME, 1982–88. *Recreations:* hill walking, woodwork. *Address:* Roedean, 25 The Avenue, Andover, Hants SP10 3EW. *T:* Andover (0264) 51196. *Club:* Army and Navy.

HOMAN, Rear-Adm. Thomas Buckhurst, CB 1978; *b* 9 April 1921; *s* of late Arthur Buckhurst Homan and Gertrude Homan, West Malling, Kent; *m* 1945, Christine Oliver; one *d. Educ:* Maidstone Grammar Sch. RN Cadet, 1939; served War of 1939–45 at sea; Comdr 1958; Captain 1965; Defence Intell. Staff, 1965; Sec. to Comdr Far East Fleet, 1967; idc 1970; Dir Naval Officer Appts (S), 1971; Captain HMS Pembroke, 1973; Rear-Adm. 1974; Dir Gen., Naval Personal Services, 1974–78. Sub-Treasurer, Inner Temple, 1978–85. *Recreations:* reading, theatre, staying at home, cooking. *Address:* 602 Hood House, Dolphin Square, SW1V 3NJ. *T:* 071–798 8434. *Clubs:* Army and Navy, Garrick.

HOMANS, Prof. George Caspar; Professor of Sociology, Harvard University, 1953–81, now Emeritus; *b* 11 Aug. 1910; *s* of Robert Homans and Abigail (*née* Adams); *m* 1941, Nancy Parshall Cooper; one *s* two *d. Educ:* St Paul's Sch., Concord, New Hampshire; Harvard Univ. (AB). Harvard Univ.: Junior Fellow, 1934–39; Instructor in Sociology, 1939–41; Associate Professor of Sociology, 1946–53; Simon Vis. Prof., Univ. of Manchester, 1953; Prof. of Social Theory, Univ. of Cambridge, 1955–56; Vis. Prof., Univ. of Kent, 1967. Overseas Fellow, Churchill Coll., Cambridge, 1972. Pres., American Sociological Assoc., 1963–64; Mem., Nat. Acad. of Sciences, USA, 1972. Officer, US Naval Reserve (Lieut-Commander), 1941–45. *Publications:* Massachusetts on the Sea, 1930; An Introduction to Pareto, 1934; Fatigue of Workers, 1941; English Villagers of the 13th Century, 1941; The Human Group, 1950; Marriage, Authority and Final Causes, 1955; Social Behaviour, 1961, rev. edn 1974; Sentiments and Activities, 1962, rev. edn 1988; The Nature of Social Science, 1967; Coming to my Senses (autobiog.), 1984; Certainties and Doubts, 1987; The Witch Hazel (poems), 1988. *Recreations:* forestry, sailing. *Address:* 11 Francis Avenue, Cambridge, Mass 02138, USA. *T:* 617–547–4737. *Club:* Tavern (Boston, USA).

HOME; *see* Douglas-Home.

HOME; *see* Milne Home.

HOME, 14th Earl of [disclaimed his peerages for life, 23 Oct. 1963]; *see under* Home of the Hirsel, Baron and Douglas-Home, Hon. D. A. C.

HOME OF THE HIRSEL, Baron *cr* 1974 (Life Peer), of Coldstream; **Alexander Frederick Douglas-Home,** KT 1962; PC 1951; DL; Chancellor, Order of the Thistle, since 1973; First Chancellor of Heriot-Watt University, 1966–77; *b* 2 July 1903; *e s* of 13th Earl of Home (*d* 1951), KT, and Lilian (*d* 1966), *d* of 4th Earl of Durham; *S* father, 1951, but disclaimed his peerages for life, 23 Oct. 1963; *m* 1936, Elizabeth Hester (*d* 1990), 2nd *d* of late Very Rev. C. A. Alington, DD; one *s* three *d. Educ:* Eton; Christ Church, Oxford. MP (U) South Lanark, 1931–45; MP (C) Lanark Div. of Lanarkshire, 1950–51; Parliamentary Private Sec. to the Prime Minister, 1937–40; Joint Parliamentary Under-Sec., Foreign Office, May-July 1945; Minister of State, Scottish Office, 1951–April 1955; Sec. of State for Commonwealth Relations, 1955–60; Dep. Leader of the House of Lords, 1956–57; Leader of the House of Lords, and Lord Pres. of the Council, 1959–60; Sec. of State for Foreign Affairs, 1960–63; MP (U) Kinross and W Perthshire, Nov. 1963–Sept. 1974; Prime Minister and First Lord of the Treasury, Oct. 1963–64; Leader of the Opposition, Oct. 1964–July 1965; Sec. of State for Foreign and Commonwealth Affairs, 1970–74. Hon. Pres., NATO Council, 1973. Captain, Royal Co. of Archers, Queen's Body Guard for Scotland, 1973. Mem., National Farmers' Union, 1964. DL Lanarkshire, 1960. Hon. DCL Oxon., 1960; Hon. Student of Christ Church, Oxford, 1962; Hon. LLD: Harvard, 1961; Edinburgh, 1962; Aberdeen, 1966; Liverpool, 1967; St Andrews, 1968; Hon. DSc Heriot-Watt, 1966. Hon. Master of the Bench, Inner Temple, 1963; Grand Master, Primrose League, 1966–84; Pres. of MCC, 1966–67. Freedom of Selkirk, 1963; Freedom of Edinburgh, 1969; Freedom of Coldstream, 1972. Hon. Freeman: Skinners' Co., 1968; Grocers' Co., 1977. *Publications:* The Way the Wind Blows (autobiog.), 1976; Border Reflections, 1979; Letters to a Grandson, 1983. *Address:* House of Lords, SW1; The Hirsel, Coldstream, Berwickshire TD12 4LP. *T:* Coldstream (0890) 2345; Castlemains, Douglas, Lanarkshire. *T:* Douglas, (Lanarks) (0555) 851241.

See also Hon. D. A. C. Douglas-Home, Hon. William Douglas-Home, Duke of Sutherland.

HOME, Anna Margaret; Head of Children's Programmes, BBC Television, since 1986; *b* 13 Jan. 1938; *d* of James Douglas Home and Janet Mary (*née* Wheeler). *Educ:* Convent of Our Lady, St Leonard's-on-Sea, Sussex; St Anne's Coll., Oxford (MA (Hons) Mod. Hist.). BBC Radio Studio Man., 1960–64; Res. Asst, Dir, Producer, Children's TV, 1966–70; Exec. Producer, BBC Children's Drama Unit, 1970–81: responsible for series such as Lizzie Dripping, Bagthorpe Saga, Moon Stallion; started Grange Hill, 1977; Controller of Programmes SE, later Dep. Dir of Programmes, TVS (one of the original franchise gp), 1981–86. FRTS 1987. Pye Award for distinguished services to children's television, 1984; Eleanor Farjeon Award for services to children's literature, 1989. *Recreations:* theatre, literature, travel, gardening. *Address:* c/o BBC Television, Television Centre, Wood Lane, W12 7RJ. *T:* 081–576 1875.

HOME, Sir David George, 13th Bt, *cr* 1671; late Temp. Major Argyll and Sutherland Highlanders; *b* 21 Jan. 1904; *o s* of Sir John Home, 12th Bt and Hon. Gwendolina H. R. Mostyn (*d* 1960), *sister* of 7th Baron Vaux of Harrowden; *S* father, 1938; *m* 1933, Sheila, *d* of late Mervyn Campbell Stephen; one *s* one *d* (and one *s* one *d* decd). *Educ:* Harrow; Jesus Coll., Cambridge (BA 1925). Member Royal Company of Archers (HM Body Guard for Scotland). FSA (Scotland). *Heir: g s* William Dundas Home, *b* 19 Feb. 1968. *Address:* Winterfield, North Berwick, East Lothian. *Clubs:* Brooks's; New (Edinburgh); Royal and Ancient (St Andrews).

See also Sir D. P. M. Malcolm, Bt.

HOME, Prof. George, BL; FIB Scot; Professor of International Banking, Heriot-Watt University, Edinburgh, 1978–85, Professor Emeritus, since 1985; *b* 13 April 1920; *s* of George Home and Leah Home; *m* 1946, Muriel Margaret Birleson; two *s* one *d. Educ:* Fort Augustus Village Sch.; Trinity Academy, Edinburgh; George Heriot's Sch., Edinburgh; Edinburgh Univ. (BL 1952). FIB(Scot); FBIM. Joined Royal Bank of Scotland, 1936; served RAF, 1940–46; Dep. Man. Dir, Royal Bank of Scotland Ltd, 1973–80; Dep. Gp Man. Dir, Royal Bank of Scotland Gp Ltd, 1976–80; Director: Williams & Glyn's Bank Ltd, 1975–80; The Wagon Finance Corp. plc, 1980–85. Vice-Pres., Inst. of Bankers in Scotland, 1977–80. Chm., George Heriot's Trust, 1989–. *Recreations:* fishing, gardening, reading, travel. *Address:* Bickley, 12 Barnton Park View, Edinburgh EH4 6HJ. *T:* 031–312 7648.

HOME, Hon. William Douglas-; dramatic author; *b* Edinburgh, 3 June 1912; *s* of 13th Earl of Home, KT; *m* 1951, Rachel Brand (*see* Baroness Dacre); one *s* three *d. Educ:* Eton; New Coll., Oxford (BA). Studied at Royal Academy of Dramatic Art, and has appeared on the West End stage. Formerly Captain RAC. Contested (Progressive Ind) Cathcart Division of Glasgow, April 1942, Windsor Division of Berks, June 1942, and Clay Cross Division of Derbyshire (Atlantic Charter), April 1944, (Liberal) South Edinburgh, 1957. Author of the following plays: Great Possessions, 1937; Passing By, 1940; Now Barabbas, The Chiltern Hundreds, 1947; Ambassador Extraordinary, 1948; Master of Arts, The Thistle and the Rose, 1949; Caro William, 1952; The Bad Samaritan, 1953; The Manor of Northstead, 1954; The Reluctant Debutante, 1955; The Iron Duchess, 1957; Aunt Edwina, 1959; Up a Gum Tree, 1960; The Bad Soldier Smith, 1961; The Cigarette Girl, 1962; The Drawing Room Tragedy, 1963; The Reluctant Peer, Two Accounts Rendered, 1964; Betzi, 1965; A Friend Indeed, 1966; The Secretary Bird, The Queen's Highland Servant, The Grouse Moor Image, The Bishop and the Actress, 1968; The Jockey Club Stakes, Uncle Dick's Surprise, 1970; The Douglas Cause, 1971; Lloyd George Knew My Father, 1972; At the End of the Day, 1973; The Bank Manager, The Dame of Sark, The Lord's Lieutenant, 1974; In The Red, The Kingfisher, Rolls Hyphen Royce, The Perch, The Consulting Room, 1977; The Editor Regrets, 1978; You're All Right: How am I?, 1981; Four Hearts Doubled, Her Mother Came Too, 1982; The Golf Umbrella, 1983;

David and Jonathan, 1984; After the Ball is Over, 1985; Portraits, 1987; A Christmas Truce, 1989. *Publications:* Half Term Report, an autobiography, 1954; Mr Home Pronounced Hume: an autobiography, 1979; Sins of Commission, 1985; Old Men Remember, 1991. *Recreations:* golf, politics. *Address:* Derry House, Kilmeston, near Alresford, Hants. *T:* Bramdean (0962771256) 256. *Club:* Travellers'.

See also Baron Home of the Hirsel.

HOME ROBERTSON, John David; MP (Lab) East Lothian, since 1983 (Berwick and East Lothian, Oct. 1978–1983); *b* 5 Dec. 1948; *s* of late Lt-Col J. W. Home Robertson and Mrs H. M. Home Robertson; *m* 1977, Catherine Jean Brewster; two *s*. *Educ:* Ampleforth Coll.; West of Scotland Coll. of Agriculture. Farmer. Mem., Berwicks DC, 1975–78; Mem., Borders Health Bd, 1976–78. Chm., Eastern Borders CAB, 1977. Chm., Scottish Gp of Labour MPs, 1983; Opposition Scottish Whip, 1983–84; opposition spokesman on agric., 1984–87, 1988–90, on Scotland, 1987–88; Mem., Select Cttee on Defence, 1990–. Founder, Paxton Trust, 1989. *Address:* House of Commons, SW1A 0AA. *T:* 071–219 4135. *Clubs:* East Lothian Labour, Prestonpans Labour.

HONDERICH, Prof. Edgar Dawn Ross, (Ted), PhD; Grote Professor of the Philosophy of Mind and Logic, and Head of Department of Philosophy, University College London, since 1988; *b* 30 Jan. 1933; *s* of John William Honderich and Rae Laura Armstrong, Baden, Canada; *m* 1st, 1964, Pauline Ann Marina Goodwin (marr. diss. 1972), *d* of Paul Fawcett Goodwin and Lena Payne, Kildare; one *s* one *d*; 2nd, 1990, Jane Elizabeth O'Grady, *d* of Major Robert O'Grady and Hon. Joan Ramsbotham, Bath. *Educ:* Kitchener Sch., Kitchener, Canada; Lawrence Park Sch., Toronto; University Coll., Univ. of Toronto (BA 1959); University Coll. London (PhD 1968). Literary Editor, Toronto Star, 1957–59; Lectr in Phil., Univ. of Sussex, 1962–64; Lectr in Phil., 1964–73, Reader in Phil., 1973–83, and Prof. of Phil., 1983–88, UCL; Chm., Bd of Phil Studies, Univ. of London, 1986–89. Vis. Prof., Yale Univ., and CUNY, 1970. Editor: Internat. Library of Philosophy and Scientific Method, 1966–; Penguin philosophy books, 1967–; The Arguments of the Philosophers, 1968–; The Problems of Philosophy: their past and present, 1984–; radio, television, journalism. *Publications:* Punishment: the supposed justifications, 1969, 4th edn 1989; (ed) Essays on Freedom of Action, 1973; (ed) Social Ends and Political Means, 1976; Violence for Equality: inquiries in political philosophy (incorporating Three Essays on Political Violence, 1976), 1980, 2nd edn 1989; (ed with Myles Burnyeat) Philosophy As It Is, 1979; (ed) Philosophy Through Its Past, 1984; (ed) Morality and Objectivity, 1985; A Theory of Determinism: the mind, neuroscience, and life-hopes, 1988, 2nd edn, as The Consequences of Determinism, 1990; Mind and Brain, 1990; Conservatism, 1990; phil articles in Amer. Phil Qly, Analysis, Inquiry, Jl of Theoretical Biol., Mind, Phil., Pol Studies, Proc. Aristotelian Soc., etc. *Recreations:* cycling, wine. *Address:* Department of Philosophy, University College London, Gower Street, WC1E 6BT. *T:* 071–380 7115/7116; 4 Keats Grove, NW3 2RT. *T:* 071–435 2687. *Clubs:* Beefsteak, Garrick.

HONDROS, Ernest Demetrios, DSc; FRS 1984; Director: Petten Establishment, Commission of European Communities' Joint Research Centre, since 1985; Institute of Advanced Materials, Petten (Netherlands) and Ispra (Italy); Visiting Professor, Department of Materials, Imperial College of Science, Technology and Medicine; *b* 18 Feb. 1930; *s* of Demetrios Hondros and Athanasia Paleologos; *m* 1968, Sissel Kristine Garder-Olsen; two *s*. *Educ:* Univ. of Melbourne (DSc MSc); Univ. of Paris (Dr d'Univ.). CEng, FIM. Research Officer, CSIRO Tribophysics Laboratory, Melbourne, 1955–59; Research Fellow, Univ. of Paris, Lab. de Chimie Minérale, 1959–62; National Physical Laboratory: Sen. Research Officer, Metallurgy Div., 1962–65; Principal Res. Fellow, 1965–68; Sen. Principal Res. Officer (Special Merit), 1974; Supt, Materials Applications Div., 1979–85. Membre d'Honneur, Société Française de Métallurgie, 1986; Mem., Academia Europaea, 1988. Rosenhain Medallist, Metals Soc., 1976; Howe Medal, Amer. Soc. for Metals, 1978; A. A. Griffiths Medal and Prize, Inst. of Metals, 1987. *Publications:* numerous research papers and reviews in learned jls. *Recreations:* music, literature, walking. *Address:* Petten Establishment, JRC, PO Box 2, 1755 ZG/Petten, The Netherlands. *T:* 31 2246 5401.

HONE, David; landscape and portrait painter; President, Royal Hibernian Academy of Arts, 1978–83; *b* 14 Dec. 1928; *s* of Joseph Hone and Vera Hone (*née* Brewster); *m* 1962, Rosemary D'Arcy; two *s* one *d*. *Educ:* Baymount School; St Columba's College; University College, Dublin. Studied art at National College of Art, Dublin, and later in Italy. Hon. RA, HRSA (ex-officio). *Recreations:* fishing, photography. *Address:* 25 Lower Baggot Street, Dublin 2, Ireland. *T:* Dublin 763746.

HONE, Maj.-Gen. Sir (Herbert) Ralph, KCMG 1951; KBE 1946 (CBE Mil. 1943); MC; TD; GCStJ 1973; QC Gibraltar 1934, QC Uganda 1938; barrister-at-law; *b* 3 May 1896; *s* of late Herbert Hone and Miriam Grace (*née* Dracott); *m* 1st, 1918, Elizabeth Daisy, *d* of James Matthews (marr. diss. 1944); one *s* one *d*; 2nd, 1945, Sybil Mary, *widow* of Wing Commander G. Simond; one *s*. *Educ:* Varndean Grammar Sch., Brighton; London Univ. LLB (Hons). Barrister-at-law, Middle Temple. Inns of Court OTC. Gazetted London Irish Rifles, 1915; Lieut, 1916; Captain, 1918; served with BEF, France, 1916 and 1917–18 (wounded, MC), Staff Captain, Ministry of Munitions, 1918–20; Major R of O (TA); Asst Treas., Uganda, 1920; called to Bar; practised and went South Eastern Circuit, 1924–25; Registrar, High Court, Zanzibar, 1925; Resident Magistrate, Zanzibar, 1928; Crown Counsel, Tanganyika Territory, 1930; acted Asst Legal Adviser to the Colonial and Dominions Offices, Jan.-Aug. 1933; Attorney-General, Gibraltar, 1933–36; Commissioner for the Revision of the laws of Gibraltar, 1934; King's Jubilee medal, 1935; Chm., Gibraltar Govt Commn on Slum Clearance and Rent Restriction, 1936; Coronation Medal, 1937; Acting Chief Justice, Gibraltar, on several occasions; Attorney-General, Uganda, 1937–43; Chairman, Uganda Government Cttee on Museum policy, 1938; Commandant, Uganda Defence Force, 1940; Chief Legal Adviser, Political Branch, GHQ, Middle East, 1941; Chief Political Officer, GHQ, Middle East, 1942–43; General Staff, War Office, 1943–45; Chief Civil Affairs Officer, Malaya, 1945–46; Maj.-Gen., 1942–46 (despatches twice, CBE (mil.)); Secretary-General to Governor-General of Malaya, 1946–48; Dep. Commissioner-General in SE Asia, 1948–49; Coronation Medal, 1953. Governor and C-in-C, North Borneo, 1949–54; Head of Legal Division, CRO, 1954–61. Resumed practice at the Bar, 1961. Retd TA with Hon. rank Maj.-Gen., 1956. GCStJ 1973; Mem. Chapter Gen. Order of St John, 1954–. Vice-Pres., Royal Commonwealth Society; Constitutional Adviser, Kenya Govt, Dec. 1961–Jan. 1962; Constitutional Adviser to Mr Butler's Advisers on Central Africa, July-Oct. 1962; Constitutional Adviser to South Arabian Government, Oct. 1965–Jan. 1966, and to Bermuda Government, July-Nov. 1966. Appeal Comr under Civil Aviation Licensing Act, 1961–71; Standing Counsel, Grand Bahama Port Authority, 1962–75. *Publications:* Index to Gibraltar Laws, 1933; revised edn of Laws of Gibraltar, 1935; revised edn of Laws of the Bahamas, 1965; Handbook on Native Courts, etc. *Recreations:* tennis, badminton and philately. *Address:* 1 Paper Buildings, Temple, EC4. *T:* 071–583 7355; 56 Kenilworth Court, Lower Richmond Road, SW15. *T:* 081–788 3367. *Clubs:* Athenæum, Commonwealth Trust.

HONE, Robert Monro, MA; Headmaster, Exeter School, 1966–79; *b* 2 March 1923; *s* of late Rt Rev. Campbell R. Hone; *m* 1958, Helen Isobel, *d* of late Col H. M. Cadell of Grange, OBE; three *d*. *Educ:* Winchester Coll. (Scholar); New Coll., Oxford (Scholar). Rifle Brigade, 1942–45. Asst Master, Clifton Coll., 1948–65 (Housemaster, 1958–65). *Address:* St Madron, Throwleigh, Okehampton, Devon EX20 2HX.

HONEY, Michael; Chief Executive, Gloucestershire County Council, since 1990; *b* 18 Nov. 1941; *s* of Denis Honey and Mary Honey (*née* Henderson); four *d*. *Educ:* Clifton College; Regent Street Polytechnic (DipArch); Columbia Univ. MArch (Urban Design); MSc (City Planning). City Planner, Boston Redevelopment Authority, 1968–70; Corporate Planning Manager, Bor. of Greenwich, 1970–74; Head, Exec. Office, Bor. of Croydon, 1974–80; Chief Executive: Bor. of Richmond upon Thames, 1980–88; LDDC, 1988–90. *Recreations:* sailing, music, people.

HONEY, Air Vice-Marshal Robert John, CB 1991; CBE 1987; Air Secretary, since 1989; *b* 3 Dec. 1936; *s* of F. G. Honey; *m* 1956, Diana Chalmers; one *s* one *d*. *Educ:* Ashford Grammar Sch. Joined RAF as pilot, 1954; served: Germany, 1956–59; Singapore, 1961–64; Canada, 1968–69; India, 1982; UK intervening years; Dep. Commander RAF Germany, 1987–89. Mountaineering expedns to Mulkila, India, 1979, Masherbrum, Pakistan, 1981. *Recreations:* climbing, mountaineering, ski-ing. *Address:* RAF Personnel Management Centre, Innsworth, Glos GL3 1EZ. *Club:* Royal Air Force.

HONEYCOMBE, Gordon; *see* Honeycombe, R. G.

HONEYCOMBE, Sir Robert (William Kerr), Kt 1990; FRS 1981; FEng 1980; Goldsmiths' Professor of Metallurgy, University of Cambridge, 1966–84, now Emeritus; *b* 2 May 1921; *s* of William and Rachel Honeycombe (*née* Kerr); *m* 1947, June Collins; two *d*. *Educ:* Geelong Coll.; Univ. of Melbourne. Research Student, Department of Metallurgy, University of Melbourne, 1941–42; Research Officer, Commonwealth Scientific and Industrial Research Organization, Australia, 1942–47; ICI Research Fellow, Cavendish Laboratory, Cambridge, 1948–49; Royal Society Armourers and Brasiers' Research Fellow, Cavendish Laboratory, Cambridge, 1949–51; Senior Lecturer in Physical Metallurgy, University of Sheffield, 1951–55; Professor, 1955–66. Fellow of Trinity Hall, Cambridge, 1966–73, Hon. Fellow, 1975; Pres. 1973–80, Fellow, 1980–88, Emeritus Fellow, 1988, Clare Hall, Cambridge. Pres., Instn of Metallurgists, 1977; Pres., Metals Soc., 1980–81; Vice-Pres., Royal Institution, 1977–78; Treas., 1986–, a Vice Pres., 1986–, Royal Soc. Visiting Professor: University of Melbourne, 1962; Stanford Univ., 1965; Monash Univ., 1974; Hatfield Meml Lectr, Kyoto Univ., 1979. Hon. Member: Iron and Steel Inst. of Japan, 1979; Soc. Française de Métallurgie, 1981; Japan Inst. of Metals, 1983 (Gold Medallist, 1983); Indian Inst. of Metals, 1984. Mem. Ct of Assts, Goldsmiths' Co., 1977– (Prime Warden, 1986–87). Hon. DAppSc Melbourne, 1974; Hon. DMet Sheffield, 1983; Dr *hc* Montan. Wiss. Leoben, 1990. Rosenhain Medal of Inst. of Metals, 1959; Sir George Beilby Gold Medal, 1963; Ste-Claire-Deville Medal, 1971; Inst. of Metals Lectr and Mehl Medallist, AIME, 1976; Sorby Award, Internat. Metallographic Soc., 1986. *Publications:* The Plastic Deformation of Metals, 1968; Steels—Microstructure and Properties, 1981; papers in Proc. Royal Soc., Metal Science, etc. *Recreations:* gardening, photography, walking. *Address:* Barrabool, 46 Main Street, Hardwick, Cambridge CB3 7QS. *T:* Madingley (0954) 210501.

HONEYCOMBE, (Ronald) Gordon; author, playwright, dramatist, television presenter, actor and narrator; *b* Karachi, British India, 27 Sept. 1936; *s* of Gordon Samuel Honeycombe and Dorothy Louise Reid Fraser. *Educ:* Edinburgh Acad.; University Coll., Oxford (MA English). National Service, RA, mainly in Hong Kong, 1955–57. Announcer: Radio Hong Kong, 1956–57; BBC Scottish Home Service, 1958; actor: with Tomorrow's Audience, 1961–62; with RSC, Stratford-on-Avon and London, 1962–63; acted in BBC TV shows, incl. That Was the Week that Was, Not so Much a Programme, 1964, TV series The Brack Report, 1982, and TV play, CQ, 1984; Newscaster with ITN, 1965–77 (twice chosen as most popular newscaster in national newspaper polls); News presenter, TV-am, 1984–89. TV Presenter: (also writer), A Family Tree and Brass Rubbing (documentaries), 1973; children's poems in Stuff and Nonsense, 1975; The Late Late Show (series), and Something Special (series), 1978; Family History (series), 1979; Close, 1981; Narrator: Arthur C. Clarke's Mysterious World (TV series), 1980; A Shred of Evidence (TV), 1984; The Black Museum (Radio 4), 1984; also narrator for indust. documentaries, trng films and cinema shorts; TV commentaries include 50th Anniversary Service of RAF, Westminster Abbey, 1968. Acted in: The Commuter (film), 1968; Play-back 625, Royal Court, 1970; Paradise Lost, York and Old Vic, 1975; Noye's Fludde (Voice of God), Putney, 1978; Suspects, Swansea, 1989; Aladdin, Wimbledon, 1989–90, Bournemouth, 1990–91; Run For Your Wife!, tour, 1990; appeared in various other television plays, series, and films (incl. The Medusa Touch, Ransom, The Fourth Protocol, and Bullseye); also appeared in charity and variety shows, Old Vic and Theatre Royal, Stratford, 1970–75; sang at Players' Theatre, 1974. Author of stage productions: The Miracles, Oxford, 1960 and (perf. by RSC), Southwark Cath., 1963 and Consett, 1970; The Princess and the Goblins (musical), Great Ayton, 1976, Ascot, 1991; Paradise Lost, York, Old Vic and Edinburgh Fest., 1975–77; Waltz of my Heart, Bournemouth, 1980; Lancelot and Guinevere, Old Vic, 1980; author of TV plays: The Golden Vision (with Neville Smith), 1968; Time and Again, 1974 (Silver Medal, Film and TV Fest., NY, 1975); The Thirteenth Day of Christmas, 1986; radio dramatisations (all Radio 4): Paradise Lost, 1975; Lancelot and Guinevere, 1976; A King shall have a Kingdom, 1977; devised Royal Gala performances: God save the Queen!, Chichester, 1977; A King shall have a Kingdom, York, 1977. Directed and prod, The Redemption, Fest. of Perth, 1990. Pres., Bournemouth Operatic Soc., 1979–81. *Publications:* *non-fiction:* Nagasaki 1945, 1981; Royal Wedding, 1981; The Murders of the Black Museum, 1982; The Year of the Princess, 1982; Selfridges, 1984; TV-am's Official Celebration of the Royal Wedding, 1986; *documentary novels:* Adam's Tale, 1974; Red Watch, 1976; Siren Song, 1991; *fiction:* The Redemption (play), 1964; Neither the Sea nor the Sand, 1969; Dragon under the Hill, 1972; The Edge of Heaven, 1981; contrib. Punch, Private Eye, national newspapers and magazines. *Recreations:* brass-rubbing, bridge, crosswords. *Address:* c/o Jon Roseman Associates, 103 Charing Cross Road, WC2H 0DT. *T:* 071–439 8245.

HONEYSETT, Martin; cartoonist and illustrator, since 1969; *b* 20 May 1943; *s* of Donovan Honeysett and Kathleen Ethel Ivy Probert; *m* 1970, Maureen Elizabeth Lonergan; one *s* one *d* (and one *s* decd). *Educ:* Selhurst Grammar Sch.; Croydon Art Coll. (for one year). After leaving Art Coll., 1961, spent several years in NZ and Canada doing variety of jobs; returned to England, 1968; started drawing cartoons part-time, 1969; became full-time freelance, working for Punch, Private Eye and other magazines and newspapers, 1972; illustrator of series of books by the author/poet, Ivor Cutler. *Publications:* Private Eye Cartoonists No 4, 1974; Honeysett at Home, 1976; The Motor Show Book of Humour, 1978; The Not Another Book of Old Photographs Book, 1981; Microphobia, 1982; The Joy of Headaches, 1983; Fit for Nothing, 1984; Animal Nonsense Rhymes, 1984; The Best of Honeysett, 1985. *Recreations:* walking, swimming. *Address:* 52 Eversfield Place, St Leonards-on-Sea, East Sussex TN37 6DB. *T:* Hastings (0424) 717266.

HONGLADAROM, Sunthorn; Knight Grand Cordon, Order of Crown of Thailand, and Order of White Elephant; Secretary-General, South-East Asia Treaty Organisation,

1972–77; Hon. Assistant Secretary-General, Thai Red Cross Society, since 1977; *b* 23 Aug. 1912; *m* 1937; five *s* one *d*. *Educ:* Trinity Coll., Cambridge. Asst Sec.-Gen. to Cabinet, 1946; Sec.-Gen., Nat. Economic Council, 1950; Ambassador to Fedn of Malaya (now Malaysia), 1957; Minister of Economic Affairs, 1959; Minister of Finance, 1960; Chairman of Boards of Governors; IBRD, IMF, IFC, and Internat. Development Assoc., 1961; Minister of Economic Affairs, 1966; Ambassador to UK, 1968–69, to USA, 1969–72. Hon. LLD, St John's Univ., NY, 1970. *Recreations:* golf, motoring. *Address:* Thai Red Cross Society, Chulalongkorn Memorial Hospital, Bangkok, Thailand. *Club:* Roehampton.

HONIG, His Honour Frederick; a Circuit Judge (formerly a County Court Judge), 1968–86; *b* 22 March 1912; 2nd *s* of late Leopold Honig; *m* 1940, Joan, *o d* of late Arthur Burkart. *Educ:* Berlin and Heidelberg Univs. LLD (Hons) Heidelberg, 1934. Barrister, Middle Temple, 1937. War service, 1940–47: Capt., JAG's Dept; Judge Advocate in civilian capacity, 1947–48; subseq. practised at Bar. *Publications:* (jtly) Cartel Law of the European Economic Community, 1963; contribs to Internat. Law Reports (ed. Lauterpacht) and legal jls, incl. Amer. Jl of Internat. Law, Internat. and Comparative Law Quarterly, Law Jl, Propriété Industrielle, etc. *Recreations:* foreign languages, country walking. *Address:* Lamb Building, Temple, EC4Y 7AS. *T:* 071–353 1612.

HONIGMANN, Prof. Ernst Anselm Joachim, DLitt; FBA 1989; Joseph Cowen Professor of English Literature, University of Newcastle upon Tyne, 1970–89, now Professor Emeritus; *b* Breslau, Germany, 29 Nov. 1927; *s* of Dr H. D. S. Honigmann and U. M. Honigmann (*née* Heilborn); *m* 1958, Dr Elsie M. Packman; two *s* one *d*. *Educ:* Glasgow Univ. (MA English Lang. and Lit. 1948; DLitt 1966); Merton Coll., Oxford (BLitt 1950). Asst Lectr, 1951, Lectr, Sen. Lectr and Reader, 1954–67, Glasgow Univ.; Fellow, Shakespeare Inst., Birmingham Univ., 1951–54; Reader, Univ. of Newcastle upon Tyne, 1968–70. Jt Gen. Ed., The Revels Plays, 1976–. *Publications:* The Stability of Shakespeare's Text, 1965; Shakespeare: Seven Tragedies, the dramatist's manipulation of response, 1976; Shakespeare's Impact on his Contemporaries, 1982; Shakespeare: the lost years, 1985; John Weever: a biography, 1987; Myriad-minded Shakespeare, 1989; *editor:* King John, 1954; Milton's Sonnets, 1966; The Masque of Flowers 1614, in A Book of Masques, 1967; Richard III, 1968; Twelfth Night, 1971; Paradise Lost, Book 10 (with C. A. Patrides), 1972; Shakespeare and his Contemporaries: essays in comparison, 1986; articles and reviews in English Studies, Erasmus, The Library, MLR, NY Rev. of Books, Philological Qly, Rev. of English Studies, Shakespeare Jahrbuch, Shakespeare Qly, Shakespeare Survey, Theatre Res., etc. *Recreations:* grandchildren, gardening, travel. *Address:* 18 Wilson Gardens, Newcastle upon Tyne NE3 4JA. *T:* 091–285 5391.

HONORÉ, Prof. Antony Maurice; QC 1987; DCL Oxon; FBA 1972; Regius Professor of Civil Law, University of Oxford, 1971–88; Fellow, 1971–89, Acting Warden, 1987–89, All Souls College, Oxford; *b* 30 March 1921; *o s* of Frédéric Maurice Honoré and Marjorie Erskine (*née* Gilbert); *m* 1st, Martine Marie-Odette Genouville; one *s* one *d*; 2nd, Deborah Mary Cowen (*née* Duncan). *Educ:* Diocesan Coll., Rondebosch; Univ. of Cape Town; New Coll., Oxford. Rhodes Scholar, 1940. Union Defence Forces, 1940–45; Lieut, Rand Light Infantry, 1942. BCL 1948. Vinerian Scholar, 1948. Advocate, South Africa, 1951; called to Bar, Lincoln's Inn, 1952, Hon. Bencher, 1971. Lectr, Nottingham Univ., 1948; Rhodes Reader in Roman-Dutch Law, 1957–70, Fellow of Queen's Coll., Oxford, 1949–64, of New Coll., 1964–70. Visiting Professor: McGill, 1961; Berkeley, 1968. Lectures: Hamlyn, Nottingham, 1982; J. H. Gray, Cambridge, 1985; Blackstone, Oxford, 1988. Hon. LLD: Edinburgh; South Africa; Stellenbosch; Cape Town. *Publications:* (with H. L. A. Hart) Causation in the Law, 1959, 2nd edn 1985; Gaius, 1962; The South African Law of Trusts, 1965, 3rd edn 1985; Tribonian, 1978; Sex Law, 1978; (with J. Menner) Concordance to the Digest Jurists, 1980; Emperors and Lawyers, 1981; The Quest for Security, 1982; Ulpian, 1982; Making Law Bind, 1987. *Address:* 94C Banbury Road, Oxford OX2 6JT. *T:* Oxford (0865) 59684.

HONOUR, (Patrick) Hugh, FRSL; writer; *b* 26 Sept. 1927; *s* of late Herbert Percy Honour and Dorothy Margaret Withers. *Educ:* King's Sch., Canterbury; St Catharine's Coll., Cambridge (BA). Asst to Dir, Leeds City Art Gall. and Temple Newsam House, 1953–54. Guest Curator for exhibn, The European Vision of America, National Gall. of Art, Washington, Cleveland Museum of Art, and, as L'Amérique vue par l'Europe, Grand Palais, Paris, 1976. FRSL 1972. Corresp. FBA 1986. *Publications:* Chinoiserie, 1961 (2nd edn 1973); Companion Guide to Venice, 1965 (rev. edn 1990); (with Sir Nikolaus Pevsner and John Fleming) The Penguin Dictionary of Architecture, 1966 (4th rev. edn 1991); Neo-classicism, 1968 (4th edn 1977); The New Golden Land, 1976; (with John Fleming) The Penguin Dictionary of Decorative Arts, 1977 (rev. edn 1989); Romanticism, 1979; (with John Fleming) A World History of Art, 1982 (Mitchell Prize, 1982) (USA as The Visual Arts: a history, rev. edn 1991); The Image of the Black in Western Art IV, from the American Revolution to World War I, 1989 (Anisfield-Wolf Book Award in Race Relations, 1990); (with John Fleming) the Venetian Hours of Henry James, Whistler and Sargent, 1991. *Recreation:* gardening. *Club:* Travellers'.

HONYWOOD, Sir Filmer (Courtenay William), 11th Bt *cr* 1660; FRICS; Company Secretary, Honywood Business Consultancy Services Ltd, since 1989; *b* 20 May 1930; *s* of Col Sir William Wynne Honywood, 10th Bt, MC, and Maud Naylor (*d* 1953), *d* of William Hodgson Wilson, Hexgreave Park, Southwell, Notts; *S* father, 1982; *m* 1956, Elizabeth Margaret Mary Cynthia, *d* of Sir Alastair George Lionel Joseph Miller of Glenlee, 6th Bt; two *s* two *d*. *Educ:* Downside; RMA Sandhurst; Royal Agricultural College, Cirencester (MRAC Diploma). Served 3rd Carabiniers (Prince of Wales' Dragoon Guards). Asst Surveyor, Min. of Agriculture, Fisheries and Food, Maidstone, 1966–73; Surveyor, Cockermouth, Cumbria, 1973–74; Senior Lands Officer, 1974–78, Regional Surveyor and Valuer, 1978–88, South Eastern Region, CEGB. Consultant on agricultural compensation/restoration, UK Nirex Ltd, 1988–90. *Heir: s* Rupert Anthony Honywood, *b* 2 March 1957. *Address:* Greenway Forstal Farmhouse, Hollingbourne, Maidstone, Kent ME17 1QA.

HOOD, family name of **Viscounts Bridport** and **Hood.**

HOOD, 7th Viscount *cr* 1796; **Alexander Lambert Hood;** Bt 1778; Baron (Ire.) 1782, (GB) 1795; Chairman, Petrofina (UK) Ltd, 1982–87 (Director, 1958–87); *b* 11 March 1914; *s* of Rear-Adm. Hon. Sir Horace Hood, KCB, DSO, MVO (*d* 1916) (3rd *s* of 4th Viscount) and Ellen Floyd (*d* 1950), *d* of A. E. Touzalin; *S* brother, 1981; *m* 1957, Diana Maud, CVO 1957, *d* of late Hon. G. W. Lyttelton; three *s*. *Educ:* RN Coll., Dartmouth; Trinity Coll., Cambridge; Harvard Business Sch. RNVR, 1939–45. Director: J. Henry Schroder Wagg & Co., 1957–75; George Wimpey, 1957–90; Tanks Consolidated Investments PLC, 1971–84 (Chm., 1976–83); Benguela Railway Co., 1979–84; Union Minière, 1973–84; Abbott Laboratories Inc., 1971–83; Abbott Laboratories Ltd, 1964–85. Part-time Mem., British Waterways Bd, 1963–73. *Heir: s* Hon. Henry Lyttelton Alexander Hood, *b* 16 March 1958. *Address:* 67 Chelsea Square, SW3 6LE. *T:* 071–352 4952; Loders Court, Bridport, Dorset DT6 3RZ. *T:* Bridport (0308) 22983. *Club:* Brooks's.

HOOD, Sir Harold (Joseph), 2nd Bt *cr* 1922, of Wimbledon, Co. Surrey; TD; Circulation Director: Universe, 1953–60; Catholic Herald, 1961–87; *b* 23 Jan. 1916; *e s* of Sir Joseph Hood, 1st Bt, and Marie Josephine (*d* 1956), *e d* of Archibald Robinson, JP, Dublin; *S* father, 1931; *m* 1946, Hon. Ferelith Rosemary Florence Kenworthy, *o d* of 10th Baron Strabolgi and Doris, *o c* of late Sir Frederick Whitley-Thomson, MP; two *s* two *d* (and one *s* decd). *Educ:* Downside Sch. Mem. Editorial Staff, The Universe, 1936–39; Asst Editor, The Catholic Directory, 1950, Managing Ed., 1959–60; Editor, The Catholic Who's Who, 1952 Edition. 2nd Lieutenant 58th Middx Battalion RE (AA) (TA) 1939; Lieut RA, 1941. GCSG (Holy See) 1986; (KSG 1964; KCSG 1978); Kt of Magistral Grace, SMO Malta, 1972. *Heir: s* John Joseph Harold Hood, *b* 27 Aug. 1952. *Address:* 31 Avenue Road, NW8 6BS. *T:* 071–722 9088. *Clubs:* Royal Automobile, MCC, Challoner.

HOOD, James; MP (Lab) Clydesdale, since 1987; *b* 16 May 1948; *m* 1967, Marion McCleary; one *s* one *d*. *Educ:* Lesmahagow Higher Grade, Coatbridge; Motherwell Tech. Coll.; Nottingham Univ. WEA. Miner, Nottingham; NUM official, 1973–85. Mem., Newark and Sherwood Dist Council, 1979–87. Mem., Select Cttee on European Legislation; Chairman: All Party Gp on ME (Myalgic Encephalomyetis); Miners Parly Gp, 1992. *Recreations:* reading, gardening. *Address:* House of Commons, SW1A 0AA; Ras-al-Ghar, 57 Biggar Road, Symington, Lanarks. *Club:* Lesmahagow Miners Welfare Social (Hon. Mem.).

HOOD, Rear-Adm. John, CBE 1981; CEng, FIMechE; Director General Aircraft (Naval), 1978–81; *b* 23 March 1924; *s* of Charles Arthur Hood, architect, and Nellie Ormiston Brown Lamont; *m* 1948, Julia Mary Trevaskis; three *s*. *Educ:* Plymouth Coll.; RN Engineering Coll., Keyham. Entered Royal Navy, 1945; RNEC, 1945–48; served in Illustrious, 1948; RN Air Stations, Abbotsinch, Anthorn, RAF West Raynham (NAFDU), 1948–51; HQ Min. of Supply, 1951–53; Air Engineer Officer, 1834 Sqdn, 1953–55, Aeroplane and Armament Experimental Estabt, 1955–57; Staff of Dir Aircraft Maintenance and Repair, 1957–59; AEO, HMS Albion, 1959–61; Sen. Air Engr, RNEC, Manadon, 1961–62; Development Project Officer, Sea Vixen 2, Min. of Aviation, 1962–65; AEO, RNAS, Lossiemouth, 1965–67; Staff of Dir of Officer Appointments (E), 1967–70; Defence and Naval Attaché, Argentina and Uruguay, 1970–73; Sen. Officers War Course, 1973; Asst Dir, Naval Manpower Requirements (Ships), 1974–75; Head of Aircraft Dept (Naval), 1975–78. Comdr 1962, Captain 1969, Rear-Adm. 1979. *Recreations:* sailing, gardening. *Club:* RN Sailing Association.

HOOD, (Martin) Sinclair (Frankland), FSA; FBA 1983; archaeologist; *b* 31 Jan. 1917; *s* of late Lt-Comdr Martin Hood, RN, and late Mrs Martin Hood, New York; *m* 1957, Rachel Simmons; one *s* two *d*. *Educ:* Harrow; Magdalen Coll., Oxford. FSA 1953. British Sch. at Athens: student, 1947–48 and 1951–53; Asst Dir, 1949–51; Dir, 1954–62. Student, British Inst. Archaeology, Ankara, 1948–49. Geddes-Harrower Vis. Prof. of Greek Art and Archaeology, Univ. of Aberdeen, 1968. Took part in excavations at: Dorchester, Oxon, 1937; Compton, Berks, 1946–47; Southwark, 1946; Smyrna, 1948–49; Atchana, 1949–50; Sakca-Gozu, 1950; Mycenae, 1950–52; Knossos, 1950–51, 1953–55, 1957–61, 1973 and 1987; Jericho, 1952; Chios, 1952–55. *Publications:* The Home of the Heroes: The Aegean before the Greeks, 1967; The Minoans, 1971; The Arts in Prehistoric Greece, 1978; various excavation reports and articles. *Address:* The Old Vicarage, Great Milton, Oxford OX9 7PB. *T:* Great Milton (0844) 279202. *Club:* Athenæum.

HOOD, Prof. Neil, FRSE; Professor of Business Policy, since 1979, Co-Director, Strathclyde International Business Unit, since 1983, and Deputy Principal (Development), since 1991, University of Strathclyde; *b* 10 Aug. 1943; *s* of Andrew Hood and Elizabeth Taylor Carruthers; *m* 1966, Anna Watson Clark; one *s* one *d*. *Educ:* Wishaw High Sch.; Univ. of Glasgow. MA, MLitt; FRSE 1987. Res. Fellow, Scottish Coll. of Textiles, 1966–68; Lectr, later Sen. Lectr, Paisley Coll. of Technol., 1968–78; Economic Advr, Scottish Economic Planning Dept, 1979; Associate Dean, 1982–85, Dean, 1985–87, Strathclyde Business Sch., Univ. of Strathclyde; Dir, Locate In Scotland, 1987–89, and Dir, Employment and Special Initiatives, 1989–90, Scottish Develt Agency (on secondment). Vis. Prof. of Internat. Business, Univ. of Texas, Dallas, 1981; Vis. Prof., Stockholm Sch. of Economics, 1983–89. Trade Adviser, UNCTAD-GATT, 1980–85; Economic Consultant to Sec. of State for Scotland, 1980–87; Consultant to: Internat. Finance Corp., World Bank, 1982–84, 1991; UN Centre on Transnational Corporations, 1982–84. Mem., Irvine Develt Corp., 1985–87. Non-executive Director: Euroscot Meat Exports Ltd, 1983–86; Scottish Develt Finance Ltd, 1984–90; Lanarkshire Industrial Field Executive Ltd, 1984–86; Prestwick Holdings PLC, 1986–87; Lamberton (Hldgs) Ltd, 1989–; GA (Hldgs) Ltd, 1990–; Shanks & McEwan Gp PLC, 1990–; First Charlotte Assets Trust plc, 1990–. Investment Advr, Castleforth Fund Managers Ltd, 1984–88. Member: various boards, CNAA, 1971–83; Industry and Employment Cttee, ESRC, 1985–87. Pres., European Internat. Business Assoc., 1986. Fellow, European Inst. of Advanced Studies in Management, Brussels, 1985–87. *Publications:* (with S. Young): Chrysler UK: Corporation in transition, 1977; Economics of Multinational Enterprise, 1979; European Development Strategies of US-owned Manufacturing Companies Located in Scotland, 1980; Multinationals in Retreat: the Scottish experience, 1982; Multinational Investment Strategies in the British Isles, 1983; (ed) Industrial Policy and the Scottish Economy, 1984; (with P. Draper, I. Smith and W. Stewart) Scottish Financial Sector, 1987; (ed with J. E. Vahlne) Strategies in Global Competition, 1987; (with S. Young and J. Hamill) Foreign Multinationals and the British Economy, Impact and Policy, 1988; articles on internat. business, marketing and business policy, in various jls. *Recreations:* reading, writing, swimming, golf, gardening. *Address:* Teviot, 12 Carlisle Road, Hamilton ML3 7DB. *T:* Hamilton (0698) 424870. *Club:* Royal Automobile (Glasgow).

HOOD, Nicholas; *see* Hood, W. N.

HOOD, Roger Grahame; University Reader in Criminology, Director of the Centre for Criminological Research, and Fellow of All Souls College, Oxford, since 1973; *b* 12 June 1936; 2nd *s* of Ronald and Phyllis Hood; *m* 1963, Barbara Blaine Young (marr. diss. 1985); one *d*; *m* 1985, Nancy Stebbing (*née* Lynah). *Educ:* King Edward's Sch., Five Ways, Birmingham; LSE (BSc Sociology); Downing Coll., Cambridge (PhD). Research Officer, LSE, 1961–63; Lectr in Social Admin, Univ. of Durham, 1963–67; Asst Dir of Research, Inst. of Criminology, Univ. of Cambridge, 1967–73; Fellow of Clare Hall, Cambridge, 1969–73. Vis. Prof., Univ. of Virginia Sch. of Law, 1980–90. Expert Consultant, UN, on death penalty, 1988. Member: Parole Bd, 1972–73; SSRC Cttee on Social Sciences and the Law, 1975–79; Judicial Studies Bd, 1979–85; Parole System Review, 1987–88; Pres., British Soc. of Criminology, 1986–89. Sellin-Glueck Award, Amer. Soc. of Criminology, 1986. Mem. Editorial Bd, Crime and Justice. *Publications:* Sentencing in Magistrates' Courts, 1962; Borstal Re-assessed, 1965; (with Richard Sparks) Key Issues in Criminology, 1970; Sentencing the Motoring Offender, 1972; (ed) Crime, Criminology and Public Policy: Essays in Honour of Sir Leon Radzinowicz, 1974; (with Sir Leon Radzinowicz) Criminology and the Administration of Criminal Justice: a bibliography, 1976; (with Sir Leon Radzinowicz) A History of English Criminal Law, vol. 5, The Emergence of Penal Policy, 1986; The Death Penalty: a world-wide perspective, 1989. *Address:* 63 Iffley Road, Oxford OX4 1EF. *T:* Oxford (0865) 246084.

HOOD, Samuel Harold; Director, Defence Operational Analysis Establishment, Ministry of Defence, 1985–86; *b* 21 Aug. 1926; *s* of Samuel N. and Annie Hood; *m* 1959, Frances Eileen Todd; two *s* four *d*. *Educ:* Larne Grammar Sch., Co. Antrim; Queen's Univ., Belfast (BA Hons Maths). Joined Civil Service, staff of Scientific Advr, Air Min., 1948; Staff of Operational Res. Br., Bomber Comd, 1950; Scientific Officer, BCDU, RAF Wittering, 1954; Operational Res. Br., Bomber Comd, 1959; Staff of Chief Scientist (RAF), 1964; joined DOAE, 1965; Supt, Air Div., DOAE, 1969; Dir, Defence Sci. Divs 1 and 7, MoD, 1974; Head, Systems Assessment Dept, RAE, 1981. *Recreations:* walking, gardening, bird watching. *Address:* The Meadow, Broadmoor Common, Woolhope, Herefordshire HR1 4QU. *T:* Fownhope (043277) 446.

HOOD, Sinclair; *see* Hood, M. S. F.

HOOD, Sir William Acland, 8th Bt *cr* 1806 and 6th Bt *cr* 1809; *b* 5 March 1901; *s* of William Fuller-Acland-Hood (*d* 1933) and Elizabeth (*d* 1966), *d* of M. Kirkpatrick, Salt Lake City, USA; *S* to baronetcies of kinsman, 2nd Baron St Audries, 1971; *m* 1925, Mary, *d* of late Augustus Edward Jessup, Philadelphia; one *d* (one *s* decd). *Educ:* Wellington; RMA Woolwich; Univ. of California (MA). Naturalized American citizen, 1926. Formerly Lieutenant RE. Professor, Los Angeles City College, retired. *Heir:* none. *Address:* HC02–Box 577, 29 Palms, California 92277, USA. *T:* 619 367–9345.

HOOD, (William) Nicholas, CBE 1991; Chairman, Wessex Water Plc, since 1989; *b* 3 Dec. 1935; *s* of Sir Tom Hood, KBE, CB, TD; *m* 1963, Angela Robinson (marr. diss. 1990); one *s* one *d*. *Educ:* Clifton Coll. CBIM 1990. Served DCLI, 1955–57. NEM General Insce Assoc. Ltd and Credit Insce Assoc. Ltd, 1958–64; G. B. Britton UK Ltd, eventually Sales and Marketing Dir, 1964–70; UBM Gp Plc, eventually Dir of Central Reg., 1970– 84; Man. Dir, UBM Overseas Ltd, 1972–82; Dir, HAT Gp Ltd, 1984–86; Chm .,Wessex Water Authy, 1987–89. Director: Bremhill Industries Plc, 1987–; Provident Life Assoc. Ltd, 1988–; Western Adv. Bd, Nat. Westminster Bank, 1990–. Chm., Water Aid Council, 1990–; Member: Water Trng Council, 1987–; Foundn for Water Res., 1989–. *Recreations:* fishing, painting. *Address:* Wessex Water Plc, Wessex House, Passage Street, Bristol BS2 0JQ. *T:* Bristol (0272) 290611. *Club:* Army and Navy.

HOOK, David Morgan Alfred, FEng 1985; Deputy Chairman, G. Maunsell & Partners, since 1989 (Managing Director, 1984–88); *b* 16 April 1931; *m* 1957, Winifred (*née* Brown); two *s* one *d*. *Educ:* Bancroft's School; Queens' College, Cambridge (MA). FICE, FIStructE. Holland & Hannen and Cubitts, 1954–58; Nuclear Civil Constructors, 1958–62; G. Maunsell & Partners (Consulting Engineers), 1962–, Partner, 1968–. *Publications:* papers in Jl of IStructE. *Recreations:* private flying, golf. *Club:* United Oxford & Cambridge University.

HOOK, Rt. Rev. Ross Sydney, MC 1945; an Assistant Bishop, Diocese of Canterbury, since 1981; *b* 19 Feb. 1917; *o s* of late Sydney Frank and Laura Harriet Hook; *m* 1948, Ruth Leslie, *d* of late Rev. Herman Masterman Biddell and Violet Marjorie Biddell; one *s* one *d*. *Educ:* Christ's Hosp.; Peterhouse, Cambridge (MA); Ridley Hall, Cambridge. Asst Curate, Milton, Hants, 1941–43. Chaplain, RNVR (Royal Marine Commandos), 1943–46. Chaplain, Ridley Hall, Cambridge, 1946–48. Select Preacher, University of Cambridge, 1948; Rector, Chorlton-cum-Hardy, Manchester, 1948–52; Rector and Rural Dean, Chelsea, 1952–61; Chaplain: Chelsea Hosp. for Women, 1954–61; St Luke's Hosp., Chelsea, 1957–61; Residentiary Canon of Rochester and Precentor, 1961–65; Treasurer, 1965; Diocesan Dir of Post Ordination Training, 1961–65; Bishop Suffragan of Grantham, 1965–72; Bishop of Bradford, 1972–80; Chief of Staff to Archbishop of Canterbury, 1980–84. Examining Chaplain to Bishop of Rochester, 1961–65, to Bishop of Lincoln, 1966–72; Prebendary of Brampton (Lincoln Cathedral), 1966–72; Dean of Stamford, 1971–72. Chm., Inspections Cttee, Central Advisory Council for the Ministry, 1966–71 (Sec., 1960–66). Hon. DLitt Bradford, 1981. *Recreation:* cricket. *Address:* Millrock, Newchurch, Romney Marsh, Kent TN29 0DN.

HOOKER, Michael Ayerst, PhD; educational consultant; Senior Educational Adviser, Jerwood Award, since 1991 (Executive Director, 1988–91); *b* 22 Jan. 1923; *s* of late Albert Ayerst Hooker, late of Bromsleigh Park, Seal Chart, Kent, and Marjorie Mitchell Hooker (*née* Gunson). *Educ:* Marlborough; St Edmund Hall, Oxford (MA 1944); Univ. of the Witwatersrand (PhD 1952). Home Guard, Oxford Univ. Sen. Trng Corps and Army Cadet Force (TARO), 1940–48. British Council, 1945–47; Schoolmaster, England and S Africa, 1947–51; London Diocesan Bd of Educn, 1952–66; Visual Aids and Public Relations, 1953–59. Chm., Fedn of Conservative Students, 1944; Parly Candidate (C) Coventry East, 1955; various offices, Conservative Commonwealth Council, 1955–60. Wells Organisation, fund raising in UK and NZ, 1957–58; Man. Dir, Hooker Craigmyle & Co. Ltd (first institutional fund raising consultants in UK), 1959–72; Man. Dir, Michael Hooker and Associates Ltd, 1972–79; Develt Dir, The Look Wide Trust, 1979–80; Chief Exec. Gov., Truman and Knightley Educn Trust, 1981–87 (Gov., 1977–87). From 1957, has helped to raise nearly £70 million for various good causes, incl. 13 historic cathedrals, univs, colleges, schools, medical causes, welfare charities, etc. Member: Adv. Cttee on Charitable Fund Raising, Nat. Council of Social Service, 1971–73; Academic Adv. Council, Prime Coll., Kuala Lumpur, 1986–. Jt Founder and Chm., Friends of Friends, subseq. Routledge Soc., 1985–90; Trustee: Ross McWhirter Foundn, 1976–; Dicey Trust, 1978–; Jerwood Oakham Foundn, 1981–; Police Convalescence and Rehabilitation Trust, 1985–; Chm. Hon. Councillor, NSPCC, 1981–; Governor: Oakham Sch., 1971–83; Shitennoji Sch., 1986–. *Publications:* various pamphlets and broadcasts on charities, historic churches, educnl issues, law and taxation, Christian stewardship of money. *Address:* Flat 8, 85 Marine Parade, Brighton BN2 1AJ. *Clubs:* Carlton, Commonwealth Trust.

HOOKER, Prof. Morna Dorothy; Lady Margaret's Professor of Divinity, University of Cambridge, since 1976; Fellow of Robinson College, Cambridge, since 1976; *b* 19 May 1931; *d* of Percy Francis Hooker, FIA, and Lily (*née* Riley); *m* 1978, Rev. Dr W. David Stacey, MA. *Educ:* Univ. of Bristol (research schol.); Univ. of Manchester (research studentship). MA (Bristol, Oxford and Cambridge); PhD (Manchester). Research Fellow, Univ. of Durham, 1959–61; Lectr in New Testament Studies, King's Coll., London, 1961–70; Lectr in Theology, Oxford, and Fellow, Linacre Coll., 1970–76 (Hon. Fellow, 1980); Lectr in Theology, Keble Coll., 1972–76. Visiting Fellow, Clare Hall, Cambridge, 1974; Visiting Professor: McGill Univ., 1968; Duke Univ., 1987 and 1989. FKC 1979. Lectures: T. W. Manson meml, 1977; A. S. Peake meml, 1978; Henton Davies, 1979; Ethel M. Wood, 1984; James A. Gray, Duke Univ., 1984; W. A. Sanderson, Melbourne, 1986; Didsbury, Manchester, 1988; Brennan, Louisville, 1989; St Paul's, 1989; Perkins, Texas, 1990. Pres., SNTS, 1988–89. Jt Editor, Jl of Theological Studies, 1985–. *Publications:* Jesus and the Servant, 1959; The Son of Man in Mark, 1967; (ed jtly) What about the New Testament?, 1975; Pauline Pieces, 1979; Studying the New Testament, 1979; (ed jtly) Paul and Paulinism, 1982; The Message of Mark, 1983; Continuity and Discontinuity, 1986; From Adam to Christ, 1990; A Commentary on the Gospel according to St Mark, 1991; contribs to New Testament Studies, Jl of Theological Studies, Theology, Epworth Review, etc. *Recreations:* Molinology, walking, music. *Address:* Divinity School, St John's Street, Cambridge CB2 1TW.

HOOKER, Ronald George, CBE 1985; FEng; FIProdE; CBIM; FRSA; Chairman: Management & Business Services Ltd, since 1972; Thomas Storey Ltd, since 1984; Co-ordinated Land and Estates, since 1985; Warner Howard plc, since 1987; company directorships; *b* 6 Aug. 1921; *m* 1954, Eve Pigott; one *s* one *d*. *Educ:* Wimbledon Technical Coll.; London Univ. (external). FIProdE 1980; FEng 1984. CBIM 1972. Apprentice, Philips Electrical Ltd, 1937–41, Develt Engr, 1945–48; FBI, 1948–50; Dir and Gen. Man., Brush Electrical Engineering Co. Ltd, 1950–60; Man. Dir, K & L Steelfounders & Engineers Ltd, 1960–65; Man. Dir, Associated Fire Alarms Ltd, 1965–68; Chm. and Man. Dir, Crane Fruehauf Trailers Ltd, 1968–71; Dir of Manufacture, Rolls Royce (1971) Ltd, 1971–73; Chm. and Man. Dir, John M. Henderson (Holdings) Ltd, 1973–75. Director: GEI Internat. plc, 1974–; Computing Devices Hldgs Ltd, 1986–. Pres., Engrg Employers' Fedn, 1986–88 (Mem. Management Bd, 1977–); Mem., Engrg Council, 1982–86. Past Pres., IProdE, 1974–75 (Hon. Life MIProdE 1980). Freeman, City of London. *Publications:* papers on management and prodn engrg to BIM, ICMA, IProdE and IMechE. *Recreations:* gardening, reading, music. *Address:* Loxborough House, Bledlow Ridge, near High Wycombe, Bucks HP14 4AA. *T:* Bledlow Ridge (024027) 486; 6 Tufton Court, Tufton Street, SW1P 3QH. *T:* 071–222 6669. *Clubs:* Athenæum, Lansdowne.

HOOKS, Air Vice-Marshal Robert Keith, CBE 1979; CEng, FRAeS; RAF retired; Deputy Managing Director, European Helicopter Industries Ltd, since 1987; *b* 7 Aug. 1929; *s* of late Robert George Hooks and Phyllis Hooks; *m* 1954, Kathleen (*née* Cooper); one *s* one *d*. *Educ:* Acklam Hall Sch.; Constantine Coll., Middlesbrough. Bsc(Eng) London. Commissioned RAF, 1951; served at RAF stations West Malling, Fassberg, Sylt, 1952–55; RAF Technical Coll., Henlow, 1956; Fairey Aviation Co., 1957–58; Air Ministry, 1958–60; Skybolt Trials Unit, Eglin, Florida, 1961–63; Bomber Command Armament Sch., Wittering, 1963–65; OC Engrg Wing, RAF Coll., Cranwell, 1967–69; HQ Far East Air Force, 1969–71; Supt of Armament A&AEE, 1971–74; Director Ground Training, 1974–76; Director Air Armament, 1976–80; Vice-Pres. (Air), Ordnance Board, 1980; Dir Gen. Aircraft 2, MoD (Procurement Exec.), 1981–84; Divl Dir (European Business), Westland Helicopters, 1984–85; Projects Dir, Helicopter Div., Westland plc, 1985–87. *Address:* c/o Lloyds Bank, Cox's & King's Branch, 7 Pall Mall, SW1Y 5NA. *Club:* Royal Air Force.

HOOKWAY, Sir Harry (Thurston), Kt 1978; Pro-Chancellor, Loughborough University of Technology, since 1987; *b* 23 July 1921; *s* of William and Bertha Hookway; *m* 1956, Barbara Olive, *o d* of late Oliver and Olive Butler; one *s* one *d*. *Educ:* Trinity Sch. of John Whitgift; London Univ. (BSc, PhD). Various posts in industry, 1941–49; DSIR, 1949–65; Asst Dir, National Chemical Laboratory, 1959; Dir, UK Scientific Mission (North America), Scientific Attaché, Washington, DC, and Scientific Adviser to UK High Comr, Ottawa, 1960–64; Head of Information Div., DSIR, 1964–65; CSO, DES, 1966–69; Asst Under-Sec. of State, DES, 1969–73; Dep. Chm. and Chief Exec., The British Library Bd, 1973–84; Chairman: Publishers Databases Ltd, 1984–87; LA Publishing Ltd, 1986–89. Chairman: UNESCO Internat. Adv. Cttee for Documentation, Libraries and Archives, 1975–79; British Council Libraries Adv. Cttee, 1982–86; President: Inst. of Information Scientists, 1973–76; Library Assoc., 1985. Mem., Royal Commn on Historical Monuments (England), 1981–89. Governor, British Inst. for Recorded Sound, 1981–86. Dir, Arundel Castle Trustees Ltd, 1976–. Hon. FLA, 1982; Hon. FIInfSc. Hon. LLD Sheffield, 1976; Hon. DLitt Loughborough, 1980. Gold Medal, Internat. Assoc. of Library Assocs, 1985. *Publications:* various contribs to jls of learned societies. *Recreations:* music, travel. *Address:* 3 St James Green, Thirsk, N Yorks YO7 1AF. *Club:* Athenæum.

HOOLAHAN, Anthony Terence, QC 1973; a Recorder of the Crown Court, since 1976; a Social Security Commissioner, since 1986; *b* 26 July 1925; *s* of late Gerald and Val Hoolahan; *m* 1949, Dorothy Veronica Connochie; one *s* one *d*. *Educ:* Dorset House, Littlehampton, Sussex; Framlingham Coll., Suffolk; Lincoln Coll., Oxford (MA). Served War, RNVR, 1943–46. Oxford Univ., 1946–48. Called to Bar, Inner Temple, 1949, Bencher, 1980; called to the Bar of Northern Ireland, 1980, QC (Northern Ireland) 1980. Chairman: Richmond Soc., 1976–80; Trustees, Richmond Museum, 1988–. Gov., St Elizabeth's Sch., Richmond, 1990–. *Publications:* Guide to Defamation Practice (with Colin Duncan, QC), 2nd edn, 1958; contrib. to Halsbury's Laws of England, Atkin's Court Forms. *Recreation:* swimming. *Address:* Harp House, 83 Farringdon Street, EC4A 4DH. *T:* 071–353 5145.

HOOLE, Alan Norman, OBE 1991; Governor and Commander-in-Chief, St Helena and its Dependencies, since 1991; *b* 25 April 1942; *s* of Walter Norman and Elsie Hoole; *m* 1st, 1962, Pauline Claire Bettison (marr. diss.); one *s* one *d*; 2nd, 1982, Delia Rose Clingham. *Educ:* Chesterfield Grammar Sch.; Lady Manners Grammar Sch., Bakewell; Sheffield Univ.; Coll. of Law, London. Admitted as Solicitor, 1964 (S. H. Clay Prize, Law Soc., 1963). Partner, Blakesley & Rooth, Solicitors, Chesterfield, 1965–78; Attorney General: St Helena, 1978–83; Anguilla, 1983–85; Chief Sec., Turks and Caicos Is, 1986–88; Attorney Gen., Anguilla, 1989–90; Dep. Gov., Anguilla, 1990–91. *Recreations:* fishing, tennis. *Address:* Plantation House, Island of St Helena, South Atlantic. *T:* 290 4444. *Club:* Commonwealth Trust.

HOOLE, Sir Arthur (Hugh), Kt 1985; Consultant, Tuck & Mann, Epsom, since 1989 (Partner, 1951–88); *b* 14 Jan. 1924; *s* of Hugh Francis and Gladys Emily Hoole; *m* 1945, Eleanor Mary Hobbs; two *s* two *d*. *Educ:* Sutton County School; Emmanuel College, Cambridge. MA, LLM. Served RAFVR, 1943–46; admitted solicitor, 1951; Mem. Council, Law Society, 1969–87 (Vice-Pres., 1983–84; Pres., 1984–85); Governor, College of Law, 1976– (Chm., 1983–90); Member: Adv. Cttee on Legal Educn, 1977–90; Common Professional Examination Bd, 1977–81 (Chm., 1978–81); Criminal Injuries Compensation Bd, 1985–. Governor: St John's Sch., Leatherhead, 1987–; Sutton Manor High Sch., 1987–. *Recreations:* cricket, books, music. *Address:* Yew Tree House, St Nicholas Hill, Leatherhead, Surrey KT22 8NE. *T:* Leatherhead (0372) 373208. *Club:* Royal Automobile.

HOOLEY, Prof. Christopher, FRS 1983; Professor of Pure Mathematics, since 1967, Head of School of Mathematics, since 1988, and Deputy Principal, since 1991, University of Wales College of Cardiff (formerly University College, Cardiff); *b* 7 Aug, 1928; *s* of Leonard Joseph Hooley, MA, BSc, and Barbara Hooley; *m* 1954, Birgitta Kniep; two *s*. *Educ:* Wilmslow Preparatory Sch.; Abbotsholme Sch.; Corpus Christi Coll., Cambridge (MA, PhD, ScD). Captain, RAEC, 1948–49 (SO III, British Troops in Egypt). Fellow, Corpus Christi Coll., Cambridge, 1955–58; Lectr in Mathematics, Univ. of Bristol, 1958–65; Prof. of Pure Mathematics, Univ. of Durham, 1965–67; University College, Cardiff: Hd of Dept of Pure Maths, 1967–88; Dean of Faculty of Science, 1973–76; Dep. Principal, 1979–81. Visiting Member: Inst. for Advanced Study, Princeton, 1970–71, and Fall Terms, 1976, 1977, 1982, 1983; Institut des Hautes Etudes Scientifiques, Paris, 1984. Adams Prize, Cambridge, 1973; Sen. Berwick Prize, London Mathematical Soc., 1980. *Publications:* Applications of Sieve Methods to the Theory of Numbers, 1976; (ed with H. Halberstam) Recent Progress in Analytic Number Theory, 1981; memoirs in diverse mathematical jls. *Recreations:* classic cars; antiquities. *Address:* Rushmoor Grange, Backwell, near Bristol. *T:* Flax Bourton (0275) 462363.

HOOLEY, Frank Oswald; retired; *b* 30 Nov. 1923; *m* 1945, Doris Irene Snook; two *d*. *Educ:* King Edward's High Sch., Birmingham; Birmingham Univ. Admin. Asst, Birmingham Univ., 1948–52; Sheffield Univ.: Asst Registrar, 1952–65; Sen. Asst Registrar, 1965–66; Registrar, Fourah Bay Coll., Sierra Leone, 1960–62 (secondment from Sheffield); Sen. Admin. Asst, Manchester Poly., 1970–71; Chief Admin. Offr, Sheffield City Coll. of Educn, 1971–74. Res. Asst to John Tomlinson, MEP, 1984–88. MP (Lab) Sheffield, Heeley, 1966–70 and Feb. 1974–1983. Chm., Parly Liaison Gp for Alternative Energy Strategies, 1978; formerly Member, Select Committees on Sci. and Technol., Overseas Aid, Foreign Affairs, and Procedure. Contested (Lab) Stratford-on-Avon, 1983. Chm., Co-ordinating Cttee, Internat. Anti-Apartheid Year, 1978. *Address:* 6 Mayland Drive, Sutton Coldfield B74 2DG. *T:* 021–353 0982.

HOOLEY, John Rouse, DL; Chief Executive, West Sussex County Council, 1975–90; Clerk to the Lieutenancy of West Sussex, 1976–90; *b* 25 June 1927; *s* of Harry and Elsie Hooley; *m* 1953, Gloria Patricia Swanston; three *s* one *d*. *Educ:* William Hulme's Sch., Manchester; Lincoln Coll., Oxford; Manchester Univ. LLB London. Admitted Solicitor (Hons), 1952. Served Lancashire Fusiliers, 1946–48. Asst Solicitor, Chester, Carlisle and Shropshire, 1952–65; Asst Clerk, Cornwall, 1965–67; Dep. Clerk and Dep. Clerk of the Peace, W Sussex, 1967–74; County Sec., W Sussex, 1974–75. Mem., Chichester HA, 1990. FRSA. DL 1991. *Recreations:* gardening, music. *Address:* Bosvigo, Lavant Road, Chichester PO19 1RQ.

HOON, Geoffrey William; Member (Lab) Derbyshire, European Parliament, since 1984; *b* 6 Dec. 1953; *s* of Ernest and June Hoon; *m* 1981, Elaine Ann Dumelow; one *s* two *d*. *Educ:* Jesus College, Cambridge (MA). Called to the Bar, Gray's Inn, 1978. Labourer at furniture factory, 1972–73; Lectr in Law, Leeds Univ., 1976–82. In practice at Nottingham, 1982–. Prospective Parly Candidate (Lab) Ashfield, 1990–. European Parliament: Mem., Legal Affairs Cttee, 1984–; President: Standing Delegn to China, 1987–89; Standing Delegn to US, 1989–. *Recreations:* football, cricket, running, squash, cinema, music. *Address:* 65a Nottingham Road, Derby DE1 3QS.

HOOPER, family name of **Baroness Hooper.**

HOOPER, Baroness *cr* 1985 (Life Peer), of Liverpool and of St James's in the City of Westminster; **Gloria Dorothy Hooper;** Parliamentary Under Secretary of State, Department of Health, since 1989; *b* 25 May 1939; *d* of late Frances and Frederick Hooper. *Educ:* University of Southampton (BA Hons Law); Universidad Central, Quito, Ecuador (Lic. de Derecho Internacional). Admitted to Law Society, Solicitor, 1973; Partner, Taylor Garrett (formerly Taylor and Humbert), 1974–84. MEP (C) Liverpool, 1979–84; Vice-Chm., Environment and Consumer Affairs Cttees, European Parlt, 1979–84; EDG Whip, European Parlt, 1982–84; contested (C) Merseyside West, European Parly elecn, 1984. Baroness in Waiting, 1985–87; Parly Under Sec. of State, DES, 1987–88, Dept of Energy, 1988–89. FRGS 1982; Fellow, Industry and Parlt Trust, 1983. *Publications:* Cases on Company Law, 1967; Law of International Trade, 1968. *Recreations:* theatre and walking. *Address:* House of Lords, Westminster, SW1A 0PW. *T:* 071–219 3000.

HOOPER, Anthony; QC 1987; a Recorder, since 1986; *b* 16 Sept 1937; *s* of late Edwin Morris Hooper and of Greta Lillian Chissim; *m* 1st, Margrethe Frances (*née* Hansen) (marr. diss. 1986); one *s* one *d*; 2nd, Heather Christine (*née* Randall). *Educ:* Sherborne; Trinity Hall, Cambridge (Scholar; MA, LLB). 2nd Lieut, 7th RTR, 1956–57. Called to the Bar, Inner Temple, 1965; admitted to Law Society of British Columbia, 1969. Asst Lectr and Lectr, Univ. of Newcastle upon Tyne, 1962–65; Asst and Associate Prof., Faculty of Law, Univ. of British Columbia, 1965–68; Prof. Associé, Univ. de Laval, 1969–70; Prof., Osgoode Hall Law Sch., York Univ., 1971–73. Visiting Professor: Univ. de Montréal, 1972, 1973; Osgoode Hall, 1984. *Publications:* (ed) Harris's Criminal Law, 21st edn 1968; articles in legal jls. *Recreation:* sailing. *Club:* Travellers'.
See also R. Hooper.

HOOPER, Ven. Charles German, MA; Archdeacon of Ipswich, 1963–76, now Archdeacon Emeritus; *b* 16 April 1911; 2nd *s* of A. C. Hooper, Solicitor; *m* 1936, Lilian Mary, *d* of late Sir Harold Brakspear, KCVO; one *s* one *d*. *Educ:* Lincoln Coll., Oxford (MA 2nd cl. English). Curacies: Corsham, Wilts, 1934–36; Claremont, CP, South Africa, 1936–39; Rector, Castle Combe, Wilts, 1940; Chaplain, RAFVR, 1942–46 (despatches); Rector, Sandy, Beds, 1946–53; Vicar and Rural Dean, Bishop's Stortford, Herts, 1953–63; Rector of Bildeston, Suffolk, 1963–67; Rector of St Lawrence's and St Stephen's, Ipswich, 1967–74. Chaplain to Cutlers Co., Sheffield, 1964–65, to Drapers Co., 1972–73. *Recreations:* painting in water colours, sailing. *Address:* East Green Cottage, Kelsale, Saxmundham, Suffolk IP17 2PJ. *T:* Saxmundham (0728) 602702.
See also Baron Methuen.

HOOPER, Sir Leonard (James), KCMG 1967 (CMG 1962); CBE 1951; idc; a Deputy Secretary, Cabinet Office, 1973–78, retired; *b* 23 July 1914. *Educ:* Alleyn's, Dulwich; Worcester Coll., Oxford. Joined Air Ministry, 1938, transferred Foreign Office, 1942; Imperial Defence Coll., 1953; Dir, Govt Communications HQ, 1965–73. *Recreation:* sport. *Address:* 9 Vittoria Walk, Cheltenham, Glos GL50 1TL. *T:* Cheltenham (0242) 511007. *Club:* New (Cheltenham).

HOOPER, Noel Barrie; Hon. Mr Justice Hooper; Judge of the High Court, Hong Kong, since 1981; *b* 9 Nov. 1931; twin *s* of late Alfred Edward Hooper and Constance Violet Hooper; *m* 1959, Pauline Mary (*née* Irwin); two *d*. *Educ:* Prince of Wales Sch., Kenya; St Peter's Hall, Oxford (BA 1954). Called to the Bar, Gray's Inn, 1956. Advocate of High Court, Uganda, 1956–61; Magistrate, Basutoland, 1961–64 and Hong Kong, 1964–68; Sen. Magistrate, Hong Kong, 1968–73; Principal Magistrate, 1973–76; Dist Judge, 1976–81; Comr of the Supreme Court of Brunei, 1983–86, 1986–89 and 1990–. *Recreations:* tennis, cricket, reading. *Address:* The Courts of Justice, Hong Kong. *Clubs:* MCC; Hong Kong Cricket, Ladies' Recreation (Hong Kong).

HOOPER, Richard; Special Adviser, Information Industry, PA Consulting Group, since 1988; Member, Radio Authority, since 1990; *b* 19 Sept. 1939; *s* of late Edwin Morris Hooper and of Greta Lillian (*née* Goode): *m* 1964, Meredith Jean Rooney; two *s* one *d*. *Educ:* Sherborne Sch.; Worcester Coll., Oxford (BA German and Russian, 1963; MA). National Service, 2nd Lieut 7th RTR, BAOR, 1958–59. Gen. trainee, BBC, 1963; Radio Producer, BBC Further Educn, 1964–66; Harkness Fellow, USA, 1967–68; Sen. Radio and TV Producer, BBC Open Univ. Prodns, 1969–72; Dir, National Develt Prog. in Computer Assisted Learning, 1973–77; Man. Dir, Mills & Allen Communications, 1978–79; Dir, Prestel, Post Office Telecommunications, 1980–81; Chief Exec., Value Added Systems and Services, BT, 1982–86; Man. Dir, Super Channel, 1986–88. Director (non-executive): G. A. Pindar & Son, 1988–; British Aerospace Communications, 1989–. Special Staff Consultant to President Lyndon Johnson's Commn on Instructional Technology, 1968. *Publications:* (ed) Colour in Britain, 1965; (ed) The Curriculum, Context, Design and Development, 1971; Unnatural Monopolies, 1991; contrib. to books and jls. *Recreations:* the family, theatre. *Address:* PA Consulting Group, 123 Buckingham Palace Road, SW1W 9SR. *T:* 071–730 9000.
See also A. Hooper.

HOOSON, family name of **Baron Hooson.**

HOOSON, Baron *cr* 1979 (Life Peer), of Montgomery in the County of Powys and of Colomendy in the County of Clwyd; **Hugh Emlyn Hooson;** QC 1960; a Recorder of the Crown Court, since 1972 (Recorder of Swansea, 1971); *b* 26 March 1925; *s* of late Hugh and Elsie Hooson, Colomendy, Denbigh; *m* 1950, Shirley Margaret Wynne, *d* of late Sir George Hamer, CBE; two *d*. *Educ:* Denbigh Gram. Sch.; University Coll. of Wales; Gray's Inn (Bencher, 1968; Vice-Treasurer, 1985; Treasurer, 1986). Called to Bar, 1949; Wales and Chester Circuit (Leader, 1971–74); Dep. Chm., Flint QS, 1960–71; Dep. Chm., Merioneth QS, 1960–67, Chm., 1967–71; Recorder of Merthyr Tydfil, 1971. MP (L) Montgomery, 1962–79. Leader, 1966–79, Pres., 1983–86, Welsh Liberal Party. Vice-Chm. Political Cttee, North Atlantic Assembly, 1975–79. Dir (non-exec.), Laura Ashley (Holdings) Ltd, 1985–. Pres., Llangollen Internat. Eisteddfod, 1987–. Hon. Professorial Fellow, University Coll. of Wales, 1971. Farms Pen-Rhiw farm, Llanidloes. *Address:* Summerfield, Llanidloes, Powys. *T:* Llanidloes (05512) 2298; 1 Dr Johnson's Buildings, Temple, EC4Y 7AX. *T:* 071–353 9328, 071–219 5226; 071–405 4160.

HOOVER, Herbert William, Jr; President, 1954–66, and Chairman of the Board, 1959–66, The Hoover Company, North Canton, Ohio; *b* 23 April 1918; *s* of late Herbert William Hoover and Grace Hoover (*née* Steele); *m* 1941, Carl Maitland Good; one *s* one *d*. *Educ:* Choate Sch., Wallingford, Conn.; Rollins Coll. (AB). Served in US Army, 1943–45. Offices held with Hoover Co.: Exec. Sales, 1941; Dir Public Relations, 1945; Asst Vice-Pres., 1948; Vice-Pres. Field Sales, 1952; Exec. Vice-Pres., 1953. The Hoover Co. Ltd, Canada: Pres., 1954; Dir, 1952; Hoover Ltd, England: Dir 1954, Chm. 1956. Hoover Inc., Panama: Dir and Pres., 1955; Hoover (America Latina) SA, Panama: Dir and Pres., 1955; Hoover Mexicana, Mexico: Dir and Pres., 1955; Hoover Industrial y Comercial SA, Colombia: Dir and Pres., 1960; Hoover Worldwide Corp., NY City: Pres. and Chm., 1960; Dir, S. A. Hoover, France, 1965. Past Regional Vice-Chm., US Cttee for the UN. Dir, Miami Heart Inst.; Mem., Bd of Trustees, Univ. of Miami. Hon. LLD, Mount Union Coll., 1959. Chevalier Légion d'Honneur, France, 1965. *Address:* 70 Park Drive, Bal Harbour, Fla 33154, USA.

HOPCROFT, George William; HM Diplomatic Service, retired; consultant on international relations; *b* 30 Sept. 1927; *s* of late Frederick Hopcroft and Dorothy Gertrude (*née* Bourne); *m* 1951, Audrey Joan Rodd; three *s* one *d*. *Educ:* Chiswick Grammar Sch.; London Univ. (BCom); Brasenose Coll., Oxford; INSEAD, Fontainebleau. Auditor with Wm R. Warner, 1946; entered Export Credits Guarantee Dept, 1946; Asst Trade Comr, Madras, 1953–57; Sen. Underwriter, ECGD, 1957–65; joined FO, 1965; First Sec. (Commercial), Amman, 1965–69; First Sec. (Econ.), Bonn, 1969–71; First Sec. (Comm.), Kuala Lumpur, 1971–75; FCO, 1975–78; Counsellor (Comm. and Econ.), Bangkok, 1978–81; FCO 1981. Lloyd's Underwriter, 1981–. Founder Mem., Export and Overseas Trade Adv. Panel (EOTAP), 1982–; operational expert in for. affairs, attached to Govt of Belize, 1982–83. *Recreations:* leisure and circumnavigation, athletics (Civil Service 880 yds champion, 1947), serendipity. *Address:* Ffrogs, Pond Road, Hook Heath, Woking, Surrey GU22 0JT. *T:* Woking (04862) 715121. *Clubs:* Commonwealth Trust; Thames Valley Harriers (Vice-Pres., 1965–); British (Bangkok).

HOPE, family name of **Baron Glendevon, Marquess of Linlithgow** and **Baron Rankeillour.**

HOPE, Rt. Hon. Lord; (James Arthur) David Hope; PC 1989; Lord Justice-General of Scotland and Lord President of the Court of Session, since 1989; *b* 27 June 1938; *s* of Arthur Henry Cecil Hope, OBE, WS, Edinburgh and Muriel Ann Neilson Hope (*née* Collie); *m* 1966, Katharine Mary Kerr, *d* of W. Mark Kerr, WS, Edinburgh; twin *s* one *d*. *Educ:* Edinburgh Acad.; Rugby Sch.; St John's Coll., Cambridge (Scholarship 1956, BA 1962, MA 1978); Edinburgh Univ. (LLB 1965). National Service, Seaforth Highlanders, 1957–59 (Lieutenant 1959). Admitted Faculty of Advocates, 1965; Standing Junior Counsel in Scotland to Board of Inland Revenue, 1974–78; Advocate-Depute, 1978–82; QC (Scotland) 1978; Dean, Faculty of Advocates, 1986–89. Chm., Med. Appeal Tribunal, 1985–86; Legal Chm., Pensions Appeal Tribunal, 1985–86. Hon. Member: Canadian Bar Assoc., 1987; SPTL, 1991; Hon. Bencher, Gray's Inn, 1989. Hon. LLD Aberdeen, 1991. *Publications:* (ed jtly) Gloag & Henderson's Introduction to the Law of Scotland, 7th edn 1968, asst editor, 8th edn 1980 and 9th edn 1987; (ed jtly) Armour on Valuation for Rating, 4th edn 1971, 5th edn 1985; (with A. G. M. Duncan) The Rent (Scotland) Act 1984, 1986; (contrib.) Stair Memorial Encyclopaedia of Scots Law. *Recreations:* walking, ornithology, music. *Address:* 34 India Street, Edinburgh EH3 6HB. *T:* 031–225 8245. *Club:* New (Edinburgh).

HOPE, Maj.-Gen. Adrian Price Webley, CB 1961; CBE 1952; *b* 21 Jan. 1911; *s* of late Adm. H. W. W. Hope, CB, CVO, DSO; *m* 1958, Mary Elizabeth (*d* 1990), *e d* of Graham Partridge, Cotham Lodge, Newport, Pembrokeshire; no *c*. *Educ:* Winchester Coll.; RMC, Sandhurst. 2/Lt KOSB, 1931; Adjt, 1/KOSB, 1937–38; Staff Capt. A, Palestine, Egypt, 1938–40; DAQMG (Plans) Egypt, 1940–41; Instructor, Staff Coll., 1941; AQMG, Egypt, Sicily, Italy, 1941–44; Col Asst Quartermaster, Plans, India, 1945; Brig., Quartermaster, SE Asia, 1946; Comdt Sch. of Military Admin., 1947–48; Instructor, jssc, 1948–50; DQMG, GHQ, MELF, 1951–53; Student, idc, 1954; Brig. Quartermaster (ops), War Office, 1955–57; BGS, HQ, BAOR, 1958–59; MGA, GHQ, FARELF, 1959–61; Dir of Equipment Policy, War Office, 1961–64; Dep. Master-Gen. of the Ordnance, Ministry of Defence, 1964–66; retd 1966. *Address:* Monks Place, Charlton Horethorne, Sherborne, Dorset. *Club:* Army and Navy.

HOPE, Alan, JP; Leader, West Midlands County Council Opposition Group (C), since 1981; *b* 5 Jan. 1933; *s* of George Edward Thomas Hope and Vera Hope; *m* 1960, Marilyn Dawson; one *s* one *d*. *Educ:* George Dixon Grammar Sch., Birmingham. Councillor, Birmingham CC, 1964–73; West Midlands County Council: Councillor, 1973; Leader, 1980–81; Chairman: Trading Standards, 1977–79; Finance, 1979–80. JP Birmingham 1974. *Address:* Whitehaven, Rosemary Drive, Little Aston Park, Sutton Coldfield, West Midlands B74 3AG. *T:* 021–353 3011. *Club:* Commonwealth Trust; Birmingham (Birmingham).

HOPE, Bob, (Leslie Townes Hope), CBE (Hon.) 1976; Congressional Gold Medal, US, 1963; film, stage, radio, TV actor; *b* England, 29 May 1903; family migrated to US, 1907; *m* 1934, Dolores Reade; two adopted *s* two adopted *d*. *Educ:* Fairmont Gram. Sch. and High Sch., Cleveland, O. Started career as dance instructor, clerk, amateur boxer; formed dancing act for Fatty Arbuckle review. After Mid-West tours formed own Company in Chicago; toured New York and joined RKO Vaudeville and Keith Circuit; first important stage parts include: Ballyhoo, 1932; Roberta, 1933; Ziegfield Follies, 1935; first radio part, 1934. Entered films, 1938. *Films include:* Big Broadcast of 1938; Some Like It Hot; The Cat and the Canary; Road to Singapore; The Ghost Breakers; Road to Zanzibar; Star Spangled Rhythm; Nothing but the Truth; Louisiana Purchase; My Favorite Blonde; Road to Morocco; Let's Face It; Road to Utopia; Monsieur Beaucaire; My Favorite Brunette; They Got Me Covered; The Princess and the Pirate; Road to Rio; Where There's Life; The Great Lover; My Favorite Spy; Road to Bali; Son of Paleface; Here Come the Girls; Casanova's Big Night; The Seven Little Foys; The Iron

Petticoat; That Certain Feeling; Beau James; The Facts of Life; Bachelor in Paradise; The Road to Hong Kong; Call Me Bwana; A Global Affair; Boy, Did I Get a Wrong Number!; Eight on the Run; How to Commit Marriage; Cancel My Reservation. *TV Series:* The Bob Hope Show, 1950–; numerous guest appearances. Five Royal Command Performances. Awarded 44 honorary degrees; more than a thousand awards and citations for humanitarian and professional services. *Publications:* They've Got Me Covered, 1941; I Never Left Home, 1944; So This is Peace, 1946; This One's on Me, 1954; I Owe Russia $1200, 1963; Five Women I Love, 1966; The Last Christmas Show, 1974; Road to Hollywood, 1977; Confessions of a Hooker, 1985. *Address:* Hope Enterprises, Inc., 3808 Riverside Drive, Burbank, Calif 91505, USA.

HOPE, Sir (Charles) Peter, KCMG 1972 (CMG 1956); TD 1945; Ambassador to Mexico, 1968–72; *b* 29 May 1912; *s* of G. L. N. Hope and H. M. V. Riddell, Weetwood, Mayfield, Sussex; *m* 1936, H. M. Turner, *d* of late G. L. Turner, company director; three *s*. *Educ:* Oratory Sch., Reading; London and Cambridge Univs. BSc (Hons), ACGI. Asst War Office, 1938; RA, TA, 1939; served until 1946 (TD). Transferred to Foreign Office and posted HM Embassy, Paris, as Temp. First Sec., 1946; transferred to United Nations Dept, Foreign Office, 1950; to HM Embassy, Bonn, as Counsellor, 1953; Foreign Office Spokesman (Head of News Dept Foreign Office), 1956–59; Minister, HM Embassy, Madrid, 1959–62; Consul-General, Houston, USA, 1963–64; Minister and Alternate UK Rep. to UN, 1965–68. Mem., Acad. of International Law. Pres., British Assoc. of Sovereign Military Order of Malta, 1983–89; KStJ 1984. Grand Cross: Order of the Aztec Eagle, 1972; Constantine Order of St George, 1981; Grand Cross, Order of Malta, 1984; Grand Officer, Order of Merito Militense, 1975. *Recreations:* shooting and fishing. *Address:* North End House, Heyshott, Midhurst, Sussex GU29 0DD. *Club:* White's.

HOPE, Christopher, FRSL; writer; *b* 26 Feb. 1944; *s* of Dennis Tully and Kathleen Mary Hope (*née* McKenna); *m* 1967, Eleanor Klein; two *s*. *Educ:* Christian Brothers College, Pretoria; Univ. of Natal (BA Hons 1970); Univ. of Witwatersrand (MA 1973). Pringle Prize, English Acad. of Southern Africa, 1972; Cholmondeley Award, Soc. of Authors, 1974; Arts Council Bursary, 1982. *Publications:* Cape Drives, 1974; A Separate Development, 1981 (David Higham Prize for Fiction); In the Country of the Black Pig, 1981; Private Parts and Other Tales, 1982 (Internat. PEN Silver Pen Award); Kruger's Alp, 1984 (Whitbread Prize for Fiction); The Hottentot Room, 1986; Black Swan, 1987; White Boy Running, 1988 (CNA Award, S Africa); My Chocolate Redeemer, 1989; Moscow! Moscow!, 1990; contribs to BBC, newspapers, jls. *Recreations:* cross country ski-ing, travel. *Address:* c/o Rogers, Coleridge & White, 20 Powis Mews, W11 1JN.

HOPE, Colin Frederick Newton, MA; CEng, FIMechE; FIMI; Chairman, T & N plc (formerly Turner & Newall), since 1989 (Group Managing Director, 1985–89); *b* 17 May 1932; *s* of Frederick and Mildred Hope; *m* 1959, Gillian Carden; two *s*. *Educ:* Stowe Sch.; St Catharine's College, Cambridge (MA). Glacier Metal Co., 1963–70; Managing Dir, 1970–73, Exec. Chm., 1973–75, Covrad; Director: Engineering Group, Dunlop, 1975–79; Tyres UK Dunlop, 1979–82; Tyres Europe Dunlop Holdings, 1982–84; Chief Exec., Dunlop Engineering International, 1984–85. *Recreations:* theatre, music, travel. *Address:* Hornby Cottage, High Street, Welford-on-Avon, Warwickshire. *T:* Stratford upon Avon (0789) 750301. *Club:* Royal Automobile.

HOPE, David; *see* Hope, Rt Hon. Lord.

HOPE, Rt. Rev. and Rt. Hon. David Michael; *see* London, Bishop of.

HOPE, James Arthur David; *see* Hope, Rt Hon. Lord.

HOPE, Sir John (Carl Alexander), 18th Bt *cr* 1628 (NS), of Craighall; *b* 10 June 1939; *s* of Sir Archibald Philip Hope, 17th Bt, OBE, DFC, AE and of Ruth, *y d* of Carl Davis; *S* father, 1987; *m* 1968, Merle Pringle, *d* of Robert Douglas, Holbrook, Ipswich; one *s* one *d*. *Educ:* Eton. *Heir:* *s* Alexander Archibald Douglas Hope, *b* 16 March 1969. *Address:* 9 Westleigh Avenue, SW15 6RF.

HOPE, Laurence Frank, OBE 1968; HM Diplomatic Service, retired; HM Consul General, Seattle, 1975–76; *b* 18 May 1918; *y s* of late Samuel Vaughan Trevylian Hope and late Ellen Edith Hope (*née* Cooler); *m* 1940, Doris Phyllis Rosa Hulbert; one *s* one *d*. Served War, reaching rank of Major, in British Army (12th (2nd City of London Regt) Royal Fusiliers, TA and York and Lancaster Regt); Indian Army (7th Rajput Regt); Mil. Govt of Germany (Economic Div.), 1939–46. Bd of Trade, London, 1946–47; Asst Brit. Trade Comr, Pretoria, 1947–51; Cape Town, 1951–53; Bd of Trade, London, 1953–56; British Trade Comr, Sydney, 1956–60; Canberra, 1960–61; Lahore, 1961–63; Singapore, 1964; transferred to HM Diplomatic Service; Head of Commercial Section, High Commn, Singapore, 1965–68; Counsellor (Economic and Commercial), Lagos, 1969–72; HM Consul-Gen., Gothenburg, 1972–75. *Recreations:* oil painting, reading. *Address:* 22 Cranford Avenue, Exmouth, Devon EX8 2HU.
See also M. L. H. Hope.

HOPE, Marcus Laurence Hulbert; HM Diplomatic Service; Deputy Head of Mission and Counsellor (Commercial and Aid), Jakarta, since 1989; *b* 2 Feb. 1942; *s* of Laurence Frank Hope, *qv*; *m* 1980, Uta Maria Luise Müller-Unverfehrt; one *s*. *Educ:* City of London Sch.; Sydney C of E Grammar Sch.; Univ. of Sydney (BA); Univ. of London (BA Hons). Joined HM Diplomatic Service, 1965; Third Sec., CRO, 1965; MECAS, 1966; Second Sec., Tripoli, 1968; FCO, 1970; First Sec., 1972; Head of Chancery, Dubai, 1974; First Sec. (Commercial), Bonn, 1976; FCO, 1980; NATO Defence Coll., Rome, 1984; Counsellor, Beirut, 1984–85; Counsellor and Head of Chancery, Berne, 1985–89. *Recreation:* classical guitar. *Address:* c/o Foreign and Commonwealth Office, King Charles Street, SW1A 2AH. *Club:* Carlton.

HOPE, Sir Peter; *see* Hope, Sir C. P.

HOPE, Sir Robert Holms-Kerr, 3rd Bt *cr* 1932; *b* 12 April 1900; *s* of Sir Harry Hope, 1st Bt and Margaret Binnie Holms-Kerr; *S* brother, 1979; *m* 1928, Eleanor (*d* 1967), *d* of late Very Rev. Marshall Lang, DD, Whittinghame, East Lothian. *Heir:* none. *Address:* Old Bridge House, Broxmouth, Dunbar, East Lothian.

HOPE-DUNBAR, Sir David, 8th Bt *cr* 1664; *b* 13 July 1941; *o s* of Sir Basil Douglas Hope-Dunbar, 7th Bt, and of his 2nd wife, Edith Maude Maclaren (*d* 1989), *d* of late Malcolm Cross; *S* father, 1961; *m* 1971, Kathleen, *yr d* of late J. T. Kenrick; one *s* two *d*. *Educ:* Eton; Royal Agricultural College, Cirencester. Qualified: ARICS 1966. *Recreations:* fishing, shooting. *Heir:* *s* Charles Hope-Dunbar, *b* 11 March 1975. *Address:* Banks Farm, Kirkcudbright. *T:* Kirkcudbright (0557) 30424.

HOPE JOHNSTONE, family name of **Earl of Annandale and Hartfell.**

HOPE-JONES, Ronald Christopher, CMG 1969; HM Diplomatic Service, retired; *b* 5 July 1920; *s* of William Hope-Jones and Winifred Coggin; *m* 1944, Pamela Hawker; two *s* one *d*. *Educ:* Eton (scholar); King's Coll., Cambridge (scholar). Served with HM Forces, 1940–45. 3rd Sec., Foreign Office, 1946, Paris, 1947; 2nd Sec., Beirut, 1949; 1st Sec., FO, 1952; Head of Chancery and Consul, Quito, 1955; Commercial Sec., Budapest, 1959; Head of Chancery, 1960; FO, 1961, Counsellor, 1963; UK Rep. to Internat. Atomic Energy Agency, Vienna, 1964–67; FCO 1967; Head of Disarmament Dept, 1967–70; Head of N African Dept, 1970–71; Counsellor, Brasilia, 1972–73; Ambassador in La Paz, 1973–77. *Address:* Wellfield House, Mill Lane, Headley, Bordon, Hants GU35 0PD. *T:* Bordon (0420) 472793.

HOPE-MORLEY, family name of **Baron Hollenden.**

HOPE-WALLACE, (Dorothy) Jaqueline, CBE 1958; *b* 1909; 2nd *d* of Charles Nugent Hope-Wallace and Mabel Chaplin. *Educ:* Lady Margaret Hall, Oxford. Entered Ministry of Labour, 1932; transferred to National Assistance Board, 1934; Under-Sec., 1958–65; Under-Sec., Min. of Housing and Local Govt, 1965–69, retired. Commonwealth Fellow, 1952–53. Comr, Public Works Loan Bd, 1974–78; Member Board: Corby Develt Corp., 1969–80; Governors, UCH, 1970–74; Inst. for Recorded Sound, 1971–74, 1979–83 (Chm. 1975–76); Nat. Corp. for Care of Old People (now Centre for Policy on Ageing), 1973–81 (Chm., 1978–80); Mem., Nat. Sound Archive Adv. Cttee, 1983–84; Chm., Friends of UCH, 1973–85. *Recreations:* arts, travel, gardening. *Address:* 17 Ashley Court, Morpeth Terrace, SW1P 1EN.

HOPETOUN, Earl of; Andrew Victor Arthur Charles Hope; *b* 22 May 1969; *s* and *heir* of Marquess of Linlithgow, *qv*. A Page of Honour to the Queen Mother, 1985–87.

HOPEWELL, John Prince; Consultant Surgeon, Royal Free Hospital, 1957–88 (Hon. Consulting Surgeon (Urology), since 1988); *b* 1 Dec. 1920; *s* of Samuel Prince and Wilhelmina Hopewell; *m* 1st, 1959, Dr Natalie Bogdan (*d* 1975); one *s* one *d*; 2nd, 1984, Dr Rosemary Radley-Smith. *Educ:* Bradfield Coll., Berks; King's Coll. Hosp., London. RAMC, 1945–48. Postgrad. education at King's Coll. Hosp. and Brighton, Sussex, and Hosp. for Sick Children, Gt Ormond Street. Formerly Cnslt Surgeon, Putney Hosp. and Frimley Hosp., Surrey. Mem., Hampstead DHA, 1982–85; Chm., Camden Div., BMA, 1985–; Past Chairman: Med. Cttee Royal Free Hosp.; N Camden Dist Med. Cttee. Founder Mem., British Transplantation Soc., 1972; Member: Internat. Soc. of Urology; British Assoc. Urol. Surgeons; Past President: Chelsea Clinical Soc.; Section of Urology, RSM, 1982–83; Fellowship of Postgrad. Medicine. Founder Mem., Assoc. of Univ. Hospitals. Hon. Mem., NY Section, AUA. Hunterian Prof., RCS, 1958. Mem. Court of Examiners, RCSE, 1969–75. Member: Friends of St Helena; Soc. of Ornamental Woodturners. *Publications:* Three Clinical Cases of Renal Transplantation, British Medical Jl, 1964, and contribs to various medical journals. *Address:* 30 Hillfield Court, Belsize Avenue, NW3 4BJ. *T:* 071–435 8809.

HOPKIN, Sir Bryan; *see* Hopkin, Sir W. A. B.

HOPKIN, Sir David (Armand), Kt 1987; Chief Metropolitan Stipendiary Magistrate, since 1982; *b* 10 Jan. 1922; *s* of Daniel and Edmée Hopkin; *m* 1948, Doris Evelyn (*née* Whitaker); one *s* three *d*. *Educ:* St Paul's Sch., W Kensington; University Coll., Aberystwyth; Corpus Christi Coll., Cambridge (BA). Called to the Bar, Gray's Inn, 1949. Served in Army, 1942–47, Hon. Major, 1947. Member of Staff of Director of Public Prosecutions, 1950–70; Metropolitan Stipendiary Magistrate, 1970–. Vice-Pres., British Boxing Board of Control, 1986– (Chm., 1983–). *Recreations:* fencing, tennis. *Address:* 8 Crane Grove, N7. *T:* 071–607 0349.

HOPKIN, John Raymond; His Honour Judge Hopkin; a Circuit Judge, since 1979; *b* 23 June 1935; *s* of George Raymond Buxton Hopkin and Muriel Hopkin; *m* 1965, Susan Mary Limb; one *s* one *d*. *Educ:* King's Sch., Worcester. Called to Bar, Middle Temple, 1958; in practice at the Bar, 1959–. A Recorder of the Crown Court, 1978–79. A Chm. of Disciplinary Tribunals, Council of Inns of Court, 1987–. Dep. Chm. of Governors, Nottingham High Sch. for Girls, 1987–. *Recreations:* fell walking and climbing, gardening, golf, the theatre. *Address:* c/o The Crown Court, Canal Street, Nottingham NG1 7EJ. *Club:* Nottingham and Notts Services.

HOPKIN, Sir (William Aylsham) Bryan, Kt 1971; CBE 1961; Hon. Professorial Fellow, University College, Swansea, since 1988; *b* 7 Dec. 1914; *s* of late William Hopkin and Lilian Hopkin (*née* Cottelle); *m* 1938, Renée Ricour; two *s*. *Educ:* Barry (Glam.) County Sch.; St John's Coll., Cambridge (Hon. Fellow, 1982); Manchester Univ. Ministry of Health, 1938–41; Prime Minister's Statistical Branch, 1941–45; Royal Commn on Population, 1945–48; Econ. Sect., Cabinet Office, 1948–50; Central Statistical Office, 1950–52; Dir, Nat. Inst. of Econ. and Soc. Research, 1952–57; Sec., Council on Prices, Productivity, and Incomes, 1957–58; Dep. Dir, Econ. Sect., HM Treasury, 1958–65; Econ. Planning Unit, Mauritius, 1965; Min. of Overseas Devlt, 1966–67; Dir-Gen. of Economic Planning, ODM, 1967–69; Dir-Gen., DEA, 1969; Dep. Chief Econ. Adviser, HM Treasury, 1970–72; Prof. of Econs, UC Cardiff, 1972–82 (on leave of absence, Head of Govt Economic Service and Chief Economic Advr, HM Treasury, 1974–77). Mem., Commonwealth Develt Corp., 1972–74. Chm., Manpower Services Cttee for Wales, 1978–79. *Address:* Aberthin House, Aberthin, near Cowbridge, South Glamorgan CF7 7HB. *T:* Cowbridge (0446) 772303.

HOPKINS, Alan Cripps Nind, MA Cantab, LLB Yale; Chairman, Wellman Engineering Corporation, 1972–83 (Director, 1968); *b* 27 Oct. 1926; *s* of late Rt Hon. Sir Richard V. N. Hopkins, GCB and Lady Hopkins; *m* 1st, 1954, Margaret Cameron (from whom divorced, 1962), *d* of E. C. Bolton, Waco, Texas, USA; one *s*; 2nd, 1962, Venetia, *d* of Sir Edward Wills, 4th Bt; twin *s*. *Educ:* Winchester Coll.; King's Coll., Cambridge; Yale University Law Sch., USA. BA Cantab 1947, MA 1950; LLB Yale 1952. Barrister, Inner Temple, 1948. MP (C and Nat L) Bristol North-East, 1959–66; PPS to Financial Sec. to Treasury, 1960–62. Dir, Dexion-Comino Internat. Ltd, 1973–85. *Recreation:* travelling. *Address:* Chalet Topaze, 1972 Anzere, Valais, Switzerland. *T:* 027–38–16–51. *Club:* Brooks's.

HOPKINS, Anthony Philip, CBE 1987; actor since 1961; *b* Port Talbot, S Wales, 31 Dec. 1937; *s* of late Richard and of Muriel Hopkins; *m* 1st, 1968, Petronella (marr. diss. 1972); one *d*; 2nd, 1973, Jennifer, *d* of Ronald Lynton. *Educ:* Cowbridge, S Wales; RADA; Cardiff Coll. of Drama. London debut as Metellus Cimber in Julius Caesar, Royal Court, 1964; National Theatre: Juno and the Paycock, A Flea in Her Ear, 1966; The Dance of Death, The Three Sisters, As You Like It (all male cast), 1967; The Architect and the Emperor of Assyria, A Woman Killed with Kindness, Coriolanus, 1971; Macbeth, 1972; Pravda, 1985 (Observer Award, Lawrence Olivier Awards, 1985; (jtly) Best Actor, British Theatre Assoc. and Drama Magazine Awards, 1985; Royal Variety Club Award, 1985); King Lear, 1986; Antony and Cleopatra, 1987. Other stage appearances include: The Taming of the Shrew, Chichester, 1972; Equus, USA, 1974–75, 1977; The Tempest, LA, 1979; Old Times, New York, 1984; The Lonely Road, Old Vic, 1985; M. Butterfly, Shaftesbury, 1989. *Films:* The Lion in Winter, 1967; The Looking Glass War, 1968; Hamlet, 1969; When Eight Bells Toll, 1971; Young Winston, 1972; A Doll's House, 1973; The Girl from Petrovka, 1973; All Creatures Great and Small, 1974; Dark Victory, 1975; Audrey Rose, 1976; A Bridge Too Far, 1976; International Velvet, 1977; Magic, 1978; The Elephant Man, 1980; A Change of Seasons, 1980; The Bounty, 1984; The Good Father, 1986; 84 Charing Cross Road, 1987; The Dawning, 1988; A Chorus of Disapproval, 1989; Desperate Hours, 1990; The Silence of the Lambs, 1991; One Man's

War, 1991; Desperate Hours, 1991. *American television films:* QB VII, 1973; Bruno Hauptmann in The Lindbergh Kidnapping Case, 1976; The Voyage of the Mayflower, 1979; The Bunker, The Acts of Peter and Paul, 1980; The Hunchback of Notre Dame, 1981; The Arch of Triumph, 1984; Hollywood Wives, 1984; Guilty Conscience, 1984; The Tenth Man, 1988; *BBC television:* Pierre Bezuhov in serial, War and Peace, 1972; Kean, 1978; Othello, 1981; Little Eyolf, 1982; Guy Burgess in Blunt (film), 1987; Donald Campbell in Across the Lake, 1988; Heartland, 1989; Indep. TV performances incl. A Married Man (series), 1983. Hon. DLitt Wales, 1988. Best TV Actor Award, SFTA, 1973; Best Actor Award, NY Drama Desk, 1975; Outer Critics Circle Award, 1975; American Authors and Celebrities Forum Award, 1975; Emmy award, 1976 and 1981; LA Drama Critics' Award, 1977; Variety Club Film Actor Award, 1984; Variety Club Stage Actor Award, 1985; Laurence Olivier/Observer Award for Outstanding Achievement, 1985; Best Actor Award, Moscow Film Fest., 1987. *Recreations:* reading, walking, piano. *Address:* c/o Peggy Thompson, 7 High Park Road, Kew, Surrey TW9 4BL.

HOPKINS, Dr Anthony Philip, MD; FRCP, FACP; Director, Research Unit, Royal College of Physicians, since 1988; Consultant Neurologist, St Bartholomew's Hospital, since 1972; *b* 15 Oct. 1937; *s* of Gerald Hopkins and Barbara Isobel Hopkins; *m* 1965, Elizabeth Ann Wood; three *s*. *Educ:* Sherborne Sch.; Guy's Hospital Med. Sch. MD London. FRCP 1976; FACP 1991. Postgraduate work: Hammersmith and National Hosps, 1961–69; Salpetrière Hosp., Paris, 1962–63; Mayo Foundn, Rochester, Minn, 1970. St Bartholomew's Hospital: Cons. Neurologist, 1972–76; Physician-in-charge, Dept of Neurological Scis, 1976–88. Res. into experimental pathology, headache, epilepsy, and into the evaluation of the effectiveness and quality of med. care. *Publications:* Epilepsy, 1987; Headache: problems in diagnosis and management, 1988; Measuring the Quality of Medical Care, 1990; contribs to sci. and med. literature. *Recreations:* walking, dining. *Address:* Research Unit, Royal College of Physicians, 11 St Andrews Place, NW1 4LE; 149 Harley Street, W1N 2DE. *T:* 071–935 4444. *Club:* Garrick.
See also M. J. Hopkins.

HOPKINS, Anthony Strother, BSc(Econ); FCA; Chief Executive, Industrial Development Board for Northern Ireland, since 1988 (Deputy Chief Executive, 1982–88); *b* 17 July 1940; *s* of Strother Smith Hopkins, OBE, and Alice Roberta Hopkins; *m* 1965, Dorothy Moira (*née* McDonough); one *s* two *d*. *Educ:* Campbell Coll., Belfast; Queen's University of Belfast (BScEcon). Manager, Thomson McLintock & Co., Chartered Accountants, London, 1966–70; Principal, Dept of Commerce, N Ireland, 1970–74; Northern Ireland Development Agency, 1975–82, Chief Executive, 1979–82; Under Secretary, 1982–88, Second Perm. Sec., 1988–, Dept of Economic Development for N Ireland. CBIM 1990. *Recreations:* golf, tennis, sailing. *Clubs:* Oriental; Royal Belfast Golf (Co. Down).

HOPKINS, Antony, CBE 1976; composer and conductor; *b* 21 March 1921; *s* of late Hugh and of Marjorie Reynolds; adopted *c* of Major and Mrs T. H. C. Hopkins since 1925; *m* 1947, Alison Purves. *Educ:* Berkhamsted Sch.; Royal Coll. of Music. Won Chappell Gold Medal and Cobbett Prize at RCM, 1942; shortly became known as composer of incidental music for radio; numerous scores composed for BBC (2 for programmes winning Italia prize for best European programme of the year, 1952 and 1957). Composed music for many productions at Stratford and in West End. Dir, Intimate Opera Co., 1952–, and has written a number of chamber operas for this group; *ballets:* Etude and Café des Sports, for Sadler's Wells; *films (music) include:* Pickwick Papers, Decameron Nights, Cast a Dark Shadow, Billy Budd; John and the Magic Music Man (narr. and orch.; Grand Prix, Besançon Film Festival, 1976). Regular broadcaster with a series of programmes entitled Talking about Music. Formerly Gresham Prof. of Music, City Univ. Hon. FRCM 1964; Hon. RAM 1979; Hon. Fellow, Robinson Coll., Cambridge, 1980. DUniv. Stirling, 1980. *Publications:* Talking about Symphonies, 1961; Talking about Concertos, 1964; Music All Around Me, 1968; Lucy and Peterkin, 1968; Talking about Sonatas, 1971; Downbeat Guide, 1977; Understanding Music, 1979; The Nine Symphonies of Beethoven, 1980; Songs for Swinging Golfers, 1981; Sounds of Music, 1982; Beating Time (autobiog.), 1982; Pathway to Music, 1983; Musicamusings, 1983; The Concertgoer's Companion: Vol. I, 1984; Vol. II, 1985; Exploring Music, 1991. *Recreations:* motoring, golf. *Address:* Woodyard Cottage, Ashridge, Berkhamsted, Herts. *T:* Little Gaddesden (044284) 2257.

HOPKINS, David Rex Eugène; Director of Quality Assurance/Administration, Ministry of Defence, 1983–90; *b* 29 June 1930; *s* of Frank Hopkins and Vera (*née* Wimhurst); *m* 1955, Brenda Joyce Phillips; two *s* one *d* (one *d* decd). *Educ:* Worthing High Sch.; Christ Church, Oxford (MA 1950; Dip. in Econs and Pol. Science, 1951). National Service Commn, RA, 1952; service in Korea. Asst Principal, WO, 1953; Principal, WO, 1957, MoD 1964; Asst Sec., 1967; Home Office, 1969–70; RCDS, 1971; Defence Equipment Secretariat, 1972; Dir, Headquarters Security, 1975; Financial Counsellor, UK Delegn to NATO, 1981–83. *Recreations:* church work, archaeological digging, fell-walking, military history. *Address:* 16 Hitherwood Drive, SE19 1XB. *T:* 081–670 7504.

HOPKINS, Douglas Edward, DMus (London); FRAM, FRCO, FGSM; Conductor, Stock Exchange Male Voice Choir, since 1956; *b* 23 Dec. 1902; *s* of Edward and Alice Hopkins; unmarried. *Educ:* St Paul's Cathedral Choir Sch.; Dulwich Coll.; Guildhall Sch. of Music (Ernest Palmer and Corporation Scholarships); Royal Academy of Music. Organist, Christ Church, Greyfriars, EC, 1921; Sub-Organist, St Paul's Cathedral, 1927; Prof., Royal Acad. of Music, 1937–78; Examr, Royal Schs of Music, 1937–81; Master of the Music, Peterborough Cathedral, 1946; Organist, Canterbury Cathedral, 1953–55; Musical Dir, St Felix Sch., Southwold, 1956–65; Organist, St Marylebone Parish Church, 1965–71. Founder, and Dir 1962–74, Holiday Course for Organists; Organist, Royal Meml Chapel, RMA Sandhurst, 1971–76. Since 1957 has done many overseas tours, inc. NZ, Africa, Malaysia, W Indies, Singapore and Hong Kong. Conductor of Handel Soc., 1928–33, and, since that, of various other musical societies. Liveryman, Worshipful Co. of Musicians. *Address:* 244 Mytchett Road, Mytchett, Camberley, Surrey GU16 6AF.

HOPKINS, Prof. Harold Horace, FRS 1973; Emeritus Professor, University of Reading, since 1984 (Professor of Applied Optics, 1967–84 and Head of Department of Physics, 1977–80); *b* 6 Dec. 1918; *s* of William Ernest and Teresa Ellen Hopkins; *m* 1950, Christine Dove Ridsdale; three *s* one *d*. *Educ:* Gateway Sch., Leicester; Univs of Leicester and London. BSc, PhD, DSc, FInstP. Physicist, Taylor, Taylor & Hobson, 1939–42; Royal Engrs, 1942; Physicist: MAP, 1942–45; W. Watson & Sons, 1945–47; Research Fellow, then Reader in Optics, Imperial Coll., 1947–67. Hon. Papers Sec. and Mem. Council, Physical Soc., 1947–59; President: Internat. Commn for Optics, 1969–72; Maths and Phys Sect., British Assoc., 1977. Thomas Young Orator, Inst. of Physics, 1960; Lister Oration, 1991. Fellow: Optical Soc. of Amer., 1972; Soc. for Photo-Instrumentation Engrs, 1975; Hon. Member: Amer. Assoc. of Gynæcologic Laparoscopy, 1977; Brit. Assoc. of Urological Surgeons, 1977; Brit. Soc. for Gastroenterology, 1980; Hon. FRCS, 1979; Hon. FRCP, 1983; Hon. FRSM, 1989; Hon. Fellow: Optical Soc. of India, 1981; Soc. for Engrg Optics, Republic of China, 1987. Hon. DèsSc Besançon, 1960; Hon. DSc: Bristol, 1980; Liverpool, 1982; Reading, 1986; Hon. Dr Med. Munich, 1980. Ives Medal, Optical Soc. of Amer., 1978; St Peter's Medal, Brit. Assoc. of Urological Surgeons, 1979; First Distinguished Service Award, Amer. Soc. for Gastrointestinal Endoscopy, 1980; Gold Medal, Internat. Soc. for Optical Engineering, 1982; Pro-Meritate Medal, Internat. Soc. of Urologic Endoscopy, 1984; Rumford Medal, Royal Soc., 1984; Distinguished Scientific Achievement Award, Amer. Urological Assoc., 1987; Founder's Medal, Eur. Urol Assoc., 1988; Lister Medal, 1990. Inventions incl. zoom lenses, fibre optics and medical endoscopes. *Publications:* Wave Theory of Aberrations, 1951; (with J. G. Gow) Handbook of Urological Endoscopy, 1978; papers in Proc. Royal Soc., Proc. Phys. Soc., Optica Acta, Jl Optical Soc. Amer., Jl of Modern Optics, Applied Optics. *Recreations:* keyboard music, sailing, languages, woodwork. *Address:* 26 Cintra Avenue, Reading, Berks RG2 7AU. *T:* Reading (0734) 871913.

HOPKINS, Sir James S. R. S.; *see* Scott-Hopkins.

HOPKINS, John; writer; *b* 27 Jan. 1931. *Plays:* This Story of Yours, Royal Court, 1968, Long Wharf Theatre, 1981, Hampstead Theatre, 1987; Find Your Way Home, Open Space, 1970, NY, 1974; Economic Necessity, Haymarket Theatre, Leicester, 1973; Next of Kin, Nat. Theatre, 1974; Losing Time, Manhattan Theatre Club, 1979, Deutsches Schauspielhaus, 1984; Valedictorian, Williston-Northampton Sch., 1982; Absent Forever, Great Lakes Theatre Festival, 1987; *TV:* includes: Talking to a Stranger (quartet), 1968; That Quiet Earth; Walk into the Dark; Some Distant Shadow; The Greeks and their Gifts, 1966; A Story to Frighten the Children, 1976; Fathers and Families (sextet), 1977; Codename Kyril, 1987; scripts for Z-Cars (series); (with John Le Carré) Smiley's People (series), 1982; adaptations of classic novels; *film scripts:* The Offence, 1973; Murder by Decree, 1979; The Holcroft Covenant, 1985. *Publications:* Talking to a Stranger, 1967; This Story of Yours, 1969; Find Your Way Home, 1971; Losing Time, 1982.

HOPKINS, Julian; *see* Hopkins, R. J.

HOPKINS, Keith; *see* Hopkins, M. K.

HOPKINS, Michael John, CBE 1989; RIBA; Founding Partner, Michael Hopkins & Partners, 1976; *b* 7 May 1935; *s* of late Gerald and Barbara Hopkins; *m* 1962, Patricia Wainwright; one *s* two *d*. *Educ:* Sherborne Sch.; Architectural Assoc. (AA Dip. 1964). RIBA 1966. Worked in offices of Sir Basil Spence, Leonard Manasseh and Tom Hancock; partnership with Norman Foster, 1969–75 and with Patricia Hopkins, 1976–; projects include: own house and studio, Hampstead, 1976; brewery bldg for Greene King, 1979; Patera Bldg System, 1984; Res. Centre for Schlumberger, Cambridge, 1984; infants sch., Hampshire, 1986; Bicentenary Stand, Lord's Cricket Ground, 1987; London office and country workshop for David Mellor, 1986–; R&D Centre, Solid State Logic, 1988–; redevelt of Bracken House, St Paul's, for Ohbayashi Corp., 1987–; master plan for: MCC, 1988–; Glyndebourne Opera House, 1987–. Consultant Architect, V&A Mus., 1985–. Mem., Royal Fine Art Commn, 1986–; Vice Pres., Architectural Assoc., 1987–; Trustee, Thomas Cubitt Trust, 1987–. Awards include: RIBA, 1977, 1980, 1988, 1989; Civic Trust, 1979, 1988; FT 1980, 1982; Structural Steel, 1980, 1988; Royal Acad. Architectural, 1982. *Recreations:* sailing, Catureglio. *Address:* 49A Downshire Hill, NW3 1NX. *T:* 071–794 1494; (office) 27 Broadley Terrace, NW1 6LG. *T:* 071–724 1751.
See also A. P. Hopkins.

HOPKINS, Prof. (Morris) Keith, FBA 1984; Professor of Ancient History, University of Cambridge, and Fellow of King's College, since 1985; *b* 20 June 1934; *s* of late Albert Thomas Hopkins and Hélène Dorothy Pratt; *m* 1963, Juliet, *d* of Sir Henry Phelps Brown, *qv;* two *s* one *d*. *Educ:* Brentwood School; King's College, Cambridge. BA 1958; MA 1961. Asst Lectr in Sociology, Leicester Univ., 1961–63; Research Fellow, King's College, Cambridge, 1963–67; Lectr and Senior Lectr in Sociology, LSE, 1963–67, 1970–72; Prof. of Sociology: Univ. of Hong Kong, 1967–69; Brunel Univ., 1972–85 (Dean, Faculty of Social Sciences, 1981–85). Mem., Inst. for Advanced Study, Princeton, 1969–70, 1974–75, 1983. *Publications:* Hong Kong: The Industrial Colony (ed), 1971; Conquerors and Slaves, 1978; Death and Renewal, 1983. *Recreation:* drinking wine. *Address:* King's College, Cambridge CB2 1ST. *T:* Cambridge (0223) 350411.

HOPKINS, (Richard) Julian; Director, CARE Britain, since 1988; *b* 12 Oct. 1940; *s* of Richard Robert Hopkins and late Grace Hilda (*née* Hatfield); *m* 1971, Maureen Mary (*née* Hoye); two *s* one *d*. *Educ:* Bedford School. Asst Manager, London Palladium, 1963; Central Services Manager, BBC, 1965; joined RSPCA as Accounts Manager, 1972, appointed Admin. and Finance Officer, 1976; Exec. Dir, 1978–82; Gen. Manager, Charity Christmas Card Council, 1982–83; Finance Dir, War on Want, 1984–88. Dir, and Mem. Exec. Cttee, World Soc. for Protection of Animals, 1980–82. Mem., Farm Animal Welfare Council, 1980–83. FBIM. *Recreation:* all theatre, but especially opera, concert-going. *Address:* Rowan, 33 Needham Terrace, NW2 6QL. *T:* 081–452 4623.

HOPKINS, Sidney Arthur; Managing Director, Guardian Royal Exchange plc, since 1990; *b* 15 April 1932; *m* 1955, Joan Marion Smith; one *d*. *Educ:* Battersea Grammar Sch. ACII. Joined Royal Exchange Assce, 1948, Man., Organisation and Methods, 1966; Guardian Royal Exchange Assurance Ltd: Chief Claims Man. (UK), 1974; Man., Home Motor, 1976; Asst Gen. Man. (Life), 1979; Guardian Royal Exchange Assurance plc: Asst Gen. Man. (Field Operations), 1983; Gen. Man. (UK), 1985; Guardian Royal Exchange (UK) Ltd: Man. Dir, 1987; Guardian Royal Exchange plc: Dir, 1986; Dep. Chief Exec., 1989. Freeman, City of London; Liveryman, Company of Insurers. *Recreations:* sports, films. *Address:* Guardian Royal Exchange plc, 68 King William Street, EC4N 7BU. *T:* 071–283 7101. *Club:* Royal Automobile.

HOPKINSON, family name of **Baron Colyton.**

HOPKINSON, Albert Cyril, CBE 1970; FRIBA; consultant architect; *b* 2 Aug. 1911; *s* of Albert Hopkinson and Isaline Pollard (*née* Cox); *m* 1943, Lesley Evelyn Hill; one *s* one *d*. *Educ:* Univs of Sheffield and London. BA 1933; MA 1934. FRIBA 1949 (ARIBA 1934); Dipl. Town Planning and Civic Architecture, London, 1938. Min. of Public Building and Works, 1937–64; Dir of Works and Chief Architect, Home Office, 1964–75. *Recreations:* reading, walking. *Address:* Frangate, Frenchlands Hatch, Ockham Road South, East Horsley, Surrey. *T:* East Horsley (04865) 4030. *Club:* Wig and Pen.

HOPKINSON, Ven. Barnabas John; Archdeacon of Sarum, since 1986; Priest-in-charge, Stratford-sub-Castle, since 1987; *b* 11 May 1939; *s* of Prebendary Stephan Hopkinson and late Mrs Anne Hopkinson; *m* 1968, Esmé Faith (*née* Gibbons); three *d*. *Educ:* Emanuel School; Trinity Coll., Cambridge (MA); Lincoln Theological Coll. Curate: All Saints and Martyrs, Langley, Manchester, 1965–67; Great St Mary's, Cambridge, 1967–70; Chaplain, Charterhouse School, 1970–75; Team Vicar of Preshute, Wilts, 1975–81; RD of Marlborough, 1977–81; Rector of Wimborne Minster, Dorset, 1981–86; RD of Wimborne, 1985–86. Canon of Salisbury Cathedral, 1983–. *Recreations:* mountaineering, camping. *Address:* Russell House, Stratford-sub-Castle, Salisbury, Wilts SP1 3LG. *T:* Salisbury (0722) 28756.

HOPKINSON, David Hugh; Chief Night Editor of The Times, since 1982; *b* 9 June 1930; *er s* of late C. G. Hopkinson. *Educ:* Sowerby Bridge Grammar Sch. Entered journalism on Huddersfield Examiner, 1950; Yorkshire Observer, 1954; Yorkshire Evening News, 1954; Evening Chronicle, Manchester, 1956; Chief Sub-Editor, Sunday Graphic, London, 1957; Asst Editor, Evening Chronicle, Newcastle upon Tyne, 1959; Chief Asst Editor, Sunday Graphic, 1960; Dep. Editor, Sheffield Telegraph, 1961, Editor, 1962–64; Editor, The Birmingham Post, 1964–73; Dir, Birmingham Post & Mail Ltd, 1967–80; Editor, Birmingham Evening Mail, 1974–79; Editor-in-Chief, Evening Mail series, 1975–79, Birmingham Post and Evening Mail, 1979–80; Asst to Editor of The Times, 1981. Member: Lord Justice Phillimore's Cttee inquiring into law of contempt; International Press Institute; Associate Mem., Justice (British br. of Internat. Commn of Jurists). National Press Award, Journalist of the Year, 1963. *Address:* c/o The Times, 1 Pennington Street, E1 9XN.

HOPKINSON, David Hugh Laing, CBE 1986; RD 1965; DL; Chairman, Harrisons and Crosfield, 1988–91 (Deputy Chairman, 1987–88, Director, 1986–91); Deputy Chairman and Chief Executive, M&G Group PLC, 1979–87; Deputy Chairman, ECC Group (formerly English China Clays), since 1986 (Director, since 1975); *b* 14 Aug. 1926; *s* of late Cecil Hopkinson and Leila Hopkinson; *m* 1951, Prudence Margaret Holmes; two *s* two *d*. *Educ:* Wellington Coll.; Merton Coll., Oxford (BA 1949). RNVR and RNR, 1944–65. A Clerk of the House of Commons, 1948–59; Robert Fleming, 1959–62; M&G Investment Management, 1963–87 (Chm., 1975–87); Director: Lloyds Bank Southern Regional Board, 1977–88; BR (Southern) Bd, 1978–87 (Chm., 1979–87); Wolverhampton and Dudley Breweries, 1987–; Mem., Adv. Gp of Governor of Bank of England, 1984. Mem., Housing Corp., 1986–88. Director: English Chamber Orchestra and Music Soc., 1970–89; Charities Investment Managers, 1970–; Merchants Trust, 1976–. Member: General Synod of C of E, 1970–90; Central Bd of Finance, 1970–90; a Church Comr, 1973–82, 1984–; Chairman: Chichester Dio. Bd of Finance, 1977–88; Church Army Bd, 1987–89. Trustee: Nat. Assoc. of Almshouses; Chichester Cathedral Development Trust; Pallant House Museum, Chichester; Royal Pavilion, Brighton; RAM Foundn; Edward James Foundn. Governor: Sherborne Sch., 1970– (Vice-Chm., Bd, 1987–); Wellington Coll., 1978–. DL 1986, High Sheriff, 1987–88, W Sussex. Hon. Fellow, St Anne's Coll., Oxford, 1984–. *Recreations:* travelling, walking, opera. *Address:* St John's Priory, Poling, Arundel, W Sussex BN18 9PS. *T:* Arundel (0903) 882393. *Club:* Brooks's.

HOPKINSON, Giles, CB 1990; Under-Secretary, Departments of the Environment and Transport, 1976–90, retired; *b* 20 Nov. 1931; *s* of late Arthur John Hopkinson, CIE, ICS, and of Eleanor (*née* Richardson); *m* 1956, Eleanor Jean Riddell; three *d*. *Educ:* Marlborough Coll.; Leeds Univ. (BSc). E. & J. Richardson Ltd, 1956–57; Forestal Land, Timber and Rly Co. Ltd, 1957–58; DSIR: Scientific Officer, 1958–61; Sen. Scientific Officer, 1961–64; Private Sec. to Perm. Sec., 1963–64; Principal, MoT, 1964–71; Asst Sec., DoE, 1971; Under-Secretary: DoE, 1976; Dept of Transport (Ports and Freight Directorate), 1979; Dir, London Region, PSA, DoE, 1983–90. *Recreations:* music, landscape gardening; restoration of antique furniture. *Address:* Digswell Water Mill, Digswell Lane, Welwyn Garden City, Herts AL7 1SW. *Club:* Commonwealth Trust.

HOPKINSON, Maj.-Gen. John Charles Oswald Rooke, CB 1984; Director, British Field Sports Society, since 1984; *b* 31 July 1931; *s* of Lt-Col John Oliver Hopkinson and Aileen Disney Hopkinson (*née* Rooke); *m* 1956, Sarah Elizabeth, *d* of Maj.-Gen. M. H. P. Sayers, *qv*; three *s* one *d*. *Educ:* Stonyhurst Coll.; RMA, Sandhurst. sc 1963, jssc 1968, rcds 1979. Commanding Officer, 1st Bn Queen's Own Highlanders, 1972–74 (despatches); Dep. Comdr 2nd Armoured Division, and Comdr Osnabrück Garrison, 1977–78; Director Operational Requirements 3 (Army), 1980–82; Chief-of-Staff, HQ Allied Forces Northern Europe, 1982–84. Colonel, Queen's Own Highlanders, 1983–. *Recreations:* shooting, fishing, sailing. *Address:* Bigsweir, Gloucestershire. *Club:* Army and Navy.

HOPKINSON, John Edmund; Judge of the High Court, Hong Kong, 1985–89, retired; *b* 25 Oct. 1924; *s* of Captain E. H. Hopkinson, OBE, RN and Mrs E. H. Hopkinson; *m* 1961, Inge Gansel; one *s* one *d*. *Educ:* Marlborough Coll., Wilts; Pembroke Coll., Cambridge (MA). Called to the Bar, Lincoln's Inn, 1949. Served War, RN, 1943–46: Ordinary Seaman, Midshipman RNVR, 1943; Sub-Lt RNVR, 1944–46. Prudential Assurance Co., 1949–50; Legal Asst, Colonial Office, 1950–55; Hong Kong, 1962–89: Crown Counsel, 1962; Principal Crown Counsel, 1972; Dist Judge, 1974. *Recreations:* golf, tennis, ski-ing, music. *Address:* 41 Clavering Avenue, SW13 9DX. *Clubs:* Roehampton; Shek O Country (Hong Kong); Royal Hong Kong Golf; Royal Cinque Ports Golf.

HOPKINSON, Prof. Ralph Galbraith; Haden-Pilkington Professor of Environmental Design and Engineering, University College London, 1965–76, now Emeritus; *b* 13 Aug. 1913; *s* of late Ralph Galbraith Hopkinson and Beatrice Frances (*née* Wright); *m* 1938, Dora Beryl (*née* Churchill); two *s* (and one *s* decd). *Educ:* Erith Grammar Sch.; Faraday House. BSc (Eng), PhD, CEng, FIEE, FRPS. Research Engr, GEC, 1934–47, lighting and radar; Principal Scientific Officer, DSIR Building Research Stn, 1947–64 (Special Merit appointment, 1960); Dean, Faculty of Environmental Studies, UCL, 1972–74. Work on: human response to buildings, leading to concept of environmental design by engr-physicists and architects in collab.; schools with Min. of Educn Develt Gp and on hosps with Nuffield Foundn, 1949–65; lighting design of Tate Gallery extension and Stock Exchange Market Hall (Design Award of Distinction, Illum. Engrg Soc. of USA, 1974); visual and noise intrusion (urban motorways) for DoE, 1970; consultant, DoE Road Construction Unit. Pres., Illuminating Engrg Soc., 1965–66 (Gold Medallist, 1972; Hon. Mem., 1976); Mem., Royal Soc. Study Gp on Human Biology in the Urban Environment, 1972–74. Trustee, British Institution Fund, 1972–77. Hon. FRIBA 1969, Hon. FCIBSE 1977. *Publications:* Architectural Physics: Lighting, 1963; Hospital Lighting, 1964; Daylighting, 1966; (with J. D. Kay) The Lighting of Buildings, 1969; Lighting and Seeing, 1969; The Ergonomics of Lighting, 1970; Visual Intrusion (RTPI), 1972; papers in Nature, Jl Optical Soc. of America, Jl Psychol., Illum. Eng, etc. *Recreations:* music, human sciences, boating, walking. *Address:* Bartlett School of Architecture and Planning, University College London, Wates House, 22 Gordon Street, WC1H 0QB.

HOPKIRK, Joyce, (Mrs W. J. Lear); Director, Editors' Unlimited, since 1990; *b* 2 March; *d* of Walter Nicholson and Veronica (*née* Keelan); *m* 1st, 1962, Peter Hopkirk; one *d*; 2nd, 1974, William James Lear; one *s*. *Educ:* Middle Street Secondary Sch., Newcastle upon Tyne. Reporter, Gateshead Post, 1955; Founder Editor, Majorcan News, 1959; Reporter, Daily Sketch, 1960; Royal Reporter, Daily Express, 1961; Ed., Fashion Magazine, 1967; Women's Ed., Sun, 1967; Launch Ed., Cosmopolitan, 1971–72 (launched 1972); Asst Ed., Daily Mirror, 1973–78; Women's Ed., Sunday Times, 1982; Editl Dir, Elle, 1984; Asst Ed., Sunday Mirror, 1985; Ed.-in-Chief, She Magazine, 1986–89. Editor of the Year, 1972; Women's Magazines Editor of the Year, 1988. FRSA. *Publications:* Successful Slimming, 1976; Successful Slimming Cookbook, 1978. *Recreations:* conversation, sleeping, gardening, hockey, ski-ing, boating. *Address:* Gadespring, 109 Piccotts End, Hemel Hempstead, Herts HP1 3AT. *T:* Hemel Hempstead (0442) 245608; Jury's Gap, Sussex; Puerto Andraitx, Mallorca. *Club:* Groucho.

HOPPE, Iver; Kt of Danish Dannebrog; Kt of Icelandic Falcon; Chairman and Chief Executive, Navalicon Ltd A/S, Denmark, 1975–84; *b* Denmark, 25 July 1920; *s* of Arthur Hans Knudsen Hoppe and Gerda (*née* Raun Byberg); *m* 1943, Ingeborg Lassen; one *d*. *Educ:* Aarhus Katedralskole; Copenhagen Univ. (Law Faculty), 1944. Acting Lecturer, Copenhagen Univ., 1946; Advocate to High Court and Court of Appeal, 1948; Jurisprudential Lecturer, Copenhagen Univ., 1952–58; study sojourn in Switzerland, 1949. A. P. Møller Concern, Copenhagen, 1955–71: Asst Dir, 1960; Man. Dir of Odense Steel Shipyard, Ltd, Odense and Lindø, 1964–71. Chm. A/S Svendborg Skibsvaerft, 1968–71; Mem. Bd of Dansk Boreselskab A/S and other cos until 1971; Man. Dir and Chief Exec., Harland and Wolff Ltd, Belfast, 1971–74; Member: Bd of Den Danske Landmandsbank A/S, 1970–72; Council of Danish National Bank, 1967–71; Bd of Danish Ship Credit Fund, 1965–71; Assoc. of Danish Shipyards, 1964–71; Assoc. of Employers within the Iron and Metal Industry in Denmark, 1967–71; Assoc. of Danish Industries, 1965–72; West of England Steam Ship Owners Protection and Indemnity Assoc., Ltd, 1960–66; Danish Acad. of Technical Sciences; Shipbuilders and Repairers Nat. Assoc. Exec. Council and Management Bd, 1971–74; British Iron and Steel Consumers' Council, 1971–74; Gen. Cttee, Lloyd's Register of Shipping; British Cttee, Det Norske Veritas; Amer. Bureau of Shipping, and other Danish and foreign instns. *Recreations:* reading, swimming, mountain walking, farming. *Address:* Malmmosegaard, Dyreborgvej 7, DK-5600 Faaborg, Denmark.

HOPPER, Prof. Frederick Ernest, MDS, FDSRCS; FFDRCSI; Professor of Dental Surgery and Dean of the School of Dentistry, University of Leeds, 1959–85, now Professor Emeritus; Consultant Dental Surgeon, Leeds Area Health Authority, 1959–85; Chairman, Board of Faculty of Medicine, University of Leeds, 1975–78; *b* 22 Nov. 1919; *s* of Frederick Ernest Hopper, MPS and Margaret Ann Carlyle; *m* 1949, Gudrun Eik-Nes, LDSRCS, *d* of Prost Knut Eik-Nes and Nina Eik-Nes, Trondheim, Norway; three *s*. *Educ:* Dame Allan's Sch., Newcastle upon Tyne; King's Coll., University of Durham. BDS (with dist.) 1943; FDSRCS 1948; MDS 1958. House Surg., Newcastle upon Tyne Dental Hosp. and Royal Dental Hospital, 1943–44; served in EMS in Maxillo-Facial Centres at E Grinstead and Shotley Bridge, 1944–46; successively Lecturer, 1946, and Sen. Lecturer, 1956, in Periodontal Diseases, King's Coll., University of Durham; Lecturer in Dental Pharmacology and Therapeutics, 1947–59; Examiner in Dental subjects, Univs of Durham, Edinburgh, St Andrews, Bristol, Liverpool; Dental Surgeon in charge Parodontal Dept, Newcastle upon Tyne Dental Hosp., and Sen. Dental Surg., Plastic and Jaw Unit, Shotley Bridge, 1946–59; Cons. Dent. Surg., United Newcastle Hosps, 1955–59. Hon. Treas., Brit. Soc. of Periodontology, 1949–53, Pres. 1954. Member: General Dental Council, 1959–85 (Chm., Educn Cttee, 1980–85); Brit. Dental Assoc., 1943–; Internat. Dental Fedn, 1948–; Pres., British Soc. for Oral Medicine, 1986. GDC Visitor, 1986–87, to Medical Univ. of Southern Africa and to Univs of Pretoria, Stellenbosch, Western Cape, the Witwatersrand, Otago, Hong Kong and Singapore. *Publications:* contribs to med. and dental jls. *Recreations:* photography (still and ciné); golf. *Address:* 23 Ancaster Road, Leeds LS16 5HH. *Clubs:* Savage; Alwoodley Golf (Leeds).

HOPPER, William Joseph; Executive Chairman, Shire Trust Ltd, since 1986; *b* 9 Aug. 1929; *s* of I. Vance Hopper and Jennie Josephine Hopper; *m* 1986, Marjorie Alice Orr; one *d* by previous *m*. *Educ:* Langside Elementary Sch., Glasgow; Queen's Park Secondary Sch., Glasgow; Glasgow Univ. (MA 1st Cl. Hons (Mod. Langs) 1953). Financial Analyst, W. R. Grace & Co., NY, 1956–59; London Office Manager, H. Hentz & Co., Members, NY Stock Exchange, 1960–66; Gen. Manager, S. G. Warburg & Co. Ltd, 1966–69; Director: Hill Samuel & Co. Ltd, 1969–74; Morgan Grenfell & Co. Ltd, 1974–79 (Adviser, 1979–86); Wharf Resources Ltd, Calgary, 1984–87; Manchester Ship Canal Co., 1985–87; Chm., Robust Mouldings, 1986–90. MEP (C), Greater Manchester West, 1979–84. Co-founder (1969) and first Chm. (now Mem., Exec. Cttee), Inst. for Fiscal Studies, London; Treasurer, Action Resource Centre, 1985–; Trustee, Hampstead, Wells and Campden Trust, 1989–. *Publication:* A Turntable for Capital, 1969. *Recreations:* listening to music, gardening. *Address:* 43 Flask Walk, NW3 1HH. *T:* 071–435 6414. *Clubs:* Carlton, Garrick.

HOPTHROW, Brig. Harry Ewart, CBE 1946 (OBE 1940); Hon. Life Member, Solent Protection Society (Member Council, 1975–85); *b* 13 Nov. 1896; *s* of Frederick Hopthrow; *m* 1925, Audrey Kassel (*d* 1975), *d* of J. Lewer; one *s* one *d*. *Educ:* Queen Elizabeth's Grammar Sch., Gainsborough; City Sch., Lincoln; Loughborough Coll. Served European War, 1915–18, RE, France and Flanders. Civil and Mechanical Engineer, ICI Ltd, 1925–39; Commanded 107 Co. RE, 1931–35, Major; Asst Dir of Works, GHQ, BEF, 1939–40, Lt-Col; served France and Flanders, 1939–40 and 1944; Dep. Chief Engineer: Home Forces, 1940–41, and Western Comd, 1941; Dep. Controller Mil. Works Services, War Office, 1941–43; Dir of Fortifications and Works, WO, 1943–45; Asst Sec., ICI Ltd, 1945–58; Hon. Secretary and a Vice-Pres., Royal Institution, 1960–68. AMIMechE 1924, FIMechE 1933. Mem. Central Advisory Water Cttee (Min. of Housing and Local Govt), 1951–69; Mem. Cttee of Inquiry into Inland Waterways (Bowes Cttee), 1956–58; Vice-Chm. IoW River and Water Authority, 1964–73; UK Rep. to Council of European Industrial Fedns; Vice-Pres., Round Tables on Pollution, 1965–73. Life Mem., Isle of Wight Soc. Officer of American Legion of Merit, 1946. *Recreations:* intellectual conversation with intelligent ladies, historical research. *Address:* Surrey House, Cowes, Isle of Wight. *T:* Isle of Wight (0983) 292430. *Clubs:* Army and Navy; Royal Engineer Yacht; Royal London Yacht, Island Sailing (Cowes).

HOPWOOD, family name of **Baron Southborough.**

HOPWOOD, Prof. Anthony George; Ernst and Young (formerly Arthur Young) Professor of International Accounting and Financial Management, London School of Economics and Political Science, University of London, since 1985; *b* 18 May 1944; *s* of late George and Violet Hopwood; *m* 1967, Caryl Davies; two *s*. *Educ:* Hanley High School; LSE (BSc Econ); Univ. of Chicago (MBA, PhD). Lectr in Management Accounting, Manchester Business Sch., 1970–73; Senior Staff, Admin. Staff Coll., Henley, 1973–76; Professorial Fellow, Oxford Centre for Management Studies, 1976–78; ICA Prof. of Accounting and Financial Reporting, London Business Sch., 1978–85. Vis. Prof. of Management, European Inst. for Advanced Studies in Management, Brussels, 1972–; Associate Fellow, Industrial Relations Research Unit, Univ. of Warwick, 1978–80; Amer. Accounting Assoc. Dist. Internat. Vis. Lectr, 1981; Distinguished Vis. Prof. of Accounting, Pennsylvania State Univ., 1983–88. Mem., Management and Industrial Relations Cttee, SSRC, 1975–79; Chm., Management Awards Panel, SSRC, 1976–79; Pres., European Accounting Assoc., 1977–79 and 1987–88; Member: Council, Tavistock Inst. of Human Relations, 1981–; Research Bd, ICA, 1982–; Dir, Greater London Enterprise Bd, 1985–87. Accounting Advr, EC, 1989–90; Accounting Cons., OECD, 1990–. Hon. DEcon Turku Sch. of Econs, Finland, 1989. Editor-in-Chief, Accounting, Organizations and Society, 1976–. *Publications:* An Accounting System and Managerial Behaviour, 1973; Accounting and Human Behaviour, 1973; (with M. Bromwich) Essays in British Accounting Research, 1981; (with M. Bromwich and J. Shaw) Auditing Research, 1982; (with M. Bromwich) Accounting Standard Setting, 1983; (with H. Schreuder) European Contributions to Accounting Research, 1984; (with C. Tomkins) Issues in Public Sector Accounting, 1984; (with M. Bromwich) Research and Current Issues in Management Accounting, 1986; Accounting from the Outside: the collected papers of Anthony G.

Hopwood, 1988; International Pressures for Accounting Change, 1989; (with M. Page and S. Turley) Understanding Accounting in a Changing Environment, 1990; articles in learned and professional jls. *Address:* Department of Accounting and Finance, London School of Economics, Houghton Street, WC2A 2AE. *T:* 071–405 7686.

HOPWOOD, Prof. David Alan, FRS 1979; John Innes Professor of Genetics, University of East Anglia, Norwich, and Head of the Genetics Department, John Innes Institute, since 1968; *b* 19 Aug. 1933; *s* of Herbert Hopwood and Dora Hopwood (*née* Grant); *m* 1962, Joyce Lilian Bloom; two *s* one *d. Educ:* Purbrook Park County High Sch., Hants; Lymm Grammar Sch., Cheshire; St John's Coll., Cambridge (MA, PhD). DSc (Glasgow). Whytehead Major Scholar, St John's Coll., Cambridge, 1951–54; John Stothert Bye-Fellow, Magdalene Coll., Cambridge, 1956–58; Res. Fellow, St John's Coll., 1958–61; Univ. Demonstrator, Univ. of Cambridge, 1957–61; Lectr in Genetics, Univ. of Glasgow, 1961–68. Pres., Genetical Soc. of GB, 1985–87. Foreign Fellow, Indian Nat. Science Acad., 1987. Hon. Professor: Chinese Acad. of Med. Scis, 1987; Insts of Microbiology and Plant Physiology, Chinese Acad. of Scis, 1987; Huazhong Agricl Univ., Wuhan, China, 1989. Hon. Fellow, UMIST, 1990. Hon. Mem., Hungarian Acad. of Scis, 1990. Hon. DSc Eidgenössische Technische Hochschule, Zürich, 1989. *Publications:* numerous articles and chapters in scientific jls and books. *Address:* John Innes Institute, Colney Lane, Norwich NR4 7UH. *T:* Norwich (0603) 52571, *Fax:* Norwich (0603) 56844.

HORAM, John Rhodes; Managing Director, CRU Holdings Ltd, since 1988; *b* 7 March 1939; *s* of Sydney Horam, Preston; *m* 1987, Judith Jackson. *Educ:* Silcoates Sch., Wakefield; Univ. of Cambridge. Market research officer, Rowntree & Co., 1960–62; leader and feature writer: Financial Times, 1962–65; The Economist, 1965–68; Man. Dir, Commodities Research Unit Ltd, 1968–70 and 1983–87. MP Gateshead West, 1970–83 (Lab, 1970–81, SDP, 1981–83). Parly Under-Sec. of State, Dept of Transport, 1976–79; Labour spokesman on econ. affairs, 1979–81; Parly spokesman on econ. affairs, SDP, 1981–83. Contested (SDP) Newcastle upon Tyne Central, 1983. Joined Conservative Party, Feb. 1987; Prospective Parly Candidate (C) Orpington, 1991–. *Address:* 6 Bovingdon Road, SW6 2AP; CRU House, 31 Mount Pleasant, WC1X 0AD. *T:* 071–278 0414.

HORAN, Rt. Rev. Forbes Trevor; *b* 22 May 1905; *s* of Rev. Frederick Seymour Horan and Mary Katherine Horan; *m* 1st, 1939, Veronica (*d* 1983), *d* of late Rt Rev. J. N. Bateman-Champain, sometime Bishop of Knaresborough; two *s* two *d*; 2nd, 1987, Elizabeth Lancaster, Cheltenham. *Educ:* Sherborne and Trinity Hall, Cambridge. RMC Sandhurst, 1924–25; Oxford and Bucks Lt Infantry, Lieutenant, 1925–29; Trinity Hall, Cambridge, 1929–32; Westcott House, Cambridge, 1932–33; Curate, St Luke's, Newcastle upon Tyne, 1933–35; Curate, St George's, Jesmond, Newcastle upon Tyne, 1935–37; Priest-in-charge, St Peter's, Balkwell, 1937–40; RNVR, 1940–45; Vicar of St Chad's, Shrewsbury, 1945–52; Vicar of Huddersfield Parish Church, 1952–60; Bishop Suffragan of Tewkesbury, 1960–73. *Recreations:* listening to the Third Programme on the radio, bicycling in order to maintain some semblance of independence, cooking and housekeeping. *Address:* 3 Silverthorn Close, Shurdington Road, Cheltenham, Glos GL53 0JL. *T:* Cheltenham (0242) 527313.

HORD, Brian Howard, CBE 1989; FRICS; Company Director; Chairman, Bexley Health Authority, since 1986; *b* 20 June 1934; *s* of late Edwin Charles and of Winifred Hannah Hord; *m* 1960, Christine Marian Lucas; two *s. Educ:* Reedham Sch.; Purley Grammar Sch. County Planning Dept, Mddx CC, 1950–51; Surveyor, private practice, 1951–57; National Service, RAF, 1957–59; Estates Surveyor, United Drapery Stores, 1959–66; Richard Costain Ltd, 1966–70; Director, Capcount UK Ltd, principal subsid. of Capital & Counties Property Co. Ltd, 1970–75; Partner, Howard Hord & Palmer, Chartered Surveyors, 1975–84. Mem., London Rent Assessment Panel, 1985–. MEP (C) London West, 1979–84; Whip of European Democratic Gp, 1982–83; Mem., Agric. and Budgets Cttees, Eur. Parlt. *Publication:* (jtly) Rates-Realism or Rebellion. *Recreations:* photography, top-fruit growing, bee-keeping. *Address:* 86 Gloucester Place, W1H 3HN. *Club:* Carlton.

HORDEN, Prof. John Robert Backhouse, FSA; FRSL; Emeritus Professor of Bibliographical Studies, University of Stirling, since 1988; Editor, Dictionary of Scottish Biography, since 1982; *o s* of late Henry Robert Horden and Ethel Edith Horden (*née* Backhouse), Warwicks; *m* 1948, Aileen Mary (*d* 1984), *o d* of late Lt Col and Mrs W. J. Douglas, Warwicks and S Wales; one *s. Educ:* Oxford, Cambridge, Heidelberg, Sorbonne, Lincoln's Inn. Revived and ed The Isis, 1945–46. Previously: Tutor and Lectr in English Literature, Christ Church, Oxford; Director, Inst. of Bibliography and Textual Criticism, Univ. of Leeds; Dir, Centre for Bibliographical Studies, Univ. of Stirling. Vis. professorial appts, Univs of Pennsylvania State, Saskatchewan, Erlangen-Nürnberg, Texas at Austin, Münster; Cecil Oldman Meml Lectr in Bibliography and Textual Criticism, 1971. Hon. Life Mem., Modern Humanities Res. Assoc., 1976. DHL (*hc*) Indiana State Univ., 1974. Marc Fitch Prize for Bibliography, 1979. Devised new academic discipline of Publishing Studies and designed first British degree course at Univ. of Leeds, 1972 (MA); initiated first British degree in Public Relations (MSc), Univ. of Stirling, 1987. Founded Stirling Univ. Press, 1985. *Publications:* Francis Quarles: a bibliography of his works to 1800, 1953; (ed) Francis Quarles' Hosanna and Threnodes, 1960, 3rd edn 1965; (ed) Annual Bibliography of English Language and Literature, 1967–75; (ed) English and Continental Emblem Books (22 vols), 1968–74; Art of the Drama, 1969; Everyday Life in Seventeenth-century England, 1974; Techniques of Bibliography, 1977; (ed) Dictionary of Concealed Authorship, vol. 1, 1980 (1st vol. of rev. Halkett and Laing); (initiator and first editor) Index of English Literary Manuscripts (7 vols), 1980–90; John Freeth: political ballad writer and inn keeper, 1985; (ed) Bibliographia, 1991; numerous contribs to learned jls. *Recreations:* golf (represented England, Warwicks, Oxford and Cambridge), music, painting. *Address:* Department of English Studies, University of Stirling, Stirling FK9 4LA. *T:* Stirling (0786) 73171. *Clubs:* Athenæum; Vincent's (Oxford); Hawks (Cambridge).

HORDER, family name of **Baron Horder.**

HORDER, 2nd Baron *cr* 1933, of Ashford in the County of Southampton; **Thomas Mervyn Horder;** Bt, of Shaston, 1923; *b* 8 Dec. 1910; *s* of 1st Baron Horder, GCVO, MD, FRCP, and Geraldine Rose (*d* 1954), *o d* of Arthur Doggett, Newnham Manor, Herts; *S* father, 1955. *Educ:* Winchester; Trinity Coll., Cambridge. BA 1932; MA 1937. Served War of 1939–45: HQ, RAF Fighter Comd, 1940–42 (despatches); Air HQ, India, 1942–44; Headquarters, South-East Asia Command, 1944–45; United Kingdom Liaison Mission, Tokyo, 1945–46; Chairman, Gerald Duckworth & Co. Ltd, 1948–70. *Publications:* The Little Genius, 1966; (ed) Ronald Firbank: memoirs and critiques, 1977; On Their Own: shipwrecks & survivals, 1988; *music:* (ed) The Orange Carol Book, 1962; Six Betjeman Songs, 1967; A Shropshire Lad (songs), 1980; (ed) The Easter Carol Book, 1982; Seven Shakespeare Songs, 1988; Black Diamonds (three Dorothy Parker songs), 1990. *Recreations:* music, idling. *Address:* 4 Hamilton Close, NW8 8QY.

HORDER, Dr John Plaistowe, CBE 1981 (OBE 1971); FRCP, FRCPE, FRCGP, FRCPsych; general practitioner of medicine, 1951–81, retired; President, Royal College of General Practitioners, 1979–82; Visiting Professor, Royal Free Hospital Medical School, since 1982; *b* 9 Dec. 1919; *s* of Gerald Morley Horder and Emma Ruth Horder; *m* 1940, Elizabeth June Wilson; two *s* two *d. Educ:* Lancing Coll.; University Coll., Oxford (BA 1945); London Hosp. (BM BCh 1948). FRCP 1972 (MRCP 1951); FRCGP 1970 (MRCGP 1957); FRCPsych 1980 (MRCPsych 1975); FRCPE 1982. Consultant, 1959, Travelling Fellow, 1964, WHO; Lectr, London School of Economics and Pol. Sci., 1964–69; Sir Harry Jeffcott Vis. Professor, Univ. of Nottingham, 1975; John Hunt Fellow, 1974–77, Wolfson Travelling Prof., 1978, Royal Coll. of Gen. Practitioners. Vis. Prof., Zagreb Univ., 1990–. Consultant Adviser, DHSS, 1978–84. Pres., Medical Art Soc., 1990–. Hon. Fellow, RSM, 1983 (Vice-Pres., 1987–89; Pres., Sect. of Gen. Practice, 1970). Hon. Fellow, Green Coll., Oxford, 1988. Hon. MD Free Univ. Amsterdam, 1985. Hon. Mem., Coll. of Family Physicians of Canada, 1982. *Publications:* ed and co-author, The Future General Practitioner—learning and teaching, 1972; articles on general practice—training for and psychiatry in. . . . , 1953–. *Recreations:* painting, music. *Address:* 98 Regent's Park Road, NW1. *T:* 071–722 3804.

HORDERN, (Alfred) Christopher (Willoughby); QC 1979; **His Honour Judge Hordern;** a Circuit Judge, since 1983; *m*; one *s* two *d. Educ:* Oxford Univ. (MA). Called to the Bar, Middle Temple, 1961; a Recorder of the Crown Court, 1974–83. *Address:* 4 King's Bench Walk, Temple, EC4Y 7DL.

HORDERN, Sir Michael (Murray), Kt 1983; CBE 1972; actor; *b* 3 Oct. 1911; *s* of Capt. Edward Joseph Calverly Hordern, CIE, RIN, and Margaret Emily (*née* Murray); *m* 1943, Grace Eveline Mortimer (*d* 1986); one *d. Educ:* Brighton Coll. Formerly in business with The Educational Supply Assoc., playing meanwhile as an amateur at St Pancras People's Theatre. First professional appearance as Lodovico in Othello, People's Palace, 1937. Two seasons of repertory at Little Theatre, Bristol, 1937–39; War service in Navy, 1940–46; demobilised as Lieut-Comdr, RNVR. Parts include: Mr Toad in Toad of Toad Hall, at Stratford, 1948 and 1949; Ivanov in Ivanov, Arts Theatre, 1950. Stratford Season, 1952: Jacques, Menenius, Caliban. Old Vic Season, 1953–54: Polonius, King John, Malvolio, Prospero. "BB" in The Doctor's Dilemma, Saville, 1956; Old Vic Season, 1958–59: Cassius, Macbeth. Ulysses (Troilus and Cressida), Edinburgh Fest., 1962; Herbert Georg Beutler in The Physicists, Aldwych, 1963; Southman in Saint's Day, St Martin's, 1965; Relatively Speaking, Duke of York's, 1967; A Delicate Balance, Aldwych, 1969; King Lear, Nottingham Playhouse, 1969; Flint, Criterion, 1970; You Never Can Tell, Haymarket, 1987; Bookends, Apollo, 1990; National Theatre: Jumpers, 1972 and 1976, Gaunt in Richard II, 1972, The Cherry Orchard, 1973, The Rivals, 1983; The Ordeal of Gilbert Pinfold, Manchester, 1977, Round House, 1979; RSC Stratford: Prospero in The Tempest, Armado in Love's Labour's Lost, 1978; also many leading parts in films, radio and television. Hon. Fellow, QMC, 1987; Hon. DLitt: Exeter, 1985; Warwick, 1987. *Recreation:* fishing. *Address:* Flat Y, Rectory Chambers, Old Church Street, SW3 5DA. *Clubs:* Garrick, Flyfishers'.

HORDERN, Sir Peter (Maudslay), Kt 1985; DL; MP (C) Horsham, 1964–74 and since 1983 (Horsham and Crawley, 1974–83); *b* 18 April 1929; British; *s* of C. H. Hordern, MBE; *m* 1964, Susan Chataway; two *s* one *d. Educ:* Geelong Grammar Sch., Australia; Christ Church, Oxford, 1949–52 (MA). Mem. of Stock Exchange, London, 1957–74. Chairman: F. & C. Smaller Cos (formerly F. & C. Alliance Investment), 1986– (Dir, 1976–); Fina (formerly Petrofina (UK)), 1987– (Dir, 1973–); Dir, TR Technology, 1975–. Chm., Cons. Parly Finance Cttee, 1970–72; Member: Exec., 1922 Cttee, 1968– (Jt Sec., 1988–); Public Accts Cttee, 1970–; Public Accounts Commn, 1984– (Chm., 1988–). DL West Sussex, 1988. *Recreations:* golf, reading and travel. *Address:* 55 Cadogan Street, SW3.

HORE-RUTHVEN, family name of **Earl of Gowrie.**

HORLICK, Vice-Adm. Sir Edwin John, (Sir Ted Horlick), KBE 1981; FEng, FIMechE, MIMarE; part-time consultant; *b* 1925; *m* Jean Margaret (*née* Covington) (*d* 1991); four *s. Educ:* Bedford Modern Sch. Joined RN, 1943; Sqdn Eng. Officer, 2nd Frigate Sqdn, 1960–63; Ship Dept, MoD, 1963–66; First Asst to Chief Engineer, HM Dockyard, Singapore, 1966–68; Asst Dir Submarines, 1969–72; SOWC 1973; Fleet Marine Engineering Officer, Staff of C-in-C Fleet, 1973–75; RCDS 1976; Dir Project Team Submarine/Polaris, 1977–79; Dir Gen. Ships, 1979–83; Chief Naval Engineer Officer, 1981–83. *Recreations:* golf, Rugby administration, DIY. *Address:* Garden Apt, 74 Great Pulteney Street, Bath BA2 4DL. *Club:* Army and Navy.

HORLICK, Sir John (James Macdonald), 5th Bt *cr* 1914; Partner, Tournaig Farming Company, since 1973; *b* 9 April 1922; *s* of Lt-Col Sir James Horlick, 4th Bt, OBE, MC, and Flora Macdonald (*d* 1955), *d* of late Col Cunliffe Martin, CB; *S* father, 1972; *m* 1948, June, *d* of late Douglas Cory-Wright, CBE; one *s* two *d. Educ:* Eton; Babson Institute of Business Admin, Wellesley Hills, Mass, USA. Served War as Captain, Coldstream Guards. Dep. Chairman, Horlicks Ltd, retired 1971. CStJ 1977. *Recreations:* shooting, model soldier collecting. *Heir:* *s* James Cunliffe William Horlick [*b* 19 Nov. 1956; *m* 1985, Fiona Rosalie, *e d* of Andrew McLaren, Alcester; three *s*]. *Address:* Tournaig, Poolewe, Achnasheen, Ross-shire. *T:* Poolewe 250; Howberry Lane Cottage, Nuffield, near Nettlebed, Oxon. *T:* Nettlebed (0491) 641454. *Clubs:* Beefsteak; Highland (Inverness).

HORLICK, Sir Ted; *see* Horlick, Sir Edwin John.

HORLOCK, Henry Wimburn Sudell; Underwriting Member of Lloyd's, since 1957; Director, Stepping Stone School, 1962–87; *b* 19 July 1915; *s* of Rev. Henry Darrell Sudell Horlock, DD, and Mary Haliburton Laurie; *m* 1960, Jeannetta Robin, *d* of F. W. Tanner, JP. *Educ:* Pembroke Coll., Oxford (MA). Army, 1939–42. Civil Service, 1942–60. Court of Common Council, City of London, 1969– (Chm., West Ham Park Cttee, 1979–82; Chm., Police Cttee, 1987–90); Deputy, Ward of Farringdon Within, 1978–; Sheriff, City of London, 1972–73; Chm., City of London Sheriffs' Soc., 1985–; Liveryman: Saddlers Co., 1937–, Master, 1976–77; Plaisterers' Co. (Hon.), 1975–; Fletchers' Co., 1977–; Gardeners' Co., 1980–; Member: Parish Clerks' Co., 1966–, Master, 1981–82; Guild of Freemen, 1972–, Master, 1986–87; Farringdon Ward Club, 1970–, Pres., 1978–79; United Wards Club, 1972–, Pres., 1980–81; City Livery Club, 1969–, Pres., 1981–82; City of London Br., Royal Soc. of St George, 1972–, Chm., 1989–90. Commander: Order of Merit, Federal Republic of Germany, 1972; National Order of the Aztec Eagle of Mexico, 1973; Order of Wissam Alouite, Morocco, 1987. *Recreations:* gardening, travel. *Address:* 97 Defoe House, Barbican, EC2Y 8DN. *T:* 071–588 1602. *Clubs:* Athenæum, Guildhall, City Livery.

HORLOCK, Prof. John Harold, FRS 1976; FEng 1977; Vice-Chancellor, 1981–90, and Fellow, since 1991, Open University; Hon. Professor of Engineering, Warwick University, since 1991; *b* 19 April 1928; *s* of Harold Edgar and Olive Margaret Horlock; *m* 1953, Sheila Joy Stutely; one *s* two *d. Educ:* Edmonton Latymer Sch.; (Scholar) St John's Coll., Cambridge (Hon. Fellow 1989). 1st Class Hons Mech. Sci. Tripos, Pt I, 1948, Rex Moir Prize; Pt II, 1949; MA 1952; PhD 1955; ScD 1975. Design and Development Engineer, Rolls Royce Ltd, Derby, 1949–51; Fellow, St John's Coll., Cambridge, 1954–57 and 1967–74; Univ. Demonstrator, 1952–56; University Lecturer, 1956–58, at Cambridge

Univ. Engineering Lab.; Harrison Prof. of Mechanical Engineering, Liverpool Univ., 1958–66; Prof. of Engineering, and Dir of Whittle Lab., Cambridge Univ., 1967–74; Vice-Chancellor, Univ. of Salford, 1974–80. Visiting Asst Prof. in Mech. Engineering, Massachusetts Inst. of Technology, USA, 1956–57; Vis. Prof. of Aero-Space Engineering, Pennsylvania State Univ., USA, 1966. Chm., ARC, 1979–80 (Mem., 1960–63, 1969–72); Member: SRC, 1974–77; Cttee of Inquiry into Engineering Profession, 1977–80; Engineering Council, 1981–83; Adv. Cttee on Safety in Nuclear Installations, 1984–. Director: BICERA Ltd, 1964–65; Cambridge Water Co., 1971–74; British Engine Insurance Ltd, 1979–84; Gaydon Technology Ltd, 1978–88; Open University Educational Enterprises Ltd, 1981–88; Co-ax Cable Communications Ltd, 1983–89 (Chm.); National Grid Co., 1989–. A Vice-Pres., Royal Soc., 1981–83. FIMechE; Fellow ASME; Foreign Associate, US Nat. Acad. of Engrg. Hon. Fellow, UMIST, 1991. Hon. DSc: Heriot-Watt, 1980; Salford, 1981; Hon. ScD East Asia, 1987; Hon. DEng Liverpool, 1987; DUniv Open, 1991. Clayton Prize, 1962; Thomas Hawksley Gold Medal, IMechE, 1969. *Publications:* The Fluid Mechanics and Thermodynamics of Axial Flow Compressors, 1958; The Fluid Mechanics and Thermodynamics of Axial Flow Turbines, 1966; Actuator Disc Theory, 1978; (ed) Thermodynamics and Gas Dynamics of Internal Combustion Engines, vol. I, 1982, vol. II, 1986; Cogeneration—Combined Heat and Power, 1987; contribs to mech. and aero. engineering jls and to Proc. Royal Society. *Recreations:* music, watching sport. *Address:* 2 The Avenue, Ampthill, Bedford MK45 2NR. *T:* Ampthill (0525) 841307. *Clubs:* Athenæum, MCC.

HORN, Alan Bowes, CVO 1971; HM Diplomatic Service, retired; *b* 6 June 1917; *m* 1946, Peggy Boocock; one *s* one *d. Educ:* London Sch. of Economics. Served in Army, 1940–46. Joined Foreign Service, 1946; Vice-Consul, Marseilles, 1948–49; 2nd Sec., HM Embassy, Tel Aviv, 1949; promoted 1st Sec. and later apptd: London, 1951–53; New York, 1953–56; Helsinki, 1957–60; FO, 1960–63; Ambassador to the Malagasy Republic, 1963–67; Counsellor, Warsaw, 1967–70; Consul-General, Istanbul, 1970–73. *Address:* Oak Trees, Shere Road, Ewhurst, Cranleigh, Surrey GU6 7PQ.

HORN, Prof. Gabriel, MA, MD, ScD; FRS 1986; Professor of Zoology, since 1978, and Head of Department, since 1979, University of Cambridge; Fellow of King's College, Cambridge, since 1978; *b* 9 Dec. 1927; *s* of late A. Horn and Mrs Horn; *m* 1st, 1952, Ann Loveday Dean Soper (marr. diss. 1979); two *s* two *d*; 2nd, 1980, Priscilla Barrett. *Educ:* Handsworth Technical Sch. and Coll., Birmingham (Nat. Cert. in Mech. Engrg); Univ. of Birmingham (BSc Anatomy and Physiology; MD, ChB). MA, ScD Cantab. Served in RAF (Educn Br.), 1947–49. House appts, Birmingham Children's and Birmingham and Midland Eye Hosps, 1955–56; Univ. of Cambridge: Univ. Demonstrator in Anat., 1956–62; Lectr in Anat., 1962–72; Reader in Neurobiology, 1972–74; Fellow of King's Coll., 1962–74; Prof. and Head of Dept of Anat., Univ. of Bristol, 1974–77. Sen. Res. Fellow in Neurophysiol., Montreal Neurol Inst., McGill Univ., 1957–58; Leverhulme Res. Fellow, Laboratoire de Neurophysiologie Cellulaire, France, 1970–71. Vis. Prof. of Physiol Optics, Univ. of Calif, Berkeley, 1963; Vis. Res. Prof., Ohio State Univ., 1965; Vis. Prof. of Zool., Makerere University Coll., Uganda, 1966; Dist. Vis. Prof., Univ. of Alberta, Edmonton, Canada, 1988; Vis. Miller Prof., Univ. of Calif, Berkeley, USA, 1989. Charnock Bradley Lectr, Edinburgh Univ., 1988; Crisp Lectr, Univ. of Leeds, 1990. Member: Biol Sciences Cttee, SRC, 1973–75; Jt MRC and SRC Adv. Panel on Neurobiol., 1971–72; Res. Cttee, Mental Health Foundn, 1973–78; Council, Anatomical Soc., 1976–78; Adv. Gp, ARC Inst. of Animal Physiology, Babraham, 1981–87. Dir, Co. of Biologists, 1980–. FIBiol 1978. Kenneth Craik Award in Physiol Psychol., 1962. *Publications:* (ed with R. A. Hinde) Short-Term Changes in Neural Activity and Behaviour, 1970; Memory, Imprinting and the Brain, 1985; (ed with J. R. Krebs) Behavioural and Neural Aspects of Learning and Memory, 1991; contrib. scientific jls, mainly on topics in neurosciences. *Recreations:* walking, cycling, music, riding. *Address:* King's College, Cambridge. *T:* Cambridge (0223) 350411.

HORNBY, Sir Derek (Peter), Kt 1990; Chairman, British Overseas Trade Board, since 1990 (Member, since 1987; Chairman, North American Group, 1987); *b* 10 Jan. 1930; *s* of F. N. Hornby and V. M. Pardy; *m* 1st, 1953, Margaret Withers (marr. diss.); one *s* one *d*; 2nd, 1971, Sonia Beesley; one *s* one *d. Educ:* Canford School. With Mobil Oil, Mars Industries and Texas Instruments; Xerox Corp., 1973 (Dir, Internat. Ops); Exec. Dir, Rank Xerox, 1980–84; Chm., Rank-Xerox (UK), 1984–90. Mem. Bd, British Rail, 1985–90; Civil Service Comr, 1986–90; Chm., NACCB. Chairman: AMRA, 1989–; Astra Training Services, 1990–; Director: Cogent Elliott, 1988–; H. Burbidge & Son Ltd, 1988–; London and Edinburgh Insurance Gp, 1989–; Kode International, 1989–; Mem. Bd, Savills, 1988–. CBIM (Chm., 1990–); FRSA. *Recreations:* Real tennis, theatre, cricket. *Address:* Badgers Farm, Idlicote, Shipston-on-Stour, Warwicks CV36 5DT. *Clubs:* Carlton, MCC; Leamington Real Tennis, Moreton Morell Real Tennis.

HORNBY, Derrick Richard; *b* 11 Jan. 1926; *s* of late Richard W. Hornby and Dora M. Hornby; *m* 1948, June Steele; two *s* one *d. Educ:* University Coll., Southampton (DipEcon). Early career in accountancy; Marketing Dir, Tetley Tea Co. Ltd, 1964–69; Man. Dir, Eden Vale, 1969–74; Chm., Spillers Foods Ltd, 1974–77; Divisional Managing Director: Spillers Internat., 1977–80; Spillers Grocery Products Div., 1979–80; Chm., Carrington Viyella Ltd, 1979–80. Pres., Food Manufrs Fedn Incorp., 1977–79; Mem., Food and Drinks EDC. Member Council: CBI, to 1979; Food and Drinks Industry Council, to 1979. Chairman: Appeal Fund, Nat. Grocers Benefit Fund, 1973–74; London Animal Trust, 1978–80. FBIM, FIGD, ACommA. *Recreations:* golf, fly-fishing. *Address:* 54 Cerne Abbas, The Avenue, Branksome Park, Poole, Dorset.

HORNBY, Prof. James Angus; Professor of Law in the University of Bristol, 1961–85, now Emeritus; *b* 15 Aug. 1922; twin *s* of James Hornby and Evelyn Gladys (*née* Grant). *Educ:* Bolton County Grammar Sch.; Christ's Coll., Cambridge. BA 1944, LLB 1945, MA 1948 Cantab. Called to Bar, Lincoln's Inn, 1947. Lecturer, Manchester Univ., 1947–61. *Publications:* An Introduction to Company Law, 1957, 5th edn 1975; contribs to legal journals. *Recreation:* hill walking. *Address:* 6 Henbury Gardens, Henbury Road, Bristol BS10 7AJ. *Club:* United Oxford & Cambridge University.

HORNBY, Lesley; *see* Twiggy.

HORNBY, Richard Phipps, MA; Chairman, Halifax Building Society, 1983–90 (Director, 1976; Vice-Chairman, 1981–83); Director, Cadbury Schweppes plc, since 1982; *b* 20 June 1922; *e s* of late Rt Rev. Hugh Leycester Hornby, MC; *m* 1951, Stella Hichens; three *s* one *d. Educ:* Winchester Coll.; Trinity Coll., Oxford (Scholar). Served in King's Royal Rifle Corps, 1941–45. 2nd Cl. Hons in Modern History, Oxford, 1948 (Soccer Blue). History Master, Eton Coll., 1948–50; with Unilever, 1951–52; with J. Walter Thompson Co., 1952–63, 1964–81 (Dir, 1974–81); Dir, McCorquodale plc, 1982–86. Contested (C) West Walthamstow: May 1955 (gen. election) and March 1956 (by-election); MP (C) Tonbridge, Kent, June 1956–Feb. 1974. PPS to Rt Hon. Duncan Sandys, MP, 1959–63; Parly Under-Sec. of State, CRO and CO, Oct. 1963–Oct. 1964. Member: BBC Gen. Adv. Council, 1969–74; Cttee of Inquiry into Intrusions into Privacy, 1970–72; British Council Exec. Cttee, 1971–74. *Recreations:* shooting, fishing, walking. *Address:* Ebble Thatch, Bowerchalke, near Salisbury, Wilts SP5 5BW.

HORNBY, Sir Simon (Michael); Kt 1988; Director, since 1974, Chairman, since 1982, W. H. Smith Group (formerly W. H. Smith & Son (Holdings) plc); Director: Pearson plc (formerly S. Pearson & Son Ltd), since 1978; Lloyds Bank, since 1988; *b* 29 Dec. 1934; *s* of late Michael Hornby and Nicolette Joan, *d* of Hon. Cyril Ward, MVO; *m* 1968, Sheran Cazalet. *Educ:* Eton; New Coll., Oxford; Harvard Business Sch. 2nd Lieut, Grenadier Guards, 1953–55. Entered W. H. Smith & Son, 1958, Dir, 1965; Gp Chief Exec., W. H. Smith & Son (Holdings), 1978–82. Mem. Exec. Cttee, 1966–, Property Cttee, 1979–86, Council 1976–, National Trust; Mem. Adv. Council, Victoria and Albert Museum, 1971–75; Council, RSA, 1985–90; Trustee, British Museum, 1975–85; Chairman: Design Council, 1986–; Assoc. for Business Sponsorship of the Arts, 1988–; President: Book Trust, 1990– (Dep. Chm., 1976–78, Chm., 1978–80, NBL); Newsvendors' Benevolent Instn, 1989–. *Recreations:* gardening, golf. *Address:* 8 Ennismore Gardens, SW7 1LN. *T:* 071–584 1597; Lake House, Pusey, Faringdon, Oxon SN7 8QB. *T:* Buckland (036787) 659. *Club:* Garrick.

HORNE, Sir (Alan) Gray (Antony), 3rd Bt *cr* 1929; *b* 11 July 1948; *s* of Antony Edgar Alan Horne (*d* 1954) (*o s* of 2nd Bt), and of Valentine Antonia, *d* of Valentine Dudensing; *S* grandfather, 1984; *m* 1981. *Heir:* none. *Address:* Château du Basty, Thenon, Dordogne, France.

HORNE, Alistair Allan; author, journalist, lecturer; *b* 9 Nov. 1925; *s* of late Sir (James) Allan Horne and Lady (Auriol Camilla) Horne (*née* Hay); *m* 1st, 1953, Renira Margaret (marr. diss. 1982), *d* of Adm. Sir Geoffrey Hawkins, KBE, CB, MVO, DSC; three *d*; 2nd, 1987, Mrs Sheelin Eccles. *Educ:* Le Rosey, Switzerland; Millbrook, USA; Jesus Coll., Cambridge (MA). Served War of 1939–45: RAF, 1943–44; Coldstream Gds, 1944–47; Captain, attached Intelligence Service (ME). Dir, Ropley Trust Ltd, 1948–77; Foreign Correspondent, Daily Telegraph, 1952–55. Founded Alistair Horne Res. Fellowship in Mod. History, St Antony's Coll., Oxford, 1969, Supernumerary Fellow, 1978–. Fellow, Woodrow Wilson Center, Washington, DC, USA, 1980–81. Lectures: Lees Knowles, Cambridge, 1982; Goodman, Univ. of West Ontario, 1983. Member: Management Cttee, Royal Literary Fund, 1969–; Franco-British Council, 1979–; Cttee of Management, Soc. of Authors, 1979–82; Trustee, Imperial War Museum, 1975–82. FRSL. *Publications:* Back into Power, 1955; The Land is Bright, 1958; Canada and the Canadians, 1961; The Price of Glory: Verdun 1916, 1962 (Hawthornden Prize, 1963); The Fall of Paris: The Siege and The Commune 1870–71, 1965, rev. 2nd edn 1990; To Lose a Battle: France 1940, 1969, rev. 2nd edn 1990; Death of a Generation, 1970; The Terrible Year: The Paris Commune, 1971; Small Earthquake in Chile, 1972, rev. 2nd edn 1990; A Savage War of Peace: Algeria 1954–62, 1977 (Yorkshire Post Book of Year Prize, 1978; Wolfson Literary Award, 1978), rev. 2nd edn 1987; Napoleon, Master of Europe 1805–1807, 1979; The French Army and Politics 1870–1970, 1984 (Enid Macleod Prize, 1985); Macmillan: the official biography, Vol. I, 1894–1956, 1988, Vol. 2, 1957–1986, 1989; contribs to books: Combat: World War I, ed Don Congdon, 1964; Impressions of America, ed R. A. Brown, 1966; Marshal V. I. Chuikov, The End of the Third Reich, 1967; Sports and Games in Canadian Life, ed N. and M. L. Howell, 1969; Decisive Battles of the Twentieth Century, ed N. Frankland and C. Dowling, 1976; The War Lords: Military Commanders of the Twentieth Century, ed Field Marshal Sir M. Carver, 1976; Regular Armies and Insurgency, ed R. Haycock, 1979; Macmillan: a life in pictures, 1983; contribs various periodicals. *Recreations:* ski-ing, painting, gardening, travel. *Address:* The Old Vicarage, Turville, near Henley-on-Thames, Oxon RG9 6QU. *Clubs:* Garrick, Beefsteak.

HORNE, David Oliver, FCA; Chairman and Chief Executive, Lloyds Merchant Bank, since 1988; *b* 7 March 1932; *s* of Herbert Oliver Horne, MBE and Edith Marion Horne (*née* Sellers); *m* 1959, Joyce Heather (*née* Kynoch); two *s* two *d. Educ:* Fettes College, Edinburgh. Director: S. G. Warburg & Co., 1966–70; Williams & Glyn's Bank, 1970–78; Lloyds Bank International, 1978–85; Managing Dir, Lloyds Merchant Bank, 1985–87. *Recreation:* golf. *Address:* Four Winds, 5 The Gardens, Esher, Surrey KT10 8QF. *T:* Esher (0372) 463510; Lloyds Merchant Bank Ltd, 48 Chiswell Street, EC1Y 4XX.

HORNE, Frederic Thomas; Chief Taxing Master of the Supreme Court, 1983–88 (Master, 1967–83); *b* 21 March 1917; *y s* of Lionel Edward Horne, JP, Moreton-in-Marsh, Glos; *m* 1944, Madeline Hatton; two *s* two *d. Educ:* Chipping Campden Grammar Sch. Admitted a Solicitor (Hons), 1938. Served with RAFVR in General Duties Branch (Pilot), 1939–56. Partner in Iliffe Sweet & Co., 1956–67. Mem., Lord Chancellor's Adv. Cttee on Legal Aid, 1983–; Chm., Working Party on the Simplification of Taxation, 1980–83 (Horne Report, 1983). *Publications:* Cordery's Law Relating to Solicitors, 7th edn (jtly) 1981, 8th edn 1987; (contrib.) Atkins Encyclopaedia of Court Forms, 2nd edn, 1983; (ed jtly) The Supreme Court Practice, 1985 and 1988 edns; (contrib.) Private International Litigation, 1987. *Recreations:* cricket, music, archaeology. *Address:* Dunstall, Quickley Lane, Chorleywood, Herts WD3 5AF. *Club:* MCC.

HORNE, Sir Gray; *see* Horne, Sir A. G. A.

HORNE, Prof. Michael Rex, OBE 1981; MA, PhD, ScD Cantab; MSc (Manchester); FRS 1981; FEng, FICE; FIStructE; Professor of Civil Engineering, University of Manchester, 1960–83 (Beyer Professor, 1978–83); *b* 29 Dec. 1921; *s* of late Rev. Ernest Horne, Leicester; *m* 1947, Molly, *d* of late Mark Hewett, Royston, Herts; two *s* two *d. Educ:* Boston (Lincs) Grammar Sch.; Leeds Grammar Sch.; St John's Coll., Cambridge. MA Cantab 1945; PhD Cantab 1950, ScD Cantab 1956. John Winbolt Prize for Research, Cambridge Univ., 1944. Asst Engineer, River Great Ouse Catchment Bd, 1941–45; Scientific Officer, British Welding Research Assoc., 1945–51; Asst Dir of Research in Engineering, 1951–56, Lectr in Engineering, 1957–60, Fellow of St John's Coll., 1957–60, Univ. of Cambridge. Royal Soc. Vis. Prof., Univ. of Hong Kong, 1986. Instn of Civil Engineers, Telford Premiums, 1956, 1966, 1978. Chm., NW Branch, 1969–70, Pres., 1980–81, IStructE; Pres., Section G, BAAS, 1981–82; Mem., Merrison Cttee on Box Girders, 1970–73; Chm., Review for Govt of Public Utility Streetworks Act, 1984. Hon. DSc Salford, 1981. Diploma, 1971, Bronze Medal, 1973, Gold Medal, 1986, IStructE; Baker Medal, ICE, 1977. *Publications:* (with J. F. Baker and J. Heyman) The Steel Skeleton, 1956; (with W. F. Merchant) The Stability of Frames, 1965; The Plastic Theory of Structures, 1971; (with L. J. Morris) Plastic Design of Low Rise Frames, 1981; contribs on structures, strength of materials and particulate theory of soils to learned journals. *Recreations:* photography, theatre-going, foreign travel. *Address:* 19 Park Road, Hale, Altrincham, Cheshire WA15 9NW.

HORNE, Dr Nigel William, FEng 1982; FIEE; Information Technology Partner, KMPG Peat Marwick McLintock, since 1990; *b* 13 Sept. 1940; *s* of late Eric Charles Henry and Edith Margaret Horne; *m* 1965, Jennifer Ann Holton; one *s* two *d. Educ:* John Lyon Sch., Harrow; Univ. of Bristol (BScEng 1962); Univ. of of Cambridge (PhD 1968). FIEE 1984. GEC Telecommunications, 1958–70; Management Systems Manager, 1970–72; Manufg Gen. Manager, 1972–75; Dir and Gen. Manager, Switching, 1976–82; Managing Dir, GEC Inf. Systems, 1982–83; Director: Technical and Corporate Develt, STC, 1983–90; Abingworth, 1985–90; LSI Logic, 1986–90. Vis. Prof., Univ. of Bristol, 1990. Mem., Nat. Electronics Council, 1985–90; Chm., Computing and Control Div., IEE,

1988–89; Chm., DTI/SERC IT Adv. Bd, 1988–; Mem., EC Esprit Adv. Bd, 1988–. FRSA. Freeman, City of London; Mem., Guild of Inf. Technologists. *Publications:* papers in learned jls. *Recreations:* piano, walking, gardening. *Address:* KPMG Peat Marwick McLintock, PO Box 486, 1 Puddle Dock, EC4V 3PD. *T:* 071–236 8000. *Club:* United Oxford & Cambridge University.

HORNE, Robert Drake; Under-Secretary, Department of Education and Science, since 1988; *b* 23 April 1945; *s* of late Harold Metcalfe Horne and of Dorothy Katharine Horne; *m* 1972, Jennifer Mary (*née* Gill); three *d*. *Educ:* Mill Hill Sch.; Oriel Coll., Oxford (MA Classics). Asst Master, Eton Coll., Windsor, 1967–68; DES, 1968–; seconded to Cabinet Office, 1979–80. *Recreations:* running, entertaining Australians. *Address:* Department of Education and Science, Sanctuary Buildings, Great Smith Street, SW1.

HORNER, Arthur William, CMG 1964; TD and clasp 1946; *b* 22 June 1909; *s* of Francis Moore and Edith Horner; *m* 1938, Patricia Denise (*née* Campbell); two *s* one *d*. *Educ:* Hardenwick; Felsted. Marine Insurance, 1926–39. Served War, 1939–46, Rifle Brigade; Lieut-Col; psc. Farming in Kenya, 1948–50. Colonial Administrative Service (later HM Overseas Civil Service), Kenya, 1950–64; Commissioner of Lands, 1955–61; Permanent Sec., 1961–64; Dir of Independence Celebrations, 1963; Principal, ODM, 1964–73; seconded Diplomatic Service, 1968–70, retired 1973. *Recreations:* music, gardening. *Address:* St Margaret's Cottage, Northiam, Rye, East Sussex TN31 6NJ.

HORNER, Douglas George, FCIB; Chairman, Mercantile Credit Company, 1980–84; Vice-Chairman, 1979–81, Director, 1975–84, Barclays Bank UK Limited; *b* Dec. 1917; *s* of Albert and Louise Horner; *m* 1941, Gwendoline Phyllis Wall; one *s*. *Educ:* Enfield Grammar Sch. Commissioned, Royal Norfolk Regt, 1940. Asst Manager/Manager at various bank branches, 1954–71; Local Dir, Lombard Street, 1971; Regional Gen. Manager, London, 1973; Gen. Man., 1975; Senior Gen. Man., 1977; Dir Barclays Bank plc, 1977–83. *Recreations:* golf, gardening. *Address:* Barclays Bank plc, 54 Lombard Street, EC3P 3AH.

HORNER, Frederick, DSc; CEng, FIEE; Director, Appleton Laboratory, Science Research Council, 1977–79; *b* 28 Aug. 1918; *s* of late Frederick and Mary Horner; *m* 1946, Elizabeth Bonsey; one *s* one *d*. *Educ:* Bolton Sch.; Univ. of Manchester (Ashbury Scholar, 1937; Fairbairn Engrg Prize, 1939; BSc 1st Cl. Hons 1939; MSc 1941; DSc 1968). CEng, FIEE 1959. On staff of DSIR, NPL, 1941–52; UK Scientific Mission, Washington DC, 1947; Radio Research Station, later Appleton Lab. of SRC, 1952–79, Dep. Dir, 1969–77; Admin. Staff Coll., Henley, 1959. Delegate: Internat. Union of Radio Science, 1950– (Chm., Commn VIII, 1966–69); Internat. Radio Consultative Cttee, 1953– (Internat. Chm., Study Group 2, 1980–90). Member: Inter-Union Commn on Frequency Allocations for Radio Astronomy and Space Science, 1965– (Sec., 1975–82); Electronics Divl Bd, IEE, 1970–76. Mem. Council: RHC, 1979–85 (Vice-Chm., 1982–85); RHBNC, 1985–89; Hon. Associate, Physics: RHC, 1975–85; RHBNC, 1985–. Diplôme d'Honneur, Internat. Radio Cons. Cttee, 1989. *Publications:* more than 50 scientific papers. *Recreations:* tennis, gardening. *Address:* Gordano Lodge, Clevedon Road, Weston-in-Gordano, Bristol BS20 8PZ.

HORNER, John; *b* 5 Nov. 1911; *s* of Ernest Charles and Emily Horner; *m* 1936, Patricia, *d* of Geoffrey and Alice Palmer; two *d*. *Educ:* elementary sch. and Sir George Monoux Grammar Sch., Walthamstow. Apprenticed Merchant Navy, 1927; Second Mate's Certificate, 1932. Joined London Fire Brigade, 1933; Gen. Sec. Fire Brigades Union, 1939–64; MP (Lab) Oldbury and Halesowen, 1964–70. Mem. Select Cttee on Nationalised Industries. *Publication:* Studies in Industrial Democracy, 1974. *Recreations:* gardening, reading history. *Address:* c/o Barclays Bank, Ross-on-Wye, Herefordshire.

HORNSBY, Timothy Richard, MA; Chief Executive, Royal Borough of Kingston upon Thames, since 1991; *b* 22 Sept. 1940; *s* of late Harker William Hornsby and Agnes Nora French; *m* 1971, Dr Charmian Rosemary Newton; one *s* one *d*. *Educ:* Bradfield Coll.; Christ Church, Oxford Univ. (MA 1st C1. Hons Modern History). Harkness Fellow, USA, at Harvard, Columbia, Henry E. Huntington Research Inst., 1961–63; Asst Prof., Birmingham Southern Coll., Alabama, 1963–64; Research Lectr, Christ Church, Oxford, 1964–65; Asst Principal, Min. of Public Building and Works, 1965–67; Private Sec. to Controller General, 1968–69; HM Treasury, 1971–73; Prin. Asst Sec., DoE, 1975; Dir, Ancient Monuments, Historic Buildings and Rural Affairs, DoE, 1983–88; Dir Gen., Nature Conservancy Council, 1988–91; Dir, Construction Policy Directorate, DoE, 1991. FRSA. *Recreations:* conservation, skiing, talking. *Address:* Royal Borough of Kingston upon Thames, Guildhall, Kingston upon Thames KT1 1EU. *T:* 081–547 5002. *Club:* Athenæum.

HOROWITZ, Michael; QC 1990; *b* 18 Oct. 1943; *s* of David Horowitz and late Irene Horowitz; *m* 1986, Gillian Mary Darley; one *d* (one *s* decd). *Educ:* St Marylebone Grammar School; Pembroke College, Cambridge (BA 1966; LLB 1967). Pres., Cambridge Union Soc., 1967; English-Speaking Union Debating Tour of USA, 1967. Called to the Bar, Lincoln's Inn, 1968; Asst Recorder, 1987. Senate of Inns of Court and Bar, 1982–85. *Recreations:* music, history. *Address:* 1 Mitre Court Buildings, Temple, EC4Y 7BS. *T:* 071–353 0434.

HOROWITZ, Prof. Myer, OC 1990; EdD; Professor Emeritus of Education, University of Alberta, Canada, since 1989; *b* 27 Dec. 1932; *s* of Philip Horowitz and Fanny Cotler; *m* 1956, Barbara, *d* of Samuel Rosen and Grace Midvidy, Montreal; two *d*. *Educ:* High Sch., Montreal; Sch. for Teachers, Macdonald Coll.; Sir George Williams Univ. (BA); Univ. of Alberta (MEd); Stanford Univ. (EdD). Teacher, Schs in Montreal, Sch. Bd, Greater Montreal, 1952–60. McGill University: Lectr in Educn, 1960–63; Asst Prof., 1963–65; Associate Prof., 1965–67; Asst to Dir, 1964–65; Prof. of Educn, 1967–69 and Asst Dean, 1965–69; University of Alberta: Prof. and Chm., Dept Elem. Educn, 1969; Dean, Faculty of Educn, 1972–75; Vice-Pres. (Academic), 1975–79; Pres. of Univ., 1979–89. Hon. Dr: McGill, 1979; Concordia, 1982; Athabasca, 1989; British Columbia, 1990; Alberta, 1990. *Address:* University of Alberta, Edmonton, Alberta T6G 2G5, Canada; 14319, 60 Avenue, Edmonton, Alberta T6H 1J8.

HORRELL, John Ray, CBE 1979; TD; DL; farmer; Leader, Cambridgeshire County Council, since 1989; *b* 8 March 1929; *er s* of late Harry Ray Horrell and of Phyllis Mary Horrell (*née* Whittome); *m* 1951, Mary Elizabeth Noëlle Dickinson; one *s* one *d*. Director: Horrell's Farmers Ltd; Horrell's Dairies Ltd. Mem., Board, Peterborough New Town Develt Corp., 1970–88; formerly Mem. Oakes and Taylor Cttees of Enquiry. Mem., Cambs (formerly Huntingdon and Peterborough) CC, 1963– (Chm., 1971–77; Chm., Educn Cttee); Chairman: Council of Local Educn Authorities, 1976–79; ACC, 1981–83 (Vice-Chm., 1979–81); E of England Agricl Soc., 1984–87. Mem. Council, CGLI, 1975–. Major, TA; a Vice-Chm., 1977–86, Chm., 1986–91, E Anglia TA&VRA. FRSA 1981. High Sheriff, Cambs, 1981–82; DL Cambs, 1973. *Address:* The Grove, Longthorpe, Peterborough PE3 6LZ. *T:* Peterborough (0733) 262618.

HORRELL, Roger William, CMG 1988; OBE 1974; HM Diplomatic Service; Counsellor, Foreign and Commonwealth Office, since 1980; *b* 9 July 1935; *s* of William John Horrell and Dorice Enid (*née* Young); *m* 1970, Patricia Mildred Eileen Smith (*née* Binns) (marr. diss. 1975); one *s* one *d*. *Educ:* Shebbear College; Exeter College, Oxford. MA. Served in Devonshire Regt, 1953–55; Colonial Administrative Service, Kenya, 1959–64; joined Foreign Office, 1964; Economic Officer, Dubai, 1965–67; FCO, 1967–70; First Sec., Kampala, 1970–73; FCO, 1973–76; First Sec., Lusaka, 1976–80. *Recreations:* cricket, reading, walking, bridge. *Address:* c/o Foreign and Commonwealth Office, SW1. *Clubs:* Reform; Frederick Pickersgill Memorial Cricket.

HORRIDGE, Prof. (George) Adrian, FRS 1969; FAA 1971; Professor, Research School of Biological Sciences, Australian National University, ACT 2601, since 1969; *b* Sheffield, England, 12 Dec. 1927; *s* of George William Horridge and Olive Stray; *m* 1954, Audrey Anne Lightburne; one *s* three *d*. *Educ:* King Edward VII Sch., Sheffield. Fellow, St John's Coll., Cambridge, 1953–56; on staff, St Andrews Univ., 1956–69; Dir, Gatty Marine Laboratory, St Andrews, 1960–69. *Publications:* Structure and Function of the Nervous Systems of Invertebrates (with T. H. Bullock), 1965; Interneurons, 1968; (ed) The Compound Eye and Vision of Insects, 1975; Monographs of the Maritime Museum at Greenwich nos 38, 39, 40, 54, 1979–; The Prahu: traditional sailing boat of Indonesia, 1982 (Oxford in Asia); Sailing Craft of Indonesia, 1985 (Oxford in Asia); Outrigger Canoes of Bali & Madura, Indonesia, 1986; contribs numerous scientific papers on behaviour and nervous systems of lower animals, to jls, etc. *Recreations:* optics, mathematics, marine biology; sailing, language, arts, boat construction in Indonesia. *Address:* PO Box 475, Canberra City, ACT 2601, Australia. *T:* Canberra 062–494532, *Fax:* 61–6–2493808.

HORROCKS, Raymond, CBE 1983; Chairman, since 1988, Chief Executive, since 1989, Chloride Group (Director, since 1986); Chairman: Owenbell Ltd, since 1987; Kay Consultancy Group plc, since 1989; Deputy Chairman, Applied Chemicals UK, since 1988; Non-executive Director: Electrocomponents plc, since 1986; Lookers plc, since 1986; SMAC Group plc, since 1989 (Chairman, 1988–89); *b* 9 Jan. 1930; *s* of Elsie and Cecil Horrocks; *m* 1953, Pamela Florence Russell; three *d*. *Educ:* Bolton Municipal Secondary School. Textile Industry, 1944–48 and 1950–51; HM Forces, Army, Intelligence Corps, 1948–50; Sales Rep., Proctor & Gamble, 1951–52; Merchandiser, Marks & Spencer, 1953–58; Sub Gp Buying Controller, Littlewoods Mail Order Stores, 1958–63; various plant, departmental and divisional management positions, Ford Motor Co., 1963–72; Regional Dir, Europe and Middle East, Materials Handling Gp, Eaton Corp., 1972–77; Chm. and Man. Dir, Austin Morris Ltd, 1978–80; Man. Dir, BL Cars, 1980–81; Chm. and Chief Exec., BL Cars Gp, 1981–82; Exec. Dir and Bd Mem., BL, 1981–86; Gp Chief Exec., Cars, 1982–86; Chairman: Unipart Group Ltd, 1981–86; Austin Rover Gp Hldgs, 1981–86; Jaguar Cars Holdings Ltd, 1982–84; non-executive Director: Jaguar plc, 1984–85; The Caravan Club, 1983–87; WOL Hldgs Ltd, 1988–89; Dir, Nuffield Services Ltd, 1982–86. Member: Council, CBI, 1981–86; Europe Cttee, CBI, 1985–86. FIMI; CBIM; FRSA. *Recreations:* fly fishing, gardening, walking. *Address:* Far End, Riverview Road, Pangbourne, Reading, Berks RG8 7AU.

HORSBRUGH, Ian Robert; Principal, Guildhall School of Music and Drama, since 1988; *b* 16 Sept. 1941; *s* of Walter and Sheila Horsbrugh; *m* 1965, Caroline Everett; two *s* two *d*. *Educ:* St Paul's Sch.; Guildhall Sch. of Music and Drama (AGSM); Royal Coll. of Music (ARCM). FGSM 1988; FRCM 1988. Head of Music: St Mary's Sch., Hendon, 1969–72; Villiers High Sch., Southall, 1972–79; Dep. Warden, ILEA Music Centre, 1979–84; Vice-Dir, Royal Coll. of Music, 1985–88. Mem., Music Panel and Chm., New Music Sub-Cttee, Arts Council, 1981–87; Member: Music Adv. Cttee, British Council, 1987–; Steering Cttee, Nat. Studio for Electronic Music, 1986–89; London Arts Bd, 1991–; Bd, City Arts Trust, 1989–; Management Bd, London Internat. String Quartet Competition, 1989–; Council, NYO, 1989–; Vice-Pres., Nat. Assoc. of Youth Orchestras, 1989–; Chm., Trustees, Parkhouse Award, 1990–. Treasurer, 1977–79, Chm., 1979–84, New Macnaghten Concerts. FRSA. *Publication:* Leoš Janáček: the field that prospered, 1981. *Recreations:* watching Rugby football and cricket, reading, walking. *Address:* Guildhall School of Music and Drama, Barbican, Silk Street, EC2Y 8DT. *T:* 071–628 2571. *Club:* MCC.

HORSBRUGH-PORTER, Sir John (Simon), 4th Bt *cr* 1902; *b* 18 Dec. 1938; *s* of Col Sir Andrew Marshall Horsbrugh-Porter, 3rd Bt, DSO and Bar, and of Annette Mary, *d* of Brig.-Gen. R. C. Browne-Clayton, DSO; *S* father, 1986; *m* 1964, Lavinia Rose, *d* of Ralph Turton; one *s* two *d*. *Educ:* Winchester College; Trinity Coll., Cambridge (BA Hons History). School Master. *Recreations:* gliding, literature, music. *Heir:* *s* Andrew Alexander Marshall Horsbrugh-Porter, *b* 19 Jan. 1971. *Address:* Bowers Croft, Coleshill, Amersham, Bucks. *T:* Amersham (0494) 724596.

HORSBURGH, John Millar Stewart, QC (Scot.) 1980; Sheriff of Lothian and Borders at Edinburgh, since 1990; *b* 15 May 1938; *s* of late Alexander Horsburgh and Helen Margaret Watson Millar or Horsburgh; *m* 1966, Johann Catriona Gardner, MB, ChB, DObst RCOG; one *s* one *d*. *Educ:* Hutchesons' Boys' Grammar Sch., Glasgow; Univ. of Glasgow (MA Hons, LLB). Admitted to Scots Bar, 1965; Advocate-Depute, 1987–89. Part-time Mem., Lands Tribunal for Scotland, 1985–87. *Address:* 8 Laverockbank Road, Edinburgh EH5 3DG. *T:* 031–552 5328.

HORSEFIELD, John Keith, CB 1957; Historian, International Monetary Fund, 1966–69; *b* 14 Oct. 1901; *s* of Rev. Canon F. J. Horsefield, Bristol; *m* 1934, Lucy G. G. Florance. *Educ:* Monkton Combe Sch.; University of Bristol; MA 1948, DSc 1971; London Sch. of Economics. Lecturer, LSE, 1939; Min. of Aircraft Production, 1940; International Monetary Fund, 1947; Under-Sec., Min. of Supply, 1951; Dep. Asst Sec.-Gen. for Economics and Finance, NATO, 1952; Supply and Development Officer, Iron and Steel Bd, 1954; Dir of Finance and Accounts, Gen. Post Office, 1955–60; Chief Editor, International Monetary Fund, 1960–66. *Publications:* The Real Cost of the War, 1940; British Monetary Experiments, 1650–1710, 1960; The International Monetary Fund, 1945–1965, 1970; articles in Economica, etc. *Address:* 60 Clatterford Road, Carisbrooke, Newport, Isle of Wight PO30 1PA. *T:* Isle of Wight (0983) 523675.

HORSEY, Gordon, JP; a District Judge, since 1991; *b* 20 July 1926; *s* of late E. W. Horsey, MBE, and of H. V. Horsey; *m* 1951, Jean Mary (*née* Favill); one *d*. *Educ:* Magnus Grammar Sch., Newark, Notts; St Catharine's Coll., Cambridge. BA, LLB. Served RN, 1944–45, RE, 1945–48 (Captain). Admitted solicitor, 1953; private practice in Nottingham, 1953–71; Registrar: Coventry County Court, 1971; Leicester County Court, 1973; a Recorder, 1978–84. JP Leics, 1975. *Recreation:* fly-fishing. *Address:* 23 The Ridgeway, Rothley, Leics LE7 7LE. *T:* Leicester (0533) 302545.

HORSFALL, Sir John (Musgrave), 3rd Bt *cr* 1909; MC 1946; TD 1949 and clasp 1951; JP; *b* 26 Aug. 1915; *s* of Sir (John) Donald Horsfall, 2nd Bt, and Henrietta (*d* 1936), *d* of William Musgrave; *S* father, 1975; *m* 1940, Cassandra Nora Bernardine, *d* of late G. E. Wright; two *s* one *d*. *Educ:* Uppingham. Major, Duke of Wellington's Regt. Dir, Skipton Building Society, 1960–85, retd. Mem. Skipton RDC, 1952–74; Pres. Skipton Divl Conservative Assoc., 1966–79. Pres., Worsted Spinners Fedn, 1961–64. JP North Yorks, 1959. *Recreation:* shooting. *Heir:* *s* Edward John Wright Horsfall [*b* 17 Dec. 1940; *m* 1965, Rosemary, *d* of Frank N. King; three *s*]. *Address:* Greenfield House, Embsay, Skipton, North Yorkshire BD23 6SD. *T:* Skipton (0756) 794560.

HORSFIELD, Maj.-Gen. David Ralph, OBE 1962; FIEE; *b* 17 Dec. 1916; *s* of late Major Ralph B. and Morah Horsfield (*née* Baynes); *m* 1948, Sheelah Patricia Royal Eagan; two *s* two *d*. *Educ*: Oundle Sch.; RMA Woolwich; Cambridge Univ. (MA). Commnd in Royal Signals, 1936; comd Burma Corps Signals, 1942; Instr, Staff Coll., 1944–45; comd 2 Indian Airborne Signals, 1946–47; Instr, RMA Sandhurst, 1950–53 (Company Comdr to HM King Hussein of Jordan); comd 2 Signal Regt, 1956–59; Principal Army Staff Officer, MoD, Malaya, 1959–61; Dir of Telecommunications (Army), 1966–68; ADC to the Queen, 1968–69; Deputy Communications and Electronics, Supreme HQ Allied Powers, Europe, 1968–69; Maj.-Gen. 1969; Chief Signal Officer, BAOR, 1969–72; Col Comdt, Royal Signals, 1972–78. Vice Pres., Nat. Ski Fedn, 1978–81. *Recreations*: ski-ing (British Ski Champion, 1949), the visual arts. *Address*: Southill House, Cranmore, Shepton Mallet, Somerset BA4 4QS. *T*: Cranmore (074988) 395. *Club*: Ski Club of Great Britain.

HORSFIELD, Peter Muir Francis, QC 1978; *b* 15 Feb. 1932; *s* of Henry Taylor Horsfield, AFC, and Florence Lily (*née* Muir); *m* 1962, Anne Charlotte, *d* of late Sir Piers Debenham, 2nd Bt, and Lady (Angela) Debenham; three *s*. *Educ*: Beaumont; Trinity Coll., Oxford (BA 1st Cl. Hons Mods and Greats). Served RNR, 1955–57; Lieut RNR, 1960. Called to the Bar, Middle Temple, 1958, Bencher, 1984; in practice at Chancery Bar, 1958–. *Recreations*: painting, observational astronomy. *Address*: (chambers) 8 Stone Buildings, Lincoln's Inn, WC2A 3TA. *Club*: Garrick.

HORSFORD, Alan Arthur; Group Chief Executive, Royal Insurance plc, 1985–89; *b* 31 May 1927; *s* of Arthur Henry Horsford and Winifred Horsford; *m* 1957, Enid Maureen Baker; one *s* one *d*. *Educ*: Holt School; Liverpool University. BA; FCII. Secretary, Royal Insurance Co. Ltd, 1970–72; Dep. General Manager, 1972–74, General Manager, 1974–79, Royal Insurance Canada; General Manager and Director, 1979–83, Dep. Chief Gen. Manager, 1983–84, Royal Insurance plc. Dep. Chm., Assoc. of British Insurers, 1985–88. *Recreations*: theatre, music, cycling, golf. *Address*: 17 Darnhills, Watford Road, Radlett, Herts WD7 8LQ.

HORSFORD, Maj.-Gen. Derek Gordon Thomond, CBE 1962 (MBE 1953); DSO 1944 and Bar 1945; *b* 7 Feb. 1917; *s* of late Captain H. T. Horsford, The Gloucestershire Regt, and Mrs V. E. Horsford; *m* 1948, Sheila Louise Russell Crawford; one *s* (and one step *s* two step *d*). *Educ*: Clifton Coll.; RMC, Sandhurst. Commissioned into 8th Gurkha Rifles, 1937; despatches 1943 and 1945; comd 4/1 Gurkha Rifles, Burma, 1944–45; transf. to RA, 1948; Instructor Staff Coll., 1950–52; transf. to King's Regt, 1950; GSO1, 2nd Infantry Div., 1955–56; comd 1st Bn, The King's Regt, 1957–59; AAG, AG2, War Office, 1959–60; Comdr 24th Infantry Brigade Group, Dec. 1960–Dec. 1962; Imperial Defence Coll., 1963; Brig., Gen. Staff, HQ, BAOR, 1964–66. Maj.-Gen. 1966; GOC 50 (Northumbrian) Div./Dist, 1966–67; GOC Yorks Dist, 1967–68; GOC 17 Div./Malaya District, 1969–70; Maj.-Gen., Brigade of Gurkhas, 1969–71; Dep. Comdr Land Forces, Hong Kong, 1970–71, retired. Col, The King's Regt, 1965–70; Col, The Gurkha Transport Regt, 1973–78. *Recreations*: travel, outdoor life. *Club*: Army and Navy.

HORSHAM, Bishop Suffragan of, since 1991; **Rt. Rev. John William Hind;** *b* 19 June 1945; *s* of Harold Hind and Joan Mary Hind; *m* 1966, Janet Helen McLintock; three *s*. *Educ*: Watford Grammar Sch.; Leeds Univ. (BA 1966). Asst Master, Leeds Modern Sch., 1966–69; Asst Lectr, King Alfred's Coll, Winchester, 1969–70; Cuddesdon Theol Coll.; Deacon 1972, Priest 1973; Asst Curate, St John's, Catford, 1972–76; Vicar, Christ Church, Forest Hill, 1976–82 and Priest-in-Charge, St Paul's, Forest Hill, 1981–82; Principal, Chichester Theol Coll., 1982–91. Canon Residentiary and Bursalis Preb., Chichester Cathedral, 1982–90. *Recreations*: judo, languages. *Address*: Bishop's Lodge, Worth, Crawley, West Sussex RH10 4RT.

HORSHAM, Archdeacon of; *see* Filby, Ven. W. C. L.

HORSHAM, Jean, CBE 1979; Deputy Parliamentary Commissioner for Administration, 1981–82, retired; Chairman, Solicitors Complaints Bureau, 1986–89; *b* 25 June 1922; *d* of Albert John James Horsham and Janet Horsham (*née* Henderson). *Educ*: Keith Grammar Sch. Forestry Commn, 1939–64, seconded to Min. of Supply, 1940–45; Min. of Land and Natural Resources, 1964–66; Min. of Housing and Local Govt, 1966; Office of Parly Comr for Administration, 1967–82. Member: Subsidence Compensation Review Cttee, 1983–84; Law Soc. Professional Purposes Cttee, 1984–86; Council on Tribunals, 1986–; Chorus Enquiry at Royal Opera House, 1988–89; Tribunals Cttee, Judicial Studies Bd, 1990–. *Address*: 14 Cotelands, Chichester Road, Croydon, Surrey CR0 5UD.

HORSLEY, Rev. Canon Alan Avery; Vicar, Mill End and Heronsgate with West Hyde, since 1991; *b* 13 May 1936; *s* of Reginald James and Edith Irene Horsley; *m* 1966, Mary Joy Marshall, MA; two *d*. *Educ*: St Chad's Coll., Durham (BA 1958); Birmingham Univ.; Pacific Western Univ., Calif (MA 1984; PhD 1985); Queen's Coll., Birmingham. Deacon 1960, priest 1961, Peterborough; Assistant Curate: Daventry, 1960–63; St Giles, Reading, 1963–64; St Paul's, Wokingham, 1964–66; Vicar of Yeadon, dio. Bradford, 1966–71; Rector of Heyford and Stowe Nine Churches, dio. Peterborough, 1971–78; RD of Daventry, 1976–78; Vicar of Oakham with Hambleton and Egleton (and Braunston and Brooke from 1980), 1978–86; Non-Residentiary Canon of Peterborough, 1979–86; Chaplain: Catmose Vale Hosp., 1978–86; Rutland Memorial Hosp., 1978–86; Vicar of Lanteglos-by-Fowey, dio. Truro, 1986–88; Canon Emeritus of Peterborough, 1986–; Provost of St Andrew's Cathedral, Inverness, 1988–91; Priest in Charge: St Mary in the Fields, Culloden, 1988–91; St Paul, Strath Nairn, 1988–91. *Publications*: (with Mary J. Horsley) A Lent Course, 1967, 2nd edn 1982; Lent with St Luke, 1978, 2nd edn 1984; Action at Lanteglos and Polruan, 1987; contribs to Rutland Record Soc. Jl. *Recreations*: music, piano and organ, cultivation of flowers, historical research. *Address*: St Peter's Vicarage, Berry Lane, Rickmansworth WD3 2HQ. *T*: Rickmansworth (0923) 772785.

HORSLEY, Air Marshal Sir (Beresford) Peter (Torrington), KCB 1974; CBE 1964; LVO 1956; AFC 1945; idc; psc; pfc; *b* 26 March 1921; *s* of late Capt. Arthur Beresford Horsley, CBE; *m* 1st, 1943, Phyllis Conrad Phinney (marr. diss. 1976); one *s* one *d*; 2nd, 1976, Ann MacKinnon, *d* of Gareth and Frances Crwys-Williams; two step *s* two step *d*. *Educ*: Wellington Coll. Joined Royal Air Force, 1940; served in 2nd TAF and Fighter Command. Adjt Oxford Univ. Air Sqdn, 1948; Commands: No 9 and No 29 Sqdns, RAF Wattisham, RAF Akrotiri. Equerry to Princess Elizabeth and to the Duke of Edinburgh, 1949–52; Equerry to the Queen, 1952–53; Equerry to the Duke of Edinburgh, 1953–56. Dep. Comdt, Jt Warfare Establishment, RAF Old Sarum, 1966–68; Asst CAS (Operations), 1968–70; AOC No 1 (Bomber) Gp, 1971–73; Dep. C-in-C, Strike Comd, 1973–75. Retired RAF, 1975. Chairman: ML Hldgs, 1988–; National Printing Ink Co., 1987–; Director: ML Aerospace and Defence, 1988–; ML Aviation, 1976–; ML Wallop Hldgs, 1988–; ML Wallop SA, 1988–; Horsley Hldgs, 1985–; RCR Internat., 1984–; IDS Aircraft, 1983–. Mem., Honeywell Adv. Council, 1978–. Pres., Yorkshire Sports, 1986–. Croix de Guerre, 1944. Holds Orders of Christ (Portugal), North Star (Sweden), and Menelik (Ethiopia). *Publication*: (as Peter Beresford) Journal of a Stamp Collector, 1972. *Recreations*: ski-ing, philately. *Address*: c/o Barclays Bank, High Street, Newmarket.

HORSLEY, Colin, OBE 1963; FRCM 1973; Hon. RAM 1977; pianist; Professor, Royal College of Music, London; *b* Wanganui, New Zealand, 23 April 1920. *Educ*: Royal College of Music. Debut at invitation of Sir John Barbirolli at Hallé Concerts, Manchester, 1943. Soloist with all leading orchestras of Great Britain, the Royal Philharmonic Soc. (1953, 1959), Promenade Concerts, etc. Toured Belgium, Holland, Spain, France, Scandinavia, Malta, Ceylon, Malaya, Australia and New Zealand. Festival appearances include Aix-en-Provence, International Contemporary Music Festival, Palermo, British Music Festivals in Belgium, Holland and Finland. Broadcasts frequently, and records for His Master's Voice and Meridian Records. *Recreation*: gardening. *Address*: Tawsden Manor, Brenchley, Kent. *T*: Brenchley (089272) 2323.

HORSLEY, (George) Nicholas (Seward); Chairman, 1970–86, Deputy Chairman, 1986–88, Northern Foods plc, retired; non-executive Chairman, Millway Foods Limited, 1988–89; *b* 21 April 1934; *s* of Alec Stewart Horsley and Ida Seward Horsley; *m* 1st, 1958, Valerie Anne Edwards (marr. diss. 1975); two *s* one *d*; 2nd, 1975, Sabita Sarkar (marr. diss. 1987); 3rd, Alwyne Marjorie Law. *Educ*: Keswick Grammar Sch.; Bootham Sch., York; Worcester Coll., Oxford (BA). Freelance journalist, 1957–58. Northern Dairies Ltd: Trainee Manager, 1958; Director, 1963; Vice-Chairman, 1968–70 (Northern Dairies Ltd changed its name to Northern Foods Ltd in 1972). Chm., News on Sunday Publishing, 1986–87. Pres., Dairy Trade Fedn, 1975–77 and 1980–85. Chm., BBC Consultative Group on Industrial and Business Affairs, 1980–83; Mem., BBC Gen. Adv. Council, 1980–83. *Recreations*: music, bridge, local pub, watching cricket, reading. *Address*: Barbados, West Indies. *Club*: Groucho.

HORSLEY, Sir Peter; *see* Horsley, Sir B. P. T.

HORSLEY, Stephen Daril; Regional Medical Officer, North Western Regional Health Authority, since 1986; *b* 23 June 1947; *s* of Donald Vincent Horsley and Marie Margaret Horsley; *m* 1974, Vivienne Marjorie Lee; one *s* two *d*. *Educ*: Guy's Hosp.; Manchester Business Sch. (MBSc 1985). FRCP 1988 (MRCP 1976); FFCM. Gen. Hosp. Medicine, Truro, 1971–75; Community Medicine, Yorks RHA, 1975–79; District Community Physician, E Cumbria HA, 1979–82; District MO, S Cumbria HA, 1982–85; Specialist in Community Medicine, Oxford RHA, 1985–86. *Publications*: contribs to BMJ, Community Medicine. *Recreations*: wind surfing, walking. *Address*: North Western Regional Health Authority, Gateway House, Piccadilly South, Manchester M60 7LP; Ulverston, Cumbria. *Club*: Border & County (Carlisle).

HORSMAN, Dame Dorothea (Jean), DBE 1986; JP; *b* 17 April 1918; *d* of Samuel Morrell and Jean (*née* Morris); *m* 1943, Ernest Alan Horsman; one *s* two *d*. *Educ*: Univ. of New Zealand (MA History); Univ. of Otago (MA Russian); Trained Teacher's Cert. Mem., Govt Working Party on Liquor Laws, 1985–86. President: NZ Fedn of University Women, 1973–76; Arthritis and Rheumatism Foundn of NZ, 1980–83; Mem., Bd of Management, 1976, Vice-Pres. 1980, Pres., 1982–86, Nat. Council of Women of NZ. Mem., Winston Churchill Meml Trust Bd, 1983–89. JP 1979. Silver Jubilee Medal, 1977. *Publications*: What Price Equality? (with J. J. Herd) (for Nat. Council of Women, NZ), 1974; Women at Home (with J. J. Herd) (for NZ Fedn of Univ. Women), 1976; (contrib. and ed) Women in Council—a History (NCW), 1982. *Recreations*: reading, listening to music. *Address*: 10 Balmoral Street, Opoho, Dunedin, New Zealand. *T*: (03) 473–7119.

HORSMAN, Malcolm; *b* 28 June 1933. Director, Slater Walker Securities Ltd, 1967–70; Chairman, Ralli International Ltd, 1969–73; Director: The Bowater Corporation Ltd, 1972–77; Tozer Kemsley & Millbourn (Holdings) Ltd, 1975–82. Member: Study Group on Local Authority Management Structures, 1971–72; South East Economic Planning Council, 1972–74; Royal Commission on the Press, 1974–77; Institute of Contemporary Arts Ltd, 1975–78; Council, Oxford Centre for Management Studies, 1973–84; Chm., British Centre, Internat. Theatre Inst., 1982–84 (Mem. Exec. Council, 1980–87). Visiting Fellow, Cranfield Institute of Technology/The School of Management, 1977–. Vis. Lectr, Univ. of Transkei, 1977. Chm., Nat. Youth Theatre, 1982–90 (Dep. Chm. 1971–82); Member: Court, RCA, 1977–80; Editorial Bd, DRAMA, 1978–81; Council, Birthright, 1974–85. *Clubs*: Reform, Royal Automobile; Harlequins Rugby Football; Knickerbocker (New York).

HORT, Sir James Fenton, 8th Bt *cr* 1767; *b* 6 Sept. 1926; *s* of Sir Fenton George Hort, 7th Bt, and Gwendolene (*d* 1982), *d* of late Sir Walter Alcock, MVO; *S* father 1960; *m* 1951, Joan, *d* of late Edwin Peat, Swallownest, Sheffield; two *s* two *d*. *Educ*: Marlborough; Trinity Coll., Cambridge. MA, MB, BChir, Cambridge, 1950. *Recreation*: fishing. *Heir*: *s* Andrew Edwin Fenton Hort, *b* 15 Nov. 1954. *Address*: Poundgate Lodge, Uckfield Road, Crowborough, Sussex.

HORTON, Dr Eric William; retired; Director of Regulatory Affairs, Glaxo Group Research Ltd, 1980–83, Member Board, 1982–83; *b* 20 June 1929; *e s* of late Harold and Agnes Horton; *m* 1956, Thalia Helen, *er d* of late Sir George Lowe; two *s* one *d*. *Educ*: Sedbergh Sch.; Edinburgh Univ. BSc, MB, ChB, PhD, DSc, MD, FRCPE. Mem. Scientific Staff, MRC, Nat. Inst. for Med. Res., London, 1958–60; Dir of Therapeutic Res. and Head of Pharmacology, Miles Labs Ltd, Stoke Poges, 1960–63; Sen. Lectr in Physiology, St Bartholomew's Hosp., London, 1963–66; Wellcome Prof. of Pharmacology, Sch. of Pharmacy, Univ. of London, 1966–69; Prof. of Pharmacology, Univ. of Edinburgh, 1969–80. Hon. Sen. Res. Fellow, Med. Coll. of St Bartholomew's Hosp., London, 1980–; Hon. Lectr in Pharmacol., Royal Free Hosp. Med. Sch., London, 1960–63. Member, Governing Body, Inveresk Res. Foundn (formerly International), 1971–80; Non-executive Director: Inveresk Res. Internat. Ltd, 1977–80; GLP Systems Ltd, 1978–80. Member: Adv. Cttee on Pesticides, MAFF, 1970–73; Biological Research and Cell Boards, MRC, 1973–75; Pharmacy Panel, SRC, 1980–81; Editorial Bd, British Jl of Pharmacology, 1960–66; Editorial Bd, Pharmacological Reviews, 1968–74. Hon. Treasurer, Brit. Pharmacological Soc., 1976–80. Baly Medal, RCP, 1973. *Publications*: Prostaglandins, 1972; papers in learned jls on peptides and prostaglandins. *Recreations*: listening to music and books on cassette, rearing beef cattle, computer programming.

HORTON, Matthew Bethell; QC 1989; *b* 23 Sept. 1946; *s* of Albert Leslie Horton, BSc, FRICS and Gladys Rose Ellen Harding; *m* 1972, Liliane Boleslawski (marr. diss. 1984); one *s* one *d*. *Educ*: Sevenoaks School; Trinity Hall, Cambridge (Open Exhibn, Hist.; Squire Law Scholar; 1st Cl. Hons Law 1967; MA 1967; LLM 1968); Astbury Scholar, Middle Temple, 1968. Called to the Bar, Middle Temple, 1969. Western Circuit; Mem., Parly Bar Mess. Member: Cttee, Jt Planning Law Conf.; Admin. Law Cttee of Justice. *Recreations*: ski-ing, windsurfing, tennis. *Address*: 2 Mitre Court Buildings, Temple, EC4Y 7BX. *T*: 071–583 1380. *Club*: Tramp.

HORTON, Robert Baynes; Chairman and Chief Executive Officer, since 1990, and a Managing Director, 1983–86 and since 1988, BP Co. plc; Chancellor, University of Kent at Canterbury, since 1990; *b* 18 Aug. 1939; *s* of late William Harold Horton and of Dorothy Joan Horton (*née* Baynes); *m* 1962, Sally Doreen (*née* Wells); one *s* one *d*. *Educ*: King's School, Canterbury; University of St Andrews (BSc); Massachusetts Inst. of Technology (SM; Sloan Fellow, 1970–71). British Petroleum, 1957–: General Manager, BP Tankers, 1975–76; General Manager, Corporate Planning, 1976–79; Man. Dir and Chief Exec. Officer, BP Chemicals, 1980–83; Chairman: Standard Oil, 1986–88; BP America, 1988–89; Dep. Chm., BP, 1989–90. Director: ICL plc, 1982–84; Pilkington

Brothers plc, 1985–86; National City Corp., 1986–88; Emerson Electric Company, 1987–. Pres., Chemicals Industry Assoc., 1982–84; Vice-Chm., BIM, 1985– (CBIM 1982); Member: SERC, 1985–86; Bd and Management Cttee, Amer. Petroleum Inst., 1986–88; Business Roundtable, 1986–88; Nat. Petroleum Council, USA, 1986–88; MIT (Sloan) Vis. Cttee, 1977–80, 1985–; MIT Corp., 1987–; UFC, 1989–. Trustee: Cleveland Orchestra, 1986–; Case Western Reserve Univ., 1987–; Chairman: Tate Foundation, 1988–; Business in the Arts, 1988–. Gov., King's Sch., Canterbury, 1984–. Hon. LLD Dundee, 1988; Hon. DCL Kent, 1990. Corporate Leadership Award, MIT, 1987; Civic Award, Cleveland, 1988. *Recreations:* music, country activities. *Address:* BP Co. plc, Britannic House, 1 Finsbury Circus, EC2M 7BA. *Clubs:* Carlton; Leander; Union, Pepper Pike (Cleveland).

HORWICH, Prof. Alan, PhD; FRCR; Professor of Radiotherapy, Institute of Cancer Research and Royal Marsden Hospital, since 1986; *b* 1 June 1948; *s* of William and Audrey Horwich; *m* 1981, Pauline Amanda Barnes; two *s* one *d*. *Educ:* William Hulme's Grammar Sch., Manchester; University College Hosp. Med. Sch. (MB BS 1971; PhD 1981). MRCP 1974; FRCR 1981. Postgrad. medicine, London, 1971– 74; Fellowship in Oncology, Harvard, 1975; res. on ribonucleic acid tumour viruses, ICRF, 1976–79; radiation oncology, Royal Marsden Hosp. and Inst. Cancer Res., 1979–. Chm., MRC Testicular Tumour Working Party, 1988–. Civilian Consultant to RN, 1989–. *Publications:* Testicular Cancer: investigation and management, 1991; numerous articles in med. jls on urological cancers and lymphomas. *Address:* Royal Marsden Hospital, Downs Road, Sutton, Surrey SM2 5PT. *T:* 081–642 6011.

HORWOOD, Hon. Owen Pieter Faure, DMS; President, Council of Governors, Development Bank of Southern Africa, since 1983; Chancellor, University of Durban-Westville, since 1973; *b* 6 Dec. 1916; *e s* of late Stanley Ebden Horwood and of Anna Johanna Horwood (*née* Faure); *m* 1946, Helen Mary Watt; one *s* one *d*. *Educ:* Boys' High Sch., Paarl, CP; University of Cape Town (BCom). South African Air Force, 1940–42. Associate Prof. of Commerce, University of Cape Town, 1954–55; Prof. of Economics, University Coll. of Rhodesia and Nyasaland, 1956–57; Univ. of Natal: William Hudson Prof. of Economics, 1957–65; Dir of University's Natal Regional Survey; Principal and Vice-Chancellor, 1966–70. Mem., 1970–80, Leader, 1978–80, South African Senate; Minister of Indian Affairs and Tourism, 1972–74; Minister of Economic Affairs, 1974–75; Minister of Finance, 1975–84. Financial Adviser to Govt of Lesotho, 1966–72. Past Chairman: Nedbank Gp; Cape Wine and Distillers Ltd; Nedbank Ltd; Finansbank Ltd; UAL Merchant Bank Ltd; Director: South African Mutual Life Assurance Soc.; South African Permanent Building Soc.; Macsteel (Pty) Ltd; TNT Skypak Internat. Patron, S Africa Sports Assoc. for Physically Disabled. Hon. DCom: Port Elizabeth, 1980; Stellenbosch, 1983; Hon. Scriptural degree, Israel Torah Res. Inst. and Adelphi Univ., 1980; Hon. DEcon Rand Afrikaans, 1981. Order of the Brilliant Star (Republic of China). *Publications:* (jtly) Economic Systems of the Commonwealth, 1962; contribs to SA Jl of Economics, SA Bankers' Jl, Economica (London), Optima, etc. *Recreations:* cricket, gardening, sailing. *Address:* PO Box 130694, Bryanston 2021, South Africa. *Clubs:* Durban (Durban); Pretoria Country; Western Province Cricket; Cape Town Cricket (Captain 1943–48).

HOSE, John Horsley, CBE 1987; Forest Craftsman, Forestry Commission, 1975–88 (Forest Worker, 1949, Skilled Forest Worker, 1950); President, National Union of Agricultural and Allied Workers, 1978–82; *b* 21 March 1928; *s* of Harry and Margaret Eleanor Hose; *m* 1st, 1967, Margaret Winifred Gaskin (marr. diss. 1987); 2nd, 1987, Linda Sharon Morris. *Educ:* Sneinton Boulevard Council Sch.; Nottingham Bluecoat Sch. Architects' Junior Asst, 1943–46. National Service, with Royal Engineers, 1946–48. Chm., Nat. Trade Gp, Agricultural and Allied Workers/TGWU, 1982–86 (Mem., 1982–89); Mem., Gen. Exec. Council, TGWU, 1986–88. *Recreations:* walking, reading, drinking real ale. *Address:* 11 Sandringham Road, Sneinton Dale, Nottingham NG2 4HH. *T:* Nottingham (0602) 580494.

HOSIE, James Findlay, CBE 1972 (OBE 1955; MBE 1946); a Director, Science Research Council, 1965–74; *b* 22 Aug. 1913; *m* 1951, Barbara Mary Mansell. *Educ:* Glasgow Univ. (MA Hons); St John's Coll., Cambridge (BA). Indian Civil Service, 1938–47; Principal, 1947–56, Asst Sec., 1956–58, Min. of Defence, London; Asst Sec. QMGF, War Office, 1958–61; Office of Minister for Science, later Dept of Educn. and Science, 1961–65. *Recreations:* bird-watching, gardening. *Address:* Flat 3, Eastbury Court, Compton, near Guildford, Surrey GU3 1EE. *T:* Guildford (0483) 810331.

HOSIER, John, CBE 1984; Director, Hong Kong Academy for Performing Arts, since 1989; *b* 18 Nov. 1928; *s* of Harry J. W. Hosier and Constance (*née* Richmond). *Educ:* Preston Manor Sch.; St John's Coll., Cambridge. MA 1954. Taught in Ankara, Turkey, 1951–53; Music Producer, BBC Radio for schools, 1953–59; seconded to ABC, Sydney, to advise on educational music programmes, 1959–60; Music Producer, subseq. Sen. and Exec. Producer, BBC TV, pioneering first regular music broadcasts to schools, 1960–73; ILEA Staff Inspector for music, and Dir of Centre for Young Musicians, 1973–76; Principal, Guildhall Sch. of Music and Drama, 1978–89. Vice-Chm., Kent Opera, 1985–87; Founder Mem. and Vice-Chm., UK Council for Music Educn and Training, 1975–81; Member: Gulbenkian Enquiry into training musicians, 1978; Music Panel, British Council, 1984–88; Music Panel, GLAA, 1984–86; Council of Management, Royal Philharmonic Soc., 1982–; Cttee, Hong Kong Philharmonic Orch., 1990–; Council for the Performing Arts, Hong Kong, 1989–; Mem. Governing Body, Chetham's Sch., 1983–88. FRSA 1976; FGSM 1978; Hon. RAM 1980; FRCM 1981; FRNCM 1985; Hon. FTCL 1986. Hon. DMus City Univ., 1986. *Compositions:* music for: Cambridge revivals of Parnassus, 1949, and Humorous Lovers, 1951; Something's Burning, Mermaid, 1974; many radio and TV productions. *Publications:* The Orchestra, 1961, revd edn 1977; various books, songs and arrangements for children; contribs on music to educnl jls. *Address:* Hong Kong Academy for Performing Arts, GPO Box 12288, Hong Kong. *Club:* City Livery.

HOSKER, Gerald Albery, CB 1987; Solicitor to the Department of Trade and Industry, since 1987; *b* 28 July 1933; *s* of Leslie Reece Hosker and Constance Alice Rose Hosker (*née* Hubbard); *m* 1956, Rachel Victoria Beatrice Middleton; one *s* one *d*. *Educ:* Berkhamsted Sch., Berkhamsted, Herts. Admitted Solicitor, 1956; Corporate Secretary 1964; Associate of the Faculty of Secretaries and Administrators 1964. Articled to Derrick Bridges & Co., 1951–56; with Clifford-Turner & Co., 1957–59; entered Treasury Solicitor's Dept as Legal Asst, 1960; Sen. Legal Asst, 1966; Asst Solicitor, 1973; Under Sec. (Legal), 1982; Dep. Treasury Solicitor, 1984–87. FRSA 1964. Hon. QC 1991. *Recreations:* the study of biblical prophecy, herbalism. *Address:* c/o Department of Trade and Industry, 10–18 Victoria Street, SW1H 0NN. *Club:* Commonwealth Trust.

HOSKING, Barbara Nancy, OBE 1985; Political Consultant to Yorkshire Television, since 1987; *b* 4 Nov. 1926; *d* of late William Henry Hosking and Ada Kathleen Hosking (*née* Murrish). *Educ:* West Cornwall School for Girls, Penzance; Hillcroft College, Surbiton; and by friends. Secretary to Town Clerk, Council of Isles of Scilly, and local corresp. for BBC and Western Morning News, 1945–47; Editl Asst, The Circle, Odeon and Gaumont cinemas, 1947–50; Asst to Inf. Officer, Labour Party, 1952–55; Asst to Gen. Manager, Uruwira Minerals Ltd, Tanzania, 1955–57; Res. Officer, Broadcasting Section, Labour Party, 1958–65; Science Press Officer, DES, 1965; Press Officer, Min. of Technology, 1967; Press and Publicity Officer, Metrication Board, 1970; Senior Inf. Officer, 10 Downing Street, 1970; Principal Inf. Officer, DoE, 1972; Private Sec. to Parly Secs, Cabinet Office, 1973; Chief Inf. Officer, DoE, 1974–77; Controller of Inf. Services, IBA, 1977–86. Pres., Media Soc., 1987–88; Mem., London Cornish Assoc.; Jt Vice-Chm., NCVO, 1987–. Trustee: Charities Aid Foundn, 1987–; 300 Gp, 1988–. Radio broadcaster, incl. BBC Radio 4 Any Questions. FRTS 1988; FRSA. Special citation, American Women's Forum, NY, 1983. *Publications:* contribs to Punch, New Scientist, Spectator. *Recreations:* opera, lieder, watching politics, watching sport. *Address:* 9 Highgate Spinney, Crescent Road, N8 8AR. *T:* 081–340 1853. *Club:* Reform.

HOSKING, Prof. Geoffrey Alan; Professor of Russian History, University of London, since 1984; *b* 28 April 1942; *s* of Stuart William Steggall Hosking and Jean Ross Hosking; *m* 1970, Anne Lloyd Hirst; two *d*. *Educ:* Maidstone Grammar Sch.; King's Coll., Cambridge (MA, PhD); St Antony's Coll., Oxford. Asst Lectr in Government, 1966–68, Lectr in Government, 1968–71, Univ. of Essex; Vis. Lectr in Political Science, Univ. of Wisconsin, Madison, 1971–72; Lectr in History, Univ. of Essex, 1972–76; Sen. Research Fellow, Russian Inst., Columbia Univ., New York, 1976; Sen. Lectr and Reader in Russian History, Univ. of Essex, 1976–84; Vis. Professor, Slavisches Inst., Univ. of Cologne, 1980–81. BBC Reith Lectr, 1988 (The Rediscovery of Politics: authority, culture and community in the USSR). Mem. Council, Writers and Scholars Educnl Trust, 1985–. Member: East-West Adv. Cttee, BCC, 1987–89; Council of Management, Keston Coll., 1987–89; Governor, Camden Sch. for Girls, 1989–. *Publications:* The Russian Constitutional Experiment: Government and Duma 1907–14, 1973; Beyond Socialist Realism: Soviet fiction since Ivan Denisovich, 1980; A History of the Soviet Union, 1985, 2nd edn 1990 (Los Angeles Times Hist. Book Prize, 1986); The Awakening of the Soviet Union, 1990, 2nd edn 1991. *Recreations:* music, chess, walking. *Address:* School of Slavonic Studies, University of London, Senate House, Malet Street, WC1E 7HU. *T:* 071–637 4934.

HOSKING, John Everard, CBE 1990; JP; Chairman, Agra Europe (London) Ltd, since 1990 (Director and Chief Executive, 1974–90); Vice-President, Magistrates' Association, since 1990 (Chairman of Council, 1987–90); *b* 23 Oct. 1929; *s* of J. Everard Hosking, OBE and E. Margaret (*née* Shaxson); *m* 1953, Joan Cecily Whitaker, BSc; two *s*. *Educ:* Marlborough Coll.; London Univ. (BScA 1953). NDA 1954. Farmer and landowner in Kent, 1953–69; Man. Dir, Eastes and Loud Ltd, 1965–69; Director: Newgrain-Kent, 1969–74; Ashford Corn Exchange Co., 1965–69; Agroup Ltd, 1987–; Bureau Européen de Recherches SA, 1987–90; European Intelligence Ltd, 1987–. Tax Comr, 1980–. Chairman: Centre for European Agricultural Studies Assoc., 1977–83; Kent Br., Magistrates' Assoc., 1973–78; Kent Magistrates' Courts Cttee, 1984–88; Member: Kent Police Authority, 1970–74; Central Council, Magistrates' Courts Cttees, 1980–83; Bar Council Professional Conduct Cttee, 1983–86; Senate of Inns of Court and the Bar Disciplinary Tribunal, 1983–86; Council, Commonwealth Magistrates' and Judges' Assoc., 1989–; Lord Chancellor's Adv. Cttee on Legal Educn and Conduct, 1991–. Member: CLA, 1958–; RASE, 1960–; NFU, 1964–. Governor, Ashford Sch., 1976–. JP Kent, 1962 (Chm., Ashford Bench, 1975–85). British Univs Ploughing Champion, 1952. *Publication:* (ed) Rural Response to the Resource Crisis in Europe, 1981. *Recreations:* the arts, the countryside. *Clubs:* Farmers', Royal Over-Seas League.

HOSKINS, Prof. Brian John, PhD; FRS 1988; FRMetS; Professor of Meteorology, since 1981, Head of Department of Meteorology, since 1990, University of Reading; *b* 17 May 1945; *s* of George Frederick Hoskins and Kathleen Matilda Louise Hoskins; *m* 1968, Jacqueline Holmes; two *d*. *Educ:* Univ. of Cambridge (MA; PhD 1970). FRMetS 1970; Fellow, Amer. Meteorol Soc, 1985. Post-doctoral Fellow, Nat. Center for Atmospheric Res., Boulder, Colo, 1970–71; Vis. Scientist, GFD Program, Univ. of Princeton, 1972–73; Univ. of Reading: Post-doctoral Fellow, 1971–72, Gp Leader, 1973–, Atmospheric Modelling Gp; Reader in Atmospheric Modelling, 1976–81. Consultant to Dept of Transport, 1990–. Chm., Atlas Supercomputer Cttee, 1990–; Member: NERC, 1988–91; Meteorol Res. Sub-Cttee, Meteorol Office, 1983–; NERC rep., Jt Policy Cttee on Advanced Res. Computing, 1987–91. Mem., Academia Europaea, 1989. Starr Meml Lecture, MIT, 1989. Royal Meteorological Society: Symons Meml Lecture, 1982; L. F. Richardson Prize, 1972; Buchan Prize, 1976; Charles Chree Silver Medal, Inst. of Physics, 1987; Carl-Gustaf Rossby Res. Medal, Amer. Meteorol Soc., 1988. *Publications:* (ed with R. P. Pearce) Large-scale Dynamical Processes in the Atmosphere, 1983; 60 papers in meteorol jls. *Recreations:* music, sport, gardening. *Address:* 32 Reading Road, Wokingham, Berks RG11 1EH. *T:* Wokingham (0734) 791015.

HOSKINS, Robert William; actor; *b* 26 Oct. 1942; *s* of Robert Hoskins and Elsie Lilian Hoskins; *m* 1st, 1970, Jane Livesey; one *s* one *d*; 2nd, 1982, Linda Banwell; one *s* one *d*. *Educ:* Stroud Green School. *Stage:* Intimate Theatre, Palmers Green, 1966; Victoria, Stoke on Trent, 1967; Century Travelling Theatre, 1969; Royal Court, 1972; Doolittle in Pygmalion, Albery, 1974; RSC season, Aldwych, 1976; The World Turned Upside Down, NT, 1978; Has Washington Legs?, NT, 1978; True West, NT, 1981; Guys and Dolls, NT, 1981; *television:* On the Move, 1976; Pennies from Heaven, 1978; Flickers, 1980; The Dunera Boys, 1985; *films:* Zulu Dawn, 1980; The Long Good Friday, 1981; The Honorary Consul, 1982; Lassiter, 1984; Cotton Club, 1984; Sweet Liberty, 1986; Mona Lisa, 1986 (Best Actor award, Cannes Fest.; Golden Globe Award); A Prayer for the Dying, 1988; The Raggedy Rawney (writer, dir, actor), 1988; Who Framed Roger Rabbit, 1988; The Lonely Passion of Judith Hearne, 1989; Heart Condition, 1990; Mermaids, 1991. *Recreations:* photography, gardening, playgoing. *Address:* c/o Anne Hutton, Hutton Management, 200 Fulham Road, SW10.

HOSKINS, Prof. William George, CBE 1971; FBA 1969; MA, PhD; *b* Exeter, 22 May 1908; *e s* of late William George Hoskins and Alice Beatrice Dymond; *m* 1933, Frances Jackson; one *d* (one *s* decd). *Educ:* Hele's Sch., Exeter; University Coll., Exeter. Lectr in Economics, University Coll., Leicester, 1931–41; 1946–48; Central Price Regulation Cttee, 1941–45; Reader in English Local History, University Coll. (now Univ.) of Leicester, 1948–51; Reader in Econ. Hist., University of Oxford, 1951–65; Hatton Prof. of English History, University of Leicester, 1965–68, retired in despair, 1968; Emeritus Professor, 1968. BBC TV Series, Landscapes of England, 1976, 1977, 1978. Mem. Royal Commission on Common Land, 1955–58; Adv. Cttee on Bldgs of Special Architectural and Historical Interest (Min. of Housing and Local Govt), 1955–64; Vice-Pres. Leicestershire Archæol and Hist. Soc., 1952; President: Dartmoor Preserv. Assoc., 1962–76; Devonshire Assoc., 1978–79; British Agricultural History Soc., 1972–74; Leverhulme Res. Fellow, 1961–63; Leverhulme Emeritus Fellowship, 1970–71. Murchison Award, RGS, 1976. Hon. FRIBA, 1973. Hon. DLitt: Exon, 1974; CNAA, 1976; DUniv Open, 1981. *Publications:* Industry, Trade and People in Exeter, 1935; Heritage of Leicestershire, 1946; Midland England, 1949; Essays in Leicestershire History, 1950; Chilterns to Black Country, 1951; East Midlands and the Peak, 1951; Devonshire Studies, (with H. P. R. Finberg), 1952; Devon (New Survey of England), 1954; The

Making of the English Landscape, 1955; The Midland Peasant, 1957; The Leicestershire Landscape, 1957; Exeter in the Seventeenth Century, 1957; Local History in England, 1959; Devon and its People, 1959; Two Thousand Years in Exeter, 1960; The Westward Expansion of Wessex, 1960; Shell Guide to Rutland, 1963; The Common Lands of England and Wales (with L. Dudley Stamp), 1963; Provincial England, 1963; Old Devon, 1966; Fieldwork in Local History, 1967; Shell Guide to Leicestershire, 1970; History from the Farm, 1970; English Landscapes, 1973; The Age of Plunder, 1976; One Man's England, 1978. *Recreations:* remembering, quietly reading.

HOSKYNS, Sir Benedict (Leigh), 16th Bt, *cr* 1676; *b* 27 May 1928; *s* of Rev. Sir Edwyn Clement Hoskyns, 13th Bt, MC, DD and Mary Trym, *d* of Edwin Budden, Macclesfield; *S* brother 1956; *m* 1953, Ann Wilkinson; two *s* two *d*. *Educ:* Haileybury; Corpus Christi Coll., Cambridge; London Hospital. BA Cantab 1949; MB, BChir Cantab 1952. House Officer at the London Hospital, 1953. RAMC, 1953–56. House Officer at Royal Surrey County Hospital and General Lying-In Hospital, York Road, SE1, 1957–58; DObstRCOG 1958; in general practice, 1958–. *Heir: s* Edwyn Wren Hoskyns [*b* 4 Feb. 1956; *m* 1981, Jane, *d* of John Sellars; one *s*. *Educ:* Nottingham Univ. Medical School (BM, BS 1979; MRCP 1984)]. *Address:* Harewood, Great Oakley, near Harwich, Essex. *T:* Ramsey (Essex) (0255) 880341.

HOSKYNS, Sir John (Austin Hungerford Leigh), Kt 1982; Director-General, Institute of Directors, 1984–89; Chairman, The Burton Group plc, since 1990; *b* 23 Aug. 1927; *s* of Lt-Colonel Chandos Benedict Arden Hoskyns and Joyce Austin Hoskyns; *m* 1956, Miranda Jane Marie Mott; two *s* one *d*. *Educ:* Winchester College. Served in The Rifle Brigade, 1945–57 (Captain); IBM United Kingdom Ltd, 1957–64; founded John Hoskyns & Co. Ltd, later part of Hoskyns Group Ltd (Chm. and Man. Dir), 1964–75; Director: ICL plc, 1982–84; AGB Research plc, later Pergamon AGB plc, 1983–89; Clerical Medical & General Life Assurance Soc., 1983–; McKechnie plc, 1983–; Ferranti Internat. Signal plc, 1986–. Hd of PM's Policy Unit, 1979–82. Hon. DSc Salford, 1985; DU Essex, 1987. *Recreations:* opera, shooting. *Address:* c/o Child & Co., 1 Fleet Street, EC4Y 1BD. *Club:* Travellers'.

HOTHAM, family name of **Baron Hotham.**

HOTHAM, 8th Baron, *cr* 1797; **Henry Durand Hotham;** Bt 1621; DL; *b* 3 May 1940; *s* of 7th Baron Hotham, CBE, and Lady Letitia Sibell Winifred Cecil, *er d* of 5th Marquess of Exeter, KG; *S* father, 1967; *m* 1972, Alexandra Stirling Home, *d* of late Maj. Andrew S. H. Drummond Moray; two *s* one *d*. *Educ:* Eton; Cirencester Agricultural Coll. Late Lieut, Grenadier Guards; ADC to Governor of Tasmania, 1963–66. DL Humberside, 1981. *Heir: s* Hon. William Beaumont Hotham, *b* 13 Oct. 1972. *Address:* Dalton Hall, Dalton Holme, Beverley, Yorks; Scorborough Hall, Driffield, Yorks.

HOTHFIELD, 6th Baron *cr* 1881; **Anthony Charles Sackville Tufton;** Bt 1851; *b* 21 Oct. 1939; *s* of 5th Baron Hothfield, TD and Evelyn Margarette (*d* 1989), *e d* of late Eustace Charles Mordaunt; *S* father, 1991; *m* 1975, Lucinda Marjorie, *d* of Captain Timothy John Gurney; one *s* one *d*. *Educ:* Eton; Magdalene Coll., Cambridge (MA). MICE. *Recreations:* Real tennis, lawn tennis, bridge, shooting. *Heir: s* Hon. William Sackville Tufton, *b* 14 Nov. 1977. *Address:* House of Lords, SW1A 0PW. *Clubs:* Hawks (Cambridge); Jesters; Cockermouth Lawn Tennis, almost every Real tennis club.

HOTSON, Leslie, LittD (Cambridge); FRSL; Shakespearean scholar and writer; *b* Delhi, Ont, Canada, 16 Aug. 1897; *s* of John H. and Lillie S. Hotson; *m* 1919, Mary May, *d* of Frederick W. Peabody. *Educ:* Harvard Univ. Sheldon Travelling Fellow, Harvard, 1923–24; Sterling Research Fellow, Yale, 1926–27; Associate Prof. of English, New York Univ., 1927–29; Guggenheim Memorial Fellow, 1929–31; Prof. of English, Haverford Coll., Pa, 1931–41; served War of 1939–45, 1st Lieut and Capt. Signal Corps, US Army, 1943–46; Fulbright Exchange Scholar, Bedford Coll., London, 1949–50; Research Associate, Yale, 1953; Fellow, King's Coll., Cambridge, 1954–60. *Publications:* The Death of Christopher Marlowe, 1925; The Commonwealth and Restoration Stage, 1928; Shelley's Lost Letters to Harriet, 1930; Shakespeare versus Shallow, 1931; I, William Shakespeare, 1937; Shakespeare's Sonnets Dated, 1949; Shakespeare's Motley, 1952; Queen Elizabeth's Entertainment at Mitcham, 1953; The First Night of Twelfth Night, 1954; Shakespeare's Wooden O, 1959; Mr W. H., 1964; Shakespeare by Hilliard, 1977. *Recreation:* boating. *Address:* Northford, Conn 06472, USA.

HOTTER, Hans; opera and concert singer, retired 1972, but still gives occasional concert performances; teaches masterclasses in USA, Japan, Great Britain, Austria, Germany and other countries; *b* Offenbach, Germany; *m* 1936, Helga Fischer; one *s* one *d*. *Educ:* Munich. Concert career began in 1929 and opera career in 1930. Prof. at Vienna Musik-Hochschule, 1977–80. Mem. of Munich, Vienna and Hamburg State Operas; guest singer in opera and concerts in all major cities of Europe and USA; concert tours in Australia; for the past 10 years, connected with Columbia Gramophone Co., England; guest singer, Covent Garden Opera, London, 1947–. Festivals: Salzburg, Edinburgh and Bayreuth. *Relevant publication:* Hans Hotter: man and artist, by Penelope Turing, 1984. *Address:* Emil Dittlerstrasse 26, 8000 München 71, West Germany.

HOTUNG, Joseph Edward; Chairman, Inter-Continental Capital Co. Ltd; *b* 25 May 1930; *s* of Edward Sai-kim Hotung and Maud Alice (*née* Newman); *m* 1st, 1957, Mary Catherine McGinley (marr. diss. 1969); two *s* two *d*; 2nd, 1970, Ann Virginia Carlo (marr. diss. 1981). *Educ:* St Francis Xavier Coll., Shanghai; St Louis Coll., Tientsin; Catholic Univ. of America (BA); Univ. of London (LLB). With Marine Midland Bank, 1957–60; Ho Hung Hing Estates Ltd, 1960–. Director: HSBC Hldgs plc; Hongkong & Shanghai Banking Corp. Ltd; Hongkong Electric Hldgs Ltd; Cavendish Internat. Hldgs Ltd; China & Eastern Investment Co. Ltd. Member: Judicial Services Commn; Inland Revenue Bd of Review. University of Hong Kong: Mem. Council; Mem., Finance Cttee; Chm. and Trustee, Staff Terminal Benefits Scheme; Mem. Council, Business Sch. Member: Internat. Council, and Trustee, Asia Soc., NY; Chm's Council and Vis. Cttee, MMA; Vis. Cttee, Freer Gall. of Art, Washington DC. *Recreation:* Oriental art. *Address:* 3310 Edinburgh Tower, The Landmark, 15 Queen's Road, Central, Hong Kong. *T:* 522–9929. *Clubs:* Hong Kong, Royal Hong Kong Jockey (Hong Kong); Century (New York).

HOUGH, George Hubert, CBE 1965; PhD; FRAeS; Chairman: Forthstar Ltd, since 1980; Abasec Ltd, since 1988; Fernan Holdings Ltd, since 1989; Fernan Avionics Ltd, since 1989; *b* 21 Oct. 1921; *m* Hazel Ayrton (*née* Russel); one *s* two *d*. *Educ:* Winsford Grammar Sch.; King's Coll., London. BSc (Hons Physics), PhD. Admiralty Signals Estabt, 1940–46. Standard Telecommunication Laboratories Ltd (ITT), 1946–51 (as external student at London Univ. prepared thesis on gaseous discharge tubes); de Havilland Propellers Ltd: early mem. Firestreak team in charge of develt of guidance systems and proximity fusing, 1951–59; Chief Engr (Guided Weapons), 1959; Chief Executive (Engrg), 1961; Dir, de Havilland Aircraft Co., 1962; Hawker Siddeley Dynamics Ltd: Technical Dir, 1963; Dep. Managing Dir, 1968; Man. Dir, 1977; Dep. Chief Exec., Dynamics Group British Aerospace, 1977. Dep. Chm., 1977, Chief Exec., 1977–80, Chm., 1978–80, British Smelter Constructions Ltd; Chm., Magnetic Components Ltd, 1986–89; Director: Sheepbridge Engrg Ltd, 1977–79; Scientific Finance Ltd, 1979–84; Programmed Neuro Cybernetics (UK) Ltd, 1979–85; Landis & Gyr Ltd, 1980–85; Leigh Instruments Ltd (Canada), 1987–88. *Publication:* (with Dr P. Morris) The Anatomy of Major Projects, 1987. *Recreation:* golf. *Address:* Trelyon, Rock, near Wadebridge, Cornwall PL27 6LB. *T:* Trebetherick (0208) 863454. *Club:* St James's.

HOUGH, John Patrick; Secretary, Institute of Chartered Accountants in England and Wales, 1972–82; *b* 6 July 1928; *s* of William Patrick Hough, MBE, Lt-Comdr RN and Eva Harriet Hough; *m* 1956, Dorothy Nadine Akerman; four *s* one *d*. *Educ:* Purbrook High School. FCA, MIMC, FBCS. Articled M. R. Cobbett & Co., Portsmouth, 1950–53; Derbyshire & Co., 1953–54; Turquand Youngs & Co., 1954–57; Computer Specialist, IBM United Kingdom Ltd, 1957–61; Consultant 1961–62, Partner 1962–69, Robson Morrow & Co.; Dep. Sec., Inst. of Chartered Accountants in England and Wales, 1969–71. *Recreations:* music, food. *Address:* 5 South Row, Blackheath, SE3; Coastguard Cottage, Newtown, Newport, Isle of Wight. *Clubs:* Travellers'; London Rowing.

HOUGH, Julia Marie, (Judy); *see* Taylor, Judy.

HOUGH, Richard Alexander; writer; *b* 15 May 1922; *s* of late George and Margaret May Hough; *m* 1st, 1943, Helen Charlotte (marr. diss.) *o d* of Dr Henry Woodyatt; four *d*; 2nd, 1980, Judy Taylor, *qv*. *Educ:* Frensham Heights. Served War, RAF Pilot, Fighter Command, home and overseas, 1941–46. Publisher, 1947–70: Bodley Head until 1955; Hamish Hamilton as Dir and Man. Dir, Hamish Hamilton Children's Books Ltd, 1955–70. Contrib. to: Guardian; Observer; Washington Post; NY Times; Encounter; History Today; New Yorker. Mem. Council, 1970–73, 1975–84, Vice-Pres., 1977–82, Navy Records Society. Chm., Auxiliary Hospitals Cttee, King Edward's Hospital Fund, 1975–80 (Mem. Council, 1975–86). *Publications:* The Fleet that had to Die, 1958; Admirals in Collision, 1959; The Potemkin Mutiny, 1960; The Hunting of Force Z, 1963; Dreadnought, 1964; The Big Battleship, 1966; First Sea Lord: an authorised life of Admiral Lord Fisher, 1969; The Pursuit of Admiral von Spee, 1969; The Blind Horn's Hate, 1971; Captain Bligh and Mr Christian, 1972 (Daily Express Best Book of the Sea Award) (filmed as The Bounty, 1984); Louis and Victoria: the first Mountbattens, 1974; One Boy's War: per astra ad ardua, 1975; (ed) Advice to a Grand-daughter (Queen Victoria's letters), 1975; The Great Admirals, 1977; The Murder of Captain James Cook, 1979; Man o' War, 1979; Nelson, 1980; Mountbatten: Hero of Our Time, 1980; Edwina: Countess Mountbatten of Burma, 1983; The Great War at Sea 1914–1918, 1983; Former Naval Person: Churchill and the Wars at Sea, 1985; The Longest Battle, 1986; The Ace of Clubs: a history of the Garrick, 1986; Born Royal, 1988; (with Denis Richards) The Battle of Britain: the jubilee history, 1989; Winston and Clementine: the triumph of the Churchills, 1990; Bless our Ship: Mountbatten and HMS Kelly, 1991; *novels:* Angels One Five, 1978; The Fight of the Few, 1979; The Fight to the Finish, 1979; Buller's Guns, 1981; Razor Eyes, 1981; Buller's Dreadnought, 1982; Buller's Victory, 1984; The Raging Sky, 1989; numerous books on motoring history and books for children under *pseudonym* Bruce Carter. *Address:* 31 Meadowbank, Primrose Hill, NW3 1AY. *T:* 071–722 5663, *Fax:* 071–722 7750. *Clubs:* Garrick, Beefsteak, MCC.

HOUGH, Stephen; concert pianist; *b* 22 Nov. 1961; *s* of Colin Hough and Annetta (*née* Johnstone). *Educ:* Chetham's Sch. Music, Manchester; Royal Northern Coll. of Music; Juilliard Sch. Numerous recitals and concerto appearances with LSO, LPO, RPO, Philharmonia, Chicago Symphony, Philadelphia Orchestra, Cleveland Orchestra, LA Philharmonic, San Francisco Symphony; festival performances incl.: Ravinia, Mostly Mozart, Hollywood Bowl, Blossom, Proms, Le Grange de Meslay. Recordings: Hummel Piano Concertos; 2 Liszt Recitals; Piano Album; Schumann Recital; Brahms Piano Concerto No 2; Complete Britten Piano Music. RNCM Dayas Gold Medal, 1981; Internat. Terence Judd Award, 1982; Naumburg Internat. Piano Competition, 1983. *Recreations:* reading, pipe-smoking. *Address:* c/o Christopher Tennant Artists' Management, 11 Lawrence Street, SW3 5NB.

HOUGHTON, family name of **Baron Houghton of Sowerby.**

HOUGHTON OF SOWERBY, Baron *cr* 1974 (Life Peer), of Sowerby, W Yorks; **Arthur Leslie Noel Douglas Houghton,** PC 1964; CH 1967; *b* 11 Aug. 1898; *s* of John and Martha Houghton, Long Eaton, Derbyshire; *m* 1939, Vera Travis (CBE 1986); no *c*. Inland Revenue, 1915–22; Civil Service Rifles, 1916–19; 1st 60th Rifles, 1919–20; Sec., Inland Revenue Staff Fedn, 1922–60. Broadcaster in "Can I Help You?" Programme, BBC, 1941–64. Alderman LCC, 1947–49; Mem. Gen. Council, TUC, 1952–60. Chm., Staff Side, Civil Service National Whitley Council, 1956–58. MP (Lab) Sowerby, WR Yorks, March 1949–Feb. 1974; Chm. Public Accounts Cttee, 1963–64; Chancellor of the Duchy of Lancaster, 1964–66; Minister Without Portfolio, 1966–67. Chm., Parly Lab. Party, 1967–70, Nov. 1970–1974. Chairman: British Parly Gp, Population and Develt, 1978–84; House of Lords Industry Study Gp, 1979–87. Member: Commn on the Constitution, 1969–73; Royal Commn on Standards of Conduct in Public Life, 1974–75. Chairman: Commonwealth Scholarships Commn, 1967–68; Young Volunteer Force Foundation, 1967–70 (Jt Vice-Chm. 1970–71); Teachers' Pay Inquiry, 1974; Cttee on aid to Political Parties, 1975–76; Cttee on Security of Cabinet Papers, 1976; Cttee for Reform of Animal Experimentation, 1977–; Vice-Pres., RSPCA, 1978–82. *Publication:* Paying for the Social Services, 2nd edn, 1968. *Address:* 110 Marsham Court, SW1. *T:* 01–834 0602; Becks Cottage, Whitehill Lane, Bletchingley, Surrey. *T:* Godstone (0883) 743340. *Club:* Reform.

HOUGHTON, Rev. Alfred Thomas, MA, LTh; General Secretary Bible Churchmen's Missionary Society, 1945–66, Vice-President 1968; Hon. Canon, Diocese of Morogoro, Central Tanganyika, 1965; *b* Stafford, 11 April 1896; *s* of Rev. Thomas Houghton (Editor of the Gospel Magazine and Vicar of Whitington, Stoke Ferry, Norfolk) and Elizabeth Ann Houghton; *m* 1924, Coralie Mary, *d* of H. W. Green, and *g d* of Maj.-Gen. Green, Indian Army; two *s* four *d*. *Educ:* Clarence Sch. (now Canford Sch.); Durham Univ. (University Coll.); London Coll. of Divinity. BA Durham, 1923; MA Durham, 1929. Commissioned 2/5th PA Som LI, Burma, 1917; Staff Officer to Inspector of Infantry, South, AHQ India, 1918; Staff Capt., QMG's Br, AHQ India, 1919; demobilised, 1919; Deacon, 1921; Priest, 1922; Missionary Sch. of Medicine, 1923–24; Supt of BCMS Mission in Burma, 1924–40; Asst Bishop-Designate of Rangoon, 1940–44 (cancelled owing to Japanese occupation of Burma); Travelling Sec., Inter-Varsity Fellowship of Evangelical Unions, 1941–44, and Asst Sec., Graduates' Fellowship, 1944–45. Pres. Missionary Sch. of Medicine, 1948–77; Trustee Keswick Convention Council, 1948, and Chm., 1951–69; Chairman: Conference of British Missionary Socs, 1960; Church of England Evangelical Council, 1960–66; Pres. Mt Hermon Missionary Training Coll., 1960–71; Vice-President: Evangelical Alliance; Lord's Day Observance Soc. *Publications:* Tailum Jan, 1930; Dense Jungle Green, 1937; Preparing to be a Missionary, 1956. *Address:* 14 Alston Court, St Albans Road, Barnet, Herts EN5 4LJ. *T:* 081–449 1741.

HOUGHTON, Brian Thomas, CB 1991; Director, International Division (formerly International Tax Policy Division), Inland Revenue, since 1987; *b* 22 Aug. 1931; *s* of Bernard Charles Houghton and Sadie Houghton; *m* 1953, Joyce Beryl (*née* Williams); three *s* one *d*. *Educ:* City Boys' Sch., Leicester; Christ's Coll., Cambridge. BA (Mod.

Langs), MA 1957. Inland Revenue, 1957; Private Sec. to Chief Sec., HM Treasury, 1966–68; Assistant Secretary: Inland Revenue, 1968–75; HM Treasury, 1975–77; Under Sec., 1977, Principal Finance Officer and Dir of Manpower, Inland Revenue, 1977–83; Policy Div. Dir, Inland Revenue, 1983–87. *Address*: 1 Barns Dene, Harpenden, Herts AL5 2HH. *T*: Harpenden (0582) 715905.

HOUGHTON, Herbert; Director: Stenhouse Holdings Ltd, 1979–83; Reed Stenhouse Cos Ltd, 1977–86; Chancellor Insurance Co. Ltd, since 1984; *b* 4 Oct. 1920; *s* of Herbert Edward and Emily Houghton; *m* 1939, Dorothy Ballantyne; one *s* one *d*. *Educ*: William Hulmes' Grammar School. Director, Cockshoots Ltd, 1955; Man. Dir, Stenhouse Northern Ltd, 1968; Chairman: Sir Wm Garthwaite (Holdings) Ltd, 1973; Sten-Re Ltd, 1973; Director and Chief Executive, A. R. Stenhouse & Partners Ltd, 1977; Dir, British Vita Co. Ltd, 1969–84. *Recreations*: overseas travel, golf, reading, gardening. *Address*: 2 Orchard Court, Grindleford, Sheffield S30 1JH. *T*: Hope Valley (0433) 31142.

HOUGHTON, Dr John, JP; Director, Teesside Polytechnic, 1971–79, retired (Principal, Constantine College of Technology, 1961–70); *b* 12 June 1922; *s* of George Stanley Houghton and Hilda (*née* Simpson); *m* 1951, Kathleen Lamb; one *s* one *d*. *Educ*: King Henry VIII Sch., Coventry; Hanley High Sch.; Coventry Techn. Coll.; King's Coll., Cambridge; Queen Mary Coll., London Univ. BSc (hons) Engrg 1949; PhD 1952. CEng, MIMechE, FRAeS. Aircraft Apprentice, Sir W. G. Armstrong-Whitworth Aircraft Ltd, 1938–43; design and stress engr, 1943–46; student at univ. (Clayton Fellow), 1946–51; Lectr, Queen Mary Coll., London Univ., 1950–52; Sen. Lectr and Head of Aero-Engrg, Coventry Techn. Coll., 1952–57; Head of Dept of Mech. Engrg, Brunel Coll. Advanced Technology, 1957–61. Freeman, City of Coventry, 1943. JP Middlesbrough, 1962. *Publications*: (with D. R. L. Smith) Mechanics of Fluids by Worked Examples, 1959; various research reports, reviews and articles in professional and learned jls. *Recreations*: keen sportsman (triple Blue), do-it-yourself activities, gardening, pottery, oil painting. *Address*: 14 Marton Moor Road, Nunthorpe, Middlesbrough, Cleveland TS7 0BH. *T*: Middlesbrough (0642) 315263. *Club*: Middlesbrough Rotary.

HOUGHTON, Sir John Theodore, Kt 1991; CBE 1983; FRS 1972; Chief Executive (formerly Director General) of the Meteorological Office, 1983–91; *b* 30 Dec. 1931; *s* of Sidney M. Houghton, schoolmaster, and Miriam Houghton; *m* 1st, 1962, Margaret Edith Houghton (*née* Broughton) (*d* 1986), MB, BS, DPH; one *s* one *d*. 2nd, 1988, Sheila Houghton (*née* Thompson). *Educ*: Rhyl Grammar Sch.; Jesus Coll., Oxford (Scholar). BA hons Physics 1951, MA, DPhil 1955. Research Fellow, RAE Farnborough, 1954–57; Lectr in Atmospheric Physics, Oxford Univ., 1958–62; Reader, 1962–76; Professor, 1976–83; Fellow, Jesus Coll., Oxford, 1960–83, Hon. Fellow 1983; on secondment as Dir (Appleton), 1979–83, and Dep. Dir, 1981–83, Rutherford Appleton Laboratory, SERC. Member: Astronomy, Space and Radio Bd, SERC (formerly SRC), 1970–73 and 1976–81; Exec. Cttee, WMO, 1983– (Vice-Pres., 1987–91); Astronomy and Planetary Sci. Bd, SERC, 1987–; Meteorological Cttee, 1975–80; Jt Organising Cttee, Global Atmospheric Res. Programme, 1976–79; Exec. Management Bd, British Nat. Space Centre, 1986–; Chairman: Jt Scientific Cttee, World Climate Research Programme, 1981–84; Earth Observation Adv. Cttee, ESA, 1982–; Scientific Assessment, Intergovtl Panel for Climate Change, 1988–. Pres., RMetS, 1976–78. FInstP; Fellow, Optical Soc. of America. Cherwell-Simon Meml Lectr, Oxford Univ., 1983–84; Bakerian Lectr, Roy. Soc., 1991. Hon. DSc Wales, 1991. Buchan Prize, RMetS, 1966; Charles Chree medal and prize, Inst. of Physics, 1979; (with F. W. Taylor, C. D. Rodgers and G. D. Peskett) Rank Prize for opto-electronics, 1989; Symons Meml Medal, RMetS, 1991; Glazebrook Medal and Prize, Inst. of Phys, 1990. *Publications*: (with S. D. Smith) Infra-Red Physics, 1966; The Physics of Atmospheres, 1977, 2nd edn 1986; (with F. W. Taylor and C. D. Rodgers) Remote Sounding of Atmospheres, 1984; Does God play dice?, 1988; papers in learned jls on atmospheric radiation, spectroscopy and remote sounding from satellites. *Recreations*: walking, gardening. *Address*: Hadley Centre for Climate Prediction and Research, Meteorological Office, London Road, Bracknell RG12 2SZ.

HOUGHTON, Maj.-Gen. Robert Dyer, CB 1963; OBE 1947; MC 1942; DL; *b* 7 March 1912; *s* of late J. M. Houghton, Dawlish, Devon; *m* 1940, Dorothy Uladh, *y d* of late Maj.-Gen. R. W. S. Lyons, IMS; two *s* one *d*. *Educ*: Haileybury Coll. Royal Marines Officer, 1930–64; Col Comdt, Royal Marines, 1973–76. Gen. Sec., Royal UK Beneficent Assoc., 1968–78. DL East Sussex, 1977. *Recreations*: gardening, sailing, model engineering. *Address*: Vert House, Whitesmith, near Lewes, East Sussex. *Club*: Army and Navy.

HOULDEN, Rev. Prof. (James) Leslie; Professor of Theology, since 1987 and Head of Department of Biblical Studies, since 1988, King's College, London; *b* 1 March 1929; *s* of James and Lily Alice Houlden. *Educ*: Altrincham Grammar Sch.; Queen's Coll., Oxford. Asst Curate, St Mary's, Hunslet, Leeds, 1955–58; Chaplain, Chichester Theological Coll., 1958–60; Chaplain Fellow, Trinity Coll., Oxford, 1960–70; Principal, Cuddesdon Theol Coll., later Ripon Coll., Cuddesdon, 1970–77; King's College, London: Lectr, 1977; Sen. Lectr in New Testament Studies, 1985; Dean, Faculty of Theology and Religious Studies, 1986–88. Hon. Canon of Christ Church Oxford, 1976–77. Member: Liturgical Commn, 1969–76; Doctrine Commn of C of E, 1969–76; Gen. Synod of C of E, 1980–90. Editor, Theology, 1983–. *Publications*: Paul's Letters from Prison, 1970; (ed) A Celebration of Faith, 1970; Ethics and the New Testament, 1973; The Johannine Epistles, 1974; The Pastoral Epistles, 1976; Patterns of Faith, 1977; Explorations in Theology 3, 1978; What Did the First Christians Believe?, 1982; Connections, 1986; Backward into Light, 1987; (ed) The World's Religions, 1988; History, Story and Belief, 1988; (ed) Dictionary of Biblical Interpretation, 1990; Truth Untold, 1991; (ed) Austin Farrer: the essential sermons, 1991; Bible and Belief, 1991; *contributed to*: The Myth of God Incarnate, 1977; Incarnation and Myth, 1979; Alternative Approaches to New Testament Study, 1985; The Reality of God, 1986; A New Dictionary of Christian Ethics, 1986; The Trial of Faith, 1988; God's Truth, 1988; Embracing the Chaos, 1990; Tradition and Unity, 1991; reviews and articles in learned jls. *Address*: 33 Raleigh Court, Lymer Avenue, SE19 1LS. *T*: 081–670 6648. *Club*: Athenæum.

HOULDER, John Maurice, CBE 1977 (MBE (mil.) 1941); Chairman, Houlder Offshore Services Ltd, since 1973; *b* 20 Feb. 1916; *m* 1981, Rody, *d* of late Major Luke White. Private Pilot's Licence, 1938–; instrument rating, 1949–; Lessee, Elstree Aerodrome, 1951–. Chairman: Houlder Diving Research Facility Ltd, 1978–; Houlder Offshore Engineering Ltd, 1984–; Administrateur, Comex SA, Marseilles. Vis. Prof., Dept of Ship and Marine Technol., Univ. of Strathclyde, 1982–. Chm., London Ocean Shipowners Joint Dock Labour Piecework Cttee, 1950–60; first Chm., River Plate Europe Freight Conf., 1961–70; Chm., Bulk Cargo Cttee, Continental River Plate Conf., 1954–70. Member: Exec. Board and Technical Cttee, Lloyds Register of Shipping, 1970–; Light Aircraft Requirements Cttee, CAA, 1955–84; Adv. Cttee on R&D to Sec. of State for Energy, 1987–90. Member, Council: RSPB, 1974–79; RINA, 1981–87; Pres., Soc for Underwater Technology, 1978–80 (President's Award, 1987). Hon. DSc Strathclyde, 1986. Stanley Gray Award, Inst. of Marine Engrs, 1982. *Recreations*: ski-ing, flying, bird-watching, computer programming. *Address*: 59 Warwick Square, SW1V 2AL. *T*: 071–834 2856. *Clubs*: Air Squadron; Kandahar Ski, 1001.

HOULDSWORTH, Sir Richard (Thomas Reginald), 5th Bt *cr* 1887, of Reddish and Coodham; Farm Manager since 1988; *b* 2 Aug. 1947; *s* of Sir Reginald Douglas Henry Houldsworth, 4th Bt, OBE, TD and of Margaret Mary, *d* of late Cecil Emilius Laurie; *S* father, 1989; *m* 1970, Jane Elizabeth (marr. diss. 1983), *o d* of Alistair Orr; two *s*. *Educ*: Bredon School, Tewkesbury, Glos; Blanerne School, Denholm, Roxburghshire. *Recreations*: shooting, fishing, tennis, squash, horse racing. *Heir*: *s* Simon Richard Henry Houldsworth, *b* 6 Oct. 1971. *Address*: Kirkbride, Glenburn, Crosshill, Ayrshire. *T*: Crosshill (06554) 202.

HOULSBY, Prof. Guy Tinmouth, PhD; Professor of Civil Engineering, and Fellow of Brasenose College, Oxford, since 1991, *b* 28 March 1954; *s* of Thomas Tinmouth Houlsby and Vivienne May Houlsby (*née* Ford); *m* 1985, Jenny Lucy Damaris Nedderman; two *s*. *Educ*: Trinity College, Glenalmond; St John's College, Cambridge (MA, PhD). CEng, MICE. Engineer, Binnie and Partners, 1975–76; Babtie Shaw and Morton, 1976–77; Research Student, Cambridge, 1977–80; Oxford University: Jun. Res. Fellow, Balliol Coll., 1980–83; Lectr in Engineering, 1983–91; Fellow, Keble College, 1983–91. *Publications*: BASIC Soil Mechanics (with G. W. E. Milligan), 1984; contribs to learned jls on soil mechanics. *Recreations*: ornithology, woodwork, Northumbrian small pipes. *Address*: 25 Purcell Road, Marston, Oxford OX3 0HB. *T*: Oxford (0865) 722128.

HOUNSFIELD, Sir Godfrey (Newbold), Kt 1981; CBE 1976; FRS 1975; Consultant to Laboratories, THORN EMI Central Research Laboratories (formerly Central Research Laboratories of EMI), Hayes, Mddx, since 1986 (Head of Medical Systems section, 1972–76; Chief Staff Scientist, 1976–77, Senior Staff Scientist, 1977–85); Consultant (part-time), National Heart & Chest Hospitals, Chelsea, since 1986; *b* 28 Aug. 1919; *s* of Thomas Hounsfield, Newark, Notts. *Educ*: Magnus Grammar Sch., Newark; City and Guilds Coll., London (Radio Communications qualif.); Faraday House Electrical Engineering Coll. (Diploma); grad. for IEE. Volunteered for RAF, 1939; served 1939–46 (incl. period as Lectr at Cranwell Radar Sch.); awarded Certificate of Merit (for work done in RAF), 1945. Attended Faraday House, where he studied elec. and mech. engrg, 1947–51. Joined EMI Ltd, 1951, working initially on radar systems and, later, on computers; led design team for the first large, all transistor computer to be built in Great Britain, the EMIDEC 1100, 1958–59; invented the EMI-scanner computerised transverse axial tomography system for X-ray examination, 1969–72 (now used at Atkinson Morley's Hosp., Wimbledon, and leading hosps in the USA and European continent, which are buying the invention); the technique can be applied to cranial examinations and the whole of the body; the system has overcome obstacles to the diagnosis of disease in the brain which have continued since Roentgen's day (1895); it includes a patient-scanning unit; developer of a new X-ray technique (the EMI-scanner system) which won the 1972 MacRobert Award of £25,000 for the invention, and a Gold Medal for EMI Ltd; working on Nuclear Magnetic Resonance Imaging, 1976–; Magnetic Resonance Imaging Advr, Nat. Heart Hosp. and Brompton Hosp. Professorial Fellow in imaging sciences, Manchester Univ., 1978–. Dr Medicine (*hc*) Universität Basel, 1975; Hon. DSc: City, 1976; London, 1976; Hon. DTech Loughborough, 1976. Hon. FRCP 1976; Hon. FRCR 1976. Wilhelm-Exner Medal, Austrian Industrial Assoc., 1974; Ziedses des Plantes Medal, Physikalisch Medizinische Gesellschaft, Würzburg, 1974; Prince Philip Medal Award, CGLI, 1975; ANS Radiation Industry Award, Georgia Inst. of Technology, 1975; Lasker Award, Lasker Foundn, 1975; Duddell Bronze Medal, Inst. Physics, 1976; Golden Plate Award, Amer. Acad. of Achievement, 1976; Reginald Mitchell Gold Medal, Stoke-on-Trent Assoc. of Engrs, 1976; Churchill Gold Medal, 1976; Gairdner Foundn Award, 1976; (jtly) Nobel Prize for Physiology or Medicine, 1979; Ambrogino d'Oro Award, City of Milan, 1980; Deutsche Roentgen Plakette, Deutsche Roentgen Museum, 1980. *Publications*: contribs: New Scientist; Brit. Jl of Radiology; Amer. Jl of Röntgenology. *Recreation*: mountain walking. *Address*: THORN EMI Central Research Laboratories, Dawley Road, Hayes, Mddx UB3 1HH. *T*: 081–848 6404; 15 Crane Park Road, Twickenham TW2 6DF. *T*: 081–894 1746. *Club*: Athenæum.

HOUSDEN, Rt. Rev. James Alan George, BA; *b* Birmingham, England, 16 Sept. 1904; *s* of William James and Jane Housden; *m* 1935, Elfreda Moira Hennessey; two *s* one *d*. *Educ*: Essendon High School; University of Queensland; St Francis College. BA 1st class, Mental and Moral Philosophy, 1928; ThL 1st Class, 1929. Deacon, 1928; Priest, 1929. Curate, St Paul's Ipswich, Qld, 1928–30; Chaplain, Mitchell River Mission, 1930–32; Curate, All Souls' Cathedral, Thursday Island, 1932–33; Rector of Darwin, NT, 1933–37; Vicar of Coolangatta, Qld, 1936–40; Rector and Rural Dean, Warwick, 1940–46; Vicar of Christ Church, S Yarra, Melbourne, 1946–47; Bishop of Rockhampton, 1947–58; Bishop of Newcastle, NSW, 1958–72. *Recreation*: bowls. *Address*: 38 Maltman Street, Caloundra, Qld 4551, Australia. *Club*: Australian (Sydney, NSW).

HOUSDEN, Peter James; Director of Education, Nottinghamshire County Council, since 1991; *b* 7 Dec. 1950; *s* of Gordon Arthur James Housden and Mary Archibald; *m* 1st, 1970, Kate Toon (marr. diss. 1974); one *s*; 2nd, 1974, Maureen McMorrow; one *s* one *d*. *Educ*: Univ. of Essex (BA Hons Sociology). Teacher, Madeley Court Sch., Telford, 1975–79; Professional Asst, Humberside LEA, 1979–82; Asst Dir of Educn, Notts LEA, 1982–86; Sen. Educn Officer, Lancs LEA, 1986–88; Dep. Chief Educn Officer, Notts LEA, 1988–91. *Recreations*: ironing, Nottingham Forest. *Address*: 12 Dovedale Road, West Bridgford, Nottingham NG2 6JA.

HOUSE, Lt-Gen. Sir David (George), GCB 1977 (KCB 1975); KCVO 1985; CBE 1967; MC 1944; Gentleman Usher of the Black Rod, House of Lords, 1978–85; Serjeant-at-Arms, House of Lords, and Secretary to the Lord Great Chamberlain, 1978–85; *b* 8 Aug. 1922; *s* of A. G. House; *m* 1947, Sheila Betty Darwin; two *d*. *Educ*: Regents Park Sch., London. War service in Italy; and thereafter in variety of regimental (KRRC and 1st Bn The Royal Green Jackets) and staff appts. Comd 51 Gurkha Bde in Borneo, 1965–67; Chief BRIXMIS, 1967–69; Dep. Mil. Sec., 1969–71; Chief of Staff, HQ BAOR, 1971–73; Dir of Infantry, 1973–75; GOC Northern Ireland, 1975–77. Colonel Commandant: The Light Division, 1974–77; Small Arms School Corps, 1974–77. Dir, Yorks and Humberside, Lloyds Bank, 1985–91. *Address*: Dormer Lodge, Aldborough, near Boroughbridge, N Yorks YO5 9EP. *Club*: Army and Navy.

HOUSE, Donald Victor; Lay Member, Restrictive Practices Court, 1962–70, retired; *b* 31 Jan. 1900; *s* of Dr S. H. House, Liverpool; *m* 1925, Cicely May Cox-Moore (*d* 1980); one *s* two *d*. *Educ*: Liverpool Coll. Lieut, Royal Garrison Artillery, 1918. Mem. (Fellow) Inst. of Chartered Accountants in England and Wales, 1922– (Mem. Council, 1942–62; Pres. 1954–55). Senior Partner, Harmood Banner & Co., 1946–62. Mem. Board of Governors, Guy's Hosp., 1955–74, and Chm. of Finance Cttee, 1957–74; Director: National Film Finance Corporation, 1954–70; Finance Cttee, Friends of the Poor and Gentlefolks Help, 1946–70; Mem., London Rent Assessment Panel, 1967–75. Hon. Sec., Herts Golf Union, 1964–75, Pres., 1976–78; Mem. Council, English Golf Union. Dir of several public and other companies (to 1962); Chm., House Cttee enquiring into Northern Ireland shipping facilities. Special Constabulary Long Service Medal, 1943. *Recreations*: golf, amateur dramatics. *Address*: Theobald House, 75 Theobald Street, Borehamwood, Herts WD6 4SL. *Clubs*: Commonwealth Trust; Sandy Lodge Golf (Hon. Mem.), Porters Park Golf (Hon. Mem.).

HOUSE, Ven. Francis Harry, OBE 1955; MA; Officer Royal (Hellenic) Order of Phoenix, 1947; Archdeacon of Macclesfield, 1967–78, now Archdeacon Emeritus; Rector of St James, Gawsworth, 1967–78; *b* 9 Aug. 1908; *s* of late Canon William Joseph House, DD; *m* 1938, Margaret Neave; two *d*. *Educ:* St George's Sch., Harpenden; Wadham Coll., Oxford; Cuddesdon Theological Coll. Sec. of Student Christian Movement of Gt Britain and Ireland, 1931–34; Deacon, 1936; Priest, 1937. Asst Missioner, Pembroke Coll. (Cambridge) Mission, Walworth, 1936–37; Travelling sec. of World's Student Christian Federation, Geneva, 1938–40; Curate of Leeds Parish Church, 1940–42; Overseas Asst, Religious Broadcasting Dept, BBC, London, 1942–44; representative of World Student Relief in Greece, 1944–46; Sec. Youth Dept World Council of Churches, Geneva, and World Conference of Christian Youth, Oslo, 1946–47; Head of Religious Broadcasting BBC, London, 1947–55; Associate Gen. Sec. of the World Council of Churches, Geneva, 1955–62; Vicar of St Giles, Pontefract, 1962–67. Select Preacher, Cambridge Univ., 1949. Member: Gen. Synod of Church of England, 1970–78; Gen. Synod's Commn on Broadcasting, 1971–73; Bd for Mission and Unity, 1971–80 (Vice-Chm., 1971–75). *Publications:* The Russian Phoenix, 1988; articles contributed to: The Student Movement, The Student World, East and West, the Ecumenical Review, Theology, Crucible, One in Christ, etc. *Address:* 11 Drummond Court, Far Headingley, Leeds LS16 5QE. *T:* Leeds (0532) 783646.

HOUSE, Dr John Peter Humphry; Reader, Courtauld Institute of Art, University of London, since 1987 (Lecturer, 1980–87); *b* 19 April 1945; *s* of Madeline Edith Church and Arthur Humphry House; *m* 1968, Jill Elaine Turner; two *s*. *Educ:* Westminster Sch.; New Coll., Oxford (BA); Courtauld Inst. of Art (MA, PhD). Lecturer: UEA, 1969–76; UCL, 1976–80. Slade Prof. of Fine Art, Univ. of Oxford, 1986–87; British Acad. Res. Reader, 1988–90. Organiser of Impressionism Exhibn, RA, 1974; Co-organiser: Post Impressionism exhibn, RA, 1979–80; Renoir exhibn, Arts Council, 1985. *Publications:* Monet, 1977, 2nd edn 1981; Monet: nature into art, 1986; (jtly) Impressionist and Post-Impressionist Masterpieces from the Courtauld Collection, 1987; author/co-author, exhibition catalogues; articles in Burlington Magazine, Art History, Art in America. *Recreation:* second hand bookshops. *Address:* Courtauld Institute of Art, University of London, Somerset House, Strand, WC2R 0RN. *T:* 071–872 0220.

See also E. H. O. Parry.

HOUSEMAN, Alexander Randolph, CBE 1984; FEng, FIMechE, FIProdE; Deputy Chairman, British Rail Engineering Ltd, since 1985 (Director, since 1979); *b* 9 May 1920; *e s* of Captain Alexander William Houseman and Elizabeth Maud (*née* Randolph); *m* 1942, Betty Edith Norrington; one *d*. *Educ:* Stockport Grammar School and College. FIMC, CBIM, FRSA. Apprenticed Crossley Motors, 1936–40; Production Engineer: Ford Motor Co. (Aero Engines) Ltd, 1940–43; Saunders-Roe Ltd, 1943–48, General Works Manager, 1948–54; Consultant, Director, Man. Dir and Dep. Chm., P-E International Ltd, 1954–81; Dir, P-E Consulting Gp Ltd, 1968–85; Chm., W. Canning Ltd, 1975–80; Dir, Record Ridgway Ltd, 1978–81. Chm., NEDO EDC for Gauge and Tool Industry, 1979–85; Institution of Production Engineers: Chm., Technical Policy Bd, 1978–82; Vice-Pres., 1982–83; Pres., 1983–84. Member: Industrial Adv. Panels of Fellowship of Engineering, 1980–; Council, Inst. of Management Consultants, 1968–83; Inst. of Directors; Life Member: Soc. of Manufg Engrs, USA, 1985; Inst. of Industrial Engrs, USA, 1985. Distinguished Engrg Management Award, Nat. Soc. of Professional Engrs, USA, 1983; Distinguished Achievements Award, LA Council of Engrs and Scientists, 1984; Nuffield Award, 1984. *Publications:* articles to learned jls and technical and management press on manufacturing technology and management. *Recreations:* DIY, sailing, photography, walking. *Address:* 11 Kings Avenue, Ealing, W5 2SJ. *T:* 081–997 3936. *Clubs:* Caledonian; Royal Anglesey Yacht (Beaumaris).

HOUSSEMAYNE du BOULAY, (Edward Philip) George, CBE 1985; FRCR, FRCP; Professor of Neuroradiology, University of London at Institute of Neurology, 1975–84, now Emeritus; Hon. Research Fellow, Zoological Society of London (Head, X-Ray Department, Nuffield Laboratories, Institute of Zoology, 1965–86); Director, Radiological Research Trust, since 1985; *b* 28 Jan. 1922; *yr s* of Philip Houssemayne du Boulay and Mercy Tyrrell (*née* Friend); *m* 1944, Vivien M. Glasson (marr. diss.); four *s* (and two *s* decd); *m* 1968, Pamela Mary Verity; two *d*. *Educ:* Christ's Hospital; King's Coll., London; Charing Cross Hosp. (Entrance Schol. 1940; MB, BS, DMRD). Served RAF (Medical), 1946–48; Army Emergency Reserve, 1952–57. House appts, Charing Cross Hosp. and Derby City Hosp., 1945–46; Registrar (Radiology), Middlesex Hosp., 1948–49; Sen. Registrar (Radiology): St Bartholomew's Hosp., 1949–54; St George's Hosp., 1951–52; Consultant Radiologist: Nat. Hosp. for Nervous Diseases, Maida Vale, 1954–68; Bartholomew's Hosp., 1954–71; Nat. Hosp. for Nervous Diseases, Queen Square, 1968–75 (Head, Lysholm Radiol Dept, 1975–84). Editor, Neuroradiology, 1974–91. Pres., Brit. Inst. of Radiology, 1976–77, Appeal Co-ordinator 1976–84; Hon. Member: Société Française de Neuroradiologie; Amer. Soc. of Neuroradiology; Swedish Soc. of Neuroradiology; German Soc. Neuroradiology. Trustee, Nat. Hosp. Develt Foundn. Glyn Evans Meml Lectr, RCR, 1970; Ernestine Henry Lectr, RCP, 1976. Hon. FACR. Barclay Medal, BIR, 1968. *Publications:* Principles of X-Ray Diagnosis of the Skull, 1965, 2nd edn 1979; (jtly) 4th edn of A Text Book of X-Ray Diagnosis by British Authors: Neuroradiology Vol. 1, 5th edn 1984; (jtly) The Cranial Arteries of Mammals, 1973; (jtly) An Atlas of Normal Vertebral Angiograms, 1976; works in specialist jls. *Recreation:* gardening. *Address:* Old Manor House, Brington, Huntingdon, Cambs PE18 0PX. *T:* Bythorn (08014) 353.

HOUSSEMAYNE du BOULAY, Sir Roger (William), KCVO 1982 (CVO 1972); CMG 1975; HM Diplomatic Service, retired; Vice Marshal of the Diplomatic Corps, 1975–82; *b* 30 March 1922; *s* of Charles John Houssemayne du Boulay, Captain, RN, and Mary Alice Veronica, *née* Morgan; *m* 1957, Elizabeth, *d* of late Brig. Home, late RM, and Molly, Lady Pile; one *d*, and two step *s*. *Educ:* Winchester; Oxford. Served RAFVR, 1941–46 (Pilot). HM Colonial Service, Nigeria, 1949–58; HM Foreign, later Diplomatic, Service, 1959; FO, 1959; Washington, 1960–64; FCO 1964–67; Manila, 1967–71; Alternate Director, Asian Development Bank, Manila, 1967–69, and Director, 1969–71; Counsellor and Head of Chancery, Paris, 1971–73; Resident Comr, New Hebrides, 1973–75. Advr, Solomon Is Govt, 1986. *Address:* Anstey House, near Buntingford, Herts SG9 0BJ.

HOUŠTECKÝ, Dr Miroslav; Ambassador of Czechoslovak Socialist Republic to the United States of America, 1986–90; *b* 10 June 1926; *s* of Josef Houštecký and Blažena Houštecká; *m* 1953, Marie Houštecká (*née* Sedlaková); one *s* two *d*. *Educ:* School of Political and Economic Sciences, Prague, 1946–50; doctorate in Social Sciences (RSDr), 1953; candidate of Historical Sciences, 1958. Lecturer and Reader, Charles Univ., Prague, and School of Political and Economic Sciences, Prague, 1950–64; Correspondent of Czechoslovak News Agency/CTK, India, 1964–69; Editor and Dep. Director General of CTK, Prague, 1969–77; Senior Official of the Central Committee of the Communist Party of Czechoslovakia, 1977–83; joined Min. of Foreign Affairs, 1983; Ambassador in UK, 1983–86. State distinction for reconstruction services. *Publications:* (jtly) History of Czechoslovak Foreign Policy (Prague), 1958; (jtly) Survey of the Modern World History, I-II (Prague), 1963. *Address:* c/o Ministry for Foreign Affairs, Prague, Czechoslovakia.

HOUSTON, Aubrey Claud D.; *see* Davidson-Houston.

HOUSTON, Maj.-Gen. David, CBE 1975 (OBE 1972); Lord-Lieutenant of Sutherland, since 1991; *b* 24 Feb. 1929; *s* of late David Houston and late Christina Charleson Houston (*née* Dunnett); *m* 1959, Jancis Veronica Burn; two *s*. *Educ:* Latymer Upper Sch. Commissioned, Royal Irish Fusiliers, 1949; served Korea, Kenya, BAOR, N Africa; Staff Coll., Camberley, 1961; commanded 1 Loyals and newly amalgamated 1st QLR, 1969–71; in comd 8th Inf. Bde, Londonderry, N Ireland, 1974–75; Mem. RCDS, 1976; Military Attaché and Commander, British Army Staff, Washington, 1977–79; HQ UKLF, 1979–80; Pres., Regular Commissions Bd, 1980–83; retd 1984. Hon. Col, Manchester and Salford Univs OTC (TA), 1985–90; Col, The Queen's Lancashire Regt, 1983–. DL Sutherland, 1991. *Recreations:* fishing, shooting, shepherding. *Address:* c/o Bank of Scotland, Bonar Bridge, Sutherland IV24 3EB.

HOUSTON, James Caldwell, CBE 1982; MD, FRCP; Physician to Guy's Hospital, 1953–82, now Emeritus Physician; Dean, United Medical and Dental Schools, Guys and St Thomas's Hospitals, 1982–84 (Dean, Medical and Dental Schools, Guy's Hospital, 1965–82); *b* 18 Feb. 1917; *yr s* of late David Houston and Minnie Walker Houston; *m* 1946, Thelma Cromarty Cruickshank, MB, ChB, 2nd *d* of late John Cruickshank, CBE; four *s*. *Educ:* Mill Hill Sch.; Guy's Hosp. Medical Sch. MRCS, LRCP 1939; MB, BS (London) 1940; MRCP 1944; MD 1946; FRCP 1956. Late Major RAMC; Medical Registrar, Guy's Hospital, 1946; Asst Ed., 1954, Jt Ed., 1958–67, Guy's Hosp. Reports; Member: Bd of Governors, Guy's Hosp., 1965–74; SE Metropolitan Regional Hosp. Bd, 1966–71; Lambeth, Lewisham and Southwark AHA (Teaching), 1974–78; Court of Governors, London Sch. of Hygiene and Tropical Med., 1969–84; Senate, Univ. of London, 1970–84; Bd of Faculty of Clinical Medicine, Cambridge Univ., 1975–81; Cttee of Vice-Chancellors and Principals, 1977–80; Special Trustee, Guy's Hosp., 1974–82; Trustee, Hayward Foundn, 1978–. Dir, Clerical, Medical & Gen. Life Assurance Soc., 1965–87; Vice-Pres., Medical Defence Union, 1970–. *Publications:* Principles of Medicine and Medical Nursing (jtly), 1956, 5th edn 1978; A Short Text-book of Medicine (jtly), 1962, 8th edn 1984; articles in Quart. Jl Med., Brit. Med. Bull., Lancet, etc. *Recreations:* golf, gardening. *Address:* Keats House, Guy's Hospital, St Thomas Street, SE1 9RT. *T:* 071–955 5000; Cockhill Farm, Detling, Maidstone, Kent ME14 3HG. *T:* Medway (0634) 31395.

HOUSTOUN-BOSWALL, Sir (Thomas) Alford, 8th Bt *cr* 1836; international economics and business consultant; *b* 23 May 1947; *s* of Sir Thomas Houstoun-Boswall, 7th Bt, and of Margaret Jean, *d* of George Bullen-Smith; *S* father, 1982; *m* 1971, Eliana Michele, *d* of Dr John Pearse, New York; one *s* one *d*. *Educ:* Lindisfarne College. Chairman, Metropolitan Car Parks and Excelsior Properties Ltd, UK; Partner, Rosedale-Engel, Houstoun-Boswall Partnership, Bermuda; Director, Stair & Co., New York (specialising in fine 18th century English furniture and works of art); Pres., Houstoun-Boswall Inc. (Fine Arts), New York. Lecturer, New York Univ. and Metropolitan Museum of Art, New York. *Heir:* *s* Alexander Alford Houstoun-Boswall, *b* 16 Sept. 1972. *Address:* 18 rue Basse, 06410 Biot, France; 15 East 77 Street, New York, NY 10021, USA.

HOVELL-THURLOW-CUMMING-BRUCE, family name of **Baron Thurlow,** and *see* Cumming-Bruce.

HOVEN, Helmert Frans van den; Knight, Order of Netherlands Lion, 1978; Commander, Order of Orange Nassau, 1984; Hon. KBE 1980; President, International Chamber of Commerce, Paris, 1985–86; Chairman, Unilever NV, 1975–84; Vice-Chairman, Unilever Ltd, 1975–84; *b* 25 April 1923; *m* 1st, 1950, Dorothy Ida Bevan (marr. diss. 1981); one *s*; 2nd, 1981, Cornelia Maria van As. *Educ:* Grammar and Trade schs in The Netherlands. Joined Unilever N. V., Rotterdam, 1938; transf. to Unilever Ltd, London, 1948, then to Turkey, 1951, becoming Chm. of Unilever's business there, 1958; Chm., Unilever's Dutch margarine business, Van den Bergh en Jurgens B. V., 1962; sen. marketing post, product gp, Margarine, Edible Fats and Oils, 1966; Mem. Bds of Unilever, and responsible for product gp, Sundry Foods and Drinks, 1970; Mem. Supervisory Bd of Shell; Chm. Supervisory Bds of Amro Bank and various other cos; Mem., Eur. Adv. Bd, Rockwell; Mem. Council, North Western (Kellogg) Business Sch. *Recreations:* summer and winter sports in general. *Address:* c/o Amro Bank, Foppingadreef 22, 1102 BS, Amsterdam, The Netherlands.

HOVING, Thomas; President, Hoving Associates, Inc., since 1977; Editor-in-Chief, Connoisseur, 1982–91; *b* 15 Jan. 1931; *s* of late Walter Hoving and Mary Osgood (*née* Field); *m* 1953, Nancy Melissa Bell; one *d*. *Educ:* Princeton Univ. BA Highest Hons, 1953; Nat. Council of the Humanities Fellowship, 1955; Kienbusch and Haring Fellowship, 1957; MFA 1958; PhD 1959. Dept of Medieval Art and The Cloisters, Metropolitan Museum of Art: Curatorial Asst, 1959; Asst Curator, 1960; Associate Curator, 1963; Curator, 1965; Commissioner of Parks, New York City, 1966; Administrator of Recreation and Cultural Affairs, New York City, 1967; Dir, Metropolitan Museum of Art, 1967–77. Distinguished Citizen's Award, Citizen's Budget Cttee, 1967. Hon. Mem. AIA, 1967. Hon. LLD, Pratt Inst., 1967; Dr *hc*: Princeton; New York Univ. Middlebury and Woodrow Wilson Awards, Princeton. *Publications:* The Sources of the Ada Group Ivories (PhD thesis), 1959; Guide to The Cloisters, 1962; The Chase and The Capture, 1976; Two Worlds of Andrew Wyeth, 1977; Tutankhamun, the Untold Story, 1978; King of the Confessors, 1981; Masterpiece (novel), 1986; Discovery (novel), 1989; articles in Apollo magazine and Metropolitan Museum of Art Bulletin. *Recreations:* sailing, ski-ing, bicycling, flying. *Address:* (office) 150 East 73rd Street, New York, NY 10021, USA.

HOWARD; *see* Fitzalan-Howard.

HOWARD, family name of **Earls of Carlisle, Effingham,** and **Suffolk,** and of **Barons Howard of Penrith** and **Strathcona.**

HOWARD DE WALDEN, 9th Baron *cr* 1597, **AND SEAFORD,** 5th Baron *cr* 1826; **John Osmael Scott-Ellis,** TD; *b* 27 Nov. 1912; *s* of 8th Baron and Margherita, CBE 1920 (*d* 1974), *d* of late Charles van Raalte of Brownsea Island, Dorset; *S* father, 1946; *m* 1st, 1934, Countess Irene Harrach (*d* 1975), *y d* of Count Hans Albrecht Harrach; four *d*; 2nd, 1978, Gillian Viscountess Mountgarret. *Educ:* Eton; Magdalene Coll., Cambridge (BA 1934, MA). Dir, Howard de Walden Estates Ltd (Chm.). Member of the Jockey Club (Senior Steward, 1957, 1964, 1976). *Heir:* (to Barony of Howard de Walden) four co-heiresses; (to Barony of Seaford) *cousin* Colin Humphrey Felton Ellis [*b* 19 April 1946; *m* 1971, Susan Magill; two *s* two *d*]. *Address:* Avington Manor, Hungerford, Berks. *T:* Kintbury (0488) 58229; Flat K, 90 Eaton Square, SW1. *T:* 071–235 7127. *Clubs:* Turf, White's.

See also Capt. D. W. S. Buchan of Auchmacoy.

HOWARD OF PENRITH, 2nd Baron, *cr* 1930; **Francis Philip Howard,** DL; Captain late RA; *b* 5 Oct. 1905; *s* of 1st Baron and Lady Isabella Giustiniani-Bandini (*d* 1963) (*d* of Prince Giustiniani-Bandini, 8th Earl of Newburgh); *S* father, 1939; *m* 1944, Anne, *widow* of Anthony Bazley; four *s*. *Educ:* Downside; Trinity Coll., Cambridge (BA); Harvard

Univ. Called to Bar, Middle Temple, 1931; served in War, 1939–42 (wounded). DL County of Glos, 1960. *Heir:* s Hon. Philip Esme Howard [b 1 May 1945; m 1969, Sarah, d of late Barclay Walker and of Mrs Walker, Perthshire; two s two d]. *Address:* Dean Farm, Coln St Aldwyns, Glos GL7 5AX.

See also Hon. Edmund B. C. Howard.

HOWARD, Alan (Mackenzie); actor; Associate Artist, Royal Shakespeare Company, since 1967; *b* 5 Aug. 1937; *s* of Arthur John Howard and Jean Compton Mackenzie; *m* 1st, Stephanie Hinchcliffe Davies (marr. diss. 1976); 2nd, Sally Beauman; one *s*. *Educ:* Ardingly Coll. Belgrade Theatre, Coventry, 1958–60, parts incl. Frankie Bryant in Roots (also at Royal Court and Duke of York's); Wesker Trilogy, Royal Court, 1960; A Loss of Roses, Pembroke, Croydon, 1961; The Changeling, Royal Court, 1961; The Chances, and The Broken Heart, inaugural season, Chichester Festival, 1962; Virtue in Danger, Mermaid and Strand, 1963; Bassanio in The Merchant of Venice, Lysander in A Midsummer Night's Dream, in tour of S America and Europe, 1964; Simon in A Heritage and its History, Phoenix, 1965; Angelo in Measure for Measure, Bolingbroke in Richard II, Nottingham, 1965–66; Cyril Jackson in The Black and White Minstrels, Traverse, Edinburgh, 1972, Hampstead, 1973; A Ride Across Lake Constance, Hampstead and Mayfair, 1973; The Silver King, Chichester, 1990; Scenes from a Marriage, Chichester, transf. Wyndhams, 1990; *Royal Shakespeare Company:* joined company, 1966, playing Orsino in Twelfth Night, Lussurioso in The Revenger's Tragedy; 1967: Jaques in As You Like It (also LA, 1968), Young Fashion in The Relapse; 1968: Edgar in King Lear, Achilles in Troilus and Cressida, Benedick in Much Ado about Nothing; 1969: Benedick (also in LA and San Francisco), Achilles, Lussurioso, and Bartholomew Cokes in Bartholomew Fair; 1970: Mephistophilis in Dr Faustus, Hamlet, Theseus/Oberon in A Midsummer Night's Dream, Ceres in The Tempest; 1971: Theseus/Oberon (NY debut); 1971–72: Theseus/Oberon, Nikolai in Enemies, Dorimant in The Man of Mode, The Envoy in The Balcony; 1972–73: Theseus/Oberon, in tour of E and W Europe, USA, Japan, Australia; 1974: Carlos II in The Bewitched; 1975: Henry V, Prince Hal in Henry IV parts I and II; 1976: Prince Hal (SWET Award for Best Actor in revival), Henry V in tour of Europe and USA, Jack Rover in Wild Oats (also Piccadilly); 1977: Henry V, Henry VI parts I, II and III, Coriolanus (Plays and Players London Critics Award, SWET Award for Best Actor in revival, Evening Standard Best Actor Award, 1978); 1978: Antony in Antony and Cleopatra; 1979: Coriolanus in tour of Europe, The Children of the Sun; 1980: title rôles in Richard II and Richard III (Variety Club Best Actor Award); 1981–82: Neschastlivsev in The Forest; Good (Standard Best Actor Award, 1981); 1985: Nikolai in Breaking the Silence. Best Actor (jt), 1981, Drama (British Theatre Assoc.) awards for Richard II, Good and The Forest. *Films include:* The Heroes of Telemark; Work is a Four Letter Word; The Return of the Musketeers; The Cook, The Thief, his Wife and her Lover. *Television appearances include:* The Way of the World; Comet Among the Stars; Coriolanus; The Holy Experiment; Poppyland; Sherlock Holmes, Evensong, The Double Helix, 1986; A Perfect Spy, 1987; The Dog it Was That Died, 1988. *Radio includes:* Soames in Forsyte Chronicles, 1990–91. *Address:* c/o Julian Belfrage Associates, 68 St James's Street, SW1. *T:* 071–491 4400.

HOWARD, Alexander Edward, CBE 1972; Lecturer in Education, London University Centre for Teachers, 1977–81; *b* 2 Aug. 1909; *o s* of Alexander Watson Howard and Gertrude Nellie Howard; *m* 1937, Phyllis Ada Adams; no *c*. *Educ:* Swindon Coll.; University Coll. and Westminster Coll., London Univ. BSc (London) 1930; Pt I, BSc (Econ.) 1934. Flt-Lieut, RAF, 1940–46. Asst Master, Sanford Boys' Sch., Swindon, 1931–34; Lectr in Maths, Wandsworth Techn. Coll., 1935–40; Maths Master, Wilson's Grammar Sch., 1946–48; Headmaster: Northfleet Sch. for Boys, Kent, 1948–51; Borough-Beaufoy Sch., London, 1951–54; Forest Hill Sch., London, 1955–63; Wandsworth Sch., 1963–74. Co-ordinating Officer Teaching Practice Organisation, London Univ. Inst. of Educn, 1975–77. Member: Naval Educn Adv. Cttee, 1966–80; Army Educational Adv. Bd, 1957–74. Academic Council, RMA, 1970–75. FRSA 1970. Hon. Mem., CGLI, 1979. *Publications:* The Secondary Technical School in England, 1955; Longman Mathematics Stages 1–5, 1962–67, new Metric edns, 1970–71; Teaching Mathematics, 1968; articles in Times Educational Supplement, The Teacher, Technology, Inside the Comprehensive Sch. *Recreations:* amateur theatre, old-time dancing, music, cricket, travel, rotary. *Address:* 19 Downsway, Sanderstead, Surrey CR2 0JB. *T:* 081–657 3399. *Club:* Surrey County Cricket.

HOWARD, Anthony Michell; political journalist; *b* 12 Feb. 1934; *s* of late Canon Guy Howard and Janet Rymer Howard; *m* 1965, Carol Anne Gaynor. *Educ:* Westminster Sch.; Christ Church, Oxford. Chm., Oxford Univ. Labour Club, 1954; Pres., Oxford Union, 1955. Called to Bar, Inner Temple, 1956. Nat. Service, 2nd Lieut, Royal Fusiliers, 1956–58; Political Corresp., Reynolds News, 1958–59; Editorial Staff, Manchester Guardian, 1959–61 (Harkness Fellowship in USA, 1960); Political Corresp., New Statesman, 1961–64; Whitehall Corresp., Sunday Times, 1965; Washington Corresp., Observer, 1966–69 and Political Columnist, 1971–72; Asst Editor, 1970–72, Editor, 1972–78, New Statesman; Editor, The Listener, 1979–81; Dep. Editor, The Observer, 1981–88. Presenter: Face the Press, Channel Four, 1982–85; The Editors, Sky News TV, 1989–90. *Publications:* (contrib.) The Baldwin Age, 1960; (contrib.) Age of Austerity, 1963; (with Richard West) The Making of the Prime Minister, 1965; (ed) The Crossman Diaries: selections from the Diaries of a Cabinet Minister, 1979; Rab: the life of R. A. Butler, 1987; Crossman: the pursuit of power, 1990. *Address:* 17 Addison Avenue, W11 4QS. *T:* 071–603 3749. *Club:* Garrick.

HOWARD, Dame Christian; *see* Howard, Dame R. C.

HOWARD, Rear-Adm. Christopher John, (Jack); management consultant; Chief of Staff, C-in-C Naval Home Command, 1987–89, retired; *b* 13 Sept. 1932; *s* of Claude Albert Howard and late Hilda Mabel Howard (*née* Norton); *m* 1st, 1960, Jean Webster (marr. diss. 1987); two *d*; 2nd, 1987, Hilary Troy; one *s* one *d*. *Educ:* Newton Abbot Grammar School; King's College London; Imperial College, London. MSc, DIC. MIEE. Entered RN 1954; served in HM Ships Ocean, Pukaki, Roebuck, Urchin, Tenby; Officer i/c RN Polaris School, 1978–80; Dean, RN Engineering College, 1980–82; Dir, Naval Officer Appts (Instructor), 1982–84; Commodore, HMS Nelson, 1985–87. NDC Latimer, 1975; Chief Naval Instructor Officer, 1987. *Recreations:* shooting, Rugby. *Club:* Army and Navy.

HOWARD, Rev. Canon Donald; Provost, St Andrew's Cathedral, Aberdeen, 1978–91, retired; *b* 21 Jan. 1927; *s* of William Howard and Alexandra Eadie (*née* Buchanan); unmarried. *Educ:* Hull Coll. of Technology; London Univ. (BD, AKC). AFRAeS, 1954–58. Design Engineer, Blackburn Aircraft, 1948–52; Hunting Percival Aircraft, 1952–54; English Electric Co., 1954–55. Assistant Minister, Emmanuel Church, Saltburn-by-the-Sea, Yorks, 1959–62; Rector and Mission Director, Dio. Kimberley and Kuruman, S Africa, 1962–65; Rector of St John the Evangelist, East London, S Africa, 1965–72; Rector of Holy Trinity Episcopal Church, Haddington, Scotland, 1972–78. Honorary Canon: Christ Church Cathedral, Hartford, Conn, USA, 1978; St Andrew's Cathedral, Aberdeen, 1991. *Address:* 42 Waterside, Bondgate, Ripon, North Yorkshire HG4 1RA. *T:* Ripon (0765) 692144.

HOWARD, Hon. Edmund Bernard Carlo, CMG 1969; LVO 1961; HM Diplomatic Service, retired; *b* 8 Sept. 1909; *s* of 1st Baron Howard of Penrith, PC, GCB, GCMG, CVO, and Lady Isabella Giustiniani-Bandini (*d* of Prince Giustiniani-Bandini, 8th Earl of Newburgh); *m* 1936, Cécile Geoffroy-Dechaume; three *s* one *d* (and one *d* decd). *Educ:* Downside Sch.; Newman Sch., Lakewood, NJ; New Coll., Oxford. Called to the Bar, 1932; Sec., Trustees and Managers, Stock Exchange, 1937. Served in HM Forces, KRRC, 1939–45. Joined HM Diplomatic Service, 1947; served in: Rome, 1947–51; Foreign Office, 1951–53; Madrid, 1953–57; Bogotá, 1957–59; Florence, 1960–61; Rome, 1961–65; Consul-Gen., Genoa, 1965–69. Comdr, Order of Merit, Italy, 1973. *Publications:* Genoa: history and art in an old seaport, 1971 (Duchi di Galliera prize, 1973); trans. The Aryan Myth, 1974. *Recreations:* travel, gardening, walking. *Address:* Jerome Cottage, Marlow Common, Bucks. *T:* Marlow (0628) 482129.

HOWARD, Sir Edward; *see* Howard, Sir H. E. de C.

HOWARD, Elizabeth Jane; novelist; *b* 26 March 1923; *d* of David Liddon and Katharine M. Howard; *m* 1st, 1942, Peter M. Scott (marr. diss. 1951; later Sir Peter Scott, CH, CBE, FRS (*d* 1989)); one *d*; 2nd, 1959, James Douglas-Henry; 3rd, 1965, Kingsley Amis (*see* Sir Kingsley Amis) (marr. diss. 1983). *Educ:* home. Trained at London Mask Theatre Sch. Played at Stratford-on-Avon, and in repertory theatre in Devon; BBC, Television, modelling, 1939–46; Sec. to Inland Waterways Assoc., 1947; subsequently writing, editing, reviewing, journalism and writing plays for television, incl. serials of After Julius in three plays and Something in Disguise in six plays. John Llewellyn Rhys Memorial Prize for The Beautiful Visit, 1950. Hon. Artistic Dir, Cheltenham Literary Festival, 1962; Artistic co-Dir, Salisbury Festival of Arts, 1973. Film script, The Attachment, 1986. *Publications:* The Beautiful Visit, 1950; The Long View, 1956; The Sea Change, 1959; After Julius, 1965; Something in Disguise, 1969 (TV series, 1982); Odd Girl Out, 1972; Mr Wrong, 1975; (ed) A Companion for Lovers, 1978; Getting It Right, 1982 (Yorkshire Post Prize) (film script, 1985); (jtly) Howard and Maschler on Food: cooking for occasions, 1987; The Light Years, 1990; Green Shades (anthology), 1991; Marking Time, 1991. *Recreations:* music, gardening, enjoying all the arts, travelling, natural history. *Address:* c/o Jonathan Clowes, Iron Bridge House, Bridge Approach, NW1 8BD.

HOWARD, Francis Alex, (Frankie Howerd), OBE 1977; *b* 6 March 1922. *Educ:* Shooters Hill Sch., Woolwich, London. *Revues:* Out of this World, 1950; Pardon my French, 1953; Way Out in Piccadilly, 1966; *one-man show:* Quite Frankly Frankie Howerd, 1990; *plays:* Charlie's Aunt, 1955; Hotel Paradiso, 1957; A Midsummer Night's Dream (playing Bottom), 1958; Alice in Wonderland, 1960; A Funny Thing Happened on the Way to the Forum, 1963 (Critics' Award for Best Musical Actor, 1964) and 1986; The Wind in the Sassafras Trees, Broadway, 1968; Simple Simon in Jack and the Beanstalk, Palladium, 1973; numerous pantomimes, 1947–83; *opera:* Frosch in Die Fledermaus, Coliseum, 1982; *films:* The Ladykillers, 1956; Runaway Bus, 1956; Touch of the Sun, 1956; Jumping for Joy, 1956; Further up the Creek, 1958; Carry On, Doctor, 1968; Carry on Up the Jungle, 1970; Up Pompeii, 1971; Up the Chastity Belt, 1972; Up the Front, 1972; The House in Nightmare Park, 1973; Sergeant Pepper's Lonely Hearts Club Band, 1978. *TV Series:* Fine Goings On, 1959; Up Pompeii, 1970–71; Up the Convicts (Australia), 1975; The Frankie Howerd Show (Canada), 1976; Frankie Howerd Strikes Again, 1981; The Blunders, 1986; in Gilbert and Sullivan series: HMS Pinafore, 1982; Trial by Jury, 1982; Frankie Howerd on Campus, 1990; All Change, 1990 and 1991. Roving reporter for TV-am, 1983–. Royal Variety Performances, 1950, 1954, 1961, 1966, 1968, 1969, 1978, 1982 Variety Club of GB Award (Show Business Personality of the Year), 1966, 1971; Radio and TV Industries Award (Show Business Personality of the Year), 1971. *Publications:* On the Way I Lost It (autobiog.), 1976; Trumps, 1982. *Recreations:* swimming, music, reading. *Address:* c/o Tessa Le Bars Management, 18 Queen Anne Street, W1M 9LB. *T:* 071–636 3191.

HOWARD, Sir (Hamilton) Edward (de Coucey), 2nd Bt *cr* 1955; GBE 1972; Director of Stockbroking Firm of Charles Stanley and Company Ltd; Chairman, LRC International Ltd, 1971–82; *b* 29 Oct. 1915; *s* of Sir (Harold Walter) Seymour Howard, 1st Bt, and Edith M. (*d* 1962), *d* of Edward Turner; *S* father 1967; *m* 1943, Elizabeth Howarth Ludlow; two *s*. *Educ:* Le Rosey, Rolle, Switzerland; Radley Coll., Abingdon; Worcester Coll., Oxford. Mem. of the Stock Exchange, London, 1946. Sheriff of the City of London, 1966 (Common Councilman, 1951; Alderman, 1963); Lord Mayor of London, 1971–72; one of HM Lieutenants, City of London, 1976–. Master of the Gardeners' Company, 1961. DSc City Univ., 1971. KStJ 1972. *Recreation:* gardening. *Heir:* *s* David Howarth Seymour Howard [*b* 29 Dec. 1945; *m* 1968, Valerie Picton, *o d* of Derek W. Crosse; two *s* two *d*]. *Address:* Courtlands, Bishops Walk, Shirley Hills, Surrey. *T:* 081–656 4444. *Clubs:* Guildhall, City Livery, United Wards.

HOWARD, Rear-Adm. Jack; *see* Howard, Rear-Adm. C. J.

HOWARD, James Boag, CB 1972; Assistant Under-Secretary of State, Home Office, 1963–75; *b* 10 Jan. 1915; *yr s* of William and Jean Howard, Greenock; *m* 1943, Dorothy Jean Crawshaw; two *d*. *Educ:* Greenock High Sch.; Glasgow Univ. (MA, BSc; 1st cl. Hons Mathematics and Natural Philosophy). Asst Principal, Home Office, 1937; Private Sec. to Permanent Sec., Ministry of Home Security, 1940–41; Principal, 1941; Asst Sec., 1948. *Address:* 12 Windhill, Bishop's Stortford, Herts CM23 2NG. *T:* Bishop's Stortford (0279) 651728.

HOWARD, Dr James Griffiths, FRS 1984; FIBiol; Programme Director (formerly Assistant Director), The Wellcome Trust, 1986–90; *b* 25 Sept. 1927; *s* of late Joseph Griffiths Howard and Kathleen Mildred Howard; *m* 1951, Opal St Clair (*née* Echalaz); two *d* (one *s* decd). *Educ:* Middlesex Hosp. Med. Sch., Univ. of London (MB, BS 1950; PhD 1957; MD 1960). FIBiol 1978. Public Health Lab. Service, 1951–53; Jun. Specialist in Pathology, RAMC, 1953–55; Res. Fellow, Wright-Fleming Inst., St Mary's Hosp., 1955–58; Edinburgh University: Immunologist (Lectr, Sen. Lectr and Reader), Dept of Surgical Science, 1958–66; Reader and Head of Immunobiology Section, Dept of Zoology, 1966–69; Wellcome Research Laboratories: Head, Experimental Immunobiology Dept, 1969–74; Head, Exp. Biology Div., 1974–83; Dir, Biomedical Res., 1984–85. *Publications:* some 130 scientific articles, reviews and chapters in books, pre-dominantly on immunology. *Recreations:* fine arts, music, cinema, cooking, hill walking. *Address:* Sarnesfield Grange, Weobly, Herefordshire HR4 8RG. *T:* Weobly (0544) 318302.

HOWARD, (James) Kenneth, RA 1991 (ARA 1983); painter; *b* 26 Dec. 1932; *s* of Frank and Elizabeth Howard; *m* Ann Howard (*née* Popham), dress designer (marr. diss. 1974). *Educ:* Kilburn Grammar School; Hornsey School of Art; Royal College of Art. ARCA. NEAC 1962, ROI 1966, RWA 1981, RWS 1983. British Council scholarship to Florence, 1958–59; taught various London Art Schools, 1959–73; Official Artist for Imperial War Museum in N Ireland, 1973, 1978; painted for the British Army in N Ireland, Germany, Cyprus, Hong Kong, Brunei, Nepal, Belize, Norway, Lebanon, Canada, Oman, 1973–; one man exhibitions: Plymouth Art Centre, 1955; John Whibley Gallery, 1966, 1968; New Grafton Gallery, 1971–; Jersey, 1978, 1980, 1983; Hong Kong, 1979; Nicosia, 1982; Delhi, 1983; Lowndes Lodge Gall., 1987, 1989, 1990, 1991; Sinfield Gall., 1991. Works purchased by Plymouth Art Gall., Imperial War Mus., Guildhall Art Gall., Ulster

Mus., Nat. Army Mus., Hove Mus., Sheffield Art Gall., Southend Mus.; commissions for UN, BAOR, Drapers' Co., Stock Exchange, States of Jersey, Banque Paribas, Royal Hosp. Chelsea. Hon. ROI 1988; Hon. RBA 1989; RSBA 1991. First Prize: Hunting Group Award, 1982; Sparkasse Karlsruhe, 1985. Gen. Editor, Art Class series, 1988. *Publications:* contribs to: The War Artists, 1983; 60th Vol. of The Old Water-Colour Societies' Club, 1985; Painting Interiors, 1989; Art of Landscape and Seascape, 1989; Visions of Venice, 1990; Venice: the artist's vision, 1990; 20th Century Painters and Sculptors, 1991. *Recreations:* cinema, opera. *Address:* 8 South Bolton Gardens, SW5 0DH. *T:* 071–373 2912 (studio); St Clements Hall, Mousehole, Cornwall. *T:* Penzance (0736) 731596. *Clubs:* Arts, Chelsea Arts.

HOWARD, John James, CBE 1985; Chief General Manager, Royal Insurance plc, 1980–84; *b* 9 March 1923; *s* of late Sir Henry Howard, KCIE, CSI, and Lady Howard; *m* 1949, Julia Tupholme Mann; one *s* one *d* (and one *d* decd). *Educ:* Rugby Sch.; Trinity Hall, Cambridge (MA). Pilot, RAFVR, 1942–46 (Flt Lieut). Royal Insurance Company Ltd: Financial Secretary, 1964–69; General Manager, 1970–80, Director, 1970–84. Chm., British Insurance Assoc., 1983–84 (Dep. Chm., 1981–83). Chm., YWCA Central Club, 1986–90. Mem. Management Cttee, Effingham Housing Assoc., 1988–. *Recreations:* golf, competitive bridge, gardening, grandchildren. *Address:* Highfields, High Barn Road, Effingham, Surrey KT24 5PX.

HOWARD, Sir John (Philip), (Sir John Howard-Lawson), 6th Bt *cr* 1841, of Brough Hall, Yorkshire; *b* 6 June 1934; *s* of Sir William Howard Lawson, 5th Bt and Joan Eleanor (*d* 1989), *d* of late Maj. Arthur Cowie Stamer, CBE; assumed surname and arms of Howard by Royal Licence, 1962; *S* father, 1990; *m* 1960, Jean Veronica (*née* Marsh); two *s* one *d*. *Educ:* Ampleforth. *Heir: s* Philip William Howard [*b* 28 June 1961; *m* 1988, Cara Margaret Browne]. *Address:* Corby Castle, Carlisle CA4 8LR. *T:* Carlisle (0228) 60246. *Club:* Farmers'.

HOWARD, Hon. John Winston; MP (Lib) for Bennelong, NSW, since 1974; Leader of the Opposition, Australia, 1985–89 (Deputy Leader, 1983–85); *b* 26 July 1939; *m* 1971, Alison Janette Parker; two *s* one *d*. *Educ:* Canterbury Boys' High Sch.; Sydney Univ. Solicitor of NSW Supreme Court. Minister for Business and Consumer Affairs, Australia, 1975; Minister assisting Prime Minister, May 1977; Minister for Special Trade Negotiations, July 1977; Federal Treasurer, 1977–83; Leader, Parly Liberal Party, Australia, 1985–89 (Dep. Leader, 1982–85). *Recreations:* reading, tennis, cricket. *Address:* 19 Milner Crescent, Wollstonecraft, NSW 2065, Australia. *T:* 02–4394360. *Club:* Australian (Sydney).

HOWARD, Kenneth; *see* Howard, J. K.

HOWARD, Leonard Henry, RD 1941; retired; *b* 5 Aug. 1904; *m* 1st, 1938, Betty Scourse; one *s* one *d*; 2nd, 1960, Barbara Davies-Colley. *Educ:* Stubbington House Sch.; Nautical Coll., Pangbourne. Sea career in Royal Navy and P&O-Orient Lines (Merchant Navy), 1922–64; commanded several RN units, War of 1939–45; Comdr, troop ship Empire Fowey, and passenger ships Strathmore, Himalaya and Arcadia, P&O Co.; Commodore, P&O-Orient Lines, 1963–64 (now P&O Steam Navigation Co.), retired. *Recreations:* golf, gardening. *Address:* Port, Heyshott, Midhurst, W Sussex. *T:* Midhurst (073081) 2560. *Club:* Cowdray Park Golf.

HOWARD, Margaret; freelance broadcaster, since 1969; *b* 29 March 1938; *d* of John Bernard Howard and Ellen Corwena Roberts. *Educ:* St Mary's Convent, Rhyl, N Wales; St Teresa's Convent, Sunbury; Guildhall Sch. of Music and Drama; Indiana Univ., Bloomington, USA. LGSM; LRAM 1960. BBC World Service Announcer, 1967–69; Reporter: The World This Weekend, BBC Radio 4, 1970–74; Edition, BBC TV, 1971; Tomorrow's World, BBC TV, 1972; Presenter: Pick of the Week, BBC Radio 4, 1974–91; It's Your World, BBC World Service, 1981–; Interviewer/Presenter, Strictly Instrumental, occasional series, 1980–85. Female UK Radio Personality of the Year, Sony Awards, 1984; Sony Radio Awards Roll of Honour, 1988. FRSA 1990. *Publications:* Margaret Howard's Pick of the Week, 1984; Court Jesting, 1986. *Recreations:* riding, tasting wine, walking the Jack Russell. *Address:* 215 Cavendish Road, SW12 0BP. *T:* 081–673 7336.

HOWARD, Rt. Hon. Michael, PC 1990; QC 1982; MP (C) Folkestone and Hythe, since 1983; Secretary of State for Employment, since 1990; *b* 7 July 1941; *s* of late Bernard Howard and of Hilda Howard; *m* 1975, Sandra Clare, *d* of Wing-Comdr Saville Paul; one *s* one *d* (and one step *s*). *Educ:* Llanelli Grammar School; Peterhouse, Cambridge. MA, LLB; President of the Union, 1962. Major Scholar, Inner Temple, 1962; called to the Bar, Inner Temple, 1964. Junior Counsel to the Crown (Common Law), 1980–82; a Recorder, 1986–. Contested (C) Liverpool, Edge Hill, 1966 and 1970; Chm., Bow Group, 1970–71. PPS to Solicitor-General, 1984–85; Parly Under-Sec. of State, DTI, 1985–87; Minister of State, DoE, 1987–90. Jt Sec., Cons. Legal Cttee, 1983–84; Jt Vice-Chm., Cons. Employment Cttee, 1983–84; Vice-Chm., Soc. of Cons. Lawyers, 1985. *Recreations:* watching football (Swansea, Liverpool) and baseball (New York Mets). *Address:* House of Commons, SW1A 0AA. *T:* 071–219 5493. *Clubs:* Carlton, Coningsby (Chm., 1972–73).

HOWARD, Sir Michael (Eliot), Kt 1986; CBE 1977; MC 1943; DLitt; FBA 1970; FRHistS; FRSL; Lovett Professor of Military and Naval History, Yale University, since 1989; *b* 29 Nov. 1922; *y s* of late Geoffrey Eliot Howard, Ashmore, near Salisbury, and of Edith Julia Emma, *o d* of Otto Edinger. *Educ:* Wellington; Christ Church, Oxford (BA 1946, MA 1948; Hon. Student, 1990). Served War, Coldstream Guards, 1942–45. Asst Lecturer in History, University of London, King's Coll., 1947; Lecturer, 1950; Lecturer in War Studies, 1953–61; Prof. of War Studies, 1963–68; University of Oxford: Fellow of All Souls Coll., 1968–80; Chichele Prof. of History of War, 1977–80; Regius Prof. of Modern History and Fellow of Oriel Coll., 1980–89 (Hon. Fellow, 1990). Vis. Prof. of European History, Stanford Univ., 1967. Ford's Lectr in English History, Oxford, 1971; Radcliffe Lectr, Univ. of Warwick, 1975; Trevelyan Lectr, Cambridge, 1977; FKC. Pres. and co-Founder, Internat. Institute for Strategic Studies; Vice-President: Council on Christian Approaches to Defence and Disarmament; Historical Assoc. For. Hon. Mem., Amer. Acad. of Arts and Scis, 1983. Hon. LittD Leeds, 1979; Hon. DLit London, 1988; Hon. DHumLit Lehigh Univ., Pa, USA, 1990. Chesney Meml Gold Medal, RUSI, 1973. *Publications:* The Coldstream Guards, 1920–46 (with John Sparrow), 1951; Disengagement in Europe, 1958; Wellingtonian Studies, 1959; The Franco-Prussian War, 1961 (Duff Cooper Memorial Prize, 1962); The Theory and Practice of War, 1965; The Mediterranean Strategy in the Second World War, 1967; Studies in War and Peace, 1970; Grand Strategy, vol IV (in UK History of 2nd World War, Military series), 1971 (Wolfson Foundn History Award, 1972); The Continental Commitment, 1972; War in European History, 1976; (with P. Paret) Clausewitz On War, 1977; War and the Liberal Conscience, 1978; (ed) Restraints on War, 1979; The Causes of Wars, 1983; Clausewitz, 1983; Strategic Deception in World War II, 1990; The Lessons of History, 1991. *Address:* The Old Farm, Eastbury, Newbury, Berks RG16 7JN. *Clubs:* Athenæum, Garrick; Yale (New York).

HOWARD, Michael Newman; QC 1986; *b* 10 June 1947; *s* of Henry Ian Howard and Tilly Celia Howard. *Educ:* Clifton College; Magdalen College, Oxford (MA, BCL). Lecturer in Law, LSE, 1970–74; called to the Bar, Gray's Inn, 1971; in practice at Bar, 1971–. Vis. Prof. of Law, Univ. of Essex, 1987–. Mem. of Panel, Lloyd's Salvage Arbitrators, 1987–. *Publications:* (ed jtly) Phipson on Evidence, 12th edn 1976 to 14th edn 1990; (contrib.) Frustration and Force Majeure (ed McKendrick), 1991; articles in legal periodicals. *Recreations:* books, music, sport. *Address:* 2 Essex Court, Temple, EC4Y 9AP. *T:* 071–583 8381. *Clubs:* United Oxford & Cambridge University, Royal Automobile.

HOWARD, Michael Stockwin; Director, Cantores in Ecclesia, since 1964; Co-founder and Artistic Director, Rye Spring Music, 1976; *b* London, 14 Sept. 1922; *er s* of late Frank Henry Howard (viola, Internat. String Quartet, Foundn principal, Beecham's Philharmonic) and Florence Mabel Howard. *Educ:* Ellesmere; Royal Acad. of Music; privately. Organist, Tewkesbury Abbey, 1943–44; Dir of Music, Ludgrove Sch.; Founder, Renaissance Society, and conductor, Renaissance Singers, 1944–64; Organist and Master of the Choristers, Ely Cath., 1953–58; Dir of Music, St George's Sch., Harpenden, 1959–61; Asst, Music Presentation, BBC, 1968–78; Dir of Music, St Marylebone Parish Church, 1971–79, Dir Emeritus, 1979; Organist to the Franciscans of Rye, 1979–83; Organist and Rector Chori, St Michael's Abbey, Farnborough, 1984–86. Freelance organist, harpsichordist, conductor, broadcaster and writer. Hon. ARAM 1976. Prix Musicale de Radio Brno, 1967; Gustave Charpentier Grand Prix du Disque, 1975. Recordings with essays include: Tallis/Byrd 1575 Cantiones Sacrae, 1969; Tallis at Waltham Abbey, 1974; Palestrina, The Garden of Love, 1974; recordings at Farnborough: Widor, Vierne, Tournemire, Saint-Saëns, Franck, all performed on England's only Cavaillé-Coll organ, 1988–89. *Principal compositions include:* Mass, Sonnet VIII, 1961; Scaena Dramatis for Antoinette Michael, 1978; Dances for a Mountain Goat, 1979; opera, The Lion's Mouth, 1980; Sequentia de Insomnia, 1981; Diptych (Arnold and St Ambrose), 1981; Discourse on Chorale by Judith Earley, 1982; Cantiones Iudithae, 1983; In Memoriam Duncan Thomson, 1983; Missa de Ecclesia Christi, 1984; *organ:* Cantique d'un Oiseau matinal, 1982; Carillon des Larmes, 1982; Te Deum Cardinalis, 1987. *Publications:* The Private Inferno (autobiog.), 1974; Tribute to Aristide Cavaillé-Coll, 1985; contrib. Musical Times, Monthly Musical Record, Dublin Review, Listener, EMG Monthly Letter, The Organists' Review. *Recreations:* steam railway traction, village fairgrounds. *Address:* 9 Wallisfield, Groombridge, Sussex TN3 9SE.

HOWARD, Air Vice-Marshal Peter, CB 1989; OBE 1957; FRCP, FRAeS; Commandant, RAF Institute of Aviation Medicine, 1975–88; The Senior Consultant, RAF, 1987–88; *b* 15 Dec. 1925; *s* of late Edward Charles Howard and Doris Mary Howard (*née* Cure); *m* 1950, Norma Lockhart Fletcher; one *s* one *d*. *Educ:* Farnborough Grammar Sch.; St Thomas's Hosp. Med. Sch. (MB BS 1949, PhD 1964); FRCP 1977; FFOM 1981; FRAeS 1973. House Physician, 1950, Registrar, 1951. St Thomas' Hosp.; RAF Medical Branch, 1951–88; RAF Consultant in Aviation Physiology, 1964; RAF Consultant Adviser in Occupational Medicine, 1983–85; Dean of Air Force Medicine, 1985–87. QHP 1982–88. Chm., Defence Med. Services Postgraduate Council, 1986–87; Registrar, Faculty of Occupational Medicine, RCP, 1986–91. *Publications:* papers and chapters in books on aviation physiology, medicine, occupational medicine. *Recreations:* fly fishing, computing. *Address:* 135 Aldershot Road, Church Crookham, Hants GU13 0JU. *T:* Fleet (0252) 617309. *Club:* Royal Air Force.

HOWARD, Philip Nicholas Charles, FRSL; Literary Editor of The Times, since 1978; *b* 2 Nov. 1933; *s* of Peter Dunsmore Howard and Doris Emily Metaxa; *m* 1959, Myrtle, *d* of Sir Reginald Houldsworth, 4th Bt, OBE, TD; two *s* one *d*. *Educ:* Eton Coll. (King's Scholar); Trinity Coll., Oxford (Major Scholar; MA). Glasgow Herald, 1959–64; The Times, 1964–: reporter, writer, columnist. Member: Classical Assoc.; Horatian Soc.; Soc. of Bookmen; Literary Soc. FRSL 1987. Liveryman, Wheelwrights' Co. London Editor, Verbatim, 1977–. *Publications:* The Black Watch, 1968; The Royal Palaces, 1970; London's River, 1975; New Words for Old, 1977; The British Monarchy, 1977; Weasel Words, 1978; Words Fail Me, 1980; A Word in Your Ear, 1983; The State of the Language, English Observed, 1984; (jtly) The Times Bicentenary Stamp Book, 1985; We Thundered Out, 200 Years of The Times 1785–1985, 1985; Winged Words, 1988; Word-Watching, 1988; (jtly) London, The Evolution of a Great City, 1989; A Word in Time, 1990; (ed) The Times Bedside Book, 1991. *Recreations:* walking, talking, music, the classics, beagles not beagling, stand at Twickenham. *Address:* Flat 1, 47 Ladbroke Grove, W11 3AR. *T:* 071–727 1077. *Clubs:* Garrick; Ad Eundem (Oxford and Cambridge).

HOWARD, Robert, (Bob); Northern Regional Secretary, Trades Union Congress, since 1980; *b* 4 April 1939; *s* of Robert and Lily Howard; *m* 1984, Valerie Stewart; two *s* one *d*. *Educ:* Gregson Lane County Primary Sch.; Deepdale Secondary Modern Sch.; Queen Elizabeth's Grammar Sch., Blackburn, Lancs; Cliff Training Coll., Calver via Sheffield, Derbyshire. British Leyland, Lancs, 1961–68: Member, Clerical and Admin. Workers' Union Br. Exec.; Councillor, Walton le Dale UDC, 1962–65; GPO, Preston, Lancs, 1969–80: Telephone Area UPW Telecomms Representative Member: Jt Consultative Council, Jt Productivity Council, Council of PO Unions Area Cttee, Delegate to Preston Trades Council; Secretary, Lancashire Assoc. of Trades Councils, 1977–79; created 14 specialist cttees for LATC; appointment as N Reg. Sec., Trades Union Congress, 1980–, by Gen. Sec., TUC, first full-time secretary to a TUC region. Member: Industrial Tribunals, 1979–80; Northumbria Regional Cttee, Nat. Trust, 1989–; Council, Northern Exams Assoc., 1986–; Bd, Durham Univ. Business Sch., 1987–; Bd, Tyneside TEC, 1989–. Northern Region Coordinator, Jobs March, 1983; Exec. Organiser, Great North Family Gala Day, 1986–90. JP Duchy of Lancaster, 1969–74. *Publications:* North-East Lancashire Structure Plan—The Trades Councils' View (with Peter Stock), 1979; Organisation and Functions of TUC Northern Regional Council, 1980. *Recreations:* fell walking, opera, ballet, classical music, camping, spectating outdoor sports, reading, chess. *Address:* 8 Caxton Way, North Lodge, Chester le Street, County Durham DH3 4BW.

HOWARD, Rev. Canon Ronald Claude; Headmaster, Hurstpierpoint College, 1945–64; *b* 15 Feb. 1902; 2nd *s* of Henry H. and Florence Howard, The Durrant, Sevenoaks. *Educ:* Sidney Sussex Coll., Cambridge; Westcott House, Cambridge. Ordained, 1926; Curate of Eastbourne, 1926–28; Chaplain, Bradfield Coll., 1928–30; Asst Master, Tonbridge Sch., 1930–37; Asst Master, Marlborough Coll., 1937, Chaplain there, 1938–43; Chaplain and Asst Master, Radley Coll., 1943–45. Canon of Chichester, 1957; Communar of Chichester Cathedral, 1964–67. Canon Emeritus, 1967. *Recreations:* painting, collecting water-colours. *Address:* 52 Wilbury Road, Hove, East Sussex BN3 3PA.

HOWARD, Dame (Rosemary) Christian, DBE 1986; *b* 5 Sept. 1916; *d* of Hon. Geoffrey Howard, *s* of 9th Earl of Carlisle, and Hon. Christian, *d* of 3rd Baron Methuen. *Educ:* Westbourne House, Folkestone; Villa Malatesta, Florence; Ozannes, Paris; and privately. STh Lambeth 1943; MA Lambeth 1979. Divinity Teacher, Chichester High Sch. for Girls, 1943–45; Licensed Lay Worker, Dio. York, 1947–; Sec., Bd of Women's Work, 1947–72; Sec., Lay Ministry, 1972–79; retired 1980. Deleg. to WCC Assemblies, 1961 and 1968; Member: Faith and Order Commn, WCC, 1961–75; BCC, 1974–87; Church Assembly, 1960–70, General Synod, 1970–85; Churches' Council for

Covenanting, 1978–82. Governor, Slingsby School. *Publications:* The Ordination of Women to Priesthood, 1972, Supplement 1978, Further Report 1984; Praise and Thanksgiving, 1972; contribs to Ecumenical Review, Year Book of Social Policy, Crucible, New Directions, Chrysalis. *Recreations:* woodwork, gardening, foreign travel. *Address:* Coneysthorpe, York YO6 7DD. *T:* Coneysthorpe (065384) 264.

HOWARD, Sir Walter Stewart, Kt 1963; MBE 1944; DL; *b* 25 Nov. 1888; *y s* of late Henry Blunt Howard; *m* 1917, Alison Mary Wall (*d* 1985), *e d* of late Herbert F. Waring, Farningham Hill, Kent. *Educ:* Wellington; Trinity Coll., Cambridge. Vice-Chm., Warwicks CC, 1955 (Chm., 1956–60); Chm. Whiteley Village Trust, 1952–62; Governor: King Edward VI Sch., Birmingham; Warwick Sch.; Pres., Association of Education Cttees, 1962–63. Trustee of Shakespeare's birthplace. JP 1931, CC 1939, CA 1948, DL 1952, Warwicks. *Recreation:* foreign travel. *Address:* Guy's Nursing Home, 26 Warwick New Road, Leamington Spa CV32 5JJ. *Club:* United Oxford & Cambridge University.

HOWARD, William Brian; Deputy Chairman, Northern Foods plc, since 1988 (Director, since 1987); Deputy Chairman, 1984–87, Joint Managing Director, 1976–86, Marks & Spencer plc; *b* 16 July 1926; *s* of William James and Annie Howard; *m* 1952, Audrey Elizabeth (*née* Jenney); one *s* one *d*. *Educ:* Revoe Junior Sch., Blackpool; Blackpool Grammar Sch.; Manchester Univ. (BA (Hons) Mod. Hist., Economics and Politics); Harvard Graduate Business Sch., 1973. Royal Signals, 1944–47. Marks & Spencer Ltd, 1951–87; Dir, 1973–87. A Church Comr, 1977–. *Address:* c/o Beverley House, St Stephen's Square, Hull HU1 3XG.

HOWARD-DOBSON, Gen. Sir Patrick John, GCB 1979 (KCB 1974; CB 1973); *b* 12 Aug. 1921; *s* of late Canon Howard Dobson, MA; *m* 1946, Barbara Mary Mills; two *s* one *d*. *Educ:* King's Coll. Choir Sch., Cambridge; Framlingham College. Joined 7th Queen's Own Hussars, Egypt, Dec. 1941; served in: Burma, 1942; Middle East, 1943; Italy, 1944–45; Germany, 1946; psc 1950; jssc 1958; comd The Queen's Own Hussars, 1963–65 and 20 Armoured Bde, 1965–67; idc 1968; Chief of Staff, Far East Comd, 1969–71; Comdt, Staff Coll., Camberley, 1972–74; Military Secretary, 1974–76; Quartermaster General, 1977–79; Vice-Chief of Defence Staff (Personnel and Logistics), 1979–81; ADC Gen. to the Queen, 1978–81. Col Comdt, ACC, 1976–82. Nat. Pres., Royal British Legion, 1981–87. Virtuti Militari (Poland), 1945; Silver Star (US), 1945. *Recreations:* sailing, golf. *Address:* 1 Drury Park, Snape, Saxmundham, Suffolk IP17 1TA. *Club:* Cavalry and Guards.

HOWARD-DRAKE, Jack Thomas Arthur; Assistant Under-Secretary of State, Home Office, 1974–78; *b* 7 Jan. 1919; *o s* of Arthur Howard and Ruby (*née* Cherry); *m* 1947, Joan Mary, *o d* of Hubert and Winifred Crook; one *s* two *d*. *Educ:* Hele's Sch., Exeter. Asst Inspector, Ministry of Health Insurance Dept, 1937–39 and 1946–47. Served War, RA, 1939–46 (Major, despatches). Colonial Office: Asst Principal, 1947; Principal, 1949; Private Sec. to Sec. of State, 1956–62; Asst Sec., 1962; Asst Sec., Cabinet Office, 1963–65; Asst Sec., Home Office, 1965–72; Asst Under-Sec. of State, NI Office, 1972–74. Chairman: Oxfordshire Local History Assoc., 1984–91; Wychwoods Local History Soc., 1984–. *Recreations:* gardening, local history, golf. *Address:* 26 Sinnels Field, Shipton-under-Wychwood, Oxon OX7 6EJ. *T:* Shipton-under-Wychwood (0993) 830792.

HOWARD-JOHNSTON, Rear-Admiral Clarence Dinsmore, CB 1955; DSO 1942; DSC 1940; *b* 13 Oct. 1903; *m* 1955, Paulette, *d* of late Paul Helleu. *Educ:* Royal Naval Colls Osborne and Dartmouth. Midshipman, 1921; Commander, 1937; Dir of Studies, Greek Naval War Coll., Athens, 1938–40; Naval staff, anti-submarine Warfare Div., Admlty, 1940; detached to set up anti-sub. trng, Quiberon, 1940; i/c ops for destruction port facilities St Malo, evacuation British troops St Malo and Jersey (despatches); anti-sub. ops, Norwegian fjords, evacuation troops and wounded, Molde and Andalsnes (DSC); in comd anti-sub. escort group, N Atlantic, 1941–42; escorted 1,229 ships (DSO for sinking U651); staff, Battle of Atlantic Comd, Liverpool, 1942–43; Captain, 1943; Dir, Anti-U-boat Div., Admlty, 1943–45, anti-sub. specialist, PM's Cabinet U-boat meetings; in Comd, HMS Bermuda, British Pacific Fleet and occupation of Japan forces, 1946–47; Naval Attaché, Paris, 1947–50; Naval ADC to the Queen, 1952; Rear-Adm., 1953; Chief of Staff to Flag Officer, Central Europe, 1953–55, retired, 1955. Inventor of simple hydraulic mechanisms; commended by Lords Comrs of the Admiralty for invention and develt of anti-submarine training devices including Johnston Mobile A/S target, 1937. Participated in and prepared maritime historical programmes on French TV, 1967–81. Order of Phœnix (Greece), 1940; Legion of Merit (USA), 1945. *Recreations:* fishing, pisiculture, hill-walking, gardening. *Address:* 45 Rue Emile Ménier, 75116 Paris, France; Le Coteau, Chambre d'Amour, 64600 Anglet, France. *Clubs:* White's, Naval and Military, (Naval Member) Royal Yacht Squadron; Jockey (Paris).

HOWARD-LAWSON, Sir John; *see* Howard, Sir J.

HOWARD-VYSE, Lt-Gen. Sir Edward (Dacre), KBE 1962 (CBE 1955); CB 1958; MC 1941; DL; *b* 27 Nov. 1905; *s* of late Lieut-Col Cecil Howard-Vyse, JP, Langton Hall, Malton, Yorks; *m* 1940, Mary Bridget, *er d* of late Col Hon. Claude Henry Comaraich Willoughby, CVO; two *s* one *d*. *Educ:* Wellington Coll., Berks; RMA. 2nd Lieut, Royal Artillery, 1925; served War of 1939–45: British Expeditionary Force, France, 1939–40; Lieut-Col, 1941; Mediterranean Expeditionary Force, 1941–44; In command 1st Royal Horse Artillery, Central Mediterranean Force, 1944–45. Brigadier, 1949; CRA 7th Armoured Division, BAOR, 1951–53; Commandant, Sch. of Artillery, 1953; Maj.-Gen., 1957; Maj.-Gen., Artillery, Northern Army Group, 1956–59; Dir, Royal Artillery, War Office, 1959–61; GOC-in-C, Western Command, 1961–64; retired, 1964. Lieut-Gen., 1961. Col Comdt: RA 1962–70; RHA 1968–70. Vice-Pres., Army Cadet Force Assoc., 1974–, Chm., 1964–74; Vice-Pres., Nat. Artillery Assoc., 1965–. DL E Riding of Yorks and Kingston upon Hull, 1964, Vice-Lieut, 1968–74; DL N Yorkshire, 1974–. Mem., British Olympic Equestrian Team, 1936 (Bronze medal). *Recreations:* country pursuits. *Address:* Langton House, Malton, North Yorks YO17 9QW. *Club:* Army and Navy.

HOWARTH, Alan Thomas, CBE 1982; MP (C) Stratford-on-Avon, since 1983; Parliamentary Under-Secretary of State, Department of Education and Science, since 1989; *b* 11 June 1944; *e s* of late T. E. B. Howarth, MC, TD and Margaret Howarth; *m* 1967, Gillian Martha, *d* of Mr and Mrs Arthur Chance, Dublin; two *s* two *d*. *Educ:* Rugby Sch. (scholar); King's Coll., Cambridge (major scholar in History; BA 1965). Sen. Res. Asst to Field-Marshal Montgomery on A History of Warfare, 1965–67; Asst Master, Westminster Sch., 1968–74; Private Sec. to Chm. of Conservative Party, 1975–79; Dir, Cons. Res. Dept, 1979–81; Vice-Chm., Conservative Party, 1980–81. PPS to Dr Rhodes Boyson, MP, 1985–87; an Asst Govt Whip, 1987–88; Lord Comr of HM Treasury, 1988–89. Sec., Cons. Arts and Heritage Cttee, 1984–85. Governor, Royal Shakespeare Theatre, 1984–. *Publications:* (jtly) Monty at Close Quarters, 1985; jt author of various CPC pamphlets. *Recreations:* books, travel, the arts, running. *Address:* House of Commons, SW1A 0AA.

HOWARTH, Elgar; freelance musician; *b* 4 Nov. 1935; *s* of Oliver and Emma Howarth; *m* 1958, Mary Bridget Neary; one *s* two *d*. *Educ:* Manchester Univ. (MusB); Royal Manchester Coll. of Music (ARMCM 1956; FRMCM 1970). Royal Opera House, Covent Garden (Orchestra), 1958–63; Royal Philharmonic Orchestra, 1963–69; Mem., London Sinfonietta, 1968–71; Mem., Philip Jones Brass Ensemble, 1965–76; freelance conductor, 1970–; Principal Guest Conductor, Opera North, 1985–88; Musical Advisor, Grimethorpe Colliery Brass Band, 1972–. *Publications:* various compositions mostly for brass instruments. *Address:* 27 Cromwell Avenue, N6.

HOWARTH, George Edward; MP (Lab) Knowsley North, since Nov. 1986; *b* 29 June 1949; *m* 1977, Julie Rodgers; two *s* one *d*. *Educ:* Liverpool Polytechnic. Formerly: engineer; teacher; Chief Exec., Wales TUC's Co-operative Centre, 1984–86. Former Mem., Huyton UDC; Mem., Knowsley Bor. Council, 1975–86 (Dep. Leader, 1982). *Address:* House of Commons, SW1A 0AA.

HOWARTH, (James) Gerald (Douglas); MP (C) Cannock and Burntwood, since 1983; *b* 12 Sept. 1947; *s* of late James Howarth and of Mary Howarth, Hurley, Berks; *m* 1973, Elizabeth Jane, *d* of Michael and Muriel Squibb, Crowborough, Sussex; two *s* one *d*. *Educ:* Haileybury and ISC Jun. Sch.; Bloxham Sch.; Southampton Univ. (BA Hons). Commnd RAFVR, 1968. Gen. Sec., Soc. for Individual Freedom, 1969–71; entered internat. banking, 1971; Bank of America Internat., 1971–77; European Arab Bank, 1977–81 (Manager, 1979–81); Syndication Manager, Standard Chartered Bank, 1981–83. Dir, Richard Unwin Internat., 1983–87. Dir, Freedom Under Law, 1973–77; estabd Dicey Trust, 1976. Mem., Hounslow BC, 1982–83. Parliamentary Private Secretary: to Parly Under-Sec. of State for Energy, 1987–90; to Minister for Housing and Planning, 1990–. Mem., Select Cttee on Sound Broadcasting, 1987–. Jt Sec., Cons. Parly Aviation Cttee, 1983–87. Britannia Airways Parly Pilot of the Year, 1988. Contributor to No Turning Back Gp pubns. *Recreations:* flying (private pilot's licence, 1965), squash, walking up hills, normal family pursuits. *Address:* House of Commons, SW1. *T:* 071–219 3580.

HOWARTH, Prof. Leslie, OBE 1955; BSc, MA, PhD; FRS 1950; FRAeS; Henry Overton Wills Professor of Mathematics, University of Bristol, 1964–76, now Emeritus; *b* 23 May 1911; *s* of late Fred and Elizabeth Ellen Howarth; *m* 1934, Eva Priestley; two *s*. *Educ:* Accrington Grammar Sch.; Manchester Univ.; Gonville and Caius Coll., Cambridge. Mathematical tripos, 1933; Smith's Prize, 1935; PhD, 1936. FRAeS 1951. Berry-Ramsey Research Fellow, King's Coll., Cambridge, 1936–45; Lecturer in Mathematics in the University of Cambridge, 1936–49; Fellow of St John's Coll., Cambridge, 1945–49; Prof. of Applied Mathematics, University of Bristol, 1949–64; Adams Prize, 1951. Worked at External Ballistics Dept, Ordnance Board, 1939–42, and at Armament Research Dept, 1942–45. Hon. FIMA 1979. *Publications:* (ed) Modern Developments in Fluid Dynamics: High Speed Flow; papers on aerodynamics. *Address:* 10 The Crescent, Henleaze, Bristol BS9 4RW. *T:* Bristol (0272) 629621.

HOWARTH, Robert Lever; Leader, Labour Group, Bolton Metropolitan Borough, since 1975; Leader, Bolton Metropolitan Borough Council, since 1980; *b* 31 July 1927; *s* of James Howarth and Bessie (*née* Pearson); *m* 1952, Josephine Mary Doyle; one *s* one *d*. *Educ:* Bolton County Grammar Sch.; Bolton Technical Coll. Draughtsman with Hawker Siddeley Dynamics. MP (Lab) Bolton East, 1964–70. Lectr in Liberal Studies, Leigh Technical Coll., 1970–76; Senior Lectr in General Studies, Wigan Coll. of Technology, 1977–87. Dep. Chm., 1986–87, Chm., 1987–88, Manchester Airport. *Recreations:* gardening, reading, walking, films. *Address:* 93 Markland Hill, Bolton, Lancs BL1 5EQ. *T:* Bolton (0204) 44121.

HOWAT, Prof. Henry Taylor, CBE 1971; MSc (Manch.); MD, FRCP, FRCPE; Professor of Gastroenterology, University of Manchester, 1972–76, now Emeritus; Physician, Manchester Royal Infirmary, 1948–76; *b* 16 May 1911; *s* of late Adam Howat, MA, and late Henrietta Howat, Pittenweem, Fife; *m* 1940, Rosaline, *o d* of late Miles Green, Auckland, NZ; two *s* one *d*. *Educ:* Cameron Public Sch. and Madras Coll., St Andrews; Univ. of St Andrews. MB, ChB (St And) 1933; MD with Hons and Univ. Gold Medal (St And), 1960; MRCP 1937, FRCP 1948; MRCPE 1961, FRCPE 1965. Resident MO, Manchester Royal Infirmary, 1938–40. Served War, MEF and BLA; RMO, Physician Specialist, Officer in charge of Med. Div., Mil. Hosps, 1940–46; temp. Lt-Col, RAMC. Univ. of Manchester: Asst Lectr in Applied Physiology, 1946–48; Lectr in Med., 1948–69 (Chm., Faculty of Med., 1968–72); Reader, 1969–72; Physician, Ancoats Hosp., Manchester, 1946–62. United Manchester Hospitals, 1948–76: Chm., Med. Exec. Cttee, 1968–73; Mem., Bd of Governors, 1966–74. President: European Pancreatic Club, 1965; British Soc. of Gastroenterology, 1968–69; Assoc. of Physicians of GB and Ireland, 1975–76; Manchester Med. Soc., 1975–76; Pancreatic Soc. of GB and Ireland, 1978–79. Hon. MD, Univ. of Louvain, Belgium, 1945. Manchester Man of the Year, 1973. Medallist, J. E. Purkyně Czechoslovak Med. Soc., 1968; Diploma and Medallion of Hungarian Gastroenterol Soc., 1988. *Publications:* (ed) The Exocrine Pancreas, 1979; articles on gastrointestinal physiology and disease. *Recreation:* golf. *Address:* 3 Brookdale Rise, Hilton Road, Bramhall, Cheshire SK7 3AG. *T:* 061–439 2853; 40 High Street, Pittenweem, Fife KY10 2PL. *T:* Anstruther (0333) 311325. *Clubs:* Athenæum; Royal and Ancient Golf (St Andrews).

HOWD, Mrs Isobel; Regional Nursing Officer, Yorkshire Regional Health Authority, 1973–83; *b* 24 Oct. 1928 (*née* Young); *m* 1951, Ralph Howd. SRN, RMN, BTA Cert. Matron, Naburn Hosp., York, 1960–63; Asst Regional Nursing Officer, Leeds Regional Hosp. Bd, 1963–70; Chief Nursing Officer, South Teesside Hosp. Management Cttee, 1970–73. Mem., Mental Health Act Commn, 1983–87. *Address:* Yew Tree Cottage, Upper Dunsforth, York YO5 9RU. *T:* Boroughbridge (0423) 322534.

HOWDEN, Timothy Simon; Managing Director, Ranks Hovis McDougall, since 1989; *b* 2 April 1937; *s* of Phillip Alexander and Rene Howden; *m* 1958, Penelope Mary Wilmott (marr. diss. 1984); two *s* one *d*. *Educ:* Tonbridge Sch. Served RA, 1955–57, 2nd Lieut. Floor Treatments Ltd, 1957–59; joined Reckitt & Colman, 1962; France, 1962–64; Germany, 1964–70; Dir, Reckitt & Colman Europe, 1970–73; Ranks Hovis McDougall, 1973–: Dir, RHM Flour Mills, 1973–75; Man. Dir, RHM Foods, 1975–81; Chm. and Man. Dir, British Bakeries, 1981–85; Planning, then Dep. Man. Dir, RHM PLC, 1985–89. *Recreations:* ski-ing, scuba diving, tennis, sailing. *Clubs:* Naval and Military, Annabel's.

HOWE, 7th Earl *cr* 1821; **Frederick Richard Penn Curzon;** Baron Howe, 1788; Baron Curzon, 1794; Viscount Curzon, 1802; a Lord in Waiting (Government Whip), since 1991; farmer; *b* 29 Jan. 1951; *s* of Chambré George William Penn Curzon (*d* 1976) (*g s* of 3rd Earl) and of Enid Jane Victoria Curzon (*née* Fergusson); *S* cousin, 1984; *m* 1983, Elizabeth Helen Stuart; two *d*. *Educ:* Rugby School; Christ Church, Oxford (MA Hons Lit. Hum.; Chancellor's Prize for Latin Verse, 1973). AIB. Entered Barclays Bank Ltd, 1973; Manager, 1982; Sen. Manager, 1984–87. Director: Adam & Co., 1987–90; Provident Life Assoc. Ltd, 1988–91. Governor: King William IV Naval Foundation, 1984–; Milton's Cottage, 1985–; Trident Trust, 1985–; President: S Bucks Assoc. for the Disabled, 1984–; Chilterns Br., RNLI, 1985–; Nat. Soc. for Epilepsy, 1986– (Vice-Pres., 1984–86); Penn Country Br., CPRE, 1986–. *Recreation:* spending time with family. *Heir: cousin* Charles Mark Penn Curzon, *b* 12 Nov. 1967. *Address:* Penn House, Amersham, Bucks HP7 0PS. *T:* High Wycombe (0494) 713366.

HOWE, Allen; Circuit Administrator, Wales and Chester Circuit, 1974–82; Chairman, Medical Appeals Tribunal for Wales, since 1982; *b* 6 June 1918; *s* of late Frank Howe and Dora Howe, Monk Bretton, Yorks; *m* 1952, Katherine, *d* of late Griffith and Catherine Davies, Pontypridd; two *d*. *Educ:* Holgate Grammar Sch., Barnsley. Served with E Yorks Regt and RWAFF, 1939–46, France, Africa, India and Burma (Major). HM Colonial Admin. Service, Gold Coast, 1946–55 (Sen. Dist Comr). Called to Bar, Middle Temple, 1953; Judicial Adviser, Ashanti, 1954–55; practised Wales and Chester Circuit, 1955–59; Legal Dept, Welsh Bd of Health, 1959–65; Legal Dept, Welsh Office, 1965–74. *Recreations:* golf, gardening, walking. *Address:* 2 Orchard Drive, Whitchurch, Cardiff CF4 2AE. *T:* Cardiff (0222) 626626. *Clubs:* Cardiff and County; Radyr Golf.

HOWE, Prof. Christopher Barry, PhD; Professor of Economics with reference to Asia, University of London, since 1979; *b* 3 Nov. 1937; *s* of Charles Roderick Howe and Patricia (*née* Creeden); *m* 1967, Patricia Anne Giles; one *s* one *d*. *Educ:* William Ellis Sch., London; St Catharine's Coll., Cambridge (MA). PhD London. Economic Secretariat, FBI, 1961–63; Sch. of Oriental and African Studies, London Univ., 1963–: Head, Contemp. China Inst., 1972–78. Member: Hong Kong Univ. and Polytechnic Grants Cttee, 1974–; UGC, 1979–84; ESRC Res. Develt Gp, 1987–88; Hong Kong Res. Grants Council, 1991–. Chm., Japan and SE Asia Business Gp, 1983–87. *Publications:* Employment and Economic Growth in Urban China 1949–57, 1971; Industrial Relations and Rapid Industrialisation, 1972; Wage Patterns and Wage Policy in Modern China 1919–1972, 1973; China's Economy: a basic guide, 1978; (ed) Studying China, 1979; (ed) Shanghai: revolution and development, 1980; (ed) The Readjustment in the Chinese Economy, 1984; (ed) China and Japan: history, trends and prospects, 1990. *Recreations:* music, Burmese cats. *Address:* 12 Highgate Avenue, N6 5RX. *T:* 081–340 8104.

HOWE, Prof. Denis; Professor of Aircraft Design, since 1973, and Dean of Engineering, since 1988, College of Aeronautics, Cranfield Institute of Technology; *b* 3 Sept. 1927; *s* of Alfred and Alice Howe; *m* 1st, 1954, Audrey Marion Wilkinson; two *s* three *d*; 2nd, 1981, Catherine Bolton. *Educ:* Watford Grammar Sch.; MIT (SM); College of Aeronautics (PhD). CEng, FIMechE, FRAeS. Project Engineer, Fairey Aviation Co., 1945–54; College of Aeronautics, Cranfield Institute of Technology: Lectr, Sen. Lectr and Reader, 1954–73; Head of College, 1986–90. *Publications:* contribs to learned jls. *Recreations:* gardening, church administration. *Address:* College of Aeronautics, Cranfield, Bedford MK43 0AL; 57 Brecon Way, Bedford MK41 8DE. *T:* Bedford (0234) 56747.

HOWE, Derek Andrew, CBE 1991; public affairs and political consultant; company director; *b* 31 Aug. 1934; *o s* of late Harold and Elsie Howe; *m* 1st, 1958, Barbara (*née* Estill); two *d*; 2nd, 1975, Sheila (*née* Digger), MBE (*d* 1990); one *s*. *Educ:* City of Leeds Sch.; Cockburn High Sch., Leeds. Journalist, Yorkshire Evening News, 1951–61; Conservative Central Office, 1962–70; Parliamentary Liaison Officer, 1970–73; Special Adviser, 1973–75; Press Officer, Leader of HM Opposition, 1975–79; special adviser to: Paymaster Gen., 1979–81; Chancellor of Duchy of Lancaster, 1981; Political Secretary, 10 Downing Street, 1981–83 and Special Adviser to Leader of the House of Commons, 1982–83. Trustee, London Youth Trust, 1985– (Chm., 1988). Freeman of the City of London. *Recreations:* gardening, reading, philately. *Address:* The Vines, Kimpton, near Andover, Hampshire. *Club:* St Stephen's Constitutional.

HOWE, Elspeth Rosamund Morton, (Lady Howe), JP; Deputy Chairman, Equal Opportunities Commission, 1975–79; Chairman of an Inner London Juvenile Court, 1970–90; *b* 8 Feb. 1932; *d* of late Philip Morton Shand and Sybil Mary (*née* Sissons); *m* 1953, Rt Hon. Sir Geoffrey Howe, *qv*; one *s* two *d*. *Educ:* Bath High Sch.; Wycombe Abbey; London Sch. of Econs and Pol Science (BSc 1985). Vice-Chm., Conservative London Area Women's Adv. Cttee, 1966–67, also Pres. of the Cttee's Contact Gp, 1973–77; Mem., Conservative Women's Nat. Adv. Cttee, 1966–71. Member: Lord Chancellor's Adv. Cttee on appointment of Magistrates for Inner London Area, 1965–75; Lord Chancellor's Adv. Cttee on Legal Aid, 1971–75; Parole Board, 1972–75. Co-opted Mem., ILEA, 1967–70; Mem., Briggs Cttee on Nursing Profession, 1970–72; Chm., Hansard Soc. Commn on Women at the Top, 1989–90. Director: Kingfisher (formerly Woolworth Holdings) PLC, 1986–; United Biscuits (Holdings) PLC, 1988–; Legal & General Group, 1989–; Chm., BOC Foundn for the Envmt and the Community, 1990–. Chm., Women's Econ. Develt Target Team, Business in the Community, 1990–. President: Women's Gas Fedn, 1979–; Fedn of Recruitment and Employment Services (formerly Fedn of Personnel Services), 1980–; Peckham Settlement, 1976–; Gov., Cumberlow Lodge Remand Home, 1967–70; Member Council: NACRO, 1974–; PSI, 1983–; St George's House, Windsor, 1987–. Vice-Pres., Pre-Sch. Playgroups Assoc., 1979–83. Has served as chm. or mem. of several sch. governing bodies in Tower Hamlets; Governor: Wycombe Abbey, 1968–90; Froebel Educn Inst., 1968–75; LSE, 1985–; Mem. Bd of Governors, James Allen's Girls' Sch., 1988–. JP Inner London Juvenile Court Panel, 1964–. Hon. LLD London, 1990. *Publication:* Under Five (a report on pre-school education), 1966. *Address:* c/o Barclays Bank, 4 Vere Street, W1.

See also B. M. H. Shand.

HOWE, Eric James, CBE 1990; Data Protection Registrar, since 1984; *b* 4 Oct. 1931; *s* of Albert Henry Howe and Florence Beatrice (*née* Hale); *m* 1967, Patricia Enid (*née* Schollick); two *d*. *Educ:* Stretford Grammar Sch.; Univ. of Liverpool (BA Econs 1954). FIDPM 1990; FBCS 1972. NCB, 1954–59; British Cotton Industry Res. Assoc., 1959–61; English Electric Computer Co., 1961–66; National Computing Centre, 1966–84: Dep. Dir, 1975–84; Mem. Bd of Dirs, 1976–84. Chairman: National Computer Users Forum, 1977–84; Focus Cttee for Private Sector Users, DoI, 1982–84; Member: User Panel, NEDO, 1983–84; Council, British Computer Soc., 1971–74 and 1980–83; NW Regional Council, CBI, 1977–83. Rep. UK, Confedn of Eur. Computer Users Assocs, 1980–83. *Recreations:* gardening, piano, local community work. *Address:* Springfield House, Water Lane, Wilmslow, Cheshire SK9 5AX. *T:* Wilmslow (0625) 535711. *Club:* Reform.

HOWE, Rt. Hon. Sir Geoffrey; *see* Howe, Rt Hon. Sir R. E. G.

HOWE, Prof. Geoffrey Leslie, TD 1962 (Bars 1969 and 1974); Professor of Oral Surgery and Oral Medicine, since 1987, and Dean, since 1988, Jordan University of Science and Technology; *b* 22 April 1924; *e s* of late Leo Leslie John Howe, Maidenhead, Berks; *m* 1948, Heather Patricia Joan Hambly; one *s*. *Educ:* Royal Dental and Middlesex Hospitals. LDS RCS 1946; LRCP, MRCS 1954; FDS RCS 1955; MDS Dunelm, 1961; FFD RCSI 1964; FICD 1981. Dental and Medical Sch. Prizeman; Begley Prize, RCS, 1951; Cartwright Prize, RCS, 1961. Dental Officer, Royal Army Dental Corps, 1946–49. House appointments, etc., Royal Dental and Middlesex Hospitals, 1949–55. Registrar in Oral Surgery, Eastman Dental Hosp. (Institute of Dental Surgery), 1955–56; Senior Registrar in Oral Surgery, Plastic and Oral Surgery Centre, Chepstow, Mon, 1956; Senior Registrar in Oral Surgery, Eastman Dental Hospital, 1956–59; Professor of Oral Surgery, University of Newcastle upon Tyne (formerly King's Coll., University of Durham), 1959–67; Prof. of Oral Surgery, Royal Dental Hosp., London Sch. of Dental Surgery, 1967–78 (Dean of School, 1974–78); Prof. of Oral Surgery and Oral Medicine, and Dean of Dental Studies, Univ. of Hong Kong, 1978–83; Dir, Prince Philip Dental Hosp., 1981–83. Cons. Oral Surgeon, United Newcastle upon Tyne Hosps, 1959–67; Chm., Central Cttee for Hosp. Dental Services, 1971–73; Vice-Pres., BDA, 1979– (Vice-Chm., 1971–73; Chm., 1973–78); Pres., Internat. Assoc. of Oral Surgeons, 1980–83. Hon. Col Comdt, RADC, 1975–89. OStJ. *Publications:* The Extraction of Teeth, 1961, 2nd edn 1970; Minor Oral Surgery, 1966, 3rd edn 1985; (with F. I. H. Whitehead) Local Anaesthesia in Dentistry, 1972, 3rd edn 1990; contribs to: Medical Treatment Yearbook, 1959; Modern Trends in Dental Surgery, 1962, and to numerous medical and dental journals. *Recreations:* sailing; Territorial Army Volunteer Reserve (lately Col, OC 217 (L) Gen. Hosp. RAMC (V), graded Cons. Dental Surgeon RADC, TAVR). *Address:* 70 Croham Manor Road, South Croydon, Surrey CR2 7BF. *Clubs:* Savage, Oral Surgery; Hong Kong; Royal Hong Kong Yacht.

HOWE, George Edward; HM Diplomatic Service, retired; Counsellor, Foreign and Commonwealth Office, 1977–82; *b* 18 June 1925; *s* of late George Cuthbert Howe and Florence May (*née* Baston); *m* 1949, Florence Elizabeth Corrish; one *s*. *Educ:* Highbury Grammar Sch.; Westminster Coll. Served British Army, 1943; Indian Army, 2nd Bn The Burma Rifles, 1945–48 (Major). HMOCS, Malaya, 1949; joined Foreign Service, later Diplomatic Service, 1957; served Pnomn Penh, Hong Kong, Singapore, Paris, Milan and FCO. Member: RUSI; NSRA. *Recreations:* fishing, shooting, military history. *Clubs:* Army and Navy, Travellers'.

HOWE, Prof. G(eorge) Melvyn, PhD, DSc; FRSE, FRGS, FRSGS, FRMetS; Professor of Geography, University of Strathclyde, 1967–85, now Emeritus; *b* Abercynon, 7 April 1920; *s* of Reuben and Edith Howe, Abercynon; *m* 1947, Patricia Graham Fennell, Pontypridd; three *d*. *Educ:* Caerphilly Boys' Grammar Sch.; UCW Aberystwyth (BSc 1940; BSc 1st cl. hons Geog. and Anthrop., 1947; MSc 1949; PhD 1957); DSc Strathclyde 1974. Served with RAF, 1940–46: Meteorological Br., 1940–42; commnd Intell. (Air Photographic Interpretation) Br., 1942–46, in Middle East Comd. Lectr, later Sen. Lectr, in Geography, UCW Aberystwyth, 1948; Reader in Geog., Univ. of Wales, 1964. Vis. Prof. (Health and Welfare, Canada), 1977. Mem. Council, Inst. of British Geographers (Pres., 1985); Mem. Medical Geography Cttee, RGS, 1960–; British Rep. on Medical Geog. Commn of IGU, 1970–; Mem., British Nat. Cttee for Geography, Royal Soc., 1978–83. Gill Memorial Award, RGS, 1964. *Publications:* Wales from the Air, 1957, 2nd edn 1966; (with P. Thomas) Welsh Landforms and Scenery, 1963; National Atlas of Disease Mortality in the United Kingdom, 1963, 2nd edn 1970; The Soviet Union, 1968, 2nd edn 1983; The USSR, 1971; Man, Environment and Disease in Britain, 1972, 2nd edn 1976; (ed and contrib.) Atlas of Glasgow and the West of Scotland, 1972; (contrib.) Wales (ed E. G. Bowen), 1958; (contrib.) Modern Methods in the History of Medicine (ed E. Clarke), 1970; (ed with J. A. Loraine, and contrib.) Environmental Medicine, 1973, 2nd edn 1980; (contrib.) Environment and Man (ed J. Lenihan and W. W. Fletcher), 1976; (ed and contrib.) A World Geography of Human Diseases, 1977; (ed and contrib.) Global Geocancerology, 1986; articles in geographical, meteorological, hydrological and medical jls. *Recreation:* travel. *Address:* Hendre, 50 Heol Croes Faen, Nottage, Porthcawl CF36 3SW. *T:* Porthcawl (0656) 772377. *Club:* Royal Air Force.

HOWE, Jack, RDI 1961; FRIBA 1953; Architect and Industrial Designer; *b* 24 Feb. 1911; *s* of Charles Henry and Florence Eleanor Howe; *m* 1960, Margaret Crosbie Corrie (*d* 1979); one *s* one *d* (by former marriage); *m* 1981, Jennifer Mary Dixon (*née* Hughes D'Aeth). *Educ:* Enfield Grammar Sch.; Polytechnic Sch. of Architecture. FSIAD 1955. Asst to E. Maxwell Fry, 1933–37; Chief Asst to Walter Gropius and Maxwell Fry, 1937–39; Drawing Office Manager to Holland, Hannan & Cubitts Ltd for Royal Ordnance Factories at Wrexham and Ranskill, 1939–43; Associate Partner, Arcon, 1944–48; private practice, 1949; Partnership with Andrew Bain, 1959–76. Architectural work includes: Highbury Quadrant Primary School, (LCC); Windmill House, Lambeth (LCC Housing Scheme); Television Research Lab. for AEI Ltd; Kodak Pavilion, Brussels Exhibn, 1958; Official Architects for British Trade Fair, Moscow, 1961; Industrial Designs include: Diesel Electric Locomotives and Express Pullman Trains; also Rly equipment. Industrial Design Consultant to various large firms and to BR Board. Mem. Design Index Cttee and Street Furniture Cttee, Design Council (formerly CoID), 1956–; Member: Cttee on Traffic Signs, Min. of Transport, 1962, 1963; Nat. Council for Diplomas in Art and Design. Pres., SIAD, 1963–64; Master of Faculty, RDI, 1975–77. Duke of Edinburgh's design prize, 1969. *Publications:* articles for various architectural and design jls. *Recreations:* music, theatre. *Address:* 4 Leopold Avenue, Wimbledon, SW19 7ET. *T:* 081–946 7116.

HOWE, John Francis, OBE 1974; Deputy Under-Secretary of State (Civilian Management), Ministry of Defence, since 1992; *b* 29 Jan. 1944; *s* of late Frank and of Marjorie Howe; *m* 1981, Angela Ephrosini (*née* Nicolaides); one *d* one step *d*. *Educ:* Shrewsbury Sch.; Balliol Coll., Oxford (Scholar; MA). Pirelli General Cable Works, 1964; joined MoD as Asst Principal, 1967; Principal, 1972; Civil Adviser to GOC NI, 1972–73; Private Sec. to Perm. Under-Sec. of State, 1975–78; Asst Sec., 1979; seconded to FCO as Defence Counsellor, UK Delegn to NATO, 1981–84; Head, Arms Control Unit, MoD, 1985–86; Private Sec. to Sec. of State for Defence, 1986–87; Asst Under-Sec. of State (Personnel and Logistics), 1988–91. *Recreation:* travel.

HOWE, Air Vice-Marshal John Frederick George, CB 1985; CBE 1980; AFC 1961; Commandant-General, RAF Regiment and Director General of Security (RAF), 1983–85, retired; *b* 26 March 1930; *m* 1961, Annabelle Gowing; three *d*. *Educ:* St Andrew's Coll., Grahamstown, SA. SAAF, 1950–54 (served in Korea, 2nd Sqdn SAAF and 19 Inf. Regt, US Army, 1951); 222 Sqdn, Fighter Comd, 1956; 40 Commando RM, Suez Campaign, 1956; Fighter Command: Flt Comdr, 222 Sqdn, 1957; Flt Comdr, 43 Sqdn, 1957–59; Sqdn Comdr, 74 Sqdn, 1960–61; Air Staff, HQ Fighter Command, 1961–63; RAF Staff Coll., 1964; USAF Exchange Tour at Air Defence Comd HQ, Colorado Springs, 1965–67; 229 Operational Conversion Unit, RAF Chivenor, 1967–68; OC 228 OCU, Coningsby, 1968–69; Central Tactics and Trials Org., HQ Air Support Comd, 1969–70; MoD, 1970–72; Station Comdr, RAF Gutersloh, 1973–74; RCDS, 1975; Gp Capt. Ops, HQ No 11 Gp, 1975–77; Comdt, ROC, 1977–80; Comdr, Southern Maritime Air Region, 1980–83. American DFC 1951; Air Medal 1951. *Recreations:* country pursuits, skiing, sailing. *Address:* c/o Barclays Bank International, Oceanic House, 1 Cockspur Street, SW1. *Club:* Royal Air Force.

HOWE, Rt. Rev. John William Alexander; Assistant Bishop, diocese of Ripon, since 1985; *b* 1920. *Educ:* Westcliff High Sch.; St Chad's Coll., Durham Univ. BA 1943; MA, BD 1948. Ordained, 1943; Curate, All Saints, Scarborough, 1943–46; Chaplain, Adisadel Coll., Gold Coast, 1946–50; Vice-Principal, Edinburgh Theological Coll., 1950–55; Hon. Chaplain, St Mary's Cathedral, Edinburgh, 1951–55; Bishop of St Andrews, Dunkeld and Dunblane, 1955–69. Hon. Canon, St Mary's Cath., Glasgow, 1969; Exec. Officer of the Anglican Communion, 1969–71; Secretary General, Anglican Consultative Council, 1971–82; Research Fellow of the Research Project, ACC, 1983–85, retd. Hon. DD: General Theological Seminary, NY, 1974; Lambeth, 1978. *Publication:* Highways and Hedges: Anglicanism and the Universal Church, 1985. *Address:* 31 Scotton Drive, Knaresborough, North Yorks HG5 9HG. *T:* Harrogate (0423) 866224.

HOWE, Josephine Mary O'C.; *see* O'Connor Howe.

HOWE, Martin, PhD; Director, Competition Policy Division, Office of Fair Trading, since 1984; *b* 9 Dec. 1936; *s* of late Leslie Wistow Howe and of Dorothy Vernon Howe (*née* Taylor Farrell); *m* 1959, Anne Cicely Lawrenson; three *s*. *Educ:* Leeds Univ. (BCom (Accountancy), PhD). Asst Lectr, Lectr, Sen. Lectr, in Economics, Univ. of Sheffield, 1959–73; Senior Economic Adviser: Monopolies Commn, 1973–77; Office of Fair Trading, 1977–80; Asst Secretary, OFT and DTI, 1980–84. *Publications:* Equity Issues and the London Capital Market (with A. J. Merrett and G. D. Newbould), 1967; articles on variety of topics in learned and professional jls. *Recreations:* theatre (including amateur dramatics), cricket, gardening. *Address:* Office of Fair Trading, Field House, Breams Buildings, EC4A 1PR. *T:* 071–242 2858.

HOWE, Rt. Hon. Sir (Richard Edward) Geoffrey, PC 1972; Kt 1970; QC 1965; MP (C) Surrey East, since 1974 (Reigate, 1970–74); *b* 20 Dec. 1926; *er s* of late B. E. Howe and Mrs E. F. Howe, JP (*née* Thomson), Port Talbot, Glamorgan; *m* 1953, Elspeth Rosamund Morton Shand (*see* Lady Howe); one *s* two *d*. *Educ:* Winchester Coll. (Exhibitioner); Trinity Hall, Cambridge (Scholar, MA, LLB); Pres., Trinity Hall Assoc., 1977–78. Lieut Royal Signals 1945–48. Chm. Cambridge Univ. Conservative Assoc., 1951; Chm. Bow Group, 1955; Managing Dir, Crossbow, 1957–60, Editor 1960–62. Called to the Bar, Middle Temple, 1952; Bencher, 1969; Mem. General Council of the Bar, 1957–61; Mem. Council of Justice, 1963–70. Dep. Chm., Glamorgan QS, 1966–70. Contested (C) Aberavon, 1955, 1959; MP (C) Bebington, 1964–66. Sec. Conservative Parliamentary Health and Social Security Cttee, 1964–65; an Opposition Front Bench spokesman on labour and social services, 1965–66; Solicitor-General, 1970–72; Minister for Trade and Consumer Affairs, DTI, 1972–74; opposition front bench spokesman on social services, 1974–75, on Treasury and economic affairs, 1975–79; Chancellor of the Exchequer, 1979–83; Sec. of State for Foreign and Commonwealth Affairs, 1983–89; Lord Pres. of the Council, Leader of H of C, and Dep. Prime Minister, 1989–90. Chm., Interim Cttee, IMF, 1982–83. Director: Sun Alliance & London Insce Co. Ltd, 1974–79; AGB Research Ltd, 1974–79; EMI Ltd, 1976–79; BICC plc, 1991–; Glaxo Hldgs, 1991–. Special Advr, Internat. Affairs, Jones, Day, Reavis and Pogue, 1991–. Member: (Latey) Interdeptl Cttee on Age of Majority, 1965–67; (Street) Cttee on Racial Discrimination, 1967; (Cripps) Cons. Cttee on Discrimination against Women, 1968–69; Chm. Ely Hospital, Cardiff, Inquiry, 1969. Visitor, SOAS, Univ. of London, 1991–; Vis. Fellow, John F. Kennedy Sch. of Govt, Harvard Univ., 1991–92; Herman Phleger Vis. Prof., Stanford Law Sch., Calif, 1992–. Mem., Internat. Adv. Council, Inst. of Internat. Studies, Stanford Univ., Calif, 1990–. President: Cons. Political Centre Nat. Adv. Cttee, 1977–79; Nat. Union of Cons. and Unionist Assocs, 1983–84; Jt Pres., Wealth of Nations Foundn, 1991–. Mem., Adv. Council, Presidium of Supreme Soviet of Ukraine, 1991–. Mem. Council of Management, Private Patients' Plan, 1969–70; Mem., Steering Cttee, Project Liberty, 1991–; Patron, Enterprise Europe, 1990–; an Hon. Vice-Pres., Consumers Assoc., 1974–. Hon. LLD Wales, 1988. *Publications:* various political pamphlets for Bow Group and Conservative Political Centre. *Address:* c/o Barclays Bank, Cavendish Square Branch, 4 Vere Street, W1. *Clubs:* Athenæum, Garrick.

HOWE, Ronald William; His Honour Judge Howe; a Circuit Judge, since 1991; *b* 19 June 1932; *s* of William Arthur and Lilian Mary Howe; *m* 1956, Jean Emily Goodman; three *s* one *d*. *Educ:* Morpeth Sch.; Coll. of Law, London. Admitted Solicitor, 1966; partner with Ronald Brooke & Co., Ilford, then Brooke, Garland & Howe, 1966–75; Registrar of County Court, subseq. Dist Judge, 1975–91. Mem., Judicial Studies Bd, 1990–91 (Mem., Civil and Family Cttee, 1988–91). *Recreations:* tennis, badminton, golf.

HOWELL, Rt. Hon. David Arthur Russell; PC 1979; MP (C) Guildford since 1966; Director, Queens Moat Houses, since 1989; journalist and economic consultant; *b* 18 Jan. 1936; *s* of late Colonel A. H. E. Howell, DSO, TD, DL and Beryl Howell, 5 Headfort Place, SW1; *m* 1967, Davina Wallace; one *s* two *d*. *Educ:* Eton; King's Coll., Cambridge. BA 1st class hons Cantab, 1959. Lieut Coldstream Guards, 1954–56. Joined Economic Section of Treasury, 1959; resigned, 1960. Leader-Writer and Special Correspondent, The Daily Telegraph, 1960; Chm. of Bow Gp, 1961–62; Editor of Crossbow, 1962–64; contested (C) Dudley, 1964. A Lord Comr of Treasury, 1970–71; Parly Sec., CSD, 1970–72; Parly Under-Sec.: Dept of Employment, 1971–72; NI Office, March-Nov. 1972; Minister of State: NI Office, 1972–74; Dept of Energy, 1974; Secretary of State: for Energy, 1979–81; for Transport, 1981–83. Chairman: Select Cttee on Foreign Affairs, 1987–; Cons. One Nation Gp, 1987–; UK-Japan 2000 Group, 1990–. Sen. Vis. Fellow, PSI, 1983–85. Dir of Conservative Political Centre, 1964–66. Mem., Internat. Adv. Council, Swiss Bank Corp., 1988–. Trustee, Federal Trust for Educn and Research. Jt Hon. Sec., UK Council of European Movement, 1968–70. *Publications:* (co-author) Principles in Practice, 1960; The Conservative Opportunity, 1965; Freedom and Capital, 1981; Blind Victory: a study in income, wealth and power, 1986; various pamphlets and articles. *Recreations:* writing, DIY, golf. *Address:* House of Commons, SW1A 0AA. *Club:* Buck's.

HOWELL, Rt. Hon. Denis Herbert, PC 1976; MP (Lab) Birmingham, Small Heath since March 1961; *b* 4 Sept. 1923; *s* of Herbert and Bertha A. Howell; *m* 1955, Brenda Marjorie, *d* of Stephen and Ruth Willson, Birmingham; two *s* one *d* (and one *s* decd). *Educ:* Gower Street Sch.; Handsworth Grammar Sch., Birmingham. Mem., Birmingham City Council, 1946–56; Hon. Sec. Birmingham City Council Labour Group, 1950–55 (served Catering Establishment, General Purposes, Health and Watch Cttees); Chm. Catering Cttee, 1952–55; Health (Gen. Purposes) Sub-Cttee for setting up of first smokeless zones. MP (Lab) All Saints Div., Birmingham, 1955–Sept. 1959; Jt Parly Under-Sec. of State, Dept of Educn and Science (with responsibility for sport), 1964–69; Minister of State, Min. of Housing and Local Govt (with responsibility for sport), 1969–70; Opposition Spokesman for Local Govt and Sport, 1970–74; Minister of State, DoE (responsible for environment, water resources and sport), 1974–79; Opposition Spokesman on Environment (Environment and Services, Water Resources, Sport, Recreation and Countryside), 1979–83, on Home Affairs, 1983–84; Opposition front bench spokesman on the Environment (specializing in Sport), 1984–. Mem., Labour Party NEC, 1982–83. Member: Dudley Road Hosp. Group Management Cttee, 1948–64; the Albemarle Cttee on the Youth Service; Management Cttee, City of Birmingham Symphony Orchestra, 1950–55; Pres., Canoldir Choir, 1979–. Governor, Handsworth Grammar Sch. Chairman: Birmingham Assoc. of Youth Clubs, 1963–64; Birmingham Settlement, 1963–64; Sports Council, 1965–70; Youth Service Develt Council, 1964–69 (report: Youth and Community Work in the 70's); Central Council of Physical Recreation, 1973–74 (Vice Pres., 1985); Cttee of Enquiry into Sponsorship of Sport, 1981–83 (report: The Howell Report on Sports Sponsorship); St Peter's Urban Village Trust, 1985–; Pres., Birmingham Olympic Council, 1985–86; Vice-President: Warwicks CCC, 1986–; Birchfield Harriers, 1987–. Pres., Assoc. of Professional, Exec. Clerical and Computer Staffs (APEX) (formerly CAWU), 1971–83. FIPR 1987 (MIPR 1961). Football League Referee, 1956–70. Hon. Freeman, City of Birmingham, 1991. Silver Medal, Olympic Order, 1981. Midlander of the Year Award, 1987. *Publications:* Soccer Refereeing, 1968; Made in Birmingham (autobiog.), 1990. *Recreations:* sport, theatre, music. *Address:* 33 Moor Green Lane, Moseley, Birmingham B13 8NE. *Clubs:* Reform; Warwickshire County Cricket (Birmingham); Birmingham Press.

HOWELL, Air Vice-Marshal Evelyn Michael Thomas, CBE 1961; CEng, FRAeS; *b* 11 Sept. 1913; *s* of Sir Evelyn Berkeley Howell, KCIE, CSI; *m* 1st, 1937, Helen Joan, *o d* of late Brig. W. M. Hayes, CBE, FRICS (marr. diss. 1972); one *s* three *d*; 2nd, 1972, Rosemary, *e d* of I. A. Cram, CEng, MICE; one *s* one *d*. *Educ:* Downside Sch.; RAF Coll., Cranwell. Commissioned, 1934; Dir of Air Armament Research and Devt, Min. of Aviation, 1960–62; Comdt, RAF Techn. Coll., 1963–65; SASO, HQ Technical Training Command RAF, 1966–67; retired, 1967. Gen. Manager, Van Dusen Aircraft Supplies, Oxford, Minneapolis, St Louis, Helsingborg, 1967–79. Mem. Livery of Clothworkers' Co., 1938. *Recreations:* swimming, rifle shooting, tennis, boating. *Address:* Bank Farm, Lorton, Cockermouth, Cumbria CA13 0RQ. *Club:* Royal Air Force.

HOWELL, Gareth, PhD; CChem; Director, British Council, Malaysia, since 1990; *b* 22 April 1935; *s* of Amwel John and Sarah Blodwen Howell; *m* 1957, Margaret Patricia Ashelford; one *s* two *d*. *Educ:* Ferndale Grammar Sch., Rhondda; University College London; Inst. of Education, Univ. of London. BSc, PhD; PGCE London. MRSC. Asst Master, Canford Sch., Wimborne, Dorset, 1957–61; Lectr, Norwich City Coll., 1961–65; British Council: Science Educn Officer, London, 1965–66; Science Educn Officer, Nigeria, 1966–70; Head, Science Educn Section, 1970–74; Director, Science and Technology Dept, 1974; Representative, Malawi, 1974–76; on secondment to Min. of Overseas Development as Educn Adviser, 1976–79; Counsellor and Dep. Educn Adviser, British Council Div., British High Commn, India, 1979–83; Controller: Sci., Technol. and Educn Div., 1983–87; Americas, Pacific and E Asia Div., 1987–90. *Recreations:* photography, philately, gardening, tennis, running, travel. *Address:* British Council, PO Box 10539, Jalan Bukit Aman 50916, Kuala Lumpur 10.01, Malaysia.

HOWELL, Gwynne Richard; Principal Bass, Royal Opera House, since 1971; *b* Gorseinon, S Wales, 13 June 1938; *s* of Gilbert and Ellaline Howell; *m* 1968, Mary Edwina Morris; two *s*. *Educ:* Pontardawe Grammar Sch.; Univ. of Wales, Swansea (BSc; Hon. Fellow 1986); Manchester Univ. (DipTP); MRTPI 1966. Studied singing with Redvers Llewellyn while at UCW; pt-time student, Manchester RCM, with Gwilym Jones, during DipTP trng at Manchester Univ.; studied with Otakar Kraus, 1968–72. Planning Asst, Kent CC, 1961–63; Sen. Planning Officer, Manchester Corp., 1965–68, meanwhile continuing to study music pt-time and giving public operatic performances which incl. the rôle of Pogner, in Die Meistersinger; as a result of this rôle, apptd Principal Bass at Sadler's Wells, 1968; also reached final of BBC Opera Singers competition for N of Eng., 1967. In first season at Sadler's Wells, sang 8 rôles, incl. Monterone and the Commendatore; appearances with Hallé Orch., 1968 and 1969; Arkel in Pelleas and Melisande, Glyndebourne and Covent Garden, 1969; Goffredo, in Il Pirato, 1969. *Royal Opera House, Covent Garden:* début as First Nazarene, Salome, 1969–70 season; the King, in Aida; Timur, in Turandot; Mephisto, in Damnation of Faust; Prince Gremin, in Eugene Onegin; High Priest, in Nabucco; Reinmar, in Tannhauser, 1973–74 (later rôle, Landgraf); Colline, in La Boheme; Pimen, in Boris Godunov; Ribbing, Un ballo in maschera; Padre Guardiano, in La forza del destino; Hobson, in Peter Grimes, 1975; Sparafucile, in Rigoletto, 1975–76 season; Ramfis in Aida, 1977; Tristan und Isolde, 1978, 1982; Luisa Miller, 1978; Samson et Delilah, 1981; Fiesco in Simon Boccanegra, 1981; Pogner in Die Meistersinger, 1982; Arkell in Pelléas et Mélisande, 1982; Dossifei in Khovanshchina, 1982; Semele, 1982; Die Zauberflöte, 1983; Raimondo, in Lucia di Lammermoor, 1985; Rocco in Fidelio, 1986; *English National Opera:* Don Carlos, Die Meistersinger, 1974–75; The Magic Flute, Don Carlos, 1975–76; Duke Bluebeard's Castle, 1978, 1991; The Barber of Seville, 1980; Tristan and Isolde, 1981; Hans Sachs in Die Meistersinger, 1984; Parsifal, 1986; *Metropolitan Opera House, New York:* début as Lódovico in Otello, and Pogner in Die Meistersinger, 1985; *sacred music:* Verdi and Mozart Requiems, Missa Solemnis, St Matthew and St John Passions; sings in Europe and USA; records for BBC and for major recording companies. *Recreations:* tennis, squash, golf, Rugby enthusiast, gardening. *Address:* 197 Fox Lane, N13 4BB. *T:* 081–886 1981.

HOWELL, Prof. John Bernard Lloyd, CBE 1991; Foundation Professor of Medicine, University of Southampton, since 1969 (Dean of the Faculty of Medicine, 1978–83); Hon. Consultant Physician, Southampton General Hospital, since 1969; *s* of late David John Howells and Hilda Mary Hill, Ynystawe, Swansea; *m* 1952, Heather Joan Rolfe; two *s* one *d*. *Educ:* Swansea Grammar Sch.; Middx Hosp. Med. Sch. (Meyerstein Scholar 1946). BSc, MB, BS, PhD; FRCP. House Officer posts, Middx and Brompton Hosps; MO RAMC, 1952–54; Lectr in Physiol Medicine, 1954–56, in Pharmacol Medicine, 1958–60, Middlesex Hosp. Med. Sch.; Manchester Royal Infirmary: Sen. Lectr in Medicine and Hon. Consultant Physician, 1960–66; Consultant Physician, 1966–69. Eli Lilly Travelling Fellow, Johns Hopkins Hospital, 1957–58; Goulstonian Lectr, RCP, 1966. Member: Physiol Soc., 1956–; Med. Res. Soc., 1956–; Assoc. of Physicians of GB and Ire., 1964–; GMC, 1978–83. Chm., Southampton and SW Hampshire DHA, 1983–. President: British Thoracic Soc., 1988–89 (Mem., 1959–); BMA, 1989–90 (Chm., Bd of Sci. and Educn, 1992–). Hon. Life Mem., Canadian Thoracic Soc., 1978; Hon. FACP 1982. *Publications:* (ed jtly) Breathlessness, 1966; chapters in: Cecil and Loeb's Textbook of Medicine, 13th edn 1970, 14th edn 1974; Recent Advances in Chest Medicine, 1976; Thoracic Medicine, 1981; Oxford Textbook of Medicine, 1982; scientific papers on respiratory physiology and medicine. *Recreations:* DIY, wine. *Address:* The Coach House, Bassett Wood Drive, Southampton SO2 3PT. *T:* Southampton (0703) 768878.

HOWELL, Prof. John Frederick; Director, Overseas Development Institute, since 1987; Visiting Professor in Agricultural Development, Wye College, University of London, since 1988; *b* 16 July 1941; *s* of Frederick John Howell and late Glenys Howell (*née* Griffiths). *Educ:* Univ. of Wales (BA Hons 1963); Univ. of Manchester (MA Econ. Dist. 1965); Univ. of Reading, (external; PhD). Lectr, Univ. of Khartoum, 1966–73; Sen. Lectr and Head of Pol. and Admin. Studies, Univ. of Zambia, 1973–77; Res. Fellow, 1977–84, Dep. Dir, 1984–87, ODI. Vis Lectr, Mananga Agric. Management Centre, Swaziland, 1978–80; Consultant on aid and agricl develt: World Bank; FAO; Commonwealth Secretariat; ODA in India, Nepal, Nigeria, Brazil, Tanzania, Sudan; Adviser: All-Party Parly Gp on Overseas Develt, 1985–86; Princess Royal's Africa Review Gp, 1987–89. Pres., UK Chapter, Soc. of Internat. Develt, 1991–. Co-editor, Develt Policy Review, 1985–87. *Publications:* Local Government and Politics in the Sudan, 1974; (ed) Borrowers and Lenders: rural financial markets and institutions in developing countries, 1980; Administering Agricultural Development for Small Farmers, 1981; (ed) Recurrent Costs and Agricultural Development, 1985; (ed) Agricultural Extension in Practice, 1988; (with Alex Duncan) Structural Adjustment and the African Farmer, 1991. *Recreations:* cricket, gardening, modern jazz, Arsenal FC. *Address:* Overseas Development Institute, Regent's College, Inner Circle, Regent's Park, NW1 4NS. *T:* 071–487 7413. *Clubs:* Commonwealth Trust, Middlesex CC.

HOWELL, Rt. Rev. Kenneth Walter, MA; *b* 4 Feb. 1909; *s* of Frederick John and Florence Sarah Howell; *m* 1st, 1937, Beryl Mary Hope (*d* 1972), *d* of late Capt. Alfred and Mrs Hope, Bedford; two *s* one *d*; 2nd, 1978, Mrs Siri Colvin. *Educ:* St Olave's; St Peter's Hall, Oxford; Wycliffe Hall, Oxford. Curate of St Mary Magdalene, Peckham, 1933–37; Chaplain of Paraguayan Chaco Mission, 1937–38; Chaplain Quepe Mission, Chile, 1938–40; Superintendent of South American Missionary Society's Mission to Araucanian Indians in S Chile, 1940–47; Vicar of Wandsworth, 1948–63, Rural Dean, 1957–63; Chaplain, Royal Hosp. and Home for Incurables, Putney, 1957–63; Hon. Canon of

Southwark, 1962–63; Bishop in Chile, Bolivia and Peru, 1963–71; Minister of St John's, Downshire Hill, Hampstead, 1972–79; an Asst Bishop, Diocese of London, 1976–79. *Address:* 96 Colney Hatch Lane, Muswell Hill, N10 1EA.

HOWELL, Maj.-Gen. Lloyd, CBE 1972; Consultant, Technical Education Development, University College, Cardiff, 1980–86 (Fellow, 1981); Director (non-executive), Building Trades Exhibitions Ltd, since 1980; *b* 28 Dec. 1923; *s* of Thomas Idris Howell and Anne Howell; *m* 1st, 1945, Hazel Barker (*d* 1974); five *s* three *d*; 2nd, 1975, Elizabeth June Buchanan Husband (*née* Atkinson); two step *s*. *Educ:* Barry Grammar Sch.; University Coll. of S Wales and Monmouthshire (BSc); Royal Military Coll. of Science. CEng, MRAeS. Commissioned RA, 1944; Field Regt, RA, E Africa, 1945–46; Staff, Divl HQ, Palestine, 1946–47; RAEC 1949; Instr, RMA Sandhurst, 1949–53; TSO II Trials Estabt, 1954–57; SO II (Educn), Divl HQ, BAOR, 1957–59; DS, Royal Mil. Coll. of Science, 1960–64; SEO, Army Apprentices Coll., 1964–67; Headmaster/Comdg, Duke of York's Royal Mil. Sch., 1967–72; Col (Ed), MoD (Army), 1972–74; Chief Educn Officer, HQ UKLF, 1974–76; Dir, Army Educn, 1976–80. Col Comdt, RAEC, 1982–86. Mem. Council, CGLI, 1977–90; Mem., Ct of Governors, University Coll., Cardiff, 1980–88. Hon. MA Open Univ., 1980. *Recreations:* gardening, golf, reading. *Address:* c/o Midland Bank, The Forum, Old Town, Swindon, Wilts SN3 1QT. *Club:* Army and Navy.

HOWELL, Michael Edward, CMG 1989; OBE 1980; HM Diplomatic Service; High Commissioner, Mauritius, since 1989; *b* 2 May 1933; *s* of Edward and Fanny Howell; *m* 1958; Joan Little; one *s* one *d*. *Educ:* Newport High Sch. Served RAF, 1951–53. Colonial Office, 1953; CRO, 1958; Karachi, 1959; 2nd Secretary: Bombay, 1962; UK Delegn to Disarmament Cttee, Geneva, 1966; 1st Sec. (Parly Clerk), FCO, 1969; Consul (Comm.), New York, 1973; ndc 1975; FCO, 1976; Hd of Chancery, later Chargé d'Affaires, Kabul, 1978; Consul-General: Berlin, 1981; Frankfurt, 1983; High Comr to Papua New Guinea, 1986. *Recreation:* tennis. *Address:* c/o Foreign and Commonwealth Office, SW1A 2AH.

HOWELL, Patrick Leonard; QC 1990; *b* 4 Dec. 1942; *s* of Leonard Howell, MC, and Mary Isobel (*née* Adam); *m* 1966, Sandra Marie McColl; two *s* one *d*. *Educ:* Radley; Christ Church, Oxford (MA); London Sch. of Econs and Pol Science (LLM). Called to the Bar: Inner Temple, 1966; Lincoln's Inn, 1968. Teaching Fellow, Osgoode Hall Law Sch., Toronto, 1965–66. *Recreation:* building things. *Address:* 7 Stone Buildings, Lincoln's Inn, WC2A 3SZ. *T:* 071–405 3886, 071–242 3546.

HOWELL, Paul Frederic; Member (C) Norfolk, European Parliament, since 1979; farmer; *b* 17 Jan. 1951; *s* of Ralph Frederic Howell, *qv*; *m* 1987, Johanna Youlten Turnbull; two *s*. *Educ:* Gresham's Sch., Holt, Norfolk; St Edmund Hall, Oxford (BA Agric. and Econ.). Conservative Research Dept, 1973–75. Prospective Parly candidate (C) Normanton, 1976–79. Mem., Agricl, Budget and Overseas Develt Cttees, European Parlt, 1979–; spokesman: on youth, culture, educn, information and sport, Eur. Democratic Gp, 1984–86; on agriculture, 1989–; Member, European Parliament's delegation: to Central America, 1987–; to Soviet Union, 1989–; Vice-Chm., EEC/Comecon Delegn, 1984; Pres., Council of Centre for Eur. Educn, 1985–87. *Recreations:* all sports. *Address:* The White House Farm, Bradenham Road, Scarning, East Dereham, Norfolk NR20 3EY. *T:* Wendling (036287) 239.

HOWELL, Paul Philip, CMG 1964; OBE 1955; *b* 13 Feb. 1917; *s* of Brig.-Gen. Philip Howell, CMG (killed in action, 1916) and Mrs Rosalind Upcher Howell (*née* Buxton); *m* 1949, Bridgit Mary Radclyffe Luard; two *s* two *d*. *Educ:* Westminster Sch.; Trinity Coll., Cambridge (Sen. Schol., MA, PhD); Christ Church, Oxford (MA, DPhil). Sudan Polit. Service, 1938; commnd in Sudan Defence Force, ADC to Gov.-Gen., 1940; Overseas Enemy Territory Administration, Eritrea, 1941; District Comr, Central Nuer, 1942; District Comr, Baggara, Western Kordofan, 1946; Chm., Jonglei Investigation, 1948; Chm. (Dep. Gov.), Southern Development Investigation, 1953; Asst Chief Sec., Uganda Protectorate, 1955; Min. of Natural Resources, 1955; Perm. Sec., Min. of Corporations and Regional Communications, 1957; Perm. Sec. Min. of Commerce and Industry, 1959; Chm., E African Nile Waters Co-ordinating Cttee, 1956–61; seconded to FO and Min. of Overseas Development; Head of Middle East Develt Div., Beirut, 1961–69. University of Cambridge: Dir of Develt Studies Courses, 1969–82; Chm., Faculty of Archaeology and Anthropology, 1977–82; Fellow of Wolfson Coll., 1969–83, Emeritus Fellow, 1983. Member: Bd of Governors, Inst. of Development Studies, 1971–85; Council, Overseas Development Inst., 1972–; Bd of Governors, Bell Educnl Trust, 1987–. Gold Medallion, La Belgique Reconnaissante, 1962. *Publications:* Nuer Law, 1954; (ed) The Equatorial Nile Project and its Effects in the Anglo-Egyptian Sudan, 1954; (ed) Natural Resources and Development Potential in the Southern Sudan, 1955; (ed) The Jonglei Canal: Impact and Opportunity, 1988; contribs to jls on social anthropology and development. *Recreations:* fishing and country pursuits. *Address:* Wolfson College, Cambridge. *T:* Cambridge (0223) 64811; Burfield Hall, Wymondham, Norfolk NR18 9SJ. *T:* Wymondham (0953) 603389. *Clubs:* Commonwealth Trust; Norfolk (Norwich).

HOWELL, Peter Adrian; Chairman, Victorian Society, since 1987; Lecturer, Department of Classics, Royal Holloway and Bedford New College, University of London, since 1985; *b* 29 July 1941; *s* of Lt-Col Harry Alfred Adrian Howell, MBE and Madge Maud Mary, *d* of Major-Gen. R. L. B. Thompson, CB, CMG, DSO. *Educ:* Downside School; Balliol College, Oxford (BA 1963; MA; MPhil 1966). Asst Lectr and Lectr, Dept of Latin, Bedford Coll., Univ. of London, 1964–85. Dep. Chm., Jt Cttee, Nat. Amenity Socs, 1991–; Member: Cttee, Victorian Soc., 1968–; Dept of Art and Architecture, Liturgy Commn , RC Bishops' Conf., 1977–84; Churches Cttee, English Heritage, 1984–88. *Publications:* Victorian Churches, 1968; (with Elisabeth Beazley) Companion Guide to North Wales, 1975; (with Elisabeth Beazley) Companion Guide to South Wales, 1977; A Commentary on Book I of the Epigrams of Martial, 1980; (ed with Ian Sutton) The Faber Guide to Victorian Churches, 1989; articles in Architectural History, Country Life. *Recreations:* art, architecture, music. *Address:* 127 Banbury Road, Oxford OX2 6JX. *T:* Oxford (0865) 515050.

HOWELL, Ralph Frederic; MP (C) North Norfolk since 1970; *b* 25 May 1923; *m* 1950, Margaret (*née* Bone); two *s* one *d*. *Educ:* Diss Grammar Sch., Norfolk. Navigator/Bomb-aimer, RAF, 1941–46; farmer, 1946–. Mem., European Parlt, 1974–79. Vice-Chm., Cons. Parly Finance Cttee, 1979–84; Mem., Treasury and Civil Service Select Cttee, 1981–87; Chairman: Cons. Parly Employment Cttee, 1984–87; Cons. Parly Agriculture Cttee, 1988; Mem. Exec., 1922 Cttee, 1984–90; Mem., Council of Europe and WEU, 1987–. *Publication:* Why Work, 1976, 2nd edn 1981. *Address:* Wendling Grange, Dereham, Norfolk NR19 2NH. *T:* Wendling (036287) 247. *Clubs:* Carlton, Farmers'.

See also P. F. Howell.

HOWELLS, Anne, (Mrs Stafford Dean), FRMCM (ARMCM); opera, concert and recital singer; *b* 12 Jan. 1941; *d* of Trevor William Howells and Mona Hewart; *m* 1st, 1966, Ryland Davies, *qv* (marr. diss. 1981); 2nd, 1981, Stafford Dean; one *s* one *d*. *Educ:* Sale County Grammar Sch.; Royal Manchester Coll. of Music. Three seasons (Chorus), with Glyndebourne, 1964–66; at short notice, given star rôle there, in Cavalli's L'Ormindo, 1967; rôles, there, also include: Dorabella in Così fan Tutte; Cathleen in (world première of) Nicholas Maw's Rising of the Moon, 1970; also the Composer in Ariadne; Diana in Calisto; Unitel Film of Salzburg prodn of Mozart's Clemenza di Tito. Royal Opera House, Covent Garden: under contract for three years, 1969–71. Rôles include: Lena in (world première of) Richard Rodney Bennett's Victory; Rosina in Barber of Seville; Cherubino in Marriage of Figaro; Der Rosenkavalier (video recording), 1985. Currently, 1973–, Guest artist with Royal Opera House. Recitals in Brussels and Vienna; operatic guest performances in Chicago, Metropolitan (NY), San Francisco, Geneva, Brussels, Salzburg, Amsterdam, Hamburg (W German début), W Berlin, Paris; sings with Scottish Opera, English Nat. Opera, major orchestras in UK. *Recreations:* cinema, tennis, reading. *Address:* c/o Harrison Parrott, 12 Penzance Place, W11 4PA.

HOWELLS, Geraint Wyn; MP Ceredigion and Pembroke North, since 1983 (Cardigan, Feb. 1974–1983) (L 1983–88, Lib Dem since 1988); *b* 15 April 1925; *s* of David John Howells and Mary Blodwen Howells; *m* 1957, Mary Olwen Hughes Griffiths; two *d*. *Educ:* Ponterwyd Primary Sch.; Ardwyn Grammar School. Farmer; former Mem., British Wool Marketing Bd (Vice-Chm., 1971–83); Chm., Wool Producers of Wales Ltd, 1977–87. Sec., Ponterwyd Eisteddfod. *Recreations:* walking, sport. *Address:* Glennydd, Ponterwyd, Ceredigion, Dyfed. *T:* Ponterwyd (097085) 258.

HOWELLS, Dr Gwyn, CB 1979; MD; FRCP, FRACP; Director-General and Permanent Head, Federal Department of Health, Canberra, Australia, 1973–83; Chairman, Cochlear Pty Ltd, Sydney, since 1984; Director, Nucleus Ltd, Sydney, since 1984; *b* 13 May 1918; *s* of Albert Henry and Ruth Winifred Howells; *m* 1942, Simone Maufe; two *s* two *d*. *Educ:* University College Sch., London; St Bartholomew's Hosp., Univ. of London (MB BS 1942, MD 1950). MRCS 1941; FRCP 1974 (MRCP 1950, LRCP 1941); FRACP 1971 (MRACP 1967). Cons. Phys., Thoracic Annexe, Toowoomba, Qld, Aust.; Chest Phys., Toowoomba Gen. Hosp., Qld, 1957–66; Federal Dept of Health, Canberra: First Asst Director-General, 1966–73; Dep. Dir-Gen., Feb.-Sept. 1973. Chairman, Nat. Health and Med. Res. Council, 1973–83; Director of Quarantine for Australia, 1973–83. *Publications:* several articles in Lancet, BMJ, Aust. Med. Jl and other specialist jls. *Recreations:* squash, tennis, reading. *Address:* 23 Beauchamp Street, Deakin, ACT 2600, Australia. *T:* Canberra 2812575. *Clubs:* Commonwealth, National Press, National Tennis and Squash Centre (Canberra).

HOWELLS, Kim Scott, PhD; MP (Lab) Pontypridd, since Feb. 1989; *b* 27 Nov. 1946; *s* of Glanville James and Joan Glenys Howells; *m* 1983, Eirlys Howells (*née* Davies); two *s* one *d*. *Educ:* Mountain Ash Grammar Sch.; Hornsey College of Art; Cambridge College of Advanced Technology (BA (Jt Hons)); Warwick Univ. (PhD). Steel-worker, 1969–70; Coal-miner, 1970–71; Lectr, 1975–79; Research Officer: Swansea Univ., 1979–82; NUM, S Wales Area, 1982–89. *Recreations:* climbing, jazz, cinema, literature. *Address:* 30 Berw Road, Pontypridd, Mid-Glamorgan CF37 2AA. *Club:* Llantwit Fadre Cricket (Pontypridd).

HOWERD, Frankie; *see* Howard, F. A.

HOWES, Prof. Christopher Kingston; Second Commissioner and Chief Executive of the Crown Estate, since 1989; *b* 30 Jan. 1942; *yr s* of Leonard Howes, OBE and Marion Howes (*née* Bussey); *m* 1967, Clare Cunliffe; two *s* one *d* (and one *d* decd). *Educ:* Gresham's Sch.; LSE; Coll. of Estate Management (BSc 1965); Univ. of Reading (MPhil 1976). ARICS 1967, FRICS 1977. Valuation and Planning Depts, GLC, 1965–67; Partner and Sen. Partner, Chartered Surveyors, Norwich, 1967–79; Department of the Environment: Dep. Dir, Land Economy, 1979–81; Chief Estates Officer, 1981–85; Dir, Land and Property Div., 1985–89. Sen. Vis. Fellow, Sch. of Envtl Scis, UEA, 1975; Vis. Lectr, Univs of Reading, 1976, Aberdeen 1980–; Vis. Prof., Bartlett Sch. of Architecture and Planning. UCL, 1984–. Member: CNAA Surveying Bd, 1978–82; Planning and Develt Divl Council, RICS, 1983–; Policy Review Cttee, RICS, 1984–90; Norfolk Archaeological Trust, 1979–; The Prince's Council, 1990–. Hon. Mem., Cambridge Univ. Land Soc., 1989–. Founder Mem., Norwich Third World Centre, 1970; dir of various housing assocs; Dir, Theatre Royal Trust, 1969–79; Steward and Hon Surveyor to Dean and Chapter, Norwich Cathedral, 1973–79; Mem., Court of Advisers, St Paul's Cathedral, 1980–. Norwich CC, 1969–73; JP Norfolk 1973–80. Mem. of various editorial bds. *Publications:* (jtly) Acquiring Office Space, 1975; Value Maps: aspects of land and property values, 1979; Economic Regeneration (monograph), 1988; Urban Revitalization (monograph), 1988; papers on land and property policy in learned jls. *Recreations:* music, esp. opera; art, esp. English water colours; sport, esp. sailing. *Address:* Highfield House, Woldingham, Surrey; Roudham Lodge, Roudham, Norfolk. *Clubs:* Athenæum; Norfolk (Norwich); Aldeburgh Yacht.

HOWES, Sally Ann; actress (stage, film and television); *b* 20 July; *d* of late Bobby Howes; *m* 1958, Richard Adler (marr. diss.); *m* 1969, Andrew Maree (marr. diss.). *Educ:* Glendower, London; Queenswood, Herts; privately. *Films include:* Thursday's Child; Halfway House; Dead of Night; Nicholas Nickleby; Anna Karenina; My Sister and I; Fools Rush In; History of Mr Polly; Stop Press Girl; Honeymoon Deferred; The Admirable Crichton; Chitty, Chitty Bang Bang. First appeared West End stage in (revue) Fancy Free, at Prince of Wales's, and at Royal Variety Performance, 1950. *Stage Shows include:* Caprice (musical debut); Paint Your Wagon; Babes in the Wood; Romance by Candlelight; Summer Song; Hatful of Rain; My Fair Lady; Kwamina, NY; What Makes Sammy Run?, NY; Brigadoon (revival), NY City Center, 1962; Sound of Music, Los Angeles and San Francisco, 1972; Lover, St Martin's; The King and I, Adelphi, 1973, Los Angeles and San Francisco, 1974; Hans Andersen, Palladium, 1977; Hamlet (tour), 1983. Has appeared on television: in England from 1949 (Short and Sweet Series, Sally Ann Howes Show, etc); in USA from 1958 (Dean Martin Show, Ed Sullivan Show, Mission Impossible, Marcus Welby MD); Play of the Week; Panel Shows: Hollywood Squares; Password; Bell Telephone Hour; US Steel Hour, etc. *Recreations:* reading, riding, theatre. *Address:* c/o Kramer and Reiss, 9100 Sunset Boulevard, Los Angeles, Calif 90069, USA.

HOWICK OF GLENDALE, 2nd Baron *cr* 1960; **Charles Evelyn Baring;** a Director, Northern Rock Building Society, since 1987; a Managing Director, Baring Brothers & Co. Ltd, 1969–82; *b* 30 Dec. 1937; *s* of 1st Baron Howick of Glendale, KG, GCMG, KCVO, and of Lady Mary Cecil Grey, *er d* of 5th Earl Grey; *S* father, 1973; *m* 1964, Clare Nicolette, *y d* of Col Cyril Darby; one *s* three *d*. *Educ:* Eton; New Coll., Oxford. Director: The London Life Association Ltd, 1972–82; Swan Hunter Group Ltd, 1972–79. Member: Exec. Cttee, Nat. Art Collections Fund, 1973–86; Council, Friends of Tate Gall., 1973–78. *Heir:* *s* Hon. David Evelyn Charles Baring, *b* 26 March 1975. *Address:* Howick, Alnwick, Northumberland. *T:* Longhoughton (0665) 577624; 42 Bedford Gardens, W8. *T:* 071–221 0880.

See also Sir E. H. T. Wakefield.

HOWIE, family name of **Baron Howie of Troon.**

HOWIE OF TROON, Baron *cr* 1978 (Life Peer), of Troon in the District of Kyle and Carrick; **William Howie;** civil engineer, publisher, journalist; Director (Internal Relations), Thomas Telford Ltd, since 1987 (General Manager, 1976–87); *b* Troon, Ayrshire, 2 March 1924; *er s* of late Peter and Annie Howie, Troon; *m* 1951, Mairi Margaret, *o d* of Martha and late John Sanderson, Troon; two *s* two *d*. *Educ:* Marr Coll.,

Troon; Royal Technical Coll., Glasgow (BSc, Diploma). MP (Lab) Luton, Nov. 1963–70; Asst Whip, 1964–66; Lord Comr of the Treasury, 1966–67; Comptroller, HM Household, 1967–68. A Vice-Chm., Parly Labour Party, 1968–70. MICE 1951, FICE 1984; Member: Council, Instn of Civil Engineers, 1964–67; Cttee of Inquiry into the Engineering Profession, 1977–80; President: Assoc. of Supervisory and Exec. Engrs, 1980–85; Assoc. for Educnl and Trng Technol., 1982–; Indep. Publishers Guild, 1987–; Vice-Pres., PPA, 1990–. Member: Governing Body, Imperial Coll. of Science and Technology, 1965–67; Pro-Chancellor, City Univ., 1984–91 (Mem. Council 1968–). MSocIS (France), 1978; FRSA 1981. *Publications:* (jtly) Public Sector Purchasing, 1968; Trade Unions and the Professional Engineer, 1977; Trade Unions in Construction, 1981; (ed jtly) Thames Tunnel to Channel Tunnel, 1987. *Recreation:* opera. *Address:* 34 Temple Fortune Lane, NW11 7UL. *T:* 081–455 0492. *Clubs:* Luton Labour, Lighthouse, Architecture.

HOWIE, Prof. Archibald, PhD; FRS 1978; Professor of Physics, since 1986, and Head of Department, since 1989, Cavendish Laboratory, University of Cambridge; Fellow of Churchill College, Cambridge, since 1960; *b* 8 March 1934; *s* of Robert Howie and Margaret Marshall McDonald; *m* 1964, Melva Jean Scott; one *d* (one *s* decd). *Educ:* Kirkcaldy High Sch.; Univ. of Edinburgh (BSc); California Inst. of Technology (MS); Univ. of Cambridge (PhD). English Speaking Union, King George VI Memorial Fellow (at Calif. Inst. of Technology), 1956–57; Cambridge University: Research Scholar, Trinity Coll., 1957–60; Research Fellow, Churchill Coll., 1960–61; Cavendish Laboratory: ICI Research Fellow, 1960–61; Demonstrator in Physics, 1961–65; Lecturer, 1965–79; Reader, 1979–86. Visiting Scientist, Nat. Research Council, Canada, 1966–67; Vis. Prof. of Physics, Univ. of Aarhus, Denmark, 1974. Hon. FRMS 1978 (Pres., 1984–86). Hon. Dr (Physics), Bologna, 1989. (Jtly with M. J. Whelan): C. V. Boys Prize, Inst. of Physics, 1965; Hughes Medal, Royal Soc., 1988. *Publications:* (co-author) Electron Microscopy of Thin Crystals, 1965, 2nd edn 1977; papers on electron microscopy and diffraction in scientific jls. *Recreations:* gardening, wine-making. *Address:* 194 Huntingdon Road, Cambridge CB3 0LB. *T:* Cambridge (0223) 276131.

HOWIE, Sir James (William), Kt 1969; MD (Aberdeen); FRCP, FRCPGlas; FRCPEd; FRCPath; Director of the Public Health Laboratory Service, 1963–73; *b* 31 Dec. 1907; *s* of late James Milne Howie and Jessie Mowat Robertson; *m* 1935, Isabella Winifred Mitchell, BSc; two *s* one *d*. *Educ:* Robert Gordon's Coll., Aberdeen; University of Aberdeen. University lectureships in Aberdeen and Glasgow, 1932–40; Pathologist, RAMC, 1941–45 (served Nigeria and War Office); Head of Dept of Pathology and Bacteriology, Rowett Research Institute, Aberdeen, 1946–51; Prof. of Bacteriology, University of Glasgow, 1951–63. Mem. Agricultural Research Council, 1957–63. Convener, Medical Research Council Working Party on Sterilisers, 1957–64; Pres., Royal College of Pathologists, 1966–69 (Vice-Pres., 1962–66); President: BMA, 1969–70; Assoc. of Clinical Pathologists, 1972–73; Inst. of Sterile Services Management, 1983–88. QHP, 1965–68. Hon. ARCVS 1977; Honorary Member: Pathological Soc. of GB and Ireland, 1977; ACP, 1977. Hon. FRCPath, 1983; Hon. LLD Aberdeen, 1969. Gold Medal, BMA, 1984. *Publications:* Portraits from Memory, 1988; various publications in medical and scientific periodicals, particularly on bacteriology and nutrition. *Recreations:* golf, music. *Address:* 34 Redford Avenue, Edinburgh EH13 0BU. *T:* 031–441 3910.

See also J. G. R. Howie.

HOWIE, Prof. John Garvie Robertson, FRCGP; FRCPE; Professor of General Practice, University of Edinburgh, since 1980; *b* 23 Jan. 1937; *s* of Sir James Howie, *qv*; *m* 1962, Elizabeth Margaret Donald; two *s* one *d*. *Educ:* High School of Glasgow; Univ. of Glasgow (MD); PhD Aberdeen; MRCPE. House officer, 1961–62; Laboratory medicine, 1962–66; General practitioner, Glasgow, 1966–70; Lectr/Sen. Lectr in General Practice, Univ. of Aberdeen, 1970–80. *Publications:* Research in General Practice, 1979, 2nd edn 1989; articles on appendicitis, prescribing and general medical practice and education, in various jls. *Recreations:* golf, gardening, music. *Address:* 4 Ravelrig Park, Balerno, Midlothian EH14 7DL. *T:* 031–449 6305.

HOWIE, Prof. John Mackintosh; Regius Professor of Mathematics, University of St Andrews, since 1970; Dean, Faculty of Science, 1976–79; *b* 23 May 1936; *s* of Rev. David Y. Howie and Janet McD. Howie (*née* Mackintosh); *m* 1960, Dorothy Joyce Mitchell Miller; two *d*. *Educ:* Robert Gordon's Coll., Aberdeen; Univ. of Aberdeen; Balliol Coll., Oxford. MA, DPhil, DSc; FRSE 1971. Asst in Mathematics: Aberdeen Univ., 1958–59; Glasgow Univ., 1961–63; Lectr in Mathematics, Glasgow Univ., 1963–67; Visiting Asst Prof., Tulane Univ., 1964–65; Sen. Lectr in Mathematics, Stirling Univ., 1967–70; Visiting Professor: Monash Univ., 1979; N Illinois Univ., 1988. Mem., Cttee to Review Examination Arrangements (Dunning Cttee), 1975–77; Chairman: Scottish Central Cttee on Mathematics, 1975–82; Cttee to Review Curriculum and Exams in Fifth and Sixth Years, Scottish Office Educn Dept, 1990–. Vice-Pres., London Mathematical Soc., 1984–86. Chm., Bd of Governors, Dundee Coll. of Educn, 1983–87. Keith Prize for 1979–81, RSE, 1982. *Publications:* An Introduction to Semigroup Theory, 1976; articles in British and foreign mathematical jls. *Recreations:* music, gardening. *Address:* Mathematical Institute, North Haugh, St Andrews, Fife KY16 9SS. *T:* St Andrews (0334) 76161.

HOWIE, Prof. Robert Andrew, PhD, ScD; FGS; FKC; Lyell Professor of Geology, Royal Holloway and Bedford New College, University of London, 1985–87, now Emeritus Professor of Mineralogy; *b* 4 June 1923; *s* of Robert Howie; *m* 1952, Honor Eugenie, *d* of Robert Taylor; two *s*. *Educ:* Bedford Sch.; Trinity Coll., Cambridge (MA, PhD, ScD). FGS 1950. Served War, RAF, 1941–46. Research, Dept of Mineralogy and Petrology, Univ. of Cambridge, 1950–53; Lectr in Geology, Manchester Univ., 1953–62; King's College, London: Reader in Geol., 1962–72; Prof. of Mineralogy, 1972–85; Fellow 1980; Dean, Faculty of Science, Univ. of London, 1979–83; Chairman: Academic Council, Univ. of London, 1983–86; Computer Policy Cttee, Univ. of London, 1987–; Vice-Chm., Bd of Management, Univ. of London Computer Centre, 1989–. Mem., Commonwealth Scholarships Commn, 1988–. Geological Society: Mem. Council, 1968–71, 1972–76; Vice-Pres., 1973–75. Mineralogical Society: Mem. Council, 1958–61, 1963–; Gen. Sec., 1965; Vice-Pres., 1975–77; Pres., 1978–80; Managing Trustee, 1978–87. Fellow, Mineral Soc. of America, 1962. Member: Council, Internat. Mineral Assoc., 1974–82; Senate, Univ. of London, 1974–78, 1980–90; Court, Univ. of London, 1984–89. Hon. Mem., Mineralogical Soc. of India, 1973, of USSR, 1982, of France, 1986. Murchison Medal, Geol Soc., 1976. Editor, Mineralogical Abstracts, 1966–. *Publications:* Rock-forming Minerals (with Prof. W. A. Deer and Prof. J. Zussman), 5 vols, 1962–63 (2nd edn, 1978–); An Introduction to the Rock-forming Minerals, 1966; scientific papers dealing with charnockites and with silicate mineralogy. *Recreations:* mineral collecting, writing abstracts. *Address:* Royal Holloway and Bedford New College, Egham Hill, Egham, Surrey TW20 0EX. *T:* Egham (0784) 443810; Gayhurst, Woodland Drive, East Horsley, Surrey. *Club:* Geological.

HOWITT, Anthony Wentworth; Senior Consultancy Partner, Peat, Marwick, Mitchell & Co., Management Consultants, 1957–84; *b* 7 Feb. 1920; *o s* of late Sir Harold Gibson Howitt, GBE, DSO, MC, and late Dorothy Radford; *m* 1951, June Mary Brent. *Educ:* Uppingham; Trinity Coll., Cambridge (MA). FCA, FCMA, JDipMA, CBIM, FIMC, FBCS. Commissioned RA; served in UK, ME and Italy, 1940–46 (Major). With Peat, Marwick, Mitchell & Co., Chartered Accountants, 1946–57. British Consultants Bureau: Vice-Chm., 1981–83; Mem. Council, 1968–75 and 1979–84; led mission to Far East, 1969. Member Council: Inst. of Management Consultants, 1964–77 (Pres., 1967–68); Inst. of Cost and Management Accountants, 1966–76 (Pres., 1972–73; Gold Medal, 1991); Management Consultants Assoc., 1966–84 (Chm., 1976); Mem., Devlin Commn of Inquiry into Industrial Representation, 1971–72. Member: Bd of Fellows of BIM, 1973–76; Adv. Panel to Overseas Projects Gp, 1973–76; Price Commn, 1973–77; Domestic Promotions Cttee, British Invisible Exports Council, 1984. Mem., Court of Assistants, Merchant Taylors' Co., 1971– (Master 1980–81). *Publications:* papers and addresses on professional and management subjects. *Recreations:* fox-hunting, tennis, golf. *Address:* 17 Basing Hill, Golders Green, NW11 8TE. *Clubs:* Army and Navy; MCC; Harlequins.

HOWITT, W(illiam) Fowler, DA (Dundee), FRIBA; architect and hospital planning consultant; Partner in Firm of Cusdin Burden and Howitt, Architects, 1965–90; *b* Perth, Scotland, May 1924; *s* of late Frederick Howitt, Head Postmaster, Forfar; *m* 1951, Ann Elizabeth, *o d* of late A. J. Hedges, Radipole, Dorset; three *s* one *d*. *Educ:* Perth Academy. Royal Marines, 1943–46. Sch. of Architecture, Dundee, 1948; RIBA Victory Scholar, 1949. Asst Louis de Soissons, London (housing and flats), 1949–52; Prin. Asst to Vincent Kelly, Dublin (hosps & offices), 1952–55; Architect to St Thomas' Hosp. (Hosp. rebuilding schemes, flats, offices), 1955–64. Projects include: design and supervision of Coll. of Medicine and King Khalid Hosp., King Saud Univ., Riyadh, Saudi Arabia; design of teaching hospitals: Abuja city and Niger State, Nigeria; children's hospitals, Anambra and Imo States, Nigeria; Addenbrooke's Hosp., Cambridge; Royal Victoria Hosp., Belfast; planning consultancy, 1980–: gen. hosps, Sharjah and Fujairah, UAE; King Fahad Medical City, Riyadh, Saudi Arabia; Polyclinico Teaching Hosp., Milan; private hosp., Milan; gen. hosps Como and Varese. *Recreations:* reading, golf. *Address:* 32 Gloucester Road, Teddington, Mddx TW11 0NU. *T:* 081–977 5772.

HOWKINS, John, MD, FRCS; Gynæcological Surgeon to St Bartholomew's Hospital, 1946–69 (Hon. Consultant Gynæcologist since 1969), to Hampstead General Hospital 1946–67 (Hon. Consultant Gynæcologist, since 1968), and to Royal Masonic Hospital, 1948–73; *b* 17 Dec. 1907; *m* 1940, Lena Brown; one *s* two *d*. *Educ:* Shrewsbury Sch.; London Univ. Arts Scholar, Middlesex Hospital, 1926; MRCS, LRCP, 1932; MB, BS, London, 1933; FRCS, 1936; MS London, 1936; MD (Gold Medal) London, 1937; MRCOG 1937, FRCOG 1947. House Surgeon and Casualty Surgeon, Middlesex Hosp., 1932–34; RMO Chelsea Hosp. for Women, 1936; Gynæcological Registrar, Middlesex Hosp., 1937–38; Resident Obstetric Surg., St Bartholomew's Hosp., 1938 and 1945; Temp. Wing-Comdr, RAFVR Med. Br., 1939–45. Hunterian Prof., RCS 1947. William Meredith Fletcher Shaw Lectr, RCOG, 1975. Sometime Examiner in Midwifery to Univs of Cambridge and London, RCOG, Conjoint Bd of England. Chm., Council Ski Club of Great Britain, 1964–67 (Hon. Life Member, 1968, Trustee, 1969–); Mem., Gynaecological Travellers' Club. *Publications:* Shaw's Textbook of Gynæcology, 7th edn 1956 to 9th edn 1971; Shaw's Textbook of Operative Gynaecology, 2nd edn 1960 to 5th edn 1983 (jtly, 4th edn–); (jtly) Bonney's Textbook of Gynæcological Surgery, 7th edn 1964, 8th edn 1974. *Recreations:* ski-ing, salmon fishing and sheep farming. *Address:* Caen Hen, Abercegir, Machynlleth, Powys, Wales SY20 8NR. *Clubs:* Ski Club of Great Britain; Wilks XV (Hon. Mem.).

HOWKINS, John Anthony; consultant and writer; *b* 3 Aug. 1945; *s* of Col Ashby Howkins and Lesley (*née* Stops); *m* 1st, 1971, Jill Liddington; 2nd, 1977, Annabel Whittet. *Educ:* Rugby Sch.; Keele Univ.; Architectural Association's Sch. of Architecture. Marketing Manager, Lever Bros, 1968–70; jt founder, TV4 Conf., 1971: TV/Radio Editor, Books Editor, Time Out, 1971–74; Sec., Standing Conf. on Broadcasting, 1975–76; Editor, InterMedia, Journal of IIC, 1975–84. Chm., London Internat. Film Sch., 1979–84; Member: Interim Action Cttee on the Film Industry, DTI, 1980–84; British Screen Adv. Council, DTI, 1985– (Dep. Chm., 1991–); Vice-Chm. (New Media), Assoc. of Independent Producers, 1984–85. Exec. Editor, National Electronics Review, 1981–; TV Columnist, Illustrated London News, 1981–83; Exec. Dir, Internat. Inst. of Communications, 1984–89. Specialist Advr, Select Cttee on European Communities, House of Lords, 1985–87; Adviser: Broadcasting Reform Commn, Poland, 1989–90; Polish-Radio-and-Television, 1991–. Associate, Coopers Lybrand Deloitte, 1990–. *Publications:* Understanding Television, 1977; The China Media Industry, 1980; Mass Communications in China, 1982; New Technologies, New Policies, 1982; Satellites International, 1987; (with Michael Foster) Television in '1992': a guide to Europe's new TV, film and video business, 1989. *Address:* 14 Balliol Road, W10 6LX. *T:* 081–960 4023, *Fax:* 081–968 7592.

HOWLAND, Lord; Andrew Ian Henry Russell; Partner, Bloomsbury Stud, since 1985; *b* 30 March 1962; *s* and *heir* of Marquess of Tavistock, *qv*. *Educ:* Heatherdown; Harrow; Harvard. *Recreations:* shooting, racing. *Address:* 6 Fairlawns, Dullingham Road, Newmarket, Suffolk CB8 9JS; (office) Tattersalls Ltd, Terrace House, High Street, Newmarket, Suffolk CB8 9BT. *Clubs:* White's; AD (Cambridge, Mass).

HOWLAND, Hon. William Goldwin Carrington; Chief Justice of Ontario, 1977–90; *b* 7 March 1915; *s* of Goldwin William Howland and Margaret Christian Carrington; *m* 1966, Margaret Patricia Greene. *Educ:* Upper Canada Coll.; Univ. of Toronto (BA 1936, LLB 1939); Osgoode Hall Law Sch. Barrister-at-law. Practised law, McMillan Binch, 1936–75; Justice of Appeal, Court of Appeal, Supreme Court of Ontario, 1975–77. Law Society of Upper Canada: Bencher, 1960, 1965; Life Bencher, 1969; (Head) Treasurer, 1968–70. President: Fedn of Law Socs of Canada, 1973–74; UN Assoc. in Canada, 1959–60. Chm., Adv. Council, Order of Ontario, 1986–90. Hon. lectr, Osgoode Hall Law Sch., 1951–67. Hon. LLD: Queen's Univ., Kingston, Ont., 1972; Univ. of Toronto, 1981; York Univ., 1984; Law Soc. of Upper Canada, 1985; Hon. DLittS Wycliffe Coll., 1985. CStJ 1984. *Publications:* special Lectures, Law Soc. of Upper Canada, 1951, 1960. *Recreation:* travel. *Address:* 2 Bayview Wood, Toronto, Ontario M4N 1R7, Canada. *T:* 483–4696. *Clubs:* Toronto, Toronto Hunt, National (Toronto).

HOWLETT, Anthony Douglas, RD 1971; Remembrancer of the City of London, 1981–86; *b* 30 Dec. 1924; *s* of late Ernest Robert Howlett and Catherine (*née* Broughton), Grantham, Lincs; *m* 1952, Alfreda Dorothy Pearce, *yr d* of Arthur W. Pearce, Hove, Sussex. *Educ:* King's Sch., Rochester; Wellingborough; King's Sch., Grantham; Trinity Coll., Cambridge. BA Hons 1948, LLB 1949, MA 1950. Served War, 1939–46, RNVR; RNVSR, 1951–60; RNR, 1960–75 (Lt Comdr 1968). Hon. Mem., HMS President. Called to the Bar, Gray's Inn, 1950; joined Legal Br., BoT, 1951; Sen. Legal Assistant, 1960; Asst Solicitor, 1972, i/c Export Credit Guarantees Br., 1972–75, i/c Merchant Shipping Br., 1975–81. UK delegate: London Diplomatic Conf. on Limitation of Liability for Maritime Claims, 1976; Geneva Diplomatic Conf. on Multi-Modal Transport, 1980, and other internat. maritime confs. Vice-Chm., Enfield HA, 1987–; Chm., Enfield Dist Res. Ethics Cttee, 1990–. Founder Mem., Sherlock Holmes Soc. of London, 1951 (Chm., 1960–63, 1986–89); Mem., City Pickwick Club, 1988–. Freedom of City of London, 1981; Liveryman, Scriveners' Co., 1981–. OStJ 1986. Order of King Abdul Aziz (II)

(Saudi Arabia), 1981; Order of Oman (III), 1982; Comdr, Order of Orange-Nassau (Netherlands), 1982; Officier, Légion d'Honneur (France), 1984; Comdr, Order of the Lion of Malaŵi, 1985; Order of Qatar (III), 1985. *Publications:* articles on Conan Doyle and Holmesiana. *Recreations:* book browsing, Sherlock Holmes, opera, photography, foreign travel. *Address:* Rivendell, 37 Links Side, Enfield, Middlesex EN2 7QZ. *T:* 081-363 5802. *Club:* Naval.

HOWLETT, Gen. Sir Geoffrey (Hugh Whitby), KBE 1984 (OBE 1972); MC 1952; Chairman: Leonard Cheshire Foundation, since 1990; Services Sound & Vision Corporation, since 1991 (Vice-Chairman, 1989–91); Regular Forces Employment Agency, since 1990 (Vice-Chairman, 1989–90); *b* 5 Feb. 1930; *s* of Brig. B. Howlett, DSO, and Mrs Joan Howlett (later Latham); *m* 1955, Elizabeth Anne Aspinal; one *s* two *d*. *Educ:* Wellington Coll.; RMA, Sandhurst. Commnd Queen's Own Royal W Kent Regt, 1950; served, 1951–69: Malaya, Berlin, Cyprus and Suez; 3 and 2 Para, 16 Parachute Bde and 15 Para (TA); RAF Staff Coll. and Jt Services Staff Coll.; Mil. Asst to CINCNORTH, Oslo, 1969–71; CO 2 Para, 1971–73; RCDS, 1973–75; Comd 16 Parachute Bde, 1975–77; Dir, Army Recruiting, 1977–79; GOC 1st Armoured Div., 1979–82; Comdt, RMA, Sandhurst, 1982–83; GOC SE District, 1983–85; C-in-C Allied Forces Northern Europe, 1986–89, retd. Colonel Commandant: ACC, 1981–89; Parachute Regt, 1983–90. Comr, Royal Hosp., Chelsea, 1989–. President: CCF, 1989–; Army Cricket Assoc., 1984–85; Combined Services Cricket Assoc., 1985; Stragglers of Asia Cricket Club, 1989–. Cross of Merit, 1st cl. (Lower Saxony), 1982. *Recreations:* cricket, shooting. *Address:* c/o Lloyds Bank, Tonbridge, Kent. *Clubs:* Naval and Military, MCC.

HOWLETT, Jack, CBE 1969; MA Oxon, PhD Manchester; MIEE, FSS, FBCS, FIMA; Consultant to International Computers Ltd, since 1975 and Editor, ICL Technical Journal, since 1978; Managing Editor, Journal of Information Technology for Development, since 1985; *b* 30 Aug. 1912; *s* of William Howlett and Lydia Ellen Howlett; *m* 1939, Joan Marjorie Simmons; four *s* one *d*. *Educ:* Stand Grammar Sch., Manchester; Manchester Univ. Mathematician, LMS Railway, 1935–40 and 1946–48; mathematical work in various wartime research estabts, 1940–46; Head of Computer Group, Atomic Energy Research Estabt, Harwell, 1948–61; Dir, Atlas Computer Lab., Chilton Didcot, Berks, 1961–75 (under SRC, 1965–75). Chm., Nat. Cttee on Computer Networks, 1976–78. Fellow by special election, St Cross Coll., Oxford, 1966. Hon. Sec., British Cttee of Honour for Celebration of 1300th Anniversary of Foundn of Bulgarian State, 1980–82; 1300th Anniversary Medal of Bulgarian State, 1982. *Publications:* reviews and gen. papers on numerical mathematics and computation; trans of French books on computational subjects. *Recreations:* hill walking, music. *Address:* 20B Bradmore Road, Oxford OX2 6QP. *T:* Oxford (0865) 52893. *Clubs:* New Arts, Savile.

HOWLETT, Air Vice-Marshal Neville Stanley, CB 1982; RAF retired, 1982; Member: Lord Chancellor's Panel of Independent Inquiry Inspectors, since 1982; Pensions Appeal Tribunal, since 1988; *b* 17 April 1927; *s* of Stanley Herbert Howlett and Ethel Shirley Howlett (*née* Pritchard); *m* 1952, Sylvia, *d* of J. F. Foster; one *s* one *d*. *Educ:* Liverpool Inst. High Sch.; Peterhouse, Cambridge. RAF pilot training, 1945–47; 32 and 64 (Fighter) Squadrons, 1948–56; RAF Staff Coll. Course, 1957; Squadron Comdr, 229 (Fighter) OCU, 1958–59; OC Flying Wing, RAF Coltishall, 1961–63; Directing Staff, RAF Staff Coll., 1967–69; Station Comdr, RAF Leuchars, 1970–72; RCDS, 1972; Dir of Operations (Air Defence and Overseas), 1973–74; Air Attaché, Washington DC, 1975–77; Dir, Management Support of Intelligence, MoD, 1978–80; Dir Gen. of Personal Services (RAF), MoD, 1980–82. Vice-Pres., RAFA, 1984–. *Recreations:* golf, fishing. *Address:* Milverton, Bolney Trevor Drive, Lower Shiplake, Oxon RG9 3PG. *Clubs:* Royal Air Force; Phyllis Court (Henley); Huntercombe Golf.

HOWLETT, Ronald William, OBE 1986; Managing Director, Cwmbran Development Corporation, 1978–88, retired; *b* 18 Aug. 1928; *s* of Percy Edward Howlett and Lucy Caroline Howlett; *m* 1954, Margaret Megan Searl; two *s*. *Educ:* University Coll. London. BSc Eng.(Hons); CEng; FICE. Crawley Develt Corp., 1953–56; Exec. Engr, Roads and Water Supply, Northern Nigeria, 1956–61; Bor. of Colchester, 1961–64; Cwmbran Develt Corp., 1964–65; Bor. of Slough, 1965–69; Dep. Chief Engr and Chief Admin. Officer, Cwmbran Develt Corp., 1969–78. *Recreations:* fishing, music. *Address:* 58 Cambria Close, Caerleon, Newport, Gwent NP6 1LF. *T:* Caerleon (0633) 422315.

HOWSE, Lt-Comdr Humphrey Derek, MBE 1954; DSC 1945; FSA, FRIN, FRAS; RN retired; Caird Research Fellow, National Maritime Museum, 1982–86; *b* Weymouth, 10 Oct. 1919; *s* of late Captain Humphrey F. Howse, RN and late Rose Chicheliana (*née* Thornton); *m* 1946, Elizabeth de Warrenne Waller; three *s* one *d*. *Educ:* RN Coll., Dartmouth. FRIN 1976; FRAS 1967; FSA 1986. Midshipman, RN, 1937–39; Sub-Lt, 1939, Lieut 1941; war service in HMS Boadicea, Sardonyx, Garth, Inconstant, Rinaldo, 1939–45; specialized in navigation, 1944, in aircraft direction, 1947 (despatches 3 times 1943–45); Lt-Comdr 1949; HMS Newcastle, Korean War, 1952–54, Inshore Flotilla, 1954–56; retd 1958. Atomic Energy Div., Gen. Electric Co., 1958–61; Associated Industrial Consultants, 1961–62; Continental Oil Co., 1962–63; Asst Keeper, Dept of Navigation and Astronomy, National Maritime Museum, 1963; Head of Astronomy, 1969; Dep. Keeper and Head of Navigation and Astronomy, 1976; Keeper, 1979–82. Clark Library Vis. Prof., UCLA, 1983–84. Member Council: IUHPS (Pres., Scientific Instrument Commn, 1977–82); British Astronomical Assoc., 1980–88 (Pres., 1980–82); Antiquarian Horological Soc., 1976–82; Royal Astronomical Soc., 1982–83; Royal Inst. of Navigation, 1982–83; Soc. for Nautical Research, 1982–86; Hakluyt Soc., 1984–88; Scientific Instrument Soc., 1987–90. Liveryman, Clockmakers' Co., 1981. *Publications:* Clocks and Watches of Captain James Cook, 1969; The Tompion Clocks at Greenwich, 1970; (with M. Sanderson) The Sea Chart, 1973; Greenwich Observatory: the buildings and instruments, 1975; Francis Place and the Early History of Greenwich Observatory, 1975; Greenwich Time and the Discovery of the Longitude, 1980; Nevil Maskelyne: the seaman's astronomer, 1989; (with N. J. W. Thrower) A Buccaneer's Atlas, 1989; (ed) Background to Discovery, 1990; papers to Mariners' Mirror, L'Astronomie, Antiquarian Horology, Jl of Navigation and Jl of British Astronomical Assoc. *Recreations:* reading, writing, sticking in photos, pottering in the vegetable beds. *Address:* 12 Barnfield Road, Riverhead, Sevenoaks, Kent TN13 2AY. *T:* Sevenoaks (0732) 454366.

HOWSON, Rear-Adm. John, CB 1963; DSC 1944; *b* 30 Aug. 1908; *s* of late George Howson and Mary Howson, Glasgow; *m* 1937, Evangeline Collins; one *s* one *d*. *Educ:* Kelvinside Academy, Glasgow; Royal Naval College, Dartmouth, 1922–25; Lieut, 1930; specialised in gunnery, 1934; Gunnery Officer, HMS Furious, 1936–38; served War of 1939–45 (despatches, DSC); HMS Newcastle, 1939–41; HMS Nelson, 1943–44; Comdr 1945; Fleet Gunnery Officer, British Pacific Fleet, 1947–48; Staff of C-in-C, Far East Stn, 1948–49; Exec. Officer, HMS Superb, 1949–50; Capt. 1951; served on Ordnance Bd, 1950–52; Comdg Officer, HMS Tamar, 1952–54; at SHAPE, 1955–57; UK Nat. Mil. Rep., RN, 1955–58; Chief of Staff to C-in-C, Plymouth, 1958–61; Rear-Adm. 1961; Comdr, Allied Naval Forces, Northern Europe, 1961–62; Naval Dep. to C-in-C Allied Forces, Northern Europe, 1963–64. Regional Officer, N Midlands, British Productivity Council, 1964–71. FRSA. *Club:* Victory Services.

HOY, Rev. David, SJ; Superior, St John's, Beaumont, since 1984; *b* 1 March 1913; *s* of Augustine Hilary Hoy and Caroline Lovelace. *Educ:* Mount St Mary's Coll. Entered Society of Jesus, 1931. Senior English Master, Wimbledon Coll., 1947, Asst Head Master, 1957–59. Rector of St Robert Bellarmine, Heythrop, Chipping Norton, 1959–64; Rector of Stonyhurst College, 1964–71 and 1980–84; Superior of Farm St Church, 1972–75. *Recreation:* walking. *Address:* St John's, Beaumont, Old Windsor, Berks SL4 2JN.

HOYES, Thomas, PhD; FRICS; Member, Lands Tribunal, since 1989; *b* 19 Nov. 1935; *s* of late Fred Hoyes and Margaret Elizabeth (*née* Hoyes); *m* 1960, Amy Joan (*née* Wood); two *d*. *Educ:* Queen Elizabeth's Grammar Sch., Alford, Lincs; Downing Coll., Cambridge (BA 1956; MA 1960; PhD 1963). FRICS 1969 (ARICS 1964). Partner, Hallam Brackett, Chartered Surveyors, Nottingham, 1963–83; Prof. of Land Management, Univ. of Reading, 1983–88 (Head of Dept, 1986–88). Royal Institution of Chartered Surveyors: Mem., Gen. Council, 1982–85; Pres., Planning and Develt Div., 1983–84. President: Cambridge Univ. Land Soc., 1973; Land Inst., 1991; Mem., Rating Surveyors Assoc., 1968–. Governor, Nottingham High Sch. for Girls (GPDST), 1976–82. *Publications:* The Practice of Valuation, 1979; articles and papers in Estates Gazette, Chartered Surveyor Weekly, and Jl of Planning and Environment Law. *Recreations:* gardening, adapting houses. *Address:* (office) 48–49 Chancery Lane, WC2A 1JR. *T:* 071–936 7200. *Club:* Farmers'.

HOYLAND, John, RA 1991 (ARA 1983); *b* 12 Oct. 1934; *s* of John Kenneth and Kathleen Hoyland; *m* 1957, Airi Karkkainen (marr. diss. 1968); one *s*. *Educ:* Sheffield Coll. of Art (NDD 1956); Royal Academy Schs (RA Cert. 1960). Taught at: Hornsey Coll. of Art, 1960–62; Chelsea Sch. of Art, 1962–69, Principal Lectr, 1965–69; St Martin's Sch. of Art, 1974–77; Slade Sch. of Art, 1974–77, 1980, 1983, resigned 1989; Charles A. Dana Prof. of Fine Arts, Colgate Univ., NY, 1972. Artist in residence: Studio Sch., NY, 1978; Melbourne Univ., 1979. Selector: Hayward Annual, 1979; RA Silver Jubilee exhibn, 1979; organized and curated Hans Hofman exhibn, Lateworks, Tate Gall., 1988. *One-man exhibitions* include: Marlborough New London Gall., 1964; Whitechapel Gall., 1967; Waddington Galls, 1967, annually 1969–71 and 1973–76, 1978, 1978, 1981, 1983, 1985; retrospective: Serpentine Gall., 1979; and in Canada, USA, Brazil, Italy, Portugal, W Germany and Australia. *Group exhibitions* include: Tate Gall., 1964; Hayward Gall., 1974; Walker Art Gall., Liverpool (in every John Moores exhibn, 1963–); British Art in the 20th Century, Royal Acad., 1987; Waddington Gall., 1987; also in Belgium, France, Japan and Norway. Work in public collections incl. RA, Tate Gall., V&A Mus. and other galls and instns in UK, Europe, USA and Australia. *TV appearances:* 6 Days in September, BBC TV, 1979; Signals, Channel 4, 1989. Designs for Zansa, Ballet Rambert, 1986. Gulbenkian Foundn purchase award, 1963; Peter Stuyvesant travel bursary, 1964, 1964; John Moores Liverpool exhibn prize, 1965, 1st prize, 1983; Open Paintings exhibn prize, Belfast, 1966; (jtly) 1st prize, Edinburgh Open 100 exhibn, 1969; 1st prize, Chichester Nat. Art exhibn, 1975; Arts Council purchase award, 1979; Athena Art Award, 1987. Order of the Southern Cross (Brazil), 1986. *Relevant publication:* John Hoyland, by Mel Gooding, 1990. *Address:* c/o Waddington Galleries, 11 Cork Street, W1X 1PD.

HOYLE, Prof. Eric; Professor of Education and Head, School of Education, University of Bristol, since 1971; *b* 22 May 1931; *s* of Percy and Bertha Hoyle; *m* 1954, Dorothy Mary Morley; one *s* two *d*. *Educ:* Preston Grammar Sch.; Univ. of London (BSc Sociology, MA). Taught, Harehills Secondary Sch., Leeds, 1953–58 (Head of English Dept, 1956–58); Head, English Dept, Batley High Sch., 1958–60; Lectr and Sen. Lectr in Educn, James Graham Coll., Leeds, 1961–64; Lectr and Sen. Lectr in Educn, Univ. of Manchester, 1965–71; Dean, Faculty of Educn, Univ. of Bristol, 1974–82, 1983–86. Member: Avon Educn Cttee, 1977–80; Educnl Res. Bd, SSRC, 1973–78 (Vice-Chm., 1976–78); Bd of Management, NFER, 1976–; Council, Exec. Council for Educn of Teachers, 1971 (Mem. Exec., 1978–81, 1987–90); Adviser to Public Schools Commn, 1968–70. Editor, World Yearbook of Educn, 1980–86; founding Co-Editor, Research in Educn, 1969. *Publications:* The Role of the Teacher, 1969; (with J. Wilks) Gifted Children and their Education, 1974; The Politics of School Management, 1986; contribs to professional jls. *Recreations:* music, reading, collecting first editions, wine-drinking, watching sport. *Address:* 1 The Crescent, Henleaze, Bristol BS9 4RN. *T:* Bristol (0272) 620614.

HOYLE, (Eric) Douglas (Harvey); MP (Lab) Warrington North, since 1983 (Warrington, July 1981–1983); consultant; *b* 17 Feb. 1930; *s* of late William Hoyle and Leah Ellen Hoyle; *m* 1953, Pauline Spencer; one *s*. *Educ:* Adlington C of E Sch.; Horwich and Bolton Techn. Colls. Engrg apprentice, British Rail, Horwich, 1946–51; Sales Engr, AEI, Manchester, 1951–53; Sales Engr and Marketing Executive, Charles Weston Ltd, Salford, 1951–74. Mem., Manchester Regional Hosp. Bd, 1968–74; Mem., NW Regional Health Authority, 1974–75. Contested (Lab): Clitheroe, 1964; Nelson and Colne, 1970 and Feb. 1974; MP (Lab) Nelson and Colne, Oct. 1974–1979; Mem., Select Cttee on Trade and Industry, 1984–. Mem. Nat. Exec., Labour Party, 1978–82, 1983–85. Pres., ASTMS, 1977–81, 1985–88 (Vice-Pres., 1981–85), MSF, 1988–; Chm., ASTMS Parly Cttee, 1975–76. Pres., Adlington Cricket Club, 1974–. JP 1958. *Recreations:* sport, cricket, theatre-going, reading. *Address:* 30 Ashfield Road, Anderton, Chorley, Lancs.

HOYLE, Prof. Sir Fred, Kt 1972; FRS 1957; MA Cantab; Hon. Research Professor: Manchester University, since 1972; University College, Cardiff, since 1975; Visiting Associate in Physics, California Institute of Technology, since 1963; *b* 24 June 1915; *s* of Ben Hoyle, Bingley, Yorks; *m* 1939, Barbara Clark; one *s* one *d*. *Educ:* Bingley Grammar Sch.; Emmanuel Coll., Cambridge (Hon. Fellow, 1983). Mayhew Prizeman, Mathematical Tripos, 1936; Smith's Prizeman, Goldsmith Exhibnr, Senior Exhibnr of Royal Commn for Exhibn of 1851, 1938. War Service for British Admiralty, 1939–45. Fellow, St John's Coll., Cambridge, 1939–72; University Lecturer in Mathematics, Cambridge, 1945–58; Plumian Prof. of Astronomy and Exptl Philosophy, Cambridge Univ., 1958–72; Dir, Inst. of Theoretical Astronomy, Cambridge, 1967–73; Prof. of Astronomy, Royal Instn of GB, 1969–72; Staff Mem., Mount Wilson and Palomar Observatories, 1957–62. California Institute of Technology: Vis. Prof. of Astrophysics, 1953, 1954; Vis. Prof. of Astronomy, 1956; Sherman Fairchild Scholar, 1974–75; Addison White Greenaway Vis. Prof. of Astronomy; Andrew D. White Prof.-at-Large, Cornell Univ., 1972–78. Mem. SRC, 1967–72. Vice-Pres., Royal Society, 1970–71; Pres., Royal Astronomical Soc., 1971–73. Hon. MRIA (Section of Science), 1977; Mem., Amer. Philos. Soc., 1980; Hon. Member: Amer. Acad. of Arts and Sciences, 1964; Mark Twain Soc., 1978; Foreign Associate, US Nat. Acad. of Sciences, 1969. Hon. Fellow, St John's Coll., Cambridge, 1973. Hon. ScD E Anglia, 1967; Hon DSc: Leeds 1969; Bradford 1975; Newcastle 1976. Royal Astronomical Soc. Gold Medal, 1968; UN Kalinga Prize, 1968; Bruce Gold Medal, 1970, Klumphe-Roberts Award, 1977, Astronomical Soc. of Pacific; Royal Medal, Royal Soc., 1974; Dag Hammarskjöld Gold Medal, Académie Diplomatique de la Paix. *Publications: general:* Some Recent Researches in Solar Physics, 1949; The Nature of the Universe, 1951; A Decade of Decision, 1953; Frontiers of Astronomy, 1955; Man and Materialism, 1956; Astronomy, 1962; Star Formation, 1963; Of Men and Galaxies, 1964; Encounter with the Future, 1965; Galaxies, Nuclei and Quasars, 1965; Man in the Universe, 1966; From Stonehenge to Modern Cosmology, 1972; Nicolaus Copernicus

1973; The Relation of Physics and Cosmology, 1973; (with J. V. Narlikar) Action-at-a-Distance in Physics and Cosmology, 1974; Astronomy and Cosmology, 1975; Highlights in Astronomy, 1975 (in England, Astronomy Today, 1975); Ten Faces of the Universe, 1977; On Stonehenge, 1977; Energy or Extinction, 1977; (with N. C. Wickramasinghe) Lifecloud, 1978; The Cosmogony of the Solar System, 1978; (with N. C. Wickramasinghe) Diseases From Space, 1979; (with G. Hoyle) Commonsense and Nuclear Energy, 1979; (with J. V. Narlikar) The Physics-Astronomy Frontier, 1980; (with N. C. Wickramasinghe) Space Travellers: the Bringers of Life, 1981; Ice, 1981; (with N. C. Wickramasinghe) Evolution from Space, 1981; The Intelligent Universe, 1983; (with N. C. Wickramasinghe) Archaeopteryx, the Primordial Bird: a case of fossil forgery, 1986; (with N. C. Wickramasinghe) Cosmic Life Force, 1988; *novels:* The Black Cloud, 1957; Ossian's Ride, 1959; (with J. Elliot) A for Andromeda, 1962; (with G. Hoyle) Fifth Planet, 1963; (with J. Elliot) Andromeda Breakthrough, 1964; October the First is Too Late, 1966; Element 79, 1967; (with G. Hoyle) Rockets in Ursa Major, 1969; (with G. Hoyle) Seven Steps to the Sun, 1970; (with G. Hoyle) The Molecule Men, 1971; (with G. Hoyle) The Inferno, 1973; (with G. Hoyle) Into Deepest Space, 1974; (with G. Hoyle) The Incandescent Ones, 1977; (with G. Hoyle) The Westminster Disaster, 1978; *children's stories with G. Hoyle:* The Energy Pirate, 1982; The Giants of Universal Park, 1982; The Frozen Planet of Azuron, 1982; The Planet of Death, 1982; Comet Halley, 1985; (with N. C. Wickramasinghe) Cosmic Life Force, 1988; *autobiography:* The Small World of Fred Hoyle, 1986; *play:* Rockets in Ursa Major, 1962; *libretto:* The Alchemy of Love; space serials for television; scientific papers. *Address:* c/o The Royal Society, 6 Carlton House Terrace, SW1Y 5AG.

HOYLE, Ven. Frederick James; Archdeacon of Bolton, 1982–85, Archdeacon Emeritus, since 1985; *b* 14 Dec. 1918; *s* of Henry and Annie Hoyle; *m* 1939, Lillian Greenlees; two *d. Educ:* S John's College, Univ. of Durham (BA 1947, DiplTh 1949, MA 1957). Served War of 1939–45; Imphal, 1944 (despatches). Asst Curate, S Paul, Withington, 1949; Curate in charge, S Martin, Wythenshawe, 1952; Vicar 1960; Vice-Chm. and Exec. Officer, Diocesan Pastoral Cttee (full-time), 1965; Hon. Canon of Manchester, 1967; Vicar of Rochdale, and Rural Dean, 1971; Rector of Rochdale Team Ministry, 1978; Team Vicar, East Farnworth and Kearsley, 1982–85. *Recreations:* rowing, sailing, boat building. *Address:* 37 Toll Bar Crescent, Scotforth, Lancaster LA1 4NR. *T:* Lancaster (0524) 37883.

HOYLE, Susan; Director of Dance, Arts Council of Great Britain, since 1989; *b* 7 April 1953; *d* of Roland and Joan Hoyle. *Educ:* Univ. of Bristol (BA Drama and French). Education Officer, London Festival Ballet, 1980–83; Administrator, Extemporary Dance Th., 1983–86; Dance and Mime Officer, Arts Council, 1986–89. *Address:* (office) 14 Great Peter Street, SW1P 3NQ.

HOYOS, Hon. Sir (Fabriciano) Alexander, Kt 1979; former Lecturer, Cave Hill, University of the West Indies; retired History Teacher, Lodge School, St John; *b* Brazil, 5 July 1912; *s* of Emigdio and Adelina Hoyos, Peru; *m* 1st, 1940, Kathleen Carmen (*d* 1970); three *s* one *d*; 2nd, 1973, Gladys Louise. *Educ:* Wesley Hall Boys' School; Harrison Coll.; Codrington Coll., Durham Univ. (Sen. Island Schol.). BA 1936; MA 1943; Hon. MEd 1963; DLitt UWI, 1982. Taught at: Combermere Sch., Barbados; St Benedict's Coll., Trinidad; Lodge Sch., 1943–72; Moderator, Caribbean History Survey Course, Cave Hill, UWI, 1963–70. Leader-writer of Daily Advocate, 1937–43; Correspondent, London Times, 1938–65. Chm., Nat. Adv. Commn on Educn, 1983–86; Member: Barbados Christian Council, 1976–80; Privy Council for Barbados, 1977–86; Constitution Review Commn, 1977–78. Queen's Jubilee Medal, 1977. *Publications:* Some Eminent Contemporaries, 1944; Two Hundred Years, 1945; Story of Progressive Movement, 1948; Our Common Heritage, 1953; Memories of Princess Margaret and Our Past, 1955; Road to Responsible Government, 1960; Barbados, Our Island Home, 1960; Rise of West Indian Democracy, 1963; Background to Independence, 1967; Builders of Barbados, 1972; Grantley Adams and the Social Revolution, 1974; Barbados: From the Amerindians to Independence, 1978; Visitor's Guide to Barbados, 1982; The Quiet Revolutionary (autobiog.), 1984; Tom Adams (biog.), 1988. *Recreations:* gardening, walking, talking, swimming. *Address:* Beachy Crest, Belair Cross Road, St Philip, Barbados, WI. *T:* 4236323. *Club:* Barbados Yacht.

HOYTE, Hugh Desmond, SC; President, Co-operative Republic of Guyana, since 1985; Leader, People's National Congress, since 1985; *b* 9 March 1929; *s* of George Alphonso Hoyte and Gladys Marietta Hoyte; *m* Joyce Hoyte. *Educ:* St Barnabas Anglican Sch.; Progressive High Sch.; Univ. of London (BA extl 1950, LLB 1959). Called to the Bar, Middle Temple, 1959. QC 1970, now SC. Civil servant and teacher; practised at Guyana Bar, 1960–; Chm., Legal Practitioners' Cttee, 1964; Mem., Nat. Elections Commn, 1966. Elected to Parliament, 1968; Minister: Home Affairs, 1969–70; Finance, 1970–72; Works and Communications, 1972–74; Economic Develt, 1974–80; Vice-Pres., Economic Planning and Finance, 1980–83, Production, 1983–84; First Vice-Pres. and Prime Minister, 1984. *Recreations:* reading, music, swimming, walking. *Address:* Office of the President, Vlissengen Road, Georgetown, Guyana. *T:* 51330.

HU DINGYI; Secretary-General, All-China Federation of Industry & Commerce, since 1988; *b* Dec. 1922; *m* Xie Heng; one *s* one *d. Educ:* Central Univ., Sichuan Province, China (graduate). 3rd Secretary, Embassy of People's Republic of China in India, 1950–54; 2nd Sec., Office of the Chargé d'Affaires of People's Republic of China in UK, 1954–58; Section Chief, Dept of Western European Affairs, Min. of Foreign Affairs, 1958–60; 1st Sec., Ghana, 1960–66; Division Chief, Dept of African Affairs, 1966–71; 1st Sec., then Counsellor, UK, 1972–79; Consul General, San Francisco, 1979–83; Minister, US, 1983–85; Ambassador to UK, 1985–87. *Recreation:* reading. *Address:* c/o All-China Federation of Industry & Commerce, 93 Bei He Yan Dajie, 100006, Beijing, China.

HUANG, Rayson Lisung, Hon. CBE 1976; DSc, DPhil; FRCPE; Vice-Chancellor, University of Hong Kong, 1972–86; *b* 1 Sept. 1920; *s* of Rufus Huang; *m* 1949, Grace Wei Li; two *s. Educ:* Munsang Coll., Hong Kong; Univ. of Hong Kong (BSc); Univ. of Oxford (DPhil, DSc); Univ. of Chicago. DSc (Malaya) 1956. FRCPE 1984. Demonstrator in Chemistry, Nat. Kwangsi Univ., Kweilin, China, 1943; Post-doctoral Fellow and Research Associate, Univ. of Chicago, 1947–50; Univ. of Malaya, Singapore: Lecturer in Chemistry, 1951–54; Reader, 1955–59; Univ. of Malaya, Kuala Lumpur: Prof. of Chemistry, 1959–69, and Dean of Science, 1962–65; Vice-Chancellor, Nanyang Univ., Singapore, 1969–72. Chm. Council, ACU, 1980–81; Pres., Assoc. of SE Asian Instns of Higher Learning, 1970–72, 1981–83. Vice Chm. Council, Shantou Univ., China; Life Member: Court, Univ. of Hong Kong; Bd of Trustees, Croucher Foundn, Hong Kong. MLC Hong Kong, 1977–83. JP. Hon. DSc Hong Kong, 1968; Hon. LLD East Asia, Macao, 1987. *Publications:* Organic Chemistry of Free Radicals, 1974 (London); about 50 research papers on chemistry of free radicals, molecular rearrangements, etc, mainly in Jl of Chem. Soc. (London). *Recreation:* music. *Address:* A7 Bellevue Court, 41 Stubbs Road, Hong Kong. *Club:* Hong Kong

HUBBARD, family name of **Baron Addington.**

HUBBARD, David; *see* Hubbard, R. D. C.

HUBBARD, Michael Joseph; QC 1985; a Recorder of the Crown Court, since 1984; *b* 16 June 1942; *s* of Joseph Thomas Hubbard and late Gwendoline Hubbard; *m* 1967, Ruth Ann; five *s. Educ:* Lancing College. Articled with Morris Bew & Baily, 1961; admitted Solicitor, 1966, Partner in Hubbard & Co., Chichester, 1966–71; called to the Bar, Gray's Inn, 1972, practising Western Circuit; Prosecuting Counsel to Inland Revenue, 1983–85. *Recreations:* messing about in boats and living on Herm Island. *Address:* (chambers) 1 Paper Buildings, Temple, EC4; Bartons, Stoughton, Chichester, West Sussex PO18 9JQ. *Club:* Chichester Sailing.

HUBBARD, (Richard) David (Cairns); Chairman, Powell Duffryn, since 1986; *b* 14 May 1936; *s* of John Cairns Hubbard and Gertrude Emilie Hubbard; *m* 1964, Hannah Neale (*née* Dennison); three *d. Educ:* Tonbridge. FCA. Commissioned, Royal Artillery, 1955–57; Peat Marwick Mitchell & Co., 1957–64; Cape Asbestos Co., 1965–74; Bache & Co., 1974–76; Powell Duffryn, 1976–; non-exec. Director: Blue Circle Industries, 1986–; London and Manchester Group, 1989–; TR City of London Trust, 1989–; Mem., Southern Adv. Bd, Nat. Westminster Bank, 1988–91. Mem., Bd of Crown Agents for Overseas Govts and Admins, 1986–88. Mem. Council, Inst. of Dirs, 1991–. Liveryman, Skinners' Co.; Freeman, City of London. *Recreation:* golf. *Address:* Meadowcroft, Windlesham, Surrey GU20 6BJ. *T:* Bagshot (0276) 72198. *Clubs:* Berkshire Golf, Lucifer Golfing Society.

HUBBARD-MILES, Peter Charles, CBE 1981; self-employed small businessman, since 1948; *b* 9 May 1927; *s* of Charles Hubbard and Agnes (*née* Lewis); *m* 1948, Pamela Wilkins; two *s* three *d. Educ:* Lewis' Sch., Pengam. Served RAF, 1945–48. County Councillor, Mid Glamorgan CC (formerly Glamorgan CC), 1967– (Leader, Conservative Group, 1974–83); Leader, Cons. Gp, Ogwr Borough Council, 1974–83, first Cons. Mayor 1979–80. Chm., Wales Cons. Local Govt Adv. Council, 1979–83. Contested (C) Bridgend, 1987. MP (C) Bridgend, 1983–87. PPS to Sec. of State for Wales, 1985–87. Chm. Governors, Bridgend Tech. Coll., 1977–81. *Recreations:* theatre, showbusiness. *Address:* 18 Lougher Gardens, Porthcawl CF36 3BJ.

HUBEL, Prof. David Hunter, MD; John Franklin Enders University Professor, Harvard Medical School, since 1982; *b* Canada, 27 Feb. 1926; US citizen; *s* of Jesse H. Hubel and Elsie M. Hunter; *m* 1953, S. Ruth Izzard; three *s. Educ:* McGill Univ. (BSc Hons Maths and Physics, 1947); McGill Univ. Med. Sch. (MD 1951). Rotating Intern, Montreal Gen. Hosp., 1951–52; Asst Resident in Neurology, Montreal Neurol Inst., 1952–53, and Fellow in Electroencephalography, 1953–54; Asst Resident in Neurol., Johns Hopkins Hosp., 1954–55; Res. Fellow, Walter Reed Army Inst. of Res., 1955–58; Res. Fellow, Wilmer Inst., Johns Hopkins Univ. Med. Sch., 1958–59; Harvard Medical School: Associate in Neurophysiology and Neuropharmacology, 1959–60; Asst Prof. of Neurophys. and Neuropharm., 1960–62; Associate Prof. of Neurophys. and Neuropharm., 1962–65; Prof. of Neurophys., 1965–67; George Packer Berry Prof. of Physiol. and Chm., Dept of Physiol., 1967–68; George Packer Berry Prof. of Neurobiol., 1968–82. George Eastman Vis. Prof., Univ. of Oxford, and Fellow, Balliol Coll., 1990–91. Sen. Fellow, Harvard Soc. of Fellows, 1971–; Mem., Bd of Syndics, Harvard Univ. Press, 1979–83. Associate, Neurosciences Res. Program, 1974. Fellow, Amer. Acad. of Arts and Sciences, 1965; Member: Amer. Physiol Soc., 1959–; National Acad. of Sciences, USA, 1971; Deutsche Akademie der Naturforscher Leopoldina, DDR, 1971; Soc. for Neuroscience, 1970; Assoc. for Res. in Vision and Ophthalmology, 1970; Amer. Philosophical Soc., 1982; Foreign Mem., Royal Soc., 1982; Hon. Member: Physiology. Soc., 1983; Amer. Neurol Assoc. Lectures: George H. Bishop, Washington Univ., St Louis, 1964; Bowditch, Amer. Physiol Soc., 1966; Jessup, Columbia Univ., 1970; Ferrier, Royal Soc., 1972; James Arthur, Amer. Mus. of Nat. Hist., 1972; Harvey, Rockefeller Univ., 1976; Grass Foundn, Soc. for Neuroscience, 1976; Weizmann Meml, Weizmann Inst. of Science, Israel, 1979; Vanuxem, Princeton Univ., 1981; Hughlings Jackson, Montreal Neurol Inst., 1982; first David Marr, Cambridge Univ., 1982; first James S. McDonnell, Washington Univ. Sch. of Medicine, 1982; James A. F. Stevenson Meml, Univ. of W Ont, 1982; Keys Meml, Trinity Coll., Toronto, 1983; Nelson, Univ. of Calif. Davis, 1983; Deane, Wellesley Coll., 1983; first James M. Sprague, Univ. of Pa, 1984; Vancouver Inst., Univ. of BC, 1985. Hon. DSc: McGill, 1978; Manitoba, 1983; Hon. DHL Johns Hopkins, 1990. Awards: Res. to Prevent Blindness Trustees, 1971; Lewis S. Rosenstiel for Basic Med. Res., Brandeis Univ., 1972; Friedenwald, Assoc. for Res. in Vision and Ophthalmol., 1975; New England Ophthalmol Soc. Annual, 1983; Paul Kayser Internat. Award of Merit for Retina Res., 1989. Prizes: Karl Spencer Lashley, Amer. Phil Soc., 1977; Louisa Gross Horwitz, Columbia Univ., 1978; Dickson in Medicine, Univ. of Pittsburgh, 1979; Ledlie, Harvard Univ., 1980; Nobel Prize in Medicine or Physiol., 1981. *Publications:* Eye, Brain and Vision, 1987; articles in scientific jls. *Recreations:* music, photography, astronomy, Japanese. *Address:* Harvard Medical School, 220 Longwood Avenue, Boston, Mass 02115, USA. *T:* (617) 732–1655.

HUBER, Prof. Robert; Director, Max-Planck-Institut für Biochemie, and Scientific Member, Max-Planck Society, since 1972; *b* 20 Feb. 1937; *s* of Sebastian and Helene Huber; *m* 1960, Christa Essig; two *s* two *d. Educ:* Grammar Sch. and Humanistisches Gymnasium, München; Technische Univ., München (Dr rer. nat. 1963). Lecturer, 1968, Associate Prof., 1976–, Technische Univ., München. Scientific Mem., Max-Planck Soc. Member: EMBO (also Mem. Council); Deutsche Chem. Ges.; Ges. für Biologische Chem.; Bavarian Acad. of Scis, 1988. Hon. Member: Amer. Soc. of Biolog. Chemists; Swedish Soc. for Biophysics. Dr *hc:* Catholic Univ. of Louvain, 1987; Univ. of Ljubljana, Jugoslavia, 1989. E. K. Frey Medal, Ges. für Chirurgie, 1972; Otto-Warburg Medal, Ges. für Biolog. Chem., 1977; Emil von Behring Medal, Univ. of Marburg, 1982; Keilin Medal, Biochem. Soc., 1987; Richard Kuhn Medal, Ges. Deutscher Chem., 1987; (jtly) Nobel Prize for Chemistry, 1988; E. K. Frey-E. Werle Gedächtnismedaille, 1989. Editor: Jl of Molecular Biology, 1976–; Biophysics of Structure and Mechanism, 1976–. *Publications:* numerous papers in learned jls on crystallography, immunology and structure of proteins. *Recreations:* cycling, hiking, ski-ing. *Address:* Max-Planck Institut für Biochemie, Am Klopferspitz 18a, 8033 Martinsried, Federal Republic of Germany. *T:* (089) 85 78 2677/8.

HUCKER, Rev. Michael Frederick, MBE 1970; Principal Chaplain, Church of Scotland and Free Churches, Royal Air Force, 1987–90; Secretary, Forces Board, Methodist Church, since 1990; *b* 1 May 1933; *s* of William John and Lucy Sophia Hucker; *m* 1961, Katherine Rosemary Parsons; one *s* one *d. Educ:* City of Bath Boys' Sch.; Bristol Univ. (MA); London Univ. (BD). Ordained Methodist minister, 1960; commnd as RAF chaplain, 1962. QHC 1987–90. *Recreations:* gardening, music. *Address:* 1 Central Buildings, Westminster, SW1H 9NH. *Club:* Royal Air Force.

HUCKFIELD, Leslie (John); Principal Officer, External Resources, St Helen's College, Merseyside, since 1989; *b* 7 April 1942; *s* of Ernest Leslie and Suvla Huckfield. *Educ:* Prince Henry's Grammar Sch., Evesham; Keble Coll., Oxford; Univ. of Birmingham. Lectr in Economics, City of Birmingham Coll. of Commerce, 1963–67. Advertising Manager, Tribune, 1983; Co-ordinator, CAPITAL (transport campaign against London Transport Bill), 1983–84. Contested (Lab) Warwick and Leamington, 1966; MP (Lab) Nuneaton, March 1967–83. PPS to Minister of Public Building and Works, 1969–70;

Parly Under-Secretary of State, Dept of Industry, 1976–79. MEP (Lab) Merseyside E, 1984–89. Member: Nat. Exec. Cttee, Labour Party, 1978–82; W Midlands Reg. Exec. Cttee, Labour Party, 1978–82; Political Sec., Nat. Union Lab. and Socialist Clubs, 1979–81. Chairman: Lab. Party Transport Gp, 1974–76; Independent Adv. Commn on Transport, 1975–76; Pres., Worcs Fedn of Young Socialists, 1962–64; Member: Birmingham Regional Hosp. Bd, 1970–72; Political Cttee, Co-op. Retail Soc. (London Regional), 1981–. *Publications:* various newspaper and periodical articles. *Recreation:* running marathons. *Address:* PO Box 200, Wigan, Lancs WN5 0LU.

HUCKLE, Sir (Henry) George, Kt 1977; OBE 1969; Chairman: Agricultural Training Board, 1970–80; Home-Grown Cereals Authority, 1977–83; *b* 9 Jan. 1914; *s* of George Henry and Lucy Huckle; *m* 1st, 1935, L. Steel (*d* 1947); one *s*; 2nd, 1949, Mrs Millicent Mary Hunter; one *d* and one step *d*. *Educ:* Latymer Sch.; Oxford Univ. (by courtesy of BRCS via Stalag Luft III, Germany). Accountant trng, 1929–33; sales management, 1933–39; RAF bomber pilot, 1940–41; POW, Germany, 1941–45; Shell Group, 1945–70: Man. Dir, Shellstar Ltd, 1965–70, retd. *Recreations:* competition bridge, gardening. *Address:* Icknield House, Saxonhurst, Downton, Wilts SP5 3JN. *T:* Downton (0725) 22754. *Club:* Farmers'.

HUCKSTEP, Prof. Ronald Lawrie, CMG 1971; MD, FRCS, FRCSE, FRACS, FTS; Professor of Traumatic and Orthopaedic Surgery, since 1972, and Chairman, School of Surgery, since 1975, University of New South Wales: Chairman of Departments of Orthopaedic Surgery and Director of Accident Services, Prince of Wales and Prince Henry Hospitals, Sydney, Australia, since 1972; Consultant Orthopaedic Surgeon, Royal South Sydney and Sutherland Hospitals, since 1974; *b* 22 July 1926; *er s* of late Herbert George Huckstep and Agnes Huckstep (*née* Lawrie-Smith); *m* 1960, Margaret Ann, *e d* of Ronald Græme Macbeth, DM, FRCS; two *s* one *d*. *Educ:* Cathedral Sch., Shanghai, China; Queens' Coll., Cambridge; Mddx Hosp. Med. Sch., London. MA, MB, BChir (Cantab) 1952; MD (Cantab) 1957; FRCS (Edinburgh) 1957; FRCS 1958; FRACS (by election) 1973. Registrar and Chief Asst, Orthopaedic Dept, St Bartholomew's Hosp., and various surgical appts Middx and Royal Nat. Orthopaedic Hosps, London, 1952–60; Hunterian Prof., RCS of Eng., 1959–60. Makerere Univ. Coll., Kampala, Uganda: Lectr, 1960–62, Sen. Lectr, 1962–65 and Reader, 1965–67, in Orthopaedic Surgery, with responsibility for starting orthopaedic dept in Uganda; Prof. of Orthopaedic Surgery, Makerere Univ., Kampala, 1967–72. Became Hon. Cons. Orthopaedic Surgeon, Mulago and Mengo Hosps, and Round Table Polio Clinic, Kampala; Adviser on Orthopaedic Surgery, Ministry of Health, Uganda, 1960–72. Corresp. Editor: Brit. and Amer. jls of Bone and Joint Surgery, 1965–72; Jl Western Pacific Orthopædic Assoc.; British Jl of Accident Surgery. Fellow, British Orthopaedic Assoc., 1967; Hon. Fellow, Western Pacific Orthopaedic Assoc., 1968. Commonwealth Foundn Travelling Lectr, 1970, 1978–79 and 1982. FRSM; FTS 1982. Patron Med. Soc., Univ. of NSW; Founder, World Orthopaedic Concern, 1973 (Hon. Mem. 1978); Vice-Pres., Australian Orthopaedic Assoc., 1982–83 (Betts Medal, 1983); Pres., Coast Med. Assoc., Sydney, 1985–86; Chairman, Fellow or Mem. various med. socs and of assocs, councils and cttees concerned with orthopaedic and traumatic surgery, accident services and rehabilitation of physically disabled. Inventions incl. Huckstep femoral fracture nail, hip, knee, shoulder and circlip. Irving Geist Award, 11th World Congress, Internat. Soc. for Rehabilitation of the Disabled, 1969; James Cook Medal, Royal Soc. of NSW, 1984; Sutherland Medal, Australian Acad. of Technological Scis, 1986; Paul Harris Fellow and Medal, Rotary Internat., 1987; Humanitarian Award, Orthopaedics Overseas, 1991. Hon. MD NSW, 1987. Hon. Mem., Mark Twain Soc., 1978. *Publications:* Typhoid Fever and Other Salmonella Infections, 1962; A Simple Guide to Trauma, 1970, 5th edn 1992 (trans. Italian 1978, Japanese 1982); Poliomyelitis A Guide for Developing Countries, Including Appliances and Rehabilitation, 1975 (ELBS and repr. edns 1979, 1983, French edn 1983); A Simple Guide to Orthopaedics, 1992; various booklets, chapters in books, papers and films on injuries, orthopaedic diseases, typhoid fever, appliances and implants. *Recreations:* photography, designing orthopaedic appliances and implants for cripples in developing and developed countries, swimming, travel. *Address:* Department of Traumatic and Orthopaedic Surgery, University of New South Wales, PO Box 1, Kensington, Sydney, NSW 2033, Australia. *T:* Sydney 3990111. *Club:* Australian (Sydney).

HUDD, Roy; actor; *b* 16 May 1936; *s* of Harold Hudd and Evelyn Barham; *m* 1st, 1963, Ann Lambert (marr. diss. 1983); one *s*; 2nd, 1988, Deborah Flitcroft. *Educ:* Croydon Secondary Technical School. Entered show business, 1957, as half of double act Hudd & Kay; Butlin Redcoats; started as a solo comedian, 1959; first pantomine, Empire Theatre, Leeds, 1959; 4 years' concert party Out of the Blue, 1960–63; first radio broadcast Workers Playtime, 1960; *stage includes:* The Merchant of Venice, 1960; The Give Away, 1969; At the Palace, 1970; Young Vic Co. seasons, 1973, 1976, 1977; Oliver!, 1977; Underneath the Arches, 1982 (SWET Actor of the Year); Run For Your Wife, 1986, 1989; The Birth of Merlin, Theatre Clwyd, 1989; The Fantasticks, 1990; Midsummer Night's Dream, 1991; *films include:* Blood Beast Terror, 1967; Up Pompeii; The Seven Magnificent Deadly Sins; Up the Chastity Belt; The Garnet Saga; An Acre of Seats in a Garden of Dreams, 1973; What'll You Have, 1974; Up Marketing, 1975; *television series include:* Not So much a Programme, More a Way of Life, 1964; Illustrated Weekly Hudd, 1966–68; Roy Hudd Show, 1971; Comedy Tonight, 1970–71; Up Sunday, 1973; Pebble Mill, 1974–75; Hold the Front Page, 1974–75; The 60 70 80 show, 1974–77; Movie Memories, 1981–85; Halls of Fame, 1985; The Puppet Man, 1985; Cinderella, 1986; Hometown, 1987, 1988–89; What's My Line?, 1990; *radio series:* The News Huddlines, 1975–; *author of stage shows:* Victorian Christmas, 1978; Just a Verse and Chorus, 1979; Roy Hudd's Very Own Music Hall, 1980; Beautiful Dreamer, 1980; Underneath the Arches, 1982; While London Sleeps, 1983; They Called Me Al, 1987; numerous pantomimes, 1980–. Chm., Entertainment Artistes Benevolent Fund, 1980–90. King Rat, Grand Order of Water Rats, 1989. Gold Badge of Merit, BASCA, 1981; Sony Gold Award, 1990; British Comedy Lifetime Achievement, LWT, 1990. *Publication:* Music Hall, 1976. *Recreations:* collecting old songs and sleeping. *Address:* 652 Finchley Road, NW11 7NT. *T:* 081–458 7288. *Club:* Green Room.

HUDDIE, Sir David (Patrick), Kt 1968; FEng 1981; retired; *b* 12 March 1916; *s* of James and Catherine Huddie; *m* 1941, Wilhelmina Betty Booth; three *s*. *Educ:* Mountjoy Sch., Dublin; Trinity Coll., Dublin. FIQA 1980; FIMechE 1974. Aero Engine Division, Rolls-Royce Ltd: Asst Chief Designer, 1947; Chief Development Engineer, 1953; Commercial Dir, 1959; General Manager, 1962; Dir, Rolls-Royce Ltd, 1961; Man. Dir, Aero Engine Div., 1965; Chm. Rolls-Royce Aero Engines Inc., 1969–70; Senior Res. Fellow, Imperial Coll., London, 1971–80, Hon. Fellow, 1981. Hon. DSc Dublin, 1968. *Recreations:* gardening, music, archaeology. *Address:* The Croft, Butts Road, Bakewell, Derbyshire DE4 1EB. *T:* Bakewell (0629) 813330.

HUDDLESTON, Most Rev. (Ernest Urban) Trevor, CR; DD; Chairman, International Defence and Aid Fund for Southern Africa, since 1983; *b* 15 June 1913; *s* of late Capt. Sir Ernest Huddleston, CIE, CBE; unmarried. *Educ:* Lancing; Christ Church, Oxford; Wells Theological College. 2nd class Hon. Mod. Hist., Oxford, 1934 (BA), MA 1937. Deacon, 1936; Priest, 1937. Joined Community of the Resurrection; Professed, 1941. Apptd Priest-in-charge Sophiatown and Orlando Anglican Missions, diocese Johannesburg, Nov. 1943; Provincial in S Africa, CR, 1949–55; Guardian of Novices, CR, Mirfield, 1956–58; Prior of the London House, Community of the Resurrection, 1958–60; Bishop of Masasi, 1960–68; Bishop Suffragan of Stepney, 1968–78; Bishop of Mauritius, 1978–83; Archbishop of the Indian Ocean, 1978–83. Provost, Selly Oak Colls, 1983–. President: Anti-Apartheid Movement, 1981– (Vice-Pres., 1969–81); Nat. Peace Council, 1983–; IVS, 1984–; Chm., Internat. Defence and Aid Fund, 1983–. Patron, Runnymede Trust, 1972–. Hon. Fellow, Queen Mary and Westfield Coll., London Univ., 1990. Hon. DD: Aberdeen, 1956; City, 1987; Hon. DLitt: Lancaster, 1972; Warwick, 1988; CNAA, 1989; City of London Polytechnic, 1989; Hon. DHL Denison Univ., USA, 1989; Hon. LLD Leeds, 1991. *Publications:* Naught for Your Comfort, 1956; The True and Living God, 1964; God's World, 1966; I Believe: reflections on the Apostles Creed, 1986. *Recreations:* walking and listening to music. *Address:* House of the Resurrection, Mirfield, W Yorks WF14 0BN.

HUDLESTON, Air Chief Marshal Sir Edmund C., GCB 1963 (KCB 1958; CB 1945); CBE 1943; Air ADC to the Queen, 1962–67, retired 1967; *b* 30 Dec. 1908; *s* of late Ven. C. Hudleston; *m* 1st, 1936, Nancye Davis (*d* 1980); one *s* one *d*; 2nd, 1981, Mrs Brenda Withrington, *d* of A. Whalley, Darwen. *Educ:* Guildford Sch., W Australia; Royal Air Force Coll., Cranwell. Entered Royal Air Force 1927; served in UK until 1933; India, NWFP, 1933–37 (despatches); RAF Staff Coll., 1938; lent to Turkish Govt 1939–40; served Middle East and N Africa, Sicily, Italy, 1941–43 (despatches thrice); AOC No 84 Group, 2 TAF, Western Front, 1944; Imperial Defence Coll., 1946; Head of UK's military delegation to the Western Union Military Staff Cttee, 1948–50; AOC No 1 Group, Bomber Command, 1950–51; Deputy Chief of Staff, Supreme Headquarters, Allied Command, Europe, 1951–53; AOC No 3 Group, Bomber Command, 1953–56; RAF Instructor, Imperial Defence Coll., 1956–57; Vice-Chief of the Air Staff, 1957–62; Air Officer Commanding-in-Chief, Transport Command, 1962–63; Comdr Allied Air Forces, Central Europe, 1964–67, and C-in-C Allied Forces Central Europe, 1964–65. Dir, Pilkington Bros (Optical Div.), 1971–79. Comdr Legion of Merit (USA), 1944; Knight Commander Order of Orange-Nassau (Netherlands), 1945; Commander Order of Couronne, Croix de Guerre (Belgium), 1945; Officer, Legion of Honour, 1956, Croix de Guerre (France), 1957. *Recreations:* cricket, squash, tennis, shooting, etc. *Address:* 156 Marine Court, St Leonards-on-Sea, East Sussex TN38 0DZ. *Club:* Royal Air Force.

HUDSON, Prof. Anne Mary, DPhil; FRHistS; FBA 1988; Professor of Medieval English, Oxford, since 1989; Fellow of Lady Margaret Hall, Oxford, since 1963; *b* 28 Aug. 1938; *d* of late R. L. and K. M. Hudson. *Educ:* Dartford Grammar Sch. for Girls; St Hugh's Coll., Oxford (BA English cl. I; MA; DPhil 1964). FRHistS 1976. Lectr in Medieval English, 1961–63, Tutor, 1963–91, LMH, Oxford; Oxford University: CUF Lectr, 1963–81; Special Lectr, 1981–83; British Acad. Reader in the Humanities, 1983–86; Lectr in Medieval English, 1986–89. Exec. Sec., 1969–82, Mem. Council, 1982–, EETS. Sir Israel Gollancz Prize, British Acad., 1985. *Publications:* (ed) Selections from English Wycliffite Writings, 1978; (ed) English Wycliffite Sermons, i, 1983, iii, 1990; Lollards and their Books, 1985; (ed jtly) From Ockham to Wyclif, 1987; The Premature Reformation, 1988. *Address:* Lady Margaret Hall, Oxford OX2 6QA.

HUDSON, Prof. Anthony Hugh, PhD; Professor of Common Law, since 1977 and Dean of Faculty of Law, 1971–78 and since 1984, Liverpool University; *b* 21 Jan. 1928; *s* of late Dr Thomas A. G. Hudson and Bridget Hudson; *m* 1962, Joan O'Malley; one *s* three *d*. *Educ:* St Joseph's Coll., Blackpool; Pembroke Coll., Cambridge (LLB 1950, MA 1953); PhD Manchester 1966. Called to Bar, Lincoln's Inn, 1954. Lecturer in Law: Hull Univ., 1951–57; Birmingham Univ., 1957–62; Manchester Univ., 1962–64; Liverpool Univ.: Sen. Lectr, 1964–71; Professor of Law, 1971–77. *Publications:* (with Prof. O. Hood Phillips) Hood Phillips: A First Book of English Law, 7th edn 1977, 8th edn 1988; (with Prof. R. R. Pennington) Commercial Banking Law, 1978; (with Prof. J. K. Macleod) Stevens and Borrie Mercantile Law, 17th edn 1978; contribs to various legal periodicals. *Recreations:* gardening, walking, history. *Address:* 18 Dowhills Road, Blundellsands, Crosby, Liverpool L23 8SW. *T:* 051–924 5830.

HUDSON, (Eleanor) Erlund, RE 1946 (ARE 1938); RWS 1949 (ARWS 1939); ARCA (London) 1937; artist; *b* 18 Feb. 1912; *d* of Helen Ingeborg Olsen, Brookline, Boston, USA, and Harold Hudson. *Educ:* Torquay; Dorking; Royal College of Art (Diploma 1937, Travelling Scholarship 1938). Mem. Chicago Print Soc. and Soc. of Artist Print-Makers. Studied and travelled in Italy summer 1939. Interrupted by war. Exhibited in London, Provinces, Scandinavia, Canada, USA, etc.; works purchased by War Artists Advisory Council, 1942–43. Artistic Dir and designer, Brooking Ballet Sch., W1, 1966–. *Recreations:* music, country life. *Address:* 6 Hammersmith Terrace, W6. *T:* 081–748 3778; Meadow House, Old Bosham, W Sussex. *T:* Bosham (0243) 573558.

HUDSON, Erlund; *see* Hudson, E. E.

HUDSON, Frank Michael Stanislaus; a Recorder of the Crown Court, 1981–87; *b* 28 Sept. 1916; *s* of Frederick Francis Hudson and Elizabeth Frances (*née* O'Herlihy); *m* 1947, Jean Colburn (*née* Gordon); one *d*. *Educ:* Wimbledon Coll.; London Univ. (BA). Called to the Bar, Middle Temple, 1961; practised Northern Circuit, 1969–86. Served War: 77th Field Regt RA, 1939–42; Glider Pilot Regt, 1942–45. Post-war employment in local govt and in trade assocs; Dep. Circuit Judge, 1977–80. *Recreations:* bee-keeping, history of English monasticism.

HUDSON, Prof. George, FRCP, FRCPath; Postgraduate Dean, since 1984, and Emeritus Professor, since 1989, University of Sheffield; *b* 10 Aug. 1924; *s* of George Hudson, blacksmith, and Edith Hannah (*née* Bennett); *m* 1955, Mary Patricia Hibbert (decd); one *d*. *Educ:* Edenfield C of E Sch.; Bury Grammar Sch.; Manchester Univ. (MSc, MB, ChB); MD, DSc Bristol. House Officer, Manchester Royal Inf., 1949–50; Demonstr in Anatomy, Univ. of Bristol, 1950–51; RAMC, 1951–53; University of Bristol: Lectr, later Reader, in Anatomy, 1953–68; Preclinical Dean, 1963–68; Vis. Prof., Univ. of Minnesota (Fulbright Award), 1959–60; Sheffield University: Admin. Dean, 1968–83; Hon. Clinical Lectr in Haematology, 1968–75; Prof. of Experimental Haematology, 1975–89; Head, Dept of Haematology, 1981–89. Hon. Cons. Haematologist, United Sheffield Hosps, 1969–89. Chm., Conf. of Deans of Provincial Med. Schs, 1980–82; Member: Sheffield RHB, 1970–74; Sheffield HA, 1974–84; DHSS Working Party on NHS Adv. and Representative Machinery, 1980–81; Council for Postgraduate Med. Educn for England and Wales, 1980–83. *Publications:* papers in medical and scientific jls on haematological subjects. *Recreations:* lay reader since 1953, badminton, cavies, garden. *Address:* The Medical School, Beech Hill Road, Sheffield S10 2RX. *T:* Sheffield (0742) 721747.

HUDSON, Sir Havelock (Henry Trevor), Kt 1977; Lloyd's Underwriter 1952–88; Chairman of Lloyd's, 1975, 1976 and 1977 (Deputy Chairman, 1968, 1971, 1973); *b* 4 Jan. 1919; *er s* of late Savile E. Hudson and Dorothy Hudson (*née* Cheetham); *m* 1st, 1944, Elizabeth (marr. diss., 1956), *d* of Brig. W. Home; two *s*; 2nd, 1957, Cathleen Blanche Lily, *d* of 6th Earl of St Germans; one *s* one *d*. *Educ:* Rugby. Merchant Service, 1937–38. Served War of 1939–45: Royal Hampshire Regt (Major), 1939–42; 9 Parachute Bn, 1942–44. Member: Cttee Lloyd's Underwriters Assoc., 1963; Cttee of Lloyd's, 1965–68,

1970–73, 1975–78; Exec. Bd, Lloyd's Register of Shipping, 1967–78. Dir, Ellerman Lines Ltd, 1979–84. Vice-Pres., Chartered Insurance Inst., 1973–76, Dep. Pres., 1976–; Chairman: Arvon Foundn, 1973–85; Oxford Artificial Kidney and Transplant Unit, 1976–90; Pres., City of London Outward Bound Assoc., 1979–88; Member, Board of Governors: Pangbourne Coll., 1976–88; Bradfield Coll., 1978–88. Lloyd's Gold Medal, 1977. *Recreation:* shooting. *Address:* The Old Rectory, Stanford Dingley, Reading, Berkshire RG7 6LX. *T:* Bradfield (0734) 744346. *Club:* Boodle's.

HUDSON, Ian Francis, CB 1976; Deputy Secretary, Department of Employment, 1976–80; *b* 29 May 1925; *s* of Francis Reginald Hudson and Dorothy Mary Hudson (*née* Crabbe); *m* 1952, Gisela Elisabeth Grettka; one *s* one *d. Educ:* City of London Sch.; New Coll., Oxford. Royal Navy, 1943–47. Customs and Excise, 1947–53; Min. of Labour, 1953–56, 1959–61, 1963–64; Treasury, 1957–58; Dept of Labour, Australia, 1961–63; Asst Sec., 1963; DEA, 1964–68; Under-Sec., 1967; Dept of Employment, 1968–73; Dep. Sec. 1973; Sec., Pay Board, 1973–74; Sec., Royal Commn on Distribution of Income and Wealth, 1974–76.
See also J. A. Hudson.

HUDSON, James Ralph, CBE 1976; FRCS; Surgeon, Moorfields Eye Hospital, 1956–81, now Honorary Consulting Surgeon; Ophthalmic Surgeon, Guy's Hospital, 1963–76; Hon. Ophthalmic Surgeon: Hospital of St John and St Elizabeth, since 1953; King Edward VII Hospital for Officers, 1970–86; Teacher of Ophthalmology, Guy's Hospital, 1964–76, Institute of Ophthalmology, University of London, 1961–81; Consultant Adviser in Ophthalmology, Department of Health and Social Security, 1969–82; *b* 15 Feb. 1916; *o s* of late William Shand Hudson and Ethel Summerskill; *m* 1946, Margaret May Oulpé; two *s* two *d. Educ:* The King's Sch., Canterbury; Middlesex Hosp. (Edmund Davis Exhibnr), Univ. of London, MRCS, LRCP 1939; MB, BS London 1940; DOMS (England) 1948; FRCS 1949; FCOphth 1988 (Hon. FCOphth 1990). Res. Med. Appts, Tindal House Emergency Hosp. (Mddx Hosp. Sector), 1939–42. RAFVR Med. Service, 1942–46; Sqdn Ldr, 1944–46. Moorfields Eye Hosp., Clin. Asst, 1947, Ho. Surg., 1947–49; Sen. Resident Officer, 1949, Chief Clin. Asst, 1950–56; Middlesex Hosp., Clin. Asst Ophth. Outpatients, 1950–51; Ophth. Surg., W Middlesex Hosp., 1950–56, Mount Vernon Hosp., 1953–59. Civil Consultant in Ophthalmology to RAF, 1970–82. Examr in Ophthalmology (Dipl. Ophth. of Examg Bd of Eng., RCP and RCS, 1960–65; Mem. Court of Examrs, RCS, 1966–72). FRSocMed 1947 (Vice-Pres. Sect. of Ophthalmology, 1965); Member: Ophthal. Soc. UK, 1948– (Hon. Sec. 1956–58, Vice-Pres., 1969–71, Pres., 1982–84); Faculty of Ophthalmologists, 1950– (Mem. Council, 1960–82; Hon. Sec. 1960–70; Vice-Pres., 1970–74; Pres., 1974–77; Rep. on Council of RCS, 1968–73; Hon. Mem., 1982–); Soc. Française d'Ophtal., 1950– (membre délégue étranger, 1970–); Cttee d'Honneur Les Entretiens Annuels d'Ophtalmologie, 1970–; Internat. Council of Ophthalmology, 1978–86; UK Rep., Union Européenne des Médecins Spécialistes (Ophthalmology Section), 1973–91 (Pres., 1982–86); Hon. Fellow, Royal Aust. Coll. Ophthalmologists; Pilgrims of Gt Britain; Hon. Steward, Westminster Abbey, 1972–88. Liveryman, Soc. of Apothecaries, and Freeman of City of London. *Publications:* (with T. Keith Lyle) chapters in Matthews's Recent Advances in the Surgery of Trauma; contrib. to chapters in Rob and Rodney Smith's Operative Surgery, 1969; articles in: Brit. Jl of Ophthalmology; Trans Ophth. Soc. UK; Proc. Royal Soc. Med. *Recreations:* motoring, travel. *Address:* 8 Upper Wimpole Street, W1M 7TD. *T:* 071–935 5038; Flat 2, 17 Montagu Square, W1H 1RD. *T:* 071–487 2680. *Club:* Garrick.

HUDSON, John Arthur, CB 1970; Deputy Under-Secretary of State, Department of Education and Science, 1969–80; *b* 24 Aug. 1920; *s* of Francis Reginald Hudson and Dorothy Mary (*née* Crabbe); *m* 1960, Dwynwen Davies; one *s* one *d. Educ:* City of London Sch.; Jesus Coll., Oxford. Served Royal Corps of Signals, 1941–45 (despatches). Entered Ministry of Education, 1946. Mem., South Bank Theatre Bd, 1967–89. *Recreations:* gardening, microscopy. *Address:* The Rosary, Green Lane, Leominster, Herefordshire HR6 8QN. *T:* Leominster (0568) 4413.
See also I. F. Hudson.

HUDSON, Prof. John Pilkington, CBE 1975 (MBE 1943); GM 1944 and Bar 1945; BSc, MSc, PhD; NDH; FIBiol; now Emeritus Professor; former Director, Long Ashton Research Station, and Professor of Horticultural Science, University of Bristol, 1967–75; *b* 24 July 1910; *o s* of W. A. Hudson and Bertha (*née* Pilkington); *m* 1936, Mary Gretta, *d* of late W. N. and Mary Heath, Westfields, Market Bosworth, Leics; two *s. Educ:* New Mills Grammar Sch.; Midland Agricultural Coll.; University Coll., Nottingham. Hort. Adviser, E Sussex CC, 1935–39. Served War of 1939–45, Royal Engineers Bomb Disposal (Major). Horticulturist, Dept of Agric., Wellington, NZ, 1945–48; Lecturer in Horticulture, University of Nottingham Sch. of Agric., 1948–50; Head of Dept of Horticulture, University of Nottingham, 1950–67 (as Prof. of Horticulture, 1958–67, Dean, Faculty of Agriculture and Horticulture, 1965–67); seconded part-time to Univ. of Khartoum, Sudan, to found Dept of Horticulture, 1961–63. Associate of Honour, Royal New Zealand Institute of Horticulture, 1948. Chm., Jt Advisory Cttee on Agricultural Education (HMSO report published, 1973); Mem., RHS Exam. Bd; PP and Hon. Mem., Hort. Educn Assoc. Hon. Fellow: RASE, 1977; Inst. of Hort., 1985. VMH, 1977. Editor, Experimental Agriculture, 1965–82; Mem. Editorial Bds, Jl Hort. Sci, SPAN. *Publications:* (ed) Control of the Plant Environment, 1957; numerous technical instructions on dealing with unexploded bomb fuses, where unambiguity is a matter of life and death; many contribs on effects of environment on plant growth and productivity to scientific jls. *Recreations:* music, gardening. *Address:* The Spinney, Wrington, Bristol BS18 7LB.

HUDSON, Keith William, FRICS; Technical Secretary, Cost Commission, Comité Européen des Economistes de la Construction, since 1989; *b* 2 June 1928; *s* of William Walter Hudson and Jessie Sarah Hudson; *m* 1952, Ailsa White; two *s* two *d. Educ:* Sir Charles Elliott Sch.; Coll. of Estate Management. FRICS 1945. Served Army, 1948–50 (Lieut). Private practice, 1945–48 and 1950–57; Min. of Works, Basic Grade, 1957–64; Min. of Health (later DHSS), 1964–: Main Grade, 1964–66; Sen. Grade, 1966–74; Superintending, 1974–76; Dir B, 1976–79; Under Sec., 1979; Dir of Construction and Cost Intelligence, and Chief Surveyor, DHSS, 1979–86, retd. *Publications:* articles in Chartered Surveyor and in Building. *Recreations:* Rugby coaching, athletics coaching. *Address:* Silver Birch, Mill Lane, Felbridge, East Grinstead, West Sussex RH19 2PE. *T:* East Grinstead (0342) 325817.

HUDSON, Prof. Liam, MA, PhD; psychologist and writer; partner, Balas Co-partnership, since 1987; *b* 20 July 1933; *er s* of Cyril and Kathleen Hudson; *m* 1st, 1955, Elizabeth Ward; 2nd 1965, Bernadine Jacot de Boinod; three *s* one *d. Educ:* Whitgift Sch.; Exeter Coll., Oxford. Post-graduate and post-doctoral research, Psychological Laboratory, Cambridge, 1957–65, and Research Centre, King's Coll., Cambridge, 1965–68; Fellow, King's Coll., Cambridge, 1966–68; Bell Prof. of Educnl Scis, Univ. of Edinburgh, 1968–77 and Dir, Res. Unit on Intellectual Develt, 1964–77; Prof. of Psychology, Brunel Univ., 1977–87. Mem., Inst. for Advanced Study, Princeton, 1974–75; Vis. Scientist, Tavistock Clinic, London, 1987–. Maurice Hille Award, SIAD, 1983. *Publications:* Contrary Imaginations, 1966; Frames of Mind, 1968; (ed) The Ecology of Human Intelligence, 1970; The Cult of the Fact, 1972; Human Beings, 1975; The Nympholepts, 1978; Bodies of Knowledge, 1982; Night Life, 1985; The Way Men Think, 1991. *Recreations:* painting and photography, making things, otherwise largely domestic. *Address:* 34 North Park, Gerrards Cross, Bucks.

HUDSON, Maurice William Petre; Hon. Consulting Anæsthetist: National Dental Hospital (University College Hospital); Westminster Hospital; St Mary's Hospital; Emeritus Consultant Anæsthetist, Princess Beatrice Hospital; Part-time Consultant Anæsthetist, Queen Mary's Hospital, Roehampton; *b* 8 Nov. 1901; *s* of late Henry Hudson, ARCA, and Anna Martha Rosa (*née* Petre); *m* 1922, Fredrica Helen de Pont; one *s* one *d* (and two *s* decd). *Educ:* Sherborne Sch.; St Thomas' Hosp. MB, BS London, 1925; MRCS, LRCP, 1924; DA England, 1936; FFARCS, 1948. Formerly: Resident House Surg., Resident Anæsthetist, and Clin. Asst, Nose and Throat Dept, St Thomas' Hosp. Fellow Assoc. Anæsthetists of Gt Brit. Mem. Royal Soc. Med. *Publications:* contrib. to med. jls. *Recreation:* swimming. *Address:* 10 Devonshire Mews South, W1N 1LA. *T:* 071–935 9665.

HUDSON, Norman Barrie; Under Secretary for Africa, Overseas Development Administration, since 1986; *b* 21 June 1937; *s* of William and Mary Hudson; *m* 1963, Hazel (*née* Cotterill); two *s* one *d. Educ:* King Henry VIII Sch., Coventry; Univ. of Sheffield (BA Hons 1958); University Coll., London (MScEcon 1960). Economist, Tube Investments Ltd, 1960; Economist, Economist Intell. Unit, 1962; National Accounts Statistician (UK Technical Assistance to Govt of Jordan), 1963; Statistician, ODM, 1966; Econ. Adviser, ME Develt Div., Beirut, 1967; Econ. Adviser, ODA, 1972, Sen. Econ. Adviser, 1973; Head, SE Asia Develt Div., Bangkok, 1974; Asst Sec., 1977; Under Sec. (Principal Establishments Officer), ODA, 1981. *Recreations:* theatre, reading, music, watching football and cricket. *Address:* The Galleons, Sallows Shaw, Sole Street, Cobham, Kent DA13 9BP. *T:* Meopham (0474) 814419.

HUDSON, Pamela May; *see* Hudson-Bendersky, P. M.

HUDSON, Lt-Gen. Sir Peter, KCB 1977; CBE 1970 (MBE 1965); DL; Lieutenant of the Tower of London, 1986–89; *b* 14 Sept. 1923; *s* of Captain William Hudson, late The Rifle Bde, and Ivy (*née* Brown); *m* 1949, Susan Anne Knollys; one adopted *s* one *d* and one adopted *d. Educ:* Wellingborough; Jesus Coll., Cambridge. Commnd into The Rifle Bde, 1944; psc 1954; comd company in Mau Mau and Malayan campaigns, 1955–57; jssc 1963; comd 3rd Bn The Royal Green Jackets, 1966–67; Regimental Col The Royal Green Jackets, 1968; Comdr 39 Infantry Bde, 1968–70; IDC 1971; GOC Eastern Dist, 1973–74; Chief of Staff, Allied Forces Northern Europe, 1975–77; Dep. C-in-C, UKLF, 1977–80; Inspector-Gen., T&AVR, 1978–80. Col Comdt, The Light Div., 1977–80; Hon. Colonel: Southampton Univ. OTC, 1980–85; 5 (Volunteer) Bn, The Royal Green Jackets, TA, 1985–. Mem., Gen. Adv. Council, BBC, 1981–85. Mem., Rifle Bde Club and Assoc. (Chm., 1979–85); Trustee, Rifle Bde Museum (Chm., Trustees, 1979–85); Chairman: Green Jacket Club, 1979–85; Council, TA&VRA, 1981–90; Pres., Reserve Forces Assoc., 1985–91. Governor: Royal Sch. Bath, 1976– (Chm., 1981–88); Bradfield Coll., 1983–. Freeman of City of London, 1965. DL Berks, 1984. FBIM. KStJ (Sec.-Gen., Order of St John, 1981–88, Mem. Council, Royal Berks, 1988–). *Recreations:* travel, fishing, most games. *Address:* Little Orchard, Frilsham, Newbury, Berks. *Clubs:* Naval and Military, MCC; I Zingari; Green Jackets; Free Foresters.

HUDSON, Peter Geoffrey; Member, Panel of Chairmen, Civil Service Selection Board, since 1987; *b* 26 July 1926; *s* of late Thomas Albert Hudson and late Gertrude Hudson; *m* 1954, Valerie Mary, *yr d* of late Lewis Alfred Hart and late Eva Mary Hart; two *s* one *d. Educ:* King Edward VII Sch., Sheffield; Queen's Coll., Oxford (Hastings Scholar, MA). Gold Medallist, Royal Schs of Music, 1940. Sub-Lt RNVR, 1944–46. Min. of Transport, 1949; Private Sec. to Minister of Transport and Civil Aviation, 1951–53; Principal, Min. of Transport and Civil Aviation, 1953–57; Admin. Staff Coll., Henley, 1957; British Civil Air Attaché, SE Asia and Far East, 1958–61; Asst Sec., Overseas Policy Div. and Estabt Div., Min. of Aviation and BoT, 1963–68; Counsellor (Civil Aviation), British Embassy, Washington, 1968–71; Under-Sec., DTI, 1971–84; Dir of Resources, British Tourist Authority and English Tourist Bd, 1984–86. Indep. Advr to Lady Marre Cttee on Future of Legal Profession, 1987–88. Vice Chm., Bromley CAB, 1989–. Governor, Coll. of Air Trng, Hamble, 1974–75. *Recreation:* music. *Address:* Candle Hill, Raggleswood, Chislehurst, Kent BR7 5NH. *T:* 081–467 1761.

HUDSON, Peter John, CB 1978; Deputy Under-Secretary of State (Finance and Budget), Ministry of Defence, 1976–79; *b* 29 Sept. 1919; *o s* of late A. J. Hudson; *m* 1954, Joan Howard FitzGerald; one *s* one *d. Educ:* Tollington Sch.; Birkbeck Coll., London. Exchequer and Audit Dept, 1938; RNVR, 1940–46 (Lieut); Asst Principal, Air Min., 1947; Private Sec. to Perm. Under Sec. of State for Air, 1948–51; Asst Sec., 1958; Head of Air Staff Secretariat, 1958–61; Imperial Defence Coll., 1962; Head of Programme and Budget Div., MoD, 1966–69; Under-Sec., Cabinet Office, 1969–72; Asst Under-Sec. of State, MoD, 1972–75; Dep. Under-Sec. of State (Air), MoD, 1975–76. *Address:* Folly Hill, Haslemere, Surrey GU27 2EY. *T:* Haslemere (042864) 2078. *Club:* Royal Air Force.

HUDSON, Prof. Robert Francis, PhD; FRS 1982; Professor of Organic Chemistry, University of Kent at Canterbury, 1967–85 (part-time, 1981–85), now Emeritus; *b* 15 Dec. 1922; *s* of late John Frederick Hudson and Ethel Hudson; *m* 1945, Monica Ashton Stray; one *s* twin *d. Educ:* Brigg Grammar Sch.; Imperial Coll. of Science and Technol., London (BSc, ARCS, PhD, DIC). Asst Lectr, Imperial Coll., London, 1945–47; Consultant, Wolsey Ltd, Leicester, 1945–50; Lectr, Queen Mary Coll., London, 1947–59; Res. Fellow, Purdue Univ., 1954; Gp Dir, Cyanamid European Res. Inst., Geneva, 1960–66. Vis. Professor: Rochester, USA, 1970; Bergen, 1971; CNRS, Thiais, Paris, 1973; Calgary, 1975; Mainz, 1979; Queen's, Kingston, Ont, 1983. Lectures: Frontiers, Case-Western Reserve Univ., USA, 1970; Nuffield, Canada, 1975; Quest, Queen's, Ont, 1983. Vice-Pres., Inst. of Science Technol., 1970–76; Member: Council, Chemical Soc., 1967–70 (Foundn Chm., Organic Reaction Mechanism Gp, 1973); Dalton Council, 1973–76; Perkin Council, 1980–83. *Publications:* (with P. Alexander) Wool—its physics and chemistry, 1954, 2nd edn 1960; Structure and Mechanism in Organophosphorus Chemistry, 1965; papers mainly in Jl of Chem. Soc., Helvetica Chemica Acta and Angewandte Chemie. *Address:* The Chemical Laboratory, University of Kent at Canterbury, Canterbury, Kent CT2 7NH. *T:* Canterbury (0227) 764000; 37 Puckle Lane, Canterbury CT1 3LA. *T:* Canterbury (0227) 761340. *Club:* Athenæum.

HUDSON, Thomas Charles, CBE 1975; Chairman, ICL Ltd, 1972–80; Chartered Accountant (Canadian); *b* Sidcup, Kent, 23 Jan. 1915; British parents; *m* 1st, 1944, Lois Alma Hudson (marr. diss. 1973); two *s* one *d*; 2nd, 1986, Susan Gillian van Kan. *Educ:* Middleton High Sch., Nova Scotia. With Nightingale, Hayman & Co, Chartered Accountants, 1935–40. Served War, Royal Canadian Navy, Lieut, 1940–45. IBM Canada, as Sales Rep., 1946–51 (transf. to IBM, UK, as Sales Manager, 1951, and Managing Dir, 1954–65). Plessey Company: Financial Dir, 1967; Dir, 1969–76; Dir, ICL, 1968. Councillor for Enfield, GLC, 1970–73. *Recreations:* tennis, ski-ing, gardening. *Address:* Hele Farm, North Bovey, Devon TQ13 8RW. *T:* Moretonhampstead (0647) 40249. *Clubs:* Carlton, American.

HUDSON, William Meredith Fisher, QC 1967; Barrister-at-law; *b* 17 Nov. 1916; *o s* of late Lt-Comdr William Henry Fisher Hudson, RN (killed in action, Jutland, 1916); *m* 1st, 1938, Elizabeth Sophie (marr. diss., 1948), *d* of late Reginald Pritchard, Bloemfontein, SA; one *s* one *d*; 2nd, 1949, Pamela Helen, *d* of late William Cecil Edwards, Indian Police; two *d*. *Educ:* Imperial Service Coll.; Trinity Hall, Cambridge. BA 1938; Harmsworth Law Scholar, 1939; MA 1940. Called to the Bar, Middle Temple, 1943, Bencher, 1972; South Eastern Circuit, 1945; Mem. of Central Criminal Court Bar Mess. Commissioned Royal Artillery (TA), 1939; served War of 1939–45, Eritrea and Sudan. Chm., Blackfriars Settlement, 1970–. *Recreations:* trains, travel, theatre; formerly athletics (Cambridge Blue, Cross Country half Blue; rep. England and Wales, European Student Games, 1938). *Address:* 5 King's Bench Walk, Temple, EC4. *T:* 071–353 4713; (home) 3 Rivercourt Road, W6. *T:* 081–741 3125. *Clubs:* Achilles; Hawks (Cambridge).

HUDSON-BENDERSKY, Pamela May, CBE 1988; JP; Regional Nursing Director, North West Thames Regional Health Authority, 1985–88, retired; *b* 1 June 1931; *d* of late Leonard Joshua Hudson and of Mabel Ellen Hudson (now Baker). *Educ:* South West Essex High School. SRN. Nursing Officer, Charing Cross Hosp., 1966–67; Matron, Fulham Hosp., 1967–70; Principal Regl Nursing Officer, SE Thames RHB, 1970–73; Area Nursing Officer, Lambeth, Southwark and Lewisham AHA(T), 1973–82; Regional Nursing Officer, NW Thames RHA, 1982–85. Member, Alcohol Education and Research Council, 1982–87. JP Inner London SE Div., 1983–88; Cheltenham Petty Sessional Div., 1989–. *Publications:* contribs to nursing profession jls. *Recreations:* embroidery, theatre. *Address:* Uluru, 13 Northcot Lane, Draycott, near Moreton-in-Marsh, Glos GL56 9LR. *T:* Blockley (0386 70) 0142.

HUDSON DAVIES, (Gwilym) Ednyfed; *see* Davies, G. E. H.

HUDSON-WILLIAMS, Prof. Harri Llwyd, MA; Professor of Greek in the University of Newcastle upon Tyne (formerly King's College, Newcastle upon Tyne, University of Durham), 1952–76 and Head of Department of Classics, 1969–76; now Emeritus Professor; *b* 16 Feb. 1911; *yr s* of late Prof. T. Hudson-Williams; *m* 1946, Joan, *er d* of late Lieut-Col H. F. T. Fisher; two *d*. *Educ:* University College of North Wales; King's Coll., Cambridge (Browne Medallist; Charles Oldham Scholar); Munich University. Asst Lectr in Greek, Liverpool Univ., 1937–40; Intelligence Corps, 1940–41; Foreign Office, 1941–45; Lectr in Greek, Liverpool Univ., 1945–50; Reader in Greek, King's Coll., Newcastle upon Tyne, 1950–52; Dean of the Faculty of Arts, 1963–66. *Publications:* contribs to various classical jls, etc. *Recreation:* gardening. *Address:* The Pound, Mill Street, Islip, Oxford OX5 2SZ. *T:* Kidlington (08675) 5893.

HUEBNER, Michael Denis; Deputy Secretary, Lord Chancellor's Department, since 1989; *b* 3 Sept. 1941; *s* of Dr Denis William Huebner and late Rene Huebner (*née* Jackson); *m* 1965, Wendy Ann, *d* of Brig. Peter Crosthwaite; one *s* one *d*. *Educ:* Rugby Sch.; St John's Coll., Oxford (BA Modern History). Called to the Bar, Gray's Inn, 1965. Lord Chancellor's Department, 1966–68, 1970–: Law Officers' Dept, 1968–70; Asst Solicitor, 1978; Under Sec., Circuit Administrator, NE Circuit, 1985–88; Prin. Estabt and Finance Officer, 1988–89; Sec. of Commns, 1989–91. *Publications:* brief guide to Ormesby Hall (Nat. Trust); contrib. (jtly) Courts, Halsbury's Laws of England, 4th edn 1975; legal articles in New Law Jl. *Recreations:* looking at pictures, architecture. *Address:* Lord Chancellor's Department, Trevelyan House, Great Peter Street, SW1P 2BY.

HUFFINLEY, Beryl; Secretary: Leeds Trades Council, since 1966; Yorkshire and Humberside TUC Regional Council, since 1974; *b* 22 Aug. 1926; *d* of Wilfred and Ivey Sharpe; *m* 1948, Ronald Brown Huffinley. Chairman: Leeds and York Dist Cttee, T&GWU, 1974–; Regional Cttee, T&GWU No 9 Region, 1972–. Member: Regional Econ. Planning Council (Yorkshire and Humberside), 1975–79; Leeds AHA, 1977–; Press Council, 1978–84. *Address:* Cornerways, South View, Menston, Ilkley, Yorks. *T:* Menston 75115. *Club:* Trades Council (Leeds).

HUFTON, Prof. Olwen, (Mrs B. T. Murphy), PhD; Professor of History, European University Institute, Florence, since 1991; *d* of Joseph Hufton and Caroline Hufton; *m* 1965, Brian Taunton Murphy; two *d*. *Educ:* Hulme Grammar Sch., Oldham; Univ. of London (BA 1959; PhD 1962). Lectr, Univ. of Leicester, 1963–66; Reading University: Lectr, then Reader, 1966–75; Prof. of Modern Hist., 1975–88; Vis. Fellow, All Souls Coll., Oxford, 1986–87; Prof. of Modern Hist. and Women's Studies, Harvard Univ., 1987–91. *Publications:* Bayeux in the Late Eighteenth Century, 1967; The Poor of Eighteenth Century France, 1974; Europe, Privilege and Protest, 1730–1789, 1980; articles in Past and Present, Eur. Studies Rev., and French Hist. Studies. *Address:* 40 Shinfield Road, Reading, Berks. *T:* Reading (0734) 871514.

HUGGINS, family name of **Viscount Malvern.**

HUGGINS, Sir Alan (Armstrong), Kt 1980; Justice of Appeal: Gibraltar, British Antarctica, Falkland Islands, and British Indian Ocean Territory, since 1988; Bermuda, since 1989; *b* 15 May 1921; *yr s* of late William Armstrong Huggins and Dare (*née* Copping); *m* 1st, 1950, Catherine Davidson (marr. diss.), *d* of late David Dick; two *s* one *d*; 2nd, 1985, Elizabeth Low, *d* of late Christopher William Lumley Dodd, MRCS, LRCP. *Educ:* Radley Coll.; Sidney Sussex Coll., Cambridge (MA). TARO (Special List), 1940–48 (Actg Major); Admiralty, 1941–46. Called to Bar, Lincoln's Inn, 1947. Legal Associate Mem., TPI, 1949–70. Resident Magistrate, Uganda, 1951–53; Stipendiary Magistrate, Hong Kong, 1953–58; District Judge, Hong Kong, 1958–65. Chm., Justice (Hong Kong Br.), 1965–68; Judicial Comr, State of Brunei, 1966–; Judge of Supreme Court, Hong Kong, 1965–76; Justice of Appeal, Hong Kong, 1976–80; Vice-Pres., Court of Appeal, Hong Kong, 1980–87. Hon. Lectr, Hong Kong Univ., 1979–87. Chm., Adv. Cttee on Legal Educn, 1972–87. Diocesan Reader, Dio. of Hong Kong and Macao, 1954–87; Reader, Dio. of Exeter, 1988–. Past Pres., YMCAs of Hong Kong. Hon. Life Governor, Brit. and For. Bible Soc; Hon. Life Mem., Amer. Bible Soc. Liveryman, Leathersellers' Company, 1942–91. *Recreations:* forestry, boating, archery, amateur theatre, tapestry. *Address:* Widdicombe Lodge, Widdicombe, Kingsbridge, Devon TQ7 2EF. *T:* Kingsbridge (0548) 580727. *Club:* Royal Over-Seas League.

HUGGINS, Prof. Charles B.; Professor Emeritus, Ben May Institute and Department of Surgery, University of Chicago, since 1969; William B. Ogden Distinguished Service Professor since 1962; *b* Halifax, Canada, 22 Sept. 1901; *s* of Charles Edward Huggins and Bessie Huggins (*née* Spencer); citizen of USA by naturalization, 1933; *m* 1927, Margaret Wellman; one *s* one *d*. *Educ:* Acadia (BA 1920; DSc 1946); Harvard (MD 1924). University of Michigan: Interne in Surgery, 1924–26; Instructor in Surgery, 1926–27; Univ. of Chicago, 1927–: Instructor in Surgery, 1927–29; Asst Prof., 1929–33; Assoc. Prof., 1933–36; Prof. of Surgery, 1936–69; Dir, Ben May Laboratory for Cancer Research, 1951–69. Chancellor, Acadia Univ., 1972–79. Alpha Omega Alpha, 1942; Mem. Nat. Acad. of Sciences, 1949; Mem. Amer. Philosophical Soc., 1962. Sigillum Magnum, Bologna Univ., 1964; Hon. Prof., Madrid Univ., 1956; Hon. FRSocMed (London), 1956; Hon. FRCSE 1958; Hon. FRCS 1959; Hon. FACS 1963; Hon. FRSE 1983. Hon. MSc, Yale, 1947; Hon. DSc: Washington Univ., St Louis, 1950; Leeds Univ., 1953; Turin Univ., 1957; Trinity Coll., Hartford, Conn., 1965; Wales, 1967; Univ. of California, Berkeley, 1968; Univ. of Michigan, 1968; Medical Coll. of Ohio, 1973; Gustavus Adolphus Coll., 1975; Wilmington Coll. of Ohio, 1980; Univ. of Louisville, 1980; Hon. LLD: Aberdeen Univ., 1966; York Univ., Toronto, 1968; Hon. DPS, George Washington Univ., 1967. Has given many memorial lectures and has won numerous gold medals, prizes and awards for his work on urology and cancer research, including Nobel Prize for Medicine (jtly), 1966. Holds foreign orders. *Publications:* Experimental Leukemia and Mammary Cancer: Induction, Prevention, Cure, 1979; over 275 articles. *Address:* Ben May Institute, University of Chicago, 5841 South Maryland Avenue, Chicago, Ill 60637, USA.

HUGGINS, Kenneth Herbert, CMG 1960; *b* 4 Dec. 1908; *m* 1934, Gladys E. Walker; one *s* one *d*. *Educ:* Hitchin Grammar Sch.; Tollington Sch.; University Coll., London. BSc London 1930; PhD Glasgow, 1940. Asst and Lecturer in Geography, Glasgow Univ., 1930–41; Ministry of Supply, 1941; Staff of Combined Raw Materials Board, Washington, 1942–46; Board of Trade, 1947; Staff of Administrative Staff Coll., Henley, 1954–55; Commercial Counsellor, British Embassy, Washington, 1957–60; UK Trade Commissioner, subsequently Consul-General, Johannesburg, 1960–62. Dir, British Industrial Develt Office, NY, 1962–68. Founder Mem. and Hon. Mem., IBG. *Publications:* atlases and articles in geographical journals. *Recreation:* computing. *Address:* 3 Skeyne Mews, Pulborough, W Sussex RH20 2BB. *T:* Pulborough (07982) 2365.

HUGGINS, Peter Jeremy William; *see* Brett, Jeremy.

HUGH-JONES, Sir Wynn Normington, (Sir Hugh Jones), Kt 1984; LVO 1961; Joint Hon. Treasurer, Liberal Party, 1984–87; *b* 1 Nov. 1923; *s* of Huw Hugh-Jones and May Normington; *m* 1st, 1958, Ann (*née* Purkiss) (marr. diss. 1987); one *s* two *d*; 2nd, 1987, Oswynne Jordan (*née* Buchanan). *Educ:* Ludlow; Selwyn Coll., Cambridge (Scholar; MA) Served in RAF, 1943–46. Entered Foreign Service (now Diplomatic Service), 1947; Foreign Office, 1947–49; Jedda, 1949–52; Paris, 1952–56; FO, 1956–59; Chargé d'Affaires, Conakry, 1959–60; Head of Chancery, Rome, 1960–64; FO, 1964–66, Counsellor, 1964; Consul, Elizabethville (later Lubumbashi), 1966–68; Counsellor and Head of Chancery, Ottawa, 1968–70; FCO, 1971, attached Lord President's Office; Cabinet Office, 1972–73; Director-Gen., E-SU, 1973–77; Sec.-Gen., Liberal Party, 1977–83. A Vice-Chm., European-Atlantic Gp, 1985–; Vice-Chm., Lib. Internat. British Gp, 1986–89. Chm., Avebury in Danger, 1988–89. Gov., Queen Elizabeth Foundn for the Disabled, 1985–. FBIM. *Recreations:* golf, gardening. *Address:* Fosse House, Avebury, Wilts SN8 1RF; 401 Beatty House, Dolphin Square, SW1. *Clubs:* English-Speaking Union; N Wilts Golf.

HUGH SMITH, Andrew Colin; Chairman, London Stock Exchange (formerly International Stock Exchange), since 1988 (Member, since 1970, Member of Council, since 1981); Chairman, Holland & Holland PLC, since 1987; *b* 6 Sept. 1931; *s* of late Lt-Comdr Colin Hugh Smith and Hon. Mrs C. Hugh Smith; *m* 1964, Venetia, *d* of Lt-Col Peter Flower; two *s*. *Educ:* Ampleforth; Trinity Coll., Cambridge (BA). Called to Bar, Inner Temple, 1956. Courtaulds Ltd, 1960–68; with Capel-Cure Carden (later Capel-Cure Myers), 1968–85. *Recreations:* gardening, shooting, fishing, reading. *Address:* London Stock Exchange, EC2N 1HP. *T:* 071–588 2355. *Clubs:* Brooks's, Pratt's.
See also H. O. Hugh Smith.

HUGH SMITH, Col Henry Owen, LVO 1976; Defence Adviser to British High Commissioner, Nairobi, 1987–90; *b* 19 June 1937; *s* of Lt-Comdr Colin Hugh Smith and late Hon. Mrs C. Hugh Smith. *Educ:* Ampleforth; Magdalene Coll., Cambridge. BA Hons 1961. Commnd Royal Horse Guards, 1957; Blues and Royals, 1969; psc 1969; served Cyprus and Northern Ireland (wounded); Equerry in Waiting to The Duke of Edinburgh, 1974–76; CO The Blues and Royals, 1978–80; GSO1, MoD, 1980–87. *Recreation:* sailing. *Address:* c/o National Westminster Bank, 1 Princes Street, EC2P 2AH. *Clubs:* Boodle's, Pratt's; Royal Yacht Squadron.
See also A. C. Hugh Smith.

HUGHES, family name of **Barons Hughes** and **Cledwyn of Penrhos.**

HUGHES, Baron, *cr* 1961, of Hawkhill (Life Peer); **William Hughes,** PC 1970; CBE 1956 (OBE 1942); DL; President: Scottish Federation of Housing Associations, since 1975; Scottish Association for Mental Health, since 1975; company director; *b* 22 Jan. 1911; *e s* of late Joseph and Margaret Hughes; *m* 1951, Christian Clacher, *o c* of late James and Sophia Gordon; two *d*. *Educ:* Balfour Street Public Sch., Dundee; Dundee Technical Coll. ARP Controller Dundee, 1939–43; Armed Forces, 1943–46; Commissioned RAOC, 1944; demobilised as Capt., 1946. Hon. City Treasurer, Dundee, 1946–47; Chairman, Eastern Regional Hospital Board, Scotland, 1948–60; Lord Provost of Dundee and HM Lieut of County of City of Dundee, 1954–60; Member: Dundee Town Council, 1933–36 and 1937–61; Court of St Andrews Univ., 1954–63; Council of Queen's Coll., Dundee, 1954–63; Cttee on Civil Juries, 1958–59; Cttee to Enquire into Registration of Title to Land in Scotland, 1960–62; North of Scotland Hydro-Electric Bd, 1957–64; Scottish Transport Council, 1960–64; Chairman: Glenrothes Develt Corp., 1960–64; East Kilbride Develt Corp., 1975–82; Royal Commn on Legal Services in Scotland, 1976–80. Contested (Lab) E Perthshire, 1945 and 1950. Jt Parly Under-Sec. of State for Scotland, 1964–69; Minister of State for Scotland, 1969–70, 1974–75. Mem., Council of Europe and WEU, 1976–87. Fellow, Inst. of Dirs. Hon. LLD St Andrews, 1960. JP County and City of Dundee, 1943–76; DL Dundee 1960. Chevalier, Légion d'Honneur, 1958. *Recreation:* gardening. *Address:* The Stables, Ross, Comrie, Perthshire PH6 2JU. *T:* Comrie (0764) 70557.

HUGHES, Andrew Anderson, MA; Chairman, Building and Estates Committee, Heriot-Watt University, since 1981; *b* Pittenweem, Fife, 27 Dec. 1915; *s* of Alexander and Euphemia Hughes; *m* 1st, 1944, Dorothy Murdoch (marr. diss. 1946); 2nd, 1946, Margaret Dorothy Aikman; no *c*. *Educ:* Waid Academy; St Andrews Univ.; Marburg Univ.; Emmanuel Coll., Cambridge. Colonial Administrative Service, 1939; Private Sec. to Governor, Gold Coast, 1940–42; Colonial Office, 1946; Dept of Health for Scotland, 1947; Asst Sec., 1956; Under-Sec., 1964; Under-Sec., Scottish Development Dept, 1966–69; Man. Dir, Crudens Ltd, 1969–71; Chm., Grampian Construction Ltd, 1971; Director: Grampian Hldgs, 1973–84; Highland Craftpoint Ltd, 1979–85; Cairngorm Chairlift Co., 1981–83; Gilmour and Dean Holdings, 1980–87. Dep. Chm., Scottish Tourist Bd, 1971–81 (Mem., 1969–81); Member: Scottish Council, CBI, 1976–82; Central Arbitration Cttee, 1977–85; Chm., Scottish Crafts Consultative Cttee, 1979–85; Mem., Crafts Council, 1981–85. Mem. Ct, Heriot-Watt Univ., 1981–. DUniv Heriot-Watt, 1988. *Recreations:* golf, fishing. *Address:* 9 Palmerston Road, Edinburgh EH9 1TL. *T:* 031–667 2353. *Club:* New (Edinburgh).

HUGHES, Aneurin Rhys; Ambassador and Head of Delegation of Commission of European Communities in Oslo, Norway, since 1987; *b* 11 Feb. 1937; *s* of William and Hilda Hughes; *m* 1964, Jill (*née* Salisbury); two *s*. *Educ:* University College of Wales, Aberystwyth (BA). President, National Union of Students, 1962–64. Research in S America, 1964–66; HM Diplomatic Service, 1967–73: served, Singapore and Rome; Commission of the European Communities, 1973–: Head of Division for Internal

Coordination in Secretariat-General, 1973–77; Adviser to Dir. Gen. for Information, 1977–80; Chef de Cabinet to Mr Ivor Richard, Comr responsible for Employment, Social Affairs and Educn, 1981–85; Adviser to Dir Gen. for Information, and Chm., Selection Bd for Candidates from Spain and Portugal, 1985–87. Organiser, Conf. on Culture, Economy and New Technologies, Florence, 1986–87. *Recreations:* squash, golf, music, hashing. *Address:* European Commission Delegation, Haakon VII's Gate 6, PO Box 1643 Vika, 0119 Oslo 1, Norway. *Clubs:* Travellers'; Norske Selskab (Oslo).

HUGHES, Anthony Philip Gilson; QC 1990; a Recorder, since 1988; *b* 11 Aug. 1948; *s* of Patrick and Patricia Hughes; *m* 1972, Susan Elizabeth March; one *s* one *d*. *Educ:* Tettenhall Coll., Staffs; Van Mildert Coll., Durham (BA 1969). Sometime Lectr, Durham Univ. and QMC. Called to the Bar, Inner Temple, 1970. *Recreations:* garden labouring and mechanics, campanology. *Address:* 1 Fountain Court, Steelhouse Lane, Birmingham B4 6DR. *T:* 021–236 5721.

HUGHES, Dr Antony Elwyn; Director, Programmes and Deputy Chairman, Science and Engineering Research Council, since 1991; *b* 9 Sept. 1941; *s* of Ifor Elwyn Hughes and Anna Betty Hughes (*née* Ambler); *m* 1963, Margaret Mary Lewis; two *s* two *d*. *Educ:* Newport High Sch., Gwent; Jesus Coll., Oxford (MA; DPhil). CPhys; FInstP. Harkness Fellow, Cornell Univ., 1967–69. United Kingdom Atomic Energy Authority, Atomic Energy Research Establishment (Harwell): Scientific Officer, 1963–67; Sen. Scientific Officer, 1969–72; Principal Scientific Officer, 1972–75; Leader: Defects in Solids Gp, 1973; Solid State Sciences Gp, 1978; Individual Merit Appointment, 1975–81; Sen. Personal Appointment, 1981–83; Head, Materials Physics Div., 1983–86; Dir, Underlying Res. and Non-Nuclear Energy Res., 1986–87; Authority Chief Scientist and Dir, Nuclear Res., 1987–88. Dir, Labs, SERC, 1988–91. *Publications:* Real Solids and Radiation, 1975; (ed) Defects and their Structure in Non-Metallic Solids, 1976; review articles in Contemporary Physics, Advances in Physics, Jl of Materials Science, Jl of Nuclear Materials, Reports on Progress in Physics. *Recreations:* hill walking, cycling, watching Rugby and cricket, music, gardening. *Address:* Science and Engineering Research Council, Polaris House, North Star Avenue, Swindon SN2 1ET. *T:* Swindon (0793) 411114.

HUGHES, Sir David (Collingwood), 14th Bt *cr* 1773; heraldic sculptor; Managing Director, Louis Lejeune Ltd, since 1978; *b* 29 Dec. 1936; *s* of Sir Richard Edgar Hughes, 13th Bt and Angela Lilian Adelaide Pell (*d* 1967); *S* father, 1970; *m* 1964, Rosemary Ann Pain, MA, LLM, *d* of Rev. John Pain; four *s*. *Educ:* Oundle and Magdalene College, Cambridge (MA). National Service, RN, 1955–57. United Steel Cos Ltd, 1960–65; Unicam Instruments Ltd (subsequently Pye Unicam Ltd), export executive, 1965–70, E Europe manager, 1970–73. Builder, 1974–76. *Recreations:* shooting, fishing. *Heir:* *s* Thomas Collingwood Hughes, *b* 16 Feb. 1966. *Address:* The Berristead, Wilburton, Ely, Cambs. *T:* Ely (0353) 740770. *Clubs:* Flyfishers'; Cambridge County (Cambridge).

HUGHES, (David Evan) Peter, MA; Director, Understanding Science Project, and Leverhulme Research Fellow, Imperial College and Westminster School, since 1989; *b* 27 April 1932; *s* of late Evan Gwilliam Forrest-Hughes, OBE; *m* 1956, Iris (*née* Jenkins); one *s* two *d*. *Educ:* St Paul's Sch.; St John's Coll., Oxford (Gibbs Schol. in Chemistry; MA). National Service, 5 RHA, 1954. Assistant Master, Shrewsbury School, 1956; Head of Chemistry, 1958, Science, 1965; Nuffield Foundation, 1967–68; Second Master, Shrewsbury Sch., 1972; Headmaster, St Peter's Sch., York, 1980–84; Head of Science, Westminster Sch., 1984–89. *Publications:* Advanced Theoretical Chemistry (with M. J. Maloney), 1964; Chemical Energetics, 1967. *Recreations:* music, bridge, hill-walking. *Address:* Flat 1, 63 Millbank, SW1P 4RW.

HUGHES, David Glyn; National Agent, 1979–88, Senior National Officer, 1986–88, the Labour Party; *b* 1 March 1928; *s* of Richard and Miriam Hughes; *m* 1958, Mary Atkinson; one *d*. *Educ:* Darwin St Secondary Modern Sch. Apprentice, later fitter and turner, 1944–52; Labour Party Agent: Northwich, Bolton, Tonbridge, Portsmouth, 1952–69; Asst Regional Organiser, 1969–75, Regional Organiser, 1975–79, Northern Region. *Recreations:* gardening, walking. *Address:* 42 Langroyd Road, SW17. *T:* 081–672 2959. *Clubs:* Stella Maris Social (Life-Mem.), Usworth and District Workmen's (Washington, Tyne and Wear).

HUGHES, David John, FRSL; writer; *b* 27 July 1930; *o s* of late Gwilym Fielden Hughes and of Edna Frances Hughes; *m* 1st, 1957, Mai Zetterling; 2nd, 1980, Elizabeth Westoll; one *s* one *d*. *Educ:* Eggar's Grammar Sch., Alton; King's College Sch., Wimbledon; Christ Church, Oxford (MA; Editor, Isis). FRSL 1986. Editorial Asst, London Magazine, 1953–55; Reader with Rupert Hart-Davis, 1956–60; Editor, Town magazine, 1960–61; script-writer and stills photographer of BBC documentaries and Scandinavian feature-films directed by Mai Zetterling, 1960–72; Editor, New Fiction Society, 1975–78, 1981–82. Asst Visiting Professor: Writers' Workshop, Univ. of Iowa, 1978–79, 1987; Univ. of Alabama, 1979; Vis. Assoc. Prof., Univ. of Houston, 1986. Film Critic, Sunday Times, 1982–83; Fiction Critic, Mail on Sunday, 1982–. *Publications: fiction:* A Feeling in the Air, 1957; Sealed with a Loving Kiss, 1958; The Horsehair Sofa, 1961; The Major, 1964; The Man Who Invented Tomorrow, 1968; Memories of Dying, 1976; A Genoese Fancy, 1979; The Imperial German Dinner Service, 1983; The Pork Butcher, 1984 (Welsh Arts Council Fiction Prize, 1984; W. H. Smith Literary Award, 1985; filmed as Souvenir, 1989); But for Bunter, 1985; (ed) Winter's Tales: New Series I, 1985; (ed with Giles Gordon) Best Short Stories, annually 1986–; *non-fiction:* J. B. Priestley, an informal study, 1958; The Road to Stockholm (travel), 1964; The Seven Ages of England (cultural history), 1967; The Rosewater Revolution, 1971; Evergreens, 1976. *Address:* c/o Anthony Sheil Associates, 43 Doughty Street, WC1N 2LF. *Club:* Savile.

HUGHES, David Morgan; His Honour Judge Morgan Hughes; a Circuit Judge, since Nov. 1972; *b* 20 Jan. 1926; *s* of late Rev. John Edward Hughes and Mrs Margaret Ellen Hughes; *m* 1956, Elizabeth Jane Roberts; one *s* two *d*. *Educ:* Beaumaris Grammar Sch.; LSE (LLB). Army, 1944–48: Captain, Royal Welch Fusiliers; attached 2nd Bn The Welch Regt; Burma, 1945–47. London Univ., 1948–51; Rockefeller Foundn Fellowship in Internat. Air Law, McGill Univ., 1951–52; called to Bar, Middle Temple, 1953; practised Wales and Chester Circuit; Dep. Chm., Caernarvonshire QS, 1970–71; a Recorder, Jan.-Nov. 1972; Dep. Chm., Agricultural Lands Tribunal, 1972; Mem., Mental Health Review Tribunal, 1989–. *Recreations:* tennis, cricket, gardening. *Address:* Bryn, Kelsall, Cheshire CW6 0PA. *T:* Kelsall (0829) 51349.

HUGHES, Hon. Sir Davis, Kt 1975; Agent-General for New South Wales, in London, 1973–78; *b* 24 Nov. 1910; *m* 1940, Joan Philip Johnson; one *s* two *d*. *Educ:* Launceston High Sch., Tasmania; Phillip Smith Teachers' Coll., Hobart, Tas. Teacher, Tasmania, incl. Friends' Sch., Hobart, 1930–35; Master, Caulfield Grammar Sch., Melbourne, 1935–40. Served War, Sqdn Ldr, RAAF, Australia and overseas, 1940–45. Dep. Headmaster, Armidale Sch., Armidale, NSW, 1946–49; Mayor of Armidale, 1953–56. MLA, NSW, 1950–53 and 1956–65; Minister for Public Works, NSW, 1965–73. Rep., Derek Crouch Aust. Ltd, 1979–. Freeman: City of Armidale, NSW, 1965; City of London, 1975. *Recreations:* tennis, golf, fishing, racing. *Address:* 68 Heath Road, Hardy's Bay, NSW 2257, Australia. *Club:* Australasian Pioneers (Sydney).

HUGHES, Desmond; *see* Hughes, F. D.

HUGHES, Rev. Edward Marshall, MTh, PhD (London); Vicar of St Mary's, Dover, 1971–84; Chaplain to the Queen, 1973–83; *b* London, 11 Nov. 1913; *o s* of late Edward William Hughes, Newhouse, Mersham, Ashford, Kent, and Mabel Frances (*née* Faggetter); descendant of Edward Hughes, *b* 1719, of Little Swanton, Mersham; unmarried. *Educ:* City of London Sch.; King's Coll., London; Cuddesdon Coll., Oxford. Deacon, 1936, Priest, 1937, Canterbury; Curate, St Martin's, Canterbury, 1936–41; Chaplain RAFVR 1941 (invalided Oct. 1941); Curate Bearsted, Kent, 1941–46; Vicar of Woodnesborough, Kent, 1946–52; Chap. St Bartholomew's Hosp., Sandwich, 1947–52; Off. Chap. RAF Station, Sandwich, 1948–52; Warden of St Peter's Theological Coll., Jamaica, 1952–61; Canon Missioner of Jamaica, 1955–61; Examining Chap. to the Bp of Jamaica, 1953–61; Hon. Chap. Jamaica, RAFA, 1954–61; Mem. Board of Governors Nuttall Memorial Hospital, Kingston, 1956–61, and St Jago High Sch., Spanish Town, 1957–61; Visiting Lecturer, McGill Univ., Canada, 1957; Hon. Lecturer, Union Theological Seminary, Jamaica, 1957–58; Visiting Lecturer, Séminaire de Théologie, Haiti, 1959; Acting Rector, St Matthew's Church, Kingston, and Chap. Kingston Public Hospital, 1959–60; JP (St Andrew, Jamaica), 1959–63; Commissary to Bishop of Jamaica, 1968–90. Fellow (Librarian, 1962–65), St Augustine's Coll., Canterbury (Central Coll. of the Anglican Communion), 1961–65; Hon. helper, RAF Benevolent Fund, for Kent, 1961–65, for London (Croydon), 1965–71, for Kent, 1971–; Divinity Master, VI Forms, The King's Sch., Canterbury, 1962–63; Officiating Chap., Canterbury Garrison, 1963–64; Vicar of St Augustine's, S Croydon, 1965–71. Proctor in Convocation, Dio. Canterbury, 1966–75. Examining Chaplain to Archbishop of Canterbury, 1967–76; Rural Dean of Dover, 1974–80; Hon. Chaplain: East and South Goodwin Lightships, 1979–85; Assoc. of Men of Kent and Kentish Men (of which his father was founder-member, 1897), 1979–. *Publications:* various papers on theological education overseas. *Recreations:* gardening, exercising the dogs, computering. *Address:* Woodlands, Sandwich Road, Woodnesborough, Sandwich, Kent CT13 0LZ. *T:* Sandwich (0304) 617098.

HUGHES, Prof. Sir Edward (Stuart Reginald), Kt 1977; CBE 1971; Chairman and Professor, Department of Surgery, Monash University, Alfred Hospital, 1973–84, now Emeritus Professor of Surgery; *b* 4 July 1919; *s* of Reginald Hawkins Hughes and Annie Grace Langford; *m* 1944, Alison Clare Lelean; two *s* two *d*. *Educ:* Melbourne C of E Grammar Sch.; Univ. of Melbourne. MB, BS 1943; MD 1945; MS 1946; FRCS 1946 (Hon. FRCS 1985); FRACS 1950. Resident Medical Officer, Royal Melbourne Hosp., 1943–45, Asst Surgeon 1950–53, Surgeon 1954–74; Surgeon, Alfred Hosp., 1973–84. Consultant Surgeon to Australian Army, 1976–82. Royal Australasian College of Surgeons: Mem. Council, 1967–78; Chm. Exec. Cttee, 1971–78; Sen. Vice-Pres., 1974–84; Pres., 1975–78. First Dir, Menzies Foundn for Health, Fitness and Physical Achievement, 1979–. Cabrini Surgical Lectures, 1989. Fellow, Queens Coll. 1955. Hon. FACS, Hon. FRCS(C), Hon. FRCSE, Hon. FRCSI; Hon. FPCS 1977. Hon. LLD Monash, 1985. Sir Hugh Devine Medal, RACS, 1977. *Publications:* Surgery of the Anal Canal and Rectum, 1957; All about an Ileostomy, 1966, 3rd edn 1971; All about a Colostomy, 1970, 2nd edn 1977; Ano-Rectal Surgery, 1972; Colo-Rectal Surgery, 1983; Rectal Cancer, 1989. *Recreations:* tennis, racing. *Address:* 24 Somers Avenue, Malvern, Victoria 3144, Australia. *T:* 20.7688. *Clubs:* Melbourne, Melbourne Cricket, Victoria Racing, Victoria Amateur Turf (Melbourne).

HUGHES, Air Vice-Marshal (Frederick) Desmond, CB 1972; CBE 1961; DSO 1945; DFC and 2 bars, 1941–43; AFC 1954; DL; *b* Belfast, 6 June 1919; *s* of late Fred C. Hughes, company dir, Donaghadee, Co. Down, and late Hilda (*née* Hunter), Ballymore, Co. Donegal; *m* 1941, Pamela, *d* of late Julius Harrison, composer and conductor; two *s* (and one *s* decd). *Educ:* Campbell Coll., Belfast; Pembroke Coll., Cambridge (MA). Joined RAF from Cambridge Univ. Air Sqdn, 1939; Battle of Britain, No. 264 Sqdn, 1940; night fighting ops in Britain and Mediterranean theatre, 1941–43; comd No. 604 Sqdn in Britain and France, 1944–45; granted perm. commn, 1946; served in Fighter Comd, 1946–53; Directing Staff, RAF Staff Coll., 1954–56; Personal Staff Off. to Chief of Air Staff, 1956–58; comd. RAF Stn Geilenkirchen, 1959–61; Dir of Air Staff Plans, Min. of Def., 1962–64; ADC to the Queen, 1963; Air Officer i/c Administration, HQ Flying Training Command, RAF, 1966–68; AOC, No 18 Group, RAF Coastal Command, and Air Officer, Scotland and N Ireland, 1968–70; Comdt, RAF Coll., Cranwell, 1970–72; SASO Near East Air Force, 1972–74, retired. Hon. Air Cdre, No 2503 RAuxAF Regt Sqdn, 1982–. Dir, Trident Trust, 1976–78. DL Lincoln 1983. *Recreations:* fishing, shooting, music. *Address:* c/o Midland Bank, Sleaford, Lincs. *Club:* Royal Air Force.

HUGHES, George; Chairman and Chief Executive, Hughes Technology Ltd, since 1984; *b* 4 May 1937; *s* of Peter and Ann Hughes; *m* 1963, Janet; two *s*. *Educ:* Liverpool Collegiate (Sen. City Scholar; Open State Schol. with 3 distinctions); Gonville and Caius Coll., Cambridge (Open Scholar; MA Hons 1st Cl. German Mod. Lang. Tripos); Harvard Business Sch. (MBA 1968). Ski instructor, 1959; lead in J. Arthur Rank film, Holiday with Pay, 1959–60; Banking, Paris, 1960; IBM, London, 1960–69 (Strategy Develt Man., 1968–69; IBM European Salesman of the Year, Rome, 1965); Merchant Banking, London, 1969–70; Vice-Chm., Chief Exec. and Gp Man. Dir, Duple Gp Ltd, 1970–71; Chairman and Chief Executive: Hughes International, 1970–83; Willowbrook International, 1970–83; Willowbrook World Wide, 1971–83; Hampton Court Farms (formerly Castle Hughes Gp), 1975–87; Hughes Truck and Bus, 1976–84. Mem., Mensa, 1961. Chm., Derbys CCC, 1976–77; Mem., TCCB, 1976–77. *Publications:* The Effective Use of Computers, 1968; Military and Business Strategy, 1968; papers on new towns; mobility: a basic human need; economic develt as strategic choice; traffic congestion in capital cities; getting action and making things happen; integrated cattle development; choosing the best way; control; scenario for the president; spare parts management; strategy for survival; road to recovery; all the milk and meat China needs; speed-thinking Kaleidoscope. *Recreations:* perception of visual patterns in thinking, creativity and innovation, historic buildings, Renoir, soccer, tennis, cricket. *Address:* Xanadu, Matthews Green Road, Wokingham RG11 1JU; Château de Beauchamps, Sarthe, France. *Clubs:* MCC, Carlton, Annabel's.

HUGHES, Prof. George Morgan; Professor of Zoology, Bristol University, 1965–85, now Emeritus; *b* 17 March 1925; *s* of James Williams Hughes and Edith May Hughes; *m* 1954, Jean Rosemary, *d* of Rowland Wynne Frazier and Jessie Frazier; two *s* one *d*. *Educ:* Liverpool Collegiate Sch.; King's Coll., Cambridge (Scholar). Martin Thackeray Studentship, 1946–48, MA, PhD, ScD (Cantab); Frank Smart Prize, 1946. Cambridge Univ. Demonstrator, 1950–55, Lectr, 1955–65; successively Bye-Fellow, Research Fellow and Fellow of Magdalene Coll., Cambridge, 1949–65; University of Bristol: Head of Dept of Zoology, 1965–70; Head of Res. Unit for Comparative Animal Respiration, 1970–90. Research Fellow, California Inst. of Technology, 1958–59; Visiting Lectr in Physiology, State Univ. of New York, at Buffalo, 1964; Visiting Professor: Duke Univ., 1969; Japan Society for the Promotion of Science, Kochi, Kyoto, Kyushu and Hokkaido Univs, 1974; Univ. of Regensburg, 1977; Univs of Bhagalpur and Bretagne Occidentale, 1979; Kuwait, 1983; Nairobi, 1985. Invited Prof., Nat. Inst. of Physiolog. Sciences, Okazaki, 1980. Mem., Internat. Cœlacanth Expdn, 1972. *Publications:* Comparative

Physiology of Vertebrate Respiration, 1963; Physiology of Mammals and other Vertebrates (jt), 1965; (ed) several symposium vols; papers in Jl of Experimental Biology and other scientific jls, mainly on respiration of fishes. *Recreations:* travel, golf, photography; hockey for Cambridge Univ., 1945, and Wales, 1952–53. *Address:* 11 Lodge Drive, Long Ashton, Bristol BS18 9JF. *T:* Bristol (0275) 393402.

HUGHES, Glyn Tegai, MA, PhD; Warden of Gregynog, University of Wales, 1964–89; *b* 18 Jan. 1923; *s* of Rev. John Hughes and Keturah Hughes; *m* 1957, Margaret Vera Herbert, Brisbane, Qld; two *s. Educ:* Newtown and Towyn County Sch.; Liverpool Institute; Manchester Grammar Sch.; Corpus Christi Coll., Cambridge (Schol., MA, PhD). Served War, Royal Welch Fusiliers, 1942–46 (Major). Lector in English, Univ. of Basel, 1951–53; Lectr in Comparative Literary Studies, Univ. of Manchester, 1953–64, and Tutor to Faculty of Arts, 1961–64. Contested (L) Denbigh Div., elections 1950, 1955 and 1959. Mem., Welsh Arts Council, 1967–76; Nat. Governor for Wales, BBC, and Chm., Broadcasting Council for Wales, 1971–79; Member: Bd, Channel Four Television Co., 1980–87; Welsh Fourth TV Channel Auth., 1981–87. Chm., Welsh Broadcasting Trust, 1988–; Vice-Pres., N Wales Arts Assoc., 1977–; Chm., Undeb Cymru Fydd, 1968–70. *Publications:* Eichendorffs Taugenichts, 1961; Romantic German Literature, 1979; (ed) Life of Thomas Olivers, 1979; Williams Pantycelyn, 1983; articles in learned journals and Welsh language periodicals. *Recreation:* book-collecting. *Address:* Rhyd-y-gro, Tregynon, Newtown, Powys SY16 3PR. *T:* Tregynon (0686) 650609.

HUGHES, (Harold) Paul; Chairman, Pan European Property Unit Trust, since 1987; Director: Lazard Select Investment Trust Ltd, since 1988; Country Mansion Hotels Ltd, since 1987; Keystone Investment Co. PLC, since 1988; *b* 16 Oct. 1926; *o s* of Edmund and Mabel Hughes; *m* 1955, Beryl Winifred Runacres; one *s* one *d. Educ:* Stand Grammar Sch., Whitefield, near Manchester. Certified Accountant. Westminster Bank Ltd, 1942–45; Royal Marines and Royal Navy, 1945–49; Arthur Guinness Son & Co. Ltd, 1950–58; British Broadcasting Corporation: Sen. Accountant, 1958–61; Asst Chief Accountant, Finance, 1961–69; Chief Accountant, Television, 1969–71; Dir of Finance, 1971–84; Pension Fund Consultant, 1984–89; Chm., BBC Enterprises Ltd, 1979–82; Chm., Visnews Ltd, 1984–85; Chief Exec., BBC Pension Trust Ltd, 1987–89; Dir, Kleinwort Benson Farmland Trust (Managers) Ltd, 1976–89. *Recreations:* opera, gardening. *Address:* 26 Downside Road, Guildford, Surrey GU4 8PH. *T:* Guildford (0483) 69166.

HUGHES, (Harold) Victor, CBE 1989; FRAgS; Principal, Royal Agricultural College, Cirencester, 1978–90, Principal Emeritus 1990; *b* 2 Feb. 1926; *s* of Thomas Brindley Hughes and Hilda Hughes (*née* Williams). *Educ:* Tenby County Grammar Sch.; UCW, Aberystwyth (BSc). FRAgS 1980. Lectr, Glamorgan Training Centre, Pencoed, 1947–49; Crop Husbandry Adv. Officer, W Midland Province, Nat. Agricultural Adv. Service, 1950; Lectr in Agric., RAC, 1950–54; Vice Principal, Brooksby Agricultural Coll., Leics, 1954–60; Royal Agricultural College: Farms Dir and Principal Lectr in Farm Management, 1960–76; Vice Principal and Farms Dir, 1976–78. Hon. ARICS 1984. *Publications:* articles in learned jls and agric. press. *Recreation:* shooting. *Address:* No 17 Quakers Row, Coates, Cirencester, Glos.

HUGHES, Herbert Delauney, MA; Principal of Ruskin College, Oxford, 1950–79; *b* 7 Sept. 1914; *s* of late Arthur Percy Hughes, BSc, and late Maggie Ellen Hughes; *m* 1937, Beryl Parker. *Educ:* Cheadle Hulme Sch.; Balliol Coll., Oxford (State and County Major Scholar). BA (Hons) in Modern History, 1936. Served War of 1939–45, with 6 Field Regt Royal Artillery. Asst Sec., New Fabian Research Bureau, 1937–39; Organising Sec., Fabian Soc., 1939–46; Mem. Exec. Fabian Soc., 1946– (Vice-Chm. 1950–52, 1958–59, Chm. 1959–60, Vice-Pres., 1971–88, Pres., 1988–); MP (Lab) Wolverhampton (West), 1945–50; Parliamentary Private Sec. to Minister of Education, 1945–47; to Financial Sec. to War Office, 1948–50; Mem. Lambeth Borough Council, 1937–42. Governor of Educational Foundation for Visual Aids, 1948–56. Member: Civil Service Arbitration Tribunal, 1955–81; Commonwealth Scholarship Commn, 1968–74; Cttee on Adult Educn, 1969–73. Vice-Pres., Workers' Educational Assoc., 1958–67, Dep. Pres., 1968–71, Pres., 1971–81, Hon. Treasurer, 1981–; Chm. Management Cttee, Adult Literacy Resource Agency, 1975–78; Mem., Adv. Council on Adult and Continuing Educn, 1978–83; Vice-Pres., Nat. Inst. of Adult and Continuing Educn, 1986–90. Chm., Webb Meml Trust, 1987–. Hon. Fellow Sheffield Polytechnic, 1979. *Publications:* (part author) Democratic Sweden, 1937, Anderson's Prisoners, 1940, Six Studies in Czechoslovakia, 1947. Advance in Education, 1947; Towards a Classless Society, 1947; A Socialist Education Policy, 1955; The Settlement of Disputes in The Public Service, 1968; (jt author) Planning for Education in 1980, 1970; (part author) Education Beyond School, 1980. *Recreations:* drinking, reading, foreign travel. *Address:* Crossways, Mill Street, Islip, Oxford OX5 2SZ. *T:* Kidlington (08675) 6935.

HUGHES, Howard; Deputy Chairman, Price Waterhouse Europe, since 1991; *b* 4 March 1938; *s* of Charles William Hughes and Ethel May Hughes (*née* Howard); *m* 1st, 1964, Joy Margaret Pilmore-Bedford (*d* 1984); two *s* one *d*; 2nd, 1988, Christine Margaret Miles. *Educ:* Rydal School. FCA. Articled Bryce Hanmer & Co., Liverpool, 1955; joined Price Waterhouse, London, 1960: Partner, 1970; Mem., Policy Cttee, 1979; Dir, London Office, 1982; Managing Partner, 1985–91. Auditor, Duchy of Cornwall, 1983–. *Recreations:* golf, music. *Address:* Witham, Woodland Rise, Seal, near Sevenoaks, Kent. *T:* Sevenoaks (0732) 61161. *Clubs:* Carlton; Wildernesse Golf (Sevenoaks).

HUGHES, Prof. Ieuan Arwel, FRCP, FRCP(C); Professor and Head of Department of Paediatrics, University of Cambridge, since 1989; *b* 9 Nov. 1944; *s* of Arwel Hughes and Enid Phillips (*née* Thomas); *m* 1969, Margaret Maureen Davies; two *s* one *d. Educ:* Univ. of Wales Coll. of Medicine, Cardiff (MB, BCh, MD). FRCP(C) 1974; FRCP 1984 (MRCP); MRSocMed. Medical Registrar, UCH, 1970–72; Senior Paediatric Resident, Dalhousie Univ., Canada, 1972–74; Endocrine Research Fellow, Manitoba Univ., Canada, 1974–76; MRC Fellow, Tenovus Inst., Cardiff, 1976–78; Consultant Paediatrician, Bristol, 1978–79; Senior Lectr in Child Health, 1979–85, Reader in Child Health, 1985–89, Univ. of Wales Coll. of Medicine, Cardiff. Sec., European Soc. for Paediatric Endocrinology, 1987–92. *Publications:* Handbook of Endocrine Tests in Children, 1986; articles on paediatric endocrine disorders, steroid biochemistry and mechanism of steroid hormone action. *Recreations:* music, travel, walking, squash. *Address:* c/o Department of Paediatrics, Level 8, Addenbrooke's Hospital, Hills Road, Cambridge CB2 2QQ.

HUGHES, Sir Jack (William), Kt 1980; chartered surveyor; Director: South Bank Estates and subsidiary companies, since 1960; TR Property Investment Trust and subsidiary companies, since 1982; Undercliff Holdings Ltd, since 1986; *b* 26 Sept. 1916; 2nd *s* of George William Hughes and Isabel Hughes, Maidstone, Kent; *m* 1939, Marie-Theresa (Slade School scholar) (*d* 1987), *d* of Graham Parmley and Jessie Thompson. *Educ:* Maidstone Grammar Sch.; Univ. of London. BSc (Est. Man.); FRICS. Served with Special Duties Br., RAF, 1940–46; demobilised Squadron Leader. A Sen. Partner, Jones, Lang, Wootton, 1949–76, Consultant, 1976–86. Chairman: Bracknell Develt Corp., 1971–82; Property Adv. Gp, DoE, 1978–82; Director: URPT, 1961–86; MEPC, 1971–86; Housing Corporation (1974) Ltd, 1974–78; BR Property Bd, 1976–86; BR Investment Co., 1981–84; Property and Reversionary Investments, 1982–87; Brighton Marina Co. (Rep., Brighton Corp.), 1974–86; Mem. Cttee, Mercantile Credit Gp Property Div.; Mem. Cttee of Management, Charities Property Unit Trust, 1967–74; Chm., South Hill Park Arts Centre Trust, 1972–79; Member: Adv. Gp to DoE on Commercial Property Develt, 1974–78; DoE Working Party on Housing Tenure, 1976–77; Adv. Bd, Continuing Professional Develt Foundn, 1980–. Trustee, New Towns Pension Fund, 1975–82. Freeman, City of London, 1959–; Liveryman, Painter Stainers Guild, 1960–. FRSA. *Publications:* (jtly) Town and Country Planning Act 1949 (RICS); (Chm. of RICS Cttee) The Land Problem: a fresh approach; techn. articles on property investment, develt and finance. *Recreations:* golf, travel, reading. *Address:* Challoners, The Green, Rottingdean, Brighton, Sussex. *Clubs:* Carlton, Royal Air Force, Buck's.

HUGHES, James Ernest, PhD; FEng 1981; Director, 1973–85 and Managing Director and Chief Executive, 1983–84, Johnson Matthey PLC; *b* 3 Nov. 1927; *s* of Herbert Thomas Hughes and Bessie Beatrice Hughes; *m* 1950, Hazel Aveline (*née* Louguet-Layton); three *d. Educ:* Spring Grove Sch.; Imperial Coll., London Univ, (BSc, ARSM (Bessemer Medalist); DIC); PhD London 1952. FIM, MIMM. Associated Electrical Industries, 1952–63; Johnson Matthey PLC, 1963–85. Vis. Professor, Univ. of Sussex, 1974–80. President: Inst. of Metals, 1972–73; Metals Soc., 1981–82; Instn of Metallurgists, 1982–83. FRSA 1978. *Publications:* scientific papers in learned jls. *Recreations:* antiques, music, gardening. *Address:* Lower Farm, Rimpton, near Yeovil, Somerset BA22 8AB.

HUGHES, John; *see* Hughes, R. J.

HUGHES, Prof. John Pinnington-, PhD; Director, Parke-Davis Research Unit, Addenbrooke's, Cambridge, since 1983; Senior Research Fellow, Wolfson College, University of Cambridge, since 1983; Vice President, Drug Discovery, Warner-Lambert, Europe, since 1988; *b* 6 Jan. 1942; *s* of Joseph and Edith Hughes; *m* 1967, Madelaine Carol Jennings (marr. diss. 1981); one *d*; and three *s* one *d* by Julie Pinnington-Hughes. *Educ:* Mitcham County Grammar Sch. for Boys; Chelsea Coll., London (BSc); Inst. of Basic Med. Sciences, London (PhD). MA Cantab, 1988. Res. Fellow, Yale Univ. Med. Sch., 1967–69; University of Aberdeen: Lectr in Pharmacology, 1969–77; Dep.-Dir, Drug Res. Unit, 1973–77; Imperial College, London University: Reader in Pharmacol Biochemistry, 1977–79; Prof. of Pharmacol Biochemistry, 1979–82; Vis. Prof., 1983–. Hon. Prof. of Neuropharmacology, Univ. of Cambridge, 1989–. Member: Substance Abuse Cttee, Mental Health Foundn, 1986–; Scientific Cttee, Assoc. of British Pharmaceutical Industry, 1990–. Mem. Council, Internat. Sch. Neuroscience, 1988–. Editor: Brit. Jl Pharmacol., 1977–83; Brain Res., 1976–; Jt Chief Exec. Editor, Neuropeptides, 1980–. Gaddum Lectr and Medal, British Parmacol Soc., 1982. Mem., Royal Acad. of Medicine, Belgium, 1983. Dr *hc* Univ. of Liège, 1978. Lasker Prize, Albert and Mary Lasker Foundn, NY, 1978; W. Feldberg Foundn Award, 1981; Lucien Dautrebande Prize, Fondation de Pathophysiologie, Belgium, 1983. *Publications:* Centrally Acting Peptides, 1978; Opioids Past, Present and Future, 1984; (ed jtly) The Neuropeptide Cholecystokinin (CCK), 1989; articles in Nature, Science, Brit. Jl Pharmacol., and Brain Res. *Recreations:* dogs, gardening. *Address:* Parke-Davis Research Unit, Addenbrooke's Hospital, Hills Road, Cambridge CB2 2QB. *T:* Cambridge (0223) 210929.

HUGHES, John; MP (Lab) Coventry North East, since 1987; *b* 29 May 1925; *m*; two *s. Educ:* Durham. Served with Fleet Air Arm, 1943–45. Apprentice joiner; then miner and mechanic; worked for GEC, and Unipart (TGWU convener). Mem., Coventry City Council, 1974–82; Chm., Coventry NE Lab Party, 1978–81. *Address:* House of Commons, SW1A 0AA.

HUGHES, Very Rev. John Chester; Vicar of Bringhurst with Great Easton and Drayton, 1978–87; *b* 20 Feb. 1924; *m* 1950, Sybil Lewis McClelland; three *s* two *d* (and one *s* decd). *Educ:* Dulwich Coll.; St John's Coll., Durham. Curate of Westcliffe-on-Sea, Essex, 1950–53; Succentor of Chelmsford Cathedral, 1953–55; Vicar of St Barnabas, Leicester, 1955–61; Vicar of Croxton Kerrial with Branston-by-Belvoir, 1961–63; Provost of Leicester, 1963–78. ChStJ 1974. *Address:* 29 High Street, Hallaton, Market Harborough, Leics LE16 8UD. *T:* Hallaton (085889) 622.

HUGHES, John Dennis; Principal, Ruskin College, Oxford, 1979–89 (Tutor in Economics and Industrial Relations, 1957–70, and Vice Principal, 1970–79); *b* 28 Jan. 1927; *s* of John (Ben) Hughes and Gwendoline Hughes; *m* 1949, Violet (*née* Henderson); four *d. Educ:* Westminster City Sch.; Lincoln Coll., Oxford (MA). Lieut, RAEC, 1949–50. Extramural Tutor, Univs of Hull and Sheffield, 1950–57. Dir, Trade Union Res. Unit, 1970–; Dep. Chm., Price Commn, 1977–79. Member: Industrial Develt Adv. Bd, 1975–79; Nat. Consumer Council, 1982–. Governor, London Business School. Mem. Council, St George's House, 1978–83; Trustee, Nat. Union of Marine, Aviation and Shipping Transport Officers (formerly Merchant Navy and Airline Officers Assoc.), 1981–. *Publications:* Trade Union Structure and Government, 1968; (with R. Moore) A Special Case? Social Justice and the Miners, 1972; (with H. Pollins) Trade Unions in Great Britain, 1973; Industrial Restructuring: some manpower aspects, 1976; Britain in Crisis, 1981; Fabian Soc. pamphlets. *Recreation:* cycling. *Address:* Rookery Cottage, Stoke Place, Old Headington, Oxford. *T:* Oxford (0865) 63076.

HUGHES, Rt. Rev. John George; *see* Kensington, Area Bishop of.

HUGHES, John Richard Poulton; DL; County Clerk and Chief Executive, Staffordshire County Council, and Clerk to the Lieutenancy, 1978–83; *b* 21 Oct. 1920; *s* of Rev. John Evan Hughes and Mary Grace Hughes; *m* 1943, Mary Margaret, *e d* of Thomas Francis Thomas; one *s. Educ:* Bromsgrove Sch.; LLB Hons London; DPA; LMRTPI. Solicitor. Served War, RN and RNVR, 1940–46; discharged with rank of Lieut, RNVR. Articled in private practice, 1937–40; Asst Solicitor: West Bromwich County Borough Council, 1947–48; Surrey CC, 1948–50; Staffs County Council: Sen. Asst Solicitor, subseq. Chief Asst Solicitor, and Dep. Clerk, 1950–74; Dir of Admin, 1974–78; Sec., Staffs Probation and After Care Cttee, 1978–83. Sec., Staffs Historic Bldgs Trust, 1983–89; Trustee and Advr, Soc. for the Prevention of Solvent Abuse, 1984– (Vice-Pres., 1989). DL Staffs, 1979. *Recreations:* forestry, antiques restoration, sailing, fishing. *Address:* Brookside, Milford, near Stafford ST17 0UL. *T:* Stafford (0785) 661005; Tyn Siglen, Cynwyd, Clwyd.

See also Sir T. P. Hughes.

HUGHES, Rt. Rev. John Taylor, CBE 1975; an Assistant Bishop, Diocese of Southwark, since 1986; *b* 12 April 1908; *s* of Robert Edward and Annie Hughes. *Educ:* Castle Hill Sch., Ealing; Uxbridge County Sch.; Bede Coll., University of Durham (BA 1931, MA 1935). Ordained 1931; Asst Chaplain and Tutor, Bede Coll., Durham, 1931–34; Lecturer, Bede Coll., 1934–35; Curate, St John's, Shildon, Co. Durham, 1934–37; Vicar, St James, West Hartlepool, 1937–48; Canon Residentiary and Missioner of Southwark Cathedral and Warden of Diocesan Retreat House, Southwark, 1948–56; Bishop Suffragan of Croydon, 1956–77; Archdeacon of Croydon, 1967–77; Bishop to the Forces, 1966–75; an Asst Bishop, Diocese of Canterbury, 1977–86. *Recreations:* music, reading. *Address:* The Hospital of the Holy Trinity, North End, Croydon CR0 1UB. *T:* 081–686 8313.

HUGHES, Prof. Leslie Ernest, FRCS, FRACS; Professor of Surgery, University of Wales College of Medicine (formerly Welsh National School of Medicine), since 1971; *b* 12

Aug. 1932; *s* of Charles Joseph and Vera Hughes; *m* 1955, Marian Castle; two *s* two *d*. *Educ:* Parramatta High Sch.; Sydney Univ. MB, BS (Sydney); DS (Queensland), 1975; FRCS, 1959; FRACS, 1959. Reader in Surgery, Univ. of Queensland, 1965–71. Hunterian Prof., RCS, 1986. Eleanor Roosevelt Internat. Cancer Fellow, 1970. President: Welsh Surgical Soc., 1991–; Surgical Res. Soc., 1992–. Audio-visual Aid Merit Award, Assoc. of Surgeons of GB and Ireland, 1983, 1986. *Publications:* (jtly) Benign Disorders of the Breast, 1988; numerous papers in medical jls, chiefly on immune aspects of cancer, and diseases of the colon. *Recreation:* music. *Address:* Department of Surgery, University Hospital of Wales, Heath Park, Cardiff CF4 4XW. *T:* Cardiff (0222) 755944.

HUGHES, Louis Ralph; Chairman, Board of Managers, Adam Opel AG, Rüsselsheim, since 1989; *b* Cleveland, Ohio, 10 Feb. 1949. *Educ:* General Motors Inst., Flint (BMechEng); Harvard Univ. (MBA). General Motors of Canada: financial staff, 1973; Asst Treasurer, 1982; Vice-Pres., of Finance, 1985; Vice-Pres. of Finance, General Motors Europe, Zürich, 1987. *Recreations:* winter sports. *Address:* Adam Opel AG, Postfach 17 10, 6090 Rüsselsheim, Germany. *T:* 06142/6 61.

HUGHES, Mark; *see* Hughes, W. M.

HUGHES, Nigel Howard; Chief Executive, Defence Research Agency, 1991; *b* 11 Aug. 1937; *s* of late William Howard Hughes and of Florence Hughes (*née* Crawshaw); *m* 1962, Margaret Ann Fairmaner; three *d*. *Educ:* St Paul's Sch.; Queen's Coll., Oxford (MA). CEng, FIMechE. Pilot Officer, RAF, 1956–58. RAE, Bedford, 1961–73; Head of Radio and Navigation Div., 1973–77, Head of Flight Systems Dept, 1977–80, RAE, Farnborough; MoD Central Staffs, 1980–82; Asst Chief Scientific Advr (Projects), MoD, 1982–84; Dep. Chief Scientific Advr, MoD, 1985–86; Dir, RSRE, 1986–89. *Recreations:* Rolls-Royce enthusiast; model engineering, amateur radio, music. *Address:* c/o Defence Research Agency HQ, Ively Road, Pyestock, Farnborough GU14 0LS.

HUGHES, Paul; *see* Hughes, H. P.

HUGHES, Peter; *see* Hughes, D. E. P.

HUGHES, Philip Arthur Booley, CBE 1982; artist; Director: Logica plc, since 1990 (Chairman, 1972–90); Thames and Hudson Ltd, since 1991; *s* of Leslie Booley Hughes and Elizabeth Alice Hughes (*née* Whyte); *m* 1964, Psiche Maria Anna Claudia Bertini; two *d* and two step-*d*. *Educ:* Bedford Sch.; Clare Coll., Cambridge (BA). Engineer, Shell Internat. Petroleum Co., 1957–61; Computer Consultant, SCICON Ltd (formerly CEIR), 1961–69; Co-Founder, Logica, 1969; Man. Dir, Logica Ltd, 1969–72. Vis. Prof., UCL, 1981–90. Member: SERC, 1981–85; Nat. Electronics Council, 1981–88. Governor, Technical Change Centre, 1980–88. Mem. Council, RCA, 1988–. Trustee: Design Museum, 1990–; Inst. for Public Policy Res., 1988–. Exhibn of paintings with Beryl Bainbridge, Monks Gall., Sussex, 1972; exhibited: Contemp. British Painting, Madrid, 1983; Contemp. Painters, Ridgeway Exhibn Museum and Art Gall., Swindon, 1986; one-man exhibitions: Parkway Focus Gall., London, 1976; Angela Flowers Gall., London, 1977; Gal. Cance Manguin, Vaucluse, 1979, 1985; Francis Kyle Gall., London, 1979, 1982, 1984, 1987, 1989, 1991; retrospective, Inverness Mus. and Art Gall., 1990. Companion of Operational Research, 1985. Hon. Fellow, QMC, 1987. DUniv Stirling, 1985; Hon. DSc Kent, 1988. *Publications:* articles in nat. press and learned jls on management scis and computing.

HUGHES, Major Richard Charles, MBE 1951; TD 1945; Director, Federation of Commodity Associations, 1973–78; *b* 24 Dec. 1915; *s* of late Frank Pemberton Hughes and Minnie Hughes, Northwich. *Educ:* Wrekin Coll., Wellington, Telford. TA commn, 4/5th (E of C) Cheshire Regt, 1935; regular commn, 22nd (Cheshire) Regt, 1939. Served War of 1939–45: 2 i/c 5th, 2nd and 1st Bns 22nd (Cheshire) Regt. Palestine, 1945–47; S/Captain MS and DAAG Western Comd, 1948–51; Korea, 1954; GSO2 Sch. of Infantry, 1955–56; Sec. of Sch. of Inf. Beagles, 1955–56; retd pay, 1958. Apptd Sec. to Sugar Assoc. of London, British Sugar Refiners Assoc. and Refined Sugar Assoc., 1958; formed British Sugar Bureau and apptd Sec., 1964–66. Hon. Treas., W Kensington Environment Cttee, 1974–75; Mem. Barons Keep Management Cttee, 1975. Member: City Liaison Cttee, Bank of England and City EEC Cttee, 1975; City Adv. Panel to City Univ., and Adviser to City of London Polytechnic, 1975; City Communications Consultative Gp, 1976. *Recreations:* travel, sailing, antiques. *Address:* 8 Barons Keep, Barons Court, W14 9AT. *T:* 071–603 0429.

HUGHES, Robert; MP (Lab) Aberdeen North since 1970; *b* Pittenweem, Fife, 3 Jan. 1932; *m* 1957, Ina Margaret Miller; two *s* three *d*. *Educ:* Robert Gordon's Coll., Aberdeen; Benoni High Sch., Transvaal; Pietermaritzburg Techn. Coll., Natal. Emigrated S Africa, 1947, returned UK, 1954. Engrg apprentice, S African Rubber Co., Natal; Chief Draughtsman, C. F. Wilson & Co. (1932) Ltd, Aberdeen, until 1970. Mem., Aberdeen Town Council, 1962–70; Convener: Health and Welfare Cttee, 1963–68; Social Work Cttee, 1969–70. Mem., AEU, 1952–. Contested (Lab) North Angus and Mearns, 1959. Member: Standing Cttee on Immigration Bill, 1971; Select Cttee, Scottish Affairs, 1971; introd. Divorce (Scotland) Bill 1971 (failed owing to lack of time); Parly Under-Sec. of State, Scottish Office, 1974–75; sponsored (as Private Member's Bill) Rating (Disabled Persons) Act 1978; Principal Opposition Spokesman: on agriculture, 1983–84; on transport, 1985–88 (Jun. Opp. Spokesman, 1981–83); Mem., PLP Shadow Cabinet, 1985–88. Chm., Aberdeen City Labour Party, 1961–69. Vice-Chm., Tribune Gp, 1984–. Founder Mem. and Aberdeen Chm., Campaign for Nuclear Disarmament; Vice-Chm., 1975–76, Chm., 1976–, Anti-Apartheid Movement; Member: Gen. Med. Council, 1976–79; Movement for Colonial Freedom, 1955– (Chm. Southern Africa Cttee); Scottish Poverty Action Group; Aberdeen Trades Council and Exec. Cttee, 1957–69; Labour Party League of Youth, 1954–57. *Recreation:* golf. *Address:* House of Commons, SW1.

HUGHES, Robert Gurth; MP (C) Harrow West, since 1987; *b* 14 July 1951; *s* of Gurth Martin Hughes and Rosemary Dorothy Hughes (*née* Brown), JP; *m* 1986, Sandra Kathleen (*née* Vaughan); one *d*. *Educ:* Spring Grove Grammar Sch.; Harrow Coll. of Technology and Art. Trainee, then Film Producer, BAC Film Unit, 1968–73; Asst News Film Editor, subseq. News Film Editor and News Picture Editor, BBC Television News, 1973–87. Greater London Council: Mem., 1980–86; Opposition Dep. Chief Whip, 1982–86; Opposition spokesman on arts and recreation, 1984–86. National Chm., Young Conservatives, 1979–80. A Governor, BFI, 1990–. *Recreations:* watching cricket, listening to music. *Address:* 34 Hatfield Road, Bedford Park, Chiswick, W4 1AF. *T:* 081–995 0075. *Clubs:* St Stephen's Constitutional; Harrow Borough Football.

HUGHES, (Robert) John; journalist; Syndicated Columnist, The Christian Science Monitor, since 1985; President, Concord Communications Inc., since 1989; *b* Neath, S Wales, 28 April 1930; *s* of Evan John Hughes and Dellis May Hughes (*née* Williams); *m* 1st, 1955, Vera Elizabeth Pockman (marr diss. 1987); one *s* one *d*; 2nd, 1988, Peggy Janeane Chu; one *s*. *Educ:* Stationers' Company's Sch., London. Reporter, sub-editor, corresp. for miscellaneous London and S African newspapers and news agencies (Natal Mercury, Durban; Daily Mirror, Daily Express, Reuter, London News Agency), 1946–54; joined The Christian Science Monitor, Boston, USA, 1954: Africa Corresp., 1955–61; Asst Foreign Editor, 1962–64; Far East Corresp., 1964–70; Man. Editor, 1970; Editor, 1970–76; Editor and Manager, 1976–79; Pres. and Publisher, Hughes Newspapers Inc., USA, 1979–81, 1984–85; Associate Dir, US Information Agency, 1981–82; Dir, Voice of America, 1982; Asst Sec. of State for Public Affairs, USA, 1982–84. Nieman Fellow, Harvard Univ., 1961–62. Pres., Amer. Soc. of Newspaper Editors, 1978–79. Pulitzer Prize for Internat. Reporting, 1967; Overseas Press Club of America award for best daily newspaper or wire service reporting from abroad, 1970; Sigma Delta Chi's Yankee Quill Award, 1977. Hon. LLD Colby Coll., 1978. *Publications:* The New Face of Africa, 1961; Indonesian Upheaval (UK as The End of Sukarno), 1967; articles in magazines and encyclopaedias. *Recreations:* reading, walking, raising Labrador retrievers. *Address:* 106 Chestnut Street, Camden, Maine 04843, USA. *T:* 207–236–0840. *Clubs:* Foreign Correspondents', Hong Kong Country (Hong Kong); Overseas Press (New York); Harvard (Boston); Army and Navy (Washington).

HUGHES, Robert Studley Forrest; Senior Writer (Art Critic), Time Magazine, New York, since 1970; *b* Sydney, Aust., 28 July 1938; *s* of Geoffrey E. F. Hughes and Margaret Sealey Vidal; *m* (marr. diss. 1981); one *s*; *m* 1981, Victoria Whistler. *Educ:* St Ignatius' Coll., Riverview, Sydney; Sydney Univ. (architecture course, unfinished). Contributed articles on art to The Nation and The Observer, Sydney, 1958–62; to Europe, 1964, living in Italy until 1966, when moved to London; freelancing for Sunday Times, BBC and other publications/instns, 1966–70. TV credits include: Landscape with Figures, ten-part series on Australian art for ABC, Australia; Caravaggio, Rubens and Bernini, for BBC, 1976–77; The Shock of the New, eight-part series for BBC, 1980. Hon. Dr Fine Arts, Sch. of Visual Arts, NY, 1982. *Publications:* The Art of Australia, 1966; Heaven and Hell in Western Art, 1969; The Shock of the New (BBC publication), 1980; The Fatal Shore, 1987; Frank Auerbach, 1990; Nothing If Not Critical, 1991. *Recreations:* gardening, shooting, river and sea fishing, cooking. *Address:* 143 Prince Street, New York, NY 10012, USA.

HUGHES, Air Marshal Sir Rochford; *see* Hughes, Air Marshal Sir S. W. R.

HUGHES, Ronald Frederick, CEng, FICE; Director and Quality Systems Manager, Mott MacDonald Consultants, since 1987; *b* 21 Oct. 1927; *s* of Harry Frederick and Kate Hughes; *m* 1957, Cecilia Patricia, *d* of Maurice Nunis, MCS, State Treasurer, Malaya, and Scholastica Nunis; two *s* one *d*. *Educ:* Birmingham Central Technical College; Bradford College of Technology. Articled pupil, Cyril Boucher and Partners, 1943; Royal Engineers Engineering Cadet, 1946; commissioned RE, 1950; service in Malaya, 1950–53. Res. Asst, BISRA, 1954; Civil Engineer, H. W. Evans & Co. Ltd, Malaya, 1955, Man. Dir, 1958; War Office, 1959; Head of War Office Works Group, Singapore, 1963; Works Adviser to C-in-C, FARELF, 1964; District Civil Engineer, Malaya, 1966; Regional Site Control Officer, Midland Region, PSA, 1969; Principal Engineer, Post Office Services, 1970; Area Works Officer, PSA Birmingham, 1977; Asst Dir, 1979, Dir, 1983–87, Civil Engineering Services, PSA. Dir, Construction Industry Computing Assoc., 1982–86; Member: Standing Cttee for Structural Safety, 1985–88; Maritime Bd, ICE, 1985–90; Nat. Jt Consultative Cttee for Building, 1986–88; Member Council: Construction Industry Res. and Inf. Assoc., 1984–88; BSI, 1985; Perm. Internat. Assoc. of Navigation Congresses, 1983–; Parly Maritime Gp, 1988–; Vice Pres., Concrete Soc., 1989–. *Recreations:* squash, photography, music. *Address:* 9A The Street, West Horsley, Surrey. *T:* East Horsley (04865) 2182. *Clubs:* Naval; Effingham (Surrey).

HUGHES, Royston John; MP (Lab) Newport East, since 1983 (Newport, Gwent, 1966–83); *b* 9 June 1925; *s* of John Hughes, Coal Miner; *m* 1957, Florence Marion Appleyard; three *d*. *Educ:* Ruskin Coll., Oxford. Mem. Coventry City Council, 1962–66; various offices in Transport and General Workers' Union, 1959–66. PPS to Minister of Transport, 1974–75; Mem., Speaker's panel, 1982–84, 1991–; opposition frontbench spokesman on Welsh affairs, 1984–88. Chairman: PLP Sports Gp, 1974–83; PLP Steel Group, 1978–87; Parly Gp, TGWU, 1979–82. Chm., Welsh Grand Cttee, 1982–84, 1991–. Exec. Mem., IPU, 1987– (Treas., 1990–). Deleg., Council of Europe, 1991–. *Recreations:* gardening, watching rugby and soccer. *Address:* Chapel Field, Chapel Lane, Abergavenny, Gwent NP7 7BT. *T:* Abergavenny (0873) 6502. *Clubs:* United Services Mess (Cardiff); Pontllanfraith Workingmen's Social.

HUGHES, Prof. Sean Patrick Francis, MS; FRCS, FRCSEd, FRCSI, FRCSEd (Orth); George Harrison Law Professor of Orthopaedic Surgery, University of Edinburgh, since 1979; *b* 2 Dec. 1941; *s* of Patrick Joseph Hughes and Kathleen Ethel Hughes (*née* Bigg); *m* 1972, Felicity Mary (*née* Anderson); one *s* two *d*. *Educ:* Downside Sch.; St Mary's Hospital, Univ. of London (MB BS, MS). Senior Registrar in Orthopaedics, Middlesex and Royal National Orthopaedic Hosp., 1974–76; Research Fellow in Orthopaedics, Mayo Clinic, USA, 1975; Sen. Lectr, and Director Orthopaedic Unit, Royal Postgraduate Medical Sch., Hammersmith Hosp., 1977–79. Hon. Civilian Consultant, RN. Member Council: RCSE, 1984–; British Orthopaedic Assoc., 1989–. Fellow: Brit. Orthopaedic Assoc.; Royal Soc. Med.; Member: Orthopaedic Research Soc.; British Orth. Res. Soc.; Soc. Internat. de Chirurgie Orth. et de Traumatologie; World Orth. Concern. *Publications:* Astons Short Text Book of Orthopaedics, 2nd edn 1976 to 4th edn 1989; Basis and Practice of Orthopaedics, 1981; Basis and Practice of Traumatology, 1983; Musculoskeletal Infections, 1986; (ed jtly) Orthopaedics: the principles and practice of musculoskeletal surgery, 1987; (ed jtly) Orthopaedic Radiology, 1987; papers on blood flow and mineral exchange, bone scanning, antibiotics in bone, external fixation of fractures, surgery of the lumbar and cervical spine. *Recreations:* sailing, golf, lying in the sun. *Address:* 9 Corrennie Gardens, Edinburgh EH10 6DG. *T:* 031–447 1443.

HUGHES, Shirley, (Mrs J. S. P. Vulliamy); free-lance author/illustrator; *b* 16 July 1927; *d* of Thomas James Hughes and Kathleen Dowling; *m* 1952, John Sebastian Papendiek Vulliamy; two *s* one *d*. *Educ:* West Kirby High Sch. for Girls; Liverpool Art Sch.; Ruskin Sch. of Art, Oxford. Illustrator/author; overseas edns or distribn in France, Spain, W Germany, Denmark, Holland, Sweden, Aust., NZ, Japan, USA, China and Canada. Lectures to Teacher Trng Colls, Colls of Further Educn, confs on children's lit. and to children in schs and libraries; overseas lectures incl. tours to Aust. and USA. Member: Cttee of Management, Soc. of Authors, 1983–86; Public Lending Right Registrar's Adv. Cttee, 1984–88; Library and Information Services Council, 1989–. Children's Rights Other Award, 1976; Kate Greenaway Award, 1978; Silver Pencil Award, Holland, 1980; Eleanor Farjeon Award for services to children's lit., 1984. *Publications:* illustrated about 200 books for children of all ages; written and illustrated: Lucy and Tom's Day, 1960, 2nd edn 1979; The Trouble with Jack, 1970, 2nd edn 1981; Sally's Secret, 1973, 3rd edn 1976; Lucy and Tom go to School, 1973, 4th edn 1983; Helpers, 1975, 2nd edn 1978; Lucy and Tom at the Seaside, 1976, 3rd edn 1982; Dogger, 1977, 4th edn 1980; It's Too Frightening for Me, 1977, 4th edn 1982; Moving Molly, 1978, 3rd edn 1981; Up and Up, 1979, 3rd edn 1983; Here Comes Charlie Moon, 1980, 3rd edn 1984; Lucy and Tom's Christmas, 1981; Alfie Gets in First, 1981, 2nd edn 1982; Charlie Moon and the Big Bonanza Bust-up, 1982, 2nd edn 1983; Alfie's Feet, 1982, 2nd edn 1984; Alfie Gives a Hand, 1983; An Evening at Alfie's, 1984; Lucy and Tom's abc, 1984; A Nursery Collection, 6 vols, 1985–86; Chips and Jessie, 1985; Another Helping of Chips, 1986; Lucy and Tom's 123, 1987; Out and About, 1988; The Big Alfie and

Annie Rose Story Book, 1988; Angel Mae, 1989; The Big Concrete Lorry, 1989; The Snowlady, 1990; Wheels, 1991. *Recreations:* looking at paintings, dressmaking, writing books for children.

HUGHES, Air Marshal Sir (Sidney Weetman) Rochford, KCB 1967 (CB 1964); CBE 1955 (OBE 1942); AFC 1947; *b* 25 Oct. 1914; *s* of late Capt. H. R. Hughes, Master Mariner, and late Mrs Hughes (*née* Brigham), Auckland, NZ; *m* 1942, Elizabeth, *d* of A. Duncum, Colombo, Ceylon; one *d*. *Educ:* Waitaki Boys' High School; Oamaru, NZ. Editorial Staff, NZ Herald, 1933–37; RNZ Air Force, 1937–38; RAF, Far East and Middle East, 1939–44 (despatches; Greek DFC); Chief Ops, USAF All Weather Centre, 1948–49; Air Min. and CO Farnborough, 1950–54; Imperial Defence Coll., 1955; CO RAF Jever, Germany, 1956–59; Air Mem. and Chm., Defence Res. Policy Staff, MoD, 1959–61; Air Officer Commanding No 19 Group, 1962–64; Dep. Controller Aircraft (RAF), Ministry of Aviation, 1964–66; Air Comdr, Far East Air Force, 1966–69, retd 1969. Air Adviser, Civil and Military, to Govt of Singapore, 1969–72; Commissioner, Northland Harbour Bd, 1974. Chm., Mazda Motors NZ, 1972–87; Director: NZ Steel, 1973–84; General Accident, 1975–84; Reserve Bank NZ, 1974–77; Whangarei Engrg Co., 1975–83; Lees Industries, 1976–84; First City Finance Corp., 1981–87. Patron, NZ Nat. Children's Health Res. Foundn. Livery, Guild of Air Pilots and Air Navigators; FRAeS. *Recreations:* yachting, motoring, fishing. *Address:* 24 Scenic Heights, Acacia Bay, Taupo, New Zealand. *Club:* Royal NZ Yacht Squadron.

HUGHES, Simon Henry Ward; MP Southwark and Bermondsey, since Feb. 1983 (L 1983–88, Lib Dem since 1988); barrister; *b* 17 May 1951; *s* of James Henry Annesley Hughes and Sylvia (Paddy) Hughes (*née* Ward). *Educ:* Llandaff Cathedral Sch., Cardiff; Christ Coll., Brecon; Selwyn Coll., Cambridge (BA 1973, MA 1978); Inns of Court Sch. of Law; Coll. of Europe, Bruges (Cert. in Higher European Studies, 1975). Trainee, EEC, Brussels, 1976; Trainee and Mem. Secretariat, Directorate and Commn on Human Rights, Council of Europe, Strasbourg, 1976–77. Called to the Bar, Inner Temple, 1974; in practice, 1978–. Vice-Pres., Southwark Chamber of Commerce, 1987– (Pres., 1984–87). Spokesman: (L), on the environment, 1983–Jan. 1987 and June 1987–March 1988; (Alliance), on health, 1987; (Lib Dem), on envmt, and on education and science, 1988–. Jun. Counsel, Lib. Party application to European Commn on Human Rights, 1978–79; Chm., Lib. Party Adv. Panel on Home Affairs, 1981–83; Vice-Chm., Bermondsey Lib. Assoc., 1981–83. Jt Pres., British Youth Council, 1983–84. President: Young Liberals, 1986–88 (Vice-Pres., 1983–86, Mem. 1973–78); Democrats Against Apartheid, 1988–; Vice-President: Union of Liberal Students, 1983–88 (Mem., 1970–73); Southwark Chamber of Commerce, 1987– (Pres., 1984–87); Student Democrats, 1988–; Vice-Chm., Parly Youth Affairs Lobby, 1984–. Member: the Christian Church; Gen. Synod of Church of England, 1984–85; Southwark Area Youth Cttee; Council of Management, Cambridge Univ. Mission, Bermondsey; Anti-Apartheid Movement. Member to Watch Award, 1985. *Publications:* pamphlets on human rights in Western Europe, the prosecutorial process in England and Wales, Liberal values for defence and disarmament. *Recreations:* music, discotheques and good parties, history, sport, theatre, the countryside and open air, travel, spending time with family and friends. *Address:* House of Commons, SW1A 0AA. *T:* 071–219 6256; 6 Lynton Road, Bermondsey, SE1 5QR.

HUGHES, Stephen Skipsey; Member (Lab) Durham, European Parliament, since 1984; *b* 19 Aug. 1952; marr. diss.; one *s* twin *d*. *Educ:* St Bede's School, Lanchester; Newcastle Polytechnic. Mem., GMBATU; local govt officer. *Address:* 2A The Leas, Darlington, Co. Durham DL1 3DD.

HUGHES, Ted, OBE 1977; author; Poet Laureate, since 1984; *b* 1930; *s* of William Henry Hughes and Edith Farrar Hughes; *m* 1956, Sylvia Plath (*d* 1963); one *s* one *d*; *m* 1970, Carol Orchard. *Educ:* Pembroke Coll., Cambridge Univ. (Hon. Fellow, 1986). Author of Orghast (performed at 5th Festival of Arts of Shiraz, Persepolis, 1971). Awards: first prize, Guinness Poetry Awards, 1958; John Simon Guggenheim Fellow, 1959–60; Somerset Maugham Award, 1960; Premio Internazionale Taormina, 1973; The Queen's Medal for Poetry, 1974. *Publications:* The Hawk in the Rain, 1957 (First Publication Award, NY, 1957); Lupercal, 1960 (Hawthornden Prize, 1961); Meet My Folks! (children's verse), 1961; The Earth-Owl and Other Moon People (children's verse), 1963 (reissued as Moon Whales, 1988); How the Whale Became (children's stories), 1963; (ed, jtly) Five American Poets, 1963; Selected Poems of Keith Douglas (ed, with Introduction), 1964; Nessie, The Mannerless Monster (children's verse story), 1964 (US as Nessie the Monster, 1974); Recklings, 1966; The Burning of the Brothel, 1966; Scapegoats and Rabies, 1967; Animal Poems, 1967; Wodwo, 1967 (City of Florence Internat. Poetry Prize, 1969); Poetry in the Making, 1967 (US as Poetry Is, 1970); The Iron Man (children's story) (US as The Iron Giant, 1968); (ed) A Choice of Emily Dickinson's Verse, 1968; Five Autumn Songs for Children's Voices, 1968; Adaptation of Seneca's Oedipus, 1969 (play, National Theatre, 1968); (libretto) The Demon of Adachigahara, 1969; The Coming of the Kings (4 plays for children), 1970 (US as The Tiger's Bones, 1974); Crow, 1970; A Few Crows, 1970; Crow Wakes, 1970; (ed) A Choice of Shakespeare's Verse, 1971 (US as With Fairest Flowers while Summer Lasts); Shakespeare's Poem, 1971; (with R. Fainlight and Alan Sillitoe) Poems, 1971; Eat Crow, 1971; Prometheus on His Crag, 1973; Spring Summer Autumn Winter, 1974; (libretto) The Story of Vasco, 1974; Cave Birds (limited edn with illustrations by Leonard Baskin), 1975; Season Songs, 1976; Earth-Moon, 1976; (introd. and trans. jtly) János Pilinsky, Selected Poems, 1976; Gaudete, 1977; (ed and introd.) Johnny Panic and the Bible of Dreams, by Sylvia Plath, 1977; Orts, 1978; Moortown Elegies, 1978; Cave Birds, 1978; Moon-Bells and other poems (verse for children), 1978 (Signal Award); (introd. and trans. jtly) Yehuda Amichai's Amen, 1978; Adam and the Sacred Nine, 1979; Remains of Elmet, 1979; Moortown, 1979 (Heinemann Bequest, RSL, 1980); 12 poems in Michael Morpurgo's All Around the Year, 1979; Henry Williamson—A Tribute, 1979; (ed) Sylvia Plath: Collected Poems, 1981; Under the North Star (poems for children), 1981 (Signal Award); Selected Poems 1957–1981, 1982; (ed with Seamus Heaney) The Rattle Bag, 1982; River, 1983; What is the Truth (for children), 1984 (Guardian Children's Fiction Award, 1985); Ffangs the Vampire Bat and the Kiss of Truth (for children), 1986; Flowers and Insects, 1987; Tales of the Early World (for children), 1988; Wolfwatching, 1989; Moortown Diary, 1989. *Address:* c/o Faber and Faber Ltd, 3 Queen Square, WC1.

HUGHES, Thomas Lowe; President and Trustee, Carnegie Endowment for International Peace, Washington, since 1971; *b* 11 Dec. 1925; *s* of Evan Raymond Hughes and Alice (*née* Lowe); *m* 1955, Jean Hurlburt Reiman; two *s*. *Educ:* Carleton Coll., Minn (BA); Balliol Coll., Oxford (Rhodes Schol., BPhil); Yale Law Sch. (LLB, JD). USAF, 1952–54 (Major). Member of Bar: Supreme Court of Minnesota; US District Court of DC; Supreme Court of US. Professional Staff Mem., US Senate Sub-cttee on Labour-Management Relations, 1951; part-time Prof. of Polit. Sci. and Internat. Relations, Univ. of Southern California, Los Angeles, 1953–54, and George Washington Univ., DC, 1957–58; Exec. Sec. to Governor of Connecticut, 1954–55; Legislative Counsel to Senator Hubert H. Humphrey, 1955–58; Admin. Asst to US Rep. Chester Bowles, 1959–60; Staff Dir of Platform Cttee, Democratic Nat. Convention, 1960; Special Asst to Under-Sec. of State, Dept of State, 1961; Dep. Dir of Intelligence and Research, Dept of State, 1961–63;

Dir of Intell. and Res. (Asst Sec. of State), 1963–69; Minister and Dep. Chief of Mission, Amer. Embassy, London, 1969–70; Mem., Planning and Coordination Staff, Dept of State, 1970–71. Chm., Nuclear Proliferation and Safeguards Adv. Panel, Office of Technology Assessment, US Congress; Chm., Bd of Editors, Foreign Policy Magazine; Sec., Bd of Dirs, German Marshall Fund of US; Dir, Arms Control Assoc. Chairman: Oxford-Cambridge Assoc. of Washington; US-UK Bicentennial Fellowships Cttee on the Arts. Member Bds of Visitors: Harvard Univ. (Center for Internat. Studies); Princeton Univ. (Woodrow Wilson Sch. of Public and Internat. Affairs); Georgetown Univ. (Sch. of Foreign Service); Bryn Mawr Coll. (Internat. Adv. Bd.); Univ. of Denver (Soc. Sci. Foundn). Member Bds of Advisers: Center for Internat. Journalism, Univ. of S Calif; Coll. of Public and Internat. Affairs, Amer. Univ., Washington, DC; Washington Strategy Seminar; Cosmos Club Jl. Member Bds of Trustees: Civilian Military Inst.; Amer. Acad. of Political and Social Sci.; Amer. Cttee, IISS; Hubert H. Humphrey Inst. of Public Affairs; Amer. Inst. of Contemp. German Studies, Washington, DC; Arthur F. Burns Fellowship Program. Mem. Adv. Bd, Fundacion Luis Munoz Marin, Puerto Rico. Member: Internat. Inst. of Strategic Studies; Amer. Assoc. of Rhodes Scholars; Amer. Political Sci. Assoc.; Amer. Bar Assoc.; Amer. Assoc. of Internat. Law; Amer. For. Service Assoc.; Amer. Acad. of Diplomacy; Internat. Studies Assoc.; Washington Inst. of Foreign Affairs; Trilateral Commn; Assoc. for Restoration of Old San Juan, Puerto Rico. Arthur S. Flemming Award, 1965. Hon. LLD Washington Coll., 1973; Denison Univ., 1979; Florida Internat. Univ., 1986; Hon. HLD: Carleton Coll., 1974; Washington and Jefferson Coll., 1979. KStJ 1984. *Publications:* occasional contribs to professional jls, etc. *Recreations:* swimming, tennis, music, 18th century engravings. *Address:* 5636 Western Avenue, Chevy Chase, Md 20815, USA. *T:* (301)6561420; 2400 N Street NW, Washington, DC 20037, USA. *T:* (office) (202) 862–7911. *Clubs:* Yale, Century Association, Council on Foreign Relations (New York); Cosmos (Washington).

HUGHES, Sir Trevor Denby L.; see Lloyd-Hughes.

HUGHES, Sir Trevor (Poulton), KCB 1982 (CB 1974); CEng, FICE; Permanent Secretary, Welsh Office, 1980–85; Chairman, B&CE Holiday Management Co., since 1987; *b* 28 Sept. 1925; *y s* of late Rev. John Evan and Mary Grace Hughes; *m* 1st, 1950, Mary Ruth Walwyn (marr. diss.); two *s*; 2nd, 1978, Barbara June Davison. *Educ:* Ruthin Sch. RE, 1945–48, Captain 13 Fd Svy Co. Municipal engineering, 1948–61; Min. of Transport, 1961–62; Min. of Housing and Local Govt: Engineering Inspectorate, 1962–70; Dep. Chief Engineer, 1970–71; Dir, 1971–72 and Dir-Gen., 1972–74, Water Engineering, DoE; Dep. Sec., DoE, 1974–77; Dep. Sec., Dept of Transport, 1977–80. Mem., British Waterways Bd, 1985–88. Vice-Chm., Public Works Congress Council, 1975–89, Chm., 1989–. Chief British Deleg., Perm. Internat. Assoc. of Navigation Congresses, 1985–. A Vice-Pres., ICE, 1984–86. Hon. Fellow, Polytechnic of Wales, 1986. Hon. FIWEM. *Recreations:* music, gardening, golf. *Address:* Clearwell, 13 Brambleton Avenue, Farnham, Surrey GU9 8RA. *T:* Farnham (0252) 714246.
    See also J. R. P. Hughes.

HUGHES, Victor; see Hughes, H. V.

HUGHES, William, CB 1953; Chairman, Tooting Youth Project, 1981–87; *b* 21 Aug. 1910; *o s* of late William Hughes, Bishop's Stortford, Herts, and of Daisy Constance, *y d* of Charles Henry Davis; *m* 1941, Ilse Erna, *o d* of late E. F. Plohs; one *s* one *d*. *Educ:* Bishop's Stortford Coll.; Magdalen Coll., Oxford (demy). Board of Trade, 1933; Asst Sec., 1942; Under-Sec., 1948–63 (Sec., Monopolies and Restrictive Practices Commission, 1952–55); Second Sec., 1963–71. Consultant to British Overseas Trade Bd, 1972–73; Under-Sec., Prices Commn, 1973–75; Dep. Sec., DTI, 1970–71. *Recreation:* music. *Address:* 250 Trinity Road, SW18. *T:* 081–870 3652; Page's, Widdington, Essex. *Clubs:* Reform; Leander.

HUGHES, Maj.-Gen. (Retd) William Dillon, CB 1960; CBE 1953; MD; FRCPI; DTM&H; Commandant, Royal Army Medical College, 1957–60; *b* 23 Dec. 1900; *s* of R. Hughes, JP; *m* 1929, Kathleen Linda Thomas; one *s*. *Educ:* Campbell Coll., Belfast; Queen's Univ., Belfast. MB, BCh, BAO, 1923; Lieut, RAMC, 1928; Officer i/c Medical Div. 64 and 42 Gen. Hosps, MEF, 1940–42; Officer i/c Medical Div. 105 Gen. Hosp., BAOR, 1944–46; Sen. MO, Belsen, 1945; consulting Physician, Far East Land Forces, 1950–53; ADMS, Aldershot Dist, 1954. Prof. in Tropical Medicine and Consulting Physician, RAM Coll., 1955–56; Vice-Pres., Royal Society of Tropical Medicine and Hygiene, 1959–60; Col Comdt RAMC, 1961–65. QHP 1957; Mitchiner Medal, RCS, 1960. *Address:* Vine House, Summer Court, Tilford Road, Farnham GU9 8DS.

HUGHES, (William) Mark, MA, PhD; *b* 18 Dec. 1932; *s* of late Edward Hughes, sometime Prof. of History at Durham, and Sarah (*née* Hughes), Shincliffe, Durham; *m* 1958, Jennifer Mary, *d* of Dr G. H. Boobyer; one *s* two *d*. *Educ:* Durham Sch.; Balliol Coll., Oxford (MA). BA Oxon 1956; PhD Newcastle 1963. Sir James Knott Research Fellow, Newcastle-upon-Tyne, 1958–60; Staff Tutor, Manchester Univ. Extra-Mural Dept, 1960–64; Lectr, Durham Univ., 1964–70. MP (Lab): Durham, 1970–83; City of Durham, 1983–87. PPS to Chief Sec. of Treasury, 1974–75; opposition spokesman on agriculture, 1980–86; Member: Select Cttee on Expenditure (Trade and Industry Sub-Cttee), 1970–74; Select Cttee on Parly Comr, 1970–75; Delegn to Consultative Assembly of Council of Europe and WEU, 1974–75; European Parlt, 1975–79 (Vice-Chm., Agric. Cttee and Chm., Fisheries Sub-Cttee, 1977–79); Exec. Cttee, British Council, 1974–85 (Vice-Chm., 1978–85); Gen. Adv. Council, BBC, 1976–84; Adv. Council on Public Records, 1984–87. An Hon. Associate, BVA, 1976–87. Fellow, Industry and Parliament Trust. *Recreations:* gardening, fishing, birdwatching.

HUGHES, William Young, CBE 1987; Chief Executive, since 1976, and Chairman, since 1985, Grampian Holdings plc; Deputy Chairman, Scottish Conservative Party, since 1989; *b* 12 April 1940; *s* of Hugh Prentice Hughes and Mary Henderson Hughes; *m* 1964, Anne Macdonald Richardson; two *s* one *d*. *Educ:* Firth Park Grammar Sch., Sheffield; Univ. of Glasgow (BSc Hons Pharmacy, 1963). MPS 1964. Research, MRC project, Dept of Pharmacy, Univ. of Strathclyde, 1963–64; Lectr, Dept of Pharmacy, Heriot-Watt Univ., 1964–66; Partner, R. Gordon Drummond (group of retail chemists), 1966–70; Man. Dir, MSJ Securities Ltd (subsid. of Guinness Gp), 1970–76; Grampian Holdings, Glasgow, 1977– (holding co. in transport, tourism, retail, sporting goods and veterinary medicines). Chm., CBI Scotland, 1987–89; Mem. Governing Council, Scottish Business in the Community, 1986–. Chm., European Summer Special Olympic Games (1990), Strathclyde, 1988–91. *Recreation:* golf. *Address:* The Elms, 12 Camelon Road, Falkirk FK1 5RX. *T:* 041–357 2000. *Club:* Glenbervie Golf.

HUGHES JONES, Dr Nevin Campbell, FRS 1985; on scientific staff, Medical Research Council, since 1954; Fellow of Hughes Hall, Cambridge, since 1987; *b* 10 Feb. 1923; *s* of William and Millicent Hughes Jones; *m* 1952, Elizabeth Helen Dufty; two *s* one *d*. *Educ:* Berkhampsted Sch., Herts; Oriel Coll., Univ. of Oxford; St Mary's Hosp. Med. School. MA, DM, PhD; FRCP. Medical posts held at St Mary's Hosp., Paddington, Radcliffe Infirmary, Oxford, and Postgrad. Med. Sch., Hammersmith, 1947–52; Member: MRC's Blood Transfusion Unit, Hammersmith, 1952–79 (Unit transferred to St Mary's Hosp. Med. Sch., Paddington, as MRC's Experimental Haematology Unit, 1960); MRC's

Mechanisms in Immunopathology (formerly in Tumour Immunity) Unit, Cambridge, 1979–. *Publication:* Lecture Notes on Haematology, 1970, 4th edn 1984. *Recreations:* making chairs, walking the Horseshoe Path on Snowdon. *Address:* 65 Orchard Road, Melbourn, Royston, Herts SG8 6BB. *T:* Royston (0763) 260471.

HUGHES-MORGAN, Maj.-Gen. Sir David (John), 3rd Bt *cr* 1925; CB 1983; CBE 1973 (MBE 1959); **His Honour Judge Hughes-Morgan;** a Circuit Judge, since 1986; *b* 11 Oct. 1925; *s* of Sir John Hughes-Morgan, 2nd Bt and Lucie Margaret (*d* 1987), *d* of late Thomas Parry Jones-Parry; *S* father, 1969; *m* 1959, Isabel Jean, *d* of J. M. Lindsay; three *s*. *Educ:* RNC, Dartmouth. Royal Navy, 1943–46. Admitted solicitor, 1950. Commissioned, Army Legal Services, 1955; Brig., Legal Staff, HQ UKLF, 1976–78; Dir, Army Legal Services, BAOR, 1978–80, MoD, 1980–84; a Recorder, 1983–86. *Heir: s* Ian Parry David Hughes-Morgan, *b* 22 Feb. 1960. *Address:* c/o National Westminster Bank, 1 High Street, Bromley BR1 1LL.

HUGHES-YOUNG, family name of **Baron St Helens.**

HUGHESDON, Charles Frederick, AFC 1944; FRAeS; *b* 10 Dec. 1909; *m* 1937, Florence Elizabeth, *widow* of Captain Tom Campbell Black (actress, as Florence Desmond); one *s*. *Educ:* Raine's Foundation School. Entered insurance industry, 1927; learned to fly, 1932; Flying Instructor's Licence, 1934; commnd RAFO, 1934; Commercial Pilot's Licence, 1936. Joined Stewart, Smith & Co. Ltd, 1936; RAF Instructor at outbreak of war; seconded to General Aircraft as Chief Test Pilot, 1939–43; rejoined RAF, 1943–45 (AFC). Rejoined Stewart, Smith & Co. Ltd, 1946; retired as Chm. of Stewart Wrightson 1976. Director: Aeronautical Trusts Ltd; Headington Brokers Ltd; Chairman: Tradewinds Helicopters Ltd; The Charles Street Co. Hon. Treas., RAeS, 1969–85. Order of the Cedar, Lebanon, 1972. *Recreations:* flying (helicopter), shooting, horseracing, riding (dressage), yachting, water ski-ing, farming. *Address:* Dunsborough Park, Ripley, Surrey GU23 6AL. *T:* Guildford (0483) 225366; Flat 12, 5 Grosvenor Square, W1. *T:* 071–493 1494. *Clubs:* Royal Air Force, Royal Thames Yacht, Lloyd's Yacht.

HUGHFF, Victor William, FIA, CBIM; Chief General Manager, Norwich Union Life Insurance Society, 1984–89; *b* 30 May 1931; *s* of William Scott Hughff and Alice Doris (*née* Kerry); *m* 1955, Grace Margaret (*née* Lambert) one *s* one *d*. *Educ:* City of Norwich School. Joined Norwich Union Life Insce Soc., 1949; Assistant Actuary, 1966; General Manager and Actuary, 1975; Main Board Director, 1981. Director: Stalwart Assurance Group, 1989–; Congregational & General Insurance, 1989–. Served in RAF, 1951–53; commnd in Secretarial Br., National Service List. Elder of United Reformed Church. *Recreations:* tennis, badminton. *Address:* 18 Hilly Plantation, Thorpe St Andrew, Norwich NR7 0JN. *T:* Norwich (0603) 34517.

HUGILL, John; QC 1976; a Recorder of the Crown Court, since 1972; *b* 11 Aug. 1930; *s* of late John A. and Alice Hugill; *m* 1956, Patricia Elizabeth Hugill (*née* Welton); two *d*. *Educ:* Sydney C of E Grammar Sch., NSW; Fettes Coll.; Trinity Hall, Cambridge (MA). 2nd Lieut RA, 1948–49. Called to the Bar, Middle Temple, 1954 (Bencher, 1984); Northern Circuit, 1954; Assistant Recorder, Bolton, 1971. Chairman: Darryn Clarke Inquiry, 1979; Stanley Royd Inquiry, 1985. Member: Senate of the Inns of Court and the Bar, 1984–86; Gen. Council of the Bar, 1987–89. *Recreation:* yachting. *Address:* 2 Old Bank Street, Manchester M2 7PF.

HUGILL, Michael James; Assistant Master, Westminster School, 1972–86; *b* 13 July 1918; 2nd *s* of late Rear-Adm. R. C. Hugill, CB, MVO, OBE. *Educ:* Oundle; King's Coll., Cambridge, Exhibitioner, King's Coll., 1936–39; MA 1943. War Service in the RN; Mediterranean, Home and Pacific Fleets, 1939–46; rank on demobilisation, Lieut-Comdr. Mathematics Master, Stratford Grammar Sch., 1947–51; Senior Mathematics Master, Bedford Modern Sch., 1951–57; Headmaster, Preston Grammar Sch., 1957–61; Headmaster, Whitgift School, Croydon, 1961–70; Lectr, Inst. of Education, Keele Univ., 1971–72. *Publication:* Advanced Statistics, 1985. *Address:* 4 Glenmore, Kersfield Road, SW15 3HL. *Club:* Army and Navy.

HUGO, Lt-Col Sir John (Mandeville), KCVO 1969 (CVO 1959); OBE 1947; Gentleman Usher to the Queen, 1952–69, an Extra Gentleman Usher since 1969; *b* 1 July 1899; *s* of R. M. Hugo; *m* 1952, Joan Winifred, *d* of late D. W. Hill; two *d*. *Educ:* Marlborough Coll.; RMA, Woolwich, Commissioned RA, 1917; transf. to Indian Cavalry, 1925; Military Sec. to Governor of Bengal, 1938–40; rejoined 7th Light Cavalry, 1940; Military Sec. to Governor of Bengal 1946–47; Asst Ceremonial Sec., Commonwealth Relations Office, 1948–52; Ceremonial and Protocol Secretary, 1952–69. *Address:* Hilltop House, Vines Cross, Heathfield, East Sussex TN21 9EN. *T:* Horam Road (04353) 2562. *Club:* Army and Navy.

HUIJSMAN, Nicolaas Basil Jacques, CMG 1973; *b* 6 March 1915; *s* of Nikolaas Kornelis Huijsman, Amsterdam and Hendrika Huijsman (*née* Vorkink). *Educ:* Selborne Coll., E London, S Africa; Univ. of Witwatersrand (BCom); Gonville and Caius Coll., Cambridge (Econ. Tripos). Commnd Royal Scots Fusiliers, 1940; HQ 17 Inf. Bde, 1940; GS03, WO, 1941–42; psc 1942; GSO2, HQ of Chief of Staff to Supreme Cmdr (Des) and SHAEF, 1943–45 (despatches 1944); Controller of Press and Publications, Control Commn for Germany, 1945–48; Colonial Office, 1948–62; Principal Private Sec. to Sec. of State for Commonwealth Relations and Colonies, 1962–64; Asst Sec., Min. of Overseas Develt, 1964–70, and 1974–75, Overseas Develt Admin/FCO, 1970–74. Bronze Star, US, 1945. *Recreations:* Byzantine history, music, opera, painting. *Address:* 13 Regent Square, Penzance TR18 4BG. *Club:* Reform.

HUISMANS, Sipko; Chief Executive, Courtaulds PLC, since 1991 (Director, since 1984; Managing Director, 1990–91); *b* 28 Dec. 1940; *s* of Jouka and Roelofina Huismans; *m* 1969, Janet; two *s* one *d*. *Educ:* primary sch., Holland; secondary sch., Standerton, S Africa; Stellenbosch Univ., S Africa (BA Com). Shift chemist, Usutu Pulp Co. Ltd, 1961–68; Gen. Man., Springwood Cellulose Co., 1968–74; Man. Dir, Courtaulds Central Trading, 1974–80; Dir, 1980–, Man. Dir, 1982–84, Courtaulds Fibres; Chairman: Internat. Paints Ltd, 1987–90; Courtaulds Chemical and Industrial Exec., 1988–. Kentucky Col, USA, 1989. *Recreations:* motor racing, sailing, competition. *Address:* Beechwood Ridge, Langley Road, Claverdon, Warwicks CV35 8PJ. *T:* Claverdon (092684) 3461. *Club:* Chichester Sailing.

HULL, Bishop Suffragan of, since 1981; **Rt. Rev. Donald George Snelgrove,** TD 1972; *b* 21 April 1925; *s* of William Henry Snelgrove and Beatrice Snelgrove (*née* Upshell); *m* 1949, Sylvia May Lowe; one *s* one *d*. *Educ:* Queens' Coll. and Ridley Hall, Cambridge (MA). Served War, commn (Exec. Br.) RNVR, 1943–46. Cambridge, 1946–50; ordained, 1950; Curate: St Thomas, Oakwood, 1950–53; St Anselm's, Hatch End, Dio. London, 1953–56; Vicar of: Dronfield with Unstone, Dio. Derby, 1956–62; Hessle, Dio. York, 1963–70; Archdeacon of the East Riding, 1970–81. Rural Dean of Hull, 1966–70; Canon of York, 1969–81. Chaplain T&AVR, 1960–73. *Recreation:* travel. *Address:* Hullen House, Woodfield Lane, Hessle, N Humberside HU13 0ES. *T:* Hull (0482) 649019.

HULL, Prof. Derek, FRS 1989; FEng 1986; FIM, FPRI; Goldsmiths' Professor of Metallurgy, University of Cambridge, since 1984; Fellow, Magdalene College, Cambridge, since 1984; *b* 8 Aug. 1931; *s* of late William and Nellie Hull (*née* Hayes); *m* 1953, Pauline Scott; one *s* four *d*. *Educ:* Baines Grammar School, Poulton-le-Fylde; Univ. of Wales. PhD, DSc. AERE, Harwell and Clarendon Lab., Oxford, 1956–60; University of Liverpool: Senior Lectr, 1960–64; Henry Bell Wortley Prof. of Materials Engineering, 1964–84; Dean of Engineering, 1971–74; Pro-Vice Chancellor, 1983–84. Dist. Vis. Prof. and Senior Vis. NSF Fellow, Univ. of Delaware, 1968–69; Monash Vis. Prof., Univ. of Monash, 1981; Hon. Fellow, University Coll. Cardiff, 1985. Andrew Laing Lecture, NEC Inst, 1989. Hon. DTech Tampere Univ. of Technology, Finland, 1987. Rosenhain Medal, 1973, A. A. Griffith Silver Medal, 1985, Inst. of Metals; Medal of Excellence in Composite Materials, Univ. of Delaware, 1990. *Publications:* Introduction to Dislocations, 1966, 3rd edn 1984; An Introduction to Composite Materials, 1981; numerous contribs to Proc. Roy. Soc., Acta Met., Phil. Mag., Jl Mat. Sci., MetalScience, Composites. *Recreations:* golf, music, fell-walking. *Address:* Department of Materials Science and Metallurgy, Pembroke Street, Cambridge CB2 3QZ. *T:* Cambridge (0223) 334305. *Clubs:* Heswall Golf, Gog Magog Golf.

HULL, John Folliott Charles; Deputy Chairman, Schroders plc, 1977–85; *b* 21 Oct. 1925; *er s* of Sir Hubert Hull, CBE, and of Judith, *e d* of P. F. S. Stokes; *m* 1951, Rosemarie Waring; one *s* three *d*. *Educ:* Downside; Jesus Coll., Cambridge (Titular Schol.; 1st cl. hons Law; MA). Captain, RA, 1944–48; served with Royal Indian Artillery, 1945–48. Called to Bar, Inner Temple, 1952, *ad eund* Lincoln's Inn, 1954. J. Henry Schroder Wagg & Co. Ltd, 1957–72, 1974–85: a Man. Dir, 1961–72; Dep. Chm., 1974–77; Chm., 1977–83; Dir, 1984–85; Dir, Schroders plc, 1969–72, 1974–85; Dep. Chm., Land Securities plc, 1976–; Director: Lucas Industries plc, 1975–90; Legal and General Assurance Soc., 1976–79; Legal & General Group plc, 1979–90; Goodwood Racecourse Ltd, 1987–. Dir-Gen., City Panel on Take-overs and Mergers, 1972–74 (Dep. Chm., 1987–); Chm., City Company Law Cttee, 1976–79. Lay Mem., Stock Exchange, 1983–84. Mem., Council, Manchester Business Sch., 1973–86. *Recreation:* reading political history and 19th century novelists. *Address:* 33 Edwardes Square, W8 6HH. *T:* 071–603 0715. *Club:* MCC.

See also Duke of Somerset.

HULL, John Grove, QC 1983; a Recorder, since 1984; *b* 21 Aug. 1931; *s* of Tom Edward Orridge Hull and Marjorie Ethel Hull; *m* 1961, Gillian Ann, *d* of Leslie Fawcett Stemp; two *d*. *Educ:* Rugby School; King's College, Cambridge. BA (1st cl. in Mech. Scis Tripos) 1953, MA 1957; LLB 1954. National Service, commissioned RE, 1954–56; called to the Bar, Middle Temple, 1958 (Cert. of Honour, Bar Final), Bencher, 1989; in practice, common law Bar, 1958–. *Recreations:* gardening, English literature. *Address:* Ravenshoe, 16 High Trees Road, Reigate, Surrey. *T:* Reigate (0737) 245181.

HULME, Bishop Suffragan of, since 1984; **Rt. Rev. Colin John Fraser Scott;** *b* 14 May 1933; *s* of Kenneth Miller Scott and Marion Edith Scott; *m* 1958, Margaret Jean MacKay; one *s* two *d*. *Educ:* Berkhamsted School; Queens' College, Cambridge; Ridley Hall, Cambridge. MA Cantab. Curate: St Barnabas, Clapham Common, 1958–61; St James, Hatcham, 1961–64; Vicar, St Mark, Kennington, 1964–71; Vice-Chm., Southwark Diocesan Pastoral Cttee, 1971–77; Team Rector, Sanderstead Team Ministry, 1977–84. *Address:* 1 Raynham Avenue, Didsbury, Manchester M20 0BW. *T:* 061–445 5922.

HULME, Geoffrey Gordon, CB 1984; Deputy Secretary, Department of Health and Social Security, since 1981, seconded to Public Finance Foundation, 1986; *b* 8 March 1931; *s* of Alfred and Jessie Hulme; *m* 1956, Shirley Leigh Cumberlidge; one *s* one *d*. *Educ:* King's Sch., Macclesfield; Corpus Christi Coll., Oxford (MA, 1st Cl Hons Mod. Langs). Nat. Service, Intelligence Corps, 1949–50; Oxford, 1950–53; Asst Principal, Min. of Health, 1953–59; Principal, 1959–64; Principal Regional Officer, W Midlands, 1964–67; Asst Sec., 1967–74; Under-Sec., 1974–81; Principal Finance Officer, 1981–86. *Recreations:* the usual things and collecting edible fungi. *Address:* Stone Farm, Little Cornard, Sudbury, Suffolk; 163A Kennington Park Road, SE11. *T:* 071–735 4461. *Club:* Royal Automobile.

HULME, Maj.-Gen. Jerrie Anthony, CB 1990; Director General of Ordnance Services, 1988–90; *b* 10 Aug. 1935; *s* of Stanley and Laurel Hulme; *m* 1st, 1959, Margaret Mary (Maureen) (*née* Turton) (marr. diss. 1974); two *s* two *d*; 2nd, 1974, Janet Kathleen (*née* Mills). *Educ:* King Henry VIII Sch., Coventry. FInstPS. jssc, psc. National Service, RAOC, 1953–56; regtl appts, Kenya, Persian Gulf, Aden, 1956–66; SC Camberley, 1966; Staff appts, 1967–70; jssc Latimer, 1970; Directing Staff, Staff Coll., 1971–74; Comdr RAOC HQ 4 Div., 1974–76; Staff appt, 1976–78; Col, Staff Coll., 1978–81; Staff appt, 1981–82; Dep. Dir Gen. of Ordnance Services, 1982–85; Dir of Logistic Ops (Army), MoD, 1985–88. Freeman, City of London, 1987. *Recreations:* music, carpentry, country pursuits. *Address:* c/o Lloyds Bank, 21–23 The Square, Kenilworth, Warwickshire CV8 1EE. *Club:* Army and Navy.

HULME, Rev. Paul; Superintendent Minister, Wesley's Chapel, London, since 1988; *b* 14 May 1942; *s* of Harry Hulme and Elizabeth Hulme; *m* 1976, Hilary Frances Martin; three *s*. *Educ:* Hatfield House, Yorks; Didsbury Theological Coll., Bristol (BA). Minister: Bungay, Suffolk, 1968–70; Brighton, 1970–75; Newquay, Cornwall, 1975–79; Taunton, 1979–86; Enfield, 1986–88. Chaplain, Sussex Univ., 1970–75. Freeman, City of London, 1990. *Recreations:* walking, music. *Address:* Wesley's Chapel, 49 City Road, EC1Y 1AU. *T:* 071–253 2262. *Clubs:* National Liberal.

HULSE, Sir (Hamilton) Westrow, 9th Bt, *cr* 1739; Barrister-at-Law, Inner Temple; *b* 20 June 1909; *o s* of Sir Hamilton Hulse, 8th Bt, and Estelle (*d* 1933) *d* of late William Lorillard Campbell, of New York, USA; *S* father, 1931; *m* 1st, 1932, Philippa Mabel (marr. diss. 1937), *y d* of late A. J. Taylor, Strensham Court, Worcs; two *s*; 2nd, 1938, Amber (*d* 1940), *o d* of late Captain Herbert Stanley Orr Wilson, RHA, Rockfield Park, Mon; 3rd, 1945 (marr. diss.); 4th, 1954, Elizabeth, *d* of late Col George Redesdale Brooker Spain, CMG, TD, FSA. *Educ:* Eton; Christ Church, Oxford. Wing Comdr RAFVR, served 1940–45 (despatches). *Heir: s* Edward Jeremy Westrow Hulse [*b* 22 Nov. 1932; *m* 1957, Verity Ann, *d* of William Pilkington, Ivy Well, St John, Jersey; one *s* one *d*]. *Address:* Breamore, Hants. *TA:* Breamore. *T:* Downton (0725) 22773. *Clubs:* Carlton; Leander.

HULSE, Sir Westrow; *see* Hulse, Sir H. W.

HULTON, Sir Geoffrey (Alan), 4th Bt, *cr* 1905; JP; DL; *b* 21 Jan. 1920; *s* of Sir Roger Braddyll Hulton, 3rd Bt and Hon. Marjorie Evelyn Louise (*d* 1970), *o c* of 6th Viscount Mountmorres; *S* father 1956; *m* 1945, Mary Patricia Reynolds. *Educ:* Marlborough. Entered Royal Marines, Sept. 1938; Lieut, 1940; sunk in HMS Repulse, Dec. 1941; prisoner-of-war, Far East, Feb. 1942–Aug. 1945; Captain, 1948; retired (ill-health), 1949. Owner of Hulton Park estate. Life Pres., Bolton West Conservative Association; Life Patron, Bolton and District Agricultural Discussion Soc.; Life Vice-Pres., Royal Lancs Agricultural Soc. (Pres., 1974–80). Chief Scout's Comr, 1964–85; President: Greater Manchester North Scout County; Bolton Scout Trust; Vice-President: Greater Manchester

West Scout County; CLA (Lancashire); Lancashire County Cricket Club; Bolton Cricket League; St Ann's Hospice Ltd; Hon. Life Vice-Pres., Westhoughton Cricket Club. JP Lancs, 1955; DL Lancs, later Greater Manchester, 1974. KCSG 1966. *Recreations:* country pursuits. *Heir:* none. *Address:* The Cottage, Hulton Park, Over Hulton, Bolton BL5 1BE. *T:* Bolton (0204) 651324. *Clubs:* Lansdowne, Royal Over-Seas League, Spanish, Victory.

HULTON, John, MA; *b* 28 Dec. 1915; *e s* of late Rev. Samuel Hulton, Knaresborough; *m* 1940, Helen Christian McFarlan; two *d. Educ:* Kingswood Sch., Bath; Hertford Coll., Oxford. DipLA; graduate of Landscape Inst. Leeds City Art Gallery and Temple Newsam House (Hon. Asst), 1937–38. Served War, RA, 1939–46. Keeper at Brighton Art Gall., Museum and Royal Pavilion, 1946–48; British Council Fine Arts Dept, 1948; Dir, 1970–75; resigned to study landscape design; now in private practice. Organised many art exhibns abroad. *Recreations:* looking at painting and sculpture; landscape and gardens. *Address:* 70 Gloucester Crescent, NW1 7EG. *T:* 071–485 6906. *Club:* Athenæum.

HUM, Christopher Owen; HM Diplomatic Service; Counsellor and Head of Chancery, UK Mission to United Nations, New York, since 1989; *b* 27 Jan. 1946; *s* of late Norman Charles Hum and of Muriel Kathleen (*née* Hines); *m* 1970, Julia Mary, second *d* of Hon. Sir Hugh Park, *qv*; one *s* one *d. Educ:* Berkhamsted Sch.; Pembroke Coll., Cambridge (Foundn Scholar; 1st Cl. Hons; MA); Univ. of Hong Kong. Joined FCO, 1967; served in: Hong Kong, 1968–70; Peking, 1971–73; Office of the UK Perm. Rep. to the EEC, Brussels, 1973–75; FCO, 1975–79; Peking, 1979–81; Paris, 1981–83; Asst Head, Hong Kong Dept, FCO, 1983–85; Counsellor, 1985; Dep. Head, Falkland Is Dept, FCO, 1985–86; Head, Hong Kong Dept, FCO, 1986–89. *Recreations:* music (piano, viola), walking. *Address:* c/o Foreign and Commonwealth Office, King Charles Street, SW1A 2AH; UK Mission to United Nations, 845 Third Avenue, New York, NY 10022, USA.

HUMBLE, James Kenneth; Chief Executive, Local Authorities Coordinating Body on Trading Standards, since 1982; *b* 8 May 1936; *s* of Joseph Humble and Alice (*née* Rhodes); *m* 1962, Freda (*née* Holden); three *d*. Fellow, Inst. of Trading Standards. Served RN, 1954–56. Weights and Measures, Oldham, 1956–62; Fed. Min. of Commerce and Industry, Nigeria, 1962–66; Chief Trading Standards Officer, Croydon, 1966–74; Asst Dir of Consumer Affairs, Office of Fair Trading, 1974–79; Dir of Metrication Bd, 1979–80; Dir, Nat. Metrological Co-ordinating Unit, 1980–87. Sec., Trade Descriptions Cttee, Inst. of Trading Standards, 1968–73; Examr, Dip. in Trading Standards, 1978–; Vice Chm., Council of Europe Cttee of Experts on Consumer Protection, 1976–79. Member: Council for Vehicle Servicing and Repair, 1972–75; Methven Cttee, 1974–76; OECD Cttee, Air Package Tours, 1978–79; BSI Divl Council, 1976–79; Eden Cttee on Metrology, 1984; Chairman: World Conf. on Safety, Sweden, 1989; Yugoslavian Conf. on 1992, 1989; Mem. Cttee, European Consumer Product Safety Assoc., 1985– (Exec., 1987–); Executive: W European Legal Metrology Co-operation, 1989–; European Forum Food Law Enforcement Practitioners, 1990–. Organiser, First European Metrology Symposium, 1988. Conf. papers to USA Western States Conf. on Weights and Measures, 1989. Sport, Devonport Services, 1954–56; Captain, Oldham Rugby Union, 1957–59; Professional Rugby, Leigh RFC, 1959–65. *Publications:* (contrib.) Marketing and the Consumer Movement, 1978; European Inspection, Protection and Control, 1990; contrib. to various jls. *Recreations:* bridge, golf, opera. *Address:* PO Box 6, Token House, 1A Robert Street, Croydon CR9 1LG. *T:* 081–688 1996.

HUME, Sir Alan (Blyth), Kt 1973; CB 1963; *b* 5 Jan. 1913; *s* of late W. Alan Hume; *m* 1943, Marion Morton Garrett; one *s* one *d. Educ:* George Heriot's Sch.; Edinburgh Univ. Entered Scottish Office, 1936. Under-Sec., Scottish Home Department, 1957–59; Asst Under-Sec. of State, Scottish Office, 1959–62; Under-Sec., Min. of Public Bldg and Works, 1963–64; Secretary, Scottish Develt Dept, 1965–73. Chairman: Ancient Monuments Bd, Scotland, 1973–81; Edinburgh New Town Conservation Cttee, 1975–90. *Recreations:* golf, fishing. *Address:* 12 Oswald Road, Edinburgh EH9 2HJ. *T:* 031–667 2440. *Clubs:* English-Speaking Union; New (Edinburgh).

HUME, His Eminence Cardinal (George) Basil; *see* Westminster, Archbishop of, (RC).

HUME, James Bell; Under-Secretary, Scottish Office, 1973–83; *b* 16 June 1923; *s* of late Francis John Hume and Jean McLellan Hume; *m* 1950, Elizabeth Margaret Nicolson. *Educ:* George Heriot's Sch., Edinburgh; Edinburgh Univ. (MA Hons History, 1st Cl.). RAF, 1942–45. Entered Scottish Office, 1947; Jt Sec., Royal Commn on Doctors' and Dentists' Remuneration, 1958–59; Nuffield Trav. Fellowship, 1963–64; Head of Edinburgh Centre, Civil Service Coll., 1969–73. *Recreations:* dance music, walking, enjoying silence. *Address:* 2/9 Succoth Court, Succoth Park, Edinburgh EH12 6BZ. *T:* 031–346 4451. *Club:* New (Edinburgh).

HUME, John; MP (SDLP) Foyle, since 1983; Member (SDLP) Northern Ireland, European Parliament, since 1979; Leader, Social Democratic and Labour Party, since 1979; *b* 18 Jan. 1937; *s* of Samuel Hume; *m* 1960, Patricia Hone; two *s* three *d. Educ:* St Columb's Coll., Derry; St Patrick's Coll., Maynooth, NUI (MA). Res. Fellow in European Studies, TCD; Associate Fellow, Centre for Internat. Affairs, Harvard, 1976. Pres., Credit Union League of Ireland, 1964–68; MP for Foyle, NI Parlt, 1969–73; Member (SDLP), Londonderry: NI Assembly, 1973–75; NI Constitutional Convention, 1975–76; NI Assembly, 1982–86; Minister of Commerce, NI, 1974. Mem. (SDLP) New Ireland Forum, 1983–84. Contested (SDLP) Londonderry, UK elections, Oct. 1974. Member: Cttee on Regl Policy and Regl Planning, European Parlt, 1979–; ACP-EEC Jt Cttee, 1979–; Bureau of European Socialist Gp, 1979–. Mem., Irish T&GWU. Hon. Dr of Letters Massachusetts, 1985. *Address:* 6 West End Park, Derry, N Ireland. *T:* Londonderry (0504) 265340.

HUME, Thomas Andrew, CBE 1977; FSA, FMA; Director, Museum of London, 1972–77; *b* 21 June 1917; *o s* of late Thomas Hume, Burnfoot, Oxton, and late Lillias Dodds; *m* 1942, Joyce Margaret Macdonald; two *s* one *d. Educ:* Heaton Grammar Sch.; King's Coll., Univ. of Durham (BA Hons Hist.). Gladstone Prizeman, Joseph Cowen Prizeman. Curator: Kirkstall Abbey House Museum, Leeds, 1949–52; Buckinghamshire County Museum, Aylesbury, 1952–60; Dir, City of Liverpool Museums, 1960–72. Member: Museums and Galleries Commn (formerly Standing Commn on Museums and Galleries), 1977–86; Adv. Cttee, London Transport Museum, 1983–90. Past Pres., NW Fedn of Museums; Past Vice-Pres., Internat. Assoc. of Transport Museums; Past Chm., ICOM British Nat. Cttee; Museum Consultant, Unesco; Dir Mus. Exchange Programme, ICOM, Unesco, 1978–79. Hon. Mem., ICOM, 1983. *Publications:* contribs Thoresby Soc., Records of Bucks; excavation reports and historical articles. *Recreations:* travel, gardening.

HUMM, Roger Frederick, FIMI; CBIM; FInstD; Managing Director, Ford Motor Co. Ltd, 1986–90; Director: Ford Motor Credit Co. Ltd, 1980–90; Henry Ford & Son Ltd (Cork), 1982–90; *b* 7 March 1937; *s* of Leonard Edward Humm, MBE, and Gladys Humm; *m* 1966, Marion Frances (*née* Czechman) (marr. diss.). *Educ:* Hampton Sch., Hampton, Mddx; Univ. of Sheffield (BAEcon Hon). Graduate trainee, Ford Motor Co. Ltd (UK), 1960, Sales Manager, 1973; Marketing Dir, 1977, Internat. Gp Dir, N Europe, 1978, Ford of Europe Inc.; Exec. Dir of Sales, Ford Motor Co. Ltd, 1980. FRSA 1987. Liveryman, Worshipful Co. of Carmen, 1986; Freeman, City of London, 1986. *Recreations:* golf, scuba diving, writing. *Address:* The Clock House, Kelvedon, Essex CO5 9DG. *Clubs:* Royal Automobile, Lord's Taverners, Variety Club of Great Britain; Harlequins.

HUMMEL, Frederick Cornelius, MA, DPhil, BSc; Head of Forestry Division, Commission of the European Communities, 1973–80, retired; *b* 28 April 1915; *s* of Cornelius Hummel, OBE, and Caroline Hummel (*née* Riefler); *m* 1st, 1941, Agnes Kathleen Rushforth (marr. diss., 1961); one *s* (and one *s* decd); 2nd, 1961, Floriana Rosemary Hollyer; three *d. Educ:* St Stephan, Augsburg, Germany; Wadham Coll., Oxford. District Forest Officer, Uganda Forest Service, 1938–46; Forestry Commn, 1946–73; Mensuration Officer, 1946; Chief, Management Sect., 1956; released for service with FAO as Co-Dir, Mexican Nat. Forest Inventory, 1961–66; Controller, Management Services, Forestry Commn, 1966–68, Comr for Harvesting and Marketing, 1968–73. Hon. Member: Société Royale Forestière de Belgique; Asociación para el Progreso Forestal, Spain; Corresponding Member: Mexican Acad. of Forest Scis; Italian Acad. of Forest Scis; Soc. of Forestry, Finland. Dr *hc* Munich, 1978. Bernard Eduard Fernow Plaquette, (jtly) Amer. Forestry Assoc. and Deutscher Forstverein, 1986. *Publications:* Forest Policy, 1984; Biomass Forestry in Europe, 1988; Forestry Policies in Europe: an analysis, 1989. *Recreations:* walking, ski-ing. *Address:* Ridgemount, 8 The Ridgeway, Guildford, Surrey GU1 2DG. *T:* Guildford (0483) 572383. *Club:* United Oxford & Cambridge University.

HUMPHREY, Arthur Hugh Peters, CMG 1959; OBE 1952; Hon. PMN (Malaya), 1958; Controller of Special Projects, Overseas Development Administration, Foreign and Commonwealth Office, 1961–71; Malayan Civil Service, 1934–60, retired; *b* 18 June 1911; *s* of late Arthur George Humphrey, Bank Manager; *m* 1948, Mary Valentine, *d* of late Lieut-Col J. E. Macpherson; three *d. Educ:* Eastbourne Coll.; Merton Coll., Oxford (Open Exhbr 1930, 1st class Maths, 1933; MA 1948). Appointed Malayan Civil Service, 1934; Private Sec. to Governor of Straits Settlements and High Comr for Malay States, 1936–38; Resident, Labuan, 1940–42; interned by Japanese in Borneo, 1942–45; idc 1948; Sec. for Defence and Internal Security, Fedn of Malaya, 1953–57; Mem. of Federal Legislative and Executive Councils, 1953–56; Sec. to the Treasury, Federation of Malaya, 1957–59; Director of Technical Assistance, Commonwealth Relations Office, 1960–61; Controller of Special Projects, ODM, 1961. Official Leader, United Kingdom delegations at Colombo Plan conferences: Tokyo, 1960, and Kuala Lumpur, 1961. Coronation Medal, 1953. *Recreations:* music, tennis. *Address:* 14 Ambrose Place, Worthing, Sussex BN11 1PZ. *T:* Worthing (0903) 33339. *Club:* East India, Devonshire, Sports and Public Schools.

HUMPHREY, (Frank) Basil, CB 1975; Parliamentary Counsel, 1967–80; *b* 21 Sept. 1918; *s* of late John Hartley Humphrey and Alice Maud Humphrey (*née* Broadbent); *m* 1947, Ol'ga Černá, *y d* of late František Černý, Trenčín, Czechoslovakia; two *s. Educ:* Brentwood Sch.; St Catharine's Coll., Cambridge (Schol.). 2nd cl. hons Pt I. Mod. Langs Tripos, 1st cl. hons Pt II Law Tripos. Served RA, 1939–45: Adjt 23rd Mountain Regt and DAAG 4 Corps, India and Burma. Called to Bar, Middle Temple, 1946 (Harmsworth Schol.). Seconded as First Parly Counsel, Fedn of Nigeria, 1961–64, and as Counsel-in-charge at Law Commn, 1971–72. *Recreations:* gardening, mountain walking, music. *Address:* 1a The Avenue, Chichester, W Sussex PO19 4PZ. *T:* Chichester (0243) 778783; Traverse des Rouvières, 83600 Bagnols-en-Forêt, France. *T:* 94 40 65 83.

HUMPHREY, William Gerald, MA Oxon and Cantab, DPhil Oxon; Assistant Secretary, University of Cambridge Appointments Board, 1962–72; Headmaster of The Leys School, Cambridge, 1934–58; Group personnel officer, Fisons Ltd, 1958–62; *b* 2 Aug. 1904; *e s* of late Rev. William Humphrey and Helen Lusher; *m* 1936, Margaret (*d* 1989), *er d* of late William E. Swift, Cornwall, Conn., USA; one *s. Educ:* King Edward VII Sch., Sheffield; Queen's Coll., Oxford (Hastings Scholar, Taberdar, University Sen. Research Student); 1st Class Final Honour Sch. of Natural Science, 1926; DPhil, 1928; Commonwealth Fund Fellow, Harvard Univ., 1929–31; Senior Science Master, Uppingham Sch., 1932–34. Mem. Ministry of Agriculture Cttee on demand for Agricultural Graduates. *Publications:* The Christian and Education, 1940; Papers in Journal of the Chemical Soc. *Recreation:* painting. *Address:* 5101 Ridgefield Road, Bethesda, Md 20816, USA. *T:* 301 913 9470.

HUMPHREYS, Arthur Leslie Charles, CBE 1970; Director, Computer Associated Systems Ltd, since 1982; Director: Charles Babbage Institute, since 1978; Computer Museum, Boston, Massachusetts, since 1985; *b* 8 Jan. 1917; *s* of late Percy Stewart Humphreys and late Louise (*née* Weston); *m* 1st, 1943, Marjorie Irene Murphy-Jones (decd); two *s* one *d*; 2nd, 1975, Audrey Norah Urquhart (*née* Dunningham) (decd). *Educ:* Catford Grammar Sch.; Administrative Staff Coll., Henley. International Computers & Tabulators Ltd: Dir 1963–83; Dep. Man. Dir 1964; Man. Dir 1967; ICL Ltd: Dir, 1968–82; Man. Dir, 1968–72; Dep. Chm., 1972–77; Dir, Data Recording Instrument Co. Ltd, 1957–84. *Recreations:* table tennis, bridge, music. *Address:* 24 Middle Street, Thriplow, Royston, Herts SG8 7RD. *T:* Fowlmere (076382) 594.

HUMPHREYS, Prof. Colin John, FIM; FInstP; Professor of Materials Science, since 1990, and Fellow of Selwyn College, since 1990, University of Cambridge; Head of Department of Materials Science and Metallurgy, since 1991; *b* 24 May 1941; *s* of Arthur William Humphreys and Olive Annie (*née* Harton); *m* 1966, Sarah Jane Matthews; two *d. Educ:* Luton Grammar Sch.; Imperial Coll., London (BSc); Churchill Coll., Cambridge (PhD); Jesus Coll., Oxford (MA). Sen. Res. Officer 1971–80, Lectr 1980–85, in Metallurgy and Science of Materials, Univ. of Oxford; Sen. Res. Fellow, Jesus Coll., Oxford, 1974–85; Henry Bell Wortley Prof. of Materials Engrg and Hd of Dept of Materials Sci. and Engrg, Liverpool Univ., 1985–89. Visiting Professor: Univ. of Illinois, 1982–86; Arizona State Univ., 1979. Chm., Commn on Electron Diffraction, and Mem. Commn on Internat. Tables, Internat. Union of Crystallography, 1984–87. Member: SERC, 1988– (Chm., Materials Sci. and Engrg Commn, 1988–; Mem., Science Bd, 1990–); Adv. Cttee, Davy-Faraday Labs, Royal Instn, 1989–; Scientific Adv. Cttee on Advanced Materials for CEC Internat. Scientific Coopn Prog., 1990–. Member Council: RMS, 1988–89; Inst. of Metals, 1989–. Mem. Court, Univ. of Bradford, 1990–. RSA Medal, 1963; Reginald Mitchell Meml Lecture and Medal, 1989; Rosenhain Medal and Prize, Inst. of Metals, 1989. *Publications:* (ed) High Voltage Electron Microscopy, 1974; (ed) Electron Diffraction 1927–77, 1978; Creation and Evolution, 1985 (trans. Chinese 1988); patents and numerous sci. and tech. pubns mainly on electron microscopy, semiconductors, superconductors and nanometre scale electron beam lithography. *Recreations:* chronology of ancient historical events, contemplating gardening. *Address:* Department of Materials Science and Metallurgy, Pembroke Street, Cambridge CB2 3QZ. *T:* Cambridge (0223) 334457.

HUMPHREYS, (David) Colin, CMG 1977; Deputy Under Secretary of State (Air), Ministry of Defence, 1979–85; *b* 23 April 1925; *s* of late Charles Roland Lloyd Humphreys and Bethia Joan (*née* Bowie); *m* 1952, Jill Allison (*née* Cranmer); two *s* one *d. Educ:* Eton Coll. (King's Scholar); King's Coll., Cambridge (MA). Served Army, 1943–46. Air Min., 1949; Private Sec. to Sec. of State for Air, 1959–60; Counsellor, UK Delegn to NATO,

1960–63; Air Force Dept, 1963–69; IDC 1970; Dir, Defence Policy Staff, 1971–72; Asst Sec. Gen. (Defence Planning and Policy), NATO, 1972–76; Asst Under Sec. of State (Naval Staff), MoD, 1977–79. Dir of Develt, RIIA, 1985–86. *Address:* Rivendell, North Drive, Virginia Water, Surrey GU25 4NQ. *T:* Wentworth (0344) 842130. *Clubs:* Royal Air Force; Wentworth.

HUMPHREYS, Emyr Owen; Author; *b* 15 April 1919; *s* of William and Sarah Rosina Humphreys, Prestatyn, Flints; *m* 1946, Elinor Myfanwy, *d* of Rev. Griffith Jones, Bontnewydd, Caerns; three *s* one *d. Educ:* University Coll., Aberystwyth; University Coll., Bangor (Hon. Fellow, Univ. of Wales, 1987). Gregynog Arts Fellow, 1974–75; Hon. Prof., English Dept, Univ. Coll. of N Wales, Bangor, 1988. Hon. DLitt Wales, 1990. *Publications:* The Little Kingdom, 1946; The Voice of a Stranger, 1949; A Change of Heart, 1951; Hear and Forgive, 1952 (Somerset Maugham Award, 1953); A Man's Estate, 1955; The Italian Wife, 1957; Y Tri Llais, 1958; A Toy Epic, 1958 (Hawthornden Prize, 1959); The Gift, 1963; Outside the House of Baal, 1965; Natives, 1968; Ancestor Worship, 1970; National Winner, 1971 (Welsh Arts Council Prize, 1972); Flesh and Blood, 1974; Landscapes, 1976; The Best of Friends, 1978; Penguin Modern Poets No 27, 1978 (Soc. of Authors Travelling Award, 1979); The Kingdom of Brân, 1979; The Anchor Tree, 1980; Pwyll a Riannon, 1980; Miscellany Two, 1981; The Taliesin Tradition, 1983 (Welsh Arts Council Non-Fiction Prize, 1984); Jones: a novel, 1984; Salt of the Earth, 1985; An Absolute Hero, 1986; Darn o Dir, 1986; Open Secrets, 1988; The Triple Net, 1988; The Crucible of Myth, 1990; Bonds of Attachment, 1991. *Recreations:* rural pursuits. *Address:* Llinon, Penyberth, Llanfairpwll, Ynys Môn, Gwynedd LL61 5YT.

HUMPHREYS, John Henry; Chairman, Industrial Tribunals (Ashford, Kent), since 1976; Legal Officer, Law Commission, since 1973; *b* 28 Feb. 1917; British; *m* 1939, Helen Mary Markbreiter; one *s* one *d. Educ:* Cranleigh School. Solicitor. Served with Co. of London Yeomanry, and Northampton Yeomanry, 1939–47; Treasury Solicitor Dept, 1947–73. *Recreations:* sailing, golf, gardening. *Address:* Gate House Cottage, Sandown Road, Sandwich, Kent CT13 9NT. *T:* Sandwich (0304) 612961. *Club:* Prince's (Sandwich).

See also Q. J. Thomas.

HUMPHREYS, Dr Keith Wood; Chairman and Managing Director, Rhône-Poulenc Ltd (formerly May & Baker), since 1984; *b* 5 Jan. 1934; *s* of William and Alice Humphreys; *m* 1964, Tessa Karen Shepherd; three *d. Educ:* Manchester Grammar School; Trinity Hall, Cambridge (MA, PhD). MRSC; CBIM. Managing Dir, Plastics Div., Ciba-Geigy (UK), 1972–78; Jt Managing Dir, Ciba-Geigy (UK), 1979–82; Managing Dir, May & Baker, 1982–84. *Recreations:* music, squash, tennis, mountain walking. *Address:* Rhône-Poulenc Ltd, Dagenham, Essex RM10 7XS.

HUMPHREYS, Kenneth William, BLitt, MA, PhD; FLA; Librarian, European University Institute, Florence, 1975–81; *b* 4 Dec. 1916; *s* of Joseph Maxmillian Humphreys and Bessie Benfield; *m* 1939, Margaret, *d* of Reginald F. Hill and Dorothy Lucas; two *s. Educ:* Southfield Sch., Oxford; St Catherine's Coll., Oxford. Library Asst, All Souls Coll., Oxford, 1933–36; Asst, Bodleian Library, 1936–50; Dep. Librarian, Brotherton Library, University of Leeds, 1950–52; Librarian, Univ. of Birmingham, 1952–75. Prof. of Library Studies, Haifa Univ., 1982. Hon. Lecturer in Palaeography: University of Leeds, 1950–52; University of Birmingham, 1952–75. Panizzi Lectr, Panizzi Trust, 1987. Hon. Sec., Standing Conf. of Nat. and University Libraries, 1954–69, Vice-Chm., 1969–71, Chm. 1971–73; Mem. Library Adv. Council for England, 1966–71; Mem. Council, Library Assoc., 1964–75, Chm. Council 1973; Chm. Exec. Cttee, West Midlands Regional Library Bureau, 1963–75; Chairman: Jt Standing Conf. and Cttee on Library Cooperation, 1965–75; Nat. Cttee on Regional Library Cooperation, 1970–75; Mem. Comité International de Paléographie, and Colloque International de Paléographie, 1955–; President: Nat. and University Libraries Section, Internat. Fedn of Library Assocs, 1968–69, Pres., University Libraries Sub-Section, 1967–73; Ligue des Bibliothèques Européennes de Recherche, 1974–80; Round Table on Library History, 1978–82. Sec. Cttee, British Acad. Corpus of British Medieval Library Catalogues, 1983–90. Editor, Studies in the History of Libraries and Librarianship; Jt Editor, Series of Reproductions of Medieval and Renaissance Texts. Hon. LittD Dublin (Trinity Coll.), 1967. Hon. FLA 1980; Socio d'onore, Italian Library Assoc., 1982. *Publications:* The Book Provisions of the Medieval Friars, 1964; The Medieval Library of the Carmelites at Florence, 1964; The Library of the Franciscans of the Convent of St Antony, Padua at the Beginning of the fifteenth century, 1966; The Library of the Franciscans of Siena in the Fifteenth Century, 1977; A National Library in Theory and in Practice, 1988; The Friars (Corpus of British Medieval Library Catalogues), 1990; articles in library periodicals. *Recreation:* collection of manuscripts. *Address:* 94 Metchley Lane, Harborne, Birmingham B17 0HS. *T:* 021–427 2785. *Clubs:* Athenæum; Kildare Street and University (Dublin).

HUMPHREYS, Sir Myles; see Humphreys, Sir R. E. M.

HUMPHREYS, Sir Olliver (William), Kt 1968; CBE 1957; BSc, FInstP, CEng, FIEE, FRAeS; *b* 4 Sept. 1902; *s* of late Rev. J. Willis Humphreys, Bath; *m* 1933, Muriel Mary Hawkins (*d* 1985). *Educ:* Caterham Sch.; University Coll., London. Joined staff GEC Research Labs, 1925, Dir, 1949–61; Director 1953, Vice-Chm., 1963–67, GEC Ltd; Chm. all GEC Electronics and Telecommunications subsidiaries, 1961–66 and GEC (Research) Ltd, 1961–67. Mem. Bd, Inst. Physics, 1951–60 (Pres., 1956–58); Mem. Coun., IEE, 1952–55 (Vice-Pres., 1959–63; Pres., 1964–65); Faraday Lectr, 1953–54. Mem., BoT Cttee on Organisation and Constitution of BSI, 1949–50; Chm., BSI Telecommunications Industry Standards Cttee, 1951–63 (Mem. Gen. Coun., 1953–56; Mem. Exec. Cttee, 1953–60); Chm., Internat. Special Cttee on Radio Interference (CISPR), 1953–61; Chm., Electrical Res. Assoc., 1958–61; Chm., DSIR Radio Res. Bd, 1954–62; Pres., Electronic Engrg Assoc., 1962–64; Founder Chm., Conf. of Electronics Industry, 1963–67; Mem., Nat. ERC, 1963–67. Fellow UCL, 1963. Liveryman, Worshipful Co. of Makers of Playing Cards. *Publications:* various technical and scientific papers in proceedings of learned societies. *Recreations:* travel, walking, reading.

HUMPHREYS, Sir (Raymond Evelyn) Myles, Kt 1977; JP; DL; Chairman: Northern Ireland Railways Co. Ltd, since 1967; Northern Ireland Transport Holding Company, since 1988 (Dir, 1968–74); *b* 24 March 1925; *s* of Raymond and May Humphreys; *m* 1st, 1963, Joan Tate (*d* 1979); two *s*; 2nd, 1987, Sheila Clements-McFarland. *Educ:* Skegoniel Primary Sch.; Londonderry High Sch.; Belfast Royal Acad. Research Engineer: NI Road Transport Bd, 1946–48; Ulster Transport Authy, 1948–55; Transport Manager, Nestle's Food Products (NI) Ltd, 1955–59; Director: Walter Alexander (Belfast) Ltd, 1959–; Quick Service Stations Ltd, 1971–85; Bowring Martin Ltd, 1978–88; Abbey National plc (formerly Abbey National Bldg Soc.), 1981– (Chm., NI Adv. Bd, 1981–); NI Railways Leasing, 1986–; Belfast Harbour Pension Fund Ltd, 1987–; NI Railways Travel Ltd, 1988–. Chm., Belfast Marathon Ltd, 1981–85. Member of Board: Ulster Transport Authority, 1966–69. Chm., NI Police Authority, 1976–86. Mem., Belfast City Council, 1964–81; Chairman: Belfast Corp. Housing Cttee, 1966–69; City Council Planning Cttee, 1973–75; City Council Town Planning and Environmental Hlth Cttee, 1973–75; Finance and Gen. Purposes Cttee, 1978–80; High Sheriff of Belfast, 1969; Dep. Lord Mayor, 1970; Lord Mayor, 1975–77. Member: Nat. Planning and Town Planning Council, 1970–81 (Chm., 1976–77); NI Tourist Bd, 1973–80; NI Housing Exec., 1975–78; Chm., Ulster Tourist Develt Assoc., 1968–78; Belfast Harbour Comr, 1979–88. Mem., May Cttee of Inquiry into UK Prison Services, 1978–79. Past Chairman: Bd of Visitors, HM Prison, Belfast; Bd of Management, Dunlambert Secondary Sch. Past-Pres., Belfast Junior Chamber of Commerce; Mem. Exec., NI Chamber of Commerce and Industry (Pres., 1982); NI Rep., Motability Internat.; Senator, Junior Chamber Internat.; Pres., Belfast Br., BIM, 1983–. Member: TA&VRA for NI, 1980; Council, Queen's Silver Jubilee Appeal. Pres., NI Polio Fellowship, 1977–. Pres., City of Belfast Youth Orch., 1980; Dir, Ulster Orch. Soc., 1980–82; Trustee, Ulster Folk & Transport Mus., 1976–81. Mem. Senate, QUB, 1975–77; Mem. Court, Ulster Univ., 1984–. District Transport Officer, St John Ambulance Brigade, 1946–66. Freeman of City of London, 1976. JP 1969; DL Belfast 1983. FCIT (Mem. Council); CBIM. OStJ. *Address:* Mylestone, 23 Massey Avenue, Belfast BT4 2JT. *T:* Belfast (0232) 761166. *Club:* Lansdowne.

HUMPHREYS, Prof. Robert Arthur, OBE 1946; MA, PhD Cantab; Director, Institute of Latin-American Studies, University of London, 1965–74; Professor of Latin-American History in University of London, 1948–74, now Emeritus; *b* 6 June 1907; *s* of late Robert Humphreys and Helen Marion Bavin, Lincoln; *m* 1946, Elisabeth (*d* 1990), *er d* of late Sir Bernard Pares, KBE, DCL. *Educ:* Lincoln Sch.; Peterhouse, Cambridge (Scholar). Commonwealth Fund Fellow, Univ. of Michigan, 1930–32. Asst Lectr in American History, UCL, 1932, Lectr 1935; Reader in American History in Univ. of London, 1942–48; Prof. of Latin-American History, UCL, 1948–70. Research Dept, FO, 1939–45. Mem., UGC Cttee on Latin American Studies, 1962–64; Chairman: Cttee on Library Resources, Univ. of London, 1969–71; Management Cttee, Inst of Archæology, 1975–80; Mem. Adv. Cttee, British Library Reference Div., 1975–79. Governor, SOAS, 1965–80, Hon. Fellow 1981. Pres., RHistS, 1964–68 (Hon. Vice-Pres., 1968). Lectures: Enid Muir Meml, Univ. of Newcastle upon Tyne, 1962; Creighton, Univ. of London, 1964; Raleigh, Brit. Acad., 1965. Corresp. Member: Hispanic Soc. of America; Argentine Acad. of History; Instituto Histórico e Geográfico Brasileiro; Academia Chilena de la Historia; Sociedad Chilena de Historia y Geografia; Instituto Ecuatoriano de Ciencias Naturales; Sociedad Peruana de Historia; Instituto Histórico y Geográfico del Uruguay; Academia Nacional de la Historia, Venezuela. Hon. DLitt: Newcastle, 1966; Nottingham, 1972; Hon. LittD Liverpool, 1972; DUniv Essex, 1973. Comdr, Order of Rio Branco, Brazil, 1972. Machado de Assis Medal, Academia Brasileira de Letras, 1974. *Publications:* British Consular Reports on the Trade and Politics of Latin America, 1940; The Evolution of Modern Latin America, 1946; Liberation in South America, 1806–1827, 1952; Latin American History: A Guide to the Literature in English, 1958; The Diplomatic History of British Honduras, 1638–1901, 1961; (with G. S. Graham), The Navy and South America, 1807–1823 (Navy Records Soc.), 1962; (with J. Lynch) The Origins of the Latin American Revolutions, 1808–1826, 1965; Tradition and Revolt in Latin America and other Essays, 1969; The Detached Recollections of General D. F. O'Leary, 1969; The Royal Historical Society, 1868–1968, 1969; Robert Southey and his History of Brazil, 1978; Latin American Studies in Great Britain (autobiog.), 1978; Latin America and the Second World War, vol. I, 1939–1942, 1981, vol. II, 1942–1945, 1982; Co-edited: (with A. D. Momigliano) Byzantine Studies and Other Essays by N. H. Baynes, 1955; (with Elisabeth Humphreys) The Historian's Business and Other Essays by Richard Pares, 1961; contrib. to The New Cambridge Modern History, vols VIII, IX and X. *Address:* 5 St James's Close, Prince Albert Road, NW8 7LG. *T:* 071–722 3628.

HUMPHRIES, Barry; *see* Humphries, J. B.

HUMPHRIES, David Ernest; Director, Australian Aeronautical Research Laboratory, Defence Science and Technology Organisation, Melbourne, since 1990; *b* 3 Feb. 1937; *er s* of late Ernest Augustus Humphries and Kathleen Humphries; *m* 1959, Wendy Rosemary Cook; one *s* one *d. Educ:* Brighton Coll.; Corpus Christi Coll., Oxford (Scholar; MA). RAE Farnborough: Materials Dept, 1961; Avionics Dept, 1966; Head of Inertial Navigation Div., 1974; Head of Bombing and Navigation Div., 1975; Head of Systems Assessment Dept, 1978; Dir Gen. Future Projects, MoD PE, 1981–83; Chief Scientist (RAF) and Dir Gen. of Res. (C), MoD, 1983–84; Dir Gen. Res. Technol., MoD (PE), 1984–86; Asst Chief Scientific Advr (Projects and Research), MoD, 1986–90. *Recreations:* music, pipe organ building and playing. *Address:* c/o DSTO Australia, ARL, 506 Lorimer Street, Fishermens Bend, Vic 3207, Australia.

HUMPHRIES, Gerard William; His Honour Judge Humphries; a Circuit Judge since 1980; *b* 13 Dec. 1928; *s* of late John Alfred Humphries and Marie Frances Humphries (*née* Whitwell), Barrow-in-Furness; *m* 1957, Margaret Valerie, *o d* of late W. W. Gelderd and Margaret Gelderd (*née* Bell), Ulverston; four *s* one *d. Educ:* St Bede's Coll., Manchester; Manchester Univ. (LLB Hons). Served RAF, 1951–53, Flying Officer. Called to Bar, Middle Temple, 1952; admitted to Northern Circuit, 1954; Asst Recorder of Salford, 1969–71; a Recorder of the Crown Court, 1974–80. Chairman: Medical Appeals Tribunal, 1976–80; Vaccine Damage Tribunals, 1979–80. Charter Mem., Serra Club, N Cheshire, 1963– (Pres. 1968, 1973). Trustee, SBC Educnl Trust, 1979 (Chm., 1979–90). Foundn Governor, St Bede's Coll., Manchester, 1978–. KHS 1986. *Recreations:* tennis, golf, music, caravanning, gardening. *Address:* 1 Deans Court, Crown Square, Manchester M3 3JL. *Clubs:* Lansdowne; Northern Lawn Tennis, Northenden Golf (Manchester).

HUMPHRIES, John Anthony Charles, OBE 1980; Chairman, Southern Council for Sport and Recreation, since 1987; *b* 15 June 1925; *s* of Charles Humphries; *m* 1951, Olga June, *d* of Dr Geoffrey Duckworth, MRCP; four *d. Educ:* Fettes; Peterhouse, Cambridge (1st Law). Served War, RNVR, 1943–46. Solicitor (Hons), 1951. Chm., Water Space Amenity Commn, 1973–83; Vice-Pres., Inland Waterways Assoc., 1973– (Chm., 1970–73); Mem. Inland Waterways Amenity Adv. Council, 1971–89; Adviser to HM Govt on amenity use of water space, 1972; Member: Nat. Water Council, 1973–83; Thames Water Authy, 1983–87. Mem., Sports Council, 1987–88. Chm., Evans of Leeds plc, 1982–; Mem., London Bd, Halifax Building Soc., 1985–; Dep. Chm., Environment Council, 1985–. *Recreations:* inland waters, gardening. *Address:* 21 Parkside, Wimbledon, SW19. *T:* 081–946 3764. *Clubs:* Naval, City.

HUMPHRIES, (John) Barry, AO 1982; music-hall artiste and author; *b* 17 Feb. 1934; *s* of J. A. E. Humphries and L. A. Brown; *m* 1st, 1959, Rosalind Tong; two *d*; 2nd, 1979, Diane Millstead; two *s*; *m* 1990, Lizzie, *d* of Sir Stephen (Harold) Spender, *qv. Educ:* Melbourne Grammar Sch.; Univ. of Melbourne. Repertory seasons, Union Theatre, Melbourne, 1953–54; Phillip Street Revue Theatre, Sydney, 1956; Demon Barber, Lyric, Hammersmith, 1959; Oliver, New Theatre, 1960. One-man shows (author and performer): A Nice Night's Entertainment, 1962; Excuse I, 1965; Just a Show, 1968; A Load of Olde Stuffe, 1971; At Least You Can Say That You've Seen It, 1974; Housewife Superstar, 1976; Isn't It Pathetic at His Age, 1979; A Night with Dame Edna, 1979; An Evening's Intercourse with Barry Humphries, 1981–82; Tears Before Bedtime, 1986; Back with a Vengeance, 1987. TV series, The Dame Edna Experience, 1987. Numerous plays, films and broadcasts. *Publications:* Bizarre, 1964; Innocent Austral Verse, 1968; (with Nicholas Garland) The Wonderful World of Barry McKenzie, 1970; (with Nicholas Garland) Bazza Holds His Own, 1972; Dame Edna's Coffee Table Book, 1976;

Les Patterson's Australia, 1979; Treasury of Australian Kitsch, 1980; A Nice Night's Entertainment, 1981; Dame Edna's Bedside Companion, 1982; The Traveller's Tool, 1985; (with Nicholas Garland) The Complete Barry McKenzie, 1988; My Gorgeous Life: the autobiography of Dame Edna Everage, 1989. *Recreations:* reading secondhand booksellers' catalogues in bed, inventing Australia. *Address:* c/o Allen, Allen and Hemsley, PO Box 50, Sydney, NSW 2001, Australia. *Clubs:* Athenæum, Garrick.

HUMPHRIES, John Charles Freeman; Editor, Western Mail, since 1988; *b* 2 Jan. 1937; *s* of Charles Montague Humphries and Lilian Clara Humphries; *m* 1959, Eliana Paola Julia Mifsud; two *s* one *d. Educ:* St Julian's High Sch., Newport, Gwent. Western Mail: News Editor, 1966–73; Dep. Editor, 1973–80; Thomson Regional Newspapers: European Bureau Chief, 1980–86; London/City Editor, 1986–87; Launch Editor, Wales on Sunday, 1989. Trustee and Founder, British Bone Marrow Donor Appeal, 1987–. *Recreations:* walking, opera, reading, Rugby, cricket. *Address:* Fairfield, Ponthir Road, Caerleon, Gwent NP6 1NH. *T:* Caerleon (0633) 420648.

HUMPHRYS, John; Presenter, Today Programme, Radio 4, since 1987; *b* 17 Aug. 1943; *s* of George and Winifred Humphrys; *m* 1965, Edna Wilding; one *s* one *d. Educ:* Cardiff High School. BBC TV: Washington Correspondent, 1971–77; Southern Africa Correspondent, 1977–80; Diplomatic Correspondent, 1980–81; Presenter, 9 o'Clock News, 1981–86. *Recreations:* music, organic dairy farming (masochism). *Address:* c/o BBC Radio, Broadcasting House, W1A 1AA.

HUNN, Sir Jack (Kent), Kt 1976; CMG 1964; LLM; Retired as Secretary of Defence, New Zealand (1963–66); *b* 24 Aug. 1906; *m* 1st, 1932, Dorothy Murray; two *s*; 2nd, 1985, Mabel Duncan. *Educ:* Wairarapa Coll.; Auckland Univ. Public Trust Office, 1924–46; Actg Sec. of Justice, 1950; Public Service Comr, 1954–61; Actg Sec. of Internal Affairs and Dir of Civil Defence, 1959; Sec. for Maori Affairs and Maori Trustee, 1960–63. Reviewed Cook Islands Public Service, 1949 and 1954; Mem. NZ delegn to Duke of Edinburgh's Conf, 1956; Mem. UN Salary Review Cttee, 1956; reviewed organisation of South Pacific Commn, Noumea and Sydney, 1957, and of SEATO, Bangkok, 1959. Chairman: Wildlife Commission of Inquiry, 1968; Fire Safety Inquiry, 1969; Fire Service Council, 1973; Fire Service Commn, 1974; Electricity Distribution Enquiry, 1987. *Publications:* Hunn Report on Maori Affairs, 1960; Not Only Affairs Of State, 1982. *Address:* 17 Kereru Street, Waikanae, Wellington, New Zealand. *T:* (058) 35033.

HUNNISETT, Dr Roy Frank, FSA, FRHistS; on staff of Public Record Office, 1953–88; *b* 26 Feb. 1928; *s* of Frank Hunnisett and Alice (*née* Budden); *m* 1st, 1954, Edith Margaret Evans (marr. diss. 1989); 2nd, 1989, Janet Heather Stevenson. *Educ:* Bexhill Grammar Sch.; New Coll., Oxford (1st Cl. Hons Mod. Hist., 1952; Amy Mary Preston Read Scholar, 1952–53; MA, DPhil 1956). FRHistS 1961; FSA 1975. Lectr, New Coll., Oxford, 1957–63. Royal Historical Society: Alexander Prize, 1957; Mem. Council, 1974–77; Vice-Pres., 1979–82; Selden Society: Mem. Council, 1975–84, 1987–; Vice-Pres., 1984–87; Treasurer, Pipe Roll Soc., 1973–87. *Publications:* Calendar of Inquisitions Miscellaneous: (ed jtly) vol. IV, 1957 and vol. V, 1962; (ed) vol. VI, 1963 and vol. VII, 1968; The Medieval Coroners' Rolls, 1960; The Medieval Coroner, 1961; (ed) Bedfordshire Coroners' Rolls, 1961; (ed) Calendar of Nottinghamshire Coroners' Inquests 1485–1558, 1969; (contrib.) The Study of Medieval Records: essays in honour of Kathleen Major, 1971; Indexing for Editors, 1972; Editing Records for Publication, 1977; (ed jtly and contrib.) Medieval Legal Records edited in memory of C.A.F. Meekings, 1978; (ed) Wiltshire Coroners' Bills, 1752–1796, 1981; (ed) Sussex Coroners' Inquests 1485–1558, 1985; articles and revs in historical and legal jls. *Recreations:* Sussex, music, cricket. *Address:* 23 Byron Gardens, Sutton, Surrey SM1 3QG. *T:* 081–661 2618.

HUNSDON OF HUNSDON, Baron; *see* Aldenham, Baron.

HUNSWORTH, John Alfred; Director, Banking Information Service, 1954–81; *b* 23 Dec. 1921; *s* of late Fred Sheard Hunsworth and Lillian Margaret (*née* Wetmon); *m* 1972, Phyllis Sparshatt. *Educ:* Selhurst Grammar Sch.; LSE (BCom). Served War, 1941–46: commnd E Surrey Regt; served 2nd Punjab Regt, Indian Army, 1942–45. Dep. Editor, Bankers' Magazine, 1948–54. Freeman, City of London. *Publications:* contrib. prof. jls. *Recreations:* gardening, world travel, philately; formerly lawn tennis and Rugby football. *Address:* 29 West Hill, Sanderstead, Surrey. *T:* 081–657 2585. *Clubs:* Reform, Royal Over-Seas League; Surrey County Cricket.

HUNT, family name of **Barons Hunt** and **Hunt of Tanworth.**

HUNT, Baron, *cr* 1966, of Llanfair Waterdine (Life Peer); **(Henry Cecil) John Hunt,** KG 1979; Kt 1953; CBE 1945; DSO 1944; *b* 22 June 1910; *s* of late Capt. C. E. Hunt, MC, IA, and E. H. Hunt (*née* Crookshank); *m* 1936, Joy Mowbray-Green; four *d. Educ:* Marlborough Coll.; RMC, Sandhurst. Commissioned King's Royal Rifle Corps, 1930; seconded to Indian Police, 1934–35 and 1938–40 (Indian Police Medal, 1940). War of 1939–45: Comd 11th Bn KRRC, 1944; Comd 11th Indian Inf. Bde, 1944–46. Staff Coll., 1946; Joint Services Staff Coll., 1949; GSO 1, Jt Planning Staffs, MELF, 1946–48; Western Europe C's-in-C Cttee, 1950–51; Allied Land Forces, Central Europe, 1951–52; Col, Gen. Staff, HQ I (British) Corps, 1952; Asst Comdt, The Staff Coll., 1953–55; Comdr 168 Inf. Bde, TA, 1955–56; retired, 1956; Hon. Brigadier. Dir, Duke of Edinburgh's Award Scheme, 1956–66. Rector, Aberdeen Univ., 1963–66. Personal Adviser to Prime Minister during Nigerian Civil War, 1968–70. Chairman: Parole Bd for England and Wales, 1967–74; Adv. Cttee on Police in N Ireland, 1969; President: Nat. Assoc. of Youth Clubs, 1954–70; Council for Volunteers Overseas, 1968–74; Nat. Assoc. of Probation Officers, 1974–80; Rainer Foundn, 1971–85; Council for Nat. Parks, 1980–86; Nat. Assoc. for Outdoor Educn, 1991–; Mem., Royal Commn on the Press, 1974–77; Pres., Britain and Nepal Soc., 1960–75. Joined Social Democratic Party, 1981, Social and Liberal Democrats, 1988. Leader, British Expedition to Mount Everest, 1952–53. President: The Alpine Club, 1956–58; Climbers' Club, 1963–66; British Mountaineering Council, 1965–68; The National Ski Fedn, 1968–72; RGS, 1977–80 (Hon. Mem., 1984). Order 1st Class Gurkha Right Hand, 1953; Indian Everest Medal, 1953; Hubbard Medal (US), 1954; Founder's Medal, RGS, 1954; Lawrence Memorial Medal, RCAS, 1954; Hon. DCL Durham 1954; Hon. LLD: Aberdeen 1954; London 1954; City 1976; Leeds 1979; Hon. DSc Sheffield, 1989. *Publications:* The Ascent of Everest, 1953; Our Everest Adventure, 1954; (with C. Brasher) The Red Snows, 1959; Life is Meeting, 1978; (ed) My Favourite Mountaineering Stories, 1978; In Search of Adventure, 1989. *Recreation:* mountain activities. *Address:* Highway Cottage, Aston, Henley-on-Thames. *Clubs:* Alpine, Ski Club of Great Britain.
See also Hugh Hunt.

HUNT OF TANWORTH, Baron *cr* 1980 (Life Peer), of Stratford-upon-Avon in the county of Warwickshire; **John Joseph Benedict Hunt,** GCB 1977 (KCB 1973; CB 1968); Secretary of the Cabinet, 1973–79; Chairman: Banque Nationale de Paris plc, since 1980; BNP UK Holdings Ltd, since 1991; Director, Prudential Corporation plc, since 1980 (Deputy Chairman, 1982–85, Chairman, 1985–90); *b* 23 Oct. 1919; *er s* of Major Arthur L. Hunt and Daphne Hunt; *m* 1st, 1941, Hon. Magdalen Mary Lister Robinson (*d* 1971), *yr d* of 1st Baron Robinson; two *s* one *d*; 2nd, 1973, Madeleine Frances, *d* of Sir William Hume, CMG, FRCP, and *widow* of Sir John Charles, KCB, FRCP; one step *s* one step *d. Educ:* Downside; Magdalene College, Cambridge (Hon. Fellow, 1977). Served Royal Naval Volunteer Reserve, 1940–46, Lieut; Convoy escort, Western Approaches and in Far East. Home Civil Service, Admin. Class, 1946; Dominions Office, 1946; Priv. Sec. to Parly Under-Sec., 1947; 2nd Sec., Office of UK High Comr in Ceylon, 1948–50; Principal, 1949; Directing Staff, IDC, 1951–52; 1st Sec., Office of UK High Comr in Canada, 1953–56; Private Secretary to: Sec. of Cabinet and Perm. Sec. to Treasury and Head of Civil Service, 1956–58; Asst Secretary: CRO 1958; Cabinet Office, 1960; HM Treasury, 1962–67, Under-Sec., 1965; Dep. Sec., 1968 and First Civil Service Comr, Civil Service Dept, 1968–71; Third Sec., Treasury, 1971–72; Second Permanent Sec., Cabinet Office, 1972–73. Dep. Chm., Prudential Assurance Co. Ltd, 1982–85; Dir, IBM (UK) Ltd, 1980–90; Adv. Dir, Unilever plc, 1980–90. Chm., Disasters Emergency Cttee, 1981–89. Chm., Inquiry into Cable Expansion and Broadcasting Policy, 1982. Chm., Ditchley Foundn, 1983–91. Chm., The Tablet Publishing Co. Ltd, 1984–. Officier, Légion d'Honneur (France), 1987. *Recreation:* gardening. *Address:* 8 Wool Road, Wimbledon, SW20 0HW. *T:* 081–947 7640.

HUNT, Alan Charles, CMG 1990; HM Diplomatic Service; Counsellor, Foreign and Commonwealth Office, since 1990; *b* 5 March 1941; *s* of John Henry Hunt and Nelly Elizabeth Hunt (*née* Hunter); *m* 1978, Meredith Margaret Claydon; two *d. Educ:* Latymer Upper School, Hammersmith; Univ. of East Anglia. First Cl. Hons BA in European Studies. Clerical Officer, Min. of Power, 1958–59; FO, 1959–62; Vice-Consul, Tehran, 1962–64; Third Sec., Jedda, 1964–65; floating duties, Latin America, 1965–67; University, 1967–70; Second, later First Sec., FCO, 1970–73; First Sec., Panama, 1973–76; FCO 1976–77; First Sec. (Commercial), Madrid, 1977–81; FCO, 1981–83; Counsellor (Econ. and Commercial), Oslo, 1983–87; Head of British Interests Section, subseq. Chargé d'Affaires, Buenos Aires, 1987–90. *Recreations:* tennis, sailing, skiing, travel, reading, music. *Address:* c/o Foreign and Commonwealth Office, SW1A 2AH.

HUNT, Arthur James, OBE 1971; FRTPI, FRICS; Chief Reporter for Public Inquiries, Scottish Office, 1974–79; *b* 18 Nov. 1915; *s* of Edward Henry and Norah Hunt; *m* 1946, Fanny Betty Bacon; one *s* three *d. Educ:* Tauntons Sch., Southampton. Ordnance Survey, 1938–44; Planning Officer with West Sussex, Kent and Bucks County Councils, 1944–48; Asst County Planning Officer, East Sussex CC, 1948–52; Town Planning Officer, City of Durban, SA, 1953–61; Sen. and Principal Planning Inspector, Min. of Housing and Local Govt, 1961–68; Mem., Roskill Commn on the Third London Airport, 1968–70; Superintending Inspector, Dept of the Environment, 1971–74. *Recreations:* sailing, gardening, caravan touring. *Address:* Pentlands, 4 West Avenue, Middleton-on-Sea, West Sussex PO22 6EF.

HUNT, Rt. Hon. David James Fletcher, PC 1990; MBE 1973; MP (C) Wirral West, since 1983 (Wirral, March 1976–1983); Secretary of State for Wales, since 1990; *b* 21 May 1942; *s* of late Alan Nathaniel Hunt, OBE and of Jessie Edna Ellis Northrop Hunt; *m* 1973, Patricia Margery (*née* Orchard); two *s* two *d. Educ:* Liverpool Coll.; Montpellier Univ.; Bristol Univ. (LLB); Guildford Coll. of Law. Solicitor of Supreme Court of Judicature, admitted 1968; Partner: Stanleys & Simpson North, 1977–88; Beachcroft Stanleys, 1988–; Partner, then Consultant, Stanley Wasbrough & Co., 1965–85; Dir, BET Omnibus Services Ltd, 1980–81. Chm., Cons. Shipping and Shipbuilding Cttee, 1977–79; Vice-Chm., Parly Youth Lobby, 1978–80; Vice-Pres., Cons. Group for Europe, 1984– (Vice-Chm., 1978–81; Chm, 1981–82); a Vice-Chm., Cons. Party, 1983–85. PPS to Sec. of State for Trade, 1979–81, to Sec. of State for Defence, 1981; an Asst Govt Whip, 1981–83; a Lord Comr of HM Treasury, 1983–84; Parly Under-Sec. of State, Dept of Energy, 1984–87; Treasurer of HM Household and Dep. Chief Whip, 1987–89; Minister for Local Govt and Inner Cities, DoE, 1989–90. Chm., Bristol Univ. Conservatives, 1964–65; winner of Observer Mace for British Universities Debating Competition, 1965–66; Nat. Vice-Chm., FUCUA, 1965–66; Chm., Bristol City CPC, 1965–68; Nat. Vice-Chm., YCNAC, 1967–69; Chm., Bristol Fedn of YCs, 1970–71; Chm., British Youth Council, 1971–74 (Pres., 1978–80); Vice-Pres., Nat. YCs, 1986–88 (Chm., 1972–73); Vice-Chm., Nat. Union of Cons. and Unionist Assocs, 1974–76. Vice-Pres., Nat. Playbus Assoc., 1981–. Contested (C) Bristol South, 1970, Kingswood, 1974. Member: South Western Economic Planning Council, 1972–76; Adv. Cttee on Pop Festivals, 1972–75. *Publications:* Europe Right Ahead, 1978; A Time for Youth, 1978. *Recreations:* cricket, walking. *Address:* Hoylake Conservative Club, Meols Drive, Hoylake, Wirral. *T:* 051–632 1052; House of Commons, SW1A 0AA. *T:* 071–219 5132. *Club:* Hurlingham.

HUNT, David Roderic Notley; QC 1987; a Recorder, since 1991; *b* 22 June 1947; *s* of Dr Geoffrey Notley Hunt and Deborah Katharine Rosamund Hunt; *m* 1974, Alison Connell Jelf; two *s. Educ:* Charterhouse School; Trinity College, Cambridge (MA Hons). Called to the Bar, Gray's Inn, 1969. *Recreations:* sailing, ski-ing, golf. *Address:* 2 Hare Court, Temple, EC4Y 7BH. *T:* 071–583 1770.

HUNT, Sir David (Wathen Stather), KCMG 1963 (CMG 1959); OBE 1943; HM Diplomatic Service, retired; Director: Observer Newspapers, since 1982; Trigraph Ltd, since 1988; *b* 25 Sept. 1913; *s* of late Canon B. P. W. Stather Hunt, DD, and late Elizabeth Milner; *m* 1st, 1948, Pamela Muriel Medawar; two *s*; 2nd, 1968, Iro Myrianthousis. *Educ:* St Lawrence Coll.; Wadham Coll., Oxford. 1st Class Hon. Mods. 1934; 1st Class Lit. Hum. 1936; Thomas Whitcombe Greene Prize, 1936; Diploma in Classical Archæology, 1937; Fellow of Magdalen Coll., 1937. Served 1st Bn Welch Regt and General Staff in Middle East, Balkans, North Africa, Sicily, Italy, 1940–46 (despatches 3 times, OBE, US Bronze Star); GSO1 18th Army Group, 1943; 15th Army Group, 1943–45; Col General Staff, Allied Force HQ, 1945–46; attached staff Governor-General Canada, 1946–47; released and granted hon. rank of Colonel, 1947. Principal, Dominions Office, 1947; 1st Secretary, Pretoria, 1948–49; Private Secretary to Prime Minister (Mr Attlee), 1950–51, (Mr Churchill) 1951–52; Asst Secretary, 1952; Deputy High Commissioner for UK, Lahore, 1954–56; Head of Central African Dept, Commonwealth Relations Office, 1956–59; Asst Under Secretary of State, Commonwealth Relations Office, 1959–60; accompanied the Prime Minister as an Adviser, on African tour, Jan.-Feb. 1960; Dep. High Comr for the UK in Lagos, Fedn of Nigeria, Oct. 1960–62; High Comr in Uganda, 1962–65; in Cyprus, 1965–67; in Nigeria, 1967–69; Ambassador to Brazil, 1969–73. Dep. Chm., Exim Credit Management and Consultants, 1974–77, Consultant, 1978–82. Chm., Bd of Governors, Commonwealth Inst., 1974–84. Mem. Appts Commn, Press Council, 1977–82. Montague Burton Vis. Prof. of Internat. Relations, Univ. of Edinburgh, 1980. President: Classical Assoc., 1981–82; Soc. for Promotion of Hellenic Studies, 1986–90. FSA 1984. Corresp. Mem., Brazilian Acad. of Arts, 1972. BBC TV Mastermind, 1977 and Mastermind of Masterminds, 1982. Hon. DHum Ball State Univ., 1991. US Bronze Star 1945; Grand Cross, Order of the Southern Cross, Brazil, 1985. *Publications:* A Don at War, 1966, 2nd edn 1990; On the Spot, 1975; Footprints in Cyprus, 1982, rev. edn 1990; (ed and trans.) Gothic Art and the Renaissance in Cyprus, by Camille Enlart, 1987; (ed with Iro Hunt) Caterina Cornaro: Queen of Cyprus, 1989; articles in Annual of British School of Archæology at Athens and Journal of Hellenic Studies; Editor, The Times Yearbook of World Affairs, 1978–81. *Recreations:*

reading, writing, roses. *Address:* Old Place, Lindfield, West Sussex RH16 2HU. *T:* Lindfield (04447) 2298. *Clubs:* Athenæum, Beefsteak; Pen Clube do Brasil.

HUNT, Derek Simpson; Chairman and Chief Executive, MFI Furniture Group Ltd, since 1987; Chairman and Managing Director, MFI Furniture Centres Ltd, since 1987; *b* 9 June 1939; *s* of John William Hunt and Elizabeth (*née* Simpson); *m* 1967, Sandra Phyllis Jones; two *s. Educ:* Queen Elizabeth Grammar Sch., Darlington, Co. Durham. Joined MFI as Retail Area Controller, 1972; Branch Ops Controller, 1973; Dir, MFI Furniture Centres, 1974; MFI Furniture Group: Dir, 1976; Man. Dir, 1981; Chm., 1984; during merger with Asda, also Chief Exec. and Dep. Chm., Asda-MFI, 1985–87; returned to MFI and effected management buy-out, 1987. Gov., Ashridge Management Coll., 1986–. Founding Fellow, Nat. Children's Home George Thomas Soc., 1989. Hon. Fellow, Manchester Polytechnic, 1988. *Recreations:* sailing, Rugby Union, fishing. *Address:* Southon House, 333 The Hyde, Edgware Road, Colindale, NW9 6TD. *T:* 081–200 8000.

HUNT, Rt. Rev. Desmond Charles; a Suffragan Bishop of Toronto, 1981–86; *b* 14 Sept. 1918; *s* of George P. and Kathleen Hunt; *m* 1944, Naomi F. Naylor; two *s* two *d. Educ:* Univ. of Toronto (BA). Rector: Trinity Church, Quebec City, 1943; St John's, Johnstown, USA, 1949; St James, Kingston, Ont., 1953; Church of the Messiah, Toronto, 1969. Hon. DD, Wycliffe Coll., Toronto, 1980. *Publication:* Benefits of His Passion, 1988. *Address:* Bishopslodge, Box 1150, Lakefield, Ontario K0L 2H0, Canada. *T:* 705–652–7372.

HUNT, Donald Frederick, FRCO; Master of the Choristers and Organist, Worcester Cathedral, since 1975; *b* 26 July 1930; *m* 1954, Josephine Benbow; two *s* two *d. Educ:* King's School, Gloucester. ARCM; ARCO 1951; FRCO(CHM) 1954. Asst Organist, Gloucester Cathedral, 1947–54; Director of Music: St John's Church, Torquay, 1954–57; Leeds Parish Church, 1957–75; Leeds City Organist, 1973–75. Chorus Dir, Leeds Festival, 1962–75; Conductor: Halifax Choral Soc., 1957–88; Leeds Philharmonic Soc., 1962–75; Worcester Festival Choral Soc., 1975–; Worcester Three Choirs Festival, 1975–; Artistic Dir, Bromsgrove Festival, 1981–91. Hon DMus Leeds 1975. *Publications:* Magnificat and Nunc Dimittis, 1972; Missa Brevis, 1973; Versicles and Responses, 1973; God be gracious, 1984; Missa Nova, 1985; Mass for Three Voices, 1986; S. S. Wesley: cathedral musician, 1990; anthems and carols. *Recreations:* cricket, poetry, travel. *Address:* 13 College Green, Worcester WR1 2LH. *T:* Worcester (0905) 23555.

HUNT, Gilbert Adams, CBE 1967; Director, Equity & General (formerly Emray) PLC, 1982–90; *b* Wolverhampton, 29 Dec. 1914; *s* of late Harold William Hunt, MBE, St Helen's, IoW; *m* 1975, Diane Rosemary, *d* of Eric O. Cook; one *d. Educ:* Old Hall, Wellington; Malvern Coll., Worcester. Director, High Duty Alloys, Slough, 1950–54; Dir and Gen. Man., High Duty Alloys (Dir, HDA, Canada, Northern Steel Scaffold & Engrg Co., all subsids Hawker Siddeley Gp), 1954–60; Man. Dir, Massey-Ferguson (UK) Ltd; Jt Man. Dir, Massey-Ferguson-Perkins; Dir, Massey-Ferguson Holdings Ltd; Chm. and Man. Dir, Massey-Ferguson (Eire) Ltd; Chm., Massey-Ferguson (Farm Services Ltd), 1960–67; Managing Dir, 1967–73, Chief Exec. Officer, 1967–76, Chm., 1973–79, Rootes Motors Ltd, later Chrysler UK Ltd (Pres., April-June 1979). Chairman: Thurgar Bardex, 1977–85 (Dep. Chm., 1985–89; non-exec. Dir, 1985–90); Hedin Ltd, 1978–85; Dir, Technology Transfer Associates, 1980–88. Chm., Cttee for Industrial Technologies, DTI, 1972–78. President: Agricultural Engrs Association Ltd, 1965; The Society of Motor Manufacturers and Traders Ltd, 1972–74. Freeman, City of London, 1968. CEng, CIMechE, FIProdE, MIBF. Hon. DSc Cranfield, 1973. *Recreations:* golfing, sailing. *Address:* The Dutch House, Sheepstreet Lane, Etchingham, E Sussex TN19 7AZ.

HUNT, (Henry) Holman, CBE 1988; Deputy Chairman, 1985–91, Member, 1980–91, Monopolies and Mergers Commission; *b* 13 May 1924; *s* of Henry Hunt and Jessie Brenda Beale; *m* 1954, Sonja Blom; one *s* two *d. Educ:* Queens Park Sch., Glasgow; Glasgow Univ. (MA). FCMA, FIMC, FBCS, FInstAM. Caledonian Insce Co., 1940–43; RAF, 1943–46; Glasgow Univ., 1946–50; Cadbury Bros, 1950–51; PA Management Consultants: Consultant, 1952–57; Manager, Office Organisation, 1958–63; Dir, Computer Div., 1964–69; Bd Dir, 1970–83; Man. Dir, PA Computers and Telecommunications, 1976–83. Pres., Inst. of Management Consultants, 1974–75. FRSA 1988. *Recreations:* music, reading, walking, travel, photography, vegetable gardening. *Address:* 28 The Ridings, Epsom, Surrey KT18 5JJ. *T:* Epsom (0372) 720974. *Club:* Caledonian.

HUNT, Hugh (Sydney), CBE 1977; MA; Professor of Drama, University of Manchester, 1961–73, now Emeritus; *b* 25 Sept. 1911; *s* of Captain C. E. Hunt, MC, and late Ethel Helen (née Crookshank); *m* 1940, Janet Mary (*née* Gordon); one *s* one *d. Educ:* Marlborough Coll.; Magdalen Coll., Oxford. BA Oxon 1934, MA Oxon 1961. Hon. MA Manchester 1965. Pres. of OUDS, 1933–34; Producer: Maddermarket Theatre, Norwich, 1934; Croydon Repertory and Westminster Theatres, 1934–35; Producer, Abbey Theatre, Dublin, 1935–38; produced The White Steed, Cort Theatre, NY. Entered HM Forces, 1939; served War of 1939–45, with Scots Guards, King's Royal Rifle Corps, and Intelligence Service; demobilised, 1945. Director of Bristol Old Vic Company, 1945–49; Director Old Vic Company, London, 1949–53; Adjudicator Canadian Drama Festival Finals, 1954; Executive Officer, Elizabethan Theatre Trust, Australia, 1955–60; Artistic Dir, Abbey Theatre, Dublin, 1969–71. Mem., Welsh Arts Council, 1979–85 (Chm., Drama Cttee, 1982–85). *Produced:* The Cherry Orchard, 1948, Love's Labour's Lost, 1949, Hamlet, 1950, New Theatre; Old Vic Seasons, 1951–53: Twelfth Night, Merry Wives of Windsor, Romeo and Juliet, Merchant of Venice, Julius Caesar; The Living Room, New York, 1954; in Australia, Medea, 1955, Twelfth Night, 1956, Hamlet, 1957, Julius Caesar, 1959; The Shaughraun, World Theatre Season, Dublin, 1968; Abbey Theatre Productions include: The Well of the Saints, 1969; The Hostage, 1970; The Morning after Optimism, 1971; Arrah-na-Pogue, 1972; The Silver Tassie, 1972; The Three Sisters, 1973; The Vicar of Wakefield, 1974; Red Roses for Me, 1980; Sydney Opera House: Peer Gynt, 1975; The Plough and the Stars, 1977. *Publications:* Old Vic Prefaces, 1954; The Director in the Theatre, 1954; The Making of Australian Theatre, 1960; The Live Theatre, 1962; The Revels History of Drama in the English Language, vol. VII, sections 1 and 2, 1978; The Abbey, Ireland's National Theatre, 1979; Sean O'Casey, 1980; author or co-author of several Irish plays including The Invincibles and In The Train. *Address:* Cae Terfyn, Criccieth, Gwynedd LL52 0SA.

See also Baron Hunt.

HUNT, James; *see* Hunt, P. J.

HUNT, James Simon Wallis; BBC television broadcaster, since 1980; *b* 29 Aug. 1947; *s* of Wallis Glyn Gunthorpe Hunt and Susan Noel Wentworth Hunt (*née* Davis); *m* 1983, Sarah Marian Lomax; two *s. Educ:* Wellington College. Racing driver with Hesketh and McLaren teams, 1973–79; world motor racing champion, 1976. *Address:* 2 Seagrave Road, SW6 1RR. *T:* 071–381 6366.

HUNT, Sir John (Leonard), Kt 1989; MP (C) Ravensbourne, since 1974 (Bromley, 1964–74); *b* 27 Oct. 1929; *s* of late William John Hunt and of Dora Maud Hunt, Keston, Kent; unmarried. *Educ:* Dulwich Coll. Councillor, Bromley Borough Council, 1953–65; Alderman, Bromley Borough Council, 1961–65; Mayor of Bromley, 1963–64. Contested (C) S Lewisham, Gen. Election, 1959. Member: Select Cttee on Home Affairs (and Mem., Sub-Cttee on Race Relations and Immigration), 1979–87; Speaker's Panel of Chairmen, 1980–. Jt-Chm., British-Caribbean Assoc., 1968–77 and 1984–; Chm., Indo-British Parly Gp, 1979–; UK Rep. at Council of Europe and WEU, 1973–77 and 1988–. Mem., BBC Gen. Adv. Council, 1975–87. Pres., Inst. of Administrative Accountants, subseq. of Financial Accountants, 1970–88. Mem. of London Stock Exchange, 1958–70. Freeman, City of London, 1986; Freeman, Haberdashers' Co., 1986. *Recreations:* foreign travel, gardening, good food. *Address:* House of Commons, SW1. *T:* 071–219 4530.

HUNT, John Maitland, MA, BLitt; Headmaster of Roedean Jan. 1971–April 1984; *b* 4 March 1932; *s* of Richard Herbert Alexander Hunt and Eileen Mary Isabelle Hunt (*née* Witt); *m* 1969, Sarah, *d* of Lt-Gen. Sir Derek Lang, *qv*; two *s. Educ:* Radley College; Wadham College, Oxford. BA 1956; BLitt 1959; MA 1960. Assistant Master, Stowe School, 1958–70 (Sixth Form tutor in Geography). Chm., Bd of Managers, Common Entrance Exam. for Girls' Schs, 1974–81. *Publications:* various articles on fine arts and architecture. *Recreations:* estate management, fine arts, writing, travel. *Address:* Logie, Dunfermline, Fife KY12 8QN. *Club:* Commonwealth Trust.

HUNT, Prof. Julian Charles Roland, PhD; FRS 1989; Professor in Fluid Mechanics, University of Cambridge, since 1990; Fellow of Trinity College, Cambridge, since 1966; *b* 5 Sept. 1941; *s* of Roland Charles Colin Hunt, *qv*; *m* 1965, Marylla Ellen Shephard; one *s* two *d. Educ:* Westminster Sch.; Trinity Coll., Cambridge (BA 1963; PhD 1967); Univ. of Warwick. Post-doctoral res., Cornell Univ., USA, 1967; Res. Officer, Central Electricity Res. Labs, 1968–70; University of Cambridge: Lectr in Applied Maths and in Engrg, 1970–78; Reader in Fluid Mechanics, 1978–90. Visiting Professor: Colorado State Univ., 1975; NC State Univ., and Envmtl Protection Agency, 1977; Univ. of Colorado, 1980; Nat. Center for Atmospheric Res., Boulder, Colo, 1983. Founder Dir, Cambridge Envmtl Res. Consultants Ltd, 1986–. Vice Pres., IMA, 1989– (Hon. Sec., 1984–89); Gen. Sec., European Res. Community for Flow Turbulence and Combustions, 1988–. Councillor, Cambridge CC, 1971–74 (Leader, Labour Gp, 1972). *Publications:* scientific pubns in Jl of Fluid Mechanics, Atmospheric Envmt, Qly Jl of Royal Meteorol Soc., etc. *Address:* Department of Applied Mathematics and Theoretical Physics, Silver Street, Cambridge CB3 9EW. *T:* Cambridge (0223) 337870.

HUNT, Brig. Kenneth, OBE 1955; MC 1943; Vice-President, International Institute for Strategic Studies, since 1988 (Deputy Director, 1967–77); *b* 26 May 1914; *s* of late John Hunt and Elizabeth Hunt; *m* 1939, Mary Mabel Crickett; two *s* (and one *d* decd). *Educ:* Chatham House Sch., Ramsgate; sc Camberley; idc. Commissioned into Royal Artillery, 1940; served, Africa, Italy, Austria, with HAC, 1 RHA and 2 RHA, 1942–46 (despatches thrice); Bt Lt-Col 1955; CO 40 Fd Regt RA, 1958–60; CRA 51 Highland Div., 1961–63; IDC 1963; Dep. Standing Gp Rep. to N Atlantic Council, 1964–66; resigned commission, 1967. Dir, British Atlantic Cttee, 1978–81. Specialist Adviser to House of Commons Defence Cttee, 1971–84. Visiting Professor: Fletcher Sch. of Law, Cambridge, Mass, 1975; Univ. of S California, 1978–79; Univ. of Surrey, 1978–87. Mem. Council, RUSI, 1977; Fellow, Inst. of Security, Tokyo, 1979–. Freeman, City of London, 1977. Hon. Dr (PolSci), Korea Univ., 1977. Order of Rising Sun, 3rd cl. (Japan), 1984. *Publications:* NATO without France, 1967; The Requirements of Military Technology, 1967; Defence with Fewer Men, 1973; (ed) The Military Balance, 1967–77; (jtly) The Third World War, 1978; (jtly) Asian Security, annually, 1979–89; Europe in the Western Alliance, 1988; contribs to learned jls, and chapters in books, in UK, USA, E Asia. *Recreations:* fly-fishing, listening to music. *Address:* 22 The Green, Ewell, Surrey KT17 3JN. *T:* 081–393 7906. *Clubs:* Army and Navy; International House of Japan (Tokyo).

HUNT, Maj.-Gen. Malcolm Peter John, OBE 1984; Commander, British Forces Falkland Islands, 1990–91; *b* 19 Nov. 1938; *s* of Peter Gordon Hunt and Rachel Margaret Hunt (*née* Owston); *m* 1962, Margaret Peat; two *s. Educ:* St John's Sch., Leatherhead; Staff Coll., Camberley. Joined Royal Marines, 1957; service in Malta, Aden and NI; OC RM Detachment, HMS Nubian, 1966–68; Instructor, Army Staff Coll., 1979–81; CO, 40 Commando RM, 1981–83 (Falklands, NI); Internat. Mil. Staff, HQ NATO, 1984–87; Dir, NATO on Defence Commitments Staff, MoD, 1987–90. *Recreations:* sport, politics, reading, theatre. *Address:* c/o National Westminster Bank, 52 Royal Parade, Plymouth, Devon PL1 1ED.

HUNT, Martin Robert, RDI 1981; Partner, Queensberry Hunt, design consultancy, since 1966; *b* 4 Sept. 1942; *s* of Frederick and Frances Hunt; *m* 1st, 1963, Pauline Hunt; one *s* one *d*; 2nd, 1980, Glenys Barton; one *s. Educ:* Monmouth. DesRCA, FCSD. Graduated RCA 1966 (Hon. Fellow 1987); formed Queensberry Hunt Partnership, 1966; part time Tutor, RCA, 1968; Head of Glass Sch., RCA, 1974–86. *Recreation:* sailing. *Address:* 24 Brook Mews North, W2. *T:* 071–724 3701. *Club:* Little Ship.

HUNT, Maurice William; Deputy Director-General since 1989, and Secretary, since 1986, Confederation of British Industry; *b* 30 Aug. 1936; *s* of Maurice Hunt and Helen Hunt (*née* Andrews); *m* 1960, Jean Mary Ellis; one *s* one *d. Educ:* Selhurst Grammar School, Croydon; LSE (BSc Econ). ACIB. Nat. Service, RAF, 1955–57. ANZ Bank, 1953–66; Joint Iron Council, 1966–67; Board of Trade, 1967; Asst Sec., DTI, 1974; RCDS 1982; Dir, Membership, CBI, 1984; Exec. Dir (Ops), CBI, 1987. *Recreations:* walking, gardening, sailing. *Address:* 24 Fairford Close, Haywards Heath, W Sussex RH16 3EF. *T:* Haywards Heath (0444) 452916. *Club:* Royal Automobile.

HUNT, Adm. Sir Nicholas (John Streynsham), GCB 1987 (KCB 1985); LVO 1961; Commander-in-Chief, Fleet, and Allied Commander-in-Chief, Channel and Eastern Atlantic, 1985–87, retired; Director-General, General Council of British Shipping, since 1991; *b* 7 Nov. 1930; *s* of Brig. and Mrs J. M. Hunt; *m* 1966, Meriel Eve Givan; two *s* one *d. Educ:* BRNC, Dartmouth. CO HMS Burnaston, HMS Palliser, HMS Troubridge, HMS Intrepid, and BRNC, Dartmouth; Asst Private Sec. to late Princess Marina, Duchess of Kent; Executive Officer, HMS Ark Royal, 1969–71; RCDS 1974; Dir of Naval Plans, 1976–78; Flag Officer, Second Flotilla, 1980–81; Dir-Gen., Naval Manpower and Training, 1981–83; Flag Officer, Scotland and NI, and Port Admiral Rosyth, 1983–85. Dep. Man. Dir (Orgn and Develt), Eurotunnel, 1987–89. Chm., SW Surrey DHA, 1990–. Comr, CWGC, 1988; Vice-Pres., E-SU of Malta, 1988. CBIM, 1988. Freeman, City of London, 1988. *Recreation:* family. *Clubs:* Boodle's, Royal Navy of 1765 and 1785 (Chm.); Woodroffs.

HUNT, Prof. Norman Charles, CBE 1975; Professor of Business Studies, 1967–84, Vice-Principal, 1980–84, University of Edinburgh, now Emeritus Professor; *b* 6 April 1918; *s* of Charles Hunt and Charlotte (*née* Jackson), Swindon, Wilts; *m* 1942, Lorna Mary, 2nd *d* of Mary and William Arthur Mann, Swindon, Wilts; two *s. Educ:* Commonweal Sch.; Swindon Coll.; University of London (Sir Edward Stern Schol., BCom 1st cl. hons); PhD (Edinburgh). On Staff (Research Dept and Personal Staff of Chief Mechanical Engineer); former GWR Co., 1934–45. Lectr in Organisation of Industry and Commerce, University of Edinburgh, 1946–53; Dir of Studies in Commerce, 1948–53; Prof. of Organisation of Industry and Commerce, 1953–66; Dean of Faculty of Social Sciences, 1962–64. Member: Departmental Cttee on Fire Service, 1967–70; Rubber Industry NEDC, 1968–71; UGC, 1969–78 (Vice-Chm., 1974–76); ODM Working Party on Management Educn and

Training in Developing Countries, 1968–69; Bd of Governors (and Chm., Management Develt Cttee), Council for Technical Educn and Training in Overseas Countries, 1971–75; Police Adv. Bd for Scotland, 1971–75; Council for Tertiary Educn in Scotland, 1979–84; CNAA, 1979–84. Consultant: UNIDO, 1973–; Hong Kong Baptist Coll., 1984–87. Chairman: R. and R. Clark Ltd, 1967–70; William Thyne Ltd, 1967–70; Director: William Thyne (Holdings) Ltd, 1963–70; William Thyne (Plastics) Ltd, 1967–70; INMAP Ltd, 1984–86; UnivEd Technologies Ltd, 1984– (Chm. 1984–86). Hon. DLitt Loughborough, 1975. *Publications:* Methods of Wage Payment in British Industry, 1951; (with W. D. Reekie) Management in the Social and Safety Services, 1974; articles in economic and management jls on industrial organisation, industrial relations, and management problems. *Recreations:* photography, motoring, foreign travel. *Address:* 65 Ravelston Dykes Road, Edinburgh EH4 3NU.

HUNT, (Patrick) James; QC 1987; a Recorder of the Crown Court, since 1982; *b* 26 Jan. 1943; *s* of Thomas Ronald Clifford Hunt and Doreen Gwyneth Katarina Hunt; *m* 1969, Susan Jennifer Goodhead; one *s* three *d*. *Educ:* Ashby de la Zouch Boys' Grammar Sch.; Keble Coll., Oxford (MA Mod. History). Called to the Bar, Gray's Inn, 1968; in practice on Midland and Oxford Circuit, from London chambers. Mem., Gen. Council of the Bar, 1989–. Legal Assessor to Disciplinary Cttee, RCVS, 1990–. *Recreations:* singing, gardening, stonework. *Address:* Easton Hall, Easton on the Hill, Stamford, Lincs PE9 3LL. *T:* Stamford (0780) 52266; (chambers) 1 King's Bench Walk, Temple, EC4.

HUNT, Peter John, FRICS; Chairman and Managing Director, Land Securities PLC, since 1987 (Managing Director, since 1978); *b* 1 July 1933; *s* of Prof. Herbert James Hunt and Sheila Jessamine Hunt; *m*; one *s*. *Educ:* Bedford Sch.; College of Estate Management (BScEstMan). Borrett and Borrett, 1956–60; Chamberlain Gp, 1960–64; Land Securities Gp, 1964–. Member: Covent Garden Market Authority, 1975–; Council, British Property Fedn, 1978–. Chm., Central London Housing Trust for the Aged, 1981–. *Recreations:* boating, tennis, squash. *Address:* 37 Devonshire Mews West, W1N 1QF.

HUNT, Philip Alexander; Director, National Association of Health Authorities and Trusts, since 1990; *b* 19 May 1949; *s* of Rev. Philip Lacey Winter Hunt and Muriel Hunt; *m* 1st, 1974 (marr. diss.); one *d*: 2nd, 1988, Selina Ruth Helen Stewart; one *s* one *d*. *Educ:* City of Oxford High Sch.; Oxford Sch.; Leeds Univ. (BA). LHSM. Oxford RHB, 1972–74; Nuffield Orthopaedic Centre, 1974–75; Mem., Oxfordshire AHA, 1975–77; Sec. Edgware/Hendon Community Health Council, 1975–78; Asst Sec., 1978–79, Asst Dir, 1979–84, Dir, 1984–90, NAHA. Member: Oxford City Council, 1973–79; Birmingham City Council, 1980–82; Council, Internat Hosp. Fedn, 1986–; King's Fund Inst. Adv. Cttee, 1991–. *Publications:* The Health Authority Member (discussion paper) (with W. E. Hall), 1978; articles in Health Service publications. *Recreations:* music, cycling, swimming. *Address:* National Association of Health Authorities and Trusts, Birmingham Research Park, Vincent Drive, Birmingham B15 2SQ; 22 Springfield Road, King's Heath, Birmingham B14 7DS. *T:* 021–471 4444.

HUNT, Philip Bodley; Director, Welsh Office Industry Department, 1975–76; *b* 28 July 1916; *s* of Bernard and Janet Hunt; *m* 1940, Eleanor Margaret Parnell (*d* 1989); three *s* one *d*. *Educ:* Sedbergh Sch.; Christ Church, Oxford (MA). Joined Board of Trade, 1946; Trade Commissioner, Montreal, 1952; Principal Trade Commissioner, Vancouver, 1955; Commercial Counsellor, Canberra, 1957; returned Board of Trade, 1962; Dept of Economic Affairs, 1964–65; Director, London & SE Region, BoT, 1968; Dir, DTI Office for Wales, 1972–75. Chm., S Wales Marriage Guidance Council, 1974–83; Mem. Nat. Exec., Nat. Marriage Guidance Council, 1977–83; Dept Mem. of Panel, County Structure Plans of S and W Glamorgan, 1978, of Gwent and Mid Glamorgan, 1979; Vice-Pres., Develt Corporation for Wales, 1980–83. Silver Jubilee Medal, 1977. *Recreations:* gardening, music. *Address:* 93 Station Road, Llanishen, Cardiff CF4 5UU. *T:* Cardiff (0222) 750480.

HUNT, Sir Rex (Masterman), Kt 1982; CMG 1980; HM Diplomatic Service, retired; Civil Commissioner, Falkland Islands, 1982–Sept. 1985, and High Commissioner, British Antarctic Territory, 1980–85 (Governor and Commander-in-Chief, Falkland Islands, 1980–82; Governor, Oct. 1985); *b* 29 June 1926; *s* of H. W. Hunt and Ivy Masterman; *m* 1951, Mavis Amanda Buckland; one *s* one *d*. *Educ:* Coatham Sch.; St Peter's Coll., Oxford (BA). Served with RAF, 1944–48; Flt Lt RAFO. Entered HM Overseas Civil Service, 1951; District Comr, Uganda, 1962; CRO, 1963–64; 1st Sec., Kuching, 1964–65; Jesselton, 1965–67; Brunei, 1967; 1st Sec. (Econ.), Ankara, 1968–70; 1st Sec. and Head of Chancery, Jakarta, 1970–72; Asst ME Dept, FCO, 1972–74; Counsellor, Saigon, 1974–75, Kuala Lumpur, 1976–77; Dep. High Comr, Kuala Lumpur, 1977–79. Hon. Air Cdre, City of Lincoln Sqn, RAuxAF, 1987–. Hon. Freeman, City of London, 1981. *Publication:* My Falkland Days, 1992. *Recreations:* golf, gardening. *Address:* Old Woodside, Broomfield Park, Sunningdale, Berks SL5 0JS. *Club:* Wentworth.

HUNT, Richard Bruce; Chairman, R. B. Hunt and Partners Ltd, since 1966; *b* 15 Dec. 1927; *s* of Percy Thompson Hunt and Thelma Constance Hunt; *m* 1972, Ulrike Dorothea Schmidt; two *d*. *Educ:* Christ's Hospital. FICS. Served Royal Signals, 1946–48; joined Merchant Bankers Ralli Brothers, 1949–66; formed own company, R. B. Hunt and Partners, 1966. Chm., Baltic Exchange Ltd, 1985–87 (Dir, 1977–80, re-elected, 1981–87); Dir, Howe Robinson and Co. Ltd, 1990–. Liveryman, Shipwrights' Co. *Recreations:* golf, ski-ing. *Address:* R. B. Hunt & Partners, 77 Mansell Street, E1 8AF. *T:* 071–488 3444. *Clubs:* Hurlingham, Royal Wimbledon Golf; Royal Lymington Yacht.

HUNT, Richard Henry; Chief Registrar of the High Court of Justice in Bankruptcy, 1980–84, retired; *b* 19 Jan. 1912; *s* of late Francis John and Lucy Edwyna Louise Hunt; *m* 1947, Peggy Ashworth Richardson; two *s*. *Educ:* Marlborough Coll.; Queen's Coll., Oxford. Called to Bar, 1936. Served with RA, 1939–45: Western Desert, Greece and Crete campaigns (PoW, Crete, 1941). Elected Bencher, Middle Temple, 1964. Registrar of the High Court of Justice in Bankruptcy, 1966–80. *Recreations:* foreign travel, languages. *Club:* Royal Ocean Racing.

HUNT, (Richard) Tim(othy), PhD; FRS 1991; Senior Scientist, Imperial Cancer Research Fund, since 1990; Fellow of Clare College, Cambridge, since 1968; *b* 19 Feb. 1943; *s* of Richard William Hunt and Katherine Eva Rowland; *m* 1971, Missy Cusick (marr. diss. 1974). *Educ:* Dragon Sch.; Magdalen Coll. Sch., Oxford; Clare Coll., Cambridge (BA Nat. Scis 1964; PhD 1968). Univ. Lectr in Biochem., Cambridge, 1981–90 (Junior Proctor, 1982–83). Mem., EMBO. *Publications:* Molecular Biology of the Cell Problems (with John Wilson), 1989; articles in cell and molecular biology jls. *Recreation:* marine stations. *Address:* Imperial Cancer Research Fund, Clare Hall Laboratories, South Mimms, Potters Bar, Herts EN6 3LD. *T:* Potters Bar (0707) 44444.

HUNT, Robert Alan, OBE 1984; Assistant Commissioner, Territorial Operations Department, Metropolitan Police, since 1990; *b* 6 July 1935; *s* of Peter and Minnie Hunt; *m* 1956, Jean White; one *s* three *d*. *Educ:* Dulwich Coll.; London Univ. (LLB external 1970). Served in RA. Joined Metropolitan Police, 1955: Chief Superintendent, 1973; Comdr, 1976; Dep. Asst Comr, 1981. *Recreations:* music—traditional and light classical, reading, the family. *Address:* New Scotland Yard, Broadway, SW1H 0BG. *T:* 071–230 1212.

HUNT, Sir Robert (Frederick), Kt 1979; CBE 1974; DL; Chairman, Dowty Group PLC, 1975–86; Deputy Chairman, Rover (formerly BL plc), since 1982 (Director, since 1980); Director, Charter Consolidated, since 1983; *b* 11 May 1918; *s* of late Arthur Hunt, Cheltenham and Kathleen Alice Cotton; *m* 1st, 1947, Joy Patricia Molly (*d* 1984), *d* of late Charles Leslie Harding, Cheltenham; four *d*; 2nd, 1987, Joyce Elizabeth Baigent, *d* of Otto Leiske. *Educ:* Pates Grammar Sch., Cheltenham; N Glos Techn. Coll. Apprenticed Dowty Equipment Ltd, 1935; Chief Instructor to Co.'s Sch. of Hydraulics, 1940; RAF Trng Comd, 1940; Export Man., Dowty Equipment Ltd, 1946; Vice-Pres. and Gen. Man., 1949, Pres., 1954, Dowty Equipment of Canada Ltd; Dir, Dowty Gp Ltd, 1956, Dep. Chm., 1959–75, Chief Exec., 1975–83. Dir, Eagle Star Hldgs plc, 1980–87. Chm., Bd of Trustees, Improvement District of Ajax, Ont., 1954; Dir, Ajax and Pickering Gen. Hosp., 1954; Chm., Cheltenham Hosp. Gp Man. Cttee, 1959; Chm., Glos AHA, 1974–81; Pres., 1967–68, Treas., 1973, Vice-Pres., 1976, Pres., 1977–78, SBAC. FEng 1982; FCASI 1976; FRAeS 1968, Hon. FRAeS 1981. Hon. DSc Bath, 1979. DL Glos, 1977; Hon. Freeman of Cheltenham, 1980. *Recreations:* family interests, golf, gardening. *Address:* Maple House, Withington, Glos GL54 4DA. *T:* Cheltenham (0242) 89344. *Club:* New (Cheltenham).

HUNT, Roger; His Honour Judge Hunt; a Circuit Judge, since 1986; *b* 15 Jan. 1935; *s* of late Richard Henry Hunt and Monica Hunt; *m* 1963, Barbara Ann Eccles; two *d*. *Educ:* Giggleswick Sch.; Pembroke Coll., Oxford (MA). Commnd Royal Signals, 1955; served Germany, HQ 4th Guards Bde, 1956; TA 49th Inf. Div., Signal Regt, 1956–63. Called to the Bar, Lincoln's Inn, 1960; joined NE Circuit, 1961; a Recorder, 1978–86. *Recreations:* golf, gardening. *Club:* Moortown Golf.

HUNT, Roland Charles Colin, CMG 1965; HM Diplomatic Service, retired; Director, British National Committee, International Chamber of Commerce, 1973–76; *b* 19 March 1916; *s* of Colin and Dorothea Hunt, Oxford; *m* 1939, Pauline (*d* 1989), 2nd *d* of late Dr J. C. Maxwell Garnett, CBE; three *s* two *d*. *Educ:* Rugby Sch. (scholar); The Queen's Coll., Oxford (scholar). Entered Indian Civil Service, 1938. Served in various districts in Madras as Sub-Collector, 1941–45; Joint Sec. and Sec., Board of Revenue (Civil Supplies), Madras, 1946–47; joined Commonwealth Relations Office, 1948; served on staff of United Kingdom High Commissioner in Pakistan (Karachi), 1948–50; Mem. UK Delegation to African Defence Facilities Conference, Nairobi, 1951; served in Office of UK High Comr in S Africa, 1952–55; Asst Sec., 1955; attached to Office of High Comr for Fedn of Malaya, Kuala Lumpur, 1956; Dep. High Commisioner for the UK in the Federation of Malaya, Kuala Lumpur, 1957–59; Imperial Defence Coll., 1960; Asst Sec., Commonwealth Relations Office, 1961; British Dep. High Comr in Pakistan, 1962–65; British High Commissioner in Uganda, 1965–67; Asst Under-Sec. of State, CO and FCO, 1967–70; High Comr, Trinidad and Tobago, 1970–73. *Publication:* (ed jtly) The District Officer in India, 1930–1947, 1980. *Recreations:* ball-games, piano-playing. *Address:* Spindlewood, Whitchurch Hill, Reading, Berks RG8 7PG.

See also Baron Hacking, J. C. R. Hunt.

HUNT, Terence; Regional General Manager, North East Thames Regional Health Authority, since 1984; *b* 8 Aug. 1943; *s* of Thomas John Hunt and Marie Louise Hunt (*née* Potter); *m* 1967, Wendy Graeme George; one *s* one *d*. *Educ:* Huish's Grammar Sch., Taunton. Associate Mem. Inst. of Health Service Management. Tone Vale Group HMC, 1963–65; NE Somerset HMC, 1965–67; Winchester Gp HMC, 1967–69; Lincoln No 1 HMC, 1969–70; Hosp. Sec., Wycombe General Hosp., 1970–73; Dep. Gp Sec., Hillingdon Hosp., 1973–74; Area General Administrator, Kensington and Chelsea and Westminster AHA(T), 1974–77; District Administrator: NW Dist of KCW AHA(T), 1977–82; Paddington and N Kensington, 1982–84. Mem., Twyford & Dist Round Table, 1975–84 (Chm., 1980–81; Pres., 1988–89). Member: Council of Govs, London Hosp. Med. Coll., 1985–; Council, UCL, 1985–. *Recreations:* sculling, cycling, Reading Town Regatta (Treasurer, 1984–86; Pres., 1989–), all things practical with metal and wood. *Address:* 36 Old Bath Road, Charvil, Reading, Berks RG10 9QR. *T:* Reading (0734) 341062.

HUNT, Tim; *see* Hunt, R. T.

HUNT, Rt. Rev. Warren; *see* Hunt, Rt Rev. W. W.

HUNT, Rt. Rev. (William) Warren, MA; Hon. Assistant Bishop to the Dioceses of Chichester and Portsmouth, since 1978; *b* 22 Jan. 1909; *s* of Harry Hunt, Carlisle; *m* 1939, Mollie, *d* of Edwin Green, Heswall, Cheshire; four *d*. *Educ:* Carlisle Grammar School; Keble College, Oxford; Cuddesdon Theological College, Oxford. Deacon 1932; Priest 1933; Curate: Kendal Parish Church, 1932–35; St Martin-in-the-Fields, London, 1935–40. Chaplain to the Forces, 1940–44. Vicar, St Nicholas, Radford, Coventry, 1944–48; Vicar, Holy Trinity, Leamington Spa, 1948–57, and Rural Dean of Leamington; Vicar and Rural Dean of Croydon, 1957–65; Bishop Suffragan of Repton, 1965–Jan. 1977. Hon. Canon Canterbury Cathedral, 1957. *Recreations:* golf, vicarage lawn croquet (own rules); travel, reading. *Address:* 15 Lynch Down, Funtington, Chichester, West Sussex PO18 9LR. *T:* Bosham (0243) 575536.

HUNTE, Joseph Alexander; Senior Community Relations Officer, Tower Hamlets, 1968–82, retired; *b* 18 Dec. 1917; *s* of Clement and Eunice Hunte; *m* 1967, Margaret Ann (formerly Jones); three *d* (and one *d* decd). *Educ:* Swansea University Coll., 1962–65 (BA Politics, Economics, Philosophy); PRO, 1964–65. West Indian Standing Conference: PRO, Sec., Chairman 1958–80; Executive Member: Jt Council for Welfare of Immigrants, 1968–74; CARD, 1969–70 (Grievance Officer); Anne Frank Foundn, 1965–70; Chm., Presentation Housing Assoc., 1981–; Governor, St Martin-in-the-Fields Girls' Sch., SW2, 1982–. Silver Jubilee Medal (for services in community relations), 1977. *Publication:* Nigger Hunting in England, 1965. *Recreations:* reading, watching television. *Address:* 43 Cambria Road, SE5 9AS. *T:* 071–733 5436.

HUNTER, family name of **Baron Hunter of Newington.**

HUNTER, Hon. Lord; John Oswald Mair Hunter, VRD; a Senator of the College of Justice in Scotland, 1961–86; *b* 21 Feb. 1913; *s* of John Mair Hunter, QC(Scot) and Jessie Donald Frew; *m* 1939, Doris Mary Simpson (*d* 1988); one *s* one *d*. *Educ:* Edinburgh Acad.; Rugby; New Coll., Oxford (BA 1934, MA 1961); Edinburgh Univ. (LLB 1936, LLD 1975). Entered RNVR, 1933; served War 1939–45 (despatches); Lt-Comdr RNVR; retired list 1949. Called to Bar, Inner Temple, 1937; admitted to Faculty of Advocates, 1937; QC(Scot) 1951. Advocate Depute (Home), 1954–57; Sheriff of Ayr and Bute, 1957–61. Chairman: Deptl Cttee on Scottish Salmon and Trout Fisheries, 1962–65; Lands Valuation Appeal Court, 1966–71; Scottish Law Commn, 1971–81; Scottish Council on Crime, 1972–75; Dep. Chm., Boundary Commn for Scotland, 1971–76. Pres., Scottish Univs Law Inst., 1972–77; Member: Scottish Records Adv. Council, 1966–81; Statute Law Cttee, 1971–81; Chm., later Hon. Pres., Cttee, RNLI (Dunbar), 1969–80 and 1981–; Hon. Pres., Scottish Assoc. for Study of Delinquency, 1971–88.

HUNTER OF NEWINGTON, Baron *cr* 1978 (Life Peer), of Newington in the District of the City of Edinburgh; **Robert Brockie Hunter,** Kt 1977; MBE (mil.) 1945; FRCP;

DL; Vice-Chancellor and Principal, University of Birmingham, 1968–81; *b* 14 July 1915; *s* of Robert Marshall Hunter and Margaret Thorburn Brockie; *m* 1940, Kathleen Margaret Douglas; three *s* one *d*. *Educ:* George Watson's Coll. MB, ChB Edinburgh, 1938; FRCPE 1950; FACP 1963; FRSEd 1964; FInstBiol 1968; FFCM 1975. Personal Physician, Field-Marshal Montgomery, NW Europe, 1944–45. Asst Dir, Edinburgh Post-Graduate Bd for Medicine, 1947; Lectr in Therapeutics, University of Edinburgh, 1947; Commonwealth (Harkness) Fellow in Medicine, 1948; Lectr in Clinical Medicine, University of St Andrews, 1948; Dean of the Faculty of Medicine, 1958–62; Prof. of Materia Medica, Pharmacology and Therapeutics, University of St Andrews, 1948–67, and in University of Dundee, 1967–68; late Consultant Physician to Dundee General Hosps and Dir, Post-graduate Medical Education. Hon. Lectr in Physiology, Boston Univ. Sch. of Medicine, USA, 1950. Member: Clinical Res. Bd, MRC, 1960–64; GMC, 1962–68; Ministry of Health Cttee on Safety of Drugs, 1963–68 (Chm., Clinical Trials Sub-Cttee); UGC, 1964–68 (Chm., Medical Sub-Cttee, 1966–68); West Midlands RHA, 1974–78; Nuffield Cttee of Inquiry into Dental Educn, 1977–80; DHSS Working Party on Medical Administrators in Health Service, 1970–72 (Chm.); DHSS Independent Scientific Cttee on Smoking and Health, 1973–80; Med. Adv. Cttee of Cttee of Vice-Chancellors and Principals, 1976–81; Management Cttee, King Edward's Hospital Fund, 1980–84; House of Lords Select Cttee on Science and Technology, 1983–87, on European Communities, 1988–. Chm., Review Cttee of Medical and Public Health Res. Progs, EEC, 1984–85. Malthe Foundation Lecturer, Oslo, 1958. Editor, Quarterly Journal of Medicine, 1957–67. Fellow (ex-President) Royal Medical Society. Major, Royal Army Medical Corps. Gained Purdue Frederick Medical Achievement Award, 1958. Senior Commonwealth Travelling Fellowship, 1960; Vis. Professor of Medicine: Post-Graduate school, University of Adelaide, 1965; McGill Univ., 1968. Christie Gordon Lectr, Birmingham, 1978; Raymond Priestley Lectr, Birmingham Univ., Goodman Lectr, Royal Soc., 1981; Wade Lectr, Keele Univ., 1982. Hon. FCP. DL West Midlands, 1975. Hon. LLD: Dundee, 1969; Birmingham, 1974; Liverpool, 1984; Hon. DSc Aston, 1981. *Publications:* Clinical Science; contrib. to Br. Med. Jl, Lancet, Edinburgh Med. Jl, Quarterly Jl of Medicine. *Recreation:* fishing. *Address:* 3 Oakdene Drive, Barnt Green, Birmingham B45 8LQ. *Club:* Oriental.

HUNTER, (Adam) Kenneth (Fisher), CBE 1990; formerly Sheriff of North Strathclyde at Paisley, now retired; *b* 1920; *o s* of late Thomas C. Hunter, MBE, AMIEE, and Elizabeth Hunter; *m* 1949, Joan Stella Hiscock, MB, ChB; one *s* two *d*. *Educ:* Dunfermline High Sch.; St Andrews Univ. (MA Hons); Edinburgh Univ. (LLB). Called to Bar, 1946; Chm. of the Supreme Court Legal Aid Cttee of the Law Society of Scotland, 1949–53; Standing Junior Counsel to HM Commissioners of Customs and Excise, 1950–53; Sheriff-Substitute, later Sheriff, of Renfrew and Argyll (subseq. N Strathclyde) at Paisley, 1953–90. *Recreations:* photography, music, philately. *Address:* Ravenswood, Bridge of Weir, Renfrewshire PA11 3AN. *T:* Bridge of Weir (0505) 612017.

HUNTER, Dr Alan, CBE 1975; Director, Royal Greenwich Observatory, 1973–75; *b* 9 Sept. 1912; *s* of late George Hunter and Mary Edwards; *m* 1937, W. Joan Portnell (*d* 1985); four *s*. *Educ:* Imperial Coll. of Science and Technology. PhD, DIC; FRAS. Research Asst, Applied Mech. Dept, RNC, 1940–46; Royal Observatory, Greenwich: Asst, 1937–61; Chief Asst, 1961–67; Dep. Dir, 1967–73. Editor, The Observatory, 1943–49. Treas., Royal Astronomical Soc., 1967–76 (Sec. 1949–56, Vice-Pres. 1957, 1965, 1976); Pres., British Astronomical Assoc., 1957–59; Chm., Large Telescope Users' Panel, 1974–75 (sec. 1969–73). Liveryman, Worshipful Co. of Clockmakers, 1975. *Recreation:* gardening. *Address:* Thatched Cottage, Frettenham Road, Hainford, Norwich NR10 3BW. *T:* Norwich (0603) 890179.

HUNTER, Sir Alexander (Albert), KBE 1976; Representative, Pecten Belize Company, since 1983; Speaker of the House of Representatives of Belize, 1974–79; *b* Belize, British Honduras, 21 May 1920; *s* of Alexander J. Hunter, KSG, and Laura Hunter (*née* Reyes); *m* 1947, Araceli Marin Sanchez, Alajuela, Costa Rica; one *s* two *d*. *Educ:* St John's Coll. (Jesuit), Belize City; Regis Coll. (Jesuit), Denver, Colo; Queen's Univ., Kingston, Ont. In Accounting Dept, United Fruit Co., Costa Rica, 1940–41 and 1945–47. Served War, NCO, Radar Br., RCAF, 1941–45: active service in UK, Azores, Gibraltar, with 220 Sqdn Coastal Comd, RAF. Joined staff of James Brodie & Co. Ltd, as Accountant, 1947; Company Sec., 1948; Dir 1952–61; Consultant: James Brodie & Co. Ltd, 1975–83; Anschutz Overseas Corp., Denver, Colo, 1975–82; Chm., Belize Airways Ltd, 1978–80. MLA (PUP), Fort George Div., 1961; Minister of Natural Resources, Commerce and Industry, March 1961; MHR (PUP), Fort George, under new Constitution, 1965; Minister of Natural Resources and Trade, 1965–69; Minister of Trade and Industry, 1969–74; Mem., Constitutional Ministerial External Affairs Cttee, 1965–74. Represented Belize: Bd of Governors, Caribbean Develt Bank, 1969–74; Council of Ministers, CARIFTA, 1971–73; Council of Ministers, Caribbean Economic Community, 1973–74. Hon. Consul of El Salvador, 1951–78. Acted as Dep. Governor, Aug.–Sept. 1975, and as Dep. Premier on several occasions, 1969–74. Official observer to Salvadoran Elections, 1982 and 1984. People's United Party: Treasurer and Mem. Central Party Council, 1961–74; Mem. Exec. Cttee, 1961–74; Chm. Fort George Div., 1961–74. Former Vice-Pres., Belize Chamber of Commerce; Member: Property Valuation Appeal Bd, 1960; Citrus Industry Investigation Cttee, 1960. Member: West India Cttee; Nat. Geographic Soc.; Belize Ex-Servicemen's League. 1939–45 Star; Atlantic Star; Defence of Britain medal; Canadian Service medal and bar; British War medal. *Recreations:* target shooting, hunting, light and heavy tackle salt-water fishing. *Address:* 6 St Matthew Street, Caribbean Shores, PO Box 505, Belize City, Belize. *T:* 44482.

HUNTER, Air Vice-Marshal Alexander Freeland Cairns, CBE 1982 (OBE 1981); AFC 1978; Commander British Forces Cyprus and Administrator of the Sovereign Base Areas, since 1990; *b* 8 March 1939; *s* of late H. A. C. Hunter and of L. E. M. Hunter; *m* 1964, Wilma Elizabeth Bruce Wilson. *Educ:* Aberdeen Grammar Sch.; Aberdeen Univ. (MA 1960, LLB 1962). Commissioned RAFVR 1959; RAF 1962; flying training 1962; Pilot, 81 (PR) Sqn, FEAF, 1964–67; Central Flying Sch., 1967–68; Instructor, Northumbrian Univ. Air Sqn, 1968–69; Asst Air Attaché, Moscow, 1971–73; RAF Staff Coll., 1974; Flight Comdr, 230 Sqn, 1975–77; OC 18 Sqn, RAF Germany, 1978–80; Air Warfare Course, 1981; MoD (Air), 1981; OC RAF Odiham, 1981–83; Gp Captain Plans, HQ Strike Comd, 1983–85; RCDS 1986; Dir of Public Relations (RAF), 1987–88; Comdt, RAF Staff Coll., 1989–90. *Recreations:* shooting, fishing, hill-walking, military history. *Address:* c/o Clydesdale Bank, Queen's Cross, Aberdeen. *Club:* Royal Air Force.

HUNTER, Alistair John, CMG 1985; HM Diplomatic Service; British Consul-General, New York, and Director-General of Trade and Investment, USA, since 1991; *b* 9 Aug. 1936; *s* of Kenneth Clarke Hunter and Joan Tunks; *m* 1st, 1963; one *s* two *d*; 2nd, 1978, Helge Milton (*née* Kahle). *Educ:* Felsted; Magdalen Coll., Oxford. Royal Air Force, 1955–57; CRO, 1961–65; Private Sec. to Permanent Under-Sec., 1961–63; 2nd Sec., Kuala Lumpur, 1963–65; 1st Sec. (Commercial), Peking, 1965–68; seconded to Cabinet Office, 1969–70; FCO, 1970–73; 1st Sec., Rome, 1973–75; FCO, 1975–80; Hd of Chancery, Bonn, 1980–85; seconded to DTI as Under Sec., Overseas Trade, 1985–88; Consul-Gen., Düsseldorf, and Dir-Gen. of British Trade and Investment Promotion in FRG, 1988–91. *Address:* c/o Foreign and Commonwealth Office, SW1.

HUNTER, Andrew Robert Frederick; MP (C) Basingstoke, since 1983; company director and consultant; *b* 8 Jan. 1943; *s* of late Sqdn Leader Roger Edward Hunter, DFC and Winifred Mary Hunter (*née* Nelson); *m* 1972, Janet, *d* of late Samuel Bourne of Gloucester; one *s* one *d*. *Educ:* St George's Sch., Harpenden; Durham Univ.; Jesus Coll., Cambridge. In industry, 1969; Asst Master, Harrow Sch., 1971–83. Contested (C) Southampton, Itchen, 1979. PPS to Minister of State, DoE, 1985–86. Member: Agriculture Select Cttee, 1985; Environment Select Cttee, 1986–. Sec., Cons. Environment Cttee, 1984–85; Vice-Chm., Cons. Agriculture Cttee, 1987–; Founding Chm., Parly British/Bophuthatswana Gp, 1987–88, Sec., 1988–; Sec., Cons. NI Cttee, 1990–; Vice Chairman: Parly British/S Africa Group, 1991–; Monday Club, 1990–91. Mem., CLA Land Usage Cttee, 1986–; Member: NFU; British Field Sports Soc. (Chm., Falconry Cttee, 1988–). Vice-Pres., Nat. Prayer Book Soc., 1987–. Mem., Court, Univ. of Southampton, 1983–. Commnd Major, TAVR, 1973 (resigned commn, 1984). Hon. Mem., Soc. of the Sealed Knot, 1990–. Order of Polonia Restituta, 1980. *Recreations:* watching cricket and Rugby football, playing with toy soldiers. *Address:* House of Commons, SW1A 0AA. *T:* 071–219 5216.

HUNTER, Rt. Rev. Anthony George Weaver; *b* 3 June 1916; *s* of Herbert George Hunter and Ethel Frances Weaver; *m* 1st, 1948, Joan Isobel Marshall (*d* 1981); 2nd, 1982, Emlyn Marianne Garton (*née* Dent). *Educ:* Wanstead; Leeds Univ. (BA); Coll. of the Resurrection, Mirfield. Deacon, 1941; Priest, 1942; Curate of St George's, Jesmond, 1941–43; Orlando Mission Dist, 1943–47; Johannesburg Coloured Mission, 1947–48; Curate of St George's, Jesmond, 1948–49; Vicar of Ashington, 1949–60; Proctor in Convocation, 1959–60; Vicar of Huddersfield, 1960–68; Rural Dean of Huddersfield, 1960–68; Hon. Canon of Wakefield, 1962–68; Proctor in Convocation, 1962–68; Bishop of Swaziland, 1968–75; Rector of Hexham, Dio. Newcastle, 1975–79; Asst Bishop, Dio. Newcastle, 1976–80; Supernumerary Bishop, 1980–81; Acting Archdeacon of Lindisfarne, 1981; retd Oct. 1981. OStJ. *Recreations:* walking, gardening, travel. *Address:* Hillside, Sheriff Hutton, N Yorks. *T:* Sheriff Hutton (03477) 226.

HUNTER, Anthony Rex; *see* Hunter, Tony.

HUNTER, Rt. Rev. Barry Russell; *see* Riverina, Bishop of.

HUNTER, Dr Colin Graeme, DSC 1939; physician, National Health Service, 1973–82; *b* 31 Jan. 1913; *s* of Robert Hunter and Evelyn Harrison; *m* 1944, Betty Louise Riley; one *s* one *d*. *Educ:* Scots Coll., Univ. of Otago, New Zealand. MD 1958, DSc 1970. Christchurch Hosp. NZ, 1937–38; Royal Naval Medical Service, 1938–55; Univ. of Toronto, Canada, 1955–58; Shell Research Ltd, 1958–73. Fellow: RCP (Lond.); Roy. Coll. of Pathologists, etc. Freeman of City of London. *Publications:* scientific papers in many jls devoted to chemical and radiation toxicology. *Recreations:* sailing, squash. *Address:* 52 Fort Picklecombe, Maker, Torpoint, Cornwall PL10 1JB. *T:* Plymouth (0752) 823419. *Club:* Royal Naval Sailing Association.

HUNTER, Hon. David Stronach, CBE 1991; **Hon. Mr Justice Hunter;** Justice of Appeal, Supreme Court of Hong Kong, since 1987; *b* 5 Oct. 1926; *s* of late Robert John Hunter and late Jayne Evelyn Hunter; *m* 1959, Janet Muriel Faulkner; one *s* two *d*. *Educ:* Harrow Sch., Hertford Coll., Oxford (Baring Scholar); MA Jurisprudence. Called to Bar, Middle Temple, 1951, Bencher, 1979; QC 1971; a Recorder of the Crown Court, 1975–81; Judge of Supreme Court of Hong Kong, 1982–87. *Recreations:* golf, gardening, painting. *Address:* Supreme Court, Hong Kong; 48 Manderly Garden, 48 Deep Water Bay Road, Hong Kong. *Clubs:* MCC; Hong Kong.

HUNTER, Evan; writer; *b* New York, 15 Oct. 1926; *s* of Charles F. Lombino and Marie Lombino; *m* 1st, 1949, Anita Melnick (marr. diss.); three *s*; 2nd, 1973, Mary Vann Finley; one step *d*. *Educ:* Cooper Union; Hunter Coll. (BA 1950). Served USNR. Literary Father of the Year, 1961; Phi Beta Kappa. Grand Master Award, Mystery Writers of America, 1986. *Publications include: as Evan Hunter:* The Blackboard Jungle, 1954; Second Ending, 1956; Strangers When We Meet, 1958; A Matter of Conviction, 1959; The Remarkable Harry, 1960; The Wonderful Button, 1961; Mothers and Daughters, 1961; Happy New Year, Herbie, 1963; Buddwing, 1964; The Paper Dragon, 1966; A Horse's Head, 1967; Last Summer, 1968; Sons, 1969; Nobody Knew They Were There, 1971; Every Little Crook and Nanny, 1972; The Easter Man, 1972; Seven, 1972; Come Winter, 1973; Streets of Gold, 1974; The Chisholms, 1976; Me and Mr Stenner, 1977; Walk Proud, 1978; Love, Dad, 1981; Far From the Sea, 1983; Lizzie, 1984; *as Ed McBain:* Cop Hater, 1956; The Mugger, 1956; The Pusher, 1956; The Con Man, 1957; Killer's Choice, 1958; Killer's Payoff, 1958; Lady Killer, 1958; Killer's Wedge, 1959; 'Til Death, 1959; King's Ransom, 1959; Give the Boys a Great Big Hand, 1960; The Heckler, 1960; See Them Die, 1960; Lady, Lady, I Did It, 1961; The Empty Hours, 1962; Like Love, 1962; Ten Plus One, 1963; Ax, 1964; The Sentries, 1965; He Who Hesitates, 1965; Doll, 1965; Eighty Million Eyes, 1966; Fuzz, 1968; Shotgun, 1969; Jigsaw, 1970; Hail, Hail, the Gang's All Here!, 1971; Sadie When She Died, 1972; Let's Hear It for the Deaf Man, 1972; Death of a Nurse, 1972; Hail to the Chief, 1973; Bread, 1974; Where There's Smoke, 1975; Blood Relatives, 1975; So Long as You Both Shall Live, 1976; Guns, 1976; Long Time No See, 1977; Goldilocks, 1978; Calypso, 1979; Ghosts, 1980; Even the Wicked, 1980; Rumpelstiltskin, 1981; Heat, 1981; Beauty and the Beast, 1982; Ice, 1983; Jack and the Beanstalk, 1984; Lightning, 1984; Snow White and Rose Red, 1985; Eight Black Horses, 1985; Cinderella, 1986; Another Part of the City, 1986; Poison, 1987; Tricks, 1987; Puss in Boots, 1987; McBain's Ladies, 1988; The House that Jack Built, 1988; Lullaby, 1989; McBain's Ladies, Too, 1989; Downtown, 1989; Vespers, 1990; *screenplays:* Strangers When We Meet, 1959; The Birds, 1962; Fuzz, 1972; Walk Proud, 1979; Dream West (TV mini-series), 1986; *plays:* The Easter Man, 1964; The Conjuror, 1969. *Recreation:* travelling. *Address:* Vanessa Holt Assoc. Ltd, 53 Crescent Road, Leigh-on-Sea, Essex SS9 2PF.

HUNTER, Guy, CMG 1973; author and consultant; Overseas Development Institute, 1967–83, retired; *b* 7 Nov. 1911; *s* of Lt-Col C. F. Hunter, DSO, and Mrs A. W. Hunter (*née* Cobbett); *m* 1941, Agnes Louisa Merrylees. *Educ:* Winchester Coll.; Trinity Coll., Cambridge. 1st cl. hons Classics, MA. Called to Bar, Middle Temple, 1935. Civil Defence, Regional Officer, Edinburgh and Principal Officer, Glasgow and W Scotland, 1939–43; Dir (Admin), Middle East Supply Centre, GHQ, Cairo, 1943–45; Dir, PEP, 1945–46; Warden, Urchfont Manor, Wilts, and Grantley Hall, Yorks, Adult Colleges, 1946–55; Dir of Studies, 1st Duke of Edinburgh's Conf., 1955–56; from 1957, research and consultancy for developing countries overseas, mainly E, W and Central Africa, India, Pakistan, SE Asia, Fiji. Launching and 1st Dir, East African Staff Coll., 1966; Inst. of Race Relations, 1959–66. Visiting Prof., Univ. of Reading, 1969–75. Member: Economic and Social Cttee, EEC, 1975–78; Council for Internat. Develt (ODM), 1977–. Bd of Governors, Inst. of Develt Studies, Sussex Univ. *Publications:* Studies in Management, 1961; The New Societies of Tropical Africa, 1962; Education for a Developing Region, 1963; (ed) Industrialization and Race Relations, 1965; South East Asia: Race, Culture and Nation, 1966; The Best of Both Worlds, 1967; Modernising Peasant Societies, 1969; The Administration of Agricultural Development, 1970; (ed jtly) Serving the Small Farmer, 1974; (ed jtly) Policy and Practice in Rural Development, 1976. *Recreations:* gardening, nature, travel. *Address:* The Miller's Cottage, Hartest, Bury St Edmunds, Suffolk. *T:* Bury St Edmunds (0284) 830334. *Club:* Travellers'.

HUNTER, Sir Ian (Bruce Hope), Kt 1983; MBE 1945; Impresario; President and Director, Harold Holt Ltd, since 1988 (Chairman and Chief Executive, 1953–88); Chairman: Tempo Video Ltd, since 1984; Musicians' Benevolent Fund, since 1987; *b* 2 April 1919; *s* of late W. O. Hunter; *m* 1st, 1949, Susan (*d* 1977), *d* of late Brig. A. G. Russell; four *d*; 2nd, 1984, Lady Showering, *widow* of Sir Keith Showering. *Educ:* Fettes Coll., Edinburgh; abroad as pupil of Dr Fritz Busch and at Glyndebourne. Served War of 1939–45, Lieut-Col. Asst to Artistic Dir, Edinburgh Festival, 1946–48; Artistic Administrator, Edinburgh Festival, 1949–50; Artistic Dir, Edinburgh Festival, 1951–55. Director, Bath Festivals, 1948, 1955, 1958–68; Adviser, Adelaide Festivals, 1960–64; Dir-Gen., Commonwealth Arts Festival, 1965; Artistic Director: Festivals of the City of London, 1962–80; Brighton Festivals, 1967–83; (with Yehudi Menuhin) Windsor Festivals, 1969–72; Hong Kong Arts Festivals, 1973–75; Malvern Festival, 1977–82; American Festival, 1985; Festival of German Arts, London, 1987. Dir, British Nat. Day Entertainment, Expo' 67. Dir, Live Music Now, 1983–. Member: Opera/Ballet Enquiry for Arts Council, 1967–69; Arts Administration Course Enquiry for Arts Council, 1970–71; Arts Council Trng Cttee, 1974–76; Centenary Appeal Cttee, RCM, 1982–; Adv. Cttee, Britain Salutes New York, 1983; Chm., Entertainments Cttee, Queen's Silver Jubilee Appeal; Pres., British Arts Festivals Assoc., 1978–81; Dep. Chm., Stravinsky Festival Trust; Trustee, Chichester Festival Theatre Trust, until 1988; Founder and Trustee, Young Concert Artists Trust, 1984–; Chm. of Governors, London Festival Ballet (later English National Ballet), 1984–89; Vice-Chm., Japan Fest. UK 1991, 1989–92; Vice-Pres., Yehudi Menuhin Sch. R. B. Bennett Commonwealth Prize for 1966. Hon. Member: Guildhall Sch. of Music and Drama, 1975; RCM 1984. FRSA (Mem. Council, 1968–73, 1976–; Chm. Council, 1981–83; a Vice-Pres., 1981–). Mem. Ct of Assistants, Musicians' Co., 1981–84. *Recreations:* gardening, painting. *Address:* Harold Holt Ltd, 31 Sinclair Road, W14 0NS. *T:* 071–603 4600. *Club:* Garrick.

HUNTER, Ian Gerald Adamson, QC 1980; a Recorder, since 1986; *b* 3 Oct. 1944; *s* of Gerald Oliver Hunter and late Jessie Hunter; *m* 1975, Maggie (*née* Reed); two *s*. *Educ:* Reading Sch.; Pembroke Coll., Cambridge (Open Scholar, Squire Univ. Law Scholar, Trevelyan Scholar, BA (double first in Law), MA, LLB); Harvard Law Sch. (Kennedy Memorial Scholar, LLM). Called to the Bar, Inner Temple, 1967 (Duke of Edinburgh Entrance Scholar, Major Scholar), Bencher, 1986. Chm., Consolidated Regulations and Transfer Cttee, Senate of Inns of Court, 1986–87 (Mem., 1982–85); Member: International Relations Cttee, Bar Council, 1982–90; Exec. Cttee, Bar Council, 1985–86. Mem. and Rapporteur, Internat. Law Assoc. Anti-Trust Cttee, 1968–72; Pres., Union Internat. des Avocats, 1989 (UK Vice-Pres., 1982–86; first Vice Pres., 1986–; Dir of Studies, 1990–). *Publications:* articles on public international law. *Recreations:* bebop, other good music, French cooking. *Address:* 4 Essex Court, Temple, EC4. *T:* 071–583 9191.

HUNTER, Brig. Ian Murray, CVO 1954; MBE 1943; psc 1943; fsc (US) 1955; FAIM 1964; Chairman and Managing Director, Allied Rubber Products (Qld) Pty Ltd; *b* Sydney, Aust., 10 July 1917; *s* of late Dr James Hunter, Stranraer, Scotland; *m* 1947, Rosemary Jane Batchelor; two *s* two *d*. *Educ:* Cranbrook Sch., Sydney; RMC, Duntroon. Lieut Aust. Staff Corps, and AIF 1939; 2/1 MG Bn, 1939–40; T/Capt. 1940; Staff Capt., 25 Inf. Bde, 1940–41; Middle East Staff Coll., Haifa, 1941; DA QMG (1), HQ 6 Div., 1941–42; T/Major 1942; AQMG, NT Force (MBE), 1942–43; Staff Sch. (Aust.), 1943; Gen. Staff 3 Corps and Advanced HQ Allied Land Forces, 1943–44; Lieut-Col 1945; Instructor, Staff Sch., 1945; AQMG, and Col BCOF, 1946–47; AQMG, AHQ and JCOSA, 1947; AA & QMG, HQ, 3 Div., 1948–50; Royal Visit, 1949; Exec. Commonwealth Jubilee Celebrations, 1950–51; CO 2 Recruit Trg Bn, 1952; CO 4 RAR, 1953; Executive and Commonwealth Marshal, Royal Visit, 1952, and 1954; Command and Gen. Staff Coll., Fort Leavenworth, USA, 1954–55; Military Mission, Washington, 1955–56; Officer i/c Admin., N Comd, 1956–59; Comd 11 Inf. Bde, 1959–60; Command 2nd RQR 1960–62; Chief of Staff 1st Div., 1963; Commandant, Australian Staff Coll., 1963–65; Comdr, Papua New Guinea Comd, 1966–69; DQMG, Army HQ, 1969. Indep. Mem., Presbyterian Church Property Commn, 1974–84. Chm., Australian Red Cross Soc. (Qld), 1990–. *Recreations:* golf, squash, swimming, riding. *Address:* PO Box 53, Stafford, Qld 4053, Australia; Garthland, 42 Charlton Street, Ascot, Brisbane, Queensland 4007, Australia; Finchley, Hargreaves Street, Blackheath, NSW 2785, Australia. *Clubs:* Australian (Sydney); Queensland (Brisbane); Royal Sydney Golf.

HUNTER, Surg. Rear-Adm. (D) John, CB 1973; OBE 1963; Director of Naval Dental Services, Ministry of Defence, 1971–74; *b* 21 Aug. 1915; *s* of Hugh Hunter and Evelyn Marian Hunter (*née* Jessop), Hale, Cheshire; *m* 1947, Anne Madelaine Hardwicke, Friarmayne, Dorset; three *s* two *d*. *Educ:* Bowdon Coll., Cheshire; Manchester Univ. LDS 1939. Surg. Lieut (D) RNVR 1940; HMS Kenya and 10th Cruiser Sqdn, 1941–42; HMS Newcastle and HMS Howe, British Pacific Fleet, 1944–47; transf. to RN; HMS Forth on Staff of Rear-Adm. Destroyers, Mediterranean (Surg. Lt-Comdr), 1948–50; Dartmouth, Royal Marines; Surg. Comdr, Staff of Flag Officer Flotillas Mediterranean, 1956; service ashore in Admty, 1960–63; Surg. Captain (D), Staff of C-in-C Mediterranean, 1965–66; Staff of C-in-C Plymouth Comd, 1967–68; Fleet Dental Surgeon on Staff of C-in-C Western Fleet, 1969–70. QHDS 1971–74. Mem., South Hams DC, 1979–83. Chm., River Yealm Harbour Authority, 1982–85. *Recreations:* ocean racing, cruising, shooting. *Address:* Horsewells, Newton Ferrers, Plymouth PL8 1AT. *T:* Plymouth (0752) 872254. *Clubs:* Royal Ocean Racing; Royal Western Yacht.

HUNTER, John; His Honour Judge Hunter; a Circuit Judge, since 1980; *b* 12 April 1921; *s* of Charles and Mary Hunter; *m* 1956, Margaret Cynthia Webb; one *s* two *d*. *Educ:* Fitzwilliam House, Cambridge (MA). Called to the Bar, Lincoln's Inn, 1952. Served War, Army, 1939–46. Industry, 1952–62; practised at the Bar, 1962–80. *Recreations:* sailing, gardening. *Address:* 6 Pump Court, Temple, EC4Y 7AP. *Clubs:* London Rowing; Sussex Yacht.

HUNTER, John Garvin; Chief Executive, Management Executive, Health and Personal Social Services, Northern Ireland, since 1990; *b* 9 Aug. 1947; *s* of Garvin and Martha Hunter; *m* 1976, Rosemary Alison Haire; one *s* two *d*. *Educ:* Merchant Taylors' Sch., Liverpool; Queen's Univ., Belfast (BA); Cornell Univ., NY (MBA). Asst Principal, NICS, 1970; Department of Health and Social Services: Dep. Principal, 1973; Harkness Fellow, 1977–79; Principal Officer, 1979; Asst Sec., 1982; Dir Gen., Internat. Fund for Ireland, 1986; Under Sec., 1988. *Publications:* contribs to conf. papers on the conflict in NI and on health service planning. *Recreations:* Corrymeela Community, church, swimming. *Address:* Department of Health and Social Services, Dundonald House, Upper Newtownards Road, Belfast BT4 3SF.

HUNTER, John Murray, CB 1980; MC 1943; Scottish Tourist Guide; *b* 10 Nov. 1920; *s* of Rev. Dr John Hunter and Frances Hunter (*née* Martin); *m* 1948, Margaret, *d* of late Stanley Cursiter, CBE, RSW, RSA, and Phyllis Eda (*née* Hourston); two *s* three *d*. *Educ:* Fettes Coll.; Clare Coll., Cambridge. Served Army, 1941–45: Captain, The Rifle Bde. Served in Diplomatic Service at Canberra, Bogotá, Baghdad, Prague, Buenos Aires and in FCO (Head of Consular Dept, 1966, and of Latin America Dept, 1971–73); idc 1961, sowc 1965, jssc (Senior Directing Staff), 1967–69. Sec., 1973–75, Comr for Admin and Finance, 1976–81, Forestry Commn. Vice- Chm., 1981–83, Chm., 1983–86, Edinburgh West End Community Council. *Recreations:* music, curling; formerly Rugby football (Cambridge 1946, Scotland 1947). *Address:* 21 Glencairn Crescent, Edinburgh EH12 5BT.

HUNTER, John Oswald Mair; *see* Hunter, Hon. Lord.

HUNTER, Keith Robert, OBE 1981; British Council Director, Italy, since 1990; *b* 29 May 1936; *s* of Robert Ernest Williamson and Winifred Mary Hunter; *m* 1959, Ann Patricia Fuller (marr. diss. 1989); one *s* two *d*; *m* 1991, Victoria Solomonidis. *Educ:* Hymers Coll., Hull; Magdalen Coll., Oxford (MA). Joined British Council, 1962; Lectr, Royal Sch. of Admin, Phnom Penh, 1960–64; Schs Recruitment Dept, 1964–66; SOAS, 1966–67; Asst Rep., Hong Kong, 1967–69; Dir, Penang, 1970–72; Dep. Rep., Kuala Lumpur, 1972–74; London Univ. Inst. of Educn, 1974–75; Rep., Algeria, 1975–78; First Sec. (Cultural), subseq. Cultural Counsellor (British Council Rep.), China, 1979–82; Sec. of Bd, and Hd of Dir-Gen.'s Dept, 1982–85; Controller, Arts Div., 1985–90. *Recreation:* music. *Address:* British Council, Palazzo del Drago, Via Quattro Fontane 20, 00184 Rome, Italy.

HUNTER, Kenneth; *see* Hunter, A. K. F.

HUNTER, Prof. Laurence Colvin, CBE 1987; FRSE 1986; Professor of Applied Economics, since 1970, and Director of External Relations, 1987–90, University of Glasgow; Chairman, Post Office Arbitration Tribunal, since 1974; *b* 8 Aug. 1934; *s* of Laurence O. and Jessie P. Hunter; *m* 1958, Evelyn Margaret (*née* Green); three *s* one *d*. *Educ:* Hillhead High Sch., Glasgow; Univ. of Glasgow (MA); University Coll., Oxford (DPhil). Asst, Manchester Univ., 1958–59; National Service, 1959–61; Post-Doctoral Fellow, Univ. of Chicago, 1961–62; University of Glasgow: Lectr, 1962; Sen. Lectr, 1967; Titular Prof., 1969; Vice-Principal, 1982–86. Member: Ct of Inquiry into miners' strike, 1972; Council, Advisory, Conciliation and Arbitration Service, 1974–86; Royal Commn on Legal Services in Scotland, 1976–80; Council, ESRC, 1989–; Chm., Police Negotiating Bd, 1987– (Dep. Chm., 1980–86). *Publications:* (with G. L. Reid) Urban Worker Mobility, 1968; (with D. J. Robertson) Economics of Wages and Labour, 1969, 2nd edn (with C. Mulvey), 1981; (with G. L. Reid and D. Boddy) Labour Problems of Technological Change, 1970; (with A. W. J. Thomson) The Nationalised Transport Industries, 1973; (with R. B. McKersie) Pay, Productivity and Collective Bargaining, 1973; (with L. Baddon *et al.*) People's Capitalism, 1989; other pubns in economics and industrial relations. *Recreations:* golf, painting. *Address:* 23 Boclair Road, Bearsden, Glasgow G61 2AF. *T:* 041–942 0793. *Club:* Commonwealth Trust.

HUNTER, Muir Vane Skerrett; QC 1965; Lt-Col (Hon.); MA Oxon; MRI; Barrister-at-Law; *b* 19 Aug. 1913; *s* of late H. S. Hunter, Home Civil Service, and Bluebell M. Hunter, novelist; *m* 1st, 1939, Dorothea Eason, JP (*d* 1986), *e d* of late P. E. Verstone; one *d*; 2nd, 1986, Gillian Victoria Joyce Petrie, *d* of late Dr Alexander Petrie, CBE, MD, FRCS, FRCP. *Educ:* Westminster Sch.; Christ Church, Oxford (Scholar). Called, Gray's Inn, 1938 (*ad eundem* Inner Temple, 1965); Holker Senior Scholar; Bencher, Gray's Inn, 1976. Served 1940–46: Royal Armoured Corps; GS Intelligence, GHQ (India); GSO 1 attd War and Legislative Depts, Govt of India; returned to the Bar, 1946; standing counsel (bankruptcy) to Bd of Trade, 1949–65; Dep. Chm., Advisory Cttee on Service Candidates, HO; Member: EEC Bankruptcy Adv. Cttee, Dept of Trade, 1973–76; Insolvency Law Review Cttee, Dept of Trade, 1977–82; Advr, Law Reform Commn, Kenya Govt, 1991–; Founder-Chairman, N Kensington Neighbourhood Law Centre, 1969–71; Mem., Exec. Cttee, British Polish Legal Assoc., 1991; Hon. Mem., Council of "Justice". Amnesty International Observer: Burundi, 1962; Rhodesia, 1969; Turkey, 1972. Governor, Royal Shakespeare Theatre, 1978–; Mem. Council, Royal Shakespeare Theatre Trust, 1978–. Chm., Gdansk Hospice Fund, 1989–. Hon. Legal Advr, Nairobi Hospice, Kenya, 1989–. Mem. Editl Board, Insolvency Law & Practice, 1985–. *Publications:* Senior Editor, Williams on Bankruptcy, 1958–78, Williams and Muir Hunter on Bankruptcy, 1979–84, Muir Hunter on Personal Insolvency, 1987–; Emergent Africa and the Rule of Law, 1963; Jt editor: Halsbury's Laws, 4th edn, Vol 3; Atkins' Forms, Vol 7; Part Editor, Kerr on Receivers, 16th edn 1983, Editor, 17th edn 1988, as Kerr on Receivers and Administrators; Part Editor, Butterworth's County Court Precedents and Pleadings, 1984–. *Recreations:* theatre, travel, music. *Address:* (chambers) 3–4 South Square, Gray's Inn, WC1R 5HP. *T:* 071–696 9900, *Fax:* 071–696 9911; 43 Church Road, Barnes, SW13 9HQ. *T:* 081–748 6693; Hunterston, Donhead St Andrew, Shaftesbury, Dorset SP7 8EB. *T:* Donhead (0747) 828779, *Fax:* Donhead (0747) 828045. *Clubs:* Commonwealth Trust; Hurlingham.

HUNTER, Dame Pamela, DBE 1981; Vice-President, National Union of Conservative and Unionist Associations, since 1985 (Vice-Chairman, 1981–84; Chairman, 1984–85); *b* 3 Oct. 1919; *d* of late Col T. G. Greenwell, TD, JP, DL, and M. W. Greenwell; *m* 1942, Gordon Lovegrove Hunter; one *s* one *d*. *Educ:* Westonbirt Sch., Tetbury; Eastbourne Sch. of Domestic Economy. Served WRNS, 1942–45. Mem., Conservative Nat. Union Exec. Cttee, 1972–88; Chairman: Northern Area Cons. Women's Adv. Cttee, 1972–75; Cons. Women's Nat. Adv. Cttee, 1978–81; Mem., Cons. Party Policy Cttee, 1978–85. President: Berwick-upon-Tweed Cons. Assoc., 1986–89; N Area Cons. Council, 1986–89. Mem., Northumbrian Water Authority, 1973–76. Member: Berwick-upon-Tweed Borough Council, 1973–83; Chatton Parish Council 1987–; Lay Chm., Parish of Chatton with Chillingham PCC, 1989–. *Recreations:* charity work for NSPCC and RNLI, antiques. *Address:* The Coach House, Chatton, Alnwick, Northumberland NE66 5PY. *T:* Chatton (06685) 259. *Club:* Lansdowne.

HUNTER, Philip Brown, TD; Chairman, John Holt & Co. (Liverpool) Ltd, 1967–71; *b* 30 May 1909; *s* of Charles Edward Hunter and Marion (*née* Harper); *m* 1937, Joyce Mary (*née* Holt); two *s* two *d*. *Educ:* Birkenhead Sch.; London University. Practised as Solicitor, 1933–80. Chm., Guardian Royal Exchange Assurance (Sierra Leone) Ltd, 1972–79; Director: Cammell Laird & Co. Ltd, 1949–70 (Chm. 1966–70); John Holt & Co. (Liverpool) Ltd, 1951–71 (Exec. Dir, 1960); Guardian Royal Exchange, 1969–79; Guardian Assurance Co. Ltd, 1967–79; Royal Exchange (Nigeria) Ltd, 1972–79; Lion of Africa Insurance Co. Ltd, 1972–79; Enterprise Insurance Co. Ltd, Ghana, 1972–79. *Recreations:* sailing, gardening. *Address:* Bryn Hyfryd, Lixwm, Holywell, Clwyd. *T:* Halkyn (0352) 780054. *Club:* Caledonian.

HUNTER, Dr Philip John: Chief Education Officer, Staffordshire, since 1985; *b* 23 Nov. 1939; *m* Ruth Bailey; two *s* one *d*. *Educ:* Univ. of Durham (BSc 1962); Univ. of Newcastle upon Tyne (PhD 1965). Lectr, Univ. of Khartoum, 1965–67; Senior Scientific Officer: ARC, Cambridge, 1967–69; DES, 1969–71; Course Dir, CS Staff Coll., 1971–73; posts at DES, including science, schools, finance and Private Office, 1973–79; Dep. Chief Educn Officer, ILEA, 1979–85. Director: Midlands Examining Gp, 1985–; Staffs TEC, 1990–; Member of Council: Keele Univ., 1987–; BTEC, 1990–; Member: Nat. Council for Educnl Technol., 1986–91; Nat. Curriculum Wkg Gp on Design and Technol., 1988–89; Design Council Educn Cttee. *Publications:* (jtly) Terrestrial Slugs; (jtly) Pulmonates;

papers on ecology of invertebrates; contrib. educnl jls on educn policy matters. *Recreation:* gardening. *Address:* Upmeads, Newport Road, Stafford ST16 1DD.

HUNTER, Rita, CBE 1980; prima donna; leading soprano, Sadler's Wells, since 1958, and Australian Opera, since 1981; *b* 15 Aug. 1933; *d* of Charles Newton Hunter and Lucy Hunter; *m* 1960, John Darnley-Thomas; one *d. Educ:* Wallasey. Joined Carl Rosa, 1950. Debut: Berlin, 1970; Covent Garden, 1972; Metropolitan, NY, 1972; Munich, 1973; Australia, 1978 (returned 1980 and 1981); Seattle Wagner Fest., 1980. Sang Brünnhilde in first complete Ring cycle with Sadler's Wells, 1973; first perf. of Norma, San Francisco then NY Metropolitan, 1975; first perf. of Tosca, Canberra, Aust., 1988. Has sung leading roles in Aida, Trovatore, Masked Ball, Cavalleria Rusticana, Lohengrin, Flying Dutchman, Idomeneo, Don Carlos, Turandot, Nabucco, Macbeth, Tristan and Isolde, Electra. Founded, 1986, and runs with husband, Maduo Sch. of Singing, Aust.; also gives world-wide master classes. Many recordings, including complete Ring, complete Euryanthe, and several recital discs. Hon. DLitt Warwick, 1978; Hon. DMus Liverpool, 1983. RAM 1978. *Publication:* Wait till the Sun Shines Nellie (autobiog.), 1986. *Recreations:* sewing, swimming, oil painting, reading, gardening (Mem. Royal Nat. Rose Soc.), caravanning (Mem. Caravan Club), swimming. *Address:* 305 Bobbin Head Road, North Turramurra, NSW 2074, Australia. *T:* Sydney 445062; (UK Rep.) Mark Bonello, 52 Dean Street, W1V 5HJ. *T:* 071–437 8564; (Aust.) Avere, 26 Oxley Drive, Bowral, NSW 2576, Australia. *T:* 048 621 688; (USA Rep.) Robert Lombardo, 61 W 62nd Street, Suite F, New York, NY 10023, USA. *T:* (2120 586 4454. *Club:* White Elephant.

HUNTER, Dr Tony, (Anthony Rex Hunter), FRS 1987; Professor, Molecular Biology and Virology Laboratory, Salk Institute, San Diego, California, since 1982; concurrently Adjunct Professor of Biology, University of California, San Diego; *b* 23 Aug. 1943; *s* of Ranulph Rex Hunter and Nellie Ruby Elsie Hunter (*née* Hitchcock); *m* 1969, Philippa Charlotte Marrack (marr. diss. 1974). *Educ:* Felsted Sch., Essex; Gonville and Caius Coll., Cambridge (BA, MA, PhD). Research Fellow: Christ's Coll., Cambridge, 1968–71 and 1973–74; Salk Inst., San Diego: Res. Associate, 1971–73; Asst Prof., 1975–78; Associate Prof., 1978–82. FRSA 1989. *Publications:* numerous, in leading scientific jls. *Recreations:* white water rafting, exploring the Baja peninsula. *Address:* Molecular Biology and Virology Laboratory, The Salk Institute, PO Box 85800, San Diego, Calif 92186, USA. *T:* 619–453–4100.

HUNTER, William Hill, CBE 1971; JP; DL; CA; Partner in McLay, McAlister & McGibbon, Chartered Accountants, since 1946; *b* 5 Nov. 1916; *s* of Robert Dalglish Hunter and Mrs Margaret Walker Hill or Hunter; *m* 1947, Kathleen, *d* of William Alfred Cole; two *s. Educ:* Cumnock Academy. Chartered Accountant, 1940. Served War: enlisted as private, RASC, 1940; commissioned RA, 1941; Staff Capt., Middle East, 1944–46. Director: Abbey National Building Soc. Scottish Adv. Bd, 1966–86; City of Glasgow Friendly Soc., 1966–88 (Pres., 1980–88); J. & G. Grant Glenfarclas Distillery, 1966–. President: Renfrew W and Inverclyde Conservative and Unionist Assoc., 1972–; Scottish Young Unionist Assoc., 1958–60; Scottish Unionist Assoc., 1964–65. Contested (U) South Ayrshire, 1959 and 1964. Chairman: Salvation Army Adv. Bd in Strathclyde, 1982– (Vice-Chm., 1972–82); Salvation Army Housing Assoc. (Scotland) Ltd, 1986–. Hon. Treasurer, Quarrier's Homes, 1979– (Acting Chm., 1989–). Deacon Convener, Trades House of Glasgow, 1986–87. JP 1970, DL 1987, Renfrewshire. *Recreations:* gardening, golf, swimming. *Address:* Armitage, Kilmacolm, Renfrewshire PA13 4PH. *T:* Kilmacolm (050587) 2444. *Clubs:* Western, Royal Scottish Automobile (Glasgow).

HUNTER, William John, MB, BS; Director, Health and Safety Commission of the European Communities, since 1988; *b* 5 April 1937; *m*; two *s* one *d. Educ:* Westminster Medical Sch. (MB, BS); LRCP, MRCS; FFOM. Commission of the European Communities: Principal Administrator, 1974–82; Hd of Div., Industrial Medicine and Hygiene, 1982–88. *Publications:* many on health and safety at work. *Recreations:* squash, jogging, music. *Address:* Commission of the European Communities, Bâtiment Jean Monnet, L2920 Luxembourg.

HUNTER-BLAIR, Sir Edward (Thomas), 8th Bt *cr* 1786, of Dunskey; landowner and forester since 1964; *b* 15 Dec. 1920; *s* of Sir James Hunter Blair, 7th Bt and Jean Galloway (*d* 1953), *d* of T. W. McIntyre, Sorn Castle, Ayrshire; *S* father, 1985; *m* 1956, Norma (*d* 1972), *d* of late W. S. Harris; one adopted *s* one adopted *d. Educ:* Balliol Coll., Oxford (BA); Univ. of Paris (Diploma, French Lang. and Lit.). Temp. Civil Servant, 1941–43; journalist (Asst Foreign Editor), 1944–49; in business in Yorkshire, manager and director of own company, 1950–63. Mem., Kirkcudbright CC, 1970–71; former Pres., Dumfries and Galloway Mountaineering Club. 1939–45 Star, Gen. Service Medal, 1946. *Publications:* Scotland Sings, and A Story of Me, 1981; A Future Time (With an Earlier Life), 1984; A Mission in Life, 1987; Nearing the Year 2000, 1990; articles on learned and other subjects. *Recreations:* gardening, hill-walking. *Heir: b* James Hunter Blair, *b* 18 March 1926. *Address:* Parton House, Castle Douglas, Scotland DG7 3NB. *T:* Parton (06447) 234. *Clubs:* Royal Over-Seas League; Western Meeting (Ayr).

HUNTER JOHNSTON, David Alan; *b* 16 Jan. 1915; *s* of James Ernest Johnston and Florence Edith Johnston (*née* Hunter); *m* 1949, Philippa Frances Ray; three *s* one *d. Educ:* Christ's Hospital; King's Coll., London. FKC 1970. Royal Ordnance Factories, Woolwich, 1936–39; S Metropolitan Gas Co., 1939–44; Min. of Economic Warfare (Economic and Industrial Planning Staff), 1944–45; Control Office for Germany and Austria, 1945–47; Sec. to Scientific Cttee for Germany, 1946; FO (German Section), Asst Head, German Gen. Economic Dept, 1947–49; HM Treasury, Supply, Estabt and Home Finance Divs, 1949–53. Central Bd of Finance of Church of England: Sec. (and Fin. Sec. to Church Assembly), 1953–59, and Investment Manager, 1959–65; concurrently, Dir, Local Authorities Mutual Investment Trust, 1961–65, and Investment Man. to Charities Official Investment Fund, 1963–65; a Man. Dir, J. Henry Schroder Wagg & Co. Ltd, 1965–74; Chairman: Schroder Executor & Trustee Co. Ltd, 1966–74; Reserve Pension Bd, 1974–75; Assoc. of Investment Trust Cos, 1975–77; Director: Trans-Oceanic Trust, subseq. Schroder Global Trust plc, 1965–88; Clerical, Medical & General Life Assurance Soc., 1970–74; Lindustries Ltd, 1970–79 and of other investment trust cos for many years. Mem., Monopolies Commn, 1969–73. A Reader, 1959–85, licensed in dio. St Albans, dio. Bath and Wells. *Address:* Eastfield, North Perrott, Crewkerne, Somerset TA18 7SW. *T:* Crewkerne (0460) 75156. *Clubs:* Farmers', City of London.

HUNTER SMART, Norman; *see* Hunter Smart, W. N.

HUNTER SMART, (William) Norman, CA; Chairman: Charterhouse Development Capital Fund Ltd, since 1987; C. J. Sims Ltd, since 1990 (Director, 1964); *b* 25 May 1921; *s* of William Hunter Smart, CA, and Margaret Thorburn Inglis; *m* 1st, 1948, Bridget Beryl Andreae (*d* 1974); four *s*; 2nd, 1977, Sheila Smith Stewart (*née* Speirs). *Educ:* George Watson's Coll., Edinburgh. Served War, 1939–45; 1st Lothians & Border Horse; Warwickshire Yeomanry; mentioned in despatches. Hays Allan, Chartered Accountants, 1950–86 (Senior Partner, 1983–86). Chm., Assoc. of Scottish Chartered Accountants in London, 1972–73; Institute of Chartered Accountants of Scotland: Council Mem., 1970–75; Vice-Pres., 1976–78; Pres., 1978–79. Member: Gaming Bd for GB, 1985–90;

Scottish Legal Aid Bd, 1986–89. *Address:* Lauriel House, Knowle Lane, Cranleigh, Surrey GU6 8JW. *T:* Cranleigh (0483) 273513. *Club:* Caledonian.

HUNTER-TOD, Air Marshal Sir John (Hunter), KBE 1971 (OBE 1957); CB 1969; Head of Engineer Branch and Director-General of Engineering (RAF), 1970–73, retired; *b* 21 April 1917; *s* of late Hunter Finlay Tod, FRCS; *m* 1959, Anne, *d* of late Thomas Chaffer Howard; one *s. Educ:* Marlborough; Trinity Coll., Cambridge (MA). DCAe 1948. Commissioned, 1940; Fighter Command and Middle East, 1939–45. Group Capt. 1958; Air Cdre 1963. Dir, Guided Weapons (Air), Min. of Aviation, 1962–65; AOEng, RAF Germany, 1965–67; AOC No 24 Group, RAF, 1967–70; Air Vice-Marshal, 1968; Air Marshal, 1971. CEng. Hon. DSc Cranfield Inst. of Technol., 1974. *Address:* 21 Ridge Hill, Dartmouth, S Devon TQ6 9PE. *T:* Dartmouth (0803) 833130. *Club:* Royal Air Force.

HUNTING, (Charles) Patrick (Maule), CBE 1975; TD 1952; FCA; Chairman of Hunting Group, 1962–74; *b* 16 Dec. 1910; *s* of late Sir Percy Hunting; *m* 1941, Diana, *d* of late Brig. A. B. P. Pereira, DSO, of Tavistock, Devon; two *s* two *d. Educ:* Rugby Sch.; Trinity Coll., Cambridge. BA (Hons) Mod. and Mediaeval Langs; MA 1975; ACA 1936, FCA 1960. Served Royal Sussex Regt, 1939–45: France and Belgium, 1940; 8th Army, Western Desert, 1942; also in Palestine and Persia; Staff Coll., Camberley (psc), 1945. Entered Hunting Group 1936, Dir, 1946, Vice-Chm., 1961; Director: Hunting Associated Industries Ltd (Chm., 1965–74); Hunting Gibson Ltd (Chm., 1970–74); Hunting Gp Ltd (Chm., 1972–74). Mem. Council, Chamber of Shipping of UK, 1960 (Chm. Tramp Tanker Section, 1962); Master, Ironmongers' Company, 1978 (Mem. Court, 1970–). *Recreations:* golf, fishing, formerly cricket. *Clubs:* Naval and Military, MCC; Hawks (Cambridge); Royal Ashdown Forest (Golf).
  See also R. H. Hunting.

HUNTING, (Lindsay) Clive; Chairman, Hunting plc, 1974–91; *b* 22 Dec. 1925; *s* of late Gerald Lindsay Hunting and Ruth (*née* Pyman); *m* 1952, Shelagh (*née* Hill Lowe); one *s* one *d. Educ:* Loretto; Trinity Hall, Cambridge (MA). Royal Navy, 1944–47; Cambridge, 1947–50; joined Hunting Group, 1950, Dir 1952, Vice-Chm. 1962, Chm., 1975. President: British Independent Air Transport Assoc., 1960–62; Fedn Internationale de Transporte Aerien Privée, 1961–63; Air Educn and Recreation Organisation, 1970–90; SBAC, 1985–86 (Treas., 1988–); Chm., Air League, 1968–71; Mem. Ct, Cranfield Inst. of Technol., 1980–. Master, Coachmakers' and Coach Harness Makers' Co., 1983–84. CBIM 1980; CRaeS 1983. Nile Gold Medal for Aerospace Educn, 1982. *Recreations:* yachting, fishing. *Address:* 14 Conduit Mews, W2 3RE. *T:* 071–402 7914; Hunting PLC, 3 Cockspur Street, SW1Y 5BQ. *T:* 071–321 0123. *Clubs:* Royal Yacht Squadron, Royal London Yacht (Cdre, 1989) (Cowes).

HUNTING, Patrick; *see* Hunting, C. P. M.

HUNTING, Richard Hugh; Chairman, Hunting plc, since 1991 (Deputy Chairman, 1989–91); *b* 30 July 1946; *s* of Charles Patrick Maule Hunting, *qv; m* 1970, Penelope, *d* of Col L. L. Fleming, MBE, MC and Mrs S. E. Fleming; one *s* two *d. Educ:* Rugby Sch.; Sheffield Univ. (BEng); Manchester Business Sch. (MBA). Joined Hunting Gp, 1972; worked at Hunting Surveys and Consultants, Field Aviation, E. A. Gibson Shipbrokers, Hunting Oilfield Services, Hunting Engineering; Director: Hunting Associated Industries, 1986–89 (Chm., 1989); Hunting Petroleum Services, 1989; Hunting plc, 1989–. Mem. Court, Ironmongers' Co., 1986–. *Recreations:* ski-ing, board sailing, computing. *Address:* (office) 3 Cockspur Street, SW1Y 5BQ. *T:* 071–321 0123. *Club:* Travellers'.

HUNTINGDON, 16th Earl of, *cr* 1529; **William Edward Robin Hood Hastings Bass;** racehorse trainer, since 1976; *b* 30 Jan. 1948; *s* of Capt. Peter Robin Hood Hastings Bass (who assumed additional surname of Bass by deed poll, 1954) (*d* 1964); *g s* of 13th Earl and of Priscilla Victoria, *d* of Capt. Sir Malcolm Bullock, 1st Bt, MBE; *S* kinsman, 1990; *m* 1989, Sue Warner. *Educ:* Winchester; Trinity Coll., Cambridge. Trainer, West Ilsley Stables, Berks, 1989–. *Heir: b* Simon Aubrey Robin Hood Hastings Bass, *b* 2 May 1950. *Address:* Hodcott House, West Ilsley, near Newbury, Berks.

HUNTINGDON, Bishop Suffragan of, since 1980; **Rt. Rev. William Gordon Roe;** *b* 5 Jan. 1932; *s* of William Henry and Dorothy Myrtle Roe; *m* 1953, Mary Andreen; two *s* two *d. Educ:* Bournemouth School; Jesus Coll., Oxford (MA, DipTh (with distinction), DPhil); St Stephen's House, Oxford. Curate of Bournemouth, 1958–61; Priest-in-charge of St Michael's, Abingdon, 1961–69; Vice-Principal of St Chad's Coll., Durham, 1969–74; Vicar of St Oswald's, Durham, 1974–80; RD of Durham, 1974–80; Chaplain of Collingwood Coll., Durham, 1974–80; Hon. Canon of Durham Cathedral, 1979–80. *Publications:* Lamennais and England, 1966; (with A. Hutchings) J. B. Dykes, Priest and Musician, 1976. *Recreations:* French literature, painting, camping. *Address:* 14 Lynn Road, Ely, Cambs CB6 1DA. *T:* Ely (0353) 662137.

HUNTINGDON, Archdeacon of; *see* Sledge, Ven. R. K.

HUNTINGFIELD, 6th Baron *cr* 1796; **Gerard Charles Arcedeckne Vanneck;** Bt 1751; international civil servant with United Nations Secretariat, 1946–75; *b* 29 May 1915; *er s* of 5th Baron Huntingfield, KCMG, and Margaret Eleanor (*d* 1943) *o d* of late Judge Ernest Crosby, Grasmere, Rhinebeck, NY; *S* father, 1969; *m* 1941, Janetta Lois, *er d* of Capt. R. H. Errington, RN, Tostock Old Hall, Bury St Edmunds, Suffolk; one *s* two *d* (and one *d* decd). *Educ:* Stowe; Trinity College, Cambridge. *Heir: s* Hon. Joshua Charles Vanneck [*b* 10 Aug. 1954; *m* 1982, Arabella, *d* of A. H. J. Fraser, MC, Moniack Castle; four *s* one *d*]. *Address:* 53 Barron's Way, Comberton, Cambridge CB3 7EQ.
  See also Hon. Sir Peter Vanneck.

HUNTINGTON-WHITELEY, Sir Hugo (Baldwin), 3rd Bt *cr* 1918; DL; *b* 31 March 1924; *e surv. s* of Captain Sir Maurice Huntington-Whiteley, 2nd Bt, RN, and Lady (Pamela) Margaret Huntington-Whiteley (*d* 1976), 3rd *d* of 1st Earl Baldwin of Bewdley, KG, PC; *S* father, 1975; *m* 1959, Jean Marie Ramsay, JP 1973, DStJ; two *d. Educ:* Eton. Royal Navy, 1942–47. Chartered Accountant; Partner, Price Waterhouse, 1963–83. Mem. Ct of Assts, Goldsmiths' Co., 1982– (Prime Warden, 1989–90). Worcs: High Sheriff 1971; DL 1972. *Recreations:* music, travel. *Heir: b* (John) Miles Huntington-Whiteley, VRD, Lieut-Comdr RNR [*b* 18 July 1929; *m* 1960, Countess Victoria Adelheid Clementine Louise, *d* of late Count Friedrich Wolfgang zu Castell-Rudenhausen; one *s* two *d*]. *Address:* Ripple Hall, Tewkesbury, Glos GL20 6EY. *T:* Tewkesbury (0684) 592431; 12 Stafford Terrace, W8 7BH. *T:* 071–937 2918. *Club:* Brooks's.

HUNTLY, 13th Marquess of, *cr* 1599 (Scot.); **Granville Charles Gomer Gordon;** Earl of Huntly, 1450; Earl of Aboyne, Baron Gordon of Strathavon and Glenlivet, 1660; Baron Meldrum (UK), 1815; Premier Marquess of Scotland; Chief of House of Gordon; *b* 4 Feb. 1944; *s* of 12th Marquess of Huntly and of Hon. Mary Pamela Berry, *d* of 1st Viscount Kemsley; *S* father, 1987; *m* 1st, 1972, Jane Elizabeth Angela (marr. diss. 1990), *d* of late Col Alistair Gibb and Lady McCorquodale of Newton; two *s* two *d*; 2nd, 1991, Mrs Catheryn Millbourn. *Educ:* Gordonstoun. *Heir:* Earl of Aboyne, *qv. Address:* Aboyne Castle, Aberdeenshire. *T:* Aboyne (0339) 2118.
  See also Baron Cranworth.

HUNTSMAN, Peter William, FRICS; FAAV; Principal, College of Estate Management, since 1981; *b* 11 Aug. 1935; *s* of late William and Lydia Irene Huntsman (*née* Clegg); *m* 1st, 1961, Janet Mary Bell (marr. diss.); one *s* one *d*; 2nd, 1984, Cicely Eleanor (*née* Tamblin). *Educ:* Hymers Coll., Hull; Coll. of Estate Management, Univ. of London (BSc Estate Man.). Agricultural Land Service: Dorset and Northumberland, 1961–69; Kellogg Foundn Fellowship, USA, 1969–70; Principal Surveyor, London, ADAS, 1971–76; Divl Surveyor, Surrey, Middx and Sussex, 1976–81. Liveryman, Chartered Surveyors' Co., 1985; Freeman, City of London, 1985. *Publications:* (contrib.) Walmsley's Rural Estate Management, 6th edn 1978; contribs to professional jls. *Recreations:* sport, Dorset countryside, reading. *Address:* College of Estate Management, Whiteknights, Reading RG6 2AW. *T:* Reading (0734) 861101. *Clubs:* Athenæum, Farmers'; Phyllis Court (Henley).

HUPPERT, Prof. Herbert Eric, ScD; FRS 1987; Professor of Theoretical Geophysics and Foundation Director, Institute of Theoretical Geophysics, Cambridge University, since 1989; Fellow of King's College, Cambridge, since 1970; *b* 26 Nov. 1943; *er c* of Leo Huppert and Alice Huppert (*née* Neuman); *m* 1966, Felicia Adina Huppert (*née* Ferster), PhD; two *s*. *Educ:* Sydney Boys' High Sch.; Sydney Univ. (BSc 1963); ANU (MSc 1964); Univ. of California at San Diego (MS 1966, PhD 1968); Univ. of Cambridge (MA 1971, ScD 1985). ICI Research Fellow, 1968–70; University of Cambridge: Asst Dir of Research, 1970–81; Lectr in Applied Maths, 1981–88; BP Venture Unit Sen. Res. Fellow, 1983–89; Reader in Geophysical Dynamics, 1988–89. Visiting research scientist: ANU; Univ. of California, San Diego; Canterbury Univ.; Caltech; MIT; Univ. of NSW; Vis. Prof., Univ. of NSW, 1991–. Woods Hole Oceanographic Inst. Co-Chm., Scientists for the Release of Soviet Refusniks, 1988– (Vice-Chm., 1985–88). Associate Editor, Jl Fluid Mechanics, 1971–90; Editor, Jl of Soviet Jewry, 1985–. *Publications:* approximately 100 papers on applied mathematics, crystal growth, fluid mechanics, geology, geophysics, oceanography and meteorology. *Recreations:* my children, squash, mountaineering, learning to play the viola. *Address:* Institute of Theoretical Geophysics, 20 Silver Street, Cambridge CB3 9EW; 46 De Freville Avenue, Cambridge CB4 1HT. *T:* Cambridge (0223) 356071; (office) Cambridge (0223) 337853, Cambridge (0223) 333463, *Fax:* Cambridge (0223) 337918.

HURD, Rt. Hon. Douglas (Richard), CBE 1974; PC 1982; MP (C) Witney, since 1983 (Mid-Oxon, Feb. 1974–1983); Secretary of State for Foreign and Commonwealth Affairs, since 1989; *b* 8 March 1930; *e s* of Baron Hurd (*d* 1966) and Stephanie Corner (*d* 1985); *m* 1st, 1960, Tatiana Elizabeth Michelle (marr. diss. 1982), *d* of A. C. Benedict Eyre, Westburton House, Bury, Sussex; three *s*; 2nd, 1982, Judy, *d* of Sidney and Pamela Smart; one *s* one *d*. *Educ:* Eton (King's Scholar and Newcastle Scholar); Trinity Coll., Cambridge (Major Scholar). Pres., Cambridge Union, 1952. HM Diplomatic Service, 1952–66; served in: Peking, 1954–56; UK Mission to UN, 1956–60; Private Sec. to Perm. Under-Sec. of State, FO, 1960–63; Rome, 1963–66. Joined Conservative Research Dept, 1966; Head of Foreign Affairs Section, 1968; Private Sec. to Leader of the Opposition, 1968–70; Political Sec. to Prime Minister, 1970–74; Opposition Spokesman on European Affairs, 1976–79; Minister of State, FCO, 1979–83; Minister of State, Home Office, 1983–84; Sec. of State for NI, 1984–85, for Home Dept, 1985–89. Vis. Fellow, Nuffield Coll., Oxford, 1978–86. *Publications:* The Arrow War, 1967; Truth Game, 1972; Vote to Kill, 1975; An End to Promises, 1979; with Andrew Osmond: Send Him Victorious, 1968; The Smile on the Face of the Tiger, 1969, repr. 1982; Scotch on the Rocks, 1971; War Without Frontiers, 1982; (with Stephen Lamport) Palace of Enchantments, 1985. *Recreation:* writing thrillers. *Address:* House of Commons, SW1. *Club:* Beefsteak.

HURFORD, Peter (John), OBE 1984; organist; *b* 22 Nov. 1930; *e c* of H. J. Hurford, Minehead; *m* 1955, Patricia Mary Matthews, *e d* of late Prof. Sir Bryan Matthews, CBE, FRS; two *s* one *d*. *Educ:* Blundells Sch.; Royal Coll. of Music; Jesus Coll., Cambridge. MA, MusB Cantab, FRCO. Director of Music, Bablake Sch., Coventry and Conductor, Leamington Spa Bach Choir, 1956–57; Master of the Music, Cathedral and Abbey Church of St Alban, 1958–78, Conductor, St Albans Bach Choir, 1958–78; Founder, Internat. Organ Festival Soc., 1963. Artist-in-Residence: Univ. of Cincinnati, 1967–68; Sydney Opera Ho., 1980, 1981, 1982; Acting Organist, St John's Coll., Cambridge, 1979–80; recital and lecture tours throughout Europe, USA, Canada, Japan, Philippines, Taiwan, Australia and NZ from 1960. Vis. Prof. of Organ, Univ. of Western Ontario, 1976–77; Prof., RAM, 1982–88, Consultant Prof., 1988–. Mem. Council, 1963–, Pres., 1980–82, RCO; Mem., Hon. Council of Management, Royal Philharmonic Soc., 1983–87. Has made numerous LP records, incl. complete organ works of J. S. Bach (Gramophone Award, 1979; Silver Disc, 1983), F. Couperin, G. F. Handel, P. Hindemith. Hon. Dr, Baldwin-Wallace Coll., Ohio, 1981. Hon. FRSCM 1977; Hon. Mem., RAM, 1981; Hon. FRCM 1987. *Publications:* Making Music on the Organ, 1988; Suite: Laudate Dominum; sundry other works for organ; Masses for Series III and Rite II of Amer. Episcopal Church; sundry church anthems. *Recreations:* walking, wine, silence. *Address:* Broom House, St Bernard's Road, St Albans, Herts AL3 5RA.

HURLEY, Dame Rosalinde, (Dame Rosalinde Gortvai), DBE 1988; LLB, MD; FRCPath; Professor of Microbiology, University of London, at Institute of Obstetrics and Gynaecology, (Royal Postgraduate Medical School), since 1975; Consultant Microbiologist, Queen Charlotte's Maternity Hospital, since 1963; *b* 30 Dec. 1929; *o d* of late William Hurley and Rose Clancey; *m* 1964, Peter Gortvai, FRCS. *Educ:* Academy of the Assumption, Wellesley Hills, Mass, USA; Queen's Coll., Harley St, London; Univ. of London; Inns of Court. Called to the Bar, Inner Temple, 1958. House Surg., Wembley Hosp., 1955; Ho. Phys., W London Hosp., 1956; Sen. Ho. Officer, 1956–57, Registrar, 1957–58, Lectr and Asst Clin. Pathologist, 1958–62, Charing Cross Hosp. and Med. Sch. Chm., Medicines Commn, 1982–; Mem., Public Health Lab. Service Bd, 1982–90. Examiner, RCPath, and univs at home and abroad; Mem. Council, 1977–, Asst Registrar, 1978–, and Vice-Pres., 1984–87, RCPath; Royal Society of Medicine: Pres., Section of Pathology, and Vice-Pres., 1979–; Mem. Council, 1980–; Hon. Sec., 1984–90; Chm., 1980–82, formerly Vice-Chm., Cttee on Dental and Surgical Materials; Pres., Assoc. of Clinical Pathologists, 1984– (Pres.-elect, 1983–84); Chm., Assoc. of Profs of Medical Microbiol., 1987–. Mem. Governing Body, Postgrad. Med. Fed., 1985–90. Hon. FFPM 1990. DUniv Surrey, 1984. *Publications:* (jtly) Candida albicans, 1964; (jtly) Symposium on Candida Infections, 1966; (jtly) Neonatal and Perinatal Infections, 1979; chapters in med. books; papers in med. and sci. jls. *Recreations:* gardening, reading. *Address:* 2 Temple Gardens, Temple, EC4Y 9AY. *T:* 071–353 0577.

HURN, (Francis) Roger; Chairman, since 1991, Chief Executive, since 1981, and Managing Director, since 1978, Smiths Industries Plc; *b* 9 June 1938; *s* of Francis James Hurn and Joyce Elsa Bennett; *m* 1980, Rosalind Jackson; one *d*. *Educ:* Marlborough Coll. Engrg apprentice, Rolls Royce Motors, 1956; joined Smiths Industries, 1958. National Service, 1959–61. Export Dir, Motor Accessory Div., Smiths Industries, 1969; Man. Dir, Internat. Operations, 1974; Exec. Dir, 1976. Non-executive Director: Ocean Transport & Trading, 1982–88; Pilkington, 1984–; S. G. Warburg Gp, 1987–; Business in the Community, 1986–; Barnet Enterprise Trust Ltd, 1987–. Mem. Council: Industrial Soc., 1982–. Gov., Henley Coll., 1986–. Liveryman, Coachmakers & Coach Harness Makers' Co., 1979–. Young Businessman of the Year, Guardian Newspaper, 1980. *Recreations:* shooting, travel. *Address:* c/o Smiths Industries Plc, 765 Finchley Road, NW11 8DS. *T:* 081–458 3232.

HURON, Bishop of, since 1990; **Rt. Rev. Percival Richard O'Driscoll;** *b* 4 Oct. 1938; *s* of T. J. O'Driscoll and Annie O'Driscoll (*née* Copley); *m* 1965, Suzanne Gertrude Savignac; one *s* one *d*. *Educ:* Bishop's Univ., Lennoxville, Quebec (BA, STB); Huron Coll., London, Ont. (DD). Ordained deacon 1964, priest 1966; Assistant Curate: St Matthias, Ottawa, 1965–67; St John Evan, Kitchener, 1967–70; Religious Educn Dir, St Paul's Cathedral and Bishop Cronyn Memorial, London, 1970; Rector: St Michael & All Angels, London, 1970–75; St Batholomew's, Sarnia, 1975–80; Rector, St Paul's Cathedral, and Dean of Huron, 1980–87; Suffragan Bishop of Huron, 1987; Coadjutor Bishop, 1989. *Recreations:* camping, hiking, photography. *Address:* 25 Cherokee Road, Ont. N6G 2N7, Canada. *T:* (519) 433–0299. *Club:* London (Ontario).

HURRELL, Sir Anthony (Gerald), KCVO 1986; CMG 1984; HM Diplomatic Service, retired; *b* 18 Feb. 1927; *s* of late William Hurrell and Florence Hurrell; *m* 1951, Jean Wyatt; two *d*. *Educ:* Norwich Sch.; St Catharine's Coll., Cambridge. RAEC, 1948–50; Min. of Labour, 1950–53; Min. of Educn, 1953–64; joined Min. of Overseas Develt, 1964; Fellow, Center for International Affairs, Harvard, 1969–70; Head of SE Asia Develt Div., Bangkok, 1972–74; Under Secretary: Internat. Div. ODM, 1974–75; Central Policy Rev. Staff, Cabinet Office, 1976; Duchy of Lancaster, 1977; Asia and Oceans Div., ODA, 1978–83; Ambassador to Nepal, 1983–86. *Recreations:* bird-ringing, bird-watching, digging ponds, music. *Address:* Lapwings, Dunwich, Saxmundham, Suffolk IP17 3DR.

HURRELL, Air Vice-Marshal Frederick Charles, CB 1986; OBE 1968; Director General, Royal Air Force Medical Services and Deputy Surgeon General (Operations), 1986–87; retired 1988; Director of Appeals, Royal Air Force Benevolent Fund, since 1988; *b* 24 April 1928; *s* of Alexander John Hurrell and Maria Del Carmen Hurrell (*née* De Biedma); *m* 1950, Jay Jarvis; five *d*. *Educ:* Royal Masonic School, Bushey; St Mary's Hosp., Paddington (MB BS 1952). MRCS, LRCP 1952; Dip Av Med (RCP) 1970; MFOM 1981, FFOM 1987. Joined RAF 1953; served UK, Australia and Singapore; Dep. Dir, Aviation Medicine, RAF, 1974–77; British Defence Staff, Washington DC, 1977–80; CO Princess Alexandra Hosp., RAF Wroughton, 1980–82; Dir, Health and Research, RAF, 1982–84; PMO Strike Command, 1984–86. QHP 1984–88. FRAeS 1987. CStJ 1986. Chadwick Gold Medal, 1970. *Recreations:* walking, climbing, painting, photography. *Address:* Hale House, 4 Upper Hale Road, Farnham, Surrey GU9 0NJ. *T:* Farnham (0252) 714190. *Club:* Royal Air Force.

HURST, George; Principal Conductor, National Symphony Orchestra of Ireland, Dublin, since 1990; *b* 20 May 1926; Rumanian father and Russian mother. *Educ:* various preparatory and public schs. in the UK and Canada; Royal Conservatory, Toronto, Canada. First prize for Composition, Canadian Assoc. of Publishers, Authors and Composers, 1945. Asst Conductor, Opera Dept, Royal Conservatory of Music, of Toronto, 1946; Lectr in Harmony, Counterpoint, Composition etc, Peabody Conservatory of Music, Baltimore, Md, 1947; Conductor of York, Pa, Symph. Orch., 1950–55, and concurrently of Peabody Conservatory Orch., 1952–55; Asst Conductor, LPO, 1955–57, with which toured USSR 1956; Associate conductor, BBC Northern Symphony Orchestra, 1957; Principal Conductor, BBC Northern Symphony Orchestra (previously BBC Northern Orchestra), 1958–68; Artistic Adviser, 1968–73, Staff Conductor, 1968–88, Vice-Pres., 1979, Western Orchestral Soc. (Bournemouth SO and Bournemouth Sinfonietta); Consultant: Nat. Centre of Orchestral Studies, 1980–87; RAM conducting studies, 1983–; Principal Guest Conductor, BBC Scottish Symphony Orchestra, 1986–89. Since 1956 frequent guest conductor in Europe, Israel, Canada. *Publications:* piano and vocal music (Canada). *Recreations:* yachting, horse-riding.

HURST, Henry Ronald Grimshaw; Overseas Labour Adviser, Foreign and Commonwealth Office, 1976–81, retired; *b* 24 April 1919; *s* of Frederick George Hurst and Elizabeth Ellen (*née* Grimshaw); *m* 1st, 1942, Norah Joyce (*d* 1984), *d* of John Stanley Rothwell; one *s* one *d*; 2nd, 1986, Joy Oldroyde (*d* 1991). *Educ:* Darwen and Blackpool Grammar Schs; St Catharine's Coll., Cambridge (MA). Served War, Army, 1940–46. Colonial Service, 1946–70: Permanent Sec., Min. of Labour, Tanzania, 1962–64; Labour Adviser, Tanzania, 1965–68, and Malaŵi, 1969–70; Dep. Overseas Labour Adviser, FCO, 1970–76. *Recreations:* cricket, gardening, golf. *Address:* Flat 1, Meriden, Weston Road, Bath, Avon BA1 2XZ. *T:* Bath (0225) 334429. *Clubs:* Civil Service; Lansdown Golf.

HURST, John Gilbert, FBA 1987; FSA 1958; Assistant Chief Inspector of Ancient Monuments, English Heritage (formerly Department of the Environment), 1980–87; *b* 15 Aug. 1927; *s* of late Charles Chamberlain and Rona Hurst; *m* 1955, Dorothy Gillian Duckett (*d* 1971); two *d*. *Educ:* Harrow; Trinity Coll., Cambridge (BA Hons Archaeol. 1951; MA 1954). Joined Ancient Monuments Inspectorate, Min. of Works, 1952; Asst Inspector, 1954, Inspector, 1964, (Medieval rescue excavations); Principal Inspector (rescue excavations), 1973–80; directed excavations: Northolt Manor, 1950–70; Norwich, 1951–55; Dir, Wharram Res. Project, 1953–90; Sec., (Deserted) Medieval Village Res. Gp, 1952–86; British Association for Advancement of Science (Sect. H Anthrop.): Sec., 1954–57; Recorder, 1958–62; Pres., 1974; Society for Medieval Archaeology: Treasurer, 1957–76; Pres., 1980–83; Hon. Vice-Pres., 1983–; Vice-Pres., Soc. of Antiquaries, 1969–73; President: Soc. for Post-Medieval Archaeology, 1970–72; Medieval Pottery Res. Gp, 1977–80; Southwark and Lambeth Arch. Soc., 1982–84; Hon. Vice-Pres., Medieval Settlement Res. Gp, 1986–. Hon. MRIA 1991. Gen. Editor, Wharram Research Project Monographs, 1979–. Legal and General Silver Trowel Award, Archaeologist of the Year, 1990. *Publications include:* Deserted Villages of Oxfordshire, 1965 and Deserted Villages of Northamptonshire, 1966 (both with K. J. A. Allison and M. W. Beresford); (with M. W. Beresford) Deserted Medieval Villages: studies, 1971, 2nd edn 1989; (ed) B. Rackham, Medieval English Pottery, 2nd edn, 1972; (ed with H. Hodges and V. Evison) Medieval Pottery from Excavations, 1974; (with D. S. Neal and H. J. E. Van Beuningen) Pottery Produced and Traded in North West Europe 1350–1650, 1986; (with M. W. Beresford) Wharram Percy: deserted medieval village, 1990; numerous contribs to learned jls. *Recreations:* listening to music, gardening. *Address:* The Old Dairy, 14 Main Street, Great Casterton, Stamford, Lincs PE9 4AP. *T:* Stamford (0780) 57072.

HURST, Peter Thomas; Master of the Supreme Court Taxing Office, since 1981; *b* Troutbeck, Westmorland, 27 Oct. 1942; *s* of Thomas Lyon Hurst and Nora Mary Hurst; *m* 1968, Diane Irvine; one *s* two *d*. *Educ:* Stonyhurst College. LLB London. Admitted as Solicitor of the Supreme Court, 1967; Partner: Hurst and Walker, Solicitors, Liverpool, 1967–77; Gair Roberts Hurst and Walker, Solicitors, Liverpool, 1977–81. Chairman: Liverpool Young Solicitors Gp, 1979; NW Young Solicitors Conf., 1980. *Publications:* Butterworth's Costs Service, vol. 2, 1986; (ed jtly) Supreme Court Practice, 1990; contribs to: Cordery on Solicitors, 8th edn 1988; Legal Aid Manual, 1990. *Recreations:* gardening, music, French food and wine. *Address:* Royal Courts of Justice, Strand, WC2A 2LL. *T:* 071–936 6000. *Club:* Athenæum (Liverpool).

HURST, Dr Robert, CBE 1973; GM 1944; FRSC; retired; *b* Nelson, NZ, 3 Jan. 1915; *s* of late Percy Cecil Hurst and late Margery Hurst; *m* 1946, Rachael Jeanette (*née* Marsh); three *s*. *Educ:* Nelson Coll.; Canterbury Coll., NZ (MSc); Cambridge Univ. (PhD). FRIC 1977. Experimental Officer, Min. of Supply, engaged in research in bomb disposal and mine detection, 1940–45. Group Leader Transuranic Elements Group, AERE, Harwell, 1948–55; Project Leader, Homogeneous Aqueous Reactor Project, AERE, Harwell, 1956–57; Chief Chemist, Research and Development Branch, Industrial Group UKAEA, 1957–58; Director, Dounreay Experimental Reactor Establishment, UKAEA, 1958–63; Dir of Res., British Ship Res. Assoc., 1963–76. *Publication:* Editor, Progress in Nuclear Engineering, Series IV (Technology and Engineering), 1957. *Recreations:* gardening, sailing. *Address:* 15 Elms Avenue, Parkstone, Poole, Dorset BH14 8EE. *Club:* Athenæum.

HURT, John; actor; stage, films and television; Director, United British Artists, since 1982; *b* 22 Jan. 1940; *s* of Rev. Arnould Herbert Hurt and Phyllis Massey; *m* 1984, Donna Peacock (marr. diss. 1990); *m* 1990, Jo Dalton; one *s*. *Educ:* The Lincoln Sch., Lincoln; RADA. Started as a painter. *Stage:* début, Arts Theatre, London, 1962; Chips With Everything, Vaudeville, 1962; The Dwarfs, Arts, 1963; Hamp (title role), Edin. Fest., 1964; Inadmissible Evidence, Wyndhams, 1965; Little Malcolm and his Struggle Against the Eunuchs, Garrick, 1966; Belcher's Luck, Aldwych (RSC), 1966; Man and Superman, Gaiety, Dublin, 1969; The Caretaker, Mermaid, 1972; The Only Street, Dublin Fest. and Islington, 1973; Travesties, Aldwych (RSC), 1974; The Arrest, Bristol Old Vic, 1974; The Shadow of a Gunman, Nottingham Playhouse, 1978; The Seagull, Lyric, Hammersmith, 1985. *Films and Television:* began films with The Wild and the Willing, 1962; A Man for All Seasons, 1966; Sinful Davey, 1967, film 1968; The Waste Places (ATV), 1968; later films and TV include: Before Winter Comes, 1969; In Search of Gregory, 1970; Mr Forbush and the Penguins, 1971; (Evans in) 10 Rillington Place, 1971; The Ghoul, 1974; Little Malcolm, 1974; The Naked Civil Servant (ITV), 1975 (Emmy Award, 1976); Caligula, in I Claudius (series BBC TV) 1976; East of Elephant Rock, 1977; Treats (TV), 1977; The Disappearance, The Shout, Spectre, The Alien, and Midnight Express (BAFTA award, 1978), all 1978; Heaven's Gate, 1979; Crime and Punishment (BBC TV series), 1979; The Elephant Man, 1980 (BAFTA award, 1981); History of the World Part 1, 1981; Partners, 1982; Champions, 1984; Nineteen Eighty-Four, 1984; The Osterman Weekend, 1984; The Hit, 1984; Jake Speed, 1986; Rocinate, 1986; Aria, 1987; Deadline (BBC TV), 1988; Poison Candy (BBC TV), 1988; White Mischief, 1988; Scandal, 1989; Frankenstein Unbound, 1990; The Field, 1990; Who Bombed Birmingham (Granada TV), 1990; King Ralph, 1991; Lapse of Memory, 1991. *Address:* c/o Julian Belfrage, 68 St James's Street, SW1. *T:* 071–491 4400.

HURWITZ, Vivian Ronald; His Honour Judge Hurwitz; a Circuit Judge, since 1974; *b* 7 Sept. 1926; *s* of Alter Max and Dora Rebecca Hurwitz; *m* 1963, Dr Ruth Cohen, Middlesbrough; one *s* two *d*. *Educ:* Roundhay Sch., Leeds; Hertford Coll., Oxford (MA). Served RNVR: Univ. Naval Short Course, Oct. 1944–March 1945, followed by service until March 1947. Called to Bar, Lincoln's Inn, 1952, practised NE Circuit. A Recorder of Crown Court, 1972–74. *Recreations:* junior cricket, bridge, music (listening), art (looking at), sport—various (watching).

HUSAIN, Abul Basher M.; *see* Mahmud Husain.

HUSBAND, Prof. Thomas Mutrie, PhD; FEng 1988; FIProdE, FIMechE; Vice-Chancellor, University of Salford, since 1990; *b* 7 July 1936; *s* of Thomas Mutrie Husband and Janet Clark; *m* 1962, Pat Caldwell; two *s*. *Educ:* Shawlands Acad., Glasgow; Univ. of Strathclyde. BSc(Eng), MA, PhD. Weir Ltd, Glasgow: Apprentice Fitter, 1953–58; Engr/Jun. Manager, 1958–62; sandwich degree student (mech. engrg), 1958–61; various engrg and management positions with ASEA Ltd in Denmark, UK and S Africa, 1962–65; postgrad. student, Strathclyde Univ., 1965–66; Teaching Fellow, Univ. of Chicago, 1966–67; Lectr, Univ. of Strathclyde, 1967–70; Sen. Lectr, Univ. of Glasgow, 1970–73; Prof. of Manufacturing Organisation, Loughborough Univ., 1973–81; Prof. of Engrg Manufacture, 1981–90, Dir of Centre for Robotics, 1982–90, Hd of Dept of Mech. Engrg, 1983–90, Imperial Coll., London Univ. Chm., Review Panel for SERC/ESRC Jt Cttee, 1990–91; Member: ETCP Cttee, Fellowship of Engrg, 1989–; ETAC Cttee, DTI, 1990–. *Publications:* Work Analysis and Pay Structure, 1976; Maintenance and Terotechnology, 1977; Education and Training in Robotics, 1986; articles in Terotechnica, Industrial Relations Jl, Microelectronics and Reliability, etc. *Recreations:* watching Arsenal FC, music, theatre. *Address:* University of Salford, Salford M5 4WT; 34 Hawthorn Lane, Wilmslow SK9 5DG.

HUSH, Prof. Noel Sydney, DSc; FRS 1988; FAA; Foundation Professor and Head of Department of Theoretical Chemistry, University of Sydney, since 1971; *b* 15 Dec. 1924; *s* of Sidney Edgar Hush and Adrienne (*née* Cooper); *m* 1949, Thea L. Warman (decd), London; one *s* one *d*. *Educ:* Univ. of Sydney (BSc 1946; MSc 1948); Univ. of Manchester (DSc 1959). FAA 1977. Res. Fellow in Chemistry, Univ. of Sydney, 1946–49; Lectr in Phys. Chem., Univ. of Manchester, 1950–54; Lectr, subseq. Reader in Chem., Univ. of Bristol, 1955–71. Visiting Professor: ANU, 1960; Florida State Univ., 1965; Case Western Reserve Univ., 1968; Cambridge Univ., 1981; Stanford Univ., 1987; Vis. Fellow, Cavendish Lab., 1971; Vis. Sen. Scientist, Brookhaven Nat. Lab., USA, 1959–. Mem., Aust. Res. Grants Cttee, 1984– (Chm., Chem. Cttee, 1987–). Adv. Editor, Chemical Physics, 1973–. *Publications:* (ed) Reactions of Molecules at Electrodes, 1971; papers in Jl of Chemical Physics, Chemical Physics, Jl of Amer. Chemical Soc. *Recreations:* literature, music, travel. *Address:* 170 Windsor Street, Paddington, Sydney, NSW 2021, Australia. *T:* 61 02 328 1685; Department of Theoretical Chemistry, University of Sydney, Sydney, NSW 2006. *T:* 61 02 692 3330. *Club:* Athenæum.

HUSKISSON, Robert Andrews, CBE 1979; Chairman, Lloyd's Register of Shipping, 1973–83 (Deputy Chairman, 1972–73); *b* 2 April 1923; *y s* of Edward Huskisson and Mary Huskisson (*née* Downing); *m* 1969, Alice Marian Swaffin. *Educ:* Merchant Taylors' Sch.; St Edmund Hall, Oxford. Served Royal Corps of Signals, 1941–47 (Major). Joined Shaw Savill & Albion Co. Ltd 1947; Dir 1966–72; Dep. Chief Exec., 1971–72; Director: Overseas Containers Ltd, 1967–72; Container Fleets Ltd, 1967–72; Cairn Line of Steamships Ltd, 1969–72. Director: SMIT Internat. Gp (UK) Ltd, 1982–87; Harland and Wolff plc, 1983–87; Lloyd's of London Press, 1983–89. President: British Shipping Fedn, 1971–72 (Chm. 1968–71); International Shipping Fedn, 1969–73; Chairman: Hotels and Catering EDC, 1975–79; Marine Technology Management Cttee, SRC, 1977–81. Dir, Chatham Historical Dockyard Trust, 1984–91; Chm., Essex Nuffield Hosp. Local Adv. Cttee, 1987–. *Recreations:* golf, gardening, music. *Address:* Lanterns, Luppitt Close, Hutton Mount, Brentwood, Essex. *Clubs:* Vincent's (Oxford); Thorndon Park Golf.

HUSSAIN, Karamat, SQA 1983; retired; Councillor (Lab) Mapesbury Ward, London Borough of Brent, 1971–86; Chairman, National Standing Conference of Afro-Caribbean and Asian Councillors, 1980–86 (Founder Member); *b* Rawalpindi, 1926; *m* Shamim. *Educ:* Aligarh Muslim Univ., India (BA Hons Humanities, MPhil). Political Educn Officer, Brent E, 1967–70. Brent Council: Chm., Planning Cttee, 1978–86; Vice Chm., Develt Cttee, 1978–86; Mem., Housing and Finance Cttees, 1978–86; Mayor of Brent, 1981–82 (Dep. Mayor, 1980–81); formerly Mem. and Vice-Chm., Brent Community Relations Council. Former Member: Regl Adv. Council on Higher Technical Educn, London and Home Counties; ASTMS. Gov., Willesden Coll. of Technology, 1971–86. *Recreation:* research in political philosophy. *Address:* Bungalow 14, Tregwilym Road, Rogerstone, Newport, Gwent NP1 9DW. *T:* Newport (0633) 892187.

HUSSEIN bin Talal; King of Jordan; *b* 14 Nov. 1935; *s* of King Talal and Queen Zein; *S* father, 1952; *m* 1st, 1955, Princess Dina (marr. diss.); one *d*; 2nd, 1961, Antoinette Gardiner (marr. diss. 1972); two *s* twin *d*; 3rd, 1972, Alia Baha Eddin Toukan (d 1977); one *s* one *d*; 4th, 1978, Lisa Hallaby, (Queen Noor); two *s* two *d*. *Educ:* Victoria Coll., Alexandria; Harrow; RMA, Sandhurst. Holds many foreign decorations. *Publication:* Uneasy Lies the Head (autobiog.), 1962. *Recreations:* water sports, karate, flying, driving, fencing, photography, ham radio. *Address:* Royal Hashemite Court, Amman, Jordan.

HUSSEY, Prof. Joan Mervyn, MA, BLitt, PhD; FSA; FRHistS; Professor of History in the University of London, at Royal Holloway College, 1950–74, now Emeritus. *Educ:* privately; Trowbridge High Sch.; Lycée Victor Duruy, Versailles; St Hugh's Coll., Oxford. Research Student, Westfield Coll., London, 1932–34; Internat. Travelling Fellow (FUW), 1934–35; Pfeiffer Research Fellow, Girton, 1934–37; Gamble Prize, 1935. Asst Lectr in Hist., Univ. of Manchester, 1937–43; Lectr in Hist., 1943–47, Reader in Hist., 1947–50, at Bedford Coll., Univ. of London. Visiting Prof. at Amer. Univ. of Beirut, 1966. Pres., Brit. Nat. Cttee for Byzantine Studies, 1961–71; Hon. Vice-Pres., Internat. Cttee for Byzantine Studies, 1976. Governor, Girton Coll., Cambridge, 1935–37; Mem. Council, St Hugh's Coll., Oxford, 1940–46; Mem. Council, Royal Holloway Coll., 1966–86. Hon. Fellow, St Hugh's Coll., Oxford, 1968; Hon. Res. Associate, RHBNC, 1986. Hon. Fellow, Instituto Siciliano de Studi Bizantini, 1975. *Publications:* Church and Learning in the Byzantine Empire 867–1185, 1937 (repr. 1961); The Byzantine World, 1957, 3rd edn 1966; Cambridge Medieval History IV, Pts I and II: ed and contributor, 1966–67; The Finlay Papers, 1973; The Orthodox Church in the Byzantine Empire, 1986, rev. edn 1990; reviews and articles in Byzantinische Zeitschrift, Byzantinoslavica, Trans Roy. Hist. Soc., Jl of Theological Studies, Enc. Britannica, Chambers's Enc., New Catholic Enc., etc. *Address:* 16 Clarence Drive, Englefield Green, Egham, Surrey TW20 0NL.

HUSSEY, Marmaduke James; Chairman, Board of Governors: BBC, since 1986; Royal Marsden Hospital, since 1985; Director, Colonial Mutual Group, since 1982; *b* 1923; *s* of late E. R. J. Hussey, CMG and Mrs Christine Hussey; *m* 1959, Lady Susan Katharine Waldegrave (*see* Lady Susan Hussey); one *s* one *d*. *Educ:* Rugby Sch.; Trinity Coll., Oxford (Scholar, MA; Hon. Fellow 1989). Served War of 1939–45, Grenadier Guards, Italy. Joined Associated Newspapers, 1949, Dir 1964; Man. Dir, Harmsworth Publications, 1967–70; joined Thomson Organisation Exec. Bd, 1971; Chief Exec. and Man. Dir, 1971–80, Dir, 1982–86, Times Newspapers Ltd; Jt Chm., Great Western Radio, 1985–86; Dir, William Collins plc, 1985–89. Mem. Bd, British Council, 1983–. Member: Govt Working Party on Artificial Limb and Appliance Centres in England, 1984–86; Management Cttee and Educn Cttee, King Edward's Hosp. Fund for London, 1987–. Pres., Royal Bath and West of England Soc., 1990–91. Trustee: Rhodes Trust, 1972–91; Royal Acad. Trust, 1988–. *Address:* Flat 15, 45/47 Courtfield Road, SW7 4DB. *T:* 071–370 1414. *Club:* Brooks's.

See also Sir Francis Brooke, Bt.

HUSSEY, Lady Susan Katharine, DCVO 1984 (CVO 1971); Lady-in-Waiting to the Queen, since 1960; *b* 1 May 1939; 5th *d* of 12th Earl Waldegrave, KG, *qv*; *m* 1959, Marmaduke James Hussey, *qv*; one *s* one *d*. *Address:* Flat 15, 45/47 Courtfield Road, SW7 4DB. *T:* 071–370 1414.

See also Sir Francis Brooke, Bt.

HUTCHINGS, Andrew William Seymour, CBE 1973; General Secretary, Assistant Masters Association, 1939–78, Joint General Secretary, Assistant Masters and Mistresses Association, Sept-Dec. 1978; Vice-President, National Foundation for Educational Research in England and Wales, since 1983 (Chairman, 1973–83); *b* 3 Dec. 1907; *o s* of William Percy and Mellony Elizabeth Louisa Hutchings; unmarried. *Educ:* Cotham Sch., Bristol; St Catharine's Coll., Cambridge (MA). Asst Master: Downside Sch., 1929–30; Methodist Coll., Belfast, 1930–34; Holt Sch., Liverpool, 1934–36; Asst Sec., Asst Masters Assoc., 1936–39; Hon. Sec., Jt Cttee of Four Secondary Assocs, 1939–78; Sec.-Gen. 1954–65, Pres. 1965–71 and 1972–73, Internat. Fedn of Secondary Teachers; Member: Exec. Cttee, World Confedn of Organisations of Teaching Profession, 1954–80; Secondary Schs Examination Council, and subseq. of Schools Council, 1939–78; Norwood Cttee on Curriculum and Examinations in Secondary Schs, 1941–43; Chm., Teachers' Panel, Burnham Primary and Secondary Cttee, 1965–78; Vice-Chm., Associated Examining Bd, 1982– (Chm., Exec. Cttee, 1979–). FEIS 1963; FCP 1975. *Publications:* educnl and professional articles and memoranda for Asst Masters Assoc. *Address:* Lower Eastacott House, Umberleigh, North Devon EX37 9AJ. *T:* Chittlehamholt (07694) 486. *Club:* Kennel.

HUTCHINGS, Gregory Frederick; Chief Executive, Tomkins PLC, since 1984 (Director, since 1983); Non-Executive Director, Mosaic Investments PLC, since 1987. *Educ:* Uppingham Sch.; University of Aston. BSc, MBA. *Address:* Tomkins PLC, East Putney House, 84 Upper Richmond Road, SW15 2ST. *T:* 081–871 4544.

HUTCHINS, Captain Ronald Edward, CBE 1961; DSC 1943; RN; *b* 7 Jan. 1912; *s* of Edward Albert Hutchins and Florence Ada (*née* Sharman); *m* 1937, Irene (*née* Wood); two *s*. *Educ:* St John's (elem. sch.), Hammersmith; TS Mercury, Hamble, Hants (C. B. Fry); RN Coll., Greenwich. Royal Navy, 1928–61, service in submarines, then Exec. Br. specialising in gunnery; Computer Industry, 1961–79: Manager and Company Dir, ICL and some of its UK subsids, and associated engrg cos. *Recreations:* walking, gardening. *Address:* 11 Virginia Beeches, Callow Hill, Virginia Water, Surrey GU25 4LT.

HUTCHINSON; *see* Hely-Hutchinson.

HUTCHINSON, family name of **Baron Hutchinson of Lullington.**

HUTCHINSON OF LULLINGTON, Baron *cr* 1978 (Life Peer), of Lullington in the County of E Sussex; **Jeremy Nicolas Hutchinson,** QC 1961; *b* 28 March 1915; *o s* of late St John Hutchinson, KC; *m* 1st, 1940, Dame Peggy Ashcroft (marr. diss. 1966; she *d* 1991); one *s* one *d*; 2nd, 1966, June Osborn. *Educ:* Stowe Sch.; Magdalen Coll., Oxford. Called to Bar, Middle Temple, 1939, Bencher 1963. RNVR, 1939–46. Practised on Western Circuit, N London Sessions and Central Criminal Court. Recorder of Bath, 1962–72; a Recorder of the Crown Court, 1972–76. Member: Cttee on Immigration Appeals, 1966–68; Cttee on Identification Procedures, 1974–76. Prof. of Law, RA, 1987–. Mem., Arts Council of GB, 1974–79 (Vice-Chm., 1977–79); Trustee: Tate Gallery, 1977–84 (Chm., 1980–84); Chantrey Bequest, 1977–. *Address:* House of Lords, Westminster, SW1A 0PW. *Club:* MCC.

HUTCHINSON, Arthur Edward; QC 1979; **His Honour Judge Arthur Hutchinson;** a Circuit Judge, since 1984; *b* 31 Aug. 1934; *s* of late George Edward Hutchinson and Kathleen Hutchinson; *m* 1967, Wendy Pauline Cordingley, one *s* two *d*.

Educ: Silcoates Sch.; Emmanuel Coll., Cambridge (MA). Commissioned, West Yorkshire Regt, 1953; served in Kenya with 5th Fusiliers, 1953–54. Called to Bar, Middle Temple, 1958; joined NE Circuit, 1959; a Recorder, 1974–84. *Recreations:* cricket, gardening, music. *Address:* c/o The Court House, Oxford Row, Leeds LS1 3BE. *T:* Leeds (0532) 451616.

HUTCHINSON, Maj.-Gen. (George) Malcolm, CB 1989; CEng, FIEE; Member, Defence Prospect Team, since 1990; *b* 24 Aug. 1935; *s* of Cecil George Hutchinson and Annie Hutchinson; *m* 1958, Irene Mary Mook; four *d*. *Educ:* Pocklington Sch.; Queen's Coll., Cambridge (MA). Develt Engr, Metropolitan Vickers, 1957; short service commn, 1958, regular commn, 1961, REME; RMCS, 1967; sc Camberley, 1968; CO 12 Armd Workshop, REME, 1968–70; Staff appts, 1970–74; British Liaison Officer, USA Army Materiel Comd, 1974–76; Comdr REME 1 British Corps troops, 1977–79; REME staff, 1979–82; Project Man., Software Systems, 1982–85; Dep. to DGEME, 1985–86; Dir Procurement Strategy MoD(PE), 1986–88; Vice Master-Gen. of the Ordnance, 1988–90. Pres., IEEIE, 1990. *Recreations:* Rugby, cricket, sailing. *Address:* c/o Barclays Bank, Benet Street, Cambridge.

HUTCHINSON, Prof. George William, MA, PhD, Cantab; Professor of Physics, Southampton University, 1960–85, now Emeritus; *b* Feb. 1921; *s* of George Hutchinson, farmer, and Louisa Ethel (*née* Saul), Farnsfield, Notts; *m* 1943, Christine Anne (marr. diss. 1970), *d* of Matthew Rymer and Mary (*née* Proctor), York; two *s*. *Educ:* Abergele Grammar Sch.; Cambridge. MA 1946, PhD 1952, Cantab. State Schol. and Schol. of St John's Coll., Cambridge, 1939–42. Research worker and factory manager in cotton textile industry, 1942–47; Cavendish Lab., Cambridge, 1947–52; Clerk-Maxwell Schol. of Cambridge Univ., 1949–52; Nuffield Fellow, 1952–53, and Lecturer, 1953–55, in Natural Philosophy, University of Glasgow; Research Assoc. of Stanford Univ., Calif, 1954. Lecturer, 1955, Sen. Lectr, 1957, in Physics, University of Birmingham. Member: Nat. Exec. Cttee, AUT, 1978–84; Nat. Council, CND, 1981–84; Nat. Co-ordinating Cttee, Scientists Against Nuclear Arms, (Internat. Sec., SANA) 1985–88, 1990–; Exec. Cttee, British Peace Assembly, 1988– (Acting Chm., 1990–); Exec. Cttee, World Disarmament Campaign UK, 1988. Exec. Cttee, Labour Action for Peace, 1990–. Duddell Medal, Physical Soc., 1959. FRAS; FRSA. *Publications:* papers on nuclear and elementary particle physics, nuclear instrumentation and cosmic rays, and disarmament and peace. *Recreations:* music, travel. *Address:* Physical Laboratory, University of Southampton, Southampton SO9 5NH. *T:* Southampton (0703) 595000.

HUTCHINSON, (John) Maxwell, RIBA; Chairman, Hutchinson and Partners Architects Ltd, since 1987; *b* 3 Dec. 1948; *s* of late Frank Maxwell Hutchinson and Elizabeth Ross Muir (*née* Wright); marr. diss. *Educ:* Wellingborough Prep. Sch.; Oundle; Scott Sutherland Sch. of Arch., Aberdeen; Architectural Assoc. Sch. of Arch. (AA Dip. 1972); RIBA 1972. Founder, Hutchinson and Partners, Chartered Architects, 1972; Chairman, Permarock Products Ltd, Loughborough, 1985. Royal Institute of British Architects: Mem. Council, 1978–, Sen. Vice Pres., 1988–89, Pres., 1989–91; Chairman: Energy Policy Cttee, 1986–89; Nat. Conf., 1982, 1983; Vice Pres., Industrial Bldg Bureau, 1988–. Vis. Prof., Arch. and Planning Dept, QUB, 1989–. Chm., London Br., Elgar Soc., 1986–; Associate Mem., PRS, 1988. Trustee, St George's, Bloomsbury, 1988–. FRSA. Freeman, City of London, 1980; Mem. Ct of Assts, Co. of Chartered Architects, 1988–. Regular radio and TV broadcaster. *Compositions:* The Kibbo Kift, Edinburgh Fest., 1976; The Ascent of Wilberforce III, Lyric Hammersmith, 1982; Requiem in a Village Church (choral), 1986; St John's Cantata, 1987. *Publications:* The Prince of Wales: right or wrong?, 1989; contrib. to technical press on architectural subjects. *Recreations:* composing, recording, playing the guitar loudly, music of Edward Elgar, opera, ballet, theatre, riding, running, Rutland. *Address:* (office) 401 St John Street, EC1V 4QE. *T:* 071–278 4477; 29 Pied Bull Court, Galen Place, WC1. *T:* 071–405 1122; Cobblers Cottage, 4 Church Street, Empingham, Rutland. *T:* Empingham (078086) 434. *Club:* Athenæum.

HUTCHINSON, Maj.-Gen. Malcolm; *see* Hutchinson, Maj.-Gen. G. M.

HUTCHINSON, Maxwell; *see* Hutchinson, J. M.

HUTCHINSON, Patricia Margaret, CMG 1981; CBE 1982; HM Diplomatic Service, retired; *b* 18 June 1926; *d* of late Francis Hutchinson and Margaret Peat. *Educ:* abroad; St Paul's Girls' Sch.; Somerville Coll., Oxford (PPE, MA, Hon Fellow, 1980). ECE, Geneva, 1947; Bd of Trade, 1947–48; HM Diplomatic Service, 1948: 3rd Sec., Bucharest, 1950–52; Foreign Office, 1952–55; 2nd (later 1st) Sec., Berne, 1955–58; 1st Sec. (Commercial), Washington, 1958–61; FO, 1961–64; 1st Sec., Lima, 1964–67 (acted as Chargé d'Affaires); Dep. UK Permanent Rep. to Council of Europe, 1967–69; Counsellor: Stockholm, 1969–72; UK Delegn to OECD, 1973–75; Consul-Gen., Geneva, 1975–80; Ambassador to Uruguay, 1980–83; Consul-Gen., Barcelona, 1983–86. Pres., Somerville ASM, 1988–. *Recreations:* music, reading. *Address:* 118A Ashley Gardens, SW1P 1HL. *Club:* United Oxford & Cambridge University.

HUTCHINSON, Prof. Philip, CPhys; Head of School of Mechanical Engineering, Cranfield Institute of Technology, since 1987; *b* 26 July 1938; *s* of George and Edna Hutchinson; *m* 1960, Joyce Harrison; one *s* one *d*. *Educ:* King James 1st Grammar Sch., Bishop Auckland, Co. Durham; King's Coll., Univ. of Durham (BSc); Univ. of Newcastle upon Tyne (PhD). MInstP. SO and SSO, Theoretical Phys. Div., AERE, Harwell, 1962–69; Vis. Fellow, Chem. Engrg Dept, Univ. of Houston, Texas, 1969–70; AERE, Harwell: SSO and PSO, Theoretical Phys Div., 1970–75; Hd of Thermodynamics and Fluid Mechanics Gp, Engrg Scis Div., 1975–80; Hd of Engrg Phys Br., Engrg Scis Div., 1980–85; Hd of Engrg Scis Div., 1985–87; Hd, Harwell Combustion Centre, 1980–87. Visiting Professor: Imperial Coll., London, 1980–85; Univ. of Leeds, 1985–. Chairman: Internat. Energy Agency Exec. Cttee on Fundamental Res. in Combustion, 1977–81; Combustion Phys Gp of InstP, 1985–89; MRI 1989; Mem., Combustion Inst., 1977–; Past Mem., Watt Cttee on Energy, representing InstP and Combustion Inst. respectively; Founding Bd Mem., Europ. Research Centre on Flow Turbulence and Combustion, 1988. 27th Leonardo da Vinci Lectr for IMechE, 1983. *Publications:* papers in learned jls on statistical mechanics, fluid mechanics, combustion and laser light scattering. *Recreations:* squash, music, reading, Go, gadgets. *Address:* School of Mechanical Engineering, Cranfield Institute of Technology, Cranfield, Beds MK43 0AL; 127 Blackmoor Gate, Furzton, Milton Keynes MK4 1DJ. *T:* Milton Keynes (0908) 504060.

HUTCHINSON, Richard Hampson; His Honour Judge Hutchinson; a Circuit Judge, since 1974; *b* 31 Aug. 1927; *s* of late John Riley Hutchinson and May Hutchinson; *m* 1954, Nancy Mary (*née* Jones); two *s* three *d*. *Educ:* St Bede's Grammar Sch., Bradford; UC Hull. LLB London. National Service, RAF, 1949–51. Called to Bar, Gray's Inn, 1949; practised on NE Circuit, 1951–74. Recorder: Rotherham, 1971–72; Crown Court, 1972–74; Hon. Recorder of Lincoln, 1991; Resident Judge, Lincoln Crown Court. Mem., County Court Rules Cttee, 1990–; Technical Rep., Central Council of Probation Cttees, 1989–. *Recreations:* reading, conversation. *Address:* c/o Crown Court, Crosstrend House, 10A Newport, Lincoln.

HUTCHINSON, Hon. Sir Ross, Kt 1977; DFC 1944; Speaker, Legislative Assembly, Western Australia, 1974–77, retired; MLA (L) Cottesloe, 1950–77; *b* 10 Sept. 1914; *s* of Albert H. Hutchinson and Agnes L. M. Hutchinson; *m* 1939, Amy Goodall Strang; one *s* one *d*. *Educ:* Wesley Coll. RAAF, 1942–45. School teacher, 1935–49. Chief Sec., Minister for Health and Fisheries, 1959–65; Minister for Works and Water Supplies, 1965–71. Australian Rules Football, former Captain Coach; East Fremantle, West Perth and South Fremantle; Captain Coach, WA, 1939. *Recreations:* tennis, reading. *Address:* 42 Griver Street, Cottesloe, WA 6011, Australia. *T:* 312680. *Club:* Royal King's Park Tennis (Perth, WA).

HUTCHISON, A(lan) Michael Clark; *b* 26 Feb. 1914; *y s* of late Sir George A. Clark Hutchison, KC, MP, of Eriska, Argyll; *m* 1937, Anne (*d* 1989), *yr d* of Rev. A. R. Taylor, DD, of Aberdeen; one *s* one *d*. *Educ:* Eton; Trinity Coll., Cambridge. Called to Bar, Gray's Inn, 1937. War of 1939–45 (despatches); served AIF, Middle East and Pacific theatres, psc (Major). Mem. Australian Mil. Mission, Washington, USA, 1945–46. Entered Colonial Admin. Service, 1946, and served as Asst Dist Comr in Palestine till 1948; thereafter as Political Officer and Asst Sec. in Protectorate and Colony of Aden; resigned, 1955. Contested (C) Motherwell Div. of Lanarks, 1955; MP (C) Edinburgh South, May 1957–79; Parliamentary Private Secretary to: Parliamentary and Financial Sec. to the Admiralty, and to the Civil Lord, 1959; the Lord Advocate, 1959–60; Sec. of State for Scotland, 1960–62. Scottish Conservative Members' Committee: Vice-Chm., 1965–66, 1967–68; Chm., 1970–71. Introduced as Private Mem.'s Bills: Solicitors (Scotland) Act; Wills Act; Intestate Succession (Scotland) Act; Confirmation to Small Estates (Scotland) Act. *Recreations:* reading, Disraeliana. *Address:* 12 Stokes View, Pangbourne Hill, Pangbourne, Berks RG8 7RP. *T:* Pangbourne (0734) 845106. *Club:* New (Edinburgh).
See also Lieut-Comdr Sir G. I. C. Hutchison.

HUTCHISON, Rt. Rev. Andrew; *see* Montreal, Bishop of.

HUTCHISON, Bruce; *see* Hutchison, W. B.

HUTCHISON, Hon. Sir Douglas; *see* Hutchison, Hon. Sir J. D.

HUTCHISON, Geordie Oliphant; Managing Director, Calders & Grandidge Ltd, timber importers and manufacturers, since 1974; *b* 11 June 1934; *s* of late Col Ronald Gordon Oliphant Hutchison and of Ruth Gordon Hutchison-Bradburne; *m* 1964, Virginia Barbezat; two *s* one *d*. *Educ:* Eton Coll. Served RN, 1952–54: commnd as aircraft pilot, 1953. Calders Ltd, 1954–59; Calders & Grandidge Ltd, 1959–: Dir, 1969. Comr, Forestry Commn, 1981–89. *Recreations:* golf, shooting. *Address:* Swallowfield House, Welby, Grantham, Lincs NG32 3LR. *T:* Loveden (0400) 30510. *Club:* Royal and Ancient Golf (St Andrews).

HUTCHISON, Lt-Comdr Sir (George) Ian Clark, Kt 1954; Royal Navy, retired; Member of the Queen's Body Guard for Scotland, Royal Company of Archers; *b* 4 Jan. 1903; *e s* of late Sir George Clark Hutchison, KC, MP, Eriska, Argyllshire; *m* 1926, Sheena (*d* 1966), *o d* of late A. B. Campbell, WS; one *d*. *Educ:* Edinburgh Academy; RN Colleges, Osborne and Dartmouth. Joined Navy as Cadet, 1916; Lieut, 1926; Lieut-Comdr 1934; specialised in torpedoes, 1929; emergency list, 1931; Mem., Edinburgh Town Council, 1935–41; Chm., Public Assistance Cttee, 1937–39; contested Maryhill Div. of Glasgow, 1935; rejoined Navy Sept. 1939; served in Naval Ordnance Inspection Dept, 1939–43; MP (U) for West Div. of Edinburgh, 1941–59. Mem. National Executive Council of British Legion (Scotland), 1943–51; Governor of Donaldson's Sch. for the Deaf, Edinburgh, 1937–75; Mem. Cttee on Electoral Registration, 1945–46; Mem. Scottish Leases Cttee, 1951–52. DL County of City of Edinburgh, 1958–84. *Recreations:* golf, fishing, walking, philately. *Address:* 16 Wester Coates Gardens, Edinburgh EH12 5LT. *T:* 031–337 4888. *Club:* New (Edinburgh).
See also A. M. C. Hutchison, J. V. Paterson.

HUTCHISON, Helena Ann, (Mrs Iain Hutchison); *see* Kennedy, H. A.

HUTCHISON, Lt-Comdr Sir Ian Clark; *see* Hutchison, Sir G. I. C.

HUTCHISON, (Joseph) Douglas, CBE 1972; MC 1944; TD 1952; Director, Ranks Hovis McDougall Ltd, 1956–83; *b* 3 April 1918; *s* of late John K. Hutchison, Kinloch, Collessie, Fife and late Ethel Rank, OBE; unmarried. *Educ:* Loretto; Clare Coll., Cambridge. BA Agric. 1939. Served Fife and Forfar Yeomanry, 1939–46 (Major); comd Regt, 1951–53. Director: R. Hutchison & Co. Ltd, 1951–73; Ranks Ltd (later RHM), 1956. Mem., ARC, 1973–78. Pres., Nat. Assoc. British and Irish Millers, 1963–64 and 1974–75; Pres., Research Assoc. Flour Millers and Bakers, 1967–72; Chm., Game Conservancy, 1970–75. *Recreations:* gardening, music. *Address:* Bolfracks, Aberfeldy, Perthshire. *Club:* New (Edinburgh).

HUTCHISON, Hon. Sir Michael, Kt 1983; **Hon. Mr Justice Hutchison;** a Judge of the High Court of Justice, Queen's Bench Division, since 1983; Presiding Judge, Western Circuit, since 1989; *b* 13 Oct. 1933; *s* of Ernest and Frances Hutchison; *m* 1957, Mary Spettigue; two *s* three *d*. *Educ:* Lancing; Clare College, Cambridge (MA). Called to Bar, Gray's Inn, 1958, Bencher, 1983; a Recorder, 1975–83; QC 1976; Judge, Employment Appeal Tribunal, 1984–87. Member: Judicial Studies Bd, 1985–87; Parole Bd, 1987–89. *Address:* Royal Courts of Justice, Strand, WC2A 2LL.

HUTCHISON, Sir Peter, 2nd Bt, *cr* 1939; *b* 27 Sept. 1907; *er s* of Sir Robert Hutchison, 1st Bt, MD, CM, and Lady Hutchison; *S* father 1960; *m* 1949, Mary-Grace (*née* Seymour); two *s* two *d*. *Educ:* Marlborough; Lincoln Coll., Oxford (MA). Admitted as a Solicitor, 1933. Dep.-Clerk of the Peace and of the CC, E Suffolk, 1947–71, Clerk of the Peace, 1971. Mem., Suffolk Coastal DC, 1973–83. Chm. of Governors, Orwell Park Prep. Sch., 1975–85. *Recreations:* gardening, reading. *Heir:* *s* Robert Hutchison [*b* 25 May 1954; *m* 1987, Anne Margaret, *er d* of Sir Michael Thomas, Bt, *qv*; two *s*]. *Address:* Melton Mead, near Woodbridge, Suffolk IP12 1PF. *T:* Woodbridge (03943) 2746.

HUTCHISON, Sir Peter Craft, 2nd Bt *cr* 1956; Chairman, Hutchison & Craft Ltd, Insurance Brokers, Glasgow, since 1979; Vice-Chairman, British Waterways Board, 1989–92 (Member, since 1987); *b* 5 June 1935; *s* of Sir James Riley Holt Hutchison, 1st Bt, DSO, TD, and Winefryde Eleanor Mary (*d* 1988), *d* of late Rev. R. H. Craft; *S* father, 1979; *m* 1966, Virginia, *er d* of late John Millar Colville, Gribloch, Kippen, Stirlingshire; one *s*. *Educ:* Eton; Magdalene Coll., Cambridge. Dir, Stakis plc and other cos; Mem., Scottish Tourist Bd, 1981–87. Chm. of Trustees, Royal Botanic Gdn, Edinburgh, 1985–. Deacon, Incorporation of Hammermen, 1984–85. *Heir:* *s* James Colville Hutchison, *b* 7 Oct. 1967. *Address:* Milton House, Milton, by Dumbarton G82 2TU.

HUTCHISON, Robert Edward; Keeper, Scottish National Portrait Gallery, 1953–82, retired; *b* 4 Aug. 1922; *y s* of late Sir William Hutchison; *m* 1946, Heather, *d* of late Major A. G. Bird; one *s* one *d*. *Educ:* Gresham's Sch., Holt. Served War, 1940–46, Infantry and RA; Asst Keeper, Scottish National Portrait Gallery, 1949. Hon. MA Edinburgh, 1972. *Publication:* (with Stuart Maxwell) Scottish Costume 1550–1850, 1958. *Address:* Ivory Court, Langriggs, Haddington, East Lothian EH41 4BY. *T:* Haddington (062082) 3213.

HUTCHISON, Sidney Charles, CVO 1977 (LVO 1967); Hon. Archivist, Royal Academy of Arts, since 1982; *b* 26 March 1912; *s* of late Henry Hutchison; *m* 1937, Nancy Arnold Brindley (*d* 1985); no *c. Educ:* Holloway Sch., London; London Univ. (Dip. in Hist. of Art, with Dist.). Joined staff of Royal Academy, 1929. Served War of 1939–45: Royal Navy, rising to Lieut-Comdr (S), RNVR. Librarian of Royal Academy, 1949–68, also Sec. of Loan Exhibitions, 1955–68; Sec., Royal Academy, 1968–82. Secretary: E. A. Abbey Meml Trust Fund for Mural Painting, 1960–87; Incorporated E. A. Abbey Scholarships Fund, 1965–; E. Vincent Harris Fund for Mural Decoration, 1970–87; British Institution Fund, 1968–82; Chantrey Trustees, 1968–82; Richard Ford Award Fund, 1977–82. Lectr in the History of Art, for Extra-Mural Dept of Univ. of London, 1957–67. Gen. Comr of Taxes, 1972–87. Governor, Holloway Sch., 1969–81. Trustee, Chantrey Bequest, 1982–; Pres., Southgate Soc. of Arts, 1983–. Organist and Choirmaster of St Matthew's, Westminster, 1933–37. Associate Mem., ICOM, 1964. FRSA 1950; FSA 1955; FMA 1962; Fellow, Assoc. of Art Historians, 1974. Officer, Polonia Restituta, 1971; Chevalier, Belgian Order of the Crown, 1972; Grand Decoration of Honour (silver), Austria, 1972; Cavaliere Ufficiale, Al Merito della Repubblica Italiana, 1980. *Publications:* The Homes of the Royal Academy, 1956; The History of the Royal Academy, 1768–1968, 1968, enl. and updated, 1768–1986, 1986; articles for Walpole Society, Museums Jl, Encyclopædia Britannica, DNB, Apollo, etc. *Recreations:* music, travel. *Address:* 60 Belmont Close, Mount Pleasant, Cockfosters, Herts EN4 9LT. *T:* 081–449 9821. *Clubs:* Athenæum, Arts.

HUTCHISON, Prof. Terence Wilmot; Professor of Economics, University of Birmingham, 1956–78, now Emeritus Professor; Dean of the Faculty of Commerce and Social Science, 1959–61; *b* 13 Aug. 1912; *m* 1st, 1935, Loretta Hack (*d* 1981); one *s* two *d*; 2nd, 1983, Christine Donaldson. *Educ:* Tonbridge Sch.; Peterhouse, Cambridge. Lector, Univ. of Bonn, 1935–38; Prof., Teachers' Training Coll., Bagdad, 1938–41. Served Indian Army, in intelligence, in Middle East and India, 1941–46; attached to Govt of India, 1945–46. Lecturer, University Coll., Hull, 1946–47; Lecturer, 1947–51 and Reader, 1951–56, London Sch. of Economics. Visiting Professor: Columbia Univ., 1954–55; Univ. of Saarbrücken, 1962, 1980; Yale Univ., 1963–64; Dalhousie Univ., 1970; Keio Univ., Tokyo, 1973; Univ. of WA, 1975; Univ. of California, Davis, 1978; Visiting Fellow: Univ. of Virginia, 1960; Aust. Nat. Univ., Canberra, 1967. Mem. Council, Royal Economic Soc., 1967–72. *Publications:* The Significance and Basic Postulates of Economic Theory, 1938 (2nd edn 1960); A Review of Economic Doctrines 1870–1929, 1953; Positive Economics and Policy Objectives, 1964; Economics and Economic Policy 1946–66, 1968; Knowledge and Ignorance in Economics, 1977; Keynes *v* the Keynesians, 1977; Revolutions and Progress in Economic Knowledge, 1978; The Politics and Philosophy of Economics, 1981; Before Adam Smith, 1988; articles, reviews in jls. *Address:* 75 Oakfield Road, Selly Park, Birmingham B29 7HL. *T:* 021–472 2020.

HUTCHISON, Thomas Oliver; Director, Imperial Chemical Industries PLC, since 1985; Deputy Governor, Bank of Scotland, since 1991 (Director, since 1985); *b* 3 Jan. 1931; *s* of late James Hutchison and Thomasina Oliver; *m* 1955, Frances Mary Ada Butterworth; three *s. Educ:* Hawick High Sch.; Univ. of St Andrews (BSc Hons First Cl. Natural Philosophy). Joined ICI General Chemicals Division, 1954; key prodn, technical and commercial appts on general chemicals side of the Company's business until apptd Head of ICI's Policy Groups Dept, London, 1974; Dep. Chm., ICI Plastics Div., 1977–79; Chairman: ICI Petrochemicals and Plastics Div., 1981–85; Phillips-Imperial Petroleum, 1982–85; Director: Océ Finance Ltd, 1977–79; ICI Australia, 1985–91; ICI Impkemix Investments Pty, 1985–91; Cadbury Schweppes, 1986–; Enterprise Oil, 1987–90. Mem. Council, British Plastics Fedn, 1977–80; Pres., Assoc. of Plastics Manufacturers in Europe, 1980–82; Mem., Cttee of Dirs and Associate, Corporate Assembly Membership, CEFIC, 1986–. *Recreations:* fishing, tennis, music. *Address:* Imperial Chemical House, Millbank, SW1P 3JF. *T:* 071–834 4444.

HUTCHISON, (William) Bruce, OC 1967; formerly Editorial Director, Vancouver Sun, now Editor Emeritus; *b* 5 June 1901; *s* of John and Constance Hutchison; *m* 1925, Dorothy Kidd McDiarmid; one *s* one *d. Educ:* Public and high schs, Victoria, BC. Political writer: Victoria Times, 1918; Vancouver Province, 1925; Vancouver Sun, 1938; editor, Victoria Times, 1950–63; associate editor, Winnipeg Free Press, 1944. Hon. LLD University of British Columbia, 1951. *Publications:* The Unknown Country, 1943; The Hollow Men, 1944; The Fraser, 1950; The Incredible Canadian, 1952; The Struggle for the Border, 1955; Canada: Tomorrow's Giant, 1957; Mr Prime Minister, 1964; Western Windows, 1967; The Far Side of the Street, 1976; Uncle Percy's Wonderful Town, 1981; The Unfinished Country, 1985; A Life in the Country, 1988. *Recreations:* fishing, gardening. *Address:* 810 Rogers Avenue, Victoria, BC, Canada. *T:* 479–2269. *Club:* Union (Victoria).

HUTCHISON, Prof. William McPhee; Personal Professor in Parasitology, University of Strathclyde, 1971–89, now Emeritus; *b* 2 July 1924; *s* of William Hutchison and Ann McPhee; *m* 1963, Ella Duncan McLaughland; two *s. Educ:* Eastwood High Sch.; Glasgow Univ. BSc, PhD, DSc; FLS, FIBiol, CBiol; FRSE. Glasgow Univ. Fencing Blue, 1949; Ford Epée Cup; Glasgow Univ. Fencing Champion, 1950 (McLure Foil Trophy, 1950). Strathclyde Univ.: Asst Lectr, 1952; Lectr, 1953; Sen. Lectr, 1969. Engaged in res. on Toxoplasma and toxoplasmosis; discoverer of life cycle of Toxoplasma, 1968–70. Robert Koch Medal, 1970. *Publications:* contrib. Trans Royal Soc. Trop. Med. and Hygiene, Ann. Tropical Med. Parasitology, BMJ. *Recreations:* general microscopy, academic heraldry, collection of zoological specimens. *Address:* 597 Kilmarnock Road, Newlands, Glasgow G43 2TH. *T:* 041–637 4882.

HUTSON, Sir Francis (Challenor), Kt 1963; CBE 1960; Senior Partner, D. M. Simpson & Co., Consulting Engineers, Barbados, 1943–70, retired; *b* 13 Sept. 1895; *s* of Francis and Alice Sarah Hutson; *m* 1st, 1925, Muriel Allen Simpkin (*d* 1945); two *s* one *d*; 2nd, 1947, Edith Doris Howell. *Educ:* Harrison Coll., Barbados; Derby Technical Coll., Derby. Resident Engineer, Booker Bros, McConnell & Co. Ltd, British Guiana, 1920–30; Consulting Engineer, Barbados, 1930–35; D. M. Simpson & Co., 1935–70. MLC, 1947–62, MEC, 1958–61, Barbados; PC (Barbados), 1961–70. FIMechE. *Recreation:* bridge. *Address:* Fleetwood, Erdiston Hill, St Michael, Barbados. *T:* 429 3905. *Clubs:* Bridgetown, Royal Barbados Yacht, Savannah (all in Barbados).

HUTSON, Maj.-Gen. Henry Porter Wolseley, CB 1945; DSO 1917; OBE 1919; MC 1915; *b* 22 March 1893; *s* of late Henry Wolseley Hutson, Wimbledon, SW19; *m* 1922, Rowena (*d* 1989), *d* of Surg.-Gen. Percy Hugh Benson, IA; two *s* one *d. Educ:* King's Coll. Sch.; RMA; 2nd Lieut RE, 1913; Capt. 1917; Major, 1929; Lieut-Col 1937; Col 1939; Temp. Brig. 1940; Maj.-Gen. 1944. Employed with Egyptian Army, 1920–24; under Colonial Office (Road Engineer Nigeria), 1926–28; Chief Instructor, Field Works and Bridging, Sch. of Military Engineering, 1934–36; Chief Engineer, Forestry Commn, 1947–58. Served European War, 1914–18, France, Belgium, Egypt and Mesopotamia (wounded, despatches thrice, DSO, OBE, MC); War of 1939–45 (despatches, CB); retired pay, 1947. *Publications:* The Birds about Delhi, 1954; (ed) The Ornithologist's Guide, 1956; Majority Rule—Why?, 1973; Rhodesia: ending an era, 1978. *Address:* David Gresham House, 226 Pollards Oak Road, Hurst Green, Oxted, Surrey RH8 0JP.

HUTSON, John Whiteford, OBE 1966; HM Diplomatic Service, retired; Consul-General, Casablanca, 1984–87; *b* 21 Oct. 1927; *s* of John Hutson and Jean Greenlees Laird; *m* 1954, Doris Kemp; one *s* two *d. Educ:* Hamilton Academy; Glasgow Univ. (MA (Hons)). MIL 1987; AITI 1987. HM Forces, 1949–51; Foreign Office, 1951; Third Secretary, Prague, 1953; FO, 1955; Second Sec., Berlin, 1956; Saigon, 1959; First Sec., 1961; Consul (Commercial) San Francisco, 1963–67; First Sec. and Head of Chancery, Sofia, 1967–69; FCO, 1969; Counsellor, 1970; Baghdad, 1971–72; Inspector, FCO, 1972–74; Head, Communications Operations Dept, FCO, 1974–76; Counsellor (Commercial), Moscow, 1976–79; Consul-Gen., Frankfurt, 1979–83.

HUTT, Rev. David Handley; Vicar of All Saints', Margaret Street, W1, since 1986; *b* 24 Aug. 1938; *s* of Frank and Evelyn Hutt. *Educ:* Brentwood; RMA Sandhurst; King's College London (Hanson Prize for Christian Ethics; Barry Prize for Theology; AKC). Regular Army, 1957–64. KCL, 1964–68. Deacon 1969, priest 1970; Curate: Bedford Park, W4, 1969–70; St Matthew, Westminster, 1970–73; Priest Vicar and Succentor, Southwark Cathedral, 1973–78; Sen. Chaplain, King's Coll., Taunton, 1978–82; Vicar, St Alban and St Patrick, Birmingham, 1982–86. *Publications:* miscellaneous theol articles and reviews. *Recreations:* gardening, cooking, music, theatre. *Address:* All Saints' Vicarage, 7 Margaret Street, W1N 8JQ. *T:* 071–636 1788/9961, *Fax:* 071–436 4470. *Club:* Athenæum.

HUTTER, Prof. Otto Fred, PhD; Regius Professor of Physiology, University of Glasgow, 1971–90, now Emeritus; *b* 29 Feb. 1924; *s* of Isak and Elisabeth Hutter; *m* 1948, Yvonne T. Brown; two *s* two *d. Educ:* Chajes Real Gymnasium, Vienna; Bishops Stortford Coll., Herts; University Coll., London (BSc, PhD). Univ. of London Postgrad. Student in Physiology, 1948; Sharpey Scholar, UCL, 1949–52; Rockefeller Travelling Fellow and Fellow in Residence, Johns Hopkins Hosp., Baltimore, 1953–55; Lectr, Dept of Physiology, UCL, 1953–61; Hon. Lectr, 1961–70. Visiting Prof., Tel-Aviv Univ., 1968, 1970; Scientific Staff, Nat. Inst. for Medical Research, Mill Hill, London, 1961–70. *Publications:* papers on neuromuscular and synaptic transmission, cardiac and skeletal muscle, in physiological jls. *Address:* Institute of Physiology, University of Glasgow, Glasgow G12 8QQ. *T:* 041–339 8855.

HUTTON, Alasdair Henry, OBE 1990 (MBE 1986); TD 1977; European Adviser, Royal Bank of Scotland; *b* 19 May 1940; *s* of Alexander Hutton and Margaret Elizabeth (*née* Henderson); *m* 1975, Deirdre Mary Cassels; two *s. Educ:* Dollar Academy; Brisbane State High Sch., Australia. Radio Station 4BH, Brisbane, 1956; John Clemenger Advertising, Melbourne, 1957–59; Journalist: The Age, Melb., 1959–61; Press and Journal, Aberdeen, Scotland, 1962–64; Broadcaster, BBC: Scotland, N Ireland, London, Shetland, 1964–79. MEP (C) S Scotland, 1979–89; European Democratic Gp spokesman on regional policy, 1983–87, on budgetary control, 1987–89; contested (C) S Scotland, European Parly Election, 1989. Bd Mem., Scottish Agricl Coll. Formerly Presenter, The Business Programme, BBC Radio Scotland. Mem., Queen's Body Guard for Scotland, Royal Co. of Archers. Life mem., John Buchan Soc.; Mem., Scots Lang. Soc. Trustee, Community Service Volunteers, 1985–. Elder, Kelso N, Church of Scotland. Editor, Turkey Today. *Recreation:* TA: Watchkeepers and Liaison Officers Pool. *Address:* Rosebank, Shedden Park Road, Kelso, Roxburghshire TD5 7PX. *T:* Kelso (0573) 24369.

HUTTON, Anthony Charles; Under Secretary, Personnel Management Division, Department of Trade and Industry, since 1989; *b* 4 April 1941; *s* of Charles James Hutton and Athene Mary (*née* Hastie); *m* 1963, Sara Flemming; two *s* one *d. Educ:* Brentwood School; Trinity College Oxford (MA). HM Inspector of Taxes, 1962; Joined Board of Trade, 1964; Private Sec. to 2nd Perm. Sec., 1967–68; Principal Private Sec. to Sec. of State for Trade, 1974–77; Asst Sec., DoT, 1977, DTI, 1983; Under Sec., DTI, 1984, External Policy Div., 1987. *Recreations:* music, reading, 20th century history. *Address:* Department of Trade and Industry, Allington Towers, 19 Allington Street, SW1E 5EB. *T:* 071–215 5000. *Club:* Athenæum.

HUTTON, Brian Gerald; County Secretary, Buckinghamshire Council for the Protection of Rural England, since 1990; *b* Barrow-in-Furness, 1 Nov. 1933; *s* of James and Nora Hutton; *m* 1958, Serena Quartermaine May; one *s* one *d. Educ:* Barrow Grammar Sch.; Nottingham Univ. (BA Hons Hist.); University Coll. London (Dip. Archive Admin.). National Service as Russian Linguist, RN, 1955–57; London Univ., 1958–59 (Churchill-Jenkinson prizeman). Asst Archivist, Herts County Record Office, 1959–60; Asst Keeper and Dep. Dir, Public Record Office, N Ireland, also Administrator, Ulster Hist. Foundn and Lectr in Archive Admin., Queen's Univ., Belfast, 1960–74; National Library of Scotland: Asst Keeper, 1974–88; Sec., 1976–88; Dep. Librarian, 1983–88. Commissioned, Kentucky Colonel, 1982. *Publications:* contribs to library and archive jls. *Recreations:* walking in Chilterns, visiting art galleries, listening to music. *Address:* Elma Cottage, The Green, Kingston Blount, Oxon OX9 4SE. *T:* Kingston Blount (0844) 54173. *Clubs:* Commonwealth Trust; New (Edinburgh).

HUTTON, Gabriel Bruce; His Honour Judge Hutton; a Circuit Judge, since 1978; *b* 27 Aug. 1932; *y s* of late Robert Crompton Hutton, and Elfreda Bruce; *m* 1st, 1963, Frances Henrietta Cooke (*d* 1963); 2nd, 1965, Deborah Leigh Windus; one *s* two *d. Educ:* Marlborough; Trinity Coll., Cambridge (BA). Called to Bar, Inner Temple, 1956; Dep. Chm., Glos QS, 1971. A Recorder of the Crown Court, 1972–77. Liaison Judge for Glos and Resident Judge for Gloucester Crown Court. *Recreations:* hunting (Chm., Berkeley Hunt), shooting, fishing. *Address:* Chestal, Dursley, Glos. *T:* Dursley (0453) 543285.

HUTTON, (Hubert) Robin; Director-General, British Merchant Banking and Securities Houses Association, since 1988; *b* 22 April 1933; *e s* of Kenneth Douglas and Dorothy Hutton; *m* 1st, 1956, Valerie Riseborough (marr. diss. 1967); one *s* one *d*; 2nd, 1969, Deborah Berkeley; two step *d. Educ:* Merchant Taylors' Sch.; Peterhouse, Cambridge (Scholar). MA Cantab 1960. Royal Tank Regt, 1952–53 (commnd). Economic Adviser to Finance Corp. for Industry Ltd, 1956–62; economic journalist and consultant; Dir, Hambros Bank Ltd, 1966–70; Special Adviser: to HM Govt, 1970–72; to Min. of Posts and Telecommunications, 1972–73. Chm., Cttee of Inquiry into Public Trustee Office, 1971; Dir of Banking, Insurance and Financial Instns in EEC, Brussels, 1973–78; Exec. Dir, S. G. Warburg & Co. Ltd, 1978–82; Chm., Soc. des Banques S. G. Warburg et Leu SA, Luxembourg, 1979–82; Director-General: Accepting Houses Cttee, 1982–87; Issuing Houses Assoc., 1983–88. Director: Ariel Exchange Ltd, 1982–86; Associated Book Publishers PLC, 1982–87; Northern Rock Building Soc, 1986– (Mem., 1978–, Chm., 1987–, London Bd); Rock Asset Management Ltd, Rock Asset Management (Unit Trust) Ltd, 1988–; Chairman: LondonClear Ltd, 1987–89; Homes Intown plc, 1989–. Dir, IMRO, 1986–; Member: Exec. Cttee, BBA, 1982– (Chm., Securities Cttee, 1987–); Council of Foreign Bondholders, 1983–89; Adv. Cttee, European Business Inst., 1983–; Chm., Nat. Adv. Cttee on Telecommunications for England, 1985–. FRSA 1990. *Recreations:* cricket, ski-ing, gardening, travel. *Address:* c/o British Merchant Banking and Securities Houses Association, 6 Frederick's Place, EC2R 8BT; Church Farm, Athelington, Suffolk. *T:* Worlingworth (072876) 361. *Club:* MCC.

HUTTON, Rt. Hon. Sir (James) Brian (Edward), PC 1988; Kt 1988; Lord Chief Justice of Northern Ireland, since 1988; *b* 29 June 1931; *s* of late James and Mabel Hutton,

Belfast; *m* 1975, Mary Gillian Murland; two *d*. *Educ:* Shrewsbury Sch.; Balliol Coll., Oxford (1st Cl. final sch. of Jurisprudence; Hon. Fellow, 1988); Queen's Univ. of Belfast. Called to Northern Ireland Bar, 1954; QC (NI) 1970; Bencher, Inn of Court of Northern Ireland, 1974; called to English Bar, 1972. Junior Counsel to Attorney-General for NI, 1969; Legal Adviser to Min. of Home Affairs, NI, 1973; Sen. Crown Counsel in NI, 1973–79; Judge of the High Court of Justice (NI), 1979–88. Hon. Bencher: Inner Temple, 1988; King's Inns, Dublin, 1988. Mem., Jt Law Enforcement Commn, 1974; Dep. Chm., Boundary Commn for NI, 1985–88. Pres., NI Assoc. for Mental Health, 1983–. *Publications:* articles in Modern Law Review. *Address:* Royal Courts of Justice (Ulster), Belfast.

HUTTON, Janet; nursing/management adviser, self-employed consultant; *b* 15 Feb. 1938; *d* of Ronald James and Marion Hutton. *Educ:* Gen. Infirmary at Leeds Sch. of Nursing. SRN 1959. Ward Sister, Leeds Gen. Infirmary, 1962–64, 1966–68; Nursing Sister, Australia, 1964–66; Commng Nurse, Lister Hosp., Stevenage, 1968–71; Planning and Develts Nurse, N London, 1971–73; Divl Nursing Officer, Colchester, 1973–79; Dist Nursing officer, E Dorset, 1979–83; Regl Nursing Officer, 1983–88, Quality Assurance Manager, 1986–88, Yorks RHA. *Recreations:* music, needlework, tennis (spectator and participant). *Club:* Soroptimist International of Great Britain and Ireland (Harrogate).

HUTTON, Prof. John Philip, MA; Professor of Economics and Econometrics, University of York, since 1982; *b* 26 May 1940; *s* of Philip Ernest Michelson Hutton and Hester Mary Black Hutton; *m* 1964, Sandra Smith Reid; one *s* one *d*. *Educ:* Daniel Stewart's Coll., Edinburgh; Edinburgh Univ. (MA 1st Cl.). York University: Junior Research Fellow, 1962; Lecturer, 1963; Sen. Lectr, 1973; Reader, 1976. Economic Adviser, HM Treasury, 1970, 1971; Advr to Malaysian Treasury, 1977, Mem., Technical Assistance Mission, Keyna, 1990, IMF; Consultant to: NEDO, 1963; Home Office, 1966; Royal Commission on Local Govt in England and Wales, 1967; NIESR, 1980. Chairman, HM Treasury Academic Panel, 1980, 1981; Mem. Council, Royal Economic Soc., 1981–86. Jt Managing Editor, Economic Journal, 1980–86; Jt Editor, Bulletin of Economic Research, 1986–; Associate Editor, Applied Economics, 1986–. *Publications:* contribs to learned jls, incl. Economic Jl, Rev. of Economic Studies, Oxford Economic Papers. *Recreation:* family. *Address:* 1 The Old Orchard, Fulford, York Y01 4LT. *T:* York (0904) 638363.

HUTTON, Kenneth; Chairman, Peterborough Development Agency, since 1987; *b* 11 May 1931; *s* of Wilks and Gertrude Hutton; *m* 1981, Georgia (*née* Hutchinson); one *s*, and two step *s* one step *d*. *Educ:* Bradford Belle Vue Grammar School; Liverpool University (Thomas Bartlett Scholar; BEng). FICE; FIHT. Graduate Asst, Halifax CBC, 1952–54; Royal Engineers, 1954–56; Sen Engineer, Halifax CBC, 1956–59; Sen. Asst Engineer, Huddersfield CBC, 1959–63; Asst Chief Engineer, Skelmersdale Develt Corp., 1963–66; Dep. Chief Engineer, Telford Develt Corp., 1966–68; Chief Engineer, 1968–84, Gen. Manager, 1984–88, Peterborough Develt Corp. Governor: Peterborough Enterprise Programme, 1988–; Peterborough Regl Coll., 1989–. *Recreations:* swimming, bridge, golf. *Address:* 4 Sunningdale, Orton Waterville, Peterborough PE2 0UB. *T:* Peterborough (0733) 233719.

HUTTON, Robin; *see* Hutton, H. R.

HUTTON, Maj.-Gen. Walter Morland, CB 1964; CBE 1960; DSO 1943; MC 1936 and bar, 1942; MA (by decree, 1967); FIL (Arabic); Fellow, 1967–72 and Home Bursar, 1966–72, Jesus College, Oxford; *b* 5 May 1912; *s* of Walter Charles Stritch Hutton and Amy Mary Newton; *m* 1945, Peronelle Marie Stella Luxmoore-Ball; two *s* one *d*. *Educ:* Parkstone Sch.; Allhallows Sch.; RMC Sandhurst. Commissioned into Royal Tank Corps, 1932; served in Palestine, 1936 (MC); 1st Class Army Interpreter in Arabic, 1937; War of 1939–45: Western Desert, Alamein and N Africa (comdg 5 RTR); Italy (comdg 40 RTR); Comdt, Sandhurst, 1944–45; Instructor, Staff Coll., Camberley, 1949–51; BGS, Arab Legion, 1953–56; Imperial Defence Coll., 1957; Deputy Comd (Land), BFAP (Aden), 1957–59; Dir of Administrative Plans, War Office, 1959–60, Dir-Gen. of Fighting Vehicles, 1961–64; Chief Army Instructor, Imperial Defence Coll., 1964–66. Mem., Bd of Governors, United Oxford Hosps, 1969–72.

HUTTON-WILLIAMS, Derek Alfred, MBE 1947; BSc, ACGI; CEng, FIMechE, MIEE; Director-General, Royal Ordnance Factories, 1969–75, retired; *b* 26 April 1914; *s* of William Hutton-Williams and Violet Woodfall Hutton-Williams; *m* 1936, Albrée Freeman; two *d*; *m* 1948, Yvonne Irene Anthony; one *s* one *d*. *Educ:* Oundle Sch.; London Univ. (Kitchener Scholar); grad. NATO Defence Coll., Paris. Pupil, Winget Ltd, Rochester, 1935; Techn. Asst, Royal Arsenal, Woolwich, 1938; Asst to Director, Small Arms and Fuzes, Ordance Factories, in charge of UK production of Sten carbine, 1939; Manager, Royal Ordnance Factory, Theale, Berks, 1942; Dep.-Dir, Housing Supplies, Ministry of Supply, 1945; Partner, Hutton-Williams and Partners (Industrial Consultant), 1946; Supt, Royal Ordnance Factory, Maltby, Yorks, 1949; NATO Defence Coll., 1957; Asst Dir, Guided Weapons Production, Min. of Aviation, 1958; Dir, Inspectorate of Armaments, 1959; Dir, Royal Small Arms Factory, Enfield, 1964. *Recreations:* gardening, building, clock repair, music; recognising and accepting the inevitable; admiring craftsmanship. *Address:* The School House, Palgrave, near Diss, Norfolk.

HUWS JONES, Robin; *see* Jones.

HUXLEY, Sir Andrew Fielding, OM 1983; Kt 1974; FRS 1955; MA, Hon. ScD Cantab; Master of Trinity College, Cambridge, 1984–90; *b* 22 Nov. 1917; *s* of late Leonard Huxley and Rosalind Bruce; *m* 1947, Jocelyn Richenda Gammell Pease; one *s* five *d*. *Educ:* University College Sch.; Westminster Sch. (Hon. Fellow, 1991); Trinity Coll., Cambridge (MA). Operational research for Anti-Aircraft Command, 1940–42, for Admiralty, 1942–45. Fellow, 1941–60, 1990–, and Dir of Studies, 1952–60, Trinity Coll., Cambridge; Hon. Fellow, Trinity Coll., 1967; Demonstrator, 1946–50, Asst Dir of Research, 1951–59, and Reader in Experimental Biophysics, 1959–60, in Dept of Physiology, Cambridge Univ.; Jodrell Prof., 1960–69 (now Emeritus), Royal Soc. Research Prof., 1969–83, UCL (Hon. Fellow, 1980). Lectures: Herter, Johns Hopkins Univ., 1959; Jesup, Columbia Univ., 1964; Alexander Forbes, Grass Foundation, 1966; Croonian, Royal Society, 1967; Review Lectr on Muscular Contraction, Physiological Soc., 1973; Hans Hecht, Univ. of Chicago, 1975; Sherrington, Liverpool, 1977; Florey, ANU, 1982; John C. Krantz Jr, Maryland Univ. Sch. of Medicine, 1982; Darwin, Darwin Coll., Cambridge, 1982; Romanes, Oxford, 1983; Fenn, IUPS XXIX Internat. Congress, Sydney, 1983; Green Coll., Oxford, 1986; Tarner, Trinity Coll., Cambridge, 1988; Maulana Abul Kalam Azad Meml, Delhi, 1991. Fullerian Prof. of Physiology and Comparative Anatomy, Royal Institution, 1967–73; Cecil H. and Ida Green Vis. Prof., Univ. of British Columbia, 1980. President: BAAS, 1976–77; Royal Soc., 1980–85 (Mem. Council, 1960–62, 1977–79, 1980–85); Internat. Union of Physiological Scis, 1986–; Vice-Pres., Muscular Dystrophy Gp of GB, 1980–. Member: ARC, 1977–81; Nature Conservancy Council, 1985–87. Trustee: BM (Nat. Hist.), 1981–91; Science Museum, 1984–88. Hon. Member: Physiolog. Soc., 1979; Amer. Soc. of Zoologists, 1985; Japan Acad., 1988; Hon. MRIA, 1986; Foreign Associate: Nat. Acad. of Scis, USA, 1979; Amer. Philosophical Soc., 1975; Foreign Hon. Member: Amer. Acad. of Arts and Sciences, 1961; Royal Acad. of Medicine, Belgium, 1978; Foreign Fellow, Indian Nat. Science Acad., 1985; Hon. MRI, 1981; Associate Mem., Royal Acad. of Scis, Letters and Fine Arts, Belgium, 1978; Mem., Leopoldina Academy, 1964; Foreign Member: Danish Acad. of Sciences, 1964; Dutch Soc. of Sciences, 1984. Hon. Fellow: Imperial Coll., London, 1980; Darwin Coll., Cambridge, 1981; QMW, London, 1987. Hon. FIBiol 1981; Hon. FRSC (Canada) 1982; Hon. FRSE 1983; Hon. FEng 1986. Hon. MD University of the Saar, 1964; Hon. DSc: Sheffield, 1964; Leicester, 1967; London, 1973; St Andrews, 1974; Aston, 1977; Western Australia, 1982; Oxford, 1983; Pennsylvania, 1984; Harvard, 1984; Keele, 1985; East Anglia, 1985; Humboldt, E Berlin, 1985; Maryland, 1987; Brunel, 1988; Hyderabad, 1991; Hon. LLD: Birmingham, 1979; Dundee, 1984; DUniv York, 1981; Hon. DHL New York, 1982; Hon. Dr Marseille Fac. of Medicine, 1979. Nobel Prize for Physiology or Medicine (jtly), 1963; Copley Medal, Royal Soc., 1973. *Publications:* Reflections on Muscle (Sherrington Lectures XIV), 1980; (contrib.) The Pursuit of Nature, 1977; papers in the Journal of Physiology, etc. *Recreations:* walking, shooting, designing scientific instruments. *Address:* Manor Field, 1 Vicarage Drive, Grantchester, Cambridge CB3 9NG. *T:* Cambridge (0223) 840207; Trinity College, Cambridge. *T:* Cambridge (0223) 338400, *Fax:* Cambridge (0223) 338564.

HUXLEY, Anthony Julian; author, free-lance writer, editor and photographer; *b* 2 Dec. 1920; *s* of Sir Julian Huxley, FRS; *m* 1st, 1943, Priscilla Ann Taylor; three *d*; 2nd, 1974, Alyson Ellen Vivian, *d* of late Beavan Archibald; one *d*. *Educ:* Dauntsey's Sch.; Trinity Coll., Cambridge (MA). Operational Research in RAF and Min. of Aircraft Production, 1941–47; Economic Research in BOAC, 1947–48; with Amateur Gardening, 1949–71 (Editor, 1967–71); Ed.-in-chief (formerly Gen. Ed.), RHS Dictionary of Gardening, 1988–. Vice Pres., RHS, 1991– (Mem., Council, 1979–91). Veitch Meml Medal, RHS, 1979; VMH 1980. *Publications:* (trans.) Exotic Plants of the World, 1955; (gen. editor) Standard Encyclopedia of the World's Mountains, 1962; (gen. editor) Standard Encyclopedia of Oceans and Islands, 1962; Garden Terms Simplified, 1962, 1971; Flowers in Greece: an outline of the Flora, 1964; (with O. Polunin) Flowers of the Mediterranean, 1965; (gen. ed.) Standard Encyclopedia of Rivers and Lakes, 1965; Mountain Flowers, 1967; (ed) Garden Perennials and Water Plants, 1971; (ed) Garden Annuals and Bulbs, 1971; House Plants, Cacti and Succulents, 1972; (ed) Deciduous Garden Trees and Shrubs, 1973; (ed) Evergreen Garden Trees and Shrubs, 1973; Plant and Planet, 1978, 2nd edn 1987; (ed) The Financial Times Book of Garden Design, 1975; (with W. Taylor) Flowers of Greece and the Aegean, 1977, 2nd edn 1989; (ed) The Encyclopedia of the Plant Kingdom, 1977; (with Alyson Huxley) Huxley's House of Plants, 1978; An Illustrated History of Gardening, 1978; (gen. editor) Success with House Plants, 1979; Penguin Encyclopedia of Gardening, 1981; (with P. and J. Davies) Wild Orchids of Britain and Europe, 1983; (ed) The Macmillan World Guide to House Plants, 1983; Green Inheritance, 1984; The Painted Garden, 1988. *Recreations:* photography, wild flowers, travel, gardening. *Address:* 50 Villiers Avenue, Surbiton, Surrey KT5 8BD. *T:* 081–390 7983.

HUXLEY, Air Vice-Marshal Brian, CB 1986; CBE 1981; Deputy Controller, National Air Traffic Services, 1985–86; retired 1987; *b* 14 Sept. 1931; *s* of Ernest and Winifred Huxley; *m* 1955, Frances (*née* Franklin); two *s*. *Educ:* St Paul's Sch.; RAF College, Cranwell. Commissioned 1952; No 28 Sqdn, Hong Kong, 1953–55; qual. Flying Instructor, 1956; Cranwell, Central Flying Sch. and No 213 Sqdn, 1956–65; MoD, 1966–68; Chief Flying Instr, Cranwell, 1969–71; Commanding RAF Valley, 1971–73; RAF Staff Coll., 1973–74; RCDS 1975; Defence Intelligence Staff, 1976–77; AOC Mil. Air Traffic Ops, 1978–80; Dir of Control (Airspace Policy), and Chm., Nat. Air Traffic Management Adv. Cttee, 1981–84. Mem., CAA Ops Adv. Cttee, 1987–. *Publications:* contribs to Children's Encyclopaedia Britannica, 1970–72, and to Railway Modeller, 1974–. *Recreations:* Flying Officer RAFVR(T), model-making. *Club:* Royal Air Force.

HUXLEY, Elspeth Josceline, (Mrs Gervas Huxley), CBE 1962; JP; *b* 23 July 1907; *d* of Major Josceline Grant, Njoro, Kenya; *m* 1931, Gervas Huxley (*d* 1971); one *s*. *Educ:* European Sch., Nairobi, Kenya; Reading Univ. (Diploma in Agriculture); Cornell Univ., USA. Asst Press Officer to Empire Marketing Board, London, 1929–32; subsequently travelled in America, Africa and elsewhere; Mem. BBC Gen. Advisory Council, 1952–59; UK Independent Mem., Monckton Advisory Commission on Central Africa, 1959. *Publications:* White Man's Country; Lord Delamere and the Making of Kenya, 2 vols, 1935; Murder at Government House (detective story), 1937, repr. 1987; Murder on Safari (detective story), 1938, repr. 1982; The African Poison Murders, 1939, repr. 1988; Red Strangers (novel), 1939; Atlantic Ordeal, 1943; (with Margery Perham) Race and Politics in Kenya, 1944; The Walled City (novel), 1948; The Sorcerer's Apprentice (travel), 1948; I Don't Mind If I Do (light novel), 1951; Four Guineas (travel), A Thing to Love, 1954; The Red Rock Wilderness, 1957; The Flame Trees of Thika, 1959 (filmed, 1981); A New Earth, 1960; The Mottled Lizard, 1962; The Merry Hippo, 1963; Forks and Hope, 1964; A Man from Nowhere, 1964; Back Street New Worlds, 1965; Brave New Victuals, 1965; Their Shining Eldorado: A Journey through Australia, 1967; Love Among the Daughters, 1968; The Challenge of Africa, 1971; Livingstone and his African Journeys, 1974; Florence Nightingale, 1975; Gallipot Eyes, 1976; Scott of the Antarctic, 1977; Nellie: letters from Africa, 1980; Whipsnade: captive breeding for survival, 1981; The Prince Buys the Manor, 1982; (with Hugo van Lawick) Last Days in Eden, 1984; Out in the Midday Sun: My Kenya, 1985; Nine Faces of Kenya (anthology), 1990. *Recreations:* resting, gossip. *Address:* Green End, Oaksey, near Malmesbury, Wilts SN16 9TL. *TA:* Oaksey, Malmesbury. *T:* Crudwell (06667) 252.

HUXLEY, Prof. George Leonard, FSA; MRIA; Hon. Professor, Trinity College Dublin, since 1989 (Research Associate, 1983–89); Professor Emeritus, Queen's University, Belfast, since 1988; *b* Leicester, 23 Sept. 1932; *s* of late Sir Leonard Huxley, KBE, DPhil, PhD, FAA and Ella M. C., *d* of F. G. and E. Copeland; *m* 1957, Davina Best; three *d*. *Educ:* Blundell's Sch.; Magdalen Coll., Oxford. 2nd Mods, 1st Greats, Derby Scholar 1955. Commnd in RE, 1951. Fellow of All Souls Coll., Oxford, 1955–61; Asst Dir, British School at Athens, 1956–58; Prof. of Greek, QUB, 1962–83; Dir, Gennadius Library, Amer. Sch. of Classical Studies, Athens, 1986–89. Harvard University: Vis. Lectr, 1958 and 1961; Loeb Lectr, 1986; Leverhulme Fellow, European Sci. Foundn, 1980–81; Vis. Lectr, St Patrick's Coll., Maynooth, 1984–85; Vis. Prof., UCSD, 1990. Mem. of Exec., NI Civil Rights Assoc., 1971–72. Member: Managing Cttee, British Sch. at Athens, 1967–79; Irish Nat. Cttee Greek and Latin Studies, 1972–86 (Chm., 1976–79); Managing Cttee, Amer. Sch. of Classical Studies, Athens, 1991–; Irish Mem., Standing Cttee on Humanities, European Science Foundn, Strasbourg, 1978–86. Royal Irish Academy: Sec., Polite Literature and Antiquities Cttee, 1979–86; Sen. Vice-Pres., 1984–85; Hon. Librarian, 1990–; Member: Bureau, Fédn Internat. d'Etudes Classiques, 1981–89 (Senior Vice-Pres. 1984–89); Academia Europaea, 1990. Hon. LittD TCD, 1984. Cromer Greek Prize, British Acad., 1963. *Publications:* Achaeans and Hittites, 1960; Early Sparta, 1962; The Early Ionians, 1966; Greek Epic Poetry from Eumelos to Panyassis, 1969; (ed with J. N. Coldstream) Kythera, 1972; Pindar's Vision of the Past, 1975; On Aristotle and Greek Society, 1979; Homer and the Travellers, 1988; articles on Hellenic and Byzantine subjects. *Recreation:* siderodromophilia. *Address:* Forge Cottage, Church Enstone, Oxfordshire OX7 4NN. *Club:* Athenæum.

HUXLEY, Mrs Gervas; *see* Huxley, Elspeth J.

HUXLEY, Hugh Esmor, MBE 1948; MA, PhD, ScD; FRS 1960; Professor of Biology, since 1987, Director, since 1988, Rosenstiel Basic Medical Sciences Research Center, Brandeis University, Boston, Mass; *b* 25 Feb. 1924; *s* of late Thomas Hugh Huxley and Olwen Roberts, Birkenhead, Cheshire; *m* 1966, Frances Fripp, *d* of G. Maxon, Milwaukee; one *d*, and two step-*s* one step-*d*. *Educ:* Park High Sch., Birkenhead; Christ's Coll., Cambridge (Exhibitioner and Scholar; Hon. Fellow 1981). Natural Science Tripos, Cambridge, 1941–43 and 1947–48 (Pt II Physics); BA 1948, MA 1950, PhD 1952, ScD 1964. Served War of 1939–45, Radar Officer, RAF Bomber Command and Telecommunications Research Establishment, Malvern, 1943–47; Mem. Empire Air Armaments Sch. Mission to Australia and NZ, 1946. Research Student, MRC Unit for Molecular Biology, Cavendish Lab., Cambridge, 1948–52; Commonwealth Fund Fellow, Biology Dept, MIT, 1952–54; Research Fellow, Christ's Coll., Cambridge, 1953–56; Mem. of External Staff of MRC, and Hon. Res. Associate, Biophysics Dept, UCL, 1956–61; Fellow, King's Coll., Cambridge, 1961–67; Scientific Staff, MRC Lab. of Molecular Biol., Cambridge, 1961–87, Dep. Dir, 1977–87; Fellow, Churchill Coll., Cambridge, 1967–87. Ziskind Vis. Prof., Brandeis Univ., 1971; Lectures: Harvey Soc., New York, 1964–65; Hooke, Univ. of Texas, 1968; Dunham, Harvard Med. Sch., 1969; Croonian, Royal Soc., 1970; Mayer, MIT, 1971; Penn, Pennsylvania Univ., 1971; Carter-Wallace, Princeton Univ., 1973; Adam Muller, State Univ. of NY, 1973; Pauling, Stanford, 1980; Jesse Beams, Virginia, 1980; Ida Beam, Iowa, 1981. Member: Council, Royal Soc., 1973–75, 1984–85; President's Adv. Bd, Rosentiel Basic Med. Scis Center, Brandeis Univ., 1971–77; Scientific Adv. Council, European Molecular Biol. Lab., 1976–81. Mem., German Acad. of Sci., Leopoldina, 1964; Hon. Member: Amer. Soc. of Biol Chem., 1976; Amer. Assoc. of Anatomy, 1981; Amer. Physiol. Soc., 1981; Amer. Soc. of Zoologists, 1986; Foreign Hon. Member: Amer. Acad. of Arts and Scis, 1965; Danish Acad. of Scis, 1971; Foreign Associate, US Nat. Acad. of Scis, 1978. Hon. ScD: Harvard, 1969; Leicester, 1989; Hon. DSc: Chicago, 1974; Pennsylvania, 1976. Feldberg Foundation Award for Experimental Medical Research, 1963; William Bate Hardy Prize (Camb. Phil. Soc.) 1965; Louisa Gross Horwitz Prize, 1971; Internat. Feltrinelli Prize, 1974; Gairdner Foundn Award, 1975; Baly Medal, RCP, 1975; Royal Medal, Royal Soc., 1977; E. B. Wilson Award, Amer. Soc. Cell Biology, 1983; Albert Einstein Award, World Cultural Council, 1987; Franklin Medal, Franklin Inst., Philadelphia, 1990. *Publications:* contrib. to learned jls. *Recreations:* ski-ing, sailing. *Address:* Rosenstiel Basic Medical Sciences Research Center, Brandeis University, Waltham, Mass 02254, USA. *T:* 617 736 2401.

HUXLEY, Rev. Keith; Rector of Gateshead, Diocese of Durham, since 1983; Rural Dean of Gateshead, since 1988; Chaplain to the Queen, since 1981; *b* 17 Sept. 1933; *s* of George and Eluned Huxley. *Educ:* Birkenhead Sch.; Christ's Coll., Cambridge (MA); Cuddesdon Theol Coll. Curate: St Mary's, Bowdon, 1959–61; Christ Church, Crewe, 1961–62; Chester Diocesan Youth Chaplain, 1962–68; Leader, Runcorn Ecumenical Team Ministry, 1968–75; Vicar, St Andrew's, Runcorn, 1968–73; Rector, East Runcorn Team Ministry, 1973–77; Home Secretary, Bd for Mission and Unity, C of E, 1977–83. Secretary: NE Ecumenical Gp, 1983–; Durham Ecumenical Relations Gp, 1985–. *Recreation:* ornithology. *Address:* Gateshead Rectory, 91 Old Durham Road, Gateshead, Tyne and Wear NE8 4BS. *T:* 091–477 3990.

HUXLEY, Paul, RA 1991 (ARA 1987); artist; Professor of Painting, Royal College of Art, since 1986; *b* 12 May 1938; *m* 1957, Margaret Doria Perryman (marr. diss. 1972); two *s*; *m* 1990, Susan Jennifer Metcalfe. *Educ:* Harrow Coll. of Art; Royal Acad. Schs (Cert.). Vis. Prof., Cooper Union, New York, 1974; Vis. Tutor, RCA, 1976. Member: Serpentine Gallery Cttee, 1971–74; Art Panel and Exhibns Sub-Cttee, Arts Council of GB, 1972–76; Trustee, Tate Gall., 1975–82. Commnd by London Transport to design 22 ceramic murals for King's Cross Underground Stn, 1984. *One-man exhibitions:* Rowan Gall., London, 1963, 1965, 1968, 1969, 1971, 1974, 1978, 1980; Juda Rowan Gall., London, 1982; Kornblee Gall., New York, 1967, 1970; Galeria da Emenda, Lisbon, 1974; Forum Kunst, Rottweil, W Germany, 1975; Mayor Rowan Gall., 1989; *group exhibitions:* Whitechapel Art Gall., London, and Albright-Knox Gall., Buffalo, NY, 1964; Paris Biennale, and Marlborough-Gerson Gall., New York, 1965; Galerie Milano, Milan, 1966; Carnegie Inst., Pittsburgh, 1967; UCLA, Calif (also USA tour), and touring show of Mus. of Modern Art, New York, 1968; Mus. am Ostwall, Dortmund (also Eur. tour), and Tate Gall., 1969; Walker Art Gall., Liverpool, 1973; Hayward Gall., 1974; São Paulo Bienal, and Forum Gall., Leverkusen, 1975; Palazzo Reale, Milan, 1976; Royal Acad., 1977; Nat. Theatre, 1979; Arts Council tour, Sheffield, Newcastle upon Tyne and Bristol, 1980; Museo Municipal, Madrid, and Eastern Arts 4th Nat. Exhibn and British tour, 1983; Juda Rowan Gall., 1985; Kunstlerhaus, Vienna, 1986; Mappin Art Gall., Sheffield, 1988; *works in public collections:* Tate Gall., V&A Mus. (prints), Arts Council of GB, British Council, Contemp. Arts Soc., Camden Council, DoE, Nuffield Foundn, and Chase Manhattan Bank, London; Swedish Lloyd, London and Stockholm; Whitworth Art Gall., Manchester; Graves Art Gall., Sheffield; Walker Art Gall., Liverpool; City Art Gall., Leeds; Creasey Collection of Modern Art, Salisbury; Leics Educn Authority; Art Gall. of NSW, and Power Inst. of Fine Arts, Sydney; Art Gall. of SA, Adelaide; Stuyvesant Foundn, Holland; Mus. of Modern Art (prints), and Bristol Myers Corp., New York; Albright-Knox Gall., Buffalo, NY; Neuberger Mus., Purchase, NY; Museo Tamayo, Mexico City; Technisches Mus., Vienna. *Publication:* (ed) Exhibition Road: painters at the Royal College of Art, 1988. *Address:* 29 St Albans Avenue, W4 5LL.

HUXLEY, Dr Peter Arthur, PhD; CBiol; FIBiol; Principal Research Adviser, International Council for Research in Agroforestry, Nairobi, since 1990; *b* 26 Sept. 1926; *s* of Ernest Henry Huxley and Florence Agnes (*née* King); *m* 1st, 1954, Betty Grace Anne Foot (marr. diss. 1980); three *s* one *d*; 2nd, 1980, Jennifer Margaret Bell (*née* Pollard); one *s* one *d*. *Educ:* Alleyn's Sch.; Edinburgh Univ.; Reading Univ. (BSc, PhD). FIBiol 1970. RNVR, 1944–46. Asst Lectr to Sen. Lectr, Makerere University Coll., Uganda, 1954–64; Dir of Res., Coffee Res. Foundn, Kenya, 1965–69; Prof. of Horticulture, Univ. of Reading, 1969–74; Prof. of Crop Science, Univ. of Dar es Salaam/FAO, 1974–76; Agric. Res. Adviser/FAO, Agric. Res. Centre, Tripoli, 1977–78; Internat. Council for Res. in Agroforestry, 1979–, Dir, Res. Develt Div., Nairobi, 1987–90. Member: Internat. Soc. Horticl Sci.; Internat. Soc. Tropical Forestry; Internat. Assoc. for Ecology; Tropical Agricl Assoc., UK; Nairobi Music Soc.; Nairobi Orchestra. FRSA. *Publications:* (ed jtly) Soils Research in Agroforestry, 1980; (ed) Plant Research and Agroforestry, 1983; (ed jtly) Manual of Research Methodology for the Exploration and Assessment of Multipurpose Trees, 1983; approx. 130 pubns in agric., horticult., agroforestry, meteorol and agricl botany jls. *Recreation:* music (double bass) and music-making. *Address:* PO Box 30677, Nairobi, Kenya. *Club:* Nairobi (Nairobi).

HUXSTEP, Emily Mary, CBE 1964; BA London: Headmistress of Chislehurst and Sidcup Girls' Grammar School, Kent, 1944–66; *b* 15 Sept. 1906; *d* of George T. and Nellie M. Huxstep (*née* Wood). *Educ:* Chatham Girls' Grammar Sch.; Queen Mary Coll. Headmistress, Hanson Girls' Grammar Sch., Bradford, Yorks, 1938–44. Hon. DCL Kent, 1974. *Address:* The Loose Valley Nursing Home, Linton Road, Loose, Maidstone, Kent ME15 0AG.

HUXTABLE, Gen. Sir Charles Richard, KCB 1984 (CB 1982); CBE 1976 (OBE 1972; MBE 1961); Commander-in-Chief, United Kingdom Land Forces, 1988–90; Aide-de-Camp General to the Queen, 1988–90; *b* 22 July 1931; *m* 1959, Mary, *d* of late Brig. J. H. C. Lawlor; three *d*. *Educ:* Wellington Coll.; RMA Sandhurst; Staff College, Camberley; psc, jssc. Commissioned, Duke of Wellington's Regt, 1952; Captain, 1958, Major, 1965; GS02 (Ops), BAOR, 1964–65; GS01 Staff College, 1968–70; CO 1 DWR, 1970–72; Col, 1973; MoD, 1974; Brig., Comd Dhofar Bde, 1976–78; Maj.-Gen., 1980; Dir, Army Staff Duties, 1982–83; Comdr, Training and Arms Dirs (formerly Training Estabts), 1983–86; QMG, 1986–88. Colonel, DWR, 1982–90; Col Comdt, The King's Div., 1983–88. *Address:* c/o Lloyds Bank, 23 High Street, Teddington, Middlesex TW11 8EX.

HUYDECOPER, Jonkheer (Jan Louis) Reinier, Hon. GCVO 1982 (Hon. KCVO 1972); Commander, Order of Orange Nassau, 1986 (Officer, 1966); Chevalier, Order of Netherlands Lion, 1980; Ambassador of the Netherlands to the Court of St James's, and concurrently to Iceland, 1982–86; *b* 23 Feb. 1922; *s* of Jonkheer Louis Huydecoper and Jonkvrouwe Laurence B. W. Ram; *m* 1944, Baroness Constance C. van Wassenaer; one *s* two *d*. *Educ:* Univ. of Utrecht (LLM). Banking, 1942–44; Legal Dept, Min. of Finance, The Hague, 1945–46; entered Min. of For. Affairs, 1946; UN, NY, 1946; Ottawa, 1947–48; Mil. Mission, Berlin, 1949–50; Bonn, 1950–52; London, 1952–56; Djakarta, 1956–59; Washington, 1959–62; Rome, 1962–66; Min. of For. Affairs, 1966–70; London, 1970–73; Ambassador, Hd of Delegn to Conf. on Security and Co-operation in Europe, Helsinki and Geneva, 1973–74; Ambassador: Moscow, 1974–77; Lisbon, 1978–80; Inspector of For. Service, Min. of For. Affairs, 1981–82. Holds various foreign orders. *Address:* Wassenaarseweg 132, 2596 EA, The Hague, Netherlands.

HUYGHE, René; Grand Officier de la Légion d'Honneur; Member of the Académie Française since 1960; Hon. Professor of Psychology of Plastic Arts, Collège de France (Professor, 1950–76); Hon. Head Keeper, Musée du Louvre; Director, Museum Jacquemart-André, Paris, since 1974; *b* Arras, Pas-de-Calais, France, 3 May 1906; *s* of Louis Huyghe and Marie (*née* Delvoye); *m* 1950, Lydie Bouthet; one *s* one *d*. *Educ:* Sorbonne; École du Louvre, Paris. Attached to Musée du Louvre, 1927; Asst Keeper, 1930; Head Keeper, Département des Peintures, Dessins, Chalcographie, 1937. Mem., Conseil Artistique de la Réunion des Musées Nationaux, 1952 (Vice-Pres. 1964, Pres. 1975–89); Pres. Assoc. internationale du Film d'Art, 1958. Holds foreign decorations. Praemium Erasmianum, The Hague, 1966. *Publications:* Histoire de l'Art contemporain: La Peinture, 1935; Cézanne 1936 and 1961; Les Contemporains, 1939 (2nd edn 1949); Vermeer, 1948; Watteau, 1950; various works on Gauguin, 1951, 1952, 1959; Dialogue avec le visible, 1955 (trans. Eng.); L'Art et l'homme, Vol. I, 1957, Vol. II, 1958, Vol. III, 1961 (trans. Eng.); Van Gogh, 1959; Merveilles de la France, 1960; L'Art et l'Ame, 1960 (trans. Eng.); La peinture française aux XVIIe et XVIIIe Siècles, 1962; Delacroix ou le combat solitaire, 1963, 2nd edn 1990 (trans. Eng.); Puissances de l'Image, 1965; Sens et Destin de l'Art, 1967; L'Art et le monde moderne, Vol. I, 1970, Vol. II, 1971; Formes et Forces, 1971; La Relève du réel, 1974; La Relève de l'imaginaire, 1976; Ce que je crois, 1976; De l'Art à la Philosophie, 1980; (with D. Ikeda) La Nuit appelle l'Aurore, 1980; Les Signes du Temps et l'Art moderne, 1985; (with M. Brion) Se perdre dans Venise, 1987; Psychologie de l'Art, 1991. *Address:* 3 rue Corneille, Paris 75006, France. *Club:* Union interalliée (Paris).

HYAM, Michael Joshua; His Honour Judge Hyam; a Circuit Judge, since 1984; *b* 18 April 1938; *s* of Isaac J. Hyam and Rachel Hyam; *m* 1968, Diana Mortimer; three *s*. *Educ:* Westminster Sch.; St Catharine's Coll., Cambridge (MA). Called to Bar, Gray's Inn, 1962; a Recorder, 1983–84; practised on SE Circuit, 1962–84. Member: Council of Legal Education, 1980–86; Ethical Cttee, Cromwell Hosp., 1983–. Gov., Dulwich Coll. Prep. Sch., 1986–. *Publication:* Learning the Skills of Advocacy, 1990. *Recreations:* book collecting, cricket, gardening. *Address:* 5 Essex Court, Temple, EC4. *T:* 071–353 2825. *Clubs:* Garrick, MCC; Norfolk (Norwich).

HYAMS, Daisy Deborah, (Mrs C. Guderley), OBE 1974; Consultant, Tesco Stores PLC; *b* 25 Nov. 1912; *d* of Hyman Hyams and Annie Burnett; *m* 1936, Sidney Hart; no *c*; *m* 1975, C. Guderley. *Educ:* Coborn Grammar Sch. for Girls, Bow. FGI. Joined Tesco, 1931; Man. Dir, Tesco (Wholesale) Ltd, 1965–82; Dir, Tesco Stores PLC, 1969–82. *Recreations:* travel, reading. *Address:* 10 Noblefield Heights, Great North Road, Highgate, N2 0NX. *T:* 081–348 1591.

HYATALI, Sir Isaac (Emanuel), Kt 1973; TC 1974; attorney-at-law; Chief Justice and President, Court of Appeal, Trinidad and Tobago, 1972–83; Legal Consultant to law firm of Hyatali and Co.; Chairman: Elections and Boundaries Commission, since 1983; Constitution Commission, since 1987; *b* 21 Nov. 1917; *s* of late Joseph Hyatali and Esther Hyatali; *m* 1943, Audrey Monica Joseph; two *s* one *d*. *Educ:* Naparima Coll., San Fernando; Gray's Inn and Council of Legal Education, London. Called to Bar, Gray's Inn, 1947. Private practice at the Bar, 1947–59; Judge, Supreme Court, 1959–62; Justice of Appeal, 1962–72; Pres., Industrial Court, 1965–72; Justice of Appeal, Seychelles Republic, 1983–86. Chairman: Arima Rent Assessment Bd, 1953–59; Agricultural Rent Bd (Eastern Counties), 1953–59; Agricultural Wages Council, 1958–59; Oil and Water Bd, 1959–62; Arbitrator and Umpire, ICAO, 1981–. Chairman: Amer. Life and Gen. Insce Co. (Trinidad) Ltd, 1983–; Ansa Foundn, 1987–; McEneaney-Alston Foundn, 1989–. Trinidad and Tobago Editor of West Indian Law Reports, 1961–65. Member: World Assoc. of Judges; Council of Management, British Inst. of Internat. and Comparative Law; Hon. Mem., World Peace through Law Center. *Recreations:* reading, social work. *Address:* (chambers) 63 Edward Street, Port of Spain, Trinidad and Tobago. *T:* (62) 34007; Election and Boundaries Commission, Salvatori Building, Port of Spain. *T:* (62) 38320; (home) 8 Pomme Rose Avenue, Cascade, St Anns, Republic of Trinidad and Tobago. *Clubs:* Commonwealth Trust; (Hon. Mem.) Union Park Turf (Trinidad); (Hon. Mem.) Union (Port of Spain).

HYATT KING, Alexander; *see* King.

HYDE, Lord; George Edward Laurence Villiers; *b* 12 Feb. 1976; *s* and *heir* of 7th Earl of Clarendon, *qv*.

HYDE, Margaret Sheila; Deputy Secretary-General, Arts Council of Great Britain, since 1991; *b* 11 Sept. 1945; *er d* of late Gerry Tomlins and Sheila (*née* Thorpe); *m* 1966, Derek Hyde (marr. diss. 1976). *Educ:* Watford Grammar Sch. for Girls; London Sch. of Econs and Political Science (DSA 1969; BSc Social Admin 1971). Blackfriars Settlement, 1965–67; Home Office, 1972–77, Private Sec. to Perm. Under Sec. of State, 1976–77; Head of Information, NCVO, 1977–85; Chief Exec., Action Resource Centre, 1985–91. Trustee: Peter Bedford Trust, 1983– (Chm., 1985–87); Charities Effectiveness Review Trust, 1986–91. Governor, LSE, 1988–. FRSA 1991. *Recreations:* walking, sailing. *Address:* 178 Dalling Road, W6 0EU. *Club:* Little Ship.

HYDE, W(illiam) Leonard, FCBSI; Director, Leeds Permanent Building Society, 1972–90 (Chief General Manager, 1973–78; Vice-President, 1978–81; President, 1981–83); Local Director, Royal Insurance Co. Ltd, since 1973. Joined Leeds Permanent Building Soc., 1936. Member Council: Building Socs Assoc., 1973–78; Nat. House Builders, 1973–78; Chm., Yorkshire County Assoc. of Building Socs, 1978–80. *Recreations:*

golf, walking. *Address:* 5 Burn Bridge Road, Harrogate, Yorks HG3 1NS. *T:* Harrogate (0423) 871748. *Clubs:* Lansdowne; Pannal Golf.

HYDE-PARKER, Sir Richard William; *see* Parker.

HYLTON, 5th Baron, *cr* 1866; **Raymond Hervey Jolliffe,** MA; ARICS; *b* 13 June 1932; *er s* of 4th Baron Hylton and of the Dowager Lady Hylton, *d* of late Raymond Asquith and *sister* of 2nd Earl of Oxford and Asquith, *qv; S* father, 1967; *m* 1966, Joanna Ida Elizabeth, *d* of late Andrew de Bertodano; four *s* one *d. Educ:* Eton (King's Scholar); Trinity Coll., Oxford (MA). Lieut R of O, Coldstream Guards. Asst Private Sec. to Governor-General of Canada, 1960–62; Trustee, Shelter Housing Aid Centre 1970–76; Chairman: Catholic Housing Aid Soc., 1972–73; Nat. Fedn of Housing Assocs, 1973–76; Housing Assoc. Charitable Trust; Help the Aged Housing Trust, 1976–82; Hugh of Witham Foundn, 1978–; Vice-Pres., Age Concern (Nat. Old People's Welfare Council), 1971–77; President: SW Reg. Nat. Soc. for Mentally Handicapped Children, 1976–79; NI Assoc. for Care and Resettlement of Offenders, 1989. Founder and Mem., Mendip and Wansdyke Local Enterprise Gp, 1979–85. Hon. Treas., Study on Human Rights and Responsibilities in Britain and N Ireland, 1985–88. Trustee: Christian Internat. Peace Service, 1977–82; Acorn Christian Healing Trust, 1983; Governor, Christian Coll. for Adult Educn, 1972–. Mem., Frome RDC, 1968–72. DL Somerset, 1975–90. *Heir: s* Hon. William Henry Martin Jolliffe, *b* April 1967. *Address:* Ammerdown, Radstock, Bath.

HYLTON-FOSTER, family name of **Baroness Hylton-Foster.**

HYLTON-FOSTER, Baroness, *cr* 1965, of the City of Westminster (Life Peer); **Audrey Pellew Hylton-Foster,** DBE 1990; British Red Cross Society: Director, Chelsea Division, 1950–60; President and Chairman, London Branch, 1960–83, Patron, since 1984; Hon. Consultant, National Headquarters, 1984–86; Convenor, Cross Bench Peers, since 1974; *b* 19 May 1908; *d* of 1st Viscount Ruffside, PC, DL (*d* 1958), and Viscountess Ruffside (*d* 1969); *m* 1931, Rt Hon. Sir Harry Hylton-Foster, QC (*d* 1965); no *c. Educ:* St George's, Ascot; Ivy House, Wimbledon. Pres., Research into Blindness Fund, 1965–76. *Recreations:* gardening, trout fishing. *Address:* The Coach House, Tanhurst, Leith Hill, Holmbury St Mary, Dorking, Surrey RH5 6LU. *T:* Dorking (0306) 711975; 54 Cranmer Court, Whiteheads Grove, SW3 3HW. *T:* 071–584 2889.

HYMAN, Joe; Underwriting member of Lloyd's; *b* 14 Oct. 1921; *yr s* of late Solomon Hyman and Hannah Hyman; *m* 1st, 1948, Corinne I. Abrahams (marriage dissolved); one *s* one *d;* 2nd, 1963, Simone Duke; one *s* one *d. Educ:* North Manchester Grammar Sch. In textiles, 1939–80; Founder, Viyella International, and Chm., 1961–69. Trustee, Pestalozzi Children's Village Trust, 1967–; Governor, LSE. FRSA 1968; FBIM. Comp. TI. *Recreations:* music, golf, gardening. *Address:* Aston Tirrold, Oxfordshire; 24 Kingston House North, Prince's Gate, SW7 1LN. *Club:* MCC.

HYMAN, Robin Philip; Chairman, John Callmann & King Ltd, since 1991; Consultant, Hambro Group Investments, since 1991; *b* 9 Sept. 1931; *s* of late Leonard Hyman and of Helen Hyman (*née* Mautner); *m* 1966, Inge Neufeld; two *s* one *d. Educ:* Henley Grammar Sch.; Christ's Coll., Finchley; Univ. of Birmingham (BA (Hons) 1955). National Service, RAF, 1949–51. Editor, Mermaid, 1953–54; Bookselling and Publishing: joined Evans Brothers Ltd, Publishers, 1955: Dir, 1964; Dep. Man. Dir, 1967; Man. Dir, 1972–77; Chm., Bell & Hyman Ltd, 1977–86, which merged with Allen & Unwin Ltd, 1986, to form Unwin Hyman Ltd, Man. Dir, 1986–88, Chm. and Chief Exec., 1989–90. Mem. Editorial Bd, World Year Book of Education, 1969–73. Publishers' Association: Mem. Council, 1975–; Treasurer, 1982–84; Vice-Pres., 1988–89, 1991–92; Pres., 1989–91; Member: Exec. Cttee, Educnl Publishers' Council, 1971–76 (Treas., 1972–75); Publishers' Adv. Cttee, British Council, 1989–. Mem., First British Publishers' Delegn to China, 1978. *Publications:* A Dictionary of Famous Quotations, 1962; (with John Trevaskis) Boys' and Girls' First Dictionary, 1967; Bell & Hyman First Colour Dictionary, 1985; Universal Primary Dictionary (for Africa), 1976; (with Inge Hyman) 11 children's books, incl. Barnabas Ball at the Circus, 1967; Runaway James and the Night Owl, 1968; The Hippo who Wanted to Fly, 1973; The Magical Fish, 1974; Peter's Magic Hide-and-Seek, 1982. *Recreations:* theatre, reading, cricket. *Address:* 101 Hampstead Way, NW11 7LR. *T:* 081–455 7055. *Clubs:* Garrick, MCC, Samuel Pepys.

HYND, Ronald; choreographer; Ballet Director, National Theater, Munich, 1970–73 and 1984–86; *b* 22 April 1931; *s* of William John and Alice Louisa Hens; *m* 1957, Annette Page, *qv;* one *d. Educ:* erratically throughout England due to multiple wartime evacuation. Joined Rambert School, 1946; Ballet Rambert, 1949; Royal Ballet (then Sadlers Well's Ballet), 1952, rising from Corps de Ballet to Principal Dancer, 1959; danced Siegfried

(Swan Lake), Florimund (Sleeping Beauty), Albrecht (Giselle), Poet (Sylphides), Tsarevitch (Firebird), Prince of Pagodas, Moondog (Lady and Fool), Tybalt (Romeo), etc; produced first choreography for Royal Ballet Choreographic Group followed by works for London Festival Ballet, Royal Ballet, Dutch National Ballet, Munich Ballet, Houston Ballet, Australian Ballet, Tokyo Ballet, Nat. Ballet of Canada, Grands Ballets Canadiens, Santiago Ballet, Cincinnati Ballet, Pact Ballet, Malmö Ballet, Ljubljania Ballet and Northern Ballet. *Ballets include:* Le Baiser de la Fée, 1968, new production 1974; Pasiphaë, 1969; Dvorak Variations, 1970; Wendekreise, 1972; In a Summer Garden, 1972; Das Telefon, 1972; Mozartiana, 1973; Charlotte Brontë, 1974; Mozart Adagio, 1974; Galileo (film), 1974; Orient/Occident, 1975; La Valse, 1975; Valses Nobles et Sentimentales, 1975; The Merry Widow, 1975; L'Eventail, 1976; The Nutcracker (new version for Festival Ballet), 1976; ice ballets for John Curry, 1977; Rosalinda, 1978; La Chatte, 1978; Papillon, 1979; The Seasons, 1980; Alceste, 1981; Scherzo Capriccioso, 1982; Le Diable a Quatre, 1984; Fanfare fur Tänzer, 1985; Coppelia (new prodn for Festival Ballet), 1985; Ludwig-Fragmente Eines Rätsels, 1986; The Hunchback of Notre Dame, 1988; Ballade, 1988; Liaisons Amoureuses, 1989; *musical:* Sound of Music, 1981. *Recreations:* the gramophone, garden. *Address:* Fern Cottage, Upper Somerton, Bury St Edmunds, Suffolk IP29 4ND.

HYND, Mrs Ronald; *see* Page, Annette.

HYNES, Prof. Richard Olding, FRS 1989; Professor of Biology, since 1983, and Director of Center for Cancer Research, since 1991, Massachusetts Institute of Technology; Investigator, Howard Hughes Medical Institute, since 1988; *b* 29 Nov. 1944; *s* of Hugh Bernard Noel and Mary Elizabeth Hynes; *m* 1966, Fleur Marshall; two *s. Educ:* Trinity Coll., Cambridge (BA 1966; MA 1970); MIT (PhD Biology 1971). Res. Fellow, Imperial Cancer Res. Fund, 1971–74; Massachusetts Institute of Technology: Asst Prof., 1975–78, Associate Prof., 1978–83, Dept of Biology and Center for Cancer Res.; Associate Hd, 1985–89, Head, 1989–91, of Biology Dept. Hon. Res. Fellow, Dept of Zoology, UCL, 1982–83. Guggenheim Fellow, 1982. FAAAS, 1987. *Publications:* (ed) Surfaces of Normal and Malignant Cells, 1979; (ed) Tumor Cell Surfaces and Malignancy, 1980; Fibronectins, 1990; over 100 articles in professional jls. *Recreations:* reading, music, gardening, ski-ing. *Address:* E17-227, Massachusetts Institute of Technology, Cambridge, Mass 02139, USA. *T:* (617) 253-6422, *Fax:* (617) 253–8357.

HYSLOP, James Telfer, OBE 1968; HM Diplomatic Service, retired; Consul General, Detroit, 1971–76; *b* 21 Sept. 1916; *s* of Mr and Mrs John J. Hyslop; *m* 1942, Jane Elizabeth Owers; one *s* one *d. Educ:* Queen Elizabeth's Grammar Sch., Hexham. Royal Navy, 1939–46. Entered Diplomatic Service, 1948; served at: Baltimore, 1948; Valparaiso, 1951; Amman, 1954; Tegucigalpa, 1958; San Francisco, 1961; Johannesburg, 1964; Bogota, 1968. *Recreations:* reading, music. *Address:* 12 Quay Walls, Berwick-on-Tweed TD15 1HB. *T:* Berwick-on-Tweed (0289) 305197.

HYSLOP, Robert John M.; *see* Maxwell-Hyslop.

HYTNER, Benet Alan, QC 1970; a Recorder of the Crown Court, since 1972; Judge of Appeal, Isle of Man, since 1980; *b* 29 Dec. 1927; *s* of late Maurice and Sarah Hytner, Manchester; *m* 1954, Joyce Myers (marr. diss. 1980); three *s* one *d. Educ:* Manchester Grammar Sch.; Trinity Hall, Cambridge (Exhibr). MA. National Service, RASC, 1949–51 (commnd). Called to Bar, Middle Temple, 1952; Bencher, 1977; Leader, Northern Circuit, 1984–88. Member: Gen. Council of Bar, 1969–73, 1986–88; Senate of Inns of Court and Bar, 1977–81, 1984–86. *Recreations:* fell walking, music, theatre, reading. *Address:* 5 Essex Court, Temple, EC4Y 9AH.
  See also N. R. Hytner.

HYTNER, Nicholas Robert; Associate Director, Royal National Theatre, since 1989; *b* 7 May 1956; *s* of Benet Hytner, *qv. Educ:* Manchester Grammar School; Trinity Hall, Cambridge (MA). Associate Dir, Royal Exchange Theatre, Manchester, 1985–89; Director of many theatre and opera productions including: *theatre:* As You Like It, 1985, Edward II, 1986, The Country Wife, 1986, Don Carlos, 1987, Royal Exchange; Measure for Measure, 1987, The Tempest, 1988, RSC; Ghetto, National Theatre, 1989; Miss Saigon, Drury Lane, 1989, Broadway, 1991; Volpone, Almeida, 1990; King Lear, RSC, 1990; The Wind in the Willows, NT, 1990; *opera:* King Priam, Kent Opera, 1983; Rienzi, 1983, Xerxes, 1985 (Laurence Olivier and Evening Standard Awards), The Magic Flute, 1988, English National Opera; Giulio Cesare, Paris Opera, Houston Grand Opera, 1987; Le Nozze di Figaro, Geneva Opera, 1989; La Clemenza di Tito, Glyndebourne, 1991. Best Director, Evening Standard Awards, 1989; Best Director, Critics Circle Awards, 1989. *Address:* The Royal National Theatre of Great Britain, South Bank, SE1 9PX.

I

IBBOTSON, Lancelot William Cripps, CBE 1971 (MBE 1948); General Manager of Southern Region, British Railways, and Chairman, Southern Railway Board, 1968–72; *b* 10 Feb. 1909; *s* of William Ibbotson, FRCS and Mrs Dora Ibbotson (*née* Chapman), London; *m* 1st, 1931, Joan Marguerite Jeffcock (*d* 1989); one *s* one *d*; 2nd, 1990, Rhoda Margot Beck. *Educ:* Radley Coll. Traffic Apprentice, LNER, 1927; Chief Clerk to Dist. Supt, Newcastle, 1939; Asst Dist Supt, York, 1942; Dist Supt, Darlington, 1945; Asst to Operating Supt, Western Region, 1950; Asst Gen. Man., Western Region, 1959; Chief Operating Officer, British Railways, 1963; Gen. Man., Western Region, BR, and Chm., Western Railway Board, 1966–68. Gen. Man., A. Pearce, Partners & Assoc., 1975–79; Dir, Flameless Furnaces Ltd, 1976–84. *Recreations:* foreign travel, photography. *Address:* 60 Carlton Hill, St John's Wood, NW8 0ET. *T:* 071–624 7853. *Club:* Naval and Military.

IBBOTSON, Peter Stamford; Corporate Consultant, Channel Four Television, since 1988; *b* 13 Dec. 1943; *s* of Arthur Ibbotson and Ivy Elizabeth (*née* Acton); *m* 1975, Susan Mary Crewdson; two *s* one *d*. *Educ:* Manchester Grammar Sch.; St Catherine's Coll., Oxford (BA Modern History). BBC: Editor, Newsweek, 1978–82; Editor, Panorama, 1983–85; Asst Head, Television Current Affairs, 1985–86; Chief Asst to Dir of Programmes, Television, 1986–87; Dep. Dir of Progs, TV, 1987–88. Director: Film and Television Completions PLC, 1990–; UK Radio Develts Ltd, 1990–. Dir, BARB, 1987–88. *Publication:* (jtly) The Third Age of Broadcasting, 1978. *Recreations:* silviculture, reading, photography. *Address:* Newnham Farm, Wallingford, Oxon OX10 8BW. *T:* Wallingford (0491) 33111. *Club:* Royal Automobile.

IBBOTT, Alec, CBE 1988; HM Diplomatic Service, retired; High Commissioner to the Republic of Gambia, 1988–90; *b* 14 Oct. 1930; *s* of Francis Joseph Ibbott and Madge Winifred Ibbott (*née* Graham); *m* 1964, Margaret Elizabeth Brown; one *s* one *d*. Joined Foreign (subseq. Diplomatic) Service, 1949; served in HM Forces, 1949–51; FCO, 1951–54; ME Centre for Arab Studies, 1955–56; Second Secretary and Vice Consul, Rabat, 1956–60; Second Secretary, FO, 1960–61; Second Sec. (Information), Tripoli, 1961; Second Sec., Benghazi, 1961–65; First Sec. (Information), Khartoum, 1965–67; First Sec., FO (later FCO), 1967–71; Asst Political Agent, Dubai, 1971; First Secretary, Head of Chancery and Consul: Dubai, 1971–72; Abu Dhabi, 1972–73; First Secretary and Head of Chancery: Nicosia, 1973–74; FCO, 1975–77; Carácas, 1977–79; Counsellor, Khartoum, 1979–82; seconded to IMS Ltd, 1982–85; Ambassador to Liberia, 1985–87. *Address:* 15a Sanderstead Hill, South Croydon, Surrey CR2 0HD.

IBBS, Sir (John) Robin, KBE 1988; Kt 1982; Deputy Chairman, Lloyds Bank, since 1988 (Director, since 1985); Chairman, Lloyds Merchant Bank Holdings, since 1989; *b* 21 April 1926; *o s* of late Prof. T. L. Ibbs, MC, DSc, FInstP and of Marjorie Ibbs (*née* Bell); *m* 1952, Iris Barbara, *d* of late S. Hall; one *d*. *Educ:* Univ. of Toronto; Trinity Coll., Cambridge (MA Mech. Scis). Instr Lieut, RN, 1947–49. Called to the Bar, Lincoln's Inn. C. A. Parsons & Co. Ltd, 1949–51; joined ICI, 1952; Dir, 1976–80 and 1982–88; on secondment as Head, Central Policy Review Staff, Cabinet Office, 1980–82; Advr to Prime Minister on Efficiency and Effectiveness in Govt, 1983–88. Dep. Chm., Lloyds Bank Canada, 1989–90. Member: Governing Body and Council, British Nat. Cttee of ICC, 1976–80; Industrial Develt Adv. Bd, DoI, 1978–80; Council, CBI, 1982–87 (Mem. Companies Cttee, 1978–80); Council, CIA, 1976–79, 1982–87 (Vice Pres., 1983–87; Hon. Mem., 1987); Chemicals EDC, NEDO, 1982–88; Council, RIIA, Chatham House, 1983–89; Top Salaries Review Body, 1983–89; Leader, Review of H of C Services, 1990. Trustee and Dep. Chm., Isaac Newton Trust, 1988–. Mem. Court, Cranfield Inst. of Technology, 1983–88; Chm. of Council, UCL, 1989–. CBIM 1985. Hon. DSc Bradford, 1986. BIM Special Award, 1989. *Address:* Lloyds Bank, 71 Lombard Street, EC3P 3BS. *Club:* United Oxford & Cambridge University (Trustee, 1989–).

IBIAM, Sir (Francis) Akanu, GCON 1963; LLD, DLit; medical missionary; Eze Ogo Isiala I: Unwana, and the Osuji of Uburu; Chairman, Imo State Council of Traditional Rulers; Chancellor, Imo State University; *b* Unwana, Afikpo Division, Nigeria, 29 Nov. 1906; *s* of late Ibiam Aka Ibiam and late Alu Owora; *m* 1939, Eudora Olayinka Sasegbon (*d* 1974); one *s* two *d*. *Educ:* Hope Waddell Training Instn Calabar; King's Coll., Lagos; University of St Andrews, Scotland. FMCP (GP) Nigeria. Medical Missionary with the Church of Scotland Mission, Calabar, Nigeria, 1936; started and built up new Hosp. in Abiriba, Bende Div., under Calabar Mission, 1936–45; Medical Supt, CSM Hosp., Itu, 1945–48; CSM Hosp., Uburu, 1952–57. MLC, Nigeria, 1947–52; MEC, 1949–52; retd from Politics, 1953; Principal, Hope Waddell Training Instn, Calabar, 1957–60; (on leave) Governor, Eastern Nigeria, 1960–66; Adviser to Military Governor of Eastern Provinces, 1966. Founder (1937) and former Pres., Student Christian Movement of Nigeria, now Hon. President; Trustee: Presbyterian Church of Nigeria, 1945–; Queen Elizabeth Hosp., Umuahia-Ibeku, 1953–; Scout Movement of Eastern Nigeria, 1957–; Mem. Bd of Governors: Hope Waddell Trng Instn, Calabar, 1945–60; Queen Elizabeth Hosp., 1950–60; Mem. Provl Council of University Coll., Ibadan, 1948–54; Mem. Privy Council, Eastern Nigeria, 1954–60; Pres., Christian Council of Nigeria, 1955–58; Mem. Calabar Mission Council, 1940–60 (now integrated with Church); Mem. Admin. Cttee of Internat. Missionary Council, 1957–61; Chm. Provisional Cttee of All Africa Churches Conf., 1958–62; Chairman: Council of University of Ibadan, Nigeria, 1958–60; Governing Council of Univ. of Nigeria, Nsukka, 1966; a Pres. of World Council of Churches, 1961; a Pres. of All Africa Church Conf., 1963; Pres., World Council of Christian Educn and Sunday Sch. Assoc.; Chm. Council, United Bible Socs, 1966–72, Vice-Pres. 1972–; Founder and Pres., Bible Soc. of Nigeria, 1963–74, Patron 1974; Founder and former Pres., All Africa Council of Churches; Founder, Nigerian SPCC; President: Soc. for Promotion of Ibo Lang. and Culture; Cancer Soc. of Nigeria. Patron, Akanu Ibiam Nat. Ambulance; Grand Patron, World Women Christian Temperance Union. Presbyterian Church of Nigeria: Mem. Educ. Authority, 1940–; Mem. Missionaries' Cttee, Med. Bd, and Standing Cttee of Synod; Advanced Training Fund Management Cttee of Synod; Elder, 1940–. Appointed OBE 1949, KBE 1951, KCMG 1962, and renounced these honours 1967 in protest at British Govt policy on Biafra. Upper Room Citation, 1966. Hon. LLD Ibadan; Hon. DSc Ife, 1966. Kt of Mark Twain. Humanitarian of Rosicrucian Order. Golden Cross with crown, Order of Orthodox Knights of Holy Sepulchre, Jerusalem, 1965; Golden Star Medal (1st degree), Order of Russian Orthodox Church, 1965. *Recreation:* reading. *Address:* Ganymede, Unwana, Afikpo Local Government Area, PO Box 240, Imo State, Nigeria.

IBRAHIM, Sir Kashim, GCON 1963; KCMG 1962; CBE 1960 (MBE 1952); Governor of Northern Nigeria, 1962–66; Chancellor, Lagos University, 1976–84; *b* 10 June 1910; *s* of Mallam Ibrahim Lakkani; *m* 1st, 1943, Halima; 2nd, 1944, Khadija; 3rd, 1957, Zainaba; four *s* three *d* (and two *d* decd). *Educ:* Bornu Provincial Sch.; Katsina Teachers' Trng Coll. Teacher, 1929–32; Visiting Teacher, 1933–49; Educ. Officer, 1949–52. Federal Minister of Social Services, 1952–55; Northern Regional Minister of Social Develt and Surveys, 1955–56; Waziri of Bornu, 1956–62. Advr to Military Governor, N Nigeria, 1966. Chm. Nigerian Coll. of Arts, Science and Technology, 1958–62; Chancellor, Ibadan Univ., 1967–75; Chm. Provisional Council of Ahmadu Bello Univ. Hon. LLD: Ahmadu Bello, 1963; Univ. of Ibadan; Univ. of Nigeria (Nsukka); University of Lagos. *Publications:* Kanuri Reader Elementary, I-IV; Kanuri Arithmetic Books, I-IV, for Elementary Schs and Teachers' Guide for above. *Recreations:* walking, riding, polo playing. *Address:* PO Box 285, Maiduguri, Bornu State, Nigeria.

IDALIE, Mme Heinric; *see* Oldenbourg-Idalie, Zoë.

IDDESLEIGH, 4th Earl of, *cr* 1885; **Stafford Henry Northcote,** DL; Bt 1641; Viscount St Cyres, 1885; Director: Television South West, since 1982; Devon & Exeter Steeplechases Ltd, since 1975 (Vice Chairman, since 1990); *b* 14 July 1932; *er s* of 3rd Earl of Iddesleigh and Elizabeth (*d* 1991), *er d* of late F. S. A. Lowndes and late Marie Belloc; *S* father, 1970; *m* 1955, Maria Luisa Alvarez-Builla y Urquijo (Condesa del Real Agrado in Spain), OBE, DL, *d* of late Don Gonzalo Alvarez-Builla y Alvera and of Viscountess Exmouth, *widow* of 9th Viscount Exmouth; one *s* one *d*. *Educ:* Downside. 2nd Lieut, Irish Guards, 1951–52. Director: UDT, 1983–87; TSB Gp, 1986–87; TSB Commercial Hldgs, 1987; Mem., SW Region, TSB GP Bd (Chm., 1983–87). DL Devon, 1979. Kt SMO Malta. *Heir:* *s* Viscount St Cyres, *qv*. *Address:* Shillands House, Upton Pyne Hill, Exeter, Devon EX5 5EB. *T:* Exeter (0392) 58916. *Club:* Army and Navy.

IDIENS, Dale; Keeper, Department of History and Applied Art, National Museums of Scotland (formerly Department of Art and Archaeology, Royal Scottish Museum), since 1983; *b* 13 May 1942; *d* of Richard Idiens and Ruth Christine Idiens (*née* Hattersley). *Educ:* High Wycombe High Sch.; Univ. of Leicester. BA (Hons); DipEd. Royal Scottish Museum, Department of Art and Archaeology: Asst Keeper in charge of Ethnography, 1964; Dep. Keeper, 1979. *Publications:* African Textiles (ed with K. G. Ponting), 1980; museum publications: Traditional African Sculpture, 1969; Ancient American Art, 1971; The Hausa of Northern Nigeria, 1981; Pacific Art, 1982; (contrib.) Indians and Europe, an Interdisciplinary Collection of Essays, 1987; Cook Islands Art, 1990; articles and papers in Jl of the Polynesian Soc., African Arts, Textile History; reviews and lectures. *Recreations:* travel, film, wine. *Address:* Sylvan House, 13 Sylvan Place, Edinburgh EH9 1LH. *T:* 031–667 2399. *Clubs:* Naval and Military; University Staff (Edinburgh).

IEVERS, Frank George Eyre, CMG 1964; Postmaster-General, East Africa, 1962–65, retired; *b* 8 May 1910; *s* of Eyre Francis and Catherine Ievers; *m* 1936, Phyllis Robinson; two *s*. *Educ:* Dover Coll. Asst Traffic Supt, Post Office, 1933; Traffic Supt, East Africa, 1946; Telecommunications Controller, 1951; Regional Dir, 1959. *Recreations:* golf, photography. *Address:* 20 Heron Close, Worcester WR2 4BW. *T:* Worcester (0905) 427121. *Clubs:* Nairobi (Kenya); Sudan (Khartoum).

IEVERS, Rear-Adm. John Augustine, CB 1962; OBE 1944; *b* 2 Dec. 1912; *s* of Eyre Francis Ievers, Tonbridge, Kent; *m* 1937, Peggy G. Marshall; one *s* two *d*. *Educ:* RN Coll., Dartmouth. CO Naval Test Squadron, Boscombe Down, 1945–47; RN Staff Coll., 1948–49; HMS Ocean, 1949; HMS Glory, 1949–50; HMS Burghead Bay, 1951–52; CO, RN Air Station, Lossiemouth, 1952–54; Dep. Dir Naval Air Warfare Div., 1954–57; Captain Air, Mediterranean, 1957–60; Deputy Controller Aircraft, Min. of Aviation, 1960–63; retd, 1964. *Recreation:* golf. *Address:* 3 Hollywood Court, Hollywood Lane, Lymington, Hants SO41 9HD. *T:* Lymington (0590) 677268.

IGGO, Prof. Ainsley, PhD, DSc; FRCPE; FRS 1978; FRSE; Professor of Veterinary Physiology, University of Edinburgh, 1962–90; *b* 2 Aug. 1924; *s* of late Lancelot George Iggo and late Catherine Josefine Fraser; *m* 1952, Betty Joan McCurdy, PhD, *d* of late Donald A. McCurdy, OBE; three *s*. *Educ:* Gladstone Sch., NZ; Southland Technical High Sch., NZ; Lincoln Coll., NZ (Sen. Scholar; MAgrSc 1947); Univ. of Otago (BSc 1949). PhD Aberdeen, 1954; DSc Edinburgh, 1962. FRSE 1962; FRCPE 1985. Asst Lectr in Physiology, Otago Univ. Med. Sch., 1948–50; NZ McMillan Brown Trav. Fellow, Rowett Inst., 1950–51; Lectr in Physiol., Univ. of Edinburgh Med. Sch., 1952–60; Nuffield Royal Soc. Commonwealth Fellow, ANU, 1959; Royal Soc. Locke Res. Fellow, 1960–62; Dean, Faculty of Veterinary Med., Univ. of Edinburgh, 1974–77 and 1985–90. Vis. Professor: Univ. of Ibadan, Nigeria, 1968; (also Leverhulme Res. Fellow) Univ. of Kyoto, 1970; Univ. of Heidelberg, 1972. Chm., IUPS Somatosensory Commn, 1974–. Mem. Council: RCVS, 1975–78 and 1985–; Royal Soc., 1982–83; Pres., Internat. Assoc. for Study of Pain, 1980–83. Governor, E of Scotland Coll. of Agriculture, 1968–77. Hon. DSc Pennsylvania. *Publications:* (ed) Sensory Physiology: Vol. II, Somatosensory System, 1973; articles on neurophysiol topics in Jl Physiol., etc. *Recreations:* bee-keeping, gardening. *Address:* 5 Relugas Road, Edinburgh EH9 2NE. *T:* 031–667 4879.

IHAKA, Ven. Sir Kingi (Matutaera), Kt 1989; MBE 1969; Archdeacon of Auckland, New Zealand, 1976–82; *b* 18 Oct. 1921; *s* of Eru Timoko Ihaka and Te Paea Ihaka; *m* Manutuke Sadlier (*d* 1972); two *s* (and one *s* decd). *Educ:* St Stephen's Sch., Bombay; St John's Theol. Coll., Auckland (LTh; Fellow). Curate, St Matthew's, Masterton, 1949–50; Pastor, Wanganui, 1951–57; Maori Missioner, Wellington, 1958–66, Auckland, 1967–75; Director, Maori work, Auckland Dio, 1976–82; Chaplain, Maori Community, Sydney, Aust., 1983–86; retired from parish work, 1987, but still active in Church and State organisations. JP 1970. *Recreations:* reading, gardening. *Address:* 9 Piccadilly Place, Kohimarama, Auckland 5, New Zealand. *T:* (09) 5213–442.

IKERRIN, Viscount; David James Theobald Somerset Butler; *b* 9 Jan. 1953; *s* and *heir* of 9th Earl of Carrick, *qv*; *m* 1975, Philippa V. J., *yr d* of Wing Commander L. V. Craxton; three *s* (including twin *s*). *Educ:* Downside. *Heir: e s* Hon. Arion Thomas Piers Hamilton Butler, *b* 1 Sept. 1975.

ILCHESTER, 9th Earl of, *cr* 1756; **Maurice Vivian de Touffreville Fox-Strangways;** Baron Ilchester of Ilchester, Somerset, and Baron Strangways of Woodsford Strangways, Dorset, 1741; Baron Ilchester and Stavordale of Redlynch, Somerset, 1747; Group Captain, Royal Air Force (rtd); Managing Director, County Border Newspapers Ltd, since 1984; *b* 1 April 1920; *s* of 8th Earl of Ilchester and Laure Georgine Emilie (*d* 1970), *d* of late Evanghelos Georgios Mazaraki, sometime Treasurer of Suez Canal Company; *S* father, 1970; *m* 1941, Diana Mary Elizabeth, *e d* of late George Frederick Simpson, Cassington, Oxfordshire. *Educ:* Kingsbridge Sch. CEng; MRAeS; FINucE (Pres., 1982–84); FBIM; FRSA; FInstD. Dir, 1982–90, Vice Chm., 1985–86, Nottingham Building Soc. Pres., Soc. of Engineers, 1974; Hon. FSE 1989. Mem., H of L Select Cttee on Science and Technology, 1984–89. President: SE Area, RAF Assoc., 1978–; Grant Maintained Schools Foundn, 1991–. Chm. of Governors, Cannock Sch., 1978–. Liveryman, GAPAN. *Recreations:* outdoor activities, enjoyment of the arts. *Heir: b* Hon. Raymond George Fox-Strangways [*b* 11 Nov. 1921; *m* 1941, Margaret Vera, *d* of late James Force, North Surrey, BC; two *s*]. *Address:* Farley Mill, Westerham, Kent TN16 1UB. *T:* Westerham (0959) 62314. *Club:* Royal Air Force.

ILERSIC, Prof. Alfred Roman; Emeritus Professor of Social Studies, Bedford College, University of London, since 1984 (Professor, 1965–84); *b* 14 Jan. 1920; *s* of late Roman Ilersic and Mary (*née* Moss); *m* 1st, 1944, Patricia Florence Bertram Liddle (marr. diss. 1976); one *s* one *d*; 2nd, 1976, June Elaine Browning. *Educ:* Polytechnic Sec. Sch., London; London Sch. of Economics, Lectr in Econs, University Coll. of S West, Exeter, 1947–53; Lectr in Social Statistics, Beford Coll., 1953; Reader in Economic and Social Statistics, Bedford Coll., London, 1963. Vis. Prof., Univ. of Bath, 1983–87. Mem., Cost of Living Adv. Cttee, 1970–88. Chm., Inst. of Statisticians, 1968–70. Mem., Wilts CC, 1989–. Hon. Mem., Rating and Valuation Assoc., 1968. *Publications:* Statistics, 1953; Government Finance and Fiscal Policy in Post-War Britain, 1956; (with P. F. B. Liddle) Parliament of Commerce 1860–1960, 1960; Taxation of Capital Gains, 1962; Rate Equalisation in London, 1968; Local Government Finance in Northern Ireland, 1969. *Recreations:* listening to music, walking. *Club:* National Liberal.

ILIFFE, family name of **Baron Iliffe.**

ILIFFE, 2nd Baron, *cr* 1933, of Yattendon; **Edward Langton Iliffe;** Vice-Chairman of the Birmingham Post and Mail Ltd, 1957–74; Chairman: Coventry Evening Telegraph, 1957–75; Cambridge News, 1959–75; *b* 25 Jan. 1908; *er s* of 1st Baron Iliffe, GBE, and Charlotte Gilding (*d* 1972); *S* father 1960; *m* 1938, Renée, *er d* of René Merandon du Plessis, Mauritius. *Educ:* Sherborne; France; Clare Coll., Cambridge. Served, 1940–46, with RAFVR (despatches). Trustee, Shakespeare's Birthplace; Mem. Council, Univ. of Warwick, 1965–71; Past Pres., Internat. Lawn Tennis Club of Gt Britain. High Sheriff of Berks, 1957. Hon. Freeman, City of Coventry. *Heir: n* Robert Peter Richard Iliffe, *qv*. *Address:* 38 St James's Place, SW1. *T:* 071–493 1938; Basildon Park, Lower Basildon, near Reading, Berks. *T:* Pangbourne (0734) 844409. *Clubs:* Brooks's, Carlton; Royal Yacht Squadron.

ILIFFE, Barrie John; Controller, Arts Division, The British Council, 1983–85; *b* 9 Jan. 1925; *s* of Edward Roy Iliffe; *m* 1959, Caroline Fairfax-Jones; three *d*. *Educ:* Westcliff High Sch.; University College London. Concerts Manager, Liverpool Philharmonic Orchestra, 1951–55; Orchestral Manager, Philharmonia Orch., 1955–56; Manager, Cape Town Orch., 1956–58; Concerts Manager, Philharmonia Orch., 1958–60; Manager, London Mozart Players, 1961–63; General Manager, New Philharmonia Orch., 1964–65; British Council: Head of Music, 1966–77; Director, Music Dept, 1977–83; Dep. Controller, Arts Div., 1981–83. Asst to Chm., John Lewis Partnership, 1988–90. Sec., William and Mary Tercentenary Trust, 1985–86. Royal Philharmonic Society: Mem., Hon. Council of Management, 1987–; Hon. Co-Treasurer, 1989–. *Recreation:* inland waterways. *Address:* 29 Murray Mews, NW1 9RH. *T:* 071–485 5154.

ILIFFE, Prof. John, FBA 1989; Professor of African History, University of Cambridge, since 1990; Fellow of St John's College, Cambridge, since 1971; *b* 1 May 1939; 2nd *s* of late Arthur Ross Iliffe and Violet Evelyn Iliffe. *Educ:* Framlingham Coll.; Peterhouse, Cambridge (BA 1961; MA; PhD 1965; LittD 1990). Lectr, then Reader, in History, Univ. of Dar-es-Salaam, 1965–71; University of Cambridge: Asst Dir of Res. in Hist., 1971–80; Reader in African Hist., 1980–90. *Publications:* Tanganyika under German Rule, 1969; A Modern History of Tanganyika, 1979; The Emergence of African Capitalism, 1983; The African Poor: a history, 1987; Famine in Zimbabwe, 1989. *Recreation:* cricket. *Address:* St John's College, Cambridge CB2 1TP. *T:* Cambridge (0223) 338714. *Club:* MCC.

ILIFFE, Robert Peter Richard; Chairman, Yattendon Investment Trust Ltd; *b* Oxford, 22 Nov. 1944; *s* of late Hon. W. H. R. Iliffe and Mrs Iliffe; *m* 1966, Rosemary Anne Skipwith; three *s* one *d* (of whom one *s* one *d* are twins). *Educ:* Eton; Christ Church, Oxford. Chairman: Cambridge Newspapers Ltd; Yattendon Estates Ltd; Dep. Chm., Chapman Industries; Director: Bemrose Corp.; Ingersoll Publications, parent co. of Birmingham Post & Mail, and Coventry Newspapers. Member of Council, Royal Agricultural Soc. of England. High Sheriff of Warwicks, 1983–84. *Recreations:* yachting, shooting, fishing and old cars. *Address:* The Old Rectory, Ashow, Kenilworth, Warwickshire CV8 2LE.

ILLINGWORTH, David Gordon, CVO 1987 (LVO 1980); MD, FRCPE; Surgeon Apothecary to HM Household at Holyrood Palace, Edinburgh, 1970–86; *b* 22 Dec. 1921; *yr s* of Sir Gordon Illingworth; *m* 1946, Lesley Beagrie, Peterhead; two *s* one *d*. *Educ:* George Watson's Coll.; Edinburgh University. MB, ChB Edinburgh, 1943; MRCPE 1949; MD (with commendation) 1963; FRCPE 1965; FRCGP 1970. Nuffield Foundn Travelling Fellow, 1966. RN Medical Service, 1944–46 (2nd Escort Gp); medical appts, Edinburgh Northern Hosps Group, 1946–82. Dep. CMO, Scottish Life Assurance Co., 1973–. Hon. Sen. Lectr in Rehabilitation Studies, Dept of Orthopaedic Surgery, Edinburgh Univ., 1977–82; Lectr in Gen. Practice Teaching Unit, Edinburgh Univ., 1965–82. Member: Cancer Planning Group, Scottish Health Service Planning Council, 1976–81; Tenovus, Edinburgh, 1978–; ASH, Royal Colleges Jt Cttee, 1978–82; Specialty Sub-Cttee on Gen. Practice, 1980–82; Nat. Med. Cons. Cttee, 1980–82. AFOM, RCP, 1980. Mem., Harveian Soc. Life Governor, Imperial Cancer Res. Fund, 1978. *Publications:* Practice (jtly), 1978; contribs to BMJ, Jl of Clinical Pathology, Gut, Lancet, Medicine. *Recreations:* golf, gardening. *Address:* 19 Napier Road, Edinburgh EH10 5AZ. *T:* 031–229 8102. *Clubs:* University (Edinburgh); Bruntsfield Links Golfing Soc.

ILLINGWORTH, Raymond, CBE 1973; cricketer; Manager, Yorkshire County Cricket Club, 1979–84; *b* 8 June 1932; *s* of late Frederick Spencer Illingworth and Ida Illingworth; *m* 1958, Shirley Milnes; two *d*. *Educ:* Wesley Street Sch., Farsley, Pudsey. Yorkshire County cricketer; capped, 1955. Captain: MCC, 1969; Leics CCC, 1969–78; Yorks CCC, 1982–83. Toured: West Indies, 1959–60; Australia twice (once as Captain), 1962–63 and 1970–71. Played in 66 Test Matches (36 as Captain). Hon. MA Hull, 1983. *Publications:* Spinners Wicket, 1969; The Young Cricketer, 1972; Spin Bowling, 1979; Captaincy, 1980; Yorkshire and Back, 1980; (with Kenneth Gregory) The Ashes, 1982; The Tempestuous Years 1977–83, 1987. *Recreations:* golf, bridge. *Address:* 386 Bradford Road, Stanningley, Pudsey, West Yorkshire LS28 7TQ. *T:* Pudsey (0532) 578137.

ILLSLEY, Eric Evlyn; MP (Lab) Barnsley Central, since 1987; *b* 9 April 1955; *s* of John and Maude Illsley; *m* 1978, Dawn Webb; two *d*. *Educ:* Barnsley Holgate Grammar Sch.; Leeds Univ. (LLB Hons 1977). NUM, Yorkshire Area: Compensation Officer, 1978–81; Asst Head of General Dept, 1981–84; Head of Gen. Dept and Chief Admin. Officer, 1984–87. Member: Select Cttee on televising proceedings of H of C, 1988–; Select Cttee on Energy, 1987–; Jt Chm., All Party Parly Glass Gp. Sec., Barnsley Constit. Lab. Pty, 1980–83 (Treas., 1979–80); Sec. and Election Agent, Yorks S Eur. Constit. Lab. Pty, 1983–87; Treas., Yorks Gp of Lab. MPs. *Recreation:* jogging. *Address:* 3 St Clements Close, Ardsley, Barnsley, S Yorks S71 5DD. *T:* (office) Barnsley (0226) 730692. *Club:* Barnsley Cricket and Athletic (Barnsley).

ILLSLEY, Prof. Raymond, CBE 1979; PhD; Professorial Fellow in Social Policy, University of Bath, since 1984; *b* 6 July 1919; *s* of James and Harriet Illsley; *m* 1948, Jean Mary Harrison; two *s* one *d*. *Educ:* St Edmund Hall, Oxford (BA 1948). PhD Aberdeen 1956. Served War, 1939–45: active service in GB and ME, 1939–42; PoW, Italy and Germany, 1942–45. Econ. Asst, Commonwealth Econ. Cttee, London, 1948; Social Res. Officer, New Town Develt Corp., Crawley, Sussex, 1948–50; Sociologist, MRC, working with Dept of Midwifery, Univ. of Aberdeen, as Mem., Social Med. Res. Unit and later Mem., Obstetric Med. Res. Unit, 1951–64; Prof. of Sociology, Univ. of Aberdeen, 1964–75, Prof. of Medical Sociology, 1975–84. Dir, MRC Medical Sociology Unit, 1965–83. Vis. Prof., Cornell Univ., NY, 1963–64; Vis. Scientist, Harvard Univ., 1968; Sen. Foreign Scientist, National Sci. Foundn, Boston Univ., 1971–72; Vis. Prof., Dept of Sociology, Boston Univ., 1971–72, Adjunct Prof., 1972–76. Chairman: Scottish TUC Inquiry on Upper Clyde Shipbuilders Ltd, 1971; Social Sciences Adv. Panel, Action for the Crippled Child, 1971–76; Health Services Res. Cttee, Chief Scientist's Org., SHHD, 1976–84. Member: Sec. of State's Scottish Council on Crime, 1972–76; Exec. Cttee, Nat. Fund for Res. into Crippling Diseases, 1972–76; Chief Scientist's Cttee, SHHD, 1973–85; EEC Cttee on Med. Res., 1974–77; SSRC, 1976–78 (Chairman: Sociol. and Soc. Admin Cttee, 1976–79; Social Affairs Cttee, 1982–85); Chief Scientist's Adv. Cttee, DHSS, 1980–81; European Adv. Cttee for Med. Res., WHO, 1981–85. Rock Carling Fellow, Nuffield Prov. Hosps Trust, 1980. Hon. DSc Univ. of Hull, 1984; DUniv Stirling, 1987. *Publications:* Mental Subnormality in the Community: a clinical and epidemiological study (with H. Birch, S. Richardson, D. Baird et al), 1970; Professional or Public Health, 1980; (with R. G. Mitchell) Low Birth Weight, 1984; articles in learned jls on reproduction, migration, social mobility, mental subnormality. *Recreation:* rough husbandry. *Address:* University of Bath, Claverton Down, Bath BA2 7AY; *T:* (office) Bath (0225) 826752; Tisbut House, Box Hill, Wilts SN14 9HG. *T:* Bath (0225) 742313.

ILLSTON, Prof. John Michael, CEng, FICE; Director of the Hatfield Polytechnic, 1982–87, Professor and Professor Emeritus, 1987; *b* 17 June 1928; *s* of Alfred Charles Illston and Ethel Marian Illston; *m* 1951, Olga Elizabeth Poulter; one *s* two *d*. *Educ:* Wallington County Grammar Sch.; King's Coll., Univ. of London (BScEng, PhD, DScEng; FKC 1985). CEng, FICE 1975. Water engr, then schoolmaster, 1949–59; Lectr, Sen. Lectr and Reader in Civil Engrg, King's Coll., London, 1959–77; Dir of Studies in Civil Engrg, Dean of Engrg, and Dep. Dir, Hatfield Polytechnic, 1977–82. Member: Commonwealth Scholarships Commn, 1983–; Engrg Bd, SERC, 1983–86; Engrg Council, 1984–90; Council, BTEC, 1986–89; Chm., CNAA Cttee for Engrg, 1987–; Visitor, Building Res. Stn, 1989–. *Publications:* (with J. M. Dinwoodie and A. A. Smith) Concrete, Timber and Metals, 1979; contrib. Cement and Concrete Res. and Magazine of Concrete Res. *Address:* 10 Merrifield Road, Ford, Salisbury, Wilts SP4 6DF.

IMBERT, Sir Peter (Michael), Kt 1988; QPM 1980; Commissioner, Metropolitan Police, since 1987 (Deputy Commissioner, 1985–87); *b* 27 April 1933; *s* of late William Henry Imbert and of Frances May (*née* Hodge); *m* 1956, Iris Rosina (*née* Dove); one *s* two *d*. *Educ:* Harvey Grammar Sch., Folkestone, Kent; Holborn College of Law, Languages and Commerce. Joined Metropolitan Police, 1953; Asst Chief Constable, Surrey Constabulary, 1976, Dep. Chief Constable, 1977; Chief Constable, Thames Valley Police, 1979–85. Metropolitan Police Anti-Terrorist Squad, 1973–75; Police negotiator at Balcome Street siege, Dec. 1975; visited Holland following Moluccan sieges, and Vienna following siege of OPEC building by terrorists, Dec. 1975. Lectures in UK to police and military on terrorism and siege situations; also in Europe (incl. Berlin, 1978); lecture tours to Australia, 1977, 1980 and 1986, to advise on terrorism and sieges, and to Canada, 1981 re practical effects on police forces of recommendations of Royal Commn on Criminal Procedure. Sec., Nat. Crime Cttee-ACPO Council, 1980–83 (Chm., 1983–85). Member: Gen. Advisory Council, BBC, 1980–87; Academic Consultative Cttee, King George VI and Queen Elizabeth Foundn of St Catharine's, Cumberland Lodge, Windsor, 1983–. Trustee, Queen Elizabeth Foundn of St Catharine's, 1988–. CBIM 1982. Hon. DLitt Reading, 1987; Hon. DBA Reading, 1989. *Publications:* book reviews re terrorism, sieges and police negotiating. *Recreations:* bad bridge, coarse golf, occasional gardening. *Address:* New Scotland Yard, Broadway, SW1H 0BG. *T:* 071–230 1212.

IMBERT-TERRY, Sir Michael Edward Stanley, 5th Bt *cr* 1917, of Strete Ralegh, Whimple, Co. Devon; *b* 18 April 1950; *s* of Major Sir Edward Henry Bouhier Imbert-Terry, 3rd Bt, MC, and of Jean (who *m* 1983, Baron Sackville, *qv*), *d* of late Arthur Stanley Garton; *S* brother, 1985; *m* 1975, Frances Dorothy, *d* of late Peter Scott, Ealing; one *s* two *d*. *Educ:* Cranleigh. *Heir: s* Brychan Edward Imbert-Terry, *b* 1975.

IMESON, Kenneth Robert, MA; Headmaster, Nottingham High School, 1954–70; *b* 8 July 1908; *s* of R. W. Imeson; *m* 1st, 1934, Peggy (*d* 1967), *d* of late A. H. Mann, Dulwich; two *d*; 2nd, Peggy (*d* 1979), *widow* of Duncan MacArthur, *d* of late Harold Pow; 3rd, 1982, Barbara Thorpe (*see* Barbara Reynolds). *Educ:* St Olave's; Sidney Sussex Coll., Cambridge (Schol.). Mathematical Tripos, Part 1 1928; Part II 1930. Asst Master, Llandovery Coll., 1930–33; Sen. Mathematical Master, Watford Grammar Sch., 1933–44; Headmaster, Sir Joseph Williamson's Mathematical Sch., 1944–53; Member: Council SCM in Schools, 1948–58; Council of Friends of Rochester Cathedral, 1947–53; Board of Visitors, Nottingham Prison, 1956–57; Teaching Cttee, Mathematical Association,

1950–58; Trustee, Nottingham Mechanics Institution, 1955–70; Court of Nottingham Univ., 1955–64, 1968–70; Lectr, Univ. of Third Age, in Cambridge, 1983–86. Member: Oxford and Cambridge Examinations Board, 1957–61, 1962–70; Council Christian Education Movement, 1965–69; Council, Arts Educational Schools, 1971–88; Cttee, Notts CCC, 1969–72; London Diocesan Bd of Educn, 1971–76; Central Council of Physical Recreation, 1971–. Governor: Lady Margaret Sch., Parson's Green; Purcell Sch. of Music, 1975–78. *Publications:* The Magic of Number, 1989; articles in Journal of Education. *Recreations:* cricket and other games; music. *Address:* 220 Milton Road, Cambridge CB4 1LQ. *T:* Cambridge (0223) 424894. *Clubs:* Royal Air Force, MCC, Yellowhammers Cricket, Forty; Cambridge Society.

IMMS, George, CB 1964; Commissioner and Director of Establishments and Organisation, HM Customs and Excise, 1965–71; *b* 10 April 1911; *o s* of late George Imms; *m* 1938, Joan Sylvia Lance; two *s. Educ:* Grange High Sch., Bradford; Emmanuel Coll., Cambridge (Scholar). Joined HM Customs and Excise, 1933; Asst Sec., 1946; Commissioner, 1957–65. Mem. Civil Service Appeals Bd, 1971–79. *Address:* 26 Lynceley Grange, Epping, Essex CM16 6RA.

IMRAN KHAN, (Imran Ahmad Khan Niazi); cricketer; Editor-in-Chief, Cricket Life International, 1989–90; *b* Lahore, 25 Oct. 1952. *Educ:* Aitchison Coll.; Keble Coll., Oxford (BA Hons; cricket blue, 1973, 1974, 1975; Captain, Oxford XI, 1974). Début for Lahore A, 1969; played first Test for Pakistan, 1970, Captain, 1982–84, 1985–87, 1988–; with Worcs CCC, 1971–76 (capped, 1976); with Sussex CCC, 1977–88 (capped, 1978; Hon. Life Mem., 1988). Hon. Fellow of Keble Coll., Oxford, 1988. Special Sports Rep., UNICEF. Pride of Performance Award, Pakistan. *Publications:* Imran, 1983; All-Round View (autobiog.), 1988; Indus Journey, 1990. *Recreations:* shooting, films, music. *Clubs:* Tramp; Gymkhana (Lahore).

IMRAY, Colin Henry, CMG 1983; HM Diplomatic Service; High Commissioner to Bangladesh, since 1989; *b* 21 Sept. 1933; *s* of late Henry Gibbon Imray and of Frances Olive Imray; *m* 1957, Shirley Margaret Matthews; one *s* three *d. Educ:* Highgate Sch.; Hotchkiss Sch., Conn; Balliol Coll., Oxford (2nd cl. Hons PPE). Served in Seaforth Highlanders and RWAFF, Sierra Leone, 1952–54. CRO, 1957; Canberra, 1958–61; CRO, 1961–63; Nairobi, 1963–66; FCO, 1966–70; British Trade Comr, Montreal, 1970–73; Counsellor, Head of Chancery and Consul-Gen., Islamabad, 1973–77; RCDS, 1977; Commercial Counsellor, Tel Aviv, 1977–80; Rayner Project Officer, 1980; Dep. High Comr, Bombay, 1980–84; Asst Under-Sec. of State (Dep. Chief Clerk and Chief Inspector), FCO, 1984–85; High Comr, Tanzania, 1986–89. *Recreations:* travel, walking. *Address:* c/o Foreign and Commonwealth Office, SW1A 2AH. *Clubs:* Commonwealth Trust, Travellers'.

INCE, Dr Basil André; High Commissioner for Republic of Trinidad and Tobago in London, 1986–87; *b* 1 May 1933; *s* of Mrs Leonora Brown and Arthur J. Ince; *m* 1961, Laurel Barnwell; two *s. Educ:* Queen's Royal Coll., Trinidad; Tufts Univ., USA (BA Pol. Sci. and Hist.); New York Univ. (PhD Internat Relations, Comparative Politics, Internat. Law, Amer. Dip. Hist.). Min. of External Affairs Mission to UN, NY, 1963–66; Asst Prof., City Univ., NY, 1966–68; Associate Prof., State Univ., Puerto Rico, 1968–70, State Univ., NY, 1970–73; Sen. Lectr, Inst. of Internat. Relations, Univ. of WI, Trinidad, 1973–81 (Acting Dir, 1978–81); Minister of External Affairs, Trinidad and Tobago, 1981–85; Minister of Sport, Culture and Youth Affairs, 1985–86. *Publications:* Decolonization and Conflict in the United Nations: Guyana's struggle for independence, 1972; (ed) Essays on Race, Economics and Politics in the Caribbean, 1972; (ed) Contemporary International Relations of the Caribbean, 1979; (ed and contrib.) Issues in Caribbean International Relations, 1983. *Recreations:* reading, sports—tennis, track, boxing. *Address:* c/o Ministry of Foreign Affairs, Knowsley Building, Queen's Park West, Port of Spain, Trinidad and Tobago. *Club:* Colonial Tennis (Port-of-Spain).

INCE, Wesley Armstrong, CMG 1968; Solicitor and Company Director; *b* 27 Nov. 1893; *s* of John and Christina Ince, Melbourne; *m* 1919, Elsie Maud Ince, *d* of Wm H. Smith, Melbourne; two *d. Educ:* Wesley Coll., Melbourne; Melbourne Univ. Admitted practice Barrister and Solicitor, 1917; Partner, Arthur Robinson & Co., 1919–67. Chm., Claude Neon Industries Ltd, 1932–70; Chm., Rheem Australia Ltd, 1937–67; Foundn Mem. Coun., Inst. of Public Affairs, 1942–; Foundn Mem., Australian-American Assoc., 1941– (Federal Pres., 1962–63, 1965–67); Chm., Petroleum Refineries (Aust.) Ltd, 1952–61; Director: International Harvester Co. of Australia Pty Ltd, 1945–74; Hoyts Theatres Ltd, 1934–76; Dulux Australia Ltd, 1945–74. *Recreations:* golf, bowls, swimming. *Address:* 372 Glenferrie Road, Malvern, Vic 3144, Australia. *T:* 20 9516. *Clubs:* Athenæum (Melbourne); Royal Melbourne Golf, Melbourne Cricket.

INCH, Sir John Ritchie, Kt 1972; CVO 1969; CBE 1958; QPM 1961; Chief Constable, Edinburgh City Police, 1955–76; *b* 14 May 1911; *s* of James Inch, Lesmahagow, Lanarkshire; *m* 1941, Anne Ferguson Shaw; one *s* two *d. Educ:* Hamilton Academy; Glasgow Univ. (MA, LLB). Joined Lanarkshire Constabulary, 1931; apptd Chief Constable, Dunfermline City Police, 1943, and of combined Fife Constabulary, 1949. OStJ 1964. Comdr, Royal Order of St Olav (Norway), 1962; Comdr, Order of Al-Kawkal Al Urdini (Jordan), 1966; Cavaliere Ufficiale, Order of Merit (Italy), 1969; Comdr, Order of Orange-Nassau (Netherlands), 1971; Order of the Oak Crown Class III (Luxembourg), 1972. *Recreations:* shooting, fishing, golf. *Address:* Fairways, 192 Whitehouse Road, Barnton, Edinburgh EH4 6DA. *T:* 031–339 3558. *Club:* Royal Scots (Edinburgh).

INCHBALD, Michael John Chantrey, FCSD; designer; *b* 8 March 1920; *s* of late Geoffrey H. E. Inchbald and Rosemary Evelyn (*née* Ilbert); *m* 1955, Jacqueline Bromley (marr. diss. 1964; *see* J. A. Thwaites); one *s* one *d*; *m* 1964, Eunice Haymes (marr. diss. 1969). *Educ:* Sherborne; Architect. Assoc. Sch. of Architecture. FSIAD 1970. Work exhibited: Triennale, Milan; V & A Mus.; Design Centres London, New York, Helsinki. Design projects for: Bank of America; Crown Estate Comrs; Cunard; Dunhill worldwide; Ferragamo; Imperial Group; Justerini & Brooks; Law Soc.; John Lewis; Manufacturers Hanover Bank; Manufacturers Hanover Trust Bank; John Player; Plessey Co.; Pratt Bernard Engineering; Savoy Group—Berkeley, Claridges and Savoy hotels, and the restaurant complex Stones Chop House; Scottish Highland Industries; Trust House Forte—Post House, London Airport and several restaurants; ships, QE2, Carmania, Franconia, Wolsey and Windsor Castle; royal and private yachts and houses. Consultant to furniture and carpet manufacturers. Consulted *re* changes at Buckingham Palace; other projects, for the Duc de la Rochefoucauld, 13th Duke of St Albans, 6th Marquess of Bristol, 17th Earl of Perth, 9th Earl of Dartmouth, 2nd Earl St Aldwyn, etc. Inchbald schs founded under his auspices, 1960. Winner of four out of four nat. design competitions entered, including: Shapes of Things to Come, 1946; Nat. Chair Design Competition, 1955. Freeman, Clockmakers' Co., 1985. *Publications:* contrib. Arch. Rev., Arch. Digest, Connaissance des Arts, Connoisseur, Country Life, Harpers/Queen, House & Garden, Internat. Lighting Rev., Tatler, and Vogue. *Recreations:* arts, travel, antiques. *Address:* Stanley House, 10 Milner Street, SW3 2PU. *T:* 071–584 8832.

INCHCAPE, 3rd Earl of, *cr* 1929; **Kenneth James William Mackay;** Viscount Glenapp of Strathnaver, *cr* 1929; Viscount Inchcape, *cr* 1924; Baron Inchcape, *cr* 1911; Chairman and Chief Executive, Inchcape PLC, 1958–82, now Life President; Chairman: P & O Steam Navigation Co., 1973–83 (Chief Executive, 1978–81; Director, 1957–83); Inchcape Family Investment Ltd, since 1985; Glenapp Estate Company, Edinburgh, since 1979; President, Commonwealth Society for the Deaf; *b* 27 Dec. 1917; *e s* of 2nd Earl and Joan (*d* 1933), *d* of late Lord Justice Moriarty; *S* father 1939; *m* 1st, 1941, Mrs Aline Thorn Hannay (marr. diss. 1954), *widow* of Flying Officer P. C. Hannay, AAF, and *d* of Sir Richard Pease, 2nd Bt; two *s* one *d*; 2nd, 1965, Caroline Cholmeley, *e d* of Cholmeley Dering Harrison, Emo Court, Co. Leix, Eire, and Mrs Corisande Harrison, Stradbally, Co. Waterford; two *s* and one adopted *s. Educ:* Eton; Trinity Coll., Cambridge (MA). Served War of 1939–45: 12th Royal Lancers BEF France; Major 27th Lancers MEF and Italy. Director: Burmah Oil Co., 1960–75; BP Co., 1965–83. Chm., Council for Middle East Trade, 1963–65; Pres., Gen. Council of British Shipping, 1976–77. Pres., Royal Soc. for India, Pakistan and Ceylon, 1970–76. Prime Warden: Shipwrights' Co., 1967; Fishmongers' Co., 1977–78. One of HM Comrs of Lieutenancy for the City of London, 1980–. Freeman, City of London. *Recreations:* all field sports. *Heir: s* Viscount Glenapp, *qv. Address:* Addington Manor, Addington, Bucks MK18 2JR; Carlock House, Ballantrae, Girvan, Ayrshire. *Clubs:* White's, Brooks's, Buck's, City, Oriental.

See also Baron Craigmyle, Baron Tanlaw.

INCHIQUIN, 18th Baron of, *cr* 1543; **Conor Myles John O'Brien;** Bt 1686; *b* 17 July 1943; *s* of Hon. Fionn Myles Maryons O'Brien (*d* 1977) (*y s* of 15th Baron) and of Josephine Reine, *d* of late Joseph Eugene Bembaron; *S* uncle, 1982; *m* 1988, Helen, *d* of Gerald Fitzgerald O'Farrell; one *d. Educ:* Eton. Served as Captain, 14th/20th King's Hussars. *Heir: cousin* Murrough Richard O'Brien [*b* 25 May 1910; *m* 1st, 1942, Irene Clarice (marr. diss. 1951), *o d* of H. W. Richards; 2nd, 1952, Joan, *d* of Charles Pierre Jenkinson and *widow* of Captain Woolf Barnato; one *s* one *d*]. *Address:* Thomond House, Dromoland, Newmarket on Fergus, Co. Clare, Ireland.

INCHYRA, 2nd Baron, *cr* 1962, of St Madoes, Co. Perth; **Robert Charles Reneke Hoyer Millar;** Secretary General, British Bankers Association, since 1988; *b* 4 April 1935; *er s* of 1st Baron Inchyra, GCMG, CVO and of Elizabeth de Marees van Swinderen; *S* father, 1989; *m* 1961, Fiona Mary, *d* of Major E. C. R. Sheffield; one *s* two *d. Educ:* Eton; New Coll. , Oxford. J. Henry Schroder Wagg & Co., 1958–64; Barclays Bank, 1964–88: Local Dir, Newcastle upon Tyne, 1967–75; Reg. Gen. Man., 1976–81; Dep. Chm., Barclays Bank Trust Co., 1982–85; Gen. Man. and Dir, UK Financial Services, 1985–88. Mem., Cttee of London and Scottish Bankers, 1988–90. *Heir: s* Hon. Christian James Charles Hoyer Millar, *b* 12 Aug. 1962. *Address:* Rookley Manor, Kings Somborne, Stockbridge, Hants SO20 6QX. *T:* Romsey (0794) 388319. *Clubs:* White's, Pratt's.

IND, Jack Kenneth; Headmaster of Dover College, 1981–91; *b* 20 Jan. 1935; *s* of late Rev. William Price Ind and Mrs Doris Maud Ind (*née* Cavell); *m* 1964, Elizabeth Olive Toombs; two *s* two *d. Educ:* Marlborough Coll.; St John's Coll., Oxford (BA Hons Mods, 2nd Cl. Class. Lit. and Lit. Hum.). Asst Master: Wellingborough Sch., 1960–63; Tonbridge Sch., 1963–81 (Housemaster, 1970–81). *Recreations:* tennis, Rugby football, music, reading. *Address:* Longridge, Dixter Road, Northiam, near Rye, East Sussex TN31 6LB. *T:* Northiam (0797) 252106.

IND, Rt. Rev. William; *see* Grantham, Bishop Suffragan of.

INDIAN OCEAN, Archbishop of the, since 1984; **Most Rev. French Kitchener Chang-Him;** Bishop of Seychelles since 1979; *m* 1975, Susan Talma; twin *d. Educ:* Lichfield Theolog. Coll.; St Augustine's Coll., Canterbury; Trinity Coll., Univ. of Toronto (LTh 1975). Deacon, Sheffield, 1962; priest, Seychelles,1963; Curate of Goole, 1962–63; Rector of Praslin, Seychelles, 1963–66 and 1969–71; Asst Priest, St Leonard's, Norwood, Sheffield, 1967–68; Vicar General, Seychelles, 1972–73; Rector, S Mahé Parish, 1973–74; Archdeacon of Seychelles, 1973–79; Priest-in-charge, St Paul's Cathedral, Mahé, 1977–79; Dean, Province of the Indian Ocean, 1983–84. *Address:* Box 44, Victoria, Mahé, Seychelles. *T:* 24242.

INGAMELLS, John Anderson Stuart; Director of the Wallace Collection, since 1978; *b* 12 Nov. 1934; *s* of late George Harry Ingamells and Gladys Lucy (*née* Rollett); *m* 1964, Hazel Wilson; two *d. Educ:* Hastings Grammar School; Eastbourne Grammar School; Fitzwilliam House, Cambridge. National Service, Army (Cyprus), 1956–58; Art Asst, York Art Gallery, 1959–63; Asst Keeper, Dept of Art, National Museum of Wales, 1963–67; Curator, York Art Gallery, 1967–77; Asst to the Director, Wallace Collection, 1977–78. FRSA 1988. *Publications:* The Davies Collection of French Art, 1967; The English Episcopal Portrait, 1981; numerous catalogues, including Philip Mercier (with Robert Raines), 1969; Portraits at Bishopthorpe Palace, 1972; museum catalogues at York, Cardiff and the Wallace Collection; articles in Apollo, Connoisseur, Burlington Magazine, Walpole Soc., etc. *Address:* 39 Benson Road, SE23 3RL.

INGE, George Patrick Francis, FRICS; Chairman, Savills Plc, since 1987; *b* 31 Aug. 1941; *s* of late John William Wolstenholme Inge and Alison Lilias Inge; *m* 1977, Joyce (*née* Leinster); one *s* one *d. Educ:* Old Malthouse Prep. Sch., Dorset; Sherborne Sch. Joined Alfred Savill & Sons, 1960; Partner, 1968; Man. Partner, Savills, 1985. Chm. of Governors, Old Malthouse Sch., Dorset, 1986–. *Recreations:* shooting, fishing, old books and porcelain. *Address:* The Old Vicarage, Little Milton, Oxford OX9 7QB. *T:* Great Milton (0844) 279538. *Clubs:* Buck's, Flyfishers', Farmers'.

INGE, Gen. Sir Peter (Anthony), KCB 1988; Chief of the General Staff, from Feb. 1992; Aide de Camp General to the Queen, since 1991; *b* 5 Aug. 1935; *s* of Raymond Albert Inge and late Grace Maud Caroline Inge (*née* Du Rose); *m* 1960, Letitia Marion Beryl, *yr d* of late Trevor and Sylvia Thornton-Berry; two *d. Educ:* Summer Fields; Wrekin College; RMA Sandhurst. Commissioned Green Howards, 1956; served Hong Kong, Malaya, Germany, Libya and UK; ADC to GOC 4 Div., 1960–61; Adjutant, 1 Green Howards, 1963–64; student, Staff Coll., 1966; MoD, 1967–69; Coy Comdr, 1 Green Howards, 1969–70; student, JSSC, 1971; BM 11 Armd Bde, 1972; Instructor, Staff Coll., 1973–74; CO 1 Green Howards, 1974–76; Comdt, Junior Div., Staff Coll., 1977–79; Comdr Task Force C/4 Armd Bde, 1980–81; Chief of Staff, HQ 1 (BR) Corps, 1982–83; GOC NE District and Comdr 2nd Inf. Div., 1984–86; Dir Gen. Logistic Policy (Army), MoD, 1986–87; Comdr 1st (Br.) Corps, 1987–89; Comdr Northern Army Gp, and C-in-C, BAOR, 1989–92. Colonel, The Green Howards, 1982–; Col Comdt: RMP, 1987–; APTC, 1988–. *Recreations:* cricket, walking, music and reading, especially military history. *Address:* c/o Barclays Bank, Leyburn, North Yorks. *Clubs:* Army and Navy, MCC.

INGE-INNES-LILLINGSTON, George David, CBE 1986; MA, DL; a Crown Estates Commissioner, since 1974; *b* 13 Nov. 1923; *s* of late Comdr H. W. Innes-Lillingston, RN, and Mrs Innes-Lillingston, formerly of Lochalsh House, Balmacara, Kyle, Ross-shire; *m* 1st, 1946, Alison Mary (*d* 1947), *er d* of late Canon F. W. Green, MA, BD, Norwich; one *d*; 2nd, 1955, Elizabeth Violet Grizel Thomson-Inge, *yr d* of late Lt-Gen. Sir William Thomson, KCMG, CB, MC; two *s* one *d. Educ:* Stowe, Buckingham; Merton Coll.,

Oxford (MA Hons Agric.). Served War as Lieut RNVR, 1942–45, Lt-Comdr RNR, 1966. Member: Agricultural Land Tribunal, 1962–72; Minister's Agricultural Panel for W Midlands, 1972–76; Council for Charitable Support, 1985–90; Chairman: N Birmingham and District Hosps, 1968–74; Agr. and Hort. Cttee, BSI, 1980–; President: Staffs Agricultural Soc., 1970–71; CLA, 1979–81 (Dep. Pres., 1977–79; Chm., 1968–71, Pres., 1983–, Staffs Br.). Dir, Lands Improvement Gp Ltd, and associated cos, 1983–; Chm., Croxden Horticultural Products Ltd, 1986–91. Chm., Midland Reg., STA, 1983–. Trustee, Lichfield Cathedral, 1980–. FRAgS 1986. JP 1967–74, DL 1969–, Staffs; High Sheriff, Staffs, 1966. *Recreation:* growing trees. *Address:* The Old Kennels, Thorpe Constantine, Tamworth, Staffs B79 0LH. *T:* Tamworth (0827) 830224. *Clubs:* Boodle's, Farmers', Royal Thames Yacht; Royal Highland Yacht (Oban).

INGESTRE, Viscount; James Richard Charles John Chetwynd-Talbot; *b* 11 Jan. 1978; *s* and *heir* of 22nd Earl of Shrewsbury and Waterford, *qv*.

INGHAM, Sir Bernard, Kt 1990; Chief Press Secretary to the Prime Minister, 1979–90; Head of Government Information Service, 1989–90; *b* 21 June 1932; *s* of Garnet and Alice Ingham; *m* 1956, Nancy Hilda Hoyle; one *s*. *Educ:* Hebden Bridge Grammar Sch., Yorks. Reporter: Hebden Bridge Times, 1948–52; Yorkshire Post and Yorkshire Evening Post, Halifax, 1952–59; Yorkshire Post, Leeds, 1959–61; Northern Industrial Correspondent, Yorkshire Post, 1961; Reporter, The Guardian, 1962–65; Labour Staff, The Guardian, London, 1965–67. Press and Public Relns Adviser, NBPI, 1967–68; Chief Inf. Officer, DEP, 1968–73; Dir of Information: Dept of Employment, 1973; Dept of Energy, 1974–77; Under Sec., Energy Conservation Div., Dept of Energy, 1978–79. Vis. Fellow, Univ. of Newcastle, 1990–. *Publication:* Kill The Messenger, 1991. *Recreations:* walking, gardening, reading. *Address:* 9 Monahan Avenue, Purley, Surrey CR2 3BB. *T:* 081–660 8970. *Club:* Reform.

INGHAM, John Henry, CMG 1956; MBE 1947; retired; *b* 1910. *Educ:* Plumtree School, S Rhodesia; Rhodes University College, S Africa; Brasenose College, Oxford. Administrative Officer, Nyasaland, 1936; Secretary for Agricultural and Natural Resources, Kenya, 1947; Administrative Secretary, 1952; Senior Secretary, East African Royal Commission, 1953–55; Secretary for African Affairs, Nyasaland, 1956–60; MEC, Nyasaland, 1961. Minister of Urban Development, Malawi, 1961. Representative of Beit Trust and Dulverton Trust in Central Africa, 1962–81. Hon. MA Rhodesia, 1979. *Address:* 25 Canterbury Road, Avondale, Harare, Zimbabwe.

INGHAM, Prof. Kenneth, OBE 1961; MC 1946; Professor of History, 1967–84, Part-time Professor of History, 1984–86, now Emeritus Professor, and Head of History Department, 1970–84, University of Bristol; *b* 9 Aug. 1921; *s* of Gladson and Frances Lily Ingham; *m* 1949, Elizabeth Mary Southall; one *s* one *d*. *Educ:* Bingley Grammar Sch.; Keble Coll., Oxford (Exhibitioner). Served with West Yorks Regt, 1941–46 (despatches, 1945). Frere Exhibitioner in Indian Studies, University of Oxford, 1947; DPhil 1950. Lecturer in Modern History, Makerere Coll., Uganda, 1950–56, Prof., 1956–62; Dir of Studies, RMA, Sandhurst, 1962–67. MLC, Uganda, 1954–61. *Publications:* Reformers in India, 1956; The Making of Modern Uganda, 1958; A History of East Africa, 1962; The Kingdom of Toro in Uganda, 1975; Jan Christian Smuts: the conscience of a South African, 1986; Politics in Modern Africa, 1990; contrib. to Encyclopædia Britannica, Britannica Book of the Year. *Address:* The Woodlands, 94 West Town Lane, Bristol BS4 5DZ.

INGHAM, Stanley Ainsworth; Deputy Director (Under Secretary), Department for National Savings, 1979–82; *b* 21 Feb. 1920; *s* of David Ingham and Ann (*née* Walshaw); *m* 1944, Ethel Clara (*née* Jordan); one *s*. *Educ:* King's School, Pontefract, Yorkshire. Clerical Officer, Post Office Savings Bank, 1937; served Royal Artillery, 1940–46; Post Office Savings Bank: Executive Officer, 1946; Higher Executive Officer, 1956; Sen. Executive Officer, 1960; Principal, 1964; Asst Sec., Dept for National Savings, 1972. *Recreations:* Church affairs, gardening. *Address:* 2 Manor Crescent, Surbiton, Surrey KT5 8LQ. *T:* 081–399 1078.

INGILBY, Sir Thomas (Colvin William), 6th Bt *cr* 1866; MRAC; ARICS; FAAV; managing own estate; *b* 17 July 1955; *s* of Sir Joslan William Vivian Ingilby, 5th Bt, DL, JP, and of Diana, *d* of late Sir George Colvin, CB, CMG, DSO; *S* father, 1974; *m* 1984, Emma Clare Roebuck, *d* of Major R. R. Thompson, Whinfield, Strensall, York; three *s* one *d*. *Educ:* Aysgarth Sch., Bedale; Eton Coll. Student Teacher, Springvale School, Marandellas, Rhodesia, Sept. 1973–April 1974. Joined Army, May 1974, but discharged on death of father; student at Royal Agricultural Coll., Cirencester, until 1978. Assistant: Stephenson & Son, York, 1978–80; Strutt & Parker, Harrogate, 1981–83. Dir, N Yorks TEC, 1989–; Founder and Nat. Co-ordinator, Stately Homes Hotline, 1988–; Council Mem., Yorks Agricl Soc., 1989–. Lecture tours, USA, speaking on castles and historic houses, 1978, 1979. Gov., Ashville Coll., Harrogate, 1987–. Internat. Hon. Citizen, New Orleans, 1979. *Recreations:* cricket, tennis, squash. *Heir:* *s* James William Francis Ingilby, *b* 15 June 1985. *Address:* Ripley Castle, Ripley, near Harrogate, North Yorkshire HG3 3AY. *T:* Harrogate (0423) 770053.

INGLEBY, 2nd Viscount, *cr* 1955, of Snilesworth; **Martin Raymond Peake;** Landowner; Director, Hargreaves Group Ltd, 1960–80; *b* 31 May 1926; *s* of 1st Viscount Ingleby, and Joan, Viscountess Ingleby (*d* 1979); *S* father, 1966; *m* 1952, Susan, *d* of late Henderson Russell Landale; four *d* (one *s* decd). *Educ:* Eton; Trinity Coll., Oxford (MA). Called to the Bar, Inner Temple, 1956. Sec., Hargreaves Group Ltd, 1958–61. Administrative Staff Coll., 1961. CC Yorks (North Riding), 1964–67. Mem., N Yorks Moors Nat. Park Planning Cttee, 1968–78. *Heir:* none. *Address:* Snilesworth, Northallerton, North Yorks DL6 3QD.

INGLEDOW, Anthony Brian, OBE 1969; HM Diplomatic Service; Counsellor, Foreign and Commonwealth Office, since 1983; *b* 25 July 1928; *s* of Cedric Francis Ingledow and Doris Evelyn Ingledow (*née* Worrall); *m* 1956, Margaret Monica, *d* of Sir Reginald Watson-Jones, FRCS; one *s* one *d*. *Educ:* St Bees School; London Univ. Served HM Forces, 1947–49. Joined Colonial Administrative Service, Nigeria, 1950; District Officer: Auchi, 1954; Oyo, 1956; Secretariat, Ibadan, 1958, retired 1960; joined HM Diplomatic Service, 1961; 2nd Secretary, Khartoum, 1962; FO, 1964; 1st Secretary, Aden, 1966; Lagos, 1967; FCO, 1970; Dakar, 1972; FCO, 1975. *Recreations:* reading, travel. *Address:* c/o Foreign and Commonwealth Office, SW1. *Clubs:* Athenæum, Commonwealth Trust.

INGLEFIELD, Sir Gilbert (Samuel), GBE 1968; Kt 1965; TD; MA, ARIBA, AADip; *b* 13 March 1909; 2nd *s* of late Adm. Sir F. S. Inglefield, KCB; *m* 1933, Laura Barbara Frances, *e d* of late Captain Gilbert Thompson, Connaught Rangers; two *s* one *d*. *Educ:* Eton; Trinity Coll., Cambridge. Architect; served War of 1939–45 with Sherwood Foresters, France, Far East. British Council Asst Rep. in Egypt, 1946–49 and in London, 1949–56. Alderman, City of London (Aldersgate Ward), 1959–79; Sheriff, 1963–64; Chm., Barbican Cttee, 1963–66; Lord Mayor of London, 1967–68; one of HM Lieutenants for City of London; Church Commissioner for England, 1962–78; Governor: Thomas Coram Foundation; Royal Shakespeare Theatre; Fedn of British Artists, 1972–; Trustee, London Symphony Orchestra; Chm., City Arts Trust, 1968–76; Member: Royal Fine Art Commission, 1968–75; Redundant Churches Fund, 1972–76. Dep. Kt Principal, Imp. Soc. of Knights Bachelor, 1972–86, now Hon. Master, Haberdashers' Co., 1972; Master, Musicians Co., 1974; Assistant, Painter Stainers Co. Chancellor of the Order of St John of Jerusalem, 1969–78; GCStJ. FRSA; Hon. RBA; Hon. GSM; Hon. FLCM. Hon. DSc City Univ., 1967. Comdr Order of the Falcon (Iceland), 1963; Order of the Two Niles, Class III (Sudan), 1964. *Recreations:* music, travel. *Address:* 6 Rutland House, Marloes Road, W8 5LE. *T:* 071–937 3458. *Clubs:* Athenæum, City Livery.

INGLEFIELD-WATSON, Lt-Col Sir John (Forbes), 5th Bt *cr* 1895, of Earnock, Co. Lanarks; *b* 16 May 1926; *s* of Sir Derrick William Inglefield Watson, Bt, TD (who changed family surname to Inglefield-Watson by Deed Poll, 1945) and of Margrett Georgina (*née* Robertson-Aikman, now Savill); *S* father, 1987. *Educ:* Eton College. MBIM. Enlisted RE, 1944; short course, Trinity Coll., Cambridge, 1944–45; commnd RE, 1946; served in Iraq, Egypt, Kenya, Libya, Cyprus, Germany, N Ireland; psc 1958; Major 1959; Lt-Col 1969; retired 1981. Association Football Referee: Class I, 1954; Chm. Army FA Referees Cttee, 1974–78; FA Staff Referee Instructor, 1978–. Mem. Council, Kent County FA, 1975–81; Hon. Vice-Pres., Army FA, 1982–. *Recreations:* Association football refereeing; philately. *Heir:* *cousin* Simon Conran Hamilton Watson [*b* 11 Aug. 1939; *m* 1971, Madeleine Stiles, *e d* of late Wagner Mahlon Dickerson]. *Address:* The Ross, Hamilton, Lanarkshire ML3 7UF. *T:* Hamilton (0698) 283734.

INGLEWOOD, 2nd Baron *cr* 1964; **(William) Richard Fletcher-Vane;** Member (C) Cumbria and Lancashire North, European Parliament, since 1989; *b* 31 July 1951; *e s* of 1st Baron Inglewood, TD and Mary (*d* 1982), *e d* of Major Sir Richard George Proby, 1st Bt, MC; *S* father, 1989; *m* 1986, Cressida, *y d* of late Desmond Pemberton-Pigott, CMG; one *s* two *d*. *Educ:* Eton; Trinity Coll., Cambridge (MA); Cumbria Coll. of Agriculture and Forestry. ARICS. Called to the Bar, Lincoln's Inn, 1975. Member: Lake Dist Special Planning Bd, 1984–90 (Chm., Devel Control Cttee, 1984–89); N W Water Authority, 1987–89. Contested (C) Houghton and Washington, 1983; Durham, European Parlt, 1984. *Heir:* *s* Hon. Henry William Frederick Fletcher-Vane, *b* 24 Dec. 1990. *Address:* Hutton-in-the-Forest, Penrith, Cumbria CA11 9TH. *T:* Skelton (08534) 500; Flat 4, 111 Alderney Street, SW1V 4HE. *Clubs:* Pratt's, Travellers'.

INGLIS, Brian (St John), PhD; FRSL; journalist; *b* 31 July 1916; *s* of late Sir Claude Inglis, CIE, FRS, and late Vera St John Blood; *m* 1958, Ruth Langdon; one *s* one *d*. *Educ:* Shrewsbury Sch.; Magdalen Coll., Oxford. BA 1939. Served in RAF (Coastal Command), 1940–46; Flight Comdr 202 Squadron, 1944–45; Squadron Ldr, 1944–46 (despatches). Irish Times Columnist, 1946–48; Parliamentary Corr., 1950–53. Trinity Coll., Dublin: PhD 1950; Asst to Prof. of Modern History, 1949–53; Lectr in Economics, 1951–53; Spectator: Asst Editor, 1954–59; Editor, 1959–62; Dir, 1962–63. TV Commentator: What the Papers Say, 1956–; All Our Yesterdays, 1962–73. Trustee, Koestler (formerly KIB) Foundn, 1983–. *Publications:* The Freedom of the Press in Ireland, 1954; The Story of Ireland 1956; Revolution in Medicine, 1958; West Briton, 1962; Fringe Medicine, 1964; Private Conscience: Public Morality, 1964; Drugs, Doctors and Disease, 1965; A History of Medicine, 1965; Abdication, 1966; Poverty and the Industrial Revolution, 1971; Roger Casement, 1973; The Forbidden Game: the social history of drugs, 1975; The Opium War, 1976; Natural and Supernatural, 1977; The Book of the Back, 1978; Natural Medicine, 1979; The Diseases of Civilisation, 1981; (with Ruth West) The Alternative Health Guide, 1983; Science and Parascience, 1984; The Paranormal: an encyclopedia of Psychic Phenomena, 1985; The Hidden Power, 1986; The Power of Dreams, 1987; The Unknown Guest, 1987; Trance, 1989; Downstart (autobiog.), 1990; Coincidence, 1990. *Address:* Garden Flat, 23 Lambolle Road, NW3 4HS. *T:* 071–794 0297.

INGLIS, Sir Brian Scott, AC 1988; Kt 1977; FTS; Chairman: Ford Motor Co. of Australia Ltd, 1981–85; Salzo Automotive Research Ltd, since 1986; Amcor, since 1989 (Deputy Chairman, 1988–89; Director, since 1984); *b* Adelaide, 3 Jan. 1924; *s* of late E. S. Inglis, Albany, WA; *m* 1953, Leila, *d* of E. V. Butler; three *d*. *Educ:* Geelong Church of England Grammar School; Trinity Coll., Univ. of Melbourne (BSc; Mem. Council, 1985). Served War of 1939–45; Flying Officer, RAAF, 453 Sqdn, 1942–45. Director and Gen. Manufacturing Manager, 1963–70, first Australian Man. Dir, Ford Motor Co. of Australia Ltd, 1970–81, Vice-Pres., 1981–83, Chm. 1981–85; Chm., Ford Asia-Pacific Inc., 1983–84. Chairman: Newmont Holdings, 1985–; Aerospace Technologies of Aust. Pty Ltd, 1987–. Chm., Defence Industry Cttee, 1984–87 (Mem., 1982–87). Chm., Centre for Molecular Biology and Medicine, Monash Univ. James N. Kirby Medal, IProdE, 1979; Kernot Medal, Faculty of Engrg, Univ. of Melbourne, 1979. *Address:* 10 Bowley Avenue, Balwyn, Victoria 3103, Australia. *Clubs:* Australian (Melbourne); Barwon Heads Golf.

INGLIS, George Bruton; Senior Partner, Slaughter and May, since 1986; *b* 19 April 1933; *s* of late Cecil George Inglis and Ethel Mabel Inglis; *m* 1968, Patricia Mary Forbes; three *s*. *Educ:* Winchester College; Pembroke College, Oxford (MA). Solicitor. Partner, Slaughter and May, 1966–. *Recreation:* gardening. *Address:* c/o Slaughter and May, 35 Basinghall Street, EC2V 5DB. *T:* 071–600 1200.

INGLIS, Ian Grahame, CB 1983; State Under Treasurer for Tasmania, 1977–89; *b* 2 April 1929; *s* of late William and Ellen Jean Inglis; *m* 1952, Elaine Arlene Connors; three *s* one *d*. *Educ:* Hutchins Sch., Hobart; Univ. of Tasmania (BComm). Agricl Economist, Tasmanian Dept. of Agric., 1951–58; Economist, State Treasury, 1958–69; Chairman: Rivers and Water Supply Commn, and Metropolitan Water Bd, 1969–77; NW Regl Water Authority, 1977; State Grants Commn, Tas, 1990–. Dir, Tasmanian Govt Insce Office, 1989–. Member: Ambulance Commn of Tasmania, 1959–65; Tasmanian Grain Elevators Bd, 1962–65; Clarence Municipal Commn, 1965–69. Dir, Comalco Aluminium (Bell Bay) Ltd, 1980–. Chm., Retirement Benefits Fund Investment Trust, 1989–. *Recreation:* yachting. *Address:* 5 Sayer Crescent, Sandy Bay, Hobart, Tas 7005, Australia. *T:* (002) 231928. *Clubs:* Tasmanian, Royal Yacht of Tasmania (Hobart).

INGLIS, James Craufuird Roger, WS; Partner, Shepherd & Wedderburn, WS, 1976–89; Chairman, British Assets Trust plc, since 1978; *b* 21 June 1925; *s* of Lt-Col John Inglis and Helen Jean Inglis; *m* 1952, Phoebe Aeonie Murray-Buchanan; two *s* four *d*. *Educ:* Winchester Coll.; Cambridge Univ. (BA); Edinburgh Univ. (LLB). Director: Scottish Provident Institution, 1962–; Selective Assets Trust plc, 1988–; Royal Bank of Scotland, 1967–89; Royal Bank of Scotland Gp plc, 1985–90. Chairman: European Assets Trust NV, 1972–; Investors Capital Trust, 1985–; Ivory & Sime Optimum Income Trust, 1989–. *Recreation:* golf. *Address:* Inglisfield, Gifford, East Lothian, Scotland. *T:* Gifford (062081) 339. *Clubs:* Army and Navy; New (Edinburgh), Royal and Ancient Golf (St Andrews), Hon. Company of Edinburgh Golfers.

INGLIS, Prof. Kenneth Stanley, DPhil; Professor of History, Australian National University, since 1977; *b* 7 Oct. 1929; *s* of S. W. Inglis; *m* 1st, 1952, Judy Betheras (*d* 1962); one *s* two *d*; 2nd, 1965, Amirah Gust. *Educ:* Univ. of Melbourne (MA); Univ. of Oxford (DPhil). Sen. Lectr in History, Univ. of Adelaide, 1956–60; Reader in History, 1960–62; Associate Prof. of History, Australian National Univ., 1962–65; Prof., 1965–66; Prof. of History, Univ. of Papua New Guinea, 1966–72, Vice-Chancellor, 1972–75;

Professorial Fellow in Hist., ANU, 1975–77. Vis. Prof. of Australian Studies, Harvard, 1982; Vis. Prof., Univ. of Hawaii, 1985; Vis. Fellow, St John's Coll., Cambridge, 1990–91. Jt Gen. Editor, Australians: a historical library, 1987–88. *Publications:* Hospital and Community, 1958; The Stuart Case, 1961; Churches and the Working Classes in Victorian England, 1963; The Australian Colonists, 1974; This is the ABC: the Australian Broadcasting Commission, 1932–1983, 1983; The Rehearsal: Australians at War in the Sudan 1885, 1985; (ed and introduced) Nation: the life of an independent journal 1958–1972, 1989. *Address:* History Department, Research School of Social Sciences, Australian National University, Canberra, ACT 2600, Australia.

INGLIS, Sheriff Robert Alexander; Sheriff of North Strathclyde (formerly Renfrew and Argyll) at Paisley, 1972–84; *b* 29 June 1918; *m* 1950, Shelagh Constance St Clair Boyd (marriage dissolved, 1956); one *s* one *d*. *Educ:* Malsis Hall, Daniel Stewart's Coll.; Rugby Sch.; Christ Church, Oxford (MA); Glasgow Univ. (LLB). Army, 1940–46; Glasgow Univ., 1946–48; called to Bar, 1948. Interim Sheriff-Sub., Dundee, 1955; perm. appt, 1956; Sheriff of Inverness, Moray, Nairn and Ross and Cromarty, 1968–72. *Recreations:* golf, fishing, bridge. *Address:* 1 Cayzer Court, Ralston, Paisley, Renfrewshire. *T:* 041–883 6498.

INGLIS of Glencorse, Sir Roderick (John), 10th Bt *cr* 1703 (then Mackenzie of Gairloch); MB, ChB; *b* 25 Jan. 1936; *s* of Sir Maxwell Ian Hector Inglis of Glencorse, 9th Bt and Dorothy Evelyn (*d* 1970), MD, JP, *d* of Dr John Stewart, Tasmania; *S* father, 1974; *m* 1960, Rachel (marr. diss. 1975), *d* of Lt-Col N. M. Morris, Dowdstown, Ardee, Co. Louth; twin *s* one *d* (and *e s* decd); *m* 1975 (marr. diss. 1977); one *d*; *m* 1986, Marilyn, *d* of A. L. Irwin, Glasgow; one *s*. *Educ:* Winchester; Edinburgh Univ. (MB, ChB 1960). *Heir: s* Ian Richard Inglis, *b* 9 Aug. 1965. *Address:* 18 Cordwalles Road, Pietermaritzburg, S Africa.

INGLIS-JONES, Nigel John, QC 1982; Barrister-at-Law; a Recorder of the Crown Court, since 1976; *b* 7 May 1935; 2nd *s* of Major John Alfred Inglis-Jones and Hermione Inglis-Jones; *m* 1st, 1965, Lenette Bromley-Davenport (*d* 1986); two *s* two *d*; 2nd, 1987, Ursula Culverwell; one *s*. *Educ:* Eton; Trinity Coll., Oxford (BA). Nat. Service with Grenadier Guards (ensign). Called to the Bar, Inner Temple, 1959, Bencher, 1981. *Publication:* The Law of Occupational Pension Schemes, 1989. *Recreations:* gardening, fishing, collecting English drinking glass, conversation. *Address:* 4 Sheen Common Drive, Richmond, Surrey. *T:* 081–878 1320. *Club:* MCC.

INGMAN, David Charles; Chairman, British Waterways Board, since 1987; *b* 22 March 1928; *s* of Charles and Muriel Ingman; *m* 1951, Joan Elizabeth Walker; two *d*. *Educ:* Grangefield Grammar Sch., Stockton-on-Tees; Durham Univ. (BSc, MSc). Imperial Chemical Industries, 1949–85: Dir, then Dep. Chm., Plastics Div., 1975–81; Gp Dir, Plastics and Petrochemicals Div., 1981–85; Chm. and Chief Exec., Bestobell, 1985–86. Dir, Engineering Services Ltd, 1975–78; Alternative Dir, AECI Ltd, SA, 1978–82; Non-exec. Dir, Negretti-Zambra, 1979–81. Mem., Nationalised Industries Chairmen's Gp, 1987–. *Recreations:* golf, walking, travel. *Address:* British Waterways Board, Greycaine Road, Watford, Herts WD2 4JR.

INGOLD, Cecil Terence, CMG 1970; DSc 1940; FLS; Professor of Botany in University of London, Birkbeck College, 1944–72; Vice-Master, Birkbeck College, 1965–70, Fellow, 1973; *b* 3 July 1905; *s* of late E. G. Ingold; *m* 1933, Leonora Mary Kemp; one *s* three *d*. *Educ:* Bangor (Co. Down) Grammar Sch.; Queen's Univ., Belfast. Graduated BSc, QUB, 1925; Asst in Botany, QUB, 1929; Lectr in Botany, University of Reading, 1930–37; Lecturer-in-charge of Dept of Botany, University Coll., Leicester, 1937–44; Dean of Faculty of Science, London Univ., 1956–60. Dep. Vice-Chancellor, London Univ., 1966–68, Chm. Academic Council, 1969–72. Chm., University Entrance and School Examinations Council, 1958–64; Vice-Chm., Inter-Univ. Council for Higher Educn Overseas, 1969–74. Chm., Council Freshwater Biolog. Assoc., 1965–74; Pres., Internat. Mycological Congress, 1971. Hooker Lectr, Linnean Soc., 1974. Linnean Medal (Botany), 1983. Hon. DLitt Ibadan, 1969; Hon. DSc Exeter, 1972; Hon. DCL Kent, 1978. *Publications:* Spore Discharge in Land Plants, 1939; Dispersal in Fungi, 1953; The Biology of Fungi, 1961; Spore Liberation, 1965; Fungal Spores: their liberation and dispersal, 1971. *Address:* 11 Buckner's Close, Benson, Oxford OX10 6LR.

INGOLD, Dr Keith Usherwood, FRS 1979; FRSC 1969; Distinguished Scientist, Steacie Institute for Molecular Sciences, since 1991; *b* Leeds, 31 May 1929; *s* of Christopher Kelk Ingold and Edith Hilda (*née* Usherwood); *m* 1956, Carmen Cairine Hodgkin; one *s* one *d* (and one *s* decd). *Educ:* University Coll. London (BSc Hons Chem., 1949; Fellow, 1987); Univ. of Oxford (DPhil 1951). Emigrated to Canada, 1951; Post-doctorate Fellow (under Dr F. P. Lossing), Div. of Pure Chem., Nat. Res. Council of Canada, 1951–53; Def. Res. Bd Post-doctorate Fellow (under Prof. W. A. Bryce), Chem. Dept, Univ. of BC, 1953–55; National Research Council of Canada: joined Div. of Appl. Chem., 1955; Head, Hydrocarbon Chem. Section of Div. of Chem., 1965; Associate Dir, Div. of Chemistry, 1977–90. Hon. Treas., RSC, 1979–81; Canadian Society for Chemistry: Vice-Pres., 1985–87, Pres., 1987–88. Hon. DSc: Univ. of Guelph, 1985; St Andrews, 1989; Hon. LLD Mount Allison, New Brunswick, 1987. Amer. Chemical Soc. Award in Petroleum Chem., 1968; Award in Kinetics and Mechanism, Chem. Soc., 1978; Medal of Chem. Inst. of Canada, 1981, Syntex Award for Physical Organic Chemistry, CIC, 1983; Centennial Medal, RSC, 1982; Henry Marshall Tory Medal, RSC, 1985; Pauling Award, ACS, 1988; Humboldt Res. Award, Alexander von Humboldt Foundn, W Germany, 1989; Alfred Bader Award in Organic Chem., Canadian Soc. for Chem., 1989; Sir Christopher Ingold Lectureship Award, RSC, 1989; VERIS Award, Vitamin E Res. Inf. Services, 1989; Lansdowne Visitor Award, Univ. of Victoria, Canada, 1990; Mangini Prize in Chem., Univ. of Bologna, 1990; Davy Medal, Royal Soc., 1990. Silver Jubilee Medal, 1977. *Publications:* over 380 scientific papers in field of physical organic chemistry, partic. free-radical chemistry. *Recreation:* ski-ing. *Address:* 72 Ryeburn Drive, Gloucester, Ont K1G 3N3, Canada. *T:* (613) 822–1123; (office) (613) 990–0938.

INGRAM; *see* Winnington-Ingram.

INGRAM, Adam Paterson, JP; MP (Lab) East Kilbride, since 1987; *b* 1 Feb 1947; *s* of Bert Ingram and Lousia Paterson; *m* 1970, Maureen Georgina McMahon. *Educ:* Cranhill Secondary School. Commercial apprentice, 1965, computer programmer, 1966–69, J. & P. Coats, Glasgow; programmer/analyst, Associated British Foods, 1969–70; programmer/systems analyst, SSEB, 1970–77; Trade Union Official, NALGO, 1977–87. Sec., Jt Trades Union Side, Gas Staffs and Senior Officers, Scottish Gas, 1978–82; Chair, East Kilbride Constituency Labour Party, 1981–85; Councillor, E Kilbride DC, 1980–87, Leader, 1984–87; Mem., Policy Cttee, COSLA, 1984–87. An Opposition Whip, Feb.–Nov. 1988 (responsible for Scottish business and Treasury matters); PPS to Leader of the Opposition, 1988–. Mem., Scottish Exec. of Labour MP's, 1987–88. JP 1980. *Recreations:* fishing, cooking, reading. *Address:* 129 Teal Crescent, East Kilbride G75 8UT. *T:* East Kilbride (03552) 35343.

INGRAM, Dr David John Edward, CBE 1991; MA, DPhil; DSc Oxon 1960; CPhys, FInstP; Vice-Chancellor, University of Kent at Canterbury, since 1980; *b* 6 April 1927; *s* of late J. E. Ingram and late Marie Florence (*née* Weller); *m* 1952, Ruth Geraldine Grace McNair; two *s* one *d*. *Educ:* King's Coll. Sch., Wimbledon; New Coll., Oxford. Postgraduate research at Oxford Univ., 1948–52; Research Fellow and Lectr, University of Southampton, 1952–57; Reader in Electronics, University of Southampton, 1957–59; Prof. and Head of Dept of Physics, Univ. of Keele, 1959–73; Dep. Vice-Chancellor, University of Keele, 1964–65, 1968–71; Principal, Chelsea Coll., London Univ., 1973–80 (Fellow, 1984). Mem., UGC, Physical Sciences Cttee, 1971–74. Chairman: London Univ. Cttee for Non-Teaching Staff, 1979–80; London Univ. Central Coordinating Cttee for Computers, 1978–80; Standing Conf. on Univ. Admissions, 1982–89; Kent County Consultative Cttee Industry Year, 1986; Hon. Treas., CVCP, 1987– (Chm., Sub-Cttee on Staff and Student Affairs, 1986–89; Chm., Universities Staff Develt Trng Unit, 1989–). Member: Carnegie UK Trust, 1980–; Camberwell DHA, 1982–85; Esso Trust for Tertiary Educn, 1978–88; Univs Authorities Panel for Staff Salaries, 1987–89; Member Council: SPCK, 1980–; CNAA, 1983–89; CET, 1983–85; UCCA, 1984–. Member, Governing Body: Wye Coll., London Univ., 1975–; King's Sch., Canterbury, 1983–; St Lawrence Coll., 1980–89 (a Vice-Pres., 1989–); Cobham Hall, 1989–; King's Coll. Hosp. Medical Sch., 1982–; Roehampton Inst., 1978–88; London Sch. of Contemporary Dance, 1983–85; South Bank Poly., 1989–; West Heath Sch., 1990–. FKC 1986; Hon. Fellow, Roehampton Inst., 1988. Hon. DSc: Clermont-Ferrand, 1965; Keele, 1983. *Publications:* Spectroscopy at Radio and Microwave Frequencies, 1955, 2nd edn, 1967; Free Radicals as Studied by Electron Spin Resonance, 1958; Biological and Biochemical Applications of Electron Spin Resonance, 1969; Radiation and Quantum Physics, 1973; Radio and Microwave Spectroscopy, 1976; various papers in Proc. Royal Soc., Proc. Phys. Soc., etc. *Recreations:* sailing, debating, DIY. *Address:* The University, Canterbury, Kent CT2 7NZ; 22 Ethelbert Road, Canterbury, Kent CT1 3NE. *Club:* Athenæum (Mem., Gen. Cttee, 1985–89).

INGRAM, Dr David Stanley; Regius Keeper, Royal Botanic Garden, Edinburgh, since 1990; *b* 10 Oct. 1941; *s* of Stanley Arthur Ingram and Vera May Ingram (*née* Mansfield); *m* 1965, Alison Winifred Graham; two *s*. *Educ:* Yardley Grammar School, Birmingham; Univ. of Hull (BSc, PhD); MA, ScD Cantab. CBiol, FIBiol. Research Fellow, Univ. of Glasgow Dept of Botany, 1966–68; ARC Unit of Develt Botany, Cambridge, 1969–74; University of Cambridge: Research Fellow, Botany Sch., 1968–69; Univ. Lectr, 1974–88; Reader in Plant Pathology, 1988–90; Mem. Gen. Board, 1984–88; Fellow, Downing Coll., Cambridge, 1974–90 (Dean, 1976–82; Tutor for Graduate Students, 1982–88; Dir of Studies in Biology, 1976–89). Member: Governing Body, John Innes Centre for Plant Science (Cambridge Lab.), 1990–; Res. Adv. Cttee, RHS, 1991–; Chairman: Scientific Adv. Cttee of Sci. and Plants for Schs Project, 1989; Scientific Council, Sainsbury Lab. for Plant Pathology, 1990. Hon. Vice-Pres., Royal Caledonian Horticl Soc, 1990; Mem., Exec. Cttee, Scotland's Nat. Gardens Scheme, 1990–; Management Cttee, Botanic Gardens Conservation Secretariat, 1991–. Trustee: Botanic Gardens, St Andrews, 1990–; Grimesthorpe and Drummond Castle Trust, 1990–. *Publications:* (with D. N. Butcher) Plant Tissue Culture, 1974; (with J. P. Helgeson) Tissue Culture Methods for Plant Pathologists, 1980; (with A. Friday) Cambridge Encyclopedia of Life Sciences, 1985; (with P. H. Williams) Advances in Plant Pathology, vol. 1, 1982—vol. 8, 1990; many papers dealing with research in plant pathology and plant tissue culture, in learned jls. *Recreations:* listening to classical music and jazz, theatre, collecting ceramics, gardening, travel, reading, strolling around capital cities. *Address:* Royal Botanic Garden, Edinburgh EH3 5LR. *T:* 031–552 7171.

INGRAM, Sir James (Herbert Charles), 4th Bt *cr* 1893; *b* 6 May 1966; *s* of (Herbert) Robin Ingram (*d* 1979) and of Shiela, *d* of late Charles Peczenik; *S* grandfather, 1980. *Educ:* Eton. *Recreations:* golf and shooting. *Heir:* half *b* Nicholas David Ingram, *b* 1975. *Address:* 8 Lochaline Street, W6 9SH.

INGRAM, Dame Kathleen Annie; *see* Raven, Dame Kathleen.

INGRAM, Paul; Head of Agricultural Services, Barclays Bank plc, since 1988; *b* 20 Sept. 1934; *s* of John Granville Ingram and Sybil Ingram (*née* Johnson); *m* 1957, Jennifer (*née* Morgan) (*d* 1988); one *s* one *d*. *Educ:* Manchester Central High School; University of Nottingham (BSc 1956). Dept of Conservation and Extension, Fedn of Rhodesia and Nyasaland, 1956–63; Nat. Agricl Adv. Service, later ADAS, MAFF, 1965–; County Livestock Officer, Lancs, 1969–70; Policy Planning Unit, MAFF, 1970–72; Farm Management Adviser, Devon, 1972–76; Regional Farm Management Adviser, Wales, 1976–77; Dep. Sen. Livestock Advr, 1977–79, Sen. Agricl Officer, 1979–85, Chief Agricl Officer, 1985–87, Dir of Farm and Countryside Service, 1987–88, ADAS. *Address:* Barclays Bank, Juxon House, 94 St Paul's Churchyard, EC4M 8EH. *T:* 071–248 9155.

INGRAM, Stanley Edward; solicitor; *b* 5 Dec. 1922; *o s* of late Ernest Alfred Stanley Ingram and Ethel Ann Ingram; *m* 1948, Vera (*née* Brown); one *s* one *d*. *Educ:* Charlton Central School. Articled clerk with Wright & Bull, Solicitors; admitted Solicitor, 1950. Served RAF, 1942–46. Legal Asst, Min. of Nat. Insurance, 1953; Sen. Legal Asst, Min. of Pensions and Nat. Insurance, 1958; Asst Solicitor, 1971, Under Sec. (Legal), 1978–83, DHSS. Member Council: Civil Service Legal Soc. and of Legal Section of First Division Assoc., 1971–82; Mem., Salaried Solicitors' Cttee of Law Society, 1978–81. Sec., Romsey Gp, CS Retirement Fellowship, 1989–. *Recreations:* gardening, country walking. *Address:* 2 Little Woodley Farm, Winchester Hill, Romsey, Hants SO51 7NU. *Club:* Law Society.

INGRAM, Prof. Vernon Martin, FRS 1970; John and Dorothy Wilson Professor of Biology, Massachusetts Institute of Technology, since 1988; *b* Breslau, 19 May 1924; *s* of Kurt and Johanna Immerwahr; *m* 1st, 1950, Margaret Young; one *s* one *d*; 2nd, 1984, Elizabeth Hendee. *Educ:* Birkbeck Coll., Univ. of London. PhD Organic Chemistry, 1949; DSc Biochemistry, 1961. Analytical and Res. Chemist, Thos Morson & Son, Mddx, 1941–45; Lecture Demonstrator in Chem., Birkbeck Coll., 1945–47; Asst Lectr in Chem., Birkbeck Coll., 1947–50; Rockefeller Foundn Fellow, Rockefeller Inst., NY, 1950–51; Coxe Fellow, Yale, 1951–52; Mem. Sci. Staff, MRC Unit for Molecular Biology, Cavendish Lab., Cambridge, 1952–58; Assoc. Prof. 1958–61, Prof. of Biochemistry, 1961–, MIT; Lectr (part-time) in Medicine, Columbia, 1961–73; Guggenheim Fellow, UCL, 1967–68. Jesup Lectr, Columbia, 1962; Harvey Soc. Lectr, 1965. Member: Amer. Acad. of Arts and Sciences, 1964; Amer. Chem. Soc.; Chemical Soc.; Biochemical Soc.; Genetical Society. Fellow, Amer. Assoc. for Advancement of Science, 1987. William Allen Award, Amer. Soc. for Human Genetics, 1967. *Publications:* Haemoglobin and Its Abnormalities, 1961; The Hemoglobins in Genetics and Evolution, 1963; The Biosynthesis of Macromolecules, 1965, new edn, 1971; articles on human genetics, nucleic acids, differentiation and molecular biology of aging and developmental neurobiology, in Nature, Jl Mol. Biol., Jl Cell Biol., Develt Biol., Jl Biol Chem., etc. *Recreations:* music; photographer of abstract images. *Address:* Massachusetts Institute of Technology, Massachusetts Avenue, Cambridge, Mass 02139, USA. *T:* 617–253–3706.

INGRAMS, family name of **Baroness Darcy de Knayth.**

INGRAMS, Richard Reid; journalist; Editor, Private Eye, 1963–86, Chairman, since 1974; *b* 19 Aug. 1937; *s* of Leonard St Clair Ingrams and Victoria (*née* Reid); *m* 1962; one *s* one *d* (and one *s* decd). *Educ:* Shrewsbury; University Coll., Oxford. Joined Private

Eye, 1962; columnist, Observer, 1988–90. *Publications:* (with Christopher Booker and William Rushton) Private Eye on London, 1962; Private Eye's Romantic England, 1963; (with John Wells) Mrs Wilson's Diary, 1965; Mrs Wilson's 2nd Diary, 1966; The Tale of Driver Grope, 1968; (with Barry Fantoni) The Bible for Motorists, 1970; (ed) The Life and Times of Private Eye, 1971; (as Philip Reid, with Andrew Osmond) Harris in Wonderland, 1973; (ed) Cobbett's Country Book, 1974; (ed) Beachcomber: the works of J. B. Morton, 1974; The Best of Private Eye, 1974; God's Apology, 1977; Goldenballs, 1979; (with Fay Godwin) Romney Marsh and the Royal Military Canal, 1980; (with John Wells) Dear Bill: the collected letters of Denis Thatcher, 1980; (with John Wells) The Other Half: further letters of Denis Thatcher, 1981; (with John Wells) One for the Road, 1982; (with John Piper) Piper's Places, 1983; (ed) The Penguin Book of Private Eye Cartoons, 1983; (with John Wells) My Round!, 1983; (ed) Dr Johnson by Mrs Thrale, 1984; (with John Wells) Down the Hatch, 1985; (with John Wells) Just the One, 1986; John Stewart Collis: a memoir, 1986; (with John Wells) The Best of Dear Bill, 1986; (with John Wells) Mud in Your Eye, 1987; The Ridgeway, 1988; You Might As Well Be Dead, 1988; England (anthology), 1989; (with John Wells) Number 10, 1989; On and On . . ., 1990. *Recreation:* bookselling. *Address:* c/o Private Eye, 6 Carlisle Street, W1. *T:* 071–437 4017.

INGRESS BELL, Philip; *see* Bell.

INGROW, Baron *cr* 1982 (Life Peer), of Keighley in the County of West Yorkshire; **John Aked Taylor;** Kt 1972; OBE 1960; TD 1951; DL; JP; Chairman and Managing Director, Timothy Taylor & Co. Ltd; Lord-Lieutenant of West Yorkshire, since 1985 (Vice Lord-Lieutenant, 1976–85); *b* 15 Aug. 1917; *s* of Percy Taylor, Knowle Spring House, Keighley, and Gladys Broster (who *m* 2nd, 1953, Sir (John) Donald Horsfall, 2nd Bt); *m* 1949, Barbara Mary, *d* of Percy Wright Stirk, Keighley; two *d*. *Educ:* Shrewsbury Sch. Served War of 1939–45: Duke of Wellington's Regt and Royal Signals, Major; Norway, Middle East, Sicily, NW Europe and Far East. Mem., Keighley Town Council, 1946–67 (Mayor, 1956–57; Chm., Educn Cttee, 1949–61; Chm., Finance Cttee, 1961–67); Mem. Council, Magistrates' Assoc., 1957–86 (Vice-Chm., Exec. Cttee, 1975–76; Chm., Licensing Cttee, 1969–76; Hon. Treasurer, 1976–86; Vice-Pres., 1986–; Past Pres. and Chm., WR Br.; Life Vice-Pres., W Yorks Br.); Chm., Keighley Conservative Assoc., 1952–56 and 1957–67 (Pres., 1971–76, Jt Hon. Treas., 1947–52, and Chm., Young Conservatives, 1946–47); Chm., Yorkshire West Conservative European Constituency Council, 1978–84 (Pres., 1984–85); Chm., Yorkshire Area, Nat. Union of Conservative and Unionist Assocs, 1966–71 (Vice-Chm., 1965–66); Chm., Exec. Cttee of Nat. Union of Conservative and Unionist Assocs, 1971–76 (Mem. 1964–83); Pres., Nat. Union of Conservative and Unionist Assocs 1982–83 (Hon. Vice-Pres., 1976–). Gen. Comr of Income Tax, 1965. Vice-Pres., Yorks and Humberside TAVRA, 1985–88, and 1991– (Pres., 1988–91). Mem. Court, Univ. of Leeds, 1986–. Pres., Council of Order of St John, S and W Yorks, 1985–; KStJ 1986. JP Borough of Keighley 1949; DL West (formerly WR) Yorks, 1971. DUniv Bradford, 1990. *Address:* Fieldhead, Keighley, West Yorkshire BD20 6LP. *T:* Keighley (0535) 603895. *Club:* Carlton.

INKIN, Geoffrey David, OBE 1974 (MBE 1971); Chairman: Cardiff Bay Development Corporation, since 1987; Land Authority for Wales, since 1986; *b* 2 Oct. 1934; *e s* of late Noel D. Inkin and of Evelyn Margaret Inkin; *m* 1961, Susan Elizabeth, *d* of Col L. S. Sheldon and late Margaret Sheldon, and step *d* of Mrs Rosemary Sheldon; three *s*. *Educ:* Dean Close Sch.; RMA, Sandhurst; Staff Coll., Camberley; Royal Agricl Coll., Cirencester. Commnd The Royal Welch Fusiliers, 1955; served Malaya, 1955–57 and Cyprus, 1958–59 (despatches); commanded 1st Bn The Royal Welch Fusiliers, 1972–74. Member: Gwent CC, 1977–83; Gwent Police Authority, 1979–83; Mem. Bd, 1980–83, Chm., 1983–87, Cwmbran Develt Corp.; Mem. Bd, Welsh Devlt Agency, 1984–87. Gov., Haberdashers' Monmouth Schs, 1977–90; Mem., Bd, WNO, 1987–; Council: UWIST, 1987–88; Univ. of Wales Coll. of Cardiff, 1988–. Parly Cand. (C) Ebbw Vale, 1977–79. FRSA. Gwent: DL, 1983–91; High Sheriff, 1987–88. *Address:* Court St Lawrence, Llangovan, Monmouth NP5 4BT. *T:* Raglan (0291) 690279. *Clubs:* Brooks's; Cardiff and County (Cardiff); Ebbw Vale Conservative.

INMAN, Edward Oliver; Director (formerly Keeper) of Duxford Airfield, Imperial War Museum, since 1978; *b* 12 Aug. 1948; *s* of John Inman and Peggy Inman (*née* Beard); *m* 1st, 1971 (marr. diss. 1982); one *s* one *d*; 2nd, 1984, Sherida Lesley (*neé* Sturton); one *d*, and two step *d*. *Educ:* King's College Sch., Wimbledon; Gonville and Caius Coll., Cambridge (BA); School of Slavonic and East European Studies, London (MA). Joined Imperial War Museum as Res. Asst, 1972; Asst Keeper 1974; Keeper of Exhibits (Duxford) 1976. *Recreations:* tennis, travel, the family. *Address:* c/o Imperial War Museum, Duxford, Cambridge CB2 4QR. *T:* Cambridge (0223) 833963.

INMAN, Herbert, CBE 1977; Regional Administrator, Yorkshire Regional Health Authority, 1973–77; Hon. Adviser to the Sue Ryder Foundation, since 1977, and Member of Council, 1986–89; Member, Executive Committee, Sue Ryder Homes, 1984–88 (Chairman, 1983–87); *b* 8 Jan. 1917; *s* of Matthew Herbert Inman and Rose Mary Earle; *m* 1939, Beatrice, *d* of Thomas Edward Lee and Florence Lee; twin *s*. *Educ:* Wheelwright Grammar Sch., Dewsbury; Univ. of Leeds. FHSM (Nat. Pres. 1968–69); DPA. Various hosp. appts, Dewsbury, Wakefield and Aylesbury, 1933–48; Dep. Gp Sec., Leeds (A) Gp HMC and Dep. Chief Admin. Officer, 1948–62; Gp Sec. and Chief Admin. Officer, Leeds (A) Gp HMC, 1962–70; Gp Sec. and Chief Admin. Officer, Leeds (St James's) Univ. HMC, 1970–73. *Publications:* occasional articles in Hospital and Health Services jls. *Recreations:* travel, gardening, Rugby football, cricket, swimming. *Address:* 7 Potterton Close, Barwick in Elmet, Leeds LS15 4DY. *T:* Leeds (0532) 812538.

INMAN, Col Roger, OBE (mil.) 1945 (MBE (mil.) 1944); TD 1945; Vice Lord-Lieutenant of South Yorkshire, 1981–90; Joint Managing Director, Harrison Fisher Group, since 1951; *b* 18 April 1915; *y s* of S. M. Inman, Sheffield; *m* 1939, Christine Lucas, *e d* of Lt-Col J. Rodgers, Sheffield; two *s*. *Educ:* King Edward VII Sch., Sheffield. Commissioned into 71st (WR) Field Bde, RA TA, 1935; served War, with RA and General Staff, Western Desert, Middle East, Italy, 1939–46; released, 1946, with rank of Lt-Col; reformed and commanded 271 (WR) Fd Regt, RA TA, 1947–51; Brevet Col 1953; Hon. Col, Sheffield Artillery Volunteers, 1964–70; Member, W Riding T&AFA, 1947–; Vice-Chm., Yorkshire and Humberside TA&VRA, 1973–80. JP 1954 (Chm. Sheffield City Bench, 1974–80), DL 1967, West Riding. General Commissioner of Income Tax, 1969–; Chm. of Comrs, Don Div. of Sheffield, 1975–90. Chm., Guardians of Standard of Wrought Plate within the Town of Sheffield, 1988–. *Recreation:* golf. *Address:* Flat 1, Mayfield View, 15 Whitworth Road, Sheffield S10 3HD. *Clubs:* Sheffield, Hallamshire Golf (Sheffield).

INNES of Coxton, Sir David (Charles Kenneth Gordon), 12th Bt *cr* 1686 (NS); Chief Engineer (Combustion Controls), Peabody Division of Dresser Holmes Ltd, since 1983; *b* 17 April 1940; *s* of Sir Charles Innes of Coxton, 11th Bt and of Margaret Colquhoun Lockhart, *d* of F. C. L. Robertson; *S* father, 1990; *m* 1969, Majorie Alison, *d* of E. W. Parker; one *s* one *d*. *Educ:* Haileybury Coll.; City & Guilds Coll. of Imperial Coll., London Univ. BSc(Eng); ACGI. Technical Dir, Peak Technologies, 1974–78; Man. Dir, Peak Combustion Controls, 1978–81. *Recreations:* electronics, aeronautics, astronomy. *Heir: s* Alastair Charles Deverell Innes, *b* 17 Sept. 1970. *Address:* 28 Wadham Close, Shepperton, Middlesex TW17 9HT. *T:* Walton-on-Thames (0932) 228273.

INNES, Fergus Munro, CIE 1946; CBE 1951; Indian Civil Service, retired; *b* 12 May 1903; *s* of late Sir Charles Innes; *m* 1st, Evangeline, *d* of A. H. Chaworth-Musters (marriage dissolved); two *d*; 2nd, Vera, *d* of T. Mahoney; one *s* one *d*. *Educ:* Charterhouse; Brasenose Coll., Oxford. Joined Indian Civil Service, 1926; various posts in Punjab up to 1937; Joint Sec., Commerce Dept, Govt of India, 1944; Mem., Central Board of Revenue, 1947; retired, 1947; Adviser in Pakistan to Central Commercial Cttee, 1947–53; Sec., The West Africa Cttee, 1956–61; Chm., India Gen. Navigation and Railway Co. Ltd, 1973–78. Company director. *Address:* The Hippins, Hook Heath Road, Woking, Surrey GU22 0DP. *T:* Woking (0483) 714626. *Club:* Oriental.

INNES, Hammond; *see* Hammond Innes, Ralph.

INNES of Edingight, Sir Malcolm Rognvald, KCVO 1990 (CVO 1981); Lord Lyon King of Arms, since 1981; Secretary to the Order of the Thistle, since 1981; *b* 25 May 1938; 3rd *s* of late Sir Thomas Innes of Learney, GCVO, LLD, and Lady Lucy Buchan, 3rd *d* of 18th Earl of Caithness; *m* 1963, Joan, *o d* of Thomas D. Hay, CA, Edinburgh; three *s*. *Educ:* Edinburgh Acad.; Univ. of Edinburgh (MA, LLB). WS 1964. Falkland Pursuivant Extraordinary, 1957; Carrick Pursuivant, 1958; Lyon Clerk and Keeper of the Records, 1966; Marchmont Herald, 1971. Mem., Queen's Body Guard for Scotland (Royal Company of Archers), 1971. Pres., Heraldry Soc. of Scotland. Trustee, Sir William Fraser's Foundn. FSA (Scot.); KStJ. Grand Officer of Merit, SMO Malta. *Recreations:* archery, fishing, shooting, visiting places of historic interest. *Address:* 35 Inverleith Row, Edinburgh EH3 5QH. *T:* 031–552 4924; Edingight House, Banffshire. *T:* Knock (046686) 270. *Clubs:* New, Puffins (Edinburgh).

INNES, Maughan William; Controller Finance, National Research Development Corporation, 1965–77; *b* 18 Nov. 1922; *s* of Leslie W. Innes and Bridget Maud (*née* Humble-Crofts); *m* 1950, Helen Mary, *d* of Roper Spyers; one *s* (and one *s* decd). *Educ:* Marlborough College. BA Open Univ., 1988. FCA; FBIM. RAF, 1941–46. Chartered Accountant, 1949; in Canada, 1953–60; retired 1977. *Recreations:* music, theatre. *Address:* Brook Cottage, Four Elms, Edenbridge, Kent TN8 6PA. *T:* Four Elms (073270) 232. *Club:* MCC.

INNES, Michael; *see* Stewart, John I. M.

INNES, Sir Peter (Alexander Berowald), 17th Bt *cr* 1628, of Balvenie; FICE; Partner, Scott Wilson Kirkpatrick and Partners, Consulting Engineers, since 1987; *b* 6 Jan. 1937; *s* of Lt-Col Sir (Ronald Gordon) Berowald Innes, 16th Bt, OBE and Elizabeth Haughton (*d* 1958), *e d* of late Alfred Fayle; *S* father, 1988; *m* 1959, Julia Mary, *d* of A. S. Levesley; two *s* one *d*. *Educ:* Prince of Wales School, Nairobi, Kenya; Bristol Univ. (BSc). Scott Wilson Kirkpatrick and Partners, 1964–; Associate, 1982–87. Responsible for several airport projects in UK, Africa and Middle East, including major military airbases. Major, Engr and Transport Staff Corps, RE(TA). *Heir: s* Alexander Guy Berowald Innes [*b* 4 May 1960; *m* 1986, Sara-Jane, *d* of late Dennis Busher]. *Address:* The Wheel House, Nations Hill, Kings Worthy, Winchester SO23 7QY. *T:* Winchester (0962) 881024.

INNES, Sheila Miriam; Deputy Chairman, The Open College, since 1989 (Chief Executive, 1987–89); *b* 25 Jan. 1931; *d* of Dr James Innes, MB, ChB, MA and Nora Innes. *Educ:* Talbot Heath School, Bournemouth; Lady Margaret Hall, Oxford (Exhibnr; BA Hons Mod. Langs; MA). BBC Radio Producer, World Service, 1955–61; BBC TV producer: family programmes, 1961–65; further education, 1965–73; exec. producer, further education, 1973–77; Head, BBC Continuing Educn, TV, 1977–84; Controller, BBC Educnl Broadcasting, 1984–87; Dir, BBC Enterprises Ltd, 1986–87. Chairman: Cross-Sector Cttee for Development and Review, BTEC, 1986–87; Cross-Sector Cttee for Product Develt, BTEC, 1989–. Member: Gen. Board, Alcoholics Anonymous, 1980–; Board of Governors, Centre for Information on Language Teaching and Research, 1981–84; Council, Open Univ., 1984–87; Council for Educational Technology, 1984–87; EBU Educational Working Party, 1984–87; RTS 1984. Pres., Educn Sect., BAAS, 1989; Mem., Clothing and Allied Products ITB Management 2000 Cttee of Enquiry, 1989. Patron, One World Broadcasting Trust, 1988–. Gov., Talbot Heath Sch., Bournemouth. FRSA 1986; FITD 1987; CBIM 1987. *Publications:* BBC publications; articles for language jls and EBU Review. *Recreations:* music (classical and jazz), country pursuits, swimming, sketching, photography, travel, languages. *Address:* The Knowle, Seer Green Lane, Jordans, Bucks HP9 2ST. *T:* Chalfont St Giles (02407) 4575; The Open College, 101 Wigmore Street, W1H 9AA. *T:* 071–935 8088. *Clubs:* Reform; Oxford Society.

INNES, Lt-Col William Alexander Disney; DL; Vice Lord-Lieutenant of Banffshire, 1971–86; *b* 19 April 1910; 2nd *s* of late Captain James William Guy Innes, CBE, DL, JP, RN, of Maryculter, Kincardineshire; *m* 1939, Mary Alison, *d* of late Francis Burnett-Stuart, Howe Green, Hertford; two *s*. *Educ:* Marlborough Coll., RMC, Sandhurst. Gordon Highlanders: 2nd Lieut, 1930; Captain 1938; Temp. Major 1941; Major, 1946; Temp. Lt-Col, 1951; retd, 1952. Served War of 1939–45: Far East (PoW Malaya and Siam, 1942–45). Chm., Banffshire T&AFA, 1959. DL 1959–87, JP 1964–86, Banffshire. *Recreations:* shooting, gardening. *Address:* Heath Cottage, Aberlour, Banffshire AB38 9QD. *T:* Aberlour (0340) 871266.

INNES, William James Alexander; Assistant Under Secretary of State, since 1985, Director of Custody, Prison Service Headquarters, since 1990, Home Office; *b* 11 Oct. 1934; *s* of late William Johnstone Innes and of Helen Margaret Meldrum Porter; *m* 1959, Carol Isabel Bruce (marr. diss. 1983); one *s* one *d*. *Educ:* Robert Gordon's Coll., Aberdeen; Aberdeen Univ. (MA). Served Royal Air Force, 1956, Officer Commanding 45 Sqdn, 1967–70. Principal, Home Office, 1972; Private Sec. to Home Sec., 1974–76; Asst Sec., 1977; Asst Under Sec. of State, seconded to NI Office, 1985–88; Dir of Operational Policy, Prison Dept, Home Office, 1988–90. *Recreations:* opera, theatre, golf. *Address:* Cleland House, Page Street, SW1P 4LN. *Clubs:* Royal Air Force; Burnham Beeches Golf.

INNES-KER, family name of **Duke of Roxburghe.**

INNISS, Sir Clifford (de Lisle), Kt 1961; Judge of the Court of Appeal of Belize, 1974–81; Chairman, Integrity Commission, National Assembly of Belize, 1981–87; Member, Belize Advisory Council, Feb.–Oct. 1985; *b* Barbados, 26 Oct. 1910; *e s* of late Archibald de Lisle Inniss and Lelia Emmaline, *e d* of Elverton Richard Springer. *Educ:* Harrison Coll., Barbados; Queen's Coll., Oxford. BA (hons jurisprudence), BCL. Called to bar, Middle Temple, 1935. QC (Tanganyika) 1950, (Trinidad and Tobago) 1953; practised at bar, Barbados; subseq. Legal Draughtsman and Clerk to Attorney-Gen., Barbados, 1938; Asst to Attorney General and Legal Draughtsman, 1941; Judge of Bridgetown Petty Debt Court, 1946; Legal Draughtsman, Tanganyika, 1947; Solicitor Gen., Tanganyika, 1949; Attorney-Gen., Trinidad and Tobago, 1953; Chief Justice, British Honduras, later Belize, 1957–72; Judge of the Courts of Appeal of Bermuda, the Bahamas, and the Turks and Caicos Is, 1974–75. *Recreations:* cricket, tennis, swimming.

Address: 11/13 Oriole Avenue, Belmopan, Belize. *Clubs:* Barbados Yacht; Kenya Kongonis (hon. mem.).

INSALL, Donald William, OBE 1981; FSA, RWA, FRIBA, FRTPI; architect and planning consultant; Principal, Donald W. Insall & Associates, since 1958; *b* 7 Feb. 1926; *o s* of late William R. Insall and Phyllis Insall, Henleaze, Bristol; *m* 1964, Amy Elizabeth, MA, *er d* of Malcolm H. Moss, Nanpantan, Leics; two *s* one *d. Educ:* private prep; Bristol Grammar Sch.; Bristol Univ.; RA; Sch. of Planning, London (Dip. (Hons)); SPAB Lethaby Schol. 1951. FRIBA 1968, FRTPI 1973. Coldstream Guards, 1944–47. Architectural and Town-Planning Consultancy has included town-centre studies, civic and univ., church, domestic and other buildings, notably in conservation of historic towns and buildings (incl. restoration of ceiling, House of Lords); Medal (Min. of Housing and Local Govt), Good Design in Housing, 1962. Visiting Lecturer: RCA, 1964–69; Internat. Centre for Conservation, Rome, 1969–; Coll. d'Europe, Bruges, 1976–81; Catholic Univ. of Leuven, 1982–; Adjunct Prof., Univ. of Syracuse, 1971–81. Mem., Council of Europe Working Party, 1969–70; Nat. Pilot Study, Chester: A Study in Conservation, 1968; Consultant, Chester Conservation Programme, 1970–87 (EAHY Exemplar; European Prize for Preservation of Historic Monuments, 1981; Europa Nostra Medals of Honour, 1983 and 1989). Member: Historic Buildings Council for England, 1971–84; Grants Panel, EAHY, 1974; UK Council, ICOMOS, 1988; Council, RSA, 1976–80 (FRSA, 1948); Council, SPAB, 1979–; Ancient Monuments Bd for England, 1980–84; Comr, Historic Blgs and Monuments Commn, 1984–89; Mem., Standing Adv. Cttee, Getty Grant Program, 1988–. Hon. Sec., Conf. on Trng Architects in Conservation, 1959–89. RIBA: Banister Fletcher Medallist, 1949; Neale Bursar, 1955; Examnr, 1957; Competition Assessor, 1971. Conferences: White House (Natural Beauty), 1965; UNESCO, 1969; Historic Architectural Interiors, USA, 1988. Lecture Tours: USA, 1964, 1972 (US Internat. Reg. Conf. on Conservation); Mexico, 1972; Yugoslavia, 1973; Canada, 1974; Argentina, 1976; India, 1979; Portugal, 1982. European Architectural Heritage Year Medal (for Restoration of Chevening), 1973; Queen's Silver Jubilee Medal, 1977. *Publications:* (jtly) Railway Station Architecture, 1966; (jtly) Conservation Areas 1967; The Care of Old Buildings Today, 1973; Historic Buildings: action to maintain the expertise for their care and repair, 1974; Conservation in Action, 1982; Conservation in Chester, 1988; contrib. to Encyclopædia Britannica, professional, environmental and internat. jls. *Recreations:* visiting, photographing and enjoying places; appreciating craftsmanship; Post-Vintage Thoroughbred Cars (Mem., Rolls Royce Enthusiasts' Club). *Address:* 73 Kew Green, Richmond, Surrey TW9 3AH; (office) 19 West Eaton Place, Eaton Square, SW1X 8LT. *T:* 071–245 9888. *Club:* Athenæum.

INSCH, James Ferguson, CBE 1974; CA; Director, Guest Keen & Nettlefolds plc, 1964–82, Deputy Chairman, 1980–82; Chairman, Birmid-Qualcast Ltd, 1977–84 (Deputy Chairman, 1975–77); *b* 10 Sept. 1911; *s* of John Insch and Edina (*née* Hogg); *m* 1937, Jean Baikie Cunningham; one *s* two *d. Educ:* Leith Academy. Chartered Accountant (Scot.). Director, number of GKN companies, 1945–66; Guest Keen & Nettlefolds Ltd: Group Man. Dir, 1967; Gp Dep. Chm. and Man. Dir, 1968–74; Jt Dep. Chm., 1979. Pres., Nat. Assoc. of Drop Forgers and Stampers, 1962–63 and 1963–64. *Recreations:* golf, fishing. *Address:* 1 Denehurst Close, Barnt Green, Birmingham B43 8HR. *T:* 021–445 2517.

INSKIP, family name of **Viscount Caldecote.**

INSKIP, John Hampden, QC 1966; **His Honour Judge Inskip;** a Circuit Judge, since 1982; *b* 1 Feb. 1924; *s* of Sir John Hampden Inskip, KBE, and Hon. Janet, *d* of 1st Baron Maclay, PC; *m* 1947, Ann Howell Davies; one *s* one *d. Educ:* Clifton Coll.; King's Coll., Cambridge. BA 1948. Called to the Bar, Inner Temple, 1949; Master of the Bench, 1975. Mem. of Western Circuit; Dep. Chm., Hants QS, 1967–71; Recorder of Bournemouth, later of the Crown Court, 1970–82. Mem., Criminal Law Revision Cttee, 1973–82; Pres., Transport Tribunal, 1982–. *Address:* Clerks, Bramshott, Liphook, Hants.

INSOLE, Douglas John, CBE 1979; Marketing Director, Trollope & Colls Ltd; *b* 18 April 1926; *s* of John Herbert Insole and Margaret Rose Insole; *m* 1948, Barbara Hazel Ridgway (*d* 1982); two *d* (and one *d* decd). *Educ:* Sir George Monoux Grammar Sch.; St Catharine's Coll., Cambridge. MA Cantab. Cricket: Cambridge Univ., 1947–49 (Captain, 1949); Essex CCC, 1947–63 (Captain, 1950–60); played 9 times for England; Vice-Captain, MCC tour of S Africa, 1956–57. Chairman: Test Selectors, 1965–68; Test and County Cricket Bd, 1975–78 (Chm., Cricket Cttee, 1968–87); Mem., MCC Cttee, 1955–; Manager, England cricket team, Australian tours, 1978–79 and 1982–83. Soccer: Cambridge Univ., 1946–48; Pegasus, and Corinthian Casuals; Amateur Cup Final medal, 1956. Member: Sports Council, 1971–74; FA Council, 1979–. JP Chingford, 1962–74. *Publication:* Cricket from the Middle, 1960. *Recreations:* cricket, soccer. *Address:* 8 Hadleigh Court, Crescent Road, Chingford, E4 6AX. *T:* 081–529 6546. *Club:* MCC.

INVERFORTH, 4th Baron *cr* 1919, of Southgate; **Andrew Peter Weir;** *b* 16 Nov. 1966; *s* of 3rd Baron Inverforth and of Jill Elizabeth, *o d* of late John W. Thornycroft, CBE; *S* father, 1982. *Educ:* Marlborough College. *Heir: uncle* Hon. John Vincent Weir, *b* 8 Feb. 1935. *Address:* 27 Hyde Park Street, W2 2JS. *T:* 071–262 5721.

INVERNESS (St Andrew's Cathedral), Provost of; *see* Grant, Very Rev. M. E.

INVERURIE, Lord; James William Falconer Keith; Master of Kintore; *b* 15 April 1976; *s* and *heir* of Earl of Kintore, *qv.*

IONESCO, Eugène; Chevalier de la Légion d'Honneur, 1970; Officier des Arts et lettres, 1961; homme de lettres; Membre de l'Académie française, since 1970; *b* 13 Nov. 1912; *m* 1936, Rodica; one *d. Educ:* Bucharest and Paris. French citizen living in Paris. Ballet: The Triumph of Death, Copenhagen, 1972. *Publications:* (most of which appear in English and American editions) Théâtre I; La Cantatrice chauve, La Leçon, Jacques ou La Soumission, Les Chaises, Victimes du devoir, Amédée ou Comment s'en débarrasser, Paris, 1956; Théâtre II: L'Impromptu de l'Alma, Tueur sans gages, Le Nouveau Locataire, L'Avenir est dans les œufs, Le Maître, La Jeune Fille à marier, Paris, 1958. Rhinocéros (play) in Collection Manteau d'Arlequin, Paris, 1959, Le Piéton de l'air, 1962, Chemises de Nuit, 1962; Le Roi se meurt, 1962; Notes et Contre-Notes, 1962; Journal en Miettes, 1967; Présent passé passé présent, 1968; Découvertes (Essays), 1969; Jeux de Massacre (play), 1970; Macbett (play), 1972; Ce formidable bordel (play), 1974; The Hermit (novel), 1975; The Man with the Suitcase, 1975; (with Claude Bonnefoy) Entre la vie et le rêve, 1977; Antidotes (essays), 1977; L'homme en question (essays), 1979; Variations sur un même thème, 1979; Voyages chez les Morts ou Thème et Variations (play), 1980; Noir et Blanc, 1980; Journeys Among The Dead (play), 1986; contrib. to: Avant-Garde (The experimental theatre in France) by L. C. Pronko, 1962; Modern French Theatre, from J. Giraudoux to Beckett, by Jean Guicharnaud, 1962; author essays and tales. *Relevant publications:* The Theatre of the Absurd, by Martin Esslin, 1961; Ionesco, by Richard N. Coe, 1961; Eugène Ionesco, by Ronald Hayman, 1972. *Address:* c/o Editions Gallimard, 5 rue Sébastien Bottin, 75007 Paris, France.

IONESCU, Prof. George Ghita; Professor of Government, University of Manchester, 1970–80, now Emeritus; Editor, Government and Opposition, since 1965; Chairman,

Research Committee, International Political Science Association, since 1975; *b* 21 March 1913; *s* of Alexandre Ionescu and Hélène Sipsom; *m* 1950, Valence Ramsay de Bois Maclaren. *Educ:* Univ. of Bucharest (Lic. in Law and Polit. Sci.). Gen. Sec., Romanian Commn of Armistice with Allied Forces, 1944–45; Counsellor, Romanian Embassy, Ankara, 1945–47; Gen. Sec., Romanian Nat. Cttee, NY, 1955–58; Dir, Radio Free Europe, 1958–63; Nuffield Fellow, LSE, 1963–68. Hon. MA(Econ) Manchester. *Publications:* Communism in Romania, 1965; The Politics of the Eastern European Communist States, 1966; (jtly) Opposition, 1967; (jtly) Populism, 1970; (ed) Between Sovereignty and Integration, 1973; Centripetal Politics, 1975; The Political Thought of Saint-Simon, 1976; (ed) The European Alternatives, 1979; Politics and the Pursuit of Happiness, 1984; Leadership in an Independent World, 1991. *Recreations:* music, bridge, racing. *Address:* 36 Sandileigh Avenue, Manchester M20 9LW. *T:* 061–445 7726. *Club:* Athenæum.

IPSWICH, Viscount; Henry Oliver Charles FitzRoy; *b* 6 April 1978; *s* and *heir* of Earl of Euston, *qv.*

IPSWICH, Bishop of; *see* St Edmundsbury.

IPSWICH, Archdeacon of; *see* Gibson, Ven. T. A.

IRBY, family name of **Baron Boston.**

IREDALE, Peter, PhD; FInstP, FIEE; Director, Culham/Harwell Sites, United Kingdom Atomic Energy Authority, since 1990; Supernumerary Fellow, Wolfson College, Oxford, since 1991; *b* Brownhills, Staffs, 15 March 1932; *s* of late Henry Iredale and Annie (*née* Kirby); *m* 1957, Judith Margaret (*née* Marshall); one *s* three *d. Educ:* King Edward VIth Grammar Sch., Lichfield; Univ. of Bristol (BSc, PhD). AERE Harwell (subseq. Harwell Laboratory), 1955–: research: on Nuclear Instrumentation, 1955–69; on Non Destructive Testing, 1969–70; Computer Storage, 1970–73; Commercial Officer, 1973–75; Gp Leader, Nuclear Instrumentation, 1975–77; Dep. Hd, Marketing and Sales Dept, 1977–79; Hd of Marine Technology Support Unit, 1979–81; Dir, Engrg, 1981–86; Dep. Dir, 1986–87, Dir, 1987–90, Harwell Lab. *Publications:* papers on high energy physics, nuclear instrumentation. *Recreations:* family, music, working with wood, gardening. *Address:* Harwell Laboratory, Harwell, Didcot, Oxfordshire OX11 0RA. *T:* Abingdon (0235) 432831.

IREDALE, Roger Oliver, PhD; Chief Education Adviser, Overseas Development Administration, Foreign and Commonwealth Office, since 1983; *b* 13 Aug. 1934; *s* of Fred Iredale and Elsie Florence (*née* Hills); *m* 1968, Mavis Potter; one *s* one *d. Educ:* Harrow County Grammar Sch.; Univ. of Reading (BA 1956, MA 1959, PhD 1971; Hurry Medal for Poetry; Early English Text Soc's Prize; Seymour-Sharman Prize for Literature; Graham Robertson Travel Award); Peterhouse Coll., Univ. of Cambridge (Cert. Ed. 1957). Teacher, Hele's Sch., Exeter, 1959–61; Lectr and Senior Lectr, Bishop Otter Coll., Chichester, 1962–70; British Council Officer and Maître de Conférences, Univ. of Algiers, 1970–72; Lectr, Chichester Coll. of Further Educn, 1972–73; British Council Officer, Madras, 1973–75; Dir of Studies, Educl Admin., Univ. of Leeds, 1975–79; Educn Adviser, ODA, 1979–83. Mem., Commonwealth Scholarship Commn, 1984–; Comr, Sino-British Friendship Scholarship Scheme Commn, 1986–. Governor: Sch. of Oriental and African Studies, 1983–; Queen Elizabeth House, Oxford, 1986–87; Commonwealth of Learning, 1988–. Poetry Society's Greenwood Prize, 1974. *Publications:* Turning Bronzes (poems), 1974; Out Towards the Dark (poems), 1978; articles in Comparative Education and other jls; poems for BBC Radio 3 and in anthologies and jls. *Recreations:* poetry writing, restoring the discarded. *Address:* Overseas Development Administration, 94 Victoria Street, SW1E 5JL. *T:* 071–273 0125.

IRELAND, Frank Edward, BSc, CChem; FRSC; FEng; FIChemE; SFInstE; consultant in air pollution control; HM Chief Alkali and Clean Air Inspector, 1964–78; *b* 7 Oct. 1913; *s* of William Edward Ireland and Bertha Naylor; *m* 1941, Edna Clare Meredith; one *s* three *d. Educ:* Liverpool Univ. (BSc). CChem, FRSC (FRIC 1945); FIChemE 1950; SFInstF 1956. Plant Superintendent, Orrs Zinc White Works, Widnes, Imperial Smelting Corp. Ltd, 1935–51; Prodn Man., Durham Chemicals Ltd, Birtley, Co. Durham, 1951–53; Alkali Inspector based on Sheffield, 1953–58; Dep. Chief Alkali Inspector, 1958–64; Pres., Inst. of Fuel, 1974–75; Vice Pres., Instn of Chem. Engrs, 1969–72. Founder Fellow, Fellowship of Engineering, 1976. Freeman 1983, Liveryman, 1986–, Engineers' Co. George E. Davis Gold Medal, Instn of Chem. Engrs, 1969. *Publications:* Annual Alkali Reports, 1964–77; (jtly) A History of Air Pollution and Its Control, 1990; contrib. Jl of IChemE; papers to nat. and internat. organisations. *Recreations:* golf, gardening. *Address:* 59 Lanchester Road, Highgate, N6 4SX. *T:* 081–883 6060.

IRELAND, Norman Charles; Chairman: Bowater plc, since 1987; London & Metropolitan, since 1986; *b* 28 May 1927; *s* of Charles and Winifred Ireland; *m* 1953, Gillian Margaret (*née* Harrison); one *s* one *d. Educ:* England, USA, India. CA (Scot.). Chartered Management Accountant. With Richard Brown & Co., Edinburgh, 1944–50; Brown Fleming & Murray, London, 1950–54; Avon Rubber Co., Melksham, 1955–64; Chief Accountant, United Glass, 1964–66; Finance Dir, BTR, 1967–87. Chairman: The Housing Finance Corp., 1988–; Intermediate Capital Gp 1989–; Director: BTR, 1969–; Meggitt, 1987–. *Recreations:* gardening, ballet, opera, music.

IRELAND, Patrick Gault de C.; *see* de Courcy-Ireland.

IRELAND, Ronald David; QC (Scotland) 1964; Sheriff Principal of Grampian, Highland and Islands, since 1988; *b* 13 March 1925; *o s* of William Alexander Ireland and Agnes Victoria Brown. *Educ:* George Watson's Coll., Edinburgh; Balliol Coll., Oxford (Scholar); Edinburgh Univ. Served Royal Signals, 1943–46. BA Oxford, 1950, MA 1958; LLB Edinburgh, 1952. Passed Advocate, 1952; Clerk of the Faculty of Advocates, 1957–58; Aberdeen University: Prof. of Scots Law, 1958–71; Dean of Faculty of Law, 1964–67; Hon. Prof., Faculty of Law, 1988–; Sheriff of Lothian and Borders (formerly Lothians and Peebles) at Edinburgh, 1972–88. Governor, Aberdeen Coll. of Education, 1959–64 (Vice-Chm., 1962–64). Comr. under NI (Emergency Provisions) Act, 1974–75. Member: Bd of Management, Aberdeen Gen. Hosps, 1961–71 (Chm., 1964–71); Departmental Cttee on Children and Young Persons, 1961–64; Cttee on the Working of the Abortion Act, 1971–74; Hon. Sheriff for Aberdeenshire, 1963–88. Member: North Eastern Regional Hosp. Bd, 1964–71 (Vice-Chm. 1966–71); After Care Council, 1962–65; Nat. Staff Advisory Cttee for the Scottish Hosp. Service, 1964–65; Chm., Scottish Hosps Administrative Staffs Cttee, 1965–72. Dir, Scottish Courts Admin, 1975–78. *Address:* The Castle, Inverness IV2 3EG. *Clubs:* New (Edinburgh); Royal Northern and University (Aberdeen); Highland (Inverness).

IREMONGER, Thomas Lascelles Isa Shandon Valiant; *o s* of Lt-Col H. E. W. Iremonger, DSO, Royal Marine Artillery, and Julia St Mary Shandon, *d* of Col John Quarry, Royal Berks Regiment; *m* Lucille Iremonger (*d* 1989), MA (Oxon), FRSL, author and broadcaster; one *d. Educ:* Oriel Coll., Oxford (MA; Rear-Cdre. Oxford Univ. Yacht Club, 1937–38). HM Overseas Service (Western Pacific, Gilbert & Ellice Islands Colony and Colony at Fiji), 1938–46. RNVR (Lt), 1942–46. MP (C) Ilford North, Feb. 1954–Feb.

1974, Redbridge, Ilford North, Feb.-Sept. 1974; PPS to Sir Fitzroy Maclean, Bt, CBE, MP, when Under-Sec. of State for War, 1954–57. Contested (C Ind. Democrat) Redbridge, Ilford N, March 1978 and (C, independently), 1979. Mem., Royal Commn on the Penal System, 1964–66. Underwriting Mem. of Lloyd's. *Publications:* Disturbers of the Peace, 1962; Money, Politics and You, 1963. *Address:* Milbourne Manor, near Malmesbury, Wilts SN16 9JA; La Voûte, Montignac-le-Coq, 16390 St Séverin, France.

IRENS, Alfred Norman, CBE 1969; Chairman: South Western Electricity Board, 1956–73; British Approvals Board for Telecommunications, 1982–84; *b* 28 Feb. 1911; *s* of Max Henry and Guinevere Emily Irens; *m* 1934, Joan Elizabeth, *d* of John Knight, FRIBA, Worsley, Manchester; two *s*. *Educ:* Blundell's Sch., Tiverton; Faraday House, London. College apprentice, Metropolitan Vickers, Ltd, Manchester. Subsequently with General Electric Co., Ltd, until joining Bristol Aeroplane Co., Ltd, 1939, becoming Chief Electrical Engineer, 1943; Consulting Engineer to Govt and other organisations, 1945–56. Part-time mem., SW Electricity Bd, 1948–56. Past Chm. IEE Utilization Section and IEE Western Sub-Centre; Chairman: British Electrical Development Assoc., 1962–63; SW Economic Planning Council, 1968–71; BEAB for Household Equipment, 1974–84. Chm., Bristol Waterworks Co., 1975–81 (Dir, 1967–81); Dir, Avon Rubber Co. Ltd, 1973–81. JP Long Ashton, Som, 1960–66. Hon. MSc Bristol, 1957. *Recreations:* general outdoor activities. *Address:* Crete Hill House, Cote House Lane, Bristol BS9 3UW. *T:* Bristol (0272) 622419.

IRESON, Rev. Canon Gordon Worley; *b* 16 April 1906; *s* of Francis Robert and Julia Letitia Ireson; *m* 1939, Dorothy Elizabeth Walker; two *s* one *d*. *Educ:* Edinburgh Theological Coll.; Hatfield Coll., Durham. Asst Curate of Sheringham, 1933–36; Senior Chaplain of St Mary's Cathedral, Edinburgh, with charge of Holy Trinity, Dean Bridge, 1936–37; Priest-Lecturer to National Soc., 1937–39; Diocesan Missioner of Exeter Diocese, 1939–46; Hon. Chaplain to Bishop of Exeter, 1941–46; Canon Residentiary of Newcastle Cathedral, 1946–58; Canon-Missioner of St Albans, 1958–73; Warden, Community of the Holy Name, 1974–82. Examining Chaplain to Bishop of Newcastle, 1949–59. *Publications:* Church Worship and the Non-Churchgoer, 1945; Think Again, 1949; How Shall They Hear?, 1957; Strange Victory, 1970; Handbook of Parish Preaching, 1982. *Recreation:* making and mending in the workshop. *Address:* St Barnabas College, Blackberry Lane, Lingfield, Surrey RH7 6NJ.

IRETON, Barrie Rowland; Under Secretary, and Principal Finance Officer, Overseas Development Administration, Foreign and Commonwealth Office, since 1988; *b* 15 Jan. 1944; *s* of Philip Thomas Ireton, CBE, and Marjorie Rosalind Ireton; *m* 1965, June Collins; one *s* one *d* (and one *s* decd). *Educ:* Alleyn's Grammar Sch., Stevenage; Trinity Coll., Cambridge (MA); London School of Economics (MSc 1970). Economic Statistician, Govt of Zambia, 1965–68; Economist, Industrial Develt Corp., Zambia, 1968–69; Development Sec., The Gambia, 1970–73; Overseas Development Administration, 1973–; Economic Advr, 1973–76; Sen. Economic Advr, 1976–84; Asst Sec., 1984–88. *Recreations:* tennis, gardening, walking. *Address:* Overseas Development Administration, Eland House, Stag Place, SW1E 5DH. *T:* 071–273 0439.

IRISH, Sir Ronald (Arthur), Kt 1970; OBE 1963; Partner, Irish Young & Outhwaite, Chartered Accountants, retired; Chairman, Rothmans of Pall Mall (Australia) Ltd, 1955–81, retired; *b* 26 March 1913; *s* of late Arthur Edward Irish; *m* 1960, Noella Jean Austin Fraser; three *s*. *Educ:* Fort Street High School. Chm., Manufacturing Industries Adv. Council, 1966–72. Pres., Inst. of Chartered Accountants in Australia, 1956–58; Pres., Tenth Internat. Congress of Accountants, 1972; Life Member: Australian Soc. of Accountants, 1972; Inst. of Chartered Accountants in Australia, 1974. Hon. Fellow, Univ. of Sydney, 1986. *Publications:* Practical Auditing, 1935; Auditing, 1947, new edn 1972. *Recreations:* walking, swimming. *Address:* 3/110 Elizabeth Bay Road, Elizabeth Bay, NSW 2011, Australia. *Clubs:* Australian, Union (Sydney).

IRONS, Jeremy; actor; *b* 19 Sept. 1948; *s* of late Paul Dugan Irons and of Barbara Anne (*née* Brereton); *m* 1st (marr. diss.); 2nd, 1978, Sinead Cusack; two *s*. *Educ:* Sherborne; Bristol Old Vic Theatre Sch. *Theatre* appearances include: Bristol Old Vic Theatre Co., 1968–71; Godspell, Round House, transf. Wyndham's, 1971; The Taming of the Shrew, New Shakespeare Co., Round House, 1975; Wild Oats, RSC, 1976–77; The Rear Column, Globe, 1978; The Real Thing, Broadway, 1984 (Tony Award for Best Actor); The Rover, Mermaid, 1986; A Winter's Tale, RSC, 1986; Richard II, RSC, 1986; *television* appearances include: The Pallisers; Love for Lydia; Brideshead Revisited, 1981; The Captain's Doll, 1983; *films* include: The French Lieutenant's Woman, 1981; Moonlighting, 1982; Betrayal, 1982; Swann in Love, 1983; The Wild Duck, 1983; The Mission, 1986; A Chorus of Disapproval, 1988; Dead Ringers, 1988; Danny Champion of the World, 1988; Reversal of Fortune, 1990; Australia, 1991. Mem., Caia Foundn. *Address:* c/o Hutton Management, 200 Fulham Road, SW10 9PN.

IRONSIDE, family name of **Baron Ironside.**

IRONSIDE, 2nd Baron, *cr* 1941, of Archangel and of Ironside; **Edmund Oslac Ironside;** Market Co-ordinator (Defence), NEI plc, 1984–89; *b* 21 Sept. 1924; *o s* of 1st Baron Ironside, Field Marshal, GCB, CMG, DSO, and Mariot Ysabel Cheyne (*d* 1984); *S* father, 1959; *m* 1950, Audrey Marigold, *y d* of late Lt-Col Hon. Thomas Morgan-Grenville, DSO, OBE, MC; one *s* one *d*. *Educ:* Tonbridge Sch. Joined Royal Navy, 1943; retd as Lt, 1952. English Electric Gp, 1952–63; Cryosystems Ltd, 1963–68; International Research and Development Co., 1968–84. Vice-Pres., Parly and Scientific Cttee, 1984–87 (Dep. Chm., 1974–77). Mem., Organising Cttee, British Library, 1971–72. President: Electric Vehicle Assoc., 1976–83; European Electric Road Vehicle Assoc., 1980–82; Vice-Pres., Inst. of Patentees and Inventors, 1977; Chm., Adv. Cttee, Science Reference Lib., 1976–84. Governor, Tonbridge Sch. and others; Member: Court, 1971–, Council, 1987–89, City Univ.; Court and Council Essex Univ., 1982–87. Master, Skinners' Co., 1981–82. Hon. FCGI (CGIA 1986). *Publication:* (ed) High Road to Command: the diaries of Major-General Sir Edmund Ironside, 1920–22, 1972. *Heir:* *s* Hon. Charles Edmund Grenville Ironside [*b* 1 July 1956; *m* 1985, Hon. Elizabeth Law, *e d* of Lord Coleraine, *qv*; one *s* one *d*]. *Address:* Priory House, Old House Lane, Boxted, Colchester, Essex CO4 5RB. *Club:* Royal Ocean Racing.

IRONSIDE, Christopher, OBE 1971; FRBS; artist and designer; *b* 11 July 1913; *s* of Dr R. W. Ironside and Mrs P. L. Williamson (2nd *m*; *née* Cunliffe); *m* 1st, 1939, Janey (*née* Acheson) (marriage dissolved, 1961); one *d*; 2nd, 1961, Jean (*née* Marsden); one *s* two *d*. *Educ:* Central Sch. of Arts and Crafts. Served War of 1939–45, Dep. Sen. Design Off., Directorate of Camouflage, Min. of Home Security. In charge of Educn Sect., Coun. of Industrial Design, 1946–48; part-time Teacher, Royal College of Art, 1953–63. Paintings in public and private collections. *One-man shows:* Redfern Gall., 1941; Arthur Jeffries Gall., 1960. *Design work includes:* Royal Coat of Arms, Whitehall and decorations in Pall Mall, Coronation, 1953; coinages for Tanzania, Brunei, Qatar, Dubai and Singapore (reverses, 1985); reverses for Decimal Coinage, UK and Jamaican; many medals, coins and awards; theatrical work (with brother, late R. C. Ironside); various clocks, coats of arms and tapestries; firegrate for Goldsmiths' Co.; brass and marble meml to 16th Duke of Norfolk, Arundel; meml to Earl and Countess Mountbatten of Burma, Westminster Abbey. FSIA 1970; FRBS 1977. *Recreation:* trying to keep abreast of modern scientific development. *Address:* 22 Abingdon Villas, W8 6BX. *T:* 071–937 9418; Church Farm House, Smannell, near Andover, Hants SP11 6JW. *T:* Andover (0264) 23909.

IRVINE, family name of **Baron Irvine of Lairg.**

IRVINE OF LAIRG, Baron *cr* 1987 (Life Peer), of Lairg in the District of Sutherland; **Alexander Andrew Mackay Irvine;** QC 1978; *b* 23 June 1940; *s* of Alexander Irvine and Margaret Christina Irvine; *m* 1974, Alison Mary, *y d* of Dr James Shaw McNair, MD, and Agnes McNair, MA; two *s*. *Educ:* Inverness Acad.; Hutchesons' Boys' Grammar Sch., Glasgow; Glasgow Univ. (MA, LLB); Christ's Coll., Cambridge (Scholar; BA 1st Cl. Hons with distinction; LLB 1st Cl. Hons; George Long Prize in Jurisprudence). Called to the Bar, Inner Temple, 1967, Bencher, 1985; a Recorder, 1985–88. Univ. Lectr, LSE, 1965–69. Contested (Lab) Hendon North, Gen. Election, 1970. Opposition front bench spokesman on legal affairs, H of L. *Recreations:* cinema, theatre, collecting paintings, travel. *Address:* 11 King's Bench Walk, Temple, EC4Y 7EQ. *T:* 071–583 0610. *Club:* Garrick.

IRVINE, Alan Montgomery, RDI; DesRCA, ARIBA; architect in private practice; *b* 14 Sept. 1926; *s* of Douglas Irvine and Ellen Marler; *m* 1st, 1955; one *s*; 2nd, 1966, Katherine Mary Buzas; two *s*. *Educ:* Regent Street Polytechnic, Secondary Sch. and Sch. of Architecture; Royal College of Art. RAF (Aircrew), 1944–47. Worked in Milan with BBPR Gp, 1954–55. In private practice since 1956, specialising in design of interiors, museums and exhibitions; partnership Buzas and Irvine, 1965–85. Work has included interior design for Schroder Wagg & Co., Lazards, Bovis, S Australian Govt, Nat. Enterprise Bd; Mem. of design team for QE2, 1966. Various exhibns for V&A Museum, Tate Gallery, Royal Academy, Imperial War Museum, RIBA, British Council, British Museum, Olivetti, Fiat etc. including: Treasures of Cambridge, 1959; Book of Kells, 1961; Architecture of Power, 1963; Mellon Collection, 1969; Age of Charles I, 1972; Pompeii AD79, 1976; Gold of El Dorado, 1978; Horses of San Marco (London, NY, Milan, Berlin), 1979–82; Great Japan Exhibition, 1981; Art and Industry, 1982; Cimabue Crucifix (London, Madrid, Munich), 1982–83; Treasures of Ancient Nigeria, 1983; The Genius of Venice, 1983; Leonardo da Vinci: studies for the Last Supper (Milan, Sydney, Toronto, Barcelona, Tokyo), 1984; Art of the Architect, 1984; Re dei Confessori (Milan, Venice), 1985; C. S. Jagger: War and Peace Sculpture, 1985; Queen Elizabeth II: portraits of 60 years, 1986; Eye for Industry, 1986; Glass of the Caesars (London, Cologne, Rome), 1988; Michaelangelo Drawings, Louvre, 1989; Conservation Today, 1989; Paul de Lamerie, 1990; Lion of Venice, London, Amsterdam, 1991. Museum work includes: Old Master Drawings Gallery, Windsor Castle, 1965; New Galleries for Royal Scottish Museum, 1968; Crown Jewels display, Tower of London, 1968; Treasuries at Winchester Cathedral, 1968, Christ Church, Oxford, 1975, and Winchester College, 1982; Heinz Gallery for Architectural Drawings, RIBA, London, 1972; Museum and Art Gallery for Harrow School, 1975; Heralds' Museum, London, 1980; Al Shaheed Museum, Baghdad, 1983; Cabinet War Rooms, London, 1984; West Wing Galls, Nat. Maritime Mus., Greenwich, 1986; Beatrix Potter Museum, Cumbria, 1988. Retrospective exhibn, RIBA Heinz Gall., 1989. Consultant designer to Olivetti, Italy; Consultant architect to British Museum, 1981–84. Mem., Crafts Council, 1984–86. Liveryman, Worshipful Co. of Goldsmiths. Hon. Fellow, RCA. *Recreations:* travel, photography. *Address:* 2 Aubrey Place, St John's Wood, NW8 9BH. *T:* 071–328 2229. *Club:* London Collie.

IRVINE, Rt. Hon. Sir Bryant Godman, Kt 1986; PC 1982; Barrister-at-Law; farmer; *b* Toronto, 25 July 1909; *s* of late W. Henry Irvine and late Ada Mary Bryant Irvine, formerly of St Agnes, Cornwall; *m* 1945, Valborg Cecilie (*d* 1990), *d* of late P. F. Carslund; two *d*. *Educ:* Upper Canada Coll.; St Paul's Sch.; Magdalen Coll., Oxford (MA). Sec. Oxford Union Soc., 1931. Called to Bar. Inner Temple, 1932. Chm. Agricultural Land Tribunal, SE Province, 1954–56. Mem. Executive Cttee, East Sussex NFU, 1947–84; Branch Chm., 1956–58. Chm. Young Conservative Union, 1946–47; Prospective Candidate, Bewdley Div. of Worcs, 1947–49; contested Wood Green and Lower Tottenham, 1951. MP (C) Rye Div., E Sussex, 1955–83; PPS to Minister of Education and to Parly Sec., Ministry of Education, 1957–59, to the Financial Sec. to the Treasury, 1959–60. Mem., Speaker's Panel of Chairmen, House of Commons, 1965–76; a Dep. Chm. of Ways and Means, and a Deputy Speaker, 1976–82; Jt Sec., Exec. Cttee, 1922 Cttee, 1965–68, Hon. Treasurer, 1974–76; Vice-Chm., Cons. Agric. Cttee, and spoke on Agriculture from Opposition Front Bench, 1964–70; Mem., House of Commons Select Cttee on Agriculture, 1967–69; Commonwealth Parliamentary Association: Hon. Treasurer, 1970–73; Mem., General Council, 1970–73; Mem., Exec. Cttee, UK Branch, 1964–76; Jt Sec. or Vice-Chm., Cons. Commonwealth Affairs Cttee, 1957–66; Jt Sec., Foreign and Commonwealth Affairs Cttee, 1967–73 (Vice-Chm., 1973–76); Chm., Cons. Horticulture Sub-Cttee, 1960–62; All Party Tourist and Resort Cttee, 1964–66. President: British Resorts Assoc., 1962–80; Southern Counties Agricl Trading Soc., 1983–86. Served War of 1939–45, Lt-Comdr RNVR, afloat and on staff of C-in-C Western Approaches and Commander US Naval Forces in Europe. Comp. InstCE, 1936–74. *Recreations:* skiing, travel by sea. *Address:* Great Ote Hall, Burgess Hill, West Sussex RH15 0SR. *T:* Burgess Hill (0444) 232179; 91 Millbank Court, 24 John Islip Street, SW1. *T:* 071–834 9221; 2 Dr Johnson's Buildings, Temple, EC4. *Clubs:* Carlton, Pratt's, Naval.

IRVINE, Dr Donald Hamilton, CBE 1987 (OBE 1979); MD; FRCGP; Principal in General Practice, Ashington, since 1960; Regional Adviser in General Practice, University of Newcastle, since 1973; *b* 2 June 1935; *s* of late Dr Andrew Bell Hamilton Irvine and of Dorothy Mary Irvine; *m* 1960; two *s* one *d*; *m* 1986, Sally Fountain. *Educ:* King Edward Sixth Grammar Sch., Morpeth; Medical Sch., King's Coll., Univ. of Durham (MB BS); DObstRCOG 1960; MD Newcastle 1964; FRCGP 1972 (MRCGP 1965). Ho. Phys. to Dr C. N. Armstrong and Dr Henry Miller, 1958–59. Chm. Council, RCGP, 1982–85 (Vice-Chm., 1981–82); Hon. Sec. of the College, 1972–78; Jt Hon. Sec., Jt Cttee on Postgraduate Trng for General Practice, 1976–82; Fellow, BMA, 1976; Mem., Gen. Medical Council, 1979– (Chm., Cttee on Standards and Medical Ethics, 1985–); Governor, MSD Foundn, 1982– (Chm., Bd of Governors, 1983). Vice-Pres., Medical Defence Union, 1974–78. Vis. Professor in Family Practice, Univ. of Iowa, USA, 1973; (first) Vis. Prof. to Royal Australian Coll. of General Practitioners, 1977; Vis. Cons. on Postgrad. Educn for Family Medicine to Virginia Commonwealth Univ., 1971, Univ. of Wisconsin-Madison, 1973, Medical Univ. of S Carolina, 1974. Mem., Audit Commn, 1990–. *Publications:* The Future General Practitioner: learning and teaching, (jtly), 1972 (RCGP); Managing for Quality in General Practice, 1990; (ed jtly) Making Sense of Audit, 1991; chapters to several books on gen. practice; papers on clinical and educnl studies in medicine, in BMJ, Lancet, Jl of RCGP. *Recreations:* bird watching, motor cars, politics, watching television. *Address:* Mole End, Fairmoor, Morpeth NE61 3JL; Flat 11, Cedarland Court, Roland Gardens, SW7 3RW.

IRVINE, Surg. Captain Gerard Sutherland, CBE 1970; RN retired; Medical Officer, Department of Health and Social Security, 1971–78; *b* 19 June 1913; *s* of Major Gerard Byrom Corrie Irvine and Maud Andrée (*née* Wylde); *m* 1939, Phyllis Lucy Lawrie (*d* 1988); one *s*. *Educ:* Imperial Service Coll., Windsor; Epsom Coll.; University Coll. and Hosp., London. MRCS, LRCP, MB, BS 1937; DLO 1940; FRCS 1967. Jenks Meml Schol. 1932; Liston Gold Medal for Surgery 1936. Surg. Sub-Lt RNVR 1935, Surg. Lt

RNVR 1937; Surg Lt RN 1939; Surg. Lt-Comdr 1944; Surg. Comdr 1953; Surg. Capt. 1963. Served War of 1939–45 (1939–45 Star, Atlantic Star with Bar for France and Germany, Burma Star, Defence Medal, Victory Medal); subseq. service: Ceylon, 1946; Haslar, 1947–49 and 1957–60; Malta, 1953–56; HMS: Maidstone (Submarine Depot Ship), 1949–51; Osprey (T&A/S Trng Sch.), 1951–53; Collingwood, 1956–57; Lion, 1960–62; Vernon (Torpedo Sch.), 1962–63; Sen. Cons. in ENT, 1953–70; Adviser in ENT to Med. Dir-Gen. (Navy), 1966–70; Sen. MO i/c Surgical Div., RN Hosp. Haslar, 1966–70; QHS 1969–70; retd 1970. Member: BMA 1938; Sections of Otology and Laryngology, RSM, 1948–77 (FRSM 1948–77); British Assoc. of Otolaryngologists, 1945–71 (Council, 1958–70); S Western Laryngological Assoc., 1951–71; Hearing Sub-Cttee of RN Personnel Res. Cttee, 1947–70; Otological Sub-Cttee of RAF Flying Personnel Res. Cttee, 1963–70. OStJ 1969. *Publications:* numerous articles in various medical jls. *Recreations:* gardening, philately, do-it-yourself. *Address:* 9 Alvara Road, Alverstoke, Gosport PO12 2HY. *T:* Gosport (0705) 580342.

IRVINE, James Eccles Malise; His Honour Judge Irvine; a Circuit Judge, since 1972 (Leicester County and Crown Courts, 1972–82; Oxford County and Northampton Crown Courts, since 1982); *b* 10 July 1925; *y s* of late Brig.-Gen. A. E. Irvine, CB, CMG, DSO, Wotton-under-Edge; *m* 1954, Anne, *e d* of late Col G. Egerton-Warburton, DSO, TD, JP, DL, Grafton Hall, Malpas; one *s* one *d*. *Educ:* Stowe Sch. (Scholar); Merton Coll., Oxford (Postmaster). MA Oxon. Served Grenadier Guards, 1943–46 (France and Germany Star); Hon. Captain Grenadier Guards, 1946. Called to Bar, Inner Temple, 1949 (Poland Prizeman in Criminal Law, 1949); practised Oxford Circuit, 1949–71; Prosecuting Counsel for Inland Revenue on Oxford Circuit, 1965–71; Dep. Chm., Glos QS, 1967–71. Lay Judge of Court of Arches of Canterbury and Chancery Court of York, 1981–. *Publication:* Parties and Pleasures: the Diaries of Helen Graham 1823–26, 1957. *Address:* 2 Harcourt Buildings, Temple, EC4; c/o Oxford Combined Courts Centre, St Aldate's, Oxford OX1 1TL.

IRVINE, Maj.-Gen. John, OBE 1955; Director of Medical Services, British Army of the Rhine, 1973–75; *b* 31 May 1914; *s* of late John Irvine and late Jessie Irvine (*née* McKinnon); *m* 1941, Mary McNicol, *d* of late Andrew Brown Cossar, Glasgow; one *d*. *Educ:* Glasgow High Sch.; Glasgow Univ. MB, ChB 1940. MFCM 1973. Commnd into RAMC, 1940; served War of 1939–45 (despatches and Act of Gallantry, 1944): Egypt, Greece, Crete, Western Desert, 1941–43; Sicily, Italy and Yugoslavia, 1943–45; served with British Troops, Austria, 1947–49; Korea, 1953–54 (OBE); Malaya, 1954–56 (despatches); Germany, 1958–61; Ghana, 1961; Germany, 1962–64; DDMS, HQ BAOR, 1968–69; DDMS, 1st British Corps, 1969–71; Dep. Dir-Gen., AMS, 1971–73. QHS 1972–75. OStJ 1971. *Recreations:* tennis, ski-ing. *Address:* Greenlawns, 11 Manor Road, Aldershot, Hants GU11 3DG. *T:* Aldershot (0252) 311524.

IRVINE, John Ferguson, CB 1983; Chief Executive, Industrial Therapy Organisation (Ulster), since 1984; *b* 13 Nov. 1920; *s* of Joseph Ferguson Irvine and Helen Gardner; *m* 1st, 1945, Doris Partridge (*d* 1973); one *s* one *d*; 2nd, 1980, Christine Margot Tudor; two *s* and two step *s*. *Educ:* Ardrossan Acad.; Glasgow Univ. (MA). RAF, 1941–46; Scottish Home Dept, 1946–48; NI Civil Service, 1948–66; Chief Exec., Ulster Transport Authority, 1966–68; Chief Exec., NI Transport Holding Co., 1968; NI Civil Service, 1969–83; Dep. Sec., DoE, NI, 1971–76; Permanent Secretary: attached NI Office, 1977–80; Dept of Manpower Services, 1980–81; DoE for NI, 1981–83. Chm. Management Cttee, 1974–75, and Vice-Chm. General Council, 1975, Action Cancer; Member: NI Marriage Guidance Council (Chm., 1976–78); Council, PHAB (NI), 1984–86; Council, PHAB (UK), 1984–86; Trustee, Heart Fund, Royal Victoria Hosp., Belfast, 1986–88. *Recreations:* distance running, yoga, Majorca, football. *Address:* c/o Allied Irish Banks, 31 High Street, Belfast BT1 5HG.

IRVINE, Prof. John Maxwell, PhD; CPhys, FInstP; FRAS; Principal and Vice-Chancellor, University of Aberdeen, since 1991; *b* 28 Feb. 1939; *s* of John MacDonald Irvine and Joan Paterson (*née* Adamson); *m* 1962, Grace Ritchie; one *s*. *Educ:* George Heriot's Sch., Edinburgh; Edinburgh Univ. (BSc Math. Phys. 1961); Univ. of Michigan (MSc 1962); Univ. of Manchester (PhD 1964). FInstP 1971; CPhys 1985; FRAS 1986. English-Speaking Union Fellow, Univ. of Michigan, 1961–62; Asst Lectr, Univ. of Manchester, 1964–66; Res. Associate, Cornell Univ., 1966–68; University of Manchester: Lectr, 1968–73; Sen. Lectr, 1973–76; Reader, 1976–83; Prof. of Theoretical Physics, 1983–91; Dean of Science, 1989–91. Mem., Nuclear Physics Bd, SERC, 1983–88 (Chm., Nuclear Structure Cttee, 1984–88). Mem. Council, Inst. of Physics, 1981–87, 1988– (Vice-Pres., 1982–87). *Publications:* The Basis of Modern Physics, 1967 (trans. Dutch and French, 1969); Nuclear Structure Theory, 1972; Heavy Nuclei, Superheavy Nuclei and Neutron Stars, 1975; Neutron Stars, 1978; research articles on nuclear physics, astrophysics and condensed matter physics. *Recreations:* hill walking, tennis, bridge. *Address:* Chanory Lodge, The Chanory, Old Aberdeen AB2 1RP; University Office, Regent Walk, Aberdeen AB9 1FY. *T:* Aberdeen (0224) 272134, *Fax:* Aberdeen (0224) 488605. *Club:* Athenæum.

IRVINE, Very Rev. (John) Murray; Provost and Rector of Southwell Minster, 1978–91, Emeritus, since 1991; Priest-in-Charge of Edingley and Halam, 1978–91; Priest-in-Charge of Rolleston with Fiskerton and Morton and Upton, 1990–91; *b* 19 Aug. 1924; *s* of Andrew Leicester Irvine and Eleanor Mildred (*née* Lloyd); *m* 1961, Pamela Shirley Brain; one *s* three *d*. *Educ:* Charterhouse; Magdalene Coll., Cambridge; Ely Theological Coll. BA 1946, MA 1949. Deacon, 1948; Priest, 1949; Curate of All Saints, Poplar, 1948–53; Chaplain of Sidney Sussex Coll., Cambridge, 1953–60; Selection Sec. of CACTM, 1960–65; Canon Residentiary, Prebendary of Hunderton, Chancellor and Librarian of Hereford Cathedral, and Dir of Ordination Training, Diocese of Hereford, 1965–78; Warden of Readers, 1976–78. *Address:* 9 Salston Barton, Strawberry Lane, Ottery St Mary, Devon EX11 1RG. *T:* Ottery St Mary (0404) 815901.

IRVINE, Michael Fraser; MP (C) Ipswich, since 1987; barrister; *b* 21 Oct. 1939; *s* of Rt Hon. Sir Arthur Irvine, PC, QC, MP, and Lady Irvine. *Educ:* Rugby; Oriel College, Oxford (BA). Called to the Bar, Inner Temple, 1964. Contested (C) Bishop Auckland, 1979. PPS to Attorney-Gen., 1990–. *Recreation:* hill walking in Scotland. *Address:* 1 Crown Office Row, Temple, EC4Y 7HH. *T:* 071-583 9292.

IRVINE, Very Rev. Murray; *see* Irvine, Very Rev. J. M.

IRVINE, Norman Forrest; QC 1973; a Recorder of the Crown Court, 1974–86; *b* 29 Sept. 1922; *s* of William Allan Irvine and Dorcas Forrest; *m* 1964, Mary Lilian Patricia Edmunds (*née* Constable); one *s*. *Educ:* High Sch. of Glasgow; Glasgow Univ. BL 1941. Solicitor (Scotland), 1943. Served War, 1942–45: Lieut Royal Signals, Staff Captain. HM Claims Commn, 1945–46; London Claims Supt, Provincial Insurance Co. Ltd, 1950–52. Called to Bar, Gray's Inn, 1955. *Recreations:* reading, piano, writing. *Address:* 11 Upland Park Road, Oxford OX2 7RU.

IRVINE, Sir Robin (Orlando Hamilton), Kt 1989; FRCP, FRACP; Vice-Chancellor, University of Otago, Dunedin, New Zealand, since 1973; *b* 15 Sept. 1929; *s* of late Claude Turner Irvine; *m* 1957, Elizabeth Mary, *d* of late Herbert Gray Corbett; one *s* two *d*. *Educ:* Wanganui Collegiate Sch.; Univ. of Otago. Otago University Med. Sch., 1948–53; MB, ChB, 1953; MD (NZ), 1958; FRCP, FRACP. House Phys., Auckland Hosp., 1954; Dept of Medicine, Univ. of Otago: Research Asst (Emily Johnston Res. Schol.), 1955; Asst Lectr and Registrar, 1956–57. Leverhulme Research Scholar, Middlesex Hosp., London, 1958; Registrar, Postgraduate Medical Sch., London, 1959–60; Isaacs Medical Research Fellow, Auckland Hosp., 1960–61; Med. Tutor and Med. Specialist, Auckland Hosp., 1962–63; Lectr, Sen. Lectr in Med., Univ. of Otago, 1963–67; Associate Prof., 1968; Clinical Dean and Personal Professor, Univ. of Otago Medical Sch., 1969–72. Girdlers' Co. Senior Vis. Res. Fellowship, Green Coll., Oxford, 1986–87. Consultant, Asian Development Bank, 1974–. Member: Selwyn Coll. Bd, 1966–; Pharmacology and Therapeutic Cttee, Min. of Health, 1967–73; Otago Hosp. Bd, 1969–88; Med. Educn Cttee of Med. Council of NZ, 1969–73; Cent. Educn Cttee, NZ Med. Assoc., 1970–73; Social Council of Nat. Develt Council of NZ, 1971–74; Cttee on Nursing Educn, Min. of Educn, 1972; Social Develt Council, 1974–79; Commn for the Future, 1976–80; NZ Planning Council, 1977–82; Council, Assoc. of Commonwealth Univs, 1979–80; Otago Polytech. Council, 1973–87; Dunedin Teachers Coll. Council, 1973–90; NZ Adv. Cttee, Nuffield Foundn, 1973–81; NZ Rhodes Scholarships Selection Cttee, 1976–81; Lottery Health Res. Distn Cttee, 1985–; Council, Dunedin Coll. of Educn, 1991–; Chairman: Otago Med. Res. Foundn, 1975–81; Ministerial working party on novel genetic techniques, 1977; NZ Vice-Chancellors' Cttee, 1979–80; Convenor, Med. Educn Mission to Univ. of S Pacific, 1971; Dir, Otago Develt Corp., 1982–85; Trustee: McMillan Trust, 1973– (Chm., 1977–86, 1990). Rowheath Trust, 1973–; NZ Red Cross Foundn. Hon. ADC 1969, and Hon. Physician 1970, to the Governor-General, Sir Arthur Porritt. Hon. Mem., Australian Soc. of Nephrology. Dr *hc* Edinburgh, 1976. FRSA 1980; FNZIM 1984. Silver Jubilee Medal, 1977. *Publications:* various papers on high blood pressure, renal med. and medical educn. *Recreations:* walking, reading, music. *Address:* University Lodge, St Leonards, Dunedin, New Zealand. *T:* 710.541. *Club:* Fernhill (Dunedin).

IRVING, Sir Charles (Graham), Kt 1990; MP (C) Cheltenham, since Oct. 1974; Consultant on Public Affairs, Dowty Group PLC; County and District Councillor. *Educ:* Glengarth Sch., Cheltenham; Lucton Sch., Hereford. Mem. Cheltenham Borough Council, 1947–74 (Alderman 1959–May 1967, and Sept. 1967–74); Mem., Cheltenham DC, 1974–; Mem. Gloucestershire CC, 1948– (Chm., Social Services Cttee, 1974–); Mayor of Cheltenham, 1958–60 and 1971–72; Dep. Mayor, 1959–63; Alderman of Gloucestershire County, 1965–74; Contested (C): Bilston, Staffs, 1970; Kingswood, Glos, Feb. 1974; Member Cons. Parly Cttees: Aviation; Social Services; Mem., Select Cttee on Administration; Chairman: Select Cttee on Catering, 1979–; All Party Mental Health Cttee, 1979–; All Party Cttee CHAR. Pres., Cheltenham Young Conservatives. Dir, Cheltenham Art and Literary Festival Co. (responsible for the only contemp. Festival of Music in England); Founder Mem., Univ. Cttee for Gloucestershire; Pres., Cheltenham and Dist Hotels' Assoc. Member: Bridgehead Housing Assoc. Ltd; Nat. Council for the Care and Resettlement of Offenders (Nat. Dep. Chm., 1974); (Chm.) NACRO Regional Council for South West; Nat. Council of St Leonard's Housing Assoc. Ltd; (Chm.) SW Midlands Housing Assoc. Ltd; SW Regional Hosp. Bd, 1971–72; Glos AHA, 1974–; (Chm.) Cheltenham and Dist Housing Assoc. Ltd, 1972; (Chm.) Cheltenham Dist Local Govt Re-Organisation Cttee, 1972; Founder and Chm., Nat. Victims Assoc., 1973; Chm., Stonham Housing Assoc., 1976–. Chairman: Irving Hotels Ltd, 1949–67; Irving Engineering Co., 1949–67; Western Travel, 1986–. Mem. NUJ; MIPR 1964. Freedom, Borough of Cheltenham, 1977. *Publications:* pamphlets (as Chm. SW Region of NACRO and SW Midlands Housing Assoc. Ltd, 1970–73) include: Prisoner and Industry; After-care in the Community; Penal Budgeting; What about the Victim; Dosser's Dream—Planner's Nightmare. Pioneered Frontsheet (1st prison newspaper); reported in national papers, Quest, Social Services, Glos. Life, etc. *Recreations:* antiques, social work. *Address:* The Grange, Malvern Road, Cheltenham, Glos. *T:* Cheltenham (0242) 523083. *Club:* St Stephen's Constitutional.

IRVING, Clifford; *see* Irving, E. C.

IRVING, Edward, ScD; FRS 1979; FRSC 1973; FRAS; Research Scientist, Pacific Geoscience Centre, Sidney, BC, since 1981; *b* 27 May 1927; *s* of George Edward and Nellie Irving; *m* 1957, Sheila Ann Irwin; two *s* two *d*. *Educ:* Colne Grammar Sch.; Cambridge Univ., 1948–54 (BA, MA, MSc, ScD). Served Army, 1945–48. Research Fellow, Fellow and Sen. Fellow, ANU, 1954–64; Dominion Observatory, Canada, 1964–66; Prof. of Geophysics, Univ. of Leeds, 1966–67; Res. Scientist, Dominion Observatory, later Earth Physics Br., Dept of Energy, Mines and Resources, Ottawa, 1967–81; Adjunct Professor: Carleton Univ., Ottawa, 1975–81; Univ. of Victoria, 1985–. FRAS 1958; Fellow: Amer. Geophysical Union, 1976 (Walter H. Bucher Medal, 1979); Geological Soc. of America, 1979. Hon. FGS 1989. Hon. DSc: Carleton, 1979; Memorial Univ. of Newfoundland, 1986. Gondwanaland Medal, Mining, Geological and Metallurgical Soc. of India, 1962; Logan Medal, Geol Assoc. of Canada, 1975; J. T. Wilson Medal, Canadian Geophys. Union, 1984. *Publications:* Paleomagnetism, 1964; numerous contribs to learned jls. *Recreations:* gardening, carpentry, choral singing. *Address:* Pacific Geoscience Centre, 9860 West Saanich Road, Box 6000, Sidney, BC V8L 4B2, Canada. *T:* (604) 363–6508; 9363 Carnoustie Crescent, Sidney, BC V8L 3S1. *T:* (604) 656–9645.

IRVING, (Edward) Clifford, CBE 1981; Member, Legislative Council, Isle of Man, since 1987; *b* 24 May 1914; *s* of late William Radcliffe Irving and Mabel Henrietta (*née* Cottier); *m* 1941, Nora, *d* of Harold Page, Luton; one *s* one *d*. *Educ:* Isle of Man; Canada. Member: House of Keys, 1955–61, 1966–81, 1984–87 (Acting Speaker, 1971–81); Executive Council, IOM Govt, 1968–81 (Chm., 1977–81). Member, IOM Government Boards: Airports, 1955–58; Assessment, 1955–56; Social Security, 1956; Local Govt, 1956–62; Tourist, 1956–62; Finance, 1966–71; Member: Industrial Adv. Council, 1961–62, 1971–81; CS Commn, 1976–81. Chairman: IOM Tourist Bd, 1971–81; IOM Sports Council, 1971–81; IOM Harbours Bd, 1985–87. Chairman: Bank of Wales (IOM), 1985–87; Etam (IOM), 1985–; Bank of Scotland (IOM) Ltd, 1987–; Bank of Scotland Nominees (IOM) Ltd, 1987–; Refuge (IOM) Ltd, 1988–. President: IOM Assoc. of Veteran Athletes; Wanderers Male Voice Choir; Manx Nat. Powerboat Club; Douglas Angling Club; Manx Parascending Club; IOM Angling Assoc.; Douglas Br., RNLI; Vice-President: Douglas Motor Boat and Sailing Club; IOM Home for Old Horses. Patron: Manx Variety Club; IOM TT Races. *Recreations:* powerboating, angling. *Address:* Highfield, Belmont Hill, Douglas, Isle of Man. *T:* Douglas (0624) 73652.

IRVING, Prof. Harry Munroe Napier Hetherington; Professor of Inorganic and Structural Chemistry, University of Leeds, 1961–71, Professor Emeritus, since 1972; Professor of Analytical Science, University of Cape Town, 1979–85 (of Theoretical Chemistry, 1978); retired; *b* 19 Nov. 1905; *s* of John and Clara Irving; *m* 1st, 1934, Monica Mary Wildsmith (*d* 1972); no *c*; 2nd, 1975, Dr Anne Mawby. *Educ:* St Bees Sch., Cumberland; The Queen's Coll., Oxford. BA 1927; First Class in Final Honour Sch. (Chemistry), 1928; MA, DPhil 1930; DSc 1958 (all Oxon); LRAM 1930. Univ. Demonstrator in Chemistry, Oxford, 1934–61; Lectr in Organic Chemistry, The Queen's Coll., 1930–34; Fellow and Tutor, St Edmund Hall, 1938–51; Vice-Principal, 1951–61; Emeritus-Fellow, 1961–. Member: Chem. Soc. 1935– (Council, 1954, Perkin Elmer

Award, 1974); Soc. Chm. Ind., 1935– (Gold Medal, 1980); Soc. for Analytical Chemists, 1950– (Council, 1952–57, 1965–67; Vice-Pres. 1955–57; Gold Medal, 1971); Fellow Royal Inst. of Chemistry, 1948– (Council, 1950–52, 1962–65; Vice-Pres. 1965–67); Mem., S African Chem. Inst., 1979. Has lectured extensively in America, Africa and Europe; broadcasts on scientific subjects. FRSSAf. Hon. DTech Brunel Univ., 1970. *Publications:* (trans.) Schwarzenbach and Flaschka's Complexometric Titrations; Short History of Analytical Chemistry, 1974; Dithizone, 1977; The Halogens in Human History, 1991; numerous papers in various learned jls. *Recreations:* music, foreign travel, ice-skating. *Address:* 1 North Grange Mount, Leeds LS6 2BY.

IRVING, James Tutin, MA Oxon and Cantab, MD, PhD Cantab; Professor of Physiology in the School of Dental Medicine at Harvard University and the Forsyth Dental Center, 1961–68, Professor Emeritus, 1968, Visiting Lecturer in Oral Biology, 1973–77; Emeritus Professor, National Institute on Aging, Baltimore, 1978–81; *b* Christchurch, New Zealand, 3 May 1902; *m* 1937, Janet, *d* of Hon. Nicholas O'Connor, New York. *Educ:* Christ's Coll., New Zealand; Caius Coll., Cambridge; Trinity Coll., Oxford; Guy's Hospital. Double First Class Hons, Nat. Sci. Tripos, Cambridge, 1923–24; Scholar and Prizeman, Caius Coll., 1923; Benn. W. Levy and Frank Smart Student, 1924–26; Beit Memorial Fellow, 1926–28; Lecturer in Physiology, Bristol Univ., 1931, and Leeds Univ., 1934; Head of Physiology Dept, Rowett Research Inst., and part-time lecturer, Aberdeen Univ., 1936; Prof. of Physiology, Cape Town Univ., 1939–53, Fellow 1948; Professor of Experimental Odontology, and Dir of the Joint CSIR and Univ. of Witwatersrand Dental Research Unit, 1953–59; Prof. of Anatomy, Harvard Sch. of Dental Med., 1959–61. Visiting Professor: Univ. of Illinois Dental Sch. 1947 and 1956; Univ. of Pennsylvania, 1951; Univ. of California, 1956. Chm., Gordon Conference on Bone and Teeth, 1969. Editor, Archives of Oral Biology, 1962–87. AM (Hon.) Harvard. Late Hon. Physiologist to Groote Schuur Hosp.; Fellow Odont. Soc. S Africa. Hon. Life Mem. of New York Academy of Sciences. Mem. of Soc. of Sigma Xi. Hon. Mem. of Soc. of Omicron Kappa Upsilon. S African Medal for war services (non-military), 1948. Isaac Schour Meml Award for Res. in Anatomical Scis, 1972. *Publications:* Calcium Metabolism, 1957; Calcium and Phosphorus Metabolism, 1973; many papers in physiological and medical journals, chiefly on nutrition, and bone and tooth formation; also publications on nautical history. *Recreations:* music, gardening, nautical research. *Address:* (home) 5 Peele House Square, Manchester, Mass 01944, USA; (office) 140 The Fenway, Boston, Mass 02115, USA. *Club:* Inanda (Johannesburg).

IRVING, Prof. John; Freeland Professor of Natural Philosophy (Theoretical Physics), University of Strathclyde, Glasgow, 1961–84; retired; *b* 22 Dec. 1920; *s* of John Irving and Margaret Kent Aird; *m* 1948, Monica Cecilia Clarke; two *s. Educ:* St John's Grammar Sch.; Hamilton Academy; Glasgow Univ. MA (1st Class Hons in Maths and Nat. Phil.), Glasgow Univ., 1940; PhD (Mathematical Physics), Birmingham Univ., 1951. FInstP 1980. Lectr, Stow Coll., Glasgow, 1944–45; Lectr in Maths, Univ. of St Andrews 1945–46; Lectr in Mathematical Physics, University of Birmingham, 1946–49; Nuffield Research Fellow (Nat. Phil.), University of Glasgow, 1949–51; Sen. Lectr in Applied Maths, University of Southampton, 1951–59; Prof. of Theoretical Physics and Head of Dept of Applied Mathematics and Theor. Physics University of Cape Town, 1959–61. Dean of Sch. of Mathematics and Physics, Strathclyde Univ., 1964–69. *Publications:* Mathematics in Physics and Engineering, 1959 (New York); contrib. to: Proc. Physical Soc.; Philosophical Magazine, Physical Review. *Recreations:* gardening, computing. *Address:* 15 Leeburn Avenue, Houston, Renfrewshire PA6 7DN. *T:* Bridge of Weir (0505) 614549.

IRVING, Prof. Miles Horsfall, MD; FRCS, FRCSE; Professor of Surgery, University of Manchester, since 1974; Hon. Consultant Surgeon, Hope Hospital, Salford, since 1974; *b* 29 June 1935; *s* of Frederick William Irving and Mabel Irving; *m* 1965, Patricia Margaret Blaiklock; two *s* two *d. Educ:* King George V Sch., Southport; Liverpool Univ. (MB, ChB 1959; MD 1962; ChM 1968); Sydney Univ., Australia; MSc Manchester Univ., 1977. FRCS 1964; FRCSE 1964. Robert Gee Fellow, Liverpool Univ., 1962; Phyllis Anderson Fellow, Sydney Univ., 1967; St Bartholomew's Hospital, London: Chief Asst in Surgery, 1969–71; Reader in Surgery, Asst Dir of Professorial Surgical Unit, and Hon. Consultant Surgeon, 1972–74. Hon. Consultant Surgeon to the Army, 1989–. Hunterian Prof., RCS, 1967; Sir Gordon Bell Meml Orator, NZ, 1982. Mem., Expert Adv. Gp on AIDS, DoH, 1991. Member: Council, RCS, 1984–91; GMC, 1989–; Pres., Ileostomy Assoc. of GB and Ireland, 1982–. Hon. Fellow, Amer. Assoc. for Surgery of Trauma, 1985. Moynihan Medal, Assoc. of Surgeons of GB and Ire., 1968; Pybus Medal, N of England Surgical Soc., 1986. *Publications:* Gastroenterological Surgery, 1983; Intestinal Fistulas, 1985. *Recreations:* thinking about and occasionally actually climbing mountains, reading The Spectator, opera. *Address:* 18 Albert Road, Heaton, Bolton, Lancs BL1 5HE. *T:* Bolton (0204) 41182.

IRWIN, Lord; James Charles Wood; *b* 24 Aug. 1977; *s* and *heir* of 3rd Earl of Halifax, *qv.*

IRWIN, Maj.-Gen. Brian St George, CB 1975; Director General, Ordnance Survey, 1969–77, retired; *b* 16 Sept. 1917; *s* of late Lt-Col Alfred Percy Bulteel Irwin, DSO, and late Eileen Irwin (*née* Holberton); *m* 1939, Audrey Lilla, *d* of late Lt-Col H. B. Steen, IMS; two *s. Educ:* Rugby Sch.; RMA Woolwich; Trinity Hall, Cambridge (MA). Commnd in RE, 1937; war service in Western Desert, 1941–43 (despatches); Sicily and Italy, 1943–44 (despatches); Greece, 1944–45; subseq. in Cyprus, 1956–59 (despatches) and 1961–63; Dir of Military Survey, MoD, 1965–69. Col Comdt, RE, 1977–82. FRICS (Council 1969–70, 1972–76); FRGS (Council 1966–70; Vice-Pres., 1974–77). *Recreations:* sailing, golf, gardening, genealogy. *Address:* 16 Northerwood House, Swan Green, Lyndhurst, Hants SO43 7DT. *T:* Lyndhurst (0703) 283499. *Club:* Army and Navy.

IRWIN, Ian Sutherland, CBE 1982; Chairman and Chief Executive, Scottish Transport Group, since 1987; *b* Glasgow, 20 Feb. 1933; *s* of Andrew Campbell Irwin and Elizabeth Ritchie Arnott; *m* 1959, Margaret Miller Maureen Irvine; two *s. Educ:* Whitehill Sen. Secondary Sch., Glasgow; Glasgow Univ. BL; CA, IPFA, FCIT, CBIM, FInstD. Commercial Man., Scottish Omnibuses Ltd, 1960–64; Gp Accountant, Scottish Bus Gp, 1964–69; Gp Sec., 1969–75, Dep. Chm. and Man. Dir, 1975–87, Scottish Transport Gp; Chairman: Scottish Bus Gp Ltd, 1975–; Caledonian MacBrayne Ltd, 1975–90; Scottish Transport Investments Ltd, 1975–; Dir, Scottish Mortgage & Trust plc, 1986–. Pres., Bus and Coach Council, 1979–80; Hon. Vice-Pres., Internat. Union of Public Transport; Mem. Council, CIT, 1978–87 (Vice Pres., 1984–87). Hon. Col, 154 Regt RCT (V), 1986–. *Publications:* various papers. *Recreations:* golf, foreign travel, gardening. *Address:* 10 Moray Place, Edinburgh EH3 6DT. *T:* 031–443 2108. *Clubs:* Caledonian, MCC.

IRWIN, John Conran; Keeper, Indian Section, Victoria and Albert Museum, 1959–78, with extended responsibility for new Oriental Department, 1970–78; *b* 5 Aug. 1917; *s* of late John Williamson Irwin; *m* 1947, Helen Hermione Scott (*née* Fletcher) (separated 1982), *d* of late Herbert Bristowe Fletcher; three *s. Educ:* Canford Sch., Wimborne, Dorset. Temp. commission, Gordon Highlanders, 1939. Private Sec. to Gov. of Bengal, 1942–45; Asst Keeper, Victoria and Albert Museum, 1946; Exec. Sec., Royal Academy

Winter Exhibition of Indian Art, 1947–48; UNESCO Expert on museum planning: on mission to Indonesia, 1956; to Malaya, 1962. British Acad. Travelling Fellowship, 1974–75; Leverhulme Res. Fellow, 1978–80; Sen. Fellow, Center for Advanced Study in the Visual Arts, Nat. Gall. of Art, Washington, DC, 1983–84; Vis. Prof., Univ. of Michigan, 1986; State visit to India, sponsored by Indian govt, 1986–87. Working with research grants from Leverhulme Trust and British Acad., 1978–84. Lectures: Birdwood Meml, 1972; Tagore Meml, 1973; Lowell Inst., Boston, Mass, 1974; guest lectr, Collège de France, 1976. Pres., Res. into Lost Knowledge Orgn, 1960; Hon. Pres., Indian Circle, SOAS, 1990. FRSA 1972; FRAS 1946; FRAI 1977; FSA 1978. *Publications:* Jamini Roy, 1944; Indian art (section on sculpture), 1947; The Art of India and Pakistan (sections on bronzes and textiles), 1951, Shawls, 1955; Origins of Chintz, 1970; (with M. Hall) Indian Painted and Printed Fabrics, 1972; Indian Embroideries, 1974; articles in Encyclopædia Britannica, Chambers's Encyclopædia, Jl of Royal Asiatic Soc., Burlington Magazine, Artibus Asiae etc. *Recreations:* music, walking. *Address:* Apt 6, Park Court, Park Road, Petersfield, Hants GU32 3DL. *T:* Petersfield (0730) 66357.

IRWIN, Dr Michael Henry Knox; Adviser, ActionAid, since 1990; Director, Health Services Department, International Bank for Reconstruction and Development (World Bank), 1989–90; *b* 5 June 1931; *s* of late William Knox Irwin, FRCS and of Edith Isabel Mary Irwin; *m* 1st, 1958, Elizabeth Miriam (marr. diss. 1982), *d* of late John and Nancie Naumann; three *d*; 2nd, 1983, Frederica Todd Harlow, *d* of Frederick and Sarah Harlow. *Educ:* St Bartholomew's Hosp. Med. Coll., London (MB, BS 1955); Columbia Univ., New York (MPH 1960). House Phys. and House Surg., Prince of Wales' Hosp., London, 1955–56; MO, UN, 1957–61; Dep. Resident Rep., UN Technical Assistance Bd, Pakistan, 1961–63; MO, 1963–66, SMO, 1966–69, and Med. Dir, 1969–73, United Nations; Dir, Div. of Personnel, UNDP, 1973–76; UNICEF Rep., Bangladesh, 1977–80; Sen. Advr (Childhood Disabilities), UNICEF, 1980–82; Sen. Consultant, UN Internat. Year of Disabled Persons, 1981; Med. Dir, UN, UNICEF and UNDP, 1982–89. Pres., Assistance for Blind Children Internat., 1978–84. Consultant, Amer. Assoc. of Blood Banks, 1984–90. Mem. Editl Adv. Panel, Medicine and War, 1985–. FRSM. Officer Cross, Internat. Fedn of Blood Donor Organizations, 1984. *Publications:* Check-ups: safeguarding your health, 1961; Overweight: a problem for millions, 1964; Travelling without Tears, 1964; Viruses, Colds and Flu, 1966; Blood: new uses for saving lives, 1967; The Truth About Cancer, 1969; What Do We Know about Allergies?, 1972; A Child's Horizon, 1982; Aspirin: current knowledge about an old medication, 1983; Can We Survive Nuclear War?, 1984; Nuclear Energy: good or bad?, 1985; *novel:* Talpa, 1990. *Recreations:* travelling, writing. *Address:* 15 Hovedene, 95 Cromwell Road, Hove, Sussex BN3 3EH.

ISAAC, Alfred James; Director of Home Regional Services, Property Services Agency, Department of the Environment, 1971–75; *b* 1 Aug. 1919; *s* of Alfred Jabez Isaac and Alice Marie Isaac (both British); *m* 1943, Beryl Marjorie Rist; one *s* two *d. Educ:* Maidenhead Grammar Sch. Post Office Engineering Dept, 1936–49. Served War, RAFVR, Flt Lt (pilot), Coastal Command, 1941–46. Min. of Works, Asst Principal, 1949; Regional Dir, Southern Region, 1960–67; Dir of Professional Staff Management, 1967. Business Coordinator, Danbury Drilling Ltd, 1977–78; Chm. (part-time), Recruitment Bds, CS Commn, 1978–87. Vice-Chm., Bigbury Parish Council, 1987–91 (part-time Clerk, 1981–83). *Recreations:* 9 grandchildren, amateur radio. *Address:* Wave Crest, Marine Drive, Bigbury on Sea, Kingsbridge, Devon TQ7 4AS. *T:* Bigbury on Sea (0548) 810387. *Club:* Civil Service.

ISAAC, Anthony John Gower, CB 1985; a Deputy Chairman, Board of Inland Revenue, 1982–91 (a Commissioner of Inland Revenue, 1973–77 and 1979–91); *b* 21 Dec. 1931; *s* of Ronald and Kathleen Mary Gower Isaac; *m* 1963, Olga Elizabeth Sibley; one *s* two *d* (and two *d* decd). *Educ:* Malvern Coll.; King's Coll., Cambridge (BA). HM Treasury, 1953–70: Private Sec. to Chief Sec. to Treasury, 1964–66; Inland Revenue, 1971; on secondment to HM Treasury, 1976–78. *Recreations:* gardening, fishing.

ISAAC, James Keith, CBE 1985; FCIT; Chairman and Chief Executive, West Midlands Travel Ltd, since 1986; *b* 28 Jan. 1932; *s* of late Arthur Burton Isaac and of Doreen (*née* Davies); *m* 1957, Elizabeth Mary Roskell; two *d. Educ:* Leeds Grammar Sch. Mem., Inst. of Traffic Admin; FCIT 1978. Asst to Traffic Manager, Aldershot and Dist Traction Co. Ltd, 1958–59; Asst Traffic Man., Jamaica Omnibus Services Ltd, Kingston, Jamaica, 1959–64; Dep. Traffic Man., Midland Red (Birmingham and Midland Motor Omnibus Co. Ltd), Birmingham, 1965–67; Traffic Manager: North Western Road Car Co. Ltd, Stockport, Cheshire, 1967–69; Midland Red, Birmingham, 1969–73; Dir of Ops, 1973–77, Dir Gen., 1977–86, W Midlands Passenger Transp. Exec., Birmingham. Chm., Bus and Coach Services Ltd, 1986–90. Hon. Chm., Internat. Commn on Transport Economics, 1988– (Chm., 1981–88); Vice-Pres., Internat. Union of Public Transport, 1989–; President: Omnibus Soc., 1982; Bus and Coach Council, 1985–86; Mem. Council, CIT, 1982–85. *Recreations:* golf, walking, travel. *Address:* 24B Middlefield Lane, Hagley, Stourbridge, West Midlands DY9 0PX. *T:* Hagley (0562) 884757. *Clubs:* Army and Navy; Rotary of Hagley (Hereford/Worcester); Churchill and Blakedown Golf (near Kidderminster).

ISAAC, Maurice Laurence Reginald, MA; Headmaster, Latymer Upper School, Hammersmith, W6, 1971–88; *b* 26 April 1928; *s* of late Frank and Lilian Isaac; *m* 1954, Anne Fielden; three *d. Educ:* Selhurst Grammar Sch., Croydon; Magdalene Coll., Cambridge. BA Hist. Tripos, 1950; MA 1955, Cambridge; Certif. in Educn, 1952. Asst Master: Liverpool Collegiate Sch., 1952–56; Bristol Grammar Sch., 1956–62; Head of History, Colchester Royal Grammar Sch., 1962–65; Headmaster, Yeovil Sch., 1966–71. *Publications:* A History of Europe, 1870–1950, 1960; contributor to The Teaching of History, 1965. *Address:* Glebe House, Crowcombe, near Taunton, Somerset TA4 4AA. *T:* Crowcombe (09848) 230.

ISAAC, Prof. Peter Charles Gerald; Professor of Civil and Public Health Engineering, 1964–81, now Emeritus, and Head of Department of Civil Engineering, 1970–81, University of Newcastle upon Tyne; Partner, Watson Hawksley (consulting engineers), 1973–83; *b* 21 Jan. 1921; *s* of late Herbert George Isaac and Julienne Geneviève (*née* Hattenberger); *m* 1950, Marjorie Eleanor White; one *s* one *d. Educ:* Felsted Sch.; London and Harvard Universities. BSc(Eng), SM. Asst Engineer, GWR, 1940–45; Lecturer in Civil Engineering, 1946; Senior Lecturer in Public Health Engineering, 1953, Reader, 1960, Univ. of Durham; Dean of Faculty of Applied Science, Univ. of Newcastle upon Tyne, 1969–73; Sandars Reader in Bibliography, Univ. of Cambridge, 1983–84. Member: Working Party on Sewage Disposal, 1969–70; WHO Expert Adv. Panel on Environmental Health, 1976–87; specialist advr, House of Lords Select Cttee on Sci. and Technol. II (Hazardous Waste), 1980–81 and House of Lords Select Cttee on Sci. and Technol. I (Water), 1982; DoE Long-Term Water-Research Requirements Cttee. Chairman: History of the Book Trade in the North, 1965–; British Book Trade Index; Printing Historical Soc., 1989–91. Member of Council: ICE, 1968–71, 1972–75, 1977–80; Bibliographical Soc., 1970–74, 1979–83 (Hon. Editor of Monographs, 1982–89; Vice-Pres., 1984–); IPHE, 1973–87 (Pres., 1977–78); Pres., British Occupational Hygiene Soc., 1962–63; Mem. Bd, CEI, 1978–79. Trustee, Asian Inst. Technology, Bangkok, 1968–82 (Vice-Chm., 1979–82). Hon. Mem., Lit. and Philos. Soc., Newcastle upon Tyne. Director:

Thorne's Students' Bookshop Ltd, 1969–74; Environmental Resources Ltd, 1972–74. Freeman, Worshipful Co. of Stationers and Newspaper Makers, 1984, Liveryman, 1986. FSA; FICE, MIWM; Hon. FIPHE 1986. Clemens Herschel Prize in Applied Hydraulics, 1952; Telford Premium, 1957; Thomas Bedford Award, 1978; Gold Medal, IPHE, 1987. *Publications:* Electric Resistance Strain Gauges (with W. B. Dobie), 1948; Public Health Engineering, 1953; Trade Wastes, 1957; Waste Treatment, 1960; River Management, 1967; William Davison of Alnwick: pharmacist and printer, 1968; Farm Wastes, 1970; Civil Engineering-The University Contribution, 1970; Management in Civil Engineering, 1971; Davison's Halfpenny Chapbooks, 1971; (ed) The Burman Alnwick Collection, 1973; William Davison's New Specimen, 1990; Six Centuries of the Provincial Book Trade in Britain, 1990; contribs to various learned and technical jls. *Recreations:* bibliography, printing, Roman engineering. *Address:* 10 Woodcroft Road, Wylam, Northumberland NE41 8DJ. *T:* Wylam (0661) 853174. *Clubs:* Commonwealth Trust; Royal Scottish Automobile (Glasgow).

ISAAC, Rear-Adm. Robert Arthur, CB 1989; Director General Marine Engineering, Ministry of Defence (Procurement Executive), 1986–89; *b* 21 Feb. 1933; *s* of Frank and Florence Isaac; *m* 1960, Joy Little; one *s* one *d*. *Educ:* Oakham Sch.; Royal Naval Engrg Coll. (Dartmouth Special Entry). CEng, FIMechE, FIMarE. Entered RN, 1951; HMS Albion, 1957–59; HM Submarines Scotsman, Aurochs, nuclear trng, and HM Submarine Warspite, 1959–69; Dir Gen. Ships, MoD, 1970–74; HMS Blake, 1974–76; 2nd Sea Lord's Dept, MoD, 1976–78; Captain 1977; Naval Attaché, Tokyo and Seoul, 1979–81; Project Dir, Surface Ships, MoD (PE), 1981–84; HMS Thunderer, RNEC in comd, 1984–86; Rear-Adm. 1986. *Recreations:* sport, gardening. *Address:* c/o Lloyds Bank, 23 Milsom Street, Bath BA1 1DF. *Clubs:* Naval, Army and Navy.

ISAACS, family name of **Marquess of Reading.**

ISAACS, Dame Albertha Madeline, DBE 1974; former Senator, now worker for the community, in the Bahamas; *b* Nassau, Bahamas, 18 April 1900; *d* of late Robert Hanna and Lilla (*née* Minns); *m*; three *s* one *d*. *Educ:* Cosmopolitan High Sch. and Victoria High Sch., Nassau. Member: Progressive Liberal Party, Senator, 1968–72; also of PLP's Nat. Gen. Council, and of Council of Women. Mem. of a Good Samaritan Group.

ISAACS, Dr Anthony John; Senior Principal Medical Officer/Under Secretary, and Head, Medical Manpower and Education Division, Department of Health (formerly of Health and Social Security), since 1986; Hon. Consultant Physician (Endocrinology), University College and Middlesex Hospitals, since 1986; *b* 22 Oct. 1942; *s* of Benjamin H. Isaacs, BSc and Lily Isaacs (*née* Rogol); *m* 1st, 1971, Jill Kathleen Elek; three *s*; 2nd, 1986, Dr Edie Friedman; one *d*. *Educ:* Wanstead County High Sch.; Hertford Coll., Oxford (Open Exhibnr; Domus Scholar; BA Animal Physiology, 1st Cl. Hons 1965; MA 1968); Westminster Med. Sch. (Barron Schol.). BM, BCh 1968; MRCP 1971. House posts, Westminster, Whittington and Hammersmith Hosps, 1968–70; Med. Registrar, Westminster Hosp., 1971–73; Research Fellow (Endocrinology), Royal Free Hosp., 1973–75; Sen. Med. Registrar, Westminster Hosp., 1975–84; SMO, Medicines Div., DHSS, 1984–85, PMO, and Med. Assessor, Cttee on Safety of Medicines, 1985–86. Vice-Chm., Jt Planning Adv. Cttee, 1986–; Member: Steering Gp for Implementation of Achieving a Balance (and Co-Chm., Technical sub-gp), 1986–; 2nd Adv. Cttee on Med. Manpower Planning, 1986–89; Steering Gp on Undergrad. Med. Educn and Res., 1987– (Chm., Implementation Task Gp, 1989–90 and Working Gp, 1990–); Ministerial Gp on Junior Doctors' Hours, 1990–. Chm., New End Sch. PTA, 1983–85; Parent Governor, Hendon Sch., 1987–. FRSocMed (Mem., Endocrinology Section). *Publications:* Anorexia Nervosa (with P. Dally and J. Gomez), 1979; papers in med. jls on rheumatol and endocrinol topics. *Recreations:* music, cinema, table tennis, chess, travel. *Address:* 158–176 Portland Court, Great Portland Street, W1N 5TB. *T:* 071–872 9302.

ISAACS, Jeremy Israel; General Director, Royal Opera House, Covent Garden, since 1988 (Member, Board of Directors, since 1985); *b* 28 Sept. 1932; *s* of Isidore Isaacs and Sara Jacobs; *m* 1st, 1958, Tamara (*née* Weinreich) (*d* 1986), Cape Town; one *s* one *d*; 2nd, 1988, Gillian Mary Widdicombe. *Educ:* Glasgow Acad.; Merton Coll., Oxford (MA). Pres. of the Union, Hilary, 1955. Television Producer, Granada TV (What the Papers Say, All Our Yesterdays), 1958; Associated-Rediffusion (This Week), 1963; BBC TV (Panorama), 1965; Controller of Features, Associated Rediffusion, 1967; with Thames Television, 1968–78: Controller of Features, 1968–74; Producer, The World at War, 1974; Director of Programmes, 1974–78; Chief Exec., Channel Four TV Co., 1981–87; TV programmes: A Sense of Freedom, STV; Ireland, a Television History, BBC. Dir, Open College, 1987–. Governor, BFI, 1979– (Chm., BFI Production Bd, 1979–81). James MacTaggart Meml Lectr, Edinburgh TV Fest., 1979. FRSA 1983; Fellow: BAFTA, 1985; BFI, 1986; FRSAMD 1989; FGSM 1989. Hon. DLitt: Strathclyde, 1984; CNAA, 1987; Bristol, 1988. Desmond Davis Award for outstanding creative contrib. to television, 1972; George Polk Meml Award, 1973; Cyril Bennett Award for outstanding contrib. to television programming, RTS, 1982; Lord Willis Award for Distinguished Service to Television, 1985; Directorate Award, Internat. Council of Nat. Acad. of TV Arts and Scis, NY, 1987; Lifetime Achievement Award, Banff, 1988. Commandeur de l'Ordre des Arts et des Lettres (France), 1988. *Publication:* Storm over Four: a personal account, 1989. *Recreations:* reading, walking. *Address:* Royal Opera House, 45 Floral Street, WC2.

ISAACS, Stuart Lindsay; QC 1991; *b* 8 April 1952; *s* of Stanley Leslie Isaacs and Marquette Isaacs. *Educ:* Haberdashers' Aske's Sch., Elstree; Downing Coll., Cambridge (Law, Double 1st cl. Hons); Univ. Libre de Bruxelles (License spécial en droit européen, grande distinction). Called to the Bar, Lincoln's Inn, 1975; admitted NY Bar, 1985. *Publications:* EEC Banking Law, 1985, 2nd edn 1991; Banking and the Competition Law of the EEC, 1978; (Consultant Editor) Butterworth's EC Case Citator, 1991; (contrib.) Commentary on the EEC Treaty, 1991. *Recreations:* travel, languages. *Address:* 4–5 Gray's Inn Square, Gray's Inn, WC1R 5AY. *T:* 071–404 5252, *Fax:* 071–242 7803. *Club:* St James's.

ISAAMAN, Gerald Michael; journalist; Editor, Hampstead and Highgate Express, since 1968; *b* 22 Dec. 1933; *s* of Asher Isaaman and Lily Finklestein; *m* 1962, Delphine Walker, *e d* of Cecile and Arnold Walker; one *s*. *Educ:* Dame Alice Owens Grammar School. Reporter, North London Observer Series, 1950, Hampstead and Highgate Express, 1955. Founder Trustee, Arkwright Arts Trust, 1971; Chairman: Camden Arts Trust Management Board, 1970–82; Exhibns Cttee, Camden Arts Centre, 1971–82; Russell Housing Soc., 1976–82; Trustees, King's Cross Disaster Fund, 1987–89; Member: Camden Festival Trust, 1982–; Council, Assoc. of British Editors, 1985–. *Recreations:* cooking breakfast, listening to jazz, work. *Address:* 9 Lyndhurst Road, NW3. *T:* 071–794 3950.

ISEPP, Martin Johannes Sebastian; Head of Music Studies, National Opera Studio, since 1979; Head of Music Staff, Glyndebourne Festival Opera, since 1973; Head of Academy of Singing, Banff School of Fine Arts, Alberta, Canada, since 1982; *b* Vienna, 30 Sept. 1930; *s* of Sebastian and Helene Isepp; *m* 1966, Rose Henrietta Harris; two *s*. *Educ:* St Paul's Sch.; Lincoln Coll., Oxford; Royal Coll. of Music, London (ARCM 1952). Studied piano with Prof. Leonie Gombrich, 1939–52. English Opera Gp, 1954–57; Glyndebourne Fest. Opera, 1957–; Head of Opera Trng Dept, Juilliard Sch. of Music, New York, 1973–78. As accompanist, began career accompanying mother, Helene Isepp (the singer and voice teacher); has accompanied many of the world's leading singers and instrumentalists, notably Elisabeth Schwarzkopf, Elisabeth Söderström, Janet Baker and John Shirley-Quirk; harpsichordist with Handel Opera Soc. of New York in most of their Handel Festivals, 1966–; master classes in opera and song at Amer. univs, incl. Southern Calif, Ann Arbor and Colorado, 1975–; coached Peking Opera and Peking Conservatory in Mozart operas, 1983. As conductor: Le Nozze di Figaro, Glyndebourne Touring Op., 1984; Don Giovanni, Glyndebourne Touring Op., 1986; Abduction from the Seraglio, Washington Op., 1986–87. Carroll Donner Stuchell Medal for Accompanists, Harriet Cohen Internat. Musical Foundn, 1965. *Recreations:* photography, walking. *Address:* 37A Steele's Road, NW3 4RG. *T:* 071–722 3085.

ISHAM, Sir Ian (Vere Gyles), 13th Bt *cr* 1627; *b* 17 July 1923; *s* of Lt-Col Vere Arthur Richard Isham, MC (*d* 1968) and Edith Irene (*d* 1973), *d* of Harry Brown; *S* cousin, Sir Gyles Isham, 12th Bt, 1976. Served War of 1939–45, Captain RAC. *Heir:* *b* Norman Murray Crawford Isham, OBE [*b* 28 Jan. 1930; *m* 1956, Joan, *d* of late Leonard James Genet; two *s* one *d*]. *Address:* 40 Turnpike Link, Croydon, Surrey CR0 5NX.

ISHIGURO, Kazuo, FRSL; author; *b* 8 Nov. 1954; *s* of Shizuo and Shizuko Ishiguro; *m* 1986, Lorna Anne MacDougall. *Educ.* Univ. of Kent (BA English/Philosophy); Univ. of East Anglia (MA Creative Writing). Began publishing short stories, articles, in magazines, 1980; writer of TV plays, 1984–. FRSL 1989. FRSA. Hon. DLitt Kent, 1990. *Publications:* A Pale View of Hills, 1982 (Winifred Holtby Prize, RSL); An Artist of the Floating World, 1986 (Whitbread Book of the Year, Whitbread Fiction Prize); The Remains of the Day, 1989 (Booker Prize). *Recreations:* music; playing piano and guitar. *Address:* c/o Faber & Faber, 3 Queen Square, WC1N 3AU.

ISHIHARA, Takashi, Hon. KBE 1990; Chairman: Nissan Motor Co., Ltd, since 1985; Nissan Motor Manufacturing Corporation, USA, 1980–82; *b* 3 March 1912; *s* of Ichiji and Shigeyo Ishihara; *m* 1943, Shizuko Nakajo; one *s*. *Educ:* Law Dept, Tohoku Univ. (grad 1937). Joined Nissan Motor Co., Ltd, 1937; promoted to Gen. Man. of Planning and Accounting Depts respectively; Dir of Finance and Accounting, 1954; Man. Dir, 1963; Exec. Man. Dir, 1969; Exec. Vice Pres., 1973; Pres., 1977; Pres., Nissan Motor Corpn in USA, 1960–65. Exec. Dir, Keidanren (Fedn of Econ. Orgns), 1977–; Chm., Keizai Doyukai (Japan Assoc. of Corporate Execs), 1985–; Dir, Nikkeiren (Japan Fedn of Employers Assocs), 1978–; President: Japan Automobile Manufacturers Assoc., Inc., 1980–86; Japan Motor Industrial Fedn, Inc., 1980–86. Hon. DCL Durham. Blue Ribbon Medal (Japan), 1974; First Order of Sacred Treasure (Japan), 1983; Grand Cross (Spain), 1985. *Recreations:* reading, golf, ocean cruising. *Address:* Nissan Motor Co., 17–1 Ginza 6–chome, Chuo-ku, Tokyo 104, Japan; 20–3, 2–chome, Shiroganedai, Minato-ku, Tokyo 108, Japan.

ISLE OF WIGHT, Archdeacon of; *see* Turner, Ven. A. H. M.

ISLES, Maj.-Gen. Donald Edward, CB 1978; OBE 1968; DL; *b* 19 July 1924; *s* of Harold and Kathleen Isles; *m* 1948, Sheila Mary Stephens (formerly Thorpe); three *s* one *d*. *Educ:* Roundhay; Leeds Univ.; RMCS. MRAeS; FBIM. Italian campaign, with 1st Bn, Duke of Wellington's Regt, 1944–45; Palestine, Egypt, Sudan, Syria, with 1DWR, 1945–47; GSO2, HQ BAOR, 1955–58; Asst Mil. Attaché, Paris, 1963–65; CO, 1DWR, BAOR and UN Forces in Cyprus, 1965–67; AMS, MoD, 1968; Col GS, MoD, 1968–71; Col GS, RARDE, 1971–72; Dir of Munitions, Brit. Defence Staff Washington, 1972–75; Dir-Gen. Weapons (Army), 1975–78, retired. Dep. Man. Dir, British Manufacture & Res. Co., 1979–89. Col, The Duke of Wellington's Regt, 1975–82; Col Comdt, The King's Div., 1975–79; Vice-Chm., Yorks and Humberside TA&VRA, 1984–87. Hon. Colonel: 3rd Bn, The Yorkshire Volunteers, 1977–83; Leeds Univ. OTC, 1985–90. Mem., Court, Leeds Univ., 1987–. DL Lincs, 1990. *Recreations:* tennis, squash. *Clubs:* Army and Navy, MCC.

ISMAY, Walter Nicholas; Managing Director, Worcester Parsons Ltd, 1975–82, retired; *b* 20 June 1921; *s* of late John Ismay, Maryport, Cumberland. *Educ:* Taunton's Sch., Southampton; King's Coll., University of London (BSc). Royal Aircraft Establishment, 1939–40; Ministry of Supply, 1940–43; Served Army (Capt., General List), 1943–46; Imperial Chemical Industries, Metals Division, 1948–58 (Technical Dir, 1957–58); Dir, Yorkshire Imperial Metals, 1958–67; Dep. Chm. Yorkshire Imperial Plastics, 1966–67; Dep. Chm. and Man. Dir, Milton Keynes Develt Corp., 1967–71; McKechnie Britain Ltd, 1972–75. FIMechE. *Recreation:* sailing. *Address:* Pitlundie, Monument Lane, Walhampton, Lymington, Hampshire SO41 5SE. *T:* Lymington (0590) 673032. *Club:* Royal Lymington Yacht.

ISOLANI, Casimiro Peter Hugh Tomasi, CBE 1975 (OBE 1960; MBE 1945); LVO 1961; HM Diplomatic Service, retired; *b* 2 Sept. 1917; *s* of late Umberto Tomasi Isolani, Bologna, and late Georgiana Eleanor Lyle-Smyth, Great Barrow, Ches; *m* 1943, Karin Gunni Signe Zetterström, *d* of Henry Zetterström, Gothenburg; one *s*. *Educ:* Aldenham Sch.; Clare Coll., Cambridge; Major open schol., 1936, 1st cl. Mod. and Med. Lang. Tripos 1; Senior Foundn schol., 1937; BA 1939. Commnd RA 1940, Intell. Corps 1941; attached 1st Canadian Div., 1943 (Sicily, Italy landings); Psychol Warfare Br., 1944; GS1 (Civil Liaison, Liaison Italian Resistance), 1945; Hon. Partisan, Veneto Corpo Volontari della Liberta; FO 1946; Vice-Consul, Bologna, 1946; Attaché, later 1st Sec. (Information), British Embassy, Rome, 1947–61; resigned Foreign Service; Dep. Dir, Inst. for Strategic Studies, 1961–63; rejoined Foreign Service; Regional Information Officer, Paris, 1963–72; Counsellor (Information), British Embassy (and UK delegn NATO and UK Representation, EEC), Brussels, 1972–77. United Nations University: Rep. (Europe), 1978–85; Sen. Consultant, 1985–87. *Address:* 44 Pont Street, SW1X 0AD. *T:* 071–584 1543. *Clubs:* Anglo-Belgian, Special Forces.

ISRAEL, Rev. Dr Martin Spencer, FRCPath; Priest-in-Charge, Holy Trinity with All Saints Church, South Kensington, since 1983; *b* 30 April 1927; *s* of Elie Benjamin Israel, ophthalmic surgeon, and Minnie Israel. *Educ:* Parktown Boys' High Sch.; Johannesburg; Univ. of the Witwatersrand (MB ChB). MRCP 1952, FRCPath 1972. Ho. Phys., Hammersmith Hosp., 1952; Registrar in Pathology, Royal Hosp., Wolverhampton, 1953–55; service in RAMC, 1955–57; Lectr and Sen. Lectr in Pathology, 1958–82, Hon. Sen. Lectr 1982–, RCS. Ordained priest in C of E, 1975. President: Guild of Health, 1983–90; Churches' Fellowship for Psychical and Spiritual Studies, 1983–. *Publications:* *medical:* General Pathology (with J. B. Walter), 1963, 6th edn 1987; *spiritual matters:* Summons to Life, 1974; Precarious Living, 1976; Smouldering Fire, 1978; The Pain that Heals, 1981; Living Alone, 1982; The Spirit of Counsel, 1983; Healing as Sacrament, 1984; The Discipline of Love, 1985; Coming in Glory, 1986; Gethsemane, 1987; The Pearl of Great Price, 1988; The Dark Face of Reality, 1989; The Quest for Wholeness, 1989; Creation, 1989; Night Thoughts, 1990; A Light on the Path, 1990. *Recreations:* music, conversation. *Address:* Flat 2, 26 Tregunter Road, SW10 9LH. *T:* 071–370 5160.

ISRAEL, Prof. Werner, FRS 1986; Professor of Physics, since 1972, University Professor, since 1985, University of Alberta; *b* 4 Oct. 1931; *s* of Arthur Israel and Marie Kappauf;

m 1958, Inge Margulies; one *s* one *d*. *Educ*: Cape Town High Sch.; Univ. of Cape Town (BSc 1951, MSc 1954); Dublin Inst. for Advanced Studies; Trinity Coll., Dublin (PhD 1960). Lectr in Applied Maths, Univ. of Cape Town, 1954–56; Asst Prof., 1958, Associate Prof., 1964, Prof. of Maths, 1968–71, Univ. of Alberta. Sherman Fairchild Dist. Schol., CIT, 1974–75; Vis. Prof., Dublin Inst. for Advanced Studies, 1966–68; Sen. Visitor, Dept of Applied Maths and Theoretical Physics, Univ. of Cambridge, 1975–76; Maître de Recherche Associé, Inst. Henri Poincaré, Paris, 1976–77; Vis. Prof., Berne, 1980, Kyoto, 1986; Vis. Fellow, Gonville and Caius Coll., Cambridge, 1985. Fellow, Canadian Inst. for Advanced Research, 1986–. Hon. DSc Queen's, Kingston, Ont., 1987. *Publications*: (ed) Relativity, Astrophysics and Cosmology, 1973; (ed with S. W. Hawking) General Relativity: an Einstein centenary survey, 1979; (ed with S. W. Hawking) 300 Years of Gravitation, 1987; numerous papers on black hole physics, general relativity, relativistic statistical mechanics. *Recreation*: music. *Address*: Avadh Bhatia Physics Laboratory, University of Alberta, Edmonton, Alberta T6G 2J1, Canada. *T*: (403) 492–3552.

ISRAELACHVILI, Prof. Jacob Nissim, FRS 1988; FAA; Professor of Chemical Engineering and Materials Science, Department of Chemical and Nuclear Engineering and Materials Department, University of California, Santa Barbara, since 1986; *b* 19 Aug. 1944; *s* of Haim and Hela Israelachvili; *m* 1971, Karina (*née* Haglund); two *d*. *Educ*: Univ. of Cambridge (MA; PhD 1972). FAA 1982. Post-doctoral res. into surface forces, Cavendish Lab., Cambridge, 1971–72; EMBO Res. Fellow, Biophysics Inst., Univ. of Stockholm, 1972–74; Res. Fellow, subseq. Professorial Fellow, Res. Sch. of Physical Scis, Inst. of Advanced Studies, ANU, Canberra, 1974–86. Council Mem., 1983–87, Vice-Pres., 1986–87, Internat. Assoc. of Colloid and Interface Scientists. Pawsey Medal, 1977, Matthew Flinders Lectr medallist, 1986, Aust. Acad. of Sci.; (jtly) David Syme Res. Prize, 1983. *Publications*: Intermolecular and Surface Forces: with applications to colloidal and biological systems, 1985; about 90 pubns in learned jls, incl. Nature, Science, Procs Royal Soc. *Recreations*: history, backgammon. *Address*: 2233 Foothill Lane, Santa Barbara, California 93105, USA. *T*: (residence) (805) 963 9545, (office) (805) 893 8407.

ISSERLIS, Steven; 'cellist; *b* 19 Dec. 1958; *s* of George and Cynthia Isserlis; lives with Pauline Mara; one *s*. *Educ*: City of London School; International 'Cello Centre; Oberlin College. London recital début, Wigmore Hall, 1977; London concerto début, with English Chamber Orchestra, 1980; concerts in Europe, N America, Australia, 1978–; tours in USSR, 1984–; débuts with Minnesota, Chicago, Boston, Montréal Orchestras, 1990; numerous recordings. *Recreations*: talking on the telephone, eating too much, regretting it, watching videos, Twin Peaks, cinema, literature, sleeping. *Address*: c/o Harrison & Parrott, 12 Penzance Place, W11 4PA. *T*: 071–229 9166.

ISTEAD, Maj.-Gen. Peter Walter Ernest, CB 1989; OBE 1978; GM 1966; Chief Executive, Institute of Brewing, since 1990; *b* 7 Aug. 1935; *s* of Walter and Marie Istead; *m* 1961, Jennifer Mary Swinson; one *s* one *d*. *Educ*: Whitgift Trinity Sch., Croydon. Enlisted as boy soldier into Scots Guards, 1952; commnd Queen's Royal Regt, 1954; seconded to KAR, 1954–56; transf. RAOC, 1957; HQ 16 Parachute Bde, 1958–62; sc 1968; Directing Staff, Staff Coll., Camberley, 1971–73; DCS, 4 Armd Div., 1978–81; RCDS, 1982; Dir, Admin. Planning (Army), 1983–86; Comdr Supply, BAOR, 1986–87; Dir Gen., Logistic Policy (Army), 1987–90. Hon. Col Comdt, RAOC, 1989–. FBIM. Freeman, City of London, 1986; Liveryman, Co. of Gold and Silver Wyre Drawers, 1990. *Recreations*: angling, squash. *Address*: Wandsworth, London. *Clubs*: Naval and Military, Special Forces.

IVAMY, Prof. Edward Richard Hardy; Professor of Law, University of London, 1960–86, now Emeritus; *b* 1 Dec. 1920; *o s* of late Edward Wadham Ivamy and late Florence Ivamy; *m* 1965, Christine Ann Frances, *o d* of William and Frances Culver; one *s*. *Educ*: Malvern Coll.; University Coll., London. Served War of 1939–45, RA: 67 Field Regt, N Africa, Italy and Middle East; 2nd Lieut 1942; Temp. Capt. 1945; Staff Capt., GHQ, Cairo, 1946. LLB (1st cl. hons) 1947; PhD 1953; LLD 1967. Barrister, Middle Temple, 1949. University Coll., London: Asst Lectr in Laws, 1947–50; Lectr, 1950–56; Reader in Law, 1956–60; Dean of Faculty of Laws, 1964 and 1965; Fellow, 1969. Hon. Sec., Soc. of Public Teachers of Law, 1960–63; Hon. Sec., Bentham Club, 1953–58; Governor, Malvern Coll., 1982–; Mem. Editorial Board: Jl of Business Law; Lloyd's Maritime and Commercial Law Quarterly; Law for Business; Consulting Editor: Banking Law Reports; Reinsurance Law Reports. *Publications*: Show Business and the Law, 1955; (ed) Payne and Ivamy's Carriage of Goods by Sea, 7th edn 1963–13th edn, 1989; Hire-Purchase Legislation in England and Wales, 1965; Casebook on Carriage of Goods by Sea, 1965 (6th edn, 1985); Casebook on Sale of Goods, 1966 (5th edn, 1987); (ed) Chalmers's Marine Insurance Act 1906, 6th edn, 1966–9th edn, 1983; General Principles of Insurance Law, 1966 (5th edn, 1985); (ed) Topham and Ivamy's Company Law, 13th edn, 1967–16th edn, 1978; Casebook on Commercial Law, 1967 (3rd edn, 1979); Fire and Motor Insurance, 1968 (4th edn, 1984); Casebook on Insurance Law, 1969 (4th edn, 1984); Marine Insurance, 1969 (4th edn, 1985); Casebook on Shipping Law, 1970 (4th edn, 1987); Casebook on Partnership, 1970 (2nd edn, 1982); Casebook on Agency, 1971 (3rd edn, 1987); Personal Accident, Life and Other Insurances, 1973 (2nd edn, 1980); (ed) Underhill's Partnership, 10th edn, 1975, 12th edn, 1985; (ed) Halsbury's Laws of England, 4th edn, 1978, vol. 25 (Insurance), 1977, vol. 43 (Shipping and Navigation), 1983; Dictionary of Insurance Law, 1981; Dictionary of Company Law, 1983, 2nd edn, 1985; Insurance Law Handbook, 1983; Dictionary of Shipping Law, 1984; Encyclopaedia of Shipping Law Sources (UK), 1985; Encyclopedia of Oil and Natural Gas Law, 1986; Encyclopedia of Carriage Law Sources, 1987; Merchant Shipping (Liner Conferences) Act 1982, 1987; Merchant Shipping Act 1970, 1987; Merchant Shipping Act 1979, 1987; (ed) Mozley and Whiteley's Law Dictionary, 10th edn 1988; contrib. to Encyclopædia Britannica, Chambers's Encyclopædia, Current Legal Problems, Jl of Business Law; Annual Survey of Commonwealth Law, 1967–77. *Recreations*: railways, cricket, tennis. *Address*: 7 Egliston Mews, SW15 1AP. *T*: 081–785 6718.

IVEAGH, 3rd Earl of, cr 1919; Arthur Francis Benjamin Guinness; Bt 1885; Baron Iveagh 1891; Viscount Iveagh 1905; Viscount Elveden 1919; Member, Seanad Eireann, 1973–77; President, Guinness PLC; *b* 20 May 1937; *o s* of Viscount Elveden (killed in action, 1945) and Lady Elizabeth Hare (*d* 1990), *yr d* of 4th Earl of Listowel; *S* grandfather, 1967; *m* 1963, Miranda Daphne Jane (marr. diss. 1984), *d* of Major Michael Smiley, Castle Fraser, Aberdeenshire; two *s* two *d*. *Educ*: Eton; Trinity Coll., Cambridge; Univ. of Grenoble. *Heir*: *s* Viscount Elveden, *qv*. *Address*: St James's Gate, Dublin 8. *Clubs*: White's; Royal Yacht Squadron (Cowes); Kildare Street and University (Dublin).

IVENS, Michael William, CBE 1983; Director, Aims of Industry, since 1971; Director of the Foundation for Business Responsibilities, since 1967; *b* 15 March 1924; *s* of Harry Guest Ivens and Nina Ailion; *m* 1st, 1950, Rosalie Turnbull (marr. diss. 1971); three *s* one *d*; 2nd, 1971, Katherine Laurence; two *s*. Jt Editor, Twentieth Century, 1967; Vice-Pres., Junior Hosp. Doctors Assoc., 1969; Director: Standard Telephone, 1970; Working Together Campaign, 1972–73. Jt Founder and Vice-Pres., Freedom Assoc.; Jt Founder and Trustee, Foundn for the Study of Terrorism, 1986; Member: Council, Efficiency in Local Govt, 1983–; Adv. Bd, US Industrial Council Educn Foundn, 1980–; Council and Hon. Treas., Poetry Soc., 1989–. *Publications*: Practice of Industrial Communication, 1963; Case Studies in Management, 1964; Case Studies in Human Relations, 1966; Case for Capitalism, 1967; Industry and Values, 1970; Which Way?, 1970; Prophets of Freedom and Enterprise, 1975; (ed jtly) Bachman's Book of Freedom Quotes, 1978; *poetry*: Another Sky, 1963; Last Waltz, 1964; Private and Public, 1968; Born Early, 1975; No Woman is an Island, 1983; New Divine Comedy, 1990; columns and articles under pseudonym Yorick. *Recreation*: campaigning. *Address*: 40 Doughty Street, WC1N 2LF. *T*: 071–405 5195. *Clubs*: Carlton, Wig and Pen, Arts.

IVERSEN, Leslie Lars, PhD; FRS 1980; Director, Merck, Sharp & Dohme Neuroscience Research Centre, Harlow, Essex, since 1982; *b* 31 Oct. 1937; *s* of Svend Iversen and Anna Caia Iversen; *m* 1961, Susan Diana (*née* Kibble); one *s* one *d* (and one *d* decd). *Educ*: Trinity Coll., Cambridge (BA Biochem, PhD Pharmacol). Harkness Fellow, United States: with Dr J. Axelrod, Nat. Inst. of Mental Health, and Dr E. Kravitz, Dept of Neurobiology, Harvard Med. Sch., 1964–66; Fellow, Trinity Coll., Cambridge, 1964–84; Locke Research Fellow of Royal Society, Dept of Pharmacology, Univ. of Cambridge, 1967–71; Dir, MRC Neurochemical Pharmacology Unit, Cambridge, 1971–82. Foreign Associate, Nat. Acad. of Scis (USA), 1986. *Publications*: The Uptake and Storage of Noradrenaline in Sympathetic Nerves, 1967; (with S. D. Iversen) Behavioural Pharmacology, 1975, 2nd edn 1981. *Recreations*: reading, gardening. *Address*: Merck, Sharp & Dohme Neuroscience Research Centre, Terlings Park, Eastwick Road, near Harlow, Essex CM20 2QR.

IVES, Arthur Glendinning Loveless, CVO 1954 (MVO 1945); *b* 19 Aug. 1904; *s* of late Rev. E. J. Ives, Wesleyan Minister; *m* 1929, Doris Marion (*d* 1987), *d* of Thomas Coke Boden; three *s* one *d*. *Educ*: Kingswood Sch.; Queen's Coll., Oxford (classical scholar); MA. George Webb Medley Junior Scholarship for Economics, Oxford Univ., 1926. London Chamber of Commerce, 1928–29; joined staff of King Edward's Hosp. Fund for London, 1929; Sec., 1938–60; retired 1960. Seriously injured in railway accident at Lewisham, Dec. 1957. A Governor of Kingswood Sch., 1954–72. *Publications*: British Hospitals (Britain in Pictures), 1948; Kingswood School in Wesley's Day and Since, 1970; contrib. to The Times, Lancet, etc, on hospital administration and allied topics. *Address*: The Cedars, Bordyke, Tonbridge, Kent. *Club*: Athenæum.
See also Rev. A. K. Lloyd.

IVES, Prof. Kenneth James, FEng 1986; FICE; Chadwick Professor of Civil Engineering, University College London, since 1984; *b* 29 Nov. 1926; *s* of Walter Ives and Grace Ives (*née* Curson); *m* 1952, Brenda Grace Tilley; one *s* one *d*. *Educ*: William Ellis Grammar School, London; University College London. BSc Eng, PhD, DSc Eng. Junior Engineer, Metropolitan Water Board, London, 1948–55; Lectr, Reader, Prof., University Coll. London, 1955–. Research Fellow, Harvard Univ., 1958–59; Visiting Professor: Univ. of North Carolina, 1964; Delft Technical Univ., 1977; Consultant Expert Adviser, WHO, 1966–. Gans Medal, Soc. for Water Treatment, 1966; Gold Medal, Filtration Soc. Internat, 1983; Jenkins Medal, IAWPRC, 1990. *Publications*: Scientific Basis of Filtration, 1975; Scientific Basis of Flocculation, 1978; Scientific Basis of Flotation, 1984; contribs to sci. and eng. jls on water purification. *Recreations*: squash, ballroom dancing. *Address*: Department of Civil and Municipal Engineering, University College London, Gower Street, WC1E 6BT. *T*: 071–380 7224.

IVISON, David Malcolm; Chief Executive, Institute of Road Transport Engineers, 1985–89; *b* 22 March 1936; *s* of John and Ruth Ellen Ivison; *m* 1961, Lieselotte Verse; one *s* one *d*. *Educ*: King Edward VI School, Lichfield; RMA Sandhurst; Staff College, Camberley. Army, Gurkha Transport Regt, 1955–83 (Lt-Col). Tate & Lyle, 1984–85. *Recreations*: learning languages, tennis, reading. *Address*: 1 Dundaff Close, Camberley, Surrey GU15 1AF. *T*: Camberley (0276) 27778.

IVORY, Brian Gammell, CA; Managing Director, The Highland Distilleries Co. plc, since 1988; *b* 10 April 1949; *s* of late Eric James Ivory and Alice Margaret Joan, *d* of Sir Sydney James Gammell; *m* 1981, Oona Mairi MacPhie, *d* of late Archibald Ian Bell-MacDonald; one *s* one *d*. *Educ*: Eton College; Magdalene College, Cambridge (MA). Director: The Highland Distilleries Co., 1978–; Matthew Gloag & Son, 1987–. Scottish Arts Council: Mem., 1983–; Chm., Combined Arts Cttee, 1984–88; Vice-Chm., 1988–; Mem., Arts Council of GB, 1988–. *Recreations*: the arts, farming, hill walking. *Address*: Brewlands, Glenisla, by Blairgowrie, Perthshire PH11 8PL. *T*: Glenisla (057582) 230. *Clubs*: New (Edinburgh); Royal Scottish Automobile (Glasgow).

IVORY, James Francis; film director; Partner in Merchant Ivory Productions, since 1961; *b* 7 June 1928; *s* of Edward Patrick Ivory and Hallie Millicent De Loney. *Educ*: Univ. of Oregon (BA Fine Arts); Univ. of Southern California (MFA Cinema). Guggenheim Fellow, 1974. Collaborator with Ruth Prawer Jhabvala and Ismail Merchant on the following films: The Householder, 1963; Shakespeare Wallah, 1965; The Guru, 1969; Bombay Talkie, 1970; Autobiography of a Princess, 1975; Roseland, 1977; Hullabaloo over Georgie and Bonnie's Pictures, 1978; The Europeans, 1979; Jane Austen in Manhattan, 1980; Quartet, 1981; Heat and Dust, 1983; The Bostonians, 1984; A Room With a View, 1986; Mr and Mrs Bridge, 1991; collaborator with Ismail Merchant (producer) on: (with Nirad Chaudhuri) Adventures of a Brown Man in Search of Civilization, 1971; (with George W. S. Trow and Michael O'Donoghue) Savages, 1972; (with Walter Marks) The Wild Party, 1975; (with Kit Hesketh-Harvey) Maurice, 1987; (with Tama Janowitz) Slaves of New York, 1989; other films: (with Terence McNally) The Five Forty Eight, 1979; documentaries: Venice, Theme and Variations, 1957; The Sword and the Flute, 1959; The Delhi Way, 1964. *Publication*: Autobiography of a Princess (Also Being the Adventures of an American Film Director in the Land of the Maharajas), 1975. *Recreation*: looking at pictures. *Address*: Patroon Street, Claverack, New York 12513, USA. *T*: 518 851 7808.

J

JACK, Hon. Sir Alieu (Sulayman), Grand Commander, 1972, and Chancellor, 1972–83, National Order of The Gambia; Kt 1970; Speaker, House of Representatives of the Republic of The Gambia, 1962–72, and 1977–83, retired; *b* 14 July 1922; *m* 1946, Yai Marie Cham; four *s* four *d* (and one *d* decd). *Educ:* St Augustine's School. Entered Gambia Civil Service, 1939; resigned and took up local appt with NAAFI, 1940–44; Civil Service, 1945–48; entered commerce, 1948; Man. Dir, Gambia National Trading Co. Ltd, 1948–72. Mem., Bathurst City Council, 1949–62. Minister for Works and Communications, The Gambia, 1972–77. Represented The Gambia Parlt at various internat. gatherings. Comdr, National Order of Senegal, 1967; Comdr, Order of Merit of Mauritania, 1967; Commander, Order of Fed. Republic of Nigeria, 1970; Kt Grand Band, Liberia, 1977. *Recreation:* golf. *Address:* PO Box 376, Banjul, The Gambia. *T:* (home) 92204, (office) 28431. *Club:* Bathurst (Banjul).

JACK, Sir David (Emmanuel), GCMG 1991; MBE 1975; Governor General, St Vincent and The Grenadines, since 1989; *b* 16 July 1918; *s* of John Fitzroy Jack and Margaret Lewis Jack; *m* 1946, Esther Veronica McKay; two *s* two *d* (and one *s* decd). *Educ:* Stubbs Govt School; La Salle Univ., Chicago (Dip. Higher Accountancy). Teacher's Cert., St Vincent Educn Dept. School Teacher, 1934–43; Engine Operator, Shell Oil Refinery, 1943–45; Commercial Accounting, 1945–69; Gen. Manager, A'Root Ind., 1969–79; in business and politics, 1979–84; elected to Parliament, 1984; Minister, 1984–89. Methodist local preacher, 1940–. *Recreations:* carpentry, music. *Address:* Government House, Montrose, St Vincent and The Grenadines. *T:* 61401.

JACK, David M.; *see* Morton Jack.

JACK, Prof. Ian Robert James, FBA 1986; Professor of English Literature, University of Cambridge, 1976–89; Fellow of Pembroke College, Cambridge, 1961–89, now Emeritus; *b* 5 Dec. 1923; *s* of John McGregor Bruce Jack, WS, and Helena Colburn Buchanan; *m* 1st, 1948, Jane Henderson MacDonald; two *s* one *d*; 2nd, 1972, Margaret Elizabeth Crone; one *s*. *Educ:* George Watson's Coll. (John Welsh Classical Schol., 1942); Univ. of Edinburgh (James Boswell Fellow, 1946; MA 1947); Merton Coll., Oxford (DPhil 1950); LittD Cantab 1973. Brasenose College, Oxford: Lectr in Eng. Lit., 1950–55; Sen. Res. Fellow, 1955–61; Cambridge University: Lectr in English, 1961–73; Reader in English Poetry, 1973–76; Librarian, Pembroke Coll., 1965–75. Vis. Professor: Alexandria, 1960; Chicago (Carpenter Prof.), 1968–69; California at Berkeley, 1968–69; British Columbia, 1975; Virginia, 1980–81; Tsuda Coll., Tokyo, 1981; New York Univ. (Berg Prof.), 1989; de Carle Lectr, Univ. of Otago, 1964; Warton Lectr in English Poetry, British Acad., 1967; Guest Speaker, Nichol Smith Seminar, ANU, 1976; Guest Speaker, 50th anniversary meeting of English Literary Soc. of Japan, 1978; numerous lecture-tours for British Council and other bodies. President: Charles Lamb Soc., 1970–80; Browning Soc., 1980–83; Johnson Soc., Lichfield, 1986–87; Vice-Pres., Brontë Soc., 1973–. *Publications:* Augustan Satire, 1952; English Literature 1815–1832 (Vol. X, Oxf. Hist. of Eng. Lit.), 1963; Keats and the Mirror of Art, 1967; Browning's Major Poetry, 1973; The Poet and his Audience, 1984; *edited:* Sterne: A Sentimental Journey, etc, 1968; Browning: Poetical Works 1833–1864, 1970; (with Hilda Marsden) Emily Brontë: Wuthering Heights, 1976; general editor: Brontë novels (Clarendon edn); The Poetical Works of Browning, vols 1–4, 1983–91; contrib. TLS, RES, etc. *Recreations:* collecting books, travelling hopefully, thinking about words. *Address:* Highfield House, High Street, Fen Ditton, Cambridgeshire CB5 8ST. *T:* Teversham (02205) 2697; Pembroke College, Cambridge CB2 1RF. *Club:* MCC.

JACK, (John) Michael, MP (C) Fylde, since 1987; Parliamentary Under-Secretary of State, Department of Social Security, since 1990; *b* 17 Sept. 1946; *m* 1976, Alison Jane Musgrave; two *s*. *Educ:* Bradford Grammar Sch.; Bradford Tech. Coll.; Leicester Univ. BA(Econs); MPhil. Shipping, subseq. Advertising, Depts, Procter & Gamble, 1970–75; PA to Sir Derek Rayner, Marks & Spencer, 1975–80; Sales Dir, L. O. Jeffs Ltd, 1980–87. Mem., Mersey RHA, 1984–87. Contested (C) Newcastle upon Tyne Central, Feb. 1974. PPS to Minister of State, DOE, 1988–89, to Minister of Agric., Fisheries and Food, 1989–90. Sec., Cons. Back-bench Transport Cttee, 1987–88; Chm., Cons. Back-bench sub-cttee on Horticulture and Markets, 1987–88; Sec., Cons. NW Members Gp, 1988–90. Vice-Pres., Think Green, 1989–90. *Recreations:* DIY, dinghy sailing, motor sport, boule. *Address:* House of Commons, SW1A 0AA.

JACK, Prof. Kenneth Henderson, PhD, ScD; FRS 1980; CChem, FRSC; Consultant, Cookson Group plc, since 1986; Professor of Applied Crystal Chemistry, University of Newcastle upon Tyne, 1964–84, and Director of Wolfson Research Group for High-Strength Materials, 1970–84; Leverhulme Emeritus Fellow, 1985–87; *b* 12 Oct. 1918; *e s* of late John Henderson Jack, DSC, and Emily (*née* Cozens), North Shields, Northumberland; *m* 1942, Alfreda Hughes (*d* 1974); two *s*. *Educ:* Tynemouth Municipal High Sch.; King's Coll., Univ. of Durham, Newcastle upon Tyne (BSc 1939, DThPT 1940, MSc 1944); Fitzwilliam Coll., Univ. of Cambridge (PhD 1950, ScD 1978). Experimental Officer, Min. of Supply, 1940–41; Lectr in Chemistry, King's Coll., Univ. of Durham, 1941–45, 1949–52, 1953–57; Sen. Scientific Officer, Brit. Iron and Steel Res. Assoc., 1945–49; research at Crystallographic Lab., Cavendish Laboratory, Cambridge, 1947–49; Research Engr, Westinghouse Elec. Corp., Pittsburgh, Pa, 1952–53; Research Dir, Thermal Syndicate Ltd, Wallsend, 1957–64. Lectures: J.W. Mellor Meml, Brit. Ceramic Soc., 1973; Harold Moore Meml, Metals Soc., 1984; W. Hume-Rothery Meml, Oxford Metallurgical Soc., 1986; Sosman Meml, Amer. Ceramic Soc., 1989. Fellow, Amer. Ceramic Soc., 1984; Membre d'Honneur, Société Française de Métallurgie, 1984; Mem., Internat. Acad. of Ceramics, 1990. Saville-Shaw Medal, Soc. of Chem. Industry, 1944; Sir George Beilby Meml Award, Inst. of Metals, RIC and Soc. of Chem. Industry, 1951; Kroll Medal and Prize, Metals Soc., 1979; (with Dr R.J. Lumby) Prince of Wales Award for Industrial Innovation and Production, 1984; Armourers & Brasiers' Co. Award, Royal Soc., 1988; World Materials Congress Award, ASM Internat., 1988; A. A. Griffith Silver Medal and Prize, Inst. of Metals, 1989. *Publications:* papers in scientific jls and conf. proc. *Address:* 147 Broadway, Cullercoats, Tyne and Wear NE30 3TA. *T:* 091–257 3664; Cookson House, Willington Quay, Wallsend, Tyne and Wear NE28 6UQ. *T:* 091–262 2211.

JACK, Dr Malcolm Roy; Clerk of Standing Committees, House of Commons, since 1991; *b* 17 Dec. 1946; *s* of late Iain Ross Jack and Alicia Maria Eça da Silva, Hong Kong. *Educ:* school in Hong Kong; Univ. of Liverpool (BA Hons 1st Class); LSE, Univ. of London (PhD). A Clerk, House of Commons, 1967–; Private Sec. to Chm. of Ways and Means, 1977–80; Clerk to Agriculture Select Cttee, 1980–88; Clerk of Supply, 1989–91. Mem., Highgate Literary and Scientific Instn. *Publications:* The Social and Political Thought of Bernard Mandeville, 1987; Corruption and Progress: the eighteenth-century debate, 1989; William Beckford: an English Fidalgo, 1991; articles and essays in books, learned and literary jls. *Recreations:* the eighteenth century, Lusitaniana, Orientalia, fine arts, music, cities. *Address:* Public Bill Office, House of Commons, SW1A 0AA. *T:* 071–219 3257. *Club:* English-Speaking Union.

JACK, Michael; *see* Jack, J. M.

JACK, Raymond Evan; QC 1982; **His Honour Judge Raymond Jack;** a Circuit Judge, since 1991; *b* 13 Nov. 1942; *s* of Evan and Charlotte Jack; *m* 1976, Elizabeth Alison, *d* of Rev. Canon James Seymour Denis Mansel, *qv*; one *s* two *d*. *Educ:* Rugby; Trinity Coll., Cambridge (MA). Called to Bar, Inner Temple, 1966; a Recorder, 1989. *Publication:* Documentary Credits, 1991. *Recreations:* words and wood. *Address:* c/o The Law Courts, Winchester, Hants.

JACK, Prof. Robert Barr, CBE 1988; Senior Partner, McGrigor Donald, Solicitors, Glasgow, Edinburgh and London, since 1990 (Partner, since 1957, Joint Senior Partner, 1986–90); Professor of Mercantile Law, Glasgow University, since 1978; *b* 18 March 1928; *s* of Robert Hendry Jack and Christina Alexandra Jack; *m* 1958, Anna Thorburn Thomson; two *s*. *Educ:* Kilsyth Acad.; High Sch., Glasgow; Glasgow Univ. MA 1948, LLB 1951. Admitted a solicitor in Scotland, 1951. Member: Company Law Cttee of Law Society of Scotland, 1971– (Convener, 1978–85); Scottish Law Commn, 1974–77. Scottish observer on Dept of Trade's Insolvency Law Review Cttee, 1977–82; Mem., DoT Adv. Panel on Company Law, 1980–83; Chm., Review Cttee on Banking Services Law, 1987–89. Lay Member: Council for the Securities Industry, 1983–85; Stock Exchange Council, 1984–86; Independent Mem., Bd of Securities Assoc., 1987–90; UK Mem., Panel of Arbitrators, ICSID, 1989–. Chairman: Brownlee plc, Timber Merchants, Glasgow, 1984–86 (Dir, 1974–86); Joseph Dunn (Bottlers) Ltd, Soft Drink Manufacturers, Glasgow, 1983–; Director: Scottish Metropolitan Property plc, 1980–; Clyde Football Club Ltd, 1980–; Bank of Scotland, 1985–; Scottish Mutual Assce Soc., 1987–. Chm., Scottish Nat. Council of YMCAs, 1966–73; Pres., Scottish Nat. Union of YMCAs, 1983–. Chm., The Turnberry Trust; Governor, Hutchesons' Educational Trust, Glasgow, 1978–87 (Chm. 1980–87); Mem. Bd of Govs, Beatson Inst. for Cancer Res., Glasgow, 1989–. *Publications:* lectures on various aspects of company, insolvency and banking law and financial services regulation law. *Recreations:* golf, hopeful support of one of Glasgow's less fashionable football teams; a dedicated lover of Isle of Arran which serves as a retreat and restorative. *Address:* (home) 39 Mansewood Road, Glasgow G43 1TN. *T:* 041–632 1659; (office) Pacific House, 70 Wellington Street, Glasgow G2 6SB. *T:* 041–248 6677. *Clubs:* Caledonian; Western (Glasgow); Pollok Golf; Shiskine Golf and Tennis (Isle of Arran) (Captain 1973–75).

JACK, Dr William Hugh, CB 1988; Comptroller and Auditor General, Northern Ireland Audit Office, since 1989; *b* 18 Feb. 1929; *s* of John Charles Jack and Martha Ann Jack; *m* 1953, Beatrice Jane Thompson; three *s* one *d*. *Educ:* Ballymena Acad.; Univ. of Edinburgh (BSc(For); PhD); Queen's Univ., Belfast (BSc (Econ)). MICFor 1959. Min. of Agriculture for NI, 1948–49; Colonial Forest Service, Gold Coast/Ghana, 1949–59 (Conservator of Forests, 1957); Dept of Agriculture for NI, 1959–89 (Permanent Sec., 1983). CBIM. *Publications:* various articles in forestry research and economic jls. *Recreations:* walking, reading. *Address:* c/o Northern Ireland Audit Office, Rosepark House, Upper Newtownards Road, Belfast BT4 3NS.

JACKAMAN, Michael Clifford John; Vice-Chairman, 1988–July 1992, Chairman from July 1992, Allied Lyons plc; *b* 7 Nov. 1935; *s* of Air Cdre Clifford Thomas Jackaman, OBE and Lily Margaret Jackaman; *m* 1960, Valerie Jane Pankhurst; one *s* one *d*. *Educ:* Felsted Sch., Essex; Jesus Coll., Cambridge (MA Hons). Dep. Man. Dir, Harveys of Bristol, 1976–78; Marketing Dir, Allied Breweries, 1978–83; Dir, Allied Lyons plc, 1978–; Chairman: Hiram Walker Allied Vintners, 1983–91; John Harvey & Sons Ltd, 1983–; Mem., Council of Admin, Château Latour, 1983–; Dir, Fintex of London Ltd, 1986–. Governor, Bristol Polytechnic, 1988–. Member: Wine Guild of UK; Keepers of the Quaich (Scotland); Commanderie des Bontemps du Médoc et des Graves (France). *Recreations:* walking, tennis, potting. *Address:* c/o Allied Lyons plc, 24 Portland Place, W1N 4BB. *T:* 071–323 9000.

JACKLIN, Anthony, CBE 1990 (OBE 1970); professional golfer, 1962–85 and since 1988; Director of Golf, San Roque Club, since 1988; *b* 7 July 1944; *s* of Arthur David Jacklin; *m* 1st, 1966, Vivien (*d* 1988); two *s* one *d*; 2nd, 1988, Astrid May Waagen; one step *s* one step *d*. Successes include: British Assistant Pro Championship, 1965; Pringle Tournament, 1967; Dunlop Masters, 1967; Greater Jacksonville Open, USA, 1968; British Open Championship, 1969; US Open Championship, 1970; Benson & Hedges, 1971; British Professional Golfers Assoc., 1972, 1982; Gtr Jacksonville Open, 1972; Bogota Open, 1973 and 1974; Italian Open, 1973; Dunlop Masters, 1973; Scandinavian Open, 1975; Kerrygold International, 1976; English National PGA Championship, 1977;

German Open, 1979; Jersey Open, 1981; PGA Champion, 1982; Ryder Cup player, 1967–80, Team Captain, Europe, 1983–89. Professional Golfers' Association: Life Vice-Pres., 1970; Hon. Life Mem., European Tournament Players Div. *Publications:* Golf with Tony Jacklin, 1969; The Price of Success, 1979; (with Peter Dobereiner) Jacklin's Golfing Secrets, 1983; Tony Jacklin: the first forty years, 1985. *Recreation:* shooting. *Address:* Quothquhan Lodge, Quothquhan, Biggar, Lanarkshire ML12 6NB. *Clubs:* Potters Bar Golf; Hon. Mem. of others.

JACKLIN, William, (Bill), RA 1991 (ARA 1989); *b* 1 Jan. 1943; *s* of Harold and Alice Jacklin; *m* 1979, Lesley Sariwa. *Educ:* Walthamstow Sch. of Art; Royal College of Art (NDD, MARCA). Part-time Lectr at various art colleges, 1967–75; Arts Council Bursary, 1975; lives and works in New York, 1985–. One man exhibns, London galleries, 1970–, USA, 1985–; frequent shows in internat. exhibns; works in major collections including Arts Council, British Mus., Metropolitan Mus. NY, Mus. of Modern Art NY, Tate Gall., V&A. *Publications:* catalogues to one man exhibns, London and New York. *Recreations:* planting trees, running. *Address:* c/o Marlborough Fine Art, 6 Albemarle Street, W1X 4BY. *T:* 071–629 5161. *Club:* Chelsea Arts.

JACKLING, Roger Tustin, CBE 1982; Deputy Under-Secretary of State (Resources and Programmes), Ministry of Defence, since 1991; *b* 23 Nov. 1943; *s* of Sir Roger Jackling, GCMG and of Joan (*née* Tustin) (Lady Jackling); *m* 1976, Jane Allen Pritchard; two *s*. *Educ:* Wellington Coll.; New York Univ. (BA); Jesus Coll., Oxford. Asst Principal, MoD, 1969, Principal, 1972; London Executive Prog., London Business Sch., 1974; Sec. of State's Office, MoD, 1976–79; Asst Sec. and Hd of DS11, 1979–82; Prime Minister's Office, 1983; Head of DS7/Resources and Programmes (Army), MoD, 1983–85; Fellow, Center for Internat. Affairs, Harvard Univ., 1985–86; Principal, CS Coll. and Under Sec., Cabinet Office (OMCS), 1986–89; Asst Under-Sec. of State (Progs), MoD, 1989–91. Mem. Council, RIPA, 1987–. *Recreations:* books, theatre, playing golf and watching cricket. *Address:* c/o Ministry of Defence, Whitehall, SW1. *Clubs:* Garrick; Highgate Golf.

JACKMAN, Air Marshal Sir Douglas, KBE 1959 (CBE 1943); CB 1946; RAF; idc 1948; Air Officer Commanding-in-Chief, Royal Air Force Maintenance Command, 1958–61, retired; *b* 26 Oct. 1902; twin *s* of late A. J. Jackman; *m* 1931, Marjorie Leonore, *d* of late A. Hyland, Kingsdown, Kent. *Educ:* HMS Worcester. Officer Royal Mail Line until 1926; joined RAF, 1926; served in Iraq, 1928–30, in No 55 Squadron; in UK with Wessex Bombing Area and at Cranwell until 1934; to Middle East Command in 1934 and served at Aboukir until 1938, when posted to HQ Middle East until 1943; with Mediterranean Air Command and Mediterranean Allied Air Forces HQ until 1944; HQ Balkan Air Force, 1944–45 (despatches five times, CB, CBE, Comdr Order George 1st of Greece with Swords, AFC [Greek]); Dir of Movements Air Ministry, 1946–47; idc 1948; Dir of Organization (forecasting and planning), Air Ministry, 1949–52; AOC No 40 Group, 1952–55; Dir-Gen. of Equipment, Air Ministry, 1955–58; Co-ordinator, Anglo-American Relations, Air Ministry, 1961–64. *Publication:* technical, on planning, 1942. *Recreations:* golf (Member: RAF Golfing Soc.; Seniors Golfing Soc., Natal); woodworking. *Address:* 226 Ninth Avenue, Greyville, Durban 4001, Republic of South Africa. *Club:* Royal Over-Seas League.

JACKS, Hector Beaumont, MA; Headmaster of Bedales School, 1946–62; *b* 25 June 1903; *s* of late Dr L. P. Jacks; *m* 1st, Mary (*d* 1959), *d* of Rev. G. N. Nuttall Smith; one *s* one *d*; 2nd, Nancy, *d* of F. E. Strudwick. *Educ:* Magdalen Coll. Sch. and Wadham Coll., Oxford. Asst master, Wellington Coll., Berks, 1925–32; Headmaster of Willaston Sch., Nantwich, 1932–37; Second Master, Cheltenham Coll. Junior Sch., 1940–46. *Recreation:* gardening. *Address:* Applegarth, Spotted Cow Lane, Buxted, Sussex. *T:* Buxted (082581) 2296.

JACKSON, Alan Robert, OA 1991; Managing Director and Chief Executive Officer, BTR plc, since 1991;*b* 30 March 1936; *m* 1962, Esme Adelia Giles; four *d*. FCA, FASA, FAIM. Accountant to Man. Dir, Mather & Platt, 1952–77; Man. Dir, BTR Nylex, 1977–90. *Recreations:* tennis, golf. *Address:* BTR, Silvertown House, Vincent Square, SW1P 2PL. *T:* 071–821 3700. *Club:* Australia.

JACKSON, Albert Leslie Samuel, JP; Chairman, Birmingham Technology Ltd (Aston Science Park), since 1984; *b* 20 Jan. 1918; *s* of Bert Jackson and Olive Powell; *m* Gladys Burley; one *s* one *d*. *Educ:* Handsworth New Road Council Sch. War service, Radio Mechanic, RAF. Mem., Birmingham CC, 1952–86; Lord Mayor, 1975–76, Dep. Lord Mayor, 1978–79, Birmingham. Dir and Cttee Chm., NEC, 1984–87. JP 1968. *Recreations:* chess, sailing. *Address:* Dickies Meadow, Dock Lane, Bredon, near Tewkesbury GL20 7LG. *T:* Tewkesbury (0684) 72541.

JACKSON, Brig. Alexander Cosby Fishburn, CVO 1957; CBE 1954 (OBE 1943); *b* 4 Dec. 1903; *s* of late Col S. C. F. Jackson, CMG, DSO, and Lucy B. Jackson (*née* Drake); *m* 1934, Margaret Hastings Hervey (*d* 1984), Montclair, NJ, USA; one *s* (and one *s* decd). *Educ:* Yardley Court, Tonbridge; Haileybury Coll.; RMC Sandhurst. 2nd Lt, R Hants Regt, 1923; Brig. 1944; employed RWAFF, 1927–33; served in Middle East, 1940–45 (despatches twice, OBE); Dep. Dir of Quartering, War Office, 1945–48; Comdr Northern Area, Kenya, 1948–51; Comdr Caribbean Area, 1951–54; HBM Military Attaché, Paris, 1954–58. ADC to the Queen, 1955–58. Order of Kutuzov 2nd Class, USSR, 1944; Comdr Legion of Honour, France, 1957. *Publications:* Rose Croix: a history of the Ancient and Accepted Rite for England and Wales, 1981; English Masonic Exposures 1760–1769, 1986; A Short Dictionary of Craft Freemasonry. *Recreation:* bowls. *Address:* Glenwhern, Grouville, Jersey.

JACKSON, Mrs (Audrey) Muriel W.; *see* Ward-Jackson.

JACKSON, Barry Trevor, MS, FRCS; Serjeant Surgeon to The Queen, since 1991; Consultant Surgeon: St Thomas' Hospital, since 1973; Queen Victoria Hospital, East Grinstead, since 1977; King Edward VII Hospital for Officers, since 1983; *b* 7 July 1936; *er s* of Arthur Stanley Jackson and Violet May (*née* Fry); *m* 1962, Sheila May Wood; two *s* one *d*. *Educ:* Sir George Monoux Grammar Sch.; King's College London; Westminster Med. Sch. (Entrance Scholar). MB, BS 1963; MRCS, LRCP 1963; MS 1972; FRCS 1967. Down Bros Ltd, 1952–54; RAF 1954–56; junior surgical appts, Gordon Hosp., St James' Hosp., Balham, St Peter's Hosp., Chertsey, St Helier Hosp., Carshalton, St Thomas' Hosp. Surgeon to the Royal Household, 1983–91; Hon. Consultant in Surgery to the Army, 1990–. Royal College of Surgeons: Arris & Gale Lectr, 1973; Examr Primary FRCS, 1977–83; Mem. Court of Examrs, 1983–89; Asst Editor 1984–91, Editor, 1992–, Annals RCS; Hon. Sec., Assoc. of Surgeons of GB and Ireland, 1986–91 (Mem. Council, 1982–85); Mem., Council, RSocMed, 1987– (Pres., Sect. of Coloproctology, 1991–92). External examr in surgery: Khartoum, 1981; Ibadan, 1982; Colombo, 1984, 1988; Abu Dhabi, 1989. Mem., W Lambeth HA, 1982–83; Special Trustee, St Thomas' Hosp., 1982–84; Chm., SE Thames Regional Med. Adv. Cttee, 1983–87. Mem. Council of Govs, UMDS of Guy's and St Thomas' Hosps, 1989–. *Publications:* contribs to surgical jls and textbooks (surgery of gastro-intestinal tract). *Recreations:* book collecting, reading, medical history, music, especially opera. *Address:* 7 St Matthew's Avenue, Surbiton, Surrey KT6 6JJ *T:* 081–399 3157; The Consulting Rooms, York House, 199 Westminster Bridge Road, SE1 7UT. *T:* 071–928 5485. *Club:* Athenæum.

JACKSON, Betty, MBE 1987; RDI 1988; Designer Director, Betty Jackson Ltd, since 1981; *b* 24 June 1947; *d* of Arthur and Phyllis Gertrude Jackson; *m* 1985, David Cohen; one *s* one *d*. *Educ:* Bacup and Rawtenstall Grammar Sch.; Birmingham Coll. of Art (DipAD fashion and textiles). Freelance fashion illustrator, 1971–73; design asst, 1973–75; chief designer, Quorum, 1975–81. Part-time Tutor, RCA, 1982–. Fellow, Birmingham Polytechnic, 1989. Hon. Fellow, RCA, 1989. Awards include: British Designer of the Year, Harvey Nichols and British Fashion Council, 1985; Viyella, 1987; Fil d'Or, Internat. Linen, 1989. *Address:* Betty Jackson Ltd, 33 Tottenham Street, W1P 9PE. *T:* 071-631 1010. *Clubs:* Groucho, Zanzibar, Moscow.

JACKSON, Very Rev. Brandon Donald; Dean of Lincoln, since 1989; *b* 11 Aug. 1934; *s* of Herbert and Millicent Jackson; *m* 1958, Mary Lindsay, 2nd *d* of John and Helen Philip; two *s* one *d*. *Educ:* Stockport School; Liverpool Univ.; St Catherine's Coll. and Wycliffe Hall, Oxford (LLB, DipTh). Curate: Christ Church, New Malden, Surrey, 1958–61; St George, Leeds, 1961–65; Vicar, St Peter, Shipley, Yorks, 1965–77; Provost of Bradford Cathedral, 1977–89. Religious Adviser to Yorkshire Television, 1969–79; Church Commissioner, 1971–73; Mem., Marriage Commn, 1975–78; Examining Chaplain to Bishop of Bradford, 1974–80; Member Council: Wycliffe Hall, Oxford, 1971–85; St John's Coll., Nottingham, 1987–89. Governor: Harrogate College, 1974–86; Bradford Grammar Sch., 1977–89; Bishop Grosseteste Coll., Lincoln, 1989–; Lincoln Christ's Hosp. Sch., 1989–. Hon. DLitt Bradford, 1990. *Recreations:* sport (cricket, squash), fell-walking, fishing. *Address:* The Deanery, Lincoln LN2 1QG. *T:* Lincoln (0522) 523608.

JACKSON, Air Chief Marshal Sir Brendan (James), KCB 1987; Air Member for Supply and Organisation, Ministry of Defence, since 1988; *b* 23 Aug. 1935. *Educ:* Chichester High Sch. for Boys; London Univ. (BA Modern Japanese); qualified Interpreter. Joined RAF, 1956; flew Meteors, Canberras, Victors, B-52s; Sqdn Leader, 1965; RAF Staff Coll., 1966; PSO to C of S, HQ 2nd ATAF, 1969; Wing Comdr, 1972; US Armed Forces Staff Coll., 1972; PSO to CAS, 1974; Group Captain, 1977; Dir of Air Staff Plans, Dept of ACAS (Policy), MoD, 1980; Air Cdre, 1981; Air Vice-Marshal, 1984; ACS (Policy), SHAPE, 1984; Air Marshal, 1986; COS and Dep. C-in-C, RAF Strike Comd, 1986–88; Air Chief Marshal, 1990. *Recreations:* reading, writing on defence, gardening, golf, ski-ing. *Address:* c/o Ministry of Defence, Main Building, Whitehall, SW1A 2HB. *Club:* Royal Air Force.

JACKSON, Caroline Frances; Member (C) Wiltshire, European Parliament, since 1984; *b* 5 Nov. 1946; *d* of G. H. Harvey; *m* 1975, Robert Victor Jackson, *qv*; one *s* decd. *Educ:* School of St Clare, Penzance; St Hugh's and Nuffield Colleges, Oxford. MA, DPhil. Elizabeth Wordsworth Research Fellow, St Hugh's College, Oxford, 1972. Oxford City Councillor, 1970–73; contested (C) Birmingham, Erdington, 1974. Secretariat of Cons. Group, European Parlt, 1974–79; Head, London Office, European Democratic Group, 1979–84. Dir, Peugeot Talbot (UK) Ltd, 1987–. Mem., Nat. Consumer Council, 1982–84. *Publications:* A Students Guide to Europe, 1988; Europe's Environment, 1989. *Recreations:* walking, painting, tennis, golf. *Address:* 74 Carlisle Mansions, Carlisle Place, SW1P 1HZ. *T:* 071–828 6113.

JACKSON, Christopher Murray; Member (C) Kent East, European Parliament, since 1979; Conservative Spokesman on Foreign Affairs, since 1991; *b* 24 May 1935; *s* of Rev. Howard Murray Jackson and Doris Bessie Jackson (*née* Grainger); *m* 1971, Carlie Elizabeth Keeling; one *s* one *d*. *Educ:* Kingswood Sch., Bath; Magdalen Coll., Oxford (Open Exhibnr, BA Hons (Physics) 1959, MA 1964); Goethe Univ., Frankfurt; London Sch. of Economics. National Service, commnd RAF, Pilot, 1954–56. Unilever, 1959–69, Sen. Man., 1967; Gen. Marketing Man., Save and Prosper Gp, 1969–71; D. MacPherson Gp, 1971–74; Dir, Corporate Development Spillers Ltd, 1974–80. Underwriting Mem., Lloyds, 1985–. Contested (C): East Ham South, 1970; Northampton North, Feb. 1974. Member, Gen. Council, Cons. Gp for Europe, 1974–76. European Parliament: EDG spokesman on develt and co-op., 1981–87; C spokesman on agric., 1987–89; Mem., Bureau of EDG, 1984–91 (Dep. Chm., 1989–91); Rapporteur-General, ACP-EEC Jt Assembly, 1985–86. Vice President: Assoc. of Dist Councils; Assoc. of Local Councils; Assoc. of Port Health Authorities. Treas. and Council Mem., St Martin-in-the-Fields, 1975–77; Member: Exec. Cttee, Soc. for Long Range Planning, 1976–79; Council, Centre for European Agricl Studies, 1981–87. Pres., Kent Hotels and Restaurants Assoc., 1988–. *Publications:* UK Apple Industry, European Democratic Group, 1980; Towards 2000—people centred development, 1986; EDG Briefs: Cars and the Uncommon Market, 1983; The EEC and the Third World, 1983, rev. edn 1986; World Hunger, 1984; (ed) Your European Watchdogs, 1990; Shaking the Foundations: Britain and the new Europe, 1990; The Measure of All Things: people-centred development, 1991. *Recreations:* music, gardening, ski-ing. *Address:* 8 Wellmeade Drive, Sevenoaks, Kent TN13 1QA. *T:* Sevenoaks (0732) 456688.

JACKSON, Daphne Diana; Assistant Personnel Officer, City Engineer's Department, City of Birmingham, since 1986; *b* 8 Oct. 1933; *d* of Major Thomas Casey, MC, South Lancs Regt, and Agnes Nora Casey (*née* Gradden); *m* 1953, John Hudleston Jackson. *Educ:* Folkestone County Grammar School for Girls; South West London College. ACIS. Westminster Bank, 1951–53; Kent Educn Cttee, 1953–57; Pfizer Ltd, Sandwich, 1957–67; Southern Transformer Products, 1967–68; Borough of Hounslow, 1968–86, Personnel and Central Services Officer, Borough Engr and Surveyor's Dept, 1978–86. Mem., NACRO Employment Adv. Cttee, 1984–86; Chm., Gen. Adv. Council to IBA, 1985–89 (Mem., 1980). Mem., Soroptimists International. Gov., Cleeve Prior C of E Controlled First Sch., 1989–. Freeman, City of London, 1980; Liveryman, Chartered Secretaries and Administrators Co., 1980. *Recreations:* bereavement counselling, learning about antiques, reading. *Address:* 3 Manor Court, Cleeve Prior, Evesham, Worcs WR11 5LQ. *T:* Bidford-on-Avon (0789) 772817.

JACKSON, Prof. David Cooper; Vice-President, Immigration Appeal Tribunal, since 1984; Professor of Law (part time), since 1984, and Director, Institute of Maritime Law, 1987–90, University of Southampton; *b* 3 Dec. 1931; *s* of late Rev. James Jackson and of Mary Emma Jackson; *m* Roma Lilian (*née* Pendergast). *Educ:* Ashville Coll., Harrogate; Brasenose Coll., Oxford. MA, BCL; Senior Hulme Scholar, 1954. Called to the Bar, Inner Temple, 1957, and Victoria, Australia, 1967. Bigelow Fellow, Univ. of Chicago, 1955; Fellow, Assoc. of Bar of City of New York, 1956; National Service, 1957–59; Senior Lectr, Univ. of Singapore, 1963–64; Sir John Latham Prof. of Law, Monash Univ., 1965–70 (Carnegie Travelling Fellow, 1969); Prof. of Law, Southampton Univ., 1970–83 (Dean of Law, 1972–75, 1978–81; Dep. Vice-Chancellor, 1982–83); Consultant, UNCTAD, 1980, 1983. Visiting Professor: Queen Mary Coll., London, 1969; Arizona State Univ., 1976; Melbourne Univ., 1976. JP Hants 1980–84. Editor, World Shipping Laws, 1979– (and contrib.). *Publications:* Principles of Property Law, 1967; The Conflicts Process, 1975; Enforcement of Maritime Claims, 1985; Civil Jurisdiction and Judgments:

maritime claims, 1987; articles in legal jls, Australia, UK, USA. *Recreations:* walking, travel, theatre. *Address:* Fleet House, 9A Captains Row, Lymington, Hants SO41 9RP.

JACKSON, Sir Edward; *see* Jackson, Sir J. E.

JACKSON, Francis Alan, OBE 1978; Organist and Master of the Music, York Minster, 1946–82, Organist Emeritus, since 1988; *b* 2 Oct. 1917; *s* of W. A. Jackson; *m* 1950, Priscilla, *d* of Tyndale Procter; two *s* one *d*. *Educ:* York Minster Choir Sch.; Sir Edward Bairstow. Chorister, York Minster, 1929–33; ARCO, 1936; BMus Dunelm 1937; FRCO (Limpus Prize), 1937; DMus Dunelm 1957. Organist Malton Parish Church, 1933–40. Served War of 1939–45, with 9th Lancers in Egypt, N Africa and Italy, 1940–46. Asst Organist, York Minster, 1946; Conductor York Musical Soc., 1947–82; Conductor York Symphony Orchestra, 1947–80. Pres. Incorp. Assoc. of Organists, 1960–62; Pres., RCO, 1972–74. Hon. FRSCM 1963; Hon. Fellow, Westminster Choir Coll., Princeton, NJ, 1970; Hon. FRNCM, 1982. DUniv York, 1983. Order of St William of York, 1983. *Publications:* organ music, including 4 sonatas, organ concerto, church music, songs, monodramas. *Recreation:* gardening. *Address:* Nether Garth, Acklam, Malton, N Yorks YO17 9RG. *T:* Burythorpe (065 385) 395.

JACKSON, Frederick Hume, CMG 1978; OBE 1966; HM Diplomatic Service, retired; Consul-General, Düsseldorf, 1975–78; *b* 8 Sept. 1918; *o s* of late Maj.-Gen. G. H. N. Jackson, CB, CMG, DSO, Rathmore, Winchcombe, Glos and Eileen, *d* of J. Hume Dudgeon, Merville, Booterstown, Co. Dublin; *m* 1950, Anne Gibson; two *s* one *d* (and one *s* decd). *Educ:* Winchester; Clare Coll., Cambridge (MA). Military service, 1939–46: GSO3 (Intelligence), HQ 1 Corps District; Colonial Service (Tanganyika), 1946–57; FO, 1957–60; Head of Chancery, Saigon, 1960–62; 1st Sec., Washington, 1962–67; Counsellor and Dep. Head, UK Delegn to European Communities, Brussels, 1967–69; UK Resident Representative, Internat. Atomic Energy Agency, 1969–75; UK Perm. Representative to UNIDO, 1971–75. Chm., Sevenoaks Cons. Assoc., 1982–85, Vice-Pres., 1985–, Pres., 1986–89. *Recreations:* fishing, sailing, shooting, riding. *Address:* Orchard Lodge, Leigh, Tonbridge, Kent TN11 8QJ. *T:* Hildenborough (0732) 833495; c/o Barclays Bank, St Nicholas Street, Scarborough, North Yorks YO11 2HS. *Club:* Flyfishers'.

JACKSON, Gerald Breck; *b* 28 June 1916; *o s* of Gerald Breck Jackson and Mary Jackson, Paterson, NJ; *m* 1940, Brenda Mary, *o d* of William and Mary Titshall; one *s*. *Educ:* various schs in USA; Canford Sch., Dorset; Faraday House Engrg Coll. Graduate Trainee, Central Electricity Bd, 1938. HM Forces, RE, 1939–43. Various appts in HV transmission with CEB and BEA, 1943–55; Overhead Line Design Engr, BEA, 1955–61; Asst Regional Dir, CEGB, 1961–64; Chief Ops Engr, CEGB, 1964–66; Regional Dir, NW Region, CEGB, 1966–68; Dir Engineering, English Electric Co. Ltd, 1968–69; Sen. Exec., Thomas Tilling Ltd, and Dir subsid. cos, 1969–71; Man. Dir, John Mowlem & Co. Ltd, 1971–72; Man. Dir, NCB (Ancillaries) Ltd, 1972–78. DFH, CEng, FIEE. *Publications:* Network for the Nation, 1960; Power Controlled, 1966. *Recreations:* photography, pen-and-ink drawing. *Address:* Larchwood, 1A Lansdowne Square, Tunbridge Wells, Kent TN1 2NF.

JACKSON, Glenda, CBE 1978; actress; Director, United British Artists, since 1983; *b* Birkenhead, 9 May 1936; *d* of Harry and Joan Jackson; *m* 1958, Roy Hodges (marr. diss. 1976); one *s*. *Educ:* West Kirby Co. Grammar Sch. for Girls; RADA. Actress with various repertory cos, 1957–63, stage manager, Crewe Rep.; joined Royal Shakespeare Co., 1963. Pres., Play Matters (formerly Toy Libraries Assoc.), 1976–. Prospective Parly Candidate (Lab), Hampstead and Highgate, 1990–. *Plays:* All Kinds of Men, Arts, 1957; The Idiot, Lyric, 1962; Alfie, Mermaid and Duchess, 1963; Royal Shakespeare Co.: Theatre of Cruelty Season, LAMDA, 1964; The Jew of Malta, 1964; Marat/Sade, 1965, NY and Paris, 1965; Love's Labour's Lost, Squire Puntila and his Servant Matti, The Investigation, Hamlet, 1965; US, Aldwych, 1966; Three Sisters, Royal Ct, 1967; Fanghorn, Fortune, 1967; Collaborators, Duchess, 1973; The Maids, Greenwich, 1974; Hedda Gabler, Australia, USA, London, 1975; The White Devil, Old Vic, 1976; Stevie, Vaudeville, 1977; Antony and Cleopatra, Stratford, 1978; Rose, Duke of York's, 1980; Summit Conference, Lyric, 1982; Great and Small, Vaudeville, 1983; Strange Interlude, Duke of York's, 1984; Phedra, Old Vic, 1984, Aldwych, 1985; Across from the Garden of Allah, Comedy, 1986; The House of Bernarda Alba, Globe, 1986; Macbeth, NY, 1988; Scenes from an Execution, Almeida, 1990; Mother Courage, Mermaid, 1990; *films:* This Sporting Life, 1963; Marat/Sade, 1967; Negatives, 1968; Women in Love (Oscar Award, 1971), 1970; The Music Lovers, 1971; Sunday, Bloody Sunday, 1971; The Boyfriend, 1972; Mary, Queen of Scots, 1972; Triple Echo, 1972; Il Sorviso de Grande Tentatore (The Tempter), 1973; Bequest to the Nation, 1973; A Touch of Class (Oscar Award, 1974), 1973; The Maids, 1974; The Romantic Englishwoman, 1974; Hedda Gabler, 1975; The Incredible Sarah, 1976; House Calls, 1978; Stevie, 1978; The Class of Miss MacMichael, 1978; Lost and Found, 1979; Hopscotch, 1980; Return of the Soldier, 1982; Health, 1982; Giro City, 1982; Sacharov, 1983; Turtle Diary, 1985; Business as Usual, 1987; Beyond Therapy, 1987; Salome's Last Dance, 1988; The Rainbow, 1989; *TV:* Elizabeth in Elizabeth R, 1971; The Patricia Neal Story (Amer.). Best film actress awards: Variety Club of GB, 1971, 1975, 1978; NY Film Critics, 1971; Nat. Soc. of Film Critics, US, 1971. *Recreations:* cooking, gardening, reading Jane Austen. *Address:* c/o Crouch Associates, 59 Frith Street, W1.

JACKSON, Gordon Noel, CMG 1962; MBE; HM Ambassador to Ecuador, 1967–70, retired; *b* 25 Dec. 1913; *m* 1959, Mary April Nettlefold, *er d* of late Frederick John Nettlefold and of Mrs Albert Coates; one *s* two *d*. Indian Political Service until 1947; then HM Foreign Service; Political Officer, Sharjah, 1947; transf. to Kuwait, Persian Gulf, 1949; transf. to Foreign Office, 1950; Consul, St Louis, USA, 1953; Foreign Service Officer, Grade 6, 1955; Consul-General: Basra, 1955–57; Lourenço Marques, 1957–60; Benghazi, 1960–63; HM Ambassador to Kuwait, 1963–67. *Publications:* Effective Horsemanship (for Dressage, Hunting, Three-day Events, Polo), 1967; (with W. Steinkraus) The Encyclopædia of the Horse, 1973. *Address:* Lowbarrow House, Leafield, Oxfordshire OX8 5NH. *T:* Asthall Leigh (099387) 443. *Club:* Travellers'.

JACKSON, Ian (Macgilchrist), BA Cantab, MB, BChir, FRCS, FRCOG; Obstetric and Gynæcological Surgeon, Middlesex Hospital, 1948–79, retired; Gynæcological Surgeon: Chelsea Hospital for Women, 1948–79; King Edward VII Hospital for Officers, 1961–84; Royal Masonic Hospital, 1963–79; Consulting Gynæcologist, King Edward VII Hospital, Midhurst, 1959; Consultant Obstetrician and Gynæcologist, RAF, 1964–83; *b* Shanghai, 11 Nov. 1914; *s* of Dr Ernest David Jackson; *m* 1943 (marr. diss., 1967); two *s* one *d*; *m* 1970, Deirdre Ruth Heitz. *Educ:* Marlborough Coll.; Trinity Hall, Cambridge (scholar; double 1st cl. hons, Nat. Sci. tripos pts I, II). London Hospital: open scholarship, 1936; house appointments, 1939; First Asst, Surgical and Obstetric and Gynæcol Depts, 1940–43. Served as Surgical Specialist, RAMC, 1943–47 (Major); Parachute Surgical Team, 224 Para. Field Amb.; Mobile Surgical Unit, 3 Commando Brigade. Royal College of Obstetricians and Gynæcologists: Council, 1951–61, 1962–70; Hon. Sec., 1954–61; Chm., Examination Cttee, 1962–65, Hon. Treas., 1966–70; Hon. Librarian, RSM, 1969–75. Examiner for Univs of Cambridge, Oxford, and London, Conjoint Bd and RCOG. Mem., Court of Assts, Worshipful Soc. of Apothecaries, 1966, Senior Warden 1977, Master 1978, Hon. Treas., 1985–89; President: Chelsea Clinical Soc., 1979; Sydenham Medical Club, 1987–90. Order of the Star of Africa (Liberia), 1969; Grand Officer of Order of Istiqlal, Jordan, 1970. *Publications:* British Obstetric and Gynæcological Practice (jtly), 1963; Obstetrics by Ten Teachers (jtly), 1966, 2nd edn 1972; Gynæcology by Ten Teachers (jtly), 1971; numerous contribs to medical literature. *Recreations:* fishing, golf, photography. *Address:* 23 Springfield Road, NW8. *T:* 071–624 3580; The Portland Hospital, 209 Great Portland Street, W1N. *T:* 071–580 4400.

JACKSON, Sir (John) Edward, KCMG 1984 (CMG 1977); HM Diplomatic Service, retired; Chairman, Spadel Ltd (formerly Brecon Beacons Natural Waters Ltd), since 1985, and director of other companies; *b* 24 June 1925; *s* of Edward Harry and Margaret Jackson; *m* 1952, Eve Stainton Harris, *d* of late George James Harris, MC and of Mrs Friede Rowntree Harris, York; two *s* one *d*. *Educ:* Ardingly; Corpus Christi Coll., Cambridge. RNVR (Sub-Lt), 1943–46; joined Foreign (now Diplomatic) Service, 1947; FO, 1947–49; 3rd Sec., Paris, 1949–52; 2nd Sec., FO, 1952–56; 1st Sec., Bonn, 1956–59; Guatemala City, 1959–62; FO, 1963–68; Counsellor, 1968; NATO Defence Coll., Rome, 1969; Counsellor (Political Adviser), British Mil. Govt, Berlin, 1969–73; Head of Defence Dept, FCO, 1973–75; Ambassador to Cuba, 1975–79; Head of UK Delegn to Negotiations on Mutual Reduction of Forces and Armaments and Associated Measures in Central Europe, with personal rank of Ambassador, 1980–82; Ambassador to Belgium, 1982–85. Director: Herbert Mueller Ltd and associated cos, 1987–90. Dir, Armistice Festival, 1986–89. Chm., Anglo-Belgian Soc., 1987–; Dep. Chm., Belgo-Luxembourg Chamber of Commerce, 1987–. Trustee, Imperial War Museum, 1986–. *Recreations:* the arts, tennis. *Address:* 17 Paultons Square, SW3 5AP. *Clubs:* Anglo-Belgian, Hurlingham.

JACKSON, John Henry; Company Secretary, British Gas, since 1990; *b* 7 Aug. 1948; *s* of John and May Jackson; *m* 1975, Patricia Mary Robinson; one *s* one *d*. *Educ:* Trinity School, Croydon; St Catherine's College, Oxford (MA). FICS. Joined SE Gas Board, 1970; Asst Sec., 1977, Sen. Asst Sec., 1983, British Gas Corp., later British Gas plc. *Address:* Rivermill House, 152 Grosvenor Road, SW1V 3JL. *T:* 071–821 1444.

JACKSON, Very Rev. Lawrence, AKC; Provost of Blackburn, since 1973; *b* Hessle, Yorks, 22 March 1926; *s* of Walter and Edith Jackson; *m* 1955, Faith Anne, *d* of Philip and Marjorie Seymour; four *d*. *Educ:* Alderman Newton's Sch.; Leicester Coll. of Technology; King's Coll., Univ. of London (AKC 1950); St Boniface Coll., Warminster. Asst Curate, St Margaret, Leicester, and Asst Chaplain, Leicester Royal Infirmary, 1951–54; Vicar of: Wymeswold, Leicester, 1954–59; St James the Greater, Leicester, 1959–65; Coventry (Holy Trinity), 1965–73. Canon of Coventry Cath., 1967–73; Rural Dean of Coventry N, 1969–73. Senior Chaplain: Leicester and Rutland ACF, 1955–65; Warwickshire ACF, 1965–73; Chaplain, Coventry Guild of Freemen, 1968–73; Dio. Chaplain, CEMS, 1969–71. Mem., Gen. Synod of C of E, 1975–; a Church Comr, 1981–. Dir, The Samaritans of Leicester, 1960–65; Pres., Coventry Round Table, 1968; Governor: Queen Elizabeth Grammar Sch., Blackburn. *Publication:* Services for Special Occasions, 1982. *Recreations:* music, archæology, architecture, countryside, after dinner speaking. *Address:* The Provost's House, Preston New Road, Blackburn BB2 6PS. *T:* Blackburn (0254) 52502. *Clubs:* Carlton, Forty, Lighthouse; Lord's Taverners'.

JACKSON, Hon. Sir Lawrence (Walter), KCMG 1970; Kt 1964; BA, LLB; Judge, 1949–77, and Chief Justice, 1969–77, Supreme Court of Western Australia; Chancellor, University of Western Australia, 1968–81; *b* Dulwich, South Australia, 27 Sept. 1913; *s* of L. S. Jackson; *m* 1937, Mary, *d* of T. H. Donaldson; one *s* two *d*. *Educ:* Fort Street High Sch., Sydney; University of Sydney. *Recreations:* swimming, golf. *Address:* 57 Lisle Street, Mount Claremont, WA 6010, Australia. *Club:* Weld (Perth, WA).

JACKSON, Hon. Dame Margaret Myfanwy Wood; *see* Booth, Hon. Dame Margaret.

JACKSON, Michael; Head of Music and Arts, BBC Television, since 1991; *b* 11 Feb. 1958; *s* of Ernest Jackson and Margaret (*née* Kearsley). *Educ:* King's Sch., Macclesfield; Poly. of Central London (BA (Hons) Media Studies). Organiser, Channel Four Gp, 1979; Producer, The Sixties, 1982; Independent Producer, Whose Town is it Anyway?, Open the Box, The Media Show, 1983–87; joined BBC Television; Editor: The Late Show (BFI Television Award), 1988–90; Late Show Productions, 1990–91, progs incl. Tales from Prague (Grierson Documentary Award), Moving Pictures, The American Late Show, Naked Hollywood. *Recreations:* reading, walking. *Address:* c/o BBC TV, Kensington House, Richmond Way, W14 0AY. *T:* 081–743 1272.

JACKSON, (Michael) Rodney; a Recorder, since 1985; Partner, Andrew M. Jackson & Co., Solicitors, since 1964; *b* 16 April 1935; *s* of John William Jackson and Nora Jackson (*née* Phipps); *m* 1968, Anne Margaret, *d* of Prof. E. W. Hawkins, *qv;* two *s*. *Educ:* Queen Elizabeth Grammar Sch., Wakefield; Queens' Coll., Cambridge (MA, LLM). Admitted Solicitor of the Supreme Court, 1962; Notary Public, 1967. *Recreations:* fell walking, visiting preserved railways. *Address:* Andrew M. Jackson & Co., PO Box 47, Victoria Chambers, Bowlalley Lane, Hull HU1 1XY. *T:* Hull (0482) 25242. *Club:* Commonwealth Trust.

JACKSON, Sir Michael (Roland), 5th Bt, *cr* 1902; MA; CEng, MIEE; FIQA; *b* 20 April 1919; *s* of Sir W. D. Russell Jackson, 4th Bt, and Kathleen (*d* 1975), *d* of Summers Hunter, CBE, Tynemouth; *S* father 1956; *m* 1st, 1942, Hilda Margaret (marr. diss. 1969), *d* of late Cecil George Herbert Richardson, CBE, Newark; one *s* one *d*; 2nd, 1969, Hazel Mary, *d* of late Ernest Harold Edwards. *Educ:* Stowe; Clare Coll., Cambridge. Served War of 1939–45; Flight-Lt, Royal Air Force Volunteer Reserve. *Heir:* *s* Thomas St Felix Jackson [*b* 27 Sept. 1946; *m* 1980, Victoria, *d* of George Scatliff, Wineham, Sussex; two *d*]. *Address:* Jolliffe's House, Stour Row, Shaftesbury, Dorset SP7 0QW.

JACKSON, Mrs Muriel W.; *see* Ward-Jackson.

JACKSON, Sir Nicholas (Fane St George), 3rd Bt *cr* 1913; organist, harpsichordist and composer; Director, Concertante of London, since 1987; *b* 4 Sept. 1934; *s* of Sir Hugh Jackson, 2nd Bt, and of Violet Marguerite Loftus, *y d* of Loftus St George; *S* father, 1979; *m* 1972, Nadia Françoise Genevieve (*née* Michard); one *s*. *Educ:* Radley Coll.; Wadham Coll., Oxford; RAM. LRAM; ARCM. Organist: St Anne's, Soho, 1963–68; St James's, Piccadilly, 1971–74; St Lawrence, Jewry, 1974–77; Organist and Master of the Choristers, St David's Cathedral, 1977–84. Musical Dir, St David's Cathedral Bach Fest., 1979; Dir, Bach Festival, Santes Creus, Spain, 1987–. Organ recitals and broadcasts: Berlin, 1967; Paris, 1972, 1975; USA (tour), 1975, 1978, 1980 and 1989; Minorca, 1977; Spain, 1979; Madrid Bach Festival, 1980; RFH, 1984; concert tours of Spain and Germany, annually 1980–. Début as harpsichordist, Wigmore Hall, 1963; appeared frequently with Soho Concertante, Queen Elizabeth Hall, 1964–72. Mem. Music Cttee, Welsh Arts Council, 1981–. Examiner, Trinity Coll. of Music, 1985–. Recordings: Mass for a Saint's Day, 1971; organ and harpsichord music, incl. works by Arnell, Bach, Couperin, Langlais, Mozart, Vierne and Walther. Liveryman, 1965, Junior Warden, 1985–86, Drapers' Co; Liveryman, Musicians' Co., 1985–. *Publications: compositions:* Mass for a Saint's Day, 1966; 20th Century Merbecke, 1967; 4 Images (for organ), 1971; Solemn Mass, 1977; Divertissement (organ), 1983; Organ Mass, 1984; 2 Organ Sonatas, 1985; Suite, for brass quintet and organ, 1986. *Recreations:* sketching, writing. *Heir:* *s* Thomas Graham St George Jackson, *b* 5 Oct. 1980. *Address:* Lloyds Bank, 39 Old Bond Street, W1.

JACKSON, Oliver James V.; *see* Vaughan-Jackson.

JACKSON, Patrick; *see* Jackson, W. P.

JACKSON, Peter John Edward; barrister; a Recorder of the Crown Court, since 1983; *b* 14 May 1944; *s* of late David Charles Jackson and of Sarah Ann (*née* Manester); *m* 1967, Ursula, *y d* of late Paul and Henny Schubert, Hamburg, W Germany; two *d*. *Educ:* Brockley County Grammar Sch.; Sprachen und Dolmetscher Inst., Hamburg; London Univ. (LLB Hons 1967); Tübingen Univ., W Germany (Dr jur. 1987). Called to the Bar, Middle Temple, 1968 (Blackstone Scholar; Churchill Prize); called to the Bar of NI, 1982. Dep. Circuit Judge, 1979–81; Asst Recorder, 1982–83; Partner, Campbell and Jackson Internat. Arbitral and Legal Consultants, Brussels, Stuttgart, Paris, 1985–90. Mem., Arbitration Panel, ICC, 1990; Co-opted Mem., Internat. Practice Cttee, Bar Council, 1991. Trustee, Newbold Coll., Bracknell. ACIArb 1983. *Recreations:* horse riding, the German language. *Address:* 3 Pump Court, Temple, EC4Y 7AJ. *T:* 071–353 0711; D7000 Stuttgart 50, Seelbergstrasse 8, W Germany. *T:* (0711) 56 14 56, *Fax:* (0711) 55 24 07.

JACKSON, Peter (Michael); Senior Lecturer, in Industrial Studies, Institute of Extra-mural Studies, National University of Lesotho, 1980; *b* 14 Oct. 1928; *s* of Leonard Patterson Jackson; *m* 1961, Christine Thomas. *Educ:* Durham Univ.; University Coll., Leicester. Lecturer, Dept of Sociology, University of Hull, 1964–66; Fellow, Univ. of Hull, 1970–72; Tutor, Open Univ., 1972–74; Senior Planning Officer, S Yorks CC, 1974–77. MP (Lab) High Peak, 1966–70; contested (Lab) Birmingham North, European Parly elecns, 1979. Member: Peak Park Jt Planning Bd, 1973–77, 1979–82; Derby CC, 1973–77. *Recreations:* numismatics, book collecting, ski-ing. *Club:* Maseru (Lesotho).

JACKSON, Air Vice-Marshal Sir Ralph (Coburn), KBE 1973; CB 1963; Honorary Civil Consultant in Medicine to RAF; Honorary Consultant (Medicine) to RAF Benevolent Fund; Medical Adviser and Director, French Hospital (La Providence), Rochester; *b* 22 June 1914; *s* of Ralph Coburn Jackson and Phillis Jackson (*née* Dodds); *m* 1939, Joan Lucy Crowley; two *s* two *d*. *Educ:* Oakmount Sch., Arnside; Guy's Hosp., London. MRCS 1937; FRCPE 1960 (MRCPE 1950); FRCP 1972 (MRCP 1968, LRCP 1937). Qualified in Medicine Guy's Hosp., 1937; House Officer appts, Guy's Hosp., 1937–38; commnd in RAF as MO, Nov. 1938; served in France, 1939–40; Russia, 1941; W Africa, 1942–43 (despatches); Sen. MO, 46 Gp for Brit. Casualty Air Evac., 1944–45 (despatches). Med. Specialist, RAF Hosps Wroughton, Aden and Halton, 1946–52 (Consultant in Med., Princess Mary's RAF Hosp. Halton, 1952–63; RAF Hosp., Wegberg, Germany, 1964–66); Consultant Advr in Medicine, 1966–74; Sen. Consultant to RAF, 1971–75; Advr in Medicine to CAA, 1966–75; Consultant Medical Referee: Confedn Life Insce Co., 1973–87; Victory Re-insurance Co., 1975–87. Chm., Defence Med. Services, Postgrad. Council, 1973–75. QHP 1969–75. MacArthur Lectr, Univ. Edinburgh, 1959. Fellow, Assurance Med. Soc.; FRSM; Fellow, Huguenot Soc., 1985; Fellow, RSPB, 1981; Member: Wild Fowl Trust, 1982; Soc. of Genealogists; RAF Histl Soc. Liveryman, Worshipful Soc. of Apothecaries; Freeman, City of London. Lady Cade Medal, RCS, 1960. *Publications:* papers on acute renal failure, the artificial kidney and routine electrocardiography in various medical books and journals, 1959–1974. *Recreations:* birdwatching, genealogy. *Address:* Cherry Trees, 15 Ball Road, Pewsey, Wiltshire SN9 5BL. *T:* Marlborough (0672) 62042. *Club:* Royal Air Force.

JACKSON, Raymond Allen, (JAK); Cartoonist, Evening Standard, since 1952; *b* 11 March 1927; *s* of Maurice Jackson and Mary Ann Murphy; *m* 1957, Claudie Sidone Grenier; one *s* two *d*. *Educ:* Lyulph Stanley Central; Willesden School of Art (NDD). Army, 1945–48. General artist, Link House Publishing, 1950–51; Keymers Advertising Agency, 1951–52; Evening Standard, 1952–. *Publications:* JAK Annual, 1969–. *Recreations:* judo, squash, walking. *Club:* St James'.

JACKSON, Richard Michael, CVO 1983; HM Diplomatic Service; Ambassador to Bolivia, since 1991; *b* 12 July 1940; *s* of Richard William Jackson and Charlotte (*née* Wrightson); *m* 1961, Mary Elizabeth Kitchin; one *s* one *d*. *Educ:* Queen Elizabeth Grammar Sch., Darlington; Paisley Grammar Sch.; Glasgow Univ. (MA Hons 1961). Joined Home Civil Service, 1961; Scottish Office, 1961–70; seconded to MAFF, 1971–72; seconded to FCO and served in The Hague, 1973–74; trans. to HM Diplomatic Service, 1974; European Integration Dept (External), FCO, 1975–76; Panama City, 1976–79; Arms Control and Disarmament Dept, FCO, 1979–81; Buenos Aires, 1981–82; Falkland Islands Dept, FCO, 1982; Stockholm, 1982–87; Dep. Head of Mission, Seoul, 1987–91. *Recreations:* birdwatching, real ale. *Address:* c/o Foreign and Commonwealth Office, King Charles Street, SW1.

JACKSON, Sir Robert, 7th Bt *cr* 1815; *b* 16 March 1910; *s* of Major Francis Gorham Jackson (*d* 1942) (2nd *s* of 4th Bt) and Ana Maria Biscar Brennan; *S* kinsman, Sir John Montrésor Jackson, 6th Bt, 1980; *m* 1943, Maria E. Casamayou; two *d*. *Educ:* St George's College. Career on estancia. *Heir: kinsman* Keith Arnold Jackson [*b* 1921; *m* Pauline Mona, *d* of B. P. Climo, Wellington, NZ; four *s* one *d*]. *Address:* Santiago de Chile 1243, Montevideo, Uruguay. *T:* 905487. *Club:* English (Montevideo).

JACKSON, Robert Victor; MP (C) Wantage, since 1983; Parliamentary Under Secretary of State, Department of Employment, since 1990; *b* 24 Sept. 1946; *m* 1975, Caroline Frances Harvey (*see* C. F. Jackson); one *s* decd. *Educ:* Falcon Coll., S Rhodesia; St Edmund Hall, Oxford (H. W. C. Davis Prize, 1966; 1st Cl. Hons Mod. Hist. 1968); President Oxford Union, 1967. Prize Fellowship, All Souls Coll., 1968 (Fellow, 1968–86). Councillor, Oxford CC, 1969–71; Political Adviser to Sec. of State for Employment, 1973–74; Member, Cabinet of Sir Christopher (now Baron) Soames, EEC Commn, Brussels, 1974–76; Chef de Cabinet, President of EEC Economic and Social Cttee, Brussels, 1976–78; Mem. (C) Upper Thames, European Parlt, 1979–84; Special Adviser to Governor of Rhodesia (Lord Soames), 1979–80; European Parlt's Rapporteur-Gen. on 1983 European Community Budget. Parly Under Sec. of State, DES, 1987–90. Contested (C) Manchester Central Div., general election, Oct. 1974. Editor: The Round Table: Commonwealth Jl of Internat. Relations, 1970–74; International Affairs (Chatham House), 1979–80. *Publications:* South Asian Crisis: India, Pakistan, Bangladesh 1972, 1975; The Powers of the European Parliament, 1977; The European Parliament: Penguin Guide to Direct Elections, 1979; Reforming the European Budget, 1981; Tradition and Reality: Conservative philosophy and European integration 1982; From Boom to Bust?—British farming and CAP reform, 1983; Political Ideas in Western Europe Today, 1984. *Recreations:* reading, music, walking. *Address:* House of Commons, SW1A 0AA. *Club:* Beefsteak.

JACKSON, Rodney; *see* Jackson, M. R.

JACKSON, Sir (Ronald) Gordon, AK 1983 (AC 1976); Chairman, Australian Industry Development Corporation, 1983–90; Member of Board, Reserve Bank of Australia, 1975–90; Chancellor, Australian National University, 1987–90; *b* 5 May 1924; *s* of late R. V. Jackson; *m* 1948, Margaret Pratley; one *s* one *d*. *Educ:* Brisbane Grammar Sch.; Queensland Univ. (BCom). FASA; FAIM. Served AIF, 1942–46. Joined CSR Ltd, 1941; Gen. Man., 1972–82; Dir, 1972–85; Dep. Chm., 1983–85. Chairman: Hampton Australia Ltd, 1984–86; Interscan Internat. Ltd, 1984–87; Austek Microsystems Ltd, 1984–87; Director: Rothmans Holdings Ltd, 1983–; Rockwell Internat. Pty Ltd, 1985–88; Mem., Pacific Adv. Council, United Technologies Corp., 1984–. Foundn Chm., Bd of Management, Aust. Graduate Sch. of Management, 1976–81; Pres., Order of Australia Assoc., 1983–86 (Foundn Chm., 1980–83); Vice-Pres., Australia/Japan Business Co-operation Cttee, 1977–; Hon. Life Mem., German–Australian Chamber of Industry and Commerce, 1986 (Foundn Pres., 1977–80; Chm. 1980–85); Member: Police Bd of NSW, 1983– (Chm., 1988–); Salvation Army Adv. Bd, 1983– (Chm., Red Shield Appeal, 1981–85, Pres. 1986–). Hon. DSc NSW, 1983. James N. Kirby Meml Award, Instn of Prodn Engrs, 1976; John Storey Medal, Aust. Inst. of Management, 1978; Prime Minister of Japan's Trade Award, 1987. Comdr, Order of Merit (FRG), 1980; Grand Cordon (first class), Order of the Sacred Treasure of Japan, 1987. *Recreations:* sailing, fishing. *Address:* 14 Nithdale Street, Pymble, NSW 2073, Australia. *Clubs:* Union, Australian (Sydney); Queensland; Royal Sydney Yacht.

JACKSON, Roy Arthur; Assistant General Secretary, Trades Union Congress, since 1984; *b* 18 June 1928; *s* of Charles Frederick Jackson and Harriet Betsy (*née* Ridewood); *m* 1956, Lilian May Ley; three *d*. *Educ:* North Paddington Central Sch.; London Univ. Extension Classes; Ruskin Coll., Oxford (DipEcon Pol Sci (Distinction); Worcester Coll., Oxford (BA Hons, PPE). Post Office Savings Bank, 1942; RN, Ord. Signalman, 1946–48; POSB, 1948–52; posts held at branch and Nat. level, CSCA, 1943–52; TUC: Educn Dept, 1956; Dir of Studies, 1964; Head of Educn, 1974–84. Member: Albemarle Cttee of Youth Service, 1958–60; Open Univ. Cttee on Continuing Educn, 1975–76; Adv. Cttee for Continuing and Adult Educn, 1977–83; Schools Council Convocation, 1978–82; Further Educn Unit, DES, 1980–; served on a number of MSC bodies, 1978–85; TUC Comr, MSC, 1987–88. *Publications:* contribs to DES Trends in Education and Joint Studies in Econ. Performance. *Recreations:* walking, reading, gardening. *Address:* 27 The Ryde, Hatfield, Herts. *T:* Hatfield (07072) 63790.

JACKSON, Rupert Matthew; QC 1987; a Recorder, since 1990; *b* 7 March 1948; *s* of late George Henry Jackson and Nancy Barbara Jackson (*née* May); *m* 1975, Claire Corinne Potter; three *d*. *Educ:* Christ's Hospital; Jesus College, Cambridge (MA, LLB). Pres., Cambridge Union, 1971. Called to the Bar, Middle Temple, 1972. FRSA 1988. *Publications:* Professional Negligence, 1982, 2nd edn 1987. *Address:* 2 Crown Office Row, Temple, EC4Y 7HJ. *T:* 071–583 8155. *Club:* Reform.

JACKSON, Sir Thomas; *see* Jackson, Sir W. T.

JACKSON, Thomas; General Secretary, Union of Communication Workers (formerly Post Office Workers), 1967–82; bookseller; *b* 9 April 1925; *s* of George Frederick Jackson and Ethel Hargreaves; *m* 1st, 1947, Norma Burrow (marr. diss. 1982); one *d*; 2nd, 1982, Kathleen Maria Tognarelli; one *d*. *Educ:* Jack Lane Elementary Sch. Boy Messenger, GPO, 1939; Royal Navy, 1943; Postman, 1946; Executive Mem., Union of Post Office Workers, 1955; Asst Sec., Union of Post Office Workers, 1964. HM Government Dir, British Petroleum, 1975–83. Member: Gen. Council of TUC, 1967–82 (Chm., 1978–79; Chm., Internat. Cttee, 1978–82); Press Council, 1973–76; Annan Cttee on the Future of Broadcasting, 1974–77; CRE, 1977–78; Broadcasting Complaints Commn, 1982–87; Yorks Water Authority, 1983–89. Non-exec. Dir, Yorks Water plc, 1989–. Member: Court and Council, Sussex Univ., 1974–78; Council, Bradford Univ., 1987–90. Vice-Pres., WEA, 1977–; Chm., Ilkley Literature Fest., 1984–87. A Governor: BBC, 1968–73; NIESR, 1974–85. *Recreations:* cooking, photography. *Address:* 22 Parish Ghyll Road, Ilkley, West Yorks LS29 9NE.

JACKSON, (Walter) Patrick, CB 1987; Under-Secretary, Department of Transport, 1981–89, retired; *b* 10 Feb. 1929; *m* 1952, Kathleen Roper; one *s* one *d*. *Educ:* University Coll., Oxford. John Lewis Partnership, 1952–66; Principal, Min. of Transport and DoE, 1966–72; Asst Sec., DoE, 1972–78; Under Sec. and Regional Dir (E Midlands), DoE and Dept of Transport, 1978–81. *Recreation:* concert- and theatre-going.

JACKSON, Gen. Sir William (Godfrey Fothergill), GBE 1975 (OBE 1958); KCB 1971; MC 1940, and Bar, 1943; Military Historian, Cabinet Office, 1977–78, and since 1982; Governor and Commander-in-Chief, Gibraltar, 1978–82; *b* 28 Aug. 1917; *s* of late Col A. Jackson, RAMC, Yanwath, Cumberland, and E. M. Jackson (*née* Fothergill), Brownber, Westmorland; *m* 1946, Joan Mary Buesden; one *s* one *d*. *Educ:* Shrewsbury; RMA, Woolwich; King's Coll., Cambridge, King's medal, RMA Woolwich, 1937. Commnd into Royal Engineers, 1937; served War of 1939–45: Norwegian Campaign, 1940; Tunisia, 1942–43; Sicily and Italy, 1943–44; Far East, 1945; GSO1, HQ Allied Land Forces SE Asia, 1945–48; Instructor, Staff Coll., Camberley, 1948–50; Instructor, RMA, Sandhurst, 1951–53; AA & QMG (War Plans), War Office, during Suez ops, 1956; Comdr, Gurkha Engrs, 1958–60; Col GS, Minley Div. of Staff Coll., Camberley, 1961–62; Dep. Dir of Staff Duties, War Office, 1962–64; Imp. Def. Coll., 1965; Dir, Chief of Defence Staff's Unison Planning Staff, 1966–68; Asst Chief of General Staff (Operational Requirements), MoD, 1968–70; GOC-in-C, Northern Command, 1970–72; QMG, 1973–76. Colonel Commandant: RE, 1971–81; Gurkha Engrs, 1971–76; RAOC, 1973–78; Hon. Col, Engineer and Rly Staff Corps, RE, TAVR, 1977–83; ADC (Gen.) to the Queen, 1974–76. Kermit Roosevelt Lectr, USA, 1975. Chm., Friends of Gibraltar's Heritage, 1990–. Reviewer of mil. books, The Times, 1987–. *Publications:* Attack in the West, 1953; Seven Roads to Moscow, 1957; The Battle for Italy, 1967; Battle for Rome, 1969; Alexander of Tunis as Military Commander, 1971; The North African Campaigns, 1975; Overlord: Normandy 1944, 1978; (ed jtly) The Mediterranean and the Middle East (British Official History, vol. VI), Pt 1, 1984, Pt 2, 1987, Pt 3, 1988; Withdrawal From Empire, 1986; The Alternative Third World War 1985–2035, 1987; The Rock of the Gibraltarians, 1988; British Defence Dilemmas, 1990; The Chiefs, 1991; contribs to Royal United Service Instn Jl (gold medals for prize essays, 1950 and 1966). *Recreations:* fishing, writing, gardening. *Club:* Army and Navy.

JACKSON, William Theodore, CBE 1967 (MBE 1946); ARIBA; MRTPI; Director of Post Office Services, Ministry of Public Building and Works, 1969–71, retired; *b* 18 July 1906; *y s* of Rev. Oliver Miles Jackson and Emily Jackson; *m* 1932, Marjorie Campbell; one *s* two *d*. *Educ:* Cheltenham Gram. Sch. Chief Architect, Iraq Govt, 1936–38; Dir, Special Repair Service, Min. of Works, 1939–45; Min. of Public Building and Works, 1946–69; Dir, Mobile Labour Force; Dir of Maintenance; seconded to World Bank as Advr to Iran Technical Bureau of Development Plan organisation, 1956–57; Regional Dir; Dir, Regional Services; Dir, Headquarters Services, 1957–69. *Recreations:* gardening, painting. *Address:* Westringes, Rowly Drive, Cranleigh, Surrey GU6 8PJ. *T:* Cranleigh (0483) 276273.

JACKSON, Sir (William) Thomas, 8th Bt *cr* 1869; farmer, declined 1990; *b* 12 Oct. 1927; *s* of Sir William Jackson, 7th Bt, and Lady Ankaret Jackson (*d* 1945), 2nd *d* of 10th Earl of Carlisle; *S* father, 1985; *m* 1951, Gilian Malise, *d* of John William Stobart, MBE; three *s*. *Educ:* Mill Hill School; Royal Agricultural Coll., Cirencester. Qualified Associate Chartered Land Agents Soc., later ARICS; resigned, 1969. Nat. Service, 1947–49, 2/Lt Border Regt; Gen. Reserve as Lieut. Land Agent in various firms and on private estates till 1969, when he left the profession and started farming. Chairman: Cumberland Branch,

CLA, 1984–86; Whitehaven Branch, NFU, 1983–85. *Recreation:* painting. *Heir: e s* (William) Roland Cedric Jackson, PhD [*b* 9 Jan. 1954; *m* 1977, Nicola Mary, *yr d* of Prof. Peter Reginald Davis, PhD, FRCS; three *s*]. *Address:* Fell End, Mungrisdale, Penrith, Cumbria CA11 0XR.

JACKSON, William Unsworth, CBE 1985; Chief Executive, Kent County Council, 1974–86; *b* 9 Feb. 1926; *s* of William Jackson and Margaret Esplen Jackson (*née* Sunderland); *m* 1952, Valerie Annette (*née* Llewellyn); one *s* one *d*. *Educ:* Alsop High Sch., Liverpool. Solicitor. Entered local govt service, Town Clerk's Office, Liverpool, 1942; Dep. County Clerk, Kent, 1970. Pres., Soc. of Local Authority Chief Execs, 1985–86 (Hon. Sec., 1980–84). Adjudicator on political restrictions in local govt in England and Wales, 1989–. Trustee, Charities Aid Foundn, 1986–. *Address:* 34 Yardley Park Road, Tonbridge, Kent TN9 1NF. *T:* Tonbridge (0732) 351078. *Club:* Royal Over-Seas League.

JACKSON, Yvonne Brenda, OBE 1985; DL; Chairman, West Yorkshire Metropolitan County Council, 1980–81; *b* 23 July 1920; *d* of Charles and Margaret Wilson; *m* 1946, Edward Grosvenor Jackson; twin *s* one *d*. *Educ:* Edgbaston C of E Coll., Birmingham; Manchester Teachers' Trng Coll. (Dip. Domestic Science and qualified teacher). School Meals Organizer, West Bromwich, Staffs, 1942–45. Mem., W Riding CC, 1967–73 (local govt reorganisation); Mem. W Yorks CC, 1973–86; Chm., Fire and Public Protection Cttee, 1977–80; Deputy Leader and Shadow Chairman: Fire Cttee, 1981–86; Trading Standards Cttee, 1981–86; Police Cttee, 1982–86. Chm., Yorks Electricity Consultative Council, 1982–90; Mem., Yorks RHA, 1982–87. Mem. Exec. Cttee, Nat. Union of Cons. Assocs, 1981–88 (Dep. Chm., Yorks Area Finance and Gen. Purposes Cttee, 1982–88; Divl Pres., Elmet, 1985–). Mem. Council and Court, Leeds Univ. DL W Yorks, 1983, High Sheriff, 1986–87. *Recreations:* badminton, fishing; formerly County hockey and tennis player; former motor rally driver (competed in nat. and internat. events inc. Monte Carlo, Alpine and Tulip rallies). *Address:* East Garth, School Lane, Collingham, W Yorks LS22 5BQ. *T:* Collingham Bridge (0937) 573452.

JACKSON-LIPKIN, Miles Henry; QC (Hong Kong) 1974; JP; a Judge of the High Court of Hong Kong, 1981–87; *b* Liverpool; *s* of late I. J. Jackson-Lipkin, MD and F.A. Patley; *m* Lucille Yun-Shim Fung, DLJ, barrister; one *s*. *Educ:* Harrow; Trinity Coll., Oxford. FCIArb 1986. Called to the Bar, Middle Temple, 1951; admitted Hong Kong Bar, 1963, NSW Bar, 1980. Comr, Supreme Court of Negara Brunei Darussalam, 1984–87. Panel Mem., Inland Revenue Bd of Review, Hong Kong, 1975; Chm. Exec. Cttee, and Man. Dir, Hong Kong Children and Youth Services, 1978–. Member: Medico-Legal Soc., 1952; Justice, 1956; Council of Honour, Monarchist League; Founder Member: Hong Kong Br., Justice, 1963; Hong Kong Medico-Legal Soc., 1974 (Mem. Cttee, 1976–). Vice-Chm., Hong Kong Island Br., Internat. Wine and Food Soc. Hon. Mem., Chinese Soc. for Wind Engrg. Liveryman: Meadmakers' Co. (Edinburgh), 1984; Arbitrators' Co., 1986; Freeman, City of London, 1986. JP Hong Kong, 1977. KCLJ 1983 (Grand Priory of Lochore) (KLJ 1977; CLJ 1973). Hon. Mem., Officers' Mess, HQBF, Hong Kong. *Publications:* The Beaufort Legitimation, 1957; Scales of Justice, 1958; Israel Naval Forces, 1959. *Recreations:* gardening, heraldry, classical music, philately, walking. *Address:* A2–19 Evergreen Villa, 43 Stubbs Road, Hong Kong; 62 Eaton Terrace, SW1W 8TZ. *Clubs:* Naval and Military, MCC; Hong Kong, Hong Kong Cricket, Royal Hong Kong Golf, Royal Hong Kong Jockey, American, Arts, China Fleet, Classic Car, Shanghai Fraternity Assoc. (Hon.) (Hong Kong).

JACKSON-STOPS, Gervase Frank Ashworth, OBE 1987; FSA 1985; Architectural Adviser, National Trust, since 1975; *b* 26 April 1947; 2nd *s* of late Anthony Ashworth Jackson-Stops and Jean Jackson-Stops, DL, JP, ARIBA. *Educ:* Harrow; Christ Church, Oxford (BA 1968; MA 1971). Museums Assoc. Studentship, V&A, 1969–71; Res. Asst, Nat. Trust, 1972–75; regular contributor to Country Life, 1973–. Trustee, Attingham Summer Sch., 1983–90; Curator, Treasure Houses of Britain exhibn, Nat. Gallery of Art, Washington, 1985–86; Curator, Robert Adam and Kedleston exhibn, Amer. Museums, 1987–89; Co-Curator, Courts and Colonies exhibn, NY and Pittsburgh, 1988–89. Member: Historic Buildings Adv. Cttee, English Heritage, 1986–88; Reviewing Cttee on Export of Works of Art, 1988–. Pres., Friends of Northampton Museum and Art Gall., 1986–. Editor, Nat. Trust Year Book, 1975–78; Nat. Trust Studies, 1979–82. *Publications:* The English Country House: a grand tour, 1985; The Country House Garden, 1987; The Country House in Perspective, 1990. *Recreations:* playing impromptus, moving at speed. *Address:* The Menagerie, Horton, Northampton NN7 2BX. *T:* Northampton (0604) 870486. *Clubs:* Travellers', Beefsteak.
See also T. W. A. Jackson-Stops.

JACKSON-STOPS, Timothy William Ashworth, FRICS; Chairman, Jackson-Stops & Staff, since 1978; *b* 1942; *s* of late Anthony and Jean Jackson-Stops; *m* 1987, Jenny MacArthur; two *s*. *Educ:* Eton; Agricultural Coll., Cirencester. Jackson-Stops & Staff, 1967–: Dir, 1974. *Recreations:* ski-ing, sailing, shooting. *Address:* Wood Burcote Court, Towcester, Northants NN12 7JP. *T:* Towcester (0327) 50443. *Club:* Buck's.
See also G. F. A. Jackson-Stops.

JACOB, Ven. Bernard Victor; Archdeacon of Reigate (title changed from Kingston-upon-Thames, 1986), 1977–88, now Archdeacon Emeritus; *b* 20 Nov. 1921; *m* 1946, Dorothy Joan Carey; one *s* two *d*. *Educ:* Liverpool Institute; St Peter's College (MA) and Wycliffe Hall, Oxford. Curate, Middleton, Lancs, 1950–54; Vicar, Ulverston, Lancs, 1954–59; Vicar, Bilston, Staffs, 1959–64; Warden of Scargill House, Yorks, 1964–68; Rector of Mortlake, 1968–77. *Recreations:* travel, reading, enjoying life. *Address:* 4 The Peacheries, Chichester, West Sussex PO19 2NP.

JACOB, David Oliver Ll.; *see* Lloyd Jacob, D. O.

JACOB, Lt-Gen. Sir (Edward) Ian (Claud), GBE 1960 (KBE 1946; CBE 1942); CB 1944; DL; late RE, Colonel, retired and Hon. Lieutenant-General; Chairman, Matthews Holdings Ltd, 1970–76; *b* 27 Sept. 1899; *s* of late Field Marshal Sir Claud Jacob, GCB, GCSI, KCMG; *m* 1924, Cecil Bisset Treherne (*d* 1991); two *s*. *Educ:* Wellington Coll.; RMA, Woolwich; King's Coll., Cambridge (BA). 2nd Lieut, Royal Engineers, 1918; Capt. 1929; Bt Major, 1935; Major, 1938; Bt Lt-Col, 1939; Col, 1943. Waziristan, 1922–23. Staff Coll., 1931–32; GSO3 War Office, 1934–36; Bde-Maj., Canal Bde, Egypt, 1936–38; Military Asst Sec., Cttee of Imperial Defence, 1938; Military Asst Sec. to the War Cabinet, 1939–46; retired pay, 1946. Controller of European Services, BBC, 1946; Dir of Overseas Services, BBC, 1947 (on leave of absence during 1952); Chief Staff Officer to Minister of Defence and Deputy Sec. (Mil.) of the Cabinet during 1952; Dir-Gen. of the BBC, 1952–60; Director: Fisons, 1960–70; EMI, 1960–73; Chm., Covent Garden Market Authority, 1961–66; a Trustee, Imperial War Museum, 1966–73. CC, E Suffolk, 1960–70, Alderman, 1970–74; CC Suffolk, 1974–77. JP Suffolk, 1961–69; DL Suffolk, 1964–84. US Legion of Merit (Comdr). *Address:* The Red House, Woodbridge, Suffolk IP12 4AD. *T:* Woodbridge (0394) 2001. *Club:* Army and Navy.

JACOB, Prof. François; Croix de la Libération; Grand-Croix de la Légion d'Honneur; President, Pasteur Institute, since 1982; Professor of Cellular Genetics, at the College of France, since 1964; *b* Nancy (Meurthe & Moselle), 17 June 1920; *m* 1947, Lysiane Bloch (*d* 1984); three *s* one *d*. *Educ:* Lycée Carnot, France. DenM 1947; DèsS 1954. Pasteur Institute: Asst, 1950; Head of Laboratory, 1956. Mem., Acad. of Scis, Paris, 1977. Charles Léopold Mayer Prize, Acad. des Sciences, Paris, 1962; Nobel Prize for Medicine, 1965. Foreign Member: Royal Danish Acad. of Letters and Sciences, 1962; Amer. Acad. of Arts and Sciences, 1964; Nat. Acad. of Scis, USA, 1969; Royal Soc., 1973; Acad. Royale de Médecine, Belgique, 1973; Acad. of Sci., Hungary, 1986; Royal Acad. of Sci., Madrid, 1987. Holds hon. doctorates from several univs, incl. Chicago, 1965. *Publications:* La Logique du Vivant, 1970 (The Logic of Life, 1974); Le Jeu des Possibles, 1981 (The Possible and the Actual, 1982); La Statue Intérieure, 1987 (The Statue Within, 1988); various scientific. *Recreation:* painting. *Address:* 25 rue du Dr Roux, 75724 Paris, Cedex 15, France.

JACOB, Frederick Henry; CBiol; retired; Director, Ministry of Agriculture, Fisheries and Food's Pest Infestation Control Laboratory, 1968–77; *b* 12 March 1915; *s* of Henry Theodore and Elizabeth Jacob; *m* 1941, Winifred Edith Sloman (decd); one *s* one *d*. *Educ:* Friars Sch., Bangor; UC North Wales. BSc, MSc; CBiol, FIBiol. Asst Entomologist: King's Coll., Newcastle upon Tyne, 1942–44; Sch. of Agriculture, Cambridge, 1944–45; Adviser in Agric. Zoology, UC North Wales, 1945–46; Adv. Entomologist, Min. of Agriculture and Fisheries, Nat. Agric. Adv. Service, N Wales, 1946–50; Head of Entomology Dept, MAFF, Plant Pathology Lab., 1950–68. Pres., Assoc. of Applied Biologists, 1976–77. *Publications:* papers mainly on systematics of Aphididae in learned jls. *Recreations:* hill walking, fishing, gardening. *Address:* Hillside, Almondbury Common, Huddersfield HD4 6SN. *T:* Huddersfield (0484) 422021. *Clubs:* Farmers', Climbers; Wayfarers (Liverpool).

JACOB, Lieut-Gen. Sir Ian; *see* Jacob, Lieut-Gen. Sir E. I. C.

JACOB, Sir Isaac Hai, (Sir Jack Jacob), Kt 1979; QC 1976; Senior Master of the Supreme Court, Queen's Bench Division, and Queen's Remembrancer, 1975–80; Director, Institute of Advanced Legal Studies, University of London, 1986–88; Fellow of University College London, 1966; *b* 5 June 1908; 3rd *s* of late Jacob Isaiah and Aziza Jacob; *m* 1940, Rose Mary Jenkins (*née* Samwell); two *s*. *Educ:* Shanghai Public Sch. for Boys; London Sch. of Economics; University Coll., London. LLB (1st class Hons), London; Joseph Hume Scholar in Jurisprudence, University Coll., London, 1928 and 1930; Arden Scholar, Gray's Inn, 1930; Cecil Peace Prizeman, 1930. Pres., Univ. of London Law Students' Soc., 1930. Called to the Bar, Gray's Inn, Nov. 1930; Hon. Bencher, 1978; Mem., Senate of Inns of Court and the Bar, 1975–78. Served in ranks from 1940 until commissioned in RAOC 1942; Staff Capt., War Office (Ord. I), 1943–45. Master, Supreme Court, Queen's Bench Div., 1957–80. Prescribed Officer for Election Petitions, 1975–80. Hon. Lectr in Law, UCL, 1959–74; teaching LLM subject, Principles in Civil Litigation, 1959–87; Hon. Lectr in Legal Ethics, Birmingam Univ., 1969–72; Hon. Visiting Lecturer: Imperial Coll. of Science and Technology, 1963–64; Birmingham Univ., 1964–65; Bedford Coll., 1969–71; European Univ. Institute, Florence, 1978; Visiting Professor: Sydney Univ., 1971; Osgoode Hall Law Sch., York Univ., Toronto, 1971; of English Law, UCL, 1974–87; Polytechnic of Central London, 1981–83. Member: Lord Chancellor's (Pearson) Cttee on Funds in Court, 1958–59; Working Party on the Revision of the Rules of the Supreme Court, 1960–65; (Payne) Cttee on Enforcement of Judgment Debts, 1965–69; (Winn) Cttee on Personal Injuries Litigation, 1966–68; (Kerr) Working Party on Foreign Judgments, 1976–80. Chm., Working Party on Form of the Writ of Summons and Appearance, 1977. Mem., Fourth Anglo-Amer. Legal Exchange on Trial of Civil Actions, 1973. Pres., Assoc. of Law Teachers, 1978–85 (Vice Pres., 1965–78); Vice-President: Industrial Law Soc.; Selden Soc., 1978–84 (Mem. Council, 1976–78, 1985–); Inst. of Legal Executives, 1978–; Mansfield Law Club, City of London Polytechnic, 1965–; Governor, Polytechnic of Central London, 1968–88; Member, Cttee of Management: Inst. of Judicial Admin, 1968–; Brit. Inst. of Internat. and Comparative Law, 1965–; Law Adv. Cttee of Associated Examining Bd, 1964–84; Friends of Hebrew Univ., Jerusalem, 1965–85; Mem. Council, Justice; Mem. Gen. Cttee, Bar Assoc. of Commerce, Finance and Industry, 1981–85. Chm., Bentham Club, UCL, 1964–84, Pres. 1985, Vice Pres. 1986–. Hon. Member: SPTL, 1981–; Council of Justice, 1988–; Internat. Assoc. of Procedural Law, 1985–. Hon. Freeman, City of London, 1976. Mem., Broderers' Co., 1977. FCIArb 1984. Hon. Fellow, Polytechnic of Central London, 1988. Hon. LLD: Birmingham, 1978; London, 1981; Dr Jur. *hc* Würzburg, Bavaria, 1982. Adv. Editor, 1962–83, Chief Adv. Editor, 1984–, Atkin's Court Forms; Editor, Annual Practice, 1961–66; General Editor: Supreme Court Practice, 1967–; Civil Justice Quarterly, 1982–; Adv. Editor, Internat. Encyclopedia of Comparative Law (Civil Procedure vol.), 1968–. *Publications:* Law relating to Rent Restrictions, 1933, 1938; Law relating to Hire Purchase, 1938; Chitty and Jacob's Queen's Bench Forms (19th, 20th and 21st edns); Bullen and Leake and Jacob's Precedents of Pleadings (12th edn, 13th edn 1990); The Reform of Civil Procedural Law and Other Essays in Civil Procedure, 1982; The Fabric of English Civil Justice (Hamlyn Lectures), 1986; (gen. ed.) Private International Litigation, 1988; (ed jtly) Trends in Enforcement of Non-Money Judgments and Orders, 1988; (with Ian Goldrein) Pleadings: principles and practice, 1990; (ed) Supreme Court Practice 1991, 1990; contributed: chapter on Civil Procedure including Courts and Evidence, in Annual Survey of Commonwealth Law, 1965–77; Discovery, Execution (jtly), Practice and Procedure, to Halsbury's Laws of England, 4th edn; Compromise and Settlement, Default Judgments, Discontinuance and Withdrawal, Discovery, Interlocutory Proceedings, Interim Orders, Issues, Judgments and Orders (part), Order 14 Proceedings, Pleadings, Service of Proceedings, Stay of Proceedings, Third Party Procedure, Writs of Summons to Atkin's Court Forms, 2d. edn. *Recreation:* painting. *Address:* 16 The Park, Golders Green, NW11 7SU. *T:* 081–458 3832. *Clubs:* City Livery, Reform, Royal Automobile.
See also R. R. H Jacob.

JACOB, Robert Raphael Hayim, (Robin Jacob), QC 1981; *b* 26 April 1941; *s* of Sir Jack I. H. Jacob, *qv*; *m* 1967, Wendy Jones; three *s*. *Educ:* King Alfred Sch., Hampstead; Mountgrace Secondary Comprehensive Sch., Potters Bar; St Paul's Sch.; Trinity Coll., Cambridge (BA, MA); LSE (LLB). Called to the Bar, Gray's Inn, 1965 (Atkin Scholar; Bencher, 1989); teacher of law, 1965–66; pupillage with Nigel (now Lord) Bridge, 1966–67, with A. M. Walton, 1967; entered chambers of Thomas Blanco White, 1967. Junior Counsel to Treasury in Patent Matters, 1976–81. Dep. Chm., Copyright Tribunal, 1989–; apptd to hear appeals to Sec. of State under the Trade Marks Acts, 1988–. *Publications:* Kerly's Law of Trade Marks (ed jtly), 1972, 1983 and 1986 edns; Patents, Trade Marks, Copyright and Designs (ed jtly), 1970, 1978, 1986; Encyclopedia of UK and European Patent Law (ed jtly), 1977; Editor, Court Forms Sections on Copyright (1978), Designs and Trade Marks (1975–); section on Trade Marks (ed jtly), 4th edn, Halsbury's Laws of England, 1984. *Recreations:* photography, country garden. *Address:* Francis Taylor Building, Temple, EC4Y 7BY. *T:* 071–353 5657.

JACOB, Rev. Canon William Mungo, PhD; Warden of Lincoln Theological College, since 1986; Canon of Lincoln, since 1986; Assistant Curate of St Michael-on-the-Mount, Lincoln, since 1987; *b* 15 Nov. 1944; *s* of John William Carey Jacob and Mary Marsters Dewar. *Educ:* King Edward VII School, King's Lynn; Hull Univ. (LLB); Linacre Coll.,

Oxford (MA); Exeter Univ. (PhD). Deacon 1970, priest 1971; Curate of Wymondham, Norfolk, 1970–73; Asst Chaplain, Exeter Univ., 1973–75; Lecturer, Salisbury and Wells Theological Coll., 1975–80, Vice-Principal, 1977–80; Sec. to Cttee for Theological Education, ACCM, 1980–86. *Address:* The Warden's House, Drury Lane, Lincoln LN1 3BP. *T:* Lincoln (0522) 538885.

JACOBI, Derek George, CBE 1985; actor; *b* 22 Oct. 1938; *s* of Alfred George Jacobi and Daisy Gertrude Masters. *Educ:* Leyton County High Sch.; St John's Coll., Cambridge (MA Hons; Hon. Fellow, 1987). Artistic Associate, Old Vic Co. (formerly Prospect Theatre Co.), 1976–81; associate actor, RSC. Vice-Pres., Nat. Youth Theatre, 1982–. *Stage:* Birmingham Repertory Theatre, 1960–63 (first appearance in One Way Pendulum, 1961); National Theatre, 1963–71; Prospect Theatre Co., 1972, 1974, 1976, 1977, 1978; Hamlet (for reformation of Old Vic Co., and at Elsinore), 1979; Royal Shakespeare Co.: Benedick in Much Ado About Nothing (Tony Award, 1985), title rôle in Peer Gynt, Prospero in The Tempest, 1982; title rôle in Cyrano de Bergerac, 1983 (SWET Award; Play and Players Award); Breaking the Code, Haymarket, 1986, Washington and NY 1987; Dir, Hamlet, Phoenix, 1988; title rôle in Kean, Old Vic, 1990; *appearances include: TV:* She Stoops to Conquer, Man of Straw, The Pallisers, I Claudius, Philby, Burgess and Maclean, Richard II, Hamlet, Inside the Third Reich; Mr Pye; *films:* 1971–: Odessa File; Day of the Jackal; The Medusa Touch; Othello; Three Sisters; Interlude; The Human Factor; Charlotte; The Man Who Went Up in Smoke; Enigma; Little Dorrit (Best Actor Award, Evening Standard); Henry V; The Fool. *Awards:* BAFTA Best Actor, 1976–77; Variety Club TV Personality, 1976; Standard Best Actor, 1983. *Address:* Duncan Heath Associates, Paramount House, 162–170 Wardour Street, W1.

JACOBI, Sir James (Edward), Kt 1989; OBE 1978; Medical Practitioner (private practice), since 1960; *b* 26 Aug. 1925; *s* of Edward William Jacobi and Doris Stella Jacobi; *m* 1946, Joy; one *s* two *d*; *m* 1974, Nora Maria; two *s*. *Educ:* Maryborough State High School; Univ. of Queensland (MB, BS, PhC). Clerk, Public Service, 1941; RAAF, 1943–46; served navigator-wireless operator, Beaufighter Sqdn, SW Pacific. Apprentice pharmaceutical chemist, 1946–50; pharm. chem., 1950–54, and Univ. student, 1954–60; Resident MO, Brisbane, 1961; MO, Dept of Health, Papua New Guinea, 1962–63; GP Port Moresby, 1963–. *Recreations:* National President, PNG Rugby Football League. *Address:* Jacobi Medical Centre, Box 1551, Boroko, Papua New Guinea. *T:* 255355. *Clubs:* United Services (Brisbane); City Tattersalls, NSW Leagues (Sydney); Brisbane Polo; Papua (Port Moresby).

JACOBS, Sir Anthony; *see* Jacobs, Sir D. A.

JACOBS, Prof. Arthur David; musicologist and critic; Member of Editorial Board, Opera, since 1961; *b* 14 June 1922; *s* of late Alexander S. and Estelle Jacobs; *m* 1953, Betty Upton Hughes; two *s*. *Educ:* Manchester Grammar Sch.; Merton Coll., Oxford (MA). Music Critic: Daily Express, 1947–52; Jewish Chronicle, 1963–75; critic, Hi-Fi News and Record Review (formerly Audio and Record Review), 1964–89; record reviewer, Sunday Times, 1968–89. Professor, RAM, 1964–79; Hd of Music Dept, Huddersfield Polytechnic, 1979–84, created Prof. 1984. Founder and Editor, British Music Yearbook (formerly Music Yearbook), 1971–79, Adv. Editor, 1979–83. Leverhulme Res. Fellow in Music, 1977–78; Leverhulme Emeritus Res. Fellow, 1991–. Vis. Fellow, Wolfson Coll., Oxford, 1979, 1984–85; Centennial Lectr, Univ. of Illinois, 1967; Vis. Professor: Univ. of Victoria, BC, 1968; Univ. of California at Santa Barbara, 1969; Temple Univ., Philadelphia, 1970, 1971; UCLA, 1973; Univ. of Western Ontario, 1974; McMaster Univ., 1975, 1983; Univ. of Queensland, 1985. Hon. RAM 1969. *Publications:* Music Lover's Anthology, 1948; Gilbert and Sullivan, 1951; A New Dictionary of Music, 1958 (also Spanish, Portuguese, Danish and Swedish edns), new edn, as The New Penguin Dictionary of Music, 1978; Choral Music, 1963 (also Spanish and Japanese edns); Libretto of opera One Man Show by Nicholas Maw, 1964; (with Stanley Sadie) Pan Book of Opera, 1966, expanded edn 1984 (US edns, Great Operas in Synopsis, The Limelight Book of Opera); A Short History of Western Music, 1972 (also Italian edn); (ed) Music Education Handbook, 1976; Arthur Sullivan: a Victorian musician, 1984; The Pan Book of Orchestral Music, 1987; Penguin Dictionary of Musical Performers, 1990; many opera translations incl. Berg's Lulu (first US perf. of complete work, Santa Fe, New Mexico, 1979); contributions to: A History of Song, 1960; Grove's Dictionary of Music and Musicians, 1980; Shakespeare and the Victorian Stage, 1986; TLS, Musical Times, foreign jls, etc. *Recreations:* puns, swimming, walking, theatre. *Address:* 10 Oldbury Close, Sevenoaks, Kent TN15 9DJ. *T:* Sevenoaks (0732) 884006. *Club:* Commonwealth Trust.

JACOBS, Sir (David) Anthony, Kt 1988; FCA; Chairman, British School of Motoring, since 1973; *b* Nov. 1931; *s* of Ridley and Ella Jacobs; *m* 1954, Evelyn Felicity Patchett; one *s* one *d*. *Educ:* Clifton Coll.; London Univ. (BCom). Chm., Nig Securities Gp, 1957–72. Contested (L) Watford, Feb. and Oct. 1974. Jt Treas., Liberal Party, 1984–87; Vice-Pres., Soc. & Lib. Dem., 1988; Chm., Federal Exec., Soc. & Lib. Dem., 1988. *Recreations:* golf, reading, theatre, opera, travel. *Address:* BSM Holdings Ltd, 9 Nottingham Terrace, NW1 4QB. *T:* 071–486 6323. *Clubs:* National Liberal; Coombe Hill Golf (Surrey); Palm Beach Country (USA).

JACOBS, David Lewis; DL; radio and television broadcaster; *b* 19 May 1926; *s* of David Jacobs and Jeanette Victoria Jacobs; *m* 1st, 1949, Patricia Bradlaw (marr. diss. 1972); three *d* (one *s* decd); 2nd, 1975, Caroline Munro (*d* 1975); 3rd, 1979, Mrs Lindsay Stuart-Hutcheson. *Educ:* Belmont Coll.; Strand Sch. RN, 1944–47. First broadcast, Navy Mixture, 1944; Announcer, Forces Broadcasting Service, 1944–45; Chief Announcer, Radio SEAC, Ceylon, 1945–47; Asst Stn Dir, Radio SEAC, 1947; News Reader, BBC Gen. Overseas Service, 1947, subseq. freelance. Major radio credits include: Book of Verse, Housewives' Choice, Journey into Space, Dateline London, Grande Gingold, Curioser and Curioser, Puffney Post Office, Follow that Man, Man about Town, Jazz Club, Midday Spin, Music Through Midnight, Scarlet Pimpernel, Radio 2 DJ Show, Pick of the Pops, Saturday Show Band Show, Melodies for You (12 years), Saturday Star Sounds, Any Questions (Chm. for 17 years), Any Answers; Internat. Fest. of Light Music. TV credits incl.: Focus on Hocus, Vera Lynn Show, Make up your Mind, Tell the Truth, Juke Box Jury, Top of the Pops, Hot Line, Miss World, Top Town, David Jacobs' Words and Music, Sunday Night with David Jacobs, Little Women, There Goes that Song Again, Make a Note, Where are they Now, What's My Line, Who What or Where, Frank Sinatra Show, Mario Lanza Show, Walt Disney Christmas Show, Wednesday Show, Wednesday Magazine, Eurovision Song Contest, TV Ice Time, Twist, A Song for Europe, Ivor Novello Awards, Aladdin, Airs and Graces, Tell Me Another, Those Wonderful TV Times, Blankety Blank, Come Dancing, Questions (TVS); Primetime. Numerous film performances incl. Golden Disc, You Must Be Joking, It's Trad Dad, Stardust; former commentator, British Movietone News. 6 Royal Command Performances; 6 yrs Britain's Top Disc Jockey on both BBC and Radio Luxembourg; Variety Club of Gt Brit., BBC TV Personality of Year, 1960, and BBC Radio Personality of the Year, 1975; Sony Gold Award for Outstanding Contribution to Radio over the Years, 1984; RSPCA Richard Martin Award, 1978. Director: Duke of York's Theatre, 1979–85; Video Travel Guides, 1990–; Chm., Kingston Theatre Trust, 1990–. Vice-Pres., Stars Organisation for Spastics (Past Chm.); Mem. Council, RSPCA, 1969–77, Vice-Chm. 1975–76; Vice-Pres., The St John Ambulance London (Prince of Wales's). Past Pres., Nat. Children's Orch.; Vice-Pres., Wimbledon Girls Choir. Chm., Think British Council, 1985–89 (Dep. Chm., 1983–85); Vice-Pres., Invest in Britain Campaign, 1989–. Pres., Kingston upon Thames Royal British Legion, 1984–; Vice-Pres., Royal Star and Garter Home, Richmond, 1988–. DL Greater London, 1983, Kingston upon Thames, 1984 (representative). *Publications:* (autobiog.) Jacobs' Ladder, 1963; Caroline, 1978; (with Michael Bowen) Any Questions?, 1981. *Recreations:* talking and listening, hotels. *Address:* 203 Pavilion Road, SW1X 0BJ. *Clubs:* Garrick, St James'; Helford River Sailing.

JACOBS, Francis Geoffrey; an Advocate General, Court of Justice of the European Communities, since 1988; *b* 8 June 1939; *s* of late Cecil Sigismund Jacobs and of Louise Jacobs (*née* Fischhof); *m* 1st, 1964, Ruth (*née* Freeman); one *s*; 2nd, 1975, Susan Felicity Gordon (*née* Cox); one *s* three *d*. *Educ:* City of London Sch.; Christ Church, Oxford; Nuffield Coll., Oxford. MA, DPhil. Called to the Bar, Middle Temple, 1964, Bencher, 1990; in practice, 1974–88; QC 1984; Lectr in Jurisprudence, Univ. of Glasgow, 1963–65; Lectr in Law, LSE, 1965–69; Secretariat, European Commn of Human Rights, and Legal Directorate, Council of Europe, Strasbourg, 1969–72; Legal Sec., Court of Justice of European Communities, Luxembourg, 1972–74; Prof. of European Law, Univ. of London, 1974–88; King's College, London: Dir, Centre of European Law, 1981–88; Vis. Prof., 1989–91; Fellow, 1990. Hon. Sec. UK Assoc. for European Law, 1974–81 (a Vice-Pres., 1988–); UK Deleg., Conf. of Supreme Administrative Courts, EEC, 1984–88; Mem., Admin. Tribunal, Internat. Inst. for Unification of Private Law, Rome. Cooley Lectr, 1983, Bishop Lectr, 1989, Univ. of Mich. Governor, British Inst. of Human Rights, 1985–. Commandeur de l'Ordre de Mérite, Luxembourg, 1983. Editor, Yearbook of European Law, 1981–88; Mem. Editorial Board: Yearbook of European Law; Common Market Law Review; European Law Review; Jl of Common Market Studies; Rivista di Diritto Europeo. Gen. Ed., Oxford European Community Law series. *Publications:* Criminal Responsibility, 1971; The European Convention on Human Rights, 1975; (jtly) References to the European Court, 1975; (ed) European Law and the Individual, 1976; (jtly) The Court of Justice of the European Communities, 1977, 3rd edn by L. Neville Brown, 1989; (jtly) The European Union Treaty, 1986; (joint editor): The European Community and GATT, 1986; The Effect of Treaties in Domestic Law, 1987. *Recreations:* family life, books, music, nature, travel. *Address:* Court of Justice of the European Communities, Kirchberg, Luxembourg; 132 Kingston Road, Teddington, Mddx TW11 9JA. *T:* 081–943 0503.

JACOBS, Prof. John Arthur; Hon. Professor, Institute of Earth Studies, University College of Wales, Aberystwyth, since 1989; Professor of Geophysics, 1974–83, and Fellow, Darwin College, since 1976 (Vice Master, 1978–82), University of Cambridge; *b* 13 April 1916; *m* 1st, 1941, Daisy Sarah Ann Montgomerie (*d* 1974); two *d*; 2nd, 1974, Margaret Jones (marr. diss. 1981); 3rd, 1982, Ann Grace Wintle. *Educ:* Univ. of London. BA 1937, MA 1939, PhD 1949, DSc 1961. Instr Lieut RN, 1941–46; Lectr, Royal Holloway Coll., Univ. of London, 1946–51; Assoc. Prof., Univ. of Toronto, 1951–57; Prof., Univ. of British Columbia, 1957–67; Dir, Inst. of Earth Sciences, Univ. of British Columbia, 1961–67; Killam Meml Prof. of Science, Univ. of Alberta, 1967–74; Dir, Inst. of Earth and Planetary Physics, Univ. of Alberta, 1970–74. Res. Fellow, RHBNC, 1987–89. Sec., Royal Astronomical Soc., 1977–82; Harold Jeffreys Lectr, RAS, 1983. FRSC 1958; DSc *hc* Univ. of BC, 1987. Centennial Medal of Canada, 1967; Medal of Canadian Assoc. of Physicists, 1975; J. Tuzo Wilson Medal, Canadian Geophys. Union, 1982. *Publications:* (with R. D. Russell and J. T. Wilson) Physics and Geology, 1959, 2nd edn 1974; The Earth's Core and Geomagnetism, 1963; Geomagnetic Micropulsations, 1970; A Textbook on Geonomy, 1974; The Earth's Core, 1975, 2nd edn 1987; Reversals of the Earth's Magnetic Field, 1984. *Recreations:* walking, music. *Address:* Institute of Earth Studies, University College of Wales, Aberystwyth, Dyfed SY23 3DB. *T:* Aberystwyth (0970) 622646.

JACOBS, John Robert Maurice; Consultant Golf Architect to John Jacobs Golf Associates, since 1988; *b* 14 March 1925; *s* of Robert and Gertrude Vivian Jacobs; *m* 1949, Rita Wragg; one *s* one *d*. *Educ:* Maltby Grammar School. Asst Professional Golfer, Hallamshire Golf Club, 1947–49; Golf Professional: Gezira Sporting Club, Cairo, 1949–52; Sandy Lodge Golf Club, 1952–64; Man. Dir, Athlon Golf, 1967–75; Professional Golfers' Association: Tournament Dir-Gen., 1971–76, Advr to Tournament Div., 1977; European Ryder Cup Captain, 1979–81 (player, 1955); Golf Instructor: Golf Digest Magazine Schs, 1971–76; Golf Magazine Schs, US, 1977. Adviser to: Walker Cup Team; Spanish and French nat. teams; Past Adviser to: Curtis Cup Team; English Golf Union team; Scottish Union team; German, Swedish and Italian teams. Golf Commentator, ITV, 1967–87. Currently associated with John Jacobs' Practical Golf Schools, based in USA. Golf adviser to Golf World Magazine, 1962–86. *Publications:* Golf, 1961; Play Better Golf, 1969; Practical Golf, 1973; John Jacobs Analyses the Superstars, 1974; Golf Doctor, 1979. *Recreations:* shooting, fishing. *Address:* Stable Cottage, Chapel Lane, Lyndhurst, Hants SO43 7FG. *T:* Southampton (0703) 282743. *Clubs:* Lucayan Country (Grand Bahamas); Sandy Lodge Golf, New Forest Golf, Brockenhurst Golf, Bramshaw Golf; Lake Nona Golf and Country (Florida).

JACOBS, Hon. Sir Kenneth (Sydney), KBE 1976; Justice of High Court of Australia, 1974–79; *b* 5 Oct. 1917; *s* of Albert Sydney Jacobs and Sarah Grace Jacobs (*née* Aggs); *m* 1952, Eleanor Mary Neal; one *d*. *Educ:* Knox Grammar Sch., NSW; Univ. of Sydney (BA, LLB). Admitted to NSW Bar, 1947; QC 1958; Supreme Court of NSW: Judge, 1960; Judge of Appeal, 1966; Pres., Court of Appeal, 1972. *Publication:* Law of Trusts, 1958. *Recreations:* printing and bookbinding; gardening. *Address:* Crooks Lane Corner, Axford, Marlborough, Wilts SN8 2HA.

JACOBS, Rabbi Dr Louis, CBE 1990; Rabbi, New London Synagogue, since 1964; Visiting Professor, University of Lancaster, since 1987; *b* 17 July 1920; *s* of Harry and Lena Jacobs; *m* 1944, Sophie Lisagorska; two *s* one *d*. *Educ:* Manchester Central High Sch.; Manchester Talmudical Coll.; BA Hons, PhD, London. Rabbinical Ordination; Rabbi, Central Synagogue, Manchester, 1948–54; New West End Synagogue, 1954–60; Tutor, Jews' Coll., London, 1959–62; Dir, Society Study of Jewish Theology, 1962–64. Vis. Prof., Harvard Divinity Sch., 1985–86. Hon. Fellow: UCL, 1988; Leo Baeck Coll., 1988. Hon. DHL: Spertus Coll., Chicago, 1987; Hebrew Union Coll., Cincinnati, 1989; Jewish Theol. Seminary, NY, 1989; Hon. DLitt Lancaster, 1991. Hon. Citizen: Texas, 1961; New Orleans, 1963. *Publications:* Jewish Prayer, 1955; We Have Reason to Believe, 1957; Guide to Rosh Hashanah, 1959; Guide to Yom Kippur, 1959; Jewish Values, 1960; (trans.) The Palm Tree of Deborah, 1960; Studies in Talmudic Logic, 1961; (trans.) Tract on Ecstasy, 1963; Principles of Jewish Faith, 1964; Seeker of Unity, 1966; Faith, 1968; Jewish Law, 1968; Jewish Ethics, Philosophy and Mysticism, 1969; Jewish Thought Today, 1970; What Does Judaism Say About . . .?, 1973; A Jewish Theology, 1973; Theology in the Responsa, 1975; Hasidic Thought, 1976; Hasidic Prayer, 1977; Jewish Mystical Testimonies, 1977; TEKYU: the unsolved problem in the Babylonian Talmud, 1981; The Talmudic Argument, 1985; A Tree of Life, 1985; Holy Living, 1990; Helping with Inquiries (autobiog.), 1989; God, Torah, Israel, 1990; Structure and Form of the Babylonian Talmud, 1991; Religion and the Individual, 1991; contribs to learned jls, collections and festschriften. *Recreations:* reading thrillers, watching television, hill walking. *Address:* 27 Clifton Hill, St John's Wood, NW8 0QE. *T:* 071–624 1299.

JACOBS, Sir Piers, KBE 1989 (OBE 1981); Financial Secretary, Hong Kong, 1986–91; *b* 27 May 1933; *s* of Dorothy and Selwyn Jacobs; *m* 1964, Josephine Lee; one *d*. *Educ:* St Paul's Sch. Solicitor (Hons), England and Wales, 1955; Solicitor, Hong Kong, 1976. Registrar General, Hong Kong, 1976; Sec. for Economic Services, Hong Kong, 1982. *Recreations:* walking, swimming, reading. *Address:* c/o Government Secretariat, Lower Albert Road, Hong Kong. *T:* 8102589. *Clubs:* Oriental; Hong Kong, Royal Hong Kong Jockey (Hong Kong).

JACOBS, Sir Wilfred (Ebenezer), GCMG 1981; GCVO 1985 (KCVO 1977); Kt 1967; OBE 1959; QC 1959; Governor-General of Antigua and Barbuda, since 1981; *b* 19 Oct. 1919; 2nd *s* of late William Henry Jacobs and Henrietta Jacobs (*née* Du Bois); *m* 1947, Carmen Sylva, 2nd *d* of late Walter A. Knight and Flora Knight (*née* Fleming); one *s* two *d*. *Educ:* Grenada Boys' Secondary Sch.; Gray's Inn, London. Called to Bar, Gray's Inn, 1946; Registrar and Additional Magistrate, St Vincent, 1946; Magistrate, Dominica, 1947, and St Kitts, 1949; Crown Attorney, St Kitts, 1952; Attorney-Gen., Leeward Is, 1957–59, and Antigua, 1960. Acted Administrator, Dominica, St Kitts, Antigua, various periods, 1947–60. MEC and MLC, St Vincent, Dominica, St Kitts, Antigua, 1947–60; Legal Draftsman and Acting Solicitor-Gen., Trinidad and Tobago, 1960. Barbados: Solicitor-Gen., and Actg Attorney-Gen., 1961–63; PC and MLC, 1962–63; Dir of Public Prosecutions, 1964; Judge of Supreme Court of Judicature, 1967; Governor of Antigua, 1967–81. KStJ. *Recreations:* swimming, gardening, golf. *Address:* Governor-General's Residence, Antigua, West Indies. *Club:* Royal Commonwealth Society.

JACOBSEN, Frithjof Halfdan; Norwegian Ambassador, retired; *b* 14 Jan. 1914; *m* 1941, Elsa Tidemand Anderson; one *s* two *d*. *Educ:* Univ. of Oslo (Law). Entered Norwegian Foreign Service, 1938; Legation, Paris, 1938–40; Norwegian Foreign Ministry, London, 1940–45; held posts in Moscow, London, Oslo, 1945–55; Director-Gen., Political Affairs, Oslo, 1955–59; Norwegian Ambassador to: Canada, 1959–61; Moscow, 1961–66; Under-Sec. of State, Oslo, 1966–70; Ambassador to Moscow, 1970–75; Ambassador to the Court of St James's and to Ireland, 1975–82. *Address:* Schwachsgate 4, Oslo 3, Norway.

JACOMB, Sir Martin (Wakefield), Kt 1985; Deputy Chairman, Barclays Bank PLC, since 1985; Chairman, British Council, from Feb. 1992; Chairman, Barclays de Zoete Wedd, 1986–91; a Director, Bank of England, since 1986; *b* 11 Nov. 1929; *s* of Hilary W. Jacomb and Félise Jacomb; *m* 1960, Evelyn Heathcoat Amory; two *s* one *d*. *Educ:* Eton Coll.; Worcester Coll., Oxford (MA Law 1953). Called to the Bar, Inner Temple, 1955. 2nd Lieut RA, 1948–49. Practised at the Bar, 1955–68; Kleinwort, Benson Ltd, 1968–85, Vice-Chm., 1976–85; Dep. Chm., Commercial Union Assurance Co., 1988– (Dir, 1984–88); Director: British Gas, 1981–88; Christian Salvesen Ltd, 1974–88; Daily Telegraph plc, 1986–; Royal Opera House, Covent Garden, 1987–; RTZ Corp., 1988–; Marks and Spencer, 1991–; Mem., Federal Reserve Bank of New York, Internat. Capital Markets Adv. Cttee, 1987–. External Mem., Finance Cttee, Delegacy of the OUP, 1971–. Trustee, Nat. Heritage Meml Fund, 1982–. Hon. Bencher, Middle Temple, 1987. *Recreations:* theatre, family bridge, tennis. *Address:* Barclays Bank, Johnson Smirke Building, 4 Royal Mint Court, EC3N 4HJ.

JACQUES, family name of **Baron Jacques.**

JACQUES, Baron *cr* 1968 (Life Peer), of Portsea Island; **John Henry Jacques;** Chairman of the Co-operative Union Ltd, 1964–70; *b* 11 Jan. 1905; *s* of Thomas Dobson Jacques and Annie Bircham; *m* 1st, 1929, Constance White (*d* 1987); two *s* one *d*; 2nd, 1989, Violet Jacques. *Educ:* Victoria Univ., Manchester; (BA(Com)); Co-operative Coll. Sec-Man., Moorsley Co-operative Society Ltd, 1925–29; Tutor, Co-operative Coll., 1929–42; Accountant, Plymouth Co-operative Soc. Ltd, 1942–45; Chief Executive, Portsea Island Co-operative Soc. Ltd, Portsmouth, 1945–65; Pres., Co-operative Congress, 1961. Pres., Retail Trades Education Council, 1971–75. A Lord in Waiting (Govt Whip), 1974–77 and 1979; a Dep. Chm. of Cttees, 1977–80. JP Portsmouth, 1951–75. *Publications:* Book-Keeping I, II and III, 1940; Management Accounting, 1966; Manual on Co-operative Management, 1969. *Recreations:* walking, snooker, gardening, West-Highland terriers. *Address:* 23 Hartford House, Blount Road, Pembroke Park, Portsmouth PO1 2TN. *T:* Portsmouth (0705) 738111. *Club:* Co-operative (Portsmouth).

JACQUES, Peter Roy Albert, CBE 1990; Secretary, TUC Social Insurance and Industrial Welfare Department, since 1971; *b* 12 Aug. 1939; *s* of George Henry Jacques and Ivy Mary Jacques (*née* Farr); *m* 1965, Jacqueline Anne Sears; one *s* one *d*. *Educ:* Archbishop Temple's Secondary Sch.; Newcastle upon Tyne Polytechnic (BSc Sociology); Univ. of Leicester. Building labourer, 1955–58; market porter, 1958–62; Asst, TUC Social Insce and Industrial Welfare Dept, 1968–71. Member: Industrial Injuries Adv. Council, 1972; Nat. Insce Adv. Cttee, 1972–78; Health and Safety Commn, 1974; Royal Commn on the Nat. Health Service, 1976–79; EEC Cttee on Health-Safety, 1976; NHS London Adv. Cttee, 1979–; Social Security Adv. Cttee, 1980–; Health Educn Council, 1984–87; Civil Justice Review Adv. Cttee, 1985–; Royal Commn on Envmtl Pollution, 1989–. Jt Sec., BMA/TUC Cttee, 1972–; Secretary: TUC Social Insurance and Industrial Welfare Cttee, 1972–; TUC Health Services Cttee, 1979–; Mem. Exec. Cttee, Royal Assoc. for Disability and Rehabilitation, 1975–. *Publications:* responsible for TUC pubns Health-Safety Handbook; Occupational Pension Schemes. *Recreations:* reading, yoga, walking, camping, vegetable growing. *Address:* TUC, Congress House, Great Russell Street, WC1B 3LS. *T:* 071–636 4030.

JACQUES, Robin; artist; illustrator of books; *b* 27 March 1920; *m* 1st, 1943, Patricia Bamford (decd); one *s*; 2nd, 1958, Azetta van der Merwe (decd); 3rd, Alexandra Mann (marr. diss.). *Educ:* Royal Masonic Schools, Bushey, Herts. Art Editor, Strand Mag., 1948–51; Principal Art Editor, COI Mags, 1951–53; *drawings for:* Hans Andersen Stories, 1953; James Joyce's Dubliners, 1954; James Joyce's Portrait of the Artist as a Young Man, 1955; Kipling's Kim, 1958; Thackeray's Vanity Fair, 1963; The Sea, Ships and Sailors, 1966; Collected Poems of W. B. Yeats, 1970; Henry James' The Europeans, 1982; Trollope's Dr Wortley's School, 1988; many illustrated books for children. *Publication:* Illustrators at Work, 1960. *Recreations:* music, travel, reading. *Address:* 5 Abbots Place, NW6 4NP. *T:* 071–624 7040.

JAEGER, Prof. Leslie Gordon, FRSE 1966; Research Professor of Civil Engineering and Applied Mathematics, Technical University of Nova Scotia, since 1988; *b* 28 Jan. 1926; *s* of Henry Jaeger; *m* 1st, 1948, Annie Sylvia Dyson; two *d*; 2nd, 1981, Kathleen Grant. *Educ:* King George V Sch., Southport; Gonville and Caius Coll., Cambridge. Royal Corps of Naval Constructors, 1945–48; Industry, 1948–52; University College, Khartoum, 1952–56; Univ. Lectr, Cambridge, 1956–62; Fellow and Dir of Studies, Magdalene Coll., Cambridge, 1959–62; Prof. of Applied Mechanics, McGill Univ., Montreal, 1962–65; Regius Prof. of Engineering, Edinburgh Univ., 1965–66; Prof. of Civil Engineering, McGill Univ., 1966–70; Dean, Faculty of Engineering, Univ. of New Brunswick, 1970–75; Academic Vice-Pres., Acadia Univ., NS, 1975–80; Vice-Pres. (Res.), Technical Univ. of NS, 1980–88.DEng *hc* Carleton Univ., Ottawa, 1991. Telford Premium, ICE, 1959; A. B. Sanderson Award, Canadian Soc. for Civil Engrg, 1983; Gzowski Medal, Engrg Inst. of Canada, 1985. *Publications:* The Analysis of Grid Frameworks and Related Structures (with A. W. Hendry), 1958; Elementary Theory of Elastic Plates, 1964; Cartesian Tensors in Engineering Science, 1965; (with B. Bakht) Bridge Analysis Simplified, 1985; (with B. Bakht) Bridge Analysis by Microcomputer, 1989; various papers on grillage analysis in British, European and American Journals. *Recreations:* golf, curling, contract bridge. *Address:* PO Box 1000, Halifax, NS B3J 2X4, Canada. *T:* 420–7757. *Club:* Saraguay (Halifax, Canada).

JAFFÉ, (Andrew) Michael, CBE 1989; LittD; Director, Fitzwilliam Museum, Cambridge, 1973–90, now Emeritus; Professor of the History of Western Art, 1973–90, now Emeritus; Fellow of King's College, Cambridge, since 1952; *b* 3 June 1923; *s* of Arthur Daniel Jaffé, OBE, and Marie Marguerite Strauss; *m* 1964, Patricia Anne Milne-Henderson; two *s* two *d*. *Educ:* Eton Coll.; King's Coll., Cambridge (MA, LittD 1980); Courtauld Inst. of Art. Lt-Comdr, RNVR, retd. Commonwealth Fund Fellow, Harvard and New York Univ., 1951–53; Asst Lectr in Fine Arts, Cambridge, 1956; Prof. of Renaissance Art, Washington Univ., St Louis, 1960–61; Vis. Prof., Harvard Univ., Summer 1961; Lectr in Fine Arts, Cambridge, 1961; Reader in History of Western Art, Cambridge, 1968; Head of Dept of History of Art, Cambridge, 1970–73; a Syndic, Fitzwilliam Museum, 1971–73. Mem., Adv. Council, V&A Museum, 1971–76. Organiser (for Nat. Gall. of Canada) of Jordaens Exhibn, Ottawa, 1968–69; Vis. Prof., Harvard Univ., Fall 1968–69. FRSA 1969. Officier, Ordre de Léopold (Belgium), 1980; Officier, Ordre des Arts et des Lettres (France), 1989. *Publications:* Van Dyck's Antwerp Sketchbook, 1966; Rubens, 1967; Jordaens, 1968; Rubens and Italy, 1977; Rubens: catalogo completo, 1989; articles and reviews (art historical) in European and N American jls, etc. *Recreation:* viticulture. *Address:* King's College, Cambridge. *Clubs:* Brooks's, Turf, Beefsteak.

JAFFRAY, Alistair Robert Morton, CB 1978; Deputy Under-Secretary of State, Ministry of Defence, 1975–84; *b* 28 Oct. 1925; *s* of late Alexander George and Janet Jaffray; *m* 1st, 1953, Margaret Betty Newman (decd); two *s* one *d*; 2nd, 1980, Edna Mary, *e d* of late S. J. Tasker, Brasted Chart. *Educ:* Clifton Coll.; Corpus Christi Coll., Cambridge. BA First Cl. Hons., Mod. Langs. Served War, RNVR, 1943–46. Apptd Home Civil Service (Admty), 1948; Private Sec. to First Lord of Admty, 1960–62; Private Sec. to successive Secretaries of State for Defence, 1969–70; Asst Under-Sec. of State, MoD, 1971, Dep. Sec. 1975; Sec. to Admty Bd, 1981–84. Governor, Clifton Coll., 1980–; Chm. Management Cttee, Royal Hospital Sch., Holbrook, 1985–91. *Address:* Okeford, Lynch Road, Farnham, Surrey.

JAFFRAY, Sir William Otho, 5th Bt, *cr* 1892; *b* 1 Nov. 1951; *s* of Sir William Edmund Jaffray, 4th Bt, TD, JP, DL; *S* father, 1953; *m* 1981, Cynthia Ross Corrington, Montreal, Canada; three *s* one *d*. *Educ:* Eton. *Heir:* *s* Nicholas Gordon Alexander Jaffray, *b* 18 Oct. 1982. *Address:* The Manor House, Priors Dean, Petersfield, Hants. *T:* Hawkley (073084) 483.

JAGAN, Cheddi, DDS; Guyanese Politician; Leader of Opposition in National Assembly, since 1964; *b* March 1918; *m* 1943; one *s* one *d*. *Educ:* Howard Univ.; YMCA Coll., Chicago (BSc); Northwestern Univ. (DDS). Member of Legislative Council, British Guiana, 1947–53; Leader of the House and Minister of Agriculture, Lands and Mines, May-Oct. 1953; Chief Minister and Minister of Trade and Industry, 1957–61; (first) Premier, British Guiana, and Minister of Development and Planning, 1961–64. Hon. Pres., Guyana Agricl and General Workers' Union; Pres., Guyana Peace Council. Order of Friendship, USSR, 1978. *Publications:* Forbidden Freedom, 1954; Anatomy of Poverty, 1964; The West on Trial, 1966; Caribbean Revolution, 1979; The Caribbean—Whose Backyard?, 1984. *Recreations:* swimming, tennis. *Address:* Freedom House, 41 Robb Street, Georgetown, Guyana.

JAGO, David Edgar John; Communar of Chichester Cathedral, since 1987; *b* 2 Dec. 1937; *s* of late Edgar George Jago and of Violet Jago; *m* 1963, Judith (*née* Lissenden); one *s* one *d*. *Educ:* King Edward's Sch., Bath; Pembroke Coll., Oxford (MA). National Service, RA, 1956–58. Asst Principal, Admiralty, 1961; Private Sec. to Permanent Under Sec. of State (RN), 1964–65; Principal 1965; Directing Staff, IDC, 1968–70; Private Sec. to Parly Under Sec. of State for Defence (RN), 1971–73; Ministry of Defence: Asst Sec., 1973; Asst Under Sec. of State: Aircraft, 1979–82; Naval Staff, 1982–84; Under Sec., Cabinet Office, 1984–1986. *Recreations:* theatre, opera, military history, supporting Arsenal FC. *Club:* United Oxford & Cambridge University.

JAHN, Dr Wolfgang; former Managing Director, Commerzbank AG, Düsseldorf; *b* 27 Sept. 1918; *s* of Dr Georg Jahn and Ella (*née* Schick); *m* 1949, Gabriele (*née* Beck); two *s* one *d*. *Educ:* Zürich Univ.; Berlin Univ.; Heidelberg Univ. (DrEcon). Industrial Credit Bank, Düsseldorf, 1949–54; IBRD, Washington, 1954–57; Commerzbank AG, Düsseldorf, 1957–84; Chm., Internat. Commercial Bank, 1984–88. *Address:* c/o Commerzbank AG, PO Box 1137, D-4000 Düsseldorf, FRG.

JAHODA, Prof. Gustav, FBA 1988; Professor of Psychology, University of Strathclyde, 1964–85, now Emeritus Professor; *b* 11 Oct. 1920; *s* of Olga and late Leopold Jahoda; *m* 1950, Jean Catherine (*née* Buchanan) (*d* 1991); three *s* one *d*. *Educ:* Vienna, Paris, Univ. of London. MScEcon, PhD. Tutor, Oxford Extra-Mural Delegacy, 1946–68; Lectr, Univ. of Manchester, 1948–51; Univ. of Ghana, 1952–56; Sen. Lectr, Univ. of Glasgow, 1956–63. Visiting Professor, Universities of: Ghana, 1968; Tilburg, 1984; Kansai, Osaka, 1985; Ecole des Hautes Etudes, Paris, 1986; Saarbrücken, 1987; New York, 1987; Geneva, 1990. Fellow, Netherlands Inst. of Advanced Studies, 1980–81; Hon. Fellow, Internat. Assoc. for Cross-Cultural Psychology (Pres., 1972–74); Membre d'Honneur, Assoc. pour la Recherche Inter-culturelle, 1986. *Publications:* White Man, 1961, 2nd edn 1983; The Psychology of Supersitition, 1969, 8th edn 1979; Psychology and Anthropology, 1982 (French edn 1989); (with I. M. Lewis) Acquiring Culture, 1988; contribs to learned jls. *Recreations:* fishing, gardening. *Address:* c/o Department of Psychology, University of Strathclyde, Glasgow G1 1RD. *Club:* University of Strathclyde Staff.

JAHODA, Prof. Marie, (Mrs A. H. Albu), CBE 1974; DPhil; Professor Emeritus, University of Sussex; *b* 26 Jan. 1907; *d* of Carl Jahoda and Betty Jahoda; *m* 1st, 1927, Paul F. Lazarsfeld; one *d*; 2nd, 1958, Austen Albu, *qv*. *Educ:* Univ. of Vienna (DPhil). Prof. of Social Psychology, NY Univ., 1949–58; Res. Fellow and Prof. of Psychol., Brunel Univ., 1958–65; Prof. of Social Psychol., Sussex Univ., 1965–73. Sen. Res. Consultant to Sci. Policy Res. Unit, Sussex Univ., 1971–83. Hon. DLit: Sussex, 1973; Leicester, 1973; Bremen, 1984; Stirling, 1988. *Publications:* Die Arbeitslosen von Marienthal, 1933 (Eng. trans. 1971); Research Methods in Human Relations, 1953; Current Concepts of Positive Mental Health, 1958; Freud and the Dilemmas of Psychology, 1977; (ed) World Futures: the great debate, 1977; Employment and Unemployment, 1982. *Recreations:* cooking, chess. *Address:* 17 The Crescent, Keymer, Sussex BN6 8RB. *T:* Hassocks (07918) 2267.

JAINE, Tom William Mahony; Editor, Good Food Guide, since 1989; *b* 4 June 1943; *s* of William Edwin Jaine and Aileen (*née* Mahony); *m* 1st, 1965, Susanna F. Fisher; 2nd, 1973, Patience Mary Welsh (decd); two *d*; 3rd, 1983, Sally Caroline Agnew; two *d*. *Educ:*

Kingswood Sch., Bath; Balliol Coll., Oxford (BA Hons). Asst Registrar, Royal Commn on Historical Manuscripts, 1967–73; Partner, Carved Angel Restaurant, Dartmouth, 1974–84; publisher, The Three Course Newsletter (and predecessors), 1980–. *Publication:* Cooking in the Country, 1986. *Recreations:* baking, buildings. *Address:* Allaleigh House, Blackawton, Totnes, Devon TQ9 7DL.

JAK; *see* Jackson, R. A.

JAKEMAN, Prof. Eric, FRS 1990; Deputy Chief Scientific Officer, Royal Signals and Radar Establishment, since 1985; *b* 3 June 1939; *s* of Frederick Leonard Jakeman and Hilda Mary Hays; *m* 1968, Glenys Joan Cooper; two *d*. *Educ:* Brunts Grammar Sch., Mansfield; Univ. of Birmingham (BSc, PhD). FInstP 1979. Asst Res. Physicist, UCLA, 1963–64. RSRE, then RRE, 1964–. Vice-Pres. for Publications, Inst. of Physics, 1989–; Chm., IOPP Ltd; Mem. Exec. Cttee, European Physical Soc., 1990–. Fellow, Optical Soc. of America, 1988. Maxwell Medal and Prize, Inst. of Physics, 1977; (jtly) MacRobert Award, 1977; (jtly) Instrument Makers' Co. Award. *Publications:* numerous contribs to learned jls. *Recreations:* gardening, music, beekeeping. *Address:* The Knell, Upper Colwall, Malvern, Worcs WR13 6PR.

JAKEWAY, Sir (Francis) Derek, KCMG 1963 (CMG 1956); OBE 1948; *b* 6 June 1915; *s* of Francis Edward and Adeline Jakeway; *m* 1941, Phyllis Lindsay Watson, CStJ; three *s*. *Educ:* Hele's Sch., Exeter; Exeter Coll., Oxford (BA Hons Mod. Hist.). Colonial Administrative Service, Nigeria, 1937–54, seconded to Seychelles, 1946–49, to Colonial Office, 1949–51; Chief Sec., British Guiana, 1954–59; Chief Sec., Sarawak, 1959–63; Governor and C-in-C, Fiji, 1964–68. Chm., Devon AHA, 1974–82. KStJ 1964. *Address:* 78 Douglas Avenue, Exmouth, Devon. *T:* Exmouth (0395) 271342.

JAKOBOVITS, family name of **Baron Jakobovits.**

JAKOBOVITS, Baron *cr* 1988 (Life Peer), of Regent's Park in Greater London; **Immanuel Jakobovits;** Kt 1981; Chief Rabbi of the United Hebrew Congregations of the British Commonwealth of Nations, 1967–91; *b* 8 Feb. 1921; *s* of Rabbi Dr Julius Jakobovits and Paula (*née* Wreschner); *m* 1949, Amelie Munk; two *s* four *d*. *Educ:* London Univ. (BA; PhD 1955; Fellow, UCL, 1984–; Hon. Fellow, QMC, 1987); Jews' Coll. and Yeshivah Etz Chaim, London. Diploma, 1944; Associate of Jews' Coll. Minister: Brondesbury Synagogue, 1941–44; SE London Synagogue, 1944–47; Great Synagogue, London, 1947–49; Chief Rabbi of Ireland, 1949–58; Rabbi of Fifth Avenue Synagogue, New York, 1958–67. Hon. DD Yeshiva Univ., NY, 1975; Hon. DLitt City, 1986; DD Lambeth, 1987. Templeton Prize for Progress in Religion, 1991. *Publications:* Jewish Medical Ethics, 1959 (NY; 4th edn 1975); Jewish Law Faces Modern Problems, 1965 (NY); Journal of a Rabbi, 1966 (NY), 1967 (GB); The Timely and the Timeless, 1977; If Only My People . . . Zionism in My Life, 1984; contrib. learned and popular jls in America, England and Israel. *Address:* Jews' College, 44 Albert Road, NW4 2SJ.

JALLAND, His Honour William Herbert Wainwright, JP; a Circuit Judge, Manchester, 1975–88 (sitting in Crown Court, Manchester, and County Courts, Manchester and Salford); *b* 1922; *o s* of Arthur Edgar Jalland, QC, JP and Elizabeth Hewitt Jalland; *m* 1945, Helen Monica, BEM 1984, *o d* of John and Edith Wyatt; one *s* one *d*. *Educ:* Manchester Grammar Sch.; Manchester Univ. LLB 1949. Served War of 1939–45, HM Forces at home and abroad, 1941–46: Captain, King's Own Royal Regt, attached 8th Bn Durham LI. Called to Bar, Gray's Inn, 1950; practised Northern Circuit; part-time Dep. Coroner, City of Salford, 1955–65; part-time Dep. Recorder, Burnley, 1962–70; part-time Dep. Chm., Lancs County Sessions, 1970–71; Recorder, 1972; a Circuit Judge, Liverpool and Merseyside, 1972–75. JP Lancs, 1970; Liaison Judge at Magistrates' Courts, Rochdale, Middleton and Heywood, 1974–86. Vice-Pres., Old Mancunians' Assoc., 1979–; Pres., Styal Sports and Social Club, 1979–88. *Recreations:* hillwalking, gardening, photography. *Address:* c/o Circuit Administrator, Northern Circuit, Aldine House, New Bailey Street, Salford M3 5EU.

JAMES, family name of **Barons James of Rusholme** and **Northbourne.**

JAMES OF HOLLAND PARK, Baroness *cr* 1991 (Life Peer), of Southwold in the County of Suffolk; **Phyllis Dorothy White,** OBE 1983; JP; FRSL; author (as P. D. James); a Governor of the BBC, since 1988; *b* 3 Aug. 1920; *d* of Sidney Victor James and Dorothy Amelia James (*née* Hone); *m* 1941, Connor Bantry White (*d* 1964); two *d*. *Educ:* Cambridge Girls' High Sch. Administrator, National Health Service, 1949–68; Civil Service: apptd Principal, Home Office, 1968; Police Dept, 1968–72; Criminal Policy Dept, 1972–79. Associate Fellow, Downing Coll., Cambridge, 1986. Member: BBC Gen. Adv. Council, 1987–88; Arts Council, 1988– (Chm., Literature Adv. Panel, 1988–); Bd, British Council, 1988– (Mem., Literature Cttee, 1988–). Chm., Booker Prize Panel of Judges, 1987. Chm., Soc. of Authors, 1984–86; Mem., Detection Club. JP: Willesden, 1979–82; Inner London, 1984. FRSL 1987; FRSA. *Publications:* Cover Her Face, 1962 (televised 1985); A Mind to Murder, 1963; Unnatural Causes, 1967; Shroud for a Nightingale, 1971 (televised 1984); (with T. A. Critchley) The Maul and the Pear Tree, 1971; An Unsuitable Job for a Woman, 1972 (filmed 1982); The Black Tower, 1975 (televised 1986); Death of an Expert Witness, 1977 (televised 1983); Innocent Blood, 1980; The Skull beneath the Skin, 1982; A Taste for Death, 1986; Devices and Desires, 1989 (televised 1991). *Recreations:* exploring churches, walking by the sea. *Address:* c/o Elaine Greene Ltd, 37a Goldhawk Road, W12 8QQ.

JAMES OF RUSHOLME, Baron *cr* 1959, of Fallowfield (Life Peer); **Eric John Francis James,** Kt 1956; Chairman, Royal Fine Art Commission, 1976–79 (Member, 1973–79); *b* 1909; *yr s* of F. W. James; *m* 1939, Cordelia, *d* of late Maj.-Gen. F. Wintour, CB, CBE; one *s*. *Educ:* Taunton's School, Southampton; Queen's Coll., Oxford (Exhibitioner and Hon. Scholar, 1927. Hon. Fellow, 1959). Goldsmiths' Exhibitioner, 1929; BA, BSc 1931; MA, DPhil 1933; Asst Master at Winchester Coll., 1933–45; High Master of Manchester Grammar Sch., 1945–62; Vice-Chancellor, Univ. of York, 1962–73. Mem. of University Grants Cttee, 1949–59; Chm. of Headmasters' Conference, 1953–54; Mem. Central Advisory Council on Education, 1957–61; Member: Standing Commission on Museums and Galleries, 1958–61; Press Council, 1963–67; SSRC, 1965–68; Chairman: Personal Social Services Council, 1973–76; Cttee to Inquire into the Training of Teachers, 1970–71. Hon. FRIBA 1979. Hon. LLD: McGill, 1957; York, (Toronto) 1970; Hon. DLitt New Brunswick, 1974; DUniv York, 1974. Fellow, Winchester Coll., 1963–69. *Publications:* (in part) Elements of Physical Chemistry; (in part) Science and Education; An Essay on the Content of Education; Education and Leadership; articles in scientific and educational journals. *Address:* Penhill Cottage, West Witton, Leyburn, N Yorks.

JAMES, Anne Eleanor S.; *see* Scott-James.

JAMES, Anthony Trafford, CBE 1979; PhD; FRS 1983; Non-Executive Director, The Wellcome Foundation, since 1985; Member of Executive Committee of Unilever Research Colworth Laboratory, also Head of Division of Biosciences, 1972–85; *b* Cardiff, Wales, 6 March 1922; *s* of J. M. and I. James; *m* 1st, 1945, O. I. A. Clayton (*d* 1980); two *s* one *d*; 2nd, 1983, L. J. Beare; one *s*. *Educ:* University College Sch.; Northern Polytechnic; University Coll. London (BSc, PhD), Fellow 1975; Harvard Business Sch. (AMP). MRC Junior Fellowship at Bedford Coll., Univ. of London (with Prof. E. E. Turner, subject: Antimalarials), 1945–47; Jun. Mem. staff, Lister Inst. for Preventive Med., London (with Dr R. L. M. Synge, Nobel Laureate, subject: Structure of Gramicidin S), 1947–50; Mem. scientific staff, Nat. Inst. for Med. Res., London (special appt awarded, 1961), 1950–62 (with Dr A. J. P. Martin, FRS, Nobel Laureate, 1950–56); Unilever Research Lab., Sharnbrook: Div. Manager and Head of Biosynthesis Unit, 1962–67; Head of Div. of Plant Products and Biochemistry, 1967–69; Gp Manager, Biosciences Gp, 1969–72. Industrial Prof. of Chemistry, Loughborough Univ. of Technology, 1966–71. Member: SRC, 1973–77; Food Sci. and Technol. Bd, MAFF, 1975–80; Manpower Cttee, SERC, 1981–84; ABRC, 1983–; Council, Royal Soc., 1988–90; Chairman: Food Composition, Quality and Safety Cttee, MAFF, 1975–80; Biotechnol. Management Cttee, SERC, 1981–85. Hon. Dr Dijon, 1981; Hon. DSc Cranfield Inst. of Technology, 1985. Has had various awards incl. some from abroad. *Publications:* New Biochemical Separations (ed A. T. James and L. J. Morris), 1964; Lipid Biochemistry—an introduction (M. I. Gurr and A. T. James), 1972. *Recreations:* glass engraving, antique collecting, gardening. *Address:* The Wellcome Foundation Ltd, Wellcome Building, 183 Euston Road, NW1.

JAMES, (Arthur) Walter; Principal, St Catharine's, Windsor, 1974–82; *b* 30 June 1912; *s* of late W. J. James, OBE; *m* 1st, 1939, Elisabeth (marr. diss. 1956), *e d* of Richard Rylands Howroyd; one *d*; 2nd, 1957, Ann Jocelyn, *y d* of late C. A. Leavy Burton; one *d* and one adopted *s* two adopted *d*. *Educ:* Uckfield Grammar Sch.; Keble Coll., Oxford (Scholar); 1st Cl. Mod. Hist.; Liddon Student; Arnold Essay Prizeman. Senior Demy of Magdalen Coll., 1935; Scholar in Mediæval Studies, British School at Rome, 1935; Editorial staff, Manchester Guardian, 1937–46. NFS 1939–45. Contested (L) Bury, Lancs, 1945. Dep. Editor, The Times Educational Supplement, 1947–51, Editor, 1952–69; Special Advisor on Educn, Times Newspapers, 1969–71; also Editor, Technology, 1957–60. Reader in Journalism, Univ. of Canterbury, NZ, 1971–74. Member: BBC Gen. Advisory Council, 1956–64; Council of Industrial Design, 1961–66; Council, Royal Society of Arts, 1964; Cttee, British-American Associates, 1964; Governor, Central School of Art and Design, 1966. Woodard Lecturer, 1965. *Publications:* (Ed.) Temples and Faiths 1958; The Christian in Politics, 1962; The Teacher and his World, 1962; A Middle-class Parent's Guide to Education, 1964; (contrib.) Looking Forward to the Seventies, 1967. *Recreation:* gardening. *Address:* 1 Cumberland Mews, The Great Park, Windsor, Berks. *T:* Egham (0784) 431377. *Club:* National Liberal.

JAMES, Aubrey Graham Wallen; Deputy Chief Land Registrar, 1975–81; *b* 5 Jan. 1918; *s* of Reginald Aubrey James and Amelia Martha James; *m* 1952, Audrey Elizabeth, *er d* of Dr and Mrs A. W. F. Edmonds; two *s*. *Educ:* Nantgyle Grammar Sch.; London Univ. (LLB 1939). Solicitor, 1940. Served Second World War, 1940–46, Major, Cheshire Regt. Legal Asst, HM Land Registry, 1948; Asst Land Registrar, 1954; Land Registrar, 1963; Dist Land Registrar, Nottingham, 1963. Chm., E Midlands Region, CS Sports Council, 1970–75. *Recreations:* gardening, motoring, golf; has played Rugby, cricket and tennis with enthusiasm and in latter years, has turned to admin of these and other sports. *Address:* 11 Playle Chase, Great Totham, Maldon CM9 8UT.

JAMES, Basil; Special Commissioner, 1963–82, Presiding Special Commissioner, 1982–83; *b* 25 May 1918; *s* of late John Elwyn James, MA (Oxon.), Cardiff, and Mary Janet (*née* Lewis), Gwaelodygarth, Glam; *m* 1943, Moira Houlding Rayner, MA (Cantab.), *d* of late Capt. Benjamin Harold Rayner, North Staffs Regt, and Elizabeth (*née* Houlding), Preston, Lancs; one *s* twin *d*. *Educ:* Llandovery Coll.; Canton High Sch., Cardiff; Christ's Coll., Cambridge (Exhibnr). Tancred Law Student, Lincoln's Inn, 1936; Squire Law Scholar, Cambridge, 1936. BA 1939; MA 1942. Called to Bar, Lincoln's Inn, 1940. Continuous sea service as RNVR officer in small ships on anti-submarine and convoy duties in Atlantic, Arctic and Mediterranean, 1940–45. King George V Coronation Scholar, Lincoln's Inn, 1946. Practised at Chancery Bar, 1946–63. Admitted to Federal Supreme Court of Nigeria, 1962. *Publications:* contrib. to Atkin's Court Forms and Halsbury's Laws of England. *Recreations:* music, gardening.

See also J. E. R. James.

JAMES, Cecil; *see* James, T. C. G.

JAMES, Charles Edwin Frederic; a Recorder of the Crown Court since 1982; *b* 17 April 1943; *s* of Frederic Crockett Gwilym James and Marjorie Peggy James (*née* Peace); *m* 1968, Diana Mary Francis (*née* Thornton); two *s*. *Educ:* Trent College, Long Eaton, Derbyshire; Selwyn College, Cambridge. MA 1968. Called to the Bar, Inner Temple, 1965; practising on Northern Circuit. *Recreation:* family pursuits. *Address:* (home) Broomlands, 38 Vyner Road South, Bidston, Birkenhead, Merseyside L43 7PR. *T:* 051–652 1951; (chambers) Refuge Assurance House, Derby Square, Liverpool L2 1TS. *T:* 051–709 4222. *Clubs:* Cambridge University Cricket; Royal Liverpool Golf, Royal Mersey Yacht.

JAMES, Christopher John; Chairman, Birmingham Midshires Building Society, since 1990; Senior Partner, Martineau Johnson, Solicitors, since 1989; *b* 20 March 1932; *s* of John Thomas Walters James, MC and Cicely Hilda James; *m* 1958, Elizabeth Marion Cicely Thomson; one *s* one *d*. *Educ:* Clifton Coll., Bristol; Magdalene Coll., Cambridge (MA). Served RA, 2nd Lieut, 1951–52; TA, 1952–60. Admitted Solicitor, 1958; Partner, Johnson & Co., Birmingham, 1960–87 (Sen. Partner, 1985–87); Dep. Sen. Partner, Martineau Johnson, 1987–89. Dir, Birmingham Midshires Building Soc. (formerly Birmingham Building Soc.), 1980– (Dep. Chm., 1988–90). Gen. Comr for Income Tax, 1974–82. Pres., Birmingham Law Soc., 1983–84. Mem. Council, Edgbaston High Sch. for Girls, 1980–90 (Chm., 1987–90); Gov., Clifton Coll. FRSA 1991. *Recreations:* photography, railways, golf. *Address:* St Philips House, St Philips Place, Birmingham B3 2PP. *T:* 021–200 3300. *Clubs:* Birmingham; Little Aston Golf.

JAMES, Christopher Philip; His Honour Judge James; a Circuit Judge, since 1980; *b* 27 May 1934; *yr s* of late Herbert Edgar James, CBE, and late Elizabeth Margaret James. *Educ:* Felsted School; Magdalene Coll., Cambridge (MA). Commnd RASC, 1953. Called to the Bar, Gray's Inn, 1959; a Recorder of the Crown Court, 1979. *Address:* Flat 8, 93 Elm Park Gardens, SW10 9QE. *Club:* United Oxford & Cambridge University.

JAMES, Clive Vivian Leopold; writer and broadcaster; feature writer for The Observer, since 1972 (also television critic, 1972–82); *b* 7 Oct. 1939; *s* of Albert Arthur James and Minora May (*née* Darke). *Educ:* Sydney Technical High Sch.; Sydney Univ.; Pembroke Coll., Cambridge. President of Footlights when at Cambridge. Record albums as lyricist for Pete Atkin: Beware of the Beautiful Stranger; Driving through Mythical America; A King at Nightfall; The Road of Silk; Secret Drinker; Live Libel; The Master of the Revels. Song-book with Pete Atkin: A First Folio. *Television series:* Cinema, Up Sunday, So It Goes, A Question of Sex, Saturday Night People, Clive James on Television, The Late Clive James, The Late Show with Clive James, Saturday Night Clive, The Talk Show with Clive James; *television documentaries:* Shakespeare in Perspective: Hamlet, 1980; The Clive James Paris Fashion Show, Clive James and the Calendar Girls, 1981; The Return of the Flash of lightning, 1982; Clive James Live in Las Vegas,1982; Clive James meets Roman Polanski, 1984; The Clive James Great American Beauty Pageant, 1984; Clive James in Dallas, 1985; Clive James Meets Katherine Hepburn, 1986; Clive James on

Safari, 1986; Clive James and the Heroes of San Francisco, 1987; Clive James in Japan, 1987; Postcard from Rio, Postcard from Chicago, and Postcard from Paris, 1989; Clive James meets Jane Fonda, Clive James on the 80s, 1989; Postcard from Miami, Postcard from Rome, Postcard from Shanghai, 1990; Postcard from Sidney, 1991. *Publications: non-fiction:* The Metropolitan Critic, 1974; The Fate of Felicity Fark in the Land of the Media, 1975; Peregrine Prykke's Pilgrimage through the London Literary World, 1976; Britannia Bright's Bewilderment in the Wilderness of Westminster, 1976; Visions Before Midnight, 1977; At the Pillars of Hercules, 1979; First Reactions, 1980; The Crystal Bucket, 1981; Charles Charming's Challenges on the Pathway to the Throne, 1981; From the Land of Shadows, 1982; Glued to the Box, 1982; Flying Visits, 1984; Snakecharmers in Texas, 1988; *fiction:* Brilliant Creatures, 1983; The Remake, 1987; *verse:* Fan-Mail, 1977; Poem of the Year, 1983; Other Passports: poems 1958–85, 1986; *autobiography:* Unreliable Memoirs, 1980; Falling Towards England: Unreliable Memoirs II, 1985; May Week Was in June: Unreliable Memoirs III, 1990. *Address:* c/o A. D. Peters & Co., 5th Floor, The Chambers, Chelsea Harbour, Lots Road, SW10 0XF.

JAMES, Rt. Rev. Colin Clement Walter; *see* Winchester, Bishop of.

JAMES, Sir Cynlais Morgan, (Sir Kenneth), KCMG 1985 (CMG 1976); HM Diplomatic Service, retired; Director General, Canning House, since 1987; Director, Latin American Investment Trust plc, since 1990; Consultant, Darwin Instruments Ltd, since 1986; *b* 29 April 1926; *s* of Thomas James and Lydia Ann James (*née* Morgan); *m* 1953, Mary Teresa, *d* of R. D. Girouard and Lady Blanche Girouard; two *d. Educ:* Trinity Coll., Cambridge. Service in RAF, 1944–47. Cambridge 1948–51. Entered Senior Branch of Foreign Service, 1951; Foreign Office, 1951–53; Third Sec., Tokyo, 1953–56; Second Sec., Rio de Janeiro, 1956–59; First Sec. and Cultural Attaché, Moscow, 1959–62; FO, 1962–65; Paris, 1965–69; promoted Counsellor, 1968; Counsellor and Consul-General, Saigon, 1969–71; Head of W European Dept, FCO, 1971–75; NATO Defence Coll., Rome, 1975–76; Minister, Paris, 1976–81; Ambassador to Poland, 1981–83; Asst Under Sec. of State, FCO, 1983; Ambassador to Mexico, 1983–86. Dir, Thomas Cook, 1986–91. Chairman: British-Mexican Soc., 1987–90; British Inst. in Paris, 1988–; Mem., Franco-British Council, 1986–. Hon. Dr Mexican Acad. of Internat. Law, 1984. Order of the Aztec, 1st cl. (Mexico), 1985; Order of Andres Bello, 1st cl. (Venezuela), 1990. *Recreation:* tennis. *Address:* 2 Belgrave Square, SW1; The Old Forge, Lower Oddington, Glos. *Clubs:* Brooks's, Beefsteak, Pratt's, MCC; Travellers' (Paris).

JAMES, Prof. David Edward; Head of Department of Educational Studies, University of Surrey, since 1982; *b* 31 July 1937; *s* of Charles Edward James and Dorothy Hilda (*née* Reeves); *m* 1963, Penelope Jane Murray; two *s* one *d. Educ:* Universities of Reading, Oxford, Durham, London (Bsc Hons Gen., BSc Hons Special, MEd, DipEd, DipFE); FRSH. Lectr in Biology, City of Bath Tech. Coll. 1961–63; Lectr in Sci. and Educn, St Mary's Coll. of Educn, Newcastle upon Tyne, 1963–64; University of Surrey: Lectr in Educnl Psych., 1964–69; Dir of Adult Educn and later Prof., 1969–. FRSA. *Publications:* A Student's Guide to Efficient Study, 1966, Amer. edn 1967; Introduction to Psychology, 1968, Italian edn 1972. *Recreation:* farming. *Address:* Department of Educational Studies, University of Surrey, Guildford, Surrey GU2 5XH.

JAMES, Dr (David) Geraint, FRCP; Consultant Physician since 1959, and Dean since 1968, Royal Northern Hospital, London; Consultant Ophthalmic Physician, St Thomas Hospital, London, since 1973; Teacher, University of London, since 1979; *b* 2 Jan. 1922; *s* of David James and Sarah (*née* Davies); *m* 1951, Sheila Sherlock, *qv*; two *d. Educ:* Jesus Coll., Cambridge (MA 1945); Mddx Hosp. Med. Sch., London (MD 1953); Columbia Univ., NYC. FRCP 1964. Adjunct Prof. of Medicine, Univ. of Miami, Fla, 1973–, and Prof. of Epidemiology, 1981–; Adjunct Prof., Royal Free Hosp. Med. Sch., 1987–; Consulting Phys. to RN, 1972–; Hon. Consultant Phys., US Veterans' Admin, 1978–; Hon. Consulting Phys., Sydney Hosp., Australia, 1969–. World Exec. Sec., 1980–, Pres., 1987–, Internat. Cttee on Sarcoidosis; President: Italian Congress on Sarcoidosis, 1983; World Assoc. of Sarcoidosis, 1987–; Vice-Pres., Fellowship of Postgrad. Medicine; Past President: Med. Soc. of London; Harveian Soc.; Osler Club (Hon. Fellow); Vice-Pres., London Glamorgan Soc., 1989–; Mem. Council, Cymmrodorion Soc. Lectures: Tudor Edwards, RCP and RCS, 1983; George Wise Meml, New York City, 1983. Foreign Corresponding Mem., French Nat. Acad. of Medicine, 1987; Hon. Corresp. Mem., Thoracic Socs of Italy, France, Dominican Republic and Portugal. Editor, Internat. Rev. of Sarcoidosis, 1984–. Freeman, City of London, 1961. Hon. LLD Wales, 1982. Chesterfield Medal, Inst. of Dermatology, London, 1957; Gold Medal, Barraquer Inst. of Ophthalmology, 1958; Carlo Forlanini Gold Medal, Italian Thoracic Soc., 1983. Gold Medal, Milan, 1987. Kt of Order of Christopher Columbus (Dominican Republic), 1987. *Publications:* Diagnosis and Treatment of Infections, 1957; Sarcoidosis, 1970; Circulation of the Blood, 1978; Atlas of Respiratory Diseases, 1981; Sarcoidosis and other Granulomatous Disorders, 1985. *Recreations:* history of medicine, international Welshness, Rugby football. *Address:* 149 Harley Street, W1N 1HG. *T:* 071–935 4444. *Club:* Athenæum.

JAMES, Dr David Gwynfor; Head of Meteorological Research Flight, Royal Aircraft Establishment, Farnborough, 1971–82; *b* 16 April 1925; *s* of William James and Margaret May Jones; *m* 1953, Margaret Vida Gower; two *d. Educ:* Univ. of Wales, Cardiff (BSc, PhD). Joined Meteorological Office, 1950; Met. Res. Flight, Farnborough, 1951; Forecasting Res., Dunstable, 1953; Christmas Island, Pacific, 1958; Satellite Lab., US Weather Bureau, 1961; Cloud Physics Res., Bracknell, 1966; Met. Res. Flight, RAE, 1971. Fellow, UC Cardiff, 1987. *Publications:* papers in Qly Jl Royal Met. Soc., Jl Atmospheric Sciences, Met. Res. Papers, and Nature. *Recreations:* golf, choral singing. *Address:* Tŷ'r Onnen, 56 Port Lion, Llangwm, Haverfordwest, Dyfed SA62 4JT.

JAMES, Dr David William Francis, OBE 1989; consultant; Chief Executive, British Ceramic Research Ltd (formerly British Ceramic Research Association), 1982–91 (Director of Research, 1978–82); *b* 29 March 1929; *s* of Thomas M. and Margaret A. James, Merthyr Tydfil; *m* 1953, Elaine Maureen, *d* of Thomas and Gladys Hewett, Swansea; two *d. Educ:* Cyfarthfa Castle Sch., Merthyr Tydfil; Univ. of Wales (BSc); Univ. of London (PhD). FICeram 1985. Research Asst, Inst. of Cancer Research, Royal Marsden Hosp., 1950–54; Flying Officer, RAF, 1954–56; Research Officer, Imperial Chemical Industries (now Mond Div.), 1956–60; Lectr and Sen. Lectr, UC North Wales, Bangor, 1960–71; Dep. Principal, Glamorgan Polytechnic, 1971–72; Principal and Director, Polytechnic of Wales, 1972–78. Council for National Academic Awards: Mem., 1976–82; Mem., Cttee for Research, 1976–83; Mem., Cttee on Entry Qualifications, 1976–79; Mem., Cttee for Academic Policy, 1979–80; Mem., Gen. Cttee, 1979–83; Chm., Sub-Cttee on College Research Degrees, 1981–85 (Mem., Working Party on Res. Policy, 1982–84); Mem., Cttee for Instns, 1982–86; Mem., Research Adv. Cttee, 1985–87; Mem., Credit Accumulation and Transfer System Adv. Bd, 1986–87. Member: WJEC Techn. Educn Cttee, 1972–78, Techn. Examns Cttee and Management Adv. Cttee, 1972–75; SRC Polytechnics Cttee, 1975–78; Mid-Glamorgan Further Educn Cttee, 1974–78; F and GP Cttee, CDRA, 1983–86 (Vice-Chm., 1985–86); Exec. Cttee, AIRTO, 1986– (Pres., 1987–88); Council, CBI, 1986–88. Pres., Inst. of Ceramics, 1989–90 (Mem. Council, 1988–). Member: Court, Univ. of Wales; Court, UWIST, 1972–78; Court, Univ. of Surrey, 1978–91; Governor, Westminster Coll., 1983–88. FRSA. Mem. Editorial Bd, Inst. of Ceramics, 1985–. *Publications:* research papers in various jls; several patents. *Recreations:* photography, reading, church work. *Address:* Fairways, Birchall, Leek, Staffs. *T:* Leek (0538) 373311.

JAMES, Derek Claude, OBE 1989; Director of Social Services, Leeds, 1978–89; *b* 9 March 1929; *s* of Cecil Claude James and Violet (*née* Rudge); *m* 1954, Evelyn (*née* Thomas); one *s* one *d. Educ:* King Edward's Grammar Sch., Camp Hill, Birmingham; Open Univ. (BA). Dip. in Municipal Admin. Local Government: Birmingham, 1946–60; Coventry, 1960–63; Bradford, 1963–69; Leeds, 1969–89. Mem., Yorks and Humberside RHA, 1976–82; Chm., Leeds Area Review Cttee (Child Abuse), 1978–89; Mem., Nat. Adv. Council on Employment of Disabled People, 1984–89; Pres., Nat. Assoc. of Nursery and Family Care, 1988–; Chm., Nightstop Homeless Persons Project, 1989–; Expert Panel Mem., Registered Homes Tribunal, 1990–; Mem., North Regl Cttee, Sanctuary Housing Assoc., 1991. Adviser: AMA Social Services Cttee, 1983–89; Physical Disablement Res. Liaison Gp, 1986–89. *Recreations:* watching sport, garden pottering. *Address:* Hill House, Woodhall Hills, Calverley, Pudsey, West Yorks LS28 5QY. *T:* Pudsey (0532) 578044.

JAMES, Air Vice-Marshal Edgar, CBE 1966; DFC 1945; AFC 1948 (Bar 1959); FRAeS; aviation consultant, retired; *b* 19 Oct. 1915; *s* of Richard George James and Gertrude (*née* Barnes); *m* 1941, Josephine M. Steel; two *s. Educ:* Neath Grammar School. Joined RAF, 1939; commnd; flying instr duties, Canada, until 1944; opl service with Nos 305 and 107 Sqdns, 1944–45. Queen's Commendation for Valuable Service in the Air (1943, 1944, 1956). Empire Flying Sch. and Fighter Comd Ops Staff, until Staff Coll., 1950. Ops Requirements, Air Min., 1951–53; 2nd TAF Germany, 1953–56; comd No 68 Night Fighter Squadron, 1954–56; CFE, 1956–58; HQ Fighter Comd Staff, 1958–59; Asst Comdt, CFS, 1959–61; CO, RAF Leeming, 1961–62; Dir Ops Requirements 1, Min. of Def. (Air Force Dept), 1962–66; Comdr British Forces, Zambia, Feb.-Sept. 1966. Dep. Controller of Equipment, Min. of Technology, 1966–69. Wing Comdr 1953; Gp Capt. 1959; Air Cdre 1963; Air Vice-Marshal 1967. FRAeS 1971. *Recreations:* sailing, golf. *Address:* Lowmead, Traine Paddock, Modbury, Devon PL21 ORN. *T:* Modbury (0548) 830492. *Clubs:* Royal Air Force; Royal Western Yacht (Plymouth).

JAMES, Edmund Purcell S.; *see* Skone James.

JAMES, Edward Foster, CMG 1968; OBE 1946; Director, Tace Plc, since 1984; *b* 18 Jan. 1917; *s* of late Arthur Foster James; *m* 1985, Janet Mary Walls; one *s* two *d* by a previous marriage. Served HM Forces, 1939–46, India, Burma, Malaya, Indonesia; Lieut-Colonel (GSO1) (OBE, despatches twice). Joined HM Diplomatic Service, 1947; Rangoon, 1948; Hong Kong, 1951; Foreign Office, 1953; Rome, 1955; Foreign Office, 1958; Berlin, 1960; FO (later FCO), 1961–74. Exec. Dir, Inst. of Directors, 1975–76; Dep. Dir-Gen., CBI, 1976–83. Chm., Coastal Pollution Control plc, 1984–85. *Address:* Flat 19, Swinton House, 95 Gloucester Terrace, W2 3HB. *T:* 071–262 0139. *Clubs:* Boodle's, Special Forces.

JAMES, Edwin Kenneth George; Chairman, Photon plc, 1986–89, retired; Chief Scientific Officer, Civil Service Department, 1970–76; *b* 27 Dec. 1916; *s* of late Edwin and Jessie Marion James; *m* 1941, Dorothy Margaret Pratt; one *d. Educ:* Latymer Upper Sch.; Northern Polytechnic. BSc London; FRSC; FOR. Joined War Office, 1938; Chem. Defence Exper. Stn, 1942; Aust. Field Exper. Stn, 1944–46; Operational Research Gp, US Army, Md, 1950–54; Dir, Biol and Chem. Defence, WO, 1961; Army (later Defence) Op. Res. Estab., Byfleet, 1965; HM Treasury (later Civil Service Dept), 1968. Chm., PAG Ltd, 1984–87 (Dir, 1977–84). Silver Medal, Op. Res. Soc., 1979. *Recreations:* writing, walking, ski-ing. *Address:* 5 Watersmeet Road, East Harnham, Salisbury, Wilts SP2 8JH. *T:* Salisbury (0722) 334099. *Club:* Athenæum.

JAMES, Eleanor Mary; Lecturer in Mathematics, University College of Wales, Aberystwyth, since 1957; *b* 31 Aug. 1935; *d* of Morris and Violet Mary Jones; *m* 1958, David Bryan James. *Educ:* Ardwyn Grammar Sch., Aberystwyth; University College of Wales, Aberystwyth (BSc 1955; PhD 1972). Member: Welsh Consumer Council, 1981–90; CECG, 1982–84; Consumer Develt Sub-Cttee, Nat. Consumer Council, 1983–85; Layfield Cttee of Enquiry, Local Govt Finance, 1974–76; Audit Commn for Local Authorities and NHS, 1988–91. Member: N Wales Area Cttee, CAB, 1987–90 (Chm., Aberystwyth, 1988–); POUNC, 1991– (Chm., Council for Wales, 1991–); Envmt and Public Affairs Sub-Cttee, NFWI, 1981–84 (Treas., Dyfed Ceredigion Fedn of WIs, 1989–); Sec., Ceredigion Br., Campaign for Protection of Rural Wales, 1989–. University College of Wales: Council, 1982–86; Court of Governors, 1982–; Treas., Old Students' Assoc., 1975–. *Publication:* (with T. V. Davies) Nonlinear Differential Equations, 1966. *Recreations:* walking, swimming, the WI. *Address:* Dolhuan, Llandre, Bowstreet, Dyfed SY24 5AB. *T:* Aberystwyth (0970) 828362.

JAMES, Rev. Canon Eric Arthur; Chaplain to HM the Queen, since 1984; Hon. Director, Christian Action, since 1990 (Director, 1979–90); *b* 14 April 1925; *s* of John Morgan James and Alice Amelia James. *Educ:* Dagenham County High School; King's Coll. London (MA, BD; FKC 1986). Asst Curate, St Stephen with St John, Westminster, 1951–55; Chaplain Trinity Coll., Cambridge, 1955–59; Select Preacher to Univ. of Cambridge, 1959–60; Vicar of St George, Camberwell and Warden of Trinity College Mission, 1959–64; Director of Parish and People, 1964–69; Proctor in Convocation, 1964–72; Canon Precentor of Southwark Cathedral, 1964–73; Canon Residentiary and Missioner, Diocese of St Albans, 1973–83; Hon. Canon, 1983–90; Canon Emeritus, 1990. Preacher to Gray's Inn, 1978–. Commissary to Bishop of Kimberley, 1965–67, to Archbishop of Melanesia, 1969–. Examining Chaplain to Bishop of St Albans, 1973–83, to Bishop of Truro, 1983–. *Publications:* The Double Cure, 1957, 2nd edn 1980; Odd Man Out, 1962; (ed) Spirituality for Today, 1968; (ed) Stewards of the Mysteries of God, 1979; A Life of Bishop John A. T. Robinson: Scholar, Pastor, Prophet, 1987; (ed) God's Truth, 1988; Judge Not: a selection of sermons preached in Gray's Inn Chapel, 1989; Collected Thoughts: fifty scripts for BBC's Thought for The Day, 1990; (ed) A Last Eccentric: a symposium concerning the Rev. Canon F. A. Simpson: historian, preacher and eccentric, 1991. *Address:* 11 Denny Crescent, SE11 4UY. *T:* 071–582 3068. *Clubs:* Reform, Commonwealth Trust.

JAMES, (Ernest) Gethin, FRICS; Director, Estate Surveying Services, Property Services Agency, 1977–84, retired; *b* 20 March 1925; *s* of Ernest Bertram James and Gwladys James; *m* 1st, 1949 (marr. diss.); 2nd, 1981, Mrs Margaret Hollis. *Educ:* Christ Coll., Brecon; Coll. of Estate Management. FRICS 1954. Defence Land Agent: Colchester, 1968–69; Aldershot, 1969–72; Dep. Chief Land Agent, MoD, 1972–74, Chief Land Agent and Valuer, 1974–75; Asst Dir (Estates), PSA, London Reg., 1975–77. *Recreations:* living each day, golf. *Address:* Heath Cottage, Church Lane, Ewshot, Farnham, Surrey GU10 5BJ. *T:* Aldershot (0252) 850548. *Club:* Army Golf (Aldershot).

JAMES, Evan Maitland; *b* 14 Jan. 1911; *er s* of late A. G. James, CBE, and late Helen James (*née* Maitland); *m* 1939, Joan Goodnow (*d* 1989), *d* of late Hon. J. V. A. MacMurray, State Dept, Washington, DC; one *s* two *d. Educ:* Durnford; Eton (Oppidan Scholar); Trinity Coll., Oxford (MA). Served War of 1939–45: War Reserve Police (Metropolitan),

1939; BBC Overseas (Propaganda Research) Dept, 1940–41; Ordinary Seaman to Lieut, RNVR, 1941–46. Clerk of the Merchant Taylors' Company, 1947–62; Steward of Christ Church, Oxford, 1962–78. *Address:* Upwood Park, Besselsleigh, Abingdon, Oxon OX13 5QE. *T:* Oxford (0865) 390535. *Club:* Travellers'.

JAMES, Geraint; *see* James, D. G.

JAMES, Geraldine; actress; *b* 6 July 1950; *d* of Gerald Trevor Thomas and Annabella Doogan Thomas; *m* 1986, Joseph Sebastian Blatchley; one *d. Educ:* Downe House, Newbury; Drama Centre London Ltd. *Stage:* repertory, Chester, 1972–74, Exeter, 1974–75, Coventry, 1975; Passion of Dracula, Queen's, 1978; The White Devil, Oxford, 1981; Turning Over, Bush, 1984; When I was a Girl I used to Scream and Shout, Whitehall, 1987; Cymbeline, National, 1988; Merchant of Venice, Phoenix, 1989, NY (Drama Desk Best Actress Award), 1990; *TV series:* The History Man, 1980; Jewel in the Crown, 1984; Blott on the Landscape, 1985; Echoes, 1988; Stanley and the Woman, 1991; *TV film:* Dummy (Best Actress, BPG), 1977; *films:* Sweet William, 1978; Night Cruiser, 1978; Gandhi, 1981; The Storm, 1985; Wolves of Willoughby Chase, 1988; The Tall Guy, 1989; She's Been Away, 1989 (Best actress, Venice Film Festival, 1989); If Looks Could Kill, 1990; The Bridge, 1990; Prince of Shadows, 1991. *Recreation:* music. *Address:* c/o Julian Belfrage Associates, 68 St James's Street, SW1A 1PH; c/o Robert Duva Gersh Agency, 130 W 42nd Street, Suite 2400, New York, NY 10036, USA.

JAMES, Gethin; *see* James, E. G.

JAMES, Henry Leonard, CB 1980; Associate Director, Godwins Ltd, since 1987; Consultant, Tolley Publishing, since 1987; Director, Pielle & Co. Ltd (PR Consultants), since 1989; *b* 12 Dec. 1919; *o s* of late Leonard Mark James and late Alice Esther James; *m* 1949, Sylvia Mary Bickell (*d* 1989). *Educ:* King Edward VI Sch., Birmingham. Entered Civil Service in Min. of Health, 1938; Founder Editor, The Window, Min. of Nat. Insce, 1948–51; Dramatic Critic and London Corresp. of Birmingham News, 1947–51; Press Officer, Min. of Pensions and Nat. Insce, 1951–55; Head of Films, Radio and Television, Admty, 1955–61; Head of Publicity, Min. of Educn, 1961–63; Chief Press Officer, Min. of Educn, 1963–64; Dep. Public Relations Adviser to Prime Minister, 1964; Dep. Press Sec. to Prime Minister, 1964–68; Chief Information Officer, Min. of Housing and Local Govt, 1969–70; Press Sec. to Prime Minister, 1970–71; Dir of Information, DoE, 1971–74; Dir-Gen., COI, 1974–78; Chief Press Sec. to the Prime Minister, 1979; Public Relations Advr to Main Bd, Vickers Ltd, 1978–80; Dir-Gen., Nat. Assoc. of Pension Funds, 1981–86; Dir-Gen., European Fedn for Retirement Provision, 1982–86. Member: Pub. Cttee, Internat. Year of the Child, 1979; Council, RSPCA, 1980–84; BOTB, 1980–83. Alumni Guest Lectr, Gustavus Adolphus Coll., Minnesota, 1977. FCAM 1980 (Dep. Chm., 1979–84; Vice-Pres., 1984–). FRSA. FIPR (Pres., 1979; President's Medal, 1976). *Recreation:* visual arts. *Address:* 53 Beaufort Road, W5 3EB. *T:* 081–997 3021.

JAMES, Howell Malcolm Plowden; Director of Corporate Affairs, BBC, since 1987; *b* 13 March 1954; *s* of late T. J. and Virginia James. *Educ:* Mill Hill Sch., London. Head of Promotions, Capital Radio, 1978–82; Organiser, Help a London Child Charity, 1979–82; Head of Press and Publicity, TV-am, 1982–85; Special Adviser: Cabinet Office, 1985; Dept of Employment, 1985–87; DTI, 1987. Dir, Broadcast Audience Res. Bd, 1987–. Dir, English Nat. Ballet Sch., 1990–; Gov., George Eliot Sch., 1989–. *Recreations:* theatre, movies, food. *Address:* c/o BBC, Broadcasting House, W1A 1AA. *T:* 071–927 5531. *Club:* Reform.

JAMES, Prof. Ioan Mackenzie, FRS 1968; MA, DPhil; Savilian Professor of Geometry, Oxford University, since 1970; Fellow of New College, Oxford, since 1970; Editor, Topology, since 1962; *b* 23 May 1928; *o s* of Reginald Douglas and Jessie Agnes James; *m* 1961, Rosemary Gordon Stewart, Fellow of Templeton College, Oxford Centre for Management Studies; no *c. Educ:* St Paul's Sch. (Foundn Schol.); Queen's Coll., Oxford (Open Schol.). Commonwealth Fund Fellow, Princeton, Berkeley and Inst. for Advanced Study, 1954–55; Tapp Res. Fellow, Gonville and Caius Coll., Cambridge, 1956; Reader in Pure Mathematics, Oxford, 1957–69, and Senior Research Fellow, St John's Coll., 1959–69, Hon. Fellow, 1988. Hon. Prof., Univ. of Wales, 1989. London Mathematical Society: Treasurer, 1969–79; Pres., 1985–87; Whitehead Prize and Lectr, 1978. Mem. Council, Royal Soc., 1982–83. Gov., St Paul's Schs, 1970–. *Publications:* The Mathematical Works of J. H. C. Whitehead, 1963; The Topology of Stiefel Manifolds, 1976; Topological Topics, 1983; General Topology and Homotopy Theory, 1984; Aspects of Topology, 1984; Topological and Uniform Spaces, 1987; Fibrewise Topology, 1988; Introduction to Uniform Spaces, 1990; papers in mathematical jls. *Address:* Mathematical Institute, 24–29 St Giles, Oxford OX1 3LB. *T:* Oxford (0865) 273541.

JAMES, John, CBE 1981; Founder and Chairman: John James Group of Companies Ltd, Bristol, 1961–79; Broadmead Group of Companies, 1946–60; Dawn Estates Ltd, since 1945; *b* 25 July 1906; *m* 1st (marr. diss.); one *s* two *d* (and one *d* decd); 2nd, Margaret Theodosia Parkes. *Educ:* Merchant Venturers, Bristol. Chm. Bd of Trustees: Dawn James Charitable Foundn, 1965–; John James (Bristol) Charitable Foundn, 1983–. Hon. LLD Bristol, 1983. *Recreations:* chess, swimming. *Address:* Tower Court, Ascot, Berks SL5 8AV.

JAMES, John A.; *see* Angell-James.

JAMES, John Anthony, CMG 1973; FRACS; Visiting Neurosurgeon, Wellington Hospital Board, Wellington, NZ, 1965–77; retired 1978; *b* 2 April 1913; *s* of Herbert L. James and Gladys E. Paton; *m* 1941, Millicent Ward, Australia; three *s* one *d. Educ:* Melbourne Grammar Sch. (Church of England); Melbourne Univ. (MB, BS). Served War: Surgeon-Lieut, RANR, 1940–43. Neurosurgeon, Neurosurgical Unit, Dunedin Hosp., 1947–52; Dir, Neurosurgical Unit, Otago Univ.; Sen. Lectr in Neurosurgery, Otago Univ., 1951–64. *Publications:* contribs to surgical jls. *Address:* 136 Vipond Road, Whangaparaoa, New Zealand. *Club:* Wellington (Wellington, NZ).

JAMES, John Christopher Urmston; Secretary, Lawn Tennis Association, since 1981 (Assistant Secretary, 1973–81); *b* 22 June 1937; *s* of John Urmston James and Ellen Irene James; *m* 1st, 1959, Gillian Mary Davies (marr. diss. 1982); two *s*; 2nd, 1982, Patricia Mary, *d* of late Arthur Leslie Walter White. *Educ:* Hereford Cathedral Sch. Harrods, 1954; Jaeger, 1961; Pringle, 1972. *Recreations:* tennis, Rugby football, walking, architecture, the countryside. *Address:* c/o Lawn Tennis Association, The Queen's Club, West Kensington, W14 9EG. *T:* 071–385 2366. *Clubs:* Queen's, Questors, London Welsh, International of GB; West Hants (Bournemouth).

JAMES, John Douglas; Executive Director, Woodland Trust, since 1985; *b* 28 July 1949; *s* of William Antony James, ERD, MA and Agnes Winifred James (*née* Mitchell); *m* 1971, Margaret Patricia Manton. *Educ:* Spalding Grammar School. Articled pupil, William H. Brown & Son, 1967–68; Marketing Dept, Geest Industries, 1969–71; Marketing Dept, John Player & Sons, 1971–77; Nat. Develt Officer, Woodland Trust, 1977; (first) Director, 1980. Nottingham Roosevelt Scholar, 1975; Churchill Fellow, 1980. Founder Mem., S Lincs Nature Reserves Ltd, 1968; Mem., Inst. of Charity Fundraising Managers. MInstD. Films: Locked up, 1964; The Story of Springfields, 1966; (producer) Woodland Rescue, BBC2 TV, 1980. Winner: Inst. of Amateur Cinematographers' Internat. Competition, 1964; Daily Mirror Childrens' Literary Competition, 1965. *Publications:* articles in countryside and gardening jls. *Recreation:* woodland walks. *Address:* The Woodland Trust, Autumn Park, Grantham, Lincs NG31 6LL. *T:* Grantham (0476) 74297.

JAMES, John Henry; General Manager: Harrow District Health Authority, since 1990; Parkside District Health Authority, since 1991; *b* 19 July 1944; step *s* of George Arthur James and *s* of Doris May James; *m* 3rd, 1987, Anita Mary Stockton, *d* of Brian Scarth, QPM and Irene Scarth. *Educ:* Ludlow Grammar Sch.; Keble Coll., Oxford (BA Mod. Hist. 1965; postgrad. dip. in Econ. and Pol. Sci. 1966). LHSM 1989. Entered Home Civil Service 1966; Asst Principal, Min. of Pensions and Nat. Insurance; Private Sec. to First Perm. Sec., 1969–71, Principal, 1971–74, DHSS; seconded to HM Treasury, 1974–76; Principal, 1976–78, Asst Sec., 1978–86, Under Sec., 1986–91, DHSS, later Dept of Health; Dir of Health Authority Finance, NHS Management Bd, 1986–89. Non-Exec. Dir, Laing Homes Ltd, 1987–89. Mem. Adv. Council, King's Fund Inst., 1990–. *Publications:* (contrib.) Oxford Textbook of Public Health, 1985; articles in jls. *Recreations:* playing chess and cricket; skibobbing, travel, food and wine, collecting edible fungi. *Address:* Northwick Park Hospital, Watford Road, Harrow, Middx HA1 3UJ.

JAMES, Prof. John Ivor Pulsford, MB, MS London; FRCS; FRCSE; George Harrison Law Professor of Orthopædic Surgery, Edinburgh University, 1958–79, now Emeritus Professor; Consultant in Orthopædic Surgery to the Navy, 1956–84; Head of Orthopaedic Services, Kuwait, 1980–84; *b* 19 Oct. 1913; *s* of late Stanley B. James and Jessica Heley; *m* 1968, Margaret Eiriol Samuel, MB, ChB; one *s* one *d. Educ:* Eggars Grammar Sch., Alton, Hants; University Coll. and Hosp., London, Hampshire County Schol., 1932–38; Ferrière Schol., University Coll., 1935; Goldsmid Schol., University Coll. Hosp., 1935; Magrath Schol., University Coll. Hosp., 1937; Rockefeller Fellowship, 1947–48; Consultant Orthopædic Surgeon, Royal National Orthopædic Hospital, 1946–58; Asst Dir of Studies, Institute of Orthopædics, University of London, 1948–58. Fellow Univ. Coll., London. Hunterian Prof., RCS, 1957; Past Pres., British Orthopædic Assoc. (Fellow); Past Pres., British Soc. for Surgery of the Hand; Mem. Société Internationale de Chirurgie Orthopédique et de Traumatologie; Corresp. Member: Amer. Orthopædic Assoc.; Austr. Orthopædic Assoc.; Scandinavian Orthopædic Assoc.; Hon. Member: Amer. Acad. of Orthopædic Surgeons; Dutch Orthopædic Assoc.; Assoc. for Orthopædic Surgery and Traumatology of Yugoslavia; Canadian Orthopædic Assoc.; New Zealand Orthopædic Assoc.; Hellenic Assoc. of Orthopædics and Traumatology; Société Française d'Orthopédie et de Traumatologie. Hon. FRACS. Late Temp. Lieut-Col RAMC. Golden Star, Order of Service to the Yugoslav People, 1970. *Publications:* Scoliosis, 1967, 2nd edn 1976; Poliomyelitis, 1987; articles relating to curvature of the spine and surgery of the hand in medical journals, etc. *Recreations:* sailing, beekeeping, gardening. *Address:* Abbey Farm, The Vatch, Slad Valley, Glos GL6 7LE. *T:* Stroud (0453) 764986.

JAMES, John Jocelyn S.; *see* Streatfeild-James.

JAMES, John Nigel Courtenay, CBE 1990; FRICS; Trustee of the Grosvenor Estate, since 1971; a Crown Estate Commissioner, since 1984; *b* 31 March 1935; *s* of Frank Courtenay James and Beryl May Wilford Burden; *m* 1961, Elizabeth Jane St Clair-Ford; one *s* one *d. Educ:* Sherborne Sch., Dorset. Chief Agent and Estate Surveyor, Grosvenor Estate, 1968–71. Director: Sun Alliance & London Insurance Gp, 1972– (a Vice-Chm., 1988–); Woolwich Equitable Building Soc., 1982–89; Williams & Glyn's Bank plc, 1983–85; Royal Bank of Scotland, 1985–. Member: Commn for the New Towns, 1978–86; Cttee of Management, RNLI, 1980–; Prince of Wales' Council, 1984–. Pres., RICS, 1980–81. *Recreation:* sailing. *Club:* Brooks's.

JAMES, Jonathan Elwyn Rayner; QC 1988; *b* 26 July 1950; *s* of Basil James, *qv*; *m* 1981, Anne Henshaw (*née* McRae); one *s. Educ:* King's College Sch., Wimbledon; Christ's Coll., Cambridge (MA, LLM); Brussels Univ. (Lic. Spécial en Droit Européen 1973). Called to Bar, Lincoln's Inn (Hardwicke Schol.), 1971. *Publications:* (co-ed) EEC Anti-Trust Law, 1975; (co-ed) Copinger and Skone James on Copyright, 13th edn 1991; (jt consulting editor) Encyclopaedia of Forms and Precedents, Vol. 15 (Entertainment), 1989. *Recreations:* DIY, opera, 007, squash, travel (in a good year). *Address:* 5 New Square, Lincoln's Inn, WC2A 3RJ. *T:* 071–404 0404.

JAMES, Sir Kenneth; *see* James, Sir C. M.

JAMES, Lionel Frederic Edward, CBE 1977 (MBE (mil.) 1944); Comptroller, Forces Help Society and Lord Roberts Workshops, 1970–82; *b* 22 Feb. 1912; *s* of late Frederic James, Westmount, Exeter; *m* 1933, Harriet French-Harley; one *s* one *d. Educ:* Royal Grammar Sch., Worcester. Investment Co., 1933–39. Served War with Royal Engineers, 1939–46: BEF; Planning Staff, Sicilian Invasion; N Africa, Sicily, Greece and Italy (Major). Dep. Dir, Overseas Service, Forces Help Soc., 1946, Dir, 1948; Asst Sec. of Society, 1953, Company Sec., 1963. *Recreation:* vetting and restoration of art and antiques.

JAMES, Michael; *see* James, R. M.

JAMES, Michael; *see* Jayston, M.

JAMES, Michael Leonard; Chairman: The Hartland Press Ltd, since 1985; Hartland Film & Television Ltd, since 1991; writer; *b* 7 Feb. 1941; *s* of late Leonard and of Marjorie James, Portreath, Cornwall; *m* 1975, Jill Elizabeth, *d* of late George Tarján, OBE and Etelka Tarján, formerly of Budapest; two *d. Educ:* Latymer Upper Sch.; Christ's Coll., Cambridge. Entered British govt service, 1963; Private Sec. to Rt Hon. Jennie Lee, MP, Minister for the Arts, 1966–68; Principal, DES, 1968–71; Planning Unit of Rt Hon. Margaret Thatcher, MP, Sec. of State for Educn and Science, 1971–73; Asst Sec., 1973; DCSO 1974; Advr to OECD, Paris, and UK Governor, IIMT, Milan, 1973–75; specialist duties, 1975–78; Director, IAEA, Vienna, 1978–83; Advr on Internat. Relations, EEC, Brussels, 1983–85. Member: Exeter Social Security Appeal Tribunal, 1986–; Devon and Cornwall Rent Assessment Panel, 1990–. Governor: East Devon Coll. of Further Educn, Tiverton, 1985–; Colyton Grammar Sch., 1985–90; Sidmouth Community Coll., 1988–; Chm., Bd of Management, Axe Vale Further Educn Unit, Seaton, 1987– (Mem., 1985–). FRSA 1982. Hon. Fellow, Univ. of Exeter, 1985. South West Arts Literary Award, 1984. *Publications:* (jtly) Internationalization to Prevent the Spread of Nuclear Weapons, 1980; articles on internat. relations and nuclear energy; five novels under a pseudonym. *Address:* Cotte Barton, Branscombe, Devon EX12 3BH. *Clubs:* Athenæum, United Oxford & Cambridge University, International PEN; Devon & Exeter Institution, Honiton Working Men's (Devon).

JAMES, Prof. Michael Norman George, DPhil, FRS 1989; FRS Canada 1985; Professor of Biochemistry, University of Alberta, since 1978; *b* 16 May 1940; *s* of Claud Stewart Murray James and Mimosa Ruth Harriet James; *m* 1961, Patricia McCarthy; one *s* one *d*; *m* 1977, Anita Sielecki. *Educ:* Univ. of Manitoba (BSc, MSc); Linacre Coll., Oxford (DPhil). Asst Prof., Associate Prof., Univ. of Alberta, 1968–78. Mem., MRC of Canada Group in Protein Structure and Function, 1974. *Publications:* contribs to learned jls. *Address:* Department of Biochemistry, University of Alberta, Edmonton, Alberta T6G 2H7, Canada. *T:* (403) 492 4550.

JAMES, Dame Naomi (Christine), (Dame Naomi Haythorne), DBE 1979; author and yachtswoman; *b* 2 March 1949; *d* of Charles Robert Power and Joan Power; *m* 1st, 1976, Robert Alan James (*d* 1983); one *d*; 2nd, 1990, Eric G. Haythorne, *o s* of G. V. Haythorne, Ottawa, Canada. *Educ:* Rotorua Girls' High Sch., NZ. Hair stylist, 1966–71; language teacher, 1972–74; yacht charter crew, 1975–77. Sailed single handed round the world via the three great Capes, incl. first woman solo round Cape Horn, on 53 ft yacht, Express Crusader, Sept. 1977–June 1978; sailed in 1980 Observer Transatlantic Race, winning Ladies Prize and achieving women's record for single-handed Atlantic crossing, on 53 ft yacht Kriter Lady; won 1982 Round Britain Race with Rob James, on multihull Colt Cars GB. Trustee, Nat. Maritime Museum, 1986–; Council Mem., Winston Churchill Meml Trust. Royal Yacht Sqdn Chichester Trophy, 1978; NZ Yachtsman of the Year, 1978. *Publications:* Woman Alone, 1978; At One with the Sea, 1979; At Sea on Land, 1981; Courage at Sea, 1987. *Recreations:* tennis, golf, skiing, antiques. *Address:* Oliver's Lodge, Painswick, Glos GL6 6TP. *Clubs:* Royal Dart Yacht (Dartmouth); Royal Lymington Yacht (Lymington); Royal Western Yacht (Plymouth); Minchinhampton Golf (Amberley Section).

JAMES, Noel David Glaves, OBE 1964; MC 1945; TD 1946; *b* 16 Sept. 1911; *o s* of late Rev. D. T. R. James, and Gertrude James; *m* 1949, Laura Cecilia (*d* 1970), *yr d* of late Sir Richard Winn Livingstone; two *s* (and one *s* decd). *Educ:* Haileybury Coll.; Royal Agricultural Coll., Cirencester (Gold Medal and Estate Management Prize). In general practice as a land agent, 1933–39. Served War, 1939–46 (MC, despatches); 68 Field Regt RA (TA), France, Middle East, Italy. Bursar, Corpus Christi Coll., Oxford, 1946–51; MA (Oxon.) 1946. Fellow, Corpus Christi Coll., Oxford, 1950–51; Land Agent for Oxford Univ., 1951–61; Estates Bursar and Agent for Brasenose Coll., 1959–61; Fellow, Brasenose Coll., Oxford, 1951–61; Agent for Clinton Devon Estates, 1961–76. President: Land Agents Soc., 1957–58; Royal Forestry Soc. of England and Wales and N Ireland, 1962–64; Member: Central Forestry Examination Bd of UK, 1951–75; Regional Advisory Cttee, Eastern Conservancy, Forestry Commn, 1951–61; Regional Advisory Cttee, SW Conservancy, Forestry Commission, 1962–75; Departmental Cttee on Hedgerow and Farm Timber, 1953; UK Forestry Cttee, 1954–59; Governor Wye Coll., Kent, 1955–61; Governor Westonbirt Sch., 1959–68. FLAS; FRICS (Diploma in Forestry and Watney Gold Medal). Gold Medal for Distinguished Service to Forestry, 1967; Royal Agricultural Coll. Bledisloe Medal for services to agriculture and forestry, 1970. *Publications:* Artillery Observation Posts, 1941; Working Plans for Estate Woodlands, 1948; Notes on Estate Forestry, 1949; An Experiment in Forestry, 1951; The Forester's Companion, 1955, 4th edn 1989; The Trees of Bicton, 1969; The Arboriculturalist's Companion, 1972, 2nd edn 1990; A Book of Trees (anthology), 1973; Before the Echoes Die Away, 1980; A History of English Forestry, 1981; A Forestry Centenary, 1982; Gunners at Larkhill, 1983; Plain Soldiering, 1987; An Historical Dictionary of Forestry and Woodland Terms, 1991. *Recreations:* forestry, shooting. *Address:* Blakemore House, Kersbrook, Budleigh Salterton, Devon EX9 7AB. *T:* Budleigh Salterton (03954) 3886. *Club:* Army and Navy.

JAMES, P. D.; *see* Baroness James of Holland Park.

JAMES, Patrick Leonard, FRCS, FDS RCS; Senior Consultant Oral and Maxillo-facial Surgeon, Royal London (formerly London) Hospital, Whitechapel, since 1963; Consultant Oral and Maxillo-facial Surgeon, North East Thames Regional Hospital Board Hospitals, since 1963; Recognized Teacher in Oral Surgery, London University, since 1965; *b* 7 Jan. 1926; *s* of late John Vincent James and Priscilla Elsie (*née* Hill), Cuffley, Herts; *m* 1951, Jean Margaret, *er d* of Leslie and Ruth Hatcher, Woking, Surrey; one *s* two *d*. *Educ:* Hertford and Cheshunt Grammar Schs; King's Coll., London; London Hosp. FDSRCS 1958; FRCS 1985 (MRCS 1956); LRCP 1956. Served RAF, Flt Lieut, ME Comd, 1949–51. Resident Ho. Surg., Ho. Phys., Cas. Officer, King George Hosp., 1956–57; Sen. Registrar, Queen Victoria Hosp., E Grinstead, 1959–63; Consultant Oral and Maxillo-facial Surgeon: to London Hosp., Honey Lane Hosp., Waltham Abbey, Herts and Essex Hosp., Bishop's Stortford, 1963–; to King George Hosp., 1967–; St Margaret's Hosp., Epping, 1966–; Black Notley Hosp., 1969–; Hon. Civil Consultant (Oral and Maxillo-facial Surgery), RAF, 1989– (Civil Consultant in Oral Surgery, 1979–89). Exchange Fellow, Henry Ford Hosp., Detroit, Mich., 1962; Hunterian Prof., RCS, 1970–71. Member: Academic Bd, London Hosp. Med. Coll., 1968–71; Adv. Cttee in Plastic Surgery, NE Met. Reg. Hosp. Bd, 1969–77; NE Thames Reg. Manpower Cttee, 1975–. Fellow: BAOS, 1963– (Mem. Council, 1971–74); Internat. Assoc. of Oral Surgs (BAOS Rep. on Council, 1974–78); Chm., Sci. Session, 6th Internat. Congress of Oral Surgs, Sydney, 1977; Associate Mem., Brit. Assoc. of Plastic Surgs, 1958–77. FRSM; Member: Council, Chelsea Clin. Soc; Bd of Governors, Eastman Hosp., 1983–84. Mem. of Lloyd's, 1984. Liveryman, Soc. of Apothecaries, 1969; Freeman, City of London, 1978. *Publications:* (chapter in Oral Surgery) Malignancies in Odontogenic Cysts, 1967; (chapter in Oral Surgery) Correction of Apertognathia with Osteotomies and Bone Graft, 1970; (chapter in Oral Surgery, vol. 7) Surgical Treatment of Mandibular Joint Disorders, 1978; numerous articles on surgical treatment of mandibular joint disorders, surgery of salivary glands and maxillo facial surgery in med. and surg. jls. *Recreations:* shooting, fishing, sailing (Cdre, United Hosps Sailing Club, 1968–75), skiing. *Address:* Meesden Hall, Meesden, Buntingford, Herts SG9 0AZ; 149 Harley Street, W1N 2DE. *T:* 071–935 4444. *Club:* Naval and Military.

JAMES, Prof. Peter Maunde Coram, VRD 1964; John Humphreys Professor of Dental Health, 1966–87, and Postgraduate Advisor in Dentistry, 1983–86, University of Birmingham (Director, Dental School, 1978–82); *b* 2 April 1922; *s* of Vincent Coram James, MRCS, LRCP, and Mildred Ivy (*née* Gooch); *m* 1945, Denise Mary Bond, LDS; four *s*. *Educ:* Westminster Sch.; Royal Dental Hosp., Univ. of London (MDS); Univ. of St Andrews (DPD). LDSRCS. House Surgeon, then Sen. House Surg., Royal Dental Hosp., 1945; Surg. Lieut (D) RNVR, 1945–48; Registrar, Res. Asst and Hon. Lectr, Inst. of Dental Surgery (Eastman Dental Hosp.), 1949–55; Gibbs Travelling Scholar, 1952; Royal Dental Hosp. Sch. of Dental Surgery, Univ. of London: Sen. Lectr, 1955–65; Asst Dean, 1958–66; Dir, Dept of Children's Dentistry, 1962–66; Hon. Cons. Dental Surg., 1961–87; Reader in Preventive Dentistry, Univ. of London, 1965; Head, Dept of Dental Health, Univ. of Birmingham, 1966–87. Consultant, Internat. Dental Fedn Commn on Dental Res., 1976–87; Cons. Advisor in Community Dentistry to DHSS, 1977–83; Reg. Advisor (W Midlands), Faculty of Dental Surgery, RCS, 1976–83. President: Brit. Paedodontic Soc., 1962; Central Counties Br., BDA, 1981–82; Founding Pres., Brit. Assoc. for Study of Community Dentistry, 1973. Chm., Specialist Adv. Cttee in Community Dental Health, 1981–86; Vice-Chm., BDA Central Cttee for Univ. Teachers and Res. Workers, 1984–87; Member: Dental Working Party, Cttee on Child Health Services, 1974–77; Standing Panel of Experts in Dentistry, Univ. of London, 1976–; Birmingham AHA (Teaching), 1979–82, Birmingham Central DHA, 1982–85; Jt Cttee for Higher Training in Dentistry, 1981–86. Ext. Assessor, Univ. of Malaya, 1977–87; ext. examr in dental subjects, univs and colls, 1955–. Editor, Community Dental Health, 1983–. *Publications:* contrib. to dental and scientific jls. *Recreations:* music, photography, camping. *Address:* The Pump House, Bishopton Spa, Stratford-upon-Avon, Warwicks. *T:* Stratford-upon-Avon (0789) 204330. *Club:* Royal Society of Medicine.

JAMES, Philip; *see* James, W. P. T.

JAMES, Prof. Philip Seaforth; Professor of English Law and Head of the Department of Law, University College at Buckingham, 1975–81, Professor Emeritus, University of Buckingham, since 1989; *b* 28 May 1914; *s* of Dr Philip William James, MC, and Muriel Lindley James; *m* 1954. Wybetty, *d* of Claas P. Gerth, Enschede, Holland; two *s*. *Educ:* Charterhouse; Trinity Coll., Oxford (MA); Research Fellow, Yale Univ., USA, 1937–38. Called to the Bar, Inner Temple, 1939. Served War of 1939–45, in Royal Artillery, India, Burma (despatches). Fellow of Exeter Coll., Oxford, 1946–49; Prof. and Hd of Dept of Law, Leeds Univ., 1952–75. Visiting Professor: Univs of Yale and of Louisville, Kentucky, USA, 1960–61; Univ. of South Carolina, 1972–73; NY Law Sch., 1981–83. Chairman: Yorks Rent Assessment Panel, 1966–75; Thames Valley Rent Assessment Panel, 1976–; Assessor to County Court under Race Relations Acts. Pres., Soc. of Public Teachers of Law, 1971–72. Governor, Swinton Conservative College, 1970–. Hon. LLD Buckingham, 1986. Hon. Mem., Mark Twain Soc., 1979. *Publications:* An Introduction to English Law, 1950 (trans. Japanese, 1985); General Principles of the Law of Torts, 1959; Shorter Introduction to English Law, 1969; Six Lectures on the Law of Torts, 1980 (trans. Spanish); various articles, notes and reviews on legal and biographical subjects. *Recreations:* golf and gardening. *Address:* Chestnut View, Mill Road, Whitfield, near Brackley, Northants NN13 5TQ. *Club:* National Liberal.

JAMES, Richard Austin, CB 1980; MC 1945; Receiver for Metropolitan Police District, 1977–80; *b* 26 May 1920; *s* of late Thomas Morris James, Headmaster of Sutton Valence Sch., and Hilda Joan James; *m* 1948, Joan Boorer; two *s* one *d*. *Educ:* Clifton Coll.; Emmanuel Coll., Cambridge. British American Tobacco Co., 1938; Royal Engrs, 1939–41; Queen's Own Royal W Kent Regt, 1941–46; Home Office, 1948; Private Sec. to Chancellor of Duchy of Lancaster, 1960; Asst Sec., 1961; Dep. Receiver for Metropolitan Police District, 1970–73; Asst Under-Sec. of State, Police Dept, Home Office, 1974–76; Dep. Under-Sec. of State, 1980. Member: Council of Management, Distressed Gentlefolk's Aid Assoc., 1982–88 (Gen. Sec., 1981–82); Cttee of Management, Sussex Housing Assoc. for the Aged, 1985–88. Pres., Brunswick Boys Club Trust, Fulham, 1990–. Freeman, City of London, 1980. *Recreation:* cricket. *Address:* 5 Gadge Close, Thame, Oxfordshire. *T:* Thame (0844) 261776. *Clubs:* Athenæum, MCC.

JAMES, (Robert) Michael; Public Relations Executive, Timber Trade Federation, since 1990; Director, Forests Forever Campaign, since 1990; *b* 2 Oct. 1934; *s* of late Rev. B. V. James and Mrs D. M. James; *m* 1959, Sarah Helen (*née* Bell); two *s* one *d*. *Educ:* St John's, Leatherhead; Trinity Coll., Cambridge (BA Hons History). Schoolmaster: Harrow Sch., 1958–60; Cranleigh Sch., 1960–62; joined CRO, 1962; 3rd Sec., Wellington, NZ, 1963–65; 1st Sec., Colombo, Sri Lanka, 1966–69; FCO, 1969–71; Dep. High Comr and Head of Chancery, Georgetown, Guyana, 1971–73; Econ. Sec., Ankara, Turkey, 1974–76; FCO, 1976–80; Commercial Counsellor and Deputy High Commissioner: Accra, 1980–83; Singapore, 1984–87; Dep. High Comr, Bridgetown, Barbados, 1987–90. *Recreations:* sport (cricket Blue, 1956–58), drawing, travel. *Address:* Timber Trade Federation, 26/27 Oxendon Street, SW1Y 4EL. *T:* 071–839 1891; 17 North Grove, Highgate, N6 4SH. *T:* 081–348 8689. *Club:* MCC.

JAMES, Sir Robert Vidal R.; *see* Rhodes James.

JAMES, Prof. Dame Sheila (Patricia Violet); *see* Sherlock, Prof. Dame S. P. V.

JAMES, Stanley Francis; Head of Statistics Division 1, Department of Trade and Industry, 1981–84; *b* 12 Feb. 1927; *s* of H. F. James; unmarried. *Educ:* Sutton County Sch.; Trinity Coll., Cambridge. Maths Tripos Pt II; Dip. Math. Statistics. Research Lectr, Econs Dept, Nottingham Univ., 1951; Statistician, Bd of Inland Revenue, 1956; Chief Statistician: Bd of Inland Revenue, 1966; Central Statistical Office, 1968; Asst Dir, Central Statistical Office, 1970–72; Dir, Stats Div., Bd of Inland Revenue, 1972–77; Head, Econs and Stats Div. 6, Depts of Industry and Trade, 1977–81. Hon. Treasurer, Royal Statistical Soc., 1978–83. *Recreations:* travel, theatre, gardening. *Address:* 23 Hayward Road, Oxford OX2 8LN. *Club:* Royal Automobile.

JAMES, Stephen Lawrence; Senior Partner, Simmons & Simmons, Solicitors, since 1980 (Partner, since 1961); *b* 19 Oct. 1930; *s* of Walter Amyas James and Cecile Juliet (*née* Hillman); *m* 1955, Patricia Eleanor Favell James (marr. diss. 1986); two *s* two *d*. *Educ:* Clifton Coll.; St Catharine's Coll., Cambridge (BA History and Law). Mem., Gray's Inn, 1953, called to the Bar, 1956; admitted Solicitor: England and Wales, 1959; Hong Kong, 1980. Director: Horace Clarkson PLC (formerly H. Clarkson (Holdings) PLC), 1975–; Sofipac (London) Ltd (formerly Intermills (London) Ltd), 1975–; Shipping Industrial Holdings Ltd, 1972–82; Tradinvest Bank & Trust Co. of Nassau Ltd, 1975–85; Nodiv Ltd, 1975–78; Silver Line Ltd, 1978–82; Thompson Moore Associates Ltd, 1984–88. Mem., Law Soc., 1961–. Freeman City of London; Mem., Glaziers' Co., 1964–. *Recreations:* yachting, gardening. *Address:* (office) Simmons & Simmons, 14 Dominion Street, EC2M 2RJ; Widden, Shirley Holms, Lymington, Hampshire SO41 8NL. *T:* Lymington (0590) 682226. *Clubs:* Royal Thames Yacht, Royal Ocean Racing; Royal Yacht Squadron (Cowes); Royal Lymington Yacht.

JAMES, Steven Wynne Lloyd; Circuit Administrator, North-Eastern Circuit, Lord Chancellor's Department, since 1988; *b* 9 June 1934; *s* of late Trevor Lloyd James and Olwen Ellis; *m* 1962, Carolyn Ann Rowlands, *d* of late James Morgan Rowlands and of Mercia Rowlands; three *s*. *Educ:* Queen Elizabeth Grammar Sch., Carmarthen; LSE. LLB 1956. Admitted solicitor, 1959. Asst Solicitor in private practice, 1959–61; Legal Asst, HM Land Registry, 1961; Asst Solicitor, Glamorgan CC, 1962–70; Asst Clerk of the Peace, 1970–71; Lord Chancellor's Dept, 1971–: Wales and Chester Circuit: Courts Administrator, (Chester/Mold), 1971–76; Asst Sec., 1976; Dep. Circuit Administrator, 1976–82; Under Sec., 1982; Circuit Adminstrator, 1982–88. *Address:* North-Eastern Circuit Office, 17th Floor, West Riding House, Albion Street, Leeds LS1 5AA. *Club:* Civil Service.

JAMES, (Thomas) Cecil (Garside), CMG 1966; Assistant Under-Secretary of State, Ministry of Defence, 1968–77; *b* 8 Jan. 1918; *s* of Joshua James, MBE, Ashton-under-Lyne; *m* 1941, Elsie Williams, Ashton-under-Lyne; one *s* two *d*. *Educ:* Manchester Grammar Sch.; St John's Coll., Cambridge. Prin. Priv. Sec. to Sec. of State for Air, 1951–55; Asst Sec., Air Min., 1955; Civil Sec., FEAF, 1963–66; Chief of Public Relations, MoD, 1966–68. *Recreation:* golf. *Address:* 9 Knoll House, Uxbridge Road, Pinner, Middx HA5 3LR. *T:* 081–868 3602.

JAMES, Thomas Garnet Henry, CBE 1984; FBA 1976; Keeper of Egyptian Antiquities, British Museum, 1974–88; *b* 8 May 1923; *s* of late Thomas Garnet James and Edith (*née* Griffiths); *m* 1956, Diana Margaret, *y d* of H. L. Vavasseur-Durell; one *s*. *Educ:* Neath Grammar Sch.; Exeter Coll., Oxford. 2nd Cl. Lit. Hum. 1947; 1st Cl. Oriental Studies 1950, MA 1948. Served War of 1939–45, RA; NW Europe; 2nd Lieut 1943; Captain 1945. Asst Keeper, Dept of Egyptian and Assyrian Antiquities, 1951; Dep. Keeper (Egyptian Antiquities), 1974. Laycock Student of Egyptology, Worcester Coll., Oxford, 1954–60; Wilbour Fellow, Brooklyn Museum, 1964; Visiting Professor: Collège de France, 1983; Memphis State Univ., 1990. Editor, Jl of Egyptian Archæology, 1960–70; Editor, Egyptological pubns of Egypt Exploration Soc., 1960–. Vice-Pres., Egypt

Exploration Soc., 1990– (Chm., 1983–89); Mem., German Archæological Inst., 1974. *Publications*: The Mastaba of Khentika called Ikhekhi, 1953; Hieroglyphic Texts in the British Museum I, 1961; The Hekanakhte Papers and other Early Middle Kingdom Documents, 1962; (with R. A. Caminos) Gebel es-Silsilah I, 1963; Egyptian Sculptures, 1966; Myths and Legends of Ancient Egypt, 1969; Hieroglyphic Texts in the British Museum, 9, 1970; Archæology of Ancient Egypt, 1972; Corpus of Hieroglyphic Inscriptions in the Brooklyn Museum, I, 1974; (ed) An Introduction to Ancient Egypt, 1979; (ed) Excavating in Egypt, 1982; (with W. V. Davies) Egyptian Sculpture, 1983; Pharaoh's People, 1984; Egyptian Painting, 1985; Ancient Egypt: the land and its legacy, 1988; (contrib.) W. B. Emery: Great Tombs of the First Dynasty II, 1954; (contrib.) T. J. Dunbabin: Perachora II, 1962; (contrib.) Cambridge Ancient History, 3rd edn, 1973; (contrib.) Encyclop. Britannica, 15th edn, 1974; (ed English trans.) H. Kees: Ancient Egypt, 1961; articles in Jl Egyptian Arch., etc; reviews in learned jls. *Recreations*: music, cooking. *Address*: 14 Turner Close, NW11 6TU. *T*: 081–455 9221. *Club*: United Oxford & Cambridge University.

JAMES, Thomas Geraint Illtyd, FRCS; Hon. Surgeon, Central Middlesex Hospital; Late Teacher of Surgery, Middlesex Hospital, and Hon. Surgical Tutor, Royal College of Surgeons of England; *b* 12 July 1900; *s* of late Evan Thomas and Elizabeth James, Barry; *m* 1932, Dorothy Marguerite, *o d* of late David John, Cardiff; two *s*. *Educ*: Barry, Glam; University Coll., Cardiff; Welsh National Sch. of Medicine; St Mary's Hosp., London; Guy's Hosp., London. BSc Wales, 1921, Alfred Sheen Prize in Anat. and Physiol.; MRCS, LRCP, 1924; MB, ChB, 1925, Maclean Medal and Prize in Obst. and Gynæcol.; FRCSE, 1927; FRCS, 1928; MCh Wales, 1932; FRSocMed; Fellow Association of Surgeons of Great Britain and Ireland; Erasmus Wilson Lectr, RCS, 1972. Mem., Internat. Soc. for Surgery; Corr. Mem. Spanish-Portuguese Soc. of Neurosurgery. Mem. Soc. of Apothecaries; Freeman of City of London. Formerly: Assoc. Examr University of London; Mem. and Chm., Court of Examiners RCS of England; Examr in Surgery, University of Liverpool; Ho. phys., Ho. surg. and Resident Surgical Officer, Cardiff Royal Infirmary; Clinical Asst St Mark's, St Peter's and Guy's Hosps, London; Asst to Neurosurg. Dept, London Hosp.; Mem., Management Cttee, Leavesden Gp of Hosps. *Publications*: in various jls on surg. and neurosurg. subjects. *Recreations*: literature, travelling. *Address*: 1 Freeland Road, W5. *T*: 081–992 2430.

JAMES, Prof. Vivian Hector Thomas; Professor and Head of Department of Chemical Pathology, St Mary's Hospital Medical School, London University, 1973–90, now Professor Emeritus; Hon. Chemical Pathologist, Paddington and North Kensington Health Authority, since 1973; *b* 29 Dec. 1924; *s* of William and Alice James; *m* 1958, Betty Irene Pike. *Educ*: Latymer Sch.; London Univ. BSc, PhD, DSc; FRCPath 1977. Flying duties, RAF, 1942–46. Scientific Staff, Nat. Inst. for Med. Res., 1952–56; St Mary's Hospital Medical School, London: Lectr, Dept of Chemical Pathol., 1956; Reader, 1962; Prof. of Chem. Endocrinol., 1967; Chm., Div. of Pathology, St Mary's Hosp., 1981. Emeritus Fellow, Leverhulme Trust, 1991. Mem., Herts AHA, 1974–77. Secretary: Clin. Endocrinol. Cttee, MRC, 1967–72; Cttee for Human Pituitary Collection, MRC, 1972–76 (Chm., 1976–82); Endocrine Sect., RSocMed, 1972–76 (Pres., 1976–78); Gen. Sec., Soc. for Endocrinology, 1979–85 (Treas., 1986–); Sec.-Gen., European Fedn of Endocrine Socs, 1986–. Editor, Clinical Endocrinology, 1972–74. Clinical Endocrinology Medal Lectr, Clin. Endocrinol. Trust, 1990. Hon. MRCP 1989. Freeman, Haverfordwest, 1946. Fiorino d'oro, City of Florence, 1977. *Publications*: (ed jtly) Current Topics in Experimental Endocrinology, 1971, 5th edn 1983; (ed) The Adrenal Gland, 1979; (ed jtly) Hormones in Blood, 1961, 3rd edn 1983; contribs to various endocrine and other jls. *Address*: Department of Chemical Pathology, St Mary's Hospital Medical School, W2 1PG. *T*: 071–723 1252. *Club*: Royal Society of Medicine.

JAMES, Walter; *see* James, Arthur Walter.

JAMES, Prof. Walter, CBE 1977; Dean and Director of Studies, Faculty of Educational Studies, 1969–77, Professor of Educational Studies, 1969–84, Open University; *b* 8 Dec. 1924; *s* of late George Herbert James and Mary Kathleen (*née* Crutch); *m* 1948, Joyce Dorothy Woollaston; two *s*. *Educ*: Royal Grammar Sch., Worcester; St Luke's Coll., Exeter; Univ. of Nottingham. BA 1955. School teacher, 1948–52; Univ. of Nottingham: Resident Tutor, Dept of Extra-Mural Studies, 1958–65; Lectr in Adult Educn, Dept of Adult Educn, 1965–69. Consultant on Adult Educn and Community Develt to Govt of Seychelles and ODA of FCO, 1973; Adviser: to Office of Educn, WCC, 1974–76; on Social Planning, to State of Bahrain, 1975; Council of Europe: UK Rep., Working Party on Develt of Adult Education, 1973–81; UK Rep. and Project Adviser, Adult Educn for Community Develt, 1982–87; Adult Educn for Social Change, 1988–; Chairman: Nat. Council for Voluntary Youth Services, 1970–76; Review of Training of part-time Youth and Community Workers, 1975–77; Religious Adv. Bd, Scout Assoc., 1977–82; Inservice Training and Educn Panel for Youth and Community Service, 1978–82; Council for Educn and Trng in Youth and Community Work, 1982–85; Nat. Adv. Council for the Youth Service, 1985–88. Member: DES Cttee on Youth and Community Work in 70s, 1967–69; ILO Working Party on Use of Radio and TV for Workers' Educn, 1968; Gen. Synod, C of E, 1970–75; Exec. Cttee, Nat. Council of Social Service, 1970–75; Univs' Council for Educn of Teachers, 1970–84; Univs Council for Adult Educn, 1971–76; BBC Further Educn Adv. Council, 1971–75; Exec. Cttee and Council, Nat. Inst. of Adult Educn, 1971–77; Library Adv. Council for England, 1974–76; Adv. Council, HM Queen's Silver Jubilee Appeal, 1976–78; Trustee: Young Volunteer Force Foundn, 1972–77; Trident Educnl Trust, 1972–86; Community Projects Foundn, 1977–90; Community Develt Foundn, 1990–; President: Inst. of Playleadership, 1972–74; Fair Play for Children, 1979–82. *Publications*: (with F. J. Bayliss) The Standard of Living, 1964; (ed) Virginia Woolf, Selections from her essays, 1966; (contrib.) Encyclopaedia of Education, 1968; (contrib.) Teaching Techniques in Adult Education, 1971; (contrib.) Mass Media and Adult Education, 1971; (with H. Janne and P. Dominice) The Development of Adult Education, 1980; (with others) The 14 Pilot Experiments, Vols 1–3, 1984; Some Conclusions from the Co-operation of 14 Development Projects, 1985; Handbook on Co-operative Monitoring, 1986; The Uses of Media for Community Development, 1988. *Recreation*: living. *Address*: 25 Kepplestone, Staveley Road, Eastbourne BN20 7JZ. *T*: Eastbourne (0323) 23376.

JAMES, Prof. (William) Philip (Trehearne), MD, DSc; FRCP, FRCPEd; FRSE; FIBiol; Director, Rowett Research Institute, Aberdeen, since 1982; Research Professor, Aberdeen University, since 1983; *b* 27 June 1938; *s* of Jenkin William James and Lilian Mary James; *m* 1961, Jean Hamilton (*née* Moorhouse); one *s* one *d*. *Educ*: Ackworth Sch., Pontefract, Yorks; University Coll. London (BSc Hons 1959; DSc 1983); University Coll. Hosp. (MB, BS 1962; MD 1968). FRCP 1978; FRCPEd 1983; FRSE 1986; FIBiol 1988. Sen. House Physician, Whittington Hosp., London, 1963–65; Clin. Res. Scientist, MRC Tropical Metabolism Res. Unit, Kingston, Jamaica, 1965–68; Harvard Res. Fellow, Mass Gen. Hosp., 1968–69; Wellcome Trust Res. Fellow, MRC Gastroenterology Unit, London, 1969–70; Sen. Lectr, Dept of Human Nutrition, London Sch. of Hygiene and Trop. Medicine, and Hon. Consultant Physician, UCH, 1970–74; Asst Dir, MRC Dunn Nutrition Unit, and Hon. Consultant Physician, Addenbrooke's Hosp., Cambridge,

1974–82. Hon. Consultant on nutrition to Army, 1989–. Chairman: FAO Consultation on internat. food needs, 1987; Nat. Food Alliance, 1988–90 (Pres., 1990–); Coronary Prevention Gp, 1988–; WHO Consultation on world food and health policies, 1989; Member: MAFF Nutrition and Food Safety Res. Cttee; DoH Cttees on Med. Aspects of Food Policy, and on Irradiated and Novel Foods. FRSA 1988. Hon. MA Cantab, 1977. *Publications*: The Analysis of Dietary Fibre in Food, 1981; The Body Weight Regulatory System: normal and disturbed mechanisms, 1981; Assessing Human Energy Requirements, 1990; documents on European national nutrition policy and energy needs for DHSS, FAO, NACNE and WHO; scientific pubns on energy metabolism, salt handling, and heart disease in Lancet, Nature, Clin. Science. *Recreations*: talking, writing reports; eating, preferably in France. *Address*: Wardenhill, Bucksburn, Aberdeen AB2 9SA. *T*: Aberdeen (0224) 712623. *Club*: Athenæum.

JAMES-MOORE, Jonathan Guy; Head of Light Entertainment, BBC Radio, since 1991; *b* 22 March 1946; *s* of Wilfrid Seward and Alana James-Moore; *m* 1975, Jenny Baynes; one *d*. *Educ*: Bromsgrove Sch.; Emmanuel Coll., Cambridge (MA). Founder Dir, Oxford & Cambridge Shakespeare Co., 1968–71; Gen. Manager, Sir Nicholas Sekers Theatre at Rosehill, 1971–72; Administrator: Mermaid Theatre, 1972–74; St George's Theatre, 1975–76; BBC Radio Light Entertainment, 1978–. *Recreations*: collecting wine labels, planning holidays. *Address*: Room 101, 16 Langham Street, W1A 1AA; 6 Legard Road, N5 1DE. *T*: 071–226 7034.

JAMESON, Derek; news, TV and radio commentator; Presenter, Radio 2 Jameson Show, since 1986; *b* 29 Nov. 1929; *e s* of Mrs Elsie Jameson; *m* 1st, 1948, Jacqueline Sinclair (marr. diss. 1966); one *s* one *d*; 2nd, 1971, Pauline Tomlin (marr. diss. 1978); two *s*; 3rd, 1988, Ellen Petrie. *Educ*: elementary schools, Hackney. Office boy rising to Chief Sub-editor, Reuters, 1944–60; Editor, London American, 1960–61; features staff, Daily Express, 1961–63; Picture Editor, Sunday Mirror, 1963–65; Asst Editor, Sunday Mirror, 1965–72; Northern Editor, Sunday and Daily Mirror, 1972–76; Managing Editor, Daily Mirror, 1976–77; Editor, Daily Express, 1977–79; Editor-in-Chief, The Daily Star, 1978–80; Editor, News of the World, 1981–84. Presenter, Jameson Tonight, Sky TV, 1989–90. *Publications*: Touched by Angels (autobiog.), 1988; Last of the Hot Metal Men (autobiog.), 1990. *Recreations*: opera, music, reading. *Address*: BBC Radio 2, Broadcasting House, W1A 1AA.

JAMESON, Air Cdre Patrick Geraint, CB 1959; DSO 1943; DFC 1940 (and Bar 1942), psa; Royal Air Force, retired, 1960; *b* Wellington, NZ, 10 Nov. 1912; *s* of Robert Delvin Jameson, Balbriggan, Ireland, and Katherine Lenora Jameson (*née* Dick), Dunedin, NZ; *m* 1941, Hilda Nellie Haiselden Webster, *d* of B. F. Webster, Lower Hutt, NZ; one *s* one *d*. *Educ*: Hutt Valley High Sch., New Zealand. Commissioned in RAF, 1936. War of 1939–45 (despatches 5 times, DFC and Bar, DSO): 46 Squadron, 1936–40, 266 Sqaudron, 1940–41; Wing Commander Flying, Wittering, 1941–42; Wing Commander (Flying), North Weald, 1942–43; Group Capt. Plans, HQ No 11 Group, 1943–44; 122 Wing in France, Belgium, Holland, Germany and Denmark, 1944–46; Staff Coll., Haifa, 1946; Air Ministry, 1946–48; CFE, West Raynham, 1949–52; Wunsdorf (2nd TAF), 1952–54; SASO, HQ No II Group, 1954–56; SASO HQ RAF Germany (2nd TAF) 1956–59; Task Force Comdr, Operation Grapple, Christmas Is., 1959–60. Norwegian War Cross, 1943; Netherlands Order of Orange Nassau, 1945; American Silver Star, 1945. *Recreations*: fishing, shooting, sailing, golf. *Address*: 70 Wai-Iti Crescent, Lower Hutt, New Zealand. *Clubs*: Royal Air Force; Hutt Golf; Hutt.

JAMIESON, Brian George, PhD; Director, Central Office, Agricultural and Food Research Council, since 1987; *b* 7 Feb. 1943; *s* of George and Amy Jamieson; *m* 1966, Helen Carol Scott. *Educ*: Boroughmuir Sch.; Edinburgh Univ. (BSc, PhD). Research Asst, Edinburgh Univ., 1967–70; Natural Environment Res. Council, 1970–73 and 1975–77; Principal, ARC, 1973–75; Cabinet Office, 1977–78; Asst Sec., 1978–87, Acting Sec., Oct.–Dec. 1990, AFRC. *Publications*: papers on the origins of igneous rocks. *Recreations*: running, keeping fit, ski-ing, travelling. *Address*: 8 Orwell Close, Caversham, Reading, Berks RG4 7PU. *T*: Reading (0734) 477780.

JAMIESON, Major David Auldjo, VC 1944; CVO 1990; Member of HM Body Guard, Hon. Corps of Gentlemen at Arms, 1968–90, Lieutenant, 1986–90; *b* 1 Oct. 1920; *s* of late Sir Archibald Auldjo Jamieson, KBE, MC; *m* 1st, 1948, Nancy Elwes (*d* 1963), *y d* of Robert H. A. Elwes, Congham, King's Lynn; one *s* two *d*; 2nd, 1969, Joanna, *e d* of Edward Woodall. *Educ*: Eton Coll. Commissioned Royal Norfolk Regt May 1939; served War of 1939–45, incl. Normandy, 1944 (VC); retired, 1948. Director: Australian Agricultural Co., 1949–78 (Governor, 1952–76); UK Branch, Australian Mutual Provident Society, 1963–89 (Dep. Chm., 1973–89); National Westminster Bank PLC, 1983–87; Steetley plc, 1976–86 (Dep. Chm., 1983–86). Clerk of the Cheque and Adjutant, Hon. Corps of Gentlemen at Arms, 1981–86. High Sheriff of Norfolk, 1980. *Recreations*: shooting, golf. *Address*: The Drove House, Thornham, Hunstanton, Norfolk PE36 6LS. *T*: Thornham (048526) 206.

JAMIESON, Air Marshal Sir (David) Ewan, KBE 1986 (OBE 1967); CB 1981; Chief of Defence Staff, New Zealand, 1983–86, retired; *b* Christchurch, 19 April 1930; *s* of R. D. Jamieson; *m* 1957, Margaret Elaine, *d* of L. J. Bridge; three *s* one *d*. *Educ*: Christchurch and New Plymouth Boys' High Sch. Joined RNZAF, 1949; OC Flying, Ohakea, 1964; CO Malaysia, 1965–66; Jt Services Staff Coll., 1969; CO Auckland, 1971–72; AOC Ops Group, 1974–76; RCDS 1977; Chief of Air Staff, RNZAF, 1979–83. *Address*: 14 Hinerau Grove, Taupo, New Zealand.

JAMIESON, Air Marshal Sir Ewan; *see* Jamieson, Air Marshal Sir D. E.

JAMIESON, Rt. Rev. Hamish Thomas Umphelby; *see* Bunbury, Bishop of.

JAMIESON, Lt-Col Harvey Morro H.; *see* Harvey-Jamieson.

JAMIESON, Rear-Adm. Ian Wyndham, CB 1970; DSC 1945; Emeritus Fellow, Jesus College, Oxford, 1986 (Home Bursar and Fellow, 1972–86); *b* 13 March 1920; *s* of late S. W. Jamieson, CBE; *m* 1949, Patricia Wheeler, Knowle, Warwickshire; two *s* one *d*. *Educ*: RNC, Dartmouth. Served War of 1939–45: Anti Submarine Warfare Specialist, 1943. Comdr, 1953; Staff of RN Tactical Sch., 1953–56; HMS Maidstone, 1956–58; Dir, Jt Tactical Sch., Malta, 1958; Capt. 1959; Asst Dir, Naval Intelligence, 1959–61; Comd HMS Nubian and 6th Frigate Sqdn, 1961–64; Dir, Seaman Officers Appts, 1964–66; Comd Britannia RN Coll., Dartmouth, 1966–68; Rear-Adm. 1968; Flag Officer, Gibraltar, and Admiral Superintendent, HM Dockyard, Gibraltar; also NATO Comdr, Gibraltar (Mediterranean Area), 1968–69; C of S to C-in-C Western Fleet, 1969–71; retired. Mem., Southern Arts Council, 1985–. Hon. MA Oxon, 1973. *Recreations*: hockey (Scotland and Combined Services), cricket, golf, tennis. *Address*: Buckels, East Hagbourne, near Didcot, Oxfordshire OX11 9LJ. *Clubs*: Army and Navy, MCC.

JAMIESON, John Kenneth; Chairman of Board and Chief Executive Officer, Exxon Corporation (formerly Standard Oil Co. (NJ)), 1969–75; *b* Canada, 28 Aug. 1910; *s* of John Locke and Kate Herron Jamieson; US citizen; *m* 1937, Ethel May Burns; one *s* one *d*. *Educ*: Univ. of Alberta; Massachusetts Inst. of Technology (BS). Northwest Stellarene

Co. of Alberta, 1932; British American Oil Co., 1934; Manager, Moose Jaw Refinery; served War of 1939–45 in Oil Controller's Dept of Canadian Govt; subseq. Manager, Manufrg Dept, British American Oil Co.; joined Imperial Oil Co., 1948: Head of Engrg and Develt Div., Sarnia Refinery, 1949; Asst Gen. Man. of Manufrg Dept, 1950; on loan to Canadian Dept of Defence Production, 1951; Dir, Imperial Oil, 1952, Vice-Pres. 1953; Pres. and Dir International Petroleum Co., 1959; Vice-Pres., Dir and Mem. Exec. Cttee Exxon Co., USA (formerly Humble Oil & Refining Co.), 1961, Exec. Vice-Pres. 1962, Pres. 1963–64; Exec. Vice-Pres. and Dir 1964, Pres. 1965–69, Jersey Standard. Dir, Raychem Corp. *Address:* 1100 Milam Building, Suite 4601, Houston, Texas 77002, USA. *Clubs:* Links (NYC); Augusta National Golf (Augusta); Ramada, Houston Country (Houston); Ristigouche Salmon (Matapedia, Quebec).

JAMIESON, Kenneth Douglas, CMG 1968; HM Diplomatic Service, retired; *b* 9 Jan. 1921; *s* of late Rt Hon. Lord Jamieson, PC, KC, Senator of College of Justice in Scotland and Violet Rhodes; *m* 1946, Pamela Hall; two *s* one *d*. *Educ:* Rugby; Balliol Coll., Oxford. War Service: 5th Regt RHA, 1941–45; HQ, RA 7th Armoured Div., 1945–46. Joined Foreign Service, 1946; served in: Washington, 1948; FO, 1952; Lima, 1954; Brussels, 1959; FO, 1961; Caracas, 1963; Dir of Commercial Training, DSAO, 1968; Head of Export Promotion Dept, FCO, 1968–70; Minister and UK Dep. Permanent Representative, UN, NY, 1970–74; Ambassador to Peru, 1974–77; Sen. Directing Staff, RCDS, 1977–80. *Address:* Mill Hill House, Bucks Green, Rudgwick, W Sussex.

JAMIESON, Rt. Rev. Penelope Ann Bansall; *see* Dunedin, Bishop of.

JAMIL RAIS, Tan Sri Dato' Abdul; *see* Abdul Jamil Rais.

JAMISON, James Hardie, OBE 1974; chartered accountant; Partner, Coopers & Lybrand, Chartered Accountants, 1939–78, retired; *b* 29 Nov. 1913; *s* of late W. I. Jamison; *m* 1940, Mary Louise, *d* of late W. R. Richardson; two *s* one *d*. *Educ:* Sydney Church of England Grammar Sch. Chm., Commn of Inquiry into Efficiency and Admin of Hosps, 1979–80. Mem., Nat. Council, Aust. Inst. of Chartered Accountants, 1969–77, Vice Pres., 1973–75, Pres., 1975–76. *Recreation:* sailing. *Address:* 8 McLeod Street, Mosman, NSW 2088, Australia. *Clubs:* Australasian Pioneers' (Pres. 1970–72), Australian, Royal Sydney Yacht Squadron (Sydney).

JAMISON, James Kenneth, OBE 1978; Director, Arts Council of Northern Ireland, 1969–91; *b* 9 May 1931; *s* of William Jamison and Alicia Rea Jamison; *m* 1964, Joan Young Boyd; one *s* one *d*. *Educ:* Belfast College of Art (DA). Secondary school teacher, 1953–61; Art Critic, Belfast Telegraph, 1956–61; Art Organiser, Arts Council of Northern Ireland, 1962–64, Dep. Director, 1964–69. Hon. DLitt Ulster, 1989. *Publications:* miscellaneous on the arts in the North of Ireland. *Recreations:* the arts, travel. *Address:* 64 Rugby Road, Belfast BT7 1PT. *T:* Belfast (0232) 323063. *Club:* Queen's University Common Room.

JANES, (John) Douglas (Webster), CB 1975; Secretary, The Bach Choir, 1981–mid 1989; Deputy Secretary, Northern Ireland Office, 1974–79; *b* 17 Aug. 1918; *s* of late John Arnold Janes and Maud Mackinnon (*née* Webster); *m* 1st, 1943, Margaret Isabel Smith (*d* 1978); one *s* two *d*; 2nd, 1986, Mrs Joan Walker (*née* Bentley). *Educ:* Southgate County Sch., Mddx; Imperial Coll. of Science and Technology. 1st cl. BSc (Eng) London, ACGI, DIC. Entered Post Office Engineering Dept, Research Branch, 1939. Served Royal Signals, RAOC, REME, 1939–45: War Office, 1941–45; Major. Min. of Town and Country Planning, 1947; Min. of Housing and Local Govt, 1951; seconded to Min. of Power, 1956–58; HM Treasury, 1960–63; Min. of Land and Natural Resources, 1964–66; Prin. Finance Officer and Accountant Gen., Min. of Housing and Local Govt, 1968–70; Prin. Finance Officer (Local Govt and Develt), DoE, 1970–73, Dep. Sec., 1973; Chief Executive, Maplin Develt Authority, 1973–74. Chm., Home Grown Timber Adv. Cttee, 1981– (Mem., 1979–); various management and organisation reviews, 1979–81. *Recreations:* singing, do-it-yourself.

JANES, Maj.-Gen. Mervyn, CB 1973; MBE 1944; *b* 1 Oct. 1920; *o s* of W. G. Janes; *m* 1946, Elizabeth Kathleen McIntyre; two *d*. *Educ:* Sir Walter St John's Sch., London. Commnd 1942; served with Essex Yeo. (104 Regt RHA), 1942–46, Middle East and Italy; psc 1951; served with 3 RHA, 1952–53; 2 Div., BMRA, 1954–55; Chief Instructor, New Coll., RMAS, 1956–57; Batt. Comd, 3 RHA, 1958–60; Asst Army Instructor (GSO1), Imperial Defence Coll., 1961–62; comd 1st Regt RHA, 1963–65; Comdr, RA, in BAOR, 1965–67; DMS2 (MoD(A)), 1967–70; GOC 5th Division, 1970–71; Dir, Royal Artillery, 1971–73. Col Comdt, RA, 1973–81. Chm. Cttee, Lady Grover's Hosp. Fund for Officers' Families, to 1991. *Recreations:* music, ornithology. *Address:* Lucy's Cottage, North Street, Theale, Reading, Berks RG7 5EX. *Club:* Army and Navy.

JANION, Rear-Adm. Sir Hugh (Penderel), KCVO 1981; Flag Officer, Royal Yachts, 1975–81; *b* 28 Sept. 1923; *s* of late Engr Captain Ralph Penderel Janion, RN, and late Mrs Winifred Derwent Janion; *m* 1956, Elizabeth Monica Ferard; one *s* one *d*. *Educ:* Malvern Link Sch., Worcs; RNC Dartmouth. Served War of 1939–45, Russian convoys, invasions of Sicily and Italy; Korean War, 1950–52, Inchon landing. Specialised in navigation; Comdr, 1958, i/c HMS Jewel, and Exec. Officer HMS Ark Royal; Captain, 1966, i/c HMS Aurora and HMS Bristol; Rear-Adm. 1975. Extra Equerry to the Queen, 1975–. Younger Brother, Trinity House, 1976–. *Recreations:* sailing, golf. *Address:* King's Hayes, Batcombe, Shepton Mallet, Somerset BA4 6HF. *T:* Upton Noble (074985) 300. *Clubs:* Naval and Military; Royal Yacht Squadron (Cowes); Royal Naval and Royal Albert Yacht (Portsmouth); Imperial Poona Yacht.

JANMAN, Timothy Simon; MP (C) Thurrock, since 1987; *b* 9 Sept. 1956; *s* of Jack and Irene Janman; *m* 1990, Shirley Buckingham. *Educ:* Sir William Borlase Grammar Sch., Marlow, Bucks; Nottingham Univ. (BSc Hons Chemistry). Ford Motor Co., 1979–83; IBM UK Ltd, 1983–87. Nat. Sen. Vice-Chm., FCS, 1980–81; Chm., Selsdon Gp, 1983–87. Mem., Southampton City Council, May–July 1987. Mem., Select Cttee on Employment, 1989–. Vice-Chm., Cons. Backbench Employment Cttee, 1988– (Sec., 1987–88); Sec., Cons. Backbench Home Affairs Cttee, 1989–. *Publications:* contribs to booklets and pamphlets. *Recreations:* restaurants, theatre. *Address:* The Green, Rectory Road, West Tilbury Village, Essex RM18 8UD. *T:* Tilbury (03752) 2597.

JANNEH, Bocar Ousman S.; *see* Semega-Janneh.

JANNER, Lady; Elsie Sybil Janner, CBE 1968; JP; *b* Newcastle upon Tyne; *d* of Joseph and Henrietta Cohen; *m* 1927, Barnett Janner (later Baron Janner) (*d* 1982); one *s* one *d*. *Educ:* Central Newcastle High Sch.; South Hampstead High Sch.; Switzerland. Founder and first Hon. Club Leader, Brady Girls' Club, Whitechapel, 1925 (now Pres., Brady Clubs and Settlement); Jt Pres., Brady/Maccabi Youth and Community Centre, Edgware, 1980–. War of 1939–45: Captain, Mechanised Transp. Corps (Def. Medal). Chm., Bridgehead Housing Assoc., to acquire property for residential purposes for homeless ex-offenders, 1967–75; Stonham Housing Assoc. (amalgamation of S Western Housing Assoc., St Leonards Housing Assoc., and Bridgehead): Chm. Adv. Bd, 1975–83; Pres., 1984–; Chm., Stonham Meml Trust. Mem., Finance and Develt Cttees; Magistrates Assoc.: Vice-Pres.; Hon. Treasurer, 1971–76; formerly Dep. Chm., Road Traffic Cttee, and Mem., Exec. Cttee; Vice Pres., Inner London Br. (former Chm.); former Mem., Jt Standing Cttee, Magistrates Assoc. and Justices' Clerks Soc. JP, Inner London, 1936; contested (Lab), Mile End, LCC, 1947; a Visiting Magistrate to Holloway Women's Prison, 1950–62; Chm., Thames Bench of Magistrates, 1975; Mem., Juvenile Courts Panel, 1944–70 (Chm. 1960–70); Former Member: Inner London and NE London Licensing Planning Cttees; Inner London Licensing Compensation Cttee; Inner London Mem., Cttee of Magistrates. Vice-Pres., Assoc. for Jewish Youth; Hon. Vice-Pres., Fedn of Women Zionists of GB and Ire.; Chm., United Jewish Educnl and Cultural Org. (internat. body to re-construct Jewish educn in countries of Europe which had been occupied by Germans), 1947–50; Member: Central Council of Jewish Religious Educn, 1945–; Bd of Deputies, British Jews Educn and Youth Cttee (Chm., 1943–66); Dep. Chm., Mitchell City of London Charity and Educnl Foundn, 1984–90 (Trustee, 1950–); Trustee, Barnett Janner Charitable Trust, from foundn, 1983–; Member: former Nat. Road Safety Adv. Council, 1965–68; Exec., Inst. Advanced Motorists, 1974–88 (Vice-Chm., 1980–84, Fellow). Freeman, City of London, 1975. *Publication:* Barnett Janner—A Personal Portrait, 1984. *Recreation:* grandchildren. *Address:* 45 Morpeth Mansions, Morpeth Terrace, SW1P 1ET. *T:* 071–828 8700; 15c Elizabeth Court, Grove Road, Bournemouth BH1 3DU. *T:* Bournemouth (0202) 293969.

See also Hon. G. E. Janner, Lord Morris of Kenwood.

JANNER, Hon. Greville Ewan, MA Cantab; QC 1971; MP (Lab) Leicester West, since 1974 (Leicester North West, 1970–74); barrister, author, lecturer, journalist and broadcaster; *b* 11 July 1928; *s* of late Baron Janner and of Lady Janner, *qv*; *m* 1955, Myra Louise Sheink, Melbourne; one *s* two *d*. *Educ:* Bishop's Coll. Sch., Canada; St Paul's Sch. (Foundn Schol.); Trinity Hall, Cambridge (Exhbnr); Harvard Post Graduate Law School (Fulbright and Smith-Mundt Schol.); Harmsworth Scholar, Middle Temple, 1955. Nat. Service: Sgt RA, BAOR, War Crimes Investigator. Pres., Cambridge Union, 1952; Chm., Cambridge Univ. Labour Club, 1952; Internat. Sec., Nat. Assoc. of Labour Students, 1952; Pres., Trinity Hall Athletic Club, 1952. Contested (Lab) Wimbledon, 1955. Mem., Select Cttee on Employment, 1982–; Chm., All-Party Industrial Safety Gp, 1975–; Founder and former Chm., All-Party Cttee for Homeless and Rootless People; Vice-Chm., All-Party Parly Cttee for Release of Soviet Jewry, 1971–; Joint Vice-Chairman: British-Israel Parly Gp, 1983–; British-India Parly Gp, 1987–; Vice-Chairman: British-Spanish Parly Gp, 1987– (Sec., 1986); All-Party British-Romanian Gp, 1990–; All-Party Parly Cttee for E Europ. Jewry, 1990–; Sec., All-Party War Crimes Gp, 1987–; Convenor and Founder, Inter-Party Council Against Anti-Semitism. Vis. Law Fellow, Lancaster Univ., 1985–88. President: National Council for Soviet Jewry, 1979–85; Bd of Deputies of British Jews, 1979–85; Commonwealth Jewish Council, 1983–; Vice-President: Assoc. for Jewish Youth, 1970–; Assoc. of Jewish Ex-Servicemen; IVS, 1983–; World Jewish Congress: European Vice-Pres., 1984–86; Mem. World Exec., 1986–; Hon. Vice-Pres., 1990–. Partner, J. S. B. Associates, 1984–; Chm., JSB Gp Ltd,. 1988–; non-exec. Dir, Ladbroke Plc, 1986–. Member: Nat. Union of Journalists; Soc. of Labour Lawyers; Magic Circle; Pres., Retired Executives, Action Clearing House, 1982–; Pres., Jewish Museum, 1985–; Mem. Bd of Dirs, Jt Israel Appeal, 1985–; Vice-Pres., Guideposts Trust, 1983–; Founder Mem., Internat. Cttee for Human Rights in USSR; Chm., Holocaust Educl Trust, 1987–. Former Dir, Jewish Chronicle Newspaper Ltd; Trustee, Jewish Chronicle Trust. Hon. Mem., Leics NUM, 1986–. Fellow, Inst. of Personnel Management, 1976. Hon. PhD Haifa Univ., 1984. Sternberg Award, CCJ, 1985. *Publications:* 64 books, mainly on employment and industrial relations law, presentational skills, and on public speaking, including: Employment Letters; Complete Speechmaker; Complete Letterwriter; Janner on Presentation; Communication; Chairing Meetings. *Recreations:* swimming, magic. *Address:* House of Commons, SW1. *T:* 071–219 3000.

JANSEN, Elly, (Mrs Elly Whitehouse-Jansen), OBE 1980; Founder and International Director, The Richmond Fellowship for community mental health, since 1959; *b* 5 Oct. 1929; *d* of Jacobus Gerrit Jansen and Petronella Suzanna Vellekoop; *m* 1969, Alan Brian Stewart Whitehouse (known as George); three *d*. *Educ:* Paedologisch Inst. of Free Univ., Amsterdam; Boerhave Kliniek (SRN); London Univ. Founded: Richmond Fellowship of America, 1968, of Australia, 1973, of New Zealand, 1978, of Austria, 1979, of Canada, 1981, of Hong Kong, of India, of Israel, 1984, and of the Caribbean, 1987. Richmond Fellowship Internat., 1981. Organised internat. confs on therapeutic communities, 1973, 1975, 1976, 1979, 1984, and 1988; acts as consultant to many govts on issues of community care. Fellowship, German Marshall Meml Fund, 1977–78. *Publications:* (ed) The Therapeutic Community Outside the Hospital, 1980; (contrib.) Mental Health and the Community, 1983; (contrib.) Towards a Whole Society: collected papers on aspects of mental health, 1985; contribs to Amer. Jl of Psychiatry, L'Inf. Psychiatrique, and other jls. *Recreations:* literature, music, interior design. *Address:* 8 Addison Road, Kensington, W14 8DL. *T:* 071–603 6373.

JANSEN, Peter Johan; Group Chief Executive, MB-Caradon (formerly MB Group), since 1989; Vice-Chairman, CMB Packaging SA; *b* 13 Feb. 1940; *s* of Eric Jansen and Elizabeth (*née* Keesman); *m* 1963, Françoise Marie-Paule; three *s*. *Educ:* Parktown Boys' High School, Johannesburg. Internat. marketing exec., Pfizer Corp., 1959–65; marketing Dir, Bristol Meyers, 1966–69; Partner, Urwick Orr & Partners, 1969–72; Senior Partner, Lee, Jansen & Partners, 1972–77; Redland plc: Divl Man. Dir, 1977–80; plc Director, 1981–85; led management buy-out and subseq. flotation, Caradon plc; Dep. Chm. and Chief Exec., 1985–89. Gov., St George's Coll., Weybridge. *Recreations:* golf, opera, theatre. *Address:* Caradon House, Queens Road, Weybridge, Surrey KT13 9UX. *T:* Weybridge (0932) 850850.

JANSEN, Sir Ross (Malcolm), KBE 1989 (CBE 1986); Chairman, Waikato Regional Council, since 1989; Mayor of Hamilton City, New Zealand, 1977–89; *b* 6 Sept. 1932; *m* 1957, Rhyl Robinson; three *s* three *d*. *Educ:* Horowhenua Coll., Levin (Dux *proxime accessit* 1950); Victoria Univ., Wellington (LLB 1957). NZ Univ. Law Moot Prize, 1956. Practised law in partnership. Hamilton, 1958–77. Hamilton City Council: Mem., 1965–74, 1977–89; Chairman: Planning Cttee, 1965–68; Works Cttee, 1968–74; Dep. Mayor, 1971–74. Chairman: Waikato United Council, 1986–89; Hamilton Industrial Develt Prog., 1966–68; NZ Bldg Industry Commn, 1986–89; Lottery Community Facilities Cttee, 1989–. President: Municipal Assoc. of NZ, 1984–89; NZ Local Govt Assoc., 1988–89. Mem. Council, Univ. of Waikato, 1977–89. Winston Churchill Trust Fellowship in Town Planning, 1968. FRSA; ACIArb. Hon. Dr Waikato Univ., 1984. Hon. Chieftain of Western Samoa (for services to the Samoan Community). Commemoration Medal, NZ, 1990. *Recreations:* reading (poetry and history), tennis, gardening. *Address:* 109 Harrowfield Drive, Hamilton, New Zealand. *T:* 558–803.

JANVRIN, Vice-Adm. Sir (Hugh) Richard Benest, KCB 1969 (CB 1965); DSC 1940; *b* 9 May 1915; *s* of late Rev. Canon C. W. Janvrin, Fairford, Glos.; *m* 1938, Nancy Fielding; two *s*. *Educ:* RNC, Dartmouth. Naval Cadet, 1929; Midshipman, 1933; Sub-Lt, 1936; Lt, 1937; Qualified Fleet Air Arm Observer, 1938. Served War of 1939–45 (took part in Taranto attack, 1940). In Command: HMS Broadsword, 1951–53; HMS Grenville, 1957–58; RNAS Brawdy, 1958; HMS Victorious, 1959–60. Imperial Defence Coll., 1961; Dir, Tactics and Weapons Policy, Admiralty, 1962–63; Flag Officer, Aircraft

Carriers, 1964–66; Dep. Chief of Naval Staff, MoD, 1966–68; Flag Officer, Naval Air Comd, 1968–70; retired 1971. Lieut-Comdr, 1945; Comdr, 1948; Capt., 1954; Rear-Adm., 1964; Vice-Adm. 1967. *Recreation:* gardening. *Address:* Allen's Close, Chalford Hill, near Stroud, Glos GL6 8QJ. *T:* Brimscombe (0453) 882336.
See also R. B. Janvrin.

JANVRIN, Robin Berry, LVO 1983; Assistant Private Secretary to the Queen, since 1990; *b* 20 Sept. 1946; *s* of Vice Adm. Sir Richard Janvrin, *qv*; *m* 1977, Isabelle de Boissonneaux de Chevigny; one *s* two *d*. *Educ:* Marlborough Coll.; Brasenose Coll., Oxford (MA). Royal Navy, 1964–75; joined Diplomatic Service, 1975; First Secretary: UK Delegn to NATO, 1976–78; New Delhi, 1981–84; Counsellor, 1985; Press Sec. to the Queen, 1987–90. *Address:* c/o Buckingham Palace, SW1 1AA.

JANZON, Mrs Bengt; *see* Dobbs, Mattiwilda.

JAPAN, Emperor of; *see* Akihito.

JAQUES, Prof. Elliott; Visiting Research Professor in Management Sciences, George Washington University, since 1989; *b* 18 Jan. 1917; one *d*. *Educ:* Univ. of Toronto (BA, MA); Johns Hopkins Med. Sch. (MD); Harvard Univ. (PhD). Qual. Psycho-analyst (Brit. Psycho-An. Soc.) 1951. Rantoul Fellow in Psychology, Harvard, 1940–41; Major, Royal Can. Army Med. Corps, 1941–45; Founder Mem., Tavistock Inst. of Human Relations, 1946–51; private practice as psycho-analyst and industrial consultant, 1952–65; Brunel University: Head of Sch. of Social Sciences, 1965–70; Prof. of Sociology, 1970–82; Dir, Inst. of Orgn and Social Studies, 1970–85, now Prof. Emeritus of Social Sciences. Adviser to BoT on organisation for overseas marketing, 1965–69; Mem. Management Study Steering Cttee on NHS Reorganisation, 1972. *Publications:* The Changing Culture of a Factory, 1951; Measurement of Responsibility, 1956; Equitable Payment, 1961; (with Wilfred Brown) Product Analysis Pricing, 1964; Time-Span Handbook, 1964; (with Wilfred Brown) Glacier Project Papers, 1965; Progression Handbook, 1968; Work, Creativity and Social Justice, 1970; A General Theory of Bureaucracy, 1976; Health Services, 1978; Levels of Abstraction and Logic in Human Action, 1978; The Form of Time, 1982; Free Enterprise, Fair Employment, 1982; Requisite Organisation, 1989; Executive Leadership, 1991; articles in Human Relations, New Society, Internat. Jl of Psycho-Analysis, etc. *Recreations:* art, music, ski-ing. *Address:* The Representative, Suite 902, 1101 South Arlington Ridge Road, Arlington, Va 22202, USA.

JARDINE, Sir Andrew (Colin Douglas), 5th Bt *cr* 1916; with Henderson Administration Group plc, since 1981; *b* 30 Nov. 1955; *s* of Brigadier Sir Ian Liddell Jardine, 4th Bt, OBE, MC, and of Priscilla Daphne, *d* of Douglas Middleton Parnham Scott-Phillips; *S* father, 1982. *Educ:* Charterhouse. Commissioned Royal Green Jackets, 1975–78. Mem., Queen's Body Guard for Scotland, Royal Company of Archers. *Heir:* *b* Michael Ian Christopher Jardine [*b* 4 Oct. 1958; *m* 1982, Maria Milky Pineda; two *s*]. *Address:* 99 Addison Road, W14 8DD. *T:* 071–603 6434. *Club:* Boodle's.
See also Sir J. R. G. Baird, Bt.

JARDINE, Sir (Andrew) Rupert (John) Buchanan-, 4th Bt *cr* 1885; MC 1944; DL; landowner and farmer; *b* 2 Feb. 1923; *s* of Sir John William Buchanan-Jardine, 3rd Bt and Jean Barbara (*d* 1989), *d* of late Lord Ernest Hamilton; *S* father, 1969; *m* 1950, Jane Fiona (marr. diss. 1975), 2nd *d* of Sir Charles Edmonstone, 6th Bt; one *s* one *d*. *Educ:* Harrow; Royal Agricultural College. Joined Royal Horse Guards, 1941; served in France, Holland and Germany; Major 1948; retired, 1949. Joint-Master, Dumfriesshire Foxhounds, 1950. JP Dumfriesshire, 1957; DL Dumfriesshire, 1978. Bronze Lion of the Netherlands, 1945. *Recreations:* country pursuits. *Heir:* *s* John Christopher Rupert Buchanan-Jardine [*b* 20 March 1952; *m* 1975, Pandora Lavinia, *d* of Peter Murray Lee; five *d*]. *Address:* Dixons, Lockerbie, Dumfriesshire DG11 2PR. *T:* Lockerbie (05762) 2508. *Club:* MCC.

JARDINE, James Christopher Macnaughton; Sheriff of Glasgow and Strathkelvin, since 1979; *b* 18 Jan. 1930; *s* of James Jardine; *m* 1955, Vena Gordon Kight; one *d*. *Educ:* Glasgow Academy; Gresham House, Ayrshire; Glasgow Univ. (BL). National Service (Lieut RASC), 1950–52. Admitted as Solicitor, in Scotland, 1953. Practice as principal (from 1955) of Nelson & Mackay, and as partner of McClure, Naismith, Brodie & Co., Solicitors, Glasgow, 1956–69; Sheriff of Stirling, Dunbarton and Clackmannan, later N Strathclyde, at Dumbarton, 1969–79. A Vice-Pres., Sheriffs' Assoc., 1976–79. Sec., Glasgow Univ. Graduates Assoc., 1956–66; Mem., Business Cttee of Glasgow Univ. Gen. Council, 1964–67. Member: Jt Probation Consultative Cttee for Strathclyde Region, 1980–; Professional Advisory Cttee, Scottish Council on Alcoholism, 1982–85. *Recreations:* boating, enjoyment of music and theatre. *Address:* Sheriff's Chambers, Sheriff Court House, 1 Carlton Place, Glasgow G5 9DA.

JARDINE, Ronald Charles C.; *see* Cunningham-Jardine.

JARDINE, Sir Rupert Buchanan-; *see* Jardine, Sir A. R. J. B.

JARDINE OF APPLEGIRTH, Sir Alexander Maule, (Sir Alec), 12th Bt *cr* 1672 (NS); 23rd Chief of the Clan Jardine; *b* 24 Aug. 1947; *s* of Col Sir William Edward Jardine of Applegirth, 11th Bt, OBE, TD, JP, DL, and of Ann Graham, *yr d* of late Lt-Col Claud Archibald Scott Maitland, DSO; *S* father, 1986; *m* 1982, Mary Beatrice, *d* of late Hon. John Michael Inigo Cross and of Mrs James Parker-Jervis; one *s* two *d*. *Educ:* Gordonstoun. Member of Queen's Body Guard for Scotland, Royal Co. of Archers. *Heir:* *s* William Murray Jardine, yr of Applegirth, *b* 4 July 1984. *Address:* Ash House, Thwaites, Millom, Cumbria LA18 5HY.

JARDINE PATERSON, Sir John (Valentine), Kt 1967; *b* 14 Feb. 1920; *y s* of late Robert Jardine Paterson, Balgray, Lockerbie, Dumfriesshire; *m* 1953, Priscilla Mignon, *d* of late Sir Kenneth Nicolson, MC; one *s* three *d*. *Educ:* Eton Coll.; Jesus Coll., Cambridge. Emergency commn, The Black Watch, RHR, 1939. Director: Jardine Henderson Ltd, Calcutta, 1952–67 (Chm. 1963–67); McLeod Russel PLC, 1967–84 (Chm., 1979–83). Chm., Indian Jute Mills Assoc., 1963; Pres., Bengal Chamber of Commerce and Industry and Associated Chambers of Commerce of India, 1966. *Recreations:* golf, shooting. *Address:* Norton Bavant Manor, Warminster, Wilts. *T:* Warminster (0985) 40378. *Clubs:* Oriental; Bengal, Royal Calcutta Turf (Calcutta).

JARMAN, Derek; painter and film maker; *b* 31 Jan. 1942; *s* of Lance Jarman and Elizabeth Evelyn Puttock. *Educ:* King's College, Univ. of London; Slade School. Designed: Jazz Calendar, Royal Ballet, 1968; Don Giovanni, ENO, 1968; The Devils, 1971, and Savage Messiah, 1972, for Ken Russell; Rake's Progress, Maggio Musicale, Florence, 1973; *films:* Sebastiane, 1975; Jubilee, 1977; The Tempest, 1979; Imagining October, 1984; The Angelic Conversation, 1985; Caravaggio, 1986; The Last of England, 1987; (jtly) Aria, 1987; War Requiem, 1989; The Garden, 1991; Edward II, 1991. Directed L'ispirazione, Florence, 1988. Painting exhibns include Edward Totah Gallery, Lisson Gallery, Internat Contemp. Art Fair, Inst. Contemp. Arts, Richard Salmon Gall. *Publications:* Dancing Ledge, 1984; The Last of England, 1987; War Requiem, 1989. *Address:* c/o British Film Institute, 29 Rathbone Place, WC2.

JARMAN, Nicholas Francis Barnaby; QC 1985; barrister; a Recorder of the Crown Court, since 1982; *b* 19 June 1938; *s* of late A. S. Jarman and of Helene Jarman; *m* 1st, 1973, Jennifer Michelle Lawrence-Smith (marr. diss. 1978); one *d*; 2nd, 1989, Julia Elizabeth MacDougall (*née* Owen-John). *Educ:* Harrow; Christ Church, Oxford (MA Jurisprudence). Commnd RA, 1956–58 (JUO Mons, 1957). Called to the Bar, Inner Temple, 1965 (Duke of Edinburgh Scholar). Bar Chm., Bucks, Berks and Oxon Jt Liaison Cttee, 1986–. *Recreations:* France, fly-fishing. *Address:* 13 Blithfield Street, W8 6RH. *T:* 071–937 0982; 4 King's Bench Walk, Temple, EC4Y 7DL. *T:* 071–353 3581.

JARMAN, Roger Whitney; Under Secretary, Housing, Health and Social Services Policy Group, Welsh Office, since 1988; *b* 16 Feb. 1935; *s* of Reginald Cecil Jarman and Marjorie Dix Jarman; *m* 1959, Patricia Dorothy Odwell; one *s*. *Educ:* Cathays High Sch., Cardiff; Univ. of Birmingham (BSocSc Hons; Cert. in Educn). Recruitment and Selection Officer, Vauxhall Motors Ltd, 1960–64; Asst Sec., Univ. of Bristol Appts Bd, 1964–68; Asst Dir of Recruitment, CSD, 1968–72; Welsh Office: Principal, European Div., 1972–74; Asst Sec., Devolution Div., 1974–78; Asst Sec., Perm. Sec.'s Div., 1978–80; Under Secretary: Land Use Planning Gp, 1980–83; Transport, Highways and Planning Gp, 1983–88; Transport, Planning, Water and Environment Gp, 1988. *Recreations:* walking, reading, cooking. *Address:* Welsh Office, Cathays Park, Cardiff CF1 3NQ. *T:* Cardiff (0222) 825257. *Club:* Civil Service.

JARRATT, Sir Alexander Anthony, (Sir Alex), Kt 1979; CB 1968; Chairman, Smiths Industries PLC, since 1985 (Director, since 1984); Joint Deputy Chairman, Prudential Corporation plc, since 1987 (Director, since 1985); Chancellor, University of Birmingham, since 1983; *b* 19 Jan. 1924; *o s* of Alexander and Mary Jarratt; *m* 1946, Mary Philomena Keogh; one *s* two *d*. *Educ:* Royal Liberty Gram. Sch., Essex; University of Birmingham. War Service, Fleet Air Arm, 1942–46. University of Birmingham, BCom, 1946–49. Asst Principal, Min. of Power, 1949, Principal, 1953, and seconded to Treas., 1954–55; Min. of Power: Prin. Priv. Sec. to Minister, 1955–59; Asst Sec., Oil Div., 1959–63; Under-Sec., Gas Div., 1963–64; seconded to Cabinet Office, 1964–65; Secretary to the National Board for Prices and Incomes, 1965–68; Dep. Sec., 1967; Dep. Under Sec. of State, Dept of Employment and Productivity, 1968–70; Dep. Sec., Min. of Agriculture, 1970. Man. Dir, IPC, 1970–73; Chm. and Chief Executive, IPC and IPC Newspapers, 1974; Chm., Reed Internat., 1974–85 (Dir, 1970–85); a Dep. Chm., Midland Bank, 1980–91; Director: ICI, 1975–91; Thyssen-Bornemisza Group, 1972–89; Mem., Ford European Adv. Council, 1983–88. Confederation of British Industry: Mem., Council, 1972–; Mem., President's Cttee, 1983–86; Chairman: Economic Policy Cttee, 1972–74; Employment Policy Cttee, 1983–86; Mem., NEDC, 1976–80. Pres., Advertising Assoc., 1979–83. Mem., Industrial Soc. (Chm., 1975–79); Chm., Henley: The Management Coll., 1977–89; Gov., Ashridge Management Coll. Pres., Periodical Publishers Assoc., 1983–85; Vice-Pres., Inst. of Marketing; Chm., Adv. Bd, Inst. of Occup. Health. FRSA. Hon. DSc Cranfield, 1973; DUniv Brunel, 1979; Hon. LLD Birmingham, 1982. *Recreations:* the countryside, reading. *Address:* c/o Smiths Industries PLC, 765 Finchley Road, Childs Hill, NW11 8DS. *T:* 081–458 3232. *Club:* Savile.

JARRATT, Prof. Peter, CEng; FBCS; FSS; FIMA; Professor of Computing and Director, Computer Centre, University of Birmingham, since 1975; *b* 2 Jan. 1935; *s* of Edward Jarratt and Edna Mary Jarratt; *m* 1972, Jeanette Debeir; one *s* two *d*. *Educ:* Univ. of Manchester (BSc, PhD). Programmer, Nuclear Power Plant Co. Ltd, 1957; Chief Programmer, Nuclear Power Gp, 1960; Lectr in Mathematics, Bradford Inst. of Technology, 1962; Asst Dir, Computing Lab., Univ. of Bradford, 1966; Dir, Computing Lab., Univ. of Salford, 1972; Dep. Dean, Faculty of Science and Engrg, 1984, first Dean of Faculty of Science, 1985–88, Birmingham Univ. Dir, Birmingham Res. and Develt Ltd, 1986–88; Chm., Birmingham Inst. for Conductive Educn, 1987–. Gov., Royal Nat. Coll. for the Blind, 1986–. *Publications:* numerous res. papers on mathematics and computer sci. *Recreations:* classical music, mountain walking, gardening, chess. *Address:* 42 Reddings Road, Moseley, Birmingham B13 8LN. *T:* 021–449 7160. *Club:* Athenæum.

JARRETT, Sir Clifford (George), KBE 1956 (CBE 1945); CB 1949; Chairman: Tobacco Research Council, 1971–78; Dover Harbour Board, 1971–80; *b* 1909; *s* of George Henry Jarrett; *m* 1st, 1933, Hilda Alice Goodchild (*d* 1975); one *s* two *d*; 2nd, 1978, Mary, *d* of C. S. Beacock. *Educ:* Dover County Sch.; Sidney Sussex Coll., Cambridge. BA 1931. Entered Civil Service, 1932; Asst Principal, Home Office, 1932–34, Admiralty, 1934–38; Private Sec. to Parl. Sec., 1936–38; Principal Private Sec. to First Lord, 1940–44; Principal Establishments Officer, 1946–50; a Dep. Sec., Admiralty, 1950–61; Permanent Sec., Admiralty, 1961–64; Permanent Under-Sec., Min. of Pensions and Nat. Insurance, later Min. of Social Security, later Dept of Health and Social Security, 1964–70. A Trustee, Nat. Maritime Museum, 1969–81. *Address:* The Coach House, Derry Hill, Menston, Ilkley, W Yorks. *Club:* United Oxford & Cambridge University.

JARRETT, Prof. William Fleming Hoggan, FRS 1980; FRSE 1965; Professor of Veterinary Pathology, University of Glasgow, since 1968; *b* 2 Jan. 1928; *s* of James and Jessie Jarrett; *m* 1952, Anna Fraser Sharp; two *d*. *Educ:* Lenzie Academy; Glasgow Veterinary Coll.; Univ. of Glasgow; PhD, FRCVS, FRCPath. Gold Medal, 1949; John Henry Steele Meml Medal, 1961; Steele Bodger Meml Schol. 1955. ARC Research Student, 1949–52; Lectr, Dept of Veterinary Pathology, Univ. of Glasgow Vet. Sch., 1952–53; Head of Hospital Path. Dept of Vet. Hosp., Univ. of Glasgow, 1953–61; Reader in Pathology, Univ. of Glasgow, 1962–65; seconded to Univ. of E Africa, 1963–64; Titular Prof. of Experimental Vet. Medicine, Univ. of Glasgow, 1965. Lectures: Leeuwenhoek, Royal Soc., 1986; McFadyean Meml, RVC, 1986. Fogarty Scholar, NIH, 1985. Hon. Doctorate Liège Univ., 1986. Centennial Award, Univ. of Pennsylvania, 1984; Makdougall Brisbane Prize, RSE, 1984; J.T. Edwards Meml Medal, RCVS, 1984; Feldberg Prize, 1987; Tenovus–Scotland Margaret McLellan Award, 1989; Saltire Award, 1989. *Publications:* various, on tumour viruses, Leukaemia and immunology. *Recreations:* sailing, skiing, mountaineering, music. *Address:* 60 Netherblane, Blanefield, Glasgow G63 9JP. *T:* Blanefield (0360) 70332. *Clubs:* Commonwealth Trust; Clyde Cruising; Glencoe Ski, Scottish Ski.

JARRING, Gunnar, PhD; Grand Cross, Order of the North Star, Sweden; Swedish Ambassador and Special Representative of the Secretary-General of the United Nations on the Middle East question, 1967–91; *b* S Sweden, 12 Oct. 1907; *s* of Gottfrid Jönsson and Betty Svensson; *m* 1932, Agnes, *d* of Prof. Carl Charlier, Lund; one *d*. *Educ:* Lund; Univ. of Lund (PhD). Family surname changed to Jarring, 1931. Associate Prof. of Turkish Langs, Lund Univ., 1933–40; Attaché, Ankara, 1940–41; Chief, Section B, Teheran, 1941; Chargé d'Affaires *ad interim:* Teheran and Baghdad, 1945; Addis Ababa, 1946–48; Minister: to India, 1948–51, concurrently to Ceylon, 1950–51; to Persia, Iraq and Pakistan, 1951–52; Dir, Polit. Div., Min. of Foreign Affairs, 1953–56; Permanent Rep. to UN, 1956–58; Rep. on Security Council, 1957–58; Ambassador to USA, 1958–64, to USSR, 1964–73, and to Mongolia, 1965–73. *Publications:* Studien zu einer osttürkischen Lautlehre, 1933; The Contest of the Fruits - An Eastern Turki Allegory, 1936; The Uzbek Dialect of Quilich, Russian Turkestan, 1937; Uzbek Texts from Afghan Turkestan, 1938; The Distribution of Turk Tribes in Afghanistan, 1939; Materials to the Knowledge of Eastern Turki (vols 1–4), 1947–51; An Eastern Turki-English Dialect

Dictionary, 1964; Literary Texts from Kashghar, 1980; Return to Kashghar, 1986. *Address:* Pontus Ols väg 7, 260 40 Viken, Sweden.

JARROLD, Kenneth Wesley; Regional General Manager, Wessex Regional Health Authority, since 1990; *b* 19 May 1948; *s* of William Stanley Jarrold and Martha Hamilton Jarrold (*née* Cowan); *m* 1973, Patricia Hadaway; two *s.* *Educ:* St Lawrence Coll., Ramsgate; Sidney Sussex Coll., Cambridge (Whittaker Schol.; BA Hons Hist. 1st cl.; Pres., Cambridge Union Soc.) Dip. IHSM (Hons Standard). E Anglian RHB, 1969–70; Briggs Cttee on Nursing, 1970–71; Dep. Supt, Royal Hosp., Sheffield, 1971–74; Hosp. Sec., Derbyshire Royal Infirmary, 1974–75; Sector Administrator, Nottingham Gen. and Univ. Hosps, 1975–79; Asst Dist Administrator (Planning), S Tees HA, 1979–82; Dist Administrator, 1982–84, Dist Gen. Manager, 1984–89, Gloucester HA. Mem., NHS Training Authy and Chm., Training Cttee, 1984–87; Chm., MESOL Project Group, 1986–89. Pres., IHSM, 1985–86 (Mem., Nat. Council, 1977–89. *Publications:* articles in professional jls. *Recreations:* being with family, fitness training. *Address:* 3 Randall Road, Chandler's Ford, Eastleigh, Hants SO5 1AJ.

JARROLD, Nicholas Robert; HM Diplomatic Service; Counsellor and Deputy Head of Mission, Havana, since 1989; *b* 2 March 1946; *s* of late A. R. Jarrold and D. V. Jarrold (*née* Roberts); *m* 1972, Anne Catherine Whitworth; two *s.* *Educ:* Shrewsbury Sch.; Western Reserve Acad., Ohio; St Edmund Hall, Oxford (Exhibnr, MA). Joined Diplomatic Service, 1968: FCO, 1968–69; The Hague, 1969–72; Dakar, 1972–75; FCO, 1975–79; Nairobi, 1979–83; FCO, 1983–89. *Address:* c/o Foreign and Commonwealth Office, King Charles Street, SW1A 2AH.

JARROW, Bishop Suffragan of, since 1990; **Rt. Rev. Alan Smithson;** *b* 1 Dec. 1936; *m* 1964, Margaret Jean; two *s* two *d.* *Educ:* Queen's Coll., Oxford (BA 1962; MA 1968); Queen's Coll., Birmingham (DipTh 1964). Deacon 1964, priest 1965; Curate: Christ Church, Skipton, 1964–68; St Mary the Virgin with St Cross and St Peter, Oxford, 1968–72; Chaplain: Queen's Coll., Oxford, 1969–72; Reading Univ., 1972–77; Vicar of Bracknell, 1977–84; Residentiary Canon, Carlisle Cathedral and Dir of Training and Diocesan Training Inst., 1984–90. *Recreations:* water colour painting, travel, camping, fell walking, 'cello playing. *Address:* The Old Vicarage, Hallgarth, Pittington, Durham DH6 1AB. *T:* Durham (091) 3720225.

JÄRVI, Neeme; Music Director, Detroit Symphony Orchestra, since 1990; Chief Conductor, Gothenburg Symphony Orchestra, Sweden, since 1982; *b* Tallinn, Estonia, 7 June 1937; *s* of August and Elss Järvi; *m* 1961, Liilia Järvi; two *s* one *d.* *Educ:* Estonia-Tallinn Conservatory of Music; Leningrad State Conservatory. Chief Conductor: Estonian Radio Symphony Orch., 1963–77 (Conductor, 1960–63); Estonia opera house, Tallinn, 1963–77; toured USA with Leningrad Phil. Orch., 1973 and 1977; Chief Conductor, Estonian State Symph. Orch., 1977–80; since emigration to USA in 1980 has appeared as Guest Conductor with New York Phil. Orch., Philadelphia Orch., Boston Symph., Chicago Symph., Los Angeles Phil., Met. Opera (New York) and in San Francisco, Cincinnati, Indianapolis, Minneapolis and Detroit; has also given concerts in Vienna, London, Canada, Sweden, Finland, Norway, Denmark, Holland, Switzerland and W Germany; Principal Guest Conductor, City of Birmingham Symph. Orch., 1981–84; Musical Dir and Principal Conductor, Scottish Nat. Orch., 1984–88, Conductor Laureate, 1989. 1st Prize, Internat. Conductors Competition, Accademia Santa Cecilia, Rome, 1971. Many recordings; current projects include: complete symphonies of Brahms, Sibelius, Glazunov, Wilhelm Stenhammar, Eduard Tubin, Berwald, Grieg, Richard Strauss, Gade (8 symphonies), Svendsen (2 symphonies); Bruckner's No 8; symphonic music by Dvorak and Prokofiev. *Recreation:* traveller. *Address:* c/o Columbia Artists Management Inc., 165 West 57th Street, New York, NY 10019, USA.

JARVIS, Frederick Frank, (Fred Jarvis); General Secretary, National Union of Teachers, 1975–89; Member of General Council, 1974–89, President, 1987, Trades Union Congress (Chairman, 1986–87); *b* 8 Sept. 1924; *s* of Alfred and Emily Ann Jarvis; *m* 1954, Elizabeth Anne Colegrove, Stanton Harcourt, Oxfordshire; one *s* one *d.* *Educ:* Plaistow Secondary Sch., West Ham; Oldershaw Grammar Sch., Wallasey; Liverpool Univ.; St Catherine's Society, Oxford. Dip. in Social Science with dist. (Liverpool Univ.); BA (Hons) in Politics, Philosophy and Economics (Oxon), MA (Oxon). Contested (Lab) Wallasey, Gen. Elec., 1951; Chm., Nat. Assoc. of Labour Student Organisations, 1951; Pres., Nat. Union of Students, 1952–54 (Dep. Pres., 1951–52); Asst Sec., Nat. Union of Teachers, 1955–59; Head of Publicity and Public Relations, 1959–70; Dep. Gen. Sec., NUT, 1970–74 (apptd Gen. Sec. Designate, March 1974). Pres., Eur. Trade Union Cttee for Educn, 1983–84, 1985–86 (Vice-Pres., 1981–83); Chairman, TUC Cttees: Local Govt, 1983–88; Educn Training, 1985–88; Chm., TUC Nuclear Energy Review Body, 1986–88; Mem., Central Arbitration Cttee. Mem., Franco-British Council, 1986–. Mem. Council, Nat. Youth Theatre. FRSA. Hon. FEIS 1980; Hon. FCP 1982. *Publications:* The Educational Implications of UK Membership of the EEC, 1972. Ed, various jls incl.: 'Youth Review', NUT Guide to Careers; NUT Univ. and Coll. Entrance Guide. *Recreations:* swimming, golf, tennis, gardening, cinema, theatre, photography. *Address:* 92 Hadley Road, New Barnet, Herts EN5 5QR. *Club:* Ronnie Scott's.

JARVIS, Hugh John, FIA; Group Chief Actuary, Prudential Corporation, 1989–91; *b* 4 July 1930; *s* of John James and Muriel Jarvis; *m* 1959, Margita; two *s* one *d.* *Educ:* Southend High School. Mercantile & General Reinsurance Co., various positions, finally Dep. General Manager, 1947–88. *Recreation:* organising and umpiring hockey. *Address:* 15 Daines Way, Thorpe Bay, Essex SS1 3PF. *T:* Southend-on-Sea (0702) 587065.

JARVIS, John Manners; QC 1989; *b* 20 Nov. 1947; *s* of Donald Edward Manners Jarvis and late Theodora Brixie Jarvis; *m* 1972, Janet Rona Kitson; two *s.* *Educ:* King's Coll. Sch., Wimbledon; Emmanuel Coll., Cambridge (MA (Law)). Called to Bar, Lincoln's Inn, 1970. Practising barrister specialising in Commercial Law, particularly banking. An Asst Recorder, 1987–. Overseas Editor, Jl of Banking and Finance—Law and Practice. Gov., King's Coll. Sch., Wimbledon, 1987–. *Recreations:* tennis, sailing, ski-ing, cycling, music. *Address:* 7 Lancaster Gardens, Wimbledon, SW19 5DG. *T:* 081–946 6603; 3 Gray's Inn Place, Gray's Inn, WC1R 5EA. *T:* 071–831 8441. *Club:* Hurlingham.

JARVIS, Martin; actor; *b* 4 Aug. 1941; *s* of Denys Jarvis and Margot Jarvis; *m*; two *s*; *m* 1974, Rosalind Ayres. *Educ:* Whitgift School; RADA (Hons Dip., 1962, Silver Medal, 1962, Vanbrugh Award, 1962; RADA Associate, 1980). Nat. Youth Theatre, 1960–62; played Henry V, Sadler's Wells, 1962; Manchester Library Theatre, 1962–63; *stage:* Cockade, Arts, 1963; Poor Bitos, Duke of York's, 1963; Man and Superman, Vaudeville, 1966; The Bandwagon, Mermaid, 1970; The Rivals, USA, 1973; Hamlet (title rôle), Fest. of British Th., 1973; The Circle, Haymarket, 1976; She Stoops to Conquer, Canada, and Hong Kong Arts Festival, 1977; Caught in the Act, Garrick, 1981; Importance of Being Earnest, NT, 1982; Victoria Station, NT, 1983; The Trojan War Will Not Take Place, NT, 1983; Woman in Mind, Vaudeville, 1986; The Perfect Party, Greenwich, 1987; Henceforward, Vaudeville, 1989; Exchange, Vaudeville, 1990; You Say Potato, Los Angeles, 1990; Twelfth Night, Playhouse, 1991; recitals of Paradise Lost, Old Vic, Chichester and QEH, 1975–77; *films:* The Last Escape, Ike, The Bunker, Taste the Blood of Dracula, Buster; *television series:* The Forsyte Saga, 1967; Nicholas Nickleby, 1968; Little Women, 1969; The Moonstone, 1971; The Pallisers, 1974; David Copperfield, 1975; Killers, 1976; Rings on Their Fingers, 1978–80; Breakaway, 1980; The Black Tower, 1985; Chelworth, 1988; Countdown, 1990; The Good Guys, 1991; Woof!, 1991; Murder Most Horrid, 1991; and numerous plays; *radio:* numerous performances, incl. one-man series, Jarvis's Frayn, as Charles Dickens in series, The Best of Times; in Redevelopment, Globe Theatre series, 1989; script writing and adaptations; commentaries for TV and film documentaries and for arts programmes; has adapted and read over 50 of Richmal Crompton's William stories for radio, TV and cassette; recorded one-man performance of David Copperfield for cassette, 1991; several further recordings of books for cassette. Mem., Stars Organisation for Spastics, 1983–. Pres., Croydon Histrionic Soc., 1984–. *Publications:* Bright Boy, 1977; short stories for radio; contribs to many anthologies; articles in The Listener and Punch. *Recreations:* Indian food, Beethoven, Mozart, people-watching. *Address:* c/o Michael Whitehall Ltd, 125 Gloucester Road, SW7. *T:* 071–244 8466. *Club:* BBC.

JARVIS, Patrick William, CB 1985; CEng, FIEE, FIMarE; FRINA; RCNC; Deputy Controller (Warships), Ministry of Defence (Procurement Executive), and Head of Royal Corps of Naval Constructors, 1983–86; *b* 27 Aug. 1926; *s* of Frederick Arthur and Marjorie Winifred Jarvis; *m* 1951, Amy (*née* Ryley); two *s.* *Educ:* Royal Naval Coll., Greenwich; Royal Naval Engrg Coll., Keyham, Devonport. BScEng. Trade apprentice, HM Dockyard, Chatham, 1942–46; Design Engineer, Admiralty, Bath, 1946–62; Warship Electrical Supt, Belfast, 1962–63; Suptg Engr, MoD(N), Bath, 1963–72; Ship Department, MoD (PE), Bath: Asst Dir and Dep. Dir, 1972–78; Under Sec., 1978; Dir of Naval Ship Production, 1979–81; Dir of Ship Design and Engrg, and Dep. Head of Royal Corps of Naval Constructors, 1981–83; Dep. Sec., 1983. *Recreations:* indoor sports, chess. *Address:* Ranworth, Bathampton Lane, Bath BA2 6ST.

JASPER, Robin Leslie Darlow, CMG 1963; HM Diplomatic Service, retired; *b* 22 Feb. 1914; *s* of T. D. Jasper, Beckenham; *m* 1st, 1940, Jean Cochrane (marr. diss.); one *d*; 2nd, 1966, Diana Speed (*née* West), two step *d.* *Educ:* Dulwich; Clare Coll., Cambridge. Apprentice, LNER Hotels Dept, 1936–39; Bursar, Dominion Students Hall Trust (London House), 1939–40; RAFVR (Wing Comdr), 1940–45; Principal, India Office (later Commonwealth Relations Office), 1945; concerned with resettlement of the Sec. of State's Services in India, 1947–48; British Dep. High Commissioner, Lahore, Pakistan, 1949–52; Adviser to London Conferences on Central African Federation, and visited Central Africa in this connection, 1952–53; Counsellor, HM Embassy, Lisbon, 1953–55; visited Portuguese Africa, 1954; Commonwealth Relations Office, 1955–60 (Head of Information Policy Dept, 1958–60); attached to the United Kingdom delegation to the United Nations, 1955 and 1956; British Dep. High Commissioner, Ibadan, Nigeria, 1960–64; Counsellor, Commonwealth Office, 1965–67; Consul-Gen., Naples, 1967–71, retired 1972. Lived in Almuñécar, Granada, Spain, 1971–79. *Recreations:* tennis, Rugby fives, wind music, 17th Century Church Sculpture, claret. *Address:* 1 Stafford Court, 50 Eversfield Place, St Leonard's-on-Sea, East Sussex TN37 6DB. *T:* Hastings (0424) 443196. *Clubs:* MCC, Jesters.

JAUNCEY, family name of **Baron Jauncey of Tullichettle.**

JAUNCEY OF TULLICHETTLE, Baron *cr* 1988 (Life Peer), of Comrie in the District of Perth and Kinross; **Charles Eliot Jauncey;** PC 1988; a Lord of Appeal in Ordinary, since 1988; *b* 8 May 1925; *s* of late Captain John Henry Jauncey, DSO, RN, Tullichettle, Comrie, and Muriel Charlie, *d* of late Adm. Sir Charles Dundas of Dundas, KCMG; *m* 1st, 1948, Jean (marr. diss. 1969), *d* of Adm. Sir Angus Cunninghame Graham of Gartmore, KBE, CB; two *s* one *d*; 2nd, 1973, Elizabeth (marr. diss. 1977), *widow* of Major John Ballingal, MC; 3rd, 1977, Camilla, *d* of late Lt-Col Charles Cathcart of Pitcairlie, DSO; one *d.* *Educ:* Radley; Christ Church, Oxford (Hon. Student, 1990); Glasgow Univ. BA 1947, Oxford; LLB 1949, Glasgow. Served in War, 1943–46, Sub-Lt RNVR. Advocate, Scottish Bar, 1949; Standing Junior Counsel to Admiralty, 1954; QC (Scotland) 1963; Kintyre Pursuivant of Arms, 1955–71; Sheriff Principal of Fife and Kinross, 1971–74; Judge of the Courts of Appeal of Jersey and Guernsey, 1972–79; a Senator of College of Justice, Scotland, 1979–88. Hon. Sheriff-Substitute of Perthshire, 1962. Mem. of Royal Co. of Archers (Queen's Body Guard for Scotland), 1951. Mem., Historic Buildings Council for Scotland, 1971–. *Recreations:* shooting, fishing, bicycling, genealogy. *Address:* Tullichettle, Comrie, Perthshire. *T:* Comrie (0764) 70349; 1 Plowden Buildings, Temple, EC4. *T:* 071–583 4246. *Club:* Royal (Perth).

JAWARA, Alhaji Sir Dawda Kairaba, Kt 1966; Hon. GCMG 1974; Grand Master, Order of the Republic of The Gambia, 1972; President of the Republic of The Gambia, since 1970; Vice-President of the Senegambian Confederation, since 1982; *b* Barajally, MacCarthy Island Div., 16 May 1924. *Educ:* Muslim Primary Sch. and Methodist Boys' Grammar Sch., Bathurst; Achimota Coll. (Vet. School); Glasgow Univ. FRCVS 1988 (MRCVS 1953); Dipl. in Trop. Vet. Med., Edinburgh, 1957. Veterinary Officer for The Gambia Govt, 1954–57, Principal Vet. Officer, 1957–60. Leader of People's Progressive Party (formerly Protectorate People's Party), The Gambia, 1960; MP 1960; Minister of Education, 1960–61; Premier, 1962–63; Prime Minister, 1963–70. Chairman: Permanent Inter State Cttee for Drought in the Sahel, 1977–79; Organisation pour la Mise en Valeur du Fleuve Gambie Conf., Heads of State and Govt, 1987–88; Authy of Heads of State and Govt, Economic Community of W African States, 1988–89. Patron, Commonwealth Vet. Assoc., 1967–. FRCVS 1988. Hon. LLD Ife, 1978; Hon. DSc Colorado State Univ., USA, 1986. Peutinger Gold Medal, Peutinger-Collegium, Munich, 1979; Agricola Medal, FAO, Rome, 1980. Grand Cross: Order of Cedar of Lebanon, 1966; Nat. Order of Republic of Senegal, 1967; Order of Propitious Clouds of China (Taiwan), 1968; Nat. Order of Republic of Guinea, 1973; Grand Officer, Order of Islamic Republic of Mauritania, 1967; Grand Cordon of Most Venerable Order of Knighthood, Pioneers of Republic of Liberia, 1968; Grand Comdr, Nat. Order of Federal Republic of Nigeria, 1970; Comdr of Golden Ark (Netherlands), 1979; Grand Gwanghwa Medal of Order of Diplomatic Service (Republic of Korea), 1984; Nishan-i-Pakistan (Pakistan), 1984. *Recreations:* golf, gardening, sailing. *Address:* State House, Banjul, The Gambia.

JAY, family name of **Baron Jay.**

JAY, Baron *cr* 1987 (Life Peer), of Battersea in Greater London; **Douglas Patrick Thomas Jay,** PC 1951; *b* 23 March 1907; *s* of Edward Aubrey Hastings Jay and Isobel Violet Jay; *m* 1st, 1933, Margaret Christian (marr. diss. 1972), *e d* of late J. C. Maxwell Garnett, CBE, ScD; two *s* two *d*; 2nd, 1972, Mary Lavinia Thomas, *d* of Hugh Lewis Thomas. *Educ:* Winchester Coll.; New Coll., Oxford (Scholar). First Class, Literæ Humaniores. Fellow of All Souls' Coll., Oxford, 1930–37, and 1968–; on the staff of The Times, 1929–33, and The Economist, 1933–37; City Editor of the Daily Herald, 1937–40; Asst Sec., Ministry of Supply, 1940–43; Principal Asst Sec., BoT, 1943–45; Personal Asst to Prime Minister, 1945–46. MP (Lab) Battersea N, July 1946–1974, Wandsworth, Battersea N, 1974–83; Economic Sec. to Treasury, 1947–50; Financial Sec. to Treasury, 1950–51; President, BoT, 1964–67. Chairman: Common Market Safeguards Campaign, 1970–77; London Motorway Action Group, 1968–80. Director: Courtaulds Ltd, 1967–70; Trades Union Unit Trust, 1967–79; Flag Investment Co., 1968–71. *Publications:* The Socialist Case,

1937; Who is to Pay for the War and the Peace, 1941; Socialism in the New Society, 1962; After the Common Market, 1968; Change and Fortune, 1980; Sterling: a plea for moderation, 1985. *Address*: Causeway Cottage, Minster Lovell, Oxon. *T*: Witney (0993) 775235.

See also Hon. Peter Jay.

JAY, Sir Antony (Rupert), Kt 1988; freelance writer and producer, since 1964; Chairman, Video Arts Ltd, 1972–89; *b* 20 April 1930; *s* of Ernest Jay and Catherine Hay; *m* 1957, Rosemary Jill Watkins; two *s* two *d*. *Educ*: St Paul's Sch.; Magdalene Coll., Cambridge (BA (1st cl. Hons) Classics and Comparative Philology, 1952; MA 1955). 2nd Lieut Royal Signals, 1952–54. BBC, 1955–64: Editor, Tonight, 1962–63; Head of Talks Features, TV, 1963–64; (with Jonathan Lynn) writer of BBC TV series, Yes, Minister and Yes, Prime Minister, 1980–88. Mem., Cttee on Future of Broadcasting, 1974–77; Hon. MA Sheffield, 1987; Hon. DBA IMCB, 1988. *Publications*: Management and Machiavelli, 1967, 2nd edn 1987; (with David Frost) To England with Love, 1967; Effective Presentation, 1970; Corporation Man, 1972; The Householder's Guide to Community Defence against Bureaucratic Aggression, 1972; (with Jonathan Lynn): Yes, Minister, Vol. 1 1981, Vol. 2 1982, Vol. 3 1983; The Complete Yes, Minister, 1984; Yes, Prime Minister, Vol. 1 1986, Vol. 2 1987; The Complete Yes, Prime Minister, 1989. *Address*: c/o Video Arts Ltd, 68 Oxford Street, W1N 9LA. *T*: 071–637 7288.

JAY, Prof. Barrie Samuel, MD, FRCS; FCOphth; Professor of Clinical Ophthalmology, University of London, since 1985; Consultant Surgeon, Moorfields Eye Hospital, since 1969; *b* 7 May 1929; *er s* of late Dr M. B. Jay and Julia Sterling; *m* 1954, Marcelle Ruby Byre; two *s*. *Educ*: Perse Sch., Cambridge; Gonville and Caius Coll., Cambridge (MA, MD); University Coll. Hosp., London. FRCS 1962. House Surgeon and Sen. Resident Officer, Moorfields Eye Hosp., 1959–62; Sen. Registrar, Ophthalmic Dept, London Hosp., 1962–65; Inst. of Ophthalmology, Univ. of London: Shepherd Res. Scholar, 1963–64; Mem., Cttee of Management, 1972–77, 1979–; Clinical Sub-Dean, 1973–77; Dean, 1980–85; Ophthalmic Surgeon, The London Hosp., 1965–79. Consultant Advr in Ophthalmol., DHSS, 1982–88. Examiner: Dip. in Ophthal., 1970–75; British Orthoptic Council, 1970–; Ophthalmic Nursing Bd, 1971–87; Mem. Ct of Examrs, RCS, 1975–80. Brit. Rep., Monospecialist Section of Ophthal., Eur. Union of Med. Specialists, 1973–85. Mem. Council: Section of Ophthal., RSM, 1965–77 (Editorial Rep., 1966–77); Faculty of Ophthalmologists, 1970–88 (Asst Hon. Sec., 1976–78; Hon. Sec., 1978–86; Pres., 1986–88); RCS (co-opted Mem. for Ophthalmology), 1983–88; Coll. of Ophthalmologists, 1988– (Vice-Pres., 1988–); Nat. Ophthalmic Treatment Bd Assoc., 1971–75; Internat. Pediatric Ophthal. Soc., 1975–; Ophthal. Soc. UK, 1985–88; Member: Ophthal. Nursing Bd, 1974–88; Orthoptists Bd, Council for Professions Supplementary to Medicine, 1977– (Vice Chm., 1982–88); Specialist Adv. Cttee in Ophthalmology, 1979–88 (Chm., 1982–88); Standing Med. Adv. Cttee, DHSS, 1980–84; Transplant Adv. Panel, DHSS, 1983–88. Trustee: Fight for Sight, 1973–; Wolfson Foundn, 1986–. Fellow, Eugenics Soc.; FRPSL; Hon. Mem., Canadian Ophthalmol Soc. Mem., Ct of Assts, Soc. of Apothecaries; Liveryman, Co. of Barbers. Mem., Bd of Governors, Moorfields Eye Hosp., 1971–90. Mem. Editorial Board: Ophthalmic Literature, 1962– (Asst Editor, 1977–78; Editor, 1978–85); British Jl of Ophthalmology, 1965–90; Jl of Medical Genetics, 1971–76; Metabolic Ophthalmology, 1975–78; Survey of Ophthalmology, 1976–; Ophthalmic Paediatrics and Genetics, 1981–. *Publications*: contrib. on ophthalmology and genetics to med. jls. *Recreations*: postal history, gardening. *Address*: 10 Beltane Drive, SW19 5JR. *T*: 081–947 1771.

JAY, Michael Hastings; HM Diplomatic Service; Assistant Under-Secretary of State for European Community Affairs, Foreign and Commonwealth Office, since 1990; *b* 19 June 1946; *s* of late Alan David Hastings Jay, DSO, DSC, RN and of Vera Frances Effa Vickery; *m* 1975, Sylvia Mylroie. *Educ*: Winchester Coll.; Magdalen Coll., Oxford (MA); School of Oriental and African Studies, London Univ. (MSc 1969). ODM, 1969–73; UK Delegn, IMF-IBRD, Washington, 1973–75; ODM, 1976–78; First Sec., New Delhi, 1978–81; FCO, 1981–85; Counsellor: Cabinet Office, 1985–87; (Financial and Commercial), Paris, 1987–90. *Address*: c/o Foreign and Commonwealth Office, SW1. *T*: 071–270 3000.

JAY, Hon. Peter; writer and broadcaster; Economics and Business Editor, BBC, since 1990; *b* 7 Feb. 1937; *s* of Baron Jay, *qv*; *m* 1st, 1961, Margaret Ann (marr. diss. 1986), *d* of Baron Callaghan of Cardiff, *qv*; one *s* two *d*; one *s*; 2nd, 1986, Emma, *d* of P. K. Thornton, *qv*; two *s*. *Educ*: Winchester Coll.; Christ Church, Oxford. MA 1st cl. hons PPE, 1960. President of the Union, 1960. Nuffield Coll., 1960. Midshipman and Sub-Lt RNVR, 1956–57. Asst Principal 1961–64, Private Sec. to Jt Perm. Sec. 1964, Principal 1964–67, HM Treasury; Economics Editor, The Times, 1967–77, and Associate Editor, Times Business News, 1969–77; Presenter, Weekend World (ITV Sunday morning series), 1972–77; The Jay Interview (ITV series), 1975–76; Ambassador to US, 1977–79; Dir Economist Intelligence Unit, 1979–83. Consultant, Economist Gp, 1979–81; Chm. and Chief Exec., TV-am Ltd, 1980–83 and TV-am News, 1982–83, Pres., TV-am, 1983–; Presenter, A Week in Politics, Channel 4, 1983–86; COS to Robert Maxwell (Chm., Mirror Gp Newspapers Ltd), 1986–89; Supervising Editor, Banking World, 1986– (Editor, 1984–86). Director: BPCC, later Maxwell Communication Corp., 1986–89; Mirror Hldgs, 1986–89; Pergamon Hldgs, 1986–89. Chm., NACRO Working Party on Children and Young Persons in Custody, 1976–77; Chairman: NCVO, 1981–86 (Vice-Pres., 1986–); United Way (UK) Ltd, 1982–83; United Way Feasibility Studies Steering Cttee, 1982–83; United Funds Ltd, 1983–85; United Funds Adv. Cttee, 1983–85; Mem. Council, Cinema and TV Benevolent Fund, 1982–83; Trustee, Charities Aid Foundn, 1981–86; Chm., Charities Effectiveness Review Trust, 1986–87. Vis. Scholar, Brookings Instn, Washington, 1979–80; Wincott Meml Lectr, 1975; Copland Meml Lectr, Australia, 1980; Shell Lectr, Glasgow, 1985. Governor, Ditchley Foundn, 1982–; Mem. Council, St George's House, Windsor, 1982–. Dir, New Nat. Theater, Washington, DC, 1979–81. Political Broadcaster of Year, 1973; Harold Wincott Financial and Economic Journalist of Year, 1973; Royal TV Soc.'s Male Personality of Year (Pye Award), 1974; SFTA Shell Internat. TV Award, 1974. FRSA 1975; FRGS 1977. Hon. DH Ohio State Univ., 1978; Hon. DLitt Wake Forest Univ., 1979; Berkeley Citation, Univ. of Calif, 1979. *Publications*: The Budget, 1972; (contrib.) America and the World 1979, 1980; The Crisis for Western Political Economy and other Essays, 1984; (with Michael Stewart) Apocalypse 2000, 1987; contrib. Foreign Affairs jl. *Recreation*: sailing. *Address*: 39 Castlebar Road, W5 2DJ. *T*: 081–998 3570. *Clubs*: Garrick; Royal Naval Sailing Association, Royal Cork Yacht.

JAYAWARDANA, Brig. Christopher Allan Hector Perera, CMG 1956; CVO 1954; OBE 1944 (MBE 1941); ED 1936; JP; FLS; KStJ; *b* 29 March 1898; 4th *s* of Gate Muhandiram Herat Perera Jayawardana; *m* 1924, Sylvia Dorothy Samarasinhe, *e d* of late Mudaliyar Soloman Dias Samarasinhe; (one *s* one *d* decd). *Educ*: Trinity Coll., Kandy, Ceylon; Keble Coll., Oxford (MA). Sen. Asst Conservator of Forests, Ceylon (retd); Dep. Warden of Wild Life, Ceylon (retd), 1924–29; served War of 1939–45; OC 1st Bn the Ceylon LI, 1938–43; Chief Comr, Ceylon Boy Scouts' Association, 1949–54; Extra Aide de Camp to HE the Governor Gen. of Ceylon, 1949; Equerry to HM the Queen, during Royal Visit to Ceylon, 1954; Hon. ADC to the Queen, 1954. Awarded Silver Wolf, 1949. FLS, 1924. Carnegie Schol., 1931; Smith-Mundt Schol., 1951; KStJ, 1959 (CStJ, 1954).

Diploma of Forestry. *Recreations*: rifle shooting, big game hunting, deep sea fishing, golf, tennis, riding, painting, camping, photography. *Clubs*: Corona; Sea Anglers' (Sri Lanka).

JAYES, Percy Harris, MB, BS, FRCS; Plastic Surgeon: St Bartholomew's Hospital, London, 1952–73; Queen Victoria Hospital, East Grinstead, 1948–73; Consultant in Plastic Surgery to the Royal Air Force, since 1960; Consultant Plastic Surgeon, King Edward VII Hospital for Officers, 1966–85; *b* 26 June 1915; *s* of Thomas Harris Jayes; *m* 1945, Kathleen Mary Harrington (*d* 1963); two *s* one *d*; *m* 1964, Aileen Mary McLaughlin; one *s* one *d*. *Educ*: Merchant Taylors' Sch.; St Bartholomew's Hosp. Resid. Plastic Surg., EMS Plastic Unit, East Grinstead, 1940–48; Surgeon in Charge, UNRRA Plastic Unit, Belgrade, 1946; Mem. Council, Brit. Assoc. Plastic Surgeons, 1954–64 (Pres., Assoc., 1960). *Publications*: contrib. British Journal of Plastic Surgery, Annals of Royal College of Surgeons and other journals. *Recreation*: tennis. *Address*: Barton St Mary, Lewes Road, East Grinstead RH19 3UB. *T*: East Grinstead (0342) 323461.

JAYEWARDENE, Junius Richard; President of Sri Lanka, 1978–88; *b* Colombo, 17 Sept. 1906; *s* of Mr Justice E. W. Jayewardene, KC and A. H. Jayewardene; *m* 1935, Elina B. Rupesinghe; one *s*. *Educ*: Royal Coll., Colombo; Ceylon University Coll.; Ceylon Law Coll. Sworn Advocate of Supreme Court of Ceylon, 1932. Ceylon National Congress, later United National Party, 1938–89: Hon. Sec., 1940–47; Hon. Treasurer, 1946–48, 1957–58; Vice-Pres., 1954–56, 1958–72; Sec., 1972–73; Pres., 1973–88. Member: Colombo Municipal Council, 1940–43; State Council, 1943–47; House of Representatives, 1947–56, 1960–77 (Leader, 1953–56); Minister of: Agriculture and Food, 1953–56; Finance, 1947–52, 1952–53, 1960; Chief Opposition Whip, 1960–65; Minister of State and Parly Sec. to Prime Minister, Minister of Defence and External Affairs, and Chief Govt Whip, 1965–70; Leader of the Opposition, House of Representatives, 1970–72, Nat. State Assembly, 1972–77; Prime Minister, and Minister of Planning and Economic Affairs, 1977; Minister of: Defence, and Plan Implementation, 1977–88; Power and Energy, 1981–88; Higher Education, Janatha Estates Develt and State Plantations. Was a co-author of Colombo Plan, 1950; has been leader of delegations to many UN and Commonwealth conferences; Governor, World Bank and IMF, 1947–52. *Publications*: Some Sermons of Buddha, 1940; Buddhist Essays; In Council, 1946; Buddhism and Marxism, 1950, 3rd edn 1957; Golden Threads, 1986; Selected Speeches. *Address*: 66 Ward Place, Colombo 7, Sri Lanka.

JAYSON, Prof. Malcolm Irving Vivian, MD; FRCP; Professor of Rheumatology and Director, University Centre for the Study of Chronic Rheumatism, University of Manchester, since 1977; *b* 9 Dec. 1937; *s* of Joseph and Sybil Jayson; *m* 1962, Judith Tauber; two *s*. *Educ*: Middlesex Hosp. Med. Sch., Univ. of London (MB, BS 1961); MD Bristol, 1969; MSc Manchester, 1977. FRCP 1976. House Physician, 1961, House Surgeon, 1962, Middlesex Hosp.; House Physician: Central Middlesex Hosp., 1962; Brompton Hosp., 1963; Sen. House Officer, Middlesex Hosp, 1963; Registrar: Westminster Hosp., 1964; Royal Free Hosp., 1965; Lectr, Univ. of Bristol, Royal Nat.. Hosp. for Rheumatic Diseases, Bath, and Bristol Royal Infirmary, 1967; Sen. Lectr, Univ. of Bristol, and Consultant, Royal Nat. Hosp. for Rheumatic Diseases, Bath, and Bristol Royal Infirmary, 1979. Vis. Professor: Univ. of Iowa, 1984; Univ. of Queensland, 1985. Gen. Sec., Internat. Back Pain Soc., 1986–; President: Soc. of Chiropodists, 1984; Arachnoiditis Self-Help Gp, 1989–. *Publications*: (with A. StJ. Dixon) Rheumatism and Arthritis, 1974, 8th edn 1991; The Lumbar Spine and Back Pain, 1976, 4th edn 1992; Back Pain: the facts, 1981, 2nd edn 1987; (with C. Black) Systemic Sclerosis: Scleroderma, 1988; contribs to Lancet, BMJ and other med. jls. *Recreations*: antiques (especially sundials), trout fishing. *Address*: The Gate House, 8 Lancaster Road, Didsbury, Manchester M20 8TY. *T*: 061–445 1729. *Club*: Royal Society of Medicine.

JAYSTON, Michael, (Michael James); actor; *b* 29 Oct. 1935; *s* of Aubrey Vincent James and Edna Myfanwy Llewelyn; *m* 1st, 1965, Lynn Farleigh (marr. diss. 1970); 2nd, 1970, Heather Mary Sneddon (marr. diss. 1977); 3rd, 1978, Elizabeth Ann Smithson; three *s* one *d*. *Educ*: Becket Grammar School, Nottingham; Guildhall Sch. of Music and Drama (FGSM). *Stage*: Salisbury Playhouse, 1962–63 (parts incl. Henry II, in Becket); Bristol Old Vic, 1963–65; RSC, 1965–69 (incl. Ghosts, All's Well That Ends Well, Hamlet, The Homecoming (NY), The Relapse); Equus, NT, 1973, Albery, 1977; Private Lives, Duchess, 1980; The Sound of Music, Apollo, 1981; The Way of the World, Chichester, 1984, Haymarket, 1985; Woman in Mind, Vaudeville, 1987; *films include*: Midsummer Night's Dream, 1968; Cromwell, 1969; Nicholas and Alexandra, 1970; *television includes*: Beethoven, 1969; Mad Jack, 1970; Wilfred Owen, 1971; The Power Game, 1978; Tinker, Tailor, Soldier, Spy, 1979; Dr Who, 1986; A Bit of a Do, 1988, 1989; Haggard, 1990. Life Mem., Battersea Dogs Home. *Recreations*: cricket, darts, chess. *Address*: c/o Michael Whitehall, 125 Gloucester Road, SW7. *Clubs*: MCC, Lord's Taverners', Cricketers'; Gedling Colliery CC (Vice-Pres.); Rottingdean CC.

JEAFFRESON, David Gregory, CBE 1981; Commissioner, Independent Commission Against Corruption, Hong Kong Government, since 1988; *b* 21 Nov. 1931; *s* of Bryan Leslie Jeaffreson, MD, FRCS, MRCOG and Margaret Jeaffreson; *m* 1959, Elisabeth Marie Jausions; two *s* two *d* (and one *d* decd). *Educ*: Bootham Sch., York; Clare Coll., Cambridge (MA). 2nd Lieut, RA, 1950. Dist Officer, Tanganyika, 1955–58; Asst Man., Henricot Steel Foundry, 1959–60; Admin. Officer, Hong Kong Govt, 1961; Dep. Financial Sec., 1972–76; Sec. for Economic Services, 1976–82; Sec. for Security, 1982–88. *Recreations*: history, music, sailing, walking. *Address*: A2 Cherry Court, 12 Consort Rise, Hong Kong. *T*: 8188025. *Club*: Royal Hong Kong Yacht.

JEANES, Leslie Edwin Elloway, CBE 1982; Chief of Public Relations, Ministry of Defence, 1978–81, retired; *b* 17 Dec. 1920; *er s* of late Edwin Eli Jubilee Jeanes and of Mary Eunice Jeanes; *m* 1942, Valerie Ruth, *d* of Ernest and Ethel Vidler; one *d*. *Educ*: Westcliff High Sch. Entered Civil Service, 1939; Inf. Officer, DSIR, 1948–65; Chief Press Officer, Min. of Technol., 1965–68; Dep. Head of Inf., MoT, 1968–70; Head of News, DoE, 1970–73; Chief Inf. Officer, MAFF, 1973–78. *Recreations*: bowls, gardening, motoring, DIY. *Address*: 14 Whistley Close, Bracknell, Berks RG12 3LQ. *T*: Bracknell (0344) 429429. *Club*: Hurst Bowling (Chm., 1987).

See also R. E. Jeanes.

JEANES, Ronald Eric; Deputy Director, Building Research Establishment, 1981–86; *b* 23 Sept. 1926; *s* of Edwin and Eunice Jeanes; *m* 1951, Helen Field (*née* Entwistle); one *s* one *d*. *Educ*: University Coll., Exeter (BSc 1951). Served HM Forces, 1945–48. Royal Naval Scientific Service, 1951–62; BRE, 1962–86. *Publications*: DoE and BRE reports. *Recreation*: amateur theatre. *Address*: 1 Wrensfield, Hemel Hempstead, Herts HP1 1RN. *T*: Hemel Hempstead (0442) 58713.

See also L. E. E. Jeanes.

JEAPES, Maj.-Gen. Anthony Showan, CB 1987; OBE 1977; MC 1960; retired; independent inquiry inspector, 1991; *b* 6 March 1935; *s* of Stanley Arthur Jeapes; *m* 1959, Jennifer Clare White; one *s* one *d*. *Educ*: Raynes Park Grammar Sch.; RMA Sandhurst. Commissioned Dorset, later Devonshire and Dorset, Regt, 1955; joined 22 SAS Regt, 1958; attached US Special Forces, 1961; Staff College, 1966; Brigade Major, 39 Inf. Bde, NI, 1967; Sqn Comdr, 22 SAS Regt, 1968; Nat. Defence Coll., 1971; Directing Staff,

Staff Coll., Camberley, 1972; CO 22 SAS Regt, 1974; Mem., British Mil. Adv. Team, Bangladesh, 1977; Dep. Comdr, Sch. of Infantry, 1979; Comdr, 5 Airborne Brigade, 1982; Comdr, Land Forces NI, 1985–87; GOC, SW Dist, 1987–90. Council, Romanian Orphanage Trust, 1991. *Publication:* SAS Operation, Oman, 1980. *Recreations:* offshore sailing, deer management, country pursuits. *Address:* c/o National Westminster Bank, Warminster, Wilts. *Club:* Army and Navy.

JEBB, family name of **Baron Gladwyn.**

JEBB, Dom (Anthony) Philip, MA; Prior, Downside Abbey, since 1991; *b* 14 Aug. 1932; 2nd *s* of late Reginald Jebb and Eleanor, *d* of Hilaire Belloc. *Educ:* Downside; Christ's Coll., Cambridge, 1957–60 (MA Classics). Professed at Downside, 1951; priest, 1956; Curate, Midsomer Norton, 1960–62; teaching at Downside, 1960–91; House master, 1962–75; Dep. Head Master, 1975–80; Headmaster, 1980–91. Archivist and Annalist, English Benedictine Congregation, 1972–; Mem., EBC Theological Commn, 1969–82 (Chm., 1979–82); Delegate to General Chapter, EBC, 1981–; Mem., Central Cttee, 1987–88, Chm., SW Div., 1988, HMC; Member: Council, Somerset Records Soc., 1975–; Cttee, Area 7, SHA, 1984–91; Court, Bath Univ., 1983–85. Trustee, Somerset Archaeol and Natural Hist. Soc., 1989–. Vice-Pres., SW Amateur Fencing Assoc., 1970–. Chaplain of Magistral Obedience, British Assoc., Sovereign Mil. Order of Malta, 1978–. *Publications:* Missale de Lesnes, 1964; Religious Education, 1968; Widowed, 1973, 2nd edn 1976; contrib. Consider Your Call, 1978, 2nd edn 1979; A Touch of God, 1982; (ed) By Death Parted, 1986; contribs to Downside Review, The Way, The Sword. *Recreations:* fencing, archaeology, astronomy, canoeing. *Address:* Downside Abbey, Stratton-on-the-Fosse, Bath BA3 4RJ. *T:* Stratton-on-the-Fosse (0761) 232295.

JEDDERE-FISHER, Arthur; Solicitor, Customs and Excise, 1982–85; *b* 15 July 1924; *s* of late Major Harry and Sarah Jeddere-Fisher; *m* 1947, Marcia Vincent, *d* of Kenneth Clarence Smith; three *s* one *d. Educ:* Harrow Sch.; Christ Church, Oxford (MA). Served War of 1939–45, Air Engineer, Royal Navy, 1942–46 (despatches). Called to Bar, Inner Temple, 1949; Magistrate, Senior Magistrate and Chairman Land Tribunal, Fiji, 1953–69; joined Solicitor's Office, HM Customs and Excise, 1970, Principal Asst Solicitor, 1977–82. *Recreations:* the collection and use of historic machinery, cricket, bird photography. *Address:* Apsley Cottage, Kingston Blount, Oxford OX9 4SJ. *T:* Kingston Blount (0844) 51300. *Clubs:* MCC, Vintage Sports Car.

JEELOF, Gerrit, CBE (Hon.) 1981; Member, Board of Directors, Philips Electronics NV, since 1990; *b* 13 May 1927; *m* 1951, Jantje Aleida Plinsinga; two *d. Educ:* Dutch Trng Inst. for Foreign Trade, Nijenrode. Philips Industries: Eindhoven, Holland, 1950–53; Spain and S America, 1953–65; Eindhoven, Holland, 1965–70; Varese, Italy, 1970–76; Chm. and Man. Dir, Philips Industries UK, 1976–80. Chm., European Community Chamber of Commerce in USA Inc.; Director: Robeco, Rolinco, Rorento, Rodamco, Netherlands; VNU Publishing, Netherlands; Central Beheer Insce, Netherlands; Cabot Corp., Boston. Chm., Bd of Trustees, Nijenrode Univ., Netherlands. Commendatore del Ordine al Merito della Repubblica Italiana, 1974; Officer, Order of Oranje-Nassau (Netherlands), 1985. *Recreations:* sailing, golf. *Address:* Apt 3F, Long Island Apts, Le Zoute, Zwinlaan 11, B-8300 Knokke-Heist, Belgium. *T:* 50 61 00 85. *Clubs:* Royal Ocean Racing; Royal Yacht Squadron; Koninklijke Nederlandsche Zeil-en Roeivereeniging (Holland).

JEEPS, Richard Eric Gautrey, CBE 1977; Chairman, Sports Council, 1978–85; *b* 25 Nov. 1931; *s* of Francis Herbert and Mildred Mary Jeeps; *m* 1954, Jean Margaret Levitt (marr. diss.); three *d. Educ:* Bedford Modern Sch. Rugby career: Cambridge City, 1948–49; Northampton, 1949–62 and 1964; Eastern Counties, 1950–62; England, 1956–62 (24 caps); Barbarians, 1958–62; British Lions: SA, 1955; NZ, 1959; SA 1962; 13 Tests. Rugby Football Union: Mem. Cttee, 1962–; Pres., 1976–77. Mem., English Tourist Bd, 1984–. Trustee, Sports Aid Trust. *Recreations:* Rugby Union football, sport. *Address:* Stocks Restaurant, 78 High Street, Bottisham, Cambridge. *Club:* Lord's Taverners.

JEEVES, Prof. Malcolm Alexander, FBPsS; FRSE; Professor of Psychology, University of St Andrews, since 1969; *b* 16 Nov. 1926; *s* of Alderman Alexander Frederic Thomas Jeeves and Helena May Jeeves (*née* Hammond); *m* 1955, Ruth Elisabeth Hartridge; two *d. Educ:* Stamford Sch.; St John's Coll., Cambridge (MA, PhD). Commissioned Royal Lincs Regt, served 1st Bn Sherwood Foresters, BAOR, 1945–48. Cambridge University: Exhibnr, St John's Coll., 1948, Res. Exhibnr, 1952; Burney Student, 1952; Gregg Bury Prizeman, 1954; Kenneth Craik Res. Award, St John's Coll., 1955. Rotary Foundn Fellow, Harvard, 1953; Lectr, Leeds Univ., 1956; Prof. of Psychology, Adelaide Univ., 1959–69, and Dean, Faculty of Arts, 1962–64; Vice-Principal, St Andrews Univ., 1981–85; Dir, MRC Cognitive Neuroscience Res. Gp, St Andrews, 1984–89. Lectures: Abbie Meml, Adelaide Univ., 1981; Cairns Meml, Aust., 1986; New Coll., Univ. of NSW, 1987. Member: SSRC Psych. Cttee, 1972–76; Biol. Cttee, 1980–84, Science Bd, 1985–89, Council, 1985–89, SERC; MRC Neuroscience and Mental Health Bd, 1985–89; Council, 1984–88, Exec., 1985–87, Vice-Pres., 1990–, RSE; Pres., Section J, BAAS, 1988. Hon. Sheriff, Fife, 1986–. Editor-in-Chief, Neuropsychologia, 1990–. *Publications:* (with Z. P. Dienes) Thinking in Structures, 1965 (trans. French, German, Spanish, Italian, Japanese); (with Z. P. Dienes) The Effects of Structural Relations upon Transfer, 1968; The Scientific Enterprise and Christian Faith, 1969; Experimental Psychology: an introduction for Biologists, 1974; Psychology and Christianity: the view both ways, 1976 (trans. Chinese); (with G. B. Greer) Analysis of Structural Learning, 1983; (with R. J. Berry and D. Atkinson) Free to be Different, 1984; Behavioural Sciences: a Christian perspective, 1984; (with D. G. Myers) Psychology—through the eyes of faith, 1987; papers in sci. jls, mainly on neuropsychology and cognition. *Recreations:* music, fly fishing, walking. *Address:* Psychology Laboratory, The University, St Andrews KY16 9JU. *T:* St Andrews (0334) 76161.

See also E. R. Dobbs.

JEEWOOLALL, Sir Ramesh, Kt 1979; *b* 20 Dec. 1940; *s* of Shivprasad Jeewoolall; *m* 1971, Usweenee (*née* Reetoo); two *s. Educ:* in Mauritius; Inns of Court Sch. of Law. Called to the Bar, Middle Temple, 1968; practising at the Bar, 1969–71; Magistrate, 1971–72; practising at the Bar and Chm., Mauritius Tea Develt Authority, 1972–76. Mem., Mauritius Parlt, 1976–82; Dep. Speaker, 1977–79; Speaker, 1979–82. *Recreations:* reading, conversation, chess. *Address:* Q1, Farquhar Avenue, Quatre Bornes, Mauritius. *T:* 4–5918.

JEFFARES, Prof. Alexander Norman, (Derry Jeffares), Hon. AM 1988; MA, PhD, DPhil; Docteur de l'Université (*hc*) Lille, 1977; Hon. DLitt Ulster, 1990; FRSA 1963; FRSL 1965; FRSE 1981; Professor of English Studies, Stirling University, 1974–86, Hon. Professor, since 1986; Managing Director, Academic Advisory Services Ltd, since 1975; Director, Colin Smythe Ltd, since 1978; *b* 11 Aug. 1920; *s* of late C. Norman Jeffares, Dublin; *m* 1947, Jeanne Agnès, *d* of late E. Calembert, Brussels; one *d. Educ:* The High Sch., Dublin; Trinity Coll., Dublin (Hon. Fellow, 1978); Oriel Coll., Oxford. Lectr in Classics, Univ. of Dublin, 1943–44; Lector in English, Univ. of Groningen, 1946–48; Lectr in English, Univ. of Edinburgh, 1949–51; Jury Prof. of English Language and Literature, Univ. of Adelaide, 1951–56; Prof. of English Lit., Leeds Univ., 1957–74. Sec., Australian Humanities Res. Council, 1954–57; Corresp. Mem. for Great Britain and Ireland, 1958–70; Hon. Fellow, Aust. Acad. of the Humanities, 1970–. Mem. Council, RSE, 1985– (a Vice-Pres., 1988–89); Scottish Arts Council: Mem., 1979–84; Vice-Chm., 1980–84; Chm., Literature Cttee, 1979–83; Chm., Touring Cttee, 1983–84; Chm., Housing the Arts, 1980–84; Mem., Arts Council of GB, 1980–84. Chm., Book Trust Scotland (formerly NBL (Scotland)), 1984–89; Mem. Exec. Cttee, NBL, 1984–86; Mem. Bd, Book Trust, 1987–88. Pres., Internat. PEN Scottish Centre, 1986–89. Vice-Pres., Film and Television Council of S Aust., 1951–56; Chairman: Assoc. for Commonwealth Literature and Language Studies, 1966–68, Hon. Fellow, 1971; Internat. Assoc. for Study of Anglo-Irish Literature, 1968–70, Co-Chm., 1971–73, Hon. Life Pres., 1973–; Dir, Yeats Internat. Summer Sch., Sligo, 1969–71. Editor, A Review of English Literature, 1960–67; General Editor: Writers and Critics, 1960–73; New Oxford English Series, 1963–; Macmillan History of Literature, 1983–; (with Michael Alexander) Macmillan Anthologies of English Literature, 1989; York Classics, 1988–; York Insights, 1989–; Joint Editor, Biography and Criticism, 1963–73; Literary Editor, Fountainwell Drama Texts, 1968–75; Co-Editor, York Notes, 1980–; Editor: Ariel, A Review of Internat. English Literature, 1970–72; York Handbooks, 1984–. *Publications:* Trinity College, Dublin: drawings and descriptions, 1944; W. B. Yeats: man and poet, 1949, rev. edn 1962; Seven Centuries of Poetry, 1955, rev. edn 1960; (with M. Bryn Davies) The Scientific Background, 1958; The Poetry of W. B. Yeats, 1961; (ed with G. F. Cross) In Excited Reverie: centenary tribute to W. B. Yeats, 1965; Fair Liberty was All His Cry: a tercentenary tribute to Jonathan Swift 1667–1743, 1967; A Commentary on the Collected Poems of W. B. Yeats, 1968; (ed) Restoration Comedy, 4 vols, 1974; (with A. S. Knowland) A Commentary on the Collected Plays of W. B. Yeats, 1975; (ed) Yeats: the critical heritage, 1977; A History of Anglo-Irish Literature, 1982; A New Commentary on the Poems of W. B. Yeats, 1984; Brought up in Dublin (poems), 1987; Brought up to Leave (poems), 1987; (ed with Antony Kamm) An Irish Childhood, 1987; (ed with Antony Kamm) A Jewish Childhood, 1988; W. B. Yeats: a new biography, 1988; also: edns of works by Congreve, Farquhar, Goldsmith, Sheridan, Cowper, Maria Edgeworth, Disraeli, Whitman and Yeats; edns of criticisms of Swift, Scott and Yeats; various monographs on Swift, Goldsmith, George Moore, Yeats, Oliver St John Gogarty; contribs to learned jls. *Recreations:* drawing, motoring. *Address:* Craighead Cottage, Fife Ness, Crail, Fife. *Clubs:* Athenæum, Commonwealth Trust.

JEFFCOATE, Sir (Thomas) Norman (Arthur), Kt 1970; Professor of Obstetrics and Gynæcology, University of Liverpool, 1945–72, now Emeritus; Hon. Consultant Obstetrical and Gynæcological Surgeon, Liverpool Area Health Authority (Teaching); *b* 25 March 1907; *s* of Arthur Jeffcoate and Mary Ann Oakey; *m* 1937, Josephine Lindsay (*d* 1981); four *s. Educ:* King Edward VI Sch., Nuneaton; University of Liverpool. MB, ChB (Liverpool) 1st class Hons 1929; MD (Liverpool) 1932; FRCS (Edinburgh) 1932; MRCOG 1932; FRCOG 1939 (Vice-Pres., 1967–69; Pres. 1969–72). Hon. Asst Surgeon: Liverpool Maternity Hosp., 1932–45; Women's Hosp., Liverpool, 1935–45. Lectures: Blair-Bell Memorial, Royal College of Obst. and Gynaec. 1938; Sir Arcot Mudalier, Univ. of Madras, 1955; Margaret Orford, S African Coll. of Physicians, Surgeons and Gynaecologists, 1969; J. Y. Simpson, RCSE, 1976. Joseph Price Orator, Amer. Assoc. of Obstetricians and Gynaecologists, 1966. Sims Black Travelling Commonwealth Prof., 1958; Visiting Professor: New York State Univ., 1955; University of Qld, 1964; Univ. of Melbourne, 1964; Univ. of Texas, 1965; Hon. Visiting Obstetrician and Gynæcologist, Royal Prince Alfred Hospital, Sydney, Australia, 1955–. Chairman, Med. Advisory Council of Liverpool Regional Hosp. Bd, 1962–69; President: N of England Obst. and Gynaec. Soc., 1960; Sect. of Obst. and Gynaec., RSM, 1965–66; Liverpool Med. Inst., 1966–67; Vice-Pres. Family Planning Assoc., 1962–79; Member: Gen. Med. Council, 1951–61; Clinical Research Bd, MRC, 1961–65; Clinical Trials Sub-Cttee of Safety of Drugs Cttee, 1963–69; Bd of Science and Educn, BMA, 1968–69; Standing Maternity and Midwifery Adv. Cttee, Dept of Health and Social Security (formerly Min. of Health), 1963–72 (Chm., 1970–72); Standing Med. Adv. Cttee and Central Health Services Council, Dept of Health and Social Security, 1969–72; Jt Sub-Cttee on Prevention of Haemolytic Disease of the Newborn, 1968–72 (Chm., 1969–72). Hon. FCOG(SA), 1972; Hon. FACOG, 1972; Hon. FRCS (C), 1973; Hon. Member: Amer. Gynec. Club; Amer. Gynec. Soc.; Amer. Assoc. Obst. and Gynec.; Central Assoc. Obst. and Gynec.; Assoc. Surg., Ceylon; Obst. and Gynaec. Socs of: Canada, Finland, Honolulu, Malta, Montreal, Panama, S Africa, Uruguay, Venezuela. Hon. LLD, TCD, 1971. Eardley Holland Gold Medal, RCOG, 1975; Simpson Gold Medal, RCSE, 1976. *Publications:* Principles of Gynæcology, 1957, 4th edn, 1975, 5th edn (rev. V. R. Tindall) as Jeffcoate's Principles of Gynaecology, 1986; communications to medical journals. *Address:* 6 Riversdale Road, Liverpool L19 3QW. *T:* 051–427 1448.

JEFFCOTT, Prof. Leo Broof, PhD, DVSc; FRCVS; Professor of Clinical Veterinary Medicine, University of Cambridge, since 1991; *b* 19 June 1942; *s* of late Edward Ian Broof Jeffcott and of Pamela Mary (*née* Hull); *m* 1969, Tisza Jacqueline (*née* Hubbard); two *d. Educ:* Univ. of London (BVMS, PhD); Univ. of Melbourne (DVSc). Animal Health Trust, Newmarket: Asst Pathologist, 1967–71; Clinician, 1972–77; Head, Clinical Dept, 1977–81; Professor: of Clinical Radiology, Uppsala, Sweden, 1981–82; of Veterinary Clinical Sciences, Univ. of Melbourne, 1982–91. Lectures: Sir Frederick Hobday Meml, 1977; Peter Hernqvist, Sweden, 1991. Norman Hall Medal for Research, RCVS, 1978; Internat. Prize of Tierklinik Hochmoor, Germany, 1981; Equine Veterinary Jl Open Award, 1982; John Hickman Orthopaedic Prize, 1991. *Publication:* (with R. K. Archer) Comparative Clinical Haematology, 1977. *Recreations:* swimming, photography, equestrian sports. *Address:* Department of Clinical Veterinary Medicine, University of Cambridge, Madingley Road, Cambridge CB3 0ES. *T:* Cambridge (0223) 337733.

JEFFERIES, David George, CBE 1990; FEng 1989; Chairman, National Grid Co., since 1990; *b* 26 Dec. 1933; *s* of Rose and George Jefferies; *m* 1959, Jeanette Ann Hanson. *Educ:* SE Coll. of Technology. CEng, FIEE, CBIM, FInstE. Southern Electricity Board: Area Manager, Portsmouth, 1967–72; Staff Coll., Henley, 1970; Chief Engr, 1972–74; Dir, NW Region, CEGB, 1974–77; Dir Personnel, CEGB, 1977–81; Chm., London Electricity Bd, 1981–86; Mem., 1981–89, Dep. Chm., 1986–89, Electricity Council. Chm., Electricity Pension Trustees, 1986–. Member: Council, IEE, 1984–; Bd of Governors, London Business Sch., 1980–84. Liveryman, Wax Chandlers' Co., 1984–. *Recreations:* golf, gardening. *Address:* Wychenwood, Gorse Hill Lane, Virginia Water, Surrey GU25 4AJ. *T:* (office) 071–620 8323. *Clubs:* Athenæum, Royal Automobile.

JEFFERIES, Roger David; Chief Executive, London Borough of Croydon, since 1990; *b* 13 Oct. 1939; *s* of George Edward Jefferies and Freda Rose Jefferies (*née* Marshall); *m* 1st, 1962, Jennifer Anne Southgate (marr. diss.); one *s* two *d;* 2nd, 1974, Margaret Sealy (marr. diss.); 3rd, 1984, Pamela Mary Elsey (*née* Holden); one *s. Educ:* Whitgift School; Balliol College, Oxford. BA, BCL; solicitor. Mem., Law Society,1965–. Asst Solicitor, Coventry Corporation, 1965–68; Asst Town Clerk, Southend-on-Sea County Borough Council, 1968–70; Director of Operations, London Borough of Hammersmith, 1970–75; Chief Exec., London Borough of Hounslow, 1975–90; Under Secretary, DoE, 1983–85 (on secondment). Member: Regl Planning Bd, Arts Council of GB, 1986–88; Council, RIPA, 1982–88; Bd, Public Finance Foundn, 1987–; Pres., SOLACE, 1990–91. Clerk:

Mortlake Crematorium Bd, 1973–90; W London Waste Authy, 1986–90. Dir, Extemporary Dance Co., 1989–. Trustee, S African Advanced Educn Project, 1989–. *Publication*: Tackling the Town Hall, 1982. *Recreations*: the novel, theatre, travel. *Address*: c/o Taberner House, Park Lane, Croydon CR9 3JY. *T*: 081–686 4433.

JEFFERIES, Sheelagh, CBE 1987; Press Consultant, Women's Royal Voluntary Service, since 1988; *b* 25 Aug. 1926; *d* of late Norman and Vera Jefferies. *Educ*: Harrogate Grammar Sch.; Girton Coll., Cambridge (MA); Smith Coll., Northampton, Mass, USA (MA). FIPR; FCAM. Archivist, RIIA, 1947–50, 1951–52; COI, 1953–60; Office of Chancellor of Duchy of Lancaster, 1960–61; Press Officer, Prime Minister's Office, 1961–67; Principal Inf. Officer, Privy Council Office, 1967–69; Chief Press Officer, Min. of Housing and Local Govt, 1969–71; Head of Parly Liaison Unit and later Head of News, DoE, 1971–74; Chief Inf. Officer, Dept of Prices and Consumer Protection, 1974–77; Central Office of Information: Dir, Overseas Press and Radio, 1977–78; Controller (Home), 1978–83; Dep. Dir Gen., 1983–87; Actg Dir Gen., Jan.–June 1987. *Recreations*: reading, conversation. *Address*: 6 Eversfield Road, Richmond, Surrey TW9 2AP. *T*: 081–940 9229.

JEFFERIES, Stephen; Senior Principal Dancer, Royal Ballet, since 1979 (Principal Dancer, 1973–76 and 1977–79); *b* 24 June 1951; *s* of George and Barbara Jefferies; *m* 1972, Rashna Homji; one *s* one *d*. *Educ*: Turves Green Sch., Birmingham; Royal Ballet Sch. ARAD (Advanced Hons). Joined Sadler's Wells Royal Ballet, 1969; created 10 leading roles whilst with Sadler's Wells; joined National Ballet of Canada as Principal Dancer, 1976; created role of Morris, in Washington Square, 1977; returned to Royal Ballet at Covent Garden, 1977; *major roles include*: Prince in Sleeping Beauty, Swan Lake and Giselle, Prince Rudolf in Mayerling, Petruchio in Taming of the Shrew, Romeo and Mercutio in Romeo and Juliet, Lescaut in Manon; lead, in Song and Dance, 1982; *roles created*: Yukinojo (mime role), in world première of Minoru Miki's opera An Actor's Revenge, 1979; male lead in Bolero, Japan, 1980 (choreographed by Yashiro Okamoto); Antonio in The Duenna, S Africa (chor. by Ashley Killar), 1980; lead, in Dances of Albion (chor. by Glen Tetley), 1980; Esenin in Kenneth Macmillan's ballet, Isadora, Covent Garden, 1981; lead, in L'Invitation au Voyage, Covent Garden, 1982; Consort Lessons, and Sons of Horos, 1986, Still Life at the Penguin Café, and The Trial of Prometheus, 1988 (chor. by David Bintley); title role in Cyrano (chor. by David Bintley), 1991. Choreographed ballets: Bits and Pieces, in Canada, 1977; Mes Souvenirs, in London, 1978; Magic Toyshop, 1987. Dances in Europe, USA, S America and Far East. *Film*: Anna, 1988. *Recreations*: golf, football, sleeping, gardening, swimming and various other sports. *Address*: c/o Royal Ballet, Royal Opera House, Covent Garden, WC2.

JEFFERS, John Norman Richard, FSS, FIS, FIBiol, FICFor; consultant; Visiting Professor: Chemical and Process Engineering Department, University of Newcastle, since 1990; Mathematical Institute, University of Kent, since 1988; *b* 10 Sept. 1926; *s* of late Lt-Col John Harold Jeffers, OBE, and Emily Matilda Alice (*née* Robinson); *m* 1951, Edna May (*née* Parratt); one *d*. *Educ*: Portsmouth Grammar Sch.; Forestry Commission Forester Trng Sch., 1944–46. Forester in Forestry Commn Research Br., 1946–55; joined Min. of Agriculture, 1955, as Asst Statistician, after succeeding in limited competition to Statistician Class; rejoined Forestry Commn as Head of Statistics Section of Forestry Commn Research Br., 1956; Dir, Nature Conservancy's Merlewood Research Station, 1968; Dep. Dir, Inst. of Terrestrial Ecology, NERC, 1973, Dir, 1976–86. Hon. Prof., Commn of Integrated Survey of Natural Resources, Academia Sinica, 1987–. Hon. DSc Lancaster, 1988. *Publications*: Experimental Design and Analysis in Forest Research, 1959; Mathematical Models in Ecology, 1972; Introduction to Systems Analysis: with ecological applications, 1978; Modelling, 1982; Practitioner's Manual on the Modelling of Dynamic Change in Ecosystems, 1988; numerous papers in stat., forestry and ecolog. jls. *Recreations*: military history and wargaming, amateur dramatics. *Address*: Ellerhow, Lindale, Grange-over-Sands, Cumbria LA11 6NA. *T*: Grange-over-Sands (05395) 3731. *Club*: Athenæum.

JEFFERSON, Bryan; *see* Jefferson, J. B.

JEFFERSON, Sir George Rowland, Kt 1981; CBE 1969; BSc Hons (London); FEng, Hon. FIMechE, FIEE, FRAeS; FRSA; CBIM; FCGI; Chairman, City Centre Communications Ltd, since 1988; Director, AMEC plc, since 1988; *b* 26 March 1921; *s* of Harold Jefferson and Eva Elizabeth Ellen; *m* 1943, Irene Watson-Browne; three *s*. *Educ*: Grammar Sch., Dartford, Kent. Engrg Apprentice, Royal Ordnance Factory, Woolwich, 1937–42; commnd RAOC, 1942; transf. REME, 1942; served 1942–45, Anti-Aircraft Comd on heavy anti-aircraft power control systems and later Armament Design Dept, Fort Halstead, on anti-aircraft gun mounting development; subseq. Mem. Min. of Supply staff, Fort Halstead, until 1952; joined Guided Weapons Div., English Electric Co. Ltd, 1952; Chief Research Engr, 1953; Dep. Chief Engr, 1958; Dir, English Electric Aviation Ltd, 1961 (on formation of co.); British Aircraft Corporation: Dir and Chief Exec., BAC (Guided Weapons) Ltd, 1963 (on formation of Corp.), Dep. Man. Dir, 1964, Mem. Board, 1965–77, Man. Dir, 1966–68, Chm. and Man. Dir, 1968–77; a Dir, British Aerospace, and Chm. and Chief Exec., Dynamics Gp, British Aerospace, 1977–80 (Mem., Organizing Cttee, 1976–77); Chm., Stevenage/Bristol and Hatfield/Lostock Divs, Dynamics Gp, 1978–80; Chm., BAC (Anti-Tank), 1968–78; Dep. Chm., Post Office, 1980; Chm., 1981–87, Chief Exec., 1981–86, British Telecommunications plc. Chm., Matthew Hall, 1987–88. Director: British Aerospace (Australia) Ltd, 1968–80; British Scandinavian Aviation AB, 1968–80; Hawker Siddeley Dynamics, 1977–80; Engineering Sciences Data Unit Ltd, 1975–80; Babcock International, 1980–87; Lloyds Bank, 1986–89. Member: NEB, 1979–80; NEDC, 1981–84; NICG, 1980–84; Member Council: SBAC, 1965–80; Electronic Engineering Assoc., 1968–72; RAeS, 1977–79 (Vice-Pres., 1979). Hon. DSc Bristol, 1984; DUniv Essex, 1985. Freeman of the City of London.

JEFFERSON, Joan Ena; Headmistress, St Swithun's School, Winchester, since 1986; *b* 15 Aug. 1946; *d* of William Jefferson and Ruth Ena Leake. *Educ*: Univ. of Newcastle (BA Hons History); Westminster Coll., Oxford (Dip Ed). Asst Mistress, 1968–70, Head of History, 1970–73, Scarborough Girls' High Sch.; Head of Humanities, Graham Sch., Scarborough, 1973–75; Dep. Head, 1975–79, Headmistress, 1979–86, Hunmanby Hall Sch., Filey. *Recreations*: drama, theatre, reading, cooking, photography; Soroptimist. *Address*: St Swithun's School, Winchester, Hants. *T*: Winchester (0962) 861316. *Club*: Commonwealth Trust.

JEFFERSON, (John) Bryan, CB 1989; CBE 1983; PPRIBA; Chairman, Property Services Agency Projects, Department of the Environment, since 1989; *b* 26 April 1928; *s* of John Jefferson and Marjorie Jefferson (*née* Oxley); *m* 1954, Alison Gray (marr. diss. 1965); three *s*. *Educ*: Lady Manners Sch., Bakewell; Sheffield Univ. DipArch 1954. ARIBA 1954. Morrison and Partners, Derby, 1955–57; established practice in Sheffield and London with Gerald F. Sheard, 1957; Sen. Partner, Jefferson Sheard and Partners, 1957–84; Dir-Gen. of Design, PSA, DoE, 1984–89. President: Sheffield Soc. of Architects, 1973–74; Concrete Soc., 1977–78; RIBA, 1979–81; Chm., RIBA Yorks Region, 1974–75. Hon. FRAIC 1980; Hon. ARICS 1987. Hon. DEng Bradford, 1986. *Publications*: broadcasts; articles in lay and professional jls. *Recreations*: music, sailing offshore. *Club*: Royal Western Yacht.

JEFFERSON, Sir Mervyn Stewart D.; *see* Dunnington-Jefferson.

JEFFERSON SMITH, Peter; Deputy Chairman, HM Customs and Excise, since 1988; *b* 14 July 1939; *m* 1964, Anna Willett; two *d*. *Educ*: Trinity College, Cambridge. HM Customs and Excise, 1960; Commissioner, 1980. *Address*: Board of Customs and Excise, New King's Beam House, 22 Upper Ground, SE1 9PJ. *T*: 071–620 1313.

JEFFERY, David John; Chief Executive, River, and Board Member, Port of London Authority, since 1986; *b* 18 Feb. 1936; *s* of late Stanley John Friend Jeffery and Sylvia May (*née* Mashford); *m* 1959, Margaret (*née* Yates); one *s* two *d*. *Educ*: Sutton High Sch., Plymouth; Croydon Coll. of Technology. Nat. Service, RAOC, 1954–56; Admiralty Dir of Stores Dept, 1956–66; RN Staff Coll., 1967; MoD, 1968–70; Treasury Centre for Admin. Studies, 1970–72; Management Science Training Adviser, Malaysian Govt, Kuala Lumpur, 1972–74; Civil Service Dept, 1974–76; MoD, 1976–83; RCDS, 1983; Dep. Dir, Supplies and Transport (Naval), 1984; Dir, Armaments and Management Services, RN Supply and Transport Service 1984–86. Chairman: Port Publishing Ltd, 1986–; Placon Ltd, 1987–; Estuary Services Ltd, 1988–. Dir, British Ports Fedn, 1988–; Trustee Dir, Pilots' Nat. Pension Fund, 1987–; Member: Internat. Assoc. of Ports and Harbours, 1986–; Co. of Watermen and Lightermen of River Thames, 1987. Freeman, City of London, 1987. *Recreations*: theatre, music, travel, children's work with the local church. *Address*: The Old Coach House, Nunney, Frome, Somerset BA11 4LZ; Flat 4, 91 Lansdowne Way, SW8 2PB.

JEFFERY, Very Rev. Robert Martin Colquhoun; Dean of Worcester, since 1987; *b* 30 April 1935; *s* of Norman Clare Jeffery and Gwenyth Isabel Jeffery; *m* 1968, Ruth Margaret Tinling; three *s* one *d*. *Educ*: St Paul's School; King's Coll., London (BD, AKC). Assistant Curate: St Aidan, Grangetown, 1959–61; St Mary, Barnes, 1961–63; Asst Sec., Missionary and Ecumenical Council of Church Assembly, 1964–68; Sec., Dept of Mission and Unity, BCC, 1968–71; Vicar, St Andrew, Headington, Oxford, 1971–78; RD of Cowley, 1973–78; Lichfield Diocesan Missioner, 1978–79; Archdeacon of Salop, 1980–87. Mem., Gen. Synod of C of E, 1982–87 and 1988–, Mem., Standing Cttee, 1990–. *Publications*: (with D. M. Paton) Christian Unity and the Anglican Communion, 1965, 3rd edn 1968; (with T. S. Garret) Unity in Nigeria, 1964; (ed) Lambeth Conference 1968 Preparatory Information; Areas of Ecumenical Experiment, 1968; Ecumenical Experiments: A Handbook, 1971; Case Studies in Unity, 1972; (ed) By What Authority?, 1987. *Recreations*: local history, cooking. *Address*: 10 College Green, Worcester WR1 2LH. *T*: Worcester (0905) 27821.

JEFFORD, Barbara Mary, OBE 1965; Actress; *b* Plymstock, Devon, 26 July 1930; *d* of late Percival Francis Jefford and Elizabeth Mary Ellen (*née* Laity); *m* 1953, Terence Longdon (marr. diss., 1961); *m* 1967, John Arnold Turner. *Educ*: Weirfield Sch., Taunton, Som. Studied for stage, Bristol and Royal Academy of Dramatic Art (Bancroft Gold Medal). *Stratford-on-Avon*: (1950–54) Isabella in Measure for Measure; Anne Bullen in Henry VIII; Hero in Much Ado About Nothing; Lady Percy in Henry IV parts I and II; Desdemona in Othello; Rosalind in As You Like It; Helena in A Midsummer Night's Dream; Katharina in The Taming of the Shrew, 1954–55; Andromache in Tiger at the Gates, London and USA, 1955 and 1956; Volumnia in Coriolanus, 1989 and 1990; *Old Vic Company*: (1956–62) Imogen in Cymbeline; Beatrice in Much Ado About Nothing; Portia in The Merchant of Venice; Julia in Two Gentlemen of Verona; Tamora in Titus Andronicus; Lady Anne in Richard III; Queen Margaret in Henry VI parts I, II and III; Isabella in Measure for Measure; Regan in King Lear; Viola in Twelfth Night; Ophelia in Hamlet; Rosalind in As You Like It; St Joan; Lady Macbeth; Gwendoline in The Importance of Being Earnest; Beatrice Cenci; Lavinia in Mourning Becomes Electra; *for Prospect, at Old Vic*: (1977–79) Gertrude in Hamlet; Cleopatra in All for Love; Cleopatra in Antony and Cleopatra; Nurse in Romeo and Juliet; Anna in The Government Inspector; RSC Nat. Tour, 1980, Mistress Quickly in Henry IV pts 1 and 2; *National Theatre*: Gertrude in Hamlet, Zabina in Tamburlaine the Great, 1976; Mother in Six Characters in Search of an Author, Arina Bazarov in Fathers and Sons, Salathiel in Ting Tang Mine (Clarence Derwent Award, 1988), 1987. *Other London stage appearances include*: Lina in Misalliance, Royal Court and Criterion, 1963; step-daughter in Six Characters in Search of an Author, Mayfair, 1963; Nan in Ride a Cock Horse, Piccadilly, 1965; Patsy Newquist in Little Murders, Aldwych, 1967; Mother Vauzou in Mistress of Novices, Piccadilly, 1973; Filumena, Lyric, 1979; Duchess of York in Richard II, and Queen Margaret in Richard III, Phoenix, 1988–89; Tatyana in Barbarians, Barbican, 1990; *other stage appearances include*: Hedda Gabler, Phèdre, Medea; has toured extensively in UK, Europe, USA, Near East, Far East, Africa, Australia, Russia, Poland and Yugoslavia. *Films*: Ulysses, 1967; A Midsummer Night's Dream, 1967; The Shoes of the Fisherman, 1968; To Love a Vampire, 1970; Hitler: the last ten days, 1973; And the Ship Sails On, 1983; Why the Whales Came, 1988; Reunion, 1988; Where Angels Fear to Tread, 1991. Has appeared in numerous television and radio plays. Silver Jubilee Medal, 1977. *Recreations*: music, swimming, gardening. *Address*: c/o Fraser and Dunlop Ltd, The Chambers, Chelsea Harbour, Lots Road, SW10 0XF.

JEFFREYS, family name of **Baron Jeffreys.**

JEFFREYS, 3rd Baron *cr* 1952, of Burkham; **Christopher Henry Mark Jeffreys;** *b* 22 May 1957; *s* of 2nd Baron Jeffreys and of Sarah Annabelle Mary, *d* of late Major Henry Garnett; *S* father, 1986; *m* 1985, Anne Elisabeth Johnson; one *s* one *d*. *Educ*: Eton. *Recreations*: country sports. *Heir*: *s* Hon. Arthur Mark Henry Jeffreys, *b* 18 Feb. 1989. *Address*: Bottom Farm, Eaton, Grantham, Lincs. *Clubs*: White's, Annabel's.

JEFFREYS, Prof. Alec John, FRS 1986; Wolfson Research Professor of the Royal Society, University of Leicester, since 1991 (Professor of Genetics, since 1987); *b* 9 Jan. 1950; *s* of Sidney Victor Jeffreys and Joan (*née* Knight); *m* 1971, Susan Miles; two *d*. *Educ*: Luton Grammar School; Luton VIth Form College; Merton College, Oxford (Postmaster; Christopher Welch Schol.; BA, MA, DPhil 1975; Hon. Fellow, 1990). EMBO Research Fellow, Univ. of Amsterdam, 1975–77; Leicester University: Lectr, Dept of Genetics, 1977–84; Reader, 1984–87; Lister Inst. Res. Fellow, 1982–91. Member: EMBO, 1983; Human Genome Orgn, 1989. Editor, Jl of Molecular Evolution, 1985. Fellow, Forensic Sci. Soc. of India, 1989. Colworth Medal for Biochemistry, Biochem. Soc., 1985; Davy Medal, Royal Soc., 1987; Linnean Soc. Bicentenary Medal, 1987; Analytika Prize, German Soc. for Clin. Chem., 1988; Press, Radio and TV Award, Midlander of the Year, 1989. UK Patents on genetic fingerprints. *Publications*: research articles on molecular genetics and evolution in Nature, Cell, etc. *Recreations*: walking, swimming, postal history, reading unimproving novels.

JEFFREYS, David Alfred, QC 1981; a Recorder of the Crown Court, since 1979; *b* 1 July 1934; *s* of Coleman and Ruby Jeffreys; *m* 1964, Mary Ann Elizabeth Long; one *s* one *d*. *Educ*: Harrow; Trinity Coll., Cambridge (BA Hons). Served, Royal Signals, 1952–54; City, 1958. Called to the Bar, Gray's Inn, 1958, Bencher, 1989; Junior Prosecuting Counsel to the Crown: Inner London Crown Court, 1974; Central Criminal Court, 1975; Sen. Prosecuting Counsel to the Crown, CCC, 1979–81. Member, Bar Council and Senate of the Inns of Court and Bar, 1977–80. *Address*: (chambers) Queen Elizabeth Building, Temple, EC4Y 9BS.

JEFFREYS, Mrs Judith Diana; Assistant Director (Keeper), the Tate Gallery, 1975–83; *b* 22 Sept. 1927; *d* of Prof. Philip Cloake, FRCP and Letitia Blanche (*née* MacDonald); *m* 1968, William John Jeffreys. *Educ:* Bedales; Courtauld Inst. of Art, Univ. of London (BA Hons History of Art). Tate Gallery: Asst Keeper, 1951–64; Publications Manager, 1960–65; Dep. Keeper, 1964–75. *Recreations:* reading, music, landscape gardening, water-colour painting. *Address:* Oak Ridge House, Sutton Mandeville, Salisbury, Wilts SP3 5LT. *Club:* Authors'.

JEFFRIES, Lionel Charles; actor since 1949, screen writer since 1959, and film director since 1970; *b* 10 June 1926; *s* of Bernard Jeffries and Elsie Jackson; *m* 1951, Eileen Mary Walsh; one *s* two *d. Educ:* Queen Elizabeth's Grammar Sch., Wimborne, Dorset; Royal Academy of Dramatic Art (Dip., Kendal Award, 1947). War of 1939–45: commissioned, Oxf. and Bucks LI, 1945; served in Burma (Burma Star, 1945); Captain, Royal West African Frontier Force. Stage: (West End) *plays:* Carrington VC; The Enchanted; Blood Wedding; Brouhaha; Hello Dolly, Prince of Wales, 1984; See How They Run, Two Into One, Rookery Nook, Shaftesbury, 1985–86; Pygmalion, Broadway, 1987; The Wild Duck, Phoenix, 1990; *films:* Colditz Story; Bhowani Junction; Lust for Life; The Baby and The Battleship; Doctor at Large; Law and Disorder; The Nun's Story; Idle on Parade; Two Way Stretch; The Trials of Oscar Wilde; Fanny; The Notorious Landlady (Hollywood); The Wrong Arm of the Law; The First Men in the Moon; The Truth about Spring; Arrivederci Baby; The Spy with a Cold Nose; Camelot (Hollywood); Chitty, Chitty, Bang Bang; Eyewitness; Baxter (also dir. 1971; Golden Bear Award for Best Film, Europe); The Prisoner of Zenda; Ménage à Trois; Chorus of Disapproval; Danny Champion of the World; Ending Up; First and Last. Wrote and directed: The Railway Children, 1970 (St Christopher Gold Medal, Hollywood, for Best Film); The Amazing Mr Blunden, 1972 (Gold Medal for Best Screen Play, Internat. Sci. Fiction and Fantasy Film Fest., Paris, 1974); Wombling Free, 1977; co-wrote and directed: The Water Babies, 1979; *television:* Cream in my Coffee, 1980; Shillingbury Tales, 1981; Father Charlie; Tom, Dick, and Harriet, 1983; Rich Tea and Sympathy, 1991. *Recreations:* swimming, painting. *Address:* c/o Denis Selinger, ICM, 388/396 Oxford Strteet, W1N 9HE.

JEFFS, Group Captain (George) James (Horatio), CVO 1960 (LVO 1943); OBE 1950; *b* 27 Jan. 1900; *s* of late James Thomas Jeffs, Chilvers Coton, Warwicks; *m* 1921, Phyllis Rosina (*née* Bell); two *s* one *d. Educ:* Kedleston Sch., Derby. Served European War: RNAS, 1916–18; RAF, 1918–19. Air Ministry, 1919–23; Croydon Airport, 1923–34; Heston Airport, 1934–37; Air Ministry, 1937–39. Served War of 1939–45, RAF: Aircrew Mem. of flights of HM King George VI and Sir Winston Churchill; Fighter, Ferry, and Transport Commands, Group Captain. UK Delegate to Civil Aviation Conf., Chicago, 1944; Ministry of Transport and Civil Aviation, 1945. Nat. Air Traffic Control Officers' Licence No 1; Airport Commandant, Prestwick, 1950–57; Airport Commandant, London-Heathrow Airport, 1957–60. Pioneered the opening and early functioning of all the major civil airports in the UK; for many years responsible for safe functioning of air traffic control in UK. Legion of Merit, USA, 1944. Liveryman, GAPAN. *Address:* Pixham Firs Cottage, Pixham Lane, Dorking, Surrey. *T:* Dorking (0306) 884084. *Club:* Naval and Military.

JEFFS, Julian, QC 1975; a Recorder of the Crown Court since 1975; *b* 5 April 1931; *s* of Alfred Wright Jeffs, Wolverhampton, and Janet Honor Irene (*née* Davies); *m* 1966, Deborah, *d* of Peter James Stuart Bevan; three *s. Educ:* Mostyn House Sch.; Wrekin Coll.; Downing Coll., Cambridge (MA; Associate Fellow, 1986). Royal Navy (nat. service), 1949–50. Sherry Shipper's Asst, Spain, 1956. Barrister, Gray's Inn, 1958 (Bencher 1981), Inner Temple, 1971; Midland and Oxford Circuit; Hong Kong Bar; retired from practice, 1991. Chm., Patent Bar Assoc., 1980–89; Member: Senate of Inns of Court and Bar, 1984–85; Bar Council, 1988–89. Gen. Comr of Income Tax, 1983–91. Editor, Wine and Food, 1965–67; Mem., Cttee of Management, International Wine & Food Soc., 1965–67, 1971–82; Chm., 1970–72, Vice-Pres., 1975–, Circle of Wine Writers. Dep. Gauger, City of London, 1979. Lauréat de l'Office International de la Vigne et du Vin, 1962; Glenfiddich wine writer awards, 1974 and 1978. General Editor, Faber's Wine Series. *Publications:* Sherry, 1961, 3rd edn 1982; (an editor) Clerk and Lindsell on Torts, 13th edn 1969 to 16th edn 1989; The Wines of Europe, 1971; Little Dictionary of Drink, 1973; (jtly) Encyclopedia of United Kingdom and European Patent Law, 1977. *Recreations:* writing, wine, walking, old cars, musical boxes, follies, Iberian things. *Address:* Church Farm House, East Ilsley, Newbury, Berks. *T:* East Ilsley (063528) 216. *Clubs:* Beefsteak, Garrick, Reform, Saintsbury.

JEFFS, Kenneth Peter, CMG 1983; FRAeS; President, MLRS International Corporation, since 1987; *b* 30 Jan. 1931; *s* of Albert Jeffs and Theresa Eleanor Jeffs; *m* Iris Woolsey; one *s* two *d. Educ:* Richmond and East Sheen County Sch. jssc. National Service, RAF, 1949–51. Entered CS as Clerical Officer, Bd of Control, 1947; Air Min., 1952; Principal, 1964; JSSC, 1966–67; Private Secretary: to Under-Sec. of State (RN), MoD, 1969–71; to Minister of Defence, 1971–72; Asst Sec., Dir Defence Sales, MoD, 1972–75; Counsellor, Defence Supply, Washington, DC, 1976–79; Dir Gen. (Marketing), MoD, 1979–83; Exec. Vice-Pres., (Mil. Affairs), 1984–87, Dir, 1985–87, British Aerospace Inc. FRAeS 1985. *Recreations:* rowing, tennis. *Address:* Old Studley, Howell Hill Grove, Ewell, near Epsom, Surrey. *Club:* Royal Automobile.

JEGER, Baroness *cr* 1979 (Life Peer), of St Pancras in Greater London; **Lena May Jeger;** *b* 19 Nov. 1915; *e d* of Charles and Alice Chivers, Yorkley, Glos; *m* 1948, Dr Santo Wayburn Jeger (*d* 1953); no *c. Educ:* Southgate County Sch., Middx; Birkbeck Coll., London University (BA). Civil Service: Customs and Excise, Ministry of Information, Foreign Office, 1936–49; British Embassy Moscow, 1947; Manchester Guardian London Staff, 1951–54, 1961–; Mem. St Pancras Borough Council, 1945–59; Mem. LCC for Holborn and St Pancras South, 1952–55. Mem., Nat. Exec. Cttee, Labour Party, 1968–80 (Vice-Chm., 1978–79; Chm., 1980). MP (Lab) Holborn and St Pancras South, Nov. 1953–1959 and 1964–74, Camden, Holborn and St Pancras South, 1974–79. Mem., Chairmen's Panel, House of Commons, 1971–79. Chm., Govt Working Party on Sewage Disposal, 1969–70. Member, Consultative Assembly: Council of Europe, 1969–71; WEU, 1969–71; UK delegate, Status of Women Commn, UN, 1967. *Address:* 9 Cumberland Terrace, Regent's Park, NW1.

JEHANGIR, Sir Hirji, 3rd Bt, *cr* 1908; *b* 1 Nov. 1915; 2nd *s* of Sir Cowasjee Jehangir, 2nd Bt, GBE, KCIE, and Hilla, MBE, *d* of late Hormarji Wadia, Lowji Castle, Bombay; *S* father, 1962; *m* 1952, Jinoo, *d* of K. H. Cama; two *s. Educ:* St Xavier Sch., Bombay; Magdalene Coll., Cambridge. Chairman: Jehangir Art Gallery, Bombay; Parsi Public School Soc.; Cowasji Jehangir Charitable Trust. *Heir: s* Jehangir [*b* 23 Nov. 1953; *m* 1988, Jasmine, *d* of Bejan Billimoria; one *s*]. *Address:* Readymoney House, 49 Nepean Sea Road, Bombay 400 036, India; 24 Kensington Court Gardens, Kensington Court Place, W8. *T:* 071–937 9587. *Clubs:* Royal Over-Seas League, English-Speaking Union; Willingdon (Bombay).

JEJEEBHOY, Sir Jamsetjee, 7th Bt *cr* 1857; *b* 19 April 1913; *s* of Rustamjee J. C. Jamsetjee (*d* 1947), and Soonabai Rustomjee Byramjee Jeejeebhoy (*d* 1968); *S* cousin, Sir Jamsetjee Jejeebhoy, 6th Bt, 1968, and assumed name of Jamsetjee Jejeebhoy in lieu of Maneckjee Rustamjee Jamsetjee; *m* 1943, Shirin J. H. Cama; one *s* one *d. Educ:* St Xavier's Coll., Bombay (BA). Chairman: Sir Jamsetjee Jejeebhoy Charity Funds; Sir J. J. Parsee Benevolent Instn; Wadiaji's Atash-behram; M. F. Cama Athornan Instn; Iran League; Rustomjee Jamsetjee Jejeebhoy Gujarat Schools' Fund; Bombay Panjrapole; Zoroastrian Bldg Fund; Parsee Dhanda Rojgar Fund; Trustee: Byramjee Jeejeebhoy Parsee Charitable Instn; A. H. Wadia Charity Trust; Parsi Surat Charity Fund; Framjee Cowasjee Inst.; Cowasji Behramji Divecha Charity Trust; Exec. Cttee, B. D. Petit Parsee Gen. Hosp.; K. R. Cama Oriental Instn (Vice Chm.). Created Special Executive Magistrate, 1977. *Heir: s* Rustom Jejeebhoy [*b* 16 Nov. 1957; *m* 1984, Delara, *d* of Jal N. Bhaisa; one *s*]. *Address:* (residence) Beaulieu, 95 Worli Sea Face, Bombay 25, India. *T:* 4930955; (office) Maneckjee Wadia Building, Mahatma Gandhi Road, Fort, Bombay 1. *T:* 273843. *Clubs:* Willingdon Sports, Royal Western India Turf, Ripon, Western India Automobile Association (Bombay); Poona (Poona).

JELF, Maj.-Gen. Richard William, CBE 1948 (OBE 1944); *b* 16 June 1904; *s* of late Sir Ernest Jelf, King's Remembrancer and Master of the Supreme Court; *m* 1928, Nowell, *d* of Major Sampson-Way, RM, Manor House, Henbury; three *s* one *d. Educ:* Cheltenham Coll.; RMA Woolwich. Commissioned Royal Artillery, 1924; Staff Coll., Quetta, 1936; Dep. Dir Staff Duties, War Office, 1946; Imperial Defence Coll., 1948; CRA 2nd Division, 1949; Dep. Chief, Organization and Training Div., SHAPE, 1951; Comdr 99 AA Bde (TA), 1953; Chief of Staff, Eastern Command, 1956; Maj.-Gen., 1957; Commandant, Police Coll., Bramshill, 1957–63; Dir of Civil Defence, Southern Region, 1963–68. ADC to the Queen, 1954. Served North-West Frontier, India (Loe Agra), 1934; NW Europe, 1939–45. Hon. Sec., Lyme Regis RNLI, 1972–84. *Address:* 10 Hill's Place, Guildford Road, Horsham, W Sussex RH12 1XT. *T:* Horsham (0403) 217071.

JELLICOE, family name of **Earl Jellicoe.**

JELLICOE, 2nd Earl, *cr* 1925; **George Patrick John Rushworth Jellicoe,** KBE 1986; DSO 1942; MC 1944; PC 1963; FRS 1990; Viscount Brocas of Southampton, *cr* 1925; Viscount Jellicoe of Scapa, *cr* 1918; Director, Tate & Lyle, since 1974 (Chairman, 1978–82); Member, Advisory Board, Sotheby's Holdings Inc., since 1987; Chancellor, Southampton University, since 1984; President, British Heart Foundation, since 1990; Chairman, Greece Fund, since 1988; *b* 4 April 1918; *o s* of Admiral of the Fleet 1st Earl Jellicoe and late Florence Gwendoline, *d* of Sir Charles Cayzer, 1st Bt; godson of King George V; *S* father, 1935; *m* 1st, 1944, Patricia Christine (marr. diss., 1966), *o d* of Jeremiah O'Kane, Vancouver, Canada; two *s* two *d*; 2nd, 1966, Philippa, *o d* of late Philip Dunne; one *s* two *d. Educ:* Winchester; Trinity Coll., Cambridge (Exhibnr). Hon. Page to King George VI; served War of 1939–45, Coldstream Guards, 1 SAS Regt, SBS Regt (despatches, DSO, MC, Légion d'Honneur, Croix de Guerre, Greek Military Cross). Entered HM Foreign Service, 1947; served as 1st Sec. in Washington, Brussels, Baghdad (Deputy Sec. General Baghdad Pact). Lord-in-Waiting, Jan.-June 1961; Jt Parly. Sec., Min. of Housing and Local Govt, 1961–62; Minister of State, Home Office, 1962–63; First Lord of the Admiralty, 1963–64; Minister of Defence for the Royal Navy, April-Oct. 1964; Deputy Leader of the Opposition, House of Lords, 1967–70; Lord Privy Seal and Minister in Charge, Civil Service Dept, 1970–73; Leader of the House of Lords, 1970–73. Chairman: Brit. Adv. Cttee on Oil Pollution of the Sea, 1968–70; 3rd Int. Conf. on Oil Pollution of the Sea, 1968. Chm., MRC, 1982–90. Chairman: Davy Corp., 1985–90; Booker Tate, 1988–91; Director: Sotheby's, 1973–85; Smiths Industries, 1973–86; Morgan Crucible, 1973–87; S. G. Warburg, 1973–88. Pres., London Chamber of Commerce and Industry, 1979–82; Mem., BOTB, 1982–86 (Chm., 1983–86); Chm., E European Trade Council, 1986–. Chm., Anglo-Hellenic League, 1978–86. A Governor, Centre for Environmental Studies, 1967–70; President: National Federation of Housing Societies, 1965–70; Parly and Scientific Cttee, 1980–83. Chm. of Council, KCL, 1977–86. FKC 1979. Hon. LLD: Southampton, 1985; Long Island Univ., 1987. *Recreation:* ski-ing. *Heir: s* Viscount Brocas, *qv. Address:* Tidcombe Manor, Tidcombe, near Marlborough, Wilts. *T:* Oxenwood (026489) 225; 97 Onslow Square, SW7. *T:* 071–584 1551. *Club:* Brooks's.

See also Adm. Sir Charles Madden, Bt.

JELLICOE, Ann; *see* Jellicoe, P. A.

JELLICOE, Sir Geoffrey (Alan), Kt 1979; CBE 1961; FRIBA (Dist TP); PPILA; FRTPI; formerly Senior Partner of Jellicoe & Coleridge, Architects; *b* London, 8 Oct. 1900; *s* of George Edward Jellicoe; *m* 1936, Ursula (*d* 1986), *d* of late Sir Bernard Pares, KBE, DCL. *Educ:* Cheltenham Coll.; Architectural Association. Bernard Webb Student at British School at Rome; RIBA Neale Bursar. Principal, Arch. Assoc. Schs, 1939–41. Pres., Inst. of Landscape Architects, 1939–49; Hon. Pres. Internat. Fed. of Landscape Architects; Mem. Royal Fine Art Commission, 1954–68; former Trustee of the Tate Gallery; Hon. Corr. Mem. American, Italian and Venezuelan Societies of Landscape Architects. Gardens for: Sandringham; Royal Lodge, Windsor; Ditchley Park; RHS central area, Wisley; Chequers; Horsted Place, Sussex; Hartwell House, Aylesbury; Shute House, Wilts; Tidcombe Manor, Wilts; St Paul's Walden, Herts; Delta Works, W Bromwich; Hilton Hotel, Stratford-upon-Avon; Dewlish House, Dorchester; The Grange, Winchester; Sutton Place, Surrey; Barnwell Manor, Northants; historical gardens for Moody Foundn, Galveston, Texas, USA, 1984; Town Plans for: Guildford, Wellington (Salop), Hemel Hempstead New Town. Arch. Cons. to N Rhodesian Govt, 1947–52. Housing for Basildon, Scunthorpe, LCC; Plymouth Civic Centre; Chertsey Civic Centre; Cheltenham Sports Centre; GLC Comprehensive Sch., Dalston; Durley Park, Keynsham; Grantham Crematorium and Swimming Pool; comprehensive plans for central area, Gloucester, and for Tollcross, Edinburgh; civic landscapes for Modena, Brescia, Asolo and Turin, Italy; Kennedy Memorial, Runnymede; Plans for Sark, Isles of Scilly, and Bridgefoot, Stratford-upon-Avon. Medal of Amer. Soc. of Landscape Architects, 1981; Medal of Landscape Inst., 1985. *Publications:* Italian Gardens of the Renaissance (joint), 1925, rev. edn 1986; (with J. C. Shepherd) Gardens and Design, 1927; Baroque Gardens of Austria, 1931; Studies in Landscape Design, Vol. I 1959, Vol. II 1966, Vol. III 1970; Motopia, 1961; (with Susan Jellicoe) Water, 1971; The Landscape of Man, 1975, rev. edn 1987; The Guelph Lectures on Landscape Design, 1983; (ed with Susan Jellicoe, Patrick Goode and Michael Lancaster) The Oxford Companion to Gardens, 1986; The Moody Historical Gardens, 1989; The Landscape of Civilisation, 1989. *Address:* 14 Highpoint, North Hill, Highgate, N6 4BA. *T:* 081–348 0123.

JELLICOE, (Patricia) Ann, (Mrs Roger Mayne), OBE 1984; playwright and director; *b* 15 July 1927; *d* of John Andrea Jellicoe and Frances Jackson Henderson; *m* 1st, 1950, C. E. Knight-Clarke (marr. diss., 1961); 2nd, 1962, Roger Mayne; one *s* one *d. Educ:* Polam Hall, Darlington; Queen Margaret's, York; Central Sch. of Speech and Drama (Elsie Fogarty Prize, 1947). Actress, stage manager and dir, London and provinces, 1947–51; privately commnd to study relationship between theatre architecture and theatre practice, 1949; founded and ran Cockpit Theatre Club to experiment with open stage, 1952–54; taught acting and directed plays, Central Sch., 1954–56; Literary Manager, Royal Court Theatre, 1973–75; Founder, 1979, Director, 1979–85 and Pres., 1986, Colway Theatre Trust to produce community plays. *Plays:* The Sport of My Mad Mother, Royal Court,

1958; The Knack, Arts (Cambridge), 1961, Royal Court, 1962, New York, 1964, Paris, 1967 (filmed, 1965); Shelley, Royal Court, 1965; The Rising Generation, Royal Court, 1967; The Giveaway, Garrick, 1969; Flora and the Bandits, Dartington Coll. of Arts, 1976; The Bargain, SW Music Theatre, 1979; *community plays:* The Reckoning, Lyme Regis, 1978; The Tide, Seaton, 1980; (with Fay Weldon and John Fowles) The Western Women, Lyme Regis, 1984; Mark og Mønt, Holbæk, Denmark, 1988; Under the God, Dorchester, 1989; *plays for children:* You'll Never Guess!, Arts, 1973; Clever Elsie, Smiling John, Silent Peter, Royal Court, 1974; A Good Thing or a Bad Thing, Royal Court, 1974; *translations include:* Rosmersholm, Royal Court, 1960; The Lady from the Sea, Queen's, 1961; The Seagull (with Ariadne Nicolaeff), Queen's, 1963; Der Freischütz, Sadlers Wells, 1964. *Principal productions include:* The Sport of My Mad Mother (with George Devine), 1958; For Children, 1959; The Knack, 1962; Skyvers, 1963; Shelley, 1965; A Worthy Guest, 1974; The Reckoning, 1978; The Tide, 1980; The Poor Man's Friend, 1981; The Garden, 1982; The Western Women, 1984; Entertaining Strangers, 1985. *Publications:* (apart from plays) Some Unconscious Influences in the Theatre, 1967; (with Roger Mayne) Shell Guide to Devon, 1975. *Address:* c/o Margaret Ramsay Ltd, 14a Goodwin's Court, St Martin's Lane, WC2.

JENCKS, Charles Alexander, PhD; Lecturer in Architecture, Architectural Association, since 1970; Professor, University of California at Los Angeles School of Architecture, since 1985 (Lecturer in Architecture, 1974–85); *b* 21 June 1939; *s* of Gardner Platt Jencks and Ruth Pearl Jencks; *m* 1st, 1960, Pamela Balding (marr. diss. 1973); two *s*; 2nd, 1978, Margaret Keswick; one *s* one *d*. *Educ:* Harvard University (BA Eng. Lit. 1961; BA, MA Arch. 1965); London University (PhD Arch. Hist., 1970). Architectural Association, 1968; writer on Post-Modern architecture, 1975–, Late-Modern architecture, 1978–; designer of furniture, and Alessi Tea and Coffee Set, 1983; numerous Univ. lectures, incl. Peking, Warsaw, Tokyo, USA, Paris; house designs incl. The Garagia Rotunda, 1976–77, The Elemental House, 1983, The Thematic House, 1984. Fulbright Schol., Univ. of London, 1965–67; Melbourne Oration, Australia, 1974; Bossom Lectr, RSA, 1980; Mem., Cttee for selection of architects, Venice Biennale, 1980; Editor at Academy Editions, 1979–; Member: Architectural Assoc.; RSA. *TV films:* (wrote) Le Corbusier, BBC, 1974; (wrote and presented) Kings of Infinite Space (Frank Lloyd Wright and Michael Graves), 1983. *Publications:* Meaning in Architecture, 1969; Architecture 2000, 1971; Adhocism, 1972; Modern Movements in Architecture, 1973, 2nd edn 1985; Le Corbusier and the Tragic View of Architecture, 1974, 2nd edn 1987; The Language of Post-Modern Architecture, 1977, 6th edn 1991; Late-Modern Architecture, 1980; Post-Modern Classicism, 1980; Free-Style Classicism, 1982; Architecture Today (Current Architecture), 1982; Abstract Representation, 1983; Kings of Infinite Space, 1983; Towards a Symbolic Architecture, 1985; What is Post-Modernism? 1986, 3rd edn 1989; Post-Modernism—the new classicism in art and architecture, 1987; The Architecture of Democracy, 1987; The Prince, The Architects and New Wave Monarchy, 1988; The New Moderns, 1990; articles in Encounter, Connoisseur, l'Oeil, TLS. *Recreations:* travel, collecting Chinese (bullet-hole) rocks. *Address:* 19 Lansdowne Walk, W11; 519 Latimer Road, Santa Monica, Calif 90402, USA.

JENKIN, family name of **Baron Jenkin of Roding.**

JENKIN OF RODING, Baron *cr* 1987 (Life Peer), of Wanstead and Woodford in Greater London; **Charles Patrick Fleeming Jenkin,** PC 1973; MA; Chairman, Friends' Provident Life Office, since 1988 (Deputy Chairman, Friends' Provident Life Office (Director, 1986–88) and UK Provident Institution (Director, 1987–88), 1987–88, when merged); *b* 7 Sept. 1926; *s* of late Mr and Mrs C. O. F. Jenkin; *m* 1952, Alison Monica Graham; two *s* two *d*. *Educ:* Dragon Sch., Oxford; Clifton Coll.; Jesus Coll., Cambridge. MA (Cantab.) 1951. Served with QO Cameron Highlanders, 1945–48; 1st Class Hons in Law, Cambridge, 1951; Harmsworth Scholar, Middle Temple, 1951; called to the Bar, 1952. Distillers Co. Ltd, 1957–70. Member: Hornsey Borough Council, 1960–63; London Coun. of Social Service, 1963–67. MP (C) Wanstead and Woodford, 1964–87. An Opposition front bench spokesman on Treasury, Trade and Economics, 1965–70; Jt Vice-Chm., Cons. Parly Trade and Power Cttee, 1966–67; Chm., All Party Parly Group on Chemical Industry, 1968–70; Financial Sec. to the Treasury, 1970–72; Chief Sec. to Treasury, 1972–74; Minister for Energy, 1974; Opposition front bench spokesman: on Energy, 1974–76; on Soc. Services, 1976–79; Secretary of State: for Social Services, 1979–81; for Industry, 1981–83; for the Environment, 1983–85. President: National CPC Cttee, 1983–86; Greater London Area, Nat. Union of Cons. Assocs, 1989– (Vice-Pres., 1987–89). Director: Tilbury Contracting Gp Ltd, 1974–79; Royal Worcester Ltd, 1975–79; Continental and Industrial Trust Ltd, 1975–79; Chairman: Crystalate Hldgs PLC, 1988–90 (Dir, 1987–90); Lamco Paper Sales Ltd, 1987–; UK Co-Chm., UK-Japan 2000 Gp, 1986–90; Vice-Pres., 1991 Japan Festival Cttee, 1987–. Adviser: Arthur Andersen & Co., Management Consultants, 1985–; Sumitomo Trust and Banking Co. Ltd, 1989–; Mem., UK Adv. Bd, Nat. Economic Res. Associates Inc., 1985–. Mem. Council: UK CEED, 1987–; Guide Dogs for the Blind Assoc., 1987–; Pres., Friends of Wanstead Hosp., 1987–; Chm., Taverner Concerts Trust, 1987–; Chm., Target Finland, 1989–; Dir, Nat. Phoenix Initiative Ltd, 1991–. Pres., British Urban Regeneration Assoc., 1990–. Chm. Trustees, Westfield Coll. Trust, 1988– (Gov., Westfield Coll., 1964–70; Fellow, QMW, 1991); Gov., Clifton Coll., 1969– (Mem. Council, 1972–79; Pres., Old Cliftonian Soc., 1987–89). Freeman: City of London, 1985; London Bor. of Redbridge, 1988. FRSA 1985. *Recreations:* music, gardening, sailing, bricklaying. *Address:* (office) 15 Old Bailey, EC4M 7AP. *T:* 071–329 4454; Home Farm, Matching Road, Hatfield Heath, Bishop's Stortford, Herts CM22 7AS; 703 Howard House, Dolphin Square, SW1V 3LX. *T:* 071–798 8724. *Club:* West Essex Conservative (Wanstead).
    See also Rear-Adm. D. C. Jenkin.

JENKIN, Conrad; *see* Jenkin, D. C.

JENKIN, Rear Adm. (David) Conrad, CB 1983; Commandant, Joint Service Defence College (formerly National Defence College), 1981–84, retired; *b* 25 Oct. 1928; *s* of Mr and Mrs C. O. F. Jenkin; *m* 1958, Jennifer Margaret Nowell; three *s* one *d*. *Educ:* Dragon Sch., Oxford; RNC, Dartmouth. Entered RN at age of 13½, 1942; qual. in Gunnery, 1953; commanded: HMS Palliser, 1961–63; HMS Cambrian, 1964–66; HMS Galatea, 1974–75; HMS Hermes (aircraft carrier), 1978–79; Flag Officer, First Flotilla, 1980–81. *Recreations:* sailing, skiing, do-it-yourself. *Address:* Knapsyard House, West Meon, Hants GU32 1LF. *T:* West Meon (073086) 227.
    See also Baron Jenkin of Roding.

JENKIN, Ian (Evers) Tregarthen, OBE 1984; Co-founder, 1986, and Vice-President, since 1991, Open College of the Arts (Director, 1986–89, retired; President, 1989–91); *b* 18 June 1920; *s* of Henry Archibald Tregarthen Jenkin, OBE and Dagmar Leggott. *Educ:* Stowe; Camberwell Sch. of Art and Crafts; Trinity Coll., Cambridge (MA Econ.); Slade Sch., University Coll. London. Royal Artillery, 1940–46. Sec. and Tutor, Slade School, 1949–75; Principal, Camberwell Sch. of Art and Crafts, 1975–85; Curator, RA Schools, 1985–86. Member: Art Panel, Arts Council (Vice-Chm.), 1979–82; Crafts Council, 1981–84 (Chm., Educn Cttee); Art and Design Working Gp, Nat. Adv. Body for Public Sector Higher Educn, 1982–85; Advisor, Member, Trustee, examiner, numerous educnl,

art and conservation bodies. Pres., Dulwich Decorative and Fine Art Soc., 1984–; Dir, Guild of St George, 1986– (Companion, 1984). FRSA. Hon. Dr Arts CNAA 1987. *Publications:* Disaster Planning and Preparedness: a survey of practices and procedures (British Liby R&D report), 1986; An Outline Disaster Control Plan (British Liby Inf. Guide), 1987; contribs to DNB. *Recreations:* gardening, painting. *Address:* Grove Farm, Fifield, Maidenhead, Berks SL6 2PF. *Clubs:* Athenæum, Arts, Buck's.

JENKIN, Simon William Geoffrey; Chief Education Officer, Devon County Council, since 1989; *b* 25 July 1943; *s* of Dudley Cyril Robert Jenkin and Muriel Grace (*née* Mather); *m* 1973, Elizabeth Tapsell; two *d*. *Educ:* Univ. of London (BSc Econs); Jesus Coll., Oxford (DipEd). Lectr, 1967–72, Sen. Lectr 1972–75, Bournemouth Coll. of Technology; Educn Officer, Essex CC, 1975–80; Area Educn Officer, NE Essex, 1980–83; Principal Educn Officer, Derbys CC, 1983–87; Dep. Chief Educn Officer, Devon CC, 1988–89. *Recreation:* my wife. *Address:* Myrtle Cottage, The Village, Clyst St Mary, Exeter, Devon EX5 1BB. *T:* Exeter (0392) 875159.

JENKINS; *see* Martin-Jenkins.

JENKINS, family name of **Barons Jenkins of Hillhead** and **Jenkins of Putney.**

JENKINS OF HILLHEAD, Baron *cr* 1987 (Life Peer), of Pontypool in the County of Gwent; **Roy Harris Jenkins,** PC 1964; Chancellor, University of Oxford, since 1987; President, Royal Society of Literature, since 1988; Leader, Social and Liberal Democratic Peers, since 1988; First Leader, Social Democratic Party, 1982–83 (Member of Joint Leadership, 1981–82); *b* 11 Nov. 1920; *o s* of late Arthur Jenkins, MP, and of Hattie Jenkins; *m* 1945, Jennifer Morris (*see* Dame Jennifer Jenkins); two *s* one *d*. *Educ:* Abersychan Grammar Sch.; University Coll., Cardiff (Hon. Fellow 1982); Balliol Coll., Oxford (Hon. Fellow 1969). Sec. and Librarian, Oxford Union Society; Chairman, Oxford Univ. Democratic Socialist Club; First Class in Hon. Sch. of Philosophy, Politics and Economics, 1941; DCL Oxford, 1987. Served War of 1939–45, in RA, 1942–46; Captain, 1944–46. Contested (Lab) Solihull Div. of Warwicks, at Gen. Election, 1945. Mem. of Staff of Industrial and Commercial Finance Corp. Ltd, 1946–48. Mem. Exec. Cttee of Fabian Soc., 1949–61; Chm., Fabian Soc., 1957–58; Mem. Cttee of Management, Soc. of Authors, 1956–60; Governor, British Film Institute, 1955–58; Adviser to John Lewis Partnership, 1954–62, Dir of Financial Operations, 1962–64. Dir, Morgan Grenfell Hldgs Ltd, 1981–82. MP (Lab): Central Southwark, 1948–50; Stechford, Birmingham, 1950–76; PPS to Sec. of State for Commonwealth Relations, 1949–50; Minister of Aviation, 1964–65; Home Sec., 1965–67, 1974–76; Chancellor of the Exchequer, 1967–70; Dep. Leader, Labour Party, 1970–72. Pres., European Commn, 1977–81. Contested: Warrington by-election as first Social Democratic candidate, July 1981; Glasgow Hillhead (SDP/Alliance), 1982. MP (SDP) Glasgow Hillhead, March 1982–1987. UK Deleg. to Council of Europe, 1955–57. Vice-Pres., Inst. of Fiscal Studies, 1970–. Formerly: Dep. Chm. Federal Union; Pres., Britain in Europe, Referendum Campaign, 1975; Chm., Labour European Cttee. A President of United Kingdom Council of the European Movement. Pres., UWIST, 1975–81. Trustee, Pilgrim Trust, 1973–. Lectures: Henry L. Stimson, Yale, 1971; Jean Monnet, Florence, 1977; Dimbleby, 1979; Churchill, Luxembourg, 1980; Rede, Cambridge, 1988; George Ball, Princeton, 1989; Goodman, 1989; Leverhulme, 1990. Liveryman, Goldsmiths' Co.; Freeman, City of London, 1965. Freeman, City of Brussels, 1980. Hon. Foreign Mem., Amer. Acad. Arts and Scis, 1973. Hon. Fellow: Berkeley Coll., Yale, 1972; St Antony's Coll., Oxford, 1987. Hon. LLD: Leeds, 1971; Harvard, 1972; Pennsylvania, 1973; Dundee, 1973; Loughborough, 1975; Bath, 1978; Michigan, 1978; Wales, 1979; Bristol, 1980; Hon. DLitt: Glasgow, 1972; City, 1976; Warwick, 1978; Reading, 1979; Hon. DCL Oxford, 1973; Hon. DSc Aston, 1977; DUniv: Keele, 1977; Essex, 1978; Open, 1979; Hon. DPhil Katholieke Univ., Leuven, 1979; Hon. doctorates: Urbino, 1979; TCD, 1979; Georgetown, 1988. Charlemagne Prize, 1972; Robert Schuman Prize, 1972; Prix Bentinck, 1978. Order of European Merit (Luxemburg), 1976; Grand Cross: Legion of Honour of Senegal, 1979; Legion of Honour of Mali, 1979; Order of Charles III (Spain), 1980; Order of Merit (Italy), 1990. *Publications:* (ed) Purpose and Policy (a vol. of the Prime Minister's Speeches), 1947; Mr Attlee: An Interim Biography, 1948; Pursuit of Progress, 1953; Mr Balfour's Poodle, 1954; Sir Charles Dilke: A Victorian Tragedy, 1958; The Labour Case (Penguin Special), 1959; Asquith, 1964; Essays and Speeches, 1967; Afternoon on the Potomac?, 1972; What Matters Now, 1972; Nine Men of Power, 1975; Partnership of Principle, 1985; Truman, 1986; Baldwin, 1987; Gallery of Twentieth Century Portraits, 1988; European Diary 1977–81, 1989; contrib. to New Fabian Essays, 1952; contrib. to Hugh Gaitskell, A Memoir, 1964. *Address:* 2 Kensington Park Gardens, W11; St Amand's House, East Hendred, Oxon. *Clubs:* Athenæum, Brooks's, Pratt's, Reform, Beefsteak, United Oxford & Cambridge University.

JENKINS OF HILLHEAD, Lady; *see* Jenkins, Dame M. J.

JENKINS OF PUTNEY, Baron *cr* 1981 (Life Peer), of Wandsworth in Greater London; **Hugh Gater Jenkins;** *b* 27 July 1908; *s* of Joseph Walter Jenkins and Florence Emily (*née* Gater), Enfield, Middlesex; *m* 1936, Marie (*née* Crosbie) (*d* 1989), *d* of Sqdn Ldr Ernest Crosbie and Ethel (*née* Hawkins). *Educ:* Enfield Grammar Sch. Personal exploration of employment and unemployment, and political and economic research, 1925–30; Prudential Assce Co., 1930–40. ROC, 1938; RAF: Fighter Comd, 1941; became GCI Controller (Flt Lt); seconded to Govt of Burma, 1945, as Dir Engl. Programmes, Rangoon Radio. Nat. Union of Bank Employees: Greater London Organiser, 1947; Res. and Publicity Officer; Ed., The Bank Officer, 1948; British Actors' Equity Assoc.: Asst Sec., 1950; Asst Gen. Sec., 1957–64; LCC: Mem. for Stoke Newington and Hackney N, 1958–65 (Public Control and Town Planning Cttees). Fabian Soc. lectr and Dir of Summer Schools in early post-war years; Chairman: H Bomb Campaign Cttee, 1954; Campaign for Nuclear Disarmament, 1979–81 (Vice-Pres., 1981–); CND, Aldermaston Marcher, 1957–63; Chm. Victory for Socialism, 1956–60; Mem. Exec. Cttee Greater London Labour Party. Contested (Lab): Enfield W, 1950; Mitcham, 1955; MP (Lab) Wandsworth, Putney, 1964–79; Minister for the Arts, 1974–76. Former Mem., Public Accounts Cttee. Member: Arts Council, 1968–71; Drama Panel, 1972–74; Nat. Theatre Bd, 1976–80; Dep. Chm., Theatres Trust, 1977–79; Dir, 1979–86, Consultant, 1986–. Theatres' Advisory Council: Jt Sec., 1963; Chm., 1964–74, 1976–86; Vice-Pres., 1986–. Occasional broadcasts and lectures on communications, theatrical and disarmament subjects. *Radio plays:* series, Scenes from an Autobiography: Solo Boy, 1983; When You and I Were Seventeen, 1985; A Day in September, 1986; In Time of War, 1986; Lost Tune from Rangoon, 1987; View to a Death, 1989. *Publications:* Essays in Local Government Enterprise (with others), 1964; The Culture Gap, 1979; Rank and File, 1980; various pamphlets; contrib. to Tribune, New Statesman, Guardian, etc. *Recreations:* reading, writing, talking, viewing, listening, avoiding retirement. *Address:* House of Lords, SW1A 0PW. *T:* 071–219 6706, (office) 071–836 8591.

JENKINS, Alan Roberts; Editorial Consultant, The New Straits Times, Malaysia; *b* 8 June 1926; *s* of Leslie Roberts Jenkins and Marjorie Kate Cawston; *m* 1st, 1949, Kathleen Mary Baker (*d* 1969); four *s*; 2nd, 1971, Helen Mary Speed; one *s*. *Educ:* Aylesbury Grammar Sch. Commnd Royal Berks Regt, 1945; Captain, W African Liaison Service,

GHQ India; Staff Captain Public Relations, Royal W African Frontier Force, Lagos; DADPR W Africa Comd (Major). Reporter, Reading Mercury and Berkshire Chronicle, 1948; Sub-editor, Daily Herald; Daily Mail: Sub-editor; Night Editor, 1962–69; Northern Editor, 1969–71; Asst Editor, Evening Standard, 1971; Dep. Editor, Sunday People, 1971–72; Asst Editor, Sunday Mirror, 1972–77; Editor, Glasgow Herald, 1978–80; Editorial exec., The Times, 1981–89. *Recreations*: golf, travel, moving house. *Address*: 6 Laman Tunku, Bukit Tunku, 50480 Kuala Lumpur, Malaysia.

JENKINS, Prof. Aubrey Dennis; Professor of Polymer Science, University of Sussex, since 1971; *b* 6 Sept. 1927; *s* of Arthur William Jenkins and Mabel Emily (*née* Street); *m* 1st, 1950, Audrey Doreen Middleton (marr. diss. 1987); two *s* one *d*; 2nd, 1987, Jitka Horská, *er d* of late Josef Horský and of Anna Horská, Hradec Králové, Czechoslovakia. *Educ*: Dartford Grammar Sch.; Sir John Cass Technical Inst.; King's Coll., Univ. of London. BSc 1948, PhD 1951; DSc 1961. FRIC 1957. Research Chemist, Courtaulds Ltd, Fundamental Research Laboratory, Maidenhead, 1950–60; Head of Chemistry Research, Gillette Industries Ltd, Reading, 1960–64 (Harris Research Labs, Washington, DC, 1963–64); University of Sussex, 1964–: Sen. Lectr in Chemistry, 1964–68; Reader, 1968–71; Dean, Sch. of Molecular Scis, 1973–78. Visiting Professor: Inst. of Macromolecular Chemistry, Prague, 1978 and 1986; Univ. of Massachusetts, Amherst, 1979. Member: Internat. Union of Pure and Applied Chemistry, Commn on Macromolecular Nomenclature, 1974–85 (Chm., 1977–85; Sec., Macromolecular Div., 1985–); GB/East Europe Centre. Mem., Brighton HA, 1983–90. Examining chaplain to Bishop of Chichester, 1980–90. Heyrovský Gold Medal for Chemistry, Czechoslovak Acad. of Scis, 1990. *Publications*: Kinetics of Vinyl Polymerization by Radical Mechanisms (with C. H. Bamford, W. G. Barb and P. F. Onyon), 1958; Polymer Science, 1972; (with A. Ledwith) Reactivity, Mechanism and Structure in Polymer Chemistry, 1974; (with J. F. Kennedy) Macromolecular Chemistry, Vol. I 1980, Vol. II 1982, Vol. III 1984; Progress in Polymer Science (12 vols), 1967–; papers in learned jls. *Recreations*: music, travel (esp. Czechoslovakia), photography. *Address*: Shoe Box Cottage, 115 Keymer Road, Keymer, Hassocks, West Sussex BN6 8QL. *T*: Hassocks (0273) 845410.

JENKINS, Sir Brian (Garton), GBE 1991; FCA; Partner, Coopers & Lybrand Deloitte, Chartered Accountants, since 1969; Lord Mayor of London, 1991–Oct. 1992; *b* 3 Dec. 1935; *s* of late Owen Garton Jenkins and Doris Enid (*née* Webber); *m* 1967, Elizabeth Ann, *d* of John Philip Manning Prentice, MSc, FRAS and Elizabeth Mason (*née* Harwood); one *s* one *d*. *Educ*: Tonbridge; Trinity Coll., Oxford (State Scholar; MA). ACA Hons 1963; FCA 1974; MBCS. Served RA, Gibraltar, 1955–57 (2nd Lieut). Joined Cooper Brothers & Co. (now Coopers & Lybrand Deloitte), 1960; Mem., Exec. Cttee, 1979–85 and 1986–88; Head of Audit, 1986–91. Dir, Royal Ordnance Factories, 1976–83. Mem., Commn for the New Towns, 1990–. Institute of Chartered Accountants in England and Wales: Mem. Council, 1976–; Vice-Pres., 1983; Dep. Pres. 1983–85; Pres., 1985–86; Chm., Courses Cttee, 1979–80; Chm., Educn and Trng Directorate, 1980–83. Chm., London and Dist Soc. of Chartered Accountants, 1975–76; Vice-Pres., Chartered Accountants Students' Soc. of London, 1978–. Alderman, City of London (Ward of Cordwainer), 1980– (Sheriff, 1987–88); Liveryman: Co. of Chartered Accountants in England and Wales, 1980– (Master, 1990–91); Merchant Taylors' Co., 1984– (Mem. Court, 1989–); Co. of Information Technologists (Mem. Court, 1985–); Mem., Court of Assts, Corp. of Sons of the Clergy, 1983–. Governor: Royal Shakespeare Theatre, 1981–; SPCK, 1987–; St Felix Sch., Southwold, 1988–; Mem. Council, RSCM, 1987–. Dir, Blackheath Preservation Trust, 1985–; Mem. Council of Management, Architectural Heritage Fund, 1987–. Trustee, Community Service Volunteers, 1987–; London House for Overseas Graduates, 1990–. Mem., Bd of Green Cloth Verge of the Palaces, 1984–. FRSA. *Publications*: An Audit Approach to Computers, 1978, 3rd edn 1986; contrib. accountancy and business magazines. *Recreations*: garden construction, old books, large jigsaw puzzles, ephemera. *Address*: Plumtree Court, EC4A 4HT. *T*: 071–583 5000. *Clubs*: Brooks's, City of London, City Livery.

JENKINS, Lt-Col Charles Peter de Brisay, MBE 1960; MC 1945; Clerk, Worshipful Company of Goldsmiths, 1975–88, retired; *b* 19 Aug. 1925; *s* of late Brig. A. de B. Jenkins and of Mrs Elizabeth Susan Jenkins; *m* 1949, Joan Mary, *e d* of late Col and Mrs C. N. Littleboy, Thirsk; one *s*. *Educ*: Cheltenham Coll.; Selwyn Coll., Cambridge. Commnd RE, 1944; served in Italy, 1944–45; subseq. Hong Kong, Kenya and Germany; jssc 1960; Instructor, Staff Coll., Camberley, 1961–63; Comdr, RE 1st Div., 1965–67; retd 1967. Asst Clerk, Goldsmiths' Co., 1968. Mem., Hallmarking Council, 1977–88; Vice-Chm., Goldsmiths' Coll. (Univ. of London) Council, 1983–. Trustee Nat. Centre for Orchestral Studies, 1980–89. *Recreations*: swimming, gardening, Wagner. *Address*: c/o Lloyds Bank, 31 Fore Street, Totnes, Devon TQ9 5MM.

JENKINS, Christopher; *see* Jenkins, J. C.

JENKINS, Clive; *see* Jenkins, D. C.

JENKINS, David, CBE 1977; MA; Librarian, National Library of Wales, 1969–79; *b* 29 May 1912; *s* of late Evan Jenkins and Mary (*née* James), Blaenclydach, Rhondda; *m* 1948, Menna Rhys, *o d* of late Rev. Owen Evans Williams, Penrhyn-coch, Aberystwyth; one *s* one *d*. *Educ*: Ardwyn Grammar Sch., Aberystwyth; UCW, Aberystwyth. BA Hons Welsh Lit. 1936, MA 1948; W. P. Thomas (Rhondda) Schol. 1936; Sir John Williams Research Student, 1937–38. Served War of 1939–45, Army; Major, 1943; NW Europe. National Library of Wales: Asst, Dept MSS, 1939–48; Asst Keeper, Dept of Printed Books, 1949, Keeper, 1957, Sen. Keeper, 1962. Professorial Fellow, UCW Aberystwyth, 1971–79. Gen. Comr of Income Tax, 1968–87; Chairman: Mid-Wales HMC, 1969–70; Welsh Books Council, 1974–80 (Vice-Chm. 1971–74); Library Adv. Council (Wales), 1979–82; Member: Court of Governors, Univ. of Wales; Ct and Council, UC Aberystwyth and Lampeter; Adv. Council, British Library, 1975–82; BBC Archives Adv. Cttee, 1976–79; Hon. Soc. of Cymmrodorion; Pantyfedwen Trust, 1969–; Coll. of Librarianship Wales; Governor: Ardwyn Grammar Sch., 1963–72; Penweddig Compreh. Sch., 1973–77. Editor: NLW Jl, 1968–79; Jl Welsh Bibliog. Soc., 1964–79; Ceredigion, Trans Cards Antiq. Soc., 1973–84. JP Aberystwyth 1959–82: Chm. Llanbadarn Bench 1965–69; Vice-Chm., Aberystwyth Bench, 1980; Member: Dyfed Magistrates' Courts Cttee, 1975–79; Dyfed-Powys Police Authority, 1977–81. Hon. DLitt Wales, 1979. Sir Ellis Griffith Meml Prize, Univ. of Wales, 1975. *Publications*: Cofiant Thomas Gwynn Jones, 1973 (biog.); Welsh Arts Council Prize, 1974); (ed) Erthyglau ac Ysgrifau Kate Roberts, 1978; Bardd a Bro: T. Gwynn Jones, Cyngor y Celfyddydau, 1984; articles in NLW Jl, Bull. Bd of Celtic Studies and many other jls; contrib. Dictionary of Welsh Biography, Cydymaith i lenyddiaeth Cymru. *Recreation*: walking. *Address*: Maesaleg, Penrhyn-coch, Aberystwyth, Dyfed SY23 3EH. *T*: Aberystwyth (0970) 828 766.

JENKINS, (David) Clive; Director, Green Independants Goshawk Trust, since 1990; Joint General Secretary, Manufacturing, Science and Finance, 1988–89, now General Secretary Emeritus (Joint General Secretary, 1968–70, General Secretary, 1970–88, Association of Scientific, Technical and Managerial Staffs); Member of the General Council of the TUC, 1974–89 (Chairman, 1987–88); *b* 2 May 1926; *s* of David Samuel Jenkins and Miriam Harris Jenkins (*née* Hughes); *m* 1963, Moira McGregor Hilley (marr.

diss. 1989); one *s* one *d*. *Educ*: Port Talbot Central Boys' Sch.; Port Talbot County Sch.; Swansea Techn. Coll. (evenings). Started work in metallurgical test house, 1940; furnace shift supervisor, 1942; i/c of laboratory, 1943; tinplate night shift foreman, 1945; Branch Sec. and Area Treas., AScW, 1946; Asst Midlands Divisional Officer, ASSET, 1947; Transport Industrial Officer, 1949; Nat. Officer, 1954; Gen. Sec., ASSET, 1961–68. Woodrow Wilson Fellow, 1968; Australian Commonwealth Fellow, 1989. Metrop. Borough Councillor, 1954–60 (Chm. Staff Cttee, St Pancras Borough Coun.); Chm., Nat. Jt Coun. for Civil Air Transport, 1967–68; Member: NRDC, 1974–80; Bullock Cttee on Industrial Democracy, 1975; Wilson Cttee to Review the Functioning of Financial Institutions, 1977–80; BNOC, 1979–82; BOTB, 1980–83; NEDC, 1983–89; Commn of Inquiry into Labour Party, 1979 (Chm., Finance Panel, 1979); TUC-Labour Party Liaison Cttee, 1980–89; Council, ACAS, 1986–89; Chairman: TUC Educnl Trust, 1979; Roosevelt Meml Trust, 1979–89; Friends of the Earth Trust, 1984–86; Trustee, Nat. Heritage Meml Fund, 1980–88; Governor, Sadler's Wells Foundn, 1985–88. Editor, Trade Union Affairs, 1961–63. Sometime columnist, Tribune, Daily Mirror, Daily Record. *Publications*: Power at the Top, 1959; Power Behind the Screen, 1961; (with J. E. Mortimer) British Trade Unions Today, 1965; (with J. E. Mortimer) The Kind of Laws the Unions Ought to Want, 1968; with B. D. Sherman: Computers and the Unions, 1977; Collective Bargaining: what you always wanted to know about trade unions and never dared ask, 1977; The Collapse of Work, 1979; The Rebellious Salariat: white collar unionism, 1979; The Leisure Shock, 1981; All Against the Collar (autobiog.), 1990. *Recreations*: working with the Green movements and keeping an eye on Diamond Island's Fairy Penguins. *Address*: Villa de l'Est, Redbill Point, Bicheno on the Pacific, Tasmania, Australia.

    See also T. H. Jenkins.

JENKINS, Rt. Rev. David Edward; *see* Durham, Bishop of.

JENKINS, David Edward Stewart; Research Consultant to HM Chief Inspector of Prisons, since 1987; *b* 9 May 1949; *s* of late William Stephen Jenkins and of Jean Nicol Downie; *m* 1972, Maggie Lack, *d* of Dr C. H. and Mrs J. D. Lack; two *s* one *d*. *Educ*: Univ. of London Goldsmiths' College (BA(Soc) 1977); LSE. Warden, Ellison Hse Adult Probation Hostel, SE17, 1973–74; Lecturer: (part-time) in Sociology, Brunel Univ., 1980–81; (part-time) in Social Administration, LSE and Goldsmiths' Coll., 1980–81; in Criminology, Univ. of Edinburgh, 1981; Dir, Howard League, 1982–86; Res. Fellow, PSI, 1986–87. Morris Ginsburg Fellow in Sociology, LSE, 1986–87. *Recreations*: music, swimming, cycling. *Address*: HM Inspectorate of Prisons, 50 Queen Anne's Gate, SW1H 9AT. *T*: 071–273 2641.

JENKINS, David John; General Secretary, Wales Trades Union Congress, since 1983; *b* 21 Sept. 1948; *s* of William and Dorothy Jenkins; *m* 1976, Felicity Anne (*née* Wood); two *s* one *d*. *Educ*: Canton High Sch., Cardiff; Liverpool Univ. (BA Hons); Garnett Coll., London (CertEd). Industrial Sales Organiser, ITT (Distributors), 1970–74; steel worker, GKN, 1974; Lectr, Peterborough Tech. Coll., 1975–78; Research and Admin. Officer, Wales TUC, 1978–83. *Recreation*: finding time to spend with family. *Address*: 1 Cathedral Road, Cardiff. *T*: Cardiff (0222) 372345.

JENKINS, Elizabeth, OBE 1981. *Educ*: St Christopher School, Letchworth; Newnham College, Cambridge. *Publications*: The Winters, 1931; Lady Caroline Lamb, a biography, 1932; Harriet (awarded the Femina Vie Heureuse Prize), 1934; The Phoenix' Nest, 1936; Jane Austen, a Biography, 1938; Robert and Helen, 1944; Young Enthusiasts, 1946; Henry Fielding (The English Novelists Series), 1947; Six Criminal Women, 1949; The Tortoise and the Hare, 1954; Ten Fascinating Women, 1955; Elizabeth the Great (biography), 1958; Elizabeth and Leicester, 1961; Brightness, 1963; Honey, 1968; Dr Gully, 1972; The Mystery of King Arthur, 1975; The Princes in the Tower, 1978; The Shadow and the Light, 1983. *Address*: 8 Downshire Hill, Hampstead, NW3. *T*: 071–435 4642.

JENKINS, Very Rev. Frank Graham; Dean of Monmouth and Vicar of St Woolos, 1976–90; *b* 24 Feb. 1923; *s* of Edward and Miriam M. Jenkins; *m* 1950, Ena Doraine Parry; two *s* one *d*. *Educ*: Cyfarthfa Sec. Sch., Merthyr Tydfil; Port Talbot Sec. Sch.; St David's Coll., Lampeter (BA Hist); Jesus Coll., Oxford (BA Theol., MA); St Michael's Coll., Llandaff. HM Forces, 1942–46. Deacon 1950, priest 1951, Llandaff; Asst Curate, Llangeinor, 1950–53; Minor Canon, Llandaff Cathedral, 1953–60; CF (TA), 1956–61; Vicar of Abertillery, 1960–64; Vicar of Risca, 1964–75; Canon of Monmouth, 1967–76; Vicar of Caerleon, 1975–76. *Address*: Rivendell, 209 Christchurch Road, Newport, Gwent NP9 7QL. *T*: Newport (0633) 255278.

JENKINS, Garth John, CB 1987; QC 1989; Deputy Secretary and Legal Adviser and Solicitor to Ministry of Agriculture, Fisheries and Food, Forestry Commission, and Intervention Board for Agricultural Produce, since 1983; *b* 7 Dec. 1933; *s* of John Ernest Jenkins and Amy Elizabeth Jenkins; *m* 1965, Patricia Margaret Lindsay; one *d*. *Educ*: Birmingham Royal Inst. for the Blind; Royal National College for the Blind; Birmingham Univ. (LLB). Called to Bar, Gray's Inn, 1963. Birmingham Corporation, 1954; South Shields Corporation, 1964; The Land Commission, 1967; MAFF, 1971–; Under Sec., 1981. *Recreations*: literature, theatre, music, chess; food, drink and conversation. *Address*: 55 Whitehall, SW1A 2EY. *T*: 071–270 8379.

JENKINS, Prof. George Charles, MB, BS, PhD; FRCPE, FRCPath; Consultant Haematologist, The Royal London (formerly London) Hospital, since 1965; Hon. Consultant, St Peter's Hospitals, 1972–86; Professor of Haematology in the University of London, since 1974; Consultant to the Royal Navy; *b* 2 Aug. 1927; *s* of late John R. Jenkins and Mabel Rebecca (*née* Smith); *m* 1956, Elizabeth, *d* of late Cecil J. Welch, London; one *s* two *d*. *Educ*: Wyggeston, Leicester; St Bartholomew's Hosp. Med. Coll. MB, BS, PhD; MRCS 1951; FRCPath 1975 (MRCPath 1964); FRCPE, FRCP 1990 (LRCP 1951). House Phys. and Ho. Surg., St Bart's Hosp., 1951–52. Sqdn Ldr, RAF Med. Br., 1952–54. Registrar in Pathology, St Bart's Hosp., 1954–57; MRC Research Fellow, Royal Postgraduate Med. Sch., 1957–60; Sen. Registrar, Haematology, London Hosp., 1960–63; Cons. Haematologist, N Middlesex Hosp., 1963–65. Examiner: Univ. of London, 1971–; Univ. of Cambridge, 1984–; Sen. Examiner, RCPath, 1971–, Mem. Council, 1979–, Vice-Pres., 1981–84. Mem. subcttee on biologicals, Cttee on Safety of Medicines, 1976–86. Pres., British Acad. of Forensic Scis, 1990– (Mem., 1977–); Chm. Exec. Council, 1985–89); Member: British Soc. for Haematology, 1962– (formerly Hon. Sec.; Pres.,1988–89); Internat. Soc. of Haematology, 1975–; Assoc. of Clinical Pathologists 1958–. *Publications*: Advanced Haematology (jtly), 1974; papers and contribs to med. and sci. books and jls. *Recreations*: theatre, music, talking to people. *Address*: The Royal London Hospital, Whitechapel, E1 1BB. *T*: 071–377 7178. *Club*: Royal Navy Medical.

JENKINS, Gilbert Kenneth; Keeper, Department of Coins and Medals, British Museum, 1965–78; *b* 2 July 1918; *s* of late Kenneth Gordon Jenkins and of Julia Louisa Jenkins (*née* Colbourne); *m* 1939, Cynthia Mary, *d* of late Dr Hugh Scott, FRS; one *s* two *d*. *Educ*: All Saints Sch., Bloxham; Corpus Christi Coll., Oxford. Open Classical Scholar (Corpus Christi Coll.), 1936; First Class Honour Mods, 1938. War Service in Royal Artillery, 1940–46 (SE Asia, 1944–46). BA, 1946. Asst Keeper, British Museum, 1947; Dep. Keeper,

1956. An Editor of Numismatic Chronicle, 1964–. Mem., German Archaeological Inst., 1967; Corresp. Mem., Amer. Numismatic Soc., 1958; Hon. Mem., Swiss Numismatic Soc., 1979; Hon. FRNS, 1980. Akbar Medal, Numismatic Soc. of India, 1966; Royal Numismatic Soc. Medal, 1975; Archer Huntington Medal, Amer. Numismatic Soc., 1976. *Publications:* Carthaginian Gold and Electrum Coins (with R. B. Lewis), 1963; Coins of Greek Sicily, 1966; Sylloge Nummorum Graecorum (Danish Nat. Museum), part 42, N Africa (ed), 1969, part 43, Spain-Gaul (ed), 1979; The Coinage of Gela, 1970; Ancient Greek Coins, 1972; (with U. Westermark) The Coinage of Kamarina, 1980; articles in numismatic periodicals. *Recreations:* music, cycling. *Address:* 3 Beechwood Avenue, Kew Gardens, Surrey.

JENKINS, Prof. Harold, MA, DLitt; FBA 1989; Professor Emeritus, University of Edinburgh; *b* 19 July 1909; *s* of Henry and Mildred Jenkins, Shenley, Bucks; *m* 1939, Gladys Puddifoot (*d* 1984); no *c*. *Educ:* Wolverton Grammar Sch.; University Coll., London. George Smith Studentship, 1930. Quain Student, University Coll., London, 1930–35; William Noble Fellow, University of Liverpool, 1935–36; Lecturer in English, University of the Witwatersrand, South Africa, 1936–45; Lecturer in English, 1945–46, Reader in English, 1946–54, UCL; Prof. of English, University of London (Westfield Coll.), 1954–67; Regius Prof. of Rhetoric and English Lit., Edinburgh Univ., 1967–71. Visiting Prof., Duke Univ., USA, 1957–58, Univ. of Oslo, 1974. Pres., Malone Soc., 1989– (Mem. Council, 1955–89). Hon. LittD Iona Coll., New Rochelle, NY, 1983. Shakespeare Prize, FVS Foundn, Hamburg, 1986. Jt Gen. Editor, Arden Shakespeare, 1958–82. *Publications:* The Life and Work of Henry Chettle, 1934; Edward Benlowes, 1952; The Structural Problem in Shakespeare's Henry IV, 1956; The Catastrophe in Shakespearean Tragedy, 1968; John Dover Wilson (British Acad. memoir), 1973; (ed) Hamlet (Arden edn), 1982; articles in Modern Language Review, Review of English Studies, The Library, Shakespeare Survey, Studies in Bibliography, etc. *Address:* 22 North Crescent, Finchley, N3 3LL. *Club:* Athenæum.

JENKINS, Hon. Dr Henry Alfred, AM 1991; retired; *b* 24 Sept. 1925; *s* of Henry Alfred Jenkins and Eileen Clare Jenkins (*née* McCormack); *m* 1951, Hazel Eileen Winter; three *s* one *d*. *Educ:* Ormond, Eltham and Heidelberg State Schools; Ivanhoe Grammar Sch.; Univ. of Melbourne (MSc, MB BS); Deakin Univ. (BA). Tutor, Univ. of Melbourne, 1946–52; RMO Alfred Hosp., 1953; Medical Practitioner, 1953–61; MLA (Lab) Reservoir Parliament of Victoria, 1961–69; MP (Lab) Scullin, Federal Parliament of Australia, 1969–85; Chm. of Committees and Dep. Speaker, House of Representatives, 1975–76, Speaker, 1983–85; Aust. Ambassador to Spain, 1986–88. *Recreations:* reading, hobby farming, community service. *Address:* 61 Mill Park Drive, Mill Park, Vic 3082, Australia. *Clubs:* Royal Automobile of Victoria, Melbourne Cricket.

JENKINS, Hugh Royston, FRICS, FPMI; Chief Executive, Prudential Portfolio Managers, and Director, Prudential Corporation, since 1989; *b* 9 Nov. 1933; *m* 1988, Mrs Beryl Kirk. *Educ:* Llanelli Grammar Sch.; National Service, Royal Artillery, 1954–56. Valuer, London County Council, 1956–62; Assistant Controller, 1962–68, Managing Director, 1968–72, Coal Industry (Nominees) Ltd; Dir Gen. of Investments, NCB, 1972–85. Vice Chm., National Assoc. of Pension Funds, 1979–80; Chief Exec. Officer, Heron Financial Corp., 1985–86; Gp Investment Dir, Allied Dunbar Assce, 1986–89; Dep. Chm. and Chief Exec., Allied Dunbar Unit Trusts, 1986–89; Chm., Dunbar Bank, 1988–89; Chm. and Chief Exec., Allied Dunbar Asset Management, 1987–89; Director: Unilever Pensions Ltd, 1985–89; IBM Pensions Trust PLC, 1985–89; Heron International, 1985–89. Chm., Property Adv. Gp, DoE, 1990–; Mem., The City Capital Markets Cttee, 1982; Lay Mem. of the Stock Exchange, 1984–85. *Recreation:* golf. *Address:* (office) 1 Stephen Street, W1P 2AP. *Club:* Garrick.

JENKINS, Dr Ivor, CBE 1970; FEng 1979; freelance Consultant, since 1979; Group Director of Research, Delta Metal Co. Ltd, 1973–78; Managing Director, 1973–77, Deputy Chairman, 1977–78, Delta Materials Research Ltd; *b* 25 July 1913; *m* 1941, Caroline Wijnanda James; two *s*. *Educ:* Gowerton Grammar Sch.; Univ. of Wales, Swansea. BSc, MSc, DSc; Hon. Fellow, UC Swansea, 1986. Bursar, GEC Research Labs, Wembley, 1934; Mem. Scientific Staff, GEC, 1935; Dep. Chief Metallurgist, Whitehead Iron & Steel Co., Newport, Mon, 1944; Head of Metallurgy Dept, 1946, Chief Metallurgist, 1952, GEC, Wembley; Dir of Research, Manganese Bronze Holdings Ltd, and Dir, Manganese Bronze Ltd, 1961–69; Dir of Research, Delta Metal Co., and Dir, Delta Metal (BW) Ltd, 1969–73. Vis. Prof., Univ. of Surrey, 1978–. FIM 1948 (Pres. 1965–66); Fellow, Amer. Soc. of Metals, 1974; Pres., Inst. of Metals, 1968–69; Mem., Iron and Steel Inst., 1937– (Williams Prize, 1946). Platinum medallist, Metals Soc., 1978. *Publications:* Controlled Atmospheres for the Heat Treatment of Metals, 1946; contribs to learned jls at home and abroad on metallurgical and related subjects. *Recreations:* music, gardening, swimming. *Address:* 31 Trotyn Croft, Aldwick Felds, Aldwick, Bognor Regis, Sussex PO21 3TX. *T:* Bognor Regis (0243) 828749. *Clubs:* Athenæum, Anglo-Belgian.

JENKINS, (James) Christopher, CB 1987; Second Parliamentary Counsel, since 1991 (Parliamentary Counsel, 1978–91); *b* 20 May 1939; *s* of Percival Si Phillips Jenkins and Dela (*née* Griffiths); *m* 1962, Margaret Elaine Edwards, *yr d* of Rt Hon. L. John Edwards and Dorothy (*née* Watson); two *s* one *d*. *Educ:* Lewes County Grammar Sch.; Magdalen Coll., Oxford. Solicitor, 1965. Joined Office of Parly Counsel, 1967; at Law Commn, 1970–72 and 1983–86. *Address:* 36 Whitehall, SW1. *Club:* United Oxford & Cambridge University.

JENKINS, Dame Jennifer; *see* Jenkins, Dame M. J.

JENKINS, John George, CBE 1971; farmer; *b* 26 Aug. 1919; *s* of George John Jenkins, OBE, FRCS and Alice Maud Jenkins, MBE; *m* 1948, Chloe Evelyn (*née* Kenward); one *s* three *d*. *Educ:* Winchester; Edinburgh University. Farmed in Scotland, 1939–62; farmed in England (Cambs and Lincs), 1957–. Pres., NFU of Scotland, 1960–61; Chm., Agricultural Marketing Development Exec. Cttee, 1967–73. Chm., United Oilseeds Ltd, 1984–87; Director: Childerley Estates Ltd, 1957–; Agricultural Mortgage Corporation Ltd, 1968–90. Compère, Anglia Television programme Farming Diary, 1963–80. *Publications:* contrib. Proc. Royal Soc., RSA Jl, etc. *Recreations:* tennis, bridge, music and the arts generally. *Address:* Childerley Hall, Dry Drayton, Cambridge CB3 8BB. *T:* Madingley (0954) 210271. *Club:* Farmers'.

JENKINS, John Owen, MBE 1978; FCSP; Chartered Physiotherapist; Senior Lecturer, St Mary's Hospital School of Physiotherapy, W2, 1975–88 (Lecturer, 1959); *b* 4 Nov. 1922; *s* of late J. O. Jenkins, JP, and M. E. Jenkins, Great House, Dilwyn, Hereford; *m* 1953, Catherine MacFarlane Baird, MCSP; three *d*. *Educ:* Worcester College for the Blind; NIB School of Physiotherapy, London. TMMG, TET, FCSP 1990. Chartered Society of Physiotherapy: Mem. Council, 1952–81; Chm., Finance and Gen. Purposes Cttee, 1955–79; Member: Education Cttee, 1953–71; Executive Cttee, 1955–79; Trustee, Members' Benevolent Fund, 1955–. CSP Examiner, 1954–88; Pres., Orgn of Chartered Physiotherapists in Private Practice, 1980–86. Physiotherapy Representative: Min. of Health Working Party on Statutory Registration, 1954; Council for Professions Supplementary to Medicine, 1961–76; Chm., Physiotherapists' Board, 1962–76. Director, LAMPS, 1969–, Chm., 1980–87, Pres., 1988–; Trustee, Moira Pakenham-Walsh Foundn, 1978–. Churchwarden, St James the Great, N20, 1974–81. *Publications:* contribs to Physiotherapy and Rehabilitation. *Recreations:* chess, rowing. *Address:* Fintray, 8 Ravensdale Avenue, N12 9HS. *T:* 081–445 6072.

JENKINS, John Robin; *b* Cambuslang, Lanarks, 11 Sept. 1912; *s* of late James Jenkins and of Annie Robin; *m* 1937, Mary McIntyre Wyllie; one *s* two *d*. *Educ:* Hamilton Academy; Glasgow Univ. (MA Hons). *Publications:* (as Robin Jenkins) Happy for the Child, 1953; The Thistle and the Grail, 1954; The Cone-Gatherers, 1955; Guests of War, 1956; The Missionaries, 1957; The Changeling, 1958; Some Kind of Grace, 1960; Dust on the Paw, 1961; The Tiger of Gold, 1962; A Love of Innocence, 1963; The Sardana Dancers, 1964; A Very Scotch Affair, 1968; The Holy Tree, 1969; The Expatriates, 1971; A Toast to the Lord, 1972; A Far Cry from Bowmore, 1973; A Figure of Fun, 1974; A Would-be Saint, 1978; Fergus Lamont, 1979; The Awakening of George Darroch, 1985; Just Duffy, 1988; Poverty Castle, 1991. *Recreations:* travel, golf. *Address:* Fairhaven, Toward, by Dunoon, Argyll PA23 7UE. *T:* Toward (036987) 288.

JENKINS, Katharine Mary; Director, Personnel, Royal Mail, since 1989; *b* 14 Feb. 1945; *d* of Daniel Jenkins and Nell Jenkins; *m* 1967, Euan Sutherland; one *s* one *d*. *Educ:* South Hampstead High Sch.; St Anne's Coll., Oxford (BA Hons); London School of Economics (MScEcon). Called to Bar, Inner Temple, 1971. Asst Principal, 1968, Principal, 1973, Dept of Employment; Central Policy Review Staff, 1976; Asst Sec., Dept of Employment, 1979; Dep. Head of Efficiency Unit, 1984; Hd, Prime Minister's Efficiency Unit, and Under Sec., Cabinet Office, 1986–89. Dir, London and Manchester Gp, 1989–. Mem., W Lambeth HA, 1990–. Mem., Ct of Governors, LSE, 1990–; Governor, Alleyn's Sch., Dulwich, 1990–. *Publications:* reports: Making Things Happen: the implementation of government scrutinies, 1985; Improving Management in Government: the next steps, 1988. *Address:* c/o Royal Mail, Royal Mail House, 148–166 Old Street, EC1V 9HQ. *T:* 071–250 2485.

JENKINS, Dame (Mary) Jennifer, (Lady Jenkins of Hillhead), DBE 1985; Member of Council, National Trust, since 1985 (Chairman, 1986–90); *b* 18 Jan. 1921; *d* of late Sir Parker Morris; *m* 1945, Baron Jenkins of Hillhead, *qv*; two *s* one *d*. *Educ:* St Mary's Sch., Calne; Girton Coll., Cambridge. Chm., Cambridge Univ. Labour Club. With Hoover Ltd, 1942–43; Min. of Labour, 1943–46; Political and Economic Planning (PEP), 1946–48; part-time extra-mural lectr, 1949–61; part-time teacher, Kingsway Day Coll., 1961–67. Chm., Consumers' Assoc., 1965–76; Historic Buildings Council for England, 1975–84; Member: Exec. Bd, British Standards Instn, 1970–73; Design Council, 1971–74; Cttee of Management, Courtauld Inst., 1981–84; Ancient Monuments Bd, 1982–84; Historic Buildings and Monuments Commn, 1984–85 (Chm., Historic Buildings Adv. Cttee, 1984–85); Pres., Ancient Monuments Soc., 1985– (Sec., 1972–75). Chm., N Kensington Amenity Trust, 1974–77. Trustee, Wallace Collection, 1977–83. Director: J. Sainsbury Ltd, 1981–86; Abbey National plc (formerly Abbey National Building Soc.), 1984–91. Freeman, City of London, 1980; Liveryman, Goldsmiths' Co. JP London Juvenile Courts, 1964–74. Hon. FRIBA, Hon. FRICS, Hon. MRTPI. Hon. LLD: London, 1988; Bristol, 1990; DUniv York, 1990. *Address:* 2 Kensington Park Gardens, W11; St Amand's House, East Hendred, Oxon.

JENKINS, Michael Nicholas Howard, OBE 1991; Chief Executive, London International Financial Futures Exchange, since 1981; *b* 13 Oct. 1932; *s* of C. N. and M. E. S. Jenkins; *m* 1957, Jacqueline Frances Jones; three *s*. *Educ:* Tonbridge School; Merton College, Oxford (MA Jurisp.). Shell-Mex & BP, 1956–61; IBM UK, 1961–67; Partner, Robson, Morrow, Management Consultants, 1967–71; Technical Dir, Stock Exchange, 1971–77; Man. Dir, European Options Exchange, Amsterdam, 1977–79. *Recreations:* games, classical music and jazz, furniture making. *Address:* London International Financial Futures Exchange, The Royal Exchange, EC3V 3PJ. *T:* 071–623 0444. *Club:* Wildernesse (Sevenoaks).

JENKINS, Sir Michael (Romilly Heald), KCMG 1990 (CMG 1984); HM Diplomatic Service; Ambassador to the Netherlands, since 1988; *b* 9 Jan. 1936; *s* of Prof. Romilly Jenkins and Celine Juliette Haeglar; *m* 1968, Maxine Louise Hodson; one *s* one *d*. *Educ:* privately; King's Coll., Cambridge (Exhibr, BA). Entered Foreign (subseq. Diplomatic) Service, 1959; served in Paris, Moscow and Bonn; Deputy Chef de Cabinet, 1973–75, Chef de Cabinet, 1975–76, to Rt Hon. George Thomson, EEC; Principal Advr to Mr Roy Jenkins, Pres. EEC, Jan–Aug. 1977; Head of European Integration Dept (External), FCO, 1977–79; Hd of Central Adv. Gp, EEC, 1979–81; Dep. Sec. Gen., Commn of the Eur. Communities, 1981–83; Asst Under Sec. of State (Europe), FCO, 1983–85; Minister, Washington, 1985–87. *Publications:* Arakcheev, Grand Vizier of the Russian Empire, 1969; contrib. History Today. *Address:* c/o Foreign and Commonwealth Office, SW1. *Clubs:* Athenæum, MCC.

JENKINS, Sir Owain (Trevor), Kt 1958; *b* 1907; 5th *s* of late Sir John Lewis Jenkins, KCSI, ICS; *m* 1940, Sybil Léonie, *y d* of late Maj.-Gen. Lionel Herbert, CB, CVO. *Educ:* Charterhouse; Balliol Coll., Oxford. Employed by Balmer Lawrie & Co. Ltd, Calcutta, 1929; Indian Army, 1940–44; Man. Dir, Balmer Lawrie, 1948–58. Pres. of the Bengal Chamber of Commerce and Industry and Pres. of the Associated Chambers of Commerce of India, 1956–57. Formerly Director: Singapore Traction Co.; Calcutta Electric Supply Corp.; Macleod Russel PLC; retd 1982. Mem., Econ. Survey Mission to Basutoland, Bechuanaland Protectorate and Swaziland, 1959. *Publication:* Merchant Prince (memoirs), 1987. *Address:* Boles House, East Street, Petworth, West Sussex GU28 0AB. *Club:* Oriental.

JENKINS, Peter; Associate Editor and Political Columnist, The Independent, since 1987; *b* 11 May 1934; *s* of Kenneth E. Jenkins and Joan E. Jenkins (*née* Croger); *m* 1st, 1960, Charlotte Strachey (decd); one *d*; 2nd, 1970, Polly Toynbee, *qv*; one *s* two *d*. *Educ:* Culford Sch.; Trinity Hall, Cambridge (BA Hist., MA). Journalist, Financial Times, 1958–60; The Guardian: Journalist, 1960; Labour Correspondent, 1963–67; Washington Correspondent, 1972–74; Political Commentator and Policy Editor, 1974–85; Political columnist, The Sunday Times, 1985–87. Theatre Critic, The Spectator, 1978–81. First stage play, Illuminations, performed at Lyric, Hammersmith, 1980; TV series, Struggle, 1983. Vis. Fellow, Nuffield Coll., Oxford, 1980–87. Awards include: Granada TV Journalist of the Year, 1978. *Publications:* The Battle of Downing Street, 1970; Mrs Thatcher's Revolution, 1987. *Address:* 1 Crescent Grove, SW4 7AF. *T:* 071–622 6492. *Club:* Garrick.

JENKINS, Peter White; management consultant; *b* 12 Oct. 1937; *s* of John White Jenkins, OBE, and Dorothy Jenkins; *m* 1961, Joyce Christine Muter; one *s* one *d*. *Educ:* Queen Mary's Grammar Sch., Walsall; King Edward VI Grammar Sch., Nuneaton. CIPFA. Local govt service in Finance Depts at Coventry, Preston, Chester, Wolverhampton; Dep. Treasurer, Birkenhead, 1969–73; County Treasurer, Merseyside CC, 1973–84; Dir. of Finance, Welsh Water Authority, 1984–87. *Recreations:* walking, gardening, reading. *Address:* 9 Camden Crescent, Brecon, Powys LD3 7BY.

JENKINS, Richard Peter Vellacott; His Honour Judge Richard Jenkins; a Circuit Judge, since 1989; *b* 10 May 1943; *s* of late Gwynne Jenkins and of Irene Lilian Jenkins;

m 1975, Agnes Anna Margaret Mullan; one *s* one *d*. *Educ:* Edge Grove School, Aldenham; Radley College; Trinity Hall, Cambridge (MA). Called to the Bar, Inner Temple, 1966; Midland Circuit, 1968–72; Midland and Oxford Circuit, 1972–89 (Remembrancer and Asst Treasurer, 1984–89); a Recorder, 1988–89. *Address:* Hall Barn, Far End, Boothby Graffoe, Lincoln LN5 0LG. *Clubs:* MCC, London Welsh Rugby Football.

JENKINS, Robin; *see* Jenkins, J. R.

JENKINS, Simon David; Editor, The Times, since 1990; *b* 10 June 1943; *s* of Dr Daniel Jenkins and Nell Jenkins; *m* 1978, Gayle Hunnicutt; one *s* and one step *s*. *Educ:* Mill Hill Sch.; St John's Coll., Oxford (BA Hons). Country Life magazine, 1965; Research Asst, Univ. of London Inst. of Educn, 1966; News Editor, Times Educational Supplement, 1966–68; Evening Standard, 1968–74; Insight Editor, Sunday Times, 1974–75; Dep. Editor, Evening Standard, 1976, Editor, 1976–78; Political Editor, The Economist, 1979–86; The Sunday Times: columnist, 1986–90; editor, Books Section, 1988–89. Member: British Railways Bd, 1979–90 (Chm., BR Environment Panel, 1984–90); LRT Bd, 1984–86; South Bank Bd, 1985–90. Director: Municipal Journal Ltd, 1980–90; Faber & Faber, 1980–90. Mem. Council, Bow Group, and Editor of Crossbow, 1968–70; Member: Cttee Save Britain's Heritage, 1976–85; Historic Buildings and Monuments Commn, 1985–90 (Dep. Chm., 1988–90); Mem. Council: Inst. of Contemporary Arts, 1976–85; Old Vic Co., 1979–81; Dep. Chm., Thirties Soc., 1979–85; Founder and Dir, Railway Heritage Trust, 1985–. Mem., Calcutt Cttee on Privacy, 1989–90; Grade Cttee on Fear of Crime, 1989. Governor: Mus. of London, 1985–87; Wycombe Abbey Sch., 1985–90; Bryanston Sch., 1986–. What The Papers Say Journalist of the Year, 1988. *Publications:* A City at Risk, 1971; Landlords to London, 1974; (ed) Insight on Portugal, 1975; Newspapers: the power and the money, 1979; The Companion Guide to Outer London, 1981; (with Max Hastings) The Battle for the Falklands, 1983; Images of Hampstead, 1983; (with Anne Sloman) With Respect Ambassador, 1985; The Market for Glory, 1986. *Recreation:* living in London. *Address:* c/o The Times, Pennington Street, E1. *Club:* Garrick.

JENKINS, Stanley Kenneth; HM Diplomatic Service, retired; *b* 25 Nov. 1920; *s* of Benjamin and Ethel Jane Jenkins; *m* 1957, Barbara Mary Marshall Webb; four *d*. *Educ:* Brecon; Cardiff Tech. Coll. President, Nat. Union of Students, 1949–51. LIOB 1950. Served War, Royal Artillery and Royal Engineers, 1942–46, retiring as Major. Joined Foreign (later Diplomatic) Service, 1951; Singapore, 1953; Kuala Lumpur, 1955; FO, 1957; Singapore, 1959; Rangoon, 1959; FO, 1964; Nicosia, 1967; FO, 1970–78, Counsellor. Chm., Ferring Sports and Leisure Assoc., 1988–. *Recreations:* gardening, tennis. *Address:* Willow Cottage, 1 Beehive Lane, Ferring, Worthing, Sussex BN12 5NL. *T:* Worthing (0903) 47356. *Club:* Commonwealth Trust.

JENKINS, Lt-Col Stephen Reginald Martin, MC 1944; farmer; Vice Lord-Lieutenant for Gloucestershire, since 1989; *b* 4 Feb. 1915; *o c* of late Capt. William Reginald Haldane Jenkins and Isabel Mary (*née* Osborne); *m* 1943, Elizabeth, *d* of Rev. A. W. Napier; two *s* two *d*. *Educ:* Eton; RMA Sandhurst; RAC, Cirencester. Commnd 4th/7th Royal Dragoon Guards, 1935; psc; Lt-Col 1954; retd 1956; Lt-Col RARO. Mem., later Alderman, Glos CC, 1964–74. DL 1969, High Sheriff 1975–76, Glos. *Address:* Hampnett Manor, Northleach, Cheltenham, Glos GL54 3NW.

JENKINS, Very Rev. Thomas Edward; *b* 14 Aug. 1902; *s* of late David Jenkins, Canon of St David's Cathedral and Vicar of Abergwili, and of Florence Helena Jenkins; *m* 1928, Annie Laura, *d* of late David Henry, Penygroes, Carms; one *s*. *Educ:* Llandyssul Grammar Sch.; St David's Coll., Lampeter; Wycliffe Hall, Oxford. St David's Coll., Lampeter, BA 1922, BD 1932, Powys Exhibitioner, 1924; Welsh Church Scholar, 1921. Ordained, 1925; Curate of Llanelly, 1925–34; Rector of Begelly, 1934–38; Vicar: Christ Church, Llanelly, 1938–46; Lampeter, 1946–55 (Rural Dean, 1949–54); Canon, St David's Cathedral, 1951–57; Vicar of Cardigan, 1955–57; Dean of St David's, 1957–72. *Address:* 18 North Road, Cardigan, Dyfed SA43 1AA.

JENKINS, Thomas Harris, (Tom), CBE 1981; General Secretary, Transport Salaried Staffs' Association, 1977–82; *b* 29 Aug. 1920; *s* of David Samuel Jenkins and Miriam Hughes (*née* Harris); *m* 1946, Joyce Smith; two *d*. *Educ:* Port Talbot Central Boys' Sch.; Port Talbot County Sch.; Shrewsbury Technical Coll. (evenings); Pitmans Coll., London (evenings). MCIT 1980. Served War, RAMC, 1941–46 (Certif. for Good Service, Army, Western Comd, 1946). Railway clerk, 1937–41; railway/docks clerk, 1946–49. Full-time service with Railway Clerks' Assoc., subseq. re-named Transport Salaried Staffs' Assoc., 1949–82: Southern Reg. Divl Sec., 1959; Western Reg. Divl Sec., 1963; LMR Divl Sec., 1966; Sen. Asst Sec., 1968; Asst Gen. Sec., 1970, also Dep. to Gen. Sec., 1973. Member: Cttee of Transport Workers in European Community, 1976–82; Transport Industry, Nationalised Industries, and Hotel and Catering Industry Cttees of TUC, 1977–82; Management and Indus. Relns Cttee, SSRC, 1979–81; Air Transport and Travel Industry Trng Bd, 1976–82; Hotel and Catering Industry Trng Bd, 1978–82; Employment Appeal Tribunal, 1982–91; British Railways Midland and NW Reg. Bd, 1982–86; Police Complaints Bd, 1983–85; Central Arbitration Cttee, 1983–90; ACAS Arbitration Bd, 1983–90. Mem. Labour Party, 1946–; Mem., Lab. Party Transport Sub-Cttee, 1970–82. *Recreations:* watching cricket, athletics and Rugby football. *Address:* 23 The Chase, Edgware, Middx HA8 5DW. *T:* 081–952 5314. *Clubs:* MCC, Middlesex County Cricket.
See also D. C. Jenkins.

JENKINS, Vivian Evan, MBE 1945; Director of Social Services, Cardiff City Council, 1971–74, retired; *b* 12 Sept. 1918; *s* of late Arthur Evan Jenkins and late Mrs Blodwen Jenkins; *m* 1946, Megan Myfanwy Evans; one *s* one *d*. *Educ:* UC Cardiff (BA). Dipl. Social Science. Army, 1940; commnd Royal Signals, 1943; served with 6th Airborne Div. as parachutist, Europe, Far East and Middle East, 1943–46 (Lieut). Child Care Officer, Glamorgan CC, 1949; Asst Children's Officer, 1951; Mem. Home Office Children's Dept Inspectorate, 1952. *Recreations:* Rugby football (former Captain of Univ. XV and Pontypridd RFC; awarded two Wales Rugby caps as schoolboy, 1933 and 1937); cricket, golf. *Address:* 24 Windsor Road, Radyr, Cardiff CF4 8BQ. *T:* Radyr (0222) 842485. *Club:* Radyr Golf.

JENKINSON, Dr David Stewart, FRS 1991; Lawes Trust Fellow, Rothamsted Experimental Station, since 1988; Visiting Professor, University of Reading, since 1992; *b* 25 Feb. 1928; *s* of Hugh McLoughlin Jenkinson and Isabel Frances (*née* Glass); *m* 1958, Moira O'Brien; three *s* one *d*. *Educ:* Armagh Royal Sch.; Trinity Coll., Dublin (BA 1950; BSc 1950; PhD 1954). MRSC 1955. Asst Lectr, Univ. of Reading, 1955–57; on scientific staff, Rothamsted Exptl Station, 1957–88. Hannaford Res. Fellow, Univ. of Adelaide, 1976–77; Vis. Scientist, CSIRO, 1977. Lectures: Hannaford, Univ. of Adelaide, 1977; Distinguished Scholars, QUB, 1989. *Publications:* Nitrogen Efficiency in Agricultural Soils, 1988; numerous papers in jls of soil science, soil biochemistry and agronomy. *Recreations:* Irish history and literature, low input gardening. *Address:* 15 Topstreet Way, Harpenden, Herts AL5 5TU. *T:* Harpenden (0582) 715744.

JENKINSON, Jeffrey Charles, MVO 1977; Chief Executive, Property, since 1987, and Board Member, since 1982, Port of London Authority; *b* 22 Aug. 1939; *s* of John Jenkinson and late Olive May Jenkinson; *m* 1962, Janet Ann (*née* Jarrett); one *s* two *d*. *Educ:* Royal Liberty Sch., Romford; City of London Coll. MCIT, MBIM. National Service, RN, 1957–59. Port of London Authority: Port operations and gen. management, 1959–71; British Transport Staff Coll., 1972; PLA Sec., 1972–81; Dir of Admin, 1982–86; Dir, Placon Ltd and other PLA gp subsid. cos, 1978–. Mem. Bd, London Chamber of Commerce and Industry Council, 1989– (Mem., 1985–); Chm., London and Reg. Affairs Cttee, 1989–; Dir, E London Small Business Centre Ltd, 1977–; Chm., Thames Riparian Housing Assoc., 1986–; Member: Newham CHC, 1974–80; Committee of Management: Seamen's Gp of Hosps, 1972–74; Seamen's Hosp. Soc., 1974–. Freeman, City of London, 1975; Mem. Ct, Co. of Watermen and Lightermen of River Thames, 1990–. *Recreations:* sailing, walking, music. *Address:* Port of London Authority, International House, World Trade Centre, St Katharine's Way, E1 9UN. *T:* 071–481 1954.

JENKINSON, Sir John (Banks), 14th Bt *cr* 1661; *b* 16 Feb. 1945; *o s* of Sir Anthony Banks Jenkinson, 13th Bt and of Frances, *d* of Harry Stremmel; *S* father, 1989; *m* 1979, Josephine Mary Marshall-Andrew; one *s* one *d*. *Educ:* Eton; Univ. of Miami. *Heir:* *s* George Samuel Anthony Banks Jenkinson, *b* 8 Nov. 1980.

JENKS, Sir Richard Atherley, 2nd Bt, *cr* 1932; *b* 26 July 1906; *er s* of Sir Maurice Jenks, 1st Bt, and Martha Louise Christabel, *d* of late George Calley Smith; *S* father 1946; *m* 1932, Marjorie Suzanne Arlette, *d* of late Sir Arthur du Cros, 1st Bt; two *s*. *Educ:* Charterhouse. Chartered Accountant, retired. *Heir:* *s* Maurice Arthur Brian Jenks [*b* 28 Oct. 1933; *m* 1962, Susan, *e d* of Leslie Allen, Surrey; one *d*]. *Address:* 42 Sussex Square, W2 2SP. *T:* 071–262 8356.

JENKYNS, Henry Leigh; Under-Secretary, Department of the Environment, 1969–75; *b* 20 Jan. 1917; *y s* of H. H. Jenkyns, Indian Civil Service; *m* 1947, Rosalind Mary Home; two *s* one *d*. *Educ:* Eton and Balliol Coll., Oxford. War Service in Royal Signals; Lt-Col, East Africa Command, 1944. Treasury, 1945–66; Private Sec. to Chancellor, 1951–53. Treasury Representative in Australia and New Zealand, 1953–56; UK Delegation to OECD, Paris, 1961–63; Asst Under-Sec. of State, DEA, 1966–69; Chm., SE Economic Planning Bd, 1968–71. Mem., Southwark Diocesan Adv. Cttee for Care of Churches, 1977–78. Mem., Exmoor Study Team, 1977. *Recreations:* music, garden, sailing, mending things. *Address:* Westcroft, Priors Hill Road, Aldeburgh, Suffolk IP15 5EP. *T:* Aldeburgh (0728) 452357.

JENNER, Ann Maureen; Director, National Theater Ballet School, Melbourne, since 1988 (Associate Director, 1987); Guest Ballet Teacher, since 1980: Victorian College of the Arts, Melbourne; Australian Ballet; Queensland Ballet; and many other schools in Sydney and Melbourne; *b* 8 March 1944; *d* of Kenneth George Jenner and Margaret Rosetta (*née* Wilson); *m* 1980, Dale Robert Baker; one *s*. *Educ:* Royal Ballet Junior and Senior Schools. Royal Ballet Co., 1961–78: Soloist 1964; Principal Dancer 1970. Australian Ballet, 1978–80. Roles include: Lise, Fille Mal Gardée, 1966; Swanhilda, Coppelia, 1968; Cinderella, 1969; Princess Aurora, Sleeping Beauty, 1972; Giselle, 1973; Gypsy, Deux Pigeons, 1974; White Girl, Deux Pigeons, 1976; Juliet, Romeo and Juliet, 1977; Countess Larisch, Mayerling, 1978; Flavia, Spartacus, 1979; Kitri, Don Quixote, 1979; Anna, Anna Karenina, 1980; Poll, Pineapple Poll, 1980; one-act roles include: Symphonic Variations, 1967; Firebird, 1972; Triad, 1973; Les Sylphides; Serenade; Les Patineurs; Elite Syncopations, Concert, Flower Festival Pas de Deux, etc. Guest Teacher, San Francisco Ballet Co. and San Francisco Ballet Sch., 1985. *Address:* National Theater Ballet School, corner of Carlisle and Barkly Street, St Kilda, Melbourne, Vic 3182, Australia.

JENNETT, Frederick Stuart, CBE 1985; consultant architect and town planner in own firm, since 1990; *b* 22 April 1924; *s* of Horace Frederick Jennett and Jenny Sophia Jennett; *m* 1948, Nada Eusebia Phillips; two *d*. *Educ:* Whitchurch Grammar School; Welsh School of Architecture, UWIST (Dip. in Architecture (dist.)). FRIBA, MRTPI, FRSA. T. Alwyn Lloyd & Gordon, Architects, Cardiff, 1949; Cwmbran Develt Corp., 1951; Louis de Soissons Peacock Hodges & Robinson, Welwyn Garden City, 1955; S. Colwyn Foukes & Partners, Colwyn Bay, 1956; Associate, 1962, Partner, 1964, Sir Percy Thomas & Son, Bristol; Chm. and Sen. Partner, Percy Thomas Partnership, 1971–89; Consultant to Studio BAAD, architects, Hebden Bridge, 1990–. Experience ranges over new town neighbourhood planning, public housing and private houses; ecclesiastical, university and hospital projects in the UK and overseas, and refurbishment of historic/listed buildings. *Publications:* papers on hospital planning. *Recreations:* running, water colour painting, hill walking. *Address:* Portland Lodge, Lower Almondsbury, Bristol BS12 4EJ. *T:* Almondsbury (0454) 615175. *Clubs:* Reform, Royal Over-Seas League.

JENNETT, Prof. (William) Bryan, FRCS; Professor of Neurosurgery, University of Glasgow, since 1968 (Dean of the Faculty of Medicine, 1981–86); *b* 1 March 1926; *s* of Robert William Jennett and Jessie Pate Loudon; *m* 1950, Sheila Mary Pope; three *s* one *d*. *Educ:* Univ. of Liverpool (MB ChB 1949, MD 1960). House Physician to Lord Cohen of Birkenhead, 1949; Ho. Surg. to Sir Hugh Cairns, 1950; Surgical Specialist, RAMC, 1951–53; Registrar in Neurosurgery, Oxford and Cardiff, 1954–56; Lectr in Neurosurgery, Univ. of Manchester, 1957–62; Rockefeller Travelling Fellow, Univ. of California, LA, 1958–59; Cons. Neurosurgeon, Glasgow, 1963–68. Member: MRC, 1979–83; GMC, 1984–; Chief Scientists' Cttee, 1983–; Inst. of Med. Ethics, 1986–. Mem. Ct, Univ. of Glasgow, 1988–. Rock Carling Fellow, London, 1983. *Publications:* Epilepsy after Blunt Head Injury, 1962, 2nd edn 1975; Introduction to Neurosurgery, 1964, 4th edn 1983; (with G. Teasdale) Management of Head Injuries, 1981; High Technology Medicine: benefits and burdens, 1984, 2nd edn 1986; many papers in Lancet, BMJ and elsewhere. *Recreations:* cruising under sail, writing. *Address:* 83 Hughenden Lane, Glasgow G12 9XN. *T:* 041–334 5148. *Club:* Royal Society of Medicine.

JENNINGS, Sir Albert (Victor), Kt 1969; Founder and Chairman, Jennings Industries Ltd (formerly A. V. Jennings (Australia) Ltd), 1932–72; *b* 12 Oct. 1896; *s* of John Thomas Jennings; *m* 1922, Ethel Sarah, *d* of George Herbert Johnson; two *s*. *Educ:* Eastern Road Sch., Melbourne. Served First World War, AIF. Council Mem., Master Builders Assoc., 1943–; Vice Pres. Housing, Master Builders Fedn of Aust., 1970–71; Member: Commonwealth Building Research and Advisory Cttee, 1948–72; Manufacturing Industries Adv. Council to Australian Govt, 1962–; Decentralisation and Develt Adv. Cttee to Victorian State Govt, 1965–; Commonwealth of Aust. Metric Conversion Bd, 1970–72; Trustee, Cttee for Economic Develt of Australia. Fellow: Aust. Inst. of Building (Federal Pres., 1964–65 and 1965–66); UK Inst. of Building, 1971. Aust. Inst. of Building Medal 1970; Urban Land Inst. Total Community Develt Award, 1973; Sir Charles McGrath Award for Services to Marketing, 1976. *Recreations:* swimming, golf. *Address:* Ranelagh House, Rosserdale Crescent, Mount Eliza, Victoria 3930, Australia. *T:* 7871350. *Clubs:* Commonwealth (Canberra); Melbourne, Savage (Melbourne).

JENNINGS, Arnold Harry, CBE 1977; MA; Headmaster, Ecclesfield School, Sheffield, 1959–79 (formerly, 1959–67, Ecclesfield Grammar School); *b* 24 May 1915; *s* of Harry Jennings and Alice Mary (*née* Northrop); *m* 1939, Elizabeth Redman; one *s* one *d*. *Educ:* Bradford Grammar Sch.; Corpus Christi Coll., Oxford (Classical Schol.; MA). Tutor,

Knutsford Ordination Test Sch., Hawarden, 1939–40. Served War, Captain RA, England, N Ireland, France, Belgium, Holland and Germany, 1940–46. Sen. Classical Master, Chesterfield Grammar Sch., 1946–53; Headmaster, Tapton House Sch., Chesterfield, 1953–58; part-time extra-mural Lectr, Sheffield Univ., 1946–54. Mem., NUT Executive, 1958–59 and 1960–72 (Chm., Secondary Adv. Cttee, 1968–72); Secondary Heads Association: Hon Sec., 1978–79; Membership Sec., 1979–81; Hon. Mem., 1981–; President: Head Masters' Assoc., 1977; Jt Assoc. of Classical Teachers, 1975–77; Mem., Secondary Schs Examinations Council, 1961–64; Schools Council: Mem., 1964–84; Dep. Chm. and Acting Chm., 1982–84; Chm., Steering Cttee 'C', 1975–78; Chm., Second Examinations Cttee, 1968–76; Jt Chm., Jt Examinations Sub-Cttee, 1971–76; Chm., Exams Cttee, 1978–83; Chm., Classics Cttee; Convenor, A-level Classics Scrutiny Panel: Secondary Examinations Council, 1984–88; Sch. Exams and Assessment Council, 1988–89. Mem. Court, Sheffield Univ., 1959–78. Governor: Richmond Further Educn Coll., Sheffield, 1986–88; High Storrs Sch., Sheffield, 1988–; Stradbrooke Tertiary Coll., Sheffield, 1989–90. Sheffield City Councillor, 1949–58 (Mem., Sheffield Educn Cttee, 1988–91); contested (Lab) Heeley, Sheffield, 1950 and 1951. *Publications:* (ed) Management and Headship in the Secondary School, 1977; (ed) Discipline in Primary and Secondary Schools Today, 1979; articles on educn *passim*. *Recreations:* work, wine, opera, photography, travel. *Address:* 74 Clarkegrove Road, Sheffield S10 2NJ. *T:* Sheffield (0742) 662520.

JENNINGS, Audrey Mary; Metropolitan Stipendiary Magistrate, since 1972; *b* 22 June 1928; *d* of Hugh and late Olive Jennings, Ashbrook Range, Sunderland; *m* 1961, Roger Harry Kilbourne Frisby, *qv* (marr. diss. 1980); two *s* one *d*. *Educ:* Durham High Sch.; Durham Univ. (BA); Oxford Univ. (DPA). Children's Officer, City and County of Cambridge, 1952–56. Called to Bar, Middle Temple, 1956 (Harmsworth Schol.); practised at Criminal Bar, London, 1956–61 and 1967–72. Mem., Criminal Law Revision Cttee, 1977–. *Recreations:* theatre, music, gardening, writing short stories.

JENNINGS, Elizabeth (Joan); author; *b* 18 July 1926; *d* of Dr H. C. Jennings, Oxon. *Educ:* Oxford High Sch.; St Anne's Coll., Oxford. Asst at Oxford City Library, 1950–58; Reader for Chatto & Windus Ltd, 1958–60. *Publications: poetry:* Poems (Arts Council Prize), 1953; A Way of Looking, 1955 (Somerset Maugham Award, 1956); A Sense of the World, 1958; (ed) The Batsford Book of Children's Verse, 1958; Song for a Birth or a Death, 1961; a translation of Michelangelo's sonnets, 1961; Recoveries, 1964; The Mind Has Mountains, 1966 (Richard Hillary Prize, 1966); The Secret Brother (for children), 1966; Collected Poems, 1967; The Animals' Arrival, 1969 (Arts Council Bursary, 1969); (ed) A Choice of Christina Rossetti's Verse, 1970; Lucidities, 1970; Relationships, 1972; Growing Points, 1975; Consequently I Rejoice, 1977; After the Ark (for children), 1978; Selected Poems, 1980; Moments of Grace, 1980; (ed) The Batsford Book of Religious Verse, 1981; Celebrations and Elegies, 1982; In Praise of Our Lady (anthology), 1982; Extending the Territory, 1985; (contrib.) A Quintet (for children), 1985; Collected Poems, 1953–86, 1986 (W. H. Smith Award, 1987); Tributes, 1989; *prose:* Let's Have Some Poetry, 1960; Every Changing Shape, 1961; Robert Frost, 1964; Christianity and Poetry, 1965; Seven Men of Vision, 1976; also poems and articles in: New Statesman, New Yorker, Botteghe Oscure, Observer, Spectator, Listener, Vogue, The Independent, etc. *Recreations:* travel, looking at pictures, the theatre, the cinema, music, collecting, conversation. *Address:* c/o David Higham Associates Ltd, 5–8 Lower John Street, W1R 4HA. *Club:* Society of Authors.

JENNINGS, James, JP; Convener, Strathclyde Regional Council, 1986–90; *b* 18 Feb. 1925; *s* of late Mark Jennings and Janet McGrath; *m* 1st, 1943, Margaret Cook Barclay (decd); three *s* two *d*; 2nd, 1974, Margaret Mary Hughes, JP; two *d*. *Educ:* St Palladius School, Dalry; St Michael's College, Irvine. In steel industry, 1946–79. Member: Ayr County Council, 1958; Strathclyde Regional Council, 1974– (Vice-Convener, 1982–86); Chairman: Ayr CC Police and Law Cttee, 1964–70; Ayrshire Jt Police Cttee, 1970–75; N Ayrshire Crime Prevention Panel, 1970–82; Police and Fire Cttee, Strathclyde Regl Council, 1978–82, 1990–. Convention of Scottish Local Authorities: Rep. for Strathclyde, 1974–; Chm., Protective Services Cttee, 1977–82; Mem., Exec. Policy Cttee, 1982–. Chm., Official Side, Police Negotiating Bd, 1986–88 (Vice-Chm., 1984–86). Chm., Garnock Valley Develt Exec., 1988–. Contested (Lab) Perth and East Perthshire, 1966. Hon. Sheriff, 1990–. Vice-Pres., St Andrew's Ambulance Assoc.; Patron, Assoc. of Youth Clubs in Strathclyde; Hon. President: Scottish Retirement Council; Princess Louise Scottish Hosp. (Erskine Hosp.); Hon. Vice-President: SNO Chorus; Royal British Legion Scotland (Dalry and District Branch). JP Cunninghame, 1969 (Chm., Cunninghame Justices Cttee, 1974–). *Recreation:* local community involvement. *Address:* 4 Place View, Kilbirnie, Ayrshire KA25 6BG. *T:* Kilbirnie (0505) 3339. *Clubs:* Royal Scottish Automobile (Glasgow); Garnock Labour (Chairman).

JENNINGS, John Southwood, CBE 1985; PhD; Managing Director, Royal Dutch/Shell Group of Companies, since 1987; *b* 30 March 1937; *s* of George Southwood Jennings and Irene Beatrice Jennings; *m* 1961, Gloria Ann Griffiths; one *s* one *d*. *Educ:* Oldbury Grammar Sch.; Univ. of Birmingham (BSc Hons Geology, 1958); Univ. of Edinburgh (PhD Geology, 1961); London Business Sch. (Sloan Fellow, 1970–71). Various posts, Royal Dutch/Shell Group, 1962–, including: Gen. Man. and Chief Rep., Shell cos in Turkey, 1976–78; Man. Dir, Shell UK Exploration and Prodn, 1979–84; Exploration and Prodn Co-ordinator, Shell Internationale Petroleum Mij., The Hague, 1985–. Hon. DSc Edinburgh, 1991. Commandeur de l'Ordre National du Mérite (Gabon), 1989. *Recreations:* fly fishing, shooting, travel. *Address:* c/o Shell Centre, SE1 7NA. *T:* 071–934 5553. *Clubs:* Brooks's, Flyfishers'.

JENNINGS, Very Rev. Kenneth Neal; Dean of Gloucester, since 1983; *b* 8 Nov. 1930; *s* of Reginald Tinsley and Edith Dora Jennings; *m* 1972, Wendy Margaret Stallworthy; one *s* one *d*. *Educ:* Hertford Grammar School; Corpus Christi College, Cambridge (MA); Cuddesdon College, Oxford. Asst Curate, Holy Trinity, Ramsgate, 1956–59; Lecturer 1959–61, Vice-Principal 1961–66, Bishop's College, Calcutta; Vice-Principal, Cuddesdon Theological Coll., 1967–73; Vicar of Hitchin, 1973–76; Team Rector of Hitchin, 1977–82. *Recreations:* music, fell-walking. *Address:* The Deanery, Miller's Green, Gloucester GL1 2BP. *T:* Gloucester (0452) 24167.

JENNINGS, Percival Henry, CBE 1953; *b* 8 Dec. 1903; *s* of late Rev. Canon H. R. Jennings; *m* 1934, Margaret Katharine Musgrave, *d* of late Brig.-Gen. H. S. Rogers, CMG, DSO; three *d*. *Educ:* Christ's Hospital. Asst Auditor, N Rhodesia, 1927; Asst Auditor, Mauritius, 1931; Auditor, British Honduras, 1934; Dep. Dir of Audit, Gold Coast, 1938; Dep. Dir of Audit, Nigeria, 1945; Dir of Audit, Hong Kong, 1948; Dep. Dir-Gen. of the Overseas Audit Service, 1955; Dir-Gen. of the Overseas Audit Service, 1960–63, retd. *Recreation:* golf. *Address:* Littlewood, Lelant, St Ives, Cornwall. *T:* Hayle (0736) 753407. *Clubs:* Commonwealth Trust, Royal Over-Seas League.

JENNINGS, Rev. Peter; Superintendent Minister, Ilford Methodist Circuit, since 1991; *b* 9 Oct. 1937; *s* of Robert William Jennings and Margaret Irene Jennings; *m* 1963, Cynthia Margaret Leicester; two *s*. *Educ:* Manchester Grammar Sch.; Keble Coll., Oxford (MA); Hartley Victoria Methodist Theological Coll.; Manchester Univ. (MA). Ordained 1965. Minister: Swansea Methodist Circuit, 1963–67; London Mission (East) Circuit, 1967–78, and Tutor Warden, Social Studies Centre, 1967–74; Gen. Sec., Council of Christians and Jews, 1974–81; Associate Minister, Wesley's Chapel, 1978–81; Asst Minister, Walthamstow and Chingford Methodist Circuit, 1981–82; Supt Minister, Whitechapel Mission, 1982–91. Hon. Treasurer, London Rainbow Group; Mem., Exec. Cttee, London Soc. of Jews and Christians. *Publications:* papers and articles on aspects of Christian-Jewish relations. *Recreations:* photography, being educated by Tim and Nick. *Address:* Methodist Church, Ilford Lane, Ilford, Essex IG1 2JZ. *T:* 081–478 5630.

JENNINGS, Peter Nevile Wake; Deputy Serjeant at Arms, House of Commons, since 1982; *b* 19 Aug. 1934; *s* of late Comdr A. E. de B. Jennings, RN and Mrs V. Jennings, MBE; *m* 1958, Shirley Anne, *d* of late Captain B. J. Fisher, DSO, RN and Mrs C. C. Fisher; one *s* two *d*. *Educ:* Marlborough College; psc (m)†, osc (US). Commissioned 2/Lt, RM, 1952; service included: 40 and 42 Commandos, Canal Zone Egypt, Malta, 1954–55; Cruiser, HMS Birmingham, 1957–58; HQ 3 Commando Bde, Malta and Singapore, 1959–62; RM Poole, 1962–64; 41 Commando Bickleigh, 1964–65; Officers' Wing, CTC RM Lympstone, 1968–70, HQ Commando Forces, 1970–71; Chief Signals Officer RM, 1972–74; SACLANT, USA, 1974–76; retired as Major (own request). Appointed to staff of House of Commons, 1976. *Address:* House of Commons, SW1A 0AA.

JENNINGS, Sir Raymond (Winter), Kt 1968; QC 1945; Master, Court of Protection, 1956–70; *b* 12 Dec. 1897; *o s* of late Sir Arthur Oldham Jennings and Mabel Winter; *m* 1930, Sheila (*d* 1972), *d* of Selwyn S. Grant, OBE; one *s* one *d*. *Educ:* Rugby; RMC, Sandhurst; Oriel Coll., Oxford (MA, BCL). Served 1916–19 in Royal Fusiliers. Called to Bar, 1922; Bencher of Lincoln's Inn, 1951. *Recreation:* fishing. *Address:* 14C Upper Drive, Hove, East Sussex BN3 6GN. *T:* Brighton (0273) 773361. *Club:* Athenæum.

JENNINGS, Sir Robert (Yewdall), Kt 1982; QC 1969; MA, LLB Cantab; a Judge, since 1982, and President, since 1991, the International Court of Justice; *b* 19 Oct. 1913; *o s* of Arthur Jennings; *m* 1955, Christine, *yr d* of Bernard Bennett; one *s* two *d*. *Educ:* Belle Vue Grammar Sch., Bradford; Downing Coll., Cambridge (scholar; 1st cl. pts I & II Law Tripos; LLB; Hon. Fellow, 1982). Served War, Intelligence Corps, 1940–46; Hon. Major, Officers' AER. Called to the Bar, Lincoln's Inn, 1943 (Hon. Bencher, 1970). Whewell Scholar in Internat. Law, Cambridge, 1936; Joseph Hodges Choate Fellow, Harvard Univ., 1936–37; Asst Lectr in Law, LSE, 1938–39; Jesus College, Cambridge: Fellow, 1939, Hon. Fellow, 1982; Sen. Tutor, 1949–55; Sometime Pres. Whewell Prof. of Internat. Law, Cambridge Univ., 1955–81; Reader in Internat. Law, Council of Legal Educn, 1959–70. Member: Permanent Court of Arbitration, 1982–; Inst. of Internat. Law, 1967– (Vice-Pres., 1979; Pres., 1981–83; Hon. Mem., 1985–); Hon. Mem., Indian Soc. of Internat. Law; Hon. Life Mem., Amer. Soc. of Internat. Law. Hon. LLD Hull, 1987; Hon. Dr jur: Saarland, W Germany, 1988; La Sapienza, Rome, 1990. Joint Editor: International and Comparative Law Quarterly, 1956–61; British Year Book of International Law, 1960–82. *Publications:* The Acquisition of Territory, 1963; General Course on International Law, 1967; articles in legal periodicals. *Address:* Jesus College, Cambridge CB5 8BL. *T:* Cambridge (0223) 62611. *Club:* United Oxford & Cambridge University.

JENOUR, Sir (Arthur) Maynard (Chesterfield), Kt 1959; TD 1950; JP; Director: Aberthaw & Bristol Channel Portland Cement Co. Ltd, 1929–83 (Chairman and Joint Managing Director, 1946–83); T. Beynon & Co. Ltd, 1938–83 (Chairman and Joint Managing Director, 1946–83); Ruthin Quarries (Bridgend) Ltd, 1947–83 (Chairman, 1947–83); Associated Portland Cement Manufacturers Ltd, 1963–75; Blue Jacket Motel (Pty) Ltd, Australia, 1964; *b* 7 Jan. 1905; *s* of Brig.-Gen. A. S. Jenour, CB, CMG, DSO, Crossways, Chepstow and Emily Anna (*née* Beynon); *m* 1948, Margaret Sophie (who *m* 1927, W. O. Ellis Fielding-Jones, *d* 1935; three *d*), *d* of H. Stuart Osborne, Sydney, NSW. *Educ:* Eton. Entered business, 1924. Served War of 1939–45, in England and Middle East, Royal Artillery, Major. High Sheriff of Monmouthshire, 1951–52; Pres., Cardiff Chamber of Commerce, 1953–54; Chm. Wales & Mon. Industrial Estates Ltd, 1954–60; Mem. Board, Development Corporation for Wales, 1958–81. JP Mon 1946; DL Mon, 1960; Vice-Lieut of Mon, 1965–74, Vice Lord-Lieut of Gwent, 1974–79. KStJ 1969. *Recreations:* walking, gardening, shooting. *Address:* Stonycroft, 13 Ridgeway, Newport, Gwent NP9 5AF. *T:* Newport (0633) 263802. *Clubs:* Cardiff and County (Cardiff); Union (Sydney, NSW).

JEPHCOTT, Sir (John) Anthony, 2nd Bt *cr* 1962; *b* 21 May 1924; *s* of Sir Harry Jephcott, 1st Bt, and Doris (*d* 1985), *d* of Henry Gregory; *S* father, 1978; *m* 1st, 1949, Sylvia Mary, *d* of Thorsten Frederick Relling, Wellington, NZ; two *d*; 2nd, 1978, Josephine Agnes Sheridan. *Educ:* Aldenham; St John's Coll., Oxford; London School of Economics (BCom). Served with REME and RAEC, 1944–47. Director, Longworth Scientific Instrument Co. Ltd, 1946; Managing Director and Chairman, 1952–73; Managing Director and Chairman, Pen Medic Ltd (NZ), 1973–78. Hon. FFARACS 1990. *Publications:* A History of Longworth Scientific Instrument Co. Ltd, 1988; correspondence in Anaesthesia (UK), and Anaesthesia and Intensive Care (Australia). *Recreations:* gardening, photography. *Heir: b* Neil Welbourn Jephcott [*b* 3 June 1929; *m* 1st, 1951, Mary Denise (*d* 1977), *d* of Arthur Muddiman; two *s* one *d*; 2nd, 1978, Mary Florence Daly]. *Address:* 26 Sage Road, Kohimarama, Auckland 5, New Zealand.

JEREMIAH, Melvyn Gwynne; Under Secretary, Department of Health (formerly of Health and Social Security), since 1987; *b* 10 March 1939; *s* of Bryn Jeremiah and Evelyn (*née* Rogers); *m* 1960, Lilian Clare (*née* Bailey) (marr. diss. 1966). *Educ:* Abertillery County Sch. Apptd to Home Office, 1958; HM Customs and Excise, 1963–75; Cabinet Office, 1975–76; Treasury, 1976–79; Principal Finance Officer (Under Sec.), Welsh Office, 1979–87; Chief Exec., Disablement Services Authy, 1987–91, on secondment from DoH. Sec., Assoc. of First Div. Civil Servants, 1967–70. *Recreations:* work, people. *Club:* Reform.

JERNE, Prof. Niels Kaj, MD; FRS 1980; *b* London, 23 Dec. 1911; *s* of Hans Jessen Jerne and Else Marie (*née* Lindberg); *m* 1964, Ursula Alexandra (*née* Kohl); two *s*. *Educ:* Univ. of Leiden, Holland; Univ. of Copenhagen, Denmark (MD). Res. worker, Danish State Serum Inst., 1943–56; Res. Fellow, Calif Inst. of Technol., Pasadena, 1954–55; CMO for Immunology, WHO, Geneva, 1956–62; Prof. of Biophysics, Univ. of Geneva, 1960–62; Chm., Dept of Microbiology, Univ. of Pittsburgh, 1962–66; Prof. of Experimental Therapy, Johann Wolfgang Goethe Univ., Frankfurt, 1966–69; Director: Paul-Ehrlich-Institut, Frankfurt, 1966–69; Basel Inst. for Immunology, 1969–80. Prof., Pasteur Inst., Paris, 1981–82. Member: Amer. Acad. of Arts and Sciences, 1967; Royal Danish Acad. of Sciences, 1968; National Acad. of Sciences, USA, 1975; Amer. Philosophical Soc., 1979; Acad. des Scis de l'Institut de France, 1981; Yugoslav Acad. of Scis and Arts, 1986. DSc *hc*: Chicago, 1972; Columbia, 1978; Copenhagen, 1979; PhD *hc*: Basel, 1981; Weizmann Inst., Israel, 1985; MD *hc* Rotterdam, 1983. Nobel Prize for Physiology or Medicine, 1984. *Publications:* scientific papers on immunology in learned jls. *Address:* Château de Bellevue, Castillon-du-Gard 30210, France. *T:* 66/370075.

JEROME, Hon. James Alexander; PC (Can.) 1981; **Hon. Mr Justice Jerome;** Associate Chief Justice, Federal Court of Canada, since 1980; lawyer, since 1958; *b*

Kingston, Ont., 4 March 1933; *s* of Joseph Leonard Jerome and Phyllis Devlin; *m* 1958, Barry Karen Hodgins; three *s* two *d*. *Educ:* Our Lady of Perpetual Help Sch., Toronto; St Michael's Coll. High Sch., Toronto; Univ. of Toronto; Osgoode Hall. Alderman, Sudbury, Ont., 1966–67. MP, Sudbury, 1968–80; Parly Sec. to President of Privy Council, 1970–74; Speaker of the House of Commons, 1974–80. QC (Can.) 1976. Pres., Commonwealth Parly Assoc., 1976. *Recreations:* golf, piano. *Address:* 1051 Cahill Drive W, Ottawa, Ontario K1V 9J1, Canada. *T:* 737–2118.

JERRAM, Maj.-Gen. Richard Martyn, CB 1984; MBE 1960; retired 1984; *b* Bangalore, India, 14 Aug. 1928; *e s* of late Brig. R. M. Jerram, DSO, MC, and late Monica (*née* Gillies); *m* 1987, Susan (*née* Roberts), *widow* of John Naylor. *Educ:* Stubbington House; Marlborough Coll.; RMA, Sandhurst. Commissioned into Royal Tank Regt, 1948; served in 2, 3 or 4 RTRs, or in Staff appts in Hong Kong, Malaya (twice) (MBE), Libya, N Ireland, USA, Germany (four times), MoD (three times). Instr, Staff Coll., Camberley, 1964–67; CO 3 RTR, 1969–71; DRAC, 1981–84. Col Comdt, RTR, 1982–88. Comr, Cornwall SJAB, 1987–. *Recreations:* travel, countryside, literature, chess. *Address:* Trehane, Trevanson, Wadebridge, Cornwall PL27 7HP. *T:* Wadebridge (0208) 812523. *Club:* Army and Navy.

JERSEY, 9th Earl of, *cr* 1697; **George Francis Child Villiers;** Viscount Grandison (of Limerick), 1620; Viscount Villiers (of Dartford), and Baron Villiers (of Hoo), 1691; *b* 15 Feb. 1910; *e s* of 8th Earl and Lady Cynthia Almina Constance Mary Needham (who *m* 2nd, 1925, W. R. Slessor (*d* 1945); she died 1947), *o d* of 3rd Earl of Kilmorey; *S* father, 1923; *m* 1st, 1932, Patricia Kenneth (who obtained a divorce, 1937; she *m* 2nd, 1937, Robin Filmer Wilson, who *d* 1944; 3rd, 1953, Col Peter Laycock, who *d* 1977; 4th, 1987, Roderick More O'Ferrall, who *d* 1990), *o d* of Kenneth Richards, Cootamundra, NSW, and of late Eileen Mary (who *m* later Sir Stephenson Kent, KCB); one *d*; 2nd, 1937, Virginia (who obtained a divorce, 1946), *d* of James Cherrill, USA; 3rd, 1947, Bianca Maria Adriana Luciana, *er d* of late Enrico Mottironi, Turin, Italy; two *s* one *d*. *Heir: s* Viscount Villiers, *qv*. *Address:* Radier Manor, Longueville, Jersey, Channel Islands JE3 9DR. *T:* Jersey (0534) 53102.

JERSEY, Dean of; *see* O'Ferrall, Very Rev. B. A.

JERUSALEM AND THE MIDDLE EAST, President Bishop of; *see* Kafity, Rt Rev. Samir.

JERVIS, family name of **Viscount St Vincent.**

JERVIS, Charles Elliott, OBE 1966; Editor-in-Chief, Press Association, 1954–65; *b* Liverpool, 7 Nov. 1907; *y s* of late J. H. Jervis, Liverpool; *m* 1931, Ethel Braithwaite (*d* 1979), Kendal, Westmorland; one *d*. Editorial Asst, Liverpool Express, 1921–23; Reporter, Westmorland Gazette, 1923–28; Dramatic Critic and Asst Editor, Croydon Times, 1928–37; Sub-Editor, Press Assoc., 1937–47; Asst Editor, 1947–54. Pres., Guild of British Newspaper Editors, 1964–65; Mem. of the Press Council, 1960–65. *Address:* The Old Vicarage, Allithwaite, Grange-over-Sands, Cumbria.

JERVIS, Roger P.; *see* Parker-Jervis.

JERVIS, Simon Swynfen, FSA 1983; Director, Fitzwilliam Museum, Cambridge, since 1990; *b* 9 Jan. 1943; *s* of late John Swynfen Jervis and Diana (*née* Marriott); *m* 1969, Fionnuala MacMahon; one *s* one *d*. *Educ:* Downside Sch.; Corpus Christi Coll., Cambridge (schol.) Student Asst, Asst Keeper of Art, Leicester Mus. and Art Gall., 1964–66; Department of Furniture, Victoria and Albert Museum: Asst Keeper, 1966–75; Dep. Keeper, 1975–89; Actg Keeper, 1989; Curator, 1989–90. Guest Schol., J. Paul Getty Mus., 1988–89; Chm., Nat. Trust Arts Panel, 1987–. Editor, Furniture History, 1987–. FRSA 1990. *Publications:* Victorian Furniture, 1968; Printed Furniture Designs Before 1650, 1974; High Victorian Design, 1983; Penguin Dictionary of Design and Designers, 1984; many articles in learned jls. *Address:* Fitzwilliam Museum, Cambridge CB2 1RB. *T:* Cambridge (0223) 332900.

JESSEL, Sir Charles (John), 3rd Bt *cr* 1883; farmer; *b* 29 Dec. 1924; *s* of Sir George Jessel, 2nd Bt, MC, and Muriel (*d* 1948), *d* of Col J. W. Chaplin, VC; *S* father, 1977; *m* 1st, 1956, Shirley Cornelia (*d* 1977), *o d* of John Waters, Northampton; two *s* one *d*; 2nd, 1979, Gwendolyn Mary (marr. diss. 1983), *d* of late Laurance Devereux, OBE, and *widow* of Charles Langer, MA. *Educ:* Eton; Balliol College, Oxford; Northants Inst. of Agric., Moulten, 1952 (Dip with distinction). Served War of 1939–45, Lieut 15/19th Hussars (despatches). Pres., British Soc. of Dowsers, 1987–. Chm., Ashford Br., NFU, 1963–64; Mem., Exec. Cttee, Kent Br., NFU, 1960–73; Mem., Canterbury Farmers' Club (Chm. 1972); Pres., Kent Br., Men of the Trees, 1979–85. Life Mem., Internat. Dendrology Soc. Hon. Fellow, Psionic Med. Soc., 1977. Dip., Inst. of Optimum Nutrition, 1988. JP Kent 1960–78. *Publication:* (ed) An Anthology of Inner Silence, 1990. *Recreations:* gardening, planting trees. *Heir: s* George Elphinstone Jessel [*b* 15 Dec. 1957; *m* 1988, Rose, *yr d* of James Coutts-Smith]. *Address:* South Hill Farm, Hastingleigh, near Ashford, Kent TN25 5HL. *T:* Elmsted (023375) 325. *Club:* Cavalry and Guards.

JESSEL, Oliver Richard; Chairman of numerous companies in the Jessel Group, since 1954; *b* 24 Aug. 1929; *s* of late Comdr R. F. Jessel, DSO, OBE, DSC, RN; *m* 1950, Gloria Rosalie Teresa (*née* Holden); one *s* five *d*. *Educ:* Rugby. Founded group of companies, 1954; opened office in City of London, 1960; Chm., London, Australian and General Exploration Co. Ltd., 1960–75; formed: New Issue Unit Trust and other trusts, 1962–68; Castle Communications, 1983; Standard Financial Holdings, 1987; responsible for numerous mergers, incl. Johnson & Firth Brown Ltd, and Maple Macowards Ltd; Chm., Charles Clifford Industries Ltd, 1978–81; reorganised Belvoir Petroleum Corp., 1987–89. *Address:* Merrington Place, Rolvenden, Cranbrook, Kent TN17 4JP. *T:* Cranbrook (0580) 241428. *Club:* Garrick.

See also T. F. H. Jessel.

JESSEL, Dame Penelope, DBE 1987; International Officer, Liberal Party, 1985–88; *b* 2 Jan. 1920; *d* of Sir Basil Blackwell and late Marion Christine, *d* of John Soans; *m* 1940, Robert George Jessel (*d* 1954); two *s*. *Educ:* Dragon Sch., Oxford; St Leonard's, St Andrews, Fife; Somerville Coll., Oxford (MA). On staff of Oxford House, London, 1940–41; ATS, 1941–43; Lecturer: William Temple Coll., 1956–62; Plater Coll., Oxford, 1968–84. Pres., Women's Liberal Fedn, 1970–72. *Publication:* Owen of Uppingham, 1965. *Recreations:* looking at old churches, music, gardening, looking at gardens. *Address:* The Cottage, The Green, Cassington, Oxford OX8 1DW. *T:* Oxford (0865) 881322. *Club:* National Liberal.

JESSEL, Toby Francis Henry; MP (C) Twickenham since 1970; *b* 11 July 1934; *y s* of late Comdr R. F. Jessel, DSO, OBE, DSC, RN; *m* 1st, 1967 (marr. diss. 1973); one *d* decd; 2nd, 1980, Eira Gwen, *y d* of late Horace and Marigwen Heath. *Educ:* Royal Naval Coll., Dartmouth; Balliol Coll., Oxford (MA). Sub-Lt, RNVR, 1954. Conservative Candidate: Peckham, 1964; Hull (North), 1966. Parly deleg. to India and Pakistan, 1971; Member: Council of Europe, 1976–; WEU, 1976–. Chm., South Area Bd GLC Planning and Transportation Cttee, 1968–70. (Co-opted) LCC Housing Cttee, 1961–65; Councillor, London Borough of Southwark, 1964–66; Mem. for Richmond-upon-Thames, GLC, 1967–73; Hon. Sec. Assoc. of Adopted Conservative Candidates, 1961–66; Chairman: Cons. Parly Arts and Heritage Cttee, 1983 (Vice-Chm., 1979); Anglo-Belgian Parly Gp, 1983; Vice-Chm., Indo-British Parly Gp, 1987– (Hon. Sec., 1972–87); Treas., Anglo-Chilean Parly Gp, 1991–. Hon. Sec., Katyn Meml Fund, 1972–75. Mem. Metropolitan Water Bd, 1967–70; Mem., London Airport Consultative Cttee, 1967–70. Mem. Council, Fluoridation Soc., 1976. Mem., Exec. Cttee and Organizing Cttee, European Music Year, 1985. Liveryman, Worshipful Co. of Musicians. Chevalier, Ordre de la Couronne (Belgium), 1980; Order of Polonia Restituta (Polish Govt in Exile); Order of Merit (Liechtenstein), 1979. *Recreations:* music (has performed Mozart, Beethoven and Schumann piano concertos), gardening, croquet (Longworth Cup, Hurlingham, 1961), ski-ing. *Address:* Old Court House, Hampton Court, East Molesey, Surrey KT8 9BW. *Clubs:* Garrick, Hurlingham.

See also O. R. Jessel, Sir A. Panufnik, J. H. Walford.

JESSOP, Alexander Smethurst; Sheriff of Grampian, Highland and Islands at Aberdeen, since 1990; *b* 17 May 1943; *s* of Thomas Alexander Jessop and Ethel Marion Jessop; *m* 1967, Joyce Isobel Duncan; two *s* one *d*. *Educ:* Montrose Acad.; Fettes Coll.; Aberdeen Univ. (MA, LLB). Solicitor in private practice, Montrose, 1966–76; Depute Procurator Fiscal, Perth, 1976–78; Asst Solicitor, Crown Office, 1978–80; Sen. Asst Procurator Fiscal, Glasgow, 1980–84; Regional Procurator Fiscal: Aberdeen, 1984–87; Glasgow, 1987–90. *Recreation:* sport. *Address:* (home) 79 Devonshire Road, Aberdeen AB1 6XP; Sheriff Court, Castle Street, Aberdeen AB9 1AP.

JEVONS, Prof. Frederic Raphael, AO 1986; Professor of Science and Technology Policy, Murdoch University, Australia, since 1988; *b* 19 Sept. 1929; *s* of Fritz and Hedwig Bettelheim; *m* 1956, Grete Bradel; two *s*. *Educ:* Langley Sch., Norwich; King's Coll., Cambridge (Major Schol.). 1st Cl. Hons Nat. Scis Pt II (Biochem) Cantab 1950; PhD Cantab 1953; DSc Manchester 1966. Postdoctoral Fellow, Univ. of Washington, Seattle, 1953–54; Fellow, King's Coll., Cambridge, 1953–59; Univ. Demonstrator in Biochem., Cambridge, 1956–59; Lectr in Biol Chem., Manchester Univ., 1959–66; Prof. of Liberal Studies in Science, Manchester Univ., 1966–75; Vice-Chancellor, Deakin Univ., Australia, 1976–85, subseq. Emeritus Prof.; consultant on distance educn in southern Africa, 1986–87. Chairman: Gen. Studies Cttee, Schools Council, 1974–75; Grad. Careers Council of Aust., 1976–80; Policy Cttee, Victorian Technical and Further Educn Off-Campus Network, 1985–88; Member: Jt Matriculation Bd, Manchester, 1969–75; Jt Cttee, SRC and SSRC, 1974–75; Educn Res. and Develt Cttee, Aust., 1980–81; Council, Sci. Mus. of Vic., 1980–83; Council, Mus. of Vic., 1983–87; Aust. Vice-Chancellors' Exec. Cttee, 1981–82; Standing Cttee on External Studies, Commonwealth Tertiary Educn Commn, Canberra, 1985–87; Aust. Sci. and Technol. Council, 1986–89. Interviewer for Civil Service Commn on Final Selection Bds, 1970–75; Adviser to Leverhulme project on educnl objectives in applied science, Strathclyde Univ., 1972–75; British Council tours in India, E Africa, Nigeria, 1972–75. Mem., Editorial Advisory Boards: R and D Management, 1972–76; Studies in Science Educn, 1974–84; Scientometrics, 1978–; Australasian Studies in History and Philosophy of Science, 1980–86. Life Gov., Geelong Hosp., 1986. DUniv Open, 1985; Hon. DLitt Deakin, 1986; Hon. DSc Manchester, 1986. *Publications:* The Biochemical Approach to Life, 1964, 2nd edn 1968 (trans. Italian, Spanish, Japanese, German); The Teaching of Science: education, science and society, 1969; (ed jtly) University Perspectives, 1970; (jtly) Wealth from Knowledge: studies of innovation in industry, 1972; (ed jtly) What Kinds of Graduates do we Need?, 1972; Science Observed: science as a social and intellectual activity, 1973; Knowledge and Power, 1976; numerous papers on biochem., history of science, science educn and science policy. *Recreations:* music, theatre, reading. *Address:* Murdoch University, WA 6150, Australia.

JEWELL, David John, MA, MSc; Master of Haileybury and Imperial Service College, since 1987; *b* 24 March 1934; *s* of late Wing Comdr John Jewell, OBE, FRAeS, and Rachel Jewell, Porthleven, Cornwall; *m* 1958, Katharine Frida Heller; one *s* three *d*. *Educ:* Blundell's Sch., Tiverton; St John's Coll., Oxford. Honours Sch. of Natural Science (Chemistry), BA 1957, MA 1961; BSc Physical Sciences, 1959, MSc 1981. National Service with RAF, 1952–54. Head of Science Dept, Eastbourne Coll., 1958–62; Winchester Coll., 1962–67; Dep. Head, Lawrence Weston Comprehensive Sch., Bristol, 1967–70; Head Master, Bristol Cathedral Sch., 1970–78; Headmaster, Repton Sch., 1979–87. Vis. Prof., Rollins Coll., Florida, 1987. Chairman: HMC, 1990 (Chairman: Direct Grant Sub-Cttee, 1977–78; Professional Develt Cttee, 1987–89); Choir Schools' Assoc., 1976–77. FRSA 1981. *Publications:* papers and articles in various scientific and educnl jls. *Recreations:* music, cricket, cooking, Cornwall. *Address:* The Master's Lodge, Haileybury, Hertford SG13 7NU. *T:* Hoddesdon (0992) 462352; Chapel Downs Cottage, Breageside, Porthleven, Cornwall. *T:* Helston (0326) 563152. *Clubs:* East India, Devonshire, Sports and Public Schools, MCC; Bristol Savages.

JEWELL, Prof. Peter Arundel, PhD; CBiol, FIBiol; Mary Marshall and Arthur Walton Professor of Physiology of Reproduction and Fellow of St John's College, University of Cambridge, since 1977; *b* 16 June 1925; *s* of Percy Arundel Jewell and Ivy Dorothea Enness; *m* 1958, Juliet Clutton-Brock; three *d*. *Educ:* Wandsworth Sch.; Reading Univ. (BSc Agric.); Cambridge Univ. (BA, MA, PhD). Lectr, Royal Veterinary Coll., 1950–60; Research Fellow, Zoological Soc. of London, 1960–66; Prof. of Biological Sciences, Univ. of Nigeria, 1966–67; Sen. Lectr and Dir of Conservation Course, University Coll. London, 1967–72; Prof. of Zoology, Royal Holloway Coll., 1972–77. *Publications:* The Experimental Earthwork on Overton Down, Wiltshire, 1960; Island Survivors: the Ecology of the Soay Sheep of St Kilda, 1974; Management of Locally Abundant Wild Mammals, 1981; scientific papers in Jl Animal Ecology, Jl Physiology, Jl Zoology, Ark, etc. *Recreations:* emulating Cornish ancestors, watching wild animals, saving rare breeds, painting and pottery, archaeology. *Address:* St John's College, Cambridge CB2 1TP.

JEWERS, William George, CBE 1982 (OBE 1976); Managing Director, Finance, and Member, British Gas plc (formerly British Gas Corporation), 1976–87; *b* 18 Oct. 1921; *s* of late William Jewers and Hilda Jewers (*née* Ellison); *m* 1955, Helena Florence Rimmer; one *s* one *d*. *Educ:* Liverpool Inst. High Sch. for Boys. Liverpool Gas Co., 1938–41. Served War: RAFVR Observer (Flying Officer), 1941–46: Indian Ocean, 265 Sqdn (Catalinas), 1943–44; Burma 194 Sqdn (Dakotas), 1945. Liverpool Gas Co./NW Gas Bd, Sen. Accountancy Asst, 1946–52; W Midlands Gas Bd: Cost Acct, Birmingham and Dist Div., 1953–62; Cost Acct, Area HQ, 1962–65; Asst Chief Acct, 1965–66; Chief Acct, 1967; Dir of Finance, 1968; Gas Council, Dir of Finance, 1969–73; British Gas Corp., Dir of Finance, 1973–76. FCMA, FCCA, JDipMA, CompIGasE. *Publications:* papers and articles to gas industry jls. *Recreations:* music, reading. *Address:* 17 South Park View, Gerrards Cross, Bucks SL9 8HN. *T:* Gerrards Cross (0753) 886169.

JEWKES, Sir Gordon (Wesley), KCMG 1990 (CMG 1980); HM Diplomatic Service, retired; Director-General of Trade and Investment, USA, and Consul-General, New York, 1989–91; *b* 18 Nov. 1931; *er s* of late Jesse Jewkes; *m* 1954, Joyce Lyons; two *s*. *Educ:* Barrow Grammar Sch.; Magnus Grammar Sch., Newark-on-Trent, and elsewhere. Colonial Office, 1948; commnd HM Forces, Army, 1950–52; Gen. Register Office,

1950–63; CS Pay Res. Unit, 1963–65; Gen. Register Office, 1965–68; transf. to HM Diplomatic Service, 1968; CO, later FCO, 1968–69; Consul (Commercial), Chicago, 1969–72; Dep. High Comr, Port of Spain, 1972–75; Head of Finance Dept, FCO, and Finance Officer of Diplomatic Service, 1975–79; Consul-General: Cleveland, 1979–82; Chicago, 1982–85; Gov., Falkland Is and High Comr, British Antarctic Territory, 1985–88. *Recreations:* music, travel, walking. *Address:* Clandon Cottage, East Brabourne, near Ashford, Kent TN25 5LP. *T:* Sellindge (030381) 3765. *Club:* Travellers'.

JEWSON, Richard Wilson; Chairman, Meyer International, since 1991; *b* 5 Aug. 1944; *s* of Charles Boardman and Joyce Marjorie Jewson; *m* 1965, Sarah Rosemary Spencer; one *s* three *d*. *Educ:* Rugby; Pembroke Coll., Cambridge (MA). Joined Jewson & Sons, 1965, Man. Dir, 1974–86; Man. Dir, Jewson Scaffold Co., 1967–72; Meyer International: Dir, 1983–; Group Man. Dir, 1986–91; Dep. Chm., 1990–91. Non-Executive Director: Eastern Daily Press, 1982–; Anglian Water, 1990–. Mem., CBI London Region Cttee, 1986–. CBIM. *Recreations:* Real tennis, golf, gardening. *Address:* Meyer International, Villiers House, 41–47 Strand, WC2N 5JG. *T:* 071–839 7766. *Clubs:* Boodle's, Queen's; Royal West Norfolk Golf.

JHABVALA, Mrs Ruth Prawer; author; *b* in Germany, of Polish parents, 7 May 1927; *d* of Marcus Prawer and Eleonora Prawer (*née* Cohn); came to England as refugee, 1939; *m* 1951, C. S. H. Jhabvala; three *d*. *Educ:* Hendon County Sch.; Queen Mary Coll., London Univ. Started writing after graduation and marriage, alternating between novels and short stories; occasional original film-scripts (with James Ivory and Ismail Merchant), including: Shakespeare-wallah, 1965; The Guru, 1969; Bombay Talkie, 1971; Autobiography of a Princess, 1975; Roseland, 1977; Hullabaloo over Georgie and Bonnie's Pictures, 1978; The Europeans (based on Henry James' novel), 1979; Jane Austen in Manhattan, 1980; Quartet (based on Jean Rhys' novel), 1981; Heat and Dust (based on own novel), 1983; The Bostonians (based on Henry James' novel), 1984; A Room with a View (based on E. M. Forster's novel), 1986 (Academy Award, 1987); film-scripts: (with John Schlesinger), Madame Sousatzka, 1988; Mr and Mrs Bridge (based on Evan Connell's novels), 1991. *Publications: novels:* To Whom She Will, 1955; The Nature of Passion, 1956; Esmond in India, 1958; The Householder, 1960; Get Ready for Battle, 1962; A Backward Place, 1965; A New Dominion, 1973; Heat and Dust, 1975 (Booker Prize, 1975); In Search of Love and Beauty, 1983; Three Continents, 1987; *short story collections:* Like Birds, like Fishes, 1964; A Stronger Climate, 1968; An Experience of India, 1971; How I became a Holy Mother and other Stories, 1976; Out of India: selected stories, 1986. *Recreation:* writing film-scripts. *Address:* 400 East 52nd Street, New York, NY 10022, USA.

See also Prof. S. S. Prawer.

JI Chaozhu; Under-Secretary General of the United Nations, since 1991; *b* Shanxi Province, 30 July 1929; *s* of Dr Chi Kung-Chuan, Commissioner of Education, and Chang Tao-Jan; *m* 1957, Wang Xiangtong; two *s*. *Educ:* Primary and secondary schools in Manhattan; Harvard Univ. (reading Chemistry); Tsinghua Univ. (graduated 1952). English stenographer at Panmunjom, Korea, for Chinese People's Volunteers, 1952–54; English interpreter for Chinese leaders, incl. Chairman Mao, Premier Chou En-Lai, 1954–73; Dep. Dir, Translation Dept, Foreign Ministry, 1970–73; Counsellor, Liaison Office, Washington DC, 1973–75; Dep. Dir, Dept of Internat. Organisations and Confs, Foreign Min., 1975–79; Dep. Dir, Dept of American and Oceanic Affairs, Foreign Min., 1979–82; Minister-Counsellor, US Embassy, 1982–85; Ambassador to Fiji, Kiribati and Vanuatu, 1985–87; Ambassador to UK, 1987–91. *Recreations:* swimming, music. *Address:* United Nations, New York, NY 10017, USA.

JILANI, Asaf; with the Eastern Service of the BBC; *b* 24 Sept. 1934; *s* of Abdul Wahid Sindhi and Noor Fatima Jilani; *m* 1961, Mohsina Jilani; two *s* one *d*. *Educ:* Jamia Millia, Delhi; Sindh Madrasa, Karachi; Karachi Univ. (BA, Economics and Persian). Sub-Editor, Daily Imroze, Karachi (Progressive Papers Ltd), 1952; Political Corresp., Daily Imroze, 1954; Special Corresp., Daily Jang, Karachi (posted in India), 1959–65; held prisoner in Delhi during India/Pakistan War, 1965; London Editor: Daily Jang (Karachi, Rawalpindi, Quetta); Daily News, Karachi, and Akhbar-Jehan, Karachi, 1965–73; Editor, Daily Jang, London (first Urdu Daily in UK), 1973–82. Iqbal Medal (Pakistan), for journalistic contribution to exposition of Islamic poetic philosopher Dr Mohammed Iqbal, during his centenary celebrations. *Recreations:* cricket, swimming, painting. *Address:* BBC, Eastern Service, Bush House, WC2. *T:* 071–257 2142; (home) 23 Horsham Avenue, N12. *T:* 081–368 5697.

JILLINGS, Godfrey Frank; Chief Executive, Financial Intermediaries, Managers and Brokers Regulatory Association, since 1990; *b* 24 May 1940; *s* of Gerald Frank Jillings and Dorothy Marjorie Jillings; *m* 1967, Moira Elizabeth McCoy (*d* 1986); one *s*. *Educ:* Tiffin's Sch., Kingston; Inst. of Personnel Management. DMS; ACIB. S. G. Warburg & Co. Ltd, 1956–58; National Westminster Bank Ltd, 1958–90: Head of Industrial Section, 1983; Sen. Project Manager, 1985–86; Director: County Unit Trust Managers Ltd, 1986–87; Natwest Stockbrokers Ltd, 1986–89; Chief Exec., Natwest Personal Financial Management Ltd, 1987–89; Senior Exec., Group Chief Exec's Office, 1989–90. *Recreations:* travel, chess. *Address:* 6 Worcester Gardens, Worcester Park, Surrey KT4 7HN. *T:* 081–337 8481.

JIMENEZ DE ARECHAGA, Eduardo, DrJur; President, Court of Arbitration for the Delimitation of Maritime areas between Canada and France; Member, World Bank Administrative Tribunal, since 1981; Professor of International Law, Montevideo Law School, since 1946; *b* Montevideo, 8 June 1918; *s* of E. Jiménez de Aréchaga and Ester Sienra; *m* 1943, Marta Ferreira; three *s* two *d*. *Educ:* Sch. of Law, Univ. of Montevideo. Under-Sec., Foreign Relations, 1950–52; Sec., Council of Govt of Uruguay, 1952–55; Mem., Internat. Law Commn of UN, 1961–69 (Pres., 1963); Cttee *Rapporteur*, Vienna Conf. on Law Treaties, 1968–69; Minister of the Interior, Uruguay, 1968; Pres. of the International Ct of Justice, The Hague, 1976–79 (Judge of the Ct, 1970–79). Inter-Amer. Bar Assoc. Book Award, 1961. *Publications:* Reconocimiento de Gobiernos, 1946; Voting and Handling of Disputes in the Security Council, 1951; Treaty Stipulations in Favour of Third States, 1956; Derecho Constitucional de las Naciónes Unidas, 1958; Curso de Derecho Internacional Público, 2 vols, 1959–61; International Law in the Past Third of a Century, vol. I, 1978; Derecho Internacional Contemporáneo, 1980. *Address:* Casilla de Correo 539, Montevideo, Uruguay.

JINKINSON, Alan Raymond; General Secretary, National and Local Government Officers' Association, since 1990; *b* 27 Feb. 1935; *s* of Raymond and Maggie Jinkinson; *m* 1968, Madeleine Gillian Douglas. *Educ:* King Edward VII Sch., Sheffield; Keble Coll., Oxford (BA Hons). National and Local Government Officers' Association: Education Dept, 1960; District Officer, 1967; District Orgn Officer, 1973; National Officer (Local Govt), 1976; Asst Gen. Sec., 1981; Dep. Gen. Sec., 1983. *Recreations:* cinema, jogging, walking. *Address:* National and Local Government Officers' Association, 1 Mabledon Place, WC1H 9AJ. *T:* 071–388 2366.

JIRIČNA, Eva Magdalena; architect; Principal of own practice, since 1984; *b* 3 March 1939; *d* of Josef Jiricny and Eva Jiricna; *m* 1963, Martin Holub (marr. diss. 1973). *Educ:* Coll. of Architecture and Town Planners, Univ. of Prague (Engr Architect 1962); Acad. of Fine Arts, Prague (Acad. Architect 1967). Professional practice and management examination, RIBA, 1973. Main projects include: Harrods Way-In; Vidal Sassoon Salons, Germany; Joseph Shops, Brompton Cross and Sloane Street; offices for Fafalios Ltd, London; Retail System for Vitra International. *Address:* 7 Dering Street, W1R 9AB. *T:* 071–629 7077.

JOACHIM, Dr Margaret Jane; Manager, UK Insurance Services, EDS (Electronic Data Systems) Ltd, since 1988; *b* 25 June 1949; *d* of Reginald Carpenter and late Joyce Margaret Carpenter; *m* 1970, Paul Joseph Joachim; one *d*. *Educ:* Brighton and Hove High School; St Hugh's College, Oxford (MA Geology); Univ. of Birmingham (PhD Geology). Grammar school teacher, 1971–76; post-doctoral research Fellow, Univ. of Birmingham, 1976–79; computer consultant, 1979–84; Futures Database Manager, Rudolf Wolff & Co., 1984–87. Training Officer, Liberal Parly Assoc., 1979–84; Mem., Exec. Cttee, Women's Liberal Fedn, 1984–85; Chair: Fawcett Soc., 1984–87 (Mem. Exec. Cttee, 1990–); internat. working gp to set up EEC Women's Lobby, 1988–90; Chair, 1989–90, Vice-Chair, 1990–91, WLD (formerly SLD Women's Orgn). Co-ordinator, Women into Public Life Campaign, 1987–88; Vice-Chair, 1989, Mem. Exec. Cttee, 1989–91, 300 Gp. Contested: (L) West Gloucestershire, 1979; (L/Alliance) Finchley, 1983; (L/Alliance) Epsom and Ewell, 1987. Mem., Exec. Cttee, Nat. Traction Engine Club, 1976–79; Founder, Steam Apprentice Club, 1978; Founder, Oxford Univ. Gilbert and Sullivan Soc., 1968. *Publications:* papers in: Studies in the Late-Glacial of North-West Europe, 1980; Holocene Palaeoecology and Palaeohydrology, 1986. *Recreations:* walking, sailing, reading, going to traction engine rallies, making jam. *Address:* 8 Newburgh Road, W3 6DQ. *T:* 081–993 0936. *Clubs:* Reform, Institute of Directors.

JOB, Rev. Canon (Evan) Roger (Gould); Canon Residentiary, Precentor and Sacrist, since 1979, Vice Dean, since 1991, Winchester Cathedral; *b* 15 May 1936; 2nd *s* of late Thomas Brian and Elsie Maud Job, Ipswich; *m* 1964, Rose Constance Mary, *o d* of late Stanley E. and Audrey H. Gordon, Hooton, Wirral; two *s*. *Educ:* Cathedral Choir School and King's Sch., Canterbury; Magdalen Coll., Oxford; Cuddesdon Theol Coll. BA 1960, MA 1964; ARCM 1955. Deacon 1962, priest 1963. Asst Curate, Liverpool Parish Church, 1962–65; Vicar of St John, New Springs, Wigan, 1965–70; Precentor of Manchester Cath., 1970–74; Precentor and Sacrist of Westminster Abbey, 1974–79; Chaplain of The Dorchester, 1976–79. *Recreations:* gardening, piano. *Address:* 8 The Close, Winchester SO23 9LS. *T:* Winchester (0962) 854771.

JOBERT, Michel; Officier de la Légion d'Honneur; Croix de Guerre (1939–45); politician, writer and lawyer; Founder and Leader, Mouvement des Démocrates, since 1974; *b* Meknès, Morocco, 11 Sept. 1921; *s* of Jules Jobert and Yvonne Babule; *m* Muriel Frances Green; one *s*. *Educ:* Lycées of Rabat and Meknès; Dip. de l'Ecole libre des sciences politiques; Ecole nationale d'Administration. Cour des comptes: Auditor, 1949; Conseiller Référendaire, 1953. Member of Ministerial Cabinets: Finance, Labour and Social Security, President of the Council, 1952–56; Director of the Cabinet of the High Commr of the Republic in French West Africa, 1956–58; Dir of Cabinet of Minister of State, 1959–61; Jt Dir, 1963–66, then Director, 1966–68, of the Prime Minister's Cabinet (Georges Pompidou); Pres., Council of Admin of Nat. Office of Forests, 1966–73; Administrator of Havas, 1968–73; Secretary-Gen., Presidency of the Republic, 1969–73; Minister for Foreign Affairs, 1973–74; Minister of State and Minister for Overseas Trade, 1981–83. Conseiller-maître, Cour des comptes, 1971– (Hon. Conseiller-maître, 1986). Former Board Member: SOFTRAD, Radio Monte-Carlo; French Radio and TV Organisation. Editor, La Lettre de Michel Jobert, 1974–84; Editorialiste, Paris ce Soir, Jan.–Feb. 1985. Prix de la Langue de France, 1989. *Publications:* Mémoires d'avenir, 1974; L'autre regard, 1976; Lettre ouverte aux femmes politiques, 1976; Parler aux Français, 1977; La vie d'Hella Schuster (novel), 1977; Maroc: extrême Maghreb du soleil couchant, 1978; La rivière aux grenades, 1982; Chroniques du Midi Libre, 1982; Vive l'Europe Libre, 1984; Par Trente-six chemins, 1984; Maghreb, à l'ombre de ses mains, 1985; Les Américains, 1987; Journal immédiat . . . et pour une petite éternité, 1987. *Address:* (home) 21 quai Alphonse-Le Gallo, 92100 Boulogne-sur-Seine, France; (office) 108 quai Louis Blériot, 75016 Paris, France.

JOBLING, Captain James Hobson, RN; Metropolitan Stipendiary Magistrate, 1973–87; *b* 29 Sept. 1921; *s* of late Captain and Mrs J. S. Jobling, North Shields, Northumberland; *m* 1946, Cynthia, *o d* of late F. E. V. Lean, Beacon Park, Plymouth; one *s* one *d*. *Educ:* Tynemouth High Sch.; London Univ. (LLB Hons, 1971). Entered Royal Navy, 1940; HMS Furious, 1941; HMS Victorious, 1941–45; awarded Gedge Medal and Prize, 1946; called to Bar, Inner Temple, 1955; Comdr, 1960; JSSC course, 1961–62; Dir, Nat. Liaison, SACLANT HQ, USA, 1962–65; Chief Naval Judge Advocate, in rank of Captain, 1969–72; retd, 1973. Planning Inspector, DoE, 1973; a Dep. Circuit Judge, 1976–82. *Recreations:* gardening, walking. *Address:* Pinewell Lodge, Wood Road, Hindhead, Surrey GU26 6PT. *T:* Hindhead (042873) 4426.

JOBSON, Roy; Chief Education Officer, Manchester Local Education Authority, since 1988; *b* 2 June 1947; *s* of James Jobson and Miriam H. Jobson; *m* 1971, Maureen Scott; one *s* two *d*. *Educ:* Bedlington Grammar Sch.; Univ. of Durham; Newcastle and Sunderland Polytechnics. King's Sch., Tynemouth, 1970–73; Norham High Sch., 1973–74; E Midland Regional Examining Bd, 1974–80; Gateshead Metropolitan Borough Council, 1980–84; Manchester City Council, 1984–. Chm., Associated Lancashire Schs Examining Bd; Member: Jt Council for GCSE; Soc. of Educn Officers. *Recreations:* children, family, church, music, Louis the Bassett Hound. *Address:* 34 Old Broadway, Didsbury, Manchester M20 9DF. *T:* 061–234 7001.

JOCELYN, family name of **Earl of Roden.**

JOCELYN, Dr Henry David, FBA 1982; Hulme Professor of Latin, University of Manchester, since 1973; *b* 22 Aug. 1933; *s* of late John Daniel Jocelyn and Phyllis Irene Burton; *m* 1958, Margaret Jill, *d* of Bert James Morton and Dulcie Marie Adams; two *s*. *Educ:* Canterbury Boys' High Sch.; Univ. of Sydney (BA); St John's Coll., Univ. of Cambridge (MA, PhD). Teaching Fellow in Latin, Univ. of Sydney, 1955; Cooper Travelling Scholar in Classics, 1955–57; Scholar in Classics, British Sch. at Rome, 1957–59; Univ. of Sydney: Lectr in Latin, 1960–64; Sen. Lectr in Latin, 1964–66; Reader in Latin, 1966–70; Prof. of Latin, 1970–73. Visiting Lectr in Classics, Yale Univ., 1967; Vis. Fellow, ANU, 1979; British Acad. Leverhulme Vis. Prof., *Thesaurus Linguae Latinae,* Munich, 1983; Vis. Lectr in Classics, Univ. of Cape Town, 1985; Professeur Invité, Univ. of Fribourg, 1990. Corresp. Fellow, Accademia Properziana del Subasio, 1985. FAHA 1970. Mem., Editorial Bd, Cambridge Classical Texts and Commentaries, 1982–. *Publications:* The Tragedies of Ennius, 1967 (corr. reprint 1969); (with B. P. Setchell) Regnier de Graaf on the Human Reproductive Organs, 1972; Philology and Education, 1988; papers on Greek and Latin subjects in various periodicals. *Address:* 4 Clayton Avenue, Manchester M20 0BN. *T:* 061–434 1526.

JOEL, Hon. Sir Asher (Alexander), KBE 1974 (OBE 1956); AO 1986; Kt 1971; Member of Legislative Council of New South Wales, 1957–78; Company Director and Public Relations Consultant; *b* 4 May 1912; *s* of Harry and Phoebe Joel, London and Sydney; *m* 1st, 1937 (marr. diss. 1948); two *s*; 2nd, 1949, Sybil, *d* of Frederick Mitchell

Jacobs; one *s* one *d*. *Educ:* Enmore Public Sch.; Cleveland Street High Sch., Sydney. Served War of 1939–45: AIF, 1942, transf. RAN; Lieut RANVR, 1943; RAN PRO staff Gen. MacArthur, 1944–45, New Guinea, Halmaheras, Philippines. Chairman: Asher Joel Media Gp; Carpentaria Newspapers Pty Ltd; Nat. Pres., Anzac Mem. Forest in Israel; Dir, Royal North Shore Hosp. of Sydney, 1959–81. Mem., Sydney Cttee (Hon. Dir, 1956–64); Hon. Dir and Organiser, Pageant of Nationhood (State welcome to the Queen), 1963; Exec. Mem., Citizens Welcoming Cttee visit Pres. Johnson, 1966; Chm., Citizens Cttee Captain Cook Bi-Centenary Celebrations, 1970; Dep. Chm., Citizens Welcoming Cttee visit Pope Paul VI to Australia, 1970; Chm., Sydney Opera Hse Official Opening Citizens Cttee, 1972; Dep. Chm., Aust. Govt Adv. Commn on US Bi-Centenary Celebrations, 1976; Mem., Nat. Australia Day Cttee. Mem., Sydney Opera Hse Trust, 1969–79; Chm., Sydney Entertainment Centre, 1979–84. Chm. Emeritus, Organising Cttee 1988 Public Relations World Congress, 1985–88; Mem., Adv. Council 31st IAA World Advertising Congress, 1984–88. Gov., Sir David Martin Foundn, 1990. Fellow: Advertising Inst. of Austr. (Federal Patron); Public Relations Inst. of Austr.; Austr. Inst. Management; FInstD; FRSA; Hon. Mem., Royal Australian Historical Soc., 1970. Hon. Fellow, Internat. Coll. of Dentists, 1975. Hon. DLitt Macquarie, 1988. US Bronze Star, 1943; Ancient Order of Sikatuna (Philippines), 1975; Kt Comdr, Order of Rizal (Philippines), 1978. *Publications:* Without Chains Free (novel), 1977; Australian Protocol and Procedures, 1982, 2nd edn 1988. *Recreations:* fishing, gardening, reading, writing. *Address:* 120 Clarence Street, Sydney, NSW 2000, Australia. *Clubs:* American, Journalists, Australasian Pioneers, Royal Agricultural Society (Sydney); Royal Sydney Yacht Squadron.

JOEL, Harry Joel; *b* 4 Sept. 1894; *o s* of Jack Barnato Joel, JP. *Educ:* Malvern Coll. Served European War 1914–18 with 15th Hussars. *Recreation:* racing. *Address:* The Stud House, Childwick Bury, St Albans, Herts. *Clubs:* Buck's; Jockey (Newmarket).

JOHANNESBURG, Bishop of, since 1986; **Rt. Rev. George Duncan Buchanan;** *b* 23 April 1935; *s* of Wyndam Kelsey Fraser Buchanan and Phyllis Rhoda Dale Buchanan (*née* Nichols); *m* 1959, Diana Margaret Dacombe; two *d*. *Educ:* St John's Coll., Johannesburg; Rhodes Univ., Grahamstown (BA 1957); Gen. Theological Seminary (MDiv 1959). Curate, St Paul's Church, Durban, 1960; Rector, Parish of Kingsway, Natal, 1961–65; Diocesan Theol Tutor, Dio. Natal, 1963–65; Sub Warden, St Paul's Theol Coll., Grahamstown, 1966–76, Warden, 1976–86; Dean, St Mary's Cathedral, Johannesburg, May–Sept. 1986; Archdeacon of Albany, Diocese of Grahamstown, 1975–86. Hon. DD General Theological Seminary, 1987. *Publication:* The Counselling of Jesus, 1985. *Recreations:* carpentry, hockey umpiring, reading. *Address:* PO Box 1131, Johannesburg 2000, South Africa; 4 Crescent Drive, Johannesburg 2193, South Africa. *T:* (office) 29–8724, (home) 486–1014.

JOHANSEN-BERG, Rev. John; Founder Member, since 1984, and Leader, since 1986, Community for Reconciliation; Moderator, Free Church Federal Council, 1987–88; *b* 4 Nov. 1935; *s* of John Alfred and Caroline Johansen-Berg, Middlesbrough; *m* 1971, Joan, *d* of James and Sally Ann Parnham, Leeds; two *s* one *d*. *Educ:* Acklam Hall Grammar Sch., Middlesbrough; Leeds Univ. (BA Hons Eng. Lit., BD); Fitzwilliam Coll., Cambridge Univ. (BA Theol Tripos, MA); Westminster Theol Coll. (Dip. Theol.). Tutor, Westminster Coll., Cambridge, 1961; ordained, 1962; pastoral charges: St Ninian's Presbyterian Church, Luton, 1962–70 (Sec., Luton Council of Churches); Founder Minister, St Katherine of Genoa Church, Dunstable (dedicated 1968); The Rock Church Centre, Liverpool (Presbyterian, then United Reformed), 1970–77, work begun in old public house, converted into Queens Road Youth Club, new Church Centre dedicated 1972, a building designed for youth, community and church use; Minister, St Andrew's URC, Ealing, 1977–86. Convener, Church and Community Cttee of Presbyterian C of E, 1970–72; Chm. Church and Society Dept, URC, 1972–79; Moderator of the Gen. Assembly of the URC, 1980–81. British Council of Churches: Mem., Assembly, 1987–90; formerly Member: Div. of Internat. Affairs; Div. of Community Affairs; Chm. Gp on Violence, Non-violence and Social Change (for Britain Today and Tomorrow Programme, 1977); Convenor, Commission on Non-Violent Action (report published 1973); Mem., Forum of Churches Together in England, 1990–. Chm., Christian Fellowship Trust, 1981–87; Trustee, Nat. Assoc. of Christian Communities and Networks, 1989–; Mem., Exec., CCJ, 1989–; Mem. Council, Centre for Study of Judaism and Jewish Christian Relns, 1989–. Founder Mem. and Sponsor, Christian Concern for Southern Africa, 1972–; Founder Sponsor, Clergy Against Nuclear Arms, 1982– (Chm., 1986–); Founder: Romania Concern, 1990; Ecumenical Order of Ministry, 1990; Jt Leader, Ecumenical Festivals of Faith in: Putney and Roehampton, 1978; Stroud, 1980; Banstead, 1983; North Mymms, 1985; Guildford, 1986; Jesmond, 1987; Worth Abbey, 1988; Palmers Green, 1990; Poole, 1991. Jt Editor, Jl of Presbyterian Historical Soc. of England, 1964–70. *Publications:* Arian or Arminian? Presbyterian Continuity in the Eighteenth Century, 1969; Prayers of the Way, 1987; Prayers of Pilgrimage, 1988; Prayers of Prophecy, 1990. *Recreations:* mountain walking, badminton, drama. *Address:* Barnes Close, Chadwich Manor Estate, Bromsgrove, Worcs B61 0RA. *T:* Romsley (0562) 710231.

JOHANSON, Rev. Dr Brian; Minister of Christ Church, United Reformed Church, Tonbridge, since 1987; *b* 8 March 1929; *s* of Bernard Johanson and Petra Johanson; *m* 1955, Marion Shirley Giles; one *s* two *d*. *Educ:* Univ. of South Africa (BA, DD); Univ. of London (BD). Parish Minister, S Africa, 1956–63; Sen. Lectr in Theology, 1964–69, Prof. of Theol., 1970–76, Univ. of SA; Minister of the City Temple, London, 1976–85; Dir of Ministerial Training, Presbyterian Church of Southern Africa, Johannesburg, 1985–86. Vis. Res. Fellow: Princeton Theol Seminary, 1970; Univ. of Aberdeen, 1976. *Publications:* univ. pubns in S Africa; booklets; essays in collections; articles in theol jls. *Address:* 25A Hadlow Road, Tonbridge, Kent.

JOHN, Arthur Walwyn, CBE 1967 (OBE 1945); FCA; company director; Underwriting Member of Lloyds, since 1977; *s* of Oliver Walwyn and Elsie Maud John; *m* 1st, 1949, Elizabeth Rosabelle (*d* 1979), *yr d* of Ernest David and Elsie Winifred Williams; one *s* two *d*; 2nd, 1986, Bonita Lynne, *e c* of Sebastian and Adela Maritano. *Educ:* Marlborough Coll. Mem. Institute of Chartered Accountants, 1934 (Mem. Council, 1965–81). Asst to Commercial Manager (Collieries), Powell Duffryn Associated Collieries Ltd, 1936. Joined Army, 1939; served War of 1939–45: commissioned, 1940; War Office, 1941; DAQMG First Army, 1942, and HQ Allied Armies in Italy; AQMG Allied Forces HQ, 1944 (despatches, 1943, 1945). Chief Accountant, John Lewis & Co Ltd, 1945; Dep. Dir-Gen. of Finance, National Coal Board, 1946; Dir-Gen. of Finance, 1955; Member, NCB, 1961–68; Chm., NCB Coal Products Div., 1962–68. Director: Unigate Ltd, 1969–75; Property Holding and Investment Trust Ltd, 1976–87 (Chm., 1977–87); Stenhouse Holdings Ltd, 1976–84 (Chm., 1982–84); Reed Stenhouse Companies Ltd, Canada, 1977–84; J. H. Sankey & Son Ltd, 1965–86; Schroder Property Fund, 1971–88; Teamdale Distribution Ltd, 1982– (Chm., 1982–); Chartered Accountants Trustees Ltd, 1982–87; Wincanton Contracts Finance Ltd, 1983–85; Dir and Chm., Chase Property Holdings plc, 1986–87. Mem., Price Commn, 1976–77. Mem. and Court, Worshipful Co. of Chartered Accts in England and Wales, 1977– (Master, 1981–82). *Address:* Limber, Top Park, Gerrards Cross, Bucks SL9 7PW. *T:* Gerrards Cross (0753) 884811. *Club:* Army and Navy.

JOHN, David Dilwyn, CBE 1961; TD; DSc; Director, National Museum of Wales, Cardiff, 1948–68; *b* 20 Nov. 1901; *e s* of Thomas John, St Bride's Major, Glam; *m* 1929, Marjorie, *d* of J. W. Page, HMI, Wellington, Salop; one *s* one *d*. *Educ:* Bridgend County Sch.; University Coll. of Wales, Aberystwyth. Zoologist on scientific staff, Discovery Investigations, engaged in oceanographical research in Antarctic waters, 1925–35; awarded Polar Medal. Appointed Asst Keeper in charge of Echinoderms at British Museum (Natural History), 1935; Deputy Keeper, 1948. Joined Territorial Army, 1936; promoted Major, RA, 1942. Hon. LLD Univ. of Wales, 1969; Hon. Fellow, UC Cardiff, 1982. *Publications:* papers, chiefly on Echinoderms, in scientific journals. *Address:* 7 Cyncoed Avenue, Cardiff CF2 6ST. *T:* Cardiff (0222) 752499.

JOHN, Elton Hercules, (Reginald Kenneth Dwight); musician, composer; *b* 25 March 1947; *s* of Stanley Dwight and Sheila (now Farebrother); *m* 1984, Renate Blauel. *Educ:* Pinner County Grammar Sch.; Royal Acad. of Music, London. Played piano in Northwood Hills Hotel, 1964; joined local group, Bluesology, 1965; signed to Dick James Music as writer and singer, 1967; visited America for concert and was overnight success, 1970; formed Elton John Band, 1970; regularly tours America, Europe, Australia and Japan; first internat. pop singer to perform in Russia, 1979. Vice-Pres. and Mem. Council, National Youth Theatre of GB, 1975–; Life Pres., Watford Football Club, 1990 (Dir, 1974; Chm., 1976–90); toured China with Watford Football Club, 1983. *Hit Records include: albums:* Empty Sky, 1969; Elton John, Tumbleweed Connection, 1970; Friends, 11.17.70, Madman Across the Water, 1971; Honky Chateau, 1972; Don't Shoot Me, Goodbye Yellow Brick Road, 1973; Caribou, Greatest Hits, 1974; Captain Fantastic, Rock of the Westies, 1975; Here and There, Blue Moves, 1976; Greatest Hits vol. II, 1977; A Single Man, 1978; Victim of Love, 1979; 21 at 33, Lady Samantha, 1980; The Fox, 1981; Jump Up, 1982; Too Low for Zero, 1983; Breaking Hearts, 1984; Ice on Fire, 1985; Leather Jackets, 1986; Live in Australia, 1987; Reg Strikes Back, 1988; Sleeping with the Past, 1989; *singles:* Your Song, 1971; Rocket Man, Crocodile Rock, 1972; Daniel, Goodbye Yellow Brick Road, 1973; Candle in the Wind, Don't Let the Sun Go Down On Me, The Bitch is Back, Lucy in the Sky with Diamonds, 1974; Philadelphia Freedom, Someone Saved My Life Tonight, 1975; Don't Go Breaking My Heart, Sorry Seems to be the Hardest Word, 1976; Ego, Part Time Love, Song for Guy, 1978; Little Jeannie, 1980; Nobody Wins, 1981; Blue Eyes, Empty Garden, Princess, 1982; I Guess that's Why They Call It the Blues, 1983; Sad Songs (Say So Much), Passengers, Who Wears These Shoes, 1984; Breaking Hearts, Act of War, Nikita, Wrap Her Up, 1985; Cry to Heaven, Heartache all over the World, Slow Rivers, 1986; Your Song (live), Candle in the Wind (live), 1987; I Don't Wanna Go On With You Like That, 1988; Healing Hands, 1989; Sacrifice, 1989. *Films:* Goodbye to Norma Jean, 1973; To Russia with Elton, 1980; played Pinball Wizard, in Tommy, 1973. Recipient of gold discs for all albums; Ivor Novello Award, Best Pop Song, 1976–77, Best Instrumental, 1978–79. *Recreations:* include playing tennis. *Address:* c/o John Reid Enterprises, 32 Galena Road, W6 0LT. *T:* 081–741 9933.

JOHN, Geoffrey Richards, CBE 1991; Chairman, Meat and Livestock Commission, since 1987; Chairman, Dairy Crest, since 1988; *b* 25 March 1934; *s* of Reginald and Mabel John; *m* 1961, Christine Merritt; two *d*. *Educ:* Bromsgrove School, Worcs; University College Cardiff (BA 1st cl. Hons Econs). Flying Officer, RAF, 1955–57; Cadbury Schweppes, 1957–74; Man. Dir, Spillers Foods, 1974–80; Chief Exec., Foods Div., Dalgety-Spillers, 1980–82; Chm. and Chief Exec., Allied Bakeries, 1982–87; Director: Associated British Foods, 1982–87; Frizzell Gp, 1991–. Mem., ARC, 1980–82. Governor, 1965–, Chm., 1982–, Bromsgrove School. *Recreations:* Rugby Football, music. *Address:* Dairy Crest House, Portsmouth Road, Surbiton, Surrey KT6 5QL. *T:* 081–398 4155. *Clubs:* Royal Air Force, Harlequin FC.

JOHN, Maldwyn Noel, FEng 1979, FIEE, FIEEE; Chairman, Kennedy & Donkin Group Ltd, since 1987; *b* 25 Dec. 1929; *s* of Thomas Daniel John and Beatrice May John; *m* 1953, Margaret Cannell; two *s*. *Educ:* University College Cardiff. BSc 1st Cl. Hons, Elec. Eng. Metropolitan Vickers Elec. Co. Ltd, Manchester, 1950–59; Atomic Energy Authy, Winfrith, 1959–63; AEI/GEC, Manchester, as Chief Engineer, Systems Dept, Chief Engineer, Transformer Div., and Manager, AC Transmission Div., 1963–69; Chief Elec. Engineer, 1969–72, Partner, 1972–86, Kennedy & Donkin. President: IEE, 1983–84; Convention of Nat. Socs of Engineering of Western Europe, 1983–84. MConsE. *Publications:* (jtly) Practical Diakoptics for Electrical Networks, 1969; (jtly) Power Circuit Breaker Theory and Design, 1st edn 1975, 2nd edn 1982; papers in IEE Procs. *Recreation:* golf. *Address:* 65 Orchard Drive, Horsell, Woking, Surrey GU21 4BS. *T:* Woking (04862) 73995.

JOHN, Michael M.; *see* Morley-John, M.

JOHN, Sir Rupert (Godfrey), Kt 1971; Governor of St Vincent, 1970–76; Director, St Vincent Building and Loan Association, since 1977; Consultant to UNITAR, since 1978; *b* 19 May 1916; 2nd *s* of late Donelley John; *m* 1937, Hepsy (*d* 1988); three *s* one *d* (and one *s* decd). *Educ:* St Vincent Grammar Sch.; Univ. of London (BA, DipEd); Gray's Inn; New York University. First Asst Master, St Kitts/Nevis Grammar Sch., 1944; Asst Master, St Vincent Grammar Sch., 1944–52; private practice at Bar of St Vincent, 1952–58; Magistrate, Grenada, 1958–60; Actg Attorney-General, Grenada, 1960–62; Human Rights Officer, UN, 1962–69; Mem. Internat. Team of Observers, Nigeria, 1969–70; Senior Human Rights Officer, 1970. Has attended numerous internat. seminars and confs as officer of UN. President: Assoc. of Sen. Citizens of St Vincent and the Grenadines, 1981–; Caribbean Inst. for Promotion of Human Rights, 1987–88 (Human Rights Award, 1988). Mem., Barclays Bank Internat. Ltd Policy Adv. Cttee (St Vincent), 1977–86. Mem. Editorial Adv. Bd, Jl of Third World Legal Studies, 1981–. KStJ 1971. *Publications:* St Vincent and its Constitution, 1971; Pioneers in Nation-Building in a Caribbean Mini-State, 1979; Racism and its Elimination, 1980; papers in various jls. *Recreations:* cricket, walking, swimming. *Address:* PO Box 677, Cane Garden, St Vincent, West Indies. *T:* 61500. *Club:* Commonwealth Trust.

JOHN CHARLES, Rt. Rev. Brother; *see* Vockler, Rt. Rev. J. C.

JOHN-MACKIE, Baron *cr* 1981 (Life Peer), of Nazeing in the County of Essex; **John John-Mackie;** Chairman, Forestry Commission, 1976–79; *b* 24 Nov. 1909; *s* of late Maitland Mackie, OBE, Farmer, and Mary Ann Mackie (*née* Yull); *m* 1934, Jeannie Inglis Milne; three *s* two *d*. *Educ:* Aberdeen Gram. Sch.; North of Scotland Coll. of Agriculture. Managing director of family farming company at Harold's Park Farm, Nazeing, Waltham Abbey, Essex, 1953–; Vicarage and Plumridge Farms, Hadley Wood, Enfield, 1968–79. MP (Lab) Enfield East, 1959–Feb. 1974; Jt Parly Sec., Min. of Agriculture, 1964–70; opposition frontbench spokesman on agriculture, food, forestry and fisheries, H of L, 1983–88. Mem., Aberdeen and Kincardine Agricl Exec. Cttee, 1939–47; Governor, North of Scotland Coll. of Agriculture, 1942–64, Vice Chm. 1956–64; Chm., Aberdeen and Kincardine Health Exec. Cttee, 1948–51; Governor, Nat. Inst. of Agricl Engrg, 1949–61; Member: Secretary of State for Scotland's Adv. Council, 1944–54; Plant Cttee on Poultry Diseases, 1963–64. Chm., Glentworth Scottish Farms Ltd, 1947–68. *Publication:* (for Fabian Soc.) Land Nationalisation. *Recreation:* tree planting. *Address:* Harold's Park,

Nazeing, Waltham Abbey, Essex EN9 2SF. *T:* Nazeing (099289) 2202. *Club:* Farmers'. *See also I. L. Aitken, Baron Mackie of Benshie, Sir Maitland Mackie.*

JOHN PAUL II, His Holiness Pope, (Karol Jozef Wojtyla); *b* Wadowice, Poland, 18 May 1920; *s* of Karol Wojtyla. *Educ:* Jagiellonian Univ., Cracow; Pontificio Ateneo 'Angelicum' (Dr in Theology). Ordained Priest, 1946; Prof. of Moral Theology, Univs of Lublin and Cracow, 1954–58; titular Bishop of Ombi, and Auxiliary Bishop of Cracow, 1958; Vicar Capitular, 1962; Archbishop and Metropolitan of Cracow, 1964–78. Cardinal, 1967; elected Pope, 16 Oct. 1978. Formerly Member, Congregations Pro Institutione Catholica, Pro Sacramentis et Cultu Divino, and Pro Clero. *Publications:* The Goldsmith Shop (play), 1960; Love and Responsibility, 1962; Person and Act, 1969; The Foundations of Renewal, 1972; Sign of Contradiction, 1976; The Future of the Church, 1979; Easter Vigil and other poems, 1979; Collected Poems (trans. Jerzy Peterkiewicz), 1982. *Address:* Apostolic Palace, 00120 Vatican City.

JOHNS, Alan Wesley, CMG 1990; OBE 1973; Executive Director, Royal Commonwealth Society for the Blind, since 1984 (Deputy Director, 1978–83); *b* 27 March 1931; *s* of Harold Wesley and Catherine Louisa Johns; *m* 1954, Joan Margaret (*née* Wheeler); one *s* one *d*. *Educ:* Farnborough Grammar Sch., Hants. BScEcon, London; CertEd, Southampton Univ. Teaching in secondary schools, Wilts LEA, 1953–61; Educn Officer, Govt of St Helena, 1961–68; Director of Education: Govt of Seychelles, 1968–74; Govt of Gibraltar, 1974–78. Official Mem., Exec. and Adv. Councils, Govt of St Helena, 1963–68. Pres., Internat. Agency for the Prevention of Blindness, 1990– (Vice-Pres., 1986–90). *Recreations:* travel in developing countries, house maintenance, sailing. *Address:* 18 Leyton Lea, Cuckfield, West Sussex RH17 5AT. *T:* Haywards Heath (0444) 413355. *Club:* Rotary (Haywards Heath).

JOHNS, Prof. David John, FEng 1990; Vice-Chancellor and Principal, University of Bradford, since 1989; *b* 29 April 1931; *m* 1954, Sheila Jean Read; one *d*. *Educ:* Univ. of Bristol (BSc Eng, MSc Eng, Aeronautical Engineering); Loughborough Univ. of Technology (PhD, DSc). FRAeS, FAeSI, FHKIE, FIOA, FCIT. Bristol Aeroplane Co., 1950–57 (section leader); Project Officer, Sir W. G. Armstrong Whitworth Co., 1957–58; Lectr, Cranfield Inst. of Technology, 1958–63; Loughborough University of Technology: Reader, 1964–68; Prof. in Transport Technology, 1968–83; Senior Pro-Vice-Chancellor, 1982–83; (Foundation) Dir, City Polytechnic of Hong Kong, 1983–89. 2nd Brunel Lectr, British Assoc. Adv. Sci., 1970. Unofficial JP Hong Kong, 1988. *Publications:* Thermal Stress Analyses, 1965; contribs to learned jls. *Recreations:* bridge, badminton, walking, music. *Address:* The University, Bradford, West Yorks BD7 1DP. *T:* Bradford (0274) 733466. *Clubs:* Athenæum; Bath and County; Hong Kong; Royal Hong Kong Jockey.

JOHNS, Glynis; actress; *b* Pretoria, South Africa; *d* of Mervyn Johns and Alice Maude (*née* Steel-Payne); *m* 1st, Anthony Forwood (marr. diss.); one *s*; 2nd, David Foster, DSO, DSC and Bar (marr. diss.); 3rd, Cecil Peter Lamont Henderson; 4th, Elliott Arnold. *Educ:* Clifton and Hampstead High Schs. First stage appearance in Buckie's Bears as a child ballerina, Garrick Theatre, London, 1935. Parts include: Sonia in Judgement Day, Embassy and Strand, 1937; Miranda in Quiet Wedding, Wyndham's, 1938 and in Quiet Weekend, Wyndham's, 1941; Peter in Peter Pan, Cambridge Theatre, 1943; Fools Rush In, Fortune; The Way Things Go, Phœnix, 1950; Gertie (title role), NY, 1952; Major Barbara (title role), NY, 1957; The Patient in Too True to Be Good, NY, 1962; The King's Mare, Garrick, 1966; Come as You Are, New, 1970; A Little Night Music, New York, 1973 (Tony award for best musical actress); Ring Round the Moon, Los Angeles, 1975; 13 Rue de l'Amour, Phœnix, 1976; Cause Célèbre, Her Majesty's, 1977 (Best Actress Award, Variety Club); Hayfever, UK; The Boy Friend, Toronto; The Circle, NY, 1989–90. Entered films as a child. *Films include:* South Riding, 49th Parallel, Frieda, An Ideal Husband, Miranda (the Mermaid), State Secret, No Highway, The Magic Box, Appointment with Venus, Encore, The Card, Sword and the Rose, Personal Affair, Rob Roy, The Weak and the Wicked, The Beachcomber, The Seekers, Poppa's Delicate Condition, Cabinet of Dr Caligari, Mad About Men, Josephine and Men, The Court Jester, Loser Takes All, The Chapman Report, Dear Bridget, Mary Poppins, Zelly and Me, Nuki. Also broadcasts; television programmes include: Star Quality; The Parkinson Show (singing Send in the Clowns); Mrs Amworth (USA); All You Need is Love; Across a Crowded Room; Little Gloria, Happy at Last; Sprague; Love Boat; Murder She Wrote; The Cavanaughs; starring role, Coming of Age (series). *Address:* c/o Gottlieb, Schiff, 555 5th Avenue, New York, NY 10017, USA.

JOHNS, Michael Alan; Director, Oil and Financial Division, Board of Inland Revenue, since 1988; *b* 20 July 1946; *s* of John and Kathleen Johns. *Educ:* Judd School, Tonbridge; Queens' College, Cambridge (MA Hist.). Inland Revenue, 1967–79; Central Policy Review Staff, 1979–80; Inland Revenue, 1980–84; seconded to Orion Royal Bank, 1985; Inland Revenue, 1986–, Under Sec., 1987. Treasurer, Working Men's College, 1986–. *Recreations:* ski-ing, teaching adults, moral philosophy. *Address:* Board of Inland Revenue, Somerset House, Strand, WC2R 1LB.

JOHNS, Rev. Patricia Holly, MA; Headmistress, St Mary's School, Wantage, Oxon, since 1980; *b* 13 Nov. 1933; *d* of William and Violet Harris; *m* 1958, Michael Charles Bedford Johns (*d* 1965), MA; one *s* one *d*. *Educ:* Blackheath High Sch.; Girton Coll., Cambridge (BA 1956, MA 1959, CertEd with distinction 1957). Asst Maths Mistress; Cheltenham Ladies' Coll., 1957–58; Macclesfield Girls' High Sch., 1958–60; Asst Maths Mistress, then Head of Maths and Dir of Studies, St Albans High Sch., 1966–75; Sen. Mistress, and Housemistress of Hopeman House, Gordonstoun, 1975–80. Ordained Deacon, 1990. *Recreations:* choral singing, walking, camping, dogs (corgis). *Address:* St Mary's School, Newbury Street, Wantage, Oxon OX12 8BZ; 8 Garden Close, Salisbury Avenue, St Albans, Herts AL1 4TX. *T:* St Albans (0727) 52185.

JOHNS, Paul; Managing Director, Traidcraft, since 1988; *b* 13 March 1934; *s* of Alfred Thomas Johns and Margherita Johns; *m* 1st, 1956, Ruth Thomas (marr. diss. 1973); two *s* one *d*; 2nd, 1984, Margaret Perry. *Educ:* Kingswood School, Bath; Oriel College, Oxford (MA Hons Modern Hist.). MIPM. Personnel Management, Dunlop Rubber Co., 1958–63 and Northern Foods Ltd, 1963–68; Senior Partner, Urwick Orr & Partners, 1968–83; Dir, Profile Consulting, 1983–89. Chairperson, 1985–87, Vice-Chairperson, 1987–88, CND. *Publications:* contribs to jls on management and on nuclear issue. *Recreations:* photography, listening to music, watching football (keen supporter of Nottingham Forest). *Address:* Flat 11, The Covers, Fox Road, West Bridgford, Nottingham NG2 6AS. *T:* Nottingham (0602) 816944.

JOHNS, Air Vice-Marshal Richard Edward, CB 1991; CBE 1985 (OBE 1978); LVO 1972; Air Officer Commanding No 1 Group, since 1991; *b* 28 July 1939; *s* of late Lt-Col Herbert Edward Johns, RM and of Marjory Harley Johns (*née* Everett); *m* 1965, Elizabeth Naomi Anne Manning; one *s* two *d*. *Educ:* Portsmouth Grammar Sch.; RAF College, Cranwell. Commissioned 1959; Flying Instructor to Prince of Wales, 1970–71; Dir, Air Staff Briefing, 1979–81; Station Comdr and Harrier Force Comdr, RAF Gütersloh, 1982–84; ADC to the Queen, 1983–84; RCDS 1985; SASO, HQ RAF Germany, 1985–88; SASO, HQ Strike Comd, 1989–91. *Recreations:* military history, Rugby, cricket. *Address:* c/o Lloyds Bank, Cox's & King's Branch, PO Box 1190, 7 Pall Mall, SW1Y 5NA. *Club:* Royal Air Force.

JOHNSON; *see* Croom-Johnson.

JOHNSON, Alan Campbell; *see* Campbell-Johnson.

JOHNSON, Air Vice-Marshal Alan Taylor, FRAeS; Director of Occupational Health, Metropolitan Police, since 1991; *b* 3 March 1931; *s* of Percy and Janet Johnson; *m* 1954, Margaret Ellen Mee; two *s* three *d* (and one *s* decd). *Educ:* Mexborough Grammar Sch.; Univ. of Sheffield (MB, ChB); DipAvMed; MFOM, MFCM. Commnd RAF, 1957; MO, RAF Gaydon, 1957–59; Princess Mary's RAF Hosp., Akrotiri, Cyprus, 1959–61; No 1 Parachute Trng Sch., RAF Abingdon, 1961–65; RAF Changi, Singapore, 1965–67; RAF Inst. of Aviation Medicine, 1967–71; RAF Bruggen, Germany, 1971–74; Med. SO (Air) HQ RAF Support Comd, 1974–77; RAF Brize Norton, 1977–78; Chief of Aerospace Medicine HQ SAC Offutt AFB, USA, 1978–81; Dep. Dir of Health and Res. (Aviation Medicine), 1981–84; OC Princess Alexandra Hosp., RAF Wroughton, 1984–86; Asst Surg.-Gen. (Environmental Medicine and Res.), MoD, 1986; PMO, HQ RAF, Germany, 1986–88; PMO, HQ Strike Comd, RAF High Wycombe, 1988–91; retired. QHS 1986–91. OStJ 1976. *Recreations:* sport parachuting, music, cricket. *Address:* c/o Lloyds Bank, 99 High Street, Huntingdon, Cambs. *Club:* Royal Air Force.

JOHNSON, Anne Montgomrey; Market Research, Harris Research Centre, 1983–91; *b* 12 June 1922; *y c* of late Frederick Harold Johnson and late Gertrude Le Quesne (*née* Martin). *Educ:* St John's, Bexhill-on-Sea; Queen Elizabeth Hosp. (SRN); Brompton Hosp. (BTA Hons); Simpson Memorial Maternity Pavilion, Edinburgh (SCM). Asst Matron, Harefield Hosp., 1956–59; Dep. Matron, St Mary's Hosp., Paddington, 1959–62; Matron, Guy's Hosp., 1962–68; Mem. Directing and Tutorial Staff, King Edward's Hosp. Fund for London, 1968–71; Regional Dir, Help the Aged, 1971–73; Matron, The Royal Star and Garter Home for Disabled Sailors, Soldiers and Airmen, 1975–82. Member: King's Fund Working Party, 'The Shape of Hospital Management 1980', 1966–67 (report publd 1967); Jt Cttee of Gen. Synod Working Party 'The Hospital Chaplain' (report publd 1974); Hosp. Chaplaincies Council, 1963–81; Nursing Cttee, Assoc. of Indep. Hosps, 1978–83. Gov., Orleans Park Sch., Twickenham, 1988–. *Recreations:* straight theatre, travel. *Address:* Flat 5, 6 Cardigan Road, Richmond-on-Thames, Surrey TW10 6BJ.

JOHNSON, WO1 Barry, GC 1990; RAOC; Warrant Officer 1 (Staff Sergeant Major), 1986; *b* 25 Jan. 1952; *s* of Charles William Johnson and Joyce Johnson; *m* 1971, Linda Maria Lane; one *s* one *d*. Mem., Inst. of Explosives Engineers. Army Apprentices College, Chepstow, 1967; Royal Army Ordnance Corps, 1970; served in UK, BAOR, NI, Canada and Belize. *Address:* RAOC Secretariat, Blackdown Barracks, Deepcut, Camberley, Surrey. *Club:* Victoria Cross and George Cross Association.

JOHNSON, Prof. Barry Edward, PhD; FRS 1978; Professor of Pure Mathematics, since 1969, and Dean of Faculty of Science since 1986, University of Newcastle upon Tyne; *b* 1 Aug. 1937; *s* of Edward Johnson and Evelyn May (*née* Bailey); *m* (marr. diss. 1979); two *s* one *d*. *Educ:* Epsom County Grammar Sch.; Hobart State High Sch.; Univ. of Tasmania (BSc 1956); Cambridge Univ. (PhD 1961). Instr, Univ. of Calif, Berkeley, 1961–62; Vis. Lectr, Yale Univ., 1962–63; Lectr, Exeter Univ., 1963–65; University of Newcastle upon Tyne: Lectr, 1965–68; Reader, 1968–69; Head of Dept of Pure Maths, 1976–83; Head of Sch. of Maths, 1983–86. Vis. Prof., Yale Univ., 1970–71. Mem., London Math. Soc. (Mem. Council, 1975–78; Pres., 1980–82). *Publications:* Cohomology of Banach Algebras, 1972; papers in Jl of London Math. Soc. and Amer. Jl of Maths. *Recreations:* reading, travel. *Address:* 12 Roseworth Crescent, Gosforth, Newcastle upon Tyne NE3 1NR. *T:* 091–284 5363.

JOHNSON, Brian; *see* Johnson, R. B.

JOHNSON, Prof. Brian Frederick Gilbert, PhD; FRS 1991; Crum Brown Professor of Inorganic Chemistry, University of Edinburgh, since 1991; *b* 11 Sept. 1938; *s* of Frank and Mona Johnson; *m* 1962, Christine Draper; two *d*. *Educ:* Northampton Grammar Sch.; Univ. of Nottingham (BSc, PhD). Lecturer: Univ. of Manchester, 1965–67; UCL, 1967–70; Cambridge University: Lectr, 1970–78; Reader, 1978–90; Fitzwilliam College: Fellow, 1970–90; Pres., 1988–89; Vice Master, 1989–90. *Publication:* Transition Metal Clusters, 1982. *Recreations:* walking, cycling. *Address:* Department of Chemistry, University of Edinburgh, West Mains Road, Edinburgh EH9 3JJ. *T:* 031–650 4706.

JOHNSON, Bruce Joseph F.; *see* Forsyth-Johnson.

JOHNSON, Carol Alfred, CBE 1951; *b* 1903; *m*. Admitted a Solicitor, 1933 (Hons); practised City of London; Hon. Solicitor to Housing Assocs in Southwark and Fulham; Asst Town Clerk, Borough of Southall, 1940–43; Secretary of the Parliamentary Labour Party, 1943–59. Alderman, Lambeth Borough Council, 1937–49 (sometime Leader). MP (Lab) Lewisham S, Sept. 1959–Feb. 1974; served on Chairman's Panel, presiding over cttees and occasionally the House; sometime Chm., History of Parliament Trust and Anglo-Italian Parly Cttee; Mem., Parly delegations to Nigeria, Persia (now Iran), the Cameroons and India. Served on Council of Europe; many years Jt Hon. Sec., British Council of European Movement, now Vice-Pres., Lab. Cttee for Europe. Sometime Hon. Sec., Friends of Africa and later Treasurer, Fabian Colonial Bureau; original Mem., Local Govt Adv. Panel, Colonial Office; Member: Fabian delegn to Czechoslovakia, 1946; British Council Lecture Tour to Finland, 1946. Exec. Mem., Commons (now Open Spaces) Soc. (formerly Chm.); Mem., Standing Cttee on Nat. Parks (now Council for Nat. Parks). Trustee, William Morris Soc.; Mem. Exec. Cttee, British-Italian Soc.; Governor, British Inst., Florence, 1965–86. Comdr, Italian Order of Merit. *Address:* 11 Cliffe House, Radnor Cliff, Folkestone, Kent CT20 2TY.

JOHNSON, Charles Ernest, JP; Councillor, Salford, since 1986; Member, Police Authority, Greater Manchester Police, since 1986; *b* 2 Jan. 1918; adopted *s* of Henry and Mary Johnson; *m* 1942, Betty, *d* of William Nelson Hesford, farmer; one *s*. *Educ:* elementary school. Commenced work as apprentice coppersmith, 1932; called up to Royal Navy, 1940, demobilised, 1946. Councillor and Alderman, Eccles Town Council, 1952–73; Mayor, 1964–65; Chm. of various cttees, incl. Housing, for 14 years, and of Local Employment Cttee, for ten years; Councillor, Greater Manchester County Council, 1974–86 (Chairman, 1982–83). Mem., Assoc. of Municipal Councils, 1958–. JP Eccles, 1965. 1939–45 Medal, Atlantic Medal, Africa Star, Victory Medal; Imperial Service Medal, 1978. *Recreations:* gardening, watching football, swimming. *Address:* 17 Dartford Avenue, Winton, Eccles, Manchester M30 8NF. *T:* 061–789 4229.

JOHNSON, Christopher Edmund; Director General, Defence Accounts, Ministry of Defence, 1984–89; *b* 17 Jan. 1934; *s* of Christopher and Phyllis Johnson; *m* 1956, Janet Yvonne Wakefield; eight *s* three *d*. *Educ:* Salesian Coll., Chertsey; Collyer's Sch., Horsham. Sub Lt, RNVR, 1952–54. Exec. Officer, 1954–58, Higher Exec. Officer, 1959–65, War Office; Principal, MoD, 1965–71; UK Jt Comd Sec., ANZUK Force, Singapore, 1971–74; Ministry of Defence: Asst Sec., 1974–84; Asst Under Sec. of State, 1984. *Recreations:*

gardening, reading. *Address:* Southcot House, Lyncombe Hill, Bath, Avon BA2 4PQ. *T:* Bath (0225) 314247.

JOHNSON, David Burnham, QC 1978; a Recorder, since 1984; *b* 6 Aug. 1930; *s* of late Thomas Burnham Johnson and of Elsie May Johnson; *m* 1968, Julia Clare Addison Hopkinson, *o d* of late Col H. S. P. Hopkinson, OBE; one *s* three *d. Educ:* Truro Sch.; Univ. of Wales. Solicitor and Notary Public, Oct. 1952. Commissioned, National Service, with Royal Artillery, 1952–54. Private practice as solicitor, Cardiff and Plymouth, 1954–67; called to Bar, Inner Temple, 1967, Bencher, 1985. *Recreations:* sailing, walking, shooting, reading, music. *Address:* 25 Murray Road, Wimbledon, SW19 4PD. *T:* 081–947 9188; (chambers) 3 Essex Court, Temple, EC4Y 9AL. *T:* 071–583 9294. *Club:* Royal Western Yacht (Plymouth).

JOHNSON, Prof. David Hugh Nevil; Professor of International Law, Sydney University, 1976–85, now Emeritus; *b* 4 Jan. 1920; 2nd *s* of James Johnson and Gladys Mary (*née* Knight); *m* 1952, Evelyn Joan Fletcher. *Educ:* Winchester Coll.; Trinity Coll., Cambridge; Columbia Univ., New York. MA, LLM Cantab. Served Royal Corps of Signals, 1940–46. Called to Bar, Lincoln's Inn, 1950. Asst Legal Adviser, Foreign Office, 1950–53; Reader in Internat. Law, 1953–59, in Internat. and Air Law, 1959–60, Prof., 1960–Dec. 1975, Dean of Faculty of Laws, 1968–72, Univ. of London. Sen. Legal Officer, Office of Legal Affairs, UN, 1956–57. Registrar, the Court of Arbitration, Argentine-Chile Frontier Case, 1965–68. *Publications:* Rights in Air Space, 1965; articles in legal jls. *Address:* 3 Flannel Flower Fairway, Shoal Bay, NSW 2315, Australia.

JOHNSON, David John; HM Diplomatic Service; Head, Conference on Security and Co-operation in Europe Unit, Foreign and Commonwealth Office, since 1990; *b* 2 March 1938; *s* of Herbert John Victor Johnson and Mildred Frances (*née* Boyd); *m* 1976, Kathleen Johanna Hicks; three *d. Educ:* Harvey Grammar Sch., Folkestone. Served RAF, 1957–59. Entered FO, 1959; Third Sec., Moscow, 1962; Third, later Second Sec., Dakar, 1965; Second Secretary: Ulan Bator, 1969; UK Mission to UN, Geneva, 1969; First Secretary: UK Mission to negotiations on mutual reduction of forces and armaments and associated measures, Vienna, 1973; Moscow, 1975; FCO, 1978; Counsellor, NATO Defence Coll., Rome, 1982; seconded to NATO Internat. Secretariat, Brussels, 1982; Counsellor and Head of Chancery, Islamabad, 1985–90. *Recreations:* marquetry, music, reading. *Address:* c/o Foreign and Commonwealth Office, SW1A 2AH.

JOHNSON, David Robert W.; see Wilson-Johnson.

JOHNSON, (Denis) Gordon, CBE 1969; Chairman, Geo. Bassett Holdings Ltd, 1955–78 (Managing Director, 1955–71); Chairman: W. R. Wilkinson & Co. Ltd, Pontefract, 1961–78; Drakes Sweets Marketing Ltd, 1961–78; B. V. de Faam, Holland, 1964–78; Barratt & Co. Ltd, London, 1968–78; *b* 8 Oct. 1911; *s* of late Percy Johnson; *m* 1986, Joan Wilde (*née* Barringham). *Educ:* Harrow; Hertford Coll., Oxford (MA). President: Cocoa, Chocolate and Confectionery Alliance, 1964–66 (Hon. Treas., 1972–77); Confectioners' Benevolent Fund, 1967–68; Member: Yorks Electricity Bd, 1965–75; Food Manufacturing Economic Develt Cttee, 1967–70; Council of CBI, 1968–78; Council, Sheffield Univ., 1972–81; Chm., S Yorks Industrialists' Council, 1976–78. Chm., Hallam Conservative Assoc., 1966–69, and 1973–76; Hon. Treas., City of Sheffield Conservative Fedn, 1969–73; Chm., City of Sheffield Cons. Assocs, 1976–78. Pres., Sheffield and Hallamshire Lawn Tennis Club. Vis. Fellow, Yorks and Humberside Regional Management Centre. CBIM; MInstD. *Publications:* address to British Assoc. (Economics Section), 1964; contributor to: Business Growth (ed Edwards and Townsend), 1966; Pricing Strategy (ed Taylor and Wills), 1969. *Recreations:* walking, travel, philosophy. *Address:* 7 Broadbent Street, W1X 9HJ. *T:* 071–629 1642; Ivy Cottage, Trolver Croft, Feock, Truro, Cornwall TR3 6RT. *T:* Truro (0872) 865669.

JOHNSON, Donald Edwin, RIBA, FRTPI; Under Secretary, 1978–80, and Deputy Chief Planner, 1975–80, Department of the Environment; *b* 4 July 1920; *s* of Henry William Johnson and Ann Catherine (*née* Lake); *m* 1947, Thérèse Andrée Simone Marquant; two *s* one *d. Educ:* Haberdashers' Aske's, Hatcham; School of Architecture, Regent Polytechnic; APRR School of Planning. Served War, Royal Artillery and Royal Engineers, 1940–45. Planning Officer, Min. of Town and Country Planning, 1947; Sen. Planning Officer, 1950, Principal Planner, 1965, Asst Chief Planner, 1972. *Publications: fiction:* Project 38, 1963; Crooked Cross, 1964; Flashing Mountain, 1965; Devil of Bruges, 1966. *Address:* Flat D, 1 Morpeth Terrace, SW1P 1EW. *T:* 071–834 7300.

JOHNSON, Prof. Douglas William John; Professor of French History, University College London, 1968–90, now Emeritus; *b* Edinburgh, 1 Feb. 1925; *o s* of John Thornburn Johnson and Christine Mair; *m* 1950, Madeleine Rébillard; one *d. Educ:* Royal Grammar Sch., Lancaster; Worcester Coll., Oxford (BA, BLitt); Ecole Normale Supérieure, Paris. Birmingham Univ.: Lectr in Modern History, 1949; Prof. of Modern History and Chm. of Sch. of History, 1963–68; Head of Dept of History, 1979–83, Dean, Faculty of Arts, 1979–82, UCL. Vis. Prof., Univs of Aix-en-Provence, Nancy, Paris, British Columbia, Toronto, Caen, Lyons, Montreal; Lectures: Zaharoff, Oxford Univ., 1989; Simon Cohen Meml, Kent Univ., 1990. Chm. Bd of Examrs in History, Univ. of London, 1973–75; Member: CNAA, 1974–79; Franco–British Council, 1976–. FRHistS. Ordre Nat. du Mérite (France), 1980; Commandeur des Palmes Académiques (France), 1987; Chevalier de la Légion d'Honneur (France), 1990. *Publications:* Guizot: Aspects of French History 1787–1874, 1963; France and the Dreyfus Affair, 1966; France, 1969; Concise History of France, 1970; The French Revolution, 1970; (ed jtly) Britain and France: Ten Centuries, 1980; (with Richard Hoggart) An Idea of Europe, 1987; (with Madeleine Johnson) The Age of Illusion, 1987; (with Geoffrey Best) The Permanent Revolution, 1988; (General Editor) The Making of the Modern World; (General Editor) The Fontana History of Modern France. *Recreations:* music, French politics. *Address:* 29 Rudall Crescent, NW3 1RR; 12 rue Delambre, Paris 75012, France. *Club:* Travellers'.

JOHNSON, Eric Alfred George, CBE 1953; retired chartered engineer; specialist in flood control, sea defences and land drainage engineering; *b* 3 Sept. 1911; *s* of Ernest George Johnson and Amelia Rhoda Johnson; *m* 1936, Barbara Mary Robin; one *d. Educ:* Taunton's Sch., Southampton; UC Southampton. Grad. Engrg, 1931; served for periods with Great Ouse and Trent Catchment Boards, 1933–37; joined Min. of Agriculture, 1937; Chief Engr, 1949–72. Has been associated with most major flood alleviation schemes carried out 1931–81, incl. Thames Barrier; Consultant, Sir Murdoch MacDonald & Partners, 1972–82; Vice-Pres., Internat. Commn of Irrigation and Drainage, 1958–61; former chm. of several internat. and nat. cttees. *Publications:* papers in ICE and other professional jls. *Recreation:* visiting the countryside and sea coast to see some of the areas with which he has been associated through floods and protection schemes. *Address:* 94 Park Avenue, Orpington, Kent BR6 9EF. *T:* Orpington (0689) 823802.

JOHNSON, Prof. Francis Rea; Professor of Anatomy, London Hospital Medical College, 1968–86, now Emeritus; Pre-clinical Sub-Dean, 1979–86; *b* 8 July 1921; *s* of Marcus Jervis Johnson and Elizabeth Johnson; *m* 1951, Ena Patricia Laverty; one *s* one *d. Educ:* Omagh Academy, N Ire.; Queen's Univ., Belfast. MB, BCh, BAO 1945, MD 1949. House appts, Belfast City Hosp., 1946; Demonstrator in Anatomy and Physiology, QUB,

1947–50; Lectr in Anatomy, Sheffield Univ., 1950–57; Reader in Anatomy, London Hosp. Med. Coll., 1957–64; Prof. of Histology, London Hosp. Med. Coll., 1964–68. *Publications:* papers on histochemistry and ultrastructure of tissues and organs in various jls. *Recreations:* motoring, camping, gardening. *Address:* 11 Beacon Rise, Sevenoaks, Kent TN13 2NJ. *T:* Sevenoaks (0732) 453343.

JOHNSON, Frank Robert; Associate Editor, The Sunday Telegraph, since 1988; *b* 20 Jan. 1943; *s* of late Ernest Johnson, pastry cook and confectioner, and Doreen (*née* Skinner). *Educ:* Chartesey Secondary Sch., Shoreditch; Shoreditch Secondary Sch. Messenger Boy, Sunday Express, 1959–60; Reporter on local and regional newspapers, 1960–69; Political Staff, Sun, 1969–72; Parly Sketch Writer and Leader Writer, Daily Telegraph, 1972–79; Columnist, Now! Magazine, 1979–81; The Times: Parly Sketch Writer, 1981–83; Paris Diarist, 1984; Bonn Corresp., 1985–86; Parly Sketch Writer, 1986–87; Associate Editor, 1987–88. Parly Sketch Writer of the Year Award, Granada, What The Papers Say, 1977; Columnist of the Year, British Press Awards, 1981. *Publications:* Out of Order, 1982; Frank Johnson's Election Year, 1983. *Recreations:* opera, ballet. *Address:* 12 Battishill Street, N1 1TE.

JOHNSON, Air Vice-Marshal Frank Sidney Roland, CB 1973; OBE 1963; CBIM; Base Manager, British Aircraft Corporation RSAF, Dhahran, Saudi Arabia, 1978–82, retired; *b* 4 Aug. 1917; *s* of Major Harry Johnson, IA, and Georgina Marklew; *m* 1943, Evelyn Hunt; two *s. Educ:* Trinity County Secondary Sch., Wood Green. Enlisted, 1935; served in UK and India; commnd, 1943; Germany (Berlin Airlift), 1948; Western Union Defence Organisation, 1955–57; Directing Staff, RAF Staff Coll., 1958–60; comd 113 MU, RAF Nicosia, 1960–63; Chief Instructor Equipment and Secretarial Wing, RAF Coll. Cranwell, 1963–64; Dep. Dir MoD, 1965–66; idc 1967; Chief Supply Officer, Fighter and Strike Comds, 1968–70; Dir-Gen. of Supply, RAF, 1971–73; Supply Manager, BAC, Saudi Arabia, 1974–76; Base Manager, BAC RSAF, Khamis Mushayt, Saudi Arabia, 1976–77. *Recreations:* golf, squash, hockey, cricket. *Address:* 9 Hazely, Tring, Herts HP23 5JH. *T:* Tring (044282) 6535. *Club:* Royal Air Force.

JOHNSON, Frederick Alistair, PhD; FInstP; Technical Director, GEC-Marconi Research Centre (formerly GEC Research), since 1987; *b* Christchurch, NZ, 9 April 1928; *s* of Archibald Frederick Johnson and Minnie, *d* of William Frederick Pellew; *m* 1952, Isobel Beth, *d* of Horace George Wilson; two *d. Educ:* Christchurch Boys' High Sch.; Univ. of Canterbury, New Zealand (MSc, PhD). Rutherford Meml Fellow, 1952; Lectr, Univ. of Otago, 1952; post graduate research, Bristol Univ., 1953–55. Royal Radar Establishment, 1956–75: Individual Merit Promotion, 1964; Head of Physics Dept, 1968–73; Dep. Director, 1973–75; Dep. Dir, Royal Armament Research & Development Estabt, 1975–77; Dir of Scientific and Technical Intell., MoD, 1977–79; Chief Scientist (Royal Navy) and Dir Gen. Research A, MoD, 1980–84; Dir, Marconi Maritime Applied Res. Lab., and Chief Scientist, Marconi Underwater Systems Ltd, 1985–87. Visiting Professor, Massachusetts Inst. of Technology, 1967–68; Hon. Prof. of Physics, Birmingham Univ., 1969–75. *Publications:* numerous papers on spectroscopy, optics and lattice dynamics in Proc. Physical Soc. and Proc. Royal Soc. *Recreation:* sailing. *Address:* Otia Tuta, Grassy Lane, Sevenoaks, Kent TN13 1PL. *Club:* Athenæum.

JOHNSON, Lt-Gen. Sir Garry (Dene), KCB 1990; OBE 1977 (MBE 1971); MC 1965; Inspector General Doctrine and Training, since 1991; *b* 20 Sept. 1937; *m* 1962, Caroline Sarah Frearson; two *s. Educ:* Christ's Hospital. psc, ndc, rcds. Commissioned 10th Princess Mary's Own Gurkha Rifles, 1956; Malaya and Borneo campaigns, 1956–67; Royal Green Jackets, 1970; command, 1st Bn RGJ, 1976–79; Comdr, 11 Armoured Brigade, 1981–82; Dep. Chief of Staff, HQ BAOR, 1983; ACDS (NATO/UK), 1985–87; Comdr, British Forces Hong Kong, and Maj.-Gen., Bde of Gurkhas, 1987–89; Comdr Trng and Arms Dirs, 1989–91. Colonel, 10th PMO Gurkha Rifles, 1985–; Col Comdt, Light Div., 1990–. *Publication:* Brightly Shone the Dawn, 1979. *Address:* HQ UK Land Forces, Erskine Barracks, Wilton, Wilts. *Clubs:* Army and Navy; Tanglin (Singapore).

JOHNSON, Gordon; see Johnson, D. G.

JOHNSON, Graham Rhodes; concert accompanist; Professor of Accompaniment, Guildhall School of Music, since 1986; *b* 10 July 1950; *s* of late John Edward Donald Johnson and of Violet May Johnson (*née* Johnson). *Educ:* Hamilton High Sch., Bulawayo, Rhodesia; Royal Acad. of Music, London. FRAM 1984; FGSM 1988. Concert début, Wigmore Hall, 1972; has since accompanied Elisabeth Schwarzkopf, Jessye Norman, Victoria de los Angeles (USA Tour 1977), Dame Janet Baker, Sir Peter Pears, Felicity Lott, Felicity Palmer, Margaret Price (USA Tour 1985), Peter Schreier, John Shirley Quirk, Valerie Masterson, Dame Kiri Te Kanawa, Mady Mesplé, Robert Holl, Tom Krause, Sergei Leiferkus, Brigitte Fassbaender. Work with contemporaries led to formation of The Songmakers' Almanac (Artistic Director); has devised and accompanied over 150 London recitals for this group since Oct. 1976. Tours of US with Sarah Walker, Richard Jackson, and of Australia and NZ with The Songmakers' Almanac, 1981. Writer and presenter of major BBC Radio 3 series on Poulenc songs, and BBC TV programmes on Schubert songs (1978) and the songs of Liszt (1986). Lectr at song courses in Savonlinna (Finland), US and at Pears-Britten Sch., Snape; Artistic advr and accompanist, Alte Oper Festival, Frankfurt, 1981–82; Festival appearances in Aldeburgh, Edinburgh, Munich, Hohenems, Bath, Hong Kong, Bermuda. Many recordings incl. those with Songmakers' Almanac, Martyn Hill, Elly Ameling, Arleen Auger, Janet Baker, Philip Langridge, Ann Murray, Sarah Walker, and of Schubert Lieder, with various artists, 1988–. Gramophone Award, 1989. *Publications:* (contrib.) The Britten Companion, ed Christopher Palmer, 1984; (contrib.) Gerald Moore, The Unashamed Accompanist, rev. edn 1984; reviews in TLS, articles for music jls. *Recreation:* eating in good restaurants with friends and fine wine. *Address:* 83 Fordwych Road, NW2 3TL. *T:* 081–452 5193.

JOHNSON, Ven. Hayman; Archdeacon of Sheffield, 1963–78, Archdeacon Emeritus 1978; a Canon Residentiary of Sheffield Cathedral, 1975–78; Chaplain to HM The Queen, 1969–82; *b* 29 June 1912; *s* of late W. G. Johnson, Exeter; *m* 1943, Margaret Louise Price; one *d. Educ:* Exeter Sch.; New Coll., Oxon. Chaplain, RAFVR, 1941–46; Chaplain and Vicar Temporal, Hornchurch, 1953–61; Examining Chaplain to Bishop of Sheffield, 1962–78. *Address:* Flat 1, Parklands, 56 Kibbles Lane, Southborough, Tunbridge Wells, Kent TN4 0LQ.

JOHNSON, Howard Sydney; solicitor; Senior Partner, Howard Johnson & McQue, 1933–83; Director, Alliance Building Society, since 1970; *b* 25 Dec. 1911; *s* of Sydney Thomas Johnson; *m* 1939, Betty Frankiss, actress. *Educ:* Brighton; Highgate. Served War of 1939–45, Africa; invalided out as Major. Joined TA before the war. Mem. of Brighton Town Council, 1945–50. MP (C) Kemptown Div. of Brighton, 1950–Sept. 1959. *Publication:* (contrib.) Against Hunting, ed Patrick Moore, 1965. *Address:* Ballakinnag Cottage, Smeale, Andreas, Isle of Man. *T:* Kirk Andreas (0624) 880712.

JOHNSON, Hugh Eric Allan; author, broadcaster and editor; *b* 10 March 1939; *s* of late Guy Francis Johnson, CBE and Grace Kittel; *m* 1965, Judith Eve Grinling; one *s* two *d. Educ:* Rugby Sch.; King's Coll., Cambridge (MA). Staff writer, Condé Nast publications, 1960–63; Editor, Wine & Food, and Sec., Wine and Food Soc., 1963–65; Wine Corresp.,

1962–67, and Travel Editor, 1967, Sunday Times; Editor, Queen, 1968–70. Pres., The Sunday Times Wine Club, 1973–. Chairman: Saling Hall Press, 1975–; Conservation Cttee, Internat. Dendrology Soc., 1979–86; Winestar Productions Ltd, 1984–; The Hugh Johnson Collection Ltd, 1985–. Dir, Société Civile du Château Latour, 1987–. Editorial Director: Jl of RHS, 1975–89, Editl Cons., 1989–; The Plantsman, 1979–. Wine Editor, Cuisine, New York, 1983–84; Wine Consultant: to Jardine Matheson Ltd, Hong Kong and Tokyo, 1985–; to British Airways, 1987–. Gardening Correspondent, New York Times, 1986–87. Video, How to Handle a Wine, 1984 (Glenfiddich Trophy, 1984; reissued as Understanding Wine, 1989); TV series: Wine—a user's guide (KQED, San Francisco), 1986; Vintage—a history of wine (Channel 4 and WGBH, Boston), 1989. Docteur ès Vins, Acad. du Vin de Bordeaux, 1987. *Publications:* Wine, 1966, rev. edn 1974; The World Atlas of Wine, 1971, 3rd edn 1985; The International Book of Trees, 1973, rev. edn 1984; (with Bob Thompson) The California Wine Book, 1976; Hugh Johnson's Pocket Wine Book, annually 1977–; The Principles of Gardening, 1979, rev. edn 1984; Understanding Wine, 1980; (with Paul Miles) The Pocket Encyclopedia of Garden Plants, 1981; Hugh Johnson's Wine Companion, 1983, 3rd edn 1991; How to Enjoy Your Wine, 1985; The Hugh Johnson Cellar Book, 1986; The Atlas of German Wines, 1986; Hugh Johnson's Wine Cellar, (US) 1986; (with Jan Read) The Wine and Food of Spain, 1987; (with Hubrecht Duijker) The Wine Atlas of France, 1987; The Story of Wine, 1989 (awards, incl. Glenfiddich Wine Award, 1990); articles on gastronomy, travel and gardening. *Recreations:* travelling, staying at home. *Address:* Saling Hall, Great Saling, Essex CM7 5DT; 73 St James's Street, SW1. *Clubs:* Garrick, Saintsbury.

JOHNSON, James, BA, DPA; *b* 16 Sept. 1908; *s* of James and Mary Elizabeth Johnson; *m* 1937, Gladys Evelyn Green; one *d. Educ:* Duke's Sch., Alnwick; Leeds Univ. BA 1st Cl. Hons Geography, 1931; Diploma in Education, 1932; Diploma in Public Administration (London), 1944. FRGS. Schoolmaster: Queen Elizabeth Grammar Sch., Atherstone, 1931; Scarborough High Sch., 1934; Bablake Sch., Coventry, 1944. Lecturer, Coventry Tech. Coll., 1948–50. MP (Lab): Rugby Div. of Warwicks, 1950–59; Kingston upon Hull West, 1964–83. Trade Union Advr, Kenya Local Govt Workers, 1959–60; Student Adviser, Republic of Liberia, 1960–64. Treasurer, Commonwealth Parly Assoc., 1979–82; Chm., Anglo-Somali Soc., 1980–. Dir, Hull City Football Club, 1982–. Freeman, City of Kingston-upon-Hull, 1982. Played soccer for British Univs and Corinthians. Grand Comdr, Order of Star of Africa (Liberia), 1967; Commander's Cross 2nd Class (Austria), 1985; Comdr, Order of Somali Star (Somalia), 1988. *Recreation:* watching soccer and snooker. *Address:* 70 Home Park Road, SW19. *T:* 081–946 6224. *Clubs:* Royal Over-Seas League; Humber St Andrews Engineering Social and Recreation.

JOHNSON, Air Vice-Marshal James Edgar, (Johnnie Johnson), CB 1965; CBE 1960; DSO 1943 and Bars, 1943, 1944; DFC 1941 and Bar, 1942; DL; Chief Executive, Johnnie Johnson Housing Trust, Ltd; Director of Companies in Canada, South Africa and UK; *m* Pauline Ingate; two *s. Educ:* Loughborough Sch.; Nottingham Univ. Civil Engr and Mem. of RAFVR until 1939; served with 616 Sqdn AAF, 1940–42; 610 Sqdn AAF, 1943; Wing Comdr Flying: Kenley, 1943; 127 Wing, 1944; Officer Comdg: 125 Wing (2nd TAF), 1944–45; 124 Wing (2nd TAF), 1945–46; RCAF Staff Coll., 1947–48; USAF (Exchange Officer), 1948–50; served Korea (with USAF), 1950–51; OC, RAF Wildenrath (2nd TAF), 1952–54; Air Ministry, 1954–57; Officer Commanding, RAF Cottesmore, Bomber Command, 1957–60; idc 1960; Senior Air Staff Officer, No 3 Group, Bomber Command, Mildenhall, Suffolk, 1960–63; AOC, Air Forces Middle East, Aden, 1963–65; retired. DL Leicester, 1967. Order of Leopold, 1945, Croix de Guerre, 1945 (Belgium); Legion of Merit, 1950, DFC 1943, Air Medal, 1950 (USA); Légion d'Honneur (France), 1988. *Publications:* Wing Leader, 1956; Full Circle, 1964; The Story of Air Fighting, 1985; (jtly) Glorious Summer, 1990. *Recreations:* shooting, golf. *Address:* The Stables, Hargate, Buxton, Derbyshire SK17 8TA. *Club:* Royal Air Force.

JOHNSON, Rt. Rev. James Nathaniel; Rector of Byfield with Boddington and Aston-le-Walls, and Assistant Bishop, Peterborough Diocese, since 1991; *b* 28 April 1932; *s* of William and Lydia Florence Johnson; *m* 1953, Evelyn Joyce Clifford; one *s* one *d. Educ:* Primary and Secondary Selective School, St Helena; Church Army College; Wells Theolog. Coll. Deacon 1864, priest 1965; Curate of St Peter's, Lawrence Weston, dio. Bristol, 1964–66; Priest-in-charge of St Paul's Cathedral, St Helena, 1966–69, Vicar 1969–71; Domestic Chaplain to Bishop of St Helena, 1967–71; USPG Area Sec. for Diocese of Exeter and Truro, 1972–74; Rector of Combe Martin dio. Exeter, 1974–80; Hon. Canon of St Helena, 1975–85; Vicar of St Augustine, Thorpe Bay, dio. Chelmsford, 1980–85; Bishop of St Helena, 1985–91. *Recreation:* music, gardening. *Address:* The Rectory, Church Street, Byfield, Daventry NN11 6XN. *Club:* Commonwealth Trust.

JOHNSON, John Robin; His Honour Judge Johnson; a Circuit Judge, since 1973; *b* 27 Nov. 1927; *s* of Sir Philip Bulmer Johnson, Hexham, Northumberland; *m* 1958, Meriel Jean, *d* of H. B. Speke, Aydon, Corbridge; one *s* one *d. Educ:* Winchester; Trinity Coll., Cambridge. Called to Bar, Middle Temple, 1950. Dep. Chm., Northumberland QS, 1966–71; a Recorder of the Crown Court, 1972–73. *Address:* c/o Crown Court, Kenton Bar, Newcastle-upon-Tyne.

JOHNSON, Sir John (Rodney), KCMG 1988 (CMG 1981); HM Diplomatic Service, retired; Director, Foreign Service Programme, and specially elected Fellow, Keble College, University of Oxford, since 1990; Chairman, Countryside Commission, since 1991; *b* 6 Sept. 1930; *s* of Edwin Done Johnson, OBE and Florence Mary (*née* Clough); *m* 1956, Jean Mary Lewis; three *s* one *d. Educ:* Manchester Grammar Sch.; Oxford Univ. (MA). HM Colonial Service, Kenya, 1955–64; Dist Comr, Thika, 1962–64; Administrator, Cttee of Vice-Chancellors and Principals of UK Univs, 1965; First Sec., FCO, 1966–69; Head of Chancery, British Embassy, Algiers, 1969–72; Dep. High Comr, British High Commn, Barbados, 1972–74; Counsellor, British High Commn, Lagos, 1975–78; Head of W African Dept, FCO, and Ambassador (non-resident) to Chad, 1978–80; High Comr in Zambia, 1980–84; Asst Under Sec. of State (Africa), FCO, 1984–86; High Comr in Kenya, 1986–90. *Recreations:* climbing, reaching remote places, conservation. *Address:* The Gables, High Street, Amersham, Bucks HP7 0DP. *Clubs:* Travellers'; Climbers; Mombasa.

JOHNSON, Air Vice-Marshal Johnnie; *see* Johnson, James Edgar.

JOHNSON, Kenneth James, OBE 1966; industrial consultant; Chairman, Crown Agents Pensions Trust, since 1984; *b* 8 Feb. 1926; *s* of Albert Percy Johnson and Winifred Florence (*née* Coole); *m* 1951, Margaret Teresa Bontoft Jenkins; three *s* two *d. Educ:* Rishworth School, near Halifax; Wadham Coll., Oxford; LSE; SOAS. Indian Army (14 Punjab Regt), 1945–47. Colonial Admin. Service, Nigeria, 1949–61, senior appts in Min. of Finance and Min. of Commerce and Industry; Head of Economic Dept, later Dir of Industrial Affairs, CBI, 1961–70; Courtaulds Ltd, 1970–73: Chm. and Man. Dir, various subsidiary cos; Dep. Chm., Pay Board, 1973–74. Dunlop Group: 1974–85: Personnel Dir, 1974–79; Overseas Dir, Dunlop Holdings plc, 1979–84; Chm., Dunlop International AG, 1984–85. Member: Bd of Crown Agents for Oversea Govts and Administrations, 1980–88; Crown Agents Hldg and Realisation Bd, 1980–88. FRSA 1972; FIPM 1976. *Recreations:* book-collecting, travel. *Address:* Woodgetters, Shipley, Horsham, West Sussex RH13 7BQ. *Clubs:* Oriental, Commonwealth Trust.

JOHNSON, Prof. Kenneth Langstreth, PhD; FRS 1982; FEng 1987; Professor of Engineering, Cambridge University, since 1977; Fellow of Jesus College, Cambridge, since 1957; *b* 19 March 1925; *s* of Frank Herbert Johnson and Ellen Howorth Langstreth; *m* 1954, Dorothy Rosemary Watkins; one *s* two *d. Educ:* Barrow Grammar Sch.; Manchester Univ. (MScTech, MA, PhD). FIMechE. Engr, Messrs Rotol Ltd, Gloucester, 1944–49; Asst Lectr, Coll. of Technology, Manchester, 1949–54; Lectr, then Reader in Engrg, Cambridge Univ., 1954–77. Tribology Trust Gold Medal, IMechE, 1985. *Publications:* Contact Mechanics, 1985; contrib. scientific and engrg jls, and Proc. IMechE. *Recreations:* mountain walking, swimming. *Address:* 13 Park Terrace, Cambridge. *T:* Cambridge (0223) 355287.

JOHNSON, Prof. Louise Napier, FRS 1990; David Phillips Professor of Molecular Biophysics, and Professorial Fellow, Corpus Christi College, Oxford, since 1990; *b* 26 Sept. 1940; *m*; one *s.* one *d. Educ:* Wimbledon High Sch. for Girls; University College London (BSc 1962); Royal Institution, London (PhD 1965). Research Asst., Yale Univ., 1966; University of Oxford: Demonstrator, Zoology Dept, 1967–73; Lectr in Molecular Biophysics, 1973–90; Reader, 1990; Additional Fellow, Somerville College, 1973–90, Hon. Fellow, 1991. Kaj Linderström-Lang Prize, 1989. *Publications:* Protein Crystallography (jtly with T. L. Blundell), 1976; papers on lysozyme, glycogen phosphorylase, protein crystallography, enzyme mechanism and allosteric mechanisms. *Recreation:* family. *Address:* Laboratory of Molecular Biophysics, Rex Richards Building, University of Oxford, South Parks Road, Oxford OX1 3QU.

JOHNSON, Merwyn; *see* Johnson, W. M.

JOHNSON, Michael Howard; a Social Security Commissioner, since 1986; a Recorder of the Crown Court, since 1980; *b* 9 May 1930; *s* of Howard Sydney Johnson and Nora Winifred Johnson; *m* 1st, 1954, Elisabeth Loewenthal (marr. diss.); two *d*; 2nd, 1962, Margaret Hazel, *d* of late Ernest Seymour Thomas and Marjorie Lillian Thomas. *Educ:* Charterhouse; Chelsea School of Art. Partner, Johnson & Hecht, Designers and Typographers, 1954–64. Called to the Bar, Gray's Inn, 1964. Asst Parliamentary Boundary Commissioner, 1976–84. Chm., Hertfordshire FPC, 1985–86. *Recreations:* painting, music, gardening. *Address:* Office of the Social Security Commissioners, 83–86 Farringdon Street, EC4A 4BL. *T:* 071–353 5145.

JOHNSON, Michael York-; *see* York, M.

JOHNSON, Dame Monica; *see* Golding, Dame (Cecilie) Monica.

JOHNSON, Nevil; Nuffield Reader in the Comparative Study of Institutions, University of Oxford, and Professorial Fellow, Nuffield College, since 1969; *b* 6 Feb. 1929; *s* of G. E. Johnson and Doris Johnson, MBE, Darlington; *m* 1957, Ulla van Aubel; two *s. Educ:* Queen Elizabeth Grammar Sch., Darlington; University Coll., Oxford (BA PPE 1952, MA 1962). Army service, 1947–49. Admin. Cl. of Home Civil Service: Min. of Supply, 1952–57; Min. of Housing and Local Govt, 1957–62; Lectr in Politics, Univ. of Nottingham, 1962–66; Sen. Lectr in Politics, Univ. of Warwick, 1966–69. Chm. Board, Faculty of Social Studies, Oxford, 1976–78. Visiting Professor: Ruhr Univ. of Bochum, 1968–69; Univ. of Munich, 1980. Mem., ESRC (formerly SSRC), 1981–87 (Chm., Govt and Law Cttee, 1982–86). Civil Service Comr (pt-time), 1982–85. Mem. Exec. Council, RIPA, 1965–87; Chm., Study of Parlt Gp, 1984–87. Hon. Editor, Public Administration, 1967–81. *Publications:* Parliament and Administration: The Estimates Committee 1945–65, 1967; Government in the Federal Republic of Germany, 1973; In Search of the Constitution, 1977 (trans. German, 1977); (with A. Cochrane) Economic Policy-Making by Local Authorities in Britain and Western Germany, 1981; State and Government in the Federal Republic of Germany, 1983; The Limits of Political Science, 1989 (trans. Spanish, 1991); articles in Public Admin, Political Studies, Parly Affairs, Ztschr. für Politik, Die Verwaltung, and Der Staat. *Recreations:* walking, swimming, gardening. *Address:* 2 Race Farm Cottages, Kingston Bagpuize, Oxon OX13 5AU. *T:* Longworth (0865) 820777.

JOHNSON, Prof. Newell Walter, MDSc, PhD; FDSRCS, FRACDS, FRCPath; Nuffield Research Professor of Dental Science, Royal College of Surgeons of England, and Hon. Director, Medical Research Council, Dental Research Unit, London Hospital Medical College, since 1984; Hon. Consultant Dental Surgeon, London Hospital, since 1968; *b* 5 Aug. 1938; *s* of Otto Johnson and Lorna (*née* Guy); *m* 1965, Pauline Margaret Trafford (marr. diss. 1984); two *d. Educ:* University High Sch., Melbourne; Univ. of Melbourne (BDSc Hons 1960; MDSc 1963); Univ. of Bristol (PhD 1967). FDSRCS 1964; FRACDS 1966; FRCPath 1982. Res. Fellow in Pathology, Univ. of Melbourne, 1961–63; Lectr in Dental Surgery, UCL, 1963–64; Scientific Officer, MRC Dental Res. Unit, Bristol, 1964–67; London Hosp. Medical College: Reader in Experimental Oral Path., 1968–76; Prof. of Oral Path., 1976–83; Governor, 1983 (Chm., Academic Div. of Dentistry, 1983); Chm., London Hosp. Div. of Dentistry, 1981–83. Consultant in Oral Health, WHO, 1984–; Consultant, Fédération Dentaire Internationale, 1984–. Chm., UK Cttee, Royal Australasian Coll. of Dental Surgeons, 1981–83; FRSM; Mem. Council, Section of Odontology, RSM, 1972– (Pres., 1988–89). Member, Editorial Board: Jl of Oral Pathology, 1982–; Jl of Periodontal Research, 1986–; Jl of Clin. Periodontology, 1990–. *Publications:* (jtly) The Oral Mucosa in Health and Disease, 1975; (jtly) The Human Oral Mucosa: structure, metabolism and function, 1976; (jtly) Dental Caries: aetiology, pathology and prevention, 1979; (ed jtly) Oral Diseases in the Tropics, 1987; (ed) Detection of High Risk Groups for Oral Diseases, 3 vols, 1991; articles in scientific jls. *Recreations:* choral singing, music, theatre, squash, the environment, the Third World. *Club:* Blizard.

JOHNSON, Patrick, OBE 1945; MA; *b* 24 May 1904; 2nd *s* of A. F. W. Johnson, JP, and F. E. L. Cocking; unmarried. *Educ:* RN Colls, Osborne and Dartmouth; Tonbridge Sch.; Magdalen Coll., Oxford. Fellow and Lecturer in Natural Science, Magdalen Coll., 1928–47, Dean, 1934–38, Vice-Pres., 1946–47. Flying Officer, RAFO, 1929–34; commissioned in RA (TA), 1938; served War of 1939–45, in Middle East and NW Europe, Lt-Col, Asst Dir of Scientific Research, 21st Army Group and comdg No. 2 operational research section. Dir of Studies, RAF Coll., Cranwell, 1947–52; Dean of Inst. of Armament Studies, India, 1952–55; Scientific Adviser to the Army Council, 1955–58; Asst Scientific Adviser, SHAPE, 1958–62; Head of Experimental Develt Unit, Educnl Foundn for Visual Aids, 1962–70. *Recreations:* rowing (rowed against Cambridge, 1927), sailing, shooting. *Address:* 5 Linley Court, Rouse Gardens, SE21 8AQ. *Club:* Leander (Henley-on-Thames).

JOHNSON, Paul (Bede); author; *b* 2 Nov. 1928; *s* of William Aloysius and Anne Johnson; *m* 1957, Marigold Hunt; three *s* one *d. Educ:* Stonyhurst; Magdalen Coll., Oxford. Asst Exec. Editor, Réalités, 1952–55; Editorial Staff, New Statesman, 1955, Dir, Statesman and Nation Publishing Co., 1965, Editor of the New Statesman, 1965–70. Member: Royal Commn on the Press, 1974–77; Cable Authority, 1984–90. *Publications:* The Suez War, 1957; Journey into Chaos, 1958; Left of Centre, 1960; Merrie England,

1964; Statesmen and Nations, 1971; The Offshore Islanders, 1972; (with G. Gale) The Highland Jaunt, 1973; Elizabeth I, 1974; A Place in History, 1974; Pope John XXIII, 1975 (Yorkshire Post Book of the Year Award, 1975); A History of Christianity, 1976; Enemies of Society, 1977; The National Trust Book of British Castles, 1978; The Recovery of Freedom, 1980; British Cathedrals, 1980; Ireland: Land of Troubles, 1980; Pope John Paul II and the Catholic Restoration, 1982; A History of the Modern World from 1917 to the 1980s, 1983; The Pick of Paul Johnson, 1985; Oxford Book of Political Anecdotes, 1986; A History of the Jews, 1987; Intellectuals, 1988; The Birth of the Modern: world society 1815–30, 1991. *Recreations:* hill-walking, painting. *Address:* 29 Newton Road, W2 5JR. *T:* 071–229 3859; The Coach House, Over Stowey, near Bridgwater, Somerset TA5 1HA. *T:* Bridgwater (0278) 732393.

JOHNSON, Sir Peter (Colpoys Paley), 7th Bt *cr* 1755, of New York in North America; author; publishing consultant; *b* 26 March 1930; *s* of Sir John Paley Johnson, 6th Bt, MBE, and of Carol, *d* of late Edmund Haas; *S* father, 1975; *m* 1st, 1956, Clare (marr. diss. 1973), *d* of Dr Nigel Bruce; one *s* two *d*; 2nd, 1973, Caroline Elisabeth, *d* of late Sir John Hodsoll, CB; one *s*. *Educ:* Wellington Coll.; Royal Military Coll. of Science. Served RA, 1949; retired 1961, Captain. Dir, Sea Sure Ltd, 1965–73; Dir and Editor, Nautical Publishing Co. Ltd, 1970–81; Publishing Dir, Nautical Books, London, 1981–86. British Delegate, Internat. Offshore (Yachting) Council, 1970–79 (Chm. Internat. Technical Cttee, 1973–76); Ocean Racing Correspondent, Yachting World, London, 1971–81. Hon. Col, King's Royal Regt of NY (Canada), 1988–. *Publications:* Ocean Racing and Offshore Yachts, 1970, 2nd edn 1972; Boating Britain, 1973; Guinness Book of Yachting Facts and Feats, 1975; Guinness Guide to Sailing, 1981; This is Fast Cruising, 1985; The Encyclopedia of Yachting, 1989. *Recreation:* sailing. *Heir:* *s* Colpoys Guy Johnson, *b* 13 Nov. 1965. *Address:* Dene End, Buckland Dene, Lymington, Hampshire SO41 9DT. *T:* Lymington (0590) 675921, *Fax:* Lymington (0590) 672885. *Clubs:* Royal Ocean Racing; Royal Yacht Squadron.

JOHNSON, Philip Cortelyou; architect, with own firm, 1953–67, with Johnson/Burgee Architects, since 1967; *b* Cleveland, Ohio, 8 July 1906; *s* of Homer H. Johnson and Louise Pope Johnson. *Educ:* Harvard (AB 1927, *cum laude*). Dir, Dept of Architecture, The Museum of Modern Art, New York, 1932–54, Trustee, 1958–; Graduate Sch. of Design, Harvard, 1940–43 (BArch). Has taught and lectured at: Yale Univ.; Cornell Univ.; Pratt Inst. (Dr Fine Arts, 1962). Mem. AIA (New York Chapter); Architectural League, NY. Hon. Dr Fine Arts Yale, 1978. Gold Medal, AIA, 1978; Pritzker Architecture Prize, 1979. *Publications:* Machine Art, 1934; Mies van der Rohe, 1st edn 1947, 2nd edn 1953; (with Henry-Russell Hitchcock) The International Style, Architecture since 1922, 1932, new edn 1966; (with others) Modern Architects, 1932; Architecture 1949–65, 1966; Philip Johnson Writings, 1979; contributor to Architectural Review. *Address:* (business) Philip Johnson, 885 Third Avenue #300, New York, NY 10022–4834, USA; (home) Ponus Ridge Road, New Canaan, Conn. *T:* (203) 966–0565. *Clubs:* Athenæum, Century.

JOHNSON, Dr Ralph Hudson, FRCPG; FRACP; FRSE; Director of Postgraduate Medical Education and Training, Oxford University, since 1987; Professorial Fellow, Wadham College, Oxford; Hon. Consultant Physician and Neurologist, Oxford Regional Health Authority and Oxfordshire Health Authority, since 1987; *b* 3 Dec. 1933; *s* of Sydney R. E. Johnson and Phyllis Johnson (*née* Hudson); *m* 1970, Gillian Sydney (*née* Keith); one *s* one *d*. *Educ:* Rugby; St Catharine's Coll., Cambridge (MA, MB, MChir, MD, Lord Kitchener Schol., Drapers' Co. Schol.); University Coll. Hosp. Med. Sch.; Worcester Coll., Oxford (MA, DPhil); DM Oxon 1966; DSc Glasgow 1976. Hosp. appts, 1958–61; Fellow, Nat. Fund for Res. into Crippling Diseases, 1961–63; Oxford Univ.: Schorstein Med. Res. Fellow, 1963–65; MRC Sci. Staff and Asst to Regius Prof., 1964–67; Dean, St Peter's Coll., 1965–68; Lectr in Neurology, 1967–68; Sen. Lectr in Neurology, Glasgow Univ., and Warden, Queen Margaret Hall, 1968–77; Hon. Consultant Neurologist, Inst. of Neurological Scis, Glasgow; Prof. of Medicine, Wellington Sch. of Medicine, Univ. of Otago, NZ, 1977–87 (Dean, 1977–86); Consultant Neurologist, Wellington Hosp. Bd, 1977–87. Wyndham Deedes Schol., Anglo-Israel Assoc., 1963; Arris and Gale Lectr, RCS, 1965; E. G. Fearnsides Schol., Cambridge, 1966–67; T. K. Stubbins Sen. Res. Fellow, RCP, 1968; Visiting Professor: McGill Univ. Montreal Neurological Inst., 1974; Baghdad, 1974, 1976; Mosul, 1979; All India Vis. Fellow, NZ, 1979. Member: Oxfordshire HA, 1989–91; GMC, 1989–, and numerous Boards and Cttees, UK and NZ. Dir, Wadham Coll., Oxford Appeal, 1989–; Trustee, Disability Information Trust, 1991–. Expeditions to Ecuador, 1960, Atlas Mountains, 1961, Jordan, 1967; Mem., exploration and expedition organisations, Oxford, 1966–68. *Publications:* (with J. M. K. Spalding) Disorders of the Automatic Nervous System, 1974; (with Gillian S. Johnson) Living with Disability, 1978; (with D. G. Lambie and J. M. K. Spalding) Neurocardiology, 1984; numerous contribs to sci. jls on clinical neurology, physiology and patient care. *Recreations:* book collecting, sailing. *Address:* Wadham College, Oxford OX1 3PN. *T:* Oxford (0865) 221517.

JOHNSON, (Reginald) Stuart, CBE 1985; Director of Education, Leeds City Council, since 1973; *b* 12 April 1933; *s* of late Reginald Johnson and Sarah Anne Johnson; *m* 1960, Dr Jennifer Johnson (*née* Craig); one *s* one *d*. *Educ:* Durham Univ. (BSc Hons); London Univ. (PGCE, DipEd). Deputy Education Officer, Leeds CC, 1968–73. Member: UGC, 1979–89 (Chm., Educn Sub-Cttee, 1985–89); Advisory Cttee on Supply and Educn of Teachers, 1980– (Chm., Teacher Trng Sub-Cttee, 1981–); PPITB, 1977–80 (Chm., Trng Cttee, 1978–80). Mem., BBC Schools and Further Educn Broadcasting Council, 1976–82. Adviser to Burnham Cttee, 1984–. Administrator, Leeds International Pianoforte Competition, 1978–81. *Publications:* frequent articles in educnl press. *Recreations:* golf, cricket, fishing. *Address:* Mickleber House, Gargrave Road, Gargrave, Skipton, W Yorks BD23 3AQ. *T:* Skipton (0756) 748423. *Clubs:* Lansdowne; Leeds (Leeds).

JOHNSON, Rex; Director of Social Services, Lancashire County Council, 1978–86; *b* 19 Aug. 1921; *s* of Samuel and Ellen Johnson; *m* 1946, Mary Elizabeth Whitney (*d* 1988); two *d*. *Educ:* Accrington Grammar Sch.; St Paul's Trng Coll., Cheltenham (qual. teacher); Leeds Univ. (MA). Served War, RAF, 1942–46; radar mechanic, educn instr; served Ireland, India, Singapore (Burma Star). Asst Master, Darwen, 1946–49; Dep. Supt, Boys' Remand Home, Lincoln, 1949–52; Head of Springfield Reception Centre, Bradford, 1953–64; Home Office Inspector, Children's Dept, 1964–65; Educnl Psychologist, Bradford, 1965–67; Univ. Lectr, Leeds, 1967–69; Social Work Service Officer, DHSS (formerly Home Office Inspector), 1969–72; Dep. Dir of Social Services, Lancs, 1972–78. Mem., Personal Social Services Council, 1977–80. *Publications:* (ed) ABC of Behaviour Problems, 1962 (2nd edn 1969); (ed) ABC of Social Problems and Therapy, 1963; (ed) ABC of Social Services, 1964; articles in Soc. Work Today, Residential Soc. Work, Community Care, Hosp. and Soc. Services Jl, and Jl RSH. *Address:* 27 St Thomas' Road, St Annes-on-Sea, Lancs FY8 1JN. *T:* St Annes (0253) 714201.

JOHNSON, Richard Keith; actor and producer; Founder Chairman and Joint Chief Executive, United British Artists, since 1983; *b* 30 July 1927; *s* of Keith Holcombe and Frances Louisa Olive Johnson; *m* 1st, 1957, Sheila Sweet (marr. diss); one *s* one *d*; 2nd, 1965, Kim Novak (marr. diss.); 3rd, 1982, Marie-Louise Norlund; one *s* one *d*. *Educ:* Parkfield School; Felsted School; RADA. RN, 1945–48. 1st stage appearance, Opera House, Manchester, 1944; repertory, Haymarket, 1944–45; *stage:* contract, Royal Shakespeare Theatre, 1957–62; Antony in Antony and Cleopatra, RSC, 1972–73; NT, 1976–78; The War That Still Goes On, Young Vic, 1991; *films:* MGM contract, 1959–65; acted in: The Haunting; Moll Flanders; Operation Crossbow; Khartoum; The Pumpkin Eater; Danger Route; Deadlier than the Male; Oedipus the King; Hennessy (also wrote original story); Aces High; The Four Feathers; produced: Turtle Diary; Castaway (Exec. Producer); The Lonely Passion of Judith Hearne. Mem. Council, BAFTA, 1977–79. *Recreations:* reading, gardening, travelling. *Address:* United British Artists, 2 Stokenchurch Street, SW6. *T:* 071–736 5920.

JOHNSON, (Robert) Brian, CBE 1990; QPM 1981; DL; Chief Constable, Lancashire Constabulary, since 1983; *b* 28 July 1932; *s* of Robert and Hilda Johnson; *m* 1954, Jean Thew; two *d*. *Educ:* Stephenson Memorial Boys' Sch.; College of Commerce, Newcastle. Newcastle City Police: Police Cadet, 1948; Police Constable, 1952; Detective Constable, 1955; Detective Sergeant, 1962; Detective Inspector, 1966; Detective Chief Inspector, 1969; Detective Supt, Northumbria Police, 1971; Chief Supt, Northumbria Police, Home Office, 1976; Asst Chief Constable, Northumbria, 1977; Dep. Chief Constable, Lancashire, 1981. President: NW Area, National Assoc. of Retired Police Officers (also Pres., Blackpool Br.), 1983–; Lancs Assoc. of Boys Clubs, 1983–; Lancs Outward Bound Assoc., 1983–; Vice-Pres., Lancs Council for Voluntary Youth Services, 1985–; Patron: NW Counties Schools ABA, 1983–; Blackburn Area, Road Safety Assoc., 1983–. DL Lancs, 1989. *Recreations:* reading, gardening. *Address:* Police Headquarters, Hutton, Preston, Lancs PR4 5SB. *Club:* Special Forces.

JOHNSON, Hon. Sir Robert (Lionel), Kt 1989; **Hon. Mr Justice Johnson;** a Justice of the High Court, Family Division, since 1989; *b* 9 Feb. 1933; *er s* of late Edward Harold Johnson, MSc, FRIC, and of Ellen Lydiate Johnson, Cranleigh; *m* 1957, Linda Mary, *er d* of late Charles William Bennie and Ena Ethel Bennie, Egglescliffe; one *s* two *d*. *Educ:* Watford Grammar Sch. (1940–51); London Sch. of Econs and Polit. Science. 5th Royal Inniskilling Dragoon Guards, 1955–57, Captain; ADC to GOC-in-C Northern Comd, 1956–57; Inns of Court Regt, 1957–64. Called to the Bar, Gray's Inn, 1957, Bencher, 1986; QC 1978; a Recorder, 1977–89. Jun. Counsel to Treasury in Probate Matters, 1975–78; Legal Assessor, GNC, 1977–82. Chairman: Bar Fees and Legal Aid Cttee, 1984–86 (Vice-Chm., 1982–84); Family Law Bar Assoc., 1984–86; Mem., Bar Council, 1981–88; Vice Chm., 1987, Chm., 1988, Gen. Council of Bar. Member: Supreme Court Procedure Cttee, 1982–87; Law Soc. Legal Aid Cttee, 1981–87; No 1 Legal Aid Area Cttee, 1980–87; Co-Chm., Civil and Family Cttee, Judicial Studies Bd, 1989–. Pres., English Chapter, Internat. Acad. of Matrimonial Lawyers, 1986–89. Sec., Internat. Cystic Fibrosis Assoc., 1984–90; Trustee: Cystic Fibrosis Res. Trust, 1964–; Robert Luff Charitable Foundn, 1977–. *Publications:* (with James Comyn) Wills & Intestacies, 1970; Contract, 1975; (with Malcolm Stitcher) Atkin's Trade, Labour and Employment, 1975. *Recreations:* charitable work, gardening. *Address:* Royal Courts of Justice, Strand, WC2A 2LL.

JOHNSON, Robert White, CBE 1962; Director, Cammell Laird & Co. Ltd, 1946–70; Chairman: Cammell Laird & Co. (Shipbuilders and Engineers) Ltd, 1957–68; Cammell Laird (Shiprepairers) Ltd, 1963–68; retired; *b* 16 May 1912; *s* of late Sir Robert (Stewart) Johnson, OBE; *m* 1950, Jill Margaret Preston; two *s* one *d*. *Educ:* Rossall Sch. Robt Bradford & Co. Ltd (Insurance Brokers), 1931–35. Served War of 1939–45, Provost Marshal's Dept, RAF, becoming Wing Comdr. Director: Patent Shaft & Axletree Co. Ltd, Wednesbury, Staffs, 1946–51; Metropolitan-Cammell Carriage and Wagon Co. Ltd, Birmingham, 1946–64; North Western Line (Mersey) Ltd, 1964–70; Bradley Shipping Ltd, 1964–70; formerly Dir, Scottish Aviation Ltd; Coast Lines Ltd; English Steel Corp. Ltd; Chm. of North West Tugs Ltd, Liverpool, 1951–66; Mem. Mersey Docks and Harbour Board, 1948–70; Pt-time Mem. Merseyside and North Wales Electricity Board, 1956–66; Chm., Merseyside Chamber of Commerce and Industry, 1972–74. Underwriting Mem., Lloyd's, 1936–. Pres., Shipbuilding Employers' Federation, 1958–59. *Recreations:* fishing, shooting, golf. *Address:* The Oaks, Well Lane, Heswall, Wirral, Merseyside L60 8NE. *T:* 051–342 3304.

JOHNSON, Sir Robin Eliot, 7th Bt *cr* 1818, of Bath; *b* 1929; *s* of Major Percy Eliot Johnson (*d* 1962) (*g g s* of 2nd Bt) and Molly, *d* of James Payn; *S* kinsman, Sir Victor Philipse Hill Johnson, 6th Bt, 1986; *m* 1954, Barbara Alfreda, *d* of late Alfred T. Brown; one *s* two *d*. *Educ:* St John's College, Johannesburg. *Heir:* *s* Patrick Eliot Johnson, *b* 1955.

JOHNSON, Prof. Roger Paul, FEng 1986; Professor of Civil Engineering, University of Warwick, since 1971; *b* 12 May 1931; *s* of Norman Eric Johnson and Eleanor Florence (*née* Paul); *m* 1958, Diana June (*née* Perkins); three *s*. *Educ:* Cranleigh Sch., Surrey; Jesus Coll., Cambridge (BA 1953; MA 1957). FIStructE 1972; FICE 1979. Holloway Bros (London), Civil Engineering Contractor, 1953–55; Ove Arup and Partners, Consulting Engineers, 1956–59; Lectr in Engineering, Cambridge Univ., 1959–71. Vis. Prof., Univ. of Sydney, 1982–83. *Publications:* Structural Concrete, 1967; Composite Structures of Steel and Concrete, vol. 1, 1975, vol. 2 (with R. J. Buckby), 1979, 2nd edn 1986; contribs to learned jls. *Recreations:* music, gardening, mountain walking. *Address:* Engineering Department, University of Warwick, Coventry CV4 7AL. *T:* Coventry (0203) 523129.

JOHNSON, Sir Ronald (Ernest Charles), Kt 1970; CB 1962; JP; *b* 3 May 1913; *o c* of Ernest and Amelia Johnson; *m* 1938, Elizabeth Gladys Nuttall; two *s* (and one *s* decd). *Educ:* Portsmouth Grammar Sch.; St John's Coll., Cambridge. Entered Scottish Office, 1935; Sec., Scottish Home and Health Dept, 1963–72. Chm., Civil Service Savings Cttee for Scotland, 1963–78. Sec. of Commissions for Scotland, 1972–78. Chm., Scottish Hosp. Centre, 1964–72. Member: Scottish Records Adv. Council, 1975–81; Cttee on Admin of Sheriffdoms, 1981–82; Chm., Fire Service Res. and Training Trust, 1976–89. Served RNVR on intelligence staff of C-in-C, Eastern Fleet, 1944–45. President: Edinburgh Bach Soc., 1973–86; Edinburgh Soc. of Organists, 1980–82. JP Edinburgh, 1972. *Publications:* articles in religious and musical jls. *Recreation:* church organ. *Address:* 14 Eglinton Crescent, Edinburgh EH12 5DD. *T:* 031–337 7733.

JOHNSON, Stanley, CBE 1970; FCA; FCIT; Managing Director, British Transport Docks Board, 1967–75; *b* 10 Nov. 1912; *s* of late Robert and Janet Mary Johnson; *m* 1940, Sheila McLean Bald; two *s* two *d*. *Educ:* King George V Sch., Southport. Served as Lieut (S) RINVR, 1942–45. Joined Singapore Harbour Board, 1939; Asst Gen. Man. 1952; Chm. and Gen. Man. 1958–59; Chief Docks Man., Hull Docks, 1962; Asst Gen. Man. 1963, Mem. and Dep. Man. Dir 1966, British Transport Docks Board. Chm. Major Ports Cttee, Dock and Harbour Authorities Assoc., 1971–72. Mem., Exec. Council, British Ports Assoc., 1973–75; Vice-Pres., Internat. Assoc. of Ports and Harbours, 1975–77. Vice-Pres., CIT, 1973–75. *Recreations:* walking, reading, travel. *Address:* The Cottage, Waldley, near Doveridge, Derbys DE6 5LR. *T:* Rocester (0889) 590442. *Club:* Naval and Military.

JOHNSON, Stanley Patrick; Director for Energy Policy, Commission of the European Communities, 1990; Special Adviser, Coopers & Lybrand, Deloitte; *b* 18 Aug. 1940; *s* of Wilfred Johnson and Irène (*née* Williams); *m* 1st, 1963, Charlotte Offlow Fawcett (marr. diss.); three *s* one *d*; 2nd, 1981, Mrs Jennifer Kidd; one *s* one *d*. *Educ:* Sherborne Sch.; Exeter Coll., Oxford (Trevelyan Schol., Sen. Classics Schol.); Harkness Fellow, USA,

1963–64. MA Oxon 1963; Dip. Agric. Econs Oxon 1965. World Bank, Washington, 1966–68; Project Dir, UNA-USA Nat. Policy Panel on World Population, 1968–69; Mem. Conservative Research Dept, 1969–70; Staff of Internat. Planned Parenthood Fedn, London, 1971–73; Consultant to UN Fund for Population Activities, 1971–73; Mem. Countryside Commn, 1971–73; Head of Prevention of Pollution and Nuisances Div., EEC, 1973–77; Adviser to Head of Environment and Consumer Protection Service, EEC, 1977–79; Member (C) Wight and Hants E, Eur. Parlt, 1979–84; Advr to Dir Gen. for Envmt, Civil Protection and Nuclear Safety, EEC, 1984–90. Newdigate Prize for Poetry, 1962; Richard Martin Award, RSPCA, 1982; Greenpeace Award, 1984. *Publications:* Life Without Birth, 1970; The Green Revolution, 1972; The Politics of the Environment, 1973; (ed) The Population Problem, 1973; The Pollution Control Policy of the EEC, 1979, 3rd edn 1989; Antarctica—the last great wilderness, 1985; *novels:* Gold Drain, 1967; Panther Jones for President, 1968; God Bless America, 1974; The Doomsday Deposit, 1980; The Marburg Virus, 1982; Tunnel, 1984; The Commissioner, 1987; Dragon River, 1989; The Warning, 1992. *Recreations:* writing, travel. *Address:* Nethercote, Winsford, Minehead, Somerset. *Club:* Savile.

JOHNSON, Stuart; *see* Johnson, R. S.

JOHNSON, Walter Hamlet; *b* Hertford, 21 Nov. 1917; *s* of John Johnson; *m* 1945. *Educ:* Devon House Sch., Margate. Councillor, Brentford and Chiswick for 6 years. Nat. Treasurer, 1965–77, Pres., 1977–81, Transport Salaried Staffs' Assoc. Joined Labour Party, 1945. Contested (Lab) Bristol West, 1955 and South Bedfordshire, 1959, in General Elections; also Acton (Lab), 1968, in by-election. MP (Lab) Derby South, 1970–83; an Assistant Govt Whip, 1974–75. Is particularly interested in welfare services, transport, labour relations and aviation matters; Chm., PLP Aviation Cttee, 1979–83. Principal Executive Assistant, London Transport, 1980–83 (formerly a Sen. Exec., Staff Trng). Governor, Ruskin Coll., Oxford, 1966–85. *Recreation:* sport. *Address:* 9 Milton Court, Haywards Heath RH16 1EY. *T:* Haywards Heath (0444) 412629.

JOHNSON, Prof. William, DSc Manchester, MA Cantab; FRS 1982; FEng 1983; FIMechE; United Technologies Distinguished Professor of Engineering, Purdue University, Indiana, 1988 and 1989; Emeritus Professor, Cambridge University; *b* 20 April 1922; *er s* of James and Elizabeth Johnson; *m* 1946, Heather Marie (*née* Thornber); three *s* two *d*. *Educ:* Central Grammar Sch., Manchester; Manchester Coll. of Science and Technology (BScTech). BSc Maths, London; CEng. Served War, Lt REME, UK and Italy, 1943–47. Asst Principal, Administrative Grade, Home Civil Service, 1948–50; Lecturer, Northampton Polytechnic, London, 1950–51; Lectr in Engineering, Sheffield Univ., 1952–56; Senior Lectr in Mechanical Engineering, Manchester Univ., 1956–60; Prof. of Mechanical Engrg, 1960–75, Chm. of Dept of Mechanical Engrg, 1960–69, 1971–73, Dir of Medical Engrg, 1973–75, UMIST; Prof. of Mechanics, Engrg Dept, CambridgeUniv., 1975–82; Professorial Fellow, Fitzwilliam Coll., 1975–82. Visiting Professor: McMaster Univ., Canada, 1969; Springer Prof., Univ. of Calif, Berkeley, 1980; Singapore, 1982; Allied Irish Banks Prof., Univ. of Belfast, 1983; Industrial Engrg Dept, Purdue Univ., Indiana, 1984 and 1985. Hon. Sec., Yorks Br. of IMechE, 1953–56, and Chm., NW Br., 1974–75; Vis. for DoI to Prodn Engrg Res. Assoc. and Machine Tool Res. Assoc., 1973–75; President: Manchester and Salford Mech. Engrs Club, 1971–72; Manchester Assoc. of Engrs, 1983–84. Founder, and Editor-in-Chief: Internat. Jl Mech. Sciences, 1960–87; Internat. Jl Impact Engineering, 1983–87; Chm., Internat. Jl Mech. Engrg Educn, 1960–84. Fellow UCL, 1982. For. Fellow, Nat. Acad. of Athens, 1982. Hon. DTech Bradford, 1976; Hon. DEng Sheffield, 1986. Premium Award, Jl RAeS, 1956; T. Constantine Medal, Manchester Assoc. of Engrs, 1962; Bernard Hall Prize (jt), IMechE, 1965–66 and 1966–67; James Clayton Fund Prize (jt), IMechE, 1972 and 1978; Safety in Mech. Engrg Prize, 1980; Silver Medal, Inst. of Sheet Metal Engrg, 1987; James Clayton Prize, 1987. *Publications:* Plasticity for Mechanical Engineers (with P. B. Mellor), 1962; Mechanics of Metal Extrusion (with H. Kudo), 1962; Slip Line Fields; Theory and Bibliography (with R. Sowerby and J. B. Haddow), 1970; Impact Strength of Materials, 1972; Engineering Plasticity (with P. B. Mellor), 1973; Lectures in Engineering Plasticity (with A. G. Mamalis), 1978; Crashworthiness of Vehicles (with A. G. Mamalis), 1978; Plane-Strain Slip-Line Fields for Metal-Deformation Processes (with R. Sowerby and R. Venter), 1982; papers in mechanics of metal forming, impact engineering, mechanics of sports and games, solids, medical and bioengineering, and history of engineering mechanics. *Recreation:* landscape gardening. *Address:* Ridge Hall, Chapel-en-le-Frith, Derbyshire SK12 6UD.

JOHNSON, His Honour William; QC (NI); County Court Judge for County Tyrone, 1947–78; *b* 1 April 1903; *s* of late William Johnson, CBE, and Ellen Johnson. *Educ:* Newry Intermediate Sch.; Portora Royal Sch., Enniskillen; Trinity Coll., Dublin (BA; Sen. Moderator Legal and Polit. Sci.; LLB (1st cl.)); King's Inns, Dublin (Certif. of Honour at Final Examinations for Call to Bar). Called to Irish Bar and Bar of N Ireland, 1924; Hon. Bencher, Inn of Court of N Ireland. Served War of 1939–45, France, Germany, Holland, Belgium (despatches); ADJAG, Actg Lt-Col. Lectr in Law, QUB, 1933–36; Chm. Court of Referees 1928–30, Dep. Umpire 1930–35, Umpire 1935–47, NI Unemployment Insce and Pensions Acts; KC (Northern Ireland) 1946; Sen. Crown Prosecutor, Co. Antrim, 1947. Chairman: Cttee on Law of Intestate Succession in NI, 1951; Cttee on Law of Family Provision in NI, 1953; Cttee on Examns for Secondary Intermediate Schs in NI, 1958; Vice-Chm., Jt Cttee on Civil and Criminal Jurisdictions in NI, 1971; Chm., Council of HM's County Ct Judges in NI, 1975–78. Has held various positions as Leader and Comr in Scout Assoc., 1923–70; Mem., NI Youth Cttee, 1939; Mem. Council, Scout Assoc., 1958–; Chief Comr for NI, Boy Scouts Assocs, 1955–65; Vice-Pres., NI Scout Council. *Publications:* contrib. NI Legal Qly. *Address:* Bar Library, Royal Courts of Justice, Belfast BT1 3JX.

JOHNSON, William Harold Barrett; Commissioner of Inland Revenue, 1965–76; *b* 16 May 1916; *s* of late William Harold Johnson and Mary Ellen (*née* Barrett); *m* 1940, Susan Gwendolen, *d* of Rev. H. H. Symonds; one *s* one *d*. *Educ:* Charterhouse; Magdalene Coll., Cambridge. Served in Royal Artillery, 1939–45. Entered Inland Revenue Dept, 1945. Vice-Pres., Cruising Assoc., 1974–77. *Recreations:* cruising under sail, gardening. *Address:* 45 Granville Park, SE13 7DY; Barrow Cottage, Ravenglass, Cumbria CA18 1ST.

JOHNSON, (Willis) Merwyn; Agent General for Saskatchewan in the United Kingdom, 1977–83; *b* 9 May 1923; *s* of Robert Arthur Johnson and Gudborg Kolbinson; *m* 1946, Laura Elaine Aseltine; two *s* two *d*. *Educ:* McKenzie High Sch., Kindersley; Univ. of Saskatchewan. BSA, BA. MP for Kindersley, Parliament of Canada, 1953–57 and 1957–58. *Recreations:* fishing, golf. *Address:* 4044 Hollydene Place, Victoria, BC V8N 3Z7, Canada. *Clubs:* Wig and Pen, Farmers', Royal Automobile, Canada.

JOHNSON-FERGUSON, Sir Neil (Edward), 3rd Bt, *cr* 1906; TD; Lt-Col Royal Corps of Signals; Vice-Lieutenant, Dumfriesshire, since 1965; *b* 2 May 1905; *s* of Sir Edward Alexander James Johnson-Ferguson, 2nd Bt, and Hon. Elsie Dorothea McLaren (*d* 1973), *d* of 1st Baron Aberconway; *S* father 1953; *m* 1931, Sheila Marion (*d* 1985), *er d* of late Col H. S. Jervis, MC; four *s*. *Educ:* Winchester; Trinity Coll., Cambridge (BA). Capt. Lanarks Yeomanry, TA, 1928; Major 1937; Major, Royal Signals, 1939; Lt-Col 1945. JP 1954, DL 1957, Dumfriesshire. American Legion of Merit. *Heir:* *s* Ian Edward Johnson-Ferguson [*b* 1 Feb. 1932; *m* 1964, Rosemary Teresa, *d* of C. J. Whitehead, Copthall Place, Clatford, Hants; three *s*]. *Address:* Springkell, Eaglesfield, Dumfriesshire.

JOHNSON-GILBERT, Ronald Stuart, OBE 1976; Secretary, Royal College of Surgeons of England, 1962–88; *b* 14 July 1925; *s* of late Sir Ian A. Johnson-Gilbert, CBE and late Rosalind Bell-Hughes; *m* 1951, Ann Weir Drummond; three *d*. *Educ:* Edinburgh Acad.; Rugby; Brasenose Coll., Oxford (Classical Exhbnr and Open Schol., 1943; MA). Intelligence Corps, 1943–46. Trainee, John Lewis Partnership, 1950–51; Admin. Staff, RCS, 1951–88; Secretary: Faculties of Dental Surgery and of Anaesthetists, 1958; Jt Conf. of Surgical Colls, 1963–88; Internat. Fedn of Surgical Colls, 1967–74; Hon. Sec., Med. Commn on Accident Prevention, 1984–88. Mem. Ct of Patrons, RCS, 1990–. Hon. FFARCS 1983; Hon. FRCS 1987; Hon. FDSRCS 1987; Hon. FRCSI 1989. John Tomes Medal, BDA, 1980; McNeill Love Medal, RCS, 1981; Royal Australasian Coll. of Surgeons Medal, 1982. *Recreations:* music, painting, literature, golf. *Address:* Home Farm, Castle Rising, near King's Lynn, Norfolk.
See also T. I. Johnson-Gilbert.

JOHNSON-GILBERT, Thomas Ian; Joint Senior Partner, Clifford Chance, Solicitors, 1987–89; *b* 2 June 1923; *s* of Sir Ian Johnson-Gilbert, CBE, LLD and late Rosalind Bell-Hughes (Lady Johnson-Gilbert); *m* 1950, Gillian June Pool; one *s* one *d*. *Educ:* Edinburgh Academy; Rugby School; Trinity College, Oxford (1942 and 1946–47); Open Classical Scholarship; MA. RAFVR, 1943–46. Admitted solicitor, 1950; Coward Chance, 1950–87 (Partner, 1954, Senior Partner, 1980–). Mem. Council, Law Society, 1970–88. *Recreations:* reading, arts, travel, spectator sport. *Clubs:* Athenæum, Garrick, City of London, MCC.
See also R. S. Johnson-Gilbert.

JOHNSON-LAIRD, Dr Philip Nicholas, FRS 1991; FBA 1986; Professor of Psychology, Princeton University, since 1989; *b* 12 Oct. 1936; *s* of Eric Johnson-Laird and Dorothy (*née* Blackett); *m* 1959, Maureen Mary Sullivan; one *s* one *d*. *Educ:* Culford Sch.; University Coll. London (Rosa Morison Medal, 1964; James Sully Schol., 1964–66; BA (Hons) 1964; PhD 1967). MBPsS 1962. 10 years of misc. jobs, as surveyor, musician, hosp. porter (alternative to Nat. Service), librarian, before going to university. Asst Lectr, then Lectr, in Psychol., UCL, 1966–73; Reader, 1973, Prof., 1978, in Exptl Psychol., Univ. of Sussex; Asst Dir, MRC Applied Psychology Unit, Cambridge, 1983–89; Fellow, Darwin Coll., Cambridge, 1984–89. Vis. Mem., Princeton Inst. for Advanced Study, 1971–72; Vis. Fellow, Stanford Univ., 1980; Visiting Professor: Stanford Univ., 1985; Princeton Univ., 1986. Member: Psychol. Cttee, SSRC, 1975–79; Linguistics Panel, SSRC, 1980–82; Adv. Council, Internat. Assoc. for Study of Attention and Performance, 1984. Member: Linguistics Assoc., 1967; Exptl Psychol. Soc., 1968; Cognitive Sci. Soc., 1980; Assoc. for Computational Linguistics, 1981. Hon. DPhil Göteborg, 1983. Spearman Medal, 1974, President's Award, 1985, BPsS. *Publications:* (ed jtly) Thinking and Reasoning, 1968; (with P. C. Wason) Psychology and Reasoning, 1972; (with G. A. Miller) Language and Perception, 1976; (ed jtly) Thinking, 1977; Mental Models, 1983; The Computer and the Mind, 1988; contribs to psychol, linguistic and cognitive sci. jls, reviews in lit. jls. *Recreations:* talking, arguing, laughing, playing modern jazz. *Address:* Department of Psychology, Princeton University, Princeton, NJ 08540, USA. *T:* (609) 258 4432.

JOHNSON-MARSHALL, Percy Edwin Alan, CMG 1975; RIBA; FRTPI; Professor of Urban Design and Regional Planning, University of Edinburgh, 1964–85; Director, Patrick Geddes Centre for Planning Studies, University of Edinburgh, since 1985; in practice as planning consultant since 1960; *b* 20 Jan. 1915; *s* of Felix William Norman Johnson-Marshall and Kate Jane Little; *m* 1944, April Bridger; three *s* four *d*. *Educ:* Liverpool Univ. Sch. of Architecture; Dip. in Arch.(Dist); (RIBA) RTPI; (RIBA) DisTP; MA (Edin). Planning Architect, Coventry, 1938–41; Served War: with Royal Engrs (India and Burma), 1942–46. Asst Regional Planner, Min. of Town and Country Planning, 1946–49; Gp Planning Officer, in charge of reconstr. areas gp, LCC, 1949–59 (Projects incl.: Lansbury and Stepney/Poplar South Bank, (jtly with City Corp.) Barbican Area, Tower Hill area, etc). Apptd Sen. Lectr, Dept of Architecture, Univ. of Edinburgh, 1959, Head, Dept of Urban Design and Regional Planning, 1967–84. Director: Architectural Research Unit, 1961–64; Planning Research Unit, 1962. Consultant on Human Settlements for UN Stockholm Conf. on Environment, 1972. Partner of Architectural and Planning Consultancy, Percy Johnson-Marshall & Partners (Projects incl. Edin. Univ. Plan, Kilmarnock and Bathgate Town Centres, Porto Regional Plan, etc). *Publications:* Rebuilding Cities, 1966; contribs to technical jls. *Address:* Bella Vista, Duddingston Village, Edinburgh EH15 3PZ. *T:* 031–661 2019.

JOHNSON SMITH, Sir Geoffrey, Kt 1982; DL; MP (C) Wealden, since 1983 (East Grinstead, Feb. 1965–1983); *b* 16 April 1924; *s* of late J. Johnson Smith; *m* Jeanne Pomeroy, MD; two *s* one *d*. *Educ:* Charterhouse; Lincoln Coll., Oxford. Served War of 1939–45: Royal Artillery, 1942–47; Temp. Capt. RA, 1946. BA Hons, Politics, Philosophy and Economics, Oxford, 1949. Mem., Oxford Union Soc. Debating Team, USA, 1949. Information Officer, British Information Services, San Francisco, 1950–52; Mem. Production Staff, Current Affairs Unit, BBC TV, 1953–54; London County Councillor, 1955–58; Interviewer, Reporter, BBC TV, 1955–59. MP (C) Holborn and St Pancras South, 1959–64; PPS, Board of Trade and Min. of Pensions, 1960–63; Opposition Whip, 1965; Parly Under-Sec. of State for Defence for the Army, MoD, 1971–72; Parly Sec., CSD, 1972–74. Chm., Cons. Back-bench Defence Cttee, 1988– (Vice-Chm., 1980–88); Chm., Select Cttee on Members' Interests, 1980–; Vice-Chm., 1922 Cttee, 1988– (Mem. Exec., 1979–). A Vice-Chm., Conservative Party, 1965–71. Member: IBA Gen. Adv. Council, 1975–80; N Atlantic Assembly, 1980– (Chm., Military Cttee, 1985–89; Leader, UK Delegn to Assembly, 1987–). Governor, BFI, 1980–88. DL East Sussex, 1986. *Address:* House of Commons, SW1. *Club:* Travellers'.

JOHNSTON; *see* Lawson Johnston.

JOHNSTON, family name of **Baron Johnston of Rockport.**

JOHNSTON OF ROCKPORT, Baron *cr* 1987 (Life Peer), of Caversham in the Royal County of Berkshire; **Charles Collier Johnston;** Kt 1973; TD; *b* 4 March 1915; *e s* of late Captain Charles Moore Johnston and Muriel Florence Mellon; *m*; two *s*; *m* 1981, Mrs Yvonne Shearman. *Educ:* Tonbridge Sch., Kent. Commissioned TA, 1938; served War of 1939–45 (TD); Major RA, retd 1946. Managing Dir, 1948–76, Chm., 1951–77, of Standex International Ltd (formerly Roehlen-Martin Ltd), Engravers and Engineers, Ashton Road, Bredbury, Cheshire; Chairman: Thames & Kennet Marina Ltd, 1982–; James Burn International, 1986–; Standex Holdings Ltd, 1986– (Dir 1983). Jt Hon. Treas., Conservative Party, 1984–87. Chm., Macclesfield Constituency Conservative Assoc., 1961–65; Hon. Treas., NW Conservatives and Mem. Conservative Bd of Finance, 1965–71; Chm., NW Area Conservatives, 1971–76; Pres., Nat. Union of Conservative and Unionist Assocs, 1986–87 (Mem. Exec. Cttee, 1965–, Chm. 1976–81). Nat. Chm., Cons. Friends of Israel, 1983–86. Mem., Boyd Commn, as official observers of elecns held in Zimbabwe/Rhodesia, April 1980. *Recreations:* spectator sports, travelling, gardening. *Address:* House of Lords, SW1.

JOHNSTON, Alan Charles Macpherson, QC (Scot.) 1980; Dean, Faculty of Advocates, since 1989 (Treasurer, 1977–89); *b* 13 Jan. 1942; *s* of Hon. Lord Dunpark, TD; *m* 1966, Anthea Jean Blackburn; three *s*. *Educ:* Edinburgh Academy; Loretto School; Jesus Coll., Cambridge (BA Hons); Edinburgh Univ. (LLB). Called to the Bar, 1967; Standing Junior, Scottish Home and Health Dept, 1974–79; Advocate Depute, 1979–82. Chairman: Industrial Tribunal, 1982–88; Med. Appeal Tribunal, 1985–89. *Publication:* (asst editor) Gloag and Henderson, Introduction to Scots Law, 7th edn 1968. *Recreations:* shooting, fishing, golf, walking. *Address:* 3 Circus Gardens, Edinburgh EH3 6TN. *Clubs:* University Pitt (Cambridge); New (Edinburgh).

JOHNSTON, Sir Alexander, GCB 1962 (CB 1946); KBE 1953; Chairman, Board of Inland Revenue, 1958–68; *b* 27 Aug. 1905; *s* of Alexander Simpson Johnston and Joan Macdiarmid; *m* 1947, Betty Joan Harris (*see* Lady Johnston); one *s* one *d*. *Educ:* George Heriot's Sch.; University of Edinburgh. Entered Home Office, 1928; Principal Asst Sec., Office of the Minister of Reconstruction, 1943–45; Under-Sec., Office of Lord Pres. of the Council, 1946–48; Dep. Sec. of the Cabinet, 1948–51; Third Sec., HM Treasury, 1951–58. Deputy Chairman: Monopolies and Mergers Commn, 1969–76; Panel on Take-overs and Mergers, 1970–83; Council for the Securities Industry, 1978–83. Hon. DSc(Econ) London, 1977; Hon. LLD Leicester, 1986. *Publications:* The Inland Revenue, 1965; The City Take-over Code, 1980; Presbyterians Awake, 1988. *Address:* 18 Mallord Street, SW3 6DU. *T:* 071–352 6840. *Club:* Reform.

JOHNSTON, Alexander Graham; Sheriff of Strathkelvin at Glasgow, since 1985; *b* 16 July 1944; *s* of Hon. Lord Kincraig, *qv*; *m* 1st, 1972, Susan (marr. diss. 1982); two *s*; 2nd, 1982, Angela; two step *d*. *Educ:* Edinburgh Acad.; Strathallan Sch.; Univ. of Edinburgh (LLB); University Coll., Oxford (BA). Admitted as Solicitor and Writer to the Signet, 1971; Partner, Hagart and Burn-Murdoch, Solicitors, Edinburgh, 1972–82. Sheriff of Grampian, Highland and Isles, 1982–85. Hon. Fellow, Inst. of Professional Investigators, 1980. *Publication:* (ed) Scottish Civil Law Reports, 1987. *Recreations:* golf, piping, curling, bridge, puzzles. *Address:* 3 North Dean Park Avenue, Bothwell, Lanarkshire. *T:* Bothwell (0698) 852177. *Clubs:* Oxford and Cambridge Golfing Society; Vincent's (Oxford); Golf House (Elie).

JOHNSTON, Most Rev. Allen Howard, CMG 1978; LTh; *b* Auckland, NZ, 1912; *s* of Joseph Howard Johnston; *m* 1937, Joyce Rhoda, *d* of John A. Grantley, Auckland; four *d*. *Educ:* Seddon Memorial Technical College; St John's College, Auckland; Auckland Univ. College. Deacon, 1935; Priest, 1936. Assistant Curate of St Mark's, Remuera, 1935–37; Vicar of Dargaville, 1937–42; Vicar of Northern Wairoa, 1942–44; Vicar of Otahuhu, 1944–49; Vicar of Whangarei, 1949–53; Archdeacon of Waimate, 1949–53; Bishop of Dunedin, 1953–69; Bishop of Waikato, 1969–80; Primate and Archbishop of New Zealand, 1972–80. Fellow, St John's Coll., Auckland, 1970. Hon. LLD Otago, 1969. ChStJ 1974. *Address:* 3 Wymer Terrace, Hamilton, New Zealand.

JOHNSTON, Betty Joan, (Lady Johnston), CBE 1989; JP; Chairman, Girls' Public Day School Trust, since 1975; *b* 18 May 1916; *d* of Edward and Catherine Anne Harris; *m* 1947, Sir Alexander Johnston, *qv*; one *s* one *d*. *Educ:* Cheltenham Ladies' Coll.; St Hugh's Coll., Oxford (1st cl. Hons Jurisprudence; MA; BCL). Called to Bar, Gray's Inn, 1940 (1st cl., Bar Final exams; Arden and Lord Justice Holker Sen. schols). Asst Parly Counsel, 1942–52; Dep. Parly Counsel, Law Commn, 1975–83; Standing Counsel to Gen. Synod of C of E, 1983–88. Vice-Chm., Direct Grant Schs Jt Cttee, 1975–81; Chm., Francis Holland (Church of England) Schs Trust, 1978–. Chairman: GBGSA, 1979–89 (Dep. Chm., 1989–); ISJC, 1983–86 (Mem., 1974–; Chm., Assisted Places Cttee, 1981–); Mem., Council, Queen's Coll., London. JP Inner London, 1966. *Address:* 18 Mallord Street, SW3 6DU. *T:* 071–352 6840.

JOHNSTON, Brian (Alexander), CBE 1991 (OBE 1983); MC 1945; freelance broadcaster and commentator; *b* 24 June 1912; *s* of Lt-Col C. E. Johnston, DSO, MC; *m* 1948, Pauline, *d* of late Col William Tozer, CBE, TD; three *s* two *d*. *Educ:* Eton; New Coll., Oxford (BA). Family coffee business, 1934–39. Served War of 1939–45: in Grenadier Guards; in 2nd Bn throughout, taking part in Normandy Campaign, advance into Brussels, Nijmegen Bridge and Crossing of Rhine into Germany. Joined BBC, 1945, retired 1972; specialises in cricket commentary for TV and radio (BBC Cricket Corresp., 1963–72), interviews, ceremonial commentary (*eg* Funeral of King George VI, 1952; Coronation of Queen Elizabeth II, 1953; Weddings of Princess Margaret, 1960, Princess Anne, 1973, Prince of Wales, 1981; Queen's Silver Jubilee, 1977); Let's Go Somewhere feature in In Town Tonight, 1948–52, Down Your Way, 1972–87, Twenty Questions, 1975–76, etc. Radio Sports Personality Award, Soc. of Authors/Pye Radio, 1981; Radio Personality of the Year Award, Sony, 1983; Radio Sports Commentator of the Year, Daily Mail, 1988. *Publications:* Let's Go Somewhere, 1952; Armchair Cricket, 1957; Stumped for a Tale, 1965; The Wit of Cricket, 1968; All About Cricket, 1972; It's Been a Lot of Fun, 1974; It's a Funny Game . . ., 1978; Rain Stops Play, 1979; Chatterboxes, 1983; Now Here's a Funny Thing, 1984; Guide to Cricket, 1986; It's Been a Piece of Cake, 1989; Down Your Way, 1990; The Tale of Billy Bouncer, 1990; Views from the Boundary, 1990; 45 Summers, 1991. *Recreations:* cricket, golf, theatre and reading newspapers. *Address:* 43 Boundary Road, NW8 0JE. *T:* 071–286 2991. *Club:* MCC.

JOHNSTON, Rear-Adm. Clarence Dinsmore H.; *see* Howard-Johnston.

JOHNSTON, Prof. David, MD, ChM; FRCS, FRCSE, FRCSGlas; Professor of Surgery and Head of Department, University of Leeds at Leeds General Infirmary, since 1977; *b* Glasgow, 4 Sept. 1936; *s* of Robert E. and Jean Johnston; *m* (marr. diss); three *s* one *d*; *m* 1987, Dr Maureen Teresa Reynolds; one *s*. *Educ:* Hamilton Acad.; Glasgow Univ. (MB, ChB Hons; MD Hons, ChM). FRCSE 1963; FRCSGlas 1964; FRCS 1979. House Surgeon, Western Infirmary, Glasgow, 1961–62; Res. Asst and Registrar, Univ. Dept of Surg., Leeds Gen. Infirm., 1962–64; Lectr in Surg., Univ. of Sheffield, 1965–68; Sen. Lectr and Consultant, Univ. Dept of Surg., Leeds Gen. Infirm., 1968–75; Prof. of Surg. and Head of Dept, Univ. of Bristol (Bristol Royal Infirm.), 1975–77. *Publications:* papers on physiology and surgery of the stomach and colon. *Recreations:* reading, running, tennis, fishing. *Address:* 23 Shire Oak Road, Headingley, Leeds LS6 2DD. *T:* Leeds (0532) 754689.

JOHNSTON, David Alan H.; *see* Hunter Johnston.

JOHNSTON, David Lawrence, CEng, FIEE; FBIM; RCNC; Director General, National Inspection Council for Electrical Installation Contracting, since 1989; Director: National Inspection Council, Quality Assurance Ltd, since 1989; National Approval Council, Security Systems Ltd, since 1990; *b* 12 April 1936; *s* of late Herbert David Johnston and of Hilda Eleanor Johnston (*née* Wood); *m* 1959, Beatrice Ann Witten; three *d*. *Educ:* Lancastrian Sch., Chichester; King's Coll., Durham (BSc). FIEE 1980. Short Service Commn (Lieut), RN, 1959–62. Joined Ministry of Defence, 1962; Overseeing, Wallsend, 1962–63; Design, Bath, 1963–66; Production and Project Management, Devonport Dockyard, 1966–73; Dockyard Policy, Bath, 1973–76; Design, Bath, 1976–79; Production and Planning, Portsmouth Dockyard, 1979–81; Planning and Production, Devonport Dockyard, 1981–84; Asst Under-Sec. of State, and Man. Dir, HM Dockyard, Devonport, 1984–87; Chm. and Man. Dir, Devonport Dockyard Ltd, Management Buy-out Co., 1985–87; Dep. Chm., Devonport Management Ltd, 1987–88; management consultant, 1988–89. Dir, Nat. Supervisory Council, Intruder Alarms Ltd, 1989–90. Chm., BASEEFA Adv. Council, HSE, 1990–; Mem., Electrical Equipment Certification Management Bd, HSE, 1990–. FBIM 1980. *Recreations:* gardening, walking, modernizing houses. *Address:* The Old Orchard, Harrowbeer Lane, Yelverton, Devon PL20 6DZ. *T:* Yelverton (0822) 854310; National Inspection Council for Electrical Installation Contracting, Vintage House, 37 Albert Embankment, SE1 7UJ. *T:* 071–582 7746.

JOHNSTON, Prof. David Lloyd; Principal and Vice-Chancellor, and Professor of Law, McGill University, since 1979; *b* 28 June 1941; *s* of Lloyd Johnston and Dorothy Stonehouse Johnston; *m* 1963, Sharon Downey; five *d*. *Educ:* Harvard Univ., Cambridge, Mass; Cambridge Univ.; Queen's Univ. at Kingston, Ont. Asst Prof., Faculty of Law, Queen's Univ., Kingston, 1966–68; Faculty of Law, Univ. of Toronto: Asst Prof., 1968–69; Associate Prof., 1969–72; Prof., 1972–74; Dean and Prof., Faculty of Law, Univ. of Western Ont, 1974–79. Chm., Nat. Round Table on Envmt and the Economy, 1988–. LLD *hc* Law Soc. of Upper Canada, 1980. *Publications:* Computers and the Law (ed), 1968; Canadian Securities Regulation, 1977; (jtly) Business Associations, 1979, rev. edn 1989; (with R. Forbes) Canadian Companies and the Stock Exchange, 1980; (jtly) Canadian Securities Regulation, Supplement, 1982; articles and reports. *Recreations:* jogging, skiing, tennis. *Address:* McGill University, 845 Sherbrooke Street West, Montreal, Que H3A 2T5, Canada. *T:* 514–398–4180, *Fax:* 514–398–4768; 18 Sunnyside Avenue, Montreal, Que H3Y 1C2. *T:* 514–485–2166. *Clubs:* University, Faculty (Montreal).

JOHNSTON, Sir (David) Russell, Kt 1985; MP Inverness, Nairn and Lochaber, since 1983 (Inverness, 1964–83) (L 1964–88, Lib Dem since 1988); Deputy Leader, Social and Liberal Democrats, since 1988; *b* 28 July 1932; *s* of late David Knox Johnston and Georgina Margaret Gerrie Russell; *m* 1967, Joan Graham Menzies; three *s*. *Educ:* Carbost Public Sch.; Portree High Sch.; Edinburgh Univ. (MA). Commissioned into Intelligence Corps (Nat. Service), 1958; subseq., Moray House Coll. of Educn until 1961; taught in Liberton Secondary Sch., 1961–63. Research Asst, Scottish Liberal Party, 1963–64. Chm., Scottish Liberal Party, 1970–74 (Vice-Chm., 1965–70), Leader, 1974–88; Pres., Scottish Social and Liberal Democrats, 1988–. Mem., UK Delegn to European Parlt, 1973–75 and 1976–79, Vice Pres., Political Cttee, 1976–79; Mem., UK Delegn to Council of Europe and WEU, 1988. Lib Dem spokesman: on foreign affairs, 1988–; on European Community affairs, 1988–. Contested (L) Highlands and Islands, European Parly elecn, 1979, 1984. Chm., All Party Scottish Gaelic Parly Gp; Vice Chm., Europe Gp; Vice-President: Liberal Gp; European Lib Dem and Reform Parties; Sec., UK-Falkland Is Parly Gp; Treasurer: All Party Photography Gp; British-Gibraltar Parly Gp. Mem., Royal Commission on Local Govt in Scotland, 1966–69. *Publications:* (pamphlet) Highland Development, 1964; (pamphlet) To Be a Liberal, 1972; Scottish Liberal Party Conf. Speeches, 1979 and 1987. *Recreations:* reading, photography. *Address:* House of Commons, SW1A 0AA. *Club:* Scottish Liberal (Edinburgh).

JOHNSTON, Sir Edward (Alexander), KBE 1989; CB 1975; Government Actuary, 1973–89; Director, Noble Lowndes Actuarial Services Ltd, since 1989; *b* 19 March 1929; 2nd *s* of Edward Hamilton Johnston, DLitt, and Iris Olivia Helena May; *m* 1st, Veronica Mary Bernays (marr. diss.); two *s* two *d*; 2nd, Christine Elizabeth Nash (*née* Shepherd). *Educ:* Groton Sch., USA; Marlborough Coll.; New Coll., Oxford. BA 1952; FIA 1957; FPMI 1976. Equity & Law Life Assce Soc., 1952–58; Govt Actuary's Dept, 1958–89. Mem. Council: Inst. of Actuaries, 1973–88; Pensions Management Inst., 1983–88 (Pres., 1985–87). *Address:* (office) Norfolk House, Wellesley Road, Croydon CR9 3EB. *Club:* Reform.

JOHNSTON, Very Rev. Frederick Mervyn Kieran; Dean of Cork, 1967–71, retired; *b* 22 Oct. 1911; *s* of Robert Mills Johnston and Florence Harriet O'Hanlon; *m* 1938, Catherine Alice Ruth FitzSimons; two *s*. *Educ:* Grammar Sch., Galway; Bishop Foy Sch., Waterford; Trinity Coll., Dublin. BA 1933. Deacon, 1934; Priest, 1936; Curate, Castlecomer, 1934–36; Curate, St Luke, Cork, 1936–38; Incumbent of Kilmeen, 1938–40; Drimoleague, 1940–45; Blackrock, Cork, 1945–58; Bandon, 1958–67; Rector of St Fin Barre's Cathedral and Dean of Cork, 1967; Examng Chaplain to Bishop of Cork, 1960–78. *Address:* 24 Lapps Court, Hartlands Avenue, Cork, Republic of Ireland.

JOHNSTON, Frederick Patrick Mair; Executive Chairman, Johnston Press plc (formerly F. Johnston & Co. Ltd), since 1973; *b* Edinburgh, 15 Sept. 1935; *e s* of late Frederick M. Johnston and of Mrs M. K. Johnston, Falkirk; *m* 1961, Elizabeth Ann Jones; two *s*. *Educ:* Morrison's Acad., Crieff; Lancing Coll., Sussex; New Coll., Oxford (MA, Mod. Hist.). Commissioned in Royal Scots Fusiliers, 1955; served in E Africa with 4th (Uganda) Bn, KAR, 1955–56. Joined Editorial Dept of Liverpool Daily Post & Echo, 1959; joined The Times Publishing Co. Ltd, as Asst Sec., 1960; Company Sec., F. Johnston & Co. Ltd, 1969–73; Managing Dir, F. Johnston & Co. Ltd, 1973–80. Chm., Dunn & Wilson Ltd, 1976–; Dir, Scottish Mortgage and Trust plc, 1991–. President: Young Newspapermen's Assoc., 1968–69; Forth Valley Chamber of Commerce, 1972–73; Scottish Newspaper Proprietors' Assoc., 1976–78; Newspaper Soc., 1989–90; Chm., Central Scotland Manpower Cttee, 1976–83; Mem., Press Council, 1974–88; Treasurer: Soc. of Master Printers of Scotland, 1981–86; CPU, 1987–91. *Recreations:* reading, travelling. *Address:* 1 Grange Terrace, Edinburgh EH9 2LD. *Clubs:* Caledonian, Commonwealth Trust; New (Edinburgh).

JOHNSTON, Henry Butler M.; *see* McKenzie Johnston.

JOHNSTON, Hugh Philip, CB 1977; FEng 1989; Deputy Secretary, Property Services Agency, Department of the Environment, 1974–87; *b* 17 May 1927; *s* of late Philip Rose-Johnston and Dora Ellen Johnston; *m* 1949, Barbara Frances Theodoridi; one *s* three *d*. *Educ:* Wimbledon Coll.; Faraday House. DFH (Hons). Air Ministry Works Dept: Asst Engr, 1951; Engr, 1956; Ministry of Public Buildings and Works: Prin. Engr, 1964; Asst Dir, 1969; Dir (Under-Sec.), Dept of Environment and Property Services Agency, Engrg Services Directorate, 1970. Pres., CIBSE, 1987–88. *Recreations:* motoring, music. *Address:* 9 Devas Road, Wimbledon, SW20 8PD. *T:* 081–946 2021.

JOHNSTON, Ian Alistair, PhD; Deputy Director General, Training Enterprise and Education Directorate, Department of Employment; *b* 2 May 1944; *s* of late Donald Dalrymple Johnston and of Muriel Joyce Johnston (*née* Hill); *m* 1973, Mary Bridget Lube; one *s* one *d*. *Educ:* Royal Grammar Sch., High Wycombe; Birmingham Univ. (BSc, PhD). Joined Dept of Employment as Assistant Principal, 1969; Private Sec. to Permanent Secretary, Sir Denis Barnes, 1972–73; Principal, 1973; First Sec. (Labour Attaché), British Embassy, Brussels, 1976–77; Asst Sec. (Director, ACAS), 1978; Under-Sec. (Dir of Planning and Resources, MSC), 1984; Chief Exec., Vocational Educn Trng Gp, MSC, 1985; Dep. Dir Gen., MSC, subseq. Training Commn, then Training Agency, now Training Enterprise and Education Directorate of Department of Employment, 1987–. Governor, Sheffield Polytechnic, 1988–. *Publications:* contribs to learned jls on atomic structure of metals, 1966–69, and subseq. on public admin. *Recreations:* birding, gardening, skiing. *Address:* Training Enterprise and Education Directorate, Department of Employment, Moorfoot, Sheffield S1 4PQ. *T:* Sheffield (0742) 594108.

JOHNSTON, Ian Henderson, CB 1981; Deputy Controller Aircraft, Procurement Executive, Ministry of Defence, 1982–84; *b* 29 April 1925; *s* of late Peter Johnston and Barbara Johnston (*née* Gifford); *m* 1949, Irene Blackburn; two *d*. *Educ:* George Heriot's Sch., Edinburgh; Edinburgh Univ. (BSc Eng); Imperial Coll., London (DIC Aeronautics). D. Napier & Sons, 1945–46; National Gas Turbine Estabt, 1947–64; Ramjet Project Officer, Min. of Aviation, 1964–66; Exchange Officer to Wright Patterson Air Force Base, Ohio, 1966–68; Asst Dir (Engine Develt), Min. of Technology, 1968–70; Dep. Dir, National Gas Turbine Estabt, 1970–73; Ministry of Defence: Dir-Gen., Multi-Role Combat Aircraft, (PE), 1973–76; Dir, Mil. Vehicles and Engrg Estabt, 1976–78; Dep. Controller, Estabts and Res. B, and Chief Scientist (Army), 1978–80; Dep. Controller, Estabt Resources and Personnel, MoD, 1980–82. *Publications:* papers on turbine research in Aeronautical Research Council Reports and Memoranda Series. *Recreations:* golf, bridge. *Address:* 49 Salisbury Road, Farnborough, Hants. *T:* Farnborough (0252) 541971.

JOHNSTON, James Campbell, CBE 1972; Chairman: Capel Court Corporation Ltd, 1969–84; Australian Foundation Investment Co., 1967–84; Director, National Mutual T&G Life Association of Australasia Ltd (formerly of T&G Mutual Life Society), 1976–84; *b* 7 July 1912; *s* of late Edwin and Estelle Johnston; *m* 1938, Agnes Emily, *yr d* of late Richard Thomas; two *s* one *d*. *Educ:* Prince Alfred Coll., Adelaide; Scotch Coll., Melbourne; University of Melbourne. Admitted to Inst. Chartered Accountants, Australia, 1933; joined J. B. Were & Son, Stock and Share Brokers, 1935, Sen. Partner, 1967–78; Stock Exchange of Melbourne: Mem., 1947; Chm., 1972–77. Comr, State Electricity Commn of Victoria, 1978–83. Chartered Accountant of the Year, 1984. *Address:* 13 Monaro Road, Kooyong, Victoria 3144, Australia. *T:* 822 2842. *Clubs:* Melbourne, Australian, Victoria Racing, Royal Melbourne Golf (Melbourne).

JOHNSTON, Maj.-Gen. James Frederick Junor, CBE 1984; Director General Army Manning and Recruiting, Ministry of Defence, since 1990; *b* 5 Aug. 1939; *s* of late William Johnston and Margaret Macrae Ward Johnston (*née* Junor). *Educ:* George Watson's College; Welbeck College; RMA Sandhurst. BSc, CEng, Eur Ing, FIMechE, psc, rcds. Commissioned REME, 1959; Comd 7 Field Workshop, 1974–76; Directing Staff, Staff Coll., 1976–79; Comd Maint., 3 Armd Div., 1979–81; Dep. Chief of Staff, 4 Armd Div., 1981–84; Asst Chief of Staff, HQ BAOR, 1986–89; Dir Manning (Army), 1989. Chm., Army Sport Control Bd, 1990. FBIM. *Recreations:* travel, photography, postal history. *Address:* c/o Royal Bank of Scotland, 22 Whitehall, SW1A 2EB. *Club:* Army and Navy.

JOHNSTON, Jennifer, (Mrs David Gilliland), FRSL; author; *b* 12 Jan. 1930; *d* of late (William) Denis Johnston, OBE; *m* 1st, 1951, Ian Smyth; two *s* two *d*; 2nd, 1976, David Gilliland, *qv*. *Educ:* Park House Sch., Dublin; Trinity Coll., Dublin. FRSL 1979. Plays: Indian Summer, performed Belfast, 1983; The Porch, prod Dublin, 1986. Hon. DLitt NUU, 1984. *Publications:* The Captains and the Kings, 1972; The Gates, 1973; How Many Miles to Babylon?, 1974; Shadows on Our Skin, 1978 (dramatised for TV, 1979); The Old Jest, 1979 (filmed as The Dawning, 1988); (play) The Nightingale and not the Lark, 1980; The Christmas Tree, 1981; The Railway Station Man, 1984; Fool's Sanctuary, 1987; The Invisible Worm, 1991. *Recreations:* theatre, cinema, gardening, travelling. *Address:* Brook Hall, Culmore Road, Derry, N Ireland BT48 8JE. *T:* Londonderry (0504) 351297.

JOHNSTON, Sir John (Baines), GCMG 1978 (KCMG 1966; CMG 1962); KCVO 1972; HM Diplomatic Service, retired; *b* 13 May 1918; *e s* of late Rev. A. S. Johnston, Banbury, Oxon; *m* 1969, Elizabeth Mary, *d* of late J. F. Crace; one *s*. *Educ:* Banbury Grammar Sch.; Queen's Coll., Oxford (Eglesfield Scholar). Served War, 1940–46: Adjt 1st Bn Gordon Highlanders, 1944; DAQMG HQ 30 Corps District, 1945. Asst Principal, Colonial Office, 1947; Principal, 1948; Asst Sec., West African Council, Accra, 1950–51; UK Liaison Officer with Commission for Technical Co-operation in Africa South of the Sahara, 1952; Principal Private Sec. to Sec. of State for the Colonies, 1953; Asst Sec., 1956; Head of Far Eastern Dept, Colonial Office, 1956; transferred to Commonwealth Relations Office, 1957; Dep. High Commissioner in S Africa, 1959–61; British High Commissioner: in Sierra Leone, 1961–63; in the Federation of Rhodesia and Nyasaland, 1963, Rhodesia, 1964–65; Asst, later Dep. Under-Secretary of State, FCO, 1968–71; British High Commissioner: in Malaysia, 1971–74; in Canada, 1974–78. A Governor, BBC, 1978–85. Chm., ARELS Exams Trust, 1982–. Mem., Disasters Emergency Cttee, 1985–. *Address:* 5 Victoria Road, Oxford OX2 7QF. *T:* Oxford (0865) 56927.

JOHNSTON, John Douglas Hartley; Under Secretary (Legal), Solicitor's Office, Inland Revenue, since 1986; *b* 19 March 1935; *s* of John Johnston and Rhoda Margaret Hartley. *Educ:* Manchester Grammar Sch.; Jesus Coll., Cambridge (MA, LLB, PhD); Harvard Law Sch. (LLM). Called to the Bar, Lincoln's Inn, 1963. Practised at Bar, 1963–67; joined Solicitor's Office, Inland Revenue, 1968; Asst Solicitor, 1976–86. *Recreations:* reading, music, gardening. *Address:* Solicitor's Office, Inland Revenue, Somerset House, WC2. *T:* 071–438 6228.

JOHNSTON, Lt-Col Sir John (Frederick Dame), GCVO 1987 (KCVO 1981; CVO 1977; MVO 1971); MC 1945; Comptroller, Lord Chamberlain's Office, 1981–87 (Assistant Comptroller, 1964–81); *b* 24 Aug. 1922; *m* 1949, Hon. Elizabeth Hardinge, JP Windsor 1971, *d* of late 2nd Baron Hardinge of Penshurst, PC, GCB, GCVO, MC, and late Lady Hardinge of Penshurst; one *s* one *d*. *Educ:* Ampleforth. Served in Grenadier Guards, 1941–64. Extra Equerry to the Queen, 1965–. Director: Theatre Royal Windsor; Claridge's Hotel; President: King George's Pension Fund for Actors and Actresses; Hearing Dogs for the Deaf; Chm., Combined Theatrical Charities Appeals Council. *Publication:* The Lord Chamberlain's Blue Pencil, 1990. *Address:* Studio Cottage, The Great Park, Windsor, Berks SL4 2HP. *T:* Egham (0784) 431627; Stone Hill, Newport, Dyfed. *Clubs:* Boodle's, Pratt's, MCC; Swinley Forest Golf.

JOHNSTON, Kenneth Robert Hope; QC 1953; *b* 18 June 1905; *e s* of Dr J. A. H. Johnston, Headmaster of Highgate Sch., 1908–36, and Kate Winsome Gammon; *m* 1937, Dr Priscilla Bright Clark, *d* of Roger and Sarah Clark, Street, Somerset; one *s* three *d*. *Educ:* Rugby Sch.; Sidney Sussex Coll., Cambridge Univ.; Harvard Univ., USA. Called to the Bar, Gray's Inn, 1933; Bencher, 1958. RAFVR, 1939–45. *Address:* 28 Leigh Road, Street, Somerset BA16 0HB. *T:* Street (0458) 43559. *Club:* MCC.

JOHNSTON, Margaret; *see* Parker, Margaret Annette McCrie J.

JOHNSTON, Lt-Gen. Sir Maurice (Robert), KCB 1982; OBE 1971; DL; Deputy Chief of Defence Staff, 1982–83, retired 1984; Chairman, The Detention Corporation, since 1988; *b* 27 Oct. 1929; *s* of late Brig. Allen Leigh Johnston, OBE, and Gertrude Geraldine Johnston (*née* Templer); *m* 1960, Belinda Mary Sladen; one *s* one *d*. *Educ:* Wellington College; RMA Sandhurst. rcds, psc. Commissioned RA, 1949; transf. The Queen's Bays, 1954; served in Germany, Egypt, Jordan, Libya, N Ireland, Borneo. Instr, Army Staff Coll., 1965–67; MA to CGS, 1968–71; CO 1st The Queen's Dragoon Guards, 1971–73; Comdr 20th Armoured Brigade, 1973–75; BGS, HQ UKLF, 1977–78; Senior Directing Staff, RCDS, 1979; Asst Chief of Gen. Staff, 1980; Dep. Chief of Defence Staff (Op. Reqs), 1981–82. Col, 1st The Queen's Dragoon Guards, 1986–. Chm., Secondary Resources plc, 1988–91; Managing Director: Freshglen Ltd, Wraxall Gp, 1984–85; Unit Security Ltd, 1985–88; Director: Multilift Ltd, 1984–; Shorrock Guards Ltd, 1988–. Governor: Dauntsey's Sch., Wilts, 1987–, St Mary's Sch., Calne, 1988–. DL Wilts, 1990. *Recreations:* fishing, shooting, gardening, music. *Address:* Ivy House, Worton, Devizes, Wilts SN10 5RU. *T:* Devizes (0380) 723727. *Clubs:* Cavalry and Guards, Army and Navy.

JOHNSTON, Very Rev. Michael Alexander Ninian C.; *see* Campbell-Johnston.

JOHNSTON, Michael Errington; Under-Secretary, Ministry of Agriculture, Fisheries and Food, 1970–76; *b* 22 Jan. 1916; *s* of late Lt-Col C. E. L. Johnston, RA, and late Beatrix Johnston; *m* 1938, Ida Brown (*d* 1988); two *d*. *Educ:* Wellington; Peterhouse, Cambridge (Scholar). BA, 1st cl. Hist. Tripos, 1937; MA 1947. Served War of 1939–45, Rifle Bde (Capt., despatches), Asst Principal, Board of Education, 1938; Principal, 1946; Asst Sec., HM Treasury, 1952, Under-Sec., 1962–68; Under-Sec., Civil Service Dept, 1968–70. *Recreations:* painting and birdwatching. *Address:* Flat 7, 151 Mortlake High Street, SW14 8SW. *T:* 081–876 5265.

JOHNSTON, Peter William; Chief Executive and Secretary, Institute of Chartered Accountants of Scotland, since 1989; *b* 8 Feb. 1943; *s* of late William Johnston and of Louisa Alice Johnston (*née* Pritchard); *m* 1967, Patricia Sandra Macdonald; one *s* one *d*. *Educ:* Univ. of Glasgow (MA, LLB). Partner, MacArthur & Co., Solicitors, Inverness, 1971–76; Procurator Fiscal Depute, Dumfries, 1976–78; Procurator Fiscal, Banff, 1978–86; Senior Procurator Fiscal Depute, Crown Office, Edinburgh, 1986–87; Asst Solicitor, Crown Office, 1987–89. Mem. Exec., Scottish Council (Develt & Industry), 1990–. FRSA. *Recreations:* music, foreign languages, sailing. *Address:* 34 York Road, Edinburgh EH5 3EQ. *T:* 031–225 5673.

JOHNSTON, Hon. Rita Margaret; Premier, Province of British Columbia, since 1991; *b* 22 April 1935; *d* of John and Annie Leichert; *m* George Johnston; one *s* two *d*. Businesswoman and Mem., Chamber of Commerce. Alderman, Surrey, BC, 1970–83; MLA for Surrey, 1983–; Parly Sec. to Minister of Energy, Mines and Petroleum Resources, then to Minister of Municipal Affairs, 1983–86; Minister: Municipal Affairs and Transit, 1986–89, also Recreation and Culture, 1988–89; Transportation and Highways, 1989–90; Dep. Premier, 1990–91. *Address:* Room 156, Parliament Buildings, Victoria, British Columbia V8V 1X4, Canada. *T:* (604) 387–1715.

JOHNSTON, Robert Alan, AC 1986; Governor, Reserve Bank of Australia, 1982–89; *b* 19 July 1924; *m* 1948, Verna, *d* of H. I. Mullin; two *s* two *d*. *Educ:* Essendon High School; University of Melbourne. BCom. Commonwealth Bank of Australia, 1940–60; RAAF, 1943–46; Reserve Bank of Australia, 1960–89: Dep. Manager and Manager, Investment Dept, 1964–70; Chief Manager, Internat. Dept, 1970–76; Adviser, 1973–82; Chief Representative, London, 1976–77; Exec. Dir, World Bank Group, Washington, 1977–79; Secretary, Reserve Bank of Aust., 1980–82. Director: Australian Mutual Prov. Soc., 1989–; John Fairfax Gp Pty, 1989–90. Pres., Cttee for Econ. Develt of Australia, 1990–.

JOHNSTON, Robert Gordon Scott; Under Secretary, Department of the Environment, and Managing Director, PSA International, since 1990; *b* 27 Aug. 1933; *s* of Robert William Fairfield Johnston, *qv*; *m* 1960, Jill Maureen Campbell; one *s* one *d*. *Educ:* Clifton; Clare Coll., Cambridge (1st Cl. Hons Classical Tripos, MA). 2/Lieut Scots Guards (National Service), 1955–57. Entered Air Min. as Asst Principal, 1957; Private Sec. to Parly Under Sec. of State for Air, 1959–62; transf. to MPBW, Def. Works Secretariat, 1963; Sec., Bldg Regulation Adv. Cttee, 1964; Principal Private Sec. to successive Ministers of Public Bldg and Works, 1965–68; seconded to Shell Internat. Chemical Co., Finance Div., 1968–70; Asst Dir of Home Estate Management, Property Services Agency, 1970–73; seconded to Cabinet Office, 1973–75; Asst Sec., Railways Directorate, Dept of Transport, 1975–79; Under Sec., seconded to Price Commn, 1979; Dir of Civil Accommodation, 1979–88, Dir, Defence Services, 1988–90, PSA, DoE. *Address:* 5 Methley Street, SE11 4AL.

JOHNSTON, Robert Smith; *see* Kincraig, Hon. Lord.

JOHNSTON, Robert William Fairfield, CMG 1960; CBE 1954; MC 1917; TD 1936 (and three Bars, 1947); Assistant Secretary, Ministry of Defence, 1946–62; retired from the Civil Service, 1962; *b* 1 May 1895; *e s* of late Capt. Robert Johnston, Army Pay Dept and Royal Scots; *m* 1922, Agnes Scott (*d* 1980), *o c* of late Peter Justice, Edinburgh; one *s*. Entered Civil Service, Dec. 1910: served in War Office, Bd of Trade, Min. of Labour, Home Office, Office of Minister without Portfolio, Min. of Defence, and seconded to FO, as Counsellor in UK Delegation in Paris to NATO and OEEC, 1953–61. Territorial Army, 1910–47; served European War, 1914–18, The Royal Scots (1st, 9th and 16th Battalions) in France, Flanders, Macedonia and Egypt; commissioned 1917; War of 1939–45, Lieut-Col, Comdg 8th Bn Gordon Highlanders, 1940–42, and 100th (Gordons) Anti-Tank Regt, RA, 1942–44, in 51st (Highland) and 2nd (British) Inf. Divs respectively; retired as Lieut-Col TA, Sept. 1947. *Address:* 8 Broad Avenue, Queen's Park, Bournemouth, Dorset.

See also R. G. S. Johnston.

JOHNSTON, Sir Russell; *see* Johnston, Sir D. R.

JOHNSTON, Sir Thomas Alexander, 14th Bt *cr* 1626, of Caskieben; *b* 1 Feb. 1956; *s* of Sir Thomas Alexander Johnston, 13th Bt, and of Helen Torry, *d* of Benjamin Franklin Du Bois; *S* father, 1984. *Heir: cousin* William Norville Johnston [*b* 11 July 1922; *m* 1952, Kathrine Pauline, *d* of Herbert Sigfred Solberg; three *s* one *d*].

JOHNSTON, Thomas Lothian, DL; Principal and Vice-Chancellor of Heriot-Watt University, 1981–88; *b* 9 March 1927; *s* of late T. B. Johnston and Janet Johnston; *m* 1956, Joan, *d* of late E. C. Fahmy, surgeon; two *s* three *d*. *Educ:* Hawick High Sch.; Univs of Edinburgh and Stockholm. MA 1951, PhD 1955, Edinburgh. FRSE 1979; FRSA 1981; CBIM 1983; FIPM 1986; FEIS 1989. Served RNVR, 1944–47 (Sub-Lt). Asst Lectr in Polit. Economy, Univ. of Edinburgh, 1953–55, Lectr 1955–65; Res. Fellow, Queen's Univ., Canada, 1965; Prof. and Hd of Dept of Econs, Heriot-Watt Univ., 1966–76. Visiting Professor: Univ. of Illinois, 1962–63; Internat. Inst. for Labour Studies, Geneva, 1973; Western Australia Inst. of Technol., 1979. Sec., Scottish Econ. Soc., 1958–65 (Pres., 1978–81); Member: Scottish Milk Marketing Bd, 1967–72; Nat. Industrial Relations Court, 1971–74; Scottish Cttee on Licensing Laws, 1971–73; Scottish Telecommunications Bd, 1977–84; Scottish Economic Council, 1977–91; Council for Tertiary Educn in Scotland, 1979–83; Chm., Manpower Services Cttee for Scotland, 1977–80; Economic Consultant to Sec. of State for Scotland, 1977–81. Trustee, Nat. Galls of Scotland, 1989–. Director: First Charlotte Assets Trust, 1981–; Universities Superannuation Scheme, 1985–88; Scottish Life Assurance, 1989–; Hodgson Martin Ltd, 1989–. A Dir, Edinburgh Sci. Festival, 1989–91. Chairman: Scottish Cttee, Industry Year 1986; Scottish Cttee, Industry Matters, 1987–89; Univ. Authorities Pay Panel, 1985–88. Chairman: Enquiry into staff representation, London Clearing Banks, 1978–79; Water Workers' Enquiry, 1983; Mem., Review Cttee for NZ Univs, 1987; Arbitrator; Overseas Corresp., Nat. Acad. of Arbitrators, USA. For. Mem., Swedish Royal Acad. of Engrg Scis, 1985. DL

Edinburgh, 1987. Dr *hc* Edinburgh, 1986; Hon. DEd CNAA, 1989; Hon. LLD Glasgow, 1989; DUniv Heriot-Watt, 1989. Comdr, Royal Swedish Order of the Polar Star, 1985. *Publications:* Collective Bargaining in Sweden, 1962; (ed and trans.) Economic Expansion and Structural Change, 1963; (jtly) The Structure and Growth of the Scottish Economy, 1971; Introduction to Industrial Relations, 1981; articles in learned jls. *Recreations:* gardening, walking. *Address:* 14 Mansionhouse Road, Edinburgh EH9 1TZ. *T:* 031–667 1439.

JOHNSTON, Very Rev. William Bryce; Minister of Colinton Parish Church, Edinburgh, since 1964; Chaplain to the Queen in Scotland, since 1981; *b* 16 Sept. 1921; *s* of William Bryce Johnston and Isabel Winifred Highley; *m* 1947, Ruth Margaret, *d* of Rev. James Arthur Cowley; one *s* two *d*. *Educ:* George Watson's Coll., Edinburgh; Edinburgh Univ. (MA Hons Classics 1942); New Coll., Edinburgh (BD (Dist.) 1945). Ordained as Chaplain to HM Forces, 1945; served in Germany and as Staff Chaplain, PoW Directorate, War Office, 1945–48; Minister: St Andrew's, Bo'ness, 1949; St George's, Greenock, 1955. Moderator of General Assembly of Church of Scotland, 1980–81. Convener: Board of St Colm's Coll., 1966–70; General Assembly: Cttee on Adult Educn, 1970; Church and Nation Cttee, 1972; Inter-Church Relations Cttee, 1978; Cttee on Role of Men and Women, 1976; Chm., Judicial Commn, 1988–. Mem., British Council of Churches, 1970–90 (Chm., Exec. Cttee, 1981–84); Delegate to 5th Assembly of World Council of Churches, 1975; Cunningham Lectr, New Coll., 1968–71; Vis. Lectr in Social Ethics, Heriot-Watt Univ., 1966–88. Mem., Broadcasting Council for Scotland, 1983–87. President, Edinburgh Rotary Club, 1975–76. Trustee, Scottish Nat. War Memorial, 1981–. Hon. DD Aberdeen, 1980; Hon. DLitt Heriot-Watt, 1989. *Publications:* (jtly) Devolution and the British Churches, 1978; (ed) Davies, Ethics and Defence, 1986; *translations:* K. Barth, Church Dogmatics, vol. 2, 1955; Calvin, Commentaries on Hebrews, 1 Peter, 1960; various Bible study pamphlets and theological articles for SCM, Scottish Jl of Theology. *Recreations:* organ-playing, bowls. *Address:* The Manse of Colinton, Edinburgh EH13 0JR. *T:* 031–441 2315. *Clubs:* New, University Staff (Edinburgh).

JOHNSTON, Ven. William Francis, CB 1983; Priest-in-charge, Winslow with Addington, diocese of Oxford, since 1987; *b* 29 June 1930; *m* 1963, Jennifer Morton; two *s* one *d*. *Educ:* Wesley Coll., Dublin; Trinity Coll., Dublin (BA 1955; MA 1969). Ordained 1955; Curate of Orangefield, Co. Down, 1955–59; commissioned into Royal Army Chaplains Dept, 1959; served, UK, Germany, Aden, Cyprus; ACG South East District, 1977–80; Chaplain-Gen. to the Forces, 1980–86; QHC 1980–86. *Recreations:* golf, fishing, gardening. *Address:* The Vicarage, Winslow, Bucks MK18 3BJ. *T:* Winslow (029671) 2564.

JOHNSTON, William James; Secretary, Association of Local Authorities of Northern Ireland, 1979–82; Chairman, National House Building Council, Northern Ireland, since 1989; *b* 3 April 1919; *s* of late Thomas Hamilton Johnston and of Mary Kathleen Johnston; *m* 1943, Joan Elizabeth Nancye (*née* Young); two *d*. *Educ:* Portora Royal Sch., Enniskillen. FCA(Ire.). Professional accountancy, 1937–44; Antrim CC, 1944–68, Dep. Sec., 1951–68; Dep. Town Clerk, Belfast, 1968–73, Town Clerk, 1973–79. Dir, NI Adv. Bd, Abbey Nat. Bldg Soc., 1982–89. Member: NI Adv. Council, BBC, 1965–69; Council, ICAI, 1967–71; NI Tourist Bd, 1980–85; Local Govt Staff Commn, 1974–85; Public Service Trng Council (formerly Public Service Trng Cttee), 1974–83 (Chm., 1974–83); Arts Council of NI, 1974–81. NI Rep., Duke of Edinburgh's Commonwealth Study Conf., Canada, 1962. *Recreations:* golf, live theatre. *Address:* 47 Layde Road, Cushendall, Co. Antrim BT44 0NQ. *T:* Cushendall (02667) 71211; Flat 4, 29 Windsor Avenue, Belfast BT9 6EJ. *T:* Belfast (0232) 660793.

JOHNSTON, William Robert Patrick K.; *see* Knox-Johnston, Robin.

JOHNSTONE; *see* Hope Johnstone, family name of Earl of Annandale and Hartfell.

JOHNSTONE, VANDEN-BEMPDE-, family name of **Baron Derwent.**

JOHNSTONE, Lord; David Patrick Wentworth Hope Johnstone; Master of Annandale and Hartfell; *b* 13 Oct. 1971; *s* and *heir* of Earl of Annandale and Hartfell, *qv*. *Educ:* Stowe; St Andrews Univ.

JOHNSTONE, Air Vice-Marshal Alexander Vallance Riddell, CB 1966; DFC 1940; AE; DL; Chairman, Climax Cleaning Co., since 1983 (Director, since 1981); *b* 2 June 1916; *s* of late Alex. Lang Johnstone and Daisy Riddell; *m* 1940, Margaret Croll; one *s* two *d*. *Educ:* Kelvinside Academy, Glasgow. 602 (City of Glasgow) Sqdn, AAF, 1934–41; CO RAF Haifa, 1942; Spitfire Wing, Malta, 1942–43 (despatches, 1942); RAF Staff Coll., 1943; OC Fairwood Common, 1943–44; HQ AEAF, 1944; Air Attaché Dublin, 1946–48; OC RAF Ballykelly, 1951–52; OC Air/Sea Warfare Devel. Unit, 1952–54; SASO HQ No 12 Gp, 1954–55; Founder and First CAS Royal Malayan Air Force, 1957; OC Middleton St George, 1958–60; idc, 1961; Dir of Personnel, Air Min., 1962–64; Comdr, Air Forces, Borneo, 1964–65; AO Scotland and N Ireland, AOC No 18 Group, and Maritime Air Comdr N Atlantic (NATO), 1965–68. Vice-Chm. Council, TA&VRA, 1969–79. DL Glasgow, 1971. Johan Mengku Negara (Malaya), 1958. *Publications:* Television Series, One Man's War, 1964; Where No Angels Dwell, 1969; Enemy in the Sky, 1976; Adventure in the Sky, 1978; Spitfire into War, 1986. *Recreations:* golf, sailing. *Address:* 36 Castle Brooks, Framlingham, Suffolk IP13 9SE. *Club:* Royal Air Force.

JOHNSTONE, David Kirkpatrick; Director of Programmes, Scottish Television plc, 1977–86; *b* 4 July 1926; *s* of John and Isabel Johnstone; *m* 1950, Kay. *Educ:* Ayr Academy; Scottish Radio College. Reporter, Ayrshire Post; Radio Officer, Blue Funnel Line; Reporter, Glasgow Herald; Night News Editor, Scottish Daily Mail; Scottish Feature Writer, News Chronicle; Scottish TV, 1958–: News Editor; Producer/Director; Head of News and Current Affairs; Asst Controller of Programmes; Controller of Programmes. Chm., Regional Programme Controllers Gp, ITV contractors Assoc., 1984–85. Member, BAFTA, 1978. Elder, Church of Scotland; Clerk to Congregational Bd, Broom Parish Church, 1989–. Pres., Eastwood Probus Club, 1989–90. *Recreations:* golf, travel, television. *Club:* Eastwood Golf (Glasgow).

JOHNSTONE, Sir Frederic (Allan George), 10th Bt of Westerhall, Dumfriesshire, *cr* 1700; *b* 23 Feb. 1906; *o s* of Sir George Johnstone, 9th Bt and Ernestine (*d* 1955), *d* of Col Porcelli-Cust; *S* father, 1952; *m* 1946, Doris, *d* of late W. L. Shortridge; two *s*. *Educ:* Imperial Service Coll. *Heir: s* George Richard Douglas Johnstone [*b* 21 Aug. 1948; *m* Gwen Bailey; one *s* one *d*].

JOHNSTONE, Isobel Theodora, PhD; Curator, Arts Council Art Collection, since 1979; *b* 1944. *Educ:* James Gillespie's High School; Edinburgh Univ.; Edinburgh Coll. of Art (MA Hons Fine Art); Glasgow Univ. (PhD). Lectr in History of Art, Glasgow School of Art, 1969–73; Scottish Arts Council, 1975–79. Painter of landscapes and portraits. *Publications:* (as Isobel Spencer): Walter Crane, 1975; articles on late 19th century and 20th century British art. *Address:* South Bank Centre, Royal Festival Hall, SE1 8XX.

JOHNSTONE, (John) Raymond, CBE 1988; Chairman, Forestry Commission, since 1989; Chairman, Murray Johnstone Ltd, since 1984 (Managing Director, 1968–88); *b* 27 Oct. 1929; *s* of Henry James Johnstone of Alva, Captain RN and Margaret Alison McIntyre; *m* 1979, Susan Sara Gore; five step *s* two step *d*. *Educ:* Eton Coll.; Trinity Coll., Cambridge (BA Maths). CA. Apprenticed Chiene & Tait, Chartered Accts, Edinburgh, 1951–54; Robert Fleming & Co. Ltd, London, 1955–59; Partner in charge of investment management, Brown Fleming & Murray CA (becoming Whinney Murray CA, 1965), Glasgow, 1959–68; Murray Johnstone Ltd, Glasgow, formed to take over investment management dept of Whinney Murray, 1968–. Chairman: Murray Technology Investments PLC, 1981-89; Murray Electronics PLC, 1983–89; Summit Gp, 1989–; Director: Shipping Industrial Holdings, 1964–75; Scottish Amicable Life Assce Soc., 1971– (Chm., 1983–85); Dominion Insurance Co. Ltd, 1973– (Chm., 1978–); Scottish Financial Enterprise, 1986– (Chm., 1989–); Glasgow Cultural Enterprise Ltd, 1988–. Hon. Pres., Scottish Opera, 1986– (Dir, 1978–86; Chm., 1983–85). Member: Scottish Adv. Cttee, Nature Conservancy Council, 1987–89; Scottish Econ. Council, 1987–. *Recreations:* fishing, music, farming. *Address:* Wards, Gartocharn, Dunbartonshire G83 8SB. *T:* Gartocharn (038983) 321. *Club:* Western (Glasgow).

JOHNSTONE, Michael Anthony; Metropolitan Stipendiary Magistrate, since 1980; *b* 12 June 1936; *s* of late Thomas Johnstone and Violet Johnstone. *Educ:* St Edmund's College, Ware. Called to the Bar, Inner Temple, 1968; formerly Solicitor of the Supreme Court, admitted 1960; former Dep. Circuit Judge. Member: Soc. for Nautical Res.; Navy Records Soc.; Army Records Soc. Mem., Campaign for Real Ale. *Recreations:* real ale (weight permitting), the study and collection of books on military and naval history. *Address:* Clerkenwell Magistrates' Court, King's Cross Road, WC1R 9QJ.

JOHNSTONE, Raymond; *see* Johnstone, J. R.

JOHNSTONE, R(obert) Edgeworth, BScTech (Manchester); MSc, DSc (London); FIChemE; FIMechE; FRSC; Lady Trent Professor of Chemical Engineering, University of Nottingham, 1960–67; *b* 4 Feb. 1900; *e s* of Lieut-Col Sir Walter Edgeworth-Johnstone, KBE, CB; *m* 1931, Jessie Marjorie (*d* 1981), *d* of late R. M. T. Greig; two *s* one *d*. *Educ:* Wellington; RMA Woolwich; Manchester Coll. of Technology; University Coll., London. Fellow Salters' Inst. of Industrial Chem., 1926–27. Held various posts at home and abroad with Magadi Soda Co., Trinidad Leaseholds, Petrocarbon, Min. of Supply and UK Atomic Energy Authority. Vice-Pres., IChemE, 1951. Liveryman, Worshipful Co. of Salters, 1956. Council Medal, IChemE, 1969, Hon. Fellow, 1981. *Publications:* Continuing Education in Engineering, 1969; (with Prof. M. W. Thring) Pilot Plants, Models and Scale-up Methods in Chemical Engineering, 1957; papers in scientific and engineering jls, especially on distillation, process development and engineering education; *as Robert Johnstone:* The Lost World, 1978; (ed) Samuel Butler on the Resurrection, 1980. *Recreations:* music, philosophy. *Address:* 3 rue Basse, 72300 Parcé, France. *Club:* Athenæum.

JOHNSTONE, William, CBE 1981; *b* 26 Dec. 1915; *s* of late David Grierson Johnstone and Janet Lang Johnstone (*née* Malcolm); *m* 1942, Mary Rosamund Rowden; one *s* two *d*. *Educ:* Dalry High Sch.; Glasgow Univ. (BSc (Agric)). NDA, NDD. Technical Officer, Overseas Dept of Deutches Kalisyndikat, Berlin, 1938–39; joined ICI Ltd, 1940; seconded to County War Agricl Exec. Cttees in SE England on food prodn campaigns, 1940–45; Reg. Sales Management, ICI, 1950–61; Commercial Dir, Plant Protection Ltd, 1961–63, Man. Dir, 1963–73; Dir, ICI Billingham/Agricl Div., 1961–73; Dep. Chm., ICI Plant Protection Div., 1974–77. Chm. Subsid. Cos: Solplant (Italy), 1967–73; Sopra (France), 1971–75; Zeltia Agraria (Spain), 1976–77; Vis. Dir, ICI (United States) Inc., 1974–77; retd from ICI, 1977. Chairman: Meat and Livestock Commn, 1977–80; British Agricl Export Council, 1977–84; Member: European Trade Cttee, BOTB, 1982–85; Sino-British Trade Council, 1983–85. *Recreations:* sheep husbandry, gardening. *Address:* Oxenbourne Farm, East Meon, Petersfield, Hants GU32 1QL. *T:* East Meon (073087) 216. *Clubs:* Caledonian, Farmers'.

JOHNSTONE, Rev. Prof. William; Professor of Hebrew and Semitic Languages, University of Aberdeen, since 1980; *b* 6 May 1936; *s* of Rev. T. K. Johnstone and Evelyn Hope Johnstone (*née* Murray); *m* 1964, Elizabeth Mary Ward; one *s* one *d*. *Educ:* Hamilton Academy; Glasgow Univ. (MA 1st Cl. Hons Semitic Langs, BD Distinction in New Testament and Old Testament); Univ. of Marburg. University of Aberdeen: Lectr 1962, Sen. Lectr 1972, in Hebrew and Semitic Languages; Dean, Faculty of Divinity, 1984–87. Member, Mission archéologique française: Ras Shamra, 1963, 1964, 1966; Enkomi, 1963, 1965, 1971; Member, Marsala Punic Ship Excavation, 1973–79. Pres., SOTS, 1990. *Publications:* Exodus, 1990; trans. Fohrer: Hebrew and Aramaic Dictionary of the Old Testament, 1973; contributions to: Ugaritica VI, 1969, VII, 1978, Alasia I, 1972; Festschrift for W. McKane, 1986; articles in Aberdeen Univ. Review, Atti del I Congresso Internazionale di Studi Fenici e Punici, Dictionary of Biblical Interpretation, Expository Times, Kadmos, Notizie degli Scavi, Palestine Exploration Qly, Trans. Glasgow Univ. Oriental Soc., Scottish Jl of Theology, Theology, Vetus Testamentum, Zeitschrift für die alttestamentliche Wissenschaft. *Recreation:* alternative work. *Address:* 37 Rubislaw Den South, Aberdeen AB2 6BD. *T:* Aberdeen (0224) 316022; Makkevet Bor, New Galloway, Castle Douglas DG7 3RN.

JOICEY, family name of **Baron Joicey.**

JOICEY, 4th Baron, *cr* 1906; **Michael Edward Joicey;** Bt 1893; DL; *b* 28 Feb. 1925; *s* of 3rd Baron Joicey and Joan (*d* 1967), *y d* of 4th Earl of Durham; *S* father, 1966; *m* 1952, Elisabeth Marion, *y d* of late Lieut-Col Hon. Ian Leslie Melville; two *s* one *d*. *Educ:* Eton; Christ Church, Oxford. DL Northumberland, 1985. *Heir: s* Hon. James Michael Joicey, [*b* 28 June 1953; *m* 1984, Harriet, *yr d* of Rev. William Thompson, Oxnam Manse, Jedburgh; one *s* one *d*]. *Address:* Etal Manor, Berwick-upon-Tweed, Northumberland TD15 2PU. *T:* Crookham (089082) 205. *Clubs:* Lansdowne, Kennel; Northern Counties (Newcastle upon Tyne).

JOLL, Prof. James Bysse, MA; FBA 1977; Stevenson Professor of International History, University of London, 1967–81, now Professor Emeritus; *b* 21 June 1918; *e s* of Lieut-Col H. H. Joll and Alice Muriel Edwards. *Educ:* Winchester; University of Bordeaux; New Coll., Oxford. War Service, Devonshire Regt and Special Ops Exec., 1939–45. Fellow and Tutor in Politics, New Coll., Oxford, 1946–50; Fellow, 1951–67, now Emeritus, and Sub-Warden, 1951–67, St Antony's Coll., Oxford. Vis. Mem., Inst. for Advanced Study, Princeton, 1954 and 1971; Visiting Professor of History: Stanford Univ., Calif., 1958; Sydney Univ., 1979; Univ. of Iowa, 1980; Vis. Lectr in History, Harvard University, 1962; Benjamin Meaker Vis. Prof., Bristol Univ., 1985. Hon. Prof. of History, Warwick Univ., 1981–87. Hon. Fellow, LSE, 1985. Hon. DLitt Warwick, 1988. *Publications:* The Second International, 1955, rev. edn 1974; Intellectuals in Politics, 1960; The Anarchists, 1964, rev. edn 1979; Europe since 1870, 1973, 4th edn 1990; Gramsci, 1977; The Origins of the First World War, 1984. *Recreation:* music. *Address:* 24 Ashchurch Park Villas, W12 9SP. *T:* 081–749 5221.

JOLLIFFE, family name of **Baron Hylton.**

JOLLIFFE, Sir Anthony (Stuart), GBE 1982; FCA; Chairman, Walker Greenbank plc, 1986–89; Consultant, Grant Thornton; Member of Governing Council, Business in the Community, since 1983 (Chairman, 1986–87); *b* Weymouth, Dorset, 12 Aug. 1938; *s* of Robert and Vi Dorothea Jolliffe. *Educ:* Porchester Sch., Bournemouth. Qualified chartered accountant, 1964; articled to Morison Rutherford & Co.; commenced practice on own account in name of Kingston Jolliffe & Co., 1965, later, Jolliffe Cork & Co., Sen. Partner, 1976. ATII. Director: Imry plc; Nikko Trading UK Ltd; JCT Internat. (UK) Ltd; Paccar UK Ltd; Chm., Causeway Capital Develt Fund. Trustee, Understanding Industry. Alderman, Ward of Candlewick, 1975–84; Sheriff, City of London, 1980–81; Lord Mayor of London, 1982–83. Pres., London Chamber of Commerce, 1985–88. Chm., Police Dependants' Trust; Trustee, Police Foundn. Pres., Soc. of Dorset Men. Member: Guild of Freemen; Ct, Worshipful Co. of Painter Stainers; Ct, Worshipful Co. of Chartered Accountants in England and Wales; Worshipful Co. of Wheelwrights. FRSA; KStJ 1983. *Clubs:* Brooks's, Garrick, City Livery (Pres., 1979–80), Saints and Sinners; Royal London Yacht (Cowes).

JOLLIFFE, Christopher, CBE 1971; Chairman, Abbeyfield Richmond Society, 1980–87; Director, Science Division, Science Research Council, 1969–72 (Director for University Science and Technology, 1965–69); *b* 14 March 1912; *s* of William Edwin Jolliffe and Annie Etheldreda Thompson; *m* 1936, Miriam Mabel Ash. *Educ:* Gresham's Sch., Holt; University Coll., London. Asst Master, Stowe Sch., 1935–37; Dept of Scientific and Industrial Research, 1937–65. Vice-Chm., Council for Science and Society, 1978–82; Dir, Leverhulme Trust Fund, 1976–77. *Address:* 8 Broomfield Road, Kew, Richmond, Surrey TW9 3HR. *T:* 081–940 4265.

JOLLIFFE, William Orlando, IPFA, FCA; County Treasurer of Lancashire, 1973–85; *b* 16 Oct. 1925; *s* of late William Dibble Jolliffe and Laura Beatrice Jolliffe; *m* 1st (marr. diss.); one *s* one *d*; 2nd, 1975, Audrey (*née* Dale); one step *d*. *Educ:* Bude County Grammar Sch. Institute of Public Finance Accountant. Chartered Accountant (first place in final exam. of (former) Soc. of Incorporated Accountants, 1956). Joined Barclays Bank Ltd, 1941. Served War of 1939–45 (HM Forces, 1944–48). Subseq. held various appts in Treasurers' depts of Devon CC, Winchester City Council, Doncaster CB Council, Bury CB Council (Dep. Borough Treas.), and Blackpool CB Council (Dep. 1959, Borough Treas., 1962). Mem. Council, Chartered Inst. of Public Finance and Accountancy, 1969–85 (Pres., 1979–80); Financial Adviser, ACC, 1976–85; Mem. Council (Pres. 1974–75), Assoc. of Public Service Finance Officers, 1963–76; Chm., Officers' Side, JNC for Chief Officers of Local Authorities in England and Wales, 1971–76; Mem. Exec. Cttee (Pres. 1970–71), NW Soc. of Chartered Accountants, 1966–76; Chm., NW and N Wales Region of CIPFA, 1974–76; Mem., Soc. of County Treasurers (Mem. Exec. Cttee, 1977–85); Hon. Treas., Lancashire Playing Fields Assoc., 1974–85. Financial Adviser to Assoc. of Municipal Corporations, 1969–74; Mem. (Govt) Working Party on Collab. between Local Authorities and the National Health Service, 1971–74. *Publications:* articles for Public Finance and Accountancy and other local govt jls. *Address:* 4 Whitewood Close, Lytham St Annes, Lancs FY8 4RN. *T:* Lytham (0253) 736201. *Clubs:* St Annes Old Links Golf, Penrith Golf.

JOLLY, Anthony Charles; His Honour Judge Jolly; a Circuit Judge since 1980; *b* 25 May 1932; *s* of Leonard and Emily Jolly; *m* 1962, Rosemary Christine Kernan; two *s* one *d*. *Educ:* Royal Naval Coll., Dartmouth; Balliol Coll., Oxford (Exhibnr history; MA). Called to Bar, Inner Temple, 1954; a Recorder, 1975–80; Hon. Recorder of Preston, 1989. *Recreations:* sailing, chess. *Address:* (home) Naze House, Freckleton, Lancs PR4 1UN. *T:* Freckleton (0772) 632285.

JOLLY, (Arthur) Richard, PhD; development economist; Deputy Executive Director, UNICEF, New York, since 1982; *b* 30 June 1934; *s* of late Arthur Jolly and Flora Doris Jolly (*née* Leaver); *m* 1963, Alison Bishop, PhD; two *s* two *d*. *Educ:* Brighton Coll.; Magdalene Coll., Cambridge (BA 1956, MA 1959); Yale Univ. (MA 1960, PhD 1966). Community Develt Officer, Baringo Dist, Kenya, 1957–59; Associate Chubb Fellow, Yale Univ., 1961–62; Res. Fellow, E Africa Inst. of Social Res., Makerere Coll., Uganda, 1963–64; Res. Officer, Dept of Applied Econs, Cambridge Univ., 1964–68 (seconded as Advr on Manpower to Govt of Zambia, 1964–66); Fellow, 1968–, Dir, 1972–81, Inst. of Develt Studies; Professorial Fellow, Univ. of Sussex, 1971–. Advr on Manpower Aid, ODM, 1968; Sen. Economist, Min. of Develt and Finance, Zambia, 1970; Advr to Parly Select Cttee on Overseas Aid and Develt, 1974–75; ILO Advr on Planning, Madagascar, 1975; Member: Triennial Rev. Gp, Commonwealth Fund for Tech. Co-operation, 1975–76; UK Council on Internat. Develt, 1974–78; UN Cttee for Develt Planning, 1978–81; Special Consultant on N-S Issues to Sec.-Gen., OECD, 1978; sometime member and chief of ILO and UN missions, and consultant to various governments and international organisations. Sec., British Alpine Hannibal Expedn, 1959. Member: Founding Cttee, European Assoc. of Develt Insts, 1972–75; Governing Council, 1976–85, and N-S Round Table, SID, 1976– (Vice-Pres., 1982–85; Chm., N-S Round Table, 1988–). Mem., Editorial Bd, World Development, 1973–. Master, Curriers' Co., 1977–78. Hon. LittD E Anglia, 1988. *Publications:* (jtly) Cuba: the economic and social revolution, 1964; Planning Education for African Development, 1969; (ed) Education in Africa: research and action, 1969; (ed jtly) Third World Employment, 1973; (jtly) Redistribution with Growth, 1974 (trans. French 1977); (ed) Disarmament and World Development, 1978, 3rd edn 1986; (ed jtly) Recent Issues in World Development, 1981; (ed jtly) Rich Country Interests in Third World Development, 1982; (ed jtly) The Impact of World Recession on Children, 1984; (ed jtly) Adjustment with a Human Face, 1987 (trans. French 1987, Spanish 1987); contributions to: Development in a Divided World, 1971; Employment, Income Distribution and Development Strategy, 1976; The Poverty of Progress, 1982; articles in professional and develt jls. *Recreations:* billiards, croquet, nearly missing trains and planes. *Address:* Institute of Development Studies, University of Sussex, Brighton, Sussex BN1 9RE. *T:* Brighton (0273) 606261; UNICEF, UNICEF House, 3 United Nations Plaza, New York 10017, USA. *T:* (212) 326-7017.

JOLLY, Richard; *see* Jolly, A. R.

JOLLY, Air Cdre Robert Malcolm, CBE 1969; retired; *b* 4 Aug. 1920; *s* of Robert Imrie Jolly and Ethel Thompson Jolly; *m* 1946, Josette Jacqueline (*née* Baindeky); no *c*. *Educ:* Skerry's Coll., Newcastle upon Tyne. Commnd in RAF, 1943; served in: Malta, 1941–45; Bilbeis, Egypt, 1945; Shaibah, Iraq, 1945–46; Malta, 1946–49; Air Cdre 1971; Dir of Personal Services, MoD, 1970–72; Dir of Automatic Data Processing (RAF), 1973–75, retd. Man. Dir, Leonard Griffiths & Associates, 1975–77; Vice-Pres., MWS Consultants Inc., 1978–80; Gen. Man., Diebold Europe SA and Dir, Diebold Research Program Europe, 1983–84. Fellow British Computer Soc., 1972; CBIM 1973. *Address:* Villa Gray Golf, Triq Galata, High Ridge, St Andrews, Malta GC. *T:* Malta 370282. *Club:* Royal Air Force.

JOLOWICZ, Prof. John Anthony; QC 1990; Professor of Comparative Law, University of Cambridge, since 1976; Fellow, Trinity College, Cambridge, since 1952; *b* 11 April 1926; *e s* of late Prof. Herbert Felix Jolowicz and Ruby Victoria Wagner; *m* 1957, Poppy Stanley; one *s* two *d*. *Educ:* Oundle Sch.; Trinity Coll., Cambridge (Scholar; MA; 1st Cl. Hons Law Tripos 1950). Served HM Forces (commnd RASC), 1944–48. Called to the Bar, Inner Temple and Gray's Inn, 1952; Bencher, Gray's Inn, 1978. Univ. of Cambridge: Asst Lectr in Law, 1955, Lectr, 1959; Reader in Common and Comparative Law, 1972. Professeur associé, Université de Paris 2, 1976; Lionel Cohen Lectr, Hebrew Univ. of Jerusalem, 1983. Pres., SPTL, 1986–87. Corresp. Mem., Institut de France, Acad. des Sciences morales et politiques, 1989. Hon. Dr Universidad Nacional Autónoma de México, 1985. Editor, Jl of Soc. of Public Teachers of Law, 1962–80. *Publications:* (ed) H. F. Jolowicz's Lectures on Jurisprudence, 1963; Winfield and Jolowicz on Tort, 1971, 13th edn (ed W. V. H. Rogers) 1989; (with M. Cappelletti) Public Interest Parties and the Active Role of the Judge, 1975; (jtly) Droit Anglais, 1986; contrib. to Internat. Encyc. of Comparative Law and to legal jls. *Address:* Trinity College, Cambridge CB2 1TQ. *T:* Cambridge (0223) 338400; West Green House, Barrington, Cambridge CB2 5SA. *T:* Cambridge (0223) 870495. *Clubs:* Royal Automobile; Leander (Henley-on-Thames).

JOLY de LOTBINIÈRE, Lt-Col Sir Edmond, Kt 1964; Chairman, Eastern Provincial Area Conservative Association, 1961–65, President, 1969–72; Chairman, Bury St Edmunds Division Conservative Association, 1953–72, President, 1972–79; *b* 17 March 1903; *er s* of late Brig.-Gen. H. G. Joly de Lotbinière, DSO; *m* 1st, 1928, Hon. Elizabeth Alice Cecilia Jolliffe (marr. diss. 1937); two *s*; 2nd, 1937, Helen Ruth Mildred Ferrar (*d* 1953); 3rd, 1954, Evelyn Adelaide (*née* Dawnay) (*d* 1985), *widow* of Lt-Col J. A. Innes, DSO. *Educ:* Eton Coll.; Royal Military Academy, Woolwich. 2nd Lieut Royal Engineers, 1923; served in India; RARO, 1928; re-employed, 1939. Served War of 1939–45: in Aden, Abyssinian Campaign and East Africa (despatches); Major 1941; Lieut-Col 1943; retired 1945. Chm. and Managing Dir of several private companies connected with the building trade. *Recreation:* bridge. *Address:* Horringer Manor, Bury St Edmunds, Suffolk. *T:* Horringer (0284) 735208. *Club:* Naval and Military.

JONAS, Peter; General Director (formerly Managing Director), English National Opera, since 1985; *b* 14 Oct. 1946; *s* of Walter Adolf Jonas and Hilda May Jonas; *m* 1989, Lucy, *d* of Christopher and Cecilia Hull. *Educ:* Worth School; Univ. of Sussex (BA Hons); Northern Coll. of Music (LRAM); Royal Coll. of Music (CAMS; Fellow, 1989); Eastman Sch. of Music, Univ. of Rochester, USA. Asst to Music Dir, 1974–76, Artistic Administrator, 1976–85, Chicago Symphony Orch.; Dir of Artistic Admin, Orchestral Assoc. of Chicago (Chicago Symph. Orch., Chicago Civic Orch., Chicago Symph. Chorus, Allied Arts Assoc., Orchestra Hall), 1977–85. Member: Bd of Management, Nat. Opera Studio, 1985–; Council, RCM, 1988–; Council, London Lighthouse, 1990–. FRSA 1989. *Recreations:* cinema, 20th century architecture. *Address:* 18 Lonsdale Place, Barnsbury Street, N1 1EL. *T:* 071–609 9427. *Club:* Athenæum.

JONES; *see* Armstrong-Jones, family name of Earl of Snowdon.

JONES; *see* Avery Jones.

JONES; *see* Gwynne Jones, family name of Baron Chalfont.

JONES; *see* Lloyd Jones and Lloyd-Jones.

JONES; *see* Mars-Jones.

JONES; *see* Morris-Jones.

JONES; *see* Owen-Jones.

JONES, Alan Payan P.; *see* Pryce-Jones.

JONES, Alan Wingate, FEng 1989; FIProdE; Chief Executive, Westland Group plc, since 1989; *b* 15 Oct. 1939; *s* of Gilbert Victor Jones and Isobel Nairn Jones; *m* 1974, Judi Ann Curtis; one *s* one *d*. *Educ:* Sutton Valence Sch.; King's Coll., Cambridge (MA MechScis). GEC, 1961–73; Plessey Co. Plc, 1973–89: Man. Dir, Plessey Marine, 1975–79; Divl Man. Dir, Plessey Displays and Sensors, 1979–85; Internat. Dir, 1985–87; Man. Dir, Plessey Electronic Systems, 1987–89; Dir, Plessey Plc, 1985–89. *Recreations:* opera, ski-ing, sailing. *Address:* The Grange, North Cadbury, near Yeovil, Somerset BA22 7BY. *Club:* Royal Automobile.

JONES, (Albert) Arthur; *b* 23 Oct. 1915; *s* of late Frederick Henry Jones and Emma (*née* Shreeves); *m* 1939, Peggy Joyce (*née* Wingate); one *s* one *d*. *Educ:* Bedford Modern Sch. (Harpur Schol.). Territorial, Beds Yeomanry, RA, 1938; Middle East with First Armd Div., 1941; captured at Alamein, 1942; escaped as POW from Italy, 600 miles walk to Allied Territory. Mem. Bedford RDC, 1946–49; Mem. Bedford Borough Council, 1949–74, Alderman, 1957–74; Mayor of Bedford, 1957–58, 1958–59; Member: Beds CC, 1956–67; Central Housing Advisory Cttee, 1959–62; Internat. Union of Local Authorities; Exec. Cttee, Nat. Union of Cons. and Unionist Assocs, 1963–73; Chm., Local Govt Nat. Adv. Cttee, Cons. Central Office, 1963–73; UK Rep., Consultative Assembly, Council of Europe and Assembly of WEU, 1971–73. Contested (C) Wellingborough, 1955; MP (C) Northants S, Nov. 1962–1974, Daventry, 1974–79; Mem., Speaker's panel of Chairmen, 1974–79. Member: Select Cttee on Immigration and Race Relations, 1969–70; Select Cttee on Expenditure, 1974–79; Chm., Environment Sub-Cttee, 1974–79; Vice-Chm., Cons. Back-Bench Cttee for the Environment, 1974–79. Dir of Private Companies. Hon. Treas., Town and Country Planning Assoc., 1975–81; Founder Mem., UK Housing Assoc., 1972–81; Member: New Towns Commn, 1980–88 (Dep. Chm., 1981–88); Anglian Water Authority, 1980–82. Vice-Pres., IWA, 1970–. Governor: Harpur Charity, 1953–89 (Chm., Estates Cttee, 1960–84; Chm., Finance Cttee, 1984–89); Centre for Policy Studies, 1980–83; St Andrew's Hosp., Northampton, 1979– (Dep. Chm., 1984–91). FSVA. *Publications:* Future of Housing Policy, 1960; War on Waste, 1965; Local Governors at Work, 1968; For the Record: Bedford 1945–74: Land Use and Financial Planning, 1981; Britain's Heritage, 1985. *Address:* Moor Farm, Pavenham, Bedford.

JONES, Prof. Albert Stanley, PhD; DSc; Professor of Chemistry, University of Birmingham, 1969–87, now Emeritus; *b* 30 April 1925; *s* of Albert Ernest Jones and Florence Jones (*née* Rathbone); *m* 1950, Joan Christine Gregg; one *s* one *d*. *Educ:* Waverley Grammar Sch.; Univ. of Birmingham (BSc (1st Cl. Hons) 1944, PhD 1947, DSc 1957). Beit Memorial Fellow for Medical Research, 1949–52; University of Birmingham: Lectr in Chemistry, 1952–61; Sen. Lectr, 1961–63; Reader in Organic Chemistry, 1963–69. Chemical Society London: Birmingham Representative, 1959–62; Mem. Council, 1966–69; Chm., Nucleotide Group, 1967–72. *Publications:* 180 papers, incl. three review articles, in scientific jls, on various aspects of organic chemistry and biological chemistry, particularly concerning nucleic acid derivatives. *Recreations:* church activities, walking, music, reading. *Address:* Waverley, 76 Manor House Lane, Yardley, Birmingham B26 1PR. *T:* 021–743 2030.

JONES, Allen, RA 1986 (ARA 1981); artist; *b* 1 Sept. 1937; *s* of William Jones and Madeline Jones (*née* Aveson); *m* 1964, Janet Bowen (marr. diss. 1978); two *d*. *Educ:* Ealing Grammar Sch. for Boys; Hornsey Sch. of Art (NDD; ATD); Royal Coll. of Art. Teacher of Lithography, Croydon Coll. of Art, 1961–63; Teacher of Painting, Chelsea Sch. of Art, 1966–68; Tamarind Fellow in Lithography, Los Angeles, 1968; Guest Professor:

Hochschule fur Bildend Kunst, Hamburg, 1968–70; Univs of S Florida, 1970, Calif at Irvine, 1973, Los Angeles, 1977; Hochschule fur Kunst Berlin, 1983; has travelled extensively. Sec., Young Contemporaries exhibn, London, 1961. One-man exhibns include: Arthur Tooth and Sons, London, 1963, 1964, 1967, 1970; Richard Feigen Gall., NY, Chicago and LA, 1964, 1965, 1970; Marlborough Fine Art, London, 1972; Arts Council sponsored exhibn tour, UK, 1974; Waddington Galls, London, 1976, 1980, 1982, 1983, 1985; James Corocan Gall., LA, 1977, 1987; UCLA Art Galls, LA, 1977; Retrospective 1958–78, ICA, 1978, tour incl. Waddington Galls, Toronto; Gall. Cavallino, Venice, 1981; Thorden and Wetterling, Gothenburg, 1983; Gall. Kammer, Hamburg, 1983, 1984; Gall. Wentzel, Cologne (sculpture), 1984; Gall. Patrice Trigano, Paris, 1985, 1986, 1989; Gall. Kaj Forsblom, Helsinki, 1985; Gall. Hete Hunermann, Dusseldorf, 1987; Charles Cowles Gall., NY, 1988; Heland Wetterling Gall., Stockholm, 1989; first Retrospective of Painting, 1959–79, Walker Art Gall., Liverpool, and tour of England and Germany, 1979; first internat. exhibn, Paris Biennale, 1961 (Prix des Jeunes Artists); first professional exhibn (with Howard Hodgkin), Two Painters, ICA, 1962; first UK mus. exhibn, Decade of Painting and Sculpture, Tate Gall., 1964; museum and group exhibns in UK and abroad include: New Generation, Whitechapel, 1964; London, The New Scene, Minneapolis, 1965; British Drawing/New Generation, NY, 1967; Documenta IV, Kassel, 1968; Pop Art Redefined, Hayward Gall., 1969; British Painting and Sculpture, Washington, 1970; Metamorphosis of Object, Brussels, and tour, 1971; Seibu, Tokyo, 1974; Hyperealist/Realistes, Paris, 1974; Arte Inglese 0991, Milan, 1976; El color en la pintura Britanica, British Council S American tour, 1977; British Painting 1952–77, Royal Academy, 1977; Arts Council sponsored exhibn tour, UK, 1978; British Watercolours, British Council tour, China, 1982; The Folding Image, Washington and Yale, 1984; Pop Art 1955–1970, NY, then Aust. tour, 1985; 40 Years of Modern Art, Tate Gall., 1986; British Art in the Twentieth Century, Royal Academy, then Stuttgart, 1987; Pop Art, Tokyo, 1987; Picturing People, British Council tour, Hong Kong, Singapore, Kuala Lumpur, 1990; New Acquisitions, Kunstmus., Dusseldorf, 1990; Seoul Internat. Art Fest., 1991; British Art since 1930, Waddington Gall., 1991; exhibited annually at Royal Acad., 1981–; murals and sculptures for public places include: Fognal, Basel and Zurich; Liverpool Garden Fest., 1984; Perseverance Works, Hackney, 1986; Citicorp/Canadian Nat. Bank, London Bridge City, 1987; Milton Keynes, 1990; BAA, Heathrow, 1990; television and stage sets include: O Calcutta!, for Kenneth Tynan, London and Europe, 1970; Manner Wir Kommen WDR, Cologne, 1970; Understanding Opera, LWT, 1988; Cinema/Eric Satie, for Ballet Rambert, 1989. Television films have been made on his work. Trustee, British Mus., 1990–. *Publications:* Allen Jones Figures, 1969; Allen Jones Projects, 1971; Waitress, 1972; Sheer Magic, 1979, UK 1980; articles in various jls. *Recreations:* very private, also gardening. *Address:* c/o Waddington Galleries, 11 Cork Street, W1X 1PD. *T:* 071–439 1866. *Clubs:* Garrick, Groucho.

JONES, Alun; *see* Jones, R. A.

JONES, Dr Alun Denry Wynn, CPhys, FInstP; Chief Executive, Institute of Physics, since 1990; *b* 13 Nov. 1939; *s* of Thomas D. and Ray Jones; *m* 1964, Ann Edwards; two *d.* *Educ:* Amman Valley Grammar Sch.; Christ Church, Oxford (MA, DPhil). CPhys, FInstP 1973. Sen. Student, Commission for Exhibn of 1851, 1964–66; Sen. Research Fellow, UKAEA, 1966–67; Lockheed Missiles and Space Co., California, 1967–70; Tutor, Open Univ., 1971–82; joined Macmillan and Co., Publishers, 1971; Dep. Editor, Nature, 1972–73; British Steel Corp., 1974–77; British Steel Overseas Services, 1977–81; Asst Dir, Technical Change Centre, 1982–85; Dep. Dir, 1986–87, Dir, 1987–90, Wolfson Foundn. Sec. of working party on social concern and biological advances, 1972–74, Mem., Section X Cttee, 1981–, BAAS. British Library: Adv. Council, 1983–85; Document Supply Centre Adv. Cttee, 1986–89; Mem. Council, Nat. Library of Wales, 1987– (Gov., 1986–). Gov., UCW, Aberystwyth, 1990–. *Publication:* (with W. F. Bodmer) Our Future Inheritance: choice or chance, 1974. *Recreations:* gardening, theatre, cricket. *Address:* Institute of Physics, 47 Belgrave Square, SW1X 8QX. *T:* 071–235 6111; 4 Wheatsheaf Close, Woking, Surrey GU21 4BP.

JONES, Rt. Rev. Alwyn Rice; *see* St Asaph, Bishop of.

JONES, Prof. Anne; Consultant, Director of Continuing Education and Professor, Brunel University, since 1991; *b* 8 April 1935; *d* of Sydney Joseph and Hilda Pickard; *m* 1958, C. Gareth Jones (marr. diss. 1989); one *s* two *d.* *Educ:* Harrow Weald County Sch.; Westfield Coll., London. BA, DipSoc, PGCE London. Assistant Mistress: Malvern Girls' Coll., 1957–58; Godolphin and Latymer Sch., 1958–62; Dulwich Coll., 1964; Sch. Counsellor, Mayfield Comprehensive Sch., 1965–71; Dep. Hd, Thomas Calton Sch., 1971–74; Head: Vauxhall Manor Sch., 1974–81; Cranford Community Sch., 1981–87; Under Sec. (Dir of Educn), Dept of Employment, 1987–91. Vis. Prof. of Educn, Sheffield Univ., 1989–. Director: CRAC, 1983–; Grubb Inst. of Behavioural Studies, 1987–. FRSA 1984 (Mem. Council, 1986–). *Publications:* School Counselling in Practice, 1970; Counselling Adolescents in School, 1977, 2nd edn as Counselling Adolescents, School and After, 1984; Leadership for Tomorrow's Schools, 1987; (with Jan Marsh and A. G. Watts): Male and Female, 1974, 2nd edn 1982; Living Choices, 1976; Time to Spare, 1980; contribs to various books. *Recreations:* walking, boating, gardening, theatre, opera. *Address:* Brunel University, Uxbridge, Middx UB8 3PH. *T:* Uxbridge (0895) 274000; 23 Southerton Road, W6 0PJ. *T:* 081–748 6399.

JONES, Maj.-Gen. Anthony George Clifford, CB 1978; MC 1945; President, Regular Commissions Board, 1975–78; *b* 20 May 1923; *s* of late Col R. C. Jones, OBE, and M. D. Jones; *m* Kathleen Mary, *d* of Comdr J. N. Benbow, OBE, RN; two *d.* *Educ:* St Paul's School; Trinity Hall, Cambridge. Commissioned RE, 1942; service includes: Troop Comdr, Guards Armd Div., Nijmegen, 1945 (MC 1945; despatches, 1947); Indian Sappers and Miners; Staff Coll., 1954; Bde Major, 63 Gurkha Inf. Bde, 1955 (despatches, 1957); jssc; OC 25 Corps Engineer Regt, 1965–67; Comdr, RE Trng Bde, 1968–72; Head of Ops Staff, Northern Army Group, 1972–74; Dep. Comdr SE District, 1974–75. Hon. Col, RE Volunteers (Sponsored Units), 1978–86. *Club:* Army and Navy.

JONES, Anthony W.; *see* Whitworth-Jones.

JONES, Arthur; *see* Jones, (Albert) Arthur.

JONES, Prof. Arthur Stanley, CBiol; Principal, Royal Agricultural College, Cirencester, since 1990; *b* 17 May 1932; *s* of John Jones and Anne Jones (*née* Hamilton); *m* 1962, Mary Margaret Smith; three *s* one *d.* *Educ:* Gosforth Grammar Sch.; Durham Univ. (BSc); Aberdeen Univ. (PhD). FIBiol; FBIM. Rowett Research Institute: Res. Scientist, 1959; Hd, Applied Nutrition Dept, 1966; Chm., Applied Scis Div., 1975; Dep. Dir, 1983; Governor, 1987–; Strathcona-Fordyce Prof. of Agriculture, Univ. of Aberdeen, 1986–90; Head, Sch. of Agriculture, Aberdeen, and Principal, N of Scotland Coll. of Agriculture, 1986–90. Chm., Scottish Beef Develts Ltd, 1988–91. FRSA. *Publications:* Nutrition of Animals of Agricultural Importance (vol. 17, Internat. Encyc. of Food and Nutrition) (ed D. P. Cuthbertson), 1967; 95 articles in learned jls. *Recreations:* yachting, flying, gardening. *Address:* Royal Agricultural College, Cirencester, Glos GL7 6JS.

JONES, Rt. Hon. Aubrey, PC 1955; Director: Thomas Tilling Ltd, 1970–82; Cornhill Insurance Company Ltd, 1971–82 (Chairman, 1971–74); *b* 20 Nov. 1911; *s* of Evan and Margaret Aubrey Jones, Merthyr Tydfil; *m* 1948, Joan, *d* of G. Godfrey-Isaacs, Ridgehanger, Hillcrest Road, Hanger Hill, W5; two *s.* *Educ:* Cyfarthfa Castle Secondary Sch., Merthyr Tydfil; London School of Economics. BSc (Econ.) 1st Cl. Hons, Gladstone Memorial Prizewinner, Gerstenberg Post-grad. Schol., LSE. On foreign and editorial staffs of The Times, 1937–39 and 1947–48. Joined British Iron and Steel Federation, 1949; General Dir, June-Dec. 1955. Served War of 1939–45, Army Intelligence Staff, War Office and Mediterranean Theatre, 1940–46. Contested (C) SE Essex in General Election, 1945 and Heywood and Radcliffe (by-election), 1946; MP (U) Birmingham, Hall Green, 1950–65; Parliamentary Private Sec. to Minister of State for Economic Affairs, 1952, and to Min. of Materials, 1953; Minister of Fuel and Power, Dec. 1955–Jan. 1957; Minister of Supply, 1957–Oct. 1959. Mem., Plowden Cttee of Inquiry into Aircraft Industry, 1965–66. Chairman: Staveley Industries Ltd, 1964–65 (Dir 1962–65); Laporte Industries (Holdings) Ltd, 1970–72; Director: Guest, Keen & Nettlefolds Steel Company Limited, 1960–65; Courtaulds Ltd, 1960–63; Black & Decker, 1977–81. Chm., Nat. Bd for Prices and Incomes, 1965–70; Vice-Pres., Consumers' Assoc., 1967–72; leading consultant to: Nigerian Public Service Commn, 1973–74; Iranian Govt, 1974–78; Plessey Ltd, 1978–80; Mem. Panel of Conciliators, Internat. Centre for Settlement of Investment Disputes, 1974–81. Pres., Oxford Energy Policy Club, 1976–88. Regent Lectr, Univ. of California at Berkeley, 1968. Vis. Fellow: New Coll., Oxford, 1978; Sci. Policy Res. Unit, Univ. of Sussex, 1986–; Sen. Res. Associate, St Antony's Coll., Oxford, 1979–82; Guest Scholar, Brookings Instn, Washington, DC, 1982. Fellow Commoner, Churchill Coll., Cambridge, 1972 and 1982–86. Hon. Fellow, LSE, 1959, Mem., Court of Governors, 1964–87. Hon. DSc Bath, 1968. Winston Churchill Meml Trust Award, 1985. *Publications:* The Pendulum of Politics, 1946; Industrial Order, 1950; The New Inflation: the politics of prices and incomes, 1973; (ed) Economics and Equality, 1976; (contrib.) My LSE, 1977; (contrib.) The End of the Keynesian Era, 1977; Oil: the missed opportunity, 1981; Britain's Economy: the roots of stagnation, 1985. *Address:* Arnen, 120 Limmer Lane, Felpham, Bognor Regis, West Sussex PO22 7LP. *T:* Middleton-on-Sea (024358) 2722.

JONES, Barry; *see* Jones, Stephen B.

JONES, Maj.-Gen. Basil Douglas, CB 1960; CBE 1950; *b* 14 May 1903; *s* of Rev. B. Jones; *m* 1932, Katherine Holberton (*d* 1986), *d* of Col H. W. Man, CBE, DSO; one *s* two *d.* *Educ:* Plymouth Coll.; RMC, Sandhurst. 2nd Lieut, Welch Regt, 1924; transferred to RAOC, 1935; Major 1939; served with Australian Military Forces in Australia and New Guinea, 1941–44; Temp. Brig. 1947; Brig. 1955; Maj.-Gen. 1958. ADC to the Queen, 1956–58; Inspector, RAOC, 1958–60, retired. Col Commandant, RAOC, 1963–67. *Recreation:* golf. *Address:* Churchfield, Sutton Courtenay, Abingdon, Oxon OX14 4AG. *T:* Abingdon (0235) 848261.

JONES, Beti, CBE 1980; *b* 23 Jan. 1919; *d* of Isaac Jones and Elizabeth (*née* Rowlands). *Educ:* Rhondda County Sch. for Girls; Univ. of Wales. BA (Hons) History, Teaching Diploma. Grammar Sch. teaching, 1941–43; S Wales Organiser, Nat. Assoc. of Girls' Clubs, 1943–47; Youth Officer, Educn Branch, Control Commission, Germany, 1947–49; Children's Officer, Glamorgan CC, 1949–68; Chief Adviser on Social Work, Scottish Office, 1968–80. Fellow, University Coll., Cardiff, 1982 (Hon. Fellow, Dept of Social Administration, 1970). *Address:* 5 Belgrave Crescent, Edinburgh EH4 3AQ. *T:* 031–332 2696; Lochside Cottage, Craigie, Blairgowrie, Perthshire. *T:* Essendy (025084) 373. *Clubs:* Royal Over-Seas League (London and Edinburgh).

JONES, Hon. Brian Leslie; Hon. Mr Justice Jones; Judge of the High Court of Justice, Hong Kong, since 1981; *b* 19 Oct. 1930; *s* of late William Leslie Jones and Gladys Gertrude Jones; *m* 1966, Yukiko Hirokane; one *s* two *d.* *Educ:* Bromsgrove Sch.; Birmingham Univ. Admitted Solicitor, 1956; called as Barrister and Solicitor, Supreme Court, Victoria, Australia, 1968. Solicitor, private practice, England, 1956–64; Asst Registrar, Supreme Court, Hong Kong, 1964–68; Legal Officer, Attorney General's Dept, Canberra, 1968–69; Asst Registrar, Hong Kong, 1969–74; District Judge, Hong Kong, 1974–81. Comr, Supreme Ct of Brunei, 1982, 1985, 1990. Chm., Standing Cttee on Company Law Reform, 1991. *Recreations:* squash, chess, walking, reading. *Address:* 16B Severn Road, The Peak, Hong Kong. *T:* Hong Kong 8496327. *Clubs:* Hong Kong; Anyos (Andorra).

JONES, Brinley; *see* Jones, Robert B.

JONES, Charles Beynon Lloyd, CMG 1978; Chairman of Directors, David Jones Ltd, 1963–80; Consul General of Finland in Sydney, since 1971; *b* 4 Dec. 1932; *s* of late Sir Charles Lloyd Jones and Lady (Hannah Beynon) Lloyd Jones, OBE. *Educ:* Cranbrook Sch., Sydney; Univ. of Sydney (not completed). Joined David Jones Ltd, 1951; Alternate Director, 1956; Director, 1957; Joint Managing Director, 1961. President: Retail Traders Assoc., NSW, 1976–78; Bd of Trustees, Art Gall. of NSW, 1980–83 (Trustee, 1972; Vice-Pres., 1976–80). Governor, London House for Overseas Graduates, 1983–. Officer, Order of Merit, Republic of Italy (Cavaliere Ufficiale); Comdr, Order of the Lion, Finland. *Address:* 294 Old South Head Road, Watsons Bay, NSW 2030, Australia; Summerlees Farm, Yarramalong, NSW 2259. *Club:* Royal Sydney Golf.

JONES, Gen. Sir (Charles) Edward (Webb), KCB 1989; CBE 1985; UK Military Representative to NATO, since 1992; *b* 25 Sept. 1936; *s* of Gen. Sir Charles Phibbs Jones, GCB, CBE, MC and of Ouida Margaret Wallace; *m* 1965, Suzanne Vere Pige-Leschallas; two *s* one *d.* *Educ:* Portora Royal School, Enniskillen. Commissioned Oxford and Bucks LI, 1956; 1st Bn Royal Green Jackets, 1958; served BAOR, 1968–70; served NI, 1971–72 (despatches 1972); Directing Staff, Staff Coll., 1972; CO 1st Bn RGJ, 1974–76; Comdr 6th Armd Brigade, 1981–83; Comdr, British Mil. Adv. and Training Team, Zimbabwe, 1983–85; Dir Gen., TA and Organisation, 1985–87; Comdr, 3rd Armoured Div., 1987–88; QMG, MoD, 1988–91. Colonel Commandant: RAEC, 1986–; RGJ, 1988–. *Recreations:* golf, tennis, fishing. *Club:* Army and Navy.

JONES, Charles Ian McMillan; Project Director, Centre for British Teachers, since 1988; *b* 11 Oct. 1934; *s* of Wilfred Charles Jones and Bessie Jones (*née* McMillan); *m* 1962, Jennifer Marie Potter; two *s.* *Educ:* Bishop's Stortford Coll.; St John's Coll., Cambridge. Certif. Educn 1959, MA 1962; FBIM, FRSA. 2nd Lieut RA, 1953–55. Head of Geog. Dept, Bishop's Stortford Coll., 1960–70, Asst to Headmaster, 1967–70; Vice-Principal, King William's Coll., IoM, 1971–75; Head Master, Bedford School, 1975–86; Dir of Studies, BRNC, Dartmouth, 1986–88. Man., England Schoolboy Hockey XI, 1967–74; Man., England Hockey XI, 1968–69; Pres., English Schoolboys Hockey Assoc., 1980–88; Mem. IoM Sports Council, 1972–75. *Publications:* articles in Guardian. *Recreations:* hockey (Captain Cambridge Univ. Hockey XI, 1959; England Hockey XI, 1959–64, 17 caps; Gt Britain Hockey XI, 1959–64, 28 caps), cricket (Captain IoM Cricket XI, 1973–75), squash, gardening. *Address:* Riverain, Staitheway Road, Wroxham, Norwich NR12 8TH. *Clubs:* MCC, East India, Devonshire, Sports and Public Schools; Hawks (Cambridge).

JONES, Sir Christopher L.; *see* Lawrence-Jones.

JONES, Clement; *see* Jones, John C.

JONES, Clive Lawson; Deputy Director General for Energy, European Commission, since 1987; *b* 16 March 1937; *s* of Celyn John Lawson Jones and Gladys Irene Jones; *m* 1961, Susan Brenda (*née* McLeod); one *s* one *d*. *Educ:* Cranleigh School; University of Wales. BSc (Chemistry). With British Petroleum, 1957–61; Texaco Trinidad, 1961–68; Principal, Min. of Power, 1968–69; Min. of Technology, 1969–70; DTI, 1970–73; Asst Sec., Oil Emergency Group, 1973–74; Department Energy: Asst Sec., 1974–77; Under Sec., Gas Div., 1981–82; Counsellor (Energy), Washington, 1977–81; Dir for Energy Policy, EC, 1982–86. *Recreations:* art, antiques. *Address:* Commission of the European Communities, 200 rue de la Loi, 1049 Brussels, Belgium.

JONES, Daniel Gruffydd; Registrar and Secretary, University College of Wales, Aberystwyth, since 1990; *b* 7 Dec. 1933; *o s* of late Ifor Ceredig Jones and Gwendolen Eluned Jones; *m* 1969, Maureen Anne Woodhall; three *d*. *Educ:* Ardwyn Grammar Sch., Aberystwyth; University Coll. of N Wales, Bangor (BA). Min. of Housing and Local Govt, 1960; Private Sec. to Sec. of Cabinet, 1967–69; Asst Sec., 1969; Sec., Water Resources Bd, 1969–73; DoE, 1973; Sec., Prime Minister's Cttee on Local Govt Rules of Conduct, 1973–74; Under Sec., 1975; Prin. Finance Officer, Welsh Office, 1975–79; Director: Local Govt Directorate, DoE, 1980–82; Central Directorate of Envmtl Protection, DoE, 1982–86; Regl Dir, SE Reg., DoE and Dept of Transport, 1986–90. *Address:* c/o University College of Wales, King Street, Aberystwyth, Dyfed SY23 2AX. *T:* Aberystwyth (0970) 622004.

JONES, David, OBE 1986; Principal, Sheffield and North Trent College of Nursing and Midwifery, since 1990; *b* 27 July 1940; *s* of John Evan Jones and Edith Catherine (*née* Edwards); *m* 1962, Janet Mary Ambler; two *s* two *d*. *Educ:* Boys' Grammar Sch., Bala, N Wales; Univ. of Wales (BEd). SRN; RMN; RNT. Divl Nursing Officer, Gwynedd, 1974–78; Chief Admin. Nursing Officer, Gwynedd HA, 1979–87; first Chm., Welsh Nat. Bd for Nursing, Midwifery and Health Visiting, 1979–86; Chief Exec., English Nat. Bd for Nursing, Midwifery and Health Visiting, 1987–89. *Recreations:* public affairs, countryside, family. *Address:* Sheffield and North Trent College of Nursing and Midwifery, 22 Collegiate Crescent, Sheffield S10 2BA. *T:* Sheffield (0742) 684604.

JONES, Sir David A.; *see* Akers-Jones.

JONES, David Charles, FCCA, FCIS; Chief Executive, Next Plc, since 1988 (Deputy Chief Executive, 1986–88); *b* 2 Feb. 1943; *s* of Frederick Charles Thomas Jones and Annie Marcella Jones; *m* 1968, Jeanette Ann Crofts; two *s* one *d*. *Educ:* King's Sch., Worcester. FCIS 1974; FCCA 1975. Joined Kays Mail Order Co. (part of Great Universal Stores), 1960, Finance Dir, 1971–77; Man. Dir, BMOC, 1977–80; Chief Exec., Grattan Plc, 1980–86. *Recreations:* golf, snooker. *Address:* Anchor House, Ingleby Road, Bradford BD99 2XG. *T:* Bradford (0274) 575511.

JONES, David Evan Alun, CBE 1985; DL; Commissioner for Local Administration in Wales, 1980–85; *b* 9 Aug. 1925; *s* of David Jacob Jones, OBE, Master Mariner, and Margaret Jane Jones; *m* 1952, Joan Margaret Erica (*née* Davies); two *s*. *Educ:* Aberaeron County Sch.; University Coll. of Wales, Aberystwyth (LLB; Sir Samuel Evans Prize, 1949). Solicitor. Served War, RAF, 1943–47 (Flt Lieut). Articled service, Exeter, 1949–52; asst solicitor posts with Ilford Bor., Southampton County Bor., Berks County and Surrey County Councils, 1952–61; Dep. Clerk, Denbighshire CC, subseq. Clerk of CC and Clerk of the Peace, 1961–74; Chief Exec., Gwynedd CC, 1974–80. Chm., All Wales Adv. Panel on Develt of Services for Mentally Handicapped People, 1985–90; Member: Broadcasting Council for Wales, 1980–85; Local Govt Boundary Commn for Wales, 1985–89; Prince of Wales's Cttee, 1985– (Chm., Gwynedd County Gp, 1990–); Gwynedd HA, 1986–88. Treasurer, UCNW, 1988–. DL Gwynedd, 1988. *Recreations:* gardening, travel, a little golf. *Address:* Min-y-Don, West End, Beaumaris, Gwynedd LL58 8BG. *T:* Beaumaris (0248) 810225. *Clubs:* National Liberal; Baron Hill Golf (Beaumaris).

JONES, David G.; *see* Gwyn Jones.

JONES, David George; Civil Secretary, British Forces Germany, since 1989; *b* 31 May 1941; *s* of Frederick George Jones and Dorothy Jones (*née* Steele); *m* 1962, Leonie Usherwood Smith; three *s*. *Educ:* High Storrs Grammar Sch., Sheffield. Joined War Office as Exec. Officer, 1960; Asst Private Sec. to Army Minister, 1970–71; Principal, MoD Central Financial Planning Div., 1973–77; Private Sec. to Minister of State for Defence, 1977–80; Regl Marketing Dir, Defence Sales Organisation, 1980–84; Asst Sec., Air Systems Controllerate, 1984–85; Dep. Dir Gen., Al Yamamah Project Office, 1985–88; Dir Gen. Aircraft 2, Air Systems Controllerate, MoD (PE), 1988–89. *Recreations:* gardening, travel. *Address:* c/o Ministry of Defence, Whitehall, SW1A 2HB. *T:* 071–218 9000. *Club:* Civil Service.

JONES, David Hugh; Associate Director, Royal Shakespeare Company, since 1966; *b* 19 Feb. 1934; *s* of John David Jones and Gwendolen Agnes Langworthy (*née* Ricketts); *m* 1964, Sheila Allen; two *s*. *Educ:* Taunton Sch.; Christ's Coll., Cambridge (MA 1st Cl. Hons English). 2nd Lieut RA, 1954–56. Production team of Monitor, BBC TV's 1st arts magazine, 1958–62, Editor, 1962–64; joined RSC, 1964; Aldwych Co. Dir, 1968–72; Artistic Dir, RSC (Aldwych), 1975–77; Producer, Play of the Month, BBC TV, 1977–78; Artistic Dir, Brooklyn Acad. of Music Theatre Co., 1979–81; Adjunct Prof. of Drama, Yale Univ., 1981. Productions for RSC incl. plays by Arden, Brecht, Gorky, Granville Barker, Günter Grass, Graham Greene, Mercer, O'Casey, Shakespeare, and Chekhov; dir. prodns for Chichester and Stratford, Ontario, Festival Theatres; other productions include: Tramway Road, Lyric Th., Hammersmith, 1984; Old Times, Theatre Royal, Haymarket, and Los Angeles (LA Dramalogue Award for direction), 1985. Dir, films for BBC TV, including: biography of poet, John Clare, 1969; adaptations of Hardy and Chekhov short stories, 1972 and 1973; Pinter's screenplay, Langrishe, Go Down, 1978; Merry Wives of Windsor, Pericles, 1982–83; The Devil's Disciple, 1987; Look Back in Anger, 1989; directed for American TV: The Christmas Wife, 1988; Sensibility and Sense, 1990; The End of a Sentence, 1991. Feature films directed: Pinter's Betrayal, 1982; 84 Charing Cross Road (royal film performance), 1987 (Christopher and Scriptor Awards, 1988); Jacknife, 1989. Obie Awards, NY, for direction of RSC Summerfolk, 1975, for innovative programming at BAM Theatre Co., 1980. *Recreations:* chess, reading modern poetry, exploring mountains and islands. *Address:* 227 Clinton Street, Brooklyn, NY 11201, USA.

JONES, Rev. David Ian Stewart; Director of the Lambeth Charities, since 1985; Hon. Priest Vicar, Southwark Cathedral, since 1985; *b* 3 April 1934; *s* of Rev. John Milton Granville Jones and Evelyn Moyes Stewart Jones (formerly Chedburn); *m* 1967, Susan Rosemary Hardy Smith; twin *s* and *d*. *Educ:* St John's Sch., Leatherhead; Selwyn Coll., Cambridge (MA). Commnd Royal Signals, 1952–54. Curate at Oldham Parish Church, 1959–62; Vicar of All Saints, Elton, Bury, 1963–66; Asst Conduct and Chaplain of Eton Coll., 1966–70; Conduct and Sen. Chaplain of Eton Coll., 1970–74; Headmaster of Bryanston School, 1974–82; Rector-designate of Bristol City, 1982–85. Spiritual Develt Advr, NABC, 1990–. Gov., Forest Sch., 1986–. *Recreations:* reading, music, education. *Address:* 127 Kennington Road, SE11 6SF. *T:* 071–735 1925. *Club:* East India, Devonshire, Sports and Public Schools.

JONES, David le Brun, CB 1975; Director, Long Term Office, International Energy Agency, 1982–88; *b* 18 Nov. 1923; *s* of Thomas John Jones and Blanche le Brun. *Educ:* City of London Sch.; Trinity Coll., Oxford. Asst Principal, Min. of Power, 1947; Principal, MOP, 1952; Asst Sec., Office of the Minister for Science, 1962; Asst Sec., MOP, 1963; Under-Sec., MOP, later Min. of Technology and DTI, 1968–73; Dep. Sec., DTI, later DoI, 1973–76; Cabinet Office, 1976–77; Dept of Energy, 1978–82. Trustee, Nat. Energy Foundn, 1989–. *Recreations:* walking, reading, chess. *Address:* 47 Grove End Road, NW8 9NB. *Club:* United Oxford & Cambridge University.

JONES, David M.; *see* Mansel-Jones.

JONES, David Martin, FIBiol; General Director, Zoological Society of London, since 1991; *b* 14 Aug. 1944; *s* of John Trevor Jones and Mair Carno Jones; *m* 1969, Janet Marian Woosley; three *s*. *Educ:* St Paul's Cathedral Choir Sch.; St John's Sch., Leatherhead; Royal Veterinary Coll., London (BSc, BVetMed). MRCVS. Veterinary Officer, Whipsnade, 1969; Sen. Veterinary Officer, 1975, Asst Dir of Zoos, 1981, Dir of Zoos, 1984, Zoological Soc. of London. Chm., Fauna and Flora Preservation Soc., 1987; Chm., Brooke Hosp. for Animals, Cairo, 1990– (Vice-Chm., 1973–90); Trustee, WWF UK, 1986–. *Publications:* over 100 papers on wild life medicine, management and conservation, in veterinary, medical and zoological jls. *Recreations:* field conservation, travel, antiquarian books, driving, gardening. *Address:* Zoological Society of London, Regent's Park, NW1 4RY.

JONES, Prof. David Morgan, MA; Professor of Classics in the University of London (Westfield College), 1953–80; *b* 9 April 1915; *m* 1965, Irene M. Glanville. *Educ:* Whitgift Sch.; Exeter Coll., Oxford (Scholar). 1st Class, Classical Hon. Mods, 1936; 1st Class, Lit Hum, 1938; Derby Scholar, 1938; Junior Research Fellow, Exeter Coll., Oxford, 1938–40; Oxford Diploma in Comparative Philology, 1940; Lecturer in Classics, University Coll. of North Wales, 1940–48; Reader in Classics in the University of London (Birkbeck Coll.), 1949–53. *Publications:* papers and reviews in classical and linguistic journals. *Address:* Kemyell Vean, 3 Laregan Hill, Penzance TR18 4NY. *T:* Penzance (0736) 63389.

JONES, Della; mezzo-soprano; *d* of Eileen Gething Jones and late Cyril Vincent Jones; *m* 1988, Paul Vigars; one *s*. *Educ:* Neath Girls' Grammar School; Royal College of Music. LRAM (singing), ARCM (piano); Kathleen Ferrier Scholarship. Mem., ENO, 1977–82, leading roles; 1982–: guest artist, ENO; sings with major British opera companies; overseas appearances include Venice, Schwetzingen, Los Angeles, Geneva, Paris, USSR, New York (Mostly Mozart Festival, 1986, 1988), Madrid, Frankfurt, Cologne, Japan (concert tour); radio and TV; numerous recordings. *Recreations:* writing cadenzas, art galleries, animal welfare, soap operas. *Address:* c/o Music International, 13 Ardilaun Road, Highbury, N5 2QR. *T:* 071–359 5183.

JONES, Sir Derek A.; *see* Alun-Jones.

JONES, Derek John Claremont, CMG 1979; Senior Fellow, Trade Policy Research Centre, 1986–90; retired; *b* 2 July 1927; *er s* of Albert Claremont Jones and Ethel Lilian Jones (*née* Hazell); *m* 1st, 1951, Jean Cynthia Withams; one *s* two *d*; 2nd, 1970, Kay Cecile Thewlis; one *s*. *Educ:* Colston Sch., Bristol; Bristol Univ.; London Sch. of Economics and Political Science. Economic Asst, Economic Section, Cabinet Office, 1950–53; Second Sec., UK Delegn to OEEC/NATO, Paris, 1953–55; Asst Principal, Colonial Office, 1955–57; Principal, Colonial Office, 1957–66; First Secretary, Commonwealth Office, 1966–67; Counsellor (Hong Kong Affairs), UK Mission, Geneva, 1967–71; Government of Hong Kong: Dep. Economic Sec., 1971–73; Sec. for Economic Services, 1973–76; Sec. for the Environment, 1976–81; Sec. for Transport, 1981–82; Minister for Hong Kong Relns with EC and Member States, 1982–86. *Recreations:* reading, travel, conversation. *Address:* Cliff House, Trevaunance Cove, St Agnes, Cornwall TR5 0RZ. *T:* St Agnes (087255) 2334. *Clubs:* Hong Kong, Royal Hong Kong Jockey.

JONES, Derek R.; *see* Rudd-Jones.

JONES, Rt. Rev. Derwyn Dixon, DD; Bishop of Huron, 1984–90; *b* 5 Aug. 1925; *s* of Rev. Walter Jones, DD, and Mary Rosalie Jones (*née* Dixon); *m* 1960, Arline Carole Dilamarter; one *s* one *d*. *Educ:* Univ. of Western Ontario (BA); Huron College (LTh, DD). Deacon 1946, priest 1947; Curate: Holy Trinity, Winnipeg, 1946–48; All Saints', Windsor, 1948–49; Rector, St Andrew's, Kitchener, 1949–52; Asst Rector, St Paul's Cathedral, London, Ont, 1952–55; Rector: Canon Davis Memorial Church, Sarnia, 1955–58; St Barnabas, Windsor, 1958–66; St Peter's, Brockville, 1966–69; St James, Westminster, London, Ont, 1969–82; Archdeacon of Middlesex, 1978–82; Suffragan Bishop of Huron, 1982; Coadjutor Bishop, 1983. *Recreation:* music. *Address:* 301–7 Picton Street, London, Ontario N6B 3N7, Canada. *T:* (519) 642–2161. *Club:* London (London, Ont).

JONES, Captain Desmond V.; *see* Vincent-Jones.

JONES, Rev. Prof. Douglas Rawlinson; Lightfoot Professor of Divinity, University of Durham, 1964–85, now Emeritus; Residentiary Canon of Durham Cathedral, 1964–85, now Emeritus; *b* 11 Nov. 1919; *s* of Percival and Charlotte Elizabeth Jones; *m* 1946, Hazel Mary Passmore; three *s* two *d*. *Educ:* Queen Elizabeth's Hosp., Bristol; St Edmund Hall, Oxford; Wycliffe Hall, Oxford. Squire Scholar, 1938; BA 1941; MA 1945; deacon, 1942; priest, 1943. Curate of St Michael and All Angels, Windmill Hill, Bristol, 1942–45; Lectr, Wycliffe Hall, Oxford, 1945–50; Chaplain, Wadham Coll., Oxford, 1945–50; Lectr in Divinity, 1948–50; University of Durham: Lectr, 1951; Sen. Lectr, 1963. Mem., Gen. Synod of C of E, 1970–80 and 1982–85. Chairman of the Liturgical Commn, 1981–86. DD Lambeth, 1985. *Publications:* Haggai, Zechariah and Malachi, 1962; Isaiah, 56–66 and Joel, 1964; Instrument of Peace, 1965; contrib. to: Peake's Commentary on the Bible, 1962; Hastings' Dictionary of the Bible, 1963; The Cambridge History of the Bible, 1963; articles in Jl of Theolog. Studies, Zeitschrift für die Alttestamentliche Wissenschaft, Vetus Testamentum, Theology, Scottish Jl of Theology. *Recreation:* carpentry. *Address:* Whitefriars, Kings Road, Longniddry, E Lothian EH32 0NN. *T:* Longniddry (0875) 52149.

JONES, Prof. Douglas Samuel, MBE 1945; FRS 1968; Ivory Professor of Mathematics, University of Dundee, since 1965; *b* 10 Jan. 1922; *s* of late J. D. Jones and B. Jones (*née* Streather); *m* 1950, Ivy Styles; one *s* one *d*. *Educ:* Wolverhampton Grammar Sch.; Corpus Christi Coll., Oxford (MA 1947; Hon. Fellow, 1980); DSc Manchester 1957. FIMA 1964; FRSE 1967; CEng, FIEE 1989. Flt-Lt, RAFVR, 1941–45. Commonwealth Fund Fellow, MIT, 1947–48; Asst Lectr in Maths, University of Manchester, 1948–51; Lectr 1951–54, Research Prof. 1955, New York Univ.; Sen. Lectr in Maths, Univ. of Manchester, 1955–57; Prof. of Maths, Univ. of Keele, 1957–64. Vis. Prof., Courant Inst., 1962–63. Member: UGC, 1976–86 (Mem., 1971–86, Chm., 1976–86, Mathematical Scis Sub-Cttee); Computer Bd, 1977–82; Open Univ. Vis. Cttee, 1982–87. Member Council:

Royal Soc., 1973–74; IMA, 1982–85, 1986– (Pres., 1988–89). Hon. DSc Strathclyde, 1975. Keith Prize, RSE, 1974; van der Pol Gold Medal, Internat. Union of Radio Sci., 1981; Naylor Prize, London Mathematical Soc., 1987. Trustee, Quarterly Jl of Mechanics and Applied Maths; Associate Editor: Jl IMA, 1964–; RSE, 1969–82; SIAM Jl on Applied Maths, 1975–; Applicable Analysis, 1976–; Mathematical Methods, 1977–; Royal Soc., 1978–83. *Publications:* Electrical and Mechanical Oscillations, 1961; Theory of Electromagnetism, 1964; Generalised Functions, 1966; Introductory Analysis, vol. 1, 1969, vol 2, 1970; Methods in Electromagnetic Wave Propagation, 1979; Elementary Information Theory, 1979; The Theory of Generalised Functions, 1982; Differential Equations and Mathematical Biology, 1983; Acoustic and Electromagnetic Waves, 1986; Assembly Programming and the 8086 Microprocessor, 1988; articles in mathematical and physical jls. *Recreations:* golf, walking, photography. *Address:* Department of Mathematics and Computer Science, The University, Dundee DD1 4HN. *T:* Dundee (0382) 23181. *Club:* United Oxford & Cambridge University.

JONES, Edgar Stafford, CBE 1960 (MBE 1953); *b* 11 June 1909; *s* of late Theophilus Jones; *m* 1938, Margaret Aldis, *d* of late Henry Charles Askew; one *s* one *d*. *Educ:* Liverpool Institute High Sch. Mem. of Local Government Service, 1925–34; joined Assistance Board, 1934. Seconded to Air Min., as Hon. Flt-Lt RAFVR, 1943; Hon. Sqdn-Ldr, 1945. Transferred to Foreign Office, 1946; transferred to Washington, 1949; Dep. Finance Officer, Foreign Office, 1953; Head of Finance Dept, Foreign Office, 1957 and Diplomatic Service Administration Office, 1965, retired 1968. *Address:* 30 Wingfield Road, Kingston upon Thames, Surrey KT2 5LR. *T:* 081–546 9812. *Clubs:* London Welsh Rugby Football, Rugby; Glamorgan County Cricket.

JONES, His Honour Judge Edward; *see* Jones, J. E.

JONES, Sir Edward; *see* Jones, Sir C. E. W.

JONES, Air Marshal Sir Edward G.; *see* Gordon Jones.

JONES, Sir Edward Martin F.; *see* Furnival Jones.

JONES, Edward W.; *see* Wilson Jones.

JONES, Rt. Hon. Sir Edward (Warburton), PC 1979; PC (N Ireland) 1965; Kt 1973; Lord Justice of Appeal, Supreme Court of Judicature, N Ireland, 1973–84 (Judge of the High Court of Justice in Northern Ireland, 1968–73); *b* 3 July 1912; *s* of late Hume Riversdale Jones and Elizabeth Anne (*née* Phibbs); *m* 1st, 1941, Margaret Anne Crosland Smellie (*d* 1953); three *s*; 2nd, 1953, Ruth Buchan Smellie (*d* 1990); one *s*. *Educ:* Portora Royal School, Enniskillen, N Ireland; Trinity Coll., Dublin. BA (TCD), with First Class Moderatorship, Legal Science, and LLB (TCD) 1935; called to Bar of Northern Ireland, 1936; QC (N Ireland), 1948; called to Bar (Middle Temple), 1964. Junior Crown Counsel: County Down, 1939; Belfast, 1945–55. Enlisted, 1939; commissioned Royal Irish Fusiliers, 1940; Staff Coll., Camberley, 1943; AAG, Allied Land Forces, SEA, 1945; released with Hon. rank Lt-Col, 1946. MP (U) Londonderry City, Parliament of Northern Ireland, 1951–68; Attorney-Gen. for Northern Ireland, 1964–68. Chancellor: Dio. Derry and Raphoe, 1945–64; Dio. Connor, 1959–64 and 1978–81; Dio. Clogher, 1973; Lay Mem. Court of Gen. Synod, Church of Ireland. Bencher, Inn of Court of NI, 1961. Hon. Bencher, Middle Temple, 1982. Vice-Pres., College Historical Soc., TCD, 1983–. *Publication:* Jones L. J.: his life and times—an autobiography, 1987. *Recreation:* golf. *Address:* Craig-y-Mor, Trearddur Bay, Anglesey. *T:* Trearddur Bay (0407) 860406. *Clubs:* Army and Navy; Ulster Reform (Belfast); Royal Portrush Golf (Captain, 1956–57).

JONES, Eifion, CMG 1964; OBE 1953; Permanent Secretary, Ministry of Works, Northern Nigeria, 1959–66; Member, Northern Nigerian Development Corporation, 1959–66; retired; *b* Llanelly, Carmarthenshire, 10 June 1912; *s* of I. J. Jones and R. A. Jones (*née* Bassett); *m* 1944, Kathleen, *d* of Donald and E. J. MacCalman, Argyllshire. *Educ:* Llanelli Grammar Sch.; University Coll., Swansea. BSc (Wales). Executive Engineer, Nigeria, 1942; Colonial Service 2nd Course, Camb. Univ., 1949–50 (Mem. Christ's Coll.). Senior Executive Engineer, 1951; Chief Engineer, 1954; Dep. Dir of Public Works, Nigeria, 1958. Member: Lagos Exec. Develt Bd, 1954–57; Governing Cttee, King's Coll., Lagos, 1956–59; Cttee for Develt of Tourism and Game Reserves in N Nigeria, 1965. Mem., West African Council, ICE, 1960–65. JP N Nigeria, 1963–66. FICE 1957; FIWEM (FIWES 1957). *Recreations:* golf, gardening, reading. *Address:* c/o Barclays Bank, Llanelli, Dyfed SA15 3UE.

JONES, Eleri Wynne; Member, Independent Television Commission, with special responsibility for Wales, since 1990; trainer and practitioner in psychotherapy and counselling; *b* 9 Aug. 1933; *d* of Ellis Edgar and Elen Mary Griffith; *m* 1960, Bedwyr Lewis Jones; two *s* one *d*. *Educ:* Howell's Sch., Denbigh (Foundn Schol.); University Coll. of Wales, Aberystwyth; University Coll., Cardiff. BA (Wales); DipIPM. Journalist, Canada, 1956–57; Careers Officer, Gwynedd, 1957–64; Tutor, Marr. Guidance Council, 1978–87; Lectr, Gwynedd Technical Coll., 1980–84; Member: Welsh Fourth Channel Authy, 1984–91; Bd of Channel Four, 1988–90. *Recreations:* walking, knitting, films. *Address:* Bodafon, Sili-wen, Bangor, Gwynedd. *T:* Bangor (N Wales) (0248) 370621.

JONES, Emlyn Bartley, MBE 1975; Director General, The Sports Council, 1978–83; sport and leisure consultant, since 1983; *s* of Ernest Jones and Sarah Bartley; *m* 1944, Constance Inez Jones; one *d*. *Educ:* Alun Grammar School, Mold, Clwyd; Bangor Normal Coll.; Loughborough Coll. of Physical Education. Diploma Loughborough Coll. (Hons). Flight Lieut, RAF, 1941–46; Teacher, Flint Secondary Modern Sch., 1946; Technical Representative, N Wales, 1947–51; Technical Adviser, Central Council of Physical Recreation, 1951–62; Dir, Crystal Palace Nat. Sports Centre, 1962–78. Dir, Jones-Hatton Internat. Ltd, 1983–. Television commentator, 1955–. Pres., British Assoc. of Nat. Sports Administrators, 1984–; Vice-Pres., NABC, 1989–. FBIM 1984. *Publications:* Learning Lawn Tennis, 1958; Sport in Space: the implications of cable and satellite television, 1984. *Recreations:* golf, ski-ing, travel, conversation. *Address:* Chwarae Teg, 1B Allison Grove, Dulwich Common, SE21 7ER. *T:* 081–693 7528. *Club:* Royal Air Force.

JONES, Emrys; *see* Jones, J. E.

JONES, Sir Emrys; *see* Jones, Sir W. E.

JONES, Prof. Emrys, MSc, PhD (Wales); FRGS; Professor of Geography, University of London, at London School of Economics, 1961–84, now Emeritus; *b* Aberdare, 17 Aug. 1920; *s* of Samuel Garfield and Anne Jones; *m* 1948, Iona Vivien, *d* of R. H. Hughes; one *d* (and one *d* decd). *Educ:* Grammar Sch. for Boys, Aberdare; University Coll. of Wales, Aberystwyth. BSc (1st Class Hons in Geography and Anthropology), 1941; MSc, 1945; PhD, 1947; Fellow of the University of Wales, 1946–47; Asst Lectr at University Coll., London, 1947–50; Fellow, Rockefeller Foundation, 1948–49; Lectr at Queen's Univ., Belfast, 1950–58, Sen. Lectr, 1958; Reader, LSE, 1959–61. O'Donnel Lectr, Univ. of Wales, 1977. Chairman: Regional Studies Assoc., 1967–69; Council, Hon. Soc. of Cymmrodorion, 1984–89 (Mem., 1977–; Pres., 1989–); Mem. Council, RGS, 1973–77 (Vice-Pres., 1978–81). Mem. Council, University Coll. of Wales, Aberystwyth, 1978–85. Consultant on urbanisation and planning. Victoria Medal, RGS, 1977. Hon. DSc Belfast, 1978; DUniv Open, 1990. *Publications:* Hon. Editor, Belfast in its Regional Setting, 1952; (jointly) Welsh Rural Communities, 1960; A Social Geography of Belfast, 1961; Human Geography, 1964; Towns and Cities, 1966; Atlas of London, 1968; (ed jtly) Man and his Habitat, 1971; (contrib.) The Future of Planning, 1973; (with E. van Zandt) The City, 1974; Readings in Social Geography, 1975; (with J. Eyles) Introduction to Social Geography, 1977; (Chief Editor) The World and its Peoples, 1979; Metropolis: the world's great cities, 1990; articles in geographical, sociological and planning jls. *Recreations:* books, music. *Address:* 2 Pine Close, North Road, Berkhamsted, Herts HP4 3BZ. *T:* Berkhamsted (0442) 875422. *Club:* Athenæum.

JONES, Prof. Emrys Lloyd, FBA 1982; Goldsmiths' Professor of English Literature, Oxford University, and Fellow, New College, Oxford, since 1984; *b* 30 March 1931; *s* of Peter Jones and Elizabeth Jane (*née* Evans); *m* 1965, Barbara Maud Everett; one *d*. *Educ:* Neath Grammar Sch.; Magdalen Coll., Oxford (BA, MA). Tutor in English, Magdalen Coll., 1955–77; Reader in Eng. Lit., Oxford Univ., 1977–84; Fellow, Magdalen Coll., Oxford, 1955–84. *Publications:* (ed) Poems of Henry Howard, Earl of Surrey, 1964; Pope and Dulness, 1972; Scenic Form in Shakespeare, 1971; The Origins of Shakespeare, 1977; (ed) Antony and Cleopatra, 1977; (ed) The New Oxford Book of Sixteenth Century Verse, 1991; contribs to jls and books. *Recreations:* looking at buildings; opera. *Address:* New College, Oxford OX1 3BN. *T:* Oxford (0865) 248451.

JONES, Eric S.; *see* Somerset Jones.

JONES, Ernest Edward; Member, Doncaster Metropolitan Borough Council, since 1980; *b* 15 Oct. 1931; *s* of William Edward Jones and Eileen Gasser; *m* 1955, Mary Armstrong; one *s* one *d*. *Educ:* Bentley Catholic Primary Sch., Doncaster; Sheffield De La Salle Coll.; Hopwood Hall Coll. of Educn, Middleton, Lancs; Manch. Univ. Sch. of Educn; Management Studies Unit, Sheffield Polytech. Min. of Educn Teaching Certif. (CertEd); Univ. Dipl. in Science Studies (DipSc); Dipl. in Educn Management (DEM). School Master, 1953–. Doncaster County Borough: Councillor, 1962–74 (Chm. Health Cttee, 1971–74; Chm. Social Services Cttee, 1972–73; served on 15 other cttees at various times). South Yorkshire CC: Mem. 1973–77; Dep. Chm., 1973–75; Chm., 1975–76; Chm., Rec., Culture and Health Cttee, 1973–75; Doncaster Metropolitan Borough Council: Chairman: Libraries, Museums and Arts Cttee, 1982–; Further Educn Cttee, 1983–85; Trent Regional Assoc. of Community Health Councils, 1988–90; Doncaster CHC, 1981–90; Vice-Chm., Educn Services Cttee, 1982–. Chairman: Co. and Council of Management, Northern Coll., 1986– (Vice-Chm., 1982–86); Doncaster College (formerly Inst. of Further and Higher Educn), 1985–. Member: Nat. Health Exec. Council, 1964–74; Doncaster and Dist Water Bd, 1972–74; AMC (Social Services), 1972–74; Peak Park Planning Bd, 1973–77; Yorks and Humberside Museum and Art Gall. Service, 1973–77, 1984–; Yorks and Humberside Jt Libraries Cttee, 1973–75, 1983–; Yorks and Humberside Assoc. of Further and High Educn, 1982–; Yorks and Humberside Assoc. of Educn Authorities, 1982– (Chm., 1988–89); Council, Museums Assoc., 1986–; S Yorks Jt Archaeol Cttee (Chm., 1987–88); S Yorks Jt Archives Cttee, 1987– (Chm., 1987–88); Exec. Mem., Nat. Field Studies Council, 1988–. Chairman: Hull Univ. Ct, 1983–85; Sheffield Univ. Council, 1983–85; Mem., Bradford Univ. Ct and Council, 1986–. Exec. Mem., Yorks Arts Assoc., 1983–85; Former Member: Yorks Regional Land Drainage Cttee; Univ. of Hull Educn Delegacy; AMA; Yorks and Humberside Museums and Art Galleries Fedn; Yorks and Humberside Regional Sports Council; Yorks, Humberside and Cleveland Tourist Bd; Exec. Mem., Youth Assoc. of South Yorks. Governor, Sheffield Polytechnic, 1982–90. MRSH; FRSA 1980. *Recreations:* music and fine arts, general interest in sport, fell-walking, keen caravanner. *Address:* 11 Norborough Road, Doncaster, South Yorks DN2 4AR. *T:* Doncaster (0302) 66122.

JONES, Eurfron Gwynne; Controller, Educational Broadcasting, BBC, since 1987; *b* 24 Sept. 1934; *d* of William Gwynne Jones and Annie (*née* Harries); *m* 1968, Michael Coyle; one *s*. *Educ:* Aberdare Girls' Grammar Sch.; University Coll., Cardiff, Univ. of Wales (BSc (Zoology); PhD). Teaching Asst, Mount Holyoke Coll., Mass, 1955–56; joined BBC as gen. trainee, 1959; Producer, BBC Sch. Radio, Sch. Television and Continuing Educn, TV, 1959–75; freelance broadcaster, writer and cons., Media Cons. Internat. Children's Centre, Educn Commn of the States, 1975–83; Asst Hd, Sch. Radio, 1983–84; Hd of Sch. Television, 1984–87. Member: Wyatt Commn on Violence, 1986–; OU Council, 1987–; Open Coll. Council, 1987–89; Council, Royal Instn, 1989–. Fellow, Smallpeice Trust, 1985–. Mem., RTS, 1984–. *Publications:* Children Growing Up, 1973; The First Five Years, 1975; How Did I Grow?, 1977; Television Magic, 1978; Lifetime I, Lifetime II, 1982; numerous articles on children and educn. *Recreations:* photography, swimming, active family life.

JONES, Ewan Perrins W.; *see* Wallis-Jones.

JONES, Sir Ewart (Ray Herbert), Kt 1963; DSc Victoria, PhD Wales, MA Oxon; FRS 1950, FRSC; Waynflete Professor of Chemistry, University of Oxford, 1955–78, now Emeritus; Fellow of Magdalen College, 1955–78, Hon. Fellow, 1978; *b* Wrexham, Denbighshire, 16 March 1911; *m* 1937, Frances Mary Copp; one *s* two *d*. *Educ:* Grove Park Sch., Wrexham; University Coll. of North Wales, Bangor; Univ. of Manchester. Fellow of Univ. of Wales, 1935–37; Lecturer, Imperial Coll. of Science and Technology, 1938; Reader in Organic Chemistry, Univ. of London, and Asst Prof., 1945; Sir Samuel Hall Prof. of Chemistry, The University, Manchester, 1947–55. Arthur D. Little Visiting Prof. of Chemistry, MIT, 1952; Karl Folkers Lectr at Univs of Illinois and Wisconsin, 1957; Andrews Lectr, Univ. of NSW, 1960. Mem. Council for Scientific and Industrial Research, and Chm., Research Grants Cttee, 1961–65; Mem. SRC and Chm., Univ. Science and Technology Bd, 1965–69; Mem., Science Bd, 1969–72. Chemical Society: Tilden Lectr, 1949; Pedler Lectr, 1959; Robert Robinson Lectr, 1978; Dalton Lectr, 1985; Award for Service to the Society, 1973; Award in Natural Product Chem., 1974; Meldola Medal, Royal Institute of Chemistry, 1940; Davy Medal, Royal Society, 1966. Fritzsche Award, American Chemical Soc., 1962. President: Chemical Soc., 1964–66; RIC, 1970–72 (Chm., Chem. Soc./RIC Unification Cttee, 1975–80); Royal Soc. of Chemistry, 1980–82. Fellow, Imperial Coll., 1967; Foreign Mem. Amer. Acad. of Arts and Sciences, 1967. Chm., Anchor and Guardian Housing Assocs, 1979–84. Hon. DSc: Birmingham, 1965; Nottingham, 1966; New South Wales, 1967; Sussex, 1969; Salford, 1971; Wales, 1971; East Anglia, 1978; Ulster, 1978; Hon. LLD Manchester, 1972. *Publications:* scientific papers in Jl of the Chem. Soc. *Address:* 6 Sandy Lane, Yarnton, Kidlington, Oxon OX5 1PB. *T:* Kidlington (08675) 2581.

JONES, Fielding; *see* Jones, N. F.

JONES, Major Francis, CVO 1969; TD (3 clasps); MA, FSA; DL; Wales Herald Extraordinary since 1963; County Archivist, Carmarthenshire, 1958–74; *b* Trevine, Pembrokeshire, 5 July 1908; *s* of James Jones, Grinston, Pembs, and Martha Jones; *m* Ethel M. S. A., *d* of late J. J. Charles, Trewilym, Pembs; two *s* two *d*. *Educ:* Fishguard County Sch., Pembs. Temp. Archivist of Pembs, 1934–36; Archivist, Nat. Library of Wales, 1936–39. Lt 4th Bn Welch Regt (TA), 1931–39; trans. Pembroke Yeomanry (RA, TA), 1939, Battery Captain; served War of 1939–45: RA (Field), N Africa (despatches), Middle

East, Italy; Battery Comdr, and 2nd-in-comd of regt; GSO2 War Office; Mil. Narrator, Hist. Section, Cabinet Office, 1945–58 (Compiled Official narrative of Sicilian and Italian Campaigns); Battery Comdr, The Surrey Yeomanry, QMR (RA, TA), 1949–56; Mil. Liaison Officer, Coronation, 1953; served on the Earl Marshal's staff, State Funeral of Sir Winston Churchill, 1965; Mem., Prince of Wales Investiture Cttee, 1967–69. Local Sec. and Mem., Cambrian Assoc.; President: Cambrian Archaeol Assoc., 1985–86; Pembrokeshire Historical Soc., 1988–89; Vice-Pres., Council, Hon. Soc. of Cymmrodorion; Member: Gorsedd, Royal National Eisteddfod of Wales; Court and Council, Nat. Library of Wales, 1967–77; Council, Nat. Museum of Wales; Historical Soc. of the Church in Wales; Carmarthenshire Local History Soc.; Pembrokeshire Records Soc. (Vice-Pres.); Croeso '69 Nat. Cttee; Academie Internationale d'Heraldique; Heraldry Soc. Trustee, Elvet Lewis Memorial (Gangell), 1967–81. Vice-Pres., Dyfed Local Councils, 1974–81. DL Dyfed, 1965. Broadcaster (TV and sound radio). Hon. MA Univ. of Wales. CStJ. *Publications:* The Holy Wells of Wales, 1954; The History of Llangunnor, 1965; God Bless the Prince of Wales, 1969; The Princes and Principality of Wales, 1969; (jtly) Royal and Princely Heraldry in Wales, 1969; Historic Carmarthenshire Homes and their Families, 1987; numerous articles on historical, genealogical and heraldic matters to learned jls. *Recreations:* genealogical research and heraldry, fly-fishing, study of ancient ruins. *Address:* Hendre, Springfield Road, Carmarthen. *T:* Carmarthen (0267) 237099.

JONES, Francis John; Chairman, Telford Development Corporation, since 1987; Chairman, Shropshire Health Authority, since 1979; *b* 26 June 1928; *s* of John Francis and Mary Emma Jones; *m* 1st, 1953, Angela Mary Kelly (marr. diss.); one *s* one *d*; 2nd, 1970, Jean Elsie Sansome; two step *s* two step *d*. *Educ:* Manchester Grammar Sch.; Manchester Univ. Various marketing and sales positions; West African Colonies, 1950–52; Proctor & Gamble, 1952–54; Beecham Group, 1954–57; Crosse & Blackwell/Nestlé, 1957–64; W. Symington, 1964–69; Chm., Telford Foods, 1970–84, retired. *Recreations:* reading, music, opera. *Address:* 2 Swan Hill Gardens, Shrewsbury SY1 1NT. *T:* Shrewsbury (0743) 362159.

JONES, Prof. F(rank) Llewellyn-, CBE 1965; MA, DPhil, DSc Oxon; Hon. LLD; Principal, University College of Swansea, 1965–74 (Vice-Principal, 1954–56 and 1960–62; Acting Principal, 1959–60); Professor Emeritus, since 1974; *b* 30 Sept. 1907; *er s* of Alfred Morgan Jones, JP, Penrhiwceiber, Glamorgan; *m* 1st, 1938, Eileen (*d* 1982), *d* of E. T. Davies, Swansea; one *s* (one *d* decd); 2nd, 1983, Mrs Gwendolen Thomas, Rhossili. *Educ:* West Monmouth Sch.; Merton Coll., Oxford. Science Exhibnr 1925; 1st Cl. Nat. Sci. physics, BA 1929; Research Scholar, Merton Coll., 1929, DPhil, MA, 1931; Senior Demy, Magdalen Coll., 1931. DSc 1955. Demonstrator in Wykeham Dept of Physics, Oxford, 1929–32; Lecturer in Physics, University Coll. of Swansea, 1932–40; Senior Scientific Officer, Royal Aircraft Establishment, 1940–45; Prof. of Physics, Univ. of Wales, and Head of Dept of Physics, University Coll. of Swansea, 1945–65. Vice-Chancellor, Univ. of Wales, 1969–71. Member: Radio Research Board, DSIR, 1951–54; Standing Conference on Telecommunications Research, DSIR, 1952–55; Board of Institute of Physics, 1947–50; Council of Physical Society, 1951–58 (Vice-Pres., 1954–59). Visiting Prof. to Univs in Australia, 1956; Supernumerary Fellow, Jesus Coll., Oxford, 1965–66, 1969–70; Hon. Professorial Res. Fellow, Univ. of Wales, 1974–; Leverhulme Emeritus Fellow, 1977–79; Fellow, UC of Swansea, 1990. Regional Scientific Adviser for Home Defence, Wales, 1952–59, Sen. and Chief Reg. Sci. Adv., 1959–77; Pres., Royal Institution of South Wales, 1957–60; Mem. of Council for Wales and Mon, 1959–63, 1963–66; Dir (Part-time), S Wales Gp, BSC, 1968–70; Chm., Central Adv. Council for Education (Wales), 1961–64. Sen. Consultant in Plasma Physics, Radio and Space Research Station of SRC, 1964–65. Vice-Pres., Hon. Soc. of Cymmrodorian, 1982. Hon. LLD Wales, 1975. C. V. Boys' Prizeman, The Physical Soc., 1960; Inaugural Ragnar Holm Scientific Achievement Award, 6th Internat. Conf. on Electric Contact Phenomena, Chicago, 1972. *Publications:* Fundamental Processes of Electrical Contact Phenomena, 1953; The Physics of Electrical Contacts, 1957; Ionization and Breakdown in Gases, 1957, 2nd edn 1966; The Glow Discharge, 1966; Ionization, Avalanches and Breakdown, 1966; papers in scientific jls on ionization and discharge physics. *Recreation:* industrial archaeology. *Address:* Brynheulog, 24 Sketty Park Road, Swansea SA2 9AS. *T:* Swansea (0792) 202344. *Club:* Athenæum.

JONES, Fred, CB 1978; CBE 1966; Deputy Secretary, HM Treasury, 1975–80, retired; *b* 5 May 1920; *s* of late Fred Jones and of Harriet (*née* Nuttall); *m* 1954, Joy (*née* Field); two *s*. *Educ:* Preston Grammar Sch.; St Catherine's Coll., Oxford. Economist, Trades Union Congress, 1951–59; Tutor in Economics and Industrial Relations, Ruskin Coll., Oxford, 1960–62; Economist, National Economic Development Office, 1962–64; Dept of Economic Affairs: Senior Economic Adviser, 1964–66; Asst Sec., 1966–68; Asst Under-Sec. of State, 1968–69; HM Treasury, Asst Under-Sec. of State, 1969–75. *Recreations:* walking, gardening, reading. *Address:* The Glen, Haighton Green Lane, Haighton, Preston, Lancs.

JONES, Gareth; *see* Jones, J. G.

JONES, Prof. Gareth (Hywel), QC 1986; FBA 1982; Fellow of Trinity College, Cambridge, since 1961; Downing Professor of the Laws of England, Cambridge University, since 1975; *b* 10 Nov. 1930; *o c* of late B. T. Jones, FRICS, and late Mabel Jones, Tylorstown, Glam; *m* 1959, Vivienne Joy, *o d* of late C. E. Puckridge, FIA, Debden Green, Loughton; two *s* one *d*. *Educ:* Porth County Sch.; University Coll. London (PhD; Fellow 1989); St Catharine's Coll., Cambridge (Scholar); Harvard Univ. (LLM). LLB London 1951; MA, LLB 1953, LLD 1972, Cantab. Choate Fellow, Harvard, 1953; Yorke Prize, 1960. Called to Bar, Lincoln's Inn, 1955 (Scholar); Hon. Bencher 1975. Lecturer: Oriel and Exeter Colls, Oxford, 1956–58; KCL, 1958–61; Trinity College, Cambridge: Lectr, 1961–74; Tutor, 1967; Sen. Tutor, 1972; Vice-Master, 1986–; Univ. Lectr, Cambridge, 1961–74; Chm., Faculty of Law, 1978–81. Vis. Professor: Harvard, 1966 and 1975; Chicago, 1976–91; California at Berkeley, 1967 and 1971; Indiana, 1971, 1975; Michigan, 1983; Georgia, 1983. Lectures: Harris, Indiana, 1981; Wright, Toronto, 1984; Lionel Cohen, Hebrew Univ., 1985; Butterworth, QMC, 1987; Nambyar, India, 1991; Richard O'Sullivan, London, 1991. Mem., American Law Inst. *Publications:* (with Lord Goff of Chieveley) The Law of Restitution, 1966, 3rd edn 1986; The History of the Law of Charity 1532–1827, 1969; The Sovereignty of the Law, 1973; (with Sir William Goodhart) Specific Performance, 1986; various articles. *Address:* Trinity College, Cambridge CB2 1TQ. *T:* Cambridge (0223) 338473; 9B Cranmer Road, Cambridge CB3 9BL. *T:* Cambridge (0223) 63932; Clay Street, Thornham Magna, Eye, Suffolk. *Club:* Beefsteak.

JONES, Geoffrey; *see* Jones, John G.

JONES, Prof. Geoffrey M.; *see* Melvill Jones.

JONES, Geoffrey Rippon R.; *see* Rees-Jones.

JONES, Air Marshal Sir George, KBE 1953 (CBE 1942); CB 1943; DFC; RAAF; *b* 22 Nov. 1896; *m* 1st, 1919, Muriel Agnes Cronan (decd), *d* of F. Stone; (two *s* decd); 2nd, 1970, Mrs Gwendoline Claire Bauer (decd). Served Gallipoli and European War, 1914–18 (despatches, DFC); joined RAAF, 1921; Dir Personnel Services, RAAF, 1936–40; Dir of Training, 1940–42; Chief of Air Staff, 1942–52. *Publication:* From Private to Air Marshal (autobiog.), 1988. *Address:* Pinehurst, 2 Jellicoe Street, Cheltenham, Vic 3192, Australia. *Club:* Naval and Military (Melbourne).

JONES, George Briscoe, CBE 1988; Director: Job Ownership Ltd, since 1983; Partnership in Business Ltd, since 1988; Chrisamer Ltd, since 1989; *b* 1 June 1929; *s* of late Arthur Briscoe Jones and Mary Alexandra Jones (*née* Taylor); *m* 1955, Audrey Patricia Kendrick; two *d*. *Educ:* Wallasey and Caldy Grammar Schools. Army, 1947–49; Unilever, 1949–84 (on secondment to CDA, 1982–84); Dir, BOCM Silcocks, 1974–82; Chm., Unitrition, 1977–82; Dir, Co-op. Develt Agency, 1982–90. Trustee, Plunkett Foundn, 1985–. *Recreations:* painting, sculpture, chess, bridge. *Address:* 3 Beverley Close, Basingstoke, Hants RG22 4BT. *T:* Basingstoke (0256) 28239. *Club:* Farmers'.

JONES, Prof. George William; Professor of Government, University of London, since 1976; *b* 4 Feb. 1938; *er s* of George William and Grace Annie Jones; *m* 1963, Diana Mary Bedwell; one *s* one *d*. *Educ:* Wolverhampton Grammar Sch.; Jesus Coll., Oxford; Nuffield Coll., Oxford. Oxf. BA 1960, MA 1965, DPhil 1965. Univ. of Leeds: Asst Lectr in Govt, 1963; Lectr in Govt, 1965; London Sch. of Economics and Political Science: Lectr in Political Science, 1966; Sen. Lectr in Polit. Sci., 1971; Reader in Polit. Sci., 1974. Sec., 1965–68, Mem. Exec. Cttee, 1969–75, Polit. Studies Assoc. of the UK; Mem., Exec. Council, Hansard Soc., 1968–70; Member, Editorial Committee: Local Government Studies, 1970–; The London Journal, 1973–80; Governance, 1987–; Korean Jl of Public Policy, 1988–; Studies in Law and Politics, 1989–; Nonprofit Management and Leadership, 1989–. Member: Layfield Cttee of Inquiry into Local Govt Finance, 1974–76; Exams Cttee, and Admin. Staff Qualifications Council, Local Govt Trng Bd, 1977–80; Political Science and Internat. Relns Cttee, SSRC, 1977–81; Chm., Central-Local Govt Relations Panel, SSRC, 1978–81; Special Adviser, Select Cttee on Welsh Affairs, 1985–87. Member: Governing Council, Wolverhampton Polytechnic, 1978–83 (Hon. Fellow, 1986); Council, RIPA, 1984–90; Nat. Consumer Council, 1991–; Vice-Pres., Assoc. of Councillors, 1980–. FRHistS 1980. Hon. Fellow, Inst. of Local Govt Studies, Birmingham Univ., 1979. *Publications:* Borough Politics, 1969; (with B. Donoughue) Herbert Morrison: portrait of a politician, 1973; (ed with A. Norton) Political Leadership in Local Authorities, 1978; (ed) New Approaches to the Study of Central-Local Government Relationships, 1980; (with J. Stewart) The Case for Local Government, 1983, 2nd edn 1985; (ed jtly) Between Centre and Locality, 1985; (ed) West European Prime Ministers, 1991; contribs to Political Studies, Public Admin., Political Qly, Parliamentary Affairs, Government and Opposition, Jl of Admin Overseas; Local Govt Chronicle. *Recreations:* cinema, politics. *Address:* Department of Government, London School of Economics, Houghton Street, WC2A 2AE. *T:* 071–955 7179.

JONES, Geraint Iwan; *b* 16 May 1917; *s* of Rev. Evan Jones, Porth, Glam; *m* 1st, 1940, M. A. Kemp; one *d*; 2nd, 1949, Winifred Roberts. *Educ:* Caterham Sch.; Royal Academy of Music (Sterndale Bennett Scholar). National Gallery Concerts, 1940–44; played complete organ works of Bach in 16 recitals in London, 1946. Musical dir of Mermaid Theatre performances of Purcell's Dido and Aeneas with Kirsten Flagstad, 1951–53. Formed Geraint Jones Singers and Orchestra, 1951, with whom many Broadcasts, and series of 12 Bach concerts, Royal Festival Hall, 1955; series of all Mozart's piano concertos, Queen Elizabeth Hall, 1969–70. Frequent European engagements, 1947– and regular US and Canadian tours, 1948–. Musical Director: Lake District Festival, 1960–78; Kirckman Concert Soc., 1963–; Artistic Director: Salisbury Festival, 1973–77; Manchester Internat. Festival, 1977–87. As consultant, has designed many organs, incl. RNCM, St Andrew's Univ., RAM, Acad. for Performing Arts, Hong Kong, and Tsim Sha Tsui culture centre, Hong Kong. Recordings as organist and conductor; Promenade Concerts; also concerts and recordings as harpsichordist, including sonatas with violinist wife, Winifred Roberts. Grand Prix du Disque, 1959 and 1966. *Publications:* translations: Clicquot's Théorie Pratique de la facture de l'orgue, 1985; Davy's Les Grandes Orgues de L'Abbatiale St Etienne de Caen, 1985. *Recreations:* motoring, photography, antiques, reading. *Address:* The Long House, Arkley Lane, Barnet Road, Arkley, Herts EN5 3JR.

JONES, Geraint Stanley; Chief Executive, S4C, since 1989; *b* 26 April 1936; *s* of Olwen and David Stanley Jones; *m* 1961, Rhiannon Williams; two *d*. *Educ:* Pontypridd Grammar Sch.; University Coll. of N Wales (BA Hons; DipEd; Hon. Fellow 1988). BBC-Wales: Studio Manager, 1960–62; Production Asst, Current Affairs (TV), 1962–65; TV Producer: Current Affairs, 1965–69; Features and Documentaries, 1969–73; Asst Head of Programmes, Wales, 1973–74; Head of Programmes, Wales, 1974–81; Controller, BBC Wales, 1981–85; Dir of Public Affairs, BBC, 1986–87; Man. Dir, Regl Broadcasting, BBC, 1987–89. Chm., Ryan Davies Trust, 1977–; Member: UK Freedom from Hunger Campaign Cttee, 1978–; Council of Management, WNO, 1985–90. Chm., Bd of Govs, Welsh Coll. of Music and Drama, 1990–. *Recreations:* music, painting, horse riding. *Address:* c/o S4C, Parc Ty Glas, Llanishen, Cardiff CF4 5DU. *Club:* Cardiff and County (Cardiff).

JONES, Dr Gerald, FRCP; Senior Principal Medical Officer, Department of Health (formerly of Health and Social Security), since 1984; *b* 25 Jan. 1939; *s* of John Jones and Gladys Jones (*née* Roberts); *m* 1964, Anne Heatley (*née* Morris) (marr. diss. 1987); one *s* two *d*; *m* 1990, Jutta Friese. *Educ:* Swansea Grammar School; Merton College, Oxford; London Hosp. Med. Coll. (BA, BM, BCh, PhD). Appointments in hosp. medicine, 1965–69; research with MRC, 1969–73; pharmaceutical industry, 1974–75; medical staff, DHSS, 1975–. *Publications:* papers on cardiopulmonary physiology, respiratory medicine, cellular immunology and drug regulation. *Recreations:* music, gardening, art history, economics, catching dragonflies, wine making. *Address:* Department of Health, Eileen House, 80–94 Newington Causeway, SE1 6EF. *T:* 071–972 2838.

JONES, Gerallt; *see* Jones, R. G.

JONES, Sir Glyn (Smallwood), GCMG 1964 (KCMG 1960, CMG 1957); MBE 1944; *b* 9 Jan. 1908; *s* of late G. I. Jones, Chester; *m* 1942, Nancy Madoc, *d* of J. H. Featherstone, CP, South Africa; one *d* (and one *s* decd). *Educ:* King's Sch., Chester; St Catherine's, Oxford Univ. (MA); Hon. Fellow, 1977. HM Colonial Service (now HM Overseas Civil Service) N Rhodesia: Cadet, 1931; District Officer, 1933; Commissioner for Native Development, 1950; Acting Development Sec., 1956; Prov. Comr, 1956; Resident Comr, Barotseland, 1957; Sec. for Native Affairs, 1958; Minister of Native Affairs and Chief Comr, 1959; Chief Sec., Nyasaland, 1960–61, Governor, 1961–64; Governor-Gen. and C-in-C of Malawi, 1964–66. Advr on Govt Admin to Prime Minister of Lesotho, 1969–71; Dep. Chm., Lord Pearce Commn on Rhodesian Opinion, 1971–72; British Govt Observer, Zimbabwe Elections, 1980. Founding Chm., Friends of Malawi Assoc, 1968–83; Chairman: Malawi Church Trust, 1970–; Friends of Jairos Jiri Assoc. (Zimbabwe), 1982–; Zimbabwe Trust (London), 1982–; Malaŵi Against Polio Trust, 1984–. Grand Cordon, Order of the Trinity of Ethiopia, 1965; Order of the Epiphany of Central Africa, 1966. KStJ. *Recreations:* shooting, fishing, golf. *Clubs:* Athenæum, Commonwealth Trust, MCC.

See also C. W. Perchard.

JONES, Rev. Canon Glyndwr; General Secretary, The Missions to Seamen, since 1990; a Chaplain to the Queen, since 1990; *b* 25 Nov. 1935; *s* of late Bertie Samuel Jones and of Elizabeth Ellen Jones; *m* 1st, 1961, Cynthia Elaine Jenkins (*d* 1964); 2nd, 1966, (Marion) Anita Morris; one *s* one *d*. *Educ:* Dynefor Sch., Swansea; St Michael's Theol Coll., Llandaff, Univ. of Wales (DipTh). Nat. Service, 1954–56: RAPC, attached 19 Field Regt RA; served Korea, Hong Kong; demobbed Sgt AER. Deacon 1962, priest 1963; Curate: Clydach, 1962–64; Llangyfelach with Morriston, 1964–67; Sketty, 1967–70; Rector, Bryngwyn with Newchurch and Llanbedr, Painscastle with Llandewi Fach, 1970–72; The Missions to Seamen: Port Chaplain, Swansea and Port Talbot, 1972–76; Sen. Chaplain, Port of London, 1976–81; Auxiliary Ministries Sec., Central Office, 1981–85; Asst Gen. Sec., 1985–90. Member Council: Merchant Navy Welfare Bd, 1990–; Marine Soc., 1990–; Partnership for World Mission, 1990–; Internat. Christian Maritime Assoc., 1990–. Hon. Chaplain, Royal Alfred Seafarers Soc., 1987–; Hon. Canon, St Michael's Cathedral, Kobe, Japan, 1988–. Freeman, City of London, 1990. Chaplain: Co. of Information Technologists, 1989–; Co. of Inn-holders, 1990–; Co. of Farriers, 1990–; Co. of Carmen, 1990–. *Recreations:* sport, music, reading, theatre, travel. *Address:* The Missions to Seamen, St Michael Paternoster Royal, College Hill, EC4R 2RL. *T:* 071–248 5202. *Club:* Commonwealth Trust.

JONES, Glynn; Circuit Administrator, Western Circuit, Lord Chancellor's Department, since 1987; *b* 5 March 1933; *s* of late Bertie Jones and Alice Maud Jones (*née* Griffiths); *m* 1957, Crystal Laura, *d* of late Edward William Kendall and Ivy Irene Kendall; one *s* one *d*. *Educ:* Pontllanfraith Grammar Technical School. Local Govt service, 1950–71; Lord Chancellor's Department: Crown Court, Newport, 1971, Winchester, 1973; Courts Administrator: Nottingham Group of Courts, 1976; South Wales Group of Courts, 1980. *Recreations:* Rugby Union football, golf. *Address:* Western Circuit Office, Bridge House, Clifton Down, Bristol. *T:* Bristol (0272) 745763. *Clubs:* Civil Service; St Pierre Golf and Country, Newport Golf.

JONES, Gordon Frederick; Editor, Product Design Review, since 1990 (Director of Research, 1985–90); *b* 25 Aug. 1929; *s* of Harold Frederick and Rose Isabel Jones; *m* 1954, Patricia Mary (*née* Rowley); one *s* one *d*. *Educ:* Saltley Grammar Sch.; The School of Architecture, Birmingham (DipArch); RIBA 1950. FRSA. Architect: in local government, 1952; War Office, 1959; Asst City Architect, Sheffield, 1966; private practice, London, 1968; Property Services Agency, DoE: Architect, 1970; Head of Student Training Office, 1976; Head of Architectural Services, 1979–85. *Recreations:* watching cats, listening to music, re-building houses. *Address:* Product Design Review, Belmont House, Station Road, Belmont, Sutton, Surrey SM2 6BS.

JONES, Sir Gordon (Pearce), Kt 1990; Chairman: Yorkshire Water, since 1983; Water Authorities Association, 1986–89; *b* 17 Feb. 1927; *s* of Alun Pearce Jones and Miriam Jones; *m* 1951, Gloria Stuart Melville; two *s* one *d*. *Educ:* Univ. of Wales (BSc (Hons) Chemistry). Royal Navy, 1947. British Iron & Steel Research Assoc., 1951; Esso Petroleum Co., 1961; English Steel Corp., 1964; Managing Director: Rotherham Tinsley Steels, 1970; Firth Vickers, 1974; Dir, T. W. Ward plc, 1979–83. *Recreations:* gardening, music, opera, travel, railway history. *Address:* Bryngower, Sitwell Grove, Rotherham, S Yorks S60 3AY. *T:* Rotherham (0709) 364588. *Club:* Naval and Military.

JONES, Graham Edward, MA; Headmaster, Repton School, since 1987; *b* 22 Sept. 1944; *s* of late Edward Thomas Jones and of Dora Rachel Jones; *m* 1976, Vanessa Mary Heloise (*née* Smith). *Educ:* Birkenhead Sch.; Fitzwilliam Coll., Cambridge (schol.; 1st cl. Hons Econs Tripos 1966). Asst Master, Hd of Economics and Politics, Housemaster, Charterhouse, 1967–87; secondment to British Petroleum, 1981. Awarder in Economics, Oxford and Cambridge Schs Examination Bd, 1979–; Reviser in Economics, JMB, 1981–. FRSA 1988. *Publications:* various articles on economics and teaching economics. *Recreations:* painting, walking, music, cooking, the classics. *Address:* The Hall, Repton, Derby DE6 6FH. *T:* Burton upon Trent (0283) 702375/702187.

JONES, Graham Julian; His Honour Judge Graham Jones; a Circuit Judge, since 1985; *b* 17 July 1936; *s* of late David John Jones, CBE, and of Edna Lillie Jones; *m* 1961, Dorothy, *o d* of late James Smith and of Doris Irene Tickle, Abergavenny; two *s* one *d*. *Educ:* Porth County Grammar Sch. (state scholarship); St John's Coll., Cambridge. MA, LLM (Cantab). Admitted Solicitor, 1961; Partner, Morgan Bruce and Nicholas, 1961 (represented Parents and Residents Assoc., Aberfan Disaster, 1966). Pres., Pontypridd Rhondda and Dist Law Soc., 1973–75; Member Council: Cardiff Law Soc., 1975–78, 1984–85; Associated Law Socs of Wales, 1974–85 (Pres., 1982–84); Mem., Lord Chancellor's Legal Aid Adv. Cttee, 1980–85. Sat as Dep. Circuit Judge, 1975–78; a Recorder, 1978–85. *Recreations:* golf, boats. *Address:* c/o Cardiff Crown Court. *Clubs:* Cardiff and County (Cardiff), Radyr Golf, Royal Porthcawl Golf.

JONES, (Graham) Wyn, QPM 1987; Assistant Commissioner of Police of the Metropolis, since 1989; *b* Ystradgynlais, Brecon, 12 Oct. 1943; *s* of Thomas James and Mary Elizabeth (*née* Almrott); *m* 1970, Joan Goodbrook. *Educ:* Thornbury Grammar Sch.; Univ. of Exeter (LLB). Joined Glos Police, 1963; Chief Inspector, Glos, 1971; Supt, 1976; Chief Supt, Oxford, 1979; Asst Chief Constable (Ops), Thames Valley Police, 1982; Dep. Asst Comr (CID), New Scotland Yard, 1984; Dep. Asst Comr, 2 Area (East), Metropolitan Police, 1985. Comd Police Ops, Greenham Common, 1983–84, Wapping, 1985–86. Vis. Lectr on policing and public disorder to Police Foundn, USA, and to Germany. *Publications:* articles and contribs to jls on public disorder, forensic investigation, police and media. *Recreations:* ballet, opera, tennis, golf, horse riding. *Address:* New Scotland Yard, Broadway, SW1H 0BG. *T:* 071–230 3228.

JONES, Griffith R.; *see* Rhys Jones.

JONES, Griffith Winston Guthrie, QC 1963; a Recorder, 1972–74 (Recorder of Bolton, 1968–71); *b* 24 Sept. 1914; second *s* of Rowland Guthrie Jones, Dolgellau, Merioneth; *m* 1st, 1959, Anna Maria McCarthy (*d* 1969); 2nd, 1978, Janet, *widow* of Commodore Henry Owen L'Estrange, DSC. *Educ:* Bootham Sch., York; University of Wales; St John's Coll., Cambridge. Called to the Bar, Gray's Inn, 1939. Dep. Chm., Cumberland QS, 1963–71. War service in Royal Artillery, 1940–46. *Recreation:* gardening. *Address:* Culleenamore, Sligo, Ireland.

JONES, Gwilym Haydn; MP (C) Cardiff North, since 1983; *s* of Evan Haydn Jones and Mary Elizabeth Gwenhwyfar Jones (*née* Moseley); *m* 1974, Linda Margaret (*née* John); one *s* one *d*. *Educ:* London and S Wales. Dir, Bowring Wales Ltd. Councillor, Cardiff CC, 1969–72 and 1973–83. PPS to Minister of State, Dept of Transport, 1991–; Mem., Select Cttee on Welsh Affairs, 1983–; Sec., Welsh Cons. Members Gp, 1984–. Founder Chm., Friendship Force in Wales, 1978–81; Vice Pres., Kidney Res. Unit for Wales Foundn, 1986–. Rowed for Wales in Speaker's Regatta, 1986. *Recreations:* golf, model railways, watching Wales win at rugby. *Address:* House of Commons, SW1A 0AA. *T:* 071–219 3000. *Clubs:* County Conservative, Cardiff and County, Rhiwbina Rugby, United Services Mess (Cardiff).

JONES, (Gwilym) Wyn, CBE 1977; Member, Gwynedd Health Authority, 1982–90, Associate Member, since 1990; *b* 12 July 1926; *s* of late Rev. John Jones, MA, BD, and Elizabeth (*née* Roberts); *m* 1951, Ruth (*née* Thomas); one *s* one *d*. *Educ:* Llanrwst Grammar Sch.; UCNW, Bangor (BA Hons); London Univ. Served RN, 1944–47. Cadet, Colonial Admin. Service, Gilbert and Ellice Islands, 1950; DO, DC and Secretariat in Tarawa, Line Islands, Phoenix Islands and Ocean Island, 1950–61; Solomon Islands, 1961; Asst Sec., 1961–67; Sen. Asst Sec., 1967–74; Dep. Chief Sec., 1974; Sec. to Chief Minister and Council of Ministers, 1974–77; Governor, Montserrat, 1977–80. Administrator, Cwmni Theatr Cymru (Welsh Nat. Theatre), 1982–85. Mem. Court, UCNW Bangor, 1980–86. *Recreation:* walking alone. *Address:* Y Frondeg, Warren Drive, Deganwy, Gwynedd. *T:* Deganwy (0492) 583377.

JONES, Gwyn; *see* Jones, Miah G.

JONES, Prof. Gwyn, CBE 1965; Professor of English Language and Literature, University College, Cardiff, 1965–75, Fellow, 1980; *b* 24 May 1907; *s* of George Henry Jones and Lily Florence (*née* Nethercott); *m* 1st, 1928, Alice (*née* Rees) (*d* 1979); 2nd, 1979, Mair (*née* Sivell), *widow* of Thomas Jones. *Educ:* Tredegar Grammar School; University of Wales. Schoolmaster, 1929–35; Lecturer, University Coll. of S Wales and Monmouthshire, 1935–40; Prof. of Eng. Language and Lit., University Coll. of Wales, Aberystwyth, 1940–64, Fellow 1987. Ida Beam Vis. Prof., Iowa Univ., 1982. Dir of Penmark Press, 1939–. Mem. of various learned societies; Pres. of Viking Soc. for Northern Research, 1950–52 (Hon. Life Mem., 1979); Mem. of Arts Council and Chm. of Welsh Arts Council, 1957–67. Gwyn Jones Annual Lecture established 1978. Hon. DLitt: Wales, 1977; Nottingham, 1978; Southampton, 1983. Fellow, Institut Internat. des Arts et des Lettres, 1960. Christian Gauss Award, 1973; Cymmrodorion Medal, 1991. Hon. Freeman of Islwyn, 1988. Commander's Cross, Order of the Falcon (Iceland), 1987 (Knight, 1963). *Publications: novels:* Richard Savage, 1935; Times Like These, 1936, repr. 1979; Garland of Bays, 1938; The Green Island, 1946; The Flowers Beneath the Scythe, 1952; The Walk Home, 1962; *short stories:* The Buttercup Field, 1945; The Still Waters, 1948; Shepherd's Hey, 1953; Selected Short Stories, 1974; *non-fiction:* A Prospect of Wales, 1948; Welsh Legends and Folk-Tales, 1955; Scandinavian Legends and Folk-Tales, 1956; The Norse Atlantic Saga, 1964, new edn 1986; A History of the Vikings, 1968, rev. and enlarged edn 1984; Kings, Beasts and Heroes, 1972; Being and Belonging (BBC Wales Annual Radio Lecture), 1977; Background to Dylan Thomas and Other Explorations, 1992; *translations:* The Vatnsdalers' Saga, 1942; (with Thomas Jones) The Mabinogion, 1948; Egil's Saga, 1960; Eirik the Red, 1961; *edited:* Welsh Review, 1939–48; Welsh Short Stories, 1956; (with I. Ff. Elis) Twenty-Five Welsh Short Stories, 1971; The Oxford Book of Welsh Verse in English, 1977; Fountains of Praise, 1983; contrib. to numerous learned and literary journals. *Address:* Castle Cottage, Sea View Place, Aberystwyth, Dyfed SY23 1DZ.

JONES, Gwyn Idris M.; *see* Meirion-Jones.

JONES, Gwyn Owain, CBE 1978; MA, DSc Oxon; PhD Sheffield; Director, National Museum of Wales, 1968–77; *b* 29 March 1917; *s* of Dr Abel John Jones, OBE, HMI, and Rhoda May Jones, Cardiff and Porthcawl; *m* 1st, 1944, Sheila Heywood (marr. diss.); two *d*; 2nd, 1973, Elizabeth Blandino. *Educ:* Monmouth Sch.; Port Talbot Secondary Sch.; Jesus Coll., Oxford (Meyricke Schol.). Glass Delegacy Research Fellow of University of Sheffield, later mem. of academic staff, 1939–41; Mem. UK Government's Atomic Energy project, 1942–46; Nuffield Foundation Research Fellow at Clarendon Laboratory, Oxford, 1946–49; Reader in Experimental Physics in University of London, at Queen Mary Coll., 1949–53; Prof. of Physics in Univ. of London, and Head of Dept of Physics at Queen Mary Coll., 1953–68; Fellow of Queen Mary and Westfield (formerly Queen Mary) Coll. Visiting Prof. Univ. of Sussex, 1964. Member: Court and Council, UWIST, 1968–74; Court, University Coll., Swansea, 1981–84; Hon. Professorial Fellow, University Coll., Cardiff, 1969–79. Yr Academi Gymreig (English Language Section) 1971 (Chm., 1978–81); Gorsedd y Beirdd (Aelod er Anrhydedd) 1974; Governor, Commonwealth Institute, 1974–77. FMA 1976. *Publications:* Glass, 1956; (in collab.) Atoms and the Universe, 1956; papers on solid-state, glass, low-temperature physics; *novels:* The Catalyst, 1960; Personal File, 1962; Now, 1965; *story sequence:* The Conjuring Show, 1981. *Address:* 12 Squitchey Lane, Summertown, Oxford OX2 7LB. *T:* Oxford (0865) 510363.

JONES, Dame Gwyneth, DBE 1986 (CBE 1976); a Principal Dramatic Soprano: Royal Opera House, Covent Garden, since 1963; Vienna State Opera, since 1966; Bavarian State Opera, since 1967; *b* 7 Nov. 1936; *d* of late Edward George Jones and late Violet (*née* Webster); *m* Till Haberfeld; one *d*. *Educ:* Twmpath Sec. Mod. Sch., Pontypool, Mon; Royal College of Music, London; Accademia Chigiana, Siena; Zürich Internat. Opera Studio; Maria Carpi Prof., Geneva. Oratorio and recitals as well as opera. Guest Artiste: La Scala, Milan; Berlin State Opera; Munich State Opera; Bayreuth Festival; Salzburg Festival; Verona; Tokyo; Zürich; Metropolitan Opera, New York; Paris; Geneva; Dallas; San Francisco; Los Angeles; Teatro Colon, Buenos Aires; Edinburgh Festival; Welsh National Opera; Rome; Hamburg; Cologne; Maggio Musicale, Florence; Chicago. Numerous recordings, radio and TV appearances. FRCM. Kammersängerin, Austria and Bavaria. Hon. DMus Wales. Shakespeare Prize, FVS Hamburg, 1987. Bundesverdienstkreuz (FRG), 1988. *Address:* PO Box, 8037 Zürich, Switzerland.

JONES, Gwynoro Glyndwr; Assistant Education Officer, Capital and Property, West Glamorgan County Council, since 1988 (Assistant Education Officer, Development Forward Planning, 1977–88); *b* 21 Nov. 1942; *s* of J. E. and late A. L. Jones, Minyrafon, Foelgastell, Cefneithin, Carms; *m* 1967, A. Laura Miles; two *s* one *d*. *Educ:* Gwendraeth Grammar Sch.; Cardiff Univ. BSc Econ (Hons) Politics and Economics. Market Research Officer with Ina Needle Bearings Ltd, Llanelli, 1966–67; Economist Section, Wales Gas Bd, 1967–69; Public Relations Officer, Labour Party in Wales, March 1969–June 1970; Dir of Res., West Glam. CC, 1974–77. Member: INLOGOV Working Gp on Res. and Intelligence Units in Local Govt, 1975–77; S Wales Standing Conf. Working Gp, 1975–77; Council of European Municipalities, 1975–77, 1980–; Local Govt Exec. Cttee of European movement, 1975–77, 1980–; MP (Lab) Carmarthen, 1970–Sept. 1974; Member: House of Commons Expenditure Cttee, 1972–74; Standing Orders Cttee, 1972–74; Council of Europe and WEU, 1974; PPS to Home Sec., 1974. Vice-Pres., District Council Assoc., 1974. Pres., Nat. Eisteddfod of Wales, 1974. Political Educn Officer, Swansea Labour Assoc., 1976–77. Mem., Soc. of Educn Officers, 1978–. Co-ordinator, Wales in Europe campaign, 1975; Sponsor, Wales Lab and TU Cttee for Europe, 1975; joined SDP, May 1981; contested: (SDP) Gower, Sept. 1982; (SDP/Alliance) Carmarthen, 1987; Prosp. Parly Cand. (Lib Dem), Hereford, 1989–. Chairman: SDP Council for Wales, 1982–85, 1987–88; Alliance Cttee for Wales, 1983–88; Interim Chm., Welsh Soc & Lib Dem Exec., 1988; Member: Council for Social Democracy, 1982–; SDP Nat. Cttee, 1982–85; SDP Orgn Cttee, 1987–88; Lib Dem Federal Exec., 1988–; Vice Chm., Lib Dem Policy Cttee, 1988–. *Publications:* booklets: The Record Put Straight, 1973; SDP and the Alliance in Wales 1981–1986, 1986; SLD Golden Opportunities, 1988; A Movement in Crisis, 1989. *Recreations:* sport (played Rugby for both 1st and 2nd class teams). *Address:* Fonthill, 24 Glanmor Park Road, Sketty, Swansea, West Glam. *T:* Swansea (0792) 202278.

JONES, Sir Harry (Ernest), Kt 1971; CBE 1955; Agent in Great Britain for Northern Ireland, 1970–76; *b* 1 Aug. 1911; *m* 1935, Phyllis Eva Dixon (*d* 1987); one *s* one *d*. *Educ:* Stamford Sch.; St John's Coll., Cambridge. Entered Northern Ireland Civil Service, 1934; Min. of Commerce: Principal Officer 1940; Asst Sec. 1942; Perm. Sec. 1955; Industrial Development Adviser to Ministry of Commerce, 1969. *Recreation:* fishing. *Address:* 51 Station Road, Nassington, Peterborough PE8 6QB. *T:* Stamford (0780) 782675.

JONES, Rt. Rev. Haydn Harold; *b* 22 Aug. 1920; *s* of Charles Samuel and Blodwen Jones (*née* Williams), Penarth, Glam. *Educ:* Brotherhood of Saint Paul, Barton. RAF, 1941–44. Deacon 1947, priest 1948, Diocese of Bradford. Curate of St Barnabas, Heaton, Bradford, 1947–49; Tor Mohun, Torquay, 1949–51; Chaplain RN, 1951–53; Licence to Officiate, Diocese of London, 1954–62, Diocese of Coventry, 1962–63; Curate of St Peter's, Coventry, 1963–64; Rector of Clutton, Diocese of Bath and Wells, 1964–76, with Cameley, 1975–76; Surrogate, 1972–76. Dean of St Mary's Cathedral, Caracas, 1976–85; Bishop of Venezuela, 1976–86. *Recreations:* formerly tennis (rep. RN 1952), bridge, films, theatre. *Address:* Apartado 17.467 Parque Central, 1015–A Caracas, Venezuela. *T:* Caracas (02) 573.1437. *Club:* Commonwealth of Venezuela.

JONES, Henry Arthur, CBE 1974; MA; Professor Emeritus, University of Leicester, since 1981 (Vaughan Professor of Education, 1967–81; Head of the Department of Adult Education, 1967–78; Pro-Vice-Chancellor, 1978–81); *b* 7 March 1917; *er s* of Henry Lloyd Jones; *m* 1st, 1942, Molly (*d* 1971), 4th *d* of Richard Shenton; two *s*; 2nd, 1972, Nancy Winifred (*née* Cox), *widow* of Lt R. B. B. Jack, RN. *Educ:* Chorlton Grammar Sch.; Manchester Univ. George Gissing Prizeman, Manchester Univ., 1936; Graduate Research Fellow, Manchester Univ., 1937, MA 1938. Served War of 1939–45 with Lancs Fusiliers and DLI, 1940–42. Sen. English Master, Chorlton Grammar Sch., 1942–47; Resident Staff Tutor, Manchester Univ., 1947–49; Asst Dir of Extra-Mural Studies, Liverpool Univ., 1949–52, Dep. Dir 1953–57; Principal, The City Literary Institute, 1957–67. Chairman: Assoc. for Adult Education, 1964–67; Adult Educn Cttee, IBA, 1973–77; Vice-Pres., Nat. Inst. of Adult Education (Exec. Chm., 1976–84); Hon. Life Mem., Educnl Centres Assoc.; Vice-Pres., Pre-retirement Assoc.; Member: Library Adv. Council, DES, 1965–68; Sec. of State's Cttee on Adult Educn, DES, 1968–72; Adv. Council for Adult and Continuing Educn, DES, 1977–83. Chm., Leics Consultative Cttee for Voluntary Orgns, 1974–77. Editor: Vaughan Papers in Educn, 1967–82; Studies in Adult Education, 1974–82. *Publications:* Adult Literacy: a study of the impact, 1978; The Concept of Success in Adult Literacy, 1978; Adult Literacy: the UK experience, 1978; Education and Disadvantage, 1978. *Address:* Stokes House, Great Bowden, Market Harborough, Leics LE16 7HF. *T:* Market Harborough (0858) 62846.

JONES, (Henry) John (Franklin); writer; *b* 6 May 1924; *s* of late Lt-Col James Walker Jones, DSO, IMS, and Doris Marjorie (*née* Franklin); *m* 1949, Jean Verity Robinson; one *s* one *d*. *Educ:* Blundell's Sch.; Colombo Public Library; Merton Coll., Oxford. Served War, Royal Navy: Ordinary Seaman, 1943; Intell. Staff, Eastern Fleet, 1944. Merton Coll., Oxford: Harmsworth Sen. Scholar, 1948; Fellow and Tutor in Jurisprudence, 1949; Univ. Sen. Lectr, 1956; Fellow and Tutor in Eng. Lit., 1962; Prof. of Poetry, Univ. of Oxford, 1979–84. Dill Meml Lectr, QUB, 1983. Football Correspondent, The Observer, 1956–59. TV appearances include The Modern World, 1988. *Publications:* The Egotistical Sublime, 1954, 5th edn 1978; (contrib.) The British Imagination, 1961; On Aristotle and Greek Tragedy, 1962, 5th edn 1980; (contrib.) Dickens and the Twentieth Century, 1962; (ed) H. W. Garrod, The Study of Good Letters, 1963; John Keats's Dream of Truth, 1969, 2nd edn 1980; (contrib.) The Morality of Art, 1969; The Same God, 1971; Dostoevsky, 1983, 2nd edn 1985. *Address:* Holywell Cottage, Oxford. *T:* Oxford (0865) 247702; Yellands, Brisworthy, Shaugh Prior, Plympton, Devon. *T:* Shaugh Prior (075539) 310.

JONES, Rev. Hugh; *see* Jones, Rev. R. W. H.

JONES, Sir Hugh; *see* Hugh-Jones, Sir W. N.

JONES, Hugh (Hugo) Jarrett H.; *see* Herbert-Jones.

JONES, Ven. Hughie; *see* Jones, Ven. T. H.

JONES, Hywel Francis; Commissioner for Local Administration in Wales, 1985–91; *b* 28 Dec. 1928; *s* of late Brynmor and Beatrice Jones, Morriston, Swansea; *m* 1959, Marian Rosser Craven; one *d*. *Educ:* Bishop Gore Grammar School, Swansea; St John's College, Cambridge (BA 1949, MA 1953). IPFA 1953. Borough Treasurer's Dept, Swansea, 1949–56; Nat. Service, RAPC, 1953–55; Dep. County Treasurer, Breconshire, 1956–59; Asst County Treasurer, Carmarthenshire, 1959–66; Borough Treasurer, Port Talbot, 1966–75; Sec., Commn for Local Administration in Wales, 1975–85. Mem., Public Works Loan Board, 1971–75; Financial Adviser, AMC, 1972–74. Treasurer, Royal National Eisteddfod of Wales, 1975–; Mem., Gorsedd of Bards, 1977. *Recreations:* music, reading, gardening. *Address:* Godre'r Rhiw, 1 Lon Heulog, Baglan, Port Talbot, West Glam SA12 8SY. *T:* Briton Ferry (0639) 813822.

JONES, Hywel Glyn; Chairman, Fixpoint Ltd, economic and marketing consultants, since 1988; Partner, Hywel Jones and Associates, economic consultants, since 1985; *b* 1 July 1948; *s* of late Thomas Glyndwr Jones and Anne Dorothy Jones (*née* Williams); *m* 1970, Julia Claire (*née* Davies). *Educ:* Trinity College, Cambridge (Open Scholar, Sen. Scholar, Res. Scholar; MA Hons Econ 1st cl; Wrenbury Scholarship in Political Economy). Lectr in Economics, Univ. of Warwick, 1971–73; Univ. Lectr in Economics of the Firm, Fellow of Linacre Coll., and Lectr, Worcester Coll., Oxford, 1973–77; Henley Centre for Forecasting: Dir of Internat. Forecasting, 1977–81; Dir and Chief Exec., 1981–85. *Publications:* Second Abstract of British Historical Statistics (jtly), 1971; An Introduction to Modern Theories of Economic Growth, 1975, trans Spanish and Japanese; Full Circle into the Future?: Britain into the 21st Century, 1984. *Recreations:* conversation, travel, military history, boating. *Address:* 59 Yarnells Hill, North Hinksey, Oxford OX2 9BE. *T:* Oxford (0865) 240916.

JONES, Rt. Rev. Hywel James; *b* 4 March 1918; *s* of Ifor James and Ann Jones; *m* 1946, Dorothy Margaret Wilcox; one *s* one *d*. *Educ:* Emmanuel Coll., Univ. of Saskatchewan (LTh). Deacon, then priest, 1942; Curate, Tofield, 1942; travelling priest, 1942–44; Incumbent of Parksville–Qualicum Beach, 1944–47; Colwood–Langford, 1947–56; Rector, St Mary the Virgin, Oak Bay, 1956–80. Hon. Canon of BC, 1959–68; Archdeacon of Quatsino, 1968–71, of Victoria, 1971–77; Archdeacon Emeritus, 1977–80; Bishop of British Columbia, 1980–84. *Recreations:* reading, music, gardening. *Address:* 2028 Frederick Norris Road, Victoria, BC V8P 2B2, Canada. *T:* 604–592–7658. *Club:* Union (Victoria, BC).

JONES, Prof. Ian C.; *see* Chester Jones.

JONES, Ian E.; *see* Edwards-Jones.

JONES, Ieuan Wyn; MP (Plaid Cymru) Ynys Môn, since 1987; *b* 22 May 1949; *s* of John Jones and Mair Elizabeth Jones; *m* 1974, Eirian Llwyd; two *s* one *d*. *Educ:* Pontardawe Grammar School; Ysgol-y-Berwyn, Y Bala, Gwynedd; Liverpool Polytechnic. LLB Hons. Qualified Solicitor, 1973; Partner in practice, 1974–87. Plaid Cymru National Vice-Chm., 1975–79, National Chm., 1980–82, 1990–. Contested (Plaid Cymru) Ynys Môn (Anglesey), 1983. *Recreations:* sport, local history. *Address:* Ty Newydd Rhosmeirch, Llangefni, Ynys Môn, Gwynedd LL77 7RZ. *T:* Llangefni (0248) 722261.

JONES, Ilston Percival Ll.; *see* Llewellyn Jones.

JONES, Ivor R.; *see* Roberts-Jones.

JONES, Jack L.; *see* Jones, James Larkin.

JONES, Sir James (Duncan), KCB 1972 (CB 1964); *b* 28 Oct. 1914; *m* 1943, Jenefer Mary Wade; one *s*. *Educ:* Glasgow High Sch.; Glasgow Univ.; University Coll., Oxford. Admiralty, 1941; Ministry of Town and Country Planning: joined 1946; Prin. Priv. Sec., 1947–50; Under-Sec., Min. of Housing and Local Govt, 1958–63; Sec., Local Govt Commn for England, 1958–61; Dep. Sec., Min. of Housing and Local Govt, 1963–66; Dep. Sec., Min. of Transport, 1966–70; Sec., Local Govt and Develt, DoE, 1970–72; Permanent Sec., DoE, 1972–75. Hon. FRIBA; Hon. FRTPI. *Recreations:* cooking, reading, looking at buildings. *Address:* The Courtyard, Ewelme, Wallingford, Oxon OX10 6HP. *T:* Wallingford (0491) 39270. *Club:* Oxford Union.

JONES, Prof. James Eirug Thomas, FRCPath; Courtauld Professor of Animal Health, Royal Veterinary College, University of London, since 1984; *b* 14 June 1927; *s* of David John and Mary Elizabeth Jones; *m* 1953, Marion Roberts; one *s* one *d*. *Educ:* Ystalyfera County Sch.; Royal Vet. Coll. MRCVS 1950; PhD 1973. Gen. vet. practice, 1950–53; vet. officer, Birmingham Corp., 1953–54; Lectr in Path., RVC, 1954–58; Res. Officer, Animal Health Trust, 1958–63; Fulbright Scholar, Univ. of Pennsylvania, 1963–64; vis. worker, 1964, Sen. Lectr, 1967, Reader in Animal Health, 1975–84, RVC. J. T. Edwards Meml Medal, 1985. *Publications:* numerous papers in sci. jls on infectious diseases of farm animals. *Recreations:* travel, reading. *Address:* 283 Bury Street West, N9 9JN. *T:* 081–360 2146.

JONES, James Larkin, (Jack), CH 1978; MBE 1950; FCIT 1970; General Secretary, Transport and General Workers' Union, 1969–78; Member, TUC General Council, 1968–78; Chairman, TUC International, Transport and Nationalised Industries Committees, 1972–78; Deputy Chairman, National Ports Council, 1967–79; *b* 29 March 1913; *m* 1938, Evelyn Mary Taylor; two *s*. *Educ:* elementary sch., Liverpool. Worked in engineering and docks industries, 1927–39. Liverpool City Councillor, 1936–39; served in Spanish Civil War; wounded Ebro battle, Aug. 1938; Coventry District Sec., Transport and General Workers' Union, also District Sec., Confedn of Shipbuilding and Engineering Unions, 1939–55; Midlands Regional Sec., Transport and General Workers' Union, 1955–63, Executive Officer, 1963–69. Mem., Midland Regional Bd for Industry, 1942–46, 1954–63; Chm., Midlands TUC Advisory Cttee, 1948–63. Coventry City Magistrate, 1950–63; Executive Chm., Birmingham Productivity Cttee, 1957–63; Member: Labour Party Nat. Exec. Cttee, 1964–67; Nat. Cttee for Commonwealth Immigrants, 1965–69; NEDC, 1969–78; Council, Advisory, Conciliation and Arbitration Service, 1974–78; Cttee of Inquiry into Industrial Democracy, 1976–77 (Chm., Labour Party Wkg Party on Industrial Democracy, 1967); Bd, Crown Agents, 1978–80; Royal Commn on Criminal Procedure, 1978–80; Jt Chm. (with Lord Aldington), Special Cttee on the Ports, 1972. Pres., EFTA Trade Union Council, 1972–73; Founder Mem., European TUC, 1973. Vice-President: ITF, 1974–79; Anti-Apartheid Movement, 1976–; Age Concern, England, 1978–; Pres., Retired Members Assocs, 1979–. Chm., Trustees, Nat. Museum of Labour History, 1988–. Vis. Fellow, Nuffield Coll., Oxford, 1970–78; Associate Fellow, LSE, 1978–82. Dimbleby Lecture, BBC, 1977. Hon. DLitt Warwick, 1978. Freeman, City of London, 1979. Award of Merit, City of Coventry, 1978. *Publications:* (contrib.) The Incompatibles, 1967; (contrib.) Industry's Democratic Revolution, 1974; (with Max Morris) A-Z of Trade Unionism and Industrial Relations, 1982; Union Man (autobiog.), 1986. *Recreation:* walking. *Address:* 74 Ruskin Park House, Champion Hill, SE5 8TH. *T:* 071–274 7067.

JONES, (James) Roger; Deputy Parliamentary Counsel, since 1991; *b* 30 May 1952; *s* of Albert James Jones and late Hilda Vera Jones (*née* Evans). *Educ:* Shrewsbury; St Catharine's Coll., Cambridge (Sen. Schol.; MA). Called to the Bar, Middle Temple, 1974 (Lloyd Jacob Meml Exhibnr; Astbury Schol.); practised Oxford and Midland Circuit, 1975–83. Joined Office of Parly Counsel, 1983; with Law Commn, 1988–91. *Recreation:* walking the dog. *Address:* 36 Whitehall, SW1. *Club:* Travellers'.

JONES, Hon. Jeffrey Richard, CBE 1978; MA; Chief Justice, 1980–85, and President of the Court of Appeal, 1982–85, Kiribati; Puisne Judge of the High Court of the Solomon Islands, 1982–85; Acting Puisne Judge of the Supreme Court of Vanuatu, 1982–85; *b* 18 Nov. 1921; *s* of Rev. Thomas Jones and Winifred (*née* Williams); *m* 1955, Anna Rosaleen Carberry; one *s* one *d*. *Educ:* Grove Park Sch., Wrexham; Denstone Coll., Staffs; Keble Coll., Oxford, 1940, 1946–49 (MA (Hons) PPE); Middle Temple, 1950–52 (Bar Finals, Council of Legal Educn; called, 1954). Served RAFVR, Flt Lieut (Pilot), 1940–46. Schoolmaster, Mountgrace Comprehensive, Potters Bar, 1953–55; private practice, Zaria, Nigeria, 1955–57; Magistrate, 1957, High Court Judge, 1965, Sen. Puisne Judge, 1970, Northern Nigeria; Chief Justice, Kano State, N Nigeria, 1975, Chief Judge (change of title, decree 41 of 1976), 1976–80. President, Rotary Club, Kano, 1977. Editor, Northern Nigeria Law Reports, 1966–74. *Publications:* Some Cases on Criminal Procedure and Evidence in Northern Nigeria 1968, 1968; Some Cases on Criminal Procedure and Evidence in Northern Nigeria 1969, 1969, 2nd edn combining 1968–69, 1970; Criminal Procedure in the Northern States of Nigeria (annotated), 1975, repr. 1978, 2nd edn 1979. *Recreations:* golf, painting, gardening, bridge, duck shooting, sea fishing. *Address:* Bradley Cottage, Bradley Lane, Holt, near Trowbridge, Wilts BA14 6QE. *T:* North Trowbridge (0225) 782004.

JONES, Jennifer, (Mrs Norton Simon); film actress (US); *b* Tulsa, Okla; *d* of Philip R. Isley and Flora Mae (*née* Suber); *m* 1st, 1939, Robert Walker (marr. diss. 1945); two *s*; 2nd, 1949, David O. Selznick (*d* 1965); one *d* decd; 3rd, 1971, Norton Simon. *Educ:* schools in Okla and Tex; Northwestern Univ., Evanston, Illinois; American Academy of Dramatic Arts, New York City. Films, since 1943, include: The Song of Bernadette; Since You Went Away; Cluny Brown; Love Letters; Duel in the Sun; We Were Strangers; Madame Bovary; Portrait of Jenny; Carrie; Wild Heart; Ruby Gentry; Indiscretion of an American Wife; Beat the Devil; Love is a Many-Splendoured Thing; The Barretts of Wimpole Street; A Farewell to Arms; Tender is the Night; The Idol; The Towering Inferno. Awards include: American Academy of Motion Pictures, Arts and Sciences Award, 1943; 4 other Academy nominations, etc. Medal for Korean War Work.

JONES, John; *see* Jones, H. J. F.

JONES, (John) Clement, CBE 1972; FRSA 1970; writer, broadcaster, technical adviser to developing countries; *b* 22 June 1915; *o s* of Clement Daniel Jones; *m* 1939, Marjorie (*d* 1991), *d* of George Gibson, Llandrindod Wells; three *s*. *Educ:* Ardwyn, Aberystwyth; BA (Hons) Open Univ., 1983. Various journalistic positions; News Editor, Express and Star, Wolverhampton, 1955; Editor, 1960–71; Editorial Director, 1971–74; Exec. Dir,

Beacon Broadcasting, Wolverhampton, 1974–83. Pres., Guild of British Newspaper Editors, 1966–67, Hon. Life Vice-Pres., 1972. Member: Press Council, 1965–74; Adv. Bd, Thomson Foundn, 1965–87; BBC W Midlands Adv. Council, 1971–75; (part-time) Monopolies and Mergers Commn (Newspaper Panel), 1973–86; W Midlands Arts Assoc., 1973–78; Exec. Cttee, Soc. Internat. Develt, 1974–78; Vice Chm., Lichfield Dio. Media Council, 1976–82; Mem. Council, and Chm. Press Freedom Cttee, Commonwealth Press Union, 1975–80; Chm., Media Panel, Commn for Racial Equality, 1981–84; Vice-Chm., British Human Rights Trust, 1975–78; Governor, British Inst. Human Rights, 1971–82. Mem. Senate, Open Univ., 1983–86. Founder Mem., Circle of Wine Writers, 1966. Pres., Staffordshire Soc., 1971–74. Founder and Pres., Frinton and Walton Heritage Trust, 1984–. *Publications:* UNESCO World Survey of Media Councils and Codes of Ethics, 1976; Racism and Fascism, 1981; Race and the Media: thirty years on, 1982; pamphlets on local history, NE Anglia. *Recreations:* travel, gardening. *Address:* 7 South View Drive, Walton on the Naze, Essex CO14 8EP. *T:* Frinton (02556) 77087. *Club:* Athenæum.

JONES, His Honour (John) Edward; a Circuit Judge (formerly County Court Judge), 1969–84; *b* 23 Dec. 1914; *s* of Thomas Robert Jones, Liverpool; *m* 1945, Katherine Elizabeth Edwards, SRN, *d* of Ezekiel Richard Edwards, Liverpool; one *s* one *d*. *Educ:* Sefton Park Council Sch.; Liverpool Institute High School. ACIS 1939–70; BCom London 1942; LLB London 1945. Called to Bar, Gray's Inn, 1945; Member of Northern Circuit, 1946; Dep. Chm., Lancs QS, 1966–69. Dep. Chm., Workmen's Compensation (Supplementation) and Pneumoconiosis and Byssinosis Benefit Boards, 1968–69; Director: Chatham Building Soc., 1955–59; Welsh Calvinistic Methodist Assurance Trust, 1953–59. Vice-Pres., Merseyside Br., Magistrates' Assoc., 1974–84. Pres., Liverpool Welsh Choral Union, 1987– (Vice Pres., 1973–87); Life Member: Welsh National Eisteddfod Court; Gorsedd of Bards (Ioan Maesgrug), 1987. Governor: Aigburth Vale Comprehensive Sch., 1976–85; Calderstones Community Comprehensive Sch., 1985–88. Pres., Merseyside Branch, British Red Cross Soc., 1980–88 (Mem. Nat. Council, 1983–86). Chm., World Friendship, 1990–. Exec. Cttee, Liverpool Free Church Federal Council, 1988–; Welsh Presbyterian Church: Deacon, 1947; Liverpool Presbytery Moderator, 1971. JP Lancs, 1966. *Address:* 45 Sinclair Drive, Liverpool L18 0HW. *Club:* Athenæum (Liverpool).

JONES, John Elfed, CBE 1987; DL; CEng, FIEE; FRSA; Chairman, Welsh Water plc (formerly Welsh Water Authority), since 1982; *b* 19 March 1933; *s* of Urien Maelgwyn Jones and Mary Jones; *m* 1957, Mary Sheila (*née* Rosser); two *d*. *Educ:* Blaenau Ffestiniog Grammar Sch.; Denbighshire Technical Coll., Wrexham; Heriot Watts Coll., Edinburgh. Student apprentice, 1949–53, graduate trainee, 1953–55, CEGB; National Service, RAF, 1955–57 (FO); Rock Climbing Instr, Outward Bound Sch., Aberdyfi, 1957; Technical Engr with CEGB, 1957–59; Dep. Project Manager, Rheidol Hydro-Electric Project, 1959–61; Sen. Elec. Engr, Trawsfynydd Nuclear Power Station, 1961–63; Deputy Manager: Mid Wales Gp of Power Stations, 1963–67; Connah's Quay Power Station, 1967–69; Anglesey Aluminium Metal Ltd: Engrg Manager, 1969–73; Production Manager, 1973–76; Admin Director, 1976–77; Dep. Man. Dir, 1977–79; Industrial Dir, Welsh Office (Under Sec. rank), 1979–82. Chm., British Water International Ltd, 1983–88. Director: HTV Cymru/Wales Ltd; W Midlands and Wales Regl Adv. Bd, National Westminster Bank. Treasurer, Urdd Gobaith Cymru, 1964–67; Chm., Welsh Language Bd, 1988–; Mem., Royal National Eisteddfod of Wales, 1981–90; Member: BBC Broadcasting Council for Wales, 1979–83; Council, Food from Britain, 1985–87; Prince of Wales Cttee, 1986–. Member: Court and Council: UCNW, Bangor, 1978–; Nat. Lib. of Wales, 1983–88; Coleg Harlech, 1983–88; Court, Univ. Coll., Aberystwyth, 1984–. Mem., Civic Trust for Wales, 1982–88. FRSA 1984; CBIM. DL Mid Glam, 1989. Hon. Col, Commonwealth of Kentucky, 1976. *Recreations:* fishing for salmon and trout, reading, attending Eisteddfodau. *Address:* Ty Mawr, Coity, Bridgend, Mid Glamorgan.

JONES, (John) Emrys, CBE 1979; Regional Organiser and Secretary, Labour Party, Wales, 1965–79, retired; *b* 12 March 1914; *s* of William Jones and Elizabeth Susan Jones; *m* 1935, Stella Davies; one *d*. *Educ:* Secondary Sch., Mountain Ash, S Wales. Shop assistant, 1928–29; railwayman, 1929–33; Rootes motor factory, 1933–36; railwayman, 1936–49. Regional Organiser, Labour Party: S West, 1949–60; W Midlands, 1960–65. *Recreations:* reading and writing. *Address:* 11 Conham Hill, Hanham, Bristol BS15 3AW. *T:* Bristol (0272) 615134.

JONES, Air Vice-Marshal John Ernest A.; *see* Allen-Jones.

JONES, John Ernest P.; *see* Powell-Jones.

JONES, Prof. (John) Gareth, MD; FRCP; Professor of Anaesthesia, Cambridge University, since 1991; *b* 20 Aug. 1936; *s* of Dr John and Catherine Jones; *m* 1964, Susan Price; three *d*. *Educ:* Welsh Nat. Sch. of Medicine (MB BCh); MD Birmingham. MRCP; FFARCS. Res. Fellow, Dept of Medicine, 1964, Lectr, Anaesthesia, 1968–70, Univ. of Birmingham; North Sen. Fellow, Cardiovascular Res. Inst., Univ. of California, San Francisco, 1970– 74; Scientific Staff, MRC, Northwick Park, 1974–86; Prof. of Anaesthesia, Univ. of Leeds, 1986–91. Vis. Scientist, Chest Service, Univ. of California, San Francisco, 1977–78. *Publications:* Effects of Anaesthesia and Surgery on Pulmonary Mechanisms, 1984; (with I. Hindmarch and E. Moss) Aspects of Recovery From Anaesthesia, 1987; Depth of Anaesthesia, 1989. *Recreations:* model engineering, moto-cross. *Address:* Cambridge University Department of Anaesthesia, Addenbrooke's Hospital, Hills Road, Cambridge CB2 2QQ. *T:* Cambridge (0223) 245151.

JONES, (John) Geoffrey; His Honour Judge Geoffrey Jones; a Circuit Judge since 1975; *b* 14 Sept. 1928; *s* of Wyndham and Lilias Jones; *m* 1954, Sheila (*née* Gregory); three *s*. *Educ:* Brighton and Hove Grammar Sch.; St Michael's Sch., Llanelli; St David's Coll., Lampeter; University Coll., London. LLB London 1955; LLM London 1985. Army service, 1946–48, commnd into RASC, 1947. Electrical wholesale business, 1948–52. Called to Bar, Gray's Inn, 1956; practised Leicester, 1958–70 and London, 1970–75. Sen. Academic Fellow, Leicester Polytechnic, 1989. *Recreation:* golf. *Address:* c/o The County Court, Lower Hill Street, Leicester LE1 3SJ.

JONES, Maj.-Gen. John H.; *see* Hamilton-Jones.

JONES, Sir John Henry H.; *see* Harvey-Jones.

JONES, John Hubert E.; *see* Emlyn Jones.

JONES, Sir (John) Kenneth (Trevor), Kt 1965; CBE 1956; QC 1976; Legal Adviser to the Home Office, 1956–77; *b* 11 July 1910; *s* of John Jones and Agnes Morgan; *m* 1940, Menna, *d* of Cyril O. Jones; two *s*. *Educ:* King Henry VIII Grammar Sch., Abergavenny; University Coll. of Wales, Aberystwyth; St John's Coll., Cambridge. Called to the Bar, Lincoln's Inn, 1937. Served Royal Artillery, 1939–45. Entered the Home Office as a Legal Asst, 1945. Mem. of the Standing Cttee on Criminal Law Revision, 1959–80. *Address:* 7 Chilton Court, Walton-on-Thames, Surrey KT12 1NG. *T:* Walton-on-Thames (0932) 226890. *Club:* Athenæum.

JONES, John Knighton C.; *see* Chadwick-Jones.

JONES, Sir John (Lewis), KCB 1983; CMG 1972; *b* 17 Feb. 1923; *m* 1948, Daphne Nora (*née* Redman). *Educ:* Christ's College, Cambridge (MA). Royal Artillery, 1942–46; Sudan Government, 1947–55; Ministry of Defence, 1955–85. *Recreation:* golf. *Club:* United Oxford & Cambridge University.

JONES, Air Vice-Marshal John Maurice, CB 1986; Royal Air Force, retired; Secretary, Ski Club of Great Britain, since 1988; *b* 27 Jan. 1931; *s* of E. Morris Jones and Gladys Jones (*née* Foulkes); *m* 1962, Joan (*née* McCallum); one *s* one *d*. *Educ:* Liverpool Institute High Sch.; Univ. of Liverpool (BDS). LDSRCS, FDSRCS 1987. FBIM. Hospital appt, Liverpool Dental Hosp., 1954; RAF Dental Branch: appts UK and abroad, incl. Christmas Island, Malta, Cyprus and Fontainebleau, 1955–73; Dep. Dir of RAF Dental Services, 1973; OC RAF Inst. of Dental Health and Training, 1976; Principal Dental Officer: HQ RAF Germany, 1979; HQ RAF Support Command, 1982; Dir, RAF Dental Services, 1982–88, and Dir, Defence Dental Services, MoD, 1985–88. QHDS, 1983–87. OBStJ 1978. *Publications:* contribs to British Dental Jl. *Recreations:* golf, shooting, fishing, skiing. *Address:* Wyckenhurst, St Michael's Close, Halton Village, Wendover, Bucks HP22 5NW. *T:* Wendover (0296) 624184. *Club:* Royal Air Force, Kandahar.

JONES, Brig. John Murray R.; *see* Rymer-Jones.

JONES, Sir John Prichard; *see* Prichard-Jones.

JONES, Rev. Prebendary John Stephen Langton; Residentiary Canon and Precentor of Wells Cathedral, 1947–67, Prebendary, since 1967; *b* 21 May 1889; *m* 1921, Jeanne Charlotte Dujardin; three *s* one *d*. *Educ:* Dover College; Jesus College, Cambridge. Asst Curate of Halifax Parish Church, 1914; Asst Curate, Hambleden, Berks, 1919; Vicar of Yiewsley, Middx, 1921; Rector of W Lydford, Taunton, 1939–47. Proctor in Convocation for Bath and Wells, 1946–50. *Address:* 16 Wimborne Road, Bournemouth BH2 6NT.

JONES, Prof. Kathleen; Professor of Social Policy, University of York, 1981–89 (Professor of Social Administration, 1965–81), now Emeritus Professor; *b* 7 April 1922; *d* of William Robert Savage and Kate Lilian Barnard; *m* 1944, Rev. David Gwyn Jones (*d* 1976); one *s*. *Educ:* North London Collegiate Sch.; Westfield Coll., Univ. of London (BA, PhD). Research Asst in Social Administration, Univ. of Manchester, 1951–53, Asst Lectr 1953–55; Sen. History Teacher, Victoria Instn, Kuala Lumpur, 1956–58, also Asst Lectr in History, Univ. of Malaya (part-time); Lectr in Social Administration, Univ. of Manchester, 1958–62, Sen. Lectr 1962–65. Chm., Social Scis Cttee, UK Commn for UNESCO, 1966–69. Mem., Gen. Synod of C of E, 1975–80; Member: Archbishop's Commn on Church and State, 1966–71; Lord Gardiner's Ctte on NI, 1974–75; Archbishop's Commn on Marriage, 1976–78; Mental Health Act Commn, 1983–86 (NE Chm., 1983–85). Pres., Assoc. of Psychiatric Social Workers, 1968–70; Chm., Social Admin Assoc., 1980–83. Hon. FRCPsych, 1976. *Publications:* Lunacy, Law and Conscience, 1955; Mental Health and Social Policy, 1960; Mental Hospitals at Work, 1962; The Compassionate Society, 1965; The Teaching of Social Studies in British Universities, 1965; A History of the Mental Health Services, 1972; Opening the Door: a study of new policies for the mentally handicapped, 1975; Issues in Social Policy, 1978; (ed) Living the Faith: a call to the Church, 1980; Ideas on Institutions, 1984; Eileen Younghusband: a biography, 1985; Experience in Mental Health, 1988; The Making of Social Policy, 1991; (series editor) International Library of Social Policy, 1968–85; (ed) Year Book of Social Policy in Britain, 1971–76. *Address:* 44 West Moor Lane, Heslington, York YO1 5ER. *T:* York (0904) 411579. *Club:* University Women's.

JONES, Keith H.; *see* Hamylton Jones.

JONES, Sir Keith (Stephen), Kt 1980; FRCSE; FRACS; *b* 7 July 1911; *s* of Stephen William and Muriel Elsy Jones; *m* 1936, Kathleen Mary Abbott; three *s*. *Educ:* Newington Coll.; Univ. of Sydney (MB, BS). General practitioner, Army MO, Surgeon; President, Aust. Medical Assoc., 1973–76; Chief MO, NSW State Emergency Service, 1966–74; Mem., NSW Medical Bd, 1971–81. Mem., Newington Coll. Council, 1951–72; Mem., Nat. Specialist Recognition Appeals Cttee, 1970–83 (Chm., 1980–83; Chm., Nat. Spec. Qualifications Cttee, 1980–83). Chairman: Australasian Medical Publishing Co., 1976–82; Manly Art Gall., 1982–85; President: Medical Benefits Fund of Aust., 1983–85; Blue Cross Assoc. of Aust., 1983–85. Acting Editor, Medical Jl of Aust., 1981. Fellow, Australian Coll. of Emergency Medicine; Hon. FRACGP 1975. Gold Medal, AMA, 1976. *Recreation:* swimming. *Address:* 123 Bayview Garden Village, Cabbage Tree Road, Bayview, NSW 2104, Australia. *T:* 997 2876.

JONES, Sir Kenneth; *see* Jones, Sir J. K. T.

JONES, Sir Kenneth (George Illtyd), Kt 1974; a Judge of the High Court, Queen's Bench Division, 1974–89; *b* 26 May 1921; *s* of late Richard Arthur Jones and Olive Jane Jones, Radyr, Cardiff; *m* 1st, 1947, Dulcie (*d* 1977); one *s* two *d*; 2nd, 1978, June Patricia (prev. marr. diss.), *o d* of late Leslie Arthur and Winifred Doxey, Harrogate. *Educ:* Brigg Gram. Sch.; University Coll., Oxford (1939–41, 1945–46), MA; Treas., Oxford Union Society, 1941; served in Shropshire Yeo. (76th Medium Regt RA), 1942–45; Staff Captain, HQ 13th Corps, 1945 (despatches). Called to Bar, Gray's Inn, 1946; joined Oxford Circuit, 1947; QC 1962; Mem. Gen. Council of the Bar, 1961–65, 1968–69; Bencher, 1969, Treas., 1987, Gray's Inn. Recorder of: Shrewsbury, 1964–66; Wolverhampton, 1966–71; the Crown Court, 1972; Dep. Chm., Herefordshire QS, 1961–71; a Circuit Judge, 1972–73. Dep. Chm., Boundary Commn for Wales, 1984–88. *Recreations:* theatre, opera, travel, fishing. *Address:* c/o Coutts & Co., 188 Fleet Street, EC4A 2HT.

JONES, Air Marshal Sir Laurence (Alfred), KCB 1987 (CB 1984); AFC 1971; Lieutenant-Governor of the Isle of Man, since 1990; *b* 18 Jan. 1933; *s* of Benjamin Howel and Irene Dorothy Jones; *m* 1956, Brenda Ann; two *d*. *Educ:* Trinity Sch., Croydon; RAF College, Cranwell. Entry to RAF Coll., 1951, graduated 1953; served as Jun. Officer Pilot with 208 Sqdn in Middle East, 1954–57; Fighter Weapons Sch., 74 Sqdn, until 1961; commanded: No 8 Sqdn, Aden, 1961–63; No 19 Sqdn, RAF Germany, 1967–70; Station Comdr, RAF Wittering, 1975–76; RCDS 1977; Director of Operations (Air Support), MoD, 1978–81; SASO, Strike Command, 1982–84; ACAS(Ops), MoD, 1984; ACDS(Progs), 1985–86; ACAS, 1986–87; Air Member for Personnel, 1987–89, retd. *Recreations:* golf, ski-ing. *Club:* Royal Air Force.

JONES, Leslie, MA; JP; Secretary for Welsh Education, Welsh Office and Department of Education and Science, 1970–77; *b* Tumble, Carms, 27 April 1917; *y s* of late William Jones, ME and Joanna (*née* Peregrine); *m* 1948, Glenys, *d* of late D. R. Davies, Swansea; one *s* one *d*. *Educ:* Gwendraeth Valley Grammar Sch.; Univ. of Wales. Served with RN, 1940–46 (Lieut RNVR). UC Swansea, 1937–40 and 1946–47 (1st cl. hons Econs); Lectr in Econs, Univ. of Liverpool, 1947–51; Lectr and Sen. Lectr in Econs, UC Cardiff, 1952–65; Dir, Dept of Extra-Mural Studies, UC Cardiff, 1965–69. Hon. Lectr, Dept of Educn, UC Cardiff, 1977–. Member: Ancient Monuments Bd for Wales, 1970–77; Court, UWIST, 1978–; Council, St David's University Coll., 1978–; Court, Nat. Library of Wales, 1978–; Court, Nat. Mus. of Wales, 1978–; Council, Dr Barnardo's, 1978–88. Hon. Fellow, UC Cardiff, 1971. JP Cardiff 1966. *Publications:* The British Shipbuilding

Industry, 1958; articles on maritime, coal, iron and steel industries; industrial economics generally. *Recreations:* walking, gardening. *Address:* 43 Cyncoed Road, Cardiff. *Club:* Naval.

JONES, Lewis C.; *see* Carter-Jones.

JONES, Lilian Pauline N.; *see* Neville-Jones.

JONES, Mark Ellis Powell; Keeper of Coins and Medals, British Museum, since 1990; *b* 5 Feb. 1951; *s* of John Ernest Powell-Jones, *qv*; *m* 1983, Ann Camilla, *d* of Stephen Edelston Toulmin, *qv*; two *s* one *d*. *Educ:* Eton College; Worcester College, Oxford (MA); Courtauld Inst. of Art. Asst Keeper, Dept of Coins and Medals, British Museum, 1974–90. Sec., British Art Medal Soc., 1982; Vice-Pres., Fédn Internat. de la Médaille; Corresp. Mem., Amer. Numismatic Soc. Editor, The Medal, 1983. *Publications:* The Art of the Medal, 1977; Impressionist Painting, 1979; Catalogue of French Medals in the British Museum, I, 1982, II, 1988; Contemporary British Medals, 1986; (ed) Fake?: the art of deception, 1990. *Address:* 88 Albion Drive, E8 4LY. *T:* 071–254 0215.

JONES, Prof. Martin Kenneth, DPhil; George Pitt-Rivers Professor of Archaeological Science, University of Cambridge, since 1990; *b* 29 June 1951; *s* of John Francis Jones and Margaret Olive (*née* Baldwin); *m* 1985, Lucy Walker; one *s* one *d*. *Educ:* Univ. of Cambridge (MA); Univ. of Oxford (DPhil 1985). Oxford Archaeological Unit, 1973–79; Res. Asst, Oxford Univ., 1979–81; Lectr, 1981–89, Sen. Lectr, 1989–90, Durham Univ. *Publications:* The Environment of Man: the Iron Age to the Anglo-Saxon period, 1981; Integrating the Subsistence Economy, 1983; England before Domesday, 1986; Archaeology and the Flora of the British Isles, 1988. *Recreations:* walking, botanising. *Address:* Department of Archaeology, Downing Street, Cambridge CB2 3DZ. *T:* Cambridge (0223) 333520.

JONES, Martyn David; MP (Lab) Clwyd South West, since 1987; *b* 1 March 1947; *m* 1974, Rhona Bellis; one *s* one *d*. *Educ:* Liverpool and Trent Polytechnics. MIBiol. Microbiologist, Wrexham Lager Beer Co., 1968–87. Mem., Clwyd CC, 1981–89. An Opposition Whip, 1988–. Mem., Select Cttee on Agriculture, 1987–; Chm., Parly Labour Party Agriculture Cttee, 1987–. *Address:* House of Commons, SW1A 0AA; 20 High Street, Johnstown, Wrexham, Clwyd.

JONES, Maude Elizabeth, CBE 1973; Deputy Director-General, British Red Cross Society, 1970–77; *b* 14 Jan. 1921; 2nd *d* of late E. W. Jones, Dolben, Ruthin, North Wales. *Educ:* Brynhyfryd Sch. for Girls, Ruthin. Joined Foreign Relations Dept, Jt War Organisation BRCS and OStJ, 1940; Dep. Dir, Jun. Red Cross, BRCS, 1949; Dir, Jun. Red Cross, 1960; Dep. Dir-Gen. for Branch Affairs, BRCS, 1966. Member: Jt Cttee (and Finance and Gen. Purposes Sub-Cttee) OStJ and BRCS, 1966–77; Council of Nat. Council of Social Service; Council of FANY, 1966–77. Governor, St David's Sch., Ashford, Mddx. SSStJ 1959. *Recreations:* music, gardening, reading. *Address:* Dolben, Ruthin, Clwyd, North Wales LL15 1RB. *T:* Ruthin (08242) 2443. *Club:* New Cavendish.

JONES, Mervyn; author; *b* 27 Feb. 1922; *s* of Ernest Jones and Katharine (*née* Jokl); *m* 1948, Jeanne Urquhart; one *s* two *d*. *Educ:* Abbotsholme School; New York University. Assistant Editor: Tribune, 1955–59; New Statesman, 1966–68; Drama Critic, Tribune, 1959–67. *Publications:* No Time to be Young, 1952; The New Town, 1953; The Last Barricade, 1953; Helen Blake, 1955; On the Last Day, 1958; Potbank, 1961; Big Two, 1962; A Set of Wives, 1965; Two Ears of Corn, 1965; John and Mary, 1966; A Survivor, 1968; Joseph, 1970; Mr Armitage Isn't Back Yet, 1971; Life on the Dole, 1972; Holding On, 1973; The Revolving Door, 1973; Strangers, 1974; Lord Richard's Passion, 1974; The Pursuit of Happiness, 1975; Scenes from Bourgeois Life, 1976; Nobody's Fault, 1977; Today The Struggle, 1978; The Beautiful Words, 1979; A Short Time to Live, 1980; Two Women and their Man, 1982; Joanna's Luck, 1985; Coming Home, 1986; Chances, 1987; That Year in Paris, 1988; A Radical Life, 1991. *Address:* 10 Waterside Place, NW1 8JT. *T:* 071–586 4404.

JONES, Miah Gwynfor, (Gwyn Jones), PhD; FBCS; Chairman, Welsh Development Agency, since 1988; *b* 2 Dec. 1948; *s* of Robert Jones and Jane Irene Jones (*née* Evans); *m* 1976, Maria Linda Johnson; two *d*. *Educ:* Ysgol Eifionydd, Porthmadog; Univ. of Manchester (BSc 1st Cl. Hons); Univ. of Essex (PhD). FBCS 1987. British Steel Corp., 1974–77; ICL, 1977–81; Chm., Business Micro Systems, 1981–85; Chm. and Chief Exec., Corporate Technology Gp, 1985–87; Chm., L. G. Software, 1985–87; Director: Apricot Computers PLC, 1989–; Welsh Water Enterprises Ltd. Member: Council, Univ. of Wales, 1989–; Court, UC of Swansea, 1989–; Prince of Wales Cttee, 1989–; Prince's Youth Business Trust, 1989–; Adv. Bd, Assoc. of MBA; Adv. Bd, British Telecom (Wales); Bd, European Business Sch., UC, Swansea. *Recreations:* golf, tennis, ski-ing. *Address:* Box Farm, Reynoldston, Gower.

JONES, Michael Abbott; Chief Executive, Association of British Insurers, since 1987; *b* 3 May 1944; *s* of Ronald and Irene Jones; *m* 1973, Wendy (*née* Saward); twin *d*. *Educ:* Felsted; Magdalen Coll., Oxford (BA, DipEd). Joined Life Offices' Assoc., 1968, Jt Sec. 1982; transf. to Assoc. of British Insurers on its formation, as Manager, Legislation, 1985. *Recreations:* reading, photography, theatre. *Address:* 51 Forest Side, E4 6BA.

JONES, Dr Michael Barry, CEng, FIMinE; HM Chief Inspector of Mines, Health and Safety Executive, since 1986; *b* 28 April 1932; *s* of Mynorydd Jones and Dorothy Anne Jones; *m* 1957, Josephine Maura (*née* Dryden); two *d*. *Educ:* Alsop High Sch., Liverpool; Leeds Univ. (BSc; PhD 1956). CEng, FIMinE 1959. Trainee, NCB, 1956; Underofficial, Whitwick Colliery, 1959; Undermanager, Rawdon, Ellistown and Donisthorpe Collieries, 1961; HM Inspector of Mines and Quarries, Lancs, 1965; HM Dist Inspector of Mines and Quarries, Yorks, 1974; HM Sen. Dist Inspector, Scotland, 1980; HM Dep. Chief Inspector, 1982. *Publications:* author and co-author of papers in The Mining Engineer. *Recreation:* growing and showing sweet peas. *Address:* St Anne's House, University Road, Bootle, Merseyside L20 3RA. *T:* 051–951 4190.

JONES, Hon. Mrs Miller; *see* Askwith, Hon. B. E.

JONES, Dr Nevin Campbell H.; *see* Hughes Jones.

JONES, Nigel John I.; *see* Inglis-Jones.

JONES, Rt. Rev. Noël Debroy; *see* Sodor and Man, Bishop of.

JONES, Norman Arthur W.; *see* Ward-Jones.

JONES, Dr (Norman) Fielding, FRCP; Consultant Physician, St Thomas' Hospital, London, since 1967; *b* 3 May 1931; *s* of William John and Winifred Jones; *m* 1958, Ann Pye Chavasse; three *s*. *Educ:* Christ Coll., Brecon; King's Coll., Cambridge (MA 1957; MD 1966); St Thomas' Hosp., London. FRCP 1970. Rockefeller Fellow, Univ. of N Carolina, 1963–64. Physician, King Edward VII's Hosp. for Officers, 1977–; Consulting Physician, Metropolitan Police, 1980–; Hon. Consulting Physician: to the Army, 1980–; to Royal Hosp., Chelsea, 1987–; CMO, Equitable Life Assurance Soc., 1985–. Royal College of Physicians: Sen. Censor and Vice Pres., 1989–90; Treasurer, 1991–; Chm., Cttee on Renal Disease, 1980–; Chm., Cttee on Legal Aspects of Medicine, 1990–. Special Trustee, St Thomas' Hosp., 1990–. *Publications:* (ed) Recent Advances in Renal Disease, 1975; (ed with Sir Douglas Black) Renal Disease, 1979; (ed with D. K. Peters) Recent Advances in Renal Medicine, 1982. *Recreations:* iconology, music. *Address:* 1 Annesley Road, SE3 0JX. *T:* 081–856 0583.

JONES, Norman Henry; QC 1985; a Recorder, since 1987; *b* 12 Dec. 1941; *s* of Henry Robert Jones and Charlotte Isobel Scott Jones; *m* 1970, Trudy Helen Chamberlain; two *s* one *d*. *Educ:* Bideford Grammar School; North Devon Tech. Coll.; Univ. of Leeds (LLB, LLM). Called to the Bar, Middle Temple, 1968. Contested Leeds NW (SDP), 1983; Mem., Nat. Cttee, SDP, 1982–84. *Recreation:* boating. *Address:* Danehurst, Greenfield Lane, Guiseley, Leeds LS20 8HF. *T:* Guiseley (0943) 78192.

JONES, Norman Stewart C.; *see* Carey Jones.

JONES, Norman William, CBE 1984; TD 1962; FCIB; Director, 1976–91 and Vice Chairman, 1989–91, Lloyds Bank plc; *b* 5 Nov. 1923; *s* of late James William Jones and Mabel Jones; *m* 1950, Evelyn June Hall; two *s*. *Educ:* Gravesend Grammar Sch. FIB 1972. Served War, Army, 1942–47: commnd Beds and Herts Regt, 1943; with Airborne Forces, 1944–47; TA, 1947–64. Entered Lloyds Bank, 1940; Gen. Man., 1973; Asst Chief Gen. Man., 1975; Dep. Group Chief Exec., 1976; Gp Chief Exec., 1978–83; a Dep. Chm., 1984–89. Chairman: Lloyds Merchant Bank (Govt Bonds) Ltd, 1986–87; Lloyds Bank (Stockbrokers) Ltd, 1986–; Director: Lloyds Bank California, 1974–83; National Bank of New Zealand, 1978–; Lloyds Bank International, 1984–85; Lloyds Bank NZA Ltd, 1985–90; Lloyds Merchant Bank Hldgs, 1985–91; Lloyds Abbey Life Group, 1988–91. Chm., Aust. and NZ Trade Adv. Cttee, 1985–88. FRSA. *Recreations:* sailing, photography, DIY. *Address:* Rowans, 21 College Avenue, Grays, Essex RM17 5UN. *T:* Grays Thurrock (0375) 373101. *Club:* Overseas Bankers.

JONES, Norvela, (Mrs Michael Jones); *see* Forster, N.

JONES, Sir (Owen) Trevor, Kt 1981; formerly Councillor, Liverpool Metropolitan District Council; *b* 1927; *s* of Owen and Ada Jones, Dyserth. Mem., Liverpool City Council, 1968, Liverpool Metropolitan District Council, 1973–91 (Leader, 1981–83). Pres., Liberal Party, 1972–73; contested (L): Liverpool, Toxteth, Feb. 1974 and Gillingham, Oct. 1974. *Address:* 221 Queen's Drive, Liverpool L15 6YE.

JONES, Penry; Chief Assistant (Television) (formerly Deputy Head of Programme Services), IBA (formerly ITA), 1971–82, retired; *b* 18 Aug. 1922; *s* of Joseph William and Edith Jones; *m* Beryl Joan Priestley; two *d*. *Educ:* Rock Ferry High Sch.; Liverpool Univ. Gen. Sec., YMCA, Altrincham, 1940; Sec., SCM, Southern Univs, 1945; Industrial Sec., Iona Community, 1948; Religious Programmes Producer, ABC Television, 1958; Religious Programmes Officer of ITA, 1964; Head of Religious Broadcasting, BBC, 1967. *Recreations:* hill-walking, swimming, watching Rugby football. *Address:* Erraid House, Isle of Iona, Argyll PA76 6SJ. *T:* Iona (06817) 448.

JONES, Brig. Percival de Courcy, OBE 1953; Chief Secretary, The Royal Life Saving Society, 1965–75; *b* 9 Oct. 1913; *s* of P. de C. Jones, Barnsley; *m* 1st, 1947, Anne Hollins (marr. diss., 1951); one *s*; 2nd, 1962, Elaine Garnett. *Educ:* Oundle; RMC, Sandhurst. Commissioned KSLI 1933; Staff Coll., 1942; comd 1st Northamptons, Burma, 1945; Staff Coll. Instructor, 1949–50; AA & QMG, 11th Armoured Div., 1951–53; comd 1st KSLI, 1953–55; AQMG, War Office, 1955–58; NATO Defence Coll., 1958–59; Bde Comdr, 1959–62; retd 1962. Mem., Aylesbury Vale DC, 1976–79. Commonwealth Chief Sec., RLSS, 1965–75. Silver Medallion, Fedn Internat. de Sauvetage, 1976. *Recreation:* gardening. *Address:* 6 Port Hill Gardens, Shrewsbury, Shropshire SY3 8SH.

JONES, Peter Benjamin Gurner, CB 1991; Under Secretary; Director of Personnel, Board of Inland Revenue, since 1984; *b* 25 Dec. 1932; *s* of Gurner Prince Jones and Irene Louise Jones (*née* Myall); *m* 1962, Diana Margaret Henly; one *s* one *d*. *Educ:* Bancroft's Sch.; St Catherine's Society, Oxford (BA (Hons) English Language and Literature). Inspector of Taxes, 1957; Inspector (Higher Grade), 1963; Sen. Inspector, 1969; Principal Inspector, 1975; Sen. Principal Inspector, 1980; Dir of Data Processing, Bd of Inland Revenue, 1981–84. *Clubs:* Hampshire Rugby Union, Swanage and Wareham RFC.

JONES, Peter Derek; Secretary: Council of Civil Service Unions, since 1980; Civil Service National Whitley Council (Trade Union Side), since 1963; *b* 21 May 1932; *s* of Richard Morgan Jones and Phyllis Irene (*née* Lloyd); *m* 1962, Noreen Elizabeth (*née* Kemp). *Educ:* Wembley County Grammar School. National Service and TA, Green Jackets/Parachute Regt, 1950–56; Civil Service, Nat. Assistance Bd, 1952–59; Asst Sec., Civil Service Nat. Whitley Council, 1959–63. Chm., Civil Service Housing Assoc. Ltd, 1988– (Dir, 1963–81; Vice Chm., 1981–88); Dir, Civil Service Building Soc., 1963–87. Vice-Pres., RIPA, 1991– (Chm., 1987–90; Vice-Chm., 1986–87; Mem. Exec. Council, 1981–85); Member: Adv. Council, Civil Service Coll., 1982–; Tourism and Leisure Industries EDC, 1987–; Adv. Council, CS Occupational Health Service, 1988–. Trustee, Inst. of Contemporary Brit. History, 1985–. Editor: Whitley Bulletin, 1963–83; CCSU Bulletin, 1984–. *Publications:* articles in RIPA and personnel management jls. *Recreations:* relaxing, reading, golf. *Address:* Highlands Farm, Cross in Hand, East Sussex TN21 0SX. *T:* Heathfield (04352) 3577. *Clubs:* Wig and Pen, Belfry; Middlesex CCC; Horam Park Golf.

JONES, Peter Eldon, FRIBA, FRTPI, FCSD, FRSA; Consultant, Department of Education and Science, since 1988; *b* 11 Oct. 1927; *s* of Wilfrid Eldon Jones and Jessie Meikle (*née* Buchanan); *m* 1st, 1954, Gisela Marie von Arnswaldt; two *s* one *d*; 2nd, 1985, Claudia Milner-Brown (*née* Laurence). *Educ:* Surbiton County Grammar Sch.; Kingston Polytechnic; University College London. DipTP. Private practice, 1950–54; joined LCC Architects Dept, 1954; Dep. Schools Architect, LCC, 1960–65; Town Development Architect/Planner, 1965–71; Technical Policy Architect, GLC, 1971–74; Education Architect, ILEA, 1974–82; Acting Director of Architecture, 1980–82, Dir of Architecture and Superintending Architect of Metrop. Bldgs, 1982–86, GLC. Director: Interior Transformation Ltd, 1985–87; Watkins Gray Peter Jones, 1986–91. Part-time Lectr in Architectl Design, Kingston Poly., 1986–90. Mem., EC Adv. Cttee on Educn and Training in Architecture, 1987–. Pres., Soc. of Chief Architects of Local Authorities, 1984–85; Mem. Council, Chm. Membership Cttee, and Vice-Pres., RIBA, 1985–87. *Publications:* articles and papers on town development, educn building, housing design and planning. *Recreations:* building, photography, travel, golf. *Address:* Pitmore Farm House, Holly Lane, Worplesdon, Surrey GU3 3PB. *T:* Worplesdon (0483) 234 367. *Club:* Woking Golf.

JONES, Peter Ferry, MA, MChir, FRCS, FRCSE; Surgeon to the Queen in Scotland, 1977–85; Honorary Consulting Surgeon, Woodend Hospital and Royal Aberdeen Children's Hospital, Aberdeen (Consultant Surgeon, 1958–85); Clinical Professor of Surgery, University of Aberdeen, 1983–85, now Emeritus; *b* 29 Feb. 1920; *s* of Ernest and Winifred Jones; *m* 1950, Margaret Thomson; two *s* two *d*. *Educ:* Emmanuel Coll., Cambridge (MA); St Bartholomew's Hosp. Med. Sch., London (MB, MChir). FRCS 1948; FRCSE 1964. Served War, RAMC, 1944–46, Captain. House Surgeon, St

Bartholomew's Hosp., 1943; Surg. Registrar, N Middlesex Hosp., 1948–51; Surg. Tutor, St Bartholomew's Hosp., 1951–53; Sen. Surg. Registrar, Central Middlesex Hosp. and the Middlesex Hosp., London, 1953–57; Reader in Surg. Paediatrics, Univ. of Aberdeen, 1965–83. *Publications:* Abdominal Access and Exposure (with H. A. F. Dudley), 1965; Emergency Abdominal Surgery in Infancy, Childhood and Adult Life, 1974, 2nd edn 1987; (jtly) Integrated Clinical Science: Gastroenterology, 1984; A Colour Atlas of Colo-Rectal Surgery, 1985; papers on paediatric and gen. surgery in Brit. Jl of Surg., BMJ, Lancet, etc. *Recreation:* hill walking. *Address:* 7 Park Road, Cults, Aberdeen AB1 9HR. *T:* Aberdeen (0224) 867702.

JONES, Peter George Edward Fitzgerald, CB 1985; Director, Atomic Weapons Research Establishment, 1982–87, retired; Consultant to the Ministry of Defence, since 1987; *b* 7 June 1925; *s* of John Christopher Jones and Isobel (*née* Howell); *m* 1st; two *s*; 2nd, Jacqueline Angela (*née* Gilbert); two *s* one *d*. *Educ:* various schs; Dulwich Coll.; London Univ. (BSc (Special) Physics 1st Cl. Hons 1951). FInstP. Served RAF, flying duties, 1943–47. GEC Res. Labs, 1951–54; AWRE and Pacific Test Site, 1955–63; Asst Dir of Res., London Communications Security, 1963; Atomic Weapons Research Establishment: Supt, Electronics Res., 1964; Head, Electronics Div., 1966; Head, Special Projs, 1971; Chief, Warhead Develt, 1974; Principal Dep. Dir, 1980. *Recreations:* flying, motoring. *Address:* Rhyd Felin, Upper Llanover, Abergavenny, Gwent NP7 9DD. *T:* Nantyderry (0873) 880779.

JONES, Peter Llewellyn G.; *see* Gwynn-Jones.

JONES, Peter Trevor S.; *see* Simpson-Jones.

JONES, Sir Philip; *see* Jones, Sir T. P.

JONES, Philip Graham, CEng, FIChemE, FIExpE; Deputy Director of Technology Division, Health and Safety Executive, since 1986; *b* 3 June 1937; *s* of Sidney and Olive Jones; *m* 1961, Janet Ann Collins; one *s* three *d*. *Educ:* Univ. of Aston in Birmingham (BSc). Eur Ing 1989. Professional position in UK explosives industry, 1961–68 and 1972–76; service with Australian Public Service, 1969–71, with UK Civil Service, 1976–; HM Chief Inspector of Explosives, HSE, 1981–86. Mem., Accreditation Bd, 1987–90, Professional Develt Cttee, 1988–91, IChemE. *Publications:* articles in The Chemical Engineer and Explosives Engineer. *Recreations:* bridge, reading, curling. *Address:* HSE Technology Division, St Anne's House, University Road, Bootle, Merseyside L20 3MF. *T:* 051–951 4695.

JONES, Philip James, DPhil; FBA 1984; FRHistS; Fellow and Tutor, Modern History, 1963–89, Librarian, 1965–89, Brasenose College, Oxford, now Emeritus Fellow; *b* 19 Nov. 1921; *s* of John David Jones and Caroline Susan Jones (*née* Davies); *m* 1954, Carla Susini; one *s* one *d*. *Educ:* St Dunstan's College; Wadham College, Oxford (1st class Hons Mod. Hist. 1945, MA, DPhil). Senior Demy, Magdalen College, Oxford, 1945–49; Amy Mary Preston Road Scholar, 1946; Bryce Research Student, 1947; Asst in History, Glasgow Univ., 1949–50; Leeds University: Lectr in Med. Hist., 1950–61; Reader in Med. Hist., 1961–63; Eileen Power Meml Student, 1956–57. Corresp. Mem., Deputazione Toscana di Storia Patria, 1975–. Serena Medal for Italian Studies, British Acad., 1988. *Publications:* The Malatesta of Rimini, 1974; Economia e Societa nell'Italia medievale, 1980; contribs to: Cambridge Economic History, Vol. 1, 2nd edn, 1966; Storia d'Italia, vol. 2, 1974; Storia d'Italia, Annali, Vol. 1, 1978; articles and reviews in hist. jls. *Address:* 167 Woodstock Road, Oxford OX2 7NA. *T:* Oxford (0865) 57953; Piazza Pitti 3, Florence, Italy. *T:* 282924.

JONES, Philip (Mark), CBE 1986 (OBE 1977); Principal, Trinity College of Music, London, since 1988; *b* 12 March 1928; *m* 1956, Ursula Strebi. *Educ:* Royal College of Music (FRCM 1983 (ARCM 1947)). Principal Trumpet with all major orchestras in London, 1949–72; Founder and Dir, 1951–86, Philip Jones Brass Ensemble; Head of Dept of Wind and Percussion, Royal Northern Coll. of Music, Manchester, 1975–77; Head of Wind and Percussion Dept, GSMD, 1983–88. Member: Arts Council of GB, 1984–88; Royal Soc. of Musicians of GB. Over 50 gramophone records. FRNCM 1977; FGSM 1984. Hon. FTCL 1988. FRSA. Freeman, City of London, 1988. Grand Prix du Disque, 1977; Composers Guild Award, 1979; Cobbett Medal, Musicians' Co., 1986. *Publications:* Joint Editor, Just Brass series (for Chester Music London), 1975–89. *Recreations:* history, ski-ing, mountain walking. *Address:* 14 Hamilton Terrace, NW8 9UG. *T:* 071–286 9155.

JONES, Piers Nicholas L.; *see* Legh-Jones.

JONES, Mrs Rachel (Marianne); *b* 4 Aug. 1908; *d* of John Powell Jones Powell, solicitor, Brecon, and Kathleen Mamie Powell; *m* 1935, Very Rev. William Edward Jones (*d* 1974); one *s* three *d*. *Educ:* Princess Helena Coll.; Bedford Coll., University of London. Subwarden, Time and Talents Settlement, Bermondsey, 1931–32; Member: Bd of Governors, Fairbridge Farm Sch., Western Australia, 1945–49; Council for Wales and Mon, 1959–66; Nat. Governor for Wales of BBC and Chm. of Broadcasting Council for Wales, 1960–65. Member: Governing Body of the Church in Wales, 1953–78; Court and Council of Nat. Museum of Wales, 1962–78; St Fagan's Welsh Folk Museum Cttee, 1978–83; Pres., St David's Diocesan Mothers' Union, 1965–70. *Recreations:* music, gardening. *Address:* 3 Albeny Gate, Belmont Hill, St Albans, Herts AL1 1BH. *T:* St Albans (0727) 69810.

JONES, Raymond Edgar; HM Diplomatic Service, retired; *b* 6 June 1919; *s* of Edgar George Jones, Portsmouth; *m* 1942, Joan Mildred Clark; one *s* two *d*. *Educ:* Portsmouth Northern Grammar Sch. Entered Admiralty service as Clerical Officer, 1936; joined RAF, 1941; commissioned, 1943; returned to Admty as Exec. Officer, 1946; transf. to Foreign Service, 1948; Singapore, 1949; Second Sec., Rome, 1950; Bahrain, 1952; Rio de Janeiro, 1955; Consul, Philadelphia, 1958; FO, 1961; First Sec., Copenhagen, 1963; Consul, Milan, 1965; Toronto (Dir of British Week), 1966; Dep. High Comr, Adelaide, 1967–71; FCO, 1971–76; Consul-Gen., Genoa, 1976–79. *Recreations:* music, gardening. *Address:* Oaklands, 3 Old Hall Drive, Dersingham, Norfolk PE31 6JT.

JONES, Reginald Ernest, MBE 1942; Chief Scientific Officer, Ministry of Technology, 1965–69, retired; *b* 16 Jan. 1904; *m* 1933, Edith Ernestine Kressig; one *s* one *d*. *Educ:* Marylebone Gram. Sch.; Imperial Coll. of Science and Technology. MSc, DIC, FIEE. International Standard Electric Corp., 1926–33; GPO, 1933–65 (Asst Engr-in-Chief, 1957). Bronze Star (US), 1943. *Recreations:* music, gardening, walking. *Address:* 22 Links Road, Epsom, Surrey. *T:* Epsom (0372) 723625.

JONES, Reginald Victor, CB 1946; CBE 1942; FRS 1965; Professor of Natural Philosophy, University of Aberdeen, 1946–81, now Emeritus; *b* 29 Sept. 1911; *s* of Harold Victor and Alice Margaret Jones; *m* 1940, Vera, *d* of late Charles and Amelia Cain; one *s* two *d*. *Educ:* Alleyn's; Wadham Coll., Oxford (Exhibitioner; MA, DPhil, 1934; Hon. Fellow, 1968); Balliol Coll., Oxford (Skynner Senior Student in Astronomy, 1934–36; Hon. Fellow 1981). Air Ministry: Scientific Officer, 1936 (seconded to Admiralty, 1938–39); Air Staff, 1939; Asst Dir of Intelligence, 1941, Dir, 1946; Dir of Scientific Intelligence, MoD, 1952–53; Mem., Carriers Panel, 1962–63; Chm., Air Defence Working Party, 1963–64; Scientific Adv. Council, War Office, 1963–66. Chairman: Infra-Red Cttee, Mins of Supply and Aviation, 1950–64; British Transport Commn Res. Adv. Council, 1954–55; Safety in Mines Res. Advisory Bd, 1956–60 (Mem., 1950–56); Electronics Res. Council, Mins of Aviation and Technol., 1964–70. Royal Society: Chm., Paul Fund Cttee, 1962–84; a Vice-Pres., 1971–72; Chairman: Inst. of Physics Cttee on Univ. Physics, 1961–63; British Nat. Cttee for History of Science, Medicine and Technol., 1970–78 (Chm., Org. Cttee, Internat. Congress, 1977); President: Crabtree Foundation, 1958; Sect. A, British Assoc., 1971. Also a mem., various cttees on electronics, scientific res., measurement, defence and educn. Rapporteur, European Convention on Human Rights, 1970. Companion, Operational Res. Soc., 1983. Governor, Dulwich Coll., 1965–79; Life Governor, Haileybury Coll., 1978. Jt Editor, Notes and Records of the Royal Society, 1969–89. Vis. Prof., Univ. of Colorado, 1982; Visitor, RMCS, 1983. Hon. Member: Manchester Lit. & Phil. Soc., 1981; American Soc. for Precision Engrg, 1990. Hon. Fellow: College of Preceptors, 1978; IERE, 1982; Inst. of Measurement and Control, 1984; British Horological Inst., 1985. Hon. Freeman, Clockmakers' Co., 1984. Hon. DSc: Strathclyde, 1969; Kent, 1980; DUniv: York, 1976; Open, 1978; Surrey, 1979; Hon. LLD Bristol, 1979. Bailie of Benachie, 1980. US Medal of Freedom with Silver Palm, 1946; US Medal for Merit, 1947; BOIMA Prize, Inst. of Physics, 1934; Duddell Medal, Physical Soc., 1960; Parsons Medal, 1967; Hartley Medal, Inst. of Measurement and Control, 1972; Mexican Min. of Telecommunications Medal, 1973; Rutherford Medal, USSR, 1977; R. G. Mitchell Medal, 1979; Old Crows Medal, 1980. Hon. Mem., US Air Force, 1982; Hon. Mayor, San Antonio, Texas, 1983. *Publications:* Most Secret War (The Wizard War, USA, La Guerre Ultra Secrète, France), 1978; Future Conflict and New Technology, 1981; Some Thoughts on 'Star Wars', 1985; Instruments and Experiences, 1988; Reflections on Intelligence, 1989; lectures and papers on scientific subjects, defence, educn, engrg, history of science and policy. *Address:* 8 Queens Terrace, Aberdeen AB1 1XL. *T:* Aberdeen (0224) 648184. *Clubs:* Athenæum, Special Forces; Royal Northern (Aberdeen).

JONES, Rhona Mary; Chief Nursing Officer, St Bartholomew's Hospital, 1969–74, retired; *b* 7 July 1921; *d* of late Thomas Henry Jones and late Margaret Evelyn King; single. *Educ:* Liverpool; Alder Hey Children's Hosp.; St Mary's Hosp., Paddington. RSCN 1943; SRN 1945; SCM 1948. Post-Registration Training, and Staff Nurse, Queen Charlotte's Hosp., 1946–48; Ward Sister, 1948–50, Departmental Sister, 1950–52, St Mary's Hosp., Paddington; General Duty Nurse, Canada, 1952–53; Asst Matron, Gen. Infirmary, Leeds, 1953–57; Dep. Matron, Royal Free Hosp., London, 1957–59; Matron, Bristol Royal Hosp., 1959–67; Matron and Superintendent of Nursing, St Bartholomew's Hosp., 1968–69. Chm., Bristol Branch, Royal Coll. of Nursing, 1962–65; Member: Standing Nursing Adv. Cttee, Central Health Services Council, 1963–74; Exec. Cttee, Assoc. Nurse Administrators (formerly Assoc. Hosp. Matrons for England and Wales), 1963–74; Area Nurse Trng Cttee, SW Region, 1965–67; NE Metropolitan Area Nurse Training Cttee, 1969–74; E London Group Hosp. Management Cttee, 1969–74. Vice-Pres., Bristol Royal Hosp. Nurses League. *Recreations:* reading, travel, listening to music. *Address:* 26 Seaton Drive, Bedford MK40 3BG. *T:* Bedford (0234) 365868.

JONES, Air Vice-Marshal Rhys Tudor Brackley, CB 1990; FRCS; Senior Consultant, Royal Air Force Medical Branch, 1988–90; *b* 16 Nov. 1925; *s* of Sir Edgar Rees Jones, KBE and Lilian May Jones; *m* 1953, Irene Lilian, *d* of late Peter Valentine Spain Gammon; two *s*. *Educ:* King's Coll. Sch., Wimbledon; St Mary's Hosp., London (qualified 1950). House Surgeon to Mr Dickson-Wright and J. C. Goligher; joined RAF, 1952; Specialist in Surgery; Consultant, 1964; Hosp. service, Aden, Singapore, Germany, as gen. surgeon, special interest oncology; Hon. Consultant, Westminster Hosp., 1982; Cade Prof., RCS, 1981; Consultant Adviser in Surgery, 1982; Dean of Air Force Medicine, 1987. QHS, 1987–90. CStJ 1986. Lady Cade Medal, RCS, 1988. *Publications:* contribs to learned jls. *Address:* Glebelands, Wiveton Road, Blakeney, Norfolk NR25 7NJ. *T:* Cley (0263) 741093. *Club:* Royal Air Force.

JONES, Rev. Richard Granville; Chairman of East Anglia District, Methodist Church, since 1983; President of the Methodist Conference, 1988–89; *b* 26 July 1926; *s* of Henry William and Ida Grace Jones; *m* 1955, Kathleen Stone; three *d*. *Educ:* Truro School, Cornwall; St John's Coll., Cambridge (MA); Manchester Univ. (BD). Instructor Officer, RN, 1947–49. Methodist Minister in Plymouth East, 1949–50; Area Sec., SCM, 1953–55; Minister: Sheffield North Circuit, 1955–59; Sheffield Carver Street, 1959–64; Birkenhead, 1964–69; Tutor, Hartley Victoria Coll., Manchester, 1969–78, Principal 1978–82; Minister, Fakenham and Wells Circuit, 1982–83. Hon. DD Hull, 1988. *Publications:* (ed) Worship for Today, 1968; (with A. Wesson) Towards a Radical Church, 1972; How goes Christian Marriage?, 1978; Groundwork of Worship and Preaching, 1980; Groundwork of Christian Ethics, 1984. *Recreations:* walking, reading, writing. *Address:* 24 Townsend Road, Norwich NR4 6RG. *T:* Norwich (0603) 52257.

JONES, Air Vice-Marshal Richard Ian, CB 1960; AFC 1948; psa; pfc; *m* 1940, Margaret Elizabeth Wright. *Educ:* Berkhamsted Sch.; Cranwell. Group Captain, 1955; Air Commodore, 1960; Air Vice-Marshal, 1965. Senior Air Staff Officer, Royal Air Force, Germany (Second Tactical Air Force), Command Headquarters, 1959–62; Dir of Flying Training, 1963–64; AOC No 25 Group, RAF Flying Training Command, 1964–67; SASO, Fighter Command, 1967–68; AOC No 11 (Fighter) Gp, Strike Command, 1969–70; retired 1970. *Recreations:* golf, ski-ing. *Clubs:* Royal Air Force; Victoria (Jersey).

JONES, Maj.-Gen. Richard K.; *see* Keith-Jones.

JONES, Richard M.; *see* Mansell-Jones.

JONES, Richard S.; *see* Stanton-Jones.

JONES, (Robert) Alun; QC 1989; *b* 19 March 1949; *s* of late Owen Glyn Jones and of Violet Marion Jones (*née* Luxton); *m* 1974, Elizabeth Clayton; one *s* three *d*. *Educ:* Oldershaw Grammar Sch., Wallasey, Cheshire; Bristol Univ. (BSc 1970). Called to the Bar, Gray's Inn, 1972. Asst Recorder, 1988. Member: Senate of Inns of Court and the Bar, 1979–82; Gen. Council of the Bar, 1986–89; Sec., Criminal Bar Assoc., 1982–86. *Recreations:* bridge, cricket, growing vegetables. *Address:* 3 Raymond Buildings, Gray's Inn, WC1R 5BH. *T:* 071–831 3833.

JONES, Robert Brannock; MP (C) Hertfordshire West, since 1983; *b* 26 Sept. 1950; *s* of Ray Elwin Jones and Iris Pamela Jones; *m* 1989, Jennifer Anne, *d* of late Lewis Emmanuel Sandercock and of Iris Delphia Sandercock, Braunton, Devon. *Educ:* Merchant Taylors' Sch.; Univ. of St Andrews (MA Hons Modern History). Marketing Develt Exec., Tay Textiles Ltd, Dundee, 1974–76; Head of Res., NHBC, 1976–78; Housing Policy Adviser, Conservative Central Office, 1978–79; Parly Adviser, Fedn of Civil Engrg Contractors, 1979–83. Member: St Andrews Burgh Council, 1972–75; Fife CC, 1973–75; Chiltern DC, 1979–83; Vice-Pres., Assoc. of Dist Councils, 1983–. Mem., Environment Select Cttee, 1983–; Chm., Cons. Party Orgn Cttee, 1986–; Vice-Chm., Cons. backbench Educn Cttee, 1989–. Mem., Inland Waterways Amenity Adv. Council, 1985–; Pres., Dacorum Sports Council, 1984–. Vice-Pres., Wildlife Hosp. Trust, 1985–. Freeman, City of London;

Liveryman, Merchant Taylors' Co. *Publications:* New Approaches to Housing, 1976; Watchdog: guide to the role of the district auditor, 1978; Ratepayers' Defence Manual, 1980; Economy and Local Government, 1981; Roads and the Private Sector, 1982; Town and Country Chaos: critique of the planning system, 1982. *Recreations:* squash, tennis, shove-halfpenny, music. *Address:* Davidson House, 168 Queensway, Hemel Hempstead, Herts. *Clubs:* Rugby; Conservative (Tring).

JONES, Dr (Robert) Brinley, FSA; Member, Broadcasting Standards Council, 1988–91; *b* 27 Feb. 1929; *yr s* of John Elias Jones and Mary Ann Jones (*née* Williams); *m* 1971, Stephanie Avril Hall; one *s*. *Educ:* Tonypandy Grammar Sch.; University Coll. Cardiff (BA Wales 1st cl. Hons 1950; DipEd 1951; Fellow 1984); Jesus Coll., Oxford (DPhil 1960). FSA 1971; FCP 1982. Commissioned RAF, 1955; Educn Officer, RAF Kidlington and Bicester, 1955–58. Asst Master, Penarth Grammar Sch., 1958–60; Lectr, UC Swansea, 1960–66; Asst Registrar, Univ. of Wales, 1966–69; Dir, Univ. of Wales Press, 1969–76; Warden, Llandovery Coll., 1976–88. Member: Literature Cttee, Welsh Arts Council, 1968–74, 1981–1987; Bd, British Council, 1987– (Chm., Welsh Adv. Cttee, 1987–). Chairman: Dinefwr Tourism Gp, 1988–; European Assoc. of Teachers, 1965. Member: Court and Council, Nat. Liby of Wales, 1974–82; Council, St David's UC, Lampeter, 1977– (Hon. Fellow 1987); Governing Body, Church in Wales, 1981–; Court, UC Swansea, 1983–; Council, Trinity Coll., Carmarthen, 1984–; Managing Trustee, St Michael's Theol Coll., 1982–; Trustee, Rhys Davies Trust, 1990–. Hon. Mem., Druidic Order, Gorsedd of Bards, 1979–; Mem., Welsh Acad., 1981–; Vice-Pres., Llangollen Internat. Musical Eisteddfod, 1989–. Fellow, Royal Commonwealth Soc., 1988–. Editor, The European Teacher, 1964–69. *Publications:* The Old British Tongue, 1970; (ed and contrib.) Anatomy of Wales, 1972; (ed with M. Stephens) Writers of Wales, 1970– (75 titles published by 1991); (ed with R. Bromwich) Astudiaethau ar yr Hengerdd: studies in old Welsh poetry, 1978; Introducing Wales, 1978, 3rd edn 1988; Prifysgol Rhydychen a'i Chysylltiadau Cymreig, 1983; Certain Scholars of Wales, 1986; (ed with D. Ellis Evans) Cofio'r Dafydd, 1987; (contrib.) C. N. D. Cole, The New Wales, 1990; (introd.) Songs of Praises: the English hymns and elegies of William Williams Pantycelyn 1717–1791, 1991; articles and reviews in learned jls. *Recreations:* music, farming, walking. *Address:* Drovers Farm, Porthyrhyd, Llanwrda, Dyfed. *T:* Pumpsaint (05585) 649. *Club:* Commonwealth Trust.

JONES, Sir Robert (Edward), Kt 1989; Chairman, Robt Jones Investments Ltd, since 1982; sporting commentator; author; *b* 24 Nov. 1939; *s* of Edward Llewyllan and Joyce Lillian Jones; *m* 1984, Patricia Anne McGowan; two *s* two *d*. *Educ:* Victoria Univ. of Wellington. Self-employed as investor, 1960–; in 1982 floated public co., Robt Jones Investments, now NZ's 8th largest company with approx. NZ$ 2 billion of commercial buildings worldwide. Leader, New Zealand Party, Gen. Elect., 1984. *Publications:* Jones on Property, 1977, 6th edn 1979; NZ The Way I Want It, 1978; Travelling, 1980; Letters, 1981; The Permit (a philosophic novel), 1984; Wimp Walloping, 1989; Prancing Pavonine Charlatons, 1990; 80's Letters, 1990; Punchlines, 1991. *Recreations:* reading, writing, gardening, trout-fishing, travel. *Address:* Melling, Lower Hutt, New Zealand; Turangi, New Zealand; Sydney, Australia.

JONES, (Robert) Gerallt; writer; Warden of Gregynog Hall, University of Wales, since 1989; *b* 11 Sept. 1934; *s* of Rev. R. E. Jones and Elizabeth Jones, Nefyn, Wales; *m* 1962, Susan Lloyd Griffith; two *s* one *d*. *Educ:* Denstone; University of Wales (University Student Pres., 1956–57). Sen. English Master, Sir Thomas Jones Sch., Amlwch, 1957–60; Lectr in Educn, University Coll., Aberystwyth, 1961–65; Prin., Mandeville Teachers' Coll., Jamaica, 1965–67; Warden and Headmaster, Llandovery Coll., 1967–76; Fellow in Creative Writing, Univ. of Wales, 1976–77; Sen. Tutor, Extra-Mural Dept, UCW, Aberystwyth, 1979–89. Director: Sgrîn 82, 1981–; S4C, 1991–. Member: Gov. Body, Church in Wales, 1959–; Welsh Acad. (Yr Academi Gymreig), 1959– (Vice-Chm., 1981; Chm., 1982–87); Broadcasting Council for Wales; Welsh Arts Council; Univ. Council, Aberystwyth. FRSA. Editor: Impact (the Church in Wales quarterly); Taliesin, 1987–. Hugh McDiarmid Trophy, 1987; Welsh Arts Council Poetry Prize, 1990. *Publications: poetry:* Ymysg Y Drain, 1959; Cwlwm, 1962; Jamaican Landscape, 1969; Cysgodion, 1973; (ed) Poetry of Wales 1930–1970, 1975; Dyfal Gerddwyr y Maes, 1981; Cerddi 1955–89, 1989 (Poetry Prize, Welsh Arts Council, 1989): *novels:* Y Foel Fawr, 1960; Naddig Gwyn, 1963; Triptych, 1978; Cafflogion, 1979; *short stories:* Gwared Y Gwirion, 1966; *criticism:* Yn Frawd i'r Eos, 1962; (ed) Fy Nghymrul, 1962; The Welsh Literary Revival, 1966; T. S. Eliot, 1981; Dathlu, 1985; Seicoleg Cardota, 1989; *autobiography:* Jamaica, Y Flwyddyn Gyntaf, 1974; Bardsey, 1976; Jamaican Interlude, 1977; Murmur Llawer Man, 1980; *travel:* Teithiau Gerallt, 1978; Pererindota, 1978; *drama:* Tair Drama, 1988. *Recreations:* cricket, journalism. *Address:* Lerry Dale, Dolybont, Borth, Aberystwyth, Wales.

JONES, Robert Gwilym L.; *see* Lewis-Jones.

JONES, Robert Hefin, CVO 1969; PhD; Under Secretary, Education Department, Welsh Office, since 1980; *b* 30 June 1932; *s* of late Owen Henry and Elizabeth Jones, Blaenau Ffestiniog. *Educ:* Ysgol Sir Ffestiniog; University Coll. of Wales, Aberystwyth (BSc); University of London (PhD). Asst Master, Whitgift Sch., 1957–63; HM Inspector of Schools (Wales), 1963; seconded to Welsh Office as Sec., Prince of Wales Investiture Cttee, and Personal Asst to the Earl Marshal, 1967; Principal, Welsh Office, 1969, Asst Sec. 1972. *Recreations:* music, reading, cooking. *Address:* 34 The Grange, Llandaff, Cardiff CF5 2LH. *T:* Cardiff (0222) 564573.

JONES, Rev. (Robert William) Hugh; Moderator of the West Midland Province of the United Reformed Church (formerly of the Congregational Church in England and Wales), 1970–78, retired; *b* 6 May 1911; *s* of Evan Hugh Jones and Sarah Elizabeth Salmon; *m* 1st, 1939, Gaynor Eluned Evans (*d* 1974); one *s* one *d*; 2nd, 1979, Mary Charlotte Pulsford, *widow* of H. E. Pulsford, FIEE. *Educ:* Chester Grammar Sch.; Univs of Wales and Manchester; Lancashire Independent College. BA Wales, History and Philosophy. Ordained, 1939; Congregational Church: Welholme, Grimsby, 1939–45; Muswell Hill, London, 1945–49; Warwick Road, Coventry, 1949–61; Petts Wood, Orpington, 1961–69; President, Congregational Church in England and Wales, 1969–70; Minister, URC, Foleshill Road, Coventry, 1978–81. Broadcaster, radio and TV; Mem., BBC/ITA Central Religious Adv. Cttee, 1971–75. Guest preacher, USA. *Recreations:* painting, photography. *Address:* 24 Ashdene Gardens, Whitemoor Road, Kenilworth, Warwicks CV8 2TR.

JONES, Robin Francis McN.; *see* McNab Jones.

JONES, R(obin) Huws, CBE 1969; Associate Director, Joseph Rowntree Memorial Trust, 1972–76 (Consultant, 1976–78); *b* 1 May 1909; *m* 1944, Enid Mary Horton; one *s* two *d*. *Educ:* Liverpool Univ. Frances Wood Prizeman, Royal Statistical Society. Lectr, Social Science Dept, Liverpool Univ., 1937–39; Staff Tutor (City of Lincoln) Oxford Univ. Extra-mural Delegacy, 1939–47; Dir of Social Science Courses, University Coll., Swansea, 1948–61; Principal, Nat. Inst. for Social Work Training, 1961–72. Visiting Prof., University of Minnesota, 1964; Heath Clark Lectr, University of London, 1969. Member: Cttee on Local Authority and Allied Personal Social Services, 1965–68; NE Metropolitan Reg. Hosp. Bd, 1967–72; Chief Scientist's Cttee, DHSS, 1971–77; Scientific Advr to DHSS and to Welsh Office, 1977–82. Mem., Ciba Foundn Cttee on Compensation in Biomedical Research, 1979–80. Founder mem., Swansea Valley Project Cttee, 1961–. Pres., Internat. Assoc. of Schools of Social Work, 1976–80. Hon. Fellow, UC Swansea, 1986. Hon. LLD Wales, 1982. *Publications:* The Doctor and the Social Services, 1971; contributions to journals. *Recreation:* gardening. *Address:* 3 Clifton Lodge, York. *T:* York (0904) 655023.

JONES, Roger; *see* Jones, James R.

JONES, Ronald Christopher H.; *see* Hope-Jones.

JONES, Brigadier Ronald M.; *see* Montague-Jones.

JONES, Group Captain Royden Anthony; RAF retired; Regional Chairman of Industrial Tribunals, London (Central) Region, 1975–86; *b* 11 June 1925; *s* of Daniel Richard Glyndwr Jones and Hilda Margaret Jones (*née* Carruthers); *m* 1st, 1948, Krystyna Emilia Kumor (decd); one *s*; 2nd, 1955, Peggy Elizabeth Martin; one *s*. *Educ:* Torquay Grammar Sch. Trooper, Household Cavalry, 1943; RMC, Sandhurst, 1944; Captain, Arab Legion armoured car squadron, 1945–48. Qualified as solicitor, 1949; joined RAF Legal Services as prosecuting officer, 1950; RAF Staff Coll., 1961; served as Dep. Dir of Legal Services (RAF), in Cyprus and Germany, retiring as Gp Captain, 1975. *Publication:* Manual of Law for Kenya Armed Forces, 1971. *Recreations:* country pursuits, reading, house maintenance, photography. *Address:* Hill Top House, Staunton Harold, Ashby-de-la-Zouch, Leics LE6 5RW. *T:* Melbourne (0332) 862583. *Club:* Royal Air Force.

JONES, Samuel; Town Clerk, City of London, since 1991; *b* 27 Dec. 1939; *s* of Samuel Jones and Sarah Johnston Jones (*née* McCulloch); *m* 1964, Jean Ann Broadhurst; two *d*. *Educ:* Morpeth Grammar Sch.; Manchester Univ. (LLB); Kent Univ. (MA). Admitted Solicitor, 1964. Asst Solicitor, Macclesfield Bor. Council, 1964–67; Asst Town Clerk, Bedford Bor. Council, 1967–71; Head of Legal Div., Coventry CBC, 1971–73; Head of Admin and Legal Dept, Sheffield Dist Council, 1973–76; Chief Exec. and County Clerk, Leics CC, and Clerk of Lieutenancy, 1976–91. *Recreations:* dog and coastal walking. *Address:* Chapel Knoll, 26 Hobbs Hill, Croyde EX33 1LZ. *T:* Croyde (0271) 890210.

JONES, Schuyler, DPhil; Curator, Pitt Rivers Museum, and Head of Department of Ethnology and Prehistory, Oxford University, since 1985; *b* 7 Feb. 1930; *s* of Schuyler Jones Jr and Ignace Mead Jones; *m* 1955, Lis Margit Søndergaard Rasmussen; one *s* one *d*. *Educ:* Edinburgh Univ. (MA Hons Anthropology); Oxford Univ. (DPhil Anthropology). Anthropological expeditions to: Atlas Mountains, Southern Algeria, French West Africa, Nigeria, 1951; French Equatorial Africa, Belgian Congo, 1952; East and Southern Africa, 1953; Morocco High Atlas, Algeria, Sahara, Niger River, 1954; Turkey, Iran, Afghanistan, Pakistan, India, Nepal, 1958–59; ten expeditions to Nuristan in the Hindu Kush, 1960–70; to Chinese Turkestan, 1985; Tibet and Gobi Desert, 1986; Southern China, Xinjiang, and Pakistan, 1988. Asst Curator, Pitt Rivers Mus., 1970–71; Asst Curator and Univ. Lectr in Ethnology, 1971–85. Mem. Council, Royal Anthropological Inst., 1986–89. Trustee, Horniman Mus., 1989–. *Publications:* Sous le Soleil Africain, 1955 (Under the African Sun, 1956); Annotated Bibliography of Nuristan (Kafiristan) and The Kalash Kafirs of Chitral, pt 1 1966, pt 2 1969; The Political Organization of the Kam Kafirs, 1967; Men of Influence in Nuristan, 1974; (jtly) Nuristan, 1979; numerous articles. *Recreation:* travel in remote places. *Address:* Old Close Cottage, Chapel Lane, Enstone OX7 4LY. *T:* Enstone (060872) 453.

JONES, Air Cdre Shirley Ann, CBE 1990; Director, Women's Royal Air Force, 1986–89; *d* of late Wilfred Esmond Jones, FRICS, and Louise May Betty Jones (*née* Dutton). *Educ:* Micklefield Sch., Seaford, Sussex. Joined Royal Air Force, 1962; commnd 1962; served UK and Libya, 1962–71; Netherlands and UK, 1971–74; sc 1975; served UK, 1975–82; Dep. Dir, 1982–86. ADC 1986–89. *Recreations:* golf, music, gardening, cookery. *Club:* Royal Air Force.

JONES, Sir Simon (Warley Frederick) Benton, 4th Bt *cr* 1919; *b* 11 Sept. 1941; *o s* of Sir Peter Fawcett Benton Jones, 3rd Bt, OBE, and Nancy (*d* 1974), *d* of late Warley Pickering; *S* father, 1972; *m* 1966, Margaret Fiona, *d* of David Rutherford Dickson; three *s* two *d*. *Educ:* Eton; Trinity College, Cambridge (MA). JP for Lincolnshire (parts of Kesteven), 1971; High Sheriff, Lincs, 1977. *Heir: s* James Peter Martin Benton Jones, *b* 1 Jan. 1973. *Address:* Irnham Hall, Grantham, Lincs. *T:* Corby Glen (047684) 212; Sopley, Christchurch, Dorset.

JONES, Stephen Barry; MP (Lab) Alyn and Deeside, since 1983 (Flint East, 1970–83); *b* 1938; *s* of late Stephen and Grace Jones, Mancot, Flintshire; *m* Janet Jones (*née* Davies); one *s*. PPS to Rt Hon. Denis Healey, 1972–74; Parly Under-Sec. of State for Wales, 1974–79; Opposition spokesman on employment, 1980–83; Chief Opposition spokesman on Wales, 1983–87, 1988–. Mem., Labour Shadow Cabinet, 1983–87 and 1988–. *Address:* House of Commons, SW1A 0AA. *T:* 071–219 3556. *Clubs:* Connah's Quay Labour Party, Shotton Royal British Legion.

JONES, Stephen Morris; Chief Executive, Wigan Metropolitan Borough Council, since 1990; *b* 12 March 1948; *s* of Owain Morris Jones and late Sylvia Blanche Jones (*née* Moss); *m* 1970, Rosemary Diana Pilgrim; one *s* two *d*. *Educ:* Univ. of Manchester (BA Hons Town Planning, 1970). MRTPI 1972. Asst Chief Exec., Bolton MBC, 1978–85; Chief Exec., Blackburn BC, 1985–90. Mem., Soc. of Local Govt Chief Execs, 1985–. *Recreations:* family, walking, sport, reading. *Address:* Wigan Metropolitan Borough Council, New Town Hall, PO Box 36, Library Street, Wigan WN1 1NN. *T:* Wigan (0942) 827000.

JONES, S(tuart) Lloyd; *b* 26 Aug. 1917; *s* of Hugh and Edna Lloyd Jones, Liverpool; *m* 1942, Pamela Mary Hamilton-Williams, Heswall; one *s* three *d*. *Educ:* Rydal Sch.; Univ. of Liverpool. Solicitor, 1940; Dep. Town Clerk, Nottingham, 1950–53; Town Clerk of Plymouth, 1953–70; Chief Exec. Officer and Town Clerk of Cardiff, 1970–74; Chm., Welsh Health Technical Services Orgn, 1973–76. Chief Counting Officer, Welsh Referendum, 1979. US State Dept Foreign Leader Scholarship, 1962. One of Advisers to Minister of Housing and Local Govt on Amalgamation of London Boroughs, 1962; Indep. Inspector, extension of Stevenage New Town, 1964; Member: Adv. Cttee on Urban Transport Manpower, 1967–69; Cttee on Public Participation in Planning, 1969; PM's Cttee on Local Govt Rules of Conduct, 1973–74. Pres., Soc. of Town Clerks, 1972. Chm. of Governors, Plymouth Polytechnic, 1982–87. Hon. Fellow, Plymouth Polytechnic, 1987. Distinguished Services Award, Internat. City Management Assoc., 1976. *Recreations:* sailing, bookbinding. *Address:* High Dolphin, Dittisham, near Dartmouth, Devon TQ6 0HR. *T:* Dittisham (080422) 224. *Club:* Royal Western Yacht Club of England (Plymouth).

JONES, Terence Leavesley; Under-Secretary, Department of the Environment, 1974–84; *b* 24 May 1926; *s* of late Reginald Arthur Jones and Grace Jones; *m* 1966, Barbara Hall; one *s*. *Educ:* Nottingham High Sch.; Jesus Coll., Cambridge (MA). RNVR, 1944–46 (Sub-Lt). Asst Inspector of Ancient Monuments, Min. of Works, 1949; Principal, 1957;

Sec., Historic Buildings Council for England, 1961–67; Asst Sec., 1967; on loan to Housing Corp., 1979–81. *Recreations:* music, archæology. *Address:* Meadow View, Woodlands Road, Mildenhall, Marlborough, Wilts SN8 2LP. *T:* Marlborough (0672) 512481.

JONES, Prof. Terence Valentine; Donald Schultz Professor of Turbomachinery, Oxford University and Professorial Fellow, St Catherine's College, since 1988; *b* 14 Feb. 1939; *s* of Albert Duncalf Jones and Frances Jones; *m* 1962, Lesley Lillian (*née* Hughes); one *s* one *d. Educ:* William Hulme's Grammar School, Manchester; Lincoln College, Oxford (MA, DPhil 1966). Lecturer: Keble College, Oxford, 1971–77; Lincoln College, Oxford, 1976–80; Jesus College, Oxford, 1977–86; Rolls Royce Tutorial Fellow, St Anne's College, Oxford, 1979–88. Senior Academic Visitor, NASA Lewis Research Center, Ohio, 1986. *Publications:* articles on turbomachinery, heat transfer and fluid dynamics in NATO, ASME and ARC jls and conf. procs. *Recreations:* running, hiking. *Address:* Department of Engineering Science, Parks Road, Oxford OX1 3PJ. *T:* Oxford (0865) 246561.

JONES, Terry, (Terence Graham Parry Jones); writer, film director and occasional performer; *b* 1 Feb. 1942; *s* of Alick George Parry Jones and Dilys Louisa Newnes; *m* Alison Telfer; one *s* one *d. Educ:* Esher C of E Primary Sch.; Royal Grammar Sch., Guildford; St Edmund Hall, Oxford. *Television:* wrote for various TV shows, 1966–68; wrote and performed in series: Do Not Adjust Your Set, 1968–69; The Complete and Utter History of Britain, 1969; Monty Python's Flying Circus, 1969–75; wrote (with Michael Palin): Secrets (play), BBC TV, 1974; Ripping Yarns, 1976–79; presented: Paperbacks, BBC TV; Victorian Values, BBC Radio; wrote and directed The Rupert Bear Story (documentary), 1981; wrote, directed and presented, So This Is Progress, BBC TV, 1991. *Films:* And Now For Something Completely Different, 1971; directed (with Terry Gilliam), co-wrote and performed, Monty Python and the Holy Grail, 1975; directed, co-wrote and performed: Monty Python's Life of Brian, 1978; Monty Python's Meaning of Life, 1983 (Grand Prix Spécial du Jury, Cannes); directed Personal Services, 1986; wrote, directed and performed, Erik the Viking, 1989. *Publications:* Chaucer's Knight, 1980, 3rd edn 1984; Fairy Tales, 1981, 4th edn 1987; The Saga of Erik the Viking, 1983, 3rd edn 1986; Nicobobinus, 1985, 2nd edn 1987; Goblins of the Labyrinth, 1986; The Curse of the Vampire's Socks, 1988; Attacks of Opinion, 1988; (with Michael Palin): Dr Fegg's Encyclopeadia (sic) of all World Knowledge, etc.; Ripping Yarns, etc.; contrib. to the various Monty Python books. *Recreation:* sleeping. *Address:* 68A Delancey Street, NW1 7RY.

JONES, Thomas E.; *see* Elder-Jones.

JONES, Thomas Glanville; a Recorder of the Crown Court, since 1972; *b* 10 May 1931; *s* of late Evan James and Margaret Olive Jones; Welsh; *m* 1964, Valma Shirley Jones; three *s. Educ:* St Clement Dane's Grammar Sch.; University Coll., London (LLB). Called to Bar, 1956. Sec., Swansea Law Library Assoc., 1963; Exec. Mem., Swansea Festival of Music and the Arts, 1967; Chm., Guild for Promotion of Welsh Music, 1970; Chm., Jt Professional Cttees of Swansea Local Bar and Swansea Law Soc. and W. Wales Law Soc.; Mem., Grand Theatre Trust. *Recreations:* Welsh culture, Rugby, reading, music, poetry, gardening. *Address:* Angel Chambers, 94 Walter Road, Swansea SA1 5QA. *T:* Swansea (0792) 464623; Gelligron, 12 Eastcliff, Southgate, Swansea SA3 2AS. *T:* Bishopston (044128) 3118. *Club:* Ffynone (Swansea).

JONES, Ven. (Thomas) Hughie; Archdeacon of Loughborough, since 1986; *b* 15 Aug. 1927; *s* of Edward Teifi Jones and Ellen Jones; *m* 1949, Beryl Joan Henderson; two *d. Educ:* William Hulme's Grammar School, Manchester; Univ. of Wales (BA); Univ. of London (BD); Univ. of Leicester (MA). Warden and Lectr, Bible Trng Inst., Glasgow, 1949–54; Minister, John Street Baptist Church, Glasgow, 1951–54; RE specialist, Leicester and Leics schs, 1955–63; Sen. Lectr in RE, Leicester Coll. of Educn, 1964–70; Vice-Principal, Bosworth Coll., 1970–75; Principal, Hind Leys College, Leics, 1975–81; Rector, The Langtons and Stonton Wyville, 1981–86. Hon. Canon of Leicester Cathedral, 1983. Vice-Chm., Ecclesiastical Law Soc.; Mem., Selden Soc. *Publications:* (contrib. OT articles) New Bible Dictionary, 1962, 2nd edn 1980; Old Testament and religious education articles in relevant jls. *Recreations:* entomology, genealogy, Welsh interests, canon law. *Address:* The Archdeaconry, 21 Church Road, Glenfield, Leicester LE3 8DP. *T:* Leicester (0533) 311632. *Clubs:* Carlton; Leicestershire (Leicester); Leicestershire County Cricket, Leicester Sporting; Millbank.

JONES, Sir (Thomas) Philip, Kt 1986; CB 1978; Chairman: Total Oil Marine plc, since 1990; Total Oil Holdings, since 1991; *b* 13 July 1931; *s* of William Ernest Jones and Mary Elizabeth Jones; *m* 1955, Mary Phillips; two *s. Educ:* Cowbridge Grammar Sch.; Jesus Coll., Oxford (MA; Hon. Fellow, 1990). 2nd Lieut, Royal Artillery, 1953–55; Asst Principal, Min. of Supply, 1955; Principal Min. of Aviation, 1959; on loan to HM Treasury, 1964–66; Principal Private Sec. to Minister of Aviation, 1966–67; Asst Sec., Min. of Technology, subseq. Min. of Aviation Supply, 1967–71; Under Secretary, DTI, 1971; Under Sec., 1974, Dep. Sec., 1976–83, Dept of Energy; Chm., Electricity Council, 1983–90. Chm., Dames, Moore, Barry; Director: Ivo Energy Ltd, 1990–; Gas Transmission Ltd, 1990–. Member: BNOC, 1980–82; BOTB, 1985–88. Chm., Nationalized Industries' Chairmen's Gp, 1986–87. Gov., Henley Management Coll., 1986–. Freeman, City of London, 1986. CBIM 1983; CompIEE 1987. FRSA 1987. *Recreations:* walking, reading, watching Rugby football. *Address:* 16 Herald's Place, Kennington, SE11 4NP. *Clubs:* Travellers', Royal Over-Seas League.

JONES, Sir Trevor; *see* Jones, Sir O. T.

JONES, Trevor David K.; *see* Kent-Jones.

JONES, Prof. Vaughan Frederick Randal, FRS 1990; Professor of Mathematics, University of California, Berkeley, since 1985; *b* Gisborne, NZ, 31 Dec. 1952; *s* of J. H. Jones and J. A. Goodfellow (*née* Collins); *m* 1979, Martha Weare Jones (*née* Myers); one *s* two *d. Educ:* St Peter's Sch., Cambridge, NZ; Auckland Grammar Sch.; Univ. of Auckland (schol.; Gillies schol.; Phillips Industries Bursary; BSc, MSc 1st Cl. Hons); Ecole de Physique, Geneva (Swiss Govt schol.; F. W. W. Rhodes Meml schol.); Ecole de Mathématiques, Geneva (DèsSc Mathematics); Vacheron Constantin Prize, Univ. de Genève. Asst, Univ. de Genève, 1975–80; E. R. Hedrick Asst Prof., UCLA, 1980–81; University of Pennsylvania: Vis. Lectr, 1981–82; Asst Prof., 1981–84; Associate Prof., 1984–85. Alfred P. Sloan Res. Fellowship, 1983; Guggenheim Fellowship, 1986. Fields Medal, 1990. *Publication:* Coxeter graphs and Towers of algebras, 1989. *Recreations:* music, tennis, squash, ski-ing. *Address:* Mathematics Department, University College Berkeley, Berkeley, Calif 94720, USA. *T:* (415) 642–4196.

JONES, Vera June, (Mrs Ernest Brynmor Jones); *see* Di Palma, V. J.

JONES, Most Rev. Walter Heath; *see* Rupert's Land, Archbishop and Metropolitan of.

JONES, Wilfred, CMG 1982; HM Diplomatic Service, retired; *b* 29 Nov. 1926; *m* 1952, Millicent Beresford; two *s.* Joined Foreign Office, 1949; served in Tamsui, Jedda, Brussels, Athens and FCO, 1950–66; First Sec. (Admin), Canberra, 1966–68; FCO, 1968–71; Copenhagen, 1971–74, Blantyre, 1974–75; Lilongwe, 1975–77; FCO, 1977–81; High Comr to Botswana, 1981–86. *Recreations:* sailing, golf, tennis. *Address:* Conifers, 16 The Hummicks, Dock Lane, Beaulieu, Hants SO4 7YJ. *Club:* RAF Yacht.

JONES, William Armand Thomas Tristan G.; *see* Garel-Jones.

JONES, Sir (William) Emrys, Kt 1971; BSc; Principal, Royal Agricultural College, Cirencester, 1973–78, now Principal Emeritus; *b* 6 July 1915; *s* of late William Jones and Mary Ann (*née* Morgan); *m* 1938, Megan Ann Morgan (marr. diss., 1966); three *s*; *m* 1967, Gwyneth George. *Educ:* Llandovery Gram. Sch.; University Coll. of Wales, Aberystwyth. Agricultural Instr, Gloucester CC, 1940–46; Provincial Grassland Adv. Officer, NAAS, Bristol, 1946–50; County Agricultural Officer, Gloucester, 1950–54; Dep. Dir, 1954–57, Dir 1957–59, NAAS, Wales; Sen. Advisory Officer, NAAS, 1959–61; Dir, 1961–66; Dir-Gen., Agricultural Develt and Adv. Service (formerly Chief Agricl Advr), MAFF, 1967–73. Mem., Adv. Council for Agriculture and Horticulture in England and Wales, 1973–79. Independent Chm., Nat. Cattle Breeders' Assoc., 1976–79. Dir, North and East Midlands Reg. Bd, Lloyds Bank, 1978–86. Hon. LLD Wales, 1973; Hon. DSc Bath, 1975. *Recreations:* golf, shooting. *Address:* 18 St Mary's Park, Louth, Lincs LN11 0EF. *T:* Louth (0507) 602043. *Club:* Farmers'.

JONES, William George Tilston; independent telecommunications consultant, since 1990; *b* 7 Jan. 1942; *s* of late Thomas Tilston Jones and of Amy Ethel Jones; *m* 1965, Fiona Mary; one *d. Educ:* Portsmouth Grammar School; Portsmouth Polytechnic (BSc; Hon. Fellow 1989). CEng, FIEE. Post Office Engineering Dept, 1960; Head, Electronic Switching Gp, 1969; Head, System X Develt Div., 1978; Dir, System Evolution and Standards, 1983; Chief Exec., Technology, BT, 1984; seconded as Exec. in Residence, Internat. Management Inst., Geneva, 1987; Sen. Strategy Adviser, BT, 1988. Member: IEE Electronics Divl Bd, 1984–89; Parly IT Cttee, 1985–87; Chairman: IT Adv. Bd, Polytechnic of Central London, 1984–87; Adv. Gp, Centre of Communication and Information Studies, 1988–89; SE Centre, IEE, 1989–90; Dir, Technology Studies, British Telecom, 1988–90. Governor, Polytechnic of Central London, 1985–89. *Publications:* contribs on telecommunications to learned jls. *Recreations:* theatre, tennis, camping, making furniture. *Address:* Primavera, 1a The Drive, Radlett, Herts WD7 7DA. *T:* Radlett (0923) 854448.

JONES, William Pearce A.; *see* Andreae-Jones.

JONES, Wyn; *see* Jones, Graham W.

JONES, Wyn; *see* Jones, Gwilym W.

JONES, Sir Wynn Normington H.; *see* Hugh-Jones.

JONES PARRY, Dr Emyr; HM Diplomatic Service; Head, European Community Department (External), Foreign and Commonwealth Office, since 1989; *b* 21 Sept. 1947; *s* of Hugh Jones Parry and Eirwen Jones Parry (*née* Davies); *m* 1971, Lynn Noble; two *s. Educ:* Gwedraeth Grammar Sch.; University Coll. Cardiff (BSc, Dip Crystallography); St Catharine's Coll., Cambridge (PhD). FO, 1973–74; First Sec., Ottawa, 1974–79; FCO, 1979–82; First Sec., UK Rep. to EC, Brussels, 1982–86; Dep. Head, Office of Pres. of European Parlt, 1987–89. *Publications:* various scientific articles. *Recreations:* gardening, theatre, reading, sport. *Address:* Foreign and Commonwealth Office, King Charles Street, SW1A 2AH. *Club:* Glamorgan County Cricket.

JONES-PARRY, Sir Ernest, Kt 1978; *b* 16 July 1908; *o s* of late John Parry and Charlotte Jones, Rhuddlan; *m* 1938, Mary Powell; two *s. Educ:* St Asaph; University of Wales; University of London. MA (Wales) 1932; PhD (London) 1934; FRHistS. Lecturer in History, University Coll. of Wales, 1935–40; Ministry of Food, 1941; Treasury, 1946–47; Asst Sec., Ministry of Food, 1948–57; Under Sec., 1957; Dir of Establishments, Ministry of Agriculture, Fisheries and Food, 1957–61. Exec. Director: Internat. Sugar Council, 1965–68; Internat. Sugar Orgn, 1969–78. *Publications:* The Spanish Marriages, 1841–46, 1936; The Correspondence of Lord Aberdeen and Princess Lieven, 1832–1854 (2 vols), 1938–39; articles and reviews in History and English Historical Review. *Recreations:* reading, watching cricket. *Address:* Flat 3, 34 Sussex Square, Brighton, Sussex BN2 5AD. *T:* Brighton (0273) 688894. *Club:* Athenæum.

JONES-WILLIAMS, Dafydd Wyn, OBE 1970; MC 1942; TD 1954; DL; Commissioner for Local Administration for Wales (Local Ombudsman), 1974–79; *b* 13 July 1916; *s* of late J. Jones-Williams, Dolgellau; *m* 1945, Rosemary Sally, *e d* of late A. E. Councell, Blaenau Hall, Rhydymain; two *d. Educ:* Dolgellau Grammar Sch.; UCW Aberystwyth (LLB). Served 1939–45 with HAC and X Royal Hussars (Western Desert). Formerly comdg 446 (Royal Welch) AB, LAA Regt, RA (TA). Solicitor, 1939. Clerk of County Council, Clerk of Peace, and Clerk to Lieutenancy, Merioneth, 1954–70; Circuit Administrator, Wales and Chester Circuit, 1970–74. Member: Hughes-Parry Cttee on Legal Status of Welsh Language, 1963–65; Lord Chancellor's Adv. Cttee on Trng of Magistrates, 1974–81; Council on Tribunals, 1980–86; BBC Gen. Adv. Council, 1979–85. Formerly: Mem., Nature Conservancy (Chm., Cttee for Wales); Mem., Nat. Broadcasting Council for Wales; Chm., Merioneth and Montgomeryshire T&AFA. DL Merioneth, 1958. *Recreations:* golf, snooker, reading. *Address:* Bryncoedifor, Rhydymain, near Dolgellau, Gwynedd LL40 2AN. *T:* Rhydymain (034141) 635. *Clubs:* Royal St Davids Golf, Dolgellau Golf.

JONKMAN, (Pieter Jan) Hans, Hon. GCVO 1982; Commander, Order of Orange Nassau; Cross of Honour, Order of House of Orange Nassau; Secretary-General of the Permanent Court of Arbitration, The Hague, since 1990; *b* 2 June 1925; *s* of Jan A. Jonkman and Johanna L. M. de Bruïne; *m* 1959, Maria Elisabeth te Winkel; one *s* two *d. Educ:* Univ. of Leyden (law degree). Entered Min. of Foreign Affairs, 1955; served Paris, Pretoria, Leopoldville, Buenos Aires; Min. of Foreign Affairs, 1962–66; Brussels, Beirut, Jakarta; Min. of Foreign Affairs, 1975–80; Grand-Officer for Special Services of HM Queen of the Netherlands, 1980–82; Grand-Master, House of The Queen, 1982–87; Ambassador of the Netherlands to UK and concurrently to Iceland, 1987–90. Holds various foreign decorations. *Address:* Peace Palace, Carnegie-plein 2, The Hague 2517 KJ, Netherlands. *T:* 3469680. *Clubs:* Dutch; Societeit de Witte (The Hague).

JONZEN, Mrs Karin, FRBS; sculptor; *b* London (Swedish parents), 22 Dec. 1914; *d* of U. Löwenadler and G. Munck av Fulkila; *m* 1944, Basil Jonzen (*d* 1967); one *s*; *m* 1972, Åke Sucksdorff. Studied Slade Sch., 1933; Slade Dipl. and Scholarship, 1937; studied Royal Academy, Stockholm, 1939. Lectr, Camden Arts Centre, 1968–72; extra mural lectures in art appreciation, London Univ., 1965–71. Mem. Accad. delle Arte e Lavore, Parma, Italy, 1980 (Gold Medal, 1980); Diploma of Merit, Università delle Arti, Parma, 1982; Gold Medal, Internat. Parliament for Safety and Peace, USA, 1983; Silver Medal, RBS, 1983. *Works in municipal museums and art galleries:* Tate Gall., Bradford, Brighton, Glasgow, Southend, Liverpool, Melbourne, Andrew White Museum, Cornell Univ., USA. *Works commissioned by:* Arts Council (reclining figure in terracotta), 1950; Festival of Britain for sports pavilion (standing figure), 1950; Modern Schs in Leics and Hertford,

1953 and Cardiff, 1954 (animals and figures in terracotta and stone); Selwyn Coll. Chapel, Cambridge (over-life size ascension group, bronze), 1956; St Michael's Church, Golders Green (carving on exterior), 1959; Arts Council (life size bronze mother and child for a housing estate in Lewisham), 1959; Guildford Cathedral (carving on exterior), 1961; WHO HQ, New Delhi (life size bronze torso), 1963 (gift of British Govt); St Mary le Bow, Cheapside (Madonna and child), 1969; City of London Corp. for London Wall site (life size bronze figure), 1971; Guildhall Forecourt (over-life size bronze group), 1972; Sadler's Wells Theatre (bronze of Dame Ninette de Valois, a gift from the sculptor), 1974; Swedish Church, Marylebone (three-quarter life size Pietà, bronze resin), 1975; Action Research (annual trophy), 1979; Cadogan Estate (figure of young girl for Sloane Gardens), 1981; St Mary and St Margaret Church, South Harting, Hants (Madonna and child), 1985; St Saviour's Church, Warwick Ave (Madonna and child), 1986; Nat. Portrait Gall. (over life size bronze of Lord Constantine), 1989; St Anne and St Mary Church, Lewes (St Anne and St Mary gp), 1990. *Works exhibited by invitation:* Battersea Park open air exhibns, 1948–51; Tate Gall., 1957–59; City of London Festival, 1968; (one man exhibn) Fieldbourne Gall., London, 1974; Poole Wills Gall., NY, 1983. *Portrait busts include:* Sir Alan Herbert, Lord Constantine (purchased by Nat. Portrait Gall.), Dame Ninette de Valois, Sir Hugh Casson, Donald Trelford, Sir Monty Finniston, Samuel Pepys (over-life size bronze, Seething Lane, EC3), Max von Sydow, Yuki. *Relevant publication:* Karin Jonzen: sculptor, introd. Carel Weight, foreword by Norman St John-Stevas, 1976. *Recreations:* music, travel. *Address:* The Studio, 6A Gunter Grove, SW10.

JOPE, Prof. Edward Martyn, FBA 1965; FSA 1946; MRIA 1973; Professor of Archæology, The Queen's University of Belfast, 1963–81, now Emeritus; Visiting Professor in Archaeological Sciences, University of Bradford, 1974–81, Honorary Visiting Professor, since 1982; *b* 28 Dec. 1915; *s* of Edward Mallet Jope and Frances Margaret (*née* Chapman); *m* 1941, Margaret Halliday; no *c.* *Educ:* Kingswood Sch., Bath; Oriel Coll., Oxford. Staff of Royal Commission on Ancient Monuments (Wales), 1938; Biochemist, Nuffield and MRC Grants, 1940; Queen's Univ., Belfast: Lectr in Archæology, 1949; Reader, 1954. Member: Ancient Monuments Adv. Coun. (NI), 1950; Royal Commission on Ancient Monuments (Wales), 1963–86; Sci.-based Archaeology Cttee, SRC, 1976–82; Ancient Monuments Bd (England), 1980–84; Pres. Section H, British Assoc., 1965. Rhys Res. Fellow and Vis. Sen. Res. Fellow, Jesus Coll., Oxford, 1977–78. Lectures: Munro, Edinburgh, 1953; O'Donnell, Oxford, 1968; Rhŷs, British Acad., 1987. Hon. DSc Bradford, 1980. *Publications:* Early Celtic Art in the British Isles, 1977; (ed) Studies in Building History, 1961; (ed and contrib.) Archaeological Survey of Co. Down, 1966; papers in Biochem. Jl, Proc. RSocMed, Phil. Trans Royal Soc., Spectrochemica Acta, Trans Faraday Soc., Proc. Prehistoric Soc., Antiquaries' Jl, Medieval Archæology, Oxoniensia, Ulster Jl of Archæology, Proc. Soc. of Antiquaries of Scotland, etc. *Recreations:* music, travel. *Address:* 1 Chalfont Road, Oxford.

JOPLING, Rt. Hon. (Thomas) Michael; PC 1979; MP (C) Westmorland and Lonsdale, since 1983 (Westmorland, 1964–83); farmer; *b* 10 Dec. 1930; *s* of Mark Bellerby Jopling, Masham, Yorks; *m* 1958, Gail, *d* of Ernest Dickinson, Harrogate; two *s.* *Educ:* Cheltenham Coll.; King's Coll., Newcastle upon Tyne (BSc Agric.). Mem., Thirsk Rural District Council, 1958–64; contested Wakefield (C), 1959; Mem. National Council, National Farmers' Union, 1962–64. Jt Sec., Cons. Parly Agric. Cttee, 1966–70; PPS to Minister of Agriculture, 1970–71; an Asst Govt Whip, 1971–73; a Lord Comr, HM Treasury, 1973–74; an Opposition Whip, March-June 1974; an Opposition spokesman on agriculture, 1974–75, 1976–79; Shadow Minister of Agriculture, 1975–76; Parly Sec. to HM Treasury, and Chief Whip, 1979–83; Minister of Agriculture, Fisheries and Food, 1983–87. Mem., Select Cttee on Foreign Affairs, 1987–. Hon. Sec., British Amer. Parly Gp, 1987– (Vice Chm., 1983–86). Mem., UK Exec., Commonwealth Parly Assoc., 1974–79, 1987– (Vice Chm., 1977–79). Pres. Councils, EEC Agric. and Fishery Ministers, July–Dec. 1986. Pres., Auto Cycle Union, 1990–. *Address:* Ainderby Hall, Thirsk, North Yorks. *T:* Thirsk (0845) 567224; Clyder Howe Cottage, Windermere, Cumbria. *T:* Windermere (09662) 2590. *Clubs:* Beefsteak, Buck's.

JORDAN, Dr Carole, FRS 1990; FInstP; Wolfson Tutorial Fellow in Natural Science, Somerville College, Oxford, and University Lecturer, Department of Theoretical Physics, Oxford, since 1976; *b* 19 July 1941; *d* of Reginald Sidney Jordan and Ethel May Jordan (*née* Waller). *Educ:* Harrow County Grammar School for Girls; University College London (BSc 1962; PhD 1965; Fellow 1991). FInstP 1973. Post-Doctoral Research Associate, Jt Inst. for Lab. Astrophysics, Boulder, Colorado, 1966; Asst Lectr, Dept of Astronomy, UCL, attached to Culham Lab., UKAEA, 1966–69; Astrophysics Research Unit, SRC, 1969–76. Mem., SERC, 1985–90 (Chm., Solar System Cttee, 1983–86; Mem., Astronomy, Space and Radio Bd, 1979–82, 1982–86). Sec., Royal Astronomical Soc., 1981–90 (Vice-Pres., 1990–91). *Publications:* scientific papers on astrophysical plasma spectroscopy and structure and energy balance in cool star coronae, in learned jls. *Address:* Department of Theoretical Physics, 1 Keble Road, Oxford OX1 3NP. *T:* Oxford (0865) 273980.

JORDAN, David Harold, CMG 1975; MBE 1962; *b* Sunderland, 27 Oct. 1924; *er s* of late H. G. Jordan, OBE, and Gwendolyn (*née* Rees); *m* 1st, 1951, Lorna Mary Holland (marr. diss.), *er d* of late W. R. Harvey; three *s* one *d*; 2nd, 1971, Penelope Amanda, *d* of late Lt-Col B. L. J. Davy, OBE, TD; one *d.* *Educ:* Roundhay Sch., Leeds; Berkhamsted; Magdalen Coll., Oxford (1st Cl. Chinese), MA 1956. 9th Gurkha Rifles, Indian Army, 1943–47. HMOCS (Hong Kong), 1951–79: Chinese Language Sch., Univ. of Hong Kong, 1951–52; Asst Sec. for Chinese Affairs, 1952–55; Colonial Secretariat, 1956–68: Asst Sec., 1956–60; jssc 1960; Defence Sec., 1961–66; Dep. Dir, Commerce and Industry, 1968–70; Dep. Economic Sec., 1970–71; Dep. Financial Sec., 1971–72; Dir of Commerce and Industry, later Trade, Industry and Customs, and MLC, Hong Kong, 1972–79. *Address:* The Lower Farm, Drayton Parslow, Milton Keynes, Bucks MK17 0JS. *T:* Mursley (0296) 720688. *Clubs:* Hong Kong; Royal Hong Kong Jockey.

JORDAN, Douglas Arthur, CMG 1977; Senior Partner, Douglas Jordan Consultants, since 1991; *b* 28 Sept. 1918; *s* of late Arthur Jordan and Elizabeth Jordan; *m* 1st, 1940, Violet Nancy (*née* Houston); one *d*; 2nd, 1970, Constance Dorothy (*née* Wallis). *Educ:* East Ham Grammar Sch., London. HM Customs and Excise: Officer, 1938; Surveyor, 1953; Inspector, 1960; Asst Collector, Manchester and London, 1962–68; Sen. Inspector, 1968–69; Chief Investigation Officer, 1969–77; Dep. Comr, 1977–79, Comr of Customs and Controls, 1979, Trade, Industry and Customs Dept, Hong Kong (Comr of Customs and Excise, Customs and Excise Dept, 1982–84); Special Anti-Piracy Advr, SE Asia, 1984, Customs and Anti-Piracy Consultant, 1985–90, Internat. Fedn of Phonogram and Videogram Producers. Freeman, City of London, 1964. *Recreations:* golf, music. *Address:* 10 Crouchmans Close, Sydenham Hill, SE26 6ST. *T:* 081–670 9638. *Clubs:* Wig and Pen, Commonwealth Trust; Dulwich and Sydenham Golf.

JORDAN, Francis Leo, (Frank), CBE 1989; QPM 1982; Chief Constable of Kent, 1982–89, retired; Member, Parole Board, since 1990; *b* 15 June 1930; *s* of Leo Thomas and Mary Jordan; *m* 1951, Ruth Ashmore; one *s* two *d.* *Educ:* St Joseph's Coll., Trent Vale, Stoke-on-Trent. CBIM. Staffordshire Police to rank of Chief Supt, 1950; seconded to Cyprus Police during EOKA emergency, 1956–58; Sen. Course in Criminology, Cambridge Univ., 1972; Sen. Comd Course, Police Staff Coll., 1973; Staff Officer to Home Office Police Inspectorate, 1975; Asst Chief Constable, West Midlands Police, 1976; Dep. Chief Constable of Kent, 1979. Mem., Kent County Cttee, SSAFA, 1985–89. FRSA 1990. OStJ 1988. *Recreations:* walking, old buildings, churches, etc, shooting. *Club:* Royal Over-Seas League.

JORDAN, Gerard Michael, CEng; Director, Dounreay Nuclear Power Establishment, United Kingdom Atomic Energy Authority, since 1987; *b* 25 Sept. 1929; *s* of Arthur Thomas and Ruby Eveline Jordan; *m* 1955, Vera Peers; one *s* one *d.* *Educ:* Grange Sch., Birkenhead; Univ. of Liverpool. BEng; CEng, MIMechE, 1974. Marine Engrg Officer, 1950–55; Gp Engr, Messrs Thomas Hedley Ltd, 1956–59; United Kingdom Atomic Energy Authority: Principal Professional and Technical Officer, 1959–73; Band Grade Officer, 1973–80; Asst Dir (Safety and Reliability Div.), 1980; Asst Dir (Engrg and Safety Dounreay), 1980–84; Dep. Dir (Engrg Northern Div.), 1984–85; Dir of Engrg (Northern Div.), 1985–87. *Publications:* Handbook on Criticality Data, 1974, 2nd edn 1979; various papers in Trans IMechE, Trans IChemE, Trans INucE. *Recreations:* hobby electronics, DIY, fishing. *Address:* Dounreay Nuclear Power Development Establishment, Thurso, Caithness KW14 7TZ.

JORDAN, Henry; Under-Secretary, Department of Education and Science, 1973–76; *b* 1919; *s* of late Henry Jordan and Mary Ann Jordan (*née* Shields); *m* 1946, Huguette Yvonne Rayée; one *s.* *Educ:* St Patrick's High Sch., Dumbarton. Served War, RA, 1939–46. Home Civil Service, Post Office, 1936; Foreign Office, 1947; Central Land Board and War Damage Commn, 1949; Min. (later Dept) of Educn, 1957. *Address:* 16 Bainfield Road, Cardross, Strathclyde.

JORDAN, Michael Anthony; Chairman and Senior Partner, Cork Gully, Chartered Accountants, since 1983; Partner, Coopers & Lybrand Deloitte (formerly Coopers & Lybrand), Chartered Accountants, since 1980; *b* 20 Aug. 1931; *s* of Charles Thomas Jordan and Florence Emily (*née* Golder); *m* 1st, 1956, Brenda Rosine Estelle Gee (marr. diss. 1989); one *s* one *d*; 2nd, 1990, Dorothea Coureau. *Educ:* Haileybury. FCA 1956. Joined R. H. March Son & Co., 1958, Partner, 1959–68; Partner: Saker & Langdon Davis, 1963–; W. H. Cork Gully & Co., 1968–80. Jt Inspector for High Court of IoM into the affairs of the Savings & Investment Bank Ltd, 1983. Gov., Royal Shakespeare Theatre, 1979–. *Publication:* (jtly) Insolvency, 1986. *Recreations:* opera, DIY, gardening. *Address:* Ballinger Farm, Ballinger, near Great Missenden, Bucks. *T:* Great Missenden (02406) 3298.

JORDAN, Air Marshal Sir Richard Bowen, KCB 1956 (CB 1947); DFC 1941; psa; RAF retired; *b* 7 Feb. 1902; *s* of late A. O. Jordan, Besford Ct, Worcestershire; *m* 1932, F. M. M. Haines (*d* 1985); one *d.* *Educ:* Marlborough Coll.; RAF Coll., Cranwell. Joined RAF, 1921. Late AOC the RAF in India and Pakistan; Air Officer Commanding RAF Gibraltar, 1948–49; Commandant of the Royal Observer Corps, 1949–51; ADC to the King, 1949–51; Air Officer Commanding No 25 Group, 1951–53; Dir-Gen. of Organisation, Air Ministry, 1953–55; Air Officer Commanding-in-Chief, Maintenance Command, 1956–58, retd. *Address:* 4 Stonegate Court, Stonegate, Wadhurst, E Sussex.

JORDAN, William Brian; President, Amalgamated Engineering Union, since 1986; a Governor, BBC, since 1988; *b* 28 Jan. 1936; *s* of Walter and Alice Jordan; *m* 1958, Jean Ann Livesey; three *d.* *Educ:* Secondary Modern Sch., Birmingham. Convener of Shop Stewards, Guest Keen & Nettlefolds, 1966; full-time AUEW Divl Organiser, 1976; Mem., TUC General Council, 1986– (Chm., Cttee on European Strategy, 1988). Member: NEDC, 1986–; Engrg Industry Training Bd, 1986–91; Council, Industrial Soc., 1987–; RIIA, 1987–; ACAS, 1987–; Nat. Trng Task Force, 1989–; Engrg Trng Authy, 1991. President: European Metal-Workers Fedn, 1986–; British Sect., Internat. Metalworkers Fedn, 1986–. Governor: London School of Economics, 1987–; Manchester Business School, 1987–. Hon. CGIA 1989. *Recreations:* reading; keen supporter, Birmingham City FC. *Address:* 110 Peckham Road, SE15 5EL. *Club:* E57 Social (King's Heath, Birmingham).

JORDAN-MOSS, Norman, CB 1972; CMG 1965; Director, Crown Financial Management, since 1984; *b* 5 Feb. 1920; *o s* of Arthur Moss and Ellen Jordan Round; *m* 1st, 1965, Kathleen Lusmore (*d* 1974); one *s* one *d*; 2nd, 1976, Philippa Rands; one *d.* *Educ:* Manchester Gram. Sch.; St John's Coll., Cambridge (MA). Ministry of Economic Warfare, 1940–44; HM Treasury, 1944–71; Asst Representative of HM Treas. in Middle East, 1945–48; Principal, 1948; First Sec. (Econ.), Belgrade, 1952–55; Financial Counsellor, Washington, 1956–60; Counsellor, UK Permanent Delegation to OECD, Paris, 1963–66; Asst Sec., 1956–68, Under-Sec., 1968–71, HM Treasury; Dep. Under-Sec. of State, DHSS, 1971–76; Dep. Sec., HM Treasury, 1976–80. *Recreations:* music, theatre. *Address:* Milton Way, Westcott, Dorking, Surrey. *Club:* Travellers'.

JORRE DE ST JORRE, Danielle Marie-Madeleine; Secretary of State, Department of Planning and External Relations, since 1986, Minister for Planning and External Relations, since 1989, Republic of Seychelles; *b* 30 Sept. 1941; *d* of Henri Jorre De St Jorre and Alice Corgat; *m* 1965 (marr. diss. 1983); one *s* one *d.* *Educ:* Univ. of Edinburgh (MA 1965); Inst. of Education, Univ. of London (PGCE 1966); Univ. of York (BPhil 1972). French Teacher, Streatham Hill and Clapham High Sch. (GPDST), 1967–69; French and English Teacher, and Hd of French Dept, Seychelles Coll., 1969–71; Principal, Teacher Training College, Seychelles, 1974–76; Principal Educn Officer, Min. of Educn, Seychelles, 1976–77; Principal Secretary: Min. of Foreign Affairs, Tourism and Aviation, 1977–79; Min. of Education and Information, 1980–82; Dept of External Relations and Co-operation, Min. of Planning and External Relations: Principal Sec., External Relns, 1982–83; Principal Sec., Planning and External Relns, 1983–86; High Comr for Seychelles in UK, concurrently Ambassador to France, Canada, Cuba, Federal Republic of Germany, Greece and USSR, 1983–85. Mem. or Head of delegn at numerous overseas meetings and conferences. Gov. for Seychelles, Bd of Governors, World Bank and African Develt Bank, 1984–; Chairperson: Seychelles Nat. Printing Co., 1977–82; Nat. Bookshop, 1977–82; Nat. Consultancy Services, 1983–88; Seychelles Hotels Ltd, 1986–91; Nat. Monument Bd, 1987–88; Develt Bank of Seychelles, 1988–91; Dir, Internat. Centre for Ocean Develt, 1987–. Vice-Pres., Comité International des Etudes Créoles, 1984–; Pres., Bannzil Kreyol, 1986–. *Publications:* Apprenons la nouvelle orthographe, 1978; Dictionnaire Créole Seychellois-français, 1982; (jtly) Lexique des Spécificités de la Langue Française aux Seychelles, 1989. *Address:* Ministry of Planning and External Relations, National House, PO Box 656, Victoria, Mahé, Republic of Seychelles.

JOSCELYNE, Richard Patrick; British Council Director, Japan, since 1991; *b* 19 June 1934; *s* of Dr Patrick C. Joscelyne and Rosalind Whitcombe; *m* 1st, 1961, Vera Lucia Mello (marr. diss. 1988); one *s* one *d*; 2nd, 1988, Irangani Dias. *Educ:* Bryanston; Queens' Coll., Cambridge. Teaching posts in France, Brazil and Britain, 1958–62. British Council: Montevideo, 1962; Moscow, 1967; Madrid, 1969; Director, North and Latin America Dept, 1973; Representative, Sri Lanka, 1977; Controller, Overseas Div. B (America, Pacific and Asia Div.), 1980; Controller, Finance Div., 1982; Representative, Spain, 1987. *Address:* c/o British Council, 10 Spring Gardens, SW1A 2BN. *T:* 071–930 8466.

JOSEPH, family name of **Baron Joseph.**

JOSEPH, Baron *cr* 1987 (Life Peer), of Portsoken in the City of London; **Keith Sinjohn Joseph,** CH 1986; PC 1962; Bt 1943; *b* 17 Jan. 1918; *o c* of Sir Samuel George Joseph, 1st Baronet, and Edna Cicely (*d* 1981), *yr d* of late P. A. S. Phillips, Portland Place, W1; *S* father 1944; *m* 1st, 1951, Hellen Louise (marr. diss. 1985), *yr d* of Sigmar Guggenheimer, NY; one *s* three *d*; 2nd, 1990, Mrs Yolanda Sheriff. *Educ:* Harrow; Magdalen Coll., Oxford. War of 1939–45, served 1939–46; Captain RA; Italian campaign (wounded, despatches). Fellow All Souls Coll., Oxford, 1946–60, 1972–; barrister, Middle Temple, 1946. Contested (C) Baron's Court, General Election, 1955. MP (C) Leeds NE, Feb. 1956–87. PPS to Parly Under-Sec. of State, CRO, 1957–59; Parly Sec., Min. of Housing and Local Govt, 1959–61; Minister of State at Board of Trade, 1961–62; Minister of Housing and Local Govt and Minister for Welsh Affairs, 1962–64; Secretary of State: for Social Services, DHSS, 1970–74; for Industry, 1979–81; for Educn and Science, 1981–86. Co-Founder and first Chm., Foundation for Management Education, 1959; Founder and first Chm., Mulberry Housing Trust, 1965–69; Founder, and Chm. Management Cttee, Centre for Policy Studies Ltd, 1974–79. Chm., Bovis Ltd, 1958–59; Dep. Chm., Bovis Holdings Ltd, 1964–70 (Dir, 1951–59); Director: Gilbert-Ash Ltd, 1949–59; Drayton Premier Investment Trust Ltd, 1975–79; Part-time Consultant: Bovis Ltd, 1986–89 (Dir, 1989–); Cable & Wireless PLC, 1986–91; Trusthouse Forte PLC, 1986–89. FIOB. Common councilman of City of London for Ward of Portsoken, 1946, Alderman, 1946–49. Liveryman, Vintners' Company. *Publications:* Reversing the Trend: a critical appraisal of Conservative economic and social policies, 1975; (with J. Sumption) Equality, 1979. *Heir* (to baronetcy): *s* Hon. James Samuel Joseph, *b* 27 Jan. 1955. *Address:* House of Lords, SW1A 0PW.

JOSEPH, Sir (Herbert) Leslie, Kt 1952; DL; Vice-Chairman, Trust Houses Forte Ltd, 1970–80; *b* 4 Jan. 1908; *s* of David Ernest and Florence Joseph; *m* 1st, 1934, Emily Irene (*d* 1987), *d* of Dr Patrick Julian Murphy, Cwmbach, Aberdare; two *d*; 2nd, 1989, Christine Jones. *Educ:* The King's Sch. Canterbury. Commissioned RE, 1940–46. Former Pres., Assoc. of Amusement Parks and Piers of Great Britain (formerly Assoc. Amusement Parks Proprietors of GB); Chairman: National Amusements Council, 1950–51; Amusement Caterers' Assoc., 1953, 1954; Housing Production Board for Wales, 1952–53. Member: Council, Swansea Univ.; Art Cttee, Nat. Museum of Wales. High Sheriff, 1975–76, DL, Mid Glamorgan. Governor, King's Sch., Canterbury, 1968–. *Recreations:* horticulture and ceramics. *Address:* Coedargraig, Newton, Porthcawl, Mid Glamorganshire CF36 5SS. *T:* Porthcawl (065671) 2610.

JOSEPH, Sir Leslie; *see* Joseph, Sir H. L.

JOSEPH, Leslie, QC 1978; *b* 13 Aug. 1925; *s* of Benjamin Francis Joseph and Sarah Edelman; *m* 1964, Ursula Mary Hamilton (*d* 1988); one *s* two *d*. *Educ:* Haberdashers' Aske's, Hampstead; University Coll. London (LLB Hons). Served Army, 1943–47: Infantry, 1943–45 (Sgt); AEC, 1945–47. Called to the Bar, Middle Temple, 1953, Bencher, 1986. *Recreations:* wine and water. *Address:* 34 Upper Park Road, NW3 2UT. *T:* 071–722 3390.

JOSEPHS, Wilfred; composer; *b* 24 July 1927; *s* of Philip Josephs and Rachel (*née* Block); *m* 1956, Valerie Wisbey; two *d*. *Educ:* Rutherford Coll. Boys' Sch.; Univ. of Durham at Newcastle (now Newcastle Univ.) (BDS Dunelm). Qual. dentistry, 1951. Army service, 1951–53. Guildhall Sch. of Music (schol. in composition, prizes), 1954; Leverhulme Schol. to study musical comp. in Paris with Maître Max Deutsch, 1958–59; Harriet Cohen Commonwealth Medal (for 1st quartet) and prizes; First Prize, La Scala, Milan, for Requiem, 1963. Abandoned dentistry completely and has since been a full-time composer, writing many concert works (incl. 10 symphonies), many film and television scores and themes, incl. music for: The Great War, I, Claudius, Disraeli, Cider with Rosie, All Creatures Great and Small, Sister Dora, Swallows and Amazons, The Brontë Series, The Somerset Maugham Series, Horizon, Chéri, A Place in Europe, The Inventing of America, The Norman Conquests, The Ghosts of Motley Hall, The House of Bernardo Alba, The Hunchback of Notre Dame, The Voyage of Charles Darwin, Enemy at the Door, People Like Us, Black Sun, The Uncanny, The Atom Spies, Churchill and the Generals, Pride and Prejudice, Strangled, A Walk in the Dark, Gift of Tongues, Miss Morison's Ghosts, The Human Race, Weekend Theatre, The Moles, The Home Front, The Making of Britain, Courts Martial series, A Married Man, The Gay Lord Quex, Pope John Paul II, Martin's Day, Mata Hari, Drummonds, Return of the Antelope, Art of the Western World, Horizon (Wasting the Alps; The Company of Ants and Bees; Red Star in Orbit), also a television opera, The Appointment; one-act opera, Pathelin; children's operas, Through the Looking-glass and What Alice Found There; Alice in Wonderland; children's musical, King of the Coast (Guardian/Arts Council Prize, 1969); Equus, the ballet (best ballet award, USA, 1980); Rebecca, 3–act opera; Cyrano de Bergerac, 3–act ballet, 1990–91. Vis. Prof. of Comp. and Composer-in-Residence at Univ. of Wisconsin-Milwaukee, 1970, at Roosevelt Univ., Chicago, 1972; Music Consultant, London Internat. Film Sch., 1988. Member: BAFTA; RSM; ISM; Composer's Guild of GB; Assoc. of Professional Composers; Producers' Assoc. Hon. DMus Newcastle, 1978. *Publications:* Requiem, Symphonies 1–10, various sonatas, quartets etc. *Recreations:* writing music, swimming, reading, opera, theatre, films. *Address:* 15 Douglas Court, Quex Road, NW6 4PT.

JOSEPHSON, Prof. Brian David, FRS 1970; Professor of Physics, Cambridge University, since 1974; Fellow of Trinity College, Cambridge, since 1962; *b* 4 Jan. 1940; *s* of Abraham Josephson and Mimi Josephson; *m* 1976, Carol Anne Olivier; one *d*. *Educ:* Cardiff High School; Cambridge Univ. BA 1960, MA, PhD 1964, Cantab. FInstP. Asst Dir of Res. in Physics, 1967–72, Reader in Physics, 1972–74, Univ. of Cambridge. Res. Asst Prof., Illinois Univ., 1965–66; Vis., Fellow, Cornell Univ., 1971; Vis. Faculty Mem., Maharishi European Res. Univ., 1975; Visiting Professor: Wayne State Univ., 1983; Indian Inst. of Sci., Bangalore, 1984. Hon. MIEEE, 1982; For. Hon. Mem., Amer. Acad. of Arts and Scis, 1974. Hon. DSc: Wales, 1974; Exeter, 1984. Awards: New Scientist, 1969; Research Corp., 1969; Fritz London, 1970; Nobel Prize for Physics, 1973. Medals: Guthrie, 1972; van der Pol, 1972; Elliott Cresson, 1972; Hughes, 1972; Holweck, 1973; Faraday, 1982; Sir George Thomson, 1984. *Publications:* Consciousness and the Physical World, 1980 (ed jtly); research papers on physics and theory of intelligence, the convergence of science and religion. *Recreations:* mountain walking, ice skating. *Address:* Cavendish Laboratory, Madingley Road, Cambridge CB3 0HE. *T:* Cambridge (0223) 337200; *Telex:* 81292 CAVLAB G.

JOSLIN, Peter David, QPM 1983; Chief Constable of Warwickshire, since 1983; *b* 26 Oct. 1933; *s* of Frederick William Joslin and Emma Joslin; *m* 1960, Kathleen Josephine Monaghan; two *s* one *d*. *Educ:* King Edward VI Royal Grammer School, Chelmsford; Essex University. BA hons. Joined Essex Police, 1954–74 (Police Constable to Superintendent); Chief Superintendent, Divl Comdr, Leicestershire Constabulary, 1974–76; Asst Chief Constable (Operations), Leics Constab., 1976–77; Dep. Chief Constable, Warwicks Constabulary, 1977–83. Chm., Traffic Cttee, ACPO, 1989–. CBIM. *Recreations:* sport (now mainly as a spectator), house renovation, good wines, after dinner speaking. *Address:* Chief Constable's Office, PO Box 4, Leek Wootton, Warwick CV35 7QB. *T:* Warwick (0926) 495431.

JOSLING, John Francis; writer on legal subjects; Principal Assistant Solicitor of Inland Revenue, 1965–71; *b* 26 May 1910; *s* of John Richard Josling, Hackney, London, and Florence Alice (*née* Robinson); *m* 1935, Bertha Frearson (*d* 1991); two *s* two *d*. *Educ:* Leyton Co. High Sch. Entered a private Solicitor's office, 1927; articled, 1937; admitted as Solicitor, 1940. Served War of 1939–45 (war stars and medals): RA, 1940–45; JAG's Br, 1945–46. Entered office of Solicitor of Inland Revenue, 1946; Sen. Legal Asst, 1948; Asst Solicitor, 1952. Mem., Law Society. Coronation Medal, 1953. *Publications:* Oyez Practice Notes on Adoption of Children, 1947, (with A. Levy) 11th edn 1991; Execution of a Judgment, 1948, 5th edn 1974; (with C. Caplin) Apportionments for Executors and Trustees, 1948, 3rd edn 1963; Change of Name, 1948, 14th edn 1989; Naturalisation, 1949, 3rd edn 1965; Summary Judgment in the High Court, 1950, 4th edn 1974; Periods of Limitation, 1951, 7th edn 1989; (with L. Alexander) The Law of Clubs, 1964, 6th edn 1987; A History of the Souvenir Normand, 1987; contribs to: Simon's Income Tax (2nd edn); Halsbury's Laws of England vol. 20 (3rd edn); Pollard's Social Welfare Law, 1977; (ed) Caplin's Powers of Attorney, 1954, 4th edn 1971; (ed) Wilkinson's Affiliation Law and Practice, 1971, 4th edn 1977; (ed) Summary Matrimonial and Guardianship Orders, 3rd edn 1973; many contribs to Solicitors' Jl and some other legal jls. *Recreations:* music and musical history; Victorian novels; Georgian children and Elizabethan grand-children. *Address:* Proton, Farley Way, Fairlight, E Sussex TN35 4AS. *T:* Hastings (0424) 812501.

JOSS, William Hay; a Recorder of the Crown Court, since 1982; *b* 20 May 1927; *s* of William Taylor Barron Joss and Elizabeth Lindsay Lillie Joss; *m* 1961, Rosemary Sarah Joss; two *s*. *Educ:* Worksop Coll., Notts; Exeter Coll., Oxon (BA Jurisprudence). Served Army, commissioned into 14th/20th King's Hussars, 1945–48. Industry, production management, 1950–62; called to the Bar, Gray's Inn, 1957; practising barrister, 1962–. *Recreations:* golf, music, literature. *Address:* 49 Village Road, Clifton Village, Nottingham NG11 8NP. *T:* Nottingham (0602) 211894. *Club:* Nottingham and Notts United Services.

JOSSET, Lawrence; RE 1951 (ARE 1936); ARCA; free-lance artist; *b* 2 Aug. 1910; *s* of Leon Antoine Hyppolite and Annie Mary Josset; *m* 1960, Beatrice, *d* of William Alford Taylor. *Educ:* Bromley County Sch. for Boys; Bromley and Beckenham Schs of Art; Royal College of Art (diploma). Engraver's Draughtsman at Waterlow and Son Ltd, Clifton Street, 1930–32; Art Master at Red Hill Sch., East Sutton, near Maidstone, Kent, 1935–36. Mem. of Art Workers' Guild. *Publications:* Mezzotint in colours; Flowers, after Fantin-Latour, 1937; The Trimmed Cock, after Ben Marshall, 1939; Brighton Beach and Spring, after Constable, 1947; Carting Timber and Milking Time, after Shayer, 1948; The Pursuit, and Love Letters, after Fragonard, 1949; Spring and Autumn, after Boucher, 1951; A Family, after Zoffany, 1953; Master James Sayer, 1954; HM The Queen after Annigoni, commissioned by the Times, 1956, and plates privately commissioned after de Lazlo, James Gunn and Oswald Birley. *Recreations:* outdoor sketching, cycling, etc. *Address:* The Cottage, Pilgrims Way, Detling, near Maidstone, Kent ME14 3JY.

JOST, H. Peter, CBE 1969; DSc; CEng; FIMechE; FIM; Hon. FIProdE; CBIM 1984; Chairman, K. S. Paul Products Ltd, since 1973 (Managing Director, 1955–89); Director of overseas companies; Hon. Industrial Professor, Liverpool Polytechnic, since 1983; Hon. Professor of Mechanical Engineering, University of Wales, since 1986; *b* 25 Jan. 1921; *o s* of late Leo and Margot Jost; *m* 1948, Margaret Josephine, *o d* of late Michael and Sara Kadesh, Norfolk Is, S Pacific; two *d*. *Educ:* City of Liverpool Techn. Coll.; Manchester Coll. of Technology. Apprentice, Associated Metal Works, Glasgow and D. Napier & Son Ltd, Liverpool; Methods Engr, K & L Steelfounders and Engrs Ltd, 1943; Chief Planning Engr, Datim Machine Tool Co. Ltd, 1946; Gen. Man. 1949, Dir 1952, Trier Bros Ltd; Lubrication Consultant: Richard Thomas & Baldwins Ltd, 1960–65; August Thyssen Hütte AG 1963–66; Chairman: Bright Brazing Ltd, 1969–76; Peppermill Brass Foundry Ltd, 1970–76; Centralube Ltd, 1974–77 (Man. Dir, 1955–77); Associated Technology Gp Ltd, 1976–; Engineering & General Equipment Ltd, 1977–; Director: Williams Hudson Ltd, 1967–75; Stothert & Pitt, 1971–85. Chairman: Lubrication Educn and Res. Working Gp, DES, 1964–65; Cttee on Tribology, DTI, 1966–74; Industrial Technologies Management Bd, DTI, 1972–74; Dep. Chm., Cttee for Industrial Technologies, DTI, 1972–74; Member: Adv. Council on Technology, 1968–70; Cttee on Terotechnology, 1971–72. Hon. Associate, Manchester Coll. of Science and Technology, 1962; Univ. of Salford: Privy Council's Nominee to Ct, 1970–; Mem. Council, 1974–84. Mem. Council: IProdE, 1973– (Vice-Pres., 1975–77, Pres., 1977–78; Chm., Technical Policy Bd and Mem., Exec. Policy Cttee, 1974; Hon. Fellow, 1980); IMechE, 1974– (Member: Technical Bd, 1975; Finance Bd, 1979– (Chm., 1988–); Disciplinary Bd, 1979–; Vice-Pres., 1987–); Council of Engineering Institutions: Mem. Bd, 1977–83; Mem. Exec., 1979–83 (Mem. External Affairs Cttee, 1974–80; Chm. Home Affairs Cttee, 1980–83); Mem., Parly and Scientific Council (formerly Parly and Scientific Cttee), 1976– (Hon. Sec., 1990–; Mem., Gen. Purposes Cttee, 1991–); Steering Cttee, 1983–; President: Internat. Tribology Council, 1973–; Manchester Technology Assoc., 1984–85; Chm., Manchester Technology Assoc. in London, 1976–. Fellow, 1970, Life Fellow, 1986, American Soc. Mechanical Engrs; Fellow, Soc. of Manufacturing Engrs, USA, 1988. Hon. MIPlantE, 1969; Hon. Member: Société Française de Tribologie, 1972; Gesellschaft für Tribologie, 1972; Amer. Soc. of Manufacturing Engrs, 1977; Chinese Mech. Engrg Soc., 1986; USSR Acad. of Engrs, 1991. Rutherford Lectr, Manchester Technology Assoc., 1979; James Clayton Lectr, IMechE, 1981. Freeman, City of London, 1984; Liveryman, Engineers' Co., 1984. Hon. DSc: Salford, 1970; Slovak Technical Univ., 1987; Bath, 1990; Hon. DTech CNAA, 1987; Hon. DEng Leeds, 1989; San Fernando Valley Engineers Council (USA) Internat. Achievement Award, 1978; State of California State Legislature Commendation, 1978; Georg Vagelpohl Insignia, Germany, 1979. Sir John Larking Medal 1944, Derby Medal 1955, Liverpool Engrg Soc.; Hutchinson Meml Medal 1952, Silver Medal for Best Paper 1952–53, 1st Nuffield Award 1981, IProdE; Merit Medal, Hungarian Scientific Soc. of Mech. Engrs, 1983; Gold Medal, Slovak Tech. Univ., 1984. Gold Insignia, Order of Merit of Poland, 1986. *Publications:* Lubrication (Tribology) Report of DES Cttee, 1966 (Jost Report); The Introduction of a New Technology, Report of DTI Cttee, 1973; Technology *vs* Unemployment, 1986; various papers in Proc. IMechE, Proc. IProdE, technical jls, etc. *Recreations:* music, opera, gardening. *Address:* Hill House, Wills Grove, Mill Hill, NW7 1QL. *T:* 081–959 3355. *Club:* Athenæum.

JOUGHIN, Sir Michael, Kt 1991; CBE 1971; JP; Chairman, Scottish Hydro-Electric plc (formerly North of Scotland Hydro-Electric Board), since 1983; farmer since 1952; *b* 26 April 1926; *s* of John Clague Joughin and May Joughin; *m* 1st, 1948, Lesley Roy Petrie; one *s* one *d*; 2nd, 1981, Anne Hutchinson. *Educ:* Kelly Coll., Tavistock. Lieut, Royal Marines, 1944–52, RM pilot with Fleet Air Arm, 1946–49. Pres., NFU of Scotland, 1964–66. Chm. of Governors: N of Scotland Coll. of Agriculture, 1969–72; Blairmore Prep. Sch., 1966–72; Chairman: N of Scotland Grassland Soc., 1970–71; Elgin Market Green Auction Co., 1969–70; Scottish Agricl Develt Council, 1971–80; N of Scotland Milk Marketing Bd, 1974–83. Governor: Rowett Research Inst., 1968–74; Scottish Plant Breeding Inst., 1969–74; Animal Diseases Research Assoc., Moredun Inst., 1969–74; Member: Intervention Bd for Agric. Produce, 1972–76; Econ. Develt Council for Agriculture, 1967–70; Agric. Marketing Develt Exec. Cttee, 1965–68; Scottish

Constitutional Cttee, 1969–70; British Farm Produce Council, 1965–66. Mem. NE Bd, Bank of Scotland, 1989–. Contested (C) Highland and Islands, European Parly Elections, 1979. FRAgS 1975. CBIM 1988 (FBIM 1979). JP Moray, 1965; DL Moray, 1974–80. *Recreation:* sailing. *Address:* Elderslie, Findhorn, Moray IV30 3TN. *T:* Findhorn (0309) 30277. *Clubs:* New (Edinburgh); Royal Naval Sailing Assoc., Royal Marines Sailing, Royal Findhorn Yacht, Goldfish.

JOWELL, Prof. Jeffrey Lionel; Professor of Public Law, University College London, since 1975; barrister-at-law; *b* 4 Nov. 1938; *s* of Jack and Emily Jowell, Cape Town; *m* 1963, Frances Barbara Suzman; one *s* one *d. Educ:* Cape Town Univ. (BA, LLB 1961); Hertford Coll., Oxford (BA 1963, MA 1969), Pres., Oxford Union Soc., 1963; Harvard Univ. Law Sch. (LLM 1966, SJD 1971). Called to Bar, Middle Temple, 1965. Research Asst, Harvard Law Sch., 1966–68; Fellow, Jt Center for Urban Studies of Harvard Univ. and MIT, 1967–68; Associate Prof. of Law and Admin. Studies, Osgoode Hall Law Sch., York Univ., Toronto, 1968–72; Leverhulme Fellow in Urban Legal Studies, 1972–74, and Lectr in Law, 1974–75, LSE; University College London: Dean, Faculty of Laws, 1979–89; Head of Dept, 1982–89. Chairman, Social Sciences and The Law Cttee, 1981–84, and Vice-Chm., Govt and Law Cttee, 1982–84, Social Science Res. Council; Asst Boundary Comr, 1976–85; Chm., Cttee of Heads of University Law Schools, 1984–86; Member: Cttee of Management, Inst. of Advanced Legal Studies, 1978–89; Standing Cttee, Oxford Centre for Socio-Legal Studies, 1980–84; Gp for Study of Comparative European Admin., 1978–86; Nuffield Cttee on Town and Country Planning, 1983–86. Lionel Cohen Lecture, Jerusalem, 1988; Vis. Prof., Univ. of Paris II, 1991. Hon. DJur: Athens, 1987; Ritsumeikan, 1988. Member Editorial Bds: Public Law, 1977–; Policy and Politics, 1976–83; Urban Law and Policy, 1978–83; Jl of Environmental Law, 1988–; Jt Editor, Current Legal Problems, 1984–89. *Publications:* author and editor of a number of books, articles and reviews on public law and planning law. *Recreations:* tennis, London, Exmoor. *Address:* 7 Hampstead Hill Gardens, NW3. *T:* 071–794 6645; Hantons, Exford, Somerset. *T:* Exford (064383) 418. *Club:* Garrick.

JOWETT, Very Rev. Alfred, CBE 1972; Dean of Manchester, 1964–83; *b* 29 May 1914; *s* of Alfred Edmund Jowett; *m* 1939, Margaret, *d* of St Clair Benford; one *s* three *d. Educ:* High Storrs Grammar Sch., Sheffield; St Catharine's Coll., Cambridge; Lincoln Theological Coll. BA 1935; Certif. Educn 1936; MA 1959. Deacon 1944; Priest 1945. Curate of St John the Evangelist, Goole, 1944–47; Sec., Sheffield Anglican and Free Church Council and Marriage Guidance Council, 1947–51; Vicar of St George with St Stephen, Sheffield, 1951–60; Part-time Lecturer, Sheffield Univ. Dept of Education, 1950–60; Vicar of Doncaster, 1960–64; Hon. Canon of Sheffield Cathedral, 1960–64. Select Preacher, Oxford Univ., 1964 and 1979. Mem., Community Relations Commn, 1968–77 (Dep. Chm., 1972–77). A Church Comr, 1978–80. Hon. Fellow, Manchester Polytechnic, 1972. OStJ 1979. Hon. LittD Sheffield, 1982. Hon. Freeman, City of Manchester, 1984. *Publication:* (Part-author) The English Church: a New Look, 1966. *Recreations:* theatre, music, walking. *Address:* 37 Stone Delf, Sheffield S10 3QX. *T:* Sheffield (0742) 305455.

JOWITT, Hon. Sir Edwin (Frank), Kt 1988; **Hon. Mr Justice Jowitt;** a Justice of the High Court, Queen's Bench Division, since 1988; *b* 1 Oct. 1929; *s* of Frank and Winifred Jowitt; *m* 1959, Anne Barbara Dyson; three *s* two *d. Educ:* Swanwick Hall Grammar Sch.; London Sch. of Economics. LLB London 1950. Called to Bar, Middle Temple, 1951, Bencher 1977; Member Midland and Oxford Circuit, 1952–80. Dep. Chm. Quarter Sessions: Rutland, 1967–71; Derbyshire, 1970–71; QC 1969; a Recorder of the Crown Court, 1972–80; a Circuit Judge, 1980–88; a Sen. Circuit Judge, 1987–88; Hon. Recorder, Birmingham, 1987–88. *Recreation:* fell walking. *Address:* Royal Courts of Justice, Strand, WC2A 2LL.

JOWITT, Juliet Diana Margaret, (Mrs Thomas Jowitt); Member, Independent Broadcasting Authority, 1981–86; Director: Yorkshire Television, since 1987; Yorkshire Television Holdings, since 1989; *b* 24 Aug. 1940; *yr d* of late Lt-Col Robert Henry Langton Brackenbury, OBE and Eleanor Trewlove (*née* Springman); *m* 1963, Frederick Thomas Benson Jowitt; one *s* one *d. Educ:* Hatherop Castle; Switzerland and Spain. Associate Shopping Editor, House and Garden and Vogue, 1966–69; Proprietor, Wood House Design (Interior Design) (formerly Colour Go Round), 1971–. Dir, Chunky Ltd; Member: Interior Decorators and Designers Assoc., 1985– (Mem. Council, 1989); Domestic Coal Consumers' Council, 1985–; Potato Marketing Bd, 1986–90. JP North Yorkshire, 1973–89. *Address:* Thorpe Lodge, Littlethorpe, Ripon, N Yorkshire HG4 3LU; 11 St George's Square, SW1.

JOY, David, CBE 1983; HM Diplomatic Service; Consul-General, Barcelona, since 1989; *b* 9 Dec. 1932; *s* of Harold Oliver Joy and late Doris Kate Buxton; *m* 1957, Montserrat Morancho Saumench, *o d* of Angel Morancho Garreta and Josefa Saumench Castells, Zaragoza, Spain; one *s* one *d. Educ:* Hulme Grammar Sch., Oldham, Lancs; St Catharine's Coll., Cambridge (MA). FBIM. HMOCS, Northern Rhodesia, 1956–64; Zambia, 1964–70: Cabinet Office, 1964; Under Sec. (Cabinet), 1968; Under Sec., Min. of Commerce and Industry, 1970; Ashridge Management Coll., 1970; joined HM Diplomatic Service, 1971; FCO, 1971–73; First Sec. (Inf.), Caracas, 1973–75; Head of Chancery, Caracas, 1975–77; Asst Head, Mexican and Caribbean Dept, FCO, 1977–78; Counsellor and Head of Chancery, Warsaw, 1978–82; Counsellor and Hd of British Interests Section, Buenos Aires, 1982–84; Head of Mexico and Central America Dept, FCO, 1984–87; Ambassador to Honduras and El Salvador, 1987–89. *Recreations:* family-life, reading, tennis, golf, music. *Address:* c/o Foreign and Commonwealth Office, SW1A 2AH. *Clubs:* United Oxford & Cambridge University; Circulo del Liceu (Barcelona).

JOY, Michael Gerard Laurie, CMG 1965; MC 1945; HM Diplomatic Service, retired; *b* 27 Oct. 1916; *s* of late Frank Douglas Howarth Joy, Bentley, Hants; *m* 1951, Ann Félise Jacomb; one *s* three *d. Educ:* Winchester; New Coll., Oxford. Served RA, 1940–46 (MC, wounded). Foreign Office, 1947; Private Sec. to Permanent Under Sec. of State, 1948–50; Saigon, 1950–53; Washington, 1953–55; IDC, 1956; Foreign Office, 1957–59; Counsellor, 1959; Addis Ababa, 1959–62; Stockholm, 1962–64; seconded to Cabinet Office, 1964–66; Foreign Office, 1966–68. *Recreation:* shooting. *Address:* Marelands, Bentley, Hants GU10 5JB. *T:* Bentley (0420) 23288.

JOY, Peter, OBE 1969; HM Diplomatic Service, retired; *b* 16 Jan. 1926; *s* of late Neville Holt Joy and Marguerite Mary Duff Beith; *m* 1953, Rosemary Joan Hebden; two *s* two *d. Educ:* Downhouse Sch., Pembridge; New Coll., Oxford. Served with RAF, 1944–47. Entered Foreign (subseq. Diplomatic) Service, 1952; 1st Sec., Ankara, 1959; 1st Sec., New Delhi, 1962; FO, 1965; 1st Sec., Beirut, 1968; FCO, 1973; Counsellor, Kuala Lumpur, 1979–80; Counsellor, FCO, 1980–86. *Recreations:* shooting, fishing. *Address:* The Old Rectory, Stoke Bliss, near Tenbury, Worcs WR15 8QJ. *T:* Kyre (0885) 410342; Carrick House, Eday, Orkney.

JOY, Thomas Alfred, LVO 1979; President, Hatchards Ltd, since 1985 (Managing Director, 1965–85); *b* 30 Dec. 1904; *s* of Alfred Joy and Annie Carpenter; *m* 1932, Edith Ellis. *Educ:* privately; Bedford House Sch., Oxford. Jun. Assistant, Bodleian Library, Oxford, 1919; indentured apprentice, 1919–25, buyer and cataloguer, 1925–35, J. Thornton & Son, University Booksellers, Oxford; Manager, Circulating Library,

1935–45, and Manager, Book Dept, 1942–45, Harrods; Army & Navy Stores: Manager, Book Dept, and founder of Library, 1945–56; Merchandise Manager, 1956; Dep. Managing Dir, 1956–65. Began Hatchards Authors of the Year parties, 1966. Employers' rep., Bookselling and Stationery Trade Wages Council, 1946–79, leader of employers' side, 1957; Member: Nat. Chamber of Trade, 1946–51; Wholesale Trades Adv. Cttee, 1946–51; 1948 Book Trade Cttee; Arts Council working party on obscene pubns, 1968–69, and sub-cttee on Public Lending Rights, 1970. President: Booksellers Assoc. of GB and Ire, 1957–58 (Hon. Life Pres., 1989); Book Trade Benevolent Soc., 1974–86 (Patron, 1986). Inaugurated Nat. Book Sale (first Chm. of Cttee, 1954–65). Hon. Life Mem., Soc. of Bookmen. FRSA 1967. Jubilee Medal, 1977. *Publications:* The Right Way to Run a Library Business, 1949; Bookselling, 1953; The Truth about Bookselling, 1964; Mostly Joy (autobiog.), 1971; The Bookselling Business, 1974; contribs to Bookseller and other trade jls. *Recreations:* reading, gardening, walking, motoring. *Address:* 13 Cole Park Gardens, Twickenham, Middlesex TW1 1JB. *T:* 081–892 5660.

JOYCE, Robert John H.; *see* Hayman-Joyce.

JOYCE, William R., Jr; lawyer, since 1951; Director and Secretary-Treasurer, Battle of Britain Museum Foundation (USA), since 1976; President, Canterbury Institute Trust (USA), since 1989; *b* 18 May 1921; *s* of William R. Joyce and Winifred Lowery; *m* 1956, Mary-Hoyt Sherman; one *s* two *d. Educ:* Loyola Univ. (BA); New York and Harvard Law Schs. JD. Lawyer, in private practice, New York City and Washington, DC; member of firm, Vance Joyce & Carbaugh, 1977–; Consul General *ad hon.*, Republic of Bolivia (Washington, DC), 1963–. Pres., Consular Corps of Washington, DC, 1982–. FRGS. Kt 1973, Kt Comdr (pro Merito Melitensi), Order of Malta, 1977; Kt, Equestrian Order of Holy Sepulchre, Jerusalem, 1976; Kt Comdr of Grace, Order of Constantine and S George (Borbon-Two Sicilies), Naples, 1977; Order of Condor of the Andes, Bolivia, 1978; Order of Simon Bolivar the Liberator, Bolivia, 1988. *Recreations:* sailing, golf. *Address:* (residence) 4339 Garfield Street NW, Washington, DC 20007, USA. *T:* 202/244–7648; (office) 1701 Pennsylvania Avenue NW, Washington, DC 20006. *T:* 202/298–7133. *Clubs:* Squash Racquets Association, Middlesex CCC; The Brook, India House, Union, New York Yacht (New York City); Metropolitan, Chevy Chase (Washington); Cooperstown Country (New York).

JOYNSON-HICKS, family name of **Viscount Brentford.**

JOYNT, Evelyn Gertrude, MBE 1967; Major (retired) WRAC; Director, World Bureau of World Association of Girl Guides and Girl Scouts, 1971–79; *b* 5 Sept. 1919; 2nd *d* of late Rev. George Joynt, Dublin. *Educ:* Collegiate Sch., Enniskillen; Banbridge Academy. Joined ATS, 1942; transf. to WRAC, 1952; jsc, WRAC Staff Coll., 1954; served Middle East and Far East; OC Drivers and Clerks Training Wing, WRAC; DAQMG, Eastern Comd; retired 1967; Nat. Gen. Sec., YWCA of GB, 1968–71. *Address:* Bowden House, West Street, Alresford, Hants SO24 9AU.

JOYNT, Rt. Rev. Michael Charles S.; *see* Scott-Joynt.

JUDD, family name of **Baron Judd.**

JUDD, Baron *cr* 1991 (Life Peer), of Portsea in the County of Hampshire; **Frank Ashcroft Judd;** Director, Oxfam, 1985–91; *b* 28 March 1935; *s* of Charles and Helen Judd; *m* 1961, Christine Elizabeth Willington; two *d. Educ:* City of London Sch.; London Sch. of Economics. Sec.-Gen., IVS, 1960–66. Contested (Lab): Sutton and Cheam, 1959; Portsmouth West, 1964; MP (Lab) Portsmouth W, 1966–74, Portsmouth N, 1974–79; PPS: to Minister of Housing, 1967–70; to the Leader of the Opposition, 1970–72; Mem., Opposition's Front Bench Defence Team, 1972–74; Parliamentary Under-Secretary of State: for Defence (Navy), MoD, 1974–76; ODM 1976; Minister of State: for Overseas Develt, 1976–77; FCO, 1977–79; Mem., British Parly Delegn to Council of Europe and WEU, 1970–73. Indep. Advr to UK Delegn to UN Special Session on Disarmament, 1982. Associate Dir, Internat. Defence Aid Fund for Southern Africa, 1979–80; Dir, VSO, 1980–85. Chairman: Centre for World Development Educn, 1980–85; Internat. Council of Voluntary Agencies, 1985–90; Mem., Steering Cttee, World Bank—NGO Cttee, 1989–. Past Chm., Fabian Soc. Member: Council, Overseas Development Inst.; ASTMS; Governing Body, Queen Elizabeth House, Oxford Univ.; Governor, LSE, 1982–. Hon. Fellow Portsmouth Poly., 1978. Hon. DLitt Bradford Univ., 1987. FRSA 1988. *Publications:* (jtly) Radical Future, 1967; Fabian International Essays, 1970; Purpose in Socialism, 1973; various papers and articles on current affairs. *Recreations:* walking, family holidays. *Address:* 21 Mill Lane, Old Marston, Oxford OX3 0PY. *Club:* Commonwealth Trust.

JUDD, Clifford Harold Alfred, CB 1987; Under Secretary, HM Treasury, 1981–87; *b* 27 June 1927; *s* of Alfred Ernest and Florence Louisa Judd; *m* 1951, Elizabeth Margaret Holmes; two *d. Educ:* Christ's Hospital; Keble Coll., Oxford. National Service, RA, 1946–48 (to 2/Lt). HM Treasury: Executive Officer, 1948, through ranks to Principal, 1964, Sen. Prin., 1969, Asst Sec., 1973. *Recreations:* cricket, golf, do-it-yourself. *Address:* 4 Colets Orchard, Otford, Kent TN14 5RA. *T:* Otford (09592) 2398. *Clubs:* Sevenoaks Vine; Knole Park Golf.

JUDD, Eric Campbell, CBE 1974; LVO 1956; Chairman, West Africa Committee, 1976–85 (Vice-Chairman, 1963–76); *b* St Thomas, Ont, 10 Aug. 1918; *s* of Frederick William Judd, PhmB (Canada), and Marjorie Katherine (*née* Bell); *m* 1947, Janet Creswell (*née* Fish); two *s* one *d. Educ:* Wellington, Canada; St Thomas Collegiate; Toronto Univ. Trainee Manager, Cities Service Oil Co., Canada, 1937–40. RCAF and RAF, 1940–45: Canada, N Atlantic Ferry Comd, Europe, Malta, Middle East, Far East, W Indies; retd Sqdn Ldr RCAF Reserve, 1945. Joined Unilever Ltd, 1946; United Africa Co. Ltd, Nigeria, 1946–60, Chm., 1957–60; Dir, UAC Ltd London, 1960, Man. Dir, 1968; Dep. Chm. and Jt Man. Dir, UAC International, 1969–77. Mem. House of Assembly, Western Nigeria, 1955–56; Chm., BNEC Africa, 1969–72; Chm., Adv. Gp Africa BOTB, 1972–74. Mem. Council, 1975–88, a Vice-Pres., 1983–88, Royal African Soc. *Recreations:* golf, tennis, theatre, music, reading. *Address:* Amberway, 23 Townsend Lane, Harpenden, Herts AL5 2PY. *T:* Harpenden (0582) 712617. *Clubs:* MCC; Mid-Herts Golf.

JUDD, Nadine; *see* Nerina, Nadia.

JUDGE, Edward Thomas, MA Cantab; FIM; Director: ETJ Consultancy Services; Cleveland Scientific Institution; *b* 20 Nov. 1908; *o s* of late Thomas Oliver and Florence Judge (*née* Gravestock); *m* 1934, Alice Gertrude Matthews; two *s. Educ:* Worcester Royal Grammar Sch.; St John's Coll., Cambridge. Joined Dorman Long, 1930, and held various appts, becoming Chief Technical Engr, 1937; Special Dir, 1944; Chief Engr, 1945; Dir, 1947; Asst Man. Dir, Dorman Long (Steel) Ltd, 1959; Jt Man. Dir, 1960; Chm. and Gen. Man. Dir, Dorman Long & Co. Ltd, 1961–67; Dir, Dorman Long Vaderbijl (SA), 1959–79. Chairman: Reyrolle Parsons Ltd, 1969–74 (Dep. Chm., 1968); A. Reyrolle & Co. Ltd, 1969–73; C. A. Parsons & Co. Ltd, 1969–73; Director: BPB Industries, 1967–79; Pilkington Bros, 1968–79; Fibreglass, 1968–79. Mem. Exec. and Develt Cttees of Brit. Iron & Steel Fedn; Rep. of Minister of Transport on Tees Conservancy Commn., 1951–66; part-time Mem. N Eastern Electricity Bd, 1952–62; Vice-Pres., Iron & Steel Inst., 1958.

President: British Iron & Steel Federation, 1965, 1966, 1967; British Electrical Allied Manufacturers' Assoc. Ltd, 1970–71 (Dep. Pres., 1969–70). Bessemer Gold Medal, Iron and Steel Inst., 1967. *Publications*: technical papers. *Recreation*: fishing. *Address*: 4 Delamores Acre, Willaston, Cheshire L64 1UB.

JUDGE, Harry George, MA Oxon, PhD London; Fellow of Brasenose College, Oxford, since 1973; Senior Research Associate, University of Oxford Department of Educational Studies, since 1988 (Director, 1973–88); Professor of Teacher Education Policy, Michigan State University, since 1988; *b* 1 Aug. 1928; *s* of George Arthur and Winifred Mary Judge; *m* 1956, Elizabeth Mary Patrick; one *s* two *d*. *Educ*: Cardiff High Sch.; Brasenose Coll., Oxford. Asst Master, Emanuel Sch. and Wallington County Grammar Sch., 1954–59; Dir of Studies, Cumberland Lodge, Windsor, 1959–62; Head Master, Banbury Grammar Sch., 1962–67; Principal, Banbury Sch., 1967–73. Vis. Professor: MIT, 1977 and 1980–82; Carnegie-Mellon Univ., 1984–86; Univ. of Virginia, 1987; Vis. Schol., Harvard Univ., 1985–87. Member: Public Schools Commission, 1966–70; James Cttee of Inquiry into Teacher Training, 1971–72; Educn Sub-Cttee, UGC, 1976–80; Oxon Educn Cttee, 1982–87. Chairman: School Broadcasting Council, 1977–81; RCN Commn on Education, 1984–85. Gen. Editor, Oxford Illus. Encyclopedia, 1985–. *Publications*: Louis XIV, 1965; School Is Not Yet Dead, 1974; Graduate Schools of Education in the US, 1982; A Generation of Schooling: English secondary schools since 1944, 1984; contribs on educational and historical subjects to collective works and learned jls. *Recreation*: canals. *Address*: Brasenose College, Oxford OX1 4AJ.

JUDGE, Hon. Sir Igor, Kt 1988; **Hon. Mr Justice Judge;** a Judge of the High Court, Queen's Bench Division, since 1988; *b* 19 May 1941; *s* of Raymond and Rosa Judge; *m* 1965, Judith Mary Robinson; one *s* two *d*. *Educ*: Oratory Sch., Woodcote; Magdalene Coll., Cambridge (Exhbnr, MA). Harmsworth Exhbnr and Astbury Scholar, Middle Temple. Called to the Bar, Middle Temple, 1963, Bencher, 1987; QC 1979. A Recorder, 1976–88; Prosecuting Counsel to Inland Revenue, Midland and Oxford Circuit, 1977–79. Leader, Midland and Oxford Circuit, 1988. Member: Senate, Inns of Court and the Bar, 1980–83, 1984–86; Bar Council, 1987–88; Judicial Studies Bd, 1984–88, 1991– (Chm. Criminal Cttee, 1991–). *Recreations*: history, music, cricket. *Address*: Royal Courts of Justice, Strand, WC2.

JUGNAUTH, Rt. Hon. Sir Aneerood, KCMG 1988; PC 1987; QC (Mauritius) 1980; Prime Minister of Mauritius, since 1982; concurrently Minister of Defence and Internal Security, Minister of Information and Minister of External Communications and the Outer Islands; *b* 29 March 1930; *m*; two *c*. *Educ*: Church of England School, Palma, Mauritius; Regent Coll., Quatre Bornes. Called to the Bar, Lincoln's Inn, 1954. Teacher, New Eton Coll., 1948; worked in Civil Service, 1949. MLA Rivière du Rempart, 1963–67, Piton-Rivière du Rempart, 1976, 1982, 1983 and 1987; Town Councillor, Vacoas-Phoenix, 1964; Minister of State for Develt, 1965–67; Min. of Labour, 1967; Leader of the Opposition, 1976–82; Minister of Finance, 1983–84. Dist Magistrate, 1967–69; Crown Counsel, 1969; Sen. Crown Counsel, 1971. Attended London Constitutional Conf., 1965. Leader, Mouvement Socialist Militant. Dr *hc* Aix-en-Provence, 1985; Hon. DCL Mauritius, 1985. Order of Rising Sun (1st cl.) (Japan), 1988; Grand Officier, Ordre de la Légion d'Honneur (France), 1990. *Address*: Office of the Prime Minister, Port Louis, Mauritius.

JUKES, Rt. Rev. John, OFMConv; STL; VG; an Auxiliary Bishop in Southwark, (RC), since 1980; Titular Bishop of Strathearn, since 1980; *b* 7 Aug. 1923; *s* of Francis Bernard Jukes and Florence Jukes (*née* Stampton). *Educ*: Blackheath; Rome. Professed in Order of Friars Minor Conventual, 1948; Priest, 1952. Lectr in Canon Law, Franciscan Study Centre, Univ. of Kent at Canterbury; Minister Provincial, English Province, 1979. Episcopal Vicar for Religious, Southwark; Area Bishop with special responsibility for Deaneries of Canterbury, Chatham, Dover, Gravesend, Maidstone, Ramsgate and Tunbridge Wells. Chm., World of Work Cttee, RC Bishops' Conf. of England and Wales. *Publications*: contribs to Misc. Francescana, Studia Canonica, New Life, Clergy Rev., etc. *Recreation*: mountain walking and climbing. *Address*: The Hermitage, More Park, West Malling, Kent ME19 6HN.

JUKES, John Andrew, CB 1968; Member, Merton and Sutton District Health Authority, 1986–90; *b* 19 May 1917; *s* of Captain A. M. Jukes, MD, IMS, and Mrs Gertrude E. Jukes (*née* King); *m* 1943, Muriel Child; two *s* two *d*. *Educ*: Shrewsbury Sch.; St John's Coll., Cambridge; London Sch. of Economics. MA in physics Cambridge, BSc (Econ.) London. Cavendish Laboratory, Cambridge, 1939; Radar and Operational Research, 1939–46; Research Dept, LMS Railway, 1946–48; Economic Adviser, Cabinet Office and Treasury, 1948–54; British Embassy, Washington, DC, 1949–51; Economic Adviser to UK Atomic Energy Authority, 1954–64 and Principal Economics and Programming Office, UKAEA, 1957–64; Dep. Dir Gen., DEA, 1964; Dep. Under-Sec. of State, Dept of Economic Affairs, 1967; Dir Gen., Research and Economic Planning, MoT, 1969–70; Dir Gen., Economics and Resources, DoE, 1970–72; Dep. Sec. (Environmental Protection), DoE, 1972–74; Chm., Steering Gp on Water Authority Econ. and Financial Objectives, 1973–74; Dir-Gen., Highways, DoE, 1974–76, Dept of Transport, 1976–77. Mem., CEGB, 1977–80. Alliance (SDP) Councillor, London Borough of Sutton, 1986–90 (Chm., Finance Sub-Cttee, 1986–90). Rep. Sutton SDP on Council for Social Democracy, 1982–86; Pres., Sutton Liberal Democrats, 1990–. *Recreations*: gardening, travelling, sometime orienteer and Himalayan trekker. *Address*: 38 Albion Road, Sutton, Surrey SM2 5TF. *T*: 081–642 5018.

JULIAN, Prof. Desmond Gareth, MD, FRCP; Consultant Medical Director, British Heart Foundation, since 1987; *b* 24 April 1926; *s* of Frederick Bennett Julian and Jane Frances Julian (*née* Galbraith); *m* 1st, 1956, Mary Ruth Jessup (decd); one *s* one *d*; 2nd, 1988, Claire Marley. *Educ*: Leighton Park Sch.; St John's Coll., Cambridge; Middlesex Hosp. MB BChir (Cantab) 1948; MA 1953; MD 1954; FRCPE 1967; FRCP 1970; FRACP 1970; FACC 1985. Surgeon Lieut, RNVR, 1949–51. Med. Registrar, Nat. Heart Hosp., 1955–56; Res. Fellow, Peter Bent Brigham Hosp., Boston, 1957–58; Sen. Reg., Royal Inf., Edinburgh, 1958–61; Cons. Cardiologist, Sydney Hosp., 1961–64, Royal Inf., Edinburgh, 1964–74; Prof. of Cardiology, Univ. of Newcastle upon Tyne, 1975–86. Mem., MRC Systems Bd, 1980–84. Pres., British Cardiac Soc., 1985–87; Second Vice-Pres., RCP. Hon. MD Gothenburg, 1987. Editor, European Heart Jl, 1980–88. *Publications*: Cardiology, 1972, 5th edn 1988; (ed) Angina Pectoris, 1975, 2nd edn 1984; Acute Myocardial Infarction, 1967; (ed) Diseases of the Heart, 1989; Coronary Heart Disease: the facts, 1991; contribs to med. jls, particularly on coronary disease and arrhythmias. *Recreations*: walking, ski-ing, writing. *Address*: Flat 1, 7 Netherhall Gardens, NW3 5RN. *T*: 071–435 8254. *Clubs*: Athenæum, Garrick.

JULIEN, Michael Frederick, FCA; FCT; Group Chief Executive, Storehouse PLC, since 1988; *b* 22 March 1938; *s* of late Robert Auguste François and Olive Rita (*née* Evans); *m* 1963, Ellen Martinsen; one *s* two *d*. *Educ*: St Edward's Sch., Oxford. Price Waterhouse & Co., 1958–67; other commercial appts, 1967–76; Gp Finance Dir, BICC, 1976–83; Exec. Dir, Finance and Planning, Midland Bank, 1983–86; Man. Dir, Finance and Administration, Guinness PLC, 1987–88. *Recreations*: family, travel. *Address*: Bendochy, Ellesmere Road, Weybridge, Surrey KT13 0HQ. *T*: Weybridge (0932) 844999. *Club*: City Livery.

JUNGELS, Dr Pierre Jean Marie Henri, Hon. CBE 1989; Executive Director Downstream, Petrofina Group, since 1989; *b* 18 Feb. 1944; *s* of Henri and Jeanne Jungels; *m* Gabrielle Winkler; one *s* one *d*; *m* 1988, Caroline Benc. *Educ*: Univ. of Liège; California Inst. of Technology (PhD 1973). Petroleum Engr, Shell, 1973–74; Dist Manager, 1975–77, General Manager and Chief Exec., 1977–80, Petrangol (Angola); Man. Dir and Chief Exec., Petrofina UK, 1980–89. Director: Fina SA, Belgium; Petrofina Refineries; Fina France SA; Fina Italiana; Fina Raffinaderij Antwerpen; Fina Europe; Deutsche Fina; Norske Fina; American Petrofina; Fina Marine; Fina Research. Past Pres., Inst. of Petroleum. *Recreation*: shooting. *Address*: Petrofina SA, 52 rue de l'Industrie, 1040 Brussels, Belgium. *T*: 322 233 9111, *Telex*: 21556, *Fax*: 322 233 9142.

JUNGIUS, Vice-Adm. Sir James (George), KBE 1977; DL; Supreme Allied Commander Atlantic's Representative in Europe, 1978–80, retired; *b* 15 Nov. 1923; *s* of Major E. J. T. Jungius, MC; *m* 1949, Rosemary Frances Turquand Matthey; three *s*. *Educ*: RNC, Dartmouth. Served War of 1939–45 in Atlantic and Mediterranean; Commando Ops in Adriatic (despatches). Specialised in Navigation in 1946, followed by series of appts as Navigating Officer at sea and instructing ashore. Comdr, Dec. 1955; CO, HMS Wizard, 1956–57; Admlty, 1958–59; Exec. Officer, HMS Centaur, 1960–61; Captain, 1963; Naval Staff, 1964–65; CO, HMS Lynx, 1966–67; Asst Naval Attaché, Washington, DC, 1968–70; CO, HMS Albion, 1971–72; Rear-Adm., 1972; Asst Chief of Naval Staff (Operational Requirements), 1972–74; Vice-Adm., 1974; Dep. Supreme Allied Comdr Atlantic, 1975–77. Chm., St John Council for Cornwall, 1987–. Fellow, Woodard Corp., 1988. Gov., Grenville Coll., 1981–. CBIM. DL Cornwall, 1982. OStJ 1987. *Address*: c/o National Westminster Bank, Wadebridge, Cornwall. *Clubs*: Royal Over-Seas League; Royal Navy Club of 1765 and 1785; Pilgrims.

JUNOR, Sir John, Kt 1980; Editor, Sunday Express, 1954–86; *b* 15 Jan. 1919; *s* of Alexander Junor, Black Isle, Ross and Cromarty; *m* 1942, Pamela Mary Welsh; one *s* one *d*. *Educ*: Glasgow Univ. (MA Hons English). Lt (A) RNVR, 1939–45. Contested (L) Kincardine and West Aberdeen, 1945, East Edinburgh, 1948, Dundee West, 1951; Asst Editor, Daily Express, 1951–53; Dep. Editor, Evening Standard, 1953–54; Director: Beaverbrook (later Express) Newspapers, 1960–86; Fleet Hldgs, 1981–85. Columnist: Sunday Express, 1973–89; Mail on Sunday, 1990–. Hon. LLD New Brunswick, 1973. *Publications*: The Best of JJ, 1981; Listening for a Midnight Tram (memoirs), 1990. *Recreations*: golf, tennis. *Address*: c/o Associated Newspapers, Northcliffe House, 2 Derry Street, W8 5AT. *Clubs*: Royal and Ancient; Walton Heath.

JUPE, George Percival; Under Secretary, Ministry of Agriculture, Fisheries and Food, 1979–90; *b* 6 April 1930; *s* of Frederick Stuart Jupe and Elizabeth (*née* Clayton); unmarried. *Educ*: Sandown Grammar Sch., IoW; Hertford Coll., Oxford. Ministry of Agriculture, Fisheries and Food: Asst Principal, 1955; Principal, 1960; Asst Sec., 1970–79: Eggs and Poultry, and Potatoes Divs, 1970–74; Internat. Fisheries Div., 1975–78; Emergencies, Food Quality and Pest Controls Gp, 1979–85; Dir, ADAS Admin, 1985–88; Horticulture, Seeds, Plant Health and Flood Defence Gp, 1988–90. *Recreations*: hill walking, gardening, music. *Address*: Briar Cottages, Brook, Isle of Wight.

JUPP, Sir Kenneth Graham, Kt 1975; MC 1943; a Judge of the High Court, Queen's Bench Division, 1975–90; *b* 2 June 1917; *s* of Albert Leonard and Marguerite Isabel Jupp; *m* 1947, Kathleen Elizabeth (*née* Richards); two *s* two *d*. *Educ*: Perse Sch., Cambridge; University Coll., Oxford (Sen. Class. Schol., 1936; 1st Cl. Hon. Mods 1938; College Prize for Greek, 1939; MA Oxon (War Degree), 1945); Lincoln's Inn (Cholmeley Schol., 1939; Cassel Schol., 1946). Regimental Service in France, Belgium, N Africa and Italy, 1939–43; War Office Selection Board, 1943–46. Called to Bar, Lincoln's Inn, 1945, Bencher, 1973; QC 1966; Dep. Chm., Cambridge and Isle of Ely QS, 1965–71; a Recorder of the Crown Court, 1972–75; Presiding Judge, NE Circuit, 1977–81. Chm., Independent Schs Tribunal, 1964–67; conducted MAFF inquiry into Wool Marketing Scheme, 1965; Chm., Public Inquiry into Fire at Fairfield Home, Nottingham, 1975. *Recreations*: playing and singing, language. *Address*: Farrer's Building, Temple, EC4. *Club*: Garrick.

JURINAC, (Srebrenka) Sena; opera singer; Member of Vienna State Opera, 1944–82, now Honorary; retired from stage, 1982; *b* Travnik, Yugoslavia, 24 Oct. 1921; *d* of Ludwig Jurinac, MD, and Christine Cerv. *Educ*: High Sch.; Musical Academy. Made first appearance on stage as Mimi with Zagreb Opera, 1942. Frequent appearances at Glyndebourne Festivals, 1949–56, as well as at the Salzburg Festivals. Guest appearances at La Scala, Covent Garden, San Francisco, Teatro Colón. Principal parts include: Donna Anna and Donna Elvira in Don Giovanni; Elisabeth in Tannhauser; Tosca; Jenufa; Marie in Wozzeck; Marschallin in Der Rosenkavalier; Composer in Ariadne auf Naxos; Elisabeth in Don Carlos; Desdemona in Othello. *Film*: Der Rosenkavalier, 1962. Singing teacher; frequent appearances as mem. of jury in singing competitions. Kammersängerin award, 1951; Ehrenkreuz für Wissenschaft und Kunst, 1961; Grosses Ehrenzeichen für Verdienste um die Republik Oesterreich, 1967. *Address*: c/o Vienna State Opera, Austria.

JURY, Archibald George, CBE 1961; FRIBA; FRIAS; City Architect, Glasgow, 1951–72, retired; *b* 23 June 1907; *s* of late George John Jury and Mabel Sophie Jury (*née* Fisher); *m* 1931, Amy Beatrice Maw (MBE 1983); one *d*. *Educ*: Mount Radford, Exeter; SW School of Art. Architect to Council, Taunton, 1938–40, and 1945. Served War, 1940–45, with Corps of Royal Engineers (rank of Major). Chief Housing Architect, Liverpool, 1946–49; Dir of Housing, Glasgow, 1949–51; Dir of Planning, Glasgow, 1951–66. Organised the building of 100,000 houses, 100,000 school places and numerous civic buildings; responsible for the Glasgow Devpt Plan, 1960–80, and implementation of urban renewal programme and official architecture. Several Saltire Soc. awards for best-designed flats in Scotland. Chairman: Technical Panel, Scottish Local Authorities Special Housing Group, 1965–72; Technical Panel, Clyde Valley Planning Adv. Cttee, 1960–70; Pres., Glasgow Inst. of Architects, 1970–72. *Publications*: contrib. professional and technical journals. *Recreations*: fishing, gardening, painting. *Address*: Redcliffe, Annan Road, Dumfries DG1 3HE.

JUSTHAM, David Gwyn; Chairman, Central Independent Television plc, 1986–91 (Director, 1981–91); *b* 23 Dec. 1923; *s* of John Farquhar Richard and Margaret Anne Justham; *m* 1950, Isobel Thelma, *d* of G. Gordon Thomson, MC; one *s* one *d*. *Educ*: Bristol Grammar School. Served RAF, Bomber Pilot (Flt Lieut), 1941–46. Admitted Solicitor, 1949; joined ICI, 1955; Asst Secretary, ICI Dyestuffs Div., 1955–59; Secretary: ICI European Council, 1960–61; ICI Nobel Div., 1961–65; Imperial Metal Industries Ltd (subseq. IMI plc), 1965–73 (Dir, 1968–85); various appts with IMI, 1965–81, incl. Chm., C. A. Norgren Co., Littleton, Colo, USA, 1974–81. Chairman: W Midlands Bd of Central Independent Television plc, 1981–85; Midland Regional Bd of National Girobank, 1982–85; Nat. Exhibition Centre Ltd, 1982–89 (Dir, 1979–89); Dir, H. Samuel plc, 1981–84; Pres., Birmingham Chamber of Industry and Commerce, 1974–75 (Mem. Council, 1969–); Chm., Birmingham Hippodrome Theatre Trust, 1979–89; Member, Council: Welsh National Opera, 1979–84; Univ. of Aston, 1982–86 (Mem.

Convocation, 1974–); Univ. of Birmingham, 1983– (Mem., 1976–, Hon. Life Mem., 1986–, Ct of Governors; Dep. Pro-Chancellor, 1987–89); City of Birmingham Symphony Orch., 1984–89; Mem., W Midlands Economic Planning Council, 1970–74. General Comr of Income Tax, 1972–77. Pres., Birmingham Press Club, 1985–86. High Sheriff of Co. of W Midlands, 1981–82. *Recreations:* opera and theatre. *Address:* 9 Birch Hollow, Edgbaston, Birmingham B15 2QE. *T:* 021–454 0688.

K

KABERRY, Hon. Sir Christopher Donald, (Hon. Sir Kit), 2nd Bt *cr* 1960, of Adel cum Eccup, City of Leeds; management consultant, since 1991; *b* 14 March 1943; *s* of Lord Kaberry of Adel (Life Peer) and of Lily Margaret, *d* of Edmund Scott; *S* to baronetcy of father, 1991; *m* 1967, Gaenor Elizabeth Vowe, *d* of C. V. Peake; two *s* one *d*. *Educ:* Repton Sch. FCA 1967. Various overseas positions, Costain Group PLC, 1969–80; Financial Manager, United Buildings Factories, Bahrain, 1980–82; Resources Manager, Balfour Beatty Group, Indonesia and Bahamas, 1983–90. *Recreations:* walking, gardening. *Heir:* *s* James Christopher Kaberry [*b* 1 April 1970; *m* 1989, Juliet Clare Hill; two *s*]. *Address:* The Croft, Rookery Lane, Wymondham, Melton Mowbray, Leics LE14 2AU.

KADOORIE, family name of **Baron Kadoorie.**

KADOORIE, Baron *cr* 1981 (Life Peer), of Kowloon in Hong Kong and of the City of Westminster; **Lawrence Kadoorie;** Kt 1974; CBE 1970; JP (Hong Kong); Joint Proprietor and Director, Sir Elly Kadoorie & Sons; Chairman: Sir Elly Kadoorie Successors Ltd; St George's Building Ltd; also chairman and director of many other companies; *b* Hong Kong, 2 June 1899; *s* of Sir Elly Kadoorie, KBE, and Laura Kadoorie (*née* Mocatta); *m* 1938, Muriel, *d* of David Gubbay, Hong Kong; one *s* one *d*. *Educ:* Cathedral Sch., Shanghai; Ascham St Vincents, Eastbourne; Clifton Coll., Bristol; Lincoln's Inn. With his brother, Horace, founded New Territories Benevolent Soc. Is also Chairman: China Light & Power Co., Ltd, Schroders Asia Ltd, Hong Kong Carpet Manufacturers Ltd, Nanyang Cotton Mill Ltd and others. Mem. Council and Court, Univ. of Hong Kong. Fellow, Mem., Patron, Governor, Chm., etc, of numerous other assocs, cttees, etc. JP Hong Kong 1936; MEC 1954, MLC 1950, 1951, 1954, Hong Kong. Hon. LLD Univ. of Hong Kong, 1961; FInstD (London). KStJ (A) (UK) 1972. Solomon Schechter Award (USA), 1959; Ramon Magsaysay Award (Philippines), 1962. Comdr, Légion d'Honneur (France), 1982 (Officier, 1975; Chevalier, 1939); Officier, Ordre de Léopold (Belgium), 1966; Comdr, Ordre de la Couronne (Belgium), 1983. *Recreations:* sports cars (Life Mem. Hong Kong AA), photography, Chinese works of art. *Address:* St George's Building, 24th floor, 2 Ice House Street, Hong Kong. *T:* 5–249221. *Clubs:* Royal Automobile; Hong Kong, Hong Kong Country, Royal Hong Kong Jockey, Jewish Recreation, American (Hong Kong); Travellers' Century (USA).

See also Sir H. Kadoorie.

KADOORIE, Sir Horace, Kt 1989; CBE 1976 (OBE); Joint Proprietor, Sir Elly Kadoorie & Sons; *b* London, 28 Sept. 1902; *s* of Sir Elly Kadoorie, KBE and Laura (*née* Mocatta). *Educ:* Cathedral Sch., Shanghai; Ascham. Hon. Life President: Hongkong and Shanghai Hotels; Peak Tramways Co.; Hon. Chm., Manila Peninsula Hotel Inc.; Director: China Light & Power Co.; Hong Kong Carpet (Hldgs); Hutchison Whampoa; Philippine Carpet Manufacturing Corp.; Rotair; St George's Building Ltd; Tai Ping Internat. (HK). Mem. Cttee, Hong Kong Agricl Show, 1956–61, 1969, 1972; Associate Mem., Hong Kong Council of Social Service; Founder Member: Conservancy Assoc.; Kadoorie Agricl Aid Loan Fund; Life Member: FPA of Hong Kong; Hong Kong Anti-Cancer Soc.; Hong Kong AA; Botanical Soc. of S Africa, Kirstenbosch; Johannesburg Garden Soc.; RSPCA (Hong Kong); St John Amb. Assoc. Hon. Pres., HKNT Fish Culture Assoc. Trustee, Ohel Leah Synagogue, Hong Kong. Patron, Alumni Assoc., Ellis Kadoorie Coll., Hong Kong. Hon. DSocScis Hong Kong, 1981. Chevalier, Legion of Honour (France); Officer, Order of Leopold (Belgium). *Publication:* The Art of Ivory Sculpture in Cathay, 1988. *Address:* St George's Building, 24th Floor, 2 Ice House Street, Hong Kong. *T:* 5–249221. *Clubs:* American, Hong Kong, Jewish Recreation, Royal Hong Kong Jockey (Hong Kong).

See also Baron Kadoorie.

KADRI, Sibghat Ullah; QC 1989; barrister-at-law; President, Standing Conference of Pakistani Organisations in UK, since 1978 (Secretary General, 1975–78); Member, Race Relations Committee, Senate, since 1983; *b* 23 April 1937; *s* of Haji Maulana Firasat Ullah Kadri and Begum Tanwir Fatima Kadri; *m* 1963, Carita Elisabeth Idman; one *s* one *d*. *Educ:* S. M. Coll., Karachi; Karachi Univ. Called to the Bar, Inner Temple, 1969. Sec. Gen., Karachi Univ. Students Union, 1957–58; jailed without trial, for opposing military regime of Ayub Khan, 1958–59; triple winner, All Pakistan Students Debates, 1960; Gen. Sec., Pakistan Students' Fedn in Britain, 1961–62, Vice Pres., 1962–63; Pres., Inner Temple Students Assoc., 1969–70. Producer and broadcaster, BBC Ext. Urdu Service, 1965–68, and Presenter, BBC Home Service Asian Prog., 1968–70. In practice at the Bar, 1969– (Head of Chambers, 11 King's Bench Walk). Chm., Soc. of Afro-Asian and Caribbean Lawyers, UK, 1979–83. Vis. Lectr in Urdu, Holborn Coll., London, 1967–70. Org. Pakistani Def. Cttees during wave of 'Paki-bashing', 1970; active in immigrant and race-relations activities, 1970–; led Asian delegn to Prime Minister, June 1976; attended UN Conf., Migrant Workers in Europe, Geneva, 1975; led Pakistan delegn to 3rd Internat. Conf., Migrant Workers in Europe, Turin, 1977. Gen. Sec., Pakistan Action Cttee, 1973; Convenor, Asian Action Cttee, 1976. Vice Chm., All Party Jt Cttee Against Racism, 1978–80. Publisher, Scopo News, London, until 1984. *Publications:* articles in ethnic minority press on immigration and race relations. *Recreations:* family and reading. *Address:* 11 King's Bench Walk, Temple, EC4Y 7EQ. *T:* 071–353 4931/2.

KAFITY, Rt. Rev. Samir; President Bishop of the Episcopal Church in Jerusalem and the Middle East, since 1986; Anglican Bishop of Jerusalem, since 1984; *b* 1933; *s* of Hanna and Nazha Kafity; *m* 1963, Najat Abed; two *d*. *Educ:* American Univ., Beirut (BA); Near East Sch. of Theol. (DipTh). Ordained deacon, 1957, priest, 1958; Parish priest: to the Arab congregation at St George's Cathedral, Jerusalem; St Andrew's Ramallah; St Peter's, Beir Zeit; All Saints, Beirut; Lectr, Beir Zeit Univ.; Archdeacon of Jerusalem, 1974; Coadjutor Bp in Jerusalem, 1982. Member: Standing Cttee, ACC; Bd of Managers and Exec. Cttee, Near East Sch. of Theol.; Council of Evangelical Community in Syria and Lebanon. Middle East Council of Churches: Sec., 1974; Pres., 1985–. Hon. Canon, Cathedral Church of St John the Divine, NY, 1988. Hon. STD Dickenson Coll., Pa, 1985; Hon. DD Virginia Theol Seminary, 1986. KHS. *Publications:* articles in Anglican and ecumenical jls. *Recreation:* travel. *Address:* PO Box 19122, Jerusalem, Israel. *T:* 972 2 287708, *Fax:* 972 2 273877. *Club:* YMCA (Jerusalem).

KAGAN, family name of **Baron Kagan.**

KAGAN, Baron *cr* 1976 (Life Peer), of Elland, W Yorks; **Joseph Kagan;** *b* 6 June 1915; *s* of late Benjamin and Miriam Kagan; *m* 1943, Margaret Stromas; two *s* one *d*. *Educ:* High School, Kaunas, Lithuania; Leeds University. BCom hons (Textiles). Founder of 'Gannex'-Kagan Textiles Limited, 1951, thereafter Chairman and Managing Director. *Recreation:* chess. *Address:* Delamere, 15 Fixby Road, Huddersfield, W Yorks HD2 2JL.

KAHAN, George; Director of Conciliation and Arbitration, Advisory, Conciliation and Arbitration Service, 1988–91; *b* 11 June 1931; *er s* of late Joseph Kahan and of Xenia (*née* Kirschner); *m* 1959, Avril Pamela Cooper; one *s*. *Educ:* St Paul's Sch. Nat. Service, RAF, 1950–51. Park Royal Woodworkers Ltd, 1951–74 (Dir, 1960–74); Principal: Dept. of Employment, 1975–76; Health and Safety Executive, Health and Safety Commn, 1976–80; Asst Sec., Dept of Employment, 1980–88. *Recreations:* lazing in the sun, reading, listening to music. *Address:* 2 Abbotsbury Close, Kensington, W14 8EG. *T:* 071–603 6752.

KAHN, Paula; Chief Executive and Chairman, Longman Group Ltd, since 1990; *b* 15 Nov. 1940; *d* of Cyril Maurice Kahn and Stella Roscoe. *Educ:* Chiswick County High Sch.; Bristol Univ. (BA Hons). Teacher, administrator, 1962–66; Longman Group, 1966–: editor, publisher, Publishing Director, Divl Man. Dir, 1966–79; Managing Director: ELT Div., Dictionaries Div. and Trade and Ref. Div., 1980–85; Internat. Sector, 1986–88; Chief Exec. (Publishing), 1988–89. English Teaching Adv. Commn, British Council, 1989; Mem. Council, Publishers Assoc., 1990. *Recreations:* cinema, theatre, France, books. *Address:* 11 Carleton Gardens, Brecknock Road, N19 5AQ. *T:* 071–485 8420.

KAHN-ACKERMANN, Georg; Secretary General, Council of Europe, 1974–79; *b* 4 Jan. 1918; *m* 1945, Rosmarie Müller-Diefenbach; one *s* three *d*. *Educ:* in Germany and Switzerland. Served in Armed Forces, 1939–45. Press Reporter and Editor from 1946; Commentator with Radio Bavaria and wrote for newspaper, Abendzeitung, 1950. Author of several books, a publisher's reader, and mem. Exec. Cttee of Bavarian Assoc. of Journalists. Dir, VG WORT, Munich, 1972–74; Vice-Chm., Bd of Deutschlandfunk (Cologne). Mem., Social Democratic Party (SDP), from 1946, and of the German Federal Parliament, 1953–57, 1962–69 and 1970–74. Previous appts include: Vice-Pres., Western European Union Assembly, 1967–70; Chm., Political Commn of Western European Union, 1971–74; Vice-Pres., Consultative Assembly of Council of Europe until elected Secretary General in 1974. Vice-Pres., Deutsche Welthunger hilfe; Pres., VG WORT. *Recreation:* ski-ing. *Address:* Sterzenweg 3, 8193 Ammerland, Bayern, Germany.

KAHURANANGA, Rt. Rev. Musa; *b* 1921; *s* of Samweli and Mariamu Kahurananga; *m* 1941, Raheli Lutozi; three *s* four *d* (and one *s* decd). *Educ:* Teachers' Training College, Katoke Bukoba. Teacher; Deacon 1952, Priest 1953; Asst Bishop in Diocese of Central Tanganyika, 1962; Archbishop of Tanzania, 1979–83; Bishop of Western Tanganyika, 1966–83. *Recreation:* farming. *Address:* PO Box 234, Kasulu, Tanzania.

KAIN, Prof. Roger James Peter, PhD; FBA 1990; Professor of Geography, Exeter University, since 1991; *b* 12 Nov. 1944; *s* of Peter Albert Kain and Ivy Kain; *m* 1970, Annmaree Wallington; one *s*. *Educ:* Harrow Weald County Grammar Sch.; University College London (BA, PhD). Tutor, Bedford Coll., London, 1971–72; Exeter University: Lectr, 1972–88; Montefiore Reader in Geography, 1988–91. Gill Meml Medal, RGS, 1990. *Publications:* Planning for Conservation: an international perspective, 1984; The Tithe Surveys of England and Wales, 1985; An Atlas and Index of the Tithe Files of Mid-Nineteenth-Century England and Wales, 1986. *Recreations:* mountain walking, gardening, cycling, angling. *Address:* Department of Geography, Exeter University, Exeter EX4 4RJ. *T:* Exeter (0392) 263333.

KAISER, Philip M.; political and economic consultant; *b* 12 July 1913; *s* of Morris Kaiser and Temma Kaiser (*née* Sloven); *m* 1939, Hannah Greeley; three *s*. *Educ:* University of Wisconsin; Balliol Coll., Oxford (Rhodes Scholar). Economist, Bd of Governors, Fed. Reserve System, 1939–42; Chief, Project Ops Staff, also Chief, Planning Staff, Bd Economic Warfare and Foreign Econ. Admin., 1942–46; Expert on Internat. Organization Affairs, US State Dept., 1946; Exec. Asst to Asst Sec. of Labor in charge of internat. labor affairs, US Dept of Labor, 1947–49; Asst Sec. of Labor for Internat. Labor Affairs, 1949–53; mem., US Govt Bd of Foreign Service, Dept of State, 1948–53; US Govt mem., Governing Body of ILO, 1948–53; Chief, US delegn to ILO Confs, 1949–53; Special Asst to Governor of New York, 1954–58; Prof. of Internat. Relations and Dir, Program for Overseas Labor and Industrial Relations, Sch. of Internat. Service, American Univ., 1958–61; US Ambassador, Republic of Senegal and Islamic Republic of Mauritania, 1961–64; Minister, Amer. Embassy, London, 1964–69. Chm., Encyclopaedia Britannica International Ltd, 1969–75; Dir, Guinness Mahon Holdings Ltd, 1975–77. US Ambassador to Hungary, 1977–80, to Austria, 1980–81. Member: US Govt Interdepartmental Cttee on Marshall Plan, 1947–48; Interdepartmental Cttee on Greek-Turkish aid and Point 4 Technical Assistance progs, 1947–49. Sen. Consultant, SRI International, 1981–. Professorial Lectr, Johns Hopkins Sch. of Adv. Internat. Studies, 1983–84; Woodrow Wilson Vis. Fellow, Hartford Univ. of W Hartford, Connecticut, 1983. Board Member: Soros Hungarian Foundn; Amer. Ditchley Foundn; Council of Amer. Ambassadors; Inst. for Diplomatic Studies; Member: Council on Foreign Relations; Washington Inst. of Foreign Affairs; IISS. *Recreations:* tennis, swimming, music. *Address:* 2101 Connecticut Avenue NW, Washington, DC 20008, USA.

KAKKAR, Prof. Vijay Vir, FRCS, FRCSE; Professor of Surgical Science, King's College School of Medicine and Dentistry, since 1975, and National Heart and Lung Institute, since 1990, University of London; Director, Thrombosis Research Institute, since 1990; b 22 March 1937; s of Dr H. B. and Mrs L. W. Kakkar; m 1962, Dr Savitri Karnani; two s. Educ: Vikram Univ., Ujjain, India (MB, BS 1960). FRCS 1964; FRCSE 1964. Junior Staff appts, 1960–64; Lectr, Nuffield Dept of Surgery, Univ. of Oxford, 1964–65; Dept of Surgery, King's Coll. Hosp., London: Pfizer Res. Fellow and Hon. Sen. Registrar, 1965–68; Sen. Registrar, 1968–69; Lectr and Hon. Sen. Registrar, 1969–71; Sen. Lectr and Hon. Consultant Surgeon, 1972–76; Dir, Thrombosis Res. Unit, 1975–; Hon. Consultant Surgeon: King's Coll. Hosp. Gp, 1972–; Mayday Hosp., Croydon, 1984–; Hon. Cons. Vascular Surgeon, Royal Brompton Nat. Heart and Lung Hosps, 1990–. Vis. Prof., Harvard Univ. Med. Sch., Boston, 1972. Pres., British Soc. for Haemostasis and Thrombosis, 1984– (Founder Mem., 1980, Sec., 1982–83); Member: Eur. Thrombosis Res. Orgn; Concerted Action Cttee on Thrombosis, EEC; Internat. Soc. on Thrombosis and Haemostasis (Chm., Cttee on Venous Thromboembolism); Internat. Surg. Soc.; Assoc. of Surgeons of GB and NI; Vascular Surg. Soc. of GB; Pan-Pacific Surg. Assoc.; Internat. Soc. for Haematology; Internat. Soc. for Angiology; Surg. Res. Soc. of GB; Hon. Mem., Assoc. of Surgeons of India; Hon. Fellow, Acad. of Medicine of Singapore. Hunterian Prof., RCS, 1969; Lectures: Gunnar Bauer Meml, Copenhagen, 1971; James Finlayson Meml, RCPGlas, 1975; Cross Meml, RCS, 1977; Wright-Schulte, Internat. Soc. on Thrombosis and Haemostasis, 1977; Freyer Meml, RCSI, 1981. David Patey Prize, Surg. Soc. of GB and Ireland, 1971. Member Editorial Board: Haemostasis, 1982–; Clinical Findings, 1982–; Internat. Angiology, 1982–; Thrombosis Research, 1990–. Publications: (jtly) Vascular Disease, 1969; (jtly) Thromboembolism: diagnosis and treatment, 1972; (jtly) Heparin: chemistry and clinical usage, 1976; (jtly) Chromogenic Peptide Substrates: chemistry and clinical usage, 1979; Atheroma and Thrombosis, 1983; 500 pubns in jls on thromboembolism and vascular disease. Recreations: golf, skiing, cricket. Address: Thrombosis Research Institute, Emmanuel Kaye Building, Manresa Road, Chelsea, SW3 6LR. T: 071–351 8301. Clubs: Athenæum; Sundridge Park Golf (Bromley, Kent).

KALISHER, Michael David Lionel; QC 1984; a Recorder, since 1985; b 24 Feb. 1941; s of Samuel and Rose Kalisher; m 1967, Helen; one s two d. Educ: Hove County Grammar Sch.; Bristol Univ. (LLB Hons 1962). Articled as solicitor to Gates & Co., Sussex, 1962–64; admitted as solicitor, 1965; practised as solicitor in London with Avery Midgen & Co., 1965–69, Partner from 1966; called to the Bar, Inner Temple, 1970, Bencher, 1989; practised first from 9 King's Bench Walk, until 1976; then in chambers of John Lloyd-Eley, QC, at 1 Hare Court, Temple. Chm., Criminal Bar Assoc., 1991–; Member: Crown Court Rules Cttee, 1989–; Lord Chancellor's Efficiency Commn, 1989–. Recreations: squash, tennis, reading. Address: 1 Hare Court, Temple, EC4Y 7BE. Club: Roehampton.

KALLIPETIS, Michel Louis; QC 1989; a Recorder, since 1989; b 29 Aug. 1941; s of Takis George Kallipetis and Sheila Gallally; m 1984, Dr Esther Inge Seidel. Educ: Cardinal Vaughan Sch.; University Coll., London. Exchequer and Audit Dept, 1960–63. Called to the Bar, Gray's Inn, 1968. Recreations: opera, cooking, travel. Address: 2 Crown Office Row, Temple, EC4Y 7HJ. T: 071–583 2681. Club: Reform.

KALMS, Stanley; Founder and Chairman, Dixons Group plc; b 21 Nov. 1931; s of Charles and Cissie Kalms; m 1953, Pamela Jimack; three s. Educ: Christ's College, Finchley. Whole career with Dixons Group: started in 1948 in one store owned by father; went public, 1962; Chairman and Chief Exec., 1967. Hon. DLitt. Recreations: communal activities, aft decking, opera, ballet. Address: Dixons Group plc, 29 Farm Street, W1X 7RD. T: 071–499 3494.

KALMUS, Prof. George Ernest, FRS 1988; Associate Director, Particle Physics Department, Rutherford Appleton Laboratory, since 1986; Visiting Professor, Physics and Astronomy Department, University College London, since 1984; b 21 April 1935; s of Hans Kalmus and Anna Kalmus; m 1957, Ann Christine Harland; three d. Educ: St Albans County Grammar Sch.; University Coll. London (BSc Hons, PhD). Res. Asst, Bubble Chamber Gp, UCL, 1959–62; Research Associate, Powell-Birge Bubble Chamber Gp, Lawrence Radiation Lab., Univ. of California, Berkeley, 1962–63 and 1964–67; Lectr, Physics Dept, UCL, 1963–64; Sen. Physicist, Lawrence Rad. Lab., 1967–71; Gp Leader, Bubble Chamber and Delphi Gps, Rutherford Appleton Lab., 1971–86. Mem., various Programme Cttees at CERN, 1974–. Publications: numerous articles on experimental particle physics in Phys. Rev., Phys. Rev. Letters, Nuclear Phys., etc. Recreations: ski-ing, cycling, reading. Address: 16 South Avenue, Abingdon, Oxon OX14 1QH. T: Abingdon (0235) 523340.

KALO, Sir Kwamala, Kt 1983; MBE 1975; Director of Administrative College, since 1987; b 28 Feb. 1929; s of Kalo Navu and Navuga Kila; m 1951, Gimaralai Samuel; two s two d. Educ: up to secondary level in Papua New Guinea. Govt Primary School teacher, 1949; served in Dept of Education as classroom teacher, Headmaster, Inspector, Supt of Schools, Asst Sec. of Technical Educn, until 1979; represented Papua New Guinea in Trusteeship Council Meeting of UN, 1963; seconded to Public Services Commn as a Comr, 1979; High Comr for Papua New Guinea in New Zealand, 1983–86. Address: PO Box 6572, Boroko, Papua New Guinea. T: 257217.

KAMBA, Prof. Walter Joseph; Vice-Chancellor, since 1981 (Vice-Principal, 1980–81), Professor of Law, since 1980, University of Zimbabwe; b 6 Sept. 1931; s of Joseph Mafara and Hilda Kamba; m 1960, Angeline Saziso Dube; three s. Educ: University of Cape Town (BA, LLB); Yale Law School (LLM). Attorney of the High Court of Rhodesia (now Zimbabwe), 1963–66; Research Fellow, Institute of Advanced Legal Studies, London Univ., 1967–68; Lecturer, then Sen. Lectr, in Comparative Law and Jurisprudence, 1969–80, Dean of the Faculty of Law, 1977–80, Univ. of Dundee. Chm., Kingstons (booksellers and distributors) (Zimbabwe), 1984–. Chm., Bd of Governors, Zimbabwe Broadcasting Corp., 1987– (Vice-Chm., 1980–87); Member: Public Service Professional Qualifications Panel, Harare, 1981–83; Council, ACU, 1981–83 (Member: Working Party on future policy, 1981–; Budget Review Cttee, 1982–83); Commonwealth Standing Cttee on student mobility, 1981–88; Exec. Bd, Assoc. of African Univs, 1984– (Chm., Finance and Admin. Cttee, 1985–); Nat. Commn, Law and Popn Studies Project, Zimbabwe, 1986–; Chm., Assoc. of Eastern and Southern African Univs, 1984–87; Vice-President: Internat. Assoc. of Univs, 1985–; ACP-EEC Foundn for Cultural Co-op., Brussels, 1986–88; Mem., Zimbabwe Nat. Commn for UNESCO, 1987–. Mem., Univ. of Swaziland Commn on Planning, 1986. Legal Adviser, ZANU (Patriotic Front), until 1980; Chm., Electoral Supervisory Commn, 1984–. Trustee: Zimbabwe Mass Media Trust, 1981–; Conservation Trust of Zimbabwe, 1981–87; Legal Resources Foundn, Zimbabwe, 1984–90; African-American Inst., NY, 1985–; Zimbabwe Cambridge Trust, 1987–; Member: Bd of Trustees, Michael Gelfand Med. Res. Foundn, Zimbabwe, 1986–; Internat. Bd, United World Colls, 1985–87; Mem. Council: Univ. for Peace, Costa Rica, 1981–86; Univ. of Zambia, 1981–86; United Nations Univ., Tokyo, 1983–89 (Chm., Council, 1985–86); Mem., Cttee on Institutional and Programmatic Develt); Univ. of Lesotho, 1987–; Mem., Internat. Adv. Cttee, Synergos Inst., NY, 1987–; Patron,

Commonwealth Legal Educn Assoc., 1986–; Governor, Ranche House Coll., Harare, 1980–; Member Board of Governors: Zimbabwe Inst. of Development Studies, 1981– (Chm. Bd, 1986–); Internat. Develt Res. Centre, Canada, 1986–; Commonwealth of Learning, 1988– (Vice-Chm., 1989–); Member: Nat. St John's Ambulance Council for Republic of Zimbabwe, 1982–87; Indep. Internat. Commn on Health Res. for Develt, 1987–; Bd, Internat. Cttee for Study of Educnl Exchange, 1988–; Exec. Cttee, Internat. Develt Res. Centre, Canada, 1989–. Hon. LLD Dundee, 1982. Officier dans l'Ordre des Palmes Académiques (France). Publications: articles in Internat. and Comparative Law Quarterly, Juridical Review. Recreation: tennis. Address: University of Zimbabwe, PO Box MP 167, Mount Pleasant, Harare, Zimbabwe. T: Harare 303211, Telex: 26580, Fax: Harare 303292.

KAMIL, Geoffrey Harvey; Stipendiary Magistrate, West Yorkshire, since 1990; b 17 Aug. 1942; s of Peter and Sadie Kamil; m 1968, Andrea Pauline Kamil (née Ellis); two d. Educ: Leeds Grammar Sch.; Leeds University (LLB). Admitted as Solicitor of the Supreme Court, 1968; Partner with J. Levi & Co., solicitors, Leeds, 1968–87; Asst Stipendiary Magistrate, 1985–87; Stipendiary Magistrate, W Midlands, 1987–90; Asst Crown Court Recorder, 1986–. Mem., Magisterial Cttee, Judicial Studies Bd, 1991–. Leeds Law Society: Mem. Cttee, 1983–87; Chm., Courts Cttee, 1983–87; Mem., Duty Solicitor Cttee, 1986–87; Mem., Leeds Bar/Law Soc. Liaison Cttee, 1983–87. Sec., Kirkstall Lodge Hostal for Ex-Offenders, 1976–87. Recreations: golf, swimming, sailing, tennis, the Lake District, classic cars. Address: The City Courts, Bradford, W Yorks BD1 1JL. Clubs: Moor Allerton Golf (Leeds); Shirley Golf (Birmingham).

KAN, Prof. Yuet Wai, FRCP 1983; FRS 1981; Louis K. Diamond Professor of Hematology, since 1984, Investigator, Howard Hughes Medical Institute Laboratory, since 1976, and Head, Division of Medical Genetics and Molecular Hematology, Department of Medicine, since 1983, University of California, San Francisco; b 11 June 1936; s of Kan Tong Po and Kan Li Lai Wan; m 1964, Alvera L. Limauro; two d. Educ: Univ. of Hong Kong (MB, BS, DSc). Research Associate, Children's Hosp. Medical Center, Dept of Pediatrics, Harvard Medical Sch., Boston, Mass; Asst Prof. of Pediatrics, Harvard Medical Sch., 1970–72; Associate Prof. of Medicine, Depts of Medicine and Laboratory Medicine, Univ. of California, San Francisco, 1972–77; Chief, Hematology Service, San Francisco General Hospital, 1972–79; Prof. of Medicine, Univ. of California, 1977–. Dir, Molecular Biology Inst., Univ. of Hong Kong, 1990– (Hon. Dir, 1988–90). Member: Nat. Acad. of Scis, USA, 1986; Academia Sinica, Taiwan, 1988. Hon. MD Univ. of Cagliari, Sardinia, 1981; Hon. DSc: Chinese Univ. of Hong Kong, 1981; Univ. of Hong Kong, 1987. Publications: contribs to: Nature, Proc. of Nat. Academy of Sciences, Jl of Clinical Investigation, Blood, British Jl of Haematology, and others. Recreations: tennis, skiing. Address: U426, University of California San Francisco, San Francisco, California 94143–0724, USA. T: (415) 476–5841, Fax: (415) 566–4969.
See also Sir Kan Yuet-Keung.

KAN Yuet-Keung, Sir, GBE 1979 (CBE 1967; OBE 1959); Kt 1972; JP; Chairman, Hong Kong Trade Development Council, 1979–83; Chairman, Bank of East Asia Ltd, 1963–83; b 26 July 1913; s of late Kan Tong Po, JP; m 1940, Ida; two s one d. Educ: Hong Kong Univ.; London Univ. BA Hong Kong 1934. Solicitor and Notary Public. Sen. Unofficial MLC 1968–72, Sen. Unofficial MEC 1974–80, Hong Kong. Pro-Chancellor, Chinese Univ. of Hong Kong, 1983– (Chm., Council, 1973–83). Hon. Fellow, LSE, 1980. Hon. LLD: Chinese Univ. of Hong Kong, 1968; Univ. of Hong Kong, 1973. Order of Sacred Treasure, 3rd Class, Japan; Officier de l'Ordre National du Mérite (France), 1978; Officer's Cross, Order of Merit 1st class (Germany), 1983; Grand Decoration of Honour in Gold with Star (Austria), 1983; Order of Sacred Treasure, 2nd class (Japan), 1983; Knight Grand Cross, Royal Order of Northern Pole Star (Sweden), 1983. Recreations: tennis, swimming, golf. Address: Swire House, 11th Floor, Chater Road, Hong Kong. T: Hong Kong 238181.
See also Yuet Wai Kan.

KANE, Professor George, FBA 1968; William Rand Kenan Jr Professor of English in the University of North Carolina at Chapel Hill, 1976–87, Chairman of the Division of the Humanities, 1980–83, Professor Emeritus, since 1987; b 4 July 1916; o s of George Michael and Clara Kane; m 1946, Katherine Bridget, o d of Lt-Col R. V. Montgomery, MC; one s one d. Educ: St Peter's Coll.; British Columbia University; Toronto Univ.; University Coll., London. BA (University of BC), 1936; Research Fellow, University of Toronto, 1936–37; MA (Toronto), 1937; Research Fellow, Northwestern Univ., 1937–38; IODE Schol., for BC, 1938–39. Served War of 1939–45: Artists' Rifles, 1939–40; Rifle Bde, 1940–46 (despatches). PhD (London), 1946; Asst Lecturer in English, University Coll., London, 1946, Lecturer, 1948, Reader in English, 1953, Fellow, 1971; Prof. of English Language and Literature and Head of English Dept, Royal Holloway College, London Univ., 1955–65; Prof. of English Language and Medieval Literature, 1965–76 and Head of English Dept, 1968–76, King's College, London, Prof. Emeritus, 1976, Fellow, 1976. Vis. Prof., Medieval Acad. of America, 1970, 1982, Corresp. Fellow, 1975, Fellow, 1978; Fellow: Amer. Acad. of Arts and Scis, 1977; Nat. Humanities Center, 1987–88; Sen. Fellow, Southeastern Inst. of Medieval and Renaissance Studies, 1978. Member: Council, Early English Text Soc., 1969–88; Governing Body, SOAS, 1970–76; Council, British Acad., 1974–76; Governing Body, Univ. of N Carolina Press, 1979–84. Sir Israel Gollancz Memorial Prize, British Acad., 1963; Haskins Medallist, Med. Acad. of Amer., 1978. Lectures: Chambers Meml, UCL, 1965; Accademia Nazionale dei Lincei, Rome, 1976; John Coffin Meml, Univ. of London, 1979; M. W. Bloomfield Meml, Harvard, 1989; Tucker-Cruse Meml, Bristol Univ., 1991; Public Orator, Univ. of London, 1962–66; Annual Chaucer Lectr, New Chaucer Soc., 1980. Gen. editor of London Edn of Piers Plowman. Publications: Middle English Literature, 1951; Piers Plowman, the A Version, 1960; Piers Plowman: The Evidence for Authorship, 1965; Piers Plowman: the B version, 1975; Geoffrey Chaucer, 1984; Chaucer and Langland, 1989; articles and reviews. Recreation: fishing. Clubs: Athenæum, Flyfishers'.

KANE, Jack, OBE 1969; DL; JP; Hon. Vice President, Age Concern, Scotland, since 1987 (Chairman, 1983–86); Lord Provost of the City of Edinburgh and Lord Lieutenant of the County of the City of Edinburgh, 1972–75; b 1 April 1911; m 1940, Anne Murphy; one s two d. Educ: Bathgate Academy. Served War, 1940–46. Librarian, 1936–55. Pres., SE of Scotland Dist, Workers' Educnl Assoc., 1983– (Sec., 1955–76). Chm., Board of Trustees for Nat. Galls of Scotland, 1975–80; Mem., South of Scotland Electricity Bd, 1975–81, Chm., Consultative Council, 1977–81. JP Edinburgh, 1945; DL City of Edinburgh, 1976. Dr hc Edinburgh, 1976. Grand Officer, Order of the Oaken Crown (Luxembourg), 1972; Grand Cross of Merit (W Germany). Recreations: reading, walking. Address: 88 Thirlestane Road, Edinburgh EH9 1AS. T: 031–447 7757. Club: Newcraighall Miners' Welfare Inst.

KANG, Dr Young Hoon; Prime Minister of the Republic of Korea, 1988–90; b 30 May 1922; m 1947, Hyo-Soo Kim; two s one d. Educ: Univ. of Manchuria (BAEcon); graduated from US Comd and Gen. Staff Coll., Kansas, 1958; Univ. of Southern California (MA Internat. Relns 1966, PhD Pol. Sci. 1973). Mil. Attaché to Korean Embassy, Washington DC, 1952–53; Korean Army Div. Comdr, 1953; Dir, Jt Staff, Korean Jt Chiefs of Staff, 1954; Asst Minister of Defence, 1955–56; Korean Army Corps

Comdr, 1959–60; Supt, Korean Mil. Acad., 1960–61; retired, rank of Lt-Gen., 1961. Staff Mem., Research Inst. on Communist Strategy and Propaganda, Univ. of S California, 1968–69; Dir, Research Inst. on Korean Affairs, Silver Spring, Md, 1970–76; Dean, Graduate Sch., Hankuk Univ. of For. Studies, Korea, 1977–78; Chancellor, Inst. of For. Affairs and Nat. Security, Min. of For. Affairs, Korea, 1978–80; Ambassador to UK, 1981–84; Ambassador to the Holy See, 1985–88. Military service medals include Ulchi with Silver Star, Chungmu with Gold Star. *Address:* c/o Office of the Prime Minister, Chang Wa Dae, 1 Sejong-no, Chongno-ku, Seoul, Republic of Korea.

KANTOROWICH, Prof. Roy Herman, BArch (Witwatersrand), MA (Manchester), RIBA, FRTPI; Professor of Town and Country Planning, 1961–84, Professor Emeritus, since 1984, Dean of the Faculty of Arts, 1975–76 and Director of Wolfson Design Unit, 1981–84, University of Manchester; *b* Johannesburg, 24 Nov. 1916; *s* of George Kantorowich and Deborah (*née* Baranov); *m* 1943, Petronella Sophie Wissema (violinist, as Nella Wissema); one *s* two *d*. *Educ:* King Edward VII Sch., Johannesburg; University of Witwatersrand. BArch 1939; ARIBA 1940; MTPI 1965 (AMTPI 1946). Post-grad. studies in Housing and Planning, MIT and Columbia Univ., 1939–41; Planning Officer: Vanderbijl Park New Town, 1942–45; directing Cape Town Foreshore Scheme, 1945–48; private practice in Cape Town, in architecture and town planning, 1948–61. Pres., S African Inst. Town and Regional Planners, 1960. Formerly Town Planning Consultant to Cape Provincial Admin., and for many cities and towns in S Africa incl. Durban, Pretoria and Port Elizabeth; Cons. for New Town of Ashkelon, Israel, 1950–56. Member: NW Econ. Planning Coun. 1965–79; Council (Chm., Educn Cttee), RTPI, 1965–70; Planning Cttee, SSRC, 1969–73; Construction and Environment Bd, and Chm., Town Planning Panel, CNAA, 1971–75; Natal Building Soc. Fellowship, 1980. Buildings include: Civic Centre, Welkom, OFS; Baxter Hall, University of Cape Town; Sea Point Telephone Exchange (Cape Province Inst. of Architects Bronze Medal Award); Architecture and Planning Building, Univ. of Manchester. FRSA 1972. *Publications:* Cape Town Foreshore Plan, 1948; (with Lord Holford) Durban 1985, a plan for central Durban in its Regional Setting, 1968; Three Perspectives on planning for the 'eighties, 1981; contribs to SAArch. Record, Jl RTPI and other professional jls. *Recreations:* music, tennis. *Address:* 3 Winster Avenue, Manchester M20 8YA. *T:* 061–445 9417. *Club:* Northern Lawn Tennis.

KAPI, Hon. Sir Mari, Kt 1988; CBE 1983; Deputy Chief Justice of Papua New Guinea, since 1982; a Justice of the Court of Appeal, Solomon Islands, since 1982; *b* 12 Dec. 1950; *s* of Kapi 'Ila and Mea Numa; *m* 1973, Tegana Kapi; two *s* three *d*. *Educ:* Univ. of Papua New Guinea (LLB); SOAS, Univ. of London (LLM). Admitted to practice in PNG and Australia, 1974. Dep. Public Solicitor, 1976; Associate Public Solicitor, 1977; Public Solicitor, 1978; a Judge of Nat. and Supreme Courts of PNG, 1979. *Recreations:* tennis, touch Rugby. *Address:* PO Box 7018, Boroko, Papua New Guinea. *T:* 259273.

KAPLAN, Prof. Joseph; Professor of Physics, University of California at Los Angeles, 1940–70, now Professor Emeritus; *b* 8 Sept. 1902; *s* of Henry and Rosa Kaplan, Tapolcza, Hungary; *m* 1st, 1933, Katherine Elizabeth Feraud (*d* 1977); no *c*; 2nd, 1978, Frances Irsak Baum (*née* Irsak). *Educ:* Johns Hopkins University, Baltimore, Md, PhD 1927; National Research Fellow, Princeton Univ., 1927–28. University of Calif. at Los Angeles: Asst Prof. of Physics, 1928–35; Associate Prof., 1935–40; Prof., 1940–. Chief, Operations Analysis Section, Second Air Force, 1943–45 (Exceptional Civilian Service Medal, US Air Corps, 1947). Chm., US Nat. Cttee for Internat. Geophysical Year, 1953–64. Fellow: Inst. of Aeronautical Sciences, 1957; Amer. Meteorological Soc., 1970 (Pres., 1963–67). Mem. Nat. Acad. of Sciences, 1957; Hon. Mem., Amer. Meteorological Soc., 1967; Vice-Pres., International Union of Geodesy and Geophysics, 1960–63, Pres., 1963–; Hon. Governor, Hebrew Univ. of Jerusalem, 1968. Hon. DSc: Notre Dame, 1957; Carleton Coll., 1957; Hon. LHD: Yeshiva Univ. and Hebrew Union Coll., 1958; Univ. of Judaism, 1959. Exceptional Civilian Service Medal (USAF), 1960; Hodgkins Prize and Medal, 1965. Exceptional Civilian Service Medal, 1969; John A. Fleming Medal, Amer. Geophysical Union, 1970; Commemorative Medal, 50th Anniversary, Amer. Meteorological Soc., 1970; Special Award, UCLA Alumni Assoc., 1970. *Publications:* Across the Space Frontier, 1950; Physics and Medicine of the Upper Atmosphere, 1952; (co-author) Great Men of Physics, 1969; publications in Physical Review, Nature, Proc. Nat. Acad. of Sciences, Jl Chemical Physics. *Recreations:* golf, ice-skating, walking. *Address:* 1565 Kelton Avenue, Los Angeles, Calif 90024, USA. *T:* (213) 477–8166. *Club:* Cosmos (Washington, DC).

KAPLAN, Neil Trevor; Hon. Mr Justice Kaplan; High Court Judge, Hong Kong, since 1990; *b* 1 Sept. 1942; *s* of Leslie Henry Kaplan and Sybil Sylvia Kaplan (*née* Gasson); *m* 1971, Barbara Jane Spector; one *s* one *d*. *Educ:* St Paul's Sch.; King's College London (LLB). FCIArb. Called to the Bar, Inner Temple, 1965, Bencher 1991; practised London, 1965–80; Dep. Principal Crown Counsel, Hong Kong, 1980, Principal Crown Counsel, 1982; QC (Hong Kong) 1982; private practice, Hong Kong Bar, 1984–90; Solicitor-barrister, Victoria, NSW, 1983; NY Bar, 1986. Chm., Hong Kong Branch, CIArb, 1984–87 and 1989–90; Dep. Chm., Justice, Hong Kong, 1988–90. JP Hong Kong, 1984. *Publications:* (jtly) Hong Kong Arbitration—Cases and Materials; articles on arbitration. *Recreations:* tennis, travel, food and wine, films, theatre, walking. *Address:* Supreme Court, 38 Queensway, Hong Kong. *T:* 8254424. *Clubs:* Royal Automobile, Old Pauline; Hong Kong, Royal Hong Kong Jockey, Hong Kong Cricket.

KAPPEL, Frederick R.; retired as Chairman of Boards, American Telephone & Telegraph Company and International Paper Company; Chairman, Board of Governors, US Postal Service; *b* Albert Lea, Minnesota, 14 Jan. 1902; *s* of Fred A. Kappel and Gertrude M. Towle Kappel; *m* 1st, 1927, Ruth Carolyn Ihm (decd); two *d*; 2nd, 1978, Alice McW. Harris. *Educ:* University of Minnesota (BSE). Northwestern Bell Telephone Company: various positions in Minnesota, 1924–33; Plant Engineer, Nebraska, S Dakota, 1934. Plant Operations Supervisor (Exec.) Gen. Staff, Omaha, Nebraska, 1937, Asst Vice-Pres. Operations, 1939, Vice-Pres. Operations and Dir, 1942. Amer. Telephone & Telegraph Co., NY: Asst Vice-Pres. (O & E), Vice-Pres. (Long Lines), Vice Pres. (O & E), 1949. Pres. Western Electric Co., 1954–56; Chm. and Chief Exec. Officer, Amer. Tel. & Tel. Co., 1956–67, Chm. Exec. Cttee, 1967–69; Chm. Bd, International Paper Co., 1969–71, Chm. Exec. Cttee 1971–74. Director: Amer. Telephone & Telegraph Co., 1956–70; Chase Manhattan Bank, 1956–72; Metropolitan Life Insurance Co., 1958–75; General Foods Corporation, 1961–73; Standard Oil Co. (NJ), 1966–70; Whirlpool Corp., 1967–72; Chase Manhattan Corp., 1969–72; Boys' Club of America; Acad. of Polit. Sciences, 1963–71; Member: Business Council (Chm., 1963–64); Advisory Board of Salvation Army, 1957–73; US Chamber of Commerce; various societies. Trustee: Presbyterian Hospital, 1949–74; Grand Central Art Galleries, Inc., 1957–70; Aerospace Corp., 1967–74; Tax Foundation, 1960–72. Trustee, University of Minnesota Foundation. Holds numerous hon. doctorates and awards, including: Cross of Comdr of Postal Award, France, 1962; Presidential Medal of Freedom, 1964. *Publications:* Vitality in a Business Enterprise, 1960; Business Purpose and Performance. *Recreation:* golf. *Address:* Apt 1101, 435 S Gulfstream Avenue, Sarasota, Fla 34236, USA. *Clubs:* Triangle, University, Economic (New York); International (Washington); Bird Key Yacht, Sarabay Country (Sarasota, Fla).

KARACHI, Archbishop of, (RC), since 1958; **His Eminence Cardinal Joseph Cordeiro;** *b* Bombay, India, 19 Jan. 1918. *Educ:* St Patrick's High School; DJ College, Karachi; Papal Seminary, Kandy, Ceylon. Priest, 1946; Asst Chaplain, St Francis Xavier's, Hyderabad, Sind, 1947; Asst Principal, St Patrick's High School, Karachi, 1948; Student at Oxford, 1948; Asst Principal, St Patrick's High Sch., 1950; Principal, Grammar Sch., and Rector, Diocesan Seminary, Quetta, 1952. Cardinal, 1973. *Address:* St Patrick's Cathedral, Karachi 3, Pakistan. *T:* 515870.

KARANJA, Hon. Dr Josphat Njuguna; Vice-President of Kenya, 1988–89; Minister of Home Affairs and National Heritage, 1988–89; *b* 5 Feb. 1931; *s* of Josphat Njuguna; *m* 1966, Beatrice Nyindombi, Fort Portal, Uganda; one *s* two *d*. *Educ:* Alliance High Sch., Kikuyu, Kenya; Makerere Coll., Kampala, Uganda; University of Delhi, India; Atlanta Univ. (MA); Princeton Univ., New Jersey, USA (PhD). Lecturer in African Studies, Farleigh Dickinson Univ., New Jersey, 1961–62; Lecturer in African and Modern European History, University College, Nairobi, Kenya, 1962–63; High Comr for Kenya in London, 1963–70; Vice-Chancellor, Univ. of Nairobi, 1970–79. MP for Mathare, Nairobi, 1986–. *Recreations:* golf, tennis. *Address:* c/o General Accident Insurance Co. (Kenya) Ltd, Icea Building, Kenyatta Avenue, PO Box 42166, Nairobi, Kenya.

KARK, (Arthur) Leslie; MA (Oxon); FRSA; author, barrister; Chairman: Lucie Clayton Secretarial College; Lucie Clayton Ltd; *b* 12 July 1910; *s* of Victor and Helena Kark, Johannesburg; *m* 1st, 1935, Joan Tetley (marr. diss., 1956); two *d*; 2nd, 1956, Evelyn Gordine (*see* E. F. Kark); one *s* one *d*. *Educ:* Clayesmore; St John's Coll., Oxford. Called to Bar, Inner Temple, 1932; Features Editor of World's Press News, 1933; Editor of Photography, 1934; Public Relations Officer to Advertising Association, 1935; Features Editor News Review, 1936–39; London Theatre Critic, New York Herald Tribune; News Editor, Ministry of Information, 1940. Served War of 1939–45, RAF, 1940–46; Air-gunner; Wing Commander in Command of Public Relations (Overseas) Unit; author, Air Ministry's official book on Air War, Far East. Short stories and novels translated into French. Swedish, German, Polish, etc. *Publications:* The Fire Was Bright, 1944; Red Rain, 1946; An Owl in the Sun, 1948; Wings of the Phœnix, 1949; On the Haycock, 1957. *Recreations:* fly-fishing, golf. *Address:* 9 Clareville Grove, SW7. *T:* 071–373 2621; Roche House, Sheep Street, Burford, Oxon. *T:* Burford (099382) 3007. *Club:* United Oxford & Cambridge University.

KARK, Austen Steven, CBE 1987; Managing Director, External Broadcasting (now World Service), BBC, 1985–86; *b* 20 Oct. 1926; *s* of Major Norman Kark and late Ethel Kark, formerly of Eaton Place, London, and Johannesburg; *m* 1st, 1949, Margaret Solomon (marr. diss. 1954); two *d*; 2nd, 1954, Nina Mary Bawden, *qv*; one *d* one step *s* (and one step *s* decd). *Educ:* Upper Canada Coll., Toronto; Nautical Coll., Pangbourne; RNC; Magdalen Coll., Oxford (MA). Served RN and RIN, 1943–46. Directed first prodn in UK of Sartre's The Flies, Oxford, 1948; trained in journalism, Belfast Telegraph, L'Illustré, Zofingen, Switzerland; Courier, Bandwagon, London Mystery Magazine; free-lance journalist and broadcaster, London and New York, 1952–54; joined BBC, 1954; scriptwriter; Producer, External Services; Head of S European Service, 1964; Head of E European (and Russian) Service, 1972; Editor, World Service, 1973; Controller, English Services, and Editor, World Service, 1974; advised Lord Soames on election broadcasting, Rhodesia, and chaired, for Prime Minister Mugabe, enquiry into future of radio and television in Zimbabwe, 1980; Dep. Man. Dir, External Broadcasting, BBC, 1981–85. Broadcasting consultant, 1987–; Chm., CPC Guidebooks, 1988–. Mem. UK Delegn, CSCE London Information Forum, 1989. Trustee, Res. Fund for Complementary Medicine, 1988–. *Recreations:* Real tennis, mosaics, Greece, grandchildren. *Address:* 22 Noel Road, N1 8HA; 19 Kapodistriou, Nauplion 21100, Greece. *Clubs:* Oriental, MCC, Queen's, Royal Tennis Court, Bushmen (ex-Chairman).

KARK, Mrs Evelyn Florence, (*nom de plume* **Lucie Clayton**); Director; *b* 5 Dec. 1928; *d* of Emily and William Gordine; *m* 1956 (Arthur) Leslie Kark, *qv*; one *s* one *d*. *Educ:* privately and inconspicuously. Asst to Editor, Courier Magazine, 1950; became Head of model school and agency (assuming name of Lucie Clayton), 1952; founded Lucie Clayton Sch. of Fashion Design and Dressmaking, 1961, and Lucie Clayton Secretarial College, 1966. *Publications:* The World of Modelling, 1968; Modelling and Beauty Care, 1985. *Recreations:* talking, tapestry, cooking. *Address:* 9 Clareville Grove, SW7. *T:* 071–373 2621; Roche House, Burford, Oxfordshire. *T:* Burford (099382) 3007.

KARK, Leslie; *see* Kark, A. L.

KARK, Mrs Nina Mary; *see* Bawden, N. M.

KARLE, Jerome, PhD; Chief Scientist, Laboratory for the Structure of Matter, since 1968; *b* NY, 18 June 1918; *s* of Louis Karfunkle and Sadie Helen Kun; *m* 1942, Isabella, *d* of Zygmunt and Elizabeth Lugoski; three *d*. *Educ:* Abraham Lincoln High Sch.; City Coll. of NY (BS 1937); Harvard Univ. (AM 1938); Univ. of Michigan (MS 1942; PhD 1943). Research Associate, Manhattan Project, Chicago, 1943–44; US Navy Project, Michigan, 1944–46; Head, Electron Diffraction Section, Naval Res. Lab., 1946–58, Head of Diffraction Branch, 1958–68. Prof. (part-time), Univ. of Maryland, 1951–70. Pres., Amer. Crystallographic Assoc., 1972; Chm., US Nat. Cttee for Crystallography, NAS and Nat. Res. Council, 1973–75; Pres., Internat. Union of Crystallography, 1981–84. Fellow, Amer. Phys. Soc.; Mem., NAS. Nobel Prize for Chemistry, 1985 (jtly). *Publications:* articles in learned jls on study of atoms, molecules, crystals and solid surfaces by diffraction methods. *Recreations:* stereo-photography, swimming, ice skating. *Address:* Laboratory for the Structure of Matter, Code 6030, Naval Research Laboratory, Washington, DC 20375, USA. *T:* (202) 767–2665.

KARMEL, His Honour Alexander D., QC 1954; an Additional Judge, Central Criminal Court, later a Circuit Judge, 1968–79; *b* 16 May 1904; *s* of Elias Karmel and Adeline (*née* Freedman); *m* 1937, Mary, *widow* of Arthur Lee and *d* of Newman Lipton; one *s*. *Educ:* Newcastle upon Tyne Royal Grammar Sch. Barrister-at-law, Middle Temple, 1932; Master of the Bench, 1962; Leader of Northern Circuit, 1966; Comr of Assize, Stafford, summer 1967; Recorder of Bolton, 1962–68. Mem., Bar Council, 1950–53, 1961–64. *Recreations:* croquet, golf. *Address:* 171 Rivermead Court, Ranelagh Gardens, SW6 3SF. *T:* 071–736 4609. *Club:* Hurlingham.

KARMEL, Emeritus Prof. Peter Henry, AC 1976; CBE 1967; Chairman: Australian Institute of Health, since 1987; Canberra Institute of the Arts, since 1988; National Council on AIDS, since 1988; *b* 9 May 1922; *s* of Simeon Karmel; *m* 1946, Lena Garrett; one *s* five *d*. *Educ:* Caulfield Grammar Sch.; Univ. of Melbourne (BA); Trinity Coll., Cambridge (PhD). Research Officer, Commonwealth Bureau of Census and Statistics, 1943–45; Lectr in Econs, Univ. of Melbourne, 1946; Rouse Ball Res. Student, Trinity Coll., Cambridge, 1947–48; Sen. Lectr in Econs, Univ. of Melbourne, 1949; Prof. of Econs, 1950–62, Emeritus, 1965, Univ. of Adelaide; Principal-designate, Univ. of Adelaide at Bedford Park (subseq. Flinders Univ. of SA), 1961–66; Vice-Chancellor, Flinders Univ. of SA, 1966–71; Chancellor, Univ. of Papua and New Guinea, 1969–70 (Chm., Interim Council, 1965–69); Chairman: Univs Commn, 1971–77; Commonwealth Tertiary Educn Commn, 1977–82; Vice-Chancellor, ANU, 1982–87. Mem. Council, Univ. of

Adelaide, 1955–69; Vis. Prof. of Econs, Queen's Univ., Belfast, 1957–58; Mem. Commonwealth Cttee: on Future of Tertiary Educn, 1961–65; of Economic Enquiry, 1963–65; Mem., Australian Council for Educn Research, 1968– (Pres., 1979–); Chairman: Cttee of Enquiry into Educn in SA, 1969–70; Interim Cttee for Aust. Schools Commn, 1972–73; Cttee of Enquiry on Med. Schs, 1972–73; Cttee of Enquiry on Open Univ., 1973–74; Australia Council, 1974–77; Cttee on Post-Secondary Educn in Tasmania, 1975–76; Quality of Educn Review Cttee, 1984–85; Member: Commonwealth Govt Cttee to Review Efficiency and Effectiveness in Higher Educn, 1985–86; Adv. Cttee of Cities Commn, 1972–74; CSIRO Adv. Council, 1979–82; Australian Stats Adv. Council, 1988–. Leader, OECD Review of US Educn Policy, 1978–79 and NZ Educn Policy, 1982. Pres., Acad. of Social Sciences in Australia, 1987–90 (FASSA 1952). Mem. Council, Chinese Univ. of Hong Kong, 1990–. FACE 1969. Hon. LLD: Univ. of Papua and New Guinea, 1970; Univ. of Melbourne, 1975; Univ. of Queensland, 1985; Hon. LittD Flinders Univ. of SA, 1971; Hon. DLit, Murdoch Univ., 1975; DU Newcastle, NSW, 1978. Mackie Medal, 1975; Aust. Coll. of Educn Medal, 1981. *Publications:* Applied Statistics for Economists, 1957, 1962 (1970 edn with M. Polasek, 4th edn 1977), Portuguese edn, 1972; (with M. Brunt) Structure of the Australian Economy, 1962, repr. 1963, 1966; (with G. C. Harcourt and R. H. Wallace) Economic Activity, 1967 (Italian edn 1969); articles in Economic Record, Population Studies, Jl Royal Statistical Assoc., Australian Jl of Education, and other learned jls. *Address:* 4/127 Hopetoun Circuit, Canberra, ACT 2600, Australia.

KARN, Prof. Valerie Ann, (Prof. Valerie Solomonides); Professor of Environmental Health and Housing, University of Salford, since 1984; Co-Director, Salford Centre for Housing Studies, since 1986; *b* 17 May 1939; *d* of Arthur and Winnifred Karn; one *d*; *m* 1989, Prof. Constantine Solomonides; one step *s* one step *d*. *Educ:* Newquay County Grammar School; Lady Margaret Hall, Oxford (BA Geography); Univ. of the Punjab, Lahore (Commonwealth scholar); Graduate Sch. of Design, Harvard Univ.; PhD Birmingham (Urban Studies). Res. Officer, ODI, 1963; Res. Fellow, Inst. of Social and Economic Res., Univ. of York, 1964–66; Res. Associate, Lectr, Sen. Lectr, Centre for Urban and Regional Studies, Univ. of Birmingham, 1966–84. Res. Officer, Central Housing Adv. Cttee, Sub-Cttee on Housing Management, 1967–69; Chair, Hulme Study, 1989–; Member: Housing Services Adv. Gp, 1976–79; Inquiry into British Housing, 1984–86; Inquiry into Glasgow's Housing, 1985–86; ESRC Social Affairs Cttee, 1985–87; Special Comr, CRE, 1987–89. BAAS Lister Lectr, 1979; Vis. Fellow, Urban Inst., Washington DC, 1979–80. *Publications:* Retiring to the Seaside, 1977 (Oddfellows Social Concern Book Prize); (jtly) Housing in Retirement, 1973; (ed jtly) The Consumers' Experience of Housing, 1980; (jtly) Home-ownership in the Inner City, Salvation or Despair, 1985; (jtly) Race, Class, and Public Housing, 1987; chapters in: The Future of Council Housing, 1982; Family Matters, 1983; Ethnic Pluralism and Public Policy, 1983; Between Centre and Locality, 1986; Low Cost Home Ownership, 1986; The Housing Crisis, 1986; The Property Owing Democracy, 1987; res. reports and articles in jls. *Recreations:* gardening, painting, walking. *Address:* 71 Barton Road, Worsley M28 4PF. *T:* (home) 061–794 7791; (office) 061–736 5843.

KARP, David; novelist; *b* New York City, 5 May 1922; *s* of Abraham Karp and Rebecca Levin; *m* 1st, 1944, Lillian Klass (*d* 1987); two *s*; 2nd, 1988, Claire Leighton. *Educ:* College of The City of New York. US Army, 1943–46, S Pacific, Japan; College, 1946–48; Continuity Dir, Station WNYC, New York, 1948–49; free-lance motion picture-television writer and motion picture producer, 1949–; President: Leda Productions Inc., 1968–; Television-Radio Branch, Writers Guild of America West, 1969–71; Member: Editorial Bd, Television Quarterly, 1966–71, 1972–77; Council, Writers Guild of America, 1966–73; Bd of Trustees, Producer-Writers Guild of America Pension Plan, 1968– (Chm., 1978, 1988; Sec., 1987); Bd of Trustees, Writers Guild-Industry Health Fund, 1973– (Chm., 1980, 1988; Sec., 1987). Guggenheim Fellow, 1956–57. *Publications:* One, 1953; The Day of the Monkey, 1955; All Honorable Men, 1956; Leave Me Alone, 1957; The Sleepwalkers, 1960; Vice-President in Charge of Revolution (with Murray D. Lincoln), 1960; The Last Believers, 1964; short stories in Saturday Eve. Post, Collier's, Esquire, Argosy, The American, etc; articles and reviews in NY Times, Los Angeles Times, Saturday Review, Nation, etc. *Recreations:* photography, reading. *Address:* 300 East 56th Street #3C, New York, NY 10022, USA. *Clubs:* Players, PEN (New York).

KARRAN, Graham, QFSM 1985; Managing Director, Able Fire Advisory Service; *b* 28 Nov. 1939; *s* of Joseph Karran and Muriel Benson; *m* 1960, Thelma Gott; one *s* one *d*. *Educ:* Bootle Grammar Sch.; Liverpool College of Building. Estate Management, 1958–60; Southport Fire Bde, 1960–63; Lancashire County Fire Bde, 1963–74; Greater Manchester Fire Service, 1974–78; Cheshire County Fire Service, 1978–80; Derbyshire Fire Service, 1980–83; Chief Fire Officer, W Yorks Fire Service, 1983–90. *Publications:* articles in English and Amer. Fire jls. *Recreations:* music, beachcombing. *T:* (business) Huddersfield (0484) 607212, *Fax:* Huddersfield (0484) 608736.

KARSH, Yousuf, CC 1990 (OC 1968); Portrait Photographer since 1932; *b* Mardin, Armenia-in-Turkey, 23 Dec. 1908; parents Armenian; Canadian Citizen; *m* 1939, Solange Gauthier (*d* 1961); *m* 1962, Estrellita Maria Nachbar. *Educ:* Sherbrooke, PQ Canada; studied photography in Boston, Mass., USA. Portrayed Winston Churchill in Canada's Houses of Parliament, 1941; King George VI, 1943; HM Queen (then Princess) Elizabeth and the Duke of Edinburgh, 1951; HH Pope Pius XII, 1951; also portrayed, among many others: Shaw, Wells, Einstein, Sibelius, Somerset Maugham, Picasso, Eden, Eisenhower, Tito, Eleanor Roosevelt, Thomas Mann, Bertrand Russell, Attlee, Nehru, Ingrid Bergmann, Lord Mountbatten of Burma, Augustus John, Pope John Paul II; 14 portraits used on postage stamps of 15 countries. One man exhibns: Men Who Make our World, Pav. of Canada, Expo. 67; Montreal Mus. of Fine Arts, 1968; Boston Mus. of Fine Arts, 1968; Corning Mus., 1968; Detroit Inst. of Arts, 1969; Corcoran Gall. of Art, Washington, 1969; Macdonald House, London, 1969; Seattle Art Museum; Japan (country-wide), and Honolulu, 1970, in Europe and USA annually, 1971–; exhibn acquired in toto by: Museum of Modern Art, Tokyo; Nat. Gall. of Australia; Province of Alberta, Canada, 1975–76; numerous exhibns throughout US, 1971–75, 1976–77; Ulrich Museum, Wichita, Kansas, 1978; Museum of Science and Industry, Chicago, 1978; Evansville Museum, Ind., 1979; Palm Springs Desert Museum, 1980; inaugural exhibn, Museum of Photography, Film and TV, Bradford, 1983; NY, 1983; Nat. Portrait Gall., 1983; Edinburgh, 1984; Internat. Center of Photography, NY, 1983; Helsinki, 1984; Minneapolis Museum, 1985; Syracuse Museum, 1985; Sarasota (Florida) Museum, 1986; 80th birthday gala exhibn, Barbican, London, and in France, Germany, Spain, Switzerland, 1988; Muscarelle Mus. of Art, William and Mary Coll., Williamsburg, Virginia, 1987; Castle Buda Palace, Budapest, 1989; Nat. Gall. of Canada, 1989; Gulbenkian Foundn, Lisbon, 1989; Copenhagen, Brussels, Zurich, 1989; Vancouver Art Mus., 1990; Vero Beach, Fla, 1991. Visiting Professor: Ohio Univ., 1967–69; Emerson Coll., Boston, 1972–73, 1973–74; Photographic Advisor, Internat. Exhibn, Expo '70, Osaka, Japan; Judge, UN 40th anniversary internat. poster contest, 1985. Trustee, Photographic Arts and Scis Foundn, 1970. FRPS; Fellow Rochester Sci. Mus. RCA 1975. Holds 22 hon. degrees. Canada Council Medal, 1965; Centennial Medal, 1967; Master of Photographic Arts, Prof. Photogrs of Canada, 1970; First Gold Medal, Nat. Assoc. Photog. Art, 1974; Life Achievement Award, Encyclopaedia Britannica, 1980; Silver Shingle Award, Law Sch., Boston Univ., 1983; Lotos Medal of Merit, Lotos Club of NY, 1989; first Creative Edge Award, NY Univ., 1989; Gold Medal, Americas Soc., 1989; Master Photographer, Internat. Center of Photography, 1990. *Publications:* Faces of Destiny, 1947; (co-author) This is the Mass, 1958; Portraits of Greatness, 1959; (co-author) This is Rome, 1960; (co-author) This is the Holy Land, 1961; (autobiog.) In Search of Greatness, 1962; (co-author) These are the Sacraments, 1963; (co-author) The Warren Court; Karsh Portfolio, 1967; Faces of our Time, 1971; Karsh Portraits, 1976; Karsh Canadians, 1979; Karsh: a fifty year retrospective, 1983. *Recreations:* tennis, bird-watching, archæology, music. *Address:* (business) Chateau Laurier Hotel, Suite 660, Ottawa K1N 8S7, Canada. *T:* AC 613–236–7181. *Clubs:* Garrick; Rideau (Ottawa); Century, Dutch Treat (NY).

KARSTEN, Ian George Francis; QC 1990; *b* 27 July 1944; *s* of Dr Frederick Karsten and Edith Karsten; *m* 1984, Moira Elizabeth Ann O'Hara; two *d*. *Educ:* William Ellis School, Highgate; Magdalen College, Oxford (MA, BCL); Diplômé, Hague Acad. of Internat. Law. Called to the Bar, Gray's Inn, 1967; Midland and Oxford Circuit; commenced practice 1970; Lectr in Law, Southampton Univ., 1966–70, LSE, 1970–88. UK Deleg. to Hague Conf. on Private Internat. Law (Convention on the Law Applicable to Agency) (Rapporteur), 1973–77; Head, UK Delegn to Unidroit Conf. on Agency in Internat. Sale of Goods, Bucharest, 1979, Geneva, 1983; Legal Assessor, UK Council for Nursing, Midwifery and Health Visiting, 1989–. *Publications:* Conflict of Laws, Halsbury's Laws of England, 4th edn (jtly), 1974; Report on the Convention on the Law Applicable to Agency (Hague Conf.), 1979; articles and notes in legal jls. *Recreations:* opera, travel, chess. *Address:* Queen Elizabeth Building, Temple, EC4Y 9BS. *T:* 071–583 7837.

KASER, Michael Charles, MA; Reader in Economics, University of Oxford, and Professorial Fellow of St Antony's College, since 1972 (Sub-Warden, 1986–87); Director, Institute of Russian, Soviet and East European Studies, University of Oxford, since 1988; *b* 2 May 1926; *er s* of Charles Joseph Kaser and Mabel Blunden; *m* 1954, Elisabeth Anne Mary, *er d* of Cyril Gascoigne Piggford; four *s* one *d*. *Educ:* King's Coll., Cambridge (Exhibr). Foreign Service, London and Moscow, 1947–51; UN Secretariat, Econ. Commn for Europe, Geneva, 1951–63; Faculty Fellow, St Antony's Coll., Oxford, 1963–72; Associate Fellow, Templeton Coll., Oxford, 1983–. Vis. Prof. of Econs, Univ. of Michigan, 1966; Vis. Fellow, Henley Management Coll., 1987–; Vis. Lectr, Cambridge Univ., 1967–68, 1977–78 and 1978–79; Vis. Lectr, INSEAD, Fontainebleau, 1959–82, 1988–. Specialist Advr, Foreign Affairs Cttee, H of C, 1985–87. Oxford Univ. Latin Preacher, 1982. Convenor/Chm., Nat. Assoc. for Soviet and East European Studies, 1965–73, Chm., Jt Cttee with BUAS, 1980–84; Gen. Editor, Internat. Econ. Assoc., 1986– (Dep. Treas., 1980–83); Vice-Chm., Internat. Activities Cttee (Vice-Chm., Area Studies Panel, SSRC) ESRC, 1980–84; Chm., Co-ordinating Council, Area Studies Assocs, 1986–88 (Sec., 1980–84, Vice-Chm., 1984–86); Governor, Plater Coll., Oxford, 1968–; Chm., Acad. Council, Wilton Park (FCO), 1986– (Mem., 1985–). Pres., British Assoc. for Soviet, Slavonic and East European Studies, 1988–91. Member: Council, Royal Econ. Soc., 1976–86, 1987–90; Council, RIIA, 1979–85, 1986–; Internat. Soc. Sci. Council, UNESCO, 1980–; Council, SSEES, 1981–87; Sec., British Acad. Cttee for SE European Studies, 1988–. Member, Editorial Boards: Soviet Studies, Energy Economics, Oxford Rev. of Educn, CUP East European Monograph Series; Steering Cttee, Königswinter Anglo-German Confs, 1969–90 (Chm., Oxford Organizing Cttee, 1975–78). KSG 1990. *Publications:* Comecon: Integration Problems of the Planned Economies, 1965, 2nd edn 1967; (ed) Economic Development for Eastern Europe, 1968; (with J. Zieliński) Planning in East Europe, 1970; Soviet Economics, 1970; (ed, with R. Portes) Planning and Market Relations, 1971; (ed, with H. Höhmann and K. Thalheim) The New Economic Systems of Eastern Europe, 1975; (ed, with A. Brown) The Soviet Union since the Fall of Khrushchev, 1975, 2nd edn 1978; Health Care in the Soviet Union and Eastern Europe, 1976; (ed with A. Brown) Soviet Policy for the 1980s, 1982; (ed jtly) The Cambridge Encyclopaedia of Russia and the Soviet Union, 1982; Gen. Ed., The Economic History of Eastern Europe 1919–1975, vols I and II (1919–49), vol. III (1949–75), 1985–86; papers in economic jls and symposia. *Address:* 7 Chadlington Road, Oxford OX2 6SY. *T:* Oxford (0865) 515581. *Club:* Reform.

KASMIN, John; art dealer since 1960; *b* 24 Sept. 1934; *s* of Vera D'Olzewski and David Kosminsky (known as Kaye); *m* 1959, Jane Nicholson (marr. diss.); two *s*. *Educ:* Magdalen College School, Oxford. Adventurous and varied jobs in New Zealand, 1952–56; art gallery assistant, London, 1956–60; Founder Director: Kasmin Ltd, 1961– (in partnership with late Marquess of Dufferin and Ava); Knoedler Kasmin Ltd, 1977–. *Recreations:* literature, wine, friendship. *Address:* c/o Kasmin Ltd, 34 Warwick Avenue, W9 2PT. *T:* 071–439 1096. *Club:* Groucho.

KASSIM bin Mohammed Hussein, Datuk, DPCM, DIMP, JMN 1978; High Commissioner for Malaysia in London, 1983–86; *b* Perak, Malaysia, 14 Feb. 1928; *s* of Mohammed Hussein and Puteh Sapiah; *m* 1962, Koeswardani; one *s* three *d*. *Educ:* Malay Coll., Kuala Kangsar, Perak; Univ. of Malaya (BA). Malayan Administrative Service, 1955; Min. of Foreign Affairs, Kuala Lumpur, 1958; Jakarta, 1959; Min. of Foreign Affairs, 1962; Karachi, 1964; Min. of Foreign Affairs, 1965; Counsellor: Manila, 1967; Cairo, 1968; Chargé d'Affaires, Addis Ababa, 1969; Counsellor, later Minister, Washington, 1971; Minister, Tokyo, 1971–74; Ambassador to Burma, 1974; Dir Gen. (ASEAN), Min. of Foreign Affairs, 1977; Ambassador to Belgium, Luxembourg and EEC, 1980–83. Hon. Fellow, Ealing Coll. of Higher Educn, 1984. *Recreations:* golf, tennis. *Address:* 1 Jalan Setia Jaya, Damansara Heights, Kuala Lumpur, Malaysia. *T:* Kuala Lumpur 949–434.

KASTNER, Prof. Leslie James, MA, ScD Cantab, FIMechE; Professor of Mechanical Engineering, King's College, University of London, 1955–76, now Emeritus; Dean of Faculty of Engineering, University of London, 1974–76; *b* 10 Dec. 1911; *o s* of late Professor Leon E. Kastner, sometime Prof. of French Language and Literature, University of Manchester, and of Elsie E. Kastner; *m* 1958, Joyce, *o d* of Lt-Col Edward Lillingston, DSO, Belstone, Devon. *Educ:* Dreghorn Castle Sch.; Colinton, Midlothian; Highgate Sch.; Clare Coll., Cambridge (Mechanical Science Tripos). Apprenticeship with Davies and Metcalfe, Ltd, Locomotive Engineers, of Romiley, Stockport, 1930–31 and 1934–36; Development Engineer, 1936–38; Osborne Reynolds Research Fellowship, University of Manchester, 1938; Lectr in Engineering, University of Manchester, 1941–46; Senior Lectr, 1946–48; Prof. of Engineering, University Coll. of Swansea, University of Wales, 1948–55. Mem. of Council, Institution of Mechanical Engineers, 1954. FKC 1974. Graduates' Prize, InstMechE, 1939; Herbert Ackroyd Stuart Prize, 1943; Dugald Clerk Prize, 1956. *Publications:* various research papers in applied thermodynamics and fluid flow. *Address:* 37 St Anne's Road, Eastbourne BN21 2HP.

KATCHALSKI-KATZIR, Prof. Ephraim; *see* Katzir, Prof. E.

KATENGA-KAUNDA, Reid Willie; Malaŵi Independence Medal, 1964; Malaŵi Republic Medal, 1966; business executive; *b* 20 Aug. 1929; *s* of Gibson Amon Katenga Kaunda and Maggie Talengeske Nyabanda; *m* 1951, Elsie Nyabanda; one *s* three *d* (and one *s* one *d* decd). *Educ:* Ndola Govt Sch., Zambia; Inst. of Public Administration, Malaŵi;

Trinity Coll., Oxford Univ.; Administrative Staff Coll., Henley. Sec., Nkhota Kota Rice Co-op. Soc. Ltd, 1952–62; Dist. Comr, Karonga, Malaŵi, 1964–65; Sen. Asst Sec., Min. of External Affairs, Zomba, Malaŵi, 1966; MP and Parly Sec., Office of the President and Cabinet, Malaŵi, 1966–68; Dep. Regional Chm., MCP, Northern Region, 1967–68; Under Sec., Office of the President and Cabinet, 1968–69; High Comr in London, 1969–70; Perm. Sec., Min. of Trade, Industry and Tourism, 1971–72; High Comr in London, 1972–73, and concurrently to the Holy See, Portugal, Belgium, Holland and France. Dep. Chm., Ncheu and Mchinji Inquiry Commn, 1967. *Recreations:* reading, walking, cinema, Association football. *Address:* c/o PO Box 511, Blantyre, Malaŵi.

KATIN, Peter Roy; concert pianist; *b* 14 Nov. 1930; *m* 1954, Eva Zweig; two *s. Educ:* Henry Thornton Sch.; Westminster Abbey; Royal Academy of Music. First London appearance at Wigmore Hall, 1948. A leading Chopin interpreter. Performances abroad include most European countries, West and East, S and E Africa, Japan, Canada, USA, Hong Kong, India, New Zealand, Singapore, Malaysia. Recordings, Decca, Everest, Unicorn, HMV, Philips, Lyrita, MFP, Pickwick International, Claudio, Olympia, Simax. Vis. Prof. in piano, Univ. of Western Ontario, 1978–84. Founder, Katin Centre for Advanced Piano Studies. Mem. Incorporated Soc. of Musicians (ISM). FRAM, ARCM. Chopin Arts Award, NY, 1977. *Recreations:* reading, writing, fishing, tape recording, photography. *Address:* c/o Helen Sykes Management, West End House, 33 Lower Richmond Road, SW14 7EZ. *T:* 081–876 8276, *Fax:* 081–876 8277; Steorra Enterprises, 243 West End Avenue, Ste. 907, New York 10023, USA. *T:* (212) 799 5783.

KATO, Tadao, Hon. KBE 1988; 1st Class Order of Sacred Treasure, 1988; Counsellor in Japan to John Swire & Sons, Imperial Chemicals, Sumitomo Metals, Suntory, Long-Term Credit Bank, since 1980; *b* 13 May 1916; *m* 1946, Yoko; two *s. Educ:* Tokyo Univ.; Cambridge Univ. Joined Japanese Diplomatic Service 1939; Singapore, 1952; London, 1953; Counsellor, Economic Affairs Bureau, Min. of Foreign Affairs, 1956–69; Counsellor, Washington, 1959–63 (Vis. Fellow, Harvard, 1959–60); Dep. Dir, Econ. Affairs Bureau, Min. of Foreign Affairs, 1963–66, Dir, 1966–67; Ambassador to OECD, 1967–70, to Mexico, 1970–74, to UK, 1975–79. Mem. Bd, Adv. Council, Texas Instruments, Dallas, 1981–; Comr, Export Import Transaction Council, Min. Internat. Trade and Industry and Econ. Council of Econ. Planning Agency, 1982–. Advisor: Hotel Okura; Nitto Kogyo Enterprise. Chm., Japan British Soc., 1981–88; Japanese Chm., UK-Japan 2000 Gp, 1985–88. Pres., Cambridge English Sch. 1st Class Order of Aztec Star, Mexico, 1972. *Recreations:* golf, goh. *Address:* 3–10–22, Shimo-Ochiai, Shinjuku-Ku, Tokyo, Japan. *Clubs:* Tokyo (Tokyo); Koganei Golf, Abiko Golf, Karuizawa Golf, Hamano Golf (Chm., 1984–), Mito Golf (Chm., 1988–), Shinyo Golf (Chm., 1989–) (Japan); Green Academy Country (Chm., 1985–) (Fukushima).

KATRITZKY, Prof. Alan Roy, DPhil, PhD, ScD; FRS 1980; FRSC; Kenan Professor of Chemistry, University of Florida, since 1980; *b* 18 Aug. 1928; *s* of Frederick Charles Katritzky and Emily Catherine (*née* Lane); *m* 1952, Agnes Juliane Dietlinde Kilian; one *s* three *d. Educ:* Oxford Univ. (BA, BSc, MA, DPhil); Cambridge Univ. (PhD, ScD). FRIC 1963. Lectr, Cambridge Univ., 1958–63; Fellow of Churchill Coll., Cambridge, 1960–63; Prof. of Chemistry, Univ. of E Anglia, 1963–80, Dean, Sch. of Chem. Sciences, UEA, 1963–70 and 1976–80. Foreign Fellow, RACI, 1983; Hon. Fellow: Italian Chem. Soc., 1978; Polish Chem. Soc., 1985. Dr *hc*: Univ. Nacional, Madrid, 1986; Univ. Poznan, Poland, 1990. Tilden Medal, Chem. Soc., 1975–76. Heterocyclic Award, RSC, 1983; Medal of Tartu State Univ., Estonia, USSR, 1986; Golden Tiger award, Exxon Corp., 1989. Cavaliere ufficiale, Order Al Merito Della Repubblica Italiana, 1975. *Publications:* (ed) Advances in Heterocyclic Chemistry, Vols 1–51, 1963–90; (ed) Physical Methods in Heterocyclic Chemistry, Vols 1–6, 1963–72; Principles of Heterocyclic Chemistry, 1968 (trans. into French, German, Italian, Japanese, Russian, Polish and Spanish); Chemistry of Heterocyclic N-Oxides (monograph), 1970; Heteroaromatic Tautomerism (monograph), 1975; Handbook of Heterocyclic Chemistry, 1985; Chm. Editorial Bd, Comprehensive Heterocyclic Chemistry (8 vols), 1985; scientific papers in Heterocyclic Chem. *Recreations:* walking, travel. *Address:* Department of Chemistry, University of Florida, Gainesville, Fla 32611, USA. *T:* 904–392–0554, *Fax:* 904–392–9199. *Club:* United Oxford & Cambridge University.

KATZ, Sir Bernard, Kt 1969; FRS 1952; Professor and Head of Biophysics Department, University College, London, 1952–78, now Emeritus, Hon. Research Fellow, 1978; *b* Leipzig, 26 March 1911; *s* of M. N. Katz; *m* 1945, Marguerite, *d* of W. Penly, Sydney, Australia; two *s. Educ:* University of Leipzig (MD 1934). Biophysical research, University Coll., London, 1935–39; PhD London, and Beit Memorial Research Fellow, 1938; Carnegie Research Fellow, Sydney Hospital, Sydney, 1939–42; DSc London, 1943. Served War of 1939–45 in Pacific with RAAF, 1942–45; Flt-Lt, 1943. Asst Dir of Research, Biophysics Research Unit, University Coll., London, and Henry Head Research Fellow (Royal Society), 1946–50; Reader in Physiology, 1950–51. Lectures: Herter, Johns Hopkins Univ., 1958; Dunham, Harvard Coll., 1961; Croonian, Royal Society, 1961; Sherrington, Liverpool Univ., 1967. A Vice-Pres., Royal Society, 1965, Biological Secretary and Vice-President, 1968–76. Mem., Agric. Research Coun., 1967–77. For. Member: Royal Danish Academy Science and Letters, 1968; Accad. Naz. Lincei, 1968; Amer. Acad. of Arts and Sciences, 1969; For. Assoc., Nat. Acad. of Scis, USA, 1976; Hon. Member: Japanese Pharmacol. Soc., 1977; American Physiolog. Soc., 1985; Assoc. Mem., European Molecular Biol. Orgn, 1978; Corresp. Mem., Australian Acad. of Science, 1987. Fellow of University Coll., London. FRCP, 1968. Hon. FIBiol, 1978. Hon. DSc: Southampton, 1971; Melbourne, 1971; Cambridge, 1980; Hon. PhD Weizmann Inst., Israel, 1979; Hon. MD Leipzig, 1990. Feldberg Foundation Award, 1965; Baly Medal, RCP, 1967; Copley Medal, Royal Society, 1967; Nobel Prize (jtly) for Physiology and Medicine, 1970; Cothenius Medal, Deutsche Akademie der Wissenschaften, Leopoldina, 1989. Foreign Mem., Orden Pour le Mérite für Wissenschaften und Künste, 1982. *Publications:* Electric Excitation of Nerve, 1939; Nerve, Muscle and Synapse, 1966; The Release of Neural Transmitter Substances, 1969; papers on nerve and muscle physiology in Jl of Physiol., Proc. Royal Society, etc. *Recreation:* chess. *Address:* University College, WC1E 6BT.

KATZ, Milton; Director, International Legal Studies, and Henry L. Stimson Professor of Law, Harvard University, 1954–78, now Emeritus; Distinguished Professor of Law, Suffolk University Law School, Boston, Mass, since 1978; *b* 29 Nov. 1907; *m* 1933, Vivian Greenberg; three *s. Educ:* Harvard Univ. AB 1927; JD 1931. Anthropological Expedition across Central Africa for Peabody Museum, Harvard, 1927–28; Mem. of Bar since 1932; various official posts, US Government, 1932–39; Prof. of Law, Harvard Univ., 1940–50; served War of 1939–45, with War Production Board and as US Executive Officer, Combined Production and Resources Board, 1941–43, thereafter Lt-Comdr, USNR, until end of war; Dep. US Special Representative in Europe with rank of Ambassador, 1949–50; Chief US Delegation, Economic Commission for Europe, and US Mem., Defense Financial and Economic Cttee under North Atlantic Treaty, 1950–51; Ambassador of the United States and US Special Representative in Europe for ECA, 1950–51; Associate Dir, Ford Foundation, 1951–54, and Consultant, 1954–66. Dir, Internat. Program in Taxation, 1961–63. Consultant, US Office of Technology Assessment, 1972–82; Chm., Energy Adv. Cttee, 1974–82. Mem. Council, Amer. Acad. of Arts and Sciences, 1982– (Pres., 1979–82); Trustee: Carnegie Endowment for Internat. Peace (Chm. Bd, 1970–78); World Peace Foundation (Exec. Cttee); Citizens Research Foundation (Pres., 1969–78); Brandeis Univ.; Case Western Reserve Univ., 1967–80; International Legal Center (Chm. Bd, 1971–78); Director, Internat. Friendship League; Member: Corp., Boston Museum of Science; Cttee on Foreign Affairs Personnel, 1961–63; Case Inst. of Technology Western Reserve Univ. Study Commn, 1966–67; Panel on Technology Assessment, Nat. Acad. of Sciences, 1968–69; Cttee on Life Sciences and Social Policy, Nat. Research Council, 1968–75 (Chm.); Vis. Cttee for Humanities, MIT, 1970–73; Adv. Bd Energy Laboratory, MIT, 1974–85; Cttee on Technology, Internat. Trade and Econ. Issues, Nat. Acad. of Engrg, 1976–; Adv. Bd, Consortium on Competitiveness and Co-operation, Univ. of California, 1986–; Co-Chm., ABA-AAAS Cttee on Science and Law, 1978–82. Sherman Fairchild Dist. Schol., Cal. Tech., 1974. John Danz Lectr, Univ. of Washington, 1974, Phi Beta Kappa Nat. Vis. Scholar, 1977–78. Hon LLD Brandeis, 1972. Legion of Merit (US Army), 1945; Commendation Ribbon (US Navy), 1945. Order of Merit, Fed. Rep. of Germany, 1968. *Publications:* Cases and Materials on Administrative Law, 1947; (Co-author and ed) Government under Law and the Individual, 1957; (with Kingman Brewster, Jr) The Law of International Transactions and Relations, 1960; The Things That are Caesar's, 1966; The Relevance of International Adjudication, 1968; The Modern Foundation: its dual nature, public and private, 1968; (contrib., jtly) Man's Impact on the Global Environment, 1970; (ed) Federal Regulation of Campaign Finance, 1972; (jtly) Assessing Biomedical Technologies, 1975; (jtly) Technology, Trade and the US Economy, 1978; (jtly) Strengthening Conventional Deterrence in Europe, 1983; (contrib.) The Positive Sum Strategy, 1986; articles in legal, business and other jls. *Address:* (business) Harvard Law Sch., Cambridge, Mass, USA; (home) 6 Berkeley Street, Cambridge, Mass, USA.

KATZIR, Prof. Ephraim (Katchalski), PhD; Institute Professor, Weizmann Institute of Science, since 1978; President, State of Israel, 1973–78; *b* Kiev, Ukraine, 16 May 1916; *s* of Yehuda and Tsila Katchalski; *m* 1938, Nina Gotlieb (decd); one *s* one *d. Educ:* Rehavia High Sch., Jerusalem; Hebrew Univ., Jerusalem (chemistry, botany, zool., bacteriol.; MSc *summa cum laude* 1937; PhD 1941). Settled in Israel with parents, 1922; involved in Labour youth movement; Inf. Comdr, Jewish Self-Defence Forces (Hagana). Asst, Dept of Theoretical and Macromolecular Chem., Hebrew Univ., 1941–45; Res. Fellow, Polytechnic Inst., and Columbia Univ., NY, 1946–48; Actg Head, Dept of Biophys., Weizmann Inst. of Science, Rehovot, Israel, 1949–51, Head 1951–73 (mem. founding faculty of Inst.); Chief Scientist, Israel Def. Min., 1966–68; Head, Dept of Biotechnology, Tel Aviv Univ., 1980–88. Vis. Prof. of Biophys., Hebrew Univ., 1953–61; Guest Scientist, Harvard Univ., 1957–59; Vis. Prof., Rockefeller Univ., NY, and Univ. of Mich, Ann Arbor, 1961–65; Sen. Foreign Scientist Fellowship, UCLA, 1964; Battelle Seattle Res. Center, Washington, 1971; Regents Prof., Univ. of Calif., San Diego, 1979; First Herman F. Mark Chair in Polymer Sci., Poly. Inst., NY, 1979. President: World ORT Union, 1986–90; Cobiotech, 1989–. Member: Biochem. Soc. of Israel; Israel Acad. of Sciences and Humanities; Israel Chem. Soc.; Council, Internat. Union of Biochem.; AAAS; Assoc. of Harvard Chemists; Leopoldina Acad. of Science, Germany; World Acad. of Art and Science; New York Acad. of Science (Life Mem.). Centennial Foreign Fellow, Amer. Chem. Soc.; For. Associate, Nat. Acad. of Sciences of USA. For. Member: The Royal Soc.; Amer. Philosoph. Soc.; Acad. des Scis, France, 1989. Hon. Fellow, Scientific Acad. of Argentina, 1986; Hon. Member: Amer. Acad. of Arts and Sciences; Amer. Soc. of Biol Chemists; Harvey Soc.; Hon. MRI 1989. Hon. Prof., Polytechnic Inst. of New York, 1975. Hon. Dr: Hebrew Univ., 1973; Brandeis Univ., Univ. of Mich, and Hebrew Union Coll., 1975; Weizmann Inst. of Science, 1976; Northwestern Univ., Evanston, 1978; Harvard, 1978; McGill, 1980; ETH Zurich, 1980; Thomas Jefferson, 1981; Oxford, 1981; Miami, 1983; Technion, Israel Inst. of Technology, 1983; Univ. of Buenos Aires, 1986. Tchernikhovski Prize, 1948; Weizmann Prize, 1950; Israel Prize in Nat. Sciences, 1959; Rothschild Prize in Nat. Sciences, 1961; Linderstrøm Lang Gold Medal, 1969; Hans Krebs Medal, 1972; Alpha Omega Achievement Medal, 1979; Underwood Prescott Award, MIT, 1982; first Japan Prize, Science and Technol. Foundn of Japan, 1985; Internat. Enzyme Engineering Award, 1987. Ephraim Katzir Chair of Biophysics, Bar Ilan Univ., Israel, founded 1976. Hon. Founding Editor, Biopolymers, 1986– (Mem., Editorial Bd, 1963–86). Comdr, Legion of Honour (France), 1990. *Address:* Weizmann Institute of Science, Rehovot 76100, Israel.

KAUFFMANN, Prof. C. Michael, MA, PhD; FBA 1987; FMA; Professor of History of Art and Director, Courtauld Institute of Art, University of London, since 1985; *b* 5 Feb. 1931; *s* of late Arthur and late Tamara Kauffmann; *m* 1954, Dorothea (*née* Hill); two *s. Educ:* St Paul's Sch.; Merton Coll., Oxford (Postmaster); Warburg Inst., London Univ. (Jun. Research Fellow). Asst Curator, Photographic Collection, Warburg Inst., 1957–58; Keeper, Manchester City Art Gall., 1958–60; Victoria and Albert Museum: Asst Keeper, 1960–75, Keeper, 1975–85, Dept of Prints & Drawings and Paintings; Asst to the Director, 1963–66; Visiting Associate Prof., Univ. of Chicago, 1969. *Publications:* The Baths of Pozzuoli: medieval illuminations of Peter of Eboli's poem, 1959; An Altar-piece of the Apocalypse, 1968; Victoria & Albert Museum: catalogue of foreign paintings, 1973; British Romanesque Manuscripts 1066–1190, 1975; Catalogue of Paintings in the Wellington Museum, 1982; John Varley, 1984; exhibn catalogues.

KAUFMAN, Rt. Hon. Gerald (Bernard); PC 1978; MP (Lab) Manchester, Gorton, since 1983 (Manchester, Ardwick, 1970–83); *b* 21 June 1930; *s* of Louis and Jane Kaufman. *Educ:* Leeds Grammar Sch.; The Queen's Coll., Oxford. Asst Gen.-Sec., Fabian Soc., 1954–55; Political Staff, Daily Mirror, 1955–64; Political Correspondent, New Statesman, 1964–65; Parly Press Liaison Officer, Labour Party, 1965–70. Parly Under-Sec. of State, DoE, 1974–75, Dept of Industry, 1975; Minister of State, Dept of Industry, 1975–79; Parly Cttee of PLP, 1980–; Shadow Home Sec., 1983–87; Shadow Foreign Sec., 1987–. *Publications:* (jtly) How to Live Under Labour, 1964; (ed) The Left, 1966; To Build the Promised Land, 1973; How to be a Minister, 1980; (ed) Renewal: Labour's Britain in the 1980s, 1983; My Life in the Silver Screen, 1985; Inside the Promised Land, 1986. *Recreations:* travel, going to the pictures. *Address:* 87 Charlbert Court, Eamont Street, NW8. *T:* 071–722 6264.

KAUFMAN, Prof. Matthew Howard, PhD, DSc; Professor of Anatomy and Head of Department of Anatomy, University of Edinburgh, since 1985; *b* 29 Sept. 1942; *s* of Benjamin and Dora Kaufman; *m* 1973, Claire Lesley Kaufman (*née* Farrow); two *s. Educ:* Westminster City Sch.; Univ. of Edinburgh (MB ChB 1967; DSc 1984); Univ. of Cambridge (PhD 1973; MA 1975). Pre- and post-registration clinical posts, 1967–69; Research Associate, Inst. of Animal Genetics, Edinburgh, 1970; MRC Jun. Research Fellow, Physiol Lab., Cambridge, 1970–73; Royal Soc./Israel Acad. of Scis Research Fellow, and MRC Travelling Fellow, Weizmann Inst. of Science, 1973–75; University of Cambridge: Univ. Demonstrator, 1975–77; Lectr in Anatomy, 1977–85; Fellow and College Lectr in Anatomy, King's Coll., 1980–85. *Publications:* Early Mammalian Development: parthenogenetic studies, 1983; research papers in the fields of experimental and descriptive embryology, cytogenetics, developmental biology and teratology. *Recreation:* history of medicine, particularly of anatomy. *Address:* Department of Anatomy, University Medical School, Teviot Place, Edinburgh EH8 9AG. *T:* 031–650 3114.

KAUL, Mahendra Nath, OBE 1975; Managing Director, Viceroy of India (Restaurants) Ltd, since 1982; UK correspondent, Daily Jagran, since 1983; *b* 28 July 1922; *s* of Dina Nath Kaul and Gauri Kaul; *m* 1955, Rajni Kapur, MA, MLS; one *d*. *Educ:* Univ. of the Punjab, India (BA). Joined Radio Kashmir of All India Radio, as news reader, actor and producer of dramas, 1949; appeared in two feature films and assisted in producing several documentaries, 1950–52; news reader and actor in three languages, also drama producer, All India Radio, New Delhi, 1952–55; joined Indian service of Voice of America, Washington DC, 1955, later becoming Editor of the service; joined external service of BBC, as newscaster, producer and dir of radio plays; producer/presenter, BBC TV prog. for Asian Viewers in UK, 1966–82. Director: Hotels & Restaurants Suppliers Ltd (formerly SK Giftware), 1985–; Arts and Crafts Emporium Ltd, 1985–; Bokhara Cuisine Ltd, 1985–. OBE awarded for services to race relations in Gt Britain. Received The Green Pennant from HRH The Duke of Edinburgh, awarded by Commonwealth Expedition (COMEX 10), 1980. *Recreations:* golf, cooking, boating, classical and light classical music, reading political works. *Address:* 50 Grove Court, Grove End Road, St John's Wood, NW8 9EP. *T:* 071–286 8131.

KAULBACK, Ronald John Henry, OBE 1946; *b* 23 July 1909; *er s* of late Lieutenant-Colonel Henry Albert Kaulback, OBE, and Alice Mary, *d* of late Rev. A. J. Townend, CF; *m* 1st, 1940, Audrey Elizabeth (marr. diss. 1984), 3rd *d* of late Major H. R. M. Howard-Sneyd, OBE; two *s* two *d*; 2nd, 1984, Joyce Norah, *widow* of Capt. H. S. Woolley, MC. *Educ:* Rugby; Pembroke Coll., Cambridge. In 1933 journeyed through Assam and Eastern Tibet with Kingdon Ward; returned to Tibet, 1935, accompanied by John Hanbury-Tracy, spending eighteen months there in an attempt to discover source of Salween River; 1938 spent eighteen months in Upper Burma hunting and collecting zoological specimens for the British Museum (Natural History); Murchison Grant of Royal Geog. Society, 1937. *Publications:* Tibetan Trek, 1934; Salween, 1938. *Address:* Altbough, Hoarwithy, Hereford. *T:* Carey (0432) 840676.

KAUNDA, David Kenneth; President of Zambia, since Oct. 1964 (Prime Minister, N Rhodesia, Jan.-Oct. 1964); Chancellor of the University of Zambia since 1966; *b* 28 April 1924; *s* of late David Julizgia and Hellen Kaunda, Missionaries; *m* 1946, Betty Banda; six *s* two *d* one adopted *s* (and one *s* decd). *Educ:* Lubwa Training Sch.; Munali Secondary Sch. Teacher, Lubwa Training Sch., 1943–44, Headmaster, 1944–47; Boarding Master, Mufulira Upper Sch., 1948–49. African National Congress: District Sec., 1950–52; Provincial Organising Sec., 1952–53; Sec.-Gen., 1953–58; Nat. Pres., Zambia African Nat. Congress, 1958–59; Nat. Pres., United Nat. Independence Party, 1960; Chm., Pan-African Freedom Movement for East, Central and South Africa, 1962; Minister of Local Government and Social Welfare, N Rhodesia, 1962–63. Chairman: Organization of African Unity, 1970, 1987; Non-aligned Countries, 1970. Hon. Doctor of Laws: Fordham Univ., USA, 1963; Dublin Univ., 1964; University of Sussex, 1965; Windsor Univ., Canada, 1966; University of Chile, 1966; Univ. of Zambia, 1974; Univ. of Humboldt, 1980; DUniv York, 1966. *Publications:* Black Government, 1961; Zambia Shall Be Free, 1962; Humanist in Africa, 1966; Humanism in Zambia and its implementation, 1967; Letter to My Children; Kaunda on Violence, 1980. *Recreations:* golf, music, table tennis, football, draughts, gardening and reading. *Address:* State House, PO Box 135, Lusaka, Zambia.

KAUNDA, Reid Willie K.; *see* Katenga-Kaunda.

KAUNTZE, Ralph, MBE 1944; MD; FRCP; Physician to Guy's Hospital, 1948–71, Consultant Physician Emeritus since 1971; *b* 5 June 1911; *s* of Charles Kauntze and Edith, *d* of Ralph Bagley; *m* 1935, Katharine Margaret, *yr d* of late Ramsay Moodie; two *s* one *d*. *Educ:* Canford Sch.; Emmanuel Coll., Cambridge; St George's Hosp., London. William Brown Sen. Schol., St George's Hosp. 1932; MRCS, LRCP 1935; MA, MB, BCh Cantab 1937; MRCP 1939; MD Cantab 1946; FRCP 1950. Served, 1939–45, RAMC, chiefly Mediterranean area, Lt-Col O i/c Med. Div. Asst Dir of Dept of Med., Guy's Hosp., 1947–48, Physician to Cardiac Dept, 1956–71; Cons. Phys. to High Wycombe War Memorial Hosp., 1948–50; Dir Asthma Clinic, 1948–52, and of Dept of Student Health, 1950–63, Guy's Hosp.; Physician to Royal Masonic Hospital, 1963–76. Former Senior Cons. Phys. to: Commercial Union Assurance Co. Ltd; British & European Assurance Co.; European Assurance Co. Ltd. Hon. Vis. Phys., Johns Hopkins Hosp., Baltimore, 1958. Examiner in Medicine: RCP; London Univ. Mem. Brit. Cardiac Soc.; Mem. Assoc. of Physicians. *Publications:* contrib. med. jls. *Recreations:* farming, walking. *Address:* Blewbury Manor, near Didcot, Oxon OX11 9QJ. *T:* Blewbury (0235) 850246.

KAVANAGH, P. J., (Patrick Joseph Gregory Kavanagh), FRSL; writer; columnist, The Spectator, since 1983; *b* 6 Jan. 1931; *s* of H. E. (Ted) Kavanagh and Agnes O'Keefe; *m* 1st, 1956, Sally Philipps (*d* 1958); 2nd, 1965, Catherine Ward; two *s*. *Educ:* Douai Sch.; Lycee Jaccard, Lausanne; Merton Coll., Oxford (MA). British Council, 1957–59. Actor, 1959–70. Mem., Kingham Cttee of Inquiry into English Lang., 1986–88. *Publications: poems:* One and One, 1960; On the Way to the Depot, 1967; About Time, 1970; Edward Thomas in Heaven, 1974; Life before Death, 1979; Selected Poems, 1982; Presences (new and selected poems), 1987; An Enchantment, 1991; Collected Poems, 1992; *novels:* A Song and Dance, 1968 (Guardian Fiction Prize, 1968); A Happy Man, 1972; People and Weather, 1979; Only by Mistake, 1986; *essays:* People and Places, 1988; *autobiography:* The Perfect Stranger, 1966 (Richard Hillary Prize, 1966); *travel autobiography:* Finding Connections, 1990; *for children:* Scarf Jack, 1978; Rebel for Good, 1980; *edited:* Collected Poems of Ivor Gurney, 1982; (with James Michie) Oxford Book of Short Poems, 1985; The Bodley Head G. K. Chesterton, 1985; Selected Poems of Ivor Gurney, 1990; Collins Book of Consolations, 1992. *Recreation:* walking. *Address:* Sparrowthorn, Elkstone, Cheltenham, Glos GL53 9PX.

KAVANAGH, Patrick Bernard, CBE 1977; QPM 1974; Deputy Commissioner, Metropolitan Police, 1977–83; *b* 18 March 1923; *s* of late Michael Kavanagh and late Violet Kavanagh (*née* Duncan); *m* Beryl (*d* 1984), *er d* of late Lt-Comdr Richard Owen Williams, RNR and Annie (*née* McShiells); one *s* two *d*. *Educ:* St Aloysius Coll., Glasgow. Rifle Bde, 1941–43; Para. Regt, 1943–46 (Lieut). Manchester City Police (Constable to Supt), 1946–64; Asst Chief Constable, Cardiff City Police, 1964–69; Asst and Dep. Chief Constable, S Wales Constabulary, 1969–73; Asst Comr (Traffic), Metropolitan Police, 1974–77. Attended Administrative Staff Coll., Henley-on-Thames, 1961. Mem., Gaming Bd for GB, 1983–91. *Recreations:* walking, bird watching, music, crosswords. *Address:* c/o Metropolitan Police, 2 Bessborough Street, SW1V 2JF. *Club:* Royal Automobile.

KAWHARU, Prof. Sir (Ian) Hugh, Kt 1989; Professor, Maori Studies, and Head of Department of Anthropology, University of Auckland, since 1985; *b* 18 Feb. 1927; *s* of Wiremu and Janet Paora Kawharu; *m* 1st, 1957, Nina; three *d*; 2nd, 1970, Freda; two *d*. *Educ:* Univ. of New Zealand (BSc); Univ. of Cambridge (MA); Univ. of Oxford (DPhil). Dept of Maori Affairs, housing welfare and trust admin, variously, 1953–65; Lectr, Dept of Anthropology, Univ. of Auckland, 1965–70; Prof. (personal chair), Social Anthropology and Maori Studies, Massey Univ., 1970–84. Consultant: FAO, 1961–63; NZ Govt, 1968–; Unesco, 1974–76; NZ Council for Educnl Res., 1976–89; NZ Maori Council, 1981–. Member: NZ Nat. Commn for Unesco, 1969–73; Royal Commn on the Courts, 1976–78; Waitangi Tribunal, 1986–; Bd of Maori Affairs, 1987–90; Council, Polynesian Soc., 1965–68; Council, Auckland Inst. and Mus., 1986–. *Publications:* Orakei, a Ngati Whatua Community, 1975; Maori Land Tenure, 1977; (ed. and co-author): Administration in New Zealand's Multiracial Society, 1967; Conflict and Compromise, 1975; Trends in Ethnic Group Relations in Asia and Oceania, 1979; Waitingi: Maori and Pakeha Perspectives of the Treaty of Waitingi, 1989. *Recreation:* music. *Address:* University of Auckland, Private Bag, Auckland, New Zealand. *T:* (Auckland) 737–999.

KAY, Sir Andrew Watt, Kt 1973; retired; Regius Professor of Surgery, University of Glasgow, 1964–81; part-time Chief Scientist, Scottish Home and Health Department, 1973–81; *b* 14 Aug. 1916; of Scottish parentage; *m* 1943, Janetta M. Roxburgh (*d* 1990); two *s* two *d*. *Educ:* Ayr Academy; Glasgow Univ. MB, ChB (Hons) with Brunton Memorial Prize, 1939; FRCSEd 1942; FRFPSG 1956 (Pres. 1972–); FRCS 1960; FRCSGlas 1967; FRSE 1971; MD (Hons) with Bellahouston Gold Medal, 1944; Major Royal Army Medical Corps i/c Surgical Div., Millbank Military Hospital, 1946–48; ChM (Hons) 1949; Consultant Surgeon in charge of Wards, Western Infirmary, Glasgow, 1956–58; Asst to Regius Prof. of Surgery, Glasgow Univ., 1942–56; Prof. of Surgery, University of Sheffield, 1958–64. Sims Travelling Prof., Australasia, 1969; McLaughlin Foundn Edward Gallie Vis. Prof., Canada, 1970. Rock Carling Fellowship, 1977. Pres., Surgical Research Soc., 1969–71. Member: Royal Commission on Medical Education, 1965–68; MRC, 1967–71; Chm., Scottish Hosps Endowment Research Trust, 1983–89; Hon. Mem., The N Pacific Surgical Assoc. FRACS 1970; FRCSCan 1972; FCS(SoAf) 1972; Hon. Fellow: Norwegian Surgical Assoc., Belgian Surgical Soc.; Amer. Surg. Assoc., 1972; Hon. FACS, 1973; Hon. FRCSI, 1979. Hon. DSc: Leicester, 1973; Sheffield, 1975; Manchester, 1981; Nebraska, 1981; Hon. MD Edinburgh, 1981. Cecil Joll Prize, RCS, 1969; Gordon-Taylor Lectureship and Medal, 1970. *Publications:* (with R. A. Jamieson, FRCS) Textbook of Surgical Physiology, 1959 (2nd edn 1964); Research in Medicine: problems and prospects, 1977; several papers in medical and surgical jls on gastroenterological subjects. *Recreation:* gardening. *Address:* 14 North Campbell Avenue, Milngavie, Glasgow G62 7AA.

KAY, Bernard Hubert Gerard; HM Diplomatic Service, retired; *b* 7 July 1925; *s* of William and Alice Kay; *m* 1957, Teresa Jean Dyer; three *d*. *Educ:* St Bede's, Bradford; Wadham Coll., Oxford (MA, MLitt). Royal Navy, 1943–46. Foreign Office, 1955; served: Hong Kong, 1958–62; Singapore, 1964; Manila, 1965; New Delhi, 1967; Vientiane, 1968; Dacca, 1972; Ulan Bator, 1973; FCO, 1973–80. *Recreations:* Asia, books, mountains, the sea. *Address:* 6 Savona Close, Wimbledon, SW19 4HT. *Club:* United Oxford & Cambridge University.

KAY, Brian Wilfrid; Senior Research Fellow, Culham College Institute, since 1982; *b* 30 July 1921; *s* of Wilfrid and Jessie Kay; *m* 1947, Dorothea Sheppard Lawson; two *d*. *Educ:* King's Sch., Chester; University Coll., Oxford (exhibnr). Classics Master, Birkenhead Sch., 1947–59; Head of Classics, Liverpool Collegiate Sch., 1959–64; HM Inspector of Schs (Wales), 1964–71; Staff Inspector, Classics, Secondary Educn, 1971–74; Head of Assessment of Performance Unit, DES, 1974–77; Chief Inspector, Res. and Planning, DES, 1977–79; Chief Inspector, Teacher Trng and Res., DES, 1979–81, retired. Co-ordinator, Hulme Project, Dept Educnl Studies, Oxford Univ., 1982–87. *Recreations:* gardening, music, architecture. *Address:* Pond Cottage, Botolph Claydon, Buckingham MK18 2NG. *T:* Winslow (029671) 3477.

KAY, Air Vice-Marshal Cyril Eyton, CB 1958; CBE 1947; DFC 1940; retired as Chief of Air Staff, with the rank of Air Vice-Marshal, RNZAF (1956–58); *b* 25 June 1902; *s* of David Kay and Mary, *d* of Edward Drury Butts; *m* 1932, Florence, *d* of Frank Armfield; two *d*. *Educ:* Auckland, NZ. Joined RAF, 1926, 5 years Short Service Commn; joined RNZAF, 1935, Permanent Commn. As Flying Officer: flew London-Sydney in Desoutter Light aeroplane, 1930 (with Flying Off. H. L. Piper as Co-pilot); first New Zealanders to accomplish this flight; also, as Flying Off. flew a De Havilland-Dragon Rapide (with Sqdn Ldr J. Hewett) in London-Melbourne Centenary Air Race, 1934; then continued over Tasman Sea to New Zealand (first direct flight England-New Zealand). Comdg Officer No 75 (NZ) Sqdn "Wellington" Bombers stationed Feltwell, Norfolk, England, 1940; IDC, 1946; Air Board Mem. for Supply, RNZAF, 1947; AOC, RNZAF, London HQ, 1950; Air Board Mem. for Personnel, 1953. *Publication:* The Restless Sky, 1964. *Recreation:* golf. *Address:* c/o Lloyds Bank, 6 Pall Mall, SW1. *Clubs:* Royal Air Force; Officers' (Wellington, NZ).

KAY, Ernest, FRGS; Founder and Director-General, International Biographical Centre, Cambridge, since 1967 (Director-General, New York, 1976–85); *b* 21 June 1915; *s* of Harold and Florence Kay; *m* 1941, Marjorie Peover (*d* 1987); two *s* one *d*. *Educ:* Spring Bank Central Sch., Darwen, Lancs. Reporter, Darwen News, 1931–34; Ashton-under-Lyne Reporter, 1934–38; Industrial Corresp., Manchester Guardian and Evening News, 1938–41; The Star, London, 1941–47; London Editor, Wolverhampton Express and Star, 1947–52, Managing Editor, 1952–54; Managing Editor, London Evening News, 1954–57; Editor and Publisher, John O'London's, 1957–61; Managing Editor, Time and Tide, 1961–67. Chairman: Kay Sons and Daughter Ltd, 1967–77; Dartmouth Chronicle Group Ltd, 1968–77; Cambridge and Newmarket Radio Ltd, 1981–; Pres., Melrose Press Ltd, 1970–77. Chm., Cambridge Symphony Orchestra Trust, 1979–83. FRSA 1967; FRGS 1975. Hon. DLitt Karachi, 1967; Hon. PhD Hong Kong, 1976. Emperor Haile Selassie Gold Medal, 1971. Key to City of: Las Vegas, 1972; New York, 1975; Miami, 1978; New Orleans (and Hon. Citizen), 1978; Beverly Hills, 1981; LA, 1981. Staff Col and ADC to Governor of Louisiana, 1979; Hon. Senator, State of La, 1986. Gold Medal, Ordre Supreme Imperial Orthodoxe Constantinian de Saint-Georges (Greece), 1977. *Publications:* Great Men of Yorkshire, 1956, 2nd edn 1960; Isles of Flowers: the story of the Isles of Scilly, 1956, 3rd edn 1977; Pragmatic Premier: an intimate portrait of Harold Wilson, 1967; The Wit of Harold Wilson, 1967; Editor, Dictionary of International Biography, 1967–; Dictionary of Caribbean Biography, 1970–; Dictionary of African Biography, 1970–; Dictionary of Scandinavian Biography, 1972–; International Who's Who in Poetry, 1970–; World Who's Who of Women, 1973–; International Who's Who in Music, 1975–; International Authors and Writers Who's Who, 1976–; Women in Education, 1977–; Who's Who in Education, 1978–; International Youth in Achievement, 1981–. *Recreations:* reading, writing, music, watching cricket, travel. *Address:* Westhurst, 418 Milton Road, Cambridge CB4 1ST. *T:* Cambridge (0223) 424893. *Clubs:* Surrey CCC; Lancashire CCC; National Arts (New York City).

KAY, Prof. Harry, CBE 1981; PhD; Vice-Chancellor, University of Exeter, 1973–84 (Hon. Professor, 1984); *b* 22 March 1919; *s* of late Williamson T. Kay; *m* 1941, Gwendolen Diana, *d* of Charles Edward Maude; one *s* one *d*. *Educ:* Rotherham Grammar Sch.; Trinity Hall, Cambridge (1938–39, 1946–51). Served War of 1939–45 with Royal Artillery. Research with Nuffield Unit into Problems of Ageing, Cambridge, 1948–51; Psychologist of Naval Arctic Expedition, 1949. Lecturer in Experimental Psychology, Univ. of Oxford, 1951–59; Prof. of Psychology, Univ. of Sheffield, 1960–73. Visiting Scientist, National Institutes of Health, Washington, DC, 1957–58. Pro-Vice-Chancellor, University of Sheffield, 1967–71. Pres., British Psychological Soc., 1971–72. Hon. Director: MRC Unit, Dept of Psychology, Sheffield; Nat. Centre of Programmed

Instruction for Industry, Sheffield. Member: SSRC, 1970–73; MRC, 1975–77 (Chm., Environmental Medicine Res. Policy Cttee, 1975–77); CNAA, 1974–79; Open Univ. Acad. Adv. Cttee; BBC Continuing Educn Adv. Cttee; Southern Univs Jt Bd (Chm., 1978–80); UCCA (Chm., 1978–84); Oakes Cttee on Management of Higher Educn, 1977–78; NATO Human Factors Panel, 1972–75; GMC, 1984–89. Chairman: Central Council for Educn and Trng in Social Work, 1980–84; Bd of Management, Northcott Theatre, 1973–84. Hon. DSc: Sheffield, 1981; Exeter, 1985. Vernon Prize, 1962. *Publication:* (with B. Dodd and M. Sime) Teaching Machines and Programmed Instruction, 1968. *Recreation:* listening. *Address:* Coastguard House, 18 Coastguard Road, Budleigh Salterton EX9 6NU.

KAY, Prof. Humphrey Edward Melville, MD, FRCP, FRCPath; Haematologist, Royal Marsden Hospital, 1956–84; Professor of Haematology, University of London, 1982–84 (Professor Emeritus, since 1984); *b* 10 Oct. 1923; *s* of late Rev. Arnold Innes and Winifred Julia Kay; *m* 1950, April Grace Lavinia Powlett (*d* 1990); one *s* two *d. Educ:* Bryanston Sch.; St Thomas's Hospital. MB, BS 1945. RAFVR, 1947–49; junior appts at St Thomas's Hosp., 1950–56. Sec., MRC Cttee on Leukaemia, 1968–84; Dean, Inst. of Cancer Research, 1970–72. Editor, Jl Clinical Pathology, 1972–80. Mem. Council, Wiltshire Trust for Nature Conservation, 1983–. *Publications:* papers and chapters on blood diseases, etc; occasional poetry. *Recreation:* natural history including gardening. *Address:* New Mill Cottage, Pewsey, Wilts SN9 5LD.

KAY, John Menzies, MA, PhD; CEng, FIMechE, FIChemE; engineering consultant; Director, GSK Steel Developments Ltd, 1976–83; *b* 4 Sept. 1920; *s* of John Aiton Kay and Isabel Kay (*née* Menzies). *Educ:* Sherborne Sch.; Trinity Hall Cambridge. University Demonstrator in Chemical Engineering, Cambridge University, 1948; Chief Technical Engineer, Division of Atomic Energy Production, Risley, 1952; Prof. of Nuclear Power, Imperial Coll. of Science and Technology, University of London, 1956; Dir of Engineering Development, Tube Investments Ltd, 1961; Chief Engineer, Richard Thomas & Baldwins Ltd, 1965; Dir-in-charge, Planning Div., BSC, 1968–70; Dir of Engrng, Strip Mills Div., BSC, 1970–76. Mem., Nuclear Safety Adv. Cttee, 1960–76; Chm., Radioactive Waste Study Gp, 1974–81; Mem., Adv. Cttee on Safety of Nuclear Installations, 1980–83. *Publications:* Introduction to Fluid Mechanics and Heat Transfer, 1957, 3rd edn 1974; Fluid Mechanics and Transfer Processes, 1985; contribs to Proc. of Institution of Mechanical Engineers. *Recreations:* hill-walking, tree planting, music. *Address:* Church Farm, St Briavels, near Lydney, Glos GL15 6QE. *Clubs:* Alpine, United Oxford & Cambridge University.

KAY, John William, QC 1984; a Recorder of the Crown Court, since 1982; *b* 13 Sept. 1943; *y s* of late C. Herbert Kay and Ida Kay; *m* 1966, Jeffa Connell; one *s* two *d. Educ:* Denstone; Christ's Coll., Cambridge (MA). Called to Bar, Gray's Inn, 1968. Tutor in Law, Liverpool Univ., 1968–69; in practice on Northern Circuit, 1968–. Mem., Gen. Council of Bar, 1988–. *Recreations:* gardening, genealogy, horse racing. *Address:* Markhams, 17 Far Moss Road, Blundellsands, Liverpool L23 8TG. *T:* 051–924 5804. *Clubs:* Athenæum, Racquet (Liverpool).

KAY, Jolyon Christopher; HM Diplomatic Service, retired; Director, Kingsfield (Middle East), since 1991; *b* 19 Sept. 1930; *s* of Colin Mardall Kay and Gertrude Fanny Kay; *m* 1956, Shirley Mary Clarke; two *s* two *d. Educ:* Charterhouse; St John's Coll., Cambridge (BA). Chemical Engr, Albright and Wilson, 1954; UKAEA, Harwell, 1958; Battelle Inst., Geneva, 1961; Foreign Office, London, 1964; MECAS, 1965; British Interests Section, Swiss Embassy, Algiers, 1967; Head of Chancery and Information Adviser, Political Residency, Bahrain, 1968; FCO, 1970; Economic Counsellor, Jedda, 1974–77; Consul-Gen., Casablanca, 1977–80; Science, later Commercial, Counsellor, Paris, 1980–84; Counsellor and Consul-Gen., Dubai, 1985–90. *Recreations:* acting, skiing, croquet. *Address:* Little Triton, Blewbury, Oxfordshire. *T:* Blewbury (0235) 850010.

KAY, Maurice Ralph; QC 1988; a Recorder, since 1988; *b* 6 Dec. 1942; *s* of Ralph and Hylda Kay; *m* 1968, Margaret Angela Alcock; four *s. Educ:* William Hulme's Grammar Sch., Manchester; Sheffield Univ. (LLB, PhD). Called to the Bar, Gray's Inn, 1975. Lecturer in Law: Hull Univ., 1967–72; Manchester Univ., 1972–73; Prof. of Law, Keele Univ., 1973–82. Practising barrister, 1975–; an Asst Recorder, 1987–88. *Publications:* (author, contributor) numerous legal books and jls. *Recreations:* music, theatre, sport. *Address:* (chambers) 3 Paper Buildings, Temple, EC4Y 7EU. *T:* 071–583 8055; 21 White Friars, Chester CH1 1NZ. *T:* Chester (0244) 323070; (home) 8 Dysart Buildings, Nantwich, Cheshire CW5 5DW. *T:* Nantwich (0270) 626278. *Club:* Reform.

KAY, Neil Vincent; Director of Social Services, Sheffield, 1979–90 (Deputy Director, 1971–79); *b* 24 May 1936; *s* of Charles Vincent Kay and Emma Kay; *m* 1961, Maureen (*née* Flemons); one *s* two *d. Educ:* Woodhouse Grammar Sch.; Downing Coll., Cambridge (MA); Birmingham Univ. (Prof. Social Work Qual.). Social Worker (Child Care), Oxford CC, and Sheffield CC, 1960–66; Lectr and Tutor in Social Work, Extramural Dept, Sheffield Univ., 1966–71. *Address:* 22 Westwood Road, Sheffield S11 7EY. *T:* Sheffield (0742) 301934.

KAY, Maj.-Gen. Patrick Richard, CB 1972; MBE 1945; RM retired; *b* 1 Aug. 1921; *y s* of late Dr and Mrs A. R. Kay, Blakeney, Norfolk; *m* 1944, Muriel Austen Smith; three *s* one *d. Educ:* Eastbourne Coll. Commissioned in Royal Marines, 1940; HMS Renown, 1941–43; 4 Commando Bde, 1944–45; Combined Ops HQ, 1945–48; Staff of Commandant-Gen., Royal Marines, 1948–50 and 1952–54; Staff Coll., Camberley, 1951; 40 Commando, RM, 1954–57; Joint Services Amphibious Warfare Centre, 1957–59; Plans Div., Naval Staff, 1959–62; CO, 43 Commando, RM, 1963–65; CO, Amphibious Training Unit, RM, 1965–66; Asst Dir (Jt Warfare) Naval Staff, 1966–67; Asst Chief of Staff to Comdt-Gen. RM, 1968; IDC, 1969; C of S to Comdt-Gen., RM, 1970–74, retired 1974. Dir of Naval Security, 1974–81. Sec., Defence, Press and Broadcasting Cttee, 1984–86. *Recreations:* gardening, golf. *Address:* c/o Barclays Bank, Fleet, Hants GU13 8BS.

KAY-SHUTTLEWORTH, family name of **Baron Shuttleworth.**

KAYE, Sir David Alexander Gordon, 4th Bt *cr* 1923, of Huddersfield; *b* 26 July 1919; *s* of Sir Henry Gordon Kaye, 2nd Bt and Winifred (*d* 1971), *d* of Walter H. Scales, Verwood, Bradford; *S* brother, 1983; *m* 1st, 1942, Elizabeth (marr. diss. 1950), *o d* of Captain Malcolm Hurtley; 2nd, 1955, Adelle, *d* of Denis Thomas, Brisbane, Queensland; two *s* four *d. Educ:* Stowe; Cambridge Univ. (BA). MRCS Eng., LRCP London 1943. *Heir: s* Paul Henry Gordon Kaye, *b* 19 Feb. 1958. *Address:* Yerinandah, 73 Moggill Road, The Gap, Brisbane, Queensland 4061, Australia.

KAYE, Col Douglas Robert Beaumont, DSO 1942 (Bar 1945); DL; JP; *b* 18 Nov. 1909; *s* of late Robert Walter Kaye, JP, Great Glenn Manor, Leics; *m* 1946, Florence Audrey Emma, *d* of late Henry Archibald Bellville, Tedstone Court, Bromyard, Herefordshire; one *s* one *d. Educ:* Harrow. 2nd Lieut Leicestershire Yeo., 1928; 2nd Lieut 10th Royal Hussars, 1931. Served War of 1939–45: Jerusalem, 1939–41; Cairo and HQ 30 Corps, 1941–42; Lieut-Col comdg 10th Royal Hussars, Africa and Italy, 1943–46 (despatches twice; wounded). Bde Major, 30 Lowland Armd Bde (TA), 1947–49; Lieut-Col comdg 16th/5th Queen's Royal Lancers, 1949–51; AA & QMG 56 London Armd Div. (TA), 1952–54; Col Comdt and Chief Instructor, Gunnery Sch., RAC Centre, 1954–56; retd 1956. Master of Newmarket and Thurlow Foxhounds, 1957–59. DL 1963, JP 1961, High Sheriff 1971, Cambridgeshire and Isle of Ely. Mem., Newmarket RDC, 1958–74 (Chm., 1972–74), E Cambridgeshire DC, 1974–84. *Recreations:* hunting, shooting. *Address:* Brinkley Hall, near Newmarket, Suffolk CB8 0SB. *T:* Stetchworth (0638) 507202. *Club:* Cavalry and Guards.

KAYE, Elaine Hilda; Headmistress, Oxford High School, GPDST, 1972–81; *b* 21 Jan. 1930; *d* of late Rev. Harold Sutcliffe Kaye and Kathleen Mary (*née* White). *Educ:* Bradford Girls' Grammar Sch.; Milton Mount Coll.; St Anne's Coll., Oxford. Assistant Mistress: Leyton County High Sch., 1952–54; Queen's Coll., Harley Street, 1954–59; South Hampstead High Sch., GPDST, 1959–65; Part-time Tutor, Westminster Tutors, 1965–67; Dep. Warden, Missenden Abbey Adult Coll., 1967–72. Project Dir, Oxford Project for Peace Studies, 1989– (Vice-Chair and Editor, 1984–89). *Publications:* History of the King's Weigh House Church, 1968; History of Queen's College, Harley St, 1972; Short History of Missenden Abbey, 1973; (contrib.) Biographical Dictionary of Modern Peace Leaders, 1985; (ed) Peace Studies: the hard questions, 1987; C. J. Cadoux: theologian, scholar and pacifist, 1988; (with Ross Mackenzie) W. E. Orchard: a study in Christian exploration, 1990. *Recreations:* music, walking, conversation. *Address:* 31 Rowland Close, Wolvercote, Oxford OX2 8PW. *T:* Oxford (0865) 53917.

KAYE, Sir Emmanuel, Kt 1974; CBE 1967; Founder and Chairman: The Kaye Organisation Ltd, 1966–89; Kaye Enterprises Ltd, since 1989; *b* 29 Nov. 1914; *m* 1946, Elizabeth Cutler; one *s* two *d. Educ:* Richmond Hill Sch.; Twickenham Technical Coll. Founded J. E. Shay Ltd, Precision Gauge, Tool and Instrument Makers, and took over Lansing Bagnall & Co. of Isleworth, 1943; then founded jtly with J. R. Sharp (*d* 1965), Lansing Bagnall Ltd, 1943–89; transf. to Basingstoke, 1949 (from being smallest manufr of electric lift trucks, became largest in Europe). Royal Warrant as supplier of Industrial Trucks to Royal Household, 1971; Queen's Awards for Export Achievement in 1969, 1970, 1971, 1979, 1980 and only co. to win Queen's Awards for both Export Achievement and Technological Innovation, 1972; Design Council Awards, 1974, 1980; winners of Gold and other Continental Awards. Chairmanships include: Elvetham Hall Ltd, 1965–; Lansing GmbH, Germany, 1966–91; Pool & Sons (Hartley Wintney) Ltd, 1967–90; Lansing Bagnall (Northern) Ltd, 1982–90; Kaye Steel Stockholders, 1978–; Lina-Loda, 1981–; Kaye Office Supplies Ltd, 1983–; Conference Booking Centre, 1986–; Pres., Lansing Linde Ltd, 1989–. Founded Unquoted Companies' Gp, 1968. Confederation of British Industry: Member: Taxation Cttee, 1970–77; Wealth Tax Panel, 1974–77; President's Cttee, 1976–85; Council, 1976–89; Econ. and Financial Policy Cttee, 1985–. Member: Council of Industry for Management Educn, 1970–87; Export Credit Guarantees Adv. Council, 1971–74; Inflation Accounting Cttee, 1974–75; Queen's Award Review Cttee, 1975; Reviewing Cttee on Export of Works of Art, 1977–80. Visiting Fellow, Univ. of Lancaster, 1970–87. Governor: Girls' High Sch., Basingstoke, 1955–70; Queen Mary's Coll., Basingstoke, 1971–75. Trustee, Glyndebourne, 1977–84; Chairman: Thrombosis Research Trust, 1985– (Vice Chm., 1981–85); Thrombosis Res. Inst., 1988–; Vice Pres., Natural Medicines Soc., 1986–. Fellow, Psionic Medical Soc., 1977–. Liveryman, Farriers' Co., 1953; Freeman, City of London, 1954. FBIM 1975; FRSA 1978. *Recreations:* chess, music, walking. *Club:* Brooks's.

KAYE, Geoffrey John; *b* 14 Aug. 1935; *s* of Michael and Golda Kaye; two *d. Educ:* Christ College, Finchley. Started with Pricerite Ltd when business was a small private company controlling six shops, 1951; apptd Manager (aged 18) of one of Pricerite Ltd stores, 1953; Supervisor, Pricerite Ltd, 1955; Controller of all stores in Pricerite Ltd Gp, 1958; Director, 1963; Chairman and Man. Dir, 1966–73. Mem. Cttee, British Assoc. Monte Carlo. *Recreations:* tennis, golf. *Address:* Europa Résidence, Place des Moulins, Monte Carlo, Monaco. *Clubs:* British Association (Monaco); Desert Highlands (Arizona).

KAYE, Sir John Phillip Lister L.; *see* Lister-Kaye.

KAYE, Mary Margaret, (Mrs G. J. Hamilton), FRSL; authoress and illustrator; *d* of late Sir Cecil Kaye, CSI, CIE, CBE, and Lady Kaye; *m* Maj.-Gen. G. J. Hamilton, CB, CBE, DSO (*d* 1985); two *d. Publications: historical novels:* Shadow of the Moon, 1957, rev. edn 1979; Trade Wind, 1963, revd edn 1981; The Far Pavilions, 1978 (televised 1984); *detective novels:* Six Bars at Seven, 1940; Death Walks in Kashmir, 1953 (republished as Death in Kashmir, 1984); Death Walks in Berlin, 1955; Death Walks in Cyprus, 1956 (republished as Death in Cyprus, 1984); Later Than You Think, 1958 (republished as Death in Kenya, 1983); House of Shade, 1959 (republished as Death in Zanzibar, 1983); Night on the Island, 1960 (republished as Death in the Andamans, 1985); Death in Berlin, 1985; *for children:* The Potter Pinner Books (series), 1937–41; The Ordinary Princess, 1980, US 1984 (shown on BBC TV Jackanory, 1983, 1984); Thistledown, 1981; *autobiography:* Vol. I, The Sun in the Morning, 1990; *edited:* The Golden Calm, 1980; Moon of Other Days, a personal choice of Kipling's verse, 1988; *illustrated:* The Story of St Francis; Children of Galilee; Adventures in a Caravan. *Recreation:* painting. *Club:* Army and Navy.

KAYE, Michael, OBE 1991; General Administrator, Young Concert Artists Trust, since 1983; Festival Director, City of London Festival, since 1984; *b* 27 Feb. 1925; *s* of Harry Kaye and Annie Steinberg; *m* 1st, 1950, Muriel Greenberg (marr. diss. 1959); one *d*; 2nd, 1962, Fay Bercovitch. *Educ:* Malmesbury Road, Bow; Cave Road, Plaistow; Water Lane, Stratford; West Ham Secondary Sch., E15. Served in Army, REME and Intelligence Corps, 1943–47. Journalism and Public Relations, 1947–53; Marketing and Public Relations in tobacco industry, 1953–61; PR Manager, later PR Director, Carreras-Rothmans, 1961–76; Director, Peter Stuyvesant Foundation, 1963–76; General Administrator, Rupert Foundn, 1972–76; Man. Dir, London Symphony Orchestra, 1976–80. Trustee: Whitechapel Art Gallery, 1964–75; Youth & Music, 1970–78; Arts Dir, GLC, and Gen. Administrator, S Bank Concert Halls, 1980–83. Chm., Educn Cttee, British Assoc. of Concert Agents, 1989–; Member: Exec. Cttee, Carl Flesch Internat. Violin Competition, 1984–; Council, Centre for Study of Judaism and Jewish/Christian Relations, 1989–. *Recreations:* photography, music (clarinet). *Address:* 3 Coppice Way, E18 2DU. *T:* 081–989 1281.

KAYE, Roger Godfrey, TD 1980 and Bar 1985; QC 1989; Barrister; *b* 21 Sept. 1946; *s* of late Anthony Harmsworth Kaye and Heidi Alice (*née* Jordy); *m* 1974, Melloney Rose, *d* of Rev. H. M. Westall. *Educ:* King's Sch., Canterbury; Birmingham Univ. (LLB 1968). Lectr in Law, Kingston Poly., 1968–73. Called to the Bar, Lincoln's Inn, 1970; Jun. Treasury Counsel in Insolvency Matters, 1978–89; Dep. High Court Registrar in Bankruptcy, 1985–89. Dep. Chm., Fees Collection Cttee, Bar Council, 1990–. Varied TA service in Europe, 1967–87. *Recreation:* going home. *Address:* 24 Old Buildings, Lincoln's Inn, WC2A 3UJ. *T:* 071–404 0946. *Clubs:* Army and Navy, Royal Automobile, Special Forces.

KAYE, Rosalind Anne, (Mrs J. A. Kaye); *see* Plowright, R. A.

KAYLL, Wing Commander Joseph Robert, DSO 1940; OBE 1946; DFC 1940; DL; JP; *b* 12 April 1914; *s* of late J. P. Kayll, MBE, The Elms, Sunderland; *m* 1940, Annette Lindsay Nisbet; two *s*. *Educ:* Aysgarth; Stowe. Timber trader; joined 607 Sqdn AAF, 1934; mobilised Sept. 1939; Commanding Officer 615 Squadron, 1940; (prisoner) 1941; OC 607 Sqdn AAF 1946. DL Durham, 1956; JP Sunderland, 1962. Mem., Wear Boating Assoc. *Recreation:* yachting. *Address:* Hillside House, Hillside, Sunderland, Tyne and Wear SR3 1YN. *T:* 091–528 3282. *Clubs:* Royal Ocean Racing; Sunderland Yacht; Royal Northumberland Yacht.

KAYSEN, Prof. Carl; David W. Skinner Professor of Political Economy, Massachusetts Institute of Technology, 1977–90, now Emeritus (Director, Program in Science, Technology, and Society, 1981–87); *b* 5 March 1920; *s* of Samuel and Elizabeth Kaysen; *m* 1940, Annette Neutra; two *d*. *Educ:* Philadelphia Public Schs; Overbrook High Sch., Philadelphia; Pennsylvania, Columbia and Harvard Univs. AB Pa 1940; MA 1947, PhD 1954, Harvard. Nat. Bureau of Economic Research, 1940–42; Office of Strategic Services, Washington, 1942–43; Intelligence Officer, US Army Air Force, 1943–45; State Dept, Washington, 1945. Dep. Special Asst to President, 1961–63. Harvard University, 1947–66: Teaching Fellow in Econs, 1947; Asst Prof. of Economics, 1950–55; Assoc. Prof. of Economics 1955–57; Prof. of Economics, 1957–66; Assoc. Dean, Graduate Sch. of Public Administration, 1960–66; Lucius N. Littauer Prof. of Political Economy, 1964–66; Jr Fellow, Soc. of Fellows, 1947–50, Actg Sen. Fellow, 1957–58, 1964–65; Syndic, Harvard Univ. Press, 1964–66; Dir, Inst. for Advanced Study, Princeton, NJ, 1966–76, Dir Emeritus, 1976; Vice Chm., and Dir of Research, Sloan Commn on Govt and Higher Educn, 1977–79. Sen. Fulbright Res. Schol., LSE, 1955–56. Trustee: Pennsylvania Univ., 1967–; Russell Sage Foundn, 1979–89. *Publications:* United States *v* United Shoe Machinery Corporation, an Economic Analysis of an Anti-Trust Case, 1956; The American Business Creed (with others), 1956; Anti-Trust Policy (with D. F. Turner), 1959; The Demand for Electricity in the United States (with F. M. Fisher), 1962; The Higher Learning, The Universities, and The Public, 1969; (contrib.) Nuclear Energy Issues and Choices, 1979; A Program for Renewed Partnership (Sloan Commn on Govt and Higher Educn Report), 1980; numerous articles on economic theory, applied economics, higher education, military strategy and arms control. *Address:* E51–208, Massachusetts Institute of Technology, Cambridge, Mass 02139, USA.

KAZAN, Elia; author; independent producer and director of plays and films; *b* Constantinople, 7 Sept. 1909; *s* of George Kazan and Athena Sismanoglou; *m* 1st, 1932, Molly Thacher (*d* 1963); two *s* two *d*; 2nd, 1967, Barbara Loden (*d* 1980); one *s*; 3rd, 1982, Frances Rudge. *Educ:* Williams Coll. (AB); 2 years postgraduate work in Drama at Yale. Actor, Group Theatre, 1932–39; first London appearance as Eddie Fuseli in Golden Boy, St James, 1938. Directed *plays:* Skin of Our Teeth, 1942; All My Sons, A Streetcar Named Desire, 1947; Death of a Salesman, 1949; Camino Real, Tea and Sympathy, 1953; Cat on a Hot Tin Roof, 1955; Dark at Top of the Stairs, JB, 1958; Sweet Bird of Youth, 1959; After the Fall, 1964; But For Whom Charlie, 1964; The Changeling, 1964; Four times won best stage Director of Year, 1942, 1947, 1948, 1949. Directed *films:* Streetcar named Desire, 1951; Viva Zapata, 1952; Pinky, 1949; Gentleman's Agreement, 1948 (won Oscar, best Dir); Boomerang, 1947; A Tree Grows in Brooklyn, 1945; On the Waterfront, 1954 (won Oscar, best Dir); East of Eden, 1954; Baby Doll, 1956; A Face in the Crowd, 1957; Wild River, 1960; Splendour in the Grass, 1962; America, America, 1964; The Arrangement, 1969; The Visitors, 1972; The Last Tycoon, 1977. Three times won Best Picture of Year from New York Film Critics, 1948, 1952, 1955. *Publications:* America, America (novel), 1963; The Arrangement (novel), 1967; The Assassins, 1972; The Understudy, 1974; Acts of Love, 1978; The Anatolian, 1982; Elia Kazan, A Life (autobiog.), 1988; magazine articles in New York Times, Theatre Arts, etc. *Recreation:* tennis.

KEABLE-ELLIOTT, Dr (Robert) Anthony, OBE 1988; FRCGP; general practitioner, 1948–87; *b* 14 Nov. 1924; *s* of Robert Keable and Jolie Buck; *m* 1953, Gilian Mary Hutchison; four *s*. *Educ:* Sherborne Sch., Dorset; Guy's Hosp., London, 1943–48 (MB BS London). Founder Mem., Chiltern Medical Soc., 1956, Vice-Pres. 1958, Pres. 1964; Member, Faculty Board of Thames Valley, Faculty of Royal Coll. of General Practitioners, 1960; Upjohn Travelling Fellowship, 1962; Member: Bucks Local Med. Cttee, 1958–75 (Chm., 1964–68; Hon. Life Mem., 1975–); GMC, 1989–. British Medical Association: Mem., 1948–; Mem. Council, 1974–; Treasurer, 1981–87; Chm., Journal Cttee, 1987–; Chm., Gen. Med. Services Cttee, 1966–72. Mem., Finance Corp. of General Practice, 1974–79. Mem., Soc. of Apothecaries, 1985–; Freeman, City of London, 1986. Asst Editor, Guy's Hospital Gazette, 1947–48. *Recreations:* sailing, golf, gardening. *Address:* Peels, Ibstone, near High Wycombe, Bucks HP14 3XX. *T:* Turville Heath (049163) 385.

KEAL, Dr Edwin Ernest Frederick, FRCP; Honorary Consulting Physician, St Mary's and Brompton Hospitals, London; *b* 21 Aug. 1921; *s* of Frederick Archibald Keal and Mabel Orange Keal; *m* 1945, Constance Mary Gilliams; one *s*. *Educ:* Kingston High Sch., Hull; London Hospital Med. Coll. MB BS London 1952, DCH 1954, MD London 1971; FRCP 1973 (MRCP 1957). Service in RNVR (Exec. Lieut), 1939–46. Junior hosp. posts, London Hosp., 1952–59; Sen. Medical Registrar, Brompton Hosp., 1959–63; Consultant Physician: St Charles Hosp., London, 1963–77; Kensington Chest Clinic, 1963–86; Brompton Hosp., 1966–86; St Mary's Hosp., London, 1977–86; Cardiothoracic Institute: Sen. Lectr, 1972–77; Hon. Sen. Lectr, 1978–86; Dean, 1979–84. Hon. Consultant in Chest Diseases to the Army, 1979–86. Member: Bd of Governors, National Heart and Chest Hosps, 1975–85; Cttee of Management, Cardiothoracic Inst., 1978–84. *Publications:* chapters in various books, and articles, mainly related to diseases of the chest. *Recreations:* gardening, travel. *Address:* 12 Dorchester Drive, Herne Hill, SE24 0DQ. *T:* 071–733 1766.

KEALY, Robin Andrew, CMG 1991; HM Diplomatic Service; Director of Trade Promotion and Investment, Paris, since 1990; *b* 7 Oct. 1944; *s* of Lt-Col H. L. B. Kealy, Royal Signals and Mrs B. E. Kealy; *m* 1987, Annabel Jane Hood; one *s*. *Educ:* Harrow Sch.; Oriel Coll., Oxford (Open Scholar; BA Lit. Hum. (1st Cl. Hons Mods); MA). Joined HM Diplomatic Service, 1967; FO, 1967; MECAS, 1968; Tripoli, 1970; Kuwait, 1972; ME Dept, FCO, 1975; Port of Spain, 1978; Commercial Sec., Prague, 1982; Asst, Aid Policy Dept, FCO, 1985; Counsellor and Consul Gen., Baghdad, 1987–90. *Recreations:* music, theatre, ski-ing, cooking, gardening. *Address:* c/o Foreign and Commonwealth Office, King Charles Street, SW1A 2AH. *Club:* Travellers'.

KEAN, Arnold Wilfred Geoffrey, CBE 1977; FRAeS; Member, UN Administrative Tribunal, since 1980 (Vice-President, 1982–88; President, 1988–89); *b* 29 Sept. 1914; *s* of late Martin Kean; *m* 1939, Sonja Irene, *d* of late Josef Andersson, Copenhagen; two *d*. *Educ:* Blackpool Gram. Sch.; Queens' Coll., Cambridge (Schol.). 1st cl. 1st div. Law Tripos, Pts I and II; Pres., Cambridge Union, 1935; Wallenberg (Scandinavian) Prize; Commonwealth Fund Fellow, Harvard Law Sch.; Yarborough-Anderson Schol., Inner Temple. Called to the Bar (studentship, certif. of honour, 1939). Wartime service on legal staff of British Purchasing Commn and UK Treas. Delegn in N America. HM Treasury Solicitor's Dept, 1945; Princ. Asst Solicitor, 1964–72; Sec. and Legal Adviser, CAA, 1972–79. Mem., Legal Cttee, Internat. Civil Aviation Organisation, 1954– (Chm., 1978–83); UK Deleg. at internat. confs on maritime, railway, atomic energy and air law. Tutor in Law, Civil Service Coll., 1963–; Visiting Lecturer: Univ. of Auckland, NZ, 1980; Univ. of Sydney, NSW, 1982; UCL, 1983–88 (Hon. Fellow). Air Law Editor, Jl of Business Law, 1970–. King Christian X Liberation Medal (Denmark), 1945. *Publications:* (ed) Essays in Air Law, 1982; articles in legal periodicals. *Recreations:* music, stamps, gardening. *Address:* Tall Trees, South Hill Avenue, Harrow HA1 3NU. *T:* 081–422 5791.

KEANE, Desmond St John; QC 1981; QC (Hong Kong) 1982; QC (NSW) 1986; a Recorder of the Crown Court, since 1979; *b* 21 Aug. 1941; *er s* of late Henry Keane, MB, BCh, and of Patricia Keane; *m* 1968, Susan Mary Little (marr. diss. 1987); two *s* two *d*. *Educ:* Downside Sch.; Wadham Coll., Oxford (Schol.; MA Mod. Hist.); Harmsworth Law Schol., 1964. Called to the Bar, Middle Temple, 1964. Dep. Judge, High Court of Hong Kong, 1983 and 1986. Hon. Lectr, Faculty of Law, Univ. of Hong Kong, 1982–88. Legal Assessor to GMC, 1982–. *Recreation:* cricket. *Address:* 2 Paper Buildings, Temple, EC4Y 7ET. *T:* 071–936 2611. *Clubs:* United Oxford & Cambridge University; Kildare Street and University (Dublin); Hong Kong (Hong Kong).

KEANE, Francis Joseph; Sheriff of Glasgow and Strathkelvin, since 1984; *b* 5 Jan. 1936; *s* of Thomas and Helen Keane; *m* 1960, Lucia Corio Morrison; two *s* one *d*. *Educ:* Blairs Coll., Aberdeen; Gregorian Univ., Rome (PhL); Univ. of Edinburgh (LLB). Solicitor; Partner, McCluskey, Keane & Co., 1959; Depute Procurator Fiscal, Perth, 1961, Edinburgh, 1963; Senior Depute PF, Edinburgh, 1971; Senior Legal Asst, Crown Office, Edinburgh, 1972; PF, Airdrie, 1976; Regional PF, S Strathclyde, Dumfries and Galloway, 1980. Pres., PF Soc., 1982–84. *Recreations:* music, painting, tennis. *Address:* Glasgow Sheriff Court, 1 Carlton Place, Glasgow G5 9DA. *T:* 041–429 8888.

KEANE, Mary Nesta, (Molly), (Mrs Robert Keane); (*nom de plume:* **M. J. Farrell**); *b* 20 July 1905; *d* of Walter Clarmont Skrine and Agnes Shakespeare Higginson; *m* 1938, Robert Lumley Keane; two *d*. *Educ:* privately. Author of plays: (with John Perry) Spring Meeting (play perf. Ambassadors Theatre and New York, 1938); Ducks and Drakes (play perf. Apollo Theatre, 1941); Guardian Angel (play perf. Gate Theatre, Dublin, 1944); Treasure Hunt (play perf. Apollo Theatre, 1949); Dazzling Prospects. *Publications: as M. J. Farrell:* The Knight of Cheerful Countenance; This Angel Knight, Young Entry; Taking Chances; Mad Puppettstown; Conversation Piece; Devoted Ladies, 1934; Full House, 1935; The Rising Tide, 1937; Two Days in Aragon, 1941; Loving Without Tears, 1951; Treasure Hunt, 1952; *as Molly Keane:* Good Behaviour, 1981 (televised 1983); Time After Time, 1983 (televised 1986); Nursery Cooking, 1985; Loving and Giving, 1988. *Address:* Dysert, Ardmore, Co. Waterford, Ireland. *TA:* Ardmore. *T:* Youghal 4225. *Clubs:* Lansdowne, Groucho.

KEANE, Major Sir Richard (Michael), 6th Bt *cr* 1801; farmer; *b* 29 Jan. 1909; *s* of Sir John Keane, 5th Bart, DSO, and Lady Eleanor Hicks-Beach (*d* 1960), *e d* of 1st Earl St Aldwyn; *S* father, 1956; *m* 1939, Olivia Dorothy Hawkshaw; two *s* one *d*. *Educ:* Sherborne Sch.; Christ Church, Oxford. Diplomatic Correspondent to Reuters 1935–37; Diplomatic Corresp. and Asst to Editor, Sunday Times, 1937–39. Served with County of London Yeomanry and 10th Royal Hussars, 1939–44; Liaison Officer (Major) with HQ Vojvodina, Yugoslav Partisans, 1944; attached British Military Mission, Belgrade, 1944–45. Publicity Consultant to Imperial Chemical Industries Ltd, 1950–62. *Publications:* Germany: What Next?, (Penguin Special), 1939; Modern Marvels of Science (editor), 1961. *Recreation:* fishing. *Heir: s* John Charles Keane [*b* 16 Sept. 1941; *m* 1977, Corinne, *d* of Jean Everard de Harzir; two *s* one *d*]. *Address:* Cappoquin House, Cappoquin, County Waterford, Ireland. *T:* 058–54004. *Club:* Cavalry and Guards.

KEAR, Graham Francis; Assistant Secretary, Abbeyfield Richmond Society, since 1984; *b* 9 Oct. 1928; *s* of Richard Walter Kear and Eva Davies; *m* 1978, Joyce Eileen Parks. *Educ:* Newport (St Julian's) High Sch., Mon; Balliol Coll., Oxford (BA). Min. of Supply, 1951–52 and 1954–57; UK Delegn to ECSC, 1953–54; Min. of Aviation, 1957–59 and 1960–63; NATO Maintenance Supply Agency, Paris, 1959–60; MoD, 1963–65; Cabinet Office, 1968–71; Min. of Aviation Supply/DTI, 1971–72; Fellow, Harvard Univ. Center for Internat. Affairs, 1972–73; Under-Sec., Dept of Energy, 1974–80. *Recreation:* music. *Address:* 28 Eastbourne Road, Brentford, Mddx TW8 9PE. *T:* 081–560 4746.

KEARLEY, family name of **Viscount Devonport.**

KEARNEY, Sheriff Brian; Sheriff of Glasgow and Strathkelvin, since 1977; *b* 25 Aug. 1935; *s* of late James Samuel and Agnes Olive Kearney; *m* 1965, Elizabeth Mary Chambers; three *s* one *d*. *Educ:* Largs Higher Grade; Greenock Academy; Glasgow Univ. (MA, LLB). Qualified solicitor, 1960; Partner, Biggart, Lumsden & Co., Solicitors, Glasgow, 1965–74. Sheriff of N Strathclyde at Dumbarton (floating sheriff), 1974–77. Sometime tutor in Jurisprudence, and external examnr in legal subjects, Glasgow Univ.; Pres., Glasgow Juridical Soc., 1964–65; Chm., Glasgow Marriage Guidance Council, 1977–90. Hon. Pres., Glasgow Marriage Counselling Service, 1990–. *Publications:* An Introduction to Ordinary Civil Procedure in the Sheriff Court, 1982; Children's Hearings and the Sheriff Court, 1987; articles in legal jls. *Recreations:* cutting sandwiches for family picnics, listening to music, reading, writing and resting. *Address:* Sheriff's Chambers, Sheriff Court House, 1 Carlton Place, Glasgow G5 9DA.

KEARNEY, Hon. Sir William (John Francis), Kt 1982; CBE 1976; Judge of the Supreme Court of the Northern Territory, since 1982; Aboriginal Land Commissioner, since 1982; *b* 8 Jan. 1935; *s* of William John Kilbeg Kearney and Gertrude Ivylene Kearney; *m* 1959, Jessie Alice Elizabeth Yung; three *d*. *Educ:* Univ. of Sydney (BA, LLB); University Coll. London (LLM). Legal Service of Papua New Guinea, 1963–75; Sec. for Law, 1972–75; dormant Commn as Administrator, 1972–73, and as High Comr, 1973–75; Judge, Supreme Ct of PNG, 1976–80; Dep. Chief Justice, 1980–82. *Recreations:* travelling, literature. *Address:* Judges' Chambers, Supreme Court, Darwin, NT 0801, Australia.

KEARNS, David Todd; Chairman since 1985, and Chief Executive since 1982, Xerox Corp.; *b* 11 Aug. 1930; *m* 1954, Shirley Cox; two *s* four *d*. *Educ:* Univ. of Rochester (BA). Served US Navy; IBM, 1954–71; Xerox Corp.: Corporate Vice Pres., 1971; Group Vice Pres. and Board of Dirs, 1976; Pres. and Chief Operating Officer, 1977. Mem. Boards of Directors: Chase Manhattan Corp.; Time Inc.; Dayton Hudson Corp; Ryder System. Member: Council on Foreign Relations; Business Roundtable; Business Council; President's Commn on Executive Exchange. Trustee: Cttee for Economic Develt; Nat. Urban League. Member: Bd of Dirs, Junior Achievement; Bd of Visitors, Fuqua Sch. of Business Administration, Duke Univ.; Mem. Exec. Adv. Commn, William E. Simon Sch. of Business, and Trustee, Univ. of Rochester. *Address:* Xerox Corporation, PO Box 1600, Stamford, Conn 06904, USA. *T:* (203) 968–3201.

KEARNS, Dr William Edward, FFPHM; Chief Medical Officer and Director of Public Health, North East Thames Regional Health Authority; *b* 10 July 1934; *s* of William Edward Kearns and Kathleen Wolfenden; *m* 1954, Beryl Cross; four *s* one *d* (and one *s* decd). *Educ:* Liverpool Coll.; Univ. of Liverpool (MB ChB); Univ. of London (MSc). MRCS, LRCP. Hosp. posts in cardiorespiratory physiology, gen. medicine and pathology,

United Liverpool Hosps, 1958–70; NW Metropolitan Regional Hospital Board: Asst SMO, 1970–73; Regional Sci. Officer, 1973–74; Dist Community Physician, Kensington and Chelsea and Westminster AHA (Teaching), 1974–82; Hon. Sen. Lectr in Community Medicine, St Mary's Hosp. Med. Sch., 1975–86; Dist MO, Paddington and N Kensington HA, 1982–86; Reginal MO and Dir of Health Care Policy, NE Thames RHA, 1986. Reader, Neasden Parish Church (S Catherine); regular volunteer driver for Gateway Clubs in Brent. *Publications:* contribs to med. jls. *Recreation:* gardening for wild life conservation. *Address:* Five Midholm, Barn Hill, Wembley Park, Middx HA9 9LJ. *T:* 081–908 1511. *Club:* Royal Society of Medicine.

KEARTON, family name of **Baron Kearton.**

KEARTON, Baron *cr* 1970 (Life Peer), of Whitchurch, Bucks; **Christopher Frank Kearton;** Kt 1966; OBE 1945; FRS 1961; Chancellor, University of Bath, since 1980; *b* 17 Feb. 1911; *s* of Christopher John Kearton and Lilian Hancock; *m* 1936, Agnes Kathleen Brander; two *s* two *d. Educ:* Hanley High Sch.; St John's Coll., Oxford. Joined ICI, Billingham Division, 1933. Worked in Atomic Energy Project, UK and USA, 1940–45. Joined Courtaulds Ltd, i/c of Chemical Engineering, 1946; Dir 1952; Dep. Chm., 1961–64; Chm., 1964–75; Chm. and Chief Exec., British Nat. Oil Corp., 1976–79. Part-time Member: UKAEA, 1955–81; CEGB, 1974–80. Dir, Hill Samuel Gp, 1970–81; Chm., British Printing Corp., 1981. Visitor, DSIR, 1955–61, 1963–68. Chairman: Industrial Reorganisation Corp., 1966–68; Electricity Supply Res. Council, 1960–77 (Mem., 1954–77); Tropical Products Inst. Cttee, 1958–79; East European Trade Council, 1975–77. Member: Windscale Accident Cttee, 1957; Special Advisory Group, British Transport Commn, 1960; Adv. Council on Technology, 1964–70; Council, RIIA, 1964–75; NEDC, 1965–71; Adv. Cttee, Industrial Expansion Bill, 1968–70 (Chm.); Central Adv. Council for Science and Technology; Cttee of Enquiry into Structure of Electricity Supply Industry, 1974–75; Offshore Energy Technology Bd, 1976–79; Energy Commn, 1977–79. Member Council: Royal Soc., 1970; British Heart Foundn, 1977–; Gov., Ditchley Foundn, 1971–91. Mem., Select Cttees, H of L, 1982–. President: Soc. of Chemical Industry, 1972–74 (Chm., Heavy Organic Chemical Section, 1961–62); RoSPA, 1973–80; BAAS, 1978–79; Aslib, 1980–82; Market Research Soc., 1983–87. Mem. Syndicate, Govt of Univ. of Cambridge, 1988–89. FIC 1976; Hon. Fellow: St John's Coll., Oxford, 1965; Manchester Coll. of Sci. and Techn., 1966; Soc. of Dyers and Colourists, 1974. Comp. TI, 1965; Hon. FIChemE 1968; Hon. LLD: Leeds, 1966; Strathclyde, 1981; Bristol, 1988; Hon. DSc: Bath, 1966; Aston in Birmingham, 1970; Reading, 1970; Keele, 1973; Ulster, 1975; Hon. DCL Oxon, 1978; DUniv Heriot-Watt, 1979. FRSA 1970; CBIM 1980. Grande Ufficiale, Order of Merit (Italy), 1977. *Address:* The Old House, Whitchurch, near Aylesbury, Bucks HP22 4JS. *T:* Aylesbury (0296) 641232. *Club:* Athenæum.

KEATING, Donald Norman, QC 1972; FCIArb; a Recorder of the Crown Court, 1972–87; *b* 24 June 1924; *s* of late Thomas Archer Keating and late Anne Keating; *m* 1st, 1945, Betty Katharine (*d* 1975); two *s* one *d*; 2nd, 1978, Kay Rosamond (*see* K. R. B. Keating); one *s* one step *d. Educ:* Roan Sch.; King's Coll., London. BA (History), 1948. RAFVR, 1943–46 (Flt Lt). Called to Bar, Lincoln's Inn, 1950; Bencher, 1979. Head of chambers, 1976–. Mem., DTI study team on Professional Liability, 1988–89. *Publications:* Building Contracts, edns 1955, 1963, 1969, 1978 and supps 1982, 1984, consultant to 5th edn 1991; Guide to RIBA Forms, 1959; various articles in legal and other jls. *Recreations:* theatre, music, travel, walking. *Address:* 10 Essex Street, WC2R 3AA. *T:* 071–240 6981. *Club:* Garrick.

KEATING, Frank; Sports Columnist, The Guardian, since 1976; *b* 4 Oct. 1937; *s* of Bryan Keating and Monica Marsh; *m* 1987, Jane Sinclair; one *s* one *d. Educ:* Belmont Abbey; Douai. Local newspapers, Stroud, Hereford, Guildford, Bristol, Southern Rhodesia, Gloucester and Slough, 1956–63; Editor, Outside Broadcasts, Rediffusion Television, 1963–67; Editor, Features, and Head of Special Projs, Thames Television, 1968–72; The Guardian, 1972–. Astroturf Sportswriter of the Year, 1978; 'What the Papers Say' Sportswriter of the Year, 1979; Sports Council Magazine Writer of the Year, 1987; Specialist Writer of Year, Magazine Publishers Awards, 1988; Sports Journalist of the Year, British Press Awards, 1988. *Television series:* Maestro, BBC, 1981–85. *Publications:* Caught by Keating, 1979; Bowled Over, 1980; Another Bloody Day in Paradise, 1981; Up and Under, 1983; Long Days, Late Nights, 1984; High, Wide and Handsome, 1986; Gents and Players, 1986; Passing Shots, 1988; Sportswriter's Eye, 1989; contrib. Punch, New Statesman, Spectator, BBC. *Recreations:* bad gardening, worse weeding. *Address:* Church House, Marden, near Hereford HR1 3EN. *T:* Sutton St Nicholas (043272) 213. *Club:* Chelsea Arts.

KEATING, Henry Reymond Fitzwalter; author; *b* 31 Oct. 1926; *s* of John Hervey Keating and Muriel Marguerita Keating (*née* Clews); *m* 1953, Sheila Mary Mitchell; three *s* one *d. Educ:* Merchant Taylors' Sch.; Trinity Coll., Dublin. Journalism, 1952–60; Crime Reviewer for The Times, 1967–83. Chairman: Crime Writers' Assoc., 1970–71; Society of Authors, 1983–84; Pres., Detection Club, 1985. FRSL 1990. *Publications:* Death and the Visiting Firemen, 1959; Zen there was Murder, 1960; A Rush on the Ultimate, 1961; The Dog it was that Died, 1962; Death of a Fat God, 1963; The Perfect Murder, 1964 (filmed 1988); Is Skin-Deep, Is Fatal, 1965; Inspector Ghote's Good Crusade, 1966; Inspector Ghote Caught in Meshes, 1967; Inspector Ghote Hunts the Peacock, 1968; Inspector Ghote Plays a Joker, 1969; Inspector Ghote Breaks an Egg, 1970; Inspector Ghote goes by Train, 1971; The Strong Man, 1971; (ed) Blood on My Mind, 1972; Inspector Ghote Trusts the Heart, 1972; The Underside, 1974; Bats Fly Up for Inspector Ghote, 1974; A Remarkable Case of Burglary, 1975; Filmi, Filmi, Inspector Ghote, 1976; Murder Must Appetize, 1976; (ed) Agatha Christie: First Lady of Crime, 1977; A Long Walk to Wimbledon, 1978; Inspector Ghote Draws a Line, 1979; Sherlock Holmes: the man and his world, 1979; The Murder of the Maharajah, 1980; Go West, Inspector Ghote, 1981; (ed) Whodunit, 1982; The Lucky Alphonse, 1982; The Sheriff of Bombay, 1984; Mrs Craggs, Crimes Cleaned Up, 1985; Under a Monsoon Cloud, 1986; Writing Crime Fiction, 1986; The Body in the Billiard Room, 1987; Crime and Mystery: the 100 best books, 1987; Dead on Time, 1988; Inspector Ghote, His Life and Crimes, 1989; (ed) Bedside Companion to Crime, 1989; The Iciest Sin, 1990. *Recreation:* popping round to the post. *Address:* 35 Northumberland Place, W2 5AS. *T:* 071–229 1100.

KEATING, Kay Rosamond Blundell; Metropolitan Stipendiary Magistrate, since 1987; *b* 3 Oct. 1943; *d* of Geoffrey Blundell Jones and Avis Blundell Jones; *m* 1st, 1965, Edmund Deighton (decd); one *d*; 2nd, 1978, Donald Norman Keating, *qv*; one *s. Educ:* St Hugh's College, Oxford (BA Jurisp. 1965; MA 1968). Called to the Bar, Gray's Inn, 1966. *Recreations:* travel, walking, tennis, riding, opera. *Address:* Greenwich Magistrates' Court, 9 Blackheath Road, SE10 8PG. *T:* 081–761 8102.

KEATING, Hon. Paul John; Federal Treasurer of Australia, 1983–91; Deputy Prime Minister, 1990–91; MP (Lab) for Blaxland, NSW, since 1969; *b* 18 Jan. 1944; *s* of Matthew and Minnie Keating; *m* 1975, Anita Johanna Maria Van Iersel; one *s* three *d. Educ:* De La Salle College, Bankstown, NSW. Research Officer, Federated Municipal and Shire Council Employees Union of Australia, 1967. Minister for Northern Australia, Oct.-Nov. 1975; Shadow Minister for Agriculture, Jan.-March 1976, for Minerals and Energy, 1976–80, for Resources and Energy, 1980–83; Shadow Treasurer, Jan.-March 1983. Member: Cabinet Expenditure Review Cttee (Dep. Chm.), 1987–91; Parly Structural Adjustment Cttee, 1987; Parly Social and Family Policy Cttee, 1983. Chm., Australian Loan Council, 1983–91. *Address:* House of Representatives, Parliament House, Canberra, ACT 2600, Australia. *T:* 062.727060, 731417.

KEATINGE, Sir Edgar (Mayne), Kt 1960; CBE 1954; *b* Bombay, 3 Feb. 1905; *s* of late Gerald Francis Keatinge, CIE; *m* 1930, Katharine Lucile Burrell (*d* 1990); one *s* one *d. Educ:* Rugby Sch.; School of Agriculture, S Africa. Diploma in Agriculture, 1925. S African Dept of Agriculture, 1926–29. Served War of 1939–45 with RA. Resigned with rank of Lieut-Col. West African Frontier Force, 1941–43; Commandant Sch. of Artillery, West Africa, 1942–43; CC West Suffolk, 1933–45. Parliamentary Candidate, Isle of Ely, 1938–44; MP (C) Bury St Edmunds, 1944–45; JP Wilts 1946; Chm. Wessex Area Nat. Union of Conservative Assocs, 1950–53; Mem. Panel, Land Tribunal, SW Area. Director: St Madeleine Sugar Co., 1944–62; Caromi Ltd, 1962–66. Governor, Sherborne Sch., 1951–74. Mem. Council, Royal African Soc., 1970–80. *Recreations:* travel, shooting. *Address:* Teffont, Salisbury, Wilts SP3 5RG. *T:* Teffont (072276) 224. *Clubs:* Carlton, Boodle's.

See also Prof. W. R. Keatinge.

KEATINGE, Prof. William Richard; MA; PhD; Professor of Physiology, Queen Mary and Westfield College, since 1990; *b* 18 May 1931; *s* of Sir Edgar Keatinge, *qv*; *m* 1955, M. E. Annette Hegarty; one *s* two *d. Educ:* Upper Canada Coll.; Rugby Sch.; Cambridge Univ.; St Thomas's Hospital. MB BChir; MRCP 1985. House Phys., St Thomas's Hospital, 1955–56; Surg.-Lt RN (Nat. Service), 1956–58; Jun. Research Fellow and Dir of Studies in Medicine, Pembroke Coll., Cambridge, 1958–60; Fellow, Cardiovascular Research Inst., San Francisco, 1960–61; MRC appt Radcliffe Infirmary, Oxford, 1961–68; Fellow of Pembroke Coll., Oxford, 1965–68; Reader in Physiology, 1968–71, Prof. of Physiol., 1971–90, London Hosp. Med. Coll. *Publications:* Survival in Cold Water, 1969; Local Mechanisms Controlling Blood Vessels, 1980; chapters in textbooks of physiology and medicine; papers in physiological and medical jls on temperature regulation and on control of blood vessels. *Recreations:* ski-ing, archaeology. *Address:* Queen Mary and Westfield College, Mile End Road, E1 4NS.

KEAY, Ronald William John, CBE 1977 (OBE 1966); DPhil; Executive Secretary, The Royal Society, 1977–85; *b* 20 May 1920; *s* of Harold John Keay and Marion Lucy (*née* Flick); *m* 1944, Joan Mary Walden; one *s* two *d. Educ:* King's College Sch., Wimbledon; St John's Coll., Oxford (BSc, MA, DPhil). Colonial Forest Service, Nigeria, 1942–62. Seconded to Royal Botanic Gardens, Kew, 1951–57; Dir, Federal Dept of Forest Research, Nigeria, 1960–62; Dep. Exec. Sec., The Royal Society, 1962–77. Leverhulme Emeritus Fellow, 1987–88; Vis. Prof., Univ. of Essex, 1991–. Pres., Science Assoc. of Nigeria, 1961–62; Vice-President: Linnean Soc., 1965–67, 1971–73, 1974–76 (Treas., 1989–); Nigerian Field Soc., 1987–; President: African Studies Assoc., 1971–72; Inst. of Biology, 1988–90. Chairman: Finance Cttee, Internat. Biological Programme, 1964–74; UK Br., Nigerian Field Soc.; Treasurer, Scientific Cttee for Problems of the Environment, 1976–77; Member: Lawes Agricl Trust Cttee, 1978–90; RHS Review Cttee, 1984–85 (Chm., RHS Liby Rev. Cttee, 1988–89); Council, Roehampton Inst. of Higher Educn, 1986–89; Council, British Initiative Against Avoidable Disablement (IMPACT Foundn), 1985–. Church Warden, St Martin-in-the-Fields, 1981–87. Hon. FIBiol 1985; Hon. FRHS 1986. *Publications:* Flora of West Tropical Africa, Vol. 1, pt 1 1954, pt 2 1958; Nigerian Trees, 1960–64, rev. and shortened edn as Trees of Nigeria, 1989; papers on tropical African plant ecology and taxonomy, and science policy. *Recreations:* gardening, walking, natural history. *Address:* 38 Birch Grove, Cobham, Surrey KT11 2HR. *T:* Cobham (0932) 865677. *Club:* Athenæum.

KEDOURIE, Prof. Elie, CBE 1991; FBA 1975; Professor of Politics in the University of London, 1965–90, now Emeritus; Founder, and Editor since 1964, Middle Eastern Studies; *b* 25 Jan. 1926; *er s* of A. Kedourie and L. Dangour, Baghdad; *m* 1950, Sylvia, *d* of Gourgi Haim, Baghdad; two *s* one *d. Educ:* Collège A-D Sasson and Shamash Sch., Baghdad; London Sch. of Economics; St Antony's Coll., Oxford (Sen. Scholar). BSc(Econ). Taught at the London Sch. of Economics, 1953–90. Visiting Lecturer: Univ. of California, Los Angeles, 1959; Univ. of Paris, 1959; Visiting Professor: Princeton Univ., 1960–61; Monash Univ., Melb., 1967 and 1989; Harvard Univ., 1968–69; Tel Aviv Univ., 1969; Brandeis Univ., 1985–86; Inst. Raymond Aron, Paris, 1990; Columbia Univ., 1991; Scholar-in-Residence, Brandeis Univ., 1982; Vis. Res. Fellow, All Souls Coll., Oxford, 1989–90; Koret Fellow, Washington Inst. for Near East Policy, 1990–91; Fellow, Woodrow Wilson Center, Washington, 1991–June 1992. Mem., Cttee of Enquiry into Validation of Acad. Degrees in Public Sector Higher Educn, 1984–85. Hist. Advr, Roads to Conflict, BBC TV, 1978. Fellow: Netherlands Inst. for Advanced Study, 1980–81; Sackler Inst. of Advanced Studies, Tel-Aviv Univ., 1983. Dr *hc* Tel-Aviv Univ., 1991. Mem. Editorial Bd, Cambridge Studies in History and Theory of Politics, 1968–82. *Publications:* England and the Middle East, 1956, new edn 1987; Nationalism, 1960 (trans. German, 1968), new edn with afterword, 1985; Afghani and 'Abduh, 1966; The Chatham House Version, 1970, new edn 1984; Nationalism in Asia and Africa, 1971; Arabic Political Memoirs, 1974; In the Anglo-Arab Labyrinth, 1976; (ed) The Middle Eastern Economy, 1977; (ed) The Jewish World, 1979; (ed jtly) Modern Egypt, 1980; Islam in the Modern World, 1980; (ed jtly) Towards a Modern Iran, 1980; (ed jtly) Palestine and Israel in the Nineteenth and Twentieth Centuries, 1982; (ed jtly) Zionism and Arabism in Palestine and Israel, 1982; The Crossman Confessions, 1984; Diamonds into Glass: the Government and the universities, 1988; (ed jtly) Studies in the Economic History of the Middle East, 1989; Perestroika in the Universities, 1989; *relevant publication:* National and International Politics in the Middle East: essays in honour of Elie Kedourie, ed Edward Ingram, 1986. *Address:* c/o London School of Economics, Houghton Street, Aldwych, WC2A 2AE. *T:* 071–405 7686.

KEE, Robert; author and broadcaster; *b* 5 Oct. 1919; *s* of late Robert and Dorothy Kee; *m* 1st, 1948, Janetta (marr. diss. 1950), *d* of Rev. G. H. Woolley, VC; one *d*; 2nd, 1960, Cynthia (marr. diss. 1989), *d* of Edward Judah; one *s* one *d* (and one *s* decd); 3rd, Kate, *yr d* of Humphrey Trevelyan. *Educ:* Stowe Sch.; Magdalen Coll., Oxford (Exhibr, MA). RAF, 1940–46. Atlantic Award for Literature, 1946. Picture Post, 1948–51; Picture Editor, WHO, 1953; Special Corresp., Observer, 1956–57; Literary Editor, Spectator, 1957; Special Corresp., Sunday Times, 1957–58; BBC TV (Panorama, etc), 1958–62; Television Reporters International, 1963–64; ITV (Rediffusion, Thames, London Week-End, ITN, Yorkshire), 1964–78; BBC, 1978–82; Presenter: Panorama, BBC1, 1982; TV-am, 1983; Channel 4's Seven Days, 1984–88. *Television series:* Ireland: a television history (13 parts), 1981. Alistair Horne Research Fellow, St Antony's Coll., Oxford, 1972–73. BAFTA Richard Dimbleby Award, 1976. *Publications:* A Crowd Is Not Company, 1947, repr. 1982; The Impossible Shore, 1949; A Sign of the Times, 1955; Broadstrop In Season, 1959; Refugee World, 1961; The Green Flag, 1972; Ireland: a history, 1980; The World We Left Behind: a chronicle of 1939, 1984; 1945: the World We Fought For, 1985; Trial and Error, 1986; Munich: the eleventh hour, 1988; The Picture Post Album, 1989;

many translations from German. *Recreations:* swimming, listening to music. *Address:* c/o Rogers, Coleridge & White, 20 Powis Mews, W11 1JN.
See also William Kee.

KEE, His Honour William; a Circuit Judge, 1972–90; *b* 15 Oct. 1921; *yr s* of Robert and Dorothy Kee; *m* 1953, Helga Wessel Eckhoff; one *s* three *d. Educ:* Rottingdean Sch.; Stowe Sch. Served War, Army, 1941–46: attached 9th Gurkha Rifles, Dehra Dun, 1943; Staff Captain, Area HQ, 1945–46. Called to Bar, Inner Temple, 1948. Principal Judge for County Courts in Kent, 1985–90. Jt Chm., Independent Schools' Tribunal, 1971–72. *Publications:* (jt) Divorce Case Book, 1950; contributor to: titles in Atkin's Encyclopaedia of Court Forms; Halsbury's Laws of England. *Recreations:* listening to music, walking.
See also Robert Kee.

KEEBLE, Sir (Herbert Ben) Curtis, GCMG 1982 (KCMG 1978; CMG 1970); HM Diplomatic Service, retired; Ambassador at Moscow, 1978–82; *b* 18 Sept. 1922; *s* of Herbert Keeble and Gertrude Keeble, BEM; *m* 1947, Margaret Fraser; three *d. Educ:* Clacton County High Sch.; London University. Served HM Forces, 1942–47. Entered HM Foreign (subsequently Diplomatic) Service, 1947; served in Djakarta, 1947–49; Foreign Office, 1949–51; Berlin, 1951–54; Washington, 1954–58; Foreign Office, 1958–63; Counsellor and Head of European Economic Organisations Dept, 1963–65; Counsellor (Commercial), Berne, 1965–68; Minister, Canberra, 1968–71; Asst Under-Sec. of State, FCO, 1971–73; HM Ambassador, German Democratic Republic, 1974–76; Dep. Under Sec. of State (Chief Clerk), FCO, 1976–78. Special Adviser, H of C Foreign Affairs Cttee, 1985–86. A Governor, BBC, 1985–90. Chm., GB-USSR Assoc., 1985–; Member Council: RIIA, 1985–90; SSEES, 1985–. *Publications:* (ed) The Soviet State, 1985; Britain and The Soviet Union, 1917–1989, 1990. *Recreations:* sailing, ski-ing. *Address:* Dormers, St Leonards Road, Thames Ditton, Surrey KT7 0RR. *T:* 081–398 7778. *Club:* Travellers'.

KEEBLE, Major Robert, DSO 1940; MC 1945; TD 1946; Director: Associated Portland Cement Manufacturers Ltd, 1970–74; Aberthaw & Bristol Channel Portland Cement Co. Ltd, 1970–74; engaged in cement manufacture; *b* 20 Feb. 1911; *s* of late Edwin Percy and Alice Elizabeth Keeble; unmarried. *Educ:* King Henry VIII's Sch., Coventry. Commanded Royal Engineer Field Company; Territorial Army Commission, passed Staff Coll., Camberley, 1939; served in War of 1939–45 (despatches twice, twice wounded, DSO, MC, 1939–45 Star, African Star, France-Germany Star and Defence Medal, TD). Mem., Inst. Quarrying. Governor, Hull Univ. Hon. Brother, Hull Trinity House. Freeman of City of London and Liveryman of Company of Fanmakers; Fellow, Drapers' Co., Coventry. *Recreation:* fishing. *Address:* 15 Fernhill Close, Kenilworth CV8 1AN. *T:* Kenilworth (0926) 55668. *Club:* Army and Navy.

KEEBLE, Thomas Whitfield; HM Diplomatic Service, retired 1976; Senior Clerk (Acting), Committee Office, House of Commons, 1976–83; *b* 10 Feb. 1918; *m* 1945, Ursula Scott Morris; two *s. Educ:* Sir John Deane's Grammar Sch., Cheshire; St John's Coll., Cambridge (MA); King's Coll., London (PhD). Served, 1940–45, in India, Persia, Iraq and Burma in RA (seconded to Indian Artillery), Captain. Asst Principal, Commonwealth Relations Office, 1948; Private Sec. to Parliamentary Under Sec. of State; Principal, 1949; First Sec., UK High Commn in Pakistan, 1950–53, in Lahore, Peshawar and Karachi; seconded to Foreign Service and posted to UK Mission to the United Nations in New York, 1955–59; Counsellor, 1958; Head of Defence and Western Dept, CRO, 1959–60; British Dep. High Comr in Ghana, 1960–63; Head of Econ. Gen. Dept, CRO, 1963–66; Minister (Commercial), British Embassy, Buenos Aires, 1966–67; Hon. Research Associate, Inst. of Latin American Studies, Univ. of London, 1967–68; Minister, British Embassy, Madrid, 1969–71; Head of UN (Econ. and Social) Dept, FCO, 1971–72, of UN Dept, 1972–74; Sen. Directing Staff (Civil), Nat. Defence Coll., Latimer, 1974–76. *Publications:* British Overseas Territories and South America, 1806–1914, 1970; articles in Hispanic reviews. *Recreations:* Hispanic history and arts, bird watching. *Address:* 49 Station Road, Oakington, Cambridge CB4 5AH. *T:* Cambridge (0223) 234922. *Club:* United Oxford & Cambridge University.

KEEFFE, Barrie Colin; dramatist; *b* 31 Oct. 1945; *s* of Edward Thomas Keeffe and Constance Beatrice Keeffe (*née* Marsh); *m* 1st, 1969, Dee Sarah Truman (marr. diss. 1979); 2nd, 1981, Verity Eileen Proud (*née* Bargate) (*d* 1981); Guardian of her two *s*; 3rd, 1983, Julia Lindsay. *Educ:* East Ham Grammar School. Formerly actor with Nat. Youth Theatre; began writing career as journalist; Thames Television Award writer-in-residence, Shaw Theatre, 1977; Resident playwright, Royal Shakespeare Co., 1978; Associate Writer, Theatre Royal, Stratford East, 1986–. Member: Board of Directors: Soho Theatre Co., 1978–; Theatre Royal, Stratford E, 1988–. French Critics Prix Revelation, 1978; Giles Cooper Best Radio Plays, 1980; Mystery Writers of America Edgar Allan Poe Award, 1982. *Theatre plays:* Only a Game, 1973; A Sight of Glory, 1975; Scribes, 1975; Here Comes the Sun, 1976; Gimme Shelter, 1977; A Mad World My Masters, 1977, 1984; Barbarians, 1977; Frozen Assets, 1978; Sus, 1979; Bastard Angel, 1980; She's So Modern, 1980; Black Lear, 1980; Chorus Girls, 1981; Better Times, 1985; King of England, 1988; My Girl, 1989; Not Fade Away, 1990; Wild Justice, 1990; I Only Want to be With You, 1991; *television plays:* Substitute, 1972; Not Quite Cricket, 1977; Gotcha, 1977; Nipper, 1977; Champions, 1978; Hanging Around, 1978; Waterloo Sunset, 1979; King, 1984; *television series:* No Excuses, 1983; *film:* The Long Good Friday, 1981; also radio plays. *Publications: novels:* Gadabout, 1969; No Excuses, 1983; *plays:* Gimme Shelter, 1977; A Mad World My Masters, 1977; Barbarians, 1977; Here Comes the Sun, 1978; Frozen Assets, 1978; Sus, 1979; Bastard Angel, 1980; The Long Good Friday, 1984; Better Times, 1985; King of England, 1988; My Girl, 1989; Wild Justice, Not Fade Away, Gimme Shelter, 1990. *Recreation:* origami. *Address:* 110 Annandale Road, SE10 0JZ.

KEEGAN, Denis Michael; Barrister; General Manager, Mercantile Credit Co. Ltd, 1975–83, retired; *b* 26 Jan. 1924; *o s* of Denis Francis Keegan and Mrs Duncan Campbell; *m* 1st, 1951, Pamela Barbara (marr. diss.), *yr d* of late Percy Bryan, Purley, Surrey; one *s*; 2nd, 1961, Marie Patricia (marr. diss.), *yr d* of late Harold Jennings; one *s*; 3rd, 1972, Ann Irene, *d* of Norman Morris. *Educ:* Oundle Sch.; Queen's University, Kingston, Ontario, Canada (BA). Served RN Fleet Air Arm, 1944–46 (petty officer pilot). Called to Bar, Gray's Inn, 1950. Mem. Nottingham City Council, 1953–55, resigned. MP (C) Nottingham Sth, 1955–Sept. 1959. Dir, HP Information PLC (Chm. 1984). Formerly Dir, Radio and Television Retailers' Assoc. *Recreations:* reading, talking, music. *Address:* 5 Paper Buildings, Temple, EC4Y 7HB. *T:* 071–353 8494.

KEEGAN, (Joseph) Kevin, OBE 1982; professional footballer, 1966–84; *b* 14 Feb. 1951; *s* of late Joseph Keegan; *m* 1974, Jean Woodhouse; two *d.* Professional footballer with: Scunthorpe Utd, 1966–71; Liverpool, 1971–77; Hamburg, 1977–80; Southampton, 1980–82; Newcastle Utd, 1982–84. Internat. appearances for England, 1973–82, Captain, 1976–82. Football expert, Thames TV. Winners' medals: League Championships, 1973, 1976; UEFA Cup, 1973, 1976; FA Cup, 1974; European Cup, 1977. European Footballer of the Year, 1978, 1979. *Publications:* Kevin Keegan, 1978; Against the World: playing for England, 1979. *Address:* c/o Thames Television, 306 Euston Road, NW1.

KEEGAN, William James Gregory; Economics Editor, since 1977, and Associate Editor, since 1983, The Observer; *b* 3 July 1938; *s* of William Patrick Keegan and Sheila Julia Keegan (*née* Buckley); *m* 1967, Tessa (*née* Young, *widow* of John Ashton) (marr. diss. 1982); two *s* two *d. Educ:* Wimbledon Coll.; Trinity Coll., Cambridge (MA). National Service (Army), 1957–59 (commissioned). Journalist, Financial Times, Daily Mail and News Chronicle, 1963–67; Economics Correspondent, Financial Times, 1967–76; Economic Intell. Dept, Bank of England, 1976–77; Asst Editor and Business Editor, The Observer, 1981–83. Member: BBC Adv. Cttee on Business and Indust. Affairs, 1981–88; Council, Employment Inst., 1987–; Adv. Bd, Dept of Applied Economics, Cambridge, 1988–; Cttee for Soc. Scis., CNAA, 1991–. Vis. Prof. of Journalism, 1989–, Hon. Res. Fellow, 1990, Sheffield Univ. *Publications:* Consulting Father Wintergreen, 1974; A Real Killing, 1976; (jtly) Who Runs the Economy?, 1978; Mrs Thatcher's Economic Experiment, 1984; Britain Without Oil, 1985; Mr Lawson's Gamble, 1989; contribs to The Tablet. *Address:* 9 Compton Road, Islington, N1; The Observer, Chelsea Bridge House, Queenstown Road, SW8 4NN. *T:* 071–627 0700. *Club:* Garrick.

KEELING, Surgeon Rear-Adm. John, CBE 1978; retired; Director of Medical Policy and Plans, Ministry of Defence, 1980–83; Chairman, NATO Joint Civil/Military Medical Group, 1981–83; *b* 28 Oct. 1921; *s* of John and Grace Keeling; *m* 1948, Olwen Anne Dix; one *s* (and one *s* decd). *Educ:* Queen Elizabeth's Sch., Hartlebury; Birmingham Univ. MRCS, LRCP; MFOM. Entered RN as Surg. Lieut, 1946; served with Fleet Air Arm, 1947–75: Pres., Central Air Med. Bd, 1954–56 and 1960–63; SMO, HMS Albion, 1956–57, HMS Victorious, 1965–67, and several Royal Naval Air Stns; Staff MO to Flag Officer Sea Trng, 1970–73; Dir of Environmental Medicine and Dep. MO i/c Inst. of Naval Medicine, 1975–77; Dep. Med. Dir-Gen. (Naval), 1977–80. Surg. Captain 1970, Surg. Cdre 1977, Surg. Rear-Adm. 1980. QHP, 1977–83. Member: BMA, 1945–; Fleet Air Arm Officers' Assoc., 1973–; Soc. of Occupational Medicine, 1976–. Membership Sec., Herefordshire Nature Trust, 1988–. *Recreations:* music, gardening, micro-computing, caravanning. *Address:* Merlin Cottage, Brockhampton, Hereford HR1 4TQ. *T:* How Caple (098986) 649. *Club:* Army and Navy.

KEELING, Robert William Maynard; a Recorder of the Crown Court, 1980–89; Consultant with Monier-Williams; *b* 16 Dec. 1917; *s* of Dr George Sydney Keeling, MD, and Florence Amy Keeling (*née* Maynard); *m* 1942, Kathleen Busill-Jones; one *s* two *d. Educ:* Uppingham; Corpus Christi Coll., Cambridge (BA 1939). Served War, RASC, 1939–46: Western Desert, Italy, Greece (despatches 1944), Berlin. FO, 1946–47. Solicitor 1950; Partner in Monier-Williams & Keeling, 1956–80; Solicitor to Vintners Company, 1953–79. Director, Sherry Producers Committee Ltd, 1967–80, Chairman 1980–. Diplôme de Grande Médaille d'Argent, Corporation des Vignerons de Champagne, 1988. Knight Comdr, Order of Civil Merit (Spain), 1967. *Recreations:* travel, painting, music. *Address:* Vale Bank, Chadlington, Oxford OX7 3LZ.

KEEMER, Peter John Charles; Assistant Auditor General, National Audit Office, since 1989; *b* 27 Jan. 1932; *s* of late Frederick and Queenie Keemer; *m* 1954, Yvonne Griffin; one *s* one *d* (and one *s* decd). *Educ:* Price's Sch., Fareham; Univ. of Bath (MPhil). Exchequer and Audit Department: Asst Auditor and Auditor, 1950–62; Private Sec. to Comptroller and Auditor Gen., 1962–65; seconded to Parly Comr for Administration as Chief Exec. Officer, 1966–70; Chief Auditor, 1970; Dep. Dir, 1973; Dir, 1978–89 (seconded to European Court of Auditors as Director, 1978–86). *Address:* How Green Cottage, How Lane, Chipstead, Surrey CR5 3LL. *T:* Downland (0737) 553711. *Club:* Anglo-Belgian.

KEEN, Kenneth Roger; QC 1991; *b* 13 May 1946; *s* of Kenneth Henry Keen and Joan Megan Keen (*née* Weetman); *m* 1969, Hilary Jane Wood; one *s* one *d. Educ:* Doncaster Grammar School. Qualified Solicitor, 1968; called to the Bar, Gray's Inn, 1976; practice on NE circuit; a Recorder, 1989. *Recreations:* everything Italian, food, drink, life. *Address:* 12 Paradise Square, Sheffield. *T:* Sheffield (0742) 738951.

KEEN, Maurice Hugh, FSA; FBA 1990; Fellow of Balliol College, Oxford, since 1961; *b* 30 Oct. 1933; *e s* of Harold Hugh Keen and Catherine Eleanor Lyle Keen (*née* Cummins); *m* 1968, Mary Agnes Keegan; three *d. Educ:* Winchester College; Balliol College, Oxford (BA 1st Cl. Mod. Hist. 1957). FSA 1987. Nat. Service 1952–54, commissioned Royal Ulster Rifles. Junior Res. Fellow, The Queen's Coll., Oxford, 1957–61; Tutor in Medieval History, Balliol Coll., Oxford, 1961–. External examr, Nat. Univ. of Ireland, 1971–78. Fellow, Winchester Coll., 1989–. Alexander Prize, RHistS, 1962. *Publications:* The Outlaws of Medieval Legend, 1961; The Laws of War in the Later Middle Ages, 1965; A History of Medieval Europe, 1968; England in the Later Middle Ages, 1973; Chivalry, 1984 (Wolfson Lit. Award for History, 1985). *Recreations:* fishing, shooting. *Address:* Balliol College, Oxford OX1 3BJ. *T:* Oxford (0865) 277735. *Club:* United Oxford & Cambridge University.

KEENE, David Wolfe; QC 1980; a Recorder, since 1989; *b* 15 April 1941; *s* of Edward Henry Wolfe Keene and Lilian Marjorie Keene; *m* 1965, Gillian Margaret Lawrance; one *s* one *d. Educ:* Hampton Grammar Sch.; Balliol Coll., Oxford (Winter Williams Prizewinner, 1962; BA 1st Cl. Hons Law, 1962; BCL 1963). Called to the Bar, Inner Temple, 1964, Bencher, 1987; Eldon Law Scholar, 1965. Chm. of Panel, Cumbria Structure Plan Examination in Public, 1980; conducted County Hall, London, Inquiry, 1987. Vice-Chm., Local Govt and Planning Bar Assoc., 1990–. *Recreations:* walking, opera, jazz. *Address:* 4 and 5 Gray's Inn Square, Gray's Inn, WC1R 5AY. *T:* 071–404 5252. *Club:* Athenæum.

KEENE, Dr Derek John; Director, Centre for Metropolitan History, Institute of Historical Research, since 1987; *b* 27 Dec. 1942; *s* of Charles Henry Keene and Edith Anne Keene (*née* Swanston); *m* 1969, Suzanne Victoria Forbes; one *s* one *d. Educ:* Ealing Grammar Sch.; Oriel Coll., Oxford (MA, DPhil). FRHistS. Researcher, 1968–74, Asst Dir, 1974–78, Winchester Research Unit; Dir, Social and Economic Study of Medieval London, Inst. of Historical Research, 1979–87. Member: RCHM, 1987–; Commn internat. pour l'histoire de villes, 1990–; Fabric Adv. Cttee, St Paul's Cathedral, 1991–. *Publications:* Winchester in the Early Middle Ages (jtly), 1976; Survey of Medieval Winchester, 1985; Cheapside Before the Great Fire, 1985; (with V. Harding) A survey of documentary sources for property holding in London before the Great Fire, 1985; (with V. Harding) Historical Gazetteer of London before the Great Fire, 1987; (ed with P. J. Corfield) Work in Towns 850–1850, 1990; contribs to learned jls and to collections of essays. *Recreations:* metropolises, walking uphill, making and repairing things. *Address:* 162 Erlanger Road, SE14 5TJ. *T:* 071–639 5371.

KEENE, John Robert R.; *see* Ruck Keene.

KEENLEYSIDE, Hugh Llewellyn, CC (Canada) 1969; consultant; *b* 7 July 1898; *s* of Ellis William Keenleyside and Margaret Louise Irvine; *m* 1924, Katherine Hall Pillsbury, BA, BSc; one *s* three *d. Educ:* Langara School and Public Schools, Vancouver, BC; University of British Columbia (BA); Clark University (MA, PhD). Holds several hon. degrees in Law, Science. Instructor and Special Lecturer in History, Brown University, Syracuse Univ., and University of British Columbia, 1923–27; Third Sec., Dept of External Affairs, 1928; Second Sec., 1929; First Sec. and First Chargé d'Affaires, Canadian

Legation, Tokyo, 1929; Dept of External Affairs and Prime Minister's Office, 1936; Chm. Board of Review to Investigate charges of illegal entry on the Pacific Coast, 1938; Sec., Cttee in charge of Royal Visit to Canada, 1938–39; Counsellor, 1940; Asst Under-Sec. of State for External Affairs, 1941–44; Mem. and Sec., Canadian Section, Canada-United States Permanent Jt Bd on Defence, 1940–44, Acting Chm., 1944–45; Member: North-West Territories Council, 1941–45; Canada-United States Joint Economic Cttees, 1941–44; Special Cttee on Orientals in BC; Canadian Shipping Board, 1939–41; War Scientific and Technical Development Cttee, 1940–45; Canadian Ambassador to Mexico, 1944–47; Deputy Minister of Resources and Development and Comr of Northwest Territories, 1947–50; Head of UN Mission of Technical Assistance to Bolivia, 1950; Dir-Gen., UN Technical Assistance Administration, 1950–58; Under-Sec. Gen. for Public Administration, UN, 1959. Chairman: BC Power Commn, 1959–62; BC Hydro and Power Authy, 1962–69. Vice-Pres. National Council of the YMCAs of Canada, 1941–45; Vice-Chm., Canadian Youth Commission, 1943–45; Head of Canadian Deleg. to UN Scientific Conf. on Conservation and Utilization of Resources, 1949. Life Mem., Asiatic Soc. of Japan; one of founders and mem. of first Board of Governors of Arctic Institute of North America; Vice-Chm., Board of Governors, Carleton Coll., 1943–50; Pres. Assoc. of Canadian Clubs, 1948–50; Mem. Bd of Trustees, Clark Univ., 1953–56; Mem. Senate, University of British Columbia, 1963–69. Hon. Life Mem., Canadian Association for Adult Education; Mem. Board of Governors, Canadian Welfare Council, 1955–69; Member: Canadian National Cttee of World Power Conference; Adv. Bd (BC), Canada Permanent Cos; Hon. Bd of Dirs, Resources for the Future; Dir, Toronto-Dominion Bank, 1960–70. Assoc. Comr General, UN Conf. on Human Settlements, 1975–76 (Hon. Chm. Canadian Nat. Cttee, 1974–77). Chancellor, Notre Dame Univ., Nelson, BC, 1969–76. Dir and Fellow, Royal Canadian Geographic Soc. Haldane Medal, Royal Inst. of Public Administration, 1954; first recipient, Vanier Medal, Inst. of Public Administration of Canada, 1962. *Publications:* Canada and the United States, 1929, revised edn 1952; History of Japanese Education (with A. F. Thomas), 1937; International Aid: a summary, 1966; Memoirs: Vol. 1, Hammer the Golden Day, 1981; Vol. 2, On the Bridge of Time, 1982; various magazine articles. *Recreations:* reading, outdoor sports, cooking, poker. *Address:* 3470 Mayfair Drive, Victoria, BC V8P 1P8, Canada. *T:* 592–9331.

KEEP, Charles Reuben; Chairman and Chief Executive, Bellair Holdings plc (formerly Bellair Cosmetics plc), since 1984; *b* 1932; *m;* one *d. Educ:* HCS, Hampstead. Joined Lloyds & Scottish Finance Ltd, 1956, Director, 1969; Man. Dir, International Factors Ltd, 1970; Group Man. Dir, Tozer Kemsley & Millbourn (Holdings) Ltd, 1973–77; Chm., Tozer Kemsley & Millbourn Trading Ltd, 1978–80; Director: Tozer Standard & Chartered Ltd, 1973–77; Barclays Tozer Ltd, 1974–77; Manufacturers Hanover Credit Corp., 1977–80; Chm., Export Leasing Ltd, Bermuda 1978–77; Pres., France Motors sa Paris, 1974–81. *Address:* The Oaks, 20 Forest Lane, Chigwell, Essex IG7 5AE. *T:* 081–504 3897. *Clubs:* Gresham; Chigwell Golf.

KEIGHLEY, Prof. Michael Robert Burch, FRCS, FRCSE; Barling Professor of Surgery, University of Birmingham, since 1988; *b* 12 Oct. 1943; *s* of late Dr Robert Arthur Spink Keighley and of Dr Jacqueline Vivian Keighley; *m* Dr Dorothy Margaret; one *s* one *d. Educ:* Monkton Combe Sch.; St Bartholomew's Hosp., Univ. of London (MB BS; MS 1976). FRCS 1970; FRCSE 1970. Prof. of Surgery, General and Dental Hosps, Univ. of Birmingham, 1984–88. Boerhaave Prof. of Surgery, Univ. of Leiden, 1985. Jacksonian Prize, RCS, 1979; Hunterian Prof., RCS, 1979. *Publications:* Antimicrobial Prophylaxis in Surgery, 1979; Inflammatory Bowel Diseases, 1981; Gastrointestinal Haemorrhage, 1983; Textbook of Gastroenterology, 1985. *Recreations:* painting, music, sailing, climbing. *Address:* Whalebone Cottage, Vicarage Hill, Tanworth in Arden, Warwickshire B94 5AN. *T:* Tanworth in Arden (05644) 2586. *Club:* Royal Society of Medicine.

KEIGHLY-PEACH, Captain Charles Lindsey, DSO 1940; OBE 1941; RN retired; *b* 6 April 1902; *s* of late Admiral C. W. Keighly-Peach, DSO; *m* 1st, V. B. Cumbers; one *s* one *d; m* 2nd, Beatrice Mary Harrison (*d* 1974). *Educ:* RN Colleges, Osborne and Dartmouth. Midshipman, 1919; Sub-Lieut 1922; Lieut 1924; 3 Squadron, RAF, 1926; HMS Eagle (402 Sqdn), 1927; H/M S/M M2, 1929; HMS Centaur, 1930; Lieut-Cdr 1932; HMS Glorious (802 Sqdn), 1932; RN Staff Coll., Greenwich, 1934; SOO to RA Destroyers, 1935; HMS London, 1937; Commander, 1938; RN Air Station Lee-on-Solent, 1939; HMS Eagle, 1940–41; Naval Assistant (Air) to 2nd Sea Lord, 1941–44; Capt. 1943; RN Air Station, Yeovilton, 1944–45; Comdg HMS Sultan, Singapore, 1945–47; in command HMS Troubridge and 3rd Destroyer Flot. Med., 1947–49; Dir Captain, Senior Officer's War Course, RN, 1949–51; Asst Chief Naval Staff (Air) on loan to Royal Canadian Navy, 1951–53. *Recreations:* golf, gardening. *Address:* Hatteras, Hall Road, Brockdish, Diss, Norfolk IP21 5JY. *T:* Harleston (0379) 853136.

KEIGHTLEY, Maj.-Gen. Richard Charles, CB 1987; Chairman, West Dorset Health Authority, since 1988; Defence Consultant, Portescap(UK), since 1987; *b* 2 July 1933; *s* of General Sir Charles Keightley, GCB, GBE, DSO, and Lady (Joan) Keightley (*née* Smyth-Osbourne); *m* 1958, Caroline Rosemary Butler, *er d* of Sir Thomas Butler, Bt, *qv;* three *d. Educ:* Marlborough Coll.; RMA, Sandhurst. Commissioned into 5th Royal Inniskilling Dragoon Guards, 1953; served Canal Zone, BAOR, N Africa, Singapore, Cyprus; sc Camberley, 1963; comd 5th Royal Inniskilling Dragoon Guards, 1972–75; Task Force Comdr, 3 Armd Div., 1978–79; RCDS 1980; Brigadier General Staff HQ UKLF, 1981; GOC Western Dist, 1982–83; Comdt, RMA Sandhurst, 1983–87. Col, 5th Royal Inniskilling Dragoon Guards, 1986–91. Pres., Dorset Br., Royal British Legion, 1990–. Chm., Combined Services Polo Assoc., 1982–86. *Recreations:* field sports, cricket, farming. *Address:* Kennels Cottage, Tarrant Gunville, Blandford, Dorset DT11 8JQ. *Club:* Cavalry and Guards.

KEIR, James Dewar; QC 1980; Director, Open University Educational Enterprises Ltd, 1983–88; Chairman, City and East London Family Practitioner Committee, 1985–89; part-time Member, Monopolies and Mergers Commission, 1987–April 1992; *b* 30 Nov. 1921; *s* of David Robert Keir and Elizabeth Lunan (*née* Ross); *m* 1948, Jean Mary, *e d* of Rev. and Mrs E. P. Orr; two *s* two *d. Educ:* Edinburgh Acad.; Christ Church, Oxford (MA 1948). Served War, 1941–46: ME, Italy; Captain, The Black Watch (RHR). Called to the Bar, Inner Temple, 1949; Yarborough-Anderson Scholar, Inner Temple, 1950. Legal Adviser, United Africa Co. Ltd, 1954–66, Sec., 1966; Dep. Head of Legal Services, Unilever Ltd, 1973; Jt Sec., Unilever PLC and Unilever NV, 1976–84; Dir, UAC Internat. Ltd, 1973–77. Chm., 1969–72, Pres., 1980–82, Bar Assoc. for Commerce, Finance and Industry; Member: Bar Council, 1971–73; Senate of Inns of Ct and Bar, 1973–78. Chm., Pharmacists Rev. Panel, 1986–. *Recreations:* ski-ing, Rugby, opera, reading. *Address:* The Crossways, High Street, Dormansland, Lingfield, Surrey RH7 6PU. *T:* Lingfield (0342) 834621. *Club:* Caledonian.

KEITH, family name of **Barons Keith of Castleacre** and **Keith of Kinkel** and of **Earl of Kintore.**

KEITH OF CASTLEACRE, Baron *cr* 1980 (Life Peer), of Swaffham in the County of Norfolk; **Kenneth Alexander Keith;** Kt 1969; merchant banker and industrialist; Director, STC (formerly Standard Telephones and Cables), since 1977 (Chairman,

1985–89); *b* 30 Aug. 1916; *er s* of late Edward Charles Keith, Swanton Morley House, Norfolk; *m* 1st, 1946, Lady Ariel Olivia Winifred Baird (marr. diss., 1958), 2nd *d* of 1st Viscount Stonehaven, PC, GCMG, DSO, and Countess of Kintore; one *s* one *d;* 2nd, 1962, Mrs Nancy Hayward (marr. diss. 1972; she *d* 1990), Manhasset, New York; 3rd, 1973, Mrs Marie Hanbury, Burley-on-the-Hill, Rutland. *Educ:* Rugby Sch. Trained as a Chartered Accountant. 2nd Lt Welsh Guards, 1939; Lt-Col 1945; served in North Africa, Italy, France and Germany (despatches, Croix de Guerre with Silver Star). Asst to Dir Gen. Political Intelligence Dept, Foreign Office, 1945–46. Vice-Chm., BEA, 1964–71; Chairman: Philip Hill Investment Trust Ltd, 1967–87; Hill Samuel Group Ltd, 1970–80; Chm. and Chief Exec., Rolls Royce Ltd, 1972–80; Director: Beecham Gp Ltd, 1949–87 (Vice-Chm., 1970–87, Chm., 1986–87); Eagle Star Insurance Co., 1955–75; Nat. Provincial Bank, 1967–69; British Airways, 1971–72; Times Newspapers Ltd, 1967–81; Bank of Nova Scotia Ltd. Member: NEDC, 1964–71; CBI/NEDC Liaison Cttee, 1974–78; Pres., BSI, 1989–; Vice-Pres., EEF. Chairman: Economic Planning Council for East Anglia, 1965–70; Governor, Nat. Inst. of Economic and Social Research. Council Mem. and Dir, Manchester Business Sch. President: Royal Norfolk Agricl Assoc., 1989; RoSPA, 1989–. FBIM; FRSA. Hon. Companion, RAeS. *Recreations:* farming, shooting, golf. *Address:* 9 Eaton Square, SW1 9DB. *T:* 071–730 4000; The Wicken House, Castle Acre, Norfolk. *T:* Swaffham (0760) 755225. *Clubs:* White's, Pratt's; Links (New York).

KEITH OF KINKEL, Baron *cr* 1977 (Life Peer), of Strathtummel; **Henry Shanks Keith,** PC 1976; a Lord of Appeal in Ordinary, since 1977; *b* 7 Feb. 1922; *s* of late Baron Keith of Avonholm, PC (Life Peer); *m* 1955, Alison Hope Alan Brown, JP, MA; four *s* (including twin *s*) one *d. Educ:* Edinburgh Academy; Magdalen Coll., Oxford (MA; Hon. Fellow 1977); Edinburgh Univ. (LLB). War of 1939–45 (despatches); commnd Scots Guards, Nov. 1941; served N Africa and Italy, 1943–45; released, 1945 (Capt.). Advocate, Scottish Bar, 1950; Barrister, Gray's Inn, 1951, Bencher 1976; QC (Scotland), 1962. Standing Counsel to Dept of Health for Scotland, 1957–62; Sheriff Principal of Roxburgh, Berwick and Selkirk, 1970–71; Senator of Coll. of Justice in Scotland, 1971–77. Chairman: Scottish Valuation Adv. Coun., 1972–76 (Mem., 1957–70); Cttee on Powers of Revenue Depts, 1980–83; Dep. Chm., Parly Boundary Commn for Scotland, 1976; Member: Law Reform Cttee for Scotland, 1964–70; Cttee on Law of Defamation, 1971–74; Mem. Panel of Arbiters: European Fisheries Convention, 1964–71; Convention for Settlement of Investment Disputes, 1968–71. *Address:* House of Lords, SW1A 0PW. *Club:* Flyfishers'.

KEITH, Hon. Brian Richard; Hon. Mr Justice Keith; a Judge of the Supreme Court of Hong Kong, since 1991; *b* 14 April 1944; *s* of Alan Keith, OBE, broadcaster, and Pearl Keith (*née* Rebuck); *m* 1978, Gilly, *d* of Air Cdre Ivan de la Plain, CBE; one *s* one *d. Educ:* University College School, Hampstead; Lincoln College, Oxford (MA). John F. Kennedy Fellow, Harvard Law School, 1966–67; called to the Bar, Inner Temple, 1968; in practice, 1969–91; Assistant Recorder, 1988; QC 1989. *Recreations:* stamp collecting, playing tennis. *Address:* The Supreme Court, Queensway, Hong Kong.

KEITH, David; *see* Steegmuller, Francis.

KEITH, Sir Kenneth (James), KBE 1988; Professor of Law, Victoria University of Wellington, since 1974; President, New Zealand Law Commission, since 1991; *b* 19 Nov. 1937; *s* of Patrick James Keith and Amy Irene Keith (*née* Witheridge); *m* 1961, Jocelyn Margaret Buckett; two *s* two *d. Educ:* Auckland Grammar Sch.; Auckland Univ.; Victoria Univ. of Wellington (LLM); Harvard Law Sch. Barrister and Solicitor, High Court of New Zealand. NZ Dept of External Affairs, 1960–62; Victoria Univ., 1962–64, 1966–; UN Secretariat, NY, 1968–70; NZ Inst. of Internat. Affairs, 1972–74. Judge: Western Samoan Court of Appeal, 1982–; Cook Is Court of Appeal, 1982–. *Publications:* (ed) Human Rights in New Zealand, 1968; The Extent of the Advisory Jurisdiction of the International Court, 1971; contrib. to Amer. Jl of Internat. Law, Internat. and Comparative Law Qly, NZ Univs Law Rev., etc. *Recreations:* walking, reading, music. *Address:* 70 Raroa Road, Wellington 6005, New Zealand. *T:* (04) 757–108.

KEITH, Penelope Anne Constance, (Mrs Rodney Timson), OBE 1989; *b* 2 April; *d* of Frederick A. W. Hatfield and Constance Mary Keith; *m* 1978, Rodney Timson. *Educ:* Annecy Convent, Seaford, Sussex; Webber Douglas Sch., London. First prof. appearance, Civic Theatre, Chesterfield, 1959; repertory, Lincoln, Salisbury and Manchester, 1960–63; RSC, Stratford, 1963, and Aldwych, 1965; rep., Cheltenham, 1967; Maggie Howard in Suddenly at Home, Fortune Theatre, 1971; Sarah in The Norman Conquests, Greenwich, then Globe Theatre, 1974; Lady Driver in Donkey's Years, 1976; Orinthia in The Apple Cart, Chichester, then Phoenix Theatre, 1977; Epifania in The Millionairess, Haymarket, 1978; Sarah in Moving, Queen's Theatre, 1981; Maggie in Hobson's Choice, Haymarket, 1982; Lady Cicely Waynflete in Captain Brassbound's Conversion, Haymarket, 1982; Judith Bliss in Hay Fever, Queen's, 1983; The Dragon's Tail, Apollo, 1985; Miranda, Chichester, 1987; The Deep Blue Sea, Haymarket, 1988; Dear Charles, Yvonne Arnaud, Guildford, 1990; The Merry Wives of Windsor, Chichester, 1990; Lady Bracknell in The Importance of Being Earnest, UK tour, 1991; *film:* The Priest of Love, 1980. Television plays and series include: The Good Life, 1974–77; The Norman Conquests, 1977; To the Manor Born, 1979, 1980 and 1981; Sweet Sixteen, 1983; Moving, 1985; Executive Stress, 1986–88; No Job for a Lady, 1990; presenter: What's My Line?, 1988; Growing Places. Pres., Actors Benevolent Fund, 1990–. Awards: BAFTA, 1976 and 1977; SWET, 1976; Variety Club of GB, 1976 and 1979. *Recreations:* gardening, theatre-going. *Address:* c/o London Management, 235/241 Regent Street, W1A 2JT. *T:* 071–493 1610.

KEITH-JONES, Maj.-Gen. Richard, CB 1968; MBE 1947; MC 1944; Manager, Management Development, Mardon Packaging International Ltd, 1969–75; *b* 6 Dec. 1913; *o s* of late Brig. Frederick Theodore Jones, CIE, MVO, VD; *m* 1938, Margaret Ridley Harrison; three *d. Educ:* Clifton Coll.; Royal Military Academy Woolwich. Commissioned into Royal Artillery, 1934; served in UK, 1934–42; 1st Airborne Div., 1943–44; War Office, 1944–47; Palestine and Egypt, 1st Regt RHA, 1947–49; Instructor Staff Coll., Camberley, 1949–52; Military Asst to F-M Montgomery, 1953–55; CO 4th Regt, RHA, 1955–57; Senior Army Instructor, JSSC, 1957–59; Dep. Comdr 17 Gurkha Div., Malaya, 1959–61; Student, Imperial Defence Coll., 1962–63; Military Adviser, High Comr, Canada, 1963–64; GOC 50 (Northumbrian) Div. (TA), 1964–66; Comdt, Jt Warfare Establishment, 1966–68; retd 1969. Col Comdt RA, 1970–78; Hon. Col, 266 (Glos Vol. Artillery) Batt., RA, T&AVR, 1975–83. *Recreations:* fishing, shooting, golf. *Address:* The White House, Brockley, Backwell, Bristol BS19 3AU. *Clubs:* MCC; Bath and County (Bath).

KEITH-LUCAS, Prof. Bryan, CBE 1983; Professor of Government, University of Kent at Canterbury, 1965–77, now Emeritus (Master of Darwin College, 1970–74); *b* 1 Aug. 1912; *y s* of late Keith Lucas, ScD, FRS, and Alys (*née* Hubbard); *m* 1946, Mary Hardwicke (MBE 1982); Sheriff of Canterbury, 1971); one *s* two *d. Educ:* Gresham's Sch., Holt; Pembroke Coll., Cambridge. MA Cantab 1937, MA Oxon 1948; DLitt Kent, 1980. Solicitor, 1937. Asst Solicitor: Kensington Council, 1938–46; Nottingham, 1946–48. Served 1939–45 in Buffs and Sherwood Foresters, N Africa and Italy (Major, despatches); DAAG Cyprus, 1945–46. Sen. Lectr in Local Govt, Oxford, 1948–65; Faculty Fellow of

Nuffield Coll., 1950–65, Domestic Bursar, 1957–65. Leverhulme Emeritus Fellow, 1983. Part-time Asst Master, King's Sch., Canterbury, 1978–83. Chm., Commn on Electoral System, Sierra Leone, 1954; Commn on local govt elections, Mauritius, 1955–56. Member: Roberts Cttee on Public Libraries, 1957–59; Commn on Administration of Lagos, 1963; Mallaby Cttee on Staffing of Local Govt, 1964–67; Local Govt Commn for England, 1965–66; Royal Commn on Elections in Fiji, 1975. Vice-Chm., Hansard Soc., 1976–80. Chairman: Nat. Assoc. of Parish Councils, 1964–70 (Vice-Pres., 1970–; Pres., Kent Assoc., 1972–81); Canterbury Soc., 1972–75; President: Kent Fedn of Amenity Socs, 1976–81; Wye Historical Soc., 1986–. City Councillor, Oxford, 1950–65. Hon. Fellow, Inst. of Local Govt Studies, Birmingham Univ., 1973. *Publications:* The English Local Government Franchise, 1952; The Mayor, Aldermen and Councillors, 1961; English Local Government in the 19th and 20th Centuries, 1977; (with P. G. Richards) A History of Local Government in the 20th Century, 1978; The Unreformed Local Government System, 1980; Parish Affairs, 1986; (with Dr G. M. Ditchfield) A Kentish Parson, 1991; various articles on local govt. *Address:* 7 Church Street, Wye, Kent TN25 5BN. *T:* Wye (0233) 812621. *Club:* National Liberal.

See also David Keith-Lucas.

KEITH-LUCAS, Prof. David, CBE 1973; MA; FEng, FIMechE, Hon. FRAeS; Chairman, Airworthiness Requirements Board, 1972–82; *b* 25 March 1911; *s* of late Keith Lucas, ScD, FRS, and Alys (*née* Hubbard); *m* 1st, 1942, Dorothy De Bauduy Robertson (*d* 1979); two *s* one *d*; 2nd, 1981, Phyllis Marion Everard (*née* Whurr). *Educ:* Gresham's Sch., Holt; Gonville and Caius Coll., Cambridge. BA (Mech Sci Tripos, 2nd Class Hons) 1933; MA 1956; FRAeS 1948, Hon. FRAeS 1979; FIMechE 1949; FAIAA 1973, Hon. FAIAA 1974; FEng 1978. Apprenticed 1933–35, design team 1935–39, C. A. Parsons & Co. Ltd; Chief Aerodynamicist, Short Bros Ltd, 1940–49; Short Bros & Harland Ltd: Chief Designer, 1949–58; Technical Dir, 1958–64; Dir of Research, 1964–65; Dir, John Brown & Co., 1970–77; Cranfield Inst. of Technology: Prof. of Aircraft Design, 1965–72; Pro-Vice-Chancellor, 1970–73; Prof. of Aeronautics and Chm. College of Aeronautics, 1972–76, now Emeritus Prof. Member: Senate, Queen's Univ., Belfast, 1955–65; Council, Air Registration Board, 1967–72; Commn on Third London Airport, 1968–70; Civil Aviation Authority, 1972–80. President: RAeS, 1968; Engrg Section, British Assoc. for the Advancement of Science, 1972. Hon. DSc: Queen's Univ., Belfast, 1968; Cranfield Inst. of Technology, 1975. Gold Medal, RAeS, 1975. *Publications:* The Shape of Wings to Come, 1952; The Challenge of Vertical Take-Off (lects IMechE), 1961–62; The Role of Jet Lift (lect. RAeS), 1962; Design Council report on design educn; papers on aircraft design, vertical take-off, engrg economics, in engrg jls. *Recreation:* small boats. *Address:* Manor Close, Emberton, Olney, Bucks MK46 5BX. *T:* Bedford (0234) 711552.

See also B. Keith-Lucas.

KEKEDO, Dame Mary (Angela), DBE 1987 (CBE); BEM; formerly Headmistress and Manageress of schools in Kokoda; retired from active public service, 1981; *b* 12 July 1919; *d* of Alphonse Natera and Lucy Silva; *m* 1939, Walter Gill Kekedo; two *s* six *d* (and two *s* decd). *Educ:* St Patrick's Sch., Yule Island, PNG. Certificated teacher. Began first sch. in Kokoda, in own private home, and first women's club in Kokoda, 1949; Headmistress of Kokoda Sch. (first female apptd in PNG), 1956; founded first Vocational Sch. in Kokoda, 1974, Manageress, 1976. Member: Kokoda Area Authority, 1975–; (first) Interim Northern Province Provincial Assembly, 1978–. Cross Pro Ecclesia et Pontifice (Holy See), 1987. *Address:* Post Office Box 10, Kokoda, Northern Province, Papua New Guinea.

KEKWICK, Prof. Ralph Ambrose, FRS 1966; Professor of Biophysics, University of London, 1966–71, now Emeritus; Member Staff, Lister Institute, 1940–71 (Head, Division of Biophysics, 1943–71); *b* 11 Nov. 1908; 2nd *s* of late Oliver A. and Mary Kekwick; *m* 1st, 1933, Barbara (*d* 1973), 3rd *d* of W. S. Stone, DD, New York; one *d*; 2nd, 1974, Dr Margaret Mackay (*d* 1982), *er d* of J. G. Mackay, MB, BS, Adelaide, Australia. *Educ:* Leyton County High Sch.; University Coll., London (Fellow, 1971). BSc 1928; MSc 1936; DSc 1941. Bayliss-Starling Scholar, University Coll. London, 1930–31. Commonwealth Fund Fellow, New York and Princeton Univs, 1931–33. Lectr in Biochemistry University Coll. London, 1933–37. Rockefeller Fellow, University of Uppsala, Sweden, 1935; MRC Fellow, Lister Inst., 1937–40. Reader in Chemical Biophysics, University of London, 1954–66. Oliver Memorial Award for Blood Transfusion, 1957. *Publications:* MRC Special Report "Separation of protein fractions from human plasma" (with M. E. Mackay), 1954. Papers on physical biochemistry and hæmatology, mostly in Biochemical Jl and Brit. Jl of Hæmatology. *Recreations:* music, gardening and bird watching. *Address:* 31 Woodside Road, Woodford Wells, Essex IG8 0TW. *T:* 081–504 4264.

KELBIE, Sheriff David; Sheriff of Grampian, Highland and Islands, at Aberdeen, and Stonehaven, since 1986; *b* 28 Feb. 1945; *s* of Robert Kelbie and Monica Eileen Pearn; *m* 1966, Helen Mary Smith; one *s* one *d*. *Educ:* Inverurie Acad.; Aberdeen Univ. (LLB Hons). Advocate; called to the Scottish Bar, 1968; Sheriff of N Strathclyde, 1979–86. Associate Lectr, Heriot-Watt Univ., 1971–75; Hon. Sec., Scottish Congregational Coll., 1975–82; Mem., Christian Aid UK/Ireland Cttee, 1986–90. *Publications:* articles in legal jls. *Recreations:* sailing, music, reading. *Address:* 38 Earlspark Drive, Bieldside, Aberdeen AB1 9AH. *T:* Aberdeen (0224) 868237.

KELBURN, Viscount of; David Michael Douglas Boyle; *b* 15 Oct. 1978; *s* and *heir* of 10th Earl of Glasgow, *qv*.

KELL, Joseph; *see* Burgess, Anthony.

KELLAND, Gilbert James, CBE 1978; QPM 1975; Assistant Commissioner (Crime), Metropolitan Police, 1977–84, retired; *b* 17 March 1924; *m* 1950, Edith Ellen Marshall; two *d*. *Educ:* Georgeham Church Sch.; Braunton Secondary Modern Sch.; National Police Coll. Served RN, Fleet Air Arm, 1942–46. Metropolitan Police, 1946–84: Police Coll. Jun. Comd (Insp.) Course, 1955, Sen. Comd Course, 1964; Chm., London Dist of Supts' Assoc. of England & Wales and Mem. Police Council of GB and of Police Adv. Bd, 1966–69; Pres., Supts' Assoc. of England & Wales, 1968; Ford (Dagenham Trust) Fellowship studying Fed. Law Enforcement in USA, 1969; Hon. Sec., London Reg. Assoc. of Chief Police Officers, 1971–77; Brit. rep., INTERPOL, 1977–84, and Mem. Exec. Cttee, 1978–81. Stated Cases: Kelland *v* de Frietas, 1961 and Kelland *v* Raymond, 1964. Member: Parole Bd, 1986–89; AAA Cttee of Enquiry into Drug Abuse, 1988. Chairman: Met. Pol. Athletic Club, 1964–84; UK Pol. Athletic Assoc. and Met. Pol. Athletic Assoc., 1977–84; Life Vice Pres., Pol. AA, and Hon. Life Mem., Met. Pol. AA, 1984. Freeman, City of London, 1983. *Publication:* Crime in London, 1986, 1987. *Recreations:* following athletics, walking, gardening, reading. *Address:* c/o Metropolitan Police Athletic Association, Wellington House, 67 Buckingham Gate, SW1E 6BE.

KELLAND, John William, LVO 1977; QPM 1975; Overseas Police Adviser and Inspector General of Dependent Territories' Police, Foreign and Commonwealth Office, since 1985; *b* 18 Aug. 1929; *s* of William John Kelland and Violet Ethel (*née* Olsen); *m* 1st, 1960, Brenda Nancy (*née* Foulsham) (decd); two *s*; 2nd, 1986, Frances Elizabeth (*née* Byrne); one step *d*. *Educ:* Sutton High Sch.; Plymouth Polytechnic. FBIM. Pilot Officer, RAF, 1947–49. Constable, later Insp., Plymouth City Police, 1950–67; Insp., later Supt, Devon & Cornwall Constabulary, 1968–72; Asst Chief Constable, Cumbria Constabulary, 1972–74; Dir, Sen. Comd Courses, Nat. Police Coll., Bramshill, 1974–75 and 1978–80; Comr, Royal Fiji Police, 1975–78; 1981–85: Management Consultant and Chm., CSSBs; Sen. Consultant, RIPA; Sen. Lectr, Cornwall Coll.; Facilitator, Interpersonal Skills, Cornwall CC Seminars. *Publications:* various articles in learned jls. *Recreations:* Rugby football, choral singing, wildlife. *Address:* c/o Foreign and Commonwealth Office, Old Admiralty Building, Whitehall, SW1A 2AF. *T:* 071–210 6330. *Club:* Royal Over-Seas League.

KELLAS, Arthur Roy Handasyde, CMG 1964; HM Diplomatic Service, retired; High Commissioner in Tanzania, 1972–74; *b* 6 May 1915; *s* of Henry Kellas and Mary Kellas (*née* Brown); *m* 1952, Katharine Bridget, *d* of Sir John Le Rougetel, KCMG, MC; two *s* one *d*. *Educ:* Aberdeen Grammar Sch.; Aberdeen Univ.; Oxford Univ.; Ecole des Sciences Politiques. Passed into Diplomatic Service, Sept. 1939. Commissioned into Border Regt, Nov. 1939. War of 1939–45: Active Service with 1st Bn Parachute Regt and Special Ops, Af. and Gr, 1941–44 (despatches twice). Third Sec. at HM Embassy, Tehran, 1944–47; First Sec. at HM Legation, Helsingfors, 1948–50; First Sec. (press) at HM Embassy, Cairo, 1951–52; First Sec. at HM Embassy, Baghdad, 1954–58; Counsellor, HM Embassy, Tehran, 1958–62; Imperial Defence Coll., 1963–64; Counsellor, HM Embassy and Consul-Gen., Tel Aviv, 1964–65; Ambassador to Nepal, 1966–70, to Democratic Yemen, 1970–72. Pres., Britain-Nepal Soc., 1975–79. *Publication:* Down to Earth (war memoir of parachute subaltern), 1990. *Recreations:* reading, reviewing books. *Address:* Inverockle, Achateny, Acharacle, Argyll PH36 4LG. *T:* Kilchoan (09723) 265. *Club:* United Oxford & Cambridge University.

KELLAWAY, (Charles) William; Secretary and Librarian, Institute of Historical Research, University of London, 1971–84; *b* 9 March 1926; *s* of late Charles Halliley Kellaway, FRS; *m* 1952, Deborah, *d* of late Sir Hibbert Alan Stephen Newton; one *s* two *d*. *Educ:* Geelong Grammar Sch.; Lincoln Coll., Oxford. BA Modern History, 1949, MA 1955. FLA, FRHistS, FSA. Asst Librarian, Guildhall Library, 1950–60; Sub-Librarian, Inst. of Historical Research, 1960–71. Hon. General Editor, London Record Society, 1964–83. *Publications:* The New England Company, 1649–1776, 1961; (ed jtly) Studies in London History, 1969; Bibliography of Historical Works Issued in UK, 1957–70, 3 vols, 1962, 1967, 1972; (ed jtly) The London Assize of Nuisance 1301–1431, 1973. *Address:* 18 Canonbury Square, N1. *T:* 071–354 0349.

KELLEHER, Dame Joan, (Joanna), DBE 1965; Hon. ADC to the Queen, 1964–67; Director, Women's Royal Army Corps, 1964–67; *b* 24 Dec. 1915; *d* of late Kenneth George Henderson, barrister-at-law, Stonehaven; *m* 1970, Brig. M. F. H. Kelleher, OBE, MC, late RAMC. *Educ:* privately at home and abroad. Joined ATS, 1941; commissioned ATS, 1941; WRAC, 1949. *Recreations:* golf and gardening. *Address:* c/o Midland Bank, 123 Chancery Lane, WC2A 1QH.

KELLER, Prof. Andrew, FRS 1972; Research Professor in Polymer Science, Department of Physics, University of Bristol, 1969–91, Professor Emeritus, since 1991; *b* 22 Aug. 1925; *s* of Imre Keller and Margit Klein; *m* 1951, Eva Bulhack; one *s* one *d*. *Educ:* Budapest Univ. (BSc); Bristol Univ. (PhD). FInstP. Techn. Officer, ICI Ltd, Manchester, 1948–55; Bristol Univ.: Min. of Supply res. appt, 1955–57; Res. Asst, 1957–63; Lectr, 1963–65; Reader, 1965–69. High Polymer Prize, Amer. Phys. Soc., 1964; Swinburne Award, Plastics Inst., 1974; Max Born Medal, Inst. Physics and Deutsche Physik Gesellschaft, 1983. *Publications:* numerous papers in Jl Polymer Science, Progress Reports in Physics, Proc. Royal Soc., Macromol. Chem., etc. *Recreations:* outdoor sports, mountain walking, concerts. *Address:* 41 Westbury Road, Bristol BS9 3AU. *T:* Bristol (0272) 629767.

KELLER, René Jacques; Ambassador of Switzerland to Austria, 1976–79, retired; *b* 19 May 1914; *s* of Jacques Keller and Marie (*née* Geiser); *m* 1942, Marion (*née* Werder); one *s* two *d*. *Educ:* Geneva; Trinity Coll., Cambridge. Vice-Consul, Prague, 1941–45; 2nd Sec. of Legation, The Hague, 1947–50; 1st Sec., London, 1950–54; Head of News Dept, Berne, 1954–56; 1st Counsellor, Swiss Embassy, Paris, 1957–60; Ambassador to Ghana, Guinea, Liberia, Mali and Togo, 1960–62; Ambassador to Turkey, 1962–65; Head of Perm. Mission of Switzerland to Office of UN and Internat. Organisations, Geneva, 1966–68; Ambassador of Switzerland to UK, 1968–71; Head of Direction for International Organisation, Foreign Ministry of Switzerland, 1971–75. *Address:* 1 Promenade du Pin, CH-1204 Geneva, Switzerland. *Club:* Cercle de la Terrase (Geneva).

KELLER, Prof. Rudolf Ernst, MA Manchester; DrPhil Zürich; Professor of German Language and Medieval German Literature, University of Manchester, 1960–82, now Emeritus; *b* 3 Feb. 1920; *m* 1947, Ivy Sparrow; two *d*. *Educ:* Kantonsschule Winterthur, Switzerland; University of Zürich. Teacher at Kantonsschule Winterthur, 1944–46; Asst, 1946–47, Asst Lecturer, 1947–49, University of Manchester; Lecturer in German, Royal Holloway College, University of London, 1949–52; Sen. Lecturer, 1952–59, Reader in German, 1959–60, Dean of Faculty of Arts, 1968–70, Pro-Vice-Chancellor, 1976–79, University of Manchester. Corresp. Mem., Inst. für deutsche Sprache, 1969; Goethe Medal, 1981. *Publications:* Die Ellipse in der neuenglischen Sprache als semantisch-syntaktisches Problem, 1944; Die Sprachen der Welt, 1955 (trans. Bodmer: The Loom of Language); German Dialects, Phonology and Morphology with Selected Texts, 1961; The German Language, 1978; articles in learned periodicals. *Recreations:* reading, travel. *Address:* 8 Wadham Way, Hale, Altrincham, Cheshire WA15 9LJ. *T:* 061–980 5237.

KELLETT, Alfred Henry, CBE 1965; Chairman, South Western Areas, National Coal Board, 1967–69, retired; *b* 2 Aug. 1904; British; *m* 1934, Astrid Elizabeth (*née* Hunter); one *s* three *d*. *Educ:* Rossall Sch.; Universities of Cambridge and Birmingham. Man. Dir, Washington Coal Co. Ltd, 1940–47; Area Gen. Man., NCB Durham Div., 1950–59; Dep. Chm., Durham Div., 1960; Chm., South Western Div., NCB, 1961–67. CStJ. *Recreation:* travel. *Address:* Pent House, Benenden, Cranbrook, Kent.

KELLETT, Sir Brian (Smith), Kt 1979; Chairman: Port of London Authority, since 1985; British Ports Federation, since 1990; Unigate PLC, since 1991 (Director, since 1974); Director: National Westminster Bank PLC, since 1981; Lombard North Central PLC, since 1985; *b* 8 May 1922; *m* 1947, Janet Lesly Street; three *d*. *Educ:* Manchester Grammar Sch.; Trinity Coll., Cambridge (MA). Wrangler and Sen. Scholar, 1942. Exper. Officer, Admty, 1942–46; Asst Principal, Min. of Transport, 1946–48; Sir Robert Watson-Watt & Partners, 1948–49; Pilkington Bros Ltd, 1949–55; joined Tube Investments Ltd, later TI Group plc, 1955, Dir 1965, a Man. Dir, 1968–82, Dep. Chm. and Chief Exec., 1974, Chm., 1976–84; Chm., British Aluminium Co. Ltd, 1972–79. Dir, IMRO, 1987–90. Member: Royal Commn on Standards of Conduct in Public Life, 1974–76; PO Review Cttee, 1976–77; Council, Industrial Soc., 1981–84. A Vice-Pres., Engineering Employers' Fedn, 1976–84. Governor: London Business Sch., 1976–84; Imperial Coll., 1979–. *Address:* The Old Malt House, Deddington, Banbury, Oxon OX15 0TG. *T:* Deddington (0869) 38257. *Club:* United Oxford & Cambridge University.

KELLETT, Sir Stanley Charles, 7th Bt *cr* 1801; *b* 5 March 1940; *s* of Sir Stanley Everard Kellett, 6th Bt, and of Audrey Margaret Phillips; *S* father, 1983; *m* 1st, 1962, Lorraine May (marr. diss. 1968), *d* of F. Winspear; 2nd, 1968, Margaret Ann (marr. diss. 1974), *d* of James W. Bofinger; 3rd, 1982, Catherine Lorna, *d* of W. J. C. Orr; one *d*. *Heir: uncle* Charles Rex Kellett [*b* 1916; *m* 1940, Florence Helen Bellamy (*d* 1984); two *s* one *d*]. *Address:* 58 Glad Gunson Drive, Eleebana, Newcastle, NSW 2280, Australia.

KELLETT-BOWMAN, Edward Thomas, JP; Member (C) Hampshire Central, European Parliament, since Dec. 1988; business and management consultant in private practice, since 1974; *b* 25 Feb. 1931; *s* of late R. E. Bowman and of M. Bowman (*née* Mathers); *m* 1st, 1960, Margaret Patricia Blakemore (*d* 1970); three *s* one *d*; 2nd, 1971, (Mary) Elaine Kellett (*see* Dame Elaine Kellett-Bowman). *Educ:* Reed's Sch.; Cranfield Inst. of Technol. MBA, DMS, FBIM. Technical and management trng in textiles, 1951–53; textile management, 1953–55; pharmaceutical man., 1955–72. Mem. (C) Lancs East, European Parlt, 1979–84; contested same seat, 1984. Liveryman, Worshipful Co. of Wheelwrights, 1979; Freeman, City of London, 1978; Hon. Citizen, New Orleans, 1960. JP Mddx, 1966. *Recreations:* shooting, tennis, swimming. *Address:* (office) 4A Desborough Road, Eastleigh, Hants SO5 5NX. *T:* Eastleigh (0703) 613452.

KELLETT-BOWMAN, Dame (Mary) Elaine, DBE 1988; MA; MP (C) Lancaster, since 1970; *b* 8 July 1924; *d* of late Walter Kay; *m* 1st, 1945, Charles Norman Kellett (decd); three *s* one *d*; 2nd, 1971, Edward Thomas Kellett-Bowman, *qv*. *Educ:* Queen Mary Sch., Lytham; The Mount, York; St Anne's Coll., Oxford; Barnett House, Oxford (post-graduate distinction in welfare diploma). Contested (C): Nelson and Colne, 1955; South-West Norfolk, March and Oct. 1959; Buckingham, 1964, 1966. Mem. (C) European Parlt, 1975–84 (Mem. for Cumbria, 1979–84); Mem. Social Affairs and Regional Policy Cttees, Europ. Parlt, 1975–84. Camden Borough Council: Alderman, 1968–74; Vice-Chm., Housing Cttee, 1968; Chm., Welfare Cttee, 1969. Called to Bar, Middle Temple, 1964. Lay Mem., Press Council, 1964–68. Governor, Culford Sch., 1963; Mem. Union European Women, 1956; Delegate to Luxemburg, 1958. No 1 Country Housewife, 1960; Christal MacMillan Law Prize, 1963. *Recreations:* gardening, collecting and repairing antiques, Morris Minors. *Address:* House of Commons, SW1A 0AA.

KELLEY, Joan, CB 1987; Member, Official Side Panel, Civil Service Appeal Board, since 1987; *b* 8 Dec. 1926; *er d* of late George William Kelley and Dora Kelley. *Educ:* Whalley Range High Sch. for Girls, Manchester; London Sch. of Econs and Polit. Science (BScEcon 1947). Europa Publications Ltd, 1948; Pritchard, Wood & Partners Ltd, 1949; joined Civil Service as Econ. Asst in Cabinet Office, 1949; admin. work in Treasury, 1954; Principal, 1956; Asst Sec., 1968; Under Sec., 1979; on secondment to NI Office, 1979–81; Under Sec., 1979–86, Principal Estabt Officer and Principal Finance Officer, 1984–86, HM Treasury. *Recreations:* gardening, map reading, drinking wine, foreign travel. *Address:* 21 Langland Gardens, NW3 6QE.

KELLEY, Mrs Joanna Elizabeth, OBE 1973; Assistant Director of Prisons (Women), 1967–74; *b* 23 May 1910; *d* of late Lt-Col William Beadon, 51st Sikhs; *m* 1934, Harper Kelley (*d* 1962); no *c*. *Educ:* Hayes Court; Girton Coll., Cambridge (MA). Souschargé, Dept of Pre-History, Musée de l'Homme, Paris, 1934–39; Mixed Youth Club Leader, YWCA, 1939–42; Welfare Officer, Admiralty, Bath, 1942–47; Prison Service, 1947–74; Governor of HM Prison, Holloway, 1959–66. Member: Council, St George's House, Windsor, 1971–77; Redundant Churches Cttee, 1974–79; Scott Holland Trust, 1978–86; Sponsor, YWCA of GB, 1979–. FSA. Hon. Fellow Girton Coll., Cambridge, 1968. Hon. LLD Hull Univ., 1960. *Publications:* When the Gates Shut, 1967; Who Casts the First Stone, 1978. *Recreation:* reading. *Address:* c/o Lloyds Bank, 6 Pall Mall, SW1V 4AQ.

KELLGREN, Prof. Jonas Henrik, FRCS, FRCP; Professor of Rheumatology, University of Manchester, 1953–76, now Emeritus; Dean, 1970–73; *b* 11 Sept. 1911; *s* of Dr Harry Kellgren and Vera (*née* Dumelunksen); *m* 1942, Thelma Marian Reynolds; four *d*. *Educ:* Bedales Sch.; University Coll., London. MB, BS, 1934; FRCS 1936; FRCP 1951. Junior clinical appointments, University Coll. Hosp., 1934–42 (Beit Memorial Fellow 1938–39); served War, 1942–46, as surgical and orthopædic specialist, RAMC; Mem. Scientific Staff, Med. Research Council, Wingfield Morris Orthopædic Hosp., Oxford, Chronic Rheumatism, University of Manchester, 1947. Pres. Heberden Soc., 1958–59. *Publications:* numerous articles in medical and scientific jls. *Recreation:* landscape painting. *Address:* Beckside Cottage, Rusland, Ulverston, Cumbria LA12 8JY. *T:* Ulverston (0229) 84244.

KELLIHER, Sir Henry (Joseph), Kt 1963; Founder, 1929, President, 1982, Dominion Breweries Ltd (Chairman to 1980, Managing Director to 1982); *b* March 1896; *s* of Michael Joseph Kelliher; *m* 1917, Evelyn J., *d* of R. S. Sproule; one *s* four *d*. *Educ:* Clyde Sch. Dir, Bank of New Zealand, 1936–42. Founded League of Health of NZ Youth, 1934 (objective, Free milk scheme for NZ children, in which it succeeded); purchased Puketutu Island, 1938; established Puketutu Ayrshire Stud, 1940, Aberdeen Angus Stud, 1942, Suffolk Stud, 1946; Thoroughbred and Standard Bred Studs, 1969. Founded: Kelliher Art Trust, 1961; Kelliher Charitable Trust, 1963. KStJ 1960. *Publications:* New Zealand at the Cross Roads, 1936; Why your £ buys Less and Less, 1954. *Recreations:* gardening, riding. *Address:* Puketutu Island, Manukau Harbour, Auckland, New Zealand. *T:* 09–2756871.

KELLOCK, Jane Ursula, JP; Member, Council on Tribunals, since 1987; *b* 21 Oct. 1925; *d* of late Arthur George Symonds and late Gertrude Frances Symonds; *m* 1967, Thomas Oslaf Kellock, *qv*. *Educ:* Priors Field Sch., Godalming. WRNS, 1943–45. Sec., Africa Bureau, London, 1957–67; Editor, Africa Digest, 1957–75; Member: Bd, Commonwealth Development Corporation, 1965–73; Police Complaints Board, 1977–85. Former Mem., S Metropolitan Conciliation Cttee, Race Relations Bd. JP: Inner London, 1968–77; Nottingham City Bench, 1977. Editor, Commonwealth Judicial Jl, 1985–89. *Recreation:* travel. *Address:* 8 King's Bench Walk, EC4Y 7DU.

KELLOCK, His Honour Thomas Oslaf; QC 1965; a Circuit Judge, 1976–91; Deputy Senior Judge (non-resident), Sovereign Base Areas, Cyprus, since 1983; *b* 4 July 1923; *s* of late Thomas Herbert Kellock, MA, MD, MCh Cambridge, FRCS LRCP; *m* 1967, Jane Ursula Kellock, *qv*. *Educ:* Rugby; Clare Coll., Cambridge. Sub-Lieut (Special Branch), RNVR, 1944–46. Called to the Bar, Inner Temple, 1949, Bencher, 1973. Admitted: Gold Coast (Ghana) Roll of Legal Practitioners, 1955; N Rhodesia (Zambia) Bar, 1956; Nigeria Bar, 1957; Ceylon (Sri Lanka) Roll of Advocates, 1960; Sierra Leone Bar, 1960; Malayan Bar, 1967; Fiji Bar, 1975. Has also appeared in courts of Kenya, Malaŵi, Pakistan, Jammu and Kashmir, Sarawak. Dir, Legal Div., Commonwealth Secretariat, 1969–72; a Recorder of the Crown Court, 1974–76. Constitutional Advr to HH Sultan of Brunei, 1975–76. Chm., Anti-Apartheid Movement, 1963–65. Contested (L) Torquay, 1959, S Kensington, 1966 and March 1968, Harwich, Oct. 1974. Gov., Nottingham Polytechnic, 1989–91. *Recreation:* travelling. *Address:* 8 King's Bench Walk, Temple, EC4Y 7DU. *T:* 071–353 6997. *Club:* Reform.

KELLOW, Kathleen; *see* Hibbert, Eleanor.

KELLY, Prof. Anthony, CBE 1988; FRS 1973; FEng; Vice-Chancellor, University of Surrey, since 1975; *s* of late Group Captain Vincent Gerald French and Mrs Violet Kelly; *m* 1956, Christina Margaret Dunleavie, BA; three *s* one *d*. *Educ:* Presentation Coll., Reading; Univ. of Reading (Schol.); Trinity Coll., Cambridge. BSc Reading 1949; PhD 1953, ScD 1968, Cantab. Research Assoc., Univ. of Illinois, 1953–55; ICI Fellow, Univ. of Birmingham, 1955; Asst, Associate Prof., Northwestern Univ., 1956–59; Univ. Lectr, Cambridge, 1959–67; Founding Fellow, 1960, Extraordinary Fellow, 1985, Churchill Coll.; Dir of Studies, Churchill Coll., 1960–67; Supt, Div. of Inorganic and Metallic Structure, 1967–69, Dep. Dir, 1969–75, Nat. Physical Lab. (seconded to ICI, 1973–75). Professor, Univ. of Surrey, 1987–. Director: Teddington Developments Ltd, 1981–; Johnson Wax Ltd, 1981–; QUO-TEC Ltd, 1984–; Chm., Surrey Satellite Technology, 1985–. Vis. Fellow, Univ. of Göttingen, 1960; Vis. Prof., Carnegie Inst. of Technol., 1967; Prof. invité, Ecole Polytechnique Fédérale de Lausanne, 1977. Chm., Jt Standing Cttee on Structural Safety, Instns of Civil and Structural Engrs, 1988–; Member: SRC Cttee, 1967–72; Council, Inst. of Metals, 1969–74; Council, British Non-Ferrous Metals Res. Assoc., 1970–73; Engrg Materials Requirements Bd, DoI, 1973–75 (Chm., 1976–80); Adv. Cttee, Community Ref. Bureau of EEC, 1973–75. Foreign Associate, Nat. Acad. of Engrg of USA, 1986. Hon. FIL 1988. William Hopkins Prize, 1967; Beilby Medal, 1967; A. A. Griffith Medal, 1974; Medal of Excellence, Univ. of Delaware, 1984. *Publications:* Strong Solids, 1966, 3rd edn (with N. H. Macmillan) 1986; (with G. W. Groves) Crystallography and Crystal Defects, 1970; many papers in jls of physical sciences. *Recreations:* science of materials, sailing. *Address:* Yardfield, Church Lane, Worplesdon, Guildford, Surrey GU3 3RU; 10 Wootton Way, Cambridge CB3 9LX. *Club:* Island Sailing (Cowes).

KELLY, Barbara Mary; Chairman, Rural Forum, since 1988; *b* 27 Feb. 1940; *d* of John Maxwell Prentice and Barbara Bain Adam; *m* 1960, Kenneth Archibald Kelly; one *s* two *d* (and one *s* decd). *Educ:* Dalbeattie High Sch.; Kirkcudbright Academy; Moray House Coll., Edinburgh. DipEd. Partner in mixed dairy farming enterprise. Chairman: Area Manpower Bd, MSC, 1987–88; Scottish Consumer Council, 1985–90; Member: Nat. Consumer Council, 1985–90; Scottish Enterprise Bd, 1990–; Priorities Bd, MAFF, 1990–; Scottish Econ. Council, 1991–; Scottish Adv. Bd, BP, 1990–. Nat. Vice-Chm., Scottish Women's Rural Insts, 1983–86. Chm., Scottish Adv. Cttee, and Mem., Nat. Adv. Cttee, Duke of Edinburgh's Award Scheme, 1980–85. Trustee: Scottish Silver Jubilee Trust; Scottish Children's Bursary Fund, 1986–. *Recreations:* home and family, music, painting, the pursuit of real food, gardening of necessity. *Address:* Barncleugh, Irongray, Dumfries DG2 9SE. *T:* Dumfries (0387) 73210.

KELLY, Rt. Hon. Sir Basil; *see* Kelly, Rt Hon. Sir J. W. B.

KELLY, Brian; *see* Kelly, H. B.

KELLY, Charles Henry, CBE 1986; QPM 1978; DL; Chief Constable of Staffordshire, since 1977; *b* 15 July 1930; *s* of Charles Henry Kelly and Phoebe Jane Kelly; *m* 1952, Doris (*née* Kewley); one *s* one *d*. *Educ:* Douglas High Sch. for Boys, IOM; London Univ. LLB (Hons). Asst Chief Constable of Essex, 1972; Dep. Chief Constable of Staffordshire, 1976. Associate Prof., Criminal Justice Dept, Michigan State Univ., 1990–. Pres., Staffordshire Small Bore Rifle Assoc.; Chairman: Staffordshire Police St John Special Centre; ACPO Communications Cttee, 1982–; No 3 Region, ACPO Cttee, 1985–. Mem. Court, Keele Univ., 1990–. DL Stafford, 1979. KStJ 1991. *Recreations:* cricket, reading, walking. *Address:* Chief Constable's Office, Cannock Road, Stafford ST17 0QG. *T:* Stafford (0785) 57717. *Club:* Special Forces.

KELLY, Christopher William; Under Secretary, Social Services and Territorial Group, HM Treasury, since 1990; *b* 18 Aug. 1946; *s* of late Reginald and of Peggy Kelly; *m* 1970, Alison Mary Collens Durant; two *s* one *d*. *Educ:* Beaumont College; Trinity College, Cambridge (MA); Manchester University (MA (Econ)). HM Treasury, 1970; Private Sec. to Financial Sec., 1971–73; Sec. to Wilson Cttee of Inquiry into Financial Instns, 1978–80; Under Sec., Pay and Industrial Relns Gp, 1987–90. *Recreations:* narrow-boating, swimming. *Address:* 22 Croftdown Road, NW5 1EH. *Club:* Camden Lifesaving.

KELLY, Edward Ronald; journalist and trout farmer; *b* 14 Oct. 1928; *s* of late William Walter Kelly and of Millicent Kelly; *m* 1954, Storm Massada. *Educ:* Honiton Sch. Journalist: Bath Evening Chronicle, 1952; East African Standard, 1953; Sunday Post, Kenya, 1954; Reuters, 1956; Central Office of Information, 1958–: Editor in Chief, Overseas Press Services Div., 1964; Asst Overseas Controller, 1968; Dir, Publications and Design Services Div., 1970; Home Controller, 1976; Overseas Controller, 1978–84. *Recreations:* fishing, fly-tying, carpentry. *Address:* Duncton Mill, near Petworth, West Sussex GU28 0LF. *T:* Petworth (0798) 42294. *Club:* Flyfishers'.

KELLY, Prof. Francis Patrick, FRS 1989; Professor of the Mathematics of Systems, University of Cambridge, since 1990; Fellow of Christ's College, Cambridge, since 1976; *b* 28 Dec. 1950; *s* of Francis Kelly and Margaret Kelly (*née* McFadden); *m* 1972, Jacqueline Pullin; two *s*. *Educ:* Cardinal Vaughan Sch.; Van Mildert Coll., Durham (BSc 1971); Emmanuel Coll., Cambridge (Knight Prize 1975; PhD 1976). Operational Research Analyst, Scicon, 1971–72; Cambridge University: Asst Lectr in Op. Res., Faculty of Engineering, 1976–78; Lectr in Statistical Lab., 1978–86; Reader in Faculty of Maths, 1986–90; variously Research Fellow, Dir of Studies, Tutor, Mem. College Council and Investments Cttee, Christ's Coll., 1976–. Nuffield Foundn Sci. Res. Fellow, 1986–87; Chm., Lyndewode Research Ltd, 1987–. Rollo Davidson Prize, Cambridge Univ., 1979; Guy Medal in Silver, Royal Statistical Soc., 1989. *Publications:* Reversibility and Stochastic Networks, 1979; articles in math. and stat. jls. *Recreations:* rewiring old houses, ski-ing, football with children. *Address:* Statistical Laboratory, 16 Mill Lane, Cambridge CB2 1SB. *T:* Cambridge (0223) 337963, 60317.

KELLY, Graham; *see* Kelly, R. H. G.

KELLY, Air Vice-Marshal (Herbert) Brian, CB 1983; LVO 1960; MD, FRCP; RAF, retired; Consultant to Civil Aviation Authority, since 1974; Consultant Medical Adviser to PPP Medical Centres, since 1983; *b* 12 Aug. 1921; *s* of late Surg. Captain James Cecil Kelly and of Meta Matheson (*née* Fraser). *Educ:* Epsom Coll.; St Thomas' Hosp. (MB, BS 1943, MD 1948). MRCP 1945, FRCP 1968; DCH 1966; MFOM 1982. House appts, St Thomas' Hosp., and St Luke's Hosp., Guildford, 1943–45; RNVR, Med. Specialist, RNH Hong Kong, 1945–48; Med. Registrar and Lectr in Medicine, St Thomas' Hosp., 1948–53; joined RAF Medical Br., 1953; Consultant in Medicine at RAF Hosps, Aden, Ely, Nocton Hall, Singapore, Cyprus, Germany, 1953–83; Consultant Adviser in Medicine to RAF, 1974, Senior Consultant, 1979–83. QHS 1978–83. FRSocMed; Fellow, Med. Soc. London; Mem., British Cardiac Soc. Liveryman, Worshipful Soc. of Apothecaries, 1978; Freeman, City of London, 1978. *Publications:* papers in BMJ, Lancet, Brit. Heart Jl, and Internat. Jl of Epidemiology. *Recreation:* choir singing. *Address:* 32 Chiswick Quay, Hartington Road, W4 3UR. *T:* 081–995 5042. *Club:* Royal Air Force.

KELLY, Rev. Canon John Norman Davidson, DD; FBA 1965; Principal of St Edmund Hall, Oxford, 1951–79, Honorary Fellow 1979; Vice-Chancellor, Oxford University, Sept.-Oct. 1966 (Pro-Vice-Chancellor, 1964–66, 1972–79); *b* 13 April 1909; *s* of John and Ann Davidson Kelly. *Educ:* privately; Glasgow Univ.; The Queen's Coll., Oxford (Ferguson Scholar; Hertford Scholar; 1st Cl. Hon. Mods, Greats and Theology; Hon.

Fellow, 1963); St Stephen's House. Deacon, 1934; priest, 1935; Curate, St Lawrence's, Northampton, 1934; Chaplain, St Edmund Hall, Oxford, 1935; Vice-Principal and Trustee, 1937. Select Preacher (Oxford), 1944–46, 1959, 1961, 1962; Speaker's Lectr in Biblical Studies, 1945–48; University Lecturer in Patristic Studies, 1948–76; Select Preacher (Cambridge), 1953; Chm. Cttee of Second Internat. Conf. on Patristic Studies, Oxford, 1955; Proctor in Convocation of Canterbury representing Oxford University, 1958–64; Chm. Archbishop's Commn on Roman Catholic Relations, 1964–68; accompanied Archbishop of Canterbury on his visit to Pope Paul VI, 1966; Mem., Academic Council, Ecumenical Theological Inst., Jerusalem, 1966–. In the War of 1939–45 did part-time work at Chatham House and collaborated in organizing the Oxford Leave Courses for United States, Allied, and Dominions Forces. Canon of Chichester and Prebendary of Wightring, 1948, Highleigh, 1964. Took lead in obtaining Royal Charter, new statutes and full collegiate status for St Edmund Hall, 1957. Mem. Governing Body: Royal Holloway Coll., London, 1959–69; King's Sch., Canterbury. Lectures: Paddock, General Theological Seminary, NY, 1963; Birkbeck, Cambridge, 1973; Hensley Henson, Oxford, 1979–80. Hon. DD: Glasgow, 1958; Wales, 1971. Dean of Degrees, St Edmund Hall, 1982–89. *Publications:* Early Christian Creeds, 1950, 3rd edn 1972; Rufinus, a Commentary on the Apostles' Creed, 1955; Early Christian Doctrines, 1958, 5th edn 1977; The Pastoral Epistles, 1963; The Athanasian Creed, 1964; The Epistles of Peter and of Jude, 1969; Aspects of the Passion, 1970; Jerome, 1975; The Oxford Dictionary of Popes, 1986; St Edmund Hall: almost seven hundred years, 1989. *Recreations:* cinema, chatting with young people. *Address:* 7 Crick Road, Oxford OX2 6QJ. *T:* Oxford (0865) 512907. *Clubs:* Athenæum; Vincent's (Oxford).

KELLY, Rt. Hon. Sir (John William) Basil, Kt 1984; PC 1984; PC (NI) 1969; **Rt. Hon. Lord Justice Kelly;** Lord Justice of Appeal, Supreme Court of Judicature, Northern Ireland, since 1984; a Judge of the High Court of Justice in Northern Ireland, 1973–84; *b* 10 May 1920; *o s* of late Thomas William Kelly and late Emily Frances (*née* Donaldson); *m* 1957, Pamela, *o d* of late Thomas Colmer and Marjorie Colthurst. *Educ:* Methodist Coll., Belfast; Trinity Coll., Dublin. BA (Mod.) Legal Science, 1943; LLB (Hons) 1944. Called to Bar: of Northern Ireland, 1944; Middle Temple, 1970; QC (N Ireland) 1958. MP (U) Mid-Down, Parliament of Northern Ireland, 1964–72; Attorney-Gen. for Northern Ireland, 1968–72. Chm., Council of Legal Educn, NI, 1989–; Mem., Law Adv. Cttee, British Council, 1982–. *Recreations:* golf, music. *Address:* Royal Courts of Justice, Belfast.

KELLY, Laurence Charles Kevin; non-executive Director, since 1972, and Vice-Chairman, since 1988, Helical Bar PLC (Deputy Chairman, 1981–84; Chairman, 1984–88); *b* 11 April 1933; *s* of late Sir David Kelly, GCMG, MC, and Lady Kelly (*née* Jourda de Vaux); *m* 1963, (Alison) Linda McNair Scott; one *s* two *d. Educ:* Downside Sch.; New Coll., Oxford (Beresford Hope Schol.; MA Hons); Harvard Business Sch. Lieut, The Life Guards, 1949–52; served (temp.) Foreign Office, 1955–56; Guest, Keen and Nettlefolds, 1956–72; Director: GKN International Trading Ltd, 1972–77; Morganite International Ltd, 1984–; Mintel Ltd; Chm., Queenborough Steel Co., 1980–89. Member: Northern Ireland Development Agency, 1972–78; Monopolies and Mergers Commn, 1982–89. Chairman, Opera da Camera Ltd (charity), 1981–87. Vice-Chm., British Iron and Steel Consumers' Council, 1976–85. Sen. Associate Mem., St Antony's Coll., Oxford, 1985. FRGS 1972. *Publications:* Lermontov, Tragedy in the Caucasus (biog.), 1978 (Cheltenham Literary Prize, 1979); St Petersburg, a Travellers' Anthology, 1981; Moscow, a Travellers' Anthology, 1983; Istanbul, a Travellers' Anthology, 1987; (with Linda Kelly) Proposals, 1989; reviews, TLS, etc. *Recreation:* opera-going. *Address:* 44 Ladbroke Grove, W11 2PA. *T:* 071–727 4663; Lorton Hall, Low Lorton, near Cockermouth, Cumbria. *T:* Cockermouth (0900) 85252. *Clubs:* Beefsteak, Brooks's, Turf; Kildare Street and University (Dublin).

KELLY, Dr Michael, CBE 1983; JP; DL; Managing Director, Michael Kelly Associates, since 1984; Chairman, Royal Scottish Society for the Prevention of Cruelty to Children, since 1987; *b* 1 Nov. 1940; *s* of David and Marguerite Kelly; *m* 1965, Zita Harkins; one *s* two *d. Educ:* Univ. of Strathclyde (BSc(Econ), PhD). FCIM (FInstM 1988). Asst Lectr in Economics, Univ. of Aberdeen, 1965–67; Lectr in Economics, Univ. of Strathclyde, 1967–84. Councillor: Anderston Ward Corp. of Glasgow, 1971–75 (Convener, Schools and Sch. Welfare; Vice-Convener, Transport); Hillington Ward, Glasgow Dist, 1977–84 (Chairman: General Purposes Cttee; Buildings and Property Cttee); Lord Provost of Glasgow, 1980–84 (masterminded "Glasgow's Miles Better" Campaign); Campaign Dir, Edinburgh—Count Me In, 1987–. Rector, Univ. of Glasgow, 1984–87. Dir, Celtic Football Club, 1990. Mem., Scottish Cttee, NACF. BBC Radio Scotland News Quiz Champion, 1986, 1987. Hon. Mem., Clan Donald, USA; Hon. Mayor, Tombstone, Ariz; Hon. Citizen: Illinois; San José; St Petersburg; Kansas City; Dallas; Fort Worth; Winnipeg. JP Glasgow 1973; DL Glasgow 1984. Hon. LLD Glasgow, 1984. Glasgow Herald Scot of the Year, 1983. OStJ 1983. Founding Editor, Jl Economic Studies. *Publication:* Studies in the British Coal Industry, 1970. *Recreations:* photography, football, philately. *Address:* 50 Aytoun Road, Glasgow G41 5HE. *T:* 041–427 1627.

KELLY, Owen, QPM 1987; Commissioner of Police for City of London, since 1985; *b* 10 April 1932; *s* of Owen Kelly and Anna Maria (*née* Hamill); *m* 1957, Sheila Ann (*née* McCarthy); five *s. Educ:* St Modan's High School, St Ninians, Stirlingshire. National Service, RAF, 1950–52; Metropolitan Police in all ranks from Police Constable to Commander, 1953–82; Asst and Dep. to Comr of Police for City of London, 1982–85; 18th Senior Command Course, Nat. Police Coll., 1981; Mem., 14th Session of Nat. Exec. Inst., FBI, USA, 1991. Hon. Sec., Chief Constables' Club, 1989–. Chm., City of London Br., Leukaemia Res. Fund, 1985. CStJ 1987 (OStJ 1986). Commendation, Order of Civil Merit, Spain, 1986; Ordre du Wissam Alouite Class III, Morocco, 1987; Ordre du Mérite, Senegal, 1988. *Recreations:* enjoying the society of a large family, do-it-yourself house and car maintenance, reading, horse riding. *Address:* 26 Old Jewry, EC2R 8DJ. *T:* 071–601 2222.

KELLY, Rt. Rev. Patrick A.; *see* Salford, Bishop of, (RC).

KELLY, Peter (John); Under-Secretary for Atomic Energy, United Kingdom Department of Energy, 1980–82; *b* 26 Nov. 1922; *s* of Thomas and Lucy Kelly; *m* 1949, Gudrun Kelly (*née* Falck); two *s* three *d* (and one *s* decd). *Educ:* Downside; Oxford Univ. (BA). RNVR, 1942–46. 3rd Secretary, Moscow Embassy, 1948–49; journalism, 1950; rejoined public service, 1956; posts in Foreign Office, Defence Dept, Dept of Trade and Industry; Asst Secretary for Internat. Atomic Affairs, 1969–71; Counsellor, Office of UK Permanent Representative to the European Communities, Brussels, 1972–75; Director, Internat. Energy Agency, 1976–79. *Publication:* Safeguards in Europe, 1985. *Recreations:* walking, music. *Address:* 2 The Crouch, Seaford, Sussex BN25 1PX. *T:* Seaford (0323) 896881.

KELLY, Philip Charles; City Treasurer, Liverpool City Council, since 1986; Treasurer, Merseyside Fire and Civil Defence Authority; *b* 23 Aug. 1948; *s* of late Charles and of Irene May Kelly; *m* 1971, Pamela (*née* Fagan); one *s* two *d. Educ:* Inst. of Science and Technology, Univ. of Wales (BSc Econ). DipM; CIPFA. Market Research, British Steel Corp., 1970–72; Economist, Coventry City Council, 1972–74; Technical Officer, 1974–78, Asst Dir of Finance, 1978–82, Kirklees MDC; Dep. City Treasurer, Liverpool CC, 1982–86. *Recreation:* family. *Address:* c/o Municipal Buildings, PO Box 1, Dale Street, Liverpool L69 2DQ. *T:* 051–225 2347.

KELLY, Philip John; Press Officer to Michael Meacher, MP, since 1991; *b* 18 Sept. 1946; *s* of late William Kelly and of Mary Winifred Kelly; *m* 1988, Dorothy Margaret Jones; two *s. Educ:* St Mary's Coll., Crosby; Leeds Univ. (BA Hons Politics). Freelance journalist and PR consultant, 1970–87; Editor, Tribune, 1987–91. Co-Founder: Leveller, 1976; State Research, 1977; Chair, London Freelance Br., NUJ, 1983. Councillor (Lab) London Borough of Islington, 1984–86, 1990–. Prospective Parly Cand. (Lab), Surrey SW. *Recreations:* railways, model railways. *Address:* 56 Windsor Road, N7 6JL. *T:* 071–219 6109. *Club:* Red Rose.

KELLY, (Robert Henry) Graham, FCIS; Chief Executive/General Secretary of the Football Association, since 1989; *b* 23 Dec. 1945; *s* of Thomas John Kelly and Emmie Kelly; *m* 1970, Elizabeth Anne Wilkinson; one *s* one *d. Educ:* Baines Grammar Sch., Poulton-le-Fylde. FCIS 1973. Barclays Bank, 1964–68; Football League, 1968–88, Sec., 1979–88. Trustee, Football Grounds Improvement Trust, 1985–88. *Address:* The Football Association, 16 Lancaster Gate, W2 3LW.

KELLY, Rosaline; publishing and industrial relations consultant; Visiting Lecturer in Journalism, London College of Printing, since 1981; *b* 27 Nov. 1922; *d* of Laurence Kelly and Ellen (*née* Fogarty), Drogheda, Co. Louth, Eire. *Educ:* St Louis Convent, Carrickmacross; University Coll., Dublin, NUI. Journalist with Woman magazine, 1958–77; local management, IPC Magazines Ltd, 1977–80. Active in NUJ, 1958–: Mem., National Exec. Council, 1972–78; first woman Pres., 1975–77; Membership of Honour, 1979; Member: NUJ Appeals Tribunal, 1978–; NUJ Standing Orders Cttee, 1978–; Trustee, NUJ Provident Fund Management Cttee, 1977– (Chairperson, 1980–82). Mem., Press Council, 1977–80 (first woman to represent Press side). Has been rejected as a catalogue holder by Empire Stores. *Recreations:* language and languages, music, compulsive reader. *Address:* c/o Robert Fleming & Co. Ltd, Hexagon House, 28 Western Road, Romford RM1 3LB; Arash Areesh, 7 Lakeview Road, Wicklow, Eire. *T:* Wicklow 69596.

KELLY, Sir Theo, (William Theodore), Kt 1966; OBE 1958; JP; Chairman, Woolworths Ltd, Australia, 1963–80, retired (Managing Director, 1945–71), and its subsidiary and associated companies; Chairman: Woolworths (NZ) Ltd, 1963–79 (Director and General Manager, 1934–71); Woolworths Properties Limited, 1963–80; retired 1980; *b* 27 June 1907; *s* of W. T. Kelly; *m* 1944, Nancy Margaret, *d* of W. E. Williams, NZ; two *s* two *d.* War of 1939–45; RAAF, 1942–44, Wing Comdr. Chm., RAAF Canteen Services Bd, 1944–59. General Manager: Woolworths Ltd (NZ), 1932; Woolworths (Australia and NZ), 1945. Mem. Board, Reserve Bank of Australia, 1961–75; Dep. Chm., Australian Mutual Provident Soc., 1972–79 (Dir, 1967–79); Chm., Aust. Mutual Provident Fire and Gen. Insurance Pty Ltd, 1967–79. Life Governor, Royal Life Saving Soc.; Vice-Pres., Royal Hort. Soc., NSW; Trustee, National Parks and Wildlife Foundn, 1969–. Mem. Board, Royal North Shore Hosp., 1969–77. Fellow, Univ. of Sydney Senate, 1968–75. FRSA 1971; FAIM 1967. JP NSW, 1946. *Recreations:* golf, boating. *Address:* 8/73 Yarranabbe Road, Darling Point, Sydney, NSW 2027, Australia. *Clubs:* Sydney Rotary, American National (Sydney); Southport Yacht (Qld).

KELLY, Sir William Theodore; *see* Kelly, Sir Theo.

KELSALL, William, OBE 1971; QPM 1969; DL; Chief Constable of Cheshire, 1974–77; retired; *b* 10 Jan. 1914. DL Cheshire, 1979. CStJ 1983. *Address:* Three Keys Cottage, Quarry Bank, Utkinton, Tarporley, Cheshire.

KELSEY, Maj.-Gen. John, CBE 1968; Director, Wild Heerbrugg (UK) Ltd, 1978–87; Director of Military Survey, 1972–77; *b* 1 Nov. 1920; *s* of Benjamin Richard Kelsey and Daisy (*née* Powell); *m* 1944, Phyllis Margaret, *d* of Henry Ernest Smith, Chingford; one *s* one *d. Educ:* Royal Masonic Sch.; Emmanuel Coll., Cambridge; Royal Mil. Coll. of Science. BSc. Commnd in RE, 1940; war service in N Africa and Europe; Lt-Col 1961; Col 1965; Dep. Dir Mil. Survey; Brig. Dir Field Survey, Ordnance Survey, 1968; Dir of Mil. Survey, Brig. 1972; Maj.-Gen. 1974. *Recreations:* Rugby football (played for Cambridge Univ., Richmond, Dorset, Wilts; Mem. RFU, 1965–66); sailing.

KELSEY, Julian George, CB 1982; Deputy Secretary (Fisheries and Food), Ministry of Agriculture, Fisheries and Food, 1980–82; *b* 1922; *s* of William and Charlotte Kelsey, Dulwich; *m* 1944, Joan (*née* Singerton); one *d.* Lord Chancellor's Dept, 1939; War Service, 1941–46: Lancs Fusiliers and RAC; SOE and Force 136; Comdg No 11 Searcher Party Team, Burma; Exec. Officer, Central Land Board, 1948; Asst Principal, MAFF, 1951; Under Sec., 1969; Dir of Establishments, 1971–76; Fisheries Sec., 1976–80. *Address:* Shaston House, St James, Shaftesbury, Dorset SP7 8HL. *T:* Shaftesbury (0747) 51147.

KELSICK, Osmund Randolph, DFC 1944; Chairman and Managing Director, Carib Holdings Ltd (owning and operating The Blue Waters Beach Hotel), 1979–85, retired; Director: Caribbean Consultants Ltd; T. H. Kelsick Ltd (Montserrat); Caribbean Hotel Association; Antigua Hotel Association; *b* 21 July 1922; *s* of T. H. Kelsick; *m* 1950, Doreen Avis Hodge; one *s* (and one *s* decd); two step *d. Educ:* private preparatory sch.; Montserrat Grammar Sch.; Oxford Univ. (Devonshire Course). RAF, Fighter Pilot, 1940–46. ADC and Personal Sec. to Governor of the Leeward Islands, 1946–47; District Commissioner, Carriacou, 1947–51; Asst Chief Sec., Governor's Office, Grenada, 1951–52; Asst Administrator and Administrator, St Vincent, 1952–57. In 1956 seconded for short periods as Asst Trade Commissioner for British West Indies, British Guiana and British Honduras in UK, and Executive Sec. of Regional Economic Cttee in Barbados. Chief Sec., Leeward Islands, 1957–60. Past Pres., Caribbean Hotel Assoc. FRSA 1973. *Recreations:* fishing, gardening, tennis. *Address:* PO Box 454, Antigua, Leeward Islands, West Indies. *Clubs:* Commonwealth Trust; New (Antigua).

KEMBALL, Prof. Charles, CBE 1991; MA, ScD Cantab; FRS 1965; FRSC; MRIA; FRSE; Hon. Fellow, Edinburgh University, since 1988 (Professor of Chemistry, 1966–83; Dean of the Faculty of Science, 1975–78); *b* 27 March 1923; *s* of late Charles Henry and Janet Kemball; *m* 1956, Kathleen Purvis, *o d* of late Dr and Mrs W. S. Lynd, Alsager, Cheshire; one *s* two *d. Educ:* Edinburgh Academy; Trinity Coll., Cambridge (Sen. Schol.). First Class Hons in Natural Sciences Tripos, Pt I, 1942, Pt II, 1943. Employed by Ministry of Aircraft Production in Dept of Colloid Science, University of Cambridge, 1943–46; Commonwealth Fund Fellow, Princeton Univ., 1946–47; Fellow of Trinity Coll., Cambridge, 1946–54 (Junior Bursar, 1949–51; Asst Lectr, 1951–54); Univ. Demonstrator in Physical Chemistry, 1951–54; Professor of Physical Chemistry, Queen's Univ., Belfast, 1954–66 (Dean of the Faculty of Science, 1957–60, Vice-Pres., 1962–65). President: RIC, 1974–76 (Vice-Pres., 1959–61); British Assoc. Section B (Chem.), 1976–77; RSE, 1988–91 (Vice-Pres., 1971–74, 1982–85); Vice-Pres., Faraday Soc., 1970–73; Chm., Publications Bd, Chem. Soc./RSC, 1973–81. Governor, East of Scotland Coll. of Agriculture, 1977–84. Hon. DSc: Heriot-Watt, 1980; QUB, 1983. Meldola Medal, 1951, Royal Inst. of Chemistry; Corday-Morgan Medal, 1958, Tilden Lectr, 1960, Surface and Colloid Chem. Award, 1972, Chemical Soc.; Ipatieff Prize, American Chemical Soc.,

1962; Gunning Victoria Jubilee Prize, RSE, 1981; Award for Service to RSC, 1985. *Publications:* contributions to various scientific jls. *Recreations:* hill walking, genealogy. *Address:* 24 Main Street, Tyninghame, Dunbar, East Lothian EH42 1XL. *T:* East Linton (0620) 860710. *Clubs:* English-Speaking Union; New (Edinburgh).

KEMBALL, Brig. Humphrey Gurdon, CBE 1971 (OBE 1966); MC 1940; *b* 6 Nov. 1919; *s* of late Brig.-Gen. Alick Gurdon Kemball (late IA) and late Evelyn Mary (*née* Synge); *m* 1945, Ella Margery Emmeline (*née* Bickham); no *c. Educ:* Trinity Coll., Glenalmond; RMC, Sandhurst. Commissioned 1939, 1st Bn The Prince of Wales's Volunteers. Served War of 1939–45 (MC); Staff Coll., 1943. JSSC, 1956; commanded 1st Bn The Lancashire Regt (PWV), 1961–63; i/c Administration, HQ Federal Regular Army, Aden, 1964–66; Asst Dir, MoD, 1966–68; Mil. Attaché, Moscow, 1968–71; HQ British Forces, Near East, 1971–73; Dep. Comdr, SW District, 1973–74, retired. *Recreations:* fishing, travelling. *Address:* 28 Windsor End, Beaconsfield, Bucks HP9 2JW. *T:* Beaconsfield (0494) 671698. *Club:* Naval and Military.

KEMBALL, Air Marshal Sir (Richard) John, KCB 1990; CBE 1981; BA; Chief of Staff and Deputy Commander-in-Chief, Strike Command and UK Air Forces, since 1989; *b* 31 Jan. 1939; *s* of Richard and Margaret Kemball; *m* 1962, Valerie Geraldine Webster; two *d. Educ:* Uppingham; Open Univ. (BA 1991). Commissioned RAF, 1957; OC No 54 Squadron, 1977; OC RAF Laarbruch, 1979; Commandant, CFS, 1983–85; Comdr, British Forces, Falkland Islands, 1985–86. ADC to HM The Queen, 1984–85. *Recreations:* shooting, tennis, cricket, gardening. *Address:* c/o Midland Bank plc, 46 Market Hill, Sudbury, Suffolk. *Club:* Royal Air Force.

KEMBALL-COOK, Brian Hartley, MA Oxon; Headmaster, Bedford Modern School, 1965–77; *b* 12 Dec. 1912; *s* of Sir Basil Alfred Kemball-Cook, KCMG, CB, and Lady (Nancy Annie) Kemball-Cook (*née* Pavitt); *m* 1947, Marian, *d* of R. C. R. Richards, OBE; three *s* one *d. Educ:* Shrewsbury Sch. (Sidney Gold Medal for Classics); Balliol Coll., Oxford (Scholar). First Class Classical Honour Mods, 1933; First Class, Litt. Hum., 1935. Sixth Form Classics Master, Repton Sch., 1936–40. Intelligence Corps, 1940–46 (despatches); Regional Intelligence Officer and Political Adviser to Regional Comr, Hanover, 1946; Principal, Min. of Transport, 1946–47. Sen. Classics Master, Repton Sch., 1947–56; Headmaster, Queen Elizabeth's Grammar Sch., Blackburn, 1956–65. Chm., Bedfordshire Musical Festival, 1967–77. Croix de Guerre with Palm, 1946. *Publications:* Ed. Shakespeare's Coriolanus, 1954; (contrib.) Education: Threatened Standards, 1972. *Recreations:* mountaineering, music, translating Homer. *Address:* 12 Francis Close, Hitchin, Herts SG4 9EJ. *T:* Hitchin (0462) 438862. *Club:* Climbers.

KEMBER, Anthony Joseph, MA; Communications Adviser, Department of Health, since 1989; *b* 1 Nov. 1931; *s* of Thomas Kingsley Kember and May Lena (*née* Pryor); *m* 1957, Drusilla Mary (*née* Boyce); one *s* two *d. Educ:* St Edmund Hall, Oxford (MA). Associate, Inst. of Health Services Management (AHSM). Deputy House Governor and Secretary to Bd of Governors, Westminster Hospital, 1961–69; Gp Secretary, Hillingdon Gp Hospital Management Cttee, 1969–73; Area Administrator, Kensington and Chelsea and Westminster AHA(T), 1973–78; Administrator, 1978–84, Gen. Man., 1984–89, SW Thames RHA. Trustee, Disabled Living Foundn (Dep. Chm.). CBIM. *Publications:* various articles for professional jls. *Recreations:* painting, inside and out; tennis, royal and common-or-garden. *Address:* 16 Orchard Rise, Richmond, Surrey TW10 5BX. *Clubs:* Roehampton; Royal Tennis Court (Hampton Court).

KEMBER, William Percy, FCA; FCT; Group Financial Controller, British Telecommunications, since 1981; *b* 12 May 1932; *s* of late Percy Kember, Purley, and Mrs Q. A. Kember, Oxted, Surrey; *m* 1982, Lynn Kirkham. *Educ:* Uppingham. Chartered Accountant; Corporate Treasurer. Various posts with Royal Dutch/Shell Group in Venezuela, 1958–63; British Oxygen Co., 1963–67; Coopers & Lybrand, 1967–72; Post Office (Telecommunications), 1972–81. Visitor, Royal Institution, 1977, Chm., 1979. *Recreations:* golf, ski-ing. *Address:* 83 Hillway, N6 6AB. *T:* 081–341 2300. *Clubs:* Royal Automobile, Highgate Golf, Ski Club of Great Britain.

KEMMER, Prof. Nicholas, FRS 1956; FRSE 1954; MA Cantab, DrPhil Zürich; Tait Professor of Mathematical Physics, University of Edinburgh, 1953–79, now Professor Emeritus; *b* 7 Dec. 1911; *o s* of late Nicholas P. Kemmer and of late Barbara Kemmer (*née* Stutzer; later Mrs Barbara Classen); *m* 1947, Margaret, *o d* of late George Wragg and late Nellie (who *m* 2nd, C. Rodway); two *s* one *d. Educ:* Bismarckschule, Hanover; Universities of Göttingen and Zürich. DrPhil Zürich, 1935; Imperial Coll., London: Beit Scientific Research Fellow, 1936–38; Demonstrator, 1938; Fellow 1971. Mem. of UK Govt Atomic Energy Research teams in Cambridge and Montreal, 1940–46; University Lecturer in Mathematics, Cambridge, 1946–53 (Stokes Lecturer since 1950). Hon. FInstP 1988. Hughes Medal, Royal Society, 1966; J. Robert Oppenheimer Meml Prize (Univ. of Miami), 1975; Max Planck Medal, German Physical Soc., 1983; Gunning Victoria Jubilee Prize, RSE, 1985. *Publications:* The Theory of Space, Time and Gravitation, 1959 (trans. from the Russian of V. Fock, 1955); What is Relativity?, 1960 (trans from the Russian, What is the theory of Relativity?, by Prof. L. D. Landau and Prof. G. B. Rumer, 1959); Vector Analysis, 1977; papers in scientific jls on theory of nuclear forces and elementary particles. *Address:* 35 Salisbury Road, Edinburgh EH16 5AA. *T:* 031–667 2893.

KEMP, family name of **Viscount Rochdale.**

KEMP, Arnold; Editor, Glasgow Herald, since 1981; *b* 15 Feb. 1939; *s* of Robert Kemp and Meta Strachan; *m* 1963, Sandra Elizabeth Shand (marr. diss.); two *d. Educ:* Edinburgh Academy; Edinburgh Univ. (MA). Sub-Editor, Scotsman, 1959–62, Guardian, 1962–65; Production Editor, Scotsman, 1965–70, London Editor, 1970–72, Dep. Editor, 1972–81. *Recreations:* jazz, reading, theatre. *Address:* Glasgow Herald, Albion Street, Glasgow G1 1QP. *T:* 041–552 6255. *Clubs:* Caledonian; Glasgow Art.

KEMP, Athole Stephen Horsford, LVO 1983; OBE 1958 (MBE 1950); Secretary General, Royal Commonwealth Society, 1967–83; *b* 21 Oct. 1917; *o s* of late Sir Joseph Horsford Kemp, CBE, KC, LLD, and Mary Stuart; *m* 1940, Alison, *yr d* of late Geoffrey Bostock, FCA; two *s* one *d. Educ:* Westminster Sch.; Christ Church, Oxford (MA). War service, RA, 1939–46; POW Far East (Thailand-Burma Railway). Malayan CS, 1940–64 (Sec. to Govt, 1955–57; Dep. Perm. Sec., PM's Dept, 1957–61). Sec., Royal Commonwealth Soc. Library Trust, 1984–90; Chief Examiner, Royal Commonwealth Soc. Essay Comp., 1986–. Chm., Oxford Fieldpaths Soc., 1991– (Mem. Exec. Cttee, 1983–); Mem., Rights of Way Cttee, CPRE (Oxon), 1983–; Local Correspondent, Open Spaces Soc., W Oxfordshire, 1985–. Clerk to Parish Council, Langford, Oxon, 1987–. Hon. Life Mem., Royal Commonwealth Society. JMN 1958. *Recreations:* gardening, public rights of way, wine. *Address:* Lockey House, Langford, Lechlade, Glos GL7 3LF. *T:* Faringdon (0367) 860239.

KEMP, Rear-Adm. Cuthbert Francis, CB 1967; Chief Service Manager, Westland Helicopters, 1968–69; *b* 15 Sept. 1913; *s* of A. E. Kemp, Willingdon; *m* 1947, Margaret Law, *d* of L. S. Law, New York; two *s. Educ:* Victoria Coll., Jersey. Joined RN, 1931; RN Engrg Coll., 1936. Served in HMS Ajax and Hood; Pilot, 1939. Served War of 1939–45: carriers and air stations at home and abroad; Naval Staff, Washington, 1945–47; Fleet Engr Officer, E Indies, 1950–52; qual. Staff Coll., 1956; Admty, 1957–59; qual. Canadian Nat. Defence Coll., 1962; Supt RN Aircraft Yard, Belfast, 1962–65; ADC 1965; Rear-Adm., Engineering, Staff of Flag Officer, Naval Air Command, 1965, retd 1967. *Recreations:* cricket, gardening, shooting. *Address:* Beech House, Marston Magna, Som BA22 8DQ. *T:* Marston Magna (0935) 850563. *Club:* Army and Navy.

KEMP, David Ashton McIntyre, QC 1973; a Recorder of the Crown Court, since 1976; *b* 14 Oct. 1921; *s* of late Sir Kenneth McIntyre Kemp and Margaret Caroline Clare Kemp; *m* 1st, 1949, Margaret Sylvia Jones (*d* 1971); 2nd, 1972, Maureen Ann Frances Stevens, *widow. Educ:* Winchester Coll.; Corpus Christi Coll., Cambridge. 1st cl. hons Law Cantab. Called to Bar, Inner Temple, 1948, Bencher, 1980. *Publications:* (with M. S. Kemp) The Quantum of Damages, Personal Injuries Claims, 1954 (4th edn 1975); (with M. S. Kemp) The Quantum of Damages, Fatal Accident Claims, 1956 (4th edn 1975). *Recreations:* ski-ing, tennis, gardening. *Address:* 63 Brixton Water Lane, SW2 1PH. *T:* 071–733 9735. *Clubs:* Hurlingham, Ski Club of Great Britain; Kandahar Ski.

KEMP, Sir (Edward) Peter, KCB 1991 (CB 1988); Second Permanent Secretary, Cabinet Office (Office of the Minister for the Civil Service), since 1988; *b* 10 Oct. 1934; *s* of late Thomas Kemp and Nancie (*née* Sargent); *m* 1961, Enid van Popta; three *s* one *d. Educ:* Millfield Sch.; Royal Naval Coll., Dartmouth. FCA (ACA 1959). Principal, later Asst Sec., Min. of Transport, 1967–73; HM Treasury, 1973, Under-Sec., 1978, Dep. Sec., 1983. *Recreations:* reading, sailing. *Address:* c/o Office of the Minister for the Civil Service, Horse Guards Road, SW1P 3AL. *Club:* Reform.

KEMP, Rt. Rev. Eric Waldram; *see* Chichester, Bishop of.

KEMP, Air Vice-Marshal George John, CB 1976; *b* 14 July 1921; *m* 1943, Elspeth Beatrice Peacock; one *s* two *d.* Commnd RAF, 1941; served in night fighter sqdns with spell on ferrying aircraft to Middle East; served in Iraq, 1953–54 and Far East, 1960–61; Stn Comdr RAF Upwood, 1968–69; Dir of Manning RAF, 1970–71; Dir of Personnel (Policy and Plans) RAF, 1972; Dir-Gen. of Personnel Management, RAF, 1973–75. *Recreations:* many and various. *Address:* Old Court, Woolley Street, Bradford on Avon, Wilts BA15 1AE. *T:* Bradford on Avon (02216) 7832. *Club:* Royal Air Force.

KEMP, Hubert Bond Stafford, MS; FRCS, FRCSE; Consultant Orthopaedic Surgeon: Royal National Orthopaedic Hospital, London and Stanmore, 1974–90; The Middlesex Hospital, 1984–90; Hon. Consultant Orthopaedic Surgeon, St Luke's Hospital for the Clergy, 1975–90; University Teacher in Orthopaedics; *b* 25 March 1925; *s* of John Stafford Kemp and Cecilia Isabel (*née* Bond); *m* 1947, Moyra Ann Margaret Odgers; three *d. Educ:* Cardiff High Sch.; Univ. of South Wales; St Thomas' Hosp., Univ. of London (MB, BS 1949; MS 1969); MRCS, LRCP 1947; FRCSE 1960; FRCS 1970. Robert Jones Gold Medal and Assoc. Prize, 1969 (Proxime Accessit, 1964); Hunterian Prof., RCS, 1969; Hon. Consultant, Royal Nat. Orthopaedic Hosp., London and Stanmore, 1965–74; Sen. Lectr, Inst. of Orthopaedics, 1965–74, Hon. Sen. Lectr, 1974–90. Vis. Professor, VII Congress of Soc. Latino Amer. de Orthopedia y Traumatologica, 1971. Member: MRC Working Party on Tuberculosis of the Spine, 1974–; MRC Working Party on Osteosarcoma, 1985. Fellow, Brit. Orthopaedic Assoc., 1972–; Chm., London Bone Tumour Unit, 1985; Member: Brit. Orthopaedic Research Soc., 1967–; Internat. Skeletal Soc., 1977–. *Publications:* (jtly) Orthopaedic Diagnosis, 1984; chapter in: A Postgraduate Textbook of Clinical Orthopaedics, 1983; Baillière's Clinical Oncology, Bone Tumours, 1987; papers on diseases of the spine, the hip, metal sensitivity, bone scanning and haemophilia. *Recreations:* fishing, painting. *Address:* 55 Loom Lane, Radlett, Herts WD7 8NX. *T:* Radlett (0923) 854265; 107 Harley Street, W1N 1DG. *T:* 071–935 2776.

See also G. D. W. Odgers.

KEMP, Prof. Kenneth Oliver, FEng 1988; Emeritus Professor of Civil Engineering and Fellow, University College London, 1984; *b* 19 Oct. 1926; *s* of Eric Austen Kemp; *m* 1952, Josephine Gloria (*née* Donovan); no *c. Educ:* University College London. BSc(Eng), PhD; FICE, FIStructE. Surveyor, Directorate of Colonial Surveys, 1947–49; Asst Engr, Collins and Mason, Consulting Engrs, 1949–54. University College London: Lectr, Sen. Lectr, Dept of Civil Engrg, 1954–69; Reader in Structural Engrg, 1969–70; Chadwick Prof. of Civil Engrg and Hd of Civil Engrg Dept, 1970–84. *Publications:* papers in: Proc. Instn of Civil Engrs; The Structural Engr; Magazine of Concrete Research; Internat. Assoc. of Bridge and Structural Engrg. *Recreation:* Norfolk. *Address:* Frenchmans, Duck Street, Wendens Ambo, Essex CB11 4JU. *T:* Saffron Walden (0799) 40966.

KEMP, Kenneth Reginald; Director, since 1962, and Hon. Life President, 1990, Smith & Nephew plc (Chairman, 1976–90); *b* 13 Nov. 1921; *s* of Philip R. Kemp and Siew Pukalanan of Thailand; *m* 1949, Florence M. Hetherington. *Educ:* Bradfield College, Berks. FCA. Joined Leeds Rifles, 1939; commissioned Royal Artillery, 1940–46; served in France, Germany, India, Far East (Captain). Peat, Marwick Mitchell & Co., 1947; qualified CA, 1950; Smith & Nephew: Company Sec., 1953, later Finance Dir; Chief Exec., 1968–76. *Recreations:* unlimited. *Address:* Smith & Nephew, 2 Temple Place, WC2R 3BP. *T:* 071–836 7922.

KEMP, Leslie Charles, CBE 1982; FCIArb, FBIM; Chairman, Griffiths McGee Ltd, Demolition Contractors, 1982–87; Proprietor, Leslie Kemp Associates, since 1976; *b* 10 Oct. 1920; *s* of Thomas and Violet Kemp. *Educ:* Hawkhurst Moor Boys' School. Apprentice blacksmith, 1934–39; served War, 1939–46: Infantry, N Africa and Italy. Civil Engrg Equipment Operator, 1947–51; District Organiser, 1951–57, Regional Organiser, 1958–63, Nat. Sec. (Construction), TGWU, 1963–76. Jt Registrar, 1975–76, Dep. Chm., 1976–81, Demolition and Dismantling Industry Registration Council. Member, Nat. Jt Council for Building Industry, 1957–76; Operatives Sec., Civil Engrg Construction Conciliation Bd for GB, 1963–76; Mem., 1964–73, Dep. Chm., 1973–76, Chm., 1976–85, Construction Industry Trng Bd (Chm., Civil Engrg Cttee, 1964–76); Member: EDC for Civil Engrg, 1964–76; Construction Ind. Liaison Gp, 1974–76; Construction Ind. Manpower Bd, 1976–; Bragg Adv. Cttee on Falsework, 1973–75; Vice-Pres., Construction Health and Safety Gp. Chm., Corby Develt Corp., 1976–80; Dep. Chm., Peterborough Develt Corp., 1974–82. Member, Outward Bound Trust, 1977–88; Pres., W Norfolk Outward Bound Assoc., 1983–88. Chm., Syderstone Parish Council, 1983–87. Construction News Man of the Year Award, 1973; in recognition of services to trng, Leslie Kemp Europ. Prize for Civil Engrg trainees to study in France, instituted 1973. CompICE. *Recreations:* travel, bird-watching, fishing. *Address:* Lamberts Yard, Syderstone, King's Lynn, Norfolk PE31 8SF. *Clubs:* Lighthouse; Fakenham Golf (Pres., 1985–88).

KEMP, Prof. Martin John, FBA 1991; Professor of Fine Arts, Department of Art History, University of St Andrews, since 1981; *b* 5 March 1942; *s* of Frederick Maurice Kemp and Violet Anne Tull; *m* 1966, Jill Lightfoot, *d* of Dennis William Lightfoot and Joan Betteridge; one *s* one *d. Educ:* Windsor Grammar Sch.; Cambridge Univ. (MA Nat. Scis and Art History); Courtauld Inst. of Art, London Univ. (Academic Dip.). Lectr in History of Art, Dalhousie Univ., Halifax, NS, Canada, 1965–66; Lectr in History of Fine Art, Univ. of Glasgow, 1966–81; Fellow, Inst. for Advanced Study, Princeton, 1984–85;

University of St Andrews: Associate Dean of Graduate Studies, Faculty of Arts, 1983–87; Mem. Court, 1988–. Prof. of History and Hon. Mem., Royal Scottish Acad., 1985–; Slade Prof. of Fine Art, Cambridge Univ., 1987–88; Benjamin Sonnenberg Vis. Prof., Inst. of Fine Arts, New York Univ., 1988. Chair, Assoc. of Art Historians, 1989–. Trustee: National Gall. of Scotland, 1982–87; V&A Museum, 1985–89. FRSA 1983. Hon. FRIAS, 1988. Mitchell Prize for best first book in English on Art History, 1981. *Publications:* Leonardo da Vinci, The Marvellous Works of Nature and Man, 1981; (jtly) Leonardo da Vinci, 1989; (jtly) Leonardo on Painting, 1989; The Science of Art, 1990; articles in Jl of Warburg and Courtauld Insts, Burlington Magazine, Art History, Art Bull., Connoisseur, Procs of British Acad., JL of RSA, L'Arte, Bibliothèque d'Humanisme et Renaissance, Med. History, TLS, London Rev. of Books, Guardian, Sunday Times, etc. *Recreations:* hockey, running, gardening, watching Dundee United, avoiding academics. *Address:* Orillia, 45 Pittenweem Road, Anstruther, Fife KY10 3DT. *T:* Anstruther (0333) 310842.

KEMP, Oliver, CMG 1969; OBE 1960; *b* 12 Sept. 1916; *s* of Walter Kemp; *m* 1940, Henrietta Taylor; two *s*. *Educ:* Wakefield Grammar Sch.; Queen's Coll., Oxford. MA Oxon (Lit. Hum.), 1939. Served in HM Forces, 1939–45. Apptd Officer in HM Foreign Service, 1945; served in Moscow, Egypt, Indonesia, Yemen, Laos, Mongolia and Foreign Office. HM Chargé d'Affaires in Yemen, 1957–58; First Secretary and Head of Chancery in Laos, 1958–60. HM Ambassador to Togo (and Consul-General), 1962–64; Deputy Head of the United Kingdom Delegation to the European Communities, Luxembourg, 1964–67; HM Ambassador to Mongolia, 1967–68; FCO, 1968–70 and 1971–73 (European affairs). Dir, BSC Office, Brussels, 1973–81. *Recreations:* music, reading, gardening. *Address:* 16 The Oval, Scarborough, N Yorks YO11 3AP. *T:* Scarborough (0723) 373354.

KEMP, Sir Peter; *see* Kemp, Sir E. P.

KEMP, Lt-Comdr Peter Kemp, OBE 1963; RN (retd); FSA, FRHistS; Head of Naval Historical Branch and Naval Librarian, Ministry of Defence, 1950–68; Editor of Journal of Royal United Service Institution, 1957–68; *b* 11 Feb. 1904; *e s* of Henry and Isabel Kemp; *m* 1st, 1930, Joyce, *d* of Fleming Kemp; 2nd, 1949, Eleanore (*d* 1987), *d* of Frederick Rothwell; two *d* (and one *s* decd). *Educ:* Royal Naval Colleges, Osborne and Dartmouth. Served in submarines till 1928 (invalided); Naval Intelligence Division, 1939–45. Asst Editor, Sporting and Dramatic, 1933–36; Member: Editorial Staff, The Times, 1936–39 and 1945–50; Council of Navy Records Society; Editorial Adv. Board of Military Affairs (US). *Publications:* Prize Money, 1946; Nine Vanguards, 1951; HM Submarines, 1952; Fleet Air Arm, 1954; Boys' Book of the Navy, 1954; HM Destroyers, 1956; Famous Ships of the World, 1956; Victory at Sea, 1958; Famous Harbours of the World, 1958; (with Prof. C. Lloyd) Brethren of the Coast, 1960; History of the Royal Navy, 1969; The British Sailor: a social history of the lower deck, 1970; Escape of the Scharnhorst and Gneisenau, 1975; A History of Ships, 1978; Merchant Ships, 1982; Seamanship, 1983; (with Richard Ormond) The Great Age of Sail, 1986; The Campaign of the Spanish Armada, 1988; regimental histories of: Staffordshire Yeomanry; Royal Norfolk Regiment; Middlesex Regiment; King's Shropshire Light Infantry; Royal Welch Fusiliers; books on sailing; children's novels; *edited:* Hundred Years of Sea Stories; Letters of Admiral Boscawen (NRS); Fisher's First Sea Lord Papers, Vol. I (NRS), 1960, Vol. II (NRS), 1964; Oxford Companion to Ships and the Sea, 1976; Encyclopædia of Ships and Seafaring, 1980; (jtly) Pocket Oxford Guide to Sailing Terms, 1987. *Recreations:* sailing, golf. *Address:* 53 Market Hill, Maldon, Essex. *T:* Maldon (0621) 852609. *Clubs:* West Mersea Yacht, Maldon Golf.

KEMP, Robert Thayer; export credit consultant; non-executive Director, Sedgwick James Credit Ltd, since 1989; *b* 18 June 1928; *s* of Robert Kemp and Ada Kemp (*née* Thayer); *m* 1951, Gwendolyn Mabel Minty; three *s*. *Educ:* Bromley Grammar Sch.; London Univ. (BA (Hons) Medieval and Mod. History). Export Credits Guarantee Department: Asst Sec., 1970; Under-Sec., 1975; Head of Project Underwriting Gp, 1981–85; Dir, Internat. Gp, 1985–88, retd. *Publication:* Review of Future Status Options (ECGD), 1989. *Recreations:* cricket, music, theatre. *Address:* 294 Tubbenden Lane South, Farnborough, Orpington, Kent BR6 7DN. *T:* Orpington (0689) 53924. *Club:* Overseas Bankers.

KEMP, Thomas Arthur, MD; FRCP; Physician, St Mary's Hospital, 1947–75, Paddington General Hospital 1950–75; *b* 12 Aug. 1915; *s* of late Fred Kemp and Edith Peters; *m* 1942, Ruth May Scott-Keat; one *s* one *d*. *Educ:* Denstone Coll.; St Catharine's Coll., Cambridge (Exhibitioner); St Mary's Hospital, London (Scholar). MB, BChir 1940; MRCP 1941; FRCP 1949; MD 1953. Examiner in Medicine, Universities of London and Glasgow. FRSM (Jt Hon. Sec., 1961–67). Served in Middle East, 1944–47; Lt-Col RAMC Officer i/c Medical Division; Hon. Cons. Physician to the Army, 1972–75. Pres. Brit. Student Health Assoc., 1962–63; Chm. Brit. Student Tuberculosis Foundation, 1963–65. Fellow, Midland Div., Woodard Schs, 1962–85; Commonwealth Travelling Fellowship, 1967. *Publications:* papers in medical journals. *Recreations:* games, especially Rugby football (played for Cambridge, 1936, for Barbarians, 1936–49, for St Mary's Hosp., 1937–43, for England, 1937–48 (Captain, 1948, Selector, 1954–61); President: Rugby Football Union, 1971–72; Students' RFU, 1980–). *Address:* 2 Woodside Road, Northwood, Mddx. *T:* Northwood (09274) 21068. *Club:* Hawks (Cambridge).

KEMP-WELCH, John; Joint Senior Partner, Cazenove & Co., since 1980; *b* 31 March 1936; *s* of Peter Wellesbourne Kemp-Welch and Peggy Penelope Kemp-Welch; *m* 1964, Diana Elisabeth Leishman; one *s* three *d*. *Educ:* Winchester Coll. CBIM 1984. Hoare & Co., 1954–58; Cazenove & Co., 1959–; Dir, Savoy Hotel PLC, 1985–. Mem., City Capital Markets Cttee, 1989–. Governor: Ditchley Foundn, 1980–; North Foreland Lodge Sch., 1980–; Trustee, King's Med. Res. Trust, 1984–; Trustee and Mem. Council, Game Conservancy Trust. FRSA 1989. *Recreations:* shooting, farming, the hills of Perthshire, cricket. *Address:* Little Hallingbury Place, Bishop's Stortford, Herts CM22 7RE. *T:* Bishop's Stortford (0279) 722455. *Clubs:* White's, City of London, MCC.

KEMPE, John William Rolfe, CVO 1980; Headmaster of Gordonstoun, 1968–78; *b* 29 Oct. 1917; *s* of late William Alfred Kempe and Kunigunda Neville-Rolfe; *m* 1957, Barbara Nan Stephen, *d* of late Dr C. R. Huxtable, MC, FRCS and Mrs Huxtable, Sydney, Australia; two *s* one *d*. *Educ:* Stowe; Clare Coll., Cambridge (Exhibitioner in Mathematics). Served war of 1939–45, RAFVR Training and Fighter Command; CO 153 and 255 Night Fighter Squadrons. Board of Trade, 1945; Firth-Brown (Overseas) Ltd, 1946–47; Head of Maths Dept, Gordonstoun, 1948–51; Principal, Hyderabad Public Sch., Deccan, India, 1951–54; Headmaster, Corby Grammar School, Northants, 1955–67. Chm., Round Square Internat. Service Cttee, 1979–87; Vice Chm., The European Atlantic Movement, 1982–. Exploration and mountaineering, Himalayas, Peru, 1952–56; Member: Cttee, Mount Everest Foundation, 1956–62; Cttee, Brathay Exploration Group, 1964–73; Foundn Trustee, Univ. of Cambridge Kurt Hahn Trust, 1986–89; Trustee: Thornton Smith Trust, 1981–; Plevins Charity, 1987–. FRGS. *Publications:* articles in Alpine Jl, Geographical Jl, Sociological Review. *Address:* Maple Tree Cottage, 24 Old Leicester Road, Wansford, near Peterborough PE8 6JR. *Clubs:* Alpine, English-Speaking Union.

KEMPNER, Prof. Thomas; Hon. Professor, Brunel University, since 1990 (Professor of Management Studies and Director of Business Studies, 1972–90); Professor Emeritus, Henley The Management College (formerly Administrative Staff College), since 1990 (Principal and Professor of Management Studies, 1972–90); Chairman, Henley Distance Learning Ltd, since 1985; *b* 28 Feb. 1930; *s* of late Martin and Rosa Kempner; *m* 1st, 1958, June Maton (*d* 1980); two *d* (and one *d* decd); 2nd, 1981, Mrs Veronica Ann Vere-Sharp. *Educ:* University Coll. London (BSc (Econ)). Asst Administrator, Hyelm Youth Hostels, 1948–49, and part-time, 1951–55; Research Officer, Administrative Staff Coll., Henley, 1954–59; Lectr (later Sen. Tutor) in Business Studies, Sheffield Univ., 1959–63; Prof. of Management Studies, Founder, and Dir of Management Centre, Univ. of Bradford, 1963–72. Member of various cttees, including: Social Studies and Business Management Cttees of University Grants Cttee, 1966–76; Management, Education and Training Cttee of NEDO, 1969– (Chm. of its Student Grants Sub-Cttee); Chm., Food Industry Manpower Cttee of NEDO, 1968–71; Jt Chm., Conf. of Univ. Management Schools, 1973–75. CBIM (FBIM 1971). Hon. DSc Cranfield, 1976; Hon. LLD Birmingham, 1983; DUniv Brunel, 1990. Burnham Gold Medal, 1970. *Publications:* editor, author, and contributor to several books, including: Bradford Exercises in Management (with G. Wills), 1966; Is Corporate Planning Necessary? (with J. Hewkin), 1968; A Guide to the Study of Management, 1969; Management Thinkers (with J. Tillet and G. Wills), 1970; Handbook of Management, 1971, 4th edn 1987; (with K. Macmillan and K. H. Hawkins) Business and Society, 1974; Models for Participation, 1976; numerous articles in Management jls. *Recreation:* travel. *Address:* Henley The Management College, Greenlands, Henley-on-Thames, Oxon RG9 3AU. *T:* Henley-on-Thames (0491) 571454; Henley Distance Learning Ltd, Craigmore House, Remenham Hill, Henley-on-Thames, Oxon RG9 3EP. *T:* Henley-on-Thames (0491) 571552.

KEMPSON, Rachel, (Lady Redgrave); actress; *b* Devon, 28 May 1910; *d* of Eric William Edward Kempson and Beatrice Hamilton Ashwell Kempson; *m* 1935, Sir Michael Redgrave, CBE (*d* 1985); one *s* two *d*. *Educ:* St Agnes Convent, East Grinstead; Colchester County High Sch.; Oaklea, Buckhurst Hill; RADA. First stage appearance in Much Ado About Nothing, Stratford, 1933; first London appearance in The Lady from Alfaqueque, Westminster, 1933; Stratford season, 1934; Liverpool Playhouse, 1935–36; Love's Labour's Lost, Old Vic, 1936; Volpone, Westminster, 1937; Twelfth Night, Oxford, 1937; The School for Scandal, Queen's, 1937; The Shoemaker's Holiday, Playhouse, 1938; Under One Roof, Richmond, 1940; The Wingless Victory, Phoenix, 1943; Uncle Harry, Garrick, 1944; Jacobowsky and the Colonel, Piccadilly, 1945; Fatal Curiosity, Arts, 1946; The Paragon, Fortune, 1948; The Return of the Prodigal, Globe, 1948; Candida, Oxford, 1949; Venus Observed, Top of the Ladder, St James's, 1950; The Happy Time, St James's, 1952; Shakespeare Meml Theatre Co., 1953; English Stage Co., 1956; The Seagull, St Joan of the Stockyards, Queen's, 1964; Samson Agonistes, Lionel and Clarissa, Guildford, 1965; A Sense of Detachment, Royal Court, 1972; The Freeway, National Theatre, 1974; A Family and a Fortune, Apollo, 1975; The Old Country, Queen's, 1977; Savannah Bay, Royal Court, 1983; Chekhov's Women, Queen's, 1986; The Cocktail Party, Phoenix, 1986; Uncle Vanya, Vaudeville, 1988; Coriolanus, Young Vic, 1989. *Films* include: The Captive Heart, 1945; Georgy Girl; The Jokers; Charge of the Light Brigade; The Virgin Soldiers; Jane Eyre; Out of Africa, 1985; The Understanding, 1985. Frequent *television* appearances include series and serials: Elizabeth R; Jennie; Love for Lydia; The Bell, 1981; The Jewel in the Crown, 1984; The Black Tower, 1985; Small World, 1988; plays: Winter Ladies, Sweet Wine of Youth, 1979; Kate, the Good Neighbour, Getting On, The Best of Everything, and Jude, 1980; Blunt Instrument, Bosom Friends, and The Box wallah, 1981; World's Beyond, 1986; *radio:* Hester, in The Forsyte Saga, 1990. *Publication:* A Family and its Fortunes (autobiog.), 1986. *Recreations:* gardening, letter writing. *Address:* c/o Philip Shaw, Creative Artists, 11–12 Betterton Street, Covent Garden, WC2H 9BP.

See also Lynn Redgrave, Vanessa Redgrave.

KEMPSON, Prof. Ruth Margaret, (Mrs M. J. Pinner), FBA 1989; Professor of General Linguistics, University of London, at School of Oriental and African Studies, since 1987; *b* 26 June 1944; *d* of Edwin Garnett Hone Kempson and Margaret Cecilia Kempson; *m* 1973, Michael John Pinner; two *s*. *Educ:* Univ. of Birmingham (BA (2 ii) Music and English); Univ. of London (MA (with dist.) Mod. English Language 1969; PhD Linguists 1972). Res. Asst to Survey of English Usage, UCL, 1969–70; Lectr in Linguistics, SOAS, 1971–85; Reader in Gen. Linguistics, Univ. of London, 1985–87. Vis. Prof. in Semantics, Univ. of Massachusetts, 1982–83. Pres., Linguistics Assoc. of GB, 1986–. *Publications:* Presupposition and the Delimitation of Semantics, 1975; Semantic Theory, 1977; Mental Representations: the interface between language and reality, 1988; articles in Linguistics and Philosophy, Jl of Linguistics and edited collections. *Recreation:* singing in Renaissance chamber choirs. *Address:* Linguistics Department, School of Oriental and African Studies, Thornhaugh Street, Russell Square, WC1H 0XG. *T:* 071–637 2388.

KEMPSTER, Hon. Michael Edmund Ivor; Hon. Mr Justice Kempster; a Justice of Appeal of the Supreme Court of Hong Kong, since 1984 (a Judge of the Supreme Court, 1982–84); Commissioner, Supreme Court of Brunei, since 1983; *b* 21 June 1923; *s* of late Rev. Ivor T. Kempster, DSO; *m* 1949, Sheila, *d* of late Dr T. Chalmers, KiH, Inverness; two *s* two *d*. *Educ:* Mill Hill Sch.; Brasenose Coll., Oxford (Scholar, MA, BCL). Royal Signals, 1943–46; commissioned in India, served 14th Army. Called to Bar, Inner Temple, 1949; Profumo Prize; Bencher 1977. QC 1969; a Recorder of the Crown Court, 1972–81. Mem., Govt Cttee on Privacy, 1971. Chm., Court of Governors, Mill Hill School, 1979–82. FCIArb, 1982. *Recreations:* fishing, hare-hunting, travel. *Address:* 53 Manderly Garden, Deepwater Bay Road, Hong Kong. *Clubs:* Travellers'; Hong Kong (Hong Kong).

KEMSLEY, 2nd Viscount *cr* 1945, of Dropmore; **(Geoffrey) Lionel Berry,** DL; Bt 1928; Baron 1936; *b* 29 June 1909; *e s* of 1st Viscount Kemsley, GBE and Mary Lilian (*d* 1928), *d* of Horace George Holmes; *S* father, 1968; *m* 1933, Lady Helen Hay, DStJ, *e d* of 11th Marquess of Tweeddale; four *d*. *Educ:* Marlborough; Magdalen Coll., Oxford. Served War of 1939–45. Capt. Grenadier Guards; invalided out of Army, 1942. MP (C) Buckingham Div. of Bucks, 1943–45. Dep. Chm., Kemsley Newspapers Ltd, 1938–59. Chm., St Andrew's Hospital, Northampton, 1973–84; Pres., Assoc. of Independent Hospitals, 1976–83. Mem. Chapter General, Order of St John. Master of Spectacle Makers' Co., 1949–51, 1959–61. CC Northants, 1964–70; High Sheriff of Leicestershire, 1967, DL 1972. FRSA; KStJ. *Heir:* *nephew* Richard Gomer Berry [*b* 17 April 1951; *m* 1981, Tana-Marie, *e d* of Clive Lester]. *Address:* Field House, Thorpe Lubenham, Market Harborough, Leics LE16 9TR. *T:* Market Harborough (0858) 462816. *Clubs:* Turf, Pratt's, Royal Over-Seas League.

See also Sir G. N. Mobbs.

KENDAL, Felicity, (Mrs Michael Rudman); actress; *d* of Geoffrey and Laura Kendal; *m* (marr. diss.); one *s*; *m* 1983, Michael Rudman, *qv*; one *s*. *Educ:* six convents in India. First appeared on stage at age of 9 months, when carried on as the Changeling boy in A Midsummer Night's Dream; grew up touring India and Far East with parents' theatre co., playing pageboys at age of eight and graduating through Puck, at nine, to parts such as Viola in Twelfth Night, Jessica in The Merchant of Venice, and Ophelia in Hamlet;

returned to England, 1965; made London debut, Carla in Minor Murder, Savoy, 1967; Katherine in Henry V, and Lika in The Promise, Leicester, 1968; Amaryllis in Back to Methuselah, Nat. Theatre, 1969; Hermia in A Midsummer Night's Dream, and Hero in Much Ado About Nothing, Regent's Park, 1970; Anne Danby in Kean, Oxford, 1970, London, 1971; Romeo and Juliet, 'Tis Pity She's A Whore, and The Three Arrows, 1972; The Norman Conquests, Globe, 1974; Viktosha in Once Upon a Time, Bristol, 1976; Arms and The Man, Greenwich, 1978; Mara in Clouds, Duke of York's, 1978; Constance Mozart in Amadeus, NT, 1979; Desdemona in Othello, NT, 1980; Christopher in On the Razzle, NT, 1981; Paula in The Second Mrs Tanqueray, NT, 1981; The Real Thing, Strand, 1982; Jumpers, Aldwych, 1985; Made in Bangkok, Aldwych, 1986; Hapgood, Aldwych, 1988; Ivanov, and Much Ado About Nothing, Strand, 1989 (Best Actress Award, Evening Standard); Hidden Laughter, Vaudeville, 1990. *Television:* four series of The Good Life, 1975–77; Viola in Twelfth Night, 1979; Solo, 1980, 2nd series 1982; The Mistress, 1985, 2nd series 1986; plays and serials. *Films:* Shakespeare Wallah, 1965; Valentino, 1976. Variety Club Most Promising Newcomer, 1974, Best Actress, 1979; Clarence Derwent Award, 1980; Variety Club Woman of the Year Best Actress Award, 1984. *Recreation:* golf. *Address:* c/o Chatto & Linnit, Prince of Wales Theatre, Coventry Street, W1V 7FE. *T:* 071–930 6677.

KENDALL, Prof. David George, DSc; ScD; FRS 1964; Professor of Mathematical Statistics, University of Cambridge, 1962–85 and Fellow of Churchill College, since 1962; *b* 15 Jan. 1918; *s* of Fritz Ernest Kendall and Emmie Taylor, Ripon, Yorks; *m* 1952, Diana Louise Fletcher; two *s* four *d. Educ:* Ripon GS; Queen's Coll., Oxford (MA, 1943; Hon. Fellow 1985); DSc Oxford, 1977; ScD Cambridge, 1988. Fellow Magdalen Coll., Oxford, and Lectr in Mathematics, 1946–62 (Emeritus Fellow, 1989). Visiting Lecturer: Princeton Univ., USA, 1952–53 (Wilks Prize, 1980); Zhong-shan Univ., Guangzhou; Xiangtan Univ.; Changsha Inst. Rlwys; Jiaotong Univ., Xi'an, 1983. Lectures: Larmor, Cambridge Philos. Soc., 1980; Milne, Wadham Coll., Oxford, 1983; Hotelling, Univ. of N Carolina, 1985; Rietz, Inst. of Math. Stats, 1989; Kolmogorov, Bernoulli Soc., 1990. Mem. Internat. Statistical Inst.; Mem. Council, Royal Society, 1967–69, 1982–83; President: London Mathematical Soc., 1972–74; Internat. Assoc. Statist. in Phys. Sci., 1973–75; Bernoulli Soc. for Mathematical Stats and Probability, 1975; Section A (Math.) and Section P (Physics), BAAS, 1982. Chm. Parish Reg. Sect., Yorks Archaeol. Soc., 1974–79. Hon. D. de l'U. Paris (René Descartes), 1976; Hon. DSc Bath, 1986. Guy Medal in Silver, Royal Statistical Soc., 1955; Weldon Meml Prize and Medal for Biometric Science, 1974; Sylvester Medal, Royal Soc., 1976; Whitehead Prize, London Math. Soc., 1980; Guy Medal in Gold, Royal Statistical Soc., 1981; De Morgan Medal, London Math. Soc., 1989. *Publications:* (jt ed) Mathematics in the Archaeological and Historical Sciences, 1971; (jt ed) Stochastic Analysis, 1973; (jt ed) Stochastic Geometry, 1974; (ed) Analytic and Geometric Stochastics, 1986. *Address:* 37 Barrow Road, Cambridge.

KENDALL, David William; Chairman, Bunzl plc, since 1990 (Director, since 1988); *b* 8 May 1935; *s* of William Jack Kendall and Alma May Kendall; *m* 1st, 1960, Delphine Hitchcock (marr. diss.); one *s* one *d*; 2nd, 1973, Elisabeth Rollison; one *s* one *d. Educ:* Enfield Grammar School; Southend High School. FCA. Elles Reeve, Shell-Mex & BP, Irish Shell & BP, 1955–70; British Petroleum Co.: Crude Oil Sales Manager, 1971–72; Manager, Bulk Trading Div., 1973–74; Organisation Planning Cttee, 1975; BP New Zealand: Gen. Manager, 1976–79; Man. Dir and Chief Exec., 1979–82; Chm., BP SW Pacific, 1979–82; BP Oil: Finance and Planning Dir, 1982–85; Man. Dir and Chief Exec., 1985–88; Director: BP Chemicals Internat., 1985–88; BP Oil Internat., 1985–88; Associated Octel Co., 1985–88; STC plc, 1988–; Dep. Chm., British Coal Corp., 1989–91. President: UK Petroleum Industries Assoc., 1987–88; Oil Industries Club, 1988. *Recreations:* golf, music, family. *Address:* Bunzl plc, Stoke House, Stoke Green, Stoke Poges, Slough SL2 4JN. *T:* Slough (0753) 693693.

KENDALL, Denis; *see* Kendall, W. D.

KENDALL, Rev. Frank; Chief Executive, St Helens Metropolitan Borough Council, since 1989; Licensed Priest, Diocese of Liverpool, since 1989; *b* 15 Dec. 1940; *s* of Norman and Violet Kendall; *m* 1965, Brenda Pickin; one *s* one *d. Educ:* Bradford Grammar School; Corpus Christi College, Cambridge (MA Classics); Southwark Ordination Course (London Univ. Dip. in Religious Studies). MPBW, 1962; DEA, 1967–68; MPBW, DoE and Dept of Transport, 1969–89; Under Secretary 1984. Hon. Curate: Lingfield, dio. Southwark, 1974–75 and 1978–82; Sketty, dio. Swansea and Brecon, 1975–78; Limpsfield, dio. Southwark, 1982–84; Licensed Preacher, dio. of Manchester, 1984–89. FRSA 1990. *Recreations:* painting: (i) pictures, (ii) decorating. *Address:* Cromwell Villa, 260 Prescot Road, St Helens WA10 3HR. *T:* St Helens (0744) 27626.

KENDALL, Graham; Chief Executive, Sheffield Development Corporation (on secondment), since 1990; *b* 24 Sept. 1943; *s* of Robert David Kendall and Phillis Margaret Moreton; *m* 1968, Helen Sheila Blackburn; two *s* two *d. Educ:* Helsby Grammar Sch.; Leicester Univ. (BSc); Liverpool Univ. (Post-grad. CertEd). Entered Civil Service as Asst Principal, 1966; DTI; Dept of Employment, 1981–; Grade 3, 1990–. *Recreations:* running, gardening, family. *Address:* 56 Blackamoor Road, Dore, Sheffield S17 3GJ. *T:* Sheffield (0742) 364533.

KENDALL, Henry Walter George, OBE 1979; Director, British Printing Industries Federation, 1972–81; *b* 21 Dec. 1916; *s* of Henry Kendall and Beatrice (Kerry) Kendall; *m* 1945, Audrey Alison Woodward; two *s* one *d. Educ:* Archbishop Temple's Sch., Lambeth. FCMA. Training with Blades, East & Blades Ltd, 1933–40. War service, RAOC; special duties, War Office, London, 1941; Mil. Coll. of Science, Inspecting Ordnance Officer Western Comd, HQ Allied Land Forces SE Asia, 1940–46. Cost accountant, British Fedn of Master Printers, 1947–55; Chief Cost Accountant, 1955; Head of Management Services, 1967. Mem. Council: CBI, 1972–81; Printing Industry Research Assoc., 1972–81; Inst. of Printing, 1972–81. *Recreations:* theatre, gardening, travel. *Address:* 28 Foxgrove Avenue, Beckenham, Kent BR3 2BA. *Clubs:* Royal Automobile, Wig and Pen.

KENDALL, Raymond Edward, QPM 1984; Secretary General, International Criminal Police Organisation (Interpol), since 1985; *b* 5 Oct. 1933; *m* Antoinette Marie. *Educ:* Simon Langton School, Canterbury; Exeter College, Oxford (MA hons). RAF, 1951–53 (principally Malaya). Asst Supt of Police, Uganda Police, 1957–62; Metropolitan Police, New Scotland Yard, 1962–85 (principally Special Branch). *Recreations:* shooting, golf. *Address:* ICPO-Interpol, 50 Quai Achille Lignon, 69006 Lyon, France. *T:* 72 44 70 00. *Clubs:* Special Forces; St James's (Paris).

KENDALL, (William) Denis, PhD; FRSA; FIMechE; MIAE; Chartered Engineer; *b* Halifax, Yorks, 27 May 1903; *yr s* of J. W. Kendall, Marton, Blackpool; *m* 1952, Margaret Hilda Irene Burden. *Educ:* Trinity Sch.; Halifax Technical Coll. MP (Ind.) Grantham Division of Kesteven and Rutland, 1942–50; Mem., War Cabinet Gun Bd, 1941–45 (decorated for bravery). Cadet in Royal Fleet Auxiliary; Asst to Chief Inspector, Budd Manufacturing Corp., Philadelphia, Pa, 1923; Dir of Manufacturing, Citroen Motor Car Co., Paris, 1929–38; Managing Director, British Manufacture and Research Co., Grantham, England (manufacturers of aircraft cannon and shells), 1938–45, and Consultant to Pentagon, Washington, on high velocity small arms. Executive Vice-Pres., Brunswick Ordnance Corp., New Brunswick, NJ, 1952–55 (also Dir and Vice-Pres. Ops, Mack Truck Corp.); President and Director: American MARC, Inc., 1955–61 (manufacturers of Diesel Engines, who developed and produced the world's first Diesel outboard engine, and also electric generators, etc), Inglewood, Calif; Dynapower Systems Corp. (Manufacturers of Electro-Medical equipment), Santa Monica, Calif, 1961–73; Pres., Kendall Medical International, Los Angeles, Calif, 1973–82. Mem. President's Council, American Management Assoc. Mem. Worshipful Co. of Clockmakers, Freeman City of London, 1943; Governor of King's Sch., Grantham, 1942–52. Mason (30° Shriner-Al Malaika Temple, LA). Religious Society of Friends (Quakers). Chevalier de l'Ordre du Ouissam Alouite Cherifien. *Address:* 1319 North Doheny Drive, Los Angeles, Calif 90069, USA. *T:* (213) 5508963. *Clubs:* Riviera Country, United British Services (Los Angeles, Calif).

KENDALL, William Leslie, CBE 1983; Secretary General, Council of Civil Service Unions (formerly Civil Service National Whitley Council, Staff Side), 1976–83; *b* 10 March 1923; *m* 1943, Irene Canham; one *s* one *d.* Clerk Insurance Cttee, 1937–41. RAF 1941–46. Entered Civil Service, 1947; Civil Service Clerical Association: Asst Sec., 1952; Dep. Gen. Sec., 1963; Gen. Sec., CPSA (formerly CSCA), 1967–76. Sec., Civil Service Alliance, 1967; Governor, Ruskin Coll., 1967–76. Member: CS Nat. Whitley Council (Chm. Staff Side, 1973–75); Advisory Council, Civil Service Coll., 1976–83; Civil Service Pay Bd, 1978–81; Vice Pres., Civil Service Council Further Educn, 1978–83. Member: Employment Appeal Tribunal, 1976–87; CS Appeal Bd, 1985–; ACAS Indep. Panel on Teachers' Dispute, 1986–87. Dir, Civil Service Building Soc., 1980–87; Mem., Management Cttee, CS Housing Assoc., 1984–87; Trustee, CS Benevolent Fund, 1987–. *Recreations:* reading, music, pottering. *Address:* 27 Moore Avenue, South Shields NE34 6AA. *T:* 091–456 9244.

KENDELL, Prof. Robert Evan, FRCP; FRCPsych; Chief Medical Officer, Scottish Office Home and Health Department, since 1991; *b* 28 March 1935; *s* of Robert Owen Kendell and Joan Evans; *m* 1961, Ann Whitfield; two *s* two *d. Educ:* Mill Hill School; Peterhouse, Cambridge. MA, MD. KCH Med. School, 1956–59; Maudsley Hosp., 1962–68; Vis. Prof., Univ. of Vermont Coll. of Medicine, 1969–70; Reader in Psychiatry, Inst. of Psychiatry, 1970–74; Prof. of Psychiatry, 1974–91, Dean, Faculty of Medicine, 1986–90, Univ. of Edinburgh. Chm., WHO Expert Cttee on Alcohol Consumption, 1979; Mem., MRC, 1984–88. Gaskell Medal, RCPsych, 1967; Paul Hoch Medal, Amer. Psychopathol Assoc., 1988. *Publications:* The Classification of Depressive Illnesses, 1968; The Role of Diagnosis in Psychiatry, 1975; (ed) Companion to Psychiatric Studies, 3rd edn 1983, 4th edn 1988. *Recreations:* overeating and walking up hills. *Address:* 3 West Castle Road, Edinburgh EH10 5AT. *T:* 031–229 4966. *Club:* Climbers'.

KENDREW, Sir John (Cowdery), Kt 1974; CBE 1963; ScD; FRS 1960; President of St John's College, Oxford, 1981–87, Hon. Fellow, since 1987; *b* 24 March 1917; *s* of late Wilfrid George Kendrew, MA, and Evelyn May Graham Sandberg. *Educ:* Dragon Sch., Oxford; Clifton Coll., Bristol; Trinity Coll., Cambridge (Hon. Fellow, 1972). Scholar of Trinity Coll., Cambridge, 1936; BA 1939; MA 1943; PhD 1949; ScD 1962. Min. of Aircraft Production, 1940–45; Hon. Wing Comdr, RAF, 1944. Fellow, Peterhouse, Cambridge, 1947–75 (Hon. Fellow, 1975); Dep. Chm., MRC Lab. for Molecular Biology, Cambridge, 1946–75; Dir Gen., European Molecular Biology Lab., 1975–82. Reader at Davy-Faraday Laboratory at Royal Instn, London, 1954–68. Mem., Council for Scientific Policy, 1965–72 (Dep. Chm., 1970–72); Sec.-Gen., European Molecular Biology Conf., 1970–74. Chm., Defence Scientific Adv. Council, 1971–74; Pres., British Assoc. for Advancement of Science, 1973–74; Trustee, British Museum, 1974–79. President: Internat. Union for Pure and Applied Biophysics, 1969–72; Confedn of Science and Technology Orgns for Develt, 1981–85; Sec. Gen, ICSU, 1974–80, first Vice-Pres., 1982–83, Pres., 1983–88, Past Pres., 1988–90; Trustee, Internat. Foundn for Science, 1975–78; Mem. Council, UN Univ., 1980–86, (Chm., 1983–85); Chm., Bd of Governors, Joint Research Centre, EEC, 1985–. Hon. MRIA 1981; Hon. Member: American Soc. of Biological Chemists, 1962; British Biophysical Soc.; Foreign Hon. Mem., Amer. Acad. of Arts and Sciences, 1964; Leopoldina Academy, 1965; Foreign Assoc., Amer. Nat. Acad. of Sciences, 1972; Hon. Fellow: Inst. of Biology, 1966; Weizmann Inst., 1970; Corresp. Mem., Heidelberg Acad. of Scis, 1978; Foreign Mem., Bulgarian Acad. of Scis, 1979; Foreign Fellow, Indian Nat. Science Acad., 1989. Lectures: Herbert Spencer, Univ. of Oxford, 1965; Crookshank, Faculty of Radiologists, 1967; Procter, Internat. Soc. of Leather Chemists, 1969; Fison Meml, Guy's Hosp., 1971; Mgr de Brún, Univ. Coll. of Galway, 1979; Saha Meml, Univ. of Calcutta, 1980. Hon. Prof., Univ. of Heidelberg, 1982. Hon. DSc: Univ. of Reading, 1968; Univ. of Keele, 1968; Exeter, 1982; Univ. of Buckingham, 1983; DUniv Stirling, 1974; Dr *honoris causa:* Pécs, Hungary, 1975; Madrid, 1987; Siena, 1991. (Jointly) Nobel Prize for Chemistry, 1962; Royal Medal of Royal Society, 1965; William Procter Prize, Sigma xi, 1988. Order of Madara Horseman, 1st degree, Bulgaria, 1980. Editor in Chief, Jl of Molecular Biology, 1959–87. *Publications:* The Thread of Life, 1966; scientific papers in Proceedings of Royal Society, etc. *Address:* The Old Guildhall, 4 Church Lane, Linton, Cambridge CB1 6JX. *T:* Cambridge (0223) 891545. *Club:* Athenæum.

KENDRICK, John Bebbington Bernard; Chief Inspector of Audit, Ministry of Housing and Local Government, 1958–65, retired; *b* 12 March 1905; 3rd *s* of late John Baker Kendrick and Lenora Teague, Leominster, Herefordshire; *m* 1932, Amelia Ruth, 4th *d* of late James Kendall, Grange-over-Sands; two *s. Educ:* Leominster Grammar Sch.; King's Sch., Chester; Queen's Coll., Oxford (MA). Called to Bar, Middle Temple. Asst District Auditor, 1926; Deputy District Auditor, 1946; District Auditor, 1953; Deputy Chief Inspector of Audit, 1958. *Recreation:* fell walking. *Address:* Green Acres, Old Hall Road, Troutbeck Bridge, Windermere, Cumbria LA23 1HF. *T:* Windermere (09662) 3705.

KENEALLY, Thomas Michael, AO 1983; FRSL; author; *b* 7 Oct. 1935; *s* of Edmond Thomas Keneally; *m* 1965, Judith Mary Martin; two *d.* Studied for NSW Bar. Schoolteacher until 1965; Commonwealth Literary Fellowship, 1966, 1968, 1972; Lectr in Drama, Univ. of New England, 1968–69. Vis. Prof., Dept of English, Univ. of California, Irvine, 1985; Berg Prof., Dept of English, New York Univ., 1988. Member: (inaugural) Australia–China Council, 1978–83; Adv. Panel, Australian Constitutional Commn, 1985–88; Literary Arts Bd, Australia, 1985–88; Chm., Aust. Soc. Authors, 1987–90 (Mem. Council, 1985–); Pres., Nat. Book Council Australia, 1985–89. FRSL 1973. Silver City (screenplay, with Sophia Turkiewicz), 1985. *Publications:* The Place at Whitton, 1964; The Fear, 1965, 2nd edn 1973; Bring Larks and Heroes, 1967, 2nd edn 1973; Three Cheers for the Paraclete, 1968; The Survivor, 1969; A Dutiful Daughter, 1971; The Chant of Jimmie Blacksmith, 1972 (filmed 1978); Blood Red, Sister Rose, 1974; Gossip from the Forest, 1975 (TV film, 1979); The Lawgiver, 1975; Season in Purgatory, 1976; A Victim of the Aurora, 1977; Ned Kelly and the City of the Bees, 1978; Passenger, 1979; Confederates, 1979; Schindler's Ark, 1982 (Booker Prize; LA Times Fiction Prize); Outback, 1983; The Cut-Rate Kingdom, 1984; A Family Madness, 1985; The Playmaker, 1987 (stage adaptation, perf. Royal Court, 1988); Towards Asmara, 1989; Flying Hero Class, 1991. *Recreations:* swimming, crosswords, hiking, cross-country ski-ing. *Address:* c/o Tessa Sayle Agency, 11 Jubilee Place, SW3 3TE.

KENILOREA, Rt. Hon. Sir Peter (Kauona Keninaraiso'ona), KBE 1982; PC 1979; MP (formerly MLA), East Are-Are, Solomon Islands, since 1976; Deputy Prime Minister of the Solomon Islands and Minister of Foreign Affairs, 1987–88 (Prime Minister, 1978–81 and 1984–86); *b* Takataka, Malaita, 23 May 1943; *m* 1971, Margaret Kwanairara; two *s* two *d*. *Educ:* Univ. and Teachers' Coll., NZ (Dip. Ed.). Teacher, King George VI Secondary Sch., 1968–70. Asst Sec., Finance, 1971; Admin. Officer, Dist Admin, 1971–73; Lands Officer, 1973–74; Dep. Sec. to Cabinet and to Chief Minister, 1974–75; Dist Comr, Eastern Solomon Is, 1975–76; Chief Minister, 1976–78; Leader of the Opposition, 1981–84. Queen's Silver Jubilee Medal, 1977; Solomon Is Indep. Medal, 1978. *Publications:* political and scientific, numerous articles. *Address:* c/o Legislative Assembly, Honiara, Guadalcanal, Solomon Islands.

KENILWORTH, 4th Baron *cr* 1937, of Kenilworth; **(John) Randle Siddeley;** Managing Director, Siddeley Landscapes, since 1976; Director, John Siddeley International Ltd; *b* 16 June 1954; *s* of John Tennant Davenport Siddeley (3rd Baron Kenilworth) and of Jacqueline Paulette, *d* of late Robert Gelpi; *S* father, 1981; *m* 1983, Kim (marr. diss.), *o d* of Danie Serfontein, Newcastle upon Tyne; *m* 1991, Mrs Kiki McDonough. *Educ:* Northease Manor, near Lewes, Sussex; West Dean College (studied Restoration of Antique Furniture); London College of Furniture. Worked at John Siddeley International as Interior Designer/Draughtsman, 1975; formed own company, Siddeley Landscapes, as Landscape Gardener, 1976. *Recreation:* ski-ing. *Address:* Unit 7, Sleaford Estate, Sleaford Street, SW8 5AB. *Clubs:* St James's; Annabel's.

KENLIS, Lord; Thomas Rupert Charles Christopher Taylour; *b* 18 June 1989; *s* and *heir* of Earl of Bective, *qv*.

KENNABY, Very Rev. Noel Martin; *b* 22 Dec. 1905; *s* of Martin and Margaret Agnes Kennaby; *m* 1st, 1933, Margaret Honess Elliman; 2nd, 1937, Mary Elizabeth Berry (*d* 1991). *Educ:* Queens' Coll., Cambridge; Westcott House, Cambridge. BA 1928; MA 1932. Deacon 1929, priest 1930, Diocese of Guildford; Curate of Epsom, 1929–32; in charge of Christ Church, Scarborough, 1932–36; Vicar of St Andrew's, Handsworth, 1936–42; Tynemouth, 1942–47; Surrogate from 1942; Rural Dean of Tynemouth, 1943–47; Provost and Vicar of Newcastle upon Tyne, 1947–61; Rural Dean of Newcastle upon Tyne, 1947–61; Senior Chaplain to the Archbishop of Canterbury, 1962–64; Hon. Canon, Newcastle Cathedral, 1962–64; Dean of St Albans and Rector of the Abbey Church, 1964–73, Dean Emeritus, 1973. Commissary, Jamaica, 1950–67. *Publication:* To Start You Praying, 1951. *Address:* Delapré House, St Andrew's Road, Bridport, Dorset DT6 3BZ.

KENNAN, Prof. George Frost; Professor, Institute for Advanced Study, Princeton, NJ, 1956–74, now Professor Emeritus; *b* 16 Feb. 1904; *m* 1931, Annelise Sorensen; one *s* three *d*. *Educ:* Princeton Univ. (AB); Seminary for Oriental Languages, Berlin. Foreign Service of the USA; many posts from 1926–52; US Ambassador to the USSR, 1952–53; Institute for Advanced Study, Princeton, 1953–61; US Ambassador to Yugoslavia, 1961–63. George Eastman Vis. Prof., Oxford, 1957–58; Reith Lectr, BBC, 1957; Prof., Princeton Univ., 1963 and 1964. Hon. LLD: Dartmouth and Yale, 1950; Colgate, 1951; Notre Dame, 1953; Kenyon Coll., 1954; New School for Social Research, 1955; Princeton, 1956; University of Michigan and Northwestern, 1957; Brandeis, 1958; Wisconsin, 1963; Harvard, 1963; Denison, 1966; Rutgers, 1966; Marquette, 1972; Catholic Univ. of America, 1976; Duke, 1977; Ripon Coll., 1978; Dickinson Coll., 1979; Lake Forest Coll., 1982; Clark Univ., 1983; Oberlin Coll., 1983; Brown Univ., 1983; New York Univ., 1985; William and Mary Coll., and Columbia Univ., 1986; Rider Coll., 1988; Hon. DCL Oxford, 1969; Dr of Politics *hc* Univ. of Helsinki, 1986. Benjamin Franklin Fellow RSA, 1968. President: Nat. Inst. of Arts and Letters, 1965–68; Amer. Acad. of Arts and Letters, 1968–72; Corresp. FBA, 1983. Pour le Mérite (Germany), 1976. Albert Einstein Peace Prize, Albert Einstein Peace Prize Foundn of Chicago, 1981; Grenville Clark Prize, Grenville Clark Fund at Dartmouth Coll., Inc., 1981; Börsenverein Peace Prize, Frankfurt, 1982; Gold Medal for History, AAIL, 1984; Creative Arts Award for Nonfiction, Brandeis Univ., 1986; Freedom from Fear Award, FDR Foundn, 1987; Physicians for Social Responsibility Award, 1988; Toynbee Prize, 1988; Encyclopeadia Britannica Award 1989; Presidential Medal of Freedom, 1989; Governor's Award of NJ, 1990. *Publications:* American Diplomacy, 1900–50, 1951 (US); Realities of American Foreign Policy, 1954 (US); Amerikanisch Russische Verhältnis, 1954 (Germany); Soviet-American Relations, 1917–20; Vol. I, Russia Leaves the War, 1956 (National Book Award; Pulitzer Prize 1957); Vol. II, The Decision to Intervene, 1958; Russia, the Atom and the West, 1958; Soviet Foreign Policy, 1917–1941, 1960; Russia and the West under Lenin and Stalin, 1961; On Dealing with the Communist World, 1964; Memoirs, vol. 1, 1925–1950, 1967 (National Book Award 1968; Pulitzer Prize 1968); Memoirs, vol. 2, 1950–1963, 1973; From Prague after Munich: Diplomatic Papers 1938–1940, 1968; Democracy and the Student Left, 1968; The Marquis de Custine and his 'Russie en 1839', 1972; The Cloud of Danger, 1977; The Decline of Bismarck's European Order, 1979; The Nuclear Delusion, 1982; The Fateful Alliance: France, Russia and the coming of the First World War, 1985; Sketches from a Life, 1989. *Club:* Century (New York City).

KENNARD, Sir George Arnold Ford, 3rd Bt *cr* 1891; *b* 27 April 1915; *s* of Sir Coleridge Kennard, 1st Bt; *S* brother, 1967; *m* 1st, 1940, Cecilia Violet Cokayne Maunsel (marr. diss. 1958); one *d*; 2nd, 1958, Jesse Rudd Miskin (marr. diss. 1974), *d* of Hugh Wyllie; 3rd, 1985, Nichola, *o d* of late Peter Carew, Tiverton. *Educ:* Eton. Commissioned 4th Queen's Own Hussars, 1939; served War of 1939–45 (despatches twice), Egypt, Greece (POW Greece); comd Regt, 1955–58; retired, 1958. Joined Cement Marketing Co., 1967, becoming Midland Representative; retired 1979. *Recreations:* hunting, shooting, fishing. *Publication:* Loopy (autobiog.), 1990. *Heir:* none. *Address:* Gogwell, Tiverton, Devon EX16 4PP. *T:* Tiverton (0884) 253153. *Club:* Cavalry and Guards.

KENNARD, Dr Olga, OBE 1988; ScD; FRS 1987; Scientific Director, Cambridge Crystallographic Data Centre, since 1965; Visiting Professor, University of London, since 1988; *b* 23 March 1924; *d* of Joir and Catherina Weisz; *m* 1948, David William Kennard (marr. diss. 1961); two *d*. *Educ:* Cambridge University (MA 1948; ScD 1973). Res. Asst, Cavendish Laboratory, Cambridge, 1944–48; MRC Scientific Staff: Inst. of Ophthalmology, London, 1948–51; Nat. Inst. for Med. Res., London, 1951–61; seconded to University Chemical Laboratory, Cambridge, 1961–71; MRC special appt, 1974–89. *Publications:* about 200 pubns in field of X-ray structure determination of organic and bioactive molecules and correlation between structure, chemical properties and biological activity, and technical innovations in X-ray crystallography; ed 20 standard reference books. *Recreations:* music, swimming, architecture, friendship and interaction with people of wit and intelligence. *Address:* University Chemical Laboratory, Lensfield Road, Cambridge CB2 1EW. *T:* Cambridge (0223) 336408.

KENNAWAY, Prof. Alexander, MA; Eur Ing, CEng, FPRI; consulting engineer, since 1966; Chairman, Terrafix Ltd, since 1983; *b* 14 Aug. 1923; *s* of late Dr and Mrs Barou; *m* 1st, 1947, Xenia Rebel (marr. diss. 1970); one *s* one *d*; 2nd, 1973, Jean Simpson. *Educ:* Downsend Sch., Leatherhead; St Paul's Sch., London; Pembroke Coll., Cambridge (MA). CEng, FIMechE 1962; FPRI 1968. Engr Officer, RN: active list, 1942–47; reserve, 1970. Imperial Chemical Industries Ltd, 1947–58; Metal Box Co., 1958–60; Director: BTR Industries, 1960–66; Allied Polymer Gp, 1972–78; Thomas Jourdan, 1976–83; Imperial Polymer Technology, 1984–86. Mem. Bd, CAA, 1979–83. Hon. medical engrg consultant, various hosps and charities, 1950–. Mem., Standing Adv. Cttee on artificial limbs, DHSS, 1964–70. Vis. Prof. of Mech. Engrg, Imp. Coll. of Science and Technology, 1976–. Interim Sec., Nat. Fedn of Zool Gardens of GB and Ireland, 1984–86. Pres., English Chess Assoc., 1988–. *Publications:* (contrib.) Advances in Surgical Materials, 1956; (contrib.) Polythene—technology and uses, 1958, 2nd edn 1960; Engineers in Industry, 1981; (contrib.) The British Malaise, 1982; some 30 papers on biomechanics, technology of use and production of rubbers and plastics, and on design of specific aids for disabled living. *Recreations:* sailing, chess, music, enlarging the limits imposed by an insular and specialist education, avoiding the natural pessimism of old(er) age, applying thought to the solution of useful problems. *Address:* 12 Fairholme Crescent, Ashtead, Surrey KT21 2HN. *T:* Ashtead (0372) 277678.

See also L. Archibald.

KENNAWAY, Sir John (Lawrence), 5th Bt, *cr* 1791; *b* 7 Sept. 1933; *s* of Sir John Kennaway, 4th Bt and Mary Felicity, *yr d* of late Rev. Chancellor Ponsonby; *S* father 1956; *m* 1961, Christina Veronica Urszenyi, MB, ChB (Cape Town); one *s* two *d*. *Educ:* Harrow; Trinity Coll., Cambridge. *Heir:* *s* John Michael Kennaway [*b* 17 Feb. 1962; *m* 1988, Lucy Frances, *yr d* of Dr Jeremy Houlton Bradshaw-Smith]. *Address:* Escot, Ottery St Mary, Devon EX11 1LU.

KENNEDY, family name of **Marquess of Ailsa.**

KENNEDY, Sir Albert (Henry), Kt 1965; KPM 1947; Hon. President, Securicor (Ulster) Ltd. Held various ranks in Royal Ulster Constabulary, incl. Inspector General, 1961–69. *Club:* Royal Belfast Golf (Ulster).

KENNEDY, A(lfred) James, CBE 1979; DSc (London), PhD (London), FEng, MIEE, FIM, FInstP; consultant; *b* 6 Nov. 1921; *m* 1950, Anna Jordan (*d* 1986); no *c*. *Educ:* Haberdashers' Aske's Hatcham Sch.; University Coll., London (Fellow 1976). BSc (Physics) 1943. Commissioned R Signals, 1944; Staff Major (Telecommunications) Central Comd, Agra, India, 1945–46 and at Northern Comd, Rawalpindi, 1946–47; Asst Lectr in Physics, UCL 1947–50; Res. Fellow, Davy-Faraday Lab. of Royal Institution, London, 1950–51; Royal Society, Armourers' and Brasiers' Research Fellow in Metallurgy (at Royal Institution), 1951–54; Head of Metal Physics Sect., BISRA, 1954–57; Prof. of Materials and Head of Dept. of Materials, Coll. of Aeronautics, Cranfield, 1957–66; Dir, British Non-Ferrous Metals Res. Assoc., later BNF Metals Technol. Centre, Wantage, 1966–78; Dir of Research, Delta Metal Co., and Man. Dir, Delta Material Research Ltd, 1978–81; Dep. Dir, Technical Change Centre, 1981–86; Dir, BL Technology Ltd, 1979–83. Vis. Prof. in Metallurgy, Imperial Coll. of Science and Technol., London, 1981–86. Institution of Metallurgists: Pres., 1976–77; a Vice Pres., 1971–74, 1975–76; Mem. Council, 1968–76. President: Inst. of Metals, 1970–71 (Mem. Council, 1968–73; Fellow, 1973); Engrg Section, BAAS, 1983; Member: Metallurgy Cttee, CNAA, 1965–71; ARC, 1967–70, 1971–74, 1977–80 (also Mem., ARC cttees); Adv. Council on Materials, 1970–71; Council, The Metals Soc., 1974–84 (Platinum Medallist, 1977); Inst. of Physics, 1968–71; SRC, 1974–78; Metall. and Mat. Cttee, SRC, 1970–75 (Chm. 1973–74); Engrg Bd, 1973–78; Council of Env. Sci. and Eng., 1973–78; Adv. Council for Applied R&D, 1976–80; Mat. and Chem. Res. Requirements Bd, DoI, 1981–83 (Chm., Non-Ferrous Metals Cttee); Chm., Council of Sci. and Tech. Insts, 1983–84. Fellow, Amer. Soc. Met., 1972. Pres., Brit. Soc. of Rheology, 1964–66; a Governor, Nat. Inst. for Agric. Engrg, 1966–74. Hon. DSc Aston, 1980. *Publications:* Processes of Creep and Fatigue in Metals, 1962; The Materials Background to Space Technology, 1964; Creep and Stress Relaxation in Metals (English edn), 1965; (ed) High Temperature Materials, 1968; research papers and articles, mainly on physical aspects of deformation and fracture in crystalline materials, particularly metals. *Recreations:* music, painting. *Address:* Woodhill, Milton under Wychwood, Oxford OX7 6EP. *T:* Shipton under Wychwood (0993) 830334. *Club:* Athenæum.

KENNEDY, Anthony McLeod; Associate Justice of the Supreme Court of the United States, since 1988; *b* 23 July 1936; *s* of Anthony J. Kennedy and Gladys Kennedy; *m* Mary Davis; two *s* one *d*. *Educ:* Stanford Univ. (AB 1958); LSE; Harvard Univ. (LLB 1961). Mem., Calif. Bar, 1962, US Tax Court Bar, 1971. Associate, Thelen Marrin John & Bridges, San Francisco, 1961–63; sole practice, 1963–67; partner Evans, Jackson & Kennedy, 1967–75. Prof. of Constitutional Law, McGeorge Sch. of Law, Univ. of Pacific, 1965–88; Judge, US Court of Appeals, 9th Circuit, Sacramento, 1976–88. *Address:* Supreme Court Building, 1 First Street NE, Washington, DC 20543, USA.

KENNEDY, Prof. Arthur Colville, FRCPE, FRCPGlas, FRCP; FRSE 1984; Muirhead Professor of Medicine, Glasgow University, 1978–88; *b* 23 Oct. 1922; *s* of Thomas and Johanna Kennedy; *m* 1947, Agnes White Taylor; two *d* (one *s* decd). *Educ:* Whitehill Sch., Glasgow; Univ. of Glasgow. MB ChB 1945; MD 1956. FRCPE 1960; FRCPGlas 1964; FRCP 1977; FRCPI 1988. Hon. Consultant in Medicine, Royal Infirmary, Glasgow, 1959–88; Titular Professor, Univ. of Glasgow, 1969–78. Mem., GMC, 1989–. Pres., RCPSG, 1986–88. Hon. FACP 1987; Hon. FRACP 1988. *Publications:* various papers on renal disease. *Recreations:* gardening, walking, reading, photography. *Address:* 16 Boclair Crescent, Bearsden, Glasgow G61 2AG. *T:* 041–942 5326. *Clubs:* Athenæum; Royal Scottish Automobile (Glasgow).

KENNEDY, Charles Peter; MP Ross, Cromarty and Skye, since 1983 (SDP 1983–88, Lib Dem since 1988); President, Liberal Democrats, 1990–Sept. 1992; *b* Inverness, 25 Nov. 1959; *yr s* of Ian Kennedy, crofter, and Mary McVarish MacEachen. *Educ:* Lochaber High Sch., Fort William; Univ. of Glasgow (joint MA Hons Philosophy and Politics). President, Glasgow Univ. Union, 1980–81; winner, British Observer Mace for Univ. Debating, 1982. Journalist, BBC Highland, Inverness, 1982; Fulbright Schol. and Associate Instructor in Dept of Speech Communication, Indiana Univ., Bloomington Campus, 1982–83. SDP spokesman on health, social services, social security and Scottish issues, 1983–87; SDP-Liberal Alliance spokesman on social security, 1987; Lib Dem spokesman on trade and industry, 1988–89, on health, 1989–. Member: Select Cttee on Social Services, 1986–87; Select Cttee on Televising of H of C, 1988–. Chm., SDP Council for Scotland, 1986–88. Occasional journalist, broadcaster and lecturer. *Address:* House of Commons, SW1A 0AA. *T:* 071–219 5090. *Club:* National Liberal.

KENNEDY, Sir Clyde (David Allen), Kt 1973; Chairman of Sydney (New South Wales) Turf Club, 1972–77 and 1980–83 (Vice-Chairman, 1967–72); company director; *b* 20 Nov. 1912; *s* of late D. H. Kennedy; *m* 1937, Sarah Stacpoole; two *s* one *d*. Member, NSW Totalisator Agency Board, 1965–82; Chairman, Spinal Research Foundation. *Address:* 13A/23 Thornton Street, Darling Point, NSW 2027, Australia. *Clubs:* Australian Jockey, Sydney Turf; Rugby, Tattersalls (all NSW).

KENNEDY, David Matthew; American Banker; Special Representative of the First Presidency of The Church of Jesus Christ of Latter-day Saints; *b* Randolph, Utah, 21 July 1905; *s* of George Kennedy and Katherine Kennedy (*née* Johnson); *m* 1925, Lenora

Bingham; four *d.* *Educ:* Weber Coll., Ogden, Utah (AB); George Washington Univ., Washington, DC (MA, LLB); Stonier Grad. Sch. of Banking, Rutgers Univ. (grad.). Special Asst to Chm. of Bd, Federal Reserve System, 1930–46; Vice-Pres. in charge of bond dept, Continental Illinois Bank and Trust Co., Chicago, 1946–53, full Vice-Pres., 1951, Pres., 1956–58, Chm. Bd and Chief Exec. Officer, 1959– (temp. resigned, Oct. 1953–Dec. 1954, to act as special Asst to Sec. of Treas., in Republican Admin.); after return to Continental Illinois Bank, still advised Treasury (also under Democrat Admin). Appointed by President Kennedy as incorporator and dir of Communication Satellite Corp.; Chm. of Commn (apptd by President Johnson) to improve drafting of Federal budget, 1967; Chm of Cttee (apptd by Mayor of Chicago) for Economic and Cultural Develt of Chicago, 1967. Again in Govt, when nominated to Nixon Cabinet, Dec. 1968; Secretary of the Treasury, 1969–70; Ambassador-at-large, USA, and Mem. President Nixon's Cabinet, 1970–73; US Ambassador to NATO, 1972. Director (past or present) of many corporations and companies including: Internat. Harvester Corp.; Abbott Laboratories; Swift & Co.; Pullman Co.; Nauvoo Restoration Inc.; Member of numerous organizations; Trustee: Univ. of Chicago; George Washington Univ.; Brookings Instn, etc. Holds hon. doctorates. *Address:* 3793 Parkview Drive, Salt Lake City, Utah 84124, USA. *Clubs:* Union League, Commercial Executives (Chicago); Old Elm Country (Fort Sheridan, Ill); Glenview Country, etc.

KENNEDY, Eamon, MA, BComm, PhD; Special Adviser, with rank of Ambassador, Permanent Mission of Ireland, United Nations, New York, since 1987; *b* 13 Dec. 1921; *s* of Luke William Kennedy and Ellen (*née* Stafford); *m* 1960, Barbara Jane Black, New York; one *s* one *d.* *Educ:* O'Connell Schools, Dublin; University Coll., Dublin (MA, BComm); National University of Ireland (PhD 1970). Entered Irish Diplomatic Service, 1943; 2nd Sec., Ottawa, 1947–49; 1st Sec., Washington, 1949–50; 1st Sec., Paris, 1950–54; Chief of Protocol, Dublin, 1954–56; Counsellor, UN Mission, New York, 1956–61; Ambassador to: Nigeria, 1961–64; Federal Republic of Germany, 1964–70; France, OECD and UNESCO, 1970–74; UN, 1974–78; UK, 1978–83; Italy, Turkey, Libya, and FAO Rome, 1983–86. Grand Cross: German Order of Merit, 1970; French Order of Merit, 1974. *Recreations:* golf, theatre, music. *Address:* The Rivergate, 401 East 34th Street, Apartment S33A, New York, NY 10016, USA; 6730 Nassau Point Road, Cutchogue, NY 11935, USA. *Club:* North Fork Country (Long Island, NY).

KENNEDY, Edward Arthur Gilbert; retired; occasional Chairman, Housing Benefit Review Boards; *b* Dublin, 5 May 1920; *s* of Captain Edward H. N. Kennedy, RN, and Frances A. Gosling, Bermuda; *m* 1944, Margarita Dagmara Hofstra; two *s* two *d.* *Educ:* Oundle; Pembroke Coll., Cambridge (BA Mod Langs). Served War, RNVR, 1941–46. Joined Northern Ireland Civil Service, 1947; served mainly in Dept of Commerce until 1970, then in Office of NI Ombudsman (Sen. Dir, 1973–83). Vice-Chm., Music Cttee, N Ireland Arts Council, 1978–83; Hon. Pres., Belfast Ballet Club, 1970–82; Chm., Belfast Picture Borrowing Gp, 1970–84. *Recreation:* interest in the arts. *Address:* 29 Tweskard Park, Belfast BT4 2JZ. *T:* Belfast (0232) 763638.

KENNEDY, Edward Moore; US Senator (Democrat) from Massachusetts, since 1962; *b* Boston, Mass, 22 Feb. 1932; *y s* of late Joseph Patrick Kennedy and of Rose Kennedy (*née* Fitzgerald); *m*; two *s* one *d.* *Educ:* Milton Acad.; Harvard Univ. (BA 1956); Internat. Law Inst., The Hague; Univ. of Virginia Law Sch. (LLB 1959). Served US Army, 1951–53. Called to Massachusetts Bar, 1959; Asst Dist Attorney, Suffolk County, Mass, 1961–62. Senate majority whip, 1969–71; Chairman: Judiciary Cttee, 1979–81; Labor and Human Resources Cttee, 1987– (Ranking Democrat, 1981–86); Member: Senate Armed Forces Cttee; Senate Jt Economic Cttee; Bd, Office of Technology Assessment. Pres., Joseph P. Kennedy Jr Foundn, 1961–; Trustee: John F. Kennedy Lib.; John F. Kennedy Center for the Performing Arts; Robert F. Kennedy Meml Foundn. Holds numerous hon. degrees, foreign decorations and awards. *Publications:* Decisions for a Decade, 1968; In Critical Condition, 1972; Our Day and Generation, 1979; (with Senator Mark Hatfield) Freeze: how you can help prevent nuclear war, 1982. *Address:* United States Senate, Washington, DC 20510, USA.

KENNEDY, Sir Francis, KCMG 1986; CBE 1977 (MBE 1958); HM Diplomatic Service, retired; Special Adviser to the Chairman and Board, British Airways, since 1986 (Director, since 1987); *b* 9 May 1926; *s* of late James Kennedy and Alice (*née* Bentham); *m* 1957, Anne O'Malley; two *s* two *d.* *Educ:* Univs of Manchester and London. RN, 1944–46. Min. of Supply, 1951–52; HM Colonial Service, Nigeria, 1953–63; Asst Dist Officer, 1953–56; Dist Officer, 1956–59; Principal Asst Sec. to Premier E Nigeria, 1961–62; Provincial Sec., Port Harcourt, 1962–63; HM Diplomatic Service, 1964; First Sec., Commercial and Economic, Dar-es-Salaam, 1965; First Sec. and Head of Post, Kuching, 1967–69; Consul, Commercial, Istanbul, 1970–73; Consul-Gen., Atlanta, 1973–78; Counsellor later Minister Lagos, 1978–81; Ambassador to Angola, 1981–83; Dir-Gen., British Trade and Investment, and Consul-Gen., NY, 1983–86. Chm., Fluor Daniel Ltd, 1989 (Dir, 1986–); Director: Leslie & Godwin Ltd, 1986–; Global Analysis Systems, 1986–88; Hambourne Development Co., 1987–; Smith & Nephew, 1988–; Fleming Overseas Investment Trust, 1988–; Mem. Bd and Council, Inward, 1986–90; Mem. Bd, Lancashire Polytechnic, 1989–. Governor, British Liver Foundn, 1990–. *Clubs:* Brooks's; Shaw Hill Golf and Country; Lancashire County Cricket.
See also Rt Rev. Mgr J. Kennedy.

KENNEDY, (George) Michael (Sinclair), OBE 1981; Associate Northern Editor, since 1986, and Staff Music Critic, since 1950 (Joint Chief Critic, 1987–89), The Daily Telegraph; Music Critic, The Sunday Telegraph, since 1989; *b* 19 Feb. 1926; *s* of Hew Gilbert Kennedy and Marian Florence Sinclair; *m* 1947, Eslyn Durdle; no *c.* *Educ:* Berkhamsted School. Joined Daily Telegraph, Manchester, 1941; served Royal Navy (BPF), 1943–46; rejoined Daily Telegraph, Manchester, serving in various capacities on editorial staff; Asst Northern Editor, 1958; Northern Ed., 1960–86. Gov., Royal Northern Coll. of Music; Mem. Cttee, Vaughan Williams Trust, 1965– (Chm., 1977–); Vice-Pres., Elgar Foundn and Elgar Soc. Hon. Mem., Royal Manchester Coll. of Music, 1971. Hon. MA Manchester, 1975. FJI 1967; FRNCM 1981. *Publications:* The Hallé Tradition, 1960; The Works of Ralph Vaughan Williams, 1964, 2nd edn 1980; Portrait of Elgar, 1968, 3rd rev. edn, 1987; Portrait of Manchester, 1970; Elgar Orchestral Works, 1970; History of Royal Manchester College of Music, 1971; Barbirolli: Conductor Laureate, 1971; (ed) The Autobiography of Charles Hallé, 1973; Mahler, 1974, 2nd edn 1990 (Japanese edn 1978); Richard Strauss, 1976; (ed) Concise Oxford Dictionary of Music, 3rd edn, 1980; Britten, 1981; The Hallé, 1858–1983, 1983; Strauss Tone Poems, 1984; Oxford Dictionary of Music, 1985; Adrian Boult, 1987; Portrait of Walton, 1989; scripts for BBC, contrib. musical jls. *Recreations:* listening to music, watching cricket. *Address:* 3 Moorwood Drive, Sale, Cheshire M33 4QA. *T:* 061–973 7225. *Club:* Portico Library (Manchester).

KENNEDY, Helena Ann; QC 1991; *b* 12 May 1950; *d* of Joshua Patrick Kennedy and Mary Veronica (*née* Jones); partner, 1978–84, (Roger) Iain Mitchell; one *s*; *m* 1986, Dr Iain Louis Hutchison; one *s* one *d.* *Educ:* Holyrood Secondary Sch., Glasgow; Council of Legal Educn. Called to the Bar, Gray's Inn, 1972; established chambers at: Garden Court, 1974; Tooks Court, 1984; Doughty St, 1990. Member: Bar Council, 1990–; Cttee, Assoc. of Women Barristers, 1991–; Nat. Bd, Women's Legal Defence Fund, 1989–; Council, Howard League for Penal Reform, 1989–; CIBA Commn into Child Sexual Abuse, 1981–83; Exec. Cttee, NCCL, 1983–85; Bd, Minority Access to Legal Profession Project, Poly. of South Bank, 1984–85; Chm., Haldane Soc., 1983–86 (Vice-Pres., 1986–); Mem. Council, Charter '88, 1988–; Patron, Civil Liberties Trust, 1991–; Comr, Hamlyn Nat. Commn on Educn, 1991–. Vis. Lectr on Criminal Law, BPMF, 1991–. Member Board: City Limits Magazine, 1982–84; New Statesman, 1990–; Counsel Magazine, 1990–; Hampstead Theatre, 1989–. FRSA. Broadcaster: first female moderator, Hypotheticals (Granada) on surrogate motherhood and artificial insemination; presenter: Heart of the Matter, BBC, 1987; Putting Women in the Picture, BBC2, 1987; The Trial of Lady Chatterley's Lover, Radio 4, 1990; Raw Deal, series of progs on med. negligence, BBC2, 1990; co-producer, Women Behind Bars, Channel 4, 1990; presenter, The Maguires: forensic evidence on trial, BBC2, 1991; creator, drama series, Blind Justice, BBC, 1988; host, After Dark, Channel 4, 1988–. *Publications:* (jtly) The Bar on Trial, 1978; (jtly) Child Abuse Within the Family, 1984; (jtly) Balancing Acts, 1989; Eve was Framed, 1991; contribs on issues connected with law, civil liberties and women. *Recreations:* theatre, spending time with family and friends. *Address:* 11 Doughty Street, WC1N 2PG. *T:* 071–404 1313.

KENNEDY, Horas Tristram, OBE 1966; HM Diplomatic Service, retired; *b* 29 May 1917; *s* of George Lawrence Kennedy and Mary Dow; *m* 1953, Maureen Beatrice Jeanne Holmes (formerly Stevens) (*d* 1976); three *d* (one *s* decd). *Educ:* Oundle; King's Coll., Cambridge. History and Mod Langs, MA. Entered HM Consular Service, 1939; Vice-Consul, Valparaiso, Chile, 1939–46; Foreign Office, 1946–48; 1st Secretary: Belgrade, 1949–52; Buenos Aires, 1952–56; Berne, 1956–61; Santiago de Chile, 1961–67; Commercial Counsellor, Warsaw, 1967–70; Consul-Gen., Barcelona, 1971–73. *Recreations:* country walking, painting, carpentry. *Address:* Borea Farm, Nancledra, Penzance, Cornwall TR20 8AY. *T:* Penzance (0736) 62722.

KENNEDY, Hon. Sir Ian (Alexander), Kt 1986; **Hon. Mr Justice Ian Kennedy;** Judge of the High Court of Justice, Queen's Bench Division, since 1986; *b* 7 Sept. 1930; *s* of late Gerald Donald Kennedy, OBE, and Elizabeth Jane (*née* McBeth); *m* 1962, Susan Margaret, *d* of late Lt-Col Edward John Hatfield, OBE, DL, and of Eileen (*née* Menneer); three *s* one *d.* *Educ:* Wellington Coll., Berks; Pembroke Coll., Cambridge (BA). Called to the Bar, Middle Temple, 1953. Dep. Chm., IoW QS, 1971; a Recorder of the Crown Court, 1972; QC 1974. Judge, Employment Appeal Tribunal, 1990–. *Recreations:* sailing, theatre, walking, gardening. *Address:* Royal Courts of Justice, Strand, WC2A 2LL. *Club:* Itchenor Sailing.

KENNEDY, Prof. Ian McColl; Professor of Medical Law and Ethics, since 1983, and Head and Dean of School of Law, since 1989, King's College London (Head, Department of Laws, 1986–89); Director, Centre of Medical Law and Ethics (formerly Centre of Law, Medicine and Ethics), King's College London, since 1978; *b* 14 Sept. 1941; *s* of Robert Charles Kennedy and late Dorothy Elizabeth Kennedy; *m* 1980, Andrea, *d* of Frederick and Barbara Gage, Ventura, Calif; two *s.* *Educ:* King Edward VI Sch., Stourbridge; University Coll. London (1st Cl. Hons LLB); Univ. of Calif, Berkeley (LLM). Called to the Bar, Inner Temple, 1974. Fulbright Fellow, 1963–65; Lectr in Law, UCL, 1965–71; Ford Foundn Fellow, Yale Univ. and Univ. of Mexico, 1966–67; Vis. Prof., Univ. of Calif, LA, 1971–72; Lectr in Law, King's Coll., London, 1973–78, Reader in English Law 1978–83; British Acad. Res. Fellow, 1978. FKC 1988. Member: Medicines Commn, 1984–; GMC, 1984–; Expert Adv. Gp on AIDS, DHSS, later Dept of Health, 1987–; Gen. Adv. Council, BBC, 1987–. Member: Editorial Bd, Jl of Medical Ethics, 1978–; Council, Open Section, RSM, 1978– (Vice-Pres., 1981–; FRSM 1985). Reith Lectr, 1980. *Publications:* The Unmasking of Medicine, 1981, rev. edn 1983; Treat Me Right, 1988; (with A. Grubb) Medical Law: cases and materials, 1989. *Address:* 10 Dartmouth Park Road, NW5 1SY.

KENNEDY, James; *see* Kennedy, A. J.

KENNEDY, Joanna Alicia Gore, CEng; Senior Engineer, Ove Arup and Partners, since 1979; *b* 22 July 1950; *d* of Captain G. A. G. Ormsby, DSO, DSC, RN and late Susan Ormsby; *m* 1979, Richard Paul Kennedy, *qv*; two *s.* *Educ:* Queen Anne's School, Caversham; Lady Margaret Hall, Oxford (Scholar, 1969; BA 1st cl. Hons Eng. Sci. 1972; MA 1976; Hon. Mem., Senior Common Room, 1985–87). MICE 1979, ACIArb 1983. Ove Arup and Partners, consulting engineers: Design Engineer, 1972; Asst Resident Engineer (Runnymede Bridge), 1977; Arup Associates, 1987; Project Management Services, 1990. Member: Engineering Council, 1984–86 and 1987–90; Council, ICE, 1984–87; Adv. Council, RNEC Manadon, 1988–; Engrg and Technol. Prog. Adv. Gp, PCFC, 1989–; Engrg Bd, SERC, 1990–. Governor: Downe House Sch.; Channing Sch. FRSA 1986. *Address:* Ove Arup & Partners, 13 Fitzroy Street, W1P 6BQ. *T:* 071–636 1531.

KENNEDY, Rt. Rev. Mgr John; Rector, Venerable English College, Rome, 1984–91; Assistant Lecturer in Theology, Gregorian University, Rome, 1984–91; *b* 31 Dec. 1930; *s* of James Kennedy and Alice Kennedy (*née* Bentham). *Educ:* St Joseph's College, Upholland; Gregorian University, Rome (STL); Oxford University (MPhil). Curate: St John's, Wigan, 1956–63; St Austin's, St Helens, 1963–65; St Edmund's, Liverpool, 1965–68; Lectr in Theology, Christ's College, Liverpool, 1968–84 (Head of Dept, 1976–84). *Recreations:* golf, squash. *Address:* Holy Family Presbytery, 1 Brompton Road, Southport, Merseyside PR8 6AS.
See also Sir Francis Kennedy.

KENNEDY, John Maxwell; Senior Partner, Allen & Overy, since 1986 (Partner, since 1962); *b* 9 July 1934; *s* of George and Betty Gertrude Kennedy; *m* 1958, Margaret Joan (*née* Davies); four *s.* *Educ:* University Coll., London (LLB). Admitted Solicitor, 1957. *Recreations:* sport, music, reading. *Address:* 16 Kensington Park Road, W11 3BU. *T:* 071–727 6929. *Clubs:* City of London, City Law, Hurlingham; Royal Wimbledon Golf.

KENNEDY, Prof. John (Stodart), FRS 1965; Research Associate, Department of Zoology, University of Oxford, since 1983; Deputy Chief Scientific Officer, Agricultural Research Council, 1967–77, and Professor of Animal Behaviour in the University of London, Imperial College at Silwood Park, Ascot, 1968–77, then Professor Emeritus; *b* 19 May 1912; *s* of James John Stodart Kennedy, MICE, and Edith Roberts Kennedy (*née* Lammers); *m* 1st, 1936, Dorothy Violet Bartholomew (divorced, 1946); one *s*; 2nd, 1950, Claude Jacqueline Bloch (*widow, née* Raphaël); one step *s*, one *s* one *d.* *Educ:* Westminster Sch.; University Coll., London. BSc (London) 1933; DSc (London) 1956. Locust Investigator for Imperial Inst. of Entomology, University of Birmingham, 1934–36, Anglo-Egyptian Sudan, 1936–37; MSc (London) 1936; London Sch. of Hygiene and Trop. Med., 1937–38; PhD (Birmingham) 1938; Rockefeller Malaria Res. Lab., Tirana, Albania, 1938–39; Wellcome Entomolog. Field Labs, Esher, Surrey, 1939–42; Res. Officer, Middle East Anti-Locust Unit, 1942–44; Chem. Defence Exptl Station, Porton, Wilts, 1944–45; ARC Unit of Insect Physiology, Cambridge, 1946–67. Sen. Res. Fellow, Imperial Coll., 1977–83. Pres. Royal Entomological Society, 1967–69 (Hon. Fellow, 1974; Wigglesworth Medal, 1985). Fellow: University (now Wolfson) Coll., Cambridge,

1966; University Coll., London, 1967; Imperial Coll., London, 1982. Gold Medal, Linnean Soc., 1984. *Publications:* The New Anthropomorphism, 1992; numerous research papers, review articles and essays on the biology of locusts, mosquitos, moths and greenfly, and insect behaviour generally. *Address:* 17 Winchester Road, Oxford OX2 6NA. *T:* Oxford (0865) 54484.

See also M. E. F. Bloch.

KENNEDY, Kevin; Chairman and Managing Director, Philips Electronics and Associated Industries Ltd, since 1991; *b* 1 March 1937; *s* of John and Cathryn Kennedy; *m* 1962, Ann Larkin; three *s*. *Educ:* Our Lady's High Sch., Motherwell. Dir and Gen. Man., Honeywell Information Systems Ltd, 1983–86; Group Man. Dir, Philips, 1986–89; Chm. and Sen. Man. Dir, Philips Information Systems, 1989–91. FBIM; MInstD. *Recreations:* golf, music. *Address:* 17 King George Square, Park Hill, Richmond, Surrey TW10 6LF. *T:* 081–940 5372.

KENNEDY, Ludovic Henry Coverley; writer and broadcaster; *b* Edinburgh, 3 Nov. 1919; *o s* of Captain E. C. Kennedy, RN (killed in action, 1939, while commanding HMS Rawalpindi against German battle-cruisers Scharnhorst and Gneisenau), and Rosalind, *d* of Sir Ludovic Grant, 11th Bt of Dalvey; *m* 1950, Moira Shearer King (*see* Moira Shearer); one *s* three *d*. *Educ:* Eton; Christ Church, Oxford (MA). Served War, 1939–46: Midshipman, Sub-Lieut, Lieut, RNVR. Priv. Sec. and ADC to Gov. of Newfoundland, 1943–44. Librarian, Ashridge (Adult Education) Coll., 1949; Rockefeller Foundation Atlantic Award in Literature, 1950; Winner, Open Finals Contest, English Festival of Spoken Poetry, 1953; Editor, feature, First Reading (BBC Third Prog.), 1953–54; Lecturer for British Council, Sweden, Finland and Denmark, 1955; Belgium and Luxembourg, 1956; Voltaire Meml Lectr, 1985; Mem. Council, Navy Records Soc., 1957–60. Contested (L) Rochdale, by-elec., 1958 and Gen. elec., 1959; Pres., Nat. League of Young Liberals, 1959–61; Mem., Lib. Party Council, 1965–67. Pres., Sir Walter Scott Club, Edinburgh, 1968–69. Columnist: Newsweek International, 1974–75; Sunday Standard, 1981–82. Chm., Royal Lyceum Theatre Co. of Edinburgh, 1977–84. Dir, The Spectator, 1988–90. Chm. of Judges, NCR Book Award, 1990–91. FRSA 1974–76. Hon. LLD Strathclyde, 1985; Dr *hc* Edinburgh, 1990; DUniv Stirling, 1991. Richard Dimbleby BAFTA Award, 1988. Cross, First Class, Order of Merit, Fed. Repub. of Germany, 1979. *TV and radio:* Introd. Profile, ATV, 1955–56; Newscaster, Independent Television News, 1956–58; Introducer of AR's feature On Stage, 1957; Introducer of AR's, This Week, 1958–59; Chm. BBC features: Your Verdict, 1962; Your Witness, 1967–70; Commentator: BBC's Panorama, 1960–63; Television Reporters Internat., 1963–64 (also Prod.); Introducer, BBC's Time Out, 1964–65, World at One, 1965–66; Presenter: Lib. Party's Gen. Election Television Broadcasts, 1966; The Middle Years, ABC, 1967; The Nature of Prejudice, ATV, 1968; Face the Press, Tyne-Tees, 1968–69, 1970–72; Against the Tide, Yorkshire TV, 1969; Living and Growing, Grampian TV, 1969–70; 24 Hours, BBC, 1969–72; Ad Lib, BBC, 1970–72; Midweek, BBC, 1973–75; Newsday, BBC, 1975–76; Tonight, BBC, 1976–78; A Life with Crime, BBC, 1979; Change of Direction, BBC, 1979; Lord Mountbatten Remembers, 1980; Did You See?, 1980–88; Timewatch, 1984; Indelible Evidence, 1987 and 1990; A Gift of the Gab, 1989; Portrait, 1989. *Television films include:* The Sleeping Ballerina; The Singers and the Songs; Scapa Flow; Battleship Bismarck; Life and Death of the Scharnhorst; U-Boat War; Target Tirpitz; The Rise of the Red Navy; Lord Haw-Haw; Coast to Coast; Who Killed the Lindbergh Baby; Elizabeth: the first thirty years; Happy Birthday, dear Ma'am. *Publications:* Sub-Lieutenant, 1942; Nelson's Band of Brothers, 1951; One Man's Meat, 1953; Murder Story (play, with essay on Capital Punishment), 1956; play: Murder Story (Cambridge Theatre), 1954; Ten Rillington Place, 1961; The Trial of Stephen Ward, 1964; Very Lovely People, 1969; Pursuit: the chase and sinking of the Bismarck, 1974; A Presumption of Innocence: the Amazing Case of Patrick Meehan, 1975; Menace: the life and death of the Tirpitz, 1979; The Portland Spy Case, 1979; Wicked Beyond Belief, 1980; (ed) A Book of Railway Journeys, 1980; (ed) A Book of Sea Journeys, 1981; (ed) A Book of Air Journeys, 1982; The Airman and the Carpenter, 1985; On My Way to the Club (autobiog.), 1989; Euthanasia: the good death, 1990; Truth to Tell (collected writings), 1991; Gen. Editor, The British at War, 1973–77. *Address:* c/o Rogers, Coleridge and White, 20 Powis Mews, W11 1JN. *Clubs:* Beefsteak, Brooks's, Army and Navy.

KENNEDY, Michael; *see* Kennedy, G. M. S.

KENNEDY, Michael Denis; QC 1979; **His Honour Judge Kennedy;** a Circuit Judge, since 1984; *b* 29 April 1937; *s* of Denis George and Clementina Catherine (*née* MacGregor); *m* 1964, Elizabeth June Curtiss; two *s* two *d*. *Educ:* Downside School; Gonville and Caius College, Cambridge (open Schol., Mod. Langs; MA). 15/19 King's Royal Hussars, 1955–57. Called to the Bar, Inner Temple, 1961; a Recorder, 1979–84. *Address:* c/o Lewes Crown Court, High Street, Lewes, E Sussex BN7 1YB. *T:* Lewes (0273) 480400.

KENNEDY, Sir Michael Edward, 8th Bt *cr* 1836, of Johnstown Kennedy, Co. Dublin; *b* 12 April 1956; *s* of Sir (George) Ronald Derrick Kennedy, 7th Bt and of Noelle Mona, *d* of Charles Henry Green; *S* father, 1988; *m* 1984, Helen Christine Jennifer, *d* of Patrick Lancelot Rae; two *d*. *Heir: uncle* Mark Gordon Kennedy, *b* 3 Feb. 1932.

KENNEDY, Moira, (Mrs L. Kennedy); *see* Shearer, M.

KENNEDY, Nigel Paul; solo concert violinist; *b* 28 Dec. 1956; *s* of John Kennedy and Scylla Stoner. *Educ:* Yehudi Menuhin School; Juilliard School of Performing Arts, NY. ARCM. Début at Festival Hall with Philharmonia Orch., 1977; regular appearances with London and provincial orchestras, 1978–; Berlin début with Berlin Philharmonic, 1980; Henry Wood Promenade début, 1981; New York début with BBC SO, 1987; tour of Hong Kong and Australia, with Hallé Orch., 1981; foreign tours, 1978–: India, Japan, S Korea, Turkey, USA; many appearances as jazz violinist with Stephane Grappelli, incl. Edinburgh Fest., 1974 and Carnegie Hall, 1976; many TV and radio appearances, incl. Vivaldi's Four Seasons and two documentaries; pop, jazz and classical recordings; Best Classical Record, 1985, British Record Industry Awards, for recording of Elgar Violin Concerto; Guinness Book of Records, 1990, for sustaining Vivaldi's Four Seasons at No 1 in UK Classical Chart for over one yr; Golden Rose of Montreaux, 1990; Variety Club Showbusiness Personality of the Year, 1991. Sen. Vice-Pres., Aston Villa FC, 1990. Hon. DLitt Bath, 1991. *Recreations:* golf, football (watching and playing), cricket. *Address:* c/o John Stanley Media Management, 28 Nottingham Place, W1M 3FD. *T:* 071–487 5665, *Fax:* 071–935 1640.

KENNEDY, Hon. Sir Paul (Joseph Morrow), Kt 1983; **Hon. Mr Justice Kennedy;** a Judge of the High Court of Justice, Queen's Bench Division, since 1983; *b* 12 June 1935; *o s* of late Dr J. M. Kennedy, Sheffield; *m* 1965 Virginia, twin *d* of Baron Devlin, *qv*; two *s* two *d*. *Educ:* Ampleforth Coll.; Gonville and Caius Coll., Cambridge (MA, LLB). Called to Bar, Gray's Inn, 1960, Bencher, 1982; a Recorder, 1972–83; QC 1973; Presiding Judge, N Eastern Circuit, 1985–89. *Address:* Royal Courts of Justice, Strand, WC2A 2LL.

KENNEDY, Richard Paul; Head Master of Highgate School, since 1989; *b* 17 Feb. 1949; *e s* of David Clifton Kennedy and Evelyn Mary Hall (*née* Tindale); *m* 1979, Joanna Alicia Gore Ormsby (*see* J. A. G. Kennedy); two *s*. *Educ:* Charterhouse; New College, Oxford (BA Maths and Phil. 1970; MA 1977). Assistant Master, Shrewsbury Sch., 1971–77, Westminster Sch., 1977–84; Dep. Headmaster, Bishop's Stortford Coll., 1984–89 (Acting Headmaster 1989). Gov., The Hall Sch., Hampstead, 1989–. GB internat. athlete (sprints), 1973–76. Mem., Acad. of St Martin-in-the-Fields Chorus, 1977–. *Recreations:* reading biographies, choral music. *Address:* 12 Bishopswood Road, N6 4NY. *T:* 081-340 7626.

KENNEDY, Thomas Alexander; economist; *b* 11 July 1920; *s* of late Rt Hon. Thomas Kennedy, PC, and Annie S. Kennedy (*née* Michie); *m* 1947, Audrey (*née* Plunkett); one *s* two *d*. *Educ:* Alleyn's Sch., Dulwich; Durham Univ. (BA). Economist: Bd of Trade, 1950–52; Colonial Office, 1952–55; Lecturer in Economics at Makerere Coll., Uganda, 1955–61; Economist: Treasury, Foreign Office, DEA, 1961–67; Economic Director, NEDO, 1967–70; Under-Sec.: DTI, 1970–74; Dept of Energy, 1974–80, resigned. Chief Tech. Adviser (Economist Planner), Min. of Petroleum and Mineral Resources, Bangladesh, 1980–81. Vis. Fellow, Clare Hall, Cambridge, 1981–82. Consultant, World Bank: Uganda, Zambia, Swaziland, 1983–86, retired 1987. *Address:* 1 Beckside Mews, Staindrop, Darlington, Co. Durham DL2 3PG. *T:* Staindrop (0833) 60616.

KENNEDY, Air Chief Marshal Sir Thomas (Lawrie), GCB 1985 (KCB 1980; CB 1978); AFC 1953 and Bar 1960; DL; Royal Air Force, retired; Controller, RAF Benevolent Fund, since 1988; *b* 19 May 1928; *s* of James Domoné Kennedy and Margaret Henderson Lawrie; *m* 1959, Margaret Ann Parker; one *s* two *d*. *Educ:* Hawick High Sch. RAF Coll., Cranwell, 1946–49; commissioned, 1949. Sqdn service, 1949–53; exchange service, RAAF, 1953–55; returned to UK, 1955; 27 Sqdn (Canberra), 1955–57; Radar Research Estabt, 1957–60; RAF Coll. Selection Bd, 1960–62; RN Staff Coll., Greenwich, 1962; HQ Middle East, 1962–64; CO, No 99 (Britannia) Sqdn, 1965–67; HQ Air Support Comd, 1967–69; CO, RAF Brize Norton, 1970–71; Dep. Comdt, RAF Staff Coll., 1971–73; Dir of Ops (AS) MoD, 1973–75; Royal Coll. of Defence Studies, 1976; Comdr, Northern Maritime Air Region, 1977–79; Deputy C-in-C, RAF Strike Command, 1979–81; C-in-C, RAF Germany, and Comdr, 2nd Allied Tactical Air Force, 1981–83; Air Mem. for Personnel, 1983–86; Air ADC to the Queen, 1983–86. Dir, Dowty Group, 1987–. Freeman, City of London, 1987; Hon. Liveryman, Fruiterers' Co., 1987. DL Leics, 1989. *Recreations:* golf, sailing. *Address:* c/o Barclays Bank, 105 London Road, Headington, Oxford OX3 9AH. *Club:* Royal Air Force.

KENNEDY, William Andrew; Metropolitan Stipendiary Magistrate, since 1991; *b* 13 Feb. 1948; *s* of Sidney Herbert and Kathleen Blanche Kennedy; *m* 1st, 1974, Alice Steen Wilkie (*d* 1987); 2nd, 1988, Lindsey Jane Sheridan; one *d*. *Educ:* Buckhurst Hill County High Sch.; College of Law, Lancaster Gate. Articled Clerk, Trotter Chapman & Whisker, Epping, Essex, 1966–72; admitted Solicitor, 1972; Partner 1972–75, Jt Sen. Partner 1975–91, Trotter Chapman & Whisker, later Whiskers. *Recreations:* golf, gentle domestic pursuits. *Address:* c/o Greenwich Magistrates' Court, Blackheath Road, SE10 8PG. *T:* 081–853 8090. *Club:* Chigwell Golf.

KENNEDY-GOOD, Sir John, KBE 1983; QSO 1977; JP; Mayor of Lower Hutt, since 1970; *b* Goulburn, NSW, 8 Aug. 1915; *s* of Charles Kennedy-Good; *m* 1940, June, *d* of Charles Mackay; four *s* three *d*. *Educ:* Southland Boys' High Sch.; Otago Univ. (BDS). Practised as dentist, 1942–72. Mem., Lower Hutt City Council, 1962–. Dir, Hutt Milk Corp., 1970–71, 1974–; Chairman: Hutt Valley Underground Water Authy, 1970–72 (Mem., 1962–72); Wellington Regl Council, 1980– (Dep. Chm., 1980–83); NZ Council of Social Services, 1975–82; Member: Wellington Harbour Bd, 1971–80; Hutt Valley Energy Bd, 1970–. Past Mem., NZ Catchment Authorities' Exec. Pres., NZ Sister Cities Inc. Chm., Dowse Art Mus. Bd, 1971–; Dep. Chm., Nat. Art Gall. and Mus. Trust Bd (Mem., 1971–). Mem., NZ Acad. Fine Arts, 1948. Founder Chm., John Kennedy-Good Human Resources Centre; Chm., Wellington Paraplegic Trust Bd (Vice-Pres., NZ Fed.); past Chm., Council for Dental Health, and past Pres., Wellington Br., NZ Dental Assoc.; Life Patron and Mem. Bd, Hutt Valley Disabled Resources Trust; Pres., Wellington Div., Order of St John; Patron, Wellington Reg. Centre, NZ Red Cross Soc.; patron, pres. or vice-pres. of numerous charity, cultural and sporting orgns. Trustee, Waiwhetu Marae, 1970–; Hon. Elder, Te Atiawa Tribe. JP Lower Hutt, 1970. *Address:* Mayoral Chambers, City Council, Private Bag, Lower Hutt, New Zealand. *T:* 666 959; Greenwood, 64 King's Crescent, Lower Hutt, New Zealand. *T:* 661 227. *Clubs:* Hutt, Hutt Rotary (past Pres.), Hutt Golf.

KENNEDY MARTIN, (Francis) Troy; writer; *b* 15 Feb. 1932; *s* of Frank Martin and Kathleen Flanagan; *m* 1967, Diana Aubrey; one *s* one *d*. *Educ:* Finchley Catholic Grammar Sch.; Trinity Coll., Dublin (BA (Hons) History). Following nat. service with Gordon Highlanders in Cyprus, wrote Incident at Echo Six, a TV play, 1959; *BBC TV:* originated: Storyboard, and The Interrogator, 1961; Z Cars, 1962; Diary of a Young Man, 1964; Man Without Papers, 1965; Edge of Darkness, 1985; *Thames TV:* Reilly, Ace of Spies, 1983; *films:* The Italian Job, 1969; Kelly's Heroes, 1970. Jt Screenwriters' Guild Award, 1962; BAFTA Scriptwriter's Award, 1962. *Publication:* Beat on a Damask Drum, 1961. *Recreation:* collecting marine models.

KENNERLEY, Prof. (James) Anthony (Machell), CEng, MIMechE; Chairman, West Surrey and North East Hampshire Health Authority, since 1986; Director, InterMatrix Ltd, Management Consultants, since 1984; Tutor to Senior Management Courses in the Public Sector; *b* 24 Oct. 1933; *s* of William James Kennerley and late Vida May (*née* Machell); *m* 1978, Dorothy Mary (*née* Simpson); one *s* one *d* (twins). *Educ:* Universities of Manchester (BSc; Silver Medallist, 1955) and London (MSc; IMechE James Clayton Fellow). AFIMA, AFRAeS. Engineer, A. V. Roe, Manchester, 1955–58; Aerodynamicist, Pratt & Whitney, Montreal, Canada, 1958–59; Jet Pilot, RCAF, 1959–62; Asst Professor of Mathematics, Univ. of New Brunswick, Canada, 1962–67; Director of Graduate Studies, Manchester Business Sch., 1967–69; Associate Professor of Business Studies, Columbia Univ., New York, 1969–70; Director, Executive Programme, London Business Sch., 1970–73; Prof. of Business Admin, and Dir, Strathclyde Business Sch., 1973–83; Vis. Prof. of Management, Univ. of Surrey, 1984–. Chairman: Management Res. Gp, Scotland, 1981–82; Scottish Milk Marketing Scheme Arbitration Panel, 1981–83; Council for Professions Supplementary to Medicine, 1990–. Member: South of Scotland Electricity Bd, 1977–84; Management Studies Bd, CNAA, 1977–84; BIM Educn Cttee, 1982–; Chm., Conf. of Univ. Management Schs, 1981–83; Director: Business Graduates Assoc., 1983–86; First Step Housing Co., Waverley BC, 1990–. Arbitrator, ACAS, 1976–. Mem., Trans-Turkey Highway World Bank Mission, 1982–83. Founder Mem., Bridgegate Trust, Glasgow, 1982–85. *Publications:* Guide to Business Schools, 1985; articles, papers on business studies, on Public Sector management, and on applied mathematics. *Recreations:* flying, travelling. *Address:* Abbey House, 282–292 Farnborough Road, Farnborough, Hants GU14 7NE. *T:* Farnborough (0252) 548881; 5 Old Rectory Gardens, Busbridge, Godalming, Surrey GU7 1XB. *T:* Godalming (0483) 428108. *Clubs:* Reform, Caledonian.

KENNET, 2nd Baron *cr* 1935; **Wayland Hilton Young;** author and politician; *b* 2 Aug. 1923; *s* of 1st Baron Kennet, PC, GBE, DSO, DSC, and of Kathleen Bruce (who *m* 1st, Captain Robert Falcon Scott, CVO, RN, and died 1947); *S* father 1960; *m* 1948, Elizabeth

Ann, *d* of late Captain Bryan Fullerton Adams, DSO, RN; one *s* five *d*. *Educ:* Stowe; Trinity Coll., Cambridge. Served in RN, 1942–45. Foreign Office, 1946–47, and 1949–51. Deleg., Parliamentary Assemblies, WEU and Council of Europe, 1962–65; Parly Sec., Min. of Housing and Local Govt, 1966–70; Opposition Spokesman on Foreign Affairs and Science Policy, 1971–74; SDP Chief Whip in H of L, 1981–83; SDP spokesman in H of L on foreign affairs and defence, 1981–90. Chairman: Adv. Cttee on Oil Pollution of the Sea, 1970–74; CPRE, 1971–72; Internat. Parly Confs on the Environment, 1972–78; Dir, Europe Plus Thirty, 1974–75; Mem., European Parlt, 1978–79. Hon. FRIBA 1970. Editor of Disarmament and Arms Control, 1962–65. *Publications:* (as Wayland Young): The Italian Left, 1949; The Deadweight, 1952; Now or Never, 1953; Old London Churches (with Elizabeth Young), 1956; The Montesi Scandal, 1957; Still Alive Tomorrow, 1958; Strategy for Survival, 1959; The Profumo Affair, 1963; Eros Denied, 1965; Thirty-Four Articles, 1965; (ed) Existing Mechanisms of Arms Control, 1965; (as Wayland Kennet) Preservation, 1972; The Futures of Europe, 1976; The Rebirth of Britain, 1982; (with Elizabeth Young) London's Churches, 1986; Northern Lazio, 1990; Fabian and SDP pamphlets on defence, disarmament, environment, multinational companies, etc. *Heir: s* Hon. William Aldus Thoby Young [*b* 24 May 1957; *m* 1987, Hon. Josephine, *yr d* of Baron Keyes, *qv*; one *d*]. *Address:* House of Lords, SW1A 0PW.

KENNETT, Ronald John, FRAeS; Director, Royal Aeronautical Society, since 1988; *b* 25 March 1935; *s* of William John and Phyllis Gertrude Kennett; *m* 1957, Sylvia Barstow; one *s* three *d*. *Educ:* Bradford Technical College. Lucas Aerospace: joined 1956; Chief Engineer, 1978–86; Quality Assurance Manager, 1986–88. FBIM. *Recreations:* reading, music, country recreation. *Address:* Royal Aeronautical Society, 4 Hamilton Place, W1V 0BQ. *T:* 071–499 3515. *Club:* Over-Seas League.

KENNETT BROWN, David, JP; a Metropolitan Stipendiary Magistrate, since 1982; a Chairman, Inner London Juvenile Panel, since 1983; a Recorder, since 1989; *b* 29 Jan. 1938; *s* of late Thomas Kennett Brown, solicitor, and of Vanda Brown; *m* 1966, Wendy Margaret Evans; one *s* two *d*. *Educ:* Monkton Combe Sch.; Lincoln Coll., Oxford. FCIArb 1982. Admitted Solicitor, 1965. Partner, Kennett Brown & Co., 1965–82. Chm., London Rent Assessment Panel, 1979–82; Pres., Central and S Mddx Law Soc., 1982. Churchwarden, St John's Church, W Ealing, 1972–86. JP Willesden, 1975–82. *Recreations:* walking, gardening. *Address:* c/o Inner London Magistrates' Courts Service, Bush House, NW Wing, Aldwych, WC2B 4PJ.

KENNEY, Anthony, FRCS; FRCOG; Consultant Obstetrician and Gynaecologist, St Thomas' Hospital, since 1980; *b* 17 Jan. 1942; *s* of Eric Alfred Allen Kenney and Doris Winifred Kenney; *m* 1973, Patricia Clare Newbery; four *s* one *d*. *Educ:* Brentwood School; Gonville and Caius College, Cambridge (MA 1967); London Hosp. Med. Coll. MB BChir 1966; FRCS 1970; MRCOG 1972, FRCOG 1987. House appts, London Hosp., Queen Charlotte's Hosp. and Chelsea Hosp. for Women, 1966–72; Registrar and Sen. Registrar, Westminster and Kingston Hosps, 1972–79. Examiner in Obstetrics and Gynaecology: Univs of London, Liverpool and Cambridge; RCOG. *Publications:* contribs to med. jls. *Recreations:* canal cruising, foreign travel. *Address:* 92 Coombe Lane West, Kingston upon Thames, Surrey KT2 7DB. *T:* 081–942 0440. *Clubs:* Royal Society of Medicine, Medical Society of London.

KENNEY, Prof. Edward John, FBA 1968; Kennedy Professor of Latin, University of Cambridge, 1974–82; Fellow of Peterhouse, Cambridge, 1953–91; *b* 29 Feb. 1924; *s* of George Kenney and Emmie Carlina Elfrida Schwenke; *m* 1955, Gwyneth Anne, *d* of late Henry Albert Harris. *Educ:* Christ's Hospital; Trinity Coll., Cambridge. BA 1949, MA 1953. Served War of 1939–45: Royal Signals, UK and India, 1943–46; commissioned 1944, Lieut 1945. Porson Schol., 1948; Craven Schol., 1949; Craven Student, 1949; Chancellor's Medallist, 1950. Asst Lectr, Univ. of Leeds, 1951–52; University of Cambridge: Research Fellow, Trinity Coll., 1952–53; Asst Lectr, 1955–60, Lectr, 1966–70; Reader in Latin Literature and Textual Criticism, 1970–74; Peterhouse: Director of Studies in Classics, 1953–74; Librarian, 1953–82, Perne Librarian, 1987–91; Tutor, 1956–62; Senior Tutor, 1962–65; Domestic Bursar, 1987–88. Jt Editor, Classical Quarterly, 1959–65. James C. Loeb Fellow in Classical Philology, Harvard Univ., 1967–68; Sather Prof. of Classical Literature, Univ. of California, Berkeley, 1968; Carl Newell Jackson Lectr, Harvard Univ., 1980. President: Jt Assoc. of Classical Teachers, 1977–79; Classical Assoc., 1982–83. For. Mem., Royal Netherlands Acad. of Arts and Scis, 1976. Treasurer and Chm., Council of Almoners, Christ's Hosp., 1984–86. *Publications:* P. Ouidi Nasonis Amores etc (ed), 1961; (with Mrs P. E. Easterling) Ovidiana Graeca (ed), 1965; (with W. V. Clausen, F. R. D. Goodyear, J. A. Richmond) Appendix Vergiliana (ed), 1966; Lucretius, De Rerum Natura III (ed), 1971; The Classical Text, 1974; (with W. V. Clausen) Latin Literature (ed and contrib.) (Cambridge History of Classical Literature II), 1982; The Ploughman's Lunch (*Moretum*), 1984; introd. and notes to Ovid, Metamorphoses, trans. A. D. Melville, 1986; Ovid, The Love Poems, 1990; Apuleius, Cupid & Psyche (ed), 1990; articles and reviews in classical jls. *Recreations:* cats and books. *Address:* Peterhouse, Cambridge CB2 1RD.

KENNEY, (William) John; United States lawyer; Partner, Squire, Sanders & Dempsey; *b* Oklahoma, 16 June 1904; *s* of Franklin R. Kenney and Nelle Kenney (*née* Torrence); *m* 1931, Elinor Craig; two *s* two *d*. *Educ:* Lawrenceville Sch., New Jersey; Stanford Univ (AB); Harvard Law Sch. (LLB). Practised law in San Francisco, 1929–36; Head of oil and gas unit, Securities and Exchange Commission, 1936–38; practised law in Los Angeles, 1938–41; Special Asst to Under-Sec. of the Navy; Chm. Navy Price Adjustment Board, General Counsel, 1941–46; Asst Sec. of the Navy, 1946–47; Under-Sec. of the Navy, 1947–49; Minister in charge of Economic Cooperation Administration Mission to the UK, 1949–50; Deputy Dir for Mutual Security, resigned 1952. Chairman: Democratic Central Cttee of DC, 1960–64; DC Chapter, American Red Cross, 1968–71. Director: Riggs National Bank, 1959–81; Merchants Fund Inc., 1954–; Porter International, 1953–; Trustee, George C. Marshall Foundn, Lexington, Va, 1963–. *Address:* 2700 Calvert Street, NW, Washington, DC 20008; (office) 1201 Pennsylvania Avenue, NW, Washington, DC 20004, USA. *Clubs:* California (Los Angeles); Alibi, Metropolitan, Chevy Chase (Washington).

KENNY, Dr Anthony John Patrick, FBA 1974; Warden, Rhodes House, since 1989; Professorial Fellow, St John's College, Oxford, since 1988; Master of Balliol College, Oxford, 1978–89 (Fellow, 1964–78; Senior Tutor, 1971–72 and 1976–78); President, British Academy, since 1989; *b* Liverpool, 16 March 1931; *s* of John Kenny and Margaret Jones; *m* 1966, Nancy Caroline, *d* of Henry T. Gayley, Jr, Swarthmore, Pa; two *s*. *Educ:* Gregorian Univ., Rome (STL); St Benet's Hall, Oxford; DPhil 1961, DLitt 1980. Ordained priest, Rome, 1955; Curate in Liverpool, 1959–63; returned to lay state, 1963. Asst Lectr, Univ. of Liverpool, 1961–63; University of Oxford: Lectr in Philosophy, Exeter and Trinity Colls, 1963–64; University Lectr, 1965–78; Wilde Lectr in Natural and Comparative Religion, 1969–72; Speaker's Lectureship in Biblical Studies, 1980–83; Mem., Hebdomadal Council, 1981–; Pro-Vice-Chancellor, 1984–87; Vice-Chm., Libraries Bd, 1985–88; Curator, Bodleian Library, 1985–88; Deleg., and Mem., Finance Cttee, OUP, 1986–. Jt Gifford Lectr, Univ. of Edinburgh, 1972–73; Stanton Lectr, Univ. of Cambridge, 1980–83; Bampton Lectr, Columbia Univ., 1983. Visiting Professor: Univs of Chicago, Washington, Michigan, Minnesota and Cornell, Stanford and Rockefeller Univs. Mem. Council, British Acad., 1985–88 (Vice-Pres., 1986–88). Chairman: Soc. for Protection of Science and Learning, 1989–; British Nat. Corpus Adv. Bd, 1990–; British Irish Assoc., 1990–. Hon. DLitt: Bristol, 1982; Liverpool, 1988; Glasgow, 1990; Hon. DHumLitt: Denison Univ., Ohio, 1986; Lafayette Univ., Penn, 1990; Hon. DCL Oxon, 1987. Editor, The Oxford Magazine, 1972–73. *Publications:* Action, Emotion and Will, 1963; Responsa Alumnorum of English College, Rome, 2 vols, 1963; Descartes, 1968; The Five Ways, 1969; Wittgenstein, 1973; The Anatomy of the Soul, 1974; Will, Freedom and Power, 1975; The Aristotelian Ethics, 1978; Freewill and Responsibility, 1978; Aristotle's Theory of the Will, 1979; The God of the Philosophers, 1979; Aquinas, 1980; The Computation of Style, 1982; Faith and Reason, 1983; Thomas More, 1983; The Legacy of Wittgenstein, 1984; A Path from Rome (autobiog.), 1985; Wyclif, 1985; The Logic of Deterrence, 1985; The Ivory Tower, 1985; A Stylometric Study of the New Testament, 1986; The Road to Hillsborough, 1987; Reason and Religion, 1987; The Heritage of Wisdom, 1987; God and Two Poets, 1988; The Metaphysics of Mind, 1989; The Oxford Diaries of Arthur Hugh Clough, 1990; Mountains: an anthology, 1991. *Address:* Rhodes House, Oxford OX1 3RG. *Clubs:* Athenæum, United Oxford & Cambridge University.

KENNY, Anthony Marriott; His Honour Judge Kenny; a Circuit Judge, since 1987; Principal Judge in Civil Matters for Berkshire and Buckinghamshire; designated Family Judge, Reading; *b* 24 May 1939; *o s* of late Noel Edgar Edward Marriott Kenny, OBE, and Cynthia Margaret Seton Kenny (*née* Melville); *m* 1969, Monica Grant Mackenzie, *yr d* of late H. B. Grant Mackenzie, Pretoria; three *s*. *Educ:* St Andrew's Coll., Grahamstown, Cape Province; Christ's Coll., Cambridge (MA). Called to the Bar, Gray's Inn, 1963; South Eastern Circuit. A Recorder, 1980–87. Governor, Scaitcliffe Sch., 1988–. *Recreations:* music, reading, tennis, skiing. *Address:* Melbury Place, Wentworth, Surrey GU25 4LB.

KENNY, Arthur William, CBE 1977; CChem, FRSC; Director in the Directorate General of Environmental Protection of the Department of the Environment, 1974–79; *b* 31 May 1918; *s* of Ernest James Kenny and Gladys Margaret Kenny; *m* 1947, Olive Edna West; one *s* two *d*. *Educ:* Canton High Sch., Cardiff; Jesus Coll., Oxford (schol.). BA (1st Cl. Hons Natural Sci.), MA, BSc, Oxon. Min. of Supply, 1941; Min. of Health, 1950; Min. of Housing and Local Govt, 1951; DoE, 1971. *Publications:* papers on disposal of radioactive and toxic wastes and on quality of drinking water. *Address:* 134 Manor Green Road, Epsom, Surrey KT19 8LL. *T:* Epsom (0372) 724850.

KENNY, Gen. Sir Brian (Leslie Graham), GCB 1991 (KCB 1985); CBE 1979; Deputy Supreme Allied Commander, Europe, since 1990; *b* 18 June 1934; *s* of late Brig. James Wolfenden Kenny, CBE, and of Aileen Anne Georgina Kenny (*née* Swan); *m* 1958, Diana Catherine Jane Mathew; two *s*. *Educ:* Canford School. Commissioned into 4th Hussars (later Queen's Royal Irish Hussars), 1954; served BAOR, Aden, Malaya and Borneo; Pilot's course, 1961; Comd 16 Recce Flt QRIH; psc 1965; MA/VCGS, MoD, 1966–68; Instructor, Staff Coll., 1971–73; CO QRIH, BAOR and UN Cyprus, 1974–76; Col GS 4 Armd Div., 1977–78; Comd 12 Armd Bde (Task Force D), 1979–80; RCDS 1981; Comdr 1st Armoured Div., 1982–83; Dir, Army Staff Duties, MoD, 1983–85; Comdr 1st (British) Corps, BAOR, 1985–87; Comdr, Northern Army Gp, and C-in-C, BAOR, 1987–89. Col QRIH, 1985; Colonel Commandant: RAVC, 1983–; RAC, 1988–. Governor, Canford Sch., 1983–. *Recreations:* ski-ing, cricket, shooting, racing, moving house. *Address:* c/o Lloyds Bank plc, Camberley, Surrey. *Clubs:* Cavalry and Guards, MCC, I Zingari, Free Foresters.

KENNY, David John, CBE 1991; Regional General Manager, North West Thames Regional Health Authority, 1984–91 (Regional Administrator, 1982–84); *b* 2 Dec. 1940; *s* of late Gerald Henry Kenny and Ellen Veronica (*née* Crosse); *m* 1964, Elisabeth Ann, *d* of late Robert and of Jean Ferris; three *s*. *Educ:* Royal Belfast Academical Instn; Queen's Univ., Belfast (LLB). FHSM. Dep. House Governor, Bd of Governors, London Hosp., 1972; Dist Administrator, Tower Hamlets Health Dist, 1974; Area Administrator, Kensington and Chelsea and Westminster AHA, 1978. Mem. Nat. Council, Inst. of Health Service Managers, 1975–86 and 1988– (Pres. 1981–82); Chm., Gen. Managers of RHAs, 1989–. Chm., Data Protection Working Gp, Internat. Med. Informatics Assoc., 1979–87. *Publications:* (jtly) Data Protection in Health Information Systems, 1980; articles on management topics, data protection and ethics. *Recreations:* cinema, theatre, athletics, rugby football. *Address:* 131 Maze Hill, SE3 7UB. *T:* 081–858 1545. *Club:* Athenæum.

KENNY, Douglas Timothy, MA, PhD; psychologist, educator; President and Vice Chancellor, University of British Columbia, 1975–83, President Emeritus, since 1989; *b* Victoria, BC, 20 Oct. 1923; *s* of John Ernest Kenny and Margaret Julia (*née* Collins); *m* 1st, 1950, Lucille Rabowski (decd); one *s* one *d*; 2nd, 1976, Margaret Lindsay Little. *Educ:* Victoria Coll.; Univ. of British Columbia (BA 1945, MA 1947); Univ. of Washington (PhD 1952). University of British Columbia: Lectr, 1950–54; Asst Prof., 1954–57; Associate Prof., 1957–64; Prof., 1965; Pres., Faculty Assoc., 1961–62; Head, Dept of Psychology, 1965–69; Acting Dean, Faculty of Arts, 1969–70, Dean, 1970–75; Hon. Pres., Alumni Assoc., 1975–83. Vis. Associate Prof., Harvard Univ., 1963–65. Member: Internat. Assoc. of Univ. Presidents, 1975–83; Social Science and Humanities Res. Council, 1978–83; BC Res. Council, 1975–; Canada Council, 1975–78; Monterey Inst. of Internat. Studies, 1980–83; Discovery Foundn, BC, 1979–83; Amer. Psychol Assoc.; Bd of Trustees, Vancouver Gen. Hosp., 1976–78; Bd of Governors, Arts, Sciences and Technol. Centre, Vancouver, 1980 (Founder Mem.); President: BC Psychol Assoc., 1951–52; Vancouver Inst., 1973–75 (Hon. Pres., 1975–83). Hon. Patron, Internat. Foundn of Learning, 1983–. Hon. LLD Univ. of BC, 1983. Park O. Davidson Meml Award for outstanding contribn to develt of psychol., 1984. Silver Jubilee Medal, 1977. *Publications:* articles in professional jls. *Address:* 4810 Crown Crescent, Vancouver, BC V6R 2A9, Canada; (office) 2136 West Mall, Vancouver, BC V6T 1Y7. *Clubs:* Vancouver, University, Faculty (Vancouver).

KENNY, Michael, RA 1986 (ARA 1976); Sculptor; Director of Fine Art Studies (formerly Head of Fine Art), Goldsmiths' College, University of London, 1983–88; *b* 10 June 1941; *s* of James Kenny and Helen (*née* Gordon); *m*; one *s* one *d* and one step *d*; *m* Angela Kenny (*née* Smith); two step *s* one step *d*. *Educ:* St Francis Xavier's Coll., Liverpool; Liverpool Coll. of Art; Slade Sch. of Fine Art (DFA London). Works in public collections of: Arts Council; V&A; British Council; British Museum; Borough of Camden; Contemporary Arts Soc.; Tate Gall.; Leicestershire Education Cttee; North West Arts Assoc.; Wilhelm Lehmbruck Museum, Duisburg; Staatsgalerie, Stuttgart; Unilever Collection, London; Hara Mus. of Contemporary Tokyo; Leeds City Art Gall.; public works sited at: Lumsden, Aberdeenshire; Addenbrooke's Hosp., Cambridge; Le Parc de la Courneuve, St Denis, Paris; Yokohama Business Park, Yokohama; works in private collections in England, Europe, Japan and America. Numerous one-man and mixed exhibitions in GB, Europe, S America, Canada, Japan, Australia and USA. Chairman, Faculty of Sculpture, British School at Rome, 1982–; Mem., Cathedrals Adv. Commn, 1988–. *Relevant publications:* Contemporary Artists, 1977, 3rd edn 1989; Contemporary British Artists, 1979; British Art in 20th Century, 1991; exhibition catalogues. *Recreation:* ornithology.

Address: c/o Annely Juda Fine Art, 23 Dering Street, W1R 9AA. *Clubs:* Chelsea Arts, Arts.

KENSINGTON, 8th Baron *cr* 1776 (Ire.); **Hugh Ivor Edwardes;** Baron Kensington (UK) 1886; *b* 24 Nov. 1933; *s* of Hon. Hugh Owen Edwardes (*d* 1937) (2nd *s* of 6th Baron) and of Angela Dorothea (who *m* 1951, Lt Comdr John Hamilton, RN retd), *d* of late Lt-Col Eustace Shearman, 10th Hussars; *S* uncle, 1981; *m* 1961, Juliet Elizabeth Massy Anderson; two *s* one *d. Educ:* Eton. *Heir: s* Hon. William Owen Alexander Edwardes, *b* 21 July 1964. *Address:* Friar Tuck, PO Box 549, Mooi River, Natal, 3300, Republic of S Africa. *Clubs:* Boodle's; Durban (Durban).

KENSINGTON, Area Bishop of, since 1987; **Rt. Rev. John George Hughes;** *b* 1935; *m* 1963, Maureen Harrison; two *s. Educ:* Queens' Coll., Cambridge (BA 1956, MA 1961); Cuddesdon Theological Coll.; Leeds Univ. (PhD 1980). Deacon 1960, priest 1961; Curate, St Martin's, Brighouse, 1960–63; Priest-in-charge, St James's, Brighouse, 1961–65; Vicar of St John's, Clifton, 1963–70; Selection Secretary, ACCM, 1970–73, Senior Selection Sec., 1973–76; Warden, St Michael's Coll., Llandaff, 1976–87; Dean of Faculty of Theology, University Coll., Cardiff, 1984–87; Hon. Canon, Llandaff Cathedral, 1980–87. Member, Governing Body 1977, and Doctrinal Commn 1980, Church in Wales. *Recreations:* music, cricket, walking, gardening, international cuisine. *Address:* 19 Campden Hill Square, W8 7JY.

KENSWOOD, 2nd Baron, *cr* 1951; **John Michael Howard Whitfield;** *b* 6 April 1930; *o s* of 1st Baron Kenswood; *S* father, 1963; *m* 1951, Deirdre Anna Louise, *d* of Colin Malcolm Methven, Errol, Perthshire; four *s* one *d. Educ:* Trinity Coll. Sch., Ontario; Harrow; Grenoble Univ.; Emmanuel Coll., Cambridge (BA). *Heir: s* Hon. Michael Christopher Whitfield, *b* 3 July 1955. *Address:* Domaine de la Forêt, 31340 Villemur sur Tarn, France. *T:* (61) 09 22 90.

KENT, Arthur William, CMG 1966; OBE 1950; Chairman, United Transport Overseas Ltd, 1980–82 (Deputy Chairman, 1978–80, Joint Managing Director, 1977–80); Managing Director, United Transport Co., 1980–82; *b* 22 March 1913; *s* of Howard and Eliza Kent; *m* 1st, 1944, Doris Jane (*née* Crowe; marr. diss., 1958); one *s* one *d;* 2nd, 1958, Mary (*née* Martin). Deputy City Treasurer, Nairobi, 1946–48, City Treasurer, 1948–65. Chief Executive: United Transport Overseas Ltd, Nairobi, 1966–69; Transport Holdings of Zambia Ltd, 1969–71; Chief Exec., United Transport Holdings (Pty) Ltd, Johannesburg, 1971–76; Dir of a number of cos owned by United Transport Overseas Ltd and other BET cos. IPFA; FCA; FCIT. *Address:* Muthaiga, Beechwood Road, Combe Down, Bath, Avon BA2 5JS. *T:* Bath (0225) 834940.

KENT, Bruce; campaigner for nuclear disarmament; Chairman, Campaign for Nuclear Disarmament, 1987–90 (General Secretary, 1980–85; Vice-Chairman, 1985–87; Hon. Vice President, 1985); *b* 22 June 1929; *s* of Kenneth Kent and Rosemary Kent (*née* Marion); *m* 1988, Valerie Flessati. *Educ:* Lower Canada Coll., Montreal; Stonyhurst Coll.; Brasenose Coll., Univ. of Oxford. LLB. Ordination, Westminster, 1958; Curate, Kensington, North and South, 1958–63; Sec., Archbishop's House, Westminster, 1963–64; Chm., Diocesan Schools Commn, 1964–66; Catholic Chaplain to Univ. of London, 1966–74; Chaplain, Pax Christi, 1974–77; Parish Priest, Somers Town, NW1, 1977–80; resigned Ministry, Feb. 1987. Pres., Internat. Peace Bureau, 1985–. Prospective Parly Candidate (Lab), Oxford West and Abingdon, 1990–. Hon LLD Manchester, 1987. *Publications:* essays and pamphlets on disarmament, Christians and peace. *Recreations:* friends, walking. *Address:* 11 Venetia Road, N4 1EJ.

KENT, Geoffrey Charles; Director, since 1988, and Chairman, since 1989, Mansfield Brewery plc (Deputy Chairman, 1988–89); Director, 1975–86, Chairman and Chief Executive, 1981–86, Imperial Group plc; *b* 2 Feb. 1922; *s* of late Percival Whitehead and Madge Kent; *m* 1955, Brenda Georgine Conisbee. *Educ:* Blackpool Grammar Sch. CBIM 1976; FCIM (FInstM 1977). Served RAF, 1939–46; Flt Lieut Coastal Comd. Advertising and marketing appts with Colman, Prentis & Varley, Mentor, and Johnson & Johnson, 1947–58; John Player & Son: Advertising Manager, 1958; Marketing Dir, 1964; Asst Man. Dir, 1969; Chm. and Man. Dir, 1975; Chm. and Chief Exec., Courage Ltd, 1978–81; Dep. Chm. and Dir, Corah plc, 1986–89. Director: Lloyds Bank plc, 1981–; Lloyds Bank International, 1983–85; Lloyds Merchant Bank Holdings Ltd, 1985–88; John Howitt Group Ltd, 1986–; Brewers' Soc., 1978–86, 1989–. Mem., Lloyd's of London, 1985–. *Recreations:* flying, ski-ing. *Address:* Hill House, Gonalston, Nottingham NG14 7JA.

KENT, Sir Harold Simcox, GCB 1963 (KCB 1954; CB 1946); QC 1973; Commissary to Dean and Chapter of St Paul's Cathedral, since 1976; *b* 11 Nov. 1903; *s* of late P. H. B. Kent, OBE, MC; *m* 1930, Zillah Lloyd (*d* 1987); one *s* (one *d* decd). *Educ:* Rugby School; Merton Coll., Oxford. Barrister-at-law, 1928; Parliamentary Counsel to the Treasury, 1940–53; HM Procurator-General and Treasury Solicitor, 1953–63; Solicitor to Vassall Tribunal, 1963; Mem., Security Commn, 1965–71; Standing Counsel to Church Assembly and General Synod, 1964–72; Vicar-General of the Province of Canterbury, 1971–76; Dean of the Arches Court of Canterbury and Auditor of the Chancery Court of York, 1972–76. Mem., Departmental Cttee to examine operation of Section 2 of Official Secrets Act, 1911, 1971–72. DCL Lambeth, 1977. *Publication:* In On the Act, 1979. *Address:* Alderley, Calf Lane, Chipping Campden, Glos GL55 6UQ. *T:* Evesham (0386) 840421. *Club:* United Oxford & Cambridge University.

KENT, John Philip Cozens, PhD; FSA; FMA; FBA 1986; Keeper, Department of Coins and Medals, British Museum, 1983–90; *b* 28 Sept. 1928; *s* of late John Cozens Kent, DCM and Lucy Ella Kent; *m* 1961, Patricia Eleanor Bunford; one *s* one *d. Educ:* Minchenden County Grammar Sch.; University Coll. London (BA 1949; PhD 1951). FSA 1961; FMA 1988. Nat. Service, 1951–53. Asst Keeper, 1953, Dep. Keeper, 1974, Dept of Coins and Medals, BM. President: British Assoc. of Numismatic Socs, 1974–78; Royal Numismatic Soc., 1984–89; London and Middlesex Archaeological Soc., 1985–88. Member: Instituto de Sintra, 1986; Internat. Numismatic Commn, 1986–91. Medallist, RNS, 1990. *Publications:* (jtly) Late Roman Bronze Coinage, 1960; (with K. S. Painter) Wealth of the Roman World, 1977; Roman Coins, 1978; 2000 Years of British Coins and Medals, 1978 (Lhotka Meml Prize, RNS); Roman Imperial Coinage, vol. VIII: the family of Constantine I 337–364, 1981; A Selection of Byzantine Coins in the Barber Institute of Fine Arts, 1985; (ed with M. R. Mays) Catalogue of the Celtic Coins in the British Museum, vol. I, 1987, vol. II, 1990; contribs to Festschriften, congress procs, and Numismatic Chronicle, British Numismatic Jl etc. *Recreations:* local history and archaeology, early (mediaeval) music, railway history and model railways, monumental brasses. *Address:* 16 Newmans Way, Hadley Wood, Barnet, Herts EN4 0LR. *T:* 081–449 8072.

KENT, Paul Welberry, DSc; FRSC; JP; Student Emeritus of Christ Church, Oxford; *b* Doncaster, 19 April 1923; *s* of Thomas William Kent and Marion (*née* Cox); *m* 1952, Rosemary Elizabeth Boutflower, *y d* of Major C. H. B. Shepherd, MC; three *s* one *d. Educ:* Doncaster Grammar Sch.; Birmingham Univ. (BSc 1944, PhD 1947); Jesus Coll., Oxford (MA 1951, DPhil 1953, DSc 1966). Asst Lectr, subseq. ICI Fellow, Birmingham Univ.,

1946–50; Vis. Fellow, Princeton Univ., 1948–49; Univ. Demonstrator in Biochem., Oxford, 1950–72; Lectr, subseq. Student, Tutor and Dr Lees Reader in Chem., Christ Church, 1955–72; Master of Van Mildert Coll. and Dir, Glycoprotein Res. Unit, Durham Univ., 1972–82. Research Assoc., Harvard, 1967; Vis. Prof., Windsor Univ., Ont, 1971, 1980. Bodleian Orator, 1959. Mem., Oxford City Council, 1964–72; Governor: Oxford Coll. of Technology, subseq. Oxford Polytechnic, 1964–72, 1983–89 (Vice-Chm. 1966–69, Chm. 1969–70); Oxford Polytechnic Higher Educn Corp., 1988– (Dep. Chm., 1988–). Member: Cttee, Biochemical Soc., 1963–67; Chemical Council, 1965–70; Res. Adv. Cttee, Cystic Fibrosis Res. Trust, 1977–82; Commn on Religious Educn in School. Sec., Foster and Wills Scholarships Bd, 1960–72; Pres., Soc. for Maintenance of the Faith, 1974–; Governor, Pusey House, 1983–. JP Oxford, 1972. Hon. DLitt Drury Coll., 1973. Hon. Fellow, Canterbury Coll., Ont, 1976. Rolleston Prize, 1952; Medal of Société de Chemie Biologique, 1969; Verdienstkreuz (Bundesrepublik), 1970. *Publications:* Biochemistry of Amino-sugars, 1955; (ed) Membrane-Mediated Information, Vols I and II, 1972; (ed) International Aspects of the Provision of Medical Care, 1976; (ed) New Approaches to Genetics, 1978; (ed with W. B. Fisher) Resources, Environment and the Future, 1982; articles in sci. and other jls. *Recreations:* music, travel. *Address:* 18 Arnolds Way, Cumnor Hill, Oxford OX2 9JB. *T:* Oxford (0865) 862087; Briscoe Gate, Cotherstone, Barnard Castle, Co. Durham. *Club:* Athenæum.

KENT, Pendarell Hugh; Associate Director, Finance and Industry, Bank of England, since 1988; *b* 18 Aug. 1937; *s* of Hugh and Ann Kent; *m* 1960, Jill George; one *s* one *d. Educ:* University College Sch.; Jesus Coll., Oxford (MA Hons). Served Intelligence Corps, 2nd Lieut, 1959–61. Bank of England, 1961–: UK Alternate Exec. Dir, IMF, 1976–79; Head: of Inf. Div., 1984–85; of Internat. Div. (Internat. Financial Instns and Developing Countries), 1985–88. Dir (non-exec.), BR Southern Region, 1986– (Chm., 1989–). *Publication:* Nursery Schools for All (with Jill Kent), 1970. *Recreations:* art, jazz, ski-ing. *Address:* c/o Bank of England, Threadneedle Street, EC2R 8AH. *T:* 071–601 4221.

KENT, Ronald Clive, CB 1965; Deputy Under-Secretary of State, MoD, 1967–76; *b* 3 Aug. 1916; *s* of Dr Hugh Braund Kent and Margaret Mary Kent; *m* 1965, Mary Moyles Havell; one step-*s* one step-*d. Educ:* Rugby Sch.; Brasenose Coll., Oxford. Air Ministry, 1939; Royal Artillery, 1940–45; Air Ministry, 1945–58; Asst Under-Sec. of State, Air Min., 1958–63, MoD, 1963–67. Dir (Admin), ICE, 1976–79, Consultant and Council Sec., 1980–85. *Address:* 21 Heathside Court, Tadworth Street, Tadworth, Surrey KT20 5RY.

KENT, Brig. Sidney Harcourt, OBE 1944; Racing consultant, Macau Jockey Club, since 1991 (Director of Racing, 1989–91); *b* 22 April 1915; *s* of Major Geoffrey Harcourt Kent, Hindhead; *m* 1945, Nina Ruth, *d* of Gen. Sir Geoffry Scoones, KCB, KBE, CSI, DSO, MC; one *s* one *d. Educ:* Wellington Coll.; RMC Sandhurst. 2nd Lieut KOYLI 1935; Lt-Col 1944; Brig. 1944; GSO1 Eighth Army, 1944; BGS Allied Land Forces, SE Asia, 1944. Comd 128 Inf. Bde (TA), 1960–63. Manager and Sec., Turf Board, 1965; Gen. Manager, 1969, Chief Executive, 1973–76, The Jockey Club. Racing Adviser, Royal Horse Soc., Iran, 1978; Consultant Steward, Jamaica Racing Commn, 1984–86. *Recreations:* farming, travel. *Address:* The Old Vicarage, Kingsey, Aylesbury, Bucks HP17 8LT. *T:* Haddenham (0844) 291411; Maroni Village, Larnaca District, Cyprus. *T:* 0433–2614.

KENT, Thomas George, CBE 1979; CEng, MIMechE, FRAeS; aerospace and defence consultant; Director: Grosvenor Technology Ltd, since 1984; Third Grosvenor Ltd, since 1987; *b* 13 Aug. 1925. *Educ:* Borden Grammar School; Medway College of Technology. Joined English Electric Co., 1951; Special Director, British Aircraft Corp., 1967; Dep. Managing Director, 1974; Director, Hatfield/Lostock Division and Stevenage/Bristol Div. of Dynamics Group, British Aerospace, 1977–79; Gp Dep. Chief Exec., BAe Dynamics Gp, 1980–85; Bd Mem., BAe, 1981–85; Director: BAe Australia Ltd, 1980–86 (Chm., 1984–86); Arab British Dynamics, 1980–85; BAJ Vickers Ltd, 1982–87 (non.-exec.). *Address:* Copper Lea, Hampton on the Hill, Warwick CV35 8QR.

KENT-JONES, Trevor David, TD; **His Honour Judge Kent-Jones;** a Circuit Judge, since 1991; *b* 31 July 1940; *s* of late David Sandford Kent-Jones and of Madeline Mary Kent-Jones (*née* Russell-Pavier); one *s* one *d. Educ:* Bedford Sch.; Liverpool Univ. (LLB). Called to the Bar, Gray's Inn, 1962; Mem., NE Circuit, 1963, Junior, 1969; a Recorder, 1985–91. Commnd KOYLI TA, 1959; served 4th Bn KOYLI, 5th Bn Light Infantry, HQ NE Dist, 1959–85; Lt-Col 1977. *Recreations:* cricket, travel, fell-walking. *Address:* 6 Beechwood Crescent, Harrogate, N Yorks HG2 0PA. *Club:* Naval and Military.

KENTFIELD, Graham Edward Alfred; Chief of Banking Department and Chief Cashier, Bank of England, since 1991; *b* 3 Sept. 1940; *s* of late E. L. H. Kentfield and F. E. M. Kentfield (*née* Tucker); *m* 1965, Ann Dwelley Hewetson; two *d. Educ:* Bancroft's Sch., Woodford Green, Essex; St Edmund Hall, Oxford (BA 1st cl. Lit.Hum.). Entered Bank of England, 1963; seconded to Dept of Applied Econs, Cambridge, 1966–67; Editor, Bank of England Qly Bull., 1977–80; Adviser: Financial Stats Div., 1980–84; Banking Dept, 1984–85; Dep. Chief of Banking Dept and Dep. Chief Cashier, 1985–91. Hon. Treas., Soc. for Promotion of Roman Studies, 1991–. *Recreations:* Roman history, genealogy, philately. *Address:* Bank of England, Threadneedle Street, EC2R 8AH. *T:* 071–601 4444.

KENTRIDGE, Sydney; QC 1984; a Judge of the Courts of Appeal of Jersey and Guernsey, since 1988; *b* Johannesburg, 5 Nov. 1922; *s* of Morris and May Kentridge; *m* 1952, Felicia Geffen; two *s* two *d. Educ:* King Edward VII Sch., Johannesburg; Univ. of the Witwatersrand (BA); Exeter Coll., Oxford Univ. (MA; Hon. Fellow, 1986). War service with S African forces, 1942–46. Advocate 1949, Senior Counsel 1965, South Africa; called to the English Bar, Lincoln's Inn, 1977, Bencher, 1986. Mem., Ct of Appeal, Botswana, 1981–. Roberts Lectr, Univ. of Pennsylvania, 1979. Hon. LLD: Seton Hall Univ., NJ, 1978; Leicester, 1985; Cape Town, 1987; Natal, 1989. Granville Clark Prize, USA, 1978. *Recreation:* opera-going. *Address:* Brick Court Chambers, 15–19 Devereux Court, WC2R 3JJ. *T:* 071–583 0777. *Club:* Athenæum.

KENWARD, Michael Ronald John, OBE 1990; science writer; *b* 12 July 1945; *s* of late Ronald Kenward and of Phyllis Kenward; *m* 1969, Elizabeth Rice. *Educ:* Wolverstone Hall; Sussex Univ. Res. scientist, UKAEA, Culham Laboratory, 1966–68; Technical editor, Scientific Instrument Res. Assoc., 1969; various editorial posts, New Scientist, 1969–79, Editor, 1979–90; Science Correspondent, The Sunday Times, 1990. Member: Royal Soc. Cttee on Public Understanding of Science, 1986–90; Public Affairs Cttee, BAAS, 1989–; Bd, Assoc. of British Editors, 1986–90. *Publications:* Potential Energy, 1976; articles on science and technology and energy in particular. *Recreations:* photography, collecting 'middle-aged' books, listening to Requiems and Texas rock-and-roll. *Address:* Grange Cottage, Staplefield, W Sussex RH17 6EL.

KENWORTHY, family name of **Baron Strabolgi.**

KENWORTHY, Cecil; Registrar of Family Division (formerly Probate and Divorce Division), of High Court of Justice, 1968–83; *b* 22 Jan. 1918; *s* of John T. and Lucy Kenworthy; *m* 1944, Beryl Joan Willis; no *c. Educ:* Manchester and Bristol Grammar Schools. Entered Principal Probate Registry, 1936. *Publications:* (co-editor) supplements to Rayden on Divorce, 1967, 1968; (co-editor) Tolstoy on Divorce, 7th edn, 1971. *Address:* Gable Lodge, 2 Zetland Road, Malvern, Worcs WR14 2JJ.

KENWORTHY, Frederick John; Chief Executive, Information Technology Services Agency, Department of Social Security, since 1990; *b* 6 Dec. 1943; *s* of late Rev. Fred Kenworthy and of Mrs Ethel Kenworthy; *m* 1968, Diana Flintham; one *d.* *Educ:* William Hulme's Grammar Sch., Manchester; Manchester Univ. (BA Econ Hons, Politics). Entered Admin. Class, Home Civil Service, as Asst Principal, MoD (Navy), 1966; Treasury Centre for Admin. Studies, 1968–69; joined BSC, Sheffield, 1969; Principal, MoD, 1972; Royal Commn on the Press Secretariat, 1974; Asst Sec., Dir, Weapons Resources and Progs (Naval), MoD, 1979–83; Head of Resources and Progs (Navy) (formerly DS4), RN Size and Shape Policy, MoD, 1983–86; Dir of Ops (Grade 4), Disablement Services Authy (formerly Div.), DHSS, 1986–88; Dir, IT Systems Directorate (Under Sec.), Dept of Social Security, 1989–90. *Recreations:* music, sport, photography. *Address:* c/o Department of Social Security, Richmond House, Whitehall, SW1. *Club:* Lansdown Lawn Tennis and Squash Racquets (Bath).

KENWORTHY, Joan Margaret, BLitt, MA; Principal, St Mary's College, University of Durham, since 1977; *b* Oldham, Lancs, 10 Dec. 1933; *o d* of late Albert Kenworthy and Amy (*née* Cobbold). *Educ:* Girls Grammar Sch., Barrow-in-Furness; St Hilda's Coll., Oxford (BLitt, MA). Henry Oliver Beckit Prize, Oxford, 1955; Leverhulme Overseas Res. Scholar, Makerere Coll., Uganda, and E African Agriculture and Forestry Res. Org., Kenya, 1956–58; Actg Tutor, St Hugh's Coll., Oxford, 1958–59; Tutorial Res. Fellow, Bedford Coll., London, 1959–60; Univ. of Liverpool: Asst Lectr in Geography, 1960–63; Lectr, 1963–73; Sen. Lectr, 1973–77; Warden of Salisbury Hall, 1966–77 and of Morton House, 1974–77. IUC short-term Vis. Lectr, Univ. of Sierra Leone, 1975; Vis. Lectr, Univ. of Fort Hare, Ciskei, 1983. Mem., NE England, Churches Regl Broadcasting Council, 1978–82. Member: Council, African Studies Assoc. of UK, 1969–71; Council, Inst. of Brit. Geographers, 1976–78; Cttee, Merseyside Conf. for Overseas Students Ltd, 1976–77; Council, RMetS, 1980–83; Treasurer, Assoc. of Brit. Climatologists, 1976–79; Northern Chm., Durham Univ. Soc., 1979–82. *Publications:* (contrib.) Geographers and the Tropics, ed R. W. Steel and R. M. Prothero, 1964; (contrib.) Oxford Regional Economic Atlas for Africa, 1965; (contrib.) Studies in East African Geography and Development, ed S. Ominde, 1971; (contrib.) An Advanced Geography of Africa, ed J. I. Clarke, 1975; (contrib.) Rangeland Management and Ecology in East Africa, ed D. J. Pratt and M. D. Gwynne, 1977; (contrib.) The Climatic Scene: essays in honour of Emeritus Prof. Gordon Manley, ed M. J. Tooley and G. Sheail,1985; articles in jls, encycs and reports of symposia. *Address:* 1 Elvet Garth, South Road, Durham DH1 3TP. *T:* Durham (091) 3843865. *Club:* Commonwealth Trust.

KENWORTHY-BROWNE, (Bernard) Peter (Francis); a District Judge (formerly Registrar) of the High Court (Family Division), since 1982; *b* 11 May 1930; *s* of late Bernard Elelyn Kenworthy-Browne and Margaret Sibylla Kenworthy-Browne; *m* 1975, Jane Elizabeth Arthur (marr. diss. 1982); *m* 1989, Elizabeth, *o d* of late Dr J. A. Bowen-Jones. *Educ:* Ampleforth; Oriel Coll., Oxford. MA. 2nd Lieut, Irish Guards, 1949–50. Called to the Bar, Lincoln's Inn, 1955; Oxford, and Midland and Oxford Circuit, 1957–82; a Recorder of the Crown Court, 1981–82. *Recreations:* music, hunting, shooting. *Address:* 30 Dewhurst Road, W14 0ES. *T:* 071–603 9580.

KENYA, Archbishop of, since 1980; **Most Rev. Manasses Kuria;** Bishop of Nairobi, since 1980; *b* 22 July 1929; *s* of John Njoroge Kuria; *m* 1947, Mary Kuria; two *s* four *d.* *Educ:* locally. Teaching, 1944–53; Deacon, 1955; ordained Priest, 1957; Archdeacon of Eldoret, 1965–70; Asst Bishop of Nakuru, 1970–75; Bishop of Nakuru, 1976–79. *Publication:* Uwakili Katika Kristo (Stewardship of Christ), 1969. *Address:* PO Box 40502, Nairobi, Kenya. *T:* 721838/723394/28146.

KENYON, family name of **Baron Kenyon.**

KENYON, 5th Baron, *cr* 1788; **Lloyd Tyrell-Kenyon,** CBE 1972; FSA; DL; Bt 1784; Baron of Gredington, 1788; Captain late Royal Artillery, TA; *b* 13 Sept. 1917; *o s* of 4th Baron and Gwladys Julia (*d* 1965), *d* of late Col H. R. Lloyd Howard, CB; *S* father, 1927; *m* 1946, Leila Mary, *d* of Comdr John Wyndham Cookson, RN, Strand Hill, Winchelsea, and Mary, *d* of Sir Alan Colquhoun, 6th Bt, KCB, JP, DL, and *widow* of Lt Hugh William Jardine Ethelston Peel, Welsh Guards; two *s* one *d* (and one *s* decd). *Educ:* Eton; Magdalene Coll., Cambridge. BA (Cambridge), 1950. 2nd Lt Shropshire Yeo. 1937; Lt RA, TA, retired (ill-health) 1943 with hon. rank of Captain. Dir, Lloyds Bank Plc, 1962–88 (Chm. North West Bd); President: University Coll. of N Wales, Bangor, 1947–82; Nat. Museum of Wales, 1952–57. Trustee, Nat. Portrait Gall., 1953–88, Chm., 1966–88; Chairman: Wrexham Powys and Mawddach Hosp. Management Cttee, 1960–74; Clwyd AHA, 1974–78; Friends of the Nat. Libraries, 1962–85; Flint Agricultural Exec. Cttee, 1964–73. Member: Standing Commn on Museums and Galleries, 1953–60; Welsh Regional Hosp. Bd, 1958–63; Council for Professions Supplementary to Medicine, 1961–65; Royal Commn on Historical MSS, 1966–; Ancient Monuments Bd for Wales, 1979–87; Bd of Governors, Welbeck Coll. Chief Comr for Wales, Boy Scouts' Assoc., 1948–65. DL Co. Flint, 1948; CC Flint, 1946 (Chm., 1954–55). Hon. LLD Wales, 1958. *Heir:* *s* Hon. Lloyd Tyrell-Kenyon, [*b* 13 July 1947; *m* 1971, Sally Carolyn, *e d* of J. F. P. Matthews; two *s*]. *Address:* Cumbers House, Gredington, Whitchurch, Salop SY13 3DH. *TA:* Hanmer 330; *T:* Hanmer (094874) 330. *Clubs:* Brooks's, Cavalry and Guards, Beefsteak.

KENYON, Clifford, CBE 1966; JP; farmer; *b* 11 Aug. 1896; *m* 1922, Doris Muriel Lewis, Herne Hill, London; three *s* two *d.* *Educ:* Brighton Grove Coll., Manchester; Manchester Univ. Joined Labour Party, 1922; Mem. Rawtenstall Council, 1923; Mayor, 1938–42, resigned from Council, 1945. MP (Lab) Chorley Div. of Lancs, 1945–70. JP Lancs, 1941.

KENYON, Sir George (Henry), Kt 1976; DL; JP; LLD; *b* 10 July 1912; *s* of George Henry Kenyon and Edith (*née* Hill); *m* 1938, Christine Dorey (*née* Brentnall); two *s* one *d.* *Educ:* Radley; Manchester Univ. Director: William Kenyon & Sons Ltd, 1942– (Chm., 1961–82); Tootal Ltd, 1971–79 (Chm., 1976–79); Manchester Ship Canal, 1972–86; Williams & Glyn's Bank, 1972–83 (Chm., 1978–83); Royal Bank of Scotland, 1978–83; Chm., Vuman Ltd, 1982–88. Gen. Comr, Inland Revenue, 1957–73. Manchester University: Chm. Bldgs Cttee, 1962–70; Treas., 1970–72, 1980–82; Chm. Council, 1972–80. Hon. Treas., Civic Trust, NW, 1962–78, Vice Pres., 1978; Member: NW Adv. Cttee, Civil Aviation, 1967–72; Manchester Reg. Hosp. Bd, 1962–68; NW Reg. Econ. Planning Council, 1970–73. JP Cheshire, 1959; Chm., S Tameside Bench, 1974–82; DL Chester, 1969, Greater Manchester, 1983. High Sheriff, Cheshire, 1973–74. Hon. LLD Manchester, 1980. *Recreations:* reading, talking, travel. *Address:* Limefield House, Hyde, Cheshire SK14 1DN. *T:* 061–368 2012.

KENYON, Ian Roy; HM Diplomatic Service; Counsellor, United Kingdom Delegation to the Conference on Disarmament, Geneva, since 1988; *b* 13 June 1939; *s* of late S. R. Kenyon and of Mrs E. M. Kenyon; *m* 1962, Griselda Rintoul; one *s* one *d.* *Educ:* Lancaster Royal Grammar School; Edinburgh University. BSc Hons. CEng, MIChemE. Lever Bros, 1962–68; Birds Eye Foods, 1968–74; First Secretary, FCO, 1974–76; Geneva, 1976–78; Head of Chancery, Bogota, 1979–81; FCO, 1982–83; Head of Nuclear Energy Dept, FCO, 1983–85; Overseas Inspectorate, 1986–88. *Recreations:* riding, carriage driving. *Address:* c/o Foreign and Commonwealth Office, SW1A 2AH. *Club:* Travellers'.

KENYON, Prof. John Philipps, FBA 1981; Joyce and Elizabeth Hall Distinguished Professor in Early Modern British History, University of Kansas, since 1987; *b* 18 June 1927; *s* of William Houston Kenyon and Edna Grace Philipps; *m* 1962, Angela Jane Ewert (*née* Venables); one *s* two *d.* *Educ:* King Edward VII Sch., Sheffield; Univ. of Sheffield (BA 1948; Hon. LittD 1980); Christ's Coll., Cambridge (PhD). Fellow of Christ's Coll., Cambridge, 1954–62; Lectr in Hist., Cambridge, 1955–62; G. F. Grant Prof. of History, Univ. of Hull, 1962–81; Prof. of Modern History, Univ. of St Andrews, 1981–87. Visiting Prof., Columbia Univ., New York, 1959–60; Junior Proctor, Cambridge, 1961–62; John U. Nef Lectr, Univ. of Chicago, 1972; Ford's Lectr in English Hist., Oxford, 1975–76; Andrew W. Mellon Fellow, Huntington Library, Calif, 1985. *Publications:* Robert Spencer Earl of Sunderland, 1958; The Stuarts, 1958, 2nd edn 1970; The Stuart Constitution, 1966, 2nd edn 1986; The Popish Plot, 1972; Revolution Principles, 1977; Stuart England, 1978, 2nd edn 1985; The History Men, 1983; The Civil Wars of England, 1988; contribs to various learned jls. *Recreation:* bridge. *Address:* Department of History, University of Kansas, 3001 Wescoe Hall, Lawrence, Kansas 66045–2130, USA. *T:* (913) 864–3569.

KENYON, Nicholas Roger; Chief Music Critic, Observer, since 1987; Editor, Early Music, since 1983; *b* 23 Feb. 1951; *s* of Thomas Kenyon and Kathleen Holmes; *m* 1976, Marie-Ghislaine Latham-Koenig; three *s* one *d.* *Educ:* Balliol College, Oxford (BA Hons 1972). English Bach Festival, 1973–76; BBC Music Div., 1976–79; music critic: The New Yorker, 1979–82; The Times, 1982–85; The Observer, 1985–87; Music Editor, The Listener, 1982–87; broadcaster, BBC Radios 2, 3 and 4, and World Service. Programme Advr, Mozart Now Fest., South Bank Centre, 1991. *Publications:* The BBC Symphony Orchestra 1930–80, 1981; Simon Rattle, 1987; (ed) Authenticity and Early Music, 1988. *Recreation:* family. *Address:* 107 Constantine Road, NW3 2LR. *T:* 071–267 5336.

KEOHANE, Desmond John, OBE 1991; FBIM; consultant in education and training, since 1991; part-time Lecturer in Educational Management, University of Leicester, since 1990; *b* 5 July 1928; *s* of William Patrick Keohane and Mabel Margaret Keohane; *m* 1960, Mary Kelliher; two *s* two *d.* *Educ:* Borden Grammar Sch., Sittingbourne; Univ. of Birmingham (BA and Baxter Prize in History, 1949); London Univ. (Postgrad. Cert. in Educn). FBIM 1981. Postgrad. res., 1949–50; Nat. Service, Educn Officer, RAF, 1950–52; sch. teacher and coll. lectr, 1953–64; Head, Dept of Social and Academic Studies, 1964–68, and Vice-Principal, 1969–71, Havering Technical Coll.; Principal, Northampton Coll. of Further Educn, 1971–76; Principal, Oxford Coll. of Further Educn, 1976–90. Vis. Fellow (Educn), Oxford Polytechnic, 1991–. Member: Council, Southern Regional Council for Further Educn, 1977–90 (Chm., Adv. Cttee for Health and Social Services, 1983–85); Secondary Exams Council, 1983–86; Berks and Oxon Area Manpower Board, 1985–88; Special Employment Measures Adv. Gp, MSC, 1986–89. Formerly governor of various educnl instns; Chm. of Govs, Thomas Becket Sch., Northampton, 1983–. *Recreations:* enjoying family and friends, watching cricket. *Address:* 14 Abington Park Crescent, Northampton NN3 3AD. *T:* Northampton 38829.

See also K. W. Keohane.

KEOHANE, Dr Kevin William, CBE 1976; Rector, Roehampton Institute of Higher Education, 1976–88, Hon. Fellow, 1988; *b* 28 Feb. 1923; *s* of William Patrick and Mabel Margaret Keohane; *m* 1949, Mary Margaret (Patricia) Ashford; one *s* three *d.* *Educ:* Borden Grammar Sch., Sittingbourne, Kent; Univ. of Bristol (BSc; PhD). FInstP. War service, RAF, Radar Br, Flt Lt. Research appts and Lectr in Anatomy, Univ. of Bristol, 1947–59; Chelsea College, London: Reader in Biophysics, 1959; Prof. of Physics and Head of Dept of Physics, 1965; Prof. of Science Educn and Dir, Centre for Science Educn, 1967–76; Vice-Principal, 1966–76. Royal Society Leverhulme Prof., Fed. Univ. of Bahia, Brazil, 1971; Visiting Professor: Chelsea College, 1977–82; KCL, 1989; Vis. Prof. of Science Educn, KCL, 1990–. Member: Academic Adv. Cttee, Open Univ., 1970–81 (Chm., 1978–81); Court, Univ. of Bristol, 1968–76; Court, 1982–, Council, 1988–, Univ. of Surrey; University of London: Member: Academic Council, 1974–76; Extra-Mural Council, 1974–76; School Examinations Council, 1975–76. Dir, Nuffield Foundn Science Projects, 1966–79; Chairman: DES Study Gp on Cert. of Extended Educn, 1978–79; Education Cttee, Commonwealth Inst., 1978–85; Nuffield-Chelsea Curriculum Trust, 1979–; Southwark Archdiocesan Educn Cttee, 1989–; Vice Chm., Internat. Adv. Panel for Provincial Univs in China, 1986–; Member: Nat. Programme Cttee for Computers in Educn, 1974–78; Royal Society/Inst. of Physics Educn Cttee, 1970–73; SSRC Educn Bd, 1971–74; BBC Further Educn Adv. Cttee, 1972–75; TEAC, RAF, 1977–79; Gen. Optical Council, 1979–84; Bd of Educn, Royal Coll. of Nursing, 1980–84; National Adv. Bd for Higher Educn, 1983–; Merton Educn Authy, 1986–; Richmond, Twickenham and Roehampton DHA, 1987–90. Dir, 1972–, and Vice-Chm., 1978–, Taylor & Francis, Scientific Pubns. Manager, Royal Instn, 1972–75. Mem. Delegacy, Goldsmiths' Coll., 1974–76; Chairman of Governors: Garnett Coll., 1974–78; St Francis Xavier VIth Form Coll., 1985–; Governor: Philippa Fawcett and Digby Stuart Colls, 1973–76; Ursuline Convent Sch., Wimbledon, 1967–; Heythrop Coll., Univ. of London, 1977–86; Wimbledon Coll., 1982–; Commonwealth Inst., 1977–85; W London Inst. of Higher Educn, 1990–. Numerous overseas consultancies and visiting professorships; Academic Mem., British Assoc. of Science Writers, 1971–; Editor, Jl of Physics Educn, 1966–69; Mem., Editorial Bd, Jl Curriculum Studies, and Studies in Sci. Educn. DUniv Surrey, 1987. Bragg Medal, Inst. of Physics, 1991. KSG 1983. *Recreations:* Rugby (spectator), railways, bee-keeping. *Address:* 3 Thetford Road, New Malden, Surrey KT3 5DN. *T:* 081–942 6861. *Club:* Athenæum.

See also D. J. Keohane.

KEPA, Sailosi Wai; Attorney-General and Minister for Justice, Fiji, since 1988; *b* 4 Nov. 1938; *m* Adi Teimumu Tuisawau; four *c.* *Educ:* Draiba Fijian Sch.; Lelean Memorial Sch.; Nasinu Training Coll.; Sydney Univ. (Dip. in Teaching of English, 1966). Called to the Bar, Middle Temple, 1972; Barrister and Solicitor, Fiji, 1974. Joined Judicial Dept, as Magistrate, 1969; served Suva, Northern Div., Sigatoka, Nadi; Chief Magistrate, July 1980; Dir of Public Prosecutions, Nov. 1980; High Comr for Fiji in London, 1985–88. Rugby player (rep. Fiji, Australia 1961), coach, manager, administrator; Chm., Fiji Rugby Union, 1983–85; Pres., Suva Rugby Union, 1989–. *Address:* Attorney-General's Chambers, Government Buildings, Suva, Fiji. *T:* 211580.

KEPPEL, family name of **Earl of Albemarle.**

KER; *see* Innes-Ker, family name of Duke of Roxburghe.

KERBY, John Vyvyan; Under Secretary and Principal Establishment Officer, Overseas Development Administration, Foreign and Commonwealth Office, since 1986; *b* 14 Dec. 1942; *s* of Theo Rosser Fred Kerby and Constance Mary (*née* Newell); *m* 1978, Shirley Elizabeth Pope; one step *s* one step *d.* *Educ:* Eton Coll.; Christ Church, Oxford (MA). Temp. Asst Principal, CO, 1965; Asst Principal, ODM, 1967; Pvte Sec. to Parly Under-

Sec. of State, FCO, 1970; Principal, ODA, 1971–74, 1975–77; CSSB, 1974–75; Asst Sec., ODA, 1977; Head of British Develt Div. in Southern Africa, 1983. *Recreations:* gardening, cricket, music, entomology. *Address:* c/o Overseas Development Administration, Eland House, Stag Place, SW1. *T:* 071–273 0380.

KERDEL-VEGAS, Francisco, Hon. CBE 1973; MD; Venezuelan Ambassador to the Court of St James's, since 1987; *b* 3 Jan. 1928; *s* of Oswaldo F. Kerdel y Sofia Vegas de Kerdel; *m* 1977, Martha Ramos de Kerdel; two *s* four *d. Educ:* Liceo Andrés Bello, Caracas (BSc); Univ. Central de Venezuela (MD); Harvard; New York Univ. (MSc). Prof. of Dermatology, Central Univ. of Venezuela, 1954–77; Vis. Scientist, Dept of Experimental Pathology, ARC Inst. of Animal Physiology, Cambridge, 1966–67; Mem., Trinity Coll, Cambridge, 1966–67; Scientific Attaché, Venezuelan Embassy, London, 1966–67; Vice-Chancellor, Simón Bolívar Univ., 1969–70; Mem. Board, Univ. Metropolitana, Caracas, 1970–. Prosser White Oration, RCP, 1972. Fellow, Venezuelan Acads of Medicine, 1967–, of Sciences, 1971–; Mem., Nat. Res. Council, Venezuela, 1969–79; Pres., FUDENA (Nat. chapter of WWF), 1974. Fellow: Amer. Coll. of Physicians; Philadelphia Coll. of Physicians; Amer. Acad. of Dermatology. Hon. Member: RSM; British Assoc. of Dermatologists; West German Assoc. of Dermatologists; Socs of Dermatology of France, Austria, Spain, Portugal, Brazil, Argentina, Mexico, Colombia, Ecuador, Peru, Central America, Cuba, Israel, S Africa. Hon. DSc California Coll. of Podiatric Medicine, 1975. Venezuelan Orders of: Andrés Bello, 1970; Cecilio Acosta, 1976; Francisco de Miranda, 1978; Diego de Losada, 1985; El Libertador, 1986; Chevalier de la Légion d'Honneur (France), 1972. *Publications:* Tratado de Dermatologia, 1959, 4th edn 1986; chapters of textbooks of Dermatology, UK, USA, Canada, Spain, Mexico. *Recreations:* travelling, swimming, photography. *Address:* Venezuelan Embassy, 1 Cromwell Road, SW7 2HR. *T:* 071–584 4206. *Clubs:* United Oxford & Cambridge University, White's; Caracas Country, Camurí Grande (Venezuela); New York University.

KERLE, Rt. Rev. Ronald Clive; Rector of St Swithun's Pymble, Diocese of Sydney, 1976–82, resident Chaplain, since 1982; *b* 28 Dec. 1915; *s* of William Alfred Ronald Kerle and Isabel Ada (*née* Turner); *m* 1940, Helen Marshall Jackson; one *s* one *d. Educ:* Univ. of Sydney (BA); Moore Theological Coll., Sydney. Sydney ACT, ThL 1937; BA 1942. Deacon 1939; Priest, 1940; Curate, St Paul's, Sydney, 1939; St Anne, Ryde, 1939–41; Rector, Kangaroo Valley, 1941–43; St Stephen, Port Kembla, 1943–47; Chaplain, AIF, 1945–47; Gen. Sec., NSW Branch, Church Missionary Society, 1947–54; Rector of Summer Hill, 1954–56; Archdeacon of Cumberland, 1954–60; Bishop Coadjutor of Sydney, 1956–65; Bishop of Armidale, 1965–76. *Address:* Gowrie Retirement Village, 10 Edward Street, Gordon, NSW 2072, Australia.

KERMACK, Stuart Ogilvy; Sheriff of Tayside, Central and Fife at Forfar and Arbroath, since 1971; *b* 9 July 1934; *s* of late Stuart Grace Kermack, CBE and of Nell P., *y d* of Thomas White, SSC; *m* 1961, Barbara Mackenzie, BSc; three *s* one *d. Educ:* Glasgow Academy; Jesus Coll., Oxford; Glasgow Univ.; Edinburgh Univ. BA Oxon (Jurisprudence), 1956; LLB Glasgow, 1959. Elected to Scots Bar, 1959. Sheriff Substitute of Inverness, Moray, Nairn and Ross, at Elgin and Nairn, 1965–71. *Publications:* articles in legal journals. *Address:* 7 Little Causeway, Forfar, Angus. *T:* Forfar (0307) 64691.

KERMAN, Prof. Joseph Wilfred; Professor of Music, University of California at Berkeley, since 1974 (Chambers Professor of Music, 1986–89); *b* 3 April 1924; *m* 1945, Vivian Shaviro; two *s* one *d. Educ:* New York Univ. (AB); Princeton Univ. (PhD). Dir of Graduate Studies, Westminster Choir Coll., Princeton, NJ, USA, 1949–51; Music Faculty, Univ. of California at Berkeley, 1951–72, 1974– (Dep. Chm., 1960–63); Heather Prof. of Music, Oxford Univ., and Fellow of Wadham Coll., Oxford, 1972–74. Co-editor, 19th Century Music, 1977–88. Guggenheim, Fulbright and NEH Fellowships; Visiting Fellow: All Souls Coll., Oxford, 1966; Society for the Humanities, Cornell Univ., USA, 1970; Clare Hall, Cambridge, 1971; Walker-Ames Vis. Prof., Univ. of Washington, 1986; Valentine Vis. Prof., Amherst Coll., 1988; Gauss Lectr, Princeton Univ., 1988. Fellow, American Academy of Arts and Sciences; Corresp. FBA 1984. Hon. FRAM. Hon. DHL Fairfield Univ., 1970. *Publications:* Opera as Drama, 1956, rev. edn 1988; The Elizabethan Madrigal, 1962; The Beethoven Quartets, 1967; A History of Art and Music (with H. W. Janson), 1968; (ed) Ludwig van Beethoven: Autograph Miscellany, 1786–99 (Kafka Sketchbook), 2 vols, 1970 (Kinkeldey Award); Listen, 1972; The Masses and Motets of William Byrd, 1981 (Kinkeldey Award; Deems Taylor Award); The New Grove Beethoven (with A. Tyson), 1983; (co-ed) Beethoven Studies, vol. 1 1973, vol 2 1977, vol. 3 1982; Musicology, 1985; essays, in music criticism and musicology, in: Hudson Review, New York Review, San Francisco Chronicle, etc. *Address:* Music Department, University of California, Berkeley, Calif 94720, USA; 107 Southampton Avenue, Berkeley, Calif 94707.

KERMODE, Sir (John) Frank, Kt 1991; MA; FBA 1973; *b* 29 Nov. 1919; *s* of late John Pritchard Kermode and late Doris Pearl Kermode; *m* 1st, 1947, Maureen Eccles (marr. diss. 1970); twin *s* and *d*; 2nd, 1976, Anita Van Vactor. *Educ:* Douglas High Sch.; Liverpool Univ. BA 1940; War Service (Navy), 1940–46; MA 1947; Lecturer, King's Coll., Newcastle, in the University of Durham, 1947–49; Lecturer in the University of Reading, 1949–58; John Edward Taylor Prof. of English Literature in the University of Manchester, 1958–65; Winterstoke Prof. of English in the University of Bristol, 1965–67; Lord Northcliffe Prof. of Modern English Lit., UCL, 1967–74; King Edward VII Prof. of English Literature, Cambridge Univ., 1974–82; Fellow, King's Coll., Cambridge, 1974–87, Hon. Fellow, 1988. Charles Eliot Norton Prof. of Poetry at Harvard, 1977–78. Co-editor, Encounter, 1966–67. Editor: Fontana Masterguides and Modern Masters series; Oxford Authors. FRSL 1958. Mem. Arts Council, 1968–71; Chm., Poetry Book Soc., 1968–76. For. Hon. Mem., Amer. Acad. of Arts and Scis. Hon. DHL Chicago, 1975; Hon. DLitt Liverpool, 1981; Hon Dr. Amsterdam, 1988. Officier de l'Ordre des Arts et des Sciences. *Publications:* (ed) Shakespeare, The Tempest (Arden Edition), 1954; Romantic Image, 1957; John Donne, 1957; The Living Milton, 1960; Wallace Stevens, 1960; Puzzles & Epiphanies, 1962; The Sense of an Ending, 1967; Continuities, 1968; Shakespeare, Spenser, Donne, 1971; Modern Essays, 1971; Lawrence, 1973; (ed, with John Hollander) Oxford Anthology of English Literature, 1973; The Classic, 1975; (ed) Selected Prose of T. S. Eliot, 1975; The Genesis of Secrecy, 1979; Essays on Fiction, 1971–82, 1983; Forms of Attention, 1985; (ed jtly) The Literary Guide to the Bible, 1987; History and Value, 1988; An Appetite for Poetry, 1989; Poetry, Narrative, History, 1990; (ed with Keith Walker) Andrew Marvell, 1990; Uses of Error, 1991; contrib. Review of Eng. Studies, Partisan Review, New York Review, New Statesman, London Rev. of Books, etc. *Address:* 27 Luard Road, Cambridge. *T:* Cambridge (0223) 247398. *Club:* Savile.

KERMODE, Hon. Sir Ronald (Graham Quayle), KBE 1986 (CBE 1975); Judge of the Court of Appeal, Republic of Fiji, since 1988; *b* 26 June 1919; *s* of George Graham Kermode and Linda Margaret (*née* McInnis); *m* 1945, Amy Rivett Marr; two *s* two *d. Educ:* Whangarei High Sch., NZ; Auckland University Coll. (LLB). Served with NZ and Fiji Mil. Forces, 1939–45. In private legal practice, 1945–75; Puisne Judge, Supreme Court of Fiji, 1976–86; Judge of the Court of Appeal: Kiribati, 1983–86; Fiji, 1985–87. Tribunal, Fiji Sugar Industry, 1985–. Elected European MLC, Fiji, 1958, and served for 15 years as Mem. of Council and Parliament; first elected Speaker of the House of Representatives, 1968–73. *Recreations:* fishing, contract bridge, reading, gardening, bird watching. *Address:* 74A Ridge Road, Howick, Auckland, New Zealand. *T:* 5375102.

KERN, Karl-Heinz; Head of Arms Control Department, Ministry of Foreign Affairs, German Democratic Republic, since 1987; *b* 18 Feb. 1930; *m* 1952, Ursula Bennmann; one *s. Educ:* King George Gymnasium, Dresden; Techn. Coll., Dresden (chem. engrg); Acad. for Polit. Science and Law (Dipl. jur., post-grad. History). Leading posts in diff. regional authorities of GDR until 1959; foreign policy, GDR, 1959–62; Head of GDR Mission in Ghana, 1962–66; Head of African Dept, Min. of For. Affairs, 1966–71; Minister and Chargé d'Affaires, Gt Britain, 1973; Ambassador to UK, 1973–80; Dep. Head of Western European Dept, Min. of Foreign Affairs, 1980–82; Ambassador to N Korea, 1982–86. Holds Order of Merit of the Fatherland, etc. *Recreations:* sport, reading, music. *Address:* Ministry of Foreign Affairs, 102 Berlin, Marx Engels Platz, Germany; Karl-Marx-Allee 70a, 1017 Berlin.

KERNOHAN, Thomas Hugh, CBE 1978 (OBE 1955); Parliamentary Commissioner for Administration and Commissioner for Complaints, Northern Ireland, 1980–87; *b* 11 May 1922; *s* of Thomas Watson Kernohan and Caroline Kernohan; *m* 1948, Margaret Moore; one *s* one *d. Educ:* Carrickfergus Model Sch.; Carrickfergus Technical Sch. On staff (admin), Harland & Wolff Ltd, Belfast, 1940–44; Engineering Employers' NI Association: Asst Sec., 1945; Sec., 1953; Dir, 1966–80; Founder, 1959, and Chm., 1961–80 and 1987–, family joinery and plastic firm, Kernohans Joinery Works Ltd. *Recreations:* Rugby (management now), boating, fishing. *Address:* Beach House, Island Park, Greenisland, Carrickfergus, N Ireland BT38 8TW. *T:* Belfast (0232) 862030.

KERR, family name of **Marquess of Lothian** and **Baron Teviot.**

KERR, Alan Grainger, FRCS, FRCSE; Consultant Otolaryngologist, Royal Victoria and Belfast City Hospitals, since 1968; *b* 15 April 1935; *s* of Joseph William and Eileen Kerr; *m* 1962, Patricia Margaret M'Neill; two *s* one *d. Educ:* Methodist College, Belfast; Queen's Univ., Belfast (MB). DObst RCOG. Prof. of Otorhinolaryngology, QUB, 1979–81. Otolaryngology Mem. Council, RCS, 1987–. Lectures, UK, Europe and USA. Prizes: Jobson Horne, BMA; Harrison, RSocMed; Howells, Univ. of London. Gen. Editor, Scott-Brown's Otolaryngology, 5th edn. *Publications:* papers on ear surgery. *Recreations:* squash, tennis, sailing, ski-ing. *Address:* 6 Cranmore Gardens, Belfast BT9 6JL. *T:* Belfast (0232) 669181. *Club:* Royal Society of Medicine.

KERR, Prof. Allen, FRS 1986; FAA; Professor of Plant Pathology, University of Adelaide, since 1980; *b* 21 May 1926; *s* of A. B. Kerr and J. T. Kerr (*née* White); *m* 1951, Rosemary Sheila Strachan; two *s* one *d. Educ:* George Heriot's Sch., Edinburgh; Univ. of Edinburgh. North of Scotland Coll. of Agric., 1947–51; University of Adelaide: Lectr, 1951–59; Sen. Lectr, 1959–67 (seconded to Tea Research Inst., Ceylon, 1963–66); Reader, 1968–80. *Recreation:* golf. *Address:* 419 Carrington Street, Adelaide, SA 5000, Australia. *T:* 232–2325.

KERR, Andrew Mark; Senior Partner, Bell & Scott, WS, Edinburgh, since 1987 (Partner, since 1969); Clerk to Society of Writers to HM Signet, since 1983; *b* Edinburgh 17 Jan. 1940; *s* of William Mark Kerr and Katharine Marjorie Anne Stevenson; *m* 1967, Jane Susanna Robertson; one *d. Educ*: Edinburgh Acad.; Cambridge Univ. (BA); Edinburgh Univ. (LLB). Served RNR, 1961–76. British Petroleum, 1961–62. Vice-Chm., Edinburgh New Town Conservation Cttee, 1972–76; Chm., Edinburgh Solicitors' Property Centre, 1976–81. Member: Council, Edinburgh Internat. Fest., 1978–82; Scottish Arts Council, 1988– (Chm., Drama Cttee, 1988–91); Sec., Edinburgh Fest. Fringe Soc. Ltd, 1969–. Mem. Council, St George's Sch. for Girls, Edinburgh, 1985–. *Recreations:* architecture, hill walking, music, ships, ski-ing, theatre. *Address:* 16 Ann Street, Edinburgh EH4 1PJ. *T:* (home) 031-332 9857; (office) 031-226 6703. *Club:* New (Edinburgh).

KERR, Andrew Stevenson, CBE 1976; arbitrator in industrial relations disputes; *b* 28 Aug. 1918; *s* of John S. Kerr and Helen L. Kerr; *m* 1946, Helen Reid Bryden; two *s* two *d. Educ:* Spiers' Sch., Beith, Ayrshire; Glasgow Univ. MA (Hons). Served Army, 1940–46. Entered Min. of Labour, 1947; general employment work in the Ministry, in Scotland, 1947–63; Industrial Relns Officer for Scotland, Min. of Labour, 1964–66; Dep. Chief Conciliation Officer, Min. of Labour, 1966–68; Chief Conciliation Officer, Dept of Employment, 1968–71; Controller (Scotland), Dept of Employment, 1972–74; Chief Conciliation Officer, ACAS, 1974–80. *Recreations:* golf, history. *Address:* The Rowans, 1 Maplewood Close, Gonerby Hill Foot, Grantham, Lincs NG31 8GY. *T:* Grantham (0476) 73370.

KERR, Brian Francis; QC (NI) 1983; Senior Crown Counsel for Northern Ireland, since 1988; *b* 22 Feb. 1948; *s* of late James William Kerr and of Kathleen Rose Kerr; *m* 1970, Gillian Rosemary Owen Widdowson; two *s. Educ:* St Colman's College, Newry, Co. Down; Queen's Univ., Belfast (LLB 1969). Called to NI Bar, 1970, to the Bar of England and Wales, Gray's Inn, 1974; Bencher, Inn of Court of NI, 1990; Junior Crown Counsel (Common Law), 1978–83. Chm., Mental Health Commn for NI, 1988. *Recreations:* outdoor activities with sons. *Address:* Royal Courts of Justice, Belfast BT1 3JY.

KERR, Clark; educator; *b* 17 May 1911; *s* of Samuel W. and Caroline Clark Kerr; *m* 1934, Catherine Spaulding; two *s* one *d. Educ:* Swarthmore Coll. (AB); Stanford Univ. (MA); Univ. of Calif., Berkeley (PhD). Actg Asst Prof., Stanford Univ., 1939–40; Asst Prof., later Assoc. Prof., Univ. of Washington, 1940–45; Prof., Dir, Inst. of Industrial Relations, Univ. of Calif, Berkeley, 1945–52; Chancellor, Univ. of Calif at Berkeley, 1952–58; Pres., Univ. of Calif, 1958–67, now Emeritus President. Chairman: Carnegie Commn on Higher Educn, 1967–74; Carnegie Council on Policy Studies in Higher Educn, 1974–80; Bd, Work in America Inst., 1975–; Bd, Global Perspectives in Educn, 1976–85, now Chm. Emeritus. Govt service with US War Labor Board, 1942–45. Mem. Pres. Eisenhower's Commn on Nat. Goals, President Kennedy and President Johnson Cttee on Labor-Management Policy; Program Dir, Strengthening Presidential Leadership Project, Assoc. of Governing Bds of Univs and Colls, 1982–85; Contract Arbitrator for: Boeing Aircraft Co. and Internat. Assoc. of Machinists, 1944–45; Armour & Co. and United Packinghouse Workers, 1945–47, 1949–52; Waterfront Employers' Assoc. and Internat. Longshoremen's and Warehousemen's Union, 1946–47, etc. Member: Amer. Acad. of Arts and Sciences; Royal Economic Society; Amer. Econ. Assoc.; Nat. Acad. of Arbitrators, etc. Phi Beta Kappa, Kappa Sigma. Trustee, Rockefeller Foundation, 1960–75; Chm., Armour Automation Cttee, 1959–79. Hon. Fellow, LSE, 1977. Hon. LLD: Swarthmore, 1952; Harvard, 1958; Princeton, 1959; Notre Dame, 1964; Chinese Univ. of Hong Kong, 1964; Rochester, 1967; Hon. DLitt, Strathclyde, 1965; Hon. Dr, Bordeaux, 1962, etc. Harold W. McGraw, Jr, Prize in Educn, 1990. *Publications:* Unions, Management and the Public (jt), 1948 (rev. edns 1960, 1967); (jtly) Industrialism and Industrial Man, 1960 (rev. edns 1964, 1973); The Uses of the University, 1963 (3rd edn 1982); Labor and Management in Industrial Society, 1964 (rev. edn 1972); Marshall, Marx and Modern Times, 1969; (jtly) Industrialism and Industrial Man Reconsidered, 1975; Labor Markets and Wage Determination, 1977; Education and National Development, 1979; The Future of Industrial Societies, 1983; (jtly) The Many Lives of

Academic Presidents, 1986; (ed jtly) Industrial Relations in a New Age, 1986; (ed jtly) Economics of Labor in Industrial Society, 1986; (jtly) How Labor Markets Work, 1988; (jtly) The Guardians: boards of trustees of American Colleges and Universities, 1989; The Great Transformation in Higher Education 1960–1980, 1991; contribs to American Economic Review, Review of Economics and Statistics, Quarterly Jl of Economics, etc. *Recreation:* gardening. *Address:* 8300 Buckingham Drive, El Cerrito, Calif 94530, USA. *T:* (415) 5291910; (office) Institute of Industrial Relations, University of California, Berkeley, Calif 94720. *T:* (415) 642 8106.

KERR, Dr David Leigh; *b* 25 March 1923; *s* of Myer Woolf Kerr and Paula (*née* Horowitz); *m* 1st, 1944, Aileen Saddington (marr. diss. 1969); two *s* one *d*; 2nd, 1970, Margaret Dunlop; one *s* two *d*. *Educ:* Whitgift Sch., Croydon; Middlesex Hosp. Med. Sch., London. Hon. Sec., Socialist Medical Assoc., 1957–63; Hon. Vice-Pres., 1963–72. LCC (Wandsworth, Central), 1958–65, and Coun., London Borough of Wandsworth, 1964–68; Mem., Herts CC (Welwyn Garden City S), 1989–. Contested (Lab) Wandsworth, Streatham (for Parlt), 1959; MP (Lab) Wandsworth Central, 1964–70. Vis. Lectr in Medicine, Chelsea Coll., 1972–82. War on Want: Dir, 1970–77; Vice-Chm., 1973–74; Chm., 1974–77. Family Doctor, Tooting, 1946–82; Chief Exec., Manor House Hosp., London, 1982–87. Mem., Inter-departmental Cttee on Death Certification and Coroners; Hon. Vice Pres. and Trustee, Health Visitors' Assoc., 1969–. FRSM. Governor, British Film Inst., 1966–71. *Recreations:* reading other people's biographies, refusing to write own. *Address:* 19 Calder Avenue, Brookmans Park, Herts AL9 7AH. *T:* Potters Bar (0707) 53954.

KERR, Prof. David Nicol Sharp, MSc; FRCP, FRCPE; Professor of Renal Medicine, Royal Postgraduate Medical School, University of London, since 1987 (Dean, 1984–91); *b* 27 Dec. 1927; *s* of William Kerr and Elsie (Ransted) Kerr; *m* 1960, Eleanor Jones; two *s* one *d*. *Educ:* George Watson's Boys' College; Edinburgh University (MB ChB); University of Wisconsin (MSc); FRCPE 1966; FRCP 1967; House Physician and Surgeon, Royal Infirmary, Edinburgh, 1951–52; Exchange scholar, Univ. of Wisconsin, 1952–53; Surgeon Lieut, RNVR, 1953–55; Asst Lectr, Univ. of Edinburgh, 1956–57; Registrar, Hammersmith Hosp., 1957–59; Lectr, Univ. of Durham, 1959–63; Consultant Physician, Royal Victoria Infirmary, Newcastle upon Tyne, 1962–83; Senior Lectr, 1963–68, Prof. of Medicine, 1968–83, Univ. of Newcastle upon Tyne. Member: Council, Internat. Soc. of Nephrology, 1984–; Council, British Heart Foundn, 1989–; NW Thames RHA, 1989–; Queen Charlotte's SHA, 1984–; Standing Med. Adv. Cttee, DHSS, 1979–90. Sen. Censor and First Vice Pres., RCP, 1990–91. *Publications:* Short Textbook of Renal Disease, 1968; chapters in numerous books incl. Cecil-Loeb Textbook of Medicine and Oxford Textbook of Medicine; articles on renal disease in med. jls. *Recreations:* fell walking, jogging. *Address:* Royal Postgraduate Medical School, Hammersmith Hospital, Du Cane Road, W12 0NN. *T:* 081–740 3200, *Fax:* 081–740 3203; 22 Carbery Avenue, W3 9AL. *T:* 081–992 3231. *Club:* Athenæum.

KERR, Deborah Jane, (Deborah Kerr Viertel); actress; *b* 30 Sept. 1921; *d* of Capt. Arthur Kerr-Trimmer; *m* 1st, 1945, Sqdn Ldr A. C. Bartley (marr. diss., 1959); two *d*; 2nd, 1960, Peter Viertel. *Educ:* Northumberland House, Clifton, Bristol. Open Air Theatre, Regent's Park, 1939, Oxford Repertory, 1939–40; after an interval of acting in films, appeared on West End Stage; Ellie Dunn in Heartbreak House, Cambridge Theatre, 1943; went to France, Belgium, and Holland for ENSA, playing in Gaslight, 1945. *Films:* Major Barbara, 1940; Love on the Dole, 1940–41; Penn of Pennsylvania, 1941; Hatter's Castle, 1942; The Day Will Dawn, 1942; Life and Death of Colonel Blimp, 1942–43; Perfect Strangers, 1944; I See a Dark Stranger, 1945; Black Narcissus, 1946; The Hucksters and If Winter Comes, 1947 (MGM, Hollywood); Edward My Son, 1948; Please Believe Me, 1949 (MGM, Hollywood); King Solomon's Mines, 1950; Quo Vadis, 1952; Prisoner of Zenda, Julius Caesar, Dream Wife, Young Bess (MGM), 1952; From Here to Eternity, 1953; The End of the Affair, 1955; The Proud and Profane, The King and I, 1956; Heaven Knows, Mr Allison, An Affair to Remember, Tea and Sympathy, 1957; Bonjour Tristesse, 1958; Separate Tables, The Journey, Count Your Blessings, 1959; The Sundowners, The Grass is Greener, The Naked Edge, The Innocents, 1961; The Chalk Garden, The Night of the Iguana, 1964; Casino Royale, 1967; Eye of the Devil, Prudence and the Pill, 1968; The Arrangement, 1970; The Assam Garden, 1985. *Stage:* Tea and Sympathy, NY, 1953; The Day After the Fair, London, 1972, tour of US, 1973–74; Seascape, NY, 1975; Candida, London, 1977; The Last of Mrs Cheyney, tour of US, 1978–79; The Day After the Fair, Melbourne and Sydney, 1979; Overheard, Haymarket, 1981; The Corn is Green, Old Vic, 1985. BAFTA Special Award, 1991. *Address:* Klosters, 7250 Grisons, Switzerland.

KERR, Desmond Moore, OBE 1970; HM Diplomatic Service, retired; *b* 23 Jan. 1930; *s* of late Robert John Kerr and Mary Elizabeth Kerr; *m* 1956, Evelyn Patricia South; one *s* two *d*. *Educ:* Methodist Coll., Belfast; Queen's Univ., Belfast. BA Hons (Classics and Ancient History). CRO, 1952; British High Commn, Karachi, 1956–59, Lagos, 1959–62; Second Sec., 1960; Commonwealth Office, 1962–66; First Sec., 1965; Dep. British Govt Rep., West Indies Associated States, 1966–70; FCO, 1970–76; Dep. High Comr, Dacca, 1976–79; High Comr, Swaziland, 1979–83; Head of Claims Dept, FCO, 1983–87. *Address:* c/o Foreign and Commonwealth Office, SW1.
See also E. Kerr.

KERR, Donald Frederick, CVO 1961; OBE 1960; Manager, Government Press Centre, Foreign and Commonwealth Office, 1976–77, retired; *b* 20 April 1915; *s* of Dr David Kerr, Cheshire; *m* 1942, Elizabeth Hayward (*d* 1978); two *s* one *d*. *Educ:* Sydney High Sch.; University of Sydney (BEcon). Served RAF (Navigator), SEAC, 1942–46. Deputy Director: British Information Services, New Delhi, 1947–53; UK Information Service, Ottawa, 1953–55; UK Information Service, Toronto, 1955–56; Dir, UK Information Service in Canada, Ottawa, 1956–59; Dir, British Information Services in India, New Delhi, 1959–63; Controller (Overseas), COI, 1963–76; on secondment, Dir of Information, Commonwealth Secretariat, Sept. 1969–Sept. 1970. *Recreation:* golf. *Address:* 4 Southdown House, 11 Lansdowne Road, Wimbledon, SW20. *Club:* Royal Wimbledon Golf.

KERR, Dr Edwin, CBE 1986; Chief Executive, College for Financial Planning, since 1988; *b* 1 July 1926; *e s* of late Robert John Kerr and Mary Elizabeth Kerr (*née* Ferguson); *m* 1949, Gertrude Elizabeth (*née* Turbitt); one *s* two *d*. *Educ:* Royal Belfast Academical Instn; Queen's Univ., Belfast (BSc, PhD). FIMA, FBCS. Asst Lectr in Maths, QUB, 1948–52; Lectr in Maths, Coll. of Technology, Birmingham (now Univ. of Aston in Birmingham), 1952–55; Lectr in Maths, Coll. of Science and Technology, Manchester (now Univ. of Manchester Inst. of Science and Technology), 1956–58; Head of Maths Dept, Royal Coll. of Advanced Technology, Salford (now Univ. of Salford), 1958–66; Principal, Paisley Coll. of Technology, 1966–72; Chief Officer, CNAA, 1972–86; Chm. and Chief Exec., Exam. Bd for Financial Planning, 1987–89. Member: Adv. Cttee on Supply and Training of Teachers, 1973–78; Adv. Cttee on Supply and Educn of Teachers, 1980–85; Bd for Local Authority Higher Educn, 1982–85; Bd for Public Sector Higher Educn, 1985–86; Mem. and Vice-Chm., Continuing Educn Standing Cttee, 1985–88. President: Soc. for Res. into Higher Educn, 1974–77; The Mathematical Assoc., 1976–77. Hon. FCP 1984; Hon. Fellow: Coventry Lanchester, Newcastle upon Tyne, Portsmouth and Sheffield Polytechnics, 1986; Huddersfield Polytechnic, and Paisley Coll. of Technol., 1987. DUniv Open, 1977; Hon. DSc Ulster, 1986; Hon. DEd CNAA, 1989. *Publications:* (with R. Butler) An Introduction to Numerical Methods, 1962; various mathematical and educational. *Recreation:* gardening. *Address:* 59 Craigdarragh Road, Helen's Bay, Co. Down BT19 1UB. *Club:* Travellers'.
See also D. M. Kerr.

KERR, Francis Robert Newsam, OBE 1962; MC 1940; JP; farmer, 1949–85, retired; Vice Lord-Lieutenant of Berwickshire, 1970–90; *b* 12 Sept. 1916; *s* of late Henry Francis Hobart Kerr and Gertrude Mary Kerr (*née* Anthony); *m* 1941, Anne Frederica Kitson; two *s* one *d*. *Educ:* Ampleforth College. Regular Officer, The Royal Scots, 1937–49; TA 1952–63; retired as Lt-Col. Member: Berwickshire County Council, 1964–75; SE Scotland Regional Hosp. Bd, 1971–74; Borders Area Health Bd, 1973–81 (Vice-Chm.); Borders Reg. Council, 1974–78; Post Office Users Nat. Council, 1972–73; Whitley Council, 1970–81; Council, Multiple Sclerosis Soc., 1973–. Sheriff of Berwick upon Tweed, 1974; JP Berwickshire, 1975. *Recreations:* country pursuits. *Address:* Howden, Jedburgh, Roxburghshire TD8 6QP. *T:* Jedburgh (0835) 64193.

KERR, James, QPM 1979; Chief Constable, Lincolnshire Police, 1977–83; *b* 19 Nov. 1928; *s* of William and Margaret Jane Kerr; *m* 1952, Jean Coupland; one *d*. *Educ:* Carlisle Grammar School. Cadet and Navigating Officer, Merchant Navy, 1945–52 (Union Castle Line, 1949–52). Carlisle City Police and Cumbria Constabulary, 1952–74; Asst Director of Command Courses, Police Staff Coll., Bramshill, 1974; Asst Chief Constable (Operations), North Yorkshire Police, 1975; Deputy Chief Constable, Lincs, 1976. Mem., Melbourne Welsh Choir. Officer Brother, OStJ, 1980. *Recreations:* music, squash. *Address:* 10 Gahnia Close, North Ringwood, Vic 3134, Australia. *Club:* Heathmont Bowling (Heathmont).

KERR, Adm. Sir John (Beverley), KCB 1989; Commander-in-Chief, Naval Home Command, since 1991; *b* 27 Oct. 1937; *s* of Wilfred Kerr and Vera Kerr (*née* Sproule); *m* 1964, Elizabeth Anne, *d* of late Dr and Mrs C. R. G. Howard, Burley, Hants; three *s*. *Educ:* Moseley Hall County Grammar Sch., Cheadle; Britannia Royal Naval Coll., Dartmouth. Served in various ships, 1958–65 (specialized in navigation, 1964); Staff, BRNC, Dartmouth, 1965–67; HMS Cleopatra, 1967–69; Staff, US Naval Acad., Annapolis, 1969–71; NDC, Latimer, 1971–72; i/c HMS Achilles, 1972–74; Naval Plans, MoD, 1974–75; Defence Policy Staff, MoD, 1975–77; RCDS, 1978; i/c HMS Birmingham, 1979–81; Dir of Naval Plans, MoD, 1981–83; i/c HMS Illustrious, 1983–84; ACNS (Op. Requirements), 1984; ACDS (Op. Requirements) (Sea Systems), 1985–86; Flag Officer First Flotilla/Flotilla One, 1986–88; MoD, 1988–91. *Recreations:* music, sailing, hill walking, history. *Address:* c/o Lloyds Bank, Dartmouth, Devon. *Club:* Army and Navy.

KERR, Sir John (Olav), KCMG 1991 (CMG 1987); HM Diplomatic Service; Ambassador and UK Permanent Representative to the European Communities, Brussels, since 1990; *b* 22 Feb. 1942; *s* of late Dr and of Mrs J. D. O. Kerr; *m* 1965, Elizabeth, *d* of Mr and Mrs W. G. Kalaugher; two *s* three *d*. *Educ:* Glasgow Academy; Pembroke Coll., Oxford (Hon. Fellow, 1991). Entered Diplomatic Service, 1966; served FO, Moscow, Rawalpindi, FCO; Private Sec. to Permanent Under Secretary, FCO, 1974–79; Head of DM1 Division, HM Treasury, 1979–81; Principal Private Sec. to Chancellor of the Exchequer, 1981–84; Hd of Chancery, Washington, 1984–87; Asst Under-Sec. of State, FCO, 1987–90. *Address:* c/o Foreign and Commonwealth Office, King Charles Street, SW1A 2AH.

KERR, Rt. Hon. Sir Michael (Robert Emanuel), Kt 1972; PC 1981; a Lord Justice of Appeal, 1981–89; *b* 1 March 1921; *s* of Alfred Kerr; *m* 1st, 1952, Julia (marr. diss. 1982), *d* of Joseph Braddock; two *s* one *d*; 2nd, 1983, Diana, *yr d* of H. Neville Sneezum; one *s* one *d*. *Educ:* Aldenham Sch.; Clare Coll., Cambridge (Hon. Fellow, 1986). Served War, 1941–45 (Pilot; Flt-Lt). BA Cantab (1st cl. Hons Law) 1947, MA 1952; called to Bar, Lincoln's Inn, 1948, Bencher 1968, Treas., 1989; QC 1961. Member: Bar Council, 1968–72; Senate, 1969–72. Dep. Chm., Hants QS, 1961–71; Mem. Vehicle and General Enquiry Tribunal, 1971–72; a Judge of the High Court of Justice, Queen's Bench Div., and of the Commercial and Admiralty Cts, 1972–78; Chm., Law Commn of England and Wales, 1978–81. Pres., London Court of Internat. Arbitration, 1985–. Mem. Council of Management: British Inst. of Internat. and Comparative Law, 1973–; Inst. of Advanced Legal Studies, 1979–85; Chairman: Lord Chancellor's inter-deptl cttee on Foreign Judgments, 1974–81; Cttee of Management, Centre of Commercial Law Studies, QMC, 1980–89; Supreme Court Procedure Cttee, 1982–86; Mem., Internat. Adv. Cttee, British Columbia Internat. Arbitration Centre, 1986–. Vice-Pres., British Maritime Law Assoc., 1977–; Pres., British-German Jurists Assoc., 1986–91. Mem., Amer. Law Inst., 1985–. Pres., CIArb., 1983–86. Hon. Life Mem., Amer. and Canadian Bar Assocs, 1976. Chorley Lectr, LSE, 1977; Alexander Lectr, CIArb, 1984. Governor, Aldenham Sch., 1959–87. Hon. Fellow, QMC, 1986. *Publications:* McNair's Law of the Air, 1953, 1965; articles and lectures on commercial law and arbitration. *Recreations:* travel, music, trying not to work, a second edition of children. *Address:* 4 Essex Court, Temple, EC4Y 9AJ. *T:* 071–583 9191, *Fax:* 071–353 3421. *Clubs:* Garrick, Pilgrims.

KERR, Robert Reid, TD; MA (Oxon), LLB; Sheriff of Tayside, Central and Fife (formerly Stirling, Dumbarton and Clackmannan) at Falkirk, 1969–83; *b* 7 May 1914; *s* of James Reid Kerr, sugar refiner, and Olive Rodger; *m* 1942, Mona Kerr; three *d*. *Educ:* Cargilfield; Trinity Coll., Glenalmond; Oxford Univ.; Glasgow Univ. Sheriff-Substitute: of Inverness, Moray, Nairn and Ross and Cromarty at Fort William, 1952–61; of Aberdeen, Kincardine and Banff at Banff, 1961–69. OStJ. *Address:* Bagatelle, 14 Rennie Street, Falkirk FK1 5QW.
See also J. K. G. Watson.

KERR, Rose; Curator of the Far Eastern Collections, Victoria and Albert Museum, since 1990; *b* 23 Feb. 1953; *d* of William Antony Kerr and Elizabeth Rendell; *m* 1990. *Educ:* SOAS, Univ. of London (BA Hons 1st Cl., Art and Archaeology of China); Languages Inst., Beijing. Fellow, Percival David Foundn of Chinese Art, 1976–78; joined Far Eastern Dept, V&A, 1978, Keeper, 1987–90. *Publications:* (with P. Hughes-Stanton) Kiln Sites of Ancient China, 1980; (with John Larson) Guanyin: a masterpiece revealed, 1985; Chinese Ceramics: porcelain of the Qing Dynasty 1644–1911, 1986; Later Chinese Bronzes, 1990; (ed and contrib.) Chinese Art and Design: the T. T. Tsui Gallery of Chinese Art, 1991; articles in Oriental Art, Orientations, Apollo, Craft Magazine, V&A Album. *Recreations:* gardening, writing, sleeping. *Address:* 109 Bow Road, E3 2AN. *T:* 071–938 8263.

KERR, Thomas Henry, CB 1983; Director, Hunting Engineering plc, since 1986 (Technical Director, 1986–88); *b* 18 June 1924; *s* of late Albert Edward Kerr and Mrs Francis Jane Kerr (*née* Simpson); *m* 1946, Myrnie Evelyn Martin Hughes; two *d*. *Educ:* Magnus Grammar, Newark; University Coll., Durham Univ. BSc 1949; CEng, FRAeS; Diplôme Paul Tissendier 1957. RAFVR pilot, 1942–46. Aero Flight, RAE, 1949–55; Head of Supersonic Flight Group, 1955–59; Scientific Adviser to C-in-C Bomber Comd, High Wycombe, 1960–64; Head of Assessment Div., Weapons Dept, RAE, 1964–66; Dep. Dir and Dir of Defence Operational Analysis Estabt, 1966–70; Head of Weapons Research Gp, Weapons Dept, RAE, 1970–72; Dir Gen. Establishments Resources

Programmes (C), MoD (PE), 1972–74; Director: Nat. Gas Turbine Estabt, 1974–80; RAE, 1980–84; R&D Dir, Royal Ordnance plc, 1984–86. Consultant, Systems Designers Scientific, 1985–88. Mem. Council, RAeS, 1979, Pres., 1985–86. *Publications:* reports and memoranda of Aeronautical Research Council, lectures to RAeS and RUSI. *Recreations:* bridge, water ski-ing, tennis, badminton. *Address:* Bundu, 013 Kingsley Avenue, Camberley, Surrey GU15 2NA. *T:* Camberley (0276) 25961.

KERR, Sir William Alexander B., (Sir Alastair); *see* Blair-Kerr.

KERR, William Francis Kennedy, OBE 1984; PhD, CEng, FIMechE; Principal, Belfast College of Technology, 1969–84; *b* 1 Aug. 1923; *m* 1953, H. Adams; two *s*. *Educ:* Portadown Technical Coll. and Queen's Univ., Belfast. BSc (Hons) in Mech. Engineering, MSc, PhD. Teacher of Mathematics, Portadown Techn. Coll., 1947–48; Teacher and Sen. Lectr in Mech. Eng, Coll. of Techn., Belfast, 1948–55; Lectr and Adviser of Studies in Mech. Eng, Queen's Univ. of Belfast, 1955–62; Head of Dept of Mech., Civil, and Prod. Eng, Dundee Coll. of Techn., 1962–67; Vice-Principal, Coll. of Techn., Belfast, 1967–69. Chm., NI Cttee for Educnl Technology, 1973–79; Member: Council for Educnl Technology, 1973–79; Belfast Educn and Library Bd, 1977–81; NI Council for Educnl Develt, 1980–84; NI Manpower Council, 1981–84; Chm., Assoc. of Principals of Colleges (NI Branch), 1982; Governor, Royal Belfast Academical Instn, 1969–84; Mem. Court, Ulster Univ., 1985–. *Publications:* contribs on environmental testing of metals, etc. *Recreations:* golf, motoring, reading. *Address:* 27 Maxwell Road, Bangor, Co. Down, Northern Ireland BT20 3SG. *T:* Bangor (0247) 465303.

KERRUISH, Sir (Henry) Charles, Kt 1979; OBE 1964; President of Tynwald and of Legislative Council, Isle of Man, since 1990; Speaker, House of Keys, 1962–90; *b* 23 July 1917; *m* 1st, 1944, Margaret Gell; one *s* three *d*; 2nd, 1975, Kay Warriner. *Educ:* Ramsey Grammar Sch. Farmer. Member, House of Keys, 1946–90; Ex-Officio MLC, 1990–. Pres., CPA, 1983–84 (Regional Councillor for British Isles and Mediterranean, 1975–77). Mem. Court, Liverpool Univ., 1974–90. Hon. LLD Lancaster, 1990. *Recreations:* horse breeding, motor cycling. *Address:* Ballafayle, Maughold, Isle of Man. *T:* Ramsey (0624) 812293. *Club:* Farmers'.

KERRY, Knight of; *see* FitzGerald, Sir G. P. M.

KERRY, Sir Michael (James), KCB 1983 (CB 1976); QC 1984; Deputy Chairman, Life Assurance and Unit Trust Regulatory Organisation, since 1987; *b* 5 Aug. 1923; *s* of Russell Kerry and Marjorie (*née* Kensington); *m* 1951, Sidney Rosetta Elizabeth (*née* Foster); one *s* two *d*. *Educ:* Rugby Sch.; St John's Coll., Oxford (MA; Hon. Fellow 1986). Served with RAF, 1942–46. Called to Bar, Lincoln's Inn, 1949, Bencher 1984. Joined BoT as Legal Asst, 1951; Sen. Legal Asst, 1959; Asst Solicitor, 1964; Principal Asst Solicitor, Dept of Trade and Industry, 1972, Solicitor, 1973–80; HM Procurator Gen. and Treasury Solicitor, 1980–84. *Recreations:* golf, tennis, gardening. *Address:* South Bedales, Lewes Road, Haywards Heath, W Sussex RH17 7TE. *T:* Scaynes Hill (0444) 831303. *Club:* Piltdown Golf.

KERSE, Christopher Stephen; Under Secretary (Legal), Department of Trade and Industry, since 1988; *b* 12 Dec. 1946; *s* of William Harold Kerse and Maude Kerse; *m* 1971, Gillian Hanks; one *s* one *d*. *Educ:* King George V Sch., Southport; Univ. of Hull (LLB). Admitted Solicitor, 1972. Lecturer in Law: Univ. of Bristol, 1968–72; Univ. of Manchester, 1972–76; Vis. Asst Prof., Faculty of Law, Univ. of British Columbia, 1974–75; Senior Legal Assistant: OFT, 1976–81; DTI, 1981–82; Asst Solicitor, DTI, 1982–88. *Publications:* The Law Relating to Noise, 1975; EEC Antitrust Procedure, 1981, 2nd edn 1988; articles in various legal jls. *Recreations:* the horn, the double bass, allotment gardening. *Address:* c/o Department of Trade and Industry, 10–18 Victoria Street, SW1H 0NN. *T:* 071–215 3500.

KERSH, Cyril; author and journalist; *b* 24 Feb. 1925; *s* of Hyman and Leah Kersh; *m* 1956, Suzanne Fajner. *Educ:* Westcliff High Sch., Essex. Served War, RN, 1943–47. Worked variously for newsagent, baker, woollen merchant and toy manufr, 1939–43; Reporter, then News and Features Editor, The People, 1943–54; Features Editor, Illustrated, 1954–59; Features staff, London Evening Standard, 1959–60; Editor, Men Only, 1960–63; Daily Express (one day), 1963; Features Editor, then Sen. Features Exec., 1963–76, Sunday Mirror; Editor, Reveille, 1976–79 (Fleet Street's 1st photocomposition editor); Asst Editor (Features), 1979–84, Man. Editor, 1984–86, Sunday Mirror. *Publications:* The Aggravations of Minnie Ashe, 1970; The Diabolical Liberties of Uncle Max, 1973; The Soho Summer of Mr Green, 1974; The Shepherd's Bush Connection, 1975; Minnie Ashe at War, 1979; A Few Gross Words, 1990. *Recreations:* talking, walking, reading, writing. *Address:* 14 Ossington Street, W2 4LZ. *T:* 071–229 6582. *Club:* Our Society.

KERSHAW, family name of **Baron Kershaw.**

KERSHAW, 4th Baron, *cr* 1947; **Edward John Kershaw;** JP; Chartered Accountant; Partner in Kidsons Impey, Chartered Accountants, 3 Beaufort Buildings, Spa Road, Gloucester; *b* 12 May 1936; *s* of 3rd Baron and Katharine Dorothea Kershaw (*née* Staines); *S* father, 1962; *m* 1963, Rosalind Lilian Rutherford; one *s* two *d*. *Educ:* Selhurst Grammar Sch., Surrey. Entered RAF Nov. 1955, demobilised Nov. 1957. Admitted to Inst. of Chartered Accountants in England and Wales, Oct. 1964. Lay Governor, The King's Sch., Gloucester, 1986–. JP Gloucester, 1982. *Heir:* *s* Hon. John Charles Edward Kershaw, *b* 23 Dec. 1971.

KERSHAW, Sir Anthony; *see* Kershaw, Sir J. A.

KERSHAW, Henry Aidan; His Honour Judge Kershaw; a Circuit Judge, since 1976; *b* 11 May 1927; *s* of late Rev. H. Kershaw, Bolton; *m* 1960, Daphne Patricia, *widow* of Dr. C. R. Cowan; four *s*. *Educ:* St John's, Leatherhead; Brasenose Coll., Oxford (BA). Served RN, 1946–48. Called to Bar, Inner Temple, 1953. Councillor, Bolton CBC, 1954–57. Asst Recorder of Oldham, 1970–71; a Recorder of the Crown Court, 1972–76. Dep. Chm., Agricultural Land Tribunal, 1972–76. Chm., Lancs Schs Golf Assoc., 1981–84; Vice-Pres., English Schs Golf Assoc., 1984–. *Recreations:* golf, ski-ing, oil-painting. *Address:* Broadhaven, St Andrew's Road, Lostock, Bolton, Lancs. *Clubs:* Royal and Ancient Golf (St Andrews); Bolton Golf; West Hill Golf.

KERSHAW, Prof. Ian, DPhil; FBA 1991; Professor of Modern History, University of Sheffield, since 1989; *b* Oldham, 29 April 1943; *s* of late Joseph Kershaw and of Alice (*née* Robinson); *m* 1966, Janet Elizabeth Murray Gammie; two *s*. *Educ:* St Bede's Coll., Manchester; Univ. of Liverpool (BA 1965); Merton Coll., Oxford (DPhil 1969). University of Manchester: Asst Lectr in Medieval Hist., 1968–70, Lectr, 1970–74; Lectr in Modern Hist., 1974–79, Sen. Lectr, 1979–87, Reader elect, 1987; Prof. of Modern History, Univ. of Nottingham, 1987–89. Vis. Prof. of Contemporary Hist., Ruhr-Univ., Bochum, 1983–84. Fellow: Alexander von Humboldt-Stiftung, 1976; Wissenschaftskolleg zu Berlin, 1989–90. *Publications:* (ed) Rentals and Ministers' Accounts of Bolton Priory 1473–1539, 1969; Bolton Priory: the economy of a Northern monastery, 1973; Der Hitler-Mythos: Volksmeinung und Propaganda im Dritten Reich, 1980, Eng. trans. 1987; Popular Opinion and Political Dissent in the Third Reich: Bavaria 1933–1945, 1983; The Nazi Dictatorship: problems and perspectives of interpretation, 1985, 2nd edn 1989; (ed) Weimar: why did German democracy fail?, 1990; Hitler: a profile in power, 1991; articles in learned jls. *Recreations:* Rugby League, cricket, music, real ale, outings in the Yorkshire dales. *Address:* Department of History, University of Sheffield, Sheffield S10 2TN. *T:* Sheffield (0742) 768555.

KERSHAW, Sir (John) Anthony, Kt 1981; MC 1943; DL; Barrister-at-Law; *b* 14 Dec. 1915; *s* of Judge J. F. Kershaw, Cairo and London, and of Anne Kershaw, Kentucky, USA; *m* 1939, Barbara, *d* of Harry Crookenden; two *s* two *d*. *Educ:* Eton; Balliol Coll., Oxford (BA). Called to the Bar 1939. Served War, 1940–46: 16th/5th Lancers. Mem. LCC, 1946–49; Westminster City Council, 1947–48. MP (C) Stroud Div. of Gloucestershire, 1955–87. Parly Sec., Min. of Public Building and Works, June-Oct. 1970; Parliamentary Under-Secretary of State: FCO, 1970–73; for Defence (RAF), 1973–74; Chm., H of C Select Cttee on Foreign Affairs, 1979–87; Mem. Exec., 1922 Cttee, 1983–87. Vice-Chm., British Council, 1974–87. DL Gloucestershire, 1989. *Address:* West Barn, Didmarton, Badminton, Avon GL9 1DT. *Club:* White's.

KERSHAW, Joseph Anthony; craftsman in wood; *b* 26 Nov. 1935; *s* of Henry and Catherine Kershaw, Preston; *m* 1959, Ann Whittle; three *s* two *d*. *Educ:* Ushaw Coll., Durham; Preston Catholic Coll., SJ. Short service commn, RAOC, 1955–58; Unilever Ltd, 1958–67; Gp Marketing Manager, CWS, 1967–69; Managing Director: Underline Ltd, 1969–71; Merchant Div., Reed International Ltd, 1971–73; Head of Marketing, Non-Foods, CWS, 1973–74; (first) Director, Nat. Consumer Council, 1975; independent management consultant, 1975–91. Chairman: Antonian Investments Ltd, 1985–87; Organised Business Data Ltd, 1987–89; Director: John Stork & Partners Ltd, 1980–85; Allia (Holdings) Ltd, 1984–88; Associate Director: Foote, Cone & Belding Ltd, 1979–84; Phoenix Advertising, 1984–86. *Recreations:* fishing, gardening, cooking; pilot of hot air balloon; CPRE. *Address:* Westmead, Meins Road, Blackburn, Lancs BB2 6QF. *T:* Blackburn (0254) 55915.

KERSHAW, Michael; *see* Kershaw, P. M.

KERSHAW, (Philip) Michael, QC 1980; **His Honour Judge Michael Kershaw;** a Circuit Commercial Judge, since 1990; *b* 23 April 1941; *s* of His Honour Philip Kershaw; *m* 1980, Anne (*née* Williams); one *s*. *Educ:* Ampleforth Coll.; St John's Coll., Oxford (MA). Called to the Bar, Gray's Inn, 1963; in practice, 1963–90; a Recorder, 1980–90. *Address:* Crown Court, Crown Square, Manchester.

KERSHAW, Mrs W. J. S.; *see* Paling, Helen Elizabeth.

KERSHAW, Prof. William Edgar, CMG 1971; VRD; Professor of Biology, University of Salford, 1966–76, now Emeritus Professor; Advisor in Tropical Medicine to Manchester Area Health Authority, since 1976. *Educ:* Manchester University. MB, ChB, 1935; MRCS, LRCP, 1936; DTM&H Eng. 1946; MD 1949; DSc 1956. Chalmers Memorial Gold Medal, Royal Society of Tropical Medicine and Hygiene, 1955. Formerly: Surgeon Captain, RNR; Demonstrator in Morbid Anatomy, Manchester Univ.; Leverhulme Senior Lectr in Med. Parasitology, Liverpool Sch. of Trop. Med. and Liverpool Univ.; Walter Myers and Everett Dutton Prof. of Parasitology and Entomology, Liverpool Univ., 1958–66. Hon. Lectr, Dept of Bacteriology, Univ. of Manchester, 1977–. *Address:* Mill Farm, Hesketh Bank, Preston PR4 6RA. *T:* Hesketh Bank (077473) 4299.

KERSS, William; Chief Executive, National Grid Co., since 1990; *b* 8 March 1931; *s* of William Kerss and Josephine Kerss (*née* Rankin); *m* 1959, Amy Murrey; two *d*. *Educ:* Durham Univ. (BSc Hons Elec. Eng). Student apprentice, NE Electricity Bd, 1948–53; power stations, research, planning and ops, transmission system design, system ops, CEGB, 1957–77; management appts, CEGB, 1963–77; Chief Engineer, SE Electricity Bd, 1977–83; Dep. Chm., S Wales Electricity Bd, 1983–88. *Recreations:* golf, gardening. *Address:* National Grid Co., National Grid House, Sumner Street, SE1 9JU. *T:* 071–620 8239.

KERWIN, Prof. Larkin, CC 1980 (OC 1977); FRSC; President, Canadian Space Agency, since 1989; *b* 22 June 1924; *s* of T. J. Kerwin and Catherine Lonergan-Kerwin; *m* 1950, Maria Guadaloupe Turcot; five *s* three *d*. *Educ:* St Francis Xavier Univ. (BSc 1944); MIT (MSc 1946); Université Laval (DSc 1949). Laval University: Dir, Dept of Physics, 1961–67; Vice-Dean, Faculty of Sciences, 1967–68; Vice-Rector, Academic, 1969–72; Rector, 1972–77. President: Royal Soc. of Canada, 1976–77; National Res. Council of Canada, 1980–89; IUPAP, 1987–90 (Sec.-Gen., 1972–84; First Vice-Pres., 1984–87). Hon. LLD: St Francis Xavier, 1970; Toronto, 1973; Concordia, 1976; Alberta, 1983; Dalhousie, 1983; Hon. DSc: British Columbia, 1973; McGill, 1974; Memorial, 1978; Ottawa, 1981; Royal Military Coll., Canada, 1982; Hon. DCL Bishop's, 1978; DSc (*hc*): Winnipeg, 1983; Windsor, 1984; Moncton, 1985. Médaille du Centenaire, 1967; Médaille de l'Assoc. Canadienne des Physiciens, 1969; Médaille Pariseau, 1965; Medal of Centenary of Roumania, 1977; Jubilee Medal, 1977; Laval Alumni Medal, 1978; Gold Medal, Canadian Council of Professional Engineers, 1982; Rousseau Medal, l'ACFAS, 1983. Kt Comdr with star, Holy Sepulchre of Jerusalem, 1974; Officier de la Légion d'Honneur, 1989. *Publications:* Atomic Physics, 1963 (trans. French, 1964, Spanish, 1970); papers in jls. *Recreation:* sailing. *Address:* 2166 Parc Bourbonnière, Sillery, Quebec G1T 1B4, Canada. *T:* (613) 993–2024. *Club:* Cercle Universitaire (Quebec).

KESSEL, Prof. William Ivor Neil, MD; FRCP, FRCPE, FRCPsych; Professor of Psychiatry, since 1965 and Dean of Postgraduate Studies, Faculty of Medicine, since 1982, University of Manchester; *b* 10 Feb. 1925; *s* of Barney Kessel and Rachel Isabel Kessel; *m* 1958, Pamela Veronica Joyce (*née* Boswell); one *s* one *d*. *Educ:* Highgate Sch.; Trinity Coll., Cambridge (MA, MD); UCH Med. Sch.; Inst. of Psychiatry. MSc Manchester. FRCP 1967; FRCPE 1968; FRCPsych 1972. Staff, Inst. of Psych., 1960; scientific staff, MRC Unit for Epidemiol. of Psych. Illness, 1961, Asst Dir 1963; Hon. Sen. Lectr, Edinburgh Univ., 1964; Dean, Faculty of Med., Univ. of Manchester, 1974–76. Member: NW RHA, 1974–77; GMC, 1974–; Adv. Council on Misuse of Drugs, 1972–80; Health Educn Council, 1979–86; Chm., Adv. Cttee on Alcoholism, DHSS, 1975–78; Cons. Adviser on alcoholism to DHSS, 1972–81, 1983–86. *Publications:* Alcoholism (with Prof. H. J. Walton), 1965, 3rd edn 1975, rev. edn 1989; articles on suicide and self-poisoning, alcoholism, psych. in gen. practice, psychosomatic disorders, psych. epidemiol., genius and mental illness *Address:* Department of Psychiatry, University Hospital of South Manchester, West Didsbury, Manchester M20 8LR. *T:* 061–447 4361. *Club:* Athenæum.

KESWICK, Henry Neville Lindley; Chairman: Matheson & Co. Ltd, since 1975; Jardine, Matheson Holdings Ltd, Hong Kong, 1972–75 and since 1989 (Director, since 1967); Jardine Strategic Holdings, since 1989 (Director, since 1988); *b* 29 Sept. 1938; *s* of Sir William Keswick and of Mary, *d* of Rt Hon. Sir Francis Lindley, PC, GCMG; *m* 1985, Tessa, Lady Reay, *y d* of 17th Baron Lovat, *qv*. *Educ:* Eton Coll.; Trinity Coll., Cambridge. BA Hons Econs and Law; MA. Commnd Scots Guards, Nat. Service, 1956–58. Director: Sun Alliance and London Insurance, 1975–; Robert Fleming Holdings Ltd; Rothmans Internat., 1988–; Hongkong Land Co., 1988–; Mandarin Oriental Internat., 1988–; Dairy Farm Internat. Hldgs, 1988–; Sun Alliance Group, 1989–; The Daily Telegraph, 1990–.

Member: London Adv. Cttee, Hongkong and Shanghai Banking Corp., 1975–; 21st Century Trust, 1987–. Proprietor, The Spectator, 1975–81. Trustee, Nat. Portrait Gall., 1982–. Chm., Hong Kong Assoc, 1988–. Vice-Chm., City and Industrial Liaison Council of Cons. Party, 1986–. *Recreation:* country pursuits. *Address:* 28 Arlington House, St James's, SW1. *Clubs:* White's, Turf; Third Guards.

See also J. C. L. Keswick, S. L. Keswick.

KESWICK, John Chippendale Lindley; Chairman, Hambros Bank Ltd, since 1986; *b* 2 Feb.1940; 2nd *s* of Sir William Keswick and of Mary, *d* of Rt Hon. Sir Francis Lindley, PC, GCMG; *m* 1966, Lady Sarah Ramsay, *d* of 16th Earl of Dalhousie, *qv*; three *s*. *Educ:* Eton; Univ. of Aix/Marseilles. Glyn Mills & Co., 1961–65; Jt Vice Chm., 1986, Jt Dep. Chm., 1990–, Hambros PLC. Director: Persimmon; Charter Consolidated. Mem. Council, Cancer Research Campaign; Hon. Treas., Children's Country Holidays Fund. Mem., Queen's Body Guard for Scotland, Royal Company of Archers. *Recreations:* bridge, field sports. *Address:* Hambros Bank, 41 Tower Hill, EC3N 4HA. *T:* 071–480 5000. *Clubs:* White's, Portland (Chm.).

KESWICK, Simon Lindley; Director: Jardine Matheson Holdings Ltd, since 1972 (Chairman, 1983–89); Jardine Strategic Holdings Ltd, since 1987 (Chairman, 1987–89); Matheson & Co. Ltd, since 1982; Chairman: Hongkong Land Holdings Ltd, since 1983; Mandarin Oriental International Ltd, since 1984; Dairy Farm International Holdings Ltd, since 1984; Fleming Mercantile Investment Trust, since 1990 (Director, since 1988); *b* 20 May 1942; *s* of Sir William Keswick and of Mary, *d* of Rt Hon. Sir Francis Lindley, PC, GCMG; *m* 1971, Emma, *d* of Major David Chetwode; two *s* two *d*. *Educ:* Eton Coll. Chm., Jardine Matheson Insurance Brokers Ltd, 1978–82; Director: Greenfriar Investment Co. Ltd, 1979–; Hongkong & Shanghai Banking Corp., 1983–88. Trustee, British Museum, 1989–. Ordinary Gov., London Hosp. Med. Coll., 1989–. Mem., the Queen's Body Guard for Scotland, Royal Co. of Archers, 1982. FRSA 1989. *Recreations:* country pursuits, Tottenham Hotspurs. *Address:* No 9, Shek O, Hong Kong; Rockcliffe, Upper Slaughter, Cheltenham, Glos GL54 2JW. *T:* Cotswold (0451) 30648. *Clubs:* White's, Turf, Portland; Union (Sydney); Shek O (Hong Kong).

See also H. N. L. Keswick, J. C. L. Keswick.

KETTLE, Captain Alan Stafford Howard, CB 1984; Royal Navy (retired); General Manager, HM Dockyard, Chatham, 1977–84; *b* 6 Aug. 1925; *s* of Arthur Stafford Kettle and Marjorie Constance (*née* Clough); *m* 1952, Patricia Rosemary (*née* Gander); two *s*. *Educ:* Rugby School. CEng, FIMechE. Joined RN, 1943; Comdr, Dec. 1959; Captain, Dec. 1968; retired, Sept. 1977. Entered Civil Service as Asst Under-Sec., Sept. 1977. *Address:* 3 Leather Tor Close, Grangelands, Yelverton PL20 6EQ. *T:* Yelverton (0822) 854249.

KETTLE, Roy Henry Richard; Group Vice Chairman, Evered Bardon plc, since 1991; *b* 2 May 1924; *s* of Arthur Charles Edwin and Emily Grace Kettle; *m* 1956, Jean Croudace; one *s* three *d*. *Educ:* Wolverhampton Grammar School. Tarmac Roadstone Ltd: Accountancy Asst, 1947; Management Acct, 1960; Chief Management Acct, 1964; Dir of Admin, 1967; Man. Dir, 1976; Tarmac plc: Dir, 1977; Gp Man. Dir, 1982–86, retd. Chm., CI Gp plc (formerly Cooper Industries), 1985–89; Dir, Evered Hldgs, subseq. Evered Bardon, 1985–; Chief Exec., Evered Hldgs, 1989–91; Dir, London and Northern Gp, 1987–91. Mem., Black Country Develt Corp., 1987–. *Recreations:* walking, gardening. *Address:* Hilbre, Watling Street South, Church Stretton, Shropshire. *T:* Church Stretton (0694) 722445; (office) Evered Bardon House, Round Green Road, Oldbury, W Midlands B69 2DH. *T:* 021–552 9977.

KETTLEWELL, Comdt Dame Marion M., DBE 1970 (CBE 1964); General Secretary, Girls' Friendly Society, 1971–78; *b* 20 Feb. 1914; *d* of late George Wildman Kettlewell, Bramling, Virginia Water, Surrey, and of Mildred Frances (*née* Atkinson), Belford, Northumberland. *Educ:* Godolphin Sch., Salisbury; St Christopher's Coll., Blackheath. Worked for Fellowship of Maple Leaf, Alta, Canada, 1935–38; worked for Local Council, 1939–41; joined WRNS as MT driver, 1941; commnd as Third Officer WRNS, 1942; Supt WRNS on Staff of Flag Officer Air (Home), 1961–64; Supt WRNS Training and Drafting, 1964–67; Director, WRNS, 1967–70. Pres., Assoc. of Wrens, 1981–. *Recreations:* needlework, walking, and country life. *Address:* Flat 2, 9 John Islip Street, SW1P 4PU.

See also R. W. Kettlewell.

KETTLEWELL, Richard Wildman, CMG 1955; Colonial Service, retired 1962; *b* 12 Feb. 1910; *s* of late George Wildman Kettlewell and of Mildred Frances Atkinson; *m* 1935, Margaret Jessie Palmer (*d* 1990); one *s* one *d*. *Educ:* Clifton Coll.; Reading and Cambridge Univs. BSc 1931; Dip. Agric. Cantab 1932; Associate of Imperial Coll. of Tropical Agriculture (AICTA), 1933. Entered Colonial Agricultural Service, 1934; appointed to Nyasaland. Served War of 1939–45 (despatches) with 2nd Bn King's African Rifles, 1939–43; rank of Major. Recalled to agricultural duties in Nyasaland, 1943; Dir of Agriculture, 1951–59; Sec. for Natural Resources, 1959–61; Minister for Lands and Surveys, 1961–62. Consultant to Hunting Technical Services, 1963–79. *Address:* Orchard Close, Over Norton, Chipping Norton, Oxon OX7 5PH. *T:* Chipping Norton (0608) 642407.

See also Comdt Dame M. M. Kettlewell.

KEVILL-DAVIES, Christopher Evelyn, CBE 1973; JP; DL; *b* 12 July 1913; 3rd *s* of William A. S. H. Kevill-Davies, JP, Croft Castle, Herefordshire; *m* 1938, Virginia, *d* of Adm. Ronald A. Hopwood, CB; one *s* one *d*. *Educ:* Radley College. Served with Suffolk Yeomanry, 1939–43 and Grenadier Gds, 1943–45, France, Belgium and Germany. Mem., Gt Yarmouth Borough Council, 1946–53; Chm., Norfolk Mental Deficiency HMC, 1950–69; Mem., East Anglian Regional Hosp. Bd, 1962 (Vice-Chm. 1967); Vice-Chm., E Anglian RHA, 1974–82. JP 1954, DL 1974–83, Norfolk; High Sheriff of Norfolk, 1965. *Address:* 11 Hale House, 34 De Vere Gardens, Kensington, W8. *T:* 071–937 5066. *Clubs:* Cavalry and Guards; Norfolk (Norwich).

KEVILLE, Sir (William) Errington, Kt 1962; CBE 1947; *b* 3 Jan. 1901; *s* of William Edwin Keville; *m* 1928, Ailsa Sherwood, *d* of late Captain John McMillan; three *s* two *d*. *Educ:* Merchant Taylors'. Pres., Chamber of Shipping, 1961 (Vice-Pres. 1960, Mem. of Council, 1940–); Chairman: Gen. Coun. of British Shipping, 1961; International Chamber of Shipping, 1963–68; Cttee of European Shipowners, 1963–65; Member: Executive Council of Shipping Federation Ltd, 1936–68; Board of PLA, 1943–59; National Maritime Board, 1945–68; Mem. of Cttee of Lloyd's Register of Shipping, 1957–68; Director: Shaw Savill & Albion Co. Ltd, 1941–68 (former Dep. Chm.); National Bank of New Zealand Ltd, 1946–75; Economic Insurance Co. Ltd, 1949–68 (Chm., 1962–68); National Mortgage & Agency Co. of NZ Ltd, 1950–68; British Maritime Trust Ltd, 1959–72 (Chm. 1962–68); Furness Withy & Co. Ltd, 1950–68 (Chm., 1962–68); Chm., Air Holdings Ltd, 1968–69. *Recreations:* walking, history. *Address:* c/o Bunts End, Leigh, Surrey RH2 8NS.

KEY, Brian Michael; Member (Lab) Yorkshire South, European Parliament, 1979–84; *b* 20 Sept. 1947; *s* of Leslie Granville Key and Nora Alice (*née* Haylett); *m* 1974, Lynn Joyce Ambler. *Educ:* Darfield County Primary Sch.; Wath upon Dearne Grammar Sch.; Liverpool Univ. (BA Hons). Careers Officer, West Riding County Council, 1970–73; Sen. Administrative Officer, South Yorkshire CC, 1973–79. *Address:* 25 Cliff Road, Darfield, Barnsley S73 9HR. *Clubs:* Darfield Working Men's; Trades and Labour (Doncaster).

KEY, Maj.-Gen. Clement Denis, MBE 1945; late RAOC; *b* 6 June 1915; *s* of late William Clement Key, Harborne, Birmingham; *m* 1941, Molly, *d* of late F. Monk, Kettering, Northants; two *s*. *Educ:* Seaford Coll. Commnd in RAOC, 1940; served in: England, 1940–44; France, Belgium, Burma, Singapore, 1944–48; Staff Coll., Camberley, 1945; England, 1948–51; USA, 1951–54; England, 1954–59; jssc 1954; Belgium, 1959–61; War Office, 1961–64; Dep. Dir of Ordnance Services, War Office, 1964–67; Dep. Dir of Ordnance Services, Southern Comd, 1967; Comdr, UK Base Organisation, RAOC, 1968–70; retd, 1970. Hon. Col, RAOC (T&AVR), 1968–71; Col Comdt, RAOC, 1972–75. Bursar, 1971–76, Clerk to Govrs, 1976–85, Tudor Hall Sch., Banbury. *Recreations:* rowing, gardening, bee-keeping. *Address:* 104 Maidenhead Road, Stratford-upon-Avon, Warwicks CV37 6XY. *T:* Stratford-upon-Avon (0789) 204345.

KEY, (Simon) Robert; MP (C) Salisbury, since 1983; *b* 22 April 1945; *s* of late Rt Rev. J. M. Key; *m* 1968, Susan Priscilla Bright Irvine, 2nd *d* of late Rev. T. T. Irvine; one *s* two *d* (and one *s* decd). *Educ:* Salisbury Cathedral Sch.; Forres Sch., Swanage; Sherborne Sch.; Clare Coll., Cambridge. MA; CertEd. Assistant Master: Loretto Sch., Edinburgh, 1967; Harrow Sch., 1969–83. Warden, Nanoose Field Studies Centre, Wool, Dorset, 1972–78; Governor: Sir William Collins Sch., NW1, 1976–81; Special Sch. at Gt Ormond Street Hosp. for Sick Children, 1976–81; Roxeth Sch., Harrow, 1979–82. Founder Chm., ALICE Trust for Autistic Children, 1977–82; Council Mem., GAP Activity Projects, 1975–84. Vice-Chm., Wembley Br., ASTMS, 1976–80. Contested (C) Camden, Holborn and St Pancras South, 1979. Political Sec. to Rt Hon. Edward Heath, 1984–85; PPS to: Minister of State for Energy, 1985–87; Minister for Overseas Develt, 1987–89; Sec. of State for the Envmt, 1989–90; Parly Under-Sec. of State, DoE, 1990–. Mem., Select Cttee on Educn, Science and the Arts, 1983–86; Sec., Cons. Parly Backbench Cttee on Arts and Heritage, 1983–84; Jt Parly Chm., Council for Educn in the Commonwealth, 1984–87; Vice-Chm., All-Party Gp on AIDS, 1988–. Chm., Harrow Central Cons. Assoc., 1980–82; Vice-Chm., Central London Cons. Euro-Constit., 1980–82; Mem., Cons. Party Nat. Union Exec., 1981–83. Member: UK Nat. Commn for UNESCO, 1984–85; MRC, 1989–90 (Mem., AIDS Cttee, 1989–90). Vice-Pres., Haemophilia Soc., 1988–90. Hon. FCollP, 1989. *Recreations:* singing, cooking, country life. *Address:* House of Commons, SW1A 0AA. *T:* 071–219 3000. *Club:* Athenæum.

KEYES, family name of **Baron Keyes.**

KEYES, 2nd Baron, *cr* 1943, of Zeebrugge and of Dover; **Roger George Bowlby Keyes;** Bt, *cr* 1919; RN, retired; *b* 14 March 1919; 2nd *s* of Admiral of the Fleet Baron Keyes, GCB, KCVO, CMG, DSO and Eva Mary Salvin Bowlby (*d* 1973), Red Cross Order of Queen Elisabeth of Belgium, *d* of late Edward Salvin Bowlby, DL, of Gilston Park, Herts, and Knoydart, Inverness-shire; *S* father 1945; *m* 1947, Grizelda Mary, 2nd *d* of late Lieut-Col William Packe, DSO; three *s* two *d*. *Educ:* King's Mead Sch., Seaford; RNC, Dartmouth. *Publication:* Outrageous Fortune, 1984 (SE Arts Literary Prize). *Heir: s* Hon. Charles William Packe Keyes, *b* 8 Dec. 1951. *Address:* Elmscroft, Charlton Lane, West Farleigh, near Maidstone, Kent. *T:* Maidstone (0622) 812477.

See also Baron Kennet.

KEYNES, Prof. Richard Darwin, CBE 1984; MA, PhD, ScD Cantab; FRS 1959; Professor of Physiology, University of Cambridge, 1973–87; Fellow of Churchill College, since 1961; *b* 14 Aug. 1919; *e s* of Sir Geoffrey Keynes, MD, FRCP, FRCS, FRCOG, and late Margaret Elizabeth, *d* of Sir George Darwin, KCB; *m* 1945, Anne Pinsent Adrian, *e d* of 1st Baron Adrian, OM, FRS, and Dame Hester Agnes Adrian, DBE, *o d* of Hume C. and Dame Ellen Pinsent, DBE; three *s* (and one *s* decd). *Educ:* Oundle Sch. (Scholar); Trinity Coll., Cambridge (Scholar). Temporary experimental officer, HM Anti-Submarine Establishment and Admiralty Signals Establishment, 1940–45. 1st Class, Nat. Sci. Tripos Part II, 1946; Michael Foster and G. H. Lewes Studentships, 1946; Research Fellow of Trinity Coll., 1948–52; Gedge Prize, 1948; Rolleston Memorial Prize, 1950. Demonstrator in Physiology, University of Cambridge, 1949–53; Lecturer, 1953–60; Fellow of Peterhouse, 1952–60 (Hon. Fellow, 1989); Head of Physiology Dept and Dep. Dir, 1960–64, Dir, 1965–73, ARC Inst. of Animal Physiology. Sec.-Gen., Internat. Union for Pure and Applied Biophysics, 1972–78, Vice-Pres., 1978–81, Pres., 1981–84; Chairman: Internat. Cell Research Orgn, 1981–83; ICSU/Unesco Internat. Biosciences Networks, 1982–. A Vice-Pres., Royal Society, 1965–68, Croonian Lectr, 1983. Fellow of Eton, 1963–78. For. Member: Royal Danish Acad., 1971; American Philosophical Soc., 1977; Amer. Acad. of Arts and Scis, 1978. Dr *hc* Univ. of Brazil, 1968. *Publications:* The Beagle Record, 1979; (with D. J. Aidley) Nerve and Muscle, 1981; (ed) Charles Darwin's Beagle Diary, 1988; (ed jtly) Lydia and Maynard: the letters of Lydia Lopokova and John Maynard Keynes, 1989; papers in Journal of Physiology, Proceedings of Royal Soc., etc. *Recreations:* sailing, gardening. *Address:* 4 Herschel Road, Cambridge CB3 9AG. *T:* Cambridge (0223) 353107; Primrose Farm, Wiveton, Norfolk NR25 7TQ. *T:* Cley (0263) 740317.

See also S. J. Keynes.

KEYNES, Stephen John; Director: Premier Consolidated Oilfields plc, since 1976; Hawkshead Ltd, since 1987; *b* 19 Oct. 1927; 4th *s* of Sir Geoffrey Keynes, MD, FRCP, FRCS, FRCOG, and late Margaret Elizabeth, *d* of Sir George Darwin, KCB; *m* 1955, Mary, *o d* of late Senator the Hon. Adrian Knatchbull-Hugessen, QC (Canada), and late Margaret, *o d* of G. H. Duggan; three *s* two *d*. *Educ:* Oundle Sch.; King's Coll., Cambridge (Foundn Scholar; MA). Royal Artillery, 1949–51. Partner, J. F. Thomasson & Co., Private Bankers, 1961–65; Director: Charterhouse Japhet Ltd and Charterhouse Finance Corp., 1965–72; Arbuthnot Latham Holdings Ltd, 1973–80; Sun Life Assce Soc. plc, 1965–89; PK English Trust Co. Ltd, 1980–90. Member: IBA (formerly ITA), 1969–74; Cttee and Treas., Islington and North London Family Service Unit, 1956–68; Adv. Cttee, Geffrye Museum, 1964–87; Trustee: Centerprise Community Project, 1971–75; Needham Research Inst. (E Asian Hist. of Science Trust); Chairman of Trustees: Whitechapel Art Gallery; English Chamber Theatre; William Blake Trust. *Recreations:* medieval manuscripts, painting, gardening, travelling. *Address:* 16 Canonbury Park South, Islington, N1. *T:* 071–226 8170; Lammas House, Brinkley, Newmarket, Suffolk CB8 0SB. *T:* Stetchworth (0638) 507268; Gunnerside, near Richmond, Yorks. *Clubs:* Cranium, Roxburghe.

See also R. D. Keynes.

KEYS, Sir (Alexander George) William, AC 1988; Kt 1980; OBE 1969; MC 1951; company director; National President, Returned Services League of Australia, 1978–88; Deputy Chairman, Canberra Permanent Building Society, since 1980; *b* 2 Feb. 1923; *s* of John Alexander Binnie Keys and Irene Daisy Keys; *m* 1950, Dulcie Beryl (*née* Stinton); three *d*. *Educ:* Hurlstone Agricultural High Sch. National Secretary, RSL, 1961–78 (Life Member); Nat. President, Korea and SE Asia Forces Assoc. of Australia, 1964–; World Pres., Internat. Fedn of Korean War Veterans Assoc., 1978–; Mem. Nat. Exec., Royal

Australian Regt Assoc., 1967–; Mem. Bd of Trustees, Aust. War Memorial, 1975; Mem. ACT, Churchill Fellows Assoc. Korean Order of National Security Merit, 1980. *Address:* Glenlee, Post Office Box 455, Queanbeyan, NSW 2620, Australia. *T:* (home) 97 5440; (office) 977877. *Clubs:* Commonwealth, National Press (Canberra); Returned Services League (Queanbeyan).

KEYS, Prof. Ivor Christopher Banfield, CBE 1976; MA, DMus Oxon; FRCO; FRCM; Hon. RAM; Professor of Music, University of Birmingham, 1968–86; *b* 8 March 1919; *er s* of Christopher Richard Keys, Littlehampton, Sussex; *m* 1944, Margaret Anne Layzell (*d* 1990); two *s* two *d. Educ:* Christ's Hospital, Horsham; Christ Church, Oxford. FRCO 1934; music scholar and asst organist, Christ Church Cathedral, Oxford, 1938–40 and 1946–47. Served with Royal Pioneer Corps, 1940–46. Lecturer in Music, Queen's University of Belfast, 1947, Reader, 1950, Sir Hamilton Harty Professor of Music, QUB, 1951–54; Prof. of Music, Nottingham Univ., 1954–68. Vis. Prof., Huddersfield Poly., 1986–89. Pres., RCO, 1968–70. Chairman: Nat. Fedn of Music Socs, 1985–88; BBC Central Music Adv. Cttee, 1985–88. Hon. DMus QUB, 1972. *Publications:* The Texture of Music: Purcell to Brahms, 1961; Brahms Chamber Music, 1974; Mozart, 1980; Johannes Brahms, 1989; *compositions:* Sonata for Violoncello and Pianoforte; Completion of Schubert's unfinished song Gretchens Bitte; Concerto for Clarinet and Strings; Prayer for Pentecostal Fire (choir and organ); The Road to the Stable (3 Christmas songs with piano); Magnificat and Nunc Dimittis (choir and organ); editions of music; reviews of music, in Music and Letters, and of books, in Musical Times. *Recreation:* bridge. *Address:* 6 Eastern Road, Birmingham B29 7JP.

KEYS, Sir William; *see* Keys, Sir A. G. W.

KHAIR-UD-DIN, Rt. Rev.; *see* Ud-Din.

KHAMENEI, Ayatollah Sayyed Ali; Leader of the Islamic Revolution, since 1989; *b* 1940; *m* 1964; four *s* two *d. Educ:* Qom; studied under Iman Khomeini, 1956–64. Imprisoned six times, 1964–78; once exiled, 1978; Mem., Revolutionary Council, 1978 until its dissolution, 1979 (Rep. in Iranian Army and Assistant of Revolutionary Affairs in Min. of Defence); Rep. of First Islamic Consultative Assembly, and of Iman Khomeini in the Supreme Council of Defence, 1980; Comdr, Revolutionary Guards, 1980; Friday Prayer Leader, Teheran, 1980–; Sec. Gen., Islamic Republic Party, 1980–87; Pres., Islamic Republic of Iran, 1981–89. *Recreations:* reading, arts, literature. *Address:* Office of Leadership, Teheran, Islamic Republic of Iran.

KHAN, Ghulam Ishaq; President of Pakistan, since 1988; *b* 20 Jan. 1915; *m* 1950; one *s* five *d. Educ:* Islamia Coll., Peshawar; Punjab Univ. Indian Civil Service, 1940–47; NWFP service, 1947–56; Government of West Pakistan: Sec. for Develt and Irrigation, 1956–58; Chm., Water and Power Develt Authy, 1961–66; Chm., Land Reforms Commn, 1978; Sec., Finance, 1966–70; Cabinet Sec., 1970; Sec.-Gen., Ministry of Defence, 1975–77; Sec.-Gen.-in-Chief, Adviser for Planning and Co-ordination, 1977–78; Adviser to Chief Martial Law Administrator, 1978; Minister for Finance and Co-ordination, 1978–79, for Finance, Econ. Affairs, Commerce and Co-ordination, 1979–85; Chairman of Senate, 1985–88. Governor, State Bank of Pakistan, 1971–75; Chm., Jt Ministerial Cttee, Board of Governors of World Bank and IMF, 1982–88. *Address:* c/o President's Secretariat, Aiwan-e-Sadr, Islamabad, Pakistan.

KHAN, Humayun; High Commissioner for Pakistan in the United Kingdom, since 1990; *b* 31 Aug. 1932; *s* of M. Safdar Khan and Mumtaz Safdar; *m* 1961, Munawar; three *d. Educ:* Trinity College, Cambridge (MA); Univ. of Southern California (MPA, Dr PA). Called to the Bar, Lincoln's Inn, 1954; Minister, Pakistan Embassy, Moscow, 1974–77; Dep. Perm. Rep., UNO, Geneva, 1977–79; Ambassador to Bangladesh, 1979–82; Additional Sec., Min. of Foreign Affairs, Pakistan, 1982–84; Ambassador to India, 1984–88; Foreign Sec. of Pakistan, 1988–89. *Recreations:* golf, shooting, fishing. *Address:* 35 Lowndes Square, SW1X 9JN. *T:* 071–235 6869; Ministry of Foreign Affairs, Islamabad, Pakistan. *Clubs:* Royal Over-Seas League, Travellers'; Islamabad.

KHAN NIAZI, Imran Ahmad; *see* Imran Khan.

KHAW, Prof. Kay-Tee, (Mrs Kay-Tee Fawcett); Professor of Clinical Gerontology, University of Cambridge, since 1989; *b* 14 Oct. 1950; *d* of Khaw Kai Boh and Tan Chwee Geok; *m* 1980, Dr James William Fawcett; one *s* one *d. Educ:* Girton Coll., Cambridge (BA, MA; MB BChir); St Mary's Hosp. Med. Sch., London; London Sch. of Hygiene and Tropical Med. (MSc). MRCP, DCH. Wellcome Trust Research Fellow, LSHTM, St Mary's Hosp. and Univ. of California San Diego, 1979–84; Asst Adjunct Prof., Univ. of California Sch. of Med., San Diego, 1985; Sen. Registrar in Community Medicine, Univ. of Cambridge Sch. of Clinical Medicine, 1986–89. Daland Fellow, Amer. Philosophical Soc., 1984. *Publications:* contribs to scientific jls on chronic disease epidemiology. *Recreation:* piano. *Address:* Clinical Gerontology Unit, University of Cambridge School of Clinical Medicine, Addenbrooke's Hospital, Cambridge CB2 2QQ.

KHOO, Francis Kah Siang; writer; General Secretary (Director), War on Want, 1988–89; *b* 23 Oct. 1947; *s* of late Teng Eng Khoo and of Swee Neo Chew; *m* 1977, Dr Swee Chai Ang, MB BS, MSc, FRCS. *Educ:* Univ. of Singapore (LLB (Hons) 1970); Univ. of London (MA 1980). Advocate and Solicitor, Singapore, 1971. Lawyer, Singapore, 1971–77; journalist, South magazine, and Mem., NUJ (UK), 1980–87. Founding Mem. and Vice-Chm. of British charity, Medical Aid for Palestinians, 1984–. *Publications:* And Bungaraya Blooms All Day: collection of songs, poems and cartoons in exile, UK, 1978; Hang On Tight, No Surrender: tape of songs, 1984. *Recreations:* photography, hill-walking, song-writing, camera designing and inventions, swimming. *Address:* 17 Knollys House, 39 Tavistock Place, WC1H 9SA. *T:* 071–380 0648.

KHORANA, Prof. Har Gobind; Sloan Professor of Chemistry and Biology, Massachusetts Institute of Technology, since 1970; *b* Raipur, India, 9 Jan. 1922; *s* of Shri Ganpat Rai and Shrimata Krishna (Devi); *m* 1952, Esther Elizabeth Sibler; one *s* two *d. Educ:* Punjab Univ. (BSc 1943; MSc 1945); Liverpool Univ. (PhD 1948; Govt of India Student). Post-doctoral Fellow of Govt of India, Federal Inst. of Techn., Zurich, 1948–49; Nuffield Fellow, Cambridge Univ., 1950–52; Head, Organic Chemistry Group, BC Research Council, 1952–60. Univ. of Wisconsin: Prof. and Co-Dir, Inst. for Enzyme Research, 1960–70; Prof., Dept of Biochemistry, 1962–70; Conrad A. Elvehjem Prof. in the Life Sciences, 1964–70. Visiting Professor: Rockefeller Inst., NY, 1958–60; Stanford Univ., 1964; Harvard Med. Sch., 1966; Andrew D. White Prof.-at-large, Cornell Univ., 1974–80. Has given special or memorial lectures in USA, Poland, Canada, Switzerland, UK and Japan. Fellow: Chem. Inst. of Canada, 1959; Amer. Assoc. for Advancement of Science, 1966; Amer. Acad. of Arts and Sciences, 1967. Overseas Fellow, Churchill Coll., Cambridge, 1967. Member: Nat. Acad. of Sciences; Deutsche Akademie der Naturforscher Leopoldina; Pontifical Acad. of Scis, Rome; Foreign Member: Indian Acad. of Scis, 1976; Royal Society, 1978; RSE, 1982. Various hon. degrees. Merck Award, Chem. Inst. Canada, 1958; Gold Medal for 1960, Professional Inst. of Public Service of Canada; Dannie-Heinneman Preiz, Germany, 1967; Remsen Award, Johns Hopkins Univ., ACS Award for Creative Work in Synthetic Organic Chemistry, Louisa Gross Horwitz Award, Lasker Foundn Award for Basic Med. Research, Nobel Prize for Medicine (jtly), 1968. US Nat.

Medal of Science, 1987. Order of San Carlos (Columbia), 1986. *Publications:* Some Recent Developments in the Chemistry of Phosphate Esters of Biological Interest, 1961; numerous papers in Biochemistry, Jl Amer. Chem. Soc., etc. *Recreations:* hiking, swimming. *Address:* Department of Biology and Chemistry, Massachusetts Institute of Technology, Cambridge, Mass 02139, USA.

KHOUINI, Hamadi; Order of Independence, Tunisia; Order of the Republic, Tunisia; Hon. CBE 1980; Minister of State, Ministry of Foreign Affairs, Tunisia, since 1990; *b* 21 May 1943; *m* 1969, Rafika Hamdi; one *s* one *d. Educ:* The Sorbonne, Paris (LèsL). Sec. Gen., Town Hall, Tunis, 1969–72; Head of Department: Min. of Foreign Affairs, 1972–73; Min. of the Interior, 1973–74; Dir of Youth, Min. of Youth and Sport, 1974–78 (Merit of Youth; Merit of Sport); Dir, Population Demographic Office, 1979–80; Governor of Sousse, 1980–83; Gov. of Tunis, 1983–87, and 1989–90; Ambassador to UK, 1987–88. Order of Civil Merit (Spain), 1983; National Order of Merit (France), 1984; Senegalese decoration. *Recreation:* sport (football in particular). *Address:* Ministry of Foreign Affairs, La Kasbah, Tunis, Tunisia.

KIBBEY, Sidney Basil; Under-Secretary, Department of Health and Social Security, 1971–76; *b* 3 Dec. 1916; *y s* of late Percy Edwin Kibbey and Winifred Kibbey, Mickleover, Derby; *m* 1939, Violet Gertrude, (Jane), Eyre; (twin) *s* and *d. Educ:* Derby Sch. Executive Officer, Min. of Health, 1936; Principal, Min. of National Insurance, 1951; Sec., Nat. Insurance Adv. Cttee, 1960–62; Asst Sec., Min. of Pensions and Nat. Insurance, 1962. *Address:* 29 Beaulieu Close, Datchet, Berks SL3 9DD. *T:* Slough (0753) 49101.

KIBBLE, Prof. Thomas Walter Bannerman, PhD; FRS 1980; Professor of Theoretical Physics, since 1970, and Head of the Department of Physics, 1983–91, Imperial College, London; *b* 1932; *s* of Walter Frederick Kibble and Janet Cowan Watson (*née* Bannerman); *m* 1957, Anne Richmond Allan; one *s* two *d. Educ:* Doveton-Corrie Sch., Madras; Melville Coll., Edinburgh; Univ. of Edinburgh (MA, BSc, PhD). Commonwealth Fund Fellow, California Inst. of Technology, 1958–59; Imperial College, London: NATO Fellow, 1959–60; Lecturer, 1961; Sen. Lectr, 1965; Reader in Theoretical Physics, 1966. Sen. Visiting Research Associate, Univ. of Rochester, New York, 1967–68. Member: Nuclear Physics Bd, SERC, 1982–86; Astronomy, Space and Radio Bd, 1984–86; Physical Sciences Sub-cttee, UGC, 1985–89. Chairman: Scientists Against Nuclear Arms, 1985– (Vice-Chm., 1981–85); Martin Ryle Trust, 1985–. Mem. Council, Royal Soc., 1987–89 (Vice-Pres., 1988–89). (Jtly) Hughes Medal, Royal Soc., 1981; (jtly) Rutherford Medal, Inst. of Physics, 1984. *Publications:* Classical Mechanics, 1966, 3rd edn 1985; papers in Phys. Rev., Proc. Royal Soc., Nuclear Physics, Nuovo Cimento, Jl Physics, and others. *Recreations:* cycling, destructive gardening. *Address:* Blackett Laboratory, Imperial College, Prince Consort Road, SW7 2BZ. *T:* 071–225 8800.

KIDD, Prof. Cecil; Regius Professor of Physiology, Marischal College, University of Aberdeen, since 1984; *b* 28 April 1933; *s* of Herbert Cecil and Elizabeth Kidd; *m* 1956, Margaret Winifred Goodwill; three *s. Educ:* Queen Elizabeth Grammar School, Darlington; King's College, Newcastle upon Tyne, Univ. of Durham (BSc, PhD). FIBiol; FRSA. Research Fellow then Demonstrator in Physiology, King's Coll., Univ. of Durham, 1954–58; Asst Lectr then Lectr in Physiol., Univ. of Leeds, 1958–68; Res. Fellow in Physiol., Johns Hopkins Univ., 1962–63; Sen. Lectr then Reader in Physiol., 1968–84, Sen. Res. Associate in Cardiovascular Studies, 1973–84, Univ. of Leeds. *Publications:* scientific papers in physiological jls. *Recreations:* squash, gardening. *Address:* School of Biomedical Sciences, Division of Physiology, Marischal College, University of Aberdeen, Aberdeen AB9 1AS. *T:* Aberdeen (0224) 273005.

KIDD, Charles William; Editor of Debrett's Peerage, since 1980; *b* 23 May 1952; *yr s* of Charles Vincent Kidd and Marian Kidd (*née* Foster), Kirkbymoorside. *Educ:* St Peter's Sch., York; Bede Coll., Durham. Assistant Editor: Burke's Peerage, 1972–77; Debrett's Peerage, 1977–80. *Publications:* Debrett's Book of Royal Children (jtly), 1982; Debrett Goes to Hollywood, 1986. *Recreations:* cinema, researching film and theatre dynasties, tennis. *Address:* Debrett's Peerage, 73–77 Britannia Road, SW6 2JR.

KIDD, Prof. Frank Forrest; Partner, Coopers & Lybrand, Chartered Accountants, since 1979; *b* 4 May 1938; *s* of Frank F. Kidd and Constance Mary Kidd (*née* Godman); *m* 1961, Beryl Ann (*née* Gillespie); two *s* two *d. Educ:* George Heriot's Sch., Ballards. CA; Mem. Inst. of Taxation. CA apprentice, 1955–60; Partner, Wylie & Hutton, 1962–79; Partner, Coopers & Lybrand, 1979– (following merger of Coopers & Lybrand with Wylie & Hutton in 1979). Pres., Inst. of Chartered Accountants of Scotland, 1988–89. Hon. Prof., Dept of Accountancy and Business Law, Univ. of Stirling, 1987–. *Recreations:* squash, golf, walking. *Address:* (home) 17 Merchiston Park, Edinburgh EH10 4PW. *T:* 031–229 3577; (business) Coopers & Lybrand, George House, 126 George Street, Edinburgh EH2 4JZ. *T:* 031-226 2595. *Clubs:* Luffness New Golf (Gullane); Edinburgh Sports.

KIDD, Sir Robert (Hill), KBE 1979; CB 1975; Head of Northern Ireland Civil Service, 1976–79; *b* 3 Feb. 1918; *s* of Andrew Kidd and Florence Hill, Belfast; *m* 1942, Harriet Moore Williamson; three *s* two *d. Educ:* Royal Belfast Academical Instn; Trinity Coll., Dublin. BA 1940, BLitt 1941. Army, 1941–46: commnd 1942, Royal Ulster Rifles, later seconded to Intell. Corps. Entered Northern Ireland Civil Service, 1947; Second Sec., Dept of Finance, NI, 1969–76. Allied Irish Banks: Dir, 1979–85; Mem., NI Local Bd, 1979–85 (Chm., 1980–85); Mem., NI Adv. Bd, 1985–88. Chairman: Ireland Co-operation North (UK) Ltd, 1982–85 (Bd Mem., 1985–89); Belfast Car Ferries Ltd, 1983–88. Board Mem., Irish Amer. Partnership, 1988–91. Governor, Royal Belfast Academical Inst., 1967–76, 1979–83; a Pro-Chancellor and Chm. Council, New Univ. of Ulster, 1980–84; Pres., TCD Assoc. of NI, 1981–83; Trustee: Scotch-Irish Trust of Ulster, 1980–; Ulster Historical Foundn, 1981– (Chm., 1987–). Hon. DLitt Ulster, 1985. *Recreation:* gardening. *Address:* 24 Massey Court, Belfast BT4 3GJ. *T:* Belfast (0232) 768694.

KIDD, Ronald Alexander; HM Diplomatic Service, retired; *b* 19 June 1926; *s* of Alexander and Jean Kidd; *m* 1st, 1954, Agnes Japp Harrower (marr. diss. 1985); two *d*; 2nd, 1985, Pamela Dempster. *Educ:* Robert Gordon's College, Aberdeen; Queens' College, Cambridge; BA Hons 1951, MA 1956. Royal Air Force, 1944–48; Foreign Office, 1951; served at Singapore, Djakarta, Osaka and Macau, 1952–56; FO, 1956–60; Second, later First Sec., Seoul, 1961–62; Djakarta, 1962–63; Tokyo, 1964–68; FCO, 1968–71; Dar Es Salaam, 1971–72; Tokyo, 1972–77; Counsellor, FCO, 1977–81. Jubilee Medal, 1977. *Recreation:* golf. *Address:* 41 Princess Road, NW1 8JS. *T:* 071–722 8406. *Club:* Royal Air Force.

KIDGELL, John Earle; Head of Division 3, Central Statistical Office, since 1991 (Assistant Director, Grade 3, since 1988); *b* 18 Nov. 1943; *s* of Gilbert James Kidgell and Cicely Alice (*née* Earle); *m* 1968, Penelope Jane Tarry; one *s* two *d. Educ:* Eton House Sch., Southend-on-Sea; Univ. of St Andrews (MA); London School of Economics and Political Science (MSc). NIESR, 1967–70; Gallup Poll, 1970–72; Statistician, CSO and Treasury, 1972–79; Chief Statistician, DoE, 1979–86; Hd of Finance Div., PSA, 1986–88; Head of Directorate D, Central Statistical Office, 1989–91. *Publications:* articles in Nat. Inst. Econ.

Rev., Econ. Trends, etc. *Recreations:* hill walking, tennis, reading. *Address:* Central Statistical Office, Great George Street, SW1. *T:* 071–270 6040.

KIDMAN, Thomas Walter, ERD 1954; Regional Administrator, East Anglian Regional Health Authority, 1973–75, retired; *b* 28 Aug. 1915; *s* of Walter James Kidman and Elizabeth Alice Kidman (*née* Littlejohns); *m* 1939, Lilian Rose Souton (*d* 1988); one *s* two *d.* *Educ:* Cambridge Central Sch.; Cambs Techn. Coll. FHSM, 1972–88. War service, 1939–46: Warrant Officer, RAMC, BEF France, 1940; Major, Suffolk Regt, seconded Corps of Mil. Police, MEF Egypt and Palestine, 1943–46; served in TA/AER, 1939–67. Local Govt Officer, Health and Educn, Cambridgeshire CC, 1930–48; East Anglian Regional Hosp. Bd: Admin. Officer, 1948; Asst Sec., 1952; Dep. Sec., 1957; Sec. of Bd, 1972. Mem., NHS Advisory Service, 1976–83; Chm., Cambs Mental Welfare Assoc., 1977–86. *Recreations:* photography, walking, gardening, golf. *Address:* Alwoodley, 225 Arbury Road, Cambridge CB4 2JJ. *T:* Cambridge (0223) 357384.

KIDU, Hon. Sir Buri (William), Kt 1980; Chief Justice of Papua New Guinea, since 1980; *b* 8 Aug. 1945; *s* of Kidu Gaudi and Dobi Vagi; *m* 1969, Carol Anne Kidu; three *s* two *d.* *Educ:* Univ. of Queensland, Australia (LLB). Barrister-at-Law of Supreme Courts of Queensland and Papua New Guinea. Legal Officer, Dept of Law, 1971; Crown Prosecutor, 1972; Deputy Crown Solicitor, 1973–74; Crown Solicitor, 1974–77; Secretary for Justice, 1977–79; Secretary of Prime Minister's Dept, 1979–80. Chancellor: Anglican Church of Papua New Guinea, 1976; Univ. of Papua New Guinea, 1981–90. Hon. LLD Univ. of Papua New Guinea, 1991. *Recreations:* reading, swimming. *Address:* Supreme Court, PO Box 7018, Boroko, Port Moresby, Papua New Guinea. *T:* 25 7099.

KIDWELL, Raymond Incledon, QC 1968; a Recorder, since 1972; *b* 8 Aug. 1926; *s* of late Montague and Dorothy Kidwell; *m* 1st, 1951, Enid Rowe (marr. diss. 1975); two *s*; 2nd, 1976, Carol Evelyn Beryl Maddison, *d* of late Warren G. Hopkins, Ontario. *Educ:* Whitgift Sch.; Magdalen Coll., Oxford. RAFVR, 1944–48. BA (Law) 1st cl. 1950; MA 1951; BCL 1st cl. 1951; Vinerian Law Schol., 1951; Eldon Law Schol., 1951; Arden Law Schol., Gray's Inn, 1952; Birkenhead Law Schol., Gray's Inn, 1955. Called to Bar, 1951; Bencher, 1978. Lectr in Law, Oriel Coll., Oxford, 1952–55; Mem., Winn Commn on Personal Injuries, 1966–68. Member: Bar Council, 1967–71; Senate, 1981–85. *Address:* Sanderstead House, Rectory Park, Sanderstead, Surrey. *T:* 081–657 4161; 2 Crown Office Row, Temple, EC4. *T:* 071–353 9337. *Club:* United Oxford & Cambridge University.

KIELY, Dr David George; Chief Naval Weapons Systems Engineer (Under Secretary), Ministry of Defence, Procurement Executive, 1983–84; consultant engineer; *b* 23 July 1925; *o s* of late George Thomas and Susan Kiely, Ballynahinch, Co. Down; *m* 1956, Dr Ann Wilhelmina (*née* Kilpatrick), MB, BCh, BAO, DCH, DPH, MFCM, Hillsborough, Co. Down; one *s* one *d.* *Educ:* Down High Sch., Downpatrick; Queen's Univ., Belfast (BSc, MSc); Sorbonne (DSci). CEng, FIEE; CPhys, FInstP; psc 1961. Appts in RN Scientific Service from 1944; Naval Staff Coll., 1961–62; Head of Electronic Warfare Div., ASWE, 1965–68; Head of Communications and Sensor Dept, ASWE, 1968–72; Dir-Gen., Telecommunications, 1972–74, Dir-Gen., Strategic Electronic Systems, 1974–76, Dir-Gen., Electronics Res., 1976–78, Exec. Officer, Electronics Research Council, 1976–78, Dir, Naval Surface Weapons, ASWE, 1978–83, MoD, PE. Gp Chief Exec. and Dir, Chemring PLC, 1984–85. Chm., R&D Policy Cttee, Gen. Lights Authorities of UK and Eire, 1974–89. Governor, Portsmouth Coll. of Technology, 1965–69. Mem., 1982–89, Chm., 1985–89, Council, Chichester Cathedral. *Publications:* Dielectric Aerials, 1953; Naval Electronic Warfare, 1988; Naval Surface Weapons, 1988; Defence Procurement, 1990; The Future for the Defence Industry, 1990; chapter: in Progress in Dielectrics, 1961; in Fundamentals of Microwave Electronics, 1963; in Naval Command and Control, 1989; papers in Proc. IEE and other learned jls, etc. *Recreations:* fly fishing, gardening. *Address:* Cranleigh, 107 Havant Road, Emsworth, Hants PO10 7LF. *T:* Emsworth (0243) 372250. *Club:* Naval and Military.

KIERNAN, Prof. Christopher Charles; Professor of Behavioural Studies in Mental Handicap, Director of the Hester Adrian Research Centre, University of Manchester, since 1984; *b* 3 June 1936; *s* of Christopher J. and Mary L. Kiernan; *m* 1962, Diana Elizabeth Maynard; two *s* one *d.* *Educ:* Nottingham Univ. (BA); London Univ. (PhD); ABPsS. Lecturer in Psychology, Birkbeck Coll., London Univ., 1961–70; Sen. Lectr, Child Development, Univ. of London Inst. of Education, 1970–74; Dep. Director, Thomas Coram Research Unit, Univ. of London Inst. of Education, 1975–84. *Publications:* Behaviour Assessment Battery, 1977, 2nd edn 1982; Starting Off, 1978; Behaviour Modification with the Severely Retarded, 1975; Analysis of Programmes for Teaching, 1981; Signs and Symbols, 1982. *Recreation:* survival. *Address:* 29 Edge Lane, Chorlton-cum-Hardy, Manchester M21 1JH.

KIKI, Hon. Sir (Albert) Maori, KBE 1975; Chairman of the Constitutional Commission, Papua New Guinea, since 1976; *b* 21 Sept. 1931; *s* of Erevu Kiki and Eau Ulamare; *m* 1957, Elizabeth Hariai Miro; two *s* three *d.* *Educ:* London Missionary Soc. Sch.; Sogeri Central Sch., Papua New Guinea; Fiji Sch. of Med. (Pathology); Papua New Guinea Admin. Coll. Medical Orderly, Kerema, Gulf Province, 1948; Teacher Trng, Sogeri, CP, 1950; Central Med. Sch., Fiji, 1951; Dept of Public Health, Port Moresby, 1954. Formed first trade union in Papua New Guinea and Pres., Council of Trade Unions; Welfare Officer, CP, Land Claims work amongst Koiari people, 1964; studied at Admin. Coll., 1964–65; Foundn Mem. and first Gen. Sec. of Pangu Pati (PNG's 1st Political League); Mem., Port Moresby CC, 1971. MP for Port Moresby, 1972; Minister for Lands, Papua New Guinea, 1972; Deputy Prime Minister and Minister for Defence, Foreign Affairs and Trade, 1975–77. Chairman of Directors, 1977–: Nat. Shipping Corp.; New Guinea Motors Pty Ltd; Credit Corp. (PNG) Ltd; Kwila Insurance Corp. Ltd; Ovameveo Develts Pty Ltd (Property Developers); Maruka Pty Ltd; On Pty Ltd; Mae Pty Ltd; Maho Investments Ltd; Consultants Pty Ltd. Hon. Dr Laws Kyung Hee Univ., South Korea, 1976. *Publications:* Ten Thousand Years in a Lifetime (autobiog.), 1970; (with Ulli Beier) HoHao: art and culture of the Orokolo people, 1972. *Recreations:* care of farm; formerly Rugby (patron and founder of PNG Rugby Union). *Address:* PO Box 1739, Boroko, Papua New Guinea; (private) Granville Farm, 8 Mile, Port Moresby, PNG.

KILBRACKEN, 3rd Baron, *cr* 1909, of Killegar; **John Raymond Godley,** DSC 1945; journalist and author; *b* 17 Oct. 1920; *er s* of 2nd Baron, CB, KC, and Elizabeth Helen Monteith, *d* of Vereker Hamilton and *widow* of Wing Commander N. F. Usborne, RNAS; *S* father 1950; *m* 1st, 1943, Penelope Anne (marr. diss., 1949), *y d* of Rear-Adm. Sir C. N. Reyne, KBE; one *s* (and one *s* decd); 2nd, 1981, Susan Lee (marr. diss. 1989), *yr d* of N. F. Heazlewood, Melbourne, Australia; one *s.* *Educ:* Eton; Balliol Coll., Oxford (MA). Served in RNVR (Fleet Air Arm), as pilot, 1940–46; commissioned 1941; Lieut-Comdr (A) 1945; commanded Nos 835 and 714 Naval Air Sqdns. A reporter for: Daily Mirror, 1947–49; Sunday Express, 1949–51; freelance, 1951–. Joined Parly Liberal Party, 1960; transferred to Labour, 1966. Hon. Sec., Connacht Hereford Breeders' Assoc., 1973–76. Pres., British-Kurdish Friendship Soc., 1975–. *Publications:* Even For An Hour (poems), 1940; Tell Me The Next One, 1950; The Master Forger, 1951; (ed) Letters From Early New Zealand, 1951; Living Like a Lord, 1955; A Peer Behind the Curtain, 1959; Shamrocks and Unicorns, 1962; Van Meegeren, 1967; Bring Back My Stringbag, 1979; The Easy Way to Bird Recognition, 1982 (TES Sen. Information Book Award, 1983); The Easy Way to Tree Recognition, 1983; The Easy Way to Wild Flower Recognition, 1984. TV documentaries: The Yemen, 1965; Morgan's Treasure, 1965; Kurdistan, 1966. *Recreations:* bird-watching, chess. *Heir:* *s* Hon. Christopher John Godley, Countertrade Manager, ICI Plant Protection Div. [*b* 1 Jan. 1945; *m* 1969, Gillian Christine, *yr d* of late Lt-Comdr S. W. Birse OBE, DSC, RN retd, Alverstoke; one *s* one *d.* *Educ:* Rugby; Reading Univ. (BSc Agric.)]. *Address:* Killegar, Cavan, Ireland. *T:* Cavan (49) 34309.

See also Hon. W. A. H. Godley.

KILBURN, Prof. Tom, CBE 1973; FRS 1965; FEng 1976; Professor of Computer Science, University of Manchester, 1964–81, now Emeritus; *b* 11 Aug. 1921; *o s* of John W. and Ivy Kilburn, Dewsbury; *m* 1943, Irene (*née* Marsden); one *s* one *d.* *Educ:* Wheelwright Grammar Sch., Dewsbury; Sidney Sussex Coll., Cambridge (MA 1944); Manchester Univ. (PhD 1948; DSc 1953). FIEE; FBCS 1970 (Distinguished Fellow, 1974). Telecommunications Research Estab., Malvern, 1942–46. Manchester Univ., 1947–81; Lecturer, 1949; Senior Lecturer, 1951; Reader in Electronics, 1955; Prof. of Computer Engineering, 1960. Foreign Associate, Nat. Acad. of Engrg, USA, 1980. Hon. Fellow, UMIST, 1984; DU Essex, 1968; DUniv Brunel, 1977; Hon. DSc Bath, 1979; Hon. DTech CNAA, 1981. McDowell Award, 1971, Computer Pioneer Award, 1982, IEEE; John Player Award, BCS, 1973; Royal Medal, Royal Society, 1978; Eckert Mauchly Award, ACM-IEEE, 1983. Mancunian of the year, Manchester Junior Chamber of Commerce, 1982. *Publications:* papers in Jl of Instn of Electrical Engineers, etc. *Address:* 11 Carlton Crescent, Urmston, Lancs. *T:* Urmston (061748) 3846.

KILBY, Michael Leopold; *b* 3 Sept. 1924; *s* of Guy and Grace Kilby; *m* 1952, Mary Sanders; three *s.* *Educ:* Luton College of Technology. General Motors, 1942–80: Apprentice; European Planning and Govt and Trade Regulations Manager; European Sales, Marketing and Service Ops Manager; Plant Manager; internat. management consultant, 1980–84. Mayor of Dunstable, 1963–64. MEP (C) Nottingham, 1984–89; contested (C) Nottingham, Eur. parly elecn, 1989. Member: SE Economic Planning Council; Industry and Economic Cttee, British Assoc. of Chambers of Commerce. *Publications:* The Man at the Sharp End, 1983; technical and political papers. *Recreations:* all sports; first love cricket; former Minor Counties cricketer. *Address:* Grange Barn, Haversham Village, Milton Keynes, Bucks MK19 7DX. *T:* Milton Keynes (0908) 313613.

KILDARE, Marquess of; Maurice FitzGerald; landscape and contract gardener; *b* 7 April 1948; *s* and *heir* of 8th Duke of Leinster, *qv*; *m* 1972, Fiona Mary Francesca, *d* of Harry Hollick; one *s* two *d.* *Educ:* Millfield School. Pres., Oxfordshire Dyslexia Assoc. *Heir:* *s* Earl of Offaly, *qv*. *Address:* Courtyard House, Oakley Park, Frilford Heath, Oxon OX13 6QW.

KILDARE AND LEIGHLIN, Bishop of, (RC), since 1987; **Most Rev. Laurence Ryan,** DD; *b* 13 May 1931; *s* of Michael Ryan and Brigid Foley. *Educ:* St Patrick's Coll., Maynooth (BA, DD). Lectr in Theology, St Patrick's Coll., Carlow, 1958–80, Pres. 1974–80; Parish Priest of Naas, Co. Kildare, 1980–85; Vicar General of Kildare and Leighlin, 1975–87; Coadjutor Bishop of Kildare and Leighlin, 1984–87. Sec. 1966–71, Pres. 1974–76, Irish Theological Assoc.; Pres., Nat. Conf. of Priests of Ireland, 1976–82. *Publications:* contribs to Irish Theological Qly, The Furrow, Irish Ecclesiastical Record, Christus Rex. *Recreation:* walking. *Address:* Bishop's House, Carlow, Ireland. *T:* 0503 31102.

KILÉNYI, Edward A.; Adjunct Professor of Music, Florida State University, since 1982 (Professor of Music, 1953–82); *b* 7 May 1911; *s* of Edward Kilényi and Ethel Frater; *m* 1945, Kathleen Mary Jones; two *d.* *Educ:* Budapest; since childhood studied piano with Ernö Dohnányi; Theory and conducting Royal Academy of Music. First concert tour with Dohnányi (Schubert Centenary Festivals), 1928; concert tours, recitals, and soloist with Principal Symphony Orchestras, 1930–39, in Holland, Germany, Hungary, Roumania, France, Scandinavia, North Africa, Portugal, Belgium; English debut, 1935, with Sir Thomas Beecham in Liverpool, Manchester, London; tours, 1940–42, and 1946–, US, Canada, Cuba. Columbia, Remington and records internationally distributed. Hon. Mem., Franz Liszt Soc., Hungary, 1987. Liszt Commemorative Medal awarded by Hungarian Govt, 1986; named Florida Ambassador of the Arts by Sec. of State for Florida, 1990. Served War of 1939–45, Capt. US Army, European theatre of operations. *Address:* 2206 Ellicott Drive, Tallahassee, Fla 32312, USA.

KILFEDDER, James Alexander; MP North Down since 1970 (UU 1970–80, UPUP since 1980) (resigned seat Dec. 1985 in protest against Anglo-Irish Agreement; re-elected Jan. 1986); Leader, Ulster Popular Unionist Party, since 1980; Barrister-at-law; *b* 16 July 1928; *yr s* of late Robert and Elizabeth Kilfedder; unmarried. *Educ:* Model Sch. and Portora Royal Sch., Enniskillen, NI; Trinity Coll., Dublin (BA); King's Inn, Dublin. Called to English Bar, Gray's Inn, 1958. MP (UU) Belfast West, 1964–66. Mem. (Official Unionist), N Down, NI Assembly, 1973–75; Mem. (UUUC) N Down, NI Constitutional Convention, 1975–76; Mem. (UPUP) N Down and Speaker, NI Assembly, 1982–86. Former Chief Whip and Hon. Sec., Ulster Unionist Parly Party. *Recreation:* walking in the country. *Address:* 96 Seacliff Road, Bangor, Co. Down B20 5EZ. *T:* Bangor (0247) 451690; House of Commons, SW1. *T:* 071–219 3563.

KILFOIL, Geoffrey Everard; His Honour Judge Kilfoil; a Circuit Judge, since 1987; *b* 15 March 1939; *s* of Thomas Albert Kilfoil and Hilda Alice Kilfoil; *m* 1962, Llinos Mai Morris; one *s* one *d.* *Educ:* Acrefair Primary Sch.; Ruabon Grammar Sch.; Jesus Coll., Oxford. Called to the Bar, Gray's Inn, 1966; practised on Wales and Chester Circuit; Dep. Circuit Judge, 1976; a Recorder, 1980–87. *Address:* Plas y Garth, Glynceiriog, Llangollen, Clwyd.

KILFOYLE, Peter; MP (Lab) Walton Division of Liverpool, since July 1991; *b* 9 June 1946; *s* of Edward and Ellen Kilfoyle; *m* 1968, Bernadette; two *s* three *d.* *Educ:* St Edward's Coll., Liverpool; Durham Univ.; Christ's Coll., Liverpool. Building labourer, 1965–70; student, 1970–73; building labourer, 1973–75; teacher/youth worker, 1975–85; Labour Party Organiser, 1985–91. *Recreations:* reading, music, spectator sport. *Address:* 24 Brockholme Road, Mossley Hill, Liverpool L18 4QQ. *T:* 071–219 3000.

KILGOUR, Dr John Lowell, CB 1987; Medical Examiner, Department of Social Security; Consultant to various commercial firms; Chairman, Civil Service Commission Recruitment Boards, since 1989; Director of Prison Medical Services, Home Office, 1983–89; *b* 26 July 1924; *s* of Ormonde John Lowell Kilgour and Catherine (*née* MacInnes); *m* 1955, Daphne (*née* Tully); two *s.* *Educ:* St Christopher's Prep. Sch., Hove; Aberdeen Grammar Sch.; Aberdeen Univ. MB, ChB 1947, MRCGP, FFCM. Joined RAMC, 1948; served in: Korea, 1950–52; Cyprus, 1956; Suez, 1956; Singapore, 1961–64 (Brunei, Sarawak); comd 23 Para. Field Amb., 1954–57; psc 1959; ADMS GHQ FARELF, 1961–64; jssc 1964; Comdt, Field Trng Sch., RAMC, 1965–66. Joined Min. of Health, 1968, Med. Manpower and Postgrad. Educn Divs; Head of Internat. Health Div., DHSS, 1971–78; Under-Sec. and Chief Med. Advr, Min. of Overseas Devel t, 1973–78;

Dir of Co-ordination, WHO, 1978–83. UK Deleg. to WHO and to Council of Europe Public Health Cttees; Chm., European Public Health Cttee, 1976; Mem. WHO Expert Panel on Communicable Diseases, 1972–78, 1983–; Chm., Cttee for Internat. Surveillance of Communicable Diseases, 1976; Consultant, WHO Special Programme on AIDS, 1987–. Vis. Lectr, 1976–89, Governor, 1987–89, LSHTM; Mem. Governing Council, Liverpool Sch. of Tropical Medicine, 1973–87; Mem. Council, 1983–89, Mem. Exec. Cttee, 1987–90, Royal Commonwealth Society for the Blind. Mem., Medico-Legal Soc. Mem., RHS, 1984–88. Winner, Cons. Constituency Speakers' Competition for London and the SE, 1968. *Publications:* chapter in, Migration of Medical Manpower, 1971; chapter in, The Global Impact of AIDS, 1988; contrib. The Lancet, BMJ, Hospital Medicine, Health Trends and other med. jls. *Recreations:* reading, gardening, travel. *Address:* Stoke House, 22 Amersham Road, Chesham Bois, Bucks HP6 5PE. *Clubs:* Athenæum, Hurlingham; Royal Windsor Racing.

KILLALOE, Bishop of, (RC), since 1967; **Most Rev. Michael Harty;** *b* Feb. 1922; *s* of Patrick Harty, Lismore, Toomevara, Co. Tipperary, Ireland. *Educ:* St Flannan's Coll., Ennis, Ire.; St Patrick's Coll., Maynooth, Ire.; University Coll., Galway. Priest, 1946; Prof., St Flannan's Coll., Ennis, 1948; Dean, St Patrick's Coll., Maynooth, 1949, 1955–67; Asst Priest, dio. Los Angeles, 1954. BA, BD, LCL, DD (Hon.); HDiplEduc. *Address:* Westbourne, Ennis, Co. Clare, Ireland. *T:* Ennis 28638.

KILLANIN, 3rd Baron, *cr* 1900; **Michael Morris;** Bt *cr* 1885; MBE 1945; TD 1945; MA; Author, Film Producer; President, International Olympic Committee, 1972–80, now Honorary Life President; *b* 30 July 1914; *o s* of late Lieut-Col Hon. George Henry Morris, Irish Guards, 2nd *s* of 1st Baron, and Dora Maryan (who *m* 2nd, 1918, Lieut-Col Gerard Tharp, Rifle Brigade (*d* 1934)), *d* of late James Wesley Hall, Mount Morgan and Melbourne, Australia; *S* uncle, 1927; *m* 1945, Mary Sheila Cathcart, MBE 1946, *o d* of late Rev. Canon Douglas L. C. Dunlop, MA, Kilcummin, Galway; three *s* one *d*. *Educ:* Eton; Sorbonne, Paris; Magdalene Coll., Cambridge. BA 1935; MA 1939. Formerly on Editorial Staff, Daily Express; Daily Mail, 1935–39; Special Daily Mail War Correspondent Japanese-Chinese War, 1937–38. Political Columnist Sunday Dispatch, 1938–39. Served War of 1939–45 (MBE, TD), KRRC (Queen's Westminsters); Brigade Maj. 30 Armd Bde, 1943–45. Past Director: Chubb (Ireland) Ltd (Chm.); Northern Telecom (Ireland) Ltd (Chm.); Gallahers (Dublin) Ltd (Chm.); Irish Shell Ltd; Hibernian Life Association Ltd (Chm.); Ulster Investment Bank (Chm.); Lombard & Ulster Banking Ireland Ltd (Chm.); Dir, Syntex Ireland Ltd. International Olympic Committee: Mem., 1952; Mem., Exec. Bd, 1967; Vice-Pres., 1968–72; President: Olympic Council of Ireland, 1950–73; Incorporated Sales Managers' Association (Ireland), 1955–58; Galway Chamber of Commerce, 1952–53; Chm. of the Dublin Theatre Festival, 1958–70. Mem., Irish Govt Commn on Film Industry, 1957; Chairman: Irish Govt Commn on Thoroughbred Horse Breeding, 1982; Nat. Heritage Council, 1988–. Member: Council Irish Red Cross Soc., 1947–72; Cttee RNLI (a Life Vice-Pres.); Cultural Adv. Cttee to Minister for External Affairs, 1947–72; Nat. Monuments of Ireland Advisory Council, 1947–80 (Chm., 1961–65); RIA, 1952; Irish Nat. Sports Council, 1970–72; Irish Turf Club (Steward 1971–73, 1981–83); Irish National Hunt Steeplechase Cttee; first President, Irish Club, London, 1947–65; Hon. Life Mem., Royal Dublin Soc., 1982; Trustee, Irish Sailors and Soldiers Land Trust, 1955–. Fellow, Irish Management Inst., 1987. Hon. LLD NUI, 1975; Hon. DLitt New Univ. of Ulster, 1977. Mem., French Acad. of Sport, 1974. Knight of Honour and Devotion, SMO, Malta, 1943; Comdr, Order of Olympic Merit (Finland), 1952; Star of Solidarity 1st Class (Italy), 1957; Comdr, Order of the Grimaldis, 1961; Medal, Miroslav Tyrš (Czechoslovakia), 1970; Commander, Order of Merit (German Federal Republic), 1972; Star of the Sacred Treasure (Japan), 1972; Order of the Madara Rider (Bulgaria), 1973; Grand Officer, Order of Merit of Rep. of Italy, 1973; Grand Cross, Order of Civil Merit (Spain), 1976; Grand Officer, Order of Republic (Tunis), 1976; Grand Officer, Order of the Phoenix of Greece, 1976; Commander, Order of Sports Merit (Ivory Coast), 1977; Chevalier, Order of Duarte Sanchez y Mella (Dominican Rep.), 1977; Commander's Order of Merit with Star (Poland), 1979; Comdr, Legion of Honour (France), 1980; Olympic Order of Merit (gold), 1980; Yugo Slav Flag with ribbon, 1984; Commander, Order of Merit (Congo); decorations from Austria, Brazil, China, Columbia, USSR etc. *Films:* (with John Ford) The Quiet Man; The Rising of the Moon; Gideon's Day; Young Cassidy; also, Playboy of the Western World; Alfred the Great; Connemara and its Pony (scriptwriter). *Publications:* contributions to: British, American and European Press; Four Days; Sir Godfrey Kneller; Shell Guide to Ireland, 1975 (with Prof. M. V. Duignan); (ed with J. Rodda) The Olympic Games, 1976; Olympic Games Moscow-Lake Placid, 1979; My Olympic Years (autobiog.), 1983; (ed with J. Rodda) Olympic Games—Los Angeles and Sarajevo, 1984; My Ireland, 1987. *Heir:* *s* Hon. (George) Redmond (Fitzpatrick) Morris, film producer [*b* 26 Jan. 1947; *m* 1972, Pauline, *o d* of late Geoffrey Horton, Dublin; one *s* one *d*. *Educ:* Ampleforth; Trinity Coll., Dublin]. *Address:* 9 Lower Mount Pleasant Avenue, Dublin 6. *T:* Dublin 972114; St Annins, Spiddal, County Galway. *T:* Galway 83103. *Clubs:* Garrick; Stephen's Green (Dublin); County (Galway).

See also W. C. R. Bryden.

KILLEARN, 2nd Baron, *cr* 1943; **Graham Curtis Lampson;** 4th Bt *cr* 1866; *b* 28 Oct. 1919; *er s* of 1st Baron Killearn, PC, GCMG, CB, MVO, and his 1st wife (*née* Rachel Mary Hele Phipps) (*d* 1930), *d* of W. W. Phipps; *S* father as 2nd Baron, 1964, and kinsman as 4th Bt, 1971; *m* 1946, Nadine Marie Cathryn, *o d* of late Vice-Adm. Cecil Horace Pilcher, DSO; two *d*. *Educ:* Eton Coll.; Magdalen Coll., Oxford (MA). Served war of 1939–45, Scots Guards (Major): served ME and N Africa with 2nd Bn, and Italy on staff of HQs 5th US and 8th British Armies, and 15th Allied Army Gp. US Bronze Star. *Heir:* *half-b* Hon. Victor Miles George Aldous Lampson, Captain RARO, Scots Guards [*b* 9 Sept. 1941; *m* 1971, Melita Amaryllis Pamela Astrid, *d* of Rear-Adm. Sir Morgan Morgan-Giles, *qv*; two *s* two *d*]. *Address:* 58 Melton Court, Old Brompton Road, SW7 3JJ. *T:* 071–584 7700.

See also Sir N. C. Bonsor, Bt, Earl of St Germans.

KILLEN, Hon. Sir (Denis) James, KCMG 1982; LLB; MP (Lib) for Moreton, Queensland, 1955–83; *b* 23 Nov. 1925; *s* of James W. Killen, Melbourne; *m* 1949, Joyce Claire; two *d*. *Educ:* Brisbane Grammar Sch.; Univ. of Queensland. Barrister-at-Law. Jackaroo; RAAF (Flight Serjeant); Mem. staff, Rheem (Aust.) Pty Ltd. Minister for the Navy, 1969–71; Opposition Spokesman: on Educn, 1973–74; on Defence, 1975; Minister for Defence, 1975–82; Vice-Pres. of Exec. Council and Leader, House of Representatives, Commonwealth of Australia, 1982–83. Foundn Pres., Young Liberals Movement (Qld); Vice-Pres., Lib. Party, Qld Div., 1953–56. *Recreations:* horseracing, golf. *Address:* 253 Chapel Hill Road, Chapel Hill, Qld 4069, Australia. *Clubs:* Johnsonian, Tattersall's, Irish Association, QTC (Brisbane), Brisbane Cricket.

KILLICK, Anthony John, (Tony); Senior Research Fellow, Overseas Development Institute, since 1987 (Director, 1982–87); *b* 25 June 1934; *s* of William and Edith Killick; *m* 1958, Ingeborg Nitzsche; two *d*. *Educ:* Ruskin and Wadham Colls, Oxford (BA Hons PPE). Lectr in Econs, Univ. of Ghana, 1961–65; Tutor in Econs, Ruskin Coll., Oxford, 1965–67; Sen. Econ. Adviser, Min. of Overseas Develt, 1967–69; Econ. Adviser to Govt of Ghana, 1969–72; Res. Fellow, Harvard Univ., 1972–73; Ford Foundn Vis. Prof., Econs Dept, Univ. of Nairobi, 1973–79; Res. Officer, Overseas Develt Inst., 1979–82. Vis. Fellow, Wolfson Coll., and Vis. Scholar, Dept of Applied Economics, Cambridge Univ., 1987–88. Vis. Prof., Dept of Economics, Univ. of Surrey, 1988–. Member: Commn of Inquiry into Fiscal System of Zimbabwe, 1984–86; Council, Royal Africa Soc. Former consultant: Govt of Sierra Leone; Govt of Kenya; Govt of Republic of Dominica; Govt of Nepal; various internat. orgns. Associate, Inst. of Develt Studies, Univ. of Sussex, 1986–. Pres., Develt Studies Assoc., 1986–88. Hon. Res. Fellow, Dept of Political Economy, UCL, 1985–. Editorial adviser: Journal of Economic Studies; Eastern Africa Economic Review, Jl of Internat. Develt. *Publications:* The Economies of East Africa, 1976; Development Economics in Action: a study of economic policies in Ghana, 1978; Policy Economics: a textbook of applied economics on developing countries, 1981; (ed) Papers on the Kenyan Economy: structure, problems and policies, 1981; (ed) Adjustment and Financing in the Developing World: the role of the IMF, 1982; The Quest for Economic Stabilisation: the IMF and the Third World, 1984; The IMF and Stabilisation: developing country experiences, 1984; A Reaction Too Far: the role of the state in developing countries, 1989; learned articles and contribs to books on Third World develt and economics. *Recreations:* gardening, music. *Address:* Karibu, 64 Thundridge Hill, Cold Christmas Lane, Ware, Herts SG12 0UF. *T:* Ware (0920) 465493.

KILLICK, Sir John (Edward), GCMG 1979 (KCMG 1971; CMG 1966); HM Diplomatic Service, retired; President, British Atlantic Committee, since 1985; *b* 18 Nov. 1919; *s* of late Edward William James Killick and Doris Marjorie (*née* Stokes); *m* 1st, 1949, Lynette du Preez (*née* Leach) (*d* 1984); no *c*; 2nd, 1985, I. M. H. Easton, OBE. *Educ:* Latymer Upper Sch.; University Coll., London, Fellow 1973; Bonn Univ. Served with HM Forces, 1939–46: Suffolk Regt, W Africa Force and Airborne Forces. Foreign Office, 1946–48; Control Commn and High Commn for Germany (Berlin, Frankfurt and Bonn), 1948–51; Private Sec. to Parly Under-Sec., Foreign Office, 1951–54; British Embassy, Addis Ababa, 1954–57; Canadian Nat. Def. Coll., 1957–58; Western Dept, Foreign Office, 1958–62; Imp. Def. Coll., 1962; Counsellor and Head of Chancery, British Embassy, Washington, 1963–68; Asst Under-Sec. of State, FCO, 1968–71; Ambassador to USSR, 1971–73; Dep. Under-Sec. of State, FCO and Permanent Rep. on Council of WEU, 1973–75; Ambassador and UK Permanent Rep. to NATO, 1975–79. Dir, Dunlop South Africa, 1980–85. *Recreations:* golf. *Address:* Challoner's Cottage, 2 Birchwood Avenue, Southborough, Kent TN4 0UE. *Clubs:* East India, Brooks's, Garrick.

KILLICK, Paul Victor St John, OBE 1969; HM Diplomatic Service, retired; Ambassador to the Dominican Republic, 1972–75; *b* 8 Jan. 1916; *s* of C. St John Killick and Beatrice (*née* Simpson); *m* 1947, Sylva Augusta Leva; one *s* two *d*. *Educ:* St Paul's School. Served with Army, N Africa and Italy, 1939–46 (despatches 1944). Diplomatic Service: Singapore, 1946–47; Tokyo, 1947–49; Katmandu, 1950–53; FO, 1953–55; Oslo, 1955–58; San Francisco, 1958–60; Djakarta, 1960–61; Rome, 1962–66; Pretoria/Cape Town, 1966–70; Tangier, 1971–72. *Recreations:* walking, gardening. *Address:* c/o Barclays Bank, 1 Brompton Road, SW3 1EB.

KILLICK, Tony; *see* Killick, A. J.

KILMAINE, 7th Baron *cr* 1789; **John David Henry Browne;** Bt 1636; Director of Fusion (Bickenhill) Ltd, since 1969; Director of Whale Tankers Ltd, since 1974; *b* 2 April 1948; *s* of 6th Baron Kilmaine, CBE, and of Wilhelmina Phyllis, *o d* of Scott Arnott, Brasted, Kent; *S* father, 1978; *m* 1982, Linda, *yr d* of Dennis Robinson; one *s* one *d*. *Educ:* Eton. *Heir:* *s* Hon. John Francis Sandford Browne, *b* 4 April 1983.

KILMARNOCK, 7th Baron *cr* 1831; **Alastair Ivor Gilbert Boyd;** Chief of the Clan Boyd; *b* 11 May 1927; *s* of 6th Baron Kilmarnock, MBE, TD, and Hon. Rosemary Guest (*d* 1971), *er d* of 1st Viscount Wimborne; *S* father, 1975; *m* 1st, 1954, Diana Mary (marr. diss. 1970, she *d* 1975), *o d* of D. Grant Gibson; 2nd, 1977, Hilary Ann, *yr d* of Leonard Sidney and Margery Bardwell; one *s*. *Educ:* Bradfield; King's Coll., Cambridge. Lieutenant, Irish Guards, 1946; served Palestine, 1947–48. Mem. SDP, 1981–; Chief SDP Whip, House of Lords, 1983–86; Dep. Leader, SDP Peers, 1986–87. Chm., All-Party Parly Gp on AIDS, 1987–. Vice-Pres., Assoc. of Dist Councils. Exec. Dir, The Social Market Foundn, 1989–; Dir, MSD Foundn, 1988–. *Publications:* Sabbatical Year, 1958; The Road from Ronda, 1969; The Companion Guide to Madrid and Central Spain, 1974, revised edn 1987; (ed) The Radical Challenge: the response of social democracy, 1987; The Essence of Catalonia, 1988. *Heir:* *b* Dr the Hon. Robin Jordan Boyd, MB BS, MRCP, MRCPEd, DCH, *b* 6 June 1941. *Address:* House of Lords, SW1A 0PW.

KILMISTER, (Claude Alaric) Anthony; Chairman, Prayer Book Society, since 1989; *b* 22 July 1931; *s* of late Dr Claude E. Kilmister and of Margaret E. Mogford, *d* of Ernest Gee; *m* 1958, Sheila, *d* of Lawrence Harwood. *Educ:* Shrewsbury Sch. National Service (army officer), 1950–52. NCB, 1952–54; Conservative Party Org., 1954–60; Asst Sec. 1960–61, Gen. Sec. 1962–72, Cinema & Television Benevolent Fund; Sec., Royal Film Performance Exec. Cttee, 1961–72; Exec. Dir, Parkinson's Disease Soc. of UK, 1972–91. Founding Cttee Mem., Action for Neurological Diseases, 1987–91; Founding Mem. and Dep. Chm., Prayer Book Soc. (and its forerunner, BCP Action Gp), 1972–89. Member: Internat. Council for Apostolic Faith, 1987–; Steering Cttee, Assoc. for Apostolic Ministry, 1989–. *Publications:* The Good Church Guide, 1982; When Will Ye be Wise?, 1983; My Favourite Betjeman, 1985; contribs to jls, etc. *Recreations:* walking, writing. *Address:* 36 The Drive, Northwood, Middlesex HA6 1HP. *T:* Northwood (09274) 24278. *Club:* Athenæum.

KILMISTER, Prof. Clive William; Professor of Mathematics, King's College, London, 1966–84; *b* 3 Jan. 1924; *s* of William and Doris Kilmister: *m* 1955, Peggy Joyce Hutchins; one *s* two *d*. *Educ:* Queen Mary Coll., Univ. of London. BSc 1944, MSc 1948, PhD 1950. King's Coll. London: Asst Lectr, 1950; Lectr, 1953; Reader, 1959; FKC 1983. Gresham Prof. of Geometry, 1972–88. President: British Soc. for History of Mathematics, 1973–76; Mathematical Assoc., 1979–80; British Soc. for Philos. of Science, 1981–83. *Publications:* Special Relativity for Physicists (with G. Stephenson), 1958; Eddington's Statistical Theory (with B. O. J. Tupper), 1962; Hamiltonian Dynamics, 1964; The Environment in Modern Physics, 1965; Rational Mechanics (with J. E. Reeve), 1966; Men of Physics: Sir Arthur Eddington, 1966; Language, Logic and Mathematics, 1967; Lagrangian Dynamics, 1967; Special Theory of Relativity, 1970; The Nature of the Universe, 1972; General Theory of Relativity, 1973; Philosophers in Context: Russell, 1984; (ed) Schrödinger: centenary celebration of a polymath, 1987. *Recreation:* opera going. *Address:* Red Tiles Cottage, High Street, Barcombe, Lewes, East Sussex BN8 5DH.

KILMORE, Bishop of, (RC), since 1972; **Most Rev. Francis J. McKiernan,** DD; *b* 3 Feb. 1926; *s* of Joseph McKiernan and Ellen McTague. *Educ:* Aughawillan National School; St Patrick's Coll., Cavan; University College, Dublin; St Patrick's Coll., Maynooth. BA, BD, HDE. St. Malachy's Coll., Belfast, 1951–52; St Patrick's Coll., Cavan, 1952–53; University Coll., Dublin, 1953–54; St Patrick's Coll., Cavan, 1954–62; Pres., St Felim's Coll., Ballinamore, Co. Leitrim, 1962–72. Editor of Breifne (Journal of Breifne Historical Society), 1958–72. *Address:* Bishop's House, Cullies, Cavan. *T:* 049–31496.

KILMORE, ELPHIN AND ARDAGH, Bishop of, since 1981; **Rt. Rev. William Gilbert Wilson,** BD, PhD; *b* 23 Jan. 1918; *s* of Adam and Rebecca R. Wilson; *m* 1944, Peggy Muriel Busby; three *s* three *d*. *Educ:* Belfast Royal Academy; Trinity Coll., Dublin. BA 1939; MA, BD 1944; PhD 1949. Curate Assistant, St Mary Magdalene, Belfast, 1941–44; St Comgall's, Bangor, 1944–47; Rector of Armoy with Loughguile, 1947–76; Prebendary of Cairncastle in Chapter of St Saviour's, Connor, 1964–76; Dean of Connor, 1976–81; Rector of Lisburn Cathedral, 1976–81; Clerical Hon. Sec. of Connor Synod and Council, 1956–81. *Publications:* A Guild of Youth Handbook, 1944; Church Teaching, A Church of Ireland Handbook, 1954, revised edn 1970; How the Church of Ireland is Governed, 1964; (jtly) Anglican Teaching—An Exposition of the Thirty-nine Articles, 1964; The Church of Ireland after 1970—Advance or Retreat?, 1968; The Church of Ireland—Why Conservative?, 1970; Is there a Life after Death?, 1974; A Critique of 'Authority in the Church', 1977; Irish Churchwardens' Handbook, 1979 (expanded, revised and rewritten edn of 1901 pubn); The Faith of an Anglican, 1980; The Way of the Church, 1982; Should we have Women Deacons?, 1984; Why no Women Priests?, 1988; Towards Accepting Women Priests, 1989; contribs to Jl of Theol Studies and The Church Qly Review. *Recreations:* gardening, woodworking. *Address:* The See House, Kilmore, Cavan, Republic of Ireland. *T:* Cavan 31336. *Club:* Dublin University.

KILMOREY, 6th Earl of; *see* Needham, Richard Francis.

KILMUIR, Countess of; *see* De La Warr, Countess.

KILNER BROWN, Hon. Sir Ralph; *see* Brown.

KILPATRICK, Prof. (George) Stewart, OBE 1986; MD; FRCP, FRCPE; David Davies Chair of Tuberculosis and Chest Diseases and Head of Department since 1968, Vice-Provost, 1987–90, University of Wales College of Medicine, Cardiff; Senior Hon. Consultant Physician to South Glamorgan Health Authority; *b* 26 June 1925; *s* of Hugh Kilpatrick and Annie Merricks Johnstone Stewart; *m* 1954, Joan Askew. *Educ:* George Watson's Coll., Edinburgh; Edinburgh Univ. Med. Sch. (MB ChB 1947, MD 1954). MRCPE 1952, FRCPE 1966; MRCP 1971, FRCP 1975. Medical posts in Edinburgh; Captain RAMC, 1949–51; Mem., Scientific Staff, MRC Pneumoconiosis Research Unit, 1952–54; med. and res. posts, London, Edinburgh and Cardiff; Dean of Clin. Studies, Univ. of Wales Coll. of Medicine, 1970–87. Chm., Sci. Cttees, Internat. Union Against Tuberculosis (formerly Chm., Treatment Cttee); Chm. Council, Assoc. for Study of Med. Educn, 1981–86; Chm., Assoc. of Medical Deans in Europe, 1982–85. Ext. Examr in Medicine, Queen's Univ. Belfast, 1986–88. Marc Daniels Lectr, RCP 1987. Pres., Cardiff Medical Soc., 1990–91. FRSocMed. Silver Jubilee Medal, 1977. *Publications:* numerous papers to med. and sci. jls; chapters in books on chest diseases, tuberculosis, heart disease, anaemia and med. educn. *Recreations:* travel, reading, photography. *Address:* Millfield, 14 Millbrook Road, Dinas Powys, South Glamorgan CF6 4DA. *T:* Cardiff (0222) 513149.

KILPATRICK, Sir Robert, Kt 1986; CBE 1979; President, General Medical Council, since 1989 (Member, 1972–76 and since 1979); *b* 29 July 1926; *s* of Robert Kilpatrick and Catherine Sharp Glover; *m* 1950, Elizabeth Gibson Page Forbes; two *s* one *d*. *Educ:* Buckhaven High Sch.; Edinburgh Univ. MB, ChB (Hons) 1949; Ettles Schol.; Leslie Gold Medallist; MD 1960; FRCP(Ed) 1963; FRCP 1975. Med. Registrar, Edinburgh, 1951–54; Lectr, Univ. of Sheffield, 1955–66; Rockefeller Trav. Fellowship, MRC, Harvard Univ., 1961–62; Commonwealth Trav. Fellowship, 1962; Prof. of Clin. Pharmacology and Therapeutics, Univ. of Sheffield, 1966–75; Dean, Faculty of Medicine, Univ. of Sheffield, 1970–73; Univ. of Leicester: Prof. and Head of Dept of Clinical Pharmacology and Therapeutics, 1975–83; Dean, Faculty of Medicine, 1975–89; Prof. of Medicine, 1984–89. Chairman: Adv. Cttee on Pesticides, 1975–87; Soc. of Endocrinology, 1975–78. Dr *hc* Edinburgh, 1987. *Publications:* articles in med. and sci. jls. *Recreations:* golf, gardening. *Address:* General Medical Council, 44 Hallam Street, W1N 6AE. *Clubs:* Reform; Royal and Ancient (St Andrews).

KILPATRICK, Stewart; *see* Kilpatrick, G. S.

KILROY, Dame Alix; *see* Meynell, Dame Alix.

KILROY-SILK, Robert; Television Presenter, Kilroy, BBC, since 1987 (Day to Day, 1986–87); Chairman, The Kilroy Television Co., since 1989; *b* 19 May 1942; *m* 1963, Jan Beech; one *s* one *d*. *Educ:* Saltley Grammar Sch., Birmingham; LSE (BScEcon). Lectr, Dept of Political Theory and Institutions, Liverpool Univ., 1966–74. MP (Lab): Ormskirk, Feb. 1974–1983; Knowsley N, 1983–86; PPS to Minister for the Arts, 1974–75; opposition frontbench spokesman on Home Office, 1984–85. Vice-Chairman: Merseyside Gp of MPs, 1974–75; PLP Home Affairs Gp, 1976–86; Chairman: Parly All-Party Penal Affairs Gp, 1979–86; PLP Civil Liberties Gp, 1979–84; Parly Alcohol Policy and Services Group, 1982–83; Mem., Home Affairs Select Cttee, 1979–84. Member: Council, Howard League for Penal Reform, 1979–; Adv. Council, Inst. of Criminology, Cambridge Univ., 1984–; Sponsor, Radical Alternatives to Prison, 1977–; Patron, APEX Trust; Chm., FARE, 1981–84. Governor, National Heart and Chest Hospital, 1974–77. Political columnist: Time Out, 1985–86; Police Review, 1983–; columnist, The Times, 1987–; Today, 1988–. *Publications:* Socialism since Marx, 1972; (contrib.) The Role of Commissions in Policy Making, 1973; The Ceremony of Innocence: a novel of 1984, 1984; Hard Labour: the political diary of Robert Kilroy-Silk, 1986; articles in Political Studies, Manchester School of Economic and Social Science, Political Quarterly, Industrial and Labor Relations Review, Parliamentary Affairs, etc. *Recreation:* gardening. *Address:* Kilroy, BBC TV, Lime Grove, W12.

KILVINGTON, Frank Ian; Headmaster of St Albans School, 1964–84; *b* West Hartlepool, 26 June 1924; *e s* of H. H. Kilvington; *m* 1949, Jane Mary, *d* of late Very Rev. Michael Clarke and of Katharine Beryl (*née* Girling); one *s* one *d*. *Educ:* Repton (entrance and foundn scholar); Corpus Christi, Oxford (open class. scholar). 2nd cl. Lit Hum, 1948; MA 1950. Served War of 1939–45: RNVR, 1943–46 (Lt); West Africa Station, 1943–45; RN Intelligence, Germany, 1945–46. Westminster School: Asst Master, 1949–64; Housemaster of Rigaud's House, 1957–64. Chairman: St Albans Marriage Guidance Council, 1968–74; St Albans CAB, 1981–86; Herts Record Soc., 1985–90; St Albans Hospice Care Team, 1988–. Pres., St Albans and Herts Architectural and Archæological Soc., 1974–77. *Publication:* A Short History of St Albans School, 1970. *Recreations:* music, local history. *Address:* 122 Marshalswick Lane, St Albans, Herts AL1 4XD.

KIM, Young Choo; Ambassador of the Republic of Korea to the Court of St James's, 1984–87, and to Dublin, 1985–87; retired; *b* 1 June 1923; *s* of late Chi Whan Kim; *m* 1950, Kwang-Ok (*née* Yoon); one *s* three *d*. *Educ:* College of Law, Seoul University. Korean Ministry of Foreign Affairs, 1950–55; served Tokyo, 1955–57; Dir-Gen. for Political Affairs, Min.of Foreign Affairs, 1957–60; served Paris, 1960–61; Dir-Gen. for Planning and Co-ordination, Min. of Foreign Affairs, 1961–62; served London, 1962–63, Bonn, 1963–64, Kampala, 1964–65; Vice-Minister of Foreign Affairs, 1965–67; Ambassador in Bonn, 1967–74, Ottawa, 1974–77; Vienna, 1977–80; Min. of Foreign Affairs, 1980–84. Korean Order of Service Merit, 1962; Korean Order of Diplomatic Service Merit, 1970. *Address:* c/o Ministry of Foreign Affairs, Seoul, Republic of Korea.

KIMBALL, family name of **Baron Kimball.**

KIMBALL, Baron *cr* 1985 (Life Peer), of Easton in the County of Leicestershire; **Marcus Richard Kimball,** Kt 1981; DL; Director, Royal Trust Bank (formerly Royal Trust Co. of Canada), since 1970; *b* 18 Oct. 1928; *s* of late Major Lawrence Kimball; *m* 1956, June Mary Fenwick; two *d*. *Educ:* Eton; Trinity Coll., Cambridge. Contested (C) Derby South, 1955; MP (C) Lincs, Gainsborough, Feb. 1956–1983. Privy Council Rep., Council of RCVS, 1969–82, Hon. ARCVS 1982. External Mem. Council, Lloyd's, 1982–90. Jt Master and Huntsman: Fitzwilliam Hounds, 1950–51 and 1951–52; Cottesmore Hounds, 1952–53, 1953–54, 1955–56 (Jt Master, 1956–58). Chm., British Field Sports Soc., 1966–82. Chairman: River Naver Fishing Bd, 1964–; Firearms Consultative Cttee, 1989–. Pres., Hunters Improvement Soc., 1990. Chm., Cambridge Univ. Vet. Sch. Trust, 1989–. Lt Leics Yeo. (TA), 1947; Capt., 1951. Mem. Rutland CC, 1955. DL Leics, 1984. *Address:* Great Easton Manor, Market Harborough, Leics LE16 8TB. *T:* Rockingham (0536) 770333; Altnaharra, Lairg, Sutherland IV27 4AE. *T:* Altnaharra (054981) 224. *Clubs:* White's, Pratt's.

KIMBER, Sir Charles Dixon, 3rd Bt, *cr* 1904; *b* 7 Jan. 1912; *o surv. s* of Sir Henry Dixon Kimber, 2nd Bt, and Lucy Ellen, *y d* of late G. W. Crookes; *S* father 1950; *m* 1st, 1933, Ursula (marr. diss., 1949; she *d* 1981), *er d* of late Ernest Roy Bird, MP; three *s*; 2nd, 1950, Margaret Bonham (marr. diss., 1965), writer; one *d* (and one *s* decd). *Educ:* Eton; Balliol Coll., Oxford (BA). Co Founder and Gen. Sec., Federal Union, 1938–41; Market Gardener, 1941–47; Diploma in Social Anthropology, 1948; collaborated in survey of Banbury, 1949–52; small holder, 1952–60; Landlord, Three Pigeons, Drayton St Leonard, 1962–65; apptd to undertake review of Parish Charities in Oxfordshire for Oxfordshire CC, 1967–77. *Heir:* *s* Timothy Roy Henry Kimber [*b* 3 June 1936; *m* 1960, Antonia Kathleen Brenda (marr. diss. 1974), *d* of Sir Francis Williams, Bt, *qv*; two *s*; *m* 1979, Susan, *widow* of Richard North, Newton Hall, near Carnforth]. *Address:* No 2 Duxford, Hinton Waldrist, near Faringdon, Oxon SN7 8SQ. *T:* Longworth (0865) 820004.

KIMBER, Derek Barton, OBE 1945; FEng; Chairman: London & Overseas Freighters plc, since 1984; Short Sea Europe Plc, since 1989; Director: Eggar Forrester (Holdings), since 1983; Wilks Shipping Co. Ltd, since 1986; Community Industry Ltd, since 1991; Trustee, AMARC Foundation, since 1986; *b* 2 May 1917; *s* of George Kimber and Marion Kimber (*née* Barton); *m* 1943, Gwendoline Margaret Maude Brotherton; two *s* two *d*. *Educ:* Bedford Sch.; Imperial Coll., London Univ; Royal Naval Coll., Greenwich. MSc(Eng), FCGI, DIC; FRINA, FIMechE, FIMarE, FNECInst, FRSA. Royal Corps of Naval Constructors, 1939–49; Consultant, Urwick, Orr & Partners Ltd, 1950–54; Fairfield Shipbuilding & Engineering Co. Ltd: Manager, 1954; Dir, 1961; Dep. Man. Dir, 1963–65; Dir, Harland & Wolff Ltd, 1966–69; Dir Gen., Chemical Industries Assoc., 1970–73; Chairman: Austin & Pickersgill, 1973–83; Bartram & Sons, 1973–83; Sunderland Shipbuilders, 1980–83; Govan Shipbuilders, 1980–83; Smith's Dock, 1980–83; Director: A. & P. Appledore International Ltd, 1974–77; British Ship Research Assoc. (Trustees) Ltd, 1973–81; R. S. Dalgliesh Ltd, 1978–80; Equity Capital for Industry Ltd, 1977–86; AMARC (T.E.S.) Ltd, 1986–91. Dir, Glasgow Chamber of Commerce, 1962–65. Chm., C. & G. Jt Adv. Cttee for Shipbuilding, 1968–70; Pres., Clyde Shipbuilders Assoc., 1964–65; Member: Shipbuilding Industry Trng Bd, 1964–69; Scottish Cttee, Lloyds Register of Shipping, 1964–65, Gen. Cttee, 1973–, Technical Cttee, 1976–80, Exec. Bd, 1978–84; Research Council, British Ship Res. Assoc., 1973–81; Brit. Tech. Cttee, Amer. Bureau of Shipping, 1976– (Chm., 1989–); Standing Cttee, Assoc. of W European Shipbuilders, 1976–89 (Chm., 1983–84); Cttee of EEC Shipbuilders' Assoc., 1985–89; Underwriting Mem., Lloyd's, 1985–; Chm., Management Bd, Shipbuilders & Repairers Nat. Assoc., 1974–76, Vice-Pres., 1976–77; Mem., Jt Industry Cons. Cttee, (SRNA/CSEU), 1966–76. Member: EDC for Chem. Industry, 1970–72; Process Plant Working Party (NEDO), 1970–72; CBI Central Council, 1970–72, 1975–84; CBI Northern Reg. Council, 1973–80 (Chm. 1975–77); Steering Cttee, Internat. Maritime Industries Forum, 1981–. Member: Council, RINA, 1961– (Chm., 1973–75, Pres. RINA 1977–81); Council, Welding Inst., 1959–74, 1976–82; Bd, CEI, 1977–81, Exec. Cttee, 1978–80; C. & G. Senior Awards Cttee, 1970–81; Council, NE Coast Inst. of Engrs and Shipbuilders, 1974– (Pres., 1982–84); Vice-Pres., British Maritime League, 1985–87. Mem., City of London Br., Royal Soc. of St George, 1985–. Liveryman: Worshipful Co. of Shipwrights, 1967 (Asst to Court 1974–, Prime Warden, 1986–87); Worshipful Co. of Engineers, 1984–. Mem., Smeatonion Soc., 1984–; Pres., Old Centralians, 1985–86. Mem. Court, City Univ., 1984–; Governor, Imperial Coll., London Univ., 1967–87. FEng 1976. Hon. FRINA 1981. RINA Gold Medallist, 1977. *Publications:* papers on shipbuilding subjects in learned soc. trans. *Recreations:* DIY, golf, rough gardening. *Address:* Broughton, Monk's Road, Virginia Water, Surrey GU25 4RR. *T:* Wentworth (0344) 844274. *Clubs:* Brooks's, Caledonian, City Livery, Aldgate Ward, Anchorites, MCC; Den Norske Klub; Yacht Club of Greece.

KIMBER, Herbert Frederick Sidney; Director, Southern Newspapers Ltd, 1975–82 (Chief Executive, 1980–81); *b* 3 April 1917; *s* of H. G. Kimber; *m* Patricia Boulton (*née* Forfar); one *s*. *Educ:* elementary sch., Southampton. Southern Newspapers Ltd, office boy, 1931. Served War, Royal Navy, 1939–46: commissioned Lieut RNVR, 1941. Manager, Dorset Evening Echo, 1960; Advertisement Manager-in-Chief, Southern Newspapers Ltd, 1961; then Dep. Gen. and Advertisement Manager, 1972; Gen. Manager, 1974. Chairman: Bird Bros, Basingstoke, 1976–81; W. H. Hallett, 1981–82; Southtel, 1981–82. Dir, Regl Newspaper Advertising Bureau, 1980–81. Member: Press Council, 1977–81; Council, Newspaper Soc., 1974–81 (Mem., Industrial Relations Cttee, 1975–81). *Recreations:* reading, travel, gardening under protest. *Address:* Pardailhan, 34360 St Chinian, France.

KIMBERLEY, 4th Earl of, *cr* 1866; **John Wodehouse;** Bt, 1611; Baron Wodehouse, 1797; Lt Grenadier Guards; *b* 12 May 1924; *o s* of 3rd Earl and Margaret (*d* 1950), *d* of late Col Leonard Howard Irby; *S* father 1941; *m* 1st, 1945; 2nd, 1949; one *s*; 3rd, 1953; two *s*; 4th, 1961; one *s*; 5th, 1970; 6th, 1982, Sarah Jane Hope Consett, *e d* of Colonel Christopher D'Arcy Preston Consett, DSO, MC. *Educ:* Eton; Cambridge. Lieut, Grenadier Guards, 1942–45; Active Service NW Europe. Member: House of Lords All Party Defence Study Gp, 1976– (Sec., 1978–); House of Lords All Party UFO Study Gp, 1979–; former Liberal Spokesman on: aviation and aerospace; defence; voluntary community services; left Liberal Party, May 1979, joined Cons. Party. Mem. Exec. Cttee, Assoc. of Cons. Peers, 1981–84; Pres., Cricklade and Latton Cons. Assoc., 1988– (Chm., 1986–88). Member: Council, The Air League; Council, British Maritime League; RUSI; IISS; British Atlantic Cttee. Delegate to N Atlantic Assembly, 1981–. Vice-Pres., World Council on Alcoholism; Chm., Nat. Council on Alcoholism, 1982–85. Mem., British Bobsleigh Team, 1949–58. ARAeS 1977. *Recreations:* shooting, fishing, all field sports, gardening, bridge. *Heir:* *s* Lord Wodehouse, *qv*. *Address:* House of Lords, Westminster, SW1A 0PW; Hailstone House, Cricklade, Swindon, Wilts SN6 6JP. *T:* Swindon (0793) 750344. *Clubs:* White's, Naval and Military, MCC; House of Lords' Yacht; Falmouth Shark Angling (Pres.).

KIMBLE, Dr David (Bryant), OBE 1962; Editor, Journal of Modern African Studies, since 1972; *b* 12 May 1921; *s* of John H. and Minnie Jane Kimble; *m* 1st, 1949, Helen

Rankin (marr. diss.); three *d* (and one *d* decd); 2nd, 1977, Margareta Westin. *Educ:* Eastbourne Grammar Sch.; Reading Univ. (BA 1942, DipEd 1943, Pres. Students Union, 1942–43); London Univ. (PhD 1961). Lieut RNVR, 1943–46. Oxford Univ. Staff Tutor in Berks, 1946–48, and Resident Tutor in the Gold Coast, 1948–49; Dir, Inst. of Extra-Mural Studies, Univ. of Ghana, 1949–62, and Master of Akuafo Hall, 1960–62; Prof. of Political Science, Univ. Coll., Dar es Salaam, Univ. of E Africa, and Dir, Inst. of Public Admin, Tanzania, 1962–68; Research Advr in Public Admin and Social Sciences, Centre africain de formation et de recherche administratives pour le développement, Tanger, Morocco, 1968–70, and Dir of Research, 1970–71; Prof. of Govt and Admin, Univ. of Botswana, Lesotho, and Swaziland, 1971–75, and Nat. Univ. of Lesotho, 1975–77, Prof. Emeritus, 1978; Tutor in Politics to King Moshoeshoe II, 1975, and Queen 'MaMohato, 1977; Vice-Chancellor, Univ. of Malaŵi, and Chm., Malaŵi Certificate Exam. and Testing Bd, 1977–86. Founder and Joint Editor (with Helen Kimble), West African Affairs, 1949–51, Penguin African Series, 1953–61, and Jl of Modern African Studies, 1963–71; Officier, Ordre des Palmes Académiques, 1982. *Publications:* The Machinery of Self-Government, 1953; (with Helen Kimble) Adult Education in a Changing Africa, 1955; A Political History of Ghana, Vol. I, The Rise of Nationalism in the Gold Coast, 1850–1928, 1963; nine University Congregation Addresses, 1978–86. *Recreations:* cricket, editing. *Address:* Huish, Chagford, Devon TQ13 8AR.

See also G. H. T. Kimble.

KIMBLE, George (Herbert Tinley), PhD; retired; *b* 2 Aug. 1908; *s* of John H. and Minnie Jane Kimble; *m* 1935, Dorothy Stevens Berry; one *s* one *d. Educ:* Eastbourne Grammar Sch.; King's Coll., London (MA); University of Montreal (PhD). Asst Lecturer in Geography, University of Hull, 1931–36; Lecturer in Geography, University of Reading, 1936–39. Served War as Lt and Lt-Comdr, British Naval Meteorological Service, 1939–44. Prof. of Geography and Chm. Dept of Geography, McGill Univ., 1945–50; Sec.-Treasurer, Internat. Geographical Union, 1949–56; Chm., Commn on Humid Tropics, Internat. Geog. Union, 1956–61. Dir, Amer. Geog. Soc., 1950–53; Dir, Survey of Tropical Africa, Twentieth Century Fund, NY, 1953–60. Chm., Dept of Geography, Indiana Univ., 1957–62; Prof. of Geography, Indiana Univ., 1957–66; Research Dir, US Geography Project, Twentieth Century Fund, 1962–68. Rushton Lecturer, 1952; Borah Lecturer, University of Idaho, 1956; Haynes Foundn Lectr, University of Redlands, 1966; Visiting Prof., University of Calif. (Berkeley), 1948–49; Stanford Univ., 1961; Stockholm Sch. of Economics, 1961. Governor, Eastbourne Sixth Form Coll., 1980–81. FRGS 1931. Hon. Mem., Inst. British Geographers. Editor, Weather Res. Bulletin, 1957–60. *Publications:* Geography in the Middle Ages, 1938; The World's Open Spaces, 1939; The Shepherd of Banbury, 1941; (with Raymond Bush) The Weather, 1943 (Eng.), 1946 (Amer.), (author) 2nd (Eng.) edn, 1951; Military Geography of Canada, 1949; (with Sir Dudley Stamp) An Introduction to Economic Geography, 1949; (with Sir Dudley Stamp) The World: a general geography, 1950; The Way of the World, 1953; Our American Weather, 1955; Le Temps, 1957; Tropical Africa (2 vols), 1960; Ghana, 1960; Tropical Africa (abridged edition), 1962; (with Ronald Steel) Tropical Africa Today, 1966; Hunters and Collectors, 1970; Man and his World, 1972; Herdsmen, 1973; From the Four Winds, 1974; This is our World, 1981; (ed for Hakluyt Soc.) Esmeraldo de Situ Orbis, 1937; (ed for American Geographical Soc. with Dorothy Good) Geography of the Northlands, 1955; articles in: Geog. Jl, Magazine, Review; Canadian Geog. Jl; Bulletin Amer. Meteorological Soc.; The Reporter; Los Angeles Times; The New York Times Magazine. *Recreations:* music, gardening. *Address:* 2 Dymock's Manor, Ditchling, E Sussex BN6 8SX. *T:* Hassocks (0273) 843157.

See also Dr D. B. Kimble.

KIMMANCE, Peter Frederick, CB 1981; Chief Inspector of Audit, Department of the Environment, 1979–82; Member, Audit Commission for Local Authorities in England and Wales, 1983–87; *b* 14 Dec. 1922; *s* of Frederick Edward Kimmance, BEM, and Louisa Kimmance; *m* 1944, Helen Mary Mercer Cooke. *Educ:* Raines Foundation, Stepney; University of London. Post Office Engineering Dept, 1939; served Royal Signals, 1943; District Audit Service, 1949; District Auditor, 1973; Controller (Finance), British Council, 1973–75; Dep. Chief Inspector of Audit, DoE, 1978. Mem. Council, CIPFA, 1979–83; Hon. Mem., British Council, 1975. *Recreations:* sailing, books, music. *Address:* Herons, School Road, Saltwood, Hythe, Kent CT21 4PP. *T:* Hythe (0303) 267921. *Clubs:* Royal Over-Seas League; Medway Yacht (Lower Upnor).

KIMMINS, Simon Edward Anthony, VRD 1967; Lt-Comdr RNR; *b* 26 May 1930; *s* of late Captain Anthony Kimmins, OBE, RN, and of Mrs Elizabeth Kimmins; *m* 1976, Jonkvrouwe Irma de Jonge; one *s* one *d. Educ:* Horris Hill; Charterhouse. Man. Dir, London American Finance Corpn Ltd (originally BOECC Ltd), 1957–73; Dir (non-exec.), Balfour Williamson, 1971–74; Chief Exec., Thomas Cook Gp, 1973–75; Director: Debenhams Ltd, 1972–85; TKM International Trade Finance, 1978–80; Aurelian Futures Fund, 1985–87; Chm., Associated Retail Develt Internat. SA Geneva, 1980–85; President: Piquet Internat. SA Geneva, 1986–; Delfinance SA. Vice-Pres., British Export Houses Assoc., 1974–80 (Chm., 1970–72). Governor, Royal Shakespeare Theatre, 1975–. *Recreations:* cricket (played for Kent), golf, shooting. *Address:* 37 Chemin de Grange Canal, Geneva 1208, Switzerland. *T:* Geneva 35 6657. *Clubs:* Garrick, MCC, The Pilgrims; Haagseclub.

KINAHAN, Charles Henry Grierson, CBE 1972; JP; DL; retired 1977; Director, Bass Ireland Ltd, Belfast, and subsidiary companies, 1956–77; *b* 10 July 1915; *e s* of Henry Kinahan, Belfast, and Ula, *d* of late Rt Rev. C. T. P. Grierson, Bishop of Down and Connor and Dromore; *m* 1946, Kathleen Blanche McClintock, MB, BS, *e d* of Rev. E. L. L. McClintock; three *s. Educ:* Stowe School. Singapore Volunteer Corps, 1939–45, POW Singapore, 1942–45. Commerce, London, 1933–38 and Malaya, 1938–56. Dir, Dunlop Malayan Estates Ltd, 1952–56; Man. Dir, Lyle and Kinahan Ltd, Belfast, 1956–63. Mem. (Alliance) Antrim S, NI Constitutional Convention, 1975–76; contested (Alliance) Antrim S, gen. election 1979. Belfast Harbour Comr, 1966–80; Chm., 1969–73, Pres., 1975–84, NI Marriage Guidance Council; Mem. Senate, QUB, 1969–82; Chairman: NI Historic Buildings Council, 1973–88; Ulster '71 Exhibn, 1971; NI Mountain Rescue: Working Party, 1976–77; Coordinating Cttee, 1978–85; Trustee, Nat. Heritage Memorial Fund, 1980–91. JP 1961, High Sheriff 1971, DL 1977, Co. Antrim; Mem., Antrim District Council (Alliance Party), 1977–81. *Recreations:* mountain trekking, farming, classical music. *Address:* Clady Cottage, 17 Clady Road, Dunadry, Antrim BT41 4QR. *T:* Templepatrick (08494) 32379. *Club:* Royal Over-Seas League.

See also Sir R. G. C. Kinahan, D. McClintock.

KINAHAN, Maj.-Gen. Oliver John, CB 1981; Paymaster-in-Chief and Inspector of Army Pay Services, 1979–83; *b* 17 Nov. 1923; *m* 1950, Margery Ellis Fisher (*née* Hill); one *s* two *d.* Commissioned Royal Irish Fusiliers, 1942; served with Nigeria Regt, RWAFF, Sierra Leone, Nigeria, India, Burma, 1943–46; Instr, Sch. of Signals, 1947–49, Sch. of Infantry, 1950–51; transf. to RAPC, 1951; Japan and Korea, 1952–53; psc 1957; Comdt, RAPC Trng Centre, 1974–75; Chief Paymaster, HQ UKLF, 1975–76; Dep. Paymaster-in-Chief (Army), 1977–78. Col Comdt RAPC, 1984–87. FBIM. *Recreations:* country pursuits. *Address:* c/o Royal Bank of Scotland, Kirkland House, Whitehall, SW1.

KINAHAN, Sir Robert (George Caldwell), (Sir Robin Kinahan), Kt 1961; ERD 1946; JP; Lord-Lieutenant, County Borough of Belfast, 1985–91 (Vice Lord-Lieutenant, 1976–85); *b* 24 Sept. 1916; *s* of Henry Kinahan, Lowwood, Belfast; *m* 1950, Coralie I., *d* of late Capt. C. de Burgh, DSO, RN; two *s* three *d. Educ:* Stowe Sch., Buckingham. Vintners' Scholar (London), 1937. Served Royal Artillery, 1939–45, Capt. Chairman: Inglis & Co. Ltd, 1962–82; E. T. Green Ltd, 1964–82; Ulster Bank Ltd, 1970–82 (Dir, 1963–85); Director: Bass Ireland, 1958–78; Gallaher Ltd, 1967–82; NI Bd, Eagle Star, 1970–81; Nat. Westminster Bank, 1973–82; Abbey Life, 1981–87; STC, 1984–87; Abbeyfield Belfast Soc., 1983–; Cheshire House (NI), 1983–. Mem., NI Adv. Commn, 1972–73. MP (NI) Clifton, 1958–59. Councillor, Belfast Corporation, 1948; Lord Mayor of Belfast, 1959–61. JP Co. Antrim, 1950, DL 1962; High Sheriff: Belfast, 1956; Co. Antrim, 1969. Hon. LLD (Belfast) 1962. *Recreations:* gardening, family life. *Address:* Castle Upton, Templepatrick, Co. Antrim BT39 0BE. *T:* Templepatrick (08494) 32466.

See also C. H. G. Kinahan, Sir A. T. C. Neave, Bt.

KINCADE, James, CBE 1988; MA, PhD; Director, Design Council, Northern Ireland, since 1990; National Governor for Northern Ireland, BBC, 1985–91; *b* 4 Jan. 1925; *s* of George and Rebecca Jane Kincade; *m* 1952, Elizabeth Fay, 2nd *d* of J. Anderson Piggot, OBE, DL, JP; one *s* one *d. Educ:* Foyle Coll.; Magee University Coll.; Trinity Coll. Dublin (Schol. and Gold Medallist, MA, Stein Research Prize); Oriel Coll., Oxford (MA, BLitt); Edinburgh Univ. (PhD). Served RAF, India and Burma, 1943–47 (commnd, 1944). Senior English Master, Merchiston Castle Sch., 1952–61; Vis. Professor of Philosophy, Indiana Univ., 1959; Headmaster: Royal Sch., Dungannon, 1961–74; Methodist Coll., Belfast, 1974–88. President, Ulster Headmasters' Assoc., 1975–77; Mem., Council for Catholic Maintained Schools, 1987–90; Mem. of Senate, Chm. External Relations Cttee, and Mem. Standing Cttee, QUB, 1982–. *Publications:* articles in Mind, Hermathena, Jl of Religion. *Recreations:* reading, writing and arithmetic. *Address:* 10A Harry's Road, Hillsborough BT26 6HJ. *T:* Hillsborough (0846) 683865.

KINCH, Anthony Alec, CBE 1987; counsellor for European Community affairs; Member, Team '92 Speakers Panel, Commission of the European Communities, since 1988; *b* 13 Dec. 1926; *s* of late Edward Alec Kinch, OBE, former Polit. Adviser, Iraq Petroleum Co. Ltd, and Catherine Teresa Kinch (*née* Cassidy); *m* 1952, Barbara Patricia (*née* Paton Walsh); four *s* two *d. Educ:* Ampleforth; Christ Church, Oxford (MA). Practised at Bar, 1951–57; Contracts Man., Electronics Div., Plessey Co. Ltd, 1957–60; Legal Adviser and Insce Consultant, R. & H. Green and Silley Weir Ltd, 1960–66; Dir, Fedn of Bakers, 1966–73; Head of Foodstuffs Div., Commn of EEC, 1973–82; Head of Div. for Project Ops, European Regl Develt Fund ops, EEC, 1982–86. Chm., Brussels Area, SDP, 1981–84; Vice Chm., SDP Europe, 1989; Mem., Council for Social Democracy, 1982–90. Contested (SDP) Kent E, 1984, London SE, 1989, European Parly elecns. Chef de Division Honoraire, EEC, 1987. Chevalier du Fourquet (Belgium), 1980. KCHS with star, 1985 (KCHS 1981). *Recreation:* living. *Address:* 36 Greenways, Beckenham, Kent BR3 3NG. *T:* 081–658 2298.

KINCHIN SMITH, Michael, OBE 1987; Appointments' Secretary to Archbishops of Canterbury and York, and Secretary, Crown Appointments Commission, 1984–87; *b* 8 May 1921; *s* of Francis John Kinchin Smith, Lectr in Classics, Inst. of Educn, London, and Dione Jean Elizabeth, *d* of Sir Francis Henry May, GCMG, sometime Governor of Hong Kong; *m* 1947, Rachel Frances, *er d* of Rt Hon. Sir Henry Urmston Willink, Bt, MC, QC, Master of Magdalene Coll., Cambridge; four *s* two *d. Educ:* Westminster Sch. (King's Schol.); Christ Church, Oxford (Schol.). 1st cl. hons Mod. History; Pres. Oxford Union, 1941. Served with 2nd and 3rd Bns, Coldstream Guards in Italian Campaign (Captain; despatches). Commercial and Admin. Trainee, ICI Ltd, 1947; admin. posts with BBC, 1950–78: Asst, Staff Admin, 1950; Admin Officer, Talks (Sound), 1954; Asst Estabt Officer, TV, 1955; Estabt Officer, Programmes, TV, 1961; Staff Admin Officer, 1962; Asst Controller, Staff Admin, 1964; Controller, Staff Admin, 1967; Controller, Development, Personnel, 1976. Lay Assistant to Archbishop of Canterbury, 1979–84. Chm. Exec. Council, RIPA, 1975–77; CIPM; Vice Pres. (Pay and Employment Conditions), IPM, 1978–80; Lay Selector, ACCM, 1963–73 (Mem. Candidates Cttee, 1966–69); Lay Chm., Richmond and Barnes Deanery Synod, 1970–76; Mem. General Synod, C of E, 1975–78. 1st Chm., Mortlake with East Sheen Soc., 1969–71; Chm., Assoc. of Amenity Societies in Richmond-upon-Thames, 1973–77. *Publication:* (jtly) Forward from Victory, 1943. *Recreations:* walking, local history. *Address:* The Old Bakery, Epwell, Banbury, Oxon OX15 6LA. *T:* Swalcliffe (029578) 773. *Club:* United Oxford & Cambridge University.

KINCRAIG, Hon. Lord; Robert Smith Johnston; a Senator of the College of Justice in Scotland, 1972–87; Chairman, Review of Parole and related matters in Scotland, since 1988; *b* 10 Oct. 1918; *s* of W. T. Johnston, iron merchant, Glasgow; *m* 1943, Joan, *d* of late Col A. G. Graham, Glasgow; one *s* one *d. Educ:* Strathallan, Perthshire; St John's Coll., Cambridge; Glasgow Univ. BA (Hons) Cantab, 1939; LLB (with distinction) Glasgow, 1942. Mem. of Faculty of Advocates, 1942; Advocate-Depute, Crown Office, 1953–55; QC (Scotland) 1955; Home Advocate Depute, 1959–62; Sheriff of Roxburgh, Berwick and Selkirk, 1964–70; Dean of the Faculty of Advocates of Scotland, 1970–72. Contested (U) Stirling and Falkirk Burghs General Election, 1959. *Recreations:* golf, curling, gardening. *Address:* Westwood Cottage, Longniddry, East Lothian EH32 0PL. *T:* Longniddry (0875) 53583. *Clubs:* Hon. Company of Edinburgh Golfers (Edinburgh); Royal Scottish Automobile (Glasgow).

See also A. G. Johnston.

KINDER, Eric; Chairman, Smith & Nephew, since 1990; *b* 26 Dec. 1927; *s* of William and Amy Kinder; *m* 1954, Isobel Margaret Barnes; one *s* one *d. Educ:* Ashton-under-Lyne and Accrington Grammar Schs. ATI. Joined Textile Div., Smith & Nephew plc, 1957; Divisional Man. Dir, 1969–72; Dir, 1972–; Chief Exec., 1982–90. *Recreations:* tennis, angling, golf, music. *Address:* Smith & Nephew plc, 2 Temple Place, Victoria Embankment, WC2R 3BP. *T:* 071–836 7922. *Club:* Queen's.

KINDERSLEY, family name of **Baron Kindersley.**

KINDERSLEY, 3rd Baron *cr* 1941; **Robert Hugh Molesworth Kindersley,** DL; Chairman, Commonwealth Development Corporation, 1980–89; Director, Lazard Bros & Co. Ltd, since 1960 (a Vice-Chairman, 1981–85); *b* 18 Aug. 1929; *s* of 2nd Baron Kindersley, CBE, MC, and Nancy Farnsworth (*d* 1977), *d* of Dr Geoffrey Boyd, Toronto; *S* father, 1976; *m* 1st, 1954, Venice Marigold (Rosie) (marr. diss. 1989), *d* of late Captain Lord (Arthur) Francis Henry Hill; two *s* one *d* (and one *s* decd); 2nd, 1989, Patricia Margaret Crichton-Stuart, *d* of late Hugh Norman. *Educ:* Eton; Trinity Coll., Oxford; Harvard Business Sch., USA. Lt Scots Guards; served Malaya, 1948–49. Director: London Assurance, 1957–; Witan Investment Co. Ltd, 1958–85; Steel Company of Wales, 1959–67; Marconi Co. Ltd, 1963–68; Sun Alliance & London Insurance Gp, 1965–; English Electric Co. Ltd, 1966–68; Gen. Electric Co. Ltd, 1968–70; British Match Corp. Ltd, 1969–73; Swedish Match Co., 1973–85; Maersk Co. Ltd, 1986–. Financial Adviser to Export Gp for the Constructional Industries, 1961–86; Mem., Adv. Panel, Overseas Projects Gp, 1975–77; Dep. Chm., ECGD Adv. Council, 1975–80; Chm., Exec. Cttee,

BBA, 1976–78; Pres., Anglo-Taiwan Trade Cttee, 1976–86. Hon. Treasurer, YWCA, 1965–76. Mem., Institut International d'Etudes Bancaires, 1971–85. Mem. Ct, Fishmongers' Co., 1973–, Prime Warden, 1989–90. DL Kent, 1986. *Recreations:* all country pursuits, including tennis and ski-ing. *Heir:* s Hon. Rupert John Molesworth Kindersley [*b* 11 March 1955; *m* 1975, Sarah, *d* of late John D. Warde; one *s* one *d*]. *Address:* West Green Farm, Shipbourne, Kent TN11 9PU. *T:* Plaxtol (0732) 810293. *Clubs:* Pratt's, MCC, All England Lawn Tennis and Croquet, Queen's.

KINDERSLEY, Lt-Col Claude Richard Henry, DSO 1944; MC 1943; DL; Vice Lord-Lieutenant, Isle of Wight, 1980–86; *b* 11 Dec. 1911; *s* of late Lt-Col Archibald Ogilvie Lyttelton Kindersley, CMG, and Edith Mary Kindersley (*née* Craven); *m* 1938, Vivien Mary, *d* of late Charles John Wharton Darwin, Elston Hall, Notts; three *d*. *Educ:* Wellington Coll.; Trinity Coll., Cambridge. MA. Commissioned HLI, 1933; served with 2nd Bn HLI, NW Frontier, Palestine and Middle East, 1936–43, and with 1st Bn HLI, France and Germany, 1944–45; commanded 1st Bn HLI, 1945; comd Infantry Boys' Batt., 1953–54; retd 1955. DL: Hants, 1962–74; Isle of Wight, 1974; High Sheriff, Isle of Wight, 1974–75. President: Country Landowners' Assoc. (IoW Branch), 1978–87; Isle of Wight Scout Assoc., 1966–86. *Recreation:* yachting. *Address:* Hamstead Grange, Yarmouth, Isle of Wight PO41 0YE. *T:* Yarmouth (0983) 760230. *Clubs:* Royal Yacht Squadron; Royal Solent (Yarmouth).

KINDERSLEY, David Guy, MBE 1979; stone-carver and designer of alphabets (self-employed); in partnership with Lida Lopes Cardozo, since 1981; *b* 11 June 1915; *s* of Guy Molesworth Kindersley and Kathleen Elton; *m* 1st, 1938, Christine Sharpe; two *s* one *d*; 2nd, 1957, Barbara Pym Eyre Petrie; 3rd, 1986, Lida Lopes Cardozo; three *s*. *Educ:* St Cyprian's, Eastbourne (prep. sch.); Marlborough Coll., Wilts. Apprenticed to Eric Gill, ARA, 1933–36. Taught at Cambridge Coll. of Arts and Technology, 1946–57; one-time adviser to MoT on street-name alphabets; adviser to Shell Film Unit on design of titles, 1949–58; consultant to Letraset Internat., 1964–88; Dir, Cambridge Super Vision Ltd, 1983–. Sen. Research Fellow, William Andrews Clark Memorial Library, Univ. of California, Los Angeles, 1967; Sen. Fellow, RCA, 1987. Hon. Pres., Wynkyn de Worde Soc. (Chm. 1976). *Publications:* Optical Letter Spacing and its Mechanical Application, 1966 (rev. and repub. by Wynkyn de Worde Soc., 1976); Mr Eric Gill, 1967, new edn (Eric Gill—Further Thoughts by an Apprentice), 1990; Graphic Variations, 1979; (with L. L. Cardozo) Letters Slate Cut, 1981, new edn 1991; contribs to Printing Technology, Penrose Annual, Visible Language. Limited edns: Variations on the Theme of 26 Letters, edn 50, 1969; Graphic Sayings, edn 130, 1973; *relevant publication:* David Kindersley: his work and workshop, by Montague Shaw, 1989. *Recreation:* archaeology. *Address:* 152 Victoria Road, Cambridge CB4 3DZ. *T:* Cambridge (0223) 62170. *Clubs:* Arts, Double Crown; (Hon. Mem.) Rounce and Coffin (Los Angeles).

KING, family name of **Baron King of Wartnaby** and **Earl of Lovelace.**

KING OF WARTNABY, Baron *cr* 1983 (Life Peer), of Wartnaby in the County of Leicestershire; **John Leonard King;** Kt 1979; Chairman, FKI Babcock plc; British Airways, since 1981; *yr s* of Albert John King and Kathleen King; *m* 1st 1941, Lorna Kathleen Sykes (*d* 1969); three *s* one *d*; 2nd, 1970, Hon. Isabel Monckton, *y d* of 8th Viscount Galway. Founded Ferrybridge Industries Ltd and Whitehouse Industries Ltd, subseq. Pollard Ball & Roller Bearing Co. Ltd, 1945 (Man. Dir 1945, Chm., 1961–69); Chairman: Dennis Motor Hldgs Ltd, 1970–72; Babcock & Wilcox Ltd, subseq. Babcock International plc now FKI Babcock plc, 1972–; Dir, David Brown Corp. Ltd, 1971–75. Current chairmanships and directorships include: SKF (UK) Ltd; Dick Corp. (USA); former directorships include: Royal Ordnance plc (Dep. Chm.); Clogau Gold Mines; National Nuclear Corp.; British Nuclear Associates Ltd; Tyneham Investments; Babcock (Plant Leasing); 1928 Investment Trust; First Union Corp. (USA). Member: Engineering Industries Council, 1975; NEDC Cttee on Finance for Investment, 1976–78; Grand Council and Financial Policy Cttee, CBI, 1976–78; Chairman: City and Industrial Liaison Council, 1973–85; Review Bd for Govt Contracts, 1975–78; British Olympic Appeals Cttee, 1975–78; Macmillan Appeal for Continuing Care, 1977–78; NEB, 1980–81 (Dep. Chm., 1979–80); Alexandra Rose Day Foundn, 1980–85; Mem. Cttee, Ranfurly Library Service; Vice-Pres., Cancer Relief Macmillan Fund (formerly Nat. Soc. for Cancer Relief), 1988; Trustee, Liver Res. Unit Trust, 1988–. Dir, Royal Opera Trust. MFH: Badsworth Foxhounds, 1949–58; Duke of Rutland's Foxhounds (Belvoir), 1958–72; Chm., Belvoir Hunt, 1972. Freeman, City of London, 1984. FBIM 1978; FCIT 1982. Hon. CRAeS, 1986. Hon. Dr Gardner-Webb Coll., USA, 1980; Hon. DSc Cranfield Inst. of Technology, 1989. Comdr, Royal Order of Polar Star (Sweden), 1983. Nat. Free Enterprise Award, 1987. *Recreations:* hunting, field sports, racing, painting. *Address:* Enserch House, 8 St James's Square, SW1Y 4JU. *T:* 071–930 4915. *Clubs:* White's, Pratts'; Brook (New York).

KING, Sir Albert, Kt 1974; OBE 1958; Leader, Labour Group, Leeds Metropolitan District Council, 1975–78, retired (Leader of the Council with one break, 1958–75); *b* 20 Aug. 1905; *s* of George and Ann King; *m* 1928, Pauline Riley; one *d*. *Educ:* Primrose Hill, Leeds. Full-time officer, engrg, 1942–70, retd. Hon. Freedom of the City of Leeds, 1976. *Recreations:* walking, reading. *Address:* 25 Brook Hill Avenue, Leeds LS17 8QA. *T:* Leeds (0532) 684684. *Clubs:* Beeston Working Men's, East Leeds Labour (Leeds).

KING, Albert Leslie, MBE 1945; *b* 28 Aug. 1911; *s* of late William John King and late Elizabeth Mary Amelia King; *m* 1938, Constance Eileen Stroud (*d* 1989); two *d*. *Educ:* University Coll. Sch., Hampstead. Joined Shell-Mex and BP Statistical Dept, 1928. Joined Territorial Army, 1939; Major, RA, 1944. Manager, Secretariat, Petroleum Board, 1947; Manager, Trade Relations Dept, Shell-Mex and BP Ltd, 1948; Gen. Manager: Administration, 1954; Sales, 1957; Operations, 1961; apptd Dir, 1962, Managing Dir, 1963–66. Dep. Dir-Gen., BIM, 1966–68. FCCA; FSS; CBIM; Hon. JDipMA. Barrister (called to the Bar 1980). *Address:* Highlands, 50 Waggon Road, Hadley Wood, Barnet, Herts EN4 0PP. *T:* 081–449 6424. *Clubs:* MCC; Surrey CCC, Saracens.

KING, Alexander, CMG 1975; CBE 1948; Co-Founder, 1968, and Hon. President, Club of Rome (President, 1984–91); *b* Glasgow, 26 Jan. 1909; *s* of J. M. King; *m* 1933, Sarah Maskell Thompson; three *d*. *Educ:* Highgate Sch.; Royal College of Science, London (DSc); University of Munich. Demonstrator, 1932, and later Senior Lecturer, until 1940, in physical chemistry, Imperial Coll. of Science; Dep. Scientific Adviser, Min. of Production, 1942; Head of UK Scientific Mission, Washington, and Scientific Attaché, British Embassy 1943–47; Head of Lord President's Scientific Secretariat, 1947–50; Chief Scientific Officer, Dept of Scientific and Industrial Research, 1950–56; Dep. Dir, European Productivity Agency, 1956–61; Dir for Scientific Affairs, OECD, 1961–68, Dir-Gen., 1968–74; Chm., Internat. Federation of Insts for Advanced Study, 1974–84. Adviser, Govt of Ontario. Assoc. Fellow, Center for the Study of Democratic Institutions, Santa Barbara, Calif; Vis. Professor: Brandeis Univ., 1978; Univ. of Montréal, 1979. Hon. Sec. Chemical Soc., 1948–50. Leader Imperial Coll. Expedition to Jan Mayen, 1938; Harrison Prize of Chemical Soc., 1938; Gill Memorial Prize, Royal Geographical Society, 1938 (Mem. Council, 1939–41); Erasmus Prize, 1987; Great Medal of Paris, 1988. DSc (hc): Ireland, 1974; Guelph, 1987; DUniv Open, 1976; Hon. LLD Strathclyde, 1982.

Publications: The International Stimulus, 1974; The State of the Planet, 1980; The First Global Revolution, 1991; various chemistry textbooks, and papers in Journal of The Chemical Soc., Faraday Soc.; numerous articles on education, science policy and management. *Address:* 168 Rue de Grenelle, Paris 75007, France. *Club:* Athenæum.

KING, Alexander Hyatt, (Alec); musical scholar; a Deputy Keeper, Department of Printed Books, British Museum, 1959–76, retired; *b* 18 July 1911; *s* of Thomas Hyatt King and Mabel Jessie (*née* Brayne); *m* 1943, Evelyn Mary Davies; two *s*. *Educ:* Dulwich Coll.; King's Coll., Cambridge (schol.; MA). Entered Dept of Printed Books, British Museum, 1934; Dep. Keeper, 1959–76; Supt of Music Room, 1944–73; Music Librarian, Ref. Div., British Library, 1973–76. Hon. Sec., British Union Catalogue of Early Music, 1948–57; Mem. Council, Royal Musical Assoc., 1949–, Editor, Proc. of the Assoc., 1952–57, Pres., 1974–78; Pres., Internat. Assoc. of Music Libraries, 1955–59 (Hon. Mem., 1968), Pres., UK Br., 1953–68, Vice-Chm. jt cttee, Internat. Musicological Soc. and IAML, for Internat. Inventory of Musical Sources, 1961–76; Chm., exec. cttee, Brit. Inst. of Recorded Sound, 1951–62. Sandars Reader in Bibliography, Univ. of Cambridge, 1962; Vice-Chm., exec. cttee, Grove's Dictionary of Music, 1970–74; Trustee, Hinrichsen Foundn, 1976–82; Hon. Librarian, Royal Philharmonic Soc., 1969–82. Mem., Zentralinst. für Mozartforschung, 1953. DUniv York, 1978; Hon. DMus St Andrews, 1981. *Publications:* Chamber Music, 1948; (jtly) catalogue: Music in the Hirsch Library, 1951; catalogue: Exhibition of Handel's Messiah, 1951; Mozart in Retrospect, 1955, 3rd edn 1976; Mozart in the British Museum, 1956, repr. 1975; exhibn catalogue: Henry Purcell—G. F. Handel, 1959; Some British Collectors of Music, 1963; 400 Years of Music Printing, 1964, 2nd edn 1968; Handel and his Autographs, 1967; Mozart Chamber Music, 1968, rev. edn 1986; Mozart String and Wind Concertos, 1978, rev. edn 1986; Printed Music in the British Museum: an account of the collections, the catalogues, and their formation, up to 1920, 1979; A Wealth of Music in the various collections of the British Library (Reference Division) and the British Museum, 1983; A Mozart Legacy: aspects of the British Library collections, 1984; Musical Pursuits: selected essays, 1987; *edited:* (jtly) Mozart's Duet Sonata in C K19d, 1953; illustr. edn of Alfred Einstein's Short History of Music, 1953; P. K. Hoffmann's Cadenzas and elaborated slow movements to 6 Mozart piano concertos, 1959; (jtly) 2nd edn of Emily Anderson's Letters of Mozart and his Family, 1966; Concert Goer's Companion series, 1970–; Auction catalogues of Music, 1973–; *contribs to:* Year's Work in Music, 1947–51; Schubert, a symposium, 1947; Music, Libraries and Instruments, 1961; Deutsch Festschrift, 1963; Essays in honour of Victor Scholderer, 1970; Grasberger Festschrift, 1975; Essays in honour of Sir Jack Westrup, 1976; The New Grove, 1980; Rosenthal Festschrift, 1984; various articles; *relevant publication* (ed by Oliver Neighbour) Music and Bibliography: Essays in honour of Alec Hyatt King, 1980. *Recreations:* watching cricket, opera, exploring Suffolk. *Address:* 37 Pier Avenue, Southwold, Suffolk IP18 6BU. *T:* Southwold (0502) 724274. *Club:* MCC.

KING, Alison, OBE 1978; Co-ordinator Properties, Women's Royal Voluntary Service, 1974–78; Director, WRVS Office Premises Ltd, 1969–78; Member, WRVS Housing Association Management Committee, 1973–83. Flight-Capt., Operations, Air Transport Auxiliary, 1940–45. Dir, Women's Junior Air Corps, 1952–58; Gen. Sec., NFWI, 1959–69. Chm., British Women Pilots' Assoc., 1956–64. *Publications:* Golden Wings, 1956 (repr. 1975); articles in Aeroplane Monthly. *Recreations:* writing, painting in oils. *Address:* 87 Kenilworth Court, SW15 1HA. *Club:* University Women's.

KING, Prof. Anthony Stephen; Professor of Government, University of Essex, since 1969; *b* 17 Nov. 1934; *o s* of late Harold and Marjorie King; *m* 1st, 1965, Vera Korte (*d* 1971); 2nd, 1980, Jan Reece. *Educ:* Queen's Univ., Kingston Ont. (1st Cl. Hons, Hist. 1956); Magdalen Coll., Oxford (Rhodes Schol.; 1st Cl. Hons, PPE, 1958). Student, Nuffield Coll., Oxford, 1958–61; DPhil (Oxon) 1962. Fellow of Magdalen Coll., Oxford, 1961–65; Sen. Lectr, 1966–68, Reader, 1968–69, Essex Univ. ACLS Fellow, Columbia Univ., NY, 1962–63; Fellow, Center for Advanced Study in the Behavioral Scis, Stanford, Calif., 1977–78; Visiting Professor: Wisconsin Univ., 1967; Princeton Univ., 1984. Elections Commentator: BBC; Daily Telegraph. *Publications:* (with D. E. Butler) The British General Election of 1964, 1965; (with D. E. Butler) The British General Election of 1966, 1966; (ed) British Politics: People, Parties and Parliament, 1966; (ed) The British Prime Minister, 1969, 2nd edn 1985; (with Anne Sloman) Westminster and Beyond, 1973; British Members of Parliament: a self-portrait, 1974; (ed) Why is Britain becoming Harder to Govern?, 1976; Britain Says Yes: the 1975 referendum on the Common Market, 1977; (ed) The New American Political System, 1978; (ed) Both Ends of the Avenue: the Presidency, the Executive Branch and Congress in the 1980s, 1983; frequent contributor to British and American jls and periodicals. *Recreations:* music, theatre, holidays, walking. *Address:* Department of Government, University of Essex, Wivenhoe Park, Colchester, Essex CO4 3SQ. *T:* Colchester (0206) 873393; The Mill House, Middle Green, Wakes Colne, Colchester, Essex CO6 2BP. *T:* Earls Colne (0787) 222497.

KING, Billie Jean; tennis player; Chief Executive Officer, Team Tennis, since 1981; *b* 22 Nov. 1943; *d* of Willard J. Moffitt; *m* 1965, Larry King. *Educ:* Los Cerritos Sch.; Long Beach High Sch.; Los Angeles State Coll. Played first tennis match at age of eleven; won first championship, Southern California, 1958; coached by Clyde Walker, Alice Marble, Frank Brennan and Mervyn Rose; won first All England Championship, 1966, and five times subseq., and in 1979 achieved record of 20 Wimbledon titles (six Singles, ten Doubles, four Mixed Doubles); has won all other major titles inc. US Singles and Doubles Championships on all four surfaces, and 24 US national titles in all. Pres., Women's Tennis Assoc., 1980–81. *Publications:* Tennis to Win, 1970; Billie Jean, 1974; (with Joe Hyams) Secrets of Winning Tennis, 1975; Tennis Love (illus. Charles Schulz), 1978; (with Frank Deford) Billie Jean King, 1982; (with Cynthia Starr) We Have Come a Long Way: the story of women's tennis, 1989. *Address:* c/o Jorgensen & Rogers, 10100 Santa Monica Boulevard, Suite #410, Los Angeles, Calif 90067, USA.

KING, Dr Brian Edmund; Director and Chief Executive, Barnsley Business and Innovation Centre, since 1987; *b* 25 May 1928; *s* of Albert Theodore King and Gladys Johnson; *m* 1952 (marr. diss.); two *s*; *m* 1972, Eunice Wolstenholme; one *d*. *Educ:* Pocklington Sch.; Leeds Univ. TMM (Research) Ltd, 1952–57; British Oxygen, 1957–67; Dir, 1967–87, and Chief Exec., 1977–87, Wira Technology Group Ltd (formerly Wool Industries Research Assoc.). *Recreations:* bridge, swimming, tennis. *Address:* Victoria Villa, Mount Street, Cleckheaton, W Yorks BD19 3QD. *T:* Cleckheaton (0274) 861170.

KING, Charles Andrew Buchanan, CMG 1961; MBE 1944; HM Diplomatic Service, retired; Chairman, Premier Sauna Ltd, 1970–81; *b* 25 July 1915; *s* of late Major Andrew Buchanan King, 7th Argyll and Sutherland Highlanders, and of Evelyn Nina (*née* Sharpe). *Educ:* Wellington Coll.; Magdalene Coll., Cambridge (MA). Vice-Consul: Zürich, 1940, Geneva, 1941; Attaché, HM Legation, Berne, 1942; transf. to FO, 1946; 2nd Sec., Vienna, 1950; transf. to FO 1953; to Hong Kong, 1958; to FO 1961; retired, 1967; Head of W European Div., Overseas Dept, London Chamber of Commerce, 1968–70. *Recreation:* travel. *Address:* 19 Archery Close, W2. *Club:* Naval and Military.

KING, Charles Martin M.; see Meade-King.

KING, Colin Sainthill W.; see Wallis-King.

KING, Prof. David Anthony, FRS 1991; FRSC, MInstP; 1920 Professor of Physical Chemistry, University of Cambridge, since 1988; Fellow of St John's College, Cambridge, since 1988; *b* 12 Aug. 1939; *s* of Arnold King and Patricia (*née* Vardy), Durban; *m* Jane Lichtenstein; one *s* one *d*, and two *s* by previous marriage. *Educ:* St John's Coll., Johannesburg; Univ. of the Witwatersrand, Johannesburg. BSc, PhD (Rand), ScD (E Anglia). Shell Scholar, Imperial Coll., 1963–66; Lectr in Chemical Physics, Univ. of E Anglia, Norwich, 1966–74; Brunner Prof. of Physical Chemistry, Univ. of Liverpool, 1974–88. Member: Comité de Direction of Centre de Cinétique Physique et Chimique, Nancy, 1974–81; Nat. Exec., Assoc. of Univ. Teachers, 1970–78 (Nat. Pres., 1976–77); British Vacuum Council, 1978– (Chm., 1982–85); Internat. Union for Vacuum Science and Technology, 1978–86; Faraday Div., Council, Chem. Soc., 1979–82; Scientific Adv. Panel, Daresbury Lab., 1980–82; Res. Adv. Cttee, Leverhulme Trust, 1980–; Beirat, Fritz Haber Inst., West Berlin, 1981–. Chairman: Gallery Cttee, Bluecoat Soc. of Arts, 1986–88; Kettle's Yard Gall., Cambridge, 1989–. Tilden Lectr, Chem. Soc., 1989. Member Editorial Board: Jl of Physics C, 1977–80; Surface Science Reports, 1983–91; Editor, Chemical Physics Letters, 1989–. Chem. Soc. Award for surface and colloid chemistry, 1978; British Vacuum Council medal and prize for research, 1991. *Publications:* papers on the physics and chemistry of solid surfaces in: Proc. Royal Soc., Surface Science, Jl Chem. Soc., Jl of Physics, etc. *Recreations:* photography, art. *Address:* 20 Glisson Road, Cambridge CB1 2HD. *T:* Cambridge (0223) 315629.

KING, (Denys) Michael (Gwilym), CVO 1989; CEng, FICE, MIMechE; Managing Director, Airports Division, BAA plc, since 1988; Director, BAA plc, since 1986 (Member, British Airports Authority, 1980–86); *b* 29 May 1929; *s* of William James King, FCIS, and Hilda May King; *m* 1st, 1956, Monica Helen (marr. diss. 1973); three *d*; 2nd, 1985, Ann Elizabeth. *Educ:* St Edmund's Sch., Canterbury; Simon Langton Sch., Canterbury; Battersea Polytechnic, London (BScEng Hons London, 1949). MIMechE 1966; FICE 1977. Engr, J. Laing Construction Ltd, 1961–71, Dir, 1971–74; Engrg Dir, BAA, 1974–77; Dir, 1977–86, Man. Dir, 1986–88, Heathrow Airport. *Recreation:* yachting. *Address:* c/o BAA plc, 130 Wilton Road, SW1V 1LQ.

KING, Douglas James Edward, FRICS; FCIArb; Senior Partner, 1963–87, Consultant, since 1987, King & Co., Chartered Surveyors; Director: Bradford & Bingley Building Society, 1982–90; Frogmore Estates plc (formerly Fairview Estates), 1982–90; *b* 12 April 1919; *s* of Herbert James King, OBE, FRICS and Gertrude Carney; *m* 1941, Betty Alice Martin; two *s* one *d*. *Educ:* Hillcrest Prep. Sch., Frinton-on-Sea; Taunton Sch. FRICS 1952. Served War, TA, 1939–46, Captain RA. Chm., Hearts of Oak & Enfield Bldg Soc., 1975–82. A Vice Pres., London Chamber of Commerce and Industry, 1980– (Chm., 1978–80); Chm., London Court of Internat. Arbitration, 1981–82, and of Jt Cttee of Management, 1987–88; Gen. Comr of Income Tax, City of London, 1978–. Master, Wheelwrights' Co., 1985–86. Governor, Queenswood Sch., 1980–. *Recreation:* lives and writings of Johnson, Boswell and Pepys. *Address:* Monkswood Cottage, 73a Camlet Way, Hadley Wood, Herts EN4 0NL. *T:* 081–449 0263. *Clubs:* Carlton, City Livery.

KING, Prof. Edmund James, MA, PhD, DLit; Professor of Education, University of London King's College, 1975–79, now Emeritus Professor; *b* 19 June 1914; *s* of James and Mary Alice King; *m* 1939, Margaret Mary Breakell; one *s* three *d*. *Educ:* Univ. of Manchester (BA, MA); Univ. of London (PhD, DLit). Taught in grammar schs, 1936–47; Asst, then Sen. Asst to Dir of Extra-Mural Studies, Univ. of London, 1947–53; Lectr, subseq. Reader, Univ. of London King's Coll., 1953–75, also Dir, Comparative Research Unit, King's Coll., 1970–73. Visiting appts at Amer., Can. and Chinese univs; also in Melbourne, Tokyo, Tehran, etc; lecturing and adv. assignments in many countries. Editor, Comparative Education, 1978–. *Publications:* Other Schools and Ours, 1958, 5th edn 1979; World Perspectives in Education, 1962, 2nd edn 1965; (ed) Communist Education, 1963; Society, Schools and Progress in the USA, 1965; Education and Social Change, 1966; Comparative Studies and Educational Decision, 1968; Education and Development in Western Europe, 1969; (ed) The Teacher and the Needs of Society, 1970; The Education of Teachers: a comparative analysis, 1970; (with W. Boyd) A History of Western Education, 1972; Post-compulsory Education, vol. I: a new analysis in Western Europe, 1974; vol. II: the way ahead, 1975 (both with C. H. Moor and J. A. Mundy); (ed) Reorganizing Education, 1977; (ed) Education for Uncertainty, 1979; Technological/occupational Challenge, Social Transformation and Educational Response, 1986. *Recreations:* gardening, music, writing. *Address:* 40 Alexandra Road, Epsom, Surrey KT17 4BT.

KING, Very Rev. Edward Laurie; Dean of Cape Town, 1958–88, Dean Emeritus since 1988; *b* 30 Jan. 1920; *s* of William Henry and Norah Alice King; *m* 1950, Helen Stuart Mathers, MB, BCh, MMed; one *s* three *d*. *Educ:* King's Coll., Taunton; University of Wales (BA). Deacon, 1945; priest, 1946, Monmouth; Associate in Theology (S Af.). Curate of Risca, 1945–48; Diocese of Johannesburg, 1948–50; Rector of Robertson, Cape, 1950–53; Rector of Stellenbosch, 1953–58. *Recreations:* cricket, reading. *Address:* 30 6th Avenue, Rondebosch East, 7700, South Africa. *T:* 021 68 68204. *Club:* City and Civil Service.

KING, Evelyn Mansfield, MA; *b* 30 May 1907; *s* of Harry Percy King and Winifred Elizabeth Paulet; *m* 1935, Hermione Edith (*d* 1989), *d* of late Arthur Felton Crutchley, DSO; one *s* two *d*. *Educ:* Cheltenham Coll.; King's Coll., Cambridge; Inner Temple. Cambridge Univ. Correspondent to the Sunday Times, 1928–30; Asst Master Bedford Sch., 1930; Headmaster and Warden, Clayesmore Sch., 1935–50; Gloucestershire Regt 1940; Acting Lt-Col 1941. MP (Lab) Penryn and Falmouth Div. of Cornwall, 1945–50; Parly Sec., Min. of Town and Country Planning, 1947–50. Resigned from Labour Party, 1951, and joined Conservative Party; contested (C) Southampton (Itchen), 1959; MP (C) Dorset S, 1964–79. Member of Parly delegations: Bermuda and Washington, 1946; Tokyo, 1947; Cairo and ME, 1967; Jordan and Persian Gulf, 1968; Kenya and Seychelles, 1969; Malta, 1970 (leader); Malawi, 1971 (leader); Mem. Select Cttee on Overseas Aid, 1971; Chm. Food Cttee, 1971–73. *Publications:* (with J. C. Trewin) Printer to the House, Biography of Luke Hansard, 1952; Closest Correspondence, 1989. *Recreations:* boats, riding. *Address:* Embley Manor, near Romsey, Hants. *T:* Romsey (0794) 512342; 11 Barton Street, SW1. *T:* 071–222 4525. *Club:* Carlton.

See also Col Rt Hon. Sir E. D. L. du Cann.

KING, Francis Henry, CBE 1985 (OBE 1979); FRSL 1948; author; Drama Critic, Sunday Telegraph, 1978–88; *b* 4 March 1923; *o s* of Eustace Arthur Cecil King and Faith Mina Read. *Educ:* Shrewsbury; Balliol Coll., Oxford. Chm., Soc. of Authors, 1975–77; Internat. Vice-Pres., PEN, 1989– (Pres., English PEN, 1978–86; Vice-Pres., 1977; Internat. Pres., 1986–89). *Publications: novels:* To the Dark Tower, 1946; Never Again, 1947; An Air That Kills, 1948; The Dividing Stream, 1951 (Somerset Maugham Award, 1952); The Dark Glasses, 1954; The Widow, 1957; The Man on the Rock, 1957; The Custom House, 1961; The Last of the Pleasure Gardens, 1965; The Waves Behind the Boat, 1967; A Domestic Animal, 1970; Flights (two short novels), 1973; A Game of Patience, 1974; The Needle, 1975; Danny Hill, 1977; The Action, 1978; Act of Darkness, 1983; Voices in an Empty Room, 1984; Frozen Music, 1987; The Woman Who Was God, 1988; Punishments, 1989; Visiting Cards, 1990; The Ant Colony, 1991; (with Tom Wakefield and Patrick Gale) Secret Lives, 1991; *short stories:* So Hurt and Humiliated, 1959; The Japanese Umbrella, 1964 (Katherine Mansfield Short Story Prize, 1965); The Brighton Belle, 1968; Hard Feelings, 1976; Indirect Method, 1980; One is a Wanderer, 1985; *poetry:* Rod of Incantation, 1952; *biography:* E. M. Forster and His World, 1978; (ed) My Sister and Myself: the diaries of J. R. Ackerley, 1982; *general:* (ed) Introducing Greece, 1956; Japan, 1970; Florence, 1982; (ed) Lafcadio Hearn: Writings from Japan, 1984; Florence: A Literary Companion, 1991. *Address:* 19 Gordon Place, W8 4JE. *T:* 071–937 5715. *Club:* PEN.

KING, Gen. Sir Frank (Douglas), GCB 1976 (KCB 1972; CB 1971); MBE 1953; Director, since 1978: Kilton Properties; Springthorpe Property Co.; PLAZA Fish Ltd; *b* 9 March 1919; *s* of Arthur King, Farmer, and Kate Eliza (*née* Sheard), Brightwell, Berks; *m* 1947, Joy Emily Ellen Taylor-Lane; one *s* two *d*. *Educ:* Wallingford Gram. Sch. Joined Army, 1939; commnd into Royal Fusiliers, 1940; Parachute Regt, 1943; dropped Arnhem, Sept. 1944; Royal Military College of Science (ptsc), 1946; Staff Coll., Camberley (psc), 1950; comd 2 Parachute Bn, Middle East, 1960–62; comd 11 Infantry Bde Gp, Germany, 1963–64; Military Adviser (Overseas Equipment), 1965–66; Dir, Land/Air Warfare, MoD, 1967–68; Dir, Military Assistance Overseas, MoD, 1968–69; Comdt, RMCS, 1969–71; GOC-in-C, Army Strategic Comd, 1971–72; Dep. C-in-C UK Land Forces, 1972–73; GOC and Dir of Ops, N Ireland, 1973–75; Comdr, Northern Army Gp, and C-in-C BAOR, 1976–78; ADC Gen. to the Queen, 1977–78. Col Comdt, Army Air Corps, 1974–79. Mil. Advr, Short Bros Ltd, 1979–85. Chairman: Assets Protection Internat. Ltd, 1981–86; John Taylor Trust, 1978–88; Dir, Control Risks Ltd, 1979–86; Director 1978–88: John Taylor Ltd; John Taylor (Worksop); Leicester Frozen Foods. Trustee, Airborne Forces Security Trust, 1981–; Mem. Council, Air League, 1982–90; Dir, Airborne Forces Charitable Trust, 1988–; Pres., Arnheim Veterans Club, 1988–. Kermit Roosevelt Lectr, 1977. *Recreations:* golf, gardening, flying. *Address:* c/o Royal Bank of Scotland, Columbia House, 69 Aldwych, WC2. *Clubs:* Army and Navy; Berkshire Golf.

KING, Frederick Ernest, FRS 1954; MA, DPhil, DSc Oxon; PhD London; Scientific Adviser to British Petroleum Co. Ltd, 1959–71, retired; *er s* of late Frederick and Elizabeth King, Bexhill, Sussex. *Educ:* Bancroft's Sch.; University of London; Oriel Coll., Oxford. Ramsay Memorial Fellow, 1930–31; Demonstrator, Dyson Perrins Laboratory, 1931–34; University Lecturer and Demonstrator in Chemistry, Oxford Univ., 1934–48, and sometime lecturer in Organic Chemistry, Magdalen Coll. and Balliol Coll.; Sir Jesse Boot Prof. of Chemistry, University of Nottingham, 1948–55; Dir in charge of research, British Celanese Ltd, 1955–59. Fellow Queen Mary Coll., 1955. Tilden Lectr, Chem. Soc., 1948. *Publications:* scientific papers mainly in Jl of Chem. Soc. *Recreation:* gardening. *Address:* 9 Saffrons Court, Compton Place Road, Eastbourne, East Sussex BN21 1DX.

KING, Hilary William, CBE 1964; HM Diplomatic Service, retired; *b* 10 March 1919; *s* of Dr W. H. King, Fowey, Cornwall; *m* 1947, Dr Margaret Helen Grierson Borrowman; one *s* three *d*. *Educ:* Sherborne; Corpus Christi Coll. Cambridge. Served War of 1939–45; Signals Officer, mission to Yugoslav Partizan GHQ, 1943–45 (MBE 1944). Apptd Mem. Foreign (subseq. Diplomatic) Service, Nov. 1946. A Vice-Consul in Yugoslavia, 1947–48; transferred to Foreign Office, 1949; promoted 1st Sec., 1950; transf. to Vienna as a Russian Sec., 1951; Washington, 1953; transf. Foreign Office, 1958; Commercial Counsellor, Moscow, 1959; acted as Chargé d'Affaires, 1960; Ambassador (and Consul-Gen.) to Guinea, 1962–65; St Antony's Coll., Oxford, Oct. 1965–June 1966; Counsellor of Embassy, Warsaw, 1966–67; Head of UN (Economic and Social) Dept, FCO, 1968–71; Consul-Gen., Hamburg, 1971–74. *Recreations:* sailing, amateur radio. *Address:* Fuaim an Sruth, South Cuan, Oban, Argyll PA34 4TU.

KING, Isobel Wilson; *see* Buchanan, I. W.

KING, Prof. James Lawrence; Regius Professor of Engineering, 1968–83, University Fellow, 1983–87, Edinburgh University; *b* 14 Feb. 1922; *s* of Lawrence Aubrey King and Wilhelmina Young McLeish; *m* 1951, Pamela Mary Ward Hitchcock; one *s* one *d*. *Educ:* Latymer Upper Sch.; Jesus Coll., Cambridge; Imperial Coll., London. Min. of Defence (Navy), 1942–68. *Recreation:* walking. *Address:* 16 Lyne Park, West Linton, Peeblesshire EH46 7HP. *T:* West Linton (0968) 60038.

KING, Prof. Jeffrey William Hitchen, MSc, CEng, FICE, FIStructE; Professor of Civil Engineering, Queen Mary College, University of London, 1953–72, now Emeritus Professor; *b* 28 Sept. 1906; *s* of George and Edith King, Wigan; *m* 1930, Phyllis Morfydd Harris (*d* 1977), *d* of Rev. W. Harris; one *s* one *d*. *Educ:* Ashton-in-Makerfield Grammar Sch.; Manchester Univ. Engineer and Agent to Cementation Co. Ltd, British Isles, Spain and Egypt, 1927–36; Research Engineer, Michelin Tyre Co. 1936–37; Lecturer in Civil Engineering, University Coll., Nottingham, 1937–47; Reader in Civil Engineering, Queen Mary Coll., London, 1947–53. Governor, Queen Mary Coll., 1962–65; formerly Mem., Academic Board and Vice-Chm., Civil Engineering Cttee of Regional Advisory Council for Higher Technological Education; formerly mem., Research Cttee, formerly Chm., Concrete Specification Cttee and Cttee on Accelerated Testing of Concrete, Instn of Civil Engineers; formerly Mem. BSI Cttees, CEB/4/4, CEB/21. *Publications:* papers in Journals of Instn of Civil Engineers, Instn of Structural Engineers, and Inst. of Mine Surveyors, and in various technical periodicals. *Recreations:* many and varied. *Address:* The Nook, Crayke Road, Easingwold, York YO6 3PN. *T:* Easingwold (0347) 21151.

KING, Jock; *see* King, John G. M.

KING, John Arthur Charles; Chairman, Analysys Ltd, since 1991; *b* 7 April 1933; *s* of late Charles William King and of Doris Frances King; *m* 1958, Ina Solavici; two *s*. *Educ:* Univ. of Bristol. BSc. IBM UK, 1956–70; Managing Director, Telex Computer Products UK Ltd, 1970–73; Dir, DP Div., Metra Consulting Gp, 1974–75; Marketing Dir, UK, later Europe (Brussels), ITT Business Systems, 1976–81; Commercial Dir, Business Communications Systems, Philips (Hilversum), 1981–83; Dir, Marketing and Corporate Strategy, subseq. Corporate Dir and Man. Dir, Overseas Div., BT plc, 1984–88; Man. Dir, Citicorp Information Business Internat., 1988–91; Chm., Quotron Internat., 1988–91. Director: Leeds Permanent BS, 1991–; Olivetti Networks and Systems, 1991–. CBIM 1986; FInstD 1986; FBCS. *Recreations:* tennis, bridge, music. *Address:* Analysys Ltd, 8–9 Jesus Lane, Cambridge CB5 8BA. *T:* Cambridge (0223) 460600.

KING, Sir John (Christopher), 4th Bt *cr* 1888, of Campsie, Stirlingshire; *b* 31 March 1933; *s* of Sir James Granville Le Neve King, 3rd Bt, TD and of Penelope Charlotte, *d* of late Capt. E. Cooper-Key, CB, MVO, RN; *S* father, 1989; *m* 1st, 1958, Patricia Foster (marr. diss. 1972); one *s* one *d*; 2nd, 1984, Aline Jane Holley (*née* Brett). *Educ:* Eton. Sub Lt, RNVR, 1952–54; Lt, Berks Yeomanry, 1955–60. Mem., Stock Exchange, 1961–73. *Recreations:* sailing, shooting, travelling. *Heir:* *s* James Henry Rupert King, *b* 24 May 1961. *Address:* c/o C. Hoare & Co., 37 Fleet Street, EC4P 4DQ. *Club:* Brooks's.

KING, John Edward; Principal Establishment Officer and Under Secretary, Welsh Office, 1977–82; Chairman, Friends of the Welsh College of Music and Drama, since 1990; *b* 30 May 1922; *s* of late Albert Edward and of Margaret King; *m* 1st, 1948, Pamela White (marr. diss.); one *d*; 2nd, 1956, Mary Margaret Beaton; two *d*. *Educ:* Penarth County

Sch.; Sch. of Oriental and African Studies, London Univ. Served with Rifle Bde, RWF and Nigeria Regt, 1941–47; Chindit campaign, Burma, with 77 Bde (despatches). Cadet, Colonial Admin. Service, N Nigeria, 1947; Permanent Sec., Fed. Govt of Nigeria, 1960; retired from HMOCS, 1963. Principal, CRO, 1963; Navy Dept, MoD, 1966–69; Private Sec. to Sec. of State for Wales, 1969–71; Asst Sec., Welsh Office, 1971–77. CS Mem., 1977–82, External Mem., 1982–86, Final Selection Bd, CS Commn. Consultant, Dept of Educn and Dir, China Studies Centre, UC, Cardiff, 1984–87. *Recreations:* books, swimming, tennis, watercolour painting. *Address:* Fairfields, Fairwater Road, Llandaff, Cardiff CF5 2LF. *T:* Cardiff (0222) 562825. *Clubs:* Civil Service; Llandaff Institute (Llandaff); Cardiff Lawn Tennis.

KING, John George Maydon, (Jock), CMG 1959; OBE 1953 (MBE 1945); retired from Colonial Agricultural Service; *b* 26 Jan. 1908; 2nd *s* of late Harold Edwin and Elizabeth Lindsay King, Durban, Natal, SA; *m* 1st, 1938, Françoise Charlotte de Rham (*d* 1966), Lausanne; two *s*; 2nd, 1970, Violet (*d* 1990), *widow* of Colin MacPherson, late of Tanganyika Administration Service. *Educ:* University Coll. Sch. (Preparatory); Oundle Sch.; London Univ. (Wye Coll.); Cambridge Univ. (Colonial Office Schol., Cambridge Univ. and Imperial Coll. of Tropical Agric.). Appointed to Colonial Agricultural Service as Agricultural Officer, Tanganyika, 1932–46; seconded to Cambridge Univ. as Lecturer in Tropical Agric. to Colonial Services Courses, 1946–48; Dir of livestock and Agricultural Services, Basutoland, 1948–54; Dir of Agriculture, Uganda, 1954–60, Swaziland, 1960–63; Regional Manager, Lower Indus Project, Hyderabad-Sind, 1964–66. *Recreations:* walking, photography. *Address:* Brockley House, Nailsworth, near Stroud, Glos GL6 0AR. *T:* Nailsworth (045383) 2407. *Club:* Farmers'.

KING, Prof. (John) Oliver (Letts), FRCVS; FIBiol; Professor of Animal Husbandry, University of Liverpool, 1969–82, now Emeritus; *b* 21 Dec. 1914; *s* of Richard Oliver King and Helen Mary (*née* Letts); *m* 1942, Helen Marion Gudgin; one *s* one *d*. *Educ:* Berkhamsted Grammar Sch.; Royal Veterinary Coll. (MRCVS); Univ. of Reading (BScAgric); Univ. of Liverpool (MVSc, PhD); FRCVS 1969. Assistant in veterinary practice, 1937; Ho. Surg., Royal Veterinary Coll., 1938; Lectr in Animal Husbandry, 1941, Sen. Lectr 1948, Reader 1961, Univ. of Liverpool. Mem. Council, British Veterinary Assoc., 1953–68; Chairman: British Council Agric. and Vet. Adv. Panel, 1978–84; Council, UFAW, 1987–90 (a Vice-Pres., 1990–); Member: Medicines Commn, 1969–71; Horserace Anti-Doping Cttee, 1973–86, Horserace Scientific Adv. Cttee, 1986–89; Farm Animal Welfare Council, 1979–84; a Vice-President: N of England Zoological Soc., 1987– (Chm. Council, 1972–86); BVA Animal Welfare Foundn, 1989–; President: Assoc. of Veterinary Teachers and Research Workers, 1961; Lancashire Veterinary Assoc., 1967; British Veterinary Zoological Soc., 1971–74; Royal Coll. of Veterinary Surgeons, 1980. Dalrymple-Champneys Cup, 1976; Bledisloe Vet. Award, 1983. *Publications:* Veterinary Dietetics, 1961; An Introduction to Animal Husbandry, 1978; papers on animal husbandry in various scientific pubns. *Recreation:* gardening. *Address:* 6 Ashtree Farm Court, Willaston, South Wirral L64 2XL. *T:* 051–327 4850. *Club:* Athenæum.

KING, Dr John William Beaufoy; Head of AFRC Animal Breeding Liaison Group, retired 1987; *b* 28 June 1927; *s* of late John Victor Beaufoy and Gwendoleen Freda King; *m* 1951, Pauline Margaret Coldicott; four *s*. *Educ:* Marling Sch., Stroud; St Catharine's Coll., Cambridge; Edinburgh Univ. BA Cantab 1947, MA Cantab 1952; PhD Edinburgh 1951; FIBiol 1974; FRSE 1975. ARC Animal Breeding Res. Organisation, 1951–82. Kellogg Foundn Schol. to USA, 1954; Genetics Cons. to Pig Industry Develt Authority, 1959; David Black Award (services to pig industry), 1966; Nuffield Foundn Fellowship to Canada, 1970; Vis. Lectr, Göttingen Univ., 1973. *Publications:* papers in scientific jls. *Recreations:* gardening, shooting, dog training. *Address:* Cottage Farm, West Linton, Peeblesshire EH46 7AS. *T:* West Linton (0968) 60448. *Club:* Farmers'.

KING, Joseph, OBE 1971; JP; Group Industrial Relations Advisor, Smith and Nephew Associated Cos Ltd, 1978–82; *b* 28 Nov. 1914; *s* of John King, coal miner, and Catherine King (*née* Thompson); *m* 1939, Lily King (*née* Pendlebury); one *s* five *d*. *Educ:* St James' RC Sch., Atherton, Lancashire. Left school at age of 14 and commenced work in cotton mill, 1929. Took active part in Union of Textile and Allied Workers from early years in industry. Elected, 1949: Labour Councillor, Tyldesley; Trades Union Organiser; Dist. Sec., NE Lancs. Gen. Sec., Nat. Union of Textile and Allied Workers, 1962–75; Jt Gen. Sec., Amalgamated Textile Workers' Union, 1974; Mem., TUC Gen. Council, 1972–75; Member, many cttees in Textile Industry. Industrial Advr ACAS NW Reg., 1975–78. Created Accrington Pakistan Friendship Association, 1961 (Pres.). Dir, Castle Cards Ltd, Preston, 1984–85. JP Accrington, 1955. *Recreations:* pleasure is in domestic work in the home and family and in trade union and political field. *Address:* 44 Southwood Drive, Baxenden, Accrington, Lancs. *T:* Accrington (0254) 394551.

KING, Hon. Leonard James, AC 1987; **Hon. Justice King;** Chief Justice of South Australia, since 1978; *b* 1 May 1925; *s* of Michael Owen and Mary Ann King; *m* 1953, Sheila Therese (*née* Keane); two *s* three *d*. *Educ:* Marist Brothers Sch., Norwood, S Aust; Univ. of Adelaide, S Aust (LLB). Admitted to Bar, 1950; QC 1967. Member, House of Assembly, Parlt of S Australia, 1970; Attorney-General and Minister of Community Welfare, 1970; additionally, Minister of Prices and Consumer Affairs, 1972. Judge of Supreme Court of S Aust, 1975. *Address:* c/o Chief Justice's Chambers, Supreme Court House, Victoria Square, Adelaide, South Australia 5000, Australia. *T:* 218 6211.

KING, Prof. Mervyn Allister; Professor of Economics, London School of Economics and Political Science, since 1984; Director, since 1990, and Chief Economist, since 1991, Bank of England; *b* 30 March 1948; *s* of Eric Frank King and Kathleen Alice Passingham. *Educ:* Wolverhampton Grammar School; King's College, Cambridge (BA 1st cl. hons 1969, MA 1973). Research Officer, Dept of Applied Economics, Cambridge, 1969–76; Kennedy Schol., Harvard Univ., 1971–72; Fellow, St John's Coll., Cambridge, 1972–77; Lectr, Faculty of Economics, Cambridge, 1976–77; Esmée Fairbairn Prof. of Investment, Univ. of Birmingham, 1977–84. Vis. Professor of Economics: Harvard Univ., 1982, 1990; MIT, 1983–84. Co-Dir, LSE Financial Markets Gp, 1987–91. Mem., City Capital Markets Cttee, 1989–. Member: Meade Cttee, 1978; Council and Exec., Royal Economic Soc., 1981–86; Fellow, Econometric Soc., 1982. Managing Editor, Review of Economic Studies, 1978–83; Associate Editor: Jl of Public Economics, 1983–; Amer. Economic Review, 1985–88. Indep. Dir, The Securities Assoc., 1987–89. Trustee, Kennedy Meml Trust, 1990–. Helsinki Univ. Medal, 1982. *Publications:* Public Policy and the Corporation, 1977; (with J. A. Kay) The British Tax System, 1978, 5th edn 1990; (with D. Fullerton) The Taxation of Income from Capital, 1984; numerous articles in economics jls. *Address:* Bank of England, Threadneedle Street, EC2R 8AH.

KING, Michael; *see* King, D. M. G.

KING, Michael, (Mike); business consultant in private practice, since 1984; *b* 31 Aug. 1934; *s* of Mac and Jessie King; *m* 1960, Teresa Benjamin; one *s* one *d*. *Educ:* Buckhurst Hill School, London Univ. (BA). Buyer, Ford Motor Co., 1958–64; Purchasing Manager, Servicing Manager, Hotpoint, 1964–68; Dir and Div. Man. Dir, Lake & Elliot, 1968–72; Chief Exec., Heatrae-Sadia International, 1972–84; Chief Exec., E Anglian RHA, 1985–88. Freeman, City of London; Liveryman, Coopers' Co. *Recreations:* tennis, skiing, music, antiques, computers. *Address:* Moat Cottage, Pleshey, Essex CM3 1HG. *T:* Chelmsford (0245) 37202. *Club:* Institute of Directors.

KING, His Honour Michael Gardner; a Circuit Judge, 1972–87; *b* 4 Dec. 1920; *s* of late David Thomson King and late Winifred Mary King, Bournemouth; *m* 1951, Yvonne Mary Lilian, *d* of late Lt-Col M. J. Ambler; two *s* one *d*. *Educ:* Sherborne Sch.; Wadham Coll., Oxford (MA). Served in RN, Lieut RNVR, 1940–46. Called to Bar, Gray's Inn, 1949. Dep. Chm., IoW QS, 1966–72; Dep. Chm., Hants QS, 1968–72. *Recreations:* sailing, shooting, golf. *Clubs:* Hampshire (Winchester); Royal Naval Sailing Association, Royal Lymington Yacht (Cdre, 1986–88), Bar Yacht; Brokenhurst Manor Golf.

KING, Vice-Adm. Sir Norman (Ross Dutton), KBE 1989; Chief of Staff to Commander Allied Naval Forces Southern Europe, 1988–91; *b* 19 March 1933; *s* of Sir Norman King, KCMG and Lady (Mona) King (*née* Dutton); *m* 1967, Patricia Rosemary, *d* of Dr L. B. Furber; two *d*. *Educ:* Fonthill School; RNC Dartmouth; graduate, Naval Command College, Newport, USA, 1969; RCDS 1978. RN Cadet, 1946; served HM Ships Indefatigable, Tintagel Castle, Ceylon, Wild Goose, Hickleton, 1951–57, and Corunna, 1957–59; long TAS course, 1960; BRNC Dartmouth, 1961–63; CO HMS Fiskerton, 1963–64; Jun. Seaman Appointer, Naval Sec's Dept, 1965–66; CO HMS Leopard, 1967–68; Staff Officer (TAS) to CBNS (Washington), 1969–71; XO HMS Intrepid, 1972–73; Staff Warfare TAS Officer, to Dir Naval Warfare, 1974–75; Naval Asst to Second Sea Lord, 1975–77; CO HMS Newcastle and Capt. 3rd Destroyer Sqn, 1979–80; CSO to CBNS (Washington), 1981–82; Dir of Naval Officer Appts (Seaman Officers), 1983–84; Comdr, British Navy Staff and British Naval Attaché, Washington, and UK Nat. Liaison Rep. to SACLANT, 1984–86; Naval Sec., 1987–88. *Publications:* (jointly) All The Queen's Men, 1967, paperback edn as Strictly Personal, 1972. *Recreations:* tennis, music, chess. *Address:* c/o Lloyd's Bank, Faversham, Kent ME13 7AP. *Club:* Royal Navy Club of 1765 and 1785.

KING, Oliver; *see* King, J. O. L.

KING, Air Vice-Marshal Peter Francis, CB 1987; OBE (mil.) 1964; FRCSE; The Senior Consultant, RAF, 1985–87; Air Vice-Marshal, Princess Mary's RAF Hospital, Halton, 1983–87; Consultant Otorhinolaryngologist, King Edward VII Hospital, Midhurst, since 1988; *b* 17 Sept. 1922; *s* of William George King, RAF, and Florence Margaret King (*née* Sell); *m* 1945, Doreen Maxwell Aaröe, 2nd *d* of Jorgen Hansen-Aaröe; one *s* one *d*. *Educ:* Framlingham Coll.; King's Coll. London, 1940–42; Charing Cross Hosp., 1942–45; Univ. of Edinburgh, 1947. DLO; MRCS, LRCP; MFOM. Kitchener Med. Services Schol. for RAF, 1941; Ho. Phys., Ho. Surg., Charing Cross Hosp., 1945; commnd RAF, 1945; specialist in Otorhinolaryngology, employed Cosford, Ely, Fayid, Halton, CME; Cons. in Otorhinolaryngology, 1955; Hunterian Prof., RCS, 1964; Cons. Adviser in Otorhinolaryngology, 1966; Air Cdre 1976; Reader in Aviation Med., Inst. of Aviation Med., 1977; Whittingham Prof. in Aviation Med., IAM and RCP, 1979; QHS 1979–87; Dean of Air Force Medicine, 1983. Cons. to Herts HA, 1963, and CAA, 1973; Examiner for Dip. in Aviation Med., RCP, 1980. Pres., Sect. of Otology, RSocMed, 1977–78 (Sec., 1972–74); Chm., Brit. Soc. of Audiology, 1979–81; Vice-Pres., RNID, 1990 (Vice-Chm., 1980–88); Member: BMA, 1945–; Scottish Otological Soc., 1955–90; Royal Aeronaut. Soc., 1976–; Council, Brit. Assoc. of Otorhinolaryngologists, 1960–89; Editorial Bd, British Jl of Audiology, 1980–88. Fellow, Inst. of Acoustics, 1977. FRSM. CStJ 1987. Lady Cade Medal, RCS, 1967. *Publications:* Noise and Vibration in Aviation (with J. C. Guignard), 1972; (with John Ernsting) Aviation Medicine, 1988; numerous articles, chapters, lectures and papers, in books and relevant jls on aviation otolaryngology, noise deafness, hearing conservation, tympanoplasty, facial paralysis, otic barotrauma, etc. *Recreations:* sculpture, looking at prints. *Address:* 5 Churchill Gate, Oxford Road, Woodstock, Oxon OX7 1QW. *T:* Woodstock (0993) 813115. *Club:* Royal Air Force.

KING, Rev. Canon Philip David; Secretary, Board of Mission, General Synod of the Church of England, since 1991 (Secretary, Board for Mission and Unity, 1989–91); *b* 6 May 1935; *s* of Frank Harman King and Gladys Winifred King; *m* 1963, Margaret Naomi Rivers Pitt; two *s* two *d*. *Educ:* Keble College, Oxford (MA Jurisp.); Tyndale Hall, Bristol. Curate, Holy Trinity, Redhill, 1960–63; Minister in charge, St Patrick's, Wallington, 1963–68; Vicar, Christ Church, Fulham, 1968–74; Gen. Sec., S American Missionary Soc., 1974–86; Vicar, Christ Church and St Peter, Harrow, 1986–89. *Publication:* Leadership Explosion, 1987. *Recreation:* hill-walking. *Address:* Board of Mission, Church House, Great Smith Street, SW1P 3NZ. *T:* 071–222 9011.

KING, Phillip, CBE 1975; RA 1991 (ARA 1977); sculptor; Professor of Sculpture, Royal College of Art, since 1980; *b* 1 May 1934; *s* of Thomas John King and of Gabrielle (*née* Liautard); *m* 1957, Lilian Odelle (marr. diss. 1987); one *s* decd. *Educ:* Mill Hill Sch.; Christ's Coll., Cambridge Univ. (languages); St Martin's Sch. of Art (sculpture). Teacher at St Martin's Sch. of Art, 1959–78; Asst to Henry Moore, 1959–60. Trustee, Tate Gallery, 1967–69; Mem. Art Panel, Arts Council, 1977–79. Vis. Prof., Berlin Sch. of Art, 1979–81. *One-man Exhibitions include:* British Pavilion, Venice Biennale, 1968; European Mus. Tour, 1974–75 (Kroller-Muller Nat. Mus., Holland; Kunsthalle, Düsseldorf; Kunsthalle, Bern; Musée Galliera, Paris; Ulster Mus., Belfast); UK Touring Exhib., 1975–76 (Sheffield, Cumbria, Aberdeen, Glasgow, Newcastle, Portsmouth); Hayward Gall. (retrospective), 1981. Commissions include: Cross Bend, European Patent Office, Munich, 1978; Hiroshima Mus. of Art, 1989. First Prize, Socha Piestanskych Parkov, Piestany, Czechoslovakia, 1969. *Address:* c/o Rowan Gallery, 31A Bruton Place, W1. *T:* 071–499 4701.

KING, Ralph Malcolm MacDonald, OBE 1968; Colonial Service, retired; *b* 8 Feb. 1911; *s* of Dr James Malcolm King and Mrs Norah King; *m* 1948, Rita Elizabeth Herring; two *s* one *d*. *Educ:* Tonbridge Sch. Solicitor (Hons) 1934. Asst to Johnson, Stokes and Master, Solicitors, Hong Kong, 1936–41. Commissioned Middx Regt, 1941; prisoner of war, 1941–45; demobilised, 1946. Colonial Legal Service, 1947; Legal Officer, Somaliland, 1947; Crown Counsel, Somaliland, 1950. Called to Bar, Gray's Inn, 1950. Solicitor-General, Nyasaland, 1953; Attorney-General, Nyasaland, 1957–61. Disbarred at his own request and since restored to Roll of Solicitors, in April 1961. Legal Draftsman to Government of Northern Nigeria, 1963–67, and to Northern States of Nigeria, 1967–73; Dir, Legislative Drafting Courses, Commonwealth Secretariat, Jamaica, 1974–75, Trinidad, 1976, and Barbados, 1977. *Recreations:* watching cricket, walking. *Address:* 36 Mill View Close, Woodbridge, Suffolk. *T:* Woodbridge (0394) 385417.

KING, Sir Richard (Brian Meredith), KCB 1976 (CB 1969); MC 1944; Adviser to Société Générale de Surveillance, since 1986; Trustee, Simon Population Trust, since 1985; Director, Rural Investment Overseas, since 1987; *b* 2 Aug. 1920; *s* of late Bernard and Dorothy King; *m* 1944, Blanche Phyllis Roberts; two *s* one *d*. *Educ:* King's Coll. Sch., Wimbledon. Air Ministry, 1939; Min. of Aircraft Prod., 1940. Army 1940–46: Major, N Irish Horse; N Af. and Ital. campaigns (MC, Cassino). Min. of Supply, 1946; Asst Principal, Ministry of Works, 1948; Principal, 1949; Asst Regional Dir (Leeds), 1949–52; seconded Treas., 1953–54; Prin. Priv. Sec. to Minister of Works, 1956–57; Asst Sec., 1957; seconded Cabinet Off., 1958 (Sec. of Commonwealth Educn. Conf. (Oxford),

1959; Constitutional Confs: Kenya, 1960; N Rhodesia, Nyasaland and Fed. Review, 1960; WI Fedn, 1961); Dept of Tech. Co-op., on its formation, 1961; Min. of Overseas Develt, on its formation, 1964: Under-Sec., 1964; Dep. Sec., 1968; Permanent Sec., 1973–76; Exec. Sec., IMF/World Bank Develt Cttee, 1976–80; Senior Advr to S. G. Warburg & Co. Ltd, 1980–85. *Publications:* The Planning of the British Aid Programme, 1971; Criteria for Europe's Development Policy to the Third World, 1974. *Recreations:* music, lawn tennis, gardening, doing-it-himself. *Address:* Woodlands Farm House, Woodlands Lane, Stoke D'Abernon, Cobham, Surrey. *T:* Oxshott (0372) 843491. *Club:* All England Lawn Tennis.

KING, Robert George Cecil; Chairman, Social Security Appeal Tribunals, since 1987; Under Secretary (Legal), HM Customs and Excise, 1985–87; *b* 21 Jan. 1927; *s* of Stanley Cecil and Kathleen Mary King; *m* 1952, Mary Marshall. *Educ:* Nunthorpe Grammar School, York. Called to the Bar, Lincolns Inn, 1965. Army, 1945–48; British Rail, 1948–53; Judicial Dept, Kenya, 1954–61; East African Common Services Organisation, 1962–64; Solicitor's Office, HM Customs and Excise, 1965–87. *Recreations:* golf, bowls, gardening, watching cricket, watching television. *Address:* 181 Greenshaw Drive, Wigginton, York YO3 8SD. *T:* York (0904) 765039. *Clubs:* MCC; Yorkshire (York); Wigginton Bowling; Royal Nairobi Golf.

KING, Robert Shirley; Under Secretary, Department of Health and Social Security, 1976–80; *b* 12 July 1920; *s* of late Rev. William Henry King, MC, TD, MA, and Dorothy King (*née* Sharpe); *m* 1st, 1947, Margaret Siddall (*d* 1956); two *d*; 2nd, 1958, Mary Rowell; one *s* two *d*. *Educ:* Alexandra Road Sch., Oldham; Manchester Grammar Sch.; Trinity Coll., Cambridge (Schol., MA). Served War, RAF, 1940–45. Colonial Service, Tanganyika, 1949–62 (Dist Comr, Bukoba, 1956–58, Geita, 1959–62); Home Office: Principal, 1962–69 (seconded to Civil Service Dept, 1968–69); Asst Sec., 1969–70; transf., with Children's Dept, to DHSS, 1971; Asst Sec., DHSS, 1971–76; Sec., Wkg Party on Role and Tasks of Social Workers, Nat. Inst. for Social Work, 1980–82; part-time Asst Sec., Home Office, 1985–86. Sec., Health Promotion Res, Trust, 1984–89. Member Council: British and Foreign Sch. Soc., 1982–89; Shape, 1982–89. Governor: Cheshunt Foundn, 1976–83; Bell Educnl Trust, 1984–89. *Recreations:* walking, cycling, gardening, African affairs. *Address:* 3 Nightingale Avenue, Cambridge CB1 4SG. *T:* Cambridge (0223) 248965.

KING, Roger Douglas; MP (C) Birmingham, Northfield, since 1983; *b* 26 Oct. 1943; *s* of Douglas and Cecilie King; *m* 1976, Jennifer Susan (*née* Sharpe); twin *s* one *d*. *Educ:* Solihull Sch. Served automobile engrg apprenticeship with British Motor Corp., 1960–66; sales rep., 1966–74; own manufg business, 1974–81; self-employed car product distributor, 1982–83. Dir (non-exec.), Nat. Express Hldgs, 1988–. PPS to Minister for Local Govt, 1987–88, for Water and Planning, 1988, DoE, to Sec. of State for Employment, 1989–. Mem., H of C Transport Select Cttee, 1984–87; Vice-Chm., All Party Motor Industry Gp, 1985–; Jt Sec., Cons. Tourism Cttee, 1985–87. FIMI 1986. *Recreations:* swimming, motoring. *Address:* c/o House of Commons, SW1A 0AA.

KING, Dame Ruth; *see* Railton, Dame R.

KING, Sir Sydney (Percy), Kt 1975; OBE 1965; JP; District Organiser, National Union of Agricultural and Allied Workers, 1946–80; Chairman, Trent Regional Health Authority, 1973–82; *b* 20 Sept. 1916; *s* of James Edwin King and Florence Emily King; *m* 1944, Millicent Angela Prendergast; two *d*. *Educ:* Brockley Central School. Member: N Midland Regional Board for Industry (Vice-Chm. 1949); Sheffield Regional Hosp. Bd, 1963–73 (Chm, 1969–73); E Midland Economic Planning Council, 1965–; E Midlands Gas Board, 1970; MAFF E Midland Regional Panel, 1972– (Chm., 1977). Pro-Chancellor, Univ. of Leicester, 1987–. JP 1956, Alderman 1967, Kesteven. Hon. LLD: Leicester, 1980; Nottingham, 1981. *Recreations:* reading, music, talking. *Address:* 49 Robertson Drive, Sleaford, Lincs NG34 7AL. *T:* Sleaford (0529) 302056.

KING, Thea, (Mrs T. Thurston), OBE 1985; FRCM; freelance musician; Professor, Guildhall School of Music, since 1988; *b* 26 Dec. 1925; *m* Jan. 1953, Frederick John Thurston (*d* Dec. 1953). *Educ:* Bedford High Sch.; Royal College of Music (FRCM 1975; ARCM 1944 and 1947). Prof. of Clarinet, RCM, 1961–87. Sadler's Wells Orchestra, 1950–52; Portia Wind Ensemble, 1955–68; London Mozart Players, 1956–84; Member: English Chamber Orchestra, Melos Ensemble of London, Vesuvius Ensemble, Robles Ensemble. Frequent soloist, broadcaster, recitalist; recordings include Mozart, Brahms, Spohr, Finzi, Bruch, Mendelssohn, Stanford and 20th Century British music. *Publications:* clarinet solos, Chester Woodwind series, 1977; arrangement of J. S. Bach, Duets for 2 Clarinets, 1979; Schumann for the Clarinet, 1991. *Recreations:* cows, pillow lace, painting, ski-ing. *Address:* 16 Milverton Road, NW6 7AS. *T:* 081–459 3453.

KING, Rt. Hon. Thomas Jeremy, (Tom); PC 1979; MP (C) Bridgwater since March 1970; Secretary of State for Defence, since 1989; *b* 13 June 1933; *s* of late J. H. King, JP; *m* 1960, Jane, *d* of late Brig. Robert Tilney, CBE, DSO, TD; one *s* one *d*. *Educ:* Rugby; Emmanuel Coll., Cambridge (MA). National service, 1951–53: commnd Somerset Light Inf., 1952; seconded to KAR; served Tanganyika and Kenya; Actg Captain 1953. Cambridge, 1953–56. Joined E.S. & A. Robinson Ltd, Bristol, 1956; various positions up to Divisional Gen. Man., 1964–69; Chm., Sale, Tilney Co Ltd, 1971–79 (Dir 1965–79). PPS to: Minister for Posts and Telecommunications, 1970–72; Minister for Industrial Develt, 1972–74; Front Bench spokesman for: Industry, 1975–76; Energy, 1976–79; Minister for Local Govt and Environmental Services, DoE, 1979–83; Sec. of State for the Environment, Jan.-June 1983, for Transport, June-Oct. 1983, for Employment, 1983–85, for NI, 1985–89. Vice-Chm., Cons. Parly Industry Cttee, 1974. *Recreations:* cricket, ski-ing. *Address:* House of Commons, SW1.

See also Mrs S. R. Clarke.

KING, Air Vice-Marshal Walter MacIan, CB 1961; CBE 1957; retired, 1967; *b* 10 March 1910; *s* of Alexander King, MB, ChB, DPH, and Hughberta Blannin King (*née* Pearson); *m* 1946, Anne Clare Hicks; two *s*. *Educ:* St Mary's Coll., Castries, St Lucia, BWI; Blundell's Sch., Tiverton, Devon. Aircraft Engineering (Messers Westland Aircraft Ltd, Handley-Page Ltd, Saunders-Roe Ltd), 1927–33; joined Royal Air Force, 1934; Overseas Service: No 8 Sqdn, Aden, 1935–37; South-east Asia, 1945–47; Middle East (Egypt and Cyprus), 1955–57. Student: RAF Staff Coll., 1944; Joint Services Staff Coll., 1947; IDC, 1954. Directing Staff, RAF Staff Coll., 1957–58; Comdt, No 16 MU, Stafford, 1958–60; Dir of Equipment (B), Air Ministry, 1961–64; Air Cdre Ops (Supply), HQ's Maintenance Command, during 1964; Senior Air Staff Officer, RAF Maintenance Command, 1964–67. Joined Hooker Craigmyle & Co. Ltd, 1967; Gen. Manager, Hooker Craigmyle (Scotland) Ltd, 1969–72; Dir, Craigmyle & Co. (Scotland) Ltd, 1972–76. *Recreations:* swimming (rep. RAF in inter-services competition, 1934); gardening. *Address:* 24 Arthur's Avenue, Harrogate HG2 0DX.

KING, Sir Wayne Alexander, 8th Bt *cr* 1815; self-employed entrepreneur; *b* 2 Feb. 1962; *s* of Sir Peter Alexander King, 7th Bt, and of Jean Margaret (who *m* 2nd, 1978, Rev. Richard Graham Mackenzie), *d* of Christopher Thomas Cavell, Deal; *S* father, 1973; *m* 1984, Laura Ellen, *d* of Donald James Lea, Almonte, Ontario; one *s*. *Educ:* Sir Roger Manwood's Sch., Sandwich, Kent; Algonquin Coll., Ottawa, Ont (majored in Accounting and Retail Management). Coach and Head Referee, Almonte Soccer (Canadian Soccer Assoc. Coaching Level I designation); Referee-in-chief, Almonte/Pakenham Minor Ice Hockey Assoc. *Recreations:* all sports. *Heir:* *s* Peter Richard Donald King, *b* 4 May 1988. *Address:* 146 High Street, Almonte, Ont K0A 1A0, Canada.

KING-HAMILTON, His Honour (Myer) Alan (Barry), QC 1954; an additional Judge of the Central Criminal Court, 1964–79; a Deputy Circuit Judge, 1979–83; *b* 9 Dec. 1904; *o s* of Alfred King-Hamilton; *m* 1935, Rosalind Irene Ellis (*d* 1991); two *d*. *Educ:* Bishop's Stortford Grammar Sch.; Trinity Hall, Cambridge (BA 1927, MA 1929; Pres. Cambridge Union Soc., 1927). Called to Bar, Middle Temple, 1929; served War of 1939–45, RAF, finishing with rank of Squadron Leader; served on Finchley Borough Council, 1938–39 and 1945–50. Recorder of Hereford, 1955–56; Recorder of Gloucester, 1956–61; Recorder of Wolverhampton, 1961–64; Dep. Chm. Oxford County Quarter Sessions, 1955–64, 1966–71; Leader of Oxford Circuit, 1961–64. Elected Bencher, Middle Temple, 1961. Elected to General Council of Bar, 1958. President: West London Reform Synagogue, 1967–75, 1977–83; Westlon Housing Assoc., 1975–; Vice-Pres., World Congress of Faiths, 1967–. Legal Member: Med. Practices Cttee, Min. of Health, 1961–64; ABTA Appeal Bd, 1980–; Member: Cttee, Birnbeck Housing Assoc., 1982–; Arts and Library Cttee, MCC, 1985–89; Chm., Mary Whitehouse Res. and Educn Trust, 1986–. Trustee, Barnet Community Trust, 1986–89. Freeman of City of London; Master, Needlemakers Co., 1969. *Publication:* And Nothing But the Truth (autobiog.), 1982. *Recreations:* cricket, gardening, the theatre. *Clubs:* Royal Air Force, MCC.

KING-HELE, Desmond George, FRS 1966; author; Deputy Chief Scientific Officer, Space Department, Royal Aircraft Establishment, Farnborough, 1968–88, retired; *b* 3 Nov. 1927; *s* of late S. G. and of B. King-Hele, Seaford, Sussex; *m* 1954, Marie Thérèse Newman; two *d*. *Educ:* Epsom Coll.; Trinity Coll., Cambridge. BA (1st cl. hons Mathematics) 1948; MA 1952. At RAE, Farnborough, 1948–88, working on space research from 1955. Mem., International Academy of Astronautics, 1961. Chairman: British Nat. Cttee for the History of Science, Medicine and Technology, 1985–89; History of Science Grants Cttee, Royal Soc., 1990–. Lectures: Symons, RMetS, 1961; Duke of Edinburgh's, Royal Inst. of Navigation, 1964; Jeffreys, RAS, 1971; Halley, Oxford, 1974; Bakerian, Royal Soc., 1974; Sydenham, Soc. of Apothecaries, 1981; H. L. Welsh, Univ. of Toronto, 1982; Milne, Oxford, 1984. FIMA; FRAS. Hon. DSc Aston, 1979; DUniv Surrey, 1986. Eddington Medal, RAS, 1971; Charles Chree Medal, Inst. of Physics, 1971; Lagrange Prize, Acad. Royale de Belgique, 1972; Nordberg Medal, Internat. Cttee on Space Res., 1990. Editor, Notes and Records of Royal Soc., 1989–. *Publications:* Shelley: His Thought and Work, 1960, 3rd edn 1984; Satellites and Scientific Research, 1960; Erasmus Darwin, 1963; Theory of Satellite Orbits in an Atmosphere, 1964; (ed) Space Research V, 1965; Observing Earth Satellites, 1966, 2nd edn 1983; (ed) Essential Writings of Erasmus Darwin, 1968; The End of the Twentieth Century?, 1970; Poems and Trixies, 1972; Doctor of Revolution, 1977; (ed) The Letters of Erasmus Darwin, 1981; (ed) The RAE Table of Earth Satellites, 1981, 4th edn 1990; Animal Spirits, 1983; Erasmus Darwin and the Romantic Poets, 1986; Satellite Orbits in an Atmosphere: theory and applications, 1987; *radio drama scripts:* A Mind of Universal Sympathy, 1973; The Lunaticks, 1978; 250 papers in Proc. Royal Society, Nature, Keats-Shelley Memor. Bull., New Scientist, Planetary and Space Science, and other scientific and literary jls. *Recreations:* tennis, reading, growing flowers, cross-country running. *Address:* 3 Tor Road, Farnham, Surrey GU9 7BX. *T:* Farnham (0252) 714755.

KING-MARTIN, Brig. John Douglas, CBE 1966; DSO 1957; MC 1953; Deputy Commander, HQ Eastern District, 1968–70, retired; *b* 9 March 1915; *s* of late Lewis King-Martin, Indian Forest Service; *m* 1940, Jeannie Jemima Sheffield Hollins, *d* of late S. T. Hollins, CIE; one *s* one *d*. *Educ:* Allhallows Sch.; RMC Sandhurst. Commnd 1935; 3rd Royal Bn 12 Frontier Force Regt, IA, 1936; Waziristan Ops, 1936–37; Eritrea, Western Desert, 1940–42 (despatches); Staff Coll., Quetta, 1944; Bde Maj., 1944–46, India, Java; GSO 2, Indian Inf. Div., Malaya, 1946–47; transf. to RA, 1948; Battery Comdr, 1948–50; DAQMG 2 Inf. Div., 1951–52; Korea, 1952–53; CO, 50 Medium Regt, RA, 1956–57; Suez, Cyprus, 1956–57; Coll. Comdr, RMA Sandhurst, 1958–60; Dep. Comdr and CRA, 17 Gurkha Div., 1961–62; Comdr, 17 Gurkha Div., 1962–64; Comdr, Rhine Area, 1964–67. Lieut-Col 1956; Brig. 1961. ADC to The Queen, 1968–70. *Recreations:* golf, painting, photography. *Address:* White House Farm, Polstead, Suffolk. *T:* Boxford (0787) 210327. *Club:* East India, Devonshire, Sports and Public Schools.

KING MURRAY, Ronald; *see* Murray.

KING-REYNOLDS, Guy Edwin, JP; Head Master, Dauntsey's School, West Lavington, 1969–85; *b* 9 July 1923; *er s* of late Dr H. E. King Reynolds, York; *m* 1st, 1947, Norma Lansdowne Russell (*d* 1949); 2nd, 1950, Jeanne Nancy Perris Rhodes; one *d*. *Educ:* St Peter's Sch., York; Emmanuel Coll., Cambridge (1944–47). Served RAF, 1942–44. BA 1946, MA 1951. Asst Master, Glenhow Prep. Sch., 1947–48; Head of Geography Dept, Solihull Sch., Warwickshire, 1948–54; family business, 1954–55; Head of Geography, Portsmouth Grammar Sch., 1955–57; Solihull School: Housemaster, 1957–63, Second Master, 1963–69. Part-time Lecturer in International Affairs, Extra-Mural Dept, Birmingham Univ.; Chm., Solihull WEA. Mem., BBC Regl Adv. Council, 1970–73. LRAM (speech and drama) 1968. Governor: St Peter's Sch., York, 1984–; Dean Close Sch., Cheltenham, 1985–; La Retraite, Salisbury, 1985–88. Mem. Cttee, GBA, 1986–89, 1990–. JP Solihull, 1965–69, Wiltshire, 1970–; Vice-Chm., Devizes Bench, 1985– (Chm., 1982–85). Freeman, City of London, 1988. *Recreations:* drama (director and actor); travel. *Address:* 14 Pulteney Mews, Great Pulteney Street, Bath, Avon BA2 4DS.

KING-TENISON, family name of **Earl of Kingston.**

KINGDON, Roger Taylor, CBE 1990; FIMechE, FIM; Chief Executive, Davy Corporation, 1987–90; *b* 27 June 1930; *s* of late Fletcher Munroe Kingdon and Laetitia May Kingdon (*née* Wissler); *m* 1956, Gaynor Mary Downs; two *s* one *d*. *Educ:* Christ's Hospital; Pembroke College, Cambridge (MA). CEng. Graduate trainee, Woodall Duckham Construction Co., 1954–58; Ashmore Benson Pease & Co., 1958–68 (Dir, 1964–68); Managing Director: Newell Dunford Group, 1968–80; Herbert Morris (Davy Group), 1980–83; Chm., Davy McKee (Stockton), 1983–87; Director: Dunford & Elliot, 1971–80; Peugeot Talbot Motor Co., 1979–; Davy Corp., 1986–90; Teesside Urban Develt Corp., 1987–. President: Process Plant Assoc., 1979–80; NE Engineering Employers' Assoc., 1986–89; Chairman: British Metallurgical Plant Constructors' Assoc., 1985–87; Latin American Trade Adv. Group, 1989–90. CBIM. *Recreations:* fell walking, tennis, sailing. *Address:* The Cottage, Butts Lane, Egglescliffe, Stockton-on-Tees, Cleveland TS16 9BU. *T:* Stockton-on-Tees (0642) 788343. *Club:* Army and Navy.

KINGHAM, His Honour James Frederick; DL; freelance lecturer and broadcaster; Teacher on Law, Selwyn College, Cambridge, since 1990; *b* 9 Aug. 1925; *s* of late Charles William and Eileen Eda Kingham; *m* 1958, Vivienne Valerie Tyrrell Brown; two *s* two *d*. *Educ:* Blaenau Ffestiniog Grammar Sch.; Wycliffe Coll.; Queens' Coll., Cambridge (MA); Graz Univ., Austria. Served with RN, 1943–47. Called to Bar, Gray's Inn, 1951; Mem. Gen. Council of Bar, 1954–58; Mem. Bar Council Sub-Cttee on Sentencing and

Penology. Dep. Recorder, Nottingham City QS, 1966–72; a Recorder, 1972–73; a Circuit Judge, 1973–90; Liaison Judge, Beds, 1981–90. Mem., Criminal Injuries Compensation Bd, 1991–. Dep. County Comr, Herts Scouts, 1971–80, formerly Asst County Comr for Venture Scouts; Venture Scout Leader: Harpenden, 1975–86; Kimpton and Wheathampstead, 1986–. DL Hertford, 1989. *Recreations:* mountain activities, squash, skiing, youth work, history, gardening, watching football. *Address:* Stone House, High Street, Kimpton, Hitchin, Herts SG4 8RJ. *T:* Kimpton (0438) 832308. *Club:* Union (Cambridge).

KINGHORN, Squadron Leader Ernest; *b* 1 Nov. 1907; *s* of A. Kinghorn, Leeds; *m* 1942, Eileen Mary Lambert Russell (*d* 1980); one *s* (and one *s* one *d* decd). *Educ:* Leeds, Basel and Lille Universities. Languages Master Ashville Coll., Doncaster Grammar Sch. and Roundhay Sch., Leeds. Served in Intelligence Branch, RAF. British Officer for Control of Manpower, SHAEF, and Staff Officer CCG. MP (Lab) Yarmouth Division of Norfolk, 1950–51, Great Yarmouth, 1945–50. *Address:* 59 Queens Avenue, Hanworth, Middx.

KINGHORN, William Oliver; Chief Agricultural Officer, Department of Agriculture and Fisheries for Scotland, 1971–75; *b* 17 May 1913; *s* of Thomas Kinghorn, Duns, and Elizabeth Oliver; *m* 1943, Edith Johnstone; one *s* two *d*. *Educ:* Berwickshire High Sch.; Edinburgh Univ. BSc (Agr) Hons, BSc Hons. Senior Inspector, 1946; Technical Develt Officer, 1959; Chief Inspector, 1970. SBStJ. *Publication:* contrib. Annals of Applied Biology, 1936. *Address:* 23 Cumlodden Avenue, Edinburgh EH12 6DR. *T:* 031–337 1435.

KINGMAN, Sir John (Frank Charles), Kt 1985; FRS 1971; Vice-Chancellor, University of Bristol, since 1985; *b* 28 Aug. 1939; *er s* of late Dr F. E. T. Kingman, FRSC; *m* 1964, Valerie, *d* of late F. Cromwell, OBE, ISO; one *s* one *d*. *Educ:* Christ's Coll., Finchley; Pembroke Coll., Cambridge. MA, ScD Cantab; Smith's Prize, 1962. Fellow of Pembroke Coll., Cambridge, 1961–65, Hon. Fellow, 1988; Asst Lectr in Mathematics, 1962–64, Lectr, 1964–65, Univ. of Cambridge; Reader in Mathematics and Statistics, 1965–66, Prof. 1966–69, Univ. of Sussex; Prof. of Maths, Univ. of Oxford, 1969–85; Fellow, St Anne's Coll., Oxford, 1978–85, Hon. Fellow, 1985. Visiting appointments: Univ. of Western Australia, 1963, 1974; Stanford Univ., USA, 1968; ANU, 1978. Chairman: Science Bd, SRC, 1979–81; SERC, 1981–85; Vice-Pres., Parly and Scientific Cttee, 1986–89 (Vice-Chm., 1983–86); Member: Council, British Technology Gp, 1984–; Bd, British Council, 1986–. Chm., Cttee of Inquiry into the Teaching of English Language, 1987–88; Director: IBM UK Holdings Ltd, 1985–; Beecham Group plc, 1986–89; SmithKline Beecham plc, 1989–90. Chm., 1973–76, Vice-Pres., 1976–, Inst. of Statisticians; President: Royal Statistical Soc., 1987–89 (Vice-Pres., 1977–79, Guy Medal in Silver, 1981); London Math. Soc., 1990–92. Mem., Brighton Co. Borough Council, 1968–71; Chm., Regency Soc. of Brighton and Hove, 1975–81. Hon. DSc: Sussex, 1983; Southampton, 1985; Hon. LLD Bristol, 1989. Royal Medal, Royal Soc., 1983. Officier des Palmes Académiques, 1989. *Publications:* Introduction to Measure and Probability (with S. J. Taylor), 1966; The Algebra of Queues, 1966; Regenerative Phenomena, 1972; Mathematics of Genetic Diversity, 1980; papers in mathematical and statistical jls. *Address:* Senate House, Tyndall Avenue, Bristol BS8 1TH. *Clubs:* Lansdowne, United Oxford & Cambridge University.

KINGS NORTON, Baron *cr* 1965, of Wotton Underwood (Life Peer); **Harold Roxbee Cox,** Kt 1953; PhD, DIC; FEng 1976; FIMechE, Hon. FRAeS; Chairman: Landspeed Ltd, since 1975; Cotswold Research Ltd, since 1978; President: Campden Food Preservation Research Association, since 1961; British Balloon Museum and Library, since 1980; Chancellor, Cranfield Institute of Technology, since 1969; *b* 6 June 1902; *s* of late William John Roxbee Cox, Birmingham, and Amelia Stern; *m* 1st, 1927, Marjorie (*d* 1980), *e d* of late E. E. Withers, Northwood; two *s*; 2nd, 1982, Joan Ruth Pascoe, *d* of late W. G. Pack, Torquay. *Educ:* Kings Norton Grammar Sch.; Imperial Coll. of Science and Technology (Schol.). Engineer on construction of Airship R101, 1924–29; Chief Technical Officer, Royal Airship Works, 1931; Investigations in wing flutter and stability of structures, RAE, 1931–35; Lectr in Aircraft Structures, Imperial Coll., 1932–38; Principal Scientific Officer. Aerodynamics Dept, RAE, 1935–36; Head of Air Defence Dept, RAE, 1936–38; Chief Technical Officer, Air Registration Board, 1938–39; Supt of Scientific Research, RAE, 1939–40; Dep. Dir of Scientific Research, Ministry of Aircraft Production, 1940–43; Dir of Special Projects Ministry of Aircraft Production, 1943–44; Chm. and Man. Dir Power Jets (Research and Development) Ltd, 1944–46; Dir National Gas Turbine Establishment, 1946–48; Chief Scientist, Min. of Fuel and Power, 1948–54. Chairman: Metal Box Co., 1961–67 (Dir, 1957–67, Dep. Chm., 1959–60); Berger Jenson & Nicholson Ltd, 1967–75; Applied Photophysics, 1974–81; Withers Estates, 1976–81; Director: Ricardo & Co. (Engrs) 1927 Ltd, 1965–77; Dowty Rotol, 1968–75; British Printing Corp., 1968–77; Hoechst UK, 1970–75. Chm. Gas Turbine Collaboration Cttee, 1941–44, 1946–48; Mem. Aeronautical Research Council, 1944–48, 1958–60; Chairman: Coun. for Scientific and Industrial Research, 1961–65; Council for National Academic Awards, 1964–71; Air Registration Bd, 1966–72; President: Royal Aeronautical Soc., 1947–49; Royal Instn, 1969–76. Fellow of Imperial Coll. of Science and Technology, 1960; FCGI 1976. Membre Correspondant, Faculté Polytechnique de Mons, 1946–. R38 Memorial Prize, 1928; Busk Memorial Prize, 1934; Wilbur Wright Lecturer, 1940; Wright Brothers Lecturer (USA), 1945; Hawksley Lecturer, 1951; James Clayton Prize, 1952; Thornton Lectr, 1954; Parsons Memorial Lectr, 1955; Handley Page Memorial Lectr, 1969. Freeman, City of London, 1987; Liveryman, GAPAN, 1987. Hon. DSc: Birmingham, 1954; Cranfield Inst. of Technology, 1970; Warwick, 1986; Hon. DTech Brunel, 1966; Hon. LLD CNAA, 1969. Bronze Medal, Univ. of Louvain, 1946; Medal of Freedom with Silver Palm, USA, 1947. *Publications:* numerous papers on theory of structures, wing flutter, gas turbines, civil aviation and airships. *Address:* Westcote House, Chipping Campden, Glos GL55 6AG. *T:* Evesham (0386) 840440. *Clubs:* Athenæum, Turf.

KINGSALE, 35th Baron *cr* 1223 (by some reckonings 30th Baron); **John de Courcy;** Baron Courcy and Baron of Ringrone; Premier Baron of Ireland; President, Impex Consultants Ltd, since 1988; Director: Marquis de Verneuil Trust, since 1971; de Courcy, Daunt Professional & Executive Agencies (Australia), since 1987; Kinsale Development Co., since 1989; Chairman, National Association for Service to the Realm; *b* 27 Jan. 1941; *s* of Lieutenant-Commander the Hon. Michael John Rancé de Courcy, RN (killed on active service, 1940), and Joan (*d* 1967), *d* of Robert Reid; *S* grandfather, 1969. *Educ:* Stowe; Universities of Paris and Salzburg. Short service commission, Irish Guards, 1962–65. At various times before and since: law student, property developer, film extra, white hunter, bingo caller, etc. Patron, L'Orchestre du Monde, 1988–. *Recreations:* shooting, food and drink, palaeontology, venery. *Heir: cousin* Nevinson Russell de Courcy [*b* 21 July 1920; *m* 1954, Nora Lydia, *yr d* of James Arnold Plint; one *s* one *d*]. *Address:* Crawley Farm House, South Brewham, Somerset. *Club:* Cavalry and Guards.

KINGSBOROUGH, Viscount; Robert Charles Henry King-Tenison; *b* 20 March 1969; *s* and *heir* of 11th Earl of Kingston, *qv*.

KINGSBURY, Derek John, CBE 1988; FEng, FIEE; Chairman, Fairey Group, since 1987 (Group Chief Executive, 1982–91); non-executive Director: Vickers, since 1981; ACAL plc, since 1991; *b* 10 July 1926; *s* of late Major Arthur Kingsbury, BEM, Virginia Water and Gwendoline Mary Kingsbury; *m* 1st, 1959, Muriel June Drake; one *s* (and one *s* decd); 2nd, 1980, Sarah Muriel Morgan; one *s*. *Educ:* Strode's Secondary Sch., City and Guilds Coll. BScEng Hons; DIC. FCGI. 2nd Lieut, REME, 1947–49. Apprentice, Metropolitan Vickers, 1949–51; Exch. Schol., Univ. of Pennsylvania, 1952–53; Associated Electrical Industries: Manager, E Canada, 1954–61; PA to Chm., 1961–63; Gen. Manager, AEI Distribution Transformers, 1963–66; Gen. Manager, Overseas Manufacturing Develt, 1966–69; Thorn Electrical Industries: Man. Dir, Foster Transformers, 1969–76; Man. Dir, Elect. & Hydr. Div., 1972–76, Exec. Dir, 1973–76; Dowty Group: Dep. Chief Exec., 1976–82; Chm., Ultra Electronics, 1977–82. Institution of Electrical Engineers: Dir Peter Peregrinus, 1976–81; Mem., Finance Cttee, 1978–80; Confederation of British Industry: Mem. Council, 1980–86; Chm., Overseas Cttee, 1980–84; missions to Japan 1981, 1983, 1985; Defence Manufacturers Association: Mem. Council, 1985–; Chm., 1987–90; Chm., F and GP Cttee, 1990–; Member: Review Bd for Govt Contracts, 1986–; Engineering Council, 1990– (Chm., CET Pilot Scheme Steering Cttee, 1988–). Pres., BHF Horse Show, 1977–. *Recreations:* golf, swimming, walking. *Address:* Fairey Group, Station Road, Egham, Surrey TW20 9NP. *T:* Egham (0784) 470470. *Clubs:* Royal Automobile, MCC; Beaconsfield Golf, St Enodoc Golf.

KINGSHOTT, (Albert) Leonard; Director, International Banking Division, Lloyds Bank Plc, 1985–89; non-executive Director, Rosehaugh plc, since 1991; Member, Monopolies and Mergers Commission, since 1990; *b* 16 Sept. 1930; *s* of A. L. Kingshott and Mrs K. Kingshott; *m* 1958, Valerie Simpson; two *s* one *d*. *Educ:* London Sch. of Economics (BSc); ACIS 1958, FCIS 1983. Flying Officer, RAF, 1952–55; Economist, British Petroleum, 1955–60; Economist, British Nylon Spinners, 1960–62; Financial Manager, Iraq Petroleum Co., 1963–65; Chief Economist, Ford of Britain, 1965; Treas., Ford of Britain, 1966–67; Treas., Ford of Europe, 1968–70; Finance Dir, Whitbread & Co., 1972; Man. Dir, Finance, BSC, 1972–77; Dir, Lloyds Bank International, responsible for Merchant Banking activities, 1977–80, for European Div., 1980–82, for Marketing and Planning Div., 1983–84; Dep. Chief Exec., Lloyds Bank International, 1985. exec. Dir, The Private Bank & Trust Co., 1989–91; Director: Bank of London and South America Ltd; Lloyds Bank California; Lloyds Bank (France) Ltd; Lloyds Bank International. Mem. Bd, Crown Agents for Oversea Govts and Admin, and Crown Agents Hldg and Realisation Bd, 1989–. Associate Mem. of Faculty, 1978, Governor, 1980–, Ashridge Management Coll. FCIS. *Publication:* Investment Appraisal, 1967. *Recreations:* golf, chess. *Address:* 4 Delamas, Beggar Hill, Fryerning, Ingatestone, Essex. *T:* Ingatestone (0277) 352077.

KINGSHOTT, Air Vice-Marshal Kenneth, CBE 1972; DFC 1953; Royal Air Force, retired 1980; *b* 8 July 1924; *s* of Walter James Kingshott and Eliza Ann Kingshott; *m* 1st, 1948, Dorrie Marie (*née* Dent) (*d* 1978); two *s*; 2nd, 1990, Valerie Rosemary Brigden. Joined RAF, 1943; served: Singapore and Korea, 1950; Aden, 1960; Malta, 1965; MoD, London, 1968; OC RAF Cottesmore, 1971; HQ 2 Allied Tactical Air Force, 1973; HQ Strike Command, 1975; Dep. Chief of Staff Operations and Intelligence, HQ Allied Air Forces Central Europe, 1977–79. *Recreations:* golf, fishing, music. *Address:* Tall Trees, Manor Road, Penn, Bucks. *Club:* Royal Air Force.

KINGSHOTT, Leonard; *see* Kingshott, A. L.

KINGSLAND, Sir Richard, Kt 1978; AO 1989; CBE 1967; DFC 1940; idc; psa; Secretary to Department of Veterans' Affairs, Canberra, 1976–81; *b* Moree, NSW, 19 Oct. 1916; *m* 1943, Kathleen Jewel, *d* of late R. B. Adams; one *s* two *d*. *Educ:* Sydney High Sch., NSW. Served War: No 10 Sqdn, Eng., 1939–41; commanded: No 11 Sqdn, New Guinea, 1941–42; RAAF Stn, Rathmines, NSW, 1942–43; Gp Captain 1943; Dir, Intell., RAAF, 1944–45. Director: Trng, 1946; Org. RAAF HQ, 1946–48; Manager, Sydney Airport, 1948–49; Airline Pilot, 1949–50; SA Reg. 1950–51, NT Reg. 1951–52, Dept of Civil Aviation; Chief Admin. Asst to CAS, RAAF, 1952–53; IDC 1955. Asst Sec., Dept of Air, Melb., 1954–58; First Asst Sec., Dept of Defence, 1958–63; Secretary: Dept of Interior, 1963–70; Dept of Repatriation, 1970–74; Repatriation and Compensation, 1974–76. Chairman: Repatriation Commn, 1970–81; ACT Arts Develt Bd (first Chm.), 1981–83; Commonwealth Films Bd of Review, 1982–86; Uranium Adv. Council, 1982–84. Hon. Nat. Sec., Nat. Heart Foundn, 1976–90. A Dir, Arts Council of Aust., 1970–72; first Chairman Council: Canberra Sch. of Music, 1970–74; Canberra Sch. of Art, 1976–83; Mem. Original Council, Australian Conservation Foundn, 1967–69; Member: Canberra Theatre Trust, 1965–75; Aust. Opera Nat. Council, 1983–; Canberra Festival Cttee, 1988–; Mem. Bd of Trustees, Aust. War Meml, Canberra, 1966–76; a Dir, Aust. Bicentennial Authority, 1983–89; Chm., ACT Health Promotion Fund, 1990–. Pres., Bd of Management, Goodwin Retirement Villages, 1984–88. Vice Pres., Australia Day in the National Capital Cttee, 1987–. *Recreations:* music, reading. *Address:* 36 Vasey Crescent, Campbell, ACT 2601, Australia. *Clubs:* Commonwealth, National Press (Canberra).

KINGSLEY, Ben; actor; *b* 31 Dec. 1943; *s* of Rahimtulla Harji Bhanji and Anna Leina Mary Bhanji; *m* 1978, Gillian Alison Macaulay Sutcliffe; two *s*, and one *s* one *d* from a previous marriage. *Educ:* Manchester Grammar Sch. Associate artist, Royal Shakespeare Co.; work with RSC includes, 1970–80; 1985–86: Peter Brook's Midsummer Night's Dream, Stratford, London, Broadway, NY; Gramsci in Occupations; Ariel in The Tempest; title role, Hamlet; Ford in Merry Wives of Windsor; title role, Baal; Squeers and Mr Wagstaff in Nicholas Nickleby; title rôle, Othello, Melons; National Theatre, 1977–78: Mosca in Volponë; Trofimov in The Cherry Orchard; Sparkish in The Country Wife; Vukhov in Judgement; additional theatre work includes: Johnny in Hello and Goodbye (Fugard), King's Head, 1973; Errol Philander in Statements After An Arrest (Fugard), Royal Court, 1974; Edmund Kean, Harrogate, 1981, Haymarket, 1983 (also televised); title role, Dr Faustus, Manchester Royal Exchange, 1981; *television* 1974–, includes The Love School (series), 1974; Silas Marner (film), 1985, Murderers Amongst Us (mini-series), 1989, and several plays; *films:* title role, Gandhi, 1980 (2 Hollywood Golden Globe awards, 1982; NY Film Critics' Award, 2 BAFTA awards, Oscar, LA Film Critics Award, 1983, Variety Club of GB Best Film Actor award, 1983); Betrayal, 1982; Turtle Diary, 1985; Harem, 1986; Testimony, 1987; Maurice, 1987; Pascali's Island, The Train, 1988; Without a Clue, 1989; The Children, 1991; The 5th Monkey, 1991; Necessary Love, 1991; Bugsie. Best Film Actor, London Standard Award, 1983; Berlin Golden Camera Award, 1990. Hon. MA Salford, 1984. Padma Shri (India), 1984. *Address:* c/o ICM Ltd, 388/396 Oxford Street, W1.

KINGSLEY, David John; consultant in management, marketing and communications, since 1975; Director, Francis Kyle Gallery Ltd, since 1978; *b* 10 July 1929; *s* of Walter John Kingsley and Margery Kingsley; *m* 1st, 1954, Enid Sophia Jones; two *d*; 2nd, 1968, Gillian Leech; two *s*; 3rd, 1988, Gisela Reichardt. *Educ:* Southend High Sch.; London School of Economics (BScEcon). Pres., Students' Union, LSE, 1952; Vice-Pres., Nat. Union of Students, 1953. Served RAF, Personnel Selection, commnd 1948. Prospective Parly Candidate (Lab) E Grinstead, 1952–54; founded Kingsley, Manton and Palmer, advertising agency, 1964; Publicity Advisor to Labour Party and Govt, 1962–70; Publicity and Election advisor to President of Republic of Zambia, 1974–; Election and

Broadcasting advisor to Govt of Mauritius, 1976–; Publicity advisor to SDP, 1981–. Mem. Boards, CNAA, 1970–82; Mem., Central Religious Adv. Cttee for BBC and IBA, 1974–82; Governor, LSE, 1966–. Chairman: Inter-Action Trust, 1981–90; Centre for World Develt Educn, 1989– (Treas., 1985–89); Vice-Chm., Royal Philharmonic Orch., 1972–77; Mem., Develt Cttee, RCM, 1985–; Trustee: Goldfields Environmental Trust, 1985–90; Schumacher Soc., 1980–. FIPA; FRSA; MCSD. Hon. RCM. Hon. doctorate, Soka Univ., Tokyo. *Publications:* Albion in China, 1979; contribs to learned jls; various articles. *Recreations:* politics, creating happy national events, music, travel, art and any books. *Address:* 99 Hemingford Road, N1 1BY. *Clubs:* Reform, Royal Automobile.

KINGSLEY, Sir Patrick (Graham Toler), KCVO 1962 (CVO 1950); Secretary and Keeper of the Records of the Duchy of Cornwall, 1954–72 (Assistant Secretary, 1930–54); *b* 1908; *s* of late Gerald Kingsley; *m* 1947, Priscilla Rosemary, *o d* of late Capt. Archibald A. Lovett Cameron, RN; three *s* one *d*. *Educ:* Winchester; New Coll., Oxford. OUCC 1928–30 (Capt. 1930), OUAFC 1927 and 1929. Served War of 1939–45 with Queen's Royal Regt. *Address:* West Hill Farm, West Knoyle, Warminster, Wilts.

KINGSLEY, Roger James, FEng, FIChemE; Chairman: LMK Engineering; UMIST Ventures Ltd; CAPCIS Ltd; Freeman Process Systems Ltd; Director, Kingsley Process & Management; *b* 2 Feb. 1922; *s* of Felix and Helene Loewenstein; changed name to Kingsley, 1942; *m* 1949, Valerie Marguerite Mary (*née* Hanna); one *s* two *d*. *Educ:* Manchester Grammar Sch.; Faculty of Technol., Manchester Univ. (BScTech); Harvard Business Sch. (Internat. Sen. Managers Program). Served War, Royal Fusiliers, 1940–46; Commando service, 1942–45; Captain; mentioned in despatches, 1946. Chemical Engr, Petrocarbon Ltd, 1949–51; technical appts, ultimately Tech. Dir, Lankro Chemicals Ltd, 1952–62; gen. management appts, Lankro Chemicals Group Ltd, 1962–77; Man. Dir, Lankro Chemicals Group Ltd, 1972–77; Director: ICI-Lankro Plasticisers Ltd, 1972–77; Fallek-Lankro Corp., Tuscaloosa, Ala, 1976–77. Dep. Chm., Diamond Shamrock Europe, 1977–82; Chm., Duolite Internat., 1978–84. Pres., IChemE, 1974–75. Member: Court of Governors, UMIST, 1969–79, 1985–. *Publications:* contrib. Chem. Engr, and Proc. IMechE. *Recreations:* skiing, riding, music. *Address:* Fallows End, Wicker Lane, Hale Barns, Cheshire WA15 0HQ. *T:* 061–980 6253. *Club:* Anglo-Belgian.

KINGSTON, 11th Earl of, *cr* 1768; **Barclay Robert Edwin King-Tenison**, Bt 1682; Baron Kingston, 1764; Viscount Kingsborough, 1766; Baron Erris, 1800; Viscount Lorton, 1806; formerly Lieutenant, Royal Scots Greys; *b* 23 Sept. 1943; *o s* of 10th Earl of Kingston and Gwyneth, *d* of William Howard Evans (who *m* 1951, Brig. E. M. Tyler, DSO, MC, late RA; she *m* 1963, Robert Woodford); *S* father 1948; *m* 1st, 1965, Patricia Mary (marr. diss. 1974), *o d* of E. C. Killip, Llanfairfechan, N Wales; one *s* one *d*; 2nd, 1974, Victoria (marr. diss. 1979), *d* of D. C. Edmonds; 3rd, 1990, Corleen Jennifer Rathbone. *Educ:* Winchester. *Heir: s* Viscount Kingsborough, *qv.*

KINGSTON (Ontario), Archbishop of, (RC), since 1982; **Most Rev. Francis John Spence**; *b* Perth, Ont., 3 June 1926; *s* of William John Spence and Rose Anna Spence (*née* Jordan). *Educ:* St Michael's Coll., Toronto (BA 1946); St Augustine's Seminary, Toronto; St Thomas Univ., Rome (JCD 1955). Ordained priest, 1950; Bishop, 1967; Mil. Vicar, Canadian Forces, 1967–70; Bishop of Charlottetown, PEI, 1970–82. *Address:* 390 Palace Road, PO Box 997, Kingston, Ont K7L 4X8, Canada.

KINGSTON-UPON-THAMES, Bishop Suffragan of, since 1984; **Rt. Rev. Peter Stephen Maurice Selby**, PhD; *b* 7 Dec. 1941. *Educ:* Merchant Taylors' School; St John's Coll., Oxford (BA 1964, MA 1967); Bishops' Coll., Cheshunt. PhD (London) 1975. Asst Curate, Queensbury, 1966–68; Assoc. Director of Training, Southwark, 1969–73; Asst Curate, Limpsfield with Titsey, 1969–77; Vice-Principal, Southwark Ordination Course, 1970–72; Asst Missioner, Dio. Southwark, 1973–77; Canon Residentiary, Newcastle Cathedral, 1977–84; Diocesan Missioner, Dio. Newcastle, 1977–84. *Publication:* Belonging, 1991. *Address:* 24 Albert Drive, SW19 6LS.

KINGTON, Miles Beresford; humorous columnist; *b* 13 May 1941; *s* of William Beresford Nairn Kington and Jean Anne Kington; *m* 1st, 1964, Sarah Paine (marr. diss. 1987); one *s* one *d*; 2nd, 1987, Mrs Hilary Caroline Maynard; one *s*. *Educ:* Trinity College, Glenalmond; Trinity College, Oxford (BAMod Langs). Plunged into free-lance writing, 1963; took up part-time gardening while starving to death, 1964; jazz reviewer, The Times, 1965; joined staff of Punch, 1967, Literary Editor, 1973, left 1980; free-lance, 1980–; regular Let's Parler Franglais column in Punch, 1977–; daily Moreover column in The Times, 1981–86; columnist, The Independent, 1986–; member, musical group Instant Sunshine on double bass; jazz player, 1970–; *television:* various programmes incl. Three Miles High (Great Railway Journeys of the World series), 1980, Steam Days, 1986, and The Burma Road, 1989. *Publications:* World of Alphonse Allais, 1977, repr. as A Wolf in Frog's Clothing, 1983; 4 Franglais books, 1979–82; Moreover, 1982; Miles and Miles, 1982; Nature Made Ridiculously Simple, 1983; Moreover, Too . . ., 1985; The Franglais Lieutenant's Woman, 1986; Welcome to Kington, 1989; Steaming Through Britain, 1990. *Recreations:* bicycling, jazz, growing parsley, meeting VAT people, trying to find something to beat friend Barlow at. *Address:* Lower Hayze, Limpley Stoke, Bath BA3 6HR. *T:* Bath (0225) 722262. *Clubs:* Garrick, 100, Ronnie Scott's.

KINLOCH, Sir David, 13th Bt *cr* 1686, of Gilmerton; *b* 5 Aug. 1951; *s* of Sir Alexander Davenport Kinloch, 12th Bt and of Anna, *d* of late Thomas Walker, Edinburgh; *S* father, 1982; *m* 1st, 1976, Susan Middlewood (marr. diss. 1986); one *s* one *d*; 2nd, 1987, Maureen Carswell; two *s*. *Educ:* Gordonstoun. Career in research into, and recovery and replacement of underground services. *Recreation:* treasure hunting. *Heir: s* Alexander Kinloch, *b* 31 May 1978. *Address:* Gilmerton House, North Berwick, East Lothian EH39 5LQ. *T:* Athelstaneford (062088) 207.

KINLOCH, Henry, (Harry); Chairman: Quartermaine & Co., since 1989; Fern Developments Ltd; KIA Securities Ltd, since 1990; *b* 7 June 1937; *s* of William Shearer Kinloch and Alexina Alice Quartermaine Kinloch; *m* 1st, 1966, Gillian Anne Ashley (marr. diss. 1979); one *s* one *d*; 2nd, 1987, Catherine Elizabeth Hossack. *Educ:* Queen's Park Sch., Glasgow; Univs of Strathclyde, Birmingham and Glasgow. MSc, PhD, ARCST, CEng, FIMechE. Lecturer in Engineering: Univ. of Strathclyde, 1962–65; Univ. of Liverpool, 1966; Vis. Associate Prof. of Engrg, MIT, 1967; Sen. Design Engr, CEGB, 1968–70; PA Management Consultants, 1970–73; Chief Exec., Antony Gibbs (PFP) Ltd, 1973–74; Chm. and Chief Exec., Antony Gibbs Financial Services Ltd, 1975–77; Man. Dir, British Shipbuilders, 1978–80; Dep. Man. Dir and Chief Exec., Liberty Life Assce Co., 1980–83; Chm. and Chief Exec., Ætna Internat. (UK), 1984–89. Dir, Slade & Kempton, 1990–. *Publications:* many publications on theoretical and applied mechanics, financial and business studies. *Recreations:* piano music, opera, political biography, ostling. *Address:* 45 Breton House, The Barbican, EC2Y 8DF. *T:* 071–628 3870. *Club:* Athenæum.

KINLOCH, Sir John, 4th Bt, of Kinloch, *cr* 1873; *b* 1 Nov. 1907; *e s* of Sir George Kinloch, 3rd Bt, OBE, and Ethel May (*d* 1959), *y d* of late Major J. Hawkins; *S* father 1948; *m* 1934, Doris Ellaline, *e d* of C. J. Head, London; one *s* two *d*. *Educ:* Charterhouse; Magdalene Coll., Cambridge. Served with British Ministry of War Transport as their repr. at Abadan, Persia, and also in London. Employed by Butterfield & Swire in China

and Hong Kong, 1931–63, and by John Swire & Sons Ltd, London, 1964–73. *Heir: s* David Oliphant Kinloch, CA [*b* 15 Jan. 1942; *m* 1st, 1968, Susan Minette (marr. diss. 1979), *y d* of Maj.-Gen. R. E. Urquhart, CB, DSO; three *d*; 2nd, 1983, Sabine, *o d* of Philippe de Loes, Geneva; one *s*]. *Address:* Aldie Cottage, Kinross, Kinross-shire KY13 7QH. *T:* Fossoway (05774) 305. *Club:* New (Edinburgh).

KINLOSS, Lady (12th in line, of the Lordship *cr* 1602); **Beatrice Mary Grenville Freeman-Grenville** (surname changed by Lord Lyon King of Arms, 1950); *b* 1922; *e d* of late Rev. Hon. Luis Chandos Francis Temple Morgan-Grenville, Master of Kinloss; *S* grandmother, 1944; *m* 1950, Dr Greville Stewart Parker Freeman-Grenville, FSA, FRAS (name changed from Freeman by Lord Lyon King of Arms, 1950), Capt. late Royal Berks Regt, *er s* of late Rev. E. C. Freeman; one *s* two *d*. *Heir: s* Master of Kinloss, *qv*. *Address:* North View House, Sheriff Hutton, York YO6 1PT. *T:* Sheriff Hutton (03477) 447. *Club:* Commonwealth Trust.

KINLOSS, Master of; **Hon. Bevil David Stewart Chandos Freeman-Grenville**; *b* 20 June 1953; *s* of Dr Greville Stewart Parker Freeman-Grenville, FSA, Capt. late Royal Berks Regt, and of Lady Kinloss, *qv*. *Educ:* Redrice Sch. *Address:* North View House, Sheriff Hutton, York YO6 1PT.

KINNAIRD, family name of **Lord Kinnaird**.

KINNAIRD, 13th Lord *cr* 1682, of Inchture; **Graham Charles Kinnaird**; Baron Kinnaird of Rossie (UK), 1860; Flying Officer RAFVR; *b* 15 Sept. 1912; *e s* of 12th Lord Kinnaird, KT, KBE, and Frances Victoria (*d* 1960), *y d* of late T. H. Clifton, Lytham Hall, Lancs; *S* father, 1972; *m* 1st, 1938, Nadia (who obtained a decree of divorce, 1940), *o c* of H. A. Fortington, OBE, Isle of Jethou, Channel Islands; 2nd, 1940, Diana, *yr d* of R. S. Copeman, Roydon Hall, Diss, Norfolk; four *d* (one *s* decd). *Educ:* Eton. Demobilised RAF, 1945. *Address:* The Garden House, Rossie Estate, Inchture, Perthshire; Durham House, Durham Place, SW3. *Clubs:* Brooks's, Pratt's.

KINNEAR, Ian Albert Clark, CMG 1974; HM Diplomatic Service, retired; *b* 23 Dec. 1924; *s* of late George Kinnear, CBE and Georgina Lilian (*née* Stephenson), Nairobi; *m* 1966, Rosemary, *d* of Dr K. W. D. Hartley, Cobham; two *d*. *Educ:* Marlborough Coll.; Lincoln Coll., Oxford (MA). HM Forces, 1943–46 (1st E Africa Reconnaissance Regt). Colonial Service (later HMOCS): Malayan Civil Service, 1951–56: District Officer, Bentong, then Alor Gajah, Asst Sec. Econ. Planning Unit; Kenya, 1956–63: Asst Sec., then Sen. Asst Sec., Min. of Commerce and Industry; 1st Sec., CRO, later Commonwealth Office, 1963–66; 1st Sec. (Commercial), British Embassy, Djakarta, 1966–68; 1st Sec. and Head of Chancery, British High Commn, Dar-es-Salaam, 1969–71; Chief Sec., later Dep. Governor, Bermuda, 1971–74; Senior British Trade Comr, Hong Kong, 1974–77; Consul-Gen., San Francisco, 1977–82. *Recreation:* painting. *Address:* Castle Hill Cottages, Castle Hill, Brenchley, Tonbridge, Kent TN12 7BS. *T:* Brenchley (089272) 3782.

KINNEAR, Nigel Alexander, FRCSI; Surgeon to Federated Dublin Voluntary Hospitals until 1974, retired; *b* 3 April 1907; *s* of James and Margaret Kinnear; *m* 1947, Frances Gardner; one *d*. *Educ:* Mill Hill Sch.; Trinity Coll., Dublin (MA, MB). Surgeon to Adelaide Hosp., Dublin, 1936; Regius Prof. of Surgery, TCD, 1967–72. President: RCSI, 1961; Royal Academy of Medicine of Ireland, 1968 (Hon. Fellow, 1983); James IV Surgical Assoc. Hon. FRCSGlas. *Publications:* articles in surgical jls. *Recreations:* salmon fishing, gardening. *Address:* Summerseat Cottage, Clonee, Co. Meath. *T:* Dunboyne 255353. *Club:* Kildare Street and University (Dublin).

KINNELL, Ian; QC 1987; professional arbitrator; Immigration Appeal Adjudicator; *b* 23 May 1943; *o s* of Brian Kinnell and Grace Madeline Kinnell; *m* 1970, Elizabeth Jane Ritchie; one *s* one *d*. *Educ:* Sevenoaks Sch., Kent. Called to the Bar, Gray's Inn, 1967. A Recorder, 1987–89. LMAA. *Recreations:* horticulture, equestrian and rural pursuits. *Address:* The Old Rectory, Little Birch, Hereford HR2 8BB. *T:* Golden Valley (0981) 540224.

KINNOCK, Rt. Hon. Neil Gordon; PC 1983; MP (Lab) Islwyn, since 1983 (Bedwellty, 1970–83); Leader of the Labour Party, and Leader of the Opposition, since 1983; *b* 28 March 1942; *s* of Gordon Kinnock, Labourer, and Mary Kinnock (*née* Howells), Nurse; *m* 1967, Glenys Elizabeth Parry; one *s* one *d*. *Educ:* Lewis Sch., Pengam; University Coll., Cardiff. BA in Industrial Relations and History, UC, Cardiff (Chm. Socialist Soc., 1963–66; Pres. Students' Union, 1965–66; Hon. Fellow, 1982). Tutor Organiser in Industrial and Trade Union Studies, WEA, 1966–70; Mem., Welsh Hosp. Bd, 1969–71. PPS to Sec. of State for Employment, 1974–75. Member: Nat. Exec. Cttee, Labour Party, 1978– (Chm., 1987–88); Parly Cttee of PLP, 1979–; Chief Opposition spokesman on educn, 1979–83. Director (unpaid): Tribune Publications, 1974–82; Fair Play for Children, 1979–; 7:84 Theatre Co. (England) Ltd, 1979–; Mem., Socialist Educational Assoc., 1975–; Pres., Assoc. of Liberal Educn, 1980–82. *Publications:* Making Our Way, 1986; contribs to Tribune, Guardian, New Statesman, etc. *Recreations:* music esp. opera and male choral, Rugby football, theatre, being with family. *Address:* House of Commons, SW1A 0AA.

KINNOULL, 15th Earl of, *cr* 1633; **Arthur William George Patrick Hay**; Viscount Dupplin and Lord Hay, 1627, 1633, 1697; Baron Hay (Great Britain), 1711; *b* 26 March 1935; *o surv. s* of 14th Earl and Mary Ethel Isobel Meyrick (*d* 1938); *S* father 1938; *m* 1961, Gay Ann, *er d* of Sir Denys Lowson, 1st Bt; one *s* three *d*. *Educ:* Eton. Chartered Land Agent, 1960; Mem., Agricultural Valuers' Assoc., 1962. Fellow, Chartered Land Agents' Soc., 1964. Pres., National Council on Inland Transport, 1964–76. Mem. of Queen's Body Guard for Scotland (Royal Company of Archers), 1965. Junior Cons. Whip, House of Lords, 1966–68; Cons. Opposition Spokesman on Aviation, House of Lords, 1968–70. Mem., British Delegn, Council of Europe, 1985–. Chm., Property Owners' Building Soc., 1976–87 (Dir, 1971–87); Dir, Woolwich Equitable Building Soc., 1987–. Mem., Air League Council, 1972; Council Mem., Deep Sea Fishermen's Mission, 1977. Vice-Pres., Nat. Assoc. of Local Councils (formerly Nat. Assoc. of Parish Councils), 1970–80. FRICS 1970. *Heir: s* Viscount Dupplin, *qv*. *Address:* 15 Carlyle Square, SW3; Pier House, Seaview, Isle of Wight. *Clubs:* Turf, Pratt's, White's, MCC.

KINROSS, 5th Baron *cr* 1902; **Christopher Patrick Balfour**; Partner in Shepherd & Wedderburn, WS, Solicitors, since 1977; *b* 1 Oct. 1949; *s* of 4th Baron Kinross, OBE, TD, and Helen Anne (*d* 1969), *d* of A. W. Hog; *S* father, 1985; *m* 1974, Susan Jane, *d* of I. R. Pitman, WS; two *s*. *Educ:* Belhaven Hill School, Dunbar; Eton College; Edinburgh Univ. (LLB). Mem., Law Soc. of Scotland, 1975; WS 1975. UK Treas., James IV Assoc. of Surgeons, 1981– (Hon. Mem., 1985–); Treas., Edinburgh Gastro-intestinal Res. Fund, 1981–. Member, Queen's Body Guard for Scotland, Royal Company of Archers, 1980–. Member: Mil. Vehicle Trust; Scottish Land Rover Owners' Club. *Recreations:* pistol, rifle and shotgun shooting, stalking, motorsport. *Heir: s* Hon. Alan Ian Balfour, *b* 4 April 1978. *Address:* 11 Belford Place, Edinburgh EH4 3DH. *T:* 031–332 9704. *Club:* New (Edinburgh).

KINSELLA, Thomas; poet; Professor of English, Temple University, Philadelphia, 1970–90; *b* 4 May 1928; *m* 1955, Eleanor Walsh; one *s* two *d*. Entered Irish Civil Service,

1946; resigned from Dept of Finance, 1965. Artist-in-residence, 1965–67, Prof. of English, 1967–70, Southern Illinois Univ. Elected to Irish Academy of Letters, 1965. J. S. Guggenheim Meml Fellow, 1968–69, 1971–72. Hon. PhD NUI, 1984. *Publications: poetry:* Poems, 1956; Another September, 1958; Downstream, 1962; Nightwalker and other poems, 1968; Notes from the Land of the Dead, 1972; Butcher's Dozen, 1972; A Selected Life, 1972; Finistère, 1972; New Poems, 1973; Selected Poems 1956 to 1968, 1973; Vertical Man and The Good Fight, 1973; One, 1974; A Technical Supplement, 1976; Song of the Night and Other Poems, 1978; The Messenger, 1978; Fifteen Dead, 1979; One and Other Poems, 1979; Poems 1956–73, 1980; Peppercanister Poems 1972–78, 1980; One Fond Embrace, 1981 (complete) 1988; Songs of the Psyche, 1985; Her Vertical Smile, 1985; St Catherine's Clock, 1987; Out of Ireland, 1987; Blood and Family, 1988; Personal Places, 1990; Poems from Centre City, 1990; *translations and general:* (trans.) The Táin, 1969; contrib. essay in Davis, Mangan, Ferguson, 1970; (ed) Selected Poems of Austin Clarke, 1976; An Duanaire—Poems of the Dispossessed (trans. Gaelic poetry, 1600–1900), 1981; (ed) Our Musical Heritage: lectures on Irish traditional music by Seán Ó Riada, 1982; (ed, with translations) The New Oxford Book of Irish Verse, 1986.

KINSEY, Thomas Richard Moseley, FEng 1982; Chairman, Deltacam Systems, since 1989; Director, Unistrut Europe PLC, since 1989; *b* 13 Oct. 1929; *s* of late Richard Moseley Kinsey and Dorothy Elizabeth Kinsey; *m* 1953, Ruth (*née* Owen-Jones); two *s*. *Educ:* Newtown Sch.; Trinity Hall, Cambridge (MA). FIMechE; CBIM. ICI Ltd, 1952–57; Tube Investments,1957–65; joined Delta plc, 1965: Director, 1973–77; Jt Man. Dir, 1977–82; Dir, 1980, Dep. Chief Exec., 1982–87, Mitchell Cotts plc, 1980–87. Chm., Birmingham Battery & Metal Co., 1984–89; Director: Gower Internat., 1984–89; Telcon, 1984–89. *Recreations:* golf, travel. *Address:* Pinewood, Poolhead Lane, Tanworth-in-Arden, Warwickshire B94 5ED. *T:* Tanworth-in-Arden (05644) 2082. *Clubs:* Athenæum; Edgbaston Golf.

KINSMAN, Surgeon Rear-Adm. Francis Michael, CBE 1982 (OBE 1972); Surgeon Rear Admiral (Ships and Establishments), 1980–82, retired; *b* 5 May 1925; *s* of Oscar Edward Kinsman and Margaret Vera Kinsman; *m* 1st, 1949, Catherine Forsyth Barr; one *s*; 2nd, 1955, Margaret Emily Hillier; two *s*. *Educ:* Rydal Sch., Colwyn Bay; St Bartholomew's Hosp. MRCS, LRCP, MFCM; DA. Joined RN, 1952; served, 1952–66: HMS Comus, HMS Tamar, HMS Centaur; RN Hosp. Malta, RN Air Med. Sch., RNAS Lossiemouth; Pres., Central Air Med. Bd, 1966–69; Jt Services Staff Coll., 1969; Staff, Med. Dir Gen. (Naval), 1970–73; Dir, Naval Med. Staff Trng, 1973–76; Comd MO to C-in-C Naval Home Comd, 1976–79; MO i/c RN Hosp. Gibraltar, 1979–80. QHP 1980–82. OStJ 1977. *Recreations:* music, painting, fishing, woodwork. *Address:* Pound House, Meonstoke, Southampton, Hants SO3 1NH.

KINTORE, 13th Earl of, *cr* 1677 (Scot.); **Michael Canning William John Keith;** Lord Keith of Inverurie and Keith Hall, 1677 (Scot.); Bt 1897; Baron 1925; Viscount Stonehaven 1938; *b* 22 Feb. 1939; *s* of 12th Earl of Kintore, and of Delia Virginia, *d* of William Loyd; assumed surname of Keith in lieu of Baird, 1967; *S* father, 1989; *m* 1972, Mary Plum, *d* of late Sqdn Leader E. G. Plum, Rumson, NJ, and of Mrs Roy Hudson; one *s* one *d*. *Educ:* Eton; RMA Sandhurst. Lately Lieutenant, Coldstream Guards. ACII. *Heir:* *s* Lord Inverurie, Master of Kintore, *qv*. *Address:* The Stables, Keith Hall, Inverurie, Aberdeenshire AB5 0LD. *T:* Inverurie (0467) 20495.

KIPKULEI, Benjamin Kipkech; Permanent Secretary, Ministry of Education, Kenya, since 1987; *b* 5 Jan. 1946; *s* of Mr and Mrs Kipkulei Chesoro; *m* 1972, Miriam; three *s* two *d*. *Educ:* BAEd Nairobi; DipEd Scotland; MEd London. Local Government, 1964 and 1965; Teacher, 1970; Education Officer, 1974; Under Secretary, 1982; High Comr in UK, and Ambassador to Italy and Switzerland, 1984–86. *Recreations:* swimming, photography. *Address:* Ministry of Education, Joogoo House B, POB 30040, Nairobi, Kenya.

KIRALFY, Prof. Albert Kenneth Roland; Professor of Law, King's College, London, 1964–81, now Emeritus Professor; *b* Toronto, 5 Dec. 1915; *s* of Bolossy Kiralfy, Theatrical Impresario, and Helen Dawnay; *m* 1960, Roberta Ann Routledge. *Educ:* Streatham Grammar Sch.; King's Coll., London Univ. LLB 1935, LLM 1936, PhD 1949. Served War of 1939–45. Called to the Bar, Gray's Inn, 1947. King's Coll., London: Asst Lectr, 1937–39 and 1947–48; Lectr, 1948–51; Reader, 1951–64; Dean of College Law Faculty, 1974–77; FKC 1971. Chm., Bd of Studies in Laws, London Univ., 1971–74; Dean of Univ. Law Faculty, 1980–81. Vis. Prof., Osgoode Hall Law Sch., Toronto, 1961–62; Exchange Scholar, Leningrad Law Sch., Spring 1964, Moscow Law Sch., April 1970; Prague Acad. of Sciences, April 1975. Dir, Comparative Law Course, Luxembourg, Aug. 1968. Chm., Council of Hughes Parry Hall, London Univ., 1970–82. Editor, Journal of Legal History, 1980–90; Mem. Editorial Bd, Internat. and Comparative Law Quarterly, 1956–86; Reviser, English trans., Polish Civil Code, 1981. *Publications:* The Action on the Case, 1951; The English Legal System, 1954 (and later edns; 8th edn 1990); A Source Book of English Law, 1957; Potter's Historical Introduction to English Law, (4th edn) 1958; (with Prof. G. Jones) Guide to Selden Society Publications, 1960 reissued as part of Selden Soc. Centenary Guide, 1987; Translation of Russian Civil Codes, 1966; chapter, English Law, in Derrett, Introduction to Legal Systems, 1968; (with Miss R. A. Routledge) Guide to Additional MSS at Gray's Inn Library, 1971; General Editor, Comparative Law of Matrimonial Property, 1972; (ed jtly): New Perspectives in Scottish Legal History, 1984; Custom, Courts and Counsel, 1985; The Burden of Proof, 1987; contributed: Encyclopædia of Soviet Law (Leiden), 1973; Contemporary Soviet Law, 1974; East-West Business Transactions, 1974; Common Law, Encyclopædia Britannica, 1974; Codification in the Communist World, 1975; Russian Law: Historical Perspectives, 1977; Le Nuove Frontiere del Diritto, 1979; André Loeber Festschrift, 1988; Nuovi Moti per la Formazione del Diritto, 1988; Internat. Encyclopedia of Comparative Law, 1989; Jean Bodin Soc., vol. 52, 1990; Jl of Legal History, NY Jl of Internat. and Comparative Law; Review of Socialist Laws; *Rapporteur*, The Child without Family Ties, Congress of Jean Bodin Soc., Strasbourg, 1972. *Recreations:* history, languages. *Address:* Law School, King's College, Strand, WC2R 2LS; 58 Cheriton Square, SW17. *Club:* National Liberal.

KIRBY, Dr Anthony John, FRS 1987; CChem, FRSC; Fellow, Gonville and Caius College, since 1962, and Reader in Organic Chemistry, since 1985, Cambridge University; *b* 18 Aug. 1935; *s* of Samuel Arthur Kirby and Gladys Rosina Kirby (*née* Welch); *m* 1962, Sara Sophia Benjamina Nieweg; one *s* two *d*. *Educ:* Eton College; Gonville and Caius College, Cambridge (MA, PhD 1962). NATO postdoctoral Fellow: Cambridge, 1962–63; Brandeis Univ., 1963–64; Cambridge University: Demonstrator, 1964–68, Lectr, 1968–85, in Organic Chemistry; Gonville and Caius College: Fellow, 1962; Dir of Studies in Natural Scis and Coll. Lectr, 1968–; Tutor, 1966–74. Visiting Professor/Scholar: Paris (Orsay), 1970; Groningen, 1973; Cape Town, 1987; Paris VI, 1987; Haifa, 1991. Fellow, Japan Soc. for Promotion of Science, 1986; Royal Society of Chemistry: Fellow, 1980; Award in Organic Reaction Mechanisms, 1983; Tilden Lectr, 1987; Chm., Organic Reaction Mechanisms Gp, 1986–90. *Publications:* The Organic Chemistry of Phosphorus (with S. G. Warren), 1967; The Anomeric Effect and Related Stereoelectronic Effects at Oxygen, 1983; papers in Jls of RSC and Amer. Chem. Soc. *Recreations:* chamber music, walking. *Address:* University Chemical Laboratory, Cambridge CB2 1EW. *T:* Cambridge (0223) 336370; 14 Tenison Avenue, Cambridge CB1 2DY. *T:* Cambridge (0223) 359343.

KIRBY, David Donald, CBE 1988; Consultant, Transmark, since 1990; *b* 12 May 1933; *s* of Walter Donald Kirby and Margaret Irene (*née* Halstead); *m* 1955, Joan Florence (*née* Dickins); one *s* one *d*. *Educ:* Royal Grammar Sch., High Wycombe; Jesus Coll., Oxford (MA). FCIT. British Rail and its subsidiaries: Divisional Shipping Manager, Dover, 1964; Operations Manager, Shipping and Continental, 1965; Asst Gen. Man., Shipping and International Services, 1966; Continental Traffic Man., BR, 1968; Gen. Man., Shipping and Internat. Services, 1974; Man. Dir, Sealink UK Ltd, 1979; Dir, London and SE, 1982–85; Mem., 1985–89, Jt Man. Dir (Rlys), 1985–87, Vice-Chm., 1987–89, BRB. *Recreations:* painting, choral singing. *Address:* Penrose, Tresarrett, Blisland, Bodmin, Cornwall PL30 4QY.

KIRBY, Dennis, MVO 1961; MBE 1955; Director, NM UK Ltd (holding co. for NM Group), since 1988; Hon. Manager, European Investment Bank, Luxembourg; Partner, McKay Management Services; *b* 5 April 1923; *s* of William Ewart Kirby and Hannah Kirby. *Educ:* Hull Grammar Sch.; Queens' Coll., Cambridge. Lt (A) RNVR (fighter pilot), 1940–46. Colonial Service, Sierra Leone, 1946–62 (District Comr, 1950; Perm. Sec., 1961–62); 1st Sec., UK Diplomatic Service, 1962; Managing Director: East Kilbride Development Corp., 1963–68; Irvine Development Corp., 1967–72; Industrial Dir, Scotland, DTI, 1972–74; European Investment Bank, 1974–87: Conseiller Principal, 1974; Dir Adjoint, 1976; Dir Associé, 1984. *Recreations:* shooting, golf. *Address:* Bowcourt, Westcott Heath, Dorking, Surrey RH4 3JZ. *T:* Dorking (0306) 889631. *Clubs:* United Oxford & Cambridge University; RNVR (Scotland) (Glasgow); Prestwick Golf, Betchworth Park Golf, Wisley Golf.

KIRBY, Prof. Gordon William, ScD, PhD; FRSC; FRSE; Regius Professor of Chemistry, University of Glasgow, since 1972; *b* 20 June 1934; *s* of William Admiral Kirby and Frances Teresa Kirby (*née* Townson); *m* 1964, Audrey Jean Rusbridge (marr. diss. 1983), *d* of Col C. E. Rusbridge; two *s*. *Educ:* Liverpool Inst. High Sch.; Gonville and Caius Coll., Cambridge (Schuldham Plate 1956; MA, PhD, ScD); FRIC 1970; FRSE 1975. 1851 Exhibn Senior Student, 1958–60, Asst Lectr, 1960–61, Lectr, 1961–67, Imperial Coll. of Science and Technology; Prof. of Organic Chemistry, Univ. of Technology, Loughborough, 1967–72; Mem., Chem. Cttee, SRC, 1971–75. Chm., Jls Cttee, Royal Chem. Soc., 1981–84. Corday-Morgan Medal, Chem. Soc., 1969; Tilden Lectr, Chem. Soc., 1974–75. *Publications:* Co-editor: Elucidation of Organic Structures by Physical and Chemical Methods, vol. IV, parts I, II, and III, 1972; Fortschritte der Chemie organischer Naturstoffe, 1971–; contributor to Jl Chem. Soc., etc. *Address:* Chemistry Department, The University, Glasgow G12 8QQ. *T:* 041–339 8855.

KIRBY, Gwendolen Maud, LVO 1969; Matron, The Hospital for Sick Children, Great Ormond Street, 1951–69; *b* 17 Dec. 1911; 3rd *d* of late Frank M. Kirby, Gravesend, Kent. *Educ:* St Mary's Sch., Calne, Wilts. State Registered Nurse: trained at Nightingale Training Sch., St Thomas' Hosp., SE1. 1933–36; The Mothercraft Training Soc., Cromwell House, Highgate, 1936; State Certified Midwife: trained at General Lying-in Hosp., York Road, Lambeth, 1938–39; Registered Sick Children's Nurse: trained at the Hospital for Sick Children, Great Ormond Street, WC1, 1942–44. Awarded Nightingale Fund Travelling Scholarship, 1948–49, and spent 1 year in Canada and United States. Member: RCN, 1936–; Gen. Nursing Council, 1955–65. *Address:* Brackenfield, Winsford, Minehead, Som TA24 7JL.

KIRBY, Louis; political consultant, Daily Mail, since 1988; *b* 30 Nov. 1928; 2nd *s* of late William Kirby and Anne Kirby; *m* 1st, 1952, Marcia Teresa Lloyd (marr. diss. 1976); two *s* three *d*; 2nd, 1976, Heather Veronica (*née* Nicholson); one *s* one *d*; 3rd, 1983, Heather McGlone; two *d*. *Educ:* Our Lady Immaculate, Liverpool; Coalbrookdale High Sch. Daily Mail: Gen. Reporter, subseq. Courts Corresp., and Polit. Corresp., 1953–62; Daily Sketch: Chief Reporter, subseq. Leader Writer and Polit. Editor, Asst Editor, Exec. Editor, and, Actg Editor, 1962–71; Daily Mail (when relaunched): Dep. Editor, 1971–74; Editor, Evening News, 1974–80; Vice-Chm., Evening News Ltd, 1975–80; Editor, The London Standard, 1980–86; Dir, Mail Newspapers plc, 1986–88; Editl Dir, Associated Newspapers, 1986–88. *Recreations:* theatre, reading. *Address:* Northcliffe House, Derry Street, W8 5EE. *Clubs:* Reform, Special Forces.

KIRBY, Michael Donald, AC 1991; CMG 1983; **Hon. Justice Kirby;** President, Court of Appeal, Supreme Court of New South Wales, Sydney, since 1984; *b* 18 March 1939; *s* of Donald Kirby and Jean Langmore Kirby. *Educ:* Fort Street Boys' High Sch.; Univ. of Sydney (BA, LLM, BEc). Admitted Solicitor, 1962; called to the Bar of NSW, 1967; Mem., NSW Bar Council, 1974; Judge, Federal Court of Australia, 1983–84; Actg Chief Justice of NSW, 1988, 1990. Dep. Pres., Aust. Conciliation and Arbitration Commn, 1974–83; Chairman: Australian Law Reform Commn, 1975–84; OECD Inter-govtl Gp on Privacy and Internat. Data Flows, 1978–80; OECD Inter-govtl Gp on Security of Information Systems, 1991–; Member: Admin. Review Council of Australia, 1976–84; Council of Aust. Acad. of Forensic Scis, 1978– (Pres., 1987–89); Aust. National Commn for Unesco, 1980–83; Aust. Inst. of Multi-cultural Affairs, 1981–84; Exec., CSIRO, 1983–86. Deleg., Unesco Gen. Conf., Paris, 1983; Chm., Unesco Expert Gp on Rights of Peoples, 1989 (Rapporteur, Budapest, 1991). International Commission of Jurists: Comr, 1984–; Mem. Exec. Cttee, 1989–; Chm.-elect, 1992–; Pres., Aust. Section, 1989–. Internat. Consultant, Commn for Transborder Data Flow Develt, Intergovtl Bureau of Information, Rome, 1985–86; Mem., Bd, Internat. Trustees, Internat. Inst. for Inf. and Communication, Montreal, 1986–; President: Criminology Sect., ANZAAS, 1981– 82; Law Sect., ANZAAS, 1984–85. Granada Guildhall Lectr, 1985; Acting Prof., Fac. of Salzburg Seminar, Salzburg, 1985. Pres., Nat. Book Council of Australia, 1980–83; Member: Library Council of NSW, 1976–85; NSW Ministerial Adv. Cttee on AIDS, 1987; Trustee, AIDS Trust of Australia, 1987–; Comr, Global Commn on AIDS, WHO, Geneva, 1989–. Mem. Council, Australian Opera, 1983–89; Patron, RSPCA, Australia. Fellow, Senate, Sydney Univ., 1964–69; Dep. Chancellor, Univ. of Newcastle, NSW, 1978–83; Chancellor, Macquarie Univ., Sydney, 1984–. Mem. Bd of Governors, Internat. Council for Computer Communications, Washington, 1984–. Hon. DLitt Newcastle, NSW, 1987. Sen. Anzac Fellow, NZ Govt, 1981; Fellow, NZ Legal Res. Foundn, 1985. *Publications:* Industrial Index to Australian Labour Law, 1978, 2nd edn 1983; Reform the Law, 1983; The Judges (Boyer Lectures), 1983; (ed jtly) A Touch of Healing, 1986; essays and articles in legal and other jls. *Recreation:* work. *Address:* 2C Dumaresq Road, Rose Bay, NSW 2029, Australia. *T:* (61–2) 230–8202, *Fax:* (61–2) 235–1006.

KIRBY, Maj.-Gen. Norman George, OBE 1971; FRCS; Consultant Accident and Emergency Surgeon, Guy's Hospital, since 1982; Director, Clinical Services, Accidents and Emergencies, since 1985; *b* 19 Dec. 1926; *s* of George William Kirby and Laura Kirby; *m* 1949, Cynthia Bradley; one *s* one *d*. *Educ:* King Henry VIII Sch., Coventry; Univ. of Birmingham (MB, ChB). FRCS 1964, FRCSE 1980; FICS 1980. Surgical Registrar: Plastic Surg. Unit, Stoke Mandeville Hosp., 1950–51; Birmingham Accident Hosp., 1953–55; Postgraduate Med. Sch., Hammersmith, 1964. Regt MO 10 Parachute

Regt, 1950–51; OC 5 Parachute Surgical Team, 1956–59 (Suez Landing, 5 Nov. 1956); Officer i/c Surg. Div., BMH Rinteln, 1959–60; OC and Surg. Specialist, BMH Tripoli, 1960–62; OC and Consultant Surgeon, BMH Dhekelia, 1967–70; Chief Cons. Surgeon, Cambridge Mil. Hosp., 1970–72; Cons. Surg. HQ BAOR, 1973–78; Dir of Army Surgery, Cons. Surg. to the Army and Hon. Surgeon to the Queen, 1978–82; Hon. Cons. Surgeon, Westminster Hosp., 1979–. Examnr in Anatomy, RCSE, 1982–90; Mem., Court of Examiners, RCS, 1988–. Chm., Army Med. Dept Working Party Surgical Support for BAOR, 1978–80; Mem., Med. Cttee, Defence Scientific Adv. Council, 1979–82. Hon. Colonel: 308 (Co. of London) Gen. Hosp. RAMC, TA, 1982–87; 144 Field Ambulance RAMC (Volunteers), TA, 1985–; Col Comdt, RAMC, 1987–. Member: Council Internat. Coll. of Surgeons; Airborne Med. Soc.; British Assoc. for Accident and Emergency Medicine (formerly Casualty Surgeons Assoc.), 1981– (Vice-Pres., 1988, Pres., 1990–); Vice-Pres., British Assoc. of Trauma in Sport, 1982–88; Chm., Accidents & Emergencies Cttee, SE Thames RHA, 1984–88. Mem. Council, TAVRA, Gtr London, 1990–. Liveryman, Soc. of Apothecaries of London, 1983–; Mem., HAC, 1988. McCombe Lectr, RCSE, 1979. Mem., Editl Bd, Brit. Jl Surg. and Injury, 1979–82. Mem., Surgical Travellers Club, 1979–. FMS London 1981. OStJ 1977 (Mem. Council, London, 1990–). Mitchener Medal, RCS, 1982. *Publications:* (ed) Field Surgery Pocket Book, 1981; Pocket Reference, Accidents and Emergencies, 1988, 2nd edn 1991; contrib. Brit. Jl Surg. and Proc. RSocMed. *Recreations:* travel, motoring, reading, archaeology. *Address:* 12 Woodsyre, Sydenham Hill, Dulwich, SE26 6SS. *T:* 081–670 5327.

KIRBY, Hon. Sir Richard (Clarence), Kt 1961; AC 1985; Chairman, Advertising Standards Council, 1973–88; *b* 22 Sept. 1904; *s* of Samuel Enoch Kirby and Agnes Mary Kirby, N Queensland; *m* 1937, Hilda Marie Ryan; two *d*. *Educ:* The King's Sch., Parramatta; University of Sydney (LLB). Solicitor, NSW, 1928; called to Bar, 1933; served AIF, 1942–44; Mem. Adult Adv. Educl Council to NSW Govt, 1944–46; Judge, Dist Court, NSW, 1944–47; Mem. Austr. War Crimes Commn, 1945, visiting New Guinea, Morotai, Singapore, taking evidence on war crimes; Australia Rep. on War Crimes, Lord Mountbatten's HQ, Ceylon, 1945; Royal Commissioner on various occasions for Federal, NSW and Tasmanian Govts, 1945–47; Acting Judge Supreme Court of NSW, 1947; Chief Judge, Commonwealth Court of Conciliation and Arbitration, 1956–73; Austr. Rep., UN Security Council's Cttee on Good Offices on Indonesian Question, 1947–48, participating in Security Council Debates, Lake Success, USA; Chm. Stevedoring Industry Commn, 1947–49; (first) Pres., Commonwealth Conciliation and Arbitration Commn, 1956–73. Chm., Nat. Stevedoring Conf., 1976–77. Pres., H. V. Evatt Meml Foundn, 1979–85. Mem. Council, Wollongong Univ., 1979–84. Hon. DLitt Wollongong Univ., 1984. *Recreation:* encouraging good will in industry. *Address:* The White House, Berrara, NSW 2540, Australia. *T:* Nowra 412171. *Club:* Athenæum (Melbourne).

KIRCHNER, Peter James, MBE 1970; HM Diplomatic Service, retired; Consul General, Berlin, 1978–79; *b* 17 Sept. 1920; *s* of late William John Kirchner and Winifred Emily Homer (*née* Adams); *m* 1952, Barbro Sarah Margareta (*née* Klockhoff); one *s* two *d*. *Educ:* St Brendan's Coll., Clifton, Bristol. Served War, RA, 1939–41. Timber production, UK and Germany, 1941–48; FO, Germany, 1948; Home Office Immigration Dept, 1952–64; Head of UK Refugee Missions in Europe, 1960–63; FCO (formerly FO): Barbados, 1965; Nairobi, 1968; Ankara, 1970; Vienna, 1973; Jerusalem, 1976. Freeman, City of London, 1963. *Recreations:* chatty golf, 18th-19th century Europe, discovering European backwaters, trying to write. *Address:* 86 York Mansions, Prince of Wales Drive, SW11 4BN. *T:* 071–622 7068.

KIRK, Prof. Geoffrey Stephen, DSC 1945; LittD; FBA 1959; Regius Professor of Greek, University of Cambridge, 1974–82, now Emeritus; Fellow of Trinity College, Cambridge, 1974–82; *b* 3 Dec. 1921; *s* of Frederic Tilzey Kirk, MC, and Enid Hilda (*née* Pentecost); *m* 1st, 1950, Barbara Helen Traill (marr. diss. 1975); one *d*; 2nd, 1975, Kirsten Jensen (Ricks). *Educ:* Rossall Sch.; Clare Coll., Cambridge. LittD Cambridge, 1965. Served War in Royal Navy, 1941–45; commissioned 1942; Temp. Lt, RNVR, 1945. Took Degree at Cambridge, 1946; Research Fellow, Trinity Hall, 1946–49; Student, Brit. Sch. at Athens, 1947; Commonwealth Fund Fellow, Harvard Univ., 1949–50; Fellow, Trinity Hall, 1950–70; Cambridge University: Asst Lecturer in Classics, 1951; Lecturer in Classics, 1952–61; Reader in Greek, 1961–65; Prof. of Classics, Yale Univ., 1965–70; Prof. of Classics, Bristol Univ., 1971–73. Visiting Lecturer, Harvard Univ., 1958; Sather Prof. of Classical Literature, University of California, Berkeley, 1968–69; Mellon Prof., Tulane Univ., 1979. Pres., Soc. for Promotion of Hellenic Studies, 1977–80. MA (Yale) 1965. *Publications:* Heraclitus, the Cosmic Fragments, 1954; (with J. E. Raven) The Presocratic Philosophers, 1958; The Songs of Homer, 1962 (abbrev., as Homer and the Epic, 1965); Euripides, Bacchae, 1970; Myth, 1970; The Nature of Greek Myths, 1974; Homer and the Oral Tradition, 1977; The Iliad: a commentary, Vol.1, books 1–4, 1985, Vol. 2, books 5–8, 1990; articles in classical, archæological and philosophical journals. *Recreation:* sailing. *Address:* 12 Sion Hill, Bath, Avon BA1 2UH.

KIRK, Grayson Louis; President Emeritus, Columbia University; *b* 12 Oct. 1903; *s* of Traine Caldwell Kirk and Nora Eichelberger; *m* 1925, Marion Louise Sands; one *s*. *Educ:* Miami Univ. (AB); Clark Univ. (AM); Ecole Libre des Sciences Politiques, Paris, 1928–29. PhD University of Wisconsin, 1930. Prof. of History, Lamar Coll., Beaumont, Tex, 1925–27; Social Science Research Coun. Fellowship (chiefly spent at London Sch. of Economics), 1936–37; Instructor in Political Science, 1929–30, Asst Prof., 1930–36, Associate Prof., 1936–38, Prof., 1938–40, University of Wisconsin; Associate Prof. of Government, Columbia Univ., 1940–43; Head, Security Section, Div. of Political Studies, US Dept of State, 1942–43; Mem. US Delegn Staff, Dumbarton Oaks, 1944; Exec. Officer, Third Commn, San Francisco Conf., 1945. Research Associate, Yale Inst. of Internat. Studies, 1943–44; Prof. of Government, Columbia Univ., 1943–47; Prof. of Internat Relations, Acting Dir of Sch. of Internat. Affairs, and Dir of European Inst., 1947–49. Appointed Provost in Nov. 1949, and also Vice-Pres in July 1950; became acting head of Columbia in President Eisenhower's absence on leave, March 1951; Pres. and Trustee of Columbia Univ., 1953–68; Bryce Prof. of History of Internat. Relations, Columbia, 1959–72, Emeritus Prof., 1972. Trustee Emeritus, The Asia Foundation; Trustee: Academy of Political Science (Chm. and Dir); American Philosophical Soc.; Pilgrims of the US (Vice-Pres.); Council on Foreign Relations; Amer. Acad. of Arts and Sciences; Amer. Soc. of French Legion of Honour. Mem. Adv. Bd, International Business Machines Corp. Hon. LLD: Miami, 1950; Waynesburg Coll., Brown Univ., Union Coll, 1951; Puerto Rico, Clark, Princeton, New York, Wisconsin, Columbia, Jewish Theol. Seminary of America, 1953; Syracuse, Williams Coll., Pennsylvania, Harvard, Washington, St Louis, Central Univ., Caracas, Univ. of the Andes, Merida, Venezuela, Univ. of Zulia, Maracaibo, Venezuela, Univ. of Delhi, India, Thamasset Univ., Bangkok, 1954; Johns Hopkins Univ., Baltimore, Amherst, 1956; Dartmouth Coll., Northwestern Univ., 1958; Tennessee, 1960; St Lawrence, 1963; Denver, Notre Dame, Bates Coll., 1964; Waseda (Japan), Michigan, 1965; Sussex, 1966; Hon. LHD N Dakota, 1958; Hon. PhD Bologna, 1951; Dr of Civil Law King's Coll., Halifax, Nova Scotia, 1958. Associate KStJ 1959. Comdr, Order of Orange-Nassau, 1952; Hon. KBE, 1955; Grand Officer, Order of Merit, of the Republic, Italy, 1956; Grand Officier Légion d'Honneur, France, 1973. Medal of the Order of Taj, Iran, 1961; Grand Cross, Order of George I (Greece), 1965; Order of the Sacred Treasure, 1st Class (Japan), 1965; Comdr, Ordre des Palmes Académiques (France), 1966. *Publications:* Philippine Independence, 1936; Contemporary International Politics (with W. R. Sharp), 1940; (with R. P. Stebbins) War and National Policy, Syllabus, 1941; The Study of International Relations in American Colleges and Universities, 1947. *Address:* 28 Sunnybrook Road, Bronxville, NY 10708, USA. *T:* 914–793 0808. *Club:* Century (New York).

KIRK, Rt. Hon. Herbert Victor, PC (N Ireland) 1962; Member (U) for South Belfast, Northern Ireland Assembly, 1973–75; *b* 5 June 1912; *s* of Alexander and Mary A. Kirk; *m* 1944, Gladys A. Dunn; three *s*. *Educ:* Queen's Univ., Belfast (BComSc). MP Windsor Div. of Belfast, NI Parlt, 1956–72; Minister of Labour and Nat. Insce, Govt of N Ireland, 1962–64; Minister of Education, 1964–65; Minister of Finance, 1965–72, Jan.-May 1974, resigned. FCA 1940. *Recreation:* golf. *Address:* 38 Massey Avenue, Belfast BT4 2JT, Northern Ireland. *Clubs:* Royal Portrush Golf, Belvoir Park Golf.

KIRK, John Henry, CBE 1957; Emeritus Professor of Marketing (with special reference to horticulture), University of London; *b* 11 April 1907; *s* of William Kirk, solicitor; *m* 1946, Wilfrida Margaret Booth; two *s*. *Educ:* Durban High Sch., S Africa; Universities of S Africa, Cambridge, North Carolina and Chicago. Ministry of Agriculture (from 1934, as economist and administrator); Under-Sec., 1959–65; Prof. of Marketing, Wye Coll., 1965–72. *Publications:* Economic Aspects of Native Segregation, 1929; Agriculture and the Trade Cycle, 1933; United Kingdom Agricultural Policy 1870–1970, 1982; contributions to journals of sociology, economics and agricultural economics. *Recreation:* gardening. *Address:* Burrington, Cherry Gardens, Wye, Ashford, Kent TN25 5AR. *T:* Wye (0233) 812640.

KIRK, Dame (Lucy) Ruth, DBE 1975; *m* 1941, Norman Eric Kirk (later, Rt Hon. Norman Kirk, PC, Prime Minister of New Zealand; *d* 1974); three *s* two *d*. Former Patron, SPUC. Awarded title, Dame of the Order of the British Empire, for public services. *Address:* Flat 1, 8(A) Ansonby Street, Avonhead, Christchurch, S Island, New Zealand.

KIRK, Raymond Maurice, FRCS; Consulting Surgeon, Royal Free Hospital, since 1989; part-time Lecturer in Anatomy, Royal Free Hospital School of Medicine, since 1989; *b* 31 Oct. 1923; *m* 1952, Margaret Schafran; one *s* two *d*. *Educ:* Mundella Sch., Nottingham; County Secondary Sch., West Bridgford; King's College London; Charing Cross Hosp. MB BS, MS, London; LRCP. RN 1942–46; Lieut RNVR. Charing Cross Hosp., 1952–53; Lectr in Anatomy, King's Coll. London, 1953–54; Hammersmith Hosp., 1954–56; Charing Cross Hosp., 1956–60; Senior Surgical Registrar, Royal Free Hosp., 1961; Consultant Surgeon, Willesden Gen. Hosp., 1962–74, Royal Free Hosp. Group, 1964–89. Dir, Overseas Doctors' Trg Scheme, RCS, 1990–. Examr to RCPSG; formerly Mem. Court of Examrs, RCS; formerly Examr to Univs of London, Liverpool, Bristol, Khartoum, Colombo; Mem. Council, RCS, 1983–; Pres., Medical Soc., 1988; FRSocMed (Pres., Surgical Section, 1986–87). Member: British Soc. of Gastroenterol.; Surg. Res. Soc.; BMA; Med. Soc. of London; Soc. of Authors. Hon. Editor, Annals of RCS, 1983–. *Publications:* Manual of Abdominal Operations, 1967; Basic Surgical Techniques, 1973, 3rd edn 1988; (jtly) Surgery, 1974; General Surgical Operations, 1978, 2nd edn 1988; (jtly) Complications of Upper Gastrointestinal Tract Surgery, 1987; papers in sci. jls and chapters in books on peptic ulcer, oesophageal, gastric and general abdominal surgery. *Recreations:* opera, theatre, squash, cycling. *Address:* 10 Southwood Lane, Highgate Village, N6 5EE. *T:* 081–340 8575. *Club:* Royal Society of Medicine.

KIRK, Dame Ruth; *see* Kirk, Dame L. R.

KIRKBY, Emma; free-lance classical concert singer; soprano; *b* 26 Feb. 1949; *d* of Geoffrey and Daphne Kirkby; one *s* by Anthony Rooley, *qv*. *Educ:* Hanford School; Sherborne School for Girls; Somerville College, Oxford (BA Classics). Private singing lessons with Jessica Cash. Regular appearances with Taverner Choir and Players, 1972–; Member: Consort of Musicke, 1973–; Academy of Ancient Music, 1975–; numerous radio broadcasts, gramophone recordings, appearances at the Proms, 1977–. Hon. DLitt Salford, 1985.

KIRKE, Rear-Adm. David Walter, CB 1967; CBE 1962 (OBE 1945), retired; *b* 13 March 1915; *s* of late Percy St George Kirke and late Alice Gertrude, *d* of Sir James Gibson Craig, 3rd Bt; *m* 1st, 1936, Tessa O'Connor (marr. diss., 1950); one *s*; 2nd, 1956, Marion Margaret Gibb; one *s* one *d*. *Educ:* RN Coll., Dartmouth. China Station, 1933–35; Pilot Training, 1937; served War of 1939–45, Russian Convoys, Fighter Sqdns; loaned RAN, 1949–50; Chief of Naval Aviation, Indian Navy, New Delhi, 1959–62; Rear-Adm. 1965; Flag Officer, Naval Flying Training, 1965–68. MBIM 1967. *Recreation:* golf. *Address:* Lismore House, Pluckley, Kent TN27 0QZ. *T:* Pluckley (023384) 439. *Club:* Army and Navy.

KIRKHAM, Donald Herbert, FCIS, FCBSI; Group Chief Executive, Woolwich Building Society, since 1991 (Chief Executive, 1986–90); *b* 1 Jan. 1936; *s* of Herbert and Hettie Kirkham; *m* 1960, Kathleen Mary Lond; one *s* one *d*. *Educ:* Grimsby Technical College. Woolwich Equitable Building Society, later Woolwich Building Society: Representative, 1959; Branch Manager, 1963; Gen. Manager's Asst, 1967; Business Planning Manager, 1970; Asst Gen. Manager, 1972; Gen. Manager, 1976; Mem. Local Board, 1979; Dep. Chief Gen. Manager, 1981; Mem. Board, 1982. Chartered Building Societies Institute: Mem. Council, 1976; Dep. Pres., 1980; Pres., 1981; Vice-Pres., 1986; Institute of Chartered Secretaries and Administrators: Mem. Council, 1979; Vice-Pres., 1985; Sen. Vice-Pres., 1990; Pres., 1991. CBIM. *Recreation:* boating. *Address:* 2 Chaundrye Close, The Court Yard, Eltham, SE9 5QB. *T:* 081–850 6144.

KIRKHAM, Rt. Rev. John Dudley Galtrey; *see* Sherborne, Area Bishop of.

KIRKHAM, Keith Edwin, OBE 1987; PhD; Administrative Director, Clinical Research Centre, Medical Research Council, since 1988; *b* 20 Oct. 1929; *s* of Thomas Kirkham and Clara Prestwich Willacy; *m* 1953, Dorothea Mary Fisher; two *s*. *Educ:* Kirkham Grammar Sch.; Birmingham Univ. (BSc); Fitzwilliam House, Cambridge (DipAgSci; T. H. Middleton Prize); MA, PhD Cantab. National Service, 2nd Lieut RA, 1955–57. Asst in Res., Cambridge, 1951–54; Univ. Demonstr, Cambridge, 1954–60; Sci. Staff, Clin. Endocrinology Res. Unit, MRC, 1960–73; Asst Dir (Admin), Clin. Res. Centre, MRC, 1973–88. Sec., Soc. for Endocrinology, 1975–79. Governor: Harrow Coll. of Higher Educn, 1983–90 (Chm. of Govs, 1986–90); Poly. of Central London, 1990–. *Publications:* contribs to sci. jls on endocrinology. *Recreations:* cruising, sport (watching). *Address:* Spring Drive, Eastcote, Pinner, Mddx HA5 1ES.

KIRKHILL, Baron *cr* 1975 (Life Peer), of Kirkhill, Aberdeen; **John Farquharson Smith;** *b* 7 May 1930; *s* of Alexander F. Smith and Ann T. Farquharson; *m* 1965, Frances Mary Walker Reid; one step-*d*. Lord Provost of the City and Royal Burgh of Aberdeen, 1971–75. Minister of State, Scottish Office, 1975–78. Chm., N of Scotland Hydro-Electric Bd, 1979–82. Mem., Council of Europe, 1987–. Hon. LLD Aberdeen, 1974. *Address:* 3 Rubislaw Den North, Aberdeen. *T:* Aberdeen (0224) 314167.

KIRKHOPE, Timothy John Robert; MP (C) Leeds North East, since 1987; an Assistant Government Whip, since 1990; *b* 29 April 1945; *s* of John Thomas Kirkhope and Dorothy Buemann Kirkhope (*née* Bolt); *m* 1969, Caroline (*née* Maling); four *s. Educ*: Royal Grammar School, Newcastle upon Tyne; College of Law, Guildford. Solicitor. Conservative Party: joined 1961 (N Area Vice-Chm of YC and Mem., Nat. Cttee); contested Durham, 1974 and Darlington, 1979; Hexham Treasurer, 1982–85; Exec., N Area, 1975–87; Mem., Nat. Exec., 1985–87. County Councillor, Northumberland, 1981–85. Mem., Newcastle Airport Bd, 1982–85; Mem., Northern RHA, 1982–86; Founder Lawyer Mem., Mental Health Act Commn, 1983–86. PPS to Minister of State for the Envmt and Countryside, 1989–90. Mem., Select Cttee on Statutory Instruments, 1987–90; Vice Chm., Backbench Legal Cttee, 1988–89; Jt Hon. Sec., Cons. Backbench Envmt Cttee, 1988–89. *Recreations*: flying (holds private pilot's licence), tennis, swimming, watching TV quiz shows. *Address*: House of Commons, SW1A 0AA. *T*: 071–219 4417. *Club*: Northern Counties (Newcastle upon Tyne).

KIRKLAND, Joseph Lane; President, American Federation of Labor & Congress of Industrial Organizations, since 1979; *b* Camden, SC, 12 March 1922; *s* of Randolph Withers Kirkland and Louise Richardson; *m* Irena Neumann; five *d. Educ*: US Merchant Marine Academy, Kings Point, NY (grad. 1942); Georgetown Univ. Sch. of Foreign Service (BS 1948). Deck officer, various merchant ships, 1942–45; Staff Scientist, US Navy Hydrographic Office, 1945–48; Staff Representative, AFL-CIO, 1948–58; Research and Information Dir, Internat. Union of Operating Engrs, 1958–60; Exec. Asst to President, AFL-CIO, 1960–69; Sec.-Treasurer, AFL-CIO, 1969–79. Member: US Delegn, ILO Confs, Geneva, 1958, 1969, 1970, 1975, 1976, 1980, 1981; Blue Ribbon Defense Panel, 1969–70; Commn on CIA Activities Within the US, 1975; Commn on Foundns and Private Philanthropy, 1969–70; Gen. Adv. Cttee on Arms Control and Disarmament, 1974–78; Nat. Commn on Productivity, 1971–74; Presidential Commn on Financial Structure and Regulation, 1970–72; President's Maritime Adv. Cttee, 1964–66; President's Missile Sites Labor Commn (Alternate), 1961–67; Commn on Exec., Legislative and Judicial Salaries; Cttee on Selection of Fed. Judicial Officers; President's Commn on Social Security, 1982–83; Bipartisan Commn on Central America, 1983–84. Director: Amer. Council on Germany; Amer. Arbitration Assoc.; Afr.-Amer. Labor Center; Asian-Amer. Free Labor Inst.; Nat. Urban League; Rockefeller Foundn; Amer. Inst. for Free Labor Develt; Council on For. Relns, Inc.; Nat. Planning Assoc. Mem., Internat. Org. of Masters, Mates and Pilots; FAAAS. *Recreation*: archaeology. *Address*: (office) 815 16th Street NW, Washington, DC 20006, USA. *T*: (202) 637–5000.

KIRKMAN, William Patrick; Secretary, University of Cambridge Careers Service, since 1968; Fellow, Wolfson College, Cambridge (formerly University College); *b* 23 Oct. 1932; *s* of late Geoffrey Charles Aylward Kirkman and Bertha Winifred Kirkman; *m* 1959, Anne Teasdale Fawcett; two *s* one *d. Educ*: Churcher's Coll., Petersfield, Hants; Oriel Coll., Oxford. 2nd cl. hons. mod. langs, 1955; MA 1959; MA (Cantab) by incorporation, 1968. National Service, 1950–52, RASC (L/Cpl). Editorial staff: Express & Star, Wolverhampton, 1955–57; The Times, 1957–64 (Commonwealth staff, 1960–64, Africa Correspondent, 1962–64). Asst Sec., Oxford Univ. Appointments Cttee, 1964–68. Chm., Standing Conf. of University Appointments Services, 1971–73; Member: Management Cttee, Central Services Unit for Univ. Careers and Appointments Services, 1971–74, 1985–87; British Cttee, Journalists in Europe, 1985–; Cambridge Univ. PR Co-ordinating Cttee, 1987–; Trng Bd, ESRC, 1990–; BBC South and East Regl Adv. Council, 1990–. Wolfson Coll: Vice-Pres., 1980–84; Mem. Council, 1969–73, 1976–80, 1988–; Dir, Press Fellowship Programme, 1982–. Churchwarden, St Mary and All Saints Willingham, 1978–85. Trustee: Sir Halley Stewart Trust, 1970– (Hon. Sec., 1978–82); Willingham British Sch. Trust, 1974–91; Homerton Coll., 1980–89; Lucy Cavendish Coll., 1989–; Mem. Cttee, Cambridge Soc., 1979–83. *Publications*: Unscrambling an Empire, 1966; contrib.: Policing and Social Policy, 1984; Models of Police/Public Consultation in Europe, 1985; Managing Recruitment, 4th edn 1988; contributor to journals incl.: Commonwealth, International Affairs, Africa Contemporary Record, Financial Times, Cambridge, and to BBC. *Recreations*: broadcasting, gardening, church activities, writing. *Address*: 19 High Street, Willingham, Cambridge CB4 5ES. *T*: Willingham (0954) 60393. *Club*: Commonwealth Trust.

KIRKNESS, Donald James, CB 1980; Deputy Secretary, Overseas Development Administration, 1977–80; *b* 29 Sept 1919; *s* of Charles Stephen and Elsie Winifred Kirkness; *m* 1947, Monica Mary Douch; one *d. Educ*: Harvey Grammar Sch., Folkestone. Exchequer and Audit Dept, 1938. Served War: RA and Royal Berkshire Regt, 1939–46. Colonial Office, 1947 (Asst Principal); Financial and Economic Adviser, Windward I, 1955–57; Dept of Economic Affairs, 1966; Civil Service Dept, 1970–73; ODA/ODM, 1973. UK Governor, Internat. Fund for Agricultural Develt, 1977–81; Mem., Exec. Bd, UNESCO, 1978–83.

KIRKPATRICK, Sir Ivone Elliott, 11th Bt, *cr* 1685; *b* 1 Oct. 1942; *s* of Sir James Alexander Kirkpatrick, 10th Bt and Ellen Gertrude, *o d* of Captain R. P. Elliott, late RNR; *S* father 1954. *Educ*: Wellington Coll., Berks; St Mark's Coll., University of Adelaide. *Heir*: *b* Robin Alexander Kirkpatrick, *b* 19 March 1944. *Address*: c/o ANZ Bank, 81 King William Street, Adelaide, SA 5000, Australia.

KIRKPATRICK, John Lister, CBE 1981; CA; Consultant, Peat Marwick McLintock, Chartered Accountants, 1987–90; *b* 27 June 1927; *s* of late Henry Joseph Rodway Kirkpatrick and Nora (*née* Lister); *m* 1977, Gay Elmslie (*née* Goudielock); one *s* one *d* of former marriage. *Educ*: Inverness Royal Acad. CA. Served RNVR, 1944–47. KMG Thomson McLintock (formerly Thomson McLintock & Co.): apprentice, 1948; qual. CA 1952; Partner, 1958; Joint Senior Partner, Glasgow and Edinburgh, 1974–80; Co-Chm., UK Policy Council, 1974–83; Sen. Partner, Scotland, 1980–87; UK Dep. Chm., 1983–87; Chm., KMG Region I, Europe, Africa, ME, Pakistan, India, 1979–85; Partner, Klynveld Main Goerdeler (KMG), 1979–87. Member: BoT Accountants' Adv. Cttee, 1967–72; Mem. (Rep. UK & Ireland), 1978–85, Chm., 1985–87, Internat. Accounting Standards Cttee; Review Body on Doctors' and Dentists' Remuneration, 1983–88; Lay Mem., Scottish Solicitors' Discipline Tribunal, 1981–. Vice-Pres., Inst. of Chartered Accountants of Scotland, 1975–77, Pres., 1977–78. FRSA. *Publications*: various papers. *Recreations*: fishing, gardening. *Address*: 1 Letham Drive, Glasgow G43 2SL. *T*: 041–633 1407. *Club*: New (Edinburgh).

KIRKPATRICK, William Brown, JP; Member, Gaming Board for Great Britain; Chairman or Director of six commercial companies; *b* 27 April 1934; *s* of late Joseph and Mary Kirkpatrick, Thornhill, Dumfriesshire; *m* 1990, Joan L. Millar. *Educ*: Morton Acad., Thornhill; George Watson's Coll., Edinburgh; Univ. of Strathclyde (BScEcon); Columbia Business Sch., NY (MS and McKinsey Scholar); Stanford Executive Program. After three years in manufacturing industry in Glasgow, Dundee and London, served 3i, 1960–85, latterly at director level, and worked in London, Scotland and Australia in investment capital, corporate finance, fixed interest capital markets, on secondment as Industrial Director of Industry Department for Scotland, in shipping finance and as a nominee director; company dir and corporate advr, 1985–90 (incl. appt within DoE on water privatisation). JP Inner London, 1985. *Recreations*: Scottish paintings, porcelain pigs,

shooting, current affairs. *Address*: 20 Abbotsbury House, Abbotsbury Road, W14 8EN. *T*: 071–603 3087; 74 Norwood Park, Bearsden, Glasgow G61 2RZ. *Club*: Caledonian.

KIRKUP, James; travel writer, poet, novelist, playwright, translator, broadcaster; *b* 23 April 1923; *o s* of James Harold Kirkup and Mary Johnston. *Educ*: South Shields High Sch.; Durham Univ. (BA). FRSL 1962. Atlantic Award in Literature (Rockefeller Foundation), 1950; Keats Prize for Poetry, 1974; Gregory Fellow in Poetry, University of Leeds, 1950–52. Visiting Poet and Head of English Dept, Bath Academy of Art, Corsham Court, Wilts, 1953–56; Lectr in English, Swedish Ministry of Education, Stockholm, 1956–57; Prof. of Eng. Lang. and Lit., University of Salamanca, 1957–58, of English, Tohoku Univ., Sendai, Japan, 1958–61; Lecturer in English Literature, University of Malaya in Kuala Lumpur, 1961–62; Literary Editor, Orient/West Magazine, Tokyo, 1963–64; Prof., Japan Women's Univ., 1964–; Poet in Residence and Visiting Prof., Amherst Coll., Mass, 1968–; Prof. of English Literature, Nagoya Univ., 1969–72. Arts Council Fellowship in Creative Writing, Univ. of Sheffield, 1974–75; Morton Vis. Prof. of Internat. Literature, Ohio Univ., 1975–76; Playwright in Residence, Sherman Theatre, University Coll., Cardiff, 1976–77; Prof. of English Lit., Kyoto Univ. of Foreign Studies, Kyoto, Japan, 1977–. President: Poets' Soc. of Japan, 1969; Blackmore Soc., 1970; Inst. of Pyschophysical Res., 1970; British Haiku Soc., 1990. Mabel Batchelder Award, 1968. *Plays performed*: Upon this Rock (perf. Peterborough Cathedral), 1955; Masque, The Triumph of Harmony (perf. Albert Hall), 1955; The True Mistery of the Nativity, 1957; Dürrenmatt, The Physicists (Eng. trans.), 1963; Dürrenmatt, The Meteor (Eng. trans.); Dürrenmatt, Play Strindberg (Eng. trans.), 1972; The Magic Drum, children's play, 1972, children's musical, 1977; Dürrenmatt, Portrait of a Planet, 1972; Dürrenmatt, The Conformer, 1974; Schiller, Don Carlos, 1975; Cyrano de Bergerac, 1975; *operas*: An Actor's Revenge, 1979; Friends in Arms, 1980; The Damask Drum, 1982; *television plays performed*: The Peach Garden, Two Pigeons Flying High, etc. Contributor to BBC, The Listener, The Spectator, Times Literary Supplement, Time and Tide, New Yorker, Botteghe Oscure, London Magazine, Japan Qly, English Teachers' Magazine (Tokyo), etc. *Publications*: The Drowned Sailor, 1948; The Cosmic Shape, 1947; The Creation, 1950; The Submerged Village, 1951; A Correct Compassion, 1952; A Spring Journey, 1954; Upon This Rock, 1955; The True Mistery of the Nativity, 1957; The Descent into the Cave, 1957; Sorrows, Passions and Alarms, 1959; These Horned Islands, A Journal of Japan, 1962; frères Gréban, The True Mistery of the Passion, 1962; Refusal to Conform, 1963; Tropic Temper: a Memoir of Malaya, 1963; Japan Industrial, 1964–65 (2 vols); Daily Life in the French Revolution, 1964; Tokyo, 1965; England, Now, 1965; Japan, Now, 1966; Frankly Speaking, I-II, 1968; Bangkok, 1968; One Man's Russia, 1968; Filipinescas, 1968; Streets of Asia, 1969; Japan Physical, 1969; Aspects of the Short Story, 1969; Hong Kong, 1970; Japan Behind the Fan, 1970; Heaven, Hell and Hara-Kiri, 1974; (with Birgit Skiöld) Zen Gardens, 1974; Scenes from Sesshu, 1977; Zen Contemplations, 1979; (with Birgit Skiöld) The Tao of Water, 1980; Folktales Japanesque, 1982; Modern American Myths, 1982; I Am Count Dracula, 1982; I Am Frankenstein's Monster, 1983; Miniature Masterpieces of Kawabata Yasunari, 1983; When I was a Child: a study of nursery-rhymes, 1983; My Way-USA, 1984; The Glory that was Greece, 1984; The Mystery & Magic of Symbols, 1987; The Cry of the Owl: Native Folktales & Legends, 1987; *poems*: The Prodigal Son, 1959; Paper Windows: Poems from Japan, 1968; Shepherding Winds (anthol.), 1969; Songs and Dreams (anthol.), 1970; White Shadows, Black Shadows: Poems of Peace and War, 1970; The Body Servant; poems of exile, 1971; A Bewick Bestiary, 1971; Modern Japanese Poetry (anthol.), 1978; Dengonban Messages (one-line poems), 1980; To the Ancestral North: poems for an autobiography, 1983; The Sense of the Visit: new poems, 1984; The Guitar-Player of Zuiganji, 1985; Fellow Feelings, 1986; *poems and translations*: Ecce Homo: My Pasolini, 1982; No More Hiroshimas, 1982; *autobiography*: The Only Child, 1957 (trans. Japanese, 1986); Sorrows, Passions and Alarms, 1987 (trans. Japanese); I, of All People: an Autobiography of Youth, 1990; A Poet could not but be Gay: some Legends of my Lost Youth, 1991; *novels*: The Love of Others, 1962; Insect Summer (for children), 1971; The Magic Drum (for children), 1973; Gaijin on the Ginza, 1991; *essays*: Eibungaku Saiken, 1980; The Joys of Japan, 1985; Lafcadio Hearn (biog.), 1985; James Kirkup's International Movie Theatre, 1985; Trends and Traditions, 1986; Portraits & Souvenirs (biog.), 1987; *opera*: The Damask Drum, 1982; *translations*: Camara Laye, The Dark Child, 1955; Ancestral Voices, 1956; Camara Laye, The Radiance of the King, 1956; Simone de Beauvoir, Memoirs of a Dutiful Daughter, 1958; The Girl from Nowhere, 1958; It Began in Babel, 1961; The Captive, 1962; Sins of the Fathers, 1962; The Gates of Paradise, 1962; The Heavenly Mandate, 1964; Daily Life of the Etruscans, 1964; Erich Kästner, The Little Man, 1966; Erich Kästner, The Little Man and The Little Miss, 1969; Heinrich von Kleist, The Tales of Hoffman, 1966; Michael Kohlhaas, 1966; Camara Laye, A Dream of Africa, 1967; The Eternal Virgin (Eng. trans. of Valéry's La Jeune Parque), 1970; (with C. Fry) The Oxford Ibsen, vol III, Brand and Peer Gynt, 1972; Selected Poems of Takagi Kyozo, 1973; Camara Laye, The Guardian of the Word, 1980; Cold Mountain Poems (trans. Han Shan), 1980; To the Unknown God, 1982; An African in Greenland, 1982; The Bush Toads, 1982; A Room in the Woods, 1991; Ito-san, 1991; Painted Shadows, 1991. *Recreation*: standing in shafts of moonlight. *Address*: British Monomarks-Box 2780, London WC1N 3XX.

KIRKWOOD, family name of **Baron Kirkwood**.

KIRKWOOD, 3rd Baron *cr* 1951, of Bearsden; **David Harvie Kirkwood**; Senior Lecturer in Metallurgy, 1976–87, Hon. Senior Lecturer and Metallurgical Consultant, since 1987, Sheffield University; *b* 24 Nov. 1931; *s* of 2nd Baron Kirkwood and of Eileen Grace, *d* of Thomas Henry Boalch; *S* father, 1970; *m* 1965, Judith Rosalie, *d* of late John Hunt; three *d. Educ*: Rugby; Trinity Hall, Cambridge (MA, PhD); CEng. Lectr in Metallurgy, Sheffield Univ., 1962; Warden of Stephenson Hall, Sheffield Univ., 1974–80. Mem., Select Cttee on Sci. and Technology, H of L. *Heir*: *b* Hon. James Stuart Kirkwood [*b* 19 June 1937; *m* 1965, Alexandra Mary, *d* of late Alec Dyson; two *d*]. *Address*: 56 Endcliffe Hall Avenue, Sheffield S10 3EL. *T*: Sheffield (0742) 663107.

KIRKWOOD, Hon. Lord; Ian Candlish Kirkwood; a Senator of the College of Justice in Scotland, since 1987; *b* 8 June 1932; *o s* of late John Brown Kirkwood, OBE, and Mrs Constance Kirkwood, Edinburgh; *m* 1970, Jill Ingram Scott; two *s. Educ*: George Watson's Boys' Coll., Edinburgh; Edinburgh Univ.; Univ. of Michigan, USA. MA (Edin) 1952; LLB (Edin) 1954; LLM (Mich) 1956. Called to Scottish Bar, 1957; apptd Standing Junior Counsel to Scottish Home and Health Dept, 1963; QC (Scot.) 1970; formerly Mem. Rules Council (Court of Session). Pres., Wireless Telegraphy Appeal Tribunal in Scotland. Chm., Med. Appeal Tribunal in Scotland. *Recreations*: fishing, golf, chess. *Address*: 58 Murrayfield Avenue, Edinburgh EH12 6AY. *T*: 031–337 3468; Knockbrex House, near Borgue, Kirkcudbrightshire. *Club*: New (Edinburgh).

KIRKWOOD, Andrew Tristram Hammett; QC 1989; a Recorder, South East Circuit, since 1987; *b* 5 June 1944; *s* of late Maj. T. G. H. Kirkwood, RE and late Lady Faulks; *m* 1968, Penelope Jane (*née* Eaton); two *s* one *d. Educ*: Radley Coll., Abingdon, Oxon; Christ Church, Oxford (MA). Called to the Bar, Inner Temple, 1966. *Address*: 4 Paper Buildings, Temple, EC4Y 7EX. *T*: 071–353 3420. *Club*: MCC.

KIRKWOOD, Archy, (Archibald Johnstone Kirkwood); MP Roxburgh and Berwickshire, since 1983 (L/Alliance 1983–88, Lib Dem since 1988); b 22 April 1946; s of David Kirkwood and Jessie Barclay Kirkwood; m 1972, Rosemary Chester; one d one s. Educ: Cranhill School; Heriot-Watt University. BSc Pharmacy. Notary Public; Solicitor. Lib Dem convenor and welfare spokesman, 1988–. Trustee, Joseph Rowntree Reform Trust, 1985–. Address: House of Commons, SW1A 0AA. T: 071–219 3000.

KIRKWOOD, Ian Candlish; see Kirkwood, Hon. Lord.

KIRKWOOD, Prof. Kenneth, MA; Rhodes Professor of Race Relations, University of Oxford, 1954–86, Professor Emeritus, since 1986; Fellow of St Antony's College, 1954–86, Emeritus Fellow, since 1986, and Sub-Warden, 1968–71; b Benoni, Transvaal, 1919; s of late Thomas Dorman Kirkwood and Lily Kirkwood (née Bewley); m 1942, Deborah Burton, d of late Burton Ireland Collings and Emily Frances Collings (née Loram); three s three d. BA; BSc Rand. Captain, South African Engineer Corps, War of 1939–45; served in East Africa, North Africa and Italy (despatches). Lecturer, University of the Witwatersrand, 1947; Lecturer, University of Natal, 1948–51; Fellowship, University of London (Inst. of Commonwealth Studies), 1952); Carnegie Travelling Fellowship, USA, 1953; Senior Research Officer, Inst. of Colonial Studies, Oxford Univ., 1953; Organiser of Institute for Social Research, University of Natal, 1954. Chm. Regional Cttee, S African Inst. of Race Relations in Natal, 1954; UK Rep. SA Inst. of Race Relations, 1955–86. Investigation on behalf UNESCO into trends in race relations in British Non-Self-Governing Territories of Africa, 1958; Visiting Prof. of Race Relations (UNESCO), University Coll. of Rhodesia and Nyasaland, 1964; composed memorandum on meaning, and procedure for further study of 'racial discrimination,' for UN Div. of Human Rights, 1966–67; Mem., Africa Educational Trust, Oxfam, etc, 1955–. Chm., UK Standing Cttee on University Studies of Africa, 1975–78; Chm. of Trustees, Oxford Project for Peace Studies, 1983–; Hon. Pres., Oxford Br., UNA, 1986–. UK Official Observer, Rhodesian Elections, March 1980. Publications: The Proposed Federation of the Central African Territories, 1952; (contrib.) Lord Hailey's An African Survey, rev. edn 1957; (ed) St Antony's Papers: African Affairs, number 1, 1961; number 2, 1963; number 3, 1969; (contrib.) Vol. VIII, Cambridge History of the British Empire, 2nd edn 1963; (ed with E. E. Sabben-Clare and D. J. Bradley) Health in Tropical Africa during the Colonial Period, 1980; (ed and contrib.) Biosocial Aspects of Ethnic Minorities, 1983; Peace within States, Ethnic, Cultural and Racial Issues (lecture), 1989; booklets and articles on race relations and internat. affairs; relevant publication: Ethnicity, Empire and Race Relations: essays in honour of Kenneth Kirkwood, ed Anthony Kirk-Greene and John Stone, 1986. Address: St Antony's College, Oxford; 233 Woodstock Road, Oxford OX2 7AD. T: Oxford (0865) 515867.

KIRSOP, Arthur Michael Benjamin; Chairman, Forth Thyme Ltd, since 1976; b 28 Jan. 1931; s of Arthur Kirsop and Sarah (née Cauthery); m 1957, Patricia (née Cooper); two s. Educ: St Paul's Sch., Brazil; Glasgow Academy; Univ. of Oxford (BA). Joined English Sewing Cotton Co. Ltd, 1955; Area Sales Man., 1957; Export Sales Man., 1961; Man. Dir., Thread Div., 1964; Dir, English Sewing Cotton Co. Ltd, 1967 (later English Calico Ltd, then Tootal Ltd); Jt Man. Dir, 1973–76; Chief Exec., 1974–76; Chm., Tootal Ltd, 1975–76; Chm. and Man. Dir, Ollerenshaw Threads Ltd, 1981–86. Hon. Consul for the Netherlands, 1971–80. CBIM (FBIM 1973). Recreations: gardening, sport. Address: Devonshire House, 237 Ashley Road, Hale, Cheshire WA15 9NE. T: 061–941 5173. Clubs: MCC; Lancs CC.

KIRSTEIN, Lincoln Edward; President, School of American Ballet; General Director, New York City Ballet; b Rochester, NY, 4 May 1907; s of Louis E. Kirstein and Rose Stein; m 1941, Fidelma Cadmus; no c. Educ: Harvard Coll.; BS 1930. Edited Hound & Horn, 1927–34; founded School of American Ballet, 1934; founded and directed American Ballet Caravan, 1936–41; Third US Army (Arts, Monuments and Archives Section), 1943–45. Editor, The Dance Index, 1941–47. Benjamin Franklin Medal, RSA, 1981; Governor's Arts Award, NY State, 1984; US Presidential Medal of Freedom, 1984; Nat. Medal of Arts, 1985; Municipal Art Soc. Award, 1985. Publications: Flesh is Heir, 1932, repr. 1975; Dance, A Short History of Theatrical Dancing, 1935; Blast at Ballet, 1938; Ballet Alphabet, 1940; Drawings of Pavel Tchelitchew, 1947; Elie Nadelman Drawings, 1949; The Dry Points of Elie Nadelman, 1952; What Ballet is About, 1959; Three Pamphlets Collected, 1967; The Hampton Institute Album, 1968; Movement and Metaphor: four centuries of ballet, 1970; Lay This Laurel, 1974; Nijinsky, Dancing, 1975; Ballet: bias and belief, 1983; verse: Rhymes of a PFC (Private First Class), 1964; monographs: Gaston Lachaise, 1935; Walker Evans, 1938; Latin American Art, 1942; American Battle Art, 1945; Henri Cartier-Bresson, 1946; Dr William Rimmer, 1946; Elie Nadelman, 1948; Pavel Tchelitchew, 1964; W. Eugene Smith, 1970; George Tooker, 1983; Paul Cadmus, 1983; edited: The Classic Dance, Technique and Terminology, 1951; William Shakespeare: A Catalogue of the Works of Art in the American Shakespeare Festival Theater, 1964; Elie Nadelman, 1973; New York City Ballet, 1973; Thirty Years: the New York City Ballet, 1978; A. Hyatt Mayor: collected writings, 1983; Quarry: a collection in lieu of memoirs, 1986; The Poems of Lincoln Kirstein, 1987. Address: School of American Ballet, 144 West 66th Street, New York, NY 10023, USA. T: 877–0600.

KIRTON, Col Hugh, TD 1952; Vice Lord-Lieutenant, County Durham, 1978–87; b Plawsworth, Co. Durham, 7 Aug. 1910; 2nd s of late Hugh Kirton and Margaretta Kirton (née Darling). Educ: Durham Sch. Chartered Accountant, 1933. Army Service: commnd in Tyne Electrical Engrs (TA), 1937; RE(TA), 1937–40; RA(TA), 1940–45 and 1951–56, Lt Col 1945; Dep. Comdr, 31AA Bde(TA), 1959–61, Col 1959; Hon. Col 439 (Tyne) Lt AD Regt RA(TA), 1961–67. With Procter & Gamble Ltd, Newcastle upon Tyne, 1934–70, Dir, 1963–70; retired 1970. Mem., North Regional Health Authority, 1973–76; General Comr of Taxes (Newcastle upon Tyne), 1965–85. Mem. Council, Inst. of Chartered Accountants in England and Wales, 1966–70; Pres., Northern Soc. of Chartered Accountants, 1968–69. Mem., St John Council for Co. Durham, 1970–, Chm., 1974–86. DL: Northumberland 1961; Durham 1974; High Sheriff Co. Durham 1973–74. KStJ 1983. Recreations: golf, gardening. Address: Ovington, Plawsworth, Chester-le-Street, Co. Durham DH2 3LE. T: Durham (091) 3710261. Clubs: Army and Navy; Northern Counties (Newcastle upon Tyne); Brancepeth Castle Golf (Captain 1969–71).

KIRWAN, Sir (Archibald) Laurence (Patrick), KCMG 1972 (CMG 1958); TD; MLitt Oxon. Hon. Vice-President, Royal Geographical Society, since 1981 (Director and Secretary, 1945–75); b 13 May 1907; 2nd s of Patrick Kirwan, Cregg, County Galway, Ireland, and Mabel Norton; m 1st, 1932, Joan Elizabeth Chetwynd; one d; 2nd, 1949, Stella Mary Monck. Educ: Wimbledon Coll.; Merton Coll., Oxford. Asst Dir of the Archaeological Survey of Nubia, Egyptian Dept of Antiquities, 1929–34; Field Dir, Oxford Univ. Expeditions to Sudan, 1934–37; Tweedie Fellowship in Archæology and Anthropology, Edinburgh Univ., 1937–39. Boston and Philadelphia Museums, 1937; Exploratory journeys, Eastern Sudan and Aden Protectorate, 1938–39. TARO Capt., General Staff, 1939; Major, 1941; Lieut-Col 1943; Joint Staffs, Offices of Cabinet and Ministry of Defence, 1942–45; Hon. Lt-Col, 1957. Editor, Geographical Journal, 1945–78; Pres., Brit. Inst. in Eastern Africa, 1961–81, Hon. Life Pres. and Hon. Mem., 1981. Pres. (Section E), British Assoc. for the Advancement of Science, 1961–62; Member: Court of

Arbitration, Argentine-Chile Frontier Case, 1965–68 (Leader, Field Mission, 1966); Sec. of State for Transport's Adv. Cttee on Landscape Treatment of Trunk Roads, 1968–81 (Dep. Chm., 1970–80); UN Register of fact-finding experts, 1968–; Court, Exeter Univ., 1969–80; a Governor, Imperial Coll. of Science and Technology, 1962–81; British Academy/Leverhulme Vis. Prof., Cairo, 1976; Mortimer Wheeler Lectr, Brit. Acad., 1977. Fellow: University Coll. London; Imperial College of Science and Technology; Hon. Fellow, SOAS. Hon. Member: Geographical Societies of Paris, Vienna, Washington; Royal Inst. of Navigation; Institut d'Egypte; Internat. Soc. for Nubian Studies; Hon. Fellow, American Geographical Society. Founder's Medal, RGS, 1975. Knight Cross of the Order of St Olav, Norway; Jubilee Medal, 1977. Publications: (with W. B. Emery) Excavations and Survey between Wadi-es-Sebua and Adindan, 1935; (with W. B. Emery) Royal Tombs of Ballana and Qustal, 1938; Oxford University Excavations at Firka, 1938; The White Road (polar exploration), 1959; papers on archæology, historical and political geography, exploration, in scientific and other publications. Recreation: travel. Address: c/o Royal Geographical Society, SW7. Club: Geographical.

KIRWAN, Sir Laurence; see Kirwan, Sir A. L. P.

KISCH, (Alastair) Royalton; Conductor of Symphony Concerts; Artistic Director, Cork Street Art Gallery; b London, 20 Jan. 1919; s of late E. Royalton Kisch, MC and Pamela Kisch; m 1940, Aline, d of late Bruce Hylton Stewart and M. F. (Molly) Hylton Stewart; one s two d. Educ: Wellington Coll., Berks; Clare Coll., Cambridge. War service, Captain, KRRC (60th Rifles), 1940–46. Has conducted Royal Festival Hall concerts with London Philharmonic Orchestra, London Symphony Orchestra, Philharmonia Orchestra, Royal Philharmonic Orchestra, etc. Guest conductor to Hallé Orchestra, Birmingham Symphony Orchestra, etc. Has also conducted concerts in Europe with Paris Conservatoire Orchestra, Palestine Symphony Orchestra, Florence Philharmonic Orchestra, Athens State Symphony Orchestra, Pasdeloup Orchestra of Paris, Royal Opera House Orchestra of Rome, San Carlo Symphony Orchestra of Naples, Vienna Symphony Orchestra, etc. Has broadcast on BBC with London Symphony Orchestra, Royal Philharmonic Orchestra, and Philharmonia Orchestra. Gramophone recordings for Decca. Specialist in English and French paintings of 20th century. Recreations: good food and wine. Address: 2 Edwardes Square, Kensington, W8. T: 071–602 6655. Clubs: Athenæum, Hurlingham.

KISCH, John Marcus, CMG 1965; b 27 May 1916; s of late Sir Cecil Kisch, KCIE, CB, and late Myra Kisch; m 1951, Gillian Poyser; four d. Educ: Rugby Sch.; King's Coll., Cambridge. Assistant Principal: Board of Inland Revenue, 1938; Colonial Office, 1939. Served Royal Corps of Signals, 1939–45. Colonial Office, 1945; seconded E Africa High Commission, 1951; Kenya Govt 1952; Asst Sec., Colonial Office, 1956; seconded CRO, 1964; transferred Min. of Defence, 1965; MoD (Navy Dept), 1965–68; Asst Sec., ODM, later ODA, 1968–72; Planning Inspector, DoE, 1972–79. Address: Westwood, Dunsfold, Surrey GU8 4LN. T: Dunsfold (048649) 252; 21 Pembroke Square, W8 6PB. T: 071–937 8590.

KISCH, Royalton; see Kisch, A. R.

KISSIN, family name of Baron Kissin.

KISSIN, Baron cr 1974 (Life Peer), of Camden in Greater London; **Harry Kissin**; Life President: GPG plc (formerly Guinness Peat Group), since 1979; Lewis & Peat Holdings Ltd, since 1987; Director: Tycon SPA Venice, since 1975, and of other public and private companies in the City of London, since 1934; b 23 Aug. 1912; s of Israel Kissin and Reusi Kissin (née Model), both of Russian nationality; m 1935, Ruth Deborah Samuel, London; one s one d. Educ: Danzig and Switzerland. Dr of Law, Basle, Swiss lawyer until 1933. Chairman: Lewis & Peat Ltd, 1961–72; Guinness Peat Group, 1973–79; Lewis & Peat Holdings Ltd, 1982–87; Linfood Holdings, 1974–81; Esperanza International Services plc, 1970–83; Dir, Transcontinental Services NV, 1982–86. Dir, Royal Opera Hse, Covent Gdn, 1973–84; Mem., Royal Opera House Trust, 1974–87 (Chm., 1974–80). Chm. Council, ICA, 1968–75. Governor: Bezalel Acad. of Arts and Design, 1975–87; Hebrew Univ. of Jerusalem, 1980. Comdr, Ordem Nacional do Cruzeiro do Sul (Brazil), 1977; Chevalier, Légion d'honneur, 1981. Address: c/o House of Lords, SW1A 0PW. Clubs: Reform, East India, Devonshire, Sports and Public Schools.

KISSINGER, Henry Alfred; Bronze Star (US); Chairman, Kissinger Associates Inc., since 1982; Counselor to Center for Strategic and International Studies, since 1977 and Trustee, since 1987; b 27 May 1923; s of late Louis Kissinger and of Paula (née Stern); m 1st, 1949, Anne Fleischer (marr. diss. 1964); one s one d; 2nd, 1974, Nancy Maginnes. Educ: George Washington High Sch., NYC; Harvard Univ., Cambridge, Mass (BA 1950, MA 1952, PhD 1954). Emigrated to United States, 1938; naturalised, 1943. Served Army, 1943–46. Teaching Fellow, Harvard Univ., 1950–54; Study Director: Council on Foreign Relations, 1955–56: Rockefeller Bros Fund, 1956–58; Associate Professor of Govt, Harvard Univ., 1958–62, Prof. of Govt, 1962–71, and Faculty Mem., Center for Internat. Affairs, Harvard; Director: Harvard Internat. Seminar, 1951–69; Harvard Defense Studies Program, 1958–69; Asst to US President for Nat. Security Affairs, 1969–75; Secretary of State, USA, 1973–77; Univ. Prof. of Diplomacy, Sch. of Foreign Service, Georgetown Univ., 1977. Chm., Nat. Bipartisan Commn on Central America, 1983–84; Member: President's Foreign Intelligence Adv. Bd, 1984–90; Commn on Integrated Long-Term Strategy of the National Security Council and Defense Dept, 1986–88; Dir, Internat. Rescue Cttee, 1987–; Hon. Gov., Foreign Policy Assoc., 1985–. Chm., Internat. Adv. Bd, American Internat. Group, Inc.; Mem., Internat. Adv. Cttee, Chase Manhattan Bank, 1977–; Director: American Express Co.; Union Pacific Corp.; R. H. Macy and Co. Trustee, Metropolitan Mus. of Art, 1977–. Syndicated writer, Los Angeles Times, 1984–. (Jtly) Nobel Peace Prize, 1973; Presidential Medal of Freedom, 1977; Medal of Liberty, 1986. Publications: A World Restored: Castlereagh, Metternich and the Restoration of Peace, 1957; Nuclear Weapons and Foreign Policy, 1957 (Woodrow Wilson Prize, 1958; citation, Overseas Press Club, 1958); The Necessity for Choice: Prospects of American Foreign Policy, 1961; The Troubled Partnership: a reappraisal of the Atlantic Alliance, 1965; Problems of National Strategy: A Book of Readings (ed), 1965; American Foreign Policy: three essays, 1969, 3rd edn 1977; White House Years (memoirs), 1979; For the Record: selected statements 1977–1980, 1981; Years of Upheaval (memoirs), 1982; Observations: selected speeches and essays 1982–1984, 1985. Address: Suite 400, 1800 K Street, NW, Washington, DC 20006, USA; 350 Park Avenue, New York, NY 10022, USA. Clubs: Century, River (New York); Metropolitan (Washington); Bohemian (San Francisco).

KITAJ, R. B., RA 1991 (ARA 1984); artist; b Ohio, 29 Oct. 1932; m (wife decd); two c; m 1983, Sandra Fisher; one s. Educ: Cooper Union Inst., NY; Acad. of Fine Art, Vienna; Ruskin Sch. of Art, Oxford; RCA (ARCA). Part-time teacher: Camberwell Sch. of Art, 1961–63; Slade Sch., 1963–67; Visiting Professor: Univ. of Calif. at Berkeley, 1968; UCLA, 1970. Lives in London. One-man Exhibitions: Marlborough New London Gall., 1963, 1970; Marlborough Gall., NY, 1965, 1974; Los Angeles County Museum of Art, 1965; Stedelijk Mus., Amsterdam, 1967; Mus. of Art, Cleveland, 1967; Univ. of Calif, Berkeley, 1967; Galerie Mikro, Berlin, 1969; Kestner Gesellschaft, Hanover, 1970; Boymans-van-Beuningen Mus., Rotterdam, 1970; (with Jim Dine) Cincinnati Art Mus.,

Ohio, 1973; Marlborough Fine Art, 1977, 1980, 1985; Retrospective Exhibitions: Hirshhorn Museum, Washington, 1981; Cleveland Museum of Art, Ohio, 1981; Kunsthalle, Düsseldorf, 1982. Member: US Inst. of Arts and Letters, NY, 1982; Nat. Acad. of Design, NY, 1982. Hon. DLit London, 1982. *Publication:* First Diasporist Manifesto, 1989; *relevant publication:* R. B. Kitaj by M. Livingstone, 1985. *Address:* c/o Marlborough Fine Art (London) Ltd, 6 Albemarle Street, W1.

KITAMURA, Hiroshi; Japanese Ambassador to the Court of St James's, since 1991; *b* 20 Jan. 1920; *s* of Teiji and Fusako Kitamura; *m* 1953, Sachiko Ito; two *d. Educ:* Univ. of Tokyo (LLB 1951); Fletcher School of Law and Diplomacy, Medford, USA, 1952. Joined Min. of Foreign Affairs, Tokyo, 1953; postings to Washington DC, New York, New Delhi, London; Dir, Policy Planning Div., Res. and Planning Dept, Tokyo, 1974; Private Sec. to Prime Minister, 1974–76; Dep. Dir-Gen., Amer. Affairs Bureau, 1977–79; Consul-Gen., San Francisco, 1979–82; Dir-Gen., American Affairs Bureau, 1982–84; Dep. Vice Minister for Foreign Affairs, 1984–87; Dep. Minister, 1987–88; Ambassador to Canada, 1988–90. *Publication:* Psychological Dimensions of US-Japanese Relations, 1977. *Recreations:* traditional Japanese music, culinary arts, golf. *Address:* Japanese Embassy, 101–104 Piccadilly, W1V 9FN. *T:* 071–465 6500. *Club:* Sunningdale Golf.

KITCATT, Peter Julian, CB 1986; Speaker's Secretary, House of Commons, since 1986; *b* 5 Dec. 1927; *s* of late Horace Wilfred Kitcatt and Ellen Louise Kitcatt (*née* Julian); *m* 1952, Audrey Marian Aylen; three *s* two *d. Educ:* Borden Grammar Sch., Sittingbourne; King's Coll., Cambridge. RASC (2nd Lt) 1948. Asst Principal, Colonial Office, 1950–53; Asst Private Sec. to Sec. of State for the Colonies, 1953–54; Principal, Colonial Office, 1954–64; Sec. to HRH The Princess Royal on Caribbean Tour, 1960; Sec., E African Econ. and Fiscal Commn, 1960; HM Treasury: Principal, 1964; Asst Sec., 1966; RCDS, 1972; Under Sec., 1973, seconded to DHSS, 1975–78. *Recreation:* golf. *Club:* Croham Hurst Golf (Croydon).

KITCHEN, Frederick Bruford, CBE 1975; *b* Melbourne, 15 July 1912; *o s* of F. W. Kitchen, Malvern, Vic, Australia; *m* 1936, Una Bernice Sloss; two *s* one *d. Educ:* Melbourne Grammar Sch.; Melbourne Univ. (BSc). Joined family firm (in Melb.), J. Kitchen and Sons Pty Ltd, which had become a Unilever soap co., 1934. Sales Dir, Lever Bros Ltd, Canada, 1946. Came to England, 1949, as Chm., Crosfields (CWG) Ltd; Chm., Lever Bros Ltd, 1957; Marketing Dir, Lever Bros & Associates Ltd, 1960; Chm., Van den Berghs & Jurgens Ltd, 1962–74; Mem., Price Commn, 1973–75. Past Pres.: Incorp. Soc. of British Advertisers; Internat. Fedn of Margarine Assocs; Margarine and Shortening Manufacturers' Assoc. Associate, Royal Australian Chemical Inst. *Recreations:* gardening, dendrology. *Address:* Southdown, Yal Yal Road, Merricks, Victoria 3916, Australia. *T:* 059–898411. *Club:* Australian (Melbourne).

KITCHEN, Michael; actor; with Royal Shakespeare Co., since 1986; *b* 31 Oct. 1948; *s* of Arthur and Betty Kitchen; partner, Rowena Miller; one *s. Educ:* City of Leicester Boys' Grammar School. Entered acting profession, 1970; *stage includes:* seasons at Belgrade Theatre, Coventry, National Youth Theatre; Royal Court, 1971–73; Big Wolf, Magnificence, Skyvers; Young Vic, 1975: Othello, Macbeth, As You Like It, Charley's Aunt; National Theatre: Spring Awakening, 1974; Romeo and Juliet, 1974; State of Revolution, 1977; Bedroom Farce, 1977; No Man's Land, 1977; The Homecoming, 1978; Family Voices, 1981; On the Razzle, 1981; The Provok'd Wife, 1981; Rough Crossing, 1984; Royal Shakespeare Co: Romeo and Juliet, Richard II, 1986; The Art of Success, 1987; *films include:* The Bunker; Breaking Glass; Towards the Morning; Out of Africa; Home Run; The Russia House; Fools of Fortune; The Dive; *television series:* Freud, 1983; The Justice Game; Steven Hind; Divorce; *television films and plays include:* Caught on a Train; Benefactors; Ball-Trap; Pied Piper; numerous other TV and radio performances. *Recreations:* piano, guitar, flying, writing, tennis, riding. *Address:* c/o Markham & Froggatt Ltd, 4 Windmill Street, W1.

KITCHEN, Stanley, FCA; *b* 23 Aug. 1913; *s* of late Percy Inman Kitchen, OBE and Elizabeth Kitchen; *m* 1941, Jean Craig; two *d. Educ:* Rugby Sch. ACA 1937, FCA 1953. Army, 1939–46: Major, RASC. Sec., British Rollmakers Corp. Ltd, Wolverhampton, 1946–48; Partner, Foster & Stephens, later Touche Ross & Co., chartered accountants, Birmingham, 1948–81. Chm., STEP Management Services Ltd, 1978–85; Dir, Cobalt (UK) Ltd, 1986–. Birmingham and West Midlands Soc. of Chartered Accountants: Mem. Cttee, 1951–81; Sec., 1953–55; Pres., 1957–58; Inst. of Chartered Accountants in England and Wales: Mem. Council, 1966–81; Vice-Pres., 1974–75; Dep. Pres., 1975–76; Pres., 1976–77. *Publications:* Learning to Live with Taxes on Capital Gains, 1967; Important Aspects of Professional Partnerships, 1974. *Recreations:* gardening, golf. *Address:* 1194 Warwick Road, Knowle, Solihull, West Midlands B93 9LL. *T:* Knowle (0564) 772360. *Clubs:* Lansdowne; Birmingham, Chamber of Commerce (Birmingham).

KITCHENER OF KHARTOUM, and of Broome; 3rd Earl, *cr* 1914; **Henry Herbert Kitchener,** TD; DL; Viscount, *cr* 1902, of Khartoum; of the Vaal, Transvaal, and Aspall, Suffolk; Viscount Broome, *cr* 1914, of Broome, Kent; Baron Denton, *cr* 1914, of Denton, Kent; late Major, Royal Corps of Signals; *b* 24 Feb. 1919; *er s* of Viscount Broome (*d* 1928) and Adela Mary Evelyn (*d* 1986), *e d* of late J. H. Monins, Ringwould House, near Dover; *S* grandfather, 1937. *Educ:* Sandroyd Sch.; Winchester Coll.; Trinity Coll., Cambridge. DL Cheshire 1972. *Heir:* none. *Address:* Westergate Wood, Eastergate, Chichester, W Sussex PO20 6SB. *T:* Eastergate (0243) 543061. *Club:* Brooks's.

KITCHIN, Prof. Laurence Tyson; university teacher, translator and critic; *b* 21 July 1913; *s* of James Tyson Kitchin, MD Edin, and Eliza Amelia Kitchin (*née* Hopps); *m* 1955, Hilary Owen, artist; one step *s. Educ:* Bootham Sch.; King's Coll., London Univ. (BA 1934); Central Sch. of Drama. Served War, RAMC and briefly, RAEC, 1941–46. Mem., univ. debates team, USA, 1933; acted in Housemaster on stage and screen, 1936, and in films, incl. Pimpernel Smith; wrote extensively for BBC Third Prog., 1948–55; The Times corresp. and drama critic, 1956–62; numerous BBC talks on literature and drama, 1962–66; UK rep., Théâtre dans le Monde, UNESCO, 1961–66; Lectr, Bristol Univ. and Tufts, London, 1966–70; Vis. Prof. of Drama, Stanford Univ., Calif, 1970–72; Vis. Prof. of Liberal Arts, City Univ. of NY, 1972–73, Prof., 1973–76; Vis. Prof. of Shakespeare Studies, Simon Fraser Univ., Canada, 1976–77. Renaissance verse translations from Italian, French and Spanish, BBC, 1978–79. Selected as one of Outstanding Educators of America, 1973. *Publications:* Len Hutton, 1953; Three on Trial, 1959; Mid-Century Drama, 1960, 2nd edn 1962; Drama in the Sixties, 1966; Love Sonnets of the Renaissance (trans. from Italian, French, Spanish and Portuguese), 1990; radio scripts, incl.: The Trial of Lord Byron, 1948, Canada 1978; The Trial of Machiavelli, 1957; The Court Lady (trans. from Castiglione), 1954; The Elizabethan, Canada 1978; The Flaming Heart (Crashaw), 1981; contrib. Shakespeare Survey, Confronto Letterario, Mod. Lang. Rev., TLS, Encounter, Observer, Listener, THES. *Recreations:* tennis, televised soccer. *Address:* c/o National Westminster Bank, 1 St James's Square, SW1Y 4JT. *Club:* Athenæum.

KITCHING, Maj.-Gen. George, CBE 1945; DSO 1943; Canadian Military Forces, retired; President, Duke of Edinburgh's Award in Canada, 1967–70, President, British Columbia and Yukon Division, 1979–82; *b* 1910; *m* 1946, Audrey Calhoun; one *s* one *d. Educ:* Cranleigh; Royal Military College. 2nd Lieut Glos Regt, 1930. Served War of 1939–45 with Royal Canadian Regt and Loyal Edmonton Regt, in Sicily, Italy and North-West Europe; commanding Canadian Infantry Brigade, 1943; actg Maj.-Gen. comdg an armoured div., 1944 (despatches, DSO, CBE). Subseq. Vice-Chief of General Staff at Army Headquarters, Ottawa; Chairman of the Canadian Joint Staff in London, 1958–62; GOC Central Command, Canada, 1962–65, retd. Col Comdt of Infantry, 1974–78. Comr, Ont Pavilion, Osaka, Japan, for Expo 1970; Chief Comr, Liquor Control Bd of Ont, 1970–76. Chm. and Patron, Gurkha Welfare Appeal (Canada), 1974–; Patron: United World Colls, 1970 (Exec. Dir, Canadian Nat. Cttee, 1968–70); Sir Edmund Hillary Foundn (Canada), 1976–; Old Fort York, Toronto, 1975–. Commander: Order of Orange Nassau (Netherlands); Military Order of Italy; Order of Merit (US). *Publication:* Mud and Green Fields (autobiog.), 1986. *Address:* 3434 Bonair Place, Victoria, BC V8P 4V4, Canada.

KITCHING, John Alwyne, OBE 1947; FRS 1960; ScD (Cambridge); PhD (London); Professor of Biology, University of East Anglia, 1963–74, now Emeritus Professor; Dean of School of Biological Sciences, 1967–70; Leverhulme Fellowship, 1974; *b* 24 Oct. 1908; *s* of John Nainby Kitching; *m* 1933, Evelyn Mary Oliver; one *s* three *d. Educ:* Cheltenham Coll.; Trinity Coll., Cambridge. BA 1930, MA 1934, ScD 1956; PhD London. Lecturer: Birkbeck Coll., London, 1931; Edinburgh Univ., 1936; Bristol Univ., 1937; Rockefeller Fellow, Princeton Univ., 1938; Research in aviation-medical problems under Canadian Nat. Research Council, 1939–45; Reader in Zoology, University of Bristol, 1948–63. Hon. DSc NUI, 1983. *Publications:* contrib. Jl of Experimental Biol., Jl of Ecology, Jl of Animal Ecology, etc. *Recreations:* travel, gardening. *Address:* 29 Newfound Drive, Cringleford, Norwich NR4 7RY. *T:* Norwich (0603) 52886.

KITSON, family name of **Baron Airedale.**

KITSON, Alexander Harper, JP; Deputy General Secretary, Transport and General Workers Union, 1980–86; *b* 21 Oct. 1921; *m* 1942, Ann Brown McLeod; two *d. Educ:* Kirknewton Sch., Midlothian, Scotland. Lorry Driver, 1935–45; Trade Union official, 1945–86. Gen. Sec., Scottish Commercial Motormens' Union, 1959–71; Chm., Scottish TUC, 1966. Mem., Freight Integration Council, 1969–78. Mem. Nat. Exec. Cttee of Labour Party, 1968–86; Chm., Labour Party, 1980–81. Mem., War on Want Council, 1986–90. Dir, Lothian Region Transport Bd, 1986–; Member: Lothian Health Challenge Cttee, 1988–; Corstorphine Community Council, Edinburgh, 1989. Fellow, Scottish Council of Develt and Industry. *Address:* 47 Craigs Crescent, Edinburgh EH12 8HU.

KITSON, Gen. Sir Frank (Edward), GBE 1985; (CBE 1972; OBE 1968; MBE 1959); KCB 1980; MC 1955 and Bar 1958; DL; *b* 15 Dec. 1926; *s* of late Vice-Adm. Sir Henry Kitson, KBE, CB and Lady (Marjorie) Kitson (*née* de Pass); *m* 1962, Elizabeth Janet, *d* of Col C. R. Spencer, OBE, DL; three *d. Educ:* Stowe. 2nd Lt Rifle Bde, 1946; served BAOR, 1946–53; Kenya, 1953–55; Malaya, 1957; Cyprus, 1962–64; CO 1st Bn, Royal Green Jackets, 1967–69; Defence Fellow, University Coll., Oxford, 1969–70; Comdr, 39 Inf. Bde, NI, 1970–72 (CBE for gallantry); Comdt, Sch. of Infantry, 1972–74; RCDS, 1975; GOC 2nd Division, later 2nd Armoured Division, 1976–78; Comdt, Staff College, 1978–80; Dep. C-in-C, UKLF, and Inspector-Gen., TA, 1980–82; C-in-C, UKLF, 1982–85. ADC Gen. to the Queen, 1983–85. 2nd Bn, The Royal Green Jackets: Col Comdt, 1979–87; Rep. Col Comdt, 1982–85; Hon. Col, Oxford Univ. OTC, 1982–87. DL 1989. *Publications:* Gangs and Counter Gangs, 1960; Low Intensity Operations, 1971; Bunch of Five, 1977; Warfare as a Whole, 1987; Directing Operations, 1989. *Address:* c/o Lloyds Bank, Farnham, Surrey. *Club:* Boodle's.

KITSON, George McCullough; Principal, Central School of Speech and Drama, London, 1978–87; *b* Castlegore, Ireland, 18 May 1922; *s* of George Kitson and Anna May McCullough-Kitson; *m* 1951, Jean Evelyn Tyte; four *s. Educ:* early educn in Ireland; London Univ. (Dip. in Child Develt, 1947); Trent Park Coll. (Teachers' Cert., 1949). Associate, Cambridge Inst. of Educn, 1956; MEd Leicester, 1960. Served War, RAF, 1940–45; Navigator, Coastal Comd. Asst Master, schs in Herts, 1949–54; Dep. Headmaster, Broadfield Sch., Hemel Hempstead, Herts, 1954–56; Lectr in Educn, Leicester Coll. of Educn, 1956–66; Tutor i/c Annexe for Mature Teachers, Northampton, 1966–71; Dep. Principal, Furzedown Coll., London, 1971–76; Vice-Principal, Philippa Fawcett and Furzedown Coll., 1976–78. Member: Nat. Council of Drama Trng, 1978–88; Conference of Drama Schs, 1980– (Chm., 1980–87). *Publications:* (contrib.) Map of Educational Research, 1969; articles on educn, social psychol., and interprofessionalism in Forum, New Era, Educn for Teaching, and Brit. Jl of Educnl Psychol. *Recreations:* book collecting (first editions), sailing, walking, music, theatre. *Address:* 24 Dovercourt Road, Dulwich, SE22 8ST. *T:* 081–299 4516. *Club:* Arts.

KITSON, Prof. Michael William Lely; Director of Studies, Paul Mellon Centre for Studies in British Art, since 1986; *b* 30 Jan. 1926; *s* of Rev. Bernard Meredyth Kitson and Helen May (*née* Lely); *m* 1950, Annabella Leslie Cloudsley (separated 1971); two *s. Educ:* Gresham's School; King's Coll., Cambridge (BA 1950; MA 1953); Courtauld Inst. of Art, Univ. of London. Served Army, 1945–48; commd RE 1946 and attached SIME, Egypt. Asst Lectr in History of Art, Slade Sch. of Art, 1952–54; Courtauld Institute of Art: Lectr, 1955–67; Reader, 1967–78; Prof., 1978–85; Dep. Dir, 1980–85. Adjunct Prof., Yale Univ., 1986–. Vice-Chm., Turner Soc., 1984–. Fellow, Courtauld Inst. of Art, 1985. *Publications:* J. M. W. Turner, 1964; The Age of Baroque, 1966; Claude Lorrain: Landscape with the Nymph Egeria (Charlton Lecture), 1968; The Art of Claude Lorrain (exhibn catalogue), 1969; The Complete Paintings of Caravaggio, 1969; Rembrandt, 1969, 4th edn 1982; Turner Watercolours from the Collection of Stephen Courtauld, 1974; Claude Lorrain: Liber Veritatis, 1978; *edited exhibition catalogues:* La Peinture romantique anglaise et les préraphaélites, 1972; Salvator Rosa, 1973; British Painting 1600–1800, 1977; Zwei Jahrhunderte Englische Malerei, 1979; contrib. Burlington Magazine, Jl of Warburg and Courtauld Insts, Walpole Soc., Turner Studies, etc. *Address:* Paul Mellon Centre, 20 Bloomsbury Square, WC1A 2NP. *T:* 071–580 0311; 72 Halton Road, N1 2AD. *T:* 071–359 6757.

KITSON, Sir Timothy (Peter Geoffrey), Kt 1974; Chairman, Provident Financial Group, since 1983; *b* 28 Jan. 1931; *s* of late Geoffrey H. and of Kathleen Kitson; *m* 1959, Diana Mary Fattorini; one *s* two *d. Educ:* Charterhouse; Royal Agricultural College, Cirencester. Farmed in Australia, 1949–51. Member: Thirsk RDC, 1954–57; N Riding CC, 1957–61. MP (C) Richmond, Yorks, 1959–83; PPS to Parly Sec. to Minister of Agriculture, 1960–64; an Opposition Whip, 1967–70; PPS to the Prime Minister, 1970–74, to Leader of the Opposition, 1974–75. Chm., Defence Select Cttee, 1982–83. *Recreations:* shooting, hunting, racing. *Address:* Leases Hall, Leeming Bar, Northallerton, North Yorks. *T:* Bedale (0677) 2180.

KITTO, Rt. Hon. Sir Frank (Walters), AC 1983; KBE 1955; PC 1963; Chancellor, University of New England, 1970–81; Chairman, Australian Press Council, 1976–82; *b* 30 July 1903; *s* of late James W. Kitto, OBE, Austinmer, New South Wales; *m* 1928, Eleanor (*d* 1982), *d* of late Rev. W. H. Howard; four *d. Educ:* North Sydney High Sch.; Sydney Univ. BA 1924; Wigram Allen Scholar, G. and M. Harris Scholar and Pitt Cobbett Prizes in Faculty of Law, and LLB first class hons, 1927; called to Bar of NSW, 1927. KC (NSW), 1942. Challis Lecturer in Bankruptcy and Probate, Sydney Univ.,

1930–33; Justice of the High Court of Australia, 1950–70. Mem. Council, University of New England, 1967–81, Deputy Chancellor, 1968–70. Hon. DLitt New England, 1982; Hon. LLD Sydney, 1982. *Address:* Unit 18, Autumn Lodge, Armidale, NSW 2350, Australia. *T:* Armidale (067) 72–1189.

KITZINGER, Sheila Helena Elizabeth, MBE 1982; author, social anthropologist and birth educator; teacher and tutor, National Childbirth Trust; *b* 29 March 1929; *d* of Alec and Clare Webster; *m* 1952, Uwe Kitzinger, *qv*; five *d*. *Educ:* Bishop Fox's Girls' Sch., Taunton; Ruskin Coll., Oxford; St Hugh's Coll., Oxford; motherhood; educn continuing. Res. Asst, Dept of Anthropology, Univ. of Edinburgh, 1952–53 (MLitt 1954; thesis on race relations in Britain). Course Team Chm., Open Univ., 1981–83. Member: Panel of Advisers, National Childbirth Trust; Advisory Cttee, Midwives Information and Resource Service (Mem. Managing Bd, 1985–87); Chairperson, Foundation for Women's Health Res. and Develt, 1985–87; Consultant, Internat. Childbirth Educn Assoc.; Adviser: Baby Milk Coalition; Maternity Alliance. Pres., Oxford Br., Royal Coll. of Midwives; Patron, Seattle Sch. of Midwifery. MRSocMed. Joost de Blank Award, to do research on problems facing West Indian mothers in Britain, 1971–73. *Publications:* The Experience of Childbirth, 1962, 6th edn 1987; Giving Birth, 1971, rev. and expanded edn 1987; Education and Counselling for Childbirth, 1977; Women as Mothers, 1978; (ed with John Davis) The Place of Birth, 1978; Birth at Home, 1979; The Good Birth Guide, 1979; The Experience of Breastfeeding, 1979, 2nd edn 1987; Pregnancy and Childbirth, 1980; Sheila Kitzinger's Birth Book, 1981; (with Rhiannon Walters) Some Women's Experiences of Episiotomy, 1981; Episiotomy: physical and emotional aspects, 1981; Birth over Thirty, 1982; The New Good Birth Guide, 1983; Woman's Experience of Sex, 1983; (ed with Penny Simkin) Episiotomy and the Second Stage of Labor, 1984; Being Born, 1986; Celebration of Birth, 1987; Freedom and Choice in Childbirth (US edn Your Baby Your Way), 1987; Giving Birth: how it really feels, 1987; Some Women's Experiences of Epidurals, 1987; (ed) The Midwife Challenge, 1988; The Crying Baby, 1989; The New Pregnancy and Childbirth, 1989; Breastfeeding Your Baby, 1989; (with Celia Kitzinger) Talking With Children About Things That Matter, 1989; (contrib.) Ethnography of Fertility and Birth, 1982; (contrib.) The Management of Labour, 1985; (contrib.) Effective Care in Pregnancy and Childbirth, 1989. *Recreations:* painting, talking. *Address:* The Manor, Standlake, Oxfordshire OX8 7RH. *T:* Oxford (0865) 300266.
See also David Webster.

KITZINGER, Uwe, CBE 1980; President, Templeton College, Oxford, 1984–91; Emeritus Fellow, Nuffield College, Oxford, since 1976; *b* 12 April 1928; *o s* of late Dr G. and Mrs L. Kitzinger, Abbots Langley, Herts; *m* 1952, Sheila Helena Elizabeth Webster (*see* S. H. E. Kitzinger); five *d*. *Educ:* Watford Grammar Sch.; Balliol Coll. and New Coll. (Foundn Schol.), Oxford. 1st in Philosophy, Politics and Economics, MA, MLitt; Pres., Oxford Union, 1950. Economic Section, Council of Europe, Strasbourg, 1951–58; Nuffield College, Oxford: Research Fellow, 1956–62, Official Fellow, 1962–76; Acting Investment Bursar, 1962–64; Investment Bursar, 1964–76; Mem., Investment Cttee, 1962–88; Assessor of Oxford University, 1967–68. Visiting Prof.: of Internat. Relations, Univ. of the West Indies, 1964–65; of Government, at Harvard, 1969–70; at Univ. of Paris (VIII), 1970–73. Leave of absence as Adviser to Sir Christopher (later Lord) Soames, Vice-Pres. of the Commn of the European Communities, Brussels, 1973–75; Dean, INSEAD (European Inst. of Business Admin), Fontainebleau, 1976–80 (Mem. Board, 1976–83); Dir, Oxford Centre for Management Studies, 1980–84; Founding Pres., Templeton Coll., 1984. Founding Pres., Internat. Assoc. of Macro-Engineering Societies Inc., 1987–. Member: ODM Cttee for University Secondment, 1966–68; British Universities Cttee of Encyclopædia Britannica, 1967–73; Nat. Council of European Movement, 1974–76; Council, RIIA, 1973–85; Court, Cranfield Inst. of Technology, 1984–85. Consultant to various nat. and internat. orgns. Founding Chm., Cttee on Atlantic Studies, 1967–70. Member: Oxfam Council, 1981–84; Major Projects Assoc., 1981–91 (Founding Chm., 1981–86); Adv. Bd, Pace Univ., NY, 1982–90; Berlin Science Centre, 1983–; Acad. Adv. Bd, World Management Council, 1989–; Bd, Jean Monnet Foundn, Lausanne, 1990–. Trustee: European Foundn for Management Educn, Brussels, 1978–80; Oxford Trust for Music and the Arts, 1986–91. Chm., Oxford Radio Consortium, 1988–. Hon. LLD, Buena Vista, 1986. *Publications:* German Electoral Politics, 1960 (German edn, 1960); The Challenge of the Common Market, 1961 (Amer. edn, The Politics and Economics of European Integration, 1963, et al); Britain, Europe and Beyond, 1964; The Background to Jamaica's Foreign Policy, 1965; The European Common Market and Community, 1967; Commitment and Identity, 1968; The Second Try, 1968; Diplomacy and Persuasion, 1973 (French edn, 1974); Europe's Wider Horizons, 1975; (with D. E. Butler) The 1975 Referendum, 1976. Founding Editor, Jl of Common Market Studies, 1962–. *Recreations:* sailing, travel, old buildings. *Address:* Nuffield College, Oxford. *T:* Oxford (0865) 278500; Standlake Manor, near Witney, Oxon OX8 7RH. *T:* Oxford (0865) 300266, *Fax:* Oxford (0865) 300438; La Rivière, 11100 Bages, France. *T:* 68412960. *Clubs:* Reform, United Oxford & Cambridge University; Royal Thames Yacht.

KLARE, Hugh John, CBE 1967; *b* Berndorf, Austria, 22 June 1916; *yr s* of F. A. Klare; *m* 1946, Eveline Alice Maria, *d* of Lieut-Col J. D. Rankin, MBE. *Educ:* privately. Came to England, 1932. Served war in Middle East and Europe; Major. Dep. Dir, Economic Organisation Br., Brit. Control Commn for Germany, 1946–48; Sec., Howard League for Penal Reform, 1950–71; seconded to Coun. of Europe as Dep. Head, Div. of Crime Problems, 1959–61; Head of Div., 1971–72; Member of Council: Internat. Soc. of Criminology, 1960–66; Inst. for Study and Treatment of Delinquency, 1964–66; Nat. Assoc. for Care and Resettlement of Offenders, 1966–71. Chm. Planning Cttee, Brit. Congress on Crime, 1966. Member: Bd of Visitors, Long Lartin Prison, 1972–76; Gloucestershire Probation and Aftercare Cttee, 1972–85; Parole Board, 1972–74. Founder and Trustee, Cheltenham and N Cotswold Eye Therapy Trust, 1976–; Chm. of Trustees, Gloucestershire Arthritis Trust, 1987– (Trustee, 1984). A Governor, British Inst. of Human Rights, 1974–80. *Publications:* Anatomy of Prison, 1960; (ed and introd) Changing Concepts of Crime and its Treatment, 1966; (ed jtly) Frontiers of Criminology, 1967; People in Prison, 1972; contribs on crime and penology to Justice of the Peace. *Address:* 34 Herriots Court, St George's Crescent, Droitwich, Worcs WR9 8HJ. *T:* Droitwich (0905) 776316.

KLEEMAN, Harry, CBE 1984; Chairman, Kleeman Plastics group of companies, since 1968; *b* 2 March 1928; *s* of Max Kleeman and Lottie Bernstein; *m* 1955, Avril Lees; two *s* two *d*. *Educ:* Westminster Sch.; Trinity Coll., Cambridge. FPRI 1980. Director, O. & M. Kleemann Ltd, 1951–65. President, British Plastics Fedn, 1979–80; Chairman: Polymer Engineering Directorate, SERC, 1980–84; Plastics Processing EDC, NEDO, 1980–85; Small Firms Cttee, OFTEL, 1985–88; Council, Plastics & Rubber Inst., 1985–87; Adv. Bd, London Sch. of Polymer Technology, 1988–; Member: CBI Smaller Firms Council, 1982–91 (Vice-Chm., 1987–88, Chm., 1988–90); CBI Council, 1984–. Treasurer, Central British Fund for World Jewish Relief, 1969–. Member: Zoological Soc., 1950–; Royal Society of Arts, 1978–; Worshipful Co. of Horners, 1954– (Upper Warden, 1991). Prison Visitor. *Recreations:* horse riding, amateur radio. *Address:* 41 Frognal, NW3 6YD. *T:* 071–794 3366.

KLEIN, Bernat, CBE 1973; FCSD (FSIAD 1974); Chairman and Managing Director, Bernat Klein Ltd, since 1973; *b* 6 Nov. 1922; *s* of Lipot Klein and Serena Weiner; *m* 1951, Margaret Soper; one *s* two *d*. *Educ:* Senta, Yugoslavia; Bezalel Sch. of Arts and Crafts, Jerusalem; Leeds Univ. Designer to: Tootal, Broadhurst, Lee, 1948–49; Munrospun, Edinburgh, 1949–51; Chm. and Man. Dir, Colourcraft, 1952–62; Man. Dir of Bernat Klein Ltd, 1962–66; Chm. and Man. Dir, Bernat Klein Design Ltd, 1966–81. Member: Council of Industrial Design, Scottish Cttee, 1965–71; Royal Fine Art Commn for Scotland, 1980–87. Exhibitions of paintings: E-SU, 1965; Alwyn Gall., 1967; O'Hana Gall., 1969; Assoc. of Arts Gall., Capetown, Goodman Gall., Johannesburg, and O'Hana Gall., 1972; Laing Art Gall., Newcastle upon Tyne, 1977; Manchester Polytechnic, 1977. Hon. FRIAS, 1990. *Publications:* Eye for Colour, 1965; Design Matters, 1976. *Recreations:* reading, tennis, walking. *Address:* High Sunderland, Galashiels, Selkirkshire. *T:* Selkirk (0750) 20730.

KLEIN, Prof. Lawrence Robert; economist; Benjamin Franklin Professor, University of Pennsylvania, since 1968; *b* Omaha, 14 Sept. 1920; *s* of Leo Byron Klein and Blanche Monheit; *m* 1947, Sonia Adelson; one *s* three *d*. *Educ:* Univ. of Calif at Berkeley (BA); MIT (PhD 1944); Lincoln Coll., Oxford (MA 1957). Chicago Univ., 1944–47; Nat. Bureau of Econ. Res., NY, 1948–50; Michigan Univ., 1949–54; Oxford Inst. of Stats, 1954–58; Prof., 1958, University Prof., 1964, Univ. of Pennsylvania. Consultant: UNCTAD, 1966, 1967, 1975; UNIDO, 1973–75; Congressional Budget Office, 1977–; Council of Econ. Advisers, 1977–80. Mem., Commn on Prices, Fed. Res. Bd, 1968–70. Member: Adv. Bd, Strategic Studies Center, Stanford Res. Inst., 1974–76; Adv. Council, Inst. for Advanced Studies, Vienna, 1977–. Corresp. FBA, 1991; Fellow: Econometric Soc. (past Pres.); Amer. Acad. of Arts and Scis; Member: Nat. Acad. of Scis; Amer. Philosophical Soc.; Amer. Economic Assoc. (Past Pres.; J. B. Clark Medal, 1959). William F. Butler Award, NY Assoc. of Business Economists, 1975; Nobel Prize for Economics, 1980. *Publications:* The Keynesian Revolution, 1947; Textbook of Econometrics, 1953; An Econometric Model of the United States 1929–52, 1955; Wharton Econometric Forecasting Model, 1967; Essay on the Theory of Economic Prediction, 1968; (ed) Econometric Model Performance, 1976. *Address:* 1317 Medford Road, Wynnewood, Pa 19096, USA; University of Pennsylvania, Philadelphia, Pa 19104, USA.

KLEIN, Prof. Rudolf Ewald; Professor of Social Policy, University of Bath, since 1978; *b* 26 Aug. 1930; *o s* of Robert and Martha Klein; *m* 1957, Josephine Parfitt; one *d*. *Educ:* Bristol Grammar Sch.; Merton Coll., Oxford (Postmaster) (Gibbs Schol. 1950; MA). Leader Writer, London Evening Standard, 1952–62; Editor, 'The Week', Leader Writer, Home Affairs Editor, The Observer, 1962–72; Research Associate, Organisation of Medical Care Unit, London Sch. of Hygiene and Tropical Medicine, 1972–73; Sen. Fellow, Centre for Studies in Social Policy, 1973–78. Member: Wiltshire AHA, 1980–82; Bath DHA, 1982–84. Jt Editor, Political Quarterly, 1981–87. *Publications:* Complaints Against Doctors, 1973; (ed) Social Policy and Public Expenditure, 1974; (ed) Inflation and Priorities, 1975; (with Janet Lewis) The Politics of Consumer Representation, 1976; The Politics of the NHS, 1983; (ed with Michael O'Higgins) The Future of Welfare, 1985; (with Patricia Day) Accountabilities, 1987; (with Linda Challis *et al*) Joint Approaches to Social Policy, 1988; (with Patricia Day) Inspecting the Inspectorates, 1990; (with Neil Carter and Patricia Day) How organisations measure success, 1991; papers on public policy, health policy and public expenditure in various jls. *Recreations:* opera, cooking, football. *Address:* 3 Macaulay Buildings, Widcombe Hill, Bath BA2 6AS. *T:* Bath (0225) 310774.

KLEINDIENST, Richard Gordon; attorney; *b* 5 Aug. 1923; *s* of Alfred R. Kleindienst and late Gladys Love, Massachusetts; *m* 1948, Margaret Dunbar; two *s* two *d*. *Educ:* Harvard Coll. (*Phi Beta Kappa, magna cum laude*); Harvard Law Sch. Associate and Partner of Jennings, Strouss, Salmon & Trask, Phoenix, Arizona, 1950–57; Sen. Partner of Shimmel, Hill, Kleindienst & Bishop, 1958–Jan. 1969. Dep. Attorney-Gen. of the US, Jan. 1969–Feb. 1972; Actg Attorney-Gen. of the US, Feb. 1972–June 1972; Attorney-Gen. of the US, 1972–73, resigned 1973; private practice of law, Washington DC, 1973–75. Pres., Federal Bar Assoc., US, 1972– (was Pres. elect, Oct. 1971–72). Hon. Dr of Laws, Susquehanna Univ., 1973. *Publication:* Justice: the memoirs of Attorney General Richard G. Kleindienst, 1985. *Recreations:* golf, chess, classical music, art. *Address:* (home) 6138 W Miramar, Tucson, Arizona 85715, USA. *T:* 602–885–3150.

KLEINPOPPEN, Prof. Hans Johann Willi, FRSE; Professor of Experimental Physics, University of Stirling, since 1968 (Head of Physics Department, 1971–73; Director of Institute of Atomic Physics, 1975–81); *b* Duisburg, Germany, 30 Sept. 1928; *m* 1958, Renate Schröder. *Educ:* Univ. of Giessen (Dipl. Physics); Univ. of Tübingen. Dr re.nat. 1961. Habilitation, Tübingen, 1967; Vis. Fellow, Univ. Colorado, 1967–68; Vis. Associate Prof., Columbia Univ., 1968; Fellow, Center for Theoretical Studies, Univ. of Miami, 1972–73; Guest Prof., Bielefeld Univ., 1978–79; Vis. Fellow, Zentrum für interdisziplinäre Forschung, Bielefeld Univ., 1979–80. Chairman: Internat. Symposium on Physics of One- and Two-Electron Atoms (Arnold Sommerfeld Centennial Meml Meeting, Munich 1968); Internat. Symposium on Electron and Photon Interactions with Atoms, in honour of Ugo Fano, Stirling, 1974; Internat. Workshop on Coherence and Correlation in Atomic Collisions, University Coll., London, 1978; Internat. Symp. on Amplitudes and State Parameters in Atomic Collisions, Kyoto, 1979; Co-Dir, Advanced Study Inst. on Fundamental Processes in Energetic Atomic Collisions, Maratea, Italy, 1982; Dir, Advanced Study Inst. on Fundamental Processes in Atomic Collision Physics, S Flavia, Sicily, 1984; Co-Dir, Advanced Study Inst. on Fundamental Processes on Atomic Dynamics, Maratea, Italy, 1987. FInstP 1969; Fellow Amer. Physical Soc. 1969; FRAS 1974; FRSE 1987. *Publications:* edited: (with F. Bopp) Physics of the One- and Two-Electron Atoms, 1969; (with M. R. C. McDowell) Electron and Photon Interactions with Atoms, 1976; Progress in Atomic Spectroscopy, (with W. Hanle) Vol. A 1978 and Vol. B 1979, (with H.-J. Beyer) Vol. C 1984 and Vol. D 1987; (with J. F. Williams) Coherence and Correlations in Atomic Collisions, 1980; (jtly) Inner-Shell and X-Ray Physics of Atoms and Solids, 1981; (jtly) Fundamental Processes in Energetic Atomic Collisions, 1983; (jtly) Fundamental Processes in Atomic Collision Physics, 1985; (jtly) Fundamental Processes in Atomic Dynamics, 1988; (with P. G. Burke) series editor, Physics of Atoms and Molecules; papers in Zeitschr. f. Physik, Z. f. Naturf., Z. f. Angew Physik, Physikalische Blätter, Physical Review, Jl of Physics, Physics Letters, Internat. Jl of Quantum Chemistry; Physics Reports, Advances of Atomic and Molecular Physics, Applied Physics; *festschrift:* (ed H. J. Beyer, K. Blum and R. Hippler) Coherence in Atomic Collision Physics, 1988. *Address:* 27 Kenningknowes Road, Stirling.

KLEINWORT, Sir Kenneth (Drake), 3rd Bt *cr* 1909; Director, Kleinwort Benson Group (formerly Kleinwort, Benson, Lonsdale plc), since 1976; *b* 28 May 1935; *s* of Ernest Greverus Kleinwort (*d* 1977) (4th *s* of 1st Bt) and Joan Nightingale Kleinwort, MBE, JP, DL (*d* 1991), *d* of late Prof. Arthur William Crossley, CMG, CBE, FRS; *S* uncle, 1983; *m* 1st, 1959, Lady Davina Pepys (*d* 1973), *d* of 7th Earl of Cottenham; one *s* one *d*; 2nd, 1973, Madeleine Hamilton, *e d* of Ralph Taylor; two *s* one *d*. *Educ:* Eton College; Grenoble Univ. Joined Kleinwort Sons & Co. Ltd, 1955; Director: Kleinwort Benson (Europe) SA, Brussels, 1970–; Banque Kleinwort Benson SA, Geneva, 1971–; Kleinwort

Benson Ltd, 1971–76; Exec. Dir, Trebol International Corp., USA, 1978–; Pres., Interalia Leasing SA, Chile, 1980–. Council Mem., WWF International, Switzerland, 1978–; Council Mem. and Hon. Treas., Wildfowl and Wetlands Trust, UK, 1982–. *Recreations:* travel, photography, skiing, tennis. *Heir: s* Richard Drake Kleinwort, [*b* 4 Nov. 1960; *m* 1989, Lucinda, *d* of William Shand Kydd]. *Address:* La Massellaz, 1126 Vaux-sur-Morges, Switzerland. *T:* (4121)–802–41–48.

KLEVAN, Rodney Conrad, QC 1984; a Recorder of the Crown Court, since 1980; *b* 23 May 1940; *s* of Sidney Leopold Klevan and late Florence Klevan (*née* Eaton); *m* 1968, Susan Rebecca (*née* Lighthill); two *s* one *d. Educ:* Temple Primary School; Manchester Central Grammar School; Birmingham Univ. (LLB Hons 1962). Pres., Birmingham Univ. Guild of Undergraduates, 1962–63. Called to the Bar, Gray's Inn, 1966; Deputy Circuit Judge, 1977. *Recreations:* theatre, television, following the fortunes of Lancashire CCC. *Address:* Beech House, 45 Manor Road, Bramhall, Stockport, Cheshire. *T:* 061–485 1847.

KLIBANSKY, Raymond, MA, PhD; FRSC; FRHistS; Frothingham Professor of Logic and Metaphysics, McGill University, Montreal, 1946–75, now Emeritus Professor; Fellow of Wolfson College, Oxford, since 1981; *b* Paris, 15 Oct. 1905; *s* of late Hermann Klibansky. *Educ:* Paris; Odenwald Sch.; Univs of Kiel, Hamburg, Heidelberg. PhD, 1928; MA Oxon by decree, 1936. Asst, Heidelberg Acad., 1927–33; Lecturer in Philosophy: Heidelberg Univ., 1931–33; King's Coll., London, 1934–36; Oriel Coll., Oxford, 1936–48; Forwood Lectr in Philosophy of Religion, Univ. of Liverpool, 1938–39. Political Intelligence Dept, FO, 1941–46. Dir of Studies, Warburg Inst., Univ. of London, 1947–48. Vis. Prof. of History of Philosophy, Université de Montréal, 1947–68; Mahlon Powell Prof., Indiana Univ., 1950; Cardinal Mercier Prof. of Philosophy, Univ. of Louvain, 1956; Vis. Prof. of Philosophy, Univ. of Rome, 1961, Univ. of Genoa, 1964, Univ. of Tokyo, 1971; Prof. Emeritus, Heidelberg Univ., 1975–, Hon. Senator, 1986–. President: Inst. Internat. de Philosophie, Paris, 1966–69 (Hon. Pres. 1969–); Société Internationale pour l'étude de la Philos. Médiévale, Louvain, 1968–72 (Hon. Pres., 1972–); Canadian Soc. for History and Philosophy of Science, 1959–72 (Pres. Emeritus, 1972–); Internat. Cttee for Anselm Studies, 1970–. Fellow: Accademia Nazionale dei Lincei, Rome; Acad. of Athens; Académie Internationale d'Histoire des Sciences, Paris; Iranian Acad. of Philosophy, Teheran; Accad. Mediterranea delle Scienze, Catania; Acad. dei Dafnici e degli Zelanti; Acireale; Corresponding Fellow: Mediaeval Acad. of America; Heidelberg Acad. of Scis; Deutsche Akad. für Sprache und Dichtung, Darmstadt. Hon. Member: Allgemeine Gesellsch. für Philosophie in Deutschland; Assoc. des Scientifiques de Roumanie, Bucarest; Hon. Foreign Mem., Amer. Acad. of Arts and Scis. Hon. Fellow: Oriel Coll., Oxford; Warburg Inst., Univ. of London; Accad. Ligure delle Scienze, Genoa; Canadian Mediterranean Inst., Athens, Rome, Cairo. Guggenheim Foundation Fellow, 1954 and 1965; Vis. Fellow, Wolfson Coll., Oxford, 1976–78. Dir, Canadian Academic Centre in Italy, Rome, 1980. Mem. Exec. Council, Union Académique Internationale, 1978–80. Comité Directeur, Fedn Internat. des Socs de Philosophie, 1958–83. DPhil *hc:* Marburg; Ottawa. Gauss Medal, Brunswick, 1990. Gen. Editor, Corpus Platonicum Medii Aevi, (Plato Latinus and Plato Arabus), Union Académique Internat., 1937–; Joint Editor and contributor to: Magistri Eckardi Opera Latina, 1933–36; Philosophy and History, 1936; Mediaeval and Renaissance Studies, 1941–68; Editor: Philosophical Texts, 1951–62; Philosophy and World Community, 1957–81; Philosophy in the Mid-Century, 1958–59; Contemporary Philosophy, 1968–71; Dir, Bibliographie de la Philosophie, 35 vols, 1954–90. *Publications:* Ein Proklos-Fund und seine Bedeutung, 1929; Heidelberg Acad. edn of Opera Nicolai de Cusa, 5 vols, 1929–82; The Continuity of the Platonic Tradition, 1939, enlarged 4th edn incl. Plato's Parmenides in the Middle Ages and the Renaissance, 1982; (with E. Panofsky and F. Saxl) Saturn and Melancholy, 1964 (enl. French and German edn, 1989–90); articles in Jahresberichte d. Heidelberger Akademie, Proceedings of British Acad., Enciclopedia Italiana, and elsewhere. *Address:* Wolfson College, Oxford OX2 6UD.

KLOOTWIJK, Jaap; Director: The Flyfishers' Co. Ltd, since 1985; Grove Holdings Ltd, since 1991; *b* 16 Nov. 1932; *s* of J. L. Klootwijk and W. J. Boer; *Educ:* Rotterdam Grammar Sch.; Technological Univ., Delft (MSc Mech. Eng., 1956). Lieut Royal Netherlands Navy, 1956–58. Joined Royal Dutch/Shell Gp, 1958; worked in various capacities in Holland, UK, France, Switzerland, Sweden, Algeria, Kenya; Area Co-ordinator, SE Asia, 1976–79; Man. Dir, Shell Internat. Gas Ltd, 1979–82; Jt Man. Dir, Shell UK, 1983–88; Man. Dir, Shell UK Oil, 1983–88; Chm., UK Oil Pipelines, 1983–88. Pres., UK Petroleum Industry Assoc., 1985–87. FRSA 1986. *Recreations:* deer-stalking, shooting, fishing, reading. *Address:* 26 Manor House Court, Warwick Avenue, W9 2PZ. *T:* 071–289 4276. *Club:* Flyfishers' (Pres., 1985–87).

KLUG, Sir Aaron, Kt 1988; PhD (Cantab); FRS 1969; Director, Medical Research Council Laboratory of Molecular Biology, Cambridge, since 1986 (member of staff, since 1962, Joint Head, Division of Structural Studies, 1978–86); Fellow of Peterhouse, since 1962; *b* 11 Aug. 1926; *s* of Lazar Klug and Bella Silin; *m* 1948, Liebe Bobrow, Cape Town, SA; two *s. Educ:* Durban High Sch.; Univ. of the Witwatersrand (BSc); Univ. of Cape Town (MSc). Junior Lecturer, 1947–48; Research Student, Cavendish Laboratory, Cambridge, 1949–52; Rouse-Ball Research Studentship, Trinity Coll., Cambridge, 1949–52; Colloid Science Dept, Cambridge, 1953; Nuffield Research Fellow, Birkbeck Coll., London, 1954–57; Head, Virus Structure Research Group, Birkbeck Coll., 1958–61. Hon. Prof., Univ. of Cambridge, 1989. Lectures: Carter-Wallace, Princeton, 1972; Leeuwenhoek, Royal Soc., 1973; Dunham, Harvard Medical Sch., 1975; Harvey, NY, 1979; Lane, Stanford Univ., 1983; Silliman, Yale Univ., 1985; Nishina Meml, Tokyo, 1986; Pauli, ETH Zürich, 1986; Cetus, Univ. of California, Berkeley, 1987; Konrad Bloch, Harvard, 1988. For. Associate, Nat. Acad. of Scis, USA, 1984; For. Mem., Max Planck Soc., Germany, 1984; For. Hon. Mem., Amer. Acad. of Arts and Scis, 1969; For. Associate Acad. des Scis, Paris, 1989. Hon. FRCP, 1987. Hon. Fellow, Trinity Coll., Cambridge, 1983. Hon. DSc: Chicago, 1978; Columbia Univ., 1978; Dr *hc* Strasbourg, 1978; Hon. Dsc: Witwatersrand, 1984; Hull, 1985; St Andrews, 1987; Hon. PhD Jerusalem, 1984; Hon. Dr Fil. Stockholm, 1980. Heineken Prize, Royal Netherlands Acad. of Science, 1979; Louisa Gross Horwitz Prize, Columbia Univ., 1981; Nobel Prize in Chemistry, 1982; Gold Medal of Merit, Univ. of Cape Town, 1983; Copley Medal, Royal Soc., 1985; Harden Medal, Biochem. Soc., 1985; Baly Medal, RCP, 1987. *Publications:* papers in scientific jls. *Recreations:* reading, gardening. *Address:* 70 Cavendish Avenue, Cambridge. *T:* Cambridge (0223) 248959.

KLYBERG, Rt. Rev. Charles John; *see* Fulham, Bishop Suffragan of.

KLYNE, Dame Barbara Evelyn; *see* Clayton, Dame B. E.

KNAGGS, Kenneth James, CMG 1971; OBE 1959; formerly overseas civil servant; *b* 3 July 1920; *e s* of late James Henry Knaggs and Elsie Knaggs (*née* Walton); *m* 1945, Barbara, *d* of late Ernest James Page; two *s. Educ:* St Paul's Sch., London. Served War, 1939–46 (Major). Northern Rhodesia Civil Service, 1946; Sec. to Govt, Seychelles, 1955 (Actg Governor, 1957–58); Northern Rhodesia: Asst Sec., 1960; Under Sec., 1961; Permanent Sec., Min. of Finance and subseq. the same in Zambia, 1964; retd 1970.

European Rep. and Manager, Zambia Airways, 1970–72; Consultant, Commonwealth Develt Corp., 1974–87. *Recreations:* walking, gardening, cooking. *Address:* High House Farm, Earl Soham, near Framlingham, Suffolk IP13 7SN. *T:* Earl Soham (072882) 416.

KNAPMAN, Dr Paul Anthony; HM Coroner for Westminster, since 1980 (Jurisdiction of Inner West London); *b* 5 Nov. 1944; *s* of Frederick Ethelbert and Myra Knapman; *m* 1970, Penelope Jane Cox; one *s* three *d. Educ:* Epsom Coll.; King's Coll., London; St George's Hosp. Med. Sch. (MB, BS 1968). MRCS, LRCP 1968; DMJ 1975. Called to the Bar, Gray's Inn, 1972. Dep. Coroner for Inner W London, 1975–80. Hon. Lectr in Med. Jurisprudence: St George's Hosp. Med. Sch., 1978–; St Mary's Hosp. Med. Sch., 1981–; Middlesex and UCH Med. Sch., 1981–; Hon. Sen. Lectr in Community Medicine, Westminster and Charing Cross Med. Sch., 1987–. Pres., S Eastern England Coroners' Soc., 1980. Gov., London Nautical Sch., 1981–. Liveryman, Worshipful Soc. of Apothecaries. *Publications:* (jtly) Coronership: the law and practice on coroners, 1985; Medicine and the Law, 1989; Casebook on Coroners, 1989; papers on medico-legal subjects. *Recreations:* squash, sailing. *Address:* Westminster Coroner's Court, Horseferry Road, SW1P 2ED. *T:* 071–834 6515. *Clubs:* Athenæum; Royal Torbay Yacht.

KNAPMAN, Roger Maurice; MP (C) Stroud, since 1987; chartered surveyor, farmer; *b* 20 Feb. 1944; *m* 1967, Carolyn Trebell (*née* Eastman); one *s* one *d. Educ:* Royal Agricl Coll., Cirencester. PPS to Min. of State for Armed Forces, 1991. Vice-Chm., Cons. backbench European Affairs Cttee, 1989–90. FRICS 1967. *Address:* House of Commons, SW1A 0AA; (office) c/o Stroud Conservative Association, Carlton Gardens, London Road, Stroud, Glos GL5 2AH.

KNAPP, David; *see* Knapp, J. D.

KNAPP, Edward Ronald, CBE 1979; Managing Director, Timken Europe, 1973–85, retired; *b* 10 May 1919; *s* of Percy Charles and Elsie Maria Knapp; *m* 1942, Vera Mary Stephenson; two *s* two *d. Educ:* Cardiff High Sch.; St Catharine's Coll., Cambridge (MA 1940); Harvard Business Sch. (AMP 1954). Served RNVR, Special Branch, Lt-Comdr, 1940–46: HMS Aurora, 1941–44; US Naval Research, Anacostia, 1944–46. Joined British Timken, 1946, Man. Dir, 1969; Dir, Timken Co., USA, 1976. Technical and Management Educnl Governor, Nene Coll., 1953–. Pres., Northampton RFC, 1986–88. *Recreations:* gardening, golf; played Rugby for Wales, 1940, Captain of Cambridge Univ. 1940 and Northampton RFC, 1948. *Address:* The Elms, 1 Millway, Duston, Northampton NN5 6ER. *T:* Northampton (0604) 584737. *Clubs:* East India, Devonshire, Sports and Public Schools; Northampton and County; Hawks (Cambridge).

KNAPP, James; General Secretary, Rail, Maritime and Transport Union, since 1990 (National Union of Railwaymen, 1983–90); *b* 29 Sept. 1940; *s* of James and Jean Knapp; *m* 1965, Sylvia Florence Yeomans; one *d. Educ:* Hurlford Primary Sch.; Kilmarnock Academy. British Rail employee (signalman), 1955–72; Hurlford NUR Branch Secretary, 1961–65; Sec., Amalgamated Kilmarnock and Hurlford NUR Br., 1965–72; Glasgow and W Scotland NUR Dist Council Sec., 1970–72; full time Divisional Officer, NUR, 1972–81; Headquarters Officer, NUR, 1981–82. Member: TUC Gen. Council, 1983–; ITF Exec. Bd, 1983–. Dir, Trade Union Unit Trust, 1984–; Pres., Unity Trust Bank, 1989– (Dir, 1984–). *Recreations:* walking, soccer, countryside. *Address:* 2 Midsummer Hill, Kennington, near Ashford, Kent.

KNAPP, (John) David, OBE 1986; Director of Conservative Political Centre, 1975–88; an Assistant Director, Conservative Research Department, 1979–88; *b* 27 Oct. 1926; *s* of late Eldred Arthur Knapp and Elizabeth Jane Knapp; *m* 1st, 1954, Dorothy Ellen May (*née* Squires) (marr. diss.); one *s*; 2nd, 1980, Daphne Monard, OBE, *widow* of Major S. H. Monard. *Educ:* Dauntsey's Sch., Wilts; King's Coll., London (BA Hons). Dir, Knapp and Bates Ltd, 1950–54. Vice-Chm., Fedn of University Conservative and Unionist Assoc., 1948–49; Conservative Publicity and Political Educn Officer, Northern Area, 1952–56; Political Educn Officer, NW Area, 1956–61, and Home Counties N Area, 1961; Dep. Dir, Conservative Political Centre, 1962–75. Member (C), Hampshire CC, 1989–. *Recreations:* philately, walking cavalier spaniels. *Address:* 71 Kirby Road, Portsmouth, Hants PO2 0PF. *T:* Portsmouth (0705) 663709. *Club:* Cosham Conservative.

KNAPP, Trevor Frederick William Beresford; Assistant Under Secretary of State (Supply and Organisation) (Air), Ministry of Defence, since 1988; *b* 26 May 1937; *s* of Frederick William Knapp and Linda Knapp (*née* Poffley); *m* 1964, Margaret Fry; one *s* one *d. Educ:* Christ's Hospital; King's College London (BSc 1958). ARIC 1960. Ministry of Aviation, 1961; Sec., Downey Cttee, 1965–66; Sec., British Defence Research and Supply Staff, Canberra, 1968–72; Asst Sec., MoD, 1974; GEC Turbine Generators Ltd, 1976; Central Policy Review Staff, 1977–79; Under-Sec., MoD, 1983; Dir Gen. (Marketing), MoD, 1983–88. *Address:* c/o Ministry of Defence, Main Building, Whitehall, SW1A 2HB.

KNAPP-FISHER, Rt. Rev. Edward George; Hon. Assistant Bishop, diocese of Chichester, since 1987; Custos of St Mary's Hospital, Chichester, since 1987; *b* 8 Jan. 1915; *s* of late Rev. George Edwin and Agatha Knapp-Fisher; *m* 1965, Joan, *d* of late R. V. Bradley. *Educ:* King's School, Worcester; Trinity College, Oxford (MA). Assistant Curate of Brighouse, Yorks, 1939; Chaplain, RNVR, 1942; Chaplain of Cuddesdon College, 1946; Chaplain of St John's College, Cambridge, 1949; Vicar of Cuddesdon and Principal of Cuddesdon Theological College, 1952–60; Bishop of Pretoria, 1960–75; Canon and Archdeacon of Westminster, 1975–87; Sub-Dean, 1982–87; Asst Bishop, Dio. Southwark 1975–87, Dio. London 1976–87. Member, Anglican Roman-Catholic Preparatory Commission, 1967–68; Member, Anglican-Roman Catholic Internat. Commn, 1969–81. *Publications:* The Churchman's Heritage, 1952; Belief and Prayer, 1964; To be or not to be, 1968; Where the Truth is Found, 1975; (ed jtly and contrib.) Towards Unity in Truth, 1981; Eucharist, Many-Sided Mystery, 1988. *Recreations:* walking, travel, gardening. *Address:* 2 Vicars' Close, Canon Lane, Chichester, West Sussex PO19 1PT. *T:* Chichester (0243) 789219.

KNARESBOROUGH, Bishop Suffragan of, since 1986; Rt. Rev. Malcolm James Menin; *b* 26 Sept. 1932; *s* of Rev. James Nicholas Menin and Doreen Menin; *m* 1958, Jennifer Mary Cullen; one *s* three *d. Educ:* Dragon School; St Edward's School; University Coll., Oxford (MA); Cuddesdon Coll. Curate: Holy Spirit, Southsea, 1957–59; St Peter and St Paul, Fareham, 1959–62; Vicar of St James, Norwich, later St Mary Magdalene with St James, Norwich, 1962–86; RD Norwich East, 1981–86; Hon. Canon, Norwich Cathedral, 1982–86. *Recreations:* walking, photography, carpentry. *Address:* 16 Shaftesbury Avenue, Leeds LS8 1DT. *T:* Leeds (0532) 664800.

KNATCHBULL, family name of **Baron Brabourne** and **Countess Mountbatten of Burma.**

KNEALE, (Robert) Bryan (Charles), RA 1974 (ARA 1970); sculptor; Professor of Drawing, Royal College of Art, since 1990; *b* 19 June 1930; *m* 1956, Doreen Lister; one *s* one *d. Educ:* Douglas High Sch.; Douglas Sch. of Art, IOM; Royal Academy Schools: Rome prize, 1949–51; RA diploma. Tutor, RCA Sculpture Sch., 1964–; Head of Sculpture Sch., Hornsey, 1967; Assoc. Lectr, Chelsea Sch. of Art, 1970. Fellow RCA, 1972; Head of

Sculpture Dept, RCA, 1985–90 (Sen. Tutor, 1980–85); Prof. of Sculpture, RA, 1985–90 (Master of Sculpture, 1982–85). Member: Fine Art Panels, NCAD, 1964–71, Arts Council, 1971–73, CNAA, 1974–82; Chm., Air and Space, 1972–73. *Organised:* Sculpture '72, RA, 1972; Battersea Park Silver Jubilee Sculpture, 1977 (also exhibited); Sade Exhbn, Cork, 1982. *Exhibitions:* at Redfern Gallery, 1954, 1956, 1958, 1960, 1962, 1964, 1967, 1970, 1976, 1978, 1981; 1983; John Moores, 1961; Sixth Congress of Internat. Union of Architects, 1961; Art Aujourd'hui, Paris, 1963; Battersea Park Sculpture, 1963, 1966; Profile III Bochum, 1964; British Sculpture in the Sixties, Tate Gall., 1965; Whitechapel Gall. 1966 (retrospective), 1981; Structure, Cardiff Metamorphis Coventry, 1966; New British Painting and Sculpture, 1967–68; City of London Festival, 1968; Holland Park, Sculpture in the Cities, Southampton, and British Sculptors, RA, 1972; Holland Park, 1973; Royal Exchange Sculpture Exhibition, 1974; New Art, Hayward Gallery, 1975; Sculpture at Worksop, 1976; Taranman Gall., 1977, 1981; Serpentine Gall., 1978; Monumental Sculpture for Manx Millenium, Ronaldsway, Isle of Man, 1979; Compass Gall., Glasgow, 1981; 51 Gall., Edinburgh, 1981; Bath Art Fair, 1981; Henry Moore Gall., RCA (retrospective), 1986; Fitzwilliam Mus., 1987; Sala Uno, Rome, 1988; Chichester Fest., 1988; Nat. History Museum, Taiwan; New Art Centre, 1990. Arts Council Tours, 1966–71. *Collections:* Arts Council of Gt Britain; Contemp. Art Soc.; Manx Museum; Leics Educn Authority; Nat. Galls of Victoria, S Australia and New Zealand; City Art Galls, York, Nottingham, Manchester, Bradford and Leicester; Tate Gall.; Beaverbrook Foundn, Fredericton; Museum of Modern Art, Sao Paulo, Brazil; Bahia Museum, Brazil; Oriel Coll., Oxford; Museum of Modern Art, New York; City Galleries, Middlesbrough, Birmingham, Wakefield; Fitzwilliam Museum, Cambridge; W Riding Educn Authority; Unilever House Collection; Walker Art Gallery. *Address:* 10A Muswell Road, N10 2BG. *T:* 081–444 7617.

KNEBWORTH, Viscount; Philip Anthony Scawen Lytton; *b* 7 March 1989; *s* and *heir* of Earl of Lytton, *qv*.

KNEIPP, Hon. Sir (Joseph Patrick) George, Kt 1982; a Judge of the Supreme Court of Queensland, since 1969; Chancellor, James Cook University of North Queensland, since 1974; *b* 13 Nov. 1922; *s* of A. G. Kneipp and K. B. McHugh; *m* 1948, Ada Joan Crawford Cattermole; two *s* one *d*. *Educ:* Downlands Coll., Toowoomba; Univ. of Queensland (LLB). Called to the Queensland Bar, 1950; in practice as Barrister-at-Law, 1950–69. *Recreations:* reading, gardening. *Address:* 20 Kenilworth Avenue, Hyde Park, Townsville, Qld 4812, Australia. *T:* 794652. *Clubs:* North Queensland, James Cook University, Townsville Turf.

KNELLER, Alister Arthur; Hon. Mr Justice Kneller; Chief Justice of Gibraltar, since 1986; *b* 11 Nov. 1927; *s* of Arthur Kneller and Hester (*née* Farr). *Educ:* King's Sch., Canterbury; Corpus Christi Coll., Cambridge (MA 1954; LLM 1985). Kenya: Resident Magistrate, 1955; Sen. State Counsel, 1962; Registrar of the High Court, 1965; Puisne Judge, 1969; Judge of the Court of Appeal, 1982. *Recreations:* music, reading. *Address:* 2 Mount Road, Gibraltar. *T:* Gibraltar 75753. *Clubs:* United Oxford & Cambridge University; Mombasa (Kenya); Royal Yacht (Gibraltar).

KNIBB, Prof. Michael Anthony, PhD; FBA 1989; Professor of Old Testament Studies, since 1986, and Head of the Department of Theology and Religious Studies, since 1989, King's College London; *b* 14 Dec. 1938; third *s* of Leslie Charles Knibb and Christian Vera Knibb (*née* Hoggar); *m* 1972, Christine Mary Burrrell. *Educ:* Wyggeston Sch., Leicester; King's Coll. London (BD, PhD; FKC 1991); Union Theol Seminary, NY (STM); Corpus Christi Coll., Oxford. Lectr in OT Studies, 1964–82, Reader, 1982–86, KCL; British Acad. Res. Reader, 1986–88. Editor, Book List of SOTS, 1980–86. *Publications:* The Ethiopic Book of Enoch: a new edition in the light of the Aramaic Dead Sea Fragments, 2 vols, 1978; Het Boek Henoch, 1983; Cambridge Bible Commentary on 2 Esdras, 1979; (ed jtly) Israel's Prophetic Tradition: essays in honour of P. R. Ackroyd, 1982; The Qumran Community, 1987; (ed with P. W. van der Horst) Studies on the Testament of Job, 1989; articles in books and learned jls. *Recreation:* walking. *Address:* 6 Shootersway Park, Berkhamsted, Herts HP4 3NX. *T:* Berkhamsted (0442) 871459. *Club:* Athenæum.

KNIGHT, Prof. Alan Sydney, DPhil; Worsham Centennial Professor of History, University of Texas at Austin, 1986–July 1992; Professor of the History of Latin America, and Fellow of St Antony's College, Oxford, from July 1992; *b* 6 Nov. 1946; *s* of William Henry Knight and Eva Maud Crandon; *m* 1st, 1969, Carole Jones (marr. diss. 1979); one *d*; 2nd, 1985, Lidia Lozano; two *s*. *Educ:* Balliol Coll., Oxford (BA Modern Hist. 1968); Nuffield Coll., Oxford (DPhil 1974). Research Fellow, Nuffield Coll., Oxford, 1971–73; Lectr in Hist., Essex Univ., 1973–85. *Publications:* The Mexican Revolution (2 vols), 1986; US-Mexican Relations 1910–40, 1987; contrib. Jl of Latin American Studies, Bull. of Latin American Res., etc. *Recreation:* kayaking. *Address:* (until July 1992) Department of History, University of Texas at Austin, Austin, Texas 78712, USA; (from July 1992) St Antony's College, Oxford OX2 6JF. *T:* Oxford (0865) 310518.

KNIGHT, Ven. Alexander Francis; Archdeacon of Basingstoke and Canon Residentiary of Winchester Cathedral, since 1990; *b* 24 July 1939; *s* of Benjamin Edward and Dorothy Mary Knight; *m* 1962, Sheelagh Elizabeth (*née* Faris); one *s* three *d*. *Educ:* Taunton Sch.; St Catharine's Coll., Cambridge (MA). Curate, Hemel Hempstead, 1963–68; Chaplain, Taunton Sch., 1968–74; Dir, Bloxham Project, 1975–81; Dir of Studies, Aston Training Scheme, 1981–83; Priest-in-charge, Easton and Martyr Worthy, 1983–90. *Publications:* contrib. SPCK Taleteller series. *Recreations:* hill walking, theatre, reading, gardening. *Address:* 1 The Close, Winchester, Hampshire SO23 9LS.

KNIGHT, Sir Allan Walton, Kt 1970; CMG 1960; Hon. FIE (Aust.); FTS; Commissioner, The Hydro-Electric Commission, Tasmania, 1946–77; Chief Commissioner, Tasman Bridge Restoration Commission, 1975–80; *b* 26 Feb. 1910; *s* of late Mr and Mrs G. W. Knight, Lindisfarne, Tasmania; *m* 1936, Margaret Janet Buchanan; two *s* one *d*. *Educ:* Hobart Technical Coll.; University of Tasmania. Diploma of Applied Science, 1929; BSc 1932; ME 1935; BCom 1946. Chief Engineer, Public Works Dept, Tasmania, 1937–46. Member: Australian Univs Commn, 1966–74; Council, Tasmanian Coll. of Advanced Education, 1968–75. Peter Nicol Russell Medal, Instn of Engrs of Australia, 1963; William Kernot Medal, Univ. of Melbourne, 1963; Wilfred Chapman Award, Inst. of Welding, Australia, 1974; John Storey Medal, Inst. of Management, Australia, 1975. Hon. DEng Tasmania, 1980. *Recreation:* royal tennis. *Address:* 64 Waimea Avenue, Sandy Bay, Hobart, Tasmania 7005, Australia. *T:* Hobart 251498. *Club:* Tasmanian (Hobart).

KNIGHT, Andrew Stephen Bower; Executive Chairman, News International plc, since 1990; Chairman, Times Newspapers Holdings, since 1990; Director, The News Corporation Ltd, since 1991; *b* 1 Nov. 1939; *s* of M. W. B. Knight and S. E. F. Knight; *m* 1st, 1966, Victoria Catherine Brittain (marr. diss.); one *s*; 2nd, 1975, Begum Sabiha Rumani Malik; two *d*. Editor, The Economist, 1974–86; Chief Exec., 1986–89, Editor-in-Chief, 1987–89, Daily Telegraph plc. Director: Tandem Computers Inc., 1984–; Reuters, 1988–. Member: Steering Cttee, Bilderberg Meetings, 1980–; Adv. Bd, Center for Economic Policy Research, Stanford Univ., 1981–; Council, Templeton Coll., Oxford, 1984–. Trustee, Harlech Scholars' Trust. Governor and Mem. Council of Management, Ditchley Foundn, 1982–; Mem., Bd of Overseers, Hoover Instn, 1989–. *Address:* Virginia Street, E1 9XY. *Clubs:* Brooks's, Royal Automobile.

KNIGHT, Sir Arthur (William), Kt 1975; Chairman, National Enterprise Board, 1979–80; Chairman, Courtaulds Ltd, 1975–79; *b* 29 March 1917; *s* of Arthur Frederick Knight and Emily Scott; *m* 1st, 1945, Beatrice Joan Osborne (*née* Oppenheim) (*d* 1968); one *s* three *d*; 2nd, 1972, Sheila Elsie Whiteman. *Educ:* Tottenham County Sch.; London Sch. of Economics (evening student) (BCom; Hon. Fellow 1984). J. Sainsbury, Blackfriars, 1933–38; LSE, Dept of Business Admin (Leverhulme Studentship), 1938–39; Courtaulds, 1939. Served War, Army, 1940–46. Courtaulds, 1946–79: apptd Dir, 1958; Finance Dir, 1961. Non-exec. Director: Pye Holdings, 1972–75; Rolls-Royce (1971), 1973–78; Richard Thomas & Baldwin, 1966–67; Dunlop Holdings, 1981–84. Member: Council of Manchester Business Sch., 1964–71; Cttee for Arts and Social Studies of Council for Nat. Academic Awards, 1965–71; Commn of Enquiry into siting of Third London Airport, 1968–70; Council of Industry for Management Educn, 1970–73; Finance Cttee, RIIA, 1971–75; Council, RIIA, 1975–85; Court of Governors, London Sch. of Economics, 1971–; Economic Cttee, CBI, 1965–72; Cairncross (Channel Tunnel) Cttee, 1974–75; NIESR Exec. Cttee, 1976–; BOTB, 1978–79; The Queen's Award Adv. Cttee, 1981–86; Cttee on Fraud Trials, 1984–85. *Publications:* Private Enterprise and Public Intervention: the Courtauld experience, 1974; various papers. *Recreations:* walking, music, reading. *Address:* Charlton End, Singleton, West Sussex PO18 0HX. *Club:* Reform.

KNIGHT, Brian Joseph; QC 1981; practising barrister, since 1966; a Recorder, since 1991; *b* 5 May 1941; *s* of Joseph Knight and Vera Lorraine Knight (*née* Docksey); *m* 1967, Cristina Karen Wang Nobrega de Lima. *Educ:* Colbayns High Sch., Clacton; University Coll. London. LLB 1962, LLM 1963. Called to the Bar, Gray's Inn, 1964; *ad eundem* Lincoln's Inn, 1979; called to the Bar of Hong Kong, 1978, of Northern Ireland, 1979. *Address:* 1 Atkin Building, Gray's Inn, WC1R 5BQ. *T:* 071–404 0102. *Club:* Garrick.

KNIGHT, Edmund Alan; Commissioner of Customs and Excise, 1971–77; *b* 17 June 1919; *s* of Arthur Philip and Charlotte Knight; *m* 1953, Annette Ros Grimmitt; one *d*. *Educ:* Drayton Manor Sch.; London Sch. of Economics. Entered Exchequer and Audit Dept, 1938; HM Customs and Excise, 1948; Asst Sec., 1957; Sec. to Cttee on Turnover Taxation, 1963–64; seconded to Inland Revenue, 1969–71; returned to Customs and Excise, 1971; Eur. Affairs Adviser to BAT Co., 1978–85; consultant on indirect taxation, 1985–87. Member: SITPRO Bd, 1971–76; EDC for Internat. Freight Movement, 1971–76. *Recreations:* gardening, local history and environment. *Address:* 40 Park Avenue North, Harpenden, Herts AL5 2ED. *Club:* Commonwealth Trust.

KNIGHT, Geoffrey Cureton, MB, BS London; FRCS; FRCPsych; Consulting Neurological Surgeon in London, since 1935; Hon. Consultant Neurosurgeon: West End Hospital for Neurology and Neurosurgery; SE Metropolitan Regional Neurosurgical Centre; Royal Postgraduate Medical School of London; formerly Teacher of Surgery, University of London; *b* 4 Oct. 1906; *s* of Cureton Overbeck Knight; *m* 1933, Betty, *d* of Francis Cooper Havell, London; two *s*. *Educ:* Brighton Coll.; St Bartholomew's Hosp. Medical Sch. Brackenbury Surgical Schol. St Bart's Hosp., 1930. Ho. Surg. and Chief Asst, Surgical Professorial Unit at St Bart's Hosp.; Demonstrator in Physiology, St Bart's Hosp. Medical Sch.; Leverhulme Research Scholar, Royal College of Surgeons, 1933–35; Mackenzie Mackinnon Research Scholar, 1936–38; Bernard Baron Research Scholar, 1938; Hunterian Prof., 1935–36 and 1963. FRSocMed; Fellow Soc. Brit. Neurological Surgeons; Fellow Med. Soc. London; Vice-Pres., Internat. Soc. for Psychosurgery. Neurological Surg. Armed Forces of Czecho-Slovakia, 1941; Hon. Fellow, Czecho-Slovak Med. Soc., Prague, 1946; Officer, Order of the White Lion of Czecho-Slovakia, 1946. *Publications:* contrib. med. jls on aetiology and surgical treatment of diseases of the spine and nervous system and the surgical treatment of mental illness. *Recreations:* gardening, swimming. *Address:* 7 Aubrey Road, Campden Hill, W8. *T:* 071–727 7719 (Sec., 071–935 7549). *Club:* Hurlingham.

KNIGHT, Geoffrey Egerton, CBE 1970; Chairman: GPG (formerly Guinness Peat Group) plc, 1989 (Director, since 1976; Joint Deputy Chairman, 1987–89); Fenchurch Insurance Group Ltd, since 1980 (Executive Vice-Chairman, 1975–80); Director: GPA Group plc, since 1977; Trafalgar House Public Limited Company, 1980–91; *b* 25 Feb. 1921; *s* of Arthur Egerton Knight and Florence Gladys Knight (*née* Clarke); *m* 1947, Evelyn Bugle; two *d*. *Educ:* Stubbington House; Brighton Coll. Royal Marines, 1939–46. Joined Bristol Aeroplane Co. Ltd, 1953; Dir, Bristol Aircraft Ltd, 1956; Dir, BAC Ltd, 1964–77, Vice Chm., 1972–76. *Publication:* Concorde: the inside story, 1976. *Address:* 33 Smith Terrace, SW3 4DH. *T:* 071–352 5391. *Clubs:* Boodle's, White's.

KNIGHT, Dr Geoffrey Wilfred; retired; Regional Medical Officer, North West Thames Regional Health Authority, 1973–76; *b* 10 Jan. 1920; *s* of Wilfred Knight and Ida Knight; *m* 1944, Christina Marion Collins Scott; one *s* one *d*. *Educ:* Leeds Univ. Med. Sch. MB, ChB, MD, DPH (Chadwick Gold Medal). County Med. Officer of Health, Herts, 1962–73. Formerly: Governor, Nat. Inst. of Social Work; Member: Personal Social Services Council; Central Midwives Bd; Exec. Cttee, Child Health Bureau; Adv. Panel, Soc. for Health Educn; formerly Mem., Govt Techn. and Sci. Cttee on Disposal of Toxic Wastes. *Recreations:* painting, golf. *Address:* 4947 197A Street, Langley, BC V3A 6W1, Canada.

KNIGHT, Gregory; MP (C) Derby North, since 1983; a Lord Commissioner of HM Treasury (Government Whip), since 1990; *b* 4 April 1949; *s* of George Knight and Isabella Knight (*née* Bell). *Educ:* Alderman Newton's Grammar School, Leicester; College of Law, Guildford. Self employed solicitor, 1973–83. Member: Leicester City Council, 1976–79; Leicestershire County Council, 1977–83 (Chm., Public Protection Cttee); PPS to the Minister of State: Home Office, 1987; Foreign Office, 1988–89; an Asst Govt Whip, 1989–90. Dir, Leicester Theatre Trust, 1979–85 (Chm., Finance Cttee, 1982–83). *Publications:* (jtly) Westminster Words, 1988; Honourable Insults: a century of political insult, 1990; pamphlets and articles for law publications. *Recreations:* music, the arts, writing, film comedy, primatology. *Address:* House of Commons, SW1A 0AA. *T:* 071–219 5099.

KNIGHT, Sir Harold (Murray), KBE 1980; DSC 1945; Chairman, IBJ Australia Bank Ltd, since 1985; Director: Western Mining Corporation, since 1982; Angus and Coote Holdings Ltd, since 1986; *b* 13 Aug. 1919; *s* of W. H. P. Knight, Melbourne; *m* 1951, Gwenyth Catherine Pennington; four *s* one *d*. *Educ:* Scotch Coll., Melbourne; Melbourne Univ. Commonwealth Bank of Australia, 1936–40. AIF (Lieut), 1940–43; RANVR (Lieut), 1943–45. Commonwealth Bank of Australia, 1946–55; Asst Chief, Statistics Div., Internat. Monetary Fund, 1957–59; Reserve Bank of Australia: Research Economist, 1960–62; Asst Manager, Investment Dept, 1962–64, Manager, 1964–68; Dep. Governor and Dep. Chm. of Board, 1968–75; Governor and Chm. of Bd, 1975–82. Chm., Mercantile Mutual Hldgs, 1985–89. Mem., Police Bd of NSW, 1988–89. Mem. Council, Macquarie Univ., 1990–. Pres., Scripture Union, NSW, 1983–. *Publication:* Introducción al Analisis Monetario (Spanish), 1959. *Address:* 76 Yarrara Road, West Pymble, NSW 2073, Australia.

KNIGHT, Jeffrey Russell, FCA; Special Adviser to Federation of Stock Exchanges in European Communities, since 1990; *b* 1 Oct. 1936; *s* of Thomas Edgar Knight and Ivy Cissie Knight (*née* Russell); *m* 1959, Judith Marion Delver Podger; four *d*. *Educ:* Bristol Cathedral Sch.; St Peter's Hall, Oxford (MA). Chartered Accountant, 1966; The Stock Exchange, subseq. Internat. Stock Exchange, 1967–90: Head of Quotations Dept, 1973; Dep. Chief Executive, 1975; Chief Exec., 1982–89. Member: City Company Law Cttee, 1974–80; Dept of Trade Panel on Company Law Revision, 1980–84; Accounting Standards Cttee, 1982–89; Special Adviser to Dept of Trade, 1975–81; Adviser to Council for the Securities Industry, 1978–85; UK Delegate: to EEC Working Parties; to Internat. Fedn of Stock Exchanges, 1973–90; to Fedn of Stock Exchanges in EEC, 1974–90 (Chm., Wking Cttee, 1980–90); to Internat. Orgn of Securities Commns, 1987–91 (Chm. Wkg Party on Capital Adequacy); Chm., Task Force on Transnational Settlement, 1987–91. *Recreations:* cricket, music. *Address:* Robin Haye, The Drive, Godalming, Surrey GU7 1PH. *T:* Godalming (0483) 424399. *Clubs:* Brooks's; Dorset Rangers (Cricket).

KNIGHT, Dame Joan Christabel Jill, (Dame Jill Knight), DBE 1985 (MBE 1964); MP (C) Birmingham, Edgbaston since 1966; *m* 1947, Montague Knight (*d* 1986); two *s*. *Educ:* Fairfield Sch., Bristol; King Edward Grammar Sch., Birmingham. Mem., Northampton County Borough Council, 1956–66. Member: Parly Select Cttee on Race Relations and Immigration, 1969–72; Council of Europe, 1977–88; WEU, 1977–88 (Chm., Cttee for Parly and Public Relations, 1984–88); Select Cttee for Home Affairs, 1980–83; Chairman: Lords and Commons All-Party Child and Family Protection Gp, 1978–; Cons. Back Bench Health and Social Services Cttee, 1982–; Mem., Exec. Cttee, 1922 Cttee, 1979– (Sec., 1983–87; Vice-Chm., 1987–88). Pres., West Midlands Conservative Political Centre, 1980–83. Vice-Pres., Townswomen's Guilds, 1986–. Kentucky Colonel, USA, 1973; Nebraska Admiral, USA, 1980. *Recreations:* music, reading, tapestry work, theatre-going, antique-hunting. *Address:* House of Commons, SW1A 0AA.

KNIGHT, Sir Michael (William Patrick), KCB 1983 (CB 1980); AFC 1964; *b* 23 Nov. 1932; *s* of William and Dorothy Knight; *m* 1967, Patricia Ann (*née* Davies); one *s* two *d*. *Educ:* Leek High Sch.; Univ. of Liverpool (BA Hons 1954; Hon. DLitt 1985). MBIM 1977; FRAeS 1984. Univ. of Liverpool Air Sqn, RAFVR, 1951–54; commnd RAF, 1954; served in Transport and Bomber Comds, and in Middle and Near East Air Forces, 1956–63; Comd No 32 Sqn, RAF Akrotiri, 1961–63; RAF Staff Coll., 1964; Min. of Aviation, 1965–66; Comd Far East Strike Wing, RAF Tengah, 1966–69; Head of Secretariat, HQ Strike Comd, 1969–70; Mil. Asst to Chm., NATO Mil. Cttee, 1970–73; Comd RAF Laarbruch, 1973–74; RCDS, 1975; Dir of Ops (Air Support), MoD, 1975–77; SASO, HQ Strike Command/DCS (Ops & Intelligence) HQ UK Air Forces, 1977–80; AOC No 1 Gp, 1980–82; Air Mem. for Supply and Organisation, 1983–86; UK Military Rep. to NATO, 1986–89. Air ADC to the Queen, 1986–89 (ADC, 1973–74). Ret'd Air Chief Marshal, 1989. Commnd Flying Officer, RAFVR (Trng Br.), 1989. Dir, Craigwell Research, 1990–; non-exec. Dir, FR Group plc, 1990–; Chm., Northern Devon Healthcare, 1991–. Member Council: RUSI, 1984–87; The Air League, 1990–. Chm., N Devon Family Support Service, Leonard Cheshire Foundn, 1989–; Devon County Rep., RAF Benev. Fund, 1990–. Adjunct Prof., Internat. Peace and Security, Carnegie Mellon Univ., Pittsburgh, 1989–. Gov. and Council Mem., Taunton Sch., 1987–; Univ. of Liverpool Develt Team, 1986–. Mem., RFU Cttee, 1977– (Chm., Internat. Sub Cttee, 1987–); President: RAF Rugby Union, 1985–89 (Chm., 1975–78); Combined Services RFC, 1987–89 (Chm., 1977–79); RAF Lawn Tennis Assoc., 1984–86. Upper Freeman, GAPAN, 1990–; Freeman City of London, 1989. *Recreations:* Rugby football, lesser sports, music, writing, after-dinner speaking. *Address:* c/o National Westminster Bank, Leek, Staffs. *Clubs:* Royal Air Force, Colonels.

KNIGHT, Dr Peter Clayton; Director, Birmingham Polytechnic, since 1985; *b* 8 July 1947; *s* of Norman Clayton Knight and Vera Catherine Knight; *m* 1977, Catherine Mary (*née* Ward); one *s* one *d*. *Educ:* Bishop Vesey's Grammar Sch., Sutton Coldfield; Univ. of York (BA 1st cl. Hons Physics; DPhil). SRC Studentship, 1968; Asst Teacher, Plymstock Comprehensive Sch., 1971; Plymouth Polytechnic: Lectr, 1972; Sen. Lectr, 1974; Head of Combined Studies, 1981; Dep. Dir, Lancashire Polytechnic, 1982–85. Nat. Pres., NATFHE, 1977; Chm., SRHE, 1987–89; Member: Burnham Cttee of Further Educn, 1976–81; Working Party on Management of Higher Educn, 1977; Nat. Adv. Body on Public Sector Higher Educn, 1982–85; PCFC, 1989–. *Publications:* articles, chapters and reviews in learned jls on educnl policy, with particular ref. to higher educn. *Recreation:* running. *Address:* Sandy Lodge, Sandy Lane, Brewood, Staffs ST19 9ET. *T:* Brewood (0902) 851339.

KNIGHT, Richard James, MA; JP; *b* 19 July 1915; *s* of Richard William Knight; *m* 1953, Hilary Marian, *d* of Rev. F. W. Argyle; two *s* one *d*. *Educ:* Dulwich Coll. (Scholar); Trinity Coll., Cambridge (Scholar; 1st class Hons Classical Tripos Pt I, 1936, Part II, 1937); BA Open Univ., 1988. Asst Master, Fettes Coll., Edinburgh, 1938–39. Served War of 1939–45 in Gordon Highlanders, Capt. Asst Master and Housemaster, Marlborough Coll., 1945–56; Headmaster of Oundle Sch., 1956–68, of Monkton Combe Sch., 1968–78. Reader, Dio. Bath and Wells. JP Northants, 1960, Bath, 1970, Avon, 1974. Hon. Liveryman, Grocers' Co., 1989–. *Recreations:* cricket and other games. *Address:* 123 Midford Road, Bath BA2 5RX. *T:* Bath (0225) 832276.

KNIGHT, Dr Roger John Beckett; Chief Curator, National Maritime Museum, since 1988; *b* 11 April 1944; *s* of John Beckett Knight and Alyson Knight (*née* Nunn); *m* 1968, Elizabeth Magowan (marr. diss. 1980); two *s*. *Educ:* Tonbridge Sch.; Trinity Coll., Dublin (MA); Sussex Univ. (PGCE); University Coll. London (PhD). Asst Master, Haberdashers' Aske's Sch., Elstree, 1972–73; National Maritime Museum: Dep. Custodian of Manuscripts, 1974–77, Custodian, 1977–80; Dep. Head, Printed Books and Manuscripts Dept, 1980–84; Head, Inf. Project Gp, 1984–86; Head, Documentation Div., 1986–88. Member: Council, Soc. for Nautical Research, 1977–81; Council, Navy Records Soc., 1974– (Vice-Pres., 1980–84). *Publications:* Guide to the Manuscripts in the National Maritime Museum, vol. 1, 1977, vol. 2, 1980; (with Alan Frost) The Journal of Daniel Paine, 1794–1797, 1983; Portsmouth Dockyard Papers, 1774–1783: the American War, 1987; articles, reviews in jls. *Recreations:* sailing, cricket, music. *Address:* National Maritime Museum, Greenwich, SE10 9NF. *T:* 081–858 4422. *Club:* West Wittering Sailing.

KNIGHT, Warburton Richard, CBE 1987; Director of Educational Services, Bradford Metropolitan District Council, 1974–91; *b* 2 July 1932; *s* of late Warburton Henry Johnston and Alice Gweneth Knight; *m* 1961, Pamela Ann (*née* Hearmon); two *s* one *d*. *Educ:* Trinity Coll., Cambridge (MA). Teaching in Secondary Modern and Grammar Schs in Middlesex and Huddersfield, 1956–62; joined West Riding in junior capacity, 1962; Asst Dir for Secondary Schs, Leics, 1967; Asst Educn Officer for Sec. Schs and later for Special and Social Educn in WR, 1970. *Recreations:* choral music, beekeeping, general cultural interests. *Address:* Thorner Grange, Sandhills, Thorner, Leeds LS14 3DE. *T:* Leeds (0532) 892356. *Club:* Royal Over-Seas League.

KNIGHT, William Arnold, CMG 1966; OBE 1954; Controller and Auditor-General of Uganda, 1962–68, retired; *b* 14 June 1915; *e s* of late William Knight, Llanfairfechan, and Clara Knight; *m* 1939, Bronwen Parry; one *s* one *d*. *Educ:* Friars' Sch., Bangor; University Coll. of North Wales (BA Hons). Entered Colonial Audit Dept as an Asst Auditor, 1938; service in Kenya, 1938–46; Mauritius, 1946–49; Sierra Leone, 1949–52; British Guiana, 1952–57; Uganda, 1957–68; Commissioner, inquiry into economy and efficiency, Uganda, 1969–70. *Recreations:* fishing and gardening. *Address:* Neopardy Mills, near Crediton, Devon EX17 5EP. *T:* Crediton (03632) 2513. *Club:* East India.

KNIGHTLEY; *see* Finch-Knightley.

KNIGHTON, William Myles, CB 1981; Principal Establishment and Finance Officer, Department of Trade and Industry, 1986–91; *b* 8 Sept. 1931; *s* of late George Harry Knighton, OBE, and Ella Knighton (*née* Stroud); *m* 1957, Brigid Helen Carrothers; one *s* one *d*. *Educ:* Bedford School; Peterhouse, Cambridge (BA). Asst Principal, Min. of Supply, 1954; Principal, Min. of Aviation, 1959; Cabinet Office, 1962–64; Principal Private Sec. to Minister of Technology, 1966–68; Asst Sec., Min. of Technology, subseq. DTI and Dept of Trade, 1967–74; Under Sec., 1974–78, Dep. Sec., 1978–83, Dept of Trade; Dep. Sec., Dept of Transport, 1983–86. *Publication:* (with D. E. Rosenthal) National Laws and International Commerce, 1982. *Recreations:* gardening, hill-walking, listening to music. *Address:* 115 Dacre Park, SE13 5BZ. *T:* 081–852 8267. *Club:* United Oxford & Cambridge University.

KNIGHTS, family name of **Baron Knights.**

KNIGHTS, Baron *cr* 1987 (Life Peer), of Edgbaston in the County of West Midlands; **Philip Douglas Knights;** Kt 1980; CBE 1976 (OBE 1971); QPM (Dist. Service) 1964; DL; Chief Constable, West Midlands Police, 1975–85; *b* 3 Oct. 1920; *s* of Thomas James Knights and Ethel Knights; *m* 1945, Jean Burman. *Educ:* King's Sch., Grantham. Lincolnshire Constabulary: Police Cadet, 1938–40; Constable, 1940. Served War, RAF, 1943–45. Sergeant, Lincs Constab., 1946; seconded to Home Office, 1946–50; Inspector, Lincs Constab., 1953, Supt 1955, Chief Supt 1957. Asst Chief Constable, Birmingham City Police, 1959; seconded to Home Office, Dep. Comdt, Police Coll., 1962–66; Dep. Chief Constable, Birmingham City Police, 1970; Chief Constable, Sheffield and Rotherham Constab., 1972–74; Chief Constable, South Yorks Police, 1974–75. Winner of Queen's Police Gold Medal Essay Competition, 1965. Mem. Lord Devlin's Cttee on Identification Procedures, 1974–75. Pres., Assoc. of Chief Police Officers, 1978–79. Member: Council, Univ. of Aston, 1985–; Adv. Council, Cambridge Univ. Inst. of Criminology, 1986–. CBIM. DL W Midlands, 1985. *Recreations:* sport, gardening. *Address:* 11 Antringham Gardens, Edgbaston, Birmingham B15 3QL. *Club:* Royal Over-Seas League.

KNIGHTS, Lionel Charles, MA, PhD; King Edward VII Professor of English Literature, University of Cambridge, 1965–73, now Emeritus Professor; Fellow, Queens' College, Cambridge, 1965–73; *b* 15 May 1906; *s* of C. E. and Lois M. Knights; *m* 1936, Elizabeth M. Barnes; one *s* one *d*. *Educ:* grammar schs; Selwyn Coll. (Hon. Fellow, 1974), and Christ's Coll., Cambridge Univ.; Charles Oldham Shakespeare Scholar, 1928; Members' Prize, 1929. Lecturer in English Literature, Manchester Univ., 1933–34, 1935–47; Prof. of English Lit., Univ. of Sheffield, 1947–52; Winterstoke Prof. of English, Bristol Univ., 1953–64. Fellow, Kenyon Sch. of Letters, 1950; Andrew Mellon Vis. Prof., Univ. of Pittsburgh, 1961–62 and 1966; Mrs W. Beckman Vis. Prof., Berkeley, 1970. Mem. of editorial board of Scrutiny, a Quarterly Review, 1932–53. For. Hon. Mem., Amer. Acad. of Arts and Sciences, 1981. Docteur (*hc*) de l'Univ. de Bordeaux, 1964; Hon. DUniv York, 1969; Hon. DLitt: Manchester, 1974; Sheffield, 1978; Warwick, 1979; Bristol, 1984. *Publications:* Drama and Society in the Age of Jonson, 1937; Explorations: Essays in Literary Criticism, 1946; Shakespeare's Politics, Shakespeare Lecture, British Academy, 1957; Some Shakespearean Themes, 1959; An Approach to Hamlet, 1960; (ed with Basil Cottle), Metaphor and Symbol, 1961; Further Explorations, 1965; Public Voices: literature and politics (Clark Lectures), 1971; Explorations 3, 1976; Hamlet and other Shakespeare Essays, 1979; Selected Essays in Criticism, 1981. *Address:* 57 Jesus Lane, Cambridge CB5 8BS. *Club:* Commonwealth Trust.

KNIGHTS, Rosemary Margaret; Deputy Chief Executive, Mersey Regional Health Authority, since 1990 (Regional Nursing Officer, 1988–90); *b* 2 Nov. 1945; *d* of Donald and Margaret Robson; *m* 1983, Michael A. Knights. *Educ:* Houghton-le-Spring Grammar School; Sunderland AHA. RGN, OND. Clinical nursing career, 1962–75 (Ward Sister posts, Sunderland and Harrogate); Nursing Officer, Harrogate, 1975–78; Sen. Nursing Officer, North Tees, Stockton, 1978–80; Dir of Nursing, Central Manchester HA, 1981–85; Unit Gen. Manager and Dist Nursing Officer, Manchester Royal Eye Hosp., 1985–88. Mem., S Manchester HA, 1983–88; Sec. and Chief Exec., Ophthalmic Nursing Bd, 1983–88. *Publications:* articles in nursing and health service papers. *Recreations:* music (piano; Friends of Hallé); the NHS!! *Address:* Mersey Regional Health Authority, Hamilton House, 24 Pall Mall, Liverpool L3 6AL. *T:* 051–236 4620. *Club:* Soroptomist International (Manchester).

KNILL, Sir John Kenelm Stuart, 4th Bt *cr* 1893, of The Grove, Blackheath; *b* 8 April 1913; *s* of Sir John Stuart Knill, 3rd Bt and Lucy Emmeline (*d* 1952), *o d* of Captain Thomas Willis, MN, FRGS; *S* father, 1973; *m* 1951, Violette Maud Florence Martin Barnes (*d* 1983); two *s*. *Educ:* St Gregory's School, Downside. Served as Lieut, RNVR, 1940–45 (Atlantic Star, Italy, France and Germany Stars). Industrial management trainee, 1945–48; canal transport proprietor, 1948–54; pig farmer, 1954–63; civil servant, MoD, 1963–77. President: Avon Transport 2000; Commercial Narrow Boat Operators' Assoc.; Vice-Pres., Thames Severn Canal Trust; Founder and Pres., Assoc. of Canal Enterprises, 1982–; Member: Kennet and Avon Canal Trust, Great Western Soc., Inland Waterways Assoc. *Recreations:* canal and railway restoration, scouting. *Heir:* *s* Thomas John Pugin Bartholomew Knill [*b* 24 Aug. 1952; *m* 1977, Kathleen Muszynski]. *Address:* Canal Cottage, Bathampton, Somerset. *T:* Bath (0225) 463603. *Club:* Victory Services.

KNILL, Prof. John Lawrence, PhD, DSc; FEng, FICE, FIGeol; Chairman, Natural Environment Research Council, since 1988; Professor of Engineering Geology, Imperial College of Science, Technology and Medicine, University of London, since 1973 (on leave of absence); *b* 22 Nov. 1934; *s* of late William Cuthbert Knill and of Mary (*née* Dempsey); *m* 1957, Diane Constance Judge; one *s* one *d*. *Educ:* Whitgift Sch.; Imperial Coll. of Science and Technol. (BSc, ARCS 1955; PhD, DIC 1957; DSc 1981). FIGeol 1985; FICE 1981; FEng 1991. Geologist, Sir Alexander Gibb & Partners, 1957; Imperial College, London: Asst Lectr, 1957; Lectr, 1959; Reader in Engrg Geology, 1965; Dean of Royal Sch. of Mines, 1980–83; Head of Dept of Geology, 1979–88; Chm., Centre for Remote Sensing, 1984–88. Member: Council, Nat. Stone Centre, 1984–; Nature Conservancy Council, 1985–91; Jt Nature Conservation Cttee, 1991–; Radioactive Waste Management Adv. Cttee, 1985– (Chm., 1987–); Univs Cttee for Non-Teaching Staffs, 1987–88; Resources Bd, BNSC, 1988–. President: Instn of Geologists, 1981–84; Geologists' Assoc., 1982–84 (Hon. Mem., 1990); Section C, BAAS, 1988–89. Manuel Rocha Lecture, 1991; F. H. Moore Lecture, 1991. Membre Correspondant, Société Geologique de Belgique, 1976. Hon. FCGI 1988. Whitaker Medal, IWEM, 1969; Aberconway Medal, Instn of Geologists, 1989. *Publications:* Industrial Geology, 1978; articles on geology of Scotland and engrg geology. *Recreation:* viticulture. *Address:* Highwood Farm, Shaw-cum-Donnington, Newbury, Berks RG16 9LB. *Clubs:* Athenæum, Chaps.

KNIPE, Sir Leslie Francis, Kt 1980; MBE; farmer; *b* Pontypool, 1913. *Educ:* West Monmouth School, Pontypool. Served War of 1939–45, Burma; RASC, attained rank of Major. President: Conservative Party in Wales (Chairman, 1972–77); Monmouth Conservative and Unionist Assoc. *Address:* Brook Acre, Llanvihangel, Crucorney, Abergavenny, Gwent NP7 8DH.

KNOLLYS, family name of **Viscount Knollys.**

KNOLLYS, 3rd Viscount, of Caversham, *cr* 1911; **David Francis Dudley Knollys;** Baron *cr* 1902; *b* 12 June 1931; *s* of 2nd Viscount Knollys, GCMG, MBE, DFC, and Margaret (*d* 1987), *o d* of Sir Stuart Coats, 2nd Bt; *S* father 1966; *m* 1959, Hon. Sheelin Virginia Maxwell (granted, 1959, title, rank and precedence of a baron's *d*, which would have been hers had her father survived to succeed to barony of Farnham), *d* of late Lt-Col Hon. Somerset Maxwell, MP and late Mrs Remington Hobbs; three *s* one *d*. *Educ:* Eton. Lt, Scots Guards, 1951. *Heir: s* Hon. Patrick Nicholas Mark Knollys, *b* 11 March 1962. *Address:* Bramerton Grange, Norwich NR14 7HF. *T:* Surlingham (05088) 266.

KNORPEL, Henry, CB 1982; QC 1988; Counsel to the Speaker, House of Commons, since 1985; *b* 18 Aug. 1924; 2nd *s* of late Hyman Knorpel and Dora Knorpel; *m* 1953, Brenda Sterling; two *d*. *Educ:* City of London Sch.; Magdalen Coll., Oxford. BA 1945, BCL 1946, MA 1949. Called to Bar, Inner Temple, 1947, Entrance Scholar, 1947–50, Bencher, 1990; practised 1947–52; entered Legal Civil Service as Legal Asst, Min. of Nat. Insce, 1952; Sen. Legal Asst, Min. of Pensions and Nat. Insce, 1958; Law Commn, 1965; Min. of Social Security, 1967; Dept of Health and Social Security: Asst Solicitor, 1968; Principal Asst Solicitor (Under-Sec.), 1971; Solicitor (also to OPCS and Gen. Register Office), 1978–85. Vis. Lecturer: Kennington Coll. of Commerce and Law, 1950–58; Holborn Coll. of Law, Languages and Commerce, 1958–70; Polytechnic of Central London, 1970–. *Publications:* articles on community law. *Recreation:* relaxing. *Address:* Conway, 32 Sunnybank, Epsom, Surrey KT18 7DX. *T:* Epsom (0372) 721394.

KNOTT, Prof. John Frederick, ScD; FRS 1990; FEng 1988; Professor and Head of the School of Metallurgy and Materials, University of Birmingham, since 1990; *b* Bristol, 9 Dec. 1938; *s* of Fred Knott and Margaret (*née* Chesney); *m* 1st, 1963, Christine Mary Roberts (marr. diss. 1986); two *s*; 2nd, 1990, Susan Marilyn Cooke (*née* Jones); two step *s*. *Educ:* Queen Elizabeth's Hosp., Bristol; Sheffield Univ. (BMet 1st cl. Hons 1959); Cambridge Univ. (PhD 1963; ScD 1991). FIM 1974; FWeldI 1985. Res. Officer, Central Electricity Res. Labs, Leatherhead, 1962–67; Cambridge University: Lectr, Dept of Metallurgy, 1967–81; Reader in Mechanical Metallurgy, 1981–90; Churchill College: Goldsmiths' Fellow, Coll. Lectr and Dir of Studies in Metallurgy and Materials Sci., 1967–90; Tutor, 1969–79; Tutor for Advanced Students, 1979–81; Vice-Master, 1988–90; Extra-Ordinary Fellow, 1991–. FRSA. LB. Pfeil Prize, 1973, Rosenhain Medal, 1978, Metals Soc.; Leslie Holliday Prize, Materials Sci. Club, 1978. *Publications:* Fundamentals of Fracture Mechanics, 1973, 2nd edn 1979; many scientific papers in Acta Met., Metal Sci., Met. Trans, Engrg Fracture Mechanics, etc. *Recreations:* bridge, crosswords, traditional jazz, playing the tenor recorder rather badly. *Address:* 6 Audley Close, St Ives, Cambs PE17 4UJ. *T:* Huntingdon (0480) 492985.

KNOTT, Sir John Laurence, AC 1981; Kt 1971; CBE 1960; *b* 6 July 1910; *s* of J. Knott, Kyneton, Victoria; *m* 1935, Jean R., *d* of C. W. Milnes; three *s* one *d*. *Educ:* Cobram State Sch.; Melbourne Univ. (Dip Com). Private Sec. to Minister for Trade Treaties, 1935–38; Sec., Aust. Delegn, Eastern Gp Supply Council, New Delhi, 1940; Exec. Officer, Secondary Industries Commn, 1943–45; Mem. Jt War Production Cttee; Dir, Defence Prod. Planning Br., Dept of Supply, 1950–52; Sec., Dept of Defence Prod., 1957–58; Mem., Aust. Defence Mission to US, 1957; Sec., Dept of Supply, Melb., 1959–65; Leader, Aust. Mission to ELDO Confs: London, 1961; Paris, 1965, 1966; Rome, 1967; Vice-Pres., ELDO Council, 1967–69. Dep. High Comr for Australia, London, 1966–68; Dir-Gen., Australian PO, 1968–72. Mem. Council, Melbourne Univ., 1973–76. Pres., ESU (Victoria); Chm., Epworth Hosp. Foundn; former Chm., Salvation Army Red Shield Appeal. Freeman, City of London. AASA, FCIS, AFAIM, LCA; idc. *Recreations:* bowls (Vice-Pres., Royal Victorian Bowling Assoc., 1957–58; Chm., World Bowls (1980) Ltd), golf, gardening. *Address:* 3 Fenwick Street, Kew, Victoria 3101, Australia. *T:* (03) 853 7777. *Clubs:* Melbourne, West Brighton (Melbourne).

KNOTT, Air Vice-Marshal Ronald George, CB 1967; DSO 1944; DFC 1943; AFC 1955; retired 1972; *b* 19 Dec. 1917; *s* of late George and Edith Rose Knott; *m* 1941, Hermione Violet (*née* Phayre); three *s* one *d*. *Educ:* Borden Grammar Sch., Sittingbourne, Kent. No 20 Sqdn RAF, 1938–40; No 5 Flight IAFVR, 1940–41; HQ Coast Defence Wing, Bombay, 1942; No 179 Sqdn, 1943–44; No 524 Sqdn, 1944–45; RAF, Gatow (Ops), 1949–50; OC, RAF Eindhoven, 1950–51; HQ 2nd TAF, 1951–52; RAF Staff Coll., 1952; Flying Trng Comd, 1953–55; Chief Flying Instructor, Central Flying Sch., 1956–58; Air Plans, Air Min., 1959; OC, RAF Gutersloh, 1959–61; ACOS Plans, 2 ATAF, 1962–63; Defence Res. Policy Staff Min. of Def. 1963; DOR2 (RAF), Min. of Def., 1963–67; SASO, HQ NEAF Cyprus, 1967–70; AOA, HQ Air Support Comd, RAF, 1970–72. *Recreations:* gardening, wine growing. *Address:* Pilgrims Cottage, Charing, Kent TN27 0DR. *T:* Charing (023371) 2723.

KNOWELDEN, Prof. John, CBE 1983; JP; MD, FRCP, FFCM, DPH; Professor of Community Medicine (formerly of Preventive Medicine and Public Health), University of Sheffield, 1960–84, retired; *b* 19 April 1919; *s* of Clarence Arthur Knowelden; *m* 1946, Mary Sweet; two *s*. *Educ:* Colfe's Grammar Sch., Lewisham; St George's Hosp. Med. Sch.; London Sch. of Hygiene and Trop. Med.; Johns Hopkins Sch. of Public Health, Baltimore. Surg. Lt, RNVR, 1942–46. Rockefeller Fellowship in Preventive Med., 1947–49; Lectr in Med. Statistics and Mem., MRC Statistical Research Unit, 1949–60. Academic Registrar, FCM, 1977–83. Civil Consultant in Community Medicine to Royal Navy, 1977–84. Editor, Brit. Jl of Preventive and Social Medicine, 1959–69 and 1973–76. Formerly Hon. Sec., Sect. of Epidemiology, Royal Society Medicine and Chm., Soc. for Social Medicine; Mem., WHO Expert Advisory Panel on Health Statistics. *Publications:* (with Ian Taylor) Principles of Epidemiology, 2nd edn, 1964; papers on clinical and prophylactic trials and epidemiological topics. *Recreations:* photography, gardening. *Address:* 2 St Helen's Croft, Grindleford, Sheffield S30 1JG. *T:* Hope Valley (0433) 30014.

KNOWLAND, Raymond Reginald; Managing Director, British Petroleum, since 1990; *b* 18 Aug. 1930; *s* of Reginald George Knowland and Marjorie Doris Knowland (*née* Alvis); *m* 1956, Valerie Mary Higgs; three *s*. *Educ:* Bristol Grammar Sch.; Sir John Cass College London. ARIC 1954; CChem. BP Chemicals: specialty plastics and PVC Plant Management, Barry Works, 1957–69; Works Gen. Manager, Barry Works, 1969–75, Baglan Bay Works, 1975–78; Man. Dir, Belgium, 1978–80; Dir, London, 1980–90; Chief Exec. Officer, London, 1983–90. *Recreations:* sailing, photography, Rugby football (spectator). *Address:* British Petroleum, Britannic House, 1 Finsbury Circus, EC2M 7BA; Heron's Wake, Flowers Hill, Pangbourne, Reading RG8 7BD. *T:* Reading (0734) 844576; 39A Devonia Road, Islington, N1 8JQ. *T:* 071–226 1038.

KNOWLES, Ann; *see* Knowles, P. A.

KNOWLES, Sir Charles (Francis), 7th Bt *cr* 1765; Senior Partner, Charles Knowles Design, since 1984; *b* 20 Dec. 1951; *s* of Sir Francis Gerald William Knowles, 6th Bt, FRS, and of Ruth Jessie, *d* of late Rev. Arthur Brooke-Smith; *S* father, 1974; *m* 1979, Amanda Louise Margaret, *d* of Lance Bromley, *qv*; two *s*. *Educ:* Marlborough Coll.; Oxford Sch. of Architecture (DipArch 1977; RIBA 1979). FRSA. *Recreations:* shooting, travel. *Heir: s* (Charles) William (Frederick Lance) Knowles, *b* 27 Aug. 1985. *Address:* Silbury Hill House, 2 Vaughan Avenue, W6 0XS.

KNOWLES, Colin George; company director; Director of Development and Public Relations, University of Bophuthatswana, since 1985; Secretary and Trustee, University of Bophuthatswana Foundation, since 1985; *b* 11 April 1939; *s* of late George William Knowles, Tarleton, Lancs; *m* 1st, 1961, Mary B. D. Wickliffe, *e d* of William Wickliffe, Co. Antrim, NI; two *d*; 2nd, 1971 (marr. diss. 1980); 3rd, 1981, Mrs Carla Johannes, *d* of Roland Stansfield Stamp, Blantyre, Malaŵi; one *d*. *Educ:* King George V Grammar Sch., Southport; CEDEP, Fontainebleau. MInstM 1966; MIPR 1970; BAIE 1972; FBIM 1972; MPRISA 1983; APR 1987. Appointed Comr of Oaths, 1991. Joined John Player & Sons, 1960; sales and marketing management appts; Head of Public Relations, 1971–73; joined Imperial Tobacco Ltd, 1973; Hd of Public Affairs, 1973–80; Company Sec., 1979–80. Chairman: Griffin Associates Ltd, 1980–84; Concept Communications (Pty) Ltd (S Africa), 1983–84; Dir, TWS Public Relations (Pty) Ltd (S Africa), 1984–85. Mem. Council, Tobacco Trade Benevolent Assoc., 1975–80; Chm., Bophuthatswana Reg., PRISA, 1988–. Dir, Bophuthatswana Council for Consumer Affairs, 1991–. Director: Nottingham Festival Assoc. Ltd, 1969–71; English Sinfonia Orchestra, 1972–80; Midland Sinfonia Concert Soc. Ltd, 1972–80; (also co-Founder) Assoc. for Business Sponsorship of The Arts Ltd, 1975–84 (Chm., 1975–80); Bristol Hippodrome Trust Ltd, 1977–81; Bath Archaeological Trust Ltd, 1978–81; The Palladian Trust Ltd, 1979–82; Mem., Chancellor of Duchy of Lancaster's Cttee of Honour on Business and the Arts, 1980–81. Arts sponsorship initiatives include responsibility for: Internat. Cello Competition (with Tortelier), Bristol, 1975 and 1977; Internat. Conductors Awards, 1978; Pompeii Exhibn, RA, 1976–77; new prodns at Royal Opera House, Covent Garden, at Glyndebourne, and at National Theatre. Governor: Manning Grammar Sch., Nottingham, 1972–73; Clayesmore Sch., Dorset, 1975–85. Chm., St John Ambulance Foundn in Bophuthatswana, 1989–. Liveryman, Worshipful Co of Tobacco Pipe Makers and Tobacco Blenders, 1973; Freeman, City of London, 1974. FRSA 1975; FRCSoc 1976. CStJ 1991 (OStJ 1977). *Publications:* papers, articles and documentary film treatments on the arts, sponsorship, and tobacco industry topics. *Recreations:* game watching, fishing, shooting, reading. *Address:* Post Bag X2046, Mmabatho 8681, Republic of Bophuthatswana, Southern Africa. *Clubs:* Carlton, MCC.

KNOWLES, George Peter; Registrar of the Province and Diocese of York, and Archbishop of York's Legal Secretary, 1968–87; *b* 30 Dec. 1919; *s* of Geoffrey Knowles and Mabel Bowman; *m* 1948, Elizabeth Margaret Scott; one *s* two *d*. *Educ:* Clifton Coll., Bristol; Queens' Coll., Cambridge. MA, LLM. Served war, Royal Artillery, 1939–46 (Lieut). Admitted a solicitor, 1948; Chm., York Area Rent Tribunal, 1959; Mem., Mental Health Review Tribunal for Yorkshire Regional Health Authority Area, 1960. *Recreations:* gardening, fishing, wildlife. *Address:* 11 Lang Road, Bishopthorpe, York YO2 1QJ. *T:* York (0904) 706443. *Club:* Yorkshire (York).

KNOWLES, Prof. Jeremy Randall, FRS 1977; Amory Houghton Professor of Chemistry and Biochemistry (formerly of Chemistry), Harvard University, since 1974; *b* 28 April 1935; *s* of late Kenneth Guy Jack Charles Knowles and of Dorothy Helen Swingler; *m* 1960, Jane Sheldon Davis; three *s*. *Educ:* Magdalen College Sch.; Balliol Coll. (Hon. Fellow 1984), Merton Coll. and Christ Church, Oxford (MA, DPhil). Sir Louis Stuart Exhibr, Balliol Coll., Oxford, 1955–59; Harmsworth Schol., Merton Coll., Oxford, and Research Lectr, Christ Church, Oxford, 1960–62; Research Associate, Calif. Inst. of Technology, 1961–62; Fellow of Wadham Coll., Oxf., 1962–74 (Hon. Fellow 1990); Univ. Lectr, Univ. of Oxford, 1966–74. Visiting Prof., Yale Univ., 1969, 1971; Sloan Vis. Prof., Harvard Univ., 1973; Newton-Abraham Vis. Prof., Oxford Univ., 1983–84. Fellow, Amer. Acad. of Arts and Scis, 1982; Foreign Associate, Nat. Acad. of Scis, USA, 1988; Mem., Amer. Philosophical Soc., 1988. Charmian Medal, RSC, 1980; Prelog Medal, ETH, 1989. *Publications:* research papers and reviews in learned jls. *Address:* 44 Coolidge Avenue, Cambridge, Mass 02138, USA. *T:* (617) 876–8469.

KNOWLES, Sir Leonard Joseph, Kt 1974; CBE 1963; barrister; Chief Justice of the Bahamas, 1973–78; *b* Nassau, 15 March 1916; *s* of late Samuel Joseph Knowles; *m* 1939, Harriet Hansen, *d* of John Hughes, Liverpool; two *s*. *Educ:* Queen's Coll., Nassau, Bahamas; King's Coll., Univ. of London (LLB); first Bahamian student to take and pass Higher Sch. Certif. in Bahamas, 1934; LLB Hons 1937, 1st cl. in Final Bar Examinations; BD London, 1985. Called to the Bar, Gray's Inn, London, 1939; Lord Justice Holker Scholar, Gray's Inn, 1940; practised law in Liverpool for some years. Served War of 1939–45, Royal Air Force (radar). Returned to Nassau, 1948, and was called to local Bar; Attorney-at-Law and Actg Attorney-Gen. of the Bahamas, 1949; Registrar-Gen., 1949–50. Past Stipendiary and Circuit Magistrate. Chm., Labour Board, Bahamas, 1953–63; MLC (Upper House of Legislature), 1960–63; President, Senate, 1964; re-elected, 1967, 1968, and continued to hold that office until 1972; returned to private law practice, 1978. Methodist local preacher. *Publications:* Elements of Bahamian Law, 1978, 2nd edn 1989; Financial Relief in Matrimonial Cases, 1980; Bahamian Real Property Law, 1989; My Life (autobiog.), 1989. *Recreations:* music, motion photography, swimming. *Address:* PO Box SS 6378, Nassau, Bahamas. *Fax:* 809–393–1651. *Club:* Commonwealth Trust.

KNOWLES, Michael; MP (C) Nottingham East, since 1983; *b* 21 May 1942; *s* of Martin Christopher and Anne Knowles; *m* 1965, Margaret Isabel Thorburn; three *d*. *Educ:* Clapham Coll. RC Grammar Sch. Sales Manager, Export & Home Sales. Mem. (C), 1971–83, Leader, 1974–83, Kingston upon Thames Borough Council. PPS to Minister for Planning and Regional Affairs, DoT, 1986–; Member: Select Cttee on European Legislation; Select Cttee on Defence. *Recreations:* walking, history. *Address:* 2 Ditton Reach, Portsmouth Road, Thames Ditton, Surrey KT7 0XB.

KNOWLES, Dr Michael Ernest, CChem, FRSC; FIFST; Chief Scientist (Fisheries and Food), Ministry of Agriculture, Fisheries and Food, since 1989; *b* 6 May 1942; *s* of late Ernest Frederick Walter Knowles and Lesley (*née* Lambert); *m* 1965, Rosalind Mary Griffiths (marr. diss. 1975); two *s*. *Educ:* Nottingham Univ. (BPharm 1st cl. Hons; PhD). CChem 1969; FRSC 1982; FIFST 1983. ICI Postdoctoral Fellow, Nottingham Univ., 1967–69; Ministry of Agriculture, Fisheries and Food: Food Sci. Unit, Norwich, 1969–74; Scientific Advr, Food Sci. Div., 1974–79; Head, Food Sci. Lab., 1979–85; Head, Food Sci. Div., 1985–89. *Publications:* series of papers on chemical aspects of food safety in learned jls. *Recreations:* target shooting, walking. *Address:* 120 Chatham Road, SW11 6HH. *T:* 071–223 3189. *Clubs:* Savage; Strangers (Norwich).

KNOWLES, (Patricia) Ann; Editor, The Universe, since 1990; *b* 31 Oct. 1944; *d* of John and Margaret Miller; *m* 1964, Leslie John Knowles; two *s* one *d*. *Educ:* Our Lady's Prep. Sch., Barrow-in-Furness; Our Lady's Convent Sch.; Open Univ. (BA). Reporter: North

Western Evening Mail, Barrow, 1962–68; North Somerset Mercury, Clevedon, 1969–70; Western Daily Press, Bristol, 1970–72; Theatre Critic, Evening Star, Burnley, 1973–77; Sub-Editor, Dep. Chief Sub-Editor, News Editor, Burnley Express, 1977–84; Asst Editor, Citizen Publications, Blackburn, 1985–87; Sub-Editor, Keighley News, 1987–89; Group Editor, Herald and Post, Burnley, 1989–90. *Recreations:* Soroptimist International, National Association of Tangent Clubs, gardening, interior decoration. *Address:* The Universe, First Floor, St James's Buildings, Oxford Street, Manchester; The Rough, Castle Road, Colne, Lancs BB8 7DS.

KNOWLES, Peter Francis Arnold; Parliamentary Counsel, since 1991; *b* 10 July 1949; *s* of Sidney Francis Knowles and Patricia Anette Knowles (*née* New); *m* 1972, Patricia Katharine Clifford; two *s. Educ:* Whitgift School, Croydon; University College, Oxford (MA). Called to the Bar, Gray's Inn, 1971. In practice at Chancery Bar, 1973–75; joined Parliamentary Counsel Office, 1975; with Law Commission, 1979–81. *Recreations:* music, sailing, ski-ing, classic car restoration. *Address:* Parliamentary Counsel Office, 36 Whitehall, SW1A 2AY.

KNOWLES, Sir Richard (Marchant), Kt 1989; Member, 1972–74 and since 1978, and Leader, since 1984, Birmingham City Council; *b* 20 May 1917; *s* of William and Charlotte Knowles; *m* 1st, 1941, Dorothy Forster (*d* 1979); one *s*; 2nd, 1981, Anne Little (*née* Macmenemey). *Educ:* village schools in Kent; WEA; technical school. Building industry, 1931–39; served RE, 1940; building and shipbuilding, 1941–50; Labour Organiser, Sevenoaks, Dover, Leeds and Birmingham, 1950–72; Nat. Organiser, Co-op Party, 1971–83. Mem., W Midlands County Council, 1973–77; Chm., Planning Cttee, Birmingham CC, 1972–74, 1980–82. Mem., Policy Cttee, AMA, 1974–77, 1984–. Dir, Nat. Exhibition Centre Ltd, 1982–. *Publications:* UNIP Election Manual, 1964; ABC of Organisation, 1977; A Voice for your Neighbourhood, 1977; contribs to local govt jls, planning and political pamphlets. *Recreations:* cycling, travel, rough gardening. *Address:* 64 Woodgate Lane, Bartley Green, Birmingham B32 3QY. *T:* 021–422 8061.

KNOWLES, Timothy; Finance Director, Insurance Services, Export Credits Guarantee Department, since 1990; *b* 17 May 1938; *s* of Cyril William Knowles and Winifred Alice Knowles (*née* Hood); *m* 1967, Gaynor Hallett; one *d. Educ:* Bishop Gore Grammar Sch., Swansea. Chartered Accountant. Company Sec./Accountant, Louis Marx & Co. Ltd, 1960–68; Controller, Modco Valenite, 1968–69; HTV Ltd: Company Sec., 1969–78; Financial Dir, 1975–81; Asst Man. Dir, 1981–86; HTV Group plc: Financial Dir, 1976–86; Gp Man. Dir., 1986–88. Director: Frost & Reed (Holdings) Ltd, 1985–88; Welsh Water Plc, 1989–. Member: S Wales Electricity Bd, 1981–82; Welsh Water Authority, 1982–89. Contested (C) Swansea East, 1966. *Recreations:* travel, walking, watching cricket. *Address:* Cae Ffynnon, 12 Ger-y-Llan, St Nicholas, Cardiff CF5 6SY. *T:* Peterston-super-Ely (0446) 760726. *Club:* Cardiff and County (Cardiff).

KNOWLES, Wyn; Editor, Woman's Hour, BBC, 1971–83; *b* 30 July 1923; *d* of Frederick Knowles and Dorothy Ellen Knowles (*née* Harrison). *Educ:* St Teresa's Convent, Effingham; Convents of FCJ in Ware and Switzerland; Polytechnic Sch. of Art, London. Cypher Clerk, War Office, 1941–45. Secretarial work, 1948–57; joined BBC, 1951; Asst Producer, Drama Dept, 1957–60; Woman's Hour: Producer, Talks Dept, 1960–65; Asst Editor, 1965–67; Dep. Editor, 1967–71. *Publication:* (ed with Kay Evans) The Woman's Hour Book, 1981. *Recreations:* travel, cooking, writing, painting, being a London Zoo Volunteer. *Address:* 80A Parkway, Regent's Park, NW1 7AN. *T:* 071–485 8258.

KNOWLTON, Richard James, CBE 1983; QFSM 1977; HM Chief Inspector of Fire Services (Scotland), 1984–89; *b* 2 Jan. 1928; *s* of Richard John Knowlton and Florence May Humby; *m* 1949, Pamela Vera Horne; one *s. Educ:* Bishop Wordsworth's Sch., Salisbury. FIFE. Served 42 Commando RM, 1945. Southampton Fire Bde, 1948; Station Officer, Worcester City and County Fire Bde, 1959; London Fire Brigade: Asst Divl Officer, 1963; Divl Officer, 1965; Divl Comdr, 1967; Winston Churchill Travelling Fellowship, 1969; Firemaster: SW Area (Scotland) Fire Bde, 1971; Strathclyde Fire Bde, 1975–84. Mem., later Chm., Bds, Fire Service Coll. Extended Interview, 1970–81; Mem., Fire Service Coll. Bd, 1978–82; Mem., later Chm., Scottish Fire Services Examinations Panel, 1971–75; Mem., Scottish Fire Service Examinations Bd, 1974–75; Fire Adviser: to Scottish Assoc. of CCs, 1974; to Convention of Scottish Local Authorities, 1975–81; Sec. to Appliances and Equipment Cttee of Chief and Asst Chief Fire Officers Assoc., 1974–81, Pres. of the Assoc., 1980; Chm., Scottish Dist Chief and Asst Chief Fire Officers Assoc., 1977–81; Zone Fire Comdr (Designate), CD for Scotland, 1975–84; Member: Scottish Central Fire Bdes Adv. Council, 1977–81 (Uniform and Personal Equipment Cttee, 1974–82); Jt Cttee on Design and Develt, 1978–82; England and Wales Central Fire Bdes Adv. Council, 1979–81; Chairman: London Branch, Instn of Fire Engineers, 1969; Scottish Assoc., Winston Churchill Fellows, 1979–81; Hazfile Cttee, 1979–81; Vice-Pres., Fire Services Nat. Benevolent Fund, 1981– (Chm. 1980). Mem., Nat. Jt Council for Chief Fire Officers, 1980–82; Mem., later Chm., Management Structures Working Gp of Nat. Jt Council for Local Authority Fire Bdes, 1980–83; British Mem., Admin. Council of European Assoc. of Professional Fire Bde Officers, 1981–85 (Vice Pres., 1984–85). *Address:* 5 Potters Way, Laverstock, Salisbury, Wilts SP1 1PY. *T:* Salisbury (0722) 326487.

KNOX, family name of **Earl of Ranfurly.**

KNOX, (Alexander) David; CMG 1988; Vice President, International Bank for Reconstruction and Development, 1980–87, retired; *b* 15 Jan. 1925; *s* of James Knox and Elizabeth Maxwell Knox; *m* 1950, Beatrice Lily (*née* Dunell); one *s* two *d. Educ:* Univ. of Toronto (BA); London School of Economics and Political Science (Hon. Fellow, 1982). LSE, 1949–63, Reader in Economics, 1955–63; International Bank for Reconstruction and Development (World Bank), 1963–87: Vice President: W Africa, 1980–84; Latin America, 1984–87. *Publications:* Latin American Debt: facing facts, 1990; articles in Economica, OECF Res. Qly (Japan), etc. *Recreations:* opera, walking. *Address:* Knights Barn, Manor Farm Lane, East Hagbourne, Oxon OX11 9ND. *T:* Didcot (0235) 817792. *Club:* Reform.

KNOX, Bryce Harry, CB 1986; a Deputy Chairman, and Director General, Internal Taxation Group, Board of Customs and Excise, 1983–88, retired; *b* 21 Feb. 1929; *e s* of Brice Henry Knox and Rose Hetty Knox; *m* Norma, *d* of late George Thomas and of Rose Thomas; one *s. Educ:* Stratford Grammar Sch.; Nottingham Univ. BA(Econ). Asst Principal, HM Customs and Excise, 1953; Principal, 1958; on loan to HM Treasury, 1963–65; Asst Sec., HM Customs and Excise, 1966; seconded to HM Diplomatic Service, Counsellor, Office of UK Perm. Rep. to European Communities, 1972–74; Under-Sec., 1974, Comr, 1975, HM Customs and Excise. *Address:* 9 Manor Way, Blackheath, SE3 9EF. *T:* 081–852 9404. *Clubs:* Reform; MCC.

KNOX, Col Sir Bryce (Muir), KCVO 1990; MC 1944 and Bar, 1944; TD 1947; Lord-Lieutenant of Ayrshire and Arran (formerly County of Ayr), 1974–91 (Vice-Lieutenant, 1970–74); Vice-Chairman, Lindustries Ltd, 1979 (Director, 1953–79); *b* 4 April 1916; *s* of late James Knox, Kilbirnie; *m* 1948, Patricia Mary Dunsmuir (*d* 1989); one *s* one *d. Educ:* Stowe; Trinity Coll., Cambridge. Served with Ayrshire (ECO) Yeomanry, 1939–45, N Africa and Italy; CO, 1953–56; Hon. Col, 1969–71; Hon. Col, The Ayrshire

Yeomanry Sqdn, Queen's Own Yeomanry, T&AVR, 1971–77; Pres., Lowlands TA&VRA, 1978–83. Member, Queen's Body Guard for Scotland, Royal Company of Archers. CStJ. *Publication:* The History of the Eglinton Hunt, 1984. *Recreation:* country sports. *Address:* Martnaham Lodge, By Ayr KA6 6ES. *T:* Dalrymple (029256) 204.

KNOX, David; *see* Knox, A. D.

KNOX, David Laidlaw; MP (C) Staffordshire Moorlands, since 1983 (Leek Division of Staffordshire, 1970–83); *b* 30 May 1933; *s* of late J. M. Knox, Lockerbie and Mrs C. H. C. Knox (*née* Laidlaw); *m* 1980, Mrs Margaret Eva Maxwell, *d* of late A. McKenzie. *Educ:* Lockerbie Academy; Dumfries Academy; London Univ. (BSc (Econ) Hons). Management Trainee, 1953–56; Printing Executive, 1956–62; O&M Consultant, 1962–70. Contested (C): Stechford, Birmingham, 1964 and 1966; Nuneaton, March 1967. PPS to Ian Gilmour, Minister of State for Defence, 1973, Sec. of State for Defence, 1974. Secretary: Cons. Finance Cttee, 1972–73; Cons. Trade Cttee, 1974; Vice-Chm., Cons. Employment Cttee, 1979–80; Member: Select Cttee on European Legislation, 1976–; House of Commons Chairmen's Panel, 1983–; Chairman: W Midlands Area Young Conservatives, 1963–64; W Midlands Area Cons. Political Centre, 1966–69; a Vice Chairman: Cons. Party Organisation, 1974–75; Cons. Gp for Europe, 1984–87. Editor, Young Conservatives National Policy Group, 1963–64. *Recreations:* watching association football, reading. *Address:* House of Commons, SW1A 0AA.

KNOX, Prof. Henry Macdonald; Professor of Education, The Queen's University of Belfast, 1951–82; *b* 26 Nov. 1916; *e s* of Rev. R. M. Knox, Edinburgh, and J. E. Church; *m* 1945, Marian, *yr d* of N. Starkie, Todmorden; one *s* one *d. Educ:* George Watson's Coll., Edinburgh; University of Edinburgh. MA 1938; MEd 1940; PhD 1949. Served as Captain, Intelligence Corps, commanding a wireless intelligence section, Arakan sector of Burma, and as instructor, War Office special wireless training wing, 1940–46. Lecturer in Education, University Coll. of Hull, 1946; Lecturer in Education, University of St Andrews, 1949; former Dean of Faculty of Education, and acting Dir, Inst. of Educn, 1968–69, QUB. Assessor in Educn, Univ. of Strathclyde, 1984–89; sometime Examiner in Educn, Universities of Durham, Leeds, Sheffield, Aberdeen, Glasgow, Strathclyde, Wales and Ireland (National); occasional Examiner, Universities of Edinburgh, Belfast, Dublin and Bristol. Chm., N Ireland Council for Educn Research, 1979–82; Member: Advisory Council on Educn for N Ireland, 1955–58, 1961–64; Senior Certificate Examination Cttee for N Ireland, 1962–65; Adv. Bd for Postgraduate Studentships in Arts Subjects, Ministry of Educn for N Ireland, 1962–74; Adv. Cttee on Supply and Training of Teachers for NI, 1976–82; NI Council for Educnl Develt, 1980–82. Mem. Governing Body: Stranmillis Coll. of Educn, Belfast, 1968–82 (Vice-Chm., 1975–82); St Joseph's Coll. of Educn, Belfast, 1968–82. *Publications:* Two Hundred and Fifty Years of Scottish Education, 1696–1946, 1953; John Dury's Reformed School, 1958; Introduction to Educational Method, 1961; Schools in Europe (ed W. Schultze): Northern Ireland, 1969; numerous articles in educational journals. *Address:* 9 Elliot Gardens, Colinton, Edinburgh EH14 1EH. *T:* 031–441 6283.

KNOX, Jean M.; *see* Swaythling, Lady.

KNOX, John; Under-Secretary, Department of Trade and Industry, retired, 1974; Head of Research Contractors Division, 1972–74; *b* 11 March 1913; *s* of William Knox and May Ferguson; *m* 1942, Mary Blackwood Johnston, *d* of late Rt Hon. Thomas Johnston, CH; one *s* one *d. Educ:* Lenzie Acad.; Glasgow Univ. (Kitchener's Schol.; MA). Business Management Trng, 1935–39; joined RAE, 1939; Op. Research with RAF, 1939–45; Asst Chief Scientific Adviser, Min. of Works, 1945–50; Dep. Dir and Dir, Intelligence Div., DSIR, 1950–58; Dep. Dir (Industry), DSIR, 1958–64; Min. of Technology, later DTI: Asst Controller, 1964–65; CSO, Head of External Research and Materials Div., 1965–68; Head of Materials Div., 1968–71; Head of Res. Div., 1971–73. *Publications:* occasional articles on management of research, development and industrial innovation. *Recreation:* golf. *Address:* 6 Mariners Court, Victoria Road, Aldeburgh, Suffolk IP15 5EH. *T:* Aldeburgh (072885) 3657.

KNOX, John, (Jack), RSA 1979 (ARSA 1972); RGI 1980; RSW 1987; Head of Painting Studios, Glasgow School of Art, since 1981; *b* 16 Dec. 1936; *s* of Alexander and Jean Knox; *m* 1960, Margaret Kyle Sutherland; one *s* one *d. Educ:* Lenzie Acad.; Glasgow Sch. of Art (DA). On the Drawing and Painting Staff at Duncan of Jordanstone Coll. of Art, Dundee, 1965–81. Work in permanent collections: Scottish Nat. Gallery of Modern Art; Arts Council; Contemporary Arts Soc.; Scottish Arts Council; Otis Art Inst., Los Angeles; Olinda Museum, São Paulo; Aberdeen, Dundee and Manchester art galleries; Hunterian Museum, Glasgow; Scottish Nat. Portrait Gall.; Kelvingrove Art Galls and Mus. Retrospective exhibn, Knox 1960–83, Scottish Arts Council, 1983. Member: Scottish Arts Council, 1974–79; Trustees Cttee, Scottish Nat. Gallery of Modern Art, 1975–81; Bd of Trustees, Nat. Galls of Scotland, 1982–87. Sec., Royal Scottish Acad., 1990–. Member: Bd of Governors, Duncan of Jordanstone Coll. of Art, Dundee, 1980–82; Bd of Governors, Glasgow Sch. of Art, 1985–88. *Address:* 31 North Erskine Park, Bearsden, Glasgow G61 4LY.

KNOX, John Andrew; Grade 3, since 1979, and Deputy Director, Serious Fraud Office; *b* 22 July 1937; *s* of late James Telford Knox and Mary Knox; *m* 1964, Patricia Mary Martin; one *s* one *d. Educ:* Dame Allan's Sch., Newcastle upon Tyne; Merton Coll., Oxford (MA). ACA 1964, FCA 1974. Cooper Brothers & Co. Chartered Accountants, 1961–65; Vickers Ltd, 1966–72; entered CS as a Sen. Accountant, 1972; Chief Accountant, 1973; Asst Sec., 1976; Head of Accountancy Services Div., 1977–85; Hd of Industrial Financial Appraisal Div, DTI, 1985–87; Chief Accountant, Serious Fraud Office, 1987. Leonard Shaw Award for Management Accountancy, Leonard Shaw Meml Fund, 1973. *Recreation:* tennis. *Address:* c/o Serious Fraud Office, Elm House, Elm Street, WC1.

KNOX, Prof. John Henderson, FRS 1984; FRSE 1971; University Fellow and Emeritus Professor of Physical Chemistry, University of Edinburgh, 1984; *b* 21 Oct. 1927; *s* of John Knox and Elizabeth May Knox (*née* Henderson); *m* 1957, Josephine Anne Wissler; four *s. Educ:* George Watson's Boys' Coll.; Univ. of Edinburgh (BSc 1949, DSc 1963); Univ. of Cambridge (PhD 1953). University of Edinburgh: Lectr in Chemistry, 1953–66; Reader in Physical Chemistry, 1966–74; Director of Wolfson Liquid Chromatography Unit, 1972–; Personal Prof. of Phys. Chem., 1974–84. Sen. Vis. Research Scientist Fellow, Univ. of Utah, 1963. *Publications:* Gas Chromatography, 1962; Molecular Thermodynamics, 1971, 2nd edn 1978; Applications of High Speed Liquid Chromatography, 1974; High Performance Liquid Chromatography, 1978, 3rd edn 1983. *Recreations:* skiing, sailing, hill walking. *Address:* 67 Morningside Park, Edinburgh EH10 5EZ. *T:* 031–447 5057.

KNOX, Hon. Sir John (Leonard), Kt 1985; **Hon. Mr Justice Knox;** a Judge of the High Court of Justice, Chancery Division, since 1985; *b* 6 April 1925; *s* of Leonard Needham Knox and Berthe Hélène Knox; *m* 1953, Anne Jacqueline Mackintosh (*d* 1991); one *s* three *d. Educ:* Radley Coll.; Worcester Coll., Oxford (Hon. Mods, 1st Cl.; Jurisprudence, 1st Cl.). Called to the Bar, Lincoln's Inn, 1953, Bencher, 1977; Member, Senate of the Inns of Court, 1975–78. QC 1979; Junior Treasury Counsel: in *bona vacantia,*

1971–79; in probate, 1978–79; Attorney-Gen., Duchy of Lancaster, 1984–85. Member: Lord Chancellor's Law Reform Cttee, 1978–; Council of Legal Educn, 1975–79; Chm., Chancery Bar Assoc., 1985. Dep. Chm., Parly Boundary Commn, 1987–. *Address:* Royal Courts of Justice, Strand, WC2. *Club:* Beefsteak.

KNOX, Robert, MA, MD, FRCP, FRCPath; Emeritus Professor of Bacteriology, University of London (Professor of Bacteriology, Guy's Hospital Medical School, 1949–69); *b* 29 May 1904; *s* of Dr Robert Knox, radiologist; *m* 1936, Bessie Lynda Crust; three *d. Educ:* Highgate; Balliol Coll., Oxford (Classical Scholar); St Bartholomew's Hosp. 1st Class Hon. Mods, 1924, 2nd Class Lit Hum, 1926; BA Oxford, 1927; MB, BS London, 1932; MD 1934; MRCS 1932; LRCP 1932, MRCP 1934, FRCP 1953; FCPath, 1964. House Physician and Chief Asst St Bartholomew's Hosp., 1932–35; MA Cambridge 1935; Demonstrator in Pathology, University of Cambridge, 1935–37; Mem. of Scientific Staff, Imperial Cancer Research Fund, 1937–39; Dir of Public Health Laboratories (Med. Research Council) at Stamford, 1939, Leicester 1940, and Oxford, 1945; MA Oxford, 1945. Fellow Royal Society Medicine; Member: Pathological Soc.; Soc. of Gen. Microbiology; Assoc. of Clinical Pathologists. *Publications:* on bacteriological subjects in medical and scientific journals. *Recreations:* coxed Oxford Univ., 1925; golf. *Address:* Five Pines, The Marld, Ashtead, Surrey KT21 1RQ. *T:* Ashtead (0372) 275102.

KNOX, Hon. Sir William Edward, Kt 1979; FCIT, FAIM; MLA (Lib), Nundah, 1957–89; Leader of Parliamentary Liberal Party, Queensland, 1983–88; *b* 14 Dec. 1927; *s* of E. Knox, Turramurra; *m* 1956, Doris Ross; two *s* two *d. Educ:* Melbourne High School. State Pres., Qld Young Liberals, 1953–56; Vice-Pres., Qld Div., Liberal Party, 1956–57, Mem. Exec., 1953–58, 1962–65; Sec., Parly Lib. Party, 1960–65. Minister for Transport, Qld, 1965–72; Minister for Justice and Attorney-Gen., Qld, 1971–76; Dep. Premier and Treasurer of Qld, 1976–78; Leader, State Parly Liberal Party, 1976–78; Minister for Health, Qld, 1978–80; Minister for Employment and Labour Relations, Qld, 1980–83. Chm., Qld Road Safety Council and Mem., Aust. Transport Adv. Council, 1965–72. Mem., Nat. Exec. Aust. Jnr Chamber of Commerce, 1961–62; Senator Jnr Chamber Internat., 1962–; State Pres., Father and Son Movement, 1965; Chm., St John Council for Qld, 1983–. CStJ. *Address:* 1621 Sandgate Road, Nundah, Queensland 4012, Australia.

KNOX-JOHNSTON, Robin, (William Robert Patrick Knox-Johnston), CBE 1969; RD (and bar) 1983; Marina Consultant since 1974; *b* 17 March 1939; *s* of late David Robert Knox-Johnston and Elizabeth Mary Knox-Johnston (*née* Cree); *m* 1962, Suzanne (*née* Singer); one *d. Educ:* Berkhamsted School. Master Mariner; FRGS; MRIN. Merchant Navy, 1957–67. First person to sail single-handed non-stop Around the World 14 June 1968 to 22 April 1969, in yacht Suhaili; won Sunday Times Golden Globe, 1969; won Round Britain Race, Ocean Spirit, 1970; won round Britain Race, British Oxygen, 1974; set British transatlantic sailing record, from NY to the Lizard, 11 days 7 hours 45 mins, 1981; established new record of 10 days 14 hours 9 mins, 1986; set world sailing record for around Ireland, 76 hours 5 mins 34 secs, May 1986; World Class II Multihull Champion, 1985; completed Guardian Columbus voyage, 1989. Man. Dir, St Katharine's Yacht Haven Ltd, 1975–76; Director: Mercury Yacht Harbours Ltd, 1970–73; Rank Marine International, 1973–75; Troon Marina Ltd, 1976–83; National Yacht Racing Centre Ltd, 1979–86; Knox-Johnston Insurance Brokers Ltd, 1983–; St Katherine's Dock. Pres., British Olympic Yachting Appeal, 1977–; Mem. Cttee of Management, RNLI, 1983–. Freeman, Borough of Bromley, Kent, 1969; Younger Brother, Trinity House, 1973. Mem., Co. of Master Mariners, 1975. Lt-Comdr RNR 1971, retired. Hon. DSc Maine Maritime Acad., 1989. Yachtsman of the Year, 1969; Silk Cut Seamanship Award, 1990; Seamanship Foundn Trophy, RYA, 1991. *Publications:* A World of my Own, 1969; Sailing, 1975; Twilight of Sail, 1978; Last but not Least, 1978; Bunkside Companion, 1982; Seamanship, 1986; The BOC Challenge 1986–1987, 1988; The Cape of Good Hope, 1989; History of Yachting, 1990. *Recreation:* sailing. *Address:* 26 Sefton Street, Putney, SW15 1LZ. *Clubs:* Royal Cruising, Royal Ocean Racing.

KNOX-LECKY, Maj.-Gen. Samuel, CB 1979; OBE 1967; BSc(Eng); CEng, FIMechE; Director-General, Agricultural Engineers Association, 1980–88; *b* 10 Feb. 1926; *s* of late J. D. Lecky, Coleraine; *m* 1947, Sheila Jones; one *s* two *d. Educ:* Coleraine Acad.; Queen's Univ., Belfast (BSc). Commnd REME, 1946; served Egypt, 1951–52; Kenya, 1953–54; jssc 1964; AA&QMG HQ 1(BR) Corps, 1965–66; CREME 4 Div., 1966–68; Sec., Principal Personnel Officers, MoD, 1968–70; RCDS, 1971; Comdt, SEME, 1972–74; DEME, BAOR, 1975; Dir, Military Assistance Office, MoD, 1976–77; Minister (DS), British Embassy, Tehran, 1977–79. Hon. Col, QUB OTC, 1978–83; Col Comdt, REME, 1980–86. *Recreations:* fishing, sailing.

KNOX-MAWER, Ronald; retired; *b* 3 Aug. 1925; *s* of George Robert Knox-Mawer and Clara Roberts; *m* 1951, June Ellis; one *s* one *d. Educ:* Grove Park Sch.; Emmanuel Coll., Cambridge (Exhibitioner; MA). Royal Artillery, 1943–47. Called to Bar, Middle Temple; Wales and Chester Circuit, 1947–52; Chief Magistrate and Actg Chief Justice, Aden, 1952–58; Sen. Magistrate, Puisne Judge, Justice of Appeal, Actg Chief Justice, Fiji, and conjointly Chief Justice, Nauru and Tonga, 1958–71; Northern Circuit, 1971–75; Metropolitan Stipendiary Magistrate, 1975–84; Dep. Circuit Judge, London, 1979–84. Various series of humorous reminiscences broadcast on BBC Radio: Tales from a Palm Court, 1984; Islands of Hope and Glory, 1985; Wretchedness in Wrexham, 1986; More Tales from a Palm Court, 1987–88; Tales of a Man called Father, 1989; The Queen Goes West, 1990. *Publications:* Palm Court, 1979 (as Robert Overton); Tales from a Palm Court, 1986; Tales of a Man Called Father, 1989; short stories and features (under different pseudonyms) in Punch, Cornhill, Argosy, The Times, Sunday Express, Blackwoods, Listener, Weekend Telegraph etc.; ed 4 vols Colonial law reports; various contribs to legal jls. *Recreation:* countryside. *Address:* c/o Midland Bank, Ruabon, N Wales. *Club:* Commonwealth Trust.

KNUDSEN, Semon Emil; retired; Chairman and Chief Executive, White Motor Corporation, 1971–80; *b* 2 Oct. 1912; *o s* of William S. and Clara Euler Knudsen; *m* 1938, Florence Anne McConnell; one *s* three *d. Educ:* Dartmouth Coll.; Mass Inst. of Technology. Joined General Motors, 1939; series of supervisory posts; Gen. Man., Detroit Diesel Div., 1955; Gen. Man., Pontiac Motor Div., 1956; Gen. Man., Chevrolet Motor Div., 1961; Dir of General Motors and Gp Vice-Pres. i/c of all Canadian and overseas activities, 1965; Exec. Vice-Pres. with added responsibility for domestic non-automotive divs, 1966, also defense activities, 1967; resigned from Gen. Motors Corp., 1968; Pres., Ford Motor Co., 1968–69. Dir, First National Bank in Palm Beach. Mem., MIT Corp. Mem. Bd of Dirs, Boys Clubs of Amer.; Trustee, Oakland (Mich) Univ. Foundn and Cleveland Clinic Fund. *Recreations:* golf, tennis, deepsea fishing, hunting. *Address:* 300 E Long Lake Road, Suite 220, Bloomfield Hills, Mich 48304, USA. *Clubs:* Detroit Athletic (Detroit); Bloomfield Hills Country (Mich); Everglades, Seminole, Bath & Tennis (Fla); Augusta National (Ga).

KNUSSEN, (Stuart) Oliver; composer and conductor; Co-Artistic Director, Aldeburgh Festival, since 1983; Co-ordinator of Contemporary Music Activities, Berkshire Music Center, Tanglewood, 1986–90; *b* Glasgow, 12 June 1952; *s* of Stuart Knussen and Ethelyn Jane Alexander; *m* 1972, Susan Freedman; one *d. Educ:* Watford Field Sch.; Watford Boys Grammar Sch.; Purcell Sch. Private composition study with John Lambert, 1963–68; Countess of Munster Awards, 1964, 1965, 1967; Peter Stuyvesant Foundn Award, 1965; début conducting Symph. no 1 with LSO, 1968; Watney-Sargent award for Young Conductors, 1969; Fellowships to Berkshire Music Center, Tanglewood, 1970, 1971, 1973; Caird Trav. Schol., 1971; Margaret Grant Composition Prize (Symph. no 2), Tanglewood, 1971; study with Gunther Schuller in USA, 1970–73; Koussevitzky Centennial Commn, 1974; Composer-in-residence: Aspen Fest., 1976; Arnolfini Gall., 1978; Instr in composition, RCM Jun. Dept, 1977–82; BBC commn for Proms 1979 (Symph. no 3); Berkshire Music Center, Tanglewood: Guest Teacher, 1981; Composer-in-residence, 1986. Arts Council Bursaries, 1979, 1981; winner, first Park Lane Gp Composer award (suite from Where the Wild Things Are), 1982; BBC commn for Glyndebourne Opera, 1983. Frequent guest conductor: London Sinfonietta, Philharmonia Orch., many other ensembles, UK and abroad, 1981–; Associate Guest Conductor, BBC SO, 1989–; Dir, Almeida Ensemble, 1986–. Mem. Executive Cttee, Soc. for Promotion of New Music, 1978–85; Member: Leopold Stokowski Soc.; International Alban Berg Soc., New York. *Publications:* Symphony no 1 op. 1, 1966–67; Symphony no 2 op. 7, 1970–71; Symphony no 3 op. 18, 1973–79; Where the Wild Things Are—opera (Maurice Sendak), op. 20, 1979–83 (staged, Glyndebourne at NT, 1984); Higglety Pigglety Pop!—opera (Sendak), op. 21, 1983–85 (staged Glyndebourne, 1984 and 1985); numerous orchestral, chamber, vocal works; articles in Tempo, The Listener, etc. *Recreations:* cinema, record collecting, record producing, visual arts. *Address:* c/o Faber Music Ltd, 3 Queen Square, WC1.

KNUTSFORD, 6th Viscount *cr* 1895; **Michael Holland-Hibbert;** Bt 1853; Baron 1888; DL; *b* 27 Dec. 1926; *s* of Hon. Wilfrid Holland-Hibbert (*d* 1961) (2nd *s* of 3rd Viscount) and of Audrey, *d* of late Mark Fenwick; *S* cousin, 1986; *m* 1951, Hon. Sheila, *d* of 5th Viscount Portman; two *s* one *d. Educ:* Eton College; Trinity Coll., Cambridge (BA). Welsh Guards, 1945–48. SW Regional Director, Barclays Bank, 1956–86. National Trust: Chm. Cttee for Devon and Cornwall, 1973–86; Mem. Exec. Cttee, 1973–86; Mem. Council, 1979–85; Mem. Finance Cttee, 1986–. DL 1977, High Sheriff 1977–78, Devon. *Heir: er s* Hon. Henry Thurstan Holland-Hibbert [*b* 6 April 1959; *m* 1988, Katherine, *d* of Sir John Ropner, Bt, *qv*; one *d*]. *Address:* Broadclyst House, Exeter, Devon EX5 3EW. *T:* Exeter (0392) 61244. *Club:* Brooks's.

KNUTTON, Maj.-Gen. Harry, CB 1975; MSc, CEng, FIEE; Director-General, City and Guilds of London Institute, 1976–85; *b* Rawmarsh, Yorks, 26 April 1921; *m* 1958, Pamela Brackley, E Sheen, London; three *s* one *d. Educ:* Wath-upon-Dearne Grammar Sch.; RMCS. Commnd RA, 1943; served with 15th Scottish and 1st Airborne Divs, NW Europe, 1944–45; India, 1945–47; Instructor in Gunnery, 1946–49; Project Officer, Min. of Supply, 1949–51; served Middle East, 1953–55; Directing Staff, RMCS, 1955–58; jssc 1958; various staff appts, MoD, 1958–60, 1962–64, 1966–67; Comdr Missile Regt, BAOR, 1964–66; Comdr Air Defence Bde, 1967–69; Fellow, Loughborough Univ. of Technology, 1969–70; Dir-Gen. Weapons (Army), 1970–73; Dir, Royal Ordnance Factories and Dep. Master-Gen. of Ordnance, 1973–75. Col Comdt, RA, 1977–82. Teacher, Whitgift Foundn, 1975–76. Member: Associated Examining Bd, 1976–85; Dep. Chm., Standing Conf. on Schools' Science and Technology, 1983–90. Governor, Imperial Coll. of Science and Technology, 1976–. CBIM 1978; FCollP 1983. FCGI 1985. Liveryman, Engineers' Co. *Publication:* contrib. to World Yearbook of Education (Vocational Education), 1987. *Address:* 43 Essendene Road, Caterham, Surrey CR3 5PB.

KOCH, Edward Irving; Mayor, City of New York, 1978–89; Partner, Robinson Silverman Pearce Aronsohn & Berman, New York, since 1990; *b* 12 Dec. 1924; *s* of Louis Koch and Joyce Silpe. *Educ:* Southside High School, Newark, NJ; City Coll. of NY; NY Univ. Law Sch. Served US Army, 1943–46, USA, France, Rhineland. Mem., NY State Bar, 1949; private law practice, 1949–64; Senior Partner, Koch, Lankenau, Schwartz & Kovner, 1965–69. Democratic dist. leader, Greenwich Village, 1963–65; Mem., NY City Council, 1967–68; NY Congressman, 1969–77. *Publications:* Mayor, 1983; Politics, 1985; (jtly) His Eminence and Hizzoner, 1989. *Address:* 2 Fifth Avenue, New York, NY 10011, USA.

KOECHLIN-SMYTHE, Patricia Rosemary, OBE 1956; President, British Show Jumping Association, 1983–86; Member of British Show Jumping Team, 1947–64; *b* 22 Nov. 1928; *d* of late Capt. Eric Hamilton Smythe, MC, Légion d'Honneur, and late Frances Monica Smythe (*née* Curtoys); *m* 1963, Samuel Koechlin (*d* 1985), Switzerland; two *d. Educ:* St Michael's Sch., Cirencester; Talbot Heath, Bournemouth. Show Jumping: first went abroad with British Team, 1947; Leading Show Jumper of the Year, 1949, 1958 (with T. Edgar), and 1962; European Ladies' Championship: Spa, 1957; Deauville, 1961; Madrid, 1962; Hickstead, 1963; Harringay: BSJA Spurs, 1949, 1951, 1952, 1954 (Victor Ludorum Championship), 1953 and 1954; Harringay Spurs, 1953; Grand Prix, Brussels, 1949, 1952 and 1956. Ladies' record for high jump (2 m. 10 cm.) Paris, 1950; won in Madrid, 1951. White City: 1951 (Country Life Cup); 1953 (Selby Cup). Was Leading Rider and won Prix du Champion, Paris, 1952; Leading Rider, etc, Marseilles, 1953; Individual Championship, etc, Harrisburg, Penn, USA, 1953; Pres. of Mexico Championship, New York, 1953; Toronto (in team winning Nations Cup), 1953; Lisbon (won 2 events), Grand Prix, Madrid, and Championship, Vichy, 1954; Grand Prix de Paris and 3 other events, 1954; Bruxelles Puissance and new ladies' record for high jump (2m. 24 cm.), Leading Rider of Show, 1954; BHS Medal of Honour, Algiers Puissance and Grand Prix, 4 events in Paris, 4 events at White City including the Championship, 1955; Grand Prix and Leading Rider of Show and 4 other events, Brussels, 1956; Grand Prix Militaire and Puissance, Lucerne; Mem. British Equestrian Olympic Team, Stockholm (Show Jumping Bronze Medal), 1956; IHS National Championship, White City; Leading Rider and other events, Palermo, 1956; won 2 Puissance events, Paris, 1957; BSJA, 1957; Ladies' National Championship in 1954–59 and 1961 and 1962 (8 times); Daily Mail Cup, White City, 1955, 1957, 1960, 1962; Mem. winning British Team, White City: 1952, 1953, 1956, 1957; Amazon Prize, Aachen, 1958; Queen's Cup, Royal Internat. Horse Show, White City, 1958; Preis von Parsenn, Davos, 1957, 1958, 1959; Championship Cup, Brussels Internat. Horse Show, 1958; Lisbon Grand Prix, 1959; Olympic Trial, British Timken Show, and Prix de la Banque de Bruxelles at Brussels, 1959. Lucerne Grand Prix; Prince Hal Stakes, Country Life and Riding Cup, White City; Pembroke Stakes, Horse Show Cttee Cup, and Leading Rider, Dublin (all in 1960). Mem. British Olympic Team in Rome, 1960. Copenhagen Grand Prix; Amazon Prize, Aachen; John Player Trophy, White City; St Gall Ladies Championship (all in 1961); Saddle of Honour and Loriners' Cup, White City, 1962; British Jumping Derby, Hickstead, 1962. Member: Internat. Council, WWF; Nat. Council, WWF UK; Bd, Earthwatch Europe; Achievement Bd, ICBP. Hon. Freeman, Worshipful Co. of Farriers, 1955; Freeman of the City of London, 1956; Hon. Freeman, Worshipful Company of Loriners, 1962; Yeoman, Worshipful Company of Saddlers, 1963. *Publications:* (as Pat Smythe): Jump for Joy; Pat Smythe's Story, 1954; Pat Smythe's Book of Horses, 1955; One Jump Ahead, 1956; Jacqueline rides for a Fall, 1957; Three Jays against the Clock, 1957; Three Jays on Holiday, 1958; Three Jays go to Town, 1959; Horses and Places, 1959; Three Jays over the Border, 1960; Three Jays go to Rome, 1960; Three Jays Lend a Hand, 1961; Jumping Round the World, 1962; Florian's Farmyard, 1962; Flanagan My Friend, 1963; Bred to Jump, 1965; Show Jumping, 1967; (with Fiona Hughes) A Pony for Pleasure, 1969; A Swiss Adventure, 1970; (with Fiona Hughes) Pony Problems, 1971; A Spanish Adventure, 1971; A Cotswold Adventure, 1972. *Recreations:* swimming, music, sailing, all sports, languages. *Address:* Sudgrove House, Miserden, near Stroud, Glos GL6 7JD. *T:* Miserden (028582) 360.

KOENIGSBERGER, Prof. Helmut Georg, MA, PhD; FBA 1989; Professor of History, King's College London, 1973–84, now Emeritus; *b* 24 Oct. 1918; *s* of late Georg Felix Koenigsberger, chief architect, borough of Treptow, Berlin, Germany, and of late Käthe Koenigsberger (*née* Born); *m* 1961, Dorothy M. Romano; two *d* (twins). *Educ:* Adams' Grammar Sch., Newport, Shropshire; Gonville and Caius Coll., Cambridge. Asst Master: Brentwood Sch., Essex, 1941–42; Bedford Sch., 1942–44. Served War of 1939–45, Royal Navy, 1944–45. Lecturer in Economic History, QUB, 1948–51; Senior Lecturer in Economic History, University of Manchester, 1951–60; Prof. of Modern History, University of Nottingham, 1960–66; Prof. of Early Modern European History, Cornell, 1966–73. Visiting Lecturer: Brooklyn Coll., New York, 1957; University of Wisconsin, 1958; Columbia University, 1962; Cambridge Univ., 1963; Washington Univ., St Louis, 1964; Fellow, Historisches Kolleg, Munich, 1984–85. Sec., 1955–75, Vice-Pres., 1975–80, Pres., 1980–85, Internat. Commn for the History of Representative and Parliamentary Institutions; Vice-Pres., RHistS, 1982–85. *Publications:* The Government of Sicily under Philip II of Spain, 1951, new edn, as The Practice of Empire, 1969; The Empire of Charles V in Europe (in New Cambridge Modern History II), 1958; Western Europe and the Power of Spain (in New Cambridge Modern History III), 1968; Europe in the Sixteenth Century (with G. L. Mosse), 1968, 2nd edn (with G. L. Mosse and G. Q. Bowler) 1989; Estates and Revolutions, 1971; The Habsburgs and Europe, 1516–1660, 1971; (ed) Luther: a profile, 1972; Politicians and Virtuosi, 1986; Medieval Europe, 1987; Early Modern Europe, 1987; (ed) Republiken und Republikanismus im Europa der frühen Neuzeit, 1988; contrib. to historical journals. *Recreations:* playing chamber music, sailing, travel. *Address:* 116 Waterfall Road, N14 7JN.

KOGAN, Prof. Maurice; Professor of Government and Social Administration, Brunel University, since 1969; *b* 10 April 1930; *s* of Barnett and Hetty Kogan; *m* 1960, Ulla Svensson; two *s*. *Educ:* Stratford Grammar Sch.; Christ's Coll., Cambridge (MA). Entered Civil Service, admin. cl. (1st in open examinations), 1953. Secretary: Secondary Sch. Exams Council, 1961; Central Advisory Council for Educn (England), 1963–66; Harkness Fellow of Commonwealth Fund, 1960–61; Asst Sec., DES, 1966. Brunel University: Head of Sch. of Social Scis, 1971–74; Dean, Faculty of Soc. Scis, 1987–89; Acting Vice-Chancellor, 1989–90. Member: Educn Sub-Cttee, Univ. Grants Cttee, 1972–75; SSRC, 1975–77; Davies Cttee on Hosp. Complaints' Procedure, 1971; Houghton Cttee on Teachers' Pay, 1974; Genetic Manipulation Adv. Gp, 1979–80; Chm., Adv. Gp, Cttee of award, Harkness Fellowship, 1989–. George A. Miller Vis. Prof., Univ. of Illinois, 1976; Vis. Scholar, Univ. of Calif, Berkeley, 1981. Hon. DSc (Econ) Hull, 1987. *Publications:* The Organisation of a Social Services Department, 1971; Working Relationships within the British Hospital Service, 1971; The Government of Education, 1971; The Politics of Education, 1971; (ed) The Challenge of Change, 1973; County Hall, 1973; Advisory Councils and Committees in Education, 1974; Educational Policy-Making, 1975; The Politics of Educational Change, 1978; The Working of the National Health Service, 1978; (with T. Becher) Process and Structure in Higher Education, 1980; The Government's Commissioning of Research, 1980; (with T. Bush) Directors of Education, 1982; (with D. Kogan) The Battle for the Labour Party, 1982; (with M. Henkel) Government and Research, 1983; (with D. Kogan) The Attack on Higher Education, 1983; (with T. Husen) Educational Research and Policy: how do they relate?, 1984; (with D. Johnson and others) School Governing Bodies, 1984; Education Accountability, 1986; (jtly) The Use of Performance Indicators in Higher Education, 1988; (jtly) Higher Education and Employment, 1988; (ed) Evaluating Higher Education, 1989; (jtly) Directors of Education Facing Reform, 1989; (jtly) Evaluation as Policy Making, 1990; contribs to TES, THES, Jl of Social Policy. *Recreations:* reading, listening to music. *Address:* 48 Duncan Terrace, Islington, N1 8AL. *T:* 071–226 0038.

KOHL, Helmut; Grosskreuz des Verdienstordens, 1979; Chancellor, Federal Republic of Germany, since 1982, re-elected, 1991, as Chancellor of the Federal Republic of Germany (reunited Germany); Chairman, Christian Democratic Union of Germany, since 1973; Member, Bundestag, since 1976; *b* 3 April 1930; *s* of Hans and Cäcilie Kohl; *m* 1960, Hannelore Renner; two *s*. *Educ:* Frankfurt Univ.; Heidelberg Univ. (Dr phil 1958 Heidelberg). On staff of a Trade Assoc., 1958–59; Mem., Parlt of Rhineland Palatinate, 1959–76; Leader, CDU Parly Party in Rhineland Palatinate Parlt, 1963–69; Mem., Federal Exec. Cttee of CDU at federal level, 1964–; Chm., CDU, Rhineland Palatinate, 1966–74; Minister-President, Rhineland Palatinate, 1969–76; Leader of the Opposition, Bundestag, 1976–82. Numerous foreign decorations. *Publications:* Die politische Entscheidung in der Pfalz und das Wiedererstehen der Parteien nach 1945, 1958; Hausputz hinter den Fassaden, 1971; Zwischen Ideologie und Pragmatismus, 1973; Die CDU: Porträt einer Volkspartei, 1981; Der Weg zur Wende, 1983; Reden 1982–1984, 1984. *Address:* Bundeskanzleramt, Adenauerallee 139/141, W-5300 Bonn 1, Federal Republic of Germany. *T:* 561; Marbacher Strasse 11, W-6700 Ludwigshafen (Rhein), Federal Republic of Germany.

KOHLER, Foy David; Associate, Advanced International Studies Institute; consultant, 1978–85; *b* 15 Feb. 1908; *s* of Leander David Kohler and Myrtle McClure; *m* 1935, Phyllis Penn. *Educ:* Toledo and Ohio State Univs, Ohio. US Foreign Service 1932–67: posts include: Amer. Emb., London, 1944; 1st Sec. Amer. Emb., Moscow, 1947; Counselor, 1948; Minister, Oct. 1948; Chief, Internat. Broadcasting Div., Dept of State, 1949; VOA 1949; Asst Administr, Internat. Information Admin, 1952; Policy Planning Staff, Dept of State, 1952; Counselor, Amer. Emb., Ankara, Turkey, 1953–56; detailed ICA, 1956–58; Deputy Asst Sec. of State for European Affairs, 1958–59; Asst Sec. of State, 1959–62; US Ambassador to USSR, 1962–66; Deputy Under-Sec. of State for Political Affairs, United States, 1966–67; Career Ambassador, USA, 1966. Prof., Univ. of Miami, 1968–80. Editor, Soviet World Outlook, 1976–85. Holds honorary doctorates. *Publications:* Understanding the Russians: a citizen's primer, 1970; (jtly) Soviet Strategy for the Seventies: from Cold War to peaceful coexistence, 1973; (jtly) The Role of Nuclear Forces in Current Soviet Strategy, 1974; (jtly) The Soviet Union: yesterday, today, tomorrow, 1975; Custine's Eternal Russia, 1976; Salt II: how not to negotiate with the Russians, 1979. *Recreations:* golf, swimming. *Address:* Waterford Tower Apt 1102, 605 South US Highway #1, Juno Beach, Fla 33408, USA.

Died 23 *Dec.* 1990.

KOHLER, Irene; pianist; Professor, Trinity College of Music, London, 1952–79; *b* London; *m* 1950, Dr Harry Waters, medical practitioner. *Educ:* Royal College of Music. Studied with Arthur Benjamin; Challen Medal, Danreuther Prize, etc; travelling scholarship to Vienna; studied there with Edward Steuermann and Egon Wellesz. BMus; Hon. FTCL, GRSM, LRAM, ARCM. First professional engagement, Bournemouth, 1933, resulting in engagement by BBC; played at first night of 40th Promenade Season, 1934. First foreign tour (recitals and broadcasts), Holland, 1938. During War of 1939–45 gave concerts for the Forces in this country and toured France and Belgium, also India and Burma, under auspices of ENSA; subsequently played in many countries of Europe and made tours. Eugene Goossens selected her for first European performance of his Phantasy Concerto; broadcast 1st performance of Sonata by Gunilla Lowenstein, Stockholm. She gave 3 concerts at the Festival Hall in Festival of Britain Year, 1951. Canadian American Tour, 1953; World Tour, 1955–56; African Tour, 1958; 2nd African Tour, 1959; Bulgarian Tour, 1959; 2nd World Tour, 1962; Czechoslovakian Tour, 1963; Scandinavian Tour, 1970; Far and Middle East Tour, 1972; recitals and master classes, Japan, 1979, 1981; Polish Tour, 1980. Film appearances include: Train of Events, Odette, Secret People, Lease of Life, and a documentary for the Ministry of Information. *Address:* 28 Castelnau, SW13 9RU. *T:* 081–748 5512.

KOHNSTAM, George, PhD; Principal of the Graduate Society, University of Durham, 1981–86 (Deputy Principal, 1972–81); Reader in Physical Chemistry, University of Durham, 1962–86; *b* 25 Dec. 1920; *s* of Emil and Margaret Kohnstam; *m* 1953, Patricia Elizabeth, *d* of Rev. A. W. G. Duffield and Margaret Duffield; one *s* three *d*. *Educ:* Royal Grammar Sch., High Wycombe; University Coll. London (BSc 1940, PhD 1948). Tuffnel Scholar, Univ. of London, 1940 (postponed); applied chemical res., 1941–45; Temp. Asst Lectr in Chemistry, UCL, 1948–50; Lectr in Phys. Chem., Univ. of Durham, 1950–59, Sen. Lectr, 1959–62. *Publications:* papers and review articles in chemical jls. *Recreations:* dinghy sailing, gardening, bridge, travel. *Address:* 67 Hallgarth Street, Durham City DH1 3AY. *T:* Durham (091) 3842018.

KOHNSTAMM, Max; Groot Officier, Order of Orange-Nassau, 1988; Comdr of the Order of House of Orange, 1949; Hon. Secretary-General, Action Committee for Europe, since 1989 (Sec.-Gen., 1985–88); *b* 22 May 1914; *s* of Dr Philip Abraham Kohnstamm and Johanna Hermana Kessler; *m* 1944, Kathleen Sillem; two *s* three *d*. *Educ:* Univ. of Amsterdam (Hist. Drs); American Univ., Washington. Private Sec. to Queen Wilhelmina, 1945–48; subseq. Head of German Bureau, then Dir of European Affairs, Netherlands FO; Sec. of High Authority, 1952–56; 1st Rep. of High Authority, London, 1956; Sec.-Gen. (later Vice-Pres.), Action Cttee for United States of Europe, 1956–75; Pres., European Community Inst. for Univ. Studies, 1958–75; Principal, Eur. Univ. Inst. of Florence, 1975–81. Co-Chm., Cttee on Soc. Develt and Peace, World Council of Churches and Pontifical Commn for Justice and Peace, 1967–75; European Pres., Trilateral Commn, 1973–75. Grande Ufficiale dell' Ordine Al Merito della Repubblica Italiana, 1981; Grosse Verdienstkreuz, 1982, mit Stern, 1989, Bundesrepublik Deutschland. *Publications:* The European Community and its Role in the World, 1963; (ed jtly) A Nation Writ Large?, 1972. *Recreations:* tennis, walking. *Address:* 20 Fenffe, 5560 Houyet, Belgium. *T:* (84) 377183.

KOHOBAN-WICKREME, Alfred Silva, CVO 1954; Member Ceylon Civil Service; Secretary to the Cabinet, 1968–70; *b* 2 Nov. 1914; *m* 1941, Mona Estelle Kohoban-Wickreme. *Educ:* Trinity Coll., Kandy; University Coll., Colombo. BA (Hons) London, 1935. Cadet, Ceylon Civil Service, 1938; served as Magistrate, District Judge, Asst Govt Agent etc, until 1948; Chief Admin. Officer, Ceylon Govt Rly, 1948; Asst Sec., Min. of Home Affairs, 1951; attached to Ceylon High Commissioner's Office in UK, May-July, 1953; Dir of Social Services and Commissioner for Workmen's Compensation, Ceylon, 1953; Conservator of Forests, Ceylon, 1958; Port Commissioner, Ceylon, 1959; Postmaster General and Dir of Telecommunications, Dec. 1962; Permanent Sec., Ministry of: Local Govt and Home Affairs, April 1964; Cultural Affairs and Social Services, June 1964; Ministry of Communications, 1965. Organised the Queen's Tour in Ceylon, April 1954 (CVO). *Recreations:* sports activities, particularly Rugby football, tennis and cricket. *Address:* 6 Kalinga Place, Jawatta Road, Colombo 5, Sri Lanka. *T:* (residence) 86385.

KOHT, Paul; Ambassador of Norway to Denmark, 1975–82; *b* 7 Dec. 1913; *s* of Dr Halvdan Koht and Karen Elisabeth (*née* Grude); *m* 1938, Grete Sverdrup; two *s* one *d*. *Educ:* University of Oslo. Law degree, 1937. Entered Norwegian Foreign Service, 1938; held posts in: Bucharest, 1938–39; London, 1940–41; Tokyo, 1941–42; New York, 1942–46; Lisbon, 1950–51; Mem. Norwegian Delegn to OEEC and NATO, Paris, and Perm. Rep. to Coun. of Europe, 1951–53; Dir General of Dept for Econ. Affairs, Min. of For. Affairs, Oslo, 1953–56; Chargé d'Affaires, Copenhagen, 1956–58; Ambassador to USA, 1958–63; Ambassador to Fed. Republic of Germany, 1963–68; Ambassador to the Court of St James's, 1968–75. Comdr, Order of St Olav; Grand Cross, Order of Dannebrog; Grand Cross, Order of Merit (Federal Republic of Germany). *Address:* Lille Frogner Allé 4b, 0263 Oslo 2, Norway.

KOLAKOWSKI, Leszek, PhD, FBA 1980; Senior Research Fellow, All Souls College, Oxford, since 1970; *b* 23 Oct. 1927; *s* of Jerzy and Lucyna (*née* Pietrusiewicz); *m* 1949, Dr Tamara Kołakowska (*née* Dynenson); one *d*. *Educ:* Łódź Univ., Poland 1945–50; Warsaw Univ. (PhD 1953). Asst in Philosophy: Łódź Univ., 1947–49; Warsaw Univ., 1950–59; Prof. and Chm., Section of History of Philosophy, Warsaw Univ., 1959–68, expelled by authorities for political reasons; Visiting Professor: McGill Univ., 1968–69; Univ. of California, Berkeley, 1969–70; Yale Univ., Conn, 1975; Univ. of Chicago, 1981–. McArthur Fellowship, 1983. Mem. Internat. Inst. of Philosophy; Foreign Mem., Amer. Academy of Arts and Science; Mem.-correspondent, Bayerische Akademie des Künste. Hon. Dr Lit. Hum Bard Coll., 1984; Hon. LLD Reed Coll., 1985. Friedenpreis des Deutschen Buchhandels, 1977; Jurzykowski Foundn award, 1968; Charles Veillou Prix Européen d'Essai, 1980; (jtly) Erasmus Prize, 1984; Jefferson Award, 1986. *Publications:* about 30 books, some of them only in Polish; trans. of various books in 14 languages; *in English:* Marxism and Beyond, 1968; Conversations with the Devil, 1972; Positivist Philosophy, 1972; Husserl and the Search for Certitude, 1975; Main Currents of Marxism, 3 vols, 1978; Religion, 1982; Bergson, 1985; Metaphysical Horror, 1988; *in French:* Chrétiens sans Eglise, 1969; *in German:* Traktat über die Sterblichkeit der Vernunft, 1967; Geist und Ungeist christlicher Traditionen, 1971; Die Gegenwärtigkeit des Mythos, 1973; Der revolutionäre Geist, 1972; Leben trotz Geschichte Lesebuch, 1977; Zweifel und die Methode, 1977. *Address:* 77 Hamilton Road, Oxford OX2 7QA. *T:* Oxford (0865) 58790.

KOLANE, John Teboho, ODSM, OL; LLD; Director of Paliamentary Affairs, Lesotho, since 1990; *b* 22 Feb. 1926; *s* of Elizabeth and Zacharia Kolane; *m* 1955, Julia; two *s* three *d*. *Educ:* National University of Lesotho; Cambridge Univ. BA South Africa; attorney's admission, Pretoria. Interpreter, District Comr's Court and Judicial Comr's Court, 1950–59; Registrar of Births, Marriages and Deaths, 1959–63; Clerk of Senate, 1965–67; Permanent Secretary: Min. of Justice, 1967–69; Cabinet Office, 1969–70; Min. of Justice, 1970–73; Speaker, National Assembly, 1973–86; High Comr to UK, 1986–89. LLD 1985. *Recreations:* golf, gardening, walking. *Address:* National Assembly, PO Box 190, Maseru, Lesotho. *Club:* Maseru Golf.

KOLBERT, Colin Francis; His Honour Judge Kolbert; a Circuit Judge, since 1988; Fellow of Magdalene College, Cambridge, since 1968; *b* 3 June 1936; *s* of Arthur Richard Alexander Kolbert and Dorothy Elizabeth Kolbert (*née* Fletcher); *m* 1959, Jean Fairgrieve Abson; two *d*. *Educ:* Queen Elizabeth's, Barnet; St Catharine's Coll., Cambridge (Harold

Samuel Schol., 1959; BA 1959; PhD 1962; MA 1963). RA, 1954–56. Called to the Bar, Lincoln's Inn, 1961. A Recorder, SE Circuit, 1985–88. Oxford University: Fellow and Tutor in Jurisprudence, St Peter's Coll., 1964–68 (MA, DPhil (Oxon) by incorp., 1964); CUF Lectr, Faculty of Law, 1965–68; Cambridge University: Tutor, Magdalene Coll., 1969–88; Univ. Lectr in Law, Dept of Land Economy, 1969–88; Sec., Faculty of Music, 1969–75; Coll. Rugby Administrator, CURUFC, 1982–88 (Trustee, 1989–). Vis. Prof. and Moderator, Univs of Ife, Lagos, Enugu, and Ahmadu Bello, Nigeria, 1970–80. Mem., Cambridge City Council, 1970–74. Member: Istituto di Diritto Agrario Internazionale e Comparato, Florence, 1964–; Secretariat, World Conf. on Agrarian Reform and Rural Develt, FAO Rome, 1978–79 (Customary Land Tenure Consultant, 1974–80). Governor: Wellingborough Sch., 1970–80; Cranleigh Sch., 1970–88; Glenalmond Coll., 1978–89; Hurstpierpont Coll., 1978–89. Violin music critic, Records and Recording, 1974–78. *Publications:* (trans. and ed) The Digest of Justinian, 1979; various legal and musical. *Recreations:* music (especially playing the violin), cricket, Rugby, military history, cooking, walking in London and Yorkshire. *Address:* Magdalene College, Cambridge, CB3 0AG; Lamb Building, Temple, EC4Y 7AS. *Clubs:* MCC, Farmers'; Hawks, CURUFC (Cambridge).

KOLO, Sule; Chairman, Alheri Enterprises; Consultant, NESCO Ltd; High Commissioner for Nigeria in London, 1970–75; *b* 1926; *m* 1957, Helen Patricia Kolo; two *s* four *d.* BSc (Econ); attended Imperial Defence College. Counsellor, Nigerian High Commn in London, 1962; Perm. Sec., Nigerian Min. of Defence, 1963; Perm. Sec., Nigerian Min. of Trade, 1966; Nigeria's Perm. Representative to European Office of UN and Ambassador to Switzerland, 1966; Chm. of GATT, 1969. Chm., Nigeria Section, Nigeria–US Business Council. Former Pres., Lions Club Internat. Dist 404, Nigeria. FREconS; FRSA 1973. Franklin Peace Medal, 1969. *Recreations:* swimming, tennis. *Address:* PO Box 1453, Jos, Nigeria. *Clubs:* Travellers'; Island (Lagos).

KOLTAI, Ralph, CBE 1983; RDI 1985; freelance stage designer; designer for Drama, Opera and Dance, since 1950; Associate Designer, Royal Shakespeare Company, 1963–66 and since 1976; *b* 31 July 1924; Hungarian-German; *s* of Dr(med) Alfred Koltai and Charlotte Koltai (*née* Weinstein); *m* 1956, Annena Stubbs. *Educ:* Central Sch. of Art and Design (Dip. with Dist.). Early work entirely in field of opera. First production, Angelique, for London Opera Club, Fortune Theatre, 1950. Designs for The Royal Opera House, Sadler's Wells, Scottish Opera, National Welsh Opera, The English Opera Group. First of 7 ballets for Ballet Rambert, Two Brothers, 1958. Head , Sch. of Theatre Design, Central Sch. of Art & Design, 1965–72. *Productions:* RSC: The Caucasian Chalk Circle, 1962; The Representative, 1963; The Birthday Party; Endgame; The Jew of Malta, 1964; The Merchant of Venice; Timon of Athens, 1965; Little Murders, 1967; Major Barbara, 1970; Too True To Be Good, 1975; Old World, 1976; Wild Oats, 1977; The Tempest, Love's Labour's Lost, 1978; Hippolytus, Baal, 1979; Romeo and Juliet, Hamlet, 1980; The Love Girl and the Innocent, 1981 (London Drama Critics Award); Much Ado About Nothing, Molière, 1982; Custom of the Country, Cyrano de Bergerac (SWET Award), 1983; Troilus and Cressida, Othello, 1985; They Shoot Horses, Don't They?, 1987; for National Theatre: an "all male" As You Like It, 1967; Back to Methuselah, 1969; State of Revolution, 1977; Brand (SWET Award), The Guardsman, 1978; Richard III, The Wild Duck, 1979; Man and Superman, 1981; *other notable productions include: opera:* for Sadler's Wells/English National Opera: The Rise and Fall of the City of Mahagonny, 1963; From the House of the Dead, 1965; Bluebeard's Castle, 1972; Wagner's (complete) Ring Cycle, 1973; Seven Deadly Sins, 1978; Anna Karenina, 1981; Pacific Overtures, 1987; for The Royal Opera House: Taverner, 1972; The Ice Break, 1977; for Sydney Opera House: Tannhäuser, 1973; for Netherlands Opera: Wozzeck, 1973; Fidelio, Munich, 1974; Verdi's Macbeth, Edinburgh Festival, 1976; Les Soldats, Lyon Opera, 1983; Italian Girl in Algiers, 1984, Tannhäuser, 1986, Geneva; (also dir.) Flying Dutchman, 1987, La Traviata, 1990, Hong Kong; *theatre:* Pack of Lies, Lyric, 1983; Across from the Garden of Allah, Comedy, 1986; for Aalborg Theatre, Denmark: Threepenny Opera, 1979; The Love Girl and the Innocent, 1980; Terra Nova, 1981; The Carmelites, 1981; Mahagonny, 1984; *musicals:* Billy, Drury Lane, 1974; Bugsy Malone, Her Majesty's, 1983; Dear Anyone, Cambridge, 1983; Carrie, Stratford, NY, 1988; Metropolis, Piccadilly, 1989; *ballet:* The Planets, Royal Ballet, 1990; The Makropulos Affair, Oslo, 1991; has worked in most countries in Western Europe, also Bulgaria, Argentine, USA, Canada, Australia. London Drama Critics Award, Designer of the Year, 1967 (for Little Murders and As You Like It); (jtly) Gold Medal, Internat. Exhibn of Stage Design, Prague Quadriennale, 1975, 1979; Individual Silver Medal, Prague Quadriennale, 1987. *Recreation:* wildlife photography. *Address:* c/o Macnaughton Lowe Representation Ltd, 200 Fulham Road, SW10. *T:* 071–351 5442.

KONSTANT, Rt. Rev. David Every; see Leeds, Bishop of, (RC).

KOOPS, Hon. Mary Claire; see Hogg, Hon. M. C.

KOOTENAY, Bishop of, since 1990; **Rt. Rev. David Crawley;** *b* 26 July 1937; *s* of Rev. Canon George Antony Crawley, LTh and Lucy Lillian Crawley (*née* Ball); *m* 1st, 1959, Frances Mary Louise Wilmot; two *d*; 2nd, 1986, Joan Alice Bubbs; one *d* decd. *Educ:* Univ. of Manitoba (BA 1958); St John's Coll., Winnipeg (LTh 1961; DD 1990); Univ. of Kent at Canterbury (MA 1967). Ordained Deacon 1961, Priest 1962. Incumbent, St Thomas', Sherwood Park, Edmonton, 1961–66; Canon Missioner, All Saints Cathedral, Edmonton, 1967–70; Rector, St Matthew's, Winnipeg, 1971–77; Archdeacon of Winnipeg, 1974–77; Archdeacon of Rupert's Land, 1977–81; Lectr, St John's College, Winnipeg, 1981–82; Rector, St Michael and All Angels, Regina, 1982–85; Rector, St Paul's, Vancouver, 1985–90. *Recreations:* ski-ing, hiking. *Address:* #201–1636 Pandosy Street, Kelowna, BC V1Y 1P7, Canada.

KOPAL, Prof. Zdeněk; Professor of Astronomy, University of Manchester, 1951–81, now Emeritus; *b* Litomyšl, 4 April 1914; 2nd *s* of Prof. Joseph Kopal, of Charles University, Prague, and Ludmila (*née* Lelek); *m* 1938, Alena, *o d* of late Judge B. Muldner; three *d. Educ:* Charles University, Prague; University of Cambridge, England; Harvard Univ., USA. Agassiz Research Fellow, Harvard Observatory, 1938–40; Research Associate in Astronomy, Harvard Univ., 1940–46; Lecturer in Astronomy, Harvard Univ., 1948; Associate Prof., Mass Institute of Technology, 1947–51. Pres., Foundation Internationale du Pic-du-Midi; Mem. Internat. Acad. of Astronautical Sciences, New York Acad. of Sciences; Chm., Cttee for Lunar and Planetary Exploration, Brit. Nat. Cttee for Space Research; Mem. Lunar-Planetary Cttee, US Nat. Space Bd. Editor-in-Chief, Astrophysics and Space Science, 1968–; Founding Editor: Icarus (internat. jl of solar system); The Moon (internat. jl of lunar studies), 1969–. Pahlavi Lectr, Iran, 1977. For. Mem., Greek Nat. Acad. of Athens, 1976; Hon. Mem., Astronomical Soc. of India, 1987. Hon. DSc Krakow, 1974. Gold Medal, Czechoslovak Acad. of Sciences, 1969; Copernicus Medal, Krakow Univ., 1974. Hon. Citizen of: Delphi, 1978; Litomyšl, 1991. *Publications:* An Introduction to the Study of Eclipsing Variables, 1946 (US); The Computation of Elements of Eclipsing Binary Systems, 1950 (US); Tables of Supersonic Flow of Air Around Cones, 3 vols, 1947–49 (US); Numerical Analysis (London), 1955; Astronomical Optics (Amsterdam), 1956; Close Binary Systems, 1959; Figures of Equilibrium of Celestial Bodies, 1960; The Moon, 1960; Physics and Astronomy of the Moon, 1962, 2nd

edn 1971; Photographic Atlas of the Moon, 1965; An Introduction to the Study of the Moon, 1966; The Measure of the Moon, 1967; (ed) Advances in Astronomy and Astrophysics, 1968; Telescopes in Space, 1968; Exploration of the Moon by Spacecraft, 1968; Widening Horizons, 1970; A New Photographic Atlas of the Moon, 1971; Man and His Universe, 1972; The Solar System, 1973; Mapping of the Moon, 1974; The Moon in the Post-Apollo Stage, 1974; Dynamics of Close Binary Systems, 1978; The Realm of Terrestrial Planets, 1978; Language of the Stars, 1979; Of Stars and Men: reminiscences of an astronomer, 1986; The Roche Problem, 1989; Mathematical Theory of Stellar Eclipses, 1990; over 400 original papers on astronomy, aerodynamics, and applied mathematics in publications of Harvard Observatory, Astrophysical Journal, Astronomical Journal, Astronomische Nachrichten, Monthly Notices of Royal Astronomical Society, Proc. Amer. Phil. Soc., Proc. Nat. Acad. Sci. (US), Zeitschrift für Astrophysik, etc. *Recreation:* mountaineering. *Address:* Greenfield, Parkway, Wilmslow, Cheshire SK9 1LS. *T:* Wilmslow (0625) 522470. *Club:* Explorers' (NY).

KOPELOWITZ, Dr (Jacob) Lionel (Garstein), JP; General Medical Practitioner, since 1953; *b* 9 Dec. 1926; *s* of Maurice and Mabel Kopelowitz; *m* 1980, Sylvia Waksman (*née* Galler). *Educ:* Clifton Coll., Bristol; Trinity Coll., Cambridge (MA 1947); University Coll. Hosp. London. MRCS, LRCP 1951; MRCGP 1964. Resident MO, London Jewish Hosp., 1951–52; Flying Officer, RAF Med. Branch, 1952–53. Member: General Medical Council, 1984–; General Optical Council, 1979–; Standing Med. Adv. Cttee, DHSS, 1974–78; British Medical Association: Fellow, 1980; Mem. Council, 1982–; Chm., Newcastle Div., 1968–69; Pres., Northern Regional Council, 1984–88; Mem., Gen. Med. Services Cttee, 1971–90 (Past Chm., Maternity Services Sub-Cttee); Chm., Central Adv. Cttee, Deputising Services, 1980–; Dep. Chm., Private Practice Cttee, 1972–89. Chm., Newcastle upon Tyne FPC, 1979–85; Pres., Soc. of FPCs of England and Wales, 1978–79; Vice-Pres., Trades Adv. Council, 1988–. President: Board of Deputies of British Jews, 1985–90; Nat. Council for Soviet Jewry, 1985–91; European Jewish Congress, 1986–91; Vice President: Conf. on Jewish Material Claims Against Germany, 1988–; Conf. on Jewish Material Claims Against Austria, 1988–. Mem. Exec. Cttee, Meml Foundn for Jewish Culture, 1988–. Mem., Chm., Pres., numerous med. bodies and Jewish organisations, UK and overseas. Vice-Pres., British Council, Share Zedek Med. Centre, 1990–. Mem. Bd of Govs, Clifton Coll., Bristol, 1988–. Liveryman, Apothecaries' Co., 1969. JP Northumberland, 1964. *Publications:* articles in med. jls; contrib. to Med. Annual. *Recreations:* foreign travel, contract bridge. *Address:* 10 Cumberland House, Clifton Gardens, W9 1DX. *T:* 071–289 6375. *Club:* Athenæum.

KORALEK, Paul George, CBE 1984; RA 1991 (ARA 1986); RIBA; Partner in Ahrends Burton and Koralek, architects, since 1961; *b* 7 April 1933; *s* of late Ernest and Alice Koralek; *m* 1958, Jennifer Chadwick; one *s* two *d. Educ:* Aldenham School; Architectural Assoc. School of Architecture. RIBA 1957; AA Dip. Hons. Architect: with Powell & Moya, London, 1956–57; with Marcel Breuer, New York, 1959–60. Part-time teaching, Sch. of Arch., Leicester Polytechnic, 1982–84. *Major projects include: public buildings:* Redcar Library, 1971; Maidenhead Libr., 1972; Roman Catholic Chaplaincy, Oxford, 1972; Nucleus Low Energy Hosp., IoW, 1982; winning entry, Nat. Gall. Extension Hampton Site Comp., 1982; Dover Heritage Centre, 1988–90; *educational buildings:* Chichester Theol Coll., 1965; Berkeley Libr., TCD, 1967 (1st Prize, Internat. Comp., 1961); Templeton Coll., Oxford, 1967; Arts Faculty Bldg, TCD, 1975–79; Portsmouth Polytechnic Libr., 1975–79; Residential bldg, Keble Coll., Oxford, 1976 (RIBA Arch. Award, 1978); *residential buildings:* houses, Dunstan Rd, Oxford, 1969; Nebenzahl House, Jerusalem, 1972; Chalvedon Housing, 1975–77; Whitmore Court Housing, Basildon, 1975 (RIBA Good Design in Housing Award, 1977); Felmore Housing, 1975–80; *commercial/industrial buildings:* Habitat Warehouse, Showroom and Offices, Wallingford, 1974 (Financial Times Indust. Arch. Award, and Structl Steel Design Award (Warehouse), 1976); factory bldgs and refurbishment, Cummins Engine Co., Shotts, Scotland, 1975–83 (Structl Steel Design Award, 1980); J. Sainsbury supermarket, Canterbury, 1984 (Structl Steel Design Award, 1985; FT Arch. at Work Award Commendation, 1986); W. H. Smith Offices, Greenbridge, 1985 (FT Arch. at Work Award Commendation, 1987); John Lewis Dept Store, Kingston-upon-Thames, 1987. *Exhibitions of drawings and works:* RIBA Heinz Gall., 1980; Douglas Hyde Gall. Dublin, 1981; Technical Univ. of Braunschweig and Tech. Univ. of Hanover, Germany, Mus. of Finnish Arch., Helsinki, Univ. of Oulu, and Alvar Aalto Mus., Jvasklya, Finland, 1982; HQ of AA, Oslo, 1983. Member: Design and Architectural Rev. Panel, Cardiff Bay Develt Corp., 1988–; ARCUK Bd of Architectural Educn, 1987–; Trustee, Bldg Industry Youth Trust, 1981–. External Examiner: Sch. of Arch., Univ. of Manchester, 1981–85; Plymouth Poly, 1988–. Competition Assessor: RIBA; ABS Housing; Irish Dept of Educn Schs comp.; Assessor, Civic Trust Awards. Papers and lectures, UK and abroad, 1964–. *Publications:* paper and articles in RIBA and other prof. jls. *Recreations:* drawing, walking, gardening. *Address:* Unit 1, 7 Chalcot Road, NW1 8LH. *T:* 071–586 3311.

KORNBERG, Prof. Arthur; Professor of Biochemistry, Stanford University, since 1959; *b* Brooklyn, 3 March 1918; *m*; three *s. Educ:* College of the City of New York (BSc 1937); University of Rochester, NY (MD 1941). Strong Memorial Hospital, Rochester, 1941–42; National Insts of Health, Bethesda, Md, 1942–52; Professor of Microbiology, Washington Univ., and Head of Dept of Microbiology, 1953–59; Head of Dept of Biochemistry, Stanford Univ., 1959–69. MNAS; MAAS; Mem. Amer. Phil. Soc. Foreign Mem., Royal Soc., 1970. Many honours and awards, including: Paul Lewis Award in Enzyme Chemistry, 1951; Nobel Prize (joint) in Medicine, 1959; Nat Medal of Science, 1979. *Publications:* DNA Synthesis, 1974; DNA Replication, 1980 (Suppl., 1982); articles in scientific jls. *Address:* Stanford University Medical Center, Palo Alto, Calif 94305–5307, USA.

KORNBERG, Prof. Sir Hans (Leo), Kt 1978; MA, DSc Oxon, ScD Cantab, PhD Sheffield; FRS 1965; FIBiol 1965; Sir William Dunn Professor of Biochemistry, University of Cambridge, and Fellow of Christ's College, since 1975; Master of Christ's College, Cambridge, since 1982; *b* 14 Jan. 1928; *o s* of Max Kornberg and Margarete Kornberg (*née* Silberbach); *m* 1956, Monica Mary King (*d* 1989); twin *s* two *d*; *m* 1991, Donna, *d* of William B. Haber. *Educ:* Queen Elizabeth Grammar Sch., Wakefield; University of Sheffield (BSc). Commonwealth Fund Fellow of Harkness Foundation, at Yale University and Public Health Research Inst., New York, 1953–55; Mem. of scientific staff, MRC Cell Metabolism Res. Unit, University of Oxford, 1955–60; Lectr, Worcester Coll., Oxford, 1958–61 (Hon. Fellow 1980); Prof. of Biochemistry, Univ. of Leicester, 1960–75. Visiting Instructor, Marine Biological Lab., Woods Hole, Mass, 1964–66, 1981–, Trustee, 1982–. Member: SRC, 1967–72 (Chm., Science Bd, 1969–72); UGC Biol. Sci. Cttee, 1967–77; NATO Adv. Study Inst. Panel, 1970–76 (Chm., 1974–75); Kuratorium, Max-Planck Inst., Dortmund, 1979–90 (Chm., Sci. Adv. Cttee); AFRC (formerly ARC), 1980–84; Priorities Bd for R & D in Agriculture, 1984–90; BP Venture Res. Council, 1981–; ACARD 1982–85; Adv. Council on Public Records, 1984–86; UK Cttee on Eur. Year of the Environment, 1986–88; Vice-Chm., EMBO, 1978–81; Chairman: Royal Commn on Environmental Pollution, 1976–81; Adv. Cttee on Genetic Manipulation, 1986–; Co-ordinating Cttee on Environmental Res., Res. Councils, 1986–88; Sci. Adv. Cttee, Inst. for Mol. Biol. and Medicine, Monash Univ., 1987–;

President: BAAS, 1984–85; Biochemical Soc., 1990–; IUB, 1991–; Assoc. for Science Educn, 1991–; Vice-Pres., Inst. of Biol., 1971–73. A Managing Trustee, Nuffield Foundn, 1973–; Trustee, Wellcome Trust, 1990–; Academic Governor, Hebrew Univ. of Jerusalem, 1976–; Governor: Weizmann Inst., 1980–; Lister Inst., 1990–. Hon. Fellow: Brasenose Coll., Oxford, 1983; Wolfson Coll., Cambridge, 1990. FRSA 1972. For Associate, Nat. Acad. of Sciences, USA, 1986; Member: Leopoldina German Acad. of Scis, 1982; Acad. Europaea, 1989; Hon. Member: Amer. Soc. Biol Chem., 1972; Biochem. Soc., FRG, 1973; Japanese Biochem. Soc., 1981; Hon. For. Mem., Amer. Acad. of Arts & Scis, 1987. Hon. ScD Cincinnati, 1974; Hon. DSc: Warwick, 1975; Leicester, 1979; Sheffield, 1979; Bath, 1980; Strathclyde, 1985; DUniv Essex, 1979; Dr med Leipzig, 1984. Colworth Medal of Biochemical Soc., 1965; Otto Warburg Medal, Biochem. Soc. of Federal Republic of Germany, 1973. *Publications:* (with Sir Hans Krebs) Energy Transformations in Living Matter, 1957; articles in scientific jls. *Recreations:* cooking and conversation. *Address:* The Master's Lodge, Christ's College, Cambridge CB2 3BU; Department of Biochemistry, Tennis Court Road, Cambridge CB2 1QW.

KÖRNER, Prof. Stephan, JurDr, PhD; FBA 1967; Professor of Philosophy, Bristol University, 1952–79, and Yale University, 1970–84; *b* Ostrava, Czechoslovakia, 26 Sept. 1913; *o s* of Emil Körner and Erna (*née* Maier); *m* 1944, Edith Laner, CBE, BSc, LLD, JP; one *s* one *d*. *Educ:* Classical Gymnasium; Charles' Univ., Prague; Trinity Hall, Cambridge. Army Service, 1936–39, 1943–46. University of Bristol: Lectr in Philosophy, 1946; Dean, Faculty of Arts, 1965–66; Pro-Vice-Chancellor, 1968–71; Hon. Fellow, 1987. Visiting Prof. of Philosophy: Brown Univ., 1957; Yale Univ., 1960; Texas Univ., 1964; Indiana Univ., 1967; Graz Univ., 1980–86 (Hon. Prof., 1982). President: Brit. Soc. for Philosophy of Science, 1965; Aristotelian Soc., 1967; Internat. Union of History and Philosophy of Science, 1969; Mind Assoc., 1973. Editor, Ratio, 1961–80. Hon. DLitt Belfast, 1981; Hon. Phil. Dr Graz, 1984. *Publications:* Kant, 1955; Conceptual Thinking, 1955; (ed) Observation and Interpretation, 1957; The Philosophy of Mathematics, 1960; Experience and Theory, 1966; Kant's Conception of Freedom (British Acad. Lecture), 1967; What is Philosophy?, 1969; Categorial Frameworks, 1970; Abstraction in Science and Morals (Eddington Meml Lecture), 1971; (ed) Practical Reason, 1974; (ed) Explanation, 1976; Experience and Conduct, 1976; Metaphysics: its structure and function, 1984; contribs to philosophical periodicals. *Recreation:* walking. *Address:* 10 Belgrave Road, Bristol BS8 2AB.

KOSSOFF, David; actor; author; illustrator; *b* 24 Nov. 1919; *s* of Louis and Anne Kossoff, both Russian; *m* 1947, Margaret (Jennie) Jenkins; one *s* (and one *s* decd). *Educ:* elementary sch.; Northern Polytechnic. Commercial Artist, 1937; Draughtsman, 1937–38; Furniture Designer, 1938–39; Technical Illustrator, 1939–45. Began acting, 1943; working as actor and illustrator, 1945–52, as actor and designer, 1952–. BBC Repertory Company, 1945–51. Took over part of Colonel Alexander Ikonenko in the Love of Four Colonels, Wyndham's, 1952; Sam Tager in The Shrike, Prince's, 1953; Morry in The Bespoke Overcoat, and Tobit in Tobias and the Angel, Arts, 1953; Prof. Lodegger in No Sign of the Dove, Savoy, 1953; Nathan in The Boychik, Embassy, 1954 (and again Morry in The Bespoke Overcoat); Mendele in The World of Sholom Aleichem, Embassy, 1955, and Johannesburg, 1957; one-man show, One Eyebrow Up, The Arts, 1957; Man on Trial, Lyric, 1959; Stars in Your Eyes, Palladium, 1960; The Tenth Man, Comedy, 1961; Come Blow Your Horn, Prince of Wales, 1962; one-man show, Kossoff at the Prince Charles, 1963, later called A Funny Kind of Evening (many countries); Enter Solly Gold, Mermaid, 1970; Cinderella, Palladium, 1971; Bunny, Criterion, 1972; own Bible storytelling programmes on radio and TV, as writer and teller, 1964–66; solo performance (stage), 'As According to Kossoff', 1970–. Has appeared in many films. Won British Acad. Award, 1956. Elected MSIA 1958. FRSA 1969. Hon. DLitt, Hatfield Poly., 1990. *Play:* Big Night for Shylock, 1968. *Publications:* Bible Stories retold by David Kossoff, 1968; The Book of Witnesses, 1971; The Three Donkeys, 1972; The Voices of Masada, 1973; The Little Book of Sylvanus, 1975; You Have a Minute, Lord?, 1977; A Small Town is a World, 1979; Sweet Nutcracker, 1985. *Recreations:* conversation, working with the hands. *Address:* 45 Roe Green Close, Hatfield, Herts AL10 9PD.

KOSTERLITZ, Hans Walter, MD, PhD, DSc; FRCPE 1981; FRS 1978; FRSE 1951; Director, Unit for Research on Addictive Drugs, University of Aberdeen, since 1973; *b* 27 April 1903; *s* of Bernhard and Selma Kosterlitz; *m* 1937, Johanna Maria Katherina Gresshöner; one *s*. *Educ:* Univs of Heidelberg, Freiburg and Berlin. MD Berlin 1929; PhD 1936, DSc 1944, Hon. LLD 1979, Aberdeen. Assistant, 1st Medical Dept, Univ. of Berlin, 1928–33; University of Aberdeen: Research Worker in Physiology, 1934–36; Asst and Carnegie Teaching Fellow, 1936–39; Lectr, 1939–45; Sen. Lectr, 1945–55; Reader in Physiology, 1955–68; Prof. of Pharmacology and Chm., 1968–73. Visiting Lecturer: in Pharmacology, Harvard Med. Sch., 1953–54; in Biology, Brown Univ., 1953; Vis. Prof. of Pharmacology, Harvard Med. Sch., 1977; Lectures: J. Y. Dent Meml, 1970; Otto Krayer, 1977; Scheele, 1977; Gen. Session, Fedn Amer. Socs for Experimental Biol., 1978; Sutcliffe Kerr, 1978; Charnock Bradley Meml, 1979; Arnold H. Maloney, 1979; Lister, 1980; Lita Annenberg Hazen, 1980; Lilly, 1980; Sherrington Meml, RSocMed, 1982; N. J. Giarman Meml, Yale Univ. Sch. of Med., 1982; Third Transatlantic, Endocrine Soc., 1982; Lorenzini, Milan, 1982; Sherrington, Univ. of Liverpool, 1989. Foreign Associate, National Acad. of Sciences, USA, 1985. Dr *hc* Liège, 1978; Hon. DSc St Andrews, 1982; Hon. LLD Dundee, 1988. Schmiedeberg Plakette, German Pharmacol Soc., 1976; Pacesetter Award, US Nat. Inst. on Drug Abuse, 1977; Nathan B. Eddy Award, US Cttee on Problems of Drug Dependence, 1978; (jtly) Albert Lasker Prize, 1978; Baly Medal, RCP, 1979; Royal Medal, 1979, Wellcome Foundn Prize, 1982, Royal Soc.; Makdougall-Brisbane Medal, RSE, 1980; Thudichum Medal, Biochem. Soc., 1980; Feldberg Foundn Prize, 1981; Harvey Prize, Technion, 1981; Prof. Lucien Dautrebande Prize, 1982; Wellcome Gold Medal, British Pharmacol Soc., 1987; Cameron Prize, Univ. of Edinburgh, 1988. *Publications:* (joint editor): Agonist and Antagonist Actions of Narcotic Analgesic Drugs, 1972; The Opiate Narcotics, 1975; Opiates and Endogenous Opioid Peptides, 1976; Pain and Society, 1980; Neuroactive Peptides, 1980; articles in Nature, Jl of Physiol, Brit. Jl of Pharmacol. *Recreations:* music, walking, travelling. *Address:* Unit for Research on Addictive Drugs, University of Aberdeen, Aberdeen AB9 1AS. *T:* Aberdeen 273000; 16 Glendee Terrace, Cults, Aberdeen AB1 9HX. *T:* Aberdeen (0224) 867366. *Club:* Lansdowne.

KOTCH, Laurie, (Mrs J. K. Kotch); *see* Purden, R. L.

KOTSOKOANE, Hon. Joseph Riffat Larry; Commander, Order of Ramatseatsana, 1982; development consultant (human and natural resources), since 1986; Minister of Education, Sports and Culture, Lesotho, 1984–86; *b* 19 Oct. 1922; *s* of Basotho parents, living in Johannesburg, South Africa; *m* 1947, Elizabeth (*née* Molise); two *s* three *d*. BSc (SA); BSc Hons (Witwatersrand); Cert. Agric. (London). Development Officer, Dept of Agric., Basutoland, 1951–54; Agric. Educn Officer i/c of Agric. Sch. for junior field staff, 1955–62; Agric. Extension Officer i/c of all field staff of Min. of Agric., 1962–63; Prin. Agric. Off. (Dep. Dir), Min. of Agric., 1964–66; High Comr for Lesotho, in London, 1966–69; Ambassador to Germany, Holy See, Rome, France, and Austria, 1968–69; Permanent Sec. and Hd of Diplomatic Service, Lesotho, 1969–70; Permanent Sec. for Health, Educn and Social Welfare, Lesotho, 1970–71; High Comr for Lesotho in East Africa, Nigeria and Ghana, 1972–74; Minister: of Foreign Affairs, Lesotho, 1974–75; of Education, 1975–76; of Agriculture, 1976–78; Perm. Rep. to UN, 1978; Sec. to the Cabinet and Head of CS (Sen. Perm. Sec.), 1978–84. Guest of Min. of Agric., Netherlands, 1955; studied agric. educn, USA (financed by Carnegie Corp. of NY and Ford Foundn), 1960–61; FAO confs in Tunisia, Tanganyika and Uganda, 1962 and 1963; Mem. Lesotho delegn to 24th World Health Assembly, 1971; travelled extensively to study and observe methods of agric. administration, 1964; meetings on nutrition, Berlin and Hamburg, 1966; diplomatic trainee, Brit. Embassy, Bonn, 1966. *Recreations:* swimming, tennis, amateur dramatics, photography, debating, reading, travelling. *Address:* PO Box 1015, Maseru 100, Lesotho, Southern Africa.

KOVACEVICH, Stephen B.; *see* Bishop-Kovacevich.

KOWALSKI, Gregor; Scottish Parliamentary Counsel, since 1987 and Assistant Legal Secretary to Lord Advocate, since 1978; *b* 7 Oct. 1949; *s* of Mieczyslaw Kowalski and Jeanie Hutcheson Kowalski (*née* MacDonald); *m* 1974, Janet McFarlane Pillatt; two *s*. *Educ:* Airdrie Academy; Strathclyde Univ. (LLB 1971). Apprentice, then Asst Solicitor, Levy & McRae, Glasgow, 1971–74; Procurator Fiscal Depute, Glasgow, 1974–78; Asst, later Deputy Parly Draftsman for Scotland and Asst Legal Sec. to Lord Advocate, 1978–87; seconded to Govt of Seychelles as Legal Draftsman, 1982–83. Founding Mem. and Sec., Soc. of Scottish Lawyers in London, 1987–89 (Vice Pres., 1989–91; Pres., 1991–). *Recreations:* singing, music. *Address:* Lord Advocate's Chambers, Fielden House, 10 Great College Street, SW1P 3SL; 5 Pine Tree Hill, Pyrford, Woking, Surrey. *T:* Woking (0483) 723173.

KRAEMER, (Thomas Whilhelm) Nicholas; conductor; *b* 7 March 1945; *s* of William Paul Kraemer and Helen Bartrum; *m* 1984, Elizabeth Mary Anderson; two *s* one *d* (and one *s* decd). *Educ:* Edinburgh Acad.; Lancing Coll.; Dartington Coll. of Arts; Nottingham Univ. (BMus 1967). ARCM. Harpsichordist with Acad. of St Martin in the Fields, 1972–80, with Monteverdi Choir and Orchestra, 1970–80; Musical Director: Unicorn Opera, Abingdon, 1971–75; West Eleven Children's Opera, 1971–88; Founder and Dir, Raglan Baroque Players, 1978–; Principal Conductor, Divertimenti, 1979–; Conductor, Glyndebourne, 1980–82; Musical Dir, Opera 80, 1980–83; Associate Conductor, BBC Scottish SO, 1983–85; Artistic Director: London Bach Orch., 1985–; Irish Chamber Orch., 1985–90. Recordings: of Vivaldi and Music from Versailles, with Raglan Baroque Players; of Mozart piano concertos, with Linda Nicolson and Capella Coloniensis. *Recreations:* theatre, badminton, holidays, active fatherhood. *Address:* 35 Glasslyn Road, N8 8RJ. *T:* 081–340 6941.

KRAFT, Rt. Rev. Richard Austin; *see* Pretoria, Bishop of.

KRAMER, Prof. Ivor Robert Horton, OBE 1984; MDS; FDSRCS, FFDRCSI, Hon. FRACDS, FRCPath; Emeritus Professor of Oral Pathology, University of London; Hon. Consultant, Mount Vernon Hospital, Northwood; *b* 20 June 1923; *yr s* of late Alfred Bertie and Agnes Maud Kramer; *m* 1st, 1946, Elisabeth Dalley; one *s*; 2nd, 1979, Mrs Dorothy Toller. *Educ:* Royal Dental Hosp. of London Sch. of Dental Surgery; MDS 1955; FDSRCS 1960 (LDSRCS 1944); FRCPath 1970 (MCRPath 1964); FFDRCSI 1973. Asst to Pathologist, Princess Louise (Kensington) Hosp. for Children, 1944–48; Wright Fleming Inst. of Microbiol., 1948–49; Instr in Dental Histology, Royal Dental Hosp. Sch. of Dental Surgery, 1944–50; Asst Pathologist, Royal Dental Hosp., 1950–56; Institute of Dental Surgery: Lectr in Dental Path., 1949–50, Sen. Lectr, 1950–57; Reader in Oral Path., 1957–62; Prof. of Oral Path., 1962–83; Sub-dean, 1950–70; Dean and Dir of Studies, 1970–83; Head, Dept of Path., Eastman Dental Hosp., 1950–83. Civilian Cons. in Dental Path., RN, 1967–83. Member: WHO Expert Adv. Panel on Dental Health, 1975–; Bd of Faculty of Dental Surgery, RCS, 1964–80, Council, RCS, 1977–80; GDC, 1973–84; Mem., Council for Postgrad. Med. Educn in Eng. and Wales, 1972–77 (Chm., Dental Cttee, 1972–77); Pres., Odontological Section, RSocMed, 1973–74; Pres., British Div., Internat. Assoc. for Dental Res., 1974–77. Hon. Pres. of the Assoc., 1974–75. Editor, Archives of Oral Biology, 1959–69. Lectures: Wilkinson, Manchester, 1962; Charles Tomes, 1969, Webb Johnson, 1981, RCS; Holme, UCH, 1969; Elwood Meml, QUB, 1970; Hutchinson, Edinburgh, 1971; Wilkinson, IDS, 1987. Hon. FRACDS 1978. Howard Mummery Prize, BDA, 1966; Maurice Down Award, Brit. Assoc. of Oral Surgeons, 1974; Colyer Gold Medal, FDS, RCS, 1985. *Publications:* (with R. B. Lucas) Bacteriology for Students of Dental Surgery, 1954, 3rd edn 1966; (with J. J. Pindborg and H. Torloni) World Health Organization International Histological Classification of Tumours: Odontogenic Tumours, Jaw Cysts and Allied Lesions, 1972; (with B. Cohen) Scientific Foundations of Dentistry, 1976; numerous papers in med. and dental jls. *Address:* 33 Sandy Lodge Road, Rickmansworth, Herts WD3 1LP. *T:* Northwood (09274) 25012.

KRAMER, Prof. Dame Leonie (Judith), DBE 1983 (OBE 1976); DPhil; Professor of Australian Literature, University of Sydney, 1968–89, now Professor Emeritus; Deputy Chancellor, University of Sydney Senate, since 1989; Director: Australia and New Zealand Banking Group, since 1983; Western Mining Corporation Ltd, since 1984; Chairman, Quadrant Magazine Co. Ltd, since 1988; *b* 1 Oct. 1924; *d* of Alfred and Gertrude Gibson; *m* 1952, Harold Kramer; two *d*. *Educ:* Presbyterian Ladies Coll., Melbourne; Univ. of Melbourne (BA 1945); Oxford Univ. (DPhil 1953); MA Sydney, 1989. FAHA; FACE. Tutor and Lectr, Univ. of Melb., 1945–49; Tutor and Postgrad. Student, St Hugh's Coll., Oxford, 1949–52; Lectr, Canberra University Coll., 1954–56; Lectr, subseq. Sen. Lectr and Associate Prof., Univ. of NSW, 1958–68. Member: Univs Council, 1977–; Bd of Studies, NSW, 1989–. Comr, Electricity Commn, NSW, 1988–. Chm., ABC, 1982–83; Chm. Bd of Dirs, Nat. Inst. of Dramatic Art, 1987–. Dir, St Vincent's Hosp., Sydney, 1988–. Mem. Council, Nat. Roads & Motorists Assoc., 1984–; Nat. Pres., Australia–Britain Soc., 1984. Sen. Fellow, Inst. of Public Affairs, 1988–. Hon. DLitt Tasmania, 1977; Hon. LLD: Melbourne, 1983; ANU, 1984. Britannica Award, 1986. *Publications:* as L. J. Gibson: Henry Handel Richardson and Some of Her Sources, 1954; as Leonie Kramer: A Companion to Australia Felix, 1962; Myself when Laura: fact and fiction in Henry Handel Richardson's school career, 1966; Henry Handel Richardson, 1967, repr. as contrib. to Six Australian Writers, 1971; (with Robert D. Eagleson) Language and Literature: a synthesis, 1976; (with Robert D. Eagleson) A Guide to Language and Literature, 1977; A. D. Hope, 1979; (ed and introd) The Oxford History of Australian Literature, 1981; (ed with Adrian Mitchell) The Oxford Anthology of Australian Literature, 1985; (ed and introd) My Country: Australian poetry and short stories—two hundred years, 1985; (ed and introd) James McAuley, 1988; (ed) Collected Poems of David Campbell, 1989. *Recreations:* gardening, music. *Address:* 12 Vaucluse Road, Vaucluse, NSW 2030, Australia. *T:* 371.9686.

KRAMRISCH, Stella, PhD; Professor of Indian Art, Institute of Fine Arts, New York University, since 1964; Curator Emeritus, Indian Art, Philadelphia Museum of Art, since 1954; *d* of Jacques Kramrisch, scientist, and Berta Kramrisch; *m* 1929, Laszlo Neményi (*d* 1950). *Educ:* Vienna University. Prof. of Indian Art, Univ. of Calcutta, 1923–50; Prof. in the Art of South Asia, Univ. of Pennsylvania, 1950–69; Lectr on Indian Art, Courtauld Inst. of Art, Univ. of London, 1937–41. Public lectures in USA, Canada, India, Nepal, W

Germany, including: Aditi Exhibn Seminar, Fest. of India, London, 1982; Fest. of India, Washington, DC, 1985. Mem., Adv. Bd, South Asian Regional Art Studies. Editor: Jl Indian Soc. of Oriental Art, 1932–50; Indian Section, Artibus Asiae, 1959–. Hon. DLit Visva Bharati Univ., 1974; Hon. LLD Pennsylvania, 1981; Hon. DHL: Smith Coll., 1982; Chicago, 1984; Hon. DLit Columbia, NY, 1985. Cross of Honour for Science and Art, Austria, 1979; Padma Bhushan Award, India, 1982; National Women's Caucus for Art Conf. Award, 1983; Prabala Gorkhadakshina Bahu Award, Nepal, 1984; Charles Lang Freer Medal, Washington, DC, 1985. *Publications:* Principles of Indian Art, 1924; Vishnudharmottara, 1924; History of Indian Art, 1929; Indian Sculpture, 1932; Asian Miniature Painting, 1932; A Survey of Painting in the Deccan, 1937; Indian Terracottas, 1939; Kantha, 1939; The Hindu Temple, 1946, repr. 1976; Arts and Crafts of Travancore, 1948; Dravida and Kerala, 1953; Art of India, 1954; Indian Sculpture in the Philadelphia Museum of Art, 1960; The Triple Structure of Creation, 1962; The Art of Nepal, 1964; Unknown India: Ritual Art in Tribe and Village, 1968; The Presence of Siva, 1981; Manifestations of Shiva, 1981; The Antelope, 1982; (contrib.) Discourses on Siva, ed Michael Meister, 1985; Painted Delight (exhibn catalogue), 1986; various articles. *Relevant publication:* Exploring India's Sacred Art: selected writings of Stella Kramrisch, by Barbara Stoler Miller, 1983. *Address:* Philadelphia Museum of Art, PO Box 7646, Philadelphia, Pa 19101, USA.

KREBS, Prof. John Richard, DPhil; FRS 1984; Royal Society Research Professor, Department of Zoology, Oxford University, since 1988; Fellow, Pembroke College, Oxford, since 1981 (E. P. Abraham Fellow, 1981–88); Director, AFRC Unit of Ecology and Behaviour, NERC Unit of Behavioural Ecology, since 1989; *b* 11 April 1945; *s* of Sir Hans Adolf Krebs, FRCP, FRS and Margaret Cicely Krebs; *m* 1968, Katherine Anne Fullerton; two *d.* *Educ:* City of Oxford High School; Pembroke College, Oxford. BA 1966; MA 1970; DPhil 1970. Asst Prof., Univ. of British Columbia, 1970–73; Lectr in Zoology, UCNW, 1973–75; Univ. Lectr in Zoology, Oxford Univ., 1976–88. Storer Lectr, Univ. of Calif, 1985. Mem., AFRC, 1988–. Pres., Internat. Soc. for Behavioral Ecology, 1988–90. Scientific Mem., Max Planck Soc., 1985–. Scientific Medal, Zool. Soc., 1981; Bicentenary Medal, Linnaean Soc., 1983. *Publications:* Behavioural Ecology, 1978, 3rd edn 1991; Introduction to Behavioural Ecology, 1981, 2nd edn 1987; Foraging Theory, 1986; articles in Animal Behaviour, Jl of Animal Ecology. *Recreations:* gardening, violin, running. *Address:* Edward Grey Institute of Field Ornithology, Department of Zoology, South Parks Road, Oxford OX1 3PS. *T:* Oxford (0865) 271166.

KREISEL, Prof. Georg, FRS 1966; Professor Emeritus of Logic and the Foundations of Mathematics, Stanford University, Stanford, California, USA; *b* 15 Sept. 1923. *Address:* Institut für Wissenschaftstheorie, Internationales Forschungszentrum, Mönchsberg 2, A-5020 Salzburg, Austria.

KRETZMER, Herbert; journalist and lyricist; *b* Kroonstad, OFS, S Africa, 5 Oct. 1925; *s* of William and Tilly Kretzmer; *m* 1st, 1961, Elisabeth Margaret Wilson (marr. diss., 1973); one *s* one *d*; 2nd, 1988, Sybil Sever. *Educ:* Kroonstad High Sch.; Rhodes Univ., Grahamstown. Entered journalism, 1946, writing weekly cinema newsreel commentaries and documentary films for African Film Productions, Johannesburg. Reporter and entertainment columnist, Sunday Express, Johannesburg, 1951–54; feature writer and columnist, Daily Sketch, London, 1954–59; Columnist, Sunday Dispatch, London, 1959–61; theatre critic, Daily Express, 1962–78; TV critic, Daily Mail, 1979–87. TV Critic of the Year, Philips Industries Award, 1980; commended in British Press Awards, 1981. As lyric writer, contributed weekly songs to: That Was The Week . ., Not So Much A Programme . ., BBC 3, That's Life. Wrote lyrics of Goodness Gracious Me, 1960 (Ivor Novello Award) and Yesterday When I was Young, 1969 (ASCAP award); Gold record for She, 1974; Our Man Crichton, Shaftesbury Theatre, 1964 (book and lyrics); The Four Musketeers, Drury Lane, 1967 (lyrics); Les Misérables, RSC, 1985 (lyrics (Tony Award, 1987; Grammy Award, 1988)); *film:* Can Heironymus Merkin Ever Forget Mercy Humppe And Find True Happiness?, 1969 (lyrics); has also written lyrics for other films, and for TV programmes. Jimmy Kennedy Award, British Acad. of Songwriters, Composers and Authors, 1989. Chevalier de L'Ordre des Arts et des Lettres, 1988. *Publications:* Our Man Crichton, 1965; (jointly) Every Home Should Have One, 1970. *Address:* c/o London Management, 235/241 Regent Street, W1A 2JT. *Club:* Royal Automobile.

KRIKLER, Dennis Michael, MD; FRCP; Consultant Cardiologist, Hammersmith Hospital, and Senior Lecturer in Cardiology, Royal Postgraduate Medical School, since 1973; *b* 10 Dec. 1928; *s* of Barnet and Eva Krikler; *m* 1955, Anne (*née* Winterstein); one *s* one *d.* *Educ:* Muizenberg High Sch.; Univ. of Cape Town, S Africa. Ho. Phys. and Registrar, Groote Schuur Hosp., 1952–55; Fellow, Lahey Clinic, Boston, 1956; C. J. Adams Meml Travelling Fellowship, 1956; Sen. Registrar, Groote Schuur Hosp., 1957–58; Consultant Physician: Salisbury Central Hosp., Rhodesia, 1958–66; Prince of Wales's Hosp., London, 1966–73; Consultant Cardiologist, Ealing Hosp., 1973–89. Expert Clinicien en Cardiologie, Ministère des Affaires Sociales, Santé, France, 1983. Visiting Professor: Baylor, Indiana and Birmingham Univs, 1985; Boston, Los Angeles and Kentucky, 1988; Lectures: Internat., Amer. Heart Assoc., 1984 (Paul Dudley White Citation for internat. achievement); George Burch Meml, Assoc. of Univ. Cardiologists, 1989; Joseph Welker Meml, Univ. of Kansas, 1989; Denolin, Eur. Soc. of Cardiology, 1990; Howard Burchell, Univ. of Minnesota, 1991. Member, British Cardiac Soc., 1971– (Treasurer, 1976–81); Hon. Member: Soc. Française de Cardiologie, 1981–; Soc. di Cultura Medica Vercellese, Italy; Soc. de Cardiologia de Levante, Spain. Editor, British Heart Journal, 1981–; Member, Editorial Committee: Cardiovascular Res., 1975–; Archives des Maladies du Coeur et des Vaisseaux, 1980–; Revista Latina de Cardiologia, 1980–; Mem. Scientific Council, Revista Portuguesa de Cardiologia, 1982–. FACC 1971; Fellow, Eur. Soc. of Cardiology, 1989 (Medal of Honour, 1990). Hon. Fellow, Council on Clin. Cardiol., Amer. Heart Assoc., 1984. Freeman, Soc. of Apothecaries, 1989. McCullough Prize, 1949; Sir William Osler Award, Miami Univ., 1981. *Publications:* Cardiac Arrhythmias (with J. F. Goodwin), 1975; (with A. Zanchetti) Calcium antagonism in cardiovascular therapy, 1981; (with D. A. Chamberlain and W. J. McKenna) Amiodarone and arrhythmias, 1983; (with P. G. Hugenholtz) Workshop on calcium antagonists, 1984; papers on cardiology in British, American and French jls. *Recreations:* reading, especially history; photography. *Address:* 55 Wimpole Street, W1M 7DF. *T:* 071–935 2098.

KRIKLER, Leonard Gideon; His Honour Judge Krikler; a Circuit Judge, since 1984; *b* 23 May 1929; *s* of late Major James Harold Krikler, OBE, ED, and Tilly Krikler; *m* 1st, 1955, Dr Thilla Krikler (*d* 1973); four *s*; 2nd, 1975, Lily Appleson; one *s*, and one step *s* two step *d.* *Educ:* Milton Sch., Bulawayo, S Rhodesia (Zimbabwe). Called to Bar, Middle Temple, 1953. Crown Counsel, Court Martial Appeals Court, 1968; Dep. Circuit Judge, 1974; a Recorder, 1980–84. Head of Chambers, London and Cambridge, 1975–84. *Recreations:* cartooning, carpentry, painting. *Address:* Lamb Building, Temple, EC4. *T:* 071–353 0774.

KRIKORIAN, Gregory, CB 1973; Solicitor for the Customs and Excise, 1971–78; *b* 23 Sept. 1913; *s* of late Kevork and late Christine Krikorian; *m* 1943, Seta Mary, *d* of Souren Djirdjirian; one *d.* *Educ:* Polytechnic Secondary Sch.; Lincoln Coll., Oxford (BA). Called to Bar, Middle Temple, 1939; practised at Bar, 1939; BBC Overseas Intell. Dept, 1940; served in RAF as Intell. Officer, Fighter Comd, 1940–45 (despatches); practised at Bar, 1945–51, Junior Oxford Circuit, 1947; joined Solicitor's Office, HM Customs and Excise, 1951. *Publication:* (jtly) Customs and Excise, in Halsbury's Laws of England, 1975. *Recreations:* gardening, bird-watching. *Address:* The Coach House, Hawkchurch, Axminster, Devon EX13 5TX. *T:* Hawkchurch (02977) 414. *Clubs:* Reform, Civil Service.

KRISH, Tanya, (Mrs Felix Krish); *see* Moiseiwitsch, T.

KRISTIANSEN, Erling (Engelbrecht), Grand Cross, Order of Dannebrog; Hon. GCVO 1974; Director, East Asiatic Co., since 1978, and other companies; *b* 31 Dec. 1912; *s* of Kristian Engelbrecht Kristiansen, Chartered Surveyor, and Andrea Kirstine (*née* Madsen); *m* 1938, Annemarie Selinko (*d* 1986), novelist. *Educ:* Herning Gymnasium; University of Copenhagen (degree awarded equiv. of MA Econ). Postgraduate Studies, Economics and Internat. Relations, Geneva, Paris, London, 1935–37. Sec.-Gen., 1935, Pres. 1936, of the Fédération Universitaire Internationale pour la Société des Nations. Danish Civil Servant, 1941; served with: Free Danish Missions, Stockholm, 1943; Washington, 1944; London, 1945; joined Danish Diplomatic Service and stayed in London until 1947; Danish Foreign Ministry, 1947–48; Head of Denmark's Mission to OEEC, Paris, 1948–50; Sec. to Economic Cttee of Cabinet, 1950–51; Asst Under-Sec. of State, 1951; Dep. Under-Sec. of State (Economic Affairs), Danish For. Min., 1954–64; Ambassador to UK, 1964–77 (concurrently accredited to Republic of Ireland, 1964–73); Doyen of the Diplomatic Corps, 1973–77; retd 1977. Dir, S. G. Warburg & Co. International Holdings Ltd, 1980–84; Mem., Internat. Adv. Bd, S. G. Warburg & Co., 1984–86, Mercury Internat. Gp, 1986–90; Nordic Investment Bank: Dir, 1977–86; Vice-Chm., 1977–78; Chm., 1978–80. Grand Officier, Légion d'Honneur; Kt Comdr: Order of St Olav; Order of White Rose of Finland; Star of Ethiopia; Knight Grand Cross, Icelandic Falcon; Comdr, Order of Northern Star of Sweden. *Publication:* Folkeforbundet (The League of Nations), 1938. *Recreations:* ski-ing, fishing and other out-door sports, modern languages. *Address:* 4 Granhøjen, DK-2900, Hellerup, Denmark. *Clubs:* MCC; Special Forces *et al.*

KROHN, Dr Peter Leslie, FRS 1963; Professor of Endocrinology, University of Birmingham, 1962–66; *b* 8 Jan. 1916; *s* of Eric Leslie Krohn and Doris Ellen Krohn (*née* Wade); *m* 1941, Joanna Mary French; two *s.* *Educ:* Sedbergh; Balliol Coll., Oxford. BA 1st Cl. Hons Animal Physiol, 1937; BM, BCh Oxon, 1940. Wartime Research work for Min. of Home Security, 1940–45; Lectr, then Reader in Endocrinology, University of Birmingham, 1946–53; Nuffield Sen. Gerontological Research Fellow and Hon. Prof. in University, 1953–62. *Publications:* contrib. to scientific jls on physiology of reproduction, transplantation immunity and ageing. *Recreations:* scuba diving, mountain walking. *Address:* Coburg House, New St John's Road, St Helier, Jersey, Channel Islands JE2 3LD. *T:* Jersey (0534) 74870.

KROLL, Natasha, RDI, FCSD; freelance television and film designer; *b* Moscow, 20 May 1914; *d* of Dr (phil.) Hermann Kroll and Sophie (*née* Rabinovich). *Educ:* Berlin. Teacher of window display, Reimann Sch. of Art, London, 1936–40; Display Manager: Messrs Rowntrees, Scarborough and York, 1940–42; Simpson Piccadilly Ltd, 1942–55; Sen. Designer, BBC TV, 1955–66: programmes include: Monitor, Panorama, science programmes, Lower Depths, Death of Danton, The Duel, Ring Round the Moon, La Traviata, Day by the Sea, The Sponge Room and many others; freelance designer, 1966–; TV designs include: The Seagull, 1966; Family Reunion, 1966; Eugene Onegin, 1967; The Soldier's Tale, 1968; La Vida Breve, 1968; Mary Stuart, 1968; Doll's House, 1969; Three Sisters, Cherry Orchard, Rasputin, Wild Duck, 1971; Summer and Smoke, Hedda Gabler, 1972; The Common, 1973; Lady from the Sea, 1974; Love's Labour's Lost, 1975; Very Like a Whale, 1980; production-designer of: The Music Lovers, 1970; The Hireling, 1973 (FTA Film award for best Art Direction); Summer Rag-time, 1976; Absolution, 1978. RDI 1966. *Publication:* Window Display, 1954. *Recreations:* painting, family, entertaining. *Address:* 5 Ruvigny Gardens, SW15 1JR. *T:* 081–788 9867.

KROLL, Rev. Dr Una (Margaret Patricia); writer and broadcaster, since 1970; Deacon of the Church in Wales, since 1988; Novice Sister of the Society of the Sacred Cross, since 1990; *b* 15 Dec. 1925; *d* of George Hill, CBE, DSO, MC, and Hilda Hill; *m* 1957, Leopold Kroll (*d* 1987); one *s* three *d.* *Educ:* St Paul's Girls' Sch.; Malvern Girls' Coll.; Girton Coll., Cambridge; The London Hosp. MB, BChir (Cantab) 1951; MA 1969. MRCGP 1967. House Officer, 1951–53; Overseas service (Africa), 1953–60; General Practice, 1960–81; Clinical MO, 1981–85, Sen. Clinical MO, 1985–88, Hastings Health Dist. Theological trng, 1967–70; worker deaconess, 1970–88; political work as a feminist, with particular ref. to status of women in the churches in England and internationally, 1970–. Mem., Provincial Validating Bd, Church in Wales. *Publications:* Transcendental Meditation: a signpost to the world, 1974; Flesh of My Flesh: a Christian view on sexism, 1975; Lament for a Lost Enemy: study of reconciliation, 1976; Sexual Counselling, 1980; The Spiritual Exercise Book, 1985; Growing Older, 1988; In Touch with Healing, 1991; contrib. Cervical Cytology (BMJ), 1969. *Recreations:* gardening, reading. *Address:* Tymawr Convent, Lydart, Monmouth, Gwent NP5 4RN. *T:* Monmouth (0600) 860244.

KROTO, Prof. Harold Walter, FRS 1990; Royal Society Research Professor, University of Sussex, Since 1991 (Professor of Chemistry, 1985–91); *b* 7 Oct. 1939; *s* of Heinz and Edith Kroto; *m* 1963, Margaret Henrietta Hunter; two *s.* *Educ:* Bolton Sch.; Univ. of Sheffield (BSc, PhD). Res. in spectroscopy (electronic microwave, infrared and photoelectron), radioastronomy, clusters and nucleation; Head, Krotographics, commercial design and graphics studio (winner, Sunday Times design competition, 1963). Res. student, Sheffield Univ., 1961–64; Postdoctoral Fellow, NRCC, 1964–66; Res. scientist, Bell Telephone Labs, NJ, 1966–67; Tutorial Fellow, 1967–68, Lectr, 1968–77, Reader, 1977–85, Univ. of Sussex. Visiting Professor: UBC 1973; USC 1981; UCLA, 1988–90. Member, SERC Committees: Phys. Chem., 1987–; Synchrotron, 1987–; Chemistry, 1988–. *Publications:* Molecular Rotation Spectra, 1975; 150 papers in chemistry, chem. physics and astronomy jls. *Recreations:* music (guitar), tennis. *Address:* School of Chemistry and Molecular Sciences, University of Sussex, Brighton BN1 9QJ. *T:* Brighton (0273) 678329.

KRUGER, Prudence Margaret; *see* Leith, P. M.

KRUSIN, Sir Stanley (Marks), Kt 1973; CB 1963; Second Parliamentary Counsel, 1970–73; *b* 8 June 1908; *m* 1st, 1937 (she *d* 1972); one *s* one *d*; 2nd, 1976 (she *d* 1988). *Educ:* St Paul's Sch.; Balliol Coll., Oxford. Called to the Bar, Middle Temple, 1932. Served RAFVR, Wing Comdr, 1944. Dep. Sec., British Tabulating Machine Co. Ltd, 1945–47. Entered Parliamentary Counsel Office, 1947; Parliamentary Counsel, 1953–69. *Address:* 5 Coleridge Walk, NW11. *T:* 081–458 1340. *Club:* Royal Air Force.

KUBELIK, Rafael; conductor and composer; Chief Conductor of Bayerischer Rundfunk, München, 1961–79; *b* Bychory, Bohemia, 29 June 1914; *s* of Jan Kubelik, violinist, and Marianne (*née* Szell); *m* 1942, Ludmila Bertlova (*decd*), violinist; one *s*; *m* 1963, Elsie Morison, soprano. *Educ:* Prague Conservatoire. Conductor, Czech Philharmonic Society,

Prague, 1936–39; Musical Director of Opera, Brno, Czechoslovakia, 1939–41; Musical Dir, Czech Philharmonic Orchestra, 1941–48; Musical Dir, Chicago Symphony Orchestra, 1950–53; Musical Dir of the Covent Garden Opera Company, 1955–58; Music Dir, Metropolitan Opera, New York, 1973–74. *Compositions* include: 5 operas; 2 symphonies with chorus; a third symphony (in one movement); Orphikon, symphony for orch.; Sequences for orch.; Peripeteia for organ and orch.; Invocation for tenor solo, boys' choir and orch.; 6 string quartets; 1 violin concerto; 1 cello concerto; 1 cantata; cantata without words for chorus and orch.; Requiems: Pro Memoria Uxoris; Libera Nos; Quattro Forme per Archi; songs; piano and violin music. Hon. RAM; Hon. Member: Bavarian Acad. of Fine Arts; Royal Swedish Acad. of Music; Italian Assoc. Anton Bruckner. Hon. Dr Amer. Conservatory of Music, Chicago; Hon. Dr Karls-Univ., Prague. Karl Amadeus Hartmann Gold Medal; Gold Medal, City of Munich; Gustav Mahler Gold Medal, Gustav Mahler Soc., Vienna; Carl Nielsen Gold Medal, Copenhagen; Medal of City of Amsterdam; Mahler Medal, Bruckner Soc. of Amer.; Golden Key, City of Cleveland. Hon. Citizen: Prague; Brno. Grosses Bundesverdienstkreuz (FRG); Bavarian Order of Merit; Chevalier, Order of the Dannebrog (Denmark); Comtur Istrucao Publica (Portugal); Commandeur de l'ordre des Arts et des Lettres (France). *Address:* 6047 Kastanienbaum, Haus im Sand, Switzerland.

KUBRICK, Stanley; producer, director, script writer; *b* 26 July 1928; *s* of Dr Jacques L. Kubrick and Gertrude Kubrick; *m* 1958, Suzanne Christiane Harlan; three *d*. *Educ:* William Howard Taft High Sch.; City Coll. of City of New York. Joined Look Magazine, 1946. At age of 21 made Documentary, Day of the Fight; made Short for RKO, Flying Padre. *Feature Films:* Fear and Desire, 1953 (at age of 24); Killer's Kiss, 1954; The Killing, 1956; Paths of Glory, 1957; Spartacus, 1960; Lolita, 1962; Dr Strangelove or How I Learned to Stop Worrying and Love the Bomb, 1964; 2001: A Space Odyssey, 1968; A Clockwork Orange, 1971; Barry Lyndon, 1975; The Shining, 1978; Full Metal Jacket, 1987. *Recreations:* literature, music, public affairs. *Address:* c/o Loeb & Loeb, 10100 Santa Monica Boulevard, Suite 2200, Los Angeles, Calif 90067, USA.

KUENSSBERG, Ekkehard von, CBE 1969; FRCGP, 1967; FRCOG (*ae*) 1981; FRCPEd 1981; President, Royal College of General Practitioners, 1976–79; *b* 1913; *s* of Prof. Eberhard von Kuenssberg; *m* 1941, Dr Constance Ferrar Hardy; two *s* two *d*. *Educ:* Schloss Schule, Salem; Univs of Innsbruck, Heidelberg and Edinburgh. MB, ChB 1939. Gen. practice throughout (Edin.). RAMC, 1944–46 (Lt-Col, DADMS E Africa Comd). Mem., Safety of Drugs Cttee, 1964–71; Chm., Gen. Med. Services Cttee, Scotland; Mem., GMSC, UK, 1960–68; RCGP: Chm. Council, 1970–73; Hon. Treas., Research Foundn Bd, 1960–77; Mackenzie Lectr, 1970; Wolfson Travelling Prof., 1974. Mem., Lothian Area Health Bd, 1974–80; Member: Council, Queen's Nursing Inst., 1972–76; Court, Edinburgh Univ., 1971–79. Foundation Council Award, RCGP, 1967; Hippocrates Medal, 1974 (SIMG). FRSocMed. *Publications:* The Team in General Practice, 1966; An Opportunity to Learn, 1977. *Recreations:* skiing, forestry. *Address:* 2 St Martin's Close, Haddington, East Lothian EH41 4BN. *T:* Haddington (062082) 2529.
See also N. C. D. Kuenssberg.

KUENSSBERG, Nicholas Christopher Dwelly; Chief Executive (UK), Dawson International, since 1991; *b* 28 Oct. 1942; *s* of Ekkehard von Kuenssberg, *qv*; *m* 1965, Sally Robertson; one *s* two *d*. *Educ:* Edinburgh Acad.; Wadham Coll., Oxford (BA Hons). FCIS; CBIM. Worked overseas, 1965–78; Director: Coats Patons Plc, 1985; Coats Viyella plc, 1986–91. Director: Scottish Power (formerly S of Scotland Electricity Bd), 1984–; W of Scotland Bd, Bank of Scotland, 1984–88; Standard Life Assce Co., 1988–. Hon. Res. Fellow, 1986, Vis. Prof., 1988, Strathclyde Business Sch. Gov., Queen's Coll., Glasgow, 1989. *Recreations:* sport, travel, opera, languages. *Address:* Dawson International, 9 Charlotte Square, Edinburgh EH2 4DR. *T:* 031–220 1919.

KUHN, Heinrich Gerhard, FRS 1954; DPhil, MA; Reader in Physics, Oxford University, 1955–71, now Emeritus; Fellow of Balliol College 1950–71, now Emeritus; *b* 10 March 1904; *s* of Wilhelm Felix and Martha Kuhn; *m* 1931, Marie Bertha Nohl; two *s*. *Educ:* High Sch., Lueben (Silesia); Universities of Greifswald and Göttingen. Lecturer in Physics, Göttingen Univ., 1931; Research at Clarendon Laboratory, Oxford, 1933–71; Lecturer, University Coll., Oxford, 1938; work for atomic energy project, 1941–45; University Demonstrator, Oxford, 1945–55. Prof. a.D, Göttingen Univ., 1957. Dr *hc* Aix-Marseille, 1958. Holweck Prize, 1967. *Publications:* Atomspektren, 1934 (Akad. Verl. Ges., Leipzig); Atomic Spectra, 1962, 2nd edn 1970; articles on molecular and atomic spectra and on interferometry. *Address:* 25 Victoria Road, Oxford OX2 7QF. *T:* Oxford (0865) 515308.

KUHN, Prof. Karl Heinz, FBA 1987; Professor of Coptic, Durham University, 1982–84, now Emeritus Professor; *b* 2 Aug. 1919; *s* of Max Kuhn and Gertrud Kuhn (*née* Hiller); *m* 1949, Rachel Mary Wilkinson; one *s* one *d*. *Educ:* school in Germany; St John's Coll., Univ. of Durham (BA 1949, PhD 1952). Scarbrough Research Studentship, Durham Univ. and abroad, 1949–53; Univ. of Durham: Research Fellow in Arts, 1953–55; Lectr, later Sen. Lectr in Hebrew and Aramaic, 1955–77; Reader in Coptic, 1977–82; Prof. of Coptic, 1982–84. Mem., editl bd, Corpus Scriptorum Christianorum Orientalium, Louvain, 1970–. *Publications:* Letters and Sermons of Besa, 1956; Pseudo-Shenoute: on Christian behaviour, 1960; A Panegyric on John the Baptist attributed to Theodosius, Archbishop of Alexandria, 1966; A Panegyric on Apollo, Archimandrite of the Monastery of Isaac by Stephen, Bishop of Heracleopolis Magna, 1978; (contrib.) Sparks, The Apocryphal Old Testament, 1984; English trans of Foerster, Gnosis, 1974, Rudolph, Gnosis, 1983; articles in Jl of Theol Studies, Le Muséon and other learned jls. *Recreations:* music. *Address:* 28 Nevilledale Terrace, Durham DH1 4QG. *T:* 091–384 2993.

KUHRT, Ven. Gordon Wilfred; Archdeacon of Lewisham, since 1989; *b* 15 Feb. 1941; *s* of Wilfred and Doris Kuhrt; *m* 1963, Olive Margaret Powell; three *s*. *Educ:* Colfe's Grammar School; London Univ. (BD Hons); Oak Hill Theol Coll. Religious Education teacher, 1963–65; Curate: Illogan, Cornwall, 1967–70; Wallington, Surrey, 1970–74; Vicar: Shenstone, Staffs, 1974–79; Emmanuel, South Croydon, Surrey, 1979–89; RD, Croydon Central, 1981–86; Hon. Canon, Southwark Cathedral, 1987–. Mem., C of E Gen. Synod, 1986– (Bd of Ministry, 1991–). Theological Lectr, London Univ. Extra-Mural Dept, 1984–. *Publications:* A Handbook for Council and Committee Members, 1985; Believing in Baptism, 1987; (contrib.) The Church and its Unity, 1991. *Address:* 3A Court Farm Road, Mottingham, SE9 4JH. *T:* 081–857 7982.

KUIPERS, John Melles; Chairman, ATT Ltd, 1984–91; *b* 7 July 1918; *s* of late Joh Kuipers and Anna (*née* Knoester); *m* 1947, Joan Lilian Morgan-Edwards; one *s* three *d*. *Educ:* Royal Masonic Sch., Bushey. Served RA, 1939–46 (Lt-Col). Ford Motor Co. Ltd, 1947–51; Treasurer, Canadian Chemical Co. Ltd, Montreal, 1951–55; Gp Manager, Halewood, and Dir, Stamping and Assembly Gp, Ford Motor Co. Ltd, 1955–67; EMI Ltd, 1967–80: Chief Exec. Electronic and Industrial Ops, 1969–72; Chm. and Chief Exec., EMI (Australia) Ltd, 1974–77; Man. Dir and Vice-Chm., 1977–79; Dir, Thames TV Ltd, 1977–81; Chm., Huntleigh Gp PLC, 1980–83. Director: Gowrings, 1980–89; Peachy Productions. *Address:* Marsh Mills Boathouse, Wargrave Road, Henley-on-Thames, Oxon RG9 3HY. *T:* Henley-on-Thames (0491) 574760.

KULUKUNDIS, Eddie, (Elias George), OBE 1988; Chairman, Knightsbridge Theatrical Productions Ltd, since 1970; Director: Rethymnis & Kulukundis Ltd, since 1964; London & Overseas Freighters, 1980–85 and since 1989; Member of Lloyd's, since 1964, Member Council, 1983–89; Member, Baltic Exchange, since 1959; *b* 20 April 1932; *s* of late George Elias Kulukundis and of Eugénie (*née* Diacakis); *m* 1981, Susan Hampshire, *qv*. *Educ:* Collegiate Sch., New York; Salisbury Sch., Connecticut; Yale Univ. Governor: Greenwich Theatre Ltd; The Raymond Mander and Joe Mitchenson Theatre Collection Ltd; Royal Shakespeare Theatre; Chm., Sports Aid Foundn Ltd, 1988–. Director: Hampstead Theatre Ltd. Member, Councils of Management: Royal Shakespeare Theatre; Royal Shakespeare Theatre Trust (Vice-Chm., 1983–); Traverse Theatre Club. Mem. Exec. Council, SWET. Trustee: Salisbury Sch., Connecticut; Theatres Trust. FRSA. As Theatrical Producer, London prodns incl. (some jtly): Enemy, 1969; The Happy Apple, Poor Horace, The Friends, How the Other Half Loves, Tea Party and The Basement (double bill), The Wild Duck, 1970; After Haggerty, Hamlet, Charley's Aunt, Straight Up, 1971; London Assurance, Journey's End, 1972; Small Craft Warnings, A Private Matter, Dandy Dick, 1973; The Waltz of the Toreadors, Life Class, Pygmalion, Play Mas, The Gentle Hook, 1974; A Little Night Music, Entertaining Mr Sloane, The Gay Lord Quex, What the Butler Saw, Travesties, Lies, The Sea Gull, A Month in the Country, A Room With a View, Too True to Be Good, The Bed Before Yesterday, 1975; Dimetos, Banana Ridge, Wild Oats, 1976; Candida, Man and Superman, Once A Catholic, 1977; Privates on Parade, Gloo Joo, 1978; Bent, Outside Edge, Last of the Red Hot Lovers, 1979; Beecham, Born in the Gardens, 1980; Tonight At 8.30, Steaming, Arms and the Man, 1981; Steafel's Variations, 1982; Messiah, Pack of Lies, 1983; Of Mice and Men, The Secret Diary of Adrian Mole Aged 13¾, 1984; Camille, 1985; The Cocktail Party, 1986; Curtains, 1987; Separation, South Pacific, Married Love, 1988; Over My Dead Body, 1989; Never the Sinner, 1990; Carmen Jones, 1991. New York prodns (jtly): How the Other Half Loves, 1971; Sherlock Holmes, London Assurance, 1974; Travesties, 1975; The Merchant, 1977; Players, 1978; Once a Catholic, 1979. *Address:* c/o Rethymnis & Kulukundis, Ltd, 15 Fetter Lane, EC4A 1JJ. *T:* 071–583 2266; c/o Knightsbridge Theatrical Productions, Ltd, 15 Fetter Lane, EC4A 1JJ. *T:* 071–583 8687. *Club:* Garrick.

KUME, Yutaka; President, Nissan Motor Co., since 1985; *b* 20 May 1921; *s* of Kinzaburo Kume and Chiyo Kume; *m* 1947, Aya Yamamoto; one *s* one *d*. *Educ:* Univ. of Tokyo (BE aircraft engineering). Joined Nissan Motor Co., 1946; General Manager, Production control and Engineering Dept, Zama Plant, 1964; Gen. Manager, Yoshiwara Plant, 1971; Dir and Mem. Bd, 1973; Managing Dir, 1977; Exec. Managing Dir, 1982; Exec. Vice-Pres., 1983. Blue Ribbon Medal from Emperor of Japan, 1986; Commander, Order of Orange Nassau, Holland, 1986. *Recreations:* photography, haiku (Japanese short poems), reading. *Address:* Nissan Motor Co. Ltd, 17–1 Ginza 6-chome, Chuo-ku, Tokyo 104, Japan. *T:* (03) 543–5523.

KUNCEWICZ, Eileen, (Mrs Witold Kuncewicz); *see* Herlie, E.

KUNERALP, Zeki, Hon. GCVO 1971; *b* Istanbul, 5 Oct. 1914; *s* of Ali Kemal and Sabiha, *d* of Mustafa Zeki Pasha; *m* 1943, Necla Ozdilci (*d* 1978); two *s*. *Educ:* Univ. of Berne. DrIuris 1938. Entered Diplomatic Service, 1940: served Bucharest, Prague, Paris, Nato Delegn and at Min. of Foreign Affairs, Ankara; Asst Sec.-Gen. 1957; Sec.-Gen. 1960; Ambassador to Berne, 1960, to Court of St James's, 1964–66; Sec.-Gen. at Min. of Foreign Affairs, Ankara, 1966–69; Ambassador to Court of St James's, 1969–72, to Spain, 1972–79, retired. Mem., Hon. Soc. of Knights of the Round Table. Holds German, Greek, Italian, Papal, Jordanian, Iranian and National Chinese orders. *Publication:* Sadece Diplomat (memoirs), 1981. *Recreations:* reading, ballet. *Address:* Fenerbahçe Cadessi 85/B, D4, Kiziltoprak, Istanbul 81030, Turkey.

KÜNG, Prof. Dr Hans; Ordinary Professor of Ecumenical Theology, since 1980 and Director of Institute for Ecumenical Research, since 1963, University of Tübingen; *b* Sursee, Lucerne, 19 March 1928. *Educ:* schools in Sursee and Lucerne; Papal Gregorian Univ., Rome (LPhil, LTh); Sorbonne; Inst. Catholique, Paris. DTheol 1957. Further studies in Amsterdam, Berlin, Madrid, London. Ordained priest, 1954. Pastoral work, Hofkirche, Lucerne, 1957–59; Asst for dogmatic theol., Univ. of Münster, 1959–60; Ord. Prof. of fundamental theol., 1960–63, Ord. Prof. of dogmatic and ecumenical theol., 1963–80, Univ. of Tübingen. Official theol. consultant (peritus) to 2nd Vatican Council, 1962–65; Guest Professor: Union Theol. Seminary, NYC, 1968; Univ. of Basle, 1969; Univ. of Chicago Divinity Sch., 1981; Univ. of Michigan, 1983; Toronto Univ., 1985; guest lectures at univs in Europe, America, Asia and Australia; Hon. Pres., Edinburgh Univ. Theol Soc., 1982–83. Editor series, Theologische Meditationen; co-Editor series, Ökumenische Forschungen and Ökumenische Theologie; Associate Editor: Tübingen Theologische Quartalschrift, 1960–80; Jl of Ecum. Studies; Mem. Exec. Editorial Cttee, Concilium. Mem., Amer. and German Pen Clubs. Holds hon. doctorates. *Publications:* (first publication in German) The Council and Reunion, 1961; That the World may Believe, 1963; The Living Church, 1963; The Changing Church, 1965; Justification: the doctrine of Karl Barth and a Catholic reflection, 1965; Structures of the Church, 1965; The Church, 1967; Truthfulness: the future of the Church, 1968; Infallible? an enquiry, 1971 (paperback 1972); Why Priests?, 1972; 20 Thesen zum Christsein, 1975; On Being a Christian, 1977 (abridged as The Christian Challenge, 1979); Was ist Firmung?, 1976; Jesus im Widerstreit: ein jüdisch-christlicher Dialog (with Pinchas Lapide), 1976; Brother or Lord?, 1977; Signposts for the Future, 1978; Freud and the Problem of God, 1979; The Church—Maintained in Truth?, 1980; Does God Exist?, 1980; Art and the Question of Meaning, 1981; Eternal Life?, 1984; (jtly) Christianity and World Religions, 1986; The Incarnation of God, 1986; Church and Change: the Irish experience, 1986; Why I am still a Christian, 1987; Theology for the Third Millennium: an ecumenical view, 1988; (with Julia Ching) Christianity and Chinese Religions, 1989; Reforming the Church Today: keeping hope alive, 1990; Global Responsibility: in search of a new world ethic, 1991; (contrib.) Theologische Meditationen, 1965 (Amer. edn as Freedom Today, 1966); (contrib.) Christian Revelation and World Religions, ed J. Neuner, 1967. *Address:* W-7400 Tübingen 1, Waldhäuserstrasse 23, Germany.

KUREISHI, Hanif; writer; *b* 5 Dec. 1954; *s* of Rafiushan Kureishi and Audrey Buss. *Educ:* King's College London. *Publications:* Outskirts, 1981; Borderline, 1981; Birds of Passage, 1983; My Beautiful Launderette, 1984; Sammy and Rosie Get Laid, 1987; The Buddha of Suburbia, 1990; London Kills Me, 1991. *Recreations:* pop music, cricket, sitting in pubs. *Address:* c/o Deborah Rogers Ltd, 20 Powis Mews, W11 1SN.

KURIA, Most Rev. Manasses; *see* Kenya, Archbishop of.

KURONGKU, Most Rev. Sir Peter; *see* Port Moresby, Archbishop of, (RC).

KUROSAWA, Akira; Japanese film director; *b* 23 March 1910. *Educ:* Keika Middle School. Assistant Director, Toho Film Co., 1936. Mem. Jury, Internat. Film Fest. of India, 1977. Directed first film, Sanshiro Sugata, 1943. *Films include:* Sanshiro Sugata; The Most Beautiful, 1944; Sanshiro Sugata II, 1945; They Who Step on the Tiger's Tail, 1945; No Regret for our Youth, 1946; One Wonderful Sunday, 1947; Drunken Angel, 1948; The Quiet Duel, 1949; Stray Dog, 1949; Scandal, 1950; Rashomon (1st prize, Venice Film Fest.), 1950; The Idiot, 1951; Ikuru, 1952; Seven Samurai, 1954; Record of a Living

Being, 1955; The Throne of Blood, 1957; The Lower Depths, 1957; The Hidden Fortress, 1958; The Bad Sleep Well, 1960; Yojimbo, 1961; Sanjuro, 1962; High and Low, 1963; Red Beard, 1965; Dodes'kaden, 1970. Dersu Uzala (Oscar award), 1975; Kagemusha (Golden Palm Award, Cannes Film Festival), 1980; Ran, 1985; Dreams, 1990; Rhapsody in August, 1991. *Publication:* Something like an Autobiography (trans. Audie Bock), 1984.

KURTI, Prof. Nicholas, CBE 1973; FRS 1956; MA Oxon; DrPhil (Berlin); FInstP; Emeritus Professor of Physics, University of Oxford; Vice-President, Royal Society, 1965–67; *b* 14 May 1908; *s* of late Károly Kürti and Margit Pintér, Budapest; *m* 1946, Giana, *d* of late Brig.-Gen. and Mrs C. T. Shipley; two *d. Educ:* Minta-Gymnasium, Budapest; University of Paris (Licence ès sci. phys.); University of Berlin (DrPhil). Asst, Techn Hochschule Breslau, 1931–33; Research Position, Clarendon Laboratory, Oxford, 1933–40; UK Atomic Bomb Project, 1940–45; University Demonstrator in Physics, Oxford, 1945–60; Reader in Physics, Oxford, 1960–67; Prof. of Physics, Oxford, 1967–75; Senior Research Fellow, Brasenose Coll., 1947–67; Professorial Fellow, 1967–75, Emeritus Fellow, 1975–. Buell G. Gallagher Visiting Prof., City Coll., New York, 1963; Vis. Prof., Univ. of Calif, Berkeley, 1964; Dist. Vis. Prof., Amherst Coll., 1979. May Lecture, Inst. of Metals, 1963; Kelvin Lecture, IEE, 1971; Larmor Lecture, Queen's Univ., Belfast, 1975; James Scott Prize and Lecture, RSE, 1976; Cherwell-Simon Lecture, Oxford Univ., 1977; Tyndall Lecture, Inst. of Physics, Royal Dublin Soc., 1980. A Governor, College of Aeronautics, Cranfield, 1953–69. Member: Electricity Supply Research Council, 1960–79; Advisory Cttee for Scientific and Technical Information, 1966–68; Comité de Direction, Service Nat. des Champs Intenses, CNRS, 1973–75; Comité, Problèmes Socio-économique de l'Energie, CNRS, 1975–78; Chairman: Adv. Cttee for Research on Measurement and Standards, DTI, 1969–73; Jt Cttee on Scientific and Technol Records, Royal Soc./Royal Commn on Historical MSS, 1970–76. Member: Council, Royal Soc., 1964–67; Council, Soc. Française de Physique, 1957–60, 1970–73; Council, Inst. of Physics and Physical Soc., 1969–73; Treasurer, CODATA (Cttee on data for sci. and technol., ICSU), 1973–80; Chm., Cttee of Management, Science Policy Foundn, 1970–75. Editor-in-Chief, Europhysics Letters, 1985–89. Emeritus Mem., Acad. Europaea, 1990; Foreign Hon. Mem., Amer. Acad. Arts and Sciences, 1968; Hon. Member: Hungarian Acad. of Sciences, 1970; Société Française de Physique, 1974; Fachverband deutscher Köche, 1978; European Physical Soc., 1989; Foreign Member: Finnish Acad. of Sciences and Letters, 1974; Akad. der Wissenschaften der DDR, 1976. Holweck Prize (British and French Physical Socs), 1955; Fritz London Award, 1957; Hughes Medal, Royal Soc., 1969. Chevalier de la Légion d'Honneur, 1976; Hungarian Order of the Star, 1988. *Publications:* (jointly) Low Temperature Physics, 1952; (ed with Giana Kurti) But the Crackling is Superb, 1988; papers on cryophysics, magnetism, energy and culinary physics; articles in the New Chambers's Encyclopædia. *Recreations:* cooking, enjoying its results and judiciously applying physics to the noble art of cookery. *Address:* 38 Blandford Avenue, Oxford OX2 8DZ. *T:* Oxford (0865) 56176; Department of Engineering Science, Parks Road, Oxford OX1 3PJ. *T:* Oxford (0865) 273115. *Club:* Athenæum.

KUSCH, Prof. Polykarp; Regental Professor Emeritus, Department of Physics, The University of Texas at Dallas, since 1982; *b* Germany, 26 Jan. 1911; *s* of John Matthias Kusch and Henrietta van der Haas; *m* 1935, Edith Starr McRoberts (*d* 1959); three *d*; *m* 1960, Betty Jane Pezzoni; two *d. Educ:* Case Inst. of Technology, Cleveland, O (BS); Univ. of Illinois, Urbana, Ill. (MS, PhD). Asst, Univ. of Illinois, 1931–36; Research Asst, Univ. of Minnesota, 1936–37; Instr in Physics, Columbia Univ., 1937–41; Engr, Westinghouse Electric Corp., 1941–42; Mem. Tech. Staff, Div. of Govt Aided Research, Columbia Univ., 1942–44; Mem. Tech. Staff, Bell Telephone Laboratories, 1944–46; Columbia University: Associate Prof. of Physics, 1946–49; Prof. of Physics, 1949–72; Exec. Officer, Dept of Physics, 1949–52, Chm. 1960–63; Exec. Dir, Columbia Radiation Laboratory, 1952–60; Vice-Pres. and Dean of Faculties, 1969–70; Exec. Vice-Pres. and Provost, 1970–71; University of Texas at Dallas: Prof. of Physics, 1972–74; Eugene McDermott Prof., 1974–80; U. T. System Chair, 1980–82. Member: Nat. Acad. of Sciences, US; American Philosophical Soc.; Amer. Acad. of Arts and Scis. Phi Beta Kappa. Hon. DSc: Case Inst. of Tech., 1956; Ohio State Univ., 1959; Colby Coll., 1961; Univ. of Illinois, 1961; Gustavus Adolphus Coll., 1963; Yeshiva Univ., 1976; Incarnate Word Coll., 1980; Columbia Univ., 1983. (Jointly) Nobel Prize in Physics, 1955. *Publications:* technical articles in Physical Review and other jls. *Address:* University of Texas at Dallas, Department of Physics, PO Box 830688, Richardson, Texas 75083–0688, USA; 7241 Paldao, Dallas, Texas 75240, USA. *T:* (214)661–1247.

KUSTOW, Michael David; writer, producer and director; *b* 18 Nov. 1939; *m* 1973, Orna, *d* of Jacob and Rivka Spector, Haifa, Israel. *Educ:* Haberdashers' Aske's; Wadham Coll., Oxford (BA Hons English). Festivals Organiser, Centre 42, 1962–63; Royal Shakespeare Theatre Company: Dir, RSC Club, Founder of Theatregoround, Editor of Flourish, 1963–67; Dir, Inst. of Contemporary Arts, 1967–70; Associate Dir, National Theatre, 1973–81; Commissioning Ed. for Arts progs, Channel Four TV, 1981–89; Dir, Michael Kustow Productions, 1990–. Lectr in Dramatic Arts, Harvard Univ., 1980–82. Chevalier de l'Ordre des Arts et des Lettres, République Française, 1980. *Productions:* Punch and Judas, Trafalgar Square, 1963; I Wonder, ICA, 1968; Nicholas Tomalin Reporting, 1975; Brecht Poetry and Songs, 1976; Larkinland, Groucho Letters, Robert Lowell, Audience, 1977–78; Miss South Africa, Catullus, A Nosegay of Light Verse, The Voice of Babel, Anatol, 1979; Iris Murdoch's Art and Eros, Shakespeare's Sonnets, Stravinsky's Soldier's Tale, 1980; Charles Wood's Has Washington Legs, Harold Pinter's Family Voices, 1981; The Mahabharata, 1989; The War that Never Ends, 1991. *Exhibitions:* Tout Terriblement Guillaume Apollinaire, ICA, 1968; AAARGH! A Celebration of Comics, ICA, 1971. *Publications:* Punch and Judas, 1964; The Book of US, 1968; Tank: an autobiographical fiction, 1975; One in Four, 1987. *Recreations:* painting, jazz. *Address:* c/o Tim Corrie, Peters, Fraser & Dunlop, The Chambers, Chelsea Harbour, Lots Road, SW10 0XF.

KUTSCHER, Hans, Dr. iur; President, Court of Justice of the European Communities, 1976–80 (Judge of Court, 1970–80), retired 1980; *b* Hamburg, 14 Dec. 1911, *m* 1946, Irmgard Schroeder; two step *d. Educ:* Univ. of Graz, Austria; Univ. of Freiburg-im-Breisgau, Berlin. Started career as civil servant; Ministry of: Commerce and Industry, Berlin, 1939; Transport, Baden Württemberg, 1946–51; Foreign Affairs, Bonn, 1951; Sec., Legal Cttee and Conf. Cttee of Bundesrat, 1951–55; Judge, Federal Constitutional Court, 1955–70. Hon. Prof., Univ. of Heidelberg, 1965. Hon. Bencher: Middle Temple, 1976; King's Inns, Dublin, 1977. Awarded Grand Cross Verdienstorden of Federal Republic of Germany, 1980. *Publications:* Die Enteignung, 1938; Bonner Vertrag mit Zusatzvereinbarungen, 1952; various contribs to professional jls. *Recreations:* literature, history. *Address:* Viertelstrasse 10, W-7506 Bad Herrenalb 5, Germany.

KWAKYE, Dr Emmanuel Bamfo; Project Coordinator, UNESCO, Nairobi, Kenya, since 1985 (Consultant Project Coordinator, 1982–85); *b* 19 March 1933; *s* of Rev. W. H. Kwakye and F. E. A. Kwakye; *m* 1964, Gloria E. (*née* Mensah); two *d. Educ:* a Presbyterian sch., Ghana; Achimota Secondary Sch., Ghana; Technical Univ., Stuttgart, West Germany (DipIng, DrIng). Development Engr, Siemens & Halske, Munich, W Germany, 1960–62; Univ. of Science and Technology, Kumasi: Lectr, 1963; Sen. Lectr, 1964; Associate Prof., 1966; Head of Dept, 1970; Dean of Faculty, 1971; Pro Vice-Chancellor, 1971; Vice-Chancellor, 1974–82. Visiting Prof., Bradley Univ., Peoria, USA, 1981. *Publications:* design and research reports on digital equipment. *Recreations:* reading, indoor games, opera and operette. *Address:* UNESCO-ROSTA, PO Box 30592, Nairobi, Kenya.

KWAPONG, Alexander Adum, MA, PhD Cantab; Lester B. Pearson Chair in Development Studies, Dalhousie University, Halifax, Canada, since 1988; *b* Akropong, Akwapim, 8 March 1927; *s* of E. A. Kwapong and Theophilia Kwapong; *m* 1956, Evelyn Teiko Caesar, Ada; six *d. Educ:* Presbyterian junior and middle schools, Akropong; Achimota Coll.; King's Coll., Cambridge (Exhibr, Minor Schol. and Foundn Schol.). BA 1951, MA 1954, PhD 1957, Cantab. 1st cl. prelims, Pts I and II, Classical Tripos, 1951; Sandys Res. Student, Cambridge Univ.; Richards Prize, Rann Kennedy Travel Fellowship, King's Coll., Cambridge. Lectr in Classics, UC Gold Coast, 1953, Sen. Lectr in Classics 1960; Vis. Prof., Princeton Univ., 1961–62; Prof. of Classics, Univ. of Ghana, 1962; Dean of Arts, Pro-Vice-Chancellor, Univ. of Ghana, 1962–65, Vice-Chancellor 1966–75; Vice-Rector for Instl Planning and Resource Develt, UN Univ., 1976–88. Chairman: Educn Review Cttee, Ghana Govt, 1966–67; Smithsonian Instn 3rd Internat. Symposium, 1969; Assoc. of Commonwealth Univs, 1971. Sir Samuel Manuwa Meml Lectr, W African Coll. of Surgeons, 1990. Member: Admin. Bd, Internat. Assoc. Univs, Paris, 1970–80; Exec. Bd, Assoc. African Univs, 1967–74; Bd of Trustees, Internat. Council for Educnl Develt, NY; Aspen Inst. for Humanistic Studies, 1972–85; Board of Directors: Internat. Assoc. for Cultural Freedom, Paris, 1967–75; Internat. Cttee for the Study of Educnl Exchange; Aspen Berlin Inst.; Consultant: World Bank, 1988–89; IDRC; Board of Trustees: Harold Macmillan Trust; Africa Leadership Forum. Fellow, Ghana Academy of Arts and Sciences. Hon. DLitt: Warwick; Ife; Ghana; Hon. LLD Princeton. Order of Volta, Ghana. *Publications:* The Role of Classical Studies in Africa Today, 1969; Higher Education and Development in Africa Today: a reappraisal, 1979; Underdevelopment and the Challenges of the 1980's: the role of knowledge, 1980; The Relevance of the African Universities to the Development Needs of Africa, 1980; What Kind of Human Beings for the 21st Century—a second look, 1981; The Humanities and National Development: a second look, 1984; The Crisis of Development: education and identity, 1985; Medical Education and National Development, 1987; Culture, Development and African Unity, 1988; African Scientific and Technical Institution—Building and the Role of International Co-operation, 1988; The Challenge of Education in Africa, 1988; *contribs to:* Grecs et Barbars, 1962; Dawn of African History (ed R. Oliver); Man and Beast: Comparative Social Behaviour (ed J. F. Eisenberg and W. S. Dillon), 1971; Pearson Notes, 1988–89; The Role of Service-Learning in International Education (procs of Wingspread conf.) (ed S. W. Showalter), 1989; various articles in classical jls, especially on Ancient and Greco-Roman Africa; various addresses and lectures on internat. higher educn in ICED pubns. *Recreations:* tennis, billiards, music and piano-playing, learning Japanese. *Address:* c/o Lester Pearson Institute for International Development, Dalhousie University, 1321 Edward Street, Halifax, Nova Scotia B3H 3H5, Canada. *T:* (902) 424–2038. *Club:* Athenæum.

KYLE, Barry Albert; freelance director; Hon. Associate Director, Royal Shakespeare Company (Associate Director, 1978–91); *b* 25 March 1947; *s* of Albert Ernest Kyle and Edith Ivy Bessie Gaskin; *m* 1971, Christine Susan Iddon (marr. diss. 1988); two *s* one *d*; *m* 1990, Lucy Joy Maycock. *Educ:* Birmingham Univ. (BA, MA). Associate Dir, Liverpool Playhouse, 1970–72; joined RSC as Asst Dir, 1973; first Artistic Dir, Swan Theatre, Stratford-upon-Avon, 1987; numerous RSC productions and directing abroad, incl. Australia, Israel, USA, Czechoslovakia; founding Artistic Dir, Dixie Nat. Forest, La, USA. Vis. Dir, Czechoslovak Nat. Theatre, Prague (first Briton to direct there). *Publications:* Sylvia Plath: a dramatic portrait, 1976; contribs to Literary Review. *Recreations:* foreign travel, reading, physical activities. *Address:* Flat 5, 20 Charing Cross Road, WC2. *T:* 071–836 5911.

KYLE, James, CBE 1989; FRCSE; FRCSI; FRCS; Chairman, Grampian Health Board, since 1989 (Member, 1973); *b* 26 March 1925; *s* of John Kyle and Dorothy Frances Kyle; *m* 1950, Dorothy Elizabeth Galbraith; two *d. Educ:* Queen's Univ., Belfast. MB BCh BAO 1947 (Gold Medal in Surgery); MCh 1956 (Gold Medal); DSc 1972. FRCSI 1953; FRCS 1954; FRCSE 1964. Mayo Clinic, USA, 1950; Tutor in Surgery, QUB, 1952; Lectr in Surgery, Univ. of Liverpool, 1957; Aberdeen University: Sen. Lectr, Surgery, 1959; Mem., Univ. Senatus, 1970; Consultant Surgeon, Aberdeen Royal Infirmary, 1959–89. Mem., GMC, 1979–; Chairman: Scottish Cttee for Hosp. Med. Services, 1977; Rep. Body, BMA, 1984–87; Scottish Jt Consultants' Cttee, 1984–89. Pres., Aberdeen Medico-Surgical Soc. Bicentenary, 1989–90. FRPSL. *Publications:* Peptic Ulceration, 1960; Pye's Surgical Handicraft, 21st edn, 1962; Scientific Foundations of Surgery, 3rd edn, 1967; Crohn's Disease, 1973; papers on surgery, history, philately. *Recreations:* amateur radio (callsign GM4 CHX), philately. *Address:* Grianan, 74 Rubislaw Den North, Aberdeen AB2 4AN. *T:* Aberdeen (0224) 317966. *Club:* Royal Northern (Aberdeen).

KYME, Rt. Rev. Brian Robert; an Assistant Bishop of Perth, Western Australia, since 1982; *b* 22 June 1935; *s* of John Robert Kyme and Ida Eileen Benson; *m* 1961, Doreen Muriel Williams; one *s* one *d. Educ:* Melbourne High School; Ridley Theological Coll., Melbourne; WA Coll. of Advanced Educn. (BA 1989); ThL Aust. Coll. of Theology, 1956; DipRE Melbourne Coll. of Divinity, 1958. MACE 1991. Deacon, 1958; priest, 1960; Curate: St John's, E Malvern, 1958–60; Glenroy and Broadmeadows, 1960–61; Morwell, 1961–63; Vicar, St Matthew's, Ashburton, 1963–69; Dean, Holy Cross Cathedral, Geraldton, WA, 1969–74; Rector, Christ Church, Claremont, Perth, 1974–82; Archdeacon of Stirling, 1977–82. ChLJ, WA, 1985–. *Recreations:* golf, reading. *Address:* 52 Swan Street, Guildford, WA 6055, Australia. *T:* (office) (09)377.4455, (home) (09)279.7790. *Club:* Rotary.

KYNASTON, Nicolas; freelance organist, since 1971; Consultant Tutor, Birmingham Conservatoire (formerly Birmingham School of Music), since 1986; *b* 10 Dec. 1941; *s* of late Roger Tewkesbury Kynaston and Jessie Dearn Caecilia Kynaston (*née* Parkes); *m* 1961, Judith Felicity Heron (marr. diss. 1989); two *s* two *d*; *m* 1989, Susan Harwood Styles. *Educ:* Westminster Cathedral Choir Sch.; Downside; Accademia Musicale Chigiana, Siena; Conservatorio Santa Cecilia, Rome; Royal Coll. of Music. Organist of Westminster Cathedral, 1961–71; concert career, 1971–, travelling throughout Europe, North America, Asia and Africa. Début recital, Royal Festival Hall, 1966; Recording début, 1968. Consultant, J. W. Walker & Sons Ltd, 1982–83 (Artistic Dir, 1978–82); Organ Consultant: Dean and Chapter, Bristol, 1986–91; Dean and Canons of Manchester, 1988–; Archbishop of Birmingham, 1989–. Jury member: Grand Prix de Chartres, 1971; St Albans Internat. Organ Festival, 1975. Pres., Incorp. Assoc. of Organists, 1983–85. Hon. FRCO 1976. Records incl. 5 nominated Critic's Choice; EMI/CFP Sales Award, 1974; MTA nomination Best Solo Instrumental Record of the Year, 1977; Deutscher Schallplattenpreis, 1978; Preis der Deutschen Schallplattenkritik, 1988. *Recreations:* walking, church architecture. *Address:* 28 High Park Road, Kew Gardens, Richmond-upon-Thames, Surrey TW9 4BH. *T:* 081–878 4455.

KYPRIANOU, Spyros; Grand Cross of the Order of George I of Greece, 1962; Grand Cross, Order of the Saviour, Greece, 1983; President of the Republic of Cyprus, 1977–88; President, Democratic Party of Cyprus, since 1976; *b* Limassol, 1932; *s* of Achilleas and Maria Kyprianou; *m* Mimi Kyprianou; two *s. Educ:* Greek Gymnasium, Limassol; City of London Coll. Called to the Bar, Gray's Inn, 1954 (Hon. Bencher, 1985); Dip. Comparative Law. Founded Cypriot Students' Union in England (first Pres. 1952–54). Sec. of Archbp Makarios, in London, 1952; Sec. of Cyprus Ethnarchy in London, 1954; left Britain for Greece, 1956, to work for world projection of Cyprus case; later in 1956, rep. Cyprus Ethnarchy, New York, until 1957; resumed London post until signing of Zürich and London Agreements, returning to Cyprus with the Archbp in 1959. On declaration of Independence, 16 Aug. 1960, following brief appt as Minister of Justice, became Foreign Minister, accompanying the Pres. on visits to countries world-wide, 1961–71; rep. Cyprus at UN Security Council and Gen. Assembly sessions, notably during debates on the Cyprus question; signed Agreement in Moscow for Soviet Military Aid to Cyprus, 1964; had several consultations with Greek Govt on Cyprus matter. Mem. Cttee of Ministers of Council of Europe at meetings in Strasburg and Paris (Pres. Cttee, April-Dec. 1967). Resigned post of Foreign Minister, 1972, after dispute with military régime in Athens. Practised law, withdrawing from politics until the coup and Turkish invasion of Cyprus, 1974; travelled between Athens, London and New York, where he led Cyprus delegn during debate on Cyprus in Gen. Assembly of UN, 1974; participated in talks between Greek Govt and Pres. Makarios, 1974; an *ad hoc* member of Cyprus delegn at Security meeting in New York, 1975. Announced estabt of Democratic Party in Cyprus, 1976, becoming Pres. of House of Reps on the party's victory in parly elections. On death of Archbp Makarios, Aug. 1977, became Actg Pres. of Republic, until elected Pres. in same month; re-elected Pres., unopposed, in Feb. 1978 for a full five-year term; re-elected for further five-year term, 1983. Holds numerous foreign decorations. *Recreations:* literature, music, sport. *Address:* Elia Papakyriakou 29, Acropolis, Nicosia, Cyprus.

KYRIAZIDES, Nikos Panayis; Comdr, Order of George I of Greece; Alternate Executive Director, IMF, since 1986; Greek Ambassador to the Court of St James's, 1982–85; *b* 3 Sept. 1927; *m* 1960, Ellie Kyrou; one *s* one *d. Educ:* Exeter Coll., Oxford Univ. (MA); Chicago Univ. Min. of Co-ordination, 1949; Head, Monetary Policy Div., 1950–51; Dir, External Payments and Trade, 1951–54; Asst Economic Advr, Bank of Greece, 1956–60; Mem., Greek Delegn, negotiations for EFTA and assoc. of Greece to EEC, 1957–61; seconded to Min. of Co-ordination as Dir Gen., relations with EEC, 1962–64; Economic Advr, Nat. Bank of Greece, 1964–67; Sen. Economist, IMF, 1968–70; Advr to Cyprus Govt, negotiations for assoc. of Cyprus to EEC, 1971–72; Dep. Governor, Bank of Greece, 1974–77; Head of Greek delegn to Accession negotiations to the EEC, 1974–77; Advr to Cyprus Govt on relations with EEC, 1979–82. Knight Commander: Order of Merit (Italy); Order of Leopold II (Belgium); Comdr, Order of Merit (FRG). *Address:* 2 Misthou Street, Athens, Greece. *Club:* Athens (Athens).

KYRLE POPE, Rear-Adm. Michael Donald, CB 1969; MBE 1946; DL; *b* 1 Oct. 1916; *e s* of late Comdr R. K. C. Pope, DSO, OBE, RN retd, and of Mrs A. J. Pope (*née* Macdonald); *m* 1947, Angela Suzanne Layton; one *s* one *d. Educ:* Wellington Coll., Berks. Joined RN, 1934; Submarine Service, 1938; HMS Vanguard, 1946–47; BJSM, Washington, 1951–53; Naval Intelligence: Germany, 1955–57, FE, 1958–60; Sen. Naval Off., Persian Gulf, 1962–64; MoD (Naval Intell.), 1965–67; Chief of Staff to C-in-C Far East, 1967–69; retd 1970. Comdr 1951; Capt. 1958; Rear-Adm. 1967. Gen. Manager, Middle East Navigation Aids Service, Bahrain, 1971–77. Dean's Administrator, St Alban's Cathedral, 1977–80. DL Herts 1983. *Recreations:* country pursuits, sailing. *Address:* Hopfields, Westmill, Buntingford, Herts SG9 9LB. *T:* Royston (0763) 71835. *Club:* Army and Navy.

See also Sir J. E. Pope.

L

LABOUCHERE, Sir George (Peter), GBE 1964; KCMG 1955 (CMG 1951); *b* 2 Dec. 1905; *s* of late F. A. Labouchere; *m* 1943, Rachel Katharine, *d* of Hon. Eustace Hamilton-Russell. *Educ:* Charterhouse Sch.; Sorbonne, Paris. Entered Diplomatic Service, 1929. Served in Madrid, Cairo, Rio de Janeiro, Stockholm, Nanking, Buenos Aires. UK Deputy-Commissioner for Austria, 1951–53; HM Minister, Hungary, 1953–55; Ambassador to Belgium, 1955–60; Ambassador to Spain, 1960–66. Retired, 1966. Member of Council, Friends of the Tate Gallery; Pres., Shropshire Br., CPRE; Mem., Dilettanti Society; FRSA. *Recreations:* shooting, fishing, Chinese ceramics, contemporary painting and sculpture. *Address:* Dudmaston, Bridgnorth, Salop WV15 6QN. *Clubs:* Brooks's, Pratt's, Beefsteak.

LABOUISSE, Mrs H. R.; *see* Curie, Eve.

LABOVITCH, Neville, MBE 1977; Chairman: Brenta Construction, since 1987 (Director, since 1985); Brenta Cogifar-Impresit, since 1990; Director, Cadogan Press, since 1979; *b* Leeds; *s* of late Mark and Anne Labovitch; *m* 1958, Sonia Deborah Barney (marr. diss. 1986); two *d*. *Educ:* Whittingehame College; Brasenose College, Oxford (MA). Treasurer, Oxford Union, 1945. Dir, 1954–82, Man. Dir, 1966–82, Darley Mills. Chairman: Trafalgar Square Assoc., 1974–; Knightsbridge Assoc., 1978–; Cleaner London Campaign, 1978–; Piccadilly Tourist Trust, 1978–82; Great Children's Party for IYC, 1979; London Environmental Campaign, 1983; Westminster Quatercentenary Cttee, 1984–; Prince of Wales Royal Parks Tree Appeal, 1987–; Mem., London Celebrations Cttee for Queen's Silver Jubilee, 1977; Chm., Silver Jubilee Exhibn, Hyde Park; Vice-Chm., Jubilee Walkway Trust, 1978–; Chm., Organizing Cttee, Queen's 60th Birthday Celebrations, 1986. Mem., Vis. Cttee, RCA, 1983–90. Dir, Nat. Children's Charities Fund, 1979–. FRSA. *Recreations:* reading and ruminating. *Club:* Brooks's.

LACEY, Ven. Clifford George; Archdeacon of Lewisham, 1985–89; *b* 1 April 1921; *s* of Edward and Annie Elizabeth Lacey; *m* 1944, Sylvia Lilian George; one *s* two *d*. *Educ:* King's College London (AKC); St Boniface Coll., Warminster. RAFVR, 1941–46. Curate: St Hilda, Crofton Park, 1950–53; Kingston-upon-Thames, 1953–56; Vicar: St James, Merton, 1956–66; Eltham, 1966–79 (Sub-dean, 1970–79); Borough Dean of Greenwich, 1979–85; Bp of Norwich's Officer for retired clergy and widows, 1991–. Hon. Canon of Southwark, 1974–. *Recreation:* photography. *Address:* 31 Kerridges, East Harling, Norwich NR16 2QA. *T:* East Harling (0953) 718458.

LACEY, Frank; Director, Metrication Board, 1976–79, retired; *b* 4 Feb. 1919; *s* of Frank Krauter and Maud Krauter (*née* Lacey); *m* 1944, Maggie Tyrrell Boyes, 2nd *d* of late Sydney Boyes; one *s* one *d*. *Educ:* St Ignatius Coll., N7. Served War, 1939–46, RAFVR. Tax Officer, Inland Revenue, 1936; joined Board of Trade, 1946, Regional Dir, E Region, 1967–70; Counsellor (Commercial), UK Mission, Geneva, 1973–76. *Recreation:* wood turning. *Address:* Alma Cottage, Whistley Green, Hurst, Berks RG10 0EH. *T:* Twyford (0734) 340880. *Club:* Commonwealth Trust.

LACEY, George William Brian; Keeper, Department of Transport, Science Museum, London, 1971–86; *b* 15 Nov. 1926; *m* 1956, Lynette (*née* Hogg); two *s*. *Educ:* Brighton, Hove and Sussex Grammar Sch., 1938–44; Brighton Technical Coll., 1944–47. BSc(Eng) 2nd Cl. Hons (External, London). National Service, REME, 1947–49. Rolls-Royce Ltd, Derby: Grad. Apprentice, Tech. Asst, Mechanical Develt and Performance Analysis, 1949–54. Asst Keeper, Science Museum, London, SW7, 1954. Chairman: Historical Gp, Royal Aeronautical Soc., 1971–78; Assoc. British Transport Museums, 1973–83; Mem. Council, Transport Trust, 1978–89. *Recreation:* golf. *Address:* Hurst Grange Cottage, Albourne Road, Hurstpierpoint, Hassocks, W Sussex BN6 9ES. *T:* Hurstpierpoint (0273) 833914.

LACEY, Prof. Richard Westgarth, MD, PhD; FRCPath; Professor of Medical Microbiology, University of Leeds, since 1983; Consultant to Leeds Health Authority, since 1983; *b* 11 Oct. 1940; *s* of Jack and Sybil Lacey; *m* 1972, Fionna Margaret Stone; two *d*. *Educ:* Felsted Sch., Essex; Cambridge Univ. (BA, MB, BChir; MD 1969); London Hosp.; Univ. of Bristol (PhD 1974). FRCPath 1985; DCH 1966. House Officer, London and Eastbourne, 1964–66; Sen. House Officer, 1966–67, Registrar, 1967–68, Bristol Royal Infirmary; Lectr, 1968–73, Reader in Clinical Microbiology, 1973–74, Univ. of Bristol; Consultant in Microbiology, 1974–83, and Consultant in Chemical Pathology, 1975–83, Queen Elizabeth Hosp., King's Lynn; Consultant in Chem. Path., E Anglian RHA, 1974–83. Consultant, WHO, 1983–. Evian Health Award, 1989; Caroline Walker Award, 1989; Freedom of Information Award, 1990. *Publications:* Safe Shopping, Safe Cooking, Safe Eating, 1989; Unfit for Human Consumption, 1991; 210 contribs to learned scientific jls. *Recreations:* antique furniture, gardening, chess, sleeping, walking, eating (not recently). *Address:* Department of Microbiology, University of Leeds, Leeds LS2 9JT. *T:* Leeds (0532) 335596.

LACHMANN, Prof. Peter Julius, FRCP; PRCPath; FRS 1982; Sheila Joan Smith Professor of Immunology (formerly Tumour Immunology), since 1977, and Fellow of Christ's College, 1962–71 and since 1976, University of Cambridge; Hon. Director of MRC Molecular Immunopathology Unit (formerly MRC Mechanisms in Tumour Immunity Unit), since 1980; President, Royal College of Pathologists, since 1990; *b* 23 Dec. 1931; *s* of late Heinz Lachmann and Thea (*née* Heller); *m* 1962, Sylvia Mary, *d* of Alan Stephenson; two *s* one *d*. *Educ:* Christ's Coll., Finchley; Trinity Coll., Cambridge; University College Hosp. MA, MB BChir, PhD, ScD (Cantab). FRCP 1973; FRCPath 1981. John Lucas Walker Student, Dept of Pathology, Cambridge, 1958–60; Vis. Investigator, Rockefeller Univ., New York, 1960–61; Empire Rheumatism Council Res. Fellow, Dept of Pathology, Cambridge, 1962–64; Asst Dir of Res. in Pathology, Univ. of Cambridge, 1964–71; Prof. of Immunology, Royal Postgraduate Med. Sch., 1971–75; Hd, 1976–77, Hon. Hd, 1977–80, MRC Gp on Mechanisms in Tumour Immunity; Hon. Clin. Immunologist, Cambridge HA, 1976–90. Member: Systems Bd, MRC, 1982–86; Med. Adv. Cttee, British Council, 1983–; Council, RCPath, 1982–85, 1989–; Chairman: Med. Res. Cttee, Muscular Dystrophy Gp, 1987–; Sci. Cttee, Assoc. Medical Res. Charities, 1988–. Vis. Investigator, Scripps Clinic and Research Foundn, La Jolla, 1966, 1975, 1980, 1986, 1989; Vis. Scientist, Basel Inst. of Immunology, 1971; Smith Kline & Beckman Vis. Prof. in USA (various centres), 1983; Smith Kline & French Vis. Prof. in Australia (various centres), 1987; Vis. Prof., Dept of Medicine, RPMS, London, 1986–89; Meyerhoff Vis. Prof., Weitzmann Inst. Rehovott, 1989; Lectures: Foundn, RCPath, 1983; Langdon-Brown, RCP, 1986; first R. R. Porter Meml, 1986; Heberden Oration, 1986. Foreign Mem., Norwegian Acad. of Science and Letters, 1991. Series Editor, Chemical Immunology (formerly Progress in Alergy), 1987–; Associate Editor, Clinical and Experimental Immunology, 1989–. *Publications:* co-ed, Clinical Aspects of Immunology, 3rd edn 1975, 4th edn 1982; papers in sci. jls on complement and immunopathology. *Recreations:* walking in mountains, keeping bees. *Address:* Conduit Head, 36 Conduit Head Road, Cambridge CB3 0EY. *T:* Cambridge (0223) 354433. *Club:* Athenæum.

LACHS, Henry Lazarus; His Honour Judge Lachs; a Circuit Judge, since 1979; *b* 31 Dec. 1927; *s* of Samuel and Mania Lachs; *m* 1959, Edith Bergel; four *d*. *Educ:* Liverpool Institute High Sch.; Pembroke Coll., Cambridge (MA, LLB). Called to Bar, Middle Temple, 1951. A Recorder of the Crown Court, 1972–79. Chm., Merseyside Mental Health Review Tribunal, 1968–79. *Address:* 41 Menlove Gardens West, Liverpool L18 2ET. *T:* 051–722 5936.

LACHS, Manfred; Judge, International Court of Justice, since 1967 (President, 1973–76); *b* 21 April 1914; *m* Halina Kirst. *Educ:* Univs of Cracow, Vienna, London and Cambridge; Univ. of Cracow, Poland (LLM 1936, Dr jur 1937); Univ. of Nancy, France (Dr); Univ. of Moscow (DSc Law). Legal Adviser, Polish Ministry Internat. Affairs, 1947–66 (Ambassador, 1960–66). Prof., Acad. Polit. Sci., Warsaw, 1949–52; Prof. Internat. Law, Univ. of Warsaw, 1952; Dir, Inst. Legal Scis, Polish Academy of Sciences, 1961–67. Röling Prof., Groningen Univ., 1990. Chm., Legal Cttee, UN Gen. Assemblies, 1949, 1951, 1955; Rep. of Poland, UN Disarmament Cttee, 1962–63; Pres. of Tribunal, Guinea/Guinea-Bissau case, 1983–85. Rapporteur, Gen. Colloque. Internat. Assoc. Juridical Sciences, UNESCO, Rome, 1948; Internat. Law Commn, UN, 1962; Chm., Legal Cttee UN Peaceful Uses of Outer Space, 1962–66; Hon. Sen. Fellow, UNITAR. Member: Inst. of Internat. Law; Ind. Commn on Internat. Humanitarian Issues, 1983–; Curatorium, Hague Acad. of Internat. Law (Vice-Pres.); Acad. of Bologna; Polish Acad. of Sciences. Hon. Mem., Amer. Soc. Internat. Law; Corr. Mem., Institut de France; Foreign Mem., Dutch Soc. of Scis, 1982. LLD (Hon.), Univs of: Budapest 1967; Algiers 1969; Delhi 1969; Nice 1972; Halifax, 1973; Bruxelles, 1973; Bucarest, 1974; New York, 1974; Southampton, 1975; Howard (Washington), 1975; Sofia, 1975; Vancouver, 1976; London, 1976; Helsinki, 1980; Vienna, 1984. Cracow, 1986; NY State, 1986; Bridgeport, 1987; Silesia, 1988. Gold medal for outstanding contribs devel. rule of law outer space, 1966; World Jurist Award for enormous contrib. to improvement of justice, Washington, 1975; Netherland's Wateler Peace Prize, 1976; Copernicus Medal, 1984; Britannica Award Laureate, 1987; First Prize, Polish Acad. of Scis, 1988; also other awards. *Publications:* War Crimes, 1945; The Geneva Agreements on Indochina, 1954; Multilateral Treaties, 1958; The Law of Outer Space, 1964; Polish-German Frontier, 1964; The Law of Outer Space—an experience in law making, 1972; Teachings and Teaching of International Law, 1977; The Teacher in International Law, 1982 (Cert. of Merit, Amer. Soc. of Internat. Law), 2nd rev. edn 1986; numerous essays and articles in eleven languages. *Address:* International Court of Justice, Peace Palace, The Hague 2517 KJ, Holland. *T:* 92–44–41.

LACKEY, Rt. Rev. Edwin Keith; *see* Ottawa, Bishop of.

LACKEY, Mary Josephine, CB 1985; OBE 1966; former Under Secretary, Department of Trade and Industry; *b* 11 Aug. 1925; *d* of William and Winifred Lackey. *Educ:* King Edward VI High Sch., Birmingham; Lady Margaret Hall, Oxford (MA). Board of Trade, 1946; Asst Principal, Central Land Bd, 1947–50; BoT, 1950–61; UK Delegn to EFTA and GATT, 1961–66; BoT, subseq. DTI and Dept of Trade, 1966–85; Asst Sec., 1968; Under Sec., 1974. *Club:* United Oxford & Cambridge University.

LACOME, Myer; professional artist/designer; Principal, Duncan of Jordanstone College of Art, Dundee, 1978–88; *b* 13 Nov. 1927; *s* of Colman Lacome and Sara (*née* Sholl); *m* 1954, Jacci Edgar; one *s* two *d*. *Educ:* Regional Coll. of Art, Liverpool. MSIAD, MSTD, MInstPkg; FRSA. National Service, RAF, 1946–48. Post-grad. course, 1948–49; designer, New York, 1949–51; consultant designer, London, 1951–59; Head of Sch. of Design, Duncan of Jordanstone Coll. of Art, Dundee, 1962–77. Vis. Fellow, Royal Melbourne Inst. of Technol., 1979. Chm., Fine Art Cttee, Scottish Arts Council, 1986–; Member: Council, CNAA, 1979–84; Higher Educn Cttee, Scottish Design Council, 1984–86; Governor, Scottish Film Council, 1982–. *Publications:* papers on crafts in Scotland and on Scandinavian design and crafts. *Recreations:* the Arts, the man-made environment, travel, swimming. *Address:* 4 Campbells Close, off Royal Mile, Edinburgh EH8 8JJ.

LACON, Sir Edmund (Vere), 8th Bt *cr* 1818; General Manager, Abdul Aziz Al-Babtain, Kuwait, since 1980; *b* 3 May 1936; *s* of Sir George Vere Francis Lacon, 7th Bt, and of Hilary Blanche (now Mrs J. D. Turner), *d* of late C. J. Scott, Adyar, Walberswick; *S* father, 1980; *m* 1963, Gillian, *d* of J. H. Middleditch, Wrentham, Suffolk; one *s* one *d*. *Educ:* Taverham Hall, Norfolk; Woodbridge School, Suffolk. RAF Regiment, 1955–59. Career in sales management and marketing, 1959–. *Recreations:* golf, water-skiing. *Heir:* *s* (Edmund) Richard (Vere) Lacon, *b* 2 Oct. 1967. *Address:* c/o Abdul Aziz Al-Babtain, PO Box 599, Kuwait. *T:* Kuwait 2412730; Milbrook, Holton St Peter, Halesworth, Suffolk. *T:* Halesworth (09867) 2536.

LACOSTE, Paul, OC 1977; DU Paris; Rector, Université de Montréal, 1975–85, Professor Emeritus since 1987; *b* 24 April 1923; *s* of Emile Lacoste and Juliette Boucher Lacoste; *m* 1973, Louise Marcil; one *s* two *d.* *Educ:* Univ. de Montréal (BA, MA, LPh, LLL). DUP 1948. Fellow, Univ. of Chicago, 1946–47; Univ. de Montréal: Prof., Faculty of Philosophy, 1948; Full Prof., 1958; Vice-Rector, 1968–75; Vis. Prof., Faculty of Law, 1962–70 and 1985–87. Practising lawyer, 1964–66. Pres., Assoc. des universités partiellement ou entièrement de langue française, 1978–81. Hon. LLD: McGill, 1975; Toronto, 1978; Hon Du Laval, 1986. Chevalier de la Légion d'Honneur, 1985. *Publications:* (jtly) Justice et paix scolaire, 1962; A Place of Liberty, 1964; Le Canada au seuil du siècle de l'abondance, 1969; Principes de gestion universitaire, 1970; (jtly) Education permanente et potentiel universitaire, 1977. *Address:* Université de Montréal, PO Box 6128, Montréal H3C 3J7, Canada. *T:* 343–7761; 2900 boulevard Edouard-Montpetit, Montréal.

LACROIX, Christian Marie Marc; designer; *b* 16 May 1951; *s* of Maxime Lacroix and Jeannette Bergier. *Educ:* Paul Valéry Univ., Montpellier; Sorbonne. History of Art degree. Assistant at Hermès, 1978; Asst for Guy Paulin, 1980; designer for Patou, 1981–86. Golden Thimble Award, 1986 and 1988; CFDA Award, NY, 1987. *Address:* 73 Faubourg St Honoré, 75008 Paris, France. *T:* 42657908.

LACY, Sir Hugh Maurice Pierce, 3rd Bt, *cr* 1921; *b* 3 Sept 1943; *s* of Sir Maurice John Pierce Lacy, 2nd Bt, and of his 2nd wife, Nansi Jean, *d* of late Myrddin Evans, Bangor, Caernarvonshire; *S* father, 1965; *m* 1968, Deanna, *d* of Howard Bailey. *Educ:* Aiglon Coll., Switzerland. *Heir:* *b* Patrick Bryan Finucane Lacy [*b* 18 April 1948; *m* 1971, Phyllis Victoria, *d* of E. P. H. James; one *s* one *d*].

LACY, John Trend, CBE 1983; General Director of Party Campaigning, Conservative Central Office, since 1989; *b* 15 March 1928; *s* of Rev. Hubert Lacy and Mrs Gertrude Lacy (*née* Markham); *m* 1956, Pamela Guerin; one *s.* *Educ:* King's Sch., Ely, Cambs. Served RN, 1945–48. Harvey & Clark (Manufrs), 1948–50; Conservative Party: London, 1950–56; Aylesbury, 1956–61; W Midlands area, 1961–64; Northern area, 1964–71; S Eastern area, 1971–85; Dir of Campaigning, 1985–89. *Recreations:* racing, fishing, philately. *Address:* 10 Sutton Close, Beckenham, Kent BR3 2UG. *T:* 081–650 5450. *Clubs:* Carlton, St Stephen's Constitutional (Vice Chm., 1988–).

LADAS, Mrs Diana Margaret; *b* 8 Feb. 1913; *er d* of late Bertram Hambro and late Mrs Charles Boyle; *m* 1945, Alexis Christopher Ladas (marr. diss. 1955); one *s.* *Educ:* Downe House Sch.; Girton Coll., Cambridge. Before the war, Sec. in Geneva, Malta and London. During War of 1939–45, worked as temp. asst Principal in Min. of Economic Warfare, Board of Trade and Political Warfare executive in Cairo. Transferred to UNRRA, worked in Athens, Washington and London; on the staff of British Information Services, in New York, 1948–50. Began teaching at Westminster Tutors, 1955; joined staff of Heathfield Sch., 1958; Dep. Head of Moira House Sch., 1959, Head Mistress, 1960; Vice-Principal of Queen's Gate Sch., 1962–65; Head Mistress, Heathfield Sch., 1965–72. Since retirement, occupied with voluntary social work and local politics. *Recreations:* gardening and travelling. *Address:* Prospect Place, 154 Peckham Rye, SE22 9QH.

LADDIE, Hugh Ian Lang; QC 1986; *b* 15 April 1946; *s* of late Bertie Daniel Laddie and of Rachel Laddie; *m* 1970, Stecia Elizabeth (*née* Zamet); two *s* one *d.* *Educ:* Aldenham Sch.; St Catharine's Coll., Cambridge (MA). Called to the Bar, Middle Temple, 1969 (Blackstone Pupillage Award); Jun. Counsel to HM Treasury in Patent Matters, 1981–86. Sec., Patent Bar Assoc., 1971–75. Asst Ed.-in-Chief, Annual of Industrial Property Law, 1975–79; UK Correspondent, European Law Rev., 1978–83. *Publications:* (jtly) Patent Law of Europe and the United Kingdom, 1978; (jtly) The Modern Law of Copyright, 1980. *Recreations:* music, gardening, fishing.

LAFITTE, Prof. François; Professor of Social Policy and Administration, University of Birmingham, 1959–80; *b* 3 Aug. 1913; *s* of John Armistead Collier and Françoise Lafitte and adopted *s* of late Havelock Ellis; *m* 1938, Eileen (*née* Saville); (one *s* decd). *Educ:* Collège Municipal, Maubeuge; George Green's Sch., Poplar; St Olave's Grammar Sch., Southwark; Worcester Coll., Oxford. Research and translating for Miners' Internat. Fed., 1936–37; on research staff, and subseq. Dep. Sec., PEP, 1938–43; on editorial staff of The Times, as special writer on social questions, 1943–59; Chm. of PEP research groups on health services, 1943–46, on housing policy, 1948–51. Dean of Faculty of Commerce and Social Science, Birmingham, Univ., 1965–68. Member: Home Office Advisory Council on the Treatment of Offenders, 1961–64; Adv. Cttees Social Science Research Council, 1966–69; Redditch New Town Corp., 1964–75; Chm., British Pregnancy Adv. Service, 1968–88. *Publications:* The Internment of Aliens, 1940, repr. 1988; Britain's Way to Social Security, 1945; Family Planning in the Sixties, 1964; (part author) Socially Deprived Families in Britain, 1970; many PEP Planning monographs; many papers on abortion and related issues; contributed to British Journal of Delinquency, Eugenics Review, Chambers's Encyclopædia. etc. *Address:* 77 Oakfield Road, Birmingham B29 7HL. *T:* 021–472 2709. *Club:* University Staff (Birmingham).

LA FRENAIS, Ian; writer, screenwriter and producer; *b* 7 Jan. 1937; *s* of Cyril and Gladys La Frenais; *m* 1984, Doris Vartan; one step *s.* *Educ:* Dame Allan's School, Northumberland. *Television:* writer or co-writer (with Dick Clement): The Likely Lads, 1965–68; The Adventures of Lucky Jim, 1968; Whatever Happened to the Likely Lads, 1971–73; Seven of One, 1973; Thick as Thieves, 1974; Comedy Playhouse, 1975; Porridge, 1974–77; Going Straight, 1978; Further Adventures of Lucky Jim, 1983; Auf Wiedersehen Pet, 1983–84; Mog, 1985; Lovejoy, 1986; Spender, 1990; Freddie and Max, 1990; Beggar Man, Thief, 1991; Old Boy Network, 1991; *US television:* On The Rocks, 1976–77; Billy, 1979; Sunset Limousine, 1983; *films:* writer or co-writer (with Dick Clement): The Jokers, 1967; The Touchables, 1968; Otley, 1968; Hannibal Brooks, 1969; The Virgin Soldiers, 1969; Villain, 1970; Catch Me a Spy, 1971; The Likely Lads, 1975; Porridge, 1979; To Russia with Elton, 1979; Prisoner of Zenda, 1981; Water, 1984; writer-producer (with Dick Clement), Vice Versa, 1987; The Commitments, 1991; *stage:* writer, Billy, 1974; co-producer, Anyone for Denis?, 1982. Partner (with Dick Clement and Allan McKeown), Witzend Productions; producer, co-producer, director, numerous productions. Awards from BAFTA, Broadcasting Guild, Evening News, Pye, Screen Writers' Guild, Soc. of TV Critics. *Publications:* novelisations of The Likely Lads, Whatever Happened to the Likely Lads, Porridge, Auf Wiedersehen Pet. *Recreations:* music, films, sports, wine, driving. *Address:* 2557 Hutton Drive, Beverly Hills, Calif 90211, USA.

LAGACOS, Eustace P.; Member of the European Parliament, since 1989; Foreign Affairs Counsellor to the Leader of the Opposition, Greece, since 1985; *b* 4 June 1921; one *d.* *Educ:* Univ. of Athens (Graduate of Law). Embassy Attaché, 1949; served Athens, Paris, Istanbul, Nicosia, London; Minister, 1969; Foreign Ministry, Athens, 1970; Ambassador to Nicosia, 1972; Dir Gen., Economic Affairs, Foreign Ministry, Athens, 1974; Permanent Representative to NATO, Brussels, 1976; Ambassador to UK, 1979–82. Grand Officer of Order of the Phoenix, Greece; Commander of Order of George I, Greece; Grand Cordon of Order of Manuel Amadoi Guerrero, Panama; Commander of Legion of Honour, France; Kt Commander of Order of Queen Isabella I, Spain; Grand Officer of Order of the Republic, Egypt. *Publication:* The Cyprus Question, 1987. *Address:* 7 Kapsali Street, Athens 10674, Greece.

LAGESEN, Air Marshal Sir Philip (Jacobus), KCB 1979 (CB 1974); DFC 1945; AFC 1959; FBIM; *b* 25 Aug. 1923; *s* of late Philip J. Lagesen, Johannesburg, South Africa; *m* 1944, Dulcie, *d* of late H. McPherson, Amanzimtoti, Natal, S Africa; one *s* one *d.* *Educ:* Jeppe, Johannesburg. Served War, 1939–45, South African Air Force. Joined RAF, 1951; Flying Instructor, Rhodesia Air Trng Gp, 1952–53; Kenya, 1953–55; No 50 Squadron, 1955–57; Staff, RAF Flying Coll., Manby, 1957–59; PSO, C-in-C Middle East, 1959–61; Comdr, No 12 (B) Sqdn, 1961–64; Wing Comdr Ops, No 1 (B) Group 1964–66; CO, RAF Tengah, Singapore, 1966–69; SPSO, Strike Comd, 1969–70; Dir Ops (S), RAF, MoD, 1970–72; SASO, HQ Strike Comd, 1972–73; Dep. Comdr, RAF Germany, 1973–75; AOC 1 Group, 1975–78; AOC 18 Group, 1978–80. *Recreations:* golf, motoring. *Address:* 10 Mayfair Mews, Heyfield Road, Kloof, Natal 3610, Republic of South Africa. *Clubs:* Royal Air Force; Kloof Country.

LAGHZAOUI, Mohammed; Ouissam El Ouala (1st class) and Commander of the Order of the Crown, Morocco; Moroccan Ambassador to France, 1971–72; *b* Fez, Morocco, 27 Sept. 1906; *m* 1940, Kenza Bouayad; three *s* three *d.* *Educ:* Moulay Idriss Coll., Fez. Founded many commercial and industrial companies; Chm., Société marocaine des Transports Laghzaoui. During French Protectorate over Morocco, he was Mem. Government's Council (many times Chm.); one of principal Signatories to Act of Independence, 1944; Dir-Gen. of Nat. Security (apptd by late Mohammed V), 1956–60. Then, as Dir-Gen. of Office chérifien des Phosphates (first nat. mining concern) he promoted production and export; later, he was responsible for Office marocain des Phosphates, and Coordinator of Nat. Mining and Industrial Cos. In charge of four ministries: Industry, Mining, Tourism and Handicraft, and was Pres. of Afro-Asiatic Assoc. for Economic Development, 1966–69; Moroccan Ambassador to UK, 1969–71. Holds foreign orders. *Recreations:* bridge, football. *Address:* Résidence Laghzaoui, Route de Suissi, Rabat, Morocco.

LAGOS, Archbishop of, (RC), since 1973 (and Metropolitan); **Most Rev. Anthony Olubunmi Okogie,** DD; *b* Lagos, 16 June 1936. *Educ:* St Gregory's Coll., Lagos; St Theresa's Minor Seminary, Ibadan; St Peter and St Paul's Seminary, Ibadan; Urban Univ., Rome. Priest, 1966; appointments include: Acting Parish Priest, St Patrick's Church, Idumagbo, 1967–71; Asst Priest, and Master of Ceremonies, Holy Cross Cathedral, Lagos, 1967–71; Religious Instructor, King's Coll., Lagos, 1967–71; Director of Vocations, Archdiocese of Lagos, 1968–71; Manager, Holy Cross Group of Schools, Lagos, 1969–71; Auxiliary Bishop of Oyo, 1971–72; Auxiliary Bishop to Apostolic Administrator, Archdiocese of Lagos, 1972–73. Vice-Pres., 1983–88, Pres., 1988–, Catholic Bishops Conf. of Nigeria; Roman Catholic Trustee of Christian Assoc. of Nigeria, 1974–; Member: State Community Relns Cttee, 1984–; Prerogative of Mercy, 1986–; Adv. Council on Religious Affairs; Chm., Christian Assoc. of Nigeria, 1989–. *Address:* Holy Cross Cathedral, PO Box 8, Lagos, Nigeria. *T:* 635729 and 633841.

LAGOS, Bishop of; *see* Nigeria, Metropolitan Archbishop and Primate of.

LAHNSTEIN, Manfred; Member of Executive Board, Bertelsmann Corporation, since 1983; President, Electronic-Media Division, since 1985; *b* 20 Dec. 1937; *s* of Walter and Hertha Lahnstein; one *s* one *d.* *Educ:* Cologne Univ. (Dipl. Kfm). German Trade Union Fedn, Dusseldorf, 1962–64; European Trade Union Office, Brussels, 1965–67; European Commn, 1967–73; German Govt service, 1973–82: served in Finance Min. and as Head of Chancellor's Office; Minister of Finance, April-Oct. 1982. Pres., Bertelsmann printing and manufacturing gp, 1983–85. *Publications:* various articles. *Recreation:* classical music. *Address:* c/o 4830 Gütersloh, Carl Bertelsmann Strasse 270, Federal Republic of Germany. *T:* 05241-801.

LAÏDI, Ahmed; Algerian Ambassador to Mexico, since 1988; *b* 20 April 1934; *m* 1964, Aicha Chabbi-Lemsine; one *s* one *d* (and one *s* decd). *Educ:* Algiers Univ. (BA); Oran Univ. (LLB). Counsellor to Presidency of Council of Algerian Republic, 1963; Head of Cabinet of Presidency, 1963–64; Dir. Gen. of Political and Economic Affairs, Min. of Foreign Affairs, 1964–66; Chm., Prep. Cttee, second Afro-Asian Conf., 1964–65; Special Envoy to Heads of States, Senegal, Mali, Ivory Coast and Nigeria, 1966; Ambassador to Spain, 1966–70; Head, Delegn to Geneva Conf. of non-nuclear countries, 1968; Wali (Governor): province Médea, 1970–74; province Tlemcen, 1975–78; Ambassador to Jordan, 1978–84; Special Envoy to Heads of States and govts, Zambia, Malaŵi, Botswana, Zimbabwe, 1985; Ambassador to UK, 1984–88, and to Ireland, 1985–88. Foreign Orders: Liberia, 1963; Bulgaria, 1964; Yugoslavia, 1964; Spain, 1970; Jordan, 1984. *Recreations:* theatre, cinema, football. *Address:* c/o Algerian Embassy, Mexico.

LAIDLAW, Sir Christophor (Charles Fraser), Kt 1982; Director: Amerada Hess Corporation, since 1983; Redland PLC, since 1984; Dalgety plc, since 1984; Mercedes-Benz (UK) Ltd, since 1986; Amerada Hess Ltd, since 1986; *b* 9 Aug. 1922; *m* 1952, Nina Mary Prichard; one *s* three *d.* *Educ:* Rugby Sch.; St John's Coll., Cambridge (MA). Served War of 1939–45: Europe and Far East, Major on Gen. Staff. Joined British Petroleum, 1948: BP Rep. in Hamburg, 1959–61; Gen. Manager, Marketing Dept, 1963–67; Dir, BP Trading, 1967; Dir (Ops), 1971–72; a Man. Dir, 1972–81, and Dep. Chm., BP, 1980–81; Dir, Soc. Française BP, 1964–85; President, BP: Belgium, 1967–71; Italiana, 1972–73; Deutsche BP, 1972–83; Chairman: BP Oil, 1977–81; BP Oil Internat., 1981; Boving & Co. Ltd, 1984–86. Chm., ICL plc, 1981–84; Pres., ICL France, 1983; Chm., Bridon, 1985–90. Director: Commercial Union Assurance, 1978–83; Barclays Bank International, 1980–87; Barclays Bank plc, 1981–88; Equity Capital for Industry Ltd, 1983–86; Barclays Merchant Bank Ltd, 1984–86; TWIL Ltd, 1985–89. Pres., German Chamber of Industry and Commerce, 1983–86; Mem., Internat. Council, 1980–, Chm. UK Adv. Bd, 1984–, Dir, INSEAD, 1987–. Master, Tallow Chandlers' Co., 1988–89. *Address:* 49 Chelsea Square, SW3 6LH. *Clubs:* Buck's, Garrick.

LAIDLAW, (Henry) Renton; golf correspondent, Evening Standard, since 1973; *b* 6 July 1939; *s* of late Henry Renton Laidlaw and of Margaret McBeath Laidlaw (*née* Raiker). *Educ:* James Gillespie's Boys' School, Edinburgh; Daniel Stewart's College, Edinburgh. Golf corresp., Edinburgh Evening News, 1957–67; news presenter and reporter, Grampian Television, Aberdeen, 1968–69; BBC news presenter, Edinburgh, 1970–72; BBC Radio golf reporter, 1976–; presenter, BBC Radio Sport on 2, 1986, 1987; ITV Eurosport and BSB golf presenter. *Publications:* Play Golf (with Peter Alliss), 1977; Jacklin—the first 40 years, 1984; Play Better Golf, 1986; Ten Years—the history of the European Open, 1988; Golf Heroes, 1989; (ed) Johnnie Walker Ryder Cup '89, 1989. *Recreations:* theatre, golf. *Address:* c/o Evening Standard, Northcliffe House, 2 Derry Street, Kensington, W8 5EE. *Clubs:* Caledonian; Sunningdale Golf, Wentworth, Royal Burgess Golf.

LAIGHT, Barry Pemberton, OBE 1970; Eur Ing; FEng, FIMechE, FRAeS; Consultant to: Design Council, since 1983; VAWT Ltd, since 1983; RES Ltd, since 1983; Production Engineering Research Association, since 1986; Department of Trade and Industry, 1988–90; *s* of Donald Norman Laight and Nora (*née* Pemberton); *m* 1951, Ruth Murton; one *s* one *d.* *Educ:* Johnston Sch., Durham; Birmingham Central Tech. Coll.; Merchant

Venturers' Tech. Coll., Bristol; Bristol Univ. MSc. FEng 1981. SBAC Scholar, apprentice, Bristol Aeroplane Co., 1937; Chief Designer, 1952, Technical Dir, 1960, Blackburn & General Aircraft (develt of Beverley and design of Buccaneer, 1953, for RN service, 1960); Chief Engineer Kingston, 1963, Dir for Military Projects, 1968, Hawker Siddeley Aviation (Harrier develt to RAF service; introd. Hawk Trainer); Exec. Dir Engineering, Short Brothers, 1977–82 (develt SD360 and Blowpipe); Sec., RAeS, 1983–85. Mem. Council, RAeS, 1955–90 (Pres., 1974–75; British Silver Medal in Aeronautics, 1963); Chairman: Educn Cttee, SBAC, 1962–67; Tech. Board, SBAC, 1967–82; Member: Aircraft Res. Assoc. Board, 1972–77 (Chm., Tech. Cttee); ARC, 1973–76; Air Educn and Recreational Organisation Council, 1969–72; CBI: Mem., Res. and Tech. Cttee; Educn Cttee; Chm., Transport Technology Panel, SRC, 1969–73; Hon. Treasurer, Internat. Council of Aero. Scis, 1978–84; AGARD Nat. Delegate, 1968–73; Sec., Bristol Gliding Club, 1949–52; Mem., Mensa, 1945; MAIAA; FInstD. *Publications:* papers in RAeS jls. *Recreations:* reading on any subject, house and car maintenance, music. *Address:* 5 Littlemead, Esher, Surrey KT10 9PE. *T:* Esher (0372) 463216.

LAINE, Cleo, (Mrs Clementine Dinah Dankworth), OBE 1979; vocalist; *b* 28 Oct. 1927; British; *m* 1st, 1947, George Langridge (marr. diss. 1957); one *s*; 2nd, 1958, John Philip William Dankworth, *qv*; one *s* one *d*. Joined Dankworth Orchestra, 1953. Melody Maker and New Musical Express Top Girl Singer Award, 1956; Moscow Arts Theatre Award for acting role in Flesh to a Tiger, 1958; Top place in Internat. Critics Poll by Amer. Jazz magazine, Downbeat, 1965. Lead, in Seven Deadly Sins, Edinburgh Festival and Sadler's Wells, 1961; acting roles in Edin. Fest., 1966, 1967, Cindy-Ella, Garrick, 1968. Many appearances with symphony orchestras performing Façade (Walton), Pierrot Lunaire and other compositions; played Julie in Show Boat, Adelphi, 1971; title role in Colette, Comedy, 1980; Hedda Gabler; Valmouth; A Time to Laugh; The Women of Troy; The Mystery of Edwin Drood, 1986; Into the Woods (US nat. tour), 1989; Noyes Fludde (proms), 1990. Frequent TV appearances. Woman of the Year, 9th annual Golden Feather Awards, 1973; Edison Award, 1974; Variety Club of GB Show Business Personality Award (with John Dankworth), 1977; TV Times Viewers Award for Most Exciting Female Singer on TV, 1978; Grammy Award for Best Female Jazz Vocalist, 1985; Theatre World Award, 1986; NARM Presidential Lifetime Achievement Award, 1990; Gold Discs: Feel the Warm; I'm a Song; Live at Melbourne; Platinum Discs: Best Friends; Sometimes When We Touch. Hon. MA Open, 1975; Hon. DMus Berklee Sch. of Music, 1982. *Recreation:* painting. *Address:* International Artistes Representation, 235 Regent Street, W1R 8AX. *T:* 071–439 8401.

LAING, family name of **Baron Laing of Dunphail**.

LAING OF DUNPHAIL, Baron *cr* 1991 (Life Peer), of Dunphail in the District of Moray; **Hector Laing,** Kt 1978; Life President, United Biscuits (Holdings) plc, 1990 (Director, 1953; Managing Director, 1964; Chairman, 1972–90); *b* 12 May 1923; *s* of Hector Laing and Margaret Norris Grant; *m* 1950, Marian Clare, *d* of Maj.-Gen. Sir John Laurie, 6th Bt, CBE, DSO; three *s*. *Educ:* Loretto Sch., Musselburgh, Scotland; Jesus Coll., Cambridge (Hon. Fellow, 1988). Served War, Scots Guards, 1942–47 (American Bronze Star, despatches, 1944); final rank, Captain. McVitie & Price: Dir, 1947; Chm., 1963. Mem. Bd, Royal Insurance Co., 1970–78; Director: Allied-Lyons, 1979–82; Exxon Corp. (USA), 1984–. A Dir, Bank of England, 1973–91. Chairman: Food and Drink Industries Council, 1977–79; Scottish Business in the Community, 1982–; Business in the Community, 1987–. Jt Treas., Cons. Party, 1988–. Mem. Council, Wycombe Abbey Sch., 1981–. FRSE 1989. DUniv Stirling, 1985; Hon. DLitt Heriot Watt, 1986. Businessman of the Year Award, 1979; National Free Enterprise Award, 1980. *Recreations:* gardening, walking, flying. *Address:* PO Box 40, Grant House, Syon Lane, Isleworth, Middx TW7 5NN. *T:* 081–560 3131. *Clubs:* White's, Boodle's.

LAING, Alastair Stuart, CBE 1980; MVO 1959; *b* 17 June 1920; *s* of Captain Arthur Henry Laing and Clare May Laing (*née* Ashworth); *m* 1946 Audrey Stella Hobbs, MCSP, *d* of Dr Frederick Hobbs and Gladys Marion Hobbs (*née* George); one *s* decd. *Educ:* Sedbergh School. Served Indian Army, 10th Gurkha Rifles, 1940–46, Captain; seconded to Civil Administration, Bengal, 1944–46. Commonwealth War Graves Commission, 1947–83 (Dep. Dir Gen., 1975–83). Chm., Vale of Aylesbury Hunt, 1981–87. *Publications:* various articles. *Recreations:* gardening, foxhunting, fell walking, history. *Address:* Wagtails, Lower Wood End, Marlow, Bucks SL7 2HN. *T:* Marlow (0628) 484481.

LAING, Austen, CBE 1973; Director General, British Fishing Federation Ltd, 1962–80; Chairman, Home-Grown Cereals Authority, 1983–89; *b* 27 April 1923; *s* of William and Sarah Ann Laing; *m* 1945, Kathleen Pearson; one *s* one *d*. *Educ:* Bede Grammar Sch., Sunderland; Newcastle Univ. BA (Social Studies) and BA (Econs). Lectr, Univ. of Durham, 1950–56; Administrator, Distant Water Vessels Develt Scheme, 1956–61. Mem. Cttee of Inquiry into Veterinary Profession, 1971–75. *Address:* Freshfields, 12 Hall Park, Swanland, North Ferriby, North Humberside HU14 3NL.

LAING, Gerald O.; *see* Ogilvie-Laing.

LAING, James Findlay; Under Secretary, Scottish Office Environment Department (formerly Scottish Development Department), since 1988; *b* 7 Nov. 1933; *s* of Alexander Findlay Laing and Jessie Ross; *m* 1969, Christine Joy Canaway; one *s*. *Educ:* Nairn Academy; Edinburgh Univ. MA (Hons History). Nat. Service, Seaforth Highlanders, 1955–57. Asst Principal and Principal, Scottish Office, 1957–68; Principal, HM Treasury, 1968–71; Asst Sec., Scottish Office, 1972–79; Under Sec., Scottish Econ. Planning Dept, later Industry Dept. for Scotland, 1979–88. *Recreations:* squash, chess. *Address:* 6 Barnton Park Place, Edinburgh EH4 6ET. *T:* 031–336 5951. *Clubs:* Commonwealth Trust; Edinburgh Sports.

LAING, Prof. John Archibald, PhD; MRCVS; Professor Emeritus, University of London, since 1984 (Courtauld Professor of Animal Husbandry and Hygiene, at Royal Veterinary College, University of London, 1959–84); *b* 27 April 1919; *s* of late John and Alexandra Laing; *m* 1946, June Margaret Lindsay Smith, *d* of Hugh Lindsay Smith, Downham Market; one *s* two *d*. *Educ:* Johnston Sch., Durham; Royal (Dick) School of Veterinary Studies, Edinburgh University; Christ's Coll. Cambridge. BSc(Edinburgh); MRCVS; PhD (Cantab). FIBiol. Aleen Cust Scholar, Royal Coll. of Veterinary Surgeons. Research Officer, 1943–46, Asst Veterinary Investigation Officer, 1946–49, Ministry of Agriculture; Lecturer in Veterinary Science, 1949–51, Senior Lecturer in Veterinary Medicine, 1951–57, Reader in Veterinary Science, 1957–59, Univ. of Bristol. Anglo-Danish Churchill Fellowship, Univ. of Copenhagen, 1954; Visiting Professor, Univs of: Munich, 1967; Mexico, 1967; Queensland, 1970 (and John Thompson Memorial Lectr); Ankara, 1977; Assiut, 1980; Consultant to FAO, UN, 1955–57; Representative of FAO in Dominican Republic, 1957–58; Consultant to UNESCO in Central America, 1963–65; Mem., British Agricultural Mission to Peru, 1970. Member: EEC Veterinary Scientific Cttee, 1981–90; Dairy Product Quota Tribunal for England and Wales, 1984. Hon. Mem., Internat. Congress on Animal Reproduction, 1988 (Sec., 1961–80; Pres., 1980–84). Chm., Melrose Meml Trust, 1984–91; Member: Governing Body, Houghton Poultry Research Station, 1968–74; Council, Royal Veterinary Coll., 1975–84; Vice-Pres., University Fedn for Animal Welfare, 1977–84 (Treasurer, 1969–75; Chm., 1975–77). Hon. Fellow Veterinary Acad., Madrid. Editor, British Veterinary Journal, 1960–84. *Publications:* Fertility and Infertility in the Domestic Animals, 1955, 4th edn 1988; papers on animal breeding and husbandry in various scientific journals. *Address:* Ayot St Lawrence, Herts AL6 9BW. *T:* Stevenage (0438) 820413. *Club:* Athenæum.

LAING, (John) Martin (Kirby), CBE 1991; DL; Chairman, John Laing, since 1985; *b* 18 Jan. 1942; *s* of Sir (William) Kirby Laing, *qv*; *m* 1965, Stephanie Stearn Worsdell; one *s* one *d*. *Educ:* St Lawrence College, Ramsgate; Emmanuel College, Cambridge (MA). FRICS. Joined Laing Group 1966; Dir, John Laing, 1980. Member: Exec. Cttee, Nat. Contractors' Group, Building Employers' Confedn, 1981– (Chm., 1987); CBI Council, 1986–; CBI Overseas Cttee, 1983– (Chm., 1989–) (Chairman: CBI Export Promotion Cttee, 1983—88; CBI Export Finance and Promotion Cttee, 1988–89); CBI Task Force on Business and Urban Regeneration, 1987–88; Cttee for Middle East Trade, 1982–86; SE Asia Trade Adv. Group, 1985–89; UK Adv. Cttee, British American Chamber of Commerce, 1985–; Adv. Council, World Economic Forum, 1986–; NEDO Construction Industry Sector Gp, 1988–; Director: Business in the Community, 1986–88 (Mem., Council, 1986–); UK–Japan 2000 Gp, 1988–; Chm., British Urban Develt, 1988–90; Mem., Business Council for Sustainable Develt, 1991–. Member: Home Office Parole Review Cttee, 1987–88; Archbishop's Council, Church Urban Fund, 1987–. Dir, City of London Sinfonia, 1988–. Dir, Herts Groundwork Trust, 1986–91; Trustee: Nat. Energy Foundn, 1988–; WWF (UK), 1988– (Chm., 1990–); WWF Internat., 1991–. Crown Mem., Court of Univ. of London, 1987–; Mem. Board of Governors, Papplewick School, Ascot, 1983–; Gov., St Lawrence Coll., Ramsgate, 1988–. CBIM 1985; CIEx 1987; FCIM 1987; FRSA 1988. DL Hertford, 1987. *Recreations:* gardening, music, travel. *Address:* John Laing plc, Page Street, NW7 2ER.

LAING, Sir (John) Maurice, Kt 1965; Director, 1939–88, and Life President, since 1988, John Laing plc (formerly John Laing & Son Ltd) (Deputy Chairman, 1966–76, Chairman, 1976–82); *b* 1 Feb. 1918; *s* of Sir John Laing, CBE, and late Beatrice Harland; *m* 1940, Hilda Violet Richards; one *s*. *Educ:* St Lawrence Coll., Ramsgate. RAF, 1941–45. Dir, Bank of England, 1963–80. Member: UK Trade Missions to Middle East, 1953, and to Egypt, Sudan and Ethiopia, 1955; Economic Planning Bd, 1961; Export Guarantees Adv. Council, 1959–63; Min. of Transport Cttee of Inquiry into Major Ports of Gt Brit. (Rochdale Cttee), 1961–62; NEDC, 1962–66. First Pres., CBI, 1965–66; President: British Employers Confederation, 1964–65; Export Group for the Constructional Industries, 1976–80; Fedn of Civil Engrg Contractors, 1977–80. Visiting Fellow, Nuffield Coll., 1965–70; A Governor: Administrative Staff Coll., 1966–72; Nat. Inst. of Economic and Social Research, 1964–82. Admiral, Royal Ocean Racing Club, 1976–82; Rear-Cdre, Royal Yacht Squadron, 1982–86; Pres., Royal Yachting Assoc., 1983–87. Hon. FCIOB 1981. Hon. LLD University of Strathclyde, 1967. Hon. FCGI 1978; winner, Aims of Industry Free Enterprise Award, 1979. Has keen interest in Church activities at home and abroad. *Recreations:* sailing, swimming. *Address:* Reculver, 63 Totteridge Village, N20 8AG. *Clubs:* Royal Yacht Squadron, Royal Ocean Racing, Arts.
See also Sir W. K. Laing.

LAING, Sir Kirby; *see* Laing, Sir W. K.

LAING, Martin; *see* Laing, J. M. K.

LAING, Sir Maurice; *see* Laing, Sir J. M.

LAING, Peter Anthony Neville Pennethorne; Adviser, European Affairs, International Centre of Social Gerontology, since 1982; *b* 12 March 1922; *s* of late Lt-Col Neville Ogilvie Laing, DSO, 4th QO Hussars, and Zara Marcella (*née* Pennethorne), Fleet, Hants; *m* 1958, Penelope Lucinda, *d* of Sir William Pennington-Ramsden, 7th Bt; two *d*. *Educ:* Eton; Paris Univ. Served War: volunteer, French Army, 1939–40, Free French Forces, 1942–44; Grenadier Guards, 1944–46. Attaché, British Embassy, Madrid, 1946; internat. marketing consultant in Western Europe, USA, Caribbean and Latin America; UN, 1975–: Dir of ITC proj. for UNDP in the Congo; Dir, Help the Aged internat. charity, 1976–82. Creator, Mediterranean Retirement Inc. (wardened housing villages for ageing Europeans of ind. means), 1985–. *Recreations:* people, foreign travel, riding any horse, fine arts. *Address:* Northfields House, Turweston, near Brackley, Northants NN13 5JX. *T:* Brackley (0280) 700049, 703498. *Club:* Turf.

LAING, (William James) Scott; consultant to motor industry publications, Economist Intelligence Unit, since 1977; special assignments for United Nations and other international agencies, since 1977; *b* 14 April 1914; *er s* of late William Irvine Laing and Jessie C. M. Laing (*née* Scott); *m* 1952, Isabelle Mary Durrant-Fox (*d* 1990); one *s*. *Educ:* George Watson's Coll., Edinburgh Univ. Appointed to Dept of Overseas Trade, 1937; Asst to Commercial Counsellor, British Embassy, Buenos Aires, 1938; Second Sec. (Commercial), Buenos Aires, 1944; First Sec. (Commercial), Helsinki, 1947; Consul, New York, 1950; Consul-Gen. (Commercial), New York, 1954; Counsellor (Commercial), Brussels and Luxembourg, 1955; Consultant to UN Secretariat, Financial Policies and Institutions Section, 1958, African Training Programme, 1960; Editor, UN Jl, 1964; Chief, Publications Sales Section, UN Secretariat, 1969–76. *Publications:* The US Market for Motor Vehicle Parts and Accessories, 1977; Concentration and Diversification of the Self-Propelled Heavy Machinery Industries in USA, 1979; (jtly) Financial Assessment of the US Automotive Industry, 1982; (jtly) Foreign Outsourcing by US Auto Manufacturers, 1983. *Address:* PO Box 384, Grand Central PO, New York, NY 10163, USA. *Club:* Caledonian.

LAING, Sir (William) Kirby, Kt 1968; JP; DL; MA; FEng, FICE; Chairman, Laing Properties plc, 1978–87, President, 1987–90; *b* 21 July 1916; *s* of late Sir John Laing, CBE, and late Lady Laing (*née* Beatrice Harland); *m* 1st, 1939, Joan Dorothy Bratt (*d* 1981); three *s*; 2nd, 1986, Dr (Mary) Isobel Lewis, *yr d* of late Edward C. Wray. *Educ:* St Lawrence Coll., Ramsgate; Emmanuel Coll., Cambridge (Hon. Fellow, 1983). Served with Royal Engineers, 1943–45. Dir John Laing plc (formerly John Laing & Son Ltd), 1939–80 (Chm., 1957–76). President: London Master Builders Assoc., 1957; Reinforced Concrete Assoc., 1960; Nat. Fedn of Building Trades Employers (now Building Employers' Confedn) 1965, 1967 (Hon. Mem., 1975); ICE, 1973–74 (a Vice-Pres., 1970–73); Construction Industry Res. and Inf. Assoc., 1984–87 (Chm., 1978–81); Chm., Nat. Jt Council for Building Industry, 1968–74. Member, Board of Governors: St Lawrence Coll. (Chm., 1977–89, Pres., 1977–); Princess Helena Coll., 1984–87; Member: Court of Governors, The Polytechnic of Central London, 1963–82; Council, Royal Albert Hall, 1970– (Pres., 1979–); Trustee, Inter-Varsity Fellowship. Hon. Mem., Amer. Assoc. of Civil Engineers. Master, Paviors' Co., 1987–88. DL Greater London, 1978. Hon. Fellow, UCNW, 1988. Hon. DTech, Poly. of Central London, 1990; Dr *hc* Edinburgh, 1991. *Publications:* papers in Proc. ICE and other jls concerned with construction. *Recreations:* flyfishing, travelling, listening to music. *Address:* 133 Page Street, NW7 2ER. *Clubs:* Naval and Military; Royal Fowey Yacht.
See also J. M. K. Laing.

LAINSON, Prof. Ralph, FRS 1982; Director, Wellcome Parasitology Unit, Instituto Evandro Chagas, Belém, Pará, Brazil, since 1965; *b* 21 Feb. 1927; *s* of Charles Harry

Lainson and Anne (*née* Denyer); *m* 1st, 1957, Anne Patricia Russell; one *s* two *d*; 2nd, 1974, Zeá Constante Lins. *Educ:* Steyning Grammar Sch., Sussex; London Univ. (BSc, PhD, DSc). Lecturer in Medical Protozoology, London Sch. of Hygiene and Tropical Medicine, London Univ., 1955–59; Officer-in-Charge, Dermal Leishmaniasis Unit, Baking-Pot, Cayo Dist, Belize, 1959–62; Attached Investigator, Dept of Medical Protozoology, London Sch. of Hygiene and Tropical Medicine, 1962–65. Career devoted to research in Medical Protozoology in the Tropics. Hon. Fellow, LSHTM, 1982; Hon. Professor, Federal Univ. of Pará, Brazil, 1982; Associate Fellow, Third World Acad. of Scis, 1989; Hon. Mem., British Soc. of Parasitology, 1984. Chalmer's Medal, Royal Soc. of Tropical Medicine and Hygiene, 1971; Oswaldo Cruz Medal, Conselho Estadual de Cultura do Pará, 1973; Manson Medal, Royal Soc. of Tropical Medicine and Hygiene, 1983; Commemorative medals: 10th anniv., Health Council for State of Pará, Brazil, 1983; 30th anniv., Fed. Univ. of Pará, Brazil, 1988. *Publications:* author, or co-author, of approximately 230 pubns in current scientific jls, on protozoal parasites of man and animals. *Recreations:* fishing, swimming, collecting South American Lepidoptera, music, philately. *Address:* Avenida Visconde de Souza Franco, 1237 (Edificio 'Visconti'), Apartamento 902, 66.030 Belém, Pará, Brazil. *T:* 223–2382 (Belém).

LAIRD, Edgar Ord, (Michael Laird), CMG 1969; MBE 1958; HM Diplomatic Service, retired; *b* 16 Nov. 1915; *s* of late Edgar Balfour Laird; *m* 1940, Heather Lonsdale Forrest; four *d*. *Educ:* Rossall; Emmanuel Coll., Cambridge. Surveyor, Uganda Protectorate, 1939. Served Army, 1939–46 (Major). Appointed to Malayan Civil Service, 1947; Sec. to Government, Federation of Malaya, 1953–55; Sec. for External Defence, Federation of Malaya, 1956; Sec., Federation of Malaya Constitutional Commission, 1956–57; Dep. Sec., Prime Minister's Dept, Federation of Malaya, 1957. Appointed to Commonwealth Relations Office, 1958; First Sec. (Finance), Office of British High Comr, Ottawa, Canada, 1960–63; High Comr in Brunei, 1963–65; Dep. High Comr, Kaduna, 1965–69; RNC Greenwich, 1969–70; Head of Hong Kong and Indian Ocean Dept, FCO, 1970–72; British Govt Rep., West Indies Associated States, 1972–75. *Recreations:* playing the piano, reading. *Address:* St Jude's Cottage, 87 Fore Street, Topsham, Exeter EX3 0HQ. *Club:* Commonwealth Trust.

LAIRD, Endell Johnston; Director and Editor in Chief: Scottish Daily Record and Sunday Mail, The Glaswegian, since 1988; *m* 1958, June Keenan; one *s* two *d*. *Educ:* Forfar Academy. Served RAF, 1952–54. Journalist: Dundee Courier, 1954–56; Scottish Daily Express, 1956–58; Evening Times, 1958–60; Sunday Mail, 1960–71; Daily Record, 1971–81; Editor, Sunday Mail, 1981–88. Chm., Scottish Editors Cttee, 1986–88; Mem., D-Notice Cttee, 1986–. *Recreations:* walking, golf, bridge. *Address:* 10 Glenburn Gardens, Bishopbriggs, Glasgow G64 3BU. *T:* 041–242 3353. *Clubs:* Bishopbriggs Golf; Bishopbriggs Bridge.

LAIRD, Gavin Harry, CBE 1988; General Secretary, since 1982, Member, Executive Council, since 1975, Amalgamated Engineering Union (formerly Amalgamated Union of Engineering Workers); Director, Bank of England, since 1986; *b* 14 March 1933; *s* of James and Frances Laird; *m* 1956, Catherine Gillies Campbell; one *d*. *Educ:* Clydebank High School. Full-time Trade Union Official, 1972–. Mem., TUC Gen. Council, 1979–82. Dir, BNOC, 1976–86; non-exec. Director: Scottish TV, 1986–; FS Assurance, then Brittania Life, 1988–; GEC Scotland, 1991–. Pt-time Mem., SDA, 1987–. Member: Arts Council of GB, 1983–86; London Cttee, Scottish Council Develt and Industry, 1984–; President's Cttee, Business in the Community, 1988–. Mem. Cttee, Strathclyde Business Sch., 1983–; Governor: Atlantic Coll., 1987–; London Business Sch., 1988–. Mem., Editl. Bd, European Business Jl, 1988–. *Recreations:* hill walking, reading, bowls. *Address:* 35 Southlands Grove, Bromley BR1 2DA.

LAIRD, John Robert, (Robin Laird), TD 1946; FRICS; chartered surveyor; Member, Lands Tribunal, England and Wales, 1956–76; retired; *b* Marlow, Bucks, 3 Sept. 1909; *o s* of late John Laird, JP, and Mary (*née* Wakelin); *m* 1st, 1940, Barbara Joyce Muir (marr. diss. 1965); one *s* one *d*; 2nd, 1966, Betty Caroline McGregor (widow). *Educ:* Sir William Borlase's Sch., Marlow; Coll. of Estate Management, London. Partner, private practice, Lawrence, Son & Laird, Chartered Surveyors, Marlow, 1938–56. Served war: 2nd Lieut RA (TA), 1939; Staff Captain 35AA Bde, RA, 1941; Acting Lt-Col Eastern Comd, 1945. *Recreations:* hockey (Scottish International; 12 caps; Captain 1935), rowing, sailing, walking. *Address:* 8 Marine Square, Kemp Town, Brighton, E Sussex BN2 1DL. *T:* Brighton (0273) 602065.

LAIRD, Margaret Heather; Third Church Estates Commissioner, since 1989; *b* 29 Jan. 1933; *d* of William Henry Polmear and Edith Polmear; *m* 1961, Rev. Canon John Charles Laird; two *s*. *Educ:* High Sch., Truro; Westfield College London (BA Hons Mediaeval History, 1954); King's College London (Cert. Rel. Know. 1955). Divinity Mistress: Grey Coat Hospital, SW1, 1955–59; Newquay Grammar Sch., 1959–60; St Albans High Sch., 1960–62; Head of Religious Studies, Dame Alice Harpur Sch., Bedford, 1969–89. Member: Gen. Synod of C of E, repr. Dio. St Albans, 1980–90 (ex officio, 1990–); Panel of Assessors, Dio. St Albans, 1988–. *Recreations:* mediaeval art, architecture, pilgrims' routes. *Address:* Church Commissioners, 1 Millbank, SW1P 3JZ. *T:* 071–222 7010. *Club:* United Oxford & Cambridge University.

LAIRD, Hon. Melvin R.; Senior Counsellor for National and International Affairs, Reader's Digest Association, since 1974; *b* 1 Sept. 1922; *s* of Melvin R. Laird and Helen Laird (*née* Connor); *m* 1945, Barbara Masters; two *s* one *d*. *Educ:* Carleton Coll., Northfield, Minn (BA 1944). Enlisted, US Navy, 1942, commissioned, 1944; served in Third Fleet and Task Force 58 (Purple Heart and other decorations). Elected: to Wisconsin State Senate, 1946 (re-elected, 1948); to US Congress, Nov. 1952 (83rd through 90th; Chm., House Republican Conf., 89th and 90th); Sec. of Defense, 1969–73; Counsellor to President of the US, 1973–74. Director: Metropolitan Life Insurance Co.; Northwest Airlines; Communications Satellite Corp.; IDS Mutual Fund Gp Inc.; Phillips Petroleum Co.; Science Applications Internat. Corp.; Martin Marietta Corp.; Public Oversight Bd (SEC Practice Sect., AICPA); DeWitt Wallace, and Lila Wallace, Reader's Digest Funds (for the promotion of the arts and humanities). Member Board of Trustees: George Washington Univ.; Kennedy Center. Various awards from Assocs, etc (for med. research, polit. science, public health, nat. educn); many hon. memberships and hon. degrees. *Publications:* A House Divided: America's Strategy Gap, 1962; Editor: The Conservative Papers, 1964; Republican Papers, 1968. *Recreations:* golf, fishing. *Address:* Suite 212, 1730 Rhode Island Avenue NW, Washington, DC 20036, USA. *Clubs:* Burning Tree (Washington, DC); Augusta National Golf.

LAIRD, Michael; *see* Laird, E. O.

LAIRD, Robin; *see* Laird, J. R.

LAISTER, Peter; company director; *b* 24 Jan. 1929; *s* of late Horace Laister and of Mrs I. L. Bates; *m* 1st, 1951, Barbara Cooke; one *s* one *d*; 2nd, 1958, Eileen Alice Goodchild (*née* Town); one *d*. *Educ:* King Edward's Sch., Birmingham; Manchester Univ., Coll. of Technology (BSc Tech, 1949; FUMIST, 1985). FInstPet, 1958; FIChemE, 1983; CEng; CBIM. RAF, 1949–51. Esso Petroleum Co. Ltd, 1951–66: Process Engr to UK Refining Co-Ordinator, 1960; Gen. Manager, Marketing Ops, 1962–66; British Oxygen Co. Ltd (BOC Intl Ltd), 1966–75 (Gp Man Dir, 1969–75); Chm., BOC Financial Corp. (USA), 1974–75; Gp Man. Dir, Ellerman Lines Ltd, 1976–79; Chairman: Tollemache and Cobbold Breweries, 1977–79; London & Hull Insce Co., 1976–79; Oceonics plc, 1986–88; Group Man. Dir, Thorn Electrical Industries, later THORN EMI, 1979–84, Chm., 1984–85. Director: (non exec.) Inchcape plc, 1982–; (non exec.) Fluor Daniel, 1985–; Maxwell Communication Corp. plc, 1985–; Mirror Hldgs Ltd, 1985–; Tower Maritime Gp Ltd, 1986–; (non exec.) A&P Appledore, 1986–87; British Cable Services, 1987–; Clyde Cable Vision, 1987–89; Metromode Ltd, 1987–; Pergamon GED Internat. Ltd, 1987–; Nimbus Records Ltd, 1987, Chm., 1988–; Pergamon Media plc, 1987–; Tower Hotels (Management), 1987–; VIP Marine and Aviation Ltd, 1987–; Laister Dickson Ltd, 1988–; Chairman: Park Hotels plc, 1985–; SelecTV plc, 1987–; MTV Europe, 1988–; Tower Gp (formerly Finance, Land & General Hldgs), 1988– (Chm., 1988–); Maxwell Satellite Communications, 1988–. Industrial Society: Council Mem., 1971–86; Mem., Industrial Develt Adv. Bd, 1981–83; Mem., BIM Exec. Bd, 1983–. Gov., BUPA, 1982–; Chm., CICI, 1988–. Vice-Pres., Research into Ageing, 1982–. Mem., Council, UCL, 1978–. *Recreations:* private flying, boating and angling, gardening, photography.

LAIT, Leonard Hugh Cecil, (Josh Lait); His Honour Judge Lait; a Circuit Judge, since 1987; *b* 15 Nov. 1930; *m* 1967, Cheah Phaik Teen; one *d*. *Educ:* John Lyon School, Harrow; Trinity Hall, Cambridge (BA). Called to the Bar, Inner Temple, 1959; Mem., SE circuit; a Recorder, 1985–87. *Recreations:* music, gardening.

LAITHWAITE, Prof. Eric Roberts; Professor of Heavy Electrical Engineering, Imperial College of Science and Technology, London, 1964–86, now Emeritus; *b* 14 June 1921; *s* of Herbert Laithwaite; *m* 1951, Sheila Margaret Gooddie; two *s* two *d*. *Educ:* Kirkham Gram. Sch.; Regent Street Polytechnic; Manchester Univ. RAF, 1941–46 (at RAE Farnborough, 1943–46). BSc 1949, MSc 1950. Manchester Univ.: Asst Lectr, 1950–53; Lectr, 1953–58; Sen. Lectr, 1958–64; PhD 1957; DSc 1964. Prof. of Royal Instn, 1967–76. Pres., Assoc. for Science Educn, 1970. FIC 1990. S. G. Brown Award and Medal of Royal Society, 1966; Nikola Tesla Award, IEEE, 1986. *Publications:* Propulsion without Wheels, 1966; Induction Machines for Special Purposes, 1966; The Engineer in Wonderland, 1967; Linear Electric Motors, 1971; Exciting Electrical Machines, 1974; (with A. Watson and P. E. S. Whalley) The Dictionary of Butterflies and Moths, 1975; (ed) Transport without Wheels, 1977; (with M. W. Thring) How to Invent, 1977; Engineer through the Looking-Glass, 1980; (with L. L. Freris) Electric Energy: its Generation, Transmission and Use, 1980; Invitation to Engineering, 1984; A History of Linear Electric Motors, 1987; many papers in Proc. IEE (7 premiums) and other learned jls. *Recreations:* entomology, gardening. *Address:* Department of Electrical Engineering, Imperial College, SW7 2BT. *T:* 071–589 5111. *Club:* Athenæum.

LAITHWAITE, John, FIMechE, FInstPet; engineering consultant; Director, Capper Neill Ltd, 1965–83 (Vice-Chairman, 1972–82); *b* 29 Nov. 1920; *s* of Tom Prescott Laithwaite and Mary Anne Laithwaite; *m* 1943, Jean Chateris; one *s* two *d*. *Educ:* Manchester Univ. (BSc Hons Mech. Eng). FIMechE 1974; FInstPet 1960; MInstW 1950. Wm Neill & Son (St Helens) Ltd, 1942–43; Dartford Shipbuilding & Engineering Co., 1943–44; Dir, Wm Neill & Son (St Helens) Ltd, 1955–58, Man. Dir, 1958–64; Man. Dir, Capper Neill Ltd, 1968–72. Mem. Council, NW Regional Management Centre. Chm., Process Plant Assoc., 1975–77, Hon. Vice-Pres., 1980–. *Publications:* articles on process plant industry and pressure vessel standardisation. *Recreations:* shooting, golf. *Address:* Gwydd Gwyllt, Malltraeth, Gwynedd LL62 5AW. *T:* Bodorgan (0407) 840586. *Clubs:* Royal Automobile; Anglesey Golf.

LAJTHA, Prof. Laszlo George, CBE 1983; MD, DPhil, FRCPE, FRCPath; Director of Paterson Laboratories, Christie Hospital and Holt Radium Institute, 1962–83; Professor of Experimental Oncology, University of Manchester, 1970–83, now Emeritus Professor; *b* 25 May 1920; *s* of Laszlo John Lajtha and Rose Stephanie Hollos; *m* 1954, Gillian Macpherson Henderson; two *s*. *Educ:* Presbyterian High School, Budapest; Medical School, Univ. of Budapest (MD 1944); Exeter Coll., Univ. of Oxford (DPhil 1950). FRCPath 1973; FRCPE 1980. Asst Prof., Dept of Physiology, Univ. of Budapest, 1944–47; Research Associate, Dept of Haematology, Radcliffe Infirmary, Oxford, 1947–50; Head, Radiobiology Laboratory, Churchill Hosp., Oxford, 1950–62; subseq. Research Fellow, Pharmacology, Yale Univ., New Haven, Conn., USA. Editor, British Jl of Cancer, 1972–82. President: British Soc. of Cell Biology, 1977–80; European Orgn for Res. on Treatment of Cancer, 1979–82. Hon. Citizen, Texas, USA; Hon. Member: Amer. Cancer Soc.; German, Italian and Hungarian Socs of Haematology; Hungarian Acad. of Sciences, 1983. Dr *hc* Szeged Univ., Hungary, 1981. *Publications:* Isotopes in Haematology, 1961; over 250 articles in scientific (medical) jls. *Recreations:* alpine gardening, medieval history, bonsai. *Address:* Brook Cottage, Little Bridge Road, Bloxham, Oxon OX15 4PU. *T:* Banbury (0295) 720311. *Club:* Athenæum.

LAKE, Sir (Atwell) Graham, 10th Bt *cr* 1711; Senior Technical Adviser, Ministry of Defence, retired 1983; *b* 6 Oct. 1923; *s* of Captain Sir Atwell Henry Lake, 9th Bt, CB, OBE, RN, and Kathleen Marion, *d* of late Alfred Morrison Turner; *S* father, 1972; *m* 1983, Mrs Katharine Margaret Lister, *d* of late D. W. Last and M. M. Last. *Educ:* Eton. British High Commission, Wellington, NZ, 1942; Gilbert and Ellice Military Forces, 1944; Colonial Administrative Service, 1945 (Secretary to Govt of Tonga, 1950–53); Norris Oakley Bros, 1957; Min. of Defence, 1959; British High Commission, New Delhi, 1966; attached Foreign and Commonwealth Office, 1969–72. *Recreations:* golf, bridge, chess, skiing. *Heir:* *b* Edward Geoffrey Lake [*b* 17 July 1928; *m* 1965, Judith Ann, *d* of John Fox; one *s* one *d*]. *Address:* Magdalen Laver Hall, Chipping Ongar, Essex CM5 0EG. *Club:* Lansdowne.

LAKEMAN, Miss Enid, OBE 1980; Editorial Consultant and a Vice-President, Electoral Reform Society, since 1979 (Director, 1960–79); *b* 28 Nov. 1903; *d* of Horace B. Lakeman and Evereld Simpson. *Educ:* Tunbridge Wells County Sch.; Bedford Coll., Univ. of London. Posts in chemical industry, 1926–41; WAAF, 1941–45; Electoral Reform Soc., 1945–. Parly candidate (L): St Albans, 1945; Brixton, 1950; Aldershot, 1955 and 1959. *Publications:* When Labour Fails, 1946; (with James D. Lambert) Voting in Democracies, 1955, (2nd edn 1959; 3rd and 4th edns, 1970 and 1974, as sole author, as How Democracies Vote); Nine Democracies, 1973, 4th edn 1991, as, Twelve Democracies; Power to Elect, 1982; pamphlets; articles in polit. jls. *Recreations:* travel, gardening. *Address:* 37 Culverden Avenue, Tunbridge Wells, Kent TN4 9RE. *T:* Tunbridge Wells (0892) 21674. *Club:* National Liberal.

LAKER, Sir Freddie, (Sir Frederick Alfred Laker), Kt 1978; *b* 6 Aug. 1922; British. *Educ:* Simon Langton Sch., Canterbury. Short Brothers, Rochester, 1938–40; General Aircraft, 1940–41; Air Transport Auxiliary, 1941–46; Aviation Traders, 1946–65; British United Airways, 1960–65; Chm. and Man. Dir, Laker Airways Ltd, 1966–82; Dir, Freddie Laker's Skytrain Ltd, 1982–83; creator of Skytrain Air Passenger Service to USA. Hon. Fellow Univ. of Manchester Inst. of Science and Technol., 1978; Hon. DSc: City, 1979; Cranfield Inst. of Technol., 1980; Hon. LLD Manchester, 1981. *Recreations:*

horse breeding, racing, sailing. *Address:* Furzegrove Farm, Chailey, near Newick, Lewes, E Sussex. *Clubs:* Eccentric, Little Ship, Jockey.

LAKES, Major Gordon Harry, CB 1987; MC 1951; Deputy Director General, Prison Service, 1985–88; *b* 27 Aug. 1928; *s* of Harry Lakes and Annie Lakes; *m* 1950, Nancy (*née* Smith); one *d. Educ:* Army Technical School, Arborfield; RMA Sandhurst. Commissioned RA 1948; service in Tripolitania, Korea, Japan, Hong Kong, Gold Coast (RWAFF), Ghana (Major), 1949–60. Middle Temple, 1960–61. Prison Service College, 1961–62; HM Borstal Feltham, 1962–65; Officers' Training Sch., Leyhill, 1965–68; Governor, HM Remand Centre, Thorp Arch, 1968–70; Prison Service HQ, 1970–74; HM Prisons: Pentonville, 1974–75; Gartree, 1975–77; Prison Service HQ, 1977–82; HM Dep. Chief Inspector of Prisons, 1982–85. Member: Council of Europe Cttee for Co-operation in Prison Affairs, 1986–; Parole Bd, 1989–. Consultant to 8th UN Congress on Prevention of Crime and Treatment of Offenders, 1989–90. Assessor to Lord Justice Woolf's Inquiry into Prison Disturbances, 1990–91. Comr, Mental Health Act, 1991–. *Recreations:* golf, photography.

LAKEY, Prof. John Richard Angwin, PhD; CEng, FINucE, FInstE; CPhys, FInstP; radiation protection consultant; founder John Lakey Associates, 1989; *b* 28 June 1929; *s* of late William Richard Lakey and Edith Lakey (*née* Hartley); *m* 1955, Dr Pamela Janet, *d* of late Eric Clifford Lancey and Florence Elsie Lancey; three *d. Educ:* Morley Grammar Sch.; Sheffield Univ. BSc (Physics) 1950, PhD (Fuel Technology) 1953. R&D posts with Simon Carves Ltd, secondment to AERE Harwell and GEC, 1953–60; Royal Naval College, Greenwich: Asst Prof., 1960–80; Prof. of Nuclear Sci. and Technol., 1980–89; Dean, 1984–86, 1988–89. Reactor Shielding Consultant, DG Ships, 1967–89; Radiation Consultant, WHO, 1973–74; Mem. and Vice-Chm., CNAA Physics Board, 1973–82; Mem., Medway Health Authy, 1981–90; Chm., UK Liaison Cttee for Scis Allied to Medicine and Biology, 1984–87. University of Surrey: External Examr, 1980–86; Hon. Vis. Prof., 1987–; Vis. Lectr, Harvard Univ., 1984–. President: Instn of Nuclear Engrs, 1988–90 (Vice-Pres., 1983–87); Internat. Radiation Protection Assoc., 1988– (Publications Dir, 1979–88); Vice-President: London Internat. Youth Science Fortnight, 1988–; European Nuclear Soc., 1989–. Liveryman, Engineers' Co. Mem. Editorial Bd, Physics in Medicine and Biology, 1980–83; News Editor, Health Physics, 1980–88. *Publications:* Protection Against Radiation, 1961; Radiation Protection Measurement: philosophy and implementation, 1975; (ed) ALARA principles and practices, 1987; IRPA Guidelines on Protection Against Non-Ionizing Radiation, 1991; papers on nuclear safety, radiological protection and management of emergencies. *Recreations:* yachting, photography, conversation. *Address:* John Lakey Associates, 5 Pine Rise, Meopham, Gravesend, Kent DA13 0JA. *T:* Meopham (0474) 812551. *Clubs:* Athenæum; Medway Yacht; Royal Naval Sailing Association.

LAKIN, Sir Michael, 4th Bt *cr* 1909; *b* 28 Oct. 1934; *s* of Sir Henry Lakin, 3rd Bt, and Bessie (*d* 1965), *d* of J. D. Anderson, Durban; *S* father, 1979; *m* 1965, Felicity Ann Murphy; one *s* one *d. Educ:* Stowe. *Heir: s* Richard Anthony Lakin, *b* 26 Nov. 1968. *Address:* Torwood, PO Box 40, Rosetta, Natal, South Africa. *T:* Rosetta 1613.

LAKING, Sir George (Robert), KCMG 1985 (CMG 1969); Chief Ombudsman, New Zealand, 1977–84, retired; *b* Auckland, NZ, 15 Oct. 1912; *s* of R. G. Laking; *m* 1940, Patricia, *d* of H. Hogg; one *s* one *d. Educ:* Auckland Grammar Sch.; Auckland Univ.; Victoria Univ. of Wellington (LLB). Prime Minister's and Ext. Affairs Depts, 1940–49; New Zealand Embassy, Washington: Counsellor, 1949–54; Minister, 1954–56. Dep. Sec. of Ext. Affairs, Wellington, NZ, 1956–58; Acting High Comr for NZ, London, 1958–61, and NZ Ambassador to European Economic Community, 1960–61; New Zealand Ambassador, Washington, 1961–67; Sec. of Foreign Affairs and Permanent Head, Prime Minister's Dept, NZ, 1967–72; Ombudsman, 1975–77; Privacy Comr, 1977–78. Member: Human Rights Commn, 1978–84; Public and Administrative Law Reform Cttee, 1980–85. Chairman: NZ-US Educnl Foundn, 1976–78; NZ Oral History Archive Trust, 1985–90; Wellington Civic Trust, 1985–86; Legislation Adv. Cttee, 1986–91; Pres., NZ Inst. of Internat. Affairs, 1980–84. Mem. Internat. Council, Asia Soc., NY, 1985–. *Address:* 3 Wesley Road, Wellington 1, New Zealand. *T:* 728–454.

LAL, Prof. Devendra, PhD; FRS 1979; Professor, Geological Research Division, Scripps Institution of Oceanography, University of California, La Jolla, since 1967; Fellow, Physical Research Laboratory, Ahmedabad, since 1990 (Director, 1972–83; Senior Professor, 1983–89); *b* 14 Feb. 1929; *s* of Radhekrishna Lal and Sita Devi; *m* 1955, Aruna L. Damany. *Educ:* Banaras Hindu Univ. (MSc); Univ. of Bombay (PhD). Fellow, Indian Acad. of Sciences, 1964. Tata Inst. of Fundamental Research, Bombay: Res. Student, 1949–50; Res. Asst, 1950–53; Res. Fellow, 1953–57; Fellow, 1957–60; Associate Prof., 1960–63; Prof., 1963–70; Sen. Prof., 1970–72. Res. Geophysicist, UCLA-IGPP, 1965–66. Vis. Prof., UCLA, 1983–84. K. S. Krishnan Meml Lect., INSA, 1981. Foreign Sec., Indian Nat. Sci. Acad., 1981–84 (Fellow, 1971); Founder Mem., Third World Acad. of Scis, Trieste, 1983; President: Internat. Assoc. of Physical Scis of the Ocean, 1979–83; Internat. Union of Geodesy & Geophysics, 1983–87. Fellow, Nat. Acad. of Scis, Allahabad, 1988; Foreign Associate, Nat. Acad. of Sciences, USA, 1975; For. Mem., Amer. Acad. of Arts and Scis, 1989; Associate, RAS, 1984; Mem., Internat. Acad. Astronautics, 1985. Mem., Sigma Xi, USA, 1984. Hon. DSc Banaras Hindu Univ., 1981. Krishnan Medal for Geochemistry and Geophysics, 1965; Shanti Swarup Bhatnagar Award for Physical Sciences, CSIR, 1967; Outstanding Scientist Award, Fedn of Indian Chambers of Commerce and Industry, 1974; Pandit Jawaharlal Nehru Award for Scis, Madhya Pradesh Govt, 1986. Padma Shri, 1971. *Publications:* (ed) Early Solar System Processes and the Present Solar System, 1980; *contributed:* Earth Science and Meteoritics, 1963; International Dictionary of Geophysics, 1968; The Encyclopedia of Earth Sciences: vol. IV, Geochemistry and Environmental Sciences, 1972; Further Advances in Lunar Research: Luna 16 and 20 samples, 1974; McGraw Hill Encyclopedia of Science and Technology, 1990; jt author of chapters in books; scientific papers to learned jls; proc. confs. *Recreations:* music, puzzles, painting, photography. *Address:* Scripps Institution of Oceanography, University of California at San Diego, La Jolla, Calif 92093–0220, USA. *T:* (office) 619 534–2134, (home) 619 587–1535.

LALANDI-EMERY, Lina, (Mrs Ralph Emery), OBE 1975; Festival Director, English Bach Festival, since 1962; *b* Athens; *d* of late Nikolas Kaloyeropoulos (former Dir of Byzantine Museum, Athens, and Dir of Beaux Arts, Min. of Educn, Athens) and Toula Gelekis. *Educ:* Athens Conservatoire (grad. with Hons in Music); privately, in England (harpsichord and singing studies). International career as harpsichordist in Concert, Radio and TV. Founded English Bach Festival Trust, 1962. Officier, l'Ordre des Arts et des Lettres, 1978. *Recreations:* cats, cooking, reading, knitting. *Address:* 15 South Eaton Place, SW1W 9ER. *T:* 071–730 5925, *Fax:* 071–730 1456.

LALANNE, Bernard Michel L.; *see* Loustau-Lalanne.

LALONDE, Hon. Marc; PC (Can.) 1972; OC 1989; QC 1971; Law Partner, Stikeman, Elliott, Montreal, since 1984; *b* 26 July 1929; *s* of late J. Albert Lalonde and Nora (*née* St Aubin); *m* 1955, Claire Tétreau; two *s* two *d. Educ:* St Laurent Coll., Montreal (BA 1950); Univ. of Montreal (LLL 1954; MA Law 1955); Oxford Univ. (Econ. and Pol. Science; MA 1957); Ottawa Univ. (Dip. of Superior Studies in Law, 1960). Prof. of Commercial Law and Econs, Univ. of Montreal, 1957–59; Special Asst to Minister of Justice, Ottawa, 1959–60; Partner, Gelinas, Bourque Lalonde & Benoit, Montreal, 1960–68; Lectr in Admin. Law for Doctorate Students, Univ. of Ottawa and Univ. of Montreal, 1961–62; Policy Advisor to Prime Minister, 1967; Principal Sec. to Prime Minister, 1968–72; MP (L) Montreal-Outremont, 1972–84; Minister of National Health and Welfare, 1972–77; Minister of State for Federal-Provincial Relations, 1977–78; Minister resp. for Status of Women, 1975–78; Minister of Justice and Attorney-Gen., 1978–79; Minister of Energy, Mines and Resources, 1980–82; Minister of Finance, 1982–84. Counsel before several Royal Commns inc. Royal Commn on Great Lakes Shipping and Royal Commn on Pilotage. Mem., Cttee on Broadcasting, 1964; Dir, Canadian Citizenship Council, 1960–65; Member, Bd of Directors: Inst. of Public Law, Univ. of Montréal, 1960–64, 1990–; Citibank Canada, 1985–; Coronet Carpets, 1986–; Chm. of Bd, Hotel-Dieu Hosp., Montreal, 1985–. Dana Award, Amer. Public Health Assoc., 1978. *Publications:* The Changing Role of the Prime Minister's Office, 1971; New Perspectives on the Health of Canadians (working document), 1974. *Recreations:* tennis, squash, skiing, jogging, sailing, reading. *Address:* 5440 Légaré, Montréal, Québec H3T 1Z4, Canada.

LALOUETTE, Marie Joseph Gerard; retired; *b* 24 Jan. 1912; 3rd *s* of late Henri Lalouette and Mrs H. Lalouette; *m* 1942, Jeanne Marrier d'Unienville; four *s* two *d. Educ:* Royal Coll., Mauritius; Exeter Coll., Oxford; London School of Economics; Middle Temple. District Magistrate, Mauritius, 1944; Electoral Commissioner, 1956; Addl. Subst. Procureur-General, 1956; Master, and Registrar, Supreme Court, 1958; Assistant Attorney-General, 1959; Solicitor-General, 1960; Puisne Judge, 1961; Senior Puisne Judge, Supreme Court, Mauritius, 1967–70; Attorney, Republic of S Africa, 1973–83; Justice of Appeal, Seychelles, 1977–82. *Publications:* Digest of Decisions of Supreme Court of Mauritius, 1926–43; The Mauritius Digest to 1950; A First Supplement to the Mauritius Digest, 1951–55; A Second Supplement to the Mauritius Digest, 1956–60; The Seychelles Digest, 1982; contrib. Internat. Encyclopedia of Comparative Law. *Recreations:* music, gardening. *Address:* 419 Windermere Centre, Windermere Road, Durban, Republic of South Africa. *T:* 031–237598.

LALUMIÈRE, Catherine; French politician; Secretary General, Council of Europe, since 1989; *b* Rennes, 3 Aug. 1935; *d* of Jacques and Andrée Bodin; *m* 1960, Pierre Lalumière. Specialist in public law; Asst Lectr, Univ. of Bordeaux and Bordeaux Inst. of Pol. Studies, 1960–71; Lectr, Univ. of Paris, 1971–81. Mem., Steering Cttee, Parti Socialiste, 1979–; Mem., National Assembly for Gironde, 1981, and 1986–June 1989 (resigned seat); Advr to Pres. on Civil Service; Sec. of State for the Civil and Admin. Reforms, May–June 1981; Minister for Consumer Affairs, 1981; Minister for Europ. Affairs, 1984–86. *Recreation:* walking. *Address:* Council of Europe, BP 431 R 6, F–67006 Strasbourg, France; (permanent political) 54 rue Camille Pelletan, F–33400 Talence, France.

LAM, Martin Philip; Associate of BIS Mackintosh, and of General Technology Systems, since 1979; Consultant, Scaneurope, since 1989; *b* 10 March 1920; *m* 1953, Lisa Lorenz; one *s* one *d. Educ:* University College Sch.; Gonville and Caius Coll., Cambridge (Scholar). Served War of 1939–45, Royal Signals. Asst Principal, Board of Trade, 1947; Nuffield Fellowship (Latin America), 1952–53; Asst Sec., 1960; Counsellor, UK Delegn to OECD, 1963–65, Advr, Commercial Policy, 1970–74, Leader UNCTAD Delegn, 1972; Under-Sec. (Computer Systems and Electronics), DoI, 1974–78; on contract to Directorate-Gen. XIII, European Commn, 1986–88. *Address:* 22 The Avenue, Wembley, Middlesex HA9 9QJ. *T:* 081–904 2584.

LAMB, family name of **Baron Rochester.**

LAMB, Sir Albert; *see* Lamb, Sir Larry.

LAMB, Sir Albert Thomas, (Sir Archie), KBE 1979 (MBE 1953); CMG 1974; DFC 1945; HM Diplomatic Service, retired; *b* 23 Oct. 1921; *s* of R. S. Lamb and Violet Lamb (*née* Haynes); *m* 1944, Christina Betty Wilkinson; one *s* two *d. Educ:* Swansea Grammar Sch. Served RAF 1941–46. FO 1938–41; Embassy, Rome, 1947–50; Consulate-General, Genoa, 1950; Embassy, Bucharest, 1950–53; FO 1953–55; Middle East Centre for Arabic Studies, 1955–57; Political Residency, Bahrain, 1957–61; FO 1961–65; Embassy, Kuwait, 1965; Political Agent in Abu Dhabi, 1965–68; Inspector, 1968–70, Sen. Inspector, 1970–73, Asst Under-Sec. of State and Chief Inspector, FCO, 1973–74; Ambassador to Kuwait, 1974–77; Ambassador to Norway, 1978–80. Mem., BNOC, 1981–82; Dir, Britoil plc, 1982–88; Mem. Bd, British Shipbuilders, 1985–87; Sen. Associate, Conant and Associates Ltd, Washington DC, 1985–; Adviser, Samuel Montagu and Co. Ltd, 1986–88. *Address:* White Cross Lodge, Zeals, Wilts BA12 6PF. *T:* Bourton (0747) 840321. *Club:* Royal Air Force.

LAMB, Air Vice-Marshal George Colin, CB 1977; CBE 1966; AFC 1947; Managing Director, Yonex (UK) Ltd, since 1990; *b* 23 July 1923; *s* of late George and Bessie Lamb, Hornby, Lancaster; *m* 1st, 1945, Nancy Mary Godsmark; two *s*; 2nd, 1981, Mrs Maureen Margaret Mepham. *Educ:* Lancaster Royal Grammar School. War of 1939–45: commissioned, RAF, 1942; flying duties, 1942–53; Staff Coll., 1953; Air Ministry, special duties, 1954–58; OC No 87 Sqdn, 1958–61; Dir Admin. Plans, MoD, 1961–64; Asst Comdt, RAF Coll., 1964–65; Dep. Comdr, Air Forces Borneo, 1965–66; Fighter Command, 1966; MoD (Dep. Command Structure Project Officer), 1967; HQ, Strike Command, 1967–69; OC, RAF Lyneham, 1969–71; RCDS, 1971–72; Dir of Control (Operations), NATS, 1972–74; Comdr, Southern Maritime Air Region, RAF Mount Batten, 1974–75; C of S, No 18 Gp Strike Comd, RAF, 1975–78. RAF Vice-Pres., Combined Cadet Forces Assoc., 1978–. Chief Exec., Badminton Assoc. of England, 1978–89; Gen. Sec., London Inst. of Sports Medicine, 1989–90. Consultant, Television, Sport and Leisure Ltd, 1989–90. Chm., Lilleshall National Sports Centre, 1984–; Member: Sports Council, 1983–88 (Mem., Drug Abuse Adv. Gp, 1988–); Sports Cttee, Prince's Trust, 1985–88; Privilege Mem. of RFU, 1985– (Mem., RFU Cttee, 1973–85); British Internat. Sports Cttee, 1989–. FBIM. *Recreations:* international Rugby football referee, cricket (former Pres., Adastrian Cricket Club). *Address:* Hambledon, 17 Meadway, Berkhamsted HP4 2PN. *T:* Berkhamsted (0442) 862583. *Club:* Royal Air Force.

LAMB, Harold Norman, CBE 1978; Regional Administrator, South East Thames Regional Health Authority, 1973–81; *b* 21 July 1922; *s* of Harold Alexander and Amelia Lamb; *m* 1946, Joyce Marian Hawkyard; one *s* one *d. Educ:* Saltley Grammar School. FHA. Served War, RAF, 1941–46. House Governor, Birmingham Gen. Hosp., 1958; Dep. Sec., United Birmingham Hosps, and House Governor, Queen Elizabeth Hosp., 1961; Sec., SE Metrop. RHB, 1968. Mem. Exec. Council, Royal Inst. of Public Admin, 1970–78. *Recreations:* golf, music. *Address:* 40 Windmill Way, Reigate, Surrey RH2 0JA. *T:* Reigate (0737) 221846. *Club:* Walton Heath Golf.

LAMB, Prof. John, CBE 1986; FEng; James Watt Professor of Electrical Engineering, since 1961, and Vice-Principal, 1977–80, University of Glasgow; *b* 26 Sept. 1922; *m* 1947, Margaret May Livesey; two *s* one *d. Educ:* Accrington Grammar Sch.; Manchester Univ. BSc (1st class Hons) Manchester Univ. 1943; Fairbairn Prizeman in Engineering;

MSc 1944, PhD 1946, DSc 1957, Manchester. Ministry of Supply Extra-Mural Res., 1943–46. Assistant Lecturer, 1946–47, Lecturer, 1947–56, Reader, 1956–61, in Electrical Engineering at Imperial Coll. (London Univ.); Assistant Director, Department of Electrical Engineering, Imperial Coll., 1958–61. Gledden Fellow, Univ. of WA, Perth, 1983. Pres., British Soc. of Rheology, 1970–72. Chm., Scottish Industry Univ. Liaison Cttee in Engrg, 1969–71; Member: Nat. Electronics Council, 1963–78; CNAA, 1964–70; Council, RSE, 1980–83, 1986–; British Nat. Cttee for Radio Sci., 1983–87. Scientific Advr, Scottish Office Industry Dept, 1987–. FInstP 1960; Fellow, Acoustical Society of America, 1960; FRSE 1968 (Vice-Pres., 1989–); FIEE 1983; FEng 1984; Hon. Fellow, Inst. of Acoustics, 1980. *Publications:* (ed jtly) Proceedings of the Fourth European Conference on Integrated Optics, 1987; numerous in Proc. Royal Society, Trans Faraday Society, Proc. Instn Electrical Engineers, Proc. Physical Society, Journal Acoustical Society of America, Quarterly Reviews of Chem. Society, Nature, Phys. Review, Journal of Polymer Science; contrib.: (The Theory and Practice of Ultrasonic Propagation) to Principles and Practice of Non-destructive Testing (ed J. H. Lamble), 1962; (Dispersion and Absorption of Sound by Molecular Processes) to Proc. International School of Physics "Enrico Fermi" Course XXVII (ed D. Sette), 1963; (Thermal Relaxation in Liquids) to Physical Acoustics, Vol. II (ed W. P. Mason), 1965; (Theory of Rheology) to Interdisciplinary Approach to Liquid Lubricant Technology (ed P. M. Ku), 1973; (Viscoelastic and Ultrasonic Relaxation Studies) to Molecular Motions in Liquids (ed J. Lascombe), 1974; (Motions in Low Molecular Weight Fluids and Glass forming Liquids) to Molecular Basis of Transitions and Relaxations (ed D. J. Meier), 1978; Shear Waves of Variable Frequency for Studying the Viscoelastic Relaxation Processes in Liquids and Polymer Melts (ed A. Kawski and A. Sliwinsky), 1979; (Development of Integrated Optical Circuits) to Integrated Optics (ed S. Martellucci and R. N. Chester), 1983; (ed jtly) Proceedings of the Fourth European Conference on Integrated Optics, 1987. *Recreations:* walking, wine-making, music. *Address:* 5 Cleveden Crescent, Glasgow G12 0PD. *T:* 041–339 2101.

LAMB, Prof. Joseph Fairweather, PhD; FRCPE; FRSE; Chandos Professor of Physiology, St Leonard's College, University of St Andrews, since 1969; *b* 18 July 1928; *s* of Joseph and Agnes May Lamb; *m* 1st, 1955, Olivia Janet Horne (marr. diss. 1989); three *s* one *d*; 2nd, 1989, Bridget Cecilia Cook; two *s*. *Educ:* Brechin High School; Edinburgh Univ. (MB ChB, BSc, PhD). FRCPE 1985. National Service, RAF, 1947–49. House Officer, Dumfries and Edinburgh, 1955–56; Hons Physiology Course, 1956–57; Univ. Junior Res. Fellow, 1957; Lectr in Physiology, Royal (Dick) Vet. Sch., 1958–61; Lectr, Sen. Lectr in Physiol., Glasgow, 1961–69. Sec., Physiol. Soc., 1984–87; Chm., Save British Science Soc., 1986–. Editor: Jl of Physiol., 1968–74; Amer. Jl of Physiol., 1985–88. FRSA; FRSE 1985. *Publications:* Essentials of Physiology, 1980, 3rd edn 1991; articles in learned jls. *Recreations:* sailing, boatbuilding, reading. *Address:* Kenbrae, Millbank, Cupar, Fife KY15 5DP. *T:* Cupar (0334) 52791. *Clubs:* Sloane, Royal Society of Medicine; Serpent Yacht.

LAMB, Hon. Kenneth Henry Lowry, CBE 1985; Secretary to the Church Commissioners, 1980–85; *b* 23 Dec. 1923; *y s* of 1st Baron Rochester, CMG; *m* 1952, Elizabeth Anne Saul; one *s* two *d*. *Educ:* Harrow; Trinity Coll., Oxford (MA). President of the Union, Oxford, 1944. Instructor-Lieut, Royal Navy, 1944–46. Lecturer, then Senior Lecturer in History and English, Royal Naval Coll., Greenwich, 1946–53. Commonwealth Fund Fellow in United States, 1953–55. Joined BBC in 1955 as a Talks Producer (Radio); became a Television Talks Producer, 1957, and then Chief Assistant, Current Affairs, TV talks, 1959–63; Head of Religious Broadcasting, BBC, 1963–66; Secretary to the BBC, 1967–68; Dir, Public Affairs, BBC, 1969–77; Special Adviser (Broadcasting Research), BBC, 1977–80. Chm., Charities Effectiveness Review Trust, 1987–. *Recreations:* cricket, walking, golf. *Address:* 25 South Terrace, Thurloe Square, SW7 2TB. *T:* 071–584 7904. *Clubs:* MCC, National Liberal; Royal Fowey Yacht.

See also Baron Rochester.

LAMB, Sir Larry, Kt 1980; Editor, Daily Express, 1983–86; Chairman, Larry Lamb Associates, since 1986; *b* Fitzwilliam, Yorks, 15 July 1929; *m* Joan Mary Denise Grogan; two *s* one *d*. *Educ:* Rastrick Grammar Sch. Worked as journalist on Brighouse Echo, Shields Gazette, Newcastle Journal, London Evening Standard; Sub-Editor, Daily Mirror; Editor: (Manchester) Daily Mail, 1968–69; The Sun, 1969–72, 1975–81; Dir, 1970–81, Editorial Dir, 1971–81, News International Ltd; Dep. Chm., News Group, 1979–81; Dir, The News Corporation (Australia) Ltd, 1980–81; Dep. Chm. and Editor-in-Chief, Western Mail Ltd, Perth, Australia, 1981–82; Editor-in-Chief, The Australian, May 1982–Feb. 1983. *Publication:* Sunrise, 1989. *Recreations:* fell-walking, cricket, fishing. *Address:* Bracken Cottage, Bratton Fleming, N Devon EX31 4TG. *Club:* Royal Automobile.

LAMB, Sir Lionel (Henry), KCMG 1953 (CMG 1948); OBE 1944; HM Diplomatic Service, retired; *b* 9 July 1900; *s* of late Sir Harry Lamb, GBE, KCMG; *m* 1927, Jean Fawcett (*née* MacDonald); one *s*. *Educ:* Winchester; Queen's Coll., Oxford. Appointed HM Consular Service in China, Dec. 1921; Consul (Gr. II), 1935; served Shanghai, 1935–37, Peking, 1937–40; Consul (Gr. I), 1938; Superintending Consul and Assistant Chinese Secretary, Shanghai, 1940; transferred to St Paul-Minneapolis, 1943; Chinese Counsellor, HM Embassy, Chungking, 1945; HM Minister, Nanking, 1947–49; Chargé d'Affaires, Peking, China, 1951–53; Ambassador to Switzerland, 1953–58, retired. *Address:* Roxford Barn, Hertingfordbury, Herts SG14 2LF.

LAMB, Captain William John, CVO 1947; OBE 1944; RN retired; *b* 26 Dec. 1906; *s* of late Sir Richard Amphlett Lamb, KCSI, CIE, ICS, and Kathleen Maud Barry; *m* 1948, Bridget, *widow* of Lieut-Commander G. S. Salt, RN; two *d*. *Educ:* St Anthony's, Eastbourne; RNC Osborne and Dartmouth. Commander, 1941; Staff of C-in-C Mediterranean Fleet, 1940–42; Staff of C-in-C, Eastern Fleet, 1942–44; Executive Officer, HMS Vanguard, 1945–47; Deputy Director of Naval Ordnance, 1948–50; Comd HMS Widemouth Bay and Captain (D) 4th Training Flotilla, Rosyth, 1951–52; Commanding Admiralty Signal and Radar Establishment, 1952–54; Commanding HMS Cumberland, 1955–56. Hon. Life Member: BIM, 1974; RNSA, 1985. *Recreation:* sailing. *Clubs:* Naval and Military; Royal Cruising.

LAMB, Prof. Willis E(ugene), Jr; Professor of Physics and Optical Sciences, University of Arizona, since 1974; *b* Los Angeles, California, USA, 12 July 1913; *s* of Willis Eugene Lamb and Marie Helen Metcalf; *m* Ursula Schaefer. *Educ:* Los Angeles High Sch.; University of California (BS, PhD). Columbia Univ.: Instructor in Physics, 1938–43, Associate, 1943–45, Assistant Professor, 1945–47, Associate Professor, 1947–48, Professor of Physics, 1948–52; Professor of Physics, Stanford Univ., California, 1951–56; Wykeham Prof. of Physics and Fellow of New Coll., University of Oxford, 1956–62; Yale University: Ford Prof. of Physics, 1962–72; Gibbs Prof. of Physics, 1972–74. Morris Loeb Lectr, Harvard Univ., 1953–54; Lectr, University of Colorado, Summer, 1959; Shrum Lectr, Simon Fraser Univ., 1972; Visiting Professor, Tata Institute of Fundamental Research, Bombay, 1960; Guggenheim Fellow, 1960–61; Visiting Professor, Columbia Univ., 1961; Fulbright Lecturer, University of Grenoble, Summer, 1964. MNAS, 1954. Hon. DSc: Pennsylvania, 1954; Gustavus Adolphus Coll., 1975; Columbia, 1990; MA (by decree), Oxford, 1956; Hon. MA Yale, 1961; Hon. LHD Yeshiva, 1965; Hon. Fellow: Institute of Physics and Physical Society, 1962; RSE, 1981; Res. Corp Award, 1954; Rumford Medal, American Academy of Arts and Sciences, 1953; (jointly) Nobel Prize in Physics, 1955; Guthrie Award, The Physical Society, 1958; Yeshiva University Award, 1962. *Publications:* (with M. Sargent and M. O. Scully) Laser Physics, 1974; contributions to The Physical Review, Physica, Science, Journal of Applied Physics, etc. *Address:* Optical Sciences Center, University of Arizona, Tucson, Arizona 85721, USA.

LAMBART, family name of **Earl of Cavan.**

LAMBERT, family name of **Viscount Lambert.**

LAMBERT, 3rd Viscount *cr* 1945, of South Molton; **Michael John Lambert;** *b* 29 Sept. 1912; *s* of 1st Viscount Lambert, PC and Barbara (*d* 1963), *d* of George Stavers; *S* brother, 1989; *m* 1939, Florence Dolores, *d* of Nicholas Lechmere Cunningham Macaskie, QC; three *d*. *Educ:* Harrow; New College, Oxford (MA). *Heir:* none. *Address:* Casanuova di Barontoli, 53010 S Rocco a Pilli, Siena, Italy.

See also Hon. Margaret Lambert.

LAMBERT, Sir Anthony (Edward), KCMG 1964 (CMG 1955); HM Diplomatic Service, retired; *b* 7 March 1911; *o s* of late R. E. Lambert, Pensbury House, Shaftesbury, Dorset; *m* 1948, Ruth Mary, *d* of late Sir Arthur Fleming, CBE; two *d*. *Educ:* Harrow; Balliol Coll., Oxford (scholar). Entered HM Foreign (subseq. Diplomatic) Service, 1934, and served in: Brussels, 1937; Ankara, 1940; Beirut and Damascus, 1942; Brussels, 1944; Stockholm, 1949; Athens, 1952; HM Minister to Bulgaria, 1958–60; HM Ambassador to: Tunisia, 1960–63; Finland, 1963–66; Portugal, 1966–70. *Club:* Brooks's.

LAMBERT, David Arthur Charles; General President, National Union of Knitwear, Footwear and Apparel Trades, since 1991 (General Secretary, 1975–82, General President, 1982–90, National Union of Hosiery and Knitwear Workers); Vice President, International Textile, Garment and Leather Workers' Federation, since 1984; *b* 2 Sept. 1933; *m*; two *s* one *d*. *Educ:* Hitchin Boys' Grammar Sch., Herts. Employed as production worker for major hosiery manufr; active as lay official within NUHKW; full-time official, NUHKW, 1964–90. Member: Employment Appeal Tribunal, 1978–; TUC Gen. Council, 1984–; CRE, 1987–. *Address:* (office) The Grange, 108 Northampton Road, Earls Barton, Northampton NN6 0JH.

LAMBERT, Sir Edward (Thomas), KBE 1958 (CBE 1953); CVO 1957; retired from Foreign Service, 1960; *b* 19 June 1901; *s* of late Brig. and Mrs T. S. Lambert; *m* 1936, Rhona Patricia Gilmore, *d* of late H. St G. Gilmore and Mrs J. H. Molyneux; one *s* one *d*. *Educ:* Charterhouse and Trinity Coll., Cambridge. Member of HM Diplomatic (formerly Foreign) Service. Entered Far Eastern Consular Service, 1926; served at Bangkok, Batavia, Medan, Curaçao, and The Hague. Consul-General, Geneva, 1949–53, Paris, 1953–59. Commandeur, Légion d'Honneur, 1957. *Recreations:* reading and travel. *Address:* Crag House, Crabbe Street, Aldeburgh, Suffolk. *T:* Aldeburgh (0728) 452296.

LAMBERT, Eric Thomas Drummond, CMG 1969; OBE 1946; KPM 1943; retd, 1968; *b* 3 Nov. 1909; *s* of late Septimus Drummond Lambert. *Educ:* Royal Sch., Dungannon; Trinity Coll., Dublin, 1928–29. Indian (Imperial) Police, 1929–47: Political Officer for Brahmaputra-Chindwin Survey, 1935–36, and Tirap Frontier Tract, 1942; District Comr, Naga Hills, 1938. Commnd General, Chinese Armed Forces, to find and evacuate Chinese Vth Army from Burma to Assam, India, June-Aug. 1942; Chief Civil Liaison Officer XIVth Army, 1944; FCO, 1947–68, with service in SE Asia, W Africa, S America, Nepal, Afghanistan. Pres., Republic of Ireland Br., Burma Star Assoc. Trustee, Nat. Library of Ireland, retired 1991. Corresp. Mem., Acad. of History, Venezuela. Chinese Armed Forces Distinguished Service, 1st Order, 1st class, 1942; Cruz Militar, Venezuela, 1983. *Publications:* Assam (jointly with Alban Ali), 1943; Carabobo 1821, 1974; Voluntarios Britanicos y Irlandeses en la Gesta Bolivariana, 1982; articles in jls of RGS and Royal Siam Soc.; Man in India; The Irish Sword. *Recreations:* historical research, lecturing a bit, golf just done with. *Address:* Drumkeen, Glenamuck Road, Dublin 18. *T:* 955887. *Club:* Stephen's Green (Dublin).

LAMBERT, Harold George; *b* 8 April 1910; *s* of late Rev. David Lambert; *m* 1934, Winifred Marthe, *d* of late Rev. H. E. Anderson, Farnham, Surrey; two *s*. *Educ:* King Edward's Sch., Birmingham; Corpus Christi Coll., Cambridge (MA); Imperial College of Science, London. Entered Ministry of Agriculture and Fisheries, 1933; Private Secretary to Parliamentary Secretary, 1938–39; Sec., Agricultural Machinery Develt Bd, 1942–45; Assistant Secretary, 1948; Under-Sec., MAFF, 1964–70, retired. Mem., panel of indep. inspectors for local enquiries, DoE and DoT, 1971–80. *Recreations:* music, art, travel. *Address:* 74 Chichester Drive West, Saltdean, Brighton.

LAMBERT, Henry Uvedale Antrobus; Chairman: Sun Alliance and London Insurance Group, since 1985 (Vice-Chairman, 1978–83; Deputy Chairman, 1983–85); Agricultural Mortgage Corporation PLC, since 1985 (Deputy Chairman, 1977–85); *b* 9 Oct. 1925; *o s* of late Roger Uvedale Lambert and Muriel, *d* of Sir Reginald Antrobus, KCMG, CB; *m* 1951, Diana, *y d* of Captain H. E. Dumbell, Royal Fusiliers; two *s* one *d*. *Educ:* Winchester College (Scholar); New College, Oxford (Exhibitioner; MA). Served War of 1939–45, Royal Navy, in HM Ships Stockham and St Austell Bay in Western Approaches and Mediterranean, subseq. RNR; Lt-Comdr (retired). Entered Barclays Bank 1948; a Local Dir at Lombard Street, 1957, Southampton, 1959, Birmingham, 1969; Vice-Chm., Barclays Bank UK Ltd, 1972; Chm., Barclays Bank Internat., 1979–83; Dep. Chm., 1979–85, Dir, 1966–91, Barclays Bank PLC. Dir, British Airways, 1985–89. Trustee: Imperial War Graves Endowment Fund, 1987–; Nat. Maritime Mus., 1990–. Vice-Pres., Navy Records Soc., 1985–89 (Treas., 1974–85). Fellow, Winchester Coll., 1979–91. *Recreations:* fishing, gardening, golf, naval history. *Address:* c/o Agricultural Mortgage Corporation PLC, Royal Bank of Canada Centre, 71 Queen Victoria Street, EC4V 4AB. *Clubs:* Brooks's, MCC.

LAMBERT, Jean Denise; Green Party (UK) representative to Green Group in European Parliament, since 1989; *b* 1 June 1950; *d* of Frederick John and Margaret Archer; *m* 1977, Stephen Lambert; one *s* one *d*. *Educ:* Palmers Grammar Sch. for Girls, Grays, Essex; University Coll., Cardiff (BA Modern Langs); St Paul's Coll., Cheltenham (PGCE). ADB(Ed). Secondary sch. teacher, Waltham Forest, 1972–89 (exmnr in spoken and written English, 1983–88). Green Party: joined 1977 (then Ecology Party); London Area Co-ordinator, 1977–81; Co-Chm. Council, 1982–85, 1986–87; Rep. to European Green Parties, 1985–86, 1988–89; Green Party Speaker, 1988–. Contested elections: GLC, 1981; local Council, 1986; European Parlt, 1984, 1989 (London NE). Founder Member: Ecology Building Soc., 1981 (Bd, 1981–84; Chm., 1982–83; now Patron); Play for Life, 1984; Council Mem., Charter 88, 1990. Radio and TV broadcaster. *Publications:* (contrib.) Into the 21st Century, 1988; articles to magazines. *Recreations:* reading (esp. detective fiction), cooking, dance. *Address:* 3 Howard Road, E17 4SH. *T:* (home) 081–520 0676; (office) 081–673 0045.

LAMBERT, Sir John (Henry), KCVO 1980; CMG 1975; HM Diplomatic Service, retired; Director, Heritage of London Trust, since 1981; Chairman, Channel Tunnel Investments plc, since 1986; *b* 8 Jan. 1921; *s* of Col R. S. Lambert, MC, and Mrs H. J. F.

Mills; *m* 1950, Jennifer Ann (*née* Urquhart); one *s* two *d*. *Educ:* Eton Coll.; Sorbonne; Trinity Coll., Cambridge. Grenadier Guards, 1940–45 (Captain). Appointed 3rd Secretary, HM Embassy, The Hague, 1945; Member of HM Foreign Service, 1947; FO, 1948; 2nd Secretary, Damascus, 1951; 1st Secretary, 1953; FO, 1954; Dep. to UK Representative on International Commn for Saar Referendum, 1955; Belgrade, 1956; Head of Chancery, Manila, 1958; UK Delegation to Disarmament Conference, Geneva, 1962; FO, 1963; Counsellor, Head of Chancery, Stockholm, 1964–67; Head of UN (Political) Dept, FCO, 1967–70; Commercial Counsellor and Consul-Gen. Vienna, 1971–74; Minister and Dep. Comdt, Berlin, 1974–77; Ambassador to Tunisia, 1977–81. *Recreations:* the arts, music, tennis, golf. *Address:* 103 Rivermead Court, SW6 3SB. *T:* 071–731 5007. *Clubs:* MCC; Hurlingham, Royal St George's Golf.

LAMBERT, John Sinclair; Director of Operations (North and West), Department of Employment, since 1990; *b* 8 April 1948; *s* of late Norman Sinclair Lambert and of Doris May Lambert; *m* 1971, Ann Dowzell; two *s*. *Educ:* Denstone Coll.; Selwyn Coll., Cambridge (MA). Department of Employment, 1970–: Private Sec. to Perm. Sec., 1973–74; on secondment to Marconi Space and Defence Systems, 1977–78; Dep. Chief Conciliation Officer, ACAS, 1982–83; Head of European Communities Branch, 1983–85; Dir of Field Ops, MSC, 1987–90. *Recreations:* birdwatching, music, reading, gardening. *Address:* c/o Department of Employment, Moorfoot, Sheffield S1 4PQ.

LAMBERT, Hon. Margaret (Barbara), CMG 1965; PhD; British Editor-in-Chief, German Foreign Office Documents, 1951–83; *b* 7 Nov. 1906; *yr d* of 1st Viscount Lambert, PC. *Educ:* Lady Margaret Hall, Oxford; London School of Economics. BA 1930, PhD 1936. Served during War of 1939–45 in European Service of BBC. Assistant Editor British Documents on Foreign Policy, 1946–50; Lecturer in Modern History, University College of the South-West, 1950–51; Lecturer in Modern European History, St Andrews University, 1956–60. *Publications:* The Saar, 1934; When Victoria began to Reign, 1937; (with Enid Marx) English Popular and Traditional Art, 1946, and English Popular Art, 1952. *Address:* 39 Thornhill Road, Barnsbury Square, N1. *T:* 071–607 2286; 1 St Germans, Exeter.

LAMBERT, Olaf Francis, CBE 1984; DL; Chairman, British Road Federation, since 1987 (Member, Executive Committee, since 1977); Vice President, The Automobile Association, since 1987; *b* 13 Jan. 1925; *s* of late Walter Lambert and Edith (*née* Gladstone); *m* 1950, Lucy, *d* of late John Adshead, Macclesfield, and Helen Seymour (*née* Ridgway); two *s* two *d*. *Educ:* Caterham Sch.; RMA, Sandhurst (war time). Commnd Royal Tank Regt, 1944; retd with rank of Major, 1959. Joined Automobile Assoc., 1959; Man. Dir, 1973–77; Dir-Gen., 1977–87. Director: Drive Publications Ltd, 1974–87; AA Insurance Services Ltd, 1974–87; AA Travel Services Ltd, 1977–87; AA Pensions Trustees Ltd, 1977–87; AA Executive Pensions Trustees Ltd, 1977–87; Mercantile Credit Co. Ltd, 1980–85; AA Re-insurance Ltd, 1982–87; AA Underwriting Services Ltd, 1982–87; Automobile Association Ltd, 1982–87; Fanum Ltd, 1982–87; AA Pension Investment Trustees Ltd, 1984–87; AA Developments Ltd, 1984–87; AA Financial Services Ltd, 1985–87. Member: Cttee of Management, AA Friendly Soc., 1982– (Chm., 1986–); AA Exec. Cttee, 1982–87; Adv. Bd, DVLA; Council, Inst. of Advanced Motorists, 1968–89; Management Cttee, Alliance Internationale de Tourisme, 1976–87 (Pres., 1983–86); Hampshire Cttee, Army Benevolent Fund, 1980–; Winchester Cathedral Trust Council, 1984–; BHS Develt Council, 1987–90. FIMI 1984 (MIMI 1977); CBIM 1980; FRSA 1984. Freeman, City of London, 1978; Liveryman, Worshipful Co. of Coachmakers and Coach Harness Makers, 1978. DL Hants, 1989. Hon. Col, RMP(TA), 1984–. Col, Commonwealth of Kentucky, 1979. *Recreations:* hunting, skiing, walking, travel, music. *Club:* Army and Navy.

LAMBERT, Patricia, OBE 1981; Public Interest Director, Life Assurance and Unit Trust Regulatory Organisation, since 1986; *b* 16 March 1926; *d* of Frederick and Elsie Burrows; *m* 1949, George Richard Lambert (marr. diss. 1983); one *s* one *d*. *Educ:* Malet Lambert High Sch., Hull; West Bridgford Grammar Sch., Nottingham; Nottingham and Dist Technical Coll. Served Royal Signals, Germany, 1944–46; medical technician, 1946–49. British Standards Institution: Member: Consumer Policy Cttee (formerly Consumer Standards Adv. Cttee), 1972–; BSI Bd, 1980–86; Quality Assce Bd, 1986–; Chm., Consumer Standards Adv. Council, 1980–86; chm. of several technical cttees. Member: National Consumer Council, 1978–82; National House Bldg Council, 1980–; Consumer Affairs, Panel, Unit Trust Assoc., 1981–; Direct Mail Services Standards Bd, 1983–. Dir and Vice-Chm., Invest in Britain (formerly Think British Campaign), 1983–. Local Govt Councillor, 1959–78. *Recreations:* driving (Mem., Inst. of Advanced Motorists), music, theatre, glass engraving. *Address:* 42 Tollerton Lane, Tollerton, Nottingham NG12 4FQ.

LAMBERT, Sir Peter John Biddulph, 10th Bt *cr* 1711, of London; archaeological consultant; *b* 5 April 1952; *s* of John Hugh Lambert (*d* 1977) (*g s* of 5th Bt) and of Edith May, *d* of late James Bance; *S* kinsman, Sir Greville Foley Lambert, 9th Bt, 1988. *Educ:* Upper Canada Coll., Toronto; Trent Univ. (BSc 1975); Univ. of Manitoba (MA 1980). *Heir: uncle* Robert William Lambert [*b* 6 June 1911; *m* 1948, Margaret Daphne Harvey].

LAMBERT, Richard Peter; Editor, Financial Times, since 1991; *b* 23 Sept. 1944; *s* of Peter and Mary Lambert; *m* 1973, Harriet Murray-Browne; one *s* one *d*. *Educ:* Fettes Coll.; Balliol Coll., Oxford (BA). Staff of Financial Times, 1966–; Lex Column, 1972; Financial Editor, 1978; New York Correspondent, 1982; Dep. Editor, 1983. *Address:* c/o Financial Times, Number One, Southwark Bridge, SE1 9HL.

LAMBERT, Prof. Thomas Howard; Professor since 1967, and Kennedy Professor since 1983, Department of Mechanical Engineering, University College London; *b* 28 Feb. 1926; *s* of Henry Thomas Lambert and Kate Lambert. *Educ:* Emanuel Sch.; Univ. of London (BSc (Eng), PhD). FIMechE; FRINA. D. Napier & Sons: Graduate Apprentice, 1946–48; Develt Engr, 1948–51; University College London: Lectr, 1951–63; Sen. Lectr, 1963–65; Reader, 1965–67; Head of Mech. Engrg Dept, 1977–89; Hon. Fellow, 1991. Hon. RCNC. *Publications:* numerous articles in learned jls, principally in Stress Analysis, Medical Engrg and Automatic Control. *Recreations:* gardening, sailing, practical engineering. *Address:* Department of Mechanical Engineering, University College London, Gower Street, WC1. *T:* 071–387 7050.

LAMBERT, Verity Ann; independent film and television producer; Director, Cinema Verity Ltd, since 1985; *b* 27 Nov.; *d* of Stanley Joseph Lambert and Ella Corona Goldburg. *Educ:* Roedean; La Sorbonne, Paris. Joined BBC Television as drama producer, 1963; first producer of Dr Who; also produced: The Newcomers, Somerset Maugham Short Stories (BAFTA Award, 1969), Adam Adamant, Detective; joined LWT as drama producer, 1970: produced Budgie and Between the Wars; returned to BBC, 1973: produced and co-created Shoulder to Shoulder; joined Thames Television as Controller of Drama Dept, 1974 (Dir of Drama, 1981–82; Dir, Thames Television, 1982–85): resp. for: Rock Follies, Rooms, Rumpole of the Bailey, Edward and Mrs Simpson, The Naked Civil Servant (many awards), Last Summer, The Case of Cruelty to Prawns, No Mama No; made creatively resp. for Euston Films Ltd, 1976 (Chief Executive, 1979–82): developed series which included Out and Danger UXB; resp. for: Minder (three series), Quatermass, Fox, The Flame Trees of Thika, Reilly: ace of spies; single films include: Charlie Muffin, Stainless Steel and the Star Spies, The Sailor's Return, The Knowledge; Dir of Prodn, THORN EMI Screen Entertainment, 1982–85: resp. for: Morons from Outer Space, Dreamchild, Restless Natives, Link, Clockwise. Executive Producer: American Roulette, 1987; May to December (series, 1989–); Producer: A Cry in the Dark, 1988; Coasting; GBH; The Boys from the Bush; Sleepers. McTaggart Lect., Edinburgh TV Fest., 1990. Governor: BFI, 1981–86 (Chairperson, Prodn Bd, 1981–82); Nat. Film and Television Sch., 1984–. Hon. LLD Strathclyde, 1988. Veuve-Clicquot Businesswoman of 1982; Woman's Own Woman of Achievement, 1983. *Recreations:* reading, eating. *Address:* (office) The Mill House, Millers Way, 1A Shepherds Bush Road, W6 7NA.

LAMBETH, Archdeacon of; *see* Bird, Ven. C. R. B.

LAMBIE, David; MP (Lab) Cunninghame South, since 1983 (Ayrshire Central, 1970–83); *b* 13 July 1925; *m* 1954, Netta May Merrie; one *s* four *d*. *Educ:* Kyleshill Primary Sch.; Ardrossan Academy; Glasgow University; Geneva University. BSc, DipEd. Teacher, Glasgow Corp., 1950–70. Chm., Glasgow Local Assoc., Educnl Inst. for Scotland, 1958–59; Chm., Scottish Labour Party, 1964; Chief Negotiator on behalf of Scottish Teachers in STSC, 1969–70; Sec., Westminster Branch, Educnl Inst. for Scotland, 1985–88, 1991–. Chm., Select Cttee on Scottish Affairs, 1981–87; Sec., Parly All-Party Cttee for Energy Studies, 1980–; Chm., PLP Aviation Cttee, 1990–. Member: Council of Europe, 1987–; WEU, 1987–. FEIS 1970. *Recreation:* watching football. *Address:* 11 Ivanhoe Drive, Saltcoats, Ayrshire KA21 6LS. *T:* Saltcoats (0294) 64843; (constituency office) 17 Townhead, Irvine, Ayrshire. *T:* Irvine (0294) 76844. *Club:* Cunninghame North Constituency Labour Social (Saltcoats).

LAMBIE-NAIRN, Martin John, RDI 1987; FCSD; Partner, Lambie-Nairn and Co. Ltd, Design Consultants (formerly Robinson Lambie-Nairn), since 1976; *b* 5 Aug. 1945; *s* of Stephen John and Joan Lois Lambie-Nairn; *m* 1970, Cordelia Margot Summers; one *s* two *d*. *Educ:* King Ethelbert Sch., Birchington, Kent; Canterbury Coll. of Art. NDD. Asst Designer, Graphic Design Dept, BBC, 1965; Designer, Rediffusion, 1966; freelance graphic designer, 1967; Art Dir, Conran Associates, 1968; Dep. to Sen. Designer, ITN, overseeing changeover from black and white to colour tv, 1968; Designer, LWT, working on light entertainment, drama and current affairs progs, 1970; formed Robinson Lambie-Nairn Ltd, design consultancy producing film and tv graphics, corporate identity, packaging and financial lit., 1976; renamed Lambie-Nairn and Co., 1990; work includes Channel 4 TV corporate identity, 1982, Anglia TV corporate identity, 1988, TFI (France) corporate identity, 1989, BSB 5 Channel identity, 1990, BBC1 and BBC2 channel identities, 1991, and design and prodn of tv commercials. Mem. Cttee, Design and Art Dirs Assoc. 1985– (Pres., 1990–91). Chm., Graphics Jury, BBC Design Awards, 1987. FCSD (FSIAD 1982). *Recreations:* opera, family, playing bagpipes. *Address:* Pirbright Manor Farmhouse, Hogscross Lane, Chipstead, Surrey.

LAMBO, Prof. Thomas Adeoye, NNOM 1979; CON 1979; OBE 1962; MD, DPM; FRCP; JP; Deputy Director-General, World Health Organization, 1973–88 (Assistant Director-General, 1971–73); Executive Director, Lambo Foundation; *b* 29 March 1923; *s* of Chief D. B. Lambo, The Otunbade of Igbore, Abeokuta, and Madam F. B. Lambo, The Iyalode of Egba Christians; *m* 1945, Dinah Violet Adams; three *s*. *Educ:* Baptist Boys' High Sch., Abeokuta; Univs of Birmingham and London. From 1949, served as House Surg. and House Phys., Birmingham, England; Med. Officer, Lagos, Zaria and Gusau; Specialist, Western Region Min. of Health, 1957–60; Consultant Psychiatrist, UCH Ibadan, 1956–63; Sen. Specialist, Western Region Min. of Health, Neuro-Psychiatric Centre, 1960–63; Prof. of Psychiatry and Head of Dept of Psychiatry and Neurology, Univ. of Ibadan, 1963–71; Dean, Medical Faculty, Univ. of Ibadan, 1966–68; Vice-Chancellor, Univ. of Ibadan, 1968–71. Member: Scientific Council for Africa (Chm., 1965–70); Expert Adv. Panel on Mental Health, WHO, 1959–71; UN Perm. Adv. Cttee on Prevention of Crime and the Treatment of Offenders (Chm. 1968–71); Exec. Cttee, World Fedn for Mental Health, 1964–; Scientific Adv. Panel, Ciba Foundn, 1966–; WHO Adv. Cttee on Med. Research, 1970–71; Scientific Cttee on Advanced Study in Developmental Sciences, 1967–; Nigeria Medical Council, 1969–; Scientific Council of the World Future Studies Fedn, 1975–; World Soc. for Ekistics (Pres., 1979–81); Adv. Bd, Earthscan, 1975–; Bd of Dirs, Internat. Inst. for Envmt and Develt; Vice-Chm., UN Adv. Cttee on Application of Science and Technology to Development, 1970–71; Co-Chm., Internat. Soc. for Study of Human Development, 1968–; Chairman: West African Examinations Council, 1969–71, co-ordinating Bd, African Chairs of Technology in Food Processing, Biotechnologies and Nutrition and Health, 1986–, etc. Founding Member: Third World Acad. of Scis, 1986–; African Acad. of Scis, 1986–. Member: Pontifical Acad. of Sciences, 1974– (first African Life Mem., 1982); Internat. Inst. for World Resources, Washington. Hon. Fellow: RCPsych, 1970 (Founding Fellow); Royal Australian and NZ Coll. of Psychiatrists. JP Western State, 1968. Hon. LLD: Kent State, Ohio, 1969; Birmingham 1971; Pennsylvania, Philadelphia; Hon. DSc: Ahmadu Bello, Nigeria; Long Island, NY, 1975; McGill, Canada, 1978; Jos, Nigeria, 1979; Nigeria, Nsukka, 1979; Hacettepe, Ankara, 1980; Hahnemann, Philadelphia, 1984; Dr *hc*: Benin, 1973; Aix-Marseille, France, 1974; Louvain, Belgium, 1976. Haile Selassie African Res. Award, 1970. *Publications:* (jtly) Psychiatric Disorders Among the Yorubas, 1963; monographs, and contribs to medical and other scientific jls. *Recreation:* tennis. *Address:* Lambo Foundation, 24A Isaac John Street, GRA Ikeja, PO Box 702, Ikeja, Lagos, Nigeria. *T:* Lagos 961102, 964351.

LAMBOLL, Alan Seymour, JP; Underwriting Member of Lloyd's; *b* 12 Oct. 1923; *s* of late Frederick Seymour and Charlotte Emily Lamboll. *Educ:* Ascham St Vincents, Eastbourne (preparatory sch.); Marlborough Coll. BBC Engineering Staff, 1941–43. Served War: Royal Signals, East Africa Command (Captain), 1943–47. Dir, family firm of wine merchants, City of London, Slack & Lamboll, Ltd, 1947–54. Lloyd's Insurance Broker, Alexr Howden, Stewart Smith (Home), 1954–57; Past Director: Anglo-Portuguese Agencies Ltd (Insurance and Reinsurance Agents), 1957–62; Aga Dictating Machine Co. Ltd, 1962–70; Roger Grayson Ltd, Wine Merchants, 1971–74; London Investment Trust Ltd; Ellinger Heath Western (Underwriting Agencies) Ltd, 1974–82; Consultant to Rank Orgn, 1970–72. Mem., Iken Parish Council, 1987–90. JP Inner London, 1965; Chm., S Westminster PSD, 1978–80; Dep. Chm., City of London Commn, 1979–82, Supplemental List, 1982. Mem. Council: City and Guilds of London Inst., 1965–79; Toynbee Hall, 1958–81 (Hon. Sec., 1968–79); Drama Centre London Ltd, 1974–82 (Chm. Council, 1975–82). Dir, City Arts Trust Ltd, 1962–77; Member: Royal Theatrical Fund (formerly Royal Gen. Theatrical Fund Assoc.), 1963– (Vice-Chm., 1967–91; Vice-Pres., 1991–); LSO Adv. Council, 1972–74; Cttee, Industrial Sponsors, 1974–84; Grand Master's Cttee, 1974–83; Governor: Mermaid Theatre Trust, 1966–77; Christ's Hospital (Donation Governor, 1971–). Secretary: Ross McWhirter Foundation, 1980–82; Dicey Trust, 1980–82. Hon. Assistant: Worshipful Co. of Distillers, 1991– (Master, 1972–73, Tercentenary Year); Worshipful Co. of Parish Clerks (Master, 1975–76); Freedom of City of London, 1947; Common Council, Ward of Langbourn, 1949–70; Alderman, Ward of Castle Baynard, 1970–78; Sheriff, City of London, 1976–77 (Silver Jubilee Year). St John Council for London, 1971–82; CStJ 1973. FRSA 1970. *Recreations:* writing, swimming, Tibetan spaniels. *Address:* Quinta Essência, Apartado 25, Estói, 8000 Faro, Algarve, Portugal. *T:* 89 97049. *Clubs:* Athenæum, Garrick, Pratt's.

LAMBTON, family name of **Earldom of Durham.**

LAMBTON, Viscount; Antony Claud Frederick Lambton; *b* 10 July 1922; *s* of 5th Earl of Durham (*d* 1970) and Diana (*d* 1924), *o d* of Granville Farquhar; disclaimed peerages for life, 1970 but allowed by Mr Speaker Lloyd to continue to sit in Parliament using courtesy title; *m* 1942, Belinda, *d* of Major D. H. Blew-Jones, Westward Ho!, North Devonshire; one *s* five *d*. MP (C) Berwick upon Tweed Div. of Northumberland, 1951–73; Parly Under-Sec. of State, MoD, 1970–May 1973; PPS to the Foreign Secretary, 1955–57. *Publications:* Snow and Other Stories, 1983; Elizabeth and Alexandra, 1985; The Abbey in the Wood, 1986; The Mountbattens, 1989; Pig and Other Stories, 1990. *Heir to disclaimed peerages: s* Hon. Edward Richard Lambton (Baron Durham) [*b* 19 Oct. 1961; *m* 1983, Christabel, *y d* of late Rory McEwen and of Mrs McEwen, Bardrochat; one *s*]. *Address:* Villa Cetinale, Sovicille, Siena, Italy; Biddick Hall, Chester-le-Street, Co. Durham.

See also Marquess of Abergavenny, Sir Edmund Fairfax-Lucy, Bt, Sir P. V. Naylor-Leyland, Bt.

LAMBTON, Prof. Ann Katharine Swynford, OBE 1942; FBA 1964; Professor of Persian, University of London, 1953–79, now Emeritus; *b* 8 Feb. 1912; *d* of late Hon. George Lambton. PhD London, 1939; DLit London, 1953. Press Attaché, British Embassy (formerly Legation), Tehran, 1939–45; Senior Lecturer in Persian, School of Oriental and African Studies, 1945–48; Reader in Persian, University of London, 1948–53. Hon. Fellow: New Hall, Cambridge, 1973; SOAS, Univ. of London, 1983. Hon. DLit Durham, 1971; Hon. LittD Cambridge, 1973. Reader Emeritus, dio. of Newcastle, 1988. *Publications:* Three Persian Dialects, 1938; Landlord and Peasant in Persia, 1953; Persian Grammar, 1953; Persian Vocabulary, 1964; The Persian Land Reform 1962–66, 1969; (ed, with others) The Cambridge History of Islam, vols 1–11, 1971; Theory and Practice in Medieval Persian Government, 1980; State and Government in Medieval Islam, 1981; Qajar Persia, 1987; Continuity and Change in Medieval Persia, 1988. *Address:* Gregory, Kirknewton, Wooler, Northumberland NE71 6XE.

LAMBURN, Patricia, (Mrs Donald Derrick), CBE 1985; Editorial Director, IPC Magazines Ltd, 1981–86; Director, IPC,1968–86; *er d* of Francis John Lamburn and Nell Winifred (*née* Kennedy); *m* 1949, Donald G. E. Douglas Derrick, DDS, LDSRCS, FRCD(Can.), FACD, FICD; one *s* one *d*. *Educ:* Queen's Gate Sch., S Kensington. Amalgamated Press, 1943–49; Curtis Publishing Co., USA, 1949–50; joined George Newnes Ltd, 1950; during ensuing yrs, edited, developed and was associated creatively with wide range of women's and teenage magazines; Dir, George Newnes Ltd, 1966–68; Gp Dir, Young Magazines Gp, 1968–71; Publishing Dir, Women's Magazines Gp, 1971–76, Asst Man. Dir (Editorial), 1976–81. Mem., Interim Licensing Authority for In Vitro Fertilisation and Embryology, 1986–91. Chm., Gen. Adv. Council, IBA, 1982–85 (Mem., 1980–82); Member: Health Educn Council, 1973–78; Information Cttee, British Nutrition Foundn, 1979–85; Periodical Publishing Trng Cttee, PPITB, 1980–82; Public Relations Cttee, RCP, 1981–88; Press Council, 1982–87; Exec. Cttee, BACUP Cancer Information Service, 1986–. Mem., Chelsea Crime Prevention Panel, 1990–. Editorial Cttee, Periodical Publishers' Assoc., 1975–87. *Address:* Chelsea, London.

LAMER, Rt. Hon. Antonio, PC (Can.) 1990; Chief Justice of Canada, since 1990; *b* 8 July 1933; *m* 1st, 1961, Suzanne Bonin; one *s*; 2nd, 1987, Danièle Tremblay; one step *s* one step *d*. *Educ;* Univ. of Montreal. Private practice, Cutler, Lamer, Bellemare & Associates; Prof., Faculty of Law, Univ. of Montreal; Judge, Superior Court and Queen's Bench, Province of Quebec, 1969; Chm., Law Reform Commn of Canada, 1976 (Vice-Chm., 1971); Justice, Quebec Court of Appeal, 1978; Justice, Supreme Court of Canada, 1980. CStJ. Order of Merit, Univ. of Montreal. *Address:* Supreme Court of Canada, Ottawa, Ontario K1A 0J1, Canada. *T:* 613–992–6940.

LAMERTON, Leonard Frederick, PhD, DSc, FInstP, FRCPath; Director, Institute of Cancer Research, London, 1977–80; Professor of Biophysics as Applied to Medicine, University of London, 1960–80; *b* 1 July 1915; *s* of Alfred Lamerton and Florence (*née* Mason); *m* 1965, Morag MacLeod. *Educ:* King Edward VI Sch., Southampton; University Coll., Southampton (PhD, DSc London). Staff member, Royal Cancer Hosp. and Inst. of Cancer Research, 1938–41 and 1946–80, Dean of the Inst., 1967–77; seconded to United Nations as a Scientific Sec. of First UN Conf. on Peaceful Uses of Atomic Energy, 1955. President: British Inst. of Radiology, 1957–58; Hosp. Physicists Assoc., 1961; Member: Bd of Governors, Royal Marsden Hosp., 1955–80; Bd of Governors, 1978–82, and Cttee of Management, 1978–82, Cardiothoracic Hosp. and Inst. Roentgen Award, 1950, Barclay Medal, 1961, British Inst. of Radiology. *Publications:* various papers on medical physics, radiation hazard, cell kinetics, experimental cancer therapy. *Recreations:* music, study of the development of Man. *Address:* 10 Burgh Mount, Banstead, Surrey SM7 1ER. *T:* Burgh Heath (0737) 353697.

LAMFORD, (Thomas) Gerald, OBE 1979; ASVU Representative, Cyprus, 1985–88; Commandant, Police Staff College, 1976–79; *b* Carmarthen, 3 April 1928; *s* of late Albert and Sarah Lamford; *m* 1952, Eira Hale; one *s* one *d*. *Educ:* Technical Coll., Swansea; London Univ. (LLB 1969); Police Coll. (Intermed. Comd Course, 1969; Sen. Comd Course, 1973). Radio Officer, Merchant Navy, 1945; Wireless Operator, RAF, 1946–48, Aden. Carmarthenshire Constab. (now Dyfed Powys Police), 1949; reached rank of Chief Inspector, CID, Crime Squad; Force Trng Officer, 1965–69; Supt, Haverfordwest, 1970; Chief Supt, Llanelli, 1971–74; Asst Chief Constable, Greater Manchester Police, 1974–79; Investigating Officer, FCO, 1981–84. Vis. Prof. of Police Science, John Jay Coll. of Criminal Justice, City Univ. of New York, 1972; sometime Vis. Lecturer: Southern Police Inst., Univ. of Louisville, Ky; N Eastern Univ., Boston; NY Univ. Sch. of Law; Rutgers Univ., NJ; Mercy Coll., Detroit. County Comr, St John Amb. Bde, Pembrokeshire, 1970; SBStJ. *Publications:* articles in Police Studies, Internat. Rev. of Police Devel̨t, Police Rev., Bramshill Jl, World Police. *Recreations:* photography, genealogy. *Address:* 11 Llwyn y Bryn, Ammanford, Dyfed. *Clubs:* Rotary (Pres., 1991–92), Probus (Ammanford).

LAMING, (William) Herbert, CBE 1985; Chief Inspector, Social Services Inspectorate, Department of Health, since 1991; *b* 19 July 1936; *s* of William Angus Laming and Lillian Laming (*née* Robson); *m* 1962, Aileen Margaret Pollard. *Educ:* Univ. of Durham (Applied Social Scis); Rainer House (Home Office Probation Trng, 1960–61); LSE (Mental Health Course, 1965–66). Notts Probation Service: Probation Officer, 1961–66; Sen. Probation Officer, 1966–68; Asst Chief Probation Officer, Nottingham City and Co. Probation Service, 1968–71; Dep. Dir, 1971–75, Dir, 1975–91, Social Services, Herts CC. Pres., Assoc. of Dirs Social Services, 1982–83. *Publications:* Lessons from America: the balance of services in social care, 1985; contribs to professional jls. *Address:* Department of Health, Richmond House, 79 Whitehall, SW1A 2NS. *T:* 071–210 5561.

LAMMIMAN, Surg. Rear Adm. David Askey, LVO 1978; QHS 1987; FFARCS; Medical Director General (Naval), since 1990; Deputy Surgeon General: Health Services, since 1990; Operations and Plans, since 1991; *b* 30 June 1932; *s* of Herbert Askey Lammiman and Lilian Elsie (*née* Park); *m* 1st, 1957, Sheila Mary Graham (marr. diss. 1984); three *s* one *d*; 2nd, 1984, Caroline Dale Brooks. *Educ:* Wyggeston Sch., Leicester; St Bartholomew's Hosp. (MB, BS 1957). DA 1962; DObstRCOG 1962; FFARCS 1969. Resident House Officer, Redhill County Hosp. and St Bartholomew's Hosp., 1957–58; joined RN, 1959; gen. service and hosp. appts at home and abroad; Clinical Asst, Southampton Gp of Hosps, Alder Hey Children's Hosp., Liverpool, and Radcliffe Infirmary, Oxford, 1966–69; served in: HMS Chaplet, 1959; HMS Eagle, 1967–68; HMY Britannia, 1976–78; Consultant Anaesthetist, RN Hospital: Malta, 1969–71; Haslar, 1971–73; Gibraltar, 1973–75; Plymouth, 1975–76; Haslar, 1978–82; Dir of Med. Personnel, MoD, 1982–84; Medical Officer i/c RN Hospital: Plymouth, 1984–86; Haslar, 1986–88; Surg. Rear Adm. (Support Med. Services), 1989–90. *Recreations:* fly fishing, golf, tennis. *Address:* c/o National Westminster Bank, St Thomas Square, Ryde, Isle of Wight PO33 2PJ. *Clubs:* Naval and Military; Royal Naval Sailing Association (Portsmouth).

LAMOND, James Alexander, JP; MP (Lab) Oldham Central and Royton, since 1983 (Oldham East, 1970–83); *b* Burrelton, Perthshire, 29 Nov. 1928; *s* of Alexander N. G. Lamond and Christina Lamond (*née* Craig); *m* 1954, June Rose Wellburn; three *d*. *Educ:* Burrelton Sch.; Coupar Angus Sch. Draughtsman. Mem., Aberdeen City Council, 1959–71; Lord Provost of Aberdeen, 1970–71; Lord Lieutenant of the County of the City of Aberdeen, 1970–71. Mem., MSF (formerly TASS), 1944– (Chm., No 1 Divisional Council of DATA, 1965–70); Pres., Aberdeen Trades Council, 1969. Mem., Chairmen's Panel, 1979–. Vice-Pres., World Peace Council. JP Aberdeen. *Recreations:* golf, travel, reading, thinking. *Address:* House of Commons, SW1A 0AA.

LAMONT, Donald Alexander; Ambassador to Uruguay, since 1991; *b* 13 Jan. 1947; *s* of Alexander Lamont and Alexa Lee Lamont (*née* Will); *m* 1981, Lynda Margaret Campbell; one *s* one *d*. *Educ:* Aberdeen Grammar Sch.; Aberdeen Univ. (MA Russian Studies). British Leyland Motor Corp., 1970; Second Sec., subseq. First Sec., FCO, 1974; First Sec., UNIDO/IAEA, Vienna, 1977; First Sec. (Commercial), Moscow, 1980; First Sec., FCO, 1982; Counsellor on secondment to IISS, 1988; Political Advr and Head of Chancery, British Mil. Govt, Berlin, 1988–91. *Address:* c/o Foreign and Commonwealth Office, SW1A 2AH. *Club:* Caledonian.

LAMONT, Rt. Hon. Norman Stewart Hughson, PC 1986; MP (C) Kingston-upon-Thames since May 1972; Chancellor of the Exchequer, since 1990; *b* Lerwick, Shetland, 8 May 1942; *s* of late Daniel Lamont and of Helen Irene; *m* 1971, Alice Rosemary, *d* of Lt-Col Peter White; one *s* one *d*. *Educ:* Loretto Sch. (scholar); Fitzwilliam Coll., Cambridge (BA). Chm., Cambridge Univ. Conservative Assoc., 1963; Pres., Cambridge Union, 1964. PA to Rt Hon. Duncan Sandys, MP, 1965; Conservative Research Dept, 1966–68; Merchant Banker, N. M. Rothschild & Sons, 1968–79. Contested (C) East Hull, Gen. Election, 1970. PPS to Norman St John-Stevas, MP, Minister for the Arts, 1974; an Opposition Spokesman on: Prices and Consumer Affairs, 1975–76; Industry, 1976–79; Parly Under Sec. of State, Dept of Energy, 1979–81; Minister of State, DTI (formerly DoI), 1981–85; Minister of State for Defence Procurement, 1985–86; Financial Sec. to HM Treasury, 1986–89; Chief Sec. to HM Treasury, 1989–90. Chairman: Coningsby Club, 1970–71; Bow Group, 1971–72. *Publications:* newspaper articles and Bow Group memoranda. *Recreations:* reading, ornithology. *Address:* House of Commons, SW1A 0AA. *Club:* Garrick.

LAMONTAGNE, Hon. (J.) Gilles, CD 1980; PC (Can.); Lieutenant-Governor of Quebec, since 1984; *b* 17 April 1919; *s* of Trefflé Lamontagne and Anna Kieffer; *m* 1949, Mary Katherine Schaefer; three *s* one *d*. *Educ:* Collège Jean-de-Bréboeuf, Montréal, Québec (BA). Served RCAF, 1941–45 (despatches, 1945). Businessman in Québec City, 1946–66. Alderman, Québec City, 1962–64, Mayor, 1965–77. MP (L) Langelier, 1977–84; Parly Sec. to Minister of Energy, Mines and Resources, 1977; Minister without Portfolio, Jan. 1978; Postmaster Gen., Feb. 1978; Actg Minister of Veterans Affairs, 1980–81; Minister of National Defence, 1980–83. Dir, Québec City Chamber of Commerce and Industry; Member: Econ. Council of Canada; Br. 260, Royal Canadian Legion. Hon. Col, Tactical Aviation Wing (Montreal), 1987. KStJ 1985. Hon. LLD Kingston Royal Mil. Coll., 1986; Hon. DAdmin St Jean Royal Mil. Coll., 1989. UN Medal 1987. Croix du Combattant de l'Europe. *Address:* (office) 1050 St-Augustin Street, Québec, PQ G1A 1A1, Canada; Government House, 1010 St Louis Road, Sillery, PQ G1S 1C7, Canada. *Clubs:* Cercle de la Garrison de Québec, Royal Québec Golf.

LAMPARD, Martin Robert; *b* 21 Feb. 1926; *s* of Austin Hugo Lampard and late Edith Gertrude Lampard (formerly White); *m* 1957, Felice MacLean; three *d*. *Educ:* Radley College, Oxford; Christ Church, Oxford (MA). Served RNVR. Admitted solicitor, 1952; joined Ashurst Morris Crisp & Co., 1954, Partner, 1957, Sen. Partner, 1974–86. Farming in East Anglia, Simmental beef herd. Dir, Allied Lyons plc, and other companies. *Address:* 507 Willoughby House, Barbican, EC2. *T:* 071–588 4048, (office) 071–247 7666; Theberton House, Theberton, near Leiston, Suffolk. *T:* Leiston (0728) 830510. *Clubs:* Royal Ocean Racing; Royal Yacht Squadron.

LAMPERT, Catherine Emily; Director, Whitechapel Art Gallery, since 1988; *b* 15 Oct. 1946; *d* of Emily F. Schubach and Chester G. Lampert; *m* 1971, Robert Keith Mason; one *d*. *Educ:* Brown Univ. (BA); Temple Univ. (MFA). UCL, 1966–67; Asst Curator, RI Sch. of Design, Mus. of Art, 1968–69; Studio Internat., 1971–72; Sen. Exhibn Organiser, Hayward Gall., 1973–88. *Publications:* Rodin: sculpture and drawings, 1986; numerous catalogue essays on Frank Auerbach, Barry Flanagan, Tony Cragg and other subjects of Twentieth Century art. *Address:* 92 Lenthall Road, E8 3JN. *T:* 071–249 7650.

LAMPL, Sir Frank (William), Kt 1990; Executive Director, Peninsular and Oriental Steam Navigation Company, since 1985; Chairman, Bovis Construction Group, since 1989; *b* 6 April 1926; adopted British nationality, 1974; *s* of Dr Otto Lampl and Olga (*née* Jelinek); *m* 1948, Blanka (*née* Kratochvílová); one *s*. *Educ:* Univ. of Brno, Czechoslovakia (Dip Eng, Faculty of Architecture and Engineering). FCIOB. Emigrated from Czechoslovakia to UK, 1968, after Russian invasion; Exec. Dir, Bovis Construction, 1974; Man. Dir, Bovis International, 1978; Dir, Bovis, 1979; Chm., Bovis Construction and Bovis International, 1985; Dep. Chm., Lehrer MacGovern-Bovis, NY, 1987. CBIM. *Recreation:* reading. *Address:* Bovis, 127 Sloane Street, SW1X 9BA. *T:* 081–422 3488. *Club:* Royal Automobile.

LAMPSON, family name of **Baron Killearn.**

LANCASTER, Bishop Suffragan of, since 1990; **Rt. Rev. John Nicholls;** *b* 16 July 1943; *s* of James William and Nellie Nicholls; *m* 1969, Judith Dagnall; two *s* two *d*. *Educ:* Bacup and Rawtenstall Grammar School; King's Coll., London (AKC); St Boniface Coll., Warminster. Curate, St Clement with St Cyprian, Salford, 1967–69; Curate, 1969–72, Vicar 1972–78, All Saints and Martyrs, Langley, Manchester; Dir of Pastoral Studies, Coll. of the Resurrection, Mirfield, 1978–83; Canon Residentiary of Manchester Cathedral, 1983–90. *Recreations:* music (listening and singing), reading, films. *Address:* 7 Dallas Road, Lancaster LA1 1TN. *T:* Lancaster (0524) 32897.

LANCASTER, Bishop of, (RC), since 1985; **Rt. Rev. John Brewer;** *b* 24 Nov 1929; *s* of Eric W. Brewer and Laura H. Brewer (*née* Webster). *Educ:* Ushaw College, Durham; Ven. English College, Rome and Gregorian Univ. PhL, STL, JCL. Ordained priest, 1956; Parish Assistant, 1959–64; Vice-Rector, Ven. English Coll., Rome, 1964–71; Parish Priest of St Mary's, Middlewich, 1971–78; Auxiliary Bishop of Shrewsbury, 1971–83; Bishop Coadjutor of Lancaster, 1984. Officiating Chaplain, Royal Navy, 1966–71; Representative of RC Bishops of England and Wales in Rome, 1964–71. Chaplain to HH Pope Paul VI, 1965. *Recreations:* reading, travel. *Address:* Bishop's House, Cannon Hill, Lancaster LA1 5NG. *T:* Lancaster (0524) 32231.

LANCASTER, Archdeacon of; *see* Gibbons, Ven. K. H.

LANCASTER, Dame Jean, DBE 1963; *b* 11 Aug. 1909; *d* of late Richard C. Davies; *m* 1967, Roy Cavander Lancaster (*d* 1981). *Educ:* Merchant Taylors' Sch., Crosby, Lancashire. Director, Women's Royal Naval Service, 1961–64. *Address:* Greathed Manor, Dormansland, Lingfield, Surrey RH7 6PA.

LANCASTER, Joan Cadogan; *see* Lancaster Lewis, J. C.

LANCASTER, Vice-Admiral Sir John (Strike), KBE 1961; CB 1958; retired 1962; *b* 26 June 1903; *s* of George Henry Lancaster; *m* 1927, Edith Laurie Jacobs (*d* 1980); two *d*. *Educ:* King Edward VI Sch., Southampton. Joined RN, 1921; Commander, 1940; Captain, 1951; Rear-Admiral, 1956; Vice-Admiral, 1959. Served War of 1939–45: HMS Gloucester; RN Barracks, Portsmouth; Persian Gulf; HMS Ocean. Rear-Admiral Personnel, Home Air Command, Lee-on-the-Solent, 1956; Director-General of Manpower, 1959–62; Chief Naval Supply and Secretariat Officer, 1959–62. *Recreation:* gardening. *Address:* Moorings, 59 Western Way, Alverstoke, Hants PO12 2NF.
See also P. M. Lancaster.

LANCASTER, Patricia Margaret; Headmistress, Wycombe Abbey School, 1974–88; a Church Commissioner, since 1989; *b* 22 Feb. 1929; *d* of Vice-Adm. Sir John Lancaster, *qv*. *Educ:* Univs of London (BA) and Southampton (Certif. Educn). English Mistress, St Mary's Sch., Calne, 1951–58; Housemistress, St Swithun's Sch., Winchester, 1958–62; Headmistress, St Michael's, Burton Park, Petworth, 1962–73. Pres., Girls' Schools' Assoc., 1979–80. *Recreation:* theatre. *Address:* 8 Vectis Road, Alverstoke, near Gosport, Hants PO12 2QF.

LANCASTER LEWIS, Joan Cadogan, CBE 1978; Director, India Office Library and Records, 1972–78; *b* 2 Aug. 1918; *yr d* of Cyril Cadogan Lancaster and Mary Ann Lancaster; *m* 1983, Rev. Kenneth Lionel Lewis, MA. *Educ:* Charles Edward Brooke Sch., London; Westfield Coll., Univ. of London. BA 1940, MA 1943; ALA 1943; FRHistS 1956; FSA 1960. Asst Librarian, University Coll., Leicester, and Asst Archivist, the Museum, Leicester, 1940–43. Served War, ATS, 1943–46. Archivist, City of Coventry, 1946–48; Asst Librarian, Inst. of Historical Research, Univ. of London, 1948–60; Asst Keeper, India Office Records, 1960–67; Dep. Librarian and Dep. Keeper, India Office Library and Records, 1968–72. Reviews Editor, Archives (Jl of British Records Assoc.), 1951–57, Editor, Archives, 1957–63. *Publications:* Guide to St Mary's Hall, Coventry, 1949, rev. edn 1981; Bibliography of historical works issued in the United Kingdom 1946–56 (Inst. of Historical Research), 1957; Guide to lists and catalogues of the India Office Records, 1966; Godiva of Coventry, 1967; India Office Records: Report for the years 1947–67 (FCO), 1970; contribs on Coventry to: Victoria County History, 1969; Historic Towns, vol. 2, 1974; Medieval Coventry—a city divided?, 1981; articles and reviews in Bulletin of Inst. of Historical Research, Archives, Asian Affairs, etc. *Recreations:* music, photography. *Address:* 9 Nostle Road, Northleach, Cheltenham, Glos GL54 3PF. *T:* Cotswold (0451) 60932.

LANCELOT, James Bennett, FRCO; Master of the Choristers and Organist, Durham Cathedral, since 1985; *b* 2 Dec. 1952; *s* of Rev. Roland Lancelot; *m* 1982, Sylvia Jane (*née* Hoare); two *d*. *Educ:* St Paul's Cathedral Choir Sch.; Ardingly Coll., Royal College of Music (ARCM); King's Coll., Cambridge (Dr Mann Organ Student; MA; BMus). Asst Organist, St Clement Danes and Hampstead Parish Ch., 1974–75; Sub-Organist, Winchester Cath., 1975–85; Asst Conductor, Winchester Music Club, 1983–85; Conductor, Durham Univ. Choral Soc., 1987–. Mem. Council, RCO, 1988–. Numerous recordings. *Recreations:* railways, walking. *Address:* 6 The College, Durham. *T:* Durham (091) 3864766.

LANCHBERY, John Arthur, OBE 1990; FRAM; Conductor; *b* London, 15 May 1923; *s* of William Lanchbery and Violet (*née* Mewett); *m* 1951, Elaine Fifield (divorced 1960); one *d*. *Educ:* Alleyn's Sch., Dulwich; Royal Academy of Music. Henry Smart Composition Scholarship, 1942. Served, Royal Armoured Corps, 1943–45. Royal Academy of Music, 1945–47; Musical Director, Metropolitan Ballet, 1948–50; Sadler's Wells Theatre Ballet, 1951–57; Royal Ballet, 1957–72 (Principal Conductor, 1959–72); Musical Director: Australian Ballet, 1972–77; American Ballet Theatre, 1978–80. ARAM 1953. Bolshoi Theatre Medal, Moscow, 1961; Queen Elizabeth II Coronation Award, Royal Acad. of Dancing, 1989; Carina Ari Medal, Stockholm, 1989. *Publications:* Arrangements and Compositions of Ballets include: Pleasuredrome, 1949; Eve of St Agnes (BBC commission), 1950; House of Birds, 1955; La Fille Mal Gardée, 1960; The Dream, 1964; Don Quixote, 1966; Giselle, 1968; La Sylphide, 1970; Tales of Beatrix Potter, 1971; Tales of Hoffman, 1972; Merry Widow, 1975; Month in the Country, 1976; Mayerling, 1978; Rosalinda, 1978; Papillon, 1979; La Bayadère, 1980; Peer Gynt, 1980; The Devil to Pay, 1982; The Sentimental Bloke, 1985; Le Chat Botté, 1985; Midsummer Night's Dream, 1985; Hunchback of Notre Dame, 1988. *Recreations:* walking, reading. *Address:* c/o Roger Stone Management, West Grove, Hammers Lane, NW7 4DY. *Club:* Garrick.

LANCHIN, Gerald; consultant; Chairman, Legislation Committee, National Federation of Consumer Groups, since 1986; Member, Data Protection Tribunal, since 1985; *b* 17 Oct. 1922; *o s* of late Samuel Lanchin, Kensington; *m* 1951, Valerie Sonia Lyons; one *s* two *d*. *Educ:* St Marylebone Grammar Sch.; London Sch. of Economics. BCom 1st cl. hons 1951; Leverhulme Schol. 1950–51. Min. of Labour, 1939–51; served with Army, RAOC and REME, 1942–46; Board of Trade (subseq. DTI and Dept of Trade): Asst Principal, 1952; Principal 1953; 1st Sec., UK Delegn to OEEC, Paris, 1955–59; Principal, Estabt and Commercial Relations and Exports Divs, 1959–66; Asst Sec., Finance and Civil Aviation Divs, 1966–71; Under-Sec., Tariff, Commercial Relations and Export, Shipping Policy, General and Consumer Affairs Divs, 1971–82. Chairman: Packaging Council, 1983–84; Direct Mail Services Standards Bd, 1983–89; Mem. Council, Consumers' Assoc., 1983–88. *Publication:* Government and the Consumer, 1985. *Recreations:* photography, reading, music. *Address:* 28 Priory Gardens, Berkhamsted, Herts HP4 2DS. *T:* Berkhamsted (0442) 875283. *Club:* Reform.

LAND, Gillian; *see* Lynne, Gillian.

LAND, Prof. Michael Francis, FRS 1982; PhD; Professor of Neurobiology, University of Sussex, since 1984; *b* 12 April 1942; *s* of late Prof. Frank William Land and of Nora Beatrice Channon; *m* 1980, Rosemary (*née* Clarke); one *s* two *d*. *Educ:* Birkenhead Sch., Cheshire; Jesus Coll., Cambridge (MA); University Coll. London (PhD). Asst Lectr in Physiology, UCL, 1966–67; Miller Fellow, 1967–79, and Asst Prof. of Physiology-Anatomy, 1979–81, Univ. of Calif, Berkeley; Lectr in Biol Sciences, 1971–77, Reader, 1977–84, Univ. of Sussex. Vis. Prof., Univ. of Oregon, 1980; Sen. Res. Fellow, ANU, 1982–84. *Publications:* numerous papers on animal vision in learned jls. *Recreations:* photography, music. *Address:* White House, Cuilfail, Lewes, East Sussex BN7 2BE. *T:* Lewes (0273) 476780.

LANDA, Hon. Abram, CMG 1968; LLB; Notary Public; Agent-General for New South Wales in London, 1965–70; *b* 10 Nov. 1902; *s* of late D. Landa, Belfast; *m* 1930, Perla (*d* 1976), *d* of late L. Levy; one *s* one *d*. *Educ:* Christian Brothers' Coll., Waverley, NSW; University of Sydney. Solicitor, 1927–. MLA for Bondi, NSW, 1930–32 and 1941–65; Minister for Labour and Industry, 1953–56; Minister for Housing and Co-operative Societies, 1956–65; Minister for Housing, NSW, 1956–65. Past Member Senate, University of Sydney; Past Trustee, NSW Public Library. *Recreations:* swimming, bowls. *Address:* 22 Coolong Road, Vaucluse, NSW, Australia. *Club:* Tattersall's (Sydney).

LANDA, Rt. Hon. Lynda; *see* Chalker, Rt Hon. L.

LANDAU, Sir Dennis (Marcus), Kt 1987; Chief Executive, Co-operative Wholesale Society Ltd, since 1980 (Deputy Chief Executive Officer, 1974–80); *b* 18 June 1927; *s* of late Michael Landau, metallurgist. *Educ:* Haberdashers' Aske's Hampstead Sch. Schweppes Ltd, 1952; Man. Dir, Schweppes (East Africa) Ltd, 1958–62; Chivers-Hartley: Prodn Dir, 1963; Man. Dir, 1966–69; Chm., Schweppes Foods Div., 1969; Dep. Chm. and Man. Dir, Cadbury Schweppes Foods, 1970; Controller, Food Div., Co-operative Wholesale Society Ltd, 1971. Chm., CWS (India) Ltd, 1980–; Dep. Chm., Co-operative Bank plc, 1989–; Vice-Chm., Lancashire Enterprises plc, 1989–; Director: Co-operative Retail Services Ltd, 1980–91; CWS (NZ Hldgs) Ltd, 1980–91; Co-operative Insce Soc. Ltd, 1980–; Unity Trust Bank plc, 1984–. Member: Metrication Bd, 1972–80; Exec. Cttee, Food & Drink Fedn (formerly Food Manufacturers' Fedn Inc.), 1972–. Mem. Council, Manchester Business Sch., 1982– (Chm., 1991–). FIGD 1977 (Pres. 1982–85); CBIM 1980. *Recreations:* Rugby, cricket, music. *Clubs:* Royal Over-Seas League; Lancashire CC.

LANDELS, William, (Willie); painter, furniture designer; *b* Venice, 14 June 1928; *s* of late Reynold Landels and Carla Manfredi; *m* 1958, Angela Ogden; two *d*. *Educ:* privately. Apprentice stage designer at La Scala, Milan, 1947; Art Director, J. Walter Thompson, 1950; Art Editor, Queen Magazine, 1965; Editor, Harpers & Queen, 1970–86; Art Dir, 1986–89, Editor, 1989–90, Departures. *Publication:* (with Alistair Burnet) The Best Years of Our Lives, 1981. *Recreation:* cooking. *Address:* 292 South Lambeth Road, SW8 1UJ.

LANDEN, Dinsdale (James); actor; *b* 4 Sept. 1932; *s* of Edward James Landen and Winifred Alice Landen; *m* 1959, Jennifer Daniel. *Educ:* King's Sch., Rochester; Hove County Grammar Sch. *Stage:* Dead Secret, Piccadilly, 1957; Auntie Mame, Adelphi; Provok'd Wife, Vaudeville; Philanthropist, May Fair, 1970; London Assurance, New, 1972; Alphabetical Order, May Fair, 1975; Bodies, Ambassadors, 1980; Taking Steps, Lyric, 1980; Loot, Lyric, 1984; Sufficient Carbohydrate, Albery, 1984; Wife Begins at Forty, Ambassadors, 1985; Selling the Sizzle, Hampstead, 1986; Dangerous Obsession, Apollo, then Fortune, 1987; Thark, Lyric, Hammersmith, 1989; Bookends, Apollo, 1990; Twelfth Night, Playhouse, 1991. *National Theatre:* Plunder; The Philanderer; On the Razzle, 1981; Uncle Vanya, 1982. *Films:* The Valiant; Every Home Should Have One; Digby the Biggest Dog in the World; Mosquito Squadron; Morons from Outer Space; *television:* Great Expectations, Mickey Dunne, The Spies, Glittering Prizes, Devenish, Two Sundays, Fathers and Families, Pig in the Middle, Radio Pictures, Absent Friends, Events in a Museum; What the Butler Saw; Some Other Spring; Fighting Against Slavery; Arms and the Man. *Recreations:* walking, golf. *Address:* 90 Felsham Road, SW15. *Club:* Stage Golfing Society.

LANDON, Dr David Neil; Dean, Institute of Neurology, London, since 1987; Reader in Neurocytology, University of London, since 1977; *b* 15 May 1936; *er s* of Christopher Guy Landon and Isabella Catherine (*née* Campbell); *m* 1960, Karen Elizabeth, *yr d* of late John Copeland and Else Margrethe Poole, Bolney, Sussex; two *s* one *d*. *Educ:* Lancing Coll.; Guy's Hospital Med. Sch. (BSc Hons Anat.; MB BS); LRCP, MRCS 1959. Ho. Officer, Guy's Hosp., 1959–60; Lectr in Anatomy, Guy's Hosp. Med. Sch., 1961–64; Lectr, later Sen. Lectr, in Neurobiology, MRC Res. Gp, Inst. of Neurology, 1964–77. Hon. Cons. in Morbid Anatomy, National Hosps for Nervous Diseases, Queen Square, 1974–. Vis. Prof., Coll. of Medicine, Lagos, 1975. Gov., National Hosps for Nervous Diseases SHA, 1988–; Mem., GMC, 1988–. Editorial Cttee, Jl of Anatomy, 1981–; Associated Editor: Jl of Neurocytol., 1980–83; Neuromuscular Disorders, 1990–. *Publications:* The Peripheral Nerve, 1976; contribs to learned jls on the fine structure, develt and pathology of nerve and muscle. *Recreations:* gardening, travel. *Address:* Woodmans, Wallcrouch, Wadhurst, East Sussex TN5 7JG. *T:* Ticehurst (0580) 200833.

LANDON, Howard Chandler Robbins; author and music historian; *b* 6 March 1926; *s* of late William Grinnell Landon and Dorothea LeBaron Robbins; *m* 1957, Else Radant. *Educ:* Aiken Preparatory Sch.; Lenox Sch.; Swarthmore Coll.; Boston Univ., USA (BMus). European rep. of Intercollegiate Broadcasting System, 1947; founded Haydn Soc. (which recorded and printed music of Joseph Haydn), 1949; became a Special Correspondent of The Times, 1957 and contrib. to that newspaper until 1961. Visiting Prof., Queen's Coll., NYC, 1969; Regents Prof. of Music, Univ. of California (Davis), 1970, 1975, 1979; John Bird Prof. of Music, UC Cardiff, 1978–; Christian Johnson Prof. of Music, Middlebury Coll., Vermont, USA, 1980–. Hon. Professorial Fellow, University Coll., Cardiff, 1971–79; Hon. Fellow, Lady Margaret Hall, Oxford, 1979–. Hon. DMus: Boston Univ., 1969; Queen's Univ., Belfast, 1974; Bristol, 1982. Verdienstkreuz für Kunst und Wissenschaft from Austrian Govt, 1972; Gold Medal, City of Vienna, 1987; Haydn Prize, Govt of Burgenland, Austria, 1990. Co-editor, The Haydn Yearbook, 1962–. *Publications:* The Symphonies of Joseph Haydn, 1955; The Mozart Companion (co-ed with Donald Mitchell), 1956; The Collected Correspondence and London Notebooks of Joseph Haydn, 1959; Essays on Eighteenth-Century Music, 1969; Ludwig van Beethoven: a documentary study, 1970; critical edn of the 107 Haydn Symphonies, (completed) 1968; five-vol. biog. of Haydn: vol. 3, Haydn in England, 1976; vol. 4, Haydn: The Years of The Creation, 1977; vol. 5, Haydn: The Late Years, 1977; vol. 1, Haydn: The Early Years, and vol. 2, Haydn in Eszterhaza, 1978–80; Haydn: a documentary study, 1981; Mozart and the Masons, 1982; Handel and his World, 1984; 1791: Mozart's Last Year, 1988; (with David Wyn Jones) Haydn: his life and music, 1988; Mozart: the golden years, 1989; (ed) The Mozart Compendium, 1990; Mozart and Vienna, 1991; Five Centuries of Music in Venice, 1991; scholarly edns of eighteenth-century music (various European publishing houses). *Recreations:* swimming, cooking, walking. *Address:* Anton Frankgasse 3, Vienna 1180, Austria. *T:* 314205; Château de Foncoussières, 81800 Rabastens (Tarn), France. *T:* (63) 40.61.45.

LANDRETH, Rev. Canon Derek, TD 1963; Vicar of Icklesham, Diocese of Chichester, 1983–89 (Priest-in-charge, 1982–83), also Priest-in-charge of Fairlight, 1984–86; Chaplain to the Queen, 1980–90; Rural Dean of Rye, 1984–89; *b* 7 June 1920; *s* of Rev. Norman Landreth and Muriel Landreth; *m* 1st, 1943, Myra Joan Brown; one *s* three *d*; 2nd, 1986, Dss Mavis Isabella White. *Educ:* Kingswood School, Bath; King's College, Cambridge (MA); Bishops' College, Cheshunt. Commissioned, Royal Artillery, 1942–46 (service India and Burma); CF (TA), 1951–67, (TAVR) 1967–70; Asst Curate, St George, Camberwell, 1948–53; Vicar, St Mark, Battersea Rise, 1953–59; Deputy Chaplain, HM Prison, Wandsworth, 1954–59; Vicar of Richmond, Surrey, and Chaplain, Star and

Garter Home for Disabled Soldiers, Sailors and Airmen, 1959–70; Rector of Sanderstead, Surrey, 1970–77; Hon. Chaplain to Bishop of Southwark, 1962–80; Hon. Canon of Southwark Cathedral, 1968–77; Canon Residentiary and Librarian, Southwark Cathedral, 1977–82; Canon Emeritus, 1982–. Proctor in Convocation, 1980–83. Indep. Mem., Richmond Borough Council, 1961–65. *Recreations:* gardening, fishing. *Address:* Gossamer Cottage, Slindon, near Arundel, W Sussex BN18 0QT. *T:* Slindon (024365) 224.

LANE, family name of **Baron Lane** and **Baron Lane of Horsell.**

LANE, Baron *cr* 1979 (Life Peer), of St Ippollitts; **Geoffrey Dawson Lane;** PC 1974; Kt 1966; AFC 1943; Lord Chief Justice of England, since 1980; *b* 17 July 1918; *s* of late Percy Albert Lane, Lincoln; *m* 1944, Jan, *d* of Donald Macdonald; one *s*. *Educ:* Shrewsbury; Trinity Coll., Cambridge (Hon. Fellow 1981). Served in RAF, 1939–45; Sqdn-Leader, 1942. Called to Bar, Gray's Inn, 1946; Bencher 1966. QC 1962. Dep. Chm., Beds. QS, 1960–66; Recorder of Bedford, 1963–66; a Judge of the High Court of Justice, Queen's Bench Div., 1966–74; a Lord Justice of Appeal, 1974–79; a Lord of Appeal in Ordinary, 1979–80. Mem., Parole Board, 1970–72 (Vice-Chm., 1972). Hon. Bencher, Inner Temple, 1980. Hon. LLD Cambridge, 1984. *Address:* Royal Courts of Justice, Strand, WC2A 2LL.

LANE OF HORSELL, Baron *cr* 1990 (Life Peer), of Woking in the County of Surrey; **Peter Stewart Lane,** Kt 1984; JP; FCA; Senior Partner, BDO Binder Hamlyn, Chartered Accountants, since 1979; Chairman, Brent Chemicals International, since 1985; Deputy Chairman, More O'Ferrall, since 1985; *b* 29 Jan. 1925; *s* of late Leonard George Lane; *m* Doris Florence (*née* Botsford) (*d* 1969); two *d*. *Educ:* Sherborne Sch., Dorset. Served RNVR (Sub-Lieut), 1943–46. Qualified as chartered accountant, 1948; Partner, Binder Hamlyn or predecessor firms, 1950–. National Union of Conservative Associations: Vice Chairman, 1981–83; Chairman, 1983–84; Chm., Exec. Cttee, 1986–; Vice President, 1984–. Governor, Nuffield Nursing Homes Trust, 1985– (Dep. Chm., 1990–). JP Surrey, 1976–; Freeman, City of London. *Address:* c/o House of Lords, SW1A 0PW. *Clubs:* Boodle's, MCC.

See also Baron Trefgarne.

LANE, Dr Anthony John, FRCP, FFPHM; Regional Medical Officer, North Western Regional Health Authority, 1974–86, retired; *b* 6 Feb. 1926; *s* of John Gill Lane and Marian (*née* Brumfield); *m* 1948, Hannah Holečková; one *s* two *d*. *Educ:* St Christopher's Sch., Letchworth; Emmanuel Coll., Cambridge. MA, MB, BChir. House posts in surgery, medicine, obstetrics and paediatrics, 1949–51; MO with Methodist Missionary Soc., Andhra State, India, 1951–57; Registrar: Tropical Diseases, UCH, 1958; Gen. Med., St James' Hosp., Balham, 1958–61; Infectious Diseases, Western Hosp., Fulham, 1961–63; MO (Trainee), Leeds RHB, 1963–64; Asst Sen. MO, Leeds RHB, 1964–66; Principal Asst Sen. MO, Leeds RHB, 1966–70; Dep. Sen. Admin. MO, SW Metrop. RHB, 1970–71; Sen. Admin. MO, Manchester RHB, 1971–74. Hon. MD Manchester, 1986. *Publications:* contrib. Positions, Movements and Directions in Health Services Research, 1974; contrib. Proc. Royal Soc. Med. *Recreations:* music, competitive indoor games, walking, gardening. *Address:* 4 Queens Road, Wilmslow, Cheshire SK9 5HS. *T:* Wilmslow (0625) 523889.

LANE, Anthony John, CB 1990; Deputy Secretary, Department of Trade and Industry, since 1990; *b* 30 May 1939; *s* of Eric Marshall Lane and Phyllis Mary Lane; *m* 1967, Judith Sheila (*née* Dodson); two *s* one *d*. *Educ:* Caterham Sch.; Balliol Coll., Oxford (BA PPE, MA). Investment Analyst, Joseph Sebag & Co., 1964–65; Asst Principal, Min. of Technology, 1965; Private Sec. to Parly Sec., 1968–69; Principal, 1969; Private Secretary: to Minister for Aerospace and Shipping, 1973–74; to Sec. of State for Prices and Consumer Protection, 1974–75; Asst Sec., Dept of Prices, 1975, Dept of Trade, 1979; Under Sec., Dept of Trade, then Dept of Transport, 1980–84; Under Sec., DTI, 1984–87; Dep. Dir Gen., OFT, 1987–90. *Recreations:* music, gardens, travel. *Address:* Department of Trade and Industry, 151 Buckingham Palace Road, SW1.

LANE, Dr Anthony Milner, FRS 1975; Deputy Chief Scientific Officer, Atomic Energy Research Establishment, Harwell, 1976–89; *b* 27 July 1928; *s* of Herbert William Lane and Doris Ruby Lane (*née* Milner); *m* 1st, 1952, Anne Sophie Zissman (*d* 1980); two *s* one *d*; 2nd, 1983, Jill Valerie Parvin; five step *d*. *Educ:* Trowbridge Boys' High Sch.; Selwyn Coll., Cambridge. BA Maths, PhD Theoretical Physics. Joined Harwell, 1953. *Publications:* Nuclear Theory, 1963; numerous research articles in Review of Modern Physics, Phys. Review, Nuclear Physics, etc. *Recreations:* gardening, bird-watching. *Address:* 6 Walton Street, Oxford OX1 2HG. *T:* Oxford (0865) 56565.

LANE, Maj.-Gen. Barry Michael, CB 1984; OBE 1974 (MBE 1965); Chief Executive, Cardiff Bay Development Corporation, since 1987; *b* 10 Aug. 1932; *m* 1st, 1956, Eveline Jean (*d* 1986), *d* of Vice-Adm. Sir Harry Koelle, KCB and Enid (*née* Corbould-Ellis); one *s* one *d*; 2nd, 1987, Shirley Ann, *d* of E. V. Hawtin. *Educ:* Dover Coll. Commissioned, 1954; served Somerset LI, 1954–59, Somerset and Cornwall LI, 1959–68, LI, 1968–75; Instructor, Staff Coll. Camberley, 1970–72; CO, 1st Bn, LI, 1972–75; Comd, 11 Armoured Bde, 1977–78; RCDS, 1979; Dep. Dir, Army Staff Duties, MoD, 1980–81; Dir, Army Quartering, 1981–82; VQMG, 1982–83; GOC SW Dist, 1984–87. Col, The LI, 1982–87. Hon. Colonel: 6th Bn, LI, 1987; Bristol Univ., OTC, 1988. *Address:* c/o National Westminster Bank, Tadworth, Surrey KT20 5AF. *Club:* Army and Navy.

LANE, David Goodwin; QC 1991; a Recorder of the Crown Court, since 1987; *b* 8 Oct. 1945; *s* of James Cooper Lane and Joyce Lilian Lane; *m* 1991, Jacqueline Elizabeth Cocks. *Educ:* Crypt Sch., Gloucester (Head Boy); King's College London (LLB, AKC). Lord Justice Holker Junior Exhibnr; Lee Essay Prizeman, H. C. Richard Ecclesiastical Law Prizeman; Albion Richardson Scholar. Called to the Bar, Gray's Inn, 1968; Asst Recorder, 1982; Head of Chambers, 1985. *Recreations:* golf, cricket, theatre, music, gardening. *Address:* All Saints' Chambers, Holbeck House, 9/11 Broad Street, Bristol BS1 2HP. *T:* Bristol (0272) 211966.

LANE, Rev. David John; Principal, College of the Resurrection, Mirfield, since 1990; *b* 12 June 1935; *s* of Rex Clayphen Fox Lane and Constance Mary Lane. *Educ:* Hurstpierpoint Coll. (Scholar); Magdalen Coll., Oxford (BA Theol 1958; Oriental Studies 1960; Pusey and Ellerton Schol., 1959; Hall Houghton Syriac Prize, 1961; MA 1962; BD 1989). Nat. Service, Royal Signals, 1953–55. Coll. of the Resurrection, Mirfield, 1960–61; Codrington Coll., Barbados, 1961–62. Deacon and Priest, Barbados, 1962; Lectr, 1961, Sen. Tutor, 1963, Codrington Coll., Barbados; Curate, St Peter's, Wolvercote, 1965–66; Associate Chaplain, and Kennicott Hebrew Fellow, 1966–68, Lectr in Theol., 1968–71, Pembroke Coll., Oxford; Lectr and Tutor, St Stephen's House, Oxford, 1968–71; Asst Prof., Near Eastern Studies, Univ. of Toronto, 1971, Associate Prof., 1974–83; Sen. Fellowship, Trinity Coll., Toronto, 1977–82; College of the Resurrection: Lectr and Tutor, 1983; Dir of Studies, 1984; Vice-Principal, 1987–90. Hon. Lectr, Dept of Theology and Religious Studies, Univ. of Leeds, 1983–. *Publications:* The Old Testament in Syriac: Part II, fasc. 5 ((ed) Ecclesiastes; (ed with J. A. Emerton) Wisdom of Solomon and Song of Songs), 1979, Part I, fasc. 2 ((ed) Leviticus), 1991; articles in learned jls. *Recreations:* garden design and maintenance, domestic planning. *Address:* College of the Resurrection, Mirfield, West Yorks WF14 0BW. *T:* Mirfield (0924) 490441. *Club:* Royal Over-Seas League.

LANE, David Neil, CMG 1983; HM Diplomatic Service, retired; Assistant Secretary-General, since 1989 and Secretary, since 1990, Order of St John; *b* 16 April 1928; *er s* of late Clive and Hilda Lane, Bath; *m* 1968, Sara, *d* of late Cecil Nurcombe, MC; two *d*. *Educ:* Abbotsholme Sch.; Merton Coll., Oxford. Army, 1946–48; Foreign (later Foreign and Commonwealth) Office: 1951–53, 1955–58, 1963–68, 1972–74; British Embassy, Oslo, 1953–55; Ankara, 1959–61, 1975–78; Conakry, 1961–63; UK Mission to the United Nations, New York, 1968–72, 1979; High Comr in Trinidad and Tobago, 1980–85; Ambassador to the Holy See, 1985–88. Pres., UN Trusteeship Council, 1971–72; UK Delegate, Internat. Exhibns Bureau, 1973–74. *Recreation:* music. *Address:* 6 Montagu Square, W1H 1RA. *T:* 071–486 1673. *Club:* Travellers'.

LANE, David Stuart, PhD, DPhil; Lecturer in Sociology, since 1990, and Official Fellow of Emmanuel College, 1974–80 and since 1990, University of Cambridge; *b* Monmouthshire (now Gwent), 24 April 1933; *s* of Reginald and Mary Lane; *m* 1962, Christel Noritzsch; one *s* one *d*. *Educ:* Univ. of Birmingham (BSocSc); Univ. of Oxford (DPhil). PhD Cantab. Graduate student, Nuffield Coll., Oxford, 1961–62, 1964–65. Formerly engrg trainee, local authority employee, sch. teacher; univ. teacher, Birmingham, Essex (Reader in Sociology) and Cambridge Univs; Prof. of Sociology, Univ. of Birmingham, 1981–90. Visiting Professor: Cornell Univ., 1987; Univ. of Graz, 1991. Mem. Exec. Cttee, British Sociol Assoc., 1987–. Vice-Chm., Birmingham Rathbone; formerly: Vice-Chm., Mencap Down's Children's Assoc.; Chm., W Midlands Council for Disabled People. Member, Editorial Boards: Sociology, 1985–88; Disability, Handicap and Society, 1987–90. *Publications:* Roots of Russian Communism, 1969, 2nd edn 1975; Politics and Society in the USSR, 1970, 2nd edn 1978; The End of Inequality?, 1971; (with G. Kolankiewicz) Social Groups in Polish Society, 1973; The Socialist Industrialist State, 1976; (with F. O'Dell) The Soviet Industrial Worker, 1978; The Work Needs of Mentally Handicapped Adults, 1980; Leninism: a sociological interpretation, 1981; The End of Social Inequality?: class status and power under state socialism, 1982; State and Politics in the USSR, 1985; Soviet Economy and Society, 1985; (ed jtly) Current Approaches to Down's Syndrome, 1985; (ed) Employment and Labour in the USSR, 1986; Soviet Labour and the Ethic of Communism, 1987; (ed) Political Power and Elites in the USSR, 1988; Soviet Society under Perestroika, 1990, 2nd edn 1991. *Recreations:* soccer, squash, films, TV. *Address:* Emmanuel College, Cambridge CB2 3AP. *T:* Cambridge (0223) 334202.

LANE, Sir David (William Stennis Stuart), Kt 1983; *b* 24 Sept. 1922; *s* of Hubert Samuel Lane, MC; *m* 1955, Lesley Anne Mary Clauson; two *s*. *Educ:* Eton; Trinity Coll., Cambridge; Yale Univ. Served War of 1939–45 (Navy). British Iron and Steel Federation, 1948 (Sec., 1956); Shell International Petroleum Co., 1959–67. Called to the Bar, Middle Temple, 1955. Chm., N Kensington Cons. Assoc., 1961–62. Contested (C) Lambeth (Vauxhall), 1964, Cambridge, 1966; MP (C) Cambridge, Sept. 1967–Nov. 1976; PPS to Sec. of State for Employment, 1970–72; Parly Under-Sec. of State, Home Office, 1972–74. Chairman: Commn for Racial Equality, 1977–82; NAYC, 1982–87. *Recreations:* walking, golf, travel. *Address:* 5 Spinney Drive, Great Shelford, Cambridge CB2 5LY. *Club:* MCC.

LANE, Frank Laurence, CBE 1961; Chairman, Elder Dempster Lines Ltd, 1963–72; *b* 1912; *s* of late Herbert Allardyce Lane, CIE, and late Hilda Gladys Duckle Lane (*née* Wraith); *m* 1938, Gwendolin Elizabeth Peterkin; one *s*. *Educ:* Wellington Coll., Berks; New Coll., Oxford. Mansfield & Co. Ltd, Singapore and Penang, 1934–42; BOAC, UK and USA, 1942–45; Mansfield & Co. Ltd, Singapore, 1945–61; Elder Dempster Lines Ltd, Liverpool, 1962–72. *Recreations:* golf, fishing. *Address:* Amberwood, Bisterne Close, Burley, Ringwood, Hampshire BH24 4AU. *T:* Burley (04253) 3249.

LANE, John, CB 1981; Deputy Director, Central Statistical Office, 1978–81; *b* 23 Oct. 1924; *e s* of R. J. I. and M. E. L. Lane; *m* 1954, Ruth Ann Crocker; one *s*. *Educ:* John Lyon Sch., Harrow; HMS Conway; Univ. of London (BSc(Econ)). Merchant Navy, 1943–47. Joined Ministry of Transport, 1950; Statistician, 1954; Asst Sec. to Council on Prices, Productivity and Incomes, 1959–61; Principal, MoT, 1962; Asst Sec., 1966; Under-Sec., DoE, 1972; Regional Dir, SE Region and Chm., SE Economic Planning Bd, 1973–76; Under Sec., Dept of Transport, 1976–78. *Address:* Fern Hill, 67 Mount Ephraim, Tunbridge Wells, Kent TN4 8BG. *T:* Tunbridge Wells (0892) 527293.

LANE, Kenneth Frederick; mining consultant; Director: RTZ Consultants, since 1988; Europa Minerals Group, since 1990; *b* 22 March 1928; British; *m* 1950, Kathleen Richards; one *s* two *d*. *Educ:* Emanuel Coll., Cambridge. Degree in Maths. Steel Industry in Sheffield, 1951–59; North America, 1959–61; Rio Tinto-Zinc Corp., 1961–65; Man. Dir, RTZ Consultants Ltd, 1965–70; Dir, RTZ Corp., 1970–75. Dir, Energy Management & Finance, 1988–89. Advisor to Civil Service, 1970–74. Vis. Prof., RSM, 1979–85. *Publication:* The Economic Definition of Ore, 1988. *Recreations:* bridge, boat building, sailing. *Address:* Down House, Lezant, Launceston, Cornwall PL15 9PR. *T:* Stoke Climsland (0579) 370495.

LANE, Margaret; novelist, biographer, journalist; *b* 23 June 1907; *o d* of late H. G. Lane; *m* 1st, 1934, Bryan (marr. diss. 1939), *e s* of Edgar Wallace; 2nd, 1944, 15th Earl of Huntingdon, (*d* 1990); two *d*. *Educ:* St Stephen's, Folkestone; St Hugh's Coll., Oxford (MA). Reporter, Daily Express, 1928–31; special correspondent: in New York and for International News Service, USA, 1931–32; for Daily Mail, 1932–38. President: Women's Press Club, 1958–60; Dickens Fellowship, 1959–61, 1970; Johnson Soc., 1971; Brontë Soc., 1975–79; Jane Austen Soc., 1985–88. *Publications:* Faith, Hope, No Charity (awarded Prix Femina-Vie Heureuse), 1935; At Last the Island, 1937; Edgar Wallace: The Biography of a Phenomenon, 1938; Walk Into My Parlour, 1941; Where Helen Lies, 1944; The Tale of Beatrix Potter, 1946, revd edn, 1985; The Brontë Story, 1953; A Crown of Convolvulus, 1954; A Calabash of Diamonds, 1961; Life With Ionides, 1963; A Night at Sea, 1964; A Smell of Burning, 1965; Purely for Pleasure, 1966; The Day of the Feast, 1968; Frances Wright and the Great Experiment, 1971; Samuel Johnson and his World, 1975; Flora Thompson, 1976; The Magic Years of Beatrix Potter, 1978; (ed) Flora Thompson's A Country Calendar and other writings, 1979; The Drug-Like Brontë Dream, 1980; Operation Hedgehog, 1981; series natural history for children: The Fox, The Spider, The Stickleback, The Squirrel, The Frog, The Beaver, 1982. *Address:* Blackbridge House, Beaulieu, Hants.

LANE, Hon. Mrs Miriam; *see* Rothschild, Hon. M. L.

LANE, Ronald Anthony Stuart, CMG 1977; MC 1945; Deputy Chairman, Chartered Trust Ltd, 1979–83; *b* 8 Dec. 1917; 2nd *s* of late Wilmot Ernest Lane and F. E. Lane (*née* Blakey); *m* 1948, Anne Brenda, 2nd *d* of E. Walsh; one *s* one *d*. *Educ:* Lancing College. FIB. Served War, 1940–45, 7th Light Cavalry, Indian Army, India and Burma (Major). Joined Chartered Bank of India, Australia & China, 1937; served in Far East, 1939–60; Gen. Manager, 1961, Chief Gen. Manager, 1972, Man. Dir, 1973–77, Vice-Chm., 1977–83, Standard Chartered Bank Ltd. Mem., Export Guarantees Adv. Council, 1973–78 (Dep. Chm., 1977–78). *Recreations:* sailing, gardening. *Address:* West Hold, By the Church, West Mersea, Essex CO5 8QD. *T:* West Mersea (0206) 2563. *Clubs:* East India, MCC; West Mersea Yacht.

LANE, Prof. Ronald Epey, CBE 1957; MD; FRCP; Emeritus Nuffield Professor of Occupational Health, University of Manchester (Professor, 1945–65); *b* 2 July 1897; *s* of E. E. Lane; *m* 1st, 1924, Winifred E. Tickner (*d* 1981); one *s* (one *d* decd); 2nd, 1982, Ida (*d* 1991), *widow* of Arnold Bailey. *Educ:* Simon Langton Sch. Canterbury; Guy's Hospital. MRCP 1925, FRCP 1938; MSc Manchester, 1946; MD London, 1947. Served European War, RFC, 1915–19. Guy's Hospital, 1919–24, qualified, 1923; General Medical practice, 1925–27; Medical Officer, Chloride Elec. Storage Co. Ltd, 1928; Physician, Salford Royal Hospital, 1935; Milroy Lecturer (Royal College of Physicians), 1947, McKenzie Lecturer, 1950. Mem. of various Govt Advisory Cttees. *Publications:* original papers on Lead Poisoning, Medical Education, Occupational Health and Universities, in Lancet, BMJ, Brit. Jl of Industrial Med., Jl of Industrial Hygiene and Toxicology, etc. *Recreations:* golf, fishing. *Address:* 3 Daylesford Road, Cheadle, Cheshire. *T:* 061–428 5738. *Club:* Athenæum.

LANE FOX, Robin James, FRSL; Fellow, New College, Oxford, since 1977; Reader in Ancient History, Oxford, since 1990; *b* 5 Oct. 1946; *s* of James Henry Lane Fox and Anne (*née* Loyd); *m* 1970, Louisa Caroline Mary, *d* of Charles and Lady Katherine Farrell; one *s* one *d*. *Educ:* Eton; Magdalen Coll., Oxford (Craven and de Paravicini scholarships, 1966; Passmore Edwards and Chancellors' Latin Verse Prize, 1968). FRSL 1974. Fellow by examination, Magdalen Coll., Oxford, 1970–73; Lectr in Classical Lang. and Lit., 1973–76, Res. Fellow, Classical and Islamic Studies, 1976–77, Worcester Coll., Oxford; Lectr in Ancient Hist., Oxford Univ., 1977–90. Weekly gardening correspondent, Financial Times, 1970–. *Publications:* Alexander the Great, 1973, 3rd edn 1978 (James Tait Black, Duff Cooper, W. H. Heinemann Awards, 1973–74); Variations on a Garden, 1974, rev. edn 1986; Search for Alexander, 1980; Better Gardening, 1982; Pagans and Christians, 1986. *Recreations:* gardening, hunting, poetry, rough travel. *Address:* New College, Oxford OX1 3BN. *T:* Shipton-under-Wychwood (0993) 830816. *Club:* Beefsteak.

LANESBOROUGH, 9th Earl of *cr* 1756; **Denis Anthony Brian Butler;** TD; DL; Baron of Newtown-Butler, 1715; Viscount Lanesborough, 1728; Major, Leicestershire Yeomanry (RA); *b* 28 Oct. 1918; *er s* of 8th Earl and Grace Lilian (*d* 1983), *d* of late Sir Anthony Abdy, 3rd Bt; *S* father 1950; *m* 1939, Bettyne Ione (marr. diss. 1950), *d* of late Sir Lindsay Everard; one *d* (and one *d* decd). *Educ:* Stowe. Leicestershire Yeomanry; Lieutenant, 1939; Major, RAC, TA, 1945. Member: Nat. Gas Consumers' Council, 1973–78; Trent RHA, 1974–82 (Vice-Chm., 1978–82). Chm., Loughborough and District Housing Assoc., 1978–85. Chm., 1953–64, Pres., 1964–86, Guide Dogs for the Blind Assoc. DL 1962, JP 1967, Leicester. *Heir: kinsman* Major Henry Arthur Brinsley Cavendish Butler [*b* 11 May 1909; *m* 1st, 1940, Ruth Ardyn (*d* 1951), *o d* of Lt-Col W. H. Barton, DSO; (one *s* decd); 2nd, 1952, Alice Isabella, *o d* of late Rev. George Watt]. *Address:* Alton Lodge, Kegworth, Derby DE7 2EU. *T:* Loughborough (0509) 672243.

LANG, Prof. Andrew Richard, FRS 1975; Professor of Physics, University of Bristol, 1979–87, now Emeritus; *b* 9 Sept. 1924; *s* of late Ernest F. S. Lang and late Susannah (*née* Gueterbock); unmarried. *Educ:* University College of South-West, Exeter, (BSc Lond. 1944; MSc Lond. 1947); Univ. of Cambridge (PhD 1953). Research Dept, Lever Bros, Port Sunlight, 1945–47; Research Asst, Cavendish Laboratory, 1947–48; North American Philips, Irvington-on-Hudson, NY, 1952–53; Instructor, Harvard Univ., 1953–54; Asst Professor, Harvard Univ., 1954–59; Lectr in Physics, 1960–66, Reader, 1966–79, Univ. of Bristol. MInstP, Mem. Geol Assoc.; Mem. Soc. Sigma Xi. Charles Vernon Boys Prize, Inst. of Physics, 1964. *Publications:* contribs to learned jls. *Address:* 1B Elton Road, Bristol BS8 1SJ. *T:* Bristol (0272) 739784.

LANG, Dr Brian Andrew; Chief Executive and Deputy Chairman, British Library, since 1991; *b* 2 Dec. 1945; *s* of Andrew Ballantyne Lang and Mary Bain Lang (*née* Smith); *m* 1st, 1975 (marr. diss. 1982); one *s*; 2nd, 1983, Caroline Susan, *e d* of David and Jean Purnell; one *s* one *d*. *Educ:* Royal High Sch., Edinburgh; Univ. of Edinburgh (MA, PhD). Social anthropological field research, Kenya, 1969–70; Lectr in social anthropology, Aarhus Univ., 1971–75; Scientific Staff, SSRC, 1976–79; Scottish Office (Sec., Historic Buildings Council for Scotland), 1979–80; Sec., Nat. Heritage Meml Fund, 1980–87; Dir of Public Affairs, Nat. Trust, 1987–91. *Recreations:* music, museums and galleries, pottering, being with my children. *Address:* British Library, 96 Euston Road, St Pancras, NW1 2DB. *T:* 071–323 7262.

LANG, Lt-Gen. Sir Derek (Boileau), KCB 1967 (CB 1964); DSO 1944; MC 1941; DL; *b* 7 Oct. 1913; *s* of Lt-Col C. F. G. Lang and Mrs Lumsden Lang (*née* M. J. L. Forbes); *m* 1st, 1942, M. Massy Dawson (*d* 1953); one *s* one *d*; 2nd, 1953, A. L. S. Shields (marr. diss. 1969); 3rd, 1969, Mrs E. H. Balfour (*d* 1982); 4th, 1983, Mrs Maartje McQueen. *Educ:* Wellington Coll.; RMC Sandhurst. Commnd, The Queen's Own Cameron Highlanders, 1933; Adjutant, TA, 1938; active service in France, E and N Africa, 1940–42; Chief Instructor, Sch. of Infantry, 1943–44; Comdr, 5th Camerons, NW Europe, 1944–45; Comdt, Sch. of Infantry, BAOR, 1945–46; Directing Staff, Staff Coll., Camberley, 1947–48; Staff, Australia, 1949–51; GSO1, War Office, 1951–53; Chief Instructor, Sch. of Infantry, 1953–55; AAG, War Office, 1955–57; NDC, 1957–58; Comd Infty Bde (153–TA), 1958–60; Chief of Staff, Scottish Comd, 1960; Gen. Officer Commanding, 51st Highland Div. and District, Perth, 1962–64; Dir of Army Training, 1964–66; GOC-in-C, Scottish Command, 1966–69; Governor of Edinburgh Castle, 1966–69; Sec., Univ. of Stirling, 1970–73; Hon. Col, 153 (Highland) Regt, RCT (Volunteers), T&AVR, 1970–76; Pres., Army Cadet Force Assoc. (Scotland), 1975–85. Associate Consultant, PA Management Consultants Ltd, 1975–84. DL Edinburgh, 1978. OStJ. *Publication:* Return to St Valéry, 1974. *Recreations:* golf, fishing, shooting. *Address:* Templeland, Kirknewton, Midlothian EH27 8DJ. *T:* Mid Calder (0506) 883211. *Clubs:* New (Edinburgh); Senior Golfers' Society; Hon. Co. of Edinburgh Golfers (Muirfield).

See also J. M. Hunt.

LANG, Henry George, ONZ 1989; CB 1977; consultant and company director, since 1977; *b* 3 March 1919; *s* of Robert and Anna Lang; *m* 1942, Octavia Gwendolin (*née* Turton); one *s* four *d*. *Educ:* Victoria Univ., Wellington. DPA, BA, BCom. Private enterprise, 1939–44; RNZAF, 1944–46. NZ government service: various economic appointments, 1946–55; Economic Advisor to High Comr in London, 1955–58; Treasury, 1958–77, Sec. to Treasury, 1968–77. Vis. Prof. of Economics, Victoria Univ. of Wellington, 1977–82, consultant, 1982–. Hon. LLD Victoria Univ., Wellington, 1984. *Publications:* (with J. V. T. Baker) Economic Policy and National Income, in, NZ Official Year Book, 1950; articles in learned journals. *Recreations:* skiing, swimming, reading. *Address:* 81 Hatton Street, Wellington, NZ. *T:* 768 788. *Club:* Wellington (Wellington, NZ).

LANG, Hugh Montgomerie, CBE 1978; Chairman, P-E International plc, since 1980 (Director, since 1972; Chief Executive since 1977); *b* Glasgow, 7 Nov. 1932; *s* of John Montgomerie Lang and Janet Allan (*née* Smillie); *m* 1st, 1959, Marjorie Jean Armour (marr. diss. 1981); one *s* one *d*; 2nd, 1981, Susan Lynn Hartley (*née* Russell). *Educ:* Shawlands Acad., Glasgow; Glasgow Univ. (BSc). ARCST 1953; CEng 1967; FIProdE 1976; FIMC 1970; CBIM 1980. Officer, REME, 1953–55 (National Service). Colvilles Ltd, 1955–56; Glacier Metal Co. Ltd, 1956–60; L. Sterne & Co. Ltd, 1960–61; P-E Consulting Group, 1961–: Manager for ME, 1965–68; Scottish Reg. Manager, 1968–72; Man. Dir, 1974–77. Chm., Brammer, 1990–; Director: Redman Heenan Internat., 1981–86 (Chm., 1982–86); Fairey Holdings Ltd, 1978–82; UKO International, 1985–86; B. Elliott, 1986–88; Siebe, 1987–91; Renaissance Hldgs, 1987–; Strong & Fisher (Hldgs), 1988–90; Co-ordinated Land and Estates, 1988–. Chairman: Food, Drink and Packaging Machinery Sector Working Party, 1976–81; Technology Transfer Services Adv. Cttee, 1982–85 (Mem., 1978–85); Member: Business Educn Council, 1980–81; CBI Industrial Policy Cttee, 1980–83; Design Council, 1983–90 (Dep. Chm., 1986–90); Engrg Council, 1984–86. FRSA 1984. *Recreations:* fishing, gardening, golf, reading. *Address:* c/o P-E International, Park House, Egham, Surrey TW20 0HW. *Clubs:* Army and Navy; Denham Golf.

LANG, Rt. Hon. Ian (Bruce), PC 1990; MP (C) Galloway and Upper Nithsdale, since 1983 (Galloway, 1979–83); Secretary of State for Scotland and Lord Keeper of the Great Seal of Scotland, since 1990; *b* 27 June 1940; *y s* of James Fulton Lang, DSC, and Maude Margaret (*née* Stewart); *m* 1971, Sandra Caroline *e d* of John Alastair Montgomerie, DSC; two *d*. *Educ:* Lathallan Sch., Kincardineshire; Rugby Sch.; Sidney Sussex Coll., Cambridge (BA 1962). Director: Hutchison & Craft Ltd, 1975–81; Hutchison & Craft (Underwriting Agents) Ltd, Lloyd's, 1976–81; P. MacCallum & Sons Ltd, 1976–81; Rose, Thomson, Young & Co. (Glasgow) Ltd, 1966–75. Member, Queen's Body Guard for Scotland (Royal Company of Archers), 1974–. Dir, Glasgow Chamber of Commerce, 1978–81; Trustee: Savings Bank of Glasgow, 1969–74; West of Scotland Trustee Savings Bank, 1974–83. Contested (C): Central Ayrshire, 1970; Glasgow Pollok, Feb. 1974. An Asst Govt Whip, 1981–83; a Lord Comr of HM Treasury, 1983–86; Parliamentary Under Secretary of State: Dept of Employment, 1986; Scottish Office, 1986–87; Minister of State, Scottish Office, 1987–90. Mem., Select Cttee on Scottish Affairs, 1979–81. Vice-Chm., Conservative Party in Scotland, 1983–87. Pres., Scottish Young Conservatives, 1982–84. OStJ 1974. *Recreations:* skiing, sailing, shooting, music. *Address:* House of Commons, SW1A 0AA. *Clubs:* Pratt's; Western (Glasgow); Prestwick Golf.

LANG, Very Rev. John Harley; Dean of Lichfield, since 1980; Chaplain to HM the Queen, 1976–80; *b* 27 Oct. 1927; *e s* of Frederick Henry Lang and Eileen Annie Lang (*née* Harley); *m* 1972, Frances Rosemary Widdowson; three *d*. *Educ:* Merchant Taylors' Sch.; King's Coll., London. MA Cantab, BD London, LRAM. Subaltern, XII Royal Lancers, 1951–52; Asst Curate, St Mary's Portsea, 1952–57; Priest Vicar, Southwark Cathedral, 1957–60; Chaplain, Emmanuel Coll., Cambridge, 1960–64; Asst Head of Religious Broadcasting, BBC, 1964–67; Head of Religious Programmes, Radio, 1967–71; Head of Religious Broadcasting, BBC, 1971–80. Member: Nat. Trust Cttee for Mercia, 1984–; Central Religious Adv. Cttee, BBC and IBA, 1985–89; Cathedrals Fabric Commn, 1991–. Mem. Court, Keele Univ., 1989–; Chm. Governors, Lichfield Cathedral Sch., 1980–; Mem. Council, Abbots Bromley Sch., 1982– (Chm., 1984–87). Hon. DLitt Keele, 1988. *Recreations:* books, music. *Address:* The Deanery, Lichfield, Staffs WS13 7LD. *Club:* Cavalry and Guards.

LANG, John Russell, CBE 1963; Deputy Chairman, The Weir Group Ltd, 1968–73; *b* 8 Jan. 1902; *s* of Chas Russell Lang, CBE; *m* 1st, 1934, Jenny (*d* 1970), *d* of Sir John Train, MP, of Cathkin, Lanarkshire; four *d* (one *s* decd); 2nd, 1973, Gay Mackie (*d* 1979); 3rd, 1981, Kay, *widow* of Norman Macfie. *Educ:* Loretto Sch., Musselburgh; France and USA. Dir, G. & J. Weir Ltd, 1930–67. Chairman, Weir Housing Corp., 1946–66. President, Scottish Engineering Employers' Association, 1963–64. Mem., Toothill Cttee and EDC for Mec. Eng. Lt-Col 277 Field Regt, RA (TA), 1937. *Recreations:* hunting, shooting, golf. *Address:* Cranford Court, The Ferns, Tetbury, Glos GL8 8JE. *T:* Tetbury (0666) 53227. *Clubs:* Royal Scottish Automobile; Prestwick Golf; Troon Golf.

LANG, Rear-Adm. William Duncan, CB 1981; retired; *b* 1 April 1925; *s* of James Hardie Lang and Elizabeth Foggo Paterson Lang (*née* Storie); *m* 1947, Joyce Rose Weeks; one *s* one *d*. *Educ:* Edinburgh Acad. Entered Royal Navy, 1943; trained as Pilot; served in 800, 816 and 825 Sqdns and as Flying Instr and Test Pilot; comd 802 Sqdn, 1958–59; Commander (Air): RNAS Culdrose, 1962–63; HMS Eagle, 1964–65; Fleet Aviation Officer, Far East Fleet, 1966–68; Captain 1969; comd RNAS Lossiemouth, 1970–72; Dep. Comdt, Jt Warfare Estabt, 1973–74; COS to Flag Officer, Naval Air Comd, 1975–76; Mil. Dep. to Hd of Defence Sales, 1978–81; Dir, Naval Security, MoD, 1981–86. Naval ADC to the Queen, 1978; Rear-Adm. 1978. *Recreation:* golf (Pres., RN Golf Soc., 1979–85). *Address:* c/o Midland Bank, 19 High Street, Haslemere, Surrey GU27 2HQ. *Club:* Army and Navy.

LANGAN, Peter St John Hevey, QC 1983; **His Honour Judge Langan;** a Circuit Judge, since 1991; *b* 1 May 1942; *s* of late Frederick Hevey Langan and of Myrrha Langan (*née* Jephson), Mount Hevey, Hill of Down, Co. Meath; *m* 1976, Oonagh May Winifred McCarthy. *Educ:* Downside School; Trinity College, Dublin (MA, LLB); Christ's College, Cambridge (PhD). Called to the Irish Bar, King's Inns, 1964; called to the Bar, Lincoln's Inn, 1967 (*ad eund*, Middle Temple, 1990); Lectr in Law, Univ. of Durham, 1966–69; in practice at the Bar, 1970–91; a Recorder, 1989–91. Legal Assessor: GMC, 1990–91; GDC, 1990–91. Chm., Eton Housing Assoc. Ltd, 1979–83. Mem., Management Cttee, Catholic Fund for Overseas Develt, 1984–91. *Publications:* Maxwell on Interpretation of Statutes, 12th edn, 1969; Civil Procedure and Evidence, 1st edn, 1970, 3rd edn (with L. D. J. Henderson) as Civil Procedure, 1983; (with P. V. Baker) Snell's Principles of Equity, 28th edn, 1982, 29th edn, 1990. *Address:* Norwich Combined Court, Bishopgate, Norwich NR3 1UR. *T:* Norwich (0603) 761776. *Club:* Athenæum.

LANGDALE, Simon John Bartholomew; Director of Educational and General Grants, The Rank Foundation, since 1988; *b* 26 Jan. 1937; *s* of late G. R. Langdale and H. J. Langdale (*née* Bartholomew); *m* 1962, Diana Marjory Hall; two *s* one *d*. *Educ:* Tonbridge Sch.; St Catharine's Coll., Cambridge. Taught at Radley Coll., 1959–73 (Housemaster, 1968–73); Headmaster: Eastbourne Coll., 1973–80; Shrewsbury Sch., 1981–88. *Recreations:* reading, gardening, golf. *Address:* Park House, Culworth, Banbury, Oxon OX17 2AP. *T:* Sulgrave (029576) 222. *Clubs:* East India; Hawks (Cambridge); Free Foresters, Jesters.

See also T. J. Langdale.

LANGDALE, Timothy James; Senior Prosecuting Counsel to the Crown, Central Criminal Court, since 1987; *b* 3 Jan. 1940; *m* twice; two *d*. *Educ:* Sevenoaks Sch.; St Andrews Univ. (MA). Called to the Bar, Lincoln's Inn, 1966. Res. Assistant, Community Justice Center, Watts, Los Angeles, 1969–70; Jun. Prosecuting Counsel to the Crown, CCC, 1979–87. *Recreations:* reading, opera, theatre, cinema. *Address:* Queen Elizabeth Building, Temple, EC4. *T:* 071–583 5766.

See also S. J. B. Langdale.

LANGDON, Anthony James; Deputy Under Secretary of State, Home Office, since 1989; *b* 5 June 1935; *s* of Dr James Norman Langdon and Maud Winifred Langdon; *m* 1969, Helen Josephine Drabble, *y d* of His Honour J. F. Drabble, QC; one *s* one *d*. *Educ:* Kingswood Sch., Bath; Christ's Coll., Cambridge. Entered Home Office, 1958; Office of

Minister for Science, 1961–63; Treasury, 1967–69; Under Sec., Cabinet Office, 1985–89. *Address:* c/o Home Office, 50 Queen Anne's Gate, SW1H 9AT.

LANGDON, (Augustus) John; chartered surveyor and land agent; *b* 20 April 1913; *e s* of late Rev. Cecil Langdon, MA and Elizabeth Mercer Langdon, MBE; *m*; two *d*; *m* 1949, Doris Edna Clinkard; one *s*. *Educ:* Berkhamsted Sch.; St John's Coll., Cambridge (Nat. Science Tripos; MA). FRICS (Chartered Land Agent); FRSA. Asst to J. Carter Jonas & Sons, Oxford, 1936–37, Partner 1945–48; Suptg Lands Officer, Admty, 1937–45; Regional Land Comr, Min. of Agriculture, 1948–65; Dep. Dir, Agric. Land Service, Min. of Agriculture, 1965–71; Chief Surveyor, Agricultural Develt and Advisory Service, MAFF, 1971–74; with the National Trust in London, 1974–76. Chm., Statutory Cttee on Agricultural Valuation; RICS: Mem., Gen. Council; Mem., Land Agency and Agricultural Divisional Council, 1971–75. *Publications:* contrib. Rural Estate Management (ed R. C. Walmsley), Fream's Elements of Agriculture, professional and agric. jls. *Recreations:* gardening, walking, collecting. *Address:* Thorn Bank, Long Street, Sherborne, Dorset DT9 3BS. *T:* Sherborne (0935) 812910. *Club:* United Oxford & Cambridge University.

LANGDON, David, OBE 1988; FRSA; Cartoonist and Illustrator; Member of Punch Table; regular contributor to Punch since 1937, to The New Yorker since 1952; Cartoonist to Sunday Mirror, since 1948; *b* 24 Feb. 1914; *er s* of late Bennett and Bess Langdon; *m* 1955, April Sadler-Phillips; two *s* one *d*. *Educ:* Davenant Gram. Sch., London. Architect's Dept, LCC, 1931–39; Executive Officer, London Rescue Service, 1939–41; served in Royal Air Force, 1941–46; Squadron Leader, 1945. Editor, Royal Air Force Jl, 1945–46. Creator of Billy Brown of London Town for LPTB. Official Artist to Centre International Audio-Visuel d'Etudes et de Recherches, St Ghislain, Belgium. Exhibitions: Oxford, New York, Lille, London. *Publications:* Home Front Lines, 1941; All Buttoned Up, 1944; Meet Me Inside, 1946; Slipstream (with R. B. Raymond), 1946; The Way I See It, 1947; Hold Tight There!, 1949; Let's Face It, 1951; Wake Up and Die (with David Clayton), 1952; Look at You, 1952; All in Fun, 1953; Laugh with Me, 1954; More in Fun, 1955; Funnier Still, 1956; A Banger for a Monkey, 1957; Langdon At Large, 1958; I'm Only Joking, 1960; Punch with Wings, 1961; How to Play Golf and Stay Happy, 1964; David Langdon's Casebook, 1969; How To Talk Golf, 1975; Punch in the Air, 1983. *Recreations:* golf, non-League soccer. *Address:* Greenlands, Honor End Lane, Great Missenden, Bucks HP16 9QY. *T:* Great Missenden (02406) 2475. *Club:* Royal Air Force.

LANGDON, John; *see* Langdon, A. J.

LANGDON, Jonathan Bertram Robert Louis; His Honour Judge Langdon; a Circuit Judge, since 1991; *b* 1 Nov. 1939; *s* of Captain John Edward Langdon, RN and Nancy Langdon; *m* 1962, Hilary Jean Fox Taylor; twin *s* one *d*. *Educ:* Hurstpierpoint Coll.; RNC Dartmouth. Entered RN, 1958; served HM Ships Bermuda, Lincoln and London, 1960–64; Supply Officer, HMS Daring, 1965–68; legal trng, 1968–70; called to the Bar, Gray's Inn, 1970; Lieut Comdr, 1970; Staff Legal Advr to FO Plymouth, 1970–73; RN FE Legal Advr, Hong Kong, 1973–75; Comdr, 1977; Supply Officer, HMS Norfolk, 1977–79; various MoD and staff appts, 1980–86; Captain, 1986; Chief Naval Judge Advocate, 1987–90; a Recorder, SE Circuit, 1989; Sec. to C-in-C Naval Home Command, 1990–91; retired voluntarily from RN, 1991. *Recreations:* sailing, gardening, croquet, travel. *Address:* c/o Lloyds Bank, 125 High Street, Sittingbourne, Kent ME10 4BD.

LANGDON, Richard Norman Darbey, FCA; chairman and director of companies; *b* 19 June 1919; *s* of Norman Langdon and Dorothy Langdon; *m* 1944, June Dixon; two *s*. *Educ:* Shrewsbury Sch. Officer, RA, 1939–46. Admitted Mem. Inst. of Chartered Accountants in England and Wales, 1947; joined Spicer and Pegler, 1949, Partner 1953, Managing Partner, 1971–82, Senior Partner, 1978–84. Chairman: Hammond and Champness Ltd, 1966–89; Aspinall Hldg, 1983–89; Finlay Packaging PLC, 1984–; Time Products PLC, 1984–; First National Finance Corp., 1985–; Beeson Gregory, 1989–; Dir, Rockware Group PLC, 1985–; Dep. Chm., Chemring Gp PLC, 1985–. Treasurer, CGLI, 1982–90. Mem. Council, Univ. of Surrey, 1988–90. *Recreations:* sailing, gardening, bricklaying. *Address:* Rough Hill House, Munstead, near Godalming, Surrey GU8 4AR. *T:* Godalming (0483) 421507. *Clubs:* City of London; Old Salopian.

LANGDON-DOWN, Antony Turnbull; Part-time Chairman, Social Security Appeals Tribunal, since 1985; Clerk to Merchant Taylors Company, 1980–85; *b* 31 Dec. 1922; *s* of Dr Reginald Langdon-Down and Ruth Langdon-Down (*née* Turnbull); *m* 1954, Jill Elizabeth Style (*née* Caruth); one *s* one *d*. *Educ:* Harrow School. Member of Lincoln's Inn, 1940–60, called to the Bar, 1948; enrolled as a solicitor, 1960; practised as solicitor, 1961–80. Pilot, Royal Air Force, 1942–47 (finally Flt Lieut). Master of Merchant Taylors Company, 1979–80. *Recreations:* sailing, tennis, bridge, music, art. *Address:* Tinley Lodge, Shipbourne, Tonbridge, Kent TN11 9QB. *T:* Plaxtol (0732) 810720. *Clubs:* Savile, Beefsteak, MCC; Bough Beech Sailing, Law Society Yacht.

LANGDON-DOWN, Barbara; *see* Littlewood, Lady (Barbara).

LANGE, Rt. Hon. David Russell, CH 1990; PC 1984; MP (Lab) Mangere, New Zealand, since 1977; Attorney General, and Minister of State, since 1989; *b* 4 Aug. 1942; *s* of Eric Roy Lange and late Phoebe Fysh Lange; *m* 1968, Naomi Joy Crampton; two *s* one *d*. *Educ:* Univ. of Auckland (LLM Hons). Called to the Bar of NZ and admitted Solicitor, 1966. Minister of Foreign Affairs, 1984–87; Prime Minister, and Minister in charge of Security Intelligence Service, 1984–89, and Minister of Education, 1987–89. Dep. Leader of the Opposition, 1979–83, Leader 1983–84. *Publication:* Nuclear-Free—the New Zealand Way, 1990. *Address:* Parliament House, Wellington, New Zealand. *T:* (04) 719998.

LANGFORD, 9th Baron, *cr* 1800; **Colonel Geoffrey Alexander Rowley-Conwy,** OBE 1943; DL; RA, retired; Constable of Rhuddlan Castle and Lord of the Manor of Rhuddlan; *b* 8 March 1912; *s* of late Major Geoffrey Seymour Rowley-Conwy (killed in action, Gallipoli, 1915), Bodrhyddan, Flints, and Bertha Gabrielle Rowley-Conwy, JP (*d* 1984), *d* of late Lieutenant Alexander Cochran, Royal Navy, Ashkirk, Selkirkshire; *S* kinsman 1953; *m* 1st, 1939, Ruth St John (marr. diss. 1956), *d* of late Albert St John Murphy, The Island House, Little Island, County Cork; 2nd, 1957, Grete (*d* 1973), *d* of late Col E. T. C. von Freiesleben, formerly Chief of the King's Adjutants Staff to the King of Denmark; three *s*; 3rd, 1975, Susan Winifred Denham, *d* of C. C. H. Denham, Chester; one *s* one *d*. *Educ:* Marlborough; RMA Woolwich. Served War of 1939–45, with RA (2nd Lieut, 1932; Lieut, 1935; Captain, 1939; Major 1941); Singapore, (POW escaped) and with Indian Mountain Artillery in Burma, 1941–45 (despatches, OBE); Staff Coll., Quetta, 1945; Berlin Airlift, Fassberg, 1948–49; GSOI 42 Inf. Div., TA, 1949–52; Lt-Col 1945; retired 1957; Colonel (Hon.), 1967. Freeman, City of London, 1986–. DL Clwyd, 1977. *Heir: s* Hon. Owain Grenville Rowley-Conwy, [*b* 27 Dec. 1958; *m* 1986, Joanna, *d* of Jack Featherstone; one *s* one *d*]. *Address:* Bodrhyddan, Rhuddlan, Clwyd. *Club:* Army and Navy.

LANGFORD, Anthony John; Deputy Chief Executive, Valuation Office Agency (formerly Deputy Chief Valuer, Valuation Office), Inland Revenue, since 1988; *b* 25 June 1936; *s* of Freeman and Ethel Langford; *m* 1957, Joan Winifred Barber; one *s* one *d*. *Educ:* Soham Grammar School. FRICS. Joined Valuation Office, 1957; District Valuer, Camden, 1976; Superintending Valuer, Northern Region, 1981; Asst Chief Valuer, 1983. *Recreations:* walking, gardening, badminton. *Address:* New Court, Carey Street, WC2A 2JE.

LANGFORD-HOLT, Sir John (Anthony), Kt 1962; Lieutenant-Commander RN (Retired); *b* 30 June 1916; *s* of late Ernest Langford-Holt; *m* 1953, Flora Evelyn Innes (marr. diss. 1969), *d* of late Ian St Clair Stuart; one *s* one *d*; *m* 1984, Irene, *d* of late David Alexander Kerr. *Educ:* Shrewsbury Sch. Joined RN and Air Branch (FAA), 1939. MP (C) Shrewsbury, 1945–83. Sec. of Conservative Parly Labour Cttee, 1945–50; Chm., Anglo-Austrian Soc., 1960–63, 1971–82; Member: CPA, 1945–83; IPU, 1945–83, and other Internat. Bodies; Parliamentary and Scientific Cttee, 1945–83; Estimates Cttee, 1964–68; Expenditure Cttee, 1977–79; Chm., Select Cttee on Defence, 1979–81. Chancellor, Primrose League, 1989–. Freeman and Liveryman of City of London. Grand Decoration of Honour, in Silver with Star (Austria), 1980. *Address:* 704 Nelson House, Dolphin Square, SW1. *T:* 071–798 8186; New Milton (0425) 621606. *Club:* White's.

LANGHAM, Sir James (Michael), 15th Bt *cr* 1660; TD 1965; *b* 24 May 1932; *s* of Sir John Charles Patrick Langham, 14th Bt, and of Rosamond Christabel (MBE 1969), *d* of late Arthur Rashleigh; *S* father, 1972; *m* 1959, Marion Audrey Eleanor, *d* of O. H. Barratt, Gararagua Estate, Tanzania; two *s* one *d*. *Educ:* Rossall School, Fleetwood. Served as Captain, North Irish Horse, 1953–67. *Recreations:* shooting, skin-diving. *Heir: s* John Stephen Langham, *b* 14 Dec. 1960. *Address:* Claranagh, Tempo, Co. Fermanagh. *T:* Tempo (036554) 247.

LANGHORNE, Richard Tristan Bailey; FRHistS; Director, Centre for International Studies, University of Cambridge, since 1987; Fellow, St John's College, Cambridge, since 1974; *b* 6 May 1940; *s* of Eadward John Bailey Langhorne and Rosemary Scott-Foster; *m* 1971, Helen Logue, *o d* of William Donaldson, CB and Mary Donaldson; one *s* one *d*. *Educ:* St Edward's Sch., Oxford; St John's Coll., Cambridge (Exhibr). BA Hist. Tripos, 1962; Certif. in Hist. Studies, 1963; MA 1965. Tutor in History, Univ. of Exeter, 1963–64; Research Student, St John's Coll., Cambridge, 1964–66; Lectr in History, 1966–74 and Master of Rutherford Coll., 1971–74, Univ. of Kent at Canterbury; St John's College, Cambridge: Steward, 1974–79; Junior Bursar, 1974–87. Vis. Prof., Univ. of Southern Calif, 1986. Freeland K. Abbott Meml Lectr, Tufts Univ., 1990. *Publications:* chapters in: The Twentieth Century Mind, 1971; British Foreign Policy under Sir Edward Grey, 1977; The Collapse of the Concert of Europe, 1890–1914, 1980; (ed) Diplomacy and Intelligence during the Second World War, 1985; reviews and articles in Historical Jl, History, and Review of International Studies. *Recreations:* music, railways. *Address:* St John's College, Cambridge; 15 Madingley Road, Cambridge. *Club:* Athenæum.

LANGLANDS, Prof. Robert Phelan, FRS 1981; Professor of Mathematics, Institute for Advanced Study, Princeton, New Jersey, since 1972; *b* 6 Oct. 1936; *s* of Robert Langlands and Kathleen Johanna (*née* Phelan); *m* 1956, Charlotte Lorraine Cheverie; two *s* two *d*. *Educ:* Univ. of British Columbia (BA 1957, MA 1958); Yale Univ. (PhD 1960). FRSC 1972. Princeton University: Instructor, 1960–61; Lectr, 1961–62; Asst Prof., 1962–64; Associate Prof., 1964–67; Prof., Yale Univ., 1967–72. Associate Prof., Ortadoğu Teknik Universitesi, 1967–68; Gast Prof., Universität Bonn, 1980–81. Hon. DSc: British Columbia, 1985; McMaster, 1985; CUNY, 1985; Paris VII, 1989; Hon. DMath Waterloo, 1988. Wilbur L. Cross Medal, Yale Univ., 1975; Cole Prize, Amer. Math. Sec., 1982; Common Wealth Award, Sigma Xi, 1984; Maths Award, Nat. Acad. of Scis, 1988. *Publications:* Automorphic Forms on GL(2) (with H. Jacquet), 1970; Euler Products, 1971; On the Functional Equations satisfied by Eisenstein Series, 1976; Base Change for GL(2), 1980; Les débuts d'une formule des traces stable, 1983; contrib. Canadian Jl Maths, Proc. Amer. Math. Soc. Symposia, Springer Lecture Notes. *Address:* Institute for Advanced Study, Princeton, NJ 08540, USA. *T:* 609–734–8106.

LANGLEY, Gordon Julian Hugh, QC 1983; a Recorder, since 1986; *b* 11 May 1943; *s* of late Gordon Thompson Langley and of Marjorie Langley; *m* 1968, Beatrice Jayanthi Langley; two *d*. *Educ:* Westminster School; Balliol College, Oxford (BA, BCL). Called to the Bar, Inner Temple, 1966. *Recreations:* music, sport. *Address:* 2 Bridgeman Road, Teddington, Mddx TW11 9AH. *T:* 071–353 1878. *Club:* Travellers'.

LANGLEY, Maj.-Gen. Sir (Henry) Desmond (Allen), KCVO 1983; MBE 1967; Governor and Commander-in-Chief of Bermuda, since 1988; *b* 16 May 1930; *s* of late Col Henry Langley, OBE, and Winsome Langley; *m* 1950, Felicity Joan, *d* of Lt-Col K. J. P. Oliphant, MC; one *s* one *d*. *Educ:* Eton; RMA Sandhurst. Commissioned The Life Guards, 1949; Adjt, Household Cavalry Regt, 1953–54; GSO3 HQ 10th Armoured Div., 1956–57; Regtl Adjt, Household Cavalry, 1959–60; psc 1961; GSO2(Ops) HQ Far East Land Forces, 1963–65; Bde Major, Household Bde, 1965–67; Comdg Officer, The Life Guards, 1969–71; Asst Sec., Chiefs of Staff Secretariat, 1971–72; Lt-Col Comdg Household Cavalry and Silver Stick-in-Waiting, 1972–75; Comdr 4th Guards Armoured Bde, 1976–77; RCDS 1978; BGS HQ UK Land Forces, 1979; GOC London District and Maj.-Gen. Comdg Household Div., 1979–83; Administrator, Sovereign Base Areas and Comdr, British Forces, Cyprus, 1983–85; retired, 1986. Gov., Church Lads' and Church Girls' Brigade, 1986–. Freeman, City of London, 1983. KStJ 1989. *Address:* Government House, Hamilton, Bermuda.

LANGRIDGE, Philip Gordon, FRAM; concert and opera singer (tenor), since 1964; *b* 16 Dec. 1939; *m* 1981, Ann Murray; one *s* (and one *s* two *d* by former marriage). *Educ:* Maidstone Grammar Sch.; Royal Academy of Music, London. ARAM 1977; FRAM 1985. Glyndebourne Festival début, 1964; BBC Promenade Concerts, 1970–; Edinburgh Fest., 1970–; Netherlands Opera, Scottish Opera, Handel Opera etc. Covent Garden: L'Enfant et les Sortilèges, Rossignole, Boris, Jenufa, Idomeneo, Peter Grimes; ENO: Turn of the Screw, Osud (Olivier Award, Outstanding Individual Performer in a New Opera Production, 1984), The Mask of Orpheus, Billy Budd, Beatrice and Benedict, Makropoulos Case; Glyndebourne, 1977–: Don Giovanni, Idomeneo, Fidelio, Jenufa, La Clemenza di Tito; La Scala, 1979–: Rake's Progress, Wozzeck, Boris Godunov, Il Sosia, Idomeneo, Oberon; Frankfurt Opera: Castor and Pollux, Rigoletto, Die Entführung; Zurich Opera: Poppea, Lucio Silla; Don Giovanni; La Fenice: Janacek's Diary; Palermo: Otello (Rossini); Pesaro: La Donna del Lago; Aix en Provence: Alcina, Les Boriades; Metropolitan Opera, NY: Così fan Tutte, Boris Godunov; Vienna State Opera: Wozzeck; Salzburg Festival: Moses und Aron, Idomeneo. Concerts with major, international orchestras and conductors including: Boston (Previn), Chicago (Solti, Abbado), Los Angeles (Christopher Hogwood), Sydney (Mackerras), Vienna Phil. (Previn), Orchestre de Paris (Barenboim, Mehta), and all major British orchestras. Many first performances of works, some dedicated to and written for him. Has made over 50 records of early, baroque, classical, romantic and modern music (Grammy Award for Schönberg's Moses und Aron, 1985). Mem., Music Panel, Arts Council of GB, 1983–86. Singer of the Year, RPS/Heidsieck Award, 1989. *Recreation:* collecting water colour paintings and Victorian postcards. *Address:* c/o Allied Artists Agency, 42 Montpelier Square, SW7 1JZ. *T:* 071–589 6243.

LANGRIDGE, Richard James; HM Diplomatic Service; Consul-General, Bordeaux, 1990–Oct. 1992; *b* 29 Oct. 1932; *m* 1965, Jeannine Louise Joosen; one *d.* HM Forces, 1951–53; joined FO 1953; served NY, Leopoldville, Athens, Dakar, Paris and FCO; Ambassador to Madagascar, 1979–84; FCO, 1985; Dep. High Comr, Colombo, 1985–89. *Address:* c/o Foreign and Commonwealth Office, SW1.

LANGRISHE, Sir Hercules (Ralph Hume), 7th Bt *cr* 1777; *b* 17 May 1927; *s* of Sir Terence Hume Langrishe, 6th Bt, and Joan Stuart (*d* 1976), *d* of late Major Ralph Stuart Grigg; *S* father, 1973; *m* 1955, Hon. Grania Sybil Enid Wingfield, *d* of 9th Viscount Powerscourt; one *s* three *d. Educ:* Summer Fields, St Leonards; Eton. 2nd Lieut, 9th Queen's Royal Lancers, 1947; Lieut, 1948; retd 1953; *Recreations:* shooting, fishing. *Heir: s* James Hercules Langrishe [*b* 3 March 1957; *m* 1985, Gemma, *d* of Patrick O'Daly; one *s* one *d*]. *Address:* Ringlestown House, Kilmessan, Co. Meath. *T:* Navan 25243. *Club:* Kildare Street and University (Dublin).

LANGSHAW, George Henry; Managing Director, Global Gas, British Gas, since 1990; *b* 6 Dec. 1939; *s* of George Henry and Florence Evelyn Langshaw; *m* 1962, Maureen Cosgrove; one *s* two *d. Educ:* Liverpool Inst. High Sch. FCMA; ACIS. Various accountancy appts, Wm Crawford & Sons, 1957–63, Littlewoods Orgn, 1963–67; British Gas: Accountant, NW, 1967–70; Develt Accountant, Southern, 1970–73; Prin. Financial Analyst, HQ, 1973–76; Chief Accountant, Wales, 1976–78; Dir of Finance, Southern, 1978–82; Dep, Chm., NW, 1982–87; Regional Chm., British Gas (Wales), 1987–89; Gp Dir of Personnel, 1989–90. Dir, Bd of Gas Consumers, Canada, 1990–. CIGasE 1988; CBIM 1991. *Recreations:* soccer, reading, golf. *Address:* British Gas, Rivermill House, 152 Grosvenor Road, SW1V 3JL.

LANGSLOW, Derek Robert, PhD; Chief Executive, English Nature, since 1990; *b* 7 Feb. 1945; *s* of Alexander Frederick Langslow and Beatrice Bibby Langslow (*née* Wright); *m* 1969, Helen Katherine (*née* Addison); one *s* one *d. Educ:* Ashville College, Harrogate; Queens' College, Cambridge (MA, PhD). Post-Doctoral Fellow, Cambridge and Univ. of Kansas; Lectr, Univ. of Edinburgh, 1972–78; Nature Conservancy Council: Senior Ornithologist, 1978–84; Asst Chief Scientist, 1984–87; Dir, Policy and Planning, 1987–90; Chief Scientist, 1990. FRSA. *Publications:* numerous papers in learned jls. *Recreations:* badminton, walking, bird watching. *Address:* 4 Engaine, Orton Longueville, Peterborough. *T:* Peterborough (0733) 232153.

LANGSTON, Group Captain John Antony S.; *see* Steff-Langston.

LANGSTONE, Rt. Rev. John Arthur William; *b* 30 Aug. 1913; *s* of Arthur James Langstone and Coullina Cook; *m* 1944, Alice Patricia Whitby; two *s. Educ:* Univ. of Toronto (BA); Trinity Coll., Toronto (LTh); Yale Univ. (MDiv). Asst Curate, St John Baptist, Toronto, 1938; Chaplain, Cdn Army, 1943; Exec. Officer, Dio. Toronto, 1947; Rector: Trinity Church, Port Credit, Toronto, 1950; St George's, Edmonton, 1958; St Faith's, Edmonton, 1969; Canon of All Saints' Cathedral, Edmonton, 1963; Archdeacon of Edmonton, 1965; Exec. Archdeacon, 1971; Bishop of Edmonton, 1976–79. Hon. DD Trinity Coll., Toronto, 1977. *Address:* 5112 109 Avenue, Edmonton, Alberta T6A 1S1, Canada. *T:* 465–4111.

LANGTON; *see* Temple-Gore-Langton, family name of Earl Temple of Stowe.

LANGTON, Bryan David, CBE 1988; FHCIMA; Director, Bass plc, since 1985; Chairman and Chief Executive, Holiday Inns, since 1990; *b* 6 Dec. 1936; *s* of Thomas Langton and Doris (*née* Brown); *m* 1960, Sylva Degenhardt; two *d. Educ:* Accrington Grammar Sch.; Westminster Tech. Coll. (Hotel Operation Dip.); Ecole Hotelière de la SSA, Lausanne (Operations Dip.). Dep. Manager, Russell Hotel, London, 1959–63; General Manager: Victoria Hotel, Nottingham, 1964–66; Grand Hotel, Manchester, 1966–71; Crest Hotels: Divl Manager, 1971–73; Ops Dir UK, 1973–75; Ops Dir Europe, 1975–77; Divl Managing Dir, Europe, 1977–81; Managing Dir, Ops, 1981–82; Man. Dir, 1982–88; Chairman, 1985–. Chairman: Holiday Inns International, 1988–; Toby Restaurants, 1988–. Hon. Fellow, Manchester Poly., 1986. *Recreations:* golf, cricket, reading, theatre. *Address:* 4185 Fairway Villas Drive, Alpharetta, Ga 30202, USA. *T:* (404) 740 9706.

LANGTON, Sir Henry Algernon; *see under* Calley, Sir H. A.

LANGTRY, Ian; *see* Langtry, J. I.

LANGTRY, (James) Ian; Education Officer, Association of County Councils, since 1988; *b* 2 Jan. 1939; *s* of late Rev. H. J. Langtry and I. M. Langtry (*née* Eagleson); *m* 1959, Eileen Roberta Beatrice (*née* Nesbitt); one *s* one *d. Educ:* Coleraine Academical Instn; Queen's Univ., Belfast (Sullivan Schol.; BSc 1st Cl., Physics). Assistant Master, Bangor Grammar Sch., 1960–61; Lectr, Belfast College of Technology, 1961–66; Asst Director of Examinations/Recruitment, Civil Service Commission, 1966–70; Principal, Dept of Educn and Science, 1970–76, Asst Sec., 1976–82, Under Sec., 1982–87; Under Sec., DHSS, 1987–88. *Recreations:* golf, sailing. *Clubs:* Royal Portrush Golf; West Kent Golf.

LA NIECE, Rear-Adm. Peter George, CB 1973; CBE 1967; *b* 23 July 1920; *s* of late George David Nelson La Niece and Gwynneth Mary (*née* Morgan); *m* 1948, Evelyn Mary Wrixon Babington (*d* 1982); two *s* one *d. Educ:* Whitgift Sch., Croydon. Entered RN, 1937; served War of 1939–45 in battleships, cruisers and destroyers; Gunnery Specialist 1945; Comdr 1953; Captain 1961; comd HMS Rame Head, 1962; Senior UK Polaris Rep., Washington, 1963–66; comd HMS Triumph, 1966–68; Cdre Clyde in Comd Clyde Submarine Base, 1969–71; Rear-Adm. 1971; Flag Officer Spithead and Port Admiral, Portsmouth, 1971–73; retired 1973. Dir in Exco Gp of Cos, 1976–85. *Recreation:* gardening. *Address:* Charltons, Yalding, Kent ME18 6DF. *T:* Maidstone (0622) 814161. *Club:* Army and Navy.

LANKESTER, Richard Shermer; Clerk of Select Committees, House of Commons, 1979–87; Registrar of Members' Interests, 1976–87; *b* 8 Feb. 1922; *s* of late Richard Ward Lankester; *m* 1950, Dorothy, *d* of late Raymond Jackson, Worsley; two *s* one *d* (and one *s* decd). *Educ:* Haberdashers' Aske's Hampstead Sch.; Jesus Coll., Oxford (MA). Served Royal Artillery, 1942–45. Entered Dept of Clerk of House of Commons, 1947; Clerk of Standing Cttees, 1973–75; Clerk of Expenditure Cttee, 1975–79. Co-Editor, The Table, 1962–67. *Address:* The Old Farmhouse, The Green, Boughton Monchelsea, Maidstone, Kent ME17 4LT. *T:* Maidstone (0622) 743749.

LANKESTER, Timothy Patrick; Permanent Secretary, Overseas Development Administration, Foreign and Commonwealth Office, since 1989; *s* of Preb. Robin Prior Archibald Lankester and Jean Dorothy (*née* Gilliat); *m* 1968, Patricia Cockcroft; three *d. Educ:* Monkton Combe Sch.; St John's Coll., Cambridge (BA); Jonathan Edwards Coll., Yale (Henry Fellow, MA). Teacher (VSO), St Michael's Coll., Belize, 1960–61; Fereday Fellow, St John's Coll., Oxford, 1965–66; Economist, World Bank, Washington DC, 1966–69; New Delhi, 1970–73; Principal 1973, Asst Sec. 1977, HM Treasury; Private Secretary to Rt Hon. James Callaghan, 1978–79; to Rt Hon. Margaret Thatcher, 1979–81; seconded to S. G. Warburg and Co. Ltd, 1981–83; Under Sec., HM Treasury, 1983–85; Economic Minister, Washington and Exec. Dir, IMF and World Bank, 1985–88; Dep. Sec., HM Treasury, 1988–89. *Address:* Overseas Development Administration, Eland House, Stag Place, SW1E 5DH.

LANSBURY, Angela Brigid; actress; *b* London, England, 16 Oct. 1925; *d* of Edgar Lansbury and late Moyna Macgill (who *m* 1st, Reginald Denham); *m* 1st, Richard Cromwell; 2nd, 1949, Peter Shaw; one *s* one *d* and one step *s*; naturalized American citizen, 1951. *Educ:* South Hampstead High Sch. for Girls; Webber Douglas Sch. of Singing and Dramatic Art, Kensington; Feagin Sch. of Drama and Radio, New York. With Metro-Goldwyn-Mayor, 1943–50; *films* included: Gaslight, 1944; National Velvet, 1944; Dorian Gray, 1944; Harvey Girls, 1946; Till the Clouds Roll By, 1946; If Winter Comes, 1947; State of the Union, 1948; Samson and Delilah, 1949. As free lance, 1950–: *films* include: Kind Lady, 1951; The Court Jester, 1956; The Long Hot Summer, 1957; The Reluctant Debutante, 1958; Summer of the 17th Doll, 1959; A Breath of Scandal, 1959; Dark at the Top of the Stairs, 1960; Blue Hawaii, 1962; All Fall Down, 1962; The Manchurian Candidate, 1963; In the Cool of the Day, 1963; The World of Henry Orient, 1964; Out of Towners, 1964; Harlow, 1965; Bedknobs and Broomsticks, 1972; Black Flowers for the Bride, 1972; Death on the Nile, 1978; The Lady Vanishes, 1979; The Mirror Crack'd, 1980; The Pirates of Penzance, 1983; The Company of Wolves, 1984; *plays:* appearances include: Hotel Paradiso (Broadway debut), 1957; Helen, in A Taste of Honey, Lyceum Theatre, New York, 1960; Anyone can Whistle (Broadway musical), 1964; Mame (Tony Award for best actress in a Broadway musical), Winter Garden, NYC, 1966–68; Dear World (Broadway), 1969 (Tony Award); Gypsy (Broadway Musical), Piccadilly, 1973, US tour, 1974 (Tony Award; Chicago, Sarah Siddons Award, 1974); Gertrude, in Hamlet, Nat. Theatre, 1975; Anna, in The King and I (Broadway), 1978; Mrs Lovett, in Sweeney Todd (Broadway), 1979 (Tony Award). TV series, Murder She Wrote, 1984–88 (Golden Globe Award, 1984, 1986). NY Drama Desk Award, 1979; Sarah Siddons Award, 1980 and 1983; inducted Theatre Hall of Fame, 1982.

LANSDOWN, Gillian Elizabeth, (Mrs Richard Lansdown); *see* Tindall, G. E.

LANSDOWNE, 8th Marquess of (GB), *cr* 1784; **George John Charles Mercer Nairne Petty-Fitzmaurice;** 29th Baron of Kerry and Lixnaw, 1181; Earl of Kerry, Viscount Clanmaurice, 1723; Viscount FitzMaurice and Baron Dunkeron, 1751; Earl of Shelburne, 1753; Baron Wycombe, 1760; Earl of Wycombe and Viscount Calne, 1784; PC 1964; *b* 27 Nov. 1912; *o s* of Major Lord Charles George Francis Mercer Nairne, MVO (killed in action, 1914; 2nd *s* of 5th Marquess), and Lady Violet Mary Elliot (she *m* 2nd, 1916, 1st Baron Astor of Hever), *d* of 4th Earl of Minto; *S* cousin, 1944; *m* 1st, 1938, Barbara, (*d* 1965), *d* of Harold Stuart Chase, Santa Barbara; two *s* one *d* (and one *d* decd); 2nd, 1969, Mrs Polly Carnegie (marr. diss. 1978), *d* of Viscount Eccles, *qv*; 3rd, 1978, Gillian Ann, (*d* 1982), *d* of Alured Morgan. *Educ:* Eton; Christ Church, Oxford. Sec. Junior Unionist League for E Scotland, 1939. Served War of 1939–45, Capt. Royal Scots Greys 1940, formerly 2nd Lt Scottish Horse (TA); Major 1944; served with Free French Forces (Croix de Guerre, Légion D'Honneur); Private Sec. to HM Ambassador in Paris (Rt Hon. A. Duff Cooper), 1944–45. Lord-in-Waiting to the Queen, 1957–58; Joint Parliamentary Under-Sec. of State, Foreign Office, 1958–62; Minister of State for Colonial Affairs, 1962–64, and for Commonwealth Relations, 1963–64. Mem. Royal Company of Archers (Queen's Body Guard for Scotland); JP, Perthshire, 1950; DL Wilts, 1952–73. Patron of two livings. Chm., Victoria League in Scotland, 1952–56; Inter-Governmental Cttee on Malaysia, 1962. Chm., Franco-British Soc., 1972–83; Pres., Franco-Scottish Soc. Prime Warden, Fishmongers' Company, 1967–68. Comdr, Légion d'Honneur, 1979. *Heir: s* Earl of Shelburne, *qv. Address:* Meikleour House, Perthshire. *Clubs:* Turf; New (Edinburgh).

See also Lady Nairne.

LANSLEY, Andrew David; Director, Conservative Research Department, since 1990; *b* 11 Dec. 1956; *s* of Thomas and Irene Lansley; *m* 1985, Marilyn Jane Biggs; two *d. Educ:* Univ. of Exeter (BA). Administration trainee, Dept of Industry, 1979; Private Sec. to Sec. of State for Trade and Industry, 1984–85; Principal Private Sec. to Chancellor of Duchy of Lancaster, 1985–87; Dir, Policy, 1987, Dep. Dir-Gen., 1989–90, ABCC, 1987–89. *Publication:* A Private Route?, 1988. *Recreations:* travel, bridge, cricket, political biography. *Address:* Conservative and Unionist Central Office, 32 Smith Square, SW1P 3HH. *T:* 071–222 9000.

LANYON, Lance Edward; Principal, Royal Veterinary College, since 1989; *b* 4 Jan. 1944; *s* of Harry Lanyon and Heather Gordon Tyrrell; *m* 1972, Mary Kear; one *s* one *d. Educ:* Christ's Hospital; Univ. of Bristol (BVSC, PhD). MRCVS. Lectr, 1967, Reader in Vet. Anatomy, 1967–79, Univ. of Bristol; Associate Prof., 1980–83, Prof., 1983–84, Tufts Sch. of Vet. Medicine, Boston, Mass; Prof. of Vet. Anatomy, Royal Vet. Coll., 1984–89 (Head, Dept of Vet. Basic Scis, 1987–88). *Publications:* chapters in books on orthopaedics, osteoporosis, and athletic training; articles in professional jls. *Recreations:* building, home improvements, sailing. *Address:* Royal Veterinary College, Royal College Street, NW1 0TU. *T:* 071–387 2898.

LAPIDGE, Michael, PhD, LittD; Reader in Insular Latin Literature, 1988–Oct. 1991, Elrington and Bosworth Professor of Anglo-Saxon, from Oct. 1991, Cambridge University; *b* 8 Feb. 1942; *s* of Rae H. Lapidge and Catherine Mary Lapidge (*née* Carruthers). *Educ:* Univ. of Calgary (BA 1962); Univ. of Alberta (MA 1965); Univ. of Toronto (PhD 1971); LittD Cantab 1988. Univ. Lectr, Cambridge, 1974–88. *Publications:* Aldhelm: the prose works, 1979; Alfred the Great, 1983; Aldhelm: the poetic works, 1985; A Bibliography of Celtic Latin Literature 400–1200, 1985; articles in learned jls. *Recreation:* mountaineering. *Address:* 9 West Road, Cambridge CB3 9DP. *T:* Cambridge (0223) 335085.

LAPOINTE, Paul André; Canadian Ambassador to Turkey, since 1990; *b* 1 Nov. 1934; *s* of Henri and Regina Lapointe; *m* 1965, Iris Donati; one *d. Educ:* Université Laval. BA, LLL. Called to the Bar, Québec, 1958. Journalist, Le Soleil, 1959–60; joined Canadian Foreign Service, 1960; served Vietnam and Laos, 1961–62, NATO, Paris, 1962–64, Geneva, 1968–72, New Delhi, 1975–76, New York, 1976–79; Dep. Perm. Rep. to UN Security Council, 1977–78; Dep. High Comr in UK, 1981–85; Consul Gen., Marseille, France, 1985–87; Sen. Negotiator, Canada-France Maritime Affairs, Dept of External Affairs, Canada, 1987–90. *Address:* Canadian Embassy, Nenehatun Caddesi 75, 06700 Gaziosmanpaşa, Ankara, Turkey. *Club:* Travellers'.

LAPOTAIRE, Jane; actress; *b* 26 Dec. 1944; *d* of unknown father and Louise Elise Lapotaire; *m* 1st, 1965, Oliver Wood (marr. diss. 1967); 2nd, 1974, Roland Joffé (marr. diss. 1982); one *s. Educ:* Northgate Grammar Sch., Ipswich; Old Vic Theatre Sch., Bristol. Bristol Old Vic Co., 1965–67; Nat. Theatre Co., 1967–71, incl. Measure for Measure, Flea in Her Ear, Dance of Death, Way of the World, Merchant of Venice, Oedipus, The Taming of the Shrew; freelance films and TV, 1971–74; RSC, 1974–75 (roles included Viola in Twelfth Night, and Sonya in Uncle Vanya); Prospect Theatre Co., West End, 1975–76 (Vera in A Month in the Country, Lucy Honeychurch in A Room with a View); freelance films and TV, 1976–78; Rosalind in As You Like It, Edin. Fest., 1977; RSC, 1978–81: Rosaline in Love's Labours Lost, 1978–79; title role in Piaf, The Other Place 1978, Aldwych 1979, Wyndhams 1980, Broadway 1981 (SWET Award 1979, London Critics Award and Variety Club Award 1980, and Broadway Tony Award

1981); National Theatre: Eileen, Kick for Touch, 1983; Belvidera, Venice Preserv'd, Antigone, 1984; Saint Joan (title rôle), Compass Co., 1985; Double Double, Fortune Theatre, 1986; RSC, 1986–87: Misalliance, 1986; Archbishop's Ceiling, 1986; Greenland, Royal Court, 1988; Shadowlands, Queen's, 1989–90 (Variety Club Best Actress Award); *television:* Marie Curie (serial), 1977; Antony and Cleopatra, 1981; Macbeth, 1983; Seal Morning (series), 1985; Napoleon and Josephine, 1987; Blind Justice (serial), 1988 (British Press Guild Best Actress Award); The Dark Angel, 1989; Love Hurts (series), 1991; *films:* Eureka, 1983; Lady Jane, 1986. Vis. Fellow, Sussex Univ., 1986–. Mem., Marie Curie Meml Foundn Appeals Cttee, 1986–88. Pres., Bristol Old Vic Theatre Club, 1985–; Hon. Pres., Friends of Southwark Globe, 1986–. *Publication:* Grace and Favour (autobiog.), 1989. *Recreation:* walking. *Address:* c/o ICM, 388 Oxford Street, W1. *T:* 071–629 8080.

LAPPER, Maj.-Gen. John; Medical Director, International Hospitals Group, 1984–1988; *b* 24 July 1921; *s* of late Col Wilfred Mark Lapper, OBE, Legion of Merit (USA), late RE, and Agnes Lapper (*née* Powner); *m* 1948, Dorothy, *d* of late Roland John and Margaret Simpson (*née* Critchlow); three *s*. *Educ:* Wolverhampton Grammar Sch.; King Edward VI Sch., Birmingham; Birmingham Univ. MB, ChB 1946; DLO 1952. House appts, Queen Elizabeth and Children's Hosp., Birmingham, and Ronkswood Hosp. and Royal Infirm., Worcester; Registrar, Royal Berks Hosp., Reading. Commnd RAMC, 1950; ENT specialist, Mil. Hosps in UK, Libya, Egypt, Germany, Singapore, Malaya; CO 14 Field Amb., BAOR, 1958; CO BMH Rinteln, BAOR, 1964; Asst Comdt, Royal Army Med. Coll., 1965–68; ADMS Hong Kong, 1969–71; CO Queen Alexandra's Mil. Hosp., Millbank, 1971–73; ADMS 3 Div., 1973; DDMS HQ UKLF, 1974–77; Dir, Med. Supply, MoD, 1977; Dir, Med. Policy and Plans, MoD, 1978–80, retired; QHS 1977–80. Hospital and Medical Dir, Nat. Guard Saudi Arabia, 1981–83. Hudson-Evans Lectr, W Kent Medico-Chirurgical Soc., 1980; Mem. Sands Cox Med. Soc., Birmingham Univ. FFCM 1980; FBIM 1980; FRSocMed; FMedSoc London; Mem. BMA; Pres. Med. Soc., Hong Kong, 1970–71; Mem., RUSI; Chm. Council, Yateley Industries for the Disabled. OStJ 1959. *Publications:* articles in professional jls. *Recreations:* travel, militaria, DIY. *Address:* Holmbush, Old School Lane, Yateley, Camberley, Surrey GU17 7NG. *T:* Yateley (0252) 874180; Rocas Del Mar, Mijas Costa, (Malaga), Spain.

LAPPERT, Prof. Michael Franz, FRS 1979; Professor of Chemistry, University of Sussex, since 1969; *b* 31 Dec. 1928; *s* of Julius Lappert and Kornelie Lappert (*née* Beran); *m* 1980, Lorna McKenzie. *Educ:* Wilson's Grammar School; Northern Polytechnic, London. BSc, PhD, DSc (London). FRSC. Northern Polytechnic, London: Asst Lecturer, 1952–53; Lecturer, 1953–55; Sen. Lectr, 1955–59. UMIST: Lectr, 1959–61; Sen. Lectr, 1961–64; Reader, Univ. of Sussex, 1964–69. SERC Sen. Res. Fellow, 1980–85. Pres., Dalton Div., RSC, 1989–91. Hon. Dr rer. nat. München, 1989. First recipient of (London) Chemical Soc. Award in Main Group Metal Chemistry, 1970; Award in Organometallic Chemistry, 1978; Tilden Lectr, 1972–73; F. S. Kipping Award of American Chem. Soc., 1976. *Publications:* (ed jtly) Developments in Inorganic Polymer Chemistry, 1962; (jtly) Metal and Metalloid Amides, 1980; (jtly) Organo-zirconium and -hafnium Compounds, 1986; approx. 500 papers in Jl Chem. Soc., etc. *Recreations:* theatre, opera, tennis, walking. *Address:* 4 Varndean Gardens, Brighton BN1 6WL. *T:* Brighton (0273) 503661.

LAPPING, Anne Shirley Lucas; independent television producer, Brook Productions, since 1982; Director, Channel Four, since 1989; *b* 10 June 1941; *d* of late Frederick Stone and of Dr Freda Lucas Stone; *m* 1963, Brian Michael Lapping; three *d*. *Educ:* City of London Sch. for Girls; London Sch. of Econs. New Society, 1964–68; London Weekend TV, 1970–73; writer on The Economist, 1974–82. Other writing and broadcasting. Member: SSRC, 1977–79; Nat. Gas Consumers' Council, 1978–79. *Recreations:* literature, housework. *Address:* 94 Highgate Hill, N6 5HE. *T:* 081–341 0523.

LAPPING, Peter Herbert; Headmaster of Sherborne, since 1988; *b* 8 Aug. 1941; *s* of late Dr Douglas James Lapping, MBE and Dorothy Lapping (*née* Horrocks) of Nhlangano, Swaziland; *m* 1967, Diana Dillworth, *d* of late Lt-Col E. S. G. Howard, MC, RA; one *s* one *d*. *Educ:* St John's College, Johannesburg; Univ. of Natal, Pietermaritzburg (BA Hons *cum laude*); Lincoln College, Oxford (MA). Asst Master, Reed's Sch., Cobham, 1966–67; Head of History, Loretto Sch., 1967–79 (Housemaster, Pinkie House, 1972–79); Headmaster, Shiplake Coll., Oxon, 1979–88. *Recreations:* cricket and other games, walking, travel. *Address:* Sherborne School, Dorset DT9 3AP. *T:* Sherborne (0935) 812646. *Clubs:* East India, Devonshire, Sports and Public Schools, MCC; Vincent's (Oxford).

LAPSLEY, Air Marshal Sir John (Hugh), KBE 1969 (OBE 1944); CB 1966; DFC 1940; AFC 1950; *b* 24 Sept. 1916; *s* of late Edward John Lapsley, Bank of Bengal, Dacca, and Norah Gladis Lapsley; *m* 1st, 1942, Jean Margaret MacIvor (*d* 1979); one *s* one *d*; 2nd, 1980, Millicent Rees (*née* Beadnell), *widow* of T. A Rees. *Educ:* Wolverhampton Sch.; Royal Air Force Coll., Cranwell. Served in Fighter Squadrons in UK, Egypt and Europe, 1938–45; psc 1946; Air Ministry Directorate of Policy, 1946–48; Commander No 74 Fighter Squadron and Air Fighting Development Squadron, 1949–52; HQ Fighter Command Staff, 1952–54; 2nd TAF Germany, 1954–58; Ministry of Defence Joint Planning Staff, 1958–60; Deputy Chief of Staff Air, 2nd Allied TAF, 1960–62; IDC, 1963; Secretary to Chiefs of Staff Cttee and Director of Defence Operations Staff, Ministry of Defence, 1964–66; No 19 Group, RAF Coastal Comd, 1967–68; AOC-in-C, RAF Coastal Comd, 1968–69; Head of British Defence Staff and Defence Attaché, Washington, 1970–73. Mem. Council, Officers' Pension Soc., 1976–87. Dir-Gen., Save the Children Fund, 1974–75. Dir, Falkland Is R&D Assoc. Ltd, 1978–83; Councillor, Suffolk Coastal District Council, 1979–87, Chm. 1983. Fellow RSPB. *Recreations:* golf, fishing, ornithology. *Address:* Milcroft, 149 Saxmundham Road, Aldeburgh, Suffolk IP15 5PB. *T:* Aldeburgh (0728) 453957. *Clubs:* Royal Air Force; Aldeburgh Golf; Suffolk Fly Fishers.

LAPUN, Sir Paul, Kt 1974; *b* 1923; *m* 1951, Lois; two *s* one *d*. *Educ:* Catholic Mission, Vunapope. Teacher, Catholic Mission, 1947–61. Under-Secretary for Forests, Papua and New Guinea, 1964–67. Founder Mem., for S Bougainville, PNG House of Assembly, 1964; Founder, Pangu Party, 1967 (Leader, 1967–68; Dep. Parly Leader, 1968); Minister: for Mines and Energy, 1972–75; for Health, 1975–77. Hon. Mem., Internat. Mark Twain Soc., USA. *Address:* Boku Patrol Post, N Solomon, Papua New Guinea.

LAQUEUR, Walter; Chairman, Research Council, Center for Strategic and International Studies, Georgetown University, since 1975; Director, Institute of Contemporary History and Wiener Library, London, since 1964; *b* 26 May 1921; *s* of late Fritz Laqueur and late Else Laqueur; *m* 1941, Barbara (*née* Koch), *d* of Prof. Richard Koch and Maria Koch (*née* Rosenthal); two *d*. Agricultural labourer during War, 1939–44. Journalist, free lance author, 1944–55; Editor of Survey, 1955–65; Co-editor of Journal of Contemporary History, 1966–. Prof., History of Ideas, Brandeis Univ., 1967–71; Prof. of Contemporary History, Tel Aviv Univ., 1970–; Vis. Professor: Chicago Univ.; Johns Hopkins Univ.; Harvard Univ. Hon. Dr Hebrew Union Coll., NY, 1988. Grand Cross of Merit, FRG, 1986. *Publications:* Communism and Nationalism in the Middle East, 1956; Young Germany, 1961; Russia and Germany, 1965; The Road to War, 1968; Europe Since Hitler, 1970; Out of the Ruins of Europe, 1971; Zionism, a History, 1972; Confrontation: the Middle East War and World Politics, 1974; Weimar: a Cultural History, 1918–33, 1974; Guerrilla, 1976; Terrorism, 1977; The Missing Years, 1980; (ed jtly) A Reader's Guide to Contemporary History, 1972; (ed) Fascism: a reader's guide, 1978; The Terrible Secret, 1980; Farewell to Europe, 1981; Germany Today: a personal report, 1985; World of Secrets: the uses and limits of intelligence, 1986; The Long Road to Freedom, 1989; Stalin: the glasnost revelations, 1991. *Recreations:* swimming, motor-boating.

LARCOM, Sir (Charles) Christopher (Royde), 5th Bt, *cr* 1868; *b* 11 Sept. 1926; *s* of Sir Philip Larcom, 4th Bt, and Aileen Monica Royde (*née* Colbeck); *S* father, 1967; *m* 1956, Barbara Elizabeth, *d* of Balfour Bowen; four *d*. *Educ:* Radley; Clare Coll., Cambridge. (Wrangler, 1947; BA, 1947; MA, 1951). Served RN (Lieutenant), 1947–50. Articled to Messrs Spicer and Pegler (Chartered Accountants), 1950–53; ACA 1954; FCA 1965; joined Grieveson, Grant and Co., 1955, Partner, 1960, retired, 1986. Member, The Stock Exchange, London, 1959 (Mem. Council, 1970–80). *Recreations:* sailing, music. *Address:* 8 The Postern, Barbican, Wood Street, EC2Y 8BJ. *T:* 071–920 0388; 4 Village Cay Marina, PO Box 145, Roadtown, Tortola, BV1. *T:* Virgin Islands 42485.

LARGE, Prof. John Barry; Professor of Applied Acoustics, since 1969, and Director of Industrial Affairs, University of Southampton; *b* 10 Oct. 1930; *s* of Thomas and Ada Large; *m* 1958, Barbara Alicia Nelson; two *s*. *Educ:* Queen Mary Coll., London Univ.; Purdue Univ., USA. BScEng (Hons), MS. Group Engr, EMI Ltd, Feltham, Mddx, 1954–56; Sen. Systems Engr, Link Aviation, Binghampton, NY, USA, 1956–58; Chief Aircraft Noise Unit, Boeing Co., Seattle, USA, 1958–69. Southampton University: Dir, Inst. of Sound and Vibration Res., 1978–82; Dean, Faculty of Engrg and Applied Sci., 1982–86. Chm., Chilworth Centre Ltd; Chief Executive: University of Southampton Hldgs Ltd; Chilworth Manor Ltd; University of Southampton Enterprises Ltd; Director: Technology Transfer South; Southampton Chamber of Commerce. Mem., Noise Adv. Council, 1976–80; Chm., Co-ordinating Cttee, BCAR-N (Noise), Air Registration Bd; Pres., Assoc. Noise Consultants, 1985–. Hon. Dep. Chief Scientific Officer, Royal Aircraft Estabt, 1974–. Corresp. Mem., Inst. Noise Control Engrg, USA, 1985–. *Publications:* contrib. (regarding aircraft noise, etc) to: Commn of European Communities, Eur 5398e, 1975; Proc. of Internoise 80, Miami, Internoise 81, Amsterdam, Internoise 82, San Francisco; Internoise 83, Edinburgh; Internoise 84, Hawaii; Internoise 85, Munich; Internoise 86, Mass, USA, Internoise 88, Lyon, Internoise 89, California; Polmet 85, Hong Kong; The Development of Criteria for Environmental Noise Control (Proc. Royal Instn, vol. 52), 1979; Internat. Congress of Acoustics, 1983. *Recreations:* skiing, gardening. *Address:* Chinook, Southdown Road, Shawford, Hants. *T:* Twyford (0962) 712307.

LARGE, Peter, CBE 1987 (MBE 1974); Chairman, Joint Committee on Mobility for the Disabled, since 1971; *b* 16 Oct. 1931; *s* of Ethel May Walters and Rosslyn Victor Large; *m* 1962, Susy Fisher (*d* 1982); one step *s* two step *d*. *Educ:* Enfield Grammar Sch.; University Coll. London. BSc Civil Eng. 1953. National Service, HM Submarines, 1953–55 (Sub Lt (E)). Joined Shell International, 1956; West Africa, 1957; Ghana, 1957–60; South East Arabia, 1960–61; Indonesia, 1961–62; paralysed by poliomyelitis, 1962; Civil Service, 1966–. Chm., Assoc. of Disabled Professionals, 1971–; Governor, Motability, 1978–; Dep. Chm., Disabled Persons Transport Adv. Cttee, 1986–; Vice-Chm., Disablement Income Group, 1985– (Parly Advr, 1973–); Mem., Nat. Adv. Council on Employment of Disabled People, 1987–. *Recreation:* conversing with Siamese cats. *Address:* 14 Birch Way, Warlingham, Surrey CR6 9DA.

LARKEN, Comdt Anthea, CBE 1991; Director, Women's Royal Naval Service, 1988–91; *b* 23 Aug. 1938; *d* of Frederick William Savill and Nance (*née* Williams); *m* 1987, Rear Adm. Edmund Shackleton Jeremy Larken, *qv*. *Educ:* Stafford Girls' High Sch. Joined WRNS as Range Assessor, 1956; commnd, 1960; qualified: as Photographic Interpreter, 1961; as WRNS Secretarial Officer, 1967; Staff Officer in Singapore, 1964–66; i/c WRNS Officers' Training, BRNC Dartmouth, 1976–78; NATO Military Agency for Standardisation, Brussels, 1981–84; CSO (Admin) to Flag Officer Plymouth, 1985–86; RCDS, 1987. ADC to the Queen, 1988–91. Governor, Royal Naval Sch., Haslemere, 1988–91. *Recreations:* theatre, music, reading, home, family and friends. *Club:* Commonwealth Trust.

LARKEN, Rear Adm. (Edmund Shackleton) Jeremy, DSO 1982; Assistant Chief of the Defence Staff (Overseas), 1988–90; advisory consultant to the Offshore Oil and Gas Industry, and to Price Waterhouse, since 1991; *b* 14 Jan. 1939, *s* of Rear Adm. Edmund Thomas Larken, CB, OBE and Eileen Margaret (*née* Shackleton); *m* 1st, 1963, Wendy Nigella Hallett (marr. diss. 1987); two *d*; 2nd, 1987, Anthea Savill (*see* Comdt Anthea Larken). *Educ:* Bryanston Sch.; BRNC, Dartmouth. Joined RN as Cadet, 1957; qualified: in Submarine Comd, 1960; in Navigation, 1965; served, 1961–84: Submarine Service (HMS Finwhale, Tudor, Ambush and Narwhal); Navigation Officer, HMS Valiant; First Lieut, HMS Otus; commanded HMS Osiris, Glamorgan and Valiant, Third Submarine Sqn, and HMS Fearless (including Falklands Campaign, 1982); exchange with USN (Submarines); Naval Plans; Dir, Naval Staff Duties, 1985; Cdre Amphibious Warfare, 1985–87. Governor, Bryanston Sch., 1988–. *Publications:* articles in military periodicals. *Recreations:* maritime and aviation interests, strategy, theatre, reading, home, family and friends. *Club:* Commonwealth Trust.

LARKIN, John Cuthbert, MA; Headmaster, Wyggeston School, Leicester, 1947–69, retired; *b* 15 Oct. 1906; *s* of J. W. Larkin; *m* 1933, Sylvia Elizabeth Pilsbury; one *s* three *d*. *Educ:* King Edward VI Sch., Nuneaton; Downing Coll., Cambridge. Assistant Master, Shrewsbury Sch., 1928–45; Headmaster, Chesterfield Grammar Sch., 1946–47. *Recreations:* cricket, gardening. *Address:* Groves Cottage, Summers Lane, Totland Bay, Isle of Wight PO39 0HQ. *T:* Isle of Wight (0983) 752506.

LARMINIE, (Ferdinand) Geoffrey, OBE 1971; Director, British Geological Survey, 1987–90; *b* 23 June 1929; *s* of late Ferdinand Samuel Larminie and of Mary Larminie (*née* Willis); *m* 1956, Helena Elizabeth Woodside Carson; one *s* one *d*. *Educ:* St Andrews Coll., Dublin; Trinity Coll., Dublin (BA 1954, MA 1972; Hon. Fellow, 1989). Asst Lectr in Geology, Univ. of Glasgow, 1954–56; Lectr in Geology, Univ. of Sydney, 1956–60; joined British Petroleum Co. Ltd, 1960: Exploration Dept in Sudan, Greece, Canada, Libya, Kuwait, California, New York, Thailand and Alaska, 1960–74; Scientific Advr, Inf. Dept, London, 1974–75; Gen. Manager, Public Affairs and Inf. Dept, London, 1975–76; Gen. Manager, Environmental Control Centre, London, 1976–84; External Affairs Co-ordinator, Health, Safety and Environmental Services, BP plc, 1984–87. Member: Royal Commn on Environmental Pollution, 1979–83; NERC, 1983–87. Council Mem., RGS, 1984–, Vice-Pres., 1987–. President: Alaska Geol Soc., 1969; Soc. of Underwater Technol., 1987–89. Trustee, Bermuda Biological Station 1978–; Member: Bd of Management, Inst. of Offshore Engrg, Heriot-Watt Univ., 1981–90; Polar Res. Bd, Nat. Res. Council, Washington, DC, 1984–88. Mem., IBA Gen. Adv. Council, 1980–85. Mem. of numerous scientific and professional socs. *Publications:* papers in scientific and technical jls on oil ind., and occasional reviews. *Recreations:* archaeology, natural history, reading, shooting. *Address:* Lane End, Lanes End, Tring, Herts. *T:* Wendover (0296) 624907.

LARMOUR, Sir Edward Noel, (Sir Nick Larmour), KCMG 1977 (CMG 1966); HM Diplomatic Service, retired; *b* 25 Dec. 1916; *s* of Edward and Maud Larmour, Belfast, N Ireland; *m* 1946, Nancy, 2nd *d* of Thomas Bill; one *s* two *d*. *Educ:* Royal Belfast Academical Institution (Kitchener Scholar); Trinity Coll., Dublin (Scholar) (1st Class Hons and University Studentship in Classics, 1939); Sydney Univ., NSW. Royal Inniskilling Fusiliers, 1940; Burma Civil Service, 1942; Indian Army, 1942–46 (Major); Dep. Secretary to Governor of Burma, 1947; Commonwealth Relations Office, 1948; served in New Zealand, Singapore, Australia and Nigeria, 1950–68; Asst Under-Secretary of State, 1964; Dep. Chief of Administration, FCO, 1968–70; High Comr, Jamaica, and non-resident Ambassador, Haiti, 1970–73; Asst Under Sec. of State, FCO, 1973–75; High Comr (non-resident) for New Hebrides, 1973–76; Dep. Under Sec. of State, FCO, 1975–76. Mem., Price Commn, 1977–80; Chm., Bermuda Constituency Boundaries Commn, 1979. *Recreations:* cricket, golf, music. *Address:* 68 Wood Vale, N10. *T:* 081–444 9744. *Clubs:* Commonwealth Trust; MCC.

LAROSIÈRE de CHAMPFEU, Jacques Martin Henri Marie de; *see* de Larosière de Champfeu.

LARSEN, Cyril Anthony; Senior Clerk, House of Commons, 1980–86, retired; *b* 29 Dec. 1919; *s* of late Niels Arthur Larsen and Ella Bessie Larsen (*née* Vaughan); *m* 1956, Patricia Sneade; two *s* three *d*. *Educ:* St Francis Xavier's College, Liverpool. Board of Trade, 1936–38; Min. of Labour, 1938–40; Royal Navy, Lieut, 1940–46; entered administrative class, Dept of Employment, 1947; seconded to HM Treasury, 1950–53; Asst Sec., 1963; seconded to Prices and Incomes Board, 1966–69; Under Sec., 1971–79. *Address:* 51 Park Hill Road, Wallington, Surrey SM6 0RJ. *T:* 081–647 9380.

LARSON, Frederick H., DFM 1943; General Manager, Business Development, Alberta Opportunity Co., Edmonton, Alberta (Alberta Crown Corporation), since 1974; *b* 24 Nov. 1913; *s* of Herman B. and Martha C. Larson; *m* 1941, Dorothy A. Layng; one *s*. *Educ:* University of Saskatchewan. Observer, RCAF, 1941–43. Member for Kindersley, Parliament of Canada, 1949–53; Delegate to UN, Paris, 1952. Ten years in oil and gas business, production refining and sales, domestic and offshore; eight years in financial trust business, representing financial interests, Canada amd Jamaica; three years in construction and engineering; agricultural interests, Saskatchewan; Agent-Gen. for Province of Saskatchewan in London, 1967–73. *Recreation:* golf. *Address:* c/o Guaranty Trust Company, 10010 Jasper Avenue, Edmonton, Alberta, Canada. *Clubs:* Ranchmen's (Calgary); Mayfair Golf (Edmonton, Alta).

LARSSON, Comr John; Territorial Commander in UK and Republic of Ireland, Salvation Army, since 1990; *b* 2 April 1938; *s* of Sture and Flora Larsson; *m* 1969, Freda Turner; two *s*. *Educ:* London Univ. (BD). Commnd as Salvation Army Officer, 1957, in corps, youth and trng work; Chief Sec., S America West, 1980–84; Principal, William Booth Meml Trng Coll., 1984–88; Admin. Planning, 1988–90. *Publications:* Doctrine Without Tears, 1974; Spiritual Breakthrough, 1983; The Man Perfectly Filled with the Spirit, 1986; How Your Corps can Grow, 1988. *Recreations:* music, walking. *Address:* Salvation Army International Headquarters, 101 Queen Victoria Street, EC4P 4EP. *T:* 071–236 5222.

LARTIGUE, Sir Louis C.; *see* Cools-Lartigue.

LASCELLES, family name of **Earl of Harewood.**

LASCELLES, Viscount; David Henry George Lascelles; *b* 21 Oct. 1950; *s* and *heir* of 7th Earl of Harewood, *qv*; *m* 1979, Margaret Rosalind Messenger; three *s* one *d*; *m* 1990, Diane Jane Howse. *Educ:* The Hall Sch.; Westminster. *Address:* Harewood House, Harewood, Leeds, West Yorks LS17 9LG.

LASCELLES, Maj.-Gen. Henry Anthony, CB 1967; CBE 1962 (OBE 1945); DSO 1944; Director-General, Winston Churchill Memorial Trust, 1967–80; *b* 10 Jan. 1912; *s* of Edward Lascelles and Leila Kennett-Barrington; *m* 1941, Ethne Hyde Ussher Charles. *Educ:* Winchester; Oriel Coll., Oxford (MA). Served War of 1939–45: Egypt, North Africa, Sicily and Italy, rising to second in command of an armoured brigade. Instructor, Staff Coll., Camberley, 1947–49; GSO 1, HQ 7th Armoured Div., BAOR, 1949–52; Comdg Officer 6th Royal Tank Regt, BAOR, 1952–55; Instructor NATO Defence Coll., 1955–56; Brigadier Royal Armoured Corps HQ 2nd Infantry Div., BAOR, 1956–57; National Defence Coll., Canada, 1958–59; BGS Military Operations, War Office, 1959–62; Chief of Staff, HQ Northern Ireland Command, 1962–63; Maj.-General, General Staff, Far East Land Forces, 1963–66. Pres., British Water Ski Fedn, 1980–. *Recreations:* squash, tennis, golf, music, gardening. *Address:* Manor Farm Cottage, Hedgerley Green, Bucks SL2 3XJ. *T:* Gerrards Cross (0753) 883582. *Club:* Naval and Military.

LASCELLES, Mary Madge, FBA 1962; Hon. Fellow, Somerville College, 1967; *b* 7 Feb. 1900; *d* of William Horace and Madeline Lascelles. *Educ:* Sherborne School for Girls; Lady Margaret Hall, Oxford. Research Studentship, Westfield Coll., 1923; Assistant Lecturer, Royal Holloway Coll., 1926; Somerville College: Tutor in English Language and Literature, 1931; Fellow, 1932–67; Vice-Principal, 1947–60; University Lecturer in English Literature, 1960–66; Reader, 1966–67. *Publications:* Jane Austen and her Art, 1939; Shakespeare's Measure for Measure, 1953; (ed) The Works of Samuel Johnson, Yale vol. ix, A Journey to the Western Islands of Scotland, 1971; The Adversaries and Other Poems, 1971; Notions and Facts, 1973; The Story-Teller Retrieves the Past, 1980; Further Poems, 1982; Selected Poems, 1990; contributions to learned journals, etc. *Address:* Valley House, Cley, Holt, Norfolk NR25 7TR. *T:* Cley (0263) 740413. *Club:* University Women's.

LASDUN, Sir Denys (Louis), Kt 1976; CBE 1965; FRIBA; architect in private practice, since 1948; with Peter Softley & Associates, since 1986; *b* 8 Sept. 1914; *s* of Norman Lasdun and Julie Abrahams; *m* 1954, Susan Bendit; two *s* one *d*. *Educ:* Rugby Sch.; Architectural Assoc. Served with Royal Engineers, 1939–45 (MBE). Practised with Wells Coates, Tecton and Drake. Hoffman Wood Professor of Architecture, University of Leeds, 1962–63. Assessor, Competitions for Belgrade Opera Hse, 1971, and new Parly Bldg, London, 1971–72. Principal works: housing and schools for Bethnal Green and Paddington; London HQ, NSW Govt; flats at 26 St James's Place; Royal College of Physicians; Fitzwilliam College, and Christ's College extension, Cambridge; new University of East Anglia and work for the Universities of London (SOAS, Inst. of Educn, Law Inst., project for Courtauld Inst.), Leicester and Liverpool; National Theatre and IBM Central London Marketing Centre, South Bank; EEC HQ for European Investment Bank, Luxembourg; design for new Hurva Synagogue, Old City, Jerusalem; Cannock Community Hosp.; Genoa Opera House competition; office buildings, Fenchurch Street, EC4 and Milton Gate, EC2. Trustee, BM, 1975–85; Member: CIAM and MARS Gp, 1935–59; V & A Adv. Cttee, 1973–83; Slade Cttee, 1976–; Arts Panel, Arts Council of GB, 1980–84; Académie d'Architecture, Paris, 1984–; Accademia Nazionale di San Luca, Rome, 1984–; Academician, Internat. Acad. of Architecture, Bulgaria, 1986. Hon. Fellow, American Institute of Architects, 1966; Hon. FRCP, 1975. Hon. DA, Manchester, 1966; Hon. DLitt: E Anglia, 1974; Sheffield, 1978. RIBA London Architecture Bronze Medallist, 1960 and 1964; Civic Trust Awards: Class I, 1967; Group A, 1969; Special Award, São Paulo Biennale, Brazil, 1969; Concrete Society Award, 1976; Royal Gold Medal for Architecture, RIBA, 1977; RIBA Architectural, Award for London Region, 1978. *Publications include:* An Architect's Approach to Architecture, 1965 (RIBA Jl); A Language and a Theme, 1976; Architecture in an Age of Scepticism, 1984. *Address:* 146 Grosvenor Road, SW1V 3JY. *T:* 071–630 8211.

LASH, Prof. Nicholas Langrishe Alleyne, DD; Norris-Hulse Professor of Divinity, University of Cambridge, since 1978; Fellow, Clare Hall, since 1988; *b* 6 April 1934; *s* of Henry Alleyne Lash and Joan Mary Lash (*née* Moore); *m* 1976, Janet Angela Chalmers; one *s*. *Educ:* Downside Sch.; Oscott Coll.; St Edmund's House, Cambridge. MA, PhD, BD, DD. Served RE, 1952–57. Oscott Coll., 1957–63; Asst Priest, Slough, 1963–68; Fellow, 1969–85, Dean, 1971–75, St Edmund's House, Cambridge; Univ. Asst Lectr, Cambridge, 1974–78. *Publications:* His Presence in the World, 1968; Change in Focus, 1973; Newman on Development, 1975; Voices of Authority, 1976; Theology on Dover Beach, 1979; A Matter of Hope, 1982; Theology on the Way to Emmaus, 1986; Easter in Ordinary, 1988. *Address:* Faculty of Divinity, St John's Street, Cambridge CB2 1TW. *T:* Cambridge (0223) 332593; 4 Hertford Street, Cambridge CB4 3AG.

LASKEY, Prof. Ronald Alfred, FRS 1984; Charles Darwin Professor of Animal Embryology, since 1983 and Fellow of Darwin College, since 1982, University of Cambridge; *b* 26 Jan. 1945; *s* of Thomas Lesley and Bessie Laskey; *m* 1971, Margaret Ann Page; one *s* one *d*. *Educ:* High Wycombe Royal Grammar Sch.; Queen's Coll., Oxford. MA, DPhil 1970. Scientific Staff: Imperial Cancer Research Fund, 1970–73; MRC Lab. of Molecular Biology, 1973–83; Co-Dir, Molecular Embryology Group, Cancer Research Campaign, 1983–. Mem., Academia Europaea, 1989. Colworth Medal, Biochem. Soc., 1979. *Publications:* articles on cell biology in scientific jls. *Recreations:* building, music, theatre. *Address:* Wellcome Trust/Cancer Research Campaign Institute for Cancer and Developmental Biology, Tennis Court Road, Cambridge CB2 1QR. *T:* Cambridge (0223) 334106.

LASKO, Prof. Peter Erik, CBE 1981; FSA; FBA 1978; Professor of the History of Art, Courtauld Institute, University of London, 1974–85; Director, Courtauld Institute, 1974–85; *b* 5 March 1924; *s* of Leo Lasko and Wally Lasko (*née* Seifert); *m* 1948, Gwendoline Joan Norman; three *d*. *Educ:* Courtauld Institute, Univ. of London. BA Hons 1949. Asst Keeper, British Museum, 1950–65; Prof. of the Visual Arts, Univ. of East Anglia, 1965–73. Member: Cathedrals Adv. Commn, 1981–91; Royal Commn on Historical Monuments (England), 1984–90; Cathedrals Fabric Commn, 1991–; Trustee: British Mus., 1981–; Royal Armouries, 1984–. *Publication:* Ars Sacra 800–1200 (Pelican History of Art), 1972. *Address:* 53 Montagu Square, W1H 1TH.

LASKY, Melvin Jonah, MA; Editor, Encounter Magazine, 1958–91; *b* New York City, 15 Jan. 1920; *s* of Samuel Lasky and Esther Lasky (*née* Kantrowitz); *m* 1947, Brigitte Newiger (marr. diss. 1974); one *s* one *d*. *Educ:* City Coll. of New York (BSS); Univ. of Michigan (MA); Columbia Univ. Literary Editor, The New Leader (NY), 1942–43; US Combat Historian in France and Germany, 1944–45; Capt., US Army, 1946; Foreign Correspondent, 1946–48; Editor and Publisher, Der Monat (Berlin), 1948–58 and 1978–83; Co-Editor, Encounter Magazine (London), 1958–91; Editorial Director, Library Press, NY, 1970–80; Publisher, Alcove Press, London, 1972–82. Regular television broadcaster, Cologne, Zürich and Vienna, 1955–. Fellow, Inst. of Advanced Study, Berlin, 1988–89. Hon. PhD York (Canada), 1990. Univ. of Michigan, Sesquicentennial Award, 1967; Distinguished Alumnus Award, City Univ., NY, 1978. *Publications:* Reisenotizen und Tagebücher, 1958; Africa for Beginners, 1962; Utopia and Revolution, 1976 (Spanish edn 1982; German edn 1989); On the Barricades, and Off, 1989; Voices in a Revolution, 1991; contributor to: America and Europe, 1951; New Paths in American History, 1965; Sprache und Politik, 1969; Festschrift for Raymond Aron, 1971; (ed) The Hungarian Revolution, 1957. *Address:* 18 Rutland Gate, Knightsbridge, SW7. *Club:* Garrick.

LASLETT, (Thomas) Peter (Ruffell), FBA 1979; Reader in Politics and the History of Social Structure, Cambridge University, 1966–83; Director, Cambridge Group for the History of Population and Social Structure, since 1964; Fellow of Trinity College, Cambridge, since 1953; *b* 18 Dec. 1915; *s* of Rev. G. H. R. Laslett and E. E. Laslett (*née* Alden); *m* 1947, Janet Crockett Clark; two *s*. *Educ:* Watford Grammar Sch.; St John's Coll., Cambridge. Served War, Royal Navy, 1940–45: Lieut RNVR, Japanese Naval Intelligence. Producer, BBC, 3rd Programme Talks, 1946–49; Fellow: St John's Coll., Cambridge, 1948–51; Inst. for Advanced Study, Princeton, 1959; Founder (with E. A. Wrigley), Cambridge Gp for the History of Population and Social Structure, 1964; Member, Working Party on Foundn of Open Univ., 1965–. Visiting Professor: Collège de France, Paris, 1976; Yale Univ., 1977. DUniv. Open, 1980. *Publications:* Locke's Two Treatises of Government, 1960, 3rd edn 1988; The World We Have Lost, 1965, 3rd edn 1983; (with R. Wall) Household and Family in Past Time, 1972; Family Life and Illicit Love in Earlier Generations, 1977; (with R. M. Smith and others) Bastardy and its Comparative History, 1980; A Fresh Map of Life, 1989. *Recreations:* book collecting, gardening. *Address:* Trinity College, Cambridge CB2 1TQ; 27 Trumpington Street, Cambridge. *T:* (Cambridge Group) Cambridge (0223) 333181.

LASOK, Prof. Dominik, QC 1982; PhD, LLD; Professor of European Law, 1973–86, and Director of Centre for European Legal Studies, 1972–86, University of Exeter; *b* 4 Jan. 1921; *s* of late Alojzy Lasok and Albina (*née* Przybyla); *m* 1952, Sheila May Corrigan; two *s* three *d*. *Educ:* secondary educn in Poland and Switzerland; Fribourg Univ. (Lic. en Droit); Univ. of Durham (LLM); Univ. of London (PhD, LLD); Universitas Polonorum in Exteris (Dr Juris). Called to the Bar, Middle Temple, 1954. Served Polish Army, Poland, France and Italy, 1939–46 (British, French and Polish mil. decorations). Industry, 1948–51; commerce, 1954–58; academic career, 1958–: Prof. of Law, Univ. of Exeter, 1968. Visiting Professor: William and Mary, Williamsburg, Va, 1966–67 and 1977; McGill, Montreal, 1976–77; Rennes, 1980–81; Fribourg, 1984; Coll. d'Europe, Bruges, 1984–86; Aix-Marseille, 1985; Marmara, Istanbul, 1987–91; Chukyo, Nagoya, 1990; Surugadi, Hanno-shi, 1990. Dhc Aix/Marseille, 1987. Officier dans l'Ordre des Palmes Académiques, 1983. *Publications:* Polish Family Law, 1968; (jtly, also ed) Polish Civil Law, 4 vols, 1973–75; (with J. W. Bridge) Law and Institutions of the European Communities, 1973, 5th edn 1991; The Law of the Economy in the European Communities, 1980; (jtly, also ed) Les Communautés Européennes en Fonctionnement, 1981; Customs Law of the European Communities, 1983, 2nd edn 1990; Professions and Services in the European Community, 1986; (with P. A. Stone) Conflict of Laws in the European Community, 1987; (contrib.) Halsbury's Laws of England, 5th edn 1991; over 120 articles in British and foreign legal jls. *Address:* Reed, Barley Lane, Exeter EX4 1TA. *T:* Exeter (0392) 72582.

LAST, Maj.-Gen. Christopher Neville, CB 1990; OBE 1976; Chief Executive, Clwyd Family Health Services Authority, since 1990; *b* 2 Sept. 1935; *s* of Jack Neville Last, MPS, FSMC, FBOA and Lorna (*née* Goodman), MPS; *m* 1961, Pauline Mary Lawton; two *d*. *Educ:* Culford Sch.; Brighton Tech. Coll. psc†, ndc. Commnd Royal Signals, 1956; Germany, Parachute Bde, Borneo, Singapore, 1956–67; OC 216 Para. Signal Sqdn, 1967;

RMCS and Staff Coll., Logistics Staff 1 (BR) Corps, 1968–71; NDC, 1972; Lt-Col, Signal Staff HQ, BAOR, 1973; CO Royal Signals NI, 1974; Staff, MoD Combat Develt, 1976, Mil. Ops, 1977; Col, Project Manager MoD (PE) for Army ADP Comd and Control, 1977; CO (Col) 8 Signal Regt Trng, Royal Signals, 1980; Brig., Comd 1 Signal Bde 1 (BR) Corps, 1981; Dir, Mil. Comd and Control Projects, MoD (PE), 1984; Head of Defence Procurement Policy (Studies Team), on Chief of Defence Procurement Personal Staff, MoD (PE), 1985; Maj.-Gen. 1986; Vice Master Gen. of the Ordnance, 1986–88; Mil. Dep. to Head of Defence Export Services, 1988–90. Col Comdt, RCS, 1990–. Mem., Co. of Information Technologists, 1988; Freeman, City of London, 1988. *Recreations:* travel, theatre, ballet, sailing, ski-ing, shooting and country pursuits, hockey (Corps, BAOR Army and Combined Services). *Address:* c/o National Westminster Bank, 34 North Street, Lancing, Sussex BN15 9AB. *Club:* Special Forces.

LAST, John William, CBE 1989; Head of Corporate Affairs, Littlewoods Organisation; *b* 22 Jan. 1940; *s* of late Jack Last (sometime Dir of Finance, Metrop. Police) and Freda Last (*née* Evans); *m* 1967, Susan Josephine, *er d* of John and late Josephine Farmer; three *s*. *Educ:* Sutton Grammar Sch., Surrey; Trinity Coll., Oxford (MA 1965). Joined Littlewoods Organisation, Liverpool, 1969. Dir, Boom, 1990–. Mem., Merseyside CC, 1973–86 (Chm., Arts Cttee, 1977–81); contested (C) Liverpool, West Derby, Feb. and Oct. 1974, Stockport N, 1979. Vis. Prof., City Univ., London, 1987. Bd Mem., Royal Liverpool Philharmonic Soc., 1973– (Chm., 1977–81, 1986–); Founder Chairman: Merseyside Maritime Museum, 1977; Empire Theatre (Merseyside) Trust, 1979–81 (Bd Mem., 1986–); Chairman: Walker Art Gall., Liverpool, 1977–81; Library Assoc./Arts Council Wkg Party on Art in Libraries, 1982–84; Wkg Party to form Merseyside TEC, 1989–90; Nat. Chm., Area Museums Councils of GB, 1979–82; Chm., Museums Training Inst., 1990–; Vice Chairman: NW Museum and Art Gall. Service, 1986– (Chm., 1977–82, 1987–); Merseyside Arts, 1985–88; Member: Museums Assoc. Council, 1978–86 (Vice-Pres., 1983); Arts Council of GB, 1980–84 (Chm., Housing the Arts Cttee, 1981–84; Chm., Regional Cttee, 1981–84); Museums and Galleries Commn, 1983– (Mem., Scottish Wkg Pty, 1984–85); Enquiry into Tyne and Wear Service, 1988–89; Chm., Enquiry into Local Authorities and Museums, 1989–91; Bd, Northern Ballet Theatre, 1986– (Vice Chm., 1986–88); Merseyside Tourism Bd, 1986–; NW Industrial Council, 1985–; Court, Liverpool Univ., 1973– (Mem. Council, 1977–81, 1986–); Calcutt Cttee on Privacy and Intrusion by the Press, 1989–90; Lay Mem., Press Council, 1980–86; Advr on Local Govt to Arts Council, 1984–; Chm., Arts, Initiative and Money Cttee, Gulbenkian Foundn, 1980–83. Mem. Bd, Charities Trust, 1990–; Trustee: Norton Priory Museum, 1983–; V&A Museum, 1984–86 (Mem., Adv. Council, 1978–84; Mem., Theatre Museum Cttee, 1983–86); Nat. Museums and Galls on Merseyside, 1986–; Gov., NYO, 1985–. FRSA 1988. Hon. FMA, 1987. Hon. Fellow, Liverpool Polytechnic, 1989. Freedom of City of London, 1985; Freeman, Barber Surgeons' Co., 1985; Liveryman 1987. *Publications:* Arts: the way forward, 1978 (jtly); A Brief History of Museums and Galleries, 1986; (jtly) A Future for the Arts, 1987; The Last Report on Local Authorities and Museums, 1991. *Recreations:* swimming, music, Victoriana. *Address:* 25 Abbey Road, West Kirby, Wirral, Merseyside L48 7EN. *T:* 051–625 5969. *Clubs:* Royal Automobile; Racquet (Liverpool).

LAST, Prof. Raymond Jack, FRCS, FRACS; Professor of Applied Anatomy, and Warden, Royal College of Surgeons, 1949–70; *b* 26 May 1903; English; *m* 1st, Vera Estella Judell; two *s*; 2nd, Margret Stewart Milne. *Educ:* Adelaide High Sch., Australia. MB, BS (Adelaide), 1924; Medical practice S. Australia, 1927–38; arrived London, 1939; Surgeon, EMS, Northern Hospital, N21, 1939–40. OC Abyssinian Medical Unit, Hon. Surgeon to Emperor Haile Selassie I, also OC Haile Selassie Hospital, Surgeon to British Legation, Addis Ababa, 1941–44; returned to London, Lieut-Colonel, RAMC, 1945; ADMS, British Borneo, 1945–46. Anatomical Curator and Bland Sutton Scholar, RCS, 1946; FRCS 1947; Adviser to Central Government of Pakistan on organization and conduct of primary FRCS instruction, Colombo Plan, 1961. Vis. Prof. of Anatomy: UCLA, 1970–87; Mt Sinai Sch. of Medicine, NY, 1971–72. *Publications:* Anatomy, Regional and Applied, 7th edn 1984; Wolff's Anatomy of Eye and Orbit, 6th edn, 1968; Aids to Anatomy, 12th edn, 1962; contrib. to Journals of Surgery; various articles. *Address:* 49 Westall Street, Unley Park, SA 5061, Australia.

LATEY, Rt. Hon. Sir John (Brinsmead), Kt 1965; MBE 1943; PC 1986; Judge of the High Court of Justice, Family Division (formerly Probate, Divorce and Admiralty Division), 1965–89; *b* 7 March 1914; *s* of late William Latey, CBE, QC, and Anne Emily, *d* of late Horace G. Brinsmead; *m* 1938, Betty Margaret (*née* Beresford); one *s* one *d*. *Educ:* Westminster; Christ Church, Oxford. MA (Hon. Sch. Jurispr.). Called to the Bar, 1936; QC 1957. Served in Army during War, 1939–45, mainly in MEF (Lieut-Colonel, 1944–). General Council of the Bar, 1952–56, 1957–61 and 1964– (Hon. Treasurer, 1959–61). Master of the Bench of the Middle Temple, 1964. Chairman, Lord Chancellor's Cttee on Age of Majority, 1965–67. Dep. Chairman, Oxfordshire QS, 1966. *Publications:* (Asst Ed.) Latey on Divorce, 14th edn, 1952; Halsbury's Laws of England (Conflict of Laws: Husband and Wife), 1956. *Recreations:* golf, bridge, chess. *Address:* 16 Daylesford Avenue, Roehampton, SW15 5QR. *T:* 081–876 6436. *Club:* United Oxford & Cambridge University.

LATHAM, family name of **Baron Latham.**

LATHAM, 2nd Baron *cr* 1942, of Hendon; **Dominic Charles Latham;** Structural Engineer with Rankine & Hill, Consulting Engineers, since 1988; *b* 20 Sept. 1954; *s* of Hon. Francis Charles Allman Latham (*d* 1959) and Gabrielle Monica (*d* 1987), *d* of Dr S. M. O'Riordan; *S* grandfather, 1970. *Educ:* Univ. of New South Wales, Australia (BEng (civil), 1977, Hons I; MEngSc 1981). Civil Engr, Electricity Commn, NSW, 1979–88. *Recreations:* tennis, squash, snooker, electronics, sailboarding. *Heir: yr* twin *b* Anthony Michael Latham, *b* 20 Sept. 1954. *Address:* PO Box 355, Kensington, NSW 2033, Australia.

LATHAM, Arthur Charles; Member, London Transport Executive, 1983–84 (part-time Member, July-Nov. 1983); *b* Leyton, 14 Aug. 1930; *m* 1951, Margaret Latham; one *s* one *d*. *Educ:* Romford Royal Liberty Sch.; Garnett Coll. of Educn. Lectr in Further Educn, Southgate Technical Coll., 1967–. Havering Council (formerly Romford Borough Council): Mem., 1952–78 and 1986–; Leader, Labour Gp, 1962–70 and 1986–; Leader of the Opposition, 1986–; Alderman, 1962–78. Mem., NE Regional Metropolitan Hosp. Bd, 1966–72. MP (Lab) Paddington N, Oct. 1969–1974, City of Westminster, Paddington, 1974–79; Jt Chm., All Party Gp for Pensioners, 1971–79; Chm., Tribune Gp, 1975–76 (Treasurer, 1977–79). Contested (Lab): Woodford, 1959; Rushcliffe, Notts, 1964; City of Westminster, Paddington, 1979; Westminster N, 1983. Chm., Greater London Lab. Party, 1977–; Vice-Chm., Nat. Cttee, Labour League of Youth, 1949–53; Vice-President: Labour Action for Peace; AMA; Treasurer, Liberation (Movement for Colonial Freedom), 1969–79; Member: British Campaign for Peace in Vietnam; Campaign for Nuclear Disarmament. Vegetarian. *Recreations:* bridge, chess, cricket. *Address:* 17 Tudor Avenue, Gidea Park, Romford RM2 5LB.

LATHAM, Cecil Thomas, OBE 1976; Stipendiary Magistrate, Greater Manchester (sitting at Salford), since 1976; *b* 11 March 1924; *s* of Cecil Frederick James Latham and Elsie Winifred Latham; *m* 1945, Ivy Frances (*née* Fowle); one *s* one *d*. *Educ:* Rochester Cathedral Choir Sch.; King's Sch., Rochester. Solicitor. War Service, 1942–45. Asst Clerk, Magistrates' Courts: Chatham, 1939–42; Maidstone, 1945; Leicester, 1948–54; Bromley, 1954–63; Dep. Justices' Clerk, Liverpool, 1963–65; Justices' Clerk, Manchester, 1965–76. Member: Magistrates' Courts Rule Cttee, 1966–; Royal Commn on Criminal Procedure, 1978–81; Criminal Law Revision Cttee, 1981–. Hon. MA Manchester, 1984. *Publications:* (ed) Stone's Justices' Manual, 101st-109th edns; How Much?: determining maintenance in magistrates' courts, 1976; Care Proceedings, 1989; (ed) Family Law Reports, 1980–86; specialist editor, Justice of the Peace Reports, 1986–; founder editor, Family Court Reporter, 1987–; contrib. Criminal Law Rev., Justice of Peace, Family Law. *Recreation:* music. *Address:* 19 Southdown Crescent, Cheadle Hulme, Cheshire SK8 6EQ. *T:* 061–485 1185.

LATHAM, Christopher George Arnot; Chairman, James Latham PLC, since 1987; *b* 4 June 1933; *s* of late Edward Bryan Latham and Anne Arnot Duncan; *m* 1963, Jacqueline Cabourdin; three *s*. *Educ:* Stowe Sch.; Clare Coll., Cambridge (MA). FCA. Articled Fitzpatrick Graham, chartered accountants, 1955; joined James Latham Ltd, timber importers, 1959, Dir 1963; Dep. Chm., 1973. A Forestry Comr, 1973–78. Dir, City and Inner London N TEC, 1991–. Pres., Inst. of Wood Sci., 1977–79; Chairman: Timber Res. and Develt Assoc., 1972–74; Commonwealth Forestry Assoc., 1975–77; Psychiatric Rehabilitation Assoc., 1983–. Mem., Worshipful Co. of Builders Merchants, 1985–. *Recreations:* tennis, beagling, forestry. *Address:* 5 Canonbury Square, N1.

LATHAM, David Nicholas Ramsay; QC 1985; a Recorder of the Crown Court, since 1983; *b* 18 Sept. 1942; *s* of Robert Clifford Latham, *qv*; *m* 1967, Margaret Elizabeth (*née* Forrest); three *d*. *Educ:* Bryanston Sch.; Queens' Coll., Cambridge (MA). Called to the Bar, Middle Temple, 1964, Bencher, 1989; one of the Junior Counsel to the Crown, Common Law, 1979–85; Junior Counsel to Dept of Trade in export credit matters, 1981–85. Member: Gen. Council of the Bar, 1987–; Judicial Studies Bd, 1988–; Council of Legal Educn, 1988–. *Recreations:* reading, music. *Address:* 1 Crown Office Row, EC4. *T:* 01–353 1801; (home) The Firs, Church Road, Sunningdale, Berks. *T:* Ascot (0990) 22686. *Club:* Leander.

LATHAM, Michael Anthony; MP (C) Rutland and Melton, since 1983 (Melton, Feb. 1974–1983); *b* 20 Nov. 1942; *m* 1969, Caroline Terry; two *s*. *Educ:* Marlborough Coll.; King's Coll., Cambridge; Dept of Educn, Oxford. BA Cantab 1964, MA Cantab 1968, CertEd Oxon 1965. Housing and Local Govt Officer, Conservative Research Dept, 1965–67; Parly Liaison Officer, Nat. Fedn of Building Trades Employers, 1967–73; Dir, House-builders Fedn, 1971–73. Westminster City Councillor, 1968–71. Contested (C) Liverpool, West Derby, 1970. Vice-Chairman: Cons. Parly Housing Cttee, 1974–76; Cons. Parly Environment Cttee, 1979–83; Member: House of Commons Expenditure Cttee, 1974–79; Jt Cttee on Statutory Instruments, 1974–75; Jt Ecclesiastical Cttee of both Houses of Parliament, 1974–; Select Cttee on Energy, 1979–82; Public Accounts Cttee, 1983–; H of C Chairmen's Panel, 1987–. Sec., British-Gibraltar Parly Gp, 1981–87; Chm., British-Israel Parly Gp, 1981–90; Pres., Anglo-Israel Assoc., 1990– (Chm. Exec. Cttee, 1986–90); Vice Pres., Cons. Friends of Israel, 1985– (Chm., 1982–85). Dir, Lovell Homes Ltd, 1975–85; Housing Adviser, Y. J. Lovell PLC, 1985–89; Dir, Lovell Partnerships, 1989–; Dir, Building (Publications) Ltd, 1988–. Mem., Adv. Council on Public Records, 1985–; Mem. Bd of Management, Shelter, 1976–82. Vice-Pres., Building Socs Assoc., 1981–91. C of E Deleg. to BCC, 1977–81; Mem., Exec. Cttee, CCJ, 1987–. C of E Lay Reader, 1988–. Trustee, Oakham Sch., 1987–. *Publications:* articles on housing, land, town planning and building. *Recreations:* gardening, fencing, listening to classical music, cricket. *Address:* House of Commons, SW1A 0AA. *Club:* Carlton.

LATHAM, Air Vice-Marshal Peter Anthony, CB 1980; AFC 1960; Senior Air Adviser, Short Bros PLC, since 1985; *b* 18 June 1925; *s* of late Oscar Frederick Latham and Rhoda Latham; *m* 1953, Barbara Mary; two *s* six *d*. *Educ:* St Phillip's Grammar Sch., Birmingham; St Catharine's Coll., Cambridge. psa 1961. Joined RAF, 1944; 1946–69: served No 26, 263, 614, and 247 Sqdns; CFE; Air Min.; Comd No 111 Sqdn; RAF Formation Aerobatic Team (Leader of Black Arrows, 1959–60); MoD Jt Planning Staff; Comd NEAF Strike and PR Wing; Coll. of Air Warfare; Ops No 38 Gp; Comd RAF Tengah, 1969–71; MoD Central Staff, 1971–73; Comd Officer and Aircrew Selection Centre, Biggin Hill, 1973–74; SASO No 38 Gp, 1974–76; Dir Def. Ops, MoD Central Staff, 1976–77; AOC No 11 Group, 1977–81. Principal, Oxford Air Trng Sch., and Dir, CSE Aviation Ltd, 1982–85. Cdre, RAF Sailing Assoc., 1974–80; Pres., Assoc. of Service Yacht Clubs, 1978–81. Liveryman, Clockmakers' Co., 1987 (Steward, 1989). *Recreations:* sailing, horology. *Address:* (office) Short Brothers, Glen House, Stag Place, Victoria, SW1E 5AG. *Club:* Royal Air Force.

LATHAM, Richard Brunton; QC 1991; a Recorder, since 1987; *b* 16 March 1947; *s* of Frederick and Joan Catherine Latham; *m* 1972, Alison Mary Goodall; three *s*. *Educ:* Farnborough Grammar School; Univ. of Birmingham (LLB 1969). Called to the Bar, Gray's Inn, 1971; practice on Midland and Oxford Circuit; Standing Prosecuting Counsel to Inland Revenue, Midland and Oxford Circuit, 1987–91. *Recreations:* sailing, opera. *Address:* 2 Crown Office Row, Temple, EC4Y 7HJ. *T:* 071–353 1365.

LATHAM, Sir Richard Thomas Paul, 3rd Bt, *cr* 1919, of Crow Clump; *b* 15 April 1934; *s* of Sir (Herbert) Paul Latham, 2nd Bt, and Lady Patricia Doreen Moore (*d* 1947), *o d* of 10th Earl of Drogheda; *S* father, 1955; *m* 1958, Marie-Louise Patricia, *d* of Frederick H. Russell, Vancouver, BC; two *d*. *Educ:* Eton; Trinity Coll., Cambridge. *Address:* 2125 Birnam Wood Drive, Santa Barbara, Calif 93108, USA.

LATHAM, Robert Clifford, CBE 1973; FBA 1982; Hon. Fellow of Magdalene College, Cambridge, since 1984 (Fellow, 1972–84; Pepys Librarian, 1972–82); *b* 11 March 1912; *s* of Edwin Latham, and Alice Latham, Audley, Staffs; *m* 1st, 1939, Eileen Frances Redding Ramsay (*d* 1969); one *s* one *d*; 2nd, 1973, Rosalind Frances Birley (*d* 1990). *Educ:* Wolstanton County Grammar Sch., Staffs; Queens' Coll., Cambridge (scholar). Hist. Tripos Pt I 1932, Pt II 1933; MA 1938. Asst Lectr in History, King's Coll., London, 1935; Lectr, 1939; University Reader in History, Royal Holloway Coll., London, 1947–72. Visiting Associate Prof., Univ. of Southern California, Los Angeles, 1955; Prof. of History, Univ. of Toronto, 1968–69; Research Fellow, Magdalene Coll., Cambridge, 1970–72. Hon. Fellow, RHBNC, 1989. Wheatley Medal, LA, 1983; Marc Fitch prize, Univ. of Leeds, 1984. *Publications:* (ed) Bristol Charters, 1509–1899 (Bristol Rec. Soc., vol. xii), 1947; (ed) The Diary of Samuel Pepys, vols i-ix (with Prof. W. Matthews), 1970–76, vols x and xi, 1983; (ed) The Illustrated Pepys, 1978; gen. editor, Catalogue of the Pepys Library at Magdalene College, Cambridge, 1978– (in progress); (ed) The Shorter Pepys, 1985; (ed with Linnet Latham) A Pepys Anthology, 1987; articles and reviews in learned and other jls. *Recreations:* music, gossip. *Address:* Magdalene College, Cambridge CB3 0AG. *T:* Cambridge (0223) 350357.

See also D. N. R. Latham.

LATHE, Prof. Grant Henry; Professor of Chemical Pathology, University of Leeds, 1957–77, now Emeritus Professor; *b* 27 July 1913; *s* of Frank Eugene and Annie Smith Lathe; *m* 1st, 1938, Margaret Eleanore Brown; one *s*; 2nd, 1950, Joan Frances Hamlin;

one *s* two *d*. *Educ:* McGill Univ.; Oxford Univ. ICI Research Fellow: Dept. of Biochemistry, Oxford Univ., 1946; Dept. of Chemical Pathology, Post Graduate Medical School of London, 1948; Lecturer in Chemical Pathology, Guy's Hospital Medical School, 1948; Biochemist, The Bernhard Baron Memorial Research Laboratories, Queen Charlotte's Maternity Hospital, London, 1949. John Scott Award (with C. R. J. Ruthven), 1971, for invention of gel filtration. *Publications:* papers in medical and biochemical journals. *Recreations:* fell-walking, campaigning against nuclear weapons. *Address:* 12A The Avenue, Leeds LS8 1EH. *T:* Leeds (0532) 661507.

LATIMER, Sir (Courtenay) Robert, Kt 1966; CBE 1958 (OBE 1948); *b* 13 July 1911; *er s* of late Sir Courtenay Latimer, KCIE, CSI; *m* 1st, 1944, Elizabeth Jane Gordon (*née* Smail) (*d* 1989); one *s* one *d*; 2nd, 1990, Frederieka Jacoba Blankert (*née* Witteween). *Educ:* Rugby; Christ Church, Oxford. ICS, 1934 (Punjab); IPS, 1939; Vice-Consul, Bushire, 1940–41; Sec. Foreign Publicity Office, Delhi, 1941–42; Sec. Indian Agency Gen., Chungking, 1944; in NW Frontier Prov., as Asst Political Agent N Waziristan, Dir of Civil Supplies, Sec. to Governor and District Comr, Bannu, 1942–43 and 1945–47. HM Overseas Service, 1948; served in Swaziland, 1948–49; Bechuanaland Protectorate, 1951–54; Office of High Comr for Basutoland, the Bechuanaland Protectorate and Swaziland, as Asst Sec., 1949–51; Sec. for Finance, 1954–60; Chief Sec., 1960–64; Minister, British Embassy, Pretoria, 1965–66; Registrar, Kingston Polytechnic, 1967–76. *Recreations:* golf, photography. *Address:* Benedicts, Old Avenue, Weybridge, Surrey.

LATIMER, Sir Graham (Stanley), KBE 1980; President, New Zealand Maori Council, since 1972 (Delegate, 1964; Vice-President, 1969–72); *b* Waiharara, N Auckland, 7 Feb. 1926; *s* of Graham Latimer and Lillian Edith Latimer (*née* Kenworth *m* 1948, Emily Patricia Moore; two *s* two *d*. *Educ:* Pukenui and Kaitaia District High School. Dairy farmer, 1961–. Member: Tai Tokerau Dist Maori Council, 1962– (Sec. 1966–75); Otamatea Maori Exec., 1959– (Sec. Treas. 1962–72, Chm. 1975–); Otamatea Maori Cttee, 1955–62; Arapaoa Maori Cttee, 1962– (Chm. 1962–69 and 1972–); N Auckland Power Bd, 1977–; Waitangi Tribunal, 1976–. Chm., since inception, Northland Community Coll.; Trustee, Maori Education Foundn; Member: Cttee, Nat. Art Gall. Museum and War Memorial; NZ Maori Arts and Crafts Inst., 1980–; Tourist Adv. Council; Northland Regional Develt Council, 1980–; Alcoholic Liquor Adv. Council, 1980–. Lay Canon, Auckland Anglican Cathedral, 1978; Mem. Gen. Synod. *Recreations:* Rugby football, tennis. *Address:* RD1, Taipuha, Northland, New Zealand. *T:* Taipuha 837.

LATIMER, Sir Robert; *see* Latimer, Sir C. R.

LATNER, Prof. Albert Louis; Professor of Clinical Biochemistry, University of Newcastle upon Tyne, 1963–78, now Emeritus Professor, and Director of Cancer Research Unit, 1967–78; Consultant Clinical Biochemist, Royal Victoria Infirmary, Newcastle upon Tyne, 1948–78, Hon. Consultant, since 1978; *b* 5 Dec. 1912; *s* of Harry Latner and Miriam Gordon; *m* 1936, Gertrude Franklin (*d* 1986). *Educ:* Imperial College of Science and University College, London; University of Liverpool. ARCSc, 1931; MSc (London) 1933; DIC, 1934; MB, ChB (Liverpool) 1939; MD (Liverpool) 1948; FRIC 1953; MRCP 1956; DSc (Liverpool) 1958; FRCPath 1963; FRCP 1964. Lectr in Physiology, Univ. of Liverpool, 1933–36 and 1939–41; Pathologist in RAMC, 1941–46; Sen. Registrar, Postgrad. Medical Sch., 1946–47; Lectr in Chem. Pathol., King's Coll., Univ. of Durham, 1947–55; Reader in Medical Biochemistry, Univ. of Durham, 1955–61; Prof. of Clin. Chem., Univ. of Durham, 1961–63. Vis. Lectr, Amer. Assoc. Clinical Chemists, 1972. Hon. Member: Assoc. of Clinical Biochemists, 1984 (Chm., 1958–61; Pres., 1961–63); British Electrophoresis Soc., 1986. Mem., Editorial Bd of Clinica Chimica Acta, 1960–68; Co-editor, Advances in Clinical Chemistry, 1971–84. Titular Member, Section of Clinical Chemistry, International Union of Pure and Applied Chemistry, 1967–73; Hon. Fellow, American Nat. Acad. of Clinical Biochemistry, 1977. Member, Editorial Board: Electrophoresis, 1980–88; Med. Sci. Res., 1981–. Wellcome Prize, 1976. *Publications:* Isoenzymes in Biology and Medicine, 1968 (co-author); Cantarow and Trumper Clinical Biochemistry, 7th edn, 1975; Chapter on Metabolic Aspects of Liver Disease in Metabolic Disturbances in Clinical Medicine (ed G. A. Smart), 1958; Chapters on Chemical Pathology and Clinical Biochemistry in British Encyclopædia of Med. Practice, Med. Progress (ed Lord Cohen of Birkenhead), 1961, 1962, 1964, 1966 and 1968; Chapter on Isoenzymes in Recent Advances in Clinical Pathology, Series IV, 1964; Section on Isoenzymes in Advances in Clinical Chemistry (ed C. P. Stewart), 1966; (ed with O. Bodansky and contrib. section on Isoelectric Focusing) Advances in Clinical Chemistry, 1975; contribs to Medical and Scientific Journals dealing with cancer, liver disease, pernicious anæmia, the serum proteins in disease and isoenzymes. *Recreations:* art, photography, gardening. *Address:* Ravenstones, Rectory Road, Gosforth, Newcastle upon Tyne NE3 1XP. *T:* 091–285 8020. *Club:* Athenæum.

LATOUR-ADRIEN, Hon. Sir (Jean François) Maurice, Kt 1971; Chief Justice of Mauritius, 1970–77; Chairman, Mauritius Union Assurance Co. Ltd, since 1982 (Director since 1978); Legal Consultant: Mauritius Commercial Bank Ltd, since 1983; Promotion and Development Ltd, since 1985; *b* 4 March 1915; 2nd *s* of late Louis Constant Emile Adrien and late Maria Ella Latour. *Educ:* Royal Coll., Mauritius; Univ. Coll., London; Middle Temple, London. LLB 1940. Called to the Bar, Middle Temple, 1940. Mauritius: Dist Magistrate, 1947; Crown Counsel, 1950; Additl Subst. Procureur and Advocate-Gen., 1954; Sen. Crown Counsel, 1958; Asst Attorney-Gen., 1960; Solicitor-Gen., 1961; Dir of Public Prosecutions, 1964; Puisne Judge, 1966–70; Acting Governor-Gen., Feb. 1973, July–Aug. 1974, Jan.–Feb. and June–Aug. 1975, July–Sept. 1976. Pres., Mauritius Red Cross Soc., 1978–; Vice-Pres., Inst. Internat. de Droit d'Expression Française (IDEF). Director: Mauritius Commercial Bank Ltd, 1980–83, 1984–87, 1988–; Mauritius Commercial Bank Finance Corp. Pres., Mental Health Assoc., 1985– (Vice-Pres., 1978–84). KLJ 1969. *Address:* Vacoas, Mauritius.

LA TROBE-BATEMAN, Richard George Saumarez; furniture designer/maker; *b* 17 Oct. 1938; *s* of John La Trobe-Bateman and Margaret (*née* Schmid); *m* 1969, Mary Elizabeth Jolly; one *s* two *d*. *Educ:* Westminster Sch.; St Martin's Sch. of Art; Royal Coll. of Art (MDesRCA). Set up workshop, 1968. Member: Council of Management, British Crafts Centre, 1975–86; Council, Contemporary Applied Arts, 1987–; Crafts Council: Mem., 1984–86; Index Selector, 1972–73; Chm., Index Selection Cttee, 1980–82. Work in: V&A Collection, 1979; Crafts Council Collection, 1981 and 1984; Keble Coll., Oxon, 1981; Temple Newsam Collection, 1983; Southern Arts Collection, 1983; Pembroke Coll., Oxon, 1984; Crafts Study Centre Collection, Bath, 1985; Northern Arts Collection, 1988; work presented by Crafts Council to the Prince of Wales, 1982. Vis. Prof., San Diego State Univ., 1986–87. *Publications:* articles in Crafts, American Crafts. *Recreations:* listening to music, hill-walking. *Address:* Elm House, Batcombe, Shepton Mallet, Somerset BA4 6AB. *T:* Upton Noble (074985) 442. *Club:* Contemporary Applied Arts.

LATTER, Leslie William; Director General, Merseyside Passenger Transport Executive, 1977–86; *b* 4 Nov. 1921; *s* of William Richard and Clara Maud Latter; *m* 1948, Pamela Jean Marsh; one *s*. *Educ:* Beckenham Grammar Sch., Kent. IPFA, FCIT. Served Royal Air Force, 1940–46. London County Council, 1947–62; Chief Asst, Beckenham Borough Council, 1962–64; Asst Borough Treasurer, Bromley, 1964–68; Dep. Borough Treasurer, Greenwich, 1968–74; Dir of Finance and Administration, Merseyside PTE, 1974–77. *Recreations:* gardening, music. *Address:* The Nursery, 19 Saxon Close, Seabrook Road, Hythe, Kent CT21 5QS. *T:* Hythe (0303) 264959.

LATTO, Dr Douglas; private medical practice; Chairman, British Safety Council, since 1971 (Vice-Chairman, 1968–71); *b* Dundee, Scotland, 13 Dec. 1913; *s* of late David Latto, Town Clerk of Dundee, and late Christina Latto; *m* 1945, Dr Edith Monica Druitt (*d* 1990); one *s* three *d*. *Educ:* Dundee High Sch.; St Andrews Univ. MB, ChB (St And.) 1939; DObst, RCOG 1944, MRCOG 1949, FRCOG 1989. During War: Ho. Surg., Dundee Royal Infirmary, 1939; Ho. Phys., Cornelia and East Dorset Hosp., Poole, 1940; Resident Obstetrician and Gynaecologist, Derbyshire Hosp. for Women, Derby, 1940; Res. Surgical Officer, Hereford Gen. Hosp., 1941; Res. Obst. and Gynaec., East End Maternity Hosp., London, 1942; Res. Obst. and Gynaec., City of London Maternity Hosp., 1943; Res. Surgical Officer, Birmingham Accident Hosp., 1944; Casualty Officer, Paddington Gen. Hosp., London, 1944; Asst Obst. and Gynaec., Mayday Hosp., Croydon, 1945. Res. Obst. and Gynaec., Southlands Hosp., Shoreham-by-Sea, Sussex, 1946–49; Asst, Nuffield Dept of Obstetrics and Gynaecology, Radcliffe Infirmary, Oxford, 1949–51. Member: BMA; Council, Soil Assoc.; Chm., Plantmilk Soc.; Vice-President: International Vegetarian Union; GB Philatelic Soc., 1986–. Governor, Internat. Inst. of Safety Management. Freeman, City of London, 1988; Liveryman, Worshipful Co. of Apothecaries. Mem., Order of the Cross. FRSocMed; FRPSL 1975. Silver Jubilee Medal, 1977; Sword of Honour, British Safety Council, 1985. *Publications:* Smoking and Lung Cancer: a report to all Members of Parliament for the British Safety Council, May 1969; contribs to BMJ; Proc. Royal Soc. Med.; Philatelic Jl; etc. *Recreations:* squash, travelling, gardening, philately (Internat. Stamp Exhibns: Large Gold Medal, London, 1970; Gold Medal, Brussels, 1972, Munich, 1973, Basle, 1974; Large Gold Medals: Paris 1975; Copenhagen, 1976 (and Prix d'Honneur); London, 1980 (and GB Philatelic Soc. Award); Vienna, 1981. *Address:* Lethnot Lodge, 4 Derby Road, Caversham, Reading, Berks RG4 0EY. *T:* Reading (0734) 472282. *Clubs:* Royal Automobile, Rolls-Royce Enthusiasts' (Paulersbury).

LATYMER, 8th Baron *cr* 1431; **Hugo Nevill Money-Coutts;** *b* 1 March 1926; *s* of 7th Baron Latymer and Patience (*d* 1982), *d* of late William Courtenay-Thompson; *S* father, 1987; *m* 1st, 1951, Hon. Penelope Ann Clare (marr. diss. 1965), *yr d* of late T. A. Emmet and Baroness Emmet of Amberley; two *s* one *d*; 2nd 1965, Jinty, *d* of late Peter George Calvert; one *s* two *d*. *Educ:* Eton. *Heir:* *s* Hon. Crispin James Alan Nevill Money-Coutts [*b* 8 March 1955; *m* 1978, Hon. Lucy Rose, *y d* of Baron Deedes, *qv*; one *s* two *d*]. *Address:* Calle Rafael Blanes 63, Arta, Mallorca, Spain.

LAUCKE, Hon. Sir Condor (Louis), KCMG 1979; Lieutenant-Governor, State of South Australia, since 1982; *b* 9 Nov. 1914; *s* of Friedrich Laucke and Marie (*née* Jungfer); *m* 19 Rose Hambour; one *s* one *d*. *Educ:* Immanuel Coll., Adelaide; South Australian School of Mines. Elected to S Australian House of Assembly, 1956, 1959, 1962; Government Whip, 1962–65; Member, Australian Senate for S Australia, 1967–81; Pres. Senate, Parlt of Commonwealth of Australia, 1976–81. Member, Liberal Party Executive, 1972–74. Joint President: CPA, 1976–79 (also Chm., Exec. Cttee, 1976–79); IPU. *Address:* Bunawunda, Greenock, SA 5360, Australia. *T:* 085 628143.

LAUDER, Sir Piers Robert Dick-, 13th Bt *cr* 1688; *S* father, 1981.

LAUDERDALE, 17th Earl of, *cr* 1624; **Patrick Francis Maitland;** Baron Maitland, 1590; Viscount Lauderdale, 1616; Viscount Maitland, Baron Thirlestane and Boltoun, 1624; Bt of Nova Scotia, 1680; Hereditary Bearer of the National Flag of Scotland, 1790 and 1952; Chief of the Clan Maitland; *b* 17 March 1911; *s* of Reverend Hon. Sydney G. W. Maitland and Ella Frances (*née* Richards); *S* brother, 1968; *m* 1936, Stanka, *d* of Professor Milivoje Lozanitch, Belgrade Univ.; two *s* two *d*. *Educ:* Lancing Coll., Sussex; Brasenose Coll., Oxford. BA Hons Oxon, 1933; Journalist 1933–59. Appts include: Balkans and Danubian Corresp., The Times, 1939–41; Special Corresp. Washington, News Chronicle, 1941; War Corresp., Pacific, Australia, New Zealand, News Chronicle, 1941–43. Foreign Office, 1943–45. MP (U) for Lanark Div. of Lanarks, 1951–Sept. 1959 (except for period May-Dec. 1957 when Ind. C). Founder and Chairman, Expanding Commonwealth Group, House of Commons, 1955–59; re-elected Chairman, Nov. 1959. Chm., Sub-Cttee on Energy, Transport and Res., House of Lords Select Cttee on EEC Affairs, 1974–79; Vice Chm. and Co-founder, Parly Gp for Energy Studies, 1980–. Dir, Elf-Aquitaine (UK) Holdings. Editor of The Fleet Street Letter Service, and of The Whitehall Letter, 1945–58. Mem., Coll. of Guardians of National Shrine of Our Lady of Walsingham, Norfolk, 1955–82 (Guardian Emeritus, 1982–). President, The Church Union, 1956–61. FRGS. *Publications:* European Dateline, 1945; Task for Giants, 1957. *Heir:* *s* The Master of Lauderdale, Viscount Maitland, *qv*. *Address:* 10 Ovington Square, SW3 1LH. *T:* 071–589 7451; 12 St Vincent Street, Edinburgh. *T:* 031–556 5692. *Clubs:* New (Edinburgh); Royal Scottish Automobile (Glasgow).
See also R. W. P. H. Hay.

LAUDERDALE, Master of; *see* Maitland, Viscount.

LAUGHARNE, Albert, CBE 1983; QPM 1978; Deputy Commissioner, Metropolitan Police, 1983–85; *b* 20 Oct. 1931; *s* of Reginald Stanley Laugharne and Jessica Simpson Laugharne; *m* 1954, Barbara Thirlwall; two *d*. *Educ:* Baines' Grammar Sch., Poulton-le-Fylde; Manchester Univ. Detective Inspector, Manchester City Police, 1952–66; Supt, Cumbria Constab., 1966–70; Chief Supt, W Yorks Constab., 1970–73; Asst Chief Constable, Cheshire Constab., 1973–76; Chief Constable: Warwicks, 1977–78; Lancashire, 1978–83. RCDS, 1975. *Publication:* Seaford House Papers, 1975. *Recreations:* gardening, painting.

LAUGHLAND, (Graham Franklyn) Bruce, QC 1977; **His Honour Judge Laughland;** a Circuit Judge, since 1989; *b* 18 Aug. 1931; 3rd *s* of late Andrew and late Constance Laughland; *m* 1969, Victoria Nicola Christina Jarman; one *s*. *Educ:* King Edward's Sch., Birmingham; Christ Church, Oxford. Stick of Honour, Mons Officer Cadet Sch., 1954; Lieut 8th RTR, 1954–56. Called to Bar, Inner Temple, 1958, Bencher, 1985; Dep. Chm., Bucks QS, 1971; Standing Counsel to the Queen's Proctor, 1968; a Recorder, 1972–89; First Prosecuting Counsel to the Inland Revenue (Midland and Oxford Circuit), 1973–77; actg Judge of the Supreme Court of the Falkland Is, 1985–. Mem., Gen. Council of the Bar, 1970; Treas., Midland and Oxford Circuit, 1986–89. Chm., Westminster Assoc. for Youth, 1984–89. *Address:* Central Criminal Court, EC4M 7EH.

LAUGHTON, Sir Anthony Seymour, Kt 1987; FRS 1980; oceanographic consultant; Director, Institute of Oceanographic Sciences, 1978–88; *b* 29 April 1927; *s* of Sydney Thomas Laughton and Dorothy Laughton (*née* Chamberlain); *m* 1st, 1957, Juliet Ann Chapman (marr. diss. 1962); one *s*; 2nd, 1973, Barbara Clare Bosanquet; two *d*. *Educ:* Marlborough Coll.; King's Coll., Cambridge (MA, PhD). RNVR, 1945–48. John Murray Student, Columbia Univ., NY, 1954–55; Nat. Inst. of Oceanography, later Inst. of Oceanographic Sciences, 1955–88: research in marine geophysics in Atlantic and Indian

Oceans, esp. in underwater photography, submarine morphology, ocean basin evolution, midocean ridge tectonics; Principal Scientist of deep sea expedns. Member: Co-ordinating Cttee for Marine Sci. and Technol., 1987–91; nat. and internat. cttees on oceanography and geophysics. Pres., Challenger Soc. for Marine Sci., 1988–90. Member Council: Royal Soc., 1986–87; Marine Biology Assoc., 1980–83, 1988–; Soc. for Underwater Technology, 1986–. Member: Governing Body, Charterhouse Sch., 1981–; Council, University Coll. London, 1983–. Trustee, Natural Hist. Mus., 1990–. Silver Medal, RSA, 1958; Cuthbert Peek grant, RGS, 1967; Prince Albert 1er Monaco Gold Medal for Oceanography, 1980; Founders Medal, RGS, 1987; Murchison Medal, Geol. Soc., 1989. *Publications:* papers on marine geophysics and oceanography. *Recreations:* music, gardening, sailing. *Address:* Okelands, Pickhurst Road, Chiddingfold, Surrey. *T:* Wormley (0428) 683941.

LAURENCE, Ven. Christopher; *see* Laurence, Ven. J. H. C.

LAURENCE, Dan Hyman; Literary and Dramatic Advisor, Estate of George Bernard Shaw, 1973–90; *b* 28 March 1920. *Educ:* New York City public schs; Hofstra Univ. (BA 1946); New York Univ. (MA 1950). First went on the stage as child actor, 1932; radar specialist with Fifth Air Force, USA, in S Pacific, 1942–45; wrote and performed for Armed Forces Radio Service in New Guinea and the Philippines during World War II, and subseq. for radio and television in USA and Australia; began teaching in 1950 as graduate asst, New York Univ.; Instr of English, Hofstra Univ., 1953–58; Editor, Readex Microprint Corp., 1959–60; Associate Prof. of English, New York Univ., 1962–67, Prof., 1967–70. Vis. Professor: Indiana Univ., 1969; Univ. of Texas at Austin, 1974–75; Tulane Univ., 1981 (Mellon Prof. in the Humanities); Univ. of BC, Vancouver, 1984; Adjunct Prof. of Drama, Univ. of Guelph, 1986– (Dist. Vis. Prof. of Drama, 1983); Vis. Fellow, Inst. for Arts and Humanistic Studies, Pennsylvania State Univ., 1976. John Simon Guggenheim Meml Fellow, 1960, 1961 and 1972; Montgomery Fellow, Dartmouth Coll., 1982. Literary Advr, Shaw Fest., Ont, 1982–90. Associate Mem., RADA, 1979. Phi Beta Kappa (hon.), 1967. President's Medal, Hofstra Univ., 1990. *Publications:* Henry James: a bibliography (with Leon Edel), 1957 (3rd edn 1981); Robert Nathan: a bibliography, 1960; (ed) Collected Letters of Bernard Shaw, vol. 1, 1874–1897, 1965, vol. 2, 1898–1910, 1972, vol. 3, 1911–1925, 1985, Vol. 4, 1926–1950, 1988; (ed) Bernard Shaw, Collected Plays with their Prefaces, 1970–74; Shaw, Books, and Libraries, 1976; Shaw: an exhibit, 1977; (dramatization) The Black Girl in Search of God, 1977; (ed) Shaw's Music, 1981, 2nd edn 1989; Bernard Shaw: a bibliography, 1983; A Portrait of the Author as a Bibliography (Engelhard Lecture on the Book, L of C, 1982), 1983; (Uncollected Writings of Shaw): How to Become a Musical Critic, 1960 (2nd edn 1968); Platform and Pulpit, 1961; (ed with David H. Greene) The Matter with Ireland, 1962; (ed with Daniel J. Leary) Flyleaves, 1977; (Gen. Editor) Bernard Shaw: Early Texts, Play Manuscripts in Facsimile, 12 vols, 1981; (with James Rambeau) Agitations: letters to the Press 1875–1950, 1985; (with Martin Quinn) Shaw on Dickens, 1985; (with Nicholas Grene) Shaw, Lady Gregory, and the Abbey, 1991. *Recreations:* theatre-going, music, book-collecting, mountain climbing. *Address:* 102 Rampart Drive (P-213), San Antonio, Texas 78216, USA.

LAURENCE, George Frederick; QC 1991; *b* 15 Jan. 1947; *s* of Dr George Bester Laurence and Anna Margaretha Laurence; *m* 1976, Ann Jessica Chenevix Trench; one *s* one *d* and one step *s*. *Educ:* Pretoria High Sch. for Boys; Univ. of Cape Town (Smuts Meml Scholarship; BA); University College, Oxford (Rhodes Scholar; MA). Called to the Bar, Middle Temple, 1972 (Harmsworth Law Scholar). *Publications:* articles in Rights of Way Law Review (Byways and Bridleways Trust). *Recreations:* communication, access to the countryside, cricket, tennis. *Address:* 12 New Square, Lincoln's Inn, WC2A 3SW. *T:* 071–405 3808.

LAURENCE, Ven. (John Harvard) Christopher; Archdeacon of Lindsey, Diocese of Lincoln, since 1985; *b* 15 April 1929; *s* of Canon H. P. Laurence and Mrs E. Laurence; *m* 1952, E. Margaret E. Chappell; one *s* one *d*. *Educ:* Christ's Hospital; Trinity Hall, Cambridge (MA); Westcott House, Cambridge. Nat. service commn, Royal Lincolnshire Regt, 1948–50. Asst Curate, St Nicholas, Lincoln, 1955–59; Vicar, Crosby St George, Scunthorpe, 1959–73; St Hugh's Missioner, Lincoln Diocese, 1974–79; Bishops' Director of Clergy Training, London Diocese, 1979–85. *Recreations:* piano, clarinet, sculpture. *Address:* The Archdeaconry, 2 Greestone Place, Lincoln LN2 1PP. *T:* Lincoln (0522) 531444.

LAURENCE, Sir Peter (Harold), KCMG 1981 (CMG 1976); MC 1944; DL; HM Diplomatic Service, retired; Chairman of Council, British Institute of Archaelogy, Ankara, since 1984; *b* 18 Feb. 1923; *s* of late Ven. George Laurence, MA, BD and late Alice (*née* Jackson); *m* 1948, Elizabeth Aïda Way; two *s* one *d*. *Educ:* Radley Coll.; Christ Church, Oxford. 60th Rifles, 1941–46 (Major). Entered Foreign Service, 1948; Western Dept, FO, 1948–50; Athens, 1950–53; Asst Political Adviser, Trieste, 1953–55; 1st Sec., Levant Dept, FO, 1955–57; Prague, 1957–60; Cairo, 1960–62; North and East African Dept, FO, 1962–65; Personnel Dept, DSAO, 1965–67; Counsellor, 1965; Political Adviser, Berlin, 1967–69; Visiting Fellow, All Souls Coll., 1969–70; Counsellor (Commercial), Paris, 1970–74; Chief Inspector, HM Diplomatic Service (Asst Under-Sec. of State), 1974–78; Ambassador to Ankara, 1980–83. Chairman: Foreign Anglican Church and Educnl Assoc. Ltd, 1976–; Community Council of Devon, 1986–; Fellow, Woodard Corp. (W Div.), 1985. Mem. Council, Univ. of Exeter, 1989–. Chm. of Governors, Grenville Coll., Bideford, 1988–. DL Devon, 1989. *Address:* Trevilla, Beaford, Winkleigh, N Devon EX19 8NS. *Club:* Army and Navy.

LAURENS, André; Editor-in-Chief of Le Monde, 1982–84; *b* 7 Dec. 1934; unmarried. Journalist: L'Eclaireur méridional, Montpellier, 1953–55; l'Agence centrale de la presse, Paris, 1958–62; joined Le Monde, 1963; Home Affairs reporter, 1969; Associate Editor, Home Affairs, 1979. Vice-Pres., Société des Rédacteurs. *Publications:* Les nouveaux communistes, 1972; D'une France à l'autre, 1974; Le métier politique, 1980. *Address:* 34 rue de Clichy, 75009 Paris, France.

LAURENSON, James Tait; Deputy Chairman since 1983 and Managing Director since 1984, Adam & Company Group; *b* 15 March 1941; *s* of James Tait Laurenson, FRCS and Vera Dorothy Kidd; *m* 1969, Hilary Josephine Thompson; one *s* three *d*. *Educ:* Eton; Magdalene College, Cambridge (MA). FCA. Ivory & Sime, investment managers, 1968–83, Partner 1970, Dir 1975; Tayburn Design Group: Man. Dir, 1983–84; Chm., 1984–89. Director: United Scientific Holdings, 1971–; First Charlotte Assets Trust, 1983–; Japan Assets Trust, 1983–88; The Life Association of Scotland, 1991–; Chm., Nippon Assets Investments, 1984–. *Recreations:* gardening, shooting, stalking, tennis, skiing. *Address:* Adam & Company Group, 22 Charlotte Square, Edinburgh EH2 4DF; Hill House, Kirknewton, Midlothian. *Club:* New (Edinburgh).

LAURIE, Sir (Robert) Bayley (Emilius), 7th Bt *cr* 1834; *b* 8 March 1931; *s* of Maj.-Gen. Sir John Emilius Laurie, 6th Bt, CBE, DSO, and Evelyn Clare, (*d* 1987), *d* of late Lt-Col Lionel James Richardson-Gardner; *S* father, 1983; *m* 1968, Laurelie, *d* of Sir Reginald Lawrence William Williams, 7th Bt, MBE, ED; two *d*. *Educ:* Eton. National Service, 1st Bn Seaforth Highlanders, 1949–51; Captain, 11th Bn Seaforth Highlanders (TA), 1951–67. Member of Lloyd's, 1955. *Heir: cousin* Andrew Ronald Emilius Laurie [*b* 20 Oct. 1944; *m* 1970, Sarah Anne, *e d* of C. D. Patterson; two *s*]. *Address:* The Old Rectory, Little Tey, Colchester, Essex CO6 1JA. *T:* Colchester (0206) 210410.

LAURIE, Robert Peter; JP; farmer, 1958–89, retired; Vice-Lord Lieutenant, Essex, since 1985; *b* 20 Aug. 1925; *s* of late Col Vernon Stewart Laurie, CBE, TD, DL, and Mary, 2nd *d* of Selwyn Robert Pryor; *m* 1952, Oonagh Margaret Faber Wild, 3rd *d* of W. P. Wild, Warcop Hall, Westmorland; three *s* one *d*. *Educ:* Eton College. Served Coldstream Guards, 1943–47, Hon. Captain. Member of Stock Exchange, 1953; Partner, Heseltine, Powell & Co., then Heseltine, Moss & Co., 1953–80, Consultant, 1980–86; Director, British Empire Securites & General Trust Ltd, 1954– (Chm., 1973–84). Governor: Brentwood Sch., 1974–; Alleyn's Sch., 1984–; Chm., 1977–86, Pres., 1986–, Essex Assoc. of Boys' Clubs; a Vice-Pres., Nat. Assoc. of Boys' Clubs, 1986–; President: Essex Agricl Soc., 1986–87; Essex Shire Horse Assoc., 1987–; Essex Home Workers, 1986–; Chelmsford and Mid Essex Samaritans, 1986–. Member: Ct, Essex Univ., 1979–; Council, CGLI, 1984–. Master, Saddlers' Co., 1981–82. Chm., Essex Co. Cttee, TAVRA, 1987–91. JP 1974, High Sheriff 1978–79, DL 1979, Essex. *Recreations:* foxhunting and field sports, gardening, reading. *Address:* Heatley's, Ingrave, Brentwood, Essex CM13 3QW. *T:* Brentwood (0277) 810224. *Club:* City Livery.

LAURIE, Robin; His Honour Judge Laurie; a Circuit Judge, South Eastern Circuit, since 1986; *b* 26 Jan. 1938; *s* of J. R. Laurie and Dr W. Metzner; *m* 1965, Susan Jane (*neé* Snelling); two *d*. *Educ:* Fettes Coll.; Geneva Univ.; Jesus Coll., Oxford (MA). Called to the Bar, Inner Temple, 1961; practice at the Bar (South Eastern Circuit), 1961–86. *Recreations:* mountaineering, mycology. *Address:* c/o 4 Paper Buildings, Temple, EC4Y 7EX. *Club:* Alpine.

LAURISTON, Alexander Clifford, QC 1972; **His Honour Judge Lauriston;** a Circuit Judge, since 1976; *b* 2 Oct. 1927; *s* of Alexander Lauriston and Nellie Lauriston (*née* Ainsworth); *m* 1954, Inga Louise Cameron; two *d*. *Educ:* Coatham Sch., Redcar, Yorks; Trinity Coll., Cambridge (MA). National Service: Army, Green Howards and RAPC, 2nd Lieut, 1948–50. Called to Bar, Inner Temple, 1952. A Recorder of the Crown Court, 1972–76. Mem., Loriners' Co., 1969. *Recreations:* outdoor activities, painting, music. *Address:* 199 Strand, WC2R 1DR. *Clubs:* United Oxford & Cambridge University; Berkshire Golf.

See also R. B. Lauriston.

LAURISTON, Richard Basil; a Permanent Chairman of Industrial Tribunals, 1976–89; formerly Senior Partner, Alex Lauriston & Son, Solicitors, Middlesbrough; *b* 26 Jan. 1917; *s* of Alexander Lauriston, MBE, and Nellie Lauriston; *m* 1944, Monica, *d* of Wilfred Leslie Deacon, BA, Tonbridge, and Dorothy Louise Deacon; three *s*. *Educ:* Sir William Turner's Sch., Redcar; St John's Coll., Cambridge (MA, LLM). Solicitor, 1948; a Recorder of the Crown Court, 1974–82. Commnd and served in War of 1939–45, Royal Corps of Signals. *Recreations:* fishing, travelling. *Address:* 26 Easby Lane, Great Ayton, North Yorks TS9 6JZ. *T:* Great Ayton (0642) 722429.

See also A. C. Lauriston.

LAUTERPACHT, Elihu, CBE 1989; QC 1970; Fellow of Trinity College, Cambridge, since 1953; Director, Research Centre for International Law, University of Cambridge, since 1983; *b* 13 July 1928; *o s* of late Sir Hersch Lauterpacht, QC and Rachel Steinberg; *m* 1955, Judith Maria (*d* 1970), *er d* of Harold Hettinger; one *s* two *d*; *m* 1973, Catherine Daly; one *s*. *Educ:* Phillips Acad., Andover, Mass; Harrow; Trinity Coll., Cambridge (Entrance Schol.). 1st cl. Pt II of Law Tripos and LLB; Whewell Schol. in Internat. Law, 1950; Holt Schol. 1948 and Birkenhead Schol. 1950, Gray's Inn; called to Bar, 1950, Bencher, 1983. Joint Sec., Interdepartmental Cttee on State Immunity, 1950–52; Cambridge University: Asst Lectr in Law, 1953; Lecturer, 1958–81; Reader in Internat. Law, 1981–88. Sec., Internat. Law Fund, 1955–85; Dir of Research, Hague Academy of Internat. Law, 1959–60; Vis. Prof. of Internat. Law, Univ. of Delhi, 1960. Chm., East African Common Market Tribunal, 1972–75; Consultant to Central Policy Review Staff, 1972–74, 1978–81; Legal Adviser to Australian Dept of Foreign Affairs, 1975–77; Consultant on Internat. Law, UN Inst. for Training and Res., 1978–79; mem. arbitration panel, Internat. Centre for Settlement of Investment Disputes; Deputy Leader: Australian Delegn to UN Law of the Sea Conf., 1975–77; Australian Delegn to UN Gen. Assembly, 1975–77. Member: Social Sciences Adv. Cttee, UK Nat. Commn for Unesco, 1980–84; World Bank Administrative Tribunal, 1980–; Panel of Arbitrators, Internat. Energy Agency Dispute Settlement Centre; Inst. of Internat. Law; Trustee, Internat. Law Fund, 1983. Editor: British Practice in International Law, 1955–68; International Law Reports, 1960–. Hon. Fellow, Hebrew Univ. of Jerusalem, 1989. Comdr, Order of Merit, Chile, 1969; awarded Annual Cert. of Merit, Amer. Soc. Internat. Law, 1972. *Publications:* Jerusalem and the Holy Places, 1968; (ed) International Law: the collected papers of Sir Hersch Lauterpacht, vol I, 1970, vol. II, 1975, vol. III, 1977, vol. IV, 1978; The Development of the Law of International Organization, 1976; Aspects of the Administration of International Justice, 1991; various articles on international law. *Address:* Research Centre for International Law, 5 Cranmer Road, Cambridge CB3 9BL. *T:* Cambridge (0223) 335358; 3 Essex Court, Temple, EC4. *T:* 071–583 9294. *Club:* Athenæum.

LAUTI, Rt. Hon. Sir Toaripi, GCMG 1990; PC 1979; MP; Governor-General of Tuvalu, since 1990; *b* Papua New Guinea, 1928; *m*; three *s* two *d*. *Educ:* Tuvalu; Fiji; Wesley Coll., Paerata, NZ; St Andrew's Coll., Christchurch, NZ; Christchurch Teacher Coll., NZ. Taught in KGV, Tarawa, Kiribati, 1953–62; Labour Relations and Trng Officer, Nauru and Ocean Islands, engaged by British Phosphate Comrs; returned to Tuvalu, 1974, and entered politics; elected unopposed to House of Assembly, May 1975; elected Chief Minister, Tuvalu, upon separation of Ellice Islands (Tuvalu) from Kiribati, Oct. 1975, re-elected Chief Minister in Sept. 1977; First Prime Minister, Tuvalu, 1978–81; Leader of the Opposition, 1981–90. Chm., 18th South Pacific Conference, Noumea, Oct. 1978. *Address:* PO Box 84, Funafuti, Tuvalu, Central Pacific.

LAVAN, Hon. Sir John Martin, Kt 1981; retired 1981 as Senior Puisne Judge of the Supreme Court of Western Australia; *b* 5 Sept. 1911; *s* of late M. G. Lavan, KC; *m* 1st, 1939, Leith Harford (decd); one *s* three *d*; 2nd, 1984, Dorothy Bell. *Educ:* Aquinas Coll., Perth; Xavier Coll., Melbourne. Barrister in private practice, 1934–69; a Judge of the Supreme Court of WA, 1969–81. Chm., Parole Bd, WA, 1969–79. Mem., Barristers' Bd, WA, 1960–69; Pres., Law Soc. of WA, 1964–66. KStJ. *Address:* 165 Victoria Avenue, Dalkeith, WA 6009, Australia. *Club:* Weld (Perth).

LAVELLE, Roger Garnett, CB 1989; Vice-President, European Investment Bank, since 1989; *b* 23 Aug. 1932; *s* of Henry Allman Lavelle and Evelyn Alice Garnett; *m* 1956, Elsa Gunilla Odeberg; three *s* one *d*. *Educ:* Leighton Park; Trinity Hall, Cambridge (BA, LLB). Asst Principal, Min. of Health, 1955; Principal, HM Treasury, 1961; Special Assistant (Common Market) to Lord Privy Seal, 1961–63; Private Sec. to Chancellor of the Exchequer, 1965–68; Asst Secretary, 1968, Under Sec., 1975, Dep. Sec., 1985, HM Treasury; Dep. Sec., Cabinet Office, 1987. *Recreations:* music and gardening. *Address:* 36 Cholmeley Crescent, Highgate, N6. *T:* 081–340 4845.

LAVENDER, Rt. Rev. Mgr Gerard; Principal Roman Catholic Chaplain (Navy), Ministry of Defence, since 1990; *b* 20 Sept. 1943; *s* of Joseph and Mary Lavender. *Educ:* Ushaw Coll., Durham. Ordained, 1969; Asst Priest, St Mary Cath., Newcastle upon Tyne, 1969–75; loaned to Royal Navy as Chaplain, 1975; completed All Arms Commando Course, 1976; served with RM, 1976–79; sea going, 1979–80, 1987–89; Exchange Chaplain to San Diego, with US Navy, 1981–83; Chaplain in: Scotland (Rosyth), 1983–85; Portsmouth, 1985–87; Plymouth, 1989–90. GSM, NI, 4 visits 1977–79. *Recreations:* golf, tennis, hill walking. *Address:* Principal RC Chaplain (Navy), Ministry of Defence, Room 725, Lacon House, Theobalds Road, WC1X 8RY. *T:* 071–430 6840. *Club:* Army and Navy.

LAVER, Frederick John Murray, CBE 1971; Member, Post Office Corporation, 1969–73, retired; *b* 11 March 1915; *er s* of late Clifton F. Laver and Elsie Elizabeth Palmer, Bridgwater; *m* 1948, Kathleen Amy Blythe; one *s* two *d*. *Educ:* Plymouth Coll. BSc London. Entered PO Engrg Dept, 1935; PO Research Stn, 1935–51; Radio Planning, 1951–57; Organization and Efficiency, 1957–63; Asst Sec., HM Treasury, 1963–65; Chief Scientific Officer, Min. of Technology, 1965–68; Director, National Data Processing Service, 1968–70; Mem., NRDC, 1974–80. Vis. Prof., Computing Lab., Univ. of Newcastle upon Tyne, 1975–79. Mem. Council: IEE, 1966–69, 1972–73; British Computer Soc., 1969–72; Nat. Computing Centre, 1966–68, 1970–73; IEE Electronic Divl Bd, 1966–69, 1970–73. Mem. Council, 1979–87, Chm., 1985–87, Pro-Chancellor, 1981–87, Exeter Univ. Pres., Devonshire Assoc., 1990–91. CEng, FIEE; Hon. FBCS. Hon. DSc Exeter, 1988. *Publications:* nine introductory books on physics and computing; several scientific papers. *Recreations:* reading, writing, and watching the sea. *Address:* 2 Park Lane, Budleigh Salterton, Devon EX9 6QT.

LAVER, Prof. John David Michael Henry, FBA 1990; Professor of Phonetics, since 1985 and Chairman, Centre for Speech Technology Research, since 1989, University of Edinburgh; *b* 20 Jan. 1938; *s* of Harry Frank Laver and Mary Laver (*née* Brearley); *m* 1st, 1961, Avril Morna Anel Macqueen Gibson; two *s* one *d*; 2nd, 1974, Sandra Traill; one *s*. *Educ:* Churcher's Coll., Petersfield; Univ. of Edinburgh (MA Hons; Postgrad. Dip. in Phonetics; PhD). Asst Lectr and Lectr in Phonetics, Univ. of Ibadan, 1963–66; University of Edinburgh: Lectr, Sen. Lectr, Reader in Phonetics, 1966–85; Dir, Centre for Speech Technology Research, 1984–89; Associate Dean, Faculty of Arts, 1989–. Member: Council, Internat. Phonetics Assoc., 1986–; Board, European Speech Communications Assoc., 1988–. Fellow, Inst. of Acoustics, 1988. *Publications:* Communication in face to face interaction, 1972; Phonetics in Linguistics, 1973; The Phonetic Description of Voice Quality, 1980; The Cognitive Representation of Speech, 1981; Aspects of Speech Technology, 1988; The Gift of Speech, 1991. *Recreations:* travel, reading, golf, building dry-stone walls. *Address:* Centre for Speech Technology Research, 80 South Bridge, University of Edinburgh, Edinburgh EH1 1HN. *T:* 031–650 2786. *Club:* Athenæum.

LAVER, Patrick Martin; HM Diplomatic Service, retired; Director of Research, Foreign and Commonwealth Office, 1980–83; *b* 3 Feb. 1932; *s* of late James Laver, CBE, RE, FRSL, and late Veronica Turleigh; *m* 1st, 1966, Marianne Ford (marr. annulled); one *d*; 2nd, 1979, Dr Elke Maria Schmitz, *d* of Thomas and Anneliese Schmitz. *Educ:* Ampleforth Coll., Yorks; New Coll., Oxford. Third Sec., Foreign Office, 1954; Second Sec., Djakarta, 1956; FO, 1957; Paris, 1958; Yaoundé, 1961; UK Delegn to Brussels Conf., 1962; First Sec., FO, 1963; UK Mission to UN, New York, 1964; Diplomatic Service Admin., 1965; Commercial Sec., Nairobi, 1968; FCO, 1970; Counsellor (Economic), Pretoria, 1973; UK Delegn to Conf. on Security and Co-operation in Europe, Geneva, 1974; Head of Rhodesia Dept, FCO, 1975–78; Counsellor, Paris, 1979–80. *Address:* 14 Hutt Street, Yarralumla, ACT 2600, Australia. *Club:* Athenæum.

LAVER, William Graeme, PhD; FRS 1987; Head, Influenza Research Unit, Australian National University, since 1983; *b* 3 June 1929; *s* of Lawrence and Madge Laver; *m* 1954, Judith Garrard Cahn; one *s* two *d*. *Educ:* Ivanhoe Grammar Sch., Melbourne; Univ. of Melbourne (BSc, MSc); Univ. of London (PhD). Technical Asst, Walter & Eliza Hall Inst. of Med. Res., Melbourne, 1947–52; Res. Asst, Dept of Biochemistry, Melbourne Univ., 1954–55; Res. Fellow, 1958–62, Fellow, 1962–64, Senior Fellow, 1964–90, Special Prof., 1990–, John Curtin Sch. of Med. Res., ANU. International Meetings: Rougemont, Switzerland, 1976; Baden, Vienna, 1977; Thredbo, Australia, 1979; Beijing, China, 1982; Banbury Center, Cold Spring Harbor, NY, 1985; Kona, Hawaii, 1989. *Publications:* papers on structure of influenza virus antigens and molecular mechanisms of antigenic shift and drift in type A influenza viruses; numerous research articles. *Recreations:* raising beef cattle, viticulture, wine-making, ski-ing, climbing volcanoes. *Address:* John Curtin School of Medical Research, PO Box 334, Canberra, ACT 2601, Australia. *T:* (062) 492397; Barton Highway, Murrumbateman, NSW 2582, Australia. *T:* (062) 275633.

LAVERICK, Elizabeth, PhD, CEng, FIEE; CPhys, FInstP, FIEEE (US); consultant; Project Director, Advanced Manufacturing in Electronics, 1985–88; *b* 25 Nov. 1925; *d* of William Rayner and Alice Garland; *m* 1946 (marr. diss. 1960); no *c*. *Educ:* Dr Challoner's Grammar Sch., Amersham; Durham Univ. Research at Durham Univ., 1946–50; Section Leader at GEC, 1950–53; Microwave Engineer at Elliott Bros, 1954; Head of Radar Research Laboratory of Elliott-Automation Radar Systems Ltd, 1959; Jt Gen. Manager, Elliott-Automation Radar Systems Ltd, 1968–69, Technical Dir, 1969–71. IEE: Mem. Electronics Divisional Bd, 1967–70; Mem. Council, 1969–70; Dep. Sec., 1971–85. Electronics CADMAT (Computer Aided Design, Manufacture and Test) Project Dir, 1982–85. Chm., Engrg Careers Co-ordinating Cttee, 1983–85; Member: DE Adv. Cttee on Women's Employment, 1970–82; Adv. Cttee for Electronic and Electrical Engrg, Sheffield Univ., 1984–87; Nat. Electronics Council, 1986–90; Pres., Women's Engineering Soc., 1967–69; Chm., Internat. Conf. of Women Engrs and Scientists 9, 1989–91. Member: Council, Inst. of Physics, 1970–73 (Chm., Women in Physics Cttee, 1985–90); Council, City and Guilds of London Inst., 1984–87; Court, Brunel Univ., 1985–88. Liveryman, Worshipful Co. of Engrs, 1985. Hon. Fellow, UMIST, 1969. Editor, Woman Engr (Jl of Women's Engrg Soc.), 1984–90. *Publications:* contribs to IEE and IEEE Jls. *Recreations:* music, gardening, careers talks, tapestry, sailing. *Address:* Lynwood, Brays Lane, Hyde Heath, Amersham, Bucks HP6 5RU.

LAVERS, Patricia Mae, (Mrs H. J. Lavers); Executive Director, Bond Street Association, 1961–76, and Regent Street Association, 1972–76; *b* 12 April 1919; *d* of Edric Allan Jordan and May Holdcraft; *m* 1st, 1945, Frederick Handel Hayward (*d* 1965); one *s*; 2nd, 1966, John Harold Ellen; 3rd, 1976, Lt-Comdr Herbert James Lavers. *Educ:* Sydenham High School. Clerk, Securities Dept, National Provincial Bank, 1938–45; Export Dir, Perth Radios, 1955–60. Alderman, St Pancras Council, 1960–66 (Libraries/Public Health). Elected to Executive of Westminster Chamber of Commerce, 1971, Chm. City Affairs Cttee, 1971–75. Chm., Sandwich Soc., 1983–. FZS. *Recreations:* swimming, collecting first editions and press books, walking. *Address:* Horse Pond Sluice, Delf Street, Sandwich, Kent. *Clubs:* Arts, Lansdowne, Players Theatre.

LAVIN, Deborah Margaret; Principal, Trevelyan College, University of Durham, since 1980; *b* 22 Sept. 1939. *Educ:* Roedean Sch., Johannesburg, SA; Rhodes Univ., Grahamstown, SA; Lady Margaret Hall, Oxford (MA, DipEd). Asst Lectr, Dept of History, Univ. of the Witwatersrand, 1962–64; Lectr, Dept of Mod. Hist., The Queen's Univ. of Belfast, 1965–78, Sen. Lectr, 1978. *Publications:* South African Memories, 1979; articles in learned jls. *Recreations:* broadcasting; the arts; passionate but unsuccessful tennis player. *Address:* Trevelyan College, Elvet Hill Road, Durham DH1 3LN. *T:* Durham (091) 3743761; Hickmans Cottages, Cat Street, East Hendred, Oxon OX12 8JT. *T:* Abingdon (0235) 833408. *Club:* Commonwealth Trust.

LAVIN, Mary, (Mrs M. MacDonald Scott); Writer; *b* East Walpole, Mass, USA, 11 June 1912; *m* 1st, 1942, William Walsh (*d* 1954), MA, NUI; three *d*; 2nd, 1969, Michael MacDonald Scott (*d* 1990), MA, MSc. *Educ:* National Univ. of Ireland, Dublin (Graduate, MA; Hon DLitt, 1968). Mem. of Irish Academy of Letters, President, 1971. Guggenheim Fellow 1959, 1962 and 1972. Katherine Mansfield Prize, 1961; Ella Lynam Cabot Award, 1971; Eire Soc. Gold Medal, Boston, 1974; Arts Award, Royal Meath Assoc., 1975; Gregory Medal, Dublin, 1975; Amer. Irish Foundn Literary Award, 1979; Allied Irish Bank Award, 1981. Personality of the Year, Royal Meath Assoc., 1976. *Publications:* Tales from Bective Bridge (short stories, awarded James Tait Black Memorial Prize), 1942 (London, 1943); The Long Ago (short stories), 1944; The House in Clewe Street (novel), 1945, repr. 1987; At Sally Gap (Boston), 1946; The Becker Wives, 1946; Mary O'Grady (novel), 1950, repr. 1986; Patriot Son (short stories), 1956; A Single Lady (short stories); A Likely Story (short novel), 1957; Selected Stories, 1959 (New York); The Great Wave (short stories), 1961; Stories of Mary Lavin, 1964; In the Middle of the Fields (short stories), 1966; Happiness (short stories), 1969; Collected Stories, 1971; A Memory and other Stories, 1972; The Second Best Children in the World, 1972; The Stories of Mary Lavin, vol. II, 1973; The Shrine and other stories, 1976; A Family Likeness, 1985; The Stories of Mary Lavin, vol. III, 1985; The House in Clewe Street, 1987. *Address:* Apt 5 Gilford Pines, Gilford Road, Sandymount, Dublin 4, Ireland. *T:* 692402.

LAW, family name of **Barons Coleraine** and **Ellenborough.**

LAW, Francis Stephen, (Frank Law), CBE 1981; Chairman, Varta Group UK, since 1971; Director: Milupa Ltd, since 1978; NFC International Holdings Ltd, since 1985; *b* 31 Dec. 1916; *s* of Henry and Ann Law-Lowensberg; *m* 1959, Nicole Vigne (*née* Fesch); one *s* (one *d* by previous *m*). *Educ:* on the Continent. War service, 1939–45. Wills Law & Co., 1947; Truvox Engrg, 1960, subseq. Dir of Controls and Communications; Dep. Chm., NFC, 1982–85 (Dir, Consortium and its predecessors, 1969–87). Chm., Rubis Investment & Cie, 1990–; Director: B. Elliott Plc, 1968–86; BMW (GB) Ltd, 1978–88; Siemens, 1984–; Aegis (formerly WCRS Gp) plc, 1988–; Mem. Adv. Bd, Berliner Bank, 1988–; Mem. Supervis. Bd, Carat, Paris, 1989–. Chm., Social Responsibilities Council, NFC, 1988–; Member: Org. Cttee, NFC, 1968; Economic and Social Cttee, EEC, 1978–86. Governor, RSC, 1985–. Trustee, Nat. AIDS Trust, 1989–. *Recreations:* music, reading, theatre, skiing, tennis, riding, swimming. *Address:* 43 Lennox Gardens, SW1X 0DF. *T:* 071–225 2142. *Clubs:* Boodle's; Pilgrims.

LAW, George Llewellyn; Senior Adviser, Morgan Grenfell Group plc, since 1989; *b* 8 July 1929; *s* of late George Edward Law and Margaret Dorothy Law, OBE (*née* Evans); *m* 1960, Anne Stewart, *d* of late Arthur Wilkinson and Ness Wilkinson (*née* Muir); one *d*. *Educ:* Westminster Sch. (Schol.); Clare Coll., Cambridge (Schol.; BA). Solicitor. Slaughter and May, Solicitors, 1952–67, Partner 1961–67; Dir, Morgan Grenfell & Co. Ltd, 1968–; Dir, 1971–89, Vice Chm., 1987–89, Morgan Grenfell Gp. Deputy Chairman: Baker Perkins plc, 1986–87 (Dir, 1981–87); Blackwood Hodge plc, 1988–90 (Dir, 1968–90); Director: Bernard Sunley Investment Trust, 1968–75; Sidlaw Group, 1974–82; APV, 1987–90. FRSA. *Recreations:* history of furniture and decorative arts, opera, reading, swimming, cricket. *Address:* 6 Phillimore Gardens Close, W8 7QA. *T:* 071–937 3061. *Clubs:* Brooks's, MCC, Surrey CC.

LAW, Adm. Sir Horace (Rochfort), GCB 1972 (KCB 1967; CB 1963); OBE 1950; DSC 1941; retired 1972; Chairman, R. & W. Hawthorn Leslie & Co., 1973–81; *b* 23 June 1911; *s* of S. Horace Law, MD, FRCSI, and Sybil Mary (*née* Clay); *m* 1941, Heather Valerie Coryton; two *s* two *d*. *Educ:* Sherborne Sch. Entered Royal Navy, 1929; gunnery specialist, 1937. Served War of 1939–45 (DSC): AA Cruisers: Cairo, 1939; Coventry, 1940; Cruiser Nigeria, 1942; Comdr 1946; Capt. 1952; comd HMS Centaur, 1958 and Britannia, RN Coll., 1960; Rear-Adm. 1961; Vice-Adm. 1965; Flag Officer Sea Training, 1961–63; Flag Officer, Submarines, 1963–65; Controller of the Navy, 1965–70; C-in-C, Naval Home Comd, and Flag Officer, Portsmouth Area, 1970–72; First and Principal Naval Aide-de-Camp to the Queen, 1970–72. Mem., Security Commn, 1973–82. President: RINA, 1975–77; Officers' Christian Union, 1976–86; Chm., Church Army Bd, 1980–87. Grand Cross, Order of the Crown (Netherlands), 1972. *Recreations:* sailing, gardening. *Address:* West Harting, Petersfield, Hants.

LAW, James, QC (Scot.) 1971; *b* 7 June 1926; *s* of late George Law, MA, and Isabella Rebecca Lamb (or Law), MA; *m* 1956, Kathleen Margaret, *d* of late Alexander Gibson; two *s* one *d*. *Educ:* Kilmarnock Academy; Girvan High Sch.; Univ. of Glasgow (MA 1948, LLB 1950). Admitted to Faculty of Advocates, 1951; Advocate-Depute, 1957–64. Mem., Criminal Injuries Compensation Bd, 1970–. *Address:* 7 Gloucester Place, Edinburgh EH3 6EE. *T:* 031–225 2974. *Clubs:* New, Caledonian (Edinburgh).

LAW, Phillip Garth, AO 1975; CBE 1961; MSc, FAIP, FTS, FAA; *b* 21 April 1912; *s* of Arthur James Law and Lillie Lena Chapman; *m* 1941, Nellie Isabel Allan; no *c*. *Educ:* Hamilton High Sch.; Ballarat Teachers' Coll.; Melbourne Univ. Science master, State secondary schs, Vic., 1933–38; Tutor in Physics, Newman Coll., Melbourne Univ., 1940–47; Lectr in Physics, 1943–48. Research Physicist and Asst Sec. of Scientific Instrument and Optical Panel of Austr. Min. of Munitions, 1940–45. Sen. Scientific Officer, ANARE, 1947–48; cosmic ray measurements in Antarctica and Japan, 1948; Dir, Antarctic Div., Dept of External Affairs, Aust., and Leader, ANARE, 1949–66; Expedition relief voyages to Heard I. and Macquarie I., 1949, 1951, 1952, 1954. Australian observer with Norwegian-British-Swedish Antarctic Exped., 1950; Leader of expedition: to establish first permanent Australian station in Antarctica at Mawson, MacRobertson Land, 1954; which established second continental station at Davis, Princess Elizabeth Land, 1957; which took over Wilkes station from USA, 1959; to relieve ANARE stations and to explore coast of Australian Antarctic Territory, annually, 1955–66. Chm., Australian Nat. Cttee for Antarctic Research, 1966–80. Exec. Vice-Pres., Victoria Inst. of Colls, 1966–77; Pres., Victorian Inst. of Marine Scis, 1978–80. Member: Council of Melbourne Univ., 1959–78; Council, La Trobe Univ., 1964–74; President: Royal Soc. of Victoria, 1967, 1968; Aust. and NZ Schs Exploring Soc., 1977–82. Dep. Pres., Science Museum of Victoria, Melbourne, 1979–82 (Trustee, 1968–83). Pres., Grad. Union, Melbourne Univ., 1972–77. Patron, British Schs Exploring Soc. Fellow: Australian Acad. of Technological Sciences; Aust. Acad. of Sci.; Aust. Inst. of Physics; ANZAAS. Hon. Fellow, Royal Melbourne Inst. of Technology. Hon. DAppSc (Melbourne); Hon. DEd (Victoria Inst. of Colls). Founder's Gold Medal, RGS, 1960; Gold Medal, Aust. Geographic Soc., 1988. *Publications:* (with John Béchervaise) ANARE, 1957; Antarctic Odyssey, 1983; chapters in: It's People that Matter, ed Donald McLean, 1969; Search for Human Understanding, ed M. Merbaum and G. Stricker, 1971; ed series of ANARE scientific reports; numerous papers on Antarctica and education. *Recreations:* tennis, ski-ing, skin diving, music, photography. *Address:* 16 Stanley Grove, Canterbury, Vic 3126, Australia. *Clubs:* Melbourne, Kelvin, Melbourne Cricket, Royal South Yarra Lawn Tennis (Melbourne).

LAW, Sylvia, OBE 1977; *b* 29 March 1931; *d* of late Reginald Howard Law and late Dorothy Margaret Law. *Educ:* Lowther Coll.; Girton Coll., Cambridge (MA); Regent Street Polytechnic (DipTP). MRTPI. Teaching, Benenden Sch., 1952–55; market research, Unilever Ltd, 1955–58; town and country planning and policy studies and research, Kent CC and GLC, 1959–86. Royal Town Planning Institute: Mem. Council, 1965–78; Chm. of Educn Cttee, 1970–73; Vice-Pres., 1972–74; Pres., 1974–75. Mem. Planning Cttee, SSRC, 1977–79. *Publications:* (contrib.) Recreational Economics and Analysis, 1974; (ed) Planning and the Future, 1976; articles in RTPI Jl, Official Architecture and Planning, Planning Outlook, Town Planning Rev., Greater London Intelligence Qly, etc. *Recreations:* music, photography, gardening.

LAW-SMITH, Sir (Richard) Robert, Kt 1980; CBE 1965; AFC 1943; Former Chairman, National Australia Bank Ltd; grazier; *b* Adelaide, 9 July 1914; *s* of W. Law-Smith; *m* 1941, Joan, *d* of Harold Gordon Darling; two *d. Educ:* St Edward's Sch., Oxford; Adelaide Univ. Served War, RAAF, 1940–46 (AFC), Sqdn Ldr. Director: Nat. Bank of Australasia, later Nat. Commercial Banking Corp. of Australia, now Nat. Australia Bank, 1959 (Vice-Chm., 1968; Chm., 1978–86); Australian Mutual Provident Soc., 1960–84 (Chm. Victoria Br., 1977–84); Broken Hill Pty Co. Ltd, 1961–84; Commonwealth Aircraft Corp., 1965–84; Blue Circle Southern Cement Ltd, 1974–84. Mem., Australian National Airlines Commn, 1962–84 (Vice-Chm., 1975–79; Chm., 1979–84). Councillor, Royal Flying Doctor Service (Victorian Div.), 1956–85. *Address:* Bolobek, Macedon, Vic 3440, Australia. *Clubs:* Australian, Melbourne (Melbourne).

LAWLER, Geoffrey John; Managing Director, The Public Affairs Company, since 1987; Vice-President, International Access Inc., since 1987; *b* 30 Oct. 1954; *s* of Major Ernest Lawler (RAEC retd) and Enid Lawler; *m* 1989, Christine, *d* of Carl Roth, Cheyenne, Wyoming. *Educ:* Richmond Sch., N Yorks; Hull Univ. (BSc (Econ); Pres., Students' Union, 1976–77). Trainee chartered accountant, 1977–78. Community Affairs Dept, 1978–80, Research Dept, 1980–82, Cons. Central Office; Public Relations Exec., 1982–83; Dir, publicity co., 1983. Contested (C) Bradford N, 1987. MP (C) Bradford N, 1983–87. Mem. Council, UKIAS, 1987–. Hon. Pres., British Youth Council, 1983–87. *Recreations:* cricket, music, travel. *Address:* 21 Kelso Gardens, Leeds, LS2 9PS. *T:* Leeds (0532) 443991.

LAWLER, Sir Peter (James), Kt 1981; OBE 1965; retired 1987; Australian Ambassador to Ireland and the Holy See, 1983–86; *b* 23 March 1921; *m*; six *s* two *d. Educ:* Univ. of Sydney (BEc). Prime Minister's Dept, Canberra, 1949–68 (British Cabinet Office, London, 1952–53); Dep. Secretary: Dept of the Cabinet Office, 1968–71; Dept of the Prime Minister and Cabinet, 1972–73; Secretary: Dept of the Special Minister of State, 1973–75; Dept of Admin. Services, Canberra, 1975–83. *Recreation:* farming. *Address:* 6 Tennyson Crescent, Forrest, ACT 2603, Australia. *T:* 062 95 1946. *Clubs:* Melbourne (Melbourne); University House, Wine and Food (Canberra).

LAWLEY, Dr Leonard Edward; Director of Kingston Polytechnic, 1969–82; *b* 13 March 1922; *yr s* of late Albert Lawley; *m* 1944, Dorothy Beryl Round; one *s* two *d. Educ:* King Edward VI Sch., Stourbridge; Univs of Wales and Newcastle upon Tyne. BSc, PhD; FInstP, CPhys. Served with RAF, 1941–46; Lectr, Univ. of Newcastle upon Tyne, 1947–53; Sen. Lectr, The Polytechnic, Regent Street, 1953–57; Kingston Coll. of Technology: Head of Dept of Physics and Maths, 1957–64; Vice-Principal, 1960–64; Principal, 1964–69. *Publications:* various papers in scientific jls on transmission ultrasonic sound waves through gases and liquids and on acoustic methods for gas analysis.

LAWLEY, Susan, (Sue); broadcaster, since 1970; presenter and interviewer, Granada Television, since 1991; *b* 14 July 1946; *d* of Thomas Clifford and Margaret Jane Lawley; *m* 1st, 1975, David Ashby (marr. diss. 1985); one *s* one *d*; 2nd, 1987, Hugh Williams. *Educ:* Dudley Girls' High Sch., Worcs; Bristol Univ. (BA Hons Modern Languages). Thomson Newspapers' graduate trainee, Western Mail and South Wales Echo, Cardiff, 1967–70; BBC Plymouth: sub-editor/reporter/presenter, 1970–72; presenter, BBC Television, London: Nationwide, 1972–75; Tonight, 1975–76; Nationwide, 1977–83; Nine O'Clock News, 1983–84; Six O'Clock News, 1984–88; Presenter, Desert Island Discs, BBC Radio Four, 1988–; other programmes, 1977–90, including: general elections; budgets; Question Time; Wogan; Royal tours; interviews. Hon. LLD Bristol, 1989; Hon. MA Birmingham, 1989; Hon. DLitt 1991. *Recreations:* family, walking, house-renovation, kettle-polishing. *Address:* c/o Noel Gay Ltd, 19 Denmark Street, WC2H 8NA.

LAWLOR, Prof. John James, MA, DLitt, FSA; Professor of English Language and Literature, University of Keele, 1950–80, now Emeritus; *b* 5 Jan. 1918; *o s* of Albert John Lawlor, Chief Armourer, RN, and Teresa Anne Clare Lawlor, Plymouth; *m* 1st, 1941, Thelma Joan Weeks, singer (marr. diss. 1979); one *s* three *d*; 2nd, 1984, Kimie Imura, Prof. Meisei Univ., Tokyo. *Educ:* Ryder's; Magdalen Coll., Oxford. BA Hons English Cl. I, 1939. Service in Devonshire Regt, 1940–45; Asst Chief Instructor, 163 Artists' Rifles OCTU, 1943–44; CMF, 1944–45; AMG Austria. Sen. Mackinnon Scholar, Magdalen Coll., 1946; Sen. Demy, 1947; Lectr in English, Brasenose and Trinity Colls, 1947–50; University Lectr in Eng. Lit., Oxford, 1949–50. Fellow of Folger Shakespeare Library, Washington, DC, 1962. Toured Australian and NZ Univs and visited Japan, 1964. Ziskind Visiting Prof., Brandeis Univ., Mass, 1966; Vis. Professor: Univ. of Hawaii, 1972; Univ. of Maryland, 1981–82; Univ. of Arizona, 1983–84. Sec.-Gen. and Treasurer, Internat. Assoc. of University Profs. of English; Contrib. Mem. Medieval Academy of America; Gov., Oswestry Sch.; Pres., N Staffs Drama Assoc.; Mem. Western Area Cttee, Brit. Drama League; Vice-Pres., The Navy League. *Publications:* The Tragic Sense in Shakespeare, 1960; Piers Plowman, an Essay in Criticism, 1962; The Chester Mystery Plays (with Rosemary Sisson), perf. Chester, 1962; The Vision of Piers Plowman, commnd, Malvern, 1964; (ed) Patterns of Love and Courtesy, 1966; (with W. H. Auden) To Nevill Coghill from Friends, 1966; Chaucer, 1968; (ed) The New University, 1968; (ed) Higher Education: patterns of change in the seventies, 1972; Elysium Revisited, 1978; (as James Dundonald): Letters to a Vice-Chancellor, 1962; La Vita Nuova, 1976; articles on medieval and modern literature in various journals and symposia. *Recreations:* travel, book-collecting, any sort of sea-faring. *Address:* Penwithian, Higher Fore Street, Marazion, Cornwall TR17 0BQ. *T:* Penzance (0736) 711180; 967-24 Misawa, Hinoshi, Tokyo 191, Japan. *T:* 0425–94–4177. *Clubs:* Athenæum; Royal Fleet (Devonport).

LAWRANCE, John Ernest; Under Secretary, Director, Technical Division 1, Inland Revenue, 1982–88, retired; *b* 25 Jan. 1928; *s* of Ernest William and Emily Lewa Lawrance; *m* 1956, Margaret Elsie Ann Dodwell; two *s* one *d. Educ:* High School for Boys, Worthing; Southampton Univ. (BA Hons Modern History). Entered Inland Revenue as Inspector of Taxes, 1951; Principal Inspector, 1968; Senior Principal Inspector on specialist technical duties, 1974. *Address:* 71A Alderton Hill, Loughton, Essex IG10 3JD. *T:* 081–508 7562.

LAWRANCE, Mrs June Cynthia; Headmistress of Harrogate Ladies' College, since 1974; *b* 3 June 1933; *d* of late Albert Isherwood and of Ida Emmett; *m* 1957, Rev. David Lawrance, MA, BD; three *d. Educ:* St Anne's Coll., Oxford (MA). Teaching appts: Univ. of Paris, 1954–57; Cyprus, 1957–58; Jordan, 1958–61; Oldham, Lancs, 1962–70; Headmistress, Broughton High Sch., Salford, 1971–73. *Recreations:* music, French literature, chess. *Address:* Harrogate Ladies' College, Clarence Drive, Harrogate, N Yorks. *T:* Harrogate (0423) 504543.

LAWRANCE, Keith Cantwell; Deputy Chairman, Civil Service Appeal Board, 1981–89 (Member 1980–89); Vice-President, Civil Service Retirement Fellowship, since 1988 (Chairman, 1982–88); *b* 1 Feb. 1923; *s* of P. J. Lawrance; *m* 1952, Margaret Joan (*née* Scott); no *c. Educ:* Latymer Sch., N9. Clerical Officer, Admiralty, 1939. Served War, RNVR, 1942–46; Sub-Lt (A), 1945. Exec. Officer, Treasury, 1947; Asst Principal, Post Office, 1954; Principal, Post Office, 1959; Asst Sec., Dept of Economic Affairs, Dec. 1966; Under-Sec., Civil Service Dept, 1971–79. Vice-Chm., Inst. of Cancer Research, 1989–. *Recreations:* model engineering, music. *Address:* White Gables, 35 Fairmile Avenue, Cobham, Surrey. *T:* Cobham (0932) 863689.

LAWRENCE, family name of **Baron Lawrence** and of **Baron Trevethin and Oaksey.**

LAWRENCE, 5th Baron *cr* 1869; **David John Downer Lawrence;** Bt 1858; *b* 4 Sept. 1937; *s* of 4th Baron Lawrence and Margaret Jean (*d* 1977), *d* of Arthur Downer, Kirdford, Sussex; *S* father, 1968. *Educ:* Bradfield College. *Address:* c/o Bird & Bird, 2 Gray's Inn Square, WC1.

LAWRENCE, Rt. Rev. Caleb James; *see* Moosonee, Bishop of.

LAWRENCE, Hon. Carmen Mary, PhD; MP (Lab) Glendalough, since 1986; Premier of Western Australia, since 1990; *b* 2 March 1948; *d* of Ern and Mary Lawrence; *m* (marr. diss.); one *s. Educ:* Univ. of Western Australia (BPsych 1st cl. Hons 1968; PhD 1983). Univ. lectr, tutor, researcher, consultant, 1968–83; Research Psychologist, Psychiatric Services Unit, Health Dept, 1983–86. Minister of Education, 1988–90. *Publications:* psychological papers. *Recreations:* literature, theatre, music. *Address:* Capita Centre, 197 St Georges Terrace, Perth, WA 6000, Australia.

LAWRENCE, Christopher Nigel, NDD, FTC; FIPG; goldsmith, silversmith; industrial designer; *b* 23 Dec. 1936; *s* of late Rev. William W. Lawrence and of Millicent Lawrence; *m* 1958, Valerie Betty Bergman; two *s* two *d. Educ:* Westborough High Sch.; Central School of Arts and Crafts. Apprenticed, C. J. Vander Ltd; started own workshops, 1968. *One man exhibitions:* Galerie Jean Renet, 1970, 1971; Hamburg, 1972; Goldsmiths' Hall, 1973; Ghent, 1975; Hasselt, 1977. Major commissions from British Govt, City Livery cos, banks, manufacturing cos; official silversmith to Bank of England. Judge and external assessor for leading art colleges; specialist in symbolic presentation pieces and limited edns of decorative pieces, *eg* silver mushrooms (creator of Capricious Mushrooms for Jone Hine Ltd). Chm., Goldsmiths, Silversmiths and Jewellers Art Council, 1976–77; Liveryman, Goldsmiths' Co., 1978–; television and radio broadcaster. Jacques Cartier Meml award for Craftsman of the Year, 1960, 1963, 1967 (unique achievement). *Recreations:* cruising on family's narrow boat, carpentry, painting. *Address:* 20 St Vincent's Road, Westcliff-on-Sea, Essex SS0 7PR. *T:* Southend-on-Sea 338443; (workshops and showroom) 172–174 London Road, Southend-on-Sea, Essex SS1 1PH. *T:* Southend-on-Sea (0702) 344897.

LAWRENCE, Prof. Clifford Hugh; Professor of Medieval History, 1970–87, now Emeritus (Head of the Department of History, Bedford College, Royal Holloway and Bedford New College (formerly at Bedford College), University of London, 1981–85); *b* 28 Dec. 1921; *s* of Ernest William Lawrence and Dorothy Estelle; *m* 1953, Helen Maud Curran; one *s* five *d. Educ:* Stationers' Co.'s Sch.; Lincoln Coll., Oxford. BA 1st Cl. Hons Mod. Hist. 1948, MA 1953, DPhil 1956. War service in RA and Beds and Herts: 2nd Lieut 1942, Captain 1944, Major 1945. Asst Archivist to Co. of Gloucester, 1949. Bedford Coll., London: Asst Lectr in History, 1951; Lectr, 1953–63; Reader in Med. History, 1963–70. External Examr, Univ. of Newcastle upon Tyne, 1972–74, Univ. of Bristol, 1975–77, Univ. of Reading, 1977–79; Chm., Bd of Examnrs in History, London Univ., 1981–83. Mem., Press Council, 1976–80; Vice-Chm. of Govs, Governing Body, Heythrop Coll., Univ. of London; Mem. Council, Westfield Coll., Univ. of London, 1981–86. FRHistS 1960; FSA 1984. *Publications:* St Edmund of Abingdon, History and Hagiography, 1960; The English Church and the Papacy in the Middle Ages, 1965; Medieval Monasticism, 1984; contribs to: Pre-Reformation English Spirituality, 1967; The Christian Community, 1971; The History of the University of Oxford, Vol. I, 1984; articles and reviews in Eng. Hist. Review, History, Jl Eccles. Hist., Oxoniensia, Encycl. Brit., Lexicon für Theol u Kirche, etc. *Recreations:* gardening, painting. *Address:* 11 Durham Road, SW20 0QH. *T:* 081–946 3820. *Club:* Reform.

See also G. C. Lawrence.

LAWRENCE, Sir David (Roland Walter), 3rd Bt, *cr* 1906; late Captain, Coldstream Guards, 1951; *b* 8 May 1929; *er s* of Sir Roland Lawrence, 2nd Bt, MC, and Susan, 3rd *d* of late Sir Charles Addis, KCMG; *S* father 1950; *m* 1955, Audrey, Duchess of Leeds, *yr d* of Brig. Desmond Young, OBE, MC. *Educ:* Radley; RMC Sandhurst. *Heir: b* Clive Wyndham Lawrence [*b* 6 Oct. 1939; *m* 1966, Sophia Annabel Stuart, *d* of late (Ian) Hervey Stuart Black, TD; three *s*]. *Address:* 28 High Town Road, Maidenhead, Berks. *Club:* Cavalry and Guards.

LAWRENCE, Dennis George Charles, OBE 1963; Director, 1978–82, Board Member, 1981–84, Cooperative Development Agency; retired; *b* 15 Aug. 1918; *s* of George Herbert and Amy Frances Lawrence; *m* 1946, Alida Jantine, *d* of Willem van den Berg, The Netherlands. *Educ:* Haberdashers' Aske's Hatcham School. Entered Civil Service as Clerical Officer, Min. of Transport, 1936; served RA, 1939–46; Exec. Officer 1946; Asst Principal, Central Land Board, 1947; Principal, 1949; GPO, 1953; Asst Sec. 1960; Sec., Cttee on Broadcasting, 1960–62; Asst Sec., GPO, 1962; Under-Secretary: GPO, 1969; Min. of Posts and Telecommunications, 1969–74; Dept of Industry, 1974–78. Chm., Working Group on a Cooperative Develt Agency, 1977. *Publications:* Democracy and Broadcasting (pamphlet), 1986; The Third Way, 1988. *Recreations:* walking, painting, travel. *Address:* Little London Farmhouse, Cann, Shaftesbury, Dorset SP7 0PZ. *T:* Shaftesbury (0747) 52252.

LAWRENCE, Geoffrey Charles, CMG 1963; OBE 1958; *b* 11 Nov. 1915; *s* of Ernest William Lawrence; *m* 1945, Joyce Acland Madge, MBE 1959, *d* of M. H. A. Madge, MC. *Educ:* Stationers' Company's Sch.; Brasenose Coll., Oxford. Served 1939–46, Middlesex Yeo. and Brit. Mil. Administration of Occupied Territories (Major). HM Overseas Civil Service (Colonial Administrative Service). Administrative Officer, Somaliland Protectorate, 1946; Asst Chief Sec., 1955; Financial Sec., 1956; Financial Sec., Zanzibar and Mem. of East African Currency Board, 1960–63; Colonial Office, 1964–66; ODM, later ODA, FCO, 1966–73; ODM, 1973–76. *Address:* c/o Barclays Bank, 42 Coombe Lane, SW20 0LB.

See also C. H. Lawrence.

LAWRENCE, Sir Guy Kempton, Kt 1976; DSO 1943; OBE 1945; DFC 1941; retired; Chairman, Eggs Authority, 1978–81; *b* 5 Nov. 1914; *s* of Albert Edward and Bianca Lawrence; *m* 1947, Marcia Virginia Powell; two *s* one *d. Educ:* Marlborough Coll. FBIM, FIGD. RAFO, 1934–45; War of 1939–45: Bomber Pilot (48 sorties), Sqdn Comdr, 78

Sqdn, Gp Captain Trng, HQ Bomber Command (DFC DSO, despatches, OBE). Contested (L) Colne Valley, 1945. Man. Dir, Chartair Ltd-Airtech Ltd, 1945–48; Chairman: Glacier Foods Ltd, 1948–75; Findus (UK) Ltd, 1967–75; Dep. Chairman: J. Lyons & Co. Ltd, 1950–75; Spillers French Holdings Ltd, 1972–75; Vice-Chm., DCA Food Industries Inc., 1973–; Dir, Eagle Aircraft Services, 1977–81. Chm., Food and Drink Industries Council, 1973–77. Member of Stock Exchange, London, 1937–45. British Ski Team, FIS, 1937–38. *Recreations:* farming, carpentry, squash, tennis. *Address:* Courtlands, Kier Park, Ascot, Berks SL5 7DS. *T:* Ascot (0990) 21074. *Club:* Royal Air Force.

LAWRENCE, (Henry) Richard (George); Chief Executive, Royal School of Church Music, since 1990; occasional writer, since 1971, and broadcaster, since 1989; *b* 16 April 1946; *s* of late George Napier Lawrence, OBE, and of Peggy Neave (*née* Breay). *Educ:* Westminster Abbey Choir Sch.; Haileybury (music schol.); Worcester Coll., Oxford (Hadow Schol.; BA 1967). Overseas Dept, Ginn & Co., educational publishers, 1968–73; Music Officer, 1973–83, Music Dir, 1983–88, Arts Council of GB. Chm., Arts Council Staff Assoc., 1974–76. Voluntary work, Friends of the Earth Trust, 1989–90. *Recreations:* travelling in Asia, pre-1914 Baedekers. *Address:* c/o Royal School of Church Music, Addington Palace, Croydon, Surrey CR9 5AD. *T:* 081–654 7676.

LAWRENCE, Ivan John, QC 1981; Barrister-at-law; MP (C) Burton, since Feb. 1974; a Recorder, since 1987; *b* 24 Dec. 1936; *o s* of late Leslie Lawrence, Brighton; *m* 1966, Gloria Hélène, *d* of Charles Crankshaw, Newcastle; one *d. Educ:* Brighton, Hove and Sussex Grammar Sch.; Christ Church, Oxford (MA). Nat. Service with RAF, 1955–57. Called to Bar, Inner Temple, 1962, Hon. Bencher, 1991; S Eastern Circuit; Asst Recorder, 1983–87. Contested (C) Peckham (Camberwell), 1966 and 1970. Chairman: Cons. Parly Legal Cttee, 1987 (Vice Chm., 1979–87); Cons. Parly Home Affairs Cttee, 1988– (Vice Chm., 1982–88); All-party Parly Anti-Fluoridation Cttee; All-party Parly Barristers Gp, 1987–; Sec., All-Party Parly Cttee for Release of Soviet Jewry; Member: Parly Expenditure Select Sub-Cttee, 1974–79; Jt Parly Cttee on Consolidation of Statutes, 1974–87; Foreign Affairs Select Cttee, 1983–. Mem. Exec., 1922 Cttee, 1988–89. Mem. Exec., CPA, 1989–. Member: Council of Justice, 1980–; Council, Statute Law Soc., 1985–; Exec., Soc. of Conservative Lawyers, 1989–. Vice-Pres., Fed. of Cons. Students, 1980–82; Mem., W Midlands Cons. Council, 1985–. Chm., Burton Breweries Charitable Trust, 1982–. *Publications:* pamphlets (jointly): Crisis in Crime and Punishment; The Conviction of the Guilty; Towards a New Nationality; Financing Strikes; newspaper articles on law and order topics and foreign affairs. *Recreations:* piano, squash, football, travel. *Address:* 1 Essex Court, Temple, EC4Y 9AR. *T:* 071–583 7759; Dunally Cottage, Lower Halliford Green, Shepperton, Mddx. *T:* Walton-on-Thames (0932) 224692; Grove Farm, Drakelow, Burton-on-Trent. *T:* Burton-on-Trent (0283) 44360.

LAWRENCE, John, OBE 1974; Director, Africa and Middle East Division, British Council, since 1990; *b* 22 April 1933; *s* of William and Nellie Lawrence. *Educ:* Queens' College, Cambridge (BA 1956, Cert. Ed. 1957, MA 1961); Indiana University (MA 1959). Teaching posts in USA and UK, 1957–60; British Council headquarters appts, 1961; Regional Representative, Sabah, 1965; Representative, Zambia, 1968, Sudan, 1974, Malaysia, 1976; Dir, South Asia Dept, 1980; Controller, America, Pacific and S Asia Div., 1982–87; Rep., Brazil, 1987–90. *Recreations:* walking and talking, simultaneously or otherwise. *Address:* c/o British Council, 10 Spring Gardens, SW1A 2BN. *T:* 071–930 8466.

LAWRENCE, Sir (John) Patrick (Grosvenor), Kt 1988; CBE 1983; Senior Partner, Wragge & Co., Solicitors, Birmingham, since 1982; *b* 29 March 1928; *s* of Ernest Victor Lawrence and Norah Grosvenor Lawrence (*née* Hill); *m* 1954, Anne Patricia (*née* Auld); one *s* one *d. Educ:* Denstone Coll., Staffs. Served RNVR, 1945–48. Admitted Solicitor 1954; Partner Wragge & Co., 1959. Chm., Midland Rent Assessment Panels, 1971–. Mem., Bromsgrove RDC, 1967–74. Vice-Pres., Nat. Union of Conservative and Unionist Assocs (Chm., 1986–87); Pres., W Midlands Conservative Council, 1988–91 (Chm., 1979–82). Vice-Chm., British Shooting Sports Council, 1985–. Member of Council: Denstone Coll., Staffs, 1989–; Birmingham Chamber of Industry and Commerce, 1989–; ABCC, 1990–; Aston Univ., 1990–. Chm., Birmingham Cathedral in Need Appeal, 1990–. *Address:* Bank House, Cherry Street, Birmingham B2 5JY. *T:* 021–632 4131. *Clubs:* Carlton; Birmingham, Bean (Birmingham); Law Society's Yacht.

LAWRENCE, Air Vice-Marshal John Thornett, CB 1975; CBE (mil.) 1967 (OBE (mil.) 1961); AFC 1945; *b* 16 April 1920; *s* of late T. L. Lawrence, JP, and Mrs B. M. Lawrence; *m* 1951, Hilary Jean (*née* Owen); three *s* one *d. Educ:* The Crypt School, Gloucester. RAFVR 1938. Served War of 1939–45 in Coastal Command (235, 202 and 86 Squadrons); Directing staff, RAF Flying Coll., 1949–53; CO 14 Squadron, 1953–55; Group Captain Operations, HQ AFME, 1962–64; CO RAF Wittering, 1964–66; AOC, 3 Group, Bomber Command, 1967; Student, IDC, 1968; Dir of Organisation and Admin Plans (RAF), 1969–71; Dir-Gen. Personnel Management (RAF), 1971–73; Comdr N Maritime Air Region and AOC Scotland and NI, 1973–75, retired 1975. Corporate Mem., Cheltenham Ladies' Coll., 1977–. Chm., Glos County SSAFA, 1980; Mem., Nat. Council, SSAFA, 1987–90. Order of Leopold II, Belgium, 1945; Croix de Guerre, Belgium, 1945. *Recreations:* golf, bridge. *Address:* The Coach House, Wightfield Manor, Apperley, Glos GL19 4DP. *Club:* Royal Air Force.

LAWRENCE, Sir John (Waldemar), 6th Bt, *cr* 1858; OBE 1945; freelance writer; Editor of Frontier, 1957–75; *b* 27 May 1907; *s* of Sir Alexander Waldemar Lawrence, 4th Bt, and Anne Elizabeth Le Poer (*née* Wynne); *S* brother, Sir Henry Eustace Waldemar Lawrence, 5th Bt, 1967; *m* 1948, Jacynth Mary (*née* Ellerton) (*d* 1987); no *c*; *m* 1988, Audrey Viola, *widow* of John Woodiwiss. *Educ:* Eton; New Coll., Oxford (MA, Lit. Hum.). Personal Asst to Dir of German Jewish Aid Cttee, 1938–39; with BBC as European Intelligence Officer and European Services Organiser, 1939–42; Press Attaché, HM Embassy, USSR, 1942–45; became freelance writer, 1946. Pres., Keston College (formerly Centre for Study of Religion and Communism), 1984– (Chm., 1969–83); Chm., GB USSR Assoc., 1970–85. Officer, Order of Orange Nassau, 1950. *Publications:* Life in Russia, 1947; Russia in the Making, 1957; A History of Russia, 1960; The Hard Facts of Unity, 1961; Russia (Methuen's Outlines), 1965; Soviet Russia, 1967; Russians Observed, 1969; Take Hold of Change, 1976; The Journals of Honoria Lawrence, 1980; The Hammer and the Cross, 1986; Lawrence of Lucknow, 1990. *Recreations:* travelling, reading in ten languages. *Heir: b* George Alexander Waldemar Lawrence [*b* 22 Sept. 1910; *m* 1949, Olga, *d* of late Peter Schilovsky; one *s* two *d*]. *Address:* 24 St Leonard's Terrace, SW3. *T:* 071–730 8033; 1 Naishes Cottages, Northstoke, Bath BA1 9AT. *Club:* Athenæum.

LAWRENCE, John Wilfred, RE 1987; book illustrator and wood engraver; *b* 15 Sept. 1933; *s* of Wilfred James Lawrence and Audrey Constance (*née* Thomas); *m* 1957, Myra Gillian Bell; two *d. Educ:* Salesian Coll., Cowley, Oxford; Hastings Sch. of Art; Central Sch. of Art. Visiting Lecturer in Illustration: Brighton Polytech., 1960–68; Camberwell Sch. of Art, 1960–; External Assessor in Illustration: Bristol Polytech., 1978–81; Brighton Polytech., 1982–85; Duncan of Jordanstone Coll. of Art, 1986–89; Exeter Coll. of Art, 1986–89; Kingston Polytechnic, 1989–; Edinburgh Coll. of Art, 1991–. Member: Art Workers Guild, 1972 (Master, 1990); Soc. of Wood Engravers, 1984. Work represented in Ashmolean Mus., V&A Mus., Nat. Mus. of Wales, and collections abroad. *Publications:* The Giant of Grabbist, 1968; Pope Leo's Elephant, 1969; Rabbit and Pork Rhyming Talk, 1975 (Francis Williams Book Illustration Award, 1977); Tongue Twisters, 1976; George, His Elephant and Castle, 1983; A Selection of Wood Engravings, 1986; Good Babies, Bad Babies, 1987; *illustrated:* more than 100 books, incl.: Colonel Jack, 1967 (Francis Williams Book Illustration Award, 1971); Diary of a Nobody, 1969; The Blue Fairy Book, 1975; The Illustrated Watership Down, 1976; Everyman's Book of English Folk Tales, 1981; The Magic Apple Tree, 1982; Mabel's Story, 1984; Entertaining with Cranks, 1985; Emily's Own Elephant, 1987; Christmas in Exeter Street, 1989; A New Treasury of Poetry, 1990; The Sword of Honour trilogy, 1990; Treasure Island, 1990; Shades of Green, 1991. *Address:* 22A Castlewood Road, N16 6DW. *T:* 081–809 3482.

LAWRENCE, Michael Hugh, CMG 1972; Head of the Administration Department, House of Commons, 1972–80; retired 1980; *b* 9 July 1920; *s* of late Hugh Moxon Lawrence and Mrs. L. N. Lawrence; *m* 1948, Rachel Mary (MA Cantab), *d* of late Humphrey Gamon, Gt Barrow, Cheshire; one *s* two *d. Educ:* Highgate (Scholar); St Catharine's Coll., Cambridge (Exhibnr; MA). Served Indian Army, 1940–45. Indian Civil Service, 1945–46; Asst Clerk, House of Commons, 1947; Senior Clerk, 1948; Deputy Principal Clerk, 1962; Clerk of the Overseas Office, 1967–72; Clerk Administrator, Services Cttee, 1972–76; Mem., Bd of Management, House of Commons, 1979–80. Sec., History of Parliament Trust, 1959–66. *Recreations:* beagling, sea bathing, looking at churches, gardening. *Address:* 22 Stradbroke Road, Southwold, Suffolk. *T:* Southwold (0502) 722794.

LAWRENCE, Murray; *see* Lawrence, W. N. M.

LAWRENCE, Sir Patrick; *see* Lawrence, Sir J. P. G.

LAWRENCE, Peter Anthony, PhD; FRS 1983; Staff Scientist, Medical Research Council Laboratory of Molecular Biology, Cambridge, since 1969; *b* 23 June 1941; *s* of Ivor Douglas Lawrence and Joy Lawrence (*née* Liebert); *m* 1971, Birgitta Haraldson. *Educ:* Wennington Sch., Wetherby, Yorks; Cambridge Univ. (MA, PhD). Harkness Fellowship, 1965–67; Dept of Genetics, Univ. of Cambridge, 1967–69. *Publications:* Insect Development (ed), 1976; The Making of a Fly, 1991; scientific papers. *Recreations:* gardening, fungi, trees, golf, theatre.

LAWRENCE, Richard; *see* Lawrence, H. R. G.

LAWRENCE, Air Vice-Marshal Thomas Albert, CB 1945; CD; RCAF, retired; *b* 1895; *s* of K. J. Lawrence; *m* 1921, Claudine Audrey Jamieson; two *s.* Served War of 1914–18, France; Flight Cadet, RFC, later 24 Fighter Sqdn, RAF. Pilot-Navigator, Canadian Air Bd; one of original gp of officers commnd into perm. RCAF, 1924; comdr, Hudson Strait Expedn, 1927; Liaison Officer, RCAF, Air Ministry, London, 1932–35; served War of 1939–45: Dir, Plans and Ops, Air Force HQ, 1939; CO Trenton, Ont., 1940; AOC, 2 Training Comd, BCATP, 1942–44; AOC, NW Air Comd, Canada, 1944–47, retd. Comdr, Legion of Merit (USA), 1945. Mem., Canada's Aviation Hall of Fame, 1980. *Address:* 10 William Morgan Drive, Toronto, Ont M4H 1E5, Canada.

LAWRENCE, Timothy; His Honour Judge Lawrence; a Circuit Judge, since 1986; President of Industrial Tribunals for England and Wales, since 1991; *b* 29 April 1942; *s* of A. Whiteman Lawrence, MBE, and Phyllis G. Lawrence (*née* Lloyd-Jones). *Educ:* Bedford School. Admitted Solicitor, 1967; with Solicitor's Dept, New Scotland Yard, 1967–70; Partner with Claude Hornby & Cox, Solicitors, 1970–86 (Sen. Partner, 1977–86). An Asst Recorder, 1980; a Recorder, 1983–86. Pres., London Criminal Courts Solicitors' Assoc., 1984–86 (Sec., 1974–84); Chm., No 14 Area, Regional Duty Solicitor Cttee, 1984–86; Legal Mem., Mental Health Review Tribunals, 1989–; Member: No 13 Area, Legal Aid Cttee, 1983–86; Law Society's Criminal Law Cttee, 1980–86; Council, Westminster Law Soc., 1979–82; Judicial Studies Bd, 1984–88; British Academy of Forensic Sciences, 1972–. Legal Assessor: Professions Supplementary to Medicine, 1976–86; Insurance Brokers Registration Council, 1983–86. FRSA. *Publications:* various articles in legal jls. *Recreations:* walking, wine, travel. *Address:* 8 Slaidburn Street, SW10 0JP; Hill Cottage, Great Walsingham, Norfolk. *Club:* Hurlingham.

LAWRENCE, (Walter Nicholas) Murray; Chairman of Lloyd's, 1988–90 (a Deputy Chairman 1982, 1984, 1985, 1986, 1987; Member: Committee of Lloyd's, 1979–82; Council of Lloyd's, annually since 1984); Chairman, Murray Lawrence Holdings LTD, since 1988; *b* 8 Feb. 1935; *s* of Henry Walter Neville Lawrence and Sarah Schuyler Lawrence (*née* Butler); *m* 1961, Sally Louise O'Dwyer; two *d. Educ:* Winchester Coll.; Trinity Coll., Oxford (BA, MA). C. T. Bowring & Co. (Ins.) Ltd, 1957–62; Asst Underwriter, H. Bowring & Others, 1962–70, Underwriter, 1970–84; Director: C. T. Bowring (Underwriting Agencies) Ltd, 1973–84; C. T. Bowring & Co. Ltd, 1976–84; Sen. Partner, Murray Lawrence & Partners, 1985–89; Chairman: Fairway (Underwriting Agencies) Ltd, 1979–85; Murray Lawrence Members Agency Ltd, 1988–; Murray Lawrence & Partners Ltd, 1989. Mem., Lloyd's Underwriters Non-Marine Assoc., 1970–84 (Dep. Chm., 1977; Chm., 1978). *Recreations:* golf, opera, travelling. *Clubs:* Boodle's, MCC; Royal & Ancient (St Andrews), Woking, Swinley, Royal St George's (Sandwich), Rye.

LAWRENCE, Sir William (Fettiplace), 5th Bt *cr* 1867, of Ealing Park, Middlesex; General Manager, Newdawn & Sun Ltd, since 1981; *b* 23 Aug. 1954; *s* of Sir William Lawrence, 4th Bt and of Pamela, *yr d* of J. E. Gordon; *S* father, 1986. *Educ:* King Edward VI School, Stratford-upon-Avon. Assistant Accountant, Wilmot Breeden Ltd/W. B. Bumpers Ltd, 1973–81. Member: Stratford-on-Avon District Council, 1982– (Chm., 1990–91); S Warwickshire CHC, 1983–84; S Warwickshire HA, 1984–; W Midlands Arts, 1989– (Mem., Management Council, 1984–89); Bd, Heart of England Tourist Bd, 1989–. Pres., Stratford and District Mencap, 1990–; Trustee, Action Unlimited Trust, 1988–. *Heir: cousin* Peter Stafford Hayden Lawrence [*b* 9 Feb. 1913; *m* 1940, Helena Francis, *d* of late Hon. George William Lyttelton; two *s* four *d*]. *Address:* The Knoll, Walcote, near Alcester, Warwickshire B49 6LZ. *T:* Great Alne (0789) 488303.

LAWRENCE, William Robert, QPM 1991; Chief Constable, South Wales Constabulary, since 1989; *b* 21 Sept. 1942; *s* of William Thomas and Norah Lawrence; *m* 1965, Kathleen Ann Lawrence; one *s* one *d. Educ:* Maesydderwen Grammar Sch. BA Open Univ., 1988. Joined Mid Wales, then Dyfed Powys Constabulary, 1961; Sergeant, 1970; Inspector, 1972; Chief Inspector, 1975; transf. to W Mercia as Supt, 1978; Chief Supt, 1982; Asst Chief Constable 1983, Dep. Chief Constable 1985, Staffordshire Police. SBStJ 1986. *Recreations:* golf, fly fishing, Rugby, amateur boxing. *Address:* Chief Constable's Office, South Wales Constabulary, Police Headquarters, Bridgend, Mid Glamorgan CF31 3SU. *T:* Bridgend (0656) 655555.

LAWRENCE-JONES, Sir Christopher, 6th Bt *cr* 1831; Chief Medical Officer, Imperial Chemical Industries, Millbank, SW1, since 1985; Chairman, Medichem, since 1986; *b* [illegible] Jan. 1940; *S* uncle, 1969; *m* 1967, Gail Pittar, Auckland, NZ; two *s. Educ:* She[illegible] Gonville and Caius Coll., Cambridge; St Thomas' Hospital. MA Cantab 1[illegible]

BChir Cantab 1964; DIH Eng. 1968. MFOM 1979, FFOM 1987. Medical adviser to various orgns, 1967–. *Recreation:* cruising under sail. *Heir: s* Mark Christopher Lawrence-Jones, *b* 28 Dec. 1968. *Club:* Royal Cruising.

LAWRENSON, Prof. Peter John, DSc; FRS 1982; FEng, FIEE, FIEEE; Professor of Electrical Engineering, Leeds University, since 1966 (Head, Department of Electrical and Electronic Engineering, 1974–84); Chairman, since 1981, and Managing Director, since 1986, Switched Reluctance Drives Ltd; *b* 12 March 1933; *s* of John Lawrenson and Emily (*née* Houghton); *m* 1958, Shirley Hannah Foster; one *s* three *d. Educ:* Prescot Grammar Sch.; Manchester Univ. (BSc, MSc; DSc 1971). FEng 1980; FIEE 1974; FIEEE 1975. Duddell Scholar, IEE, 1951–54; Res. Engr, Associated Electrical Industries, 1956–61; Univ. of Leeds: Lectr, 1961–65; Reader, 1965–66; Chm., Jt Faculties of Science and Applied Science, 1978–80; Chm., Shadow Faculty of Engrg, 1981. Science and Engineering Research Council: Mem., Electrical and Systems Cttee, 1971–; Chm., Electrical Engrg Sub-Cttee, 1981–84; Mem., Machines and Power Cttee, 1981–84; Mem., Engrg Bd, 1984–87; Organiser, National Initiative, Integrated Drive Systems, 1984–. Director: Allenwest Ltd, 1988–; Dale Electric Internat., 1988–. Institution of Electrical Engineers: Mem. Council, 1966–69 and 1981–; Chm., Accreditation Cttee, 1979–83; Chm., Power Divisional Bd, 1985–86; Dep. Pres., 1990–Sept. 1992. Mem. of cttees, Engrg Council, 1983–. Mem. Council, Buckingham Univ., 1987–. IEE Awards: Premia-Crompton, 1957 and 1967; John Hopkinson, 1965; The Instn, 1981; Faraday Medal, 1990. James Alfred Ewing Medal, ICE and Royal Soc., 1983; Royal Soc. Esso Energy Award, 1985. *Publications:* (with K. J. Binns) Analysis and Computation of Electromagnetic Field Problems, 1963, 2nd edn 1973; (with M. R. Harris and J. M. Stephenson) Per Unit Systems, 1970; papers and patents in areas of electromagnetism, electromechanics and control. *Recreations:* lawn tennis, squash, chess, bridge, jewelry making. *Address:* Spen Watch, 318 Spen Lane, Leeds LS16 5BA. *T:* Leeds (0532) 755849.

LAWREY, Keith, JP; Secretary and Registrar, Royal College of Veterinary Surgeons, since 1990; *b* 21 Aug. 1940; *s* of George William Bishop Lawrey and Edna Muriel (*née* Gass); *m* 1969, Helen Jane Marriott, BA; two *s* two *d. Educ:* Colfe's Sch.; Birkbeck Coll., Univ. of London (MSc Econ; LLB). Barrister-at-Law; called to Bar, Gray's Inn, 1972. Education Officer, Plastics and Rubber Inst., 1960–68; Lectr and Sen. Lectr, Bucks Coll. of Higher Educn, 1968–74; Head of Dept of Business Studies, Mid-Kent Coll. of Higher and Further Educn, 1974–78; Sec.-Gen., Library Assoc., 1978–84; Dean, Faculty of Business and Management, Harrow Coll. of Higher Educn, subseq. Head, Sch. of Business and Management, Polytechnic of Central London/Harrow Coll., 1984–90. FCollP (Hon. Treas., 1987–); FCIS. Gov., Cannock Sch. Mem., Worshipful Co. of Chartered Secretaries and Administrators. JP Inner London, 1974. *Publications:* papers in Jl, Coll. of Preceptors, Jl Assoc. of Law Teachers, Trans and Jl of Plastics Inst. *Recreations:* preaching, sailing, swimming, theatre, gardening. *Clubs:* Old Colfeians; Dell Quay Sailing.

LAWS, Courtney Alexander, OBE 1987; OD 1978; Director, Brixton Neighbourhood Community Association, since 1971; *b* Morant Bay, St Thomas, Jamaica, 16 June 1934; *s* of Ezekiel Laws and Agatha Laws; *m* 1955, Wilhel, (Rubie), Brown, JP; one *s* two *d. Educ:* Morant Bay Elem. Sch.; Jones Pen and Rollington Town Elem. Sch.; Lincoln Coll.; Nat. Coll. for Youth Workers, Leicester; Cranfield Coll., Bedford. Rep., Works Cttee, Peak Freans Biscuit Co., 1960–69; Shop Steward, TGWU, 1960–70. Member: Lambeth Council for Community Relations, 1964–; Consortium of Ethnic Minorities, Lambeth, 1978–; W Indian Standing Conf., 1959–; Campaign against Racial Discrimination, 1960–; NCCI, 1960–; Commn for Racial Equality, 1977–80; Central Cttee, British Caribbean Assoc. (Exec. Mem.), 1960–; Assoc. of Jamaicans (Founder Mem.), 1965; Geneva and Somerleyton Community Assoc., 1966–; Consultative Cttee, ILEA, Lambeth, 1975–; Consultative Council, City and E London Coll., 1975–; South Eastern Gas Consumers' Council, 1980–; Governor, Brixton Coll. of Further and Higher Educn, 1970–; Member: W Indian Sen. Citizens' Assoc. (Pres.), 1973–; St John's Interracial Club, 1958–; Brixton United Cricket Club, 1968– (Pres.); Brixton Domino Club (Chm.); Oasis Sports and Social Club, 1969–. Medal of Appreciation, Prime Minister of Jamaica, 1987; Community of Brixton Award, 1987. *Recreations:* reading, music. *Address:* 71 Atlantic Road, SW9 8PU. *T:* 071–274 0011.

LAWS, Frederick Geoffrey; Vice-Chairman, Commission for Local Administration in England, since 1984; *b* Blackpool, 1 Aug. 1928; *s* of Frederick and Annetta Laws; *m* 1955, Beryl Holt; two *d. Educ:* Arnold School; Manchester Univ.; London Univ. (LLB); solicitor 1952. Asst Solicitor, Blackpool Corp., 1952–54, Bournemouth Corp., 1954–59; Southend-on-Sea Corporation: Asst Sol., 1959–62; Dep. Town Clerk and Clerk of the Peace, 1962–71; Town Clerk, 1971–74; Chief Exec., Southend-on-Sea Borough Council, 1974–84. Pres., Southend-on-Sea Law Soc., 1981. Hon. Freeman, Southend-on-Sea Borough Council, 1985. *Recreations:* Rugby football, golf. *Address:* 270 Maplin Way North, Southend-on-Sea, Essex. *T:* Southend (0702) 587459. *Clubs:* Athenæum; Thorpe Hall Golf (Captain, 1983); Southend Rugby Football.

LAWS, John Grant McKenzie; First Junior Treasury Counsel, Common Law, since 1984; a Recorder, since 1985; *b* 10 May 1945; *s* of late Dr Frederic Laws and Dr Margaret Ross Laws, *d* of Prof. John Grant McKenzie; *m* 1973, Sophie Susan Sydenham Cole Marshall, BLitt, MA; one *d. Educ:* Durham Cathedral Choir Sch.; Durham Sch. (King's Scholar); Exeter Coll., Oxford (Sen. Open Classical Scholar; BA 1967, Hon. Sch. of Lit. Hum. 1st Cl.; MA 1976). Called to the Bar, Inner Temple, 1970, Bencher, 1985; practice at Common Law Bar, 1971–; Asst Recorder, 1983–85; admitted to Bar: New South Wales, 1987; Gibraltar, 1988. *Publications:* (contrib.) Halsbury's Laws of England, 4th edn 1973; (contrib.) Dict. of Medical Ethics, 1977; reviews for Theology, Law & Justice; contribs to legal jls. *Recreations:* Greece, living in London, philosophy, writing verse, painting. *Address:* 39 Essex Street, WC2R 3AT. *Club:* United Oxford & Cambridge University.

LAWS, Dr John William, CBE 1982; FRCP; FRCR; consultant diagnostic radiologist; Director of Radiology, King's College Hospital, and Director of Radiological Studies, King's College Hospital Medical School, 1967–86; *b* 25 Oct. 1921; *s* of Robert Montgomery Laws and Lucy Ibbotson; *m* 1st, 1945, Dr Pamela King, MRCS, LRCP (*d* 1985); one *s* one *d*; 2nd, 1986, Dr Diana Brinkley (*née* Rawlence), FRCR. *Educ:* The Leys Sch., Cambridge; Sheffield Univ. Med. Sch. MB ChB 1944; DMRD 1952; MRCP 1951; FRCR (FFR 1955); FRCP 1967. Nat. service, 1947–49 (Captain RAMC). House Physician and House Surg., Royal Hosp., Sheffield, 1944–45; Res. Surgical Officer, Salisbury Gen. Infirmary, 1945–47; Med. Registrar, 1949–51, Radiology Registrar and Sen. Registrar, 1951–55, United Sheffield Hosps; Consultant Radiologist, Dep. Dir, Hammersmith Hosp., and Hon. Lectr, RPMS, 1955–67. Consultant Civilian Advr to Army, 1976–86; Med. Dir, King's Centre for Assessment of Radiol Equipment, 1979–86. Chm., Radiol Equipment Sub-Cttee, DHSS, 1972–81; Member: Central Adv. Cttee on Hosp. Med. Records, DHSS, 1969–74; Radiol Adv. Cttee, DHSS, 1972–86; Consultant Advr in Radiol., DHSS, 1982–86. Chm., British Delegn, XV Internat. Congress of Radiol., 1981. Royal College (formerly Faculty) of Radiologists: Mem. Fellowship Bd, 1966–71; Hon. Sec., 1974–75; Registrar, 1975–76; Warden of Fellowship, 1976–80; Pres., 1980–83; Knox Lectr, 1984. Mem. Council, RCS, 1981–84. Vis Prof. and Lectr at academic instns and congresses worldwide. Member Editorial Board: Clin. Radiol., 1960–63; Gut, 1970–74; Gastrointestinal Radiol., 1975–85; Asst, later Hon., Editor, British Jl of Radiol., 1961–71. Hon. FACR 1973; Hon. FFR RCSI 1975; Hon. FRACR 1979. Barclay Prize, British Inst. of Radiol., 1964. *Publications:* numerous papers and pubns on various aspects of clinical radiology, particularly gastrointestinal and hepatic radiology and the radiology of pulmonary disease, in medical journals and books. *Recreations:* listening to music, sculpting, golf. *Address:* 5 Frank Dixon Way, Dulwich, SE21 7BB. *T:* 081–693 4815.

LAWS, Richard Maitland, CBE 1983; PhD; FRS 1980; Director, British Antarctic Survey, 1973–87; Master, St Edmund's College, Cambridge, since 1985; *b* 23 April 1926; *s* of Percy Malcolm Laws and Florence May (*née* Heslop); *m* 1954, Maureen Isobel Winifred (*née* Holmes); three *s. Educ:* Dame Allan's Sch., Newcastle-on-Tyne; St Catharine's Coll., Cambridge (Open Scholar, 1944; Res. Scholar, 1952–53; Hon. Fellow, 1982). BA Cantab 1947, MA 1952, PhD 1953; FInstBiol 1973. Biologist and Base Leader, Falkland Is Dependencies Survey, 1947–53; Biologist and Whaling Inspector, F/F Balaena, 1953–54; Principal Sci. Officer, Nat. Inst. of Oceanography, 1954–61; Dir, Nuffield Unit of Tropical Animal Ecology, Uganda, 1961–67; Dir, Tsavo Research Project, Kenya, 1967–68; Smuts Meml Fund Fellowship, 1968–69; Leverhulme Research Fellowship, 1969; Head, Life Sciences Div., British Antarctic Survey, 1969–73. Dir, NERC Sea Mammal Res. Unit, 1977–87; Scientific Committee for Antarctic Research: Convener, Gp of Specialists on Seals, 1972–88; Pres., Biology Working Gp, 1990– (Mem., 1972–; Chm., 1980–86); UK Delegate, 1984–. Food and Agriculture Organization: Mem., 1974–77, Chm., 1976–77, Working Party on Marine Mammals; Chm., Scientific Consultation on Conservation and Management of Marine Mammals and their Environment, 1976. Zoological Society of London: Mem. Council, 1982–84; Vice-Pres., 1983–84; Sec., 1984–88. University of Cambridge: Mem., Financial Bd, 1988–; Mem., Council of Senate, 1989–; Chm., Local Examinations Syndicate, 1990–. Vice-Pres., Inst. Biol., 1984–85. 36th annual Lectr, CIBA Foundn, 1984. Hon. DSc Bath, 1991. Bruce Medal, RSE, 1954; Scientific Medal, Zool Soc. London, 1965; Polar Medal, 1976. *Publications:* (with I. S. C. Parker and R. C. B. Johnstone) Elephants and their Habitats, 1975; (ed) Scientific Research in Antarctica, 1977; (ed) Antarctic Ecology, 1984; (co-ed) Antarctic Nutrient Cycles and Food Webs, 1985; Antarctica: the last frontier, 1989; (ed jtly) Life at Low Temperatures, 1990; papers in biol jls. *Recreations:* walking, photography, painting. *Address:* St Edmund's College, Cambridge CB3 0BN. *T:* Cambridge (0223) 350398; 3 The Footpath, Coton, Cambridge CB3 7PX. *T:* Madingley (0954) 210567.

LAWS, Stephen Charles; Parliamentary Counsel, since 1991; *b* 28 Jan. 1950; *s* of Dennis Arthur Laws and Beryl Elizabeth Laws (*née* Roe); *m* 1972, Angela Mary Deardon; two *s* three *d. Educ:* St Dunstan's College, Catford; Bristol Univ. (LLB Hons 1972). Called to the Bar, Middle Temple, 1973. Asst Lectr, Univ. of Bristol, 1972; Legal Asst, Home Office, 1975; Asst, Sen. Asst, then Dep. Parly Counsel, 1976–91. *Publications:* (with Peter Knowles) Statutes title in Halsbury's Laws of England, 4th edn, 1983. *Address:* Office of the Parliamentary Counsel, 36 Whitehall, SW1A 2AY. *T:* 071–210 6611.

LAWSON, family name of **Baron Burnham.**

LAWSON, Sir Christopher (Donald), Kt 1984; management consultant; Director, Communications Centre, since 1984; *b* 31 Oct. 1922; *s* of James Lawson and Ellen de Verrine; *m* 1945, Marjorie Bristow; two *s* one *d. Educ:* Magdalen Coll., Oxford. Served RAF, 1941–49: Pilot, Sqdn Leader. Thomas Hedley (Proctor and Gamble), 1949–57; Cooper McDougal Robertson, 1958–61; Managing Dir, TMC, 1961–63; Director: Mars Ltd, 1965–81; Mars Inc., USA, 1975–82; Pres., Mars Snackmaster, USA, 1977–82; Chm. and Man. Dir, Goodblue Ltd, 1981–; Chm., Spearhead Ltd, 1983–; Dir of Marketing, 1982–83, Dir of Special Services, 1986–87, Cons. and Unionist Party. *Recreations:* collecting antiques and new artists' work; all sport, particularly golf, cricket, hockey. *Address:* Church Cottage, Great Witcombe, Glos GL3 4TT. *Clubs:* Royal Air Force, Carlton, MCC; Lillybrook Golf (Cheltenham); Doublegate Country (Ga, USA).

LAWSON, Prof. David Hamilton; Consultant Physician, Glasgow Royal Infirmary, since 1973; *b* 27 May 1939; *s* of David Lawson and Margaret Harvey Lawson (*née* White); *m* 1963, Alison Diamond; three *s. Educ:* High Sch. of Glasgow; Univ. of Glasgow. MB, ChB 1962; MD 1973. FRCPE 1975; FRCPGlas 1986; FFPM 1989. Junior medical posts in Royal Infirmary and Western Infirmary, Glasgow; Boston Collaborative Drug Surveillance Prog., Boston, Mass, 1970–72; Attending Physician, Lemuel Shattuck Hosp., Boston, 1971; Adviser on Adverse Drug Reactions, Wellcome Foundn, 1975–87; Vis. Prof., Faculty of Sci., Univ. of Strathclyde, 1976–. Member: Health Services Res. Cttee of Chief Scientist Office, SHHD, 1984–88; Cttee on Safety of Medicines, Dept of Health (formerly DHSS), 1987–; Mem., 1979–, Chm., 1987–, Cttee on Review of Medicines, Dept of Health (formerly DHSS). Examiner, Final MB, Univs of Glasgow, Dundee, Birmingham, London. *Publications:* Clinical Pharmacy and Hospital Drug Management (ed with R. M. E. Richards), 1982; Current Medicine 2, 1990; (ed jtly) Risk Factors for Adverse Drug Reactions: epidemiological approaches, 1990; papers on clinical pharmacol, haematol and renal topics. *Recreations:* hill-walking, photography, bird-watching. *Address:* 43 Drumlin Drive, Milngavie, Glasgow G62 6NF. *T:* 041–956 2962. *Club:* Commonwealth Trust.

LAWSON, Dominic Ralph Campden; Editor, The Spectator, since 1990; *b* 17 Dec. 1956; *s* of Rt Hon. Nigel Lawson, *qv* and late Vanessa Mary Addison Lawson (*née* Salmon); *m* 1982, Jane Fiona Wastell Whytehead (marr. diss. 1991). *Educ:* Westminster Sch.; Christ Church, Oxford (exhibnr; Hons PPE). Researcher, BBC TV and radio, 1979–81; Financial Times: joined 1981; energy corresp., 1983–86; columnist (Lex), 1986–87; Dep. Editor, The Spectator, 1987–90; columnist: Sunday Correspondent, 1990; Financial Times, 1991–. Harold Wincott Prize for financial journalism, 1987. *Publications:* (with Raymond Keene) Kasparov-Korchnoi, the London Contest, 1983; (jtly) Britain in the Eighties, 1989. *Recreations:* playing cricket, watching chess. *Address:* The Spectator, 56 Doughty Street, WC1N 2LL. *Clubs:* Academy, MCC.

LAWSON, Prof. Donald Douglas; Professor of Veterinary Surgery, University of Glasgow, 1974–86; *b* 25 May 1924; *s* of Alexander Lawson and Jessie Macnaughton; *m* 1949, Barbara Ness; two *s* two *d. Educ:* Whitehill Sch., Glasgow; Glasgow Veterinary Coll. MRCVS, BSc, DVR. Asst in Veterinary Practice, 1946–47; Asst, Surgery Dept, Glasgow Vet. Coll., 1947–49; Glasgow Univ.: Lectr, Vet. Surgery, 1949–57; Sen. Lectr, 1957–66; Reader, 1966–71; Titular Prof., 1971–74. *Publications:* many articles in Veterinary Record and Jl of Small Animal Practice. *Recreations:* gardening, motoring. *Address:* The Cottage, Mill of Lumphart, Oldmeldrum, Aberdeenshire AB5 0EA. *T:* Oldmeldrum (06512) 2688.

LAWSON, Edmund James, QC 1988; *b* 17 April 1948; *s* of Donald and Veronica Lawson; *m* 1973, Jennifer Cleary; three *s. Educ:* City of Norwich Sch.; Trinity Hall, Cambridge (BA Hons, Law). Called to the Bar, Gray's Inn, 1971; in chambers of: Dr F. Hallis, 1971–76; Sir Arthur Irvine, QC, subseq. Gilbert Gray, QC, 1976–; Head of Chambers, 1990–. *Recreations:* music, family. *Address:* 4 Paper Buildings, Temple, EC4Y 7EX. *T:* 071–583 7765.

LAWSON, Elizabeth Ann; QC 1989; *b* 29 April 1947; *d* of Alexander Edward Lawson, FCA, and Helen Jane Lawson (*née* Currie). *Educ:* Croydon High School for Girls (GPDST); Nottingham Univ. (LLB). Called to Bar, Gray's Inn, 1969. Chm., Leeways Enquiry for London Borough of Lewisham, 1985; Chm., Liam Johnson Review for Islington Area Child Protection Cttee, 1989. *Recreations:* knitting, reading, cake decoration. *Address:* Cloisters, Temple, EC4Y 7AA. *T:* 071–583 0303.

LAWSON, Rear-Adm. Frederick Charles William, CB 1971; DSC 1942 and Bar, 1945; Chief Executive, Royal Dockyards, Ministry of Defence, 1972–75; *b* 20 April 1917; *s* of M. L. Lawson, formerly of Public Works Dept, Punjab, India; *m* 1945, Dorothy (*née* Norman) (*d* 1986), Eastbourne; one *s* three *d*. *Educ:* Eastbourne Coll.; RNEC. Joined RN, 1935; specialised in engrg; Cmdr 1949; Captain 1960; Cdre Supt Singapore, 1965–69; Rear-Adm. 1969; Flag Officer, Medway and Adm. Supt, HM Dockyard, Chatham, 1969–71, retired. *Recreation:* golf. *Address:* Weaverhoult, Woolley Street, Bradford-on-Avon, Wilts.
See also Rear-Adm. M. A. C. Moore.

LAWSON, Prof. Gerald Hartley; Professor of Business Finance, Manchester Business School, University of Manchester, 1969–88, now Emeritus; financial and economic consultant; *b* 6 July 1933; of English parents; *m* 1957, Helga Elisabeth Anna Heine; three *s*. *Educ:* King's Coll., Univ. of Durham. BA (Econ), MA (Econ); MBA Manchester; FCCA. Accountant in industry, 1957–59; Lectr in Accountancy and Applied Economics, Univ. of Sheffield, 1959–66; Prof. of Business Studies, Univ. of Liverpool, 1966–69. Prof., Univ. of Augsburg, Germany, 1971–72; Prof., Univ. of Texas, 1977, 1981; Prof., Ruhr Univ., Bochum, 1980; British Council Scholar, Hochschule für Welthandel, Vienna, 1967, and Univ. of Louvain, 1978. Visiting Professor: Southern Methodist Univ., Dallas, 1989–; Nanyang Technological Univ., Singapore, 1989. Dir, Dietsmann (UK), 1984–89. *Publications:* (with D. W. Windle): Tables for Discounted Cash Flow, etc, Calculations, 1965 (5th repr. 1978); Capital Budgeting in the Corporation Tax Regime, 1967; many articles and translations. *Recreations:* cricket, skiing. *Address:* c/o Manchester Business School, Booth Street West, Manchester M15 6PB. *T:* 061–275 6333. *Club:* Manchester Business School.

LAWSON, Hugh McDowall, BScEng London; CEng, FICE; Director of Leisure Services, Nottingham City Council, 1973–76; *b* Leeds, 13 Feb. 1912; *s* of late John Lawson, Pharmaceutical Chemist; *m* 1st, 1937, Dorothy (*d* 1982), *d* of late Rev. T. H. Mallinson, BA; two *s*; 2nd, 1988, Eva (*d* 1991), *widow* of Richard Koch, *d* of late Prof. David Holde, Berlin. *Educ:* Nottingham High Sch.; University Coll., Nottingham. Served in Royal Engineers, 1940–44. MP (Common Wealth) Skipton Div. of Yorks, 1944–45. Contested (Common Wealth) Harrow West Div., 1945; (Lab) Rushcliffe Div., 1950; (Lab) King's Lynn Div., 1955; joined SDP, 1981, SLD, 1988. Dep. City Engr, Nottingham, 1948–73. Mem. Council, ICE, 1972–75. *Address:* 68 Marshall Hill Drive, Mapperley, Nottingham NG3 6FS. *T:* Nottingham (0602) 605241.

LAWSON, Air Vice-Marshal Ian Douglas Napier, CB 1965; CBE 1961; DFC 1941, Bar 1943; AE 1945; RAF, retired; *b* 11 Nov. 1917; *y s* of late J. L. Lawson and Ethel Mary Lawson (*née* Ludgate); *m* 1945, Dorothy Joyce Graham Nash; one *s* one *d*. *Educ:* Brondesbury Coll.; Polytechnic, Regent Street. Aircraft Industry, 1934–39. Joined RAFVR 1938. Served War of 1939–45 (despatches thrice): Bomber Comd, 1940–41; Middle East Comd, 1941–45. Permanent Commission, 1945. Bomber Comd, 1945–46; Staff Coll., 1946; Air Ministry, 1946–49; Transport Comd, 1949–50; Middle East Comd, 1950–52; JSSC, 1953; Ministry of Defence, 1953–56; Flying Coll., Manby, 1956–57; Transport Comd, 1957–62; Air Forces Middle East, 1962–64; Commandant, RAF Coll., Cranwell, 1964–67; Asst Chief Adviser (Personnel and Logistics), MoD, 1967–69. Joined BAC, 1969, Chief Sales Exec., Weybridge, Bristol Div., 1974–79; Gen. Marketing Manager (civil), BAe, 1979–81; non-exec. Dir, Glos Air (Holdings) Ltd, 1981–82. FBIM. US Legion of Merit. *Recreations:* gardening, motor sport. *Address:* The Dower Cottage, Bewley Lane, Lacock, Wilts SN15 2PG. *T:* Lacock (024973) 307. *Club:* Royal Air Force.

LAWSON, James Robert; Regional Nursing Officer, Mersey, 1985–89; *b* 29 Dec. 1939; *s* of James and Grace Lawson; *m* 1962, Jean; two *d*. *Educ:* Keswick High School; Royal Albert Hosp. (Registered Nurse of Mentally Handicapped); Cumberland Infirmary (Registered Gen. Nurse). Chief Nurse, 1972; Area Nurse, Personnel, 1974; Divl Nursing Officer, 1976; District Nursing Officer, 1982–85. *Recreations:* fellwalking, caravaning, active sports. *Address:* Browside Cottage, Tanhouse Lane, Burtonwood, Warrington, Cheshire. *T:* Warrington (0925) 32735.

LAWSON, John Alexander Reid, OBE 1979; FRCGP; General Medical Practitioner, 1948–86, retired; Regional Adviser in General Practice, Tayside Region, 1972–82; *b* 30 Aug. 1920; *s* of Thomas Reid Lawson and Helen Scrimgour Lawson; *m* 1944, Pat Kirk; two *s* two *d*. *Educ:* High Sch. of Dundee; Univ. of St Andrews (MB, ChB). RAMC, 1944–47 (Major). Surgical Registrar, Royal Infirmary, Dundee, 1947–48. Royal College of General Practitioners: Mem., 1952; Fellow, 1967; Chm. Council, 1973–76; Pres., 1982–85. Mem. Cttee of Enquiry into Competence to Practice, 1974–76; Chairman: Jt Cttee on Postgraduate Training for General Practice, 1975–78; Armed Service Gen. Practice Approval Bd, 1979–87. *Recreations:* shooting, fishing, golf, gardening. *Address:* The Ridges, 458 Perth Road, Dundee. *T:* Dundee (0382) 66675. *Clubs:* New (Edinburgh); Royal and Ancient Golf (St Andrews).

LAWSON, Col Sir John Charles Arthur Digby, 3rd Bt, *cr* 1900; DSO 1943; MC 1940; Colonel 11th Hussars, retired; former Chairman, Fairbairn Lawson Ltd, Leeds; *b* 24 Oct. 1912; *e s* of Sir Digby Lawson, Bt, TD, JP, and late Mrs Gerald Wallis (*née* Iris Mary Fitzgerald); *S* father 1959; *m* 1st, 1945, Rose (marr. diss., 1950; she *d* 1972), *widow* of Pilot Officer William Fiske, RAF, and *er d* of late D. C. Bingham and late Lady Rosabelle Brand; 2nd, 1954, Tresilla Ann Elinor (de Pret Roose) (*d* 1985), *d* of late Major E. Buller Leyborne Popham, MC; one *s*. *Educ:* Stowe; RMC, Sandhurst; commissioned 11th Hussars (PAO), 1933; Palestine, 1936–37; Transjordan Frontier Force, 1938; Western Desert, 1940–43 (despatches twice, MC, DSO); Armoured Adviser to Gen. Patton, N Africa, 1943; Staff Coll., 1943; US Marines Staff Course, 1944; Special Liaison Officer to Gen. Montgomery, NW Europe, 1944; Comd Inns of Court Regt, 1945–47; retired, 1947. Colonel, 11th Hussars (PAO), 1965–69; Col, The Royal Hussars (PWO), 1969–73. Legion of Merit (US). *Heir: s* Charles John Patrick Lawson [*b* 19 May 1959; *m* 1987, Lady Caroline Lowther, *d* of Earl of Lonsdale, *qv*; one *s* one *d*. *Educ:* Harrow; Royal Agricl Coll., Cirencester]. *Clubs:* Cavalry and Guards, MCC.

LAWSON, John David, ScD; FRS 1983; Deputy Chief Scientific Officer, Rutherford Appleton Laboratory, Science and Engineering Research Council, Chilton, Oxon, 1978–87, retired, now Hon. Scientist; *b* 4 April 1923; *s* of Ronald L. Lawson and Ruth (*née* Houseman); *m* 1949, Kathleen (*née* Wyllie); two *s* one *d*. *Educ:* Wolverhampton Grammar Sch.; St John's Coll., Cambridge (BA, ScD). FInstP. TRE Malvern, Aerials group, 1943; AERE Malvern Br., Accelerator gp, 1947; AERE Harwell, Gen. Physics Div., 1951–62; Microwave Laboratory, Stanford, USA, 1959–60; Rutherford Laboratory (later Rutherford Appleton Laboratory), Applied Phys. Div., and later Technology Div., 1962–87, except, Vis. Prof., Dept of Physics and Astronomy, Univ. of Maryland, USA, 1971; Culham Lab., Technology Div., 1975–76. *Publications:* The Physics of Charged Particle Beams, 1977, 2nd edn 1988; papers on various topics in applied physics in several jls. *Recreations:* travel, mountain walking, collecting old books. *Address:* 7 Clifton Drive, Abingdon, Oxon OX14 1ET. *T:* Abingdon (0235) 521516.

LAWSON, Lesley, (Mrs Leigh Lawson); *see* Twiggy.

LAWSON, Hon. Sir Neil, Kt 1971; Judge of High Court of Justice, Queen's Bench Division, 1971–83; *b* 8 April 1908; *s* of late Robb Lawson and Edith Marion Lawson (*née* Usherwood); *m* 1933, Gweneth Clare (*née* Wilby); one *s* one *d*. Called to Bar, Inner Temple, 1929; QC 1955; Recorder of Folkestone, 1962–71; a Law Commissioner, 1965–71. RAFVR, 1940–45. Hon. Fellow, LSE, 1974. Foreign decorations: DK (Dato' Peduka Kerubat), 1959, DSN (Dato' Setia Negara), 1962, PSMB (Dato' Sri Mahota), 1969, Brunei. *Recreations:* literature, music, the country. *Address:* 30a Heath Drive, Hampstead, NW3.

LAWSON, Rt. Hon. Nigel, PC 1981; MP (C) Blaby, Leicestershire, since Feb. 1974; Chairman, Central Europe Trust Co. Ltd, since 1990; Director: Barclays Bank plc, since 1990; GPA Group plc, since 1990; Member, International Advisory Board, Creditanstalt, since 1991; *b* 11 March 1932; *o s* of late Ralph Lawson and of Joan Elisabeth Lawson (*née* Davis); *m* 1st, 1955, Vanessa Salmon (marr. diss. 1980; she *d* 1985); one *s* three *d*; 2nd, 1980, Thérèse Mary Maclear; one *s* one *d*. *Educ:* Westminster; Christ Church, Oxford (Scholar). 1st class hons PPE, 1954. Served with Royal Navy (Sub-Lt RNVR), 1954–56. Mem. Editorial Staff, Financial Times, 1956–60; City Editor, Sunday Telegraph, 1961–63; Special Assistant to Prime Minister (Sir Alec Douglas-Home), 1963–64; Financial Times columnist and BBC broadcaster, 1965; Editor of the Spectator, 1966–70; regular contributor to: Sunday Times and Evening Standard, 1970–71; The Times, 1971–72; Fellow, Nuffield Coll., Oxford, 1972–73; Special Pol Advr, Cons. Party HQ, 1973–74. Contested (C) Eton and Slough, 1970. An Opposition Whip, 1976–77; an Opposition Spokesman on Treasury and Economic Affairs, 1977–79; Financial Sec. to the Treasury, 1979–81; Sec. of State for Energy, 1981–83; Chancellor of the Exchequer, 1983–89. Chm., Coningsby Club, 1963–64. Vice-Chm., Cons. Political Centre Nat. Adv. Cttee, 1972–75. *Publications:* (jtly) Britain and Canada, 1976; (with Jock Bruce-Gardyne) The Power Game, 1976; (jtly) The Coming Confrontation, 1978; The New Conservatism (pamphlet), 1980. *Address:* c/o House of Commons, SW1. *Clubs:* Garrick, Pratt's, Political Economy.
See also D. R. C. Lawson.

LAWSON, Gen. Sir Richard (George), KCB 1980; DSO 1962; OBE 1968; Commander-in-Chief, Allied Forces Northern Europe, 1982–86; *b* 24 Nov. 1927; *s* of John Lawson and Florence Rebecca Lawson; *m* 1956, Ingrid Lawson; one *s*. *Educ:* St Alban's Sch.; Birmingham Univ. CO, Independent Squadron, RTR (Berlin), 1963–64; GSO2 MoD, 1965–66; CofS, South Arabian Army, 1967; CO, 5th RTR, 1968–69; Comdr, 20th Armoured Bde, 1972–73; Asst Military Deputy to Head of Defence Sales, 1975–77; GOC 1st Armoured Div., 1977–79; GOC Northern Ireland, 1980–82. Col Comdt, RTR, 1980–82. Leopold Cross (Belgium), 1963; Knight Commander, Order of St Sylvester (Vatican), 1964. *Publications:* Strange Soldiering, 1963; All the Queen's Men, 1967; Strictly Personal, 1972. *Address:* c/o Royal Bank of Scotland, Kirkland House, SW1. *Club:* Army and Navy.

LAWSON, Richard Henry; Chairman: Greenwell Montagu, Stockbrokers, 1987–91; Securities and Futures Authority, 1991; *b* 16 Feb. 1932; *s* of Sir Henry Brailsford Lawson, MC, and Lady (Mona) Lawson; *m* 1958, Janet Elizabeth Govier; three *s* (one *d* decd). *Educ:* Lancing College. ICI, 1952–54; W. Greenwell & Co. (now Greenwell Montagu & Co.), 1954–91; Jt Sen. Partner, 1980–86. Deputy Chairman: Stock Exchange, 1985–86; Securities Assoc., 1986–91. Dir, Investors Compensation Scheme, 1989–. *Recreations:* golf, tennis, walking, birdwatching, skiing. *Address:* Cherry Hill, Burrows Lane, Gomshall, Guildford, Surrey GU5 9QE. *Club:* Naval and Military.

LAWSON, Sonia, RA 1991 (ARA 1982); RWS 1988 (ARWS 1985); artist; Tutor, Royal Academy Schools; Visiting Tutor, Royal College of Art; *b* 2 June 1934; *d* of Frederick Lawson and Muriel (*née* Metcalfe), artists; *m* 1969, C. W. Congo; one *d*. *Educ:* Leyburn; Southwick Girls' Sch.; Doncaster Sch. of Art; Royal Coll. of Art (ARCA 1st cl. 1959). Postgraduate year, RCA; Travelling Scholarship, France, 1960. *Solo exhibitions:* Zwemmer, London, 1960; New Arts Centre, London, 1963; Queen's Sq. Gall., Leeds, 1964; Trafford Gall., London, 1967; Bradford New Liby, 1972; Middlesbrough and Billingham, 1977; Open Univ., Darlington and Harrogate Art Galls, 1979; Harrogate Northern Artists, 1980; Manchester City Art Gall., 1987; Wakefield City Art Gall., 1988; Cartwright Hall, Bradford, 1989; Boundary Gall., London, 1989; Galerie zur alten deutschen schule, Thun, Switzerland, 1990; retrospective exhibn, Shrines of Life, toured 1982–83, Sheffield (Mappin), Hull (Ferens), Bradford (Cartwright), Leicester Poly., Milton Keynes (Exhibn Gall); *mixed exhibitions,* 1960–: Arts Council of GB Touring Exhibns (Fragments against Ruin, The Subjective Eye); Tolly Cobbold National Exhibns; Moira Kelly Fine Art; Hayward Annual; Green Street, New York (8 in the 80s); Fruitmarket Gall., Edinburgh; Royal Acad. Annual; John Moores, Liverpool; London Gp; RCA (Exhibition Road, to celebrate 150 years of RCA), 1988; Smith Gall., London, 1988, 1989; Olympia Fest., London, 1988, 1989; Bath Fest., 1989; Faces of Britain, China (British Council Touring Exhibn), 1989–90; Glasgow Royal Inst. of Fine Art, 1990; Royal Academy (The Infernal Method, etchings by Academicians), 1991. Works in public collections: Arts Council of GB; Graves Art Gall., Sheffield; Huddersfield, Carlisle, Belfast, Middlesbrough, Bradford, Dewsbury, Rochdale, Wakefield, and Harrogate Art Galls; Imperial War Mus.; Min. of Educn; Min. of Works; Leeds Univ.; Open Univ.; Cranfield Inst. of Technol.; RCA; St Peter's Coll., Oxford; Nuffield Foundn; Augustine (commissioned), presented by Archbishop of Canterbury to Pope John Paul II, Vatican Collection, Rome, 1989; private collections in UK, Germany, Australia, USA. BBC TV, Monitor, 1960, John Schlesinger's doc. "Private View". Visual records of preparations for Exercise Lionheart, BAOR, 1984 (Imperial War Mus. commn). Rowney Prize, Royal Acad., 1984; Gainsborough House Drawing Prize, Eastern Arts, 1984; Lorne Award, Slade Sch. of Fine Art, 1986; Lady Evershed Drawing Prize, Eastern Arts Open, 1990. *Recreation:* denizen watching. *Address:* c/o Royal Academy of Arts, Burlington House, Piccadilly, W1V 0DS. *T:* 071–439 7438. *Club:* Arts.

LAWSON JOHNSTON, family name of **Baron Luke.**

LAWSON JOHNSTON, Hon. Hugh de Beauchamp, TD 1951; DL; *b* 7 April 1914; *yr s* of 1st Baron Luke of Pavenham, KBE, and *b* of 2nd Baron Luke, *qv*; *m* 1946, Audrey Warren, *d* of late Colonel F. Warren Pearl and late Mrs A. L. Pearl; three *d*. *Educ:* Eton; Chillon Coll.; Corpus Christi, Cambridge. BA 1934, MA (Cantab), 1938. With Bovril Ltd, 1935–71, finally as Chm. Territorial Service with 5th Bn Beds and Herts Regt, 1935–; Captain, 1939, and throughout War. Chm., Tribune Investment Trust Ltd, 1951–86; Chm., Pitman Ltd, 1973–81. Chm. of Cttees, United Soc. for Christian Literature, 1949–82. High Sheriff of Bedfordshire, 1961–62; DL Beds, 1964. *Recreations:* walking, gardening, photography. *Address:* Flat 1, 28 Lennox Gardens, SW1X 0DQ. *T:*

071–584 1446; Woodleys Farm House, Melchbourne, Bedfordshire MK44 1AG. *T:* Bedford (0234) 708282.

LAWSON-TANCRED, Sir Henry, 10th Bt, *cr* 1662; JP; *b* 12 Feb. 1924; *e surv. s* of Major Sir Thomas Lawson-Tancred, 9th Bt, and Margery Elinor (*d* 1961), *d* of late A. S. Lawson, Aldborough Manor; *S* father, 1945; *m* 1st, 1950, Jean Veronica (*d* 1970), 4th and *y d* of late G. R. Foster, Stockeld Park, Wetherby, Yorks; five *s* one *d*; 2nd, 1978, Mrs Susan Drummond, *d* of Sir Kenelm Cayley, 10th Bt. *Educ:* Stowe; Jesus Coll., Cambridge. Served as Pilot in RAFVR, 1942–46. JP West Riding, 1967. *Heir: s* Andrew Peter Lawson-Tancred, *b* 18 Feb. 1952. *Address:* Aldborough Manor, Boroughbridge, Yorks YO5 9EP. *T:* Boroughbridge (0423) 322716.

LAWTHER, Prof. Patrick Joseph, CBE 1978; DSc; FRCP; Professor of Environmental and Preventive Medicine, University of London, at St Bartholomew's Hospital Medical College, 1968–81, also at London Hospital Medical College, 1976–81, now Professor Emeritus; Member, Medical Research Council Scientific Staff, 1955–81; *b* 9 March 1921; *s* of Joseph and Winefride Lawther; *m* 1944, Kathleen May Wilkowski, MB BS; two *s* one *d*. *Educ:* Carlisle and Morecambe Grammar Schs; King's Coll., London; St Bartholomew's Hosp. Med. Coll. MB BS 1950; DSc London 1971. FRCP 1963 (MRCP 1954); FFOM 1981 (MFOM 1980). St Bartholomew's Hospital: Ho. Phys., Med. Professorial Unit, 1950; Cooper & Coventson Res. Schol., 1951–53; Associate Chief Asst, 1952–62; Hon. Cons. and Phys.-in-Charge, Dept of Envir. and Prev. Med., 1962–81; Consulting Physician, 1981–. Director, MRC Air Pollution Unit (later Envir. Hazards Unit), 1955–77; Head of Clinical Sect., MRC Toxicology Unit, 1977–81. Cons. Expert, WHO, 1960–; Civilian Cons. in Envir. Medicine, RN, 1975–. Chairman: DHSS Cttee on Med. Aspects of Contamination of Air and Soil, 1973–83; DHSS Working Party on Lead and Health, 1978–80; Environmental Dirs Gp, MRC, 1981–85; Cttee on Environmental and Occupational Health, MRC, 1985–; Assessor, Inquiry on Lorries, People and Environment, (Armitage Inquiry), 1979–80. Pres., Nat. Soc. for Clean Air, 1975–77. Sir Arthur Thomson Vis. Prof., Univ. of Birmingham, 1975–76; RCP Marc Daniels Lectr, 1970; Harben Lectr, RIPH&H, 1970; Guymer Meml Lectr, St Thomas' Hosp., 1979. RSA Silver Medal, 1964; Acad. Nat. de Médecine Bronze Medal, 1972; RCP Bissett Hawkins Medal, 1974; RSM Edwin Stevens Gold Medal, 1975. *Publications:* various papers and chapters in books relating to environmental and occupational medicine. *Recreations:* almost everything. *Address:* Apple Trees, Church Road, Purley, Surrey CR2 3QQ. *T:* 01–660 6398. *Club:* Surrey CCC.

LAWTON, Alistair; *see* Lawton, J. A.

LAWTON, Prof. Denis; Chairman, University of London School Examinations Board; *b* 5 April 1931; *s* of William Benedict Lawton and Ruby (*née* Evans); *m* 1953, Joan Weston; two *s*. *Educ:* St Ignatius Coll.; Univ. of London Goldsmiths' Coll. (BA); Univ. of London Inst. of Education (PhD). Asst Master, Erith Grammar Sch., 1958–61; Head of English/Housemaster, Bacon's Sch., SE1, 1961–63; University of London Institute of Education: Research Officer, 1963–64; Lectr in Sociology, 1964–67; Sen. Lectr in Curriculum Studies, 1967–72; Reader in Education, 1972–74; Professor of Education, 1974; Dep. Dir, 1978–83; Dir, 1983–89. Hon. Fellow, College of Preceptors, 1983. *Publications:* Social Class, Language and Education, 1968; Social Change, Education Theory and Curriculum Planning, 1973; Class, Culture and the Curriculum, 1975; Social Justice and Education, 1977; The Politics of the School Curriculum, 1980; An Introduction to Teaching and Learning, 1981; Curriculum Studies and Educational Planning, 1983; (with P. Gordon) HMI, 1987; Education, Culture and the National Curriculum, 1989. *Recreations:* walking German Shepherd dogs, photographing bench-ends, sampling real ale, music. *Address:* Laun House, Laundry Lane, Nazeing, Essex EN9 2DY.

LAWTON, Prof. Sir Frank (Ewart), Kt 1981; DDS; FDSRCS; Professor of Operative Dental Surgery, University of Liverpool, 1956–80, now Emeritus Professor; *b* 23 Oct. 1915; *s* of Hubert Ralph Lawton and Agnes Elizabeth (*née* Heath); *m* 1943, Muriel Leonora Bacon; one *s* one *d*. *Educ:* Univ. of Liverpool (BDS 1937); Northwestern Univ., Chicago (DDS 1948). FDSRCS 1948. Lectr, 1939, and Dir of Dental Educn, 1957–80, Univ. of Liverpool. President: BDA, 1973–74; GDC, 1979–89. Editor, Internat. Dental Jl, 1963–81. Hon. DDSc Newcastle, 1981; Hon. DDS Birmingham, 1982; Hon. DSc Manchester, 1984. *Publications:* (ed with Ed Farmer) Stones Oral and Dental Diseases, 1966; contrib. scientific and prof. jls. *Recreation:* music. *Address:* Newcroft, Castle Bolton, Leyburn, N Yorks DL8 4EX. *T:* Wensleydale (0969) 22802.

LAWTON, Rt. Hon. Sir Frederick (Horace), PC 1972; Kt 1961; a Lord Justice of Appeal, 1972–86; *b* 21 Dec. 1911; *o s* of William John Lawton, OBE; *m* 1937, Doreen (*née* Wilton) (*d* 1979); two *s*. *Educ:* Battersea Grammar Sch.; Corpus Christi Coll., Cambridge (Hon. Fellow, 1968). Barrister, Inner Temple, 1935; Bencher, 1961. Served with London Irish Rifles, 1939–41; invalided out of Army, 1941, and returned to practice at the Bar. QC 1957; Judge of the High Court of Justice, Queen's Bench Div., 1961–72. Recorder of City of Cambridge, 1957–61; Dep. Chm., Cornwall QS, 1968–71. Member: Bar Council, 1957–61; Departmental Cttee on Proceedings before Examining Justices, 1957–58; Standing Cttee on Criminal Law Revision, 1959–86 (Chm., 1977–86); Inter-departmental Cttee on Court of Criminal Appeal, 1964–65; Chm., Adv. Cttee on Legal Educn, 1976–86. Presiding Judge, Western Circuit, 1970–72. President, British Academy of Forensic Sciences, 1964. *Address:* 1 The Village, Skelton, York YO3 6XX. *T:* York (0904) 470441. *Clubs:* Garrick; Yorkshire (York).

LAWTON, Harold Walter, MA; Docteur de l'Université de Paris; Officier d'Académie; Emeritus Professor, University of Sheffield, since 1964; *b* Stoke-on-Trent, 27 July 1899; *y s* of late William T. C. and Alice Lawton; *m* 1933, Bessie (*d* 1991), *y d* of T. C. Pate; two *s* one *d*. *Educ:* Middle Sch., Newcastle under Lyme; Rhyl Grammar Sch.; Universities of Wales and Paris. BA Hons (Wales) 1921; MA (Wales) 1923; Fellow University of Wales, 1923–26; Docteur de l'Univ. de Paris, 1926. University College, Southampton: Lecturer in French, 1926–37; Professor of French, 1937–50; Dean of Faculty of Arts, 1945–49; first Warden of New, later Connaught, Hall, 1930–33; University of Sheffield: Professor of French, 1950–64; Warden of Ranmoor House, 1957–63; Deputy Pro-Vice-Chancellor, 1958–61; Pro-Vice-Chancellor, 1961–64. Transcriber, the Gladstone Diaries, 1933–36. Médaille d'Argent de la Reconnaissance Française, 1946; Officier d'Académie, 1948. *Publications:* Térence en France au XVIe Siècle: éditions et traductions (Paris), 1926; repr. 1970; Handbook of French Renaissance Dramatic Theory, 1950, repr. 1972; J. du Bellay, Poems, selected with introduction and notes, 1961; Térence en France au XVIe Siècle: imitation et influence, 1972; articles and reviews to British and French periodicals. *Address:* 1 The Pastures, Toll Bar, Cottesmore, near Oakham, Leics LE15 7DZ. *T:* Oakham (0572) 812265.

LAWTON, (John) Alistair, CBE 1981; DL; with Sea Properties Ltd, since 1955; *b* 1 Oct. 1929; *s* of Richard Geoffrey Lawton and Emma Lawton; *m* 1952, Iris Lilian Barthorpe; one *s* two *d*. *Educ:* Crewkerne Sch., Somerset. Southern Rhodesia Govt, 1946–55. Member: Deal Borough Council, 1956–74 (Mayor, 1966–68); Kent County Council, 1966–89 (Chm., 1977–79); Chairman: Kent Police Authority, 1987–89; SE Kent HA, 1988–. Comr, Manpower Services Commn, 1983–85. Treas., Kent CCC, 1988–. DL Kent, 1983. Hon. DCL Kent, 1982. *Recreations:* cricket, Rugby (non-participating now). *Address:* 6 Archery Square, Walmer, Deal, Kent CT14 7HP. *T:* Deal (0304) 375060.

LAWTON, Ven. John Arthur; Rector of Winwick, 1969–87; Archdeacon of Warrington, 1970–81, Archdeacon Emeritus since 1986; *b* 19 Jan. 1913; *s* of Arthur and Jennie Lawton; unmarried. *Educ:* Rugby; Fitzwilliam House, Cambridge (MA); Cuddesdon Theological College, Oxford. Curate, St Dunstan, Edgehill, Liverpool, 1937–40; Vicar of St Anne, Wigan, 1940–56; Vicar of St Luke, Southport, 1956–60; Vicar of Kirkby, Liverpool, 1960–69; Canon Diocesan of Liverpool, 1963–87. *Address:* 32 Ringwood Close, Gorse Covert, Warrington WA3 6TQ. *T:* Warrington (0925) 818561.

LAWTON, Prof. John Hartley, FRS 1989; Professor of Community Ecology, and Director, Interdisciplinary Research Centre in Population Biology, Imperial College of Science, Technology and Medicine, University of London, since 1989; *b* 24 Sept. 1943; *s* of Frank Hartley Lawton and Mary Lawton; *m* 1966, Dorothy (*née* Grimshaw); one *s* one *d*. *Educ:* Balshaw's Grammar Sch., Leyland, Lancs; University Coll. and Dept of Zoology, Univ. of Durham (BSc, PhD). Res. Student, Univ. of Durham, 1965–68; Deptl Demonstrator in Animal Ecology, Oxford Univ., 1968–71; College Lectr in Zoology, St Anne's and Lincoln Colls, Oxford, 1970–71; University of York: Lectr, 1971–78; Sen. Lectr, 1978–82; Reader, 1982–85; Personal Chair, 1985–89. Mem., Royal Commn on Envmtl Pollution, 1989–. *Publications:* Insects on Plants: community patterns and mechanisms (with D. R. Strong and T. R. E. Southwood), 1984; over 150 sci. papers in specialist jls. *Recreations:* bird watching, natural history photography, travel, gardening, walking. *Address:* 21 Lime Avenue, York YO3 0BT. *T:* York (0344) 424873; 17 Course Road, Ascot, Berks SL5 7HQ. *T:* Ascot (0344) 26819.

LAWTON, Louis David, QC 1973; Barrister-at-Law; a Recorder of the Crown Court, since 1972; *b* 15 Oct. 1936; *m* 1959, Helen Margaret (*née* Gair); one *s* two *d*. *Educ:* Repton Sch.; Sidney Sussex Coll., Cambridge (MA). Called to Bar, Lincoln's Inn, 1959; Bencher, Lincoln's Inn, 1981. Mem. Criminal Injuries Compensation Bd, 1981–83. *Address:* 2 Harcourt Buildings, Temple, EC4. *Club:* United Oxford & Cambridge University.

LAWTON, Philip Charles Fenner, CBE 1967; DFC 1941; Group Director and Chairman, BEA, 1972–73; Member: British Airways Board, 1972–73; Board, BOAC, 1972–73; *b* Highgate, London, 18 Sept. 1912; *o s* of late Charles Studdert Lawton and late Mabel Harriette Lawton; *m* 1941, Emma Letitia Gertrude, *y d* of late Lieut-Colonel Sir Henry Kenyon Stephenson, 1st Bt, DSO, and Frances, Hassop Hall, Bakewell, Derbyshire; one *s* one *d*. *Educ:* Westminster Sch. Solicitor, 1934–39. Joined AAF, 1935. Served War of 1939–45 (despatches twice, Group Captain): Pilot with 604 Aux. Sqdn (night fighters), 1939–41; Staff Officer HQ, Fighter Command, 1942; Station Commander, RAF Predannock; RAF Portreath; RAF Cranfield and Special Duties for Inspector-General, RAF, 1943–45. Joined BEA, 1946; Commercial and Sales Dir, 1947–71, Mem. Corporation 1964, Exec. Bd Member 1971; Chm., BEA Airtours, 1969–72. LLB Hons Degree, 1933; FCIT (MInstT 1955). *Address:* Fenner House, Glebe Way, Wisborough Green, West Sussex. *T:* Wisborough Green (0403) 700606; 17 Pembroke Walk, W8. *T:* 071–937 3091. *Club:* RAF.

LAXNESS, Halldor Kiljan; Icelandic writer; *b* 23 April 1902; *s* of Gudjon Helgason and Sigridur Halldorsdottir, Iceland; *m* 1st, Ingibjörg Einarsdottir; one *s*; 2nd, Audur Sveinsdottir; two *d*. Awarded Nobel literary prize, 1955; Sonning Prize, 1969. *Publications* (many of which have been translated into English) include: *novels:* Barn náttúrunnar, 1919; Undir Helgahnúk (Under the Holy Mountain), 1924; Vefarinn mikli frá Kasmir (The Great Weaver from Kashmir), 1927; Salka Valka, 1934 (first published as þu vínviður hreini, 1931, and Fuglinn í fjörunni, 1932); Sjálfstætt fólk (Independent People), 2 vols, 1934–35; Ljós heimsins, 1937, Höll sumarlandsins, 1938, Hús skáldsins, 1939, Fegurð himinsins, 1940 (these four republished as Heimsljos (The Light of the World), 2 vols, 1955); Íslandsklukkan, 1943; Hið ljósa man, 1944; Eldur í Kaupinhafn, 1946; Atómstöðin (The Atom Station), 1948; Gerpla (Happy Warriors), 1952; Brekkukotsannáll (Fish Can Sing), 1957; Paradísarheimt (Paradise Reclaimed), 1960; Kristnihald undir Jökli, 1968; Guðsgjafathula, 1972; *autobiography:* Skáldatími, 1963; Í túninu heima, 1975; Úngur eg var, 1976; Sjömeistarasagan, 1978; Grikklandsárið, 1980; collections of short stories, essays, poems and plays; translations into Icelandic include: Farewell to Arms by Ernest Hemingway; Candide by Voltaire. *Address:* PO Box 664, Reykjavik, Iceland.

LAY, Richard Neville; Chairman, Debenham Tewson & Chinnocks Holdings plc and subsidiary companies, since 1987; *b* 18 Oct. 1938; *s* of Edward John Lay and late Nellie Lay; *m* 1964; one *s* one *d*. *Educ:* Whitgift School. FRICS. Partner, Debenham Tewson & Chinnocks, 1965–87. Mem., West End Board, Sun Alliance and London Insurance Group, 1975–; Surveyor, Armourers' and Brasiers' Co., 1983–. Trustee, Tate Gall. Foundn, 1989–. Governor, Belmont Sch., Surrey, 1983–88. *Recreations:* gardening, walking. *Address:* 15 Clareville Grove, SW7 5AU. *T:* 071–408 1161. *Club:* Royal Automobile.

LAYARD, Rear-Adm. Michael Henry Gordon, CBE 1982; Director General, Naval Manpower and Training, since 1990; *b* Sri Lanka, 3 Jan. 1936; *s* of late Edwin Henry Frederick and Doris Christian Gordon (*née* Spence); *m* 1966, Elspeth Horsley Fisher; two *s*. *Educ:* Pangbourne Coll.; RN Coll., Dartmouth. Joined RN, 1954; specialised in aviation, 1958; Fighter Pilot, 1960–72; Air Warfare Instructor, 1964; Commanded: 899 Naval Air Sqn, in HMS Eagle, 1970–71; HMS Lincoln, 1971–72; ndc, 1974–75; Directorate, Naval Air Warfare, MoD, 1975–77; Comdr (Air), HMS Ark Royal, 1977–78; CSO (Air), FONAC, 1979–82; Sen. Naval Officer, SS Atlantic Conveyor, Falklands conflict, 1982 (CBE); Commanded: RNAS Culdrose, 1982–84; HMS Cardiff, 1984–85; Task Gp Comdr, Persian Gulf, 1984; Dep. Dir, Naval Warfare (Air), MoD, 1985–88; Flag Officer Naval Aviation (formerly Air Comd), 1988–90. Chm. of Trustees, FAA Mus., 1988–. Mem., FAA Officers' Assoc. Chevalier Bretvin, 1984. *Recreations:* painting, sailing, music, history. *Address:* c/o Lloyds Bank plc, Cheapside, Langport, Somerset. *Clubs:* Commonwealth Trust, Royal Navy of 1765 and 1785; Royal Navy Sailing Association; Royal Navy Golfing Society (Pres.).

LAYARD, Prof. (Peter) Richard (Grenville); Professor of Economics, London School of Economics, since 1980, and Director, Centre for Economic Performance, since 1990; Chairman of Employment Institute, since 1987; *b* 15 March 1934; *s* of Dr John Layard and Doris Layard. *Educ:* Eton Coll.; King's Coll., Cambridge (BA); London School of Economics (MScEcon). History Master: Woodberry Down Sch., 1959–60; Forest Hill Sch., 1960–61; Senior Research Officer, Robbins Cttee on Higher Educn, 1961–63; London School of Economics: Dep. Director, Higher Educn Research Unit, 1964–74 (part-time from 1968); Lectr in Economics, 1968–75; Reader in the Economics of Labour, 1975–80; Hd, Centre for Labour Econs, 1974–90. Mem., UGC, 1985–89. *Publications:* (jtly) The Causes of Graduate Unemployment in India, 1969; (jtly) The Impact of Robbins: Expansion in Higher Education, 1969; (jtly) Qualified Manpower and Economic Performance: An Inter-Plant Study in the Electrical Engineering Industry, 1971; (ed) Cost-Benefit Analysis, 1973; (jtly) Microeconomic Theory, 1978; (jtly) The Causes of Poverty, 1978; More Jobs, Less Inflation, 1982; How to Beat Unemployment, 1986; (jtly) Handbook of Labour Economics, 1986; (jtly) The Performance of the British

Economy, 1988. *Recreations:* walking, tennis, the clarinet. *Address:* 18 Provost Road, NW3. *T:* 071–722 6347.

LAYCRAFT, Hon. James Herbert; Chief Justice of Alberta, since 1985; *b* 5 Jan. 1924; *s* of George Edward Laycraft and Hattie Cogswell Laycraft; *m* 1948, Helen Elizabeth Bradley; one *s* one *d*. *Educ:* University of Alberta (BA, LLB 1951). Admitted to Bar, 1952; law practice, 1952–75; Trial Div. Judge, Supreme Court of Alberta, 1975; Judge, Court of Appeal, Alberta, 1979–85. Hon. LLD Calgary, 1986. *Publications:* articles in Canadian Bar Review and Alberta Law Review. *Recreations:* outdoor activities. *Address:* 8952 Bayridge Drive SW, Calgary, Alberta, Canada; Court House, 611 4th Street SW, Calgary. *T:* (403) 297 7434. *Club:* Ranchman's (Calgary).

LAYDEN, Anthony Michael; HM Diplomatic Service; Counsellor (Economic and Commercial), Copenhagen, since 1991; *b* 27 July 1946; *s* of Sheriff Michael Layden, SSC, TD and Eileen Mary Layden; *m* 1969, Josephine Mary McGhee; three *s* one *d*. *Educ:* Holy Cross Academy, Edinburgh; Edinburgh Univ. (LLB Hons Law and Econ. 1968). Lieut, 15th (Scottish Volunteer) Bn, Parachute Regt, 1966–69. Foreign Office, 1968; MECAS, Lebanon, 1969; Jedda, 1971; Rome, 1973; FCO, Middle East, Rhodesia, Personnel Ops Depts, 1977–82; Head of Chancery, Jedda, 1982–85; Hong Kong Dept, FCO, 1985–87; Counsellor and Head of Chancery, Muscat, 1987–91. *Recreations:* sailing, walking, music, bridge. *Address:* c/o Foreign and Commonwealth Office, SW1A 2AH.
See also P. J. Layden.

LAYDEN, Sir John, Kt 1988; JP; miner; Councillor, Rotherham Metropolitan Borough Council, since 1974, Leader since 1974; *b* 16 Jan. 1926; *m* 1949, Dorothy Brenda McLean; two *s*. Joined Labour Party, 1944. Elected to Maltby UDC, 1953 (Chm., 1959–60 and 1970–71). Chm., Assoc. of Metropolitan Authorities, 1984–91; Vice-Chm., British Section, IULA/CEM, 1974–; Mem., Bd of Trustees, Municipal Mutual Insurance Co., 1983–. Freeman, City of London, 1988. JP Rotherham Borough, 1965. *Recreations:* music, sport (particularly football). *Address:* 9 Lilac Grove, Maltby, Rotherham, South Yorkshire S66 8BX. *T:* Rotherham (0709) 812481.

LAYDEN, Patrick John, TD 1981; Scottish Parliamentary Counsel and Senior Assistant Legal Secretary, Lord Advocate's Department, since 1987; *b* 27 June 1949; *s* of Sheriff Michael Layden, SSC, TD and Eileen Mary Layden; *m* 1984, Patricia Mary Bonnar; two *s* one *d*. *Educ:* Holy Cross Acad., Edinburgh; Edinburgh Univ. (LLB Hons). Called to the Scottish Bar, 1973; Dep. Scottish Parly Counsel and Asst Legal Sec., Lord Advocate's Dept, 1977–87. Univ. of Edinburgh OTC, 1967–71; 2/52 Lowland Vol., TA, 1971–77; 1/51 Highland Vol., 1977–81 (OC London Scottish, 1978–81); OC 73 Ord. Co. (V), 1981–84. *Recreations:* reading, walking. *Address:* 38 Milner Road, Kingston upon Thames, Surrey KT1 2AU. *T:* 081–541 1586.
See also A. M. Layden.

LAYE, Evelyn, CBE 1973; actress; singer; *b* London, 10 July 1900; *o d* of Gilbert Laye and Evelyn Froud; *m* 1st, 1926, Sonnie Hale (from whom she obtained a divorce, 1931); 2nd, 1934, Frank Lawton (*d* 1969). *Educ:* Folkestone; Brighton. Made first appearance on stage, Theatre Royal, Brighton, 1915, in Mr Wu. First London appearance in The Beauty Spot, Gaiety, 1918; first big success in title-role of The Merry Widow, Daly's, 1923; subsequently starred in London in Madame Pompadour, Daly's, 1923; The Dollar Princess, Daly's, 1925; Cleopatra, Daly's, 1925; Betty in Mayfair, Adelphi, 1925; Merely Molly, Adelphi, 1926; Princess Charming, Palace, 1927; Lilac Time, Daly's, 1927; Blue Eyes, Piccadilly, 1928; The New Moon, Drury Lane, 1929; Bitter Sweet, His Majesty's, 1930; Helen!, Adelphi, 1932; Give Me A Ring, Hippodrome, 1933; Paganini, Lyceum, 1937; Lights Up, Savoy, 1940; The Belle of New York, Coliseum, 1942; Sunny River, Piccadilly, 1943; Cinderella, His Majesty's, 1943; Three Waltzes, Prince's, 1945; Cinderella, Palladium, 1948; Two Dozen Red Roses, Lyric, 1949; Peter Pan, Scala, 1953; Wedding in Paris, Hippodrome, 1954–56; Silver Wedding, Cambridge, 1957; The Amorous Prawn, Saville/Piccadilly, 1959–62; Never Too Late, Prince of Wales, 1964; The Circle, Savoy, 1965; Strike A Light!, Piccadilly, 1966; Let's All Go Down the Strand, Phoenix, 1967; Charlie Girl, Adelphi, 1969; Phil the Fluter, Palace, 1969; No Sex, Please-We're British, Strand, 1971–73; A Little Night Music (revival), Exeter, 1979, 1981, on tour, 1979, Nottingham, 1980–81, 1982; one woman show, 1983; Babes in the Wood, Chichester, 1984, Richmond, 1985. First New York appearance in Bitter Sweet, Ziegfeld Theatre, 1929; subsequently on Broadway in Sweet Aloes, Booth, 1936; Between the Devil, Majestic, 1937. Film début in silent production, The Luck of the Navy, 1927. Films include: One Heavenly Night (Hollywood), 1932; Waltz Time, 1933; Princess Charming, 1934; Evensong, 1935; The Night is Young (Hollywood), 1936; Make Mine A Million, 1959; Theatre of Death, 1967; Within and Without, 1969; Say Hello to Yesterday, 1971. Numerous broadcasts and television appearances incl. rôles in Dizzy, Tales of the Unexpected, The Gay Lord Quex, 1983; My Family and Other Animals, 1987. *Publication:* Boo, to my Friends (autobiography), 1958. *Address:* c/o Jeremy Conway Ltd, 109 Jermyn Street, SW1Y 6HB.

LAYFIELD, Sir Frank (Henry Burland Willoughby), Kt 1976; QC 1967; *b* Toronto, 9 Aug. 1921; *s* of late H. D. Layfield; *m* 1965, Irene Patricia, *d* of late Captain J. D. Harvey, RN (retired); one *s* one *d*. *Educ:* Sevenoaks Sch. Army, 1940–46. Called to the Bar, Gray's Inn, 1954, Bencher, 1974; a Recorder, 1979–82. Chairman: Inquiry into Greater London Development Plan, 1970–73; Cttee of Inquiry into Local Government Finance, 1974–76; Inspector, Inquiry into Sizewell B Nuclear Power Station, 1983–85. Associate, RICS, 1977; Hon. FSVA 1978; Hon. Fellow, Coll. of Estate Management, 1982. Gold Medal, Lincoln Inst. of Land Policy, 1984. *Publications:* (with A. E. Telling) Planning Applications, Appeals and Inquiries, 1953; (with A. E. Telling) Applications for Planning Payments, 1955; Engineering Contracts, 1956. *Recreations:* walking, tennis. *Address:* 2 Mitre Court Buildings, Temple, EC4Y 7BX. *T:* 071–583 1355. *Clubs:* Garrick, United Oxford & Cambridge University.

LAYMAN, Rear-Adm. Christopher Hope, CB 1991; DSO 1982; LVO 1977; Assistant Director (Communications and Information Systems), International Military Staff, NATO, Brussels, 1988–91; *b* 9 March 1938; *s* of late Captain H. F. H. Layman, DSO, RN and Elizabeth Hughes; *m* 1964, Katharine Romer Ascherson; one *s* one *d*. *Educ:* Winchester. Joined Royal Navy, 1956; specialised Communications and Electronic Warfare, 1966; commanded HM Ships: Hubberston, 1968–70; Lynx, 1972–74; Exec. Officer, HM Yacht Britannia, 1976–78; Captain, 7th Frigate Sqn, 1981–83; commanded HM Ships: Argonaut, 1981–82; Cleopatra, 1982–83; Invincible, 1984–86; Commander, British Forces Falkland Islands, 1986–87. *Publication:* Man of Letters, 1990. *Recreations:* fishing, archaeology. *Address:* c/o Drummonds, 49 Charing Cross, SW1A 2DX. *Club:* New (Edinburgh).

LAYTON, family name of **Baron Layton.**

LAYTON, 3rd Baron *cr* 1947, of Danehill; **Geoffrey Michael Layton;** Director, The Toxbox Co. Ltd, since 1986; *b* 18 July 1947; *s* of 2nd Baron Layton and of Dorothy Rose, *d* of Albert Luther Cross; *S* father, 1989; *m* 1st, 1969, Viviane Cracco (marr. diss. 1970); 2nd, 1989, Caroline Jane Soulis. *Educ:* St Paul's School; Stanford Univ., California; Univ. of Southern California. *Recreation:* riding. *Heir: uncle* Hon. David Layton, MBE [*b* 5 July 1914; *m* 1st, 1939, Elizabeth (marr. diss. 1972), *d* of Robert Gray; two *s* one *d*; 2nd, 1972, Joy Parkinson].
See also Hon. C. W. Layton.

LAYTON, Hon. Christopher Walter; Director, World Order Project, Federal Trust, since 1987; Editor, Alliance, 1982–83, Associate Editor, New Democrat, 1983–85; *b* 31 Dec. 1929; *s* of 1st Baron Layton; *m* 1st, 1952, Anneliese Margaret, *d* of Joachim von Thadden, Hanover (marr. diss. 1957); one *s* one *d*; 2nd, 1961, Margaret Ann, *d* of Leslie Moon, Molesey, Surrey; three *d*. *Educ:* Oundle; King's Coll., Cambridge. Intelligence Corps, 1948–49; ICI Ltd, 1952; The Economist Intelligence Unit, 1953–54; Editorial writer, European affairs,The Economist, 1954–62; Economic Adviser to Liberal Party, 1962–69; Dir, Centre for European Industrial Studies, Bath Univ., 1968–71; Commission of European Communities: Chef de Cabinet to Commissioner Spinelli, 1971–73; Dir, Computer Electronics, Telecomms and Air Transp. Equipment Manufg, Directorate-Gen. of Internal Market and Industrial Affairs, 1973–81; Hon. Director-General, EEC, 1981–. Contested (SDP) London W, European Parly Elecn, 1984. *Publications:* Transatlantic Investment, 1966; European Advanced Technology, 1968; Cross-frontier Mergers in Europe 1970; (jtly) Industry and Europe, 1971; (jtly) Ten Innovations: International Study on Development Technology and the Use of Qualified Scientists and Engineers in Ten Industries, 1972; Europe and the Global Crisis, 1987; A Step Beyond Fear, 1989; The Healing of Europe, 1990. *Recreations:* painting, sculpture, healing. *Address:* 6 Northumberland Place, Richmond, Surrey TW10 6TS.

LAZARUS, Sir Peter (Esmond), KCB 1985 (CB 1975); FCIT; Member, Civil Aviation Authority, since 1986; Director, Manchester Ship Canal Co., since 1986; *b* 2 April 1926; *er s* of late Kenneth M. Lazarus and Mary R. Lazarus (*née* Halsted); *m* 1950, Elizabeth Anne Marjorie Atwell, *e d* of late Leslie H. Atwell, OBE; three *s*. *Educ:* Westminster Sch.; Wadham Coll., Oxford (Open Exhibition). Served RA, 1945–48. Entered Ministry of Transport, 1949: Secretary, London and Home Counties Traffic Advisory Cttee, 1953–57; Private Secretary to Minister, 1961–62; Asst Sec., 1962; Under-Sec., 1968–70; Under-Sec., Treasury, 1970–72; Deputy Secretary: DoE, 1973–76; Dept of Transport, 1976–82; Perm. Sec., Dept of Transport, 1982–85. Chairman: Assoc. of First Div. Civil Servants, 1969–71; Cttee for Monitoring Agreements on Tobacco Advertising and Sponsorship, 1986–91. Chm., Council, Liberal Jewish Synagogue, St John's Wood, 1972–75, and 1987–; Comdt, Jewish Lads' and Girls' Brigade, 1987–. FRSA 1981. *Recreations:* music, reading. *Address:* 28 Woodside Avenue, N6 4SS. *T:* 081–883 3186. *Club:* Athenæum.

LAZENBY, Prof. Alec, AO 1988; FTS, FIBiol; Vice-Chancellor, University of Tasmania, 1982–91; *b* 4 March 1927; *s* of G. and E. Lazenby; *m* 1957, Ann Jennifer, *d* of R. A. Hayward; one *s* two *d*. *Educ:* Wath on Dearne Grammar Sch.; University Coll. of Wales, Aberystwyth. BSc 1949, MSc 1952, Wales; MA 1954, PhD 1959, ScD 1985, Cantab. Scientific Officer, Welsh Plant Breeding Station, 1949–53; Demonstr in Agricultural Botany, 1953–58, Lectr in Agricultural Botany, 1958–65, Univ. of Cambridge; Fellow and Asst Tutor, Fitzwilliam Coll., Cambridge, 1962–65; Foundation Prof. of Agronomy, Univ. of New England, NSW, 1965–70, now Professor Emeritus; Vice-Chancellor, Univ. of New England, Armidale, NSW, 1970–77; Dir, Grassland Res. Inst., 1977–82. Vis. Prof., Reading Univ., 1978; Hon. Professorial Fellow, Univ. of Wales, 1979. Hon DRurSci New England, NSW, 1981. *Publications:* (jt Editor) Intensive Pasture Production, 1972; (jt Editor) Australian Field Crops, vol. I, 1975, vol. II, 1979; Australia's Plant Breeding Needs, 1986; (jt Editor) The Grass Crop, 1988; papers on: pasture plant breeding; agronomy; weed ecology, in various scientific jls. *Recreation:* golf. *Address:* University of Tasmania, Box 252C, GPO, Hobart, Tasmania 7001, Australia.

LEA, His Honour Christopher Gerald, MC; a Circuit Judge, 1972–90; *b* 27 Nov. 1917; *y s* of late George Percy Lea, Franche, Kidderminster, Worcs; *m* 1952, Susan Elizabeth Dorrien Smith, *d* of Major Edward Pendarves Dorrien Smith, Greatwood, Restronguet, Falmouth, Cornwall; two *s* one *d* (and one *d* decd). *Educ:* Charterhouse; RMC, Sandhurst. Commissioned into XX The Lancashire Fusiliers, 1937, and served with Regt in UK until 1939. Served War of 1939–45 (despatches, MC): with Lancashire Fusiliers, No 11 Special Air Service Commando, and Parachute Regt in France, Italy and Malaya. Post-war service in Indonesia, Austria and UK; retired, 1948. Called to Bar, Inner Temple, 1948; Oxford Circuit. Mem. Nat. Assistance Bd Appeal Tribunal (Oxford Area), 1961–63; Mem. Mental Health Review Tribunal (Oxford Region), 1962–68, 1983–July 1992. A Metropolitan Magistrate, 1968–72; Dep. Chm., Berks QS, 1968–71. *Address:* Simms Farm House, Mortimer, Berks RG7 2JP. *T:* Mortimer (0734) 332360. *Club:* English-Speaking Union.

LEA, David Edward, OBE 1978; Assistant General Secretary of the Trades Union Congress, since 1977; *b* 2 Nov. 1937; *s* of Edward Cunliffe Lea and Lilian May Lea. *Educ:* Farnham Grammar Sch.; Christ's Coll., Cambridge. Economist Intelligence Unit, 1961; Economic Dept, TUC, 1964, Asst Sec., 1967, Sec. 1970. Jt Sec., TUC-Labour Party Liaison Cttee, 1972–; Secretary: TUC Cttee on European Strategy, 1989–; Envmt Action Gp, 1989–. Chm., Econ. Cttee, ETUC, 1980–; Member: Royal Commn on the Distribution of Income and Wealth, 1974–79; Adv. Gp on Channel Tunnel and Cross-Channel Services, 1974–75; Cttee of Inquiry on Industrial Democracy, 1975–77; Energy Commn, 1977–79; Retail Prices Index Adv. Cttee, 1977–; Delors Cttee on Economic and Social Concepts in the Community, 1977–79; NEDC Cttee on Finance for Investment, 1978–; Kreisky Commn on Unemployment in Europe, 1986–89; Franco-British Council, 1982–; Expert Adviser, UN Commn on Transnational Corporations, 1977–81; Governor, NIESR, 1981–. *Publications:* Trade Unionism, 1966; contrib. The Multinational Enterprise, 1971; Industrial Democracy (TUC), 1974; Keynes Plus: a participatory economy (ETUC), 1979. *Address:* 17 Ormonde Mansions, 106 Southampton Row, WC1B 4BP. *T:* 071–405 6237; South Court, Crondall, near Farnham, Surrey GU9 7JJ. *T:* Farnham (0252) 850711.

LEA, Vice-Adm. Sir John (Stuart Crosbie), KBE 1979; retired; Director, GEC Marine & Industrial Gears Ltd, 1986–88 (Chm., 1980–86); *b* 4 June 1923; *m* 1947, Patricia Anne Thoseby; one *s* two *d*. *Educ:* Boxgrove Sch., Guildford; Shrewsbury Sch.; RNEC, Keyham. Entered RN, 1941; Cruisers Sheffield and Glasgow, 1943; RNEC, 1942–45; HMS Birmingham, 1945; entered Submarines, 1946; HMS/Ms Talent, Tireless, Aurochs, Explorer; Sen. Engr, HMS Forth (Depot Ship), 1952–53; on Staff, RNEC, 1954–57; psc 1958; Sqdn Engr Officer, 2nd Destroyer Sqdn and HMS Daring, 1959–61; Staff of CinC Portsmouth, 1961–62; Naval Staff in Ops Div., 1963–65; Engr Officer, HMS Centaur, 1966; Staff of Flag Officer Submarines; Dep. Supt, Clyde Submarine Base, 1967–68; idc 1969; Dir of Naval Admin. Planning, 1970–71; Cdre HMS Nelson, 1972–75; Asst Chief of Fleet Support, 1976–77; Dir Gen., Naval Manpower and Trng, 1977–80. Comdr 1957; Captain 1966; Rear-Adm. 1976; Vice-Adm. 1978. Chairman: Portsmouth Naval Heritage Trust, 1983–87; Regular Forces Employment Assoc., 1986–89; Hayling Island Horticultural Soc., 1980–; Pres., Hants Autistic Soc., 1988–. Trustee, Hayling Island Community Centre, 1981–. Master, Worshipful Co. of Plumbers, 1988–89. *Recreations:* walking, woodwork, gardening. *Address:* Springfield, Brights Lane, Hayling Island, Hants PO11 0JX.

LEA, Sir Thomas (William), 5th Bt *cr* 1892, of The Larches, Kidderminster and Sea Grove, Dawlish; *b* 6 Sept. 1973; *s* of Sir Julian Lea, 4th Bt and of Gerry Valerie, *d* of late Captain Gibson C. Fahnestock; *S* father, 1990. *Educ:* Uppingham Sch. *Heir: b* Alexander Julian Lea, *b* 28 Oct. 1978. *Address:* Bachelors Hall, Hundon, Sudbury, Suffolk C10 8DY.

LEACH, Allan William, FLA; Director-General and Librarian, National Library for the Blind, since 1982; *b* 9 May 1931; *yr s* of Frank Leach, MBE and Margaret Ann Bennett; *m* 1962, Betty, *e d* of William George Gadsby and Doris Cree; one *s* one *d. Educ:* Watford Grammar Sch.; Loughborough Coll. BA Open; DPA London. Various posts with Hertfordshire County Library, 1948–59; Librarian, RAF Sch. of Educn, 1949–51; Regional Librarian, Warwickshire County Libr., 1959–65; County Librarian, Bute County Libr., 1965–71; Librarian and Curator, Ayr Burgh, 1971–74; Dir of Library Services, Kyle and Carrick District, 1974–82. Mem., Standing Cttee, Section of Libraries for the Blind, IFLA, 1983– (Chm., 1985–87; Ed., Newsletter, 1985–). Editor: Rickmansworth Historian, 1961–66; Ayrshire Collections, 1973–82. *Publications:* Begin Here, 1966; Rothesay Tramways, a brief history, 1969; Round old Ayr (with R. Brash and G. S. Copeland), 1972; Libraries in Ayr, 1975; Looking Ahead, 1987; articles on libraries, local history, literature and educn. *Recreations:* music, the countryside, books, people. *Address:* 4 Windsor Road, Hazel Grove, Stockport, Cheshire SK7 4SW. *T:* 061–483 6418.

LEACH, (Charles Guy) Rodney, MA; Director, Jardine Matheson Holdings Ltd, since 1984; Chairman, Jardine Insurance Brokers, since 1984; *b* 1 June 1934; *s* of late Charles Harold Leach and Nora Eunice Ashworth; *m*; two *s* three *d. Educ:* Harrow; Balliol Coll., Oxford (1st Cl. Hon. Mods, 1st Cl. Lit. Hum.). N. M. Rothschild & Sons, 1963–76: Partner, 1968; Dir, 1970; Director: Rothschild Investment Trust, 1970–76; Trade Development Bank, 1976–83; Matheson & Co., 1983–; Hong Kong Land, 1985–; Dairy Farm, 1987–; Mandarin Oriental, 1987–; Kwik Save Gp, 1987–; Safra Republic Hldgs. Trustee, PO Staff Superannuation Fund, 1976–; Chm., Res. Cttee, Mental Health Foundn, 1984–. *Recreations:* the humanities, tennis, bridge. *Address:* 3 Lombard Street, EC3V 9AQ. *T:* 071–528 4000. *Clubs:* White's, Portland, Queen's, Vanderbilt.

LEACH, Clive William; Managing Director, Yorkshire Television plc, since 1988; *b* 4 Dec. 1934; *s* of Stanley and Laura Leach; *m* 1st, 1958, Audrey (*née* Parker) (*d* 1978); three *s*; 2nd, 1980, Stephanie (*née* McGinn); one *s. Educ:* Sir John Leman Grammar Sch., Beccles, Suffolk. DipM. Gen. Sales Manager, Tyne Tees Television, 1968–74; Sales Dir, 1974–79, Dir of Sales and Marketing, 1979–82, Trident Television; Man. Dir, Link Television, 1982–85; Dir of Sales and Marketing, Yorkshire Television, 1985–88; Man. Dir, 1985–88, Chm., 1988–, Yorkshire Television Enterprises. Chm., Yorkshire Television Internat., 1988–; Director: ITN, 1988–; New Era Television, 1988–. *Recreations:* golf, cricket, travel. *Address:* The White House, Barkston Ash, Tadcaster, W Yorks; Yorkshire Television plc, The Television Centre, Leeds LS3 1JS. *Clubs:* MCC, Clermont; Harewood Downs Golf.

LEACH, David Andrew, OBE 1987; potter, designer, lecturer; *b* 7 May 1911; *e s* of Bernard Leach, CH, CBE, and Edith Muriel, *o d* of Dr William Evans Hoyle; *m* 1938, Mary Elizabeth Facey; three *s. Educ:* Prep. Sch., Bristol; Dauntsey's Sch., Wilts; Blundell's Sch., Devon. At age of 19, began to work in his father's pottery at St Ives, Cornwall (tuition from him and associates); Manager and Partner, 1946–55; took Manager's course, N Staffs Technical Coll., Stoke-on-Trent, to 1937; taught pottery at Dartington Hall Progressive Sch., 1933. Served War, DCLI, 1941–45. Taught at Penzance Sch. of Art and St Ives, 1945. Designed and made David Leach Electric Kiln, 1950; helped to start a pottery in Norway, 1951; in charge of Ceramic Dept, and taught, at Loughborough Coll. of Art, 1953 (later Vis. Lectr). Started workshop at Bovey Tracey, 1956; researched into glazes and changed from slipware to stoneware, 1961; now makes a large percentage of porcelain. Late Mem. Council, Craftsmen Potters Assoc. of GB (Past Chm.), late Mem. Grants Cttee of the Crafts Adv. Commn; Mem. Council, Crafts Council, 1977; Chm., Devon Guild of Craftsmen, 1986–; Adviser, Dartington Pottery Trng Workshop. Has exhibited in Europe, USA and Far East; first major one-man show, CPA, 1966; Internat. Ceramics Exhibn, 1972, and Craftsmen's Art, 1973, V&A Mus., 1973; major one-man show, NY, 1978; exhibitions in Germany (Darmstadt, Munich, Deidesheim, Sandhausen-bei-Heidelberg, and Hanover), Holland (Amsterdam), Belgium (Brussels), USA (San Francisco), Japan (Osaka) and Norway (Oslo); Joint Exhibitions: New Ashgate Gall., Farnham, 1982, 1983, (3 Generations Leach) 1986; Beaux Arts Gall., Bath, 1984; (with John Leach) Peter Dingley Gall., Stratford, 1985; Solus Exhibitions: NY, and lecture tour, USA, 1978; Washington DC, and 2nd lecture tour, USA, 1979; British Crafts Centre, London, 1979. Galerie St Martin, Cologne, 1982; St Paul's Sch., Barnes, 1982; Robert Welch Gall., Chipping Campden, 1982; Frontroom Gall., Dallas, 1983; Chestnut Gall., Bourton-on-the-Water, 1984; Century Gall., Henley-on-Thames, 1984; Castle Mus., Norwich, 1985; Galerie F15, Oslo, 1986; Elaine Potter Gall., San Francisco, 1986; Greenwich House Gall., NY, 1987; New Ashgate Gall., Farnham, 1988; Lecture demonstration tours: in USA, 1985, 1986, 1987 and 1988; in Caracas, Venezuela, 1987. Craft of the Potter, BBC, 1976. Gold Medal, Istanbul, 1967. *Publications:* David Leach: A Potter's Life, with Workshop Notes (introd. by Bernard Leach), 1977. *Address:* Lowerdown Pottery, Bovey Tracey, Devon. *T:* Bovey Tracey (0626) 833408.

LEACH, Admiral of the Fleet Sir Henry (Conyers), GCB 1978 (KCB 1977); Chairman, St Dunstan's, since 1983 (Member of Council, since 1982); *b* 18 Nov. 1923; 3rd *s* of Captain John Catterall Leach, MVO, DSO, RN and Evelyn Burrell Leach (*née* Lee), Yarner, Bovey Tracey, Devon; *m* 1958, Mary Jean (*d* 1991), *yr d* of Adm. Sir Henry McCall, KCVO, KBE, CB, DSO; two *d. Educ:* St Peter's Court, Broadstairs; RNC Dartmouth. Cadet 1937; served in: cruiser Mauritius, S Atlantic and Indian Ocean, 1941–42; battleship Duke of York, incl. Scharnhorst action, 1943–45; destroyers in Mediterranean, 1945–46; spec. Gunnery, 1947; various gunnery appts, 1948–51; Gunnery Officer, cruiser Newcastle, Far East, 1953–55; staff appts, 1955–59; comd destroyer Dunkirk, 1959–61; comd frigate Galatea as Captain (D) 27th Sqdn and Mediterranean, 1965–67; Dir of Naval Plans, 1968–70; comd Commando Ship Albion, 1970; Asst Chief of Naval Staff (Policy), 1971–73; Flag Officer First Flotilla, 1974–75; Vice-Chief of Defence Staff, 1976–77; C-in-C, Fleet, and Allied C-in-C, Channel and Eastern Atlantic, 1977–79; Chief of Naval Staff and First Sea Lord, 1979–82. First and Principal Naval ADC to the Queen, 1979–82. psc 1952; jssc 1961. President: RN Benevolent Soc., 1983–; Sea Cadets Assoc., 1984–; Naval Pres., Officers' Assoc., 1985–; Vice Pres., SSAFA, 1984. Chm. Council, King Edward VII Hosp., 1987–. Governor: Cranleigh Sch.; St Catherine's Sch., Bramley. Freeman: City of London; Shipwrights' Co.; Hon. Freeman, Merchant Taylors' Co. *Recreations:* fishing, gardening, antique furniture repair. *Address:* Wonston Lodge, Wonston, Winchester, Hants SO21 3LS.

LEACH, Norman, CMG 1964; Under-Secretary, Foreign and Commonwealth Office (Overseas Development Administration), 1970–72; *b* 8 March 1912; *s* of W. M. Leach. *Educ:* Ermysted's Gram. Sch., Skipton in Craven, Yorks; St Catharine's Coll., Cambridge (Scholar). 1st Class Hons, Pts I and II English Tripos, 1933 and 1934; Charles Oldham Shakespeare Schol., 1933. Asst Principal, Inland Revenue Dept, 1935; Under-Secretary: Ministry of Pensions and National Insurance, 1958–61; Dept of Technical Co-operation, 1961–64; ODM, 1964–70. *Address:* Low Bank, 81 Gargrave Road, Skipton in Craven, North Yorks BD23 1QN. *T:* Skipton (0756) 793719.

LEACH, Paul Arthur; General Consultant to The Law Society, 1980–81, retired; *b* 10 July 1915; *s* of Rev. Edward Leach and Edith Swannell Leach; *m* 1st, 1949, Daphne Copeland (marr. diss. 1957); one *s* one *d*; 2nd, 1958, Rachel Renée Lachmann. *Educ:* Marlborough Coll.; Keble Coll., Oxford (1st Cl. Hons BA Mod. Hist., 1937; MA 1945); Birmingham Univ. (2nd Cl. Hons LLB 1940). Law Soc. Finals, 1940; admitted Solicitor, 1946. Served War, RA, 1940–45: Staff Captain 1st AA Bde; attached SO II, RAEC, 1945–46. Private practice as solicitor, 1946–48; Talks Producer, BBC Home Talks, 1949; joined Law Soc. staff, 1950; Clerk and later Sec., Professional Purposes Cttee, 1950–71; Secretary: Future of the Profession Cttee, 1971–80; Internat. Relations Cttee, 1975–80; Dep. Sec.-Gen., 1975–80. Secretary: UK Delegn to Commn Consultative des Barreaux de la Communauté Européenne, 1975–81; Inter-Professional Gp, 1978–81; UK Vice-Pres., Union Internationale des Avocats, 1978–81. *Publications:* (ed) Guide to Professional Conduct of Solicitors, 1974; articles in Law Society's Gazette. *Recreations:* foreign travel, gardening, history, listening to classical music. *Address:* c/o 14 Cavendish Road, W4 3UH; 5333 Myrtlewood, The Meadows, Sarasota, Fla 34235, USA.

LEACH, Rodney; *see* Leach, C. G. R.

LEACH, Rodney, PhD; CEng; FRINA; FIIM; FCIM; company director; Chief Executive and Managing Director, VSEL Consortium plc, 1986–88; Chief Executive, 1985–88, and Chairman, 1986–88, Vickers Shipbuilding and Engineering Ltd; Chairman, Cammell Laird Shipbuilders Ltd, 1985–88; *b* 3 March 1932; *s* of Edward and Alice Leach; *m* 1958, Eira Mary (*née* Tuck); three *s* one *d. Educ:* Baines Grammar Sch., Poulton Le Fylde, Lancs; Birmingham Univ. (BSc, PhD). CEng, FRINA 1987; FCIM (FInstM 1972); FIIM 1987. Radiation Physicist, Nuclear Power Plant Co. Ltd, 1957; Physicist, UKAEA, 1960; Sen. Physicist, South of Scotland Electricity Board, 1963; Associate, McKinsey & Co. Inc., 1965, Partner, 1970; Peninsular & Oriental Steam Navigation Co.: Hd of European and Air Transport Div., 1974; Dir, 1978–85; Chairman: P&O European Transport Services Ltd, 1979–83; P&O Cruises Ltd, 1980–85. Director: Jasmin plc, 1989–; North West Water Group plc, 1989–; Mem., NW Water Authority, 1989. Mem., Gen. Council, Cumbria Tourist Bd, 1986–. Dir, Renaissance Theatre Trust Co. Ltd, 1989–. Conseiller Spécial, Chambre de Commerce et d'Industrie de Boulogne-sur-Mer et de Montreuil, 1989–. Mem., RYA, 1977–. Liveryman: Worshipful Company of Carmen, 1976; Worshipful Company of Shipwrights, 1988–; Freeman, City of London, 1976. FRSA 1989. *Publications:* (jtly) Containerization: the key to low cost transport, 1965; frequent papers in scientific and technical jls, 1965–72. *Recreations:* fell-walking, sailing, gardening, literature. *Address:* Cleeve Howe, Windermere, Cumbria LA23 1AS. *T:* Windermere (09662) 4199. *Club:* Royal Automobile.

LEACH, Sir Ronald (George), GBE 1976 (CBE 1944); Kt 1970; FCA; Chairman: Standard Chartered Bank(CI), since 1980; Standard Chartered Trust (CI) Ltd, since 1980; *b* 21 Aug. 1907; *s* of William T. Leach, 14 Furze Croft, Hove; *m* Margaret Alice Binns. *Educ:* Alleyn's. Dep. Financial Sec. to Ministry of Food, Sept. 1939–June 1946. Sen. Partner in firm of Peat, Marwick, Mitchell & Co., Chartered Accountants, 1966–77; Dir, Samuel Montagu & Co., 1977–80. Director: Internat. Investment Trust of Jersey, 1980–; Ann Street Brewery, 1981–; Barrington Management (CI), 1984–87; Berkeley Australian Develt Capital, 1985–90; Govett American Endeavour Fund Ltd. Member: Cttee on Coastal Flooding, 1953; Inquiry into Shipping, 1967–70; National Theatre Board, 1972–79; Chairman: Consumer Cttee for GB (Agricultural Marketing Acts, 1931–49), 1958–67; Accounting Standards Steering Cttee, 1970–76. Pres. Inst. of Chartered Accountants in England and Wales, 1969–70. Hon. LLD Lancaster, 1977. *Publication:* (with Prof. Edward Stamp) British Accounting Standards: the first ten years, 1981. *Address:* La Rosière, St Saviour, Jersey, CI. *T:* Jersey (0534) 77039 or 78427.

LEADBEATER, Howell; Under/Deputy Secretary, Department of the Environment, retired 1976; *b* 22 Oct. 1919; *s* of late Thomas and Mary Ann Leadbeater; *m* 1946, Mary Elizabeth Roberts; two *s* one *d. Educ:* Pontardawe Secondary Sch.; University College, Swansea. Army Service, 1940–46: Adjt 11th E African Div. Signals. Min. of Works, later MPBW and Dept of Environment: Asst Principal, 1948; Asst Sec., 1958; Under Sec., 1968; Under/Dep. Sec., 1973. Design Coordinator for Caernarfon Castle, Investiture of Prince of Wales, 1969. Mem., Crafts Adv. Cttee, 1978–80. *Address:* Tides Reach, Llansteffan, Carmarthen, Dyfed SA33 5EY. *T:* Llansteffan (026783) 375.

LEADBETTER, Alan James, DSc; Director, Daresbury Laboratory, Science and Engineering Research Council, since 1988; *b* 28 March 1934; *s* of Robert and Edna Leadbetter; *m* 1957, Jean Brenda Williams; one *s* one *d. Educ:* Liverpool Univ. (BSc 1954; PhD 1957); Bristol Univ. (DSc 1971). CPhys 1972; FInstP 1972; CChem 1980; FRSC 1980. Fellow, NRCC, 1957–59; Res. Asst, Lectr and Reader, Univ. of Bristol, 1959–74; Prof. of Phys. Chem., Univ. of Exeter, 1975–82; Associate Dir, Science, Rutherford Appleton Lab., SERC, 1982–88. Hon. Professor: Univ. of Hull, 1986–; Univ. of Manchester, 1989–. *Publications:* res. papers in chem. and phys in learned jls. *Recreations:* gardening, walking, cooking. *Address:* Daresbury Laboratory, Warrington WA4 4AD. *T:* Warrington (0925) 603119.

LEADBETTER, David Hulse, CB 1958; Assistant Under-Secretary of State, Department of Education and Science, 1964–68 (Under Secretary, Ministry of Education, 1953–64); *b* 14 Aug. 1908; *s* of late Harold Leadbetter; *m* 1933, Marion, *d* of late Horatio Ballantyne, FRIC, FCS; two *s* two *d* (and one *d* decd.). *Educ:* Whitgift; Merton Coll., Oxford (Classical Postmaster). Entered Board of Education, 1933. *Recreations:* photography, gardening. *Address:* Ryall's Ground, Queen Street, Yetminster, Sherborne, Dorset DT9 6LL. *T:* Yetminster (0935) 872216.

LEADBITTER, Edward; MP (Lab) The Hartlepools, since 1964; *b* 18 June 1919; *s* of Edward Leadbitter, Easington, Durham; *m* 1940, Phyllis Irene Mellin, Bristol; one *s* one *d. Educ:* State Schs; Teachers' Training Coll. Served War, 1939–45, with RA; commissioned 1943; War Office Instructor in Gunnery. Became a teacher. Joined Labour Party, 1938; Pres., Hartlepools Labour Party, 1958–62; Mem., West Hartlepool Borough Council, 1954–67 (sometime Mem., Town Planning, Finance, Housing, Industrial Develt, and Educn Cttees). Member: Estimates Cttee, 1966–69; Select Cttee on Science and Technology, 1970–80; Select Cttee on Energy, 1980–; Chairmens' Panel, House of Commons, 1980–; Chm., Anglo-Tunisian Parly Group, 1974–. Sponsored Children's Homes Registration Bill, 1982. Mem. NUPE, 1963–. Organizer of Exhibition on History of Labour Movement, 1956. Pres., Hartlepool Football Club, 1983–. First Hon. Freeman, Co. Borough of Hartlepool, 1981; Freeman of City of London, 1986. *Address:* 8 Warkworth Drive, Hartlepool, Cleveland. *T:* Hartlepool (0429) 263404.

LEAHY, Sir John (Henry Gladstone), KCMG 1981 (CMG 1973); HM Diplomatic Service, retired; *b* 7 Feb. 1928; *s* of late William Henry Gladstone and late Ethel Leahy; *m* 1954, Elizabeth Anne, *d* of J. H. Pitchford, *qv*; two *s* two *d. Educ:* Tonbridge Sch.; Clare Coll., Cambridge; Yale University. RAF, 1950–52; FO, 1952–54 (Asst Private Sec. to Minister of State, 1953–54); 3rd, later 2nd Sec., Singapore, 1955–57; FO, 1957–58; 2nd, later 1st Sec., Paris, 1958–62; FO, 1962–65; Head of Chancery, Tehran, 1965–68; Counsellor, FCO, 1969; Head of Personnel Services Dept, 1969–70; Head of News Dept, FCO, 1971–73; Counsellor and Head of Chancery, Paris, 1973–75; seconded as Under Sec., NI Office, 1975–76; Asst Under-Sec. of State, FCO, 1977–79; Ambassador to South Africa, 1979–82; Dep. Under- Sec. of State, FCO, 1982–84; High Comr, Australia, 1984–88. Dir, The Observer, 1989–. Exec. Dir, Urban Foundn (London), 1989–. Pro-Chancellor, City Univ., 1991– (Council Mem.). Vice-Chm., Maritime Trust, 1990–. Chm., Franco-British Council, 1989–. Gov., ESU, 1989–. Gov., Skinners' Sch. for Girls, Hackney, 1988–. Warden, Skinners' Co., 1988–. *Recreation:* tennis. *Address:* Manor Stables, Bishopstone, near Seaford, East Sussex BN25 2UD. *T:* Seaford (0323) 898898. *Club:* United Oxford & Cambridge University.

LEAKE, Prof. Bernard Elgey, PhD, DSc, FRSE, FGS; Head of Department of Geology and Applied Geology, and Keeper of Geological Collections in Hunterian Museum, University of Glasgow, since 1974; *b* 29 July 1932; *s* of late Norman Sidney Leake and Clare Evelyn (*née* Walgate); *m* 1955, Gillian Dorothy Dobinson; five *s*. *Educ:* Wirral Grammar Sch., Bebington, Cheshire; Liverpool Univ. (1st Cl. Hons BSc, PhD); Bristol Univ. (DSc 1974). Leverhulme post-doctoral Res. Fellow, Liverpool Univ., 1955–57; Asst Lectr, subseq. Lectr in Geology, Bristol Univ., 1957–68, Reader in Geol., 1968–74. Res. Associate, Berkeley, Calif, 1966; Gledden Sen. Vis. Fellow, Univ. of W Australia, 1986. Chm., Cttee on amphibole nomenclature, Internat. Mineral Assoc., 1982– (Sec., 1968–79); Member: NERC, 1978–84 (Chm., Vis. Gp to Brit. Geol Survey, formerly Inst. of Geological Sciences, 1982–84; Chm., Isotope Facilities Prog. Cttee, 1987–); Council, Mineral Soc., 1965–68, 1978–80 (Vice-Pres., 1979–80); Council, Geol Soc., 1971–74, 1979–85, 1989– (Vice-Pres., 1980, Treasurer, 1981–85, 1989–, Pres., 1986–88; Lyell Medal, 1977); Council, RSE, 1988–90; publication cttees, Mineral Soc., 1970–85, Geol Soc., 1970–85, and 1986–; Chm., Geol Soc. Publication Bd, 1987–. FRSE 1978. Editor: Mineralogical Magazine, 1970–83; Jl of Geol Soc., 1973 and 1974. *Publications:* A Catalogue of analysed calciferous and sub-calciferous amphiboles, 1968; The Geology of South Mayo, 1989; over 100 papers in geol, mineral and geochem. jls on geol. of Connemara, study of amphiboles, X-ray fluorescence anal. of rocks and use of geochem. in identifying origins of highly metamorphosed rocks; maps: The geological map of Connemara, 1982; The geological map of South Mayo, 1985. *Recreations:* walking, reading, theatre, gardening, museums, genealogy, study of railway and agricultural development. *Address:* Geology and Applied Geology Department, The University, Glasgow G12 8QQ. *T:* 041–339 8855, ext. 7435; 2 Garngaber Avenue, Lenzie, Kirkintilloch, Dunbartonshire. *Club:* Geological Society.

LEAKE, Rt. Rev. David; *see* Argentina, Bishop of.

LEAKEY, Maj.-Gen. Arundell Rea, CB 1967; DSO 1945; MC 1941 (Bar 1942); Director and Secretary, Wolfson Foundation, 1968–80; *b* 30 Dec. 1915; parents British; *m* 1950, Muriel Irene Le Poer Trench; two *s*. *Educ:* Weymouth Coll.; Royal Military Coll., Sandhurst. Command of 5th Royal Tank Regt, 1944; Instructor at Staff Coll., Camberley, 1951–52; Comdr, 1st Arab Legion Armoured Car Regt, 1954–56; Instructor (Col), Staff Coll., Camberley, 1958–60; Comdr, 7th Armoured Brigade, 1961–63; Dir-Gen. of Fighting Vehicles, 1964–66; GOC Troops in Malta and Libya, 1967–68; retired 1968. Czechoslovakian Military Cross, 1944. *Recreations:* gardening, enjoying retirement. *Address:* Ladymead Cottage, Houghton, Stockbridge, Hants SO20 6LU. *T:* Romsey (0794) 388396. *Club:* Naval and Military.

LEAKEY, Dr David Martin, FEng 1979; Group Technical Adviser, British Telecom, since 1990; *b* 23 July 1932; *s* of Reginald Edward and Edith Doris Leakey; *m* 1957, Shirley May Webster; one *s* one *d*. *Educ:* Imperial College, Univ. of London (BScEng, PhD, DIC). FCGI, FIEE. GEC Coventry, 1953–57; GEC Hirst Research Centre, 1957–63; Tech. Manager, Public Exchange Div., GEC Coventry, 1963–66; Head, Elect. Eng. Dept, Lanchester Polytechnic, 1966–67; Advanced Product Planning Manager, 1967–69, Technical Dir, 1969–84, GEC Coventry; Dep. E-in-C, 1984–86, Chief Scientist, 1986–90, British Telecom. Director: Fulcrum Ltd, 1985–; Mitel Inc., 1986–. Vice-Pres., IEE, 1984–87. Liveryman, Worshipful Co. of Engineers, 1985–. *Publications:* papers to professional journals. *Recreations:* horticulture, wine. *Address:* Rocheberie, Grassy Lane, Sevenoaks, Kent TN13 1PW.

LEAKEY, Prof. Felix William; author; *b* 29 June 1922; *s* of Hugh Leakey and Kathleen Leakey (*née* March); *m* 1947, Daphne Joan Sleep (*née* Salter); one *s* two *d*. *Educ:* St Christopher Sch., Letchworth; Queen Mary Coll., London. BA, PhD (London). Asst Lectr, then Lectr in French, Univ. of Sheffield, 1948–54; Univ. of Glasgow: Lectr in French, 1954–64; Sen. Lectr, 1964–68; Reader, 1968–70; Prof. of French, Univ. of Reading, 1970–73; Prof. of French Lang. and Lit., Bedford Coll., London, 1973–84 (Head of Department, 1973–79 and 1982–84). Carnegie Research Fellow, 1961–62; Leverhulme Research Fellow, 1971–72. Assoc. of University Profs of French: Hon. Sec., 1972–73; Jt Hon. Sec., 1973–75; Vice-Chm., 1975–76; Chm., 1976–77. Public performances as poetry speaker: Baudelaire's Les Fleurs du Mal, French Inst., London, 1984, and Glasgow Univ., 1985; bilingual recital, Chants/Songs, univ. centres in Britain, France and W Germany, 1976–. *Publications:* Baudelaire and Nature, 1969; (ed jtly) The French Renaissance and its Heritage: essays presented to Alan Boase, 1968; Sound and Sense in French Poetry (Inaugural Lecture, with readings on disc), 1975; (ed jtly) Samuel Beckett, Drunken Boat, 1977; Baudelaire: Love Poems (videotape), 1989; Baudelaire: Selected Poems from Les Fleurs du Mal (audiotape), 1989; Baudelaire: collected essays 1953–1988, 1990; Baudelaire: Les Fleurs du Mal, 1992; contribs to: French Studies; Rev. d'hist. litt. de la France; Rev. de litt. comparée; Rev. des sciences humaines; Etudes baudelairiennes; etc. *Recreations:* foxhunting, beagling, riding, poetry, art, music, especially opera.

LEAKEY, Mary Douglas, FBA 1973; FRAI; former Director, Olduvai Gorge Excavations; *b* 6 Feb. 1913; *d* of Erskine Edward Nicol and Cecilia Marion Frere; *m* 1936, Louis Seymour Bazett Leakey, FBA (*d* 1972); three *s*. *Educ:* privately. Hon. Mem., American Assoc. for Arts and Sciences, 1979–; Foreign Associate, Amer. Nat. Acad. of Science, 1987; For. Mem., Royal Swedish Acad. of Scis., 1978. Hon. FSA. Geological Soc. of London, Prestwich Medal and Nat. Geographic Soc. Hubbard Medal (jointly with late L. S. B. Leakey); Gold Medal, Soc. of Women Geographers, USA; Linneus Gold Medal, Royal Swedish Acad., 1978. Elizabeth Blackwell Award, Mary Washington Coll., 1980; Bradford Washburn Award, Boston, 1980. Hon. DSc: Witwatersrand, 1968; Western Michigan, 1980; Chicago, 1981; Cambridge, 1982; Emory, 1988; Massachusetts, Amherst, 1988; Hon. DSSc Yale, 1976; Hon. DLitt Oxford, 1981; Brown Univ., 1990. *Publications:* Olduvai Gorge, vol. 3, Excavation in Beds I and II, 1971; Africa's Vanishing Art: the rock paintings of Tanzania, 1983; Disclosing the Past (autobiog.), 1984; various papers in Nature and other scientific jls. *Recreations:* reading, game watching. *Address:* c/o National Museum, Box 30239, Nairobi, Kenya.

See also R. E. F. Leakey.

LEAKEY, Richard Erskine Frere; Director, Wildlife and Conservation Management Service, Kenya, since 1989; *b* 19 Dec. 1944; *s* of late Louis Seymour Bazett Leakey, FBA, and of Mary Leakey, *qv*; *m* 1970, Dr Meave (*née* Epps); three *d*. *Educ:* Nairobi Primary Sch.; Lenana (formerly Duke of York) Sch., Nairobi. Self employed tour guide and animal trapper, 1961–65; Dir, Photographic Safaris in E Africa, 1965–68; Administrative Dir, 1968–74, Dir, 1974–89, Nat. Museums of Kenya. Co-leader, palaeontol expedn to Lake Natron, Tanzania, 1963–64; expedn to Lake Baringo, Kenya, in search of early man, 1966; Co-leader, Internation Omo River Expedn, Ethiopia, in search of early man, 1967; Leader, E Turkana (formerly E Rudolf) Res. Proj. (multi-nat., interdisciplinary sci. consortium investigation of Plio/Pleistocene, Kenya's northern Rift Valley), 1968–. Chairman: Bd of Govs, Nat. Museums of Kenya; Bd of Trustees, Kenya Wildlife Service. Chairman: Foundn for Res. into Origin of Man (FROM), 1974–81; E African Wild Life Soc., 1984– (Vice-Chm., 1978–84); Kenya Cttee, United World Colls, 1987; Bd of Governors and Council, Regent's Coll., London, 1985–; Trustee: Nat. Fund for the Disabled; Rocklord Coll., Illinois, 1983–85; Wildlife Clubs of Kenya, 1985–. Presenter, The Making of Mankind, BBC TV series, 1981. Mem., Selection Cttee, Beyond War Award, 1985–; Juror: Kalinga Prize, Unesco, 1986–88; Rolex Awards, 1990. Hon. Mem., Bd of Dirs, Thunderbird Res. Corp., USA, 1988–. Hon. degrees from Wooster Coll., Rochford Coll. and Univ. of Kent. Golden Ark Medal for Conservation, 1989. *Publications:* (contrib.) General History of Africa, vol. 1, 1976; (with R. Lewin) Origins, 1978; (with R. Lewin) People of the Lake, 1979; (with M. G. Leakey) Koobi Fora Research Project, vol. I, 1979; The Making of Mankind, 1981; Human Origins, 1982; One Life, 1984; articles on palaeontol. in Nature, Jl of World Hist., Science, Amer. Jl of Phys. and Anthropol. *Address:* PO Box 24926, Nairobi, Kenya.

LEANING, Very Rev. David; Provost and Rector of Southwell, since 1991. *Educ:* Keble Coll., Oxford, 1957–58; Lichfield Theological Coll. Deacon 1960, priest 1961, dio. Lincoln; Curate of Gainsborough, 1960–65; Rector of Warsop with Sookholme, 1965–76; Vicar of Kington and Rector of Huntington, Diocese of Hereford, 1976–80; RD of Kington and Weobley, 1976–80; Archdeacon of Newark, 1980–91; Warden, Community of St Laurence, Belper, 1984–. Mem., Bd of Selectors, ACCM, 1988–. *Address:* The Residence, Southwell, Notts NG25 0HP. *T:* Southwell (0636) 812593.

LEAPER, Prof. Robert Anthony Bernard, CBE 1975; Professor of Social Administration, University of Exeter, 1970–86, Professor Emeritus 1987; *b* 7 June 1921; *s* of William Bambrick Leaper and Gertrude Elizabeth (*née* Taylor); *m* 1950, Elizabeth Arno; two *s* one *d*. *Educ:* Ratcliffe Coll., Leicester; St John's Coll., Cambridge (MA); Balliol Coll., Oxford (MA). Dipl. Public and Social Admin. (Oxon). Coal miner, 1941–44. Warden, St John Bosco Youth Centre, Stepney, 1945–47; Cadet officer, Civil Service, 1949–50; Co-operative Coll., Stanford Hall, 1950–56; Principal, Social Welfare Trng Centre, Zambia, 1956–59; Lectr, then Sen. Lectr, then Acting Dir, Social Admin., UC, Swansea, 1960–70. Vis. Lectr, Roehampton Inst., Univ. of Surrey, 1986–90. Exec., later Vice-Chm., Nat. Council of Social Service, 1964–80; Pres., European Region, Internat. Council on Social Welfare, 1971–79; Chm., Area Bd, MSC, 1975–86; Governor, Centre for Policy on Ageing, 1982–88. Editor, Social Policy and Administration. Dr *hc* Univ. de Rennes, 1987. Médaille de l'Ecole Nationale de Santé, France, 1975. *Publications:* Communities and Social Change, 1966; Community Work, 1969, 2nd edn 1972; Health, Wealth and Housing, 1980; Change and Continuity, 1984; At Home in Devon, 1986; Age Speaks for Itself, 1988. *Recreations:* walking, railways, wine. *Address:* Birchcote, New North Road, Exeter EX4 4AD. *T:* Exeter (0392) 72565.

LEAR, Joyce, (Mrs W. J. Lear); *see* Hopkirk, J.

LEARMONT, Gen. Sir John (Hartley), KCB 1989; CBE 1980 (OBE 1975); Quarter Master General, Ministry of Defence, since 1991; *b* 10 March 1934; *s* of Captain Percy Hewitt Learmont, CIE, RIN and Doris Orynthia Learmont; *m* 1957, Susan (*née* Thornborrow); three *s*. *Educ:* Fettes College; RMA Sandhurst. Commissioned RA, 1954; Instructor, RMA, 1960–63; student, Staff Coll., 1964; served 14 Field Regt, Staff Coll. and 3 RHA, 1965–70; MA to C-in-C BAOR, 1971–73; CO 1 RHA, 1974–75 (despatches 1974); HQ BAOR, 1976–78; Comdr, 8 Field Force, 1979–81; Dep. Comdr, Commonwealth Monitoring Force, Rhodesia, Nov. 1979–March 1980; student RCDS, 1981; Chief of Mission, British Cs-in-C Mission to Soviet Forces in Germany, 1982–84; Comdr Artillery, 1 (British) Corps, 1985–87; COS, HQ UKLF, 1987–88; Comdt, Staff Coll. Camberley, 1988–89; Mil. Sec., MoD, 1989–91. Colonel Commandant: Army Air Corps, 1988–; RA, 1989–; RHA, 1990–; Hon. Col, 2nd Bn Wessex Regt (Vols), 1990–. Pres., Army Athletics Assoc., 1989–. *Recreations:* fell walking, golf, theatre. *Address:* Ministry of Defence, Main Building, Whitehall, SW1A 2HB. *Club:* Naval and Military.

LEAROYD, Wing Comdr Roderick Alastair Brook, VC 1940; RAF; *b* 5 Feb. 1913; *s* of late Major Reginald Brook Learoyd and Marjorie Scott Boadle. *Educ:* Wellington Coll. *Address:* 12 Fittleworth Gardens, Rustington, W Sussex BN16 3EW.

LEARY, Brian Leonard; QC 1978; *b* 1 Jan. 1929; *o s* of late A. T. Leary; *m* 1965, Myriam Ann Bannister, *d* of Kenneth Bannister, CBE, Mexico City. *Educ:* King's Sch. Canterbury; Wadham Coll., Oxford. MA Oxon. Called to the Bar, Middle Temple, 1953; Harmsworth Scholar; Bencher, 1986. Senior Prosecuting Counsel to the Crown at Central Criminal Court, 1971–78. Chm., British-Mexican Soc., 1989–. *Recreations:* travel, sailing, growing herbs. *Address:* East Farleigh House, Lower Road, East Farleigh, Kent ME15 0JW. *T:* Maidstone (0622) 726295; 5 Paper Buildings, Temple, EC4. *T:* 071–353 7811.

LEASK, Lt-Gen. Sir Henry (Lowther Ewart Clark), KCB 1970 (CB 1967); DSO 1945; OBE 1957 (MBE 1945); GOC Scotland and Governor of Edinburgh Castle, 1969–72, retired; *b* 30 June 1913; *s* of Rev. James Leask, MA; *m* Zoë de Camborne, *d* of Col W. P. Paynter, DSO, RHA; one *s* two *d*. 2nd Lt Royal Scots Fusiliers, 1936. Served War of 1939–45 in Mediterranean and Italy; Staff College Camberley, 1942; GSO 1942; Bde Major Inf. Bde 1943; 2nd in Comd and CO, 8 Bn Argyll and Sutherland Highlanders, 1944–45; Comd 1st Bn London Scottish, 1946–47; RAF Staff College, 1947; Gen. Staff Mil. Ops, WO, 1947–49; Instr Staff Coll., 1949–51; Comd 1st Bn The Parachute Regt, 1952–54; Asst Military Sec. to Sec. of State for War, 1955–57; Comdt, Tactical Wing Sch. of Inf., 1957–58; Comd Infantry Bde, 1958–61; idc 1961; Dep. Mil. Sec. to Sec. of State for War, 1962–64; GOC 52 Lowland Div., 1964–66; Dir of Army Training, MoD (Army), 1966–69. Brig. 1961, Maj.-Gen. 1964, Lt-Gen. 1969. Col of the Royal Highland Fusiliers, 1964–69; Col Comdt, Scottish Div. of Infantry, 1968–72. Chm., Army Benevolent Fund, Scotland, 1972–88. *Recreation:* field sports. *Clubs:* Carlton, Hurlingham; New (Edinburgh).

LEASOR, (Thomas) James; author; *b* 20 Dec. 1923; *s* of late Richard and Christine Leasor, Erith, Kent; *m* 1951, Joan Margaret Bevan, LLB, Barrister-at-law, *o d* of late Roland S. Bevan, Crowcombe, Somerset; three *s*. *Educ:* City of London Sch.; Oriel Coll., Oxford. Kentish Times, 1941–42. Served in Army in Burma, India, Malaya, 1942–46, Capt. Royal Berks Regt. Oriel Coll., Oxford, 1946–48, BA 1948; MA 1952; edited The Isis. On staff Daily Express, London, 1948–55, as reporter, foreign correspondent, feature writer. Contrib. to many American and British magazines, newspapers and periodicals; scriptwriter for TV series The Michaels in Africa. FRSA. OStJ. *Publications: novels:* Not Such a Bad Day, 1946; The Strong Delusion, 1951; NTR-Nothing to Report, 1955; Passport to Oblivion, 1964; Spylight, 1966; Passport in Suspense, 1967; Passport for a

Pilgrim, 1968; They Don't Make Them Like That Any More, 1969; A Week of Love, 1969; Never had a Spanner on Her, 1970; Love-all, 1971; Follow the Drum, 1972; Host of Extras, 1973; Mandarin Gold, 1973; The Chinese Widow, 1974; Jade Gate, 1976; Love and the Land Beyond, 1979; Open Secret, 1982; Ship of Gold, 1984; Tank of Serpents, 1986; Frozen Assets, 1989; Love Down Under, 1991; *as Andrew Macallan*: Succession, 1989; Generation, 1990; Diamond-Hard, 1991; Fusillade, 1992; *non-fiction*: Author by Profession, The Monday Story, 1951; Wheels to Fortune, The Serjeant Major, 1954; The Red Fort; (with Kendal Burt) The One That Got Away, 1956; The Millionth Chance, 1957; War at the Top, 1959; (with Peter Eton) Conspiracy of Silence, 1959; Bring Out Your Dead, 1961; Rudolf Hess: The Uninvited Envoy, 1961; Singapore: The Battle that Changed the World, 1968; Green Beach, 1975; Boarding Party, 1977; The Unknown Warrior, 1980; Who Killed Sir Harry Oakes?, 1983; The Marine from Mandalay, 1988. *Recreation*: vintage sports cars. *Address*: Swallowcliffe Manor, Salisbury, Wilts SP3 5PB; Casa do Zimbro, Praia da Luz, Lagos, Algarve, Portugal. *Club*: Garrick.

LEATES, Margaret; parliamentary and pensions consultant; *d* of Henry Arthur Sargent Rayner and Alice (*née* Baker); *m* 1973, Timothy Philip Leates; one *s* one *d. Educ*: Lilley and Stone Girls' High Sch., Newark; King's Coll., London (LLB, LLM; undergrad. and postgrad. entrance schol.; AKC). Admitted Solicitor, 1975; joined Office of Parliamentary Counsel, 1976; seconded to Law Commn, 1981–83 and 1987–89; Dep. Parly Counsel, 1987–90. *Recreations*: son and daughter; junk. *Address*: Crofton Farm, 161 Crofton Lane, Orpington, Kent. *T*: Orpington (0689) 820192. *Club*: Whitstable Yacht.

LEATHAM, Dr Aubrey (Gerald), FRCP; cardiologist; Hon. Consulting Physician: St George's Hospital, London; National Heart Hospital; King Edward VII Hospital, London; *b* 23 Aug. 1920; *s* of Dr H. W. Leatham (*d* 1973), Godalming and Kathleen Pelham Burn (*d* 1971), Nosely Hall, Leicester; *m* 1954, Judith Augustine Savile Freer; one *s* three *d. Educ*: Charterhouse; Trinity Hall, Cambridge; St Thomas' Hospital. BA Cambridge 1941; MB, BChir 1944; MRCP 1945; FRCP 1957. House Phys., St Thomas' Hosp., 1944; RMO, Nat. Heart Hosp., 1945; Phys., RAMC, 1946–47; Sherbrook Research Fellow, Cardiac Dept, and Sen. Registrar, London Hosp., 1948–50; Asst Dir, Inst. of Cardiology, 1951–54, Dean, 1962–69. Goulstonian Lectr, RCP, 1958. R. T. Hall Travelling Prof., Australia and NZ, 1963. Member: Brit. Cardiac Soc.; Sociedad Peruana de Cardiologia, 1966; Sociedad Colombiana de Cardiologia, 1966. Hon. FACC 1986. Royal Order of Bhutan, 1966. *Publications*: Auscultation of the Heart and Phonocardiography, 1970; (jtly) Lecture Notes in Cardiology, 1990; articles in Lancet, British Heart Jl, etc, on auscultation of the heart and phonocardiography, artificial pacemakers, coronary artery disease, etc. *Recreations*: ski-ing and ski-touring, mountain walking, tennis, racquets, gardening, photography. *Address*: 27 Sulivan Road, SW6 3DT. *T*: 071–736 2237; 45 Wimpole Street, W1M 7D9. *T*: 071–935 5295; Rookwood Lane House, West Wittering, Sussex. *T*: Birdham (0243) 514649.

LEATHART, Air Cdre James Anthony, CB 1960; DSO 1940; *b* 5 Jan. 1915; *s* of P. W. Leathart, BSc, MD, Ear, Nose and Throat Specialist, Liverpool; *m* 1939, E. L. Radcliffe, Birkenhead; two *s* one *d. Educ*: St Edward's, Oxford; Liverpool Univ. Joined Auxiliary Air Force (610 County of Chester Squadron), 1936; transferred RAF, 1937, CO 54 Sqn, Battle of Britain, 1940; Chief of Staff Headquarters, 12 Group, RAF, 1959–61; Dir of Operational Requirements, Air Ministry, 1961–62, retd. Oct. 1962. *Recreations*: fly-fishing, motoring, ornithology, gardening. *Address*: Wortley Farmhouse, Wotton-under-Edge, Glos GL12 7QP. *T*: Dursley (0453) 842312.

LEATHER, Sir Edwin (Hartley Cameron), KCMG 1974; KCVO 1975; Kt 1962; Governor and C-in-C of Bermuda, 1973–77; writer and broadcaster; *b* 22 May 1919; *s* of Harold H. Leather, MBE, Hamilton, Canada, and Grace C. Leather (*née* Holmes); *m* 1940, Sheila A. A. (CStJ), *d* of Major A. H. Greenlees, Hamilton; two *d. Educ*: Trinity College Sch., Canada; Royal Military Coll., Kingston, Canada. Commnd RCHA; served overseas; served War of 1939–45 with Canadian Army, UK and in Europe, 1940–45. Contested (C) South Bristol, 1945; MP (C) N Somerset, 1950–64. Mem., Exec. Cttee, British Commonwealth Producers Organisation, 1960–63; Chairman: Bath Festival Soc., 1960–65; Horder Centre for Arthritics, 1962–65; Cons. and Unionist Assocs, 1969–70 (Mem. Nat. Exec. Cttee, 1963–70); Mem. Cons. Party Bd of Finance, 1963–67; Mem., Bd of Dirs, Yehudi Menuhin Sch., 1967–; Dir, N. M. Rothschild (Bermuda), 1978–91, and other cos. Canadian Legion rep. on Exec. Cttee of Brit. Commonwealth Ex-Servicemen's League, 1954–63; Pres., Institute of Marketing, 1963–67. Lay reader, in Church of England, 1950–. Chm., Bermuda Cttee, United World Colls, 1975–91; Mem. Council, Imp. Soc. of Knights Bachelor, 1969–; Nat. Gov., Shaw Fest., Niagara-on-the-Lake, Ontario, 1990–; Trustee, Menuhin Foundn of Bermuda Comm., 1975–; Hon. Patron, Bermuda Fest., 1975–; Hon. Cttee Canada Meml Foundn, 1991–; Grand Senechal Confrerie des Chevaliers du Tastevin, 1990. FRSA 1969; Hon. LLD Bath, 1975. KStJ 1974. Hon. Citizen, Kansas City, USA, 1957; Gold Medal, Nat. Inst. Social Sciences, NY, 1977. Medal of Merit, Royal Canadian Legion, 1963. *Publications*: The Vienna Elephant, 1977; The Mozart Score, 1978; The Duveen Letter, 1980. *Address*: Chelsea, Inwood Close, Paget, Bermuda PG05. *Clubs*: Carlton; York (Toronto); Hamilton (Canada); Royal Bermuda Yacht.

LEATHER, Ted; *see* Leather, Sir E. H. C.

LEATHERLAND, Baron, *cr* 1964, of Dunton (Life Peer); **Charles Edward Leatherland,** OBE 1951; Treasurer and Member of Council, University of Essex, from foundation until 1973; *b* 18 April 1898; *e s* of John Edward Leatherland, Churchover, Warwicks; *m* 1922, Mary Elizabeth (*d* 1987), *d* of Joseph Henry Morgan, Shareshill, Staffs; one *s* one *d. Educ*: Harborne, Birmingham; University Extension Courses. Asst Editor, Daily Herald, until retirement, 1963. Served European War, 1914–19 (despatches, MSM); enlisted, 1914, aged 16; served in France, Belgium, Germany; Company Sgt Major, Royal Warwicks Regt; Essex TA Assoc., 1946–68, and E Anglian TA Assoc., 1968. Chm., Essex County Council, 1960–61 (Vice-Chm. 1952–55 and 1958–60); CA Essex, 1946–68. Dep. Chm., Epping Magistrates Bench. JP (Essex) 1944–70; DL Essex, 1963. Mem. Bd of Basildon Development Corporation, 1967–71. Additional Mem., Monopolies Commn, to consider newspaper mergers, 1969. Chm., E Counties Regional Council of the Labour Party, 1950–66. DUniv. Essex, 1973. *Publications*: (part author) The Book of the Labour Party, 1925; Labour Party pamphlets; contribs on local govt affairs in Municipal Jl and general press; 4 Prince of Wales Gold Medals 1923 and 1924 for essays on: Measures that may be taken by other countries to promote an improvement in the economic condition of Czecho-Slovakia, 1923; The possibilities of the cinema in the development of commercial education, 1923; Difficulties attending the economic position of Czecho-Slovakia after the Peace Treaty, and the methods adopted to remove them, 1924; Home and foreign trade: their relative importance and interdependence, 1924. *Recreations*: formerly fox hunting, now walking. *Address*: 19 Starling Close, Buckhurst Hill, Essex. *T*: 081–504 3164.

LEATHERS, family name of Viscount Leathers.

LEATHERS, 2nd Viscount, *cr* 1954; **Frederick Alan Leathers;** Baron Leathers, 1941; *b* 4 April 1908; *er s* of 1st Viscount Leathers, PC, CH, LLD; *S* father, 1965; *m* 1st, 1940,

Elspeth Graeme (marr. diss. 1983; she *d* 1985), *yr d* of late Sir Thomas (Alexander) Stewart; two *s* two *d*; 2nd, 1983, Mrs Lorna M. Barnett. *Educ*: Brighton Coll.; Emmanuel Coll., Cambridge (MA (hons) in Economics). Mem. of Baltic Exchange. Director: Wm Cory & Son Ltd, 1929–72 (Chm.); Cory Mann George Ltd, 1941–72 (Chm.); Cory Ship Towage Ltd, 1941–72 (Chm.); Smit & Cory International Port Towage Ltd, 1970–72 (Chm.); Hull Blyth & Co. Ltd, 1949–72 (Chm.); Rea Ltd, 1941–72 (Chm.); St Denis Shipping Co. Ltd, 1957–72 (Chm.); Laporte Industries Ltd, 1959–71; Laporte Industries (Holdings) Ltd, 1959–71; Tunnel Cement Ltd, 1960–74; Guardian Cement Co. Ltd, 1963–71; New Zealand Cement Holdings Ltd, 1963–71; National Westminster Bank, Outer London Region, 1968–78. Member: Court of Worshipful Company of Shipwrights; Court of Watermen's and Lightermen's Company; Fellow Institute of Chartered Shipbrokers; FRPSL; FRSA; MInstPet. *Heir*: *s* Hon. Christopher Graeme Leathers [*b* 31 Aug. 1941; *m* 1964, Maria Philomena, *yr d* of Michael Merriman, Charlestown, Co. Mayo; one *s* one *d*]. *Address*: Park House, Chiddingfold, Surrey GU8 4TS. *T*: Wormley (042879) 3222. *Club*: Royal Automobile.

LEATHWOOD, Barry; National Secretary, Agricultural and Allied Workers National Trade Group, Transport and General Workers' Union, since 1987; *b* 11 April 1941; *s* of Charles and Dorothy Leathwood; *m* 1963, Veronica Ann Clarke; one *d*. Apprentice Toolmaker, 1956–62; Toolmaker/Fitter, 1962–73; District Organiser, Nat. Union of Agric. and Allied Workers, 1973–83; Regional Officer, TGWU Agric. Group, 1983–87. *Recreations*: socialist politics, reading, photography. *Address*: Transport House, Smith Square, SW1P 3JB. *T*: 071–828 7788.

LEAVER, Sir Christopher, GBE 1981; JP; Chairman, Russell & McIver Group of Companies (Wine Merchants); *b* 3 Nov. 1937; *s* of Dr Robert Leaver and Mrs Audrey Kerpen; *m* 1975, Helen Mireille Molyneux Benton; one *s* two *d. Educ*: Eastbourne Coll. Commissioned (Army), RAOC, 1956–58. Member, Retail Foods Trades Wages Council, 1963–64. JP Inner London, 1970–83, City, 1974–; Member: Council, Royal Borough of Kensington and Chelsea, 1970–73; Court of Common Council (Ward of Dowgate), City of London, 1973; Alderman (Ward of Dowgate), City of London, 1974; Sheriff of the City of London, 1979–80; Lord Mayor of London, 1981–82; HM Lieutenant, City of London, 1982–. Chm., London Tourist Bd, 1983–89; Deputy Chairman: Thames Water Authority, 1983–89; Thames Water plc, 1989–; Chm., Thames Line Plc, 1987–89; Director: Bath & Portland Gp, 1983–85; Thermal Scientific plc, 1986–88. Member: Bd of Brixton Prison, 1975–78; Court, City Univ., 1978– (Chancellor, 1981–82); Council of the Missions to Seamen, 1983–; Council, Wine and Spirit Benevolent Soc., 1983–88; Finance Cttee, London Diocesan Fund, 1983–86; Trustee: Chichester Festival Theatre, 1982–; LSO, 1983–91; Vice-President: Bridewell Royal Hosp., 1982–89; NPFA, 1983–; Governor: Christ's Hospital Sch., 1975–; City of London Girls' Sch., 1975–78; City of London Freemen's Sch., 1980–81; Chm., Council, Eastbourne Coll., 1989– (Mem., 1988–); Almoner Trustee, St Paul's Cathedral Choir Sch. Foundn, 1986–90. Trustee, Music Therapy Trust, 1981–89; Chairman, Young Musicians' Symphony Orch. Trust, 1979–81; Hon. Mem., Guildhall Sch. of Music and Drama, 1982–. Church Warden, St Olave's, Hart Street, 1975–90 (Chm., Patronage Trust, 1990–); Church Comr, 1982–. Mem., Ct of Assistants, Carmen's Co., 1973 (Master, 1987–88); Hon. Liveryman, Farmers' Company; Freeman, Co. of Watermen and Lightermen; Hon. Mem., Co. of Environmental Cleaners, 1983–; Hon. Col, 151 (Greater London) Tpt Regt RCT (V), 1983–88; Hon. Col Comdt, RCT, 1988–91. Hon. DMus City, 1981. KStJ 1982. Order of Oman Class II. *Recreations*: gardening, music. *Address*: The Rectory, St Mary-at-Hill, EC3R 8EE. *T*: 071–283 3575.

LEAVER, Prof. Christopher John, FRS 1986; FRSE; Sibthorpian Professor of Plant Sciences, since 1990, and Fellow, St John's College, University of Oxford; *b* 31 May 1942; *s* of Douglas Percy Leaver and Elizabeth Constance Leaver; *m* 1971, Anne (*née* Huggins); one *s* one *d. Educ*: Imperial College, University of London (BSc, ARCS, DIC, PhD); MA 1990. Fulbright Scholar, Purdue Univ., 1966–68; Scientific Officer, ARC Plant Physiology Unit, Imperial Coll., 1968–69; University of Edinburgh: Lectr, Dept of Botany, 1969–80; Reader, 1980–86; SERC Sen. Res. Fellow, 1985–89; Prof. of Plant Molecular Biol., 1986–89. Member: AFRC, 1990–; Priorities Bd for R & D in Agriculture and Food. Trustee, John Innes Foundn, 1987–. Mem., Academia Europaea, 1988. T. H. Huxley Gold Medal, Imperial Coll., 1970; Tate & Lyle Award, Phytochem. Soc. of Europe, 1984. *Publications*: numerous papers in internat. sci. jls. *Recreations*: walking and talking in Upper Coquetdale. *Address*: Department of Plant Sciences, University of Oxford, South Parks Road, Oxford OX1 3RA. *T*: Oxford (0865) 275143, *Fax*: Oxford (0865) 275144.

LEAVER, Peter Lawrence Oppenheim; QC 1987; *b* 28 Nov. 1944; *er s* of Marcus Isaac Leaver and Lena Leaver (*née* Oppenheim); *m* 1969, Jane Rachel, *o d* of Leonard and Rivka Pearl; three *s* one *d. Educ*: Aldenham Sch., Elstree; Trinity Coll., Dublin. Called to the Bar, Lincoln's Inn, 1967. Chairman: Bar Cttee, 1989; Internat. Practice Cttee, 1990. Member: Gen. Council of the Bar, 1987–90; Cttee on the Future of the Legal Profession, 1986–88; Council of Legal Educn, 1986–. *Recreations*: sport, theatre, wine. *Address*: 1 Essex Court, Temple, EC4Y 9AR. *T*: 071–583 2000; 5 Hamilton Terrace, NW8 9RE. *T*: 071–286 0208. *Clubs*: Athenæum, MCC.

LEAVETT, Alan; Member, Woodspring District Council, since 1986; *b* 4 May 1924; *s* of George and Mabel Dorothy Leavett; *m* 1948, Jean Mary Wanford; three *d. Educ*: Gosport County Sch.; UC, Southampton. BA Hons 1943. MAP (RAE), 1943; HM Customs and Excise, 1947; HM Foreign Service, 1949; Rio de Janeiro, 1950–53; Bangkok, 1955–59; UK Perm. Delegate to ECAFE, 1958; Cabinet Office, 1961; Min. of Housing and Local Govt, 1963; Sec., Noise Adv. Council, 1970; Under-Sec., Civil Service Selection Bd, 1973, Dept of Environment, 1974–81. Gen. Sec., Avon Wildlife Trust, 1981–84; Member: Rural Develt Commn, 1982–91; Council, World Wildlife Fund UK, 1983–86; Vice-Pres., ACRE, 1987–; Vice-Chm., Avon Community Council, 1981–89. *Publication*: Historic Sevenoaks, 1969. *Recreations*: book-collecting, music. *Address*: Darenth House, St Martins, Long Ashton, Bristol BS18 9HP. *T*: Long Ashton (0275) 392876.

LEAVEY, John Anthony, BA; *b* 3 March 1915; *s* of George Edwin Leavey and Marion Louise Warnock; *m* 1952, Lesley Doreen, *d* of Rt Hon. Sir Benjamin Ormerod. *Educ*: Mill Hill Sch.; Trinity Hall, Cambridge. Served War, 1939–46; 5th Royal Inniskilling Dragoon Guards. MP (C) Heywood and Royton Div. of Lancashire, 1955–64. PPS to Minister of Defence, 1956–57, to Chancellor of Exchequer, 1959–60. Chairman: Wilson (Connolly) Hldgs, 1966–82 (Dir, 1966–85); Robert Moss, 1981–82 (Dir, 1981–86); Edward Barber & Co., 1982–88; Director: Smith & Nephew, 1948–80 (Dep. Chm., 1962–72); BIA, 1976–85; Fläkt, 1976–85; CSE Aviation, 1986–88. Panel Mem., SE London Indust. Tribunal, 1978–84. Mem. Council, Outward Bound Trust, 1974–; Trustee, Kurt Hahn Trust, 1987–. *Recreation*: fishing. *Address*: 30 Pembroke Gardens Close, W8 6HR. *Club*: Army and Navy.

LE BAILLY, Vice-Adm. Sir Louis (Edward Stewart Holland), KBE 1972 (OBE 1952); CB 1969; DL; Director-General of Intelligence, Ministry of Defence, 1972–75; *b* 18 July 1915; *s* of Robert Francis Le Bailly and Ida Gaskell Le Bailly (*née* Holland); *m* 1946, Pamela Ruth Berthon; three *d. Educ*: RNC Dartmouth. HMS Hood, 1932; RNEC,

1933–37; HMS Hood, 1937–40; HMS Naiad, 1940–42; RNEC, 1942–44; HMS Duke of York, 1944–46; Admiralty, 1946–50; HMS Bermuda, 1950–52; RNEC, 1955–58; Admiralty: Staff Officer to Dartmouth Review Cttee, 1958; Asst Engineer-in-Chief, 1958–60; Naval Asst to Controller of the Navy, 1960–63; IDC, 1963; Dep. Dir of Marine Engineering, 1963–67; Naval Attaché, Washington, DC, and Comdr, British Navy Staff, 1967–69; Min. of Defence, 1970–72; Vice-Adm. 1970, retired 1972. Mem. Council, Inst. for Security and Conflict Studies (formerly Inst. for Study of Conflict), 1976–. DL Cornwall, 1982. FIMechE; FInstPet; MIMarE. *Publication:* The Man Around the Engine, 1990. *Address:* Garlands House, St Tudy, Bodmin, Cornwall PL30 3NN. *Club:* Naval and Military.

LEBETER, Fred; Keeper, Department of Transport and Mining, Science Museum, 1953–67; *b* 27 Dec. 1903; *e s* of Arthur Lebeter, Mining Engineer, and Lucy Wilson; *m* 1926, Sybil Leah, *o d* of Henry Ward; one *d* decd. *Educ:* Rotherham and Bridgnorth Gram. Schs; Birmingham Univ. BSc 1925; MSc (Research on Classification of British Coals) 1926. Manager, Magnesite Mines and Works, Salem, S India, 1926–31; Lecturer in Mining, Heanor Mining Sch., 1931–33; Sen. Lectr in Mining, Chesterfield Tech. Coll., 1933–37; Asst Keeper, Science Museum, 1937–39; Dep. Chief Mining Supplies Officer, Min. of Fuel and Power, 1939–47; Asst Keeper, Science Museum, 1947–49, Dep. Keeper, 1949–53. Consultant on Mine Ventilation and Underground Transport, 1931–; Mem. Council Nat. Assoc. of Colliery Managers (Midland Br.), 1935–37; Adviser to Coal Commission, Germany, on Mining Supplies, 1944; UK rep. to European Coal Organisation, 1945–47. United Kingdom delegate to European Coal Organisation, Paris, 1946. Mem., Industrial Cttee, National Museum of Wales, 1959–67. Retired 1967. *Publications:* contributor of many technical articles to Colliery Engineering, Mine and Quarry Engineering, historical articles in Zeitschrift für Kunst und Kultur im Bergbau, etc. *Recreations:* sport and gardening. *Address:* 6 Bay House, Pelham Road, Seaford, E Sussex BN25 1EP. *T:* Seaford (0323) 894751.

LEBLANC, Rt. Rev. Camille André; Chaplain at Caraquet Hospital; *b* Barachois, NB, 25 Aug. 1898. *Educ:* Collège Sainte-Anne, Church Point, NS; Grand Séminaire Halifax, NS. Priest, 1924; Subseq. Curé at Shemogue and the Cathedral of Nôtre Dame de l'Assomption, Moncton; Bishop of Bathurst, 1942–69. *Address:* c/o Hôpital de l'Enfant-Jésus, Caraquet, NB E0B 1K0, Canada.

LEBLOND, Prof. C(harles) P(hilippe), OC 1977; MD, PhD, DSc; FRSC 1951; FRS 1965; Professor of Anatomy, McGill University, Canada, since 1948; *b* 5 Feb. 1910; *s* of Oscar Leblond and Jeanne Desmarchelier; *m* 1936, Gertrude Elinor Sternschuss; three *s* one *d*. *Educ:* Sch. St Joseph, Lille, France; Univs. of Lille, Nancy, Paris, Montreal. L-ès-S, Nancy 1932; MD Paris 1934; PhD Montreal 1942; DSc Sorbonne 1945. Asst in Histology, Med. School, Univ. of Paris, 1934–35; Rockefeller Fell., Sch. of Med., Yale Univ., 1936–37; Asst, Laboratoire de Synthése Atomique, Paris, 1938–40; McGill Univ.: Lectr in Histology and Embryology, 1941–42; Asst Prof. of Anatomy, 1942–43; Assoc. Prof. of Anatomy, 1946–48; Prof. of Anatomy, 1948–; Chm. of Dept of Anatomy, 1957–75. Mem. Amer. Assoc. of Anatomists; Fellow, Amer. Acad. of Arts and Scis. Hon. DSc: Acadia, 1972; McGill, 1982; Montreal, 1985; York, 1986. *Publications:* over 300 articles, mainly on radio-autography, in anatomical journals. *Recreation:* country. *Address:* (home) 68 Chesterfield Avenue, Westmount, Montreal, Quebec H3Y 2M5, Canada. *T:* 514– 486–4837; (office) Department of Anatomy, McGill University, 3640 University Street, Montreal, Quebec H3A 2B2, Canada. *T:* 514–398–6340

LE BRETON, David Francis Battye, CBE 1978; HM Diplomatic Service, retired; Financial Adviser/Sales Associate, Allied Dunbar Assurance plc, since 1987; *b* 2 March 1931; *e s* of late Lt-Col F. H. Le Breton, MC, and Elisabeth Le Breton (*née* Trevor-Battye), Endebess, Kenya; *m* 1961, Patricia June Byrne; one *s* two *d*. *Educ:* Winchester; New Coll., Oxford. Colonial Administrative Service, Tanganyika, 1954; Private Sec. to Governor, 1959–60; Magistrate, 1962; Principal, CRO, 1963; HM Diplomatic Service, 1965; First Sec., Zanzibar, 1964; Lusaka, 1964–68; FCO, 1968–71; Head of Chancery, Budapest, 1971–74; HM Comr in Anguilla, 1974–78; Counsellor and Head of Chancery, Nairobi, 1978–81; High Comr in The Gambia, 1981–84; Head of Commonwealth Co-ordination Dept, FCO, 1984–86; Head of Nationality and Treaty Dept, FCO, 1986–87. *Recreations:* travel, African affairs. *Address:* Brackenwood, French Street, near Westerham, Kent TN16 1PN.

le BROCQUY, Louis, FCSD (FSIAD 1960); HRHA 1983; painter since 1939; *b* Dublin, 10 Nov. 1916; *s* of late Albert le Brocquy, MA, and late Sybil Staunton; *m* 1st, 1938, Jean Stoney (marr. diss., 1948); one *d*; 2nd, 1958, Anne Madden Simpson; two *s*. *Educ:* St Gerard's Sch., Wicklow, Ireland. Self-taught. Founder-mem. of Irish Exhibn of Living Art, 1943; Visiting Instructor, Central Sch. of Arts and Crafts, London, 1947–54; Visiting Tutor, Royal Coll. of Art, London, 1955–58. Member: Irish Council of Design, 1963–65; Adv. Council, Guinness Peat Awards, 1980–85. Director: Kilkenny Design Workshops, 1965–77; Irish Mus. of Modern Art, 1989–. Represented Ireland, Venice Biennale (awarded internat. prize), 1956. Work exhibited in: "50 Ans d'Art Moderne", Brussels, 1958; Painting since World War II, Guggenheim Mus., New York, 1987–88; Olympiad of Art, Seoul, 1988; L'Europe des Grands Maîtres 1870–1970, Inst. de France, 1989; Internat. Art Fest., Seoul, 1991; Premiers Chefs d'Oeuvres des Grands Maîtres, Mus. Art, Tokyo, Osaka, Kyoto. One Man Shows: Leicester Galleries, London, 1948; Gimpel Fils, London, 1947, 1949, 1951, 1955, 1956, 1957, 1959, 1961, 1966, 1968, 1971, 1974, 1978, 1983, 1988, 1991; Waddington, Dublin, 1951; Robles Gallery, Los Angeles, 1960; Gallery Lienhard, Zürich, 1961; Dawson/Taylor Gallery, Dublin, 1962, 1966, 1969, 1971, 1973, 1974, 1975, 1981, 1985, 1986, 1988; Municipal Gallery of Modern Art, Dublin, 1966, 1978; Ulster Mus., Belfast, (retrospective) 1966–67, 1987; Gimpel-Hanover, Emmerich Zürich, 1969, 1978 1983; Gimpel, NY, 1971, 1978, 1983; Fondation Maeght, 1973; Bussola, Turin, 1974; Arts Council, Belfast, 1975, 1978; Musée d'Art Moderne, Paris, 1976; Giustiniani, Genoa, 1977; Waddington, Montreal, Toronto, 1978; Maeght, Barcelona, Madrid, Granada, 1978–79; Jeanne Bucher, Paris, 1979, 1982; NY State Mus., 1981; Boston Coll. 1982; Westfield Coll., Mass, 1982; Palais des Beaux Arts, Charleroi, 1982; Chicago Internat. Expo (Brownstone Gall.), 1986; Arts Council, Dublin, 1987; Nat. Gall. of Vic, Melbourne, Festival Centre, Adelaide, and Mus. of Contemp. Art, Brisbane, 1988; Musée Picasso, Antibes, 1989; Kerlin, Dublin, 1991; Mus. of Modern Art, Kamakura, 1991; Itami City Mus. of Art, Osaka, 1991; City Mus. of Contemp. Art, Hiroshima, 1991. Public Collections possessing work include: Albright Museum, Buffalo; Arts Council, London; Carnegie Inst., Pittsburgh; l'Etat Français; Chicago Arts Club; Columbus Mus., Ohio; Detroit Inst. of Art; Dublin Municipal Gallery; Fort Worth Center, Texas; Foundation of Brazil Museum, Bahia; Gulbenkian Mus., Lisbon; Guggenheim Museum, NY; J. H. Hirshhorn Foundation, Washington; Ho-Am Mus., Seoul; Itami Mus., Osaka; Kunsthaus, Zürich; Fondation Maeght, St Paul; Leeds City Art Gallery; Musée d'Art Moderne, Paris; Musée Picasso, Antibes; Mus. of Contemp. Art, Hiroshima; Mus. of Modern Art, Kamakura; NY State Mus.; San Diego Mus., Calif.; Tate Gallery; Uffizi, Florence; Ulster Museum, Belfast; Vatican Mus.; V&A Museum. RHA 1950–69. Film, An Other Way of Knowing, RTE, 1986. Chevalier de la Légion d'Honneur, 1975. Hon. DLitt Dublin, 1962; Hon. LLD NUI, 1988. Commandeur du Bontemps de Médoc et des Graves, 1969. *Illustrated work:* The Táin, trans. Thomas Kinsella, 1969; The Playboy of the Western World, Synge, 1970; The Gododdin, 1978; Dubliners, Joyce, 1986; Stirrings Still, Samuel Beckett, 1988. *Relevant publication:* Louis le Brocquy by D. Walker, introd. John Russell, Ireland 1981, UK 1982. *Address:* c/o Gimpel Fils, 30 Davies Street, W1Y 1LG.

LE CARRÉ, John; *see* Cornwell, David John Moore.

LE CHEMINANT, Peter, CB 1976; Director-General, General Council of British Shipping, 1985–91; *b* 29 April 1926; *s* of William Arthur Le Cheminant and Agnes Ann Le Cheminant (*née* Wilson); *m* 1959, Suzanne Elisabeth Horny; three *s*. *Educ:* Holloway Sch.; London Sch. of Economics. Sub-Lt, RNVR, 1944–47. Min. of Power, 1949; Cabinet Office, 1950–52 and 1964–65; UK Delegn to ECSC, 1962–63; Private Sec. to Prime Minister, 1965–68; Min. of Power, later Min. of Technology, 1968–71; Under-Sec., DTI, 1971–74; Deputy Secretary: Dept of Energy, 1974–77; Cabinet Office, 1978–81; CSD, subseq. HM Treas., 1981–83; Second Perm. Sec., Cabinet Office (MPO), 1983–84. Member, Council: Inst. of Manpower Studies, 1983–; King George's Fund for Sailors, 1987–. Liveryman, Worshipful Co. of Shipwrights, 1987. CBIM 1984; FCIT 1987. *Recreations:* reading, walking, history. *Club:* Reform.

LE CHEMINANT, Air Chief Marshal Sir Peter (de Lacey), GBE 1978; KCB 1972 (CB 1968); DFC 1943, and Bar, 1951; Lieutenant-Governor and Commander-in-Chief of Guernsey, 1980–85; *b* 17 June 1920; *s* of Lieut-Colonel Keith Le Cheminant and Blanche Etheldred Wake Le Cheminant (*née* Clark); *m* 1940, Sylvia, *d* of J. van Bodegom; one *s* two *d*. *Educ:* Elizabeth Coll., Guernsey; RAF Coll., Cranwell. Flying posts in France, UK, N Africa, Malta, Sicily and Italy, 1940–44; comd No 223 Squadron, 1943–44; Staff and Staff Coll. Instructor, 1945–48; Far East, 1949–53; comd No 209 Sqn, 1949–51; Jt Planning Staff, 1953–55; Wing Comdr, Flying, Kuala Lumpur, 1955–57; jssc 1958; Dep. Dir of Air Staff Plans, 1958–61; comd RAF Geilenkirchen, 1961–63; Dir of Air Staff Briefing, 1964–66; SASO, HQ FEAF, 1966–67, C of S, 1967–68; Comdt Joint Warfare Estabt, MoD, 1968–70; Asst Chief of Air Staff (Policy), MoD, 1971–72; UK Mem., Perm. Mil. Deputies Gp, CENTO, Ankara, 1972–73; Vice-Chief of Defence Staff, 1974–76; Dep. C-in-C, Allied Forces, Central Europe, 1976–79. KStJ 1980. *Recreations:* golf, sailing, reading. *Address:* La Madeleine De Bas, Ruette de la Madeleine, St Pierre du Bois, Guernsey, CI. *Club:* Royal Air Force.

LECHIN-SUAREZ, Brigadier General Juan, Condor de los Andes, Guerrillero José Miguel Lanza, Mérito Aeronautico, Mérito Naval (Bolivia); *b* 8 March 1921; *s* of Juan Alfredo Lechín and Julia Suárez; *m* 1947, Ruth Varela; one *s* three *d*. *Educ:* Bolivian Military College. Chief of Ops, Bolivian Army HQ, 1960–61; Military and Air Attaché, Bolivian Embassy, Bonn, 1962–63; Comdr, Bolivian Army Fifth Inf. Div., 1964; Pres., Bolivian State Mining Corp. (with rank of Minister of State), 1964–68; Comdr, Bolivian Army Third Inf. Div., 1969; Bolivian Ambassador to the UK and to the Netherlands, 1970–74; Minister for Planning and Co-ordination, 1974–78; Chm., Nat. Adv. and Legislation Council, 1980–81. Das Grosse Verdienstkreuz (FRG). *Publications:* La Estrategia del Altiplano Boliviano, 1975; La Batalla de Villa Montes, 1989. *Recreations:* tennis, swimming. *Address:* Casilla 4405, La Paz, Bolivia.

LECHMERE, Sir Berwick (Hungerford), 6th Bt, *cr* 1818; JP; Vice Lord-Lieutenant, Hereford and Worcester, since 1977; Land Agent; *b* 21 Sept. 1917; *s* of Sir Ronald Berwick Hungerford Lechmere, 5th Bt, and Constance Marguerite (*née* Long) (*d* 1981); *S* father, 1965; *m* 1954, Norah Garrett Elkington; no *c*. *Educ:* Charterhouse; Magdalene Coll., Cambridge. High Sheriff of Worcs, 1962, JP, 1966, DL 1972. FRICS. CStJ. *Heir:* *cousin* Reginald Anthony Hungerford Lechmere [*b* 24 Dec. 1920; *m* 1956, Anne Jennifer Dind; three *s* one *d*]. *Address:* Church End House, Hanley Castle, Worcester. *T:* Upton-on-Severn (06846) 2130.

LECKIE, John, CB 1955; *b* 2 Sept. 1911; *o s* of late Alexander M. Leckie; *m* 1937, Elizabeth Mary Murray Brown; two *s*. *Educ:* Hamilton Academy; Glasgow Univ. (MA, BSc). Entered Administrative Class, Home Civil Service, by competitive examination, 1934; Customs and Excise Dept, 1934; transferred to Board of Trade, 1940; Head of Board of Trade Delegation, Washington, USA, 1943–45; Adviser on Commercial Policy, 1950; Under-Sec., 1950–60, Second Sec., 1960–64, BoT; Deputy Secretary: Min. of Technology, 1964–70; DTI, 1970–72, retd 1972. *Address:* 1 The Wedges, West Chiltington Lane, Itchingfield, Horsham, Sussex RH13 7TA.

LECKY, Arthur Terence, CMG 1968; HM Diplomatic Service, retired; *b* 10 June 1919; *s* of late Lieut-Colonel M. D. Lecky, DSO, late RA, and late Bertha Lecky (*née* Goss); *m* 1946, Jacqualine (*d* 1974), *d* of late Dr A. G. Element; three *s*. *Educ:* Winchester Coll.; Clare Coll., Cambridge (1938–39). Served RA, 1939–46. FO (Control Commission for Germany), 1946–49; FO, 1950–54; Vice-Consul, Zürich, 1954–56; FO, 1957–61; First Secretary, The Hague, 1962–64, FCO (formerly FO), 1964–70, retired. Mem., Hants CC, 1981–89. Vice-Chm., Hants Police Authority, 1988–89. *Address:* Springfield, Mill End, Damerham, near Fordingbridge, Hants SP6 3HU. *T:* Rockbourne (07253) 595.

LECKY, Maj.-Gen. Samuel K.; *see* Knox-Lecky.

LECONFIELD, Baron; *see* Egremont.

LECOURT, Robert; Commandeur, Legion of Honour; Croix de Guerre; Rosette de la Résistance; Member, Constitutional Council of the French Republic, 1979–89; *b* 19 Sept. 1908; *s* of Léon Lecourt and Angèle Lépron; *m* 1932, Marguerite Chabrerie; one *d*. *Educ:* Rouen; Univ. de Caen (DenDroit). Advocate, Court of Appeal: Rouen, 1928; Paris, 1932. Served with French Air Force, 1939–40; Mem. Resistance Movt, 1942–44; Deputy for Paris, 1945–58 and for Hautes Alpes, 1958–61, National Assembly; Pres., Parly Gp, MRP, 1945–48 and 1952–57; Minister of Justice, 1948–49 and 1957–58; Minister of State responsible for co-operation with Africa, 1958–61. Judge, Court of Justice, European Community, 1962, President 1967–76; Hon. Bencher, Gray's Inn, 1972; DUniv Exeter, 1975. Holds numerous foreign decorations. *Publications:* Nature juridique de l'action en réintégrande, 1931; Code pratique du travail, Responsabilité des architectes et entrepreneurs, etc, 1932–39; Le Juge devant le marché commun, 1970; L'Europe des juges, 1976; Concorde sans concordat 1952–57, 1978; contrib. Le Monde, Figaro, Aurore, and other European jls. *Address:* 11 Boulevard Suchet, 75016 Paris, France.

LEDERBERG, Prof. Joshua, PhD; University Professor, Rockefeller University, since 1990; consultant; *b* Montclair, NJ, USA, 23 May 1925; *s* of Zwi H. and Esther Lederberg (*née* Goldenbaum); *m* 1968, Marguerite Stein Kirsch, MD; one *d*, one step *s*. *Educ:* Stuyvesant High Sch., NYC; Columbia Coll. (BA); Yale Univ. (PhD). Assistant Professor of Genetics, University of Wisconsin, 1947; Associate Professor, 1950; Professor, 1954; Fulbright Vis. Prof. of Bacteriology, Univ. of Melbourne, Aust., 1957; Prof. and Exec. Head, Dept of Genetics, Sch. of Medicine, Stanford Univ., 1959–78; Pres., Rockefeller Univ., 1978–90. Dir, Inst. for Sci. Inf., Philadelphia, 1970–; Mem. Bd, Center for Advanced Study in the Behavioral Sciences, Stanford, 1975–81. Dir, Procter & Gamble Co., Cincinnati, Ohio, 1984–; Consultant: Cetus Cos, Berkeley, Calif, 1972–; J. D. Wolfensohn Assoc., NY, 1983–; Celanese Corp., 1981–. Shared in discoveries concerning genetic re-combination, and organization of genetic material of bacteria, contributing to cancer research; discovered a method of artificially introducing new genes into bacteria in investigation of hereditary substance. Chm., President's Cancer Panel (US), 1980–81. Member: Defense Sci. Bd, USA, 1979–; Chief of Naval Ops Exec. Panel, USN, 1981–; Council of Scholars, US Library of Congress, 1985–; Tech. Assessment Adv. Cttee, Office of Technology Assessment, US Congress, 1988–; Adv. Cttee for Med. Res., WHO, 1971–76; Chm. Bd, Annual Reviews, Palo Alto, Calif, 1972–; Member Board: Chemical Industry Inst. for Toxicology, 1980–; Dreyfus Foundn, 1983–; Revson Foundn, 1986–; Trustee, Carnegie Corp., NYC, 1985–. Columnist, Science and Man (Washington Post Syndicate), 1966–71. Mem., National Academy of Sciences, United States, 1957. For. Mem., Royal Society, 1979. ScD (*hc*): Yale Univ.; Columbia Univ.; Univ. of Wisconsin; Mt Sinai Sch. of Medicine; Rutgers; New York Univ.; MD (*hc*): Tufts Univ.; Univ. of Turin; LittD (*hc*) Jewish Theol Seminary; LLD (*hc*) Univ. of Pennsylvania. (Jointly) Nobel Prize in Medicine, 1958. US Nat. Medal of Science, 1989. *Publications:* contribs to learned journals on genetics, bacteria and general biological problems. *Address:* Rockefeller University, 1230 York Avenue, New York, NY 10021, USA. *T:* 212.570.8000.

LEDERMAN, David; QC 1990; a Recorder, since 1987; *b* 8 Feb. 1942; *s* of Eric Kurt Lederman and Marjorie Alice Lederman; *m* 1974, Georgina Anne Rubin; one *s* two *d*. *Educ:* Clayesmore School, Dorset; Gonville and Caius College, Cambridge. Called to the Bar, Inner Temple, 1966; general common law practice, particularly crime. *Recreations:* tennis, squash, horses, France, family. *Address:* 1 Dr Johnson's Buildings, Temple, EC4Y 7AX.

LEDERMAN, Dr Leon Max; Director, Fermi National Accelerator Laboratory, since 1979; Professor of Physics, Columbia University, since 1958; *b* 15 July 1922; *s* of Minnie Rosenberg and Morris Lederman; *m* 1st, Florence Gordon; one *s* two *d*; 2nd, 1981, Ellen. *Educ:* City College of New York (BS 1943); Columbia Univ. (AM 1948; PhD 1951). US Army, 1943–46. Columbia University: Research Associate, Asst Prof., Associate Prof., 1951–58; Associate Dir, Nevis Labs, 1953, Director, 1962–79. Ford Foundn Fellow, 1958–59; John Simon Guggenheim Foundn Fellow, 1958–59; Ernest Kempton Adams Fellow, 1961. Fellow, Amer. Physical Soc.; Mem., Nat. Acad. of Scis, 1965. Numerous hon. degrees. Nat. Medal of Science, 1965; (jtly) Nobel Prize in Physics, 1988. *Publications:* papers and contribs to learned jls on high energy physics. *Recreations:* mountain hiking, ski-ing, jogging, piano, riding, gardening. *Address:* Fermi National Accelerator Laboratory, PO Box 500, Batavia, Illinois 60510, USA. *T:* (312) 840–3211.

LEDGER, Frank, OBE 1985; Deputy Chairman, Nuclear Electric plc, since 1990; *b* 16 June 1929; *s* of Harry and Doris Ledger; *m* 1953, Alma Moverley; two *s*. *Educ:* Leeds College of Technology (BSc Eng). FEng; FIMechE; FIEE; CBIM. Student Apprentice, Leeds Corp. Elect. Dept, 1947; appts in power station construction and generation operation in CEA then CEGB, 1955–65; Station Manager, Cottam Power Station, 1965; Central Electricity Generating Board: Group Manager, Midlands Region, 1968; System Operation Engineer, 1971; Dir, Resource Planning, Midlands Region, 1975; Dir of Computing, 1980; Dir of Operations, 1981; Exec. Bd Mem. for Prodn, 1986. *Recreations:* music, photography, gardening, walking. *Address:* (office) 123 Pall Mall, SW1Y 5EA. *T:* 071–389 3402.

LEDGER, Sir Frank, (Joseph Francis), Kt 1963; retired Company Director (engineering etc); *b* 29 Oct. 1899; *s* of Edson and Annie Frances Ledger; *m* 1923, Gladys Muriel Lyons (*d* 1981); one *s* two *d*. *Educ:* Perth Boys' Sch., Perth, WA. President: J. E. Ledger Cos; Mitchell Cotts Gp; Dir, Mitchell Cotts Australia; Governing Dir, Ledger Investments; Past Chm. of Dirs, S Australian Insurance Co.; Director: Chamber of Manufrs Insurance Co.; ARC Engineering Co.; Winget Moxey (WA) Pty Ltd; Lake View and Star Ltd; Member, Past Chairman: WA Branch of Inst. of Directors (London); WA Govt Industrial Develt Adv. Cttee; Pres., Royal Commonwealth Society (WA Branch); Past President: WA Chamber of Manufacturers; WA Employers Federation; Ironmasters Assoc. (WA); Metal Industries Assoc. (WA); Inst. of Foundrymen (WA); Past Vice-Pres., Associated Chamber of Manufacturers (Canberra). Pres., WA Trotting Assoc.; Vice-Pres., Australian Trotting Council. *Recreations:* golfing, sailing. *Address:* 2 The Esplanade, Peppermint Grove, WA 6011, Australia. *Clubs:* Weld, Perth, Royal Freshwater Bay Yacht, Cottesloe Golf; WA Turf, WA Cricket Association (all in Perth, WA).

LEDGER, Sir Joseph Francis; *see* Ledger, Sir Frank.

LEDGER, Philip (Stevens), CBE 1985; Principal, Royal Scottish Academy of Music and Drama, since 1982; *b* 12 Dec. 1937; *s* of Walter Stephen Ledger and Winifred Kathleen (*née* Stevens); *m* 1963, Mary Erryl (*née* Wells); one *s* one *d*. *Educ:* Bexhill Grammar Sch.; King's Coll., Cambridge (Maj. Schol.); John Stewart of Rannoch Schol. in Sacred Music; 1st Cl. Hons in Pt I and Pt II, of Music Tripos; MA, MusB. FRCO (Limpus and Read prizes); FRCM 1983; FRNCM 1989; FRSE 1990. Master of the Music, Chelmsford Cathedral, 1962–65; Dir of Music, Univ. of East Anglia, 1965–73 (Dean of Sch. of Fine Arts and Music, 1968–71); Dir of Music and Organist, King's Coll., Cambridge, 1974–82; Conductor, CU Musical Soc., 1973–82. Artistic Dir, 1968–89, Vice-Pres., 1989–, Aldeburgh Festival of Music and the Arts. Hon. RAM 1984; Hon. GSM 1989. Hon. LLD Strathclyde, 1987. *Publications:* (ed) Anthems for Choirs 2 and 3, 1973; (ed) The Oxford Book of English Madrigals, 1978; other edns of Byrd, Handel and Purcell; carol arrangements. *Recreations:* swimming, theatre, membership of Sette of Odd Volumes. *Address:* 322 Albert Drive, Pollokshields, Glasgow G41 5DZ. *T:* 041–429 0967. *Club:* Athenæum.

LEDGER, Ronald Joseph; Casino Proprietor and Manager; *b* 7 Nov. 1920; *s* of Arthur and Florence Ledger; *m* 1946, Madeleine Odette de Villeneuve; three *s* one *d*. *Educ:* Skinners Grammar Sch., Tunbridge Wells; Nottingham Univ. Toolroom Engineer, 1938–42. Served RAF, 1942–47, fitter, Leading Aircraftsman; India three years. Univ. of Nottingham, 1947–49 (Diploma in Social Science); Staff Training Officer, Enfield Highway Co-op. Society, 1949; Business Partner, 1950, Company Director, 1953, Employment Specialists. Mem. Herts CC, 1952–54. Contested (Lab) Rushcliffe Div. of Nottingham, 1951; MP (Lab and Co-op) Romford, 1955–70. Director: Enfield Electronics (CRT) Ltd, 1958; London Co-operative Society Ltd, 1961. Chairman, Hairdressing Council, 1966–79. *Recreations:* tennis, cricket, golf, snooker. *Address:* Pomona, Shanklin, Isle of Wight. *Clubs:* Shanklin and Sandown Golf, Enfield Golf.

LEDINGHAM, Prof. John Gerard Garvin, DM; FRCP; May Reader in Medicine, since 1974, Professor of Clinical Medicine, since 1989, and Director of Clinical Studies, 1977–82 and since 1991, University of Oxford; Fellow of New College, Oxford, since 1974; Hon. Clinical Director, Biochemical and Clinical NMR Unit, Medical Research Council, Oxford, since 1988; *b* 1929; *s* of late John Ledingham, MB BCh, DPH, and late Una Ledingham, MD, FRCP, *d* of J. L. Garvin, CH, Editor of The Observer; *m* 1961, Elaine Mary, *d* of late R. G. Maliphant, MD, FRCOG, and of Dilys Maliphant, Cardiff; four *d*. *Educ:* Rugby Sch.; New Coll., Oxford; Middlesex Hosp. Med. Sch. (1st Cl. Physiol.; BM BCh; DM 1966). FRCP 1971 (MRCP 1959). Junior appts, Middlesex, London Chest, Whittington, and Westminster Hospitals, London, 1957–64; Travelling Fellow, British Postgraduate Med. Fedn, Columbia Univ., New York, 1965–66; Consultant Physician, Oxford AHA(T), 1966–82, Hon. Consultant Physician, Oxfordshire HA, 1982–. Chm., Medical Staff Council, United Oxford Hosps, 1970–72. Chm., Medical Res. Soc., 1988–; Hon. Sec., Assoc. of Physicians of Gt Britain and Ireland 1977–82, Hon. Treas., 1982–88; Pro-Censor, RCP, 1983–84, Censor, 1984–85. Governing Trustee, Nuffield Provincial Hosps Trust, 1978–; Trustee, Beit Trust, 1989–. *Publications:* (ed jtly) Oxford Textbook of Medicine, 1982, 2nd edn 1987; contribs to med. books and scientific jls in the field of hypertension and renal diseases. *Recreations:* music, golf. *Address:* 22 Hid's Copse Road, Cumnor Hill, Oxford OX2 9JJ. *T:* Oxford (0865) 862023. *Club:* Vincent's (Oxford).

LEDINGHAM, Prof. John Marshall, MD, FRCP; Consultant Physician, The London Hospital, 1954–81, now Consulting Physician; Professor of Medicine, University of London, at London Hospital Medical College, 1971–81, now Emeritus; *b* 1916; *s* of late Prof. Sir John C. G. Ledingham, CMG, FRS, of The Lister Institute, London, and late Lady Barbara Ledingham; *m* 1950, Josephine, *d* of late Matthew and Jane Metcalf, Temple Sowerby, Westmorland; two *s*. *Educ:* Whitgift Sch.; University College, London; The London Hospital. BSc (London) First Class Hons in Physics, 1936; MRCS, LRCP, 1942; MD (London) Gold Medal, 1951, FRCP, 1957. Service in RAMC as Graded Clinical and Experimental Pathologist, in UK, France, Middle and Far East, 1942–47. Lectr in Medicine, London Hosp. Med. Sch., 1948–53; Univ. Reader in Medicine, 1953–64; Prof. of Experimental Medicine, 1964–71, London Hosp. Med. Coll., London Univ. Vis. Prof., Maiduguri Univ., Nigeria, 1982. Mem., Professional and Linguistic Assessment Bd, GMC, 1984–90. Past Pres., Section of Exptl Med. and Therapeutics, RSM; Bertram Louis Abrahams Lectr, RCP, 1970; Censor, RCP, 1975. Editor, Dep. Chm. and Chm. Editl Bd, Clinical Science, 1965–70. *Publications:* numerous scientific, mainly in field of hypertension and renal disease, 1938–. *Address:* 11 Montpelier Walk, SW7 1JL. *T:* 071–584 7976.

LEDLIE, John Kenneth, OBE 1977; Deputy Secretary, Northern Ireland Office, since 1990; *b* 19 March 1942; *s* of late Reginald Cyril Bell Ledlie and Elspeth Mary Kaye; *m* 1965, Rosemary Julia Allan; three *d*. *Educ:* Westminster School (Hon. Schol.); Brasenose Coll., Oxford (Triplett Exbnr; MA Lit Hum). Solicitor of the High Court; articles with Coward Chance, 1964–67; Min. of Defence, 1967; Asst Private Sec. to Minister of State for Equipment and Sec. of State for Defence, 1969–70; First Sec., UK Delegn to NATO, Brussels, 1973–76; Dep. Chief, Public Relations, 1977–79; NI Office and Cabinet Office, 1979–81; Procurement Exec., MoD, 1981–83; Head, Defence Secretariat 19, MoD, 1983; Regional Marketing Dir, Defence Sales Orgn, 1983–85; Chief of PR, MoD, 1985–87; Fellow, Center for Internat. Affairs, Harvard Univ., 1987–88; Asst Under-Sec. of State, MoD, 1988–90. *Recreations:* ornithology, cricket, tennis, squash, theatre, opera. *Address:* Northern Ireland Office, Whitehall SW1A 2AZ. *T:* 071–210 3000. *Club:* United Oxford & Cambridge University.

LEDSOME, Neville Frank, CB 1988; Member, Civil Service Appeal Board, since 1990; Under Secretary, Personnel Management Division, Department of Trade and Industry, 1983–89, retired; *b* 29 Nov. 1929; *s* of late Charles Percy Ledsome and Florence Ledsome; *m* 1953, Isabel Mary Lindsay; three *s*. *Educ:* Birkenhead Sch. Exec. Officer, BoT, 1948; Monopolies Commn, 1957; Higher Exec. Officer, BoT, 1961; Principal, 1964; DEA, 1967; HM Treasury, 1969; DTI, 1970; Asst Sec., 1973; Under Sec., 1980. *Recreations:* gardening, theatre.

LEDWIDGE, Sir (William) Bernard (John), KCMG 1974 (CMG 1964); writer; HM Diplomatic Service, retired; Chairman, United Kingdom Committee for UNICEF, 1976–89; *b* 9 Nov. 1915; *s* of late Charles Ledwidge and Eileen O'Sullivan; *m* 1st, 1948, Anne Kingsley (marr. diss. 1970); one *s* one *d*; 2nd, 1970, Flora Groult. *Educ:* Cardinal Vaughan Sch.; King's Coll., Cambridge; Princeton Univ., USA. Commonwealth Fund Fellow, 1937–39; served War of 1939–45: RA 1940; Indian Army, 1941–45. Private Secretary to Permanent Under-Secretary, India Office, 1946; Secretary, Frontier Areas Cttee of Enquiry, Burma, 1947; Foreign Office, 1947–49; British Consul, St Louis, USA, 1949–52; First Secretary, British Embassy, Kabul, 1952–56; Political Adviser British Military Govt, Berlin, 1956–61; Foreign Office, 1961–65; Minister, Paris, 1965–69; Ambassador to Finland, 1969–72; Ambassador to Israel, 1972–75. Mem., Police Complaints Bd, 1977–82. *Publications:* Frontiers (novel), 1979; (jtly) Nouvelles de la Famille (short stories), 1980; De Gaulle, 1982; De Gaulle et les Américains, 1984; Sappho, La première voix de femme, 1987. *Recreation:* drinking and talking. *Address:* 54 rue de Bourgogne, 75007 Paris, France. *T:* 705 8026; 19 Queen's Gate Terrace, SW7. *T:* 071–584 4132. *Clubs:* Travellers', MCC.

LEDWITH, Dr Anthony; Director of Group Research, Pilkington plc, since 1988; *b* 14 Aug. 1933; *s* of Thomas Ledwith and Mary (*née* Coghlan); *m* 1960, Mary Clare Ryan; one *s* three *d*. *Educ:* BSc (external) London 1954; PhD 1957, DSc 1970, Liverpool Univ. FRSC 1986. Liverpool University: Lectr, 1959, Prof., 1976, Campbell Brown Prof. of Industrial Chem., 1980, Dept of Inorganic Physical and Industrial Chem.; Dean, Faculty of Sci., 1980–83; Dep. Dir, Group R&D, Pilkington plc, 1984–88. Member: DSAC, 1988–; SERC, 1990–. *Publications:* (with A. D. Jenkins) Reactivity, Mechanism and Structure in Polymer Chemistry, 1974; (with A. M. North) Molecular Behaviour and the Development of Polymeric Materials, 1975; (with S. J. Moss) The Chemistry of the Semiconductor Industry, 1987; (ed jtly) Comprehensive Polymer Science, 7 vols, 1989. *Recreations:* squash, tennis, golf. *Address:* Pilkington Group Research, Hall Lane, Lathom, near Ormskirk L40 5UF. *T:* Skelmersdale (0695) 54230.

LEE, Hon. Allen; *see* LEE PENG-FEI, A.

LEE, Sir Arthur (James), KBE 1966 (CBE 1959); MC and Bar (1939–45); Company Director; National President, Returned Services League, Australia, 1960–74 (State President, 1954–60); *b* 30 July 1912; *s* of Arthur James and Kathleen Maud Lee; *m* 1945, Valerie Ann Scanlan; three *s* one *d*. *Educ:* Collegiate School of St Peter, Adelaide. Chm., War Veterans Home, SA, 1967–. Trustee, Aust. War Meml, 1960–74. *Recreation:* golf. *Address:* 2 Arthur Street, Toorak Gardens, SA 5065, Australia. *T:* 35106. *Clubs:* Naval and Military, Royal Adelaide Golf (Adelaide).

LEE, Arthur James, CBE 1979; DSC (and Bar); Controller of Fisheries Research and Development, Ministry of Agriculture, Fisheries and Food, 1977–80; *b* 17 May 1920; *s* of Arthur Henry and Clara Lee; *m* 1953, Judith Graham; three *d*. *Educ:* City Boys' Sch., Leicester; St Catharine's Coll., Cambridge (MA). Served War of 1939–45 (DSC and Bar). Apptd: Scientific Officer at Fisheries Laboratory, Lowestoft, 1947; Dep. Dir of Fishery Research, 1965, Dir, 1974–77. *Publications:* (ed) Atlas of the Seas around the British Isles, 1981; contribs to various marine science jls. *Recreation:* gardening. *Address:* 191 Normanston Drive, Oulton Broad, Lowestoft, Suffolk NR32 2PY. *T:* Lowestoft (0502) 574707.

LEE, Christopher Frank Carandini; actor; entered film industry, 1947; *b* 27 May 1922; *s* of Geoffrey Trollope Lee (Lt-Col 60th KRRC), and Estelle Marie Carandini; *m* 1961, Birgit, *d* of Richard Emil Kroencke; one *d*. *Educ:* Wellington Coll. RAFVR, 1941–46 (Flt Lieut; mentioned in despatches, 1944). Films include: Moulin Rouge; Tale of Two Cities; Dracula; Rasputin; The Devil Rides Out; Private Life of Sherlock Holmes; The Wicker Man; The Three Musketeers; The Four Musketeers; The Man with the Golden Gun; To the Devil, a Daughter; Airport '77; The Passage; Bear Island; 1941; The Serial; The Last Unicorn; Safari 3000, The Salamander; Goliath Awaits; An Eye for an Eye; Charles and Diana; The Return of Captain Invincible; The House of the Long Shadows; The Far Pavilions; The Disputation; Mio My Mio; The Return of the Musketeers; The French Revolution; Gremlins II. OStJ 1986. Officier des Arts et des Lettres, France, 1973. *Publications:* Christopher Lee's 'X' Certificate, 1975 (2nd edn 1976); Christopher Lee's Archives of Evil, USA 1975 (2nd edn 1976); (autobiog.) Tall, Dark and Gruesome, 1977. *Recreations:* travel, opera, golf, cricket. *Address:* c/o James Sharkey & Associates, 15 Golden Square, W1; c/o Irv Schechter Co., 9300 Wilshire Boulevard, Beverly Hills, Calif 90212, USA. *Clubs:* Buck's, MCC; Honourable Company of Edinburgh Golfers; Travellers' (Paris).

LEE, David John, CBE 1989; FEng 1980; Chairman: G. Maunsell and Partners, Consulting Engineers, since 1984 (Partner since 1966); Maunsell Structural Plastics Ltd; Director of Maunsell Group cos; *b* 28 Aug. 1930; *s* of Douglas and Mildred Lee; *m* 1957, Helga Bass; one *s* one *d. Educ:* Manchester Univ. (BSc Tech 1950); Imperial Coll. of Science and Technol. (DIC 1954). MICE 1957, FICE 1966; MIStructE 1960, FIStructE 1968. National Service, RE, 1950–52. Engr, Reinforced Concrete Steel Co. Ltd, 1952–53 and 1954–55; G. Maunsell and Partners, Consulting Engineers: Resident Engr, 1955–59; Sen. Engr, 1960–65; Associate, 1965–66. Visiting Professor: Imperial College, London, 1987–; Univ. of Newcastle upon Tyne, 1989–. Engr and Transport Staff Corps, RE (TA), 1977– (Col). Member: General Cttee, Parly and Scientific Cttee; Standing Cttee on Structural Safety. Mem. Council, IStructE, 1974–77, 1978–, Pres., 1985–86; Mem. Council, Concrete Soc., 1968–71, Vice Pres. 1977–78. Chm., Council, CIRIA, 1989–; Member: Overseas Project Bd, DTI, 1989–; British Nat. Cttee for Internat. Engrg Affairs, 1989–. George Stephenson Medal, ICE, 1969; Medal, Fedn Internationale de la Précontrainte, 1974. *Publications:* The Theory and Practice of Bearings and Expansion Joints for Bridges, 1971; (contrib. chapter on bridges) The Civil Engineer's Reference Book, 3rd edn 1975, 4th edn 1989; (contrib. chapter on bridges) Developments in Pre-stressed Concrete, vol. 2 1978; papers in Proc. ICE and Proc. IStructE. *Recreations:* art, music, simple barbecuing. *Address:* G. Maunsell and Partners, Maunsell House, 154–160 Croydon Road, Beckenham, Kent BR3 4DE. *T:* 081–663 6565, *Telex:* 946171, *Fax:* 081–663 6723. *Club:* East India.

LEE, Air Chief Marshal Sir David (John Pryer), GBE 1969 (KBE 1965; CBE 1947; OBE 1943); CB 1953; retired, 1971; *b* 4 Sept. 1912; *s* of late John Lee, Byron Crescent, Bedford; *m* 1938, Denise, *d* of late Louis Hartoch; one *s* one *d. Educ:* Bedford Sch.; RAF Coll., Cranwell. NWFP, India, 1933–36; Central Flying Sch., Upavon, 1937; RAF Examining Officer, Supt. of Reserve, 1938–39; Bomber Command, Hemswell, 1939–40; RAF Staff Coll. (student), 1942; Deputy Director Plans, Air Ministry, 1943–44; OC 904 Fighter Wing, Batavia, Java, 1945–46; Directing Staff, RAF Staff Coll., 1948–50; Deputy Director Policy, Air Ministry, 1951–53; OC RAF Scampton, Lincs, 1953–55; Secretary, Chiefs of Staff Cttee, Ministry of Defence, 1956–59; AOC, AFME (Aden), 1959–61; Comdt, RAF Staff Coll., 1962–65; Air Member for Personnel, MoD, 1965–68; UK Military Rep. to NATO, 1968–71. Vice-Pres., RAF Benevolent Fund, 1988–; Chm., Governing Trustees, Nuffield Trust for Armed Forces, 1975–; Dir, Utd Services Trustee, 1971–88; Pres., Corps of Commissionaires, 1984–88. *Publications:* Flight from the Middle East, 1981; Never Stop the Engine When It's Hot, 1983; Eastward: a history of the Royal Air Force in the Far East 1945–1972, 1984; Wings in the Sun, 1989; And We Thought the War was Over, 1990. *Address:* Danemore Cottage, South Godstone, Surrey RH9 8JF. *T:* South Godstone (0342) 893162. *Club:* Royal Air Force.

LEE, Sir Desmond; *see* Lee, Sir H. D. P.

LEE, Edward, MSc, PhD; Director, Admiralty Research Laboratory, Teddington, 1971–74, retired; *b* 2 March 1914; *s* of Thomas and Florence Lee; *m* 1942, Joan Pearson; three *d. Educ:* Consett Grammar Sch.; Manchester Univ.; Pembroke Coll., Cambridge. Admiralty Research Laboratory, 1939–46; Ministry of Defence, 1946–48; Dept of Physical Research, Admiralty, 1948–51; Admiralty Research Laboratory, 1951–55; Dir of Operational Research, Admty, 1955–58; Dep. Dir, Nat. Physical Laboratory, 1958–60; Director, Stations and Industry Div., DSIR, 1960–65; Dep. Controller (R), Min. of Technology, 1965–70; Head of Res. Services, Dept of Trade and Industry, 1970–71. *Publications:* scientific papers. *Recreation:* golf. *Address:* 17 Farington Acres, Vale Road, Weybridge, Surrey KT13 9NH. *T:* Weybridge (0932) 841114.

LEE, (Edward) Stanley, FRCS; Consulting Surgeon Westminster Hospital; formerly Civilian Consultant in Surgery of Neoplastic Diseases, Queen Alexandra Military Hospital; Surgeon Emeritus, Guildford Radiotherapy Centre; *b* 1907. *Educ:* Westminster Hospital. MB, BS 1931; FRCS, 1933; MS London, 1936. Past Member of Court of Examiners, Royal College of Surgeons, England, 1953–59; Past Member: Grand Council British Empire Cancer Campaign; Internat. Union against Cancer; Assoc. of Head and Neck Oncologists of GB. FRSM; Sen. Fellow, Assoc. of Surgeons. Hon. Mem. Royal College of Radiologists. *Publications:* contributions to medical literature, etc. *Address:* Ingram, The Grand, Folkestone, Kent CT20 2LR.

LEE, George Ranson, CVO 1980; CBE 1983; HM Diplomatic Service, retired; *b* 26 Sept. 1925; *s* of late Wilfred Lee and Janet (*née* Ranson); *m* 1955, Anne Christine Black; one *d.* Served Indian Army, 6th Gurkha Rifles, NW Frontier Prov., 1945–47; TA, W Yorks Regt, 1948–53. Employed in Trng Dept, Min. of Food, 1948–53; joined CRO, 1954; Karachi, 1955–58; First Sec., Madras, 1959–63; CRO, 1964; Head of Chancery: Singapore, 1965–69; Santiago, 1969–72; FCO, 1972–74; Dep. UK Perm. Rep. to Council of Europe, Strasbourg, 1974–78; Counsellor, Berne, 1978–83. Council of Europe Medal, *pro merito,* 1978. *Address:* Garthmynd, Trevor Hill, Church Stretton, Shropshire SY6 6JH. *Club:* Commonwealth Trust.

LEE, George Russell, CMG 1970; Acting Assistant Director, Ministry of Defence, 1967–78, retired; *b* 11 Nov. 1912; *s* of Ernest Harry Lee and Alice Mary Lee (*née* Russell); *m* 1947, Annabella Evelyn (*née* Dargie); one *s* one *d. Educ:* Birkenhead Sch., Cheshire. WO and MoD, 1940–78. *Address:* 13 Abberbury Road, Iffley, Oxford OX4 4ET.

LEE, Brig. Sir Henry; *see* Lee, Brig. Sir L. H.

LEE, Sir (Henry) Desmond (Pritchard), Kt 1961; MA; President, Hughes Hall, Cambridge, 1973–78, Hon. Fellow 1978; *b* 30 Aug. 1908; *s* of Rev. Canon Henry Burgass Lee; *m* 1935, Elizabeth, *d* of late Colonel A. Crookenden, CBE, DSO; one *s* two *d. Educ:* Repton Sch. (George Denman Scholar); Corpus Christi Coll., Cambridge (Entrance Scholar). 1st Class Part 1 Classical Tripos, 1928; Foundation Scholar of the College; 1st Class Part 2 Classical Tripos, 1930; Charles Oldham Scholar; Fellow of Corpus Christi Coll., 1933, Life Fellow, 1948–68, 1978–; Tutor, 1935–48; University Lecturer in Classics, 1937–48; Headmaster of Clifton Coll., 1948–54; Headmaster of Winchester Coll., 1954–68. Fellow, University Coll., later Wolfson Coll., Cambridge, 1968–73, Hon. Fellow, 1974. Regional Comr's Office, Cambridge, 1941–44; Mem. Council of the Senate, 1944–48. Mem. Anderson Cttee on Grants to Students, 1958–59; Chm., Headmasters' Conference, 1959–60, 1967. Hon. DLitt (Nottingham), 1963. *Publications:* Zeno of Elea: a Text and Notes, 1935; Aristotle, Meteorologica, 1952; Plato, Republic, 1955, rev. edn 1974; Plato, Timæus and Critias, 1971; Entry and Performance at Oxford and Cambridge, 1966–71, 1972; (ed) Wittgenstein's Lectures 1930–32, 1980. *Address:* 8 Barton Close, Cambridge CB3 9LQ.

LEE, James Giles; Director and Vice President, Boston Consulting Group, since 1987; *b* 23 Dec. 1942; *s* of John Lee, CBE and Muriel Giles; *m* 1966, Linn Macdonald; one *s* two *d. Educ:* Trinity Coll., Glenalmond; Glasgow Univ.; Harvard Univ., USA. Consultant, McKinsey & Co., 1969–80; Mem., Central Policy Review Staff, 1972. Dep. Chm. and Chief Exec., Pearson Longman, 1980–83; Chairman: Penguin Publishing Co., 1980–84; Longman Gp, 1980–84; Direct Broadcasting by Satellite Consortium, 1986–87; Deputy Chairman: Westminster Press, 1980–84; Financial Times, 1980–84; Yorkshire TV, 1982–85; Dir, S. Pearson & Son, 1981–84; Chm., 1981–85, Chief Exec., 1983–85, Goldcrest Films and Television. *Publications:* Planning for the Social Services, 1978; The Investment Challenge, 1979. *Recreations:* photography, travelling, sailing. *Address:* Meadow Wood, Penshurst, Kent. *T:* Penshurst (0892) 870309. *Clubs:* Reform; Harvard (New York, USA).

LEE, Hon. James Matthew, PC 1982; MLA; Leader, Progressive Conservative Party, Prince Edward Island, since 1981; Commissioner, Canadian Pension Commission, since 1986; *b* Charlottetown, 26 March 1937; *s* of late James Matthew Lee and of Catherine Blanchard Lee; *m* 1960, Patricia, *d* of late Ivan Laurie; one *s* two *d. Educ:* Queen's Square Sch.; St Dunstan's Univ. Architectural draftsman. First elected MLA (PC) for 5th Queens Riding, by-election, 1975; re-elected since; former Minister: of Health and Social Services; of Tourism, Parks and Conservation; Premier and Pres. Exec. Council, PEI, 1981–86. Jaycee Internat. Senator, 1983. *Address:* 25 Ash Drive, Sherwood, Prince Edward Island, Canada. *T:* 902–892–6653.

LEE, Maj.-Gen. James Stuart, CB 1990; MBE 1970; Director of Army Education, 1987–90; *b* 26 Dec. 1934; *s* of George Lee and Elizabeth (*née* Hawkins); *m* 1960, Alice Lorna; one *s. Educ:* Normanton Grammar Sch.; Leeds Univ. (BA Hons); King's Coll., London (MA War Studies, 1976). Pres., Leeds Univ. Union, 1958–59. Educn Officer in UK Trng Units, Catterick, Taunton, Bovington, 1959–64; Mil. Trng Officer, Beaconsfield, 1964; RMCS and Staff Coll., 1964–65; DAQMG HQ Cyprus Dist, 1966 and HQ NEARELF, 1967; SO2 MoD (Army Educn 1), 1968–70; DAA&QMG HQ FARELF, 1970 and GSO2 HQ FARELF, 1970–71; OC Officer Wing, Beaconsfield, 1971–74; Gp Educn Officer, 34 AEC, Rheindahlen, 1974–75; Chief Educn Officer, HQ NE Dist, 1976–78; Hd, Officer Educn Br., 1978–79; SO1 Trng HQ UKLF, 1979; Chief Inspector of Army Educn and Col Res., 1980–82; Res. Associate, IISS, 1982–83; Comdr Educn, HQ BAOR, 1983–87. Dep. Comr, British Scouts Western Europe, 1983–87; Mem., Management Bd, NFER, 1987–90. Non-Exec. Dir, Exhibition Consultants Ltd, 1990–. Member: Nat Adv. Bd, Duke of Edinburgh Award Scheme, 1987–90; Council, Scout Assoc., 1988–; Council, CGLI, 1989– (Chm., Sen. Awards Cttee, 1990–). Trustee and Sec., Gallipoli Meml Lecture Trust, 1987–90. FRSA 1987. *Publication:* contrib. Arms Transfers in Third World Development, 1984. *Recreations:* theatre, boats. *Address:* c/o Royal Bank of Scotland, Holt's Branch, Whitehall, SW1A 2EB.

LEE, John Michael Hubert; Barrister-at-Law; *b* 13 Aug. 1927; *s* of late Victor Lee, Wentworth, Surrey, and late Renee Lee; *m* 1960, Margaret Ann, *d* of James Russell, ICS, retired, and late Kathleen Russell; one *s* one *d. Educ:* Reading Sch.; Christ's Coll., Cambridge (Open Exhibnr Modern Hist.; 2nd Cl. Hons Pts I and II of Hist. Tripos; MA). Colonial Service: Administrative Officer, Ghana, 1951–58; Principal Assistant Secretary, Min. of Communications, Ghana, 1958. On staff of BBC, 1959–65. Called to the Bar, Middle Temple, 1960; practising, Midland and Oxford Circuit, 1966–; Dep. Circuit Judge, 1978–81; Assistant Recorder, 1981–87. MP (Lab) Reading, 1966–70; MP (Lab) Birmingham, Handsworth, Feb. 1974–1979; Chm., W Midland Gp of Labour MPs, 1974–75. *Recreations:* watching tennis, watching cricket, walking, studying philosophy. *Address:* 2 Dr Johnson's Buildings, EC4Y 7AY. *Club:* Royal Over-Seas League.

LEE, John Robert Louis; MP (C) Pendle, since 1983 (Nelson and Colne, 1979–83); *b* 21 June 1942; *s* of late Basil and Miriam Lee; *m* 1975, Anne Monique Bakirgian; two *d. Educ:* William Hulme's Grammar Sch., Manchester. FCA. Accountancy Articles, 1959–64; Henry Cooke, Lumsden & Co., Manchester, Stockbrokers, 1964–66; Founding Dir, Chancery Consolidated Ltd, Investment Bankers; Dir, Paterson Zochonis (UK) Ltd, 1975–76, 1990–; Chm., Country Holidays Ltd, 1989–; Consultant: Trust House Forte, 1990–; P. S. Turner (Hldgs), 1989–. Vice-Chm., NW Conciliation Cttee, Race Relations Bd, 1976–77; Chm. Council, Nat. Youth Bureau, 1980–83. Political Sec. to Rt Hon. Robert Carr (now Lord Carr of Hadley), 1974; contested (C) Manchester, Moss Side, Oct. 1974; PPS to Minister of State for Industry, 1981–83, to Sec. of State for Trade and Industry, 1983; Parly Under Sec. of State, MoD, 1983–86, Dept of Employment, 1986–89 (Minister for Tourism, 1987–89). Jt Sec., Conservative Back Benchers' Industry Cttee, 1979–80. *Recreations:* fly fishing, collecting. *Address:* House of Commons, SW1A 0AA.

LEE, John (Thomas Cyril); His Honour Judge John Lee; Circuit Judge (attached Midland Oxford Circuit), since Sept. 1972; *b* 14 Jan. 1927; *s* of Cyril and Dorothy Lee; *m* 1956, Beryl Lee (*née* Haden); one *s* three *d. Educ:* Holly Lodge Grammar Sch., Staffs; Emmanuel Coll., Cambridge (MA, LLB). Called to Bar, Gray's Inn, 1952. Practised, Oxford Circuit, 1952–72. Chairman various Tribunals. *Recreation:* golf. *Address:* The Red House, Upper Colwall, Malvern, Worcs. *T:* Colwall (0684) 40645. *Clubs:* Union and County (Worcester); Worcester Golf and Country.

LEE KUAN YEW; Prime Minister, Singapore, 1959–90; Senior Minister, Prime Minister's Office, since 1990; *b* 16 Sept. 1923; *s* of Lee Chin Koon and Chua Jim Neo; *m* 1950, Kwa Geok Choo; two *s* one *d. Educ:* Raffles Coll., Singapore; Fitzwilliam Coll., Cambridge (class 1 both parts of Law Tripos). Called to Bar, Middle Temple, 1950, Hon. Bencher, 1969. Advocate and Solicitor, Singapore, 1951. Formed People's Action Party, 1954, Sec.-Gen., 1954–; People's Action Party won elections, 1959; became PM, 1959, re-elected 1963, 1968, 1972, 1976, 1980, 1984, 1988; MP Fed. Parlt of Malaysia, 1963–65. Hon. Freeman, City of London, 1982. Hon. CH 1970; Hon. GCMG 1972. Hon. FRCPE 1988. Bintang Republik Indonesia Adi Pradana, 1973; Order of Sikatuna, The Philippines, 1974; Most Honourable Order of Crown of Johore (1st Cl.), Malaysia, 1984. *Recreations:* jogging, swimming. *Address:* Prime Minister's Office, Istana Annexe, Singapore 0923.

LEE, Laurie, MBE 1952; poet and author; *m* 1950, Catherine Francesca Polge; one *d. Educ:* Slad Village Sch.; Stroud Central Sch. Travelled Mediterranean, 1935–39; GPO Film Unit, 1939–40; Crown Film Unit, 1941–43; Publications Editor, Ministry of Information, 1944–46; Green Park Film Unit, 1946–47; Caption Writer-in-Chief, Festival of Britain, 1950–51. Freeman of City of London, 1982. *Publications:* The Sun My Monument (Poems), 1944; Land at War (HMSO), 1945; (with Ralph Keene) A Film in Cyprus, 1947; The Bloom of Candles (Poems), 1947; The Voyage of Magellan, 1948; My Many-Coated Man (Poems), 1955; A Rose for Winter, 1955; Cider With Rosie (autobiography), 1959; Pocket Poets (Selection), 1960; The Firstborn, 1964; As I Walked Out One Midsummer Morning (autobiography), 1969; I Can't Stay Long, 1975; Selected

Poems, 1983; Two Women, 1983. *Recreations*: indoor sports, music, travel. *Address*: 9/40 Elm Park Gardens, SW10. *T*: 071–352 2197. *Clubs*: Chelsea Arts, Garrick.

LEE, Brig. Sir (Leonard) Henry, Kt 1983; CBE 1964 (OBE 1960); Deputy Director, Conservative Board of Finance, since 1970; *b* 21 April 1914; *s* of late Henry Robert Lee and Nellie Lee; *m* 1949, Peggy Metham. *Educ*: Portsmouth Grammar Sch.; Southampton Univ. (Law). Served War, 1939–45; with BEF in France, ME and NW Europe (despatches, 1945); Royal Scots Greys, Major; Staff Lt-Col 1954: Chief of Intelligence to Dir of Ops, Malaya, 1957–60; Mil. and Naval Attaché, Saigon, S Vietnam, 1961–64; Chief of Personnel and Admin, Allied Land Forces Central Europe, France, 1964–66; Chief of Intelligence, Allied Forces Central Europe, Netherlands, 1966–69; retd 1969. *Recreations*: gardening, golf. *Address*: Fairways, Sandy Lane, Kingswood, Surrey KT20 6ND. *T*: Mogador (0737) 832577. *Club*: Kingswood Golf.

LEE, Malcolm Kenneth, QC 1983; a Recorder of the Crown Court, since 1980; *b* 2 Jan. 1943; 2nd *s* of late Thomas Marston Lee, solicitor, Birmingham, and of Fiona Margaret Lee, JP (*née* Mackenzie); *m* 1970, Phyllis Anne Brunton Speed, *er d* of Andrew Watson Speed, Worcs; three *s* three *d* (and one *d* decd). *Educ*: King Edward's Sch., Birmingham (Foundation Schol.); Worcester Coll., Oxford (Schol.; MA Class. Hon. Mods and Lit.Hum.). Assistant Master: Marlborough Coll., 1965; King Edward's Sch., Birmingham, 1966; Major Schol., Inner Temple, 1967; called to the Bar, Inner Temple, 1967; practised on Midland Circuit, 1968–71, Midland and Oxford Circuit, 1972–. Dep. Chm., Agricl Land Tribunal, E Midland Area, 1979–82, Midland Area, 1982–; Prosecuting Counsel to DHSS, Midland and Oxford Circuit, 1979–83. *Recreations*: squash, tennis, walking, reading. *Address*: (chambers) 4 Fountain Court, Steelhouse Lane, Birmingham B4 6DR. *T*: 021–236 3476; Goldsmith Building, Temple, EC4Y 7BL. *T*: 071–353 6802; (home) 24 Estria Road, Edgbaston, Birmingham B15 2LQ. *T*: 021–440 4481. *Club*: Edgbaston Priory (Birmingham).

LEE, Michael Charles M.; *see* Malone-Lee.

LEE, Maj.-Gen. Patrick Herbert, CB 1982; MBE 1964; CEng, FIMechE; Vice-Chairman, Road Haulage Association, since 1990 (Director, since 1988); Director, Wincanton Distribution Services (formerly Wincanton Transport) Ltd, since 1983; *b* 15 March 1929; *s* of Percy Herbert and Mary Dorothea Lee; *m* 1952, Peggy Eveline Chapman; one *s* one *d*. *Educ*: King's Sch., Canterbury; London Univ. (BSc (Gen.), BSc (Special Physics)). Commnd RMA Sandhurst, 1948; Staff Coll., 1960; WO Staff Duties, 1961–63; CO, Parachute Workshop, 1964–65; JSSC, 1966; Military Asst to Master General of Ordnance, 1966–67; Directing Staff, Staff Coll., 1968–69; Commander, REME 2nd Div., 1970–71; Col AQ 1 British Corps, 1972–75; Dep. Comdt, Sch. of Electrical and Mechanical Engrg, 1975–77; Comdt, REME Trng Centre, 1977–79; Dir Gen., Electrical and Mechanical Engrg (Army), 1979–83. Col Comdt, REME, 1983–89. Mem., Wessex Water Authy, 1983–88. FBIM, FInstD. *Recreations*: gardening, railways, Roman history, industrial archaeology. *Address*: c/o Royal Bank of Scotland, Holts Branch, Farnborough, Hants. *Club*: Army and Navy.

LEE, Rt. Rev. Paul Chun Hwan, CBE 1974; Bishop of Seoul, 1965–83; *b* 5 April 1922; unmarried. *Educ*: St Michael's Theological Seminary, Seoul; St Augustine's College, Canterbury. Deacon, 1952 (Pusan Parish); Priest, 1953 (Sangju and Choungju Parish). Director of Yonsei University, Seoul, 1960–, Chm., Bd of Trustees, 1972–, Hon. DD 1971. Chairman: Christian Council of Korea, 1966–67; Christian Literature Soc. of Korea, 1968–83; Korean Bible Soc., 1972–83 (Vice-Pres., 1969–72); Nat. Council of Churches in Korea, 1976–78. Hon. LLD Korea, 1978. *Recreation*: reading. *Address*: 3–403 Shinbanpo Apartments, 2–1 Banpo-dong, Soch'o-ku, Seoul 137–042, Korea. *T*: 02–599–1123.

LEE, Peter Gavin; Senior Partner, Strutt & Parker, since 1979; *b* 4 July 1934; *s* of Mr and late Mrs J. G. Lee; *m* 1963, Caroline Green; two *s* one *d*. *Educ*: Midhurst Grammar School; College of Estate Management; Wye College. FRICS. Joined Strutt & Parker, 1957; became full partner, 1972. High Sheriff, Essex, 1990. *Recreations*: the restoration and enjoyment of vintage cars and aircraft, flying, country pursuits. *Address*: Fanners, Great Waltham, Chelmsford, Essex CM3 1EA. *T*: Chelmsford (0245) 360470. *Club*: Boodle's.

LEE, Rowland Thomas Lovell; a Recorder of the Crown Court, since 1979; *b* 7 March 1920; *s* of late Ronald Lovell Lee and of Jessie Maude Lee; *m* 1944, Marjorie Betty, *d* of late William Holmes and Clare Johnston Braid Holmes; two *d*. *Educ*: Bedford Modern School. Served Royal Navy, 1939–48; POW, Sept. 1942–March 1943. Bedfordshire Constabulary, 1948–52; Articles with E. A. S. Barnard, Dunstable, 1954; qualified as solicitor, 1957; Principal, Wynter Davies & Lee, Hertford, 1959–89, Consultant, 1989–. Chairman: Medical Services Cttee, Hertfordshire Family Practitioners Cttee, 1970–77; N Herts HA (formerly Herts AHA), 1977–84. *Address*: Culpepers, 5 Letty Green, Hertford, Herts SG14 2NZ. *T*: Hatfield (0707) 261445.

LEE, Stanley; *see* Lee, (Edward) S.

LEE, Tsung-Dao; Enrico Fermi Professor of Physics, since 1964, and University Professor, since 1984, Columbia University, USA; *b* 25 Nov. 1926; 3rd *s* of C. K. and M. C. Lee; *m* 1950, Jeannette H. C. Chin; two *s*. *Educ*: National Chekiang Univ., Kweichow, China; National Southwest Associated Univ., Kunming, China; University of Chicago, USA. Research Associate: University of Chicago, 1950; University of California, 1950–51; Member, Inst. for Advanced Study, Princeton, 1951–53. Columbia University: Asst Professor, 1953–55; Associate Professor, 1955–56; Professor, 1956–60; Member, Institute for Advanced Study, Princeton, 1960–63; Columbia Univ.: Adjunct Professor, 1960–62; Visiting Professor, 1962–63; Professor, 1963–. Hon. Professor: Univ. of Sci and Technol. of China, 1981; Jinan Univ., China, 1982; Fudan Univ., China, 1982; Qinghua Univ., 1984; Peking Univ., 1985; Nanjing Univ., 1985. Member: Acad. Sinica, 1957; Amer. Acad. of Arts and Scis, 1959; Nat. Acad of Scis, 1964; Amer. Philosophical Soc., 1972; Acad. Nazionale dei Lincei, Rome, 1982. Hon. DSc: Princeton, 1958; City Coll., City Univ. of NY, 1978; Bard Coll., 1984; Hon. LLD Chinese Univ. of Hong Kong, 1969; Hon. LittD Drexel Univ., 1986; Dip. di Perfezionamento in Physics, Scuola Normale Superiore, Pisa, 1982. Nobel Prize for the non-conservation of parity (with C. N. Yang), 1957; Albert Einstein Award in Science, 1957. *Publications*: Particle Physics: an introduction to field theory, 1981; papers mostly in Physical Review, and Nuclear Physics. *Address*: Department of Physics, Columbia University, New York, New York 10027, USA.

LEE, Sir William (Allison), Kt 1975; OBE 1945; TD 1948; DL; Chairman, Northern Regional Health Authority, 1973–78; *b* 31 May 1907; *s* of Samuel Percy and Florence Ada Lee, Darlington; *m* 1st, 1933, Elsa Norah (*d* 1966), *d* of late Thomas Hanning, Darlington; 2nd, 1967, Mollie Clifford (*d* 1989), *d* of late Sir Cuthbert Whiteside, Knysna, S Africa; no *c*. *Educ*: Queen Elizabeth Grammar Sch., Darlington. Insurance Branch Manager, retd. Served R Signals, 1935–53; Dep. Comdr, 151 Inf. Bde (TA), 1953–58; County Comdt, Durham ACF, 1962–70. Mem., Darlington RDC, 1949–61, Chm. 1957–60. Chairman: Winterton HMC, 1967–70 (Mem., 1954–70); Newcastle Reg. Hosp. Bd, 1973–74 (Mem., 1956–74). Pres., Darlington Div., SSAFA. DL County of

Durham, 1965; High Sheriff, Durham, 1978. *Recreations*: fell walking, gardening. *Address*: Whiteside, 23 Low Green, Gainford, Co. Durham DL2 3DS. *T*: Darlington (0325) 730564.

LEE YONG LENG, Dr; Professor of Geography, National University of Singapore, 1970–90, retired; *b* 26 March 1930; *m* Wong Loon Meng; one *d*. *Educ*: Univs of Oxford, Malaya and Singapore. BLitt (Oxon), MA (Malaya), PhD (Singapore). Research Asst, Univ. of Malaya, 1954–56; University Lectr/Sen. Lectr, Univ. of Singapore, 1956–70; Associate Prof., Univ. of Singapore, 1970–71; High Comr for Singapore in London, 1971–75; Ambassador to Denmark, 1974–75, and Ireland, 1975; Min. of Foreign Affairs, Singapore, 1975–76. Mem., Govt Parly Cttee on Defence and For. Affairs, 1987–90. Chm., Singapore Nat. Library Bd, 1978–80. Dir, Centre for Advanced Studies, National Univ. of Singapore, 1983–85. *Publications*: North Borneo, 1965; Sarawak, 1970; Southeast Asia and the Law of the Sea, 1978; The Razor's Edge: boundaries and boundary disputes in Southeast Asia, 1980; Southeast Asia: essays in political geography, 1982; articles in: Population Studies; Geog. Jl; Erdkunde; Jl Trop. Geog., etc. *Recreations*: swimming, tennis, travelling, reading.

LEE, Prof. Yuan Tseh; Professor of Chemistry, University of California, Berkeley, since 1974; *b* 29 Nov. 1936; *s* of Tse Fan Lee and Pei Tsai; *m* 1963, Bernice Chinli Wi; two *s* one *d*. *Educ*: Nat. Taiwan Univ. (BSc 1959); Nat. Tsinghua Univ., Taiwan (MSc 1961); Univ. of California (PhD 1965). Military service, 1961–62. University of California, Berkeley: Postdoctoral Fellow, 1965–67; Research Fellow, 1967–68; James Franck Inst. and Dept of Chemistry, Univ. of Chicago: Asst Prof. of Chemistry, 1968–71; Associate Prof. of Chemistry, 1971–72; Prof. of Chemistry, 1973–74. Principal Investigator, Materials and Molecular Research Div., Lawrence Berkeley Lab., 1974–. Vis Lectr, US and overseas univs. Mem., editl boards, chem. and sci. jls. Mem., Nat. Acad. of Sciences, 1979, and other learned bodies. Nobel Prize in Chemistry (jtly), 1986; numerous awards from US and foreign instns. *Publications*: papers on molecular chemistry and related subjects. *Recreations*: sports (baseball, ping pong, tennis), classical music. *Address*: Department of Chemistry, University of California, Berkeley, Calif 94720, USA. *T*: (415) 486–6154, 642–3861.

LEE-BARBER, Rear-Adm. John, CB 1959; DSO 1940 and Bar 1941; Admiral Superintendent, HM Dockyard, Malta, 1957–59, retired; *b* 16 April 1905; *s* of Richard Lee-Barber, Herringfleet, near Great Yarmouth; *m* 1939, Suzanne (*d* 1976), *d* of Colonel Le Gallais, ADC, MC, La Moye, Jersey, CI; two *d*. *Educ*: Royal Naval Colleges, Osborne and Dartmouth. Service in destroyers and in Yangtze gunboat until 1937; CO Witch, 1937–38; CO Griffin, 1939–40–41; Commander, 1941; CO Opportune, 1942–44; 2nd in Command, HMS King Alfred, 1945; CO, HMS St James, 1946–47; Captain, 1947; Senior Officer Reserve Fleet, Harwich, 1948–49; Naval Attaché, Chile, 1950–52; CO Agincourt and Captain D4, 1952–54; Commodore, Inshore Flotilla, 1954–56; Rear-Admiral, 1957. Polish Cross of Valour, 1940. *Recreation*: sailing. *Address*: Ferry House, The Quay, Wivenhoe, Essex. *T*: Wivenhoe (0206) 822592.
See also D. R. W. Harrison.

LEE CHU-MING, Martin; QC (Hong Kong) 1979; JP; *b* 8 June 1938; *m* 1969, Amelia Lee; one *s*. *Educ*: Wah Yan College, Kowloon; Univ. of Hong Kong (BA 1960). Called to the Bar, Lincoln's Inn, 1966. Member: Hong Kong Legislative Council, 1985–Aug. 1991; Hong Kong Law Reform Commn, 1985–July 1991; Hong Kong Fight Crime Cttee, 1986–; Basic Law Drafting Cttee, 1985–90; numerous groups and cttees advising on Govt, law, nationality and community matters. JP Hong Kong, 1980. *Publication*: The Basic Law: some basic flaws (with Szeto Wah), 1988. *Address*: Admiralty Centre, Room 704A, Tower I, 18 Harcourt Road, Hong Kong. *T*: 529–0864. *Clubs*: Hong Kong; Royal Hong Kong Golf, Royal Hong Kong Jockey.

LEE PENG-FEI, Hon. Allen, (Hon. Allen Lee), CBE 1988 (OBE 1982); JP; Senior Member, Hong Kong Legislative Council, since 1988; President, Meadville, since 1984; *b* 24 April 1940; *m* Maria Lee; two *s* one *d*. *Educ*: Univ. of Michigan (BSc Engineering Maths). Test Engineer Supervisor, Lockheed Aircraft International, 1966–67; Engineering Ops Manager, Fabri-teck, 1967; Test Engineer Manager, Lockheed Aircraft International, 1968–70; Test Manager, Ampex Ferrotec, 1970–72; Gen. Manager, Dataproducts HK, 1972–74; Managing Dir, Ampex Ferrotec, 1974–79; Gen. Manager, Ampex World Operations, 1979–83; Managing Dir, Ampex Far East Operations, 1983–84. MLC, 1978–, MEC, 1985–, Hong Kong. JP Hong Kong, 1980. FHKIE, 1985. Nat. Award, Asian Productivity Organization, 1986; Outstanding Young Persons Award, Hong Kong, 1977. *Recreations*: swimming, tennis. *Address*: 609–610 Cheung Sha Wan Plaza, Tower 1, 833 Cheung Sha Wan Road, Kowloon, Hong Kong. *T*: 7457488. *Clubs*: Royal Hong Kong Jockey; Dynasty (Hong Kong).

LEE-POTTER, Jeremy Patrick, FRCPath; Consultant Haematologist, Poole General Hospital, since 1969; Chairman of Council, British Medical Association, since 1990; *b* 30 Aug. 1934; *s* of Air Marshal Sir Patrick Lee Potter, KBE, MD, QHS and Audrey Mary (*née* Pollock); *m* 1957, Lynda Higginson; one *s* two *d*. *Educ*: Epsom Coll.; Guy's Hosp. Med. Sch. MB BS 1958; MRCS, LRCP 1958; DTM&H 1963; DCP 1965; FRCPath 1979. Specialist in Pathology, 1960, Sen. Specialist, 1965, RAF (Sqn Ldr); in charge of Haematology Dept, Inst. of Pathology and Tropical Medicine; Lectr in Haematology, St George's Hosp. Med. Sch., 1968–69. Mem., Standing Med. Adv. Cttee, 1990–. British Medical Association: Dep. Chm., Central Consultants and Specialists Cttee, 1988–90; Mem. Council, 1988–. *Recreations*: printing, printmaking, visual arts. *Address*: Poole General Hospital, Longfleet Road, Poole, Dorset. *T*: Poole (0202) 675100. *Club*: Parkstone Golf.

LEE-STEERE, Sir Ernest (Henry), KBE 1977 (CBE 1963); JP; Lord Mayor of Perth, Western Australia, 1972–78; company director, pastoralist and grazier; *b* Perth, 22 Dec. 1912; *s* of Sir Ernest Lee-Steere, JP, KStJ; *m* 1942, Jessica Margaret, *d* of Frank Venn; two *s* three *d*. *Educ*: Hale Sch., Perth; St Peter's Coll., Adelaide. Served War: Captain Army/Air Liaison Group, AIF; SW Pacific Area, 1944–45. President (for WA): Pastoralists and Graziers Assoc., 1959–72; Boy Scout Assoc., 1957–64; National Trust, 1969–72. Vice-Pres., Council of Royal Flying Doctor Service of WA, 1954–59 and 1962–74. Chairman: State Adv. Cttee, CSIRO, 1962–71 (Councillor, Fed. Adv. Council, 1960–71); WA Soil Conservation Adv. Cttee, 1955–72; Aust. Capital Cities Secretariat, 1975–76; WA Turf Club, 1963–84 (Vice-Chm., 1959–63). Member: Nat. Council of Aust. Boy Scouts Assoc., 1959–64; Exec. Cttee of WA State Cttee, Freedom from Hunger Campaign; WA State Adv. Cttee, Aust. Broadcasting Commn, 1961–64; Aust. Jubilee Cttee for the Queen's Silver Jubilee Appeal for Young Australians, 1977; Aust. Wool Industry Conf., 1971–74 (also Mem. Exec. Cttee). Councillor: Aust. Wool Growers and Graziers Council (Pres., 1972–73); St George's Coll., Univ. of WA, 1945–81. Chm. and dir of several cos. Leader, Trade Mission to India, 1962. JP Perth, 1965. *Recreation*: polo (played in WA Polo Team in Australasian Gold Cup). *Address*: Dardanup, 26 Odern Crescent, Swanbourne, WA 6010, Australia. *T*: 384–2929. *Club*: Weld (Perth).

LEECH, Air Vice-Marshal David Bruce, CBE 1978 (OBE 1976); Commandant General, RAF Regiment and Director General of Security (RAF), 1985–87; retired, 1988;

b 8 Jan. 1934; *s* of Mrs S. A. Leech; *m* 1958, Shirley Anne (*née* Flitcroft); two *d*. *Educ:* Bolton School, Lancs. Joined RAF 1954, and served with Nos 11 and 20 Sqns, 1956–58; Pilot attack instr, APC Sylt, 1958–61; Mem., RAF 2 TAF Air Gunnery Team, Cazaux, 1958; qualified flying instr, RAF Coll., Cranwell, CFS and Church Fenton, 1961–66; Chief Instr, Canadian Tactical Air Ops Sch., Rivers, Manitoba, 1966–69; RAF Staff Coll., 1969–70; HQ 38 Gp, Ops Staff, 1970–72; OC Ops Wing, RAF Wittering, 1973–75; Stn Comdr, RAF Wildenrath, RAF Gutersloh and Comdr RAF Germany Harrier Force, 1975–77; Dir, Dept of Warfare, RAF Coll., 1977–79; Inspector of Flight Safety, 1979–81; RCDS 1982; Comdr, Allied Sector Ops Centre No 1, Brockzetel, 1983–85. *Recreations:* golf, country pursuits. *Address:* National Westminster Bank, 196 Monton Road, Monton, Eccles, Greater Manchester M30 9PY. *Club:* Royal Air Force.

LEECH, Prof. Geoffrey Neil, FBA 1987; Professor of Linguistics and Modern English Language, University of Lancaster, since 1974; *b* 16 Jan. 1936; *s* of Charles Richard Leech and Dorothy Eileen Leech; *m* 1961, Frances Anne Berman; one *s* one *d*. *Educ:* Tewkesbury Grammar School; University College London (BA 1959; MA 1963; PhD 1968). Asst Lectr, UCL, 1962–64; Harkness Fellow, MIT, 1964–65; Lectr, UCL, 1965–69; Reader, Univ. of Lancaster, 1969–74. Visiting Professor: Brown Univ., 1972; Kobe Univ., 1984. Hon. Fil Dr Lund, 1987. *Publications:* English in Advertising, 1966; A Linguistic Guide to English Poetry, 1969; Towards a Semantic Description of English, 1969; Meaning and the English Verb, 1971, 2nd edn 1987; (with R. Quirk, S. Greenbaum and J. Svartvik) A Grammar of Contemporary English, 1972; Semantics, 1974, 2nd edn 1981; (with J. Svartvik) A Communicative Grammar of English, 1975; Explorations in Semantics and Pragmatics, 1980; (ed with S. Greenbaum and J. Svartvik) Studies in English Linguistics: for Randolph Quirk, 1980; (with M. Short) Style in Fiction, 1981; (with R. Hoogenraad and M. Deuchar) English Grammar for Today, 1982; Principles of Pragmatics, 1983; (with R. Quirk, S. Greenbaum, and J. Svartvik) A Comprehensive Grammar of the English Language, 1985; (ed with C. N. Candlin) Computers in English Language Teaching and Research, 1986; (ed with R. Garside and G. Sampson) The Computational Analysis of English: a corpus-based approach, 1987; An A-Z of English Grammar and Usage, 1989. *Recreations:* music, esp. playing the piano in chamber music groups. *Address:* Department of Linguistics, University of Lancaster, Bailrigg, Lancaster LA1 4YT.

LEECH, John, (Hans-Joachim Freiherr von Reitzenstein); Head of External Relations and Member of Management Board, Commonwealth Development Corporation, 1981–85; Chairman, Farm Services Co. BV, since 1988; Deputy Chairman, Rural Investment Overseas Ltd, since 1990 (Chairman, 1985–90); *b* 21 April 1925; *s* of Hans-Joachim and Josefine von Reitzenstein; *m* 1st, 1949, Mair Eiluned Davies (marr. diss. 1958); one *d*; 2nd, 1963, Noretta Conci, concert pianist. *Educ:* Bismarck Gymnasium, Berlin; Whitgift, Croydon. L. G. Mouchel & Partners, Consulting Civil Engineers, 1942–52; Bird & Co. Ltd, Calcutta, 1953–57; Dir, Europe House, London, and Exec. Mem. Council, Britain in Europe Ltd, 1958–63; Pres., Internat. Fedn of Europe Houses, 1961–65; Dir, Joint Industrial Exports Ltd, 1963–65; with Commonwealth Develt Corp., London and overseas, 1965–85; Co-ordinator, Interact Gp of European develt finance instns, 1973–85. Asst Dir, NATO Parliamentarians' Conf., 1959–60. Vice-Chairman: Indian Concrete Soc., 1953–57; Anglo-Ivory Coast Soc., 1981–; Member: Council, Federal Trust for Educn and Research, 1985–; Exec. Cttee, London Symphony Orch., 1979–; Royal Commonwealth Soc. for the Blind, 1983–; Music Industry Trust for Young Professional Pianists, 1991–. Liveryman, Worshipful Co. of Paviors, 1968–. FRSA. *Publications:* The NATO Parliamentarians' Conference 1955–59, 1960; Europe and the Commonwealth, 1961; Aid and the Community, 1972; Halt! Who Goes Where?: the future of NATO in the new Europe, 1991; contrib. to jls on aspects of overseas develt, European matters and arts subjects. *Recreations:* music, travel, Italy. *Address:* 8 Chester Square Mews, SW1W 9DS. *T:* 071–730 2307. *Club:* Travellers'.

LEECH, Rev. Kenneth; M. B. Reckitt Urban Fellow, St Botolph's Church, Aldgate, since 1991; *b* 15 June 1939; *s* of John and Annie Leech; *m* 1970, Rheta Wall; one *s*. *Educ:* King's College London (BA Hons Mod. History, AKC 1961); Trinity Coll., Oxford (BA Hons Theol. 1961, MA 1968); St Stephen's House, Oxford. Deacon 1964, priest 1965; Curate: Holy Trinity, Hoxton, N1, 1964–67; St Anne, Soho, W1, 1967–71; Sec., Soho Drugs Group, 1967–71; Dir, Centrepoint, Soho, 1969–71; Chaplain and Tutor, St Augustine's Coll., Canterbury, 1971–74; Rector of St Matthew, Bethnal Green, 1974–80; Field Work Sec., BCC, 1980; Race Relations Field Officer, C of E Bd for Social Responsibility, 1981–87; Dir, Runnymede Trust, 1987–90. Vis. Lectr, St Stephen's House, Chicago, 1978–90. *Publications:* Pastoral Care and the Drug Scene, 1970; A Practical Guide to the Drug Scene, 1972; Keep the Faith, Baby, 1972; Youthquake, 1973; Soul Friend, 1977; True Prayer, 1980; The Social God, 1981; True God, 1984; Spirituality and Pastoral Care, 1986; Struggle in Babylon: Racism in the Cities and Churches of Britain, 1988; Care and Conflict, 1990. *Recreations:* cartoon drawing, Lancashire dialect poetry, pubs. *Address:* St Botolph's Crypt, Aldgate, EC3N 1AB. *T:* 071–283 6810.

LEECH, His Honour Robert Radcliffe; a Circuit Judge (formerly Judge of County Courts), 1970–86; *b* 5 Dec. 1919; *s* of late Edwin Radcliffe Leech; *m* 1951, Vivienne Ruth, *d* of A. J. Rickerby, Carlisle; two *d*. *Educ:* Monmouth Sch.; Worcester Coll., Oxford (Open Classics Exhibnr 1938). Served War, 1940–44, Border Regt (despatches twice). Called to Bar, Middle Temple, 1949 (Harmsworth Law Scholar); Dep. Chm., Cumberland QS, 1966–71; Hon. Recorder of Carlisle, 1985–86. *Recreations:* sailing, golf. *Address:* Scaur House, Cavendish Terrace, Stanwix, Carlisle, Cumbria CA3 9ND. *Clubs:* Oriental; County and Border (Carlisle).

LEEDS, Bishop of, (RC), since 1985; **Rt. Rev. David Every Konstant;** *b* 16 June 1930; *s* of Antoine Konstant and Dulcie Marion Beresford Konstant (*née* Leggatt). *Educ:* St Edmund's College, Old Hall Green, Ware; Christ's College, Cambridge (MA); Univ. of London Inst. of Education (PGCE). Priest, dio. Westminster, 1954; Cardinal Vaughan School, Kensington, 1959; Diocesan Adviser on Religious Education, 1966; St Michael's School, Stevenage, 1968; Director, Westminster Religious Education Centre, 1970; Auxiliary Bishop of Westminster (Bishop in Central London) and Titular Bishop of Betagbara, 1977–85. Chm., Dept for Catholic Education and Formation (formerly Dept for Christian Doctrine and Formation), Bishops' Conf. of Eng. and Wales, 1984–. *Publications:* various books on religious education and liturgy. *Recreation:* music. *Address:* Bishop's House, 13 North Grange Road, Headingley, Leeds LS6 2BR. *T:* Leeds (0532) 304533.

LEEDS, Archdeacon of; *see* Comber, Ven. A. J.

LEEDS, Sir Christopher (Anthony), 8th Bt *cr* 1812; Senior Lecturer, University of Nancy II; *b* 31 Aug. 1935; *s* of Geoffrey Hugh Anthony Leeds (*d* 1962) (*b* of 6th Bt) and Yoland Thérèse Barré (*d* 1944), *d* of James Alexander Mitchell; *S* cousin, 1983; *m* 1974, Elaine Joyce (marr. diss. 1981), *d* of late Sqdn Ldr C. H. A. Mullins. *Educ:* King's School, Bruton; LSE, Univ. of London (BSc Econ. 1958); Univ. of Southern California (Sen. Herman Fellow in Internat. Relations, MA 1966). Assistant Master: Merchant Taylors' School, Northwood, 1966–68; Christ's Hospital, 1972–75; Stowe School, 1978–81. Publisher, 1975–78. Vis. Lectr, Univ. of Strasbourg I, 1983–87. *Publications include:* Political Studies, 1968, 3rd edn 1981; European History 1789–1914, 1971, 2nd edn 1980; Italy under Mussolini, 1972; Unification of Italy, 1974; Historical Guide to England, 1976; (with R. S. Stainton and C. Jones) Management and Business Studies, 1974, 3rd edn 1983; Basic Economics Revision, 1982; Politics in Action, 1986; World History—1900 to the present day, 1987; Peace and War, 1987; English Humour, 1989. *Recreations:* tennis, modern art, travel. *Heir: cousin* Aubrey Leeds [*b* 4 Aug. 1903; *m* 1933, Barbara, *o c* of J. Travis, Lightcliffe, Yorks; one *s* two *d*]. *Address:* c/o 45A High Street, Wimbledon Village, SW19 5AU; 7 rue de Turique, 54000 Nancy, France. *Club:* Lansdowne.

LEEMING, Geraldine Margaret; *see* Coleridge, G. M.

LEEMING, Ian; QC 1988; a Recorder, since 1989; *b* Preston, Lancs, 10 April 1948; *s* of late Thomas Leeming (Bombing Leader, RAF), and of Lilian (*née* Male); *m* 1973, Linda Barbara Cook; one *s* two *d*. *Educ:* The Catholic Coll., Preston; Manchester Univ. (LLB 1970). Called to the Bar: Gray's Inn, 1970; Lincoln's Inn (*ad eundem*), 1981. In practice at Chancery Bar, 1971–; Lectr in Law (part-time), Manchester Univ., 1971–75. Chm., Heaton Conservatives, Bolton, 1986–88; Vice-Chm., Northern Soc. of Cons. Lawyers, 1985–88. *Publications:* (with James Bonney) Observations upon the Insolvency Bill, 1985; articles, notes and reviews in legal jls and specialist periodicals. *Recreations:* squash, real tennis, occasional racquets. *Address:* 11 Stone Buildings, Lincoln's Inn, WC2A 3TG; Crown Square Chambers, 1 Deans Court, Crown Square, Manchester M3 3HA. *T:* 061–833 9801. *Clubs:* Carlton; Manchester Tennis and Racquet.

LEEMING, John Coates; space consultant; Director General, British National Space Centre, 1987–88 (Director, Policy and Programmes, 1985–87); *b* 3 May 1927; *s* of late James Arthur Leeming and Harriet Leeming; *m* 1st, 1949 (marr. diss. 1974); two *s*; 2nd, 1985, Cheryl Gillan. *Educ:* Chadderton Grammar Sch., Lancs; St John's Coll., Cambridge (Schol.). Teaching, Hyde Grammar Sch., Cheshire, 1948. Asst Principal, HM Customs and Excise, 1950 (Private Sec. to Chm.); Principal: HM Customs and Excise, 1954; HM Treasury, 1956; HM Customs and Excise, 1958; Asst Sec., HM Customs and Excise, 1965; IBRD (World Bank), Washington, DC, 1967; Asst Sec., 1970, Under Sec., 1972, CSD; a Comr of Customs and Excise, 1975–79; Dept of Industry (later DTI), 1979–85. *Recreation:* golf. *Address:* 9 Walnut Close, Epsom, Surrey. *T:* Epsom (0372) 725397. *Club:* Royal Automobile.

LEES, Prof. Anthony David, FRS 1968; Senior Research Fellow, Imperial College at Silwood Park, since 1982; *b* 27 Feb. 1917; *s* of Alan Henry Lees, MA and Mary Hughes Bomford; *m* 1943, Annzella Pauline Wilson; one *d*. *Educ:* Clifton Coll., Bristol; Trinity Hall, Cambridge (Schol.). BA 1939; PhD (Cantab) 1943; ScD 1966. Mem., ARC Unit of Insect Physiology at Zoology Dept, Cambridge, 1945–67; Lalor Fellow, 1956; Vis. Prof., Adelaide Univ., 1966; Hon. Lectr, London Univ., 1968; DCSO and Prof. of Insect Physiology, ARC at Silwood Park Field Station, Ascot, 1969–82, now Prof. Emeritus. Pres., Royal Entomological Soc., 1973–75, Hon. Fellow 1984. Leverhulme Res. Fellow, 1988–89. *Publications:* scientific papers. *Recreations:* gardening, fossicking. *Address:* Wells Lane Corner, London Road, Ascot, Berks SL5 7DY.

LEES, Sir Antony; *see* Lees, Sir W. A. C.

LEES, C(harles) Norman; His Honour Judge Lees; a Circuit Judge since 1980; *b* 4 Oct. 1929; *s* of late Charles Lees, Bramhall, Cheshire; *m* 1961, Stella (*d* 1987), *d* of late Hubert Swann, Stockport; one *d*. *Educ:* Stockport Sch.; Univ. of Leeds. LLB 1950. Called to Bar, Lincoln's Inn, 1951. Dep. Chm., Cumberland County QS, 1969–71; a Recorder of the Crown Court, 1972–80; Chm., Mental Health Review Tribunal, Manchester Region, 1977–80 (Mem., 1971–80). *Recreations:* squash rackets, music, history. *Address:* 1 Deans Court, Crown Square, Manchester M3 3JL. *T:* 061–834 4097. *Clubs:* Lansdowne; Northern Lawn Tennis.

LEES, Sir David (Bryan) Kt 1991; FCA; Chairman and Chief Executive, GKN plc, since 1988; a Director, Bank of England, since 1991; *b* 23 Nov. 1936; *s* of late Rear-Adm. D. M. Lees, CB, DSO, and C. D. M. Lees; *m* 1961, Edith Mary Bernard; two *s* one *d*. *Educ:* Charterhouse. Qualified as a chartered accountant, 1962. Chief Accountant, Handley Page Ltd, 1964–69; GKN Sankey Ltd: Chief Accountant, 1970–72; Dep. Controller, 1973; Director and Controller, 1974–76; Guest Keen and Nettlefolds, later GKN plc: Group Finance Executive, 1977; General Manager Finance, 1978–81; Finance Dir, 1982–87; Man. Dir, 1987–88. Non-Exec. Dir, Courtaulds, 1991–. Chm., Economic and Financial Policy Cttee, CBI, 1988–; Pres., EEF, 1990–; Member: Audit Commission, 1983–90; Exec. Cttee and Council, SMMT, 1987–89. Mem. Governing Body, Shrewsbury Sch., 1986–. *Recreations:* walking, golf, opera, music. *Address:* GKN plc, PO Box 55, Redditch, Worcs B98 0TL. *Club:* MCC.

LEES, Prof. Dennis Samuel, CBE 1980; Emeritus Professor of Industrial Economics, University of Nottingham, since 1983 (Professor, 1968–82); *b* 20 July 1924; *s* of late Samuel Lees and Evelyn Lees (*née* Withers), Borrowash, Derbyshire; *m* 1950, Elizabeth Bretisch, London; two *s* one *d*. *Educ:* Derby Technical Coll.; Nottingham Univ. BSc(Econ), PhD. Lecturer and Reader in Economics, Keele Univ., 1951–65; Prof. of Economics, University Coll., Swansea, 1965–67. Exchange Lectr, Reed Coll., Portland, Ore, 1958–59; Visiting Prof. of Economics: Univ. of Chicago, 1963–64; Univ. of California, Berkeley, 1971; Univ. of Sydney, 1975. Chairman: Nat. Ins. Advisory Committee, 1972–80; Industrial Injuries Advisory Council, 1973–78; Mem., Adv. Council, Inst. of Econ. Affairs, 1974–. Freeman, City of London, 1973. *Publications:* Local Expenditure and Exchequer Grants, 1956; Health Thru Choice, 1961; Economic Consequences of the Professions, 1966; Economics of Advertising, 1967; Financial Facilities for Small Firms, 1971; Impairment, Disability, Handicap, 1974; Economics of Personal Injury, 1976; Solicitors' Remuneration in Ireland, 1977; articles on industrial and social policy in: Economica, Jl of Political Economy, Amer. Econ. Rev., Jl of Law and Econ., Jl Industrial Econ., Jl Public Finance. *Recreations:* cricket and pottering. *Address:* 8 Middleton Crescent, Beeston, Nottingham NG9 2TH. *T:* Nottingham (0602) 258730.

LEES, Geoffrey William; Headmaster, St Bees School, 1963–80; *b* 1 July 1920; *o s* of late Mr and Mrs F. T. Lees, Manchester; *m* 1949, Joan Needham, *yr d* of late Mr and Mrs J. Needham, Moseley, Birmingham. *Educ:* King's Sch., Rochester; Downing Coll., Cambridge. Royal Signals, 1940–46 (despatches): commissioned 1941; served in NW Europe and Middle East, Captain. 2nd Class Hons English Tripos, Pt I, 1947; History Tripos, Part II, 1948; Asst Master, Brighton Coll., 1948–63. Leave of absence in Australia, Asst Master, Melbourne Church of England Gram. Sch., 1961–62. *Recreations:* reading, lepidoptera, walking. *Address:* 10 Merlin Close, Upper Drive, Hove, Sussex BN3 6NU. *Clubs:* MCC; Hawks', Union (Cambridge).

LEES, Capt. Nicholas Ernest Samuel; Clerk of the Course and Managing Director, Leicester Racecourse, since 1972 (Assistant Manager, 1970–71); Chief Executive and Clerk of the Course, Newmarket, since 1974; *b* 3 May 1939; *s* of Ernest William Lees and Marjorie May Lees; *m* 1st, 1969, Elizabeth Helen Spink (marr. diss. 1985); one *d*; 2nd, 1985, Jocelyn Kosina; one *d*. *Educ:* Abbotsholme Sch., Rocester, Staffs. Shell Oil, 1956–59; commnd 17/21 Lancers, 1959; retd from Army, 1967; studied for Chartered Surveyors exams, 1967–69 (passed final exams but never practised); auctioneer, Warner, Sheppard

& Wade Ltd, Leicester, 1969–73; Clerk of the Course: Teesside Park, 1972–73; Great Yarmouth, 1977–91. *Recreations:* horse racing, point to pointing, antique furniture, silver, sporting art. *Address:* Capers End, Bradfield St George, Bury St Edmunds, Suffolk IP30 0AY. *T:* Bury St Edmunds (0284) 86651.

LEES, Norman; *see* Lees, C. N.

LEES, Air Vice-Marshal Robin Lowther, CB 1985; MBE 1962; FIPM, FBIM; RAF retired; Chief Executive, British Hotels, Restaurants and Caterers Association, since 1986; *b* 27 Feb. 1931; *e s* of late Air Marshal Sir Alan Lees, KCB, CBE, DSO, AFC, and Norah Elizabeth (*née* Thompson); *m* 1966, Alison Mary Benson, *o d* of late Col C. B. Carrick, MC, TD, JP; three *s*. *Educ:* Wellington Coll.; RAF Coll., Cranwell. Commissioned RAF, 1952; served AAFCE Fontainebleau, 1953–56; Waterbeach, 1956–58; UKSLS Ottawa, 1958–61; DGPS(RAF) Staff MoD, 1962–66; Wyton, 1966–68; HQ Far East Comd, 1968–70; Directing Staff RAF Staff Coll., 1971–74; RAF PMC, 1974–76; Dir of Personnel (Ground) MoD, 1976; Dir of Personal Services (2) (RAF) MoD, 1976–80; RCDS 1980; Dir of Personnel Management (Policy and Plans) (RAF) MoD, 1981–82; AOA RAF Support Comd, 1982–85, and Head of Admin. Br., RAF, 1983–85. Mem. Council, CBI, 1990–. Gov., Wellington Coll., 1990–. *Recreations:* real tennis, lawn tennis, squash, golf. *Address:* c/o Barclays Bank, 6 Market Place, Newbury, Berks. *Clubs:* Royal Air Force (Chairman, 1977–82); Jesters', All England Lawn Tennis and Croquet.

LEES, Sir Thomas (Edward), 4th Bt, *cr* 1897; landowner; *b* 31 Jan. 1925; 2nd *s* of Sir John Victor Elliott Lees, 3rd Bt, DSO, MC, and Madeline A. P. (*d* 1967), *d* of Sir Harold Pelly, 4th Bt; *S* father 1955; *m* 1949, Faith Justin, *d* of G. G. Jessiman, OBE, Great Durnford, Wilts; one *s* three *d*. *Educ:* Eton; Magdalene Coll., Cambridge. Served War in RAF; discharged 1945, after losing eye. Magdalene, Cambridge, 1945–47; BA Cantab 1947 (Agriculture). Since then has farmed at and managed South Lytchett estate. Chm., Post Green Community Trust Ltd. Mem., General Synod of C of E, 1970–90. JP 1951, CC 1952–74, High Sheriff 1960, Dorset. *Recreation:* sailing. *Heir: s* Christopher James Lees [*b* 4 Nov. 1952; *m* 1st, 1977, Jennifer (marr. diss. 1987), *d* of John Wyllie; 2nd, 1989, Clare, *d* of Austen Young, FRCS, Aberystwyth; one *d*]. *Address:* Post Green, Lytchett Minster, Poole, Dorset. *T:* Lytchett Minster (0202) 622048. *Club:* Royal Cruising.

LEES, Sir Thomas Harcourt Ivor, 8th Bt *cr* (UK) 1804, of Black Rock, County Dublin; *b* 6 Nov. 1941; *s* of Sir Charles Archibald Edward Ivor Lees, 7th Bt, and Lily, *d* of Arthur Williams, Manchester; *S* father, 1963. *Heir: kinsman* John Cathcart d'Olier-Lees [*b* 12 Nov. 1927; *m* 1957, Wendy Garrold, *yr d* of late Brian Garrold Groom; two *s*].

LEES, Dr William, CBE 1970; TD 1962; FRCOG; Medical Manpower Consultant to South West Thames Regional Health Authority, 1981; retired; *b* 18 May 1924; *s* of William Lees and Elizabeth Lees (*née* Massey); *m* 1947, Winifred Elizabeth (*née* Hanford); three *s*. *Educ;* Queen Elizabeth's, Blackburn; Victoria Univ., Manchester. MB ChB; LRCP; MRCS; MRCOG, FRCOG; DPH; MFCM. Obstetrics and Gynaecology, St Mary's Hosps, Manchester, 1947–58; Min. of Health, later DHSS, 1959–81; Under Sec., (SPMO) 1977–81. QHP, 1969–72. Col, 10th, later no 257, Gen. Hosp., TAVR RAMC, 1966–71; Col Comdt, NW London Sector, ACF, 1971–76; Mem. for Greater London, TA&VRA, 1966–. OStJ 1967. *Publications:* numerous contribs on: intensive therapy, progressive patient care, perinatal mortality, day surgery, district general hospital. *Recreations:* music, golf, travel. *Address:* 13 Hall Park Hill, Berkhamsted, Herts. *T:* Berkhamsted (04427) 3010. *Clubs:* Athenæum, St John's.

LEES, Sir (William) Antony Clare, 3rd Bt *cr* 1937; *b* 14 June 1935; *s* of Sir (William) Hereward Clare Lees, 2nd Bt, and of Lady (Dorothy Gertrude) Lees, *d* of F. A. Lauder; *S* father, 1976; *m* 1986, Joanna Olive Crane. *Educ:* Eton; Magdalene Coll., Cambridge (MA). *Heir:* none.

LEES-MILNE, James; *b* 6 Aug. 1908; *er s* of George Crompton Lees-Milne, Crompton Hall, Lancs and Wickhamford Manor, Worcs; *m* 1951, Alvilde, formerly wife of 3rd Viscount Chaplin and *d* of late Lt-Gen. Sir Tom Molesworth Bridges, KCB, KCMG, DSO; no *c*. *Educ:* Eton Coll.; Magdalen Coll., Oxford. Private Sec. to 1st Baron Lloyd, 1931–35; on staff, Reuters, 1935–36; on staff, National Trust, 1936–66; Adviser on Historic Buildings to National Trust, 1951–66. 2nd Lieut Irish Guards, 1940–41 (invalided). FRSL 1957; FSA 1974. *Publications:* The National Trust (ed), 1945; The Age of Adam, 1947; National Trust Guide: Buildings, 1948; Tudor Renaissance, 1951; The Age of Inigo Jones, 1953; Roman Mornings, 1956 (Heinemann Award, 1956); Baroque in Italy, 1959; Baroque in Spain and Portugal, 1960; Earls of Creation, 1962; Worcestershire: A Shell Guide, 1964; St Peter's, 1967; English Country Houses: Baroque 1685–1714, 1970; Another Self, 1970; Heretics in Love, 1973; Ancestral Voices, 1975; William Beckford, 1976; Prophesying Peace, 1977; Round the Clock, 1978; Harold Nicolson, vol. I, 1980, vol. II, 1981 (Heinemann Award, RSL, 1982); (with David Ford) Images of Bath, 1982; The Country House (anthology), 1982; Caves of Ice, 1983; The Last Stuarts, 1983; Midway on the Waves, 1985; The Enigmatic Edwardian, 1986; Some Cotswold Country Houses, 1987; Venetian Evenings, 1988; The Fool of Love, 1990; The Bachelor Duke, 1991. *Address:* Essex House, Badminton, Avon GL9 1DD. *T:* Badminton (045421) 288. *Club:* Brooks's.

LEES-SPALDING, Rear-Adm. Ian Jaffery, (Tim), CB 1973; RN retd; Joint Editor, Macmillan and Silk Cut Nautical Almanac, since 1980; *b* London, 16 June 1920; *s* of Frank Souter Lees-Spalding and Joan (*née* Bodilly); *m* 1946, June Sandys Lyster Sparkes; two *d*. *Educ:* Blundells Sch.; RNEC. Served War of 1939–45 (King's Commendation for Bravery, 1941; Royal Lifesaving Inst. medal, 1942); served in HMS Sirius, HM S/Ms Trespasser, Teredo, Truculent and Andrew, HMS Cleopatra and Tiger; Chief of Staff to C-in-C Naval Home Comd, 1969; CSO (Technical) to C-in-C Fleet, 1971; retd 1974. Administrator, London Internat. Film Sch., 1975–79. *Recreations:* music, travelling. *Address:* St Olaf's, Wonston, Winchester, Hants S021 3LP. *T:* Winchester (0962) 760249. *Club:* Army and Navy.

LEESE, John Arthur; Editor-in-Chief, Evening Standard, 1986–91; *b* 4 Jan. 1930; *s* of late Cyril Leese and May Leese; *m* 1959, Maureen Jarvis; one *s* one *d*. *Educ:* Bishop Vesey's School, Warwicks. Editor, Coventry Evening Telegraph, 1964–70; Dep. Editor, Evening News, 1970–76, Editor, 1980; Editor-in-Chief and Publisher, Soho News, NY, 1981–82; Editl Dir, Harmsworth Publishing, 1975–82; Editor, You Magazine and Editor-in-Chief and Man. Dir, Associated Magazines, 1983–86; Editor, Evening News, 1987; Dir, Associated Newspaper Hldgs, 1989–.

LEESE, Sir John Henry Vernon, 5th Bt *cr* 1908; *b* 7 Aug. 1901; *s* of Vernon Francis Leese, OBE (*d* 1927) and Edythe Gwendoline (*d* 1929), *d* of Charles Frederick Stevenson; *g s* of Sir Joseph Francis Leese, 1st Bt; *S* cousin, 1979. *Heir:* none.

LeFANU, Dame Elizabeth; *see* Maconchy, Dame E.

LE FANU, Sir (George) Victor (Sheridan), KCVO 1987; Serjeant at Arms, House of Commons, 1982–89; *b* 1925; *s* of late Maj.-Gen. Roland Le Fanu, DSO, MC, and Marguerite (*née* Lumsden); *m* 1956, Elizabeth, *d* of late Major Herbert Hall and Kitty (*née* Gauvain); three *s*. *Educ:* Shrewsbury School. Served Coldstream Guards, 1943–63; Asst-Adjt, Royal Military Academy, Sandhurst, 1949–52; Adjt 2nd Bn Coldstream Guards, 1952–55; sc Camberley, 1959; Staff Captain to Vice-Quartermaster-General to the Forces, War Office, 1960–61; GSO2, Headquarters London District, 1961–63; Dep. Asst Serjeant at Arms, House of Commons, 1963–76; Asst Serjeant at Arms, 1976–81; Deputy Serjeant at Arms, 1981–82.

LE FANU, Mark; General Secretary, The Society of Authors, since 1982; *b* 14 Nov. 1946; *s* of Admiral of the Fleet Sir Michael Le Fanu, GCB, DSC and Prudence, *d* of Admiral Sir Vaughan Morgan, KBE, CB, MVO, DSC; *m* 1976, Lucy Cowen; three *s* one *d*. *Educ:* Winchester; Univ. of Sussex. Admitted Solicitor, 1976. Served RN, 1964–73; McKenna & Co., 1973–78; The Society of Authors, 1979–. *Recreations:* canals, travel, washing up. *Address:* 25 St James's Gardens, W11 4RE. *T:* 071–603 4119. *Club:* PEN.

LeFANU, Nicola Frances; composer; Senior Lecturer in Music, King's College London, since 1977; *b* 28 April 1947; *d* of William Richard LeFanu and Dame Elizabeth Violet Maconchy, *qv*; *m* 1979, David Newton Lumsdaine; one *s*. *Educ:* St Mary's Sch., Calne; St Hilda's Coll., Oxford (BA Hons 1968, MA 1972); Royal Coll. of Music; DMus London, 1988. Cobbett Prize for chamber music, 1968; BBC Composers' Competition, 1st Prize, 1971; Mendelssohn Scholarship, 1972; Harkness Fellowship for composition study, Harvard, 1973–74. Dir of Music, St Paul's Girls' Sch., 1975–77; Composer in Residence (jtly with David Lumsdaine), NSW Conservatorium of Music, Sydney, 1979. Deleg. to Moscow Internat. New Music Festival, 1984. Leverhulme Res. Award, 1989. *Publications:* numerous compositions, incl. opera, orchestral works, chamber music with and without voice, choral music and solo pieces. *Recreations:* natural history, and therefore conservation; peace movement, women's movement. *Address:* 9 Kempe Road, NW6 6SP. *T:* 081–960 0614.

LE FANU, Sir Victor; *see* Le Fanu, Sir G. V. S.

LEFEBVRE, Prof. Arthur Henry; Distinguished Reilly Professor of Combustion Engineering, School of Mechanical Engineering, Purdue University, since 1979 (Professor and Head of School, 1976–80); *b* 14 March 1923; *s* of Henri and May Lefebvre; *m* 1952, Elizabeth Marcella Betts; two *s* one *d*. *Educ:* Long Eaton Grammar Sch; Nottingham Univ.; Imperial Coll., London. DSc (Eng), DIC, PhD, CEng, FIMechE, FRAeS. Ericssons Telephones Ltd: Engrg apprentice, 1938–41; Prodn Engr, 1941–47; res. work on combustion and heat transfer in gas turbines, Rolls Royce, Derby, 1952–61; Prof. of Aircraft Propulsion, Coll. of Aeronautics, 1961–71; Prof. and Hd of Sch. of Mechanical Engrg, Cranfield Inst. of Technol., 1971–76. Mem., AGARD Combustion and Propulsion Panel, 1957–61; Mem., AGARD Propulsion and Energetics Panel, 1970–76; Chm., Combustion Cttee, Aeronautical Res. Council, 1970–74. Hon. DSc Cranfield Inst. of Technology, 1989. Gas Turbine Award, ASME, 1982; R. Tom Sawyer Award, ASME, 1984; inaugural AIAA Propellants and Combustion Award, 1990. *Publications:* Gas Turbine Combustion, 1983; Selected Papers on Fundamentals of Gas Turbine Combustion, 1988; Atomization and Sprays, 1989; papers on combustion and heat transfer in Proc. Royal Soc., internat. symposium vols on combustion, combustion and flame, combustion science and technology. *Recreations:* music, reading, golf. *Address:* 1741 Redwood Lane, Lafayette, Indiana 47905, USA. *T:* (317) 447–0117.

LEFEVER, Kenneth Ernest, CB 1974; Deputy Chairman, Civil Service Appeal Board, 1978–80 (Official Side Member, 1976–78); *b* 22 Feb. 1915; *s* of E. S. Lefever and Mrs E. E. Lefever; *m* 1939, Margaret Ellen Bowley; one *s* one *d*. *Educ:* County High Sch., Ilford. Board of Customs and Excise: joined Dept as Officer, 1935; War Service, 1942–46 (Captain, RE); Principal Inspector, 1966; Dep. Chief Inspector, 1969; Collector, London Port, 1971; Chief Inspector, 1972; Dir of Organisation and Chief Inspector, 1974; Comr, Bd of Customs and Excise, 1972–75, retd. *Recreations:* gardening, walking, cricket. *Address:* Trebarwith, 37 Surman Crescent, Hutton Burses, Brentwood, Essex CM13 2PW. *T:* Brentwood (0277) 212110. *Clubs:* MCC, Civil Service.

LEFF, Prof. Gordon; Professor of History, University of York, 1969–88, now Emeritus; *b* 9 May 1926; *m* 1953, Rosemary Kathleen (*née* Fox) (marr. diss 1980); one *s*. *Educ:* Summerhill Sch.; King's Coll., Cambridge. BA 1st Cl. Hons, PhD, LittD. Fellow, King's Coll., Cambridge, 1955–59; Asst Lectr, Lectr, Sen. Lectr, in History, Manchester Univ., 1956–65; Reader in History, Univ. of York, 1965–69. Carlyle Vis. Lectr, Univ. of Oxford, 1983. *Publications:* Bradwardine and the Pelagians, 1957; Medieval Thought, 1958; Gregory of Rimini, 1961; The Tyranny of Concepts, 1961; Richard Fitzralph, 1963; Heresy in the Later Middle Ages, 2 vols, 1967; Paris and Oxford Universities in 13th and 14th Centuries, 1968; History and Social Theory, 1969; William of Ockham: the metamorphosis of scholastic discourse, 1975; The Dissolution of the Medieval Outlook, 1976. *Recreations:* walking, gardening, watching cricket, listening to music. *Address:* The Sycamores, 12 The Village, Strensall, York Y03 5XS. *T:* York (0904) 490358.

le FLEMING, Morris John; DL; Chief Executive, Hertfordshire County Council, and Clerk to the Lieutenancy, Hertfordshire, 1979–90; *b* 19 Aug. 1932; *s* of late Morris Ralph le Fleming and Mabel le Fleming; *m* 1960, Jenny Rose Weeks; one *s* three *d*. *Educ:* Tonbridge Sch.; Magdalene Coll., Cambridge (BA). Admitted Solicitor, 1958. Junior Solicitor, Worcester CC, 1958–59; Asst Solicitor: Middlesex CC, 1959; Nottinghamshire CC, 1959–63; Asst Clerk, Lindsey (Lincolnshire) CC, 1963–69; Hertfordshire CC: Second Dep. Clerk, 1969–74; County Secretary, 1974–79; Clerk, Magistrates' Courts Cttee, 1979–90; Sec., Probation Care Cttee, 1979–90. Dir, Herts TEC, 1989–90. DL Herts, 1991. *Address:* 14 Swangleys Lane, Knebworth, Herts SG3 6AA. *T:* Stevenage (0438) 813152. *Club:* Royal Over-Seas League.

LE FLEMING, Peter Henry John; health management consultant, since 1988; Regional General Manager, South East Thames Regional Health Authority, 1984–88; *b* 25 Oct. 1923; *s* of late Edward Ralph Le Fleming and Irene Louise Le Fleming (*née* Adams); *m* 1st, 1949, Gudrun Svendsen (marr. diss. 1981); two *s*; 2nd, 1987, Jean, *yr d* of Edgar and Alice Price, Llangenny, Wales. *Educ:* Addison Gardens Sch., Hammersmith; Pembroke Coll., Cambridge. MA; FHSM. Served 1942–47, RTR and Parachute Regt, MEF, CMF, Palestine; commnd 1943. Sudan Political Service, Equatoria, Kassala, Blue Nile Provinces, 1949–55; NHS, 1955–: Redevelt Sec., St Thomas's Hosp., London, 1955–57; Hosp. Sec., The London Hosp., 1957–61; Dep. Clerk to the Governors, Guy's Hosp., 1961–69; Gp Sec., Exeter and Mid Devon Hosp. Management Cttee, 1969–74; Area Administrator, Kent AHA, 1974–81; Regional Administrator, SE Thames RHA, 1981–84. Mem., Health Service Supply Council, 1982–86. Clerk to Special Trustees, Guy's Hosp., 1988–. *Recreations:* long distance fell walking, breeding and showing dogs, trad jazz and serious music. *Address:* Lilacs, Leys Road, Tostock, near Bury St Edmunds, Suffolk IP30 9PN. *T:* Beyton (0359) 71015.

le FLEMING, Sir Quentin (John), 12th Bt *cr* 1705, of Rydal, Westmorland; Taxi Proprietor, Palmerston North Taxis Ltd, since 1982; *b* 27 June 1949; *s* of Sir William Kelland le Fleming, 11th Bt and of Noveen Avis, *d* of C. C. Sharpe; *S* father, 1988; *m* 1971, Judith Ann, *d* of C. J. Peck; two *s* one *d*. *Recreations:* flying modern and vintage aircraft (private pilot), Scouting, caravanning, restoration of vintage cars. *Heir: s* David

Kelland le Fleming, *b* 12 Jan. 1976. *Address:* 147 Stanford Street, Ashhurst, Manawatu, New Zealand. *T:* 063–268–406.

LEGARD, Sir Charles Thomas, 15th Bt *cr* 1660; *S* father, 1984. *Heir: s* Christopher John Charles Legard.

LÉGER, His Eminence Cardinal Paul-Émile; *b* Valleyfield, Quebec, Canada, 26 April 1904; *s* of Ernest Léger and Alda Beauvais. *Educ:* Ste-Thérèse Seminary; Grand Seminary, Montreal. Seminary of Philosophy, Paris, 1930–31; Seminary of Theology, Paris, 1931–32; Asst Master of Novices, Paris, 1932–33; Superior Seminary of Fukuoka, Japan, 1933–39; Prof., Seminary of Philosophy, Montreal, 1939–40; Vicar-Gen., Diocese of Valleyfield, 1940–47; Rector, Canadian Coll., Rome, 1947–50; consecrated bishop in Rome and apptd to See of Montreal, 1950; elevated to Sacred Coll. of Cardinals and given titular Church of St Mary of the Angels, 1953; Archbishop of Montreal, 1950–67; resigned to work as a missionary in Africa; Parish Priest, St Madeleine Sophie Barat parish, Montreal, 1974–75. Hon. Pres., Jules and Paul-Émile Léger Foundn and its subsidiaries, that help the poorest of world. Variety Club award, 1976. Has several hon. doctorates both from Canada and abroad. Holds foreign decorations. *Address:* CP1500–Succursale A, Montréal, PQ H3C 2Z9, Canada.

LEGG, Allan Aubrey R.; *see* Rowan-Legg.

LEGG, Prof. Brian James; Director, Silsoe Research Institute, Agricultural and Food Research Council, since 1990; *b* 20 July 1945; *s* of Walter and Mary Legg; *m* 1972, Philippa Whitehead; one *s* one *d. Educ:* Balliol Coll., Oxford (BA Physics 1966); Imperial Coll. London (PhD 1972). FInstP, FIAgrE, CPhys. Voluntary Service Overseas, The Gambia, 1966–67; Res. Scientist, Rothamsted Exptl Station, 1967–83; Head, Res. Divs, Silsoe Res. Inst., 1983–90. Vis. Scientist, CSIRO Div. of Envtl Mechanics, Camberra, 1980–82; Vis. Prof., Silsoe Coll., Cranfield Inst. of Technology, 1990. *Publications:* contribs to learned jls. *Recreations:* sailing, ski-ing, music. *Address:* Silsoe Research Institute, Wrest Park, Silsoe, Bedford MK45 4HS. *T:* Silsoe (0525) 60000.

LEGG, Cyrus Julian Edmund; Secretary, The Natural History Museum (formerly British Museum (Natural History)), since 1987; *b* 5 Sept. 1946; *s* of Cyrus and Eileen Legg; *m* 1967, Maureen Jean (*née* Lodge); two *s. Educ:* Tiffin School. Agricultural and Food Research Council, 1967–83; HM Treasury, 1983–87. *Recreation:* gardening. *Address:* The Natural History Museum, Cromwell Road, SW7 5DB. *T:* 071–938 8733.

LEGG, Keith (Leonard Charles), OBE 1981; PhD, MSc (Eng); CEng, FIMechE, FRAeS, FCIT; FHKIE; Hon. Professor and Advisor to Xian Jiaotung University, Shanghai Polytechnic University and South China Institute of Technology, China; consultant on aerospace engineering and on higher education; *b* 24 Oct. 1924; *s* of E. H. J. Legg; *m* 1947, Joan, *d* of H. E. Green; two *s. Educ:* London Univ. (External); Cranfield Inst. of Technology. Engineering apprenticeship, 1940–45; Dep. Chief Research and Test Engr, Asst Chief Designer, Chief Project and Structural Engr, Short Bros & Harland Ltd, Belfast, 1942–56; Chief Designer and Prof., Brazilian Aeronautical Centre, São Paulo, 1956–60; Head of Dept, 1960–72, and Prof., 1965–72, Loughborough Univ. of Technology (Sen. Pro Vice-Chancellor, 1967–70); Dir, Lanchester Polytechnic, 1972–75; Dir, Hong Kong Polytechnic, 1975–84. Chm., Internat. Directing Cttee, CERI/OECD Higher Educn Institutional Management, 1973–75; Member: Road Transport Industrial Trng Bd, 1966–75; Bd of Educn, 1975–84; World Council for Co-operative Educn, 1979–; Adv. Cttee on Environmental Protection, 1977–84; Council, Royal Aeronautical Soc.; Hong Kong Management Assoc. Council, 1982–84; Environmental and Pollution Council of Hong Kong; Indust. Develt Bd, 1982–84; Council of City Polytechnic of Hong Kong, 1984; Court, Cranfield Inst. of Technology, 1987– (Hon. Vice-Pres. of Convocation, 1987–). Adviser to OECD in Paris; Mem. various nat. and professional cttees. Fellow, Hong Kong Management Assoc. Hon. DTech Loughborough, 1982; Hon. LLD Hong Kong, 1984. *Publications:* numerous: on aerospace structures and design, transport systems, higher educn and educnl analytical models. *Recreations:* most sports, classical music, theatre, walking, aid to the handicapped. *Address:* 19 Broom Park, Broom Road, Teddington, Middx TW11 9RS. *T:* 081–977 8215.

LEGG, Thomas Stuart, CB 1985; QC 1990; Permanent Secretary, Lord Chancellor's Department, and Clerk of the Crown in Chancery, since 1989; *b* 13 Aug. 1935; *e s* of Stuart Legg and Margaret Legg (*née* Amos); *m* 1st, 1961, Patricia Irene Dowie (marr. diss.); two *d*; 2nd, 1983, Marie-Louise Clarke, *e d* of late Humphrey Jennings. *Educ:* Horace Mann-Lincoln Sch., New York; Frensham Heights Sch., Surrey; St John's Coll., Cambridge (MA, LLM). Royal Marines, 1953–55. Called to the Bar, Inner Temple, 1960, Bencher, 1984; joined Lord Chancellor's Dept, 1962; Private Secretary to Lord Chancellor, 1965–68; Asst Solicitor, 1975; Under Sec., 1977–82; SE Circuit Administrator, 1980–82; Dep. Sec., 1982–89; Dep. Clerk of the Crown in Chancery, 1986–89; Sec. of Commns, 1989. *Address:* Lord Chancellor's Department, House of Lords, SW1. *Club:* Garrick.

LEGGATT, Rt. Hon. Sir Andrew (Peter), Kt 1982; PC 1990; **Rt. Hon. Lord Justice Leggatt;** a Lord Justice of Appeal, since 1990; *b* 8 Nov. 1930; *er s* of late Captain William Ronald Christopher Leggatt, DSO, RN and of Dorothea Joy Leggatt (*née* Dreyer); *m* 1953, Gillian Barbara Newton; one *s* one *d. Educ:* Eton; King's Coll., Cambridge (Exhibr). MA 1957. Commn in Rifle Bde, 1949–50; TA, 1950–59. Called to the Bar, Inner Temple, 1954, Bencher, 1976. QC 1972; a Recorder of the Crown Court, 1974–82; Judge, High Court of Justice, QBD, 1982–90. Chm., Supreme Court Procedure Cttee, 1990–. Mem., Bar Council, 1971–82; Mem. Senate, 1974–83; Chm. of the Bar, 1981–82. Hon. Member: American Bar Assoc.; Canadian Bar Assoc.; non-resident mem., American Law Inst.; Mem., Top Salaries Review Body, 1979–82. *Recreations:* listening to music, personal computers. *Address:* Royal Courts of Justice, Strand, WC2A 2LL. *Clubs:* MCC, Pilgrims.

LEGGATT, Sir Hugh (Frank John), Kt 1988; art dealer; *b* 27 Feb. 1925; 2nd *s* of late Henry and Beatrice Leggatt; *m* 1st, 1953, Jennifer Mary Hepworth (marr. diss. 1990); two *s*; 2nd, 1991, Gaynor, *yr d* of late W. L. Tregoning, CBE and D. M. E. Tregoning. *Educ:* Eton; New Coll., Oxford. RAF, 1943–46. Chm., Soc. of London Art Dealers, 1966–70; Mem., Museums and Galleries Commn, 1983–. Hon. Sec., Heritage in Danger, 1974–. *Address:* 17 Duke Street, St James's, SW1Y 6DB. *T:* 071–930 3772. *Club:* White's.

LEGGE, family name of **Earl of Dartmouth**.

LEGGE, (John) Michael; Assistant Secretary General for Defence Planning and Policy, NATO, since 1988; *b* 14 March 1944; *s* of Alfred John Legge and Marion Frances Legge (*née* James); *m* 1971, Linda (*née* Bagley); two *s. Educ:* Royal Grammar Sch., Guildford; Christ Church Oxford (BA, MA). Ministry of Defence: Asst Principal, 1966; Asst Private Sec. to Sec. of State for Defence, 1970; Principal, 1971; 1st Sec., UK Delegn to NATO, 1974–77; Asst Sec., MoD, 1979–87; Rand Corp., Santa Monica, California, 1982; Asst Under Sec. of State (Policy), MoD, 1987–88. *Publication:* Theatre Nuclear Weapons and the NATO Strategy of Flexible Response, 1983. *Recreations:* golf, gardening. *Address:* c/o NATO HQ, 1110 Brussels, Belgium. *Club:* Puttenham Golf.

LEGGE, Rt. Rev. William Gordon, DD; *b* 20 Jan. 1913; *s* of Thomas Legge and Jane (*née* Gill); *m* 1941, Hyacinth Florence Richards; one *s* one *d. Educ:* Bishop Feild and Queen's Colls, St John's, Newfoundland. Deacon 1938, priest 1939; Curate, Channel, 1938–41; Incumbent of Botwood, 1941–44; Rector, Bell Island, 1944–55; Sec., Diocesan Synod, 1955–68; Archdeacon of Avalon, 1955–68; Canon of Cathedral, 1955–76; Diocesan Registrar, 1957–68; Suffragan Bishop, 1968; Bishop of Western Newfoundland, 1976–78. DD *hc*, Univ. of King's College, Halifax, NS, 1973. *Address:* 52 Glenhaven Boulevard, Corner Brook, Newfoundland A2H 4P6, Canada.

LEGGE-SCHWARZKOPF, Elisabeth; *see* Schwarzkopf.

LEGGETT, Sir Clarence (Arthur Campbell), Kt 1980; MBE (mil.) 1943; FRACS, FACS; Surgeon; Hon. Consulting Surgeon, Princess Alexandra Hospital, Brisbane, since 1968; *b* 24 July 1911; *s* of late A. J. Leggett; *m* 1939, Avril, *d* of late R. L. Bailey; one *s* two *d. Educ:* Sydney Univ. (MA, MB BS; 1st cl. Hons, Univ. Medallist, 1936); Queensland Univ. (MS). RMO, Royal Prince Alfred Hosp., Sydney, 1937–38; Asst Dep. Med. Supt, 1939. Major, AAMC, 1941–46. Asst Surgeon, Royal Brisbane Hosp., 1941–51; Junior Surg., 1951–56; Senior Surg., Princess Alexandra Hosp., Brisbane, 1956–68. University of Queensland: Hon. Demonstrator and Examiner, Anatomy Dept, 1941–47; Chief Asst, Dept of Surgery, 1947–51; Mem. Faculty Bd, 1947–51; Special Lectr, 1951–68. Member of Council: Queensland Inst. for Med. Research, 1948–65; RACS, 1966–75 (Gordon Craig Schol.; Chm. Court of Examiners, 1971–75; Junior Vice-Pres., 1973–75; Mem. Ct of Honour). FAMA 1985; Hon. FRCS 1983. *Publications:* numerous surgical and historical papers, orations and theses. *Recreations:* breeding Arabian horses and Hereford cattle; univ. blue, and mem., Australian hockey team, 1934. *Address:* Craigston, 217 Wickham Terrace, Brisbane, Queensland 4000, Australia. *T:* 07-831-0031. *Club:* Queensland (Brisbane).

LEGGETT, Douglas Malcolm Aufrère, MA, PhD, DSc; FRAeS; FIMA; Vice-Chancellor, University of Surrey, 1966–75; *b* 27 May 1912; *s* of George Malcolm Kent Leggett and Winifred Mabel Horsfall; *m* 1943, Enid Vida Southall; one *s* one *d. Educ:* Rugby Sch.; Edinburgh Univ.; Trinity Coll., Cambridge. Wrangler, 1934; Fellow of Trinity Coll., Cambridge, 1937; Queen Mary Coll., London, 1937–39; Royal Aircraft Establishment, 1939–45; Royal Aeronautical Society, 1945–50; King's Coll., London, 1950–60; Principal, Battersea Coll. of Technology, 1960–66. FKC 1974; DUniv Surrey 1975. *Publications:* (with C. M. Waterlow) The War Games that Superpowers Play, 1983; (with M. G. Payne) A Forgotten Truth, 1986; The Sacred Quest, 1987; Facing the Future, 1990; contrib. to scientific and technical jls. *Address:* Southlands, Fairoak Lane, Oxshott, Surrey KT22 0TW. *T:* Oxshott (0372) 843061.

LEGH; *see* Cornwall-Legh, family name of Baron Grey of Codnor.

LEGH, family name of **Baron Newton.**

LEGH-JONES, Piers Nicholas; QC 1987; an Assistant Recorder, since 1984; *b* 2 Feb. 1943; *s* of late John Herbert Legh-Jones and of Elizabeth Anne (*née* Halford). *Educ:* Winchester College; New College, Oxford (MA Hist. 1964, Jurisp. 1966). Legal Instructor, Univ. of Pennsylvania, 1966–67; Lectr in Law, New College, Oxford, 1967–71; Eldon Law Scholar, Univ. of Oxford, 1968. Called to the Bar, Lincoln's Inn, 1968. *Publications:* (ed) MacGillivray and Parkington on Insurance Law, 6th edn, to 8th edn 1988; contribs to Modern Law Review and Cambridge Law Jl. *Recreations:* vintage motorcars, cycling, modern history. *Address:* 3 Essex Court, Temple, EC4Y 9AL. *T:* 071–583 9294. *Club:* Travellers'.

LE GOY, Raymond Edgar Michel, FCIT; a Director General, Commission of the European Communities, since 1981; *b* 1919; *e s* of J. A. S. M. N. and May Le Goy; *m* 1960, Ernestine Burnett, Trelawny, Jamaica; two *s. Educ:* William Ellis Sch.; Gonville and Caius Coll., Cambridge (MA). 1st cl. hons Hist. Tripos, 1939, 1940. Sec. Cambridge Union; Chm., Union Univ. Liberal Socs. Served Army, 1940–46: Staff Captain, HQ E Africa, 1944; Actg Major, 1945. LPTB, 1947; Min. of Transport, 1947; UK Shipping Adviser, Japan, 1949–51; Far East and SE Asia, 1951; Dir, Goeland Co., 1952; Asst Secretary: MoT, 1958; Min. of Aviation, 1959; BoT and DEA, 1966; Under-Sec., 1968, BoT, later DTI; Dir Gen. for Transport, EEC, 1973–81. *Publication:* The Victorian Burletta, 1953. *Recreations:* theatre, music, race relations. *Address:* c/o Société Générale de Banque, 10 Rond Point Schuman, Brussels 1040, Belgium.

LE GRICE, Very Rev. F(rederick) Edwin, MA; Dean Emeritus of Ripon Cathedral, since 1984 (Dean, 1968–84); *b* 14 Dec. 1911; *s* of Frederick and Edith Le Grice; *m* 1940, Joyce Margaret Hildreth; one *s* two *d. Educ:* Paston Sch., North Walsham; Queens' Coll., Cambridge; Westcott House, Cambridge. BA (2nd class hons Mathematics, 2nd class hons Theology) 1934; MA 1946. Asst Curate: St Aidan's, Leeds, 1935–38; Paignton, 1938–46; Vicar of Totteridge, N20, 1946–58; Canon Residentiary and Sub-Dean of St Albans Cathedral, 1958–68; Examining Chaplain to the Bishop of St Albans, 1958–68. A Church Comr, 1973–82; Mem., Church Commn on Crown Appts, 1977–82. *Publications:* Sharp Reflections (poetry), 1989; Five Instant Glorias and a Creed, 1991. *Address:* The West Cottage, Markenfield Hall, Ripon, N Yorks HG4 3AD.

LEHANE, Maureen, (Mrs Peter Wishart); concert and opera singer; *d* of Christopher Lehane and Honor Millar; *m* 1966, Peter Wishart (*d* 1984), composer. *Educ:* Queen Elizabeth's Girls' Grammar Sch., Barnet; Guildhall Sch. of Music and Drama. Studied under Hermann Weissenborn, Berlin (teacher of Fischer Dieskau); also under John and Aida Dickens (Australian teachers of Joan Sutherland); gained Arts Council award to study in Berlin. Speciality is Handel; has sung numerous leading roles (operas inc. Ezio, Ariadne and Pharamondo) with Handel opera societies of England and America, in London, and in Carnegie Hall, New York, also in Poland, Sweden and Germany; gave a number of master classes on the interpretation of Handel's vocal music (notably at s'Hertogenbosch Festival, Holland, July 1972; invited to repeat them in 1973); masterclasses on Handel and Purcell, The Hague and Maastricht, 1991. Debut at Glyndebourne, 1967. Festival appearances include: Stravinsky Festival, Cologne; City of London; Aldeburgh; Cheltenham; Three Choirs; Bath; Oxford Bach; Göttingen Handel Festival, etc; has toured N America; also 3–month tour of Australia at invitation of ABC and 2–month tour of Far East and ME, 1971; sang in Holland, and for Belgian TV, 1978; visits also to Berlin, Lisbon, Poland and Rome, 1979–80, to Warsaw, 1981. Title rôle in: Handel's Ariodante, Sadler's Wells, 1974; (her husband's 4th opera) Clytemnaestra, London, 1974; Purcell's Dido and Aeneas, Netherlands Opera, 1976; castrato lead in J. C. Bach's Adriano in Siria, London, 1982; female lead in Hugo Cole's The Falcon, Somerset, 1983; Peter Wishart's The Lady of the Inn, Reading Univ., 1983. Cyrus in first complete recording of Handel's Belshazzar. Appears regularly on BBC; also in promenade concerts. Has made numerous recordings (Bach, Haydn, Mozart, Handel, etc). Mem. Jury, Internat. Singing Comp., s'Hertogenbosch Fest., Holland, 1982–. Musical Dir and Founder, Great Elm Music Festival, 1987–. *Publication:* (ed with Peter Wishart) Songs of Purcell. *Recreations:* cooking, gardening, reading. *Address:* Bridge House, Great Elm, Frome, Somerset BA11 3NY. *T:* Mells (0373) 812383.

LEHMAN, Prof. Meir, (Manny), DSc, PhD; FEng, FBCS, FIEE, FIEEE, MACM; Managing and Technical Director, Lehman Software Technology Associates Ltd, since

1985; Professor of Computing Science, Imperial College of Science and Technology, University of London, 1972–84, now Emeritus Professor; *b* 24 Jan. 1925; *s* of late Benno and Theresa Lehman; *m* 1953, Chava Robinson; three *s* two *d*. *Educ:* Letchworth Grammar Sch.; Imperial Coll. of Science and Technol. (BSc Hons, PhD, ARCS, DIC); DSc (London) 1987. FIEE 1972; FBCS 1968; MACM 1955; FIEEE 1985; FEng 1989. Murphy Radio, 1941–50; Imperial Coll., 1950–56; London Labs, Ferranti, 1956–57; Scientific Dept, Israeli Defence Min., 1957–64; Res. Div., IBM, 1964–72; Dept of Computing, Imperial Coll., 1972–84 (part-time 1984–87, and 1989–), Hd of Dept, 1979–84, Sen. Res. Fellow, 1989–; Imperial Software Technology: Founder, 1982; Chm., 1982–84; Dir, 1984–87; Exec. Dir, 1987–88. Vice-Chm. of Exec., Kisharon Day Sch. for Special Educn, 1976–. *Publications:* Software Evolution—Processes of Program Change, 1985; over 100 refereed pubns and some 6 book chapters. *Recreations:* family, Talmudic studies, classical orchestral music, gardening, DIY. *Address:* 5 Elm Close, NW4 2PH. *T:* (office) 071–589 5111.

LEHMANN, Prof. Andrew George; Emeritus Professor, University of Buckingham; *b* 17 Feb. 1922; *m* 1942, Alastine Mary, *d* of late K. N. Bell; two *s* one *d*. *Educ:* Dulwich Coll.; The Queen's Coll., Oxford. MA, DPhil Oxon. Served with RCS and Indian Army, 6th Rajputana Rifles. Fenced for England (Sabre), 1939. Asst lecturer and lecturer, Manchester Univ., 1945–51; Prof. of French Studies, 1951–68, Dean of Faculty of Letters and Soc. Scis, Univ. of Reading, 1960–66. Hon. Prof., Univ. of Warwick, 1968–78; various industry posts, 1968–78; Dir, Inst. of European Studies, Hull Univ., 1978–83; Rank Foundn Prof. of European Studies, and Dean, Sch. of Humanities, Univ. of Buckingham, 1983–88. Mem., Hale Cttee on University Teaching Methods, 1961–63; Chm., Industrial Council for Educnl and Trng Technology, 1974–76 (Pres., 1979–81, Vice-Pres., 1981–85); Mem., Anglo-French Permanent Mixed Cultural Commission, 1963–68. Adviser: Chinese Univ. of Hong Kong, 1964; Haile Selassie I Univ., Ethiopia, 1965. Member: Hong Kong Univ. Grants Cttee, 1966–73; Academic Planning Board and Academic Adv. Cttee, New Univ. of Ulster, 1966–77; Court and Council, Bedford Coll., London Univ., 1971–78; British Library Adv. Cttee (Reference), 1975–78; Princeton Univ. Academic Adv. Council, 1975–81. Shakespeare-Preis-Kuratorium, FVS Foundn, Hamburg, 1984–90. Governor, Ealing Tech. Coll., 1974. *Publications:* The Symbolist Aesthetic in France, 1950 and 1967; Sainte-Beuve, a portrait of the Critic, 1962; The European Heritage, 1984; articles in various periodicals and learned reviews. *Recreations:* music, travel, gardening. *Address:* Westway Cottage, West Adderbury, Banbury, Oxon OX17 3EU. *T:* Banbury (0295) 810272. *Club:* Athenæum.

LEHN, Prof. Jean-Marie; Chevalier, Ordre National du Mérite, 1976; Officier, Légion d'Honneur, 1988 (Chevalier, 1983); Professor of Chemistry, Collège de France, Paris, since 1979; *b* Rosheim, Bas-Rhin, 30 Sept. 1939; *s* of Pierre Lehn and Marie Lehn (*née* Salomon); *m* 1965, Sylvie Lederer; two *s*. *Educ:* Univ. of Strasbourg (PhD); Research Fellow, Harvard, 1964. CNRS, 1960–66; Asst Prof., Univ. of Strasbourg, 1966–69; University Louis Pasteur, Strasbourg: Associate Prof., 1970; Prof. of Chemistry, 1970–79. Visiting Professor, 1972–: Harvard, Zürich, Cambridge, Barcelona, Frankfurt. Mem. or Associate, and Hon. Degrees from professional bodies in Europe and USA; Hon. FRSC 1987. Nobel Prize for Chemistry (jtly), 1987, and numerous awards from sci. instns. Orden pour le mérite für Wissenchaften und Künste (FRG), 1990. *Publications:* many chapters in books and contribs to learned jls on supramolecular chemistry, physical organic chemistry and photochemistry. *Recreation:* music. *Address:* Institut le Bel, Université Louis Pasteur, 4 rue Blaise Pascal, 67000 Strasbourg, France. *T:* 88 416056; Collège de France, 11 place Marcelin Berthelot, 75005 Paris, France. *T:* 44271360.

LEHRER, Thomas Andrew; writer of songs since 1943; *b* 9 April 1928; *s* of James Lehrer and Anna Lehrer (*née* Waller). *Educ:* Harvard Univ. (AB 1946, MA 1947); Columbia Univ.; Harvard Univ. Student (mathematics, especially probability and statistics) till 1953. Part-time teaching at Harvard, 1947–51. Theoretical physicist at Baird-Atomic, Inc., Cambridge, Massachusetts, 1953–54. Entertainer, 1953–55, 1957–60. US Army, 1955–57. Lecturer in Business Administration, Harvard Business Sch., 1961; Lecturer: in Education, Harvard Univ., 1963–66; in Psychology, Wellesley Coll., 1966; in Political Science, MIT, 1962–71; Vis. Lectr, Univ. of Calif, Santa Cruz, 1972–. *Publications:* Tom Lehrer Song Book, 1954; Tom Lehrer's Second Song Book, 1968; Too Many Songs by Tom Lehrer, 1981; contrib. to Annals of Mathematical Statistics, Journal of Soc. of Industrial and Applied Maths. *Recreation:* piano. *Address:* PO Box 121, Cambridge, Massachusetts 02138, USA. *T:* (617) 354–7708.

LEICESTER, 6th Earl of, *cr* 1837; **Anthony Louis Lovel Coke;** Viscount Coke 1837; farmer, since 1976; *b* 11 Sept. 1909; *s* of Hon. Arthur George Coke (killed in action, 1915) (2nd *s* of 3rd Earl) and of Phyllis Hermione (Lady Howard-Vyse), *d* of late Francis Saxham Elwes Drury; *S* cousin, 1976; *m* 1st, 1934, Moyra Joan (marr. diss. 1947, she *d* 1987), *d* of late Douglas Crossley; two *s* one *d*; 2nd, 1947, Vera Haigh (*d* 1984), Harare, Zimbabwe; 3rd, 1985, Elizabeth Hope Johnstone, Addo, Eastern Province, South Africa, *d* of late Clifford Arthur Johnstone. *Educ:* Gresham's School, Holt. Served War of 1939–45 in RAF. Career spent ranching. *Recreations:* general. *Heir:* *s* Viscount Coke, *qv*. *Address:* Hillhead, PO Box 544, Plettenberg Bay, 6600, South Africa. *T:* (04457) 32255.

LEICESTER, Bishop of, since 1991; **Rt. Rev. Thomas Frederick Butler;** *b* 1940; *s* of Thomas John Butler and Elsie Butler (*née* Bainbridge); *m* 1964, Barbara Joan Clark; one *s* one *d*. *Educ:* Univ. of Leeds (BSc 1st Cl. Hons, MSc, PhD). CEng; MIEE. College of the Resurruection, Mirfield, 1962–64; Curate: St Augustine's, Wisbech, 1964–66; St Saviour's, Folkestone, 1966–68; Lecturer and Chaplain, Univ. of Zambia, 1968–73; Acting Dean of Holy Cross Cathedral, Lusaka, Zambia, 1973; Chaplain to Univ. of Kent at Canterbury, 1973–80; Archdeacon of Northolt, 1980–85; Area Bishop of Willesden, 1985–91. Six Preacher, Canterbury Cathedral, 1979–84. *Recreations:* reading, mountain walking. *Address:* Bishop's Lodge, 10 Springfield Road, Leicester LE2 3BD. *T:* Leicester (0533) 708985.

LEICESTER, Provost of; *see* Warren, Very Rev. A. C.

LEICESTER, Archdeacon of; *see* Silk, Ven. R. D.

LEIFLAND, Leif, Hon. GCVO 1983; Ambassador of Sweden to the Court of St James's, 1982–90; *b* 30 Dec. 1925; *s* of Sigfrid and Elna Leifland; *m* 1954, Karin Abard; one *s* two *d*. *Educ:* Univ. of Lund (LLB 1950). Joined Ministry of Foreign Affairs, 1952; served: Athens, 1953; Bonn, 1955; Stockholm, 1958; Washington, 1961; Stockholm, 1964; Washington, 1970; Stockholm, 1975. Secretary, Foreign Relations Cttee, Swedish Parliament, 1966–70; Under Secretary for Political Affairs, 1975–77; Permanent Under-Secretary of State for Foreign Affairs, 1977–82. *Publications:* books and articles on foreign policy and national security questions. *Address:* c/o Ministry of Foreign Affairs, Gustav Adolfstorg 1, POB 16121, 103 23 Stockholm, Sweden.

LEIGH, family name of **Baron Leigh.**

LEIGH, 5th Baron *cr* 1839; **John Piers Leigh;** *b* 11 Sept. 1935; *s* of 4th Baron Leigh, TD and Anne (*d* 1977), *d* of Ellis Hicks Beach; *S* father, 1979; *m* 1st, 1957, Cecilia Poppy (marr. diss. 1974), *y d* of late Robert Cecil Jackson; one *s* one *d* (and one *d* decd); 2nd, 1976, Susan (marr. diss. 1982), *d* of John Cleave, Whitnash, Leamington Spa; one *s*; 3rd, 1982, Mrs Lea Hamilton-Russell, *o d* of Col Noel Wild, OBE. *Educ:* Eton; Oxford and London Universities. *Recreations:* horses, hunting, racing, sport, country pursuits. *Heir:* *s* Hon. Christopher Dudley Piers Leigh [*b* 20 Oct. 1960; *m* 1990, Sophy-Ann, *d* of Richard Burrows]. *Address:* Unicorn Lodge, 12 Briar Walk, Putney, SW15.

LEIGH, (Archibald) Denis, MD, FRCP; Consultant Physician, Bethlem Royal and Maudsley Hospitals, 1949–80, now Emeritus; Secretary-General, World Psychiatric Association, 1966–78; Hon. Consultant in Psychiatry to the British Army, 1969–80; Lecturer, Institute of Psychiatry; *b* 11 Oct. 1915; *o s* of Archibald Leigh and Rose Rushworth; *m* 1941, Pamela Parish; two *s* three *d*. *Educ:* Hulme Grammar Sch.; Manchester Univ.; University of Budapest. Manchester City Schol. in Medicine, 1932; BSc 1936; MB, ChB (1st class hons) 1939; Dauntesey Med. Sen. Schol., Prof. Tom Jones Exhibitioner in Anatomy; Sidney Renshaw Jun. Prize in Physiol.; Turner Med. Prize; John Henry Agnew Prize; Stephen Lewis Prize; Prize in Midwifery; MRCP 1941; MD (Manchester), 1947; FRCP, 1955. RAMC, 1940–45 (Lt-Col); Adviser in Neurology, Eastern Army, India. 1st Assistant, Dept of Neurology, London Hospital; Nuffield Fellow, 1947–48; Clinical Fellow, Harvard Univ., 1948. Recognised Clinical Teacher, London Univ.; Founder European Society of Psychosomatic Research; Editor-in-Chief and Founder, Journal of Psychosomatic Res.; Editorial Bd, Japanese Journal of Psychosomatic Medicine, Medicina Psychosomatica, Psychosomatic Medicine, Behaviour Therapy; Examiner in Psychological Med., Edinburgh Univ., 1958–65; Beattie Smith Lectr, Melbourne Univ., 1967. Governor, Bethlem Royal and Maudsley Hospitals, 1956–62; President Sect. of Psychiatry, Royal Society Med., 1967–68. Hon. Member: Deutschen Gesellschaft für Psychiatrie und Nervenheilkunde; Italian Psychosomatic Soc.; Assoc. Brasileira de Psiquiatria; Sociedad Argentina de Medicina Psicosomática; Polish Psychiatric Assoc.; Corresp. Mem., Pavlovian Soc. of N America; Hon. Corresp. Mem., Austn Acad. of Forensic Scis; Hon Fellow: Swedish Soc. of Med. Scis; Soc. Colombiana de Psiquiatría; Soviet Soc. of Neurologists and Psychiatrists; Czechoslovak Psychiatric Soc.; Finnish Psychiatric Soc. Distinguished Fellow: Amer. Psychiatric Assoc.; Hong Kong Psychiatric Assoc. *Publications:* (trans. from French) Psychosomatic Methods of Painless Childbirth, 1959; The Historical Development of British Psychiatry, Vol. I, 1961; Bronchial Asthma, 1967; A Concise Encyclopaedia of Psychiatry, 1977; chapters in various books; papers on neurology, psychiatry, history of psychiatry and psychosomatic medicine. *Recreations:* fishing, collecting. *Address:* 152 Harley Street, W1. *T:* 071–935 8868; The Grange, Otford, Kent. *T:* Otford (09592) 3427.

LEIGH, Christopher Humphrey de Verd; QC 1989; a Recorder of the Crown Court, since 1985; *b* 12 July 1943; *s* of late Wing Commander Humphrey de Verd Leigh and of Johanna Leigh; *m* 1970, Frances Powell. *Educ:* Harrow. Called to the Bar, Lincoln's Inn, 1967. *Recreations:* fishing, travel. *Address:* 1 Paper Buildings, Temple, EC4Y 7EP. *T:* 071–353 3728. *Club:* Hampshire (Winchester).

LEIGH, Edward Julian Egerton; MP (C) Gainsborough and Horncastle, since 1983; Parliamentary Under Secretary of State, Department of Trade and Industry, since 1990; *b* 20 July 1950; *s* of Sir Neville Egerton Leigh, *qv*; *m* 1984, Mary Goodman; one *s* three *d*. *Educ:* St Philip's Sch., Kensington; Oratory Sch.; French Lycée, London; UC, Durham Univ. (BA Hons). Called to the Bar, Inner Temple, 1977. Mem., Cons. Res. Dept, seconded to office of Leader of Opposition, GLC, 1973–75; Prin. Correspondence Sec. to Rt Hon. Margaret Thatcher, MP, 1975–76. Member (C): Richmond Borough Council, 1974–78; GLC, 1977–81. Contested (C) Teesside, Middlesbrough, Oct. 1974. PPS to Minister of State, Home Office, 1990. Sec., Conservative Backbench Cttees on agric., defence and employment, 1983–90. Chm., Nat. Council for Civil Defence, 1980–82; Dir, Coalition for Peace Through Security, 1982–83. *Publications:* Right Thinking, 1979; (jtly) Onwards from Bruges: the state as enabler not provider. *Recreations:* walking, reading. *Address:* House of Commons, SW1A 0AA.

LEIGH, Sir Geoffrey (Norman), Kt 1990; Chairman, Allied London Properties, since 1987 (Managing Director, 1970–87); *b* 23 March 1933; *s* of late Rose Leigh and of Morris Leigh; *m* 1st, 1955, Valerie Lennard (marr. diss. 1975; she *d* 1976); one *s* two *d*; 2nd, 1976, Sylvia Pell; one *s* one *d*. *Educ:* Haberdashers' Aske's Hampstead Sch.; Univ. of Michigan. Man. Dir, 1965, Chm., 1980–, Sterling Homes. Founder and First Pres., Westminster Junior Chamber of Commerce, 1959–63; Underwriting Mem., Lloyd's, 1973–. Member: Cttee, Good Design in Housing for Disabled, 1977; Cttee, Good Design in Housing, 1978–79; British ORT Council, 1979–80; Internat. Adv. Bd, American Univ., Washington, 1983–; Adv. Council, Prince's Youth Business Trust, 1985–; Main Finance Bd, NSPCC, 1985–; Royal Vet. Coll. Appeal Cttee, 1985–88; London Historic House Museums Trust, 1987–; Governing Council, Business in the Community, 1987–; Somerville Coll. Appeal, 1987–; Royal Fine Art Commn Art and Arch. Educn Trust, 1988–; Per Cent Club, 1988–; Council, City Technology Colls Trust; City Appeal Cttee, Royal Marsden Hosp., 1990–; Review Body on Doctors' and Dentists' Remuneration, 1990–; Chancellor's Ct of Benefactors, Oxford Univ., 1991–; Comr and Trustee, Fulbright Commn, 1991–; Sponsor, Leigh City Technology Coll., Dartford (Chm. of Govs, 1988–); Founder/Sponsor, Friends of British Liby, 1987–; Founder, Margaret Thatcher Centre, Somerville Coll., Oxford, 1991; Treasurer: Commonwealth Jewish Council, 1983–89; Commonwealth Jewish Trust, 1983–89; Patron, Hampstead and Highgate Cons. Assoc., 1991–; Treas. and Trustee, Action Addiction, 1991–; Trustee, Margaret Thatcher Foundn, 1991–. Freeman, City of London, 1976; Liveryman, Furniture Makers' Co. FRSA. Presidential Citation, The American Univ., 1987. *Recreations:* photography, reading, golf. *Address:* 26 Manchester Square, W1A 2HU. *T:* 071–486 6080. *Clubs:* Carlton, United and Cecil, Royal Automobile, Savile, Hurlingham, Pilgrims.

LEIGH, Sir John, 2nd Bt, *cr* 1918; *b* 24 March 1909; *s* of Sir John Leigh, 1st Bt, and Norah Marjorie, CBE (*d* 1954); *S* father 1959; *m* 1959, Ariane, *d* of late Joseph Wm Allen, Beverly Hills, California, and *widow* of Harold Wallace Ross, NYC. *Educ:* Eton; Balliol Coll., Oxford. *Heir:* *nephew* Richard Henry Leigh [*b* 11 Nov. 1936; *m* 1st, 1962, Barbro Anna Elizabeth (marr. diss. 1977), *e d* of late Stig Carl Sebastian Tham, Sweden; 2nd, 1977, Chérie Rosalind, *e d* of D. D. Dale and *widow* of A. Reece, RMS]. *Clubs:* Brooks's; Travellers' (Paris).

LEIGH, Prof. Leonard Herschel; Professor of Criminal Law in the University of London, at the London School of Economics and Political Science, since 1982; *b* 19 Sept. 1935; *s* of Leonard William and Lillian Mavis Leigh; *m* 1960, Jill Diane Gale; one *s* one *d*. *Educ:* Univ. of Alberta (BA, LLB); Univ. of London (PhD 1966). Admitted to Bar: Alberta, 1959; NW Territories, 1961. Private practice, Province of Alberta, 1958–60; Dept of Justice, Canada, 1960–62; London School of Economics: Asst Lectr in Law, 1964–65; Lectr, 1965–71; Reader, 1971–82. Vis. Prof., Queen's Univ., Kingston, Ont, 1973–74; British Council Lecturer: Univ. of Strasbourg, 1978; National Univ. of Mexico, 1980; UN Asia and Far East Inst., Tokyo, 1986; South India, 1989. Mem., Canadian Govt Securities Regulation Task Force, 1974–78; UK Convenor, Université de l'Europe Steering Cttee, 1987–90; Chm., English Nat. Section, 1988–, Mem., Conseil de Direction, 1989–, Internat. Assoc. of Penal Law. *Publications:* The Criminal Liability of Corporations in English Law, 1969; (jtly) Northey and Leigh's Introduction to Company

Law, 1970, 4th edn 1987; Police Powers in England and Wales, 1975, 2nd edn 1986; Economic Crime in Europe, 1980; (jtly) The Companies Act 1981, 1981; (jtly) The Management of the Prosecution Process in Denmark, Sweden and the Netherlands, 1981; The Control of Commercial Fraud, 1982; Strict and Vicarious Liability, 1982; (jtly) A Guide to the Financial Services Act, 1986; articles in British, European, Amer. and Canadian jls. *Recreations:* music, walking. *Address:* London School of Economics and Political Science, Houghton Street, WC2A 2AE. *T:* 071–405 7686.

LEIGH, Mike; dramatist; theatre, television and film director; *b* 20 Feb. 1943; *s* of late Alfred Abraham Leigh, MRCS, LRCP and of Phyllis Pauline Leigh (*née* Cousin); *m* 1973, Alison Steadman; two *s.* *Educ:* North Grecian Street County Primary Sch.; Salford Grammar Sch.; RADA; Camberwell Sch. of Arts and Crafts; Central Sch. of Art and Design (Theatre Design Dept); London Film Sch. Sometime actor, incl. Victoria Theatre, Stoke-on-Trent, 1966; Assoc. Dir, Midlands Arts Centre for Young People, 1965–66; Asst Dir, RSC, 1967–68; Drama Lectr, Sedgley Park and De La Salle Colls, Manchester, 1968–69; Lectr, London Film Sch., 1970–73. Arts Council of GB: Member: Drama Panel, 1975–77; Dirs' Working Party and Specialist Allocations Bd, 1976–84; Member: Accreditation Panel, Nat. Council for Drama Trng, 1978–; Gen. Adv. Council, IBA, 1980–82. NFT Retrospective, 1979; BBC TV Retrospective (incl. Arena: Mike Leigh Making Plays), 1982. Hon. MA Salford, 1991. George Devine Award, 1973. Productions of own plays and films evolved from scratch entirely by rehearsal through improvisation; *stage plays:* The Box Play, 1965, My Parents Have Gone To Carlisle, The Last Crusade Of The Five Little Nuns, 1966, Midlands Arts Centre; Nenaa, RSC Studio, Stratford-upon-Avon, 1967; Individual Fruit Pies, E15 Acting Sch., 1968; Down Here And Up There, Royal Ct Th. Upstairs, 1968; Big Basil, 1968, Glum Victoria And The Lad With Specs, Manchester Youth Theatre, 1969; Epilogue, Manchester, 1969; Bleak Moments, Open Space, 1970; A Rancid Pong, Basement, 1971; Wholesome Glory, Dick Whittington and his Cat, Royal Ct Th. Upstairs, 1973; The Jaws of Death, Traverse, Edinburgh Fest., 1973; Babies Grow Old, Other Place, 1974, ICA, 1975; The Silent Majority, Bush, 1974; Abigail's Party, Hampstead, 1977; Ecstasy, Hampstead, 1979; Goose-Pimples, Hampstead, Garrick, 1981 (Standard Best Comedy Award); Smelling a Rat, Hampstead, 1988; Greek Tragedy, Sydney, 1989, Edinburgh Fest. and Theatre Royal, Stratford East, 1990. *BBC radio play:* Too Much Of A Good Thing (banned), 1979; *feature films:* Bleak Moments, 1971 (Golden Hugo, Chicago Film Fest., 1972; Golden Leopard, Locarno Film Fest., 1972); High Hopes, 1989 (Critics' Award, Venice Film Fest., 1988; Stars de Demain Coup de Coeur, 1989; Evening Standard Peter Sellers Comedy Award, 1989); Life is Sweet, 1991; *BBC TV plays and films:* A Mug's Game, 1972; Hard Labour, 1973; The Permissive Society, Afternoon, A Light Snack, Probation, Old Chums, The Birth Of The 2001 FA Cup Final Goalie, 1975; Nuts in May, Knock For Knock, 1976; The Kiss Of Death, Abigail's Party, 1977; Who's Who, 1978; Grown-Ups, 1980; Home Sweet Home, 1982; Four Days In July, 1984; *Channel Four films:* Meantime, 1983; The Short and Curlies, 1987. Directed and designed orig. prodn of Halliwell's Little Malcolm And His Struggle Against The Eunuchs, Unity, 1965. *Relevant publication:* The Improvised Play: the work of Mike Leigh, by Paul Clements, 1983. *Address:* c/o A. D. Peters & Co. Ltd, The Chambers, Chelsea Harbour, Lots Road, SW10 0XF.

LEIGH, Sir Neville (Egerton), KCVO 1980 (CVO 1967); Clerk of the Privy Council, 1974–84; *b* 4 June 1922; *s* of late Cecil Egerton Leigh; *m* 1944, Denise Margaret Yvonne, *d* of late Cyril Denzil Branch, MC; two *s* one *d.* *Educ:* Charterhouse. RAFVR, 1942–47 (Flt-Lt). Called to Bar, Inner Temple, 1948. Legal Asst, Treasury Solicitors Dept, 1949–51; Senior Clerk, Privy Council Office, 1951–65; Deputy Clerk of Privy Council, 1965–74. Member: Investigation Cttee, ICA, 1985–90; Press Council, 1986–88; Chm., Central London Valuation and Community Charge Tribunal, 1990– (Mem., Central London Valuation Panel, 1986–90). Pres., British Orthoptic Soc., 1984–91. Consultant, Royal Coll. of Nursing of UK, 1985–88. Trustee: R&D Trust for the Young Disabled, Royal Hosp. and Home, Putney, 1986–90; Coll. of Arms Trust, 1987–; Gov., Suttons Hosp., Charterhouse, 1986–. Hon. FCIOB 1982. *Address:* 11 The Crescent, Barnes, SW13 0NN. *T:* 081–876 4271. *Club:* Army and Navy.
See also Edward Leigh.

LEIGH, Peter William John, FRICS; chartered surveyor and property consultant; *b* 29 June 1929; *s* of John Charles Leigh and Dorothy Grace Leigh; *m* 1956, Mary Frances (*née* Smith); two *s* one *d.* *Educ:* Harrow Weald County Grammar Sch.; Coll. of Estate Management (ext.). National Service, Royal Signals, 1947–49. Private surveying practice, 1949–53; Valuation Asst, Mddx CC, 1953–60; Commercial Estates Officer, Bracknell Develt Corp., 1960–66; sen. appts, Valuation and Estates Dept, GLC, 1966–81; Dir of Valuation and Estates, GLC, 1981–84; Dir of Property Services, Royal County of Berks, 1984–88. Member: Gen. Council, RICS, 1984–86; Govt Property Adv. Gp, 1984–88. Exec. Mem., Local Authority Valuers Assoc. (formerly Assoc. of Local Authority Valuers and Estate Surveyors), 1981–88. *Recreations:* exploring Cornwall, drawing, gardening (therapy). *Address:* 41 Sandy Lane, Wokingham, Berks RG11 4SS. *T:* Wokingham (0734) 782732.

LEIGH-PEMBERTON, John, AFC 1945; artist painter; *b* 18 Oct. 1911; *s* of Cyril Leigh-Pemberton and Mary Evelyn Megaw; *m* 1948, Doreen Beatrice Townshend-Webster. *Educ:* Eton. Studied Art, London, 1928–31. Past Member Royal Institute of Painters in Oils and other Societies. Served 1940–45 with RAF as Flying Instructor. Series of pictures for Coldstream Guards, 1950. Festival Almanack, 1951, for Messrs Whitbread; Royal Progress, 1953, for Shell Mex & BP Ltd. Works in public and private collections, UK and America; decorations for ships: City of York, City of Exeter, Britannic, Caledonia, Corfu, Carthage, Kenya, Uganda. Many series of paintings, chiefly of natural history subjects, for Midland Bank Ltd. *Publications:* A Book of Garden Flowers, 1960; A Book of Butterflies, Moths and other Insects, 1963; British Wildlife, Rarities and Introductions, 1966; Garden Birds, 1967; Sea and Estuary Birds, 1967; Heath and Woodland Birds, 1968; Vanishing Wild Animals of the World, 1968; Pond and River Birds, 1969; African Mammals, 1969; Australian Mammals, 1970; North American Mammals, 1970; Birds of Prey, 1970; European Mammals, 1971; Asian Mammals, 1971; South American Mammals, 1972; Sea and Air Mammals, 1972; Wild Life in Britain, 1972; Disappearing Mammals, 1973; Ducks and Swans, 1973; Lions and Tigers, 1974; Baby Animals, 1974; Song Birds, 1974; Leaves, 1974; Big Animals, 1975; Apes and Monkeys, 1975; Reptiles, 1976; Seals and Whales, 1976; Butterflies and Moths, 1978; Hedges, 1979; Birds of Britain and Northern Europe, 1979; Bears and Pandas, 1979. *Address:* 5 Roehampton Gate, Roehampton, SW15 5JR. *T:* 081–876 3332.

LEIGH-PEMBERTON, Rt. Hon. Robert, (Robin), PC 1987; Governor, Bank of England, since 1983; Lord-Lieutenant of Kent, since 1982 (Vice Lord-Lieutenant, 1972–82); *b* 5 Jan. 1927; *e s* of late Robert Douglas Leigh-Pemberton, MBE, MC, Sittingbourne, Kent; *m* 1953, Rosemary Davina, *d* of late Lt-Col D. W. A. W. Forbes, MC, and late Dowager Marchioness of Exeter; five *s.* *Educ:* St Peter's Court, Broadstairs; Eton; Trinity Coll., Oxford (MA; Hon. Fellow, 1984). Grenadier Guards, 1945–48. Called to Bar, Inner Temple, 1954 (Hon. Bencher, 1983); practised in London and SE Circuit until 1960. National Westminster Bank: Dir, 1972–83; Dep. Chm., 1974; Chm., 1977–83. Director: Birmid Qualcast, 1966–83 (Dep. Chm., 1970; Chm., 1975–77); University Life Assce Soc., 1967–78; Redland Ltd, 1972–83; Equitable Life Assce Soc., 1979–83 (Vice-Pres., 1982–83). County Councillor (Chm. Council, 1972–75), 1961–77, CA 1965, Kent. Member: SE Econ. Planning Council, 1972–74; Medway Ports Authority, 1974–76; NEDC, 1982–; Prime Minister's Cttee on Local Govt Rules of Conduct, 1973–74; Cttee of Enquiry into Teachers' Pay, 1974; Cttee on Police Pay, 1977–79. Chm., Cttee of London Clearing Bankers, 1982–83. Trustee: Glyndebourne Arts Trust, 1978–83; RA Trust, 1982–88 (hon. Trustee Emeritus, 1988–). Pro-Chancellor, Univ. of Kent at Canterbury, 1977–83; Seneschal, Canterbury Cathedral, 1983–. Hon. Colonel: Kent and Sharpshooters Yeomanry Sqn, 1979–; 265 (Kent and Co. of London Yeo.) Signal Sqn (V); 5th (Volunteer) Bn, The Queen's Regt, 1987–. Gov., Ditchley Foundn, 1987–. Hon. DCL Kent, 1983; Hon. DLitt City, 1988. FRSA 1977; FBIM 1977. JP 1961–75, DL 1970, Kent. KStJ 1983. *Recreation:* country life. *Address:* Bank of England, EC2R 8AH. *T:* 071–601 4444. *Clubs:* Brooks's, Cavalry and Guards.

LEIGHTON OF ST MELLONS, 2nd Baron, *cr* 1962; **John Leighton Seager;** Bt 1952; *b* 11 Jan. 1922; *er s* of 1st Baron Leighton of St Mellons, CBE, JP, and of Marjorie, *d* of William Henry Gimson, Breconshire; *S* father, 1963; *m* 1st, 1953, Elizabeth Rosita (*d* 1979), *o d* of late Henry Hopgood, Cardiff; two *s* one *d* (and one *d* decd); 2nd, 1982, Ruth Elizabeth Hopwood. *Educ:* Caldicott Sch.; The Leys Sch., Cambridge. Director: Principality Building Soc.; Watkin Williams & Co; formerly Partner, Probity Industrial Maintenance Services. *Heir:* *s* Hon. Robert William Henry Leighton Seager, *b* 28 Sept. 1955. *Address:* 346 Caerphilly Road, Birchgrove, Cardiff CF4 4NT.

LEIGHTON, Leonard Horace; Under Secretary, Department of Energy, 1974–80; *b* 7 Oct. 1920; *e s* of Leonard and Pearl Leighton, Bermuda; *m* 1945, Mary Burrowes; two *s.* *Educ:* Rossall Sch.; Magdalen Coll., Oxford (MA). FInstF. Royal Engrs, 1940–46; Nat. Coal Bd, 1950–62; Min. of Power, 1962–67; Min. of Technology, 1967–70; Dept of Trade and Industry, 1970–74. *Publications:* papers in various technical jls. *Address:* Hither Mickley, Lower Grinsty Lane, Callow Hill, Worcs B97 5PJ.

LEIGHTON, Sir Michael (John Bryan), 11th Bt, *cr* 1693; *b* 8 March 1935; *o s* of Colonel Sir Richard Tihel Leighton, 10th Bt, and Kathleen Irene Linda, *o d* of Major A. E. Lees, Rowton Castle, Shrewsbury; *S* father 1957; *m* 1974 (marr. diss. 1980). *Educ:* Stowe; Tabley House Agricultural Sch.; Cirencester Coll. *Address:* Loton Park, Shrewsbury, Salop SY5 9AG.

LEIGHTON, Ronald; MP (Lab) Newham North-East, since 1979; *b* 24 Jan. 1930; *s* of Charles Leighton and Edith (*née* Sleet); *m* 1951, Erika Wehking; two *s.* *Educ:* Monteagle and Bifrons Sch., Barking. Newspaper printer. Secretary, Labour Cttee for Safeguards on Common Market, 1967–70; Director, All-Party Common Market Safeguards Campaign, 1970–73; Editor, Resistance News, 1973–74; Secretary, Get Britain Out Campaign, 1974–75; National Organiser, National Referendum Campaign, which campaigned for 'No' vote in Referendum, 1975; Chairman: Labour Common Market Safeguards Cttee, 1975–; Select Cttee on Employment, 1984–. An Opposition Whip on Employment, 1981–84. Sponsored member, Sogat '82. *Publications:* The Labour Case Against Entry to the Common Market; What Labour Should Do About the Common Market; also pamphlets (1963–). *Recreations:* reading, footpath walking. *Address:* c/o House of Commons, SW1A 0AA.

LEIGHTON WILLIAMS, John; *see* Williams.

LEINSDORF, Erich; orchestral and operatic conductor; *b* Vienna, 4 Feb. 1912; *s* of Ludwig Julius Leinsdorf and Charlotte (*née* Loebl); *m* 1st, 1939, Anne Frohnknecht (marr. diss. 1968); three *s* two *d*; 2nd, 1968, Vera Graf. *Educ:* University of Vienna; State Academy of Music, Vienna (dipl.). Assistant conductor: Salzburg Festival, 1934–37; Metropolitan Opera, NY, 1937–39; Chief Conductor, German operas, 1939–43; Conductor, Rochester Philharmonic, 1947–56; Director, NYC Opera, 1956; Music Cons. Director, Metropolitan Opera, 1957–62; Music Director, Boston Symphony Orchestra, 1962–69. Director: Berkshire Music Center, Berkshire Music Festival, 1963–69; American Arts Alliance, 1979–; Mem., Nat. Endowment for the Arts, 1980–. Guest appearances with virtually every major orchestra in the USA and Europe, incl. Philadelphia Orchestra, Los Angeles, St Louis, New Orleans, Chicago, Minneapolis, Cleveland, New York, Concertgebouw Amsterdam, Israel Philharmonic, London Symphony, New Philharmonia, San Francisco Opera, Bayreuth, Holland and Prague Festivals, BBC. Records many symphonies and operas. Former Member Executive Cttee, John F. Kennedy Center for Performing Arts. Fellow, American Academy of Arts and Sciences. Holds hon. degrees. *Publications:* Cadenza (autobiog.), 1976; The Composer's Advocate, 1981; transcriptions of Brahms Chorale Preludes; contribs. to Atlantic Monthly, Saturday Review, New York Times, High Fidelity. *Address:* 1016 Fifth Avenue, New York, NY 10028, USA.

LEINSTER, 8th Duke of, *cr* 1766; **Gerald FitzGerald;** Baron of Offaly, 1205; Earl of Kildare, 1316; Viscount Leinster (Great Britain), 1747; Marquess of Kildare, 1761; Earl of Offaly, 1761; Baron Kildare, 1870; Premier Duke, Marquess, and Earl, of Ireland; Major late 5th Royal Inniskilling Dragoon Guards; *b* 27 May 1914; *o s* of 7th Duke of Leinster and May (*d* 1935), *d* of late Jesse Etheridge; *S* father, 1976; *m* 1st, 1936, Joane (who obtained a divorce, 1946), *e d* of late Major McMorrough Kavanagh, MC, Borris House, Co. Carlow; two *d*; 2nd, 1946, Anne Eustace Smith; two *s.* *Educ:* Eton; Sandhurst. *Heir:* *s* Marquess of Kildare, *qv.* *Recreations:* fishing, shooting. *Address:* Kilkea House, Ramsden, Oxford OX7 3BA.

LEISHMAN, Frederick John, CVO 1957; MBE 1944; *b* 21 Jan. 1919; *s* of Alexander Leishman and Freda Mabel (*née* Hood); *m* 1945, Frances Webb, Evanston, Illinois, USA; two *d.* *Educ:* Oundle; Corpus Christi, Cambridge. Served RE, 1940–46, and with Military Government, Germany, 1945–46; Regular Commission, 1945; resigned 1946. Joined Foreign Service, 1946; FO, 1946–48; Copenhagen, 1948–51; CSSB, 1951; Asst Private Sec. to Foreign Sec., 1951–53; First Sec., Washington, 1953–58; First Sec. and Head of Chancery, Teheran, 1959–61; Counsellor, 1961; HM Consul-General, Hamburg, 1961–62; FO, 1962–63. Dir, Hill Samuel & Co. Ltd, 1965–80; Dep. Chm. and Chief Exec., Hill Samuel Gp (SA) Ltd, 1969–72; Partner and Chm., Hill Samuel & Co. oHG, Germany, 1975–77; Dir and Exec. Vice-Pres., Saehan Merchant Banking Corp., Seoul, 1977–80. Chm., The Friends of the Bowes Museum, 1985–90. FRSA. *Recreations:* golf, fishing, hill walking. *Address:* Saltoun House, Cotherstone, Barnard Castle, Co. Durham DL12 9PF. *T:* Teesdale (0833) 50671. *Clubs:* Hawks (Cambridge); Cambridge University Rugby Union Football; London Scottish Football; Barnard Castle Rugby (Pres.); Royal Ashdown Forest Golf, Barnard Castle Golf.

LEITCH, David Alexander; Under Secretary, Social Work Services Group, Scottish Education Department, 1983–89; *b* 4 April 1931; *s* of Alexander and Eileen Leitch; *m* 1954, Marie (*née* Tain); two *s* one *d.* *Educ:* St Mungo's Acad., Glasgow. Min. of Supply, 1948–58; Dept of Agriculture and Fisheries for Scotland: Asst Principal, 1959; Principal, 1963; Asst Sec., 1971; Asst Sec., Local Govt Finance, Scottish Office (Central Services),

1976–81, Under Sec., 1981–83. *Recreations:* climbing, hill-walking. *Address:* 3 The Glebe, Cramond, Edinburgh EH4 6NW.

LEITCH, Sir George, KCB 1975 (CB 1963); OBE 1945; retired; *b* 5 June 1915; *er s* of late James Simpson and Margaret Leitch; *m* 1942, Edith Marjorie Maughan; one *d. Educ:* Wallsend Grammar Sch.; King's Coll., University of Durham. Research and teaching in mathematics, 1937–39. War Service in Army (from TA), 1939–46 (despatches, OBE): Lieut-Colonel in charge of Operational Research in Eastern, then Fourteenth Army, 1943–45; Brigadier (Dep. Scientific Adviser, War Office), 1945–46; entered Civil Service, as Principal, 1947; Ministry of Supply, 1947–59 (Under-Secretary, 1959); War Office, 1959–64; Ministry of Defence: Asst Under-Secretary of State, 1964–65; Dep. Under-Sec. of State, 1965–72; Procurement Executive, MoD: Controller (Policy), 1971–72; 2nd Permanent Sec., 1972–74; Chief Exec. (Permanent Sec.), 1974–75; Chm., Short Brothers Ltd, 1976–83. Chm., Adv. Cttee on Trunk Rd Assessment, 1977–80. Commonwealth Fund Fellow, 1953–54. Hon. DSc (Durham), 1946. *Recreations:* swimming, gardening. *Address:* 10 Elmfield Road, Gosforth, Newcastle upon Tyne NE3 4AY. *T:* Tyneside (091) 2846559.

LEITCH, William Andrew, CB 1963; Law Reform Consultant, Government of Northern Ireland, 1973–78; Examiner of Statutory Rules, Northern Ireland Assembly, 1974–78, retired; *b* 16 July 1915; *e s* of Andrew Leitch, MD, DPH, Castlederg, Co. Tyrone, and May, *d* of W. H. Todd, JP, Fyfin, Strabane, Co. Tyrone; *m* 1939, Edna Margaret, *d* of David McIlvennan, Solicitor, Belfast; one *s* two *d. Educ:* Methodist Coll., Belfast; Queen's Univ., Belfast; London Univ. (LLB). Admitted Solicitor, NI, 1937; Asst Solicitors Dept, Ministry of Finance, NI, 1937–43; Asst Parly Draftsman, 1944–56; First Parly Draftsman, 1956–74. Hon. LLM, Queen's Univ., Belfast, 1967. *Publications:* A Handbook on the Administration of Estates Act (NI), 1955, 1957; (jointly) A Commentary on the Interpretation Act (Northern Ireland) 1954, 1955; articles in various legal publications. *Recreations:* fishing, golf, reading. *Address:* 53 Kensington Road, Belfast BT5 6NL. *T:* Belfast (0232) 794784.

LEITH, family name of **Baron Burgh.**

LEITH, Sir Andrew George F.; *see* Forbes-Leith.

LEITH, Prudence Margaret, (Mrs Rayne Kruger), OBE 1989; Managing Director, Prudence Leith Ltd (parent company of the Leith's Group), since 1972; *b* 18 Feb. 1940; *d* of late Sam Leith and of Margaret Inglis; *m* Rayne Kruger; one *s* one *d. Educ:* Hayward's Heath, Sussex; St Mary's, Johannesburg; Cape Town Univ.; Sorbonne, Paris; Cordon Bleu, London. French studies at Sorbonne, and preliminary cooking apprenticeship with French families; Cordon Bleu sch. course; small outside catering service from bedsitter in London, 1960–65; started Leith's Good Food (commercial catering co.), 1965, and Leith's (restaurant), 1969; Cookery Corresp., Daily Mail, 1969–73; opened Leith's Sch. of Food and Wine, 1975; added Leith's Farm, 1976; Cookery Corresp., Sunday Express, 1976–80; Cookery Editor, 1980–85, Columnist, 1986–90, The Guardian. Bd Mem., British Transport Hotels, 1977–83; pt-time Mem., BRB, 1980–85. Member: Food from Britain Council, 1983–86; Leisure Industries EDC, NEDO, 1986–90; Nat. Trng Task Force, 1989–. Chm., Restaurateurs' Assoc. of GB, 1990–; Mem. Council, Museum of Modern Art, Oxford, 1984–. FRSA 1984. Business Woman of the Year, 1990. *Publications:* Leith's All-Party Cook Book, 1969; Parkinson's Pie (in aid of World Wild Life Fund), 1972; Cooking For Friends, 1978; The Best of Prue Leith, 1979; (with J. B. Reynaud) Leith's Cookery Course (3–part paperback), 1979–80, (comp. hardback with C. Waldegrave), 1980; The Cook's Handbook, 1981; Prue Leith's Pocket Book of Dinner Parties, 1983; Dinner Parties, 1984; (with Caroline Waldegrave) Leith's Cookery School, 1985; (with Polly Tyrer) Entertaining with Style, 1986; Confident Cooking (52 issue part-work), 1989–90. *Recreations:* riding, tennis, old cookbooks and kitchen antiques. *Address:* 94 Kensington Park Road, W11 2PN. *T:* 071–221 5282.

LEITH-BUCHANAN, Sir Charles (Alexander James), 7th Bt *cr* 1775; President, United Business Machines Inc., Alexandria, Va, since 1978; *b* 1 Sept. 1939; *s* of John Wellesley MacDonald Leith-Buchanan (*g s* of 4th Bt) (*d* 1956) and Jane Elizabeth McNicol (*d* 1955), *d* of Ronald McNicol; *S* cousin, 1973; *m* 1962, Mary Anne Kelly (marr. diss. 1987); one *s* one *d. Heir: s* Gordon Kelly McNicol Leith-Buchanan, *b* 18 Oct. 1974. *Address:* 7510 Clifton Road, Clifton, Va 22024, USA.

LEITHEAD, James Douglas; *b* 4 Oct. 1911; *s* of late William Leithead, Berwick-on-Tweed; *m* 1936, Alice (*d* 1989), *d* of late Thomas Wylie, Stirling, Scotland; one *s. Educ:* Bradford Grammar Sch. Accountant, 1927–32; ACA 1932; FCA 1960; Chartered Accountant, 1932–39. Lecturer Bradford Technical Coll., 1934–39; Secretarial Assistant, Midland (Amalgamated) District (Coal Mines) Scheme, 1939–42; Ministry of Supply, 1942–45; BoT, 1945–64; HM Diplomatic Service, 1965–68; BoT, later DTI, 1968–72, retired. British Trade Commissioner: Australia, 1950–63; New Zealand, 1963–67. Vice-Pres., W Australian Branch of Royal Commonwealth Soc., 1957–63. *Recreation:* chess. *Address:* 48 Eaton Road, Appleton, Oxon OX13 5JH.

LELLO, Walter Barrington, (Barry); Deputy Director, North-West Region, Department of Trade and Industry, since 1988; *b* 29 Sept. 1931; *o s* of Walter Joseph Lello and Louisa (*née* McGarrigle); *m* 1959, Margaret, *o d* of Alexander and Alice McGregor. *Educ:* Liverpool Institute High School. Nat. Service, RN, 1950–52. Open Exec. Comp. to Civil Service, 1949; Min. of Supply, later Aviation, 1952–64; Asst British Civil Aviation Rep., Far East, Hong Kong, 1964–67; BoT, later Dept of Trade, 1967–71; Civil Air Attaché, Middle East, Beirut, 1971–76; DTI, 1976–78; Dir Gen., Saudi–British Economic Co-operation Office, Riyadh, 1978–81; seconded to British Electricity International as Dir, Middle East Ops, 1981–83; DTI, 1983; Commercial Counsellor, Cairo, 1984–88. *Recreations:* mountaineering, reading, theatre. *Address:* 15 Long Meadow, Gayton, Wirral, Merseyside L60 8QQ.

LE MARCHANT, Sir Francis (Arthur), 6th Bt *cr* 1841, of Chobham Place, Surrey; *b* 6 Oct. 1939; *s* of Sir Denis Le Marchant, 5th Bt and of Elizabeth Rowena, *y d* of late Arthur Hovenden Worth; *S* father, 1987. *Educ:* Gordonstoun; Royal Academy Schools. *Heir: cousin* Michael Le Marchant [*b* 28 July 1937; *m* 1st, 1963, Philippa Nancy (marr. diss.), *er d* of late R. B. Denby; two *s* two *d*; 2nd, 1981, Sandra Elisabeth Champion (*née* Kirby)]. *Address:* c/o Midland Bank, 88 Westgate, Grantham, Lincs NG31 6LF.

LE MARECHAL, Robert Norford; Deputy Comptroller and Auditor General, National Audit Office, since 1989; *b* 29 May 1939; *s* of late Reginald Le Marechal and of Margaret Le Marechal; *m* 1963, Linda Mary (*née* Williams); two *d. Educ:* Tauntons School, Southampton. Joined Exchequer and Audit Dept, 1957; Nat. Service, RAEC, 1958–60; Senior Auditor, Exchequer and Audit Dept, 1971; Chief Auditor, 1976; Dep. Dir of Audit, 1980; Dir of Audit, 1983; Dir of Policy and Planning, 1984–86, Asst Auditor General, 1986–89, Nat. Audit Office. *Recreations:* reading poetry, gardening. *Address:* 62 Woodcote Hurst, Epsom, Surrey. *T:* Epsom (0372) 721291.

LE MASURIER, Sir Robert (Hugh), Kt 1966; DSC 1942; Bailiff of Jersey, 1962–74; *b* 29 Dec. 1913; *s* of William Smythe Le Masurier and Mabel Harriet Briard; *m* 1941, Helen Sophia Sheringham; one *s* two *d. Educ:* Victoria Coll., Jersey. MA 1935; BCL 1936. Sub-Lieut RNVR, 1939; Lieut RNVR, 1943; Lieut-Commander RNVR, 1944. Solicitor-General, Jersey, 1955; Attorney-General, Jersey, 1958. *Recreations:* sailing, carpentry. *Address:* 4 La Fantasie, Rue du Hucquet, St Martin, Jersey, CI. *T:* Jersey 52748. *Clubs:* St Helier Yacht, United (Jersey).

LEMIEUX, Most Rev. (M.) Joseph; *b* Quebec City, 10 May 1902; *s* of Joseph E. Lemieux and Eva (*née* Berlinguet). *Educ:* College of St Anne de la Pocatière; Dominican House of Studies, Ottawa; College of Angelico, Rome; Blackfriars, Oxford. Missionary to Japan, 1930; Parish Priest, Miyamaecho, Hakodate, Japan, 1931–36; First Bishop of Sendai, 1936; resigned, 1941; Administrator of Diocese of Gravelbourg, Sask., 1942; Bishop of Gravelbourg, 1944–53; Archbishop of Ottawa, 1953–66; Apostolic Nuncio to Haiti, 1966–69; Apostolic Pro-Nuncio in India, 1969–71; Delegate of St Peter's Basilica in Vatican, 1971–73. *Address:* 143 St Patrick, Ottawa, Ontario K1N 5J9, Canada.

LEMIEUX, Prof. Raymond Urgel, OC (Canada), 1968; FRS 1967; Professor of Organic Chemistry, University of Alberta, 1961–80, University Professor, 1980–85, now Emeritus; *b* 16 June 1920; *s* of Octave Lemieux; *m* 1948, Virginia Marie McConaghie; one *s* five *d* (and one *s* decd). *Educ:* Edmonton, Alberta. BSc Hons (Chem.) Alta, 1943; PhD (Chem.) McGill, 1946. Research Fellow, Ohio State Univ., 1947; Asst Professor, Saskatchewan Univ., 1948–49; Senior Research Officer, National Research Council, Canada, 1949–54, Member, 1976–81; Professor, Ottawa Univ., 1954–61. Pres., Chem. Inst. of Canada, 1984–85. Rhône-Poulenc Lectr, RSC, 1989. FRSC 1955. Hon. Mem., Canadian Soc. for Chemistry, 1986. Hon. DSc: New Brunswick Univ., 1967; Laval Univ., 1970; Univ. de Provence, 1973; Univ. of Ottawa, 1975; Waterloo Univ., 1980; Meml Univ., Newfoundland, 1981; Quebec, 1982; Queen's Univ., Kingston, Ont, 1983; McGill, 1984; McMaster, 1986; Sherbrooke, 1986; Hon. LLD Calgary, 1979; Hon. PhD Stockholm, 1988. Chem. Inst. of Canada Medal, 1964; C. S. Hudson Award, Amer. Chem. Soc., 1966; W. N. Haworth Medal, Chem. Soc., 1978; Izaak Walton Killam Award, Canada Council, 1981; Diplôme d'Honneur, Groupe Français des Glucides, 1981; Sir Frederick Haultain Prize, Alberta, 1982; Tischler Award, Harvard Univ., 1983; Medal of Honor, CMA, 1985; Gairdner Foundn Internat. Award in Medical Science, 1985; LeSueur Award, SCI, 1989; King Faisal Internat. Prize for Science, 1990; Alberta Order of Excellence, 1990; Canada Gold Medal for Science and Engrg, 1991. *Publications:* over 200 research papers mainly in area of carbohydrate chemistry in Canadian Journal of Chemistry, etc. *Recreations:* golf, curling, fishing. *Address:* 7602, 119th Street, Edmonton, Alberta T6G 1W3, Canada. *T:* 436–5167. *Clubs:* University of Alberta Faculty (Edmonton); Lake Edith Golf (Jasper).

LEMKIN, James Anthony, CBE 1986; Consultant, Field Fisher Waterhouse, Solicitors (Senior Partner, 1985–90); *b* 21 Dec. 1926; *s* of William Lemkin, CBE, and Rachel Irene (*née* Faith); *m* 1960, Joan Dorothy Anne Casserley, FFARCS, MRCPsych; two *s* two *d. Educ:* Charterhouse; Merton Coll., Oxford (MA). Admitted solicitor, 1953; RN, 1945–47. Greater London Council: Additional Mem., 1970–73, Mem. for Hillingdon, Uxbridge, 1973–86; Chm., Legal and Parly Cttee, 1977–78; Chm., Scrutiny Cttee, 1978–81; Cons. spokesman on police, 1981–82; Opposition Chief Whip, 1982–86. Contested: (C and NL) Chesterfield, 1959; (L) Cheltenham, 1964. Chm., Bow Gp, 1952, 1956, 1957 (Founder Chm., Crossbow, 1957–60); Vice-Chm., Soc. of Cons. Lawyers, 1990–92 (Treasurer, 1978–82, 1985–88). Member: N London Hosp. Management Cttee, 1971–74; NW Thames RHA, 1980–84; Royal Marsden Hosp. SHA, 1982–89; Appeal Cttee, Cancer Res. Campaign, 1967–81; Chm., Barnet FPC, 1985–. Governor: Westfield Coll., London Univ., 1970–83; Commonwealth Inst., 1985–. Trustee, Whitechapel Art Gall., 1983–90. Co-founder, Africa Confidential, 1960. High Sheriff, Gtr London, 1992–93. *Publication:* (ed) Race and Power, 1956. *Recreation:* umpiring cricket. *Address:* 4 Frognal Close, NW3 6YB. *T:* 071–435 6499. *Clubs:* Athenæum, Carlton.

LEMLEY, Jack Kenneth; Chief Executive Officer, Transmanche-Link, Channel tunnel contractors, since 1989; *b* 2 Jan. 1935; *s* of Kenneth Clyde Lemley and Dorothy Whitsitte; *m* 1st, 1961, Georgia Marshall (marr. diss. 1978); two *s* one *d*; 2nd, 1983, Pamela (*née* Hroza). *Educ:* Coeur d'Alene High Sch., Idaho; Univ. of Idaho (BA Architecture 1960). Asst Project Engineer, Guy F. Atkinson Co., 1960–69; Pres., Healthcare, 1969–70; Manager, Indust. and Power Construction Div., Guy F. Atkinson Co., 1971–77; Sen. Vice-Pres., Constr. Div., Morrison-Knudsen Co., 1977–87; Pres. and Chief Exec., Blount Construction Gp, 1987–88; Management Consultant, Lemley & Associates, 1988–89. *Publications:* numerous papers on underground construction projects and international tunnelling. *Recreations:* snow ski-ing, sailing, white water rafting, reading. *Address:* The Penthouse, One The Leas, Folkestone, Kent CT20 2DR. *T:* Folkestone (0303) 221606; 2145 Table Rock Road, Boise, Idaho, Id 83712, USA. *T:* (208) 383–9253. *Club:* Arid (Boise, Idaho).

LEMMON, Cyril Whitefield, FRIBA, FAIA; Architect, Honolulu, Hawaii (Private Practice), 1946–69, retired; Chairman of the Board, Architects Hawaii Ltd; *b* Kent, 27 Oct. 1901; *s* of T. E. Lemmon and Catherine Whitefield; *m* 1st, 1921, Ethel Belinda Peters, artist (marr. diss., 1936); no *c*; 2nd, 1938, Rebecca Robson Ramsay; two *d. Educ:* University of Pennsylvania, Philadelphia, Pa. Fifth-year Studio Instructor and Lecturer in the School of Architecture, University of Liverpool, 1933–36; Consulting Architect to Government of India for Rebuilding of Quetta, 1936; Consulting Architect to MES for all military buildings in India, 1938. Lieut-Colonel, Royal Indian Engineers, 1941; Director of Civil Camouflage in India, 1943; GSO 1, GHQ, India and 11th Army Group, 1943–44. President, Hawaii Chapter, AIA, 1950; AIA Honour Award, Hawaii State Capitol. Exhibited paintings in Salon des Tuileries, Paris, 1933; travel in United States, Mexico, Europe, N Africa and Asia. Public Lectures on Architecture and Painting. 32° Mason; Potentate, Aloha Temple, AONMS, 1970. *Publications:* contributions to professional journals on Architecture. *Recreations:* golf, swimming. *Address:* 1434 Punahou Street, #1016 Honolulu, Hawaii 96822, USA. *Clubs:* Pacific, Waialae Country.

LEMMON, David Hector; writer; *b* 4 April 1931; *s* of Frederick Robert Lemmon and Sophie Elizabeth Lemmon (*née* Beadle); *m* 1958, (Jean) Valerie Fletcher; two *s. Educ:* Southgate Grammar Sch.; Coll. of St Mark and St John, Chelsea. Teacher's Cert., 1953; BA Hons London 1968. ACP 1968. Shell Mex & BP Co., 1947–49; RAF, 1949–51; Master, Bound's Green Sch., 1953–57; Ankara Coll., Turkey, 1957–60 (Dir, Amer. Little Theatre, 1958–59); Head of English: Kingsbury High Sch., Warwicks, 1960–63; Torells Girls Sch., Thurrock, 1963–68; Nicholas Sch., Basildon, 1968–73 (and Dir of Studies, 1973–83); full-time writer, 1983–. Examnr, Advanced Level Theatre Studies Practical, 1980–. Mem. Editl Bd, Cricket World, 1991–. *Publications:* Summer of Success, 1980; Great One-Day Cricket Matches, 1982, 1984; Tich Freeman, 1982; Wisden Book of Cricket Quotations, 1, 1982, 2, 1990; The Book of One-Day Internationals, 1983; Johnny Won't Hit Today, 1983; The Great Wicket-Keepers, 1984; Percy Chapman, 1985; Ken McEwan, 1985; (with Ted Dexter) A Walk to the Wicket, 1984; (ed) Cricket Heroes, 1984; (with Ken Kelly) Cricket Reflections, 1985; Cricket Mercenaries, 1987; (with Mike Marshall) The Official History of Essex CCC, 1987; The Crisis of Captaincy, 1988; One-Day Cricket, 1988; The Official History of Middlesex CCC, 1988, of Worcestershire CCC, 1989, of Surrey CCC, 1989; (with Chris Cowdrey) Know Your Sport—Cricket,

1989; British Theatre Yearbook, 1989, 2nd edn 1990; Len Hutton, a Pictorial Biography, 1990; Cricket's Champion Counties, 1991; The Cricketing Greigs, 1991; Pelham Cricket Year, then Benson and Hedges Cricket Year, annually 1979–90. *Recreations:* work—theatre and sport; music, literature, art, people, entertaining. *Address:* 26 Leigh Road, Leigh-on-Sea, Essex SS9 1LD. *T:* Southend-on-Sea (0702) 79640. *Clubs:* MCC, Cricket Writers'; Essex County Cricket.

LEMMON, Rt. Rev. George Colborne; *see* Fredericton, Bishop of.

LEMON, Sir (Richard) Dawnay, Kt 1970; CBE 1958; QPM 1964; Chief Constable of Kent, 1962–74; *b* 1912; *o s* of late Lieut-Colonel F. J. Lemon, CBE, DSO, and of Mrs Laura Lemon; *m* 1939, Sylvia Marie Kentish; one *s* one *d* (and one *d* decd). *Educ:* Uppingham Sch.; RMC, Sandhurst. Joined West Yorks Regt, 1932; retired 1934. Metropolitan Police, 1934–37; Leicestershire Constabulary, 1937–39; Chief Constable of East Riding of Yorkshire, 1939–42; Chief Constable of Hampshire and Isle of Wight, 1942–62. *Recreations:* cricket, golf, shooting. *Address:* Rosecroft, Ringwould, Deal, Kent CT14 8HR. *T:* Deal (0304) 367554. *Clubs:* Naval and Military; Royal Yacht Squadron (Cowes (hon.)); Royal St Georges Golf (Sandwich).

LENDRUM, Prof. Alan Chalmers, MA, MD, BSc, ARPS; FRCPath; Professor of Pathology, University of Dundee, 1967–72, Professor Emeritus, 1972, Honorary Research Fellow, 1972; *b* 3 Nov. 1906; *yr s* of late Rev. Dr Robert Alexander Lendrum and Anna, *e d* of late James Guthrie of Pitforthie, Angus; *m* 1st, 1934, Elizabeth Bertram (*d* 1983), *e d* of late Donald Currie, BA, LLB; two *s* one *d*; 2nd, 1984, Dr Ann Brougham Sandison. *Educ:* High Sch., Glasgow; Ardrossan Acad.; University of Glasgow. Asst to Sir Robert Muir, MD, FRS, 1933; Lecturer in Pathology, University of Glasgow; Prof. of Pathology, Univ. of St Andrews, 1947–67. Visiting Prof. of Pathology, Yale, 1960. Kettle Meml Lecture, RCPath, 1973. Hon. For. Mem. Argentine Soc. of Normal and Pathological Anatomy; Hon. Member: Pathol Soc. of GB and Ireland; Nederlandse Patholoog Anatomen Vereniging; Dialectic Soc., Glasgow Univ.; Forfarshire Medical Assoc.; Hon. Fellow, and ex-Pres., Inst. Med. Lab. Sci. Dean of Guildry of Brechin, 1971–73. Capt. RAMC (TA) retd. Sims Woodhead Medal, 1971. Chm. of Governors, Duncan of Jordanstone Coll. of Art, Dundee, 1975–77. *Publications:* (co-author) Recent Advances in Clinical Pathology, 1948; Trends in Clinical Pathology, 1969; publications in medical journals. *Address:* Hobstones, Gawthrop, Dent, Sedbergh, Cumbria LA10 5TA. *T:* Dent (05875) 238.

LENG, Gen. Sir Peter (John Hall), KCB 1978 (CB 1975); MBE 1962; MC 1945; Master-General of the Ordnance, 1981–83, retired; *b* 9 May 1925; *s* of J. Leng; *m* 1st, Virginia Rosemary Pearson (marr. diss. 1981); three *s* two *d*; 2nd, 1981, Mrs Flavia Tower, *d* of late Gen. Sir Frederick Browning and Lady Browning (Dame Daphne du Maurier, DBE). *Educ:* Bradfield Coll. Served War of 1939–45: commissioned in Scots Guards, 1944; Guards Armoured Div., Germany (MC). Various post-war appts; Guards Independent Parachute Company, 1949–51; commanded: 3rd Bn Royal Anglian Regt, in Berlin, United Kingdom and Aden, 1964–66; 24th Airportable Bde, 1968–70; Dep. Military Sec., Min. of Defence, 1971–73; Comdr Land Forces, N Ireland, 1973–75; Dir, Mil. Operations, MoD, 1975–78; Comdr 1 (Br) Corps, 1978–80. Colonel Commandant: RAVC, 1976–83; RMP, 1976–83. Fund Raising Dir, Jubilee Sailing Trust, 1984–85. Chm., Racecourse Assoc., 1985–89. *Recreations:* fishing, shooting, painting. *Address:* c/o Barclays Bank, 1 Brompton Road, SW3 1EB. *Club:* Naval and Military.
See also V. H. A. Leng.

LENG, Virginia Helen Antoinette, MBE 1986; equestrian event rider; *b* 1 Feb. 1955; *d* of late Col Ronald Morris Holgate, RM and of Heather Holgate; *m* 1985, Hamish Julian Peter Leng, *s* of Gen. Sir Peter Leng, *qv*. *Educ:* Bedgebury Park, Goudhurst, Kent. Three day event wins: Junior European Champion, 1973 (Dubonnet); Mini Olympics, 1975 (Jason); Burghley, 1983 (Priceless), 1984 (Nightcap), 1985 (Priceless), 1986 (Murphy Himself), 1989 (Master Craftsman); Badminton, 1985 (Priceless), 1989 (Master Craftsman); European Championship, 1985 (Priceless), 1987 (Nightcap), 1989 (Master Craftsman); World Championship, 1986 (Priceless); Team Silver Olympic Medal, 1984 and 1988; Bronze Individual Olympic Medal, 1984 (Priceless), and 1988 (Master Craftsman). *Publications:* (with Genevieve Murphy) Ginny, 1986; (with Nancy Roberts) Priceless, 1987; (with Genevieve Murphy) Ginny and Her Horses, 1987; (with Genevieve Murphy) Training the Event Horse, 1990. *Recreations:* ski-ing, cooking, art, theatre. *Address:* Ivyleaze, Acton Turville, Badminton, Avon. *T:* Badminton (045421) 681.

LENIHAN, Brian Joseph; Teachta Dala (TD) for Dublin (West County), Parliament of Ireland, since 1977 (TD for Roscommon/Leitrim, 1961–73); *b* 17 Nov. 1930; *s* of Patrick Lenihan (TD Longford-Westmeath, 1965–70); *m* 1958, Ann Devine; four *s* one *d*. *Educ:* St Mary's Coll. (Marist Brothers), Athlone; University Coll., Dublin. Member: Roscommon CC, 1955–61; Seanad Eireann (FF), 1957–61 and (as Leader in Seanad, Fianna Fáil), 1973–77; Parly Sec. to Minister for Lands, 1961–64; Minister for: Justice, 1964–68; Educn, 1968–69; Transport and Power, 1969–73; Foreign Affairs, 1973; Fisheries and Forestry, 1977–79; Foreign Affairs, 1979–81; Agriculture, 1982; Foreign Affairs, 1987–89; Defence, 1989–90; Tánaiste (Dep. Prime Minister), 1987–90. Mem., European Parlt, 1973–77. Dep. Leader, Fianna Fáil Party, 1983–. Contested (FF), Presidency of Ireland, 1990. *Publication:* For the Record, 1991. *Address:* Leinster House, Dublin 2, Eire.

LENNARD, Rev. Sir Hugh Dacre B.; *see* Barrett-Lennard.

LENNIE, Douglas; *b* 30 March 1910; *e s* of Magnus S. Lennie; *m* 1941, Rhona Young Ponsonby; two *s*. *Educ:* Berkhamsted Sch.; Guy's Hospital, LDS, RCS, 1934; Northwestern University, Chicago, DDS, 1938. Served War of 1939–45, Temporary Surg. Lt-Comdr (D) RNVR; formerly Surgeon Dentist to Queen Mary. *Address:* 72 Chiltley Way, Liphook, Hants GU30 7HE.

LENNON, Prof. (George) Gordon; retired gynæcologist; Professor Emeritus, University of Western Australia, Perth, 1974; *b* 7 Oct. 1911; *s* of late J. Lennon; *m* 1940, Barbara Brynhild (*née* Buckle); two *s*. *Educ:* Aberdeen Academy; Aberdeen Univ. MB, ChB Aberdeen, 1934; served in hospital posts in Aberdeen, Glasgow, London, Birmingham; MRCOG 1939; FRCOG 1952; MMSA 1943; ChM (Hons) Aberdeen, 1945. Served War of 1939–45, Sqdn-Ldr in charge of Surgical Div., RAFVR, 1942–46. First Asst, Nuffield Dept of Obstetrics and Gynæcology, Radcliffe Infirmary (University of Oxford), 1946–51; Prof. of Obstetrics and Gynæcology, Univ. of Bristol, 1951–67; Dean, Faculty of Med., Univ. of WA, Perth, 1967–74. Visiting Professor: Iraq and Turkey, 1956; South Africa and Uganda, 1958; Iran, 1965. *Publications:* Diagnosis in Clinical Obstetrics; articles in British Medical Journal, Proceedings of the Royal Society of Medicine, Journal of Obstetrics and Gynæcology of the British Empire, etc. *Recreation:* golf. *Address:* 246 Melksham Road, Holt, Wilts. *T:* North Trowbridge (0225) 782935.

LENNOX; *see* Gordon-Lennox and Gordon Lennox.

LENNOX, Lionel Patrick Madill; Registrar of the Province and Diocese of York, and Registrar of the Convocation of York, since 1987; *b* 5 April 1949; *s* of Rev. James Lennox and Mrs May Lennox; *m* 1979, Barbara Helen Firth; two *s* one *d*. *Educ:* St John's Sch., Leatherhead; Univ. of Birmingham (LLB). Admitted Solicitor, 1973; Ecclesiastical Notary, 1987. Solicitor in private practice, 1973–81; Asst Legal Advr to Gen. Synod, 1981–87. Secretary: Archbishop of Canterbury's Gp on Affinity, 1982–84; Legal Adv. Commn, Gen. Synod of C of E, 1986–. Trustee, Yorks Historic Churches Trust, 1988–. *Address:* 1 Peckitt Street, York YO1 1SG. *T:* York (0904) 623487.

LENNOX, Robert Smith, CBE 1978; JP; Lord Provost of Aberdeen, 1967–70 and 1975–77; *b* 8 June 1909; *m* 1963, Evelyn Margaret; no *c*. *Educ:* St Clement Sch., Aberdeen. Hon. LLD Aberdeen, 1970. JP Aberdeen. *Address:* 7 Gillespie Crescent, Ashgrove, Aberdeen. *T:* Aberdeen (0224) 43862.

LENNOX-BOYD, family name of **Viscount Boyd of Merton.**

LENNOX-BOYD, Hon. Mark Alexander; MP (C) Morecambe and Lunesdale, since 1983 (Morecambe and Lonsdale, 1979–83); Parliamentary Under Secretary of State, Foreign and Commonwealth Office, since 1990; *b* 4 May 1943; 3rd *s* of 1st Viscount Boyd of Merton, CH, PC and of Lady Patricia Guinness, 2nd *d* of 2nd Earl of Iveagh, KG, CB, CMG, FRS; *m* 1974, Arabella Lacloche; one *d*. *Educ:* Eton Coll.; Christ Church, Oxford. Called to the Bar, Inner Temple, 1968. Parliamentary Private Secretary: to Sec. of State for Energy, 1981–83; to the Chancellor of the Exchequer, 1983–84; Asst Govt Whip, 1984–86; a Lord Comr of HM Treasury (Govt Whip), 1986–88; PPS to Prime Minister, 1988–90. *Recreation:* travel. *Clubs:* Pratt's, Beefsteak.

LENTON, (Aylmer) Ingram, PhD; Chairman: John Heathcoat and Co. (Holdings) Ltd, since 1984; Compass Group plc, since 1987; Deputy Chairman, Board of Crown Agents for Oversea Governments and Administrations, since 1990 (Member, since 1987); *b* 19 May 1927; *s* of Albert Lenton and Olive Lenton; *m* 1951, Ursula Kathleen King; one *s* two *d*. *Educ:* Leeds Grammar Sch.; Magdalen Coll., Oxford (MA); Leeds Univ. (PhD). Richard Haworth & Co. Ltd, 1951; British Nylon Spinners Ltd, 1956; Managing Director, S African Nylon Spinners Ltd, 1964; Director, ICI Fibres Ltd, 1966; Director, John Heathcoat & Co. Ltd, 1967, Man. Dir, 1971; Bowater Corporation Ltd: Dir, 1979; Man. Dir, 1981–84; Chm. and Man. Dir, Bowater Industries plc (formerly Bowater Corp.), 1984–87; Chairman: Bowater UK Paper Co., 1976; Bowater UK Ltd, 1979; Inveresk Ltd, 1991–; Watts Blake Bearne & Co., 1991– (Dir, 1987–; Dep. Chm., 1988–91); Director: Atkins Holdings, 1987– (Chm., 1989–); Scapa Gp, 1988–. CBIM. Hon. Fellow, British Orthopaedic Assoc., 1990. Court Asst, Stationers' & Newspaper Makers' Co. *Recreations:* golf, fencing, fell walking, fishing. *Address:* Compass Group, Queen's Wharf, Queen Caroline Street, W6 9RJ.

LEO, Dame Sister Mary, DBE 1973 (MBE 1963), **(Kathleen Agnes Niccol);** of Auckland, New Zealand; Member of the Sisters of Mercy' Auckland. Specialised in vocal training. Entered Order of Sisters of Mercy, 1923. Has been a singing teacher for over 40 years; pupils who have gained international success include Dame Kiri Te Kanawa, DBE, Heather Begg, Mina Foley and Malvina Major. Biography in preparation. *Address:* St Mary's Convent, PO Box 47025, Ponsonby, Auckland 1, New Zealand.

LEON, Sir John (Ronald), 4th Bt, *cr* 1911; actor (stage name, **John Standing**); *b* 16 Aug. 1934; *er s* of 3rd Bt and late Kay Hammond; *S* father, 1964; *m* 1961, Jill (marr. diss. 1972), *d* of Jack Melford; one *s*; *m* 1984, Sarah, *d* of Bryan Forbes, *qv*; one *s* two *d*. *Educ:* Eton. Late 2nd Lt, KRRC. *Plays include:* Darling Buds of May, Saville, 1959; leading man, season, Bristol Old Vic, 1960; The Irregular Verb to Love, Criterion, 1961; Norman, Duchess, 1963; So Much to Remember, Vaudeville, 1963; The Three Sisters, Oxford Playhouse, 1964; See How They Run, Vaudeville, 1964; Seasons at Chichester Theatre, 1966, 1967; The Importance of Being Earnest, Haymarket 1968; Ring Round the Moon, Haymarket, 1968; The Alchemist, and Arms and the Man, Chichester, 1970; Popkiss, Globe, 1972; A Sense of Detachment, Royal Court, 1972; Private Lives, Queen's and Globe, 1973, NY and tour of USA, 1974; Jingo, Aldwych, 1975; Plunder, The Philanderer, NT, 1978; Close of Play, NT, 1979; Tonight at 8.30, Lyric, 1981; The Biko Inquest, Riverside, 1984; Rough Crossing, National, 1984. *Films:* The Wild and the Willing, 1962; Iron Maiden, 1962; King Rat, 1964; Walk, Don't Run, 1965; Zee and Co., 1973; The Eagle has Landed, 1976; The Class of Miss MacMichael, 1977; The Legacy, 1977; The Elephant Man, 1979; The Sea Wolves, 1980; (TV film) The Young Visiters, 1984; Nightflyers. Television appearances incl.: for British TV: Arms and the Man; The First Churchills; Charley's Aunt; Rogue Male; The Sinking of HMS Victoria; Home and Beauty; Tinker, Tailor, Soldier, Spy; The Other 'Arf; Old Boy Network; Tonight at 8.30; Count of Solar; for American TV: Lime Street; Hotel; Flap Jack Floozie; Visitors; Murphy's Law; The Endless Game; Murder She Wrote; LA Law; Windmills of the Gods. *Recreation:* painting. *Heir:* *s* Alexander John Leon, *b* 3 May 1965. *Address:* c/o James Sharkey, 15 Golden Square, W1R 3AG; c/o Agency for Performing Arts, 9000 Sunset Boulevard, Los Angeles, Calif., USA.

LEONARD, Dick; *see* Leonard, Richard Lawrence.

LEONARD, Rt. Rev. and Rt. Hon. Sir Graham Douglas, KCVO 1991; Bishop of London, 1981–91; *b* 8 May 1921; *s* of late Rev. Douglas Leonard, MA; *m* 1943, Vivien Priscilla, *d* of late M. B. R. Swann, MD, Fellow of Gonville and Caius Coll., Cambridge; two *s*. *Educ:* Monkton Combe Sch.; Balliol Coll., Oxford (Hon. Fellow, 1986). Hon. Sch. Nat. Science, shortened course. BA 1943, MA 1947. Served War, 1941–45; Captain, Oxford and Bucks Light Infantry; Army Operational Research Group (Ministry of Supply), 1944–45. Westcott House, Cambridge, 1946–47. Deacon 1947, Priest 1948; Vicar of Ardleigh, Essex, 1952–55; Director of Religious Education, Diocese of St Albans, 1955–58; Hon. Canon of St Albans, 1955–57; Canon Residentiary, 1957–58; Canon Emeritus, 1958; General Secretary, Nat. Society, and Secretary, C of E Schools Council, 1958–62; Archdeacon of Hampstead, Exam. Chaplain to Bishop of London, and Rector of St Andrew Undershaft with St Mary Axe, City of London, 1962–64; Bishop Suffragan of Willesden, 1964–73; Bishop of Truro, 1973–81. Dean of the Chapels Royal, 1981–91; Prelate of the Order of the British Empire, 1981–91; Prelate of the Imperial Soc. of Knights Bachelor, 1986–91. Chairman: C of E Cttee for Social Work and the Social Services, 1967–76; C of E Board for Social Responsibility, 1976–83; Churches Main Cttee, 1981–91; C of E Board of Education, 1983–88; BBC and IBA Central Religious Adv. Cttee, 1984–89. Member: Churches Unity Commn, 1977–78, Consultant 1978; Churches Council for Covenanting, 1978–82; PCFC, 1989–. An Anglican Mem., Commn for Anglican Orthodox Jt Doctrinal Discussions, 1974–81; one of Archbp of Canterbury's Counsellors on Foreign Relations, 1974–81. Elected delegate, 5th Assembly WCC, Nairobi, 1975. House of Lords, 1977–91. Select Preacher to University of Oxford, 1968, 1984 and 1989; Hensley Henson Lectr, Univ. of Oxford, 1991–92. Lectures: John Findley Green Foundn, Fulton, Missouri, 1987; Earl Mountbatten Meml, Cambridge Union, 1990. Freeman, City of London, 1970. President: Middlesex Assoc., 1970–73; Corporation of SS Mary and Nicholas (Woodard Schools), 1973–78, Hon. Fellow, 1978. Member Court of City Univ., 1981–91. Hon. DD: Episcopal Seminary, Kentucky, 1974; Westminster Coll., Fulton, Missouri, 1987; Hon. DCnL Nashotah, USA, 1983; STD Siena Coll., USA, 1984; Hon. LLD, Simon Greenleaf Sch. of Law, USA, 1987; Hon. DLitt CNAA, 1989. Episcopal Canon of Jerusalem, 1982; Hon. Bencher, Middle Temple,

1982. *Publications:* Growing into Union (Jt author), 1970; The Gospel is for Everyone, 1971; God Alive: Priorities in Pastoral Theology, 1981; Firmly I Believe and Truly, 1985; Life in Christ, 1986; (jtly) Let God be God, 1990; contrib. to: The Christian Religion Explained, 1960; Retreats Today, 1962; Communicating the Faith, 1969; A Critique of Eucharistic Agreement, 1975; Is Christianity Credible?, 1981; The Price of Peace, 1983; The Cross and the Bomb, 1983; Unholy Warfare, 1983; Synod of Westminster, 1986; After the Deluge, 1987; (ed) Faith and the Future, 1988. *Recreations:* reading, especially biographies; music. *Address:* 25 Woodlands Road, Witney, Oxon OX8 6DR. *Clubs:* Garrick, Royal Green Jackets.

LEONARD, Hon. Sir (Hamilton) John, Kt 1981; **Hon. Mr Justice Leonard;** a Judge of the High Court, Queen's Bench Division, since 1981; Presiding Judge, Wales and Chester Circuit, 1982–86; *b* 28 April 1926; *s* of late Arthur and Jean Leonard, Poole, Dorset; *m* 1948, Doreen Enid, *yr d* of late Lt-Col Sidney James Parker, OBE, and May Florence Parker, Sanderstead, Surrey; one *s* one *d*. *Educ:* Dean Close Sch., Cheltenham; Brasenose Coll., Oxford (MA). Coldstream Guards (Captain), 1944–47. Called to Bar, Inner Temple, 1951; Master of the Bench, 1977; practised on South-Eastern Circuit; 2nd Junior Prosecuting Counsel to the Crown at Central Criminal Court, 1964–69; QC 1969; Dep. Chm., Surrey QS, 1969–71; Comr, CCC, 1969–71; a Recorder of the Crown Court, 1972–78; a Circuit Judge, 1978–81; Common Serjeant in the City of London, 1979–81. Member: General Council of the Bar, 1970–74, Senate, 1971–74, Senate of Four Inns and the Bar, 1974–77. Chm., Criminal Bar Assoc., 1975–77. Member: Home Sec.'s Adv. Bd on Restricted Patients, 1973–78; Deptl Cttee to Review Laws on Obscenity, Indecency and Censorship, 1977–79; Judicial Studies Bd, 1979–82. Mem. Council, Hurstpierpoint Coll., 1975–83; Gov., Dean Close Sch., Cheltenham, 1986–. Liveryman, Plaisterers' Co.; HM Lieutenant, City of London, 1980–81. *Recreations:* books, music, painting. *Address:* Royal Courts of Justice, WC2A 2LL. *Club:* Garrick.

LEONARD, Hugh, (John Keyes Byrne); playwright since 1959; Programme Director, Dublin Theatre Festival, since 1978; Literary Editor, Abbey Theatre, 1976–77; *b* 9 Nov. 1926; *m* 1955, Paule Jacquet; one *d*. *Educ:* Presentation College, Dun Laoghaire. Hon. DHL Rhode Island, 1980; Hon. DLitt TCD, 1988. *Stage plays:* The Big Birthday, 1956; A Leap in the Dark, 1957; Madigan's Lock, 1958; A Walk on the Water, 1960; The Passion of Peter Ginty, 1961; Stephen D, 1962; The Poker Session, and Dublin 1, 1963; The Saints Go Cycling In, 1965; Mick and Mick, 1966; The Quick and the Dead, 1967; The Au Pair Man, 1968; The Barracks, 1969; The Patrick Pearse Motel, 1971; Da, 1973; Thieves, 1973; Summer, 1974; Times of Wolves and Tigers, 1974; Irishmen, 1975; Time Was, 1976; A Life, 1977; Moving Days, 1981; Kill, 1982; Scorpions (3 stage plays), 1983; The Mask of Moriarty, 1985; Moving, 1991. *TV plays:* Silent Song (Italia Award, 1967); The Last Campaign, 1978; The Ring and the Rose, 1978; A Life, 1986; Hunted Down, 1989. *TV serials:* Nicholas Nickleby, 1977; London Belongs to Me, 1977; Wuthering Heights, 1978; Strumpet City, 1979; The Little World of Don Camillo, 1980; Good Behaviour, 1983; O'Neill, 1983; The Irish RM, 1985; Troubles, 1987; Parnell and the Englishwoman, 1991. *Films:* Herself Surprised, 1977; Da, 1988. *Publications:* Home Before Night (autobiog.), 1979; Out After Dark (autobiog.), 1988; Parnell and the Englishwoman (novel), 1990. *Recreations:* chess, travel, living. *Address:* 6 Rossaun, Pilot View, Dalkey, Co. Dublin. *T:* Dublin 809590. *Clubs:* Dramatists'; Players' (NY).

LEONARD, His Honour James Charles Beresford Whyte, MA Oxon; a Circuit Judge (formerly Deputy Chairman of Quarter Sessions, Inner London and Middlesex), 1965–79; Judge of the Mayor's and City of London Court, 1972–79; *b* 1905; *s* of Hon. J. W. Leonard, Middle Temple, KC (S Africa); *m* 1939, Barbara Helen (*d* 1989), *d* of late Capt. William Incledon-Webber; two *s* one *d*. *Educ:* Clifton Coll.; Christ Church, Oxford. Called to the Bar, Inner Temple, 1928, Bencher 1961. Served 1940–45, with RAF (Sqdn Ldr). Recorder of Walsall, Staffs, 1951–64; Junior Counsel to Ministry of Agriculture, Fisheries and Food, Forestry Commission and Tithe Redemption Commission, 1959–64; Deputy Chairman of QS: Co. of London, 1964–65; Oxfordshire, 1962–71. Chairman: Disciplinary Cttee, Pharmaceutical Soc. of GB, 1960–64; Adv. Cttee dealing with internment under Civil Authorities (Special Powers) Act (NI) 1962, April-Nov. 1972; Comr under Terrorism (N Ireland) Order 1972, 1972–74; Dep. Chm., Appeal Tribunal, 1974–75. *Address:* Cross Trees, Sutton Courtenay, Oxon OX14 4AD. *T:* Abingdon (0235) 848230.

See also Earl of Westmeath.

LEONARD, Hon. Sir John; *see* Leonard, Hon. Sir H. J.

LEONARD, Michael William, CVO 1984; BSc(Eng), FEng, FICE, MIMechE, FCIArb; Consultant; Founder Secretary, The Fellowship of Engineering, 1976–83; Founder Clerk to the Worshipful Company of Engineers, 1983–86; *b* 25 Dec. 1916; *e s* of late Frank Leonard and Marguerite Leonard (*née* Holborow); *m* 1945, Rosalinna Cushnir; three *s*. *Educ:* Haberdashers' Aske's; Pupilage in Mechanical Engineering, Messrs Fraser & Chalmers Ltd, Erith; University College London (Pres., Union Society, 1939). Civil Engineer, Mowlem Group of Companies, to 1968; Dir, later Chief Exec., Soil Mechanics Ltd; Dir, Soil Mechanics-Soletanche Ltd; Chm., Engineering Laboratory Equipment Ltd. Mem., BSI Code of Practice Cttee on Site Investigations; Mem., later Chm., Tip Safety Cttee (post Aberfan); Sec., Council of Engineering Institutions, 1969–82; Chm., BSI Code of Practice Cttee on Foundations; Design Council Engineering Design, later Industrial, Adv. Cttee; DoI Cttee for Industrial Technologies. Parliamentary and Scientific Committee: formerly Hon. Treasurer; Hon. Sec., 1987; Vice-Pres., 1990; Mem. Council, 1991. Vice Pres., Fédération Européenne d'Associations Nationales d'Ingenieurs; Sec., Commonwealth Engineers' Council; Mem., Executive Cttee, World Fedn of Engineering Organizations (Vice-Pres., 1987–). Hon. Prof., Dept of Civil and Structural Engrg, Sheffield Univ. FEng 1983. *Publications:* papers and articles on Foundation and Geotechnical Engineering, and on Professional Engineering, for jls and confs. *Recreations:* touring, golf, fishing. *Address:* 5 Havelock Road, Croydon CR0 6QQ. *T:* 081–654 4493. *Club:* Athenæum.

LEONARD, Richard Lawrence, (Dick Leonard); writer and political consultant; *b* 12 Dec. 1930; *s* of late Cyril Leonard, Pinner, Mddx, and Kate Leonard (*née* Whyte); *m* 1963, Irène, *d* of late Dr Ernst Heidelberger and of Dr Gertrud Heidelberger, Bad Godesberg, Germany; one *s* one *d*. *Educ:* Ealing Grammar Sch.; Inst. of Education, London Univ.; Essex Univ. (MA). School teacher, 1953–55; Dep. Gen. Sec., Fabian Society, 1955–60; journalist and broadcaster, 1960–68; Sen. Research Fellow (Social Science Research Council), Essex Univ., 1968–70. Mem., Exec. Cttee, Fabian Soc., 1972–80 (Chm., 1977–78); Chm., Library Adv. Council, 1978–81. Trustee, Assoc. of London Housing Estates, 1973–78. Vis. Prof., Free Univ. of Brussels, 1988–; Res. Advr, Univ. of S Carolina, 1988–; European Advr, Publishers Assoc., 1987–. Contested (Lab) Harrow W, 1955; MP (Lab) Romford, 1970–Feb. 1974; PPS to Rt Hon. Anthony Crosland, 1970–74; Mem., Speaker's Conf. on Electoral Law, 1972–74. Introduced Council Housing Bill, 1971; Life Peers Bill, 1973. Asst Editor, The Economist, 1974–85; Brussels and EC correspondent, The Observer, 1989–. *Publications:* Guide to the General Election, 1964; Elections in Britain, 1968; (ed jtly) The Backbencher and Parliament, 1972; Paying for Party Politics, 1975; BBC Guide to Parliament, 1979; (ed jtly) The Socialist Agenda, 1981; (jtly) World Atlas of Elections, 1986; Pocket Guide to the EEC, 1988; Das EG Handbuch, 1989; Elections in Britain Today; contrib.: Guardian, Financial Times, TLS, The Bulletin, Encounter and leading newspapers in USA, Canada, Japan, India, Australia and New Zealand. *Recreations:* walking, book-reviewing, family pursuits. *Address:* 22 rue du Gruyer, 1170 Brussels, Belgium. *T:* 660 2662. *Club:* Reform.

LEONARD-WILLIAMS, Air Vice-Marshal Harold Guy, CB 1966; CBE 1946; DL; retired; *b* 10 Sept. 1911; *s* of late Rev. B. G. Leonard-Williams; *m* 1937, Catherine Estelle, *d* of late G. A. M. Levett; one *d*. *Educ:* Lancing Coll.; RAF Coll., Cranwell. 58 Sqdn, 1932–33; 208 Sqdn, Middle East, 1933–36; No 17 Signals Course, 1936–37; Instructor, RAF Coll., 1937–38; Advanced Air Striking Force, France, 1939–40 (despatches, 1940); Air Min. (Signals), 1940–43; Chm., Brit. Jt Communications Bd, 1943–46; RAF Staff Coll., 1947; Dep. CSO, RAF Middle East, 1947–50; Jt Services Staff Coll., 1950–51; CO Radio Engrg Unit, 1951–53; Dep. Dir Signals, Air Min., 1953–56; Sen. Techn. Staff Off., 90 Signals Gp, 1956–57; Dir of Signals, Air Min., 1957–59; Comdt No 1 Radio Sch., 1959–61; Comd. Electronics Off., Fighter Comd., 1961–63; AOA, HQ Far East Air Force, and AOC, HQ Gp, 1963–65; Dir-Gen. of Manning (RAF), Air Force Dept, 1966–68. Warden, St Michael's Cheshire Home, Axbridge, 1968–72. Mem., Somerset CC, 1973–85 (Chm. 1978–83). Chm., Exmoor Nat. Park, 1978–85. DL Somerset 1975. Officer, Legion of Merit (US), 1945. *Recreations:* gardening, do-it-yourself. *Address:* Openbarrow, Barrows Park, Cheddar, Somerset BS27 3AZ. *T:* Cheddar (0934) 742474. *Club:* Royal Air Force.

LEONTIEF, Prof. Wassily; Economist, New York University, since 1975 (Founder, 1978, Director, 1978–85, Institute for Economic Analysis; Member of Research Staff, since 1986); *b* Leningrad, Russia, 5 Aug. 1906; *s* of Wassily Leontief and Eugenia Leontief (*née* Bekker); *m* 1932, Estelle Helena Marks; one *d*. *Educ:* Univ. of Leningrad (Learned Economist, 1925; MA); Univ. of Berlin (PhD 1928). Research Associate, Inst. of World Econs, Univ. of Kiel, Germany, 1927–28; Economic Adviser to Chinese Govt, Nanking, 1928–29; Res. Associate, Nat. Bureau of Econ. Res., NY, 1931; Harvard University: Instr Economics, 1932–33; Asst Prof., 1933–39; Associate Prof., 1939–46; Prof. of Econs, 1946–53; Henry Lee Prof. of Pol. Econ., 1953–75; Sen. Fellow, Soc. of Fellows, 1956–75 (Chm., 1965–75); Dir, Harvard Economic Research Project, 1948–72; Guggenheim Fellow, 1940, 1950. Gen. Consultant: US Dept of Labor, 1941–47 and 1961–65; US Dept of Commerce, 1966–82; Office of Technology Assessment, 1980–; Econ. Consultant, Russian Econs Sub-Div., Office of Strategic Services, 1943–45; Consultant: UN Sec.-Gen.'s Consultative Gp of Econ. and Social Consequences of Disarmament, 1961–62; UN Develt Prog., 1980–; Mem., Exec. Bd, Science Adv. Council, Environmental Protection Agency, 1975–80. President: Amer. Econ. Assoc., 1970; Sect. F, BAAS, 1976; Mem., Nat. Acad. of Sciences, 1974; FAAAS 1977; Foreign Mem., USSR Acad. of Sciences, 1988; Mem., Soc. of the Optimate, Italian Cultural Inst., NY, 1989; Corr. Mem., Institut de France, 1968; Corr. FBA, 1970; Hon. MRIA, 1976. Dr *hc*: Brussels, 1962; York, 1967; Louvain, 1971; Paris (Sorbonne), 1972; Pennsylvania, 1976; Lancaster, 1976; Toulouse, Louisville, Vermont, Long Island, 1980; Karl Marx Univ., Budapest, 1981; Adelphi Coll., 1988; Cordoba, 1990; Hon. DHL Rensselaer Polytechnic Inst., 1988. Nobel Prize in Economic Science, 1973. Order of the Cherubim, Univ. of Pisa, 1953. Officier, Légion d'Honneur, 1968; Order of the Rising Sun, Japan, 1984; Commandeur des Arts et des Lettres, France, 1985. *Publications:* The Structure of the American Economy 1919–29, 1941, 2nd edn 1953; Studies in the Structure of the American Economy, 1953; Input-Output Economics, 1966, 2nd edn, 1986; Essays in Economics, vol. I 1966, vol. II 1977; The Future of the World Economy, 1977; (with F. Duchin) Military Spending: facts and figures, worldwide implications and future outlook, 1983; (jtly) The Future of Non-Fuel Minerals in the US and World Economy, 1983; (with F. Duchin) The Impact of Automation on Workers, 1986; contribs to learned jls. *Recreation:* fly fishing. *Address:* Institute for Economic Analysis, 269 Mercer Street, 2nd floor, New York, NY 10003, USA.

LEORO-FRANCO, Dr Galo; Gran Cruz, National Order Al Mérito of Ecuador, 1970; Ambassador and Permanent Representative of Ecuador to the Office of the United Nations in Switzerland, since 1984; *s* of José Miguel Leoro and Albertina Franco de Leoro; *m* 1957, Aglae Monroy de Leoro; one *s* two *d*. *Educ:* Central Univ., Quito. Licenciado in Political and Soc. Scis, 1949; Dr in Jurisprudence, Faculty of Law, 1951. Third Sec., Washington, 1955–56, Second Sec., 1956–58; First Sec., Ministry of Foreign Affairs, 1960; Counsellor, Mexico, 1961, Chargé d'Affaires, 1962; Counsellor, Alternate Rep. of Ecuador to OAS, Washington, DC, 1962–64, Minister, 1964–68; Ambassador, 1968–; Chief Legal Advisor to Ministry of Foreign Affairs, 1969–70; Undersec. Gen., Ministry of Foreign Affairs, 1970–71; Ambassador to the Dominican Republic, 1971–72; Perm. Rep. of Ecuador to OAS, 1972–79; Advisor on Internat. Orgns, Ministry of Foreign Affairs, 1979–81; Advisor on Nat. Sovereignty, Ministry of Foreign Affairs, and Rep. of the Ministry in Nat. Congress, 1981–83; Ambassador to UK, 1983–84. Chairman: OAS Permanent Council, 1972–78 (Chm. of several Cttees of OAS Council and Gen. Assembly); Cttee II, Special Commn for Study of Interamerican System, Economic Co-operation problems, Washington, DC, 1973–75; INTELSAT Panel of Jurisexperts, Washington, DC, 1983–85; Rapporteur, Interamerican Conf. for Revision of TIAR; elected mem., Interamerican Juridical Cttee, Rio de Janeiro, 1981–84, Vice-Chm., 1982–83, Chm., 1984–85; Conciliator, Internat. Center for Settlement of Investment Disputes, IMF, Washington, DC, 1986–; Ecuadorian Mem., National Gp of Arbiters, Internat. Court of Arbitration, The Hague, 1987. Representative of Ecuador at over 90 internat. conferences and Chm. of the Delegation at various of them. Gran Cruz: Iron Cross, Fed. Repub. of Germany, 1970; Order of Duarte, Sánchez and Mella, Dominican Repub., 1972; Order of the Sun, Perú, 1976; 1st Class, Order of Francisco de Miranda, Venezuela, 1976. *Publications:* various papers for Ecuadorean Year Book of Internat. Law. *Recreations:* chess, tennis. *Address:* 139 rue de Lausanne, 1202 Geneva, Switzerland. *Club:* Quito Tennis and Golf.

LE POER, Baron; Richard John Beresford; *b* 19 Aug. 1987; *s* and *heir* of Earl of Tyrone, *qv*.

LE POER TRENCH, family name of **Earl of Clancarty.**

LE POER TRENCH, Brinsley; *see* Clancarty, 8th Earl of.

LE PORTZ, Yves; Comdr Légion d'Honneur 1978; Grand Officier de l'Ordre National du Mérite; French financial executive; Inspector-General of Finances, 1971; *b* Hennebont, 30 Aug. 1920; *m* 1946, Bernadette Champetier de Ribes; five *c*. *Educ:* Univ. de Paris à la Sorbonne; Ecole des Hautes Etudes Commerciales; Ecole Libre des Sciences Politiques. Attached to Inspection Générale des Finances, 1943; Directeur Adjoint du Cabinet, Président du Conseil, 1948–49; Sous-Directeur, then Chef de Service, Min. of Finance and Economic Affairs, 1949–51; Directeur du Cabinet: Sec. of State for Finance and Economic Affairs, 1951–52; Minister for Posts, Telegraphs and Telephones (PTT), 1952–55; Minister for Reconstruction and Housing, 1955–57; French Delegate to UN Economic and Social Council, 1957–58; Dir-Gén., Finance, Algeria, 1958–62; Administrateur-Gén., Development Bank of Algeria, 1959–62. European Investment Bank: Vice-Pres. and

Vice-Chm., Bd of Dirs, 1962–70; Pres. and Chm. Bd of Dirs, 1970–84; Hon. Pres., 1984. Chm., Commn des Opérations de Bourse, Paris, 1984–88. *Address:* Tour Mirabeau, 39 quai André Citroën, 75015 Paris, France. *T:* (33) 1 4578 3997.

LEPPARD, Captain Keith André, CBE 1977; RN; Secretary, Institute of Brewing, 1977–90; Director Public Relations (Royal Navy), 1974–77; *b* 29 July 1924; *s* of Wilfred Ernest Leppard and Dora Gilmore Keith; *m* 1954, Betty Rachel Smith; one *s* one *d*. *Educ:* Purley Grammar Sch. MRAeS 1973; FBIM 1973; FSAE 1985. Entered RN, FAA pilot duties, 1943; Opnl Wartime Service, Fighter Pilot, N Atlantic/Indian Oceans, 1944–45; Fighter Pilot/Flying Instr, Aircraft Carriers and Air Stns, 1946–57; CO 807 Naval Air Sqdn (Aerobatic Display Team, Farnborough), 1958–59; Air Org./Flying Trng Staff appts, 1959–63; Comdr (Air), HMS Victorious, 1963–64; Jt Services Staff Coll., 1964–65; Dir, Naval Officer Appts (Air), 1965–67; Chief Staff Officer (Air), Flag Officer Naval Air Comd, 1967–69; Chief Staff Officer (Ops/Trng), Far East Fleet, 1969–71; CO, Royal Naval Air Stn, Yeovilton, and Flag Captain to Flag Officer Naval Air Comd, 1972–74. Naval ADC to the Queen, 1976–77. *Recreations:* country life, tennis, golf. *Address:* Little Holt, Kingsley Green, Haslemere, Surrey. *T:* Haslemere (0428) 2797. *Club:* Naval and Military.

LEPPARD, Raymond John, CBE 1983; conductor, harpsichordist, composer; Music Director, Indianapolis Symphony Orchestra, since 1987; Principal Guest Conductor, St Louis Symphony Orchestra, since 1984; *b* 11 Aug. 1927; *s* of A. V. Leppard. *Educ:* Trinity Coll., Cambridge. Fellow of Trin. Coll., Cambridge, Univ. Lecturer in Music, 1958–68. Hon. Keeper of the Music, Fitzwilliam Museum, 1963–82. Conductor: Covent Garden, Sadler's Wells, Glyndebourne, and abroad; Principal Conductor, BBC Northern Symphony Orchestra, 1972–80. Hon. RAM 1972; Hon. GSM 1983; Hon. FRCM 1984. Hon. DLitt Univ. of Bath, 1972. Commendatore al Merito della Repúbblica Italiana, 1974. *Publications:* realisations of Monteverdi: Il Ballo delle Ingrate, 1958; L'Incoronazione di Poppea, 1962; L'Orfeo, 1965; Il Ritorno d'Ulisse, 1972; realisations of Francesco Cavalli: Messa Concertata, 1966; L'Ormindo, 1967; La Calisto, 1969; Magnificat, 1970; L'Egisto, 1974; L'Orione, 1983; realisation of Rameau's Dardanus, 1980; British Academy Italian Lecture, 1969, Procs Royal Musical Assoc. *Recreations:* music, theatre, books, friends. *Address:* c/o Colbert Artists Management, 111 West 57th Street, New York, NY 10019, USA.

LEPPING, Sir George (Geria Dennis), GCMG 1988; MBE 1981; Governor-General of the Solomon Islands, since 1988; *b* 22 Nov. 1947; *e s* of Chief Dionisio Tanutanu, BEM and Regina Suluki; *m* 1972, Margaret Kwalea Teioli; two *s* four *d* (incl. twins) and one adopted *d*. *Educ:* St John's and St Peter's Primary Schs; King George VI Secondary Sch.; Agricl Coll., Vudal, PNG (Dip. Tropical Agric.); Reading Univ. (Dip. Agric.; MSc). Joined Solomon Is Public Service as Field Officer, Dept of Agric. and Rural Economy, 1968; Sen. Field Officer, then Under-Sec. (Agricl), Min. of Agric., 1979–80; Permanent Secretary: Min. of Home Affairs and Nat. Develt, 1981–84; Special Duties, as Project Dir, Rural Services Project (Develt), 1984–87; Min. of Finance, 1988. Sometime Dir, Chm. or Mem., various govt cos and authorities; Chm., Nat. Disaster Council, 1981–84. Pres., Solomon Is Amateur Athletics Union, 1970–73, 1981–82 (first Solomon Is athlete to win internat. sports medals). *Recreations:* reading, swimming, lawn tennis, snooker, snorkelling, high-speed boat driving, fishing. *Address:* Government House, PO Box 252, Honiara, Solomon Islands. *T:* 22222, 21777.

LEPSCHY, Prof. Giulio Ciro, FBA 1987; Professor of Italian, University of Reading, since 1975; *b* 14 Jan. 1935; *s* of Emilio Lepschy and Sara Castelfranchi; *m* 1962, Anna Laura Momigliano. *Educ:* Univ. of Pisa (Dott. Lett.); Scuola Normale Superiore, Pisa (Dip. Lic. and Perf.). Lib. Doc., Italy. Research, 1957–64, at Univs of Zurich, Oxford, Paris, London, Reading; Lectr 1964, Reader 1967, Univ. of Reading. Mem. Council, Philological Soc., 1984–89. Member editorial boards: Historiographia Linguistica; Italian Studies; The Italianist; Jl of Italian Linguistics; Linguistica e Letteratura; Quaderni di Semantica; Rivista di Grammatica Generativa; Rivista di Linguistica; Romance Philology; Spunti e Ricerche; Stanford Italian Review; Studi Linguistici e Semiologici. *Publications:* A Survey of Structural Linguistics, 1970, new edn 1982; (jtly) The Italian Language Today, 1977, 2nd edn 1988; Saggi di linguistica italiana, 1978; Intorno a Saussure, 1979; Mutamenti di prospettiva nella linguistica, 1981; Nuovi saggi di linguistica italiana, 1989; Sulla linguistica moderna, 1989; Storia della linguistica, 1990; contribs to learned jls. *Address:* Department of Italian Studies, The University, Whiteknights, Reading RG6 2AA. *T:* Reading (0734) 875123.

LE QUESNE, Sir (Charles) Martin, KCMG 1974 (CMG 1963); Member of the States of Jersey, 1978–90 (Deputy for St Saviour's parish); HM Diplomatic Service, retired; *b* 10 June 1917; *s* of C. T. Le Quesne, QC; *m* 1948; three *s*. *Educ:* Shrewsbury; Exeter Coll., Oxford (Hon. Fellow, 1990). Served in Royal Artillery, 1940–45. Apptd HM Foreign Service, 1946; 2nd Sec. at HM Embassy, Baghdad, 1947–48; 1st Secretary: Foreign Office, 1948–51, HM Political Residency, Bahrain, 1951–54; attended course at NATO Defence Coll., Paris, 1954–55; HM Embassy, Rome, 1955–58; Foreign Office, 1958–60; apptd HM Chargé d'Affaires, Republic of Mali, 1960, subsequently Ambassador there, 1961–64; Foreign Office, 1964–68; Ambassador to Algeria, 1968–71; Dep. Under-Sec. of State, FCO, 1971–74; High Comr in Nigeria, 1974–76. Mem. Council, Royal African Soc. Mem. Council, Southampton Univ. *Recreations:* gardening, books. *Address:* Beau Désert, St Saviour, Jersey, Channel Islands. *T:* Jersey 22076. *Clubs:* Reform (Chairman 1973–74), MCC; United (Jersey); Royal Channel Islands Yacht.

See also Sir J. G. Le Quesne, L. P. Le Quesne.

LE QUESNE, Sir (John) Godfray, Kt 1980; QC 1962; Judge of Courts of Appeal of Jersey and Guernsey, since 1964; a Recorder, since 1972; *b* 1924; 3rd *s* of late C. T. Le Quesne, QC; *m* 1963, Susan Mary Gill; two *s* one *d*. *Educ:* Shrewsbury Sch.; Exeter Coll., Oxford (MA). Pres. of Oxford Union, 1943. Called to Bar, Inner Temple, 1947; Master of the Bench, Inner Temple, 1969, Reader, 1988, Treasurer, 1989; admitted to bar of St Helena, 1959. Dep. Chm., Lincs (Kesteven) QS, 1963–71. Chm., Monopolies and Mergers Commn, 1975–87 (a part-time Mem., 1974–75). Chm. of Council, Regent's Park Coll., Oxford, 1958–87. *Recreations:* music, walking. *Address:* 1 Crown Office Row, Temple, EC4. *T:* 071–583 9292.

See also Sir C. M. Le Quesne, L. P. Le Quesne.

LE QUESNE, Prof. Leslie Philip, CBE 1984; DM, MCh, FRCS; Medical Administrator, Commonwealth Scholarship Commission, 1984–91; *b* 24 Aug. 1919; *s* of late C. T. Le Quesne, QC; *m* 1969, Pamela Margaret, *o d* of late Dr A. Fullerton, Batley, Yorks; two *s*. *Educ:* Rugby; Exeter Coll., Oxford; Middlesex Hosp. Med. Sch. Jun. Demonstrator, Path. and Anat., 1943–45; House Surgeon, Southend Hosp. and St Mark's Hosp., 1945–47; Appointments at Middlesex Hospital: Asst, Surgical Professorial Unit, 1947–52; Asst Dir, Dept of Surgical Studies, 1952–63; Surgeon, 1960–63; Prof. of Surgery, Med. Sch., and Dir, Dept of Surgical Studies, 1963–84; Dep. Vice-Chancellor and Dean, Fac. of Medicine, Univ. of London, 1980–84. Sir Arthur Sims Commonwealth Travelling Prof., 1975. Mem. GMC, 1979–84. Editor, Post Graduate Med. Jl, 1951–52. Arris and Gale Lectr, RCS, 1952; Baxter Lectr, Amer. Coll. Surgs, 1960. Mem., Ct of Examrs, RCS, 1971–77. Formerly Chm., Assoc. of Profs of Surgery; Pres., Surgical Res. Soc. Chm., The British Jl of Surgery. Hon. FRACS, 1975; Hon. FACS, 1982; Hon. Fellow RPMS, 1985. Moynihan Medal, 1953. *Publications:* medical articles and contribs to text books; Fluid Balance in Surgical Practice, 2nd edn, 1957. *Recreations:* fishing, reading. *Address:* 8 Eton Villas, NW3 4SX.

See also Sir C. M. Le Quesne, Sir J. G. Le Quesne.

LE QUESNE, Sir Martin; *see* Le Quesne, Sir C. M.

LERNER, Max; author; Syndicated newspaper column appears New York Post, Los Angeles Times Syndicate and elsewhere; Professor of American Civilization and World Politics, Brandeis University, USA, 1949–73, now Emeritus; Professor of Human Behavior, Graduate School of Human Behavior, US International University, San Diego, since 1974; *b* 20 Dec. 1902; *s* of Benjamin Lerner and Bessie Podel; *m* 1st; two *d* (and one *d* decd); 2nd, 1941, Edna Albers; three *s*. *Educ:* Yale Univ. (BA); Washington Univ., St Louis (MA); Robert Brookings Graduate Sch. of Economics and Government (PhD). Encyclopædia of Social Sciences, 1927, managing editor; Sarah Lawrence Coll., 1932–36, Prof. of Social Science; Harvard, 1935–36, Prof. of Government; Prof. of Political Science, Williams Coll., 1938–43; Ford Foundation Prof. of Amer. Civilization, Sch. of Internat. Studies, University of Delhi, 1959–60; Ford Foundn res. project on European unity, 1963–64. Welch Prof. of Amer. Studies, Univ. of Notre Dame, 1982–84. Editor of the Nation, 1936–38; Editorial Director PM, 1943–48; Columnist for the New York Star, 1948–49. *Publications:* It is Later Than You Think, 1938, rev. edn, 1943, new edn with afterword, 1989; Ideas are Weapons, 1939, new edn with afterword, 1990; (ed) Machiavelli, Prince and Discourses, 1940; Ideas for the Ice Age, 1941; The Mind and Faith of Justice Holmes, 1943, new edn with afterword, 1989; (ed) Aristotle's Politics, 1943; Public Journal, 1945; The Third Battle for France, 1945; The World of the Great Powers, 1947; The Portable Veblen, 1948; Actions and Passions, 1949; America as a Civilization, 1957, rev. edn, 1987; The Unfinished Country, 1959; Education and a Radical Humanism, 1962; The Age of Overkill, 1962; Tocqueville and American Civilization, 1966; (ed) Essential Works of John Stuart Mill, 1961; (ed) Tocqueville, Democracy in America, 1966; Values in Education, 1976; Ted and the Kennedy Legend, 1980; Wrestling with the Angel, 1990. *Address:* 25 East End Avenue, New York, NY 10028, USA; (office) New York Post, 210 South Street, New York, NY 10002, USA.

LE ROY LADURIE, Prof. Emmanuel Bernard; Officier de la Légion d'Honneur; Professor of History of Modern Civilisation, Collège de France, since 1973; General Administrator, Bibliothèque Nationale, since 1987; *b* 19 July 1929; *s* of Jacques Le Roy Ladurie and Léontine (*née* Dauger); *m* 1955, Madeleine Pupponi; one *s* one *d*. *Educ:* Univ. of Sorbonne (agrégé d'histoire); DèsL 1952. Teacher, Lycée de Montpellier, 1953–57; Res. Assistant, CNRS, 1957–60; Assistant, Faculté des Lettres de Montpellier, 1960–63; Asst Lectr, 1963, Dir of Studies, 1965–, Ecole Pratique des Hautes Etudes; Lectr, Faculté des Lettres de Paris, 1969; UER Prof. of Geography and Social Sci., Univ. de Paris VII, 1970–. Hon. FBA 1985. Hon. Dr: Michigan; Geneva; Leeds; Hull; Leicester. *Publications:* Les Paysans du Languedoc, 1966; Histoire du climat depuis l'an mil, 1967; Le Territoire de l'historien, vol. 1 1973, vol. 2 1978; Montaillou: village occitan 1294–1324, 1975; (jtly) Histoire économique et sociale de la France, vol. 1 1450–1660, vol. 2 Paysannerie et Croissance, 1976; Le Carnaval de Romans (Prix Pierre Lafue), 1979; L'Argent, l'Amour et la Mort en pays d'Oc, 1980; (jtly) Inventaire des campagnes, 1980; (jtly) L'Histoire urbaine de la France, vol. 3, 1981; Parmi les historiens, 1983; Pierre Prion: scribe, 1987; (jtly) L'Histoire de France: l'état royal 1460–1610, 1987; (ed) Monarchies, 1987; L'Ancien Régime, 1991. *Address:* Collège de France, 11 place Marcelin-Berthelot, 75005 Paris, France; Bibliothèque Nationale, 58 rue Richelieu, 75084 Paris Cedex 02, France. *T:* 47.03.82.50; (home) 88 rue d'Alleray, 75015 Paris, France.

LeROY-LEWIS, David Henry, FCA; Director, Touche, Remnant & Co., 1974–88 (Deputy Chairman, 1981–88); Chairman, Henry Ansbacher Holdings plc, 1982–88; *b* 14 June 1918; *er s* of late Stuyvesant Henry LeRoy-Lewis and late Bettye LeRoy-Lewis; *m* 1953, Cynthia Madeleine, *er d* of late Comdr John C. Boldero, DSC, RN (Retd); three *d*. *Educ:* Eton. FCA 1947. Chairman: TR North America Trust PLC (formerly Continental Union Trust Ltd) 1974–88 (Dir, 1948–88); R. P. Martin plc, 1981–85; Hill Martin, 1989–; Director: TR Industrial & General Trust PLC, 1967–88; Akroyd & Smithers Ltd, 1970–81 (Chm., 1976–81); TR Trustees Corp. PLC, 1973–88; TR Energy PLC, 1981–88. Mem., 1961–81, a Dep. Chm., 1973–76, Stock Exchange Council. *Recreation:* fishing. *Address:* Stoke House, Stoke, Andover, Hants SP11 0NP. *T:* St Mary Bourne (0264) 738548. *Clubs:* Naval and Military, MCC.

LESLIE, family name of **Earl of Rothes.**

LESLIE, Lord; James Malcolm David Leslie; *b* 4 June 1958; *s* and *heir* of 21st Earl of Rothes, *qv*. *Educ:* Eton. Graduated Parnham House, 1990. *Address:* Littlecroft, West Milton, Bridport, Dorset DT6 3SL.

LESLIE, Sir Alan; *see* Leslie, Sir C. A. B.

LESLIE, Ann Elizabeth Mary, (Mrs Michael Fletcher); journalist and broadcaster; *b* Pakistan; *d* of Norman Leslie and Theodora (*née* McDonald); *m* 1969, Michael Fletcher; one *d*. *Educ:* Presentation Convent, Matlock, Derbyshire; Convent of the Holy Child, Mayfield, Sussex; Lady Margaret Hall, Oxford (BA). Daily Express, 1962–67; freelance, 1967–: regular contributor to Daily Mail. Broadcasting includes Stop the Week, Any Questions, TV-am and Question Time. British Press Awards Commendation, 1980; Variety Club Women of the Year Award for journalism and broadcasting, 1981; British Press Awards Feature Writer of the Year, 1981, 1989; British Press Awards Commendation, 1983, 1985, 1987. *Recreations:* family life, photography. *Address:* c/o Daily Mail, Northcliffe House, 2 Derry Street, Kensington, W8 5TS. *T:* 071–938 6000, *Fax:* 071–937 3251.

LESLIE, Sir (Colin) Alan (Bettridge), Kt 1986; Commissioner, Foreign Compensation Commission, 1986–90; *b* 10 April 1922; *s* of Rupert Colin Leslie and Gladys Hannah Leslie (*née* Bettridge); *m* 1st, 1953, Anne Barbara (*née* Coates) (*d* 1982); two *d*; 2nd, 1983, Jean Margaret (Sally), widow of Dr Alan Cheatle. *Educ:* King Edward VII School, Lytham; Merton College, Oxford (MA Law). Solicitor. Commissioned, The Royal Scots Fusiliers, 1941–46. Legal practice, Stafford Clark & Co., Solicitors, 1948–60; Head of Legal Dept and Company Secretary, British Oxygen Co., later BOC International, then BOC Group, 1960–83. Law Society: Vice-Pres., 1984–85; Pres., 1985–86. *Recreation:* fishing. *Address:* Tile Barn Cottage, Alfriston, E Sussex. *T:* Alfriston (0323) 870388; 36 Abingdon Road, W8. *T:* 071–937 2874. *Club:* United Oxford & Cambridge University.

LESLIE, Prof. David Clement; consultant engineer; Senior Consultant, Turbulence Unit, Queen Mary College, London, since 1990 (Director, 1975–90); Professor Emeritus, London University, since 1984; *b* Melbourne, 18 Dec. 1924; *o s* of Clement and Doris Leslie; *m* 1952, Dorothea Ann Wenborn; three *s* two *d*. *Educ:* Westminster; Leighton Park; Wadham Coll., Oxford (MA, DPhil). Royal Navy, 1944–47. Postgrad. research in physics, 1948–50; Sir W. G. Armstrong Whitworth Aircraft, Coventry, 1951–54; Guided Weapons Div., RAE Farnborough, 1954–58; UKAEA Harwell and Winfrith,

1958–68; Prof. of Nuclear Engrg, 1968–84 (Hd of Dept, 1968–80), Dean, Faculty of Engrg, 1980–83, QMC. Member: Scientific and Technical Cttee, EEC, 1973–86 (Chm. 1980–84); Electricity Supply Res. Council, 1981–89 (Dep. Chm. 1984–89); Machines and Power Cttee, SERC, 1985–87. Safety Adviser to the Local Authorities for the Sizewell Inquiry, 1981–87. *Publications:* Developments in the Theory of Turbulence, 1973; papers in Proc. Royal Soc., Jl of Fluid Mechanics, Nature, Nuclear Science and Engrg, etc. *Address:* 22 Piercing Hill, Theydon Bois, Essex CM16 7JW. *T:* Theydon Bois (0992) 813249.

LESLIE, Rt. Rev. (Ernest) Kenneth, OBE 1972; *b* 14 May 1911; *s* of Rev. Ernest Thomas Leslie and Margaret Jane Leslie; *m* 1941, Isabel Daisy Wilson; two *s* one *d* (and one *s* decd). *Educ:* Trinity Gram. Sch., Kew, Vict.; Trinity Coll., University of Melbourne (BA). Aust. Coll. of Theology. ThL, 2nd Cl. 1933, Th Schol. 1951, 2nd Cl. 1952. Deacon, 1934; Priest, 1935; Asst Curate, Holy Trinity, Coburg, 1934–37; Priest-in-Charge, Tennant Creek, Dio. Carpentaria, 1937–38; Alice Springs with Tennant Creek, 1938–40; Rector of Christ Church, Darwin, 1940–44; Chaplain, AIF, 1942–45; Rector of Alice Springs with Tennant Creek, 1945–46; Vice-Warden, St John's Coll., Morpeth, NSW, 1947–52; Chap. Geelong Church of Eng. Gram. Sch., Timbertop Branch, 1953–58; Bishop of Bathurst, 1959–81. *Recreations:* walking, woodwork, cycling. *Address:* PO Box 737, Bathurst, NSW 2250, Australia.

LESLIE, His Honour Gilbert Frank; retired Circuit Judge (formerly Judge of County Courts); *b* 25 Aug. 1909; *e s* of late F. L. J. Leslie, JP and M. A. Leslie (*née* Gilbert), Harrogate; *m* 1947, Mary Braithwaite, MD, JP, *e d* of late Col W. H. Braithwaite, MC, TD, DL and Mrs E. M. Braithwaite, Harrogate; three *d.* *Educ:* St Christopher Sch., Letchworth; King's Coll., Cambridge (MA). Called to the Bar, Inner Temple, 1932; joined North-Eastern Circuit. Served War of 1939–45; Private Sherwood Foresters, 1939; commissioned West Yorkshire Regt, 1940; on Judge-Advocate-General's staff from Nov. 1940; finally ADJAG, HQ BAOR; released Nov. 1945 (Lt-Col). Asst Recorder, Newcastle upon Tyne City Quarter Sessions, 1954–60, Sheffield City Quarter Sessions, 1956–60; Recorder of Pontefract, 1958–60; Recorder of Rotherham, 1960; Dep. Chm., West Riding Quarter Sessions, 1960–63; Judge of County Court Circuit 14, 1960; Circuit 46, 1960–63; Circuit 42 (Bloomsbury and Marylebone), 1963–80 (Circuit Judge, 1972); Dep. Chm., Inner London Area Sessions, 1965–71. Dep. Chm., Agricultural Lands Tribunal (Yorkshire Area), 1958–60. Jt Pres., Council of HM Circuit Judges, 1978. Manager, 1974–77, 1980–83, Vice-Pres., 1975–77, 1980–83, Royal Institution. Mem. Board of Faculty of Law and Court of Governors, Sheffield Univ., 1958–61; Governor, 1964–87, Chm. of Governors, 1974–84, Parsons Mead Sch. for Girls. Liveryman, Worshipful Co. of Gardeners, 1963– (Mem. Court, 1978–, Master, 1987–88). FRSA. *Recreations:* gardening, horticultural history. *Address:* Ottways, 26 Ottways Lane, Ashtead, Surrey KT21 2NZ. *T:* Ashtead (0372) 274191. *Club:* Reform.

LESLIE, James Bolton, AO 1984; MC 1944; Chairman, Christies Australia Ltd, since 1990; director of companies; Chancellor, Deakin University, since 1987; *b* 27 Nov. 1922; *s* of Stuart Deacon Leslie and Dorothy Clare (*née* Murphy); *m* 1955, Alison Baker three *s* one *d.* *Educ:* Trinity Grammar Sch., Melbourne; Harvard Business Sch., Boston, USA. Served war, Australian Infantry, Pacific Theatre, 1941–46. Mobil Oil Australia Ltd: joined, 1946; Manager, Fiji, 1947–50; various postings, Australia, 1950–59; Mobil Corp., New York, 1959–61; Gen. Manager, New South Wales, 1961–66; Director, Mobil Australia, 1966–68; Chm. and Chief Exec., Mobil New Zealand, 1968–72; Chairman: Mobil Australia and Pacific, 1972–80; Qantas Airways, 1980–89. Chm., Internat. Culture Corp. of Australia, 1980–; Director: Nat. Mutual Life Assoc., 1983–; Equity Trustees, 1980–; Newmont Australia Ltd, 1987–; Boral Ltd, 1984–. *Recreations:* farming, horse breeding. *Address:* 42 Grey Street, East Melbourne, Victoria 3002, Australia. *T:* 03 4196149. *Clubs:* Melbourne, Australian, Melbourne Cricket, Beefsteak, Victoria Racing (Melbourne).

LESLIE, Sir John (Norman Ide), 4th Bt *cr* 1876; *b* 6 Dec. 1916; *s* of Sir (John Randolph) Shane Leslie, 3rd Bt and Marjorie (*d* 1951), *y d* of Henry C. Ide, Vermont, USA; *S* father, 1971. *Educ:* Downside; Magdalene College, Cambridge (BA 1938). Captain, Irish Guards; served War of 1939–45 (prisoner-of-war). Kt of Honour and Devotion, SMO Malta, 1947; KCSG 1958. *Recreations:* ornithology, ecology. *Heir:* *b* Desmond Arthur Peter Leslie [*b* 29 June 1921; *m* 1st, 1945, Agnes Elizabeth, *o d* of late Rudolph Bernauer, Budapest; two *s* one *d*; 2nd, 1970, Helen Jennifer, *d* of late Lt-Col E. I. E. Strong; two *d*]. *Address:* 19 Piazza in Piscinula, Trastevere, 00153 Rome, Italy. *Clubs:* Travellers'; Circolo della Caccia (Rome).

LESLIE, Rt. Rev. Kenneth; *see* Leslie, Rt Rev. E. K.

LESLIE, (Percy) Theodore; retired British Aerospace engineer; *b* 19 Nov. 1915; *s* of Frank Harvey Leslie (*d* 1965) (*g g s* of 4th Bt), Christ's Hospital, and Amelia Caroline (*d* 1918), *d* of Alexander Russon; *heir* to the Leslie of Wardis and Findrassie baronetcy (*cr* 1625). *Educ:* London and privately. FSA Scot 1983. Freeman, City of London, 1978. Mem. Knightly Assoc. of St George (USA), 1983. *Recreations:* chess, gardening and visiting places of historic interest. *Address:* c/o National Westminster Bank, 5 Market Place, Kingston upon Thames, Surrey.

LESLIE, Sir Peter (Evelyn), Kt 1991; Chairman, Commonwealth Development Corporation, since 1989; *b* 24 March 1931; *s* of late Patrick Holt Leslie, DSc and Evelyn (*née* de Berry); *m* 1975, Charlotte, former wife of W. N. Wenban-Smith, *qv* and *d* of Sir Edwin Chapman-Andrews, KCMG, OBE and of Lady Chapman-Andrews; two step *s* two step *d.* *Educ:* Dragon Sch., Oxford; Stowe Sch.; New Coll., Oxford (Exhbnr; MA). Commnd Argyll and Sutherland Highlanders, 1951; served 7th Bn (TA), 1952–56. Entered Barclays Bank DCO, 1955; served in Sudan, Algeria, Zaire, Kenya and the Bahamas, 1956–71; Gen. Manager, Barclays Bank and Barclays Bank Internat., 1973–81, Sen. Gen. Manager, 1981–84; Dir, 1980–91, Chief Gen. Man., 1985–87, Man. Dir, 1987–88, Dep. Chm., 1987–91, Barclays Bank plc. Dep. Chm., Midland Gp, 1991–. Mem., Bd of Banking Supervision, Bank of England, 1989–. Chm., Export Guarantees Adv. Council, 1987–July 1992 (Mem., 1978–81, Dep. Chm., 1986–87); Mem., Matthews Cttee on ECGD, 1983. Chairman: Exec. Cttee, British Bankers Assoc., 1978–79; Cttee, London and Scottish Clearing Bankers, 1986–88; Overseas Develt Inst., 1988–. Member: Council for Ind. and Higher Educn, 1987–91; CARE Britain Bd, 1988–. Chm. Council, Queen's Coll., London, 1989–; Governor: Stowe Sch., 1983–; National Inst. of Social Work, 1973–83. *Recreations:* natural history, historical research. *Address:* c/o Commonwealth Development Corporation, 1 Bessborough Gardens, SW1V 2JQ.

LESLIE, Theodore; *see* Leslie, P. T.

LESLIE MELVILLE, family name of **Earl of Leven and Melville.**

LESOURNE, Jacques François; Chevalier de la Légion d'Honneur; Commandeur de l'ordre National de Mérite; Chevalier des Palmes Académiques; Directeur-gérant, Le Monde, since 1991; Professor of Economics, Conservatoire National des Arts et Métiers, since 1974; *b* 26 Dec. 1928; *s* of André Lesourne and Simone Guille; *m* 1961, Odile Melin; one *s* two *d* (and one *s* decd). *Educ:* Ecole Polytechnique; Ecole Nationale Supérieure des Mines, Paris. Head, Econ. Dept, French Coal Mines, 1954–57; Directeur général, later Pres., SEMA, 1958–75; Dir, Interfutures Project, OECD, 1976–79. Pres., Internat. Fedn of OR Socs, 1986–88; Vice-President: Internat. Inst. for Applied Systems Analysis, 1973–79; Centre for European Policy Studies, 1987–; Member Council: Inst. of Management Science, 1976–79; Eur. Econ. Assoc., 1984–89. Harold Lander Prize, Canadian OR Soc., 1991. *Publications:* Technique économique et gestion industrielle, 1958 (Economic Technique and Industrial Management); Le Calcul économique, 1964; Du bon usage de l'étude économique dans l'entreprise, 1966; (jtly) Matière grise année O, 1970 (The Management Revolution); Le Calcul économique, théorie et applications, 1972 (Cost-Benefit Analysis and Economic Theory); Modèles économiques de croissance de l'entreprise, 1972; (jtly) Une Nouvelle industrie: la matière grise, 1973; Les Systèmes de destin, 1976; A Theory of the Individual for Economic Analysis, 1977; (jtly) L'Analyse des décisions d'aménagement regional, 1979; Demain la France dans le monde, 1980; Les Mille Sentiers de l'avenir, 1981 (World Perspectives—a European Assessment); (jtly) Facilitating Development in a Changing Third World, 1983; Soirs et lendemains de fête: journal d'un homme tranquille, 1981–84 (autobiog.), 1984; (jtly) La gestion des villes, analyse des décisions d'économie urbaine, 1985; (jtly) La Fin des habitudes, 1985; L'Entreprise et ses futurs, 1985; L'après-Communisme, de l'Atlantique à l'Oural; The Economics of Order and Disorder, 1991. *Recreation:* piano. *Address:* 52 rue de Vaugirard, 75006 Paris, France; Le Monde, 15 rue Falguière, 75015 Paris. *T:* 40.65.25.25.

LESSELS, Norman; Partner, Chiene & Tait, CA, since 1980; Chairman, Standard Life Assurance Co., since 1988 (Deputy Chairman, 1982–88); *b* 2 Sept. 1938; *s* of John Clark Lessels and Gertrude Margaret Ellen Lessels (*née* Jack); *m* 1st, 1960, Gillian Durward Lessels (*née* Clark) (*d* 1979); one *s* (and one *s* one *d* decd); 2nd, 1981, Christine Stevenson Lessels (*née* Hitchman). *Educ:* Melville Coll.; Edinburgh Acad. CA (Scotland) 1961. CA apprentice with Graham Smart & Annan, Edinburgh, 1955–60; with Thomson McLintock & Co., London, 1960–61; Partner, Wallace & Somerville, Edinburgh, merged with Whinney Murray & Co., 1969, latterly Ernst & Whinney, 1962–80. Director: Standard Life Assurance Co., 1978–; Scottish Eastern Investment Trust, 1980–; Bank of Scotland, 1988–; SIB, 1989–; Cairn Energy, 1988–; Havelock Europa, 1989–; NWS Bank, 1989–; BUPA, 1990–. Mem., Scottish Homes, 1988–. Pres., Inst. of Chartered Accountants of Scotland, 1987–88. *Recreations:* golf, bridge, music. *Address:* 11 Forres Street, Edinburgh EH3 6BJ. *T:* 031–225 5596. *Clubs:* New (Edinburgh); Hon. Company of Edinburgh Golfers, Royal and Ancient Golf, Bruntsfield Links.

LESSER, Sidney Lewis; Vice-President, Royal Automobile Club, since 1979 (Executive Chairman, 1978–79); *b* 23 March 1912; *s* of Joseph and Rachel Lesser; *m* 1938, Nina Lowenthal; two *d.* Solicitor of Supreme Court of Judicature; Comr for Oaths. In sole practice, 1935–82. *Recreations:* golf, travel, reading. *Address:* 37 Fairfax Place, Hampstead, NW6 4EJ. *T:* 071–328 2607. *Clubs:* Royal Automobile; Coombe Hill Golf; Propeller of the United States.

LESSING, Charlotte; Editor of Good Housekeeping, 1973–87; freelance writer; publishing and public relations consultant; *b* 14 May; *m* 1948, Walter B. Lessing (*d* 1989); three *d.* *Educ:* Henrietta Barnet Sch.; evening classes. Univ. of London Dipl. Eng. Lit. Journalism and public relations: New Statesman and Nation; Royal Society of Medicine; Lilliput (Hulton Press); Notley Public Relations; Good Housekeeping, 1964–87; Editor-in-Chief, Country Living, 1985–86. *Publications:* short stories, travel, wine and feature articles. *Recreations:* travel, wine. *Address:* 2 Roseneath Road, SW11 6AH.

LESSING, Mrs Doris (May); author; *b* Persia, 22 Oct. 1919; *d* of Captain Alfred Cook Tayler and Emily Maude McVeagh; lived in Southern Rhodesia, 1924–49; *m* 1st, 1939, Frank Charles Wisdom (marr. diss., 1943); one *s* one *d*; 2nd, 1945, Gottfried Anton Nicholas Lessing (marr. diss., 1949); one *s.* Associate Member: AAAL, 1974; Nat. Inst. of Arts and Letters (US), 1974. Mem., Inst. for Cultural Res., 1974. Hon. Fellow, MLA (Amer.), 1974. Hon. DLitt Princeton, 1989. Austrian State Prize for European Literature, 1981; Shakespeare Prize, 1982; Grinzane Cavour Award, Italy, 1989. *Publications:* The Grass is Singing, 1950 (filmed 1981); This Was the Old Chief's Country, 1951; Martha Quest, 1952; Five, 1953 (Somerset Maugham Award, Soc. of Authors, 1954); A Proper Marriage, 1954; Retreat to Innocence, 1956; Going Home, 1957; The Habit of Loving (short stories), 1957; A Ripple from the Storm, 1958; Fourteen Poems, 1959; In Pursuit of the English, 1960 (adapted for stage, 1990); The Golden Notebook, 1962 (Prix Médicis 1976 for French trans., Carnet d'or); A Man and Two Women (short stories), 1963; African Stories, 1964; Landlocked, 1965; The Four-Gated City, 1969; Briefing for a Descent into Hell, 1971; The Story of a Non-Marrying Man (short stories), 1972; The Summer Before the Dark, 1973; The Memoirs of a Survivor, 1975 (filmed 1981); Collected Stories: Vol. I, To Room Nineteen, 1978; Vol. II, The Temptation of Jack Orkney, 1978; Canopus in Argos: Archives: Re Planet 5, Shikasta, 1979; The Marriages Between Zones Three, Four and Five, 1980; The Sirian Experiments, 1981; The Making of the Representative for Planet 8, 1982 (libretto, 1988); The Sentimental Agents in the Volyen Empire, 1983; The Diaries of Jane Somers, 1984 (Diary of a Good Neighbour, 1983; If the Old Could . . . ., 1984; published under pseudonym Jane Somers); The Good Terrorist, 1985 (W. H. Smith Literary Award, 1986; Palermo Prize and Premio Internazionale Mondello, 1987); The Fifth Child, 1988; Doris Lessing Reader, 1990; *non-fiction:* Going Home, 1957; Particularly Cats, 1966, rev. edn as Particularly Cats and More Cats, 1990; Prisons We Choose to Live Inside, 1986; The Wind Blows Away Our Words, 1987; *play:* play with a Tiger, 1962. *Address:* c/o Jonathan Clowes Ltd, Iron Bridge House, Bridge Approach, NW1 8BD.

LESSOF, Prof. Maurice Hart, FRCP; Professor of Medicine, University of London at United Medical and Dental Schools (Guy's Hospital), 1971–89, now Emeritus; *b* 4 June 1924; *s* of Noah and Fanny Lessof; *m* 1960, Leila Liebster; one *s* two *d.* *Educ:* City of London Sch.; King's Coll., Cambridge. Appts on junior staff of Guy's Hosp., Canadian Red Cross Memorial Hosp., Johns Hopkins Hosp., etc.; Clinical Immunologist and Physician, Guy's Hosp., 1967. Chm., SE Thames Regl Med. Audit Cttee, 1990–91; Dep. Chm., Guy's and Lewisham NHS Trust, 1991–. Adviser on Allergy, DHSS, 1982–. Vice-Pres. and Sen. Censor, RCP, 1987–88; Past Pres., British Soc. for Allergy. Mem. Senate, London Univ., 1981–85. *Publications:* (ed) Immunological Aspects of Cardiovascular Diseases, 1981; (ed) Immunological and Clinical Aspects of Allergy, 1984 (Spanish and Portuguese edns, 1987); (ed) Clinical Reactions to Food, 1983; (ed) Allergy: an international textbook, 1987; Food Reactions, 1992. *Recreation:* painting. *Address:* 8 John Spencer Square, Canonbury, N1 2LZ. *T:* 071–226 0919, *Fax:* 071–354 8913. *Club:* Athenæum.

LESSORE, Helen, OBE 1958; RA 1986; painter; *b* 31 Oct. 1907; *d* of Alfred Brook and Edith Berliner; *m* 1934, Frederick Lessore (*d* 1951); two *s.* *Educ:* Slade School of Fine Art. Began working at Beaux Arts Gallery, 1931 (founder, Frederick Lessore); director of gallery, 1952–65; full-time artist, 1965–. Exhibitions: with Marlborough Fine Art, Helen Lessore and the Beaux Arts Gallery, 1968; 12 Duke Street, 1981; retrospective, Fine Art Soc., 1987. *Publication:* A Partial Testament, 1986. *Address:* c/o Royal Academy, Burlington House, Piccadilly, W1V 0DS.

LESTER, Anthony Paul, QC 1975; QC (NI); a Recorder, since 1987; *b* 3 July 1936; *e s* of Harry and Kate Lester; *m* 1971, Catherine Elizabeth Debora Wassey; one *s* one *d.* *Educ:*

City of London Sch.; Trinity Coll., Cambridge (Exhibnr) (BA); Harvard Law Sch. (Harkness Commonwealth Fund Fellowship) (LLM). Served RA, 1955–57, 2nd Lieut. Called to Bar, Lincoln's Inn, 1963 (Mansfield scholar), Bencher, 1985; called to Bar of N Ireland, 1984; Irish Bar, 1983. Special Adviser to: Home Secretary, 1974–76; Standing Adv. Commn on Human Rights, 1975–77. Hon. Vis. Prof., UCL, 1983–. Lectures: Owen J. Roberts, Univ. of Pennsylvania Law Sch., 1976; F. A. Mann, London, 1983; Rubin, Columbia Law Sch., 1988. Member: Bd of Overseers, Univ. of Pennsylvania Law Sch., 1978–89; Court of Governors, LSE. Chairman: Interights, 1983–; Runnymede Trust; Member: Internat. Law Assoc. Cttee on Human Rights; Amer. Law Inst., 1985–; Council, PSI; Council, Inst. of Advanced Legal Studies; Nat. Cttee for Electoral Reform; Adv. Bd, Constitutional Reform Centre. Governor, British Inst. of Human Rights. Chm., Bd of Govs, James Allen's Girls' Sch., 1987–. *Publications:* Justice in the American South, 1964 (Amnesty Internat.); (co-ed.) Shawcross and Beaumont on Air Law, 3rd edn, 1964; (co-author) Race and Law, 1972; contributor to: British Nationality, Immigration and Race Relations, in Halsbury's Laws of England, 4th edn, 1973; The Changing Constitution (ed Jowell and Oliver), 1985, 2nd edn 1990. *Address:* 2 Hare Court, Temple, EC4Y 7BH. *T:* 071–583 1770. *Club:* Garrick.

LESTER, James Theodore; MP (C) Broxtowe, since 1983 (Beeston, Feb. 1974–1983); *b* 23 May 1932; *s* of Arthur Ernest and Marjorie Lester; *m*; two *s*. *Educ:* Nottingham High School. Mem. Notts CC, 1967–74. An Opposition Whip, 1976–79; Parly Under-Sec. of State, Dept of Employment, 1979–81. Mem., Select Cttee on Foreign affairs, 1982–; Vice-Chm., All Party Gp on overseas develt, 1983–. Deleg. to Council of Europe and WEU, 1975–76. *Recreations:* reading, music, motor racing, travelling. *Address:* 4 Trevose House, Orsett Street, SE11.

LESTER, Richard; film director; *b* 19 Jan. 1932; *s* of Elliott and Ella Young Lester; *m* 1956, Deirdre Vivian Smith; one *s* one *d*. *Educ:* Wm Penn Charter Sch.; University of Pennsylvania (BSc). Television Director: CBS (USA), 1951–54; AR (Dir TV Goon Shows), 1956. Directed The Running, Jumping and Standing Still Film (Acad. Award nomination; 1st prize San Francisco Festival, 1960). *Feature Films directed:* It's Trad, Dad, 1962; Mouse on the Moon, 1963; A Hard Day's Night, 1964; The Knack, 1964 (Grand Prix, Cannes Film Festival); Help, 1965 (Best Film Award and Best Dir Award, Rio de Janeiro Festival); A Funny Thing Happened on the Way to the Forum, 1966; How I won the War, 1967; Petulia, 1968; The Bed Sitting Room, 1969 (Gandhi Peace Prize, Berlin Film Festival); The Three Musketeers, 1973; Juggernaut, 1974 (Best Dir award, Teheran Film Fest.); The Four Musketeers, 1974; Royal Flash, 1975; Robin and Marian, 1976; The Ritz, 1976; Butch and Sundance: the early days, 1979; Cuba, 1979; Superman II, 1981; Superman III, 1983; Finders Keepers, 1984; The Return of the Musketeers, 1989; Get Back, 1991. *Recreations:* composing, playing popular music. *Address:* Twickenham Film Studios, St Margaret's, Twickenham, Mddx.

LESTER SMITH, Ernest; *see* Smith, E. L.

LESTOR, Joan; MP (Lab) Eccles, since 1987; freelance lecturer; *b* Vancouver, British Columbia, Canada; one *s* one *d* (both adopted). *Educ:* Blaenavon Secondary Sch., Monmouth; William Morris Secondary Sch., Walthamstow; London Univ. Diploma in Sociology. Nursery Sch. Teacher, 1959–66. Chairman: Council, Nat. Soc. of Children's Nurseries, 1969–70; UK Branch, Defence for Children International; Member: Wandsworth Borough Council, 1958–68; LCC, 1962–64; Exec. Cttee of the London Labour Party, 1962–65; Nat. Exec., Labour Party, 1967–82 (Chm., 1977–78) and 1987–; Chm., Internat. Cttee, Labour Party, 1978–. MP (Lab) Eton and Slough, 1966–83; Parliamentary Under-Secretary: Dept of Educn and Science, Oct. 1969–June 1970; FCO, 1974–75; DES, 1975–76; resigned from Labour Govt on cuts policy, 1976; frontbench spokesperson on overseas aid and develt co-operation, 1988–89, on children's affairs, 1989–90 (backbench, 1990–). Contested (Lab): Lewisham W, 1964; Slough, 1983. Dir, Trade Unions Child Care Project, 1986–87. Co-Chm., Jt Cttee against Racialism, 1978–; Mem., CND Nat. Council, 1983–. *Recreations:* theatre, reading, playing with children and animals.

L'ETANG, Hugh Joseph Charles James; medical editor and writer; *b* 23 Nov. 1917; *s* of late Dr J. G. L'Etang and Frances L'Etang; *m* 1951, Cecily Margaret Tinker, MD, MRCP; one *s* one *d*. *Educ:* Haileybury Coll.; St John's Coll., Oxford; St Bartholomew's Hosp.; Harvard Sch. of Public Health. BA 1939, BM, BCh 1942, DIH 1952. War Service, 1943–46, RMO 5th Bn Royal Berks Regt; TA from 1947, RAMC; Lt-Col 1953–56. Medical Adviser: North Thames Gas Bd, 1948–56; British European Airways, 1956–58; John Wyeth & Brother Ltd, 1958–69; Asst and Dep. Editor, The Practitioner, 1969–72, Editor 1973–82. Hira S. Chouké Lectr, Coll. of Physicians of Philadelphia, 1972 (Hon. Fellow, 1985); Henry Cohen Hist. of Medicine Lectr, Univ. of Liverpool, 1986. Member: RUSI; IISS; Military Commentators' Circle; Amer. Civil War Round Table, London; Sherlock Holmes Soc. Editor, Travel Medicine International, 1983–; Consultant Editor, The Physician, 1983–; Editor-in-Chief: RSM International Congress and Symposium Series, 1983–89; RSM Round Table Series, 1989–. *Publications:* The Pathology of Leadership, 1969; Fit to Lead?, 1980; (ed) Regulation and Restraint in Contemporary Medicine in the UK and USA, 1983; (Consultant Editor) Fontana Dictionary of Modern Thought, 1988; (Specialist Corresp.) Chronicle of the 20th Century, 1988; (ed) Health Care Provision under Financial Constraint: a decade of change, 1990; articles in Practitioner, Jl RAMC, Jl RUSI, Army Qly, Brassey's Annual, Navy Internat., NATO's Fifteen Nations, Politics and the Life Sciences. *Recreation:* medical aspects of military and foreign affairs. *Address:* 27 Sispara Gardens, West Hill Road, SW18 1LG. *T:* 081–870 3836. *Club:* United Oxford & Cambridge University.

LETHBRIDGE, Sir Thomas (Periam Hector Noel), 7th Bt *cr* 1804; *b* 17 July 1950; *s* of Sir Hector Wroth Lethbridge, 6th Bt, and of Evelyn Diana, *d* of late Lt-Col Francis Arthur Gerard Noel, OBE; *S* father, 1978; *m* 1976, Susan Elizabeth Rocke; four *s* two *d*. *Educ:* Milton Abbey. Studied farming, Cirencester Agricultural Coll., 1969–70; Man. Dir, Art Gallery, Dorset and London, 1972–77; also fine art specialist in sporting paintings and engravings. *Recreations:* shooting, swimming, hunting. *Heir:* *s* John Francis Buckler Noel Lethbridge, *b* 10 March 1977. *Address:* Lloyds House, Honeymead, Simonsbath, Minehead, Somerset TA24 7JX. *Clubs:* Farmers', Naval and Military.

LE TOCQ, Eric George, CMG 1975; HM Diplomatic Service, retired; British Government Representative in the West Indies Associated States, 1975–78; *b* 20 April 1918; *s* of Eugene Charles Le Tocq; *m* 1946, Betty Esdaile; two *s* one *d*. *Educ:* Elizabeth Coll., Guernsey; Exeter Coll., Oxford (MA). Served War of 1939–45: commissioned in Royal Engineers, 1939; North Africa, 1942–43; Italy, 1943; Austria and Greece; major. Taught Modern Languages and Mathematics at Monmouth Sch., 1946–48; Assistant Principal, Commonwealth Relations Office, 1948; Karachi, 1948–50; Principal, 1950; Dublin, 1953–55; Accra, 1957–59; Assistant Secretary, 1962; Adviser on Commonwealth and External Affairs, Entebbe, 1962; Deputy High Commissioner, Uganda, 1962–64; Counsellor, British High Commission, Canberra, 1964–67; Head of E African Dept, FCO, 1968–71; High Comr in Swaziland, 1972–75. *Address:* Forest Edge, May Lane, Pilley, Hants SO41 5QR.

LETSON, Major-General Harry Farnham Germaine, CB 1946; CBE 1944; MC; ED; CD; *b* Vancouver, BC, 26 Sept. 1896; *e s* of late J. M. K. Letson, Vancouver, BC; *m* 1928, Sally Lang Nichol; no *c*. *Educ:* McGill Univ.; University of British Columbia; University of London. BSc (UBC) 1919; PhD (Eng) London, 1923. Active Service Canadian Army, 1916–19; Associate Professor Mechanical and Electrical Engineering, University of BC, 1923–36; on Active Service Canadian Army, 1939–46; Adjt-General Canadian Army, 1942–44; Commander of Canadian Army Staff in Washington, 1944–46; Secretary to Governor-General of Canada, 1946–52; Adviser on Militia, Canadian Army, 1954–58, retired. Hon. Colonel British Columbia Regt, 1963. LLD (University of BC), 1945. *Recreation:* fishing. *Address:* 474 Lansdowne Road, Ottawa K1M 0X9, Canada. *Clubs:* Rideau (Ottawa); Vancouver (Vancouver, BC).

LETTS, Anthony Ashworth; Chairman, Charles Letts Holdings Ltd, since 1977; *b* 3 July 1935; *s* of Leslie Charles Letts and Elizabeth Mary (*née* Gibson); *m* 1962, Rosa Maria Ciarrapico; one *s* one *d*. *Educ:* Marlborough Coll.; Cambridge Univ. (MAEcon); Yale Univ. (Industrial Admin). National Service, RE, 2 Lieut, 1954–56. Joined Charles Letts & Co. Ltd, 1960; Man. Dir, 1965. Charles Letts family business founded by John Letts (g g g grandfather), 1796. *Recreations:* tennis, sailing, hill walking, theatre. *Address:* Fairlight, Kingston Hill, Kingston upon Thames, Surrey KT2 7LX. *T:* 081–546 5757. *Club:* Hurlingham.

LETTS, Charles Trevor; Underwriting Member of Lloyd's, since 1944; Deputy Chairman of Lloyd's, 1966 (entered Lloyd's, 1924; Member, 1941; Committee, 1964–67); *b* 2 July 1905; *o s* of late Charles Hubert and Gertrude Letts; *m* 1942, Mary R. (Judy), *o d* of late Sir Stanley and late Lady (Hilda) Woodwark; two *s* one *d*. *Educ:* Marlborough Coll. Served RNVR, Lieut-Commander, 1940–45. Member: Cttee, Lloyd's Underwriters' Assoc., 1960–70 (Chairman, 1963–64); Council, Lloyd's Register of Shipping, 1964–77 (Chairman, Yacht Sub-Cttee, 1967–75); Salvage Association, 1963–70. Dir, Greig Fester (Agencies) Ltd, 1980–85. *Recreations:* sailing, golf. *Address:* Bearwood, Holtye, Edenbridge, Kent TN8 7EG. *T:* Cowden (0342) 850472. *Club:* Royal Ocean Racing.

LETWIN, Prof. William; Professor Emeritus, London School of Economics, since 1988; Senior Advisor, Putnam, Hayes & Bartlett, since 1988; Director, FPL Financial Ltd, since 1988; *b* 14 Dec. 1922; *s* of Lazar and Bessie Letwin; *m* 1944, Shirley Robin; one *s*. *Educ:* Univ. of Chicago (BA 1943, PhD 1951); London Sch. of Economics (1948–50). Served US Army, 1943–46. Postdoctoral Fellow, Economics Dept, Univ. of Chicago, 1951–52; Research Associate, Law Sch., Univ. of Chicago, 1953–55; Asst. Prof. of Industrial History, MIT, 1955–60; Associate Prof. of Economic History, MIT, 1960–67; Reader in Political Science, 1966–76, Prof. of Pol Science, 1976–88, LSE. Chm., Bd of Studies in Economics, Univ. of London, 1971–73. *Publications:* (ed) Frank Knight, on The History and Method of Economics, 1956; Sir Josiah Child, 1959; Documentary History of American Economic Policy, 1961, 2nd edn 1972; Origins of Scientific Economics 1660–1776, 1963; Law and Economic Policy in America, 1965; (ed) Against Equality, 1983; Freeing the Phones, 1991; articles in learned jls. *Address:* 15 Arlington Road, NW1 7ER. *T:* 071–387 6715.

LEUCHARS, Maj.-Gen. Peter Raymond, CBE 1966; Chief Commander, St John Ambulance, 1980–89 (Commissioner-in-Chief, 1978–80 and 1985–86); *b* 29 Oct. 1921; *s* of late Raymond Leuchars and Helen Inez Leuchars (*née* Copland-Griffiths); *m* 1953, Hon. Gillian Wightman Nivison, *d* of 2nd Baron Glendyne; one *s*. *Educ:* Bradfield College. Commnd in Welsh Guards, 1941; served in NW Europe and Italy, 1944–45; Adjt, 1st Bn Welsh Guards, Palestine, 1945–48; Bde Major, 4 Guards Bde, Germany, 1952–54; GSO1 (Instr.), Staff Coll., Camberley, 1956–59; GSO1 HQ 4 Div. BAOR, 1960–63; comd 1st Bn Welsh Guards, 1963–65; Principal Staff Off. to Dir of Ops, Borneo, 1965–66; comd 11 Armd Bde BAOR, 1966–68; comd Jt Operational Computer Projects Team, 1969–71; Dep. Comdt Staff Coll., Camberley, 1972–73; GOC Wales, 1973–76. Col, The Royal Welch Fusiliers, 1974–84. Pres., Guards' Golfing Soc., 1977. BGCStJ 1989. Order of Istiqlal (Jordan), 1946. *Recreations:* golf, shooting, travel, photography. *Address:* 5 Chelsea Square, SW3 6LF. *T:* 071–352 6187. *Clubs:* Royal and Ancient Golf; Royal Wimbledon Golf; Sunningdale Golf (Captain 1975).

LEUCHARS, Sir William (Douglas), KBE 1984 (MBE (mil.) 1959); ED (2 bars); Dominion President, New Zealand Returned Services Association Inc., 1974–88; *b* 8 Aug. 1920; *s* of late James and Isabella Leuchars; *m* 1947, Mary Isbister Walter; three *s* one *d*. *Educ:* Scots College, NZ. New Zealand Army: Territorial Force, 1939–41; NZEF (to Captain), 1941–46; NZ Scottish Regt, Territorial Force (to Lt-Col), 1946–71; Returned Services Association: Pres., Tawa Branch, Wellington RSA, 1949–60, Life Mem., 1981; Mem. Council, Wellington RSA, 1950–57, 1967–71, Life Mem., 1981 (Mem. numerous Cttees, 1955–); Mem., Dominion Exec. Cttee, 1965–68, Dominion Vice-Pres., 1968–74; NZRSA Rep. on numerous bodies and overseas confs; Gold Star and Cert. of Merit, 1966, Gold Badge and Life Mem., 1985, NZRSA. Chm., Scots Coll. Bd of Governors, 1974–91 (Mem., 1968–); Founder Trustee, Nat. Paraplegic Trust, 1973–90; President: Wellington Regional Employers' Assoc., 1975–77, 1983–84 (Mem., 1973–); NZ Employers' Fedn, 1984–86 (Mem. Exec., 1975–87; Vice-Pres., 1975–77, 1984); Director: Tolley & Son Ltd, 1957–66 (Chm., 1963–66); Tolley Holdings Ltd, 1963–85; Tolley Industries Ltd, 1966–82; ASEA Tolley Electric Co. (subseq. ASEA Electric Co. Ltd), 1985–88; Norwich Winterthur Insurance NZ Ltd, 1977–91. *Recreation:* bowling (Patron, Tawa Services Bowling). *Address:* 45 Lohia Street, Khandallah, Wellington 4, New Zealand. *T:* 792.391. *Clubs:* various service clubs, NZ.

LEUCKERT, Jean Elizabeth, (Mrs Harry Leuckert); *see* Muir, J. E.

LEUPENA, Sir Tupua, GCMG 1986; MBE 1977; Governor General of Tuvalu, 1986–90; *b* 2 Aug. 1922; *s* of Leupena Vaisua, Vaitupu, and Tolotea Vaisua (*née* Tavita), Niutao; *m* 1947, Annie Nitz, Vaitupu; four *s* three *d* (and one *s* decd). *Educ:* Ellice Is Govt Sch., Vaitupu; King George V Secondary Sch., Tarawa, Gilbert Is (now Republic of Kiribati). Clerk, Gilbert and Ellice Is Colony, 1941; Sgt, GEIC Labour Corps, 1944; Clerk 1945, Chief Clerk 1953, Resident Comr's office; transf. to Dist Admin as Asst Admin Officer, 1957, frequently serving in Gilbert Is and Ellice Is Dists, 1958–64 and 1967–69; District Commissioner: Phoenix Is Dist, 1965–66; Ocean Is, 1970–72; Dist Officer, Ellice Is District, 1973–75; acted as Sec. to Govt on Separation of Tuvalu from Kiribati in 1976 and retired from service same year; re-employed on contract as Sec. Reserved Subjects in Queen's Comr's Office, 1977; Speaker of Tuvalu Parlt, 1978; Man., Vaitupu's Private Commercial Enterprise, 1979–81; Chm., Tuvalu's Public Service Commn, 1982–86. *Recreations:* fishing, gardening, cricket, football. *Address:* Vaiaku, Funafuti Island, Tuvalu. *T:* 714.

LEUTWILER, Fritz, PhD; Chairman of the Board of Directors, BBC Brown, Boveri Ltd, Baden, since 1985; Co-Chairman of the Board of Directors, ABB Asea Brown Boveri Ltd, Zurich, since 1988; *b* 30 July 1924; *m* 1951, Andrée Cottier; one *s* one *d*. *Educ:* Univ. of Zürich (PhD 1948). Sec., Assoc. for a Sound Currency, 1948–52; Swiss National Bank, Zürich: Econ. Scientist, 1952–59; Manager, 1959–66; Dep. Gen. Man., 1966–68; Mem., Governing Bd, and Head, Dept III, 1968–74; Chm., Governing Bd, and Head, Dept I, 1974–84; Chm. and Pres., BIS, Basle, 1982–84. Hon. Dr: Berne, 1978; Zürich, 1983;

Lausanne, 1984. *Recreations:* golf; collector of rare books (Helvetica, Economica). *Address:* Zumikon, Switzerland. *Club:* Golf and Country (Zumikon).

LEVEN, 14th Earl of, **AND MELVILLE,** 13th Earl of, *cr* 1641; **Alexander Robert Leslie Melville;** Baron Melville, 1616; Baron Balgonie, 1641; Earl of Melville, Viscount Kirkcaldie, 1690; Lord-Lieutenant of Nairn since 1969; *b* 13 May 1924; *e s* of 13th Earl and Lady Rosamond Sylvia Diana Mary Foljambe (*d* 1974), *d* of 1st Earl of Liverpool; *S* father, 1947; *m* 1953, Susan, *er d* of Lieut-Colonel R. Steuart-Menzies of Culdares, Arndilly House, Craigellachie, Banffshire; two *s* one *d*. *Educ:* Eton. ADC to Governor General of New Zealand, 1951–52. Formerly Capt. Coldstream Guards; retired, 1952. Vice-Pres., Highland Dist TA. Pres., British Ski Fedn, 1981–85. DL, County of Nairn, 1961; Convener, Nairn CC, 1970–74. Chm. Governors, Gordonstoun Sch., 1971–89. *Heir: s* Lord Balgonie, *qv*. *Address:* Glenferness House, Nairn IV12 5VP. *T:* Glenferness (03095) 202. *Club:* New (Edinburgh).

LEVENE, Ben, RA 1986 (ARA 1975); painter; *b* 23 Dec. 1938; *s* of Mark and Charlotte Levene. *Educ:* Slade School (DFA). Boise Scholarship, 1961; lived in Spain, 1961–62. First one-man show, Thackeray Gall., 1973; shows at Browse & Darby, London, 1986–. *Address:* c/o Royal Academy of Arts, Piccadilly, W1.

LEVENE, Prof. Malcolm Irvin, MD; FRCP; Professor of Paediatrics and Child Health, University of Leeds, since 1989; *b* 2 Jan. 1951; *s* of Maurice Levene and Helen Levene (*née* Kutner); *m* 1st, 1972, Miriam Bentley (marr. diss. 1990); three *d*; 2nd, 1991, Susan Anne Cave. *Educ:* Varndean Grammar Sch., Brighton; Guy's Hosp. Med. Sch., London Univ. (MB BS 1972); MD 1981. MRCS, LRCP, 1972; MRCP 1978; FRCP 1988. Junior posts at Royal Sussex, Northampton General and Charing Cross Hosps, 1974–77; Registrar, Derby Children's and Charing Cross Hosps, 1977–79; Res. Lectr, RPMS, Hammersmith Hosp., 1979–82; Sen. Lectr and Reader, Dept of Paediatrics, Univ. of Leicester, 1982–88. Hancock Prize, RCS, 1974; British Paediatric Association: Donald Paterson Prize, 1982; Michael Blecklow Meml Prize, 1982; Guthrie Medal, 1987; Ronnie MacKeith Prize, British Paed. Neurology Assoc., 1984; BUPA Res. Prize, 1988. *Publications:* (with H. Nutbeam) A Handbook for Examinations in Paediatrics, 1981; (jtly) Ultrasound of the Infant Brain, 1985; (jtly) Essentials of Neonatal Medicine, 1987; (ed jtly) Fetal and Neonatal Neurology and Neurosurgery, 1988; Diseases of Children, 6th edn, 1990; chapters in books and articles in learned jls on paed. topics, esp. neurology of new-born. *Recreations:* music, occasional gentle golf and gardening. *Address:* Monkswood, 45 Vesper Road, Leeds LS5 3QT. *T:* Leeds (0532) 755337.

LEVENE, Sir Peter (Keith), KBE 1989; Deputy Chairman, Wasserstein Perella & Co. International Ltd, since 1991; Special Adviser to Secretary of State for the Environment, since 1991; *b* 8 Dec. 1941; *s* of late Maurice Levene and Rose Levene; *m* 1966, Wendy Ann (*née* Fraiman); two *s* one *d*. *Educ:* City of London School; Univ. of Manchester. BA Econ. Joined United Scientific Holdings, 1963; Man. Dir, 1968–85; Chm., 1982–85; Chief of Defence Procurement, MoD, 1985–91; UK Nat. Armaments Dir, 1988–91; Chm., European Nat. Armaments Dirs, 1989–90. Member: SE Asia Trade Adv. Group, 1979–83; Council, Defence Manufacturers' Assoc., 1982–85 (Vice-Chm., 1983–84; Chm., 1984–85); Personal Adviser to Sec. of State for Defence, 1984. Mem., Bd of Management, London Homes for the Elderly, 1984–91 (Chm., 1990–91). Governor: City of London Sch. for Girls, 1984–85; City of London Sch., 1986–; Sir John Cass Primary Sch., 1985– (Dep. Chm., 1990–). Mem. Court, HAC, 1984–; Mem., Court of Common Council, City of London, 1983–84 (Ward of Candlewick); Alderman (Ward of Portsoken), 1984–; Liveryman, Carmen's Co., 1984– (Hon. Mem., Ct of Assistants, 1987–). CBIM, FRSA. *Recreations:* skiing, watching association football, travel. *Address:* c/o Wasserstein Perella & Co. International Ltd, 10–11 Park Place, SW1A 1LP. *Clubs:* Guildhall, City Livery.

LEVENTHAL, Colin David; Director of Acquisition and Sales, Channel Four Television Co. Ltd, since 1987; Director, Channel Four Television Co. Ltd, since 1988; *b* 2 Nov. 1946; *s* of Morris and Olga Leventhal. *Educ:* Carmel Coll., Wallingford, Berks; King's Coll., Univ. of London (BA Philosophy). Solicitor of Supreme Court of England and Wales. Admitted Solicitor, 1971; BBC, 1974–81: Asst Head of Programme Contracts, 1977; Head of Copyright, 1978; Head of Prog. Acquisition, Channel Four TV, 1981–87. *Recreations:* theatre, film. *Address:* 60 Charlotte Street, W1. *T:* 071–631 4444.

LEVER, family name of **Baron Lever of Manchester** and of **Viscount Leverhulme.**

LEVER OF MANCHESTER, Baron *cr* 1979 (Life Peer), of Cheetham in the City of Manchester; **Harold Lever,** PC 1969; *b* Manchester, 15 Jan. 1914; *s* of late Bernard and Bertha Lever; *m* 1962, Diane, *d* of Saleh Bashi; three *d* (and one *d* from late wife). *Educ:* Manchester Grammar Sch.; Manchester Univ. Called to Bar, Middle Temple, 1935. MP (Lab) Manchester Exchange, 1945–50, Manchester, Cheetham, 1950–74, Manchester Central, 1974–79. Promoted Defamation Act, 1952, as a Private Member's Bill. Joint Parliamentary Under-Secretary, Dept of Economic Affairs, 1967; Financial Sec. to Treasury, Sept. 1967–69; Paymaster General, 1969–70; Mem., Shadow Cabinet, 1970–74; Chancellor of the Duchy of Lancaster, 1974–79. Chm., Public Accounts Cttee, 1970–73. Chairman: SDS Bank Ltd (formerly London Interstate Bank) (Sparekassen SDS), 1984–90; Stormgard, 1985–87; Pres., Authority Investments PLC, 1986–91 (Chm., 1984–86); Mem., Internat. Adv. Bd, Creditanstalt-Bankverein, 1982–90; Director: The Guardian and Manchester Evening News, 1979–90; INVESCO MIM (formerly Britannia Arrow Hldgs), 1983–. Treasurer, Socialist International, 1971–73. Governor: LSE, 1971–; ESU, 1973–86; Trustee, Royal Opera House, 1974–82; Mem. Ct, Manchester Univ., 1975–. Hon. Fellow, and Chm. Trustees, Royal Acad., 1981–87. Hon. doctorates in Law, Science, Literature and Technology. Grand Cross, Order of Merit, Germany, 1979. *Publication:* (jtly) Debt and Danger, 1985. *Address:* House of Lords, SW1.

LEVER, Sir Christopher; *see* Lever, Sir T. C. A. L.

LEVER, Jeremy Frederick; QC 1972; *b* 23 June 1933; *s* of late A. Lever. *Educ:* Bradfield Coll.; University Coll., Oxford; Nuffield Coll., Oxford. Served RA, 1951–53. 1st cl. Jurisprudence, 1956, MA Oxon; Pres., Oxford Union Soc., 1957, Trustee, 1972–77 and 1988–. Fellow, All Souls Coll., Oxford, 1957– (Sub-Warden, 1982–84; Sen. Dean, 1988–). Called to Bar, Gray's Inn, 1957, Bencher, 1985. Mem. Council, British Inst. of Internat. and Comparative Law, 1987–. Director (non-exec.): Dunlop Holdings Ltd, 1973–80; Wellcome plc, 1983–. Mem., Arbitral Tribunal, US/UK Arbitration concerning Heathrow Airport User Charges, 1989–. Governor, Berkhamsted Schs, 1985–. *Publications:* The Law of Restrictive Practices, 1964; other legal works. *Recreations:* walking, music. *Address:* 4 Raymond Buildings, Gray's Inn, WC1R 5BP. *T:* 071–405 7211, *Fax:* 071–405 2084. *Club:* Garrick.

LEVER, (John) Michael, QC 1977; **His Honour Judge Lever;** a Circuit Judge, since 1981; *b* 12 Aug. 1928; *s* of late John and Ida Donaldson Lever; *m* 1964, Elizabeth Marr; two *s*. *Educ:* Bolton Sch.; Gonville and Caius Coll., Cambridge (Schol.). BA (1st cl. hons Law Tripos), 1949. Flying Officer, RAF, 1950–52. Called to Bar, Middle Temple, 1951 (Blackstone Schol.); practised Northern Circuit from 1952; Asst Recorder, Salford, 1969–71; a Recorder of the Crown Court, 1972–81. Governor, Bolton Sch. *Recreations:* theatre, fell-walking. *Address:* Lakelands, Rivington, near Bolton, Lancs BL6 7RT.

LEVER, Paul, CMG 1991; Ambassador and Head, UK Delegation to Conventional Arms Control Negotiations, Vienna, since 1990; *b* 31 March 1944; *s* of John Morrison Lever and Doris Grace (*née* Battey); *m* 1990, Patricia Anne, *d* of John and Anne Ramsey. *Educ:* St Paul's Sch.; The Queen's Coll., Oxford (MA). 3rd Secretary, Foreign and Commonwealth Office, 1966–67; 3rd, later 2nd Secretary, Helsinki, 1967–71; 2nd, later 1st Secretary, UK Delegn to NATO, 1971–73; FCO, 1973–81; Asst Private Sec. to Sec. of State for Foreign and Commonwealth Affairs, 1978–81; Chef de Cabinet to Christopher Tugendhat, Vice-Pres. of EEC, 1982–84; Head of UN Dept, FCO, 1985–86; Head of Defence Dept, 1986–87; Head of Security Policy Dept, FCO, 1987–90. *Recreations:* squash, walking, art deco pottery. *Address:* c/o Foreign and Commonwealth Office, SW1A 2AH; Mas La Nogarède, 66150 Montferrer, France.

LEVER, Sir (Tresham) Christopher (Arthur Lindsay), 3rd Bt *cr* 1911; *b* 9 Jan. 1932; *s* of Sir Tresham Joseph Philip Lever, FRSL, 2nd Bt, and Frances Yowart (*d* 1959), *d* of Lindsay Hamilton Goodwin; step *s* of Pamela Lady Lever, *d* of late Lt-Col Hon. Malcolm Bowes Lyon; *S* father, 1975; *m* 1st, 1970; 2nd, 1975, Linda Weightman McDowell, *d* of late James Jepson Goulden, Tennessee, USA. *Educ:* Eton; Trinity Coll., Cambridge (BA 1954, MA 1957). MBOU; FLS. Commissioned, 17th/21st Lancers, 1950. Peat, Marwick, Mitchell & Co., 1954–55; Kitcat & Aitken, 1955–56; Dir, John Barran & Sons Ltd, 1956–64. Consultant, Zoo Check Charitable Trust, 1984–; Chairman: African Fund for Endangered Wildlife (UK), 1987–90; Mem., IUCN Species Survival Commn, 1988–; Trustee: Internat. Trust for Nature Conservation, 1980– (Vice-Pres. 1986–); Migraine Trust, 1983–89; Rhino Rescue Trust, 1986–91 (Patron 1985–); Nat. Eczema Soc., 1989–; Chm. and Patron, Tusk Trust, 1990–; Chm., Ruaha Trust, 1990–; Member Council: Soc. for Protection of Animals in N Africa, 1986–88; British Trust for Ornithology, 1988–91 (Chm., Nat. Centre Appeal, 1987–92); Patron, Lynx Educnl Trust for Animal Welfare, 1991–. Hon. Life Mem., Brontë Soc., 1988. *Publications:* Goldsmiths and Silversmiths of England, 1975; The Naturalized Animals of the British Isles, 1977; (contrib.) Wildlife '80: the world conservation yearbook, 1980; (contrib.) Evolution of Domesticated Animals, 1984; Naturalized Mammals of the World, 1985; Naturalized Birds of the World, 1987; (contrib.) Beyond the Bars: the zoo dilemma, 1987; (contrib.) For the Love of Animals, 1989; The Mandarin Duck, 1990; They Dined on Eland: the story of the acclimatisation societies, 1992; contribs to various fine art, scientific and general publications. *Recreations:* watching and photographing wildlife, golf, fishing. *Heir:* none. *Address:* Newell House, Winkfield, Windsor, Berks SL4 4SE. *T:* Winkfield Row (0344) 882604. *Club:* Buck's.

LEVERHULME, 3rd Viscount, *cr* 1922, of the Western Isles; **Philip William Bryce Lever,** KG 1988; TD; Baron, *cr* 1917; Bt, *cr* 1911; Knight of Order of St John of Jerusalem; Major, Cheshire Yeomanry; Lord-Lieutenant of City and County of Chester, 1949–90; Advisory Director of Unilever Ltd; Chancellor of Liverpool University, since 1980; *b* 1 July 1915; *s* of 2nd Viscount and Marion, *d* of late Bryce Smith of Manchester; *S* father, 1949; *m* 1937, Margaret Ann (*d* 1973), *o c* of John Moon, Tiverton; three *d*. *Educ:* Eton; Trinity Coll., Cambridge. Hon. Air Commodore 663 Air OP Squadron, RAuxAF; Hon. Air Commodore 610 (County of Chester) Squadron, Royal Auxiliary Air Force; Dep. Hon. Col, Cheshire Yeomanry, T&AVR, 1971–72, Hon. Col, 1972–81; Hon. Col, The Queen's Own Yeomanry, 1979–81. Pres. Council, Liverpool Univ., 1957–63, Sen. Pro-Chancellor, 1963–66. Member: National Hunt Cttee, 1961 (Steward, 1965–68); Deputy Senior Steward, Jockey Club, 1970–73, Senior Steward, 1973–76; Council of King George's Jubilee Trust; Chairman, Exec. Cttee Animal Health Trust, 1964. Hon. FRCS 1970; Hon. ARCVS 1975. Hon. LLD Liverpool, 1967. *Recreations:* shooting, fishing. *Heir:* none. *Address:* Thornton Manor, Thornton Hough, Wirral, Merseyside L63 1JB; Badanloch, Kinbrace, Sutherland; Flat 6, Kingston House East, Prince's Gate, Kensington, SW7 1LJ. *Clubs:* Boodle's, Jockey.

LEVERSEDGE, Leslie Frank, CMG 1955; MA Cantab; Economic Secretary to Northern Rhodesia Government, 1956–60, retired; *b* 29 May 1904; *s* of F. E. Leversedge, UP, India; *m* 1945, Eileen Melegueta Spencer Payne; two *s* three *d*. *Educ:* St Paul's Sch., Darjeeling, India; St Peter's Sch., York; St John's Coll., Cambridge; Inner Temple, London. Cadet in Colonial Administrative Service, Northern Rhodesia, Dec. 1926; District Officer, Dec. 1928; Provincial Commissioner, Jan. 1947; Senior Provincial Commissioner, Dec. 1948. Development Secretary to Northern Rhodesia Government, 1951–56. MLC 1951; MEC 1951. British Council Local Correspondent for Kent, 1963–75. FRSA 1973. *Recreations:* walking, overseas travelling. *Address:* 24 Ashley Brake, West Hill, Ottery St Mary, Devon EX11 1TW. *T:* Ottery St Mary (0404) 813956.

LEVERTON, Colin Allen H.; *see* Hart-Leverton.

LEVESON, Lord; Granville George Fergus Leveson Gower; *b* 10 Sept. 1959; *s* and *heir* of 5th Earl Granville, *qv*.

LEVESON, Brian Henry; QC 1986; a Recorder, since 1988; *b* 22 June 1949; *er s* of late Dr Ivan Leveson and Elaine Leveson, Liverpool; *m* 1981, Lynne Rose (*née* Fishel); two *s* one *d*. *Educ:* Liverpool College, Liverpool; Merton College, Oxford (MA). Called to the Bar, Middle Temple, 1970; Harmsworth Scholar, 1970; practised Northern Circuit, 1971; University of Liverpool: Lectr in Law, 1971–81; Mem. Council, 1983–. *Recreation:* golf. *Address:* 5 Essex Court, Temple, EC4Y 9AH. *T:* 071–353 4363; 25 Byrom Street, Manchester M3 4PF. *T:* 061–834 5238. *Club:* Athenæum (Liverpool).

LEVESON GOWER, family name of **Earl Granville.**

LEVESQUE, Most Rev. Louis, ThD; Archbishop Emeritus of Rimouski, since 1973; *b* 27 May 1908; *s* of Philippe Levesque and Catherine Levesque (*née* Beaulieu). *Educ:* Laval Univ. Priest, 1932; Bishop of Hearst, Ontario, 1952–64; Archbishop of Rimouski, 1967–73. Chm., Canadian Cath. Conf., 1965–67; Mem. Congregation Bishops, Rome, 1968–73. *Address:* 300 avenue du Rosaire, Rimouski, PQ G5L 3E3, Canada.

LEVEY, Sir Michael (Vincent), Kt 1981; LVO 1965; MA Oxon and Cantab; FRSL; FBA 1983; Director of the National Gallery, 1973–87 (Deputy Director, 1970–73); *b* 8 June 1927; *s* of O. L. H. Levey and Gladys Mary Milestone; *m* 1954, Brigid Brophy, *qv*; one *d*. *Educ:* Oratory Sch.; Exeter Coll., Oxford, Hon. Fellow, 1973. Served with Army, 1945–48; commissioned, KSLI, 1946, and attached RAEC, Egypt. National Gallery: Asst Keeper, 1951–66, Dep. Keeper, 1966–68, Keeper, 1968–73. Slade Professor of Fine Art, Cambridge, 1963–64; Supernumerary Fellow, King's Coll., Cambridge, 1963–64; Hon. Fellow, Royal Acad., 1986; Foreign Mem., Ateneo Veneto, 1986. Hon. DLitt Manchester, 1989. *Publications:* Six Great Painters, 1956; National Gallery Catalogues: 18th Century Italian Schools, 1956; The German School, 1959; Painting in 18th Century Venice, 1959, rev. edn 1980; From Giotto to Cézanne, 1962; Dürer, 1964; The Later Italian Paintings in the Collection of HM The Queen, 1964, rev. edn 1991; Canaletto Paintings in the Royal Collection, 1964; Tiepolo's Banquet of Cleopatra (Charlton Lecture, 1962), 1966; Rococo to Revolution, 1966; Bronzino (The Masters), 1967; Early Renaissance, 1967 (Hawthornden Prize, 1968); Fifty Works of English Literature We Could Do Without (co-author), 1967; Holbein's Christina of Denmark, Duchess of Milan, 1968; A History of Western Art, 1968; Painting at Court (Wrightsman Lectures), 1971; 17th and 18th

Century Italian Schools (Nat. Gall. catalogue), 1971; The Life and Death of Mozart, 1971, 2nd edn 1988; The Nude: Themes and Painters in the National Gallery, 1972; (co-author) Art and Architecture in 18th Century France, 1972; The Venetian Scene (Themes and Painters Series), 1973; Botticelli (Themes and Painters Series), 1974; High Renaissance, 1975; The World of Ottoman Art, 1976; Jacob van Ruisdael (Themes and Painters Series), 1977; The Case of Walter Pater, 1978; Sir Thomas Lawrence (Nat. Portrait Gall. exhibn), 1979; The Painter Depicted (Neurath Lect.), 1981; Tempting Fate (fiction), 1982; An Affair on the Appian Way (fiction), 1984; (ed) Pater's Marius the Epicurean, 1985; Giambattista Tiepolo, 1986 (Banister Fletcher Prize, 1987); The National Gallery Collection: a selection, 1987; Men at Work (fiction), 1989; (ed) The Soul of the Eye: anthology of painters and painting, 1990; contributions Burlington Magazine, etc. *Address:* 36 Little Lane, Louth, Lincs LN11 9DU.

LEVI, Prof. Edward Hirsch; Glen A. Lloyd Distinguished Service Professor, University of Chicago, 1977–84, now Emeritus; *b* 26 June 1911; *s* of Gerson B. Levi and Elsa B. Levi (*née* Hirsch); *m* 1946, Kate Sulzberger; three *s*. *Educ:* Univ. of Chicago; Yale Univ. Law Sch. Univ. of Chicago: Asst Prof. of Law, 1936–40; Prof. of Law, 1945–75; Dean of the Law School, 1950–62; Provost, 1962–68; President, 1968–75; Pres. emeritus, 1975; Attorney-Gen. of US, 1975–77. Public Dir, Chicago Bd of Trade, 1977–80. Herman Phleger Vis. Prof., Stanford Law Soc., 1978. Special Asst to Attorney-Gen., Washington, DC, 1940–45; 1st Asst, War Div., Dept of Justice, 1943; 1st Asst, Anti-trust Div., 1944–45; Chm., Interdeptl Cttee on Monopolies and Cartels, 1944; Counsel, Subcttee on Monopoly Power Judiciary Cttee, 81st Congress, 1950; Chm., Council on Educn in Professional Responsibility, 1965–69; Member: Nat. Council on Legal Clinics, 1960–76; White House Task Force on Educn, 1966–67; President's Task Force on Priorities in Higher Educn, 1969–70; White House Central Gp in Domestic Affairs, 1964; Citizens Commn on Graduate Medical Educn, 1963–66; Sloan Commn on Cable Communications, 1970–71; Nat. Commn on Productivity, 1970–75; Commn on Foundations and Private Philanthropy, 1969–70; Martin Luther King, Jr, Federal Holiday Commn, 1985–86. Mem. Council, American Law Inst., 1965–; American Bar; Illinois Bar; Chicago Bar; Supreme Court, 1945–; Amer. Judicature Soc.; Council on Legal Educn for Profl. Responsibility, 1968–74; Order of Coif; Phi Beta Kappa; res. adv. bd, Commn Econ. Develt, 1951–54; bd Dirs, SSRC, 1959–62; Nat. Commn on Productivity, 1970–75; Nat. Council on the Humanities, 1974–75. Dir Emeritus, MacArthur Foundn, 1984– (Dir, 1979–84); Trustee: Internat. Legal Center; Museum of Science and Industry, 1971–75; Russell Sage Foundn, 1971–75; Aspen Inst. for Humanist Studies, 1970–75, 1977–79; Univ. Chicago, 1966; Woodrow Wilson Nat. Fellowship Foundn, 1972–75, 1977–79; Inst. Psycho-analysis, Chicago, 1961–75; Skadden Fellowship Foundn, 1988–; Member Board of Trustees: Nat. Humanities Center, 1978– (Chm., 1979–83); The Aerospace Corp., 1978–80 (Life Trustee, 1989); William Benton Foundn, 1980–; Mem. Bd of Dirs, Continental Illinois Holding Corp., 1985–. Salzburg Seminar in Amer. Studies, 1980; Mem. Bd of Overseers, Univ. of Pennsylvania Law Sch., 1978–82; Mem. Bd of Governors, Univ. of Calif Humanities Res. Inst., 1988–; Pres., Amer. Acad. of Arts and Scis, 1986–89; Hon. Trustee: Inst. of Internat. Educn; Univ. of Chicago, 1975. Fellow: Amer. Bar Foundn; Amer. Acad. Arts and Scis; Amer. Philos. Soc. Chubb Fellow, Yale, 1977. Hon. degrees: LHD: Hebrew Union Coll.; Loyola Univ.; DePaul Univ.; Kenyon Coll.; Univ. of Chicago; Bard Coll.; Beloit Coll.; LLD: Univ. of Michigan; Univ. of California at Santa Cruz; Univ. of Iowa; Jewish Theological Seminary of America; Brandeis Univ.; Lake Forest Coll.; Univ. of Rochester; Univ. of Toronto; Yale Univ.; Notre Dame; Denison Univ., Nebraska Univ. Law Sch.; Univ. of Miami; Boston Coll.; Ben N. Cardozo Sch. of Law, Yeshiva Univ., NYC; Columbia Univ., Dropsie Univ., Pa; Univ. of Pa Law Sch.; Brigham Young Univ.; Duke Univ.; Ripon Coll.; Georgetown Univ.; Claremont Univ. Center and Grad. Sch.; DCL NY Univ. Legion of Honour (France); Chicago Bar Assoc. Centennial Award, 1975; Distinguished Citizen Award, Ill St Andrews Soc., 1976; Herbert H. Lehman Ethics Medal, Jewish Theol. Seminary, 1976; Learned Hand Medal, Fedn Bar Council, NYC, 1976; Wallace Award, Amer.-Scottish Foundn, 1976; Morris J. Kaplun Meml Prize, Dropsie, 1976; Fed. Bar Assoc. Award, 1977; Fordham-Stein Prize, Fordham, 1977; Citation of Merit, Yale, 1977; Louis Dembitz Brandeis Award, 1978; Illinois Bar Assoc. Award of Honor, 1983. *Publications:* Introduction to Legal Reasoning, 1949; Four Talks on Legal Education, 1952; Point of View, 1969; The Crisis in the Nature of Law, 1969; Elements of the Law (ed, with Roscoe Steffen), 1936; Gilbert's Collier on Bankruptcy (ed, with James W. Moore), 1936; Member, editorial board: Jl Legal Educn, 1956–68; Encyclopaedia Britannica, 1968–75. *Address:* (office) 1116 East 59th Street, Chicago, Illinois 60637, USA. *T:* (312) 702–8588; (home) 4950 Chicago Beach Drive, Chicago, Illinois 60615. *Clubs:* Quadrangle, Columbia Yacht, Mid-America (Chicago); Commercial, Century (New York); Chicago (DC).

LEVI, Peter Chad Tigar, FSA; FRSL; Professor of Poetry, University of Oxford, 1984–89; Fellow of St Catherine's College, Oxford, 1977–91; *b* 16 May 1931; *s* of Herbert Simon Levi and Edith Mary Tigar; *m* 1977, Deirdre, *o d* of Hon. Dennis Craig, MBE, and *widow* of Cyril Connolly, CBE, CLit. *Educ:* Beaumont; Oxford Univ. (MA). FSA 1976; FRSL 1985. Society of Jesus, 1948–77: priest, 1964; resigned priesthood, 1977. Tutor and Lectr in Classics, Campion Hall, Oxford, 1965–77; student, Brit. Sch. of Archaeol., Athens, 1965–68; Lectr in Classics, Christ Church, Oxford, 1979–82. The Times Archaeol Correspondent, 1977–78. Mem., Kingman Cttee on English, 1987–88. Corres. mem., Soc. of Greek Writers, 1983. Television films: Ruined Abbeys, 1966; Foxes have holes, 1967; Seven black years, 1975; presenter of TV series, Art, Faith and Vision, 1989. *Publications: poetry:* The Gravel Ponds, 1960; Water, Rock and Sand, 1962; The Shearwaters, 1965; Fresh Water, Sea Water, 1966; Ruined Abbeys, 1968; Pancakes for the Queen of Babylon, 1968; Life is a Platform, 1971; Death is a Pulpit, 1971; Collected Poems, 1976; Five Ages, 1978; Private Ground, 1981; The Echoing Green, 1983; (ed) The Penguin Book of English Christian Verse, 1985; Shakespeare's Birthday, 1985; (ed) New Verses by Shakespeare, 1988; Shadow and Bone, 1989; Goodbye to the Art of Poetry, 1989; *prose:* Beaumont, 1961; *Ὁ τόνος τῆς φωνῆς τοῦ Σεφέρη* (Mr Seferis' Tone of Voice), 1970; The Lightgarden of the Angel King, 1973; The English Bible (1534–1859), 1974; In Memory of David Jones, 1975; John Clare and Thomas Hardy, 1975; The Noise made by Poems, 1976; The Hill of Kronos, 1980; Atlas of the Greek World, 1980; The Flutes of Autumn, 1983; (ed) Johnson and Boswell, Western Islands, 1984; The Lamentation of the Dead, 1984; A History of Greek Literature, 1985; The Frontiers of Paradise: a study of monks and monasteries, 1987; Life and Times of Shakespeare, 1988; To the Goat (novella), 1988; Boris Pasternak, 1990; The Art of Poetry (lectures), 1991; *thrillers:* The Head in the Soup, 1979; Grave Witness, 1985; Knit One, Drop One, 1987; (with Cyril Connolly) Shade Those Laurels, 1990; *translations:* Yevtushenko, 1962; Pausanias, 1971; Pavlopoulos, The Cellar, 1976; The Psalms, 1976; Marko the Prince (Serbo-Croat heroic verse), 1983; Papadiamantis, The Murderess, 1983; The Holy Gospel of John, a New Translation, 1985. *Recreations:* elderly. *Address:* Prospect Cottage, The Green, Frampton on Severn, Glos. *Club:* Beefsteak.

LEVI, Renato, (Sonny), RDI 1987; freelance powerboat designer; *b* 3 Sept. 1926; *s* of Mario Levi and Eleonora Ciravegna; *m* 1954, Ann Watson; two *s* one *d*. *Educ:* Collège de Cannes; St Paul's, Darjeeling. Over 30 years contributing to development of fast planing craft. *Publication:* Dhows to Deltas, 1971. *Recreation:* the Far East. *Address:* Sandhills, Porchfield, Isle of Wight PO30 4LH. *T:* Isle of Wight (0983) 524713. *Club:* Royal London Yacht (Cowes).

LEVI-MONTALCINI, Prof. Rita; research scientist; *b* 22 April 1909; *d* of Adamo Levi and Adele Montalcini; *Educ:* Turin Univ. Med. Sch. Neurological research, Turin and Brussels, 1936–41, Piemonte, 1941–43; in hiding in Florence, 1943–44; worked among war refugees, Florence, 1944–45; Univ. of Turin, 1945; with Prof. Viktor Hamburger, St Louis, USA, at Washington Univ., 1947–77 (Associate Prof., 1956, Prof., 1958–77); Dir, Inst. of Cell Biology, Italian Nat. Council of Research, Rome, 1969–79, Guest Prof., 1979–. (Jtly) Nobel Prize for Physiology or Medicine, 1986. *Publications:* articles in learned jls on chemical growth factors controlling growth and development of different cell lines. *Address:* Institute of Neurobiology, CNR, Viale Marx 15, 00156 Rome, Italy.

LÉVI-STRAUSS, Claude; Grand Croix de la Légion d'Honneur, 1991; Commandeur, Ordre Nationale du Mérite, 1971; Member of French Academy, since 1973; Professor, Collège de France, 1959–82, Hon. Professor, since 1983; *b* 28 Nov. 1908; *s* of Raymond Lévi-Strauss and Emma Lévy; *m* 1st, 1932, Dina Dreyfus; 2nd, 1946, Rose-Marie Ullmo; one *s*; 3rd, 1954, Monique Roman; one *s*. *Educ:* Lycée Janson-de-Sailly, Paris; Sorbonne. Prof., Univ. of São Paulo, Brazil, 1935–39; Vis. Prof., New School for Social Research, NY, 1941–45; Cultural Counsellor, French Embassy, Washington, 1946–47; Associate Curator, Musée de l'Homme, Paris, 1948–49. Corresp. Member: Royal Acad. of Netherlands; Norwegian Acad.; British Acad.; Nat. Acad. of Sciences, USA; Amer. Acad. and Inst. of Arts and Letters; Amer. Philos. Soc.; Royal Anthrop. Inst. of Great Britain; London Sch. of African and Oriental Studies. Hon. Dr: Brussels, 1962; Oxford, 1964; Yale, 1965; Chicago, 1967; Columbia, 1971; Stirling, 1972; Univ. Nat. du Zaïre, 1973; Uppsala, 1977; Johns Hopkins, 1978; Laval, 1979; Mexico, 1979; Visva Bharati, India, 1980; Harvard, 1986. *Publications:* La Vie familiale et sociale des Indiens Nambikwara, 1948; Les Structures élémentaires de la parenté, 1949 (The Elementary Structures of Kinship, 1969); Race et histoire, 1952; Tristes Tropiques, 1955 (A World on the Wane, 1961; complete English edn as Tristes Tropiques, 1973); Anthropologie structurale, Vol. 1, 1958, Vol. 2, 1973 (Structural Anthropology, Vol. 1, 1964, Vol. 2, 1977); Le Totémisme aujourd'hui, 1962 (Totemism, 1963); La Pensée sauvage, 1962 (The Savage Mind, 1966); Le Cru et le cuit, 1964 (The Raw and the Cooked, 1970); Du Miel aux cendres, 1967 (From Honey to Ashes, 1973); L'Origine des manières de table, 1968 (The Origin of Table Manners, 1978); L'Homme nu, 1971 (The Naked Man, 1981); La Voie des masques, 1975 (The Way of the Masks, 1982); Le Regard éloigné, 1983 (The View from Afar, 1985); Paroles Données, 1984 (Anthropology and Myth, 1987); La Potière Jalouse, 1985 (The Jealous Potter, 1988); (with D. Eribon) De Près et de loin, 1988; *relevant publications:* Conversations with Lévi-Strauss (ed G. Charbonnier), 1969; by Octavio Paz: On Lévi-Strauss, 1970; Claude Lévi-Strauss: an introduction, 1972. *Address:* 2 rue des Marronniers, 75016 Paris, France. *T:* 42.88.34.71.

LEVICK, William Russell, FRS 1982; FAA; Professor, John Curtin School of Medical Research, Australian National University, since 1983; *b* 5 Dec. 1931; *s* of Russell L. S. Levick and Elsie E. I. (*née* Nance); *m* 1961, Patricia Jane Lathwell; two *s* one *d*. *Educ:* Univ. of Sydney (BSc 1st Cl. Hons, MSc, MB, BS 1st Cl. Hons). Registered Medical Practitioner, State of NSW. FAA 1973. RMO, Royal Prince Alfred Hosp., Sydney, 1957–58; National Health and Med. Res. Council Fellow, Univ. of Sydney, 1959–62; C. J. Martin Travelling Fellow, Cambridge Univ. and Univ. of Calif, Berkeley, 1963–64; Associate Res. Physiologist, Univ. of Calif, Berkeley, 1965–66; Sen. Lectr in Physiol., Univ. of Sydney, 1967; Professorial Fellow of Physiology, John Curtin Sch. of Medicine, ANU, 1967–83. Fellow, Optical Soc. of America, 1977. *Publications:* articles on neurophysiology of the visual system in internat. scientific jls. *Address:* John Curtin School of Medical Research, Australian National University, Canberra, ACT 2601, Australia. *T:* (62)-49-2525.

LEVIN, (Henry) Bernard, CBE 1990; journalist and author; *b* 19 Aug. 1928; *s* of late Phillip Levin and Rose (*née* Racklin). *Educ:* Christ's Hospital; LSE, Univ. of London. BSc (Econ.). Has written regularly or irregularly for many newspapers and magazines in Britain and abroad, 1953–, principally The Times, Sunday Times, Observer, Manchester Guardian, Truth, Spectator, Daily Express, Daily Mail, Newsweek, International Herald-Tribune; has written and broadcast for radio and television, 1952–, incl. BBC and most ITV cos. Sir Dorab Tata Trust Lectr, India, 1990. Pres., English Assoc., 1984–85, Vice-Pres., 1985–88. Various awards for journalism. Hon. Fellow, LSE, 1977–. Mem., Order of Polonia Restituta (by Polish Government-in-Exile), 1976. *Publications:* The Pendulum Years, 1971; Taking Sides, 1979; Conducted Tour, 1981; Speaking Up, 1982; Enthusiasms, 1983; The Way We Live Now, 1984; A Shakespeare Mystery (English Assoc. Presidential address), 1985; Hannibal's Footsteps, 1985; In These Times, 1986; To The End Of The Rhine, 1987; All Things Considered, 1988; A Walk Up Fifth Avenue, 1989; Now Read On, 1990. *Address:* c/o Curtis Brown Ltd, 162–168 Regent Street, W1R 5TB.

LEVIN, Richard, OBE 1952; RDI 1971; photographer, since 1975; *b* 31 Dec. 1910; *s* of Henry Levin and Margaret Sanders; *m* 1st, 1932, Evelyn Alexander; two *d*; 2nd, 1960, Patricia Foy, Producer, BBC TV. *Educ:* Clayesmore; Slade, UC London. Assistant Art Director, Gaumont British, 1928; private practice; exhibition; graphic and industrial designer working for BBC, C. C. Wakefield Ltd, Bakelite Ltd, LEB, etc, 1931–39; Camouflage Officer, Air Ministry, 1940; MOI Exhibn Div.; Designer, British Army Exhibns, UK and Paris, 1943; private practice, 1946; Designer, Festival of Britain, Land Travelling Exhibn, 1951; Head of Design, BBC Television, 1953–71. FSIAD 1955. Silver Medal, Royal Television Soc., 1972. *Publications:* Television by Design, 1960; Design for Television (BBC lunch-time lecture), 1968. *Recreation:* fishing. *Address:* Sandells House, West Amesbury, Wilts SP4 7BH. *T:* Amesbury (0980) 623857.

LEVINE, Sir Montague (Bernard), Kt 1979; FRCGP; general practitioner, 1956–87; HM Coroner, Inner South District, Greater London, since 1987; Clinical Tutor in General Practice, St Thomas' Hospital, since 1972; *b* 15 May 1922; *s* of late Philip Levine and of Bessie Levine; *m* 1959, Dr Rose Gold; one *s* one *d*. *Educ:* Royal Coll. of Surgeons in Ireland (LRCSI); Royal Coll. of Physicians in Ireland (MRCPI, LRCPI, LM). DMJ Clin.; FRCGP 1988. Licentiate of Rubber Industry, 1944. Industrial physicist, rubber industry, 1939–45; House Surgeon: Royal Victoria Hosp., Bournemouth, 1955; Meath Hosp., Dublin, 1955; Metrop. Police Surg., 1960–66; Asst Dep. Coroner, Inner South London, 1974. Hon. Lectr in Coroners' Law, St Thomas' Hosp. and Guy's Hosp., 1987–. Fellow, Hunterian Soc. Royal Coll. of Surgeons in Ireland: Stoney Meml Gold Medal in Anatomy, 1951; Silver Medallist, Medicine, 1953, Pathology, 1953, and Medical Jurisprudence, 1954; Macnaughton Gold Medal in Obs and Gynae., 1955; Lectr in Anat., 1956. *Publication:* Inter-parental Violence and its Effect on Children, 1975. *Recreations:* fishing, photography, painting. *Address:* Gainsborough House, 120 Ferndene Road, Herne Hill, SE24 0AA. *T:* 071–274 9196. *Club:* Organon.

LEVINE, Sydney; a Recorder, North-Eastern Circuit, since 1975; *b* 4 Sept. 1923; *s* of Rev. Isaac Levine and Mrs Miriam Levine; *m* 1959, Cécile Rona Rubinstein; three *s* one *d*. *Educ:* Bradford Grammar Sch.; Univ. of Leeds (LLB). Called to the Bar, Inner Temple,

1952; Chambers in Bradford, 1953–. *Recreations:* music, gardening, amateur theatre. *Address:* 2A Primley Park Road, Leeds LS17 7HS. *T:* Leeds (0532) 683769.

LEVINGE, Sir Richard (George Robin), 12th Bt *cr* 1704; farming since 1968; *b* 18 Dec. 1946; *s* of Sir Richard Vere Henry Levinge, 11th Bt, MBE, TD, and of Barbara Mary, *d* of late George Jardine Kidston, CMG; *S* father, 1984; *m* 1st, 1969, Hilary (marr. diss. 1978), *d* of Dr Derek Mark; one *s*; 2nd, 1978, Donna Maria d'Ardia Caracciolo; one *s* one *d*. *Educ:* Brook House, Bray, Co. Wicklow; Hawkhurst Court, West Sussex; Mahwah High School, New York; Craibstone Agricultural Coll. *Heir: s* Richard Mark Levinge, *b* 15 May 1970. *Address:* Clohamon House, Bunclody, Co. Wexford, Ireland. *T:* 054–77253.

LEVINSON, Dr Stephen Curtis, FBA 1988; Reader, Linguistics Department, Cambridge, since 1991; Director, Max Planck Research Group for Cognitive Anthropology, since 1991; *b* 6 Dec. 1947; *s* of Dr Gordon A. Levinson and Dr Mary C. Levinson; *m* 1976, Dr Penelope Brown; one *s*. *Educ:* Bedales Sch.; King's Coll., Cambridge (Sen. Schol.; 1st Cl. Hons. Archaeology and Anthropology Tripos 1970); PhD Linguistics Anthropology, Calif., 1977. Asst Lectr, 1975–78, Lectr, 1978–91, Linguistics Dept, Cambridge. Vis. Res. Fellow, ANU, 1980–82; Vis. Associate Prof., Stanford Univ., 1987–88. Dir, Max Planck Project Gp for Cognitive Anthropology, 1989–91. *Publications:* Pragmatics, 1983; (with Dr P. Brown) Politeness, 1987; articles in books and jls. *Recreations:* Sunday painting, hiking. *Address:* Payensweg 7, 6523 MB Nijmegen, The Netherlands; Research Group for Cognitive Linguistics, Max Planck Institute for Psycholinguistics, PB 310, NL 6500 AH Nijmegen, The Netherlands.

LEVIS, Maj.-Gen. Derek George, CB 1972; OBE 1951; DL; retired; *b* 24 Dec. 1911; *er s* of late Dr George Levis, Lincoln; *m* 1st, 1938, Doris Constance Tall (*d* 1984); one *d*; 2nd, 1984, Charlotte Anne Nichols, *y d* of late Charles Pratt, Lincoln. *Educ:* Stowe Sch.; Trinity Coll., Cambridge; St Thomas' Hospital, London. BA Cantab 1933; MRCS, LRCP 1936; MB, BChir (Cantab), 1937; DPH 1949. Commnd into RAMC, 1936; house appts, St Thomas' Hospital, 1936–37; served in: China, 1937–39; War of 1939–45 (1939–45 Star, Pacific Star, France and Germany Star, Defence and War Medal): Malaya and Java, 1939–42; Ceylon, 1942–43; NW Europe, 1944–45; qualified as specialist in Army Health, RAM Coll., 1949; Asst Director Army Health, HQ British Troops Egypt, 1949–51; Deputy Asst Dir Army Health, HQ British Commonwealth Forces, Korea, 1952–53 (Korean Co. Medal and UN Medal); Asst Dir Army Health: Malaya Comd, 1953–55 (Gen. Service Medal, Clasp Malaya, despatches); War Office, 1956–58; Deputy Director, Army Health, HQ, BAOR, 1958–62; Comdt Army School of Health, 1962–66; Director of Army Health, Australian Military Forces, Melbourne, 1966–68; Dep. Director Army Health, HQ Army Strategic Comd, 1968; Director of Army Health, MoD (Army), 1968–70; Dep. Dir, Medical Services, Southern Comd, 1970–71. QHP 1969–71. Col Comdt, RAMC, 1973–76. Co. Comr, St John Ambulance Brigade, Lincs, 1972–85. Mem., Faculty of Community Physicians, RCP, 1971. DL Lincs, 1976. KStJ 1983. *Publications:* contribs to Journal RAMC and Proc. Royal Society Med. *Recreations:* fishing, reading. *Address:* 27 The Green, Welbourn, Lincoln LN5 0NJ. *T:* Loveden (0400) 72673.

LEVISON, Rev. Mary Irene; Chaplain to the Queen in Scotland, since 1991; *b* 8 Jan. 1923; *d* of late Rev. David Colville Lusk and Mary Theodora Lusk (*née* Colville); *m* 1965, Rev. Frederick Levison. *Educ:* St Leonard's Sch., St Andrews; Lady Margaret Hall, Oxford (BA); Univ. of Edinburgh (BD). Deaconess in the parish of Inveresk, Musselburgh, 1954–58; Tutor, St Colm's Coll., Edinburgh, 1958–61; Asst Chaplain, Univ. of Edinburgh, 1961–64; Asst Minister, St Andrew's and St George's Church, Edinburgh and Chaplain to the retail trade, 1978–83. Moderator of the Presbytery of Edinburgh, 1988. *Recreations:* music, gardening, golf. *Address:* 2 Gillsland Road, Edinburgh EH10 5BW. *T:* 031–228 3118.

LEVY, Allan Edward; QC 1989; barrister; author; *b* 17 Aug. 1942; *s* of Sidney Levy and Mabel (*née* Lewis). *Educ:* Bury Grammar Sch.; Hull Univ. (LLB Hons); Inns of Court Law School. Called to the Bar, Inner Temple, 1969; Asst Recorder, 1990–. Member: Family Law Bar Assoc. Cttee, 1987–; Council, Justice, 1988–; Bar Council Law Reform Cttee, 1989–; Council, Medico-Legal Soc., 1990–. Speaker at seventh Internat. Congress on Child Abuse, Rio de Janeiro, 1988; Chm., Staffs Child Care Inquiry, 1990. Hon. Legal Advr, Nat. Children's Bureau, 1990–. *Publications:* Wardship Proceedings, 1982, 2nd edn 1987; Custody and Access, 1983; (with J. F. Josling) Adoption of Children, 10th edn 1985; (ed and contrib.) Focus on Child Abuse, 1989; The Pindown Experience, 1991. *Recreations:* travel, writing, watching sport. *Address:* 1 Temple Gardens, Temple, EC4Y 9BB. *T:* 071–353 3737, *Fax:* 071–583 0018. *Clubs:* Reform, Wig and Pen.

LEVY, Dennis Martyn; QC 1982; a Recorder, since 1989; *b* 20 Feb. 1936; *s* of Conrad Levy and Tillie (*née* Swift); *m* 1967, Rachel Jonah; one *s* one *d*. *Educ:* Clifton Coll.; Gonville and Caius Coll., Cambridge (MA). Called to the Bar, Gray's Inn, 1960, Hong Kong, 1985, Turks and Caicos Is, 1987. Granada Group Ltd, 1960–63; Time Products Ltd, 1963–67; in practice at the Bar, 1967–. *Recreations:* living in London and travelling abroad. *Address:* 24 Old Buildings, Lincoln's Inn, WC2A 3UJ. *T:* 071–404 0946.

LEVY, Sir Ewart Maurice, 2nd Bt *cr* 1913; *b* 10 May 1897; *o s* of Sir Maurice Levy, 1st Bt; *S* father, 1933; *m* 1932, Hylda (*d* 1970), *e d* of late Sir Albert Levy; one *d*. *Educ:* Harrow. High Sheriff of Leicestershire, 1937; served, 1940–45, Royal Pioneer Corps, Lieut-Colonel, 1944; BLA, 1944–45 (despatches). JP Co. Leicester. *Heir:* none. *Address:* Welland House, Weston-by-Welland, Market Harborough, Leicestershire LE16 8HS. *Club:* Reform.

LEVY, George Joseph; Chairman, H. Blairman & Sons Ltd, since 1965; *b* 21 May 1927; *s* of Percy and Maude Levy; *m* 1952, Wendy Yetta Blairman; one *s* three *d*. *Educ:* Oundle Sch. Joined H. Blairman & Sons Ltd (Antique Dealers), 1950, Dir, 1955. Pres., British Antique Dealers Assoc., 1974–76. Chairman: Grosvenor House Antiques Fair, 1978–79; Somerset Hse Art Treasures Exhibn, 1979; Burlington Hse Fair, 1980–82; Friends of the Iveagh Bequest, Kenwood, 1978–; London Historic House Museums Liaison Gp, English Heritage, 1985–; Mem. Council, Jewish Museum, 1980–. *Recreations:* tennis, photography. *Address:* Apartment 4, 6 Aldford Street, W1Y 5PS. *T:* 071–495 1730.

LEVY, Prof. John Court, (Jack), OBE 1984; FEng 1988; FIMechE, FRAeS; FCGI; engineering consultant, since 1990; Director, Engineering Profession, Engineering Council, 1983–90; *b* London, 16 Feb. 1926; *s* of Alfred and Lily Levy; *m* 1952, Sheila Frances Krisman; two *s* one *d*. *Educ:* Owens Sch., London; Imperial Coll., Univ. of London (BScEng, ACGI, PhD); Univ. of Illinois, USA (MS). Stressman, Boulton-Paul Aircraft, 1945–47; Asst to Chief Engr, Fullers Ltd, 1947–51. Asst Lectr, Northampton Polytechnic, London, 1951–53; Fulbright Award to Univ. of Illinois, for research into metal fatigue, 1953–54; Lectr, Sen. Lectr, Reader, Northampton Polytechnic (later City Univ.), 1954–66; also a Recognised Teacher of the Univ. of London, 1958–66; Head of Department of Mechanical Engineering, 1966–83 (now Prof. Emeritus), and Pro-Vice-Chancellor, 1975–81, City Univ. Consultant to Shell International Marine, 1963–85; Chairman, 1st Panel on Marine Technology, SRC, 1971–73; Chm., Chartered Engr Section, Engineers Registration Bd, CEI, 1978–82; non-exec. Dir, City Technology Ltd, 1980–. Freeman, City of London, 1991; Liveryman, Co. of Engineers, 1991. DTech CNAA, 1990. *Publications:* papers on metal fatigue, marine technology, engrg educn, IMechE, RAeS, etc. *Recreations:* theatre, chess, exploring cities. *Address:* 18 Woodberry Way, Finchley, N12 0HG. *T:* 081–445 5227. *Club:* Island Sailing (Cowes, IoW).

LEVY, Paul, PhD; FRSL; Food and Wine Editor, The Observer, since 1982 (Food Correspondent, 1980–82); author and broadcaster; *b* 26 Feb. 1941; *er s* of late H. S. Levy and of Mrs Shirley Meyers (*née* Singer), Lexington, Ky, USA; *m* 1977, Penelope, *o c* of late Clifford and of Ruby Marcus; two *d*. *Educ:* Univ. of Chicago (AB); University Coll. London; Harvard Univ. (PhD 1979); Nuffield Coll., Oxford. FRSL 1980. Teaching Fellow, Harvard, 1966–68; lapsed don, 1971–; freelance journalist, 1974–80; frequent radio and television broadcasting. Member: Soc. of Authors; PEN; Location Register of Manuscripts Panel, SCONUL. Trustee: Strachey Trust, 1972–; Jane Grigson Trust, 1990–. Corning Award for food writing, 1980, 1981; Glenfiddich Food Writer of the Year, 1980, 1983; Glenfiddich Restaurant Critic of the Year, 1983; Specialist Writer Commendation, British Press Awards, 1985, 1987; Wine Journalist of the Year, Wine Guild of the UK, 1986. Confrèrie des Mousquetaires, 1981; Chevalier du Tastevin, 1987. *Publications:* (ed) Lytton Strachey: the really interesting question, 1972; The Bloomsbury Group, in Essays on John Maynard Keynes, ed Milo Keynes, 1975; G. E. Moore and the Cambridge Apostles, 1979, 3rd edn 1989; (ed with Michael Holroyd) The Shorter Strachey, 1980, 2nd edn 1989; (with Ann Barr) The Official Foodie Handbook, 1984; Out to Lunch, 1986 (Seagrams/Internat. Assoc. of Cookery Professionals Award, USA, 1988); Finger-Lickin' Good: a Kentucky childhood (autobiog.), 1990; contribs to Metropolitan Home, New York Times, Wall Street Jl, TLS, Petits Propos Culinaires, Harpers & Queen, Vogue, Elle, A la Carte, New Statesman, Punch, Homes and Gardens, Decanter, Connoisseur, Paris en Cuisine. *Recreations:* being cooked for, drinking better wine. *Address:* c/o The Observer, Chelsea Bridge House, Queenstown Road, SW8 4NN. *T:* 071–627 0700. *Club:* Groucho.

LEVY, Prof. Philip Marcus, PhD; CPsychol, FBPsS; Professor of Psychology, University of Lancaster, since 1972; *b* 4 Feb. 1934; *s* of late Rupert Hyam Levy and of Sarah Beatrice Levy; *m* 1958, Gillian Mary (*née* Harker); two *d*. *Educ:* Leeds Modern School; Univ. of Leeds (BA 1955); Univ. of Birmingham (PhD 1960). FBPsS. Res. Fellow, Birmingham Univ., 1955–59; Psychologist, RAF, 1959–62; Sen. Res. Fellow, Lectr, Sen. Lectr, Birmingham Univ., 1962–72. Economic and Social Research Council (formerly Social Science Research Council): Mem. Council, 1983–86; Mem., Psychol. Cttee, 1976–82 (Chm., 1979–82); Chm., Educn and Human Develt Cttee, 1982–87; Chm., Human Behaviour and Develt R&D Gp, 1987–89 (Mem. Council, 1987–89). British Psychological Society: Mem. Council, 1973–80; Pres., 1978–79. Editor, Brit. Jl of Mathematical and Statistical Psychology, 1975–80. *Publications:* (jtly) Tests in Education, 1984; (jtly) Cognition in Action, 1987; numerous in psychol jls. *Address:* Department of Psychology, University of Lancaster, Lancaster LA1 4YF. *T:* Lancaster (0524) 65201.

LEWANDO, Sir Jan (Alfred), Kt 1974; CBE 1968; *b* 31 May 1909; *s* of Maurice Lewando and Eugenie Lewando (*née* Goldsmid); *m* 1948, Nora Slavouski; three *d*. *Educ:* Manchester Grammar Sch.; Manchester University. Served War of 1939–45, British Army: British Army Staff, Washington DC and British Min. of Supply Mission, 1941–45 (Lt-Col, 1943). Marks & Spencer Ltd, 1929–70 (Dir 1954–70); Chairman: Carrington Viyella Ltd, 1970–75; Consolidated Textile Mills Ltd, Canada, 1972–75; Penn Consultants Ltd, 1975–; Pres., Carrington Viyella Inc. (USA), 1971–75; Director: Carrington Tesit (Italy), 1971–75; Heal and Son Holdings, 1975–82 (Dep. Chm., 1977–82); Bunzl PLC (formerly Bunzl Pulp & Paper Ltd), 1976–86; W. A. Baxter & Sons Ltd, 1975–; Johnston Group Inc. (USA) (formerly Johnston Industries Inc.), 1976–85; Edgars Stores Ltd (South Africa), 1976–82; Royal Worcester Spode Ltd, 1978–79; Bunzl and Biach AG (Austria), 1979–80; Johnston Industries Ltd, 1980–85; Chm., Gelvenor Textiles Ltd, S Africa, 1973–75. Vice Chm., Clothing Export Council, 1966–70; Pres., British Textile Confedn, 1972–73; Vice Pres., Comitextil, Brussels, 1972–73; Member: British Overseas Trade Bd, 1972–77 (Mem., European Trade Cttee, 1973–83); British Overseas Trade Adv. Council, 1975–77; BNEC, 1969–71 (Chm., Area Export Cttee for Israel, 1968–71); British Overseas Trade Group for Israel, 1977–; Council, UK-S Africa Trade Assoc., 1973–; Export Council for Europe, 1965–69; European Steering Cttee, CBI, 1968–71; Grand Council, CBI, 1971–75. Pres., Transport Trust, 1989–91 (Vice Pres., 1973–88). Chm., Appeal Cttee, British Inst. of Radiology, 1979–84. CBIM 1980 (FBIM 1972); FRSA 1973. Companion, Textile Inst., 1972. Order of Legion of Merit (USA), 1946. *Address:* Davidge House, Knotty Green, Beaconsfield, Bucks HP9 1XL. *T:* Beaconsfield (0494) 674987. *Clubs:* Carlton, Royal Automobile, Pilgrims, Institute of Directors, MCC; Wentworth, Beaconsfield Golf, Stoke Poges Golf.

LEWEN, John Henry, CMG 1977; HM Diplomatic Service, retired; Ambassador to the People's Republic of Mozambique, 1975–79; *b* 6 July 1920; *s* of Carl Henry Lewen and Alice (*née* Mundy); *m* 1945, Emilienne Alette Julie Alida Galant; three *s*. *Educ:* Christ's Hospital; King's Coll., Cambridge. Royal Signals, 1940–45. HM Foreign (subseq. Diplomatic) Service, 1946; HM Embassy: Lisbon, 1947–50; Rangoon, 1950–53; FO, 1953–55; HM Embassy: Rio de Janeiro, 1955–59; Warsaw, 1959–61; FO, 1961–63; Head of Chancery, HM Embassy, Rabat, 1963–67; Consul-General, Jerusalem, 1967–70; Inspector of HM Diplomatic Estabts, 1970–73; Dir, Admin and Budget, Secretariat-Gen. of Council of Ministers of European Communities, 1973–75. OStJ 1969. *Recreations:* singing, history. *Address:* 1 Brimley Road, Cambridge CB4 2DQ. *T:* Cambridge (0223) 359101.

LEWER, Michael Edward; QC 1983; a Recorder of the Crown Court, since 1983; *b* 1 Dec. 1933; *s* of late Stanley Gordon Lewer and Jeanie Mary Lewer; *m* 1965, Bridget Mary Gill; two *s* two *d*. *Educ:* Tonbridge Sch.; Oriel Coll., Oxford (MA). Called to Bar, Gray's Inn, 1958. Territorial Army: Captain, 300 LAA Regt, RA, 1955–64; APIS, Intelligence Corps, 1964–67. Chm., Home Secretary's Adv. Cttee on Local Govt Electoral Arrangements for England, 1971–73; Asst Comr, Parly Boundary Commn for England, 1965–69, 1976–88. Member: Bar Council, 1978–81; Criminal Injuries Compensation Bd, 1986–. *Address:* Farrar's Building, Temple, EC4Y 7BD. *T:* 071–583 9241. *Club:* Western (Glasgow).

LEWERS, Very Rev. Benjamin Hugh; Provost of Derby, since 1981; *b* 25 March 1932; *s* of Hugh Bunnett Lewers and Coral Helen Lewers; *m* 1957, Sara Blagden; three *s*. *Educ:* Sherborne School; Selwyn Coll., Cambridge (MA); Lincoln Theological Coll. Employee, Dunlop Rubber Co., 1953–57. Curate, St Mary, Northampton, 1962–65; Priest-in-charge, Church of the Good Shepherd, Hounslow, 1965–68; Industrial Chaplain, Heathrow Airport, 1968–75; Vicar of Newark, 1975–80, Rector 1980–81. A Church Commissioner, 1985–. *Recreations:* cricket, music, gardening, wine and rug making, photography. *Address:* The Provost's House, 9 Highfield Road, Derby DE3 1GX. *T:* Derby (0332) 42971.

LEWES, Suffragan Bishop of, since 1977; **Rt. Rev. Peter John Ball,** CGA; Prebendary of Chichester Cathedral, since 1978; *b* 14 Feb. 1932; *s* of Thomas James and Kathleen Obena Bradley Ball. *Educ:* Lancing; Queens' Coll., Cambridge; Wells Theological

College. MA (Nat. Sci.). Ordained, 1956; Curate of Rottingdean, 1956–58; Co-founder and Brother of Monastic Community of the Glorious Ascension, 1960 (Prior, 1960–77). Fellow of Woodard Corporation, 1962–71; Member: Archbishops' Council of Evangelism, 1965–68; Midlands Religious Broadcasting Council of the BBC, 1967–69; Admin. Council, Royal Jubilee Trusts, 1986–88. Archbishop of Canterbury's Adviser to HMC, 1985–90. Governor: Wellington Coll., 1985–; Radley Coll., 1986–; Lancing Coll. *Recreations:* squash (Cambridge Blue, 1953) and music. *Address:* Beacon House, Berwick, Polegate, East Sussex BN26 6ST. *T:* Alfriston (0323) 870387.

See also Bishop of Truro.

LEWES, John Hext, OBE 1944; Lieutenant of Dyfed, 1974–78 (Lord Lieutenant of Cardiganshire, 1956–74); *b* 16 June 1903; *s* of late Colonel John Lewes, RA, and of Mrs Lewes (*née* Hext); *m* 1929, Nesta Cecil, *d* of late Captain H. Fitzroy Talbot, DSO, RN; one *s* two *d*. *Educ:* RN Colleges Osborne and Dartmouth. Sub-Lieut, 1923, Lieut, 1925; specialised in Torpedoes, 1928; Commander, 1939; commanded: HMS Shikari, Intrepid, 1941–42 (despatches); Ameer, 1944–45 (despatches); retired 1947, with war service rank of Captain, RN. Now farming. FRAgSs 1972. KStJ 1964. *Address:* Llanllyr, near Lampeter, Dyfed. *T:* Aeron (0570) 470323.

LEWES AND HASTINGS, Archdeacon of; *see* Glaisyer, Ven. H.

LEWIN, family name of **Baron Lewin.**

LEWIN, Baron *cr* 1982 (Life Peer), of Greenwich in Greater London; **Admiral of the Fleet Terence Thornton Lewin,** KG 1983; GCB 1976 (KCB 1973); LVO 1958; DSC 1942; Chief of the Defence Staff, 1979–82; *b* Dover, 19 Nov. 1920; *m* 1944, Jane Branch-Evans; two *s* one *d*. *Educ:* The Judd Sch., Tonbridge. Joined RN, 1939; War Service in Home and Mediterranean Fleets in HMS Valiant, HMS Ashanti in Malta Convoys, N Russian Convoys, invasion N Africa and Channel (despatches); comd HMS Corunna, 1955–56; Comdr HM Yacht Britannia, 1957–58; Captain (F) Dartmouth Training Squadron and HM Ships Urchin and Tenby, 1961–63; Director, Naval Tactical and Weapons Policy Division, MoD, 1964–65; comd HMS Hermes, 1966–67; Asst Chief of Naval Staff (Policy), 1968–69; Flag Officer, Second-in-Comd, Far East Fleet, 1969–70; Vice-Chief of the Naval Staff, 1971–73; C-in-C Fleet, 1973–75; C-in-C Naval Home Command, 1975–77; Chief of Naval Staff and First Sea Lord, 1977–79. Flag ADC to the Queen, 1975–77; First and Principal ADC to the Queen, 1977–79. Mem. Council, White Ensign Assoc. Ltd, 1982– (Chm. Council and Assoc., 1983–87); Chm., Trustees, National Maritime Museum, 1987– (Trustee, 1981–; Dep. Chm., 1986–87); Mem., Museums and Galleries Commn, 1983–87; President: Shipwrecked Fishermen and Mariners' Royal Benevolent Soc., 1984–; British Schools Exploring Soc., 1985–; Soc. for Nautical Res., 1990–. Elder Brother of Trinity House, 1975; Hon. Freeman: Skinners' Co., 1976; Shipwrights' Co., 1978. Hon. DSc City, 1978. *Address:* House of Lords, SW1A 0PW.

LEWINTON, Christopher; Chief Executive since 1986, and Chairman since 1989, TI Group plc (Deputy Chairman, 1986–89); *b* 6 Jan. 1932; *s* of Joseph and Elizabeth Lewinton; *m* 1st, Jennifer Alcock (marr. diss.); two *s*; 2nd, 1979, Louise Head; two step *s*. *Educ:* Acton Technical College; Univ. of London. CEng, MIMechE. Army Service, Lieut REME. Pres., Wilkinson Sword, N America, 1960–70; Chm., Wilkinson Sword Group, 1970–85; Pres., Internat. Gp, Allegheny International, 1976–85 (Exec. Vice-Pres., Mem. Board). Dir, Reed Internat., 1990–. *Recreations:* golf, tennis, travel, reading. *Address:* TI Group, 50 Curzon Street, W1Y 7PN. *T:* 071–499 9131. *Clubs:* Buck's; Sunningdale Golf; Metropolitan (New York); Key Biscayne Yacht (Florida).

LEWIS, family name of **Baron Lewis of Newnham** and of **Barony of Merthyr.**

LEWIS OF NEWNHAM, Baron *cr* 1989 (Life Peer), of Newnham in the County of Cambridgeshire; **Jack Lewis;** Kt 1982; FRS 1973; FRSC; Professor of Chemistry, University of Cambridge, since 1970; Hon. Fellow of Sidney Sussex College (Fellow, 1970–77); (first) Warden of Robinson College, Cambridge, since 1975; *b* 13 Feb. 1928; *m* 1951, Elfreida Mabel (*née* Lamb); one *s* one *d*. *Educ:* Barrow Grammar Sch. BSc London 1949; PhD Nottingham 1952; DSc London 1961; MSc Manchester 1964; MA Cantab 1970; ScD Cantab 1977. Lecturer: Univ. of Sheffield, 1953–56; Imperial Coll., London, 1956–57; Lecturer-Reader, University Coll., London, 1957–62; Prof. of Chemistry: Univ. of Manchester, 1962–67; UCL, 1967–70. Firth Vis. Prof., Univ. of Sheffield, 1969; Lectures: Frontiers of Science, Case/Western Reserve, 1963; Tilden, RIC, 1966; Miller, Univ. of Illinois, 1966; Shell, Stanford Univ., 1968; Venables, Univ. of N Carolina, 1968; A. D. Little, MIT, 1970; Boomer, Univ. of Alberta, 1971; AM, Princeton, 1972; Baker, Cornell, 1974; Nyholm, Chem. Soc., 1974; Chini, Italian Chem. Soc., 1981; Bailar, Illinois Univ., 1982; Dwyer, NSW Inst. of Tech., 1982; Powell, Queensland Univ., 1982; Mond, Chem. Soc., 1984; Leeumaker, Wesleyan Univ., 1984; Pettit May, Texas, 1985; Wheeler, Dublin, 1986; Bakerian, Roy. Soc., 1989. Member: CNAA Cttee, 1964–70; Exec. Cttee, Standing Cttee on Univ. Entry, 1966–76; Schs Council, 1966–76; SERC (formerly SRC): Polytechnics Cttee, 1973–; Chemistry Cttee (Chm., 1975–82); Science Bd, 1975–82; Council, 1980–; SERC/SSRC Jt Cttee, 1981–84; UGC (Phy. Sci.), 1975–81; Council, Royal Soc., 1982–84 (a Vice-Pres., 1984); Vis. Cttee, Cranfield Inst. of Tech., 1983– (Chm., 1985–); Royal Commn on Environmental Pollution, 1985– (Chm., 1986–); Pres., Royal Soc. of Chemistry, 1986–88; Sci. Rep. for UK on NATO Sci. Cttee, 1985–. Patron, Student Community Action Develt Unit, 1985–. For. Mem., Amer. Acad. of Arts and Science, 1984; For. Associate, Nat. Acad. of Sciences, USA, 1987. FNA 1980 (For. Fellow 1986). Hon. Fellow: UCL, 1990; UMIST, 1990. Dr *hc* Rennes, 1980; DUniv Open, 1982; Hon. DSc: Nottingham, 1983; Keele, 1984; Leicester, 1988; Birmingham, 1988; Waterloo, Canada, 1988; Manchester, 1990; Wales (Swansea), 1990; Hon. ScD East Anglia, 1983. American Chem. Soc. Award in Inorganic Chemistry, 1970; Transition Metal Award, Chem. Soc., 1973; Davy Medal, Royal Soc., 1985; Mallinckrodt Award in Inorganic Chemistry, American Chem. Soc., 1986. *Publications:* papers, mainly in Jl of Chem. Soc. *Address:* Chemistry Department, University Chemical Laboratory, Lensfield Road, Cambridge CB2 1EW. *Clubs:* Athenæum, United Oxford & Cambridge University.

LEWIS, Adam Anthony Murless, FRCSE, FRCS; Surgeon to the Royal Household, since 1991; Consultant Surgeon, Royal Free Hospital, since 1975; Surgeon: St John and Elizabeth Hospital, London; King Edward VII Hospital for Officers, London; *s* of Bernard S. Lewis and Mary Lewis (*née* Murless); *m* 1964, Margaret Catherine Ann Surgey; two *s* two *d*. *Educ:* St Bartholomew's Hosp. Med. Coll. (MB, BS London 1963); FRCSE 1968; FRCS 1969. Formerly: Sen. Registrar (Surg.), Royal Free Hosp.; Post Doctoral Fellow, Stanford Univ.; Sen. Lectr (Surg.), Univ. of Benin. *Publications:* papers on general and gastro-intestinal surgery. *Address:* 8 Upper Wimpole Street, W1M 7TD. *T:* 071–935 1956.

LEWIS, Maj.-Gen. Alfred George, CBE 1969; *b* 23 July 1920; *s* of Louis Lewis; *m* 1946, Daye Neville, *d* of Neville Greaves Hunt; two *s* two *d*. *Educ:* St Dunstan's Coll.; King's Coll., London. Served War of 1939–45, India and Burma. Commanded 15th/19th Hussars, 1961–63; Dir, Defence Operational Requirements Staff, MoD, 1967–68; Dep. Comdt, Royal Mil. Coll. of Science, 1968–70; Dir Gen., Fighting Vehicles and Engineer Equipment, 1970–72, retired 1973. Man. Dir, 1973–80, Dep. Chm., 1980–81, Alvis Ltd; Dep. Chm., Self Changing Gears Ltd, 1976–81; Company Secretary: Leyland Vehicles, 1980–81; Bus Manufacturers (Hldgs), 1980–84; Staff Dir, BL plc, 1981–84. Hon. Col, Queen's Own Mercian Yeomanry, 1977–82. *Recreations:* shooting, golf, gardening. *Club:* Cavalry and Guards.

LEWIS, Sir Allen (Montgomery), GCSL 1986; GCMG 1979; GCVO 1985; Kt 1968; Governor-General of St Lucia, 1982–87 (first Governor-General, 1979–80; Governor, 1974–79); *b* 26 Oct. 1909; *s* of George Ferdinand Montgomery Lewis and Ida Louisa (*née* Barton); *m* 1936, Edna Leofrida Theobalds; three *s* two *d*. *Educ:* St Mary's Coll., St Lucia. LLB Hons (external) London, 1941. Admitted to practice at Bar of Royal Court, St Lucia (later Supreme Court of Windward and Leeward Islands), 1931; called to English Bar, Middle Temple, 1946; in private practice, Windward Islands, 1931–59; Acting Magistrate, St Lucia, 1940–41; Acting Puisne Judge, Windward and Leeward Islands, 1955–56; QC 1956; Judge: of Federal Supreme Court, 1959–62; of British Caribbean Court of Appeal, 1962; of Court of Appeal, Jamaica, 1962–67; Acting President, Court of Appeal, 1966; Acting Chief Justice of Jamaica, 1966; Chief Justice, West Indies Associated States Supreme Court, 1967–72; Chm., Nat. Develt Corp., St Lucia, 1972–74. MLC, St Lucia, 1943–51; Member, Castries Town Council, 1942–56 (Chairman six times); President W Indies Senate, 1958–59. Served on numerous Government and other public cttees; Comr for reform and revision of laws of St Lucia, 1954–58; rep. St Lucia, Windward Islands, and W Indies at various Conferences. Director, St Lucia Branch, British Red Cross Society, 1955–59; President: Grenada Boy Scouts' Assoc., 1967–72; St John Council for St Lucia, 1975–80. Served as President and/or Cttee Member, cricket, football and athletic associations, St Lucia, 1936–59. Chancellor, Univ. of WI, 1975–89; Hon. LLD Univ. of WI, 1974. Chief Scout, St Lucia, 1976–80, 1984–87. Coronation Medal, 1953; Silver Jubilee Medal, 1977. KStJ. *Publication:* Revised Edition of Laws of St Lucia, 1957. *Recreation:* gardening. *Address:* Beaver Lodge, The Morne, PO Box 1076, Castries, St Lucia. *T:* 809–45–27285. *Club:* St Lucia Yacht.

LEWIS, (Alun) Kynric, QC 1978; QC (NI) 1988; a Recorder of the Crown Court, since 1979; *b* Harlech, 23 May 1928; 3rd *s* of late Rev. Cadwaladr O. Lewis and Ursula Lewis; *m* 1955, Bethan, *er d* of late Prof. Edgar Thomas, CBE, and Eurwen Thomas; one *s* two *d*. *Educ:* The Grammar School, Beaumaris; University Coll. of N Wales (BSc); London School of Economics (LLB). Barrister, Middle Temple, 1954, Bencher, 1988; Gray's Inn, 1961. Member: Cttees of Investigation for GB and England and Wales under Agricl Marketing Act, 1979–88; Parole Bd, 1982–85; Welsh Arts Council, 1986. *Recreations:* walking, fishing, tending vines. *Address:* Penrallt, Llys-faen, Caerdydd; Francis Taylor Building, Temple, EC4Y 7BY. *Club:* Reform.

LEWIS, Adm. Sir Andrew (Mackenzie), KCB 1971 (CB 1967); JP; Lord-Lieutenant and Custos Rotulorum of Essex, since 1978; Commander-in-Chief, Naval Home Command, 1972–74; Flag ADC to The Queen, 1972–74; *b* 24 Jan. 1918; *s* of late Rev. Cyril Lewis; *m* 1st, 1943, Rachel Elizabeth Leatham (*d* 1983); two *s*; 2nd, 1989, Primrose Robinson (*née* Sadler-Phillips). *Educ:* Haileybury. Director of Plans, Admiralty, 1961–63; in command of HMS Kent, 1964–65; Director-General, Weapons (Naval), 1965–68; Flag Officer, Flotillas, Western Fleet, 1968–69; Second Sea Lord and Chief of Naval Personnel, 1970–71. DL Essex 1975. DU Essex, 1990. KStJ 1978. *Address:* Coleman's Farm, Finchingfield, Braintree, Essex CM7 4PE. *Club:* Brooks's.

LEWIS, Anthony; *see* Lewis, J. A.

LEWIS, Anthony Meredith; Joint Senior Partner, Taylor Joynson Garrett, Solicitors, since 1989; *b* 15 Nov. 1940; *s* of Col Glyndwr Vivian Lancelot Lewis and Gillian Lewis (*née* Fraser); *m* 1970, Mrs Ewa Maria Anna Strawinska; one *s* one *d*. *Educ:* Rugby School; St Edmund Hall, Oxford (MA Law). Freshfields, 1964–70; Partner, Joynson-Hicks, 1970–86, Senior Partner, 1986–89. *Recreations:* opera, tennis, ski-ing, shooting, cricket. *Address:* Hampnett House, Northleach, Glos. *Clubs:* Buck's, Wig and Pen.

LEWIS, Anthony Robert, (Tony Lewis); writer and broadcaster on cricket; BBC TV presenter of cricket and commentator, since 1974; Sunday Telegraph Cricket Correspondent, since 1974; *b* 6 July 1938; *s* of Wilfrid Llewellyn Lewis and Florence Marjorie Lewis (*née* Flower); *m* 1962, Joan (*née* Pritchard); two *d*. *Educ:* Neath Grammar Sch.; Christ's Coll., Cambridge (MA). Double Blue, Rugby football, 1959, cricket, 1960–62, Captain of cricket, 1962, Cambridge Univ. Glamorgan CCC: cricketer, 1955–74; Captain, 1967–72; Chm., 1988–; 9 Tests for England, 1972–73 (Captain of 8); Captained MCC to India, Ceylon and Pakistan, 1972–73. Presenter: sports and arts magazine programmes, HTV, 1971–82; Sport on Four, BBC Radio, 1977–86. Chm. Cttee, Assoc. of Business Sponsorship of the Arts (Wales), 1988–. *Publications:* A Summer of Cricket, 1976; Playing Days, 1985; Double Century, 1987. *Recreations:* classical music, golf. *Address:* Ewenny Isaf, Ewenny, Mid Glamorgan CF35 5BN. *Clubs:* East India, MCC; Cardiff and County; Royal Porthcawl Golf, Royal Worlington & Newmarket Golf.

LEWIS, Arthur William John; ex-Trade Union Official (National Union of General and Municipal Workers); *b* 21 Feb. 1917; *s* of late J. Lewis; *m* 1940, Lucy Ethel Clack; one *d*. *Educ:* Elementary Sch.; Borough Polytechnic. Shop steward of his Dept of City of London Corporation at 17; Vice-Chairman of TU branch (City of London NUGMW) at 18; full-time London district official NUGMW 1938–48; Member of London Trades Council and Holborn City Trades Council, various joint industrial councils, Government cttees, etc; Member: ASTMS; APEX; G&MWU. MP (Lab): West Ham, Upton, 1945–50; W Ham N, 1950–74; Newham NW, 1974–83; contested (Ind. Lab) Newham NW, 1983. Mem., Expenditure Cttee. Formerly Member Exec. Cttee, London Labour Party; Chairman Eastern Regional Group of Labour MPs, 1950–83; Member Eastern Regional Council of Labour Party and Exec. Cttee of that body, 1950–83. Served in the Army. *Recreations:* swimming, motoring, boxing, general athletics.

LEWIS, Prof. Barry, MD, PhD; FRCP; FRCPath; Consultant Physician and Professor Emeritus, University of London; *b* 16 March 1929; *s* of George Lewis and Pearl Lewis; *m* 1972, Eve Simone Rothschild; three *c*. *Educ:* Rondebosch School, Cape Town; University of Cape Town. PhD, MD. Training posts, Groote Schuur Hosp., Cape Town, 1953; lectureship and fellowships, St George's Hosp., 1959; MRC, 1963; Consultant Pathologist, St Mark's Hosp., 1967; Sen. Lectr in Chemical Pathology, hon. consultant chem. pathologist and physician, Hammersmith Hosp., 1971; Chm., Dept of Chem. Path. and Metabolic Disorders, St Thomas' Hosp., and Dir of Lipid Clinic, 1976–88. Present research interests: causes and prevention of atherosclerosis. Chm., Internat. Taskforce for Prevention of Coronary Heart Disease, 1987–91. Heinrich Wieland Prize, 1980. *Publications:* The Hyperlipidaemias: clinical and laboratory practice, 1976; (with Eve Lewis) The Heart Book, 1980; (with N. Miller) Lipoproteins, Atherosclerosis and Coronary Heart Disease, 1981; (jtly) Metabolic and Molecular Bases of Acquired Disease, 1990; Handbook on Prevention of Coronary Heart Disease, 1990; (with G. Assmann) Social and Economic Contexts of Coronary Disease Prevention, 1990; numerous papers on heart disease, nutrition and lipoproteins in med. and sci. jls. *Recreations:* music, travel, reading. *Address:* York House, Westminster Bridge Road, SE1 7UT. *T:* 071–928 5485.

LEWIS, Bernard, BA, PhD; FBA 1963; FRHistS; Cleveland E. Dodge Professor of Near Eastern Studies, Princeton University, 1974–86, now Emeritus; Director of Annenberg Research Institute, Philadelphia, since 1986; *b* London, 31 May 1916; *s* of H. Lewis, London; *m* 1947, Ruth Hélène (marr. diss. 1974), *d* of late Overretsagfrer M. Oppenhejm, Copenhagen; one *s* one *d*. *Educ:* Wilson Coll.; The Polytechnic; Universities of London and Paris (Fellow UCL 1976). Derby Student, 1936. Asst Lecturer in Islamic History, Sch. of Oriental Studies, University of London, 1938; Prof. of History of Near and Middle East, SOAS, London Univ., 1949–74 (Hon. Fellow, 1986). Served RAC and Intelligence Corps, 1940–41; attached to a dept of Foreign Office, 1941–45. Visiting Prof. of History, University of Calif, Los Angeles, 1955–56, Columbia Univ., 1960 and Indiana Univ., 1963; Class of 1932 Lectr, Princeton Univ., 1964; Vis. Mem., 1969, Long-term Mem., 1974–86, Inst. for Advanced Study, Princeton, New Jersey; Gottesman Lectr, Yeshiva Univ., 1974; Visiting Professor: Collège de France, 1980; Ecoles des Hautes Etudes, Paris, 1983–86; A. D. White Prof.-at-Large, Cornell Univ., 1984–. Mem., Amer. Acad. of Arts and Scis, 1983; Membre Associe, Institut d'Egypte, Cairo, 1969; For. Mem., Amer. Philosophical Soc., 1973. Hon. Fellow, Turkish Historical Soc., Ankara, 1972; Hon. Dr: Hebrew Univ., Jerusalem, 1974; Tel Aviv Univ., 1979; State Univ. of NY, Univ. of Penn, Hebrew Union Coll., 1987. Certificate of Merit for services to Turkish Culture, Turkish Govt, 1973. Harvey Prizewinner, 1978. *Publications:* The Origins of Ismā'īlism, 1940; Turkey Today, 1940; British contributions to Arabic Studies, 1941; Handbook of Diplomatic and Political Arabic, 1947, 1956; (ed) Land of Enchanters, 1948; The Arabs in History, 1950 (5th rev. edn, 1970); Notes and Documents from the Turkish Archives, 1952; The Emergence of Modern Turkey, 1961 (rev. edn, 1968); The Kingly Crown (translated from Ibn Gabirol), 1961; co-ed. with P. M. Holt, Historians of the Middle East, 1962; Istanbul and the Civilization of the Ottoman Empire, 1963; The Middle East and the West, 1964; The Assassins, 1967; Race and Colour in Islam, 1971; Islam in History, 1973; Islam to 1453, 1974; Islam from the Prophet Muhammad to the Capture of Constantinople, 2 vols, 1974; History, Remembered, Recovered, Invented, 1975; (ed) The World of Islam: Faith, People, Culture, 1976; Studies in Classical and Ottoman Islam, 7th-16th centuries, 1976; (with Amnon Cohen) Population and Revenue in the Towns of Palestine in the Sixteenth Century, 1978; The Muslim Discovery of Europe, 1982; The Jews of Islam, 1984; Semites and Anti-Semites, 1986; The Political Language of Islam, 1988; co-ed, Encyclopaedia of Islam, 1956–87; (ed, with others) The Cambridge History of Islam, vols 1–11, 1971; articles in learned journals. *Address:* Near Eastern Studies Department, Jones Hall, Princeton University, Princeton, NJ 08540, USA. *Club:* Athenæum.

LEWIS, His Honour Bernard; a Circuit Judge (formerly a County Court Judge), 1966–80; *b* 1 Feb. 1905; 3rd *s* of late Solomon and Jeannette Lewis, London; *m* 1934, Harriette, *d* of late I. A. Waine, Dublin, London and Nice; one *s*. *Educ:* Trinity Hall, Cambridge (MA). Called to the Bar, Lincoln's Inn, 1929. Mem. S-E Circuit. Hon. Mem., Central Criminal Court Bar Mess. *Recreations:* revolver shooting, bricklaying. *Address:* Trevelyan House, Arlington Road, Twickenham, Middx TW1 2AS. *T:* 081–892 1841. *Clubs:* Reform, Aula; Cambridge Society; Ham and Petersham Rifle and Pistol.

LEWIS, Very Rev. Bertie; Dean of St Davids, since 1990; *b* 24 Aug. 1931; *m* 1958, Rayann Pryce; one *s* three *d*. *Educ:* St David's Coll., Lampeter (BA); St Catherine's Coll., Oxford (MA); Wycliffe Hall, Oxford. Priest 1957; Curate: Cwmaman, 1957–60; Aberystwyth St Michael, 1960–62; Vicar: Llanddewibrefi, 1962–65; Henfynyw with Aberaeron, 1965–75; Lampeter, 1975–80; Canon, St Davids Cathedral, 1978–86; Rector, Rectorial Benefice of Aberystwyth, 1980–88; Archdeacon of Cardigan, 1986–90; Vicar of Nevern, 1988–90. *Recreations:* rugby, music, books. *Address:* The Deanery, St Davids, Dyfed SA62 6RH. *T:* St Davids (0437) 720202.

LEWIS, Cecil Arthur, MC; Author; *b* Birkenhead, 29 March 1898; *m* 1921 (marr. diss. 1940); one *s* one *d*; *m* 1942 (marr. diss. 1950); no *c*; *m* 1960. *Educ:* Dulwich Coll.; University Coll. Sch.; Oundle. Royal Flying Corps, 1915 (MC, despatches twice); Manager Civil Aviation, Vickers, Ltd, 1919; Flying Instructor to Chinese Government, Peking, 1920, 1921; one of four founders of BBC, Chm. of Programme Board, 1922–26; Varied Literary Activities: stage, screen (first two adaptations of Bernard Shaw's plays to screen, 1930–32), and television plays (Nativity, Crucifixion and Patience of Job, 1956–59) and production connected therewith. RAF, 1939–45. Sheep farming, South Africa, 1947–50. United Nations Secretariat, New York, radio and television, 1953–55. Commercial television, London, 1955–56. Daily Mail, 1956–66; retd. *Publications:* Broadcasting From Within, 1924; The Unknown Warrior, trans. from French of Paul Raynal, 1928; Sagittarius Rising, 1936, repr. 1966 and 1983; The Trumpet is Mine, 1938; Challenge to the Night, 1938; Self Portrait: Letters and Journals of the late Charles Ricketts, RA (Editor), 1939 (filmed for TV, 1979); Pathfinders, 1943, rev. edn 1986; Yesterday's Evening, 1946; Farewell to Wings, 1964; Turn Right for Corfu, 1972; Never Look Back (autobiog.), 1974 (filmed for TV, 1978); A Way to Be, 1977; Gemini to Joburg, 1984; The Gospel According to Judas, 1989; The Dark Sands of Shambala, 1990; Sagittarius Surviving, 1991. *Address:* c/o National Westminster Bank, 34 Henrietta Street, WC2E 8NL.

LEWIS, Prof. Dan, PhD; DSc; FRS 1955; Quain Professor of Botany, London University, 1957–78, now Emeritus; Hon. Research Fellow, University College, London, since 1978; *b* 30 Dec. 1910; *s* of Ernest Albert and Edith J. Lewis; *m* 1933, Mary Phœbe Eleanor Burry; one *d*. *Educ:* High Sch., Newcastle-under-Lyme, Staffs; Reading University (BSc); PhD, DSc (London). Research Scholar, Reading Univ., 1935–36; Scientific Officer, Pomology Dept, John Innes Hort. Inst., 1935–48; Head of Genetics Dept, John Innes Horticultural Institution, Bayfordbury, Hertford, Herts, 1948–57. Rockefeller Foundation Special Fellowship, California Inst. of Technology, 1955–56; Visiting Prof. of Genetics, University of Calif, Berkeley, 1961–62; Royal Society Leverhulme Visiting Professor: University of Delhi, 1965–66; Singapore, 1970; Vis. Prof., QMC, 1978–. Pres., Genetical Soc., 1968–71; Mem., UGC, 1969–74. *Publications:* Sexual Incompatibility in Plants, 1979; Editor, Science Progress; scientific papers on Genetics and Plant Physiology. *Recreations:* swimming, gardening, music. *Address:* 56/57 Myddelton Square, EC1R 1YA. *T:* 071–278 6948.

LEWIS, David Courtenay M.; *see* Mansel Lewis.

LEWIS, Very Rev. David Gareth; Dean of Monmouth, since 1990; *b* 13 Aug. 1931; *s* of Mordecai Lewis and Bronwen May Lewis (*née* Evans). *Educ:* Cyfarthfa Grammar Sch., Merthyr Tydfil; Bangor Coll., Univ. of Wales (BA); Oriel Coll., Oxford (MA); St Michael's Coll., Llandaff. Deacon 1960, priest 1961; Curate of Neath, 1960–63; Vice-Principal, Salisbury Theol Coll., 1963–69; Dean of Belize, 1969–78; Vicar of St Mark, Newport, 1978–82; Canon Residentiary of Monmouth, 1982–90. Clerical Sec., Governing Body of the Church in Wales, 1986–. Mem., BCC, 1985–90. *Publication:* The History of St John's Cathedral, Belize, 1976. *Recreations:* swimming, travelling. *Address:* The Deanery, Stow Hill, Newport, Gwent NP9 4ED. *T:* Newport (0633) 263338.

LEWIS, David Henry L.; *see* LeRoy-Lewis.

LEWIS, David Malcolm, MA, PhD; FBA 1973; Professor of Ancient History, University of Oxford, since 1985; Student of Christ Church, Oxford, since 1956; *b* London, 7 June 1928; *s* of William and Milly Lewis; *m* 1958, Barbara, *d* of Prof. Samson Wright, MD, FRCP; four *d*. *Educ:* City of London Sch.; Corpus Christi Coll., Oxford (MA); Princeton Univ. (PhD). National Service with RAEC, 1949–51. Mem., Inst. for Advanced Study, Princeton, 1951–52, 1964–65. Student, British Sch. at Athens, 1952–54; Junior Research Fellow, Corpus Christi Coll., Oxford, 1954–55; Tutor in Ancient History, Christ Church, Oxford, 1955–85; Univ. Lectr in Greek Epigraphy, Oxford, 1956–85. Corr. Mem., German Archaeol Inst., 1985. *Publications:* (with John Gould) Pickard-Cambridge: Dramatic Festivals of Athens (2nd edn), 1968; (with Russell Meiggs) Greek Historical Inscriptions, 1969; Sparta and Persia, 1977; Inscriptiones Graecae I, 1981; (ed) Cambridge Ancient History, vol IV, 1988; articles in learned jls. *Recreations:* opera, gardening. *Address:* Christ Church, Oxford OX1 1DP. *T:* Oxford (0865) 276212.

LEWIS, David Thomas, CB 1963; Hon. Professorial Fellow, Department of Chemistry, University College of Wales, Aberystwyth, 1970–78; *b* 27 March 1909; *s* of Emmanuel Lewis and Mary (*née* Thomas), Breconshire, Wales; *m* 1st, 1934, Evelyn (*née* Smetham); one *d*; 2nd, 1959, Mary (*née* Sadler). *Educ:* Brynmawr County Sch.; University Coll. of Wales, Aberystwyth. BSc (Wales), 1st Class Hons in Chemistry, 1930; PhD (Wales), 1933; DSc (Wales), 1958. Senior Chemistry Master, Quakers' Yard Secondary Sch., 1934–38; Asst Lecturer, University Coll., Cardiff, 1938–40. Various scientific posts finishing as Principal Scientific Officer, Ministry of Supply, Armaments Research Establishment, 1941–47, and as Senior Superintendent of Chemistry Div., Atomic Weapons Research Establishment, Aldermaston, 1947–60; Govt Chemist, 1960–70. FRIC 1940; FRSH 1964. Dawes Memorial Lectr, 1965. Scientific Governor, British Nutrition Foundn, 1967; Member: British National Cttee for Chemistry (Royal Society), 1961–70; British Pharmacopœia Commission, 1963–73. *Publications:* Ultimate Particles of Matter, 1959; Mountain Harvest (Poems), 1964. Analytical Research Investigations in learned jls; scientific articles in encyclopædias, scientific reviews, etc. *Recreations:* writing, fishing, shooting. *Address:* Green Trees, 24 Highdown Hill Road, Emmer Green, Reading, Berks RG4 8QP. *T:* Reading (0734) 471653.

LEWIS, Dr Dennis Aubrey, BSc; FIInfSc; Director, Aslib, the Association for Information Management, 1981–89; *b* 1 Oct. 1928; *s* of Joseph and Minnie Lewis; *m* 1956, Gillian Mary Bratby; two *s*. *Educ:* Latymer Upper Sch.; Univ. of London (BSc 1st Cl. Hons Chemistry, 1953; PhD 1956). FIInfSc 1984. Res. Chemist, 1956–68, Intelligence Manager, 1968–81, ICI Plastics Div. Member: Adv. Council, British Library, 1976–81; Library Adv. Cttee, British Council, 1981–. Member: Welwyn Garden UDC, 1968–74; Welwyn Hatfield DC, 1974– (Chm., 1976–77). *Publications:* Index of Reviews in Organic Chemistry, annually 1963–; (ed jtly) Great Information Disasters, 1991; pubns on information management in Aslib Procs and other journals. *Recreations:* music, old churches, 'futurology'. *Address:* c/o National Westminster Bank, Welwyn Garden City, Herts.

LEWIS, Derek (Compton); Group Chief Executive, Granada Group PLC, 1990–91; *b* 9 July 1946; *s* of Kenneth Compton Lewis and Marjorie Lewis; *m* 1969, Louise (*née* Wharton); two *d*. *Educ:* Wrekin Coll., Telford; Queens' Coll., Cambridge (MA); London Business Sch. (MSc). Ford Motor Co., 1968–82, Dir of Finance, Ford of Europe, 1978–82; Dir of Corporate Develt and Gp Planning Man., Imperial Gp, 1982–84; Finance Dir, 1984–87, Man. Dir, 1988–89, Granada Gp. Dir, Courtaulds Textiles, 1990–. *Club:* Caledonian.

LEWIS, Donald Gordon, OBE 1988; Director, National Exhibition Centre, 1982–84; General Sales Manager, Birmingham Dairies, since 1961; *b* 12 Sept. 1926; *s* of late Albert Francis Lewis and Nellie Elizabeth Lewis; *m* 1950, Doreen Mary (*née* Gardner); one *d*. *Educ:* King Edward's Sch., Birmingham; Liverpool Univ. Dairy Industry, 1947–. Councillor (C) Birmingham CC, Selly Oak Ward, 1959, Alderman 1971–74; past Chairman, Transport and Airport Committees; West Midlands County Council: Mem., 1974–81; Chm., 1980–81; Chairman, Airport Cttee, 1974–80; Sec., Conservative Group, 1974–80; City of Birmingham District Council: Mem., 1982–; Chm., Nat. Exhibn Centre Cttee, 1982–84; Chm., Birmingham Housing Cttee, 1983–84. Director: West Midlands Travel Ltd; Birmingham International Airport plc. Chm., Selly Oak (Birmingham) Constituency Conservative Assoc., 1975–80, Pres., 1980–; Vice-Pres., Birmingham Cons. Assoc., 1987– (Chm., 1984–87). Mem., West Midlands Passenger Transport Authority, 1984–. Governor: Dame Elizabeth Cadbury Sch., 1979–; Selly Park Girls Sch.; St Mary's C of E Sch., 1966–. *Recreation:* eating out. *Address:* 8 Pavenham Drive, Edgbaston, Birmingham B5 7TW. *T:* 021–471 3139. *Club:* Selly Oak (Birmingham) Conservative.

LEWIS, Ernest Gordon, (Toby), CMG 1972; OBE 1958; HM Diplomatic Service, retired; *b* New Zealand, 26 Sept. 1918; *s* of George Henry Lewis; *m* 1949, Jean Margaret, *d* of late A. H. Smyth. *Educ:* Otago Boys' High Sch.; Otago Univ., NZ. Served War, Army, with 2nd NZ Div., Middle East, 1939–46 (Lt-Col; despatches, MBE). Joined Colonial Service, Nigeria, 1947; Administrator, Turks and Caicos Is, 1955–59; Permanent Sec., to Federal Govt of Nigeria, 1960–62; First Sec., Pakistan, 1963–66; Foreign and Commonwealth Office, 1966–69; Kuching, Sarawak, 1969–70; Governor and C-in-C, Falkland Islands, and High Comr, British Antarctic Territory, 1971–75; Head of Gibraltar and General Dept, FCO, 1975–77. *Recreation:* golf. *Address:* 5 Smith Street, Chelsea, SW3 4EE. *Club:* Army and Navy.

LEWIS, Esyr ap Gwilym; QC 1971; **His Honour Judge Esyr Lewis;** a Circuit Judge (Official Referee), since 1984; *b* 11 Jan. 1926; *s* of late Rev. T. W. Lewis, BA, and Mary Jane May Lewis (*née* Selway); *m* 1957, Elizabeth Anne Vidler Hoffmann, 2nd *d* of O. W. Hoffmann, Bassett, Southampton; four *d*. *Educ:* Salford Grammar Sch.; Mill Hill Sch.; Trinity Hall, Cambridge (MA, LLM). Served in Intelligence Corps, 1944–47. Exhibitioner, 1944, Scholar, 1948, at Trinity Hall (Dr Cooper's Law Studentship, 1950); 1st cl. hons, Law Tripos II, 1949, 1st cl. LLB, 1950, Cambridge. Holker Sen. Schol., Gray's Inn, 1950; Called to Bar, Gray's Inn, 1951; Bencher, 1978. Law Supervisor, Trinity Hall, 1950–55; Law Lectr, Cambridgeshire Technical Coll., 1949–50. A Recorder, 1972–84; Leader, Wales and Chester Circuit, 1978–81. Member: Bar Council, 1965–68; Council of Legal Education, 1967–73; Criminal Injuries Compensation Bd, 1977–84. Contested (L) Llanelli, 1964. *Publication:* contributor to Newnes Family Lawyer, 1963. *Recreations:* reading, gardening, watching Rugby football. *Address:* 2 South Square, Gray's Inn, WC1. *T:* 071–405 5918; The High Court of Justice, Official Referees' Courts, St Dunstan's House, 133–137 Fetter Lane, EC4A 1HD. *T:* 071–936 6466. *Clubs:* Garrick; Old Millhillians.
See also M. ap G. Lewis.

LEWIS, Prof. Geoffrey Lewis, FBA 1979; Professor of Turkish, University of Oxford, 1986, now Emeritus; Fellow, St Antony's College, Oxford, 1961, now Emeritus; *b* 19 June 1920; *s* of Ashley Lewis and Jeanne Muriel (*née* Sintrop); *m* 1941, Raphaela Rhoda Bale Seideman; one *s* (one *d* decd). *Educ:* University Coll. Sch.; St John's Coll., Oxford (MA 1945, DPhil 1950; James Mew Arabic Scholar, 1947). Lectr in Turkish, 1950–54,

Sen. Lectr in Islamic Studies, 1954–64, Sen. Lectr in Turkish, 1964–86, Oxford Univ. Vis. Professor: Robert Coll., Istanbul, 1959–68; Princeton Univ., 1970–71, 1974; UCLA, 1975; British Acad. Leverhulme Vis. Prof., Turkey, 1984. Vice-Pres., Anglo-Turkish Soc., 1972–; Mem., British-Turkish Mixed Commn, 1975–; Pres., British Soc. for Middle Eastern Studies, 1981–83. Corresp. Mem., Turkish Language Soc., 1953–. DUniv, Univ. of the Bosphorus, Istanbul, 1986. Turkish Govt Cert. of Merit, 1973; Turkish Min. of For. Affairs Exceptional Service Plaque 1991. *Publications:* Teach Yourself Turkish, 1953, rev. edn 1989; Modern Turkey, 1955, 4th edn 1974; (trans., with annotations) Katib Chelebi, The Balance of Truth, 1957; Plotiniana Arabica, 1959; (with Barbara Hodge) A Study in Education for International Misunderstanding (Cyprus School History Textbooks), 1966; Turkish Grammar, 1967, rev. edn 1988; (with M. S. Spink) Albucasis on Surgery and Instruments, 1973; The Book of Dede Korkut, 1974; The Atatürk I Knew, 1981; articles on Turkish language, history and politics, and on Arab alchemy. *Recreations:* bodging, etymology. *Address:* St Antony's College, Oxford OX2 6JF; 25 Warnborough Road, Oxford OX2 6JA. *T:* Oxford (0865) 57150; Le Baousset, 06500 Menton, France.

LEWIS, Gillian Marjorie, FMA, FIIC, FRSA; Head of Conservation and Registration, National Maritime Museum, since 1988; *b* 10 Oct. 1945; *d* of late William Lewis and of Marjorie Lewis (*née* Pargeter). *Educ:* Tiffin Sch., Kingston upon Thames; Univ. of Newcastle upon Tyne (BA 1967). DCP, Gateshead Tech. Coll., 1969; FIIC 1977; FMA 1988. Shipley Art Gallery, Co. Durham, 1967–69; free-lance conservator, 1969–73; Nat. Maritime Mus., 1973–; Keeper of Conservation, 1978; Hd, Div. of Conservation and Technical Services, 1978–88; Asst Dep. Dir, 1982–86. Vice-Chm., UK Inst. for Conservation, 1983–84 (Mem. Cttee, 1978–80). Member: Cttee, Dulwich Picture Gall., 1983–; Wallpaintings Conservation Panel, Council for Care of Churches, 1985–88; Volunteer Steering Cttee, Office of Arts and Libraries, 1988–90; Trng Standards Panel, Museums and Galleries Commn Museums Trng Inst., 1990–; Council, Leather Conservation Centre, 1991–; Visitor, City and Guilds of London Sch. of Art, 1981–90; Trustee, Whatmore Trust, 1988–. Examiner, London Inst., Camberwell Sch. of Art, 1991–. FRSA 1987. *Publications:* official publications of the National Maritime Museum. *Address:* c/o National Maritime Museum, SE10 9NF. *T:* 081–312 6663. *Clubs:* Arts; Civil Service Riding.

LEWIS, Prof. Graham Pritchard; Dean, Hunterian Institute (formerly Institute of Basic Medical Sciences), 1982–89, Vandervell Professor of Pharmacology, 1974–89, now Emeritus, Royal College of Surgeons; *b* 5 Aug. 1927; *s* of George Henry and Ruth Lewis; *m* 1973, Averil Priscilla Myrtle; two *s* two *d*. *Educ:* Monkton House School, Cardiff; University College Cardiff (BPharm, PhD). Mem., Scientific Staff, Nat. Inst. for Med. Research, MRC, 1953–63; Dep. Dir, Research, and Dir, Biological Research, Ciba-Geigy Pharmaceuticals, 1964–73. *Publications:* 5-Hydroxytryptamine, 1958; The Role of Prostaglandins in Inflammation, 1976; Mechanisms of Steroid Action, 1981; Mediators of Inflammation, 1986; numerous contribs to British and overseas sci. jls, esp. Jl Physiol., BJ Pharmacol. *Recreations:* writing unfathomable stories, painting indescribable paintings and cooking excruciating dishes. *Address:* The Noke, 6 Chantry Close, Storrington, West Sussex RH20 4BX.

LEWIS, Gwynedd Margaret; a Recorder of the Crown Court, 1974–81; barrister-at-law; *b* 9 April 1911; *d* of late Samuel David Lewis and Margaret Emma Lewis. *Educ:* King Edward's High Sch., Birmingham; King's Coll., Univ. of London. BA. Called to Bar, Gray's Inn, 1939; Mem., Midland and Oxford Circuit; Dep. Stipendiary Magistrate for City of Birmingham, 1962–74. Legal Mem., Mental Health Review Tribunal for the W Midlands Region, 1972–83. *Recreations:* archaeology, bird-watching. *Address:* Berringtons, Burley Gate, Hereford HR1 3QS.

LEWIS, Henry Nathan; Deputy Chairman, Berisford International (formerly S & W Berisford) plc, 1987–90; director of companies; *b* 29 Jan. 1926; *m* 1953, Jenny Cohen; one *s* two *d*. *Educ:* Hollywood Park Council Sch., Stockport; Stockport Sch.; Manchester Univ. (BA Com); LSE. Served RAF (Flt Lt), 1944–48. Joined Marks & Spencer, 1950; Dir, 1965; Jt Man. Dir responsible for textiles, 1973–76, 1983–85, for foods, 1976–83; retired 1985. Director: Dixons Group, 1985–; Hunter Saphir, 1987–; Porter Chadburn (formerly LDH Group), 1987–; Delta Galil, 1988–. Mem. Adv. Bd, Bank of Hapoalim BM, 1973–. Governor, Jerusalem Inst. of Management; Mem., Policy Adv. Gp, Inst. of Jewish Affairs. *Address:* 62 Frognal, NW3 6XG.

LEWIS, H(erbert) J(ohn) Whitfield, CB 1968; *b* 9 April 1911; *s* of Herbert and Mary Lewis; *m* 1963, Pamela (*née* Leaford); one *s* three *d*. *Educ:* Monmouth Sch.; Welsh Sch. of Architecture. Associate with Norman & Dawbarn, Architects and Consulting Engineers; in charge of housing work, 1945–50; Principal Housing Architect, Architects Dept, London County Council, 1950–59; County Architect, Middlesex County Council, 1959–64; Chief Architect, Ministry of Housing and Local Govt, 1964–71. FRIBA; FRTPI, DisTP 1957. *Recreations:* music, electronics. *Address:* 8 St John's Wood Road, NW8.

LEWIS, Rt. Rev. Hurtle John; *see* Queensland, North, Bishop of.

LEWIS, Prof. Hywel David, MA, BLitt; Professor of History and Philosophy of Religion, in the University of London, 1955–77; *b* 21 May 1910; *s* of Rev. David John and Rebecca Lewis, Waenfawr, Cærnarvon; *m* 1943, Megan Elias Jones, MA (*d* 1962), *d* of J. Elias Jones, Bangor; *m* 1965, K. A. Megan Pritchard, *d* of T. O. Pritchard, Pentrefoelas. *Educ:* University Coll., Bangor; Jesus Coll., Oxford (Hon. Fellow, 1986). Lecturer in Philosophy, University Coll., Bangor, 1936; Senior Lecturer, 1947; Prof. of Philosophy, 1947–55; Fellow of King's Coll., London, 1963; Dean of the Faculty of Theology in the University of London, 1964–68; Dean of the Faculty of Arts, King's Coll., 1966–68, and Faculty of Theology, 1970–72. President: Mind Association, 1948–49, Aristotelian Soc., 1962–63; Chm. Council, Royal Inst. of Philosophy, 1965–88; Soc. for the Study of Theology, 1964–66; President: Oxford Soc. for Historical Theology, 1970–71; London Soc. for Study of Religion, 1970–72; Inst. of Religion and Theology, 1972–75; International Soc. for Metaphysics, 1974–80. Editor, Muirhead Library of Philosophy, 1947–78; Editor, Religious Studies, 1964–79; Leverhulme Fellow, 1954–55; Visiting Professor: Brynmawr Coll., Pa, USA, 1958–59; Yale, 1964–65; University of Miami, 1968; Boston Univ., 1969; Kyoto Univ., 1976; Santiniketan Univ., 1977; Surrey Univ., 1977–83; Emory Univ., 1977–81; Jadavpur Univ., 1979; Vis. Professorial Fellow, UCW Aberystwyth, 1979–84; Lectures: Robert McCahan, Presbyterian Coll., Belfast, 1960; Wilde, in Natural and Comparative Religion, Oxford, 1960–63; Edward Cadbury, Birmingham, 1962–63; Centre for the Study of World Religions, Harvard, 1963; Ker, McMaster Divinity Coll., Ont, 1964; Owen Evans, University Coll., Aberystwyth, 1964–65; Firth Meml, Nottingham, 1966; Gifford, Edinburgh, 1966–68; L. T. Hobhouse Meml, London, 1966–68; Elton, George Washington Univ., 1969; Otis Meml, Wheaton Coll., 1969; Drew, London, 1973–74; Laidlaw, Toronto, 1979. Commemoration Preacher, University of Southampton, 1958; Commemoration Lectr, Cheshunt Coll., Cambridge, 1960, and Westminster Coll., 1964. Warden, Guild of Graduates, University of Wales, 1974–77; Mem., Advisory Council for Education (Wales), 1964–67. Mem., Gorsedd of Bards. Hon. Vice-Pres., FISP, 1984. Hon. DD St Andrews, 1964; Hon. DLit Emory Univ., USA, 1978. *Publications:* Morals and the New Theology, 1947; Morals and Revelation, 1951; (ed) Contemporary British Philosophy, Vol. III, 1956, Vol. IV, 1976; Our Experience of God, 1959; Freedom and History, 1962; (ed) Clarity is not Enough, 1962; Teach yourself the Philosophy of Religion, 1965; World Religions (with R. L. Slater), 1966; Dreaming and Experience, 1968; The Elusive Mind, 1969; The Self and Immortality, 1973; (ed) Philosophy East and West, 1975; (ed with G. R. Damodaran) The Dynamics of Education, 1975; Persons and Life after Death, 1978; Jesus in the Faith of Christians, 1980; The Elusive Self, 1982; Freedom and Alienation, 1985; Gweriniaeth, 1940; Y Wladwriaeth a'i Hawdurdod (with Dr J. A. Thomas), 1943; Ebyrth, 1943; Diogelu Diwylliant, 1945; Crist a Heddwch, 1947; Dilyn Crist, 1951; Gwybod am Dduw, 1952; Hen a Newydd, 1972; Pwy yw Iesu Grist?, 1979; Gofidiau Patsi, 1988; *festschrift:* ed S. Sutherland and T. A. Roberts, Religion, Reason and the Self, 1990; contributions to Mind, Proc. of Aristotelian Society, Philosophy, Ethics, Hibbert Jl, Philosophical Quarterly, Analysis, Efrydiau Athronyddol, Llenor, Traethodydd, etc. *Address:* 1 Normandy Park, Normandy, near Guildford, Surrey GU3 2AL. *T:* Aldershot (0252) 26673.

LEWIS, Ian Talbot; Under Secretary (Legal), Treasury Solicitor's Office, 1982–91; *b* 7 July 1929; *s* of late Cyril Frederick Lewis, CBE and Marjorie (*née* Talbot); *m* 1st, 1962, Patricia Anne (*née* Hardy) (marr. diss. 1978); two *s*; 2nd, 1986, Susan Lydia Sargant. *Educ:* Marlborough Coll. Admitted Solicitor, 1951. National Service, 3rd The King's Own Hussars, 1952–53. Solicitor, private practice, London, 1954–57; Treasury Solicitor's Office: Legal Asst, 1957; Sen. Legal Asst, 1963; Asst Treasury Solicitor, 1977. Liveryman, Merchant Taylors' Co., 1966. *Recreations:* sport, the countryside, reading, theatre, cinema. *Address:* South Cottage, Fordcombe, near Tunbridge Wells, Kent TN3 0RY. *T:* Fordcombe (0892) 740413. *Clubs:* Cavalry and Guards, MCC; Blackheath Football (Rugby Union) (Past Pres.); Blackheath Cricket (Hon. Vice Pres.); Piltdown Golf.

LEWIS, Prof. Ioan Myrddin, DPhil; FBA 1986; Professor of Anthropology, London School of Economics and Political Science, since 1969; Hon. Director, International African Institute, since 1981; *b* 30 Jan. 1930; *s* of John Daniel Lewis and Mary Stevenson Scott (*née* Brown); *m* 1954, Ann Elizabeth Keir; one *s* three *d*. *Educ:* Glasgow High Sch.; Glasgow Univ. (BSc 1951); Oxford Univ. (Dip. in Anthrop., 1952; BLitt 1953; DPhil 1957). Res. Asst to Lord Hailey, Chatham House, 1954–55; Colonial SSRC Fellow, 1955–57; Lectr in African Studies, University Coll. of Rhodesia and Nyasaland, 1957–60; Lectr in Social Anthrop., Glasgow Univ., 1960–63; Lectr, then Reader in Anthrop., UCL, 1963–69. Hitchcock Prof., Univ. of Calif at Berkeley, 1977; Vis. Professor: Univ. of Helsinki, Finland, 1982; Univ. of Rome, 1983; Univ. of Malaya, 1986; Univ. of Kyoto, 1986. Malinowski Meml Lectr, London, 1966. Hon. Sec., Assoc. of Social Anthropologists of the Commonwealth, 1964–67; Member: Council and Standing Cttee of Council, Royal Anthropol Inst., 1965–67 and 1981–84; Court of Governors and Standing Cttee, LSE, 1984–88; Editor, Man (Jl of RAI), 1969–72. *Publications:* Peoples of the Horn of Africa, 1955, 2nd rev. edn 1969; A Pastoral Democracy: pastoralism and politics among the Northern Somali of the Horn of Africa, 1961, 2nd edn 1982 (trans. Italian); (with B. W. Andrzejewski) Somali Poetry, 1964, 2nd edn 1968; The Modern History of Somaliland: from nation to state, 1965, 3rd rev. edn 1988; Ecstatic Religion, 1971, 4th rev. edn 1989 (trans. Dutch, Italian, French, Portuguese and Japanese); Social Anthropology in Perspective, 1976, 4th edn 1990 (trans. Italian and Chinese); Religion in Context: cults and charisma, 1986 (trans. German); (ed and introd): Islam in Tropical Africa, 1966, 3rd edn 1980; History and Anthropology, 1968 (trans. Spanish); Symbols and Sentiments: cross-cultural studies in symbolism, 1977; (co-ed with Fred Eggan and C. von Fürer-Haimendorf), Atlas of Mankind, 1982; Nationalism and Self-Determination in the Horn of Africa, 1983; (co-ed with Gustav Jahoda) Acquiring Culture: cross cultural studies in child development, 1988; (ed jtly) Women's Medicine: the Zar-Bori Cult in Africa and beyond, 1991; contrib. learned jls. *Recreations:* travel, fishing. *Address:* 26 Bramshill Gardens, NW5 1JH. *T:* 071–272 1722.

LEWIS, Joan; *see* Lancaster Lewis, J. C.

LEWIS, Ven. John Arthur; Archdeacon of Cheltenham, since 1988; *b* 4 Oct. 1934; *s* of Lt-Col Harry Arthur Lewis and Evaline Helen Ross Lewis; *m* 1959, Hazel Helen Jane Morris; one *s* one *d*. *Educ:* Jesus College, Oxford (MA); Cuddesdon College. Assistant Curate: St Mary, Prestbury, Glos, 1960–63; Wimborne Minster, 1963–66; Rector, Eastington with Frocester, 1966–70; Vicar of Nailsworth, 1970–78; Vicar of Cirencester, 1978–88; RD of Cirencester, 1984–88. Hon. Canon, 1985–88, Canon, 1988–, Gloucester Cathedral. Hon. Chaplain, Glos Constabulary, 1988–. Chairman: Diocesan Stewardship Cttee, 1988–; Diocesan Redundant Church Uses Cttee, 1988–; Diocesan Educn Cttee, 1990–. *Recreations:* travel, music, walking, gardening. *Address:* Westbourne, 283 Gloucester Road, Cheltenham, Glos GL51 7AD. *T:* Cheltenham (0242) 522923.

LEWIS, John Elliott, MA; Head Master, Geelong Grammar School, Australia, since 1980; *b* 23 Feb. 1942; *s* of John Derek Lewis and Margaret Helen (*née* Shaw); *m* 1968, Vibeke Lewis (*née* Johansson). *Educ:* King's College, Auckland, NZ; Corpus Christi Coll., Cambridge (Girdlers' Company Schol.; MA Classics). Assistant Master, King's Coll., Auckland, 1964, 1966–70; Jun. Lecturer in Classics, Auckland Univ., 1965; Asst Master, 1971–80, Master in College, 1975–80, Eton College. *Address:* Geelong Grammar School, Corio, Victoria 3214, Australia. *T:* 052 (Geelong) 739200.

LEWIS, Ven. (John Hubert) Richard; Archdeacon of Ludlow, since 1987; *b* 10 Dec. 1943; *s* of John Wilfred and Winifred Mary Lewis; *m* 1968, Sara Patricia Hamilton; three *s*. *Educ:* Radley; King's Coll., London (AKC). Curate of Hexham, 1967–70; Industrial Chaplain, Diocese of Newcastle, 1970–77; Communications Officer, Diocese of Durham, 1977–82; Agricultural Chaplain, Diocese of Hereford, 1982–87. Nat. Chm., Small Farmers' Assoc., 1984–88. Mem., Gen. Synod of C of E, 1990–. *Publication:* (ed jtly) The People, the Land and the Church, 1987. *Recreations:* printing, bricklaying, bumble bees. *Address:* 51 Gravel Hill, Ludlow, Shropshire SY8 1QS. *T:* Ludlow (0584) 872862.

LEWIS, Maj.-Gen. (Retd) John Michael Hardwicke, CBE 1970 (OBE 1955); *b* 5 April 1919; *s* of late Brig. Sir Clinton Lewis, OBE, and Lilian Eyre (*née* Wace); *m* 1942, Barbara Dorothy (*née* Wright); three *s*. *Educ:* Oundle; RMA, Woolwich. Commissioned, 2nd Lieut, RE, 1939. Served War: in 18 Div. and Special Force (Chindits), in Far East, 1940–45. Staff Coll., Camberley, 1949; CRE, Gibraltar, 1959–61; Instr, JSSC, 1961–63; IDC, 1966; Asst Chief of Staff (Ops), HQ Northern Army Gp, 1967–69; Brig. GS (Intell.), MoD, 1970–72; ACOS (Intelligence), SHAPE, 1972–75. *Publications:* Michiel Marieschi: Venetian artist, 1967; J. F. Lewis, RA (1805–1876): a monograph, 1978. *Recreations:* English water-colours, Swiss painters, picture framing. *Address:* Bedford's Farm, Frimley Green, Surrey. *T:* Deepcut (0252) 835188.

LEWIS, (Joseph) Anthony; Chief London Correspondent, New York Times, 1965–72, editorial columnist, since 1969; Lecturer in Law, Harvard Law School, since 1974; James Madison Visiting Professor, Columbia University, since 1983; *b* 27 March 1927; *s* of Kassel Lewis and Sylvia Lewis (*née* Surut), NYC; *m* 1st, 1951, Linda (marr. diss. 1982), *d* of John Rannells, NYC; one *s* two *d*; 2nd, 1984, Margaret, *d* of Bernard Charles Marshall, Osterville, Mass. *Educ:* Horace Mann Sch., NY; Harvard Coll. (BA). Sunday Dept, New

York Times, 1948–52; Reporter, Washington Daily News, 1952–55; Legal Corresp., Washington Bureau, NY Times, 1955–64; Nieman Fellow, Harvard Law Sch., 1956–57. Governor, Ditchley Foundation, 1965–72. Pulitzer Prize for Nat. Correspondence, 1955 and 1963; Heywood Broun Award, 1955; Overseas Press Club Award, 1970. Hon. DLitt: Adelphi Univ. (NY), 1964; Rutgers Univ., NJ, 1973; NY Med. Coll., 1976; Williams Coll., Mass, 1978; Clark Univ., Mass, 1982; Hon. LLD: Syracuse, 1979; Colby Coll., 1983; Northeastern Univ., Mass, 1987. *Publications:* Gideon's Trumpet, 1964; Portrait of a Decade: The Second American Revolution, 1964; Make No Law: the Sullivan case and the First Amendment, 1991; articles in American law reviews. *Recreation:* dinghy sailing. *Address:* 2 Faneuil Hall Marketplace, Boston, Mass 02109, USA. *Clubs:* Garrick; Tavern (Boston).

LEWIS, Keith William, CB 1981; Chairman, Pipelines Authority of South Australia, since 1987; *b* 10 Nov. 1927; *s* of Ernest John and Alinda Myrtle Lewis; *m* 1958, Alison Bothwell Fleming; two *d. Educ:* Adelaide High Sch.; Univ. of Adelaide (BE Civil); Imperial Coll., Univ. of London (DIC). FTS; FIE(Aust); FAIM. Engineer for Water and Sewage Treatment, E and WS Dept, 1968–74; Dir Gen. and Engr in Chief, Engrg and Water Supply Dept, SA, 1974–87. Chairman: S Australian Water Resources Council, 1976–87; Australian Water Res. Adv. Council, 1985–90; Murray-Darling Basin Freshwater Res. Centre, 1986–; Energy Planning Exec., SA, 1987–; SA Urban Land Trust, 1990–; Member: Standing Cttee, Australian Water Resources Council, 1974–87; Electricity Trust of S Australia, 1974–84; State Planning Authority 1974–82; Golden Grove Jt Venture Cttee, 1984–; SA Natural Gas Task Force, 1987–; Bd, Amdel Ltd, 1987–; Seaford Jt Venture Cttee, 1990–. River Murray Commissioner, representing SA, 1982–87. Silver Jubilee Medal, 1977. *Recreations:* reading, ornithology, golf, tennis, skiing. *Address:* 24 Delamere Avenue, Netherby, SA 5062, Australia. *T:* (home) 338 1507; (office) 226 5500. *Clubs:* Adelaide, Kooyonga Golf (South Australia).

LEWIS, Sir Kenneth, Kt 1983; DL; *b* 1 July 1916; *s* of William and Agnes Lewis, Jarrow; *m* 1948, Jane (*d* 1991), *d* of Samuel Pearson, of Adderstone Mains, Belford, Northumberland; one *s* one *d. Educ:* Jarrow; Edinburgh Univ. Served War of 1939–45. RAF, 1941–46; Flt Lt. Chm. Business and Holiday Travel Ltd. Contested (C) Newton-le-Willows, 1945 and 1950, Ashton-under-Lyne, 1951. MP (C): Rutland and Stamford, 1959–83; Stamford and Spalding, 1983–87. Chm., Cons. Back Bench Labour Cttee, 1962–64. CC Middx, 1949–51; Mem., NW Metropolitan Hosp. Management Cttee, 1949–62. DL Rutland 1973. *Recreations:* music, travel. *Address:* 96 Green Lane, Northwood, Middx. *T:* Northwood (09274) 23354; Redlands, Preston, Rutland. *Clubs:* Carlton, Pathfinder, Royal Air Force.

LEWIS, Maj.-Gen. Kenneth Frank Mackay, CB 1951; DSO 1944; MC 1918; retired; *b* 29 Jan. 1897; *s* of Frank Essex Lewis and Anne Florence Mackay; *m* 1930, Pamela Frank Menzies Pyne, *d* of Lt-Col C. E. Menzies Pyne; two *s. Educ:* privately. Commissioned 2nd Lt RH & RFA, 1916; served with 9th Scottish Div., France and Belgium, 1916–18; ADC to GOC Lowland Div., 1921; ADC to GOC Upper Silesia Force, 1922; Iraq Levies, 1923–25; Adjutant, Portsmouth and IOW, 1926–29; Royal West African Frontier Force, Nigeria Regt, 1929–30; Colchester, 1930–33; India, School of Artillery, Quetta 22 Mountain Battery, 1933–37; Military Coll. of Science, UK, 1938; School of Artillery, Larkhill, 1939–41; CO 7th Survey Regt, 1942; CO 185 Field Regt, 1943; CRA 43 and 49 Divisions, 1944 and 1945 (despatches 1946); CCRA Palestine, 1947 and 1948 (despatches 1949); BRA Western Command, UK, 1948; GOC 4th Anti-Aircraft Group, 1949–50; Dir of Royal Artillery, War Office, Dec. 1950–54; retired, 1954; Col Comdt RA, 1957–. OStJ 1955. Order of Leopold, Croix de Guerre (Belgium). *Recreations:* sailing, shooting, books and music. *Address:* 18 Beverley Road, Colchester CO3 3NG. *T:* Colchester (0206) 76507. *Club:* Army and Navy.

LEWIS, Kynric; *see* Lewis, A. K.

LEWIS, Leonard; QC 1969; retired 1982; *b* 11 May 1909; *e s* of Barnet Lewis; *m* 1939, Rita Jeanette Stone; two *s* one *d. Educ:* Grocer's Company Sch.; St John's Coll., Cambridge (Major Schol.). Wrangler, Wright's Prizeman, MA Cantab; BSc 1st class Hons London. Called to Bar, 1932 and started to practise. Served War of 1939–45, RAF. *Address:* East Park House, Newchapel, near Lingfield, Surrey RH7 6HS. *T:* Lingfield (0342) 832114.

LEWIS, Prof. Leonard John, CMG 1969; BSc; DipEd; Professor of Education, with special reference to Education in Tropical Areas, in the University of London, 1958–73, now Emeritus; *b* 28 Aug. 1909; of Welsh-English parentage; *s* of Thomas James Lewis and Rhoda Lewis (*née* Gardiner); *m* 1940, Nora Brisdon (marr. diss. 1976); one *s* (and one *s* decd); *m* 1982, Gwenda Black (decd). *Educ:* Lewis Sch., Pengam; University Coll., of South Wales and Monmouth (BSc); University of London Institute of Education (DipEd). Lecturer, St Andrew's Coll., Oyo, Nigeria, 1935–36; Headmaster, CMS Gram. Sch., Lagos, Nigeria, 1936–41; Education Sec., CMS Yoruba Mission, 1941–44; Lectr, University of London Institute of Education, 1944–48; Editorial staff, Oxford Univ. Press, 1948–49; Prof. of Educn and Dir of Institute of Educn, University Coll. of Ghana, 1949–58. Principal and Vice-Chancellor, Univ. of Zimbabwe, 1980–81; Vice-Chancellor, PNG Univ. of Technology, 1982–83. Nuffield Visiting Prof., University of Ibadan, 1966. Hon. Professorial Fellow, University Coll., Cardiff, 1973; Hon. FCP 1974. Coronation Medal, 1953; Zimbabwe Independence Medal, 1980. *Publications:* Equipping Africa, 1948; Henry Carr (Memoir), 1948; Education Policy and Practice in British Tropical Areas, 1954; (ed and contrib.) Perspectives in Mass Education and Community Development, 1957; Days of Learning, 1961; Education and Political Independence in Africa, 1962; Schools, Society and Progress in Nigeria, 1965; the Management of Education (with A. J. Loveridge), 1965. *Address:* Flat 1, 6 Stanwell Road, Penarth, S Glamorgan CF6 2EA. *T:* Cardiff (0222) 702299.

LEWIS, Martyn John Dudley; journalist and broadcaster; Presenter, BBC Television Nine O'Clock News, since 1987; *b* 7 April 1945; *s* of late Thomas John Dudley Lewis and of Doris (*née* Jones); *m* 1970, Elizabeth Anne Carse; two *d. Educ:* Dalriada High Sch., Ballymoney, NI; Trinity Coll., Dublin (BA 1967). Reporter: BBC, Belfast, 1967–68; HTV, Cardiff, 1968–70; Independent Television News; reporter, 1970–86; Head, Northern Bureau, 1971–78; presenter, News at Ten, 1981–86; Presenter, BBC One O'Clock News, 1986–87. Documentaries include: Battle for the Falklands; The Secret Hunters; Fight Cancer; Living with Dying; Great Ormond Street—a Fighting Chance; Health UK. Occasional presenter, Songs of Praise, 1990–. Chm., Drive for Youth, 1990–; Mem., Policy Adv. Cttee, Tidy Britain Gp, 1988–; Director: Hospice Arts, 1989–; CLIC UK, 1990–; Cities in Schools, 1989–; Adopt-A-Student, 1988–; Pres., United Response, 1989–; Vice-President: Cancer Relief Macmillan Fund, 1988– (Dir, 1990–); Marie Curie Cancer Care, 1990–; Help the Hospices, 1990–; British Soviet Hospice Soc., 1990–; Patron: Cambridge Children's Hospice, 1989–; SW Children's Hospice, 1991–; London Lighthouse, 1990–. Liveryman, Patternmakers' Co., 1989; Freeman, City of London, 1989. FRSA 1990. *Publications:* And Finally, 1983; Tears and Smiles—the Hospice Handbook, 1989; Cats in the News, 1991; Youth Opportunities Handbook, 1992. *Recreations:* tennis, photography, piano, good food. *Address:* c/o BBC Television News,

BBC Television Centre, Wood Lane, W12 7RJ. *T:* 081–743 8000. *Clubs:* Annabel's, Vanderbilt.

LEWIS, Michael ap Gwilym; QC 1975; a Recorder of the Crown Court, since 1976; *b* 9 May 1930; *s* of Rev. Thomas William Lewis and Mary Jane May Selway; *m;* two *d* three *s. Educ:* Mill Hill; Jesus Coll., Oxford (Scholar). MA (Mod. History). 2nd Royal Tank Regt, 1952–53. Called to Bar, Gray's Inn, 1956, Bencher, 1986; Mem., Senate, 1979–82; South Eastern Circuit. *Address:* 3 Hare Court, Temple, EC4Y 7BJ. *T:* 071–353 7561.

See also E. ap G. Lewis.

LEWIS, Michael Samuel, PhD; FGS; educational consultant; *b* 18 Oct. 1937; *s* of Nicholas Samuel Japolsky and Annie Catherine Lewis (Japolsky); *m* 1962, Susan Mary Knowles; one *s* one *d. Educ:* St Paul's Sch., London; Balliol Coll., Oxford (BA Geology); King's Coll., London (PhD). National Service, RN rating, 1956–58. Management trng, United Steel Cos Ltd, Sheffield, 1961–62; Res. Studentship, KCL, res. into carbonate sediments of The Seychelles, 1962–65; Asst Lectr in Geol., Univ. of Glasgow, 1965–68; Gen. Service Officer, Brit. Council, 1968–75; Asst Rep., Calcutta, 1969–73; Science Officer, Benelux, 1973–75; Asst Sec., S Bank Poly., 1975–78; Asst Registrar, CNAA, 1978–80; Registrar, Oxford Poly., 1980–83; Sec., Cttee of Dirs of Polytechnics, 1983–91; Sec. and a Dir, Polys Central Admissions System, 1984–89. *Publications:* sci. papers on carbonate sedimentology. *Recreations:* music, geology, shaping gardens. *Address:* 50 Denton Road, Twickenham, Middx TW1 2HQ. *T:* 081–892 1519.

LEWIS, Naomi, FRSL; author, critic and broadcaster; *b* coastal Norfolk. Contributor at various times to Observer, New Statesman, New York Times, Listener, Encounter, TLS, TES, etc. *Publications:* A Visit to Mrs Wilcox, 1957; A Peculiar Music, 1971; The Silent Playmate, 1979; Leaves, 1980; Come With Us (poems), 1982; Once upon a Rainbow, 1981; A Footprint on the Air (poems), 1983; Messages (poems), 1985; A School Bewitched, 1985; Arabian Nights, 1987; Cry Wolf!, 1988; Proud Knight, Fair Lady, 1989; Johnny Longnese, 1989; *translations:* Hans Andersen's Fairy Tales, 1981; The Snow Queen, 1988; The Frog Prince, 1990. *Recreation:* trying in practical ways to alleviate the lot of pigeons, wolves, camels, horses and other ill-used fellow mortals in a human world. *Address:* 13 Red Lion Square, WC1R 4QF. *T:* 071–405 8657.

LEWIS, Norman; author; *s* of Richard and Louise Lewis. *Educ:* Enfield Grammar Sch. Served War of 1939–45, in Intelligence Corps. *Publications:* Sand and Sea in Arabia, 1938; Samara, 1949; Within the Labyrinth, 1950, new edn 1985; A Dragon Apparent, 1951, new edn 1982; Golden Earth, 1952, repr. 1983; A Single Pilgrim, 1953; The Day of the Fox, 1955, new edn 1985; The Volcanoes Above Us, 1957; The Changing Sky, 1959, repr. 1984; Darkness Visible, 1960; The Tenth Year of the Ship, 1962; The Honoured Society, 1964, rev. edn 1984; A Small War Made to Order, 1966; Every Man's Brother, 1967; Flight from a Dark Equator, 1972; The Sicilian Specialist, 1974, new edn 1985; The German Company, 1979; Cuban Passage, 1982; A Suitable Case for Corruption, 1984; A View of the World, 1986; The March of the Long Shadows, 1987; To Run Across the Sea, 1989; A Goddess in the Stones, 1991; *autobiography:* Naples '44, 1978, repr. 1983; Voices of the Old Sea, 1984, new edn 1985; Jackdaw Cake, 1985; The Missionaries, 1988. *Address:* c/o Jonathan Cape, 20 Vauxhall Bridge Road, SW1V 2SA.

LEWIS, Peter; Director, Personal Tax Division (formerly Personal Tax, Policy Division), Inland Revenue, since 1986; *b* 24 June 1937; *s* of Reginald George and Edith Lewis; *m* 1962, Ursula Brigitte Kilian; one *s* one *d. Educ:* Ealing Grammar School; St Peter's Hall, Oxford. Royal Navy, 1955–57. Inland Revenue Inspector of Taxes, 1960–69; Inland Revenue Policy Div., 1969–. *Address:* Inland Revenue, New Wing, Somerset House, Strand, WC2R 1LB. *T:* 071–438 6371.

LEWIS, Peter Ronald; Director General, Bibliographic Services, British Library, 1980–89; *b* 28 Sept. 1926; *s* of Charles Lewis and Florence Mary (*née* Kirk); *m* 1952, June Ashley; one *s* one *d. Educ:* Royal Masonic Sch.; Belfast Univ. (MA). FLA; Hon. FLA 1989. Brighton, Plymouth, Chester public libraries, 1948–55; Head, Bibliographic Services, BoT Library, 1955–65; Lectr in Library Studies, QUB, 1965–69; Librarian: City Univ., 1969–72; Univ. of Sussex, 1972–80. Vice-Pres., 1979–85 and Hon. Treasurer, 1980–82, Library Assoc. (Chm., Bd of Fellowship, 1979–87); Mem., IFLA Professional Bd, 1985–87. Chm., LA Publishing Co., 1983–85. *Publications:* The Literature of the Social Sciences, 1960; The Fall and Rise of National Bibliography (Bangalore), 1982; numerous papers on librarianship and bibliography, 1963–. *Recreation:* wild life photography. *Address:* Wyvern, Blackheath, Wenhaston, Suffolk.

LEWIS, Peter Tyndale; Chairman, John Lewis Partnership, since 1972; *b* 26 Sept. 1929; *s* of Oswald Lewis and Frances Merriman Lewis (*née* Cooper); *m* 1961, Deborah Anne, *d* of late Sir William (Alexander Roy) Collins, CBE and Priscilla Marian, *d* of late S. J. Lloyd; one *s* one *d. Educ:* Eton; Christ Church, Oxford. National service, Coldstream Guards, 1948–49; MA (Oxford) 1953; called to Bar (Middle Temple) 1956; joined John Lewis Partnership, 1959. Member: Council, Industrial Soc., 1968–79; Design Council, 1971–74; Chm., Retail Distributors' Assoc., 1972. Trustee, Jt Educnl Trust, 1985–87. Governor: NIESR, 1983; Windlesham Hse Sch., 1979–; The Bell Educnl Trust, 1987–. CBIM; FRSA. *Address:* John Lewis Partnership, 171 Victoria Street, SW1E 5NN.

LEWIS, Ven. Richard; *see* Lewis, Ven. J. H. R.

LEWIS, Very Rev. Richard; Dean of Wells, since 1990; *b* 24 Dec. 1935; *m* 1959, Jill Diane Wilford; two *s. Educ:* Royal Masonic Sch.; Fitzwilliam House, Cambridge (BA 1958; MA 1961). Ripon Hall, Oxford. Asst Curate, Hinckley, Leicester, 1960–63; Priest-in-Charge, St Edmund, Riddlesdown, 1963–66; Vicar: All Saints, South Merstham, 1966–72; Holy Trinity and St Peter, Wimbeldon, 1972–79; St Barnabas, Dulwich and Foundation Chaplain of Alleyn's College of God's Gift at Dulwich, 1979–90. *Recreations:* music of all sorts, walking, gardening, reading. *Address:* The Dean's Lodging, 25 The Liberty, Wells, Somerset BA5 2SZ. *T:* Wells (0749) 72192.

LEWIS, Rev. Canon Robert Hugh Cecil; Chaplain to the Queen, since 1987; *b* 23 Feb. 1925; *s* of Herbert Cecil and Olive Frances Lewis; *m* 1948, Joan Dorothy Hickman; one *s* one *d. Educ:* Manchester Grammar School; New Coll., Oxford (BA 1950, MA 1950); Westcott House, Cambridge. Deacon 1952, priest 1953; Curate: St Mary, Crumpsall, 1952–54; New Bury, 1954–56; Incumbent, Bury St Peter, 1956–63; Vicar, Poynton, dio. of Chester, 1963–91; RD of Stockport, 1972–85, of Cheadle, 1985–87. Diocesan Ecumenical Officer, 1987–91; County Ecumenical Officer for Cheshire, 1987–91; Hon. Canon, Chester Cathedral, 1975–. *Recreations:* gardening, poetry. *Address:* 78 Dean Drive, Wilmslow, Cheshire SK9 2EY. *T:* Wilmslow (0625) 524761.

LEWIS, Captain Roger Curzon, DSO 1939; OBE 1944; RN retired; *b* 19 July 1909; *s* of late F. W. and K. M. Lewis; *m* 1944, Marguerite Christiane (*d* 1971), *e d* of late Captain A. D. M. Cherry, RN, retd; two *s. Educ:* Royal Naval Coll., Dartmouth. HMS Lowestoft, Africa Station, 1927–29; HMS Vivien and HMS Valentine, 6th Flotilla Home Fleet, 1930–32; Qualifying Lt T 1933; HMS Enterprise, East Indies Station, 1935–37; Staff of HMS Vernon, 1938–39; HMS Florentino, 1939–40; HMS Rodney, 1940–42; Staff of

Comdr-in-Chief Mediterranean, 1942–45; HMS Lioness, Sen. Officer, 11th Minesweeping Flotilla, 1945–46; Admiralty, Bath, 1946–48; HMS Seahawk, 1948–49; Superintendent of Torpedo Experimental Establishment, Greenock, 1950–53; CSO to FO, ME, 1953–55; Capt. of the Dockyard and Queen's Harbourmaster, Chatham, 1955–58; retired, 1959. *Address:* 3 Albion Street, Shaldon, Teignmouth, Devon TQ14 0DF.

LEWIS, Roland Swaine, FRCS; Honorary Consultant Surgeon to the ENT Department, King's College Hospital, since 1973 (Consultant Surgeon, 1946–65, Senior Consultant Surgeon, 1965–73); Honorary Consultant ENT Surgeon: to Mount Vernon Hospital and The Radium Institute; to Norwood and District Hospital; *b* 23 Nov. 1908; *s* of Dr William James Lewis, MOH, and Constance Mary Lewis, Tyrwaun, Ystalyfera; *m* 1936, Mary Christianna Milne (Christianna Brand) (*d* 1988); one adopted *d. Educ:* Epsom Coll.; St John's Coll., Cambridge; St George's Hospital. BA Cantab 1929; FRCS 1934; MA Cantab 1945; MB BCh Cantab 1945. Surgical Chief Asst, St George's Hospital, 1935. Major, RAMC (ENT Specialist), 1939–45. *Publications:* papers to medical journals. *Recreations:* ornithology, fishing. *Address:* 88 Maida Vale, W9 1PR. *T:* 071–624 6253; Aberdar, Cwrt y Cadno, Llanwrda, Dyfed.

LEWIS, Séan D.; *see* Day-Lewis.

LEWIS, Terence; MP (Lab) Worsley, since 1983; *b* 29 Dec. 1935; *s* of Andrew Lewis; *m* 1958, Audrey, *d* of William Clarke; one *s. Educ:* Mt Carmel Sch., Salford. Nat. service, RAMC, 1954–56. Personnel Officer. Sponsored by TGWU. Member: Kearsley UDC, 1971–74; Bolton BC, 1975– (Chm., Educn Cttee, 1982–83). *Address:* House of Commons, SW1; 54 Greenmount Park, Kearsley, Bolton, Lancs. *Labour Clubs:* Astley, Higher Folds, Mosley Common, Little Hulton, Armitage, Walkden, Cadishead.

LEWIS, Sir Terence (Murray), Kt 1986; OBE 1979; GM 1960; QPM 1977; Commissioner of Police, Queensland, 1976–89; *b* 29 Feb. 1928; *s* of late George Murray Lewis and of Monica Ellen Lewis (*née* Hanlon); *m* 1952, Hazel Catherine Lewis (*née* Gould); three *s* two *d. Educ:* Univ. of Queensland (DPA 1974; BA 1978). Queensland Police Force, 1948; Criminal Investigation Br., 1950–63; Juvenile Aid Bureau, 1963–73; Inspector of Police, 1973. Member: Royal Aust. Inst. of Public Admin, 1964; Internat. Police Assoc., 1968; Internat. Assoc. of Chiefs of Police, 1977. Churchill Fellow, 1968; FAIM 1978. Hon. Correspondent for Royal Humane Soc. of Australasia, 1981. Patron, Vice-Patron, Pres., Trustee, or Mem., numerous Qld organisations. Queensland Father of the Year, 1980. Silver Jubilee Medal, 1977. *Recreation:* reading. *Address:* 12 Garfield Drive, Paddington Heights, Qld 4064, Australia.

LEWIS, Thomas Loftus Townshend, CBE 1979; FRCS; Consultant Obstetric and Gynæcological Surgeon at Guy's Hospital, Queen Charlotte's Maternity Hospital and Chelsea Hospital for Women, 1948–83; Hon. Consultant in Obstetrics and Gynaecology, to the Army, 1973–83; *b* 27 May 1918; *e s* of late Neville Lewis and his first wife, Theodosia Townshend; *m* 1946, Kathleen Alexandra Ponsonby Moore; five *s. Educ:* Diocesan Coll., Rondebosch, S Africa; St Paul's Sch.; Cambridge Univ.; Guy's Hospital. BA Cantab (hons in Nat. Sci. Tripos), 1939; MB, BChir Cantab, 1942. FRCS 1946; MRCOG 1948; FRCOG 1961. House Appointments Guy's Hospital, 1942–43; Gold Medal and Prize in Obstetrics, Guy's Hospital, 1942. Volunteered to join South African Medical Corps, 1944; seconded to RAMC and served as Capt. in Italy and Greece, 1944–45. Returned to Guy's Hospital; Registrar in Obstetrics and Gynæcology, 1946, Obstetric Surgeon, 1948; Surgeon, Chelsea Hosp. for Women, 1950; Surgeon, Queen Charlotte's Maternity Hosp., 1952. Examiner in Obstetrics and Gynæcology: University of Cambridge, 1950; University of London, 1954; Royal College of Obstetricians and Gynæcologists, 1952; London Soc. of Apothecaries, 1955; University of St Andrews, 1960. Hon. Sec. and Mem. Council, Royal College of Obstetricians and Gynæcologists, 1955–68, 1971–, Vice-Pres., 1976–78; Mem. Council Obstetric Section, Royal Society of Med., 1953– (Pres. 1981); co-opted Mem. Council, RCS, 1978–81. Guest Prof. to Brisbane, Australia, Auckland, New Zealand, 1959, Johns Hopkins Hosp., Baltimore, 1966; Litchfield Lectr, University of Oxford, 1968; Sims-Black Prof. to Australia, NZ and Rhodesia, 1970. *Publications:* Progress in Clinical Obstetrics and Gynæcology, 2nd edn 1964; (ed jtly and contrib.) Obstetrics by Ten Teachers, 11th edn 1966 to 15th edn 1990; (jtly) Queen Charlotte's Textbook of Obstetrics, 12th edn 1970; (ed jtly and contrib.) Gynaecology by Ten Teachers, 12th edn 1970 to 15th edn 1990; (contrib.) French's Index of Differential Diagnosis, 10th edn 1973 to 12th edn 1984; contributions to: Lancet, BMJ, Practitioner, Proc. Roy. Soc. Med., Encyclopædia Britannica Book of the Year (annual contrib.), etc. *Recreations:* ski-ing, sailing, tennis, golf, croquet, wind-surfing, underwater swimming, photography, viniculture on the Isle of Elba. *Address:* 13 Copse Hill, Wimbledon, SW20. *T:* 081–946 5089. *Clubs:* Old Pauline; Royal Wimbledon Golf; Guy's Hospital Rugby Football (ex-Pres.).

LEWIS, Tony; *see* Lewis, A. R.

LEWIS, Dr Trevor; Director, AFRC Institute of Arable Crops Research, since 1989; Head of Rothamsted Experimental Station, since 1987; Visiting Professor in Invertebrate Zoology, University of Nottingham, since 1977; *b* 8 July 1933; *s* of Harold and Maggie Lewis; *m* 1959, Margaret Edith Wells; one *s* one *d. Educ:* Univ. of Nottingham (DSc 1986); Imperial Coll. of Science and Technol., Univ. of London (PhD, DIC 1958); MA Cambridge, 1960. University Demonstr in Agricl Zoology, Sch. of Agriculture, Cambridge, 1958–61; scientific staff, Rothamsted Experimental Station, 1961–; seconded to ODA as Sen. Res. Fellow, Univ. of WI, Trinidad, 1970–73; Head, Entomology Dept, 1976–83; Dep. Dir, 1983–87; Hd of Crop and Envmt Protection Div., 1983–89. Special Lectr in Invertebrate Zool., Univ. of Nottingham, 1968–69 and 1973–75. AFRC Assessor to MAFF Adv. Cttee on Pesticides, 1984–89; Member: Management Bd, British Crop Protection Council, 1985–; R&D Cttee, Potato Marketing Bd, 1985–89. Mem. Council, British Ecological Soc., 1982–84; Pres., Royal Entomol Soc. of London, 1985–87. FRSA 1989. Huxley Gold Medal, Imperial Coll. of Science and Technol., Univ. of London, 1977. *Publications:* (with L. R. Taylor) Introduction to Experimental Ecology, 1967; Thrips—their biology, ecology and economic importance, 1973; (ed) Insect Communication, 1984; contribs to scientific jls on topics in entomology. *Recreations:* music, gardening. *Address:* 41 Tennyson Road, Harpenden, Herts AL5 4BD. *T:* Harpenden (05827) 5861.

LEWIS, Trevor Oswin, CBE 1983; JP; *b* 29 Nov. 1935; *s* of 3rd Baron Merthyr, PC, KBE, TD, and of Violet, *y d* of Brig.-Gen. Sir Frederick Charlton Meyrick, 2nd Bt, CB, CMG; *S* father, 1977, as 4th Baron Merthyr, but disclaimed his peerage for life; also as 4th Bt (*cr* 1896) but does not use the title; *m* 1964, Susan Jane, *yr d* of A. J. Birt-Llewellin; one *s* three *d. Educ:* Downs Sch.; Eton; Magdalen Coll., Oxford; Magdalene Coll., Cambridge. Mem. Countryside Commn, 1973–83 (Dep. Chm., 1980–83); Chm., Countryside Commn's Cttee for Wales, 1973–80. JP Dyfed, formerly Pembs, 1969. *Heir (to disclaimed peerage):* *s* David Trevor Lewis, *b* 21 Feb. 1977. *Address:* Hean Castle, Saundersfoot, Dyfed SA69 9AL. *T:* Saundersfoot (0834) 812222.

LEWIS, Dame Vera Margaret; *see* Lynn, Dame Vera.

LEWIS-BOWEN, Thomas Edward Ifor; His Honour Judge Lewis-Bowen; a Circuit Judge, since 1980; *b* 20 June 1933; *s* of late Lt-Col J. W. Lewis-Bowen and K. M. Lewis-Bowen (*née* Rice); *m* 1965, Gillian, *d* of late Reginald Brett, Puckington, Som; one *s* two *d. Educ:* Ampleforth; St Edmund Hall, Oxford. Called to Bar, Middle Temple, 1958. A Recorder of the Crown Court, 1974–80. *Address:* Flat 4, Asquith Court, Eaton Crescent, Swansea, West Glamorgan SA1 4QL. *T:* Swansea (0792) 473736; Clynfyw, Boncath, Dyfed SA37 0HF. *T:* Boncath (0239) 841236.

LEWIS-JONES, Captain (Robert) Gwilym, CBE 1969; RN retired; Chairman, Meirionydd Citizens' Advice Bureau, since 1988; Member, Clwyd Social Security Appeals Tribunal, since 1988; *b* 22 Feb. 1922; *s* of Captain David Lewis Jones and Olwen Lewis Jones (*née* Evans), Corris and Dolgellau; *m* 1946, Ann Mary, *d* of David and Margaret Owen, Dolgellau; two *s. Educ:* Tywyn Grammar Sch.; Gonville and Caius Coll., Cambridge. CEng, MRAeS, FBIM. FAA Observers Course, 1942–43; 842 Sqdn in HM Ships Indefatigable, Furious and Fencer on Murmansk and Atlantic convoys, 1943–45; Long Air Communications Course, 1945–46; Long Air Electronics/Electrical Course, 1946–47; RRE Malvern, 1947–49; Long Ships Electrical Course, 1950; RAE Farnborough, 1950–53; Sen. Aircraft Engr Off., HMS Albion, 1953–56; Dep. Comd Engr Off., Staff of Flag Officer Naval Air Comd, 1956–58; Head of Air Electrical Comd, RN Air Stn Brawdy, 1958–61; Sqdn Weapons Off., HMS Caesar and 8th Destroyer Sqdn, 1961–63; Exec. Off. and 2nd in Comd, HMS Condor, 1963–65; Gen. Man., RN Aircraft Yard, Belfast, 1965–67; Dir of Aircraft Armament, MoD (N), 1967–68; Jt Services Planning and Co-ordinating Off. responsible for Armed Forces participation in Investiture of Prince of Wales, 1967–69; Sen. Officers War Course, RNC Greenwich, 1969–70; Staff of Dir Gen. Ships (Directorate Naval Ship Production), 1970–72; Dir, Fleet Management Services, 1973–75; Dir, Naval Management and Orgn, 1975–76. ADC to HM the Queen, 1976. Lt-Comdr 1952; Comdr 1958; Captain 1967. Member: (C) for Carshalton, GLC, 1977–81; Mayor of Dolgellau and Chm., Dolgellau Town Council, 1987–88 (Dep. Mayor, 1986–87). Chm., Merioneth SSAFA, 1984–; Dep. Chm., 1984–88, Chm., 1988–89, Gwynedd Valuation Panel; Pres., Gwynedd Valuation and Community Charge Tribunal, 1989–; Member: Snowdonia Nat. Park Cttee, 1982–88; Prince of Wales' Cttee (Mid Wales Gp), 1988–. Deacon, Welsh Presbyterian Church, 1983–. JP SE London, 1979–81. High Sheriff of Gwynedd, 1991–92. *Recreations:* golf, choral music, Welsh culture. *Address:* Mansiriol, Dolgellau, Gwynedd LL40 2YS. *T:* Dolgellau (0341) 422526.

LEWISHAM, Viscount; William Legge; Chartered Accountant; *b* 23 Sept. 1949; *e s* and *heir* of 9th Earl of Dartmouth, *qv* and of Countess Spencer, *qv. Educ:* Eton; Christ Church, Oxford; Harvard Business Sch. Secretary, Oxford Union Soc., 1969. Contested (C): Leigh, Lancs, Feb. 1974; Stockport South, Oct. 1974. Chm. and Founder, Kirklees Cable. *Recreations:* squash, supporting American football. *Address:* Blakelea House, Marsden, near Huddersfield, W Yorks. *Clubs:* Turf; Harvard (New York); Stockport County Football.

LEWISHAM, Archdeacon of; *see* Kuhrt, Ven. G. W.

LEWISOHN, His Honour Anthony Clive Leopold; a Circuit Judge, 1974–90; *b* 1 Aug. 1925; *s* of John Lewisohn and Gladys (*née* Solomon); *m* 1957, Lone Ruthwen Jurgensen; two *s. Educ:* Stowe; Trinity Coll., Oxford (MA). Royal Marines, 1944–45; Lieut, Oxf. and Bucks LI, 1946–47. Called to Bar, Middle Temple, 1951; S Eastern Circuit.

LEWISOHN, Neville Joseph; Director of Dockyard Manpower and Productivity (Under Secretary), Ministry of Defence, 1979–82; *b* 28 May 1922; *s* of Victor and Ruth Lewisohn; *m* 1944, Patricia Zeffertt; two *d* (and one *d* decd). *Educ:* Sutton County Sch., Surrey. Entered Admiralty as Clerical Officer, 1939; promoted through intervening grades to Principal, 1964; Dir of Resources and Progs (Ships), 1972 (Asst Sec.); Head of Civilian Management (Specialists), 2 Div., 1976. *Recreations:* music, drama. *Address:* 46 Middle Stoke, Limpley Stoke, Bath BA3 6JG. *T:* Limpley Stoke (0225) 723357.

LEWISON, Kim Martin Jordan; QC 1991; *b* 1 May 1952; *s* of Anthony Frederick Lewison and Dinora Lewison (*née* Pines); *m* 1979, Helen Mary Janecek; one *s* one *d. Educ:* St Paul's Sch., London; Downing Coll., Cambridge (MA 1973); Council of Legal Education. Called to the Bar, Lincoln's Inn, 1975. Mem. Council, Liberal Jewish Synagogue, 1990. *Publications:* Development Land Tax, 1978; Drafting Business Leases, 1979, 3rd edn 1989; Lease or Licence, 1985; The Interpretation of Contracts, 1989; (Gen. Editor) Woodfall on Landlord and Tenant, 1990–. *Recreation:* visiting France. *Address:* Falcon Chambers, Falcon Court, EC4Y 1AA. *T:* 071–353 2484.

LEWISON, Peter George Hornby, CBE 1977; Chairman, National Dock Labour Board, 1969–77; Member, National Ports Council, 1972–77; *b* 5 July 1911; *s* of late George and Maud Elizabeth Lewison; *m* 1937, Lyndsay Sutton Rothwell; one *s* one *d. Educ:* Dulwich; Magdalen Coll., Oxford. Dunlop Rubber Co., Coventry, 1935–41; Min. of Supply (seconded), 1941–44; RNVR (Special Br.), 1944–46. Min. of Labour, 1946–47; Personnel Manager, British-American Tobacco Co. Ltd, 1947–68, retd. *Recreations:* music, cricket, maintaining a sense of curiosity. *Address:* Court Hill House, East Dean, Chichester, Sussex. *T:* Singleton (024363) 200. *Club:* MCC.

LEWITTER, Prof. Lucjan Ryszard; Professor of Slavonic Studies, University of Cambridge, 1968–84; *b* 1922. *Educ:* schools in Poland; Perse Sch., Cambridge; Christ's Coll., Cambridge. PhD 1951. Univ. Asst Lectr in Polish, 1948; Fellow of Christ's Coll., 1951; Dir of Studies in Modern Languages, 1951–64; Tutor, 1960–68; Vice-Master, 1977–80; Univ. Lectr in Slavonic Studies (Polish), 1953–68. *Publications:* (ed, with A. P. Vlasto) Ivan Pososhkov, The Book of Poverty and Wealth, 1987; articles in learned jls. *Address:* Christ's College, Cambridge CB2 3BU. *T:* Cambridge (0223) 357320. *Club:* United Oxford & Cambridge University.

LEWTHWAITE, Brig. Rainald Gilfrid, CVO 1975; OBE 1974; MC 1943; *b* 21 July 1913; 2nd *s* of Sir William Lewthwaite, 2nd Bt of Broadgate, Cumberland, and Beryl Mary Stopford Hickman; *b* of Sir William Anthony Lewthwaite, 3rd Bt, *qv*; *m* 1936, Margaret Elizabeth Edmonds, MBE 1942 (*d* 1990), 2nd *d* of late Harry Edmonds and Florence Jane Moncrieffe Bolton, High Green, Redding, Conn, USA; one *s* one *d* (and one *s* one *d* decd). *Educ:* Rugby Sch.; Trinity Coll., Cambridge. BA (Hons) Law 1934. Joined Scots Guards, 1934. Served War of 1939–45 (MC, despatches twice). Retired as Defence and Military Attaché, British Embassy, Paris, 1968. Dir of Protocol, Hong Kong, 1969–76. French Croix-de-Guerre with Palm, 1945. *Recreation:* country life. *Address:* Broadgate, Millom, Cumbria LA18 5JY. *T:* Broughton-in-Furness (0229) 716295; 14 Earl's Walk, W8 6LP. *T:* 071–602 6323. *Clubs:* Cavalry and Guards, The Pilgrims.

LEWTHWAITE, Sir William Anthony, 3rd Bt, *cr* 1927; Solicitor, 1937–75; *b* 26 Feb. 1912; *e s* of Sir William Lewthwaite, 2nd Bt, JP, and Beryl Mary Stopford (*d* 1970), *o c* of late Major Stopford Cosby Hickman, JP, DL, of Fenloe, Co. Clare; *S* father, 1933; *m* 1936, Lois Mairi, *o c* of late Capt. Robertson Kerr Clark (brother of 1st Baron Inverchapel, PC, GCMG) and Lady Beatrice Minnie Ponsonby, *d* of 9th Earl of Drogheda (who *m* 2nd, 1941, 1st Baron Rankeillour, PC; she *d* 1966); one *d* (and one *d* decd). *Educ:* Rugby; Trinity Coll., Cambridge, BA. Lt, Grenadier Guards, 1943–46. Mem. Council, CLA,

1949–64. Mem. Cttee, Westminster Law Society, 1964–73. *Heir:* b Brig. Rainald Gilfrid Lewthwaite, *qv*. *Address:* 114 Cranmer Court, SW3 3HE. *T:* 071–584 2088.

LEY, Arthur Harris, FRSA; FRIBA, AADip, FIStructE, MRAeS; former Partner, Ley Colbeck & Partners, Architects; *b* 24 Dec. 1903; *s* of late Algernon Sydney Richard Ley, FRIBA, and Esther Eliza Harris; *m* 1935, Ena Constance Riches (*d* 1988); one *d*. *Educ:* Westminster City Sch.; AA Coll. of Architecture. Architect for: Principal London Office Barclays Bank DCO; Head Office Nat. Mutual Life Assce Soc.; Palmerston Hse, EC2; Baltic Hse, EC3; Bishops House, Bishopsgate; Broad Street House; Hqrs Marine Soc.; Hqrs SBAC; Hqrs RAeS; Hqrs Instn Struct. Engrs; York Hall, Windsor Gt Park; Aircraft Research Assoc. Estab., Bedford. Factories and Office Blocks for: Vickers Ltd, at Barrow, etc.; British Aircraft Corporation at Weybridge and Hurn; Wallpaper Manufrs Ltd; Sir Isaac Pitman & Sons; Decca Radar Ltd; Ever Ready Co.; Charter Consolidated, Ashford, Kent; also numerous office blocks in the City of London, Leeds, Inverness and Vancouver. Banks for: Hambro; Nat. Provincial; Barclays; Bank of Scandinavia; Head London office, Hongkong and Shanghai Bank. Central area develt, Watford and Ashford, Kent. Hospitals: Watford and Harrow. Schools: London, Hertfordshire, Barrow in Furness and Surrey. Mem. Council: Architects Registr. Coun. of UK, 1958–60; Instn Struct. Engrs, 1951–54; London Chamber of Commerce, 1955–79; Associated Owners of City Properties (Pres., 1971–77). Consultant, Bishopsgate Foundn; Mem. Court, City Univ., to 1988; Liveryman: Worshipful Co. of Paviors (Master, 1962), and of Upholders (Master, 1966); Hon. Liveryman, Co. of Constructors; Freeman, City of London; Sheriff 1964–65, and Mem. Court of Common Council, City of London, 1964–80; Churchwarden of St Mary-le-Bow, 1960–83. Grand Officer of the Order of Merit (Chile). *Publications:* contributions to journals and technical press. *Address:* 14 Fox Close, off Queens Road, Weybridge, Surrey KT13 0AX. *T:* Weybridge (0932) 842701. *Clubs:* City Livery (Pres., 1968–69), Guildhall, United Wards (Pres., 1961), Bishopsgate Ward (Pres., 1966).

LEY, Sir Francis (Douglas), 4th Bt *cr* 1905; MBE 1961; TD; DL; JP; *b* 5 April 1907; *yr s* of Major Sir Gordon Ley, 2nd Bt (*d* 1944); *S* brother, 1980; *m* 1931, Violet Geraldine Johnson (*d* 1991); one *s* one *d*. *Educ:* Eton; Magdalene Coll., Cambridge (MA). JP 1939, DL 1957, Derbyshire. High Sheriff of Derbyshire, 1956. *Heir:* *s* Ian Francis Ley [*b* 12 June 1934; *m* 1957, Caroline Margaret, *d* of Major George Henry Errington, MC; one *s* one *d*]. *Address:* Pond House, Shirley, Derby DE6 3AZ. *T:* Ashbourne (0335) 60327.

LEY, Prof. Steven Victor, FRS 1990; Professor of Organic Chemistry, since 1983 and Head of Chemistry Department, since 1989, Imperial College, London; *b* 10 Dec. 1945; *s* of Mary Ley (*née* Hall) and Ralph Gilbert Ley; *m* 1970, Rosemary Ann Jameson; one *d*. *Educ:* Loughborough Univ. of Technology (BTech 1st cl. Hons 1969; PhD 1972); DSc London 1983. Res. Fellow, Ohio State Univ., 1972–74; Res. Asst, 1974–75, Lectr, 1975–83, Imperial Coll. Vis. Lectr and Vis. Prof., overseas estabts. Chm., Organic Chem. Cttee, SERC, 1985–89. Royal Society of Chemistry: Hickinbottom Res. Fellow, 1981–83 (1st recipient); Corday Morgan Medal Prize, 1982; Pfizer Res. Award, 1983 (1st recipient); Tilden Lectr and Medal, 1988; Award for Synthetic Chem., 1989. *Publications:* over 200 papers in internat. jls of chemistry. *Recreations:* walking, ski-ing, listening to music. *Address:* Department of Chemistry, Imperial College of Science, Technology and Medicine, SW7 2AY. *T:* 071–225 8330.

LEYLAND, Sir Philip Vyvian N.; *see* Naylor-Leyland.

LEYLAND, Ronald Arthur; Chief Executive, North Yorkshire County Council, since 1990; *b* 23 Aug. 1940; *s* of Arthur and Lucy Leyland; *m* 1962, Joan Virginia Sinclair; three *s*. *Educ:* Merchant Taylors' Sch., Crosby; Liverpool Univ. (LLB Hons 1961). Solicitor (Hons 1964). Assistant Solicitor: Bootle CBC, 1964–65; Nottingham City Council, 1965–68; Sen. Asst Solicitor, then Dir of Admin, Leeds MDC, 1968–75; County Sec., Hampshire CC., 1975–90. Chm., Soc. of County Secretaries, 1986–87. *Recreation:* walking. *Address:* County Hall, Northallerton, North Yorks DL7 8AD; White House, Maunby, near Thirsk YO7 4HG.

LEYSER, Prof. Karl Joseph, TD 1963; FBA 1983; Chichele Professor of Medieval History, Oxford University, 1984–88; Fellow, All Souls College, Oxford, 1984–88; *b* 24 Oct. 1920; *s* of late Otto Leyser and Emmy Leyser; *m* 1962, Henrietta Louise Valerie Bateman; two *s* two *d*. *Educ:* Hindenburg Gymnasium, Düsseldorf; St Paul's School; Magdalen College, Oxford. Gibbs Scholar in History, 1946, Bryce Research Student, 1948. FRHistS 1960, FSA 1980. War service: Pioneer Corps, 1940–43 (Cpl); The Black Watch (RHR), 1943; commissioned 1944; service with 7th Bn, 51 Div., NW Europe, 1944–45 (despatches 1945) (Captain); Territorial, 1949–63, 6/7 The Black Watch and HQ 153 Bde (Major 1961). Official Fellow and Tutor in History, Magdalen Coll., Oxford, 1948–84, Senior Dean of Arts, 1951–55, Vice-Pres., 1971–72; University Lectr, 1950–65, and 1975–84 (CUF); Special Lectr, Medieval European Hist., 1965–75; Chm., Faculty of Modern Hist., 1980–82, Vice-Chm. Bd, 1985–88. Distinguished Vis. Prof. of Medieval Studies, Univ. of California, Berkeley, 1987; Vis. Prof., Harvard, 1989. Lectures: Dark Age, Univ. of Kent, 1981; Raleigh, British Acad., 1983; Collège de France, 1984; Denys Hay Seminar in Medieval and Renaissance Hist., Univ. of Edinburgh, 1986; Medieval Acad. of America, 1987 (Corresp. Fellow, 1988); Reichenau, 1988, 1990; Centre d'Etudes Supérieures de Civilisation Médiévale, 1989; Theodor-Schieder-Gedächtnisvorlesung, 1991. Governor: Magdalen Coll. Sch., Oxford, 1971–84; St Paul's Schs, 1974–. Mem. Council: Max-Planck-Inst. für Geschichte, Göttingen, 1978–; RHistS, 1985–89; German Historical Inst., London, 1985–; Corresp. Mem., Zentral-Direktion, Monumenta Germaniae Historica, 1979–; Kuratorium, Historisches Kolleg, Munich, 1985–; Corresp. Mem., Akademie der Wissenschaften, Göttingen, 1991. *Publications:* Rule and Conflict in an Early Medieval Society: Ottonian Saxony, 1979; Medieval Germany and its Neighbours 900–1250, 1982; articles in learned jls. *Address:* Manor House, Islip, Oxford. *T:* Kidlington (08675) 3177. *Club:* Athenæum.

LI, Fook Kow, CMG 1975; JP; Chairman, Public Service Commission, Hong Kong, 1980–87, retired; *b* 15 June 1922; *s* of Tse Fong Li; *m* 1946, Edith Kwong Li; four *c*. *Educ:* Massachusetts Inst. of Technology (BSc,MSc). Mem. Hong Kong Admin. Service; Teacher, 1948–54; various departmental posts and posts in the Government Secretariat, 1955–60; Asst Financial Sec., Asst Estabt Officer, Dep. Financial Sec. and Estabt Officer, 1961–69; Dep. Dir of Commerce and Industry, 1970; Dep. Sec. for Home Affairs, 1971–72; Dir of Social Welfare, 1972; Sec. for Social Services, 1973; Sec. for Home Affairs, 1977–80. JP Hong Kong, 1959. *Address:* D21 Carolina Garden, 32 Coombe Road, Hong Kong. *Clubs:* Royal Hong Kong Jockey, Hong Kong Country.

LI, Simon Fook Sean; Director: The Bank of East Asia Ltd, Hong Kong, since 1987; Hong Kong Telephone Co. Ltd, since 1988; *b* 19 April 1922; 3rd *s* of late Koon Chun Li and late Tam Doy Hing Li; *m* Marie Veronica Lillian Yang; four *s* one *d*. *Educ:* King's Coll., Hong Kong; Hong Kong Univ.; Nat. Kwangsi Univ.; University Coll., London Univ. (LLB 1950; Fellow, 1991). Barrister-at-Law, Lincoln's Inn, 1951. Crown Counsel, Attorney-General's Chambers, Hong Kong, 1953; Senior Crown Counsel, 1962; District Judge, 1966–71, Puisne Judge, 1971–80, Justice of Appeal, 1980–84, Vice-Pres., Court of Appeal, 1984–87, Hong Kong. Chm., Insce Claims Complaints Bd, 1990–; Mem., Hong Kong Special Admin. Region Basic Law Drafting Cttee, 1985–90. Hon. LLD Chinese Univ., Hong Kong, 1986. *Recreations:* hiking, swimming. *Address:* Room 1104/5, Hing Wai Building, 36 Queen's Road, Central, Hong Kong. *T:* 5232541. *Clubs:* Commonwealth Trust; Hong Kong, Chinese, Royal Hong Kong Jockey (Steward) (Hong Kong).

LIAO Poon-Huai, Hon. Donald, CBE 1983 (OBE 1972); Director: HSBC Holdings plc, since 1990; Shun Hing Group, Hong Kong, since 1991; Kumagai Gurni (HK) Ltd, since 1990; Provincial Insurance plc (Hong Kong Branch), since 1990; Morgan Crucible Company Plc, since 1991; *b* 29 Oct. 1929; *s* of late Liao Huk-Koon and Yeo Tsai-Hoon; *m* 1963, Christine Yuen Ching-Me; two *s* one *d*. *Educ:* Univ. of Hong Kong (BArch Hons); Univ. of Durham (Dip. Landscape Design). Architect, Hong Kong Housing Authority, 1960, Housing Architect, 1966; Commissioner for Housing and Member, Town Planning Board, 1968; Director of Housing and Vice-Chm., Hong Kong Housing Authority, 1973; Sec. for Housing and Chm., Hong Kong Housing Authority, 1980; Sec. for Dist Admin, Hong Kong, 1985. MLC, Hong Kong, 1980; MEC, 1985. Mem., Sino-British Jt Liaison Gp, 1987. Fellow, Hong Kong Inst. of Architects. Hon. FIH. *Recreations:* golf, skiing, riding. *Address:* (residence) 95A Kadoorie Avenue, Kowloon, Hong Kong. *T:* 7155822; (office) 801–2 East Ocean Centre, 98 Granville Road, Kowloon, Hong Kong. *T:* 3693949. *Clubs:* Athenæum; Royal Hong Kong Golf, Royal Hong Kong Jockey (Hong Kong).

LIARDET, Rear-Adm. Guy Francis, CB 1990; CBE 1985; Director of Public Affairs, Chemical Industries Association, since 1990; *b* 6 Dec. 1934; *s* of Maj.-Gen. Henry Maughan Liardet, *qv*; *m* 1962, Jennifer Anne O'Hagan; one *s* two *d*. *Educ:* Royal Naval Coll., Dartmouth. Trng Comdr, BRNC, Dartmouth, 1969–70; comd HMS Aurora, 1970–72; Exec. Officer, HMS Bristol, 1974–76; Defence Policy Staff, MoD, 1978–79; RCDS, 1980; CSO (Trng), C-in-C Naval Home Comd, 1981–82; comd HMS Cleopatra and Seventh Frigate Sqn, 1983–84; Dir of Public Relations (Navy), MoD, 1984–86; Flag Officer Second Flotilla, 1986–88; Comdt, JSDC, 1988–90, retd. *Publications:* contrib. Naval Review. *Recreation:* sailing. *Address:* c/o Royal Bank of Scotland, Holt's Branch, Kirkland House, Whitehall, SW1A 2EB.

LIARDET, Maj.-Gen. Henry Maughan, CB 1960; CBE 1945 (OBE 1942); DSO 1945; DL; *b* 27 Oct. 1906; *s* of late Maj.-Gen. Sir Claude Liardet, KBE, CB, DSO, TD, DL; *m* 1933, Joan Sefton, *d* of Major G. S. Constable, MC, JP; three *s*. *Educ:* Bedford School. 1st Commission for Territorial Army, 1924, Royal Artillery; Regular Commission, Royal Tank Corps, 1927; service UK, India, Egypt, 1927–38; Staff Coll., Camberley, 1939; War of 1939–45: War Office, 1939–41; active service in Egypt, N Africa, Italy, 1941–45; General Staff appointments, command of 6th RTR, 1942–44; GSO1, 10th Armoured Div., Alamein; Comdr, 1st Armoured Replacement Gp, 1944; 2nd in Comd, 25th Tank Brigade (later Assault Brigade), 1944–45; Commander: 25th Armoured Engr Brigade, April–Sept. 1945 (despatches twice); Detachment, 1st Armoured Div., Palestine, 1947; Brig., RAC, MELF, 1947–49; Comdr, 8th RTR, 1949–50; Dep. Dir, Manpower Planning, War Office, 1950–52; Comdr, 23 Armd Bde, 1953–54; idc, 1955; Chief of Staff, British Joint Services Mission (Army Staff), Washington, DC, 1956–58; ADC to the Queen, 1956–58; Director-General of Fighting Vehicles, WO, 1958–61; Deputy Master-General of the Ordnance, War Office, 1961–64, retired. Colonel Comdt, Royal Tank Regt, 1961–67. Dir, British Sailors' Soc., 1961–78; Chm., SS&AFA W Sussex Cttee, 1966–85. DL, Sussex, 1964–74, W Sussex 1974–. W Sussex CC, 1964–74; Alderman, 1970–74. Pres. Sussex Council, Royal British Legion, 1975–81. *Recreations:* shooting, gardening. *Address:* Warningcamp House, Arundel, West Sussex BN18 9QY. *T:* Arundel (0903) 882533. *Clubs:* Army and Navy; Sussex.

See also G. F. Liardet.

LIBBY, Donald Gerald, PhD; Under Secretary, Department of Education and Science, since 1980; *b* 2 July 1934; *s* of late Herbert Lionel Libby and of Minnie Libby; *m* 1st, 1961, Margaret Elizabeth Dunlop McLatchie (*d* 1979); one *d*; 2nd, 1982, June Belcher. *Educ:* RMA, Sandhurst; London Univ. (BSc, PhD Physics). CEng, MIEE. Dept of Educn and Science: Principal Scientific Officer, 1967–72; Principal, 1972–74; Asst Sec., 1974–80; Under Sec., Planning and Internat. Relations Br., 1980–82, Architects, Bldg and Schs Br., 1982–86, Further and Higher Educn Br. 2, 1986–91; Sec., ABRC., 1991–. FRSA. *Recreations:* music, rowing, tennis. *Address:* Lygon Cottage, 26 Wayneflete Tower Avenue, Esher, Surrey KT10 8QG.

LICHFIELD, 5th Earl of, *cr* 1831; **Thomas Patrick John Anson;** Viscount Anson and Baron Soberton, 1806; *b* 25 April 1939; *s* of Viscount Anson (Thomas William Arnold) (*d* 1958) and Princess Anne of Denmark (*née* Anne Fenella Ferelith Bowes-Lyon) (*d* 1980); *S* grandfather, 1960; *m* 1975, Lady Leonora Grosvenor (marr. diss. 1986), *d* of 5th Duke of Westminster, TD; one *s* two *d*. *Educ:* Harrow Sch.; RMA, Sandhurst. Joined Regular Army, Sept. 1957, as Officer Cadet; Grenadier Guards, 1959–62 (Lieut). Now Photographer (known professionally as Patrick Lichfield). FBIPP; FRPS. *Publications:* The Most Beautiful Women, 1981; Lichfield on Photography (also video cassettes), 1981; A Royal Album, 1982; Patrick Lichfield's Unipart Calendar Book, 1982; Patrick Lichfield Creating the Unipart Calendar, 1983; Hot Foot to Zabriskie Point, 1985; Lichfield on Travel Photography, 1986; Not the Whole Truth (autobiog.), 1986; (ed) Courvoisier's Book of the Best, 1986, 3rd edn, 1990; Lichfield in Retrospect, 1988. *Heir:* *s* Viscount Anson, *qv*. *Address:* 133 Oxford Gardens, W10 6NE. *T:* 081–969 6161; (seat) Shugborough Hall, Stafford. *T:* Little Haywood (0889) 881454. *Club:* White's.

LICHFIELD, Bishop of, since 1983; **Rt. Rev. Keith Norman Sutton;** *b* 23 June 1934; *s* of Norman and Irene Sutton; *m* 1963, Edith Mary Jean Geldard; three *s* one *d*. *Educ:* Jesus College, Cambridge (MA 1959). Curate, St Andrew's, Plymouth, 1959–62; Chaplain, St John's Coll., Cambridge, 1962–67; Tutor and Chaplain, Bishop Tucker Coll., Mukono, Uganda, 1968–73; Principal of Ridley Hall, Cambridge, 1973–78; Bishop Suffragan of Kingston-upon-Thames, 1978–83. Chairman: Gen. Synod Bd for Mission and Unity, 1989–91; Gen. Synod Bd of Mission, 1991–; Mem., Gen. Synod Standing Cttee, 1989–. Select Preacher, Univ. of Cambridge, 1987. Pres., Queen's Coll., Birmingham, 1986–. Entered House of Lords, 1989. Gov., St John's Coll., Durham, 1987–. *Publication:* The People of God, 1983. *Recreations:* Russian literature, third world issues, music. *Address:* Bishop's House, 22 The Close, Lichfield, Staffs WS13 7LG.

LICHFIELD, Dean of; *see* Lang, Very Rev. J. H.

LICHFIELD, Archdeacon of; *see* Ninis, Ven. R. B.

LICHFIELD, Prof. Nathaniel; Professor Emeritus, University of London, since 1978; Chairman, Nathaniel Lichfield & Partners Ltd, Planning, Development, Urban Design and Economic Consultants, since 1989 (Senior Partner, 1962–89); *b* 29 Feb. 1916; 2nd *s* of Hyman Lichman and Fanny (*née* Grecht); *m* 1st, 1942, Rachel Goulden (*d* 1968); two *d*; 2nd, 1970, Dalia Kadury; one *s* one *d*. *Educ:* Raines Foundn Sch.; University of London. BSc (EstMan), PhD (Econ), PPRTPI, FRICS, CEng, MICE. From 1945 has worked continuously in urban and regional planning, specialising in econs of planning from 1950, with particular reference to social cost-benefit in planning, land policy and urban conservation; worked in local and central govt depts and private offices. Consultant commns in UK and all continents. Special Lectr, UCL, 1950; Prof. of Econs of

Environmental Planning, UCL, 1966–79. Visiting Professor: Univ. of California, 1976–78; Univ. of Tel Aviv, 1959–60, 1966; Technion—Israel Inst. of Technol., 1972–74; Hebrew Univ., Jerusalem, 1980–; Univ. of Naples, 1986–; Special Prof., Univ. of Nottingham, 1989. Chm., Econs Cttee, and Co-Chm., Strategic Planning Gp, Internat. Council for Monuments and Sites, 1988–; Member: Exec. Cttee, Internat. Centre for Land Policy Studies, 1975–; Council, Tavistock Inst. of Human Relations, 1970–; formerly Member: SSRC; CNAA; SE Econ. Planning Council. *Publications:* Economics of Planned Development, 1956; Cost Benefit Analysis in Urban Redevelopment, 1962; Cost Benefit Analysis in Town Planning: A Case Study of Cambridge, 1966; Israel's New Towns: A Development Strategy, 1971; (with Prof. A. Proudlove) Conservation and Traffic: a case study of York, 1975; (with Peter Kettle and Michael Whitbread) Evaluation in the Planning Process, 1975; (with Haim Darin-Drabkin) Land Policy in Planning, 1980; (with Leslie Lintott) Period Buildings: evaluation of development–conservation options, 1985; (with Prof. J. Schweid) Conservation of the Built Heritage, 1986; Economics in Urban Conservation, 1988; Land Policy in Israel, 1991; papers in Urban Studies, Regional Studies, Land Economics, Town Planning Review, Restauro, Built Environment. *Recreations:* finding out less and less about more and more, countering advancing age. *Address:* 13 Chalcot Gardens, Englands Lane, NW3 4YB. *T:* 071–586 0461. *Club:* Reform.

LICHINE, Mme David; *see* Riabouchinska, Tatiana.

LICHTENSTEIN, Roy; American painter and sculptor; *b* 27 Oct. 1923; *s* of Milton Lichtenstein and Beatrice (*née* Werner); *m* 1st, 1949, Isabel Wilson (marr. diss.); two *s*; 2nd, 1968, Dorothy Herzka. *Educ:* Art Students League, NY; Ohio State Univ. (BFA 1946; MFA 1949). Cartographical draughtsman, US Army, 1943–46; Instructor, Fine Arts Dept, Ohio State Univ., 1946–51; product designer for various cos, Cleveland, 1951–57; Asst Prof., Fine Arts Dept, NY State Univ., 1957–60, Rutgers Univ., 1960–63. Mem., Amer. Acad. and Inst. of Arts and Letters, 1979. Hon. degrees in Fine Arts. Skowhegan Medal for Painting, 1977. Works in Pop Art and other themes derived from comic strip techniques. One-man shows include: Carlebach Gall., NY, 1951; Leo Castelli Gall., NY, 1962, 1963, 1965, 1967, 1971–75, 1977, 1979, 1981, 1983, 1985, 1986, 1987; Galerie Illeana Sonnabend, Paris, 1963, 1965, 1970, 1975; Venice Biennale, 1966; Pasadena Art Museum, 1967; Walker Art Center, Minneapolis, 1967, 1986; Stedelijk Museum, Amsterdam, 1967; Tate Gall., London, 1968; Guggenheim Museum, NY, 1969; Nelson Gall., Kansas City, 1969; Museum of Contemporary Art, Chicago, 1970; Centre Nat. d'Art Contemporain, Paris, 1975, travelling to Berlin; Seattle Art Museum, 1976; Inst. of Contemp. Art, Boston, 1979; Portland Center for Visual Arts, 1980; St Louis Art Museum, 1981; Fundación Juan March, Madrid, 1982; Seibu Mus., Takanawa, 1983; Mus. of Modern Art, NY, 1987, travelling to Amsterdam and Tel Aviv, 1987, to Frankfurt, Oxford and Washington, 1988. Group shows include: Nat. Collection of Fine Art, Washington, 1966; Venice Biennale, 1966; 36th Biennial Exhibn of Contemp. Amer. Painting, Corcoran Gall., Washington, DC, 1979; Nat. Mus. of Amer. Art, Smithsonian Instn, Washington, 1984. Created outside wall for Circarama of NY State Pavilion, NY World's Fair, 1963; large painting for Expo '67, Montreal, 1967; brushstroke murals for Düsseldorf Univ. Med. Centre, 1970; public sculpture, Mermaid, for Theater of Performing Arts, Miami, 1979; Brushstrokes in Flight, Port Columbus Airport, Columbus, Ohio, 1984; Mural with Blue Brushstrokes, Equitable Life Tower, NY, 1985; Coups de Pinceau, Caisse des Dépôts et Consignations, Paris, 1988; Tel Aviv Mural, Tel Aviv Mus. of Art, 1989. Represented in permanent collections: Albright Knox Gall., Buffalo; Chicago Art Inst.; Corcoran Gall. of Art, Washington; Hirschorn Mus. and Sculpture Garden, Washington; Liby of Congress, Washington; Ludwig Mus., Cologne; Mus. of Modern Art, NY; Nat. Gall. of Art, Washington; Norton Simon Mus., Pasedena; San Francisco Mus. of Modern Art; Seibu Art Mus., Tokyo; Smithsonian Instn, Washington; Stedelijk Mus., Amsterdam; Tate Gall.; V&A Mus.; Walker Art Center, Minneapolis; Whitney Mus. of Amer. Art, NY; Yale Univ. *Address:* PO Box 1369, Southampton, New York, NY 11969, USA.

LICKISS, Michael Gillam; Senior Partner, Grant Thornton, since 1989; *b* 18 Feb. 1934; *s* of Frank Gillam and Elaine Rheta Lickiss; *m* 1st, 1959, Anita (marr. diss. 1979); two *s* two *d*; 2nd, 1987, Anne; one *s*. *Educ:* Bournemouth Grammar Sch.; LSE, London Univ. (BSc Econ 1955). FCA. Articled, Bournemouth, 1955–58; commissioned, Army, 1959–62; practised Bournemouth, 1962–68; Partner, Thornton Baker, Bournemouth, 1968–73, London, 1973–: Exec. Partner, 1975; Managing Partner, 1985; firm's name changed to Grant Thornton, 1986. DTI Inspector, jtly with Hugh Carlisle, QC, 1986–88; Lectr, UK and overseas. Chairman: Family Planning Sales; Crighton Gp; Dir of other cos. Institute of Chartered Accountants: Mem. Council, 1971–81, 1983–; Vice-Pres., 1988–89; Dep. Pres., 1989–90; Pres., 1990–91; Past Chairman: Educn and Training, Tech. Cttee and Ethics Cttee; Professional Conduct Directorate. Chm., CCAB, 1990–91; Dep. Chm., Financial Reporting Council, 1990–91; Mem. Council, BTEC (Chm., Finance Cttee, 1985–); Founder President, Assoc. of Accounting Technicians, 1980–82. *Publications:* articles in learned jls. *Recreations:* gardening in Somerset, walking in the Lake District. *Address:* Grant Thornton House, Melton Street, Euston Square, NW1 2EP. *Club:* Royal Automobile.

LICKLEY, Sir Robert (Lang), Kt 1984; CBE 1973; BSc; DIC; FRSE; FEng; Hon. FIMechE; FRAeS; FIProdE; consultant; *b* Dundee, 19 Jan. 1912. *Educ:* Dundee High Sch.; Edinburgh Univ. (Hon. DSc 1972); Imperial Coll. (Fellow, 1973); FCGI 1976. Formerly: Professor of Aircraft Design, College of Aeronautics, Cranfield; Managing Director, Fairey Aviation Ltd; Hawker Siddeley Aviation Ltd, 1960–76 (Asst Man. Dir, 1965–76); Head, Rolls Royce Support Staff, NEB, 1976–79. President: IMechE, 1971; IProdE, 1981–82. FRSE 1977. Hon. FIMechE 1982; Hon. MIED. Hon. DSc: Edinburgh, 1973; Strathclyde, 1987. *Recreation:* golf. *Address:* Foxwood, Silverdale Avenue, Walton-on-Thames, Surrey KT12 1EQ.

LICKORISH, Leonard John, CBE 1975; *b* 10 Aug. 1921; *s* of Adrian J. and Josephine Lickorish; *m* 1945, Eileen Maris Wright (*d* 1983); one *s*. *Educ:* St George's Coll., Weybridge; University Coll., London (BA). Served RAF, 1941–46. British Travel Assoc., 1946–70; Dir-Gen., BTA, 1970–86; Dir of Studies (Tourism), RIPA, 1986–89. Vis. Prof., Univ. of Strathclyde, 1989–. Chm., European Travel Commn, 1984–86 (Hon. Vice-Chm., 1986); Vice-Pres., Exhibition Industry Federation, 1989– (Chm., 1987–89); Sec., European Tourism Action Group, 1986. Officer of Crown of Belgium, 1967. *Publications:* The Travel Trade, 1955; The Statistics of Tourism, 1975; Tourism Marketing, 1989; numerous for nat. and internat. organisations on internat. travel. *Recreation:* gardening. *Address:* 46 Hillway, Highgate, N6 6EP. *Club:* Royal Over-Seas League.

LIDBURY, Sir John (Towersey), Kt 1971; FRAeS; Vice-Chairman, Hawker Siddeley Group PLC, 1974–83 (Director, 1960; Deputy Managing Director, 1970–81; Consultant, 1983–85); *b* 25 Nov. 1912; *m* 1939, Audrey Joyce (*née* Wigzell); one *s* two *d*. *Educ:* Owen's Sch. Joined Hawker Aircraft Ltd, 1940; Dir, 1951, Gen. Manager, 1953, Man. Dir, 1959, Chm., 1961; Jt Man. Dir, Hawker Siddeley Aviation Ltd, 1959, Dir and Chief Exec., 1961, Dep. Chm. and Man. Dir, 1963–77; Chairman: Hawker Siddeley Dynamics Ltd, 1971–77 (Dep. Chm., 1970); High Duty Alloys Ltd, 1978–79 (Dep. Chm., 1971); High Duty Alloys Castings Ltd, 1978–79; High Duty Alloys Extrusions Ltd, 1978–79; High Duty Alloys Forgings Ltd, 1978–79; Carlton Industries PLC, 1981–82 (Dir, 1978–82); Director: Hawker Siddeley International Ltd, 1963–82; Smiths Industries PLC, 1978–85; Invergordon Distillers (Hldgs) PLC, 1978–82. Dir, Hawker Siddeley Pensions Trustees Ltd, 1968–82 (Chm., 1975–82). Pres., 1969–70, Mem. Council, 1959–77, Soc. of British Aerospace Companies Ltd. Trustee, Science Museum, 1984–85. CBIM. JP Kingston-upon-Thames, 1952–62.

LIDDELL, family name of **Baron Ravensworth.**

LIDDELL, Alasdair Donald MacDuff; Regional General Manager, East Anglian Regional Health Authority, since 1988; *b* 15 Jan. 1949; *s* of late Donald Liddell and of Barbara Liddell (*née* Dixon); *m* 1976, Jennifer Abramsky, *qv*; one *s* one *d*. *Educ:* Balliol College, Oxford (BA Hons Jurisp. 1970); DMS Thames Polytechnic; LHA. King's College and Royal Free Hosps, 1972–77; Administrator (Planning and Policy), Tower Hamlets HA, 1977–79; Area Gen. Administrator, Kensington and Chelsea and Westminster AHA (T), 1979–82; District Administrator, Hammersmith and Fulham HA, 1982–84; District Administrator later District Gen. Manager, Bloomsbury HA, 1984–88. King's Fund Internat. Fellow, 1987–88. *Publication:* contrib. to In Dreams Begins Responsibility: a tribute to Tom Evans, 1987. *Recreations:* ski-ing, playing with computers, buying French wine. *Address:* East Anglian RHA, Union Lane, Chesterton, Cambridge CB4 1RF. *T:* Cambridge (0223) 375266. *Club:* Royal Society of Medicine.

LIDDELL, Dr Donald Woollven, FRCP 1964; FRCPsych; Head of Department of Psychological Medicine, King's College Hospital, 1961–79; *b* 31 Dec. 1917; *m* 1954, Emily (*née* Horsfall) (marr. diss. 1977); one *s* one *d*. *Educ:* Aldenham Sch.; London Hospital. MRCP 1941; Neurological training as RMO, The National Hospital, Queen Square, 1942–45; Psychiatric training, Edinburgh and Maudsley Hospital. Medical Superintendent, St Francis Hospital, Haywards Heath, 1957–61; retired as Physician to Bethlem and Maudsley Hosps, 1968. Examr to RCP and RCPsych. Founder FRCPsych, 1971. *Publications:* contrib. Journal of Mental Science, Journal of Neurology, Psychiatry and Neuro-surgery, American Journal of Mental Diseases, Journal of Social Psychology. *Address:* 8 Newmarket Street, Usk, Gwent NP5 1AT.

LIDDELL, Helen Lawrie; Director of Personnel and Public Affairs, Scottish Daily Record and Sunday Mail (1986) Ltd, since 1988; *b* 6 Dec. 1950; *d* of Hugh Reilly and Bridget Lawrie Reilly; *m* 1972, Dr Alistair Henderson Liddell; one *s* one *d*. *Educ:* St Patrick's High Sch., Coatbridge; Strathclyde Univ. Head, Econ. Dept, 1971–75, and Asst Sec., 1975–76, Scottish TUC; Econ. Correspondent, BBC Scotland, 1976–77; Scottish Sec., Labour Party, 1977–88. *Publication:* Elite, 1990. *Recreations:* cooking, hill-walking, music, writing. *Address:* Glenisla, Langbank, Renfrewshire, Scotland PA14 6XP. *T:* Langbank (047554) 344.

LIDDELL, Jennifer, (Mrs Alasdair Liddell); *see* Abramsky, Jennifer.

LIDDELL, (John) Robert; author; *b* 13 Oct. 1908; *e s* of late Major J. S. Liddell, CMG, DSO, and Anna Gertrude Morgan. *Educ:* Haileybury Coll.; Corpus Christi Coll., Oxford (MA, BLitt). Lecturer in Universities of Cairo and Alexandria, 1942–51, and assistant professor of English, Cairo Univ., 1951; Head of English Dept, Athens Univ., 1963–68. FRSL. Hon. DLitt Athens, 1987. *Publications: fiction:* The Last Enchantments, 1948; The Rivers of Babylon, 1959; An Object for a Walk, 1966; The Deep End, 1968; Stepsons, 1969; The Aunts, 1987, and other novels; *non-fiction:* A Treatise on the Novel, 1947; Aegean Greece, 1954; The Novels of I. Compton-Burnett, 1955; Byzantium and Istanbul, 1956; The Morea, 1958; The Novels of Jane Austen, 1963; Mainland Greece, 1965; Cavafy: a critical biography, 1974; The Novels of George Eliot, 1977; Elizabeth and Ivy, 1986; A Mind at Ease: Barbara Pym and her novels, 1989; Twin Spirits: Emily and Anne Brontë, 1990; *translation:* Ferdinand Fabre, The Abbé Tigrane, 1988.

LIDDELL, Robert; *see* Liddell, J. R.

LIDDERDALE, Sir David (William Shuckburgh), KCB 1975 (CB 1963); TD; Clerk of the House of Commons, 1974–76; *b* 30 Sept. 1910; *s* of late Edward Wadsworth and Florence Amy Lidderdale; *m* 1943, Lola, *d* of late Rev. Thomas Alexander Beckett, Tubbercurry and Ballinew; one *s*. *Educ:* Winchester; King's Coll., Cambridge (MA). Assistant Clerk, House of Commons, 1934. Served War of 1939–45, The Rifle Brigade (TA); active service, N Africa and Italy. Senior Clerk, 1946, Fourth Clerk at the Table, 1953, Second Clerk Assistant, 1959, Clerk Assistant, 1962, House of Commons. Joint Secretary, Assoc. of Secretaries-General of Parliaments (Inter-Parliamentary Union), 1946–54, Mem., 1954–76, Vice-Pres., 1973–76, Hon. Vice-Pres., 1976. *Publications:* The Parliament of France, 1951; (with Lord Campion) European Parliamentary Procedure, 1953; (ed) Erskine May's Parliamentary Practice, 19th edn, 1976. *Recreation:* walking. *Address:* 46 Cheyne Walk, SW3. *Clubs:* Travellers', MCC.

LIDDIARD, Richard England, CBE 1978; non-executive Director, Lion Mark Holdings Ltd (Chairman, 1983–87); Chairman, Bart's Research Development Trust, since 1988; *b* 21 Sept. 1917; *s* of late E. S. Liddiard, MBE, and M. A. Brooke; *m* 1943, Constance Lily, *d* of late Sir William J. Rook; one *s* three *d*. *Educ:* Oundle; Worcester Coll., Oxford (MA). Lt-Col, Royal Signals, 1939–46. Chairman: C. Czarnikow Ltd, 1958–74; Czarnikow Group Ltd, 1974–83; Sugar Assoc. of London, 1960–78; British Fedn of Commodity Assocs, 1962–70, Vice-Chm., 1970–77; London Commodity Exchange, 1972–76; Mem., Cttee on Invisible Exports, 1966–70. Mem. Ct of Assts, Worshipful Co. of Haberdashers, 1958, Master 1978. FRSA. MC (Poland), 1941; Silver Jubilee Medal, 1977. *Recreation:* walking. *Address:* Oxford Lodge, 52 Parkside, Wimbledon, SW19 5NE. *T:* 081–946 3434.

LIDDIARD, Ronald; social work and management consultant, flying instructor and airline pilot; *b* 26 July 1932; *s* of Tom and Gladys Liddiard; *m* 1957, June Alexandra (*née* Ford); two *d*. *Educ:* Canton High Sch., Cardiff; Colleges of Commerce and Technology, Cardiff; Inst. of Local Govt Studies, Birmingham Univ. Dip. Municipal Admin, Certif. Social Work. Health Administrator, 1958–60; Social Worker, 1960–64; Sen. Welfare Administrator, 1964–70; Dir of Social Services: Bath, 1971–74; Birmingham, 1974–85. Hon. Kentucky Col, 1977. *Publications:* How to Become an Airline Pilot, 1989; chapters in: Innovations in the Care of the Elderly, 1984; Self-Care and Health in Old Age, 1986; articles in social work, aviation, management and health jls. *Recreations:* travel, freelance journalism, wines. *Address:* Whitefriars, Portway, Worcs B48 7HP. *T:* Wythall (0564) 826235.

LIESNER, Hans Hubertus, CB 1980; Deputy Chairman, Monopolies and Mergers Commission, since 1989; *b* 30 March 1929; *e s* of Curt Liesner, lawyer, and Edith L. (*née* Neumann); *m* 1968, Thelma Seward; one *s* one *d*. *Educ:* German grammar schs; Bristol Univ. (BA); Nuffield Coll., Oxford; MA Cantab. Asst Lectr, later Lectr, in Economics, London Sch. of Economics, 1955–59; Lectr in Economics, Univ. of Cambridge; Fellow, Dir of Studies in Economics and some time Asst Bursar, Emmanuel Coll., Cambridge, 1959–70; Under-Sec. (Economics), HM Treasury, 1970–76; Dep. Sec., and Chief Econ. Advr, DTI (formerly Industry, Trade and Prices and Consumer Protection), 1976–89, retd. *Publications:* The Import Dependence of Britain and Western Germany, 1957; Case Studies in European Economic Union: the mechanics of integration (with J. E. Meade and S. J. Wells), 1962; Atlantic Harmonisation: making free trade work, 1968; Britain and the Common Market: the effect of entry on the pattern of manufacturing production (with S. S. Han), 1971; articles in jls, etc. *Recreations:* ski-ing, walking, gardening. *Address:* c/o Monopolies and Mergers Commission, New Court, 48 Carey Street, WC2A 2JT. *Club:* Reform.

LIFFORD, 9th Viscount *cr* 1781 (Ire.); **Edward James Wingfield Hewitt;** Director, Neilson Cobbold, Stockbrokers; *b* 27 Jan. 1949; *s* of 8th Viscount Lifford and of Alison Mary Patricia, *d* of T. W. Ashton; *S* father, 1987; *m* 1976, Alison Mary, *d* of Robert Law; one *s* two *d. Educ:* The Old Malthouse, Dorset; Aiglon College, Switzerland. Mem., Stock Exchange; Director: Hampshire Building Soc.; City of Winchester Assured Tenancies; Winchester Cottage Improvement Soc. plc. *Recreations:* country sports. *Heir: s* Hon. James Thomas Wingfield Hewitt, *b* 29 Sept. 1979. *Address:* Field House, Hursley, Hants SO21 2LE. *T:* Hursley (0962) 75203. *Clubs:* Boodle's, Pratt's; Hampshire (Winchester).

LIGETI, Prof. György Sándor; Member, Order of Merit, Germany, 1975; music composer; Professor for Composition, Hamburg Academy of Music, 1973–89; *b* 28 May 1923; *s* of Dr Sándor Ligeti and Dr Ilona Somogyi; *m* 1957, Dr Vera Spitz; one *s. Educ:* Budapest Academy of Music (Dipl. in composition). Lecturer for harmony and counterpoint, Budapest Acad. of Music, 1950–56; Guest Prof., Stockholm Acad. of Music, 1961–71; composer in residence, Stanford Univ., Calif, 1972. Member: Swedish Royal Acad. of Music, 1964; Acad. of Arts, Berlin, 1968; Free Acad. of Arts, Hamburg, 1971; Bavarian Acad. of Fine Arts, Munich, 1978. Hon. Mem., Amer. Acad. and Inst. of Arts and Letters, 1984. Dr *hc* Hamburg, 1988. Grawemeyer Award, 1986. *Main compositions:* Apparitions, for orch., 1959; Atmosphères, for orch., 1961; Aventures, for 3 singers and 7 instrumentalists, 1962; Requiem, for 2 soli, chorus and orch., 1965; Cello concerto, 1966; Chamber concerto, 1970; Melodien, for orch., 1971; Le Grand Macabre, opera, 1977; Trio, for violin, horn, piano, 1982; Piano études, 1985; Piano concerto, 1986; Nonsense madrigals, 1988; Violin concerto, 1991. *Address:* Himmelhofgasse 34, A-1130 Vienna, Austria; Mövenstrasse 3, W-2000 Hamburg 60, Germany.

LIGGINS, Sir Edmund (Naylor), Kt 1976; TD 1947; Solicitor; *b* 21 July 1909; *s* of Arthur William and Hannah Louisa Liggins; *m* 1952, Celia Jean Lawrence (CBE 1991), *d* of William Henry and Millicent Lawrence; three *s* one *d. Educ:* King Henry VIII Sch., Coventry; Rydal Sch. Joined TA, 1936; commissioned 45th Bn (RWR), RE; served War: comd 399 Battery, RA, subseq. 498 LAA Battery, RA, 1942–45. Subseq. commanded 853 Indep. Battery, RA, 1948–51. Consultant, Blythe Liggins, Solicitors, Coventry, Leamington Spa, Balsall Common, Kenilworth, Nuneaton and Warwick. Elected Mem. Council, Law Society, 1963, Vice-Pres., 1974–75, Pres., 1975–76 (Chm., Non-Contentious Business Cttee of Council, 1968–71; Chm., Educn and Trng Cttee, 1973–74); Chm., West Midland Legal Aid Area Cttee, 1963–64; Pres., Warwickshire Law Soc., 1969–70. Mem. Court, Univ. of Warwick, 1964–; Hon. LLD Warwick, 1988. Hon. Mem., Amer. Bar Assoc. *Recreations:* cricket, rugby football, squash rackets; amateur theatre. *Address:* Hareway Cottage, Hareway Lane, Barford, Warwickshire CV35 8DB. *T:* Barford (0926) 624246. *Clubs:* Army and Navy, MCC, Forty; Coventry and North Warwickshire Cricket, Drapers' (Coventry).

LIGGINS, Sir Graham Collingwood, Kt 1991; CBE 1983; FRCSE, FRACS, FRCOG; FRS 1980; FRSNZ 1976; Professor of Obstetrics and Gynaecological Endocrinology, University of Auckland, New Zealand, 1968–87, now Professor Emeritus (formerly Senior Lecturer); Consultant to National Women's Hospital, Auckland. *Educ:* Univ. of NZ. MB, ChB, Univ. NZ, 1949; PhD, Univ. of Auckland, 1969. MRCOG Lond. 1956; FRCSE 1958; FRACS 1960. Is distinguished for his work on the role of foetal hormones in the control of parturition. Hon. FAGS, 1976; Hon. FACOG, 1978. Hon. MD Lund, 1983. Hector Medal, RSNZ, 1980. *Publications:* approx. 200 published papers. *Recreations:* forestry, sailing, fishing. *Address:* Postgraduate School of Obstetrics and Gynaecology, National Women's Hospital, Claude Road, Auckland 3, New Zealand. *T:* 775–127; 3/38 Awatea Road, Parnell, Auckland 1, New Zealand.

LIGHT, (Sidney) David; a Civil Service Commissioner, 1978–79; Member, Civil Service Commission's Panel of Selection Board Chairmen, 1980–89; *b* 9 Dec. 1919; *s* of late William Light; *m* Edna Margaret Honey; one *s. Educ:* King Edward VI Sch., Southampton. RAF, 1940–46. HM Customs and Excise, 1938; HM Treasury, 1948–68; Asst Sec., CS Commn, 1969–75; Under Sec., CSD, 1975–78. *Recreations:* bricolage, watching cricket, travel. *Address:* Oakhanger, Vicarage Hill, Farnham, Surrey GU9 8HJ. *T:* Farnham (0252) 721522. *Clubs:* Commonwealth Trust; Hampshire Cricket.

LIGHTBODY, Ian (Macdonald), CMG 1974; *b* 19 Aug. 1921; *s* of Thomas Paul Lightbody and Dorothy Marie Louise Lightbody (*née* Cooper); *m* 1954, Noreen, *d* of late Captain T. H. Wallace, Dromore, Co. Down; three *s* one *d. Educ:* Queens Park Sch., Glasgow; Glasgow Univ. (MA). War service, Indian Army, India and Far East, 1942–46 (Captain); Colonial Admin. Service, Hong Kong, 1945; various admin. posts; District Comr, New Territories, 1967–68; Defence Sec., 1968–69; Coordinator, Festival of Hong Kong, 1969; Comr for Resettlement, 1971; Sec. for Housing and Chm., Hong Kong Housing Authority, 1973–77; Sec. for Admin, Hong Kong, 1977–78; Chm., Public Services Commn, Hong Kong, 1978–80. MLC 1971; MEC 1977; retd from Hong Kong, 1980. Mem., Arun DC, 1983–91. *Recreations:* walking, politics, Japanese prints. *Address:* Two Stacks, Lake Lane, Barnham, Sussex PO22 0AD. *Clubs:* Hong Kong, Royal Hong Kong Jockey.

LIGHTBOWN, David Lincoln; MP (C) Staffordshire South East, since 1983; Comptroller of HM Household, since 1990; *b* 30 Nov. 1932; *m* Margaret Ann. Former Engrg Dir, a public limited co. in West Midlands. Member: Lichfield Dist Council, 1975–86 (Leader of Council, 1977–83); Staffs CC, 1977–85 (formerly Chm., Educn and Finance Cttees). An Assistant Govt Whip, 1986–87; a Lord Comr of HM Treasury (Govt Whip), 1987–90; Vice-Chamberlain, HM Household, 1990. *Address:* House of Commons, SW1A 0AA. *T:* 071–219 6241/4212.

LIGHTBOWN, Ronald William, MA; FSA, FRAS; art historian and author; Keeper of the Department of Metalwork, Victoria and Albert Museum, 1985–89; *b* Darwen, Lancs, 2 June 1932; *s* of late Vincent Lightbown and of Helen Anderson Lightbown (*née* Burness); *m* 1962, Mary Dorothy Webster; one *s. Educ:* St Catharine's Coll., Cambridge (MA). FSA, FRAS. Victoria and Albert Museum: Asst Keeper, Library, 1958–64; Asst Keeper, Dept of Metalwork, 1964–73; Dep. Keeper, 1973–76, Keeper, 1976–85, Library. Fellow, Inst. for Res. in the Humanities, Wisconsin Univ., 1974. Pres., Jewellery History Soc., 1990; a Vice-Pres., Soc. of Antiquaries, 1986–90 (Sec., 1979–86); Associate Trustee, Soane Mus., 1981–. Socio dell' Ateneo Veneto, for contrib. to study of culture of Venice and the Veneto, 1987; Socio dell' Accademia Clementina, Bologna, for contribns to study of Italian art, 1988. *Publications:* French Secular Goldsmith's work of the Middle Ages, 1978; Sandro Botticelli, 1978, 2nd edn, 1989 (Prix Vasori, 1990); (with M. Corbett) The Comely Frontispiece, 1978; (ed and trans. with A. Caiger-Smith) Piccolpasso: the art of the potter, 1980; Donatello and Michelozzo, 1980; Andrea Mantegna, 1986; (ed and introd) History of Art in 18th Century England (series of source-books on 18th century British art), 14 vols, 1970–71; V&A Museum catalogues and publications: (pt author) Italian Sculpture, 1964; Tudor Domestic Silver, 1970; Scandinavian and Baltic Silver, 1975; French Silver, 1979; (with M. Archer) India Observed, 1982; many articles in learned jls, incl. Burlington Magazine, Warburg Jl and Art Bulletin. *Recreations:* reading, travel, music, conversation. *Address:* Barronmount, Goresbridge, Co. Kilkenny, Ireland.

LIGHTFOOT, George Michael; His Honour Judge Lightfoot; a Circuit Judge, since 1986; *b* 9 March 1936; *s* of Charles Herbert Lightfoot and Mary Lightfoot (*née* Potter); *m* 1963, Dorothy (*née* Miller); two *s* two *d. Educ:* St Michael's Catholic College, Leeds; Exeter College, Oxford (MA). Schoolmaster, 1962–66. Called to the Bar, Inner Temple, 1966; practised on NE circuit. A Recorder, 1985–86. Mem., Home Farm Trust, 1980–; President: Leeds Friends of Home Farm Trust, 1987–; Mencap, Leeds, 1987–. *Recreations:* cricket and sport in general, gardening (labourer), learning to listen to music. *Address:* 4 Shadwell Park Close, Leeds LS17 8TN. *T:* Leeds (0532) 665673. *Clubs:* Lansdowne; Catenian Association (City of Leeds Circle).

LIGHTHILL, Sir (Michael) James, Kt 1971; FRS 1953; FRAeS; Provost of University College London, 1979–89, Hon. Fellow, 1982, Hon. Research Fellow, 1989; *b* 23 Jan. 1924; *s* of E. B. Lighthill; *m* 1945, Nancy Alice Dumaresq; one *s* four *d. Educ:* Winchester Coll.; Trinity Coll., Cambridge (Hon. Fellow, 1986). Aerodynamics Division, National Physical Laboratory, 1943–45; Fellow, Trinity Coll., Cambridge, 1945–49; Sen. Lectr in Maths, Univ. of Manchester, 1946–50; Beyer Prof. of Applied Mathematics, Univ. of Manchester, 1950–59; Dir, RAE, Farnborough, 1959–64; Royal Soc. Res. Prof., Imperial Coll., 1964–69; Lucasian Prof. of Mathematics, Univ. of Cambridge, 1969–79. Chm., Academic Adv. Cttee, Univ. of Surrey, 1964; Member: Adv. Council on Technology, 1964; NERC, 1965–70; Shipbuilding Inquiry Cttee, 1965; (part-time) Post Office Bd, 1972–74; First Pres., Inst. of Mathematics and its Applications, 1964–66; a Sec. and Vice-Pres., Royal Soc., 1965–69; President: Internat. Commn on Mathematical Instruction, 1971–74; Internat. Union of Theoretical and Applied Mechanics, 1984–88. FRAeS 1961, Hon. FRAeS 1990. Foreign Member: American Academy of Arts and Sciences, 1958; American Philosophical Soc., 1970; US Nat. Acad. of Sciences, 1976; US Nat. Acad. of Engineering, 1977. Associate Mem., French Acad. of Sciences, 1976. FIC 1991; Hon. Fellow American Inst. of Aeronautics and Astronautics, 1961. Hon. DSc: Liverpool, 1961; Leicester, 1965; Strathclyde, 1966; Essex, 1967; Princeton, 1967; East Anglia, 1968; Manchester, 1968; Bath, 1969; St Andrews, 1969; Surrey, 1969; Cranfield, 1974; Paris, 1975; Aachen, 1975; Rensselaer, 1980; Leeds, 1983; Brown, 1984; Southern California, 1984; Ludwig-Prandtl-Ring, 1984; Lisbon, 1986; Rehovot, 1987. Royal Medal, Royal Society, 1964; Gold Medal, Royal Aeronautical Society, 1965; Harvey Prize for Science and Technol., Israeli Inst. of Technol., 1981; Gold Medal, Inst. of Maths and Its Applications, 1982. Comdr Order of Léopold, 1963. *Publications:* Introduction to Fourier Analysis and Generalised Functions, 1958; Mathematical Biofluiddynamics, 1975; Newer Uses of Mathematics, 1977; Waves in Fluids, 1978; An Informal Introduction to Theoretical Fluid Mechanics, 1986; articles in Royal Soc. Proc. and Trans, Qly Jl of Mechanics and Applied Maths, Philosophical Magazine, Jl of Aeronautical Scis, Qly Jl of Maths, Aeronautical Qly, Communications on Pure and Applied Maths, Proc. Cambridge Philosophical Soc., Jl of Fluid Mechanics, Reports and Memoranda of ARC; contrib. to Modern Developments in Fluid Dynamics: High Speed Flow; High Speed Aerodynamics and Jet Propulsion; Surveys in Mechanics; Laminar Boundary Layers. *Recreations:* music and swimming. *Address:* Department of Mathematics, University College London, Gower Street, WC1E 6BT. *Club:* Athenæum.

LIGHTMAN, Gavin Anthony, QC 1980; *b* 20 Dec. 1939; *s* of Harold Lightman, *qv*; *m* 1965, Naomi Ann Claff; one *s* two *d. Educ:* Univ. of London (LLB); Univ. of Michigan (LLM). Called to the Bar, Lincoln's Inn, 1963, Bencher 1987. Dep. Pres., Anglo Jewish Assoc. *Publications:* (with G. Battersby) Cases and Statutes on Real Property, 1965; (with G. Moss) The Law Relating to the Receivers of Companies, 1986; A Report on the National Union of Miners, 1990. *Recreations:* reading, walking, eating. *Address:* 5B Prince Arthur Road, Hampstead, NW3. *T:* 071–794 5180. *Clubs:* Athenæum, Royal Automobile.

LIGHTMAN, Harold, QC 1955; Master of the Bench of Lincoln's Inn; *b* 8 April 1906; *s* of Louis Lightman, Leeds; *m* 1936, Gwendoline Joan, *d* of David Ostrer, London; three *s. Educ:* City of Leeds Sch.; privately. Accountant, 1927–29. Barrister, Lincoln's Inn, 1932. Home Guard, 1940–45. Defence Medal, 1946. Liveryman, Company of Glovers, 1960. *Publication:* (ed) 40th edn, Gore Browne, Company Law and Emergency War Legislation, 1945. *Recreation:* reading. *Address:* Stone Buildings, Lincoln's Inn, WC2. *T:* 071–242 3840. *Club:* Royal Automobile.
See also G. A. Lightman.

LIGHTMAN, Ivor Harry, CB 1984; Public Affairs Adviser, Touche Ross Management Consultants, since 1989; Hon. Research Fellow, Cardiff Business School, since 1989; Member, Parole Board, since 1990; *b* 23 Aug. 1928; *s* of late Abraham Lightman, OBE and Mary (*née* Goldschneider); *m* 1950, Stella Doris Blend; one *s. Educ:* Abergele Grammar Sch. Clerical Officer, Min. of Food, 1946; Nat. Service, RAOC (Corp.), 1946–49; Officer of Customs and Excise, 1949–56; Asst Principal, Ministry of Works, 1957; Principal: Ministry of Works, 1961–65; HM Treasury, 1965–67; Assistant Secretary: MPBW, 1967–70; CSD, 1970–73; Under Secretary: Price Commn, 1973–76; Dept of Prices and Consumer Protection, 1976–78; Dept of Industry, 1978–81; Dep. Sec., Welsh Office, 1981–88, retd. Chairman: First Choice Housing Assoc., 1989–; All-Wales Adv. Panel on Services for Mentally Handicapped People, 1990–. *Address:* 6 Clos Coedydafarn, Lisvane, Cardiff CF4 5ER.

LIGHTMAN, Lionel; Lay Observer attached to Lord Chancellor's Department, 1986–90; *b* 26 July 1928; *s* of late Abner Lightman and late Gitli Lightman (*née* Szmul); *m* 1952, Helen, *y d* of late Rev. A. Shechter and late Mrs Shechter; two *d. Educ:* City of London Sch.; Wadham Coll., Oxford (MA). Nat. Service, RAEC, 1951–53 (Temp. Captain). Asst Principal, BoT, 1953; Private Sec. to Perm. Sec., 1957; Principal 1958; Trade Comr, Ottawa, 1960–64; Asst Sec. 1967; Asst Dir, Office of Fair Trading, 1973–75; Under Sec., Dept of Trade, 1975–78, DoI, 1978–81; Dir of Competition Policy, OFT, 1981–84. *Address:* 73 Greenhill, NW3 5TZ. *T:* 071–435 3427.

LIGHTON, Sir Christopher Robert, 8th Bt, *cr* 1791; MBE 1945; *b* 30 June 1897; *o s* of 7th Bt and Helen (*d* 1927), *d* of late James Houldsworth, Coltness, Lanarkshire; *S* father, 1929; *m* 1st, 1926, Rachel Gwendoline (marr. diss. 1953; she *d* 1991), *yr d* of late Rear-Admiral W. S. Goodridge, CIE; two *d*; 2nd, 1953, Horatia Edith (*d* 1981), *d* of A. T. Powlett, Godminster Manor, Bruton, Somerset; one *s*; 3rd, 1985, Eve, *o d* of late Rear-Adm. A. L. Mark-Wardlaw, *widow* of Maj. Stopford Ram. *Educ:* Eton Coll.; RMC. Late The King's Royal Rifle Corps; rejoined the Army in Aug. 1939 and served War of 1939–45. *Heir: s* Thomas Hamilton Lighton [*b* 4 Nov. 1954; *m* 1990, Belinda, *d* of John Fergusson; one *d*]. *Address:* Fairview, Dirleton, East Lothian.

LIKAKU, Victor Timothy; General Manager, The New Building Society, Blantyre, since 1985; Mayor of City of Blantyre, since 1981; *b* 15 Oct. 1934; *m* 1959, Hilda; one *s* two *d.* Malaŵi Civil Service, Min. of Finance, 1957–62; Malaŵi Govt Schol., St Steven's

Coll., Univ. of Delhi, India, 1962 (BA Econ.); Dept of Customs and Excise, 1966; Customs and Admin. Courses, New Zealand, 1967, Vienna 1972; UN Fellowship, GATT, Geneva, 1973; Controller of Customs and Excise, Malaŵi Govt, 1973; High Comr for Malaŵi in London, 1976–78. Mayor, City of Blantyre, 1981–83. *Recreations:* reading, soccer. *Address:* The New Building Society, Building Society House, Victoria Avenue, PO Box 466, Blantyre, Malaŵi. *T:* 634 753. *Clubs:* Hurlingham (Hon. Mem.), International Sporting, Penthouse.

LIKIERMAN, Prof. (John) Andrew; Professor of Accounting and Financial Control, since 1987, Dean of External Affairs, since 1989, and Deputy Principal, since 1990, London Business School; *b* 30 Dec. 1943; *s* of Dolek and Olga Likierman; *m* 1987, Meira, *d* of Joshua and Miriam Gruenspan; one step *s* one step *d. Educ:* Stowe Sch.; Univ. of Vienna; Balliol Coll., Oxford (MA). FCMA, FCCA. Divl Management Accountant, Tootal Ltd, 1965–68; Asst Lectr, 1968–69, Lectr, 1972–74, Dept of Management Studies, Leeds Univ.; Qualitex Ltd, 1969–72 (Man. Dir, Overseas Div., 1971–72); Vis. Fellow, Oxford Centre for Management Studies, 1972–74; Chm., Ex Libris Ltd, 1973–74; London Business Sch., 1974–76 and 1979–: Dir, Part-time Masters Programme, 1981–85; Dir, Inst. of Public Sector Management, 1983–88; Chm., Faculty Bd, 1986–89; Elected Governor, 1986–89, Governor, 1990–. Asst Sec., Cabinet Office (Mem., Central Policy Review Staff), 1976–79, Advr, 1979–82; Advisor, H of C Select Committees: Treasury and CS, 1981–; Employment, 1985–; Transport, 1981, 1987–; Social Services, 1988; Social Security, 1991; Mem., various govt inquiries, 1975–; Chm., Inquiry into Professional Liability, 1989. Member: Finance Cttee, Oxfam, 1974–84; Cttee on med. costs, London Univ., 1980–81; Current Affairs Adv. Gp, Channel 4, 1986–87; Acad. Adv. Panel, Accounting Standards Cttee, 1987–90 (Mem., Public Sector Liaison Gp, 1984–86); Audit Commn, 1988–91; Financial Reporting Council, 1990–; Exec. Cttee, British Acad. of Management, 1988–90; Consultative Cttee of Accountancy Bodies, 1989–; Council: RIPA, 1982–88; Consumers' Assoc., 1983–85; Chartered Inst. of Management Accountants, 1985– (Pres., 1991–); Civil Service Coll., 1989–; Scientific Council, Eur. Inst. of Public Admin, 1990–. Chm. Editl Bd, Public Money and Management, 1988–; non-exec. Dir, Economists' Bookshop, 1981–91 (non-exec. Chm., 1987–91). *Publications:* The Reports and Accounts of Nationalised Industries, 1979; Cash Limits and External Financing Limits, 1981; (jtly) Public Sector Accounting and Financial Control, 1983; (with P. Vass) Structure and Form of Government Expenditure Reports, 1984; Public Expenditure, 1988; (jtly) Accounting for Brands, 1989; contribs to academic and professional jls. *Recreations:* ski-ing, cycling, choral singing, architecture, wine. *Address:* 5 Downshire Hill, NW3 1NR. *T:* 071–435 9888. *Club:* Reform.

LILFORD, 7th Baron, *cr* 1797; **George Vernon Powys;** *b* 8 Jan. 1931; *s* of late Robert Horace Powys (*g g grandson* of 2nd Baron) and of Vera Grace Bryant, Rosebank, Cape, SA; *S* kinsman, 1949; *m* 1st, 1954, Mrs Eve Bird (marr. diss.); 2nd, 1957, Anuta Merritt (marr. diss., 1958); 3rd, 1958, Norma Yvonne Shell (marr. diss., 1961); 4th, 1961, Mrs Muriel Spottiswoode (marr. diss., 1969); two *d*; 5th, 1969, Margaret Penman; one *s* two *d. Educ:* St Aidan's Coll., Grahamstown, SA; Stonyhurst Coll. *Recreations:* golf, cricket. *Heir: s* Hon. Mark Vernon Powys, *b* 16 Nov. 1975. *Address:* Le Grand Câtelet, St John, Jersey, Channel Islands.

LILL, John Richard, OBE 1978; concert pianist; Professor at Royal College of Music; *b* 17 March 1944; *s* of George and Margery Lill. *Educ:* Leyton County High Sch.; Royal College of Music. FRCM; Hon. FTCL; FLCM; Hon. RAM 1988. Gulbenkian Fellowship, 1967. First concert at age of 9; Royal Festival Hall debut, 1963; Promenade Concert debut, 1969. Numerous broadcasts on radio and TV; has appeared as soloist with all leading British orchestras. Recitals and concertos throughout Great Britain, Europe, USA, Canada, Scandinavia, USSR, Japan and Far East, Australia, New Zealand, etc. Overseas tours as soloist with many orchestras including London Symphony Orchestra and London Philharmonic Orchestra. Complete recordings of Beethoven sonatas and concertos; complete Beethoven cycle, London, 1982, 1986, and Tokyo, 1988. Chappell Gold Medal; Pauer Prize; 1st Prize, Royal Over-Seas League Music Competition, 1963; Dinu Lipatti Medal in Harriet Cohen Internat. Awards; 1st Prize, Internat. Tchaikowsky Competition, Moscow, 1970. Hon. DSc Aston, 1978; Hon. DMus Exeter, 1979. *Recreations:* amateur radio, chess, walking. *Address:* c/o Harold Holt Ltd, 31 Sinclair Road, W14 0NS. *T:* 071–603 4600.

LILLEY, Prof. Geoffrey Michael, OBE 1981; CEng, FRSA, FRAeS, MIMechE, FIMA; Professor of Aeronautics and Astronautics, University of Southampton, 1964–82, now Emeritus Professor (Head of Department of Aeronautics and Astronautics, 1963–82); Director and Deputy Chairman, Hampshire Technology Centre, since 1985; *b* Isleworth, Mddx, 16 Nov. 1919; *m* 1948, Leslie Marion Wheeler; one *s* two *d. Educ:* Isleworth Grammar Sch.; Battersea and Northampton Polytechnics; Imperial Coll. BSc(Eng) 1944, MSc(Eng) 1945, DIC 1945. Gen. engrg trg, Benham and Kodak, 1936–40; Drawing Office and Wind Tunnel Dept, Vickers Armstrong Ltd, Weybridge, 1940–46; Coll. of Aeronautics: Lectr, 1946–51; Sen. Lectr, 1951–55; Dep. Head of Dept of Aerodynamics, 1955, and Prof. of Experimental Fluid Mechanics, 1962–64. Visiting Professor: Stanford Univ., 1977–78; ME Technical Univ., Ankara, Turkey, 1983–90; Univ. of the Witwatersrand, 1990. Past Member: Aeronautical Res. Council (past Mem. Council and Chm. Aerodynamics, Applied Aerodynamics, Noise Res., Fluid Motion and Performance Cttees); Noise Advisory Council (Chm., Noise from Air Traffic Working Group); Past Chm., Aerodynamics Cttee, Engrg Sci. Data Unit. Consultant to: Rolls Royce, 1959–61, 1967–84; AGARD, 1959–63 andd 1988–89; OECD, 1969–71. Gold Medal for Aeronautics, RAeS, 1983; Aerodynamic Noise Medal, AIAA, 1985. *Publications:* (jt editor) Proc. Stanford Conf. on Complex Turbulent Flows; articles in reports and memoranda of: Aeronautical Research Council; Royal Aeronautical Soc., and other jls. *Recreations:* music, chess, walking. *Address:* Highbury, Pine Walk, Chilworth, Southampton SO1 7HQ. *T:* Southampton (0703) 769109. *Club:* Athenæum.

LILLEY, Rt. Hon. Peter Bruce, PC 1990; MP (C) St Albans, since 1983; Secretary of State for Trade and Industry, since 1990; *b* 23 Aug. 1943; *s* of Arnold Francis Lilley and Lillian (*née* Elliott); *m* 1979, Gail Ansell. *Educ:* Dulwich Coll.; Clare Coll., Cambridge. MA; FInstPet 1978. Economic consultant in underdeveloped countries, 1966–72; investment advisor on energy industries, 1972–84. Chm., London Oil Analysts Gp, 1979–80; Partner, 1980–86, Dir, 1986–87, W. Greenwell & Co., later Greenwell Montagu. Consultant Dir, Cons. Res. Dept, 1979–83. Chm., Bow Group, 1972–75. Contested (C) Tottenham, Oct. 1974. PPS to Ministers for Local Govt, Jan.–Oct. 1984, to Chancellor of the Exchequer, 1984–87; Economic Sec. to HM Treasury, 1987–89, Financial Sec., 1989–90. *Publications:* Do You Sincerely Want to Win?, 1972, 2nd edn 1973; Lessons for Power, 1974; (with S. Brittan) Delusion of Incomes Policy, 1977; (contrib.) Skidelsky: End of the Keynesian Era, 1980. *Address:* House of Commons, SW1. *T:* 071–219 3000. *Club:* Carlton.

LILLICRAP, Harry George, CBE 1976; Chairman, Cable and Wireless, 1972–76; *b* 29 June 1913; *s* of late Herbert Percy Lillicrap; *m* 1938, Kathleen Mary Charnock; two *s. Educ:* Erith County Sch.; University College London. BSc (Eng) 1934. Post Office Telecommunications, 1936–72; Sen. Dir Planning, Sen. Dir Customer Services, 1967–72. Dir, Telephone Rentals Ltd, 1976–84. *Address:* Lower Flat, Leysters, Highfield Road, East Grinstead, West Sussex RH19 2DX. *T:* East Grinstead (0342) 325811.

LILLINGSTON, George David I. I.; *see* Inge-Innes-Lillingston.

LILLY, Prof. Malcolm Douglas, FRS 1991; FEng 1982; Professor of Biochemical Engineering, University College London, since 1979; *b* 9 Aug. 1936; *s* of Charles Victor Lilly and Amy Gardiner; *m* 1959, Sheila Elizabeth Stuart; two *s. Educ:* St Olave's Grammar Sch.; University College London (BSc, PhD, DSc). FIChemE, FIBiotech. University College London: Lecturer in Biochemical Engrg, 1963–72; Reader in Enzyme Technology, 1972–79; Dir, Centre for Biochem. Engrg and Biotechnol., 1982–89; Fellow, 1988. Director, Whatman Biochemicals, 1968–71. Vis. Prof., Univ. of Pennsylvania, 1969; Vis. Engrg Fellow, Merck & Co., USA, 1987 (Vice-Dean, Faculty of Engrg, 1987). Past Chm., Internat. Orgn for Biotechnology and Bioengineering, 1980– (Chm, 1972–80); Dir, Internat. Inst. of Biotechnology, 1989–; Member: Council, Soc. for Gen. Microbiol., 1979–83; Research Cttee, British Gas, 1982–; Bd of Management and Executive Cttee, Inst. for Biotechnological Studies, 1983–89; Bd, PHLS, 1988–. Hartley Lecture, Royal Soc., 1988. Food, Pharmaceutical and Bioengrg Award, Amer. Inst. of Chem. Engrs, 1976. *Publications:* (jtly) Fermentation and Enzyme Technology, 1979; (jtly) OECD Report, Biotechnology: international trends and perspectives, 1982; numerous papers on biochemical engrg, fermentation and enzyme technology. *Recreations:* sailing, advanced motoring (IAM Observer), voluntary countryside ranger. *Address:* 8 Tower Road, Orpington, Kent BR6 0SQ. *T:* Orpington (0689) 21762.

LIM, Sir Han-Hoe, Kt 1946; CBE 1941; Hon. LLD (Malaya); MB, ChB (Edinburgh); JP; Pro-Chancellor, University of Malaya, 1949–59; *b* 27 April 1894; 2nd *s* of late Lim Cheng Sah, Singapore; *m* 1920, Chua Seng Neo; two *s* two *d. Educ:* St Andrew's Sch. and Raffles Institution; University of Edinburgh. RMO North Devon General Hospital, with charge of Military Auxiliary Hospital, 1919; Municipal Commissioner, Singapore, 1926–31; Member of Legislative Council, Straits Settlements, 1933–42, and its Finance Cttee, 1936–42; Member of Exec. Council, Straits Settlements, 1939–42; Member of Advisory Council, Singapore, 1946–48; Member of Exec. Council, Singapore, 1948–50. Member of Council, King Edward VII College of Medicine, Singapore, 1930–42; Mem. and Chm., Public Services Commission, Singapore, 1952–56. *Recreations:* tennis, chess. *Address:* 758 Mountbatten Road, Singapore 15. *T:* 40655. *Club:* Garden (Singapore).

LIM FAT, Sir (Maxime) Edouard (Lim Man), Kt 1991; Professor Emeritus, University of Mauritius, since 1975; company director; *s* of V. Lim Fat and S. Lifo; *m* 1952, Y. H. Chan Wah Hak; two *s* one *d. Educ:* Univ. of London (BSc Chem. Eng.); Univ. of Newcastle (MSc Agric. Eng.). AEE Harwell, 1950–51; Engineer, Min. of Agriculture, Mauritius, 1951–63; Principal, Mauritius Coll. of Agriculture, 1963–68; Head, Sch. of Industrial Technology, Univ. of Mauritius, 1968–80; Director, 1980–: Bank of Mauritius; Develt Bank of Mauritius; four factories. *Publications:* numerous articles, mainly on industrial develt and educn. *Recreations:* golf, economics, music. *Address:* 19 Rev. Lebrun Street, Rose-hill, Mauritius. *T:* (home) 230–454–7680, (office) 230–454–8288. *Clubs:* Gymkhana, Vacoas.

LIM PIN, Professor, MD; FRCP, FRCPE, FRACP, FACP; Vice-Chancellor, National University of Singapore, since 1981; *b* 12 Jan. 1936; *s* of late Lim Lu Yeh and of Choo Siew Kooi; *m* 1964, Shirley Loo; two *s* one *d. Educ:* Univ. of Cambridge (MA; MD 1970). FRCP 1976; FRCPE 1981; FRACP 1978; FACP 1981. MO, Min. of Health, Singapore, 1965–66; Univ. of Singapore: Lectr in Medicine, 1966–70; Sen. Lectr in Medicine, 1971–73; Associate Prof. of Medicine, 1974–77; Prof. and Head, Dept of Medicine, 1978–81; Dep. Vice-Chancellor, 1979–81. Eisenhower Fellow, USA, 1982. Chm., Applied Res. Corp., 1982–; Director: Neptune Orient Lines, 1981–; Nat. Univ. Hosp., 1985–; Member: Nat. Productivity Council, 1981–; Cttee on Nat. Computerisation, 1985–; Econ. Develt Bd, 1989–; Founder Pres., Endocrine and Metabolic Soc. of Singapore. Chm., Bd of Govs, Raffles Instn, 1988–; Member, Board of Governors: Inst. of E Asian Philosophies, 1987–; Inst. of Policy Studies, 1988–; Member: Admin Bd, Assoc. of SE Asian Instns of Higher Learning, 1988–; Bd of Advrs, Mendaki, 1989–; Bd of Govs, Singapore Inst. of Labour Studies; Adv. Council, Canada—ASEAN Centre; Bd of Dirs, Overseas Union Bank; Bd of Dirs, Lee Kuan Yew Exchange Fellowship. Hon. Fellow, Coll. of Gen. Practitioners of Singapore, 1982. Public Administration Medal (Gold), Singapore, 1984; Meritorious Service Medal, Singapore, 1990. Officier, Ordre des Palmes Académiques (France), 1988. *Publications:* articles in New England Jl of Medicine, Med. Jl of Australia, BMJ, Qly Jl of Medicine, and Tissue Antigens. *Recreations:* swimming, badminton. *Address:* National University of Singapore, 10 Kent Ridge Crescent, Singapore 0511, Republic of Singapore. *T:* 7756666. *Club:* Singapore Island Country.

LIMANN, Dr Hilla, Hon. GCMG 1981; President of Ghana, 1979–81; *b* 1934; *m*; five *c. Educ:* Lawra Primary Boarding Sch.; Tamale Middle Boarding Sch.; Govt Teacher Trng Coll.; London Sch. of Economics (Hon. Fellow, 1982); Sorbonne; Univ. of London; Faculty of Law and Econ. Sciences, Univ. of Paris. BSc(Econ.) 1960; BA Hons (Hist.), 1964; PhD (Polit. Sci. and Law), 1965. Teacher, 1952–55; examiner for Civil Service grad. entry, W African Exams Council. Councillor, Tumu Dist Council, 1952 (Chm., 1953–55); contested (Indep.) Constituency, Party Elec., 1954. Head of Chancery and Official Sec., Ghana Embassy, Lomé, Togo, 1968–77; Mem., Constitutional Commn on 1969 Constitution for Ghana; Mem. Govt Delegns for opening of borders of Ghana with the Ivory Coast/Upper Volta; Mem./Sec. to Ghana delegns, OAU and Non-aligned States, Confs of ILO, WHO, Internat. Atomic Energy Agency. Leader, People's National Party.

LIMBU; *see* Rambahadur Limbu.

LIMERICK, 6th Earl of, *cr* 1803 (Ire.); **Patrick Edmund Pery,** KBE 1983; DL; MA, CA; Baron Glentworth, 1790 (Ire.); Viscount Limerick, 1800 (Ire.); Baron Foxford, 1815 (UK); Director: TR Pacific Investment Trust PLC, since 1976; De La Rue Company plc, since 1983; Chairman: Polymeters Response International, since 1988; Pirelli UK, since 1989; Chairman, Board of Governors, City of London Polytechnic, since 1984; *b* 12 April 1930; *e s* of 5th Earl of Limerick, GBE, CH, KCB, DSO, TD, and Angela Olivia, Dowager Countess of Limerick, GBE, CH (*d* 1981); *S* father, 1967; *m* 1961, Sylvia Rosalind Lush (*see* Countess of Limerick); two *s* one *d. Educ:* Eton; New Coll., Oxford. CA 1957. Chm., Mallinson–Denny Ltd, 1979–81; Director: Kleinwort Benson Ltd, 1967–87 (Vice Chm., 1983–85; Dep Chm., 1985–87); Kleinwort Benson Gp, 1982–90; Commercial Bank of Australia Ltd (London Adv. Bd), 1969–72; Brooke Bond Gp, 1981–84. Parly Under-Sec. of State for Trade, DTI, 1972–74; Chairman: BOTB, 1979–83; BIEC, 1984–91; Pres., Inst. of Export, 1983–; Vice-Pres., Assoc. of British Chambers of Commerce, 1977– (Pres., 1974–77); Member: Cttee for ME Trade, 1968– (Chm., 1975–79); Council, London Chamber of Commerce, 1968–79. Trustee, City Parochial Foundn, 1971–. President: Anglo-Swiss Soc., 1984–; Ski Club of Gt Britain, 1974–81; Alpine Ski Club, 1985–87 (Vice-Pres., 1975–77); Vice-Pres., Alpine Club, 1989–. DL W Sussex, 1988. *Recreations:* skiing, mountaineering. *Heir: s* Viscount Glentworth, *qv. Address:* Chiddinglye, West Hoathly, East Grinstead, West Sussex RH19 4QT. *T:* Sharpthorne (0342) 810214; 30 Victoria Road, W8 5RG. *T:* 071–937 0573.

LIMERICK, Countess of; Sylvia Rosalind Pery, CBE 1991; MA; Chairman, British Red Cross Society, since 1985; President, Health Visitors' Association, since 1984 (a Vice President, 1978–84); Vice-Chairman, Foundation for the Study of Infant Deaths, since 1971; *b* 7 Dec. 1935; *e d* of Maurice Stanley Lush, CB, CBE, MC; *m* 1961, Viscount Glentworth (now 6th Earl of Limerick, *qv*); two *s* one *d*. *Educ:* St Swithun's, Winchester; Lady Margaret Hall, Oxford (MA). Research Asst, Foreign Office, 1959–62. Mem., Bd of Governors, St Bartholomew's Hosp., 1970–74; Vice-Chm., Community Health Council, S District of Kensington, Chelsea, Westminster Area, 1974–77; Mem., Kensington, Chelsea and Westminster AHA, 1977–82. British Red Cross Society: Nat. HQ Staff, 1962–66; Pres., Kensington and Chelsea Div., 1966–72; a Vice-Pres., London Br., 1972–85; Vice President: UK Cttee for UN Children's Fund, 1979– (Pres., 1972–79); Nat. Assoc. for Maternal and Child Welfare, 1985– (Pres., 1973–84). Member: Cttee of Management, Inst. of Child Health, 1976–; Council, King Edward's Hospital Fund (Mem., Cttee of Management, 1977–81, 1985–89); Maternity Services Adv. Cttee, DHSS, 1981–84; CS Occupational Health Service Adv. Bd, 1989; Eastman Dental Hosp., SHA, 1990–. Trustee, Child Accident Prevention Trust, 1979–87. Reviewed National Association of Citizens Advice Bureaux, 1983. FRSM 1977; Hon. MRCP 1990; Hon. Mem., BPA, 1986. Hon. DLitt CNAA, 1990. *Publication:* (jtly) Sudden Infant Death: patterns, puzzles and problems, 1985. *Recreations:* music, mountaineering, ski-ing. *Address:* 30 Victoria Road, W8 5RG. *T:* 071–937 0573; Chiddinglye, West Hoathly, East Grinstead, W Sussex RH19 4QT. *T:* Sharpthorne (0342) 810214.

LIMERICK AND KILLALOE, Bishop of, since 1985; **Rt. Rev. Edward Flewett Darling;** *b* 24 July 1933; *s* of late Ven. Vivian W. Darling and Honor F. G. Darling; *m* 1958, E. E. Patricia Mann; three *s* two *d*. *Educ:* Cork Grammar School; Midleton Coll., Co. Cork; St John's School, Leatherhead, Surrey; Trinity Coll., Dublin (MA). Curate: St Luke's, Belfast, 1956–59; St John's, Orangefield, Belfast, 1959–62; Incumbent, St Gall's, Carnalea, Co. Down, 1962–72; Chaplain, Bangor Hosp., Co. Down, 1963–72; Rector, St John's, Malone, Belfast, 1972–85; Chaplain, Ulster Independent Clinic, Belfast, 1981–85. *Publications:* Choosing the Hymns, 1984; (ed) Irish Church Praise, 1990. *Recreations:* music, gardening. *Address:* Bishop's House, North Circular Road, Limerick, Ireland. *T:* Limerick 51532.

LIMON, Donald William; Clerk Assistant, House of Commons, since 1990; *b* 29 Oct. 1932; *s* of late Arthur and Dora Limon; *m* 1987, Joyce Beatrice Clifton. *Educ:* Durham Cathedral Chorister Sch.; Durham Sch.; Lincoln Coll., Oxford (MA). A Clerk in the House of Commons, 1956–: Sec. to House of Commons Commn, 1979–81; Clerk of Financial Cttees, 1981–84; Principal Clerk, Table Office, 1985–89; Clerk of Cttees, 1989–90. *Recreations:* cricket, golf, singing. *Address:* Wicket Gate, Churt, Farnham, Surrey GU10 2HY. *T:* Headley Down (0428) 714350.

LINACRE, Sir (John) Gordon (Seymour), Kt 1986; CBE 1979; AFC 1943; DFM 1941; CBIM; Deputy Chairman, United Newspapers plc, since 1981 (Director, since 1969; Joint Managing Director, 1981–83; Chief Executive, 1983–88); President, Yorkshire Post Newspapers Ltd, since 1990 (Managing Director, 1965–83; Deputy Chairman, 1981–83; Chairman, 1983–90); *b* 23 Sept. 1920; *s* of John James Linacre and Beatrice Barber Linacre; *m* 1943, Irene Amy (*née* Gordon); two *d*. *Educ:* Firth Park Grammar Sch., Sheffield. CBIM (FBIM 1973). Served War, RAF, 1939–46, Sqdn Ldr. Journalistic appts, Sheffield Telegraph/Star, 1937–47; Kemsley News Service, 1947–50; Dep. Editor: Newcastle Journal, 1950–56; Newcastle Evening Chronicle, 1956–57; Editor, Sheffield Star, 1958–61; Asst Gen. Man., Sheffield Newspapers Ltd, 1961–63; Exec. Dir, Thomson Regional Newspapers Ltd, London, 1963–65. Chairman: United Provincial Newspapers Ltd, 1983–88; Sheffield Newspapers Ltd, 1981–88; Lancashire Evening Post Ltd, 1982–88; Northampton Mercury Co. Ltd, 1983–88; The Reporter Ltd, 1970–88; Blackpool Gazette & Herald Ltd, 1984–88; Dep. Chm., Express Newspapers, 1985–88; Director: United Newspapers (Publications) Ltd, 1969–88; Trident Television Ltd, 1970–84; Yorkshire Television Ltd, 1967–. Dir, INCA/FIEJ Res. Assoc., Darmstadt, Germany, 1971–79 (Pres., 1974–77); Pres. FIEJ, 1984–88 (Mem. Bd, 1971–). Member: Newspaper Soc. Council, 1966– (Pres., Newspaper Soc., 1978–79); Press Assoc., 1967–74 (Chm., 1970–71); Reuters Ltd, 1970–74 (Trustee, 1974–); Evening Newspaper Advertising Bureau Ltd, 1966–78 (Chm., 1975–76); English National Opera, 1978–81; Opera North (formerly English National Opera North), 1978– (Chm.); N Eastern Postal Bd, 1974–80; Adv. Bd, Yorks and Lincs, BIM, 1973–75; Health Educn Council, 1973–77; Leeds TEC, 1989– (Chm.). Governor, Harrogate Festival of Arts and Sciences Ltd, 1973–. Trustee, Yorks and Lincs Trustee Savings Bank, 1972–78; Mem. Council, 1985–, Chm. Foundation, 1989–, Leeds Univ. Kt, Order of White Rose (Finland), 1987; Grande Ufficiale al Merito della Repubblica Italiana, 1988 (Commendatore, 1973). *Recreations:* golf, fishing, walking. *Address:* White Windows, Staircase Lane, Bramhope, Leeds LS16 9JD. *T:* Arthington (0532) 842751. *Clubs:* Alwoodley Golf; Kilnsey Angling.

LINAKER, Lawrence Edward, (Paddy); Deputy Chairman and Chief Executive, M & G Group, since 1987; *b* 22 July 1934; *s* of late Lawrence Wignall and Rose Linaker; *m* 1963, Elizabeth Susan Elam; one *s*. *Educ:* Malvern College. FCA. Esso Petroleum, 1957–63; joined M & G Group, 1963; Man. Dir, 1972, Chm., 1987–, M & G Investment Management. Member: Council, RPMS, 1977–; Governing Body, SPCK, 1976–; Council, Malvern College. *Recreations:* music, wine, gardening. *Address:* Swyre Farm, Aldsworth, near Cheltenham, Glos. *T:* Windrush (04514) 466. *Club:* Athenæum.

LINCOLN, 18th Earl of, *cr* 1572; **Edward Horace Fiennes-Clinton;** retired; *b* 23 Feb. 1913; *s* of Edward Henry Fiennes-Clinton (killed in action, 1916) and Edith Annie (*née* Guest) (*d* 1965); *S* to earldom of 10th Duke of Newcastle, 1988; *m* 1st, 1940, Leila Ruth Millen (*d* 1947); one *s* one *d*; 2nd, 1953, Linda Alice O'Brien. *Educ:* Hale School; Govt Schools; Junior Technical Coll., Perth. In goldmining industry, Kalgoorlie, 1935–53; Public Works Dept (water supply) and farming (mainly wheatbelt), 1956–76. *Recreations:* boating, gardening. *Heir:* *s* Hon. Edward Gordon Fiennes-Clinton [*b* 7 Feb. 1943; *m* 1970, Julia, *d* of William Howson; two *s* one *d*]. *Address:* Flat 45, Elanora Villas, 37 Hastie Street, Bunbury, WA 6230, Australia. *T:* 211223.

LINCOLN, Bishop of, since 1986; **Rt. Rev. Robert Maynard Hardy;** Bishop to HM Prisons, since 1985; *b* 5 Oct. 1936; *s* of Harold and Monica Mavie Hardy; *m* 1970, Isobel Mary, *d* of Charles and Ella Burch; two *s* one *d*. *Educ:* Queen Elizabeth Grammar School, Wakefield; Clare College, Cambridge (MA). Deacon 1962, priest 1963; Assistant Curate, All Saints and Martyrs, Langley, Manchester, 1962; Fellow and Chaplain, Selwyn College, Cambridge, 1965 (Hon. Fellow, 1986); Vicar of All Saints, Borehamwood, 1972; Priest-in-charge, Aspley Guise, 1975; Course Director, St Albans Diocese Ministerial Training Scheme, 1975; Incumbent of United Benefice of Aspley Guise with Husborne Crawley and Ridgmont, 1980; Bishop Suffragan of Maidstone, 1980–86. *Recreations:* walking, gardening, reading. *Address:* Bishop's House, Eastgate, Lincoln LN2 1QQ. *T:* Lincoln (0522) 534701.

LINCOLN, Dean of; *see* Jackson, Very Rev. B. D.

LINCOLN, Archdeacon of; *see* Brackenbury, Ven. M. P.

LINCOLN, Sir Anthony (Handley), KCMG 1965 (CMG 1958); CVO 1957; Ambassador to Venezuela, 1964–69; *b* 2 Jan. 1911; *s* of late J. B. Lincoln, OBE; *m* 1948, Lisette Marion Summers; no *c*. *Educ:* Mill Hill Sch.; Magdalene Coll., Cambridge (BA). Prince Consort and Gladstone Prizes, 1934. Appointed Asst Principal, Home Civil Service, 1934; subsequently transferred to Foreign Service; served in Foreign Office; on UK Delegation to Paris Peace Conf., 1946, and in Buenos Aires. Counsellor, and Head of a Dept of Foreign Office, 1950. Dept. Sec.-Gen., Council of Europe, Strasbourg, France, 1952–55; Counsellor, British Embassy, Copenhagen, 1955–58; British Ambassador to Laos, 1958–60; HM Minister to Bulgaria, 1960–63; Officer Order of Orange Nassau, 1950; Comdr Order of Dannebrog, 1957. *Publication:* Some Political and Social Ideas of English Dissent, 1937. *Recreations:* country pursuits. *Clubs:* Brooks's, Reform.

LINCOLN, Prof. Dennis William; Director, Medical Research Council Reproductive Biology Unit, Edinburgh, since 1982; *b* 21 July 1939; *s* of late Ernest Edward Lincoln and Gertrude Emma Holmes; one *s* one *d*. *Educ:* Bracondale Sch., Norwich; Essex Inst. of Agriculture; Univ. of Nottingham (BSc); Univ. of Cambridge (MA, PhD); Univ. of Bristol (DSc). Agricl labourer, 1955–57; Research Technician, Univ. of Nottingham, 1957–59; Res. Fellow, Corpus Christi Coll., Cambridge, 1966–67; Lectr, 1967–74, Reader, 1974–81, Prof., 1981–82, Univ. of Bristol. Short-term appts in Switzerland, The Netherlands, USA, Australia; numerous nat. and internat. duties related to promotion of reproductive health. Hon. Prof., Univ. of Edinburgh, 1984. *Publications:* papers on reproductive biology, esp. on neural mechanisms in control of lactation and fertility. *Recreations:* ornithology, international travel, wildlife photography. *Address:* Centre for Reproductive Biology, 37 Chalmers Street, Edinburgh EH3 9EW. *T:* Edinburgh 031–229 2575, *Fax:* 031–228 5571.

LINCOLN, F(redman) Ashe, QC 1947; MA, BCL; Captain RNVR; a Recorder, 1972–79 (Recorder of Gravesend, 1967–71); Master of the Bench, Inner Temple, since 1955; Master of the Moots, 1955–64, and 1968–70; *s* of Reuben and Fanny Lincoln; *m* 1933, Sybil Eileen Cohen; one *s* one *d*. *Educ:* Hoe Gram. Sch., Plymouth; Haberdashers' Aske's Sch.; Exeter Coll., Oxford. Called to Bar, Inner Temple, Nov. 1929. Joined RNV(S)R, 1937; served in Royal Navy (RNVR), Sept. 1939–May 1946: Admiralty, 1940–42; in parties to render mines safe, May 1940; rendered safe first type G magnetic mine (King's Commendation for bravery); Mediterranean, 1943, with commandos in Sicily and Italy at Salerno landings, 1943; Seine Bay (D-day) Landings, 1944; assault crossing of Rhine, March 1945 (despatches twice). Dep. World Pres., Internat. Assoc. of Jewish Lawyers and Jurists, 1973–. Renter Warden of Worshipful Company of Plaisterers, 1946–47, Master, 1949–50; Freeman and Liveryman of City of London; fought general election 1945 (C) Harrow East Div. (Middx.); Chm. Administrative Law Cttee of Inns of Court Conservative Association, 1951; Mem. Exec., Gen. Council of the Bar, 1957–61. Associate MNI, 1976; Pres., RNR Officers' Club, 1981–; Member: Council, British Maritime League, 1983–; Exec., London Flotilla, 1984–. Mem., RNSA. Chm., London Devonian Assoc., 1965–85, Pres., 1985–. Trustee: British Maritime Charitable Fund, 1983; Associated Marine and Related Charities (Trng, Educn and Safety), 1985–. KStJ 1980. *Publications:* The Starra, 1939; Secret Naval Investigator, 1961. *Recreations:* yachting, tennis. *Address:* 9 King's Bench Walk, Temple, EC4Y 7DX. *T:* 071–353 7202. *Clubs:* Athenæum, Royal Automobile, MCC, Naval, City Livery; Royal Corinthian Yacht (Burnham-on-Crouch and Cowes); Bar Yacht; RNVR Yacht.

LIND, Per; Swedish Ambassador to the Court of St James's, 1979–82, retired; *b* 8 Jan. 1916; *s* of Erik and Elisabeth Lind; *m* 1942, Eva Sandström; two *s* two *d*. *Educ:* Univ. of Uppsala. LLB 1939. Entered Swedish Foreign Service as Attaché, 1939; served in Helsinki, 1939–41; Berlin, 1942–44; Second Sec., Stockholm Foreign Ministry, 1944–47; First Sec., Swedish Embassy, Washington, 1947–51; Personal Asst to Sec.-General of UN, 1953–56; re-posted to Swedish Foreign Ministry: Chief of Div. of Internat. Organisations, 1956–59; Dep. Dir Political Affairs, 1959–64; Ambassador with special duties (*ie* disarmament questions) and actg Chm., Swedish Delegation in Geneva, 1964–66; Ambassador to Canada, 1966–69; Under-Sec. of State for Administration at Foreign Ministry, Stockholm, 1969–75; Chm. Special Political Cttee of 29th Session of Gen. Assembly of UN, 1974; Ambassador to Australia, 1975–79. *Recreation:* golf. *Address:* Gyllenstiernsgatan 7, S-115 26 Stockholm, Sweden.

LINDAHL, Tomas Robert, MD; FRS 1988; Head, Imperial Cancer Research Fund, Clare Hall Laboratories, since 1983; *b* 28 Jan. 1938; *s* of Robert and Ethel Lindahl; *m* 1967, Alice Adams (marr. diss. 1979); one *s* one *d*. *Educ:* Karolinska Inst., Stockholm (MD). Research Fellow, Princeton Univ., 1964–67; Helen Hay Whitney Fellow, 1967–69, Asst Prof., 1968–69, Rockefeller Univ.; Asst Prof., 1969–75, Associate Prof., 1975–77, Karolinska Inst.; Prof. of Medical Biochemistry, Univ. of Gothenburg, 1978–81; Imperial Cancer Research Fund: Staff Scientist, 1981–83; Asst Dir of Research, 1985–89; Associate Dir of Research, 1989–91; Dep Dir, Lab. Res., 1991–. Member: EMBO; Royal Swedish Acad. of Scis; Academia Europaea. *Publications:* res. papers in biochem. and molecular biol. *Recreations:* piano, wine, modern art.

LINDARS, Rev. Prof. Frederick Chevallier, (Barnabas Lindars, SSF), DD; Rylands Professor of Biblical Criticism and Exegesis, University of Manchester, 1978–90 (Dean, Faculty of Theology, 1982–84), now Professor Emeritus; *b* 11 June 1923; *s* of Walter St John Lindars and Rose Lindars. *Educ:* Altrincham Grammar Sch.; St John's Coll., Cambridge (Rogerson Scholar, 1941; BA 1945 (1st Cl. Oriental Langs Tripos, Pt I, 1943; 1st Cl. Theol Tripos, Pt I, 1946, 2nd Cl. Pt II, 1947); MA 1948, BD 1961, DD 1973). Served War, 1943–45. Westcott House, Cambridge, 1946–48; Deacon 1948, Priest 1949; Curate of St Luke's, Pallion, Sunderland, 1948–52; joined Soc. of St Francis (Anglican religious order), taking the name of Barnabas, 1952; Asst Lectr in Divinity, Cambridge Univ., 1961–66, Lectr, 1966–78; Fellow and Dean, Jesus Coll., Cambridge, 1976–78. Proctor for Northern Univs in Convocation of York and Gen. Synod of C of E, 1980–July 1990. Lectures: T. W. Manson Meml, Manchester Univ., 1974; Ethel M. Wood, London Univ., 1983; Peake Meml, Methodist Conf., 1986. Canon Theologian (hon.), Leicester Cathedral, 1977–. Member: Studiorum Novi Testamenti Societas; Soc. for Old Testament Study (Pres., 1986). *Publications:* New Testament Apologetic, 1961 (2nd edn 1973); (ed and contrib.) Church without Walls, 1968; (ed with P. R. Ackroyd, and contrib.) Words and Meanings, 1968; Behind the Fourth Gospel, 1971 (also French edn 1974; Italian edn 1978); The Gospel of John, 1972 (2nd edn 1977); (ed with S. S. Smalley, and contrib.) Christ and Spirit in the New Testament, 1973; Jesus Son of Man, 1983; (with J. Rogerson and C. Rowland) The Study and Use of the Bible, 1988; (ed and contrib.) Law and Religion: essays on the place of the law in Israel and Early Christianity, 1988; John, 1990; The Theology of the Letter to the Hebrews, 1991; articles in Jl Theol Studies, New Testament Studies, Vetus Testamentum, and Theol. *Recreations:* walking, music. *Address:* The Friary, Hilfield, Dorchester, Dorset DT2 7BE. *T:* Cerne Abbas (0300) 341345.

LINDBERGH, Anne Spencer Morrow; author, United States; *b* 1906; *d* of Dwight Whitney Morrow and Elizabeth Reeve Morrow (*née* Cutter); *m* 1929, Col Charles Augustus Lindbergh, AFC, DFC (*d* 1974); three *s* two *d* (and one *s* decd). *Educ:* Miss Chapin's Sch., New York City; Smith Coll., Northampton, Mass (two prizes for literature). Received Cross of Honour of United States Flag Association for her part in survey of air route across Atlantic, 1933; received Hubbard Gold Medal of National Geographical Soc. for work as co-pilot and radio operator in flight of 40,000 miles over five continents, 1934. Hon. MA, Smith Coll., Mass., 1935. *Publications:* North to the Orient, 1935; Listen, the Wind, 1938; The Wave of the Future, 1940; The Steep Ascent, 1944; Gift from the Sea, 1955; The Unicorn and other Poems, 1935–55, 1958; Dearly Beloved, 1963; Earth Shine, 1970; Bring Me a Unicorn (autobiog.), 1972; Hour of Gold, Hour of Lead (autobiog.), 1973; Locked Rooms and Open Doors: diaries and letters 1933–35, 1974; The Flower and the Nettle: diaries and letters 1936–39, 1976; War Within and Without: diaries and letters 1939–44, 1980.

LINDEN, Anya, (Lady Sainsbury of Preston Candover); Ballerina, Royal Ballet, 1958–65, retired; *b* 3 Jan. 1933; English; *d* of George Charles and Ada Dorothea Eltenton; *m* 1963, John Davan Sainsbury (*see* Baron Sainsbury of Preston Candover); two *s* one *d*. *Educ:* Berkeley, Calif; Sadler's Wells Sch., 1947. Entered Sadler's Wells Co. at Covent Garden, 1951; promoted Soloist, 1952; Ballerina, 1958. Principal rôles in the ballets: Coppelia; Sylvia; Prince of Pagodas; Sleeping Beauty; Swan Lake; Giselle; Cinderella; Agon; Solitaire; Noctambules; Fête Etrange; Symphonic Variations; The Invitation; Firebird; Lady and the Fool; Antigone; Ondine; Seven Deadly Sins. Member: Nat. Council for One-Parent Families, 1978– (Hon. Vice-Pres., 1985–; Mem. Appeal Cttee, 1966–); Adv. Council, British Theatre Museum, 1975–83; Drama and Dance Adv. Cttee, British Council, 1981–83; Theatre Museum Assoc., 1984–86. Dep.-Chm. and Dir, Rambert Dance Co. (formerly Ballet Rambert), 1975–89; Governor: Royal Ballet Sch., 1977–; Rambert Sch. of Ballet Charitable Trust Ltd, 1983–; Dep. Chm. and Mem. Council of Management, Benesh Inst. of Choreology (formerly Benesh Inst. of Movement Notation), 1986–. *Recreations:* gardening, painting, photography. *Address:* c/o Stamford House, Stamford Street, SE1.

LINDESAY-BETHUNE, family name of **Earl of Lindsay.**

LINDISFARNE, Archdeacon of; *see* Bowering, Ven. M. E.

LINDLEY, Sir Arnold (Lewis George), Kt 1964; DSc; FCGI; FEng, FIMechE, FIEE; Chairman, GEC, 1961–64, retired; *b* 13 Nov. 1902; *s* of George Dilnot Lindley; *m* 1927, Winifred May Cowling (*d* 1962); one *s* one *d*; *m* 1963, Mrs Phyllis Rand. *Educ:* Woolwich Polytechnic. Chief Engineer BGEC, South Africa, 1933; Director: East Rand Engineering Co., 1943; BGEC, S Africa, 1945; Gen. Manager Erith Works, GEC, 1949; GEC England, 1953; Vice-Chm. 1959, Managing Dir, 1961–62, GEC. Chairman: BEAMA, 1963–64; Internat. Electrical Assoc., 1962–64; Engineering Industry Trng Bd, 1964–74; Dep. Chm., Motherwell Bridge (Holdings) Ltd, 1965–84. President, Instn of Mechanical Engineers, 1968–69; Chm., Council of Engineering Instns, 1972–73 (Vice-Chm., 1971–72); Member: Council, City Univ., 1969–78; Design Council, 1971–. Appointed by Govt to advise on QE2 propulsion turbines, 1969; Associate Consultant, Thames Barrier, 1970–. *Recreations:* sailing, golf. *Address:* Heathcote House, 18 Nab Lane, Shipley, W Yorks BD18 4HJ.

LINDLEY, Bryan Charles, CBE 1982; Chief Executive, National Advanced Robotics Research Centre, since 1989; *b* 30 Aug. 1932; *m* 1987; one *s* by former *m*. *Educ:* Reading Sch.; University Coll., London (Fellow 1979). BSc (Eng) 1954; PhD 1960; FIMechE 1968; FIEE 1968; FInstP 1968; FInstD 1968; FPRI 1984. National Gas Turbine Establishment, Pyestock, 1954–57; Hawker Siddeley Nuclear Power Co. Ltd, 1957–59; C. A. Parsons & Co. Ltd, Nuclear Research Centre, Newcastle upon Tyne, 1959–61; International Research and Development Co. Ltd, Newcastle upon Tyne, 1962–65; Man., R&D Div., C. A. Parsons & Co. Ltd, Newcastle upon Tyne, 1965–68; Electrical Research Assoc. Ltd: Dir, 1968–73; Chief Exec. and Man. Dir, ERA Technology Ltd, 1973–79; Dir, ERA Patents Ltd, 1968–79; Chm. and Man. Dir, ERA Autotrack Systems Ltd, 1971–79. Director: Dunlop Ltd, 1982–85; Soil-Less Cultivation Systems, 1980–85; Chm. and Dir, Thermal Conversions (UK), 1982–85; Dir of Technology, Dunlop Holdings, 1979–85; Director: BICC Cables Ltd, 1985–88; BICC Research and Engineering Ltd, 1985–88; Thomas Bolton & Johnson Ltd, 1986–88; Chm., Optical Fibres, 1985–87. Vis. Prof., Univ. of Liverpool, 1989–. Chairman: Materials, Chemicals and Vehicles Requirements Bd, DTI, 1982–85; RAPRA Council, 1984–85; Dir, RAPRA Technology Ltd, 1985–; Member: Nat. Electronics Council, 1969–79; Res. and Technol. Cttee, CBI, 1974–80; Design Council, 1980–86 (Mem., Design Adv. Cttee, 1980–86); Cttee of Inquiry into Engineering Profession, 1977–80; Adv. Council for Applied Research and Develt, 1980–86; Adv. Cttee for Safety of Nuclear Installations, 1987–; Chm., Sci. Educn and Management Div., IEE, 1974–75; Dep. Chm., Watt Cttee on Energy Ltd, 1976–80. Mem., SAE, 1984. *Publications:* articles on plasma physics, electrical and mechanical engineering, management science, impact of technological innovation, etc, in learned jls. *Recreations:* music, ski-ing, walking. *Address:* 1 Edgehill Chase, Wilmslow, Cheshire SK9 2DJ. *Club:* Institute of Directors.

LINDLEY, Prof. Dennis Victor; Professor and Head of Department of Statistics and Computer Science, University College London, 1967–77; *b* 25 July 1923; *s* of Albert Edward and Florence Louisa Lindley; *m* 1947, Joan Armitage; one *s* two *d*. *Educ:* Tiffin Boys' Sch., Kingston-on-Thames; Trinity Coll., Cambridge. MA Cantab 1948. Min. of Supply, 1943–45; Nat. Physical Lab., 1945–46 and 1947–48; Statistical Lab., Cambridge Univ., 1948–60 (Dir, 1957–60); Prof. and Head of Dept of Statistics, UCW, Aberystwyth, 1960–67, Hon. Professorial Fellow, 1978–. Hon. Prof., Univ. of Warwick, 1978–. Vis. Professor: Chicago and Stanford Univs, 1954–55; Harvard Business Sch., 1963; Univ. of Iowa, 1974–75; Univ. of Bath, 1978–81. Wald Lectr, Inst. Math. Statistics, 1988. Guy Medal (Silver), Royal Statistical Soc., 1968. Fellow, Inst. Math. Statistics; Fellow, American Statistical Assoc. *Publications:* (with J. C. P. Miller) Cambridge Elementary Statistical Tables, 1953; Introduction to Probability and Statistics (2 vols), 1965; Making Decisions, 1971, rev. edn 1985; Bayesian Statistics, 1971; (with W. F. Scott) New Cambridge Elementary Statistical Tables, 1985; contribs to Royal Statistical Soc., Biometrika, Annals of Math. Statistics. *Address:* 2 Periton Lane, Minehead, Somerset TA24 8AQ. *T:* Minehead (0643) 705189.

LINDNER, Dr Gerhard; Director, Northern Europe/Great Britain Division, Ministry of Foreign Affairs, German Democratic Republic, 1989–90; *b* 26 Feb. 1930; *m* Edeltraut; two *s*. *Educ:* Leipzig University. Entered Diplomatic Service, DDR, 1956; Counsellor: Czechoslovakia, 1964; Finland, 1965–68; Head of Trade Mission, Denmark, 1970–71; Ambassador: in Australia, 1977–81; in UK, 1984–89. Holder of awards and medals. *Recreations:* sport, classical music.

LINDOP, Sir Norman, Kt 1973; DL; MSc; CChem, FRSC; *b* 9 March 1921; *s* of Thomas Cox Lindop and May Lindop, Stockport, Cheshire; *m* 1974, Jenny C. Quass; one *s*. *Educ:* Northgate Sch., Ipswich; Queen Mary Coll., Univ. of London (BSc, MSc). Various industrial posts, 1942–46; Lectr in Chemistry, Queen Mary Coll., 1946; Asst Dir of Examinations, Civil Service Commn, 1951; Sen. Lectr in Chemistry, Kingston Coll. of Technology, 1953; Head of Dept of Chemistry and Geology, Kingston Coll. of Technology, 1957; Principal: SW Essex Technical Coll. and Sch. of Art, 1963; Hatfield Coll. of Technology, 1966; Dir, Hatfield Polytechnic, 1969–82; Principal, British Sch. of Osteopathy, 1982–90. Chairman: Cttee of Dirs of Polytechnics, 1972–74; Council for Professions Supplementary to Medicine, 1973–81; Home Office Data Protection Cttee, 1976–78; Cttee of Enquiry into Public Sector Validation, DES, 1984–85; British Library Adv. Council, 1986–; Herts Area Manpower Bd, 1986–88; Res. Council for Complementary Medicine, 1989–90; Member: CNAA, 1974–81; US-UK Educn (Fulbright) Commn, 1971–81; SRC, 1974–78; GMC, 1979–84. Chm. Council, Westfield Coll., London Univ., 1983–89. FCP 1980; Fellow: QMC, 1976; Hatfield Polytechnic, 1983; Hon. Fellow, Brighton Polytechnic, 1990. FRSA. DL Hertford, 1989. Hon. DEd CNAA, 1982. *Recreations:* mountain walking, music (especially opera). *Address:* 36 Queens Road, Hertford, Herts SG13 8AZ. *Club:* Athenæum.

LINDOP, Prof. Patricia Joyce, (Mrs G. P. R. Esdale); Professor of Radiation Biology, University of London, 1970–84, now Emeritus; *b* 21 June 1930; 2nd *c* of Elliot D. Lindop and Dorothy Jones; *m* 1957, Gerald Paton Rivett Esdale; one *s* one *d*. *Educ:* Malvern Girls' Coll.; St Bartholomew's Hospital Med. Coll.; BSc (1st cl. Hons), MB, BS, PhD; DSc London 1974; MRCP 1956; FRCP 1977. Registered GP, 1954. Research and teaching in physiology and medical radiobiology at Med. Coll. of St Bartholomew's Hosp., 1955–84. UK Mem., Council of Pugwash Confs on Science and World Affairs, 1982–87 (Asst Sec. Gen., 1961–71); Mem., Royal Commn on Environmental Pollution, 1974–79; Chm. and Trustee, Soc. for Education in the Applications of Science, 1968–; Member: Cttee 10 of ICRU, 1972–79; ESRO-NASA, 1970–74; Soc. for Radiol Protection, 1987–. Member Council: Science and Society, 1975–; Soc. for Protection of Science and Learning, 1974–86; formerly Mem. Council, British Inst. of Radiology; Chairman: Univ. of London Bd of Studies in Radiation Biology, 1979–81; Interdisciplinary Special Cttee for the Environment, 1979–81. Governor, St Bartholomew's Hosp. Med. Coll. Hon. Member: RCR, 1972; ARR, 1984. Ciba Award, 1957; Leverhulme Res. Award, 1984. *Publications:* in field of radiation effects. *Recreation:* watching events. *Address:* 58 Wildwood Road, NW11 6UP. *T:* 081–455 5860. *Club:* Royal Society of Medicine.

LINDSAY, family name of **Earl of Crawford** and **Baron Lindsay of Birker.**

LINDSAY, 16th Earl of, *cr* 1633 (Scot.); **James Randolph Lindesay-Bethune;** Lord Lindsay of The Byres, 1445; Lord Parbroath, 1633; Viscount of Garnock, Lord Kilburnie, Kingsburn and Drumry, 1703; landscape designer and consultant; *b* 19 Nov. 1955; *s* of 15th Earl of Lindsay and of Hon. Mary Clare Douglas-Scott-Montagu, *y d* of 2nd Baron Montagu of Beaulieu; *S* father, 1989; *m* 1982, Diana, *er d* of Major Nigel Chamberlayne-Macdonald, Cranbury Park, Winchester; one *s* two *d*. *Educ:* Eton; Univ. of Edinburgh (MA Hons); Univ. of Calif, Davis. Trustee, Gardens for the Disabled Trust; Mem. Council and Trustee, London Gardens Soc. Pres., Brighter Kensington and Chelsea Scheme. *Publication:* (jtly) Garden Ornament. *Heir:* *s* Viscount Garnock, *qv*. *Address:* Lahill, Upper Largo, Fife.

LINDSAY OF BIRKER, 2nd Baron, *cr* 1945; **Michael Francis Morris Lindsay;** Professor Emeritus in School of International Service, The American University, Washington, DC; *b* 24 Feb. 1909; *e s* of 1st Baron Lindsay of Birker, CBE, LLD, and Erica Violet (*née* Storr) (*d* 1962); *S* father 1952; *m* 1941, Li Hsiao-li, *d* of Col Li Wen-chi of Lishih, Shansi; one *s* two *d*. *Educ:* Gresham's Sch., Holt; Balliol Coll., Oxford. Adult education and economic research work in S Wales, 1935–37; Tutor in Economics, Yenching Univ., Peking, 1938–41; Press Attaché, British Embassy, Chungking, 1940. Served War of 1939–45, with Chinese 18th Group Army, 1942–45. Vis. Lectr at Harvard Univ., 1946–47; Lectr in Econs, University Coll., Hull, 1948–51; Sen. Fellow of the Dept of Internat. Relations, ANU, Canberra, 1951–59 (Reader in Internat. Relations, 1959); Prof. of Far Eastern Studies, Amer. Univ., Washington, 1959–74, Chm. of E Asia Programme, 1959–71. Visiting Professor: Yale Univ., 1958; Ball State Univ., Indiana, 1971–72. *Publications:* Educational Problems in Communist China, 1950; The New China, three views, 1950; China and the Cold War, 1955; Is Peaceful Co-existence Possible?, 1960; The Unknown War: North China 1937–45, 1975; Kung-ch'an-chu-i Ts'o-wu ts'ai Na-li, 1976; articles in learned journals. *Heir:* *s* Hon. James Francis Lindsay [*b* 29 Jan. 1945; *m* 1966, Mary Rose, *d* of W. G. Thomas]. *Address:* 6812 Delaware Street, Chevy Chase, Md 20815, USA. *T:* (301)-656–4245.

LINDSAY, Master of; Alexander Thomas Lindsay; *b* 5 Aug. 1991; *s* and *heir* of Lord Balniel, *qv*.

LINDSAY, Maj.-Gen. Courtenay Traice David, CB 1963; Director-General of Artillery, War Office, 1961–64, retired; *b* 28 Sept. 1910; *s* of late Courtenay Traice Lindsay and Charlotte Editha (*née* Wetenhall); *m* 1934, Margaret Elizabeth, *d* of late William Pease Theakston, Huntingdon; two *s*. *Educ:* Rugby Sch.; RMA Woolwich. 2nd Lt RA, 1930. Mem., Ordnance Board (Col), 1952; Dir of Munitions, British Staff (Brig.), Washington, 1959; Maj.-Gen. 1961. *Address:* Huggits Farm, Stone-in-Oxney, Tenterden, Kent. *Club:* Rye Golf.

LINDSAY, Crawford Callum Douglas; QC 1987; barrister; a Recorder of the Crown Court, since 1982; *b* 5 Feb. 1939; *s* of Douglas Marshall Lindsay, FRCOG and Eileen Mary Lindsay; *m* 1963, Rosemary Gough; one *s* one *d*. *Educ:* Whitgift Sch., Croydon; St John's Coll., Oxford. Called to the Bar, Lincoln's Inn, 1961. Mem., Criminal Injuries Compensation Bd, 1988–. *Address:* 6 King's Bench Walk, Temple, EC4Y 7DR. *Club:* MCC.

LINDSAY, Donald Dunrod, CBE 1972; *b* 27 Sept. 1910; *s* of Dr Colin Dunrod Lindsay, Pres. BMA 1938, and Mrs Isabel Baynton Lindsay; *m* 1936, Violet Geraldine Fox; one *s* one *d*. *Educ:* Clifton Coll., Bristol; Trinity Coll., Oxford. Asst Master, Manchester Gram. Sch., 1932; Asst Master, Repton Sch., 1935; temp. seconded to Bristol Univ. Dept of Education as lecturer in History, 1938; Senior History Master, Repton Sch., 1938–42; Headmaster: Portsmouth Gram. Sch., 1942–53; Malvern Coll., 1953–71. Dir, Independent Schs Information Service, 1972–77. Chm., Headmasters' Conference, 1968. Governor, Harrow Sch., 1977–82. *Publications:* A Portrait of Britain Between the Exhibitions, 1952; A Portrait of Britain, 1688–1851, 1954; A Portrait of Britain Before 1066, 1962; Authority and Challenge, Europe 1300–1600, 1975; Europe and the World, 1979; Friends for Life: a portrait of Launcelot Fleming, 1981; Forgotten General, 1986; Sir Edmund Bacon: a Norfolk life, 1988. *Recreations:* walking, theatre, music. *Address:* 29 Teme Avenue, Malvern, Worcs WR14 2XA.

LINDSAY, Rt. Rev. Hugh; *see* Hexham and Newcastle, Bishop of, (RC).

LINDSAY, Sir James Harvey Kincaid Stewart, Kt 1966; President and Board Member, Institute of Cultural Affairs International, Brussels, 1982–89; *b* 31 May 1915; *s* of Arthur Harvey Lindsay and Doris Kincaid Lindsay; *m* Marguerite Phyllis Boudville (one *s* one *d* by previous marriage). *Educ:* Highgate Sch. Joined Metal Box Co. Ltd, 1934; joined Metal Box Co. of India Ltd, 1937; Man. Dir, 1961; Chm., 1967–69; Dir of Internat. Programmes, Admin. Staff Coll., Henley-on-Thames, 1970–79. Vis. Lectr, Univ. of Buckingham, 1984–89. President: Bengal Chamber of Commerce and Industry; Associated Chambers of Commerce and Industry of India, 1965; Rotary Club of Calcutta, 1965. Director: Indian Oxygen Co., 1966; Westinghouse, Saxon Farmer Ltd, Hindusthan Pilkington, 1966. Pres., Calcutta Management Association, 1964; Pres. (and elected Life Mem., 1984), All India Management Assoc., 1964–69; Mem. of Governing Body: Indian

Inst. of Management, Calcutta, 1964; Administrative Staff Coll. of India, 1965; Indian Institutes of Technology, 1966; National Council of Applied Economic Research, 1966; All-India Board of Management Studies, 1964; Indian Inst. of Foreign Trade, 1965; Member: BoT, Central Adv. Council of Industries, Direct Taxes Adv. Cttee, 1966; National Council on Vocational and Allied Trades, 1963. Convener, Internat. Exposition of Rural Develt, 1980–86; Trustee, Inst. of Family and Environmental Research, 1971–. FCIM (FInstM 1975); CBIM (FBIM 1971). *Recreations:* music, table tennis. *Address:* Christmas Cottage, Lower Shiplake, near Henley-on-Thames, Oxon. *T:* Reading (0734) 402859. *Club:* East India, Devonshire, Sports and Public Schools.

LINDSAY, Hon. James Louis; *b* 16 Dec. 1906; *yr s* of 27th Earl of Crawford and Balcarres; *m* 1933, Bronwen Mary, *d* of 8th Baron Howard de Walden; three *s* one *d. Educ:* Eton; Magdalen Coll., Oxford. Served 1939–45 war, Major KRRC. Contested (C) Bristol South-East, 1950 and 1951; MP (C) N Devon, 1955–Sept. 1959. *Address:* Pound House, Nether Cerne, Dorchester, Dorset DT2 7AJ.

LINDSAY, John Edmund Fredric, QC 1981; *b* 16 Oct. 1935; *s* of late George Fredric Lindsay and Constance Mary Lindsay (*née* Wright); *m* 1967, Patricia Anne Bolton; three *d. Educ:* Ellesmere Coll.; Sidney Sussex Coll., Cambridge (BA 1959; MA). Fleet Air Arm, 1954–56; Sub-Lt, RNVR. Called to the Bar, Middle Temple, 1961, Bencher, 1987; joined Lincoln's Inn (*ad eundem*); Junior Treasury Counsel, *bona vacantia*, 1979–81. Chm., Employed Barristers' Registration Cttee, 1982–89; Member: Senate of Inns of Court and Bar, 1979–82; Legal Panel, Insolvency Law Review Cttee (Cork Report), 1980–82; Insolvency Rules Adv. Cttee, 1985–. *Address:* 7 Stone Buildings, Lincoln's Inn, WC2A 3SZ.

LINDSAY, (John) Maurice, CBE 1979; TD 1946; Consultant, The Scottish Civic Trust, since 1983 (Director, 1967–83); *b* 21 July 1918; *s* of Matthew Lindsay and Eileen Frances Brock; *m* 1946, Aileen Joyce Gordon; one *s* three *d. Educ:* Glasgow Acad.; Scottish National Acad. of Music (now Royal Scottish Acad. of Music, Glasgow). Drama Critic, Scottish Daily Mail, Edinburgh, 1946–47; Music Critic, The Bulletin, Glasgow, 1946–60; Prog. Controller, 1961–62, Prodn Controller, 1962–64, and Features Exec. and Chief Interviewer, 1964–67, Border Television, Carlisle. Mem., Historic Buildings Council for Scotland, 1976–87; Pres., Assoc. for Scottish Literary Studies, 1988–; Trustee, National Heritage Meml Fund, 1980–84; Hon. Sec.-Gen., Europa Nostra, 1983–91. Hon. FRIAS 1985. Hon. DLitt Glasgow, 1982. Atlantic Rockefeller Award, 1946. Editor: Scots Review, 1949–50; The Scottish Review, 1975–85. *Publications: poetry:* The Advancing Day, 1940; Perhaps To-morrow, 1941; Predicament, 1942; No Crown for Laughter: Poems, 1943; The Enemies of Love: Poems 1941–1945, 1946; Selected Poems, 1947; Hurlygush: Poems in Scots, 1948; At the Wood's Edge, 1950; Ode for St Andrews Night and Other Poems, 1951; The Exiled Heart: Poems 1941–1956, 1957; Snow Warning and Other Poems, 1962; One Later Day and Other Poems, 1964; This Business of Living, 1969; Comings and Goings: Poems, 1971; Selected Poems 1942–1972, 1973; The Run from Life, 1975; Walking Without an Overcoat, Poems 1972–76, 1977; Collected Poems, 1979; A Net to Catch the Winds and Other Poems, 1981; The French Mosquitoes' Woman and Other Diversions and Poems, 1985; Requiem for a Sexual Athlete and Other Poems and Diversions, 1988; Collected Poems 1940–1990, 1990; *prose:* A Pocket Guide to Scottish Culture, 1947; The Scottish Renaissance, 1949; The Lowlands of Scotland: Glasgow and the North, 1953, 3rd edn, 1979; Robert Burns: The Man, His Work, The Legend, 3rd edn, 1980; Dunoon: The Gem of the Clyde Coast, 1954; The Lowlands of Scotland: Edinburgh and the South, 1956, 3rd edn, 1979; Clyde Waters: Variations and Diversions on a Theme of Pleasure, 1958; The Burns Encyclopedia, 1959, 3rd edn, 1980; Killochan Castle, 1960; By Yon Bonnie Banks: A Gallimaufry, 1961; Environment: A Basic Human Right, 1968; Portrait of Glasgow, 1972, rev. edn, 1981; Robin Philipson, 1977; History of Scottish Literature, 1977; Lowland Scottish Villages, 1980; Francis George Scott and the Scottish Renaissance, 1980; (with Anthony F. Kersting) The Buildings of Edinburgh, 1981, 2nd edn 1987; Thank You For Having Me: a personal memoir, 1983; (with Dennis Hardley) Unknown Scotland, 1984; The Castles of Scotland, 1986; Count All Men Mortal—A History of Scottish Provident 1837–1987, 1987; Victorian and Edwardian Glasgow, 1987; Glasgow 1837, 1989; (with David Bruce) Edinburgh Past and Present, 1990; *editor:* Poetry Scotland One, Two, Three, 1943, 1945, 1946; Sailing Tomorrow's Seas: An Anthology of New Poems, 1944; Modern Scottish Poetry: An Anthology of the Scottish Renaissance 1920–1945, 1946, 4th edn, 1986; (with Fred Urquhart) No Scottish Twilight: New Scottish Stories, 1947; Selected Poems of Sir Alexander Gray, 1948; Poems, by Sir David Lyndsay, 1948; (with Hugh MacDiarmid) Poetry Scotland Four, 1949; (with Helen Cruickshank) Selected Poems of Marion Angus, 1950; John Davidson: A Selection of His Poems, 1961; (with Edwin Morgan and George Bruce) Scottish Poetry One to Six 1966–72; (with Alexander Scott and Roderick Watson) Scottish Poetry Seven to Nine, 1974, 1976, 1977; (with R. L. Mackie) A Book of Scottish Verse, 1967, 3rd edn 1983; The Discovery of Scotland: Based on Accounts of Foreign Travellers from the 13th to the 18th centuries, 1964, 2nd edn 1979; The Eye is Delighted: Some Romantic Travellers in Scotland, 1970; Scotland: An Anthology, 1974, 2nd edn 1989; As I Remember, 1979; Scottish Comic Verse 1425–1980, 1980; (with Joyce Lindsay) The Scottish Dog, 1989; (with Alexander Scott) The Comic Poems of William Tennant, 1990; (with Joyce Lindsay) A Book of Scottish Quotation, 1991; Thomas Hamilton, The Youth and Manhood of Cyril Thornton, 1991. *Recreations:* enjoying and adding to compact disc collection, walking. *Address:* 7 Milton Hill, Milton, Dumbarton G82 2TS. *T:* Dumbarton (0389) 62655.

LINDSAY, John Vliet; Mayor of New York City, 1965–73 (elected as Republican-Liberal, Nov. 1965, re-elected as Liberal-Independent, Nov. 1969); *b* 24 Nov. 1921; *s* of George Nelson and Eleanor (Vliet) Lindsay; *m* 1949, Mary Harrison; one *s* three *d. Educ:* St Paul's Sch., Concord, NH; Yale Univ. BA 1944; LLB 1948. Lt US Navy, 1943–46. Admitted to: NY Bar, 1949; Fed. Bar, Southern Dist NY, 1950; US Supreme Court, 1955; DC Bar, 1957. Mem., law firm of Webster, Sheffield, NYC, 1949–55, 1957–61, 1974–. Exec. Asst to US Attorney Gen., 1955–57; Mem., 86th-89th Congresses, 17th Dist, NY, 1959–66. Bd Mem., Lincoln Center for Performing Arts; Chm. Bd, Lincoln Center Theatre Co. (the Beaumont), 1985–. Hon. LLD: Williams Coll., 1968; Harvard, 1969. *Publications:* Journey into Politics, 1967; The City, 1970; The Edge, 1976.

LINDSAY, Maurice; *see* Lindsay, J. M.

LINDSAY, Most Rev. Orland Ugham; *see* West Indies, Archbishop of.

LINDSAY of Dowhill, Sir Ronald Alexander, 2nd Bt *cr* 1962, of Dowhill; 23rd Representer of Baronial House of Dowhill; *b* 6 Dec. 1933; *er s* of Sir Martin Lindsay of Dowhill, 1st Bt, CBE, DSO, and of Joyce Lady Lindsay, *d* of late Major Hon. Robert Lindsay, Royal Scots Greys; *S* father, 1981; *m* 1968, Nicoletta, *yr d* of late Captain Edgar Storich, Royal Italian Navy and late Mrs Storich; three *s* one *d. Educ:* Eton College; Worcester Coll., Oxford (MA). National service in Grenadier Guards (Lieut), 1952–54. Insurance executive, 1958–; Dir, Oxford Members' Agency, 1989–. Chairman: Standing Council of the Baronetage, 1987–89 (Vice-Chm., 1984–86); The Baronets Trust, 1990–; Vice-Chm., Anglo-Spanish Soc., 1985–. Member of Queen's Body Guard for Scotland (Royal Company of Archers). FCII 1963. Encomienda, Orden de Isabel la Católica (Spain), 1988. *Heir: s* James Martin Evelyn Lindsay, *b* 11 Oct. 1968. *Address:* Courleigh, Colley Lane, Reigate, Surrey RH2 9JJ. *T:* Reigate (0737) 243290.

LINDSAY-HOGG, Sir Edward William, 4th Bt *cr* 1905, of Rotherfield Hall, Sussex; Hereditary Cavaliere d'Italia; dramatist and scriptwriter; *b* 23 May 1910; *s* of William Lindsay Lindsay-Hogg (*d* 1918) (1st *s* of 1st Bt) and Nora Cicely (*d* 1929), *d* of John James Barrow; *S* nephew, 1988; *m* 1st, 1936, Geraldine (marr. diss. 1946), *d* of E. M. Fitzgerald; one *s*; 2nd, 1957, Kathleen Mary, *widow* of Captain Maurice Cadell, MC and *d* of James Cooney. *Educ:* Eton. Former racehorse trainer and amateur jockey when living at the Curragh. *Publications:* contrib. to literary periodicals, mainly in Ireland. *Recreations:* gardening, reading, walking. *Club:* Stephen's Green (Dublin). *Heir: s* Michael Edward Lindsay-Hogg [*b* 5 May 1940; *m* 1967, Lucy Mary (marr. diss. 1971), *o d* of Donald Davies].

LINDSAY-SMITH, Iain-Mór; Chief Executive and Managing Director, Lloyd's of London Press Ltd, since 1991 (Executive Director, 1984–87; Deputy Managing Director, 1987–90); Publisher, since 1984, and Chairman, since 1990, Lloyds List Ltd; Chairman and Chief Executive, Lloyd's Information Services Ltd, since 1990; Chairman, LLP Business Publishing Ltd, since 1990; *b* 18 Sept. 1934; *s* of Edward Duncanson Lindsay-Smith and Margaret Anderson; *m* 1960, Carol Sara (*née* Paxman); one *s. Educ:* High Sch. of Glasgow; London Univ. (diploma course on Internat. Affairs). Scottish Daily Record, 1951–57; Commissioned 1st Bn Cameronians (Scottish Rifles), 1953–55; Daily Mirror, 1957–60; Foreign Editor, subseq. Features Editor, Daily Mail, 1960–71; Dep. Editor, Yorkshire Post, 1971–74; Editor, Glasgow Herald, 1974–77; Exec. Editor, The Observer, 1977–84. Director: Lloyd's of London Press Incorporated, USA, 1985–; Lloyd's of London Press (Far East) Ltd, Hong Kong, 1989–; Lloyd's of London Press GmbH, Germany, 1989–; Lloyd's Maritime Information Services Ltd, 1990–; Lloyd's Maritime Information Services Inc., USA, 1990–; Lutine Publications Ltd, 1984–; Internat. Art & Antique Loss Register Ltd, 1990–; Colchester Mercury Theatre Ltd, 1985–. Member: Little Horkesley Parish Council, 1987–91; PCC, 1985–. *Publication:* article in Electronics and Power. *Recreations:* shooting (game and clay), playing Highland bagpipe, the outdoors. *Address:* Lloyd's of London Press, One Singer Street, EC2A 4LQ; Sheepen Place, Colchester, Essex CO3 3LP. *Club:* Travellers'.

LINDSEY, 14th Earl of, *cr* 1626, **AND ABINGDON,** 9th Earl of, *cr* 1682; **Richard Henry Rupert Bertie;** Baron Norreys, of Rycote, 1572; *b* 28 June 1931; *o s* of Lt-Col Hon. Arthur Michael Bertie, DSO, MC (*d* 1957) and Aline Rose (*d* 1948), *er d* of George Arbuthnot-Leslie, Warthill, Co. Aberdeen, and *widow* of Hon. Charles Fox Maule Ramsay, MC; *S* cousin, 1963; *m* 1957, Norah Elizabeth Farquhar-Oliver, *yr d* of late Mark Oliver, OBE; two *s* one *d. Educ:* Ampleforth. Lieut, Royal Norfolk Regt (Supplementary Reserve of Officers), 1951–52. Underwriting Member of Lloyd's, 1958–; company director, 1965–; Chm., Dawes and Henderson (Agencies), 1988–. Chm., Anglo-Ivory-Coast Soc., 1974–77. High Steward of Abingdon, 1963–. *Heir: s* Lord Norreys, *qv. Address:* Gilmilnscroft, Sorn, Mauchline, Ayrshire; 3 Westgate Terrace, SW10. *Clubs:* White's, Turf, Pratt's.

LINDSEY, Archdeacon of; *see* Laurence, Ven. J. H. C.

LINDT, Auguste Rudolph, LLD; retired as Swiss Ambassador; *b* Berne, Switzerland, 5 Aug. 1905. Studied law at Universities of Geneva and Berne. Special correspondent of several European newspapers, in Manchuria, Liberia, Palestine, Jordan, the Persian Gulf, Tunisia, Roumania and Finland, 1932–40. Served in Swiss Army, 1940–45. Special delegate of International Cttee of the Red Cross at Berlin, 1945–46. Press Attaché, 1946, Counsellor, 1949, Swiss Legation in London. Switzerland's Permanent Observer to the United Nations (appointed 1953) and subseq. Minister plenipotentiary (1954); appointments connected with work of the United Nations: Chairman Exec. Board of UNICEF, 1953 and 1954; President, UN Opium Conference, 1953; Head of Swiss Delegation to Conference on Statute of International Atomic Energy Agency, held in New York, 1956. United Nations High Commissioner for Refugees (elected by acclamation), Dec. 1956–60; Swiss Ambassador to USA, 1960–63; Delegate, Swiss Fed. Council for Technical Co-operation, 1963–66; Swiss Amassador to Soviet Union and Mongolia, 1966–69, on leave as International Red Cross Comr-Gen. for Nigeria-Biafra relief operation, 1968–69; Swiss Ambassador to India and Nepal, 1969–70. Adviser to Pres. of Republic of Rwanda, 1973–75. Pres., Internat. Union for Child Welfare, Geneva, 1971–77. Hon. DrUniv Geneva, 1960; Hon. Dr, Coll. of Wilmington, Ohio, 1961. *Publications:* Special Correspondent with Bandits and Generals in Manchuria, 1933; Generäle hungern nie: Geschichte einer Hilfsaktion in Afrika, 1983. *Address:* Jolimontstrasse 2, CH-3006 Bern, Switzerland.

LINE, Frances Mary, (Mrs James Lloyd); Controller, BBC Radio 2, since 1990; *b* 22 Feb. 1940; *d* of Charles Edward Line and Leoni Lucy Line (*née* Hendriks); *m* 1972, James Richard Beilby Lloyd. *Educ:* James Allen's Girls' Sch., Dulwich. Joined BBC as clerk/typist, 1957; Sec. in TV and Radio, 1959–67; Radio 2 producer, 1967–73; senior producer, 1973–79; Chief Assistant: Radio 2, 1979–83; Radio 4, 1983–85; Head, Radio 2 Music Dept, 1985–89. *Recreations:* theatre, Sussex, happy-snaps. *Address:* BBC, Broadcasting House, W1A 1AA. *T:* 071–580 4468.

LINE, Maurice Bernard, MA; FRSA; FLA, FIInfSc, FBIM; Director General (Science, Technology and Industry), British Library, 1985–88 (Deputy Director General, 1973–74, Director General, 1974–85, Lending Division); *b* 21 June 1928; *s* of Bernard Cyril and Ruth Florence Line; *m* 1954, Joyce Gilchrist; one *s* one *d. Educ:* Bedford Sch.; Exeter Coll., Oxford (MA). Library Trainee, Bodleian Library, 1950–51; Library Asst, Glasgow Univ., 1951–53; Sub-Librarian, Southampton Univ., 1954–65; Dep. Librarian, Univ. of Newcastle upon Tyne, 1965–68; Librarian, Univ. of Bath, 1968–71; Librarian, Nat. Central Library, 1971–73; Project Head, DES Nat. Libraries ADP Study, 1970–71. Prof. Associate, Sheffield Univ., 1977–; Vis. Prof., Loughborough Univ. of Technol., 1986–. Member: Library Adv. Council for England, 1972–75; British Library Board, 1974–88; Pres., Library Assoc., 1990. Hon. DLitt Heriot Watt, 1980; Hon. DSc Southampton, 1988. *Publications:* Library Surveys, 1967, 2nd edn 1982; National Libraries, 1979; Universal Availability of Publications, 1983; National Libraries II, 1987; Academic Library Management, 1990; contribs to: Jl of Documentation; Aslib Proc.; Jl of Librarianship, etc. *Recreations:* music, walking, other people. *Address:* 10 Blackthorn Lane, Burn Bridge, Harrogate, North Yorks HG3 1NZ. *T:* Harrogate (0423) 872984.

LINEHAN, Anthony John; HM Chief Inspector of Factories, Health and Safety Executive, since 1988; Director of Field Operations, Health and Safety Executive, since 1990; *b* 27 June 1931; *s* of Daniel and Ada Linehan; *m* 1955, Oonagh Patricia FitzPatrick; two *s* two *d. Educ:* Bristol Univ. (BA Hons 1952). Short Service Commission, RN, 1953–57. HM Factory Inspectorate: joined 1958; HM District Inspector, 1969; Labour Adviser, Hong Kong Govt, 1973–76; Health and Safety Executive: HQ, 1976–79; Area Dir, Wales, 1979–84; HM Dep. Chief Inspector of Factories, 1984–88. *Recreations:* walking, reading, watching rugby. *Address:* 35 Weld Road, Birkdale, Southport PR8 2DR. *T:* Southport (0704) 67421.

LINES, (Walter) Moray, CBE 1969; Chairman, Lines Brothers Ltd, 1962–71 (Joint Managing Director, 1962–70); *b* 26 Jan. 1922; *er s* of late Walter Lines; *m* 1955, Fiona Margaret Denton; three *s* one *d*. *Educ:* Gresham Sch. Joined Board of Lines Bros Ltd, 1946; Chm., British Toy Manufacturers Assoc., 1968–70. *Address:* Stable Cottage, Shirwell, near Barnstaple, N Devon. *T:* Shirwell (0271) 850265.

LINFORD, Alan C.; *see* Carr Linford.

LING, Arthur George, FRIBA; PPRTPI; architect and town planner in practice with Arthur Ling and Associates; *b* 20 Sept. 1913; *s* of George Frederick Ling and Elsie Emily (*née* Wisbey); *m* 1939, Marjorie Tall; one *s* three *d*. *Educ:* Christ's Hospital; University College, London (Bartlett School of Architecture). BA (Architecture), London. Architect in Office of E. Maxwell Fry and Walter Gropius, 1937–39; Structural Engineer with Corporation of City of London (Air raid shelters and War debris clearance), 1939–41; Member town planning team responsible for preparation of County of London Plan, 1943, under direction of J. H. Forshaw and Sir Patrick Abercrombie, 1941–45; Chief Planning Officer, London County Council, 1945–55; Head of Department of Town Planning, University College, London Univ., 1947–48; Sen. Lecturer in Town Planning, 1948–55; City Architect and Planning Officer, Coventry, 1955–64; Prof. and Head of Dept of Architecture and Civic Planning, Univ. of Nottingham, 1964–69, Special Prof. of Environmental Design, 1969–72. Visiting Professor: University of Santiago, Chile, 1963; Univ. of NSW, Australia, 1969; Chancellor Lectures, Univ. of Wellington, NZ, 1969. Joint Architect for Development Plan for University of Warwick. Cons. Architect Planner, Runcorn New Town Corporation. UN (Habitat) Project Manager, Physical Perspective Plan, 1981–2000, Libyan Jamahiriya, 1977–80. Former Chairman, Board of Chief Officers, Midlands Housing Consortium; Past Vice-Pres., RIBA; President: RTPI, 1968–69; Commonwealth Assoc. of Planners, 1968–76. Mem., Sports Council, 1968–71; Vice-Chm., E Midlands Sports Council, 1968–76. Pres., Heckington Village Trust, 1974–84. RIBA Dist. in Town Planning, 1956; Silver Medallist (Essay), 1937; Hunt Bursary, 1939. Fellow University College, London, 1967. *Publications:* Urban and Regional Planning and Development in the Commonwealth, 1988; contrib. to professional journals on architecture and town planning. *Address:* The Old Rectory, Howell, Sleaford, Lincolnshire NG34 9PT.

LING, Maj.-Gen. (Retd) Fergus Alan Humphrey, CB 1968; CBE 1964; DSO 1944; Defence Services Consultant, Institute for the Study of Conflict, since 1970; *b* 5 Aug. 1914; 3rd *s* of John Richardson and Mabel Ling; *m* 1940, Sheelah Phyllis Sarel (*d* 1990); two *s* three *d*. *Educ:* Stowe Sch.; Royal Military Coll., Sandhurst. Comd 2nd/5th Queen's, 1944; GSO 1 (Ops), GHQ, Middle East, 1945–46; British Liaison Officer, US Infantry Centre, 1948–50; Comd Regt Depot, Queen's Royal Regt, 1951; Directing Staff, Staff Coll., Camberley, 1951–53; comd 5th Queen's, 1954–57; Asst Military Secretary, War Office, 1957–58; comd 148 North Midland Brigade (TA), 1958–61; DAG, HQ, BAOR, 1961–65; GOC: 54 (East Anglian) Division/District, 1965–67; East Anglian District, 1967–68; Eastern District, 1968–69. Col, The Queen's Regt, 1973–77 (Dep. Col, 1969–73). Chairman: Surrey T&AVR Cttee, 1973–80; SE T&AVR Assoc., 1978–79. DL Surrey, 1970, Vice Lord-Lieutenant 1975–82. *Recreations:* home, garden, fifteen grandchildren. *Address:* Mystole Coach House, near Canterbury CT4 7DB. *T:* Canterbury (0227) 738496.

LING, Jeffrey, CMG 1991; HM Diplomatic Service; Director of Information Systems, Foreign and Commonwealth Office, since 1989; *b* 9 Sept. 1939; *s* of Frank Cecil Ling and Mary Irene Nixon; *m* 1967, Margaret Anne Tatton; one *s*. *Educ:* Bristol Univ. BSc (Hons); FInstP; FBIM. FCO, 1966–69; Private Sec. to HM Ambassador, Washington, 1969–71; First Sec., Washington, 1971–73; Perm. Delegn to OECD, Paris, 1973–77; FCO, 1977–79; on secondment as Special Adviser to HM the Sultan of Brunei, 1979–82; Counsellor (Technology), Paris, 1982–86; Dir of Res., FCO, 1986–89; Asst Under-Sec. of State and Dir of Communications, 1989. *Recreations:* travel, old cars. *Address:* c/o Foreign and Commonwealth Office, SW1A 2AH.

LING, John de Courcy; *see* de Courcy Ling.

LINGARD, (Peter) Anthony, CBE 1977; TD; Director General, St John Ambulance Association, 1978–82; *b* 29 Feb. 1916; *s* of late Herbert Arthur Lingard and Kate Augusta Burdett; *m* 1946, Enid Nora Argile; two *d*. *Educ:* Berkhamsted Sch.; London Univ. (BCom). Served RA, 1939–46; Major, 1941 (despatches twice). Co. of London Electric Supply Gp, 1936; Area Manager Lambeth and Camberwell, County Group, 1947; Commercial Officer, S Western Sub-Area, 1948, Chief Commercial Officer, 1959–62, London Electricity Board; Commercial and Development Adviser, Electricity Council, 1962–65; Mem., Electricity Council, 1965–77; Chm., E Midlands Electricity Bd, 1972–77. Member: CEGB, 1972–75; Directing Cttee, Internat. Union of Producers and Distributors of Electrical Energy, 1973–77. County Dir, Suffolk, St John Ambulance, 1982–85. Member until 1977: Ct of Governors, Admin. Staff Coll.; Council, IEE; Council of Industrial Soc.; E Midlands Econ. Planning Council; Mem. Nottingham Univ. Ct, 1975–77. CompIEE 1967. FBIM 1973. KStJ. *Recreations:* photography, painting, sailing, reading. *Address:* The Dumble, High Street, Orford, Woodbridge, Suffolk IP12 2NW. *T:* Orford (0394) 450622. *Clubs:* Army and Navy; Aldeburgh Yacht, Aldeburgh Golf.

LINGARD, Robin Anthony; Director of Training and Development, Highlands and Islands Enterprise, since 1991; *b* 19 July 1941; *s* of late Cecil Lingard and Lucy Lingard; *m* 1968, Margaret Lucy Virginia Elsden; two *d*. *Educ:* Felsted School; Emmanuel College, Cambridge (Exhibnr, MA). Min. of Aviation, 1963–66; Min. of Technology, 1966–70 (Private Sec. to Jt Parly Sec., 1966–68); DTI, 1971–74; DoI, 1974–83, Asst Sec., 1976; Under Sec., DTI, 1984, Cabinet Office (Enterprise Unit), 1984–85; Hd, Small Firms and Tourism Div., Dept of Employment, 1985–87; Mem. Bd, Highlands and Islands Develt Bd, 1988–91. Member: NEDC Sector Gp for Tourism and Leisure Industries, 1987–; Scottish Tourist Bd, 1988–; Management Bd, Prince's Trust and Royal Jubilee Trusts, 1989–. FTS 1988. *Recreations:* reading, walking, watching birds, aviation history. *Address:* Kinnairdie House, Dingwall, Ross-shire IV15 9LL. *T:* Dingwall (0349) 61044.

LINGS, Dr Martin; Keeper Emeritus of Oriental Manuscripts and Printed Books, British Library; *b* 24 Jan. 1909; *e s* of late George Herbert Lings and late Gladys Mary Lings (*née* Greenhalgh), Burnage, Lancs; *m* 1944, Lesley, 3rd *d* of late Edgar Smalley. *Educ:* Clifton Coll.; Magdalen Coll., Oxford; Sch. of Oriental and African Studies, Univ. of London. Class. Mods 1930, BA English 1932, MA 1937, Oxon; BA Arabic 1954, PhD 1959, London. Lectr in Anglo-Saxon and Middle English, Univ. of Kaunas, 1935–39; Lectr in English Lit., Univ. of Cairo, 1940–51; Asst Keeper, Dept of Oriental Printed Books and Manuscripts, British Museum, 1955–70; Deputy Keeper, 1970; Keeper, 1971; seconded to the British Library, 1973. FRAS. *Publications:* The Book of Certainty, 1952 (trans. Spanish and French); (with A. S. Fulton) Second Supplementary Catalogue of Arabic Printed Books in the British Museum, 1959; A Moslem Saint of the Twentieth Century, 1961 (trans. French and Arabic); Ancient Beliefs and Modern Superstitions, 1965 (trans. Turkish, Portuguese, French and Greek); Shakespeare in the Light of Sacred Art, 1966; The Elements and Other Poems, 1967; The Heralds and Other Poems, 1970; A Sufi Saint of the Twentieth Century, 1971 (trans. Urdu, Persian, Spanish, Turkish and French); What is Sufism?, (trans. French, Italian, Spanish, German, Portuguese and Croatian); (with Y. H. Safadi) Third Supplementary Catalogue of Arabic Printed Books in the British Library, 1976; (with Y. H. Safadi) The Qur'ān, Catalogue of an Exhibition at the British Library, 1976; The Quranic Art of Calligraphy and Illumination, 1977; Muhammad: his life based on the earliest sources, 1983 (trans. French, Urdu, Tamil, Spanish, Arabic and Italian); The Secret of Shakespeare, 1984 (trans. Italian, Spanish, Persian and French); The Eleventh Hour, 1987 (trans. German and French); Collected Poems, 1987; Symbol and Archetype: studies in the meaning of existence, 1990 (trans. French); articles in Encycl. Britannica, Encycl. Islam, Studies in Comparative Religion, Cambridge History of Arabic Literature, etc. *Recreations:* walking, gardening, music. *Address:* 3 French Street, Westerham, Kent TN16 1PN. *T:* Westerham (0959) 62855.

LINKIE, William Sinclair, CBE 1989; Controller, Inland Revenue (Scotland), 1983–90; *b* 9 March 1931; *s* of late Peter Linkie and of Janet Black Linkie (*née* Sinclair; she *m* 2nd, John McBryde); *m* 1955, Elizabeth Primrose Marion (*née* Reid); one *s* one *d*. *Educ:* George Heriot's Sch., Edinburgh. Dept of Agriculture and Fisheries for Scotland, 1948; Inland Revenue (Scotland), 1952–90: HM Inspector of Taxes, 1961; Dist Inspector, Edinburgh 6, 1964; Principal Inspector i/c Centre I, 1975; Dist Inspector, Edinburgh 5, 1982. Pres., Inland Revenue Sports Assoc. (Scotland), 1983. Elder, Church of Scotland. *Recreations:* golf, badminton, choral singing.

LINKLATER, Magnus Duncan; Editor, The Scotsman, since 1988; *b* 21 Feb. 1942; *s* of late Eric Robert Linklater, CBE, TD, and of Marjorie MacIntyre; *m* 1967, Veronica Lyle; two *s* one *d*. *Educ:* Eton Coll.; Freiburg Univ.; Sorbonne; Trinity Hall, Cambridge (BA 2nd Cl. Hons (Mod. Lang.)). Reporter, Daily Express, Manchester, 1965–66; Diary Reporter, London Evening Standard, 1966–67; Editor: Londoner's Diary, Evening Standard, 1967–69; 'Spectrum', Sunday Times, 1969–72; Sunday Times Colour Magazine, 1972–75; Assistant Editor: News, Sunday Times, 1975–79; Features, Sunday Times, 1979–81; Exec. Editor (Features), Sunday Times, 1981–83; Man. Editor (News), The Observer, 1983–86; Editor, London Daily News, 1987. Vice Chm., Scottish Daily Newspaper Soc. *Publications:* (with Stephen Fay and Lewis Chester) Hoax—The Inside Story of the Howard Hughes/Clifford Irving Affair, 1972; (with Lewis Chester and David May) Jeremy Thorpe: a secret life, 1979; Massacre: the story of Glencoe, 1982; (with the Sunday Times Insight Team) The Falklands War, 1982; (with Isabel Hilton and Neal Ascherson) The Fourth Reich—Klaus Barbie and the Neo-Fascist Connection, 1984; (with Douglas Corrance) Scotland, 1984; (contrib.) A Scottish Childhood, 1985; (with David Leigh) Not With Honour: inside story of the Westland Scandal, 1986; (with Christian Hesketh) For King and Conscience: the life of John Graham of Claverhouse, Viscount Dundee, 1989. *Recreations:* cricket, fishing, book-collecting. *Address:* c/o The Scotsman, 20 North Bridge, Edinburgh EH1 1YT. *T:* 031–225 2468. *Clubs:* Caledonian, MCC.

LINKLATER, Nelson Valdemar, CBE 1974 (OBE 1967); Drama Director, Arts Council of Great Britain, 1970–77; *b* 15 Aug. 1918; *s* of Captain Arthur David Linklater and Elsie May Linklater; *m* 1944, Margaret Lilian Boissard; two *s*. *Educ:* Imperial Service Coll.; RADA. RNVR, 1939–46 (final rank Lieut (S)). Professional theatre as actor and business manager, 1937–39. Documentary Films Manager, Army Kinema Corp., 1946–48; Arts Council of Great Britain: Asst Regional Dir (Nottingham), 1948–52; Asst and Dep. Drama Dir (London), 1952–70. Mem., Southern Arts Gen. Council and Exec. Cttee, 1978–89. Chm., CPRE, Wallingford Area Cttee, 1977–80. Member: Bd, Anvil Productions (Oxford Playhouse), 1977–88; Trent Polytechnic Theatre Design Adv. Cttee, 1980–83; Develt Panel, Cheek by Jowl Theatre Co., 1988–. Mem., London Inst. Formation Cttee, 1985; Governor: Central Sch. of Art and Design, London, 1978–87; Wyvern Arts Trust (Swindon), 1978–91; Theatre Design Trust, 1988–91; Trustee, Arts Council Trust for Special Funds, 1981–. *Publication:* (contrib.) The State and the Arts, 1980. *Recreations:* painting, reading, gardening. *Address:* 1 Church Close, East Hagbourne, Oxon OX11 9LP. *T:* Didcot (0235) 813340.

LINKS, Mary, (Mrs J. G. Links); *see* Lutyens, Mary.

LINLEY, Viscount; David Albert Charles Armstrong-Jones; *b* 3 Nov. 1961; *s* and *heir* of 1st Earl of Snowdon, *qv*, and *s* of HRH the Princess Margaret. *Educ:* Bedales; Parnham School for Craftsmen in Wood. Designer and Cabinet maker; Chairman: David Linley Furniture Ltd, 1985–; David Linley Company Ltd, 1985–; Dir, Lachmead Group, 1988–. Vogue—Sotheby's Cecil Beaton Award for portrait photograph, 1983.
See under Royal Family.

LINLITHGOW, 4th Marquess of, *cr* 1902; **Adrian John Charles Hope;** Bt (NS) 1698; Baron Hope, Viscount Aithrie, Earl of Hopetoun 1703 (Scot.); Baron Hopetoun 1809 (UK); Baron Niddry 1814 (UK); Stockbroker; *b* 1 July 1946; *s* of 3rd Marquess of Linlithgow, MC, TD, and Vivienne (*d* 1963), *d* of Capt. R. O. R. Kenyon-Slaney and of Lady Mary Gilmour; *S* father, 1987; *m* 1st, 1968, Anne (marr. diss. 1978), *e d* of A. Leveson, Hall Place, Hants; two *s*; 2nd, 1980, Peta C. Binding; one *s* one *d*. *Educ:* Eton. Joined HM Navy, 1965. *Heir:* *s* Earl of Hopetoun, *qv*. *Address:* Hopetoun House, South Queensferry, West Lothian EH30 9SL. *T:* 031–331 1169. *Club:* White's.
See also Baron Glendevon.

LINNANE, Prof. Anthony William, FAA; FRS 1980; Professor of Biochemistry, since 1965, Director, Centre for Molecular Biology and Medicine, since 1983, Monash University, Australia; *b* 17 July 1930; *s* of late W. Linnane, Sydney; *m* 1956, Judith Neil (marr. diss. 1980); one *s* one *d*; *m* 1980, Daryl, *d* of A. Skurrie. *Educ:* Sydney Boys' High School; Sydney Univ. (PhD, DSc); Univ. of Wisconsin, USA. Lecturer, then Senior Lectr, Sydney Univ., 1958–62; Reader, Monash Univ., Aust., 1962. Visiting Prof., Univ. of Wisconsin, 1967–68. President: Aust. Biochemical Soc., 1974–76; Fedn of Asian and Oceanic Biochemical Socs, 1975–77; 12th Internat. Congress of Biochemistry, 1982; Treasurer, Internat. Union of Biochemistry, 1988–. Work concerned especially with the biogenesis and genetics of mitochondria and molecular biol. of interferons and mucinous cancers. Editor-in-Chief, Biochemistry Internat. *Publications:* Autonomy and Biogenesis of Mitochondria and Chloroplasts, 1971; many contributions to learned journals. *Address:* Department of Biochemistry, Monash University, Clayton, Victoria 3168, Australia. *T:* Melbourne 565 3721, *Telex:* AA32691, *Fax:* G3 (3) 565–4699; 25 Canterbury Road, Camberwell, Vic 3124, Australia. *Clubs:* Athenæum; Moonee Valley Race; VRC; VATC.

LINNELL, David George Thomas, CBE 1987; Chairman, Birkdale Group PLC (formerly Brunning Group), since 1987; *b* 28 May 1930; *s* of George and Marguerite Linnell; *m* 1953, Margaret Mary Paterson; one *s* one *d*. *Educ:* Leighton Park School, Reading. Managing Dir, Thomas Linnell & Sons, 1964–75; Chief Exec., Linfood Holdings, 1975–79; Chm., Spar Food Holdings, 1975–81. Pres., Inst. of Grocery Distribution, 1980–82; Chm., Eggs Authority, 1981–86; Chm., Neighbourhood Stores, 1983–87. *Recreations:* shooting, ski-ing, boats. *Address:* The Old Rectory, Titchmarsh, Kettering, Northants NN14 3DG. *Club:* Carlton.

LINNETT, Dr Michael Joseph, OBE 1975; FRCGP; Apothecary to the Prince and Princess of Wales, 1983–90; general medical practitioner, 1957–90, retired; *b* 14 July 1926; *s* of Joseph Linnett and Dora Alice (*née* Eabry); *m* 1950, Marianne Patricia, *d* of Aubrey Dibdin, CIE; two *d* (and one *s* decd). *Educ:* Wyggeston Grammar School for Boys, Leicester; St Bartholomew's Hosp. Med. Coll., London (MB BS 1949; Wix Prize Essay 1947). FRCGP 1970 (MRCGP 1957). House Physician, 1949, Demonstrator in Pharmacology, 1954, Jun. Registrar, 1955, St Bartholomew's Hosp., London; Ho. Phys., Evelina Children's Hosp., 1950; RAF Medical Br., Sqdn Ldr, 1950–54. Chm. Council, RCGP, 1976–79; Member: Cttee on Safety of Medicines, 1970–75; Medicines Commn, 1976– (Vice-Chm., 1984–); Med. Adv. Panel, IBA, 1979–; Pres., Chelsea Clinical Soc., 1987–88; Governor: National Hosp. for Nervous Diseases, 1974–82; Sutton's Hosp., Charterhouse, 1985–. Freeman, City of London, 1980; Chm., Livery Cttee, Worshipful Soc. of Apothecaries, 1982–84, Mem., Ct of Assts, 1985–. Chm., Editorial Bd, Prescribers' Jl, 1973–74. FRSocMed 1958. *Publications:* chapter, People with Epilepsy—the Burden of Epilepsy, in A Textbook of Epilepsy, ed Laidlaw & Richens, 1976; chapter, Ethics in General Practice, in Doctors' Decisions—Ethical Conflicts in Medical Practice, ed Dunstan and Shinebourne, 1989; contrib. BMJ (jtly) Drug Treatment of Intractable Pain, 1960. *Recreation:* music. *Address:* 37 Ashcombe Street, SW6 3AW. *T:* 071–736 2487.

LINSTEAD, Stephen Guy; Director, Department of Trade and Industry, West Midlands Region, since 1990; *b* 23 June 1941; *s* of late George Frederick Linstead and of May Dorothy Linstead (*née* Griffiths); *m* 1st, 1971 (marr. diss.); two *s*; 2nd, 1982, Rachael Marian Feldman; two *d*. *Educ:* King Edward VII Sch., Sheffield; Corpus Christi Coll., Oxford (MA Mod. Hist.; Dipl. Public and Social Admin.); Carleton Univ., Ottawa (MA Political Sci.). Board of Trade, 1964–76 (Private Sec. to Minister of State, 1967–69); Asst Sec., Dept of Prices and Consumer Protection, 1976–79; Dept of Trade, 1979–82; Office of Fair Trading, 1982–90; Under-Sec., DTI, 1990–. Vice-Chm., Assoc. of First Div. Civil Servants, 1982–84. *Publication:* contrib. Ottawa Law Review. *Recreations:* biblical criticism, swimming, travel, entertainment. *Address:* Department of Trade and Industry, 77 Paradise Circus, Queensway, Birmingham B1 2DT. *T:* 021–212 5000. *Club:* Royal Over-Seas League.

LINTON, Alan Henry Spencer, LVO 1969; HM Diplomatic Service, retired; Consul-General, Detroit, USA, 1976–79; *b* Nottingham, 24 July 1919; *s* of Rt Rev. James Henry Linton, DD and Alicia Pears (*née* Aldous); *m* 1959, Kaethe Krebs (*d* 1990); four *d*. *Educ:* St Lawrence, Ramsgate; Magdalen Coll., Oxford (MA). Served War, RA, 1940–46. HM Overseas Civil Service, Tanganyika, 1947–62; FO, 1963–65; First Sec. (Inf.), Vienna, 1965–69; Head of Chancery, Lusaka, Zambia, 1970–73; First Sec. (Commercial), Kingston, Jamaica, 1973–75; Dep. High Comr, Kingston, 1975–76. *Recreations:* skiing, sailing, photography. *Address:* 29 The Avenue, Poole BH13 6LH. *Club:* Royal Over-Seas League.

LINTOTT, Sir Henry, KCMG 1957 (CMG 1948); *b* 23 Sept. 1908; *s* of late Henry John Lintott, RSA, and of Edith Lunn; *m* 1949, Margaret Orpen; one *s* one *d*. *Educ:* Edinburgh Acad.; Edinburgh Univ.; King's Coll., Cambridge. Entered Customs and Excise Dept, 1932; Board of Trade, 1935–48; Dep. Secretary-General, OEEC, 1948–56. Dep. Under-Secretary of State, Commonwealth Relations Office, 1956–63; British High Commissioner in Canada, 1963–68. *Address:* 47 Grantchester Street, Cambridge CB3 9HZ. *T:* Cambridge (0223) 312410.

LINTOTT, Robert Edward, FInstPet; Chief Executive, Coverdale Organisation, since 1987; *b* 14 Jan. 1932; *s* of Charles Edward and Doris Mary Lintott; *m* 1958, Mary Alice Scott; three *s*. *Educ:* Cambridgeshire High School; Trinity College, Cambridge. BA Nat. Scis 1955, MA. Served RAF, 1950–52 (Flying Officer); joined Esso Petroleum Co. Ltd, 1955; Corporate Planning Dept, Exxon Corp., 1975–78; Exec. Asst to Chm., Exxon Corp., 1978–79; Director: Esso Petroleum Co. Ltd, 1979–84; Esso Pension Trust, 1979–87; Esso Exploration & Production UK, 1984–87; Esso UK plc, Esso Petroleum, 1984–87 (Man. Dir, 1984–86); Matthew Hall Engineering Holdings Ltd, 1987–89; Chairman: Irish Refining Co., 1979–82; Esso Teoranta, 1982–84. Vice-Pres., UK Petroleum Industry Assoc., 1985–86; Pres., Oil Industries Club, 1986–88. Council Mem., 1979–, and Chm. Exec. Cttee, 1987–, Foundn for Management Educn; Member: Council for Management Educn and Develt, 1989–; Steering Cttee, Oxford Summer Business Sch., 1979– (Chm., 1987–); Council, Manchester Business Sch., 1985–. Councillor, Royal Bor. of Windsor and Maidenhead, 1987–91. *Recreations:* cricket, vintage and modern motoring. *Address:* The Coverdale Organisation Ltd, Dorland House, 14–16 Regent Street, SW1Y 4PH. *T:* 071–925 0099. *Clubs:* Royal Air Force, MCC.

LION, Jacques Kenneth, OBE 1979; President, The London Metal Exchange Ltd, since 1987; *b* 18 Dec. 1922; *s* of Felix J. Lion and Ethel (*née* Myers); *m* 1947, Jean Elphinstone (*née* Mackenzie); two *s* one *d*. *Educ:* St Paul's Sch. Pres., Non-Ferrous Div., Bureau Internationale de la Récupération, 1970–74; Mem. Council, British Secondary Metals Assoc., 1956–77 (Pres., 1959 and 1964). Dir, 1972, Chm., 1984, Metal Market & Exchange Co. Ltd. *Recreations:* music, gardening, golf. *Address:* c/o The London Metal Exchange Ltd, Plantation House, Fenchurch Street, EC3M 3AP. *T:* 071–626 3311. *Clubs:* City of London, Gresham.

LIPFRIEND, Alan; His Honour Judge Lipfriend; Circuit Judge since 1974; *b* 6 Oct. 1916; 2nd *s* of I. and S. Lipfriend; *m* 1948, Adèle Burke (*d* 1986); one *s*. *Educ:* Central Foundation Sch., London, Queen Mary Coll., London (BSc(Eng) (Hons) 1938; Fellow, 1987). Design Staff, Hawker Aircraft Ltd, 1939–48. Called to Bar, Middle Temple, 1948; Pres., Appeal Tribunal, under Wireless and Telegraphy Act, 1949, 1971–73; Mem. Parole Bd, 1978–81. A Governor, Queen Mary Coll., Univ. of London, 1981–89; Trustee and Gov., Central Foundation School for Boys, 1985–. *Recreations:* theatre and all sport. *Address:* 27 Edmunds Walk, N2 0HU. *T:* 081–883 4420. *Club:* Royal Automobile.

LIPKIN, Miles Henry J.; *see* Jackson-Lipkin.

LIPMAN, Maureen Diane, (Mrs J. M. Rosenthal); actress; *b* 10 May 1946; *d* of Maurice and Zelma Lipman; *m* 1973, Jack Morris Rosenthal, *qv*; one *s* one *d*. *Educ:* Newland High Sch. for Girls, Hull; London Acad. of Music and Dramatic Art. Professional début in The Knack, Watford, 1969; Stables Theatre, Manchester, 1970; National Theatre (Old Vic), 1971–73: Molly, in The Front Page; Long Day's Journey into Night; The Good Natur'd Man; *West End:* Candida, 1976; Maggie, in Outside Edge, 1978; Meg, in Meg and Mog, 1982; Messiah, 1983; Miss Skillen, in See How They Run, 1984 (Laurence Olivier Award; Variety Club of GB Award); Wonderful Town, Queen's, 1986; Re: Joyce!, Fortune, 1988, Vaudeville, 1989 and 1991, Long Wharf, Conn, USA, 1990; other plays include: Celia, in As You Like It, RSC, 1974; Jenny, in Chapter Two, Hammersmith, 1981; Kitty McShane, in On Your Way, Riley, Stratford East, 1983; *television:* plays, series and serials include: The Evacuees; Smiley's People; The Knowledge; Rolling Home; Outside Edge; Princess of France, in Love's Labour's Lost; Absurd Person Singular; Shift Work; Absent Friends; Jane Lucas, in 3 series of Agony; All at No 20 (TV Times Award, 1989); About Face, 1989 and 1990; *films:* Up the Junction, 1969; Educating Rita, 1983; Water, 1984. TV Times Award, for BT Commercials, 1988. Magazine columnist: Options, 1983–88; Riva, She, 1988–91. *Publications:* How Was it for You?, 1985; Something to Fall Back On, 1987; You Got an 'Ology?, 1989; Thank You for Having Me, 1990. *Recreations:* the radio, other people's problems, yoga, full-time guilt.

LIPSCOMB, Air Vice-Marshal (retired) Frederick Elvy, CB 1958; CBE 1953; *b* 2 Sept. 1902; *s* of late Arthur Bossley Lipscomb, St Albans; *m* 1931, Dorothy May (*d* 1964), *d* of Frederick Foskett, Berkhamsted, Herts; no *c*. *Educ:* Aldenham Sch.; Middlesex Hospital. MRCS LRCP 1927; DTM&H (Eng.), 1933; DPH (London) 1934. Commnd RAF 1927; psa 1946. Served Aden, Malta, Palestine; War of 1939–45, Mediterranean and West Africa (despatches thrice). Director of Hygiene and Research, Air Ministry, 1950; Principal Medical Officer, Far East Air Force, 1951–54; Dep. Director General RAF Medical Services, 1954–55; Principal Medical Officer, Home Command, 1955–57. KHP 1952; QHP 1952–57. CStJ 1952. *Publications:* Tropical Diseases section, Conybeare's Textbook of Medicine, 6th to 9th edns. Contributions to British Medical Journal, RAF Quarterly, etc. *Address:* Kilfillan House, Graemsdyke Road, Berkhamsted, Herts HP4 3LZ. *T:* Berkhamsted (0442) 862387.

LIPSCOMB, Prof. William Nunn; Abbott and James Lawrence Professor of Chemistry, Harvard University, 1971–90, now Emeritus; Nobel Laureate in Chemistry, 1976; *b* 9 Dec. 1919; *s* of late William Nunn Lipscomb Sr, and of Edna Patterson Porter; *m* 1983, Jean Craig Evans; one *s* one *d* by previous marriage. *Educ:* Univ. of Kentucky (BS); California Inst. of Technology (PhD). Univ. of Minnesota, Minneapolis: Asst Prof. of Physical Chem., 1946–50; Associate Prof., 1950–54; Actg Chief, Physical Chem. Div., 1952–54; Prof. and Chief of Physical Chem. Div., 1954–59; Harvard Univ.: Prof. of Chemistry, 1959–71 (Chm., Dept of Chem., 1962–65). Member: Bd of Dir's, Dow Chemical Co., USA, 1982–89; Scientific Adv. Bd, Robert A. Welch Foundn, 1982–. Member: Amer. Chemical Soc. (Chm., Minneapolis Section, 1949); Amer. Acad. of Arts and Sciences, 1959–; Nat. Acad. of Sciences, USA, 1961–; Internat. Acad. of Quantum Molecular Science, 1980; Académie Européenne des Scis, des Arts et des Lettres, Paris, 1980; Foreign Mem., Netherlands Acad. of Arts and Sciences, 1976; Hon. Member: Internat. Assoc. of Bioinorganic Scientists, 1979; RSC, 1983. MA (hon.) Harvard, 1959; Hon. DSc: Kentucky, 1963; Long Island, 1977; Rutgers, 1979; Gustavos Adolphus, 1980; Marietta, 1981; Miami, 1983; Dr *hc* Munich, 1976. *Publications:* Boron Hydrides, 1963 (New York); (with G. R. Eaton) Nuclear Magnetic Resonance Studies of Boron and Related Compounds, 1969 (New York); chapters in: The Aesthetic Dimensions of Science, ed D. W. Curtin, 1982; Crystallography in North America, ed D. Mchachlan and J. Glusker, 1983; contribs to scientific jls concerning structure and function of enzymes and natural products in inorganic chem. and theoretical chem. *Recreations:* tennis, chamber music. *Address:* Gibbs Chemical Laboratory, Harvard University, 12 Oxford Street, Cambridge, Mass 02138, USA. *T:* 617–495–4098.

LIPSEY, David Lawrence; Associate Editor, The Times, since 1990; *b* 21 April 1948; *s* of Lawrence and Penelope Lipsey; *m* 1982, Margaret Robson; one *d*. *Educ:* Bryanston Sch.; Magdalen Coll., Oxford (1st Cl. Hons PPE). Research Asst, General and Municipal Workers' Union, 1970–72; Special Adviser to Anthony Crosland, MP, 1972–77 (Dept of the Environment, 1974–76; FCO, 1976–77); Prime Minister's Staff, 10 Downing Street, 1977–79; Journalist, New Society, 1979–80; Sunday Times: Political Staff, 1980–82; Economics Editor, 1982–86; Editor, New Society, 1986–88; Co-founder and Dep. Editor, The Sunday Correspondent, 1988–90. Secretary, Streatham Labour Party, 1970–72; Chm., Fabian Soc., 1981–82; Mem., Exec. Cttee, Charter for Jobs, 1984–86. *Publications:* Labour and Land, 1972; (ed, with Dick Leonard) The Socialist Agenda: Crosland's Legacy, 1981; Making Government Work, 1982. *Recreation:* family life. *Address:* 44 Drakefield Road, SW17 8RP. *T:* 081–767 3268.

LIPSEY, Prof. Richard George, FRSC; Professor of Economics, Simon Fraser University, Burnaby, BC, since 1989; Fellow, Canadian Institute for Advanced Research, since 1989; *b* 28 Aug. 1928; *s* of R. A. Lipsey and F. T. Lipsey (*née* Ledingham); *m* 1960, Diana Louise Smart; one *s* two *d*. *Educ:* Univ. of British Columbia (BA 1st Cl. Hons 1950); Univ. of Toronto (MA 1953); LSE (PhD 1957). Dept of Trade and Industry, British Columbia Provincial Govt, 1950–53; LSE: Asst Lectr, 1955–58; Lectr, 1958–60; Reader, 1960–61; Prof. 1961–63; Univ. of Essex: Prof. of Economics, 1963–70; Dean of School of Social Studies, 1963–67; Sir Edward Peacock Prof. of Econs, Queen's Univ., Kingston, Ont, 1970–87. Vis. Prof., Univ. of California at Berkeley, 1963–64; Simeon Vis. Prof., Univ. of Manchester, 1973; Irving Fisher Vis. Prof., Yale Univ., 1979–80. Economic Consultant, NEDC, 1961–63; Sen. Econ. Advr, C. D. Howe Inst., Toronto, 1984–89. Member of Council: SSRC, 1966–69; Royal Economic Soc., 1968–71. President: Canadian Economics Assoc., 1980–81; Atlantic Economic Assoc., 1986–87. Editor, Review of Economic Studies, 1960–64. Fellow, Econometric Soc., 1972. FRSC 1980. Hon. LLD: McMaster, 1984; Victoria, 1985; Carleton, 1987; Queen's Univ. at Kingston, 1990. *Publications:* An Introduction to Positive Economics, 1963, 7th edn 1989; (with P. O. Steiner) Economics, 1966, 9th edn 1990; (with G. C. Archibald) An Introduction to a Mathematical Treatment of Economics, 1967, 3rd edn 1977; The Theory of Customs Unions: a general equilibrium analysis, 1971; (with G. C. Archibald) An Introduction to Mathematical Economics, 1975; (with C. Harbury) An Introduction to the UK Economy, 1983, 3rd edn 1989; (with F. Flatters) Common Ground for the Canadian Common Market, 1984; (with M. Smith): Canada's Trade Options in a Turbulent World, 1985; Global Imbalance and US Policy Response, 1987; (with R. York) A Guided Tour through the Canada—US Free Trade Agreement, 1988; (with C. Harbury) First Principles of Economics, 1988; articles in learned jls on many branches of theoretical and applied economics. *Recreations:* skiing, sailing, film making. *Address:* Economic Growth and Policy Program, Simon Fraser University at Harbour Centre, 515 W Hastings Street, Vancouver, BC V6B 5K3, Canada.

LIPSTEIN, Prof. Kurt; Professor of Comparative Law, Cambridge University, 1973–76; Fellow of Clare College, Cambridge, since 1956; *b* 19 March 1909; *e s* of Alfred Lipstein, MD and Hilda (*née* Sulzbach); *m* 1944, Gwyneth Mary Herford; two *d*. *Educ:* Goethe Gymnasium, Frankfurt on Main; Univs of Grenoble and Berlin; Trinity Coll., Cambridge. Gerichtsreferendar 1931; PhD Cantab 1936; LLD 1977. Called to Bar, Middle Temple, 1950, Hon. Bencher, 1966. Univ. Lectr, Cambridge, 1946; Reader in Conflict of Laws, Cambridge Univ., 1962–73. Dir of Research, Internat. Assoc. Legal Science, 1954–59. Vis. Professor: Univ. of Pennsylvania, 1962; Northwestern Univ., Chicago, 1966, 1968; Paris I, 1977. Humboldt Prize, Alexander von Humboldt Stiftung, Bonn, 1981. *Publications:* The Law of the EEC, 1974; Principles of the Conflict of Laws, National and International, 1981; joint editor and contributor: Dicey's Conflict of Laws, 6th edn, 1948—8th edn, 1967; Leske-Loewenfeld, Das Eherecht der europäischen Staaten, 1963; (ed) International Encyclopaedia of Comparative Law, vol. Private International Law, 1972; Harmonization of Private International Law by the EEC, 1978; contrib. English and foreign legal periodicals. *Address:* Clare College, Cambridge CB2 1TL. *T:* Cambridge (0223) 333200; 7 Barton Close, Cambridge CB3 9LQ. *T:* (0223) 357048; 13 Old Square, Lincoln's Inn, WC2A 3UA. *T:* 071–404 4800.

LIPTON, Stuart Anthony; Chief Executive, Stanhope Properties PLC, since 1983; Member, Royal Fine Art Commission, since 1988; *b* 9 Nov. 1942; *s* of Bertram Green and Jeanette Lipton; *m* 1966, Ruth Kathryn Marks; two *s* one *d*. *Educ:* Berkhamsted Sch. Director: Sterling Land Co., 1971–73; First Palace Securities Ltd, 1973–76; Man. Dir,

Greycoat PLC, 1976–83. Advr to Hampton Site Co. for Sainsbury Bldg, Nat. Gall., 1985–; Member: Adv. Bd, Dept of Construction Management, Reading Univ., 1983–; Property Adv. Gp, DoE, 1986–; Mil. Bldgs Cttee, MoD, 1987–. Mem. Council, British Property Fedn, 1987–. Trustee, Whitechapel Art Gall., 1987–; Member: Bd, Nat. Theatre, 1988–; Adv. Bd, RA, 1987–. Mem., Governing Body, Imperial Coll., 1987–. Hon. RIBA 1986. *Recreations:* architecture, crafts, art and technology, wine. *Address:* (office) Lansdowne House, Berkeley Square, W1.

LIPWORTH, Sir (Maurice) Sydney, Kt 1991; Chairman, Monopolies and Mergers Commission, since 1988 (Member, since 1981); *b* 13 May 1931; *s* of Isidore and Rae Lipworth; *m* 1957, Rosa Liwarek; two *s. Educ:* King Edward VII Sch., Johannesburg; Univ. of the Witwatersrand, Johannesburg (BCom, LLB). Admitted Solicitor, Johannesburg, 1955; called to the South African Bar, 1956. Barrister, Johannesburg, 1956–64; Non-Exec. Dir, Liberty Life Assoc. of Africa Ltd, 1956–64; Director: private trading/financial gps, 1965–67; Abbey Life Assurance Gp, 1968–70; Allied Dunbar Assurance plc (formerly Hambro Life Assurance), 1971–88 (Jt Man. Dir, 1980–84; Dep. Chm., 1984–87); Chm., Allied Dunbar Unit Trusts, 1985–88 (Man. Dir, 1983–85); Director: J. Rothschild Holdings plc, 1984–87; BAT Industries plc, 1985–88. Chm., BreakThrough Breast Cancer Res. Trust, 1990–; Trustee: Allied Dunbar Charitable Trust, 1971–; Philharmonia Orchestra, 1982– (Dep. Chm. of Trustees, 1986–); Royal Acad. Trust, 1988–; Governor, Sadler's Wells Foundn, 1987–90. Hon. Bencher, Inner Temple, 1989. *Publications:* chapters and articles on investment, taxation, life insurance and pensions. *Recreations:* tennis, music, theatre. *Address:* Monopolies and Mergers Commission, 48 Carey Street, WC2A 2JT. *Clubs:* Reform, Queen's.

LISBURNE, 8th Earl of, *cr* 1776; **John David Malet Vaughan;** Viscount Lisburne and Lord Vaughan, 1695; barrister-at-law; *b* 1 Sept. 1918; *o s* of 7th Earl of Lisburne; *S* father, 1965; *m* 1943, Shelagh, *er d* of late T. A. Macauley, 1266 Redpath Crescent, Montreal, Canada; three *s. Educ:* Eton; Magdalen Coll., Oxford (BA, MA). Called to Bar, Inner Temple, 1947. Captain, Welsh Guards. Director: British Home Stores Ltd, 1964–87; S Wales Regional Bd, Lloyds Bank Ltd, 1978–; Divisional Dir for Wales, Nationwide Building Soc., 1982–. Chm., Wales Council for Voluntary Action (formerly Council of Social Service for Wales), 1976–; Hon. Life Mem., AA (Mem. Exec. Cttee, 1981–88). *Heir: s* Viscount Vaughan, *qv. Address:* Cruglas, Ystrad Meurig, Dyfed SY25 6AN. *T:* Pontrhydfendigaid (09745) 230. *Clubs:* Buck's, Pratt's, Turf.

LISHMAN, Prof. William Alwyn, MD, DSc; FRCP, FRCPsych; Professor of Neuropsychiatry, Institute of Psychiatry, University of London, since 1979; Consultant Psychiatrist, Bethlem Royal and Maudsley Hospitals, since 1967; *b* 16 May 1931; *s* of George Hackworth Lishman and Madge Scott (*née* Young); *m* 1966, Marjorie Loud; one *s* one *d. Educ:* Houghton-le-Spring Grammar Sch.; Univ. of Birmingham (BSc Hons Anatomy and Physiology, 1953; MB, ChB Hons 1956; MD 1965). DPM London, 1963; DSc London, 1985. MRCP 1958, FRCP 1972; FRCPsych 1972. House Phys. and House Surg., Queen Elizabeth Hosp., Birmingham, 1956–57; MO Wheatley Mil. Hosp., 1957–59 (Major, RAMC); Registrar, United Oxford Hosps, 1959–60; Registrar, later Sen. Registrar, Maudsley Hosp., London, 1960–66; Consultant in Psychol Medicine, Nat. Hosp. and Maida Vale Hosp., London, 1966–67; Sen. Lectr in Psychol Medicine, Hammersmith Hosp. and RPMS, 1967–69; Consultant Psychiatrist, Bethlem Royal and Maudsley Hosps, 1967–74; Reader in Neuropsychiatry, Inst. of Psychiatry, 1974–79. Vis. Fellow, Green Coll., Oxford, 1983. Advisor to Bermuda Hosps Bd, 1971; Scientific Advisor, DHSS, 1979–82; Civilian Consultant, RAF, 1987–. Member: Neurosciences Bd, MRC, 1976–78 (Dep. Chm., 1976–77); Scientific Adv. Panel, Brain Res. Trust, 1986–; Adv. Cttee, Mason Med. Res. Trust, 1986–. Examiner: Univ. of Oxford (also Mem. Bd of Examrs), 1975–79; Univ. of Birmingham, 1984–87; Nat. Univ. of Malaysia, 1989. Chm., British Neuropsychiatry Assoc., 1987–; Member: Experimental Psychology Soc., 1975–; Assoc. of British Neurologists, 1979–. Gaskell Gold Medal, Royal Medico-Psychol Assoc., 1965. Member, Editorial Boards: Psychological Medicine, 1970–; Psychiatric Developments, 1983–; Neuropsychiatry, Neuropsychology and Behavioral Neurology, 1988–. Guarantor of Brain, 1984–. *Publications:* Organic Psychiatry: the psychological consequences of cerebral disorder, 1978, 2nd edn 1987; physiol and psychol papers on brain maturation, cerebral dominance, organisation of memory; clinical papers on head injury, dementia, epilepsy, neuroimaging, and alcoholic brain damage. *Recreations:* organ, piano, harpsichord, travelling. *Address:* 9 Elwill Way, Beckenham, Kent BR3 3AB.

LISLE; *see* Orchard-Lisle.

LISLE, 7th Baron, *cr* 1758; **John Nicholas Horace Lysaght;** *s* of late Hon. Horace G. Lysaght and Alice Elizabeth, *d* of Sir John Wrixon Becher, 3rd Bt; *b* 10 Aug. 1903; *S* grandfather, 1919; *m* 1st, 1928, Vivienne Brew (who obtained a divorce, 1939; she *died* 1948); 2nd, 1939, Mary Helen Purgold, Shropshire. *Heir: nephew* Patrick James Lysaght [*b* 1 May 1931; *m* 1957, Mrs Mary Louise Shaw-Stewart (marr. diss.); two *s* one *d*]. *Address:* The Chestnuts, Barge Farm, Taplow, Bucks.

LISSMANN, Hans Werner, FRS 1954; Reader, Department of Zoology, Cambridge, 1966–77, now Emeritus, and Director, Sub-Department of Animal Behaviour, 1969–77; Fellow of Trinity College, Cambridge, since 1955; *b* 30 April 1909; *s* of Robert and Ebba Lissmann; *m* 1949, Corinne Foster-Barham; one *s. Educ:* Kargala and Hamburg. Dr.rer.nat., Hamburg, 1932; MA, Cantab, 1947. Asst Director of Research, Dept of Zoology, Cambridge, 1947–55; Lecturer, 1955–66. *Address:* 9 Bulstrode Gardens, Cambridge CB3 0EN. *T:* Cambridge (0223) 356126.

LISTER; *see* Cunliffe-Lister, family name of Earl of Swinton.

LISTER, Geoffrey Richard, FCA; Chief Executive, since 1985, Director, since 1988, Bradford & Bingley Building Society; *b* 14 May 1937; *s* of Walter and Margaret Lister; *m* 1962, Myrtle Margaret (*née* Cooper); one *s* two *d. Educ:* St Bede's Grammar Sch., Bradford. Articled clerk, J. Pearson & Son, 1955–60, qual. chartered accountant, 1960; Computer and Systems Sales, Burroughs Machines Ltd, 1961–63; Audit Man., Thos Gardner & Co., 1963–65; Bradford & Bingley Building Society: Asst Accountant, 1965–67; Computer Man., 1967–70; Chief Accountant, 1970–73; Asst Gen. Man., 1973–75; Dep. Gen. Man., 1975–80; Gen. Man., 1980–84; Dep. Chief Exec., 1984–85. Dir, EFT Ltd, 1984–. Mem. Council, Bldg Socs Assoc., 1984–; Governor: Nab Wood Grammar Sch., Bingley, 1977–; Beckfoot Grammar Sch., Bingley, 1985–. *Recreations:* shooting, boating, fishkeeping, gardening. *Address:* Mandalay, Longwood Hall, Longwood Avenue, Bingley, W Yorks BD16 2RX. *T:* Bradford (0274) 562276. *Clubs:* Beckfoot Golf, Bradford and Bingley Rugby Union Football (Bingley).

LISTER, Prof. James, MD, FRCS; Professor of Paediatric Surgery, University of Liverpool, 1974–86, now Emeritus; *b* 1 March 1923; *s* of Thomas and Anna Rebecca Lister; *m* 1946, Greta Redpath; three *d. Educ:* St Paul's Sch., London; Edinburgh Univ. (MB, ChB 1945; MD 1972). FRCS 1975, FRCSE 1950, FRCSGlas 1969. Surg. Lieut, RNVR, 1945–48. Surgical training posts, Edinburgh and Dundee, 1948–58; Halstead Res. Fellow, Colorado Univ., 1959; Sen. Lectr in Paediatric Surgery and Consultant Surgeon, Hosp. for Sick Children, Great Ormond St, and Queen Elizabeth Hosp., Hackney Rd, 1960–63; Consultant Paediatric Surgeon, Sheffield Children's Hosp., 1963–74. Civil Consultant in Paediatric Surgery to RN, 1979–86. Past Examiner: Univs of Glasgow and Sheffield (in paediatric surgery); DCH London; Part I and Part II FRCSE. Mem. Council, RCSE, 1977– (Convenor of Examinations Cttee, 1986–90; a Vice-Pres., 1988–91); Mem., St Helens & Knowsley DHA, 1983–86. Chm., European Union of Paediatric Surgical Assocs, 1983–86; Hon. Member, Paediatric Assocs of Brazil, Chile, Germany, Greece, Hungary, Peru, Poland, Scandinavia, Yugoslavia. Hon. Fellow: Amer. Acad. of Paediatrics, 1976; Assoc. of Surgeons of India, 1985. Member of Editorial Board: Jl of RCSEd; Jl of Paediatric Surgery; Consultant editor, Annals of Tropical Paediatrics, 1985–. *Publications:* Neonatal Surgery, ed jtly 2nd edn 1978 and 3rd edn, 1990; Complications in Paediatric Surgery, 1986; papers on neonatal surgery and myelomeningocele. *Recreations:* gardening, hill walking. *Address:* Kailheugh, Hownam, Kelso, Roxburghshire TD5 8AL. *T:* Morebattle (05734) 224.

LISTER, Very Rev. John Field, MA; *b* 19 Jan. 1916; *s* of Arthur and Florence Lister. *Educ:* King's Sch., Worcester; Keble Coll., Oxford; Cuddesdon Coll., Oxford. Asst Curate, St Nicholas, Radford, Coventry, 1939–44; Asst Curate, St John Baptist, Coventry, 1944–45; Vicar of St John's, Huddersfield, 1945–54; Asst Rural Dean of Halifax, 1955–61; Archdeacon of Halifax, 1961–72; Vicar of Brighouse, 1954–72; Provost of Wakefield, 1972–82. Examng Chaplain to Bishop of Wakefield, 1972–78. Hon. Canon of Wakefield Cathedral, 1961, Canon, 1968; RD of Wakefield, 1972–80. Chaplain to The Queen, 1966–72. *Address:* 5 Larkcliff Court, The Parade, Birchington, Kent CT7 9NB.

LISTER, Prof. (Margot) Ruth (Aline); Professor of Applied Social Studies, University of Bradford, since 1987; *b* 3 May 1949; *d* of Dr Werner Bernard Lister and Daphne (*née* Carter). *Educ:* Univ. of Essex (BA Hons Sociology); Univ. of Sussex (MA Multi-Racial Studies). Child Poverty Action Group: Legal Res. Officer, 1971–75; Asst Dir, 1975–77; Dep. Dir, 1977–79; Dir, 1979–87. Eleanor Rathbone Meml Lecture, Univ. of Leeds, 1989. Hon. LLD Manchester, 1987. *Publications:* Supplementary Benefit Rights, 1974; Welfare Benefits, 1981; The Exclusive Society, 1990; chapters in: Justice, Discretion and Poverty, 1975; Labour and Equality, 1980; The Economics of Prosperity, 1980; Taxation and Social Policy, 1981; Families in Britain, 1982; The New Politics of Welfare, 1989; The Social Economy and the Democratic State, 1989; The Economics of Social Security; Year Book of Social Work, 1989; pamphlets and articles on poverty and social security. *Recreations:* relaxing—with friends, music, and through walking, meditation and Tai Chi; reading. *Address:* University of Bradford, Richmond Road, Bradford, W Yorks BD7 1DP; 26 Lynton Drive, Bradford BD9 5JT.

LISTER, Patrick; *see* Lister, R. P.

LISTER, Raymond (George), MA, LittD Cantab; President, Royal Society of Miniature Painters, Sculptors and Gravers, 1970–80; Chairman, Board of Governors, Federation of British Artists, 1976–80 (Governor, 1972–80); *b* 28 March 1919; *s* of late Horace Lister and Ellen Maud Mary Lister (*née* Arnold); *m* 1947, Pamela Helen, *d* of late Frank Bishop Brutnell; one *s* one *d. Educ:* St John's Coll. Choir Sch., Cambridge; Cambridge and County High Sch. for Boys. Served apprenticeship in family firm (architectural metalworking), 1934–39; specialised war service (engrg), 1939–45; Dir of family firm, 1941–; Man. Editor, Golden Head Press, 1952–72; Dir, John P. Gray and Son, craft bookbinders, 1978–82. Hon. Senior Mem., University Coll., subseq. Wolfson Coll., Cambridge, 1971–75, Mem. Coll. Council, 1983–85, Emeritus Fellow (Fellow, 1975–86); a Syndic, Fitzwilliam Mus., Cambridge, 1981–89. Liveryman, Blacksmiths' Co., 1957, Mem. Ct of Assistants, 1980, Prime Warden, 1989–90. Associate Mem. 1946, Mem. 1948, Royal Soc. of Miniature Painters; Pres., Private Libraries Assoc., 1971–74; Vice-Pres., Architectural Metalwork Assoc., 1970–75, Pres., 1975–77. *Publications:* Decorative Wrought Ironwork in Great Britain, 1957; Decorative Cast Ironwork in Great Britain, 1960; Edward Calvert, 1962; Beulah to Byzantium, 1965; Victorian Narrative Paintings, 1966; William Blake, 1968; Hammer and Hand, 1969; Samuel Palmer and his Etchings, 1969; A Title to Phoebe, 1972; British Romantic Art, 1973; Samuel Palmer: a biography, 1974; (ed) The Letters of Samuel Palmer, 1974; Infernal Methods: a Study of William Blake's art techniques, 1975; Apollo's Bird, 1975; For Love of Leda, 1977; Great Images of British Printmaking, 1978; (jtly) Samuel Palmer: a vision recaptured, 1978; Samuel Palmer in Palmer Country, 1980; George Richmond, 1981; Bergomask, 1982; There was a Star Danced, 1983; Prints and Printmaking, 1984; Samuel Palmer and 'The Ancients', (catalogue of exhibn at Fitzwilliam Mus., Cambridge, also selected by R. Lister), 1984; The Paintings of Samuel Palmer, 1985; The Paintings of William Blake, 1986; Samuel Palmer, his Life and Art, 1987; A Catalogue Raisonné of the Works of Samuel Palmer, 1988; British Romantic Painting, 1989; contrib. Climbers' Club Jl, The Irish Book, Blake Studies, Blake Quarterly, Gazette des Beaux-arts, Connoisseur, Studies in Romanticism, Book Collector and TLS. *Recreations:* mountaineering in the fens, merels. *Address:* Windmill House, Linton, Cambs CB1 6NS. *T:* Cambridge (0223) 891248. *Clubs:* Athenæum, Sette of Odd Volumes (Pres. 1960, 1982).

LISTER, (Robert) Patrick; retired; *b* 6 Jan. 1922; *s* of Robert B. Lister; *m* 1942, Daphne Rosamund, *d* of Prof. C. J. Sisson; three *s* one *d* (and one *s* decd). *Educ:* Marlborough College; Cambridge University (MA); Harvard Business School (MBA). Captain Royal Engineers, 1942–46; Massey Harris, Toronto, 1949–51; joined Coventry Climax Ltd, 1951, Managing Director, 1971–80, Deputy Chairman, 1980–81; Dir, Climax Fork Trucks, 1981–83; Dir and Chief Exec., Engrg Employers W Midlands Assoc., 1983–84. President: Fedn Européenne de la Manutention, 1978–80; Coventry and Dist Engineering Employers' Assoc., 1979–80 and 1983; British Indust. Truck Assoc., 1980–81; Vice-Pres., Inst. of Materials Handling, later Inst. of Materials Management, 1982–. Chm., Bd of Governors, Coventry Polytechnic, 1986– (Mem., 1984–); Gov., Coventry Technical Coll., 1984–; Chm. Trustees, St Joseph's Sch., Kenilworth. *Recreations:* marriage counselling, ex-offenders' hostels, travel, gardening, DIY. *Address:* 35 Warwick Avenue, Coventry CV5 6DJ. *T:* Coventry (0203) 73776.

LISTER, Ruth; *see* Lister, M. R. A.

LISTER, Tom, CBE 1978; QFSM 1977; Chief Fire Officer, West Midlands County Council, 1975–81, retired; *b* 14 May 1924; *s* of late T. Lister and of Mrs E. Lister; *m* 1954, Linda, *d* of late T. J. and Mrs H. Dodds; one *d. Educ:* Charter House, Hull. Hull Fire Service, 1947–60; divisional officer, Lancs, 1960–62; Asst Chief Fire Officer, Warwicks, 1962–68; Chief Fire Officer, Glos, 1968–71, Bristol and Avon, 1972–75.

LISTER, Dame Unity (Viola), DBE 1972 (OBE 1958); Member of Executive, European Union of Women, since 1971 (Vice-Chairman, 1963–69); Member: European Movement, since 1970; Conservative Group for Europe, since 1970; *b* 19 June 1913; *d* of Dr A. S. Webley; *m* 1940, Samuel William Lister. *Educ:* St Helen's, Blackheath; Sorbonne Univ. of Paris. Member, London County Council, 1949–65 (Dep.-Chm., 1963–64); Chairman: Women's Nat. Advisory Cttee, 1966–69; Nat. Union of Conservative and Unionist Assocs, 1970–71 (Mem. Exec); Mem., Inner London Adv. Cttee on Appt of Magistrates, 1966–. Vice-Chm., Horniman Museums (Chm., 1967–70); Governor: Royal Marsden Hosp., 1952–; various schools and colleges. *Recreations:* languages, travel, music, gardening, theatre, museums, reading, walking. *Address:* 32 The Court Yard, Eltham, SE9 5QE. *T:* 081–850 7038. *Club:* St Stephen's Constitutional.

LISTER-KAYE, Sir John (Phillip Lister), 8th Bt *cr* 1812, of Grange, Yorks; Director of the Aigas Trust, since 1979; *b* 8 May 1946; *s* of Sir John Christopher Lister Lister-Kaye, 7th Bt and Audrey Helen (*d* 1979), *d* of E. J. Carter; *S* father, 1982; *m* 1972, Sorrel Deirdre (marr. diss. 1987), *d* of Count Henry Noel Bentinck; one *s* two *d*; 2nd, 1989, Lucinda Anne (formerly Hon. Mrs Evan Baillie), *d* of Robin Law, Withersfield; one *d*. *Educ:* Allhallows School. Naturalist, author, farmer, lecturer. Created first field studies centre in Highlands of Scotland, 1970; Founder Director of Scottish conservation charity, the Aigas Trust, 1979. Mem., Internat. Cttee, World Wilderness Foundn, 1983–; Chairman: Scottish Adv. Cttee, RSPB, 1986–; NW Region, NCC for Scotland, 1991–. *Publications:* The White Island, 1972; Seal Cull, 1979; The Seeing Eye, 1980. *Recreations:* breeding and showing pedigree highland cattle. *Heir:* *s* John Warwick Noel Lister-Kaye, *b* 10 Dec. 1974. *Address:* Aigas House, Beauly, Inverness-shire IV4 7AD. *T:* Beauly (0463) 782729. *Club:* Caledonian.

LISTON, James Malcolm, CMG 1958; Chief Medical Adviser, Foreign and Commonwealth Office, Overseas Development Administration, 1970–71; *b* 1909; *m* 1935, Isobel Prentice Meiklem, Edinburgh; one *s* one *d*. *Educ:* Glasgow High Sch.; Glasgow Univ. MB, ChB, Glasgow, 1932; DTM & H Eng., 1939; DPH University of London, 1947; FRCP Glasgow, 1963. Medical Officer, Kenya, 1935; Director of Medical and Health Services, Sarawak, 1947–52; Deputy Director of Medical Services, Hong Kong, 1952–55; Director of Medical Services, Tanganyika, 1955–59; Permanent Secretary to Ministry of Health, Tanganyika, 1959–60; Deputy Chief Medical Officer: Colonial Office, 1960–61; Dept of Tech. Co-op., 1961–62; Chief Medical Adviser, Dept of Tech. Co-op., 1962–64; Medical Adviser, Min. of Overseas Develt, 1964–70. *Address:* 6A Western Terrace, Murrayfield, Edinburgh EH12 5QF. *T:* 031–337 4236.

LISTOWEL, 5th Earl of, *cr* 1822; **William Francis Hare,** PC 1946; GCMG 1957; Baron Ennismore, 1800; Viscount Ennismore, 1816; Baron Hare (UK), 1869; Chairman of Committees, House of Lords, 1965–76; *b* 28 Sept. 1906; *e s* of 4th Earl and Hon. Freda Vanden-Bempde-Johnstone (*d* 1968), *y d* of 2nd Baron Derwent; *S* father, 1931; *m* 1st, 1933, Judith (marr. diss., 1945), *o d* of R. de Marffy-Mantuano, Budapest; one *d*; 2nd, 1958, Stephanie Sandra Yvonne Wise (marr. diss., 1963), Toronto; one *d*; 3rd, 1963, Mrs Pamela Read; two *s* one *d*. *Educ:* Eton; Balliol Coll., Oxford. PhD London Univ. Lieut, Intelligence Corps; Whip of Labour Party in House of Lords, 1941–44; Parliamentary Under-Secretary of State, India Office, and Deputy Leader, House of Lords, 1944–45; Postmaster-General, 1945–47; Secretary of State for India, April-Aug. 1947; for Burma, 1947–Jan. 1948; Minister of State for Colonial Affairs, 1948–50; Joint Parliamentary Secretary, Ministry of Agriculture and Fisheries, 1950–51; Member (Lab) LCC for East Lewisham, 1937–46, for Battersea North, 1952–57. Governor-General of Ghana, 1957–60. Jt Patron, British Tunisian Soc.; President: British-Cameroon Soc.; Council for Aid to African Students; Jt Pres., Anti-Slavery Soc. for Protection of Human Rights; Vice-Pres., European-Atlantic Gp. *Publications:* The Values of Life, 1931; A Critical History of Modern Æsthetics, 1933 (2nd edn, as Modern Æsthetics: an Historical Introduction, 1967). *Heir:* *s* Viscount Ennismore, *qv*. *Address:* 10 Downshire Hill, NW3. *Club:* Reform.
See also Baron Grantley, Hon. A. V. Hare, Earl of Iveagh.

LITCHFIELD, Jack Watson, FRCP; retired; Consulting Physician, St Mary's Hospital, since 1972 (Physician, 1946–72 and Physician i/c Cardiac Department, 1947–72); *b* 7 May 1909; *s* of H. L. Litchfield, Ipswich; *m* 1941, Nan (*d* 1984), *d* of A. H. Hatherly, Shanghai; two *s* one *d*. *Educ:* Ipswich Sch.; Oriel Coll., Oxford (Scholar); St Mary's Hospital. Theodore Williams Schol. in Physiology, 1929, in Pathology, 1931; Radcliffe Schol. in Pharmacology, 1932; BA (2nd class hons) 1930; BM, BCh 1933; University schol. at St Mary's Hospital Medical Sch., 1931; MRCP 1936; FRCP 1947. Medical Registrar: St Mary's Hospital, 1936; Brompton Hospital, 1938; Physician, King Edward Memorial Hosp., W13, 1947–69. Served in RAMC in N Africa, Italy, etc (despatches), Lt-Col i/c Medical Div. *Publications:* papers on various subjects in medical journals. *Recreations:* gardening, conservation. *Address:* 2 Pound Cottages, The Green, Long Melford, Sudbury, Suffolk CO10 9DX. *T:* Sudbury (0787) 312730.

LITCHFIELD, Captain John Shirley Sandys, OBE 1943; RN; *b* 27 Aug. 1903; *e s* of late Rear-Admiral F. S. Litchfield-Speer, CMG, DSO, and late Cecilia Sandys; *m* 1939, Margaret, *d* of late Sir Bertram Portal, KCB, DSO, and late Hon. Lady Portal; one *s* two *d*. *Educ:* St Aubyns, Rottingdean; RN Colleges Osborne and Dartmouth. Midshipman and Lieut in HMS Renown during Royal Cruise to India and Japan, 1921–22 and to Australia and NZ, 1927; Yangtse river gunboat, 1929–31; RN Staff Coll., 1935; comd naval armoured trains and cars, Palestine, 1936 (despatches); Staff Officer (Ops) to C-in-C Mediterranean, 1936–38; comd HMS Walker, 1939, HMS Norfolk 1943, HMS Tyne, 1946–47 and HMS Vanguard, 1951–53; Naval SO, Supreme War Council, 1939, Joint Planning Staff, 1940; SO (O) Western Approaches, 1941; Russian Convoys and N Africa landings, 1941–43; planning staff, Normandy ops, 1944; Combined Chiefs of Staff, Washington, 1945; National War College of US, 1947–48; Dep. Director Naval Intelligence, 1949–50; idc 1951; Director of Ops, Admiralty, 1953–54; retired 1955. CC Kent, 1955–58. MP (C) Chelsea, 1959–66. Liveryman, Vintner's Company. *Address:* Snowfield, Bearsted, Kent ME14 4DH. *Clubs:* Royal Navy Club of 1765 and 1785; Bearsted Cricket.

LITCHFIELD, Dame Ruby (Beatrice), DBE 1981 (OBE 1959); Director, Festival City Broadcasters Ltd, 1975–86, retired (first woman appointed); Trustee, Adelaide Festival Centre, 1971–82, retired (first woman to be appointed to this position) (Life Member, 1982); *b* 5 Sept. 1912; *d* of Alfred John Skinner and Eva Hanna (*née* Thomas); *m* 1940, Kenneth Lyle Litchfield (*d* 1976); one *d*. *Educ:* North Adelaide Primary Sch.; Presbyterian Girls' Coll., Glen Osmond. Bd Mem., Kidney Foundn, 1968–; Chairperson: Carclew Youth Performing Arts Centre, 1972–88 (Life Patron, 1988); Families, Religion, Cultural Cttee, S Aust. Jubilee 150th, 1980–86; Women's Cttee, Nat. Heart Foundn. First woman Mem., Bd of S Aust. Housing Trust, 1962–70; Life Member: Queen Victoria Maternity Hosp., 1972 (Mem. Bd and Vice-Pres., 1953–72); Adelaide Rep. Th., 1967 (Mem. Bd, 1951–68); Spastic Paralysis Welfare Assoc. Inc. (Mem. Cttee, Miss South Australia Quest, Spastic PWA). Mayoress of Prospect, 1954–57; Pres., Sportswomen's Assoc., 1969–74; Mem., Divl Council, Aust. Red Cross, S Aust. Div., 1955–71; Councillor, Royal Dist Bush Nursing Soc., 1957–66; Member: S Aust. Davis Cup Cttee, 1952, 1963, 1968; SA Cttee of Royal Acad. of Dancing, 1961–66; Bd, Telethon Channel 9, 1969–86; Mem. Cttee, Adelaide Festival of Arts, 1960 (Mem. Bd of Govs, 1966–90); Sponsorship Cttee, Constitutional Mus., 1979–80; Council, Sudden Infant Death Res. Foundn, 1979–; Bd, Mary Potter Foundn (Chair, Hospice Appeal Cttee, 1988–); numerous charitable and med. appeal cttees; Mem. Bd, Crippled Children's Assoc., 1976–. Silver Jubilee Medal, 1977; Advance Australia Award, 1985; S Australia Great Award, 1987. *Recreation:* tennis (SA Hardcourt Champion, 1932–35). *Address:* 33 Hallett Road, Burnside, SA 5066, Australia. *Club:* Royal Commonwealth Society (Adelaide).

LITHERLAND, Prof. Albert Edward, FRS 1974; FRSC 1968; University Professor, since 1979 and Professor of Physics, since 1966, University of Toronto; *b* 12 March 1928; *e s* of Albert Litherland and Ethel Clement; *m* 1956, (Elizabeth) Anne Allen; two *d*. *Educ:* Wallasey Grammar Sch.; Univ. of Liverpool (BSc, PhD). State Scholar to Liverpool Univ., 1946; Rutherford Memorial Scholar to Atomic Energy of Canada, Chalk River, Canada, 1953; Scientific Officer at Atomic Energy of Canada, 1955–66. Guggenheim Fellow, Toronto Univ., 1986–87. Canadian Assoc. of Physicists Gold Medal for Achievement in Physics, 1971; Rutherford Medal and Prize of Inst. of Physics (London), 1974; JARI Silver Medal, Pergamon Press, 1981. Izaac Walton Killam Memorial Scholarship, 1980. *Publications:* numerous, in scientific jls. *Address:* 3 Hawthorn Gardens, Toronto, Ontario M4W 1P4, Canada. *T:* 416–923–5616.

LITHERLAND, Robert Kenneth; MP (Lab) Manchester Central, since Sept. 1979; *b* 1930; *s* of Robert Litherland and Mary (*née* Parry); *m* 1953, Edna Litherland; one *s* one *d*. *Educ:* North Manchester High Sch. for Boys. Formerly sales representative for printing firm. Mem., Manchester City Council (Dep. Chm., Housing Cttee; former Chm., Manchester Direct Works Cttee); Dep. Chm., Public Works Cttee, Assoc. of Municipal Authorities. Member: Council of Europe; WEU. *Address:* House of Commons, SW1; 32 Darley Avenue, Didsbury, Manchester M20 8YD.

LITHGOW, Sir William (James), 2nd Bt of Ormsary, *cr* 1925; DL; CEng; industrialist and farmer; Chairman, 1959–84 and since 1988, Director, since 1956, Lithgows Ltd; *b* 10 May 1934; *o s* of Colonel Sir James Lithgow, 1st Bt of Ormsary, GBE, CB, MC, TD, DL, JP, LLD, and Gwendolyn Amy, *d* of late John Robinson Harrison of Scalesceugh, Cumberland; *S* father, 1952; *m* 1964, Valerie Helen (*d* 1964), 2nd *d* of late Denis Scott, CBE and Mrs Laura Scott; *m* 1967, Mary Claire, *d* of Colonel F. M. Hill, CBE and Mrs Hill; two *s* one *d*. *Educ:* Winchester Coll. CEng; FRINA; CBIM 1980 (FBIM 1969). Chm., Lithgow Drydocks Ltd, 1967–78; Vice-Chm., Scott Lithgow Ltd, 1968–78; Chairman: Western Ferries (Argyll) Ltd, 1972–85; Hunterston Develt Co. Ltd, 1987– (Dir, 1971–); Director: Bank of Scotland, 1962–86; Campbeltown Shipyard Ltd, 1970–; Lithgows Pty Ltd, 1972–; Landcatch, 1981–. Member: British Cttee, Det Norske Veritas, 1966–; Exec. Cttee, Scottish Council Develt and Industry, 1969–85; Scottish Regional Council of CBI, 1969–76; Clyde Port Authority, 1969–71; Bd, National Ports Council, 1971–78; West Central Scotland Plan Steering Cttee, 1970–74; General Board (Royal Soc. nominee), Nat. Physical Lab., 1963–66; Greenock Dist Hosp. Bd, 1961–66; Scottish Milk Marketing Bd, 1979–83. Chm., Iona Cathedral Trustees Management Bd, 1979–83; Mem. Council, Winston Churchill Meml Trust, 1979–83. Hon. Pres., Students Assoc., and Mem. Court, Univ. of Strathclyde, 1964–69. Petitioner in case of Lithgow and others *v* UK, at Eur. Court of Human Rights, 1986. Member, Queen's Body Guard for Scotland (Royal Company of Archers), 1964. Fellow, Scottish Council, 1988. FRSA 1990. DL Renfrewshire, 1970. Hon. LLD Strathclyde, 1979. *Recreations:* rural life, invention, photography. *Heir:* *s* James Frank Lithgow, *b* 13 June 1970. *Address:* Ormsary House, by Lochgilphead, Argyllshire PA31 8PE. *T:* Ormsary (08803) 252; Drums, Langbank, Renfrewshire PA14 6YH. *T:* Langbank (047554) 606; RMB 125A, Karridale, WA 6288, Australia. *T:* 758–2297; (office) PO Box 7, Lochgilphead, Argyllshire PA31 8JH. *T:* Ormsary (08803) 244. *Clubs:* Oriental; Western, Royal Scottish Automobile (Glasgow).

LITTLE, Ian Malcolm David, AFC 1943; FBA 1973; *b* 18 Dec. 1918; *s* of Brig.-Gen. M. O. Little, CB, CBE, and Iris Hermione Little (*née* Brassey); *m* 1946, Doreen Hennessey; one *s* one *d*. *Educ:* Eton; New Coll., Oxford (MA, DPhil). RAF Officer, 1939–46. Fellow: All Souls Coll., Oxford, 1948–50; Trinity Coll., Oxford, 1950–52; Nuffield Coll., Oxford, 1952–76, Emeritus Fellow, 1976. Dep. Dir, Economic Section, Treasury, 1953–55; Mem., MIT Centre for Internat. Studies, India, 1958–59 and 1965; Vice-Pres., OECD Develt Centre, Paris, 1965–67; Prof. of Economics of Underdeveloped Countries, Oxford Univ., 1971–76. Dir, Investing in Success Ltd, 1960–65; Bd Mem., British Airports Authority, 1969–74. Dir, Gen. Funds Investment Trust, 1974–76; Special Adviser, IBRD, 1976–78. Hon. DSc(SocSci) Edinburgh, 1976. *Publications:* A Critique of Welfare Economics, 1950; The Price of Fuel, 1953; (jtly) Concentration in British Industry, 1960; Aid to Africa, 1964; (jtly) International Aid, 1965; (jtly) Higgledy-Piggledy Growth Again, 1966; (jtly) Manual of Industrial Project Analysis in Developing Countries, 1969; (jtly) Industry and Trade in Some Developing Countries, 1970; (jtly) Project Analysis and Planning, 1974; Economic Development: theory, policy and international relations, 1982; (jtly) Small Manufacturing Enterprises, 1987; many articles in learned jls. *Address:* 43 Blandford Avenue, Oxford OX2 8EB.

LITTLE, John Eric Russell, OBE 1961 (MBE 1943); HM Diplomatic Service, retired; *b* 29 Aug. 1913; *s* of William Little and Beatrice Little (*née* Biffen); *m* 1945, Christine Holt; one *s* one *d*. *Educ:* Strand Sch. Served in FO, 1930–40, and in Army, 1940–41. Transferred to Minister of State's Office, Cairo, 1941, and seconded to Treasury. Returned to FO and appointed to British Middle East Office, 1946. Transferred to FO, 1948; Consul, Milan, 1950 (acting Consul-General, 1951, 1952); Bahrain as Asst Political Agent, 1952 (acting Political Agent, 1953, 1954, 1955); 1st Secretary, Paris, 1956; Asst Finance Officer, Foreign Office, 1958; HM Consul-General: Basra, 1962–65; Salonika, 1965–70; Counsellor, British Embassy, Brussels, 1970–72. *Recreations:* walking, reading, music. *Address:* Golna, Stonestile Lane, Hastings, East Sussex TN35 4PE.

LITTLE, John Philip Brooke B.; *see* Brooke-Little.

LITTLE, Dr Robert Clement; Head of Chemistry Division, Agricultural Science Service, Ministry of Agriculture, Fisheries and Food, 1979–85; *b* 8 Nov. 1925; *s* of Ernest William Little and Hannah Little; *m* 1950, Margaret Isobel Wilson; two *d*. *Educ:* Carlisle Grammar Sch.; Manchester Univ. (BScTech); Glasgow Univ. (PhD). W of Scotland Agricultural Coll., 1946–55; Agricultural Develt and Adv. Service (formerly National Agricl Adv. Service), MAFF, 1955–85. *Recreations:* golf, gardening, fell walking. *Address:* 9 Ashcroft Close, Harpenden, Herts AL5 1JJ. *T:* Harpenden (0582) 715613.

LITTLE, Most Rev. Thomas Francis; *see* Melbourne, Archbishop of, (RC).

LITTLECHILD, Prof. Stephen Charles; Director General of Electricity Supply, since 1989; Professor of Commerce and Head of Department of Industrial Economics and Business Studies, University of Birmingham, since 1975 (on leave of absence); *b* 27 Aug. 1943; *s* of Sidney F. Littlechild and Joyce M. Littlechild (*née* Sharpe); *m* 1974, Kate Crombie (*d* 1982); two *s* one *d*. *Educ:* Wisbech Grammar Sch.; Univ. of Birmingham (BCom); Univ. of Texas (PhD). Temp. Asst Lectr in Ind. Econs, Univ. of Birmingham, 1964–65; Harkness Fellow, Stanford Univ., 1965–66; Northwestern Univ., 1966–68; Univ. of Texas at Austin, 1968–69; ATT Post-doctoral Fellow, UCLA and Northwestern Univ., 1969; Sen. Res. Lectr in Econs, Graduate Centre for Management Studies, Birmingham, 1970–72; Prof. of Applied Econs and Head of Econs, Econometrics, Statistics and Marketing Subject Gp, Aston Management Centre, 1972–75; Vis. Scholar, Dept of Econs, Univ. of California at Los Angeles, 1975; Vis. Prof., New York, Stanford and Chicago Univs, and Virginia Polytechnic, 1979–80. Member: Monopolies and Mergers Commn, 1983–89; Sec. of State for Energy's Adv. Council on R&D, 1987–89. *Publications:* Operational Research for Managers, 1977; The Fallacy of the Mixed Economy, 1978, 2nd edn 1986; Elements of Telecommunications Economics, 1979; Energy Strategies for the UK, 1982; Regulation of British Telecommunications' Profitability, 1983; Economic Regulation of Privatised Water Authorities, 1986; over 50 articles in econs and ops res.

jls. *Recreations:* football, genealogy. *Address:* Office of Electricity Regulation, Hagley House, Hagley Road, Birmingham B16 8QG. *T:* 021–456 2100.

LITTLEJOHN, Alan Morrison; Director, Shipbuilders and Shiprepairers Association (formerly Shiprepairers and Shipbuilders Independent Association), 1977–90; Secretary General, UK Land and Hydrographic Survey Association Limited, 1980–90; retired; *b* 17 Oct. 1925; *s* of Frank Littlejohn and (Ethel) Lucy (*née* Main); *m* 1955, Joy Dorothy Margaret (*née* Till); one *d*. *Educ:* Dame Allan's Boys' Sch., Newcastle upon Tyne; King's Coll., Durham Univ. (BScAgric); Lincoln Coll. and Agricultural Economics Res. Inst., Oxford Univ. (BLitt, DipAgEcon). Asst Agric. Economist: King's Coll., Durham Univ., 1945–47; Wye Coll., London Univ., 1950–51; Agric. Chemical Div., Shell Internat. Chemical Co., London, 1951–67; Economist, Agric. Engineers Assoc., 1968–73; Dir Gen., Clay Pipe Develt Assoc., 1973–77; Dir, Assoc. of High Pressure Water Jetting Contractors, 1980–87. Chm., Catherine Place Personnel Services Ltd, 1981–89. Member: Chorleywood Parish Council, 1979– (Chm., 1985–87); (C) Three Rivers Dist Council, 1988– (Chm., Resources Cttee, 1990–91). *Recreations:* current affairs, gardening, photography. *Address:* 5 The Readings, Chorleywood, Herts WD3 5SY. *T:* Chorleywood (0923) 284420.

LITTLEJOHN, Doris; President, Industrial Tribunals (Scotland), since 1991; *b* 19 March 1935; *m* 1958, Robert White Littlejohn; three *d*. *Address:* 125 Henderson Street, Bridge of Allan, Stirlingshire. *T:* Bridge of Allan (0786) 832032.

LITTLEJOHN, William Hunter, RSA 1973 (ARSA 1966); Head of Fine Art Department, 1982–85, Head of Drawing and Painting Department, 1970–85, Gray's School of Art, Aberdeen, (Lecturer, 1966–70); *b* Arbroath, 16 April 1929; *s* of late William Littlejohn and Alice Morton King. *Educ:* Arbroath High Sch.; Dundee Coll. of Art (DA). National Service, RAF, 1951–53; taught Art at Arbroath High Sch. until 1966. *One man exhibitions:* The Scottish Gallery, Edinburgh, 1962, 1967, 1972, 1977, 1984, 1989. Exhibits in RA, RSA, SSA, etc. *Address:* 16 Colvill Place, Arbroath, Angus, Scotland. *T:* Arbroath (0241) 74402.

LITTLEJOHN COOK, George Steveni; HM Diplomatic Service, retired; *b* 29 Oct. 1919; *s* of late William Littlejohn Cook, OBE, and Xenia Steveni, BEM; *m* 1st, 1949, Marguerite Teresa Bonnaud; one *d*; 2nd, 1964, Thereza Nunes Campos; one *s*. *Educ:* Wellington Coll.; Trinity Hall, Cambridge. Served with 2nd Bn Cameronians (Scottish Rifles), 1939–46, rank of Capt.; POW Germany; Political Intelligence Dept, Foreign Office, 1945–46. Entered Foreign Service, 1946; Third Secretary, Foreign Office, 1946–47; Second Secretary, Stockholm, 1947–49; Santiago, Chile, 1949–52; First Secretary, 1950; Foreign Office, 1952–53; Chargé d'Affaires, Phnom-Penh, 1953–55; Berne, 1956–58; Director of British Information Service in Brazil, 1959–64; Head of Information Depts, FO (and FCO), 1964–69; Counsellor and Consul-General, Bangkok, 1969–71. *Recreations:* painting, sailing, ski-ing. *Address:* Quinta da Madrugada, Lagos 8600, Algarve, Portugal. *Clubs:* Brooks's, Royal Automobile.

LITTLER, Sir (James) Geoffrey, KCB 1985 (CB 1981); Chairman, National Westminster Investment Bank, since 1991 (Director, since 1989); *b* 18 May 1930; *s* of late James Edward Littler and Evelyn Mary Littler (*née* Taylor); *m* 1958, Shirley Marsh (*see* Shirley Littler); one *s*. *Educ:* Manchester Grammar Sch.; Corpus Christi Coll., Cambridge (MA). Asst Principal, Colonial Office, 1952–54; transf. to Treasury, 1954; Principal 1957; Asst Sec. 1966; Under-Sec. 1972; Dep. Sec., 1977; Second Permanent Sec. (Overseas Finance), 1983–88. Chairman: EC Monetary Cttee Deputies, 1974–77; Working Party 3, OECD, 1985–88; EC Monetary Cttee, 1987–88. Chm., TR European Growth Trust plc, 1990–; Dir, Maritime Transport Services Ltd, 1990–. *Recreation:* music. *Address:* National Westminster Bank, 6 Tothill Street, SW1H 9ND. *Club:* Reform.

LITTLER, Shirley, (Lady Littler); retired; *b* 8 June 1932; *d* of late Sir Percy William Marsh, CSI, CIE, and late Joan Mary Beecroft; *m* 1958, Sir (James) Geoffrey Littler, *qv*; one *s*. *Educ:* Headington Sch., Oxford; Girton Coll., Cambridge (MA). Assistant Principal, HM Treasury, 1953; Principal: HM Treasury, 1960; Dept of Trade and Industry, 1964; HM Treasury, 1966; Asst Secretary, National Board for Prices and Incomes, 1969; Secretary, V&G Tribunal, 1971; transf. to Home Office, 1972, Asst Under-Sec. of State, 1978–83. Joined IBA, 1983; Dep. Dir Gen., 1986–90; Dir Gen., 1990. *Recreations:* history, reading.

LITTLER, William Brian, CB 1959; MSc, PhD; *b* 8 May 1908; *s* of William Littler, Tarporley, Ches; *m* 1937, Pearl Davies (*d* 1990), Wrexham; three *d*. *Educ:* Grove Park, Wrexham; Manchester Univ.; BSc (1st Class), Chemistry, 1929; MSc, 1930; PhD, 1932; Beyer Fellow, 1930–31. Joined Res. Dept, Woolwich, 1933; loaned by Min. of Supply to Defence Res. Bd, Canada; Chief Supt, Cdn Armament Research and Devel. Establishment, Valcartier, Quebec, 1947–49; Supt of Propellants Research, Explosives Research and Devel. Estab., Waltham Abbey, 1949–50; in industry (Glaxo Laboratories Ltd, Ulverston), 1950–52; Dir of Ordnance Factories (Explosives), Min. of Supply, 1952–55; Principal Dir of Scientific Research (Defence), Ministry of Supply, 1955–56; Dir-Gen. of Scientific Research (Munitions), Ministry of Supply, 1956–60; Dep. Chief Scientist, Min. of Defence (Army), 1960–65; Minister, and Head of Defence R&D Staff, British Embassy, Washington, DC, 1965–69; Chemist-in-Charge, Quality Assurance Directorate (Materials), Royal Ordnance Factory, Bridgwater, 1969–72. *Publications:* Papers on Flame and Combustion in Proc. Royal Society and Jour. Chem. Soc. *Recreations:* golf, swimming. *Address:* Arkley Lawn Nursing Home, Arkley, High Barnet, Herts.

See also Philip Attenborough.

LITTLETON, family name of **Baron Hatherton.**

LITTLEWOOD, Lady (Barbara); Consultant with Barlows, Solicitors, of Guildford; *b* 7 Feb. 1909; *d* of Dr Percival Langdon-Down, Teddington; *m* 1934, Sir Sydney Littlewood (*d* 1967); one *s*. *Educ:* Summerleigh Sch., Teddington; King's Coll., London, (BSc). Admitted solicitor, 1936. Pres. West Surrey Law Soc., 1952–53; Mem. Home Office Departmental Committees on: the Summary Trial of Minor Offences, 1954–55; Matrimonial Proceedings in Magistrates' Courts, 1958–59; Financial Limits prescribed for Maintenance Orders made in Magistrates' Courts, 1966–68. Pres., Nat. Fedn of Business and Professional Women's Clubs of Gt Brit. and N Ire., 1958–60; Pres. Internat. Fedn of Business and Professional Women, 1965–68; Lay Member, Press Council, 1968–74. JP Middx, 1950–. *Recreation:* occasional golf. *Address:* 26 St Margarets, London Road, Guildford, Surrey GU1 1TT. *T:* Guildford (0483) 504348.

LITTLEWOOD, James, CB 1973; Director of Savings, Department for National Savings, 1972–81; *b* Royton, Lancashire, 21 Oct. 1922; *s* of late Thomas and Sarah Littlewood; *m* 1950, Barbara Shaw; two *s* one *d*. *Educ:* Manchester Grammar Sch.; St John's Coll., Cambridge (Scholar, MA). Army (Captain), 1942–46. HM Treasury, 1947–67; Civil Service Selection Bd, 1951–52; Sec. to Cttee on Administrative Tribunals and Enquiries, 1955–57; Colombo Plan Conf. Secretariat, 1955 and 1959; Dept for Nat. Savings, 1967–81. *Recreations:* golf, bridge. *Address:* 3 Smugglers Lane South, Highcliffe, Christchurch, Dorset BH23 4NF. *Club:* United Oxford & Cambridge University.

LITTLEWOOD, Joan (Maud); theatre artist. *Educ:* London. Dir, Theatre of Action, Manchester (street theatre), 1931–37; founder, Theatre Union, Manchester, introducing individual work system, 1937–39; freelance writer, 1939–45 (banned from BBC and ENSA for political opinions); founded Theatre Workshop with Gerry Raffles, 1945; touring in GB, Germany, Norway, Sweden with original works, 1945–53; moved to Theatre Royal, Stratford, London, with classics, 1953; invited to Theatre of the Nations, Paris, 1955, then yearly (Best Production of the Year three times); Centre Culturel, Hammamet, Tunisia, 1965–67; Image India, Calcutta, 1968; creation of Children's Environments, Bubble Cities linked with Music Hall, around Theatre Royal, Stratford, 1968–75. Left England to work in France, 1975; Seminar Relais Culturel, Aix-en-Provence, 1976. Productions include: Lysistrata, 1958 (Gold Medal, East Berlin, 1958; Olympic Award, Taormina, 1959), transferred to London and Broadway from Stratford, 1960–61; Sparrers Can't Sing (film), 1962; O What a Lovely War (with Gerry Raffles and the Company), 1963. Mem., French Academy of Writers, 1964. SWET Special Award, 1983. Dr *hc*, Univ. of the Air, 1977. *Recreation:* theatre. *Address:* 1 Place Louis Revol, 38200 Vienne, France.

LITTMAN, Mark; QC 1961; Director: Rio Tinto-Zinc Corporation PLC, since 1968; Granada Group PLC, since 1977; Burton Group plc, since 1983; *b* 4 Sept. 1920; *s* of Jack and Lilian Littman; *m* 1965, Marguerite Lamkin, USA. *Educ:* Owen's Sch.; London Sch. of Economics; The Queen's Coll., Oxford. BScEcon. (first class hons) 1939; MA Oxon 1941. Served RN, Lieut, 1941–46. Called to Bar, Middle Temple, 1947, Bencher, 1970, Treas., 1988; practised, as Barrister-at-law, 1947–67 and 1979–; Member: General Council of the Bar, 1968–72; Senate of Inns of Court and the Bar, 1968–. Dep. Chm., BSC, 1970–79. Mem. Royal Commn on Legal Services, 1976–79. Director: Commercial Union Assurance Co. Ltd, 1970–81; Amerada Hess Corp. (US), 1973–86; British Enkalon Ltd, 1976–80; Envirotech Corp. (US), 1974–78. Mem., Internat. Council for Commercial Arbitration, 1978–. Mem., Ct of Governors, LSE, 1980–. *Address:* 79 Chester Square, SW1W 9DU. *Clubs:* Garrick, Reform, United Oxford & Cambridge University, Royal Automobile; Century Association, Harmonie (New York).

LITTON, Peter Stafford; Under Secretary, Department of Education and Science, 1978–81; a General Commissioner of Income Tax, Epsom Division, since 1983; *b* 26 Oct. 1921; *s* of late Leonard Litton and Louisa (*née* Horn); *m* 1942, Josephine Peggy Bale; one *d*. *Educ:* Barnstaple Grammar School. Clerical Officer, Board of Education, 1938. Served in Royal Corps of Signals, 1941–46. Min. of Education, 1946; Principal Private Sec. to Secretary of State for Educn and Science, 1965–66. Mem. Council, British and Foreign School Soc., 1983–. *Recreations:* gardening, armchair astronomy. *Address:* 14 Guillards Oak, Midhurst, W Sussex GU29 9JZ. *T:* Midhurst (0730) 815491.

LIU, Tsz-Ming, Benjamin; Hon. Mr Justice Liu; a Judge of the High Court of Hong Kong, since 1980; *b* 17 May 1931; *s* of late Dr Y. T. Liu and of Dorothy Mei-Kow (*née* Kwok); *m* 1954, Annemarie Marent; one *s* one *d*. *Educ:* Wah Yan College. Called to the Bar, Lincoln's Inn, 1957; QC (Hong Kong) 1973; Judge of the District Court, Hong Kong, 1973–79; Judicial Comr, Supreme Ct, State of Brunei, 1978–89. Panel Mem., Inland Revenue Bd of Review, Hong Kong, 1972; Chm., Sub-Cttee on Bail in Criminal Proceedings, Law Reform Commn, 1985–89. *Address:* Supreme Court, Hong Kong. *T:* 8498539. *Clubs:* Hong Kong, Chinese, Hong Kong Country (Hong Kong).

LIVELY, Penelope Margaret, OBE 1989; writer; *b* 17 March 1933; *d* of Roger Low and Vera Greer; *m* 1957, Jack Lively; one *s* one *d*. *Educ:* St Anne's Coll., Oxford (BA Mod. History). Member: Soc. of Authors, 1973–; PEN, 1985–. FRSL 1985. *Publications: children's books:* Astercote, 1970; The Whispering Knights, 1971; The Wild Hunt of Hagworthy, 1971; The Driftway, 1972; The Ghost of Thomas Kempe, 1973 (Carnegie Medal); The House in Norham Gardens, 1974; Going Back, 1975; Boy Without a Name, 1975; A Stitch in Time, 1976 (Whitbread Award); The Stained Glass Window, 1976; Fanny's Sister, 1976; The Voyage of QV66, 1978; Fanny and the Monsters, 1979; Fanny and the Battle of Potter's Piece, 1980; The Revenge of Samuel Stokes, 1981; Fanny and the Monsters (three stories), 1983; Uninvited Ghosts and other stories, 1984; Dragon Trouble, 1984; Debbie and the Little Devil, 1987; A House Inside Out, 1987; *non-fiction:* The Presence of the Past: an introduction to landscape history, 1976; *fiction:* The Road to Lichfield, 1976; Nothing Missing but the Samovar and other stories, 1978 (Southern Arts Literature Prize); Treasures of Time, 1979 (National Book Award); Judgement Day, 1980; Next to Nature, Art, 1982; Perfect Happiness, 1983; Corruption and other stories, 1984; According to Mark, 1984; Pack of Cards, collected short stories 1978–86, 1986; Moon Tiger, 1987 (Booker Prize); Passing On, 1989; City of the Mind, 1991; television and radio scripts. *Recreations:* gardening, landscape history, talking and listening. *Address:* c/o Murray Pollinger, 222 Old Brompton Road, SW5 0BZ. *T:* 071–373 4711.

LIVERMAN, John Gordon, CB 1973; OBE 1956; Deputy Secretary, Department of Energy, 1974–80; *b* London, 21 Oct. 1920; *s* of late George Gordon Liverman and Hadassah Liverman. *Educ:* St Paul's Sch.; Trinity Coll., Cambridge (BA). Served with RA, 1940–46. Civil servant in various government departments, 1947–80. Mem., British Nat. Oil Corp., 1976–80. *Address:* 24 Graces Mews, Camberwell, SE5 8JF. *T:* 071–708 5017. *Club:* Commonwealth Trust.

LIVERPOOL, 5th Earl of, *cr* 1905 (2nd creation); **Edward Peter Bertram Savile Foljambe;** Baron Hawkesbury, 1893; Viscount Hawkesbury, 1905; Joint Chairman and Managing Director, Melbourns Brewery Ltd, since 1975; Chairman and Managing Director, Rutland Properties Ltd, since 1987 (Director, since 1986); *b* posthumously, 14 Nov. 1944; *s* of Captain Peter George William Savile Foljambe (killed in action, 1944) and of Elizabeth Joan (who *m* 1947, Major Andrew Antony Gibbs, MBE, TD), *d* of late Major Eric Charles Montagu Flint, DSO; *S* great uncle, 1969; *m* 1970, Lady Juliana Noel, *e d* of Earl of Gainsborough, *qv*; two *s*. *Educ:* Shrewsbury School; Univ. for Foreigners, Perugia. Director: Rutland Properties Ltd, 1985–; Hart Hambleton Plc, 1986–; Hilstone Developments Ltd, 1987–; Rutland Management Ltd, 1989–; Naylor Automatics Ltd, 1988–. *Heir: s* Viscount Hawkesbury, *qv*. *Address:* Barham Court, Exton, Oakham, Rutland LE15 8AP. *Clubs:* Turf, Pratt's, Air Squadron.

LIVERPOOL, Archbishop of, (RC), and Metropolitan of Northern Province with Suffragan Sees, Hallam, Hexham, Lancaster, Leeds, Middlesbrough and Salford, since 1976; **Most Rev. Derek John Harford Worlock;** *b* 4 Feb. 1920; 2nd *s* of Captain Harford Worlock and Dora (*née* Hoblyn). *Educ:* St Edmund's Coll., Ware, Herts. Ordained RC Priest, 1944. Curate, Our Lady of Victories, Kensington, 1944–45; Private Secretary to Archbishop of Westminster, 1945–64; Rector and Rural Dean, Church of SS Mary and Michael, London, E1, 1964–65; Bishop of Portsmouth, 1965–76. Privy Chamberlain to Pope Pius XII, 1949–53; Domestic Prelate of the Pope, 1953–65; *Peritus* at Vatican Council II, 1963–65; Consultor to Council of Laity, 1967–76; Episcopal Secretary to RC Bishops' Conference, 1967–76, Vice-Pres., 1979–. Member: Synod Council, 1976–77; Holy See's Laity Council, 1977– (formerly Mem., Cttee for the Family); English delegate to Internat. Synod of Bishops, 1974, 1977, 1980, 1983, 1987 and 1990. Chm., Nat. Pastoral Congress, 1980. Hon. Fellow, Portsmouth Polytechnic, 1988. Hon. LLD Liverpool, 1981; Hon. DTech Liverpool Polytechnic, 1987; Hon. DD

Cambridge, 1990. Knight Commander of Holy Sepulchre of Jerusalem, 1966. *Publications:* Seek Ye First (compiler), 1949; Take One at Bedtime (anthology), 1962; English Bishops at the Council, 1965; Turn and Turn Again, 1971; Give Me Your Hand, 1977; (with Rt Rev. D. Sheppard) Better Together, 1988; (with Rt Rev. D. Sheppard) With Christ in the Wilderness, 1990. *Address:* Archbishop's House, 87 Green Lane, Liverpool L18 2EP. *T:* 051–722 2379.

LIVERPOOL, Bishop of, since 1975; **Rt. Rev. David Stuart Sheppard;** *b* 6 March 1929; *s* of late Stuart Morton Winter Sheppard, Solicitor, and Barbara Sheppard; *m* 1957, Grace Isaac; one *d. Educ:* Sherborne; Trinity Hall, Cambridge (MA; Hon. Fellow, 1983); Ridley Hall Theological Coll. Asst Curate, St Mary's, Islington, 1955–57; Warden, Mayflower Family Centre, Canning Town, E16, 1957–69; Bishop Suffragan of Woolwich, 1969–75. Chairman: Central Religious Adv. Cttee for BBC and IBA, 1989–; Gen. Synod Bd for Social Responsibility, 1991–. Cricket: Cambridge Univ., 1950–52 (Captain 1952); Sussex, 1947–62 (Captain 1953); England (played 22 times) 1950–63 (Captain 1954). Hon. LLD Liverpool, 1981; Hon. DTech Liverpool Polytechnic, 1987. *Publications:* Parson's Pitch, 1964; Built as a City, 1974; Bias to the Poor, 1983; The Other Britain (Richard Dimbleby Lecture), 1984; (with Most Rev. D. Worlock) Better Together, 1988; (with Most Rev. D. Worlock) With Christ in the Wilderness, 1990. *Recreations:* family, reading, music, painting, theatre. *Address:* Bishop's Lodge, Woolton Park, Woolton, Liverpool L25 6DT.

LIVERPOOL, Auxiliary Bishops of, (RC); *see* Malone, Rt Rev. Vincent; O'Connor, Rt Rev. Kevin; Rawsthorne, Rt Rev. John.

LIVERPOOL, Dean of; *see* Walters, Very Rev. R. D. C.

LIVERPOOL, Archdeacon of; *see* Durant, Ven. S. V.

LIVESAY, Adm. Sir Michael (Howard), KCB 1989; Chief of Naval Personnel, Second Sea Lord and Admiral President, Royal Naval College, Greenwich, since 1991; *b* 5 April 1936; *s* of William Lindsay Livesay and Margaret Eleanor Chapman Steel; *m* 1959, Sara House; two *d. Educ:* Acklam Hall Grammar Sch.; Britannia Royal Naval Coll. Joined RN, 1952; training appts, 1954–57; commnd 1957; qual. Aircraft Direction Specialist, 1959; Direction Officer, HMS Hermes, HMS Aisne, Fighter Direction Sch., and 893 Sqdn, 1959–66; i/c HMS Hubberston, 1966–68, HMS Plymouth, 1970–72; Captain Fishery Protection/Captain Mine Counter Measures, 1975–77; 1st CO HMS Invincible, 1979–82; Dir of Naval Warfare, 1982–84; Flag Officer Sea Training, 1984–85; ACNS, 1986–88; Flag Officer Scotland and NI, 1989–91. *Recreations:* gliding, sailing, skiing, fishing, golf. *Address:* c/o The Naval Secretary, Old Admiralty Building, Ministry of Defence, SW1A 2BL. *Clubs:* Army and Navy, Royal Navy of 1765 and 1785; Royal Yacht Squadron.

LIVESEY, Bernard Joseph Edward; QC 1990; a Recorder, since 1987; *b* 21 Feb. 1944; *s* of Joseph Augustine Livesey and Marie Gabrielle Livesey (*née* Caulfield); *m* 1971, Penelope Jean Harper; two *d. Educ:* Cardinal Vaughan Sch., London; Peterhouse, Cambridge (MA, LLB). Called to the Bar, Lincoln's Inn, 1969. *Recreations:* music, gardening, ski-ing, bellringing. *Address:* 2 Crown Office Row, Temple, EC4Y 7HJ. *T:* 071–353 1365.

LIVESEY, Ronald John Dearden, QC 1981; a Recorder of the Crown Court, since 1981; Deputy Senior Judge, Sovereign Base Areas, Cyprus, since 1983; *b* 11 Sept. 1935; *s* of John William and Una Florence Livesey; *m* 1965, Elizabeth Jane Coutts; one *s* one *d. Educ:* Malvern Coll.; Lincoln Coll., Oxford (BA). Called to the Bar, Lincoln's Inn, 1962, Bencher, 1989. *Recreation:* golf. *Address:* 46A Grosvenor Road, Birkdale, Southport L68 2ET. *T:* Southport (0704) 60561. *Clubs:* Athenæum (Liverpool); Union (Southport).

LIVINGS, Henry; *b* 20 Sept. 1929; *m* 1957, Judith Francis Carter; one *s* one *d. Educ:* Park View Primary Sch.; Stand Grammar Sch.; Liverpool Univ. Served in RAF. Joined Puritex, Leicester. Theatre Royal Leicester, then many Repertories; Theatre Workshop, 1956. 1st TV play, 1961; 1st stage play, 1961. *Publications:* contribs to Penguin New English Dramatists 5 and 6; Kelly's Eye and Other Plays, 1964; Eh?, 1965; Good Grief!, 1968; The Little Mrs Foster Show, 1969; Honour and Offer, 1969; Pongo Plays 1–6, 1971; This Jockey Drives Late Nights, 1972; The Ffinest Ffamily in the Land, 1973; Jonah, 1974; Six More Pongo Plays, 1975; That the Medals and the Baton be Put on View, 1975; Cinderella, 1976; Pennine Tales, 1983; Flying Eggs and Things, 1986. *Recreations:* dominoes, walking. *Address:* 49 Grains Road, Delph, Oldham, Lancs OL3 5DS. *T:* Saddleworth (04577) 70854. *Clubs:* Dobcross Band, Delph Band.

LIVINGSTON, Air Vice-Marshal Graham; Consultant Occupational Health Physician, North-West Herts Health Authority, since 1989; *b* 2 Aug. 1928; *s* of late Neil Livingston and Margaret Anderson (*née* Graham); *m* 1970, Carol Judith Palmer; one *s* one *d* (and one *s* one *d* (and one *d* decd) of former marriage). *Educ:* Bo'ness Academy; Edinburgh Univ. (MB ChB 1951, DPH 1963); DIH (Conjoint) 1963; MFPHM (MFCM 1974); MFOM 1981. Joined RAF 1952; served N Ireland and Egypt, 1952–55; civilian GP and obst., 1956–57; rejoined RAF 1958; served Lindholme and Honington, 1958–62; post grad. study in public and indust. health, Edinburgh Univ., 1962–63; SMO, RAF Laarbruch, 1963–66; RAF Coll., Cranwell, 1966–70; served Cosford, Halton and Akrotiri, 1970–74; OC RAF Hosps, Cosford, 1974–76, Wegberg, 1976–79; Dep. Dir. Med. Personnel and Dep. Dir Med. Orgn, MoD, 1979–80; Dep. PMO, Strike Command, 1981–83; Principal Medical Officer: RAF Germany, 1983–84; RAF Support Comd, 1984–89; QHS 1985–89. Consultant in community medicine, 1984. FBIM 1986. *Recreations:* golf, ski-ing, caravanning. *Address:* c/o Lloyds Bank, Cox's and King's Branch, PO Box 1190, 7 Pall Mall, SW1Y 5NA. *Clubs:* Royal Air Force; Ashridge Golf.

LIVINGSTON BOOTH, John Dick, OBE 1976; charity consultant, since 1981; Chairman, Legislation Monitoring Service for Charities, since 1981; Patron, International Standing Conference on Philanthropy, since 1987 (President, 1975–87); Member of Lloyd's, since 1979; *b* 7 July 1918; *o s* of late Julian Livingston Booth and late Grace Marion (*née* Swainson); *m* 1st, 1941, Joan Ashley Tabrum (d 1976), *d* of Ashley Tabrum, OBE, LLM, MA; two *s* one *d*; 2nd, 1979, Audrey Betty Hope Harvey, PhD, AcDipEd (Psych), DipHEd, DipSoc, SRN, FRSH, MIHE, *d* of Sqdn Leader John James Haslett, RAF. *Educ:* Melbourne Church of England Grammar Sch.; Sidney Sussex Coll., Cambridge (MA). Served War, 1940–43; T/Captain RA; RWAFF; Instructor, 121 HAC OCTU RHA. Nigerian Administrative Service, 1943–57; Perm. Sec., Min. of Local Govt, Eastern Nigeria, 1956–57; Dir, Charities Aid Foundn, 1957–81. Member: Exec. Cttee, Nat. Council for Voluntary Organisations, 1974–81; Exec. Cttee, Christian Orgs Research and Adv. Trust, 1975–88; Develt and Stewardship Cttee, Central Bd of Finance, 1977–80. Trustee, Europhil Trust, 1987–90 (Chm., 1986–87). Lay Reader, Church of England, 1955–83. *Publications:* Directory of Grant-Making Trusts, 1968, 7th edn 1981; Trusts and Foundations in Europe, 1971; Report on Foundation Activity, 1977; Charity Statistics (annual), 1978–81; articles and booklets on charity. *Recreations:* home-making, travel, philately. *Address:* Mullions, Trulls Hatch, Argos Hill, Rotherfield, Crowborough, E Sussex TN6 3QL. *T:* Rotherfield (089285) 3205. *Clubs:* Garrick, Commonwealth Trust.

LIVINGSTONE, James, CMG 1968; OBE 1951; British Council service, retired; *b* 4 April 1912; *e s* of late Angus Cook Livingstone, sometime Provost of Bo'ness, Scotland, and Mrs Jean Fraser Aitken Wilson Livingstone; *m* 1945, Dr Mair Eleri Morgan Thomas, MB ChB, BSc, DPH, FRCPath, *e d* of late John Thomas, DSc, Harlech and Mrs O. M. Thomas, Llanddewi Brefi and Wilmslow; one *d* (one *s* decd). *Educ:* Bo'ness Acad.; Edinburgh Univ.; Moray House Trng Coll., Edinburgh. Adult Educn and School Posts, Scotland and Egypt, 1936–42; British Coun. Service, Egypt and Iran, 1942–45; Middle East Dept, 1945–46; Asst Rep., Palestine, 1946–48; Dep. Dir, 1949, Dir, 1956, Personnel Dept; Controller: Establishments Div., 1962; Overseas A Div. (Middle East and Africa), 1969–72. Mem. Council, British Inst. of Persian Studies, 1977–88 (Hon. Treasurer, 1977–82). *Recreations:* photography, exploring the West Highlands and Islands. *Address:* 21 Park Avenue, NW11 7SL. *T:* 081–455 7600; Tan yr Allt, Llangeitho, Dyfed. *Clubs:* Commonwealth Trust, Travellers'.

LIVINGSTONE, Ken; MP (Lab) Brent East, since 1987; *b* 17 June 1945; *s* of Robert Moffat Livingstone and Ethel Ada Livingstone; *m* 1973, Christine Pamela Chapman (marr. diss. 1982). *Educ:* Tulse Hill Comprehensive Sch.; Philippa Fawcett Coll. of Educn (Teacher's Cert.). Technician, Chester Beatty Cancer Res. Inst., 1962–70. Joined Labour Party, 1969; Reg. Exec., Greater London Lab. Party, 1974–86; Lambeth Borough Council: Councillor, 1971–78; Vice-Chm., Housing Cttee, 1971–73; Camden Borough Council: Councillor, 1978–82; Chm., Housing Cttee, 1978–80; Greater London Council: Mem. for Norwood, 1973–77, for Hackney N, 1977–81, for Paddington, 1981–86; Lab. Transport spokesman, 1980–81; Leader of Council and of Lab. Gp, 1981–86. Mem., NEC, Labour Party, 1987–89. Contested (Lab) Hampstead, gen. elec., 1979. *Publications:* If voting changed anything they'd abolish it, 1987; Livingstone's Labour, 1989. *Recreations:* cinema, science fiction. *Address:* House of Commons, SW1A 0AA.

LIVSEY, Richard Arthur Lloyd; MP Brecon and Radnor, since July 1985 (L 1985–88, Lib Dem since 1988); *b* 2 May 1935; *s* of Arthur Norman Livsey and Lilian Maisie (*née* James); *m* 1964, Irene Martin Earsman; two *s* one *d. Educ:* Talgarth County Primary Sch.; Bedales Sch.; Seale-Hayne Agricl Coll.; Reading Univ. (MSc Agric.). Develt Officer, Agric. Div., ICI, 1961–67; Farm Manager, Blairdrummond, 1967–71; farmer at Llanon; Sen. Lectr in Farm Management, Welsh Agricl Coll., Aberystwyth, 1971–85. Joined Liberal party, 1960; contested (L): Perth and E Perth, 1970; Pembroke, 1979; Brecon and Radnor, 1983. Liberal Parly spokesman on agric., 1985–87; Alliance spokesman on the countryside and on agric. in Wales, and on Wales, 1987; Leader, Welsh Liberal Democrats and Parly Spokesman on Wales, 1988–. *Recreations:* cricket, fishing. *Address:* House of Commons, SW1.

LLANDAFF, Bishop of, since 1985; **Rt. Rev. Roy Thomas Davies;** *b* 31 Jan. 1934; *s* of Hubert and Dilys Davies; unmarried. *Educ:* St David's Coll., Lampeter (BA); Jesus Coll., Oxford (BLitt); St Stephen's House, Oxford. Asst Curate, St Paul's, Llanelli, 1959–64; Vicar of Llanafan, 1964–67; Chaplain to Anglican Students, University Coll. of Wales, Aberystwyth, 1967–73; Sec., Provincial Council for Mission and Unity of Church in Wales, 1973–79; Vicar of St David's, Carmarthen, 1979–83; Vicar of Llanegwad, 1983–85; Archdeacon of Carmarthen, 1982–85; Clerical Sec., Governing Body of Church in Wales, 1983–85. ChStJ 1986. *Recreations:* walking, reading. *Address:* Llys Esgob, Llandaff, Cardiff CF5 2YE. *T:* Cardiff (0222) 562400.

LLANDAFF, Dean of; *see* Davies, Very Rev. A. R.

LLEWELLIN, Rt. Rev. John Richard Allan; *see* St Germans, Bishop Suffragan of.

LLEWELLYN, Bryan Henry; Director, Granada Travel PLC, since 1989; *b* 1 May 1927; *s* of Nora and Charles Llewellyn; *m* 1983, Joanna (*née* Campbell); two *s. Educ:* Charterhouse; Clare Coll., Cambridge (BA). Commissioned, The Queen's, 1946. Research Asst, Dept of Estate Management, Cambridge, 1954; joined Fisons Ltd, 1955; Marketing Manager, Greaves & Thomas Ltd, 1960; Regional Marketing Controller, Thomson Regional Newspapers Ltd, 1962; Marketing Dir, TRN Ltd, 1966; Managing Director: Thomson Holidays Ltd, 1969; Thomson Travel Ltd, 1972 (Chm., 1977–78); Exec. Dir, Thomson Organisation Ltd, 1972–80; Man. Dir and Chief Exec., Thomson Publications Ltd, 1977–80; Man. Dir, The Kitchenware Merchants Ltd, 1985–88. Non-Exec. Dir, Orion Insurance Ltd, 1976. *Address:* 10 Lisgar Terrace, W14 8SE.

LLEWELLYN, Prof. David Thomas; Professor of Money and Banking, Head of the Economics Department, and Chairman of the Banking Centre, Loughborough University of Technology, since 1976; *b* 3 March 1943; *s* of Alfred George Llewellyn and Elsie Alexandria Frith; *m* 1970, Wendy Elizabeth James; two *s. Educ:* William Ellis Grammar Sch., London; London Sch. of Econs and Pol Science (BSc Econ). Economist: Unilever NV, Rotterdam, 1964; HM Treasury, London, 1965–67; Lectr in Econs, Nottingham Univ., 1967–73; Economist, IMF, Washington, 1973–76. Consultant Economist to Butler Harlow Ueda, 1981–; Mem., London Bd of Dirs, Halifax Building Soc., 1988–; formerly Consultant to World Bank, Building Societies Assoc., bldg socs and banks. Mem., Bank of England Panel of Academic Consultants. TV and radio broadcasts on financial issues. *Publications:* International Financial Integration, 1980; Framework of UK Monetary Policy, 1984; The Evolution of the British Financial System, 1985; Prudential Regulation and Supervision of Financial Institutions, 1986; Reflections on Money, 1989; articles in academic and professional jls and books on monetary policy and instns, and on internat. finance. *Recreations:* DIY, culinary arts, travels, boating. *Address:* 8 Landmere Lane, Ruddington, Notts NG11 6ND. *T:* Nottingham (0602) 216071.

LLEWELLYN, Sir David (Treharne), Kt 1960; Captain, late Welsh Guards; journalist; *b* Aberdare, 17 Jan. 1916; 3rd *s* of Sir David Richard Llewellyn, 1st Bt, LLD, JP, and of Magdalene Anne (*d* 1966), *yr d* of late Rev. Henry Harries, DD, Porthcawl; *m* Joan Anne Williams, OBE, 2nd *d* of R. H. Williams, Bonvilston House, Bonvilston, near Cardiff; two *s* one *d. Educ:* Eton; Trinity Coll., Cambridge. BA 1938; MA 1979. Served War of 1939–45; enlisted Royal Fusiliers, serving in ranks; commissioned Welsh Guards; North-West Europe, 1944–45. Contested (Conservative) Aberavon Div. of Glamorgan, 1945. MP (C) Cardiff, North, 1950–Sept. 1959; Parliamentary Under-Sec. of State, Home Office, 1951–52 (resigned, ill-health). *Publications:* Nye: The Beloved Patrician, 1961; The Adventures of Arthur Artfully, 1974; Book of Racing Quotations, 1988. *Address:* Yattendon, Newbury, Berks.

LLEWELLYN, David Walter, CBE 1983; Managing Director, Walter Llewellyn & Sons Ltd, and other Companies in the Llewellyn Group, since 1953; *b* 13 Jan. 1930; *s* of late Eric Gilbert and Florence May Llewellyn; *m* 1st, 1955, Josephine Margaret Buxton (marr. diss. 1985); three *s*; 2nd, 1986, Tessa Caroline Sandwith. *Educ:* Radley College. FCIOB. Commissioned Royal Engineers, 1952. Industrial Adviser to Minister of Housing and Local Govt, 1967–68; Mem., Housing Corp., 1975–77; Pres., Joinery and Timber Contractors' Assoc., 1976–77; Chm., Nat. Contractors' Gp of Nat. Fedn of Building Trades Employers (now Building Employers Confedn), 1977; Chm., Building Regulations Adv. Cttee, 1977–85 (Mem. 1966–74); Dep. Chm., Nat. Building Agency, 1977–82 (Dir. 1968–82). Underwriting Member of Lloyd's, 1978–. Pres., CIOB, 1986–87. Master, Worshipful Co. of Tin Plate Workers alias Wireworkers, 1985. Governor, St Andrew's

Sch., Eastbourne, 1966–78; Trustee, Queen Alexandra Cottage Homes, Eastbourne, 1973–. *Recreation:* the use, restoration and preservation of historic vehicles. *Address:* (office) 16/20 South Street, Eastbourne BN21 4XE; (home) Cooper's Cottage, Chiddingly, near Lewes, East Sussex BN8 6HD. *Clubs:* Reform, City Livery; Devonshire (Eastbourne), Eastbourne.

LLEWELLYN, Dr Donald Rees; JP; Vice-Chancellor, University of Waikato, 1964–85; *b* 20 Nov. 1919; *s* of late R. G. Llewellyn, Dursley; *m* 1943, Ruth Marian, *d* of late G. E. Blandford, Dursley; one *s* one *d*. *Educ:* Dursley Grammar Sch.; Univ. of Birmingham, 1939–41, BSc 1st cl. hons Chem. 1941, DSc 1957; Oxford 1941–44, DPhil 1943. Research Fellow, Cambridge Univ., 1944–46; Lectr in Chemistry, UC of N Wales, 1946–49; ICI Research Fellow, UCL, 1949–52; Lectr in Chemistry, UCL, 1952–57; Prof. of Chemistry and Dir of Labs, Univ. of Auckland, 1957–64; Asst Vice-Chancellor, Univ. of Auckland, 1962–64. Mem., NZ Atomic Energy Cttee, 1958–85. Pres., NZ Inst. Chemistry, 1967 and 1988 (Vice-Pres., 1965–67, 1986–88). Member: Council, Hamilton Teachers Coll., 1965–85; Council, Waikato Tech. Inst., 1968–85; Pres., NZ Nat. Field Days Soc., 1969–75 and 1978–81 (Life Mem., 1981); Patron, Waikato Med. Res. Foundn, 1990–. JP Waikato, 1971. Freeman, City of Hamilton, 1985. CChem, FRSC (FRIC 1952); FNZIC 1957 (Hon. FNZIC 1985); FRSA 1960. Hon. Dr Waikato, 1985. Waikato Business Pioneer, 1990. *Publications:* numerous papers on application of stable isotopes in Jl Chem. Soc. and others. *Recreations:* squash, tennis, showjumping (FEI Judge), photography, travel. *Address:* Hamilton RD4, New Zealand. *T:* (071) 69172. *Club:* Hamilton (NZ).

LLEWELLYN, Sir Henry Morton, (Sir Harry Llewellyn), 3rd Bt *cr* 1922; Kt 1977; CBE 1953 (OBE (mil.) 1944); MA; late Warwicks Yeomanry; President, Whitbread Wales Ltd, since 1972 (Chairman, 1958–72); Director, Chepstow Racecourse Co. Ltd; Vice-Chairman, Civic Trust for Wales, since 1960; *b* 18 July 1911; 2nd *s* of Sir David Llewellyn, 1st Bt, and Magdalene (*d* 1966), *d* of Dr H. Hiley Harries, DD, Porthcawl; *S* brother, 1978; *m* 1944, Hon. Christine Saumarez, 2nd *d* of 5th Baron de Saumarez; two *s* one *d*. *Educ:* Oundle; Trinity Coll., Cambridge (MA). Joined Warwickshire Yeo., Sept. 1939; Iraq-Syria Campaign, 1941; Middle East Staff Coll., Haifa, 1942; 8th Army from El Alamein to Tunis as GSO II Ops (Liaison) (despatches), 1942–43; Sicily, Italy (despatches), 1943; MA Chief of Staff HQ 21 Army Gp, 1943; NW Europe GSO I Ops (Liaison), 1943–44; OBE 1944; US Legion of Merit, 1945; Hon. Lt Col. Riding Ego, came 2nd in Grand National 'chase, 1936, 4th, 1937. Nat. Hunt Cttee, 1946– (Steward, 1948–50); The Jockey Club, 1969–. Jt Master Monmouthshire Hounds, 1952–57, 1963–65. Captain winning Brit. Olympic Show-Jumping Team, Helsinki (riding Foxhunter), 1952; Chm., Brit. Show Jumping Assoc., 1967–69; Pres./Chm., British Equestrian Fedn, 1976–81; Pres., Royal Internat. Horse Show, 1989–. Chm., Welsh Sports Council, 1971–81; Mem., GB Sports Council, 1971–81. President: Inst. of Directors (Wales), 1963–65; Inst. of Marketing, Wales, 1965–67. Chm., C. L. Clay & Co. Ltd (Coal Exporters), 1936–47. Chairman: Wales Bd, Nationwide Building Soc., 1972–86; Eagle Star Assurance Co. (Wales Bd), 1963–81; formerly Director: North's Navigation Colliery Ltd; TWW Ltd; Rhigos Colliery Ltd; S Wales Reg. Bd, Lloyds Bank, 1963–82. Member: Wales Tourist Board, 1969–75; WWF Council, 1986–; Pres., Royal Welsh Agricl Show, 1985. Hon. Deleg., FEI, 1983. DL Monmouthshire, 1952, JP 1954–68, High Sheriff 1966. Royal Humane Soc. Medal for Life-saving, 1956; FEI Gold Medal, 1962. *Publications:* Foxhunter in Pictures, 1952; Passports to Life, 1980. *Recreations:* hunting, all sports, wild life photography. *Heir:* *s* David St Vincent Llewellyn [*b* 2 April 1946; *m* 1980, Vanessa Mary Theresa (marr. diss. 1987), *y d* of Lieut-Comdr Peregrine and Lady Miriam Hubbard; two *d*. *Educ:* Eton]. *Address:* Ty'r Nant, Llanarth, Raglan, Gwent NP5 2AR. *Clubs:* Cavalry and Guards; Shikar.

LLEWELLYN, Rear-Adm. Jack Rowbottom, CB 1974; Assistant Controller of the Navy, 1972–74; retired; *b* 14 Nov. 1919; *s* of Ernest and Harriet Llewellyn, Ashton under Lyne, Lancs; *m* 1944, Joan Isabel, *d* of Charles and Hilda Phillips, Yelverton, Devon; one *s*. *Educ:* Purley County Sch. Entered RN, 1938; RNEC, Keyham, 1939. Served War of 1939–45: HMS Bermuda, 1942; RNC, Greenwich, 1943; HMS Illustrious, 1945. Engr in Chief's Dept, Admlty, 1947; HMS Sluys, 1949; HMS Thunderer, 1951; HMS Diamond, 1953; Comdr, 1953; Asst Engr in Chief, on loan to Royal Canadian Navy, 1954; in charge Admty Fuel Experimental Station, Haslar, 1958; HMS Victorious, 1960; Asst Dir, Marine Engrg, MoD (N), 1963; Captain, 1963; in command, HMS Fisgard, 1966; Dep. Dir, Warship Design, MoD (N), 1969; Rear-Adm., 1972. *Recreations:* travel, gardening. *Address:* 3 Jubilee Terrace, Chichester, W Sussex PO19 1XL. *T:* Chichester (0243) 780180.

LLEWELLYN, His Honour John Desmond S.; *see* Seys-Llewellyn.

LLEWELLYN, Rev. John Francis Morgan, LVO 1982; MA; Chaplain at the Chapel Royal of St Peter ad Vincula within HM Tower of London, 1974–89; Officiating Chaplain, Order of St John of Jerusalem, since 1974; *b* 4 June 1921; *s* of late Canon D. L. J. Llewellyn; *m* 1955, Audrey Eileen (*née* Binks). *Educ:* King's College Sch., Wimbledon; Pembroke Coll., Cambridge (MA); Ely Theological Coll. Served War, 1941–45, in Royal Welch Fusiliers and in India (Captain). Curate of Eltham, 1949–52; Chaplain and Asst Master, King's College Sch., Wimbledon, 1952–58; Headmaster, Cathedral Choir Sch., and Minor Canon of St Paul's Cathedral, 1958–74; Sacrist and Warden of College of Minor Canons, 1968–74; Dep. Priest-in-Ordinary to the Queen, 1968–70, 1974–, Priest-in-Ordinary, 1970–74; Asst Master, Dulwich Coll. Prep. Sch., 1974–86. Sub-Chaplain, Order of St John of Jerusalem, 1970–74; Chaplain: City Solicitor's Co., 1975–; Builders' Merchants' Co., 1986–. *Publications:* (contrib.) The Tower of London: Its Buildings and Institutions, 1978; The Chapel Royal in the Tower, 1987. *Recreations:* golf, fishing. *Address:* The Gate House, Ouseley Lodge, Ouseley Road, Old Windsor, Berks SL4 2SQ. *T:* Windsor (0753) 855681. *Clubs:* MCC; Hawks (Cambridge).

LLEWELLYN, Lt-Col Sir Michael (Rowland Godfrey), 2nd Bt *cr* 1959, of Baglan, Co. Glamorgan; JP; Lord-Lieutenant of West Glamorgan, since 1987 (Vice Lord-Lieutenant, 1985–87); *b* 15 June 1921; *s* of Sir (Robert) Godfrey Llewellyn, 1st Bt, CB, CBE, MC, TD, JP, DL, and Frances Doris (*d* 1969), *d* of Rowland S. Kennard; *S* father, 1986; *m* 1956, Janet Prudence Edmondes; three *d*. *Educ:* Harrow. Commissioned Grenadier Guards, 1941; served Italian campaign, 1943–44; retired from Army, 1949; Comd 1st Bn Glamorgan Army Cadet Force, 1951–59. Director of companies, 1949–; Gen. Comr of Income Tax, 1965–. Pres., Gower Cons. Assoc., 1967–85; Chm., W Wales Gp of Cons Assocs, 1975–78; Chm., 1978–83, Pres., 1983–85, Mid and W Wales Cons. European Assoc. Chm., 1967–79, Vice-Pres., 1979–87, Pres., 1987–, St John Council for W Glamorgan. President: W Glamorgan SSAFA, 1987–; W Glamorgan County Scout Council, 1987–; Swansea Br., Royal British Legion, 1987–; TA&VRA for Wales, 1990–; W Glamorgan Magistrates' Assoc., 1988–. KStJ 1991. High Sheriff of W Glamorgan, 1980–81, DL 1982; JP Swansea, 1984. *Recreations:* shooting, gardening. *Heir:* none. *Address:* Glebe House, Penmaen, Swansea, West Glamorgan SA3 2HH. *T:* Penmaen (0792) 371232. *Clubs:* Cardiff and County (Cardiff); Bristol Channel Yacht.

LLEWELLYN, Maj.-Gen. Richard Morgan, OBE 1979 (MBE 1976); Chief of Staff, HQ United Kingdom Land Forces, 1990–91, retired; *b* 22 Aug. 1937; *s* of Griffith Robert Poyntz Llewellyn and Bridget Margaret Lester Llewellyn (*née* Karslake); *m* 1964, Elizabeth Lamond (Polly) Sobey; three *s* one *d* (and one *d* decd). *Educ:* Haileybury; Imperial Service College; rcds, psc. Enlisted Royal Welch Fusiliers (Nat. Service), 1956; active service, Malaya and Cyprus, 1957–59; Instructor, Army Outward Bound Sch., 1962–63; Staff Coll., 1970; MA to CGS, 1971–72; Brigade Major, 1974–76; CO, 1st Bn RWF, 1976–79; Directing Staff, RCDS, 1979–81; Comdr, Gurkha Field Force, 1981–84; Dir, Army Staff Duties, 1985–87; GOC Wales, 1987–90. Regtl Col, Gurkha Transport Regt, 1984–; Col, RWF, 1990–. Chm., Army Mountaineering Assoc., 1988–91; Vice-Pres., Operation Raleigh; Council Mem., Soldiers' and Airmen's Scripture Readers Assoc. FBIM. *Recreations:* most outdoor pursuits, gardening, reading. *Address:* c/o Lloyds Bank, High Street, Crickhowell, Powys. *Clubs:* Army and Navy; Cardiff and County.

LLEWELLYN, Timothy David; Chief Executive, Sotheby's, since 1991 (Managing Director, 1984–91); *b* 30 May 1947; *s* of Graham David Llewellyn and Dorothy Mary Driver; *m* 1st, 1970, Irene Sigrid Mercy Henriksen (marr. diss.); one *s*; 2nd, 1978, Elizabeth Hammond. *Educ:* St Dunstan's College; Magdalene College, Cambridge. Old Master Painting Dept, 1969, Director, 1974, Sotheby's. Chm., Friends of the Courtauld Inst., 1986–. Order of Cultural Merit, Min. of Culture and Fine Arts, Poland, 1986. *Recreations:* music, fishing, travel, tennis. *Address:* 3 Cranley Mansion, 160 Gloucester Road, SW7 4QF. *T:* 071–373 2333; Sotheby's, 34 & 35 New Bond Street, W1A 2AA. *T:* 071–408 5373. *Clubs:* Brooks's, Queen's.

LLEWELLYN, Rt. Rev. William Somers; Assistant Curate of Tetbury with Beverston, since 1977; *b* 16 Aug. 1907; *s* of Owen John and Elizabeth Llewellyn; *m* 1947, Innis Mary, *d* of Major Arthur Dorrien Smith, Tresco Abbey, Isles of Scilly; three *s*. *Educ:* Eton; Balliol and Wycliffe Hall, Oxford. BA 1929; diploma in Theology (with dist.) 1934; MA 1937. Priest, 1936; Curate of Chiswick, 1935–37; Vicar of Badminton, with Acton Turville, 1937–49. CF 1940–46; served with Royal Gloucestershire Hussars in Egypt and Western Desert, and as Senior Chaplain with 8th Army HQ, Canal Area and East Africa; Vicar of Tetbury with Beverston, 1949–61; Rural Dean of Tetbury, 1955–61; Archdeacon of Lynn, 1961–72; first Suffragan Bishop of Lynn, 1963–72; Priest-in-charge of Boxwell with Leighterton, 1973–77. *Address:* Glebe House, Leighterton, Tetbury, Glos GL8 8UW. *T:* Leighterton (066689) 236.

LLEWELLYN-JONES, Frank; *see* Jones, F. Ll.

LLEWELLYN JONES, His Honour Ilston Percival; a Circuit Judge, 1978–88; *b* 15 June 1916; *s* of Rev. L. Cyril F. Jones and Gertrude Anne Jones; *m* 1963, Mary Evelyn; one *s* (by a former *m*). *Educ:* Baswich House and Fonthill prep. schs; St John's Sch., Leatherhead. Admitted Solicitor, Nov. 1938; practised privately until served Sussex Yeomanry RA and 23rd Field Regt RA (commnd), 1939–42; Solicitors Dept, Metropolitan Police, New Scotland Yard, 1942–48; private practice, Torquay, 1948–52; Devon County Prosecuting Solicitor, 1952–56; Clerk to N Devon Justices, 1956–62; private practice, 1962–77; a Recorder of the Crown Court, 1972–78. *Recreations:* now mainly golf; formerly Rugby football, tennis, squash, swimming, cross country running. *Address:* Stonecroft, The Hayes, Cheddar, Somerset BS27 3HP. *T:* Cheddar (0934) 743524.

LLEWELLYN SMITH, Prof. Christopher Hubert, DPhil; FRS 1984; Chairman of Physics, University of Oxford, since 1987; Fellow of St John's College, Oxford, since 1974; *b* 19 Nov. 1942; *s* of late J. C. and of M. E. F. Llewellyn Smith; *m* 1966, Virginia Grey; one *s* one *d*. *Educ:* Wellington College; New College, Oxford (Scholar). BA 1964, DPhil 1967; full Blue for cross-country running, 1961–63, Captain 1963; full Blue for Athletics, 1963. Royal Society Exchange Fellow, Lebedev Inst., Moscow, 1967; Fellow, CERN, Geneva, 1968; Research Associate, SLAC, Stanford, Calif, 1970; Staff Mem., CERN, 1972; Oxford University: Lectr, 1974; Reader in Theoretical Physics, 1980; Professor, 1987. Mem. of various policy and programme cttees for CERN (Chm., Scientific Policy Cttee, 1990–), SLAC, Deutsches Elektronen-Synchrotron Hamburg and SERC, 1972–; Mem., ACOST, 1989–. Maxwell Prize and Medal, Inst. of Physics, 1979. *Publications:* numerous articles in Nuclear Physics, Physics Letters, Phys. Rev., etc. *Recreations:* books, travel, opera. *Address:* 3 Wellington Place, Oxford OX1 2LD. *T:* Oxford (0865) 57145.

See also E. M. Llewellyn-Smith, M. J. Llewellyn Smith.

LLEWELLYN-SMITH, Elizabeth Marion, CB 1985; Principal, St Hilda's College Oxford, since 1990; *b* 17 Aug. 1934; *d* of late John Clare Llewellyn Smith and of Margaret Emily Frances (*née* Crawford). *Educ:* Christ's Hospital, Hertford; Girton Coll., Cambridge (MA). Joined Board of Trade, 1956; various appointments in Board of Trade, Cabinet Office, Dept of Trade and Industry, Dept of Prices and Consumer Protection, 1956–76; Royal Coll. of Defence Studies, 1977; Under Sec., Companies Div., Dept of Trade, later DTI, 1978–82; Dep. Dir Gen., OFT, 1982–87; Dep. Sec., DTI, 1987–90. UK Dir, EIB, 1987–90. *Recreations:* travel, books, entertaining. *Address:* The Principal's Lodgings, St Hilda's College, Oxford OX4 1DY. *T:* Oxford (0865) 276814; 1 Charlwood Road, Putney, SW15 1PJ. *T:* 081–789 1572. *Clubs:* United Oxford & Cambridge University, Players Theatre.

See also C. H. Llewellyn Smith, M. J. Llewellyn Smith.

LLEWELLYN SMITH, Michael John, CMG 1989; HM Diplomatic Service; Ambassador to Poland, since 1991; *b* 25 April 1939; *s* of late J. C. Llewellyn Smith and of M. E. F. Crawford; *m* 1967, Colette Gaulier; one *s* one *d*. *Educ:* Wellington Coll.; New Coll., Oxford; St Antony's Coll., Oxford. BA, DPhil. FCO, 1970; Cultural Attaché, Moscow, 1973; Paris, 1976; Royal Coll. of Defence Studies, 1979; Counsellor and Consul Gen., Athens, 1980–83; Hd of Western European Dept, FCO, 1984–85; Hd of Soviet Dept, FCO, 1985–87; Minister, Paris, 1988–91. *Publications:* The Great Island: a study of Crete, 1965, 2nd edn 1973; Ionian Vision: Greece in Asia Minor 1919–22, 1973. *Recreations:* music, walking, wine. *Address:* c/o Foreign and Commonwealth Office, King Charles Street, SW1A 2AH. *Club:* United Oxford & Cambridge University.

See also C. H. Llewellyn Smith, E. M. Llewellyn-Smith.

LLEWELYN, Sir John Michael D. V.; *see* Venables-Llewelyn.

LLEWELYN-DAVIES, family name of **Baroness Llewelyn-Davies of Hastoe.**

LLEWELYN-DAVIES OF HASTOE, Baroness *cr* 1967 (Life Peer), of Hastoe; **Patricia Llewelyn-Davies,** PC 1975; a Deputy Speaker, House of Lords, since 1987; Principal Deputy Chairman of Committees and Chairman, Select Committee on European Communities, House of Lords, 1982–87; *b* 16 July 1915; *d* of Charles Percy Parry and Sarah Gertrude Parry (*née* Hamilton); *m* 1943, Richard Llewelyn-Davies (later Baron Llewelyn-Davies) (*d* 1981); three *d*. *Educ:* Liverpool Coll., Huyton; Girton Coll., Cambridge (Hon. Fellow, 1979). Civil Servant, 1940–51 (Min. of War Transp., FO, Air Min., CRO). Contested (Lab) Wolverhampton S-W, 1951, Wandsworth Cent., 1955, 1959. A Baroness-in-Waiting (Govt Whip), 1969–70; Dep. Opposition Chief Whip, House of Lords, 1972–73; Opposition Chief Whip, 1973–74, 1979–82; Captain of the Gentlemen at Arms (Govt Chief Whip), 1974–79. Hon. Sec., Lab. Parly Assoc., 1960–69. Chm., Women's National Cancer Control Campaign, 1972–75; Member: Bd of Govs, Hosp. for Sick Children, Gt Ormond Street, 1955–67 (Chm. Bd, 1967–69); Court, Univ.

of Sussex, 1967–69. Dir, Africa Educnl Trust, 1960–69. Co.-Chm., Women's Nat. Commn, 1976–79. *Address:* Flat 15, 9–11 Belsize Grove, NW3 4UU. *T:* 071–586 4060.

LLOWARCH, Martin Edge, FCA; Chief Executive, British Steel plc (formerly British Steel Corporation), 1986–91; *b* 28 Dec. 1935; *s* of Wilfred and Olga Llowarch; *m* 1965, Ann Marion Buchanan; one *s* two *d. Educ:* Stowe Sch., Buckingham. Coopers & Lybrand, 1962–68; British Steel Corporation, subseq. British Steel plc: Hd of Special Projects, 1968; Man. Dir (S Africa), 1971; Dir, Finance and Admin (Internat.), 1973; Finance Dir, Tubes Div., 1975; Finance Controller, Strip Products Gp, 1980; Man. Dir, Finance, 1983; Mem., Main Bd, 1984–91; Dep. Chief Exec., 1986. Mem., Accounting Standards Cttee, 1985–87. FICA 1973. CBIM 1985. *Recreations:* most forms of sport, music, gardening, reading. *Address:* c/o British Steel, 9 Albert Embankment, SE1 7SN. *T:* 071–735 7654. *Club:* Rand (Johannesburg).

LLOYD, family name of **Baron Lloyd of Hampstead.**

LLOYD OF HAMPSTEAD, Baron *cr* 1965 (Life Peer); **Dennis Lloyd,** QC 1975; Quain Professor of Jurisprudence in the University of London (University College), 1956–82, now Emeritus; Hon. Research Fellow, University College London, since 1982; *b* 22 Oct. 1915; 2nd *s* of Isaac and Betty Lloyd; *m* 1940, Ruth Emma Cecilia Tulla; two *d. Educ:* University Coll. Sch.; University Coll., London; Gonville and Caius Coll., Cambridge. LLB (London) 1935; BA 1937, MA 1941, LLD 1956 (Cantab). Called to Bar, 1936; Yorke Prize, 1938; in practice in London, 1937–39 and 1946–82. Served War of 1939–45 in RA and RAOC, Liaison Officer (DADOS) with Free French Forces in Syria and Lebanon, 1944–45. Reader in English Law, University Coll., London, 1947–56; Fellow of University Coll., London; Dean of Faculty of Laws, University of London, 1962–64; Head of Dept of Law, University Coll., 1969–82. Hon. Fellow, Ritsumeikan Univ., Kyoto, Japan, 1978. Member: Law Reform Cttee, 1961–82; Consolidation Bills Cttee, 1965–77; European Communities Cttee, 1973–79, 1984–90; Joint Cttee on Theatre Censorship; Joint Cttee on Broadcasting, 1976–81; Select Cttee on Bill of Rights; Interim Action Cttee on Film Industry, 1976–85; Conseil de la Fédération Britannique de l'Alliance Française, 1970–78; Council, BAFTA, 1985–86; British Screen Adv. Council, 1985–; Council, Anglo-Jewish Assoc., 1989–; Chairman: Nat. Film Sch. Cttee; Planning for Nat. Film Sch.; Governors, Nat. Film School, 1970–88 (Hon. Pres., 1988); British Film Inst., 1973–76 (Governor, 1968–76); Brighton and Hove Arts Trust, 1989–. Pres., Bentham Club (University Coll. London), 1983; Chm. Council, University Coll. Sch., 1971–79. Hon. LLD Ritsumeikan Univ., Kyoto, Japan, 1986. *Publications:* Unincorporated Associations, 1938; Rent Control, 1949, 2nd edition, 1955; Public Policy: A Comparative Study in English and French Law, 1953; United Kingdom: Development of its Laws and Constitution, 1955; Business Lettings, 1956; Introduction to Jurisprudence, 1959, 5th edn 1985; The Idea of Law, 1964, 9 rev. imps, 1968–87, Japanese trans., 1969, Spanish trans., 1987; Law (Concept Series), 1968; contrib. to periodicals. *Recreations:* painting, listening to music, modern Greek. *Address:* House of Lords, SW1A 0PW. *Clubs:* Athenæum, Royal Automobile, PEN (Hon. Life Mem.).

LLOYD, Rev. (Albert) Kingsley; President of the Conference of the Methodist Church, 1964; *b* 1903; *s* of Rev. Albert Lloyd; *m* 1926, Ida Marian (*née* Cartledge) (*d* 1969); one *s* one *d;* 2nd, 1972, Katharine G., *d* of A. G. L. Ives, *qv. Educ:* Kingswood Sch., Bath; Richmond Coll., Surrey (University of London). Methodist Circuit Minister: London, Bedford, Cambridge, 1926–52; Chm., London N Dist, 1951–53. Secretary, Dept of Connexional Funds of the Methodist Church, 1952–69. Wesley Historical Soc. Lectr, 1968. *Recreation:* gardening. *Address:* 13 High Street, Orwell, Royston, Herts.

LLOYD, Rt. Hon. Sir Anthony (John Leslie), Kt 1978; PC 1984; DL; **Rt. Hon. Lord Justice Lloyd;** a Lord Justice of Appeal, since 1984; *b* 9 May 1929; *o s* of late Edward John Boydell Lloyd and Leslie Johnston Fleming; *m* 1960, Jane Helen Violet, *er d* of C. W. Shelford, Chailey Place, Lewes, Sussex. *Educ:* Eton (Schol.); Trinity Coll., Cambridge (Maj. Schol.). 1st cl. Classical Tripos Pt I; 1st cl. with distinction Law Tripos Pt II. National Service, 1st Bn Coldstream Guards, 1948. Montague Butler Prize, 1950; Sir William Browne Medal, 1951. Choate Fellow, Harvard, 1952; Fellow of Peterhouse, 1953 (Hon. Fellow, 1981); Fellow of Eton, 1974. Called to Bar, Inner Temple, 1955; QC 1967; Bencher, 1976. Attorney-General to HRH The Prince of Wales, 1969–77; Judge of the High Court of Justice, Queen's Bench Div., 1978–84. Vice-Chairman: Parole Bd, 1984–85 (Mem., 1983–); Security Commn, 1985–; Mem., Criminal Law Revision Cttee, 1981–. Chm., Sussex Assoc. for Rehabilitation of Offenders, 1985–; Vice-Pres., British Maritime Law Assoc., 1983–. Mem., Top Salaries Review Body, 1971–77. Trustee: Smiths Charity, 1971–; Glyndebourne Arts Trust, 1973 (Chm., 1975–); Dir, RAM, 1979– (Hon. FRAM 1985); Chm., Chichester Diocesan Bd of Finance, and Mem., Bishop's Council, 1972–76. Hon. Mem., Salters' Co., 1988. DL E Sussex, 1983. *Recreations:* music, carpentry; formerly running (ran for Cambridge in Mile, White City, 1950). *Address:* 68 Strand-on-the-Green, Chiswick, W4. *T:* 081–994 7790; Ludlay, Berwick, East Sussex. *T:* Alfriston (0323) 870204. *Club:* Brooks's.

LLOYD, Anthony Joseph; MP (Lab) Stretford, since 1983; *b* 25 Feb. 1950; *s* of late Sydney and Ciceley Beaumont Lloyd; *m* 1974, Judith Ann Tear; three *d* one *s. Educ:* Stretford Grammar Sch.; Nottingham Univ. (BSc Hons); Manchester Business Sch. (DipBA). Lectr, Dept of Business and Administration, Salford Univ., 1979–83. *Address:* 117 Derbyshire Lane, Stretford, Manchester M32 8DG.

LLOYD, Prof. Antony Charles; Professor of Philosophy, Liverpool University, 1957–83, now Emeritus; *b* 15 July 1916; *s* of Charles Mostyn Lloyd and Theodosia Harrison-Rowson. *Educ:* Shrewsbury Sch.; Balliol Coll., Oxford. Asst to Prof. of Logic and Metaphysics, Edinburgh Univ., 1938–39 and 1945; served in Army, 1940–45; Lecturer in Philosophy, St Andrews Univ., 1946–57. Visiting Professor: Kansas Univ., 1967; Berkeley, Calif., 1982. *Publications:* Form and Universal in Aristotle, 1981; Anatomy of Neoplatonism, 1990; chapters in Cambridge History of Later Ancient Philosophy, 1967. *Address:* 11 Palmeira Court, 25–28 Palmeira Square, Hove, E Sussex BN3 2JP.

LLOYD, Ven. (Bertram) Trevor; Archdeacon of Barnstaple, since 1989; *b* 15 Feb. 1938; *s* of Bertram and Gladys Lloyd; *m* 1962, Margaret Eldey; two *s* one *d* (and one *s* decd). *Educ:* Highgate School; Hertford Coll., Oxford (schol; BA History 1960, Theology 1962; MA 1962). Clifton Theol Coll., Bristol. Curate, Christ Church, Barnet, 1964–69; Vicar, Holy Trinity, Wealdstone, 1970–84; Priest-in-charge, St Michael and All Angels, Harrow Weald, 1980–84; Vicar, Trinity St Michael, Harrow, 1984–89; Area Dean of Harrow, 1977–82. Member: C of E Liturgical Commn, 1981–; Gen. Synod of C of E, 1990–; Central Bd of Finance, C of E, 1990–. *Publications:* Informal Liturgy, 1972; Institutions and Inductions, 1973; The Agape, 1973; Liturgy and Death, 1974; Ministry and Death, 1974; Lay Presidency at the Eucharist?, 1977; Evangelicals, Obedience and Change, 1977; (ed) Anglican Worship Today, 1980; Ceremonial in Worship, 1981; Introducing Liturgical Change, 1984; Celebrating Lent, Holy Week and Easter, 1985; Celebrating the Agape today, 1986; The Future of Anglican Worship, 1987. *Recreations:* hill walking, photography, swimming, caravanning, making things from wood. *Address:* Stage Cross, Whitemoor Hill, Bishop's Tawton, Barnstaple, Devon EX32 0BE. *T:* Barnstaple (0271) 75475.

LLOYD, Dr Brian Beynon, CBE 1983; Chairman of Directors, Oxford Gallery, since 1967; Chairman, Trumedia Study Oxford Ltd, since 1985; Director, International Nutrition Foundation, since 1990; *b* 23 Sept. 1920; *s* of David John Lloyd, MA Oxon and Olwen (*née* Beynon); *m* 1949, Reinhild Johanna Engeroff; four *s* three *d* (inc. twin *s* and twin *d*). *Educ:* Newport High Sch.; Winchester Coll. (Schol.); Balliol Coll., Oxford (Domus and Frazer Schol.). Special Certif. for BA (War) Degree in Chem., 1940; took degrees BA and MA, 1946; Theodore Williams Schol. and cl. I in Physiology, 1948; DSc 1969. Joined Oxford Nutrition Survey after registration as conscientious objector, 1941; Pres., Jun. Common Room, Balliol, 1941–42; Chm., Undergraduate Rep. Coun., 1942; Biochemist: SHAEF Nutrition Survey Team, Leiden, 1945; Nutrition Survey Group, Düsseldorf, 1946. Fellow of Magdalen by exam. in Physiology, 1948–52, by special election, 1952–70; Senior Tutor, 1963–64; Vice-Pres., 1967 and 1968; Emeritus Fellow, 1970; Chemist, Laboratory of Human Nutrition, later Univ. Lectr in Physiology, Univ. of Oxford, 1948–70; Senior Proctor, 1960–61; Dir, Oxford Polytechnic, 1970–80. Chairman: CNAA Health and Med. Services Bd, 1975–80; Health Educn Council, 1979–82 (Mem., 1975–82); Mem., Adv. Council on Misuse of Drugs, 1978–81. Vis. Physiologist, New York, 1963. Pres., Section I, 1964–65, Section X, 1980, British Assoc. for the Advancement of Science. Chm. of Govs, Oxford Coll. of Technology, 1963–69. Chairman: Oxford-Bonn Soc., 1973–81; Oxford Management Club, 1979–80; Pullen's Lane Assoc., 1985–; Pres., Oxford Polytechnic Assoc., 1984–90. *Publications:* Gas Analysis Apparatus, 1960; (jt ed) The Regulation of Human Respiration, 1962; Cerebrospinal Fluid and the Regulation of Respiration, 1965; Sinclair, 1990; articles in physiological and biochemical jls. *Recreations:* Klavarskribo, Correggio, round tables, the analysis of running records, slide rules, ready reckoners. *Address:* High Wall, Pullen's Lane, Oxford OX3 0BX. *T:* Oxford (0865) 63353.

See also Sir J. P. D. Lloyd.

LLOYD, Charles William, JP; MA; Master, Dulwich College, 1967–75; *b* 23 Sept. 1915; *s* of late Charles Lloyd and late Frances Ellen Lloyd, London; *m* 1939, Doris Ethel, *d* of late David Baker, Eastbourne; one *s* one *d* (and one *d* decd). *Educ:* St Olave's Sch.; Emmanuel Coll., Cambridge. Asst Master Buckhurst Hill Sch., 1938–40. War Service with RA, 1940–46 (despatches). Asst Master Gresham's Sch., Holt, 1946–51; Headmaster, Hutton Gram. Sch., near Preston, 1951–63; Headmaster, Alleyn's Sch., London, 1963–66. Trustee, Nat. Maritime Museum, 1974–86. JP Inner London, 1970. *Recreations:* reading, travel, golf. *Address:* 16 Tavistock, Devonshire Place, Eastbourne, E Sussex BN21 4AG. *T:* Eastbourne (0323) 20577.

LLOYD, Christopher, VMH 1979; MA, BSc (Hort.); writer on horticulture; regular gardening correspondent, Country Life, since 1963; *b* 2 March 1921; *s* of late Nathaniel Lloyd and Daisy (*née* Field). *Educ:* Wellesley House, Broadstairs, Kent; Rugby Sch.; King's Coll., Cambridge (MA Mod Langs); Wye Coll., Univ of London (BSc Hort.). Asst Lectr in Decorative Horticulture, Wye Coll., 1950–54. Then returned to family home at Great Dixter and started Nursery in clematis and uncommon plants. *Publications:* The Mixed Border, 1957; Clematis, 1965, rev. edn (with Tom Bennett), 1989; Shrubs and Trees for Small Gardens, 1965; Hardy Perennials, 1967; Gardening on Chalk and Lime, 1969; The Well-Tempered Garden, 1970, rev. edn 1985; Foliage Plants, 1973, rev. edn 1985; The Adventurous Gardener, 1983; The Well-Chosen Garden, 1984; The Year at Great Dixter, 1987; (with Richard Bird) The Cottage Garden, 1990; (with Graham Rice) Garden Flowers from Seed, 1991; regular gardening contributor to The Observer Magazine, The Guardian, American Horticulture, Country Life. *Recreations:* walking, entertaining and cooking for friends, canvas embroidery. *Address:* Great Dixter, Northiam, Rye, East Sussex TN31 6PH. *T:* Northiam (0797) 253107.

LLOYD, Christopher Hamilton, Surveyor of The Queen's Pictures, since 1988; *b* 30 June 1945; *s* of Rev. Hamilton Lloyd and Suzanne Lloyd (*née* Moon); *m* 1967, Christine Joan Frances Newth; four *s. Educ:* Marlborough Coll.; Christ Church, Oxford (BA 1967; MA 1971; BLitt 1972). Asst Curator of Pictures, Christ Church, Oxford, 1967–68; Dept of Western Art, Ashmolean Museum, 1968–88. Fellow of Villa I Tatti, Florence (Harvard Univ.), 1972–73; Vis. Res. Curator of Early Italian Painting, Art Inst., Chicago, 1980–81. *Publications:* Art and its Images, 1975; Catalogue of Earlier Italian Paintings in the Ashmolean Museum, 1977; Camille Pissarro (cat. of retr. exhbn, 1980–81); (with Richard Brettell) Catalogue of Drawings by Camille Pissarro in the Ashmolean Museum, 1980; Camille Pissarro, 1981; (with Richard Thomson) Impressionist Drawings from British Collections, 1986; (introd. and ed) Catalogue of Old Master Drawings at Holkham Hall, by A. E. Popham, 1986; (ed) Studies on Camille Pissarro, 1986; (with Simon Thurley) Henry VIII—images of a Tudor King (cat. of exhbn, Hampton Court Palace, 1990–91); reviews and contribs to learned jls. *Recreations:* books, theatre, cinema, music, real tennis. *Address:* 179 Woodstock Road, Oxford OX2 7NB. *T:* Oxford (0865) 59133.

LLOYD, Clive Hubert, AO 1985; OJ 1985; OB 1986; Executive Promotion Officer, Project Fullemploy, since 1987; Director, Red Rose Radio PLC, since 1981; Manager, West Indies cricket tour in Australia, winter 1988–89; *b* Georgetown, Guyana, 31 Aug. 1944; *er s* of late Arthur Christopher Lloyd and of Sylvia Thelma Lloyd; *m* 1971, Waveney Benjamin; one *s* two *d. Educ:* Chatham High Sch., Georgetown (schol). Clerk, Georgetown Hosp., 1960–66. Began cricket career, Demarara CC, Georgetown, 1959; début for Guyana, 1963; first Test Match, 1966; played for Haslingden, Lancs League, 1967; Lancashire County Cricket Club: Mem., 1968–86, capped 1969; Captain, 1981–84 and 1986; Captain, WI cricket team, 1974–78 and 1979–85; World Series Cricket in Australia, 1977–79. Made first 1st class century, 1966; passed total of 25,000 runs (incl. 69 centuries), 1981; captained WI teams which won World Cup, 1975, 1979. First Pres., WI Players' Assoc., 1973. Mem. (part-time), Commn for Racial Equality, 1987–90. Hon. Fellow: Manchester Polytechnic, 1986; Lancashire Polytechnic, 1986. Hon. MA: Manchester; Hull; Hon. Dr of Letters, Univ. of West Indies, Mona. Golden Arrow of Achievement (Guyana), 1975; Cacique Crown of Honours, Order of Rorima (Guyana), 1985. *Publications:* (with Tony Cozier) Living for Cricket, 1980; *relevant publication:* Clive Lloyd, by Trevor McDonald, 1985. *Address:* c/o Harefield, Harefield Drive, Wilmslow, Cheshire SK9 1NJ.

LLOYD, Air Vice-Marshal Darrell Clive Arthur, CB 1980; Commander, Northern Maritime Air Region, 1981–83; retired; *b* 5 Nov. 1928; *s* of Cecil James Lloyd and Doris Frances Lloyd; *m* 1957, Pamela (*née* Woodside); two *s. Educ:* Stowe; RAF Coll., Cranwell. Commnd 1950; ADC to C-in-C, ME Air Force, 1955–57; Instr, Central Flying Sch., 1958–60; Personal Air Sec. to Sec. of State for Air, 1961–63; CO, RAF Bruggen, 1968–70; RCDS, 1972; Dir of Defence Policy, UK Strategy Div., 1973–75; Dep. Comdr, RAF Germany, 1976–78; ACAS (Ops), 1978–81. FBIM 1972. *Recreations:* travel, golf (Sec., Tandridge Golf Club), painting. *Address:* c/o Lloyds Bank, 6 Pall Mall, SW1. *Clubs:* Royal Air Force; Royal Cinque Ports Golf (Deal); Tandridge Golf (Oxted).

LLOYD, David Bernard; Secretary, Royal College of Physicians and Faculty of Occupational Medicine, since 1986; *b* 14 Jan. 1938; *s* of George Edwards and Lilian Catherine Lloyd; *m* 1968, Christine Vass; three *d. Educ:* Presteigne Grammar Sch.; Hereford High Sch. FCCA. Early posts in local govt, UCL, UCH Med. Sch.; Royal College of Obstetricians and Gynaecologists: Accountant, 1971–76; Secretary, 1976–82;

Secretary, Nat. Inst. of Agricultural Engineering, 1982–86. Chm., Management Cttee, St Albans CAB, 1990– (Mem., 1985–). Governor: Sir John Lawes Sen. Sch., 1986–87 (also Chm.); Roundwood Jun. Sch., 1980–89 (Chm., 1985–88). *Recreations:* local charity, garden. *Address:* 29 Bloomfield Road, Harpenden, Herts AL5 4DD. *T:* Harpenden (0582) 761292.

LLOYD, David Mark; Senior Commissioning Editor, News and Current Affairs, Channel Four Television, since 1988; *b* 3 Feb. 1945; *s* of late Maurice Edward and Roma Doreen Lloyd; *m* 1982, Jana Tomas; one *s* one *d* and one step *s. Educ:* Felsted Sch.; Brentwood Sch.; Brasenose Coll., Oxford (MA 1967). Joined BBC as Gen. Trainee, 1967: Dep. Ed., Nationwide, 1978; Editor: Money Prog., 1980; Newsnight, 1982; Sixty Minutes, 1983; Breakfast Time, 1984. Shell Film and TV Award, 1982. *Recreations:* cricket, golf, music, travel. *Address:* Channel Four Television Co. Ltd, 60 Charlotte Street, W1. *T:* 071–927 8759.

LLOYD, David Richard, (Denys Lloyd); *b* 28 June 1939; *s* of Richard Norman Lloyd and Grace Enid Lloyd. *Educ:* Brighton College (George Long Scholar); Trinity Hall, Cambridge (Exhibitioner; BA 1961, MA 1965); Leeds Univ. (MA 1969). Deacon, 1963; Priest, 1964; Asst Curate, St Martin's, Rough Hills, Wolverhampton, 1963–67; professed as Mem. of Community of Resurrection, 1969 (taking name Denys); Tutor, Coll. of Resurrection, 1970–75, Vice-Principal, 1975–84; Principal, 1984–90; Associate Lecturer, Dept of Theology and Religious Studies, Univ. of Leeds, 1972–90. Received into Roman Catholic Church, 1990. *Publications:* contribs to theolog. jls. *Recreations:* walking, domestic architecture. *Address:* Quarr Abbey, Ryde, Isle of Wight PO33 4ES.

LLOYD, Denis Thelwall; His Honour Judge Denis Lloyd; a Circuit Judge, since 1972; *b* 3 Jan. 1924; *s* of late Col Glyn Lloyd, DSO, FRCVS, Barrister-at-Law and Olga Victoria Lloyd (*née* Roberts); *m* 1st, 1950, Margaret Sheila (*d* 1976), *d* of Bernard Bushell, Wirral, Ches; one *s* two *d*; 2nd, 1983, Ann, *d* of John and Georgia Cunningham, Montana and Hawaii, USA. *Educ:* Wellington College. Enlisted KRRC, 1942; commnd KRRC Dec. 1942; Central Mediterranean Force, (Italy, S France, Greece) 1943–45; attached 1st York and Lancaster Regt and then joined Parachute Regt, 1944 (wounded); Palestine, 1945–46; GSO3 (ops) HQ British Troops Austria, 1946; Staff Captain British Mil. Mission to Czechoslovakia, 1947. Called to the Bar, Gray's Inn, 1949; joined NE Circuit, 1950; Asst Recorder, Leeds, 1961–67; Recorder of Pontefract, 1971; Dep. Chm., WR Yorks QS, 1968–71; Sen. Resident Judge, Knightsbridge Crown Court, 1988–. Dep. Chm., Agricultural Land Tribunal, Yorks and Lancs, 1968–71; Legal Chm., Mental Health Review Tribunal, 1983–86. Contested (L): York, 1964; Hallam Div. of Sheffield, 1966. Czech War Cross, 1946. *Recreations:* gardening, fishing. *Address:* c/o Knightsbridge Crown Court, 1 Hans Crescent, SW1X 0LQ. *T:* 071–589 4500.

LLOYD, Denys; *see* Lloyd, David Richard.

LLOYD, Eve, (Lady Lloyd); *see* Pollard, E.

LLOYD, Frances Mary, (Mrs James Lloyd); *see* Line, F. M.

LLOYD, Frederick John, CBE 1977; FIA; Chairman, Road Transport Industry Training Board, 1978–83; *b* 22 Jan. 1913; *m* 1942, Catherine Johnson (*née* Parker); one *s* one *d. Educ:* Ackworth Sch., Yorks; Liverpool Univ. (BSc). FIA 1947; FIS 1949; FSS 1953; FCIT 1968. War Service, Operational Research, Bomber Comd, 1942–45. Royal Insurance Co., 1933–47; London Passenger Transport Bd, 1947–69: Staff Admin Officer, 1952; Divl Supt (South), 1957; Chief Operating Manager (Central Buses), 1961; Chief Commercial and Planning Officer, 1965–69; Dir Gen., West Midlands Passenger Transport Exec., 1969–78. *Publications:* contribs to actuarial and transport jls. *Recreations:* golf, gardening. *Address:* 8 Cliveden Coppice, Sutton Coldfield, West Midlands B74 2RG. *T:* 021–308 5683. *Club:* Whittington Barracks Golf (Lichfield, Staffs).

LLOYD, Prof. Geoffrey Ernest Richard, PhD; FBA 1983; Professor of Ancient Philosophy and Science, University of Cambridge, since 1983; Master of Darwin College, Cambridge, since 1989; *b* 25 Jan. 1933; *s* of William Ernest Lloyd and Olive Irene Neville Lloyd; *m* 1956, Janet Elizabeth Lloyd; three *s. Educ:* Charterhouse; King's Coll., Cambridge. BA 1954, MA 1958, PhD 1958. Cambridge University: Asst Lectr in Classics, 1965–67; Lectr, 1967–74; Reader in Ancient Philosophy and Science, 1974–83; Fellow, 1957–89 (Hon. Fellow, 1990), and Sen. Tutor, 1969–73, King's Coll. Bonsall Prof., Stanford Univ., 1981; Sather Prof., Berkeley, 1983–84. Fellow, Japan Soc. for the Promotion of Science, 1981. Sarton Medal, History of Science Soc., USA, 1987. *Publications:* Polarity and Analogy, 1966; Aristotle: the growth and structure of his thought, 1968; Early Greek Science: Thales to Aristotle, 1970; Greek Science after Aristotle, 1973; (ed) Hippocratic Writings, 1978; (ed) Aristotle on Mind and the Senses, 1978; Magic, Reason and Experience, 1979; Science, Folklore and Ideology, 1983; Science and Morality in Greco-Roman Antiquity, 1985; The Revolutions of Wisdom, 1987; Demystifying Mentalities, 1990; Methods and Problems in Greek Science, 1991; contribs to classical and philosophical jls. *Recreation:* travel. *Address:* 2 Prospect Row, Cambridge CB1 1DU; Darwin College, Cambridge CB3 9EU.

LLOYD, (George) Peter, CMG 1965; CVO 1983; Governor, Cayman Islands, 1982–87, retired; *b* 23 Sept. 1926; *er s* of late Sir Thomas Ingram Kynaston Lloyd, GCMG, KCB; *m* 1957, Margaret Harvey; two *s* one *d. Educ:* Stowe Sch.; King's Coll., Cambridge. Lieut, KRRC, 1945–48; ADC to Governor of Kenya, 1948; Cambridge, 1948–51 (MA; athletics blue); District Officer, Kenya, 1951–60; Principal, Colonial Office, 1960–61; Colonial Secretary, Seychelles, 1961–66; Chief Sec., Fiji, 1966–70; Defence Sec., Hong Kong, 1971–74; Dep. Governor, Bermuda, 1974–81. *Address:* Watch house, 13 Fort Hamilton Drive, Pembroke HM 19, Bermuda. *Clubs:* Commonwealth Trust; Royal Bermuda Yacht (Bermuda); Hong Kong (Hong Kong); Muthaiga (Nairobi, Kenya).

LLOYD, George Walter Selwyn; composer and conductor; *b* 28 June 1913; *s* of William Alexander Charles Lloyd and Constance Priestley Rawson; *m* 1937, Nancy Kathleen Juvet. *Educ:* privately, and with Albert Sammons for violin, Harry Farjeon for composition. Works composed and conducted: Symphony No 1, Bournemouth, 1933; Symphony No 2, Eastbourne, 1935; opera Iernin, Lyceum, London, 1935; Symphony No 3, BBC Symph. Orch., 1935; composed 2nd opera The Serf, perf. Convent Garden, 1938; during 1939–45 war served in Royal Marines Band aboard HMS Trinidad, severely shell-shocked 1942, whilst on Arctic convoy; composed opera John Scoman, 1st perf. Bristol, 1951; due to poor health lived in Dorset growing carnations and mushrooms, only composing intermittently; health improved; subseq. composed many more symphonies, concertos (Symphonies No 11 and 12 commissioned and recorded by Albany Symph. Orch, NY; first perf. of No 11, 1986, of No 12, 1990); numerous recordings. *Publications:* The Vigil of Venus, 1981; A Miniature Tryptich, 1981; Royal Parks, 1985; Diversions on a Bass Theme, 1986; Aubade, 1987; The Forest of Arden, 1988; English Heritage, 1990. *Recreation:* reading. *Address:* 199 Clarence Gate Gardens, Glentworth Street, NW1 6AU. *T:* 071–262 7969.

LLOYD, Very Rev. Henry Morgan, DSO 1941; OBE 1959; MA; *b* 9 June 1911; *y s* of late Rev. David Lloyd, Weston-super-Mare, Somerset. *m* 1962, Rachel Katharine, *d* of late

J. R. Wharton, Haffield, nr Ledbury; one *d. Educ:* Canford Sch.; Oriel Coll., Oxford; Cuddesdon Theological Coll. Deacon, 1935; priest, 1936; Curate of Hendon Parish Church, Middlesex, 1935–40. Served War as Chaplain RNVR, 1940–45. Principal of Old Rectory Coll., Hawarden, 1946–48; Secretary of Central Advisory Council of Training for the Ministry, 1948–50; Dean of Gibraltar, 1950–60; Dean of Truro and Rector of St Mary, Truro, 1960–81; Dean Emeritus, 1981. Hon. Citizen of the City of Truro, 1978. *Recreations:* walking, reading. *Address:* 3 Hill House, The Avenue, Sherborne, Dorset. *T:* Sherborne (0935) 812037. *Club:* Commonwealth Trust (Fellow).

LLOYD, Humphrey John; QC 1979; a Recorder, since 1990; *b* 16 Nov. 1939; *s* of Rees Lewis Lloyd of the Inner Temple, barrister-at-law, and Dorothy Margaret Ferry (*née* Gibson); *m* 1969, Ann Findlay; one *s* one *d. Educ:* Westminster; Trinity Coll., Dublin (BA (Mod), LLB; MA). Called to the Bar, Inner Temple, 1963, Bencher, 1985. Pres., Soc. of Construction Law, 1985–88. Hon. Senior Vis. Fellow, QMC, 1987. Editor-in-chief: Building Law Reports, 1977–; The Internat. Construction Law Rev., 1983–. *Publication:* (ed) The Liability of Contractors, 1986. *Address:* 1 Atkin Building, Gray's Inn, WC1R 5BQ. *Club:* Reform.

LLOYD, Sir Ian (Stewart), Kt 1986; MP (C) Havant, since 1983 (Portsmouth, Langstone, 1964–74, Havant and Waterloo, 1974–83); *b* 30 May 1921; *s* of late Walter John Lloyd and Euphemia Craig Lloyd; *m* 1951, Frances Dorward Addison, *d* of late Hon. W. Addison, CMG, OBE, MC, DCM; three *s. Educ:* Michaelhouse; University of the Witwatersrand; King's Coll., Cambridge. President, Cambridge Union, and Leader, Cambridge tour of USA, 1947; MA 1951; MSc 1952. Econ. Adviser, Central Mining and Investment Corporation, 1949–52; Member, SA Board of Trade and Industries, 1952–55; Director, Acton Soc. Trust, 1956; Dir of Res., 1956–64, Economic Advr, 1956–83, British and Commonwealth Shipping. Chairman, UK Cttee and Vice-Chairman, International Exec., International Cargo Handling Co-ordination Assoc., 1961–64. Chairman: Cons. Parly Shipping and Shipbuilding Cttee, 1974–77; Select Cttee on Sci. Sub-Cttee, 1975–77; Select Cttee on Sci. Sub-Cttee on Technological Innovation, 1977–79; Select Cttee on Energy, 1979–89; All-Party Cttee on Information Technology, 1979–87; Pres., Parly and Scientific Cttee, 1990– (Vice-Pres., 1983–87; Vice-Chm., 1988–90); Chm. Bd, Parly Office of Science and Technology. Member, UK Delegation, Council of Europe, Western European Union, 1968–72; UK rep., Internat. Parly Conf., Bucharest, 1975; Leader, UK Delegn, OECD Conf. on Energy, 1981. *Publications:* Rolls-Royce, 3 vols, 1978; contribs to various journals on economics, politics and information technology. *Recreations:* yachting, ski-ing, good music. *Clubs:* Brooks's, Army and Navy, Royal Yacht Squadron.

LLOYD, Illtyd Rhys; HM Chief Inspector of Schools (Wales), 1982–90, retired; *b* 13 Aug. 1929; *s* of John and Melvina Lloyd; *m* 1955, Julia Lewis; one *s* one *d. Educ:* Port Talbot (Glan-Afan) County Grammar Sch.; Swansea UC (Hon. Fellow, Univ. of Wales, 1987). BSc, MSc; DipStat, DipEd. Commnd Educn Br., RAF, 1951–54 (Flt Lieut). Second Maths Master, Howardian High Sch. for Boys, Cardiff, 1954–57; Hd of Maths Dept, Pembroke Grammar Sch., 1957–59; Dep. Headmaster, Howardian High Sch., 1959–63; Welsh Office: HM Inspector of Schs, 1964–70; Staff Inspector (Secondary Educn), 1971–82. Member: S Glam FHSA; Council, Baptist Union of Wales; Council, Cardiff Theol Coll.; Council, Council for Educn in World Citizenship–Cymru. Hon. Mem., Gorsedd of Bards. *Recreation:* walking. *Address:* 134 Lake Road East, Roath Park, Cardiff CF2 5NQ. *T:* Cardiff (0222) 755296.

LLOYD, James Monteith, CD 1979; CMG 1961; Deputy Chairman, Industrial Disputes Tribunal, Jamaica, 1976–78; *b* 24 Nov. 1911; *s* of late Jethro and Frances Lloyd; *m* 1936, Mavis Anita Frankson; two *s* two *d. Educ:* Wolmer's High Sch., Jamaica. Called to Bar, Lincoln's Inn, 1948. Jamaica: entered Public Service as Asst, Registrar-General's Dept, 1931 (2nd Class Clerk, 1939, 1st Class Clerk, 1943, Asst Registrar-General, 1947); Asst Secretary, Secretariat, 1950; Principal Asst Secretary, Secretariat, 1953 (seconded to Grenada on special duty, Dec. 1955–May 1956); Permanent Secretary, Jamaica, 1956; Administrator, Grenada, 1957–62; Permanent Secretary, Jamaica, 1962–72; Chm., Ombudsman Working Party, Jamaica, 1972; retired from Civil Service, 1975. Chief Comr, Scouts, Jamaica, 1973–78. Coronation Medal, 1953; Jamaica Independence Medal, 1962. *Recreations:* cricket, tennis, golf. *Address:* 5 Melwood Avenue, Kingston 8, Jamaica. *Clubs:* Jamaica; Kingston CC; YMCA.

LLOYD, John Graham; Executive Officer/Commercial Surveyor, Commission for the New Towns, Corby, since 1981; *b* Watford, 18 Feb. 1938; *s* of late Richard and Edith Lloyd; *m* 1960, Ann (*née* Plater); three *s. Educ:* City of London Sch.; College of Estate Management, London Univ. (BSc Estate Management). FRICS. In private practice, London and Leamington Spa, 1959–75. Commercial and Industrial Manager, Hemel Hempstead, Commission for the New Towns, 1975–78, Manager, 1978–81. *Recreations:* soccer, motor racing, jazz and popular music, gardening. *Address:* 10 Polhill Avenue, Bedford MK41 9DS. *T:* Bedford (0234) 56089.

LLOYD, John Nicol Fortune; journalist; Moscow Correspondent, Financial Times, since 1991; *b* 15 April 1946; *s* of Joan Adam Fortune and Christopher Lloyd; *m* 1st, 1974, Judith Ferguson (marr. diss. 1979); 2nd, 1983, Marcia Levy. *Educ:* Waid Comprehensive School; Edinburgh Univ. (MA Hons). Editor, Time Out, 1972–73; Reporter, London Programme, 1974–76; Producer, Weekend World, 1976–77; industrial reporter, labour corresp., industrial and labour editor, Financial Times, 1977–86; Editor, New Statesman, 1986–87; with Financial Times, 1987–. Journalist of the Year, Granada Awards, 1984; Specialist Writer of the Year, IPC Awards, 1985. *Publications:* (with Ian Benson) The Politics of Industrial Change, 1982; (with Martin Adeney) The Miners' Strike: loss without limit, 1986; (with Charles Leadbeater) In Search of Work, 1987; (contrib.) Counterblasts, 1989. *Recreations:* opera, hill walking, squash. *Address:* Flat 1, 14 Kutuzovsky Prospekt, Moscow, USSR. *T:* Moscow 230.2267.

LLOYD, Sir (John) Peter (Daniel), Kt 1971; Chancellor, University of Tasmania, 1982–85; *b* 30 Aug. 1915; *s* of late David John Lloyd; *m* 1947, Gwendolen, *d* of late William Nassau Molesworth; two *s* four *d. Educ:* Rossall Sch.; Brasenose Coll., Oxford (MA). Royal Artillery, 1940–46 (despatches, Order of Leopold, Belgian Croix de Guerre). Joined Cadbury Bros Ltd, Birmingham, 1937; served in UK and Australia; Dir, Cadbury Fry Pascall Australia Ltd, 1949, Chm., 1953–71. Member: Council, Univ. of Tasmania, 1957–85; Council, Australian Admin. Staff Coll., 1959–71; Board, Commonwealth Banking Corp., 1967–82; Board, Goliath Cement Holdings, 1969–88; Board, Australian Mutual Provident Society, 1970–88. Member: Australian Taxation Review Cttee, 1972–74; Cttee of Inquiry into Educn and Training, 1976–78. Hon. LLD Tasmania, 1986. *Address:* 12 Curtis Court, Gisborne, Vic 3437, Australia. *Club:* Australian (Sydney). *See also* B. B. Lloyd.

LLOYD, Prof. John Raymond; *see under* Lloyd, M. R.

LLOYD, John Wilson; Deputy Secretary, Welsh Office, since 1988; *b* 24 Dec. 1940; *s* of late Dr Ellis Lloyd and of Mrs Dorothy Lloyd; *m* 1967, Buddug Roberts; two *s* one *d. Educ:* Swansea Grammar Sch.; Clifton Coll., Bristol; Christ's Coll., Cambridge (MA).

Asst Principal, HM Treasury, 1962–67 (Private Sec. to Financial Sec., 1965–67); Principal, successively HM Treasury, CSD and Welsh Office, 1967–75 (Private Sec. to Sec. of State for Wales, 1974–75); Welsh Office: Asst Sec., 1975–82; Under Sec., 1982–88; Principal Establishment Officer, 1982–86; Hd, Housing, Health and Social Servs Policy Gp, 1986–88. *Recreations:* golf, squash, swimming. *Address:* c/o Welsh Office, Cathays Park, Cardiff CF1 3NQ. *T:* Cardiff (0222) 825111.

LLOYD, Dame June (Kathleen), DBE 1990; FRCP, FRCPE; FRCGP; Nuffield Professor of Child Health, British Postgraduate Medical Federation, London University, since 1985; *b* 1928; *d* of Arthur Cresswell Lloyd and Lucy Bevan Lloyd. *Educ:* Royal School, Bath; Bristol Univ. (MD); Durham Univ. (DPH). FRCP 1969; FRCPE 1989; FRCGP 1990. Junior Hosp. appts, Bristol, Oxford and Newcastle, 1951–57; Res. Fellow and Lectr in Child Health, Univ. of Birmingham, 1958–65; Sen. Lectr, Reader in Paediatrics, Inst. of Child Health, 1965–73; Prof. of Paediatrics, London Univ., 1973–75; Prof. of Child Health, St George's Hosp. Med. Sch., London Univ., 1975–85. Vis. Examr in Paediatrics in Univs in UK and abroad. Member: Council, RCP, 1982–85, 1986–88; MRC, 1984–88; ABRC, 1989–90; DHSS Cttees. Pres., British Paediatric Assoc., 1988–91. *Publications:* research articles, reviews and leading articles in sci. jls. *Recreations:* cooking, gardening, walking. *Address:* Institute of Child Health, 30 Guilford Street, WC1N 1EH.

LLOYD, Rev. Kingsley; *see* Lloyd, Rev. A. K.

LLOYD, Leslie, CBE 1981; FCIT; General Manager, Western Region, British Rail, 1976–82; *b* 10 April 1924; *s* of Henry Lloyd and Lilian Wright; *m* 1953, Marie Snowden; one *s* two *d*. *Educ:* Hawarden Grammar Sch. RAF, 1943–47. British Rail: Management Trainee, Eastern Reg., 1949–52; Chief Controller, Manchester, 1953–56; Freight Officer, Sheffield, 1956–59; Modernisation Asst, King's Cross, 1959–61; Dist Manager, Marylebone, 1961–63; Movements Supt, Great Northern Line, 1963–64; Ops Officer, Eastern Reg., 1964–67; Man., Sundries Div., 1967; Movements Man., Western Reg., 1967–69; Chief Ops Man., British Rail HQ, 1969–76. *Recreations:* golf, gardening. *Address:* 73 The Fairway, Burnham, Bucks SL1 8DY. *Club:* Burnham Beeches Golf (Burnham).

LLOYD, Prof. Michael Raymond; Professor, Bergen School of Architecture, since 1986; Executive Architect/Planner, Norconsult Associates, Oslo, since 1981; *b* 20 Aug. 1927; *s* of W. R. Lloyd; *m* 1957, Berit Hansen; one *s* two *d*. *Educ:* Wellington Sch., Somerset; AA School of Architecture. AA Dipl. 1953; ARIBA 1954; MNAL 1960. Private practice and Teacher, State School of Arts and Crafts, Oslo, 1955–60 and 1962–63; First Year Master, AA School of Architecture, 1960–62; Dean, Faculty of Arch., and Prof. of Arch., Kumasi Univ. of Science and Technology, 1963–66; Principal, AA Sch. of Architecture, 1966–71; Consultant, Land Use Consultants (Internat.) Lausanne, 1971–72; Senior Partner, Sinar Associates, Tunbridge Wells, 1973–78; Consultant Head, Hull Sch. of Architecture, 1974–77; Technical Officer, ODA, Central America, 1979–81. Leverhulme Sen. Res. Fellow, UCL, 1976–78. *Publications:* (as J. R. Lloyd) Tegning og Skissing; ed World Architecture, Vol. I Norway, Vol. III Ghana; Shelter in Society: Norwegian Laftehus; Environmental Impact of Development Activities. *Recreations:* sailing, ski-ing. *Address:* Setravn 11B, 0390 Oslo 3, Norway.

LLOYD, Sir Nicholas (Markley), Kt 1990; MA; Editor, Daily Express, since 1986; *b* 9 June 1942; *s* of Walter and Sybil Lloyd; *m* 1st, 1968, Patricia Sholliker (marr. diss. 1978); two *s* one *d*; 2nd, 1979, Eve Pollard, *qv*; one *s*. *Educ:* Bedford Modern Sch.; St Edmund Hall, Oxford (MA Hons History); Harvard Univ., USA. Reporter, Daily Mail, 1964; Educn Correspondent, Sunday Times, 1966; Dep. News Editor, Sunday Times, 1968; News Editor, The Sun, 1970; Asst Editor, News of the World, 1972; Asst Editor, The Sun, 1976; Dep. Editor, Sunday Mirror, 1980; Editor: Sunday People, 1982–83; News of the World, 1984–85. *Recreations:* football, golf, tennis, cinema, theatre. *Address:* Ludgate House, 245 Blackfriars Road, SE1 9UX. *T:* 071–928 8000.

LLOYD, Peter, CBE 1957; Director, Booth International Holdings Ltd, 1973–79 (Consultant, 1980); *b* 26 June 1907; *s* of late Godfrey I. H. Lloyd and late Constance L. A. Lloyd; *m* 1st, 1932, Nora K. E. Patten; one *s* one *d*; 2nd, 1951, Joyce Evelyn Campbell. *Educ:* Gresham's Sch.; Trinity Coll., Cambridge (MA). Industrial Research in Gas Light and Coke Co., London, 1931–41; Royal Aircraft Establishment, 1941–44; Power Jets (Research and Development), 1944–46. National Gas Turbine Establishment, Pyestock, 1946–60, Deputy Director, 1950; Dir-Gen. Engine R&D, Mins of Aviation and Technology, 1961–69; Head of British Defence Research and Supply Staff, Canberra, 1969–72. Chm., Gas Turbine Collaboration Cttee, 1961–68. CEng, FRAeS, SFInstE. Pres., Cambridge Univ. Mountaineering Club, 1928–29; Chm., Mount Everest Foundn, 1982–84 (Vice Chm., 1980–82). Himalayan expeditions: Nanda Devi, 1936; Everest, 1938; Langtang Himal, 1949; Kulu, 1977. *Publications:* various papers in scientific and technical journals. *Recreations:* mountaineering, fishing, gardening. *Address:* 121 Tourist Road, Toowoomba, Qld 4350, Australia. *Clubs:* Athenæum, Alpine (Vice-Pres., 1961–63, Pres., 1977–80); Queensland (Brisbane).
See also T. A. Evans.

LLOYD, Peter; *see* Lloyd, G. P.

LLOYD, Sir Peter; *see* Lloyd, Sir J. P. D.

LLOYD, Peter Gordon, CBE 1976 (OBE 1965); retired; British Council Representative, Greece, 1976–80; *b* 20 Feb. 1920; *s* of Peter Gleave Lloyd and Ellen Swift; *m* 1952, Edith Florence (*née* Flurey); two *s* one *d*. *Educ:* Royal Grammar Sch., Newcastle upon Tyne; Balliol Coll., Oxford (Horsley Exhibnr, 1939; BA, MA 1948). RA (Light Anti-Aircraft), subseq. DLI, 1940–46, Captain. British Council, 1949–: Brit. Council, Belgium and Hon. Lector in English, Brussels Univ., 1949–52; Reg. Dir, Mbale, Uganda, 1952–56; Dep. Dir Personnel, 1956–60; Representative: Ethiopia, 1960–68; Poland, 1969–72; Nigeria, 1972–76. *Publications:* (introd) Huysmans, A Rebours, 1940; The Story of British Democracy, 1959; Perspectives and Identities, 1989; critical essays on literature in periodicals. *Recreations:* literature, music, travel. *Address:* 111 Sussex Road, Petersfield, Hants GU31 4LB. *T:* Petersfield (0730) 62007. *Club:* United Oxford & Cambridge University.

LLOYD, Peter Robert Cable; MP (C) Fareham, since 1979; Parliamentary Under Secretary of State, Home Office, since 1989; *b* 12 Nov. 1937; *s* of David and late Stella Lloyd; *m* 1967, Hilary Creighton; one *s* one *d*. *Educ:* Tonbridge Sch.; Pembroke Coll., Cambridge (MA). Formerly Marketing Manager, United Biscuits Ltd. Sec., Cons. Parly Employment Cttee, 1979–81; Vice-Chm., Cons. European Affairs Cttee, 1980–81; PPS to Minister of State, NI Office, 1981–82, to Sec. of State for Educn and Sci., Sir Keith Joseph, 1983–84; Asst Govt Whip, 1984–86; a Lord Comr of HM Treasury (Govt Whip), 1986–88; Parly Under-Sec. of State, Dept of Social Security, 1988–89. Chairman, Bow Group, 1972–73; Editor of Crossbow, 1974–76. *Recreations:* theatre, gardening. *Address:* House of Commons, SW1A 0AA.

LLOYD, Sir Richard (Ernest Butler), 2nd Bt *cr* 1960, of Rhu, Co. Dunbarton; Chairman, Vickers plc, since 1991 (Director, since 1978; Deputy Chairman, 1989–91); Deputy Chairman, Hill Samuel & Co. Ltd, 1978–87 and since 1991 (Chief Executive, 1980–87, Chariman, 1987–91); *b* 6 Dec. 1928; *s* of Major Sir (Ernest) Guy Richard Lloyd, 1st Bt, DSO, and Helen Kynaston (*d* 1984), *yr d* of Col E. W. Greg, CB; *S* father, 1987; *m* 1955, Jennifer Susan Margaret, *e d* of Brigadier Ereld Cardiff, CB, CBE; three *s*. *Educ:* Wellington Coll.; Hertford Coll., Oxford (MA). Nat. Service (Captain, Black Watch), 1947–49. Joined Glyn, Mills & Co., 1952; Exec. Dir, 1964–70; Chief Executive, Williams & Glyn's Bank Ltd, 1970–78. Director: Legal & Gen. Gp, 1966–; SIEBE, 1988–; Simon Engineering, 1988–; Harrisons & Crosfield, 1988–. Member: CBI Council, 1978–; Industrial Develt Adv. Bd, 1972–77; Nat. Econ. Develt Council, 1973–77; Cttee to Review the Functioning of Financial Institutions, 1977–80; Overseas Projects Bd, 1981–85; Advisory Bd, Royal Coll. of Defence Studies, 1987–. Hon. Treas., British Heart Foundn, 1989–; Mem. Council and Chm., F and GP Cttee, Ditchley Foundn, 1985–. *Recreations:* walking, fishing, gardening. *Heir:* *s* Richard Timothy Butler Lloyd [*b* 12 April 1956; *m* 1989, Wilhelmina, *d* of Henri Schut]. *Address:* Sundridge Place, Sundridge, Sevenoaks, Kent TN14 6DD. *T:* Westerham (0959) 63599. *Club:* Boodle's.

LLOYD, Richard Hey; *b* 25 June 1933; *s* of Charles Yates Lloyd and Ann Lloyd; *m* 1962, Teresa Morwenna Willmott; four *d*. *Educ:* Lichfield Cathedral Choir Sch.; Rugby Sch. (Music Scholar); Jesus Coll., Cambridge (Organ Scholar). MA, FRCO, ARCM. Asst Organist, Salisbury Cath., 1957–66; Organist and Master of the Choristers, Hereford Cath., 1966–74; Conductor, Three Choirs Festival, 1966–74 (Chief Conductor 1967, 1970, 1973); Organist and Master of the Choristers, Durham Cathedral, 1974–85; Dep. Headmaster, Salisbury Cathedral Choir Sch., 1985–88. Examiner, Associated Bd of Royal Schs of Music, 1967–. Mem. Council, RCO, 1974–. *Publications:* church music. *Recreations:* cricket, theatre, travel, reading. *Address:* Refail Newydd, Pentraeth, Anglesey LL75 8YF. *T:* Pentraeth (024870) 220.

LLOYD, Robert Andrew, CBE 1991; freelance opera singer, broadcaster and writer; *b* 2 March 1940; *s* of William Edward Lloyd and May (*née* Waples); *m* 1964, Sandra Dorothy Watkins (marr. diss. 1990); one *s* three *d*. *Educ:* Southend-on-Sea High Sch.; Keble Coll., Oxford (BA Hons Mod. History; Hon. Fellow, 1990). Instructor Lieut RN (HMS Collingwood), 1963–66; Civilian Tutor, Police Staff Coll., Bramshill, 1966–68; studied at London Opera Centre, 1968–69; début in Leonore, Collegiate Theatre, 1969; Principal Bass: Sadler's Wells Opera, Coliseum, 1969–72; Royal Opera House, 1972–82; Parsifal, Covent Garden, 1988; Flying Dutchman, La Scala, 1988; début at Metropolitan Opera, NY, in Barber of Seville, 1988; début at Vienna State Opera in La Forza del Destino. Guest appearances in Amsterdam, Berlin, Hamburg, Aix-en-Provence, Milan (La Scala), San Francisco, Florence, Paris, Munich, Nice, Boston, Toronto, Salzburg; soloist with major orchestras; over 50 recordings; associated with rôles of King Philip, Boris Godunov (first British bass to sing this rôle at Kirov Opera), Gurnemanz, Fiesco, Banquo, King Henry; film, Parsifal; TV productions: Six Foot Cinderella, 1988; Bluebeard's Castle (opera), 1988. *Publications:* contrib. miscellaneous jls. *Recreations:* sailing, straight theatre. *Address:* c/o Harrison Parrott Ltd, 12 Penzance Place, W11 4PA. *T:* 071–229 9166. *Club:* Garrick.

LLOYD, Prof. Seton Howard Frederick, CBE 1958 (OBE 1949); FBA 1955; Archæologist; Professor of Western Asiatic Archæology, University of London, 1962–69, now Emeritus; *b* 30 May 1902; *s* of John Eliot Howard Lloyd and Florence Louise Lloyd (*née* Armstrong); *m* 1944, Margery Ulrica Fitzwilliams Hyde (*d* 1987); two *s* one *d*. *Educ:* Uppingham; Architectural Assoc. ARIBA 1926; Asst to Sir Edwin Lutyens, PRA, 1926–28; excavated with Egypt Exploration Society, 1928–30; excavated in Iraq for University of Chicago Oriental Institute, 1930–37; excavated in Turkey for University of Liverpool, 1937–39; FSA 1938 (Vice-Pres., 1965–69); Technical Adviser, Government of Iraq; Directorate-General of Antiquities, 1939–49; Director British Institute of Archæology, Ankara, Turkey, 1949–61. Hon. MA (Edinburgh), 1960. Lawrence of Arabia Meml Medal, RCAS, 1971; Gertrude Bell Meml Medal, British Sch. of Archaeology in Iraq, 1979. *Publications:* Mesopotamia (London), 1936; Sennacherib's Aqueduct at Jerwan (Chicago), 1935; The Gimilsin Temple (Chicago), 1940; Presargonid Temples (Chicago), 1942; Ruined Cities of Iraq (Oxford), 1942; Twin Rivers, (Oxford), 1942; Foundations in the Dust (London), 1947, rev. edn 1980; Early Anatolia (Pelican), 1956; Art of the Ancient Near East (London), 1961; Mounds of the Ancient Near East (Edinburgh) 1963; Highland Peoples of Anatolia (London), 1967; Archaeology of Mesopotamia (London), 1978; The Interval (London), 1986; Ancient Turkey, 1989; Excavation Reports and many articles in journals. *Recreation:* mnemonics. *Address:* Woolstone Lodge, Faringdon, Oxon SN7 7QL. *T:* Uffington (036782) 248. *Club:* Chelsea Arts.

LLOYD, Timothy Andrew Wigram; QC 1986; *b* 30 Nov. 1946; *s* of late Thomas Wigram Lloyd and of Margo Adela Lloyd (*née* Beasley); *m* 1978, Theresa Sybil Margaret Holloway. *Educ:* Winchester College; Lincoln College, Oxford. MA. Called to the Bar, Middle Temple, 1970; Mem., Middle Temple and Lincoln's Inn. *Publication:* (ed) Wurtzburg & Mills, Building Society Law, 15th edn 1989. *Recreations:* music, travel. *Address:* 11 Old Square, Lincoln's Inn, WC2A 3TS. *T:* 071–430 0341.

LLOYD, Ven. Trevor; *see* Lloyd, Ven. B. T.

LLOYD DAVIES, John Robert; *see* Davies.

LLOYD DAVIES, Trevor Arthur, MD; FRCP; *b* 8 April 1909; *s* of Arthur Lloyd Davies and Grace Margret (*née* Bull); *m* 1936, Joan (*d* 1972), *d* of John Keily, Co. Dublin; one *d*; *m* 1975, Margaret, *d* of Halliday Gracey, Woodford. *Educ:* Woking Grammar Sch.; St Thomas' Hospital, SE1. MRCS, LRCP 1932; MB, BS London (gold medal and hons in surgery, forensic med., obst. and gynæc.); MRCP 1933; MD London 1934; FRCP 1952. Resident Asst Physician, St Thomas' Hospital, 1934–36; MO, Boots Pure Drug Co., 1937–53; Prof. of Social Medicine, University of Malaya, 1953–61; Senior Medical Inspector of Factories, Min. of Labour and Dept of Employment and Productivity, 1961–70; Chief Med. Adviser, Dept of Employment, 1970–73. QHP 1968–71. *Publications:* The Practice of Industrial Medicine, 2nd edn, 1957; Respiratory Diseases in Foundrymen, 1971; Whither Occupational Medicine?, 1973; numerous papers on industrial and social medicine, in Lancet and Medical Journal of Malaya. *Recreations:* gardening, carpentry and bricklaying. *Address:* The Old Bakery, High Street, Elmdon, Saffron Walden, Essex CB11 4NL. *Club:* Athenæum.

LLOYD-EDWARDS, Captain Norman, RD 1971 and Bar 1980, RNR; Lord-Lieutenant of South Glamorgan, since 1990 (Vice Lord-Lieutenant, 1986–90); *b* 13 June 1933; *s* of Evan Stanley Edwards and Mary Leah Edwards. *Educ:* Monmouth School for Boys; Quaker's Yard Grammar School; Univ. of Bristol (LLB). Joined RNVR 1952, RN 1958–60; RNR 1960–86; CO S Wales Div., RNR, 1981–84; Naval ADC to the Queen, 1984. Partner, Cartwrights, later Cartwrights, Adams & Black, Solicitors, Cardiff, 1960–. Cardiff City Councillor, 1963–87; Dep. Lord Mayor, 1973–74; Lord Mayor, 1985–86. Member: Welsh Arts Council, 1983–89; BBC Adv. Council (Wales), 1987–90. Chapter Clerk, Llandaff Cathedral, 1975–90. Chm. of Wales, Duke of Edinburgh's Award, 1981–; Nat. Rescue Training Council, 1983–. Chm., Glamorgan TAVRA, 1987–90; President: S Glam Scouts, 1989–; Cardiff Assoc., National Trust, 1990–. DL S Glamorgan 1978.

KStJ 1988 (Prior of Wales, 1989–). *Recreations:* music, gardening, table talk. *Address:* Hafan Wen, Llantrisant Road, Llandaff CF5 2PU. *Clubs:* Army and Navy; Cardiff and County, United Services Mess (Cardiff).

LLOYD-ELEY, John, QC 1970; a Recorder of the Crown Court, since 1972; *b* 23 April 1923; *s* of Edward John Eley; *m* 1946, Una Fraser Smith; two *s*. *Educ:* Xaverian Coll., Brighton; Exeter Coll., Oxford (MA). Served War, 1942–46, Lieut 50th Royal Tank Regt and 7th Hussars, N Africa, Sicily and Italy. Barrister, Middle Temple, 1951; South-Eastern Circuit; Mem., Bar Council, 1969. *Recreations:* farming, travel. *Address:* 1 Hare Court, Temple, EC4Y 7BE. *T:* 071–353 5324; Luxfords Farm, East Grinstead. *T:* East Grinstead (0342) 21583.

LLOYD GEORGE, family name of **Earl Lloyd George of Dwyfor.**

LLOYD-GEORGE, family name of **Viscount Tenby.**

LLOYD GEORGE OF DWYFOR, 3rd Earl, *cr* 1945; **Owen Lloyd George;** Viscount Gwynedd, 1945; *b* 28 April 1924; *s* of 2nd Earl Lloyd George of Dwyfor, and Roberta Ida Freeman, 5th *d* of Sir Robert McAlpine, 1st Bt; *S* father, 1968; *m* 1st, 1949, Ruth Margaret (marr. diss. 1982), *o d* of Richard Coit; two *s* one *d*; 2nd, 1982, Cecily Josephine, *d* of late Sir Alexander Gordon Cumming, 5th Bt, MC, and of Elizabeth Countess Cawdor, *widow* of 2nd Earl of Woolton and former wife of 3rd Baron Forres. *Educ:* Oundle. Welsh Guards, 1942–47. Italian Campaign, 1944–45. Formerly Captain Welsh Guards. An Underwriting Member of Lloyd's. Carried the Sword at Investiture of HRH the Prince of Wales, Caernarvon Castle, 1969. Mem., Historic Buildings Council for Wales, 1971. Mem. Court, Nat. Mus. of Wales, 1978. *Heir: s* Viscount Gwynedd, *qv*. *Recreations:* shooting, gardening. *Address:* Ffynone, Boncath, Pembrokeshire SA37 0HQ; 47 Burton Court, SW3. *Clubs:* White's, City of London, Pratt's.

LLOYD-HUGHES, Sir Trevor Denby, Kt 1970; author and consultant in Government/industry relations; Chairman, Lloyd-Hughes Associates Ltd, International Consultants in Public Affairs, 1970–89; *b* 31 March 1922; *er s* of late Elwyn and Lucy Lloyd-Hughes, Bradford, Yorks; *m* 1st, 1950, Ethel Marguerite Durward (marr. diss., 1971), *o d* of late J. Ritchie, Dundee and Bradford; one *s* one *d*; 2nd, 1971, Marie-Jeanne, *d* of Marcel and late Helene Moreillon, Geneva; one *d* (and one adopted *d*— a Thai girl). *Educ:* Woodhouse Grove Sch., Yorks; Jesus Coll., Oxford (MA). Commissioned RA, 1941; served with 75th (Shropshire Yeomanry) Medium Regt, RA, in Western Desert, Sicily and Italy, 1941–45. Asst Inspector of Taxes, 1948; freelance journalist, 1949; joined staff of Liverpool Daily Post, 1949; Political Corresp., Liverpool Echo, 1950, Liverpool Daily Post, 1951. Press Secretary to the Prime Minister, 1964–69; Chief Information Adviser to Govt, 1969–70. Dir, Trinity International Holdings plc (formerly Liverpool Daily Post and Echo Ltd), 1978–91. Member of Circle of Wine Writers, 1961, Chm., 1972–73. *Recreations:* yoga, gardening, playing the Spanish guitar, golf, walking, travel. *Address:* Au Carmail, Labarrere, 32250 Montréal du Gers, France. *T:* (33) 62 29 45 31. *Clubs:* Mosimann's, Wellington; Golf de Guinlet.

LLOYD-JACOB, David Oliver, CBE 1984; Executive Chairman, Butte Mining plc, since 1991; *b* 30 March 1938; *s* of Sir George and Lady Lloyd-Jacob; *m* 1st, 1961, Clare Bartlett; two *d*; 2nd, 1982, Carolyn Howard. *Educ:* Westminster; Christ Church, Oxford. Pres., Azcon Corp., USA, 1974–79; Man. Dir, Consolidated Gold Fields plc, 1979–81; Chm., Amcon Group Inc., USA, 1979–82; Chm. and Chief Exec. Officer, Levinson Steel Co., Pittsburgh, 1983–90. Chm., Britain Salutes NY, 1981–83. *Recreations:* opera, theatre, restoring old houses. *Address:* 3 Neal Street, WC2H 9PU. *T:* 071–240 5776. *Clubs:* Garrick; Leander (Henley-on-Thames); River (New York).

LLOYD JONES, Charles Beynon; *see* Jones, C. B. L.

LLOYD-JONES, David Mathias; freelance conductor; *b* 19 Nov. 1934; *s* of late Sir Vincent Lloyd-Jones, and of Margaret Alwena, *d* of late G.H. Mathias; *m* 1964, Anne Carolyn Whitehead; two *s* one *d*. *Educ:* Westminster Sch.; Magdalen Coll., Oxford (BA). Repetiteur, Royal Opera House, Covent Garden, 1959–60; Chorus Master, New Opera Co., 1961–64; conductor: Bath Fest., 1966; City of London Fest., 1966; Wexford Fest., 1967–70; Scottish Opera, 1968; WNO, 1968; Royal Opera House, 1971; ENO (formerly Sadler's Wells Opera), 1969 (Asst Music Dir, 1972–78); Artistic Dir, Opera North, 1978–90; also conductor of BBC broadcasts, TV operas (Eugene Onegin, The Flying Dutchman, Hansel and Gretel), and operas in Amsterdam, Paris, Karlsruhe, Nice and Leningrad; has appeared with most British symph. orchs; recordings with LPO and English Northern Philharmonia (Founder Conductor). Hon. DMus Leeds, 1986. *Publications:* (trans.) Boris Godunov (vocal score), 1968; (trans.) Eugene Onegin (vocal score), 1971; Boris Godunov (critical edn of original full score), 1975; The Gondoliers (first ever pubn of a Gilbert and Sullivan full score), 1986; contrib. 6th edn Grove's Dictionary of Music and Musicians, 1980; contrib. Musik in Geschichte und Gegenwart, Music and Letters, and The Listener. *Recreations:* theatre, old shrub roses, French cuisine. *Address:* 9 Clarence Road, Leeds LS18 4LB; 94 Whitelands House, Cheltenham Terrace, SW3 4RA. *T:* 071–730 8695.

LLOYD-JONES, His Honour David Trevor, VRD 1958; a Circuit Judge, 1972–88; *b* 6 March 1917; *s* of Trevor and Anne Lloyd-Jones, Holywell, Flints; *m* 1st, 1942, Mary Violet (marr. diss.; she *d* 1980), *d* of Frederick Barnardo, CIE, CBE, MD, London; one *d*; 2nd, 1958, Anstice Elizabeth, MB, BChir (*d* 1981), *d* of William Henry Perkins, Whitchurch; one *s* one *d*; 3rd, 1984, Florence Mary, *d* of William Fairclough, MM, Wallasey. *Educ:* Holywell Grammar School. Banking, 1934–39 and 1946–50. Called to the Bar, Gray's Inn, 1951; practised Wales and Chester Circuit, 1952–71; Prosecuting Counsel to Post Office (Wales and Chester Circuit), 1961–66; Dep. Chm., Caerns QS, 1966–70, Chm, 1970–71; Legal Mem., Mental Health Appeal Tribunal (Wales Area), 1960–72; Dep. Chm., Agricultural Land Tribunal (Wales Area), 1968–72. Served War of 1939–45, RNVR and RNR, Atlantic, Mediterranean and Pacific; Lt-Comdr, RNR, retd. *Recreations:* golf, music. *Address:* 29 Curzon Park North, Chester. *T:* Chester (0244) 675144. *Clubs:* Army and Navy; Royal Dornoch Golf.

LLOYD-JONES, Sir (Peter) Hugh (Jefferd), Kt 1989; FBA 1966; Regius Professor of Greek in the University of Oxford and Student of Christ Church, 1960–89, now Emeritus Professor and Emeritus Student; *b* 21 Sept. 1922; *s* of Major W. Lloyd-Jones, DSO, and Norah Leila, *d* of F. H. Jefferd, Brent, Devon; *m* 1st, 1953, Frances Elisabeth Hedley (marr. diss. 1981); two *s* one *d*; 2nd, 1982, Mary Lefkowitz (Andrew W. Mellon Professor in the Humanities, Wellesley College, Mass), *d* of Harold and Mena Rosenthal, New York. *Educ:* Lycée Français du Royaume Uni, S Kensington; Westminster Sch.; Christ Church, Oxford. Served War of 1939–45, 2nd Lieut, Intelligence Corps, India, 1942; Temp. Captain, 1944. 1st Cl. Classics (Mods), 1941; MA 1947; 1st Cl., LitHum, 1948; Chancellor's Prize for Latin Prose, 1947; Ireland and Craven Schol., 1947; Fellow of Jesus Coll., Cambridge, 1948–54; Asst Lecturer in Classics, University of Cambridge, 1950–52, Lecturer, 1952–54; Fellow and E. P. Warren Praelector in Classics, Corpus Christi Coll., Oxford, 1954–60; J. H. Gray Lecturer, University of Cambridge, 1961; Visiting Prof., Yale Univ., 1964–65, 1967–68; Sather Prof. of Classical Literature, Univ. of California at Berkeley, 1969–70; Alexander White Vis. Prof., Chicago, 1972; Vis. Prof., Harvard Univ., 1976–77. Fellow, Morse Coll., Yale Univ. Hon. Mem., Greek Humanistic Soc., 1968; Corresponding Member: Acad. of Athens, 1978; Rheinisch-Westfälische Akad. der Wissenschaften, 1983; Accademia di Archeologia Lettere e Belle Arti, Naples, 1984; Hon. Foreign Mem., Amer. Acad. of Arts and Scis, 1978. Hon. DHL Chicago, 1970; Hon. DPhil Tel Aviv, 1984. *Publications:* Appendix to Loeb Classical Library edn of Aeschylus, 1957; Menandri Dyscolus (Oxford Classical Text), 1960; Greek Studies in Modern Oxford, 1961; (trans.) Paul Maas, Greek Metre, 1962; (ed) The Greeks, 1962; Tacitus (in series The Great Historians), 1964; (trans.) Aeschylus: Agamemnon, The Libation-Bearers, and The Eumenides, 1970, 2nd edn 1979; The Justice of Zeus, 1971, 2nd edn 1983; (ed) Maurice Bowra, 1974; Females of the Species: Semonides of Amorgos on Women, 1975; (with Marcelle Quinton) Myths of the Zodiac, 1978; (with Marcelle Quinton) Imaginary Animals, 1979; Blood for the Ghosts, 1982; Classical Survivals, 1982; (with P. J. Parsons) Supplementum Hellenisticum, 1983; (with N. G. Wilson) Sophoclis Fabulae, 1990; (with N. G. Wilson) Sophoclea, 1990; Academic Papers (2 vols), 1990; Greek in a Cold Climate, 1990; contribs to periodicals. *Recreations:* cats, remembering past cricket. *Address:* 15 West Riding, Wellesley, Mass 02181, USA. *T:* 617.237.2212; Christ Church, Oxford OX1 1DP. *T:* Oxford (0865) 791063. *Club:* United Oxford & Cambridge University.

LLOYD JONES, Sir Richard (Anthony), KCB 1988 (CB 1981); Permanent Secretary, Welsh Office, since 1985; *b* 1 Aug. 1933; *s* of Robert and Anne Lloyd Jones; *m* 1955, Patricia Avril Mary Richmond; two *d*. *Educ:* Long Dene Sch., Edenbridge; Nottingham High Sch.; Balliol Coll., Oxford (MA). Entered Admiralty, 1957; Asst Private Sec. to First Lord of the Admiralty, 1959–62; Private Sec. to Secretary of the Cabinet, 1969–70; Asst Sec., Min. of Defence, 1970–74; Under Sec., 1974–78, Dep. Sec. 1978–85, Welsh Office. Chm., Civil Service Benevolent Fund, 1987–. Hon. Fellow, UCW Aberystwyth, 1990. *Recreations:* music, walking. *Address:* c/o Welsh Office, Cathays Park, Cardiff CF1 3NQ. *Club:* United Oxford & Cambridge University.

LLOYD-JONES, Robert; Director-General, Brick Development Association, since 1984; *b* 30 Jan. 1931; *s* of Robert and Edith Lloyd-Jones; *m* 1958, Morny Baggs-Thompson (marr. diss. 1977); two *s* one *d*. *Educ:* Wrekin Coll.; Queens' Coll., Univ. of Cambridge (MA Hons); Harvard Business School. Short Service Commission, RN, 1956; Shell International, 1959; BTR Industries Ltd, 1962; International Wool Secretariat, 1964; Schachenmayr, Germany, 1971; British Textile Employers Association, 1977–81; Dir-Gen., Retail Consortium, 1981–83. Governor, Coll. for Distributive Trades, 1982–84; Founder Chm., Nat. Retail Trng Council, 1982–84. Mem., BFI. Member: RN Golf Soc.; China Golfing Soc. Friend of Royal Acad. and of Tate Gall. FRSA. *Recreations:* golf, squash, tennis, music, chess, art, and the general pursuit of pleasure. *Address:* Newell Cottage, Winkfield, Windsor, Berks SL4 4SE. *T:* (office) Winkfield Row (0344) 885651. *Clubs:* Lansdowne, Institute of Directors; Dormy House (Rye); Royal Birkdale Golf, Rye Golf, Formby Golf, Liphook Golf; Royal Ascot Squash, Royal Ascot Tennis.

LLOYD-MOSTYN, family name of **Baron Mostyn.**

LLOYD OWEN, Maj.-Gen. David Lanyon, CB 1971; DSO 1945; OBE 1954; MC 1942; Chairman, Long Range Desert Group Association, since 1945; *b* 10 Oct. 1917; *s* of late Capt. Reginald Charles Lloyd Owen, OBE, RN; *m* 1947, Ursula Evelyn, *d* of late Evelyn Hugh Barclay and Hon. Mrs Barclay, MBE; three *s*. *Educ:* Winchester; RMC, Sandhurst. 2nd Lieut, The Queen's Royal Regt, 1938. Comdr, Long Range Desert Group, 1943–45. Military Asst to High Commissioner in Malaya, 1952–53; Comdg 1st Queen's, 1957–59; Comdr 24 Infantry Bde Group, 1962–64; GOC Cyprus District, 1966–68; GOC Near East Land Forces, 1968–69. Pres., Regular Commns Bd, 1969–72, retd. Kt of Cross of Merit, SMO Malta, 1946. *Publications:* The Desert My Dwelling Place, 1957; Providence Their Guide, 1980. *Address:* Violet Bank, Swainsthorpe, Norwich NR14 8PR. *T:* Swainsthorpe (0508) 470468.

LLOYD WEBBER, Andrew; composer; *b* 22 March 1948; *s* of late William Southcombe Lloyd Webber, CBE, DMus, FRCM, FRCO, and of Jean Hermione Johnstone; *m* 1st, 1971, Sarah Jane Tudor (*née* Hugill) (marr. diss. 1983); one *s* one *d*; 2nd, 1984, Sarah Brightman (marr. diss. 1990); 3rd, 1991, Madeleine Astrid Gurdon. *Educ:* Westminster Sch.; Magdalen Coll., Oxford; Royal Coll. of Music (FRCM 1988). Composer: (with lyrics by Timothy Rice): Joseph and the Amazing Technicolour Dreamcoat, 1968 (rev. 1973); Jesus Christ Superstar, 1970; Evita, 1976 (stage version, 1978); (with lyrics by Alan Ayckbourn) Jeeves, 1975; (with lyrics by Don Black) Tell Me on a Sunday, 1980; Cats, 1981 (based on poems by T. S. Eliot); (with lyrics by Don Black) Song and Dance, 1982; (with lyrics by Richard Stilgoe) Starlight Express, 1984; (with lyrics by Richard Stilgoe and Charles Hart) The Phantom of the Opera, 1986; (with lyrics by Don Black and Charles Hart) Aspects of Love, 1989. Producer: Daisy Pulls It Off, 1983; The Hired Man, 1984; Lend Me a Tenor, 1986. Film scores: Gumshoe, 1971; The Odessa File, 1974. Composed "Variations" (based on A minor Caprice No 24 by Paganini), 1977, symphonic version, 1986; Requiem Mass, 1985. Awards include Tony, Drama Desk, and Grammy. *Publications:* (with Timothy Rice) Evita, 1978; (with Timothy Rice) Joseph and the Amazing Technicolour Dreamcoat, 1982; The Complete Phantom of the Opera, 1987. *Recreation:* architecture. *Address:* Palace Theatre, Shaftesbury Avenue, W1V 8AY.

See also J. Lloyd Webber.

LLOYD WEBBER, Julian; 'cellist; *b* 14 April 1951; *s* of late William Southcombe Lloyd Webber, CBE, DMus, FRCM, FRCO, and of Jean Hermione Johnstone; *m* 1st, 1974, Celia Mary Ballantyne (marr. diss. 1989); 2nd, 1989, Princess Zohra Mahmud Ghazi. *Educ:* University College Sch., London; Royal College of Music. ARCM. Studied 'cello with: Douglas Cameron, 1965–68; Pierre Fournier, Geneva, 1972. Début, Queen Elizabeth Hall, 1972; USA début, Lincoln Center, NY, 1980. Has performed with all major British orchestras; toured: USA, Germany, Holland, Africa, Bulgaria, S America, Spain, Belgium, France, Scandinavia, Portugal, Denmark, Australasia, Singapore, Japan, Korea, Czechoslovakia, Austria, Canada, Hong Kong and Taiwan. Has made first recordings of works by Benjamin Britten, Frank Bridge, Delius, Rodrigo, Holst, Vaughan Williams, Haydn, Sullivan, John McCabe, Malcolm Arnold; recorded: Elgar Cello Concerto (cond. Menuhin), 1985 (British Phonographic Industry Award for Best Classical Recording, 1986); Dvořák Cello Concerto with Czech Philharmonic Orchestra, 1988; also concertos by Delius, Haydn, Honneger, Lalo and Saint-Saens. *Publications:* Travels with My Cello, 1984; Song of the Birds, 1985; edited: series, The Romantic 'Cello, 1978, The Classical 'Cello, 1980, The French 'Cello, 1981; Frank Bridge 'Cello Music, 1981; Young Cellist's Repertoire, Books 1, 2, 3, 1984; Holst, Invocation, 1984; Vaughan Williams, Fantasia on Sussex Folk Tunes, 1984; Recital Repertoire for Cellists, 1987; Short, Sharp Shocks, 1990; contribs to music jls and national Press in UK, US, Canada and Australia. *Recreations:* countryside (especially British), keeping turtles, reading horror stories, beer, Orient FC. *Address:* c/o Patrick Garvey Management, 32 Bigwood Avenue, Hove, E Sussex BN3 6FQ.

See also A. Lloyd Webber.

LO, Kenneth Hsiao Chien; author, Chinese food critic and consultant; *b* 12 Sept. 1913; *s* of Lo Tsung Hsien and Wei Ying; *m* 1954, Anne Phillipe Brown; two *s* two *d*. *Educ:* Yenching Univ., Peking (BA); Cambridge Univ. (MA). Student-Consul for China,

Liverpool, 1942–46; Vice-Consul for China, Manchester, 1946–49. Man. Director, Cathay Arts Ltd (Chinese Fine Art Publishers), 1951–66; Founder Director: Memories of China restaurant, 1980; Ken Lo's Kitchen, chinese cookery sch., 1980. Chm., Chinese Gourmet Club, London, 1975–. *Publications include:* Chinese Food, 1972; Peking Cooking, 1973; Chinese Vegetarian Cooking, 1974; Encyclopedia of Chinese Cookery, 1975; Quick and Easy Chinese Cooking, 1973; Cheap Chow, 1977; Love of Chinese Cooking, 1977; Chinese Provincial Cooking, 1979; Chinese Eating and Cooking for Health, 1979; Wok Cookbook, 1981; Chinese Regional Cooking, 1981. *Recreation:* tennis (Davis cup for China, 1946; Veteran Doubles Champion of Britain, 1976, 1979, 1981, 1982, 1984; Single for UK in Britannia Cup and Crawford Cup (World Super-Veteran Championships), 1981, 1983, 1984, 1985, 1986. *Address:* 60 Sussex Street, SW1. *Clubs:* Hurlingham, Queen's.

LOACH, Kenneth; television and film director; *b* 17 June 1936. *Educ:* King Edward VI School, Nuneaton; St Peter's Hall, Oxford. BBC Trainee, Drama Dept, 1963. Television: Diary of a Young Man, 1964; 3 Clear Sundays, 1965; The End of Arthur's Marriage, 1965; Up The Junction, 1965; Coming Out Party, 1965; Cathy Come Home, 1966; In Two Minds, 1966; The Golden Vision, 1969; The Big Flame, 1969; After A Lifetime, 1971; The Rank and File, 1972; Days of Hope, 1975; The Price of Coal, 1977; The Gamekeeper, 1979; Auditions, 1980; A Question of Leadership, 1981; Questions of Leadership, 1983 (banned from TV); The Red and the Blue, 1983; Which Side Are You On?, 1985. Films: Poor Cow, 1968; Kes, 1970; In Black and White, 1970; Family Life, 1972; Black Jack, 1979; Looks and Smiles, 1981; Fatherland, 1987; The View from the Woodpile, 1988; Hidden Agenda, 1990; Riff-Raff, 1991. *Address:* c/o Judy Daish Associates, 83 Eastbourne Mews, W2.

LOADER, Sir Leslie (Thomas), Kt 1987; CBE 1980; retired company chairman; *b* 27 April 1923; *s* of Edward Robert Loader and Ethel May Loader (*née* Tiller); *m* 1st, 1957, Jennifer; three *d*; 2nd, 1981, Elizabeth. *Educ:* Bitterne Park; Bournemouth Municipal Coll.; London Sch. of Economics and Political Science (occasional student). Served War of 1939–45; commnd Hampshire Regt (now Royal Hampshire Regt); saw active service in Italy. Mem., Southampton Borough Council, 1947–59; contested (C) Southampton, Itchen, 1955; Chairman: Southampton Young Conservatives, 1947; Southampton Itchen Cons. Assoc., 1964–70; Wessex Area Cons. Party, 1972–75; Euro-Cons. Assoc. for Wight and Hants E, 1979–82 (Hon. Treas., 1984–87); Pres., Eastleigh Cons. Assoc., 1985; Founder Chairman: Southern Parishes Cons. Club, Eastleigh; Cosham Cons. Club, Portsmouth N; Hon. Life Vice Pres., Wessex Area, Nat. Union of Cons. and Unionist Assocs, 1990. Founded Rotary Club of Bitterne and Woolston Housing Assoc., 1962 (Chm., 1962–83; Pres., 1983–); Pres., Swaythling Housing Soc. Ltd, 1983– (Chm., 1976–83); Chm., Wessex Body Scanner Appeal, 1980–83; Member: Southampton Harbour Bd, 1951–56; Southampton and SW Hampshire HA, 1981–86; Trustee, Wessex Med. Sch. Trust, 1983–86. Formerly Mem. Ct of Governors, UC Southampton, later Univ. of Southampton. Founder, S Hampshire Aviation Historical Soc., 1980. Freeman, City of London; Liveryman, Painter-Stainers' Co. *Publications:* booklets and articles on housing and political matters. *Recreations:* relaxation, especially sitting; being with nice people. *Club:* Carlton.

LOADES, David Henry, FIA; Directing Actuary (Under Secretary), Government Actuary's Department, since 1983; *b* 16 Oct. 1937; *s* of John Henry Loades and Evelyn Clara Ralph; *m* 1962, Jennifer Glenys Stevens; one *s* two *d*. *Educ:* Beckenham and Penge County Grammar Sch. for Boys. FIA 1961. Govt Actuary's Dept, 1956–. Medal of Merit for services to the Scout Assoc., 1986. *Publications:* papers in actuarial jls. *Recreations:* painting, visiting art galleries, supporting the Institute of Actuaries. *Address:* 22 Kingsway, WC2B 6LE.

LOANE, Most Rev. Marcus Lawrence, KBE 1976; DD; *b* 14 Oct. 1911; *s* of K. O. A. Loane; *m* 1937, Patricia Evelyn Jane Simpson Knox; two *s* two *d*. *Educ:* The King's School, Parramatta, NSW; Sydney University (MA). Moore Theological College, 1932–33; Australian College of Theology (ThL, 1st Class, 1933; Fellow, 1955). Ordained Deacon, 1935, Priest, 1936; Resident Tutor and Chaplain, Moore Theological College, 1935–38; Vice-Principal, 1939–53; Principal, 1954–59. Chaplain AIF, 1942–44. Canon, St Andrew's Cathedral, 1949–58; Bishop-Coadjutor, diocese of Sydney, 1958–66; Archbishop of Sydney and Metropolitan of Province of NSW, 1966–82; Primate of Australia, 1978–82. Hon. DD Wycliffe College, Toronto, 1958. *Publications:* Oxford and the Evangelical Succession, 1950; Cambridge and the Evangelical Succession, 1952; Masters of the English Reformation, 1955; Life of Archbishop Mowll, 1960; Makers of Religious Freedom, 1961; Pioneers of the Reformation in England, 1964; Makers of Our Heritage, 1966; The Hope of Glory, 1968; This Surpassing Excellence, 1969; They Were Pilgrims, 1970; Hewn from the Rock, 1976; Men to Remember, 1987. *Address:* 18 Harrington Avenue, Warrawee, NSW 2074, Australia.

LOBB, Howard Leslie Vicars, CBE 1952; FRIBA, AIStructE, FRSA; architect; *b* 9 March 1909; *e s* of late Hedley Vicars Lobb and Mary Blanche (*née* Luscombe); *m* 1949, Charmian Isobel (*née* Reilly); three *s*. *Educ:* privately; Regent Street Polytechnic School of Architecture. Senior Partner, Howard Lobb Partnership, 1950–74. During War of 1939–45, Architect to various ministries: subseq. built numerous schools for County Authorities; HQ of City and Guilds of London Inst., W1; British Pavilion Brussels International Exhibition, 1958; Cons. Architect for Hunterston Nuclear Power Station, Ayrshire; Dungeness Nuclear Power Station; Newcastle Racecourse; Newmarket Rowley Mile, for Jockey Club; Car park, Savile Row, for City of Westminster; HQ for British Council, SW1; Calgary Exhbn and Stampede, Upper Alberta, Canada. Chairman Architectural Council, Festival of Britain, and later Controller (Constr.) South Bank Exhibition. Member RIBA Council and Executive, 1953–56; Life Vice-Pres. (formerly Chm.), London Group of Building Centres; Chm., Architects' Registr. Council, UK, 1957–60; Vice-Pres., Architects' Benevolent Society, 1980– (Hon. Sec., 1953–80). Freeman of City of London; Master, Worshipful Co. of Masons, 1974–75. Chm., Solent Protection Soc. *Publications:* contrib. various Arch. Journals, Reviews, etc. *Recreations:* sailing, gardening, colour photography, model railways. *Address:* Shallows Cottage, Pilley Hill, Pilley, near Lymington, Hants SO41 5QF. *T:* Lymington (0590) 677595. *Clubs:* Royal Corinthian Yacht (Vice-Cdre 1960–63); Tamesis (Teddington) (Cdre, 1954–57); Royal Lymington Yacht.

LOBO, Sir Rogerio Hyndman, (Sir Roger Lobo), Kt 1985; CBE 1978 (OBE 1972); JP; Chairman, P. J. Lobo & Co. Ltd, Hong Kong, since 1960; Chairman, Broadcasting Authority of Hong Kong, since 1989; *b* 15 Sept. 1923; *s* of Dr P. J. Lobo and Branca Helena (*née* Hyndman); *m* 1947, Margaret Mary (*née* Choa); five *s* five *d*. *Educ:* Escola Central, Macao; Seminario de S Jose, Macao; Liceu Nacional Infante Dom Henrique, Macao; La Salle Coll., Hong Kong. Director: Associated Liquor Distributors, 1975–; Danish Fancy Food Group (HK), 1982–; HK Macao Hydrofoil Co., 1970–; dir of 14 other cos. Unofficial MLC, Hong Kong, 1972–85 (Sen. Mem., 1980–85); Unofficial MEC, 1978–85. Member: Urban Council, 1965–78; Housing Authority, 1967–83; Chm., Adv. Cttee on Post-Retirement Employment, 1987–; Comr, Civil Aid Services, 1977– (Mem., 1955–). Hon. LLD Univ. of Hong Kong, 1982. JP Hong Kong, 1963. Silver Jubilee Medal, 1977; Civil Aid Services Long Service Medal, 1970; Civil Defence Long Service Clasp, 1982. Comdr, Order of St Gregory the Great, The Vatican, 1969. *Recreation:* golf. *Address:* Woodland Heights, E1, 2 Wongneichong Gap Road, Hong Kong. *T:* 574 0779; (business) 33/F New World Tower, 16–18 Queen's Road, C., Hong Kong. *T:* 526 9418/521 8302. *Clubs:* Dynasty, Hong Kong, Rotary, Royal Hong Kong Jockey, Royal Hong Kong Golf, Hong Kong Country, Shek O Country (Hong Kong).

LOCK, Lt-Comdr Sir Duncan; *see* Lock, Lt-Comdr Sir J. D.

LOCK, (George) David; Secretary, Frizzell Foundation, since 1989; *b* 24 Sept. 1929; *s* of George Wilfred Lock and Phyllis Nita (*née* Hollingworth); *m* 1965, Ann Elizabeth Biggs; four *s* one *d*. *Educ:* Haileybury and ISC; Queens' Coll., Cambridge (MA). British Tabulating Machine Co. Ltd (now ICL), 1954–59; Save & Prosper Group Ltd, 1959–69; American Express, 1969–74; Private Patients Plan Ltd, 1974–85 (Man. Dir, 1975–85); Dir, Plan for Active Retirement, Frizzell Insce and Financial Services Ltd (formerly New Business Ventures, Frizzell Consumer Services Ltd), 1986–89. Director: Priplan Investments Ltd, 1979–85; Priplan Services Ltd, 1979–85; PPP Medical Centre Ltd (incorp. Cavendish Medical Centre), 1981–85. Director: Home Concern for the Elderly, 1985–87, 1989–; The Hosp. Management Trust, 1985–; Bd of Management, St Anthony's Hosp., Cheam, 1986–. Sec., Friends of Children of Great Ormond Street, 1986. Trustee, Eynsham Trust, 1975–83; Gov., PPP Medical Trust Ltd (Dir, 1983–89). Member: Nuffield Nursing Homes Trust, 1979–; Exec. Cttee, Assoc. of Independent Hosps, 1981–87. Mem., RSocMed., 1979–. Freeman, Barbers' Co., 1982–. *Recreations:* bridge, music, family activities, entertaining. *Address:* Buckhurst Place, Horsted Keynes, Sussex RH17 7AH. *T:* Danehill (0825) 790599.

LOCK, Graham; *see* Lock, T. G.

LOCK, John Arthur, QPM 1975; Deputy Assistant Commissioner, Metropolitan Police, and National Co-ordinator, Regional Crime Squads of England and Wales, 1976–79, retired; *b* 20 Oct. 1922; *s* of Sidney George Lock and Minnie Louise Lock; *m* 1950, Patricia Joyce Lambert; two *d*. *Educ:* George Palmer Central School, Reading. Royal Air Force, 1941–46; Wireless Operator/Air Gunner; Flying Officer. Joined Metropolitan Police, 1946. *Recreations:* Association football (Vice-Chm., Met. Police FC), golf. *Club:* Royal Air Force.

LOCK, Lt-Comdr Sir (John) Duncan, Kt 1978; RN; Chairman, Association of District Councils of England and Wales, 1974–79; *b* 5 Feb. 1918; *s* of Brig. Gen. F. R. E. Lock, DSO, and Mary Elizabeth Lock; *m* 1947, Alice Aileen Smith (*d* 1982); three *d*. *Educ:* Royal Naval Coll., Dartmouth. Served as regular officer in Royal Navy (retiring at his own request), 1931–58: specialised in navigation and navigated Battleships HMS King George V and Howe, the Cruiser Superb, destroyers and minesweepers. Served War of 1939–45: took part in Battle of Atlantic, Norwegian and N African campaigns, Pacific War and Normandy and Anzio landings. Farmed family estate in Somerset, 1958–61. Admty Compass Observatory as specialist in magnetic compasses, 1962–83. Member of Lloyd's. Eton RDC, 1967–74; Chairman: Bucks Br., RDC Assoc., 1969–74; S Bucks Dist Council, 1985–87 (Mem., 1973–); Assoc. of Dist Councils of England and Wales Council and Policy Cttee, 1974–79 (Chm. Bucks Br., 1974–); Rep. Body for England, 1977–89; Local Authorities Management Services and Computer Cttee, 1981–86; Mem., Adv. Cttee on Local Govt Audit, 1979–82; British Rep., Conference of Local and Reg. Authorities of Europe, 1979–. Chm., Beaconsfield Constituency Conservative Assoc., 1972–75; Mem., S Bucks Housing Assoc., 1990– (Chm., 1990–91). *Recreations:* gardening, shooting. *Address:* Fen Court, Oval Way, Gerrards Cross, Bucks SL9 8QD. *T:* Gerrards Cross (0753) 882467.

LOCK, Stephen Penford, CBE 1991; MA, MD; FRCP; Editor, British Medical Journal, 1975–91; Governor, Brendoncare Foundation, since 1984; *b* 8 April 1929; *er s* of Wallace Henry Lock, Romford, Essex; *m* 1955, Shirley Gillian Walker, *d* of E. W. Walker, Bridlington, Yorks; one *d* (one *s* decd). *Educ:* City of London Sch.; Queens' Coll., Cambridge; St Bartholomew's Hosp., London. MA 1953; MB 1954; MD 1987; MRCP 1963; FRCP 1974; FACP 1989; FRCPE 1989. Jun. hosp. appts, 1954–63; Asst Editor, British Med. Jl, 1964–69, Sen. Asst Editor, 1969–74, Dep. Editor, 1974–75. Med. Corresp., BBC Overseas Service, 1966–74. Chm., Internat. Gp on Medical Jl Style, 1978. Organiser and/or participant in numerous Postgrad. Courses in Med. Writing and confs in scientific editing worldwide, 1971–. Member: RCP cttee on dietary fibre, 1978, on smoking, 1982, on relations with the pharmaceutical industry, 1984, on medical fraud, 1989 (Hon. Sec.); Med. Inf. Review Panel, 1979–; Managing Cttee, Bureau of Hygiene and Tropical Diseases, 1981–; Council, Inst. of Med. Ethics, 1986–; KCH Delegacy, 1989–. Vice-Pres., Internat. Union of the Medical Press, 1976–; Pres., 1982–85, Mem. Council, 1985–91, European Assoc. of Sci. Editors. Vis. Prof. in Medicine, McGill Univ., 1978; Visitor, Acad. Dept of Medicine, Monash Univ., 1982; Foundn Vis. Prof. in Medicine, RCSI, 1986; Lectures: Wade, Keele Univ., 1980; Morgan, Royal Cornwall Hosp., 1984; Rock Carling, Nuffield Provincial Hosps Trust, 1985; Maurice Bloch, Glasgow Univ., 1986; Wolfson, Wolfson Coll., Oxford, 1986; Estelle Brodman, Washington Univ., St Louis, 1989; Sarah Davies, TCD, 1990; William Hey, Leeds Univ., 1990. Vice-Pres., Friends of Norham Gardens, 1986–. Hon. FRCPI 1987; Hon. Mem., BPA, 1991. Hon. MSc Manchester, 1985. Donders Medal, Ned. Tijdsch. Geneesk, 1981; Internat. Medal, Finnish Med. Soc. Duodecim, 1981; Medal of Honour, Finnish Med. Jl, 1987. Officer, first cl., White Rose of Finland, 1982. *Publications:* An Introduction to Clinical Pathology, 1965; Health Centres and Group Practices, 1966; The Enemies of Man, 1968; Better Medical Writing, 1970; Family Health Guide, 1972; Medical Risks of Life, 1976; Thorne's Better Medical Writing, 2nd edn 1977; (ed) Adverse Drug Reactions, 1977; (ed) Remembering Henry, 1977; A Difficult Balance: editorial peer review in medicine, 1985; chapter on jls and journalism in Oxford Companion to Medicine, 1983. *Recreations:* as much opera as possible (before Stockhausen), hill walking, gardening. *Address:* 115 Dulwich Village, SE21 7BJ. *T:* 081–693 6317. *Club:* Athenæum.

LOCK, (Thomas) Graham; Chief Executive, Amalgamated Metal Corporation plc, 1983–91; *b* 19 Oct. 1931; *s* of Robert Henry Lock and Morfydd Lock (*née* Thomas); *m* 1954, Janice Olive Baker Lock (*née* Jones); two *d*. *Educ:* Whitchurch Grammar School; University College of South Wales and Monmouthshire (BSc Metall); College of Advanced Technology, Aston; Harvard Business School. CEng, FIM, CBIM. Instructor Lieut, RN, 1953–56; Lucas Industries and Lucas Electrical, 1956–61; Dir, Girling Bremsen GmbH, 1961–66; Gen. Man. and Overseas Ops Dir, Girling Ltd, 1966–73; Gen. Man. and Dir, Lucas Service Overseas Ltd, 1973–79; Man. Dir, Industrial Div., Amalgamated Metal Corp., 1979–83; non-exec. Director: Marshall's Universal plc, 1983–86; Evode Gp plc, 1985–. Liveryman, Co. of Gold and Silver Wyre Drawers, 1988–. Freeman, City of London, 1987. *Recreations:* sailing, music, skiing. *Address:* The Cottage, Fulmer Way, Gerrards Cross, Bucks SL9 8AJ. *T:* Gerrards Cross (0753) 883200. *Clubs:* Royal Naval Sailing Association (Portsmouth), Royal Southern Yacht (Hamble).

LOCKE, John Howard, CB 1984; Chairman, National Examination Board in Occupational Safety and Health, since 1986; *b* 26 Dec. 1923; *s* of Percy Locke and Josephine Locke (*née* Marshfield); *m* 1948, Eirene Sylvia Sykes; two *d*. *Educ:* Hymers

Coll., Hull; Queen's Coll., Oxford. MIOSH. Ministry of Agriculture, Fisheries and Food, 1945–65; Under-Secretary: Cabinet Office, 1965–66; MoT, 1966–68; Dept of Employment and Productivity, 1968–71; Dep. Sec., Dept of Employment, 1971–74; Dir, Health and Safety Exec., 1975–83. *Address:* 4 Old Palace Terrace, The Green, Richmond-on-Thames, Surrey TW9 1NB. *T:* 081–940 1830; Old Box Trees, East Preston, Sussex BN16 1JP.

LOCKETT, Reginald; His Honour Judge Lockett; a Circuit Judge, since 1981; *b* 24 June 1933; *s* of George Alfred Lockett and Emma (*née* Singleton); *m* 1959, Edna (*née* Lowe); one *s* one *d. Educ:* Ashton-in-Makerfield Grammar Sch.; Manchester Univ.; London Univ. (LLB 1954). Solicitor, 1955. Asst Coroner for Wigan, 1963–70; Dist Registrar and County Court Registrar, Manchester, 1970–81; a Recorder of the Crown Court, 1978–81. Pres., Manchester Law Students' Soc., 1975–77. Vice Pres., The Boys' Bde, 1978– (Dist Pres., NW Dist, 1973–90). Reader, Anglican Church, 1970–. Editor, Butterworths Family Law Service, 1983–90; Consultant Editor, Sweet-Maxwell's High Court Litigation Manual, 1990. *Recreations:* music, photography. *Address:* c/o The Sessions House, Lancaster Road, Preston PR1 2PD. *T:* Preston (0772) 21451.

LOCKHART, Brian Alexander; Sheriff in Glasgow and Strathkelvin, since 1981 (in North Strathclyde, 1979–81); *b* 1 Oct. 1942; *s* of John Arthur Hay Lockhart and Norah Lockhart; *m* 1967, Christine Ross Clark; two *s* two *d. Educ:* Glasgow Academy; Glasgow Univ. (BL). Qualified as solicitor, 1964; Partner in Robertson Chalmers & Auld, Solicitors, Glasgow, 1966–79. *Recreations:* fishing, golf, family. *Address:* 18 Hamilton Avenue, Glasgow G41 4JF. *T:* 041–427 1921.

LOCKHART, Frank Roper; His Honour Judge Lockhart; a Circuit Judge, since 1988; *b* 8 Dec. 1931; *s* of Clement and Betsy Lockhart; *m* 1958, Brenda Harriett Johnson; one *s* one *d. Educ:* King Edward VI Sch., Retford; Doncaster Grammar Sch.; Univ. of Leeds (LLB Hons). Asst Town Clerk, Southend-on-Sea, 1960–65; Partner, Jefferies, Solicitors, 1965–87. Chairman: Industrial Tribunal, 1983–87; Social Security Tribunal, 1970–87; a Recorder, 1985–88. *Recreations:* golf, tennis, Rack. *Address:* Snaresbrook Crown Court, The Court House, Hollybush Hill, Snaresbrook, E11 1QW. *Clubs:* Thorpe Hall Golf, Hazards Golf, Chigwell Golf.

LOCKHART, Harry Eugene, (Gene), CPA; Chief Executive, Group Operations, since 1988, and UK Banking, since 1990, Midland Bank plc; *b* 4 Nov. 1949; *s* of Harry Eugene Lockhart, Sen., Austin, Texas, and Gladys Cummings Lockhart; *m* 1974, Terry Lockhart; one *s* three *d. Educ:* Univ. of Virginia (MechEng degree); Darden Graduate Bus. Sch. (MBA). CPA 1976. Sen. Cons., Arthur Anderson & Co., 1974–77; Man. Principal, Europe, Nolan Norton & Co., 1977–82; Gp Dir, Management Services, C. T. Bowring & Co., 1982–85; Vice Pres., First Manhattan Consulting Gp, 1985–87; Chief Exec., IT, Midland Bank, 1987–88. *Recreations:* tennis, golf, running, ski-ing, photography, riding, classical music, ballet. *Address:* Midland Bank plc, 27–32 Poultry, EC2P 2BX. *T:* 071–260 7358. *Clubs:* Royal Automobile, Annabel's, Vanderbilt; St George's Hill (Liphook).

LOCKHART, James Lawrence, FRCM, FRCO(CHM); Director of Opera, Royal College of Music, since 1986; *b* 16 Oct. 1930; *s* of Archibald Campbell Lockhart and Mary Black Lawrence; *m* 1954, Sheila Margaret Grogan; two *s* one *d. Educ:* George Watson's Boys' College; Edinburgh Univ. (BMus); Royal College of Music (ARCM, FRCM). Yorkshire Symphony Orchestra, 1954–55; Münster City Opera, 1955–56; Bavarian State Opera, 1956–57; Glyndebourne Festival Opera, 1957, 1958, 1959; Opera Workshop, Univ. of Texas, 1957–59; Royal Opera House, Covent Garden, 1959–60; BBC Scottish Orchestra, 1960–61; Scottish Opera, 1960–61; Conductor, Sadler's Wells Opera, 1961–62; Conductor and Repetiteur, Royal Opera House, Covent Garden, 1962–68; Music Dir, Welsh National Opera, 1968–73; General-musikdirektor: Staatstheater, Kassel, 1972–80; Koblenz Opera, 1981–88; Rheinische Philharmonie, 1981–91. *Recreations:* swimming, hill-walking, driving fast cars. *Address:* 105 Woodcock Hill, Harrow, Middx HA3 0JJ. *T:* 081–907 2112. *Club:* Savage.

LOCKHART, Sir Simon John Edward Francis S.; *see* Sinclair-Lockhart.

LOCKHART-MUMMERY, Christopher John; QC 1986; *b* 7 Aug. 1947; *s* of Sir Hugh Lockhart-Mummery, KCVO, MD, MChir, FRCS and late Elizabeth Jean Crerar, *d* of Sir James Crerar, KCSI, CIE; *m* 1971, Elizabeth Rosamund, *d* of N. P. M. Elles, *qv* and of Baroness Elles, *qv*; one *s* two *d. Educ:* Stowe; Trinity College, Cambridge (BA). Called to the Bar, Inner Temple, 1971 (Bencher, 1991). Specialist Editor, Hill and Redman's Law of Landlord and Tenant, 1974–89. *Recreations:* fishing, listening to music, opera, gardening.

LOCKLEY, Andrew John Harold; Director, Legal Practice, The Law Society, since 1987; *b* 10 May 1951; *s* of Ven. Harold Lockley, *qv*; *m* 1974, Ruth Mary Vigor; two *s* one *d. Educ:* Marlborough Coll.; Oriel Coll., Oxford (BA Lit. Hum. 1973; MA 1982). Admitted a Solicitor, 1979. Res. Fellow, World Council of Churches, 1973–75; Solicitor in private practice, 1979–82; Asst Sec., 1982–85, Sec., 1985–87, Contentious Business Dept, The Law Soc. Mem., Commn on Efficiency in the Criminal Courts, 1986–. A Dir, Solicitors' Financial and Property Services Ltd, 1988–. *Publications:* Christian Communes, 1976; contribs to legal periodicals. *Recreations:* growing fruit and vegetables, swimming, walking, cooking. *Address:* The Law Society, 113 Chancery Lane, WC2A 1PL. *T:* 071–242 1222.

LOCKLEY, Ven. Harold; Archdeacon of Loughborough, 1963–86, Archdeacon Emeritus since 1986; Post-graduate research student, Emmanuel College, Cambridge, since 1986; *b* 16 July 1916; *s* of Harry and Sarah Elizabeth Lockley; *m* 1947, Ursula Margaret, JP (*d* 1990), *d* of Rev. Dr H. Wedell and Mrs G. Wedell (*née* Bonhoeffer); three *s. Educ:* Loughborough Coll. (Hons Dip. Physical Education); London University; Westcott House, Cambridge. BA Hons 1937, BD Hons 1943, MTh 1949, London Univ.; PhD 1955, Nottingham Univ.; MLitt Cantab 1990. Served RN, 1940–46. Chaplain and Tutor, Loughborough Coll., 1946–51; Vicar of Glen Parva and South Wigston, 1951–58; Canon Chancellor of Leicester Cathedral, 1958–63; Vicar of All Saints, Leicester, 1963–78. OCF Royal Leics Regt, 1951–58; Chaplain, Leics Yeomanry Assoc., 1968–; Chaplain, Leicester Royal Infirmary Maternity Hospital, 1967–74; Proctor in Convocation of Canterbury, 1960–80. Sen. Examining Chaplain to Bishop of Leicester, 1951–79; part-time Lectr in Divinity, Univ. of Leicester, 1953–86; Mem., Leics Educn Cttee, 1973–85. Chm., Anglican Young People's Assoc., 1966–86. Founder Governor, Leicester Grammar Sch., 1981–. *Publications:* Editor, Leicester Cathedral Quarterly, 1960–63. *Recreations:* walking and foreign travel. *Address:* 7 Dower House Gardens, Quorn, Leics LE12 8DE. *T:* Quorn (0509) 412843; Emmanuel College, Cambridge. *Club:* Leicestershire (Leicester).

See also Prof. E. A. O. G. Wedell, A. J. H. Lockley.

LOCKLEY, Ronald Mathias; author and naturalist; *b* 8 Nov. 1903. Hon. MSc Wales, 1977. *Publications:* Dream Island, 1930, rev. 1988; The Island Dwellers, 1932; Island Days, 1934; The Sea's a Thief, 1936; Birds of the Green Belt, 1936; I Know an Island, 1938; Early Morning Island, 1939; A Pot of Smoke, 1940; The Way to an Island, 1941; Shearwaters, 1942; Dream Island Days, 1943; Inland Farm, 1943; Islands Round Britain, 1945; Birds of the Sea, 1946; The Island Farmers, 1947; Letters from Skokholm, 1947; The Golden Year, 1948; The Cinnamon Bird, 1948; Birds of Pembrokeshire, 1949; The Charm of the Channel Islands, 1950; (with John Buxton) Island of Skomer, 1951; Travels with a Tent in Western Europe, 1953; Puffins, 1953; (with Rosemary Russell) Bird Ringing, 1953; The Seals and the Curragh, 1954; Gilbert White, 1954; (with James Fisher) Sea-Birds, 1954; Pembrokeshire, 1957; The Pan Book of Cage Birds, 1961; Britain in Colour, 1964; The Private Life of the Rabbit, 1964; Wales, 1966; Grey Seal, Common Seal, 1966; Animal Navigation, 1967; The Book of Bird-Watching, 1968; The Channel Islands, 1968, rev. edn, A Traveller's Guide to the Channel Islands, 1971; The Island, 1969; The Naturalist in Wales, 1970; Man Against Nature, 1970; Seal Woman, 1974; Ocean Wanderers, 1974; Orielton, 1977; Myself when Young, 1979; Whales, Dolphins & Porpoises, 1979; (with Noel Cusa) New Zealand Endangered Species, 1980; The House Above the Sea, 1980; (with Richard Adams) Voyage Through the Antarctic, 1982; Flight of the Storm Petrel, 1983; (with Geoff Moon) New Zealand's Birds, 1983; The Lodge above the Waterfall, 1987; (with Betty Brownlie) Secrets of Natural New Zealand, 1987; Birds and Islands: travels in far places, 1991; *edited:* Natural History of Selborne, by G. White, 1949, rev. edn 1976; Nature Lover's Anthology, 1951; The Bird-Lover's Bedside Book, 1958; *compiled:* In Praise of Islands, 1957. *Address:* 6 Calder Place, Auckland 6, New Zealand.

LOCKLEY, Stephen Randolph, FCIT; Director General, Strathclyde Passenger Transport Executive, since 1986; *b* 19 June 1943; *s* of Randolph and Edith Lockley; *m* 1968, Angela; two *d. Educ:* Manchester Univ. (BScCivEng, 1st Cl. Hons). MICE; MIHT; FCIT 1987. Lancashire County Council: North West Road Construction Unit, Highway Engrg and Planning, 1964–72; Highway/Transportation Planning, 1972–75; Lanarkshire CC, Strathclyde Regional Council: Prin. Engr (Transportation), 1975–77; Depute Dir of Policy Planning, 1977–80; Prin. Exec. Officer, 1980–86. *Address:* 64 Townhead Street, Strathaven ML10 6DJ. *T:* Strathaven (0357) 21774.

LOCKWOOD, Baroness *cr* 1978 (Life Peer), of Dewsbury, W Yorks; **Betty Lockwood;** DL; President, Birkbeck College, London, 1983–89; a Deputy Speaker, House of Lords, since 1989; *b* 22 Jan. 1924; *d* of Arthur Lockwood and Edith Alice Lockwood; *m* 1978, Lt-Col Cedric Hall (*d* 1988). *Educ:* Eastborough Girls' Sch., Dewsbury; Ruskin Coll., Oxford. Chief Woman Officer and Asst Nat. Agent of Labour Party, 1967–75; Chm., Equal Opportunities Commn, 1975–83. Vice-Chm., Internat. Council of Social Democratic Women, 1969–75; Chm., Adv. Cttee to European Commn on Equal Opportunities for Women and Men, 1982–83. Chm., Mary Macarthur Educnl Trust, 1971–; Pres., Mary Macarthur Holiday Homes, 1990– (Chm., 1971–90). Member: Dept of Employment Adv. Cttee on Women's Employment, 1969–83; Adv. Council on Energy Conservation, 1977–80; Council, Advertising Standards Authority, 1983–; Leeds Urban Develt Corp., 1988–. Pres., Hillcroft Coll., 1987–. Member, Council: Bradford Univ., 1983– (a Pro-Chancellor, 1988–); Leeds Univ., 1985–. Hon. Fellow: UMIST, 1986; Birkbeck Coll., 1987. Hon. DLitt Bradford, 1981; Hon. LLD Strathclyde, 1985. DL W Yorks, 1987. Editor, Labour Woman, 1967–71. *Recreations:* walking and country pursuits, music. *Address:* 6 Sycamore Drive, Addingham, Ilkley LS29 0NY. *Club:* Soroptomist.

LOCKWOOD, Prof. David, FBA 1976; Professor of Sociology, since 1968, and Pro-Vice-Chancellor, since 1989, University of Essex; *b* 9 April 1929; *s* of Herbert Lockwood and Edith A. (*née* Lockwood); *m* 1954, Leonore Davidoff; three *s. Educ:* Honley Grammar Sch.; London Sch. of Economics. BSc(Econ) London, 1st Cl. Hons 1952; PhD London, 1957. Trainee, textile industry, 1944–47; Cpl, Intell. Corps, Austria, 1947–49. Asst Lectr and Lectr, London Sch. of Economics, 1953–60; Rockefeller Fellow, Univ. of California, Berkeley, 1958–59; Univ. Lectr, Faculty of Economics, and Fellow, St John's Coll., Cambridge, 1960–68. Visiting Professor: Dept of Sociology, Columbia Univ., 1966–67; Delhi Univ., 1975; Stockholm Univ., 1989. Mem., SSRC (Chm., Sociol. and Soc. Admin Cttee), 1973–76. Mem., Academia Europaea, 1990. *Publications:* The Blackcoated Worker, 1958, 2nd edn 1989; (jtly) The Affluent Worker in the Class Structure, 3 vols, 1968–69; Solidarity and Schism, 1991; numerous articles in jls and symposia. *Address:* 82 High Street, Wivenhoe, Essex. *T:* Wivenhoe (020622) 3530.

LOCKWOOD, Robert; General Director, Overseas Planning and Project Development, General Motors Corporation, 1982–85, retired; *b* 14 April 1920; *s* of Joseph A. Lockwood and Sylvia Lockwood; *m* 1947, Phyllis M. Laing; one *s* one *d. Educ:* Columbia Univ. (AB); Columbia Law Sch. (LLB). Attorney, Bar of New York, 1941; US Dist of New York and US Supreme Court, 1952. Pilot, USAAF (8th Air Force), 1944–45. Attorney: Ehrich, Royall, Wheeler & Holland, New York, 1941 and 1946–47; Sullivan & Cromwell, New York, 1947–54; Sec. and Counsel, Cluett, Peabody & Co., Inc., New York, 1955–57; Man. Dir, Cluett, Peabody & Co., Ltd, London, 1957–59; General Motors: Overseas Ops, Planning and Develt, 1960–61; Asst to Man. Dir, GM Argentina, Buenos Aires, 1962; Asst to Man. Dir, and Manager, Parts, Power and Appliances, GM Continental, Antwerp, 1964–66; Branch Man., Netherlands Br., GM Continental, Rotterdam, 1967–68; Man., Planning and Develt, GM Overseas Ops, New York, 1969–73; Vice Pres., GM Overseas Corp., and Gen. Man., Japan Br., 1974–76; Exec. Vice Pres., Isuzu Motors Ltd, Tokyo, 1976; Chm., GM European Adv. Council, 1977–82. Mem., Panel of Arbitrators, Amer. Arbitration Assoc., 1989–. *Recreations:* tennis, chess, reading. *Address:* 126 Littlefield Road, Monterey, Calif 93940, USA. *Clubs:* Royal Air Force, Hurlingham; Monterey Peninsula Country, Spanish Bay, Beach and Tennis (Pebble Beach).

LOCKYER, Rear-Adm. (Alfred) Austin, LVO 1973; Chief Staff Officer (Engineering) to Commander-in-Chief Fleet, 1982–84, retired; Director General, Timber Trade Federation, since 1985; *b* 4 March 1929; *s* of Austin Edmund Lockyer and late Jane Russell (*née* Goldman); *m* 1965, Jennifer Ann Simmons; one *s. Educ:* Frome County School; Taunton School; Royal Naval Engineering College. Entered RN 1947; Comdr 1965; Staff of Commander Far East Fleet, 1965–67; jssc, 1968–69; Ship Dept, 1969–71; HMY Britannia, 1971–73; Captain 1973; sowc, 1973–74; Naval Ship Production Overseer, Scotland and NI, 1974–76; Dep. Dir, Fleet Maintenance, 1976–78; Dir, Naval Officers Appointments (Engrg), 1978–80; HMS Sultan in Comd, 1980–82; ADC to the Queen, 1981; Rear-Adm. 1982. Governor: Forres Sch., Swanage, 1980– (Chm., 1983–); Sherborne Sch., 1981–. *Recreations:* gardening, listening to good music and watching sport. *Address:* 8 Darlington Place, Bath, Avon BA2 6BX. *Clubs:* Army and Navy, Commonwealth Trust.

LODER, family name of **Baron Wakehurst.**

LODER, Sir Giles Rolls, 3rd Bt, *cr* 1887; DL; *b* 10 Nov. 1914; *o s* of late Capt. Robert Egerton Loder, *s* of 2nd Bt, and late Muriel Rolls, *d* of J. Rolls-Hoare; *S* grandfather, 1920; *m* 1939, Marie, *o c* of Bertram Hanmer Bunbury Symons-Jeune; two *s. Educ:* Eton; Trinity Coll., Cambridge (MA). High Sheriff of Sussex, 1948–49; DL West Sussex, 1977. Vice-Pres., RHS, 1983–. VMH 1971. *Recreations:* sailing, horticulture. *Heir:* *s* Edmund Jeune Loder [*b* 26 June 1941; *m* 1966, Penelope Jane (marr. diss. 1971), *d* of Ivo Forde; one *d*]. *Address:* Ockenden House, Cuckfield, Haywards Heath, West Sussex RH17 5LD. *T:* Haywards Heath (0444) 459433; Leonardslee Gardens, Horsham, Sussex. *Club:* Royal Yacht Squadron.

LODGE, Anton James Corduff; QC 1989; *b* 17 April 1944; *s* of Sir Thomas Lodge, *qv*. *Educ:* Ampleforth College; Gonville and Caius College, Cambridge (MA). Called to the Bar, Gray's Inn, 1966; a Recorder, 1985. *Recreations:* cricket, tennis, ski-ing, music, theatre. *Address:* Park Court Chambers, Park Cross Street, Leeds LS1 2QH. *T:* Leeds (0532) 433277. *Club:* Yorkshire (York).

LODGE, Prof. David John, MA, PhD; FRSL 1976; Professor 1976–87, Hon. Professor, since 1987, of Modern English Literature, University of Birmingham; *b* 28 Jan. 1935; *s* of William Frederick Lodge and Rosalie Marie Lodge (*née* Murphy); *m* 1959, Mary Frances Jacob; two *s* one *d*. *Educ:* St Joseph's Acad., Blackheath; University College, London (Fellow, 1982). BA hons, MA (London); PhD (Birm). National Service, RAC, 1955–57. British Council, London, 1959–60. Univ. of Birmingham: Asst Lectr in English, 1960–62; Lectr, 1963–71; Sen. Lectr, 1971–73; Reader in English, 1973–76. Harkness Commonwealth Fellow, 1964–65; Visiting Associate Prof., Univ. of California, Berkeley, 1969; Henfield Writing Fellow, Univ. of E Anglia, 1977. Yorkshire Post Fiction Prize, 1975; Hawthornden Prize, 1976; Whitbread Book of the Year Award, 1980; Sunday Express Book of the Year Award, 1988. Stage play, The Writing Game, Birmingham Rep., 1990. *Publications: novels:* The Picturegoers, 1960; Ginger, You're Barmy, 1962; The British Museum is Falling Down, 1965; Out of the Shelter, 1970, rev. edn 1985; Changing Places, 1975; How Far Can You Go?, 1980; Small World, 1984 (televised 1988); Nice Work, 1988 (adapted for television, 1989); Paradise News, 1991; *criticism:* Language of Fiction, 1966; The Novelist at the Crossroads, 1971; The Modes of Modern Writing, 1977; Working with Structuralism, 1981; Write On, 1986; After Bakhtin (essays), 1990; *edited:* Jane Austen's Emma: a casebook, 1968; Twentieth Century Literary Criticism, 1972; Modern Criticism and Theory, 1988. *Recreations:* tennis, television, cinema. *Address:* c/o Department of English, University of Birmingham, Birmingham B15 2TT. *T:* 021–414 3344.

LODGE, Prof. Geoffrey Arthur, BSc, PhD, FIBiol; FRSE 1986; Professor of Animal Science, Sultan Qaboos University, Muscat, 1986–90, retired; *b* 18 Feb. 1930; *m* 1956, Thelma (*née* Calder); one *s* two *d*. *Educ:* Durham University (BSc). PhD Aberdeen. Formerly Reader in Animal Production, Univ. of Nottingham School of Agriculture, and Principal Research Scientist, Animal Research Inst., Ottawa; Strathcona-Fordyce Prof. of Agriculture, Univ. of Aberdeen, and Principal, North of Scotland Coll. of Agriculture, 1978–86. FRSA. *Publications:* (ed jointly) Growth and Development of Mammals, 1968; contribs to journals and books. *Recreations:* food, malt whisky, travelling, house restoration. *Address:* The Shoemaker's, Glenkindie, Alford, Aberdeenshire. *Club:* Farmers'.

LODGE, Oliver Raymond William Wynlayne; Regional Chairman of Industrial Tribunals, London (South), since 1980; *b* Painswick, Glos, 2 Sept. 1922; *e s* of Oliver William Foster Lodge and Winifred, (Wynlayne), *o d* of Sir William Nicholas Atkinson, ISO, LLD; *m* 1953, Charlotte (*d* 1990), *o d* of Col Arthur Davidson Young, CMG; one *s* two *d*. *Educ:* Bryanston Sch.; King's Coll., Cambridge. BA 1943, MA 1947. Officer-cadet, Royal Fusiliers, 1942. Called to the Bar, Inner Temple, 1945; admitted *ad eundem*, Lincoln's Inn, 1949, Bencher, 1973; practised at Chancery Bar, 1945–74; Permanent Chairman of Industrial Tribunals, 1975–. Member: Bar Council, 1952–56, 1967–71; Supreme Court Rules Cttee, 1968–71. Gen. Comr of Income Tax, Lincoln's Inn, 1983–91. *Publications:* (ed) Rivington's Epitome of Snell's Equity, 3rd edn, 1948; (ed) Fraudulent and Voidable Conveyances, article in Halsbury's Laws of England, 3rd edn, 1956; contribs to legal periodicals. *Recreations:* walking, bell-ringing, reading history, formerly sailing. *Address:* Southridge House, Hindon, Salisbury, Wilts. *T:* Hindon (074789) 238; 8 Stone Buildings, Lincoln's Inn, WC2. *T:* 071–831 0681. *Clubs:* Garrick; Bar Yacht.

LODGE, Sir Thomas, Kt 1974; Consultant Radiologist, United Sheffield Hospitals, 1946–74, retired; Clinical Lecturer, Sheffield University, 1960–74; *b* 25 Nov. 1909; *s* of James Lodge and Margaret (*née* Lowery); *m* 1940, Aileen Corduff (*d* 1990); one *s* one *d*. *Educ:* Univ. of Sheffield. MB, ChB 1934, FFR 1945, FRCP 1967, FRCS 1967. Asst Radiologist: Sheffield Radium Centre, 1936; Manchester Royal Infirmary, 1937–38; 1st Asst in Radiology, United Sheffield Hosps, 1938–46; Cons. Adviser in Radiology, DHSS, 1965–74. Fellow, BMA, 1968; Hon. FRSocMed; Hon. FFR RCSI; Hon. FRACR 1963; Hon. FACR 1975; Hon. MSR 1975; Hon. Mem., British Inst. of Radiology, 1990. Twining Medal, 1945, Knox Lectr, 1962, Pres., 1963–66, Faculty of Radiologists. Gold Medal, RCR, 1986. Hon. Editor, Clinical Radiology, 1954–59. Hon. MD Sheffield, 1985. *Publications:* Recent Advances in Radiology, 3rd edn 1955, 4th edn 1964, 5th edn 1975, 6th edn 1979; articles in Brit. Jl Radiology, Clinical Radiology, etc. *Recreation:* gardening. *Address:* 46 Braemore Court, Kingsway, Hove, E Sussex BN3 4FG. *T:* Brighton (0273) 724371.

See also A. J. C. Lodge.

LODGE, Thomas C. S.; *see* Skeffington-Lodge.

LOEHNIS, Anthony David, CMG 1988; Director, S. G. Warburg Group plc, since 1989; a Vice-Chairman, S. G. Warburg & Co., since 1989; *b* 12 March 1936; *s* of Sir Clive Loehnis, *qv*; *m* 1965, Jennifer Forsyth Anderson; three *s*. *Educ:* Eton; New Coll., Oxford (BA); Harvard Sch. of Public Administration. HM Diplomatic Service, 1960–66; J. Henry Schroder Wagg & Co. Ltd, 1967–80 (on secondment to Bank of England, 1977–79); Bank of England: Associate Dir (Overseas), 1980–81; Exec. Dir, 1981–89. *Address:* c/o S. G. Warburg & Co. Ltd, 2 Finsbury Avenue, EC2M 2PA. *Club:* Garrick.

LOEHNIS, Sir Clive, KCMG 1962 (CMG 1950); Commander RN (retired); *b* 24 Aug. 1902; *s* of H. W. Loehnis, Barrister-at-Law, Inner Temple; *m* 1929, Rosemary Beryl, *d* of late Major Hon. R. N. Dudley Ryder, 8th Hussars; one *s* one *d*. *Educ:* Royal Naval Colls, Osborne, Dartmouth and Greenwich. Midshipman, 1920; Lt, 1924; qualified in signal duties, 1928; Lt-Comdr, 1932; retired, 1935; AMIEE 1935. Re-employed in Signal Div. Admiralty, 1938; Comdr on retd List, 1942; Naval Intelligence Div., 1942; demobilised and entered Foreign Office, 1945; Dep. Dir, Government Communications Headquarters, 1952–60; Dir, Government Communications HQ, 1960–64. Dep. Chm., Civil Service Selection Bd, 1967–70. *Address:* 12 Eaton Place, SW1X 8AD. *T:* 071–235 6803. *Clubs:* White's, MCC.

See also A. D. Loehnis, Baron Remnant.

LOFTHOUSE, Geoffrey; JP; MP (Lab) Pontefract and Castleford, since Oct. 1978; *b* 18 Dec. 1925; *s* of Ernest and Emma Lofthouse; *m* 1946, Sarah Lofthouse (*d* 1985); one *d*. *Educ:* Featherstone Primary and Secondary Schs; Leeds Univ. MIPM 1984. Haulage hand in mining industry at age of 14. Personnel Manager, NCB Fryston, 1970–78. Member: Pontefract Borough Council, 1962–74 (Mayor, 1967–68); Wakefield Metropolitan District Council, 1974– (Chm., Housing Cttee). Mem., NUM, 1939–64, APEX, 1970–. JP Pontefract, 1970. *Publication:* A Very Miner MP (autobiog.), 1986. *Recreations:* Rugby League, cricket. *Address:* 67 Carleton Crest, Pontefract, West Yorkshire.

LOFTHOUSE, John Alfred, (Jack), OBE 1967; Member, British National Oil Corporation, 1980–82; *b* 30 Dec. 1917; *s* of John Duncan Lofthouse and Clara Margaret Smith; *m* 1950, Patricia Ninette Mann (*d* 1956); one *d*. *Educ:* Rutlish Sch., Merton; St Catharine's Coll., Cambridge (BA Hons, MA). Joined ICI Ltd as engr, 1939; Engrg Manager, Petrochemicals Div., 1958; Technical Dir, Nobel Div., 1961; Chm., Petrochems Div., 1967; Dir, Main Bd of ICI Ltd, 1970–80: responsibilities included Personnel Dir, Petrochems, Oil, and Explosives businesses, and Chm., ICI Americas Ltd; Dir, Britoil, 1983–88. *Publications:* contrib. Geographical Jl and engrg jls. *Recreations:* gardening, hill-walking, music. *Address:* Little Paddocks, Streatley, Berks RG8 9RD.

LOFTHOUSE, Reginald George Alfred, FRICS; Chairman, Advisory Committee, Centre for Agricultural Strategy, Reading University, since 1982 (Member, since 1980); Vice-Chairman, Standing Conference on Countryside Sports, since 1988 (Convener, 1978–88); *b* Workington, 30 Dec. 1916; *m* 1939, Ann Bernardine Bannan; three *d*. *Educ:* Workington Secondary Sch.; with private land agent, Cockermouth. Chartered Surveyor and Land Agent (Talbot-Ponsonby Prizeman). Asst District Officer, Penrith, 1941–42; District Officer, Carlisle, for Cumberland War Agric. Exec. Cttee, 1942–43; Asst Land Comr, West Riding, 1943–46; Land Commissioner: N and E Ridings, 1946–48; Derbs, Leics, Rutland, Northants, 1948–50; Somerset and Dorset, 1950–52; Regional Land Comr, Hdqtrs, 1952–59, and SE Region, 1959–71; Regional Officer, SE Region, Agric., Develt and Adv. Service, 1971–73; Chief Surveyor, MAFF, 1973–76. Chairman: UK Jt Shelter Res. Cttee, 1958–71; Statutory Cttee on Agricl Valuations, 1973–76. Mem., Farming and Wildlife Adv. Gp, 1966–81. Adviser to: Lord Porchester's Exmoor Study, 1977; Nature Conservancy Council, 1978–82; Council for Environmental Conservation, 1980–81. Vis. Lectr in Rural Estate Management and Forestry, Regent Street Polytechnic, 1954–62. Member: Bd of Governors, Coll. of Estate Management, 1963–85 (Chm., 1972–77; Research Fellow, 1982–85, Hon. Fellow 1985; Chm., Centre for Advanced Land Use Studies, 1972–81); Court and Council, Reading Univ., 1973–; Delegacy for Nat. Inst. for Res. in Dairying, Shinfield, 1974–80; Gen. Council, RICS, 1974–76; RICS Land Agency and Agric. Div. Council, 1974–77. Hon. Life Mem., Cambridge Univ. Land Soc.; Chm. Farm Bldgs Cttee 1973–80, Mem. Engrg and Bldgs Res. Bd 1973–80, Jt Consultative Organisation. Liveryman, Loriners' Co., 1976; Freeman, City of London, 1976. *Publications:* The Berwyn Mountains Area of Wales, 1979; contrib. professional, techn. and countryside jls. *Address:* c/o College of Estate Management, Whiteknights, Reading RG6 2AW. *Clubs:* Athenæum, MCC.

LOFTUS, Viscount; Charles John Tottenham; Head of French Department, Strathcona-Tweedsmuir School, Calgary; *b* 2 Feb. 1943; *e s* and *heir* of 8th Marquess of Ely, *qv*; *m* 1969, Judith Marvelle, *d* of Dr J. J. Porter, FRS, Calgary, Alberta; one *s* one *d*. *Educ:* Trinity Coll. Sch., Port Hope, Ont; Ecole Internationale de Genève; Univ. of Toronto (MA). *Address:* 1424 Springfield Place SW, Calgary, Alberta T2W 0Y1, Canada.

LOGAN, David Brian Carleton, CMG 1991; HM Diplomatic Service; Minister and Deputy Head of Mission, Moscow, since 1989; *b* 11 Aug. 1943; *s* of Captain Brian Ewen Weldon Logan, RN (Retd) and Mary Logan (*née* Fass); *m* 1967, Judith Margaret Walton Cole; one *s* one *d* (and one *s* decd). *Educ:* Charterhouse; University College, Oxford. MA. Foreign Office, 1965; served Istanbul, Ankara and FCO, 1965–70; Private Sec. to Parly Under Sec. of State for Foreign and Commonwealth Affairs, 1970–73; First Sec., 1972; UK Mission to UN, 1973–77; FCO, 1977–82; Counsellor, Hd of Chancery and Consul-Gen., Oslo, 1982–86; Hd of Personnel Ops Dept, FCO, 1986–88; Sen. Associate Mem., St Antony's Coll., Oxford, 1988–89. *Recreations:* music, reading, sailing. *Address:* c/o Foreign and Commonwealth Office, King Charles Street, SW1A 2AH. *Club:* Royal Ocean Racing.

LOGAN, Sir Donald (Arthur), KCMG 1977 (CMG 1965); HM Diplomatic Service, retired; Chairman, Jerusalem and East Mission (formerly Middle East) Trust Ltd, since 1981; Chairman, St Clare's College, Oxford, since 1984; *b* 25 Aug. 1917; *s* of late Arthur Alfred Logan and Louise Anne Bradley; *m* 1957, Irène Jocelyne Angèle, *d* of Robert Everts (Belgian Ambassador at Madrid, 1932–39) and Alexandra Comnène; one *s* two *d*. *Educ:* Solihull. Fellow, Chartered Insurance Institute, 1939. War of 1939–45: Major, RA; British Army Staff, Washington, 1942–43; Germany, 1945. Joined HM Foreign (subseq. Diplomatic) Service, Dec. 1945; Foreign Office, 1945–47; HM Embassy, Tehran, 1947–51; Foreign Office, 1951–53; Asst Political Agent, Kuwait, 1953–55; Asst Private Sec. to Sec. of State for Foreign Affairs, 1956–58; HM Embassy, Washington, 1958–60; HM Ambassador to Guinea, 1960–62; Foreign Office, 1962–64; Information Counsellor, British Embassy, Paris, 1964–70; Ambassador to Bulgaria, 1970–73; Dep. Permanent UK Rep. to NATO, 1973–75; Ambassador and Permanent Leader, UK Delegn to UN Conf. on Law of the Sea, 1976–77. Leader, UK delegn to Conf. on Marine Living Resources of Antarctica, Buenos Aires and Canberra, 1978–80. Dir, GB/E Europe Centre, 1980–87. Vice-Pres., Internat. Exhibitions Bureau, Paris, 1963–67. *Address:* 6 Thurloe Street, SW7 2ST. *Clubs:* Brooks's, Royal Automobile.

LOGAN, Sir Douglas; *see* Logan, Sir R. D.

LOGAN, James, OBE 1988; CChem; Director, Scotland The What? Revue Company, since 1970; *b* 28 Oct. 1927; *s* of John and Jean Logan; *m* 1959, Anne Brand, singer; one *s* one *d*. *Educ:* Robert Gordon's Inst., Aberdeen. MRIC. Member, Sen. Scientific Staff, Macaulay Inst. for Soil Research, 1949–81. Chm., Voluntary Service Aberdeen, 1989–. Member: Arts Council of Great Britain, 1984–88; Scottish Arts Council, 1983–88 (Vice-Chm., 1984–88); Founder/Chm., Friends of Aberdeen Art Gallery and Museums, 1975–77. Queen's Jubilee Medal, 1978. *Recreation:* theatre. *Address:* 53 Fountainhall Road, Aberdeen AB2 4EU. *T:* Aberdeen (0224) 646914.

LOGAN, Prof. Malcolm Ian, PhD; Vice-Chancellor, Monash University, since 1987; *b* 3 June 1931; *m* 1954, Antoinette, *d* of F. Lalich; one *d*. *Educ:* Univ. of Sydney (BA Hons 1951, DipEd 1952, PhD 1965). Lectr in Geography, Sydney Teachers Coll., 1956–58; Lectr in Geog., 1959–64, Sen. Lectr, 1965–67, Univ. of Sydney; Prof. of Geog. and of Urban and Regional Planning, Univ. of Wisconsin, Madison, USA, 1967–71; Monash University: Prof. of Geog., 1971–81; Pro Vice-Chancellor, 1982–85; Dep. Vice-Chancellor, 1986. Visiting Professor: Univ. of Ibadan, Nigeria, 1970–71; LSE, 1973; Nanyang Univ., Singapore, 1979. *Publications:* (jtly) New Viewpoints in Economic Geography, 1966; Studies in Australian Geography, 1968; New Viewpoints in Urban and Industrial Geography, 1971; Urban and Regional Australia, 1975; Urbanisation, the Australian Experience, 1980; (jtly) The Brittle Rim, 1989; contribs to Aust. Geographical Studies, Regional Studies, Land Econs, and Econ. Geography. *Address:* Vice Chancellor's Residence, Monash University, Clayton, Vic 3168, Australia. *T:* 565 2000. *Club:* Athenæum (Melbourne).

LOGAN, Sir (Raymond) Douglas, Kt 1983; grazier (sheep and cattle), since 1944; *b* 31 March 1920; *s* of Raymond Hough Logan and Agnes Eleanor Logan; *m* 1944, Florence Pearl McGill (MBE 1975); one *s* one *d* (and one *s* decd). *Educ:* Thornburgh College, Charters Towers. Served RAAF, 1941–44 (Flying Officer, pilot; trained EATS, Australia, 1941–42; served with 66 Sqdn RAF, 1942–44). Member: Qld Govt Beef Cttee of Enquiry, 1975–77; Qld Meat Industry Orgn and Marketing Authority (now Livestock and Meat Authority of Qld), 1978–; United Graziers Assoc. of Qld; Cattlemen's Union, Qld. *Recreations:* tennis, horse riding, sailing, flying. *Address:* Richmond Downs, Richmond, Qld 4822, Australia.

LOGAN, Robert Faid Bell; Group Chief Executive and Deputy Chairman, Samuel Montagu & Co. (Holdings), 1985–86; Chairman, Samuel Montagu & Co. Ltd, 1986; *b* 30 Nov. 1932; *s* of John Logan and Mary Logan (*née* Bell); *m* 1958, Susan Elizabeth Vokes; three *d*. *Educ:* Berwickshire High School, Duns. British Linen Bank, 1949–50 and 1952–55; RAF, 1950–52; Bank of London & South America, 1955–60; Citibank NA, 1960–81 (Exec. Vice-Pres. Merchant Banking Group); Chief Financial Officer, Continental Grain Co., 1981–83; Group Chief Exec., Grindlays Bank, 1983–85. *Recreations:* shooting, tennis, diving. *Clubs:* Marks; Piping Rock (New York).

LOGAN, Rt. Rev. Vincent; *see* Dunkeld, Bishop of, (RC).

LOGAN, William Philip Dowie, MD, PhD, BSc, DPH, FRCP; epidemiological consultant to various national and international organisations, since 1974; Director, Division of Health Statistics, WHO, 1961–74; *b* 2 Nov. 1914; *s* of late Frederick William Alexander Logan and late Elizabeth Jane Dowie; *m* 1st, Pearl (*née* Piper) (marr. diss.); four *s* two *d* (and one *s* decd); 2nd, Barbara (*née* Huneke). *Educ:* Queen's Park Sch., Glasgow; Universities of Glasgow and London. RAF Med. Branch, 1940–46 (Squadron Leader). Hospital appointments in Glasgow, 1939–40 and 1946. Gen. practice in Barking, Essex, 1947–48; General Register Office, 1948–60 (Chief Medical Statistician, Adviser on Statistics to Ministry of Health, Head of WHO Centre for Classification of Diseases, and Member, WHO panel of experts on Health Statistics). *Publications:* contribs on epidemiology, vital and health statistics in official reports and medical jls. *Address:* 164 Elmer Road, Bognor Regis, West Sussex PO22 6JA; 10 chemin de la Tourelle, 1209 Geneva, Switzerland.

LOGSDAIL, (Christopher) Nicholas (Roald); Managing Director, Lisson Gallery, since 1967; *b* 21 June 1945; *s* of late John Logsdail and of Else Logsdail (*née* Dahl); *m* 1st, 1968, Fiona McLean; one *s*; 2nd, 1985, Caroline Mockett; two *s* one *d*. *Educ:* Bryanston Sch.; Slade Sch., University College London. Opened Lisson Gallery, 1967; organised numerous exhibns, representing work of British and internat. artists; instrumental in introducing new generation of British sculptors, 1979–; Mem., Soc. of London Art Dealers. *Publications:* monographs and artists books, 1970–. *Recreations:* collecting 20th century art and furniture, sailing. *Address:* Lisson Gallery, 67 Lisson Street, NW1 5DA. *T:* 071–724 2739.

LOGUE, Christopher; *b* 23 Nov. 1926; *s* of John Logue and Molly Logue (*née* Chapman); *m* 1985, Rosemary Hill. *Educ:* Prior Park Coll., Bath; Portsmouth Grammar Sch. Mem., Equity. *Plays:* The Story of Mary Frazer, 1962; trans. Brecht, Baal, 1985. *Screen plays:* Savage Messiah (dir Ken Russell), 1972; (with Walon Green) Crusoe (based on Defoe's novel), 1989. *Broadcast:* The Arrival of the Poet in the City: a melodrama for narrator and seven musicians (music by George Nicholson), 1985; *Recordings:* (with Tony Kinsey and Bill Le Sage) Red Bird (poetry and jazz), 1960; Songs from The Establishment (singer Annie Ross), 1962; The Death of Patroclus (with Vanessa Redgrave, Alan Dobie and others), 1963; Strings (melodrama for voice and 14 musicians, with music by Jason Osborn), 1988. *Film roles:* Swinburne, in Ken Russell's Dante's Inferno, 1966; John Ball, in John Irvin's The Peasants' Revolt, 1969; Cardinal Richelieu, in Ken Russell's The Devils, 1970; TV and stage roles. *Publications: verse:* Wand & Quadrant, 1953; Devil, Maggot & Son, 1956; Songs, 1959; Patrocleia, 1962; ABC, 1966; Pax, 1967; New Numbers, 1969; Twelve Cards, 1972; The Crocodile (illus. Binette Schroeder), 1976; Abecedary (illus. Bert Kitchen), 1977; War Music, 1981; Ode to the Dodo, 1981; Kings, 1991; *prose:* Ratsmagic (illus. Wayne Anderson), 1976; The Magic Circus (illus. Wayne Anderson), 1979; The Bumper Book of True Stories (illus. Bert Kitchen), 1980; *plays:* The Trial of Cob & Leach, 1959; (with Harry Cookson) The Lilywhite Boys, 1959; trans. Hugo Claus, Friday, 1971; trans. Brecht and Weill, The Seven Deadly Sins, 1986; *anthologies:* The Children's Book of Comic Verse, 1979; London in Verse, 1982; Sweet & Sour, 1983; The Oxford Book of Pseuds, 1983; The Children's Book of Children's Rhymes, 1986; contrib. Private Eye, The Times, The Sunday Times, etc; *as Count Palmiro Vicarion:* Lust, a pornographic novel, 1957; (ed) Count Palmiro Vicarion's Book of Limericks, 1957; (ed) Count Palmiro Vicarion's Book of Bawdy Ballads, 1957. *Address:* 41 Camberwell Grove, SE5 8JA.

LOISELLE, Gilles; MP Langelier Constituency, since 1988; Minister of State for Finance, Canada, since 1989; President, Treasury Board of Canada, since 1990; *b* 20 May 1929; *s* of Arthur Loiselle and Antoinette Lethiecq; *m* 1962, Lorraine Benoît; one *s* one *d*. *Educ:* Sacred-Heart Coll., Sudbury, Ont. BA Laval. Tafari Makonnen Sch., Addis Ababa, 1951–53; Journalist, Le Droit, Ottawa, 1953–56; Haile Selassie First Day Sch., Addis Ababa, 1956–62; Dir, Behrane Zarie Néo Inst., Addis Ababa, 1958–62; Canadian Broadcasting Corporation: Editor, TV French Network, 1962–63; Quebec and Paris correspondent, French Radio and TV Network, 1963–67; Counsellor, Quebec House, Paris, 1967–72; Dir Gen. of Quebec Govt Communications, 1972–76; Pres., Intergovt Deptl Cttee for Olympic Year, 1976; Dir, Interparly Relations, Quebec Nat. Assembly, 1977; Agent General for Quebec in London, with responsibility for Scandinavian countries, Iceland, and Ireland, 1977–83; Dep. Minister for federal provincial relations, 1983–84, for Cultural Affairs, Quebec, 1984–85; Agent Gen. for Quebec in Rome, 1985–88. Founder Mem., Assoc. France-Québec, 1969–72; Member: Council, Office franco-québécois pour la Jeunesse, 1973–76; Inst. of Public Admin; RIIA. *Recreations:* reading, gardening. *Address:* House of Commons, Ottawa, Ont K1A 0A6, Canada.

LOKOLOKO, Sir Tore, GCMG 1977; GCVO 1982; OBE; Chairman, Indosuez Niugini Bank, 1983–89; *b* 21 Sept. 1930; *s* of Loko Loko Tore and Kevau Sarufa; *m* 1950, Lalahaia Meakoro; four *s* six *d*. *Educ:* Sogeri High Sch., PNG. Dip. in Cooperative, India. Chm., PNG Cooperative Fedn, 1965–68; MP, 1968–77 (two terms); Minister for Health, and Dep. Chm. of National Exec. Council, 1968–72. Rep. PNG: Co-op. Conf., Australia, 1951; S Pacific Conf., Lae, 1964; attended UN Gen. Assembly, 1969, and Trusteeship Council, 1971. Governor-General of Papua New Guinea, 1977–82. KStJ 1979. *Address:* c/o Indosuez Niugini Bank, Burns House, Port Moresby, Papua New Guinea.

LOMAS, Alfred; Member (Lab) London North East, European Parliament, since 1979; Leader, British Labour Group, European Parliament, since 1985; *b* 30 April 1928; *s* of Alfred and Florence Lomas; one *s* one *d*. *Educ:* St Paul's Elem. Sch., Stockport; various further educnl estabs. Solicitor's clerk, 1942–46; Radio Telephony Operator, RAF, 1946–49; various jobs, 1949–51; railway signalman, 1951–59; Labour Party Sec./Agent, 1959–65; Polit. Sec., London Co-op., 1965–79. *Publication:* The Common Market—why we should keep out, 1970. *Recreations:* chess, jogging, arts, sport. *Address:* 28 Brookway, SE3 9BJ. *T:* 081–852 6689. *Club:* Hackney Labour.

LOMAX, (Janis) Rachel; Deputy Chief Economic Adviser, HM Treasury, since 1990; *b* 15 July 1945; *d* of William and Dilys Salmon; *m* 1967, Michael Acworth Lomax (marr. diss. 1990); two *s*. *Educ:* Cheltenham Ladies' Coll.; Girton Coll., Cambridge (MA); LSE (MSc). HM Treasury: Econ. Assistant, 1968; Econ. Advr, 1972; Sen. Econ. Advr, 1978; Principal Pvte Sec. to Chancellor of the Exchequer, 1985–86; Under-Sec., 1986–90. Mem. Council, REconS, 1989–. *Address:* HM Treasury, Parliament Street, SW1P 3AG. *T:* 071–270 4409.

LOMAX, Rachel; *see* Lomax, J. R.

LOMBARD, Rt. Rev. Charles F.; *see* Fitzgerald-Lombard.

LOMBE, Edward Christopher E.; *see* Evans-Lombe.

LOMER, Dennis Roy, CBE 1984; Adviser, Balfour Beatty; *b* 5 Oct. 1923; *s* of Bertie Cecil Lomer and Agnes Ellen Coward; *m* 1949, Audrey May Bick; one *s* one *d*. With Consulting Engineers, 1948–50; joined Electricity Supply Industry, 1952; Project Engr, Transmission Div., 1961; Asst Chief Transmission Engr, 1965; Generation Construction Div. (secondment at Dir level), 1972; Dep. Dir-Gen. (Projects), 1973; Dir-Gen., Transmission Div., 1975; Member: CEGB, 1977–83; Technical Review Gp for Eurotunnel, 1988–. Dir, Davidson Gp Ltd, 1983–88. Pres., Welding Inst., 1985–87 (non-exec. Dir, 1988–); Hon. FWeldI. FIEE; CBIM. *Recreations:* golf, sailing. *Address:* Henley House, Heathfield Close, Woking, Surrey GU22 7JQ. *T:* Woking (0483) 764656. *Club:* West Hill Golf (Surrey).

LOMER, Geoffrey John, CBE 1985; MA; FEng 1984; FIEE; Technical Director, Racal Electronics plc, since 1977; *b* 5 Jan. 1932; *s* of Frederick John Lomer and Dorothy Lomer; *m* 1st, 1955, Pauline Helena May (*d* 1974); one *s* one *d*; 2nd, 1977, Antoinette Ryall; one step *s* one step *d*. *Educ:* St Austell Grammar School; Queens' College, Cambridge (MA). Research Engineer, EMI Research Laboratories, 1953–57; Head of Radio Frequency Div., Broadcast Equipment Dept, EMI Electronics, 1957–63; Head of Transmitter Lab., Racal Communications, 1963–68; Technical Dir, Racal Mobilcal, 1968–70; Dir in Charge, Racal Communications Equipment, 1970–76; Dep. Man. Dir, Racal Tacticom, 1976–77. *Recreations:* music, theatre. *Address:* Racal Electronics plc, Bracknell, Berks RG12 1RG. *T:* Bracknell (0344) 481222.
See also W. M. Lomer.

LOMER, William Michael, PhD; Director, Culham Laboratory, United Kingdom Atomic Energy Authority, 1981–90, retired; *b* 2 March 1926; *s* of Frederick John Lomer and Dorothy Lomer; *m* 1952, Pamela Anne Wakelin; one *s* two *d*. *Educ:* St Austell County School; University College of the South West, Exeter (MSc London); Queens' College, Cambridge (MA, PhD). Research Scientist, UKAEA, 1952; AERE Harwell: Divison Head, Theory Div., 1958–62; Division Head, Solid State Physics, 1962–68; Research Director, 1968–81; Dep. Dir, Inst. Laue Langevin, Grenoble, 1973–74. Hon. Treasurer, Inst. of Physics, 1980–82. FInstP. *Publications:* papers in physics and metallurgical jls. *Recreations:* gardening, walking, painting. *Address:* 7 Hids Copse Road, Cumnor Hill, Oxford OX2 9JJ. *T:* Oxford (0865) 862173.
See also G. J. Lomer.

LONDESBOROUGH, 9th Baron, *cr* 1850; **Richard John Denison;** *b* 2 July 1959; *s* of John Albert Lister, 8th Baron Londesborough, TD, AMICE, and of Elizabeth Ann, *d* of late Edward Little Sale, ICS; *S* father, 1968; *m* 1987, Rikki Morris, *d* of J. E. Morris, Bayswater; one *s*. *Educ:* Wellington College; Exeter Univ. *Heir: s* Hon. James Frederick Denison, *b* 4 June 1990. *Address:* Edw Cottage, Aberedw, Builth Wells, Powys LD2 3UR.

LONDON, Bishop of, since 1991; **Rt. Rev. and Rt. Hon. David Michael Hope;** PC 1991; DPhil; Prelate of the Order of the British Empire, since 1991; Dean of the Chapels Royal, since 1991; *b* 14 April 1940. *Educ:* Nottingham Univ. (BA Hons Theol); Linacre Coll., Oxford (DPhil). Curate of St John, Tuebrook, Liverpool, 1965–70; Chaplain, Church of Resurrection, Bucharest, 1967–68; Vicar, St Andrew, Warrington, 1970–74; Principal, St Stephen's House, Oxford, 1974–82; Warden, Community of St Mary the Virgin, Wantage, 1980–87; Vicar of All Saints', Margaret Street, 1982–85; Bishop of Wakefield, 1985–91. Examining Chaplain to: Bp of Bath and Wells, 1976–85; Bp of Wakefield, 1979–85; Bp of Norwich, 1981–85; Bp of London, 1984–85. *Publication:* The Leonine Sacramentary, 1971. *Address:* London House, 8 Barton Street, Westminster, SW1P 3NE. *T:* 071–222 8661.

LONDON, Archdeacon of; *see* Cassidy, Ven. G. H.

LONDON, CENTRAL, Bishop in, (RC); *see* Crowley, Rt Rev. John.

LONDON, EAST, Bishop in, (RC); *see* Guazzelli, Rt Rev. Victor.

LONDON, NORTH, Bishop in, (RC); *see* Harvey, Rt Rev. Philip.

LONDON, WEST, Bishop in, (RC); *see* Mahon, Rt Rev. Gerald Thomas.

LONDONDERRY, 9th Marquess of, *cr* 1816; **Alexander Charles Robert Vane-Tempest-Stewart;** Baron Londonderry, 1789; Viscount Castlereagh, 1795; Earl of Londonderry, 1796; Baron Stewart, 1814; Earl Vane, Viscount Seaham, 1823; *b* 7 Sept. 1937; *s* of 8th Marquess of Londonderry and Romaine (*d* 1951), *er d* of Major Boyce Combe, Great Holt, Dockenfield, Surrey; *S* father 1955; *m* 1st, 1958, Nicolette (marr. diss. 1971), *d* of Michael Harrison, Netherhampton, near Salisbury, Wilts; two *d*; 2nd, 1972, Doreen Patricia Wells, *qv*; two *s*. *Educ:* Eton. *Heir: s* Viscount Castlereagh, *qv*. *Address:* PO Box No 8, Shaftesbury, Dorset SP7 0LR.

LONDONDERRY, Marchioness of; *see* Wells, Doreen P.

LONG, family name of **Viscount Long.**

LONG, 4th Viscount, *cr* 1921, of Wraxall; **Richard Gerard Long;** a Lord in Waiting (Government Whip), since 1979; *b* 30 Jan. 1929; *s* of 3rd Viscount and Gwendolyn (*d* 1959), *d* of Thomas Reginald Hague Cook; *S* father, 1967; *m* 1957, Margaret Frances (marr. diss. 1984), *d* of late Ninian B. Frazer; one *s* one *d* (and one *d* decd); *m* 1984, Catherine Patricia Elizabeth Mier-Woolf (marr. diss. 1990), *d* of C. T. Mills-Ede, S Africa; *m* 1990, Helen Fleming-Gibbons. *Educ:* Harrow. Wilts Regt, 1947–49. Opposition Whip, 1974–79. Vice-Pres. and formerly Vice-Chm., Wilts Royal British Legion; Pres., Bath Gliding Club. *Heir: s* Hon. James Richard Long, *b* 31 Dec. 1960. *Address:* House of Lords, SW1A 0PW. *Club:* Pratt's.

LONG, Athelstan Charles Ethelwulf, CMG 1968; CBE 1964 (MBE 1959); President, United Bank International, Cayman Islands, since 1975; Chairman: International Management Group, since 1988; Casualty Underwriters Inc., since 1989; Chairman and Director of some twelve companies; Chairman, Public Service Commission, since 1987; *b* 2 Jan. 1919; *s* of Arthur Leonard Long and Gabrielle Margaret Campbell (historical writer and novelist, Marjorie Bowen); *m* 1948, Edit Majken Zadie Harriet Krantz, *d* of late Erik Krantz, Stockholm; two *s*. *Educ:* Westminster Sch.; Brasenose Coll., Oxford. Served War of 1939–45: commnd into RA, 1940; seconded 7th (Bengal) Battery, 22nd Mountain Regt, IA, 1940; served Malaya; POW as Capt., 1942–45; appointed to Indian Political Service, 1946. Cadet, Burma Civil Service, 1947–48; Colonial Admin. Service (N Nigeria), 1948; Sen. District Officer, 1958; Resident, Zaria Province, 1959; Perm. Sec., Min. of Animal Health and Forestry, 1959; started new Min. of Information as Perm. Sec., 1960; Swaziland: appointed Govt Sec., 1961; Chief Sec., 1964; Leader of Govt business in Legislative Council and MEC, 1964–67; HM Dep. Comr, 1967–68; Administrator, later Governor, of the Cayman Is, 1968–71; Comr of Anguilla, March–July 1972; Admin. Sec., Inter-University Council, 1972–73. Man. Dir, Anegada Corp.

Ltd, 1973–74; Dir and Chm., Cayman Airways, 1977–81. Chairman: Planning Appeals Tribunal, 1982–84; Coastal Works Adv. Cttee, 1986–91. Chm. Governing Council, Waterford Sch., Swaziland, 1963–68. FRAS; FRGS. *Recreations:* travel, tropical farming, reading. *Address:* Box 131, Savannah, Grand Cayman, Cayman Islands, West Indies.

LONG, Christopher William, CMG 1986; HM Diplomatic Service; Ambassador to Switzerland, since 1988; *b* 9 April 1938; *s* of late Eric and May Long; *m* 1972, Patricia, *d* of Dennis and late May Stanbridge; two *s* one *d. Educ:* King Edward's Sch., Birmingham; Balliol Coll., Oxford (Deakin Scholar); Univ. of Münster, W Germany. Served RN, 1956–58. HM Diplomatic Service, 1963–: FO, 1963–64; Jedda, 1965–67; Caracas, 1967–69; FCO, 1969–74; Budapest, 1974–77; Belgrade (CSCE), 1977; Counsellor, Damascus, 1978–80; Counsellor and Dep. Perm. Rep., UKMIS, Geneva, 1980–83; Head, Near East and N Africa Dept, FCO, 1983–85; Asst Under-Sec. of State (Dep. Chief Clerk and Chief Inspector), FCO, 1985–88. *Address:* c/o Foreign and Commonwealth Office, King Charles Street, SW1A 2AH; Thunstrasse 50, 3005 Berne, Switzerland. *T:* 031 44 50 21.

LONG, Gerald; *b* 22 Aug. 1923; *o s* of Fred Harold Long and Sabina Long (*née* Walsh); *m* 1951, Anne Hamilton Walker; two *s* three *d. Educ:* St Peter's Sch., York; Emmanuel Coll., Cambridge. Army Service, 1943–47. Joined Reuters, 1948: served as Reuter correspondent in Germany, France and Turkey, 1950–60; Asst General Manager, 1960; Chief Exec., 1963–81 (Gen. Manager, 1963–73; Man. Dir., 1973–81); Man. Dir, Times Newspapers Ltd, 1981–82; Dep. Chm., News International plc, 1982–84. Chairman: Visnews Ltd, 1968–79; Exec. Cttee, Internat. Inst. of Communications Ltd, 1973–78. Mem., Design Council, 1974–77; Council Mem., Journalists in Europe, 1974– (Exec. Dir, 1987–88). CBIM (FBIM 1978). Commander, Royal Order of the Phoenix, Greece, 1964; Grand Officer, Order of Merit, Italy, 1973; Commander, Order of the Lion of Finland, 1979; Chevalier de la Légion d'Honneur, France, 1979; Commander's Cross, Order of Merit, Federal Republic of Germany, 1983. *Recreation:* cooking. *Address:* 15 rue d'Aumale, 75009 Paris, France. *T:* 48 74 67 26; 51 route de Caen, 14400 St Martin des Entrees, France. *T:* 31 92 47 12.

LONG, Hubert Arthur, CBE 1970; Deputy Secretary, Exchequer and Audit Department, 1963–73; *b* 21 Jan. 1912; *s* of Arthur Albert Long; *m* 1937, Mary Louise Parker; three *s. Educ:* Taunton's Sch., Southampton. Entered Exchequer and Audit Department, 1930. *Address:* 2A Hawthorndene Road, Hayes, Kent. *T:* 081–462 4373.

LONG, John Richard, CBE 1987; freelance consultant on National Health Service management and state regulation of medicines; *b* 9 March 1931; *s* of late Thomas Kendall Long and Jane Long; *m* 1952, Margaret (*née* Thistlethwaite); one *s* two *d. Educ:* Kirkham Grammar School. Clerical Officer, Customs and Excise, 1947; Exec. Officer, Min. of Pensions, subseq. DHSS, 1949; various posts on health functions; Asst Sec., 1978 (posts on regulation and pricing of medicines, maternity and child health, and communicable diseases); Under Sec., 1987 (NHS Personnel Div.), resigned 1988. *Publications:* co-author, articles on regulation of medicines. *Recreations:* vegetable growing, wild life, writing fiction. *Address:* 77 Prospect Road, Farnborough, Hants GU14 8NT. *T:* Farnborough (0252) 548525.

LONG, Ven. John Sanderson, MA; Archdeacon of Ely, Hon. Canon of Ely and Rector of St Botolph's, Cambridge, 1970–81; Archdeacon Emeritus, 1981; *b* 21 July 1913; *s* of late Rev. Guy Stephenson Long and Ivy Marion Long; *m* 1948, Rosamond Mary, *d* of Arthur Temple Forman; one *s* three *d. Educ:* St Edmund's Sch., Canterbury; Queens' Coll., Cambridge; Cuddesdon Theological Coll. Deacon, 1936; Priest, 1937; Curate, St Mary and St Eanswythe, Folkestone, 1936–41. Chaplain, RNVR, 1941–46. Curate, St Peter-in-Thanet, 1946; Domestic Chaplain to the Archbishop of Canterbury, 1946–53; Vicar of: Bearsted, 1953–59; Petersfield with Sheet, 1959–70; Rural Dean of Petersfield, 1962–70. *Recreations:* walking, gardening. *Address:* 23 Thornton Road, Girton, Cambridge CB3 0NP. *T:* Cambridge (0223) 276421.

LONG, Olivier; Ambassador; President, Graduate Institute of Public Administration, Lausanne, 1981–89; *b* 1915; *s* of Dr Edouard Long and Dr Marie Landry; *m* 1946, Francine Roels; one *s* two *d. Educ:* Univ. de Paris, Faculté de Droit et Ecole des Sciences Politiques; Univ. de Genève. PhD Law, 1938; Rockefeller Foundn Fellow, 1938–39; PhD Pol. Sc., 1943. Swiss Armed Forces, 1939–43; International Red Cross, 1943–46; Swiss Foreign Affairs Dept, Berne, 1946–49; Washington Embassy, 1949–54; Govt Delegate for Trade Agreements, 1955–66; Head of Swiss Delegn to EFTA, 1960–66; Ambassador to UK and Malta, 1967–68; Dir-Gen., GATT, 1968–80. Prof., Graduate Inst. of Internat. Studies, Geneva, 1962–85. Mem., Internat. Red Cross Cttee, 1980–. Trustee, Foundn for Internat. Conciliation, Geneva, 1984–. *Publications:* Law and its Limitations in the GATT Multilateral Trade System, 1985; Le dossier secret des Accords d'Evian—une mission suisse pour la paix en Algérie, 1988. *Address:* 6 rue Constantin, 1206 Geneva, Switzerland.

LONG, Pamela Marjorie, (Mrs John Nichols); Metropolitan Stipendiary Magistrate, since 1978; *b* 12 Sept. 1930; *d* of late John Holywell Long, AMICE, and Emily McNaughton; *m* 1966, Kenneth John Heastey Nichols, *qv. Educ:* Carlisle and County High School for Girls. Admitted Solicitor of Supreme Court, 1959; private practice, 1959–63; Solicitor's Dept, New Scotland Yard, 1963–77. Mem., Cttee of Magistrates for Inner London, 1984–. *Recreations:* music, riding, watching cricket. *Address:* Horseferry Road Magistrates' Court, 70 Horseferry Road, SW1P 2AX.

LONG, Captain Rt. Hon. William Joseph, OBE 1985; PC (N Ireland) 1966; JP; Minister of Education, Northern Ireland, 1969–72; MP (Unionist) Ards, Parliament of Northern Ireland, 1962–72; *b* 23 April 1922; *s* of James William Long and Frederica (Walker); *m* 1942, Dr Elizabeth Doreen Mercer; one *s. Educ:* Friends' Sch., Great Ayton, Yorks; Edinburgh Univ.; RMC, Sandhurst. Served Royal Inniskilling Fusiliers, 1940–48. Secretary: NI Marriage Guidance Council, 1948–51; NI Chest and Heart Assoc., 1951–62. Parliamentary Secretary, Min. of Agriculture, NI, 1964–66; Sen. Parliamentary Secretary, Min. of Development, NI, Jan.–Oct. 1966; Minister of Educn, 1966–68; Minister of Home Affairs, Dec. 1968–March 1969; Minister of Develt, March 1969–May 1969. *Recreations:* cricket, horticulture, angling, sailing, model engineering, aviation. *Address:* Lisvarna, Warren Road, Donaghadee, Co. Down. *T:* Donaghadee (0247) 2538.

LONGAIR, Prof. Malcolm Sim, PhD; FRSE 1981; Jacksonian Professor of Natural Philosophy, University of Cambridge, since 1991; Professorial Fellow, Clare Hall, Cambridge; *b* 18 May 1941; *s* of James Sim Longair and Lily Malcolm; *m* 1975, Dr Deborah Janet Howard; one *s* one *d. Educ:* Morgan Acad., Dundee; Queen's Coll., Dundee, Univ. of St Andrews (BSc Electronic Physics, 1963); Cavendish Lab., Univ. of Cambridge (MA, PhD 1967). Res. Fellow, Royal Commn for Exhibn of 1851, 1966–68; Royal Soc. Exchange Fellow to USSR, 1968–69; University of Cambridge: Res. Fellow, 1967–71, and Official Fellow, 1971–80, Clare Hall; Univ. Demonstrator in Phys., 1970–75; Univ. Lectr in Phys., 1975–80; Astronomer Royal for Scotland, Regius Prof. of Astronomy, Univ. of Edinburgh, and Dir, Royal Observatory, Edinburgh, 1980–90. Vis. Professor: of Radio Astronomy, Calif Inst of Technol., 1972; of Astronomy, Inst. for Advanced Study, Princeton, 1978. Editor, Monthly Notices of RAS, 1974–78. Hon. LLD Dundee, 1982.

Britannica Award, 1986. *Publications:* (ed) Confrontation of Cosmological Theories with Observational Data, 1974; (ed with J. Einasto) The Large-Scale Structure of the Universe, 1978; (with J. E. Gunn and M. J. Rees) Observational Cosmology, 1978; (ed with J. Warner) The Scientific Uses of the Space Telescope, 1980; High Energy Astrophysics: an informal introduction, 1980; (ed with H. A. Brück and G. Coyne) Astrophysical Cosmology, 1982; Theoretical Concepts in Physics, 1984; Alice and the Space Telescope, 1989; The Origins of Our Universe, 1991; over 100 papers, mostly in Monthly Notices of RAS. *Recreations:* music, art, architecture. *Address:* c/o Cavendish Laboratory, Madingley Road, Cambridge CB3 0HE. *T:* Cambridge (0223) 332385.

LONGBOTTOM, Charles Brooke; Chairman, Acorn Christian Healing Trust, since 1988; *b* 22 July 1930; *s* of late William Ewart Longbottom, Forest Hill, Worksop; *m* 1962, Anita, *d* of G. Trapani and Mrs Basil Mavroleon; two *d. Educ:* Uppingham. Contested (C) Stockton-on-Tees, 1955; MP (C) York, 1959–66; Parly Private Secretary to Mr Iain Macleod, Leader of the House, 1961–63. Barrister, Inner Temple, 1958; Chairman: Austin & Pickersgill, Shipbuilders, Sunderland, 1966–72; A&P Appledore International Ltd, 1970–79; Seascope Holdings Ltd, 1970–82; Seascope Sale & Purchase, 1970–87; Seascope Shipping Ltd, 1982–87; Seascope Insurance Holdings Ltd, 1984–86; Seascope Insurance Services Ltd, 1984–87; Illingworth Morris Pension Trustees Ltd, 1990–; Director: Henry Ansbacher Hldgs Ltd, 1982–87; Henry Ansbacher & Co., 1982–87; Ansbacher (Guernsey) Ltd, 1982–87; British Shipbuilders, 1986–; MC Shipping Inc., 1989–. Member: General Advisory Council, BBC, 1965–75; Community Relations Commn, 1968–70. *Recreations:* shooting, golf and racing. *Address:* 66 Kingston House North, Princes Gate, SW7. *Clubs:* White's, Carlton.

LONGCROFT, James George Stoddart, FCA; FInstPet; Managing Director, Tournesol Ltd, Bermuda, since 1984; Senior Partner, Longcrofts, Chartered Accountants, since 1969; *b* 25 Oct. 1929; *s* of Reginald Stoddart Longcroft and Annie Mary Longcroft (*née* Thompson); *m*; four *s* one *d. Educ:* Wellington Coll., Crowthorne, Berks. FBIM. Partner, Longcrofts, Chartered Accountants, 1955; Director 1964, Managing Director 1969, Chairman, 1980–88, Tricentrol plc. Master, Worshipful Company of Founders, 1978; Mem., Honourable Artillery Co., 1957–. FRSA 1985. *Recreations:* skiing, tennis. *Address:* La Tour St Georges, 1815 Clarens-Montreux, Switzerland. *Club:* City of London.

LONGDEN, Sir Gilbert (James Morley), Kt 1972; MBE 1944; MA (Cantab), LLB; *b* 16 April 1902; *e s* of late Lieut-Colonel James Morley Longden, Castle Eden, Co. Durham, and of late Kathleen, *d* of George Blacker Morgan, JP; unmarried. *Educ:* Haileybury; Emmanuel Coll., Cambridge. Secretary ICI (India) Ltd, 1930–37; travelled throughout Asia (Middle and Far East) and in North and South America. Student at University of Paris, 1937. Called up from AOER into DLI, 1940; served with 2nd and 36th Divisions in Burma campaigns (MBE (mil.)). Adopted Parliamentary Candidate for Morpeth, 1938; contested (C) Morpeth, 1945; MP (C) SW Herts, 1950–Feb. 1974. UK Representative to Council of Europe, 1953–54; United Kingdom Delegate to 12th and 13th Sessions of United Nations; Past Chairman: British Atlantic Cttee; Conservative Gp for Europe; Great Britain-East Europe Centre. Vice-Chm., British Council. *Publications:* A Conservative Philosophy, 1947; and (jointly): One Nation, 1950; Change is our Ally, 1954; A Responsible Society, 1959; One Europe, 1969. *Recreations:* reading, writing, gardening. *Address:* 89 Cornwall Gardens, SW7 4AX. *T:* 071–584 5666. *Clubs:* Brooks's, Hurlingham.

LONGDEN, Henry Alfred, FEng, FICE, FIMinE; FGS; Director, Trafalgar House Investments Ltd, 1970–76; *b* 8 Sept. 1909; *s* of late Geoffrey Appleby Longden and late Marjorie Mullins; *m* 1935, Ruth, *d* of Arthur Gilliat, Leeds; one *s* four *d. Educ:* Oundle; Birmingham Univ. (BSc Hons). Served in Glass Houghton and Pontefract Collieries, 1930; Asst Gen. Manager, Stanton Ironworks Co., 1935; Gen. Manager, Briggs Colliers Ltd, 1940; Director: Blackwell Colliery Co., 1940; Briggs Collieries Co., 1941; New Hucknell Colliery Co., 1941; Area Gen. Manager, 1947, and Production Dir, 1948, NE Div., NCB; Dir-Gen., Production, NCB, 1955; Chm., W Midlands Div., NCB, 1960; Chm. and Chief Exec., Cementation Co. Ltd, 1963–70 (Dep. Chm. and Chief Exec., 1961–63). President: Instn of Mining Engineers, 1958; Engineering Industries Assoc., 1965–71; Member: Engineering Industry Trg Bd, 1967–70; Confedn of British Industry, 1968. Fellow, Fellowship of Engineering, 1977. *Publication:* Cadman Memorial Lecture, 1958. *Recreations:* Rugby football, cricket, tennis, shooting, fishing, sailing. *Address:* Raeburn, Northdown Road, Woldingham, Surrey. *T:* Woldingham (088385) 2245.

LONGDEN, Wilson, JP; education and training consultant; *b* 26 May 1936; *s* of late Harold and Doris Longden; *m* 1st, 1966 (marr. diss. 1982); two *s*; 2nd, 1985, Olga Longden. *Educ:* Chesterfield Grammar Sch.; Univ. of Hull (BA Hons, Dip Ed); Univ. of Bradford (MSc). National service, RAF, 1955–57; Teacher, Northmount High Sch., Canada, 1961–62; Lecturer: Matthew Boulton Tech. Coll., Birmingham, 1962–66; Bingley Coll. of Educn, 1966–67; Margaret McMillan Coll. of Educn, 1967–68; Hatfield Polytechnic, 1968–69; Coventry (Lanchester) Polytechnic, 1969–73; Vice-Principal, Barnfield College, Luton, 1973–87. Sec., Assoc. of Vice-Principals of Colleges, 1986–87 (Pres., 1982–84). Comr, MSC, 1983–85. JP Luton, 1980. *Publications:* The School Manager's and the School Governor's Handbook, 1977; Meetings, 1977; Making Secondments Work, 1990. *Recreations:* music, playing the organ and the piano. *Address:* 311 Turnpike Drive, Luton LU3 3RE. *T:* Luton (0582) 573905.

LONGFIELD, Dr Michael David; Director, Teesside Polytechnic, since 1980; *b* 28 April 1928; *s* of Edric Douglas Longfield and Dorothy Longfield (*née* Hennessey); *m* 1st, 1952, Ann McDonnell; two *s* two *d*; 2nd, 1970, June Shirley, *d* of late Levi and of Esther Beman; two *s. Educ:* Prince Henry's Grammar Sch., Otley; Leeds Univ. BSc, PhD; CEng, MIMechE. Lectr in Mech. Engrg, Univ. of Leeds, 1960–68; Manager, Leeds Univ. Industrial Unit of Tribology, 1968–70; Head of Dept of Mech., Marine and Production Engrg, Liverpool Polytechnic, 1970–72; Asst Dir, Teesside Polytechnic, 1972–80. *Publications:* contribs to engineering and medical engineering journals. *Address:* Plum Tree House, Thirlby, Thirsk, N Yorks YO7 2DJ.

LONGFORD, 7th Earl of, *cr* 1785, **Francis Aungier Pakenham,** KG 1971; PC 1948; Baron Longford, 1759; Baron Silchester (UK), 1821; Baron Pakenham (UK), 1945; *b* 5 Dec. 1905; 2nd *s* of 5th Earl of Longford, KP, MVO; *S* brother (6th Earl) 1961; *m* 1931, Elizabeth (*see* Countess of Longford); four *s* three *d* (and one *d* decd). *Educ:* Eton; New Coll., Oxford, MA. 1st Class in Modern Greats, 1927. Tutor, University Tutorial Courses, Stoke-on-Trent, 1929–31; Cons. Party Economic Res. Dept, 1930–32. Christ Church, Oxford: Lecturer in Politics, 1932; Student in Politics, 1934–46, and 1952–64. Prospective Parliamentary Labour Candidate for Oxford City, 1938. Enlisted Oxford and Bucks LI (TA), May 1939; resigned commission on account of ill-health, 1940. Personal assistant to Sir William Beveridge, 1941–44; a Lord-in-Waiting to the King, 1945–46; Parliamentary Under-Secretary of State, War Office, 1946–47; Chancellor of the Duchy of Lancaster, 1947–48; Minister of Civil Aviation, 1948–51; First Lord of the Admiralty, May–Oct. 1951; Lord Privy Seal, 1964–65; Secretary of State for the Colonies, 1965–66; Leader of the House of Lords, 1964–68; Lord Privy Seal, 1966–68; Chm., The National Bank Ltd, 1955–63; Dir, Sidgwick and Jackson, 1980–85 (Chm., 1970–80). Chm., Nat. Youth

Employment Council, 1968–71; Joint Founder: New Horizon Youth Centre, 1964; New Bridge for Ex-Prisoners, 1956; (also Dir) The Help Charitable Trust, 1986. *Publications*: Peace by Ordeal (The Anglo-Irish Treaty of 1921), 1935 (repr. 1972); (autobiog.) Born to Believe, 1953; (with Roger Opie), Causes of Crime, 1958; The Idea of Punishment, 1961; (autobiog.) Five Lives, 1964; Humility, 1969; (with Thomas P. O'Neill) Eamon De Valera, 1970; (autobiog.) The Grain of Wheat, 1974; Abraham Lincoln, 1974; Jesus Christ, 1974; Kennedy, 1976; St Francis of Assisi, 1978; Nixon, 1980; (with Anne McHardy) Ulster, 1981; Pope John Paul II, 1982; Diary of a Year, 1982; Eleven at No. 10: a personal view of Prime Ministers, 1984; One Man's Faith, 1984; The Search for Peace, 1985; The Bishops, 1986; Saints, 1987; A History of the House of Lords, 1989; Suffering and Hope, 1990; Punishment and the Punished, 1991. *Heir*: s Thomas (Frank Dermot) Pakenham, *qv*. *Address*: Bernhurst, Hurst Green, East Sussex TN19 7QN. *T*: Hurst Green (058086) 248; 18 Chesil Court, Chelsea Manor Street, SW3. *T*: 071–352 7794; The Help Charitable Trust, 287 Goldhawk Road, W12. *Club*: Garrick.
See also Lady Rachel Billington, Lady Antonia Fraser, Hon. M. A. Pakenham, A. D. Powell.

LONGFORD, Countess of; Elizabeth Pakenham, CBE 1974; *b* 30 Aug. 1906; *d* of late N. B. Harman, FRCS, 108 Harley Street, W1, and of Katherine (*née* Chamberlain); *m* 1931, Hon. F. A. Pakenham (*see* 7th Earl of Longford); four *s* three *d* (and one *d* decd). *Educ*: Headington Sch., Oxford; Lady Margaret Hall, Oxford (MA). Lectr for WEA and Univ. Extension Lectr, 1929–35. Contested (Lab) Cheltenham, 1935, Oxford, 1950; candidate for King's Norton, Birmingham, 1935–43. Mem., Rent Tribunal, Paddington and St Pancras, 1947–54; Trustee, National Portrait Gall., 1968–78; Member: Adv. Council, V&A Museum, 1969–75; Adv. Bd, British Library, 1976–80; Hon. Life Pres., Women Writers and Journalists, 1979. Hon. DLitt Sussex 1970. *Publications*: (as Elizabeth Pakenham): Points for Parents, 1956; Catholic Approaches (ed), 1959; Jameson's Raid, 1960, new edn 1982; (as Elizabeth Longford) Victoria RI, 1964 (James Tait Black Memorial Prize for Non-Fiction, 1964); Wellington: Years of the Sword, 1969 (Yorkshire Post Prize); Wellington: Pillar of State, 1972; The Royal House of Windsor, 1974; Churchill, 1974; Byron's Greece, 1975; Life of Byron, 1976; A Pilgrimage of Passion: the life of Wilfrid Scawen Blunt, 1979; (ed) Louisa: Lady in Waiting, 1979; Images of Chelsea, 1980; The Queen Mother, a biography, 1981; Eminent Victorian Women, 1981; Elizabeth R, 1983; The Pebbled Shore (autobiog.), 1986; The Oxford Book of Royal Anecdotes, 1989. *Recreations*: gardening, reading. *Address*: Bernhurst, Hurst Green, East Sussex. *T*: Hurst Green (058086) 248; 18 Chesil Court, Chelsea Manor Street, SW3. *T*: 071–352 7794.
See also Lady Rachel Billington, Lady Antonia Fraser, Hon. M. A. Pakenham, T. F. D. Pakenham.

LONGFORD, Elizabeth; *see* Longford, Countess of.

LONGHURST, Andrew Henry, FCBSI; Chief Executive and Managing Director, Cheltenham & Gloucester Building Society, since 1982; *b* 23 Aug. 1939; *s* of Henry and Connie Longhurst; *m* 1962, Margaret; one *s* two *d*. *Educ*: Nottingham University (BSc Hons). FBCS 1968; FCBSI 1990; CBIM 1989. Computer systems consultancy, 1961; Cheltenham & Gloucester Building Society: Data Processing Manager, 1967; Asst Gen. Man. (Admin), 1970; Dep. Gen. Man., 1977. *Recreation*: golf. *Address*: Cheltenham & Gloucester Building Society, Barnett Way, Gloucester GL4 7RL. *T*: Gloucester (0452) 372372.

LONGLAND, Sir Jack, (Sir John Laurence Longland), Kt 1970; Director of Education, Derbyshire, 1949–70; *b* 26 June 1905; *e s* of late Rev. E. H. Longland and late Emily, *e d* of Sir James Crockett; *m* 1934, Margaret Lowrey, *y d* of late Arthur Harrison, Elvet Garth, Durham; two *s* two *d*. *Educ*: King's Sch., Worcester; Jesus Coll., Cambridge (Rustat Exhibitioner and Scholar). 2nd Class, 1st Part Classical Tripos, 1925; 1st Class, 1st Division, Historical Tripos, Part II, 1926; 1st Class with special distinction, English Tripos, 1927; Charles Kingsley Bye-Fellow at Magdalene Coll., Cambridge, 1927–29; Austausch-student, Königsberg Univ., 1929–30; Lectr in English at Durham Univ., 1930–36; Dir Community Service Council for Durham County, 1937–40; Regional Officer of Nat. Council of Social Service, 1939–40; Dep. Educn Officer, Herts, 1940–42; County Educn Officer, Dorset CC, 1942–49. Athletic Blue; Pres., Cambridge Univ. Mountaineering Club, 1926–27; Member: Mount Everest Expedn, 1933; British East Greenland Expedn, 1935; Pres., Climbers' Club, 1945–48 and Hon. Mem., 1964; Pres., Alpine Club, 1973–76 (Vice-Pres., 1960–61); Member: Colonial Office Social Welfare Adv. Cttee, 1942–48; Develt Commn, 1948–78; Adv. Cttee for Educn in RAF, 1950–57; Adv. Cttee for Educn in Germany, 1950–57; Central Adv. Council for Educn in England and Wales, 1948–51; Nat. Adv. Council on the Training and Supply of Teachers, 1951–; Children's Adv. Cttee of the ITA, 1956–60; Wolfenden Cttee on Sport, 1958–60; Outward Bound Trust Council, 1962–73; Central Council of Physical Recreation Council and Exec., 1961–72; Electricity Supply Industry Training Bd, 1965–66; Royal Commn on Local Govt, 1966–69; The Sports Council, 1966–74 (Vice-Chm. 1971–74); Countryside Commn, 1969–74; Commn on Mining and the Environment, 1971–72; Water Space Amenity Commn, 1973–76; President: Assoc. of Educn Officers, 1960–61; British Mountaineering Council, 1962–65 (Hon. Mem., 1983); Chairman: Mountain Leadership Training Bd, 1964–80; Council for Environmental Educn, 1968–75. Chm., My Word, BBC, 1956–76. *Publications*: literary and mountaineering articles in various books and journals. *Recreations*: walking, books. *Address*: Bridgeway, Bakewell, Derbyshire. *T*: Bakewell (062981) 2252. *Clubs*: Savile, Alpine, Achilles.

LONGLAND, Sir John Laurence; *see* Longland, Sir Jack.

LONGLEY, Mrs Ann Rosamund; Head Mistress, Roedean School, since 1984; *b* 5 March 1942; *d* of late Jack Gilroy Dearlove and of Rhoda E.M. Dearlove (*née* Billing); *m* 1964, Stephen Roger Longley (*d* 1979); one *s* two *d*. *Educ*: Walthamstow Hall School, Sevenoaks; Edinburgh University (MA 1964); PGCE Bristol University, 1984. Wife and mother, 1964–; Teacher, Toorak Coll., Victoria, Australia, 1964–65; Asst Housemistress, Peninsula C of E Sch., Victoria, 1966–67; Residential Teacher, Choate School, Conn, USA, 1968–73; Teacher, Webb School, Calif, 1975–78; Headmistress, Vivian Webb School, Calif, 1981–84. *Recreations*: tennis, swimming, fishing, walking. *Address*: Roedean House, Roedean School, Brighton, Sussex BN2 5RQ. *T*: Brighton (0273) 680791. *Clubs*: New Cavendish; University (Los Angeles).

LONGLEY, Sir Norman, Kt 1966; CBE; DL; retired as Chairman, James Longley (Holdings) Ltd, Building and Civil Engineering Contractors, Crawley, Sussex; *b* 14 Oct. 1900; *s* of Charles John Longley and Anna Gibson Marchant; *m* 1925, Dorothy Lilian Baker; two *s* one *d*. *Educ*: Clifton. West Sussex County Council, 1945–61, Alderman 1957–61. President: National Federation of Building Trades Employers, 1950; International Federation of Building and Public Works Contractors, 1955–57. Hon. Fellow, Institute of Builders. DL West Sussex, 1975. Hon. DSc: Heriot-Watt, 1968; Sussex, 1986. Coronation Medal, 1953. *Recreation*: horticulture. *Address*: The Beeches, Crawley, Sussex. *T*: Crawley (0293) 20253.

LONGMAN, Peter Martin; Director (formerly Secretary), Museums and Galleries Commission, since 1984; *b* 2 March 1946; *s* of Denis Martin Longman and Mary Joy

Longman (*née* Simmonds); *m* 1976, Sylvia June Prentice; two *d*. *Educ*: Huish's School, Taunton; University College, Cardiff; Univ. of Manchester. Finance Dept and Housing the Arts Officer, Arts Council, 1968–78; Dep. Dir, Crafts Council, 1978–83; Dep. Sec., Museums and Galleries Commn, 1983–84. Dir, Caryl Jenner Productions Ltd, 1983–87. Mem. Council, Textile Conservation Centre Ltd, 1983– (Mem., Exec. Cttee, 1983–85). Trustee, Theatres Trust, 1991–. FRSA 1989. *Publications*: Working Party Reports: Training Arts Administrators, Arts Council, 1971; Area Museum Councils and Services, HMSO, 1984; Museums in Scotland, HMSO, 1986; articles on theatre, the arts, museums. *Recreations*: discovering Britain, listening to music. *Address*: Museums and Galleries Commission, 16 Queen Anne's Gate, SW1H 9AA. *T*: 071–233 4200, *Fax*: 071–233 3686.

LONGMORE, Andrew Centlivres; QC 1983; *b* 25 Aug. 1944; *s* of John Bell Longmore and Virginia Longmore (*née* Centlivres); *m* 1979, Margaret Murray McNair; one *s*. *Educ*: Winchester College; Lincoln College, Oxford. MA. Called to the Bar, Middle Temple, 1966, Bencher, 1990. Chm., Law Reform Cttee, Bar Council, 1987–90. *Publications*: (co-editor) MacGillivray and Parkington, Law of Insurance, 6th edn 1975, 8th edn 1988. *Recreation*: fell-walking. *Address*: 7 King's Bench Walk, Temple, EC4Y 7DS. *T*: 071–583 0404.

LONGRIGG, John Stephen, CMG 1973; OBE 1964; HM Diplomatic Service, retired; *b* 1 Oct. 1923; *s* of late Brig. Stephen Hemsley Longrigg, OBE; *m* 1st, 1953, Lydia Meynell (marr. diss. 1965); one *s* one *d*; 2nd, 1966, Ann O'Reilly; one *s* decd. *Educ*: Rugby Sch.; Magdalen Coll., Oxford (BA). War Service, Rifle Bde, 1942–45 (despatches). FO, 1948; Paris, 1948; Baghdad, 1951; FO, 1953; Berlin, 1955; Cabinet Office, 1957; FO, 1958; Dakar, 1960; Johannesburg, 1962; Pretoria, 1962; Washington, 1964; FO, 1965–67; Bahrain, 1967–69; FCO, 1969–73; seconded to HQ British Forces, Hong Kong, 1974–76; FCO, 1976–82; Administrator, Common Law Inst. of Intellectual Property, 1983–88. *Recreation*: golf. *Address*: 2 The Cedars, 3 Westcombe Park Road, Blackheath, SE3 7RE. *T*: 081–858 1604. *Clubs*: Reform; Royal Blackheath Golf, Littlestone Golf.
See also R. E. Longrigg.

LONGRIGG, Roger Erskine; author; *b* 1 May 1929; *s* of Brig. S. H. Longrigg, OBE; *m* 1957, Jane Chichester; three *d*. *Educ*: Bryanston Sch.; Magdalen Coll., Oxford (BA Hons Mod. Hist.). *Publications*: A High Pitched Buzz, 1956; Switchboard, 1957; Wrong Number, 1959; Daughters of Mulberry, 1961; The Paper Boats, 1963; The Artless Gambler, 1964; Love among the Bottles, 1967; The Sun on the Water, 1969; The Desperate Criminals, 1971; The History of Horse Racing, 1972; The Jevington System, 1973; Their Pleasing Sport, 1975; The Turf, 1975; The History of Foxhunting, 1975; The Babe in the Wood, 1976; The English Squire and his Sport, 1977; Bad Bet, 1982. *Recreations*: trout fishing, racing. *Address*: Orchard House, Crookham, Hants. *T*: Aldershot (0252) 850333. *Clubs*: Brooks's, Pratt's.
See also J. S. Longrigg.

LONGSTRETH THOMPSON, Francis Michael; *see* Thompson, F. M. L.

LONGUET-HIGGINS, Prof. Hugh Christopher, DPhil (Oxon); FRS 1958; Professor Emeritus, University of Sussex, 1989 (Royal Society Research Professor, 1974–88); *b* 11 April 1923; *e s* of late Rev. H. H. L. Longuet-Higgins. *Educ*: Winchester (schol.); Balliol Coll., Oxford (schol., MA). Research Fellow of Balliol Coll., 1946–48; Lecturer and Reader in Theoretical Chemistry, University of Manchester, 1949–52; Prof. of Theoretical Physics, King's Coll., University of London, 1952–54; FRSE; John Humphrey Plummer Professor of Theoretical Chemistry, University of Cambridge, 1954–67; Royal Soc. Res. Prof., Univ. of Edinburgh, 1968–74; Fellow of Corpus Christi Coll., 1954–67, Life Fellow 1968; Hon. Fellow: Balliol Coll., Oxford, 1969; Wolfson Coll., Cambridge, 1977. A Governor, BBC, 1979–84. Warden, Leckhampton House, 1961–67. Editor of Molecular Physics, 1958–61. For. Mem., Amer. Acad. of Arts and Scis, 1961; Foreign Associate, US National Academy of Sciences, 1968. DUniv York, 1973; DU Essex, 1981; Hon. DSc: Bristol, 1983; Sussex, 1989. Harrison Meml Prize, Chemical Soc., 1950; Naylor Prize, London Mathematical Soc., 1981. *Publications*: co-author, The Nature of Mind (Gifford Lectures), 1972; Mental Processes, 1987; papers on theoretical physics, chemistry and biology in scientific journals. *Recreations*: music and arguing. *Address*: Centre for Research on Perception and Cognition, Laboratory of Experimental Psychology, University of Sussex, Falmer, Brighton BN1 9QY. *T*: Brighton (0273) 678341.

LONGUET-HIGGINS, Michael Selwyn, FRS 1963; Royal Society Research Professor, University of Cambridge, 1969–89; Fellow, Trinity College, Cambridge, since 1969; *b* 8 Dec. 1925; *s* of late Henry Hugh Longuet and Albinia Cecil Longuet-Higgins; *m* 1958, Joan Redmayne Tattersall; two *s* two *d*. *Educ*: Winchester Coll. (Schol.); Trinity Coll., Cambridge (Schol.). (BA). Admiralty Research Lab., Teddington, 1945–48; Res. Student, Cambridge, 1948–51; PhD Cambridge, 1951; Rayleigh Prize, 1951; Commonwealth Fund Fellowship, 1951–52; Res. Fellow, Trinity Coll., Cambridge, 1951–55; Nat. Inst. of Oceanography, 1954–69. Visiting Professor: MIT, 1958; Institute of Geophysics, University of California, 1961–62; Univ. of Adelaide, 1964. Prof. of Oceanography, Oregon State Univ., 1967–69. Foreign Associate, US Nat. Acad. of Sci., 1979. Hon. DTech Tech. Univ. of Denmark, 1979; Hon. LLD Glasgow, 1979. Sverdrup Gold Medal, Amer. Meteorolog. Soc., 1983; Internat. Coastal Engrg Award, Amer. Soc. of Civil Engineers, 1984; Oceanography Award, Soc. for Underwater Technol., 1990. *Publications*: papers in applied mathematics, esp. physical oceanography, dynamics of sea waves and currents. *Recreations*: music, mathematical toys. *Address*: Gage Farm, Comberton, Cambridge CB3 7DH.

LONGWORTH, Ian Heaps, PhD; FSA, FSAScot; Keeper of Prehistoric and Romano-British Antiquities, British Museum, since 1973; *b* 29 Sept. 1935; *yr s* of late Joseph Longworth and Alice (*née* Heaps); *m* 1967, Clare Marian Titford; one *s* one *d*. *Educ*: King Edward VII, Lytham; Peterhouse, Cambridge. Open and Sen. Scholar, Matthew Wren Student, 1957, MA, PhD, Cantab. Temp. Asst Keeper, Nat. Museum of Antiquities of Scotland, 1962–63; Asst Keeper, Dept of British and Medieval Antiquities, Brit. Mus., 1963–69; Asst Keeper, Dept of Prehistoric and Romano-British Antiquities, Brit. Mus., 1969–73. Mem., Ancient Monuments Bd for England, 1977–84. Chm., Area Archaeol. Adv. Cttee for NW England, 1978–79. Hon. Sec., Prehistoric Soc., 1966–74, Vice-Pres., 1976–80; Sec., Soc. of Antiquaries of London, 1974–79, Vice-Pres., 1985–89. *Publications*: Yorkshire (Regional Archaeologies Series), 1965; (with G. J. Wainwright) Durrington Walls—excavations 1966–68, 1971; Collared Urns of the Bronze Age in Great Britain and Ireland, 1984; Prehistoric Britain, 1985; (with I. A. Kinnes) Catalogue of the Excavated Prehistoric and Romano-British Material in the Greenwell Collection, 1985; (ed with J. Cherry) Archaeology in Britain since 1945, 1986; (with A. Ellison and V. Rigby) Excavations at Grimes Graves, Norfolk, 1972–76, Fasc. 2, 1988, (et al.) Fasc. 3, 1991; articles in various learned jls on topics of prehistory. *Address*: 2 Hurst View Road, South Croydon, Surrey CR2 7AG. *T*: 081–688 4960. *Club*: MCC.

LONGWORTH, Wilfred Roy, AM 1986; MSc, PhD; FRSC, FRACI, FACE; Principal Director (formerly Director), Swinburne Institute of Technology and College of Technical and Further Education, 1970–86, retired; *b* 13 Dec. 1923; *s* of Wilfred Arnold Longworth and Jessie Longworth; *m* 1951, Constance Elizabeth Dean; two *d. Educ:* Bolton Sch.; Manchester Univ. (BSc, MSc, PhD). FRIC 1963; FRACI 1970; FACE 1976. Works Manager and Chief Chemist, Blackburn & Oliver, 1948–56; postgrad. res., Univ. of Keele, 1956–59; Lectr in Physical Chemistry, Huddersfield Coll. of Technol., 1959–60; Sen. Lectr in Phys. Chem., Sunderland Technical Coll., 1960–64; Head, Dept of Chem. and Biol., Manchester Polytechnic, 1964–70. Pres., World Council on Co-op. Educn, 1983–85. *Publications:* articles on cationic polymerisation in learned jls. *Recreations:* lawn bowls, gardening. *Address:* 35 Fairmont Avenue, Camberwell, Vic 3124, Australia. *T:* 809 1145. *Club:* Naval and Military (Melbourne).

LONSDALE, 7th Earl of (UK), *cr* 1807; **James Hugh William Lowther,** Viscount and Baron Lowther, 1797; Bt 1764; *b* 3 Nov. 1922; *er s* of Anthony Edward, Viscount Lowther (*d* 1949), and Muriel Frances, Viscountess Lowther (*d* 1968), 2nd *d* of late Sir George Farrar, Bt, DSO, and Lady Farrar; *S* grandfather, 1953; *m* 1975, Caroline, *y d* of Sir Gerald Ley, 3rd Bt, TD; one *s* one *d* (and three *s* three *d* of previous marriages). *Educ:* Eton. Armed Forces, 1941–46; RAC and East Riding Yeo. (despatches, Captain). Structural engineering, 1947–50; farmer and forester; Chm. of family co., Lakeland Investments Ltd, and of three subsidiaries; otherwise retired. CBIM; FRSA 1984. *Heir: s* Viscount Lowther, *qv. Address:* Askham Hall, Penrith, Cumbria CA10 2PF. *T:* Hackthorpe (09312) 208. *Clubs:* Brooks's, Turf.

LONSDALE, Maj.-Gen. Errol Henry Gerrard, CB 1969; MBE 1942; Transport Officer-in-Chief (Army) 1966–69; *b* 26 Feb. 1913; 2nd *s* of Rev. W. H. M. Lonsdale, Arlaw Banks, Barnard Castle; *m* 1944, Muriel Allison, *d* of E. R. Payne, Mugswell, Chipstead; one *s* one *d. Educ:* Westminster Sch.; St Catharine's Coll., Cambridge (MA). 2nd Lt, RASC, 1934; Bt Lt-Col 1952; Col 1957; Brig. 1961; Maj.-Gen. 1965. Sudan Defence Force, 1938–43 (despatches); Chief Instr, RASC Officers Trng Centre, 1944–45; AQMG FARELF, 1945–47; CRASC 16 Airborne Div., 1947–48; GSOI, 1948–51; AA & QMG, War Office, 1951–53; Korea, 1953–54; Malaya, 1954–56 (despatches); ACOS, G4 Northern Army Group, 1957–60; DDST, 1st Corps, 1960–62; Comdt RASC Trng Centre, 1962–64; Inspector, RASC, 1964–65; ADC to the Queen, 1964–66; Inspector, RCT, 1965–66; psc; jssc. Col Comdt, RCT, 1969–74. Hon. Colonel: 160 Regt RCT(V), 1967–74; 562 Para Sqdn RCT(V), 1969–78. FCIT (MInstT) 1966. Vice-President: Transport Trust, 1969; Internat. Union for Modern Pentathlon and Biathlon, 1976–80; Pres., Modern Pentathlon Assoc. of Great Britain, 1977–88, Hon. Pres., 1988– (Chm., 1967); Chm., Inst. of Advanced Motorists, 1971–79, Vice-Pres., 1979. *Recreations:* modern pentathlon, photography, driving. *Address:* Windleys, Podgers Lane, Ilton, Ilminster, Somerset TA19 9HE.

LONSDALE, Robert Henry H.; *see* Heywood-Lonsdale.

LONSDALE, Dr Roger Harrison, FBA 1991; Fellow and Tutor in English, Balliol College, Oxford, since 1963; Reader in English Literature, University of Oxford, since 1990; *b* 6 Aug. 1934; *s* of Arthur John Lonsdale and Phebe (*née* Harrison); *m* 1964, Anne Mary Menzies; one *s* one *d. Educ:* Hymers Coll., Hull; Lincoln Coll., Oxford (BA 1st class Hons 1957); DPhil (Oxon) 1962. National Service, RAF, commnd as Navigator, 1952–54. English Dept, Yale Univ., 1958–60; Bradley Jun. Res. Fellow, Balliol Coll., Oxford, 1960–63. *Publications:* Dr Charles Burney: a literary biography, 1965; *edited:* The Poems of Gray, Collins and Goldsmith, 1969; Vathek, by William Beckford, 1970; Dryden to Johnson, 1971; The New Oxford Book of Eighteenth-century Verse, 1984; The Poems of John Bampfylde, 1988; Eighteenth-century Women Poets: an Oxford anthology, 1989. *Recreations:* music, book-collecting. *Address:* Balliol College, Oxford OX1 3BJ. *T:* Oxford (0865) 277777.

LOOSLEY, Brian; Metropolitan Stipendiary Magistrate, since 1989; *b* 20 Dec. 1948; *s* of Bernard Allan Loosley and Barbara Clara Randle; *m* 1971, Christine Mary Batt; one *s* one *d. Educ:* Sir William Borlase Grammar Sch., Marlow; Leeds Univ. (LLB 1971). Admitted Solicitor 1974. Prosecuting Solicitor, Thames Valley Police, 1975–78; Solicitor and Partner: Kidd Rapinet Badge & Co., High Wycombe, 1978–83; Allan Janes & Co., High Wycombe, 1983–89. *Recreations:* fishing, Russian history and literature, foreign travel. *Address:* Greenwich Magistrates' Court, 9 Blackheath Road, SE10 8PG. *T:* 081–853 8090.

LOPES, family name of **Baron Roborough.**

LORAM, Vice-Adm. Sir David (Anning), KCB 1979; LVO 1957; Deputy Supreme Allied Commander Atlantic, 1977–80, retired; Gentleman Usher to The Queen, since 1982; *b* 24 July 1924; *o surv. s* of late Mr and Mrs John A. Loram; *m* 1st, 1958, Fiona Beloe (marr. diss. 1981); three *s*; 2nd, 1983, Diana Keigwin (marr. diss. 1990). *Educ:* Royal Naval Coll., Dartmouth (1938–41). Awarded King's Dirk. Served War: HMS Sheffield, Foresight, Anson, Zealous, 1941–45. ADC to Governor-Gen. of New Zealand, 1946–48; specialised in Signal Communications, 1949; served in HMS Chequers, 1951; Equerry to the Queen, 1954–57; qualified helicopter pilot, 1955; commanded HMS Loch Fada, 1957; Directing Staff, JSSC, 1959–60; served in HMS Belfast, 1961; Naval Attaché, Paris, 1964–67; commanded HMS Arethusa, 1967; Dir, Naval Ops and Trade, 1970–71; commanded HMS Antrim, 1971; ADC to The Queen, 1972–73; Comdr British Forces, FO Malta, and NATO Comdr SE Mediterranean, 1973–75; Comdt, Nat. Defence Coll., 1975–77. Mem., RN Cresta Team, 1954–59. *Recreation:* fishing. *Address:* Sparkford Hall, Sparkford, Yeovil, Somerset BA22 7LD. *T:* North Cadbury (0963) 40834. *Club:* Chesapeake.

LORANT, Stefan; *b* 22 Feb. 1901; *m* 1963, Laurie Robertson (marr. diss. 1978); one *s* (and one *s* decd). *Educ:* Evangelical Gymnasium, Budapest; Academy of Economics, Budapest; Harvard Univ. (MA 1961). Editor: Das Magazin, Leipzig, 1925; Bilder Courier, Berlin, 1926; Muenchner Illustrierte Presse, Munich, 1928–33; Editor, in England: Weekly Illustrated, 1934 (also Creator); Picture Post, 1938–48; Founding editor and creator of Lilliput, Editor, 1937–40. Hon. LLD, Knox Coll., Galesburg, Ill., 1958; DHL *hc* Syracuse Univ., NY, 1985; Hon. Dr Univ. of Bradford, 1989. *Publications:* Wir vom Film, 1928, repr. 1986; I Was Hitler's Prisoner, 1935 (trans. of Ich war Hitlers Gefangener, German edn first pubd 1985); Chamberlain and the Beautiful Llama, 1940; Lincoln, His Life in Photographs, 1941; The New World, 1946, rev. edn 1965; F.D.R., a pictorial biography, 1950; The Presidency, a pictorial history of presidential elections from Washington to Truman, 1951; Lincoln: a picture story of his life, 1952, rev. and enl. edns 1957, 1969; The Life of Abraham Lincoln, 1954; The Life and Times of Theodore Roosevelt, 1959; Pittsburgh, the story of an American city, 1964, rev. and enl. edns 1975, 1980, 1988; The Glorious Burden: the American Presidency, 1968, rev. and enl. edn, 1976; Sieg Heil: an illustrated history of Germany from Bismarck to Hitler, 1974 (German trans. 1976); Pete: the story of Peter F. Flaherty, 1978; My Years in England, fragments to an autobiography, 1991; Mark I Love You (a memorial to my son), 1991. *Address:* Farview, Lenox, Mass 01240, USA. *T:* Lenox 637–0666.

LORD, Alan, CB 1972; Deputy Chairman and Chief Executive, Lloyd's of London, since 1986; *b* 12 April 1929; *er s* of Frederick Lord and Anne Lord (*née* Whitworth), Rochdale; *m* 1953, Joan Ogden; two *d. Educ:* Rochdale; St John's Coll., Cambridge (BA 1950 (1st Cl. Hons); MA 1987). Entered Inland Revenue, 1950; Private Sec. to Dep. Chm. and to Chm. of the Board, 1952–54; HM Treasury, 1959–62; Principal Private Sec. to First Secretary of State (then Rt Hon. R. A Butler), 1962–63; Comr of Inland Revenue, 1969–73, Dep. Chm. Bd, 1971–73; Principal Finance Officer to DTI, subseq. to Depts of Industry, Trade, and Prices and Consumer Protection, 1973–75; Second Permanent Sec. (Domestic Econ.), HM Treasury, 1975–77. Man. Dir, 1980, Chief Exec., 1982–84, Dunlop Hldgs plc; formerly: Exec. Dir, Dunlop Hldgs; Man. Dir, Dunlop Internat. Ltd, 1978. Director: Allied-Lyons plc, 1979–86; Bank of England, 1983–86; Johnson Matthey Bankers, 1985–86. Chm., CBI Taxation Cttee, 1979–81. Mem. Council of Management, Henley Centre for Forecasting, 1977–82. Governor, NIESR. Pres., Johnian Soc., 1985–86. *Publications:* A Strategy for Industry (Sir Ellis Hunter Meml Lecture, Univ. of York), 1976; Earning an Industrial Living (1985 Johnian Society Lecture). *Recreations:* reading, gardening, rough-shooting. *Address:* Mardens, Hildenborough, Tonbridge, Kent. *T:* Hildenborough (0732) 832268. *Club:* Reform.

LORD, Geoffrey, OBE 1989; Secretary and Treasurer, Carnegie United Kingdom Trust, since 1977; *b* 24 Feb. 1928; *s* of Frank Lord and Edith Lord; *m* 1955, Jean; one *s* one *d. Educ:* Rochdale Grammar Sch.; Univ. of Bradford (MA Applied Social Studies). AIB. Midland Bank Ltd, 1946–58; Probation and After-Care Service, 1958–76: Dep. Chief Probation Officer, Greater Manchester, 1974–76. Chairman: Unemployed Voluntary Action Fund (Scotland), 1990–; Pollock Meml Missionary Trust, 1985–. FRSA 1985. Hon. Fellow, Manchester Polytechnic, 1987. *Publication:* The Arts and Disabilities, 1981. *Recreations:* philately, walking, appreciation of the arts. *Address:* 9 Craigleith View, Ravelston, Edinburgh EH4 3JZ. *T:* 031–337 7623. *Club:* New (Edinburgh).

LORD, John Herent; His Honour Judge Lord; a Circuit Judge, since 1978; *b* 5 Nov. 1928; *s* of late Sir Frank Lord, KBE, JP, DL, and Lady Lord (*née* Rosalie Jeanette Herent), Brussels; *m* 1959, June Ann, *d* of late George Caladine and of Ada Caladine, Rochdale; three *s. Educ:* Manchester Grammar Sch.; Merton Coll., Oxford (BA (Jurisprudence), MA). Half Blue, Oxford Univ. lacrosse XII, 1948 and 1949; represented Middlesex, 1950. Called to Bar, Inner Temple, 1951; The Junior of Northern Circuit, 1952; Asst Recorder of Burnley, 1971; a Recorder of the Crown Court, 1972–78. Chm. of Governors, Bramcote Sch.; Trustee, Frank Lord Postgraduate Med. Centre. *Recreations:* photography, shooting. *Address:* Three Lanes, Greenfield, Oldham, Lancs OL3 7PB. *T:* Saddleworth (0457) 872198. *Clubs:* St James's (Manchester); Leander.
See also P. H. Lord.

LORD, Michael Nicholson; MP (C) Suffolk Central, since 1983; *b* 17 Oct. 1938; *s* of John Lord and Jessie Lord (*née* Nicholson); *m* 1965, Jennifer Margaret (*née* Childs); one *s* one *d. Educ:* Christ's College, Cambridge. MA. FArborA. Arboricultural consultant. PPS: to Minister of State, MAFF, 1984–85; to Chief Secretary to the Treasury, 1985–87. Member: Select Cttee on Parly Comr for Admin, 1990–; Council of Europe, 1987–; WEU, 1987–. *Recreations:* golf, sailing, gardening, trees. *Address:* House of Commons, SW1A 0AA.

LORD, Peter Herent, OBE 1991; FRCS; Consultant Surgeon, Wycombe General Hospital, High Wycombe, 1964–90; *b* 23 Nov. 1925; *s* of Sir Frank Lord, KBE, JP, DL and Rosalie Jeanette Herent; *m* 1952, Florence Shirley Hirst; two *s* two *d. Educ:* Manchester Grammar Sch.; St John's Coll., Cambridge (MA, MChir). St George's Hosp., Salford Royal Hosp., Christie Hosp., Manchester, St Margaret's, Epping, St George's Hosp., 1949–63 (Captain, RAMC, 1952–53). Royal College of Surgeons: H. N. Smith Research Fellow, 1964; Penrose May Teacher, 1970; Mem. Council, 1978–90; Vice-Pres., 1986–87. *Publications:* Cardiac Pacemakers, 1964; Pilonidal Sinus, 1964; Wound Healing, 1966; Haemorrhoids, 1969; Hydrocoele, 1972, Surgery in Old Age, 1980. *Recreations:* sailing, fishing. *Address:* Holly Tree House, 39 Grove Road, Beaconsfield, Bucks HP9 1PE. *T:* Beaconsfield (0494) 674488.
See also J. H. Lord.

LORD, William Burton Housley, CB 1979; scientific and technological consultant; *b* 22 March 1919; *s* of Arthur James Lord and Elsie Lord (*née* Housley); *m* 1942, Helena Headon Jaques; two *d. Educ:* King George V Sch., Southport; Manchester Univ.; London Univ. (External MSc); Trinity Coll., Cambridge (MA). Enlisted Royal Fusiliers, commn S Lancs Regt (served Middle East and N Africa), 1941–46. Cambridge Univ., 1946. Entered Civil Service, 1949; joined Atomic Weapons Res. Estab., 1952; Head of Metallurgy Div., AWRE, 1958; moved to MoD, 1964; Asst Chief Scientific Adviser (Research), 1965; Dep. Chief Scientist (Army), 1968–71; Dir Gen., Establishments, Resources and Programmes (B), MoD, 1971–76; Dir, RARDE, 1976–79. Award for wartime invention of radio proximity fuse, 1952. *Recreations:* amateur radio, walking, orienteering, water sports. *Address:* c/o Barclays Bank, 2 Victoria Street, SW1H 0ND.

LOREN, Sophia; film actress; *b* 20 Sept. 1934; *d* of Ricardo Scicolone and Romilda Villani; *m* 1957, Carlo Ponti, film producer (marriage annulled in Juarez, Mexico, Sept. 1962; marriage in Paris, France, April 1966); two *s. Educ:* parochial sch. and Teachers' Institute, Naples. First leading role in, Africa sotto i Mari, 1952; acted in many Italian films, 1952–55; subsequent films include: The Pride and the Passion; Boy on a Dolphin; Legend of the Lost; The Key; Desire under the Elms; Houseboat; The Black Orchid (Venice Film Festival Award, 1958); That Kind of Woman; It Started in Naples; Heller in Pink Tights; The Millionairess; Two Women (Cannes Film Festival Award, 1961); A Breath of Scandal; Madame sans Gêne; La Ciociara; El Cid; Boccaccio 70; Five Miles to Midnight; Yesterday, Today and Tomorrow; The Fall of the Roman Empire; Marriage, Italian Style; Operation Crossbow; Lady L; Judith; A Countess from Hong Kong; Arabesque; Sunflower; The Priest's Wife; The Man of La Mancha; The Verdict; The Voyage; Una Gionnata Particolare; Firepower; Blood Feud. *Publications:* Eat with Me, 1972; Sophia Loren on Woman and Beauty, 1984; *relevant publication:* Sophia: living and loving, by A. E. Hotcher, 1979. *Address:* Chalet Daniel Burgenstock, Luzern, Switzerland.

LORIMER, Dr George Huntly, FRS 1986; Research Leader, Central Research Department, E. I. Du Pont de Nemours & Co., since 1978; *b* 14 Oct. 1942; *s* of Gordon and Ellen Lorimer; *m* 1970, Freia (*née* Schulz-Baldes); one *s* one *d. Educ:* George Watson's College, Edinburgh; Univ. of St Andrews (BSc); Univ. of Illinois (MS); Michigan State Univ. (PhD). Scientist, Max-Planck Society, Berlin, 1972–74; Research Fellow, Inst. for Advanced Studies, ANU, Canberra, 1974–77; Scientist, Society for Radiation and Environmental Research, Munich, 1977. Mem., Amer. Soc. of Biological Chemists. *Publications:* contribs to Biochemistry, Jl of Biological Chemistry. *Recreations:* music, philately. *Address:* 2025 Harwyn Road, Wilmington, Delaware 19810, USA. *T:* (home) (302) 475–6748; (office) (302) 695–4584.

LORIMER, Hew Martin, OBE 1986; RSA; Sculptor; Representative in Fife of National Trust for Scotland; *b* 22 May 1907; 2nd *s* of late Sir Robert Stodart Lorimer, KBE, Hon. LLD, ARA, RSA, architect, and of Violet Alicia (*née* Wyld); *m* 1936, Mary McLeod Wylie (*d* 1970), 2nd *d* of H. M. Wylie, Edinburgh; two *s* one *d. Educ:*Loretto; Edinburgh Coll. of Art, Andrew Grant Scholarship, 1933 and Fellowship, 1934–35. National Library of Scotland, Edinburgh, sculptor of the 7 allegorical figures, 1952–55; Our Lady of the Isles, South Uist, 1955–57; St Francis, Dundee, 1957–59. Hon. LLD Dundee, 1983.

Recreations: music, travel, home. *Address:* Kellie Castle, Pittenweem, Anstruther, Fife KY10 2RF. *T:* Arncroach (03338) 323.

LORIMER, Sir (Thomas) Desmond, Kt 1976; Chairman, Northern Bank Ltd, since 1986 (Director, since 1983; Deputy Chairman, 1985); *b* 20 Oct. 1925; *s* of Thomas Berry Lorimer and Sarah Ann Lorimer; *m* 1957, Patricia Doris Samways; two *d.* *Educ:* Belfast Technical High Sch. Chartered Accountant, 1948; Fellow, Inst. of Chartered Accountants in Ireland, 1957. Practised as chartered accountant, 1952–74; Sen. Partner, Harmood, Banner, Smylie & Co., Belfast, Chartered Accountants, 1960–74; Chm., Lamont Holdings PLC, 1973–; Dir, Irish Distillers PLC, 1986–. Chm., Industrial Develt Bd for NI, 1982–85; Pres., Inst. of Chartered Accountants in Ireland, 1968–69; Chairman: Ulster Soc. of Chartered Accountants, 1960; NI Housing Exec., 1971–75; Mem., Rev. Body on Local Govt in NI, 1970. *Recreations:* gardening and golf. *Address:* Windwhistle Cottage, 6A Circular Road West, Cultra, Holywood, Co. Down BT18 0AT. *T:* Holywood (02317) 3323. *Clubs:* Carlton; Royal Belfast Golf, Royal Co. Down Golf (Co. Down).

LÖRINCZ-NAGY, János, Golden Grade of Order of Merit for Labour; Head of Department, Ministry of Foreign Affairs, Hungary, since 1981; *b* 19 Dec. 1931; *m* Ida Lörincz-Nagy; one *d.* *Educ:* Foreign Affairs Acad., Budapest; Coll. of Polit. Sciences, Budapest. Entered Diplomatic Service, 1953; Press Attaché, Peking, 1953–55; 2nd Sec., Djakarta, 1957–61; Dep. Head of Personnel Dept, 1964–68; Ambassador to Ghana, 1968–72; Head of Press Dept, 1972–74; Ambassador, Head of Hungarian Delegn to Internat. Commn of Control and Supervision in Saigon, 1974; Ambassador: to Sweden, 1975–76; to the Court of St James's, 1976–81. *Recreations:* reading and walking. *Address:* Ministry of Foreign Affairs, II Bem József rakpart 47, H-1394 Budapest, Hungary.

LORNE, Marquess of; Torquhil Ian Campbell; *b* 29 May 1968; *s* and *heir* of 12th Duke of Argyll, *qv.* *Educ:* Craigflower; Cargilfield; Glenalmond Coll. A Page of Honour to the Queen, 1981–83. *Address:* Inveraray Castle, Inveraray, Argyll.

LOSINSKA, Kathleen Mary, (Kate), OBE 1986; Senior Vice-President, Civil and Public Services Association, 1986–88 (President, 1979–82 and 1983–86, a Vice-President, 1982–83); *b* Croydon, Surrey, 5 Oct. 1924; *d* of late James Henry Conway, Border Regt and Dorothea Marguerite Hill; *m* 1942, Stanislaw Losinski (formerly serving Officer, Polish Air Force, subseq. 301 Bomber Sqdn, RAF, retd with rank of Sqdn Leader; awarded Polish Virtuti Militari Cross, Croix de Guerre, Cross of Lorraine, Yugoslav Cross of Valour, etc); one *s.* *Educ:* Selhurst Grammar Sch., Croydon (matriculation); university of life generally. Entered Civil Service, 1939; with Office of Population Censuses and Surveys. Delegate Mem., Council of Civil Service Unions, 1970–87 (Chm. 1980–81); Vice-Chm., CS Retirement Fellowship, 1988–. Commissioner: Trade Union TUC Nuclear Energy Review; CS Appeals BD, 1988–. Chairman: White Eagle Trust, 1985–; Solidarnosc Foundn. Has held all honorary positions, CFSA. Founder Mem., Resistance Internat., 1983–. Governor, Ruskin Coll., 1976, 1979–86. Silver Jubilee Medal, 1977. Kt Comdr, Order of Polonia Restituta, 1987. *Recreations:* journalism, reading, music, history, travel; work for the Christian Trade Union and Moderate Trade Union Movements. *Address:* Ballinard, Herbertstown, Co. Limerick, Eire. *T:* Limerick (61) 46177. *Club:* Civil Service.

LOSOWSKY, Prof. Monty Seymour, FRCP; Professor of Medicine and Head of University Department of Medicine, St James's University Hospital, Leeds, since 1969; Dean, Faculty of Medicine, Leeds University, since 1989; *b* 1 Aug. 1931; *s* of Dora and Myer Losowsky; *m* 1971, Barbara Malkin; one *s* one *d.* *Educ:* Coopers' Company's Sch., London; Univ. of Leeds (Hons MB, ChB; MD). House appts, Leeds Gen. Infirmary, 1955–56; Registrar in Medicine, Epping, 1957–59; Asst, Externe Hôpital St Antoine, Paris, 1960; Research Fellow, Harvard Med. Unit, 1961–62; Lectr, Sen. Lectr, Reader in Medicine, Univ. of Leeds, 1962–69. Member: Leeds Eastern Health Authy, 1981–89; Specialist Adv. Cttee on General (Internal) Medicine, 1984–88; Systems Bd Grants Cttee B, MRC, 1984–88; Panel of Studies Allied to Medicine, UGC, 1982–89; British Digestive Foundn Sci. and Res. Awards Cttee, 1987–90; Yorks RHA, 1989–90; Working Gp, France Steering Gp on Undergrad. Medical and Dental Educn, DoH, 1990–; Council, British Nutrition Foundn, 1991– (Mem. Scientific Adv. Cttee, 1987–91; Scientific Governor, 1991–); CVCP Rep., Acad. and Res. Staff Cttee of DoH Jt Planning and Adv. Cttee, 1990– (Mem., General Purposes Working Gp, 1989–). Chm., Coeliac Trust, 1983–. Examr for Membership, RCP. *Publications:* (jtly) Malabsorption in Clinical Practice, 1974; (ed) The Gut and Systemic Disease, 1983; (ed jtly) Advanced Medicine, 1983; (jtly) The Liver and Biliary System, 1984; (jtly) Clinical Nutrition in Gastroenterology, 1986; (jtly) Gut Defences in Clinical Practice, 1986; (jtly) Gastroenterology, 1988; papers relating to hepatology and gastroenterology. *Recreations:* table tennis, watching cricket, walking, DIY, medical biography. *Address:* Department of Medicine, St James's University Hospital, Leeds LS9 7TF. *T:* Leeds (0532) 433144. *Club:* Royal Society of Medicine.

LOSTY, Howard Harold Walter, FEng, FIEE; Secretary, Institution of Electrical Engineers, 1980–89; *b* 1 Aug. 1926; *s* of Patrick J. Losty and Edith E. Wilson; *m* 1950, Rosemary L. Everritt; two *d.* *Educ:* Harvey Grammar Sch, Folkestone; Sir John Cass Coll., London. BSc. GEC Research Laboratories, 1942–53; GEC Nuclear Power Programme, 1953–66; Head of Engineering Div., GEC Research Centre, 1966–71; Dir, GEC Hirst Research Centre, 1971–77; Man. Dir, GEC Electronic Devices Ltd, 1977–80. Hon. DEng Bradford, 1986. *Publications:* (co-author) Nuclear Graphite, 1962; some forty technical papers. *Recreations:* walking, listening to music (opera), reading history. *Address:* Shandon, 14 Wyatts Road, Chorleywood, Herts WD3 5TE. *T:* Chorleywood (0923) 283568.

LOTEN, Alexander William, CB 1984; FCIBSE; Under Secretary, Department of the Environment, and Director, Mechanical and Electrical Engineering Services, Property Services Agency, 1981–85, retired; *b* 11 Dec. 1925; *s* of late Alec Oliver Loten and Alice Maud Loten; *m* 1954, Mary Diana Flint; one *s* one *d.* *Educ:* Churcher's Coll., Petersfield; Corpus Christi Coll., Cambridge Univ. (BA). CEng, FIMechE 1980; FCIBSE 1970. Served War, RNVR, 1943–46 (Air Engr Officer). Engineer: Rolls-Royce Ltd, Derby, 1950–54; Benham & Sons, London, 1954–58; Air Min. Work Directorate, 1958–64; Sen. Engr, 1964–70, Superintending Engr (Mechanical Design), 1970–75, MPBW; Dir of Works, Civil Accommodation, PSA, 1975–81. Pres., CIBS, 1976–77. Lt-Col, Engr and Railway Staff Corps RE, T&AVR, 1979–. *Recreations:* walking, gardening. *Address:* Hockridge House, London Road, Maresfield, E Sussex TN22 2EH.

LOTHIAN, 12th Marquess of *cr* 1701; **Peter Francis Walter Kerr,** KCVO 1983; DL; Lord Newbattle, 1591; Earl of Lothian, 1606; Baron Jedburgh, 1622; Earl of Ancram, Baron Kerr of Nisbet, Baron Long-Newton and Dolphingston, 1633; Viscount of Brien, Baron Kerr of Newbattle, 1701; Baron Ker (UK), 1821; Lord Warden of the Stannaries and Keeper of the Privy Seal of the Duke of Cornwall, 1977–83; *b* 8 Sept. 1922; *s* of late Captain Andrew William Kerr, RN, and Marie Constance Annabel, *d* of Capt. William Walter Raleigh Kerr; *S* cousin, 1940; *m* 1943, Antonella, *d* of late Maj.-Gen. Sir Foster Newland, KCMG, CB, and Mrs William Carr, Ditchingham Hall, Norfolk; two *s* four *d.* *Educ:* Ampleforth; Christ Church, Oxford. Lieut, Scots Guards, 1943. Mem. Brit. Delegation: UN Gen. Assembly, 1956–57; European Parliament, 1973; UK Delegate, Council of Europe and WEU, 1959. PPS to Foreign Sec., 1960–63; a Lord in Waiting (Govt Whip, House of Lords), 1962–63, 1972–73; Joint Parliamentary Sec., Min. of Health, April-Oct. 1964; Parly Under-Sec. of State, FCO, 1970–72. Chm., Scottish Council, British Red Cross Soc., 1976–86. Mem., Queen's Body Guard for Scotland (Royal Company of Archers). Mem., Prince of Wales Council, 1976–83. DL, Roxburgh, 1962. Kt, SMO Malta. *Heir:* *s* Earl of Ancram, *qv.* *Address:* Ferniehirst Castle, Jedburgh, Roxburghshire. *T:* Jedburgh (0835) 64021; 54 Upper Cheyne Row, SW3. *Clubs:* Boodle's, Beefsteak; New (Edinburgh).

See also Col Sir D. H. Cameron of Lochiel, Earl of Dalkeith, Earl of Euston.

LOTON, Brian Thorley, AC 1989; FTS; Managing Director, since 1982, and Chief Executive Officer, since 1984, Broken Hill Proprietary Co. Ltd; Director, National Australia Bank, since 1988; *b* Perth, WA, 17 May 1929; *s* of Sir (Ernest) Thorley Loton and Grace (*née* Smith); *m* 1956, Joan Kemelfield; two *s* two *d.* *Educ:* Hale Sch., Perth; Trinity Coll., Melbourne Univ. (BMetEng 1953). Joined BHP as Cadet 1954; Technical Asst, 1959; Asst Chief Engr, 1961; Gen. Manager Planning and Develt, 1969, Gen. Manager Newcastle Steel Works, 1970; Exec. Gen. Manager Steel Div., 1973; Dir, 1976; Chief Gen. Manager, 1977. Pres., Australian Mining Industry Council, 1983–84; Mem. Council (Pres., 1982), Aust. Inst. of Mining and Metallurgy; Vice-Chm., Defence Industry Cttee, 1976–88; Member: Aust. Sci. and Tehnol. Council, 1977–80; Aust. Manufg Council, 1977–81; Vict. Govt Long Range Policy Planning Cttee, 1980–82; Aust. Council on Population and Ethnic Affairs, 1980–82. Internat. Counsellor, The Conf. Bd, 1984–. Mem. Faculty Engrg, Melbourne Univ., 1980–83. FIE (Aust) 1984 (Hon. Fellow); FAIM 1973; FIDA 1980. *Address:* c/o GPO Box 86A, Melbourne, Vic 3001, Australia. *Clubs:* Melbourne, Australian (Melbourne).

LOTT, Dr Bernard Maurice, OBE 1966; Research Fellow, University College London, since 1980; *b* 13 Aug. 1922; *s* of late William Lott and of Margaret Lott (*née* Smith); *m* 1949, Helena, *d* of late Clarence Winkup; one *s* one *d* (and one *s* decd). *Educ:* Bancroft's Sch.; Keble Coll., Oxford (MA); Univ. of London (MA Distinction, PhD); Univ. of Edinburgh (Dip. in Applied Linguistics, Dist.). RN, 1942–46. Brit. Council Lectr in English, Ankara Univ. and Gazi Inst. of Educn, Turkey, 1949–55; Brit. Council Asst Rep., Finland, 1955–57; Prof. of Eng. and Head of Dept, Univ. of Indonesia, 1958–61; Dir of Studies, Indian Central Inst. of Eng., 1961–66; Dep. Controller, Educn Div., Brit. Council, 1966–72; Controller, Eng. Teaching Div., Brit. Council, 1972–75; Brit. Council Representative, Poland, 1975–77; English Language Teaching Develt Adviser, British Council, 1977–79; Course Tutor, Open Univ., 1979–86; Lectr in Applied Linguistics, Poly. of Central London, 1989–90. *Publications:* A Course in English Language and Literature, 1986; Gen. Editor, New Swan Shakespeare series, and edited: Macbeth, 1958, Twelfth Night, 1959, Merchant of Venice, 1962, Hamlet, 1968 (also Open Univ. edn 1970), King Lear, 1974, Much Ado About Nothing, 1977; contribs on teaching of English as foreign lang. to Times Educnl Supp. and Eng. Lang. Teaching Jl. *Recreations:* local studies, music. *Address:* 8 Meadway, NW11 7JT. *T:* 081–455 0918.

LOTT, Felicity Ann Emwhyla, CBE 1990; soprano; *b* 8 May 1947; *d* of John Albert Lott and Whyla (*née* Williams); *m* 1st, 1973, Robin Mavesyn Golding (marr. diss. 1982); 2nd, 1984, Gabriel Woolf; one *d.* *Educ:* Pate's Grammar Sch. for Girls, Cheltenham; Royal Holloway Coll., Univ. of London (BA Hons French); Royal Acad. of Music (LRAM; ARAM 1976; FRAM 1986). Principal rôles with English National Opera, Glyndebourne, Welsh National Opera, Covent Garden, Scottish Opera; opera and recitals all over Europe and USA; Australian tour, 1985; many recordings. Founder Mem., The Songmakers' Almanac. Dr *hc* Sussex, 1989. *Recreations:* reading, sleeping. *Address:* c/o Lies Askonas, 186 Drury Lane, WC2B 5QD. *T:* 071–405 1808.

LOTZ, Prof. Dr Kurt; German business executive; *b* 18 Sept. 1912; *m* Elizabeth Lony; two *s* one *d.* *Educ:* August-Vilmar-Schule, Homberg. Joined Police Service, 1932; Lieut 1934. Served Luftwaffe (Gen. Staff; Major), 1942–45. Employed by Brown Boveri & Cie, Dortmund, 1946; Head of Business Div., Mannheim, 1954; Dir 1957; Chm. 1958–67; Mem. Board of Directors in parent company, Baden, Switzerland, 1961; Managing Director, 1963–67. Dep. Chm., 1967–68, Chm., 1968–71, Volkswagenwerk AG. Member: Deutscher Rat für Landespflege. Chm., World Wildlife Fund, Germany, 1980. Mem., Rotary Internat. Hon. Senator, Heidelberg Univ., 1963; Hon. Prof., Technische Universität Carolo Wilhelmina, Brunswick, 1970. Dr rer. pol. *hc* Mannheim, 1963. *Publication:* Lebenserfahrungen: Worüber man in Wirtschaft und Politik auch sprechen sollte, 1978. *Recreations:* hiking, hunting, golf. *Address:* W-6900 Heidelberg, Bergstrasse 110, Germany.

LOUDON, George Ernest; Director, Midland Group, and Chief Executive, Midland Montagu, since 1988; *b* 19 Nov. 1942; *m* 1968, Angela Mary Goldsbrough; one *s* one *d.* *Educ:* Christelijk Lyceum, Zeist; Balliol Coll., Oxford (BA); Johns Hopkins Univ., Washington (MA). Lazard Frères & Cie, Paris, 1967–68; Ford Foundn, New York and Jakarta, 1968–71; McKinsey & Co., Amsterdam, 1971–76; Amro Bank, Amsterdam: Gen. Man., 1976–83; Mem., Bd of Man. Dirs, 1983–88. *Address:* Chief Executive's Office, Midland Montagu, 10 Lower Thames Street, EC3R 6AE. *T:* 071–260 9500.

LOUDON, John Duncan Ott, OBE 1988; FRCSE, FRCOG; retired; Consultant Obstetrician and Gynaecologist, Eastern General Hospital, Edinburgh, 1960–87; Senior Lecturer, University of Edinburgh, since 1962; *b* 22 Aug. 1924; *s* of late James Alexander Law Loudon and Ursula (*née* Ott) *m* 1953, Nancy Beaton (*née* Mann); two *s.* *Educ:* John Watson's Sch., Edinburgh; Wyggeston Sch., Leicester; Univ. of Edinburgh (MB, ChB 1947). FRCSE 1954; FRCOG 1973 (MRCOG 1956). National Service, RAF, 1948–50. House appts, Edinburgh and Cambridge, 1948–52; Registrar, Sen. Registrar and Consultant Obstetrician and Gynaecologist, Simpson Maternity Pavilion and Royal Infirm., Edinburgh, 1954–66. Formerly Examiner in Obstetrics and Gynaecology: Univs of Cardiff, Manchester, Leeds, Dundee, Glasgow, Aberdeen, Newcastle upon Tyne, Cape Town, RCSI, RCSE, RCOG and RACOG. Adviser in Family Welfare to Govt of Malta, 1976–81. Vice Pres., RCOG, 1981–84 (Mem. Council, 1966–72 and 1976–81). Member: Interim Licensing Authority for IVF, 1985–; GMC, 1986–. *Publications:* papers to obstetric and gynaecol jls. *Recreations:* gardening, golf, travel, food and wine. *Address:* Ardbeg, 4 Kinnear Road, Edinburgh EH3 5PE. *T:* 031–552 1327. *Clubs:* Royal Air Force; Bruntsfield Links Golfing Society (Edinburgh).

LOUDON, John Hugo; Jonkheer (Netherlands title); Knight in the Order of the Netherlands Lion, 1953; Grand Officer, Order of Orange-Nassau, 1965; KBE (Hon.) (Gt Brit.), 1960; Officer, Légion d'Honneur, 1963; holds other decorations; *b* 27 June 1905; *s* of Jonkheer Hugo Loudon and Anna Petronella Alida Loudon (*née* van Marken); *m* 1931, Baroness Marie Cornelie van Tuyll van Serooskerken (*d* 1988); three *s* (and one *s* decd). *Educ:* Netherlands Lyceum, The Hague; Utrecht Univ., Holland. Doctor of Law, 1929. Joined Royal Dutch/Shell Group of Cos, 1930; served in USA, 1932–38; Venezuela, 1938–47 (Gen. Man., 1944–47); Man. Dir, 1947–52, Pres., 1952–65, Chm., 1965–76, Royal Dutch Petroleum Co.; former Chm., Shell Oil Co. (New York); Vice-Chm. Bd, Royal Netherlands Blast-furnaces & Steelworks, NV, 1971–76; Director: Orion Bank Ltd, 1971–81; Chase Manhattan Corp., 1971–76; Estel NV Hoesch-Hoogovens, 1972–76; Russell Reynolds Assocs Inc., 1977–; Adv. Dir, Bd, Arrow Partners CV, NY, 1983–.

Chairman: Internat. Adv. Cttee, Chase Manhattan Bank, 1965–77; Bd, Atlantic Inst., 1969–84; European Adv. Cttee, Ford Motor Co., 1976–83. Bd Mem., Institut Européen d'Administration des Affaires, 1971–89; Mem., Rockefeller Univ. Council, NY, 1978–; Mem. Bd Trustees, Ford Foundation, 1966–75; Internat. Pres., World Wildlife Fund, 1977–81. *Recreations:* golf, yachting. *Address:* 48 Lange Voorhout, 2514 EG The Hague, Holland. *T:* 3453755; Koekoeksduin, 5 Vogelenzangseweg 2111 HP, Aerdenhout, Holland. *T:* Haarlem 245924. *Clubs:* White's; Royal Yacht Squadron.

LOUDON, Prof. Rodney, FRS 1987; Professor of Physics, Essex University, since 1967; *b* 25 July 1934; *s* of Albert Loudon and Doris Helen (*née* Blane); *m* 1960, Mary Anne Philips; one *s* one *d*. *Educ:* Bury Grammar Sch.; Brasenose Coll., Oxford (MA, DPhil). Postdoctoral Fellow, Univ. of California, Berkeley, 1959–60; Scientific Civil Servant, RRE Malvern, 1960–65; Member, Technical Staff: Bell Labs, Murray Hill, NJ, 1965–66, 1970; RCA Labs, Zurich, 1975; Essex University: Reader in Physics, 1966–67; Dean of Sch. of Physical Scis, 1972–74; Chm. of Physics Dept, 1976–79 and 1988–89. Visiting Professor: Yale Univ., 1975; Univ. of California, Irvine, 1980; Ecole Polytechnique, Lausanne, 1985; Univ. of Rome, 1988. Chm., Bd of Editors of Optica Acta, 1984–87. Thomas Young Medal and Prize, Inst. of Physics, 1987. *Publications:* The Quantum Theory of Light, 1973, 2nd edn 1983; (with W. Hayes) Scattering of Light by Crystals, 1978; (ed with V. M. Agranovich) Surface Excitations, 1984; (with D. J. Barber) An Introduction to the Properties of Condensed Matter, 1989; papers in Nature, Phys. Rev., Optica Acta, Jl Phys., etc. *Recreation:* music, particularly choral singing and instrument making. *Address:* 3 Gaston Street, East Bergholt, Colchester, Essex CO7 6SD. *T:* Colchester (0206) 298550.

LOUDOUN, Countess of (13th in line) *cr* 1633; **Barbara Huddleston Abney-Hastings;** Lady Campbell Baroness of Loudoun, 1601; Lady Tarrinzean and Mauchline, 1638; the 3 English baronies of Botreaux 1368, Stanley 1456, and Hastings 1461, which were held by the late Countess, are abeyant, the Countess and her sisters being *co-heiresses*; *b* 3 July 1919; assumed by deed poll, 1955, the surname of Abney-Hastings in lieu of that of Griffiths; *S* mother, 1960; *m* 1st, 1939 (marr. diss., 1945), Capt. Walter Strickland Lord; one *s*; 2nd, 1945, Capt. Gilbert Frederick Greenwood (*d* 1951); one *s* one *d*; 3rd, 1954, Peter Griffiths (who assumed by deed poll the surname of Abney-Hastings in lieu of his patronymic, 1958); three *d*. *Heir:* *s* Lord Mauchline, *qv*. *Address:* Mount Walk, Ashby-de-la-Zouch, Leics. *T:* Ashby-de-la-Zouch (0530) 415844.

LOUDOUN, Maj.-Gen. Robert Beverley, CB 1973; OBE 1965; Director, Mental Health Foundation, 1977–90; *b* 8 July 1922; *s* of Robert and Margaret Loudoun; *m* 1950, Audrey Stevens; two *s*. *Educ:* University College Sch., Hampstead. Served War of 1939–45 (despatches): enlisted Royal Marines, 1940; commissioned, 1941; 43 Commando, Central Mediterranean, 1943–45; 45 Commando, Hong Kong, Malta and Palestine, 1945–48. Instructor, RNC Greenwich, 1950–52; Staff of C-in-C America and West Indies, 1953–55; RN Staff Coll., 1956; Adjt, 40 Commando, Malta and Cyprus, 1958–59; USMC Sch., Quantico, Virginia, 1959–60; MoD, 1960–62; Second-in-Command, 42 Commando, Singapore and Borneo, 1963–64; CO, 40 Commando, Far East, 1967–69; Brig., UK Commandos, Plymouth, 1969–71; Maj.-Gen. RM Training Gp, Portsmouth, 1971–75, retired 1975. Representative Col Comdt, RM, 1983–84. Chairman: Jt Shooting Cttee for GB, 1977–82; British Yugoslav Soc., 1989–. Freeman, City of London, 1979; Mem., Guild of Freemen, 1982–. *Address:* 2 Warwick Drive, Putney, SW15 6LB. *Club:* Army and Navy.

LOUGH, Prof. John, FBA 1975; Professor of French, University of Durham (late Durham Colleges), 1952–78; *b* 19 Feb. 1913; *s* of Wilfrid Gordon and Mary Turnbull Lough, Newcastle upon Tyne; *m* 1939, Muriel Barker; one *d*. *Educ:* Newcastle upon Tyne Royal Grammar Sch.; St John's Coll., Cambridge; Sorbonne. Major Schol., St John's Coll., 1931; BA, First Cl. Hons Parts I and II Mod. and Medieval Langs Tripos, 1934; Esmond Schol. at British Inst. in Paris, 1935; Jebb Studentship, Cambridge, 1936; PhD 1937, MA 1938, Cambridge. Asst (later Lectr), Univ. of Aberdeen, 1937; Lectr in French, Cambridge, 1946. Leverhulme Res. Fellow, 1973. Hon. Dr, Univ. of Clermont, 1967; Hon. DLitt Newcastle, 1972. Officier de l'Ordre National du Mérite, 1973. *Publications:* Locke's Travels in France, 1953; (ed) selected Philosophical Writings of Diderot, 1953; (ed) The Encyclopédie of Diderot and d'Alembert: selected articles, 1954; An Introduction to Seventeenth Century France, 1954; Paris Theatre Audiences in the 17th and 18th centuries, 1957; An Introduction to Eighteenth Century France, 1960; Essays on the Encyclopédie of Diderot and D'Alembert, 1968; The Encyclopédie in 18th Century England and other studies, 1970; The Encyclopédie, 1971; The Contributors to the Encyclopédie, 1973; (ed with J. Proust) Diderot: Œuvres complètes, vols V-VIII, 1977; (with M. Lough) An Introduction to Nineteenth Century France, 1978; Writer and Public in France, 1978; Seventeenth Century French Drama: the background, 1979; The Philosophes and Post-Revolutionary France, 1982; France Observed in the Seventeenth Century by British Travellers, 1985; France on the Eve of Revolution: observations by British travellers 1763–1788, 1987; (with E. Merson) John Graham Lough (1798–1876), a Northumbrian Sculptor, 1987; articles on French literature and ideas in 17th and 18th centuries in French and English learned jls. *Address:* 1 St Hild's Lane, Durham DH1 1QL. *T:* Durham (091) 3848034.

LOUGHBOROUGH, Lord; Jamie William St Clair-Erskine; *b* 28 May 1986; *s* and *heir* of Earl of Rosslyn, *qv*.

LOUGHBOROUGH, Archdeacon of; *see* Jones, Ven. T. H.

LOUGHEED, Hon. (Edgar) Peter, CC (Can.) 1987; PC (Can.) 1982; QC (Can.) 1972; Partner, Bennett Jones Verchere, barristers and solicitors, Calgary and Edmonton; *b* Calgary, 26 July 1928; *s* of late Edgar Donald Lougheed and Edna Bauld; *m* 1952, Jeanne Estelle Rogers, Edmonton; two *s* two *d*. *Educ:* public and secondary schs, Calgary; Univ. of Alberta (BA, LLB); Harvard Grad. Sch. of Business (MBA). Read law with Calgary firm of lawyers; called to Bar of Alberta, 1955, and practised law with same firm, 1955–56. Joined Mannix Co. Ltd, as Sec., 1956 (Gen. Counsel, 1958, Vice-Pres., 1959, Dir, 1960). Entered private legal practice, 1962. Director: ATCO Ltd; Luscar Ltd; Canadian Pacific; Royal Bank of Canada; Princeton Developments; Northern Telecom; Brascan Ltd; Bombardier Inc.; Quorum Capital Corp.; Reed Stenhouse Cos Ltd; The Matthews Gp; Norcen Energy Resources Ltd; Carlson Construction Ltd; CFCN Telecommunications Ltd; PWA Corporation Ltd; Bechtel Canada Inc., DMR Gp Inc. Adviser to: Morgan Grenfell & Co. Ltd; Govt of Northwest Territories. Lectr, Calgary Univ. Elected: Provincial Leader of Progressive Conservative Party of Alberta, also Member for Calgary West, 1965; Leader of the Official Opposition, 1967; Premier of Alberta, 1971–85 (re-elected 1975, 1979 and 1982). Hon. LLD: St Francis Xavier, 1983; Alberta, 1986; Calgary, 1987; Windsor, Lethbridge, 1988. *Recreations:* golf, ski-ing. *Address:* (office) 4500 Bankers Hall East, 855 2nd Street SE, Calgary, Alberta T2P 4J8, Canada.

LOUGHLIN, Charles William; trade union official; retired 1974; *b* 16 Feb. 1914; *s* of late Charles Loughlin, Grimsby; *m* 1945, May, *d* of David Arthur Dunderdale, Leeds; one *s* (one *d* decd). *Educ:* St Mary's Sch., Grimsby; National Council of Labour Colls; Leeds Polytechnic (BA History and Politics, 1989). Area Organiser, Union of Shop, Distributive and Allied Workers, 1945–74. MP (Lab) Gloucestershire West, 1959–Sept. 1974; Parly Sec., Min. of Health, 1965–67; Jt Parly Sec., Min. of Social Security, then Dept of Health and Social Security, 1967–68; Parly Sec., Min. of Public Building and Works, 1968–70. *Address:* Flat 25, Richmond House, Street Lane, Leeds LS8 1BW. *T:* Leeds (0532) 665327.

LOUGHRAN, James; Principal Conductor and Musical Adviser, Hallé Orchestra, 1971–83, Conductor Laureate, since 1983; *b* 30 June 1931; *s* of James and Agnes Loughran; *m* 1st, 1961, Nancy Coggon (marr. diss. 1983); two *s*; 2nd, 1985, Ludmila (*née* Navratil). *Educ:* St Aloysius' Coll., Glasgow; Bonn, Amsterdam and Milan. FRNCM 1976; FRSAMD 1983. 1st Prize, Philharmonia Orchestra's Conducting Competition, 1961. Associate Conductor, Bournemouth Symphony Orchestra, 1962–65; Principal Conductor: BBC Scottish Symphony Orchestra, 1965–71; Bamberg Symphony Orchestra, 1979–83; Musical Dir, English Opera Gp, 1966 (Festivals of Drottningholm, Versailles and Aldeburgh). Guest conductor of principal orchestras of Europe, America, Australia and Japan. Internat. festivals and tours with Bamberg and Hallé orchestras, as well as Munich Philharmonic, BBC Symphony, Stockholm Philharmonic, London Philharmonic and Scottish Chamber orchestras. Many recordings, including complete Beethoven and Brahms symphonies. Gold Disc, EMI, 1983. Hon. DMus Sheffield, 1983. *Address:* The Rookery, Bollington Cross, Macclesfield, Cheshire SK10 5EL.

LOUIS, John Jeffry, Jr; Director: Air Wisconsin, Inc., since 1984; Baxter Travenol Laboratories, since 1984; Gannett Company, Inc., since 1984; Johnson's Wax, since 1961; *b* 10 June 1925; *s* of John Jeffry Louis and Henrietta Louis (*née* Johnson); *m* 1953, Josephine Peters; one *s* two *d*. *Educ:* Deerfield Academy, Mass; Northwestern Univ., 1943 and 1946; Williams Coll., Mass (BA 1947); Dartmouth Coll., New Hampshire (MBA 1949). Served with AUS, 1943–45. Account Executive, Needham, Louis & Brorby, Inc., Chicago, 1952–58; Director, International Marketing, Johnson's Wax, Wis, 1958–61; Chairman Board: KTAR Broadcasting Co., Ariz., 1961–68; Combined Communications Corp., Chicago, 1968–80. US Ambassador to UK, 1981–83. Trustee: Northwestern Univ., 1967–81, 1984–; Deerfield Acad., 1963–81; Foxcroft Sch., 1975–79; Williams Coll., 1979–81. Trustee, Evanston Hosp., 1959–81, 1984– (Chm., 1962–68). Hon. Master of The Bench, Middle Temple, 1981. *Recreations:* golf, tennis, skiing, shooting. *Address:* Suite 510, One Northfield Plaza, Northfield, Illinois 60093, USA. *Clubs:* Old Elm (Illinois); Pine Valley Golf (New Jersey); Augusta National Golf (Georgia); Gulfstream Golf (Florida).

LOUISY, Rt. Hon. Allan (Fitzgerald Laurent), CBE 1983; PC 1981; Leader of St Lucia Labour Party. Prime Minister of St Lucia, and Minister of Finance, Home Affairs, Information and Tourism, 1979–81; Minister without Portfolio, 1981–82; Minister of Legal Affairs, Jan.-May 1982. *Address:* Laborie, St Lucia, West Indies.

LOUSADA, Sir Anthony (Baruh), Kt 1975; Solicitor; Partner in Stephenson Harwood, 1935–73; Consultant, 1973–81; *b* 4 Nov. 1907; *s* of Julian George Lousada and Maude Reignier Conder; *m* 1st, 1937, Jocelyn (marr. diss. 1960), *d* of late Sir Alan Herbert, CH; one *s* three *d*; 2nd, 1961, Patricia, *d* of late C. J. McBride, USA; one *s* one *d*. *Educ:* Westminster; New Coll., Oxford. Admitted Solicitor, 1933. Min. of Economic Warfare, 1939–44; Min. of Production and War Cabinet Office, 1944–45. Member: Council, Royal College of Art, 1952–79 (Hon. Fellow, 1957; Sen. Fellow, 1967; Vice-Chm., 1960–72; Treasurer, 1967–72; Chm., 1972–79; Hon. Dr 1977); Cttee, Contemp. Art Soc., 1955–71 (Vice-Chm., 1961–71); Fine Arts Cttee, British Council (visited Japan on behalf of Council, 1970, to set up exhibn of sculpture by Barbara Hepworth); GPO Adv. Cttee on Stamp Design, 1968–80; Chairman: Adv. Cttee, Govt Art Collection, 1976–83; British Art Market Standing Cttee, 1984–90. Council, Friends of Tate Gallery, 1958– (Hon. Treasurer, 1960–65, Chm., 1971–77); Trustee, Tate Gallery, 1962–69 (Vice-Chm., 1965–67; Chm., 1967–69). One-man exhibns of drawings, Covt Gdn Gall., 1977, 1981. Officer, Order of Belgian Crown, 1945. *Recreations:* painting, music, travel. *Address:* The Tides, Chiswick Mall, W4. *T:* 081–994 2257. *Clubs:* Garrick; London Corinthian Sailing.

LOUSTAU-LALANNE, Bernard Michel; Secretary-General, European Federation of Management Consulting Associations, since 1991; *b* 20 June 1938; *s* of Joseph Antoine Michel Loustau-Lalanne, OBE, and Marie Therese Madeleine (*née* Boullé); *m* 1974, Debbie Elizabeth Temple-Brown (marr. diss. 1982); one *d*. *Educ:* Seychelles Coll.; St Mary's Coll., Southampton; Imperial Coll., London. Called to the Bar, Middle Temple, London, 1969. Assistant Inspector, Northern Rhodesia Police, 1962–64; Crown Counsel, Seychelles, 1970–72; Sen. State Counsel and Official Notary, 1972–76; Attorney-General, Seychelles, 1976–78; High Comr for Seychelles, in London, 1978–80; concurrently Seychelles Ambassador to USA, and Seychelles Perm. Rep. to UN; Internat. Rep., PRS, 1980–90. *Recreations:* international affairs, French literature, theatre, tennis, ski-ing. *Address:* FEACO, 79 avenue de Cortenbergh, 1040 Brussels, Belgium. *T:* (322) 736 6001, *Fax:* (322) 736 3008. *Club:* Seychelles Yacht.

LOUTH, 16th Baron, *cr* 1541, **Otway Michael James Oliver Plunkett;** *b* 19 Aug. 1929; *o s* of Otway Randal Percy Oliver Plunkett, 15th Baron, and Ethel May, *d* of Walter John Gallichen, Jersey, Channel Islands; *S* father, 1950; *m* 1951, Angela Patricia Cullinane, Jersey; three *s* two *d*. *Heir:* *s* Hon. Jonathan Oliver Plunkett, BSc, AMIEE [*b* 4 Nov. 1952; *m* 1981, Jennifer, *d* of Norman Oliver Hodgetts, Weston-super-Mare; one *s* one *d*]. *Address:* Les Sercles, La Grande Pièce, St Peter, Jersey, Channel Islands.

LOUTIT, John Freeman, CBE 1957; FRS 1963; MA, DM, FRCP; External Scientific Staff Medical Research Council, 1969–75, Visitor at Radiobiology Unit, 1975–88; *b* 19 Feb. 1910; *s* of John Freeman Loutit, Perth, WA; *m* 1941, Thelma Salusbury; one *s* two *d*. *Educ:* C of E Grammar Sch., Guildford, W Australia; Univs of W Australia, Melbourne, Oxford, London. Rhodes Scholar (W Australia), 1930; BA Oxon 1933, BM, BCh Oxon 1935. Various appointments, London Hosp., 1935–39; MA (Oxon) 1938; Director, South London Blood Supply Depot, 1940–47; DM Oxon, 1946; Dir, Radiobiological Research Unit, AERE Harwell, 1947–69. FRCP 1955. VMD (*hc*) Stockholm, 1965; Hon. DSc St Andrews, 1988. Officer, Order of Orange-Nassau (Netherlands) 1951. *Publications:* Irradiation of Mice and Men, 1962; Tissue Grafting and Radiation (jointly), 1966; articles in scientific journals. *Recreations:* cooking, gardening. *Address:* 22 Milton Lane, Steventon, Oxon OX13 6SA. *T:* Abingdon (0235) 831279.

LOVAT, 17th Baron (S) *cr* before 1440 (*de facto* 15th Baron, 17th but for the Attainder); **Simon Christopher Joseph Fraser,** DSO 1942; MC; TD; JP; DL; Baron (UK) 1837; 24th Chief of Clan Fraser of Lovat; *b* 9 July 1911; *s* of 16th Baron and Hon. Laura Lister (*d* 1965), 2nd *d* of 4th Baron Ribblesdale; *S* father, 1933; *m* 1938, Rosamond, *o d* of Sir Delves Broughton, 11th Bt; four *s* two *d*. *Educ:* Ampleforth; Magdalen Coll., Oxford, BA. Lt, Scots Guards, 1932–37, retd. Served War of 1939–45: Capt. Lovat Scouts, 1939; Lt-Col 1942; Brig. Commandos, 1943 (wounded, MC, DSO, Order of Suvarov, Légion d'Honneur, Croix de Guerre avec palme; Norway Liberation Cross). Under-Sec. of State for Foreign Affairs, 1945. DL 1942, JP 1944, Inverness. Awarded LLD (Hon.) by Canadian universities. Order of St John of Jerusalem; Knight of Malta; Papal Order of St Gregory with Collar. *Publication:* March Past, 1978. *Heir:* *s* Master of Lovat, *qv*. *Address:* Balblair,

Beauly, Inverness-shire. *Club*: Cavalry and Guards.
See also Earl of Eldon, Sir Fitzroy Maclean of Dunconnel, Bt, Lord Reay.

LOVAT, Master of; Hon. Simon Augustine Fraser; *b* 28 Aug. 1939; *s* of 17th Baron Lovat, *qv*; *m* 1972, Virginia, *d* of David Grose; two *s* one *d*. *Educ*: Ampleforth Coll. Lieut Scots Guards, 1960. *Address*: Beaufort Castle, Beauly, Inverness-shire.

LOVAT, Sheriff Leonard Scott; Sheriff of South Strathclyde, Dumfries and Galloway at Hamilton, since 1978; *b* 28 July 1926; *s* of late Charles Lovat and Alice (*née* Hunter); *m* 1960, Elinor Frances, *d* of late J. A. McAlister and Mary McAlister; one *s* one *d*. *Educ*: St Aloysius Coll., Glasgow; Glasgow Univ. (BL 1947). Solicitor, 1948; in partnership, 1955–59. Asst to Prof. of Roman Law, Glasgow Univ., 1954–63; Cropwood Fellow, Inst. of Criminology, Univ. of Cambridge, 1971. Procurator Fiscal Depute, Glasgow, 1960; Sen. Asst Procurator Fiscal, Glasgow and Strathkelvin, 1976. Mem. Cttee, W of Scotland Br., CCJ. *Publications*: Climbers' Guide to Glencoe and Ardgour, 2 vols, 1959, 1965; articles and reviews in legal jls. *Recreations*: music, mountaineering, bird-watching. *Address*: 38 Kelvin Court, Glasgow G12 0AE. *T*: 041–357 0031. *Club*: Alpine.

LOVE, Prof. Andrew Henry Garmany, MD; FRCP, FRCPI; Professor of Medicine since 1983, and Dean of Faculty of Medicine, 1981–86, Queen's University of Belfast; *b* 28 Sept. 1934; *s* of Andrew and Martha Love; *m* 1963, Margaret Jean Lennox; one *s*. *Educ*: Bangor Endowed Sch., NI; Queen's Univ. of Belfast (BSc Hons 1955; MD 1963). FRCP 1973; FRCPI 1972. Lectr in Physiology, 1960–63 and Lectr in Medicine, 1963–64, QUB; MRC Travelling Fellow, and Hon. Consultant, US Naval Med. Res. Unit-2, Taipei, Taiwan, 1964–65; Sen. Lectr in Medicine, 1966–73 and Prof. of Gastroenterology, 1973–83, QUB (on leave of absence, Res. Fellow, Boston City Hosp., Mass, 1966). Hon. Consultant, SEATO Cholera Labs, Pakistan, 1967–70. Mem., GMC, 1981–87. Pres., Assoc. of Medical Deans of Europe, 1988–. *Publications*: articles in learned jls on gen. medicine, intestinal function, trace element metabolism and nutrition. *Recreations*: golf, sailing. *Address*: The Lodge, New Road, Donaghadee, Co. Down, Northern Ireland BT21 0DU. *T*: Donaghadee (0247) 883507. *Clubs*: East India, Devonshire, Sports and Public Schools; Royal Ulster Yacht (Bangor, Co. Down); Royal County Down Golf (Newcastle).

LOVE, Sir (Makere Rangiatea) Ralph, Kt 1987; QSO; JP; Department of Maori Affairs (welfare, Maori Land Court and other administration divisions), New Zealand, 1925–65, retired; *b* 16 Sept. 1907; *s* of Wi Hapi Love, OBE and Ripeka Love, OBE; *m* 1933, Flora Heberley; one *s* one *d*. *Educ*: Petone District High Sch. Public Service cadet in Native Trust Office, 1925; Accounts; Administrator for Maori lands, Native Dept, 1932; Secretarial Corps of Parlt, 1946. Councillor, Wellington CC, 1962–65; Mayor of Bor. of Petone, 1965–68; Member: Wellington Reg. Authority; Envmt and Planning Services Cttee, Wellington Regl Council. Jt Patron, Wellington 1990 Trust. PM, William Ferguson Massey Lodge no 282. Sir Ralph belongs to the Maori Te Atiawa tribe on his father's side and to the Taranaki tribe on his mother's side. *Recreations*: participant in cricket, rugby, swimming; later an administrator in all these sports (Executive and Council, NZ Rugby Union). *Address*: 17 Rakeiora Grove, Korokoro, Petone, New Zealand. *T*: (04) 691–924. *Clubs*: Petone Workingmen's (Life Member), and others.

LOVE, Prof. Philip Noel, CBE 1983; Professor of Conveyancing and Professional Practice of Law, University of Aberdeen, since 1974 (Dean of Faculty of Law, 1979–82, Vice-Principal, 1986–90); Member, Scottish Law Commission, since 1986; *b* 25 Dec. 1939; *o s* of Thomas Isaac and Ethel Violet Love; *m* 1963, Isabel Leah, *yr d* of Innes Taylor and Leah Wallace Mearns; three *s*. *Educ*: Aberdeen Grammar Sch.; Aberdeen Univ. (MA 1961, LLB 1963). Admitted Solicitor in Scotland, 1963; Advocate in Aberdeen, 1963–; Partner, Campbell Connon & Co., Solicitors, Aberdeen, 1963–74, Consultant, 1974–. Law Society of Scotland: Mem. Council, 1975–86; Examr, 1975–83 (Chm. Examrs, 1977–80); Vice-Pres., 1980–81; Pres., 1981–82. Local Chm., Rent Assessment Panel for Scotland, 1972–; Chairman: Sec. of State for Scotland's Expert Cttee on house purchase and sale, 1982–84; Scottish Conveyancing and Executory Services Bd, 1991–; Vice-Pres., Scottish Law Agents Soc., 1970; Member: Jt Standing Cttee on Legal Educn in Scotland, 1976–85 (Chm., 1976–80); Rules Council, Court of Session, 1968–; Council, Internat. Bar Assoc., 1983–87 (Vice-Chm., Legal Educn Div., 1983–87); Jt Ethical Cttee, Grampian Health Bd, 1984– (Vice-Chm., 1985; Chm., 1986). Chm., Aberdeen Home for Widowers' Children, 1971–. Pres., Aberdeen Grammar Sch. Former Pupils' Club, 1987–88. Hon. Sheriff of Grampian, Highland and Islands, 1978–. Chm., Registers of Scotland Customer Adv. Gp, 1990–. Trustee, Grampian and Islands Family Trust, 1988–. Gov., Inst. of Occupational Medicine Ltd, 1990–. Mem., Editl Consultative Bd for Scotland, Butterworth & Co. (Publishers) Ltd, 1990–. *Recreations*: Rugby (Golden Oldies variety now), keep-fit (FRS Club, Aberdeen). *Address*: 3A Rubislaw Den North, Aberdeen AB2 4AL. *T*: Aberdeen (0224) 313339. *Clubs*: New (Edinburgh); Royal Aberdeen Golf, Aberdeen Grammar School Former Pupils' Club Centre (Aberdeen).

LOVE, Sir Ralph; *see* Love, Sir M. R. R.

LOVEDAY, Alan (Raymond); Solo Violinist; *b* 29 Feb. 1928; *s* of Leslie and Margaret Loveday; *m* 1952, Ruth Stanfield; one *s* one *d*. *Educ*: privately; Royal College of Music (prizewinner). Made debut at age of 4; debut in England, 1946; has given many concerts, broadcasts, and made TV appearances, in this country and abroad, playing with all leading conductors and orchestras; repertoire ranges from Bach (which he likes to play on an un-modernised violin), to contemporary music. Prof., RCM, 1955–72. Full-time Mem. and Soloist, Acad. of St Martin-in-the-Fields. *Recreations*: chess, bridge.

LOVEGROVE, Geoffrey David, QC 1969; His Honour Judge Lovegrove; a Circuit Judge (formerly County Court Judge), since 1971; *b* 22 Dec. 1919; *s* of late Gilbert Henry Lovegrove; *m* 1959, Janet, *d* of John Bourne; one *s* two *d*. *Educ*: Haileybury; New College, Oxford (MA). Army, 1940–46. Called to the Bar, Inner Temple, 1947; Dep. Chairman, W Sussex Quarter Sessions, 1965–71; Master, Innholders' Company, 1980–81. *Address*: 1 King's Bench Walk, Temple, EC4.

LOVELACE, 5th Earl of, *cr* 1838; **Peter Axel William Locke King;** Baron King and Ockham, 1725; Viscount Ockham, 1838; *b* 26 Nov. 1951; *s* of 4th Earl of Lovelace and Manon Lis (*d* 1990), *d* of Axel Sigurd Transo, Copenhagen, Denmark; *S* father, 1964. *Address*: Torridon House, Torridon, Ross-shire.

LOVELL, Sir (Alfred Charles) Bernard, Kt 1961; OBE 1946; FRS 1955; Director of Jodrell Bank Experimental Station, Cheshire, now Nuffield Radio Astronomy Laboratories, 1951–81; Professor of Radio Astronomy, University of Manchester, 1951–80, now Emeritus Professor; *b* 31 Aug. 1913; *s* of G. Lovell, Oldland Common, Gloucestershire; *m* 1937, Mary Joyce Chesterman; two *s* three *d*. *Educ*: Kingswood Grammar Sch., Bristol; University of Bristol. Asst Lectr in Physics, Univ. of Manchester, 1936–39; Telecommunication Res. Establishment, 1939–45; Physical Laboratories, Univ. of Manchester and Jodrell Bank Experimental Station, Cheshire; Lectr, 1945, Sen. Lectr, 1947, Reader, 1949, in Physics. Reith Lectr, 1958; Lectures: Condon, 1962; Guthrie, 1962; Halley, 1964; Queen's, Berlin, 1970; Brockington, Kingston, Ont, 1970; Bickley, Oxford, 1977; Crookshank, RCR, 1977; Angel Meml, Newfoundland, 1977; Blackett Meml, Operational Res. Soc., 1987. Vis. Montague Burton Prof. of Internat. Relations,

Univ. of Edinburgh, 1973. Member: Air Navigation Cttee, 1953–56 (Vice-Chm., 1955–56); Air Warfare Cttee, 1954–60; ARC, 1955–58; Radar & Signals Adv. Bd, 1956–59; Sci. Adv. Council, 1957–60; Guided Weapons Adv. Bd, 1958–60; SRC, 1965–70; Amer. Philosophical Soc., 1974–. Pres., RAS, 1969–71; Vice-Pres., Internat. Astronomical Union, 1970–76; Pres., British Assoc., 1975–76. Pres., Guild of Church Musicians, 1976–89; Jun. Warden, 1984–85, Sen. Warden, 1985–86, Master, 1986–87, Musicians' Co. Hon. Freeman, City of Manchester, 1977. Hon. Fellow, Society of Engineers, 1964; Hon. Foreign Member American Academy of Arts and Sciences, 1955; Hon. Life Member, New York Academy, 1960; Hon. Member: Royal Swedish Academy, 1962; RNCM, 1981; Manchester Lit. & Philos. Soc., 1988. Hon. LLD: Edinburgh, 1961; Calgary, 1966; Hon. DSc: Leicester, 1961; Leeds, 1966; London, 1967; Bath, 1967; Bristol, 1970; DUniv Stirling, 1974; DUniv Surrey, 1975; Hon. FIEE, 1967; Hon. FInstP, 1976. Duddell Medal, 1954; Royal Medal, 1960; Daniel and Florence Guggenheim International Astronautics Award, 1961; Ordre du Mérite pour la Recherche et l'Invention, 1962; Churchill Gold Medal, 1964; Maitland Lecturer and Silver Medallist, Institution of Structural Engineers, 1964; Second RSA American Exchange Lectr, Philadelphia, 1980; Benjamin Franklin Medal, RSA, 1980; Gold Medal, Royal Astronomical Soc., 1981; Rutherford Meml Lectr, Royal Soc., 1984. Commander's Order of Merit, Polish People's Republic, 1975. *Publications*: Science and Civilisation, 1939; World Power Resources and Social Development, 1945; Radio Astronomy, 1951; Meteor Astronomy, 1954; The Exploration of Space by Radio, 1957; The Individual and The Universe, (BBC Reith Lectures, 1958); The Exploration of Outer Space (Gregynog Lectures, 1961); Discovering the Universe, 1963; Our Present Knowledge of the Universe, 1967; (ed with T. Margerison) The Explosion of Science: The Physical Universe, 1967; The Story of Jodrell Bank, 1968; The Origins and International Economics of Space Exploration, 1973; Out of the Zenith, 1973; Man's Relation to the Universe, 1975; P. M. S. Blackett: a biographical memoir, 1976; In the Centre of Immensities, 1978; Emerging Cosmology, 1981; The Jodrell Bank Telescopes, 1985; Voice of the Universe, 1987; (with Sir Francis Graham Smith) Pathways to the Universe, 1988; Astronomer by Chance (autobiog.), 1990; many publications in Physical and Astronomical journals. *Recreations*: cricket, gardening, music. *Address*: The Quinta, Swettenham, Cheshire. *T*: Lower Withington (0477) 71254. *Clubs*: Athenæum, MCC; Lancashire County Cricket (Vice-Pres., 1981–).

LOVELL, Kenneth Ernest Walter; Treasurer to the Greater London Council, 1977–80, retired; *b* 25 Oct. 1919; *s* of Ernest John and Alice Lovell; *m* 1946, Vera Mary Pithouse; one *s* two *d*. *Educ*: Ashford County Grammar School. Mem. Chartered Inst. of Public Finance and Accountancy. Middlesex County Council (Finance Dept): Computer Manager, 1961; Asst County Treasurer, 1963. Greater London Council: Asst Treasurer, 1965; Finance Officer, ILEA, 1972. *Recreations*: gardening, cricket, hockey, photography; study of social and economic development of British Isles; study of landscape of British Isles. *Address*: 15 Meadway Close, Staines, Mddx TW18 2PR. *T*: Staines (0784) 452806.

LOVELL-DAVIS, family name of **Baron Lovell-Davis.**

LOVELL-DAVIS, Baron *cr* 1974 (Life Peer), of Highgate; **Peter Lovell Lovell-Davis;** Member: Commonwealth Development Corporation, 1978–84; London Consortium, since 1978; *b* 8 July 1924; *s* of late William Lovell Davis and late Winifred Mary Davis; *m* 1950, Jean Graham; one *s* one *d*. *Educ*: Christ's Coll., Finchley; King Edward VI Sch., Stratford-on-Avon; Jesus Coll., Oxford. BA Hons English, MA. Served War, RAF (Pilot), to Flt-Lt, 1943–47. Oxford, 1947–50. Managing Dir, Central Press Features Ltd, 1952–70; Dir, various newspaper and printing cos. Chm., Colour Features Ltd; Chairman: Davis & Harrison Ltd, 1970–73; Features Syndicate, 1971–74; Lee Cooper Licensing Services, 1983–90; Pettifor, Morrow & Associates, 1986–. Mem., Islington DHA, 1982–85. A Lord in Waiting (Govt Whip), 1974–75; Parly Under-Sec. of State, Dept of Energy, 1975–76. Adviser to various Govt Cttees, Health Educn Council, Labour Party and Govt, on media. Vice-Pres., YHA, 1978–; Trustee, Whittington Hosp. Academic Centre, 1980–. *Recreations*: industrial archaeology, inland waterways, bird-watching, walking, sketching. *Address*: 80 North Road, Highgate, N6 4AA. *T*: 081–348 3919.

LOVELOCK, Sir Douglas (Arthur), KCB 1979 (CB 1974); First Church Estates Commissioner, since 1983; Chairman, Central Board of Finance of the Church of England, since 1983; *b* 7 Sept. 1923; *s* of late Walter and Irene Lovelock; *m* 1961, Valerie Margaret (*née* Lane); one *s* one *d*. *Educ*: Bec Sch., London. Entered Treasury, 1949; Min. of Supply, 1952; Private Sec. to Permanent Sec., 1953–54; Principal, 1954; Private Sec. to successive Ministers of Aviation (Rt Hon. Peter Thorneycroft and Rt Hon. Julian Amery), 1961–63; Asst Sec., 1963; Under-Sec. (Contracts), Min. of Technology, subseq. Min. of Aviation Supply, 1968–71; Asst Under-Sec. of State (Personnel), MoD, 1971–72; Dep. Sec., DTI, 1972–74, Depts of Trade, Industry, Prices and Consumer Protection, 1974–77; Chm., Bd of Customs and Excise, 1977–83. Chm., Civil Service Benevolent Fund, 1980–83. Chm., Review of Citizens' Advice Bureaux Service, 1983–84. Governor: Whitgift Foundn, 1986–; Whitgift Sch., 1986–; Trinity Sch., 1986–. *Recreations*: walking, gardening, outdoor activities generally. *Address*: The Old House, 91 Coulsdon Road, Old Coulsdon, Surrey CR3 2LD. *T*: Downland (07375) 55211.

LOVELOCK, Prof. James Ephraim, CBE 1990; FRS 1974; independent scientist, since 1964; Visiting Professor, University of Reading, 1967–90; *b* 26 July 1919; *s* of Tom Arthur Lovelock and Nellie Ann Elizabeth (*née* March); *m* 1942, Helen Mary Hyslop (*d* 1989); two *s* two *d*; *m* 1991, Sandra Jean Orchard. *Educ*: Strand Sch., London; Manchester and London Univs. BSc, PhD, DSc, ARIC. Staff Scientist, Nat. Inst. for Med. Research, 1941–61; Rockefeller Fellow, Harvard Univ., 1954–55; Yale Univ., 1958–59; Prof. of Chemistry, Baylor Univ. Coll. of Medicine, Texas, 1961–64. Pres., Marine Biol Assoc., 1986–90. Mem. Sigma Xi, Yale Chapter, 1959. Hon. ScD East Anglia, 1982; Hon. DSc: Exeter, 1988; Plymouth Polytechnic, 1988. Amsterdam Prize, Roy. Netherlands Acad. of Arts and Scis, 1990. *Publications*: Gaia, 1979; (with Michael Allaby) The Great Extinction, 1983; The Ages of Gaia, 1988; numerous papers and patents. *Recreations*: walking, painting, computer programming, reading. *Address*: Coombe Mill, St Giles on the Heath, Launceston, Cornwall PL15 9RY.

LOVEMAN, Stephen Charles Gardner; Under Secretary, Department of Employment, since 1989; *b* 26 Dec. 1943; *s* of Charles Edward Loveman and Edith Mary Gardner; *m* 1972, Judith Pamela Roberts; one *s* one *d*. *Educ*: Arnold Sch., Blackpool; Emmanuel College, Cambridge (BA). Dept of Employment, 1967; Private Sec. to Minister of State for Employment, 1972–74; Health and Safety Exec., 1974–77; Dept of Employment, 1977–80; Manpower Services Commn, 1980–84; Dept of Employment, 1987–88; Cabinet Office, 1988–89. *Recreations*: walking, opera, light reading, swimming. *Address*: 24 Brincliffe Crescent, Sheffield S11 9AW.

LOVERIDGE, Sir John (Henry), Kt 1975; CBE 1964 (MBE 1945); Bailiff of Guernsey, 1973–82; Barrister-at-Law; Judge of Appeal for Jersey, 1974–82; *b* 2 Aug. 1912; *e s* of late Henry Thomas and Vera Lilian Loveridge; *m* 1946, Madeleine Melanie, *o d* of late Eugene Joseph C. M. Tanguy; one *s* one *d*. *Educ*: Elizabeth Coll., Guernsey; Univ. of Caen. Called to Bar, Middle Temple, 1950. Advocate of Royal Court of Guernsey, 1951; HM Solicitor-General, Guernsey, 1954–60; HM Attorney-General, Guernsey, 1960–69;

Deputy Bailiff of Guernsey, 1969–73. RAFVR, 1954–59. KStJ 1980. *Recreations:* reading, swimming, sport. *Address:* Kinmount, Sausmarez Road, St Martin's, Guernsey. *T:* Guernsey (0481) 38038. *Club:* Royal Guernsey Golf.

LOVERIDGE, Sir John (Warren), Kt 1988; JP; senior partner of family businesses in agriculture, education and property; *b* 9 Sept. 1925; *s* of C. W. Loveridge and Emily (Mickie), *d* of John Malone; *m* 1954, Jean Marguerite, *d* of E. J. Chivers; three *s* two *d*. *Educ:* St John's Coll., Cambridge (MA). Mem., Hampstead BC, 1953–59. Contested (C) Aberavon, 1951, Brixton (LCC), 1952. MP (C) Hornchurch, 1970–74, Upminster, 1974–83. Member: Parly Select Cttee on Expenditure (Mem. General Purposes Sub-Cttee); Procedure Cttee; Chm., Cons. Smaller Business Cttee, 1979–83). Treasurer/Trustee, Hampstead Conservative Assoc., 1959–74; Pres., Hampstead and Highgate Conservative Assoc., 1986–91; Vice-Pres., Greater London Area Conservatives, 1984–. Vice-Pres., Nat. Council for Civil Protection (formerly Civil Defence), 1980–. JP West Central Division, 1963. FRAS; FRAgS; MRIIA. Liveryman, Girdlers' Co. *Publications:* (jtly) Moving Forward: small businesses and the economy, 1983; *poems:* God Save the Queen: Sonnets of Elizabeth I, 1981; Hunter of the Moon, 1983; Hunter of the Sun, 1984. *Recreations:* painting, writing, historic houses, shooting. *Address:* c/o The Private Office, 2 Arkwright Road, NW3 6AD.

LOVERING, Prof. John Francis, FAA; Vice-Chancellor and Professor of Geology, Flinders University of South Australia, since 1987; *b* 27 March 1930; *s* of George Francis Lovering and Dorothy Irene Mildwater; *m* 1954, Jennifer Kerry FitzGerald; two *s* one *d*. *Educ:* Canterbury High Sch., Sydney; Univ. of Sydney (MSc); Univ. of Melbourne (MSc); California Inst. of Technology (PhD). FAA 1982. Asst Curator of Minerals, Australian Museum, 1951–55; Research Fellow, Fellow and Sen. Fellow, Dept of Geophysics and Geochemistry, ANU, 1956–69; University of Melbourne: Prof. of Geology, 1969–87; Dean of Science, 1983–85; Dep. Vice-Chancellor (Research), 1985–87. Chairman of Directors: Comlabs Ltd, 1985–; Geotrack International Pty Ltd, 1987–. Chevalier des Palmes Académiques, 1981. *Publications:* Last of Lands: Antarctica (with J. R. V. Prescott), 1979; contribs to learned jls. *Recreations:* music, wine, food. *Address:* Flinders University of South Australia, GPO Box 2100, Adelaide, SA 5001, Australia. *T:* (08) 201–2061. *Clubs:* Adelaide (Adelaide); Antarctic, Banool Ski, Melbourne, Wallaby (Melbourne).

LOVICK, Albert Ernest Fred; retired; Chairman, 1964–68, Director, 1950–68 and 1969–78, Co-operative Insurance Society Ltd; Chairman, Cumbrian Co-operative Society Ltd, Carlisle, 1972–86; Director: CWS Ltd, 1949–78; Shoefayre Ltd, 1975–78; *b* 19 Feb. 1912; *s* of late Arthur Alfred Lovick and late Mary Lovick (*née* Sharland); *m* 1934, Florence Ena Jewell; no *c*. *Educ:* Elementary Sch., Eastleigh, Hants; Peter Symonds, Winchester. Hearne & Partner, rating surveyors, 1928; Eastleigh Co-operative Society, 1929–33; Harwich, Dovercourt and Parkeston CS, 1933–35; Managing Secretary, Basingstoke CS, 1935–49. During War of 1939–45, government cttees. Member, Basingstoke Borough Council, 1946–49. Former Chm., Centratours Ltd. Member: Export Credits Guarantees Advisory Council, 1968–73; Bristol Rent Assessment Cttee, 1973–; Bristol Rent Tribunal, 1973–. Fellow, Co-operative Secretaries Assoc.; FCIS; FCIArb. *Recreations:* golf, gardening. *Address:* Coedway, Bristol Road, Stonehouse, Glos GL10 2BQ. *T:* Stonehouse (045382) 3167. *Club:* Commonwealth Trust.

LOVILL, Sir John (Roger), Kt 1987; CBE 1983; DL; Chairman, Sloane Square Investments, since 1980 (Director since 1960); *b* 26 Sept. 1929; *s* of Walter Thomas Lovill and Elsie Lovill (*née* Page); *m* 1958, Jacqueline (*née* Parker); two *s* one *d*. *Educ:* Brighton Hove and Sussex Grammar School. S. G. Warburg, 1951–55; Dep. Gen. Manager, Securicor Ltd, 1955–60; Dir, Municipal Gen. Insce Co., 1984–; Managing Trustee, Municipal Mutual Insce, 1988–. Contested (C) Ebbw Vale, 1966; Mem., East Sussex CC, 1967–89, Leader, 1973–77; Chairman: Sussex Police Authority, 1976–79; Local Authority Conditions of Service Adv. Bd, 1978–83; ACC, 1983–86; Pres., Sussex Assoc. of Local Councils, 1987–; Leader, Conservative Assoc. of County Councils, 1981–83. DL E Sussex 1983. *Recreations:* opera, politics, marine paintings. *Address:* Beddingham, near Lewes, Sussex. *T:* Glynde (0273) 858212.

LOW, family name of **Baron Aldington.**

LOW, Sir Alan (Roberts), Kt 1977; retired; Governor, Reserve Bank of New Zealand, 1967–77; *b* 11 Jan. 1916; 4th *s* of Benjamin H. Low and Sarah Low; *m* 1940, Kathleen Mary Harrow; one *s* two *d*. *Educ:* Timaru Main Sch.; Timaru Boys' High Sch.; Canterbury University College. MA 1937. Joined Reserve Bank of New Zealand, 1938; Economic Adviser, 1951; Asst Governor, 1960; Deputy Governor, 1962; Governor, 1967. Army Service, 1942–44; on loan to Economic Stabilisation Commission, 1944–46. Hon. Fellow, Bankers' Inst. of NZ, 1977. Hon. LLD Canterbury, 1977. *Publications:* No Free Lunch, 1983; Where DO We Go For Lunch, 1984; contributions to many economic and financial jls. *Recreations:* gardening, music, reading. *Address:* 171 Muritai Road, Eastbourne, Wellington, New Zealand. *T:* 628–861.

LOW, Prof. Donald Anthony, DPhil; PhD; FAHA, FASSA; President of Clare Hall, since 1987, and Smuts Professor of the History of the British Commonwealth, since 1983, University of Cambridge; *b* 22 June 1927; *o s* of late Canon Donald Low and Winifred (*née* Edmunds); *m* 1952, Isobel Smails; one *s* two *d*. *Educ:* Haileybury and ISC; Univ. of Oxford (MA, DPhil); PhD Cantab 1983. Open Scholar in Modern History, 1944 and Amelia Jackson Sen. Student, 1948, Exeter Coll., Oxford; Lectr, subseq. Sen. Lectr, Makerere Coll., University Coll. of E Africa, 1951–58; Uganda corresp., The Times, 1952–58; Fellow, subseq. Sen. Fellow in History, Res. Sch. of Social Sciences, ANU, 1959–64; Founding Dean of Sch. of African and Asian Studies, and Prof. of Hist., Univ. of Sussex, 1964–72; Australian National University: Prof. of History, 1973–83; Dir, Res. Sch. of Pacific Studies, 1973–75; Vice Chancellor, 1975–82; University of Cambridge: Fellow, Churchill Coll., 1983–87; Dir, Centre of Internat. Studies, 1985–87; Mem., Council of Senate, 1985–88. Chm., Educn Adv. Cttee, Aust. Develt Assistance Bureau, 1979–82; Mem. Exec., 1976–82, Dep. Chm., 1980, Aust. Vice-Chancellors' Cttee; Member: Council, Univ. of Papua New Guinea, 1974–82; Standing Cttee, Aust. Univs Internat. Develt Program, 1975–82; Council, ACU, 1980–82; Cttee, Australian Studies Centre, London Univ., 1983–; Governing Body: SOAS, 1983–; Inst. of Develt Studies, Sussex Univ., 1984–; Haileybury, 1985–; Chm., Cttee of Management, Inst. of Commonwealth Studies, London Univ., 1984–. Sen. Visitor Nuffield Coll., Oxford, 1956–57; Smuts Fellow and Vis. Fellow, Clare Hall, Cambridge, 1971–72. Hon. Fellow: Inst. of Develt Studies, UK, 1972; University House, ANU 1983. President: African Studies Assoc. of Aust. and Pacific, 1979–82; Asian Studies Assoc. of Aust., 1980–82; British Australian Studies Assoc., 1984–86; Chm., Co-ordinating Council, Area Studies Assoc., 1988–. Commander of the Order of Civil Merit (Spain), 1984. *Publications:* Buganda and British Overrule, 1900–1955 (with R. C. Pratt), 1960; (ed) Soundings in Modern South Asian History, 1968; (with J. C. Iltis and M. D. Wainwright) Government Archives in South Asia, 1969; Buganda in Modern History, 1971; The Mind of Buganda, 1971; Lion Rampant, 1973; (ed) Congress and the Raj 1917–1947, 1977; Oxford History of East Africa: (contrib.) Vol. I, 1963 and Vol. II, 1965; (contrib. and ed jtly) Vol. III, 1976; (ed) Constitutional Heads and Political Crises, 1988; (ed) The Indian National Congress, 1988; (ed jtly) Sovereigns and Surrogates, 1990; Eclipse of Empire, 1991; (ed) Political Inheritance of Pakistan, 1991; articles on internat. history in jls. *Address:* Clare Hall, Cambridge CB3 9AL. *T:* Cambridge (0223) 332370.

LOW, Dr (George) Graeme (Erick), CBE 1989; Member, 1986–91, Managing Director, Site Operations, 1990–91, United Kingdom Atomic Energy Authority; *b* Palmerston North, NZ, 29 Nov. 1928; *s* of George Eric Low and Evelyn Edith Low (*née* Gillman); *m* 1st, 1952, Marion Townsend (marr. diss. 1977); two *d*; 2nd, 1985, Joan Kathleen Swinburne. *Educ:* New Plymouth Boys' High Sch., NZ; Canterbury Coll., Univ. of NZ (BSc, MSc); Univ. of Reading (PhD, DSc). FInstP. Special Branch, RNZN, 1952–58; Research Scientist, 1958–68, Head of Materials Physics Div., 1968–70, AERE Harwell; Special Asst to Dir, UKAEA Research Gp, 1970–73; Programme Dir (Applied Nuclear), 1973–76, Research Dir (Industry), 1976–81, Dir of Environmental Research, 1981–83, AERE Harwell; Dir, AEE, Winfrith, 1983–86; Dir, AERE Harwell, 1986–87; Mem. for Estabts, UKAEA, 1987–90. Dir, UK Nirex Ltd, 1986–91. *Publications:* papers on semi-conductors, neutron beam studies of the solid state, magnetism and management. *Recreations:* reading, walking, family and friends. *Address:* UKAEA, 11 Charles II Street, SW1Y 4QP. *T:* 071–389 6565.

LOW, Sir James (Richard) Morrison-, 3rd Bt, *cr* 1908; DL; DFH, CEng, MIEE; Director, Osborne & Hunter Ltd, Glasgow, 1956–89 (Electrical Engineer with firm, since 1952); *b* 3 Aug. 1925; *s* of Sir Walter John Morrison-Low, 2nd Bt and Dorothy Ruth de Quincey Quincey (*d* 1946); *S* father 1955; *m* 1953, Ann Rawson Gordon; one *s* three *d*. *Educ:* Ardvreck; Harrow; Merchiston. Served Royal Corps of Signals, 1943–47; demobilised with rank of Captain. Faraday House Engineering Coll., 1948–52. Chm., Scottish Cttee, Nat. Inspection Council for Electrical Installation Contracting, 1982–88; Pres., Electrical Contractors Assoc. of Scotland, 1982–84. Chm., Fife Area Scout Council, 1966–84. Hon. Pipe-Major, Royal Scottish Pipers Soc., 1981–83. Eur Ing, 1990. DL Fife, 1978. *Recreations:* shooting, piping. *Heir:* *s* Richard Walter Morrison-Low, *b* 4 Aug. 1959. *Address:* Kilmaron Castle, Cupar, Fife. *T:* Cupar (0334) 52248. *Clubs:* New, Royal Scottish Pipers Society (Edinburgh).

LOWDEN, Gordon Stuart; President, Institute of Chartered Accountants of Scotland, 1989–90 (Senior Vice-President, 1988–89); Chairman, Dundee Port Authority, since 1979; *b* 22 May 1927; *s* of James Soutar Lowden and Jean Lowden; *m* 1953, Kathleen Arnot; two *s* one *d*. *Educ:* Dundee High Sch.; Strathallan Sch.; St John's Coll., Cambridge (MA); Univ. of St Andrews (LLB). CA. Moody Stuart & Robertson, later Peat Marwick McLintock: training, 1949–53; Partner, 1959; Office Managing Partner, 1985; retired 1988. University of Dundee: Lectr, Sen. Lectr, 1955–83; Hon. Vis. Prof., Dept of Accountancy and Business Finance, 1987. *Recreations:* golf, watching sport, bridge. *Address:* 169 Hamilton Street, Barnhill, Dundee. *T:* Dundee (0382) 78360. *Clubs:* New (Edinburgh); Royal and Ancient Golf.

LOWE, David Alexander; QC 1984; *b* Kilbirnie, Ayrshire, 1 Nov. 1942; *o s* of late David Alexander Lowe and of Rea Sadie Aitchison Lowe (*née* Bridges); *m* 1972, Vivian Anne Langley; three *s* two *d*. *Educ:* Pocklington Sch., York; St John's Coll., Cambridge (schol.; MA; MacMahon Law Student). Called to Bar, Middle Temple, 1965 (Harmsworth Schol.); *ad eundem,* Lincoln's Inn, 1975. In practice at the Chancery Bar, 1966–. *Address:* 3 New Square, Lincoln's Inn, WC2A 3RS. *T:* 071–405 5296.

LOWE, David Bruce Douglas; His Honour Judge Lowe; a Circuit Judge, since 1983; *b* 3 April 1935; *o s* of late Douglas Gordon Arthur Lowe, QC, and of Karen, *e d* of Surgeon Einar Thamsen; *m* 1978, Dagmar, *o d* of Horst and Anneliese Bosse; one *s* three *d* (and one *s* one *d* by a previous marriage). *Educ:* Winchester College; Pembroke Coll., Cambridge (MA). National service, RN, 1953–55. Profumo Scholar, Inner Temple. Called to the Bar, Inner Temple, 1960; Midland and Oxford Circuit (formerly Midland); Prosecuting Counsel to Dept of Trade, 1975–83; a Recorder of the Crown Court, 1980–83. *Recreations:* music, tennis, gardening (formerly rackets and real tennis). *Address:* Crown Court at Middlesex Guildhall, Broad Sanctuary, SW1P 3BB. *Club:* Hawks (Cambridge).

LOWE, David Nicoll, OBE 1946; MA, BSc; FRSE; Secretary, Carnegie United Kingdom Trust, 1954–70; *b* 9 Sept. 1909; *s* of George Black Lowe and Jane Nicoll, Arbroath, Angus; *m* 1939, Muriel Enid Bryer, CSP; one *s* three *d*. *Educ:* Arbroath High Sch.; St Andrews Univ. (Kitchener Scholar). MA 1931; BSc (1st Class Hons Botany) 1934; President Union, 1933–34; President Students' Representative Council, 1934–35; Founder President, University Mountaineering Club; Asst Secretary British Assoc. for the Advancement of Science, 1935–40, Secretary 1946–54. War Cabinet Secretariat, 1940–42 and 1945–46; Ministry of Production, 1942–45. Joint Hon. Secretary, Society of Visiting Scientists, 1952–54; Member Executive Cttee: Scottish Council of Social Service, 1953–71; Nat. Trust for Scotland, 1971–81; Member, Countryside Commn for Scotland, 1968–78. Chairman: Scottish Congregational Coll., 1961–68; Pollock Meml Missionary Trust, 1973–84; Governor, Scottish Nat. Meml to David Livingstone, 1974–80. Contributor to Annual Register, 1947–59. Queen's Silver Jubilee Medal, 1977. *Recreations:* gardening, choral music. *Address:* Caddam, Perth Road, Crieff, Perthshire.

LOWE, Hon. Douglas Ackley; MLC (Ind.) for Buckingham, Tasmania, since 1986; Deputy Leader for Government, Legislative Council, since 1989; *b* 15 May 1942; *s* of Ackley Reginald Lowe and Dulcie Mary Lowe (*née* Kean); *m* 1963, Pamela June (*née* Grant); two *s* two *d*. *Educ:* St Virgil College, Hobart. Mem. Tasmanian House of Assembly, for Franklin, 1969–86: ALP, 1969–82; Ind., 1982–86. Minister for Housing, 1972; Chief Secretary, 1974; Deputy Premier, 1975–77; Chief Sec. and Minister for Planning and Reorganisation, 1975; Premier, 1977–81; Treasurer, 1980–81; Minister for: Industrial Relations, Planning and the Environment, 1976; Industrial Relations and Health, Aug. 1976; Industrial Relations and Manpower Planning, 1977–79; Economic Planning and Development, 1979–80; Energy, 1979–81. Australian Labor Party: State Sec. 1965–69, State Pres. 1974–75, Tasmanian Section. Tasmanian Deleg. to Aust. Constitutional Convention. Queen's Silver Jubilee Medal, 1977. *Publication:* The Price of Power, 1984. *Address:* (home) 15 Tooma Avenue, Chigwell, Hobart, Tasmania; (office) Parliament House, Hobart, Tasmania. *T:* (002) 302348.

LOWE, Air Chief Marshal Sir Douglas (Charles), GCB 1977 (KCB 1974; CB 1971); DFC 1943; AFC 1946; Chairman, Band III Holdings Ltd, since 1986; Director, Rolls-Royce, since 1984; *b* 14 March 1922; *s* of John William Lowe; *m* 1944, Doreen Elizabeth (*née* Nichols); one *s* one *d*. *Educ:* Reading School. Joined RAF, 1940; No 75 (NZ) Sqdn, 1943; Bomber Comd Instructors' Sch., 1945; RAF Coll., Cranwell, 1947; Exam. Wing CFS, 1950; Air Min. Operational Requirements, 1955; OC No 148 Sqdn, 1959; Exchange Officer, HQ SAC, USAF, 1961; Stn Comdr Cranwell, 1963; idc 1966; DOR 2 (RAF), MoD (Air), 1967; SASO, NEAF, 1969–71; ACAS (Operational Requirements), 1971–73; AOC No 18 Group, RAF, 1973–75; Controller, Aircraft, MoD Procurement Executive, 1975–82; Chief of Defence Procurement, MoD, Sept. 1982–June 1983. Air ADC to the Queen, 1978–83. Chm., Mercury Communications Ltd, 1984–85; Dir, Royal Ordnance plc, 1984–7. Mem. Council, St John's Sch., Leatherhead, 1984–. CRAeS 1982; CBIM 1984. *Recreations:* gardening, domestic odd-jobbing, photography, theatre, music. *Address:*

c/o Lloyds Bank, Byfleet, Surrey. *Club:* Royal Air Force.
See also Baron Glanusk.

LOWE, Air Vice-Marshal Sir Edgar (Noel), KBE 1962 (CBE 1945); CB 1947; Director General of Supply Co-ordination, Ministry of Defence, 1966–70, retired (Inspector General of Codification and Standardisation, 1964); *b* 1905; *s* of late Albert Henry Lowe, Church Stretton, Shropshire; *m* 1948, Mary McIlwraith, *o d* of George M. Lockhart, Stair House, Stair, Ayrshire; one *s* one *d.* Served India, 1934–38; psa 1939; served in France 1939–40 (despatches); Air Commodore, Director of Organisation (Forecasting and Planning), Air Ministry, 1945–47; idc 1949; ADC to the King, 1949–52, to the Queen, 1952–57; Directing Staff, RAF Staff Coll., Bracknell, 1950–51; Director of Organisation, Air Ministry, 1951–53; Deputy Asst Chief of Staff (Logistics), SHAPE, 1953–56; Senior Air Staff Officer, HQ No 41 Group, RAF, 1956–58; AOC No 40 Group, RAF, 1958–61; Director-General of Equipment, Air Ministry, 1961–64. *Address:* Wyndford, 97 Harestone Hill, Caterham, Surrey CR3 6DL. *Club:* Royal Air Force.

LOWE, Frank Budge; Founder, 1981, and Chairman of The Lowe Group Plc; Chairman of Lowe International, since 1985; Director, Interpublic, since 1990; *b* 23 Aug. 1941; *s* of Stephen and Marion Lowe; one *s* one *d.* *Educ:* Westminster School. Managing Director, Collett Dickenson Pearce, 1972–79. *Recreations:* tennis, ski-ing, shooting. *Address:* The Lowe Group Plc, Bowater House, Knightsbridge, SW1X 7LT.

LOWE, Geoffrey Colin; aviation consultant, 1980–88; *b* 7 Sept. 1920; *s* of late Colin Roderick and late Elsie Lowe; *m* 1948, Joan Stephen (*d* 1985); one *d*; *m* 1988, Jean Marion Bailey (*née* Wigginton). *Educ:* Reigate Grammar Sch. GPO, 1937; Exchequer and Audit Dept, 1939. Served War, RAFVR, 1941–46 (Flt-Lt). Asst Principal, Min. of Civil Aviation, 1947; Private Sec. to Permanent Sec., MCA, 1950; Principal, 1950; Colonial Office, 1954–57; Min. of Transport and Civil Aviation, 1957–61; Civil Air Attaché, SE Asia, 1961–64; Asst Sec., Overseas Policy Div., Min. of Aviation, 1964–68; Investment Grants Div., Bd of Trade, 1968–71; Counsellor (Civil Aviation), British Embassy, Washington, 1971–73, Counsellor (Civil Aviation and Shipping), Washington, 1973–74; Under Sec. (Management Services and Manpower), Depts of Industry and Trade, 1974–80. *Recreations:* theatre, crossword puzzles. *Address:* 13 Highwood, Sunset Avenue, Woodford Green, Essex IG8 0SZ. *T:* 081–504 7035.

LOWE, Prof. Gordon, FRS 1984; CChem, FRSC; Professor of Biological Chemistry, University of Oxford, since 1989; Official Fellow and Tutor, Lincoln College, Oxford, since 1962; *b* 31 May 1933; *s* of Harry Lowe and Ethel (*née* Ibbetson); *m* 1956, Gwynneth Hunter; two *s.* *Educ:* Imperial Coll. of Science and Technol., Univ. of London (Governors Prize and Edmund White Prize, 1954; Edmund White Prize, 1957; BSc 1954; ARCS 1954; PhD 1957; DIC 1957). DSc Oxon 1985 (MA 1960). CChem, FRSC 1981. University of Oxford: Pressed Steel Res. Fellow, 1957–59; Deptl Demonstrator, 1959–65; Weir Jun. Res. Fellow, University Coll., 1959–61; Lectr, Organic Chemistry, 1965–88; Aldrichian Praelector in Chemistry, 1988–89; Sub-Rector, Lincoln Coll., 1986–89. Irvine Lectr, Univ. of St Andrews, 1984; Upper Rhine Lectr, Univs of Basle, Mulhouse, Strasbourg, Freiburg and Karlsruhe, 1989; Liversidge Lectr, Univ. of Sydney, 1990. Member: Biochemistry and Biophysics Cttee, SERC, 1979–82; Molecular Enzymology Cttee, Biochemical Soc., 1978–84; Editorial Adv. Panel, Biochemical Jl, 1981–; Editorial Bd, Bio-organic Chemistry, 1983–. FRSA 1986. Charmian Medal, RSC, 1983. *Publications:* reports on the cysteine proteinases, β-Lactam antibiotics, and chiral phosphate and sulphate esters; articles in primary chemical and biochemical jls. *Address:* 17 Norman Avenue, Abingdon, Oxon OX14 2HQ. *T:* Abingdon (0235) 23029.

LOWE, Dr John; Head, Country Educational Policy Reviews, Education and Training Division, OECD, 1973–87; *b* 3 Aug. 1922; *s* of John Lowe and Ellen (*née* Webb); *m* 1949, Margaret James (*d* 1982); two *s* one *d.* *Educ:* Univ. of Liverpool (BA Hons 1950); Univ. of London (CertEd 1951, PhD 1960). Served War of 1939–45 and Control Commn for Germany, 1945–47 (Captain). Lectr, subseq. Sen. Lectr, Univ. of Liverpool, 1955–63; Dir, Extra-Mural Studies, Univ. of Singapore, 1963–64; Dir, Dept of Adult Educn and Extra-Mural Studies, subsequently Head, Dept of Educnl Studies, Univ. of Edinburgh, 1964–72; Consultant in field, 1964–. Sec./Treas., Internat. Congress of Univ. Adult Educn, 1972–76. Hon. Prof., Warwick Univ., 1990–. *Publications:* On Teaching Foreign Languages to Adults (ed jtly), 1965; Adult Education in England and Wales, 1970; (ed) Adult Education and Nation-Building, 1970; (ed) Education and Nation-Building in the Third World, 1971; The Education of Adults: a world perspective, 1975, rev. edn, 1982; (ed) The Clanricarde Letter Book, 1983; Compulsory Schooling in a Changing World, 1983; (jtly) Schools and Quality, 1989; articles in educnl and hist. jls. *Recreations:* reading, music, theatre, swimming. *Address:* 3 Rue Ribera, 75016 Paris, France. *T:* 4520.2515.

LOWE, John Eric Charles, LVO 1965; MBE 1937; *b* 11 Aug. 1907; 6th *s* of late John Frederick Lowe; *m* 1935, Trudy (*née* Maybury); one *s* two *d.* *Educ:* Burghley Road Sch., Highgate. Vice-Consul, Jibuti, 1930–37, Harar, 1940; Political Officer, Aden Protectorate, 1940; served in HM Forces, Somaliland and Ethiopia, 1941–46; Senior Asst, Foreign Office, 1947–49; Acting Consul, Suez, 1949; Vice-Consul, Beira, 1950; Vice-Consul, Hamburg, 1951 and Frankfurt, 1953; 2nd Secretary, Helsinki, 1953; Political Agent's Representative, Mina-Al-Ahmadi (Kuwait), 1956; Vice-Consul, Leopoldville, 1959; Consul, Khartoum, 1962; Consul-General, Basra, 1965–67; retired, Sept. 1967. Order of the Two Niles (Sudan), 1965. *Recreations:* gardening, golf, sailing. *Address:* 16 Oakfield, Hawkhurst, Kent TN18 4JR. *T:* Hawkhurst (0580) 753405.

LOWE, John Evelyn, MA, FSA, FRSA; cultural consultant and author, since 1978; foreign travel specialist, journalist and photographer; *b* 23 April 1928; *s* of late Arthur Holden Lowe; *m* 1st, 1956, Susan Helen Sanderson (marr. diss. 1981); two *s* one *d*; 2nd, 1989, Yukiko Nomura; one *d.* *Educ:* Wellington Coll., Berks; New Coll., Oxford. Served in RAEC, 1947–49 (Sgt Instructor). Victoria and Albert Museum, Dept of Woodwork, 1953–56; Deputy Story Editor, Pinewood Studios, 1956–57; Victoria and Albert Museum: Dept of Ceramics, 1957–61; Assistant to the Director, 1961–64; Dir, City Museum and Art Gall., Birmingham, 1964–69; Dir, Weald and Downland Open Air Museum, 1969–74; Principal, West Dean College, Chichester, West Sussex, 1972–78; Literary Editor, Kansai Time Out, 1983–88. Hofer-Hecksher Bibliographical Lectr, Harvard, 1974; Vis. Prof. in British Cultural Studies, Doshisha Univ., Japan, 1979–81. Pres., Midlands Fedn of Museums, 1967–69. Member: Exec. Cttee, Midland Arts Centre for Young People, 1964–69; Council of the British School at Rome, 1968–70; Crafts Adv. Cttee, 1973–78. Consultant to: Seibu Ltd, Tokyo, 1968–72; Specialtours, London, 1969–74. Trustee: Sanderson Art in Industry Fund, 1968–; Edward James Foundn, 1972–73; Idlewild Trust, 1972–78. Hon. Fellow, RCA, 1988. Asst Ed., Collins Crime Club, 1953–54; Founding Ed., Faber Furniture Series, 1954–56. *Publications:* Thomas Chippendale, 1955; Cream Coloured Earthenware, 1958; Japanese Crafts, 1983; Into Japan, 1985; Into China, 1986; Corsica: a traveller's guide, 1988; A Surrealist Life—Edward James—Poet, Patron & Eccentric, 1991; major contribs to Encyclopædia Britannica and OUP Junior Encyclopedia; articles on applied arts, foreign travel, social history and Japan. *Recreations:* Japan, music, reading, book-collecting, travel. *Address:* La Paillole Basse, Cours, 47360 Prayssas, France. *T:* 53.68.86.45; 6–15 Daini Kume Mansion, 1-Banchi, Nishihiraki-cho, Takano, Sakyo-ku, Kyoto 606, Japan. *T:* 075.721.5948.

LOWE, Prof. Kenneth Gordon, CVO 1982; MD; FRCP, FRCPE, FRCPGlas; Physician to the Queen in Scotland, 1971–82; Formerly Consultant Physician, Royal Infirmary and Ninewells Hospital, Dundee; Hon. Professor of Medicine, Dundee University, since 1969; *b* 29 May 1917; *s* of Thomas J. Lowe, MA, BSc, Arbroath, and Flora MacDonald Gordon, Arbroath; *m* 1942, Nancy Young, MB, ChB, twin *d* of Stephen Young, Logie, Fife; two *s* one *d.* *Educ:* Arbroath High Sch.; St Andrews Univ. (MD Hons). Served with RAMC, 1942–46; Registrar, Hammersmith Hosp., Royal Postgrad. Med. Sch., 1947–52; Sen. Lectr in Medicine, St Andrews Univ., 1952–61. *Publications:* (jtly) Regional Anatomy Illustrated, 1983; contribs to med. and scientific jls, mainly on renal, metabolic and cardiac disorders. *Recreations:* reading, fishing. *Address:* 36 Dundee Road, West Ferry, Dundee DD5 1HY. *T:* Dundee (0382) 78787. *Club:* Flyfishers'.

LOWE, Philip Martin; Chef de Cabinet to Rt Hon. Bruce Millan, European Commissioner for regional policies, Commission of the European Communities, since 1989; *b* 29 April 1947; *s* of late Leonard Ernest Lowe and Marguerite Helen Lowe (*née* Childs); *m* 1st, 1967, Gillian Baynton Forge (marr. diss. 1980); two *s*; 2nd, 1984, Nora Mai O'Connell. *Educ:* Leeds Grammar Sch.; Reading Sch.; St John's Coll., Oxford (Trevelyan Scholar, Casberd Exhibnr; MA in PPE); London Business Sch. (MSc Business Studies). Tube Investments, production planning and financial analyst, 1968–73; Commission of the European Communities: Directorate-Gen. for Credit and Investments, Luxembourg, 1973–82; Mem., Cabinet of President Gaston Thorn, 1982–85, of Alois Pfeiffer, European Comr for economic and financial affairs, 1985–86; Directorate-Gen. for co-ordination of Structural Investments, 1986–89. *Recreations:* music, theatre, running, hillwalking, languages. *Address:* avenue Michel-Ange 18, 1040 Brussels, Belgium. *T:* (office) 2359207; (home) 7349665.
See also Ven. S. R. Lowe.

LOWE, Dr Robert David; Medical Research Consultant, National Heart Foundation of Australia, 1986–89, retired; *b* 23 Feb. 1930; *s* of John Lowe and Hilda Althea Mead; *m* 1952, Betty Irene Wheeler; one *s* three *d.* *Educ:* Leighton Park Sch.; Emmanuel Coll., Cambridge; UCH Medical School. BCh, MB, MA, MD, PhD Cantab; FRCP, LMSSA. Medical Specialist, RAMC, 1955–59; Research Asst, UCH Med. Sch., 1959–61; St George's Hosp. Med. Sch.: MRC Res. Fellow, 1961–62; Wellcome Sen. Res. Fellow in Clinical Science, 1963–64; Sen. Lectr in Medicine, St Thomas' Hosp. Med. Sch., 1964–70; Hon. Consultant to St Thomas' Hosp., 1966–70; Dean, St George's Hosp. Med. Sch., 1971–82. AUCAS: Exec. Mem., 1967–; Chm., 1972–78. *Publications:* (with B. F. Robinson) A Physiological Approach to Clinical Methods, 1970; papers on peripheral circulation, hypertension, adrenergic mechanisms, central action of angiotensin, control of cardiovascular system. *Recreations:* bridge, squash, hill-walking, sailing. *Address:* Te Uenga, RD4 Hikurangi, Northland, New Zealand. *T:* 0940 37416.

LOWE, Robson; philatelist, publisher, editor, author, auctioneer; *b* 7 Jan. 1905; *s* of John Lowe and Gertrude Lee; *m* 1928, Winifred Marie Denne (*d* 1973); two *d.* *Educ:* Fulham Central Sch. Started own business, 1920; worked on PO Records, 1926; purchased control of Woods of Perth (Printers), 1964; formed Australian co., 1967; joined bd of Christie, Manson & Woods, 1968; formed Italian co., 1969 (founded Il Piccolo for Italian collectors). Chm., Expert Cttee of British Philatelic Assoc., 1941–61; Past Pres., British Philatelic Fedn, 1979–81; Co-founder, Postal History Soc., 1935; Founder: Soc. of Postal Historians, 1950; annual British Philatelic Exhibn, 1965. Mem. jury at internat. philatelic exhibns: first, Durban, 1928; Chm., Cape Town, 1979. Over 1000 lectures. Took over Philatelic Jl of GB, 1958 (still the publisher); Editor, The Philatelist, 1934–74 (centenary, 1966), 1986–. *Publications:* Philatelic Encyclopaedia (ed), 1935; Handstruck Stamps of the Empire, 1937, 4th edn 1941; Sperati and his Craft, 1953; British Postage Stamps, 1968; (jtly) St Vincent, 1971; Encyclopaedia of Empire Stamps: Europe, 1947, 2nd edn 1951; Africa, 1949; Asia, 1951; Australia, 1962; North America, 1973; Leeward Islands, 1991; monographs (latest, US Military Mail, WW II); articles in philatelic pubns. *Recreations:* history, philately, study of forgers and forgery. *Address:* Robson Lowe, 8 King Street, St James's, SW1Y 6QT. *Clubs:* East India; Collectors (New York).

LOWE, Ven. Stephen Richard; Archdeacon of Sheffield, since 1988; *b* 3 March 1944; *s* of Leonard Ernest Lowe and Marguerite Helen Lowe; *m* 1967; one *s* one *d.* *Educ:* Leeds Grammar School; Reading School; London Univ. (BSc Econs); Ripon Hall, Oxford. Curate, St Michael's Anglican Methodist Church, Gospel Lane, Birmingham, 1968–72; Minister-in-Charge, Woodgate Valley Conventional District, 1972–75; Team Rector of East Ham, 1975–88. Hon. Canon, Chelmsford Cathedral, 1985–88; Chelmsford Diocesan Urban Officer, 1986–88. Travelling Fellowship, Winston Churchill Meml Trust, 1980. Mem., Gen. Synod of C of E, 1991–. *Publication:* Churches' Role in Care of the Elderly, 1974. *Recreations:* football, music, cinema, theatre and travel. *Address:* 23 Hill Turrets Close, Ecclesall, Sheffield S11 9RE. *T:* Sheffield (0742) 350191, *fax:* Sheffield (0742) 352275.
See also P. M. Lowe.

LOWE, Sir Thomas (William Gordon), 4th Bt *cr* 1918, of Edgbaston, City of Birmingham; *b* 14 Aug. 1963; *s* of Sir Francis Reginald Gordon Lowe, 3rd Bt and of Franziska Cornelia, *d* of Siegfried Steinkopf; *S* father, 1986. *Educ:* Stowe School; London School of Economics (LLB 1984); Jesus Coll., Cambridge (LLM 1986). Called to the Bar, Inner Temple, 1985. *Publications:* articles in various legal periodicals. *Heir:* *b* Christopher Colin Francis Lowe, *b* 25 Dec. 1964. *Address:* 8 Seymour Walk, SW10 9NF; 8 New Square, Lincoln's Inn, WC2.

LOWE, Veronica Ann; Director, Solicitors Complaints Bureau, since 1990; *b* 29 June 1951; *d* of Arthur Ernest Bagley and late Agatha (*née* Blackham); *m* 1977, Ian Stanley Lowe; one *d.* *Educ:* King Edward VI Grammar Sch. for Girls, Handsworth, Birmingham; St Hugh's Coll., Oxford (MA); Oxford Polytechnic (MIL Exams); City of Birmingham Polytechnic. Articled Clerk, Ryland, Martineau & Co., Birmingham, 1976–78; Lectr in Labour Law, Univ. of Aston in Birmingham, 1978–80; admitted solicitor, 1979; solicitor in private practice, 1979–86; Asst Area Dir, Legal Aid Area No 8, 1986–88; Area Dir (W Midlands), Legal Aid Area No 6, 1988–89; Gp Manager (Midlands), Legal Aid Bd, 1989–90. *Publications:* contribs to publications on law for accountants and businessmen. *Recreations:* cooking, eating and drinking, reading, writing unfinished novels, listening to music, travel, talking, current affairs, being with my daughter, all historical subjects. *Address:* Phoenix Cottage, 6 Rugby Road, Dunchurch, Warwicks CV22 6PE.

LOWENSTEIN, Prof. Otto Egon, FRS 1955; FRSE; DSc (Glasgow); PhD (Birmingham); DrPhil (Munich); Honorary Senior Research Fellow, Pharmacology Department (formerly at Neurocommunications Research Unit), Birmingham University Medical School, since 1976 (Leverhulme Emeritus Research Fellow, 1974–76); *b* 24 Oct. 1906; *s* of Julius Lowenstein and Mathilde Heusinger; *m* 1st, Elsa Barbara, *d* of R. Ritter; two *s*; 2nd, Gunilla Marika (*d* 1981), *d* of Prof. Gösta Dohlman; one step *s*; 3rd, Maureen Josephine, *d* of K. McKernan. Educ: Neues Realgymnasium, Munich; Munich Univ. Asst, Munich Univ., 1931–33; Research Scholar, Birmingham Univ., 1933–37; Asst Lecturer,

University College, Exeter, 1937–38; Senior Lecturer, Glasgow Univ., 1938–52; Mason Prof. of Zoology and Comparative Physiology, Birmingham Univ., 1952–74. President: Assoc. for the Study of Animal Behaviour, 1961–64; Section D, British Assoc., 1962; Institute of Biology, 1965–67; Member Council, Royal Society, 1968–69. *Publications:* Revision of 6th edn of A Textbook of Zoology (Parker and Haswell), Vol. I; The Senses, 1966; papers in various learned journals on Electrophysiology and Ultrastructure of Sense Organs, esp. inner ear of vertebrates. *Recreations:* music, mountain walking, painting. *Address:* 22 Estria Road, Birmingham B15 2LQ. *T:* 021–440 2526.

LOWES, Peter Donald; Director, Anti-Slavery Society for Protection of Human Rights, 1987–89; *b* 13 Sept. 1926; *s* of Col J. H. Lowes and Queenie Frances Lowes (*née* Bowyer); *m* 1954, Linnea Newton (marr. diss. 1980); one *s* two *d. Educ:* Bradfield Coll.; Emmanuel Coll., Cambridge (MA); Univ. of British Columbia (LLB); Geneva Univ. (PhD). Served with Royal Engineers, 1946–48. Master, Wanganui Collegiate Sch., NZ, 1949, Upper Canada Coll., Toronto, 1950–51; practised law, Vancouver, 1953–55; UNRWA, Jordan, 1955–58; journalist, Canadian Broadcasting Corp., 1958; UN Narcotic Drugs, Geneva, 1959–65; External Aid, Canadian Govt, Ottawa, 1965–66; Resident Representative, United Nations Development Programme: Lesotho, 1966–68; Swaziland, 1968–71; Malaŵi, 1971–74; HQ, NY, 1974–75; Morocco, 1975–79; Co-ordinator, Internat. Drinking Water Supply and Sanitation Decade, Geneva, 1979–86. Mem. Bd, 1980–86, Consultant, 1987, Internat Reference Centre, The Hague; UNDP Consultant, 1987. Adviser: CARE (UK); Help the Aged. *Publication:* The Genesis of International Narcotics Control, 1965. *Recreations:* walking, mountaineering, history. *Address:* Apartment 34, 4 Clos Belmont, Geneva 1208, Switzerland. *T:* 735 03 13. *Clubs:* Commonwealth Trust, Climbers'.

LOWNIE, Ralph Hamilton; His Honour Judge Lownie; a Circuit Judge, since 1986; *b* 27 Sept. 1924; *yr s* of James H. W. Lownie and Jesse H. Aitken; *m* 1960, Claudine Therese, *o d* of Pierre Lecrocq, Reims; one *s* one *d. Educ:* George Watson's Coll.; Edinburgh Univ. (MA, LLB, Dip. Admin. Law and Practice); Kent Univ. (PhD 1989). Royal Engineers, 1943–47, NW Europe. WS 1952; enrolled as solicitor, 1953; Mem. Faculty of Advocates 1959; called to Bar, Inner Temple, 1962. Dep. Registrar, Supreme Court of Kenya, 1954–56; Resident Magistrate, 1956–61, Sen. Resident Magistrate, 1961–63, Dep. Registrar-Gen., Kenya, 1963–65; Sen. Magistrate, Bermuda, 1965–72; a Metropolitan Stipendiary Magistrate, 1974–86; a Deputy Circuit Judge, 1976–82; a Recorder, 1983–86. Chm. of Juvenile Courts, 1976–85. Lectr, Kenya Sch. of Law, 1963–65. *Recreations:* hill-walking, military heraldry. *Address:* Law Courts, Barker Road, Maidstone, Kent ME16 8EW.

LOWREY, Air Comdt Dame Alice, DBE 1960; RRC 1954; Matron-in-Chief, Princess Mary's Royal Air Force Nursing Service, 1959–63 (retired); *b* 8 April 1905; *d* of William John Lowrey and Agnes Lowrey (formerly Walters). *Educ:* Yorkshire; Training Sch., Sheffield Royal Hospital. Joined PMRAFNS, 1932; served in Iraq and Aden. Principal Matron: HQ, MEAF and FEAF, 1956–58; HQ, Home Command and Technical Training Command, 1958–59. Air Commandant, 1959. Officer Sister Order of St John, 1959. *Address:* c/o Midland Bank, Attleborough, Norfolk.

LOWRY, family name of **Baron Lowry.**

LOWRY, Baron *cr* 1979 (Life Peer), of Crossgar in the County of Down; **Robert Lynd Erskine Lowry;** PC 1974; PC (NI) 1971; Kt 1971; a Lord of Appeal in Ordinary, since 1988; *b* 30 Jan. 1919; *o s* of late William Lowry (Rt Hon. Mr Justice Lowry) and Catherine Hughes Lowry, 3rd *d* of Rev. R. J. Lynd, DD; *m* 1945, Mary Audrey (*d* 1987), *o d* of John Martin, 12 Deramore Park, Belfast; three *d. Educ:* Royal Belfast Academical Institution (Porter exhibnr, 1937); Jesus Coll., Cambridge (Hon. Fellow 1977). Entrance Exhibn. (Classics); Scholar, 1939; 1st Class Classical Tripos, Part I, 1939, Part II 1940; MA 1944. Served HM Forces, 1940–46; enlisted Royal Inniskilling Fusilers, 1940; Tunisia, 1942–43 with 38 Irish Inf. Bde; commissioned Royal Irish Fusiliers, 1941; Major, 1945; Hon. Colonel: 7th Bn Royal Irish Fusiliers, 1969–71 (5th Bn, 1967–68); 5th Bn Royal Irish Rangers, 1971–76. Called to the Bar of N Ireland, 1947; Bencher of the Inn of Court, 1955–; Hon. Bencher, Middle Temple, 1973; Hon. Bencher, King's Inns, Dublin, 1973; QC (N Ireland), 1956. Counsel to HM Attorney-General, 1948–56; Judge of the High Court of Justice (NI), 1964–71; Lord Chief Justice of N Ireland, 1971–88. Member Departmental Cttees on Charities, Legal Aid and Registration of Title; Dep. Chm., Boundaries Commn (NI) 1964–71; Chairman: Interim Boundary Commn (NI Constituencies), 1967; Permanent Boundary Commn, 1969–71; Dep. Chm., Lord Chancellor's Cttee on NI Supreme Court; Member, Jt Law Enforcement Commn, 1974; Chairman: N Ireland Constitutional Convention, 1975; Council of Legal Educn (NI), 1976–79. Governor, Royal Belfast Academical Instn, 1956–71, Chm., Richmond Lodge Sch., 1956–77; Chm. Governing Bodies Assoc. (NI), 1965; Visitor, Univ. of Ulster, 1989–. Hon. LLD QUB, 1980; Hon. DLitt NUU, 1981. *Recreations:* golf (Pres., Royal Portrush GC, 1974–); showjumping (Chm., SJAI Exec., 1969–72; Mem. Nat. Equestrian Fedn, 1969–78; Internat. Showjumping Judge, 1973, Official Internat. Judge, 1987). *Address:* House of Lords, SW1A 0PW; White Hill, Crossgar, Co. Down BT30 9HJ. *T:* Crossgar (0396) 830397. *Clubs:* Army and Navy, MCC; Royal and Ancient (St Andrews).

LOWRY, Sir (John) Patrick, (Sir Pat), Kt 1985; CBE 1978; President, Institute of Personnel Management, 1987–89; *b* 31 March 1920; *s* of John McArdle and Edith Mary Lowry; *m* 1952, Sheilagh Mary Davies; one *s* one *d. Educ:* Wyggeston Grammar Sch., Leicester; London Sch. of Economics (evening student). BCom London; CIPM, CBIM. Statistical Clerk, Engineering Employers' Fedn, 1938; served Army, 1939–46; various posts in EEF, 1946–70, Dir 1965–70; Dir of Industrial Relations, British Leyland Motor Corp., 1970, Board Dir 1972; Dir of Personnel, 1975–77, of Personnel and Admin, British Leyland Ltd, 1977–78, of Personnel and External Affairs, 1978–81; Chairman: ACAS, 1981–87; Nat. Jt Council for Engineering Construction Industry, 1987–; Univs Academic Salaries Cttee, 1987–. Hon. Prof., Sch. of Industrial and Business Studies, Warwick Univ., 1983. Member: UK Employers' Delegn, ILO, 1962, 1963, 1967; Court of Inquiry, Barbican and Horseferry Road Building Disputes, 1967; Court of Inquiry, Grunwick Dispute, 1977. Pres., Inst. of Supervisory Management, 1972–74. FRSA 1984. Hon. LLD Leicester, 1984. *Recreation:* theatre. *Address:* 31 Seaton Close, Lynden Gate, SW15 3TJ. *T:* 081–785 6199.

LOWRY, Mrs Noreen Margaret, (Nina); Her Honour Judge Lowry; a Circuit Judge, since 1976; *b* 6 Sept. 1925; *er d* of late John Collins, MC, and Hilda Collins; *m* 1st, 1950, Edward Lucas Gardner, QC (marr. diss., 1962); one *s* one *d*; 2nd, 1963, Richard John Lowry, *qv*; one *d. Educ:* Bedford High Sch.; Birmingham Univ. LLB Birmingham, 1947. Called to the Bar, Gray's Inn, 1948. Criminal practice on S Eastern Circuit, Central Criminal Court, Inner London Sessions, etc., practising as Miss Nina Collins; Metropolitan Stipendiary Magistrate, 1967–76. Mem. Criminal Law Revision Cttee, 1975–. *Recreations:* theatre, travel. *Address:* Central Criminal Court, EC4M 7EH.

LOWRY, Sir Pat; *see* Lowry, Sir J. P.

LOWRY, Richard John; QC 1968; **His Honour Judge Richard Lowry;** a Circuit Judge, since 1977; *b* 23 June 1924; *s* of late Geoffrey Charles Lowry, OBE, TD, and late Margaret Spencer Lowry; *m* 1963, Noreen Margaret Lowry, *qv*; one *d. Educ:* St Edward's Sch.; University College, Oxford. RAF, 1943; qualified as pilot and commnd, 1944; No 228 Group Staff Officer, India, 1945; Flt-Lieut, 1946. University College, Oxford, 1942–43 and 1946–48; BA, 1948, MA 1949. Called to Bar, Inner Temple, 1949; Bencher 1977; Member, General Council of Bar, 1965–69. Dep. Chm., Herts QS, 1968; a Recorder, 1972–77. Mem., Home Office Adv. Council on Penal System, 1972–78. *Recreations:* theatre, swimming, fossicking; formerly rowing (Oxford Univ. wartime VIII, 1943). *Address:* Central Criminal Court, EC4M 7EH. *Clubs:* Garrick; Leander (Henley-on-Thames).

LOWRY-CORRY, family name of **Earl of Belmore.**

LOWSON, Sir Ian (Patrick), 2nd Bt *cr* 1951; *b* 4 Sept. 1944; *s* of Sir Denys Colquhoun Flowerdew Lowson, 1st Bt and of Patricia, OStJ, *yr d* of 1st Baron Strathcarron, PC, KC; *S* father, 1975; *m* 1979, Mrs Tanya Du Boulay, *d* of R. F. A. Judge; one *s* one *d. Educ:* Eton; Duke Univ., USA. OStJ. *Heir: s* Henry William Lowson, *b* 10 Nov. 1980. *Address:* 23 Flood Street, SW3 5ST. *Clubs:* Boodle's, Pilgrims; Brook (NY).

LOWTHER, family name of **Earl of Lonsdale** and **Viscount Ullswater.**

LOWTHER, Viscount; Hugh Clayton Lowther; *b* 27 May 1949; *s* and *heir* of 7th Earl of Lonsdale, *qv*, and Tuppina Cecily, *d* of late Captain G. H. Bennet; *m* 1971, Pamela Middleton; *m* 1986, Angela M., *d* of Captain Peter J. Wyatt, RN and Mrs Christine Wyatt; one *d*.

LOWTHER, Col Sir Charles (Douglas), 6th Bt *cr* 1824; Officer in charge, Household Cavalry and Royal Armoured Corps Manning and Record Office, since 1989; *b* 22 Jan. 1946; *s* of Lt-Col Sir William Guy Lowther, 5th Bt, OBE, and of Grania Suzanne, *d* of late Major A. J. H. Douglas Campbell, OBE; *S* father, 1982; *m* 1975, Florence Rose, *y d* of Colonel Alexander James Henry Cramsie, O'Harabrook, Ballymoney, Co. Antrim; one *s* one *d. Educ:* Winchester College. Commissioned, Queen's Royal Irish Hussars, 1966; Regimental Duty UK and BAOR, including ADC to Chief of Defence Staff, 1974–76; Army Staff College, Camberley, 1978–79; Staff appointment, 1981; CO, QRIH, 1986–89. *Recreations:* fieldsports, travel. *Heir: s* Patrick William Lowther, *b* 15 July 1977. *Club:* Cavalry and Guards.

LOWTHER, John Luke, CBE 1983; JP; Lord Lieutenant for Northamptonshire, since 1984; *b* 17 Nov. 1923; *s* of Col J.G. Lowther, CBE, DSO, MC, TD and the Hon. Mrs Lowther; *m* 1952, Jennifer Jane Bevan; one *s* two *d. Educ:* Eton; Trinity College, Oxford. MA 1949. Served King's Royal Rifle Corps, 1942–47; worked for Singer Sewing Co., USA, 1949–51; Managing Dir, own manufacturing Co., 1951–60; farmer, 1960–. CC Northants, 1970–84 (Leader of Council, 1977–81); High Sheriff 1971, DL 1977, JP 1984, Northants. Hon. Col, Royal Anglian Regt (Northamptonshire), TA, 1986–89. *Recreations:* shooting, countryman. *Address:* Guilsborough Court, Northampton NN6 8QW. *T:* Northampton (0604) 740289. *Club:* Boodle's.

LOXAM, John Gordon; Director of Veterinary Field Services, Ministry of Agriculture, Fisheries and Food, 1983–86, retired; *b* 26 April 1927; *s* of John Loxam and Mary Elizabeth Loxam (*née* Rigby); *m* 1950, Margaret Lorraine Smith; one *d* (and one *s* decd). *Educ:* Lancaster Royal Grammar Sch.; Royal (Dick) Veterinary Coll., Edinburgh. MRCVS. General veterinary practice: Marlborough, 1949–51; Carlisle, 1951–53; Vet. Officer, MAFF, Lincoln, 1953–63; Divisional Veterinary Officer: Tolworth, Surrey, 1963–66; Bury St Edmunds, 1966–71; Dep. Regl Vet. Officer, Leeds, 1971–76; Regl Vet. Officer, Tolworth, 1976–78; Asst Chief Vet. Officer, Tolworth, 1979–83. Hon. Sec., 1987–90, Pres., 1990–, Vet. Benevolent Fund. Churchwarden, All Saints, Chelsworth, 1990–. *Recreations:* gardening, golf; spectator sports, particularly Rugby football. *Address:* Riverside, Chelsworth, Ipswich, Suffolk IP7 7HU. *T:* Bildeston (0449) 740619. *Clubs:* Farmers'; Stowmarket Golf.

LOY, Francis David Lindley; Stipendiary Magistrate at Leeds since 1974; a Recorder of the Crown Court, since 1983; *b* 7 Oct. 1927; *s* of late Archibald Loy and late Sarah Eleanor Loy; *m* 1954, Brenda Elizabeth Walker; three *d. Educ:* Repton Sch.; Corpus Christi Coll., Cambridge. BA Hons (Law) 1950. Royal Navy, 1946–48. Called to the Bar, Middle Temple, 1952; practised North-Eastern Circuit, 1952–72; Recorder (Northern Circuit), 1972; Stipendiary Magistrate of Leeds, 1972–74. Hon. Sec., Soc. of Provincial Stipendiary Magistrates, 1980–89, Chm., 1990–. *Recreations:* reading, English History, walking, travel. *Address:* 4 Wedgewood Drive, Roundhay, Leeds LS8 1EF; 14 The Avenue, Sheringham, Norfolk. *T:* Sheringham (0263) 822697. *Club:* Leeds (Leeds).

LOYD, Christopher Lewis, MC 1943; *b* 1 June 1923; 3rd and *o* surv. *s* of late Arthur Thomas Loyd, OBE, JP, Lockinge, Wantage, Berks, and Dorothy, *d* of late Paul Ferdinand Willert, Headington, Oxford; *m* 1957, Joanna, *d* of Captain Arthur Turberville Smith-Bingham, Milburn Manor, Malmesbury, Wilts; two *s* one *d. Educ:* Eton; King's Coll., Cambridge (MA). Served 1942–46, with Coldstream Guards, Captain. ARICS 1952, FRICS 1955. Mem., Jockey Club. Trustee, Wallace Collection, 1973–90. JP 1950, DL 1954, Oxfordshire (formerly Berks); High Sheriff of Berkshire, 1961. *Address:* Lockinge, Wantage, Oxfordshire OX12 8QL. *T:* Abingdon (0235) 833265. *Club:* Boodle's.

LOYD, Sir Francis Alfred, KCMG 1965 (CMG 1961); OBE 1954 (MBE 1951); *b* 5 Sept. 1916; *s* of Major A. W. K. Loyd, Royal Sussex Regt; *m* 1st, 1946, Katharine Layzell (*d* 1981), *d* of Lt Col S. C. Layzell, MC, Mwatati, Kenya; two *d*; 2nd, 1984, Helen Monica, *widow* of Lt Col C. R. Murray Brown, DSO, Worlington, Suffolk. *Educ:* Eton; Trinity Coll., Oxford (MA). District Officer, Kenya, 1939; Mil. Service, E Africa, 1940–42; Private Secretary to Governor of Kenya, 1942–45; HM Consul, Mega, Ethiopia, 1945; District Comdr, Kenya, 1947–55; Commonwealth Fund Fellowship to USA, 1953–54; Provincial Commissioner, 1956; Permanent Secretary, Governor's Office, 1962–63; HM Commissioner for Swaziland, 1964–68. Dir, London House for Overseas Graduates, 1969–79; Chm., Oxfam Africa Cttee, 1979–85. *Recreations:* golf, gardening. *Address:* 53 Park Road, Aldeburgh, Suffolk IP15 5EN. *T:* Aldeburgh (0728) 452478. *Clubs:* Army and Navy; Vincent's (Oxford).

LOYD, John Anthony Thomas; QC 1981; **His Honour Judge Loyd;** a Circuit Judge, assigned to Official Referees' business, London, since 1990; *b* 18 July 1933; *e s* of Leslie William Loyd and Joan Louisa Loyd; *m* 1963, Rosaleen Iona Ward; one *d* (and one *d* decd). *Educ:* Wycliffe Coll.; Gonville and Caius Coll., Cambridge (BA 1956, MA 1959). RAF Regt, 1951–53. Called to the Bar, Gray's Inn, 1958; a Recorder, 1985–90. *Recreations:* viticulture, sailing. *Address:* 9 Coldharbour, E14 9NS; Segos, Le Boulvé, Lot, France.

LOYD, Sir Julian (St John), KCVO 1991 (CVO 1979); DL; FRICS; Land Agent to HM The Queen, Sandringham Estate, 1964–91; *b* 25 May 1926; *s* of General Sir Charles Loyd, GCVO, KCB, DSO, MC and Lady Moyra Loyd; *m* 1960, Mary Emma, *d* of Sir Christopher Steel, GCMG, MVO and Lady Steel; one *s* two *d. Educ:* Eton Coll.; Magdalene Coll., Cambridge (MA). FRICS 1955. Partner in Savills, Norwich, 1955–64.

DL Norfolk, 1983. *Recreation:* fishing. *Address:* Perrystone Cottage, Burnham Market, King's Lynn PE31 8HA. *Club:* Army and Navy.

LOYDEN, Edward; MP (Lab) Liverpool, Garston, Feb. 1974–1979 and since 1983; *b* 3 May 1923; *s* of Patrick and Mary Loyden; *m* 1944, Rose Ann; one *s* two *d* (and one *d* decd). *Educ:* Friary RC Elem. School. Shop boy, margarine factory, 1937; Able-Seaman, MN, 1938–46; Seaman Port Worker, Mersey Docks & Harbour Co., 1946–74. Member: Liverpool City Council, 1960 (Dep. Leader, 1983–); Liverpool District Council, 1973; Merseyside Met. CC, 1973; Liverpool Met. Dist Council (St Mary's Ward), 1980–83. Shop Steward, TGWU, 1954, Branch Chm. 1959; Mem. District Cttee, Docks and Waterways, 1967; Mem. Nat. Cttee, TGWU, 1968; Pres., Liverpool Trades Council, 1967; Pres., Merseyside Trades Council, 1974. *Recreations:* full-time political. *Address:* 456 Queens Drive, Walton, Liverpool L4 8UA. *T:* 051–226 4478. *Clubs:* Gillmoss Labour, Woolton Labour.

LOYN, Prof. Henry Royston, DLitt; FSA, FRHistS; FBA 1979; Professor Emeritus, University of London; Professor of History, Westfield College, University of London, 1977–87 (Vice-Principal, 1980–86; Fellow, 1989); *b* 16 June 1922; *s* of late Henry George Loyn and Violet Monica Loyn; *m* 1950, Patricia Beatrice, *d* of late R. S. Haskew; three *s*. *Educ:* Cardiff High Sch.; University Coll., Cardiff (MA 1949, DLitt 1968). FRHistS 1958; FSA 1968. Dept of History, University Coll., Cardiff: Asst Lectr, 1946; Lectr, 1949; Sen. Lectr, 1961; Reader, 1966; Prof. of Medieval Hist., 1969–77; Dean of Students, 1968–70 and 1975–76; Fellow, 1981. President: Historical Assoc., 1976–79; Glam Hist. Soc., 1975–77; Cardiff Naturalists Soc., 1975–76; Soc. for Medieval Archaeol., 1983–86 (Vice-Pres., 1971–74); St Albans and Herts Architectural and Archaeolog. Soc., 1990–; Vice-President: Soc. of Antiquaries, 1983–87; RHistS, 1983–86. Mem., Ancient Monuments Bd for England, 1982–84. W. N. Medlicott Medal for service to history, Historical Assoc., 1986. *Publications:* Anglo-Saxon England and the Norman Conquest, 1962; Norman Conquest, 1965; Norman Britain, 1966; Alfred The Great, 1967; A Wulfstan MS, Cotton, Nero Ai, 1971; (ed with H. Hearder) British Government and Administration, 1974; (with J. Percival) The Reign of Charlemagne, 1975; The Vikings in Britain, 1977; (with Alan and Richard Sorrell) Medieval Britain, 1977; The Governance of England, vol. 1, 1984; (introd.) facsimile edn, Domesday Book, 1987; (ed) The Middle Ages: a concise encyclopaedia, 1989; The Making of the English Nation, 1991; contribs to Eng. Hist. Rev., History, Antiquaries Jl, and Med. Archaeol. *Recreations:* natural history, gardening. *Address:* Queen Mary and Westfield College, Kidderpore Avenue, NW3 7ST. *Club:* Athenæum.

LU, Dr Gwei-Djen; Associate Director, East Asian History of Science Library, Needham Research Institute, Cambridge, since 1976; Fellow of Robinson College, Cambridge, 1979–80, Emeritus Fellow, since 1980; *b* 1 Sept. 1904; *d* of Mou-T'ing Lu and Hsiu-Ying Lu; *m* 1989, Joseph Needham, *qv*. *Educ:* Ming-Tê Sch., Nanking; Ginling Coll., Nanking (BA). PhD Cambridge. Trained as clin. pathologist, Peking Union Med. Coll.; Lectr in Physiology and Biochemistry, St John's Univ., Shanghai; Res. Fellow, Lester Inst. of Med. Research, Shanghai (nutritional biochemistry); research, Cambridge Biochemical Lab., 1937–39, followed by research at Univ. of Calif, Berkeley, Birmingham City Hosp., Alabama, and at Coll. of Physicians and Surgeons, Columbia Univ., NY; staff mem., Sino-British Science Co-operation Office, HM Embassy, Chungking, later Nanking; Prof. of Nutritional Science, Ginling Coll., Nanking, 1947; staff mem., Secretariat, UNESCO, Paris (i/c Nat. Sci. Div., Field Science Co-operation Offices); working with Dr Joseph Needham on Science and Civilisation in China proj., Cambridge, 1957–. Hon. Prof. of History of Science, Academia Sinica, Beijing, China, 1990. Medal for Literature, Ministry of Educn, China. *Publications:* Epicure in China, 1942; (with Dr J. Needham and others) Clerks and Craftsmen in China and the West, 1970; (with Dr J. Needham and others) Science and Civilisation in China, 1971–: Vol. 4, pt 3; Vol. 5, pts 2, 3, 4, 5 and 7; Vol. 6, pts 1, 3 and 4; (with Dr J. Needham) Celestial Lancets: a history and rationale of Acupuncture and Moxa, 1980; Trans-Pacific Echoes and Resonances; Listening Once Again, 1985; The Hall of Heavenly Records: Korean astronomical instruments and clocks 1380–1780, 1986; papers in biochem. and historical jls. *Recreation:* reading, esp. history, economics, politics and sociology. *Address:* 2A Sylvester Road, Cambridge CB3 9AF. *T:* Cambridge (0223) 352183; 8 Sylvester Road, Cambridge CB3 9AF. *T:* Cambridge (0223) 311545.

LUBBOCK, family name of **Baron Avebury.**

LUBBOCK, Christopher William Stuart; a Master of the Supreme Court (Queen's Bench Division), 1970–90; *b* 4 Jan. 1920; 2nd *s* of late Captain Rupert Egerton Lubbock, Royal Navy; *m* 1947, Hazel Gordon, *d* of late Gordon Chapman; one *s* one *d*. *Educ:* Charterhouse; Brasenose Coll., Oxford. Served 1939–46, RNVR. Called to Bar, Inner Temple, 1947. *Address:* Great Horkesley, Essex.

LUCAN, 7th Earl of, *cr* 1795; **Richard John Bingham;** Bt 1632; Baron Lucan, 1776; Baron Bingham (UK), 1934; *b* 18 Dec. 1934; *e s* of 6th Earl of Lucan, MC; *S* father, 1964; *m* 1963, Veronica, *d* of late Major C. M. Duncan, MC, and of Mrs J. D. Margrie; one *s* two *d*. *Educ:* Eton. Lieut (Res. of Officers) Coldstream Guards. *Heir: s* Lord Bingham, *qv*.

LUCAS, family name of **Baron Lucas of Chilworth.**

LUCAS; *see* Keith-Lucas.

LUCAS OF CHILWORTH, 2nd Baron *cr* 1946, of Chilworth; **Michael William George Lucas;** *b* 26 April 1926; *er s* of 1st Baron and Sonia (*d* 1979), *d* of Marcus Finkelstein, Libau, Latvia; *S* father, 1967; *m* 1955, Ann-Marie, *o d* of Ronald Buck, Southampton; two *s* one *d*. *Educ:* Peter Symond's Sch., Winchester; Luton Technical Coll. Served with Royal Tank Regt. A Lord in Waiting (Govt Whip), 1983–84; Parly Under-Sec. of State, DTI, 1984–87. Mem., House of Lords Select Cttee on Science and Technol., 1980–83, on European Communities, 1988–; UK deleg., N Atlantic Assembly, 1981–83, 1988–. TEng(CEI); FIMI (Mem. Council, 1972–76); FInstTA; President: League of Safe Drivers, 1976–80; Inst. of Transport Administration, 1980–83; Vice-Pres., RoSPA, 1980; Mem., Public Policy Cttee, RAC, 1981–83, 1988–. Governor, Churcher's Coll., Petersfield, 1985–. *Heir: s* Hon. Simon William Lucas, late Capt. RE [*b* 6 Feb. 1957. *Educ:* Churcher's Coll., Petersfield; Leicester Univ. (BSc). Geophysicist, USA]. *Address:* House of Lords, SW1A 0PW.

See also Hon. I. T. M. Lucas.

LUCAS OF CRUDWELL, Baroness (10th in line) *cr* 1663 **AND DINGWALL,** Lady (13th in line) *cr* 1609; **Anne Rosemary Palmer;** *b* 28 April 1919; *er d* of Group Captain Howard Lister Cooper, AFC, and Baroness Lucas and Dingwall; *S* mother, 1958; is a *co-heir* to Barony of Butler; *m* 1950, Major the Hon. Robert Jocelyn Palmer, MC, DL, late Coldstream Guards, 3rd *s* of 3rd Earl of Selborne, PC, CH; two *s* one *d*. *Heir: er s* Hon. Ralph Matthew Palmer [*b* 7 June 1951; *m* 1978, Clarissa Marie, *d* of George Vivian Lockett, TD; one *s* one *d*]. *Address:* The Old House, Wonston, Winchester, Hampshire.

LUCAS, Ven. Brian Humphrey; QHC 1989; Chaplain-in-Chief, Royal Air Force, since 1991; *b* 20 Jan. 1940; *s* of Frederick George Humphrey Lucas and Edith Mary Lucas; *m* 1966, Joy Penn; two *s* one *d*. *Educ:* St David's Coll., Lampeter (BA); St Stephen's House, Oxford. Ordained deacon 1964, priest 1965; Curate: Llandaff Cathedral, 1964–67; Parish of Neath, 1967–70; Royal Air Force: Chaplain, 1970–87; Asst Chaplain-in-Chief, 1987–91. *Recreations:* archaeology of the Near East, travel (excluding tourist areas), watching Welsh Rugby football. *Address:* Ministry of Defence, Adastral House, Theobalds Road, WC1X 8RU. *T:* 071–430 7268. *Club:* Royal Air Force.

LUCAS, (Charles) Vivian; Chief Executive, Devon County Council, 1974–79; solicitor; *b* 31 May 1914; *s* of Frank and Mary Renshaw Lucas, Malvern, Worcs; *m* 1941, Oonah Holderness; two *s* two *d*. *Educ:* Malvern Coll.; abroad; London Univ. (LLB). Clerk, Devon County Council, 1972–74; Clerk to the Lieutenancy of Devon, 1972–79. *Recreations:* sport, bridge. *Address:* Highfield Lodge, 7 Salterton Road, Exmouth EX8 2BR. *Club:* Golf and Country (Exeter).

LUCAS, Christopher Charles; Under Secretary, Community and International Policy Division, Department of Energy, 1977–80, retired; *b* 5 June 1920; *s* of Charles Edwin Lucas and Mabel Beatrice Read; *m* 1945, Beryl June Vincent; two *d*. *Educ:* Devonport High Sch.; Balliol Coll., Oxford (Newman Exhibnr). Min. of Fuel, 1946; Central Econ. Planning Staff, 1948; HM Treasury, 1950–70; Cabinet Office, 1970–72; Sec., NEDC, 1973–76; Under-Sec., Dept of Energy, 1976–. *Recreation:* riding. *Address:* Orchard Croft, Withycombe, near Minehead, Somerset. *T:* Dunster (0643) 821551.

LUCAS, Sir Cyril (Edward), Kt 1976; CMG 1956; FRS 1966; Director of Fisheries Research, Scotland (Department of Agriculture and Fisheries for Scotland) and Director Marine Laboratory Aberdeen, 1948–70; *b* Hull, Yorks, 30 July 1909; *o s* of late Archibald and Edith Lucas, Hull; *m* 1934, Sarah Agnes (*d* 1974), *o d* of late Henry Alfred and Amy Rose; two *s* one *d*. *Educ:* Grammar Sch., Hull; University Coll., Hull. BSc (London) 1931, DSc (London) 1942. FRSE 1939; Vice-Pres., 1962–64; Neill Prize, 1960. Research Biologist, University Coll., Hull, 1931; Head of Dept of Oceanography, University Coll., Hull, 1942. UK Expert or Delegate to various internat. confs on Marine Fisheries and Conservation, 1948–, and Chm. of research cttees in connexion with these; Chm., Consultative and Liaison Cttees, Internat. Council for Exploration of Sea, 1962–67; Member: Adv. Cttee on Marine Resources Research, FAO, 1964–71 (Chm. 1966–71); Council for Scientific Policy, 1968–70; Nat. Environmental Res. Council, 1970–78. Hon. DSc Hull, 1975; Hon. LLD Aberdeen, 1977. *Publications:* various scientific, particularly on marine plankton and fisheries research in Bulletins of Marine Ecology (Joint Editor), Jl of Marine Biological Assoc., etc and various international jls. *Address:* 16 Albert Terrace, Aberdeen AB1 1XY. *T:* Aberdeen (0224) 645568.

LUCAS, George; film director, producer and screenwriter; Chairman, Lucasfilm, since 1974; *b* 14 May 1944; *s* of George and Dorothy Lucas. *Educ:* Univ. of Southern California (Bachelor of Fine Arts, 1966). Asst to Francis Ford Coppola on The Rain People, 1967 (winner, Grand Prize, Nat. Student Film Festival for short film, THX-1138, 1967); director, co-author of screenplays: THX-1138, 1970; American Graffiti, 1973; dir, author, Star Wars, 1977; executive producer, author: More American Graffiti, 1979; The Empire Strikes Back, 1980; Return of the Jedi, 1983; Indiana Jones and the Temple of Doom, 1984; Willow, 1988; co-executive producer: Raiders of the Lost Ark (and co-author), 1981; Land Before Time, 1988; Indiana Jones and the Last Crusade, 1989; executive producer: Mishima, 1985; Howard the Duck, 1986; Labyrinth, 1986; Tucker, the Man and his Dream, 1988. *Publication:* Star Wars, 1976. *Address:* Lucasfilm Ltd, PO Box 2009, San Rafael, Calif 94912, USA. *T:* (415) 662–1800.

LUCAS, Prof. Ian Albert McKenzie, CBE 1977; Principal of Wye College, 1977–88, Professor, 1988, University of London, now Professor Emeritus; *b* 10 July 1926; *s* of Percy John Lucas and Janie Inglis (*née* Hamilton); *m* 1950, Helen Louise Langerman; one *s* two *d*. *Educ:* Clayesmore Sch.; Reading Univ.; McGill Univ. BSc, MSc; FIBiol; FRAgS. Lectr, Harper Adams Agricl Coll., 1949–50; pig nutrition res., Rowett Res. Inst., Aberdeen, 1950–57 and 1958–61; Res. Fellow, Ruakura Res. Station, New Zealand, 1957–58; Prof. of Agriculture, UCNW, Bangor, 1961–77. Chm., Agricl and Vet. Cttee, British Council, 1978–87. Member: MAFF Adv. Council for Agric. and Hortic., 1969–79; Agric. and Vet. Sub-Cttee, UGC, 1972–77; CVCP, 1985–88; Cttee, Internat. Co-operation in Higher Educn, British Council, 1986–90. President: Sect. M, BAAS, 1983; Agricl Educn Assoc., 1987. Member Governing Body: Grassland Res. Inst., 1970–79; Rydal Sch., 1975–77; RVC, 1978–88; E Malling Res. Station, 1978–87; Hadlow Agric. Coll., 1978–88; Inst. for Grassland and Animal Production Research, 1987–89. Hon. Life Mem., British Council, 1987. *Publications:* scientific papers in Jl Agricl Science, Animal Production, Brit. Jl Nutrition and others. *Recreations:* sailing. *Address:* Valley Downs, Brady Road, Lyminge, Folkestone, Kent CT18 8DU. *T:* Lyminge (0303) 863053. *Clubs:* Farmers'; Hollowshore Cruising (Oare, Kent).

LUCAS, Hon. Ivor Thomas Mark, CMG 1980; HM Diplomatic Service, retired; Assistant Secretary-General, Arab-British Chamber of Commerce, 1985–87; *b* 25 July 1927; 2nd *s* of George William Lucas, 1st Baron Lucas of Chilworth, and Sonia Lucas; *m* 1954, Christine Mallorie Coleman; three *s*. *Educ:* St Edward's Sch., Oxford; Trinity Coll., Oxford (MA). Served in Royal Artillery, 1945–48 (Captain). BA Oxon 1951. Entered Diplomatic Service, 1951; Middle East Centre for Arab Studies, Lebanon, 1952; 3rd, later 2nd Sec., Bahrain, Sharjah and Dubai, 1952–56; FO, 1956–59; 1st Sec., Karachi, 1959–62; 1st Sec. and Head of Chancery, Tripoli, 1962–66; FO, 1966–68; Counsellor, Aden, 1968–69 (Chargé d'Affaires, Aug. 1968–Feb. 1969); Dep. High Comr, Kaduna, Nigeria, 1969–71; Counsellor, Copenhagen, 1972–75; Head of Middle East Dept, FCO, 1975–79; Ambassador to Oman, 1979–81, to Syria, 1982–84. Mem., Central Council, Royal Over-Seas League, 1988–; Chm., Anglo-Omani Soc., 1990–; Vice-Pres., RSAA, 1990–. *Publications:* chapters in: The Middle East: a handbook, 1988; Politics and the Economy in Syria, 1991. *Recreations:* music, cricket, tennis. *Clubs:* Royal Over-Seas League, Commonwealth Trust.

LUCAS, Ven. John Michael; Archdeacon of Totnes, 1976–81, now Archdeacon Emeritus; *b* 13 June 1921; *s* of Rev. Stainforth John Chadwick Lucas and Dorothy Wybray Mary Lucas; *m* 1952, Catharina Madeleine Bartlett; three *s* (one *d* decd). *Educ:* Kelly Coll., Tavistock; Lichfield Theological Coll. Deacon 1944, priest 1945, dio. Exeter; Asst Curate: Parish of Wolborough, 1944; Parish of Ashburton, 1950; Rector of Weare Giffard with Landcross and Vicar of Monkleigh, 1952; Vicar of Northam, 1962; Vicar of Chudleigh Knighton, 1976–83. *Recreations:* family recreations, garden. *Address:* Wybray House, Shobrooke, Crediton, Devon.

LUCAS, John Randolph, FBA 1988; Fellow and Tutor of Merton College, Oxford, since 1960; *b* 18 June 1929; *s* of late Rev. E. de G. Lucas, sometime Archdeacon of Durham and Joan Mary Lucas; *m* 1961, Morar Portal, *er d* of Sir Reginald Portal, KCB, DSC; two *s* two *d*. *Educ:* St Mary's Coll., Winchester; Balliol Coll., Oxford (John Locke Schol., 1952; MA). Jun. Res. Fellow, Merton Coll., Oxford, 1953–56; Fellow and Asst Tutor, Corpus Christi Coll., Cambridge, 1956–59. Jane Eliza Procter Vis. Fellow, Princeton Univ., 1957–58; Leverhulme Res. Fellow, Leeds Univ., 1959–60. Chm., Oxford Consumers' Gp,

1961–63, 1965. Member: Archbishops' Commn on Christian Doctrine, 1967–76; Lichfield Commn on Divorce and Remarriage, 1975–78. Lectures: (jtly) Gifford, Univ. of Edinburgh, 1971–73; Margaret Harris, Univ. of Dundee, 1981; Harry Jelema, Calvin Coll., Grand Rapids, 1987. *Publications:* Principles of Politics, 1966, 2nd edn 1985; The Concept of Probability, 1970; The Freedom of the Will, 1970; (jtly) The Nature of Mind, 1972; (jtly) The Development of Mind, 1973; A Treatise on Time and Space, 1973; Essays on Freedom and Grace, 1976; Democracy and Participation, 1976 (trans. Portuguese, 1985); On Justice, 1980; Space, Time and Causality, 1985; The Future, 1989; (jtly) Space, Time and Electromagnetism, 1990; various articles in learned jls. *Recreation:* walking and talking. *Address:* Merton College, Oxford OX1 4JD. *T:* Oxford (0865) 276327; Postmasters' Hall, Merton Street, Oxford OX1 4JE. *T:* Oxford (0865) 276321; Lambrook House, East Lambrook, South Petherton, Som TA13 5HW. *T:* South Petherton (0460) 40413.

LUCAS, Keith Stephen; artist and teacher; Head of Radio, Film and Televison Studies, Christ Church College, Canterbury, 1984–89; *b* 28 Aug. 1924; *m* 1969, Rona Stephanie Lucas (*née* Levy); two *s* one *d* (and two step *s*). *Educ:* Royal Coll. of Art (ARCA). London Press Exchange, 1956–64; Prof. of Film and Television, Royal Coll. of Art, 1964–72 (first holder of Chair); Dir, British Film Institute, 1972–78; Television Consultant, BFI, 1979–84. Artistic Dir, Commonwealth Film and TV Fest. and supporting arts prog., Cyprus, 1980. Chairman: Canterbury New Theatre Ltd, 1979–83; Canterbury Theatre and Festival Trust, 1983–86 (Pres., 1986); Vice-Pres., Centre Internat. de Liaison des Ecoles de Cinéma et de Télévision, 1970–72. Governor: North East London Poly., 1971–72; Canterbury Coll. of Art (formerly Canterbury Sch. of Art), 1971–74, 1981–87; Maidstone Coll. of Art, 1982–87; Kent Inst. of Art and Design, 1987–89. Exhibitions: retrospective 1956–86, Poor Priests Hosp., Canterbury, 1986; John Nevill Gall., Canterbury, 1988; Royal Mus., Canterbury, 1990. Hon. Fellow, Royal Coll. of Art, 1972. *Recreations:* writing, listening to music. *Address:* The Old School House, Bishopsbourne, Canterbury, Kent CT4 5JB. *T:* Canterbury (0227) 830026. *Clubs:* Athenæum, Chelsea Arts.

LUCAS, Percy Belgrave, CBE 1981; DSO 1943 and Bar 1945; DFC 1942; Chairman: GRA Property Trust Ltd, 1965–75 (Managing Director, 1957–65); John Jacobs Golf Consultants Ltd, since 1978; John Jacobs Golf Associates Ltd, since 1985; *b* Sandwich Bay, Kent, 2 Sept. 1915; *y s* of late Percy Montagu Lucas, Prince's, Sandwich, form. of Filby House, Filby, Norfolk; *m* 1946, Jill Doreen, *d* of Lt-Col A. M. Addison, Ascot; two *s* (and one *s* decd). *Educ:* Stowe; Pembroke Coll., Cambridge. Editorial Staff, Express Newspapers, 1937–40. Joined RAFVR, 1939; Commanded: 249 (Fighter) Sqdn, Battle of Malta, 1942; 616 (Fighter) Sqdn, 1943; Coltishall Wing, Fighter Command, 1943; 613 (Mosquito) Sqdn, 2 Gp, 2nd TAF, North-West Europe, 1944–45; Fighter Command, HQ Staff, 1942; Air Defence of Great Britain HQ Staff, 1944; demobilised with rank of Wing Comdr, 1946. Contested (C) West Fulham, 1945; MP (C) Brentford and Chiswick, 1950–59. Capt. Cambridge Univ. Golf team, 1937; Pres. Hawks Club, Cambridge, 1937; English International Golf team, 1936, 1948, 1949 (Capt. 1949); British Walker Cup team, 1936, 1947, 1949 (Capt. 1949); Capt., Walker Cup Society, 1986–88. Vice-President: Golf Foundation Ltd, 1983– (Mem. Council, 1966–83; Pres., 1963–66); Nat. Golf Clubs Advisory Assoc., 1969– (Pres., 1963–69); Assoc. of Golf Club Secretaries, 1974– (Pres., 1968–74). Member: General Advisory Council, BBC, 1962–67; Council, National Greyhound Racing Soc. of Great Britain, 1957–72; Policy Cttee, Nat. Greyhound Racing Club Ltd, 1972–77; AAA Cttee of Inquiry, 1967; Exec. Cttee, General Purposes and Finance Cttee; Central Council of Physical Recreation; Management Cttee, Crystal Palace Nat. Sports Centre, 1961–73; Sports Council, 1971–83 (Chm., Finance Cttee, 1978–82; Chm., Sports Trade Adv. Panel, 1972–83); Governor, Stowe Sch., 1964–79. Pres., Old Stoic Soc., 1979–81. Croix de Guerre avec Palme, 1945. *Publications:* Five-Up (autobiography), 1978, 2nd edn 1991; The Sport of Prince's (reflections of a golfer), 1980; Flying Colours: the epic story of Douglas Bader, 1981, 2nd edn 1990; Wings of War: airmen of all nations tell their stories 1939–1945, 1983; Out of the Blue: the role of luck in air warfare 1917–66, 1985; John Jacobs' Impact on Golf: the man and his methods, 1987; Thanks for the Memory: unforgettable characters in air warfare 1939–1945, 1989; (with Air Vice-Marshal J. E. Johnson) Glorious Summer: the story of the Battle of Britain, 1990. *Recreations:* golf, photography. *Address:* 11 Onslow Square, SW7 3NJ. *T:* 071–584 8373. *Clubs:* Naval and Military, Royal Air Force; Sandy Lodge Golf; Walton Heath Golf; Prince's Golf; Royal West Norfolk Golf.

LUCAS, Prof. Raleigh Barclay; Professor of Oral Pathology, University of London, 1954–79, now Emeritus; Consultant Pathologist, Royal Dental Hospital of London, 1950–79; *b* 3 June 1914; *s* of H. Lucas; *m* 1942, Violet Sorrell; one *d* (one *s* decd). *Educ:* George Watson's Coll.; Univ. of Edinburgh. MB, ChB (Edinburgh) 1937; DPH 1939; MD 1945; MRCP 1946; FRCPath 1963; FRCP 1974; FDS RCS 1974. Asst Bacteriologist, Edinburgh Royal Infirmary, 1939–40; Pathologist, Stoke Mandeville Hosp. and Royal Buckinghamshire Hospital, 1947–49; Reader in Pathology, University of London, 1950–54; Dean, Sch. of Dental Surgery, Royal Dental Hospital of London, 1958–73. Examiner in Pathology and Bacteriology for dental degrees, Univs of London, Glasgow, Birmingham, Sheffield, Liverpool and Wales. Served War of 1939–45, Major RAMC; FRSocMed; Fellow and Past Pres., Royal Medical Society; Mem. Pathological Soc. of Great Britain and Ireland; Mem. BMA. *Publications:* (jtly) Bacteriology for Students of Dental Surgery, 1954; Pathology of Tumours of the Oral Tissues, 1964; (jtly) Tumors of the Major Salivary Glands, 1974; (jtly) Atlas of Oral Pathology, 1985; various articles in medical and scientific journals.

LUCAS, Sir Thomas (Edward), 5th Bt *cr* 1887; MA; Research Director, TLA Communications Group; *b* 16 Sept. 1930; *s* of late Ralph John Scott Lucas (killed in action, 1941), and Dorothy (*d* 1985), *d* of late H. T. Timson, Tatchbury Mount, Hants; *S* cousin, 1980; *m* 1958, Charmian (*d* 1970), *d* of late Col J. S. Powell; one *s*; *m* 1980, Ann Graham Moore. *Educ:* Wellington College; Trinity Hall, Cambridge. FRSA. *Publications:* Handbook of Vacuum Physics, Vol. 1, part 2, 1964; Patterns of World Social and Economic Change—the next 15 years, 1984; articles in scientific and technical jls. *Heir: s* Stephen Ralph James Lucas, *b* 11 Dec. 1963. *Clubs:* Athenæum, Ski Club of Great Britain.

LUCAS, Vivian; *see* Lucas, C. V.

LUCAS-TOOTH, Sir (Hugh) John, 2nd Bt *cr* 1920, of Bught; *b* 20 Aug. 1932; *s* of Sir Hugh Vere Huntly Duff Munro-Lucas-Tooth of Teananich, 1st Bt and Laetitia Florence, OBE (*d* 1978), *er d* of Sir John Ritchie Findlay, 1st Bt, KBE; *S* father, 1985; *m* 1955, Hon. Caroline, *e d* of Baron Poole, *qv*; three *d*. *Educ:* Eton College; Balliol Coll., Oxford. *Heir: cousin* James Lingen Warrand [*b* 6 Oct. 1936; *m* 1960, Juliet Rose, *yr d* of late T. A. Pearn; two *s* one *d*]. *Address:* Parsonage Farm, East Hagbourne, Didcot, Oxon OX11 9LN. *Clubs:* Brooks's, Beefsteak.

LUCE, Rt. Hon. Sir Richard (Napier), Kt 1991; PC 1986; MP (C) Shoreham, since 1974 (Arundel and Shoreham, Apr. 1971–1974); *b* 14 Oct. 1936; *s* of late Sir William Luce, GBE, KCMG, and Margaret, *d* of late Adm. Sir Trevylyan Napier, KCB; *m* 1961, Rose, *d* of Sir Godfrey Nicholson, 1st Bt; two *s*. *Educ:* Wellington Coll.; Christ's Coll., Cambridge. 2nd cl. History. Nat. Service officer, 1955–57, served in Cyprus. Overseas Civil Service, served as District Officer, Kenya, 1960–62; Brand Manager, Gallaher Ltd, 1963–65; Marketing Manager, Spirella Co. of GB; Dir, National Innovations Centre, 1968–71; Chairman: IFA Consultants Ltd, 1972–79; Selanex Ltd, 1973–79; Courtenay Stewart International Ltd, 1975–79; Mem. European Adv. Bd, Corning Glass International, 1975–79. Contested (C) Hitchin, 1970. PPS to Minister for Trade and Consumer Affairs, 1972–74; an Opposition Whip, 1974–75; an Opposition spokesman on foreign and commonwealth affairs, 1977–79; Parly Under Sec. of State, 1979–81, Minister of State, 1981–82 and 1983–85, FCO; Minister of State, Privy Council Office (Minister for the Arts), 1985–90. *Recreations:* tennis, walking, reading, etc. *Address:* House of Commons, Westminster, SW1A 0AA.

LUCE, Thomas Richard Harman; Under Secretary, Community Services Division, Department of Health, since 1990; *b* 11 July 1939; *s* of late Air Cdre Charles Luce, DSO, and of Mrs J. M. E. Luce (*née* Johnson); *m* Virginia Manson Hunt; two step *s*. *Educ:* Clifton Coll.; Christ's Coll., Cambridge (BA Hons); Indiana Univ., USA. HM Inspector of Taxes, 1965–67; Asst Principal, Ministries of Aviation and Technology, 1967–69; Principal, CSD, 1969–72; Department of Health and Social Security: Principal, 1972–75; Asst Sec., 1975–84; Under Sec., 1984–; seconded to HM Treasury (Head of Management Policy and Running Costs Gp), 1987–90. *Publications:* occasional music criticism. *Recreations:* music, reading, walking, swimming. *Address:* Department of Health, Richmond House, Whitehall, SW1. *Clubs:* Athenæum, Royal Automobile.

LUCEY, Rear-Adm. Martin Noel, CB 1973; DSC 1944; RN retired; *b* 21 Jan. 1920; *s* of A. N. Lucey; *m* 1947, Barbara Mary Key; two *s* one *d*. *Educ:* Gresham's Sch., Holt. Entered RN, 1938. Served War of 1939–45: qualif. in navigation, 1944; "N" 10th Destroyer Sqdn, 1944. Comdr, 1953; Mem. NATO Defence Coll., 1954; Captain, 1961; Captain "F7" HMS Puma, 1964; Cdre, Sen. Naval Officer, West Indies, 1968; Rear-Adm., 1970; Adm. President, RNC Greenwich, 1970–72; Flag Officer, Scotland and NI, 1972–74. Dir Gen., Nat. Assoc. of British and Irish Millers, 1975–84. *Recreation:* painting. *Address:* Oldways, Houghton, Arundel, West Sussex.

LUCIE-SMITH, (John) Edward (McKenzie); poet and art critic; *b* Kingston, Jamaica, 27 Feb. 1933; *s* of John Dudley Lucie-Smith and Mary (*née* Lushington); unmarried. *Educ:* King's Sch., Canterbury; Merton Coll., Oxford (MA). Settled in England, 1946. Education Officer, RAF, 1954–56; subseq. worked in advertising and as free-lance journalist and broadcaster. FRSL. *Publications:* A Tropical Childhood and other poems, 1961 (jt winner, John Llewellyn Rhys Mem. Prize; winner, Arts Coun. Triennial Award); (ed, with Philip Hobsbaum) A Group Anthology, 1963; Confessions and Histories, 1964; (with Jack Clemo, George MacBeth) Penguin Modern Poets 6, 1964; (ed) Penguin Book of Elizabethan Verse, 1965; What is a Painting?, 1966; (ed) The Liverpool Scene, 1967; (ed) A Choice of Browning's Verse, 1967; (ed) Penguin Book of Satirical Verse, 1967; Thinking about Art, 1968; Towards Silence, 1968; Movements in Art since 1945, 1969; (ed) British Poetry Since 1945, 1970; (with Patricia White) Art in Britain 69–70, 1970; (ed) A Primer of Experimental Verse, 1971; (ed with S. W. Taylor) French Poetry: the last fifteen years, 1971; A Concise History of French Painting, 1971; Symbolist Art, 1972; Eroticism in Western Art, 1972; The First London Catalogue, 1974; The Well Wishers, 1974; The Burnt Child (autobiog.), 1975; The Invented Eye (early photography), 1975; World of the Makers, 1975; (with Celestine Dars) How the Rich Lived, 1976; Joan of Arc, 1976; (with Celestine Dars) Work and Struggle, 1977; Fantin-Latour, 1977; The Dark Pageant (novel), 1977; Art Today, 1977; A Concise History of Furniture, 1979; Super Realism, 1979; Cultural Calendar of the Twentieth Century, 1979; Art in the Seventies, 1980; The Story of Craft, 1981; The Body, 1981; A History of Industrial Design, 1983; Art Terms: an illustrated dictionary, 1984; Art in the Thirties, 1985; American Art Now, 1985; Lives of the Great Twentieth Century Artists, 1986; Sculpture since 1945, 1987; (ed) The Essential Osbert Lancaster, 1988; (with Carolyn Cohen, Judith Higgins) The New British Painting, 1988; Art in the Eighties, 1990; Art Deco Painting, 1990; Fletcher Benton, 1990; Jean Rustin, 1991; contribs to Times, Sunday Times, Independent, Mail-on-Sunday, Listener, Spectator, New Statesman, Evening Standard, Encounter, London Magazine, Illustrated London News, etc. *Recreations:* walking the dog, malice. *Address:* c/o Rogers, Coleridge & White, 20 Powis Mews, W11.

LUCKHOO, Hon. Sir Edward Victor, Kt 1970; QC (Guyana); Order of Roraima, 1979; attached to Luckhoo and Luckhoo, Guyana, 1949–66 and 1984–87; *b* Guyana (when Br. Guiana), 24 May 1912; *s* of late E. A. Luckhoo, OBE and *g s* of Moses Luckhoo, official interpreter to the courts; *m* 1981, Maureen Moxlow, Batley, Yorks. *Educ:* New Amsterdam Scots Sch.; Queen's Coll., Guyana; St Catherine's Coll., Oxford (BA). Called to Bar, Middle Temple, 1936; QC Guyana 1965. Began career in magistracy as acting Magistrate, Essequibo District, 1943; Magistrate, 1944–47; Judge of Appeal, 1966; Chancellor and President of Court of Appeal, Guyana, 1968–76; Actg Governor-General, 1969–70; Actg Pres. of Guyana, Feb.–March, 1970; High Comr in India and Sri Lanka, 1976–83. Chairman: Customs Tariff Tribunal, 1954–56; Judicial Service Commn, 1966–75; Honours Adv. Council, 1970–76. Mem. Exec. Bd, UNESCO, 1983–87. *Address:* 43 Penn Drive, Liversedge, W Yorks WF15 8DB.

See also Sir J. A. Luckhoo, Sir L. A. Luckhoo.

LUCKHOO, Hon. Sir Joseph (Alexander), Kt 1963; Judge, Belize Court of Appeal, since 1987; *b* 8 June 1917; *e s* of late Joseph Alexander Luckhoo, KC and Irene Luckhoo; *g s* of Moses Luckhoo, official interpreter to the Courts; *m* 1964, Leila Patricia Singh; three *s* one *d*. *Educ:* Queen's Coll., British Guiana; University Coll., London; Middle Temple. BSc London, 1939. Barrister, Middle Temple, 1944; practised at Bar, British Guiana. Crown Counsel, British Guiana, 1949; Legal Draftsman, 1953; acted as Solicitor Gen., British Guiana, 1952, 1954 and 1955; Puisne Judge, British Guiana, 1956; Acting Chief Justice, 1959; Chief Justice, 1960–66; Chief Justice Guyana, 1966; Judge, Court of Appeal, Jamaica, 1967–76; Acting Pres., Court of Appeal, Jamaica, 1972, 1973, and 1974–76; Reserve Judge, 1978–81, Judge, 1981–82, President, 1982–87, Bahamas Court of Appeal; Judge of Ct of Appeal, Turks and Caicos, 1979, Pres., 1982–87. Chairman: Judicial Service Commission, 1961–66; Law Reform Cttee, Jamaica, 1973–76. *Publications:* Editor: Law Reports of British Guiana, 1956–58; British Guiana section of West Indian Reports, 1958–61, Jamaica section, 1970–72; Dominion Report Service (Canada), 1977–87. *Recreation:* watching sport. *Address:* 31 Aldenham Crescent, Don Mills, North York, Ontario M3A 1S3, Canada.

See also Hon. Sir E. V. Luckhoo, Sir L. A. Luckhoo.

LUCKHOO, Sir Lionel (Alfred), KCMG 1969; Kt 1966; CBE 1962; QC (Guyana) 1954; Judge of Supreme Court, Guyana, 1980, retired; *b* 2 March 1914; 2nd *s* of late Edward Alfred Luckhoo, OBE, Solicitor, and Evelyn Luckhoo; *g s* of Moses Luckhoo, official interpreter to the Courts; *m* Sheila Chamberlin; two *s* three *d*. *Educ:* Queen's Coll., Georgetown, Brit. Guiana; Middle Temple, London. MLC, 1949–51; Mem. State Coun., 1952–53; Minister without Portfolio, 1954–57; Mem. Georgetown Town Council, 1950–64; Mayor, City of Georgetown, 1954, 1955, 1960, 1961 (Dep. Mayor three times); High Comr in UK, for Guyana, May 1966–70; for Barbados, Nov. 1966–70; Ambassador of Guyana and Barbados, to Paris, Bonn and The Hague, 1967–70. Pres., MPCA Trade

Union, Brit. Guiana, 1949–52; Pres. of several Unions; has served on Commns of Enquiry, Public Cttees, Statutory Bodies, Legal Cttees, Drafting Cttees, Disciplinary Cttees, etc. Head of Luckhoo & Luckhoo, Legal Practitioners. Chm., Red Cross Soc., 1978. Pres., Guyana Olympic Assoc., 1974–79. Mem. of the Magic Circle. Listed in the Guinness Book of Records as the world's most successful advocate with 245 successful defences in murder cases. Has travelled more than one million miles around the world speaking of Jesus. *Publications:* (jtly) The Fitzluck Theory of Breeding Racehorses, 1960; I Believe, 1968; God is Love, 1975; Life After Death, 1975; The Xmas Story, 1975; Sense of Values, 1975; Dear Atheist, 1977; Dear Boys and Girls, 1978; Dear Adults, 1979; God and Science, 1980; Dear Muslims, 1980; The Question Answered, 1984; The Verdict is Yours, 1985. *Recreation:* cricket. *Address:* Lot 1, Croal Street, Georgetown, Guyana. *Club:* Commonwealth Trust.

See also Hon. Sir E. V. Luckhoo, Hon. Sir Joseph A. Luckhoo.

LUCY, Sir Edmund J. W. H. C. R. F.; *see* Fairfax-Lucy.

LUDDINGTON, Sir Donald (Collin Cumyn), KBE 1976; CMG 1973; CVO 1974; retired; *b* 18 Aug. 1920; *s* of late F. Norman John Luddington, Ceylon Civil Service, and late M. Myrtle Amethyst Payne; *m* 1945, Garry Brodie Johnston; one *s* one *d.* *Educ:* Dover Coll.; St Andrews Univ. (MA). Served War, Army, 1940–46, KOYLI and RAC, Captain. Hong Kong Govt, 1949–73; Sec. for Home Affairs, 1971–73; Governor, Solomon Islands, 1973–76. Chm., Public Services Commn, Hong Kong, 1977–78; Comr, Indep. Commn against Corruption, Hong Kong, 1978–80. *Recreation:* walking. *Address:* The Firs, Little Lane, Easingwold, York YO6 3AQ. *Clubs:* Commonwealth Trust; Hong Kong (Hong Kong).

LUDER, (Harold) Owen, CBE 1986; PPRIBA; architect and construction industry consultant; Principal, Owen Luder Consultancy, Communication in Construction Ltd, since 1987; *b* London, 7 Aug. 1928; *s* of late Edward Charles and Ellen Clara Luder; *m* 1st, 1951, Rose Dorothy (Doris) Broadstock (marr. diss. 1988); four *d* (one *s* decd); 2nd, 1989, Jacqueline Ollerton. *Educ:* Deptford Park Primary Sch.; Peckham Sch. for Girls; Brixton Sch. of Building; Regent St Polytechnic Sch. of Architecture. ARIBA 1954, FRIBA 1967, PRIBA 1981–83. Private practice in architecture, 1957–87; Founder and Sen. Partner, Owen Luder Partnership, 1958–78, when it became one of the first architectural partnerships to convert to an unlimited co., Chm. and Man. Dir, 1978–87; on withdrawal from architectural practice, set up Owen Luder Consultancy (specialising in communication in construction), 1987; Dir, Communication in Construction Ltd, 1990–. Principal architectural works in commercial and industrial architecture and environmental and urban planning in UK and abroad; consultant: to NCB for Vale of Belvoir coal mining project, 1975–87; to BR for re-use of Engrg Works, Shildon and Swindon, 1985–86; Consultant Architect, RCS, 1974–87; Architect/Planning Consultant, Marine Soc., 1990–. Royal Institute of British Architects: Mem. Council, 1967–89; Hon. Treasurer, 1975–78; Vice-Pres., Membership Communications, 1989–90; Hon. Sec./Treasurer, Commonwealth Assoc. of Architects, 1985–87; Chm. Organising Cttee, IUA Congress 1987. Pres., Norwood Soc., 1981–. Columnist, Building magazine, 1983–; Editor and Presenter, Architectural Practice Video Magazine, 1987–. Occasional radio and TV broadcaster, UK and USA. British Kart Racer, 1961–63; survivor, Lakonia cruise-liner disaster, 1963. FRSA 1984. RIBA Architecture Bronze Medal, 1963; various Civic Trust architectural and housing awards and commendations; Silver Jubilee Medal, for Housing Strategy for the 80s, Town Planning Assoc., 1981; Business Columnist of the Year, Publisher magazine, 1985. Arkansas Traveller, USA, 1971. *Publications:* Sports Stadia after Hillsborough, 1990; contribs on architectural, planning and building matters to various jls. *Recreations:* writing, swimming, photography, theatre, playing golf badly, supporting Arsenal FC avidly. *Address:* 2 Smith Square, SW1P 3HS. *Clubs:* Savage, Royal Automobile.

LUDLOW, Bishop Suffragan of, since 1987; **Rt. Rev. Ian Macdonald Griggs;** *b* 17 May 1928; *s* of late Donald Nicholson Griggs and of Agnes Elizabeth Griggs; *m* 1953, Patricia Margaret Vernon-Browne; two *s* three *d* (and one *s* decd). *Educ:* Brentwood School; Trinity Hall, Cambridge (MA); Westcott House, Cambridge. Curate, St Cuthbert, Copnor, dio. Portsmouth, 1954–59; Domestic Chaplain to Bishop of Sheffield, 1959–64; Diocesan Youth Chaplain (part-time), 1959–64; Vicar of St Cuthbert, Fir Vale, dio. Sheffield, 1964–71; Vicar of Kidderminster, 1971–83; Hon. Canon of Worcester Cathedral, 1977–83; Archdeacon of Ludlow, 1984–87; Priest-in-Charge, St Michael, Tenbury, 1984–88. Chm., Churches' Council for Health and Healing, 1990–. *Recreations:* mountaineering and hill-walking. *Address:* Bishop's House, Halford, Craven Arms, Shropshire SY7 9BT. *T:* Craven Arms (0588) 673571.

LUDLOW, Archdeacon of; *see* Lewis, Ven. J. H. R.

LUDLOW, (Ernest John) Robin, TD 1979; Managing Consultant, Euro Management Search, since 1990; *b* 2 May 1931; *s* of late Donald Ernest Ludlow, Blandford, Dorset, and Buxted, Sussex; *m* 1970, Sonia Louise Hatfeild; one *s* one *d.* *Educ:* Framlingham Coll., Suffolk. RMA Sandhurst, 1949–52; commissioned RASC, 1952; Staff, RMA Sandhurst, 1954–57; retd 1957. J. Lyons & Co. Ltd, 1957–59; The Economist, 1959–72; Press Sec. to the Queen, 1972–73; Dep. Dir, Aims of Industry, 1973–77; Head of Publicity, Strutt and Parker, 1977; Man. Dir, Kiernan and Co. Ltd (Exec. Search), 1977–79; Partner, Boyden Internat. (Exec. Search), 1979–81; Managing Director: Robin Ludlow & Associates (Exec. Search), 1981–89; Management Search Internat., 1985–89. Governor: Clergy Orphan Corp., 1973–83; Royal Star and Garter Home for Disabled Servicemen, 1987–91; Chairman: The Yeomanry Benevolent Fund, 1981–90; Sharpshooters Yeomanry Assoc., 1973–83. Kent and Co. of London Yeomanry (Sharpshooters), TA, 1959–69; The Queen's Regt, TA, 1971–78 (Maj.). Vice Chm., SE, TA&VRA, 1988–91 (Mem., F and GP Cttee, 1973–86; Mem., 1973–86, Chm., 1988–91, Kent Cttee). *Recreations:* shooting, gardening, Territorial Army. *Club:* Cavalry and Guards.

LUDMAN, Harold, FRCS; Consultant Surgeon to Ear, Nose and Throat Department, King's College Hospital, since 1965; Consultant Surgeon in Neuro-otology, National Hospital for Neurology and Neurosurgery, since 1967; *b* 23 Feb. 1933; *s* of Nathan Ludman and Fanny Dinah Jerome; *m* 1957, Lorraine Israel; one *s* one *d.* *Educ:* Bradford Grammar Sch.; Sidney Sussex Coll., Cambridge (BA 1954; MB, BChir 1957; MA 1958). FRCS 1961. House Physician, UCH, 1957; House Surgeon: Royal Ear Hosp., UCH, 1957; Edgware Gen. Hosp., 1958; Royal Marsden Hosp., 1958–59; Registrar and Sen. Registrar, Ear, Nose and Throat Dept, KCH, 1960–65. President: British Assoc. Otolaryngology, 1990–; Section of Otology, RSocMed, 1985; Chm., Soc. Audiology Technicians, 1967–75. Chm., Specialist Adv. Cttee in Otolaryngology, Jt Cttee Higher Surgical Trng, 1988–; Mem., Intercollegiate Bd in Otolaryngology, RCS (formerly Mem. Court of Examiners); Chm., working party on deafness, MRC, 1973–77; formerly Mem., Hearing Aid Council. W. J. Harrison Prize, RSocMed, 1987; W. Jobson Horne Prize, BMA, 1990. *Publications:* (jtly) Diseases of the Ear, 1963, 5th edn 1988; (contrib.) Scott-Brown's Diseases of the Ear, Nose and Throat, 4th edn 1979, 5th edn 1987; contribs to books on ear diseases; numerous papers to learned jls on diseases of the ear. *Recreations:* computers, reading, theatre, walking on the flat. *Address:* 149 Harley Street, W1N 2DE. *T:* 071–935 4444.

LUDWIG, Christa; singer; *b* Berlin, 16 March; *d* of Anton Ludwig, singer, stage director and opera general manager and Eugenie (*née* Besalla), singer; *m* 1st, 1957, Walter Berry (marr. diss. 1970), baritone; one *s*; 2nd, 1972, Paul-Emile Deiber, actor and stage-director. *Educ:* Matura. Staedtische Buehnen, Frankfurt; Landestheater Darmstadt; Landestheater, Hannover; Vienna State Opera; guest appearances in New York, Chicago, London, Berlin, Munich, Tokyo, Milan, Rome, Lucerne, Salzburg, Epidauros, Zürich, Holland, Los Angeles, Cleveland, Saratoga, Bayreuth, Copenhagen, Gent, Montreal, Prague, Budapest and others. Kammersängerin, Austria, 1962; Grand Prix du Disque, 1966; Mozart Medal, Mozartgemeinde, Vienna, 1969; First Class Art and Science, Austria, 1969; Deutscher Schallplattenpreis, 1970; Orphée d'Or, 1970; Prix des Affaires Culturelles, 1972; Vienna Philharmonic Silver Rose, 1980; Hugo Wolf Medal, 1980; Gustav Mahler Medal, 1980; Ehrenring, Staatsoper Vienna, 1980, Hon. Mem., 1981; Golden Medal, City of Salzburg, 1987, and Vienna, 1987. Commandeur des Arts et des Lettres (France), 1988; Chevalier, Légion d'Honneur (France), 1989. *Recreations:* listening to music, theatre, concerts, reading. *Address:* c/o Heidrun Artmüller, Goethegasse 1, A-1010 Wien, Austria; Rigistrasse 14, CH-6045 Meggen, Switzerland.

LUFF, Rev. Alan Harold Frank; Precentor of Westminster Abbey, since 1979 (Precentor and Sacrist, 1979–86); *b* 6 Nov. 1928; *s* of Frank Luff and late Elsie Lilian Luff (*née* Down), Bristol; *m* 1956, Enid Meirion, *d* of late Robert Meirion Roberts and Daisy Harker Roberts; three *s* one *d.* *Educ:* Bristol Grammar School; University Coll., Oxford (BA 1951, Dip. Theol. 1952, MA 1954); Westcott House, Cambridge. ARCM 1977. Deacon, 1956; priest, 1957; Assistant Curate: St Mathew, Stretford, Manchester, 1956–59; St Peter, Swinton, Manchester (with charge of All Saints, Wardley), 1959–61; Precentor of Manchester Cathedral, 1961–68; Vicar of Dwygyfylchi (otherwise Penmaenmawr), Gwynedd, dio. Bangor, 1968–79. Chm., Hymn Soc. of Great Britain and Ireland, 1987– (Hon. Sec., 1973–86). *Publications:* Hymns and Psalms (composer and author), 1981; Welsh Hymns and their tunes, 1990; contribs to New Christian, Musical Times, Organist's Review, etc. *Recreations:* singing, conducting, cooking. *Address:* 7 Little Cloister, Westminster Abbey, SW1P 3PL. *T:* 071–222 1386.

LUFF, Geoffrey Shadrack, IPFA, FCCA; County Treasurer, Nottinghamshire County Council, 1984–91; *b* 12 July 1933; *s* of Shadrack Thomas Luff and Rosie Winifred Luff (*née* Lister); *m* 1956, Gloria Daphne Taylor; one *s* one *d.* *Educ:* Mundella Grammar Sch., Nottingham. Various posts in City Treasury, Nottingham CC, 1949–67; Sen. Technical Asst and Asst Bor. Treasurer, Derby CBC, 1967–73; Asst County Treasurer, Derbyshire CC, 1973–78; Dep. County Treasurer, Nottinghamshire CC, 1978–84. *Recreations:* bowls, gardening, birdwatching, photography.

LUFF, Richard William Peter, FRICS; FRSA; Member Board, Commission for New Towns, since 1987; Deputy Chairman, London Regional Transport Property Board, since 1988 (Member, since 1987); Director, Housing Standards Co. Ltd, since 1988; *b* 11 June 1927; *s* of Victor and Clare Luff; *m* 1st, 1950, Betty Chamberlain (*d* 1989); no *c*; 2nd, 1990, Daphne Olivia Louise Andrews (*née* Brough). *Educ:* Hurstpierpoint Coll., Sussex; Coll. of Estate Management. Service in RA, India and UK, 1945–48. Estates and Valuation Dept, MCC, 1949–65; Asst Valuer, GLC, 1968–75; City Surveyor, Corp. of London, 1975–84; Dir of Property, British Telecom, 1984–87. Royal Institution of Chartered Surveyors: Mem., Gen. Practice Divl Council, 1973–83; Chm., Valuation and Rating Cttee, 1974–79; Mem., Gen. Council, 1975–86; Dep. Chm., Public Affairs Cttee, 1975–79; Pres., 1982–83; Pres., Assoc. of Local Authority Valuers and Estate Surveyors, 1978–79; Hon. Vice-Pres., 1983–89, Hon. Mem., 1989–, Cambridge Univ. Land Soc. Dir, London Wall Litigation Claims Ltd, 1988–. Mem., Furniture History Soc. Master, Chartered Surveyors' Co., 1985. Hon. FISM 1983. *Publications:* Furniture in England—the age of the joiner (with S. W. Wolsey), 1968; articles and papers on compensation and allied property matters; nearly 50 articles on furniture history in Antique Collector, Country Life, and Connoisseur, 1961–73. *Recreations:* collecting antiquarian objects, writing and lecturing on English furniture. *Address:* Blossoms, Broomfield Park, Sunningdale, Ascot, Berks SL5 0JT. *T:* Ascot (0344) 23806. *Clubs:* MCC; Surrey County Cricket.

LUFFINGHAM, Prof. John Kingley, FDS RCSE; Professor of Orthodontics, University of Glasgow, since 1976; *b* 14 Aug. 1928; *s* of Alfred Hulbert Carr Luffingham and Frances Tugby; *m* 1968, Elizabeth Margaret Anderson; two *s* one *d.* *Educ:* Haileybury; London Hosp. Med. Coll. (BDS, PhD London); Dip. Orth RCSE. House Surgeon, London Hosp. Med. Coll., 1957–58; Registrar, KCH, 1959–61; Clinical Research Fellow, MRC, 1961–64; Sen. Registrar, Guy's Hosp., 1965–67; Sen. Lectr, Glasgow Univ., 1968–76; Consultant Orthodontist, Greater Glasgow Health Board, 1968–76. *Publications:* articles in dental jls, incl. British Jl of Orthodontics, European Jl of Orthodontics, Archives of Oral Biology. *Recreations:* sailing, skiing. *Address:* Orthodontic Department, University of Glasgow, Glasgow G12 8QQ.

LUFT, His Honour Arthur Christian, CBE 1988; Member, Legislative Council, Isle of Man, since 1988; *b* 21 July 1915; *e s* of late Ernest Christian Luft and late Phoebe Luft; *m* 1950, Dorothy, *yr d* of late Francis Manley; two *s.* *Educ:* Bradbury Sch., Cheshire. Served Army, 1940–46. Admitted to Manx Bar, 1940; Attorney-Gen., IOM, 1972–74; Second Deemster, 1974–80; HM's First Deemster, Clerk of the Rolls, and Dep. Governor, IOM, 1980–88. Chairman: IOM Criminal Injuries Compensation Tribunal, 1974–80; Prevention of Fraud (Unit Trust) Tribunal, 1974–80; IOM Licensing Appeal Court, 1974–80; Wireless Telegraphy Appeal Bd for IOM, 1974–80; IOM Income Tax Appeal Comrs, 1980–88; IOM Gaming Control Comrs, 1980–90; Rivers Pollution Cttee, 1989–; Data Protection Tribunal, 1990–; Mem., Dept of Local Govt and Envmt, IOM, 1988–. Pres., Youth Adv. Gp. Pres., Manx Deaf Soc., 1975–. Pres., IOM Cricket Club, 1980. *Recreations:* theatre, watching cricket, gardening. *Address:* Leyton, Victoria Road, Douglas, Isle of Man. *T:* Douglas (0624) 621048. *Clubs:* Ellan Vannin, Manx Automobile (Douglas).

LUKE, 2nd Baron *cr* 1929, of Pavenham; **Ian St John Lawson Johnston,** KCVO 1976; TD; DL; JP; *b* 7 June 1905; *e s* of 1st Baron and Hon. Edith Laura (*d* 1941), *d* of 16th Baron St John of Bletsoe; *S* father, 1943; *m* 1932, Barbara, *d* of Sir FitzRoy Hamilton Anstruther-Gough-Calthorpe, 1st Bt; four *s* one *d.* *Educ:* Eton; Trinity Coll., Cambridge, MA. Life President, Electrolux Ltd, 1978– (Chm., 1963–78); Chm., Gateway Building Society, 1978–86; Dir, Ashanti Goldfields Corporation Ltd and other companies; Chm., Bovril Ltd, 1943–70. One of HM Lieutenants, City of London, 1953–. Hon. Col 5th Bn Beds Regt, 1947–62; OC 9th Bn Beds and Herts Regt, 1940–43; Chairman: Area Cttee for National Fitness in Herts and Beds, 1937–39; London Hospitals Street Collections Cen. Cttee, 1943–45; Beds TAA, 1943–46; Duke of Gloucester's Red Cross and St John Fund, 1943–46; Nat. Vice-Pres., Royal British Legion; Chm., National Playing Fields Assoc., 1950–76 (a Vice-Pres., 1977–); an Hon. Sec., Assoc. of British Chambers of Commerce, 1944–52; Mem. of Church Assembly (House of Laity), 1935; Lay Reader, St Alban's dio., 1933–; Mem., International Olympic Cttee, 1951–88, Hon. Mem., 1988–;

President: Incorporated Sales Managers Assoc., 1953–56; Advertising Assoc., 1955–58; Outdoor Advertising Council, 1957; Operation Britain Organisation, 1957–62; London Chamber of Commerce, 1952–55; Inst. of Export, 1973–83; Chm. Governors, Queen Mary Coll., Univ. of London, 1963–82, Fellow, 1980. MFH Oakley Hunt, 1947–49. CC, DL, JP, Bedfordshire. *Heir: s* Hon. Arthur Charles St John Lawson Johnston, DL [*b* 13 Jan. 1933; *m* 1st, 1959, Silvia Maria (marr. diss. 1971), *yr d* of Don Honorio Roigt and Doña Dorothy Goodall de Roigt; one *s* two *d*; 2nd, 1971, Sarah, *d* of Richard Hearne; one *s*]. *Address:* Odell Castle, Odell, Beds MK43 7BB. *T:* Bedford (0234) 720240. *Club:* Carlton.

See also Hon. H. de B. *Lawson Johnston.*

LUKE, Peter (Ambrose Cyprian), MC 1944; writer and dramatist, freelance since 1967; *b* 12 Aug. 1919, *e s* of late Sir Harry Luke, KCMG, DLitt Oxon and Joyce Fremlin; *m* 1st, Carola Peyton-Jones (decd); 2nd, Lettice Crawshaw (marr. diss.); one *d* (one *s* decd); 3rd, June Tobin; two *s* three *d*. *Educ:* Eton; Byam Shaw Sch. of Art; Atelier André Lhote, Paris. Served War, 1939–46 with Rifle Bde in ME, Italy and NW Europe. Sub-Editor, Reuters News Desk, 1946–47; wine trade, 1947–57; Story Editor, ABC TV, 1958–62; Editor, The Bookman (ABC TV), 1962–63; Editor, Tempo (ABC TV Arts Programme), 1963–64; Drama Producer, BBC TV, 1963–67. Dir, Edwards-Mac Liammoir Dublin Gate Theatre Co., 1977–80; Directed, Abbey Theatre, Dublin: Hadrian VII, 1970; directed, Gaiety Theatre, Dublin: Rings for a Spanish Lady, 1978. Author TV plays: Small Fish are Sweet, 1958; Pigs Ear with Flowers, 1960; Roll on Bloomin' Death, 1961; (with William Sansom) A Man on Her Back, 1965; Devil a Monk Wou'd Be, 1966; Honour, Profit and Pleasure, 1985. Produced, Silent Song, BBC TV (Prix Italia, 1967). Wrote and directed films: Anach Cuan (about Sean O Riada), BBC TV, 1967; Black Sound—Deep Song (about Federico Garcia Lorca), BBC TV, 1968; wrote stage plays: Hadrian the Seventh, prod. Birmingham Rep. 1967, Mermaid 1968, Theatre Royal, Haymarket and Broadway, 1969 (Antoinette Perry Award nomination, 1968–69); Bloomsbury, Phoenix, 1974; Proxopera (adaptation), Dublin Gate Theatre, 1979; Married Love, Thorndyke, Leatherhead, 1985, Wyndham's, 1988; (trans.) Yerma, by Federico García Lorca, NT, 1987; wrote BBC Radio Plays: Nymphs and Satyrs Come Away, 1984; The Last of Baron Corvo, 1989; It's a Long Way to Talavera and The Long Road to Waterloo, 1991. OStJ 1940. *Publications:* The Play of Hadrian VII, 1968; Sisyphus and Reilly, an autobiography, 1972; (ed) Enter Certain Players, Edwards-Mac Liammoir 1928–1978, 1978; Paquito and the Wolf (children), 1981; Telling Tales: selected short stories, 1981; The Other Side of the Hill, a novel of the Peninsular War, 1984; The Mad Pomegranate & the Praying Mantis, Adventure in Andalusia, 1985; translations from the Spanish: Yerma, by Federico García Lorca; Rings for a Spanish Lady (Anillos para Una Dama) by Antonio Gala; short stories in: Envoy, Cornhill, Pick of Today's Short Stories, Winter's Tales, Era, New Irish Writing, etc. *Recreations:* conviviality, tauromachy. *Address:* c/o Lemon Unna & Durbridge Ltd, 24 Pottery Lane, Holland Park, W11 4LZ.

LUKES, Prof. Steven Michael, DPhil; FBA 1987; Professor of Political and Social Theory, European University Institute, Florence, since 1987; *b* 8 March 1941; *o s* of S. Lukes; *m* 1977, Nina Vera Mary Stanger; two *s* one *d*. *Educ:* Royal Grammar School, Newcastle upon Tyne; Balliol Coll., Oxford (MA 1965; DPhil 1968). Student, 1962–64, Res. Fellow, 1964–66, Nuffield Coll., Oxford; Fellow of Balliol Coll., Oxford, 1966–88; Lectr in Politics, Oxford Univ., 1967–88. *Publications:* (ed jtly) The Good Society, 1972; Emile Durkheim: his life and work, 1972; Individualism, 1973; Power: a radical view, 1974; Essays in Social Theory, 1976; (ed) Durkheim: Rules of Sociological Method, 1982; (ed jtly) Rationality and Relativism, 1982; (ed jtly) Durkheim and the Law, 1984; Marxism and Morality, 1985; (jtly) No Laughing Matter: a collection of political jokes, 1985; (ed) Power, 1986; Moral Conflict and Politics, 1990. *Recreation:* playing jazz piano. *Address:* European University Institute, Badia Fiesolana, Via dei Roccetini 9, 50016 San Domenico di Fiesole, Florence, Italy. *T:* (55) 50921. *Club:* Zanzibar.

LUMET, Sidney; film director; *b* Philadelphia, 25 June 1924; *o s* of Baruch and Eugenia Lumet; *m* Rita Gam (marr. diss.); *m* 1956, Gloria Vanderbilt (marr. diss. 1963); *m* 1963, Gail Jones (marr. diss. 1978); two *d*; *m* 1980, Mary Gimbel. *Educ:* Professional Children's Sch., NY; Columbia Univ. Served US Army, SE Asia, 1942–46. Appeared as child actor: Dead End; The Eternal Road; Sunup to Sunday; Schoolhouse on the Lot; My Heart's in the Highlands; Dir, Summer Stock, 1947–49; taught acting, High Sch. of Professional Arts; Associate Dir, CBS, 1950, Dir, 1951–57. *TV shows include:* Danger; Your Are There; Alcoa: The Sacco and Vanzetti Story; Goodyear Playhouse; Best of Broadway; Omnibus. *Films directed include:* Twelve Angry Men, 1957; Stage Struck, 1958; That Kind of Woman, 1959; The Fugitive Kind, 1960; A View from the Bridge, Long Day's Journey into Night, 1962; Fail Safe, 1964; The Pawnbroker, The Hill, 1965; The Group, 1966; The Deadly Affair, 1967; Bye Bye Braverman, Last of the Mobile Hot Shots, Child's Play, The Seagull, 1969; The Anderson Tapes, 1971; The Offence, 1973; Serpico, Murder on the Orient Express, 1974; Dog Day Afternoon, 1975; Network, 1977; Equus, 1977; The Wiz, 1979; Just Tell Me What You Want, 1979; Prince of the City, 1980; Deathtrap, 1981; The Verdict, 1982; Daniel, 1983; Garbo Talks, 1984; Power, 1985; The Morning After, 1987; Family Business, 1990; Q & A, 1991; *play:* Caligula, 1960. *Address:* c/o 1775 Broadway, New York, NY 10019, USA.

LUMLEY, family name of **Earl of Scarbrough.**

LUMLEY, Viscount; Richard Osbert Lumley; *b* 18 May 1973; *s* and *heir* of 12th Earl of Scarbrough, *qv.*

LUMLEY-SAVILE, family name of **Baron Savile.**

LUMSDAINE, Nicola Frances; *see* LeFanu, N. F.

LUMSDEN, Sir David (James), Kt 1985; Principal, Royal Academy of Music, since 1982; *b* Newcastle upon Tyne, 19 March 1928; *m* 1951, Sheila Daniels; two *s* two *d*. *Educ:* Dame Allan's Sch., Newcastle upon Tyne; Selwyn Coll., Cambridge (Hon. Fellow, 1986). Organ scholar, Selwyn Coll., Cambridge, 1948–51; BA Class I, 1950; MusB (Barclay Squire Prize) 1951; MA 1955; DPhil 1957. Asst Organist, St John's Coll., Cambridge, 1951–53; Res. Student, 1951–54; Organist and Choirmaster, St Mary's, Nottingham, 1954–56; Founder and Conductor, Nottingham Bach Soc., 1954–59; Rector Chori, Southwell Minster, 1956–59; Dir of Music, Keele, 1958–59; Prof. of Harmony, Royal Academy of Music, 1959–61; Fellow and Organist, New Coll., Oxford, and Lectr in the Faculty of Music, Oxford Univ., 1959–76; Principal, RSAMD, Glasgow, 1976–82. Conductor: Oxford Harmonic Soc., 1961–63; Oxford Sinfonia, 1967–70; BBC Scottish Singers, 1977–80; Organist, Sheldonian Theatre, 1964–76; Choragus, Oxford Univ., 1968–72. Harpsichordist to London Virtuosi, 1972–75. Member of Board: Scottish Opera, 1977–83; ENO, 1983–88. President: Inc. Assoc. of Organists, 1966–68; ISM, 1984–85; RCO, 1986–88; Chairman: NYO, 1985–; Early Music Soc., 1985–89. Hugh Porter Lectr, Union Theological Seminary, NY, 1967; Vis. Prof., Yale Univ., 1974–75. Hon. Editor, Church Music Soc., 1970–73. Hon. FRCO 1976; Hon. RAM 1978; FRCM 1980; FRNCM 1981; FRSAMD 1982; Hon. GSM 1984; FLCM 1985; FRSA 1985; FRSCM 1987; Hon. FTCL 1988; FKC 1991. Hon. DLitt Reading, 1990. *Publications:* An Anthology of English Lute Music, 1954; Thomas Robinson's Schoole of Musicke, 1603,

1971; Articles in: The Listener; The Score; Music and Letters: Galpin Soc. Jl; La Luth et sa Musique; La Musique de la Renaissance, etc. *Recreations:* reading, theatre, photography, travel, hill-walking, etc. *Address:* 47 York Terrace East, NW1 4PT; Royal Academy of Music, Marylebone Road, NW1 5HT; Melton House, Soham, Cambs CB7 5DB.

LUMSDEN, George Innes, FRSE; Member, Civil Service Commission Science Division's Panel of Chairmen, since 1988; *b* 27 June 1926; *s* of George Lumsden and Margaret Ann Frances Lumsden (*née* Cockburn); *m* 1958, Sheila Thomson; two *s* one *d*. *Educ:* Banchory Academy; Aberdeen University (Lyon Prize in Geol.; BSc). MIGeol. Geological Survey of GB, 1949; District Geologist S Scotland, 1970, Asst Dir and Sen. Officer Scotland, 1980, Inst. of Geol Scis; British Geological Survey: CSO and Dep Dir, 1982–85; Dir, 1985–87. Member: Council of Management, Macaulay Inst. for Soil Research, 1980–87; Engineering and Sci. Adv. Cttee, Derby Coll. of Higher Educn, 1983–87; Geol. Museum Adv. Panel, 1985–87; Chm., Dirs of Western European Geol Surveys' Standing Gp on Envmtl Geology, 1984–87, Hon. Pres., 1987–, Hon. Sec., 1988–. *Publications:* maps, papers and books on geol topics in official Geol Survey. *Recreations:* music, theatre, sport, gardening, word processing. *Address:* 15 Ockham Court, 24 Bardwell Road, Oxford OX2 6SR. *T:* Oxford (0865) 57427.

LUMSDEN, James Alexander, MBE 1945; TD 1962; DL; Partner, Maclay, Murray & Spens, Solicitors, Glasgow and Edinburgh, 1947–82; *b* 24 Jan. 1915; *s* of late Sir James Robert Lumsden and Lady (Henrietta) Lumsden (*née* Macfarlane Reid); *m* 1947, Sheila, *d* of late Malcolm Cross and Evelyn Cross (*née* Newlands); three *s*. *Educ:* Rugby Sch.; Corpus Christi Coll., Cambridge. BA Cantab, LLB. Director: Bank of Scotland, 1958–85; Weir Group PLC, 1957–84; William Baird PLC, 1959–84; Murray Growth Trust PLC and other companies in Murray Johnstone Group, 1967–85 (Chm., 1971–84); Scottish Provident Instn, 1968–85 (Chm., 1977–83); Burmah Oil Co. Ltd, 1957–76 (Chm., 1971–75). Mem. Jenkins Cttee on Company Law. DL Dunbartonshire, 1966. *Recreations:* shooting and other country pursuits. *Address:* Bannachra, Helensburgh, Dunbartonshire. *T:* Arden (038985) 653. *Clubs:* Caledonian; New (Edinburgh); Western (Glasgow).

LUMSDEN, Prof. Keith Grant; Director, The Esmée Fairbairn Research Centre, Heriot-Watt University, since 1975; *b* 7 Jan. 1935; *s* of Robert Sclater Lumsden and Elizabeth Brow; *m* 1961, Jean Baillie Macdonald; one *s*. *Educ:* Univ. of Edinburgh (MA Hons Econ 1959); Stanford Univ., California (PhD 1968). Stanford University: Instructor, Dept of Econs, 1960–63; Asst Prof., Graduate Sch. of Business, 1964–67; Research Associate, Stanford Res. Inst., 1965–71; Associate Prof., Grad. Sch. of Business, 1968–75. Vis. Prof., Heriot-Watt Univ., 1969–70; Affiliate Prof. of Econs, INSEAD, 1975; Acad. Dir, Sea Transport Exec. Programme, 1979; Prof. of Econs, Advanced Management Coll., Stanford Univ., 1971. Director: Economic Educn Project, 1969–74; Behavioral Res. Labs, 1970–72; Capital Preservation Fund, 1971–75; Nielsen Engineering Research, 1972–75; Hewlett-Packard Ltd, 1981. *Publications:* The Free Enterprise System, 1963; The Gross National Product, 1964; International Trade, 1965; (jtly) Macroeconomics, 1966, 4th edn 1981; (jtly) Macroeconomics, 1966, 4th edn 1981; (ed) New Development in the Teaching of Economics, 1967; Excess Demand and Excess Supply in World Tramp Shipping Markets, 1968; (ed) Recent Research in Economics Education, 1970; (jtly) Basic Economics: theory and cases, 1973, 2nd edn 1977; (ed) Efficiency in Universities: the La Paz papers, 1974; (jtly) Division Management Simulation, 1978; (jtly) Economics Education in the UK, 1980; (jtly) Basic Macroeconomic Models, 1981; (jtly) Running the British Economy, 1981, 6th edn 1990; (jtly) Managing the Australian Economy, 1985; (jtly) Shipping Management Model—Stratship, 1983; (jtly) Macroeconomic Database, 1984; (jtly) Strategies for Life—Stratlife, 1988; articles in professional jls. *Recreations:* tennis, deep sea game fishing. *Address:* 40 Lauder Road, Edinburgh EH9 1UE. *Clubs:* Waverley Lawn Tennis & Squash (Edinburgh); Dalmahoy Golf and Leisure (Kirknewton).

LUNCH, John, CBE 1975; VRD 1965; FCA, FCIT; Director-General of the Port of London Authority, and Board Member, 1971–76; Chairman: Comprehensive Shipping Group, 1973–75; Transcontinental Air Ltd, 1973–75; *b* 11 Nov. 1919; *s* of late Percy Valentine Lunch and late Amy Lunch (*née* Somerville); *m* 1943, Joyce Barbara Clerke (*d* 1989); two *s*. *Educ:* Roborough Sch., Eastbourne. Served War, Lt RNVR, Medit. and Home Fleets, 1939–46 (N Atlantic convoys, Crete, N Africa, Malta convoys, Sicily D-Day landings; Torpedo specialist, 1944), subseq. Permanent RNVR, later RNR; Lt-Comdr RNR, retd list, 1969; Lt-Col RE (TA), Engr and Transport Staff Corps (formerly Engr and Railway Staff Corps), 1971, Col, 1976. In business in City, 1946–48: Asst Man. Dir, Tokenhouse Securities Corp. Ltd, 1947, and dir several cos; British Transport Commn, 1948–61: road and rail transport and ancillary businesses; PLA, 1961; Dir of Finance, also Dir of Commerce, 1966; Asst Dir-Gen., responsible docks and harbour, 1969; Chairman: (and founder) PLA Port Users Consultative Cttee, 1966–71; Internat. Port Develt Cttee, Internat. Assoc. of Ports and Harbors, 1972–76; Pres., Inst. of Freight Forwarders, 1972–73. Chm., London Industrial Chartered Accountants, 1971–72; Member Council: Inst. of Chartered Accountants, 1970–77; Chartered Inst. of Transport, 1973–76. Mem. Cttee of Management, 1977–, a Vice-Pres., 1987–, RNLI; Founder Chm., RNLI Manhood Br., 1976–78; Pres., RNLI, Hayling Island Lifeboat Station, 1978–88; Hon. Art Adviser, RNLI, 1981–. Hon. Life Mem. Internat. Assoc. of Airport and Seaport Police, 1974. CBIM (FBIM 1971); FCIM (FInstM 1973); FRSA (Council nominee) 1976; Hon. FIFF 1986. Freeman: City of London, 1970; Watermen & Lightermen's Co. of River Thames, 1970 (Court Mem., 1976–80, Hon. Court Mem., 1980–). ADC to Governor of Louisiana, with rank Adm., 1971–. *Publications:* The Chartered Accountant in Top Management, 1965; A Plan for Britain's Ports, 1975. *Recreations:* sailing, art. *Address:* Twittens, Itchenor, Chichester, West Sussex PO20 7AN. *T:* Birdham (0243) 512105; 97A York Mansions, Prince of Wales Drive, SW11 4BN. *T:* 071–622 8100. *Clubs:* Army and Navy; West Sussex County (Chichester); Itchenor Sailing (West Sussex).

LUND, John Walter Guerrier, CBE 1975; FRS 1963; DSc, PhD; Botanist, at Windermere Laboratory of Freshwater Biological Association, 1945–78; Deputy Chief Scientific Officer; *b* 27 Nov. 1912; *s* of George E. Lund and Kate Lund (*née* Hardwick); *m* 1949, Hilda M. Canter; one *s* one *d*. *Educ:* Sedbergh Sch.; Univ. of Manchester; London Univ. (PhD 1939; DSc 1951). Demonstrator in Botany, Univ. of Manchester, also Queen Mary Coll. and Chelsea Polytechnic, Univ. of London, 1935–38; Temp. Lectr in Botany, Univ. of Sheffield, 1936; Staff Biologist, W Midland Forensic Science Laboratory, Birmingham, 1938–45. Hon. DSc Buckingham, 1988. *Publications:* papers and articles in scientific jls, symposium vols, etc. *Recreation:* gardening. *Address:* Ellerbeck, Ellerigg Road, Ambleside, Cumbria LA22 9EU. *T:* Ambleside (05394) 32369.

LUND, Rodney Cookson; Chairman, Enterprise Support Ltd, since 1991; a Director: Short Brothers, since 1988 (Chairman, 1988–90); Hazlewood Foods plc, since 1991; *b* 16 June 1936; *s* of late Arthur and Doris Lund; *m* 1st, 1964, Lynda Brooks (marr. diss. 1973); one *s*; 2nd, 1988, Hyacinth, (Miki), Wallace. *Educ:* Wallasey Grammar School; Liverpool University (BCom Hons). Served RAPC, 1957–59 (commissioned). Evans Medical, 1959; Carreras Rothmans, 1960–64; Partner, Urwick Orr & Partners, 1964–66 and 1969–73; Man. Dir, The Mace Voluntary Gp, 1966–69; Vice-Chm., Produce Importers Alliance, 1966–69; Exec. Director: Rank Radio International, 1973–75; British Sugar

Corp., 1976–82; Woolworth Holdings, 1982–86; Chm., Nat. Bus Co., 1986–88 (Part-time Mem., 1989–). Mem., Nationalised Industries Chairmen's Gp, 1986–88. CBIM. *Recreations:* travel, opera, cooking. *Address:* 18 Billing Road, Chelsea, SW10 9UL. *T:* 071–352 2641.

LUNKOV, Nikolai Mitrofanovich; Soviet Ambassador to Italy, since 1980; *b* Pavlovka, Ryazan Region, 7 Jan. 1919; *Educ:* Lomonosov Technical Inst., Moscow. Diplomatic Service, 1943–; Asst Minister of Foreign Affairs, 1951–52; Dep. Political Counsellor, Soviet Control Commn in Germany, 1952–54; Counsellor, Stockholm, 1954–57; Dep. Head, Dept of Internat. Organizations, Ministry of Foreign Affairs, 1957; 3rd European Dept, 1957–59; Head of Scandinavian Dept, Min. of Foreign Affairs, 1959–62; Ambassador to Norway, 1962–68; Head of Dept of Cultural Relations with Foreign Countries, 1968–71; Head of 2nd European Dept, 1971–73; Ambassador to the Court of St James's, 1973–80. Mem. of Collegium of Min. of Foreign Affairs, 1968–73. Awarded orders and medals. *Address:* Embassy of the USSR, Via Gaeta 5, Rome, Italy.

LUNN, Rt. Rev. David Ramsay; *see* Sheffield, Bishop of.

LUNN, Peter Northcote, CMG 1957; OBE 1951; HM Diplomatic Service, retired 1972; *b* 15 Nov. 1914; *e s* of late Sir Arnold Lunn; *m* 1939, Hon. (Eileen) Antoinette (*d* 1976), *d* of 15th Viscount Gormanston; three *s* two *d* (and one *d* decd). *Educ:* Eton. Joined RA, 1940; served 1940–46 (Malta, Italy and BAOR); entered FO, 1947; Vienna, 1948–50; Berne, 1950–53; Germany, 1953–56; London, 1956–57; Bonn, 1957–62; Beirut, 1962–67; FCO, 1967–72. Mem., Brit. International Ski team, 1931–37, Capt. 1934–37; Capt. British Olympic Ski team, 1936. *Publications:* High-Speed Skiing, 1935; Evil in High Places, 1947; A Skiing Primer, 1948, rev. edn 1951; The Guinness Book of Ski-ing, 1983. *Club:* Ski Club of Great Britain.

LUNNY, William Francis; Sheriff of South Strathclyde, Dumfries and Galloway, since 1984; *b* 10 Dec. 1938; *s* of James F. Lunny and Sarah Ann Crawford or Lunny; *m* 1967, Elizabeth McDermott; two *s* one *d*. *Educ:* Our Lady's High School, Motherwell; Glasgow Univ. (MA, LLB). Solicitor, 1961–67; Depute Procurator Fiscal, 1967–74; Crown Counsel/Legal Draftsman, Antigua, 1974–76; Advocate, 1977. Barrister, Antigua, 1981. KHS 1989. *Recreations:* walking, travelling. *Address:* Sheriff's Chambers, Sheriff Court, Hamilton, Lanarkshire ML3 6AA. *T:* Hamilton (0698) 282957.

LUNS, Dr Joseph Marie Antoine Hubert; Officer, Order of Orange-Nassau, 1947; Knight Grand Cross, Order of the Netherlands Lion, 1971; Hon. GCMG; Hon. CH 1971; Secretary-General of NATO, 1971–84; *b* 28 Aug. 1911; *m* Baroness E. C. van Heemstra; one *s* one *d*. *Educ:* sec. schs, Amsterdam and Brussels; universities of Leyden, Amsterdam, London and Berlin. Attaché of Legation, 1938; 2nd Sec., 1942; 1st Sec., 1945; Counsellor, 1949. Served in: Min. for For. Affairs, 1938–40; Berne, 1940–41; Lisbon, 1941–43; London, at Netherlands Min. for For. Affairs, 1943–44, and at Netherlands Embassy, 1944–49; Netherlands Delegn to UN, NY, 1942–52; Minister of Foreign Affairs, The Netherlands, 1952–71. MP (Second Chamber, Netherlands), July-Oct. 1956 and March-June 1959. Hon. Fellow, London Sch. of Economics, 1969. Prix Charlemagne, Aachen, 1967; Gustav Stresemann Medal, 1968. Hon. DCL: Harvard, 1970; Oxon, 1972; Exeter, 1974; Dr Humanities, Hope Coll., USA, 1974. Holds numerous foreign orders. *Publications:* The Epic of The Royal Netherlands Navy; articles on Royal Netherlands Navy in Dutch and foreign jls, and articles on international affairs in International Affairs, La Revue Politique, and others. *Recreation:* swimming. *Address:* 117 Avenue Franklin Roosevelt, 1050 Brussels, Belgium. *Clubs:* Athenæum, Reform (Hon. Mem.); Haagsche, De Witte (Netherlands).

LUNT, Maj.-Gen. James Doiran, CBE 1964 (OBE 1958); MA (Oxon); FRGS; FRHistS; Domestic Bursar, and Fellow, Wadham College, Oxford, 1973–83, now Emeritus Fellow; *b* 13 Nov. 1917; *s* of late Brig. W. T. Lunt, MBE, Camberley, Surrey; *m* 1940, Muriel, *d* of late A. H. Byrt, CBE, Bournemouth; one *s* one *d*. *Educ:* King William's Coll., IOM; RMC, Sandhurst. 2nd Lieut, Duke of Wellington's Regt, 1937; served with 4th Bn Burma Rifles, 1939–41; Burma Campaign, 1942; transf. to 16/5th Queen's Royal Lancers, 1949; served with Arab Legion, 1952–55; comd 16/5th Queen's Royal Lancers, 1957–59; comd Fed. Regular Army, Aden, 1961–64; Dir of Admin. Planning (Army), MoD, 1964–66; Defence Adviser to British High Commissioner, India, 1966–68; Chief of Staff, Contingencies Planning, SHAPE, 1969–70; Vice-Adjt-Gen., MoD, 1970–72; Col, 16th/5th The Queen's Royal Lancers, 1975–80. Order of Independence (Jordan), 1956; Commander, Order of South Arabia, 1964. *Publications:* Charge to Glory, 1961; Scarlet Lancer, 1964; The Barren Rocks of Aden, 1966; Bokhara Burnes, 1969; From Sepoy to Subedar, 1970; The Duke of Wellington's Regiment, 1971; 16th/5th The Queen's Royal Lancers, 1973; John Burgoyne of Saratoga, 1975; Imperial Sunset, 1981; Glubb Pasha, 1984; A Hell of a Licking: the retreat from Burma 1941–42, 1986; Hussein of Jordan, 1989. *Recreations:* fly fishing, writing. *Address:* Hilltop House, Little Milton, Oxon OX9 7PU. *T:* Great Milton (0844) 279242. *Clubs:* Cavalry and Guards, Flyfishers'.

LUNT, Rev. Canon Ronald Geoffrey, MC 1943; MA, BD; Rector of Martley, 1974–78; Chief Master, King Edward's School, Birmingham, 1952–74; *b* 25 June 1913; *s* of late Rt Rev. G. C. L. Lunt, DD, Bishop of Salisbury; *m* 1945, Veslemoy Sopp Foss, Oslo, Norway; one *s* two *d*. *Educ:* Eton (King's Scholar); The Queen's Coll., Oxford (Scholar, 1st class Lit. Hum.); Westcott House, Cambridge. Assistant Master, St George's Sch., Harpenden, 1935; Haberdashers' Sch., Hampstead, 1936–37; Deacon, 1938; Priest, 1939; Master in Orders at Radley Coll., Abingdon, 1938–40; CF 1940–45; Middle East, 1941–44 (MC); CF 3rd class, SCF 1 Airborne Division, 1945; Headmaster, Liverpool Coll., 1945–52. Won Cromer Greek Prize, 1937; Page Scholar to USA, 1959; Select Preacher: University of Cambridge, 1948, 1960, Oxford, 1951–53, 1983. Chm., Birmingham Council of Churches, 1957–60; Hon. Canon, Birmingham Cathedral, 1969. Mem., Birmingham Educn Cttee, 1952–74. Life Governor, Queen's Coll., Birmingham, 1957; Trustee, 1954, Chm., 1971–74, E. W. Vincent Trust; Governor, 1952, Sen. Vice-Pres., 1971–72, Pres., 1973, Birmingham and Midland Inst. Pres., Incorporated Assoc. of Head Masters, 1962. Mem., Press Council, 1964–69. BD (Oxon), 1967. *Publications:* Edition of Marlowe's Dr Faustus, 1937, Edward II, 1938; contrib. to Arts v. Science, 1967; articles in Theology, Expository Times, and other journals. *Address:* The Station House, Ledbury, Herefordshire HR8 1AR. *T:* Ledbury (0531) 3174.

See also Julian Hall.

LUPTON, Prof. Thomas; Professor of Organisational Behaviour, University of Manchester, 1966–86; Visiting Professor, Instituto de Estudios Superiores de la Empresa, Barcelona, since 1987; Director of International Programmes, Escuela de Alta Dirección y Administración, Barcelona, since 1990; *b* 4 Nov. 1918; *s* of Thomas Lupton, blacksmith, and Jane Lupton (*née* Vowell); *m* 1st, 1942, Thelma Chesney; one *d*; 2nd, 1963, Dr Constance Shirley Wilson; one *s* one *d*; 3rd, 1988, Dorothy Joyce Meredith. *Educ:* Elem. and Central Sch.; Technical Coll.; Ruskin Coll.; Oriel Coll., Oxford; Univ. of Manchester. DipEconPolSci (Oxon), MA (Oxon), PhD (Manch.). Served War, HM Forces, 1939–41 and 1944–46; Marine Engr, 1932–39, 1941–44. Research Posts: Liverpool Univ., 1951–54; Manchester Univ., 1954–57; Lectr in Sociology, Manchester Univ., 1957–59; Head of Dept of Industrial Admin, Coll. of Advanced Techn., Birmingham, 1959–64; Montague Burton Prof. of Ind. Rel., Univ. of Leeds, 1964–66; Dir, Manchester Business Sch., 1977–83. Gen. Editor, Jl of Management Studies, 1966–76; Dir, Pirelli General Cables Ltd, 1970–77; Member: Civil Service Arbitration Tribunal, 1967–70; Arbitration Panel, Dept of Employment, 1969–; various official commns and tribunals, 1960–. Hon. DSc Aston, 1987. *Publications:* On the Shop Floor, 1963; Industrial Behaviour and Personnel Management, 1964; Management and the Social Sciences, 1966, 3rd edn, 1983; Selecting a Wage Payment System (with D. Gowler), 1969; Job and Pay Comparisons (with A. M. Bowey), 1973; Wages and Salaries (with A. M. Bowey), 1974, rev. edn 1983; Achieving Change (with I. R. Tanner), 1987; articles in Jl of Management Studies, Manchester Sch., Production Engineer, etc. *Recreations:* golf, Association Football.

LUPU, Radu; pianist; *b* 30 Nov. 1945; *s* of Mayer Lupu, lawyer, and Ana Gabor, teacher of languages; *Educ:* Moscow Conservatoire. Debut at age of twelve with complete programme of own music; studied with Florica Muzicescu, Cella Delavrancea, Heinrich Neuhaus and Stanislav Neuhaus. 1st prize: Van Cliburn Competition, 1966; Enescu Internat. Competition, 1967; Leeds Internat. Pianoforte Competition, 1969. Numerous recordings include complete Mozart violin and piano sonatas, complete Beethoven Piano Concertos, 1979. *Recreations:* history, art, sport. *Address:* c/o Terry Harrison Artists Management, 9a Penzance Place, W11 4PE. *T:* 071–221 7741.

LURGAN, 5th Baron *cr* 1839; **John Desmond Cavendish Brownlow,** OBE 1950; Lieut-Colonel, Grenadier Guards, retired; *b* 29 June 1911; *s* of Captain Hon. Francis Cecil Brownlow (*d* 1932) (3rd *s* of 2nd Baron) and Angela (*d* 1973), *d* of Samuel Radcliffe Platt; *S* cousin, 1984. *Educ:* Eton. *Address:* Pennington House, Lymington, Hants.

LURIE, Prof. Alison; writer; Professor of English, Cornell University, since 1976; *b* 3 Sept. 1926; *d* of Harry Lurie and Bernice Stewart; *m* 1948, Jonathan Bishop (marr. diss. 1985); three *s*. *Educ:* Radcliffe Coll., Cambridge, Mass (AB). *Publications:* Love and Friendship, 1962; The Nowhere City, 1965; Imaginary Friends, 1967 (televised, 1987); Real People, 1969; The War Between the Tates, 1974; Only Children, 1979; Foreign Affairs, 1984 (Pulitzer Prize, 1985); The Truth About Lorin Jones, 1988; *non-fiction:* The Language of Clothes, 1981; Don't Tell the Grown-ups, 1990; *children's books:* Clever Gretchen, 1980; The Heavenly Zoo, 1980; Fabulous Beasts, 1981. *Address:* c/o English Department, Cornell University, Ithaca, NY 14853, USA.

LUSBY, John Martin; General Manager and Member, since 1990, Chief Executive and an Executive Director, since 1991, Lothian Health Board (Member, 1990–91); *b* 27 April 1943; *s* of William Henry Lusby and Florence Mary (*née* Wharam); *m* 1966, Clare (*née* Gargan); one *s* one *d*. *Educ:* Marist Coll., Hull; Ushaw Coll., Durham. DipHSM 1972; MHSM 1972. Entered NHS, 1961; junior appointments: De la Pole Hosp., Hull, 1961–66; County Hosp., York, 1966–67; Kettering Gen. Hosp., 1967–68; Admin. Asst, United Sheffield Hosps, 1968–70; Dep. Hosp. Sec., E Birmingham Hosp, 1970–72; Hosp. Sec., Pontefract Gen. Infirmary and Headlands Hosp., Pontefract, 1972–74; Area Gen. Administrator, Kirklees AHA, 1974–76; Asst Dist Administrator (Patient Services), 1976–79, Dist Administrator, Wandsworth and E Merton Dist, 1979–81, Merton, Sutton and Wandsworth AHA(T); Area Administrator, Doncaster AHA, 1981; Dist Administrator, 1981–84, Dist. Gen. Man., 1984–90, Exec. Dir, 1990, Doncaster HA. *Recreations:* music, reading, walking. *Address:* 95/6 Grange Loan, Edinburgh EH9 3ED.

LUSCOMBE, Prof. David Edward, LittD; FSA; FRHistS; FBA 1986; Professor of Medieval History, since 1972, and Pro-Vice-Chancellor, since 1990, University of Sheffield; *b* 22 July 1938; *s* of Edward Dominic and Nora Luscombe; *m* 1960, Megan Phillips; three *s* one *d*. *Educ:* St Michael's Sch., North Finchley; Finchley Catholic Grammar Sch.; King's Coll., Cambridge (BA, MA, PhD, LittD). Fellow, King's Coll., Cambridge, 1962–64; Fellow and Dir of Studies in History, Churchill Coll., Cambridge, 1964–72; Sheffield University: Head of Dept of History, 1973–76, 1979–84; Dean, Faculty of Arts, 1985–87. External examiner for higher degrees in Univs. of Cambridge, Oxford, London, Liverpool, Bangor, ANU, Toronto, Groningen, for BA degrees at Bangor, Leicester and Leeds. Leverhulme European Fellow, 1973. Raleigh Lectr, British Acad., 1988. Member: Assoc. (formerly Governing Body), St Edmund's House, Cambridge, 1971–84; Cttee, Ecclesiastical History Soc., 1976–79; Council, RHistS, 1981–85; Council, British Acad., 1989– (Publications Sec., 1990–; Member: Medieval Texts Cttee, 1982–; Publications Cttee, 1987–; Postgrad. Studies Cttee, 1988–90); Vice-Pres., Soc. Internat. pour l'étude de la philosophie médiévale, 1987–. Gen. Editor, Cambridge Studies in Medieval Life and Thought, 4th series, 1988– (Adv. Editor, 1983–88). *Publications:* The School of Peter Abelard, 1969; Peter Abelard's Ethics, 1971 (trans. Italian, 1976); (ed jtly) Church and Government in the Middle Ages, 1976; (ed jtly) Petrus Abaelardus 1079–1142: Person, Werk und Wirkung, 1980; (jtly) David Knowles Remembered, 1991; articles in learned jls. *Recreations:* walking a spaniel, swimming, using libraries. *Address:* 4 Caxton Road, Broomhill, Sheffield S10 3DE. *T:* Sheffield (0742) 686355.

LUSCOMBE, Rt. Rev. Lawrence Edward; Bishop of Brechin, 1975–90; Primus of the Episcopal Church in Scotland, 1985–90; *b* 10 Nov. 1924; *s* of Reginald John and Winifred Luscombe; *m* 1946, Doris Carswell Morgan, BSc, MB, ChB; one *d*. *Educ:* Torquay Grammar Sch.; Kelham Theological Coll.; King's Coll., London. CA 1952, ASAA 1957. FSAScot 1980. Served Indian Army, 1942–47, Major. Partner, Galbraith, Dunlop & Co., Chartered Accountants, Glasgow, 1952–63. Ordained deacon, 1963; priest, 1964; Curate, St Margaret's, Glasgow, 1963–66; Rector, St Barnabas', Paisley, 1966–71; Provost of St Paul's Cathedral, Dundee, 1971–75. Hon. Canon, Trinity Cathedral, Davenport, Iowa, 1983. Chm. of Council, Glenalmond Coll., 1987–. FRSA 1987. Hon. DLitt Geneva Theological Coll., 1972; Hon. LLD Dundee, 1987. OStJ 1986. *Address:* Woodville, Kirkton of Tealing, by Dundee DD4 0RD. *T:* Tealing (082 621) 331.

LUSH, Christopher Duncan, CMG 1983; HM Diplomatic Service, retired; Governor, British Institute of Human Rights, since 1988; Editor, Human Rights Case Digest, since 1989; *b* 4 June 1928; *s* of late Eric Duncan Thomas Lush and Iris Leonora (*née* Greenfield); *m* 1967, Marguerite Lilian, *d* of Frederick Albert Bolden; one *s*. *Educ:* Sedbergh; Magdalen Coll., Oxford. Called to Bar, Gray's Inn, 1953. Asst Legal Adviser, FO, 1959–62; Legal Adviser, Berlin, 1962–65, Dep. Political Adviser, Berlin, 1965–66; FO (later FCO), 1966–69; Head of Chancery, Amman, 1969–71; Head of Aviation and Telecommunications Dept, FCO, 1971–73; Canadian Nat. Defence Coll., 1973–74; Counsellor, Paris, 1974–78; Counsellor, Vienna, 1978–82; Ambassador and UK Perm. Rep. to Council of Europe, Strasbourg, 1983–86. Médaille de Vermeil, Société d'Encouragement au Progrès, 1978. *Publications:* articles in Internat. and Compar. Law Qly, Connoisseur. *Club:* Travellers'.

LUSH, Hon. Sir George (Hermann), Kt 1979; Justice, Supreme Court of Victoria, 1966–83; *b* 5 Oct. 1912; *s* of John Fullarton Lush and Dora Louise Emma Lush; *m* 1943, Winifred Betty Wragge; three *d*. *Educ:* Carey Grammar Sch.; Ormond Coll., Melbourne Univ. (LLM). Admitted, Victorian Bar, 1935; served War, Australian Imperial Forces, 1940–45; Lecturer, Mercantile Law, Melbourne Univ., 1947–55; QC: Victoria 1957, Tasmania 1958. Chairman, Victorian Bar Council, 1964–66; President: Medico-Legal Soc., Victoria, 1962–63; Australian Bar Assoc., 1964–66; Commissioner, Overseas

Telecommunications Commn, 1961–66. Chancellor, Monash Univ., 1983– (Mem. Council, 1969–74); Chm. Council, Ormond Coll., 1981–90. *Recreations:* tennis, walking. *Address:* 37 Rochester Road, Canterbury, Victoria 3126, Australia. *Clubs:* Melbourne, Melbourne Cricket (Melbourne); Lorne Country (Lorne, Vic.).

LUSHINGTON, Sir John (Richard Castleman), 8th Bt *cr* 1791, of South Hill Park, Berkshire; *b* 28 Aug. 1938; *s* of Sir Henry Edmund Castleman Lushington, 7th Bt and of Pamela Elizabeth Daphne, *er d* of Major Archer Richard Hunter; *S* father, 1988; *m* 1966, Bridget Gillian Margaret, *d* of late Colonel John Foster Longfield; three *s*. *Educ:* Oundle. Mem., Management and Skills Trng Orgn. *Heir: s* Richard Douglas Longfield Lushington, *b* 29 March 1968. *Address:* The Glebe House, Henham, Bishops Stortford, Herts CM22 6AH.

LÜST, Prof. Reimar; Director General, European Space Agency, 1984–89; President, Alexander von Humboldt Foundation, Bonn, since 1989; *b* 25 March 1923; *s* of Hero Lüst and Grete (*née* Strunck); *m* 1986, Nina Grunenberg; two *s* by a previous marriage. *Educ:* Univ. of Frankfurt; Univ. of Göttingen (Dr rer. nat.). Max-Planck-Institut of Physics: Staff Scientist, 1950–60; Head of Astrophysics Dept, 1960–63; Dir, Max-Planck-Institut of Extraterrestrial Physics, 1963–. Vis. Prof., Univs of Princeton, Chicago, New York, MIT, CIT, 1955–63; Hon. Prof., Technical Univ. of Munich, 1965. Chm., German Science Council, 1969–72; President: Max-Planck-Gesellschaft zur Förderung der Wissenschaften, 1972–84. Mem. and Hon. Mem. of eight academies. Grand Cross, Order of Merit (FRG), 1984; Officier, Légion d'Honneur (France), 1984; Grand Cross of Merit with Star and Shoulderblade (FRG), 1990. *Publications:* Hydrodynamik, 1955; articles in scientific jls. *Recreations:* tennis, history, ski-ing. *Address:* Max-Planck-Institute of Meterology, Bundesstrasse 55, 2000 Hamburg 13, Germany. *T:* (040) 411 73–300.

LUSTIGER, His Eminence Cardinal Jean-Marie; Archbishop of Paris, since 1981; *b* Paris, 1926. *Educ:* Carmelite Seminary; Institut Catholique de Paris; Sorbonne (Lèsl, LenThéol). Ordained priest, 1954. Chaplain to students, Sorbonne, Paris; Dir, Centre d'étudiants Richelieu, Paris, 1959–69; Parish Priest, Sainte Jeanne de Chantal, Paris, 1969–79; Bishop of Orléans, 1979–81. Cardinal, 1983. *Publications:* Sermons d'un curé de Paris, 1978; Pain de vie, Peuple de Dieu, 1981; Osez croire—Osez vivre, 1985; Freude der Weihnacht, 1985; Premiers pas dans la prière, 1986 (trans. as First Steps in Prayer, 1988); Six sermons aux élus de la nation, 1987; The Mass, 1987; Le choix de Dieu, 1987; The Lord's Prayer, 1988; La Messe, 1988; Le Sacrement de l'Onction des Malades, 1990; Dieu merci, les droits de l'homme, 1990. *Address:* Maison diocésaine, 8 rue de la Ville-l'Evêque, 75008 Paris, France.

LUSZTIG, Prof. George, PhD; FRS 1983; Professor of Mathematics, Massachusetts Institute of Technology, Cambridge, USA, since 1978; *b* 20 May 1946; *s* of Akos and Erzsébet Lusztig; *m* 1972, Michal-Nina Abraham; two *d*. *Educ:* Univ. of Bucharest, Rumania; Princeton Univ. (MA, PhD). Asst, Univ. of Timisoara, Rumania, 1969; Mem., Inst. for Advanced Study Princeton, 1969–71; Univ. of Warwick: Res. Fellow, 1971–72; Lectr in Maths, 1972–74; Prof. of Maths, 1974–78. *Publications:* The Discrete Series of GL_n over a Finite Field, 1974; and Characters of Reductive Groups over a Finite Field, 1984. *Address:* 106 Grant Avenue, Newton, Mass 02159, USA. *T:* (617) 964–8579.

LUTHER, Rt. Rev. Arthur William; retired; *b* 21 March 1919; *s* of William and Monica Luther; *m* 1946, Dr Kamal Luther; one *s* two *d*. *Educ:* Nagpur University; India (MA, BT); General Theological Seminary, New York (STD 1957). Deacon, 1943; Priest, 1944; in USA and Scotland for study and parish work, 1952–54; Chaplain to Bishop of Nagpur, 1954; Head Master, Bishop Cotton School, Nagpur, 1954–57; Bishop of Nasik, 1957–70; Bishop of Bombay, 1970–73; held charge of Kolhapur Diocese concurrently with Bombay Diocese, Dec. 1970–Feb. 1972; Bishop, Church of North India, and Reg. Sec. of the Leprosy Mission, 1973–80; Promotional Sec., 1980–84. *Address:* Convent of St Mary, 5 Guruwar Peth, Panchhowd, Pune 411 042, Maharashtra, India. *T:* 423897.

LUTOSŁAWSKI, Witold; composer and conductor; *b* Warsaw, 25 Jan. 1913; *m* 1946, Maria Danuta Dygat. *Educ:* Warsaw Conservatoire. Dep. Chief of Music Dept, Polish Radio, 1945–46; teacher of composition: Berkshire Music Center, USA, 1962; Dartington, 1963, 1964; Aarhus, 1968; composer-in-residence: Hopkins Center, USA, 1966; Aldeburgh Fest., 1983. Vice-Pres., Polish Composers' Union, 1973–79. Hon. RAM, 1976; Hon. GSM, 1978. Member: Swedish Royal Acad. of Music; Free Acad. of Arts, Hamburg; Acad. of Arts, Berlin; German Acad. of Arts, E Berlin; Bavarian Acad. of Fine Arts; Amer. Acad. of Arts and Letters; Nat. Inst. of Arts and Letters, NY; Acad. of Fine Arts, France; Acad. Européenne des Scis et des Lettres; Acad. Royale des Sciences, des Lettres et des Beaux Arts de Belgique; Associate Mem., Acad. Naz. di Santa Cecilia. Hon. Member: Polish Composers' Union; Polish Soc. of Contemp. Music; ISCM; Konzerthausges., Vienna; Assoc. of Professional Composers; Serbian Acad. of Sci.; Internat. Music Council; Soc. of Norwegian Composers. FRCM; FRNCM, GSMD. Hon. Dr: Cleveland Inst. of Music; Northwestern; Evanston, Chicago; Warsaw; Lancaster; Glasgow; Torún; Durham; Cracow; Cambridge; Duquesnes Univ., Pittsburgh; QUB; Warsaw Acad. of Music; New England Conservatoire of Music, Boston; Univ. des Scis Humaines de Strasbourg. Many prizes include: City of Warsaw Music Prize, 1948; state prizes; Sonning Music Prize, Copenhagen, 1967; Ravel Prize, 1971; Sibelius Prize, 1972; Ernst von Siemens Music Prize, 1983; Solidarność (Solidarity) Prize, 1984 (Poland); Univ. of Louisville Grawemeyer Award for music composition, 1985; (jtly) Gold Medal, Royal Philharmonic Soc., 1985; Queen Sofia of Spain, 1985; High Fidelity Internat. Record Critics' Award for Symphony No 3, 1986; Grammy Award, USA, 1986; Pittsburgh Symphony Orch. Signature Award. Order of Builder of People's Poland, 1977; Comdr des Arts et des Lettres (France). *Compositions* include: *orchestral:* Symphonic Variations, 1938; 1st Symphony, 1947; Concerto for Orchestra, 1954; Musique Funèbre, 1958; Jeux vénitiens, 1961; 2nd Symphony, 1967; Livre pour orchestre, 1968; Cello concerto, 1970; Mi-parti, 1976; Novelette, 1979; 3rd Symphony, 1983; Chain 2 for violin and orchestra, 1985; Chain 3 for orchestra, 1986; Concerto for Piano and Orchestra, 1988; Interlude for orch., 1990; *chamber:* Overture, 1949; Three Poems of Henri Michaux for choir and orch., 1963; String Quartet, 1964; Paroles tissées for tenor and chamber orch., 1965; Preludes and Fugues for 13 solo strings, 1972; Les espaces du sommeil for baritone and orch., 1975; Double Concerto, 1980; Chain 1, 1983; Partita for violin and piano, 1984 (version for violin and orch., 1988); Tarantella for baritone and piano, 1990; vocal and choral works, compositions for piano, and children's music; scores and incidental music for theatre, films and radio. Has made many recordings, conducting own compositions. *Address:* Ul. Smiała 39, 01–523 Warsaw, Poland.

LUTTRELL, Col Geoffrey Walter Fownes, MC 1945; JP; Lord-Lieutenant of Somerset, since 1978; *b* 2 Oct. 1919; *s* of late Geoffrey Fownes Luttrell of Dunster Castle, Somerset; *m* 1942, Hermione Hamilton, *er d* of late Capt. Cecil Gunston, MC, and Lady Doris Gunston. *Educ:* Eton; Exeter Coll., Oxford. Served War of 1939–45, with 15th/19th King's Royal Hussars, 1940–46; North Somerset Yeomanry, 1952–57; Lt-Col 1955; Hon. Col, 6th Bn LI, TAVR, 1977–87; Col 1987. Liaison Officer, Ministry of Agriculture, 1965–71. Regional Dir, Lloyds Bank, 1972–83. Member: National Parks Commn, 1962–66; Wessex Regional Cttee, Nat. Trust, 1970–85; SW Electricity Bd, 1969–78;

UGC, 1973–76. Pres., Royal Bath and West and Southern Counties Soc., 1983. DL Somerset, 1958–68, Vice Lord-Lieutenant, 1968–78; High Sheriff of Somerset, 1960; JP 1961. Hon. Col Somerset ACF, 1982–89. KStJ. *Address:* Court House, East Quantoxhead, Bridgwater, Somerset TA5 1EJ. *T:* Holford (027874) 242. *Club:* Cavalry and Guards.

LUTYENS, Mary, (Mrs J. G. Links), FRSL; writer since 1929; *b* 31 July 1908; *γ d* of late Sir Edwin Lutyens, OM, KCIE, PRA, and late Lady Emily Lutyens; *m* 1st, 1930, Anthony Sewell (marr. diss. 1945; decd); one *d*; 2nd, 1945, J. G. Links, OBE. *Educ:* Queen's Coll., London; Sydney, Australia. FRSL 1976. *Publications: fiction:* Forthcoming Marriages, 1933; Perchance to Dream, 1935; Rose and Thorn, 1936; Spider's Silk, 1939; Family Colouring, 1940; A Path of Gold, 1941; Together and Alone, 1942; So Near to Heaven, 1943; And Now There is You, 1953; Week-End at Hurtmore, 1954; The Lucian Legend, 1955; Meeting in Venice, 1956; Cleo, 1973; *for children:* Julie and the Narrow Valley, 1944; *autobiography:* To Be Young, 1959, repr. 1989; *edited:* Lady Lytton's Court Diary, 1961; (for Krishnamurti) Freedom from the Known, 1969; The Only Revolution, 1970; The Penguin Krishnamurti Reader, 1970; The Urgency of Change, 1971; (with Malcolm Warner) Rainy Days at Brig O'Turk, 1983; *biography:* Effie in Venice, 1965; Millais and the Ruskins, 1967; The Ruskins and the Grays, 1972; Krishnamurti: the years of awakening, 1975; The Lyttons in India, 1979; Edwin Lutyens, 1980, repr. 1991; Krishnamurti: the years of fulfilment, 1982; Krishnamurti: the open door, 1988; The Life and Death of Krishnamurti, 1990, repr. 1991; also numerous serials, afterwards published, under pseudonym of Esther Wyndham; contribs to TLS, Apollo, The Cornhill, The Walpole Soc. Jl. *Recreations:* reading, cinema-going. *Address:* 8 Elizabeth Close, Randolph Avenue, W9 1BN. *T:* 071–286 6674.

LUTZ, Marianne Christine, (Mrs C. A. Whittington-Smith); Headmistress, Sheffield High School for Girls (Girls' Public Day School Trust), 1959–83; *b* 9 Dec. 1922; *d* of Dr H. Lutz; *m* 1981, Charles Alexander Whittington-Smith, LLM, FCA. *Educ:* Wimbledon High Sch., GPDST; Girton Coll., Cambridge (Schol.); University of London (DipEd, DipTh). Asst Mistress (History) at: Clergy Daughters' Sch., Bristol, 1946–47; South Hampstead High Sch., GPDST, 1947–59. Former Member: History Textbooks Panel for W Germany (under auspices of FO and Unesco); Professional Cttee, Univ. of Sheffield; Historical Assoc.; Secondary Heads' Assoc.; Schnauzer Club of Great Britain. *Publications:* several in connection with Unesco work and Historical Assoc. *Recreations:* travel, crosswords, books, opera, art and theatre. *Address:* Grendon, Hydro Close, Baslow, Bakewell, Derbyshire DE4 1SH. *T:* Baslow (0246) 582152.

LUXMOORE, Rt. Rev. Christopher Charles; Bishop of Bermuda, 1984–89; *b* 9 April 1926; *s* of Rev. William Cyril Luxmoore and Constance Evelyn Luxmoore; *m* 1955, Judith, *d* of late Canon Verney Johnstone; four *s* one *d*. *Educ:* Sedbergh School, Yorks; Trinity Coll., Cambridge; Chichester Theol Coll. Deacon 1952, priest 1953; Asst Curate, St John the Baptist, Newcastle upon Tyne, 1952–55; Priest-in-Charge, St Bede's Ecclesiastical Dist, Newsham, 1955–57; Vicar of Newsham, 1957–58; Rector of Sangre Grande, Trinidad, 1958–66; Vicar of Headingley, Leeds, 1967–81; Proctor in Convocation and Mem. Gen. Synod, 1975–81; Hon. Canon of Ripon Cathedral, 1980–81; Precentor and Canon Residentiary of Chichester Cathedral, 1981–84; Dean of Bermuda Cathedral, 1984–89; Archdeacon of Lewes and Hastings, 1989–91. Commissary for Bishop of Trinidad and Tobago, 1968–84. Provost, Woodard Schools Southern Div., 1989–. *Recreations:* music, church history, winemaking. *Address:* 42 Willowbed Drive, Chichester, W Sussex PO19 2JB. *T:* Chichester (0243) 784680.

LUXON, Benjamin Matthew, CBE 1986; FGSM; baritone; *b* Camborne, Cornwall, 1937; *m* 1969, Sheila Amit; two *s* one *d*. *Educ:* Truro Sch.; Westminster Trng Coll.; Guildhall Sch. of Music. Teacher of Physical Education until becoming professional singer, 1963. Repertoire includes lieder, folk music, Victorian songs and duets, oratorio (Russian, French and English song), and operatic rôles at major opera houses at home and abroad. Major rôles include: Eugene Onegin, Don Giovanni, Wozzeck, Papageno, Julius Caesar, Posa, Gianni Schicchi, Falstaff. Numerous recordings. Appointed Bard of the Cornish Gorsedd, 1974. Third prize, Munich Internat. Festival, 1961; Gold Medal GSM, 1963. FGSM 1970; Hon. RAM, 1980; Hon. DMus Exeter, 1980. *Recreations:* collecting English water-colours and drawings; tennis, swimming. *Address:* Lower Cox Street Farm, Detling, Maidstone, Kent ME14 3HE.

LUXTON, William John, CBE 1962; Director, London Chamber of Commerce and Industry, 1964–74 (Secretary, 1958–74); *b* 18 March 1909; *s* of late John Luxton and Emma Luxton (*née* Webber); *m* 1942, Megan, *d* of late John M. Harries and Mary Ann Harries (*née* Lewis); one *s* one *d*. *Educ:* Shebbear Coll., N Devon; London Univ. Wallace Brothers & Co. Ltd (merchant bankers), 1926–38. Called to the Bar, Lincoln's Inn, 1938; Chancery Bar, 1938–40. Served with Royal Armoured Corps, 1940–45. Legal Parliamentary Secretary, Association of British Chambers of Commerce, 1947–53 (Vice-Pres., 1974); Secretary Birmingham Chamber of Commerce, 1953–58; Dir, Fedn of Commonwealth Chambers of Commerce, 1958–74. *Address:* 19 Brookfields, Crickhowell, Powys NP8 1DJ. *T:* Crickhowell (0873) 811493.

LUYT, Sir Richard (Edmonds), GCMG 1966 (KCMG 1964; CMG 1960); KCVO 1966; DCM 1942; Vice-Chancellor and Principal, University of Cape Town, 1968–80; *b* 8 Nov. 1915; *m* 1st, 1948, Jean Mary Wilder (*d* 1951); one *d*; 2nd, 1956, Eileen Betty Reid; two *s*. *Educ:* Diocesan Coll., Rondebosch, Cape, SA; Univ. of Cape Town (BA); Trinity Coll., Oxford (MA). Rhodes Scholar from S Africa, 1937. Entered Colonial Service and posted to N Rhodesia, 1940; War Service, 1940–45: with Mission 101, in Ethiopia, 1941; remained in Ethiopia with British Military Mission, for remainder of War. Returned to N Rhodesia, Colonial Service, 1945; transferred to Kenya, 1953; Labour Commissioner, Kenya, 1954–57; Permanent Secretary to various Ministries of the Kenya Government, 1957–60; Secretary to the Cabinet, 1960–61; Chief Secretary, Northern Rhodesia, 1962–64; Governor and C-in-C, British Guiana, 1964–66, until Guyana Independence; Governor-General of Guyana, May–Oct. 1966. Vice-Pres., South African Inst. of Race Relations, 1983–85; Nat. Pres., Friends of the Nat. Union of South African Students, 1980–88; Governor, Africa Inst. of South Africa, 1968–; Pres. (formerly Patron), Civil Rights League, 1968–. Hon. LLD: Natal, 1972; Witwatersrand, 1980; Hon. DAdmin Univ. of South Africa, 1980; Hon. DLitt Cape Town, 1982. *Recreations:* gardening, sport, particularly Rugby (Oxford Blue, 1938) and cricket (Oxford Captain 1940) (also played for Kenya at cricket). *Address:* Allandale, 64 Alma Road, Rosebank, Cape, 7700, South Africa. *T:* 6866765. *Clubs:* Commonwealth Trust; Nairobi (Kenya); City and Civil Service (Cape Town).

LUZZATTO, Prof. Lucio, FRCP, FRCPath; Professor of Haematology, Royal Postgraduate Medical School, since 1981; Hon. Director, Medical Research Council/Leukaemia Research Fund's Leukaemia Unit, since 1987; *b* 28 Sept. 1936; *s* of Aldo and Anna Luzzatto; *m* 1963, Paola Caboara; one *s* one *d*. *Educ:* Genoa Univ. (MD 1959); Pavia Univ. (Spec. Haematology 1962); Lib. Doc. Italy, 1965. FRCPath 1982; FRCP 1983. Research Fellow in Haematology, Columbia Univ., 1963–64; Lectr, then Prof. of Haematology, Univ. of Ibadan, 1964–74; Dir, Internat. Inst. of Genetics and Biophysics, Naples, 1974–81. Pius XI Medal, 1976; Laurea ad hon., Univ. of Urbino,

1990. *Publications:* numerous contribs to learned jls. *Address:* Department of Haematology, Royal Postgraduate Medical School, Hammersmith Hospital, W12 0NN. *T:* 081–740 3234.

LWOFF, Prof. André Michel; Grand-Croix de la Légion d'Honneur, 1982 (Grand Officier; Commandeur, 1966; Officier, 1960; Chevalier, 1947); Médaille de la Résistance, 1946; Directeur de l'Institut de Recherches Scientifiques sur le Cancer, 1968–72; Professor of Microbiology, Faculté des Sciences, Paris, 1959–68, and Head of Department of Microbial Physiology, Pasteur Institute, 1938–68; *b* Ainay-le-Château, Allier, France, 8 May 1902; *m* 1925, Marguerite Bourdaleix. *Educ:* (Fac. des Sciences et de Méd.) Univ. of Paris. MD (Paris) 1927; DSc (Paris) 1932. With the Pasteur Institute, 1921–. Fellow: Rockefeller Foundn, 1933 and 1935; Salk Inst., 1967; Vis. Professor: MIT, 1960; Harvard Univ., Albert Einstein Med. Sch., New York, 1964. Lectures: Dunham, Harvard, 1947; Marjory Stephenson, Soc. for Gen. Microbiol.; Harvey, 1954; Leuwenhoek, Royal Soc., 1966; Dyer, 1969; Penn, University of Pennsylvania, 1969; MacCormick, Univ. of Chicago, 1969. Hon. Member: Soc. for Gen. Microbiol.; Amer. Soc. of Microbiol.; Amer. Botanical Soc.; Amer. Soc. of Biochem.; Corresp. Mem., Acad. of Med. Sciences of USSR; Foreign Member: Royal Soc., 1958; Hungarian Acad. of Science; Indian Acad. of Science; For. Associate, Nat. Acad. of Scis, USA; For. Associate Mem., Amer. Acad. of Arts and Scis. President: Internat. Assoc. of Societies of Microbiology, 1962; Mouvement Français pour le Planning Familial, 1970–. Exhibitions of paintings: Galerie Alex Maguy, 1960; Galerie Aleph, 1978, 1985. Holds hon. doctorates in science and law at British and other foreign univs. Awarded several prizes and medals from 1928 onwards, both French and foreign, for his work; Nobel Prize for Medicine (jointly), 1965; Leuwenhoek Medal, Royal Netherlands Acad. of Science; Keilin Medal, Biochemical Soc. *Publications:* (with L. Justin-Besançon) Vitamine antipellagreuse et avitaminoses nocotiniques, 1942; L'Evolution physiologique, Collection de microbiologie, Hermann éd., 1944; Problems of Morphogenesis in Ciliates, The Kinetosomes in Development, Reproduction and Evolution, 1950; Biological Order, 1960; Jeux et combats, 1981. *Recreation:* painting. *Address:* 69 avenue de Suffren, 75007 Paris, France. *T:* 47.83.27.82.

LYALL, Andrew Gardiner, CMG 1976; Under Secretary, Department of Transport, 1981–86, retired; *b* 21 Dec. 1929; *s* of late William and Helen Lyall (*née* Gardiner); *m* 1953, Olive Leslie Gennoe White; one *s* one *d*. *Educ:* Kirkcaldy High Sch. Joined MoT, 1951; Asst Shipping Attaché, British Embassy, Washington, DC, 1961–64; Principal, Nationalised Industry Finance and Urban Transport Planning, 1965–70; Asst Sec., Railways Div., 1970–72; seconded to FCO as Counsellor, UK Representation to European Communities, 1972–75; Assistant Secretary: Land Use Planning, DoE, 1975–76; Central Unit on Environmental Pollution, 1976–77; Under Sec., PSA, 1978–81. *Recreations:* photography, travel, historical research. *Address:* 5 Barrowfield, Cuckfield, Haywards Heath, West Sussex. *T:* Haywards Heath (0444) 454606. *Club:* Civil Service.

LYALL, Gavin Tudor; author; *b* 9 May 1932; *s* of J. T. and A. A. Lyall; *m* 1958, Katharine E. Whitehorn, *qv*; two *s*. *Educ:* King Edward VI Sch., Birmingham; Pembroke Coll., Cambridge (MA). RAF, 1951–53 (Pilot Officer, 1952). Journalist with: Picture Post, 1956–57; BBC, 1958–59; Sunday Times, 1959–63. Hon. Consultant, Air Transport Users' Cttee, CAA, 1985– (Mem., 1979–85); Mem., Air Travel Trust Cttee, 1986–. *Publications:* The Wrong Side of the Sky, 1961; The Most Dangerous Game, 1964; Midnight Plus One, 1965; Shooting Script, 1966; Venus with Pistol, 1969; Blame the Dead, 1972; Judas Country, 1975; Operation Warboard, 1976; The Secret Servant, 1980 (televised, 1984); The Conduct of Major Maxim, 1982; The Crocus List, 1985; Uncle Target, 1988; (as Editor) Freedom's Battle: The RAF in World War II, 1968. *Recreations:* cooking, military history, model making. *Address:* 14 Provost Road, NW3 4ST. *T:* 071–722 2308. *Clubs:* Royal Air Force, Detection.

LYALL, Katharine Elizabeth; *see* Whitehorn, K.

LYALL, William Chalmers, MBE 1952; HM Diplomatic Service, retired; *b* 6 Aug. 1921; *s* of John Brown Lyall and Margaret Angus Leighton Stevenson Lyall; *m* 1948, Janet Lawson McKechnie; two *s* one *d*. *Educ:* Kelty Public and Beath Secondary schools. Min. of Labour, 1940–48; HM Forces, 1941–47; FO, 1948; Hankow, 1948–51; São Paulo, 1952–53; Manila, 1953–55; FO, 1955–57; Caracas, 1957–60; Bahrain, 1960–64; FO, 1964–65; DSAO, 1965–68; FCO, 1968–69; Consul-General, Genoa, 1969–73; FCO, 1973; Counsellor (Administration), Bonn, 1974–78. *Recreations:* music, photography. *Address:* 30 Charles Way, Limekilns, Dunfermline, Fife KY11 3JN. *T:* Limekilns (0383) 872044.

LYALL GRANT, Maj.-Gen. Ian Hallam, MC 1944; Director General, Supply Co-ordination, Ministry of Defence, 1970–75; retired; *b* 4 June 1915; *s* of Col H. F. Lyall Grant, DSO; *m* 1951, Mary Jennifer Moore; one *s* two *d*. *Educ:* Cheltenham Coll.; RMA, Woolwich; Cambridge Univ. (MA). Regular Commission, RE, 1935; service in: India, Burma and Japan, 1938–46 (MC; twice mentioned in despatches); Cyprus and Egypt, 1951–52; Imperial Defence Coll., 1961; Aden, 1962–63; Comdt, Royal School of Mil. Engineering, 1965–67; Maj.-Gen. 1966; Dep. QMG, 1967–70, retired 1970. Col Comdt, RE, 1972–77. *Recreations:* sailing, fishing, paintings, gemmology. *Club:* Naval and Military.

LYDDON, (William) Derek (Collier), CB 1984; Chief Planning Officer, Scottish Development Department, 1967–85; *b* 17 Nov. 1925; *s* of late A. J. Lyddon, CBE, and E. E. Lyddon; *m* 1949, Marian Louise Kaye Charlesworth, *d* of late Prof. J. K. Charlesworth, CBE; two *d*. *Educ:* Wrekin Coll.; University Coll., London. BA (Arch.) 1952; ARIBA 1953; DipTP 1954; AMTPI 1963; FRTPI 1973. Depute Chief Architect and Planning Officer, Cumbernauld Development Corp., 1962; Chief Architect and Planning Officer, Skelmersdale Development Corp., 1963–67. Vice-Chm., Planning Exchange, 1984–88; Chairman: Edinburgh Old Town Cttee for Conservation and Renewal, 1988–; Edinburgh Sch. of Environmental Design, 1988–. Pres., Internat. Soc. of City and Regional Planners, 1981–84. Hon. Prof., Heriot-Watt Univ., 1986; Vis. Prof., Strathclyde Univ., 1986–89; Hon. Fellow: Univ. of Edinburgh, 1986–; Duncan Jordanstone Coll. of Art, Dundee, 1986–. Hon. DLitt Heriot-Watt, 1981. *Recreations:* walking, reading. *Address:* 38 Dick Place, Edinburgh EH9 2JB. *T:* 031–667 2266.

LYELL, family name of **Baron Lyell.**

LYELL, 3rd Baron *cr* 1914, of Kinnordy; **Charles Lyell;** Bt, 1894; DL; *b* 27 March 1939; *s* of 2nd Baron, VC (killed in action, 1943), and Sophie, *d* of Major S. W. and Lady Betty Trafford; *S* father, 1943. *Educ:* Eton; Christ Church, Oxford. 2nd Lieut Scots Guards, 1957–59. CA Scotland. An Opposition Whip, 1974–79; a Lord in Waiting (Govt Whip), 1979–84; Parly Under-Sec. of State, NI Office, 1984–89. Mem., Queen's Body Guard for Scotland (Royal Company of Archers). DL Angus, 1988. *Heir:* none. *Address:* Kinnordy House, Kirriemuir, Angus. *T:* Kirriemuir (0575) 72848; 20 Petersham Mews, SW7. *T:* 071–584 9419. *Clubs:* Turf, White's.

LYELL, Rt. Hon. Sir Nicholas (Walter), Kt 1987; PC 1990; QC 1980; MP (C) Mid Bedfordshire, since 1983 (Hemel Hempstead, 1979–83); Solicitor General, since 1987; *b* 6 Dec. 1938; *s* of late Sir Maurice Legat Lyell and Veronica Mary Lyell; *m* 1967, Susanna Mary Fletcher; two *s* two *d*. *Educ:* Stowe Sch.; Christ Church, Oxford (MA Hons Mod. Hist.). National Service, commnd Royal Artillery, 1957–59; Walter Runciman & Co., 1962–64; called to the Bar, Inner Temple, 1965, Bencher, 1986; private practice, London (Commercial and Industrial Law), 1965–86; a Recorder, 1985–. Jt Sec., Constitutional Cttee, 1979; PPS to the Attorney General, 1979–86; Parly Under-Sec. of State (Social Security), DHSS, 1986–87. Chm., Soc. of Cons. Lawyers, 1985–86 (Vice-Chm., 1982–85). Vice-Chm., BFSS, 1983–86. Governor, Stowe Sch., 1990–. *Recreations:* gardening, shooting, drawing. *Address:* House of Commons, SW1. *Clubs:* Brooks's, Pratt's, Beefsteak.

LYGO, Adm. Sir Raymond (Derek), KCB 1977; CBIM; aerospace, defence and industrial consultant; Chief Executive, British Aerospace PLC, 1986–89 (Managing Director, 1983–86); Board Member, British Aerospace PLC, 1980–89; Director: James Capel Corporate Finance, since 1990; LET, since 1990; *b* 15 March 1924; *s* of late Edwin T. Lygo and of Ada E. Lygo; *m* 1950, Pepper Van Osten, USA; two *s* one *d*. *Educ:* Valentine's Sch., Ilford; Ilford County High Sch.; Clark's Coll., Bromley. The Times, 1940; Naval Airman, RN, 1942; CO, HMS Ark Royal, 1969–71; Vice Chief of Naval Staff, 1975–78 and Chief of Naval Staff, 1978. British Aerospace: Man. Dir, Hatfield/Lostock Div., 1978–79, Group Dep. Chm., 1980; Chm. and Chief Exec., Dynamics Gp, 1980–82; Chairman: BAe Inc., 1983–88; Royal Ordnance, 1987–88; BAe Enterprises Ltd, BAe (Space Systems) Ltd, BAe Hldgs Inc., 1988–89; Mem., Supervisory Bd, Airbus Industrie, 1987–89. Dir, CBI Educn Foundn, 1985–; Mem., NEDC, 1989–91. Freeman, City of London, 1985; Liveryman: Coachmakers' and Coach Harness Makers' Co., 1986–; Shipwrights' Co., 1988–. Appeal Pres., SENSE (Nat. Deaf-Blind & Rubella Assoc.), 1983–; Appeal Chm., Industrial Soc., 1989–. FRSA. Hon. FRAeS; Hon. Fellow, Poly. of Central London, 1989. *Recreations:* building, gardening, joinery. *Address:* c/o Barclays Bank, 54 Lombard Street, EC3. *Clubs:* Royal Automobile, City Livery, Ambassadeurs; Royal Naval and Royal Albert Yacht (Portsmouth).

LYLE, Alexander Walter Barr, (Sandy), MBE 1987; professional golfer, since 1977; *b* 9 Feb. 1958; *s* of Alex and Agnes Lyle; *m* (marr. diss.); two *s*; *m* 1989, Brigitte Jolande Huurman. *Educ:* Shrewsbury local sch. Rookie of the Year, 1978; 1st in European order of merit, 1979, 1980, 1985; Open Champion, Royal St George's, 1985; won US Masters, 1988. *Publication:* Learning Golf the Lyle Way, 1986. *Recreation:* cars. *Address:* c/o IMG, The Pier House, Strand on the Green, Chiswick, W4 3NN. *Club:* Turnberry Hotel and Golf Courses.

LYLE, Lt-Col (Archibald) Michael; JP; Vice Lord-Lieutenant, Perth and Kinross, since 1984; farmer and landowner; *b* 1 May 1919; 3rd *s* of Col Sir Archibald Lyle, 2nd Bt, MC, TD and Lady Lyle; *m* 1942, Hon. Elizabeth Sinclair, *yr d* of 1st Viscount Thurso, KT, CMG, PC; three *d* (and one *d* decd). *Educ:* Eton College; Trinity College, Oxford (BA; MA). Hon. Attaché, Rome, 1938–39; served 1939–45 with The Black Watch, RHR (wounded Normandy, 1944 and discharged, 1945); Lt-Col, The Scottish Horse RAC (TA), 1953–56. Chm., T&AFA, 1959–64. Mem., Royal Company of Archers, Queen's Body Guard for Scotland. Member: Perth and Kinross CC, 1946–74; Tayside Regional Council, 1974–79. Chm., Perth Coll. of Further Educn, 1978–. JP Perth 1950; DL Perthshire 1961. *Recreations:* fishing, shooting, music. *Address:* Riemore Lodge, Dunkeld, Perthshire PH8 0HP. *T:* Butterstone (03504) 205. *Clubs:* Brooks's, MCC; Puffin's (Edinburgh); Royal Perth Golfing Society.

LYLE, Sir Gavin Archibald, 3rd Bt *cr* 1929; estate manager, farmer; company director; *b* 14 Oct. 1941; *s* of late Ian Archibald de Hoghton Lyle and of Hon. Lydia Yarde-Buller (who *m* 1947, as his 2nd wife, 13th Duke of Bedford; marr. diss. 1960; now Lydia Duchess of Bedford), *d* of 3rd Baron Churston; *S* grandfather, 1946; *m* 1967, Suzy Cooper (marr. diss. 1985); five *s* one *d*. *Heir:* *s* Ian Abram Lyle, *b* 25 Sept. 1968. *Address:* Glendelvine, Caputh, Perthshire PH1 4JN.

LYLE, Lt-Col Michael; *see* Lyle, Lt-Col A.M.

LYLE, Sandy; *see* Lyle, A. W. B.

LYMBERY, Robert Davison; QC 1967; **His Honour Judge Lymbery;** a Circuit Judge (formerly Judge of County Courts), since 1971; Common Serjeant in the City of London, since 1990; *b* 14 Nov. 1920; *s* of late Robert Smith Lymbery and late Louise Lymbery; *m* 1952, Pauline Anne, *d* of late John Reginald and of Kathleen Tuckett; three *d*. *Educ:* Gresham's Sch.; Pembroke Coll., Cambridge. Served Army, 1940–46; commissioned 17/21 Lancers, 1941; Middle East, Italy, Greece (Royal Tank Regt), 1942–46, Major. Pembroke Coll., 1939–40, 1946–48 (MA, LLB 1st class hons). Foundation Exhibn. 1948; called to Bar, Middle Temple, 1949, Bencher, 1990; Harmsworth Law Scholar, 1949; practice on Midland Circuit, 1949–71. Recorder of Grantham, 1965–71, now Honorary Recorder; Chairman: Rutland QS, 1966–71 (Dep. Chm., 1962–66); Bedfordshire QS, 1969–71 (Dep. Chm., 1961–69); Commissioner of Assize, 1971. Freeman, City of London, 1983. *Recreations:* various. *Address:* Central Criminal Court, EC4. *Club:* Hawks (Cambridge).

LYMINGTON, Viscount; Oliver Henry Rufus Wallop; *b* 22 Dec. 1981; *s* and *heir* of Earl of Portsmouth, *qv*.

LYMPANY, Miss Moura, CBE 1979; FRAM 1948; concert pianist; *b* Saltash, Cornwall, 18 Aug. 1916; British; *d* of John and Beatrice Johnstone; *m* 1944, Lt-Col Colin Defries (marr. diss. 1950); *m* 1951, Bennet H. Korn, American Television Executive (marr. diss. 1961); one *s* decd. *Educ:* Belgium, Austria, England. First public performance at age of 12, 1929, at Harrogate, playing Mendelssohn G Minor Concerto. Won second prize out of 79 competitors at Ysaye International Pianoforte Competition at Brussels, 1938. Has played in USA, Canada, South America, Australia, New Zealand, India, and all principal European countries. Records for HMV and Decca. Commander of the Order of the Crown, Belgium, 1980. *Publication:* Moura Lympany: her autobiography, 1991. *Recreations:* gardening, tapestry, reading. *Address:* c/o Miss Jennings, 2 Hereford House, Links Road, W3 0HX.

LYNAM, Desmond Michael; sports broadcaster, BBC, since 1969; *b* 17 Sept. 1942; *s* of Edward Lynam and Gertrude Veronica Lynam (*née* Malone); *m* 1965, Susan Eleanor Skinner (marr. diss. 1974); one *s*. *Educ:* Varndean Grammar Sch., Brighton; Brighton Business Coll. ACII. Business career in insurance, until 1967; also freelance journalist; reporter for local radio, 1967–69; reporter, presenter and commentator, BBC Radio, 1969–78; presenter and commentator, BBC TV Sport, 1978–, incl. Grandstand, Commonwealth and Olympic Games, and World Cup; presenter, Holiday, BBC TV, 1988–. TV Sports Presenter of the Year, TV and Radio Industries Club, 1985, 1987, 1988; Radio Times Male TV Personality, 1989. *Publications:* Guide to Commonwealth Games, 1986; The 1988 Olympics, 1988. *Recreations:* golf, tennis, Brighton and Hove Albion, reading, theatre. *Address:* c/o BBC, Richmond Way, Shepherds Bush, W14.

LYNCH, David; His Honour Judge Lynch; a Circuit Judge, since 1990; *b* 23 Aug. 1939; *s* of Henry and Edith Lynch; *m* 1974, Ann Knights; two *s*. *Educ:* Liverpool Collegiate Grammar School. LLB London. Called to the Bar, Middle Temple, 1968; a

Recorder, 1988–90. *Recreations:* classical guitar, archery, golf. *Address:* The Queen Elizabeth II Law Courts, Derby Square, Liverpool L2 1XA. *T:* 051–473 7373.

LYNCH, Rev. Prebendary Donald MacLeod, CBE 1972; MA; *b* 2 July 1911; *s* of Herbert and Margaret Lynch; *m* 1st, 1941, Ailsa Leslie Leask; three *s* one *d*; 2nd, 1963, Jean Wileman. *Educ:* City of London Sch.; Pembroke Coll., Cambridge; Wycliffe Hall, Oxford. Curate, Christ Church, Chelsea, 1935; Tutor, Oak Hill Theological Coll., 1938; Curate, St Michael's, Stonebridge Park, 1940; Minister, All Saints, Queensbury, 1942; Vicar, St Luke's, Tunbridge Wells, 1950; Principal, Church Army Training Coll., 1953; Chief Sec., Church Army, 1960–76; Preb. of Twiford, St Paul's Cathedral, 1964–76, now Emeritus; Priest-in-Charge of Seal, St Lawrence, dio. Rochester, 1974–85, also of Underriver, 1980–85; RD, Sevenoaks, 1979–84. Chaplain to the Queen, 1969–81. *Publications:* Action Stations, 1981; Chariots of the Gospel, 1982. *Recreations:* reading, walking. *Address:* Flat 2, 20 Grassington Road, Eastbourne, Sussex BN20 7BJ. *T:* Eastbourne (0323) 20849.

LYNCH, John; *b* 15 Aug. 1917; *y s* of Daniel Lynch and Norah O'Donoghue; *m* 1946, Mairin O'Connor. *Educ:* Christian Brothers' Schools, N Monastery, Cork; University College, Cork; King's Inns, Dublin. Entered Civil Service (Dept of Justice), 1936; called to Bar, 1945; resigned from Civil Service, became Mem. Munster Bar and commenced practice in Cork Circuit, 1945. Teachta Dala (TD) for Cork, Parlt of Ireland, 1948–81; Parly Sec. to Govt and to Minister for Lands, 1951–54; Minister for: Education, 1957–59; Industry and Commerce, 1959–65; Finance, 1965–66; Leader of Fianna Fail, 1966–79; Taoiseach (Head of Government of Ireland), 1966–73 and 1977–79; Pres., European Council (EEC), July–Dec. 1979. Alderman, Co. Borough of Cork, 1950–57; Mem. Cork Sanatoria Board and Cttee of Management, N Infirmary, Cork, 1950–51 and 1955–57; Mem. Cork Harbour Comrs, 1956–57; Vice-Pres., Consultative Assembly of Council of Europe, 1958; Pres., Internat. Labour Conf., 1962. Freeman, City of Cork, 1980. Hon. LLD: Univ. of Dublin, 1967; Nat. Univ. of Ireland, 1969; Rhode Island Coll., USA, 1980; Hon. DCL N Carolina, 1971. Grand Cross, Order of the Crown (Belgium), 1968. Robert Schumann Gold Medal, 1973; Mérite Européen Gold Medal, 1981. *Address:* 21 Garville Avenue, Rathgar, Dublin 6, Ireland.

LYNCH, Prof. John; Director of Institute of Latin American Studies, 1974–87 and Professor of Latin American History, 1970–87, University of London, now Professor Emeritus; *b* 11 Jan. 1927; *s* of late John P. Lynch and of Teresa M. Lynch, Boldon Colliery, Co. Durham; *m* 1960, Wendy Kathleen, *d* of late Frederick and of Kathleen Norman; two *s* three *d*. *Educ:* Corby Sch. Sunderland; Univ. of Edinburgh; University College, London. MA Edinburgh 1952; PhD London 1955. FRHistS 1958. Army, 1945–48. Asst Lectr and Lectr in Modern History, Univ. of Liverpool, 1954–61; Lectr in Hispanic and Latin American History, University Coll. London, Reader 1964. Harrison Vis. Prof., Coll. of William and Mary, Williamsburg, 1991–92. Corresp. Member: Academia Nacional de la Historia, Argentina, 1963, Academia Nacional de la Historia, Venezuela, 1980; Academia Panameña de la Historia, 1981; Academia Chilena de la Historia, 1985; Real Academia de la Historia, Spain, 1986; Sociedad Boliviana de Historia, 1987. Dr *hc* Seville, 1990. Order of Andrés Bello (Venezuela), 1979; Comdr, Order of Isabel la Católica (Spain), 1988. *Publications:* Spanish Colonial Administration 1782–1810, 1958; Spain under the Habsburgs, vol. 1 1964, vol. 2 1969; (with R. A. Humphreys) The Origins of the Latin American Revolutions, 1808–1826, 1965; The Spanish American Revolutions 1808–1826, 1973; Argentine Dictator: Juan Manuel de Rosas, 1829–52, 1981; (ed) Andrés Bello: the London years, 1982; (ed) Past and Present in the Americas, 1984; Hispanoamérica 1750–1850, 1987; Bourbon Spain 1700–1808, 1989; (contrib.) Cambridge History of Latin America, vol. III 1985, vol. IV 1986. *Address:* 8 Templars Crescent, N3 3QS. *T:* 081–346 1089.

LYNCH, Martin Patrick James; Under Secretary, Overseas Development Administration, Foreign and Commonwealth Office, 1975–83, retired; *b* 4 June 1924; 2nd *s* of late Frederick Lynch, DSM, and late Elizabeth Yeatman; *m* 1959, Anne, *d* of late Major Gerald McGorty, MC, RAMC; two *s* one *d* (and one *s* decd). *Educ:* London Oratory School. BA Hons London. RAF, 1942–49; Exec. Officer, HM Treasury, 1950; Asst Private Sec. to Financial Sec., 1953–54; Private Sec. to Minister Without Portfolio, 1954–55; Principal, 1958; Asst Sec., Min. of Overseas Develt, 1966 and 1971–75; Counsellor, UK Treasury and Supply Delegn, Washington, and UK Alternate Dir, World Bank, 1967–71. Asst Sec. (Admin), British Coll. of Optometrists (formerly British Coll of Ophthalmic Opticians), 1984–87; Asst to Optical Services Audit Cttee, Gen. Optical Council, 1989–. FRSA 1973; Mem. Council, Assoc. for Latin Liturgy, 1973– (Chm., 1976–88). *Address:* Hillside, Combe Hill, Combe St Nicholas, Chard, Somerset TA20 3NW. *T:* Chard (0460) 50239. *Clubs:* Reform; Somerset CC.

LYNCH, Patrick, MA; MRIA; Professor of Political Economy (Applied Economics), University College, Dublin, 1975–80, now Emeritus; *b* 5 May 1917; *s* of Daniel and Brigid Lynch, Co. Tipperary and Dublin; *m* Mary Crotty (*née* Campbell), MA. *Educ:* Univ. Coll., Dublin. Fellow Commoner, Peterhouse, Cambridge, 1956. Entered Irish Civil Service, 1941; Asst Sec. to Govt, 1950; Univ. Lectr in Econs, UC Dublin, 1952, Associate Prof., 1966–75. Chm., Aer Lingus, 1954–75; Jt Dep. Chm., Allied Irish Banks, 1976–84. Has acted as economic consultant to OECD, Council of Europe, Dept of Finance, Dublin, Gulbenkian Inst., Lisbon. Directed surveys sponsored by Irish Govt with OECD into long-term Irish educnl needs, 1965, and into requirements of Irish economy in respect of scientific res., develt and technology, 1966; estab. Science Policy Res. Centre in Dept of Applied Econs, UC Dublin, 1969. Mem., various Irish Govt Commns and Cttees, 1952–; Member: Club of Rome, 1973; EEC Economic and Monetary Union 1980 Group, 1974; Nat. Science Council, 1968–78; Higher Educn Authority, 1968–72; Nat. Economic and Social Council, 1973–76; European Science Foundn, 1974–77; Chairman: Medico-Social Research Board, 1966–72; Public Service Adv. Council, 1973–77; Exec. Cttee, Econ. and Social Res. Inst., 1983–88; Editl Bd, Economic and Social Review; Mem. Editorial Bd, University Review. Chm., Nat. Library of Ireland Soc., 1969–72; Chm., Irish Anti-Apartheid Movement, 1972; Member: Irish Assoc. for Civil Liberty; Movement for Peace in Ireland. Chm., Inst. of Public Administration, 1973–77. Member: Governing Body UC Dublin, 1963–75; Senate NUI, 1972–77; Treasurer, RIA, 1972–80. Hon. DUniv Brunel, 1976; Hon. LLD: Dublin, 1979; NUI, 1985. *Publications:* Planning for Economic Development in Ireland, 1959; (with J. Vaizey) Guinness's Brewery in the Irish Economy, 1960; (jtly) Economics of Educational Costing, 1969; (with Brian Hillery) Ireland in the International Labour Organisation, 1969; (with B. Chubb) Economic Development Planning, 1969; Whither Science Policy, 1980; (ed with J. Meenan) Essays in Memory of Alexis Fitzgerald, 1987; essays in various symposia, etc; articles in Administration, The Bell, Encycl. Britannica, Econ. History Review, Irish Hist. Studies, Irish Jl of Educn, Statist, Studies, University Review, etc. *Address:* 68 Marlborough Road, Dublin 4, Ireland.

LYNCH-BLOSSE, Sir Richard Hely, 17th Bt *cr* 1622; RAMC, 1975–85, retired; general medical practioner, since 1985; *b* 26 Aug. 1953; *s* of Sir David Edward Lynch-Blosse, 16th Bt, and of Elizabeth, *er d* of Thomas Harold Payne, Welwyn Garden City; *S* father, 1971; *m* 1976, Cara, *o d* of George Sutherland, St Ives, Cambs; two *d*. *Educ:* Royal Free Hosp. Sch. of Medicine. Commnd RAMC, July 1975; LRCP MRCS 1978; MB BS 1979; DRCOG 1983; MRCGP 1984. *Publication:* contrib. to Jl of RAMC. *Heir: cousin* (Eric) Hugh Lynch-Blosse, OBE [*b* 30 July 1917; *m* 1946, Jean Evelyn, *d* of Commander Andrew Robertson Hair, RD, RNR; one *s* one *d* (and one *d* decd)]. *Address:* The Surgery, Watery Lane, Clifton Hampden, Oxon.

LYNCH-ROBINSON, Sir Niall (Bryan), 3rd Bt *cr* 1920; DSC 1941; late Lieut RNVR; one time Chairman, Leo Burnett Ltd, 1969–78; *b* 24 Feb. 1918; *s* of Sir Christopher Henry Lynch-Robinson, 2nd Bt and Dorothy (*d* 1970), *d* of Henry Warren, Carrickmines, Co. Dublin; *S* father 1958; *m* 1940, Rosemary Seaton, *e d* of Mrs M. Seaton Eller; one *s* one (adopted) *d*. *Educ:* Stowe. Sub-Lieut 1939, Lieut 1940, RNVR; served War of 1939–45 (DSC, Croix de Guerre). Mem. Exec. Cttee, Nat. Marriage Guidance Council, 1961–86. Chm. of Governors, Cranbourne Chase School, 1970–82. *Recreations:* fishing, gardening. *Heir:* *s* Dominick Christopher Lynch-Robinson [*b* 30 July 1948; *m* 1973, Victoria, *d* of Kenneth Weir; one *s* one *d*]. *Address:* The Old Vicarage, Ampfield, Romsey, Hants SO51 9BQ.

LYNDEN-BELL, Prof. Donald, FRS 1978; Professor of Astrophysics, University of Cambridge, since 1972; Director, Institute of Astronomy, Cambridge, 1972–77 and 1982–87; *b* 5 April 1935; *s* of late Lt-Col L. A. Lynden-Bell, MC and of M. R. Lynden-Bell (*née* Thring); *m* 1961, Ruth Marion Truscott, MA, PhD; one *s* one *d*. *Educ:* Marlborough; Clare Coll., Cambridge (MA, PhD). Harkness Fellow of the Commonwealth Fund, NY, at the California Inst. of Technology and Hale Observatories, 1960–62; Research Fellow and then Fellow and Dir of studies in mathematics, Clare Coll., Cambridge, 1960–65; Asst Lectr in applied mathematics, Univ. of Cambridge, 1962–65; Principal Scientific officer and later SPSO, Royal Greenwich Observatory, Herstmonceux, 1965–72. Visiting Associate, Calif. Inst. of Technology and Hale Observatories, 1969–70. Pres., RAS, 1985–87. FHMAAAS 1985. For. Associate, US NAS, 1990. Hon. DSc Sussex, 1987. Eddington Medal, RAS, 1984; Brouwer Prize, AAS, 1990. *Publications:* contrib. to Monthly Notices of Royal Astronomical Soc. *Recreations:* hill walking, golf, squash racquets. *Address:* Institute of Astronomy, The Observatories, Madingley Road, Cambridge CB3 0HA. *T:* Cambridge (0223) 337525.

LYNE, Air Vice-Marshal Michael Dillon, CB 1968; AFC (two Bars); DL; *b* 23 March 1919; *s* of late Robert John Lyne, Winchester; *m* 1943, Avril Joy Buckley, *d* of late Lieut-Colonel Albert Buckley, CBE, DSO; two *s* two *d*. *Educ:* Imperial Service Coll.; RAF Coll., Cranwell. Fighter Comd and Middle East, 1939–46; Comdg No 54 Fighter Squadron, 1946–48; Comdg RAF Wildenrath, 1958–60; Air Attaché, Moscow, 1961–63; Commandant, Royal Air Force Coll., Cranwell, 1963–64; Air Officer Commanding No 23 Group, RAF Flying Training Command, 1965–67; Senior RAF Instructor, Imperial Defence Coll., 1968–69; Dir-Gen. Training, RAF, 1970–71; retired. Sec., Diocese of Lincoln, 1971–76. Vice-Chm. (Air), TAVR Assoc. for East Midlands, 1977–84. Vice Chm., Governing Body, Bishop Grosseteste Coll., 1976–86. Vice-President: RAF Gliding and Soaring Assoc.; RAF Motor Sport Assoc.; Old Cranwellian Assoc., 1982–. Founder and first Chm., Lincs Microprocessor Soc., 1979–83; Mem. Council, British Computer Soc., 1980–83. President: Lincoln Branch, SCF, 1977–89; Grantham Constituency Liberal Assoc., 1979–88; Grantham Constituency Liberal Democrats, 1990–; No 54 Squadron Assoc., 1981–. DL Lincs, 1973. *Recreations:* sailing, gardening. *Address:* Far End, Far Lane, Coleby, Lincoln LN5 0AH. *T:* Lincoln (0522) 810468. *Club:* Royal Air Force.

See also R. M. J. Lyne.

LYNE, Roderic Michael John; HM Diplomatic Service; Head of Soviet Department, Foreign and Commonwealth Office, since 1990; *b* 31 March 1948; *s* of Air Vice-Marshal Michael Dillon Lyne, *qv*; *m* 1969, Amanda Mary, *d* of Sir Howard Frank Trayton Smith, *qv*; two *s* one *d*. *Educ:* Legbourne County Primary Sch., Lincs; Highfield Sch., Hants; Eton Coll.; Leeds Univ. (BA Hist. 1970). FCO 1970; Army Sch. of Langs, 1971; Moscow, 1972–74; Dakar, 1974–76; Eastern European and Soviet Dept, FCO, 1976–79; Rhodesia Dept, FCO, 1979; Asst Pvte Sec. to Sec. of State for Foreign and Commonwealth Affairs, 1979–82; UK Mission to UN, NY, 1982–86; Vis. Res. Fellow, RIIA, 1986–87; Counsellor and Hd of Chancery, Moscow, 1987–90. *Recreation:* sport. *Address:* c/o Foreign and Commonwealth Office, SW1A 2AH.

LYNK, Roy, OBE 1990; National President, Union of Democratic Mineworkers, since 1987 and General Secretary, Nottingham Section, since 1985; *b* 9 Nov. 1932; *s* of John Thomas Lynk and Ivy Lynk; *m* 1978, Sandra Ann; three *s* three *d*. *Educ:* Station Road Higher Sch. and Healdswood Sch., Sutton-in-Ashfield; Nottingham Univ. Cert. in Industrial Relations. Miner at Teversal Colliery, Nottingham, 1947; RN 1948; Miner at various collieries, Nottingham, 1950–79. National Union of Mineworkers: Branch Sec., Sutton Colliery, 1958–79; full time Area Official, Nottingham, 1979–83; Financial Sec., Nottingham Area, 1983–85, Gen. Sec., 1985; Union of Democratic Mineworkers: formed, Dec. 1985; Nat. Gen. Sec., 1985–86. Mem., European Coal and Steel Community's Consultative Cttee, 1988–. *Recreation:* watching football. *Address:* Columbia House, 143 Huthwaite Road, Sutton-in-Ashfield, Notts.

LYNN, Bishop Suffragan of, since 1986; **Rt. Rev. David Edward Bentley;** *b* 7 Aug. 1935; *s* of William Bentley and Florence (*née* Dalgleish); *m* 1962, Clarice Lahmers; two *s* two *d*. *Educ:* Gt Yarmouth Grammar School; Univ. of Leeds (BA English); Westcott House, Cambridge. Deacon 1960, priest 1961; Curate: St Ambrose, Bristol, 1960–62; Holy Trinity with St Mary, Guildford, 1962–66; Rector: Headley, Bordon, 1966–73; Esher, 1973–86. Hon. Canon of Guildford Cathedral, 1980; RD of Emly, 1977–82. Warden, Community of All Hallows, Ditchingham, 1989–. Chairman: Guildford dio. Council of Social Responsibility, 1980–86; Guildford dio. House of Clergy, 1977–86; ACCM Candidates Cttee, 1987–. *Recreations:* music; sport, especially cricket; theatre. *Address:* The Old Vicarage, Castle Acre, King's Lynn, Norfolk PE32 2AA. *T:* Swaffham (0760) 755553. *Clubs:* MCC; Norfolk (Norwich).

LYNN, Archdeacon of; *see* Foottit, Ven. A. C.

LYNN, Jonathan Adam; director, writer and actor; *b* 3 April 1943; *s* of Robin and Ruth Lynn; *m* 1967, Rita Merkelis; one *s*. *Educ:* Kingswood Sch., Bath; Pembroke Coll., Cambridge (MA). Acted in Cambridge Circus, New York, 1964; TV debut, Ed Sullivan Show, 1964; actor in repertory, Leicester, Edinburgh and Bristol Old Vic, and in London; performances include: Green Julia, 1965; Fiddler on the Roof, 1967–68; Blue Comedy, 1968; The Comedy of the Changing Years, 1969; When We Are Married, 1970; Dreyfus, 1982; actor in TV comedy programmes and plays, including: Barmitzvah Boy, 1975; The Knowledge, 1979; Outside Edge, 1982; Diana, 1984; actor in films including: Prudence and the Pill, 1967; Into the Night, 1984; Three Men and a Little Lady, 1990; Artistic Dir, Cambridge Theatre Co., 1977–81 (dir. 19 prodns); *director: London:* The Plotters of Cabbage Patch Corner, 1970; The Glass Menagerie, 1977; The Gingerbread Man, 1977 and 1978; The Unvarnished Truth, 1978; The Matchmaker, 1978; Songbook, 1979 (SWET Award, Best Musical, 1979); Tonight at 8.30, 1981; Arms and the Man, 1981; Pass the Butler, 1982; Loot, 1984; *National Theatre:* A Little Hotel on the Side, 1984; Jacobowski and the Colonel, 1986; Three Men on a Horse, 1987 (Olivier Award for Best Comedy); *RSC:* Anna Christie, Stratford 1979, London 1980; *Broadway:* The

Moony Shapiro Songbook, 1981; *short film:* Mick's People, 1982. *TV scriptwriter:* situation comedies, including: My Brother's Keeper, 2 series, 1974 and 1975 (also co-starred); Yes, Minister (also radio scripts), 3 series, 1980, 1981 and 1982; Yes, Prime Minister, 1986, 1987; Life After Life, 1990; *film scriptwriter:* The Internecine Project, 1974; Clue (wrote and dir.), 1986; Nuns on the Run (wrote and dir.), 1990; My Cousin Vinny (dir), 1991. Writer's Award, BAFTA, 1987; Pye TV Writers Award (for Yes, Minister and Yes, Prime Minister), 1981, 1986; Broadcasting Press Guild Award, 1980, 1986; ACE Award for Amer. Cable TV Best Comedy Writing (for Yes, Prime Minister), 1988. Hon. MA Sheffield. *Publications:* A Proper Man (novel), 1976; with Antony Jay: Yes, Minister, The Diaries of a Cabinet Minister: Vol. I, 1981; Vol. II, 1982; Vol. III, 1983; The Complete Yes Minister, 1984; Yes, Prime Minister, the Diaries of the Rt Hon. James Hacker: Vol. I, 1986; Vol. II, 1987; The Complete Yes Prime Minister, 1989. *Recreation:* changing weight. *Address:* c/o A. D. Peters & Co. Ltd, The Chambers, Chelsea Harbour, Lots Road, SW10 0XF.

LYNN, Maurice Kenneth, MA; Headmaster, The Oratory School, since 1989; *b* 3 March 1951. *Educ:* Thornleigh Salesian College, Bolton; Magdalen College, Oxford (Open Scholar; BA Hons 1973; MA 1977). Asst Master, Oratory Sch., 1973–79; Asst Master, Radley Coll., 1979–83; Head of French, Westminster Sch., 1983–88. *Recreations:* English Catholic poetry, twentieth century French drama, soccer, ski-ing, cricket, acting and producing, cycling, travel. *Address:* The Oratory School, Woodcote, near Reading RG8 0PJ. *T:* Checkendon (0491) 680207. *Club:* East India.

LYNN, Prof. Richard; Professor of Psychology, University of Ulster, since 1972; *b* 20 Feb. 1930; *s* of Richard and Ann Lynn; *m* 1st, 1956, Susan Maher (marr. diss. 1978); one *s* two *d*; 2nd, 1990, Susan Hampson. *Educ:* Bristol Grammar Sch.; King's Coll., Cambridge (Passingham prizeman). Lectr in Psychology, Univ. of Exeter, 1956–67; Prof. of Psychology, Dublin Economic and Social Res. Inst., 1967–72. US Mensa Award for Excellence, for work on intelligence, 1985, 1988. *Publications:* Attention, Arousal and the Orientation Reaction, 1966; The Irish Braindrain, 1969; The Universities and the Business Community, 1969; Personality and National Character, 1971; An Introduction to the Study of Personality, 1972; (ed) The Entrepreneur, 1974; (ed) Dimensions of Personality, 1981; Educational Achievement in Japan, 1987; The Secret of the Miracle Economy, 1991; articles on personality, intelligence and social psychology. *Recreation:* do-it-yourself house renovation. *Address:* Dunderg House, Coleraine, Co. Londonderry. *Club:* Northern Counties (Londonderry).

LYNN, Dame Vera, (Dame Vera Margaret Lewis), DBE 1975 (OBE 1969); singer; *b* 20 March 1917; *d* of Bertram Samuel Welch and Annie Welch; *m* 1941, Harry Lewis; one *d*. *Educ:* Brampton Rd Sch., East Ham. First public appearance as singer, 1924; joined juvenile troupe, 1928; ran own dancing school, 1932; broadcast with Joe Loss and joined Charlie Kunz, 1935; singer with Ambrose Orch., 1937–40, then went solo; voted most popular singer, Daily Express comp., 1939, and named Forces Sweetheart; own radio show, Sincerely Yours, 1941–47; starred in Applesauce, London Palladium, 1941; sang to troops in Burma, etc, 1944 (Burma Star, 1985); subseq. Big Show (radio), USA; London Laughs, Adelphi; appeared at Flamingo Hotel, Las Vegas, and many TV shows, USA and Britain, including own TV series on Rediffusion, 1955; BBC TV, 1956; BBC 2, 1970; also appearances in Holland, Denmark, Sweden, Norway, Germany, Canada, NZ and Australia; in seven Command Performances, also films and own shows on radio. 14 Gold Records; records include Auf Wiederseh'n (over 12 million copies sold), became first British artiste to top American Hit Parade. Pres., Printers' Charitable Corp., 1980. Internat. Ambassador, Variety Club Internat., 1985. Hon. Citizen: Winnipeg, 1974; Nashville, Tennessee, 1977. Hon. LLD Memorial Univ. of Newfoundland, 1977 (founded Lynn Music Scholarship, first award, 1982). Freedom: City of London, 1978; City of Corner Brook, Newfoundland, 1981. FInstD. Music Publishers' Award, 1975; Show Business Personality of the Year, Grand Order of Water Rats, 1975; Ivor Novello Award, 1975; Humanitarian Award, Variety Club Internat., 1985. Comdr, Order of Orange-Nassau, Holland. *Publications:* Vocal Refrain (autobiog.), 1975; (jtly) We'll Meet Again, 1989; Unsung Heroines, 1991. *Recreations:* gardening, painting, sewing, swimming.

LYNN, Wilfred; Director, National Westminster Bank Ltd (Outer London Board), 1969–73; *b* 19 May 1905; *s* of late Wilfred Crosland Lynn and Alice Lynn; *m* 1936, Valerie, *e d* of late B. M. A. Critchley; one *s* one *d* (twins). *Educ:* Hull Grammar School. Entered National Provincial Bank Ltd, 1921; Asst General Manager, 1952; Joint General Manager, 1953; Chief General Manager, 1961; Director, 1965–69; Dir, North Central Finance Ltd, 1962–70. FIB. *Recreation:* golf. *Address:* c/o National Westminster Bank, 15 Bishopsgate, EC2.

LYNNE, Gillian, (Mrs Peter Land); director, choreographer, dancer, actress; *d* of late Leslie Pyrke and Barbara (*née* Hart); *m* 1980, Peter Land, actor. *Educ:* Baston Sch., Bromley, Kent; Arts Educnl Sch. Leading soloist, Sadler's Wells Ballet, 1944–51; star dancer, London Palladium, 1951–53; role in film, Master of Ballantrae, 1952; lead in Can-Can, Coliseum, 1954–55; Becky Sharp in Vanity Fair, Windsor, 1956; guest principal dancer: Samson and Delilah, Sadler's Wells, 1957; Aida, and Tannhauser, Covent Garden, 1957; Puck in A Midsummer Night's Dream, TV, 1958; star dancer in Chelsea at Nine (featured dance segments), TV, 1958; lead in New Cranks, Lyric, Hammersmith, 1959; roles in Wanda, Rose Marie, Cinderella, Out of My Mind, and lead in revue, 1960–61; leading lady, 5 Past Eight Show, Edinburgh, 1962; conceived, dir., chor. and starred in Collages (mod. dance revue), Edinburgh Fest., 1963, transf. Savoy; *choreographed:* The Owl and the Pussycat (1st ballet), Western Theatre Ballet, 1962; Queen of the Cats, London Palladium, 1962–63; Wonderful Life (1st film), 1963–64; Every Day's a Holiday, and Three Hats for Lisa (musical films), 1964; The Roar of the Greasepaint, and Pickwick, Broadway, 1965; The Flying Dutchman, Covent Garden, 1966; Half a Sixpence (film), 1966–67 (also staged musical nos); How Now Dow Jones, Broadway, 1967; Midsummer Marriage, Covent Garden, 1968; The Trojans, Covent Garden, 1969, 1977; Breakaway (ballet), Scottish Theatre Ballet, 1969; Phil the Fluter, Palace, 1969; Ambassador, Her Majesty's, 1971; Man of La Mancha (film), 1972; The Card, Queen's, 1973; Hans Andersen, London Palladium, 1975; The Way of the World, Aldwych, 1978; My Fair Lady, national tour and Adelphi, 1979; Parsifal, Covent Garden, 1979; (also Associate Dir) Cats, New London, 1981 (Olivier Award, 1981), Broadway 1982, nat. tour, 1983, Los Angeles, Sydney, 1985, East Berlin, 1987, Canada, Japan, Australia, Holland, Paris, 1989 (Molière Award, Best Musical); Café Soir (ballet), Houston Ballet Co., 1985; Cabaret, Strand, 1986; The Phantom of the Opera, Her Majesty's, 1986, Broadway, Japan, Vienna, 1989, Stockholm, Chicago, Hamburg, Australia, Canada, 1990; A Simple Man (ballet), Sadler's Wells, 1988. *directed and choreographed* The Match Girls, Globe, 1966; Bluebeard, Sadler's Wells Opera, 1966, new prodn, Sadler's Wells Opera, Coliseum, 1969; Love on the Dole (musical), Nottingham Playhouse, 1970; Liberty Ranch, Greenwich, 1972; Once Upon a Time, Duke of York's, 1972; Jasperina, Amsterdam, 1978; Cats, Vienna, 1983 (1st proscenium arch prodn; Silver Order of Merit, Austria, 1984), Paris, 1989; *directed:* Round Leicester Square (revue), Prince Charles, 1963; Tonight at Eight, Hampstead, 1970 and Fortune, 1971; Lillywhite Lies, Nottingham, 1971; A Midsummer Night's Dream (co-dir.), Stratford, 1977; Tomfoolery, Criterion, 1980; Jeeves Takes

Charge, Fortune, 1980, off-Broadway, 1983, Los Angeles, 1985; To Those Born Later, New End, 1981; (Additional Dir) La Ronde, RSC, Aldwych, 1982; (also appeared in) Alone Plus One, Newcastle, 1982; The Rehearsal, Yvonne Arnaud, Guildford and tour, 1983; Cabaret, Strand, 1986; *staged:* England Our England (revue), Princes, 1961; 200 Motels (pop-opera film), 1971; musical nos in Quilp (film), 1974; A Comedy of Errors, Stratford, 1976 (TV musical, 1977); musical As You Like It, Stratford, 1977; Songbook, Globe, 1979; Once in a Lifetime, Aldwych, 1979; new stage act for Tommy Steele, 1979; wedding sequence in Yentl (film), 1982; European Vacation II (film); Pirelli Calendar, 1988; *choreographed for television:* Peter and the Wolf (narrated and mimed all 9 parts), 1958; At the Hawk's Well (ballet), 1975; There was a Girl, 1975; The Fool on the Hill (1st Colour Special for ABC), with Australian Ballet and Sydney Symph. Orch., staged Sydney Opera House, 1975; Muppet Show series, 1976–80; (also musical staging) Alice in Wonderland, 1985; shows and specials for Val Doonican, Perry Como, Petula Clark, Nana Mouskouri, John Curry, Harry Secombe, Ray Charles, and Mike Burstein; also produced and devised Noel Coward and Cleo Laine specials; *directed for television:* Mrs F's Friends, 1981; Easy Money, 1982; Le Morte d'Arthur (also devised), 1983; A Simple Man; The Look of Love, 1989. *Publications:* (contrib.) Cats, The Book of the Musical; articles in Dancing Times. *Club:* Pickwick.

LYNTON, Norbert Casper; Professor of the History of Art, 1975–89, and Dean of the School of European Studies, 1985–88, University of Sussex; *b* 22 Sept. 1927; *s* of Paul and Amalie Christiane Lynton; *m* 1st, 1949, Janet Irving; two *s*; 2nd, 1969, Sylvia Anne Towning; two *s*. *Educ:* Douai Sch.; Birkbeck Coll., Univ. of London (BA Gen.); Courtauld Inst., Univ. of London (BA Hons). Lectr in History of Art and Architecture, Leeds Coll. of Art, 1950–61; Sen. Lectr, then Head of Dept of Art History and Gen. Studies, Chelsea Sch. of Art, 1961–70. London Corresp. of Art International, 1961–66; Art Critic, The Guardian, 1965–70; Dir of Exhibitions, Arts Council of GB, 1970–75; Vis. Prof. of History of Art, Open Univ., 1975. Trustee, National Portrait Gallery, 1985–. *Publications:* (jtly) Simpson's History of Architectural Development, vol. 4 (Renaissance), 1962; Kenneth Armitage, 1962; Paul Klee, 1964; The Modern World, 1968; The Story of Modern Art, 1980, 2nd edn 1989; Looking at Art, 1981; (jtly) Looking into Paintings, 1985; articles in Burlington Mag., TLS, Studio International, Architectural Design, Art in America, Smithsonian, Leonardo, etc. *Recreations:* art, people, music, travel. *Address:* 28 Florence Road, Brighton BN1 6DJ. *T:* Brighton (0273) 509478.

LYON; see Bowes Lyon.

LYON, Alexander Ward; Chairman, UK Immigrants Advisory Service, 1978–84; *b* 15 Oct. 1931. Called to the Bar, Inner Temple, 1954. Contested (Lab) York, 1964, 1983. MP (Lab) York, 1966–83; addtl PPS to the Treasury Ministers, 1969; PPS to Paymaster General, 1969; Opposition Spokesman: on African Affairs, 1970; on Home Affairs, 1971; Min. of State, Home Office, 1974–76. Member: Younger Cttee on Intrusions into Privacy; Select Cttee on Home Affairs, 1979; Chm., PLP Home Affairs Gp, 1979. *Address:* 23 Larkhall Rise, SW4 6JB. *T:* 071–720 1525.

LYON, Prof. Christina Margaret; Professor of Law, Head of Department of Law, and Head of School of Law, Keele University, since 1987; *b* 12 Nov. 1952; *d* of Edward Arthur Harrison and Kathleen Joan Harrison; *m* 1976, Adrian Pirrie Lyon, LLB, Barrister; one *s* one *d*. *Educ:* Wallasey High Sch. for Girls; University Coll. London. LLB (1st Cl. Hons) 1974; admitted Solicitor, 1977. Tutor and sometime Lectr in Law, University Coll. London, 1974–75; Trainee and Asst Solicitor, Bell & Joynson, 1975–77; Liverpool University: part-time Tutor in Law, 1976–77; Lectr in Law, 1977–80; Manchester University: Lectr in Law and Law and Social Work, 1980–86; Sub-Dean, Law Faculty, 1986. Member: ESRC Res. Grants Bd, 1988–91; Child Policy Review Gp, Nat. Children's Bureau, 1989–; Trustee, Independent Representation for Children in Need, 1989–; Nat. Exec. Cttee, Relate, 1990– (Pres., N Staffs Relate, 1987–). Dr Barnardo's Research Fellow, 1987–. Jt Editor, Jl of Social Welfare Law, 1984–. FRSA 1991. *Publications:* Matrimonial Jurisdiction of Magistrates' Courts, 1981; Cohabitation without Marriage, 1983; (ed) Butterworth's Family Law Service Encyclopaedia, 1983, rev. edn 1990; Law of Residential Homes and Day Care Establishments, 1984; Child Abuse, 1990; The Law Relating to Children in Principles and Practice of Forensic Psychiatry, 1990; Butterworths Family Law Handbook, 1991. *Recreations:* riding, swimming, foreign travel, reading, theatre, opera. *Address:* 54 Cromptons Lane, Calderstones, Liverpool L18 3EX.

LYON, Clare; see Short, C.

LYON, (Colin) Stewart (Sinclair), FIA; FSA, FRNS; General Manager (Finance), Group Actuary and Director, Legal & General Group Plc, 1980–87; company director; *b* 22 Nov. 1926; *s* of late Col Colin Sinclair Lyon, OBE, TD and Mrs Dorothy Winstanley Lyon (*née* Thomason); *m* 1958, Elizabeth Mary Fargus Richards; four *s* one *d*. *Educ:* Liverpool Coll.; Trinity Coll., Cambridge (MA). FIA 1954; FSA 1972; FRNS 1955. Chief Exec., Victory Insurance Co. Ltd, 1974–76; Chief Actuary, Legal & General Assurance Soc. Ltd, 1976–85. Director: Lautro Ltd, 1987–; Cologne Reinsurance Co. Ltd, 1987–; City of Birmingham Touring Opera Ltd, 1987–90; Ætna Internat. (UK) Ltd, 1988–91. Member: Occupational Pensions Bd, 1979–82; Inquiry into Provision for Retirement, 1983–85; Treasure Trove Reviewing Cttee, 1986–. President: Inst. of Actuaries, 1982–84; British Numismatic Soc., 1966–70 (Sanford Saltus Gold Medal, 1974); Vice-Pres., Guildford Philharmonic Soc., 1974–. Trustee, Disablement Income Gp Charitable Trust, 1967–84; Dir, Disablement Income Gp, 1984–; Trustee, Independent Living Fund, 1988–. *Publications:* (with C. E. Blunt and B. H. I. H. Stewart) Coinage in Tenth-Century England, 1989; papers on Anglo-Saxon coinage, particularly in British Numismatic Jl; contrib. Jl of Inst. of Actuaries and Trans Internat. Congress of Actuaries. *Recreations:* numismatics, music, amateur radio (call sign G3EIZ). *Address:* Cuerdale, White Lane, Guildford, Surrey GU4 8PR. *T:* Guildford (0483) 573761. *Club:* Actuaries'.

LYON, (John) David (Richard); Chief Executive, Bowater plc (formerly Bowater Industries), since 1987; *b* 4 June 1936; *s* of John F. A. Lyon and Elizabeth Lyon (*née* Owen); *m* 1st, 1960, Nicola M. E. Bland (marr. diss. 1986); two *s* (and one *s* decd); 2nd, 1987, Lillis Lanphier. *Educ:* Wellington College; Magdalen College, Oxford (BA Modern History 1959); Harvard Business Sch. (Advanced Management Programme, 1973). 1st Bn The Rifle Brigade, Kenya and Malaya, 1954–56 (despatches). Courtaulds, 1959–70; Rank Organisation, 1970–71; Redland, 1971–87 (Dir 1976; Man. Dir, 1982); Dir, Smiths Industries, 1991–. *Recreations:* stalking, opera, old fashioned roses, bonfires, and much else. *Address:* Oaktree House, Amberley, Arundel, West Sussex BN18 9ND. *Club:* Special Forces.

LYON, Mary Frances, ScD; FRS 1973; Deputy Director, Medical Research Council Radiobiology Unit, Harwell, 1982–90, retired; *b* 15 May 1925; *e d* of Clifford James Lyon and Louise Frances Lyon (*née* Kirby). *Educ:* King Edward's Sch., Birmingham; Woking Grammar Sch.; Girton Coll., Cambridge (ScD 1968; Hon. Fellow 1985). FIBiol. MRC Scientific Staff, Inst. of Animal Genetics, Edinburgh, 1950–55; MRC Radiobiology Unit, Harwell, 1955–90, Hd Genetics Div., 1962–87. Clothworkers Visiting Research Fellow, Girton Coll., Cambridge, 1970–71. Foreign Hon. Mem., Amer. Acad. Arts and Scis, 1980 (Amory Prize, 1977). Foreign Associate, US Nat. Acad. of Scis, 1979. Royal

Medal, Royal Soc., 1984; Prize for Genetics, Sanremo, Italy, 1985; Gairdner Foundn Award, 1985; Allan Award, Amer. Soc. of Human Genetics, 1986. *Publications:* papers on genetics in scientific jls. *Address:* MRC Radiobiology Unit, Chilton, Oxon OX11 0RD. *T:* Abingdon (0235) 834393.

LYON, Maj.-Gen. Robert, CB 1976; OBE 1964 (MBE 1960); Bursar, Loretto School, Musselburgh, 1979–91; *b* Ayr, 24 Oct. 1923; *s* of David Murray Lyon and Bridget Lyon (*née* Smith); *m* 1951, Constance Margaret Gordon (*d* 1982); one *s* one *d*. *Educ:* Ayr Academy. Commissioned, Aug. 1943, Argyll and Sutherland Highlanders. Served Italy, Germany, Palestine, Greece; transf. to Regular Commn in RA, 1947; Regtl Service, 3 RHA in Libya and 19 Field in BAOR, 1948–56; Instr, Mons Officer Cadet Sch., 1953–55; Staff Coll., 1957; DAQMG, 3 Div., 1958–60; jssc, 1960; BC F (Sphinx) Bty 7 PARA, RHA, 1961–62 (Bt Lt-Col); GSO1, ASD2, MoD, 1962–65 (Lt-Col); CO 4 Lt Regt, RA, 1965–67, Borneo (despatches), UK and BAOR (Lt-Col); as Brig.: CRA 1 Div., 1967–69, BAOR; IDC, 1970; Dir Operational Requirements, MoD, 1971–73; DRA (Maj.-Gen.), 1973–75; GOC SW District, 1975–78; retired 1979. Pres., Army Hockey Assoc., 1974–76; Chm., Army Golf Assoc., 1977–78. Chm., RA Council of Scotland, 1984–90. Col Comdt RA. Director: Braemar Civic Amenities Trust, 1986–; Edinburgh Military Tattoo Ltd, 1988–. HM Comr, Queen Victoria Sch., Dunblane, 1984–. FBIM (MBIM 1978). *Publication:* Irish Roulette, 1991. *Recreations:* golf, fishing, ski-ing, writing. *Address:* Woodside, Braemar, Aberdeenshire AB3 5YB. *T:* Braemar (03397) 41667; Appt 6 La Punta, Los Cristianos, Tenerife, Canary Is. *Club:* New (Edinburgh); Hon. Company of Edinburgh Golfers.

LYON, Stanley Douglas; Deputy Chairman, Imperial Chemical Industries Ltd, 1972–77 (Director, 1968–77); *b* 22 June 1917; *s* of late Ernest Hutcheon Lyon and Helen Wilson Lyon; *m* 1941, May Alexandra Jack; three *s*. *Educ:* George Heriot's Sch., Edinburgh; Edinburgh Univ. (BSc Hons Engrg). MICE, CBIM. Major, Royal Engrs, 1939–46. ICI Ltd: Engr, Dyestuffs Div., 1946; Engrg Dir, Wilton Works, 1957; Prodn Dir, Agricl Div., 1962; Dep. Chm. 1964, Chm. 1966, Agric. Div. *Recreations:* golf, tennis, gardening, sculpture. *Address:* Ghyll Close, West Lane, Danby, Whitby, N Yorks YO21 2LY.

LYON, Hon. Sterling, PC 1982; **Hon. Mr Justice Lyon;** a Judge of the Manitoba Court of Appeal, since 1986; *b* 30 Jan. 1927; *s* of David Rufus Lyon and Ella May (*née* Cuthbert); *m* 1953, Barbara Jean Mayers; two *s* three *d*. *Educ:* Portage Collegiate (Governor-General's Medal); United College (BA 1948); Univ. of Manitoba Law Sch. (LLB 1953). Crown Attorney, Manitoba, 1953–57; QC (Canada) 1960. Member, Manitoba Legislative Assembly, and Executive Council, 1958–69; Attorney-General, 1958–63 and 1966–69; Minister of: Municipal Affairs, 1960–61; Public Utilities, 1961–63; Mines and Natural Resources, 1963–66; Tourism and Recreation, Commissioner of Northern Affairs, 1966–68; Govt House Leader, 1966–69; Leader, Progressive Cons. Party of Manitoba, 1975–83; MLA: for Fort Garry, 1958–69; for Souris-Killarney, 1976–77; for Charleswood, 1977–86; Leader of the Opposition, Manitoba, 1976–77 and 1981–83; Premier of Manitoba and Minister of Dominion-Provincial Affairs, 1977–81. *Recreations:* hunting, fishing. *Address:* Law Courts, Winnipeg, Manitoba R3C 0V8, Canada. *T:* (204) 94592050. *Club:* Albany (Toronto).

LYON, Stewart; *see* Lyon, C. S. S.

LYON-DALBERG-ACTON, family name of **Baron Acton.**

LYONS, Bernard, CBE 1964; JP; DL; Chairman: UDS Group PLC, 1972–82 (Director, 1954–83; Joint Managing Director, 1966; Managing Director, 1972–79); Colmore Trust Ltd, since 1984; *b* 30 March 1913; *m* 1938, Lucy Hurst; three *s* one *d*. *Educ:* Leeds Grammar Sch. Chairman: Yorkshire and City Properties Ltd, 1956–73; Glanfield Securities, 1958–74. Chm., Yorkshire and NE Conciliation Cttee, Race Relations Bd, 1968–70; Member: Leeds City Council, 1951–65; Community Relations Commn, 1970–72; Govt Adv. Cttee on Retail Distribution, 1970–76. Mem. Court and Council, Univ. of Leeds, 1953–58; Chm., Swarthmore Adult Educn Centre Appeal for Building Extensions, 1957–60. Chm., Leeds Judean Youth Club, 1955–70; Jt Chm., Leeds Br., CCJ, 1955–60; Life Pres., Leeds Jewish Representative Council, 1960–. JP Leeds, 1960; DL West Riding, Yorks, 1971. Hon. LLD Leeds, 1973. *Publications:* The Thread is Strong, 1981; The Narrow Edge, 1985. *Recreations:* farming, forestry, travel, writing. *Address:* Upton Wood, Fulmer, Bucks SL3 6JJ. *T:* Fulmer (0753) 662404.
See also S. R. Lyons.

LYONS, Charles Albert; General Secretary, Transport Salaried Staffs' Association, 1982–89, retired; *b* Liverpool, 13 Aug. 1929; *s* of Maurice Lyons and Catherine Jones; *m* 1958, Judith Mary Robinson; three *s*. *Educ:* St Mary's RC Secondary Modern Sch., Fleetwood. Wages Clerk, fishing industry, 1943–47; National Service, RAPC, 1947–49; Clerical Officer, British Rail, 1950–59; Transport Salaried Staffs' Association: Clerical Asst, 1959–64; Scottish Sec., 1965–68; London Midland Div. Officer, 1968–73; Asst Gen. Sec., 1973–77; Senior Asst Gen. Sec., 1977–82; Member: TUC Gen. Council, 1983–89 (Mem. Committees: Finance and Gen. Purposes; Equal Rights; Transport; Public Enterprise; Social Insurance and Indust. Welfare; Employment, Policy and Orgn); Hotels and Catering Industrial Training Bd, 1982–84; Railway Industry Adv. Cttee, 1982–86; Jt Council for Railways, EEC; Vice-Chm., ITF Travel Bureau Section, 1979–89; individual Mem., Labour Party, 1950–. *Address:* 55 Cardy Road, Hemel Hempstead, Herts HP1 1SQ. *T:* Hemel Hempstead (0442) 212300.

LYONS, Dennis John, CB 1972; CEng, FRAeS; Director General of Research, Department of the Environment, 1971–76; *b* 26 Aug. 1916; *s* of late John Sylvester Lyons and of Adela Maud Lyons; *m* 1939, Elisabeth, *d* of Arnold and Maria Friederika Müller Haefliger, Weggis, Switzerland; five *s* two *d*. *Educ:* Grocers' Company School; Queen Mary Coll., London Univ. (Fellow, 1969). Aerodynamics Dept, Royal Aircraft Estabt, 1937; RAFVR, 1935–41; Aerodynamics Flight Aero Dept, RAE, 1941–51; Head of Experimental Projects Div., Guided Missiles Dept, RAE, 1951; Head of Ballistic Missile Group, GW Dept, 1956; Head of Weapons Dept, RAE, 1962; Dir., Road Research Laboratory, 1965–72. Member: Adv. Board for Res. Councils, 1973–76; SRC, 1973–76; Engineering Bd, SRC, 1970–76; Natural Environment Res. Council, 1973–76. Pres. OECD Road Research Unit, 1968–72. Hon. Mem., Instn Highway Engineers. *Publications:* papers in scientific jls. *Recreations:* ski-ing, pottery-making, philately. *Address:* Summerhaven, Gough Road, Fleet, Hants. *T:* Fleet (0252) 4773.

LYONS, Edward; QC 1974; LLB; a Recorder of the Crown Court, since 1972; *b* 17 May 1926; *s* of late A. Lyons and of Mrs S. Taylor; *m* 1955, Barbara, *d* of Alfred Katz; one *s* one *d*. *Educ:* Roundhay High Sch.; Leeds Univ. LLB (Hons) 1951. Served Royal Artillery, 1944–48; Combined Services Russian Course, Cambridge Univ., 1946; Interpreter in Russian, Brit. CCG, 1946–48. Called to Bar, Lincoln's Inn, 1952, Bencher, 1983. MP (Lab 1966–81, SDP 1981–83) Bradford E, 1966–74, Bradford W, 1974–83; PPS at Treasury, 1969–70; SDP Parly spokesman: on home affairs, 1981–82; on legal affairs, 1982–83. Member: H of C Select Cttee on European Legislation, 1975–83; SDP Nat. Cttee, 1984–90; Chairman: PLP Legal and Judicial Gp, 1974–77; PLP Home Office Gp, 1974–79 (Dep. Chm., 1970–74). Contested: (Lab) Harrogate, 1964; (SDP) Bradford W, 1983; (SDP) Yorkshire West, European Parly Elecn, 1984. Member: Exec. of Justice, 1974–89; Amnesty. *Recreations:* history, opera. *Address:* 4 Brick Court, Temple, EC4Y 9AD. *T:* 01–353 1492; 59 Westminster Gardens, Marsham Street, SW1P 4JG. *T:* 071–834 1960; 4 Primley Park Lane, Leeds LS17 7JR. *T:* Leeds (0532) 685351; 6 Park Square, Leeds LS1 2NG. *T:* Leeds (0532) 459763.

LYONS, Sir Edward Houghton, Kt 1977; FAIM; Chairman, Totalisator Administration Board, Queensland, 1981–85. Formerly Chairman, Katies Ltd, and Gen. Manager, Industrial Acceptance Corp. Ltd; Dir, Bruck (Australia) Ltd. Trustee, National Party. *Address:* 47 Kneale Street, Holland Park Heights, Queensland 4121, Australia. *T:* 49 6461.

LYONS, Hamilton; *b* 3 Aug. 1918; *s* of Richard Lyons and Annie Cathro Thomson; *m* 1943, Jean Cathro Blair; two *s*. *Educ:* Gourock High Sch.; Greenock High Sch.; Glasgow Univ. (BL 1940). Practised as Solicitor, Greenock, until 1966; Sheriff Substitute of Inverness, Moray, Nairn and Ross and Cromarty at Stornoway and Lochmaddy, 1966–68; Sheriff of N Strathclyde (formerly Renfrew and Argyll, and Ayr and Bute), 1968–84, retd; Temp. Sheriff, 1984–88. Member: Coun. of Law Soc. of Scotland, 1950–66 (Vice-Pres., 1962–63); Law Reform Cttee for Scotland, 1954–64; Cttee of Inquiry on Children and Young Persons, 1961–64; Cttee of Inquiry on Sheriff Courts, 1963–67; Sheriff Court Rules Coun., 1952–66; Scottish Probation Adv. and Trng Coun., 1959–69. *Address:* 14 Cloch Road, Gourock, Inverclyde PA19 1AB. *T:* Gourock (0475) 32566.

LYONS, (Isidore) Jack; Chairman: J. E. London Properties Ltd, since 1986; Natural Nutrition Company Ltd, 1989–91; Advisor, Cranbury Group, 1981–89; Director of other companies; *b* 1 Feb. 1916; *s* of Samuel H. Lyons and Sophia Niman; *m* 1943, Roslyn Marion Rosenbaum; two *s* two *d*. *Educ:* Leeds Grammar Sch. Dir, UDS Gp, 1955–80. Chm., Leeds Musical Festival, 1955–72, Vice-Pres., 1973; Chm., London Symphony Orchestra Trust, 1970–91 (Jt Chm., 1963–70), Trustee, 1970– (Hon. Mem., LSO, 1973); Jt Chm., Southwark Rehearsal Hall Trust, 1974–; Chm., Shakespeare Exhibn (quatercentenary celebrations Stratford-upon-Avon), 1964; Mem. Exec. Cttee, Royal Acad. of Dancing, 1964; Life Trustee, Shakespeare Birthplace Trust, 1967; Mem., Culture Adv. Cttee, UNESCO, 1973–, Dep. Chm., Fanfare for Europe, 1972–73; Chm., FCO US Bicentennial Cttee for the Arts, 1973–; Mem., Adv. Cttee of Honour, Britain's Salute to NY 1983 Bicentennial. Chairman: Sir Jack Lyons Charitable Trust; Musical Therapy Charity, 1984–85; Trustee, Heslington Foundn for Music and Associated Arts, 1987–; Dir, Wolf Trap Foundn, USA. Vice-Pres., Anglo-Italian Chamber of Commerce, 1977–. Vice-Pres., Jt Israel Appeal, 1972 (Dep. Chm. 1957); Chm., Fedn of Jewish Relief Organisations, 1958–86. Member: Canadian Veterans' Assoc., 1964; Pilgrims, 1965. Mem. Council, Internat. Triangle Res. Inst., 1983–. Patron, St Gemma's Hospice. Dep. Chm., Governors of Carmel Coll., 1961–69; Mem. Ct, York Univ., 1965. FRSA 1973. Hon. FRAM, 1972. DUniv York, 1975. *Recreations:* music, the arts and swimming.

LYONS, Sir James (Reginald), Kt 1969; JP; Chairman and Company Director, Park Lodge Property Company; Airport Manager, Cardiff Airport, 1955–75; *b* 15 March 1910; *s* of James Lyons; *m* 1937, Doreen Mary Fogg; one *s*. *Educ:* Howard Gardens High Sch.; Cardiff Technical Coll. Served War of 1939–45: Royal Tank Regt, 1940–46 (1939–45 Star, Africa Star, Italy Star, Defence Medal, War Medal of 1939–45). Civil Service, 1929–65: Post Office, Min. of Supply, Min. of Aviation. Mem., Wales Tourist Bd. Glamorgan CC, 1965–74; Cardiff City Council: Councillor, 1949–58; Alderman, 1958–74; Lord Mayor of Cardiff, 1968–69. Mem., Norfolk Cttee for investiture of Prince of Wales, 1968–69. Mem., BBC Broadcasting Council. Assessor under Race Relations Act, 1976. President: Welsh Games Council, 1985– (Life Vice-Pres., 1975); Cardiff Horticultural Soc., 1962–. Trustee, Wales and Border Counties TSB. Chairman of Governors: UC Cardiff, 1955–70; St Illtyd's Coll., 1956–; Governor, De La Salle Prep. Sch. JP Cardiff, 1966–. OStJ; KCSG. *Recreations:* Rugby football, swimming, tennis. *Address:* 101 Minehead Avenue, Sully, S Glam CF6 2TL. *T:* Sully (0222) 530403.

LYONS, Sir John, Kt 1987; FBA 1973; Master of Trinity Hall, Cambridge, since 1984; *b* 23 May 1932; *s* of Michael A. Lyons and Mary B. Lyons (*née* Sullivan); *m* 1959, Danielle J. Simonet; two *d*. *Educ:* St Bede's Coll., Manchester; Christ's Coll., Cambridge. MA; PhD 1961; LittD 1988. Lecturer: in Comparative Linguistics, SOAS, 1957–61; in General Linguistics, Univ. of Cambridge, 1961–64; Prof. of General Linguistics, Edinburgh Univ., 1964–76; Prof. of Linguistics, 1976–84, Pro-Vice-Chancellor, 1981–84, Sussex Univ. DèsL (*hc*) Univ. Catholique de Louvain, 1980; Hon. DLitt: Reading, 1986; Edinburgh, 1988; Sussex, 1990. *Publications:* Structural Semantics, 1964; Introduction to Theoretical Linguistics, 1968; New Horizons in Linguistics, 1970; Chomsky, 1970, 3rd edn 1991; Semantics, vols 1 and 2, 1977; Language and Linguistics, 1981; Language, Meaning and Context, 1981, 2nd edn 1991; Natural Language and Universal Grammar, 1991; articles and reviews in learned journals. *Address:* The Master's Lodge, Trinity Hall, Cambridge CB2 1TJ.

LYONS, John, CBE 1986; General Secretary, Engineers' and Managers' Association, 1977–91, and Electrical Power Engineers' Association, 1973–91; *b* 19 May 1926; *s* of Joseph and Hetty Lyons; *m* 1954, Molly McCall; two *s* two *d*. *Educ:* St Paul's Sch.; Polytechnic, Regent Street; Cambridge Univ. (BA Econ). RN 1944–46. Asst. to Manager of Market Research Dept, Vacuum Oil Co., 1950; Research Officer: Bureau of Current Affairs, 1951; Post Office Engineering Union, 1952–57; Asst. Sec., Instn of Professional Civil Servants 1957–66, Dep. Gen. Sec. 1966–73. Member: TUC Gen. Council, 1983–91; Nat. Enterprise Bd, 1975–79; Exec. Cttee PEP, 1975–78; Council, PSI, 1978–80; Adv. Council for Applied R&D, 1978–81; Engrg Council, 1982–86; PO Bd, 1980–81, British Telecommunications Bd, 1981–83; Sec., Electricity Supply Trade Union Council (formerly Employees' Nat. Cttee for Electricity Supply Industry), 1976–91; Chm., NEDO Working Party on Industrial Trucks, 1977–80. A Vice-Pres., Industrial Participation Assoc., 1976–90; Mem., Econ. and Social Cttee, EC, 1990–. Governor, Kingsbury High School, 1974–86; Member: Court of Governors, LSE, 1978–84; Bd of Governors, London Business Sch., 1987–88. Hitachi Lectr, Sussex Univ., 1983; addresses and papers to: British Assoc., 1973; IEE, 1977; Internat. Monetary Conference, 1984; Newcastle Univ., 1989. FRSA. *Publications:* various papers and articles. *Recreation:* family. *Address:* 305 Salmon Street, Kingsbury, NW9 8YA.

LYONS, Prof. Malcolm Cameron; Sir Thomas Adams's Professor of Arabic, University of Cambridge, since 1985; Fellow, since 1957, President, since 1989, Pembroke College, Cambridge; *b* Indore, India, 11 Feb. 1929; *s* of Harold William Lyons and Florence Katharine (*née* Cameron); *m* 1961, Ursula Schedler. *Educ:* New Park Sch., St Andrews; Fettes Coll.; Pembroke Coll., Cambridge (Major Open Classical Schol., 1946; John Stewart of Rannoch Classical Schol. in Latin and Greek, 1948; Browne Medallist, 1948, 1949; 1st cl. hons Pts I and II, Classical Tripos, 1948, 1949; 1st cl. hons Pts I and II, Oriental Studies, Arabic and Persian, 1953; E. G. Browne Prize, 1953; MA 1954; PhD 1957). RAF, 1949–51, commissioned 1950. University of Cambridge: Asst Lectr in Arabic, 1954–59; Lectr, 1959–84; Reader in Medieval Islamic Studies, 1984–85. Seconded to FO as Principal Instructor, MECAS, Lebanon, 1961–62. Founder Editor: Arabic Technical and Scientific Texts, 1966–78; Jl of Arabic Literature, 1970–. *Publications:* Galen on Anatomical Procedures (with W. Duckworth and B. Towers), 1962; In

Hippocratis de Officina Medici, 1963, and De Partibus Artis Medicativae, De Causis Contentivis, De Diaeta in Morbis Acutis (in Corpus Medicorum Graecorum), 1967; An Arabic Translation of Themistius' Commentary on Aristotle's De Anima, 1973; Aristotle's Ars Rhetorica, Arabic version, 1982; (with E. Maalouf) The Poetic Vocabulary of Michel Trad, 1968; (with J. Riley-Smith and U. Lyons) Ayyubids, Mamlukes and Crusaders, 1971; (with D. Jackson) Saladin, The Politics of the Holy War, 1982; articles and reviews in learned jls. *Recreations:* golf, ski-ing, walking. *Address:* Pembroke College, Cambridge CB1 2RF. *T:* Cambridge (0223) 352241. *Club:* Royal and Ancient Golf (St Andrews).

LYONS, Michael Thomas; Chief Executive, Nottinghamshire County Council, since 1990; *b* West Ham, 15 Sept. 1949; *s* of Thomas Lyons and Lillian Lyons (*née* Stafford); *m* Gwendolene Jane Calvert; two *s* one *d*. *Educ:* Stratford Grammar Sch.; Middlesex Polytechnic (BA Soc. Scis Hons); Queen Mary Coll., London (MSc Econ). Street market trader, 1970–72; Brand Manager, Crookes-Anestan, 1971–72; Lectr and Res. Fellow, Dept of Industrial Econs, Univ. of Nottingham, 1973–75; Sen. Res. Officer, DoE, 1975–78; W Midlands County Council: Principal Economist, 1978–82; Dep. Dir and Dir, Economic Develt, 1982–85; Chief Exec., Wolverhampton MBC, 1985–90. Councillor, Birmingham City Council, 1980–83. FRSA. *Publications:* (ed with A. Johnson) The Winning Bid, 1991; contribs to professional jls. *Recreations:* a young and energetic family, cinema, walking. *Address:* Nottinghamshire County Council, County Hall, West Bridgeford, Notts. *T:* Nottingham (0602) 823823.

LYONS, Stuart Randolph; Chairman and Chief Executive, Royal Doulton Ltd, since 1987 (Managing Director, 1985–87); Chairman: Lawleys Ltd, since 1985; The Royal Crown Derby Porcelain Co. Ltd, Minton Ltd, China Millers Ltd, Royal Doulton subsidiaries in USA, Canada, Australia, Belgium and Hong Kong, since 1987; *b* 24 Oct. 1943; 3rd *s* of Bernard Lyons, *qv*; *m* 1969, Ellen Harriet Zion; two *s* one *d*. *Educ:* Rugby (Scholar); King's Coll., Cambridge (Major Scholar; 1st Cl. Hons Pt I Classical Tripos, Cl. II(I) Pt II Classical Tripos; BA 1965, MA 1969). Man. Dir, John Collier Tailoring Ltd, 1969–74 (Chm., 1975–83); Dir, UDS Group plc, 1974–83 (Man. Dir, 1979–83); Chairman: Wm Timpson, 1976–83; Richard Shops, 1982–83. Director: British Ceramic Res. Ltd, 1987–; Royal Doulton Dodwell KK (Japan), 1988–; estabd Sir Henry Doulton Sch. of Sculpture, 1986, Trustee, 1987–. Member: Leeds CC, 1970–74; Yorkshire and Humberside Econ. Planning Council, 1972–75; Clothing EDC, 1976–79; Ordnance Survey Review Cttee, 1978–79; Monopolies and Mergers Commn, 1981–85; Dir, Staffs TEC, 1990–. Pres., BCMF, 1989–90; Chm., British Ceramic Confedn, 1989–. Mem. Council, Keele Univ., 1989–. Contested (C) Halifax, Feb. and Oct. 1974. *Address:* Minton House, London Road, Stoke-on-Trent ST4 7QD. *T:* Stoke-on-Trent (0782) 744766. *Clubs:* Carlton, Hurlingham.

LYONS, Terence Patrick; a consultant, since 1983; Director, Industrial Training Services Ltd, since 1980; *b* 2 Sept. 1919; *s* of Maurice Peter Lyons and Maude Mary Elizabeth Lyons (*née* O'Farrell); *m* 1945, Winifred Mary Normile; two *d*. *Educ:* Wimbledon Coll.; King's College, London; London Sch. of Economics. CompIPM, FCIB. Indian Armd Corps, 1940–46. Unilever Ltd, 1948–54; Philips Electrical Industries Ltd, 1954–60; Ilford Ltd, 1960–66; Dir of Personnel, Staveley Industries Ltd, 1966–69; Exec. Dir (Personnel), 1969–81, Dir, 1981–82, Williams & Glyn's Bank Ltd. Associate Dir, Hurst Associates (Europe), 1989–. Sen. Vis. Fellow, City Univ. Business Sch., 1983–86. Pres., Inst. of Personnel Management, 1971–73; Mem. Council, Inst. Bankers, 1975–81; Chairman: Manpower Services Adv. Panel, CBI, 1975–82; Educn and Trng Cttee, CBI, 1976–77 (Vice-Chm., 1977–82); Council, Fedn of London Clearing Bank Employers, 1976–78 (Mem., 1971–81); IPM Career Counselling and Outplacement Forum, 1990–. Member: Monopolies and Mergers Commn, 1975–81; MSC, 1981–82; EEC Vocational Trng Cttee, 1981–84. Member Council: Open Univ., 1980–90 (Chm., Council's Staff Cttee, 1980–90); CBI Educn Foundn, 1976–86. DUniv Open, 1990. *Publications:* The Personnel Function in a Changing Environment, 1971, 2nd edn 1985; contrib. newspapers and personnel management and banking jls. *Recreations:* sailing, golf, music. *Address:* Winter Ride, 2 Rosefield, Kippington Road, Sevenoaks, Kent TN13 2LJ. *Clubs:* Army and Navy; Wildernesse Golf; Royal Eastbourne Golf; Chipstead Sailing.

LYSAGHT, family name of **Baron Lisle.**

LYTHALL, Basil Wilfrid, CB 1966; MA; occasional research consultant; *b* 15 May 1919; *s* of Frank Herbert Lythall and Winifred Mary (*née* Carver); *m* 1942, Mary Olwen Dando; one *s*. *Educ:* King Edward's Sch., Stourbridge; Christ Church, Oxford. Joined Royal Naval Scientific Service, 1940; Admiralty Signal and Radar Establishment, 1940–53; Admiralty Research Laboratory, 1954–57; Asst Dir of Physical Research, Admty, 1957–58; a Dep. Chief Scientist, Admty Signal and Radar Estabt (later Admty Surface Weapons Estabt), 1958–60; first Chief Scientist of Admty Underwater Weapons Estabt, Portland, 1960–64; Member of Admiralty Bd of Defence Council and Chief Scientist (Royal Navy), 1964–78; Dep. Controller, R&D Estab., Procurement Exec., 1971–78; Dir, SACLANT Anti-Submarine Warfare Res. Centre, La Spezia, Italy, 1978–81. Chm., Policy Bd, Centre for Operational Res. and Defence Analysis, CAP Scientific Ltd, 1986–88. Technical Advr, Monopolies and Mergers Commn, 1989, 1990. Trustee, National Maritime Museum, 1974–80. UK Mem., Editorial Bd, Naval Forces, 1986–. *Publications:* occasional articles in learned jls. *Recreations:* gardening, sculpting, genealogy. *Address:* 48 Grove Way, Esher, Surrey KT10 8HL. *T:* 081–398 2958.

LYTHGO, Wilbur Reginald, OBE 1964; HM Diplomatic Service, retired; *b* 7 June 1920; *yr s* of late Alfred and Marion Lythgo, Monkton, Ayrshire; *m* 1943, Patricia Frances Sylvia Smith; two *s*. *Educ:* Palmer's Sch., Grays, Essex. Joined Home Office, 1937. Served in RASC, 1939–41 and Indian Army, 1941–46. Rejoined Home Office, 1946; British Information Services, New Delhi, 1948–54; UK High Commn, New Delhi, 1956–59; British High Commn, Ottawa, 1962–66; Head of Office Services and Supply Dept, DSAO, 1966–68; Counsellor, British Embassy, and Consul-Gen., Washington DC, 1968–71; Consul-Gen., Cleveland, Ohio, 1971–73. Hon. Kentucky Col, 1971. *Recreations:* reading, gardening. *Address:* 200 Dovercourt Avenue, Ottawa, Ontario K1Z 7H2, Canada. *T:* (613) 722 3242.

LYTHGOE, Prof. Basil, FRS 1958; Professor of Organic Chemistry, Leeds University, 1953–78, now Emeritus; *b* 18 Aug. 1913; 2nd *s* of Peter Whitaker and Agnes Lythgoe; *m* 1946, Kathleen Cameron, *er d* of H. J. Hallum, St Andrews; two *s*. *Educ:* Leigh Grammar Sch.; Manchester Univ. Asst Lectr, Manchester Univ., 1938; Univ. Lectr, Cambridge Univ., 1946. Fellow of King's Coll., Cambridge, 1950. *Publications:* papers on chemistry of natural products, in Jl of Chem. Soc. *Recreation:* mountaineering. *Address:* 113 Cookridge Lane, Leeds LS16 7NB. *T:* Leeds (0532) 678837.

LYTHGOE, Ian Gordon, CB 1975; company director, retired; *b* 30 Dec. 1914; *s* of John and Susan Lythgoe; *m* 1st, 1939, Marjory Elsie Fleming; three *s*; 2nd, 1971, Mary Margaret Pickard, CBE 1980. *Educ:* Southland Boys' High Sch., Invercargill; Victoria UC, Wellington. MComm (Hons); FCA(NZ). Private Sec., Ministers of Finance, 1944–53; Asst Sec., Treasury, 1962; State Services Commission: Mem., 1964–66; Dep. Chm., 1967–70; Chm., 1971–74. NZ Soc. of Accountants: Mem. Council, 1966–76; Vice-Pres., 1973–74; Pres., 1974–75; Chm., Disciplinary Cttee, 1982–87 (Mem., 1979–87). Mem. Council, Central Inst. of Technology, 1977–86 (Vice Chm., 1978–80, Chm., 1980–86). Member: Commn of Enquiry into Rescue and Fire Safety at Internat. Airports (NZ); Information Authority, 1982–88; Commn of Enquiry concerning Ian David Donaldson, 1983. Director: Fletcher Challenge Corp. Ltd (formerly Challenge Corp. Ltd), 1975–84; Philips Electrical Industries Ltd, 1975–87. *Recreations:* gardening, reading. *Address:* 6A/19 Cottleville Terrace, Wellington 711–961, New Zealand. *Club:* Wellington (Wellington, NZ).

LYTTELTON, family name of **Viscount Chandos** and of **Viscount Cobham.**

LYTTELTON, Humphrey Richard Adeane; musician; band-leader (specializing in Jazz); journalist; *b* Eton, Bucks, 23 May 1921; *s* of late Hon. George William Lyttelton; *m* 1st, 1948, Patricia Mary Braithwaite (marr. diss. 1952); one *d*; 2nd, 1952, Elizabeth Jill, *d* of Albert E. Richardson; two *s* one *d*. *Educ:* Sunningdale Sch.; Eton Coll.; Camberwell Sch. of Art; self-taught as regards musical educn. Served War of 1939–45: Grenadier Guards, 1941–46. Cartoonist, Daily Mail, 1949–53. Formed his own band, 1948; leader of Humphrey Lyttelton's Band, and free-lance journalist, 1953–; founded: own record label, Calligraph, 1984; own music publishers, Humph Music. Has composed over 150 original works for his band; numerous recordings and television appearances; jazz festival appearances, Nice, Bracknell, Zürich, Camden, Montreux, Newcastle, Warsaw. Compère, BBC radio jazz programmes: Jazz Scene, Jazz Club, The Best of Jazz, etc. Pres., Soc. for Italic Handwriting, 1990–. Hon. DLitt: Warwick, 1987; Loughborough, 1988; Hon. DMus Durham, 1989. *Publications:* I Play as I Please, 1954; Second Chorus, 1958; Take It from the Top (autobiog.), 1975; The Best of Jazz: Basin Street to Harlem, 1978; Humphrey Lyttelton's Jazz and Big Band Quiz, 1979; The Best of Jazz 2—Enter the Giants, 1981; Why No Beethoven? the diary of a vagrant musician, 1984; contributor: Melody Maker, 1954–; Reynolds News, 1955–62; Sunday Citizen, 1962–67; Harper's & Queen's, Punch, The Field, High Life. *Recreations:* birdwatching, calligraphy. *Address:* BBC Light Music Department, Broadcasting House, Portland Place, W1A 4WW. *T:* 071–580 4468; (home) Alyn Close, Barnet Road, Arkley, Herts.

LYTTLE, James Brian Chambers; Secretary, Probation Board for Northern Ireland, since 1987; *b* 22 Aug. 1932; *s* of late James Chambers Lyttle and Margaret Kirkwood Billingsley; *m* 1957, Mary Alma Davidson; four *d*. *Educ:* Bangor Grammar Sch.; Trinity Coll., Dublin (BA 1st Cl. Hons Classics). Entered NI Civil Service as Asst Principal, 1954; Private Sec. to Minister of Commerce, 1960–62; Chief Exec., Enterprise Ulster, 1972–75; Dir, Employment Service, Dept of Manpower Services, 1975–77; Dir, Industrial Develt Orgn, Dept of Commerce, 1977–81; Under Secretary, Dept of Commerce, later Dept of Economic Develt, 1977–84; Under Sec., Dept of Finance and Personnel, 1984–87. *Recreations:* reading, walking, music.

LYTTLETON, Prof. Raymond Arthur, MA, PhD; FRS 1955; Emeritus Professor of Theoretical Astronomy, University of Cambridge; Fellow of St John's College, Cambridge; Member, Institute of Astronomy (formerly Institute of Theoretical Astronomy), University of Cambridge, since 1967; *b* 7 May 1911; *o s* of William John Lyttleton and Agnes (*d* of Patrick Joseph Kelly), Warley Woods, near Birmingham, formerly of Ireland; *m* Meave Marguerite, *o d* of F. Hobden, Parkstone, formerly of Shanghai; no *c*. *Educ:* King Edward's Grammar Sch., Five Ways; King Edward's Sch., Birmingham; Clare Coll., Cambridge. Wrangler; Tyson Medal for Astronomy. Procter Visiting Fellowship, Princeton Univ., USA; Exptl Officer, Min. of Supply, 1940–42; Technical Asst to Scientific Adviser to the Army Council, War Office, 1943–45. Lectr in Mathematics, 1937–59, Stokes Lectr, 1954–59, Reader in Theoretical Astronomy, 1959–69 (resigned), Univ. of Cambridge. Jacob Siskind Vis. Prof., Brandeis Univ., USA, 1965–66; Vis. Prof., Brown Univ., USA, 1967–68; Halley Lectr, Oxford Univ., 1970; Milne Lectr, Oxford, 1978. Mem. of Council, Royal Society, 1959–61; Geophysical Sec. of Royal Astronomical Soc., 1949–60 and Mem. of Council, 1950–61, 1969–72; Fellow, 1934–; Pres., Milne Soc., 1977–88. Hon. Mem., Mark Twain Soc., 1977. Hopkins Prize (for 1951) of Cambridge Philosophical Soc.; Gold Medallist of Royal Astronomical Soc., 1959; Royal Medallist of Royal Society, 1965. *Publications:* The Comets and their Origin, 1953; The Stability of Rotating Liquid Masses, 1953; The Modern Universe, 1956; Rival Theories of Cosmology, 1960; Man's View of the Universe, 1961; Mysteries of the Solar System, 1968; (Play) A Matter of Gravity (produced by BBC, 1968); Cambridge Encyclopædia of Astronomy (co-ed and contrib.), 1977; The Earth and Its Mountains, 1982; papers on astrophysics, cosmogony, cosmology, physics, dynamics, and geophysics in Proc. Royal Soc., Monthly Notices of Royal Astron. Soc., Proc. Camb. Phil Soc., etc. *Recreations:* motoring, music; wondering about it all. *Address:* 48 St Alban's Road, Cambridge. *T:* Cambridge (0223) 354910; St John's College, Cambridge. *T:* Cambridge (0223) 338600; Institute of Astronomy, Madingley Road, Cambridge. *T:* Cambridge (0223) 337548, ext. 7506.

LYTTON, family name of **Earl of Lytton.**

LYTTON, 5th Earl of, *cr* 1880; **John Peter Michael Scawen Lytton;** Baron Wentworth, 1529; Bt 1838; Baron Lytton, 1866; Viscount Knebworth, 1880; Sole practitioner, John Lytton & Co., Chartered Surveyors and Valuers, since 1988; *b* 7 June 1950; *s* of 4th Earl of Lytton, OBE, and of Clarissa Mary, *d* of Brig.-Gen. C. E. Palmer, CB, CMG, DSO, RA; *S* father, 1985; *m* 1980, Ursula Alexandra (*née* Komoly); one *s* one *d*. *Educ:* Downside; Reading Univ. (BSc, Estate Management). FRICS 1987 (ARICS 1976); IRRV 1990. *Heir:* *s* Viscount Knebworth, *qv*. *Address:* (office) Estate Office, Newbuildings Place, Shipley, Horsham, West Sussex RH13 7JQ. *T:* Coolham (0403) 741650.

LYTTON COBBOLD, family name of **Baron Cobbold.**

LYVEDEN, 6th Baron *cr* 1859; **Ronald Cecil Vernon;** retired; *b* 10 April 1915; *s* of 5th Baron Lyveden and Ruby (*née* Shanley) (*d* 1932); *S* father 1973; *m* 1938, Queenie Constance, *d* of Howard Ardern; three *s*. *Educ:* Te Aroha College. *Heir:* *e s* Hon. Jack Leslie Vernon [*b* 10 Nov. 1938; *m* 1961, Lynette June, *d* of William Herbert Lilley; one *s* two *d*]. *Address:* 20 Farmer Street, Te Aroha, New Zealand. *T:* 410. *Club:* RSA (Te Aroha).

M

MA LIN, Hon. CBE 1983; PhD; JP; Emeritus Professor of Biochemistry, and Chairman of Board of Trustees of Shaw College, since 1986, The Chinese University of Hong Kong; *b* 8 Feb. 1925; *s* of late Prof. Ma Kiam and Sing-yu Cheng; *m* 1958, Dr Meng-Hua Chen; three *d. Educ:* West China Union Univ., China (BSc); Univ. of Leeds (PhD). Post-doctorate Fellow, University College Hosp. Med. Sch., London, and St James's Hosp., Leeds, 1955–56. Assistant Lectr, 1957–59, and Lectr, 1959–64, in Clinical Chemistry, Dept of Pathology, Univ. of Hong Kong; Chinese University of Hong Kong: part-time Lectr in Chemistry, 1964; Sen. Lectr, 1965–72, Reader, 1972–73, Prof., 1973–78, in Biochemistry; Dean of Faculty of Science, 1973–75; Vice-Chancellor, 1978–87. Visiting Biochemist, Hormone Research Laboratory, Univ. of California, San Francisco, 1969. FRSA 1982. Unofficial JP, 1978. Hon. DSc Sussex, 1984; Hon. DLit East Asia, 1987; Hon. LLD Chinese Univ. of Hong Kong, 1987; Hon. DHL SUNY, 1989. Order of the Rising Sun, Gold Rays, with neck ribbon (Japan), 1986; Commander's Cross, Order of Merit (FRG), 1988. *Publications:* various research papers in academic jls. *Recreations:* swimming, table-tennis. *Address:* 95 Sunderland Estate, Hereford Road, Kowloon, Hong Kong.

MAAN, Bashir Ahmed, JP; DL; Chairman: Strathcylde Community Relations Council, since 1986; Strathclyde Interpreting Services Advisory Committee, since 1988; Bailie, City of Glasgow, 1980–84; Judge, City of Glasgow District Courts; *b* Maan, Gujranwala, Pakistan, 22 Oct. 1926; *s* of Choudhry Sardar Khan Maan and late Mrs Hayat Begum Maan; *m*; one *s* three *d. Educ:* D. B. High Sch., Qila Didar Singh; Panjab Univ. Involved in struggle for creation of Pakistan, 1943–47; organised rehabilitation of refugees from India in Maan and surrounding areas, 1947–48; emigrated to UK and settled in Glasgow, 1953; Glasgow Founder Sec., Pakistan Social and Cultural Soc., 1955–65, Pres., 1966–69; Vice-Chm., Glasgow Community Relations Council, 1970–75; Pres., Standing Conf. of Pakistani Orgns in UK, 1974–77; a Dep. Chm., Commn for Racial Equality, 1977–80; Founder Chm., Scottish Pakistani Assoc., 1984–. Hon. Res. Fellow, Univ. of Glasgow, 1988–. Councillor, Glasgow Corp., 1970–75, City of Glasgow Dist, 1974–84; Magistrate, City of Glasgow, 1971–74; Vice-Chm. 1971–74, Chm. 1974–75, Police Cttee, Glasgow Corp.; Police Judge, City of Glasgow, 1974–75; Mem. Exec. Cttee, Glasgow City Labour Party, 1969–70. Contested (Lab) East Fife, Feb. 1974. Mem., BBC Immigrants Programme Adv. Cttee, 1972–80; Convener, Pakistan Bill Action Cttee, 1973; Member: Nat. Road Safety Cttee, 1971–75; Scottish Accident Prevention Cttee, 1971–75; Scottish Gas Consumers' Council, 1978–81; Greater Glasgow Health Bd, 1981–91; Management Bd, Scottish Council for Voluntary Orgns, 1988–. Chm., Organising Cttee, Glasgow Internat. Sports Festival Co. Ltd, 1987–89. Mem. Bd of Governors, Jordanhill Coll. of Educn, Glasgow, 1987–. JP 1968, DL 1982, Glasgow. *Publications:* articles, contrib. to press. *Recreations:* golf, reading. *Address:* 8 Riverview Gardens, Flat 6, Glasgow G5 8EL. *T:* 041–429 7689. *Club:* Douglas Park Golf.

MAAZEL, Lorin; symphony conductor; Music Director, Pittsburgh Symphony Orchestra, since 1988; *b* 6 March 1930; *s* of Lincoln Maazel and Marie Varencove; *m* 3rd, 1986, Dietlinde Turban; two *s*, and one *s* three *d* by previous marriages. *Educ:* Pittsburgh University. FRCM 1981. Début as a conductor at age of 9, as violinist a few years later; by 1941 had conducted foremost US Orchestras, including Toscanini's NBC; European début as conductor, 1953; active as conductor in Europe, Latin America, Australia, Japan and USA, 1954–; performances at major festivals, including Edinburgh, Bayreuth, Salzburg and Lucerne; in USA: conducted Boston Symphony, New York Philharmonic, Philadelphia Orchestra, and at Metropolitan, 1960 and 1962; Covent Garden début, 1978. Artistic Director of Deutsche Oper Berlin, 1965–71; Chief Conductor, Radio Sinfonie Orchester, Berlin, 1965–75; Associate Principal Conductor, Philharmonia (formerly New Philharmonia) Orchestra, 1970–72, Principal Guest Conductor, 1976–80; Music Director, Cleveland Orchestra, 1972–82, Conductor Emeritus, 1982; Principal Guest Conductor, 1977–88, Music Director, 1988–90, Orchestre National de France; Director, Vienna State Opera, 1982–84. Has made numerous recordings. Hon. Dr of Music Pittsburgh Univ., 1968; Hon. Dr of Humanities Beaver Coll., 1973; Hon. Dr of Fine Arts, Carnegie-Mellon Univ., Pennsylvania; Hon. Dr of Music, RCM, 1984; Hon. DCL Univ. of South, Sewanee, 1988; Hon. Dr Indiana Univ., 1988. Sibelius Medal, Finland, 1969. Commander's Cross of Order of Merit, Federal Republic of Germany, 1977; Officier, Légion d'Honneur, France, 1981. *Address:* c/o Helga Hazelrig, Holbeinstrasse 14, D-8000 Munich 80, Federal Republic of Germany.

MABBS, Alfred Walter, CB 1982; Keeper of Public Records, 1978–82; *b* 12 April 1921; *e s* of James and Amelia Mabbs; *m* 1942, Dorothy Lowley; one *s. Educ:* Hackney Downs Sch. Served War, RAF, 1941–46. Asst Keeper, Public Record Office, 1950–66; Principal Asst Keeper, 1967–69; Records Admin. Officer, 1970–73; Dep. Keeper of Public Records, 1973–78. Pres., Internat. Council on Archives, 1980–82. FRHistS 1954. FSA 1979. *Publications:* Guild Stewards Book of the Borough of Calne (vol. vii, Wilts Arch. and Record Soc.), 1953; The Records of the Cabinet Office to 1922, 1966; Guide to the Contents of the Public Record Office, vol. iii (main contributor), 1968; Exchequer of the Jews, vol. iv (jt contrib.), 1972; The Organisation of Intermediate Records Storage (with Guy Duboscq), 1974; articles and reviews in various jls. *Recreations:* golf, reading. *Address:* 32 The Street, Wallington, Herts SG7 6SW.

MABEY, Richard Thomas; writer and broadcaster; *b* 20 Feb. 1941; *s* of late Thomas Gustavus Mabey and of Edna Nellie (*née* Moore). *Educ:* Berkhamsted Sch.; St Catherine's Coll., Oxford (BA Hons 1964, MA 1971). Lectr in Social Studies, Dacorum Coll. of Further Educn, 1963–65; Sen. Editor, Penguin Books, 1966–73; freelance writer, 1973–. Pres., London Wildlife Trust, 1982–; Member: Nature Conservancy Council, 1982–86; Council, Botanical Soc. of the British Isles, 1981–83. Dir, Common Ground, 1988–. Patron, Thomas Bewick Trust, 1986–. Leverhulme Trust Res. Award, 1983–84. *Publications:* (ed) Class, 1967; The Pop Process, 1969; Food for Free, 1972, 2nd edn 1989; Children in Primary School, 1972; The Unofficial Countryside, 1973; The Pollution Handbook, 1973; The Roadside Wildlife Book, 1974; Street Flowers, 1976 (TES Inf. Book Award); Plants with a Purpose, 1977; The Common Ground, 1980; The Flowering of Britain, 1980; (ed) Landscape with Figures, 1983; Oak and Company, 1983 (NY Acad. of Sci. Children's Book Award, 1984); In a Green Shade, 1983; Back to the Roots, 1983; (ed) Second Nature, 1984; The Frampton Flora, 1985; Gilbert White: a biography, 1986 (Whitbread Biography Award); Gen. Ed., The Journals of Gilbert White, 1986–89; (ed) The Gardener's Labyrinth, 1987; The Flowering of Kew, 1988; Home Country, 1989; (ed) The Flowers of May, 1990. *Recreations:* food, woods, walking, gardening. *Address:* 10 Cedar Road, Berkhamsted, Herts HP4 2LA. *Club:* Groucho.

MABON, Rt. Hon. (Jesse) Dickson, PC 1977; company director and physician; *b* 1 Nov. 1925; *s* of Jesse Dickson Mabon and Isabel Simpson Montgomery; *m* 1970, Elizabeth, *o d* of Maj. William Zinn; one *s. Educ:* Possilpark, Cumbrae, North Kelvinside Schools. Worked in coalmining industry before Army service, 1944–48. MB, ChB (Glasgow); DHMSA; MFHom; Visiting Physician, Manor House Hospital, London, 1958–64. Political columnist, Scottish Daily Record, 1955–64; studied under Dr Kissinger, Harvard, 1963. President: Glasgow University Union, 1951–52; Scottish Union of Students, 1954–55; Chairman: Glasgow Univ. Labour Club, 1948–50; National Assoc. of Labour Students, 1949–50. Contested: (Lab) Bute and N Ayrshire, 1951; (Lab and Co-op) W Renfrewshire, 1955; Renfrew W and Inverclyde (SDP) 1983, (SDP/Alliance) 1987; (SDP) Lothians, European Parly Election, 1984. MP (Lab and Co-op 1955–81, SDP 1981–83) Greenock, Dec. 1955–1974, Greenock and Port Glasgow, 1974–83; Joint Parly Under-Sec. of State for Scotland, 1964–67; Minister of State, Scottish Office, 1967–70; Dep. Opposition Spokesman on Scotland, 1970–72 (resigned over Labour's attitude to Common Mkt); Minister of State, Dept of Energy, 1976–79. Chairman: UK Labour Cttee for Europe, 1974–76; Scottish Parly Labour Party, 1972–73, 1975–76; Member: Council of Europe, 1970–72 and 1974–76; Assembly, WEU, 1970–72 and 1974–76; North Atlantic Assembly, 1980–82; Chm., European Movement, 1975–76, Dep. Chm., 1979–83. Founder Chm., Manifesto Gp, Parly Lab. Party, 1974–76. Founder Mem., SDP, 1981; Mem., SDP Nat. Cttee, 1984–88; Chm., Scottish Social and Liberal Democrats, 1988. Chm., Young Volunteer Force Foundn, 1974–76. Fellow: Inst. of Petroleum; Inst. of Directors; Faculty of History of Medicine (Pres. 1990–); Soc. of Apothecaries; FRSA. Freeman of City of London. *Recreations:* gardening, theatre. *Address:* 57 Hillway, N6 6AD. *T:* 081–340 5189; 2 Sandringham, Largs, Ayrshire KA30 8BT. *T:* Largs (0475) 672293.

MABY, (Alfred) Cedric, CBE 1962; HM Diplomatic Service, retired; *b* 6 April 1915; 4th *s* of late Joseph Maby, Penrose, Monmouthshire; *m* 1944, Anne-Charlotte, *d* of Envoyén Einar Modig, Stockholm; one *s* two *d. Educ:* Cheltenham; Keble Coll., Oxford. Joined HM Consular Service, 1939. Served at Peking, 1939, Chungking, 1940, Tsingtao, 1941, Istanbul, 1943, Angora, 1944, Buenos Aires, 1946, Caracas, 1949, Singapore, 1954; Counsellor and Consul-General, Peking, 1957–59 (Chargé d'Affaires, 1957 and 1958); Deputy Consul-General, New York, 1959–62; Counsellor (Commercial) at Vienna, 1962–64; Asst Sec., Min. of Overseas Development, 1964–67; Consul-General, Zürich and Liechtenstein, 1968–71; Dir, Trade Promotion for Switzerland, 1970–71. Member: Governing Body, Church in Wales, 1975–78; Church in Wales Adv. Commn on Church and Society, 1977–86. Fellow, Huguenot Soc., London, 1977. High Sheriff of Gwynedd, 1976. *Publications:* Dail Melyn o Tseina, 1983; Y Cocatŵ Coch, 1987; contribs to Planet, Y Faner and other Welsh periodicals. *Address:* Cae Canol, Minffordd, Penrhyn-Deudraeth, Gwynedd LL48 6EN.

McADAM, Sir Ian (William James), Kt 1966; OBE 1957; FRCS, FRCSE; *b* 15 Feb. 1917; *s* of W. J. McAdam and Alice Culverwell; *m* 1st, 1939, Hrothgarde Gibson (marr. diss. 1961); one *s* two *d*; 2nd, 1967, Lady (Pamela) Hunt (*née* Medawar). *Educ:* Plumtree Sch., S Rhodesia; Edinburgh Univ. MB, ChB. Cambridge Anatomy Sch., 1940; Dept of Surgery, Edinburgh, 1942; Wilkie Surgical Research Fellow, 1942; Clinical Tutor, Royal Infirmary, Edinburgh, 1942; Surgical Specialist, Uganda, 1946; Senior Consultant, Uganda, 1957; Prof. of Surgery, Makerere Univ., Univ. of E Africa, 1957–72, also Consultant Surgeon Uganda Govt and Kenyatta Hosp., Kenya; Consultant to Nat. Insts of Health, Bethesda, Md, 1973–74. *Publications:* various papers in medical jls. *Recreations:* golf, gardening. *Address:* Box 166, Plettenberg Bay, Cape Province, South Africa.

See also K. P. W. J. McAdam.

McADAM, James; Deputy Chairman, Coats Viyella plc, since 1986; *b* 10 Dec. 1930; *s* of John Robert McAdam and Helen McAdam (*née* Cormack); *m* 1955, Maisie Una Holmes; two *d. Educ:* Lenzie Academy. Joined J. & P. Coats Ltd, 1945; Finance Dir, Coats Chile, 1962–66, Coats India, 1966–70, Coats Patons UK, 1972–75; Dir, 1975, Chief Exec., 1985–86, Chm., 1986–, Coats Patons plc; Chief Operating Officer, Coats Viyella (merged co.), 1986–90. Director: London Region Post Office, 1985–87; Textile Pensions Trust Ltd, 1985–; Scottish Business in the Community, 1986–. Mem., Exec. Cttee, Scottish Council Develt and Industry, 1988–. FRSA; CBIM. *Recreations:* theatre, gardening, travel. *Address:* Coats Viyella, 28 Savile Row, W1X 2DD. *T:* 071–734 5321.

McADAM, Prof. Keith Paul William James, FRCP; Wellcome Professor of Tropical Medicine, since 1984, and Head of Department of Clinical Sciences, since 1988, London School of Hygiene and Tropical Medicine, London University; Consultant Physician, Hospital for Tropical Diseases, NW1, since 1984; *b* 13 Aug. 1945; *s* of Sir Ian William James McAdam, *qv*, and Mrs L. M. Hrothgaarde Bennett (*neé* Gibson); *m* 1968, Penelope Ann (*neé* Spencer); three *d. Educ:* Prince of Wales School, Nairobi; Millfield School, Som.; Clare Coll., Cambridge (MA, MB BChir); Middlesex Hosp. Med. Sch. FRSTM&H; Fellow, London Med. Soc.; Dip. Amer. Bd of Internal Medicine, Dip. Amer. Bd of Allergy and Clinical Immunology. Medical posts at Middlesex Hosp., Royal Northern

Hosp., Brompton Hosp., Nat. Hosp. for Nervous Diseases, 1969–73; Lectr in Medicine, Inst. of Med. Research, Goroka, Papua New Guinea, 1973–75; MRC Travelling Fellow, 1975–76; Vis. Scientist, Immunology Branch, Nat. Cancer Inst., NIH, Bethesda, 1976–77; Asst Prof., Tufts Univ. Sch. of Medicine, 1977–82; Associate Prof., Divs of Allergy, Exptl Medicine and Geographic Medicine, Tufts Univ., 1982–84. *Publications:* scientific articles on immunology and tropical medicine, esp. on amyloidosis, acute phase proteins, leprosy, tuberculosis, AIDS, inflammation. *Recreations:* cricket, squash, tennis, golf, ski-ing. *Address:* Department of Clinical Sciences, London School of Hygiene and Tropical Medicine, Keppel Street, WC1E 7HT. *T:* 071–636 8636. *Club:* MCC.

MACADAM, Sir Peter, Kt 1981; Chairman: BAT Industries plc, 1976–82; Libra Bank, 1984–90; *b* 9 Sept. 1921; *s* of late Francis Macadam and Marjorie Mary Macadam (*née* Browne); *m* 1949, Ann Musson; three *d. Educ:* Buenos Aires, Argentina; Stonyhurst Coll., Lancs. Served as Officer in Queen's Bays, 1941–46. Joined BAT Gp tobacco co., Argentina, 1946; Chm. and Gen. Man., gp co., Argentina, 1955–58; PA in London to Dir resp. for Africa, 1959–60 (travelled widely in Africa); Chm., BAT Hong Kong, 1960–62; BAT Main Bd, 1963 (resp. at times for interest in S and Central Africa, S and Central America and Caribbean); Mem., Chm.'s Policy Cttee with overall resp. for tobacco interests and special interest, USA, Canada and Mexico, 1970; Chm., Tobacco Div. Bd and Dir, Gp HQ Bd, 1973; Vice-Chm., 1975. Dir, National Westminster Bank, 1978–84. Chm., British Nat. Cttee, ICC, 1978–85; Mem. Exec. Cttee, ICC, Paris, 1982–85. Pres., Hispanic and Luso Brazilian Council, 1982–87; Chm., Anglo-Argentine Soc., 1987–. Hon. FBIM; FRSA 1975. *Recreations:* golf, shooting. *Address:* Layham Hall, Layham, near Hadleigh, Suffolk IP7 5LE. *T:* Hadleigh (0473) 822137. *Club:* Canning.

McADAM CLARK, James; *see* Clark, James McAdam.

McADOO, Most Rev. Henry Robert, PhD, STD, DD; *b* 1916; *s* of James Arthur and Susan McAdoo; *m* 1940, Lesley Dalziel Weir; one *s* two *d. Educ:* Cork Grammar School; Mountjoy School, Dublin. Deacon, 1939; Priest, 1940; Curate of Holy Trinity Cathedral, Waterford, 1939–43; Incumbent of Castleventry with Ardfield, 1943–48 (with Kilmeen, 1947–48); Rector of Kilmocomogue, Diocese of Cork, 1948–52; Rural Dean of Glansalney West and Bere, 1948–52; Canon of Kilbrittain in Cork Cathedral, and Canon of Donoughmore in Cloyne Cathedral, 1949–52; Dean of Cork, 1952–62; Canon of St Patrick's Cathedral, Dublin, 1960–62; Bishop of Ossory, Ferns and Leighlin, 1962–77; Archbishop of Dublin and Primate of Ireland, 1977–85. Member, Anglican-Roman Catholic Preparatory Commission, 1967–68; Jt Chm., Anglican-Roman Catholic International Commission, 1969–81 (Canterbury Cross). Hon. Fellow, TCD, 1989. *Publications:* The Structure of Caroline Moral Theology, 1949; John Bramhall and Anglicanism, 1964; The Spirit of Anglicanism, 1965; Modern Eucharistic Agreement, 1973; Modern Ecumenical Documents on Ministry, 1975; Being an Anglican, 1977; Rome and the Anglicans, 1982; The Unity of Anglicanism: Catholic and Reformed, 1983; The Eucharistic Theology of Jeremy Taylor Today, 1988; contribs to: Authority in the Anglican Communion, 1987; Christian Authority, 1988. *Address:* 2 The Paddocks, Dalkey, Co. Dublin. *Club:* Kildare Street and University (Dublin).

McALISKEY, (Josephine) Bernadette, (Mrs Micheal McAliskey); Chairman, Independent Socialist Party, Ireland; *b* 23 April 1947; *d* of late John James Devlin and Elizabeth Devlin; *m* 1973, Micheal McAliskey; three *c. Educ:* St Patrick's Girls' Acad., Dungannon; psychology student at Queen's Univ., Belfast, 1966–69. Youngest MP in House of Commons when elected at age of 21; MP (Ind. Unity) Mid Ulster, Apr. 1969–Feb. 1974. Founder Member and Mem. Exec., Irish Republican Socialist Party, 1975–76. Contested: (Ind) N Ireland, European Parlt, 1979; (People's Democracy), Dublin N Central, Dáil Eireann, Feb. and Nov. 1982. *Publication:* The Price of my Soul (autobiog.), 1969. *Recreations:* walking, folk music, doing nothing, swimming.

McALISTER, Michael Ian, FCA; Chairman, International Dynamics Ltd, since 1989; a Director, Cluff Resources PLC (formerly Cluff Oil Holdings), since 1979; *b* Leeds, Yorkshire, 23 Aug. 1930; *s* of S. McAlister, CBE, and J. A. McAlister (*née* Smith); *m* 1st, 1953, Patricia (*née* Evans) (marr. diss. 1983); four *s* three *d*; 2nd, 1984, Elizabeth Anne, *o d* of Mr and Mrs Ludwig Hehn. *Educ:* Brazil; France; St John's Coll., Oxford (MA). National Service, Lieut, Intelligence Corps (MI8), 1950–51 (Acting Capt). Articled Clerk, Price Waterhouse, London, 1954–58; Private Sec. to the Duke of Windsor, 1959–61; Investment Manager, Ionian Bank Ltd, London, 1961–67; Managing Dir, Ionian Bank Trustee Co, London, 1967–68; Slater Walker Securities (Australia): Dep. Chm., 1969–70, Chm., 1970–72; Pres., Aust. Associated Stock Exchanges, 1972–74; Dir (Middle Est), Lester B. Knight and Associates, USA, 1975–79. Chm., Woking Cons. Assoc., 1967–68. *Recreations:* game fishing, carpentry, DIY. *Address:* Two Berwick Cottages, Terling Hall Road, Hatfield Peveral, Chelmsford, Essex CM3 2EY. *T:* Chelmsford (0245) 380158. *Club:* Royal Automobile.

McALISTER, Maj.-Gen. Ronald William Lorne, CB 1977; OBE 1968 (MBE 1959); Bursar, Wellesley House School, Broadstairs, 1977–88; *b* 26 May 1923; 2nd *s* of late Col R. J. F. McAlister, OBE and Mrs T. M. Collins, Bath; *m* 1964, Sally Ewart Marshall; two *d. Educ:* Dreghorn Castle Sch., Edinburgh; Sedbergh School. Commnd 3rd QAO Gurkha Rifles, 1942; Adjt 1/3 GR Burma, 1945 (despatches); Adjt 2/10 GR Malaya, 1950–52 (despatches); Instructor, Sch. of Infantry, 1953–55; psc 1956; Bde Major 99 Gurkha Bde, Malaya, 1957–59 (MBE); jssc 1961–62; Asst Sec., Chiefs of Staff Cttee, 1962–64; 2nd in comd and CO 10th PMO Gurkha Rifles, Borneo, 1964–66 (despatches); Internal Security Duties, Hong Kong, 1967–68 (OBE); Instructor, Jt Services Staff Coll., 1968; comd Berlin Inf. Bde, 1968–71; ndc, Canada, 1971–72; Exercise Controller UK Cs-in-C Cttee, 1972–75; Dep. Commander Land Forces Hong Kong and Maj.-Gen. Brigade of Gurkhas, 1975–77; retired 1977. Col, 10th Princess Mary's Own Gurkha Rifles, 1977–85; Chm., Gurkha Brigade Assoc., 1980–90. Chm., Buckmaster Meml Home, Broadstairs, 1980–. *Publication:* (ed and contrib.) Bugle and Kukri, Vol. 2, 1986. *Recreations:* golf, gardening. *Address:* The Chalet, 41 Callis Court Road, Broadstairs, Kent. *T:* Thanet (0843) 62351. *Clubs:* Army and Navy; Royal St George's Golf (Captain, 1989–90; Hon. Treas., 1991–), Senior Golfers' Society.

McALISTER, William Harle Nelson; Director, Creative Research Ltd, since 1989; *b* 30 Aug. 1940; *s* of Flying Officer William Nelson (*d* 1940) and Marjorie Isobel (*née* McIntyre); adopted by William Edwyn McAlister (whom she *m* 2nd); *m* 1968 (marr. diss. 1985); two *s* two *d. Educ:* Sorbonne, Paris; Univ. of Copenhagen (BA Hons Psychology, 1967); University Coll. London. Dir, Almost Free Theatre, 1968–72; Dep. Dir, Inter-Action Trust, 1968–72; Founder Dir, Islington Bus Co., 1972–77; Director: Battersea Arts Centre, 1976–77; ICA, 1977–90. Dir, Sense of Ireland Fest., 1980; Bd Dir, London International Theatre Fest., 1983; Chm. for the Arts, IT 82 Cttee, 1982. Chm., Recreational Trust, 1972–88; Co-Founder, Fair Play for Children, 1974–75; Advr, Task Force Trust, 1972–74; Trustee: Circle 33 Housing Trust, 1972–75; Moving Picture Mime Trust, 1978–80; Shape (Arts for the Disadvantaged), 1979–81. Trustee, International House, 1989–. Governor, Holloway Adult Educn Inst., 1974–76. Mem. Court, RCA, 1980–. British Deleg. to Ministerial Conf. on cultural policy, Bulgaria, 1980; British Cultural Deleg., China, 1982. *Publications:* Community Psychology, 1975; EEC and the Arts, 1978; articles on Arts Policy. *Recreations:* angling, tennis, travel. *Address:* 151c Grosvenor Avenue, N5 2NH. *T:* 071–226 0205.

MACALLAN, Andrew; *see* Leasor, T. J.

McALLION, John; MP (Lab) Dundee East, since 1987; *b* 13 Feb. 1948; *s* of Joseph and Norah McAllion; *m* 1971, Susan Jean Godlonton; two *s. Educ:* St Augustine's Comprehensive School, Glasgow; St Andrews Univ. (MA Hons 2nd cl. Modern and Medieval Hist. 1972); Dundee Coll. of Education. Civil Servant, Post Office, 1967–68; History Teacher, St Saviour's High Sch., Dundee, 1973–78; Social Studies Teacher, Balgowan Sch., Dundee, 1978–82; Research Asst to Bob McTaggart, 1982–86. Regional Councillor, 1984–87, Convener, 1986–87, Tayside Regional Council. *Recreations:* sport, reading, music. *Address:* 3 Haldane Street, Dundee. *T:* Dundee (0382) 826678; House of Commons, SW1. *T:* 071–219 5048.

McALLISTER, John Brian; Chief Executive, Cresta Holdings Ltd, since 1990 (Group Managing Director, 1988–90); *b* 11 June 1941; *s* of late Thomas McAllister and of Jane (*née* McCloughan); *m* 1966, Margaret Lindsay Walker; two *d. Educ:* Royal Belfast Academical Instn; Queen's Univ., Belfast (BA Hons). Joined NI Civil Service as Asst Principal, Dept of Educn, 1964; Dep. Principal, Higher Educn Div., 1968; Principal: Secondary Schs Br., 1969; Re-Organisation of Local Govt Br., 1970; Principal, Dept of Finance, 1971, Dept's Central Secretariat, 1972; Asst Sec. 1973, Sen. Asst Sec. 1976, Dep. Sec., 1978–80, Dept of Educn; Dep. Sec., later Under Sec., Dept of Finance, 1980–83; Under Sec., DoE, NI, 1983–84; Dep. Chief Exec., 1984–85, Chief Exec., 1985–88, Industrial Develt Bd for NI. *Recreations:* watching sport of all kinds, reading, walking the dog. *Address:* Cresta Holdings Ltd, Cresta House, 2 Circular Road, Douglas, Isle of Man.

McALPINE, family name of **Baron McAlpine of West Green.**

McALPINE OF WEST GREEN, Baron *cr* 1984 (Life Peer), of West Green in the County of Hampshire; **Robert Alistair McAlpine;** Director, Sir Robert McAlpine & Sons Ltd, since 1963; *b* 14 May 1942; *s* of Lord McAlpine of Moffat and Ella Mary Gardner Garnett (*d* 1987); *m* 1964, Sarah Alexandra Baron (marr. diss. 1979); two *d*; *m* 1980, Romilly, *o d* of A. T. Hobbs, Cranleigh, Surrey; one *d. Educ:* Stowe. Joined Sir Robert McAlpine & Sons Ltd, 1958. Hon. Treasurer: Europ. Democratic Union, 1978–; Europ. League for Econ. Co-operation, 1974–75 (Vice Pres., 1975–); Conservative and Unionist Party, 1975–90 (Dep. Chm., 1979–83). Director: George Weidenfeld Holdings Ltd, 1975–83; ICA, 1972–73. Mem., Arts Council of GB, 1981–82; Vice-President: Friends of Ashmolean Museum, 1969–; Greater London Arts Assoc., 1971–77; Vice-Chm., Contemporary Arts Soc., 1973–80. Pres., British Waterfowl Assoc., 1978–81, Patron 1981–. Member: Friends of V&A Museum, 1976–; Council, English Stage Co., 1973–75. Trustee, Royal Opera House Trust, 1974–80; Dir, Theatre Investment Fund, 1981– (Chm., 1985–90). Governor: Polytechnic of the South Bank, 1981–82; Stowe Sch., 1981–84. *Recreations:* the arts, horticulture, aviculture, agriculture. *Address:* House of Lords, SW1. *Clubs:* Garrick, Carlton, Buck's, Pratt's, Beefsteak.
See also Hon. Sir W. H. McAlpine, Bt.

McALPINE, Christopher; *see* McAlpine, R. D. C.

McALPINE, Robert Douglas Christopher, CMG 1967; HM Diplomatic Service, retired; Director: Baring Brothers, 1969–79; H. Clarkson (Holdings) plc, 1980–87; *b* 14 June 1919; *s* of late Dr Douglas McAlpine, FRCP and late Elizabeth Meg Sidebottom; *m* 1943, Helen Margery Frances Cannan; two *s* one *d* (and one *d* decd). Educ: Winchester; New Coll., Oxford. RNVR, 1939–46. Entered Foreign Service, 1946. FO, 1946–47; Asst Private Sec. to Sec. of State, 1947–49; 2nd Sec. and later 1st Sec., UK High Commn at Bonn, 1949–52; FO, 1952–54; Lima, 1954–56; Moscow, 1956–59; FO, 1959–62; Dep. Consul-Gen. and Counsellor, New York, 1962–65; Counsellor, Mexico City, 1965–68. Town Councillor, Tetbury, 1987–. *Recreations:* sailing, tennis, fishing. *Address:* Longtree House, Cutwell, Tetbury, Glos GL8 8EB. *Club:* United Oxford & Cambridge University.

McALPINE, Robert James, FCIOB; Chairman, Alfred McAlpine plc, since 1983 (Director since 1957); *b* 6 May 1932; *s* of Alfred James McAlpine and Peggy (*née* Saunders); *m* 1st, Mary Jane Anton; two *s* one *d*; 2nd, Angela Bell (*née* Langford Brooke); one *d. Educ:* Harrow Sch. FCIOB. Director: Haynes Hanson & Clarke, 1978–; Hall Engrg, 1985–. Chm., Export Gp for Constructional Industries, 1975–77. Mem., Jockey Club. *Recreations:* racing, shooting, golf, bridge. *Address:* Alfred McAlpine plc, Hooton, South Wirral, Cheshire L66 7ND. *T:* 051–339 4141. *Clubs:* White's, Turf, Portland, MCC.

McALPINE, Sir Robin, Kt 1969; CBE 1957; Director, Newarthill plc, 1972 (Chairman, 1972–77); Chairman, Sir Robert McAlpine & Sons Ltd, 1967–77; *b* 18 March 1906; *s* of late Sir (Thomas) Malcolm McAlpine, KBE, and late Lady (Maud) McAlpine; *m* 1st, 1939, Nora Constance (*d* 1966), *d* of F. H. Perse; 2nd, 1970, Mrs Philippa Nicolson (*d* 1987), *d* of Sir Gervais Tennyson D'Eyncourt, 2nd Bt. *Educ:* Charterhouse. Pres., Federation of Civil Engineering Contractors, 1966–71. *Recreation:* owner and breeder of racehorses. *Address:* Aylesfield, Alton, Hants. *Club:* Jockey.

McALPINE, Hon. Sir William (Hepburn), 6th Bt *cr* 1918, of Knott Park; FRSE; FCIT; RSA; company director; *b* 12 Jan. 1936; *s* of Lord McAlpine of Moffat (Life Peer) and Ella Mary Gardner Garnett (*d* 1987); *S* to baronetcy of father, 1990; *m* 1959, Jill Benton, *o d* of Lt-Col Sir Peter Fawcett Benton Jones, 3rd Bt, OBE, ACA; one *s* one *d. Educ:* Charterhouse. Life Guards, 1954–56. Dir, Sir Robert McAlpine & Sons Ltd, 1956–. *Recreation:* steam railways (owner of the famous 4472 Flying Scotsman). *Heir: s* Andrew William McAlpine [*b* 22 Nov. 1960; *m* 1991, Caroline Claire, *yr d* of Frederick Hodgson]. *Address:* (office) 40 Bernard Street, WC1N 1LG. *Clubs:* Garrick, Caledonian; Western (Glasgow).
See also Baron McAlpine of West Green.

MacANDREW, family name of **Baron MacAndrew.**

MacANDREW, 3rd Baron *cr* 1959, of the Firth of Clyde; **Christopher Anthony Colin MacAndrew;** farmer; *b* 16 Feb. 1945; *s* of 2nd Baron MacAndrew and Ursula Beatrice (*d* 1986), *d* of Captain Joseph Steel; *S* father, 1989; *m* 1975, Sarah, *o d* of Lt-Col P. H. Brazier; one *s* two *d. Educ:* Malvern. *Heir: s* Hon. Oliver Charles Julian MacAndrew, *b* 3 Sept. 1983. *Recreations:* cricket, golf, tennis. *Address:* Hall Farm, Archdeacon Newton, Darlington, Co. Durham.

MACARA, Sir Hugh Kenneth, 4th Bt *cr* 1911, of Ardmore, St Anne-on-the-Sea, Co. Lancaster; *b* 17 Jan. 1913; 4th *s* of Sir William Cowper Macara, 2nd Bt and Lilian Mary (*d* 1971), *d* of John Chapman; *S* brother, 1982. *Heir:* none.

McARDLE, Rear-Adm. Stanley Lawrence, CB 1975; LVO 1952; GM 1953; JP; Flag Officer, Portsmouth, and Port Admiral, Portsmouth, 1973–75; retired; *b* 1922; *s* of Theodore McArdle, Lochmaben, Dumfriesshire; *m* 1st, 1945, (Helen) Joyce, *d* of Owen Cummins, Wickham, Hants; one *d*; 2nd, 1962, Jennifer, *d* of Walter Talbot Goddard, Salisbury, Wilts; one *d. Educ:* Royal Hospital Sch., Holbrook, Suffolk. Joined RN, 1938;

served War, 1939–45. Lieut 1945; Comdr 1956; Captain 1963. Directorate of Naval Operations and Trade, 1969; Comd HMS Glamorgan, 1970; Dir Naval Trng, Director General, Personal Services and Trng (Naval), 1971–73; Rear Admiral 1972. Dir, Endless Holdings Ltd, 1985–. JP Wilts, 1977. *Address:* Barn Ridge Cottage, Farley, Salisbury, Wilts.

MACARTHUR, Rev. Arthur Leitch, OBE 1981; MA, MLitt; inducted, Christ Church, Marlow-on-Thames, 1980, retired 1986; *b* 9 Dec. 1913; *s* of Edwin Macarthur and Mary Macarthur (*née* Leitch); *m* 1950, Doreen Esmé Muir; three *s* one *d*. *Educ:* Rutherford Coll.; Armstrong Coll., Durham Univ. (MA, MLitt Dunelm); Westminster Coll., Cambridge. Ordained, 1937; inducted, Clayport, Alnwick, 1937; served with YMCA in France, 1940. Inducted: St Augustine's, New Barnet, 1944; St Columba's, North Shields, 1950. Gen. Sec., Presbyterian Church of England, 1960–72; Moderator, Presbyterian Church of England, 1971–72; Jt Gen.-Sec., URC, 1972–74; Moderator, URC, 1974–75; Gen. Sec., URC, 1975–80; Moderator, Free Church Federal Council, 1980–81. Vice-Pres., BCC, 1974–77 (Chm., Admin. Cttee, 1969–74). Director: Tavistock Court Ltd; URC Insurance Co., etc. *Recreations:* gardening, golf, walking. *Address:* Haywards Corner, Randalls Green, Chalford Hill, near Stroud, Glos GL6 8LH. *T:* Brimscombe (0453) 883700.

MacARTHUR, Brian; Assistant Editor, The Sunday Times, since 1990 (Executive Editor, 1987–90); *b* 5 Feb. 1940; *o s* of late S. H. MacArthur and of Mrs M. MacArthur; *m* 1975, Bridget Trahair; two *d*. *Educ:* Brentwood Sch.; Helsby Grammar Sch.; Leeds Univ. (BA). Yorkshire Post, 1962–64; Daily Mail, 1964–66; The Guardian, 1966–67; The Times: Education Correspondent, 1967–70; Dep. Features Editor, 1970–71; Founder Editor, The Times Higher Educn Supplement, 1971–76; Home News Editor, 1976–78; Dep. Editor, Evening Standard, 1978–79; Chief Asst to the Editor, The Sunday Times, 1979–81; Exec. Editor (News), The Times, 1981–82; Jt Dep. Editor, The Sunday Times, 1982–84; Editor, Western Morning News, 1984–85; Editor-in-Chief, Today, 1986–87. Hon. MA, Open Univ., 1976. *Publications:* The National Press in Political Communications: the general election campaign of 1987, 1988; Eddy Shah: Today and the Newspaper Revolution, 1988; Deadline Sunday, 1991; Gulf War Despatches, 1991. *Recreations:* reading, gardening. *Address:* (office) 1 Pennington Street, E1 9XW. *T:* 071–782 5801; (home) 50 Lanchester Road, N6 4TA. *T:* 081–883 1855. *Club:* Garrick.

MacARTHUR, Mrs Charles; *see* Hayes, Helen.

MACARTHUR, Charles Ramsay, QC (Scot.) 1970; Sheriff of Tayside, Central and Fife, 1981–91; *s* of late Alastair and late Joan Macarthur; *m* 1973, Rosemary Valda Morgan (marr. diss. 1982), Edinburgh. *Educ:* Glasgow Univ. (MA, LLB). Served War of 1939–45: joined Royal Navy, 1942; demobilised as Lieut, RNVR, 1946. Solicitor, 1952–59; admitted Scottish Bar, 1960; Standing Junior Counsel, Highlands and Islands Development Board, 1968–70; Sheriff of the Lothians and Borders, 1974–76. *Recreations:* travel, talking. *Club:* New (Edinburgh).

MacARTHUR, Ian, OBE 1988; Director, British Textile Confederation, 1977–89; *b* 17 May 1925; *yr s* of late Lt-Gen. Sir William MacArthur, KCB, DSO, OBE, MD, DSc, FRCP, KHP; *m* 1957, Judith Mary, (RGN 1976), *d* of late Francis Gavin Douglas Miller; four *s* three *d*. *Educ:* Cheltenham Coll.; The Queen's Coll., Oxford (Scholar, MA). Contested (U), Greenock Gen. Election, May 1955, also by-election, Dec. 1955; MP (C) Perth and E Perthshire, 1959–Sept. 1974; an Asst Government Whip (unpaid), 1962–63; a Lord Comr of the Treasury and Govt Scottish Whip, 1963–64; Opposition Scottish Whip, 1964–65; an Opposition Spokesman on Scottish Affairs, 1965–70 (Opposition front bench, 1965–66, 1969–70). Former Member: Speaker's Conf. on Electoral Law; Select Cttees on European Legislation, on Scottish Affairs, and on Members' Interests. Chm., Scottish Cons. Mems' Cttee, 1972–73. Introduced, as Private Member's Bills: Law Reform (Damages and Solatium) (Scotland) Act, 1962; Interest on Damages (Scotland) Act, 1971; Social Work (Scotland) Act, 1972; Domicile and Matrimonial Proceedings Act, 1973. Personal Asst to the Prime Minister, Rt Hon. Sir Alec Douglas-Home, Kinross and W Perthshire By-Election, Nov. 1963. Hon. Pres., Scottish Young Unionists, 1962–65; Vice-Chm., Cons. Party in Scotland, 1972–75. Formerly Dir of Administration, J. Walter Thompson Co. Ltd. Served War of 1939–45, with RN (Ord. Seaman) and RNVR, 1943–46 (King's Badge; Flag Lieut to C-in-C Portsmouth, 1946). FRSA 1984. Gold Cross of Merit, Polish Govt in Exile, 1971. *Address:* 15 Old Palace Lane, Richmond, Surrey. *Clubs:* Naval; Puffin's (Edinburgh).
See also R. A. G. Douglas Miller.

McARTHUR, Dr John Duncan, FRCPGlas; Consultant Physician and Cardiologist, Western Infirmary, Glasgow, since 1978; *b* 7 Jan. 1938; *s* of Neil McPhail McArthur and Elizabeth Duncan; *m* 1963, Elizabeth Agnew Bowie; two *s* one *d*. *Educ:* Univ. of Glasgow (BSc Hons 1960; MB ChB Hons 1963); DM Madras 1970. DObstRCOG 1965; MRCP 1966; MRCPG 1966; MRCPE 1967; FRCPGlas 1980. Junior House Officer, Glasgow Royal Infirmary and Ayrshire Hosps, 1963–65; Senior House Officer and Registrar, Glasgow Royal Inf., 1965–67; Lectr, Sen. Lectr, Reader, Christian Med. Coll. Hosp., Vellore, India, as Missionary, Church of Scotland, 1968–73; Sen. Registrar, Medicine/Cardiology, Glasgow Teaching Hosps, 1973–78. *Publications:* articles on valvular heart disease and pacemakers. *Recreations:* DIY, gardening. *Address:* 8 Durness Avenue, Bearsden, Glasgow G61 2AQ. *T:* 041–942 7330.

McARTHUR, Dr Thomas Burns, (Tom); English teacher, since 1959; feature writer, since 1962; lecturer and writer on yoga and Indian philosophy, since 1962; author and language consultant, since 1970; Editor: English Today, since 1984; Oxford Companion to the English Language, since 1988; *b* 23 Aug. 1938; *s* of Archibald McArthur and Margaret Burns; *m* 1963, Fereshteh Mottahedin; one *s* two *d*. *Educ:* Glasgow Univ. (MA 1958); Edinburgh Univ. (MLitt 1970; PhD 1978). Officer-Instr, RAEC, 1959–61; Asst Master, Riland Bedford Sch., Warwicks, 1961–63; Head of English, Cathedral and John Connon Sch., Bombay, India, 1965–67; Vis. Prof. in the English of the Media, Rajendra Prasad College of Mass Communication (Bharatiya Vidya Bhavan), Univ. of Bombay, 1965–67; Dir of Extra-Mural English Language Courses, Univ. of Edinburgh, 1972–79; Associate Prof. of English, Université du Québec à Trois-Rivières, Canada, 1979–83. Co-founder (with Reinhard Hartmann), Internat. Lexicography Course, Univ. of Exeter, 1987–. Consultant: Min. of Educn, Quebec, 1980–81; Société pour la promotion de l'enseignement de l'anglais (langue seconde) au Québec, 1980–83; Henson International Television (the Muppets), 1985–86; Dictionary Res. Centre, Exeter Univ., 1987–; also on dictionaries and ELT books published by Century Hutchinson, Chambers, Collins, CUP, Longman and OUP. The Story of English (BBC radio series with D. Crystal), 1987. Mem., Editl Bd, Internat. Jl of Lexicography, 1988–. *Publications:* Patterns of English series, 1972–74; English for Students of Economics, 1973; (with Beryl Atkins) Collins Dictionary of English Phrasal Verbs, 1974; (ed with A. J. Aitken) Languages of Scotland, 1979; Longman Lexicon of Contemporary English, 1981; A Foundation Course for Language Teachers, 1983; The Written Word, Books 1 and 2, 1984; Worlds of Reference, 1986; Yoga and the Bhagavad-Gita, 1986; Understanding Yoga, 1986; Unitive Thinking, 1988 (Beyond Logic and Mysticism, USA, 1990); The English Language as Used in Quebec: a survey, 1989. *Recreations:* reading, television, walking, cycling, travel. *Address:* 22–23 Ventress Farm Court, Cherry Hinton Road, Cambridge CB1 4HD. *T:* Cambridge (0223) 245934.

MACARTNEY, Sir John Barrington, 6th Bt *cr* 1799, of Lish, Co. Armagh; dairy farmer, retired; *b* 21 Jan. 1917; *s* of John Barrington Macartney (3rd *s* of Sir John Macartney, 3rd Bt; he *d* 1951) and Selina Koch, Hampden, Mackay, Qld, Australia; *S* uncle, Sir Alexander Miller Macartney, 5th Bt, 1960; *m* 1944, Amy Isobel Reinke (*d* 1978); one *s*. *Heir:* *s* John Ralph Macartney [*b* 24 July 1945; *m* 1966, Suzanne Marie Fowler; four *d*]. *Address:* 37 Meadow Street, North Mackay, Qld 4740, Australia.

MACAULAY OF BRAGAR, Baron *cr* 1989 (Life Peer), of Bragar in the county of Ross and Cromarty; **Donald Macaulay.** *Educ:* Univ. of Glasgow (MA, LLB). Admitted to Faculty of Advocates, 1963; QC (Scot.) 1975. *Address:* House of Lords, SW1.

MACAULAY, Janet Stewart Alison, MA; Headmistress of St Leonards and St Katharines Schools, St Andrews, 1956–70; *b* 20 Dec. 1909; 3rd *d* of late Rev. Prof. A. B. Macaulay, DD, of Trinity Coll., Glasgow. *Educ:* Laurel Bank Sch., Glasgow; Glasgow Univ.; Somerville Coll., Oxford. BA Oxon 1932; BLitt Oxon 1934; MA Oxon 1936. Asst Mistress, Wycombe Abbey Sch., Bucks, 1933–36; Sutton High Sch. (GPDST), Sutton, Surrey, 1937–45; Headmistress, Blackheath High Sch. (GPDST), 1945–Dec. 1955. Hon. LLD St Andrews, 1977. *Address:* 3 Drummond Place, Edinburgh EH3 6PH.

McAVOY, Sir (Francis) Joseph, Kt 1976; CBE 1969; Chairman: Queensland and Australian Canegrowers Councils, 1963–82 (Member, 1952–82); Australian Canegrowers Council, 1952–82; retired; *b* 26 Feb. 1910; *s* of William Henry McAvoy and Hanorah Catherine McAvoy; *m* 1936, Mary Irene Doolan; four *s* (one *d* decd). *Educ:* Nudgee Coll., Brisbane; Sacred Heart Convent, Innisfail, Qld. Member: Goondi Mill Suppliers Cttee, 1947–82; Innisfail Canegrowers Exec., 1949–82; Metric Conversion Bd (Aust.), 1970–78; Aust. Immigration Adv. Council, 1964–72; Exec. Council of Agriculture, 1963–82; Exec., Aust. Farmers Fedn, 1969–77, Nat. Farmers Fedn, 1977–82. Vice-Pres., Internat. Fedn of Agricultural Producers, 1968–74. Paul Harris Fellow, Rotary Internat., USA, 1986. *Recreation:* lawn bowls. *Address:* PO Box 95, Innisfail, Qld 4860, Australia. *T:* 633724. *Clubs:* Rotary, IDB (Innisfail, Qld).

McAVOY, Thomas McLaughlin; MP (Lab and Co-op) Glasgow, Rutherglen, since 1987; *b* 14 Dec. 1943; *m* Eleanor Kerr; four *s*. Employee, Hoover, Cambuslang; shop steward, AEU. Mem., Strathclyde Regl Council, 1982–87; former Chm., Rutherglen Community Council. An Opposition Whip, 1990–. *Address:* House of Commons, SW1A 0AA; 9 Douglas Avenue, Rutherglen, Glasgow G73 4RA.

McBAIN, (David) Malcolm, LVO 1972; HM Diplomatic Service, retired; Ambassador to Madagascar, 1984–87; *b* 19 Jan. 1928; *s* of David Walker McBain and Lilian J. McBain; *m* 1951, Audrey Yvonne Evison; one *s* three *d*. *Educ:* Sutton County School; London School of Economics (evening student). Min. of Civil Aviation appts in Tripoli, Libya, 1949–51, New Delhi, 1953–54; Diplomatic Service: New Delhi, 1958–61; Kenya, 1963–67; Thailand, 1968–75; Brunei, 1978–81; Texas, 1981–84. Order of Crown of Thailand, 1972. *Recreations:* golf, fishing. *Address:* Edmeads Cottage, Teffont Magna, Salisbury, Wilts SP3 5QY.

McBAIN, Ed; *see* Hunter, Evan.

McBAIN, Malcolm; *see* McBain, D. M.

MACBEATH, Prof. Alexander Murray, PhD (Princeton, NJ); MA (Cantab); Professor of Mathematics and Statistics, University of Pittsburgh, 1979–90; *b* 30 June 1923; *s* of late Prof. Alexander Macbeath, CBE; *m* 1951, Julie Ormrod, Lytham St Anne's; two *s*. *Educ:* Royal Belfast Academical Inst.; Queen's Univ., Belfast; Clare Coll., Cambridge. Entrance Schol., Dixon Prize in Maths, Purser Studentship, 1st class hons in Maths, BA, QUB. Temp. post with Foreign Office, 1943–45. Cambridge, 1945–48; Maj. Entrance Schol., Wrangler Math. Tripos, Part II, dist. Part III, BA, Owst Prize. Commonwealth Fund Fellowship, Princeton, NJ, 1948–50; Smith's Prize, 1949; PhD Princeton, 1950. Research Fellow, Clare Coll., Cambridge, 1950–51; MA Cambridge, 1951. Lectr in Maths, Univ. Coll. of North Staffordshire, 1951–53; Prof. of Maths, Queen's Coll., Dundee, 1953–62; Mason Prof. of Pure Maths, Univ. of Birmingham, 1962–79. Visiting Professor: California Inst. of Technology, 1966–67; Univ. of Pittsburgh, 1974–75. *Publications:* Elementary Vector Algebra, 1964; papers in: Jl London Mathematical Soc.; Proc. London Math. Soc.; Proc. Cambridge Philosophical Soc.; Quarterly Jl of Mathematics; Annals of Mathematics; Canadian Jl of Mathematics. *Recreation:* Scottish country dancing. *Address:* 30 Grey Street, Tayport, Fife DD6 9HW.

MacBETH, George Mann; writer; *b* Scotland, 1932; *s* of George MacBeth and Amelia Morton Mary Mann; *m* 1955, Elizabeth Browell Robson, *qv* (marr. diss. 1975); *m* 1982, Lisa St Aubin de Téran (marr. diss. 1989); one *s*; *m* 1989, Penelope Ronchetti-Carpenter; one *d*. *Educ:* New Coll., Oxford (read Classics and Philosophy). BBC, 1955–76: Producer, Overseas Talks Dept, 1957; Producer, Talks Dept, 1958; Editor: Poet's Voice, 1958–65; New Comment, 1959–64; Poetry Now, 1965–76. Cholmondeley Award (jtly), 1977. *Publications: poems:* A Form of Words, 1954; The Broken Places, 1963 (Sir Geoffrey Faber Meml Award (jtly), 1964); A Doomsday Book, 1965; The Colour of Blood, 1967; The Night of Stones, 1968; A War Quartet, 1969; The Burning Cone, 1970; Collected Poems 1958–1970, 1971; The Orlando Poems, 1971; Shrapnel, 1973; A Poet's Year, 1973; In The Hours Waiting For The Blood To Come, 1975; Buying a Heart, 1978; Poems of Love and Death, 1980; Poems from Oby, 1982; The Long Darkness, 1983; The Cleaver Garden, 1986; Anatomy of a Divorce, 1988; Collected Poems 1958–82, 1989; Trespassing, 1991; *prose poems:* My Scotland, 1973; *prose:* The Transformation, 1975; The Samurai, 1975; The Survivor, 1977; The Seven Witches, 1978; The Born Losers, 1981; A Kind of Treason, 1982; Anna's Book, 1983; The Lion of Pescara, 1984; Dizzy's Woman, 1986; Another Love Story, 1991; *anthologies:* The Penguin Book of Sick Verse, 1963; (with J. Clemo and E. Lucie-Smith) Penguin Modern Poets VI, 1964; The Penguin Book of Animal Verse, 1965; (with notes) Poetry, 1900–1965, 1967; The Penguin Book of Victorian Verse, 1968; The Falling Splendour, 1970; The Book of Cats, 1976; Poetry, 1900–1975, 1980; Poetry for Today, 1984; *children's books:* Noah's Journey, 1966; Jonah and the Lord, 1969; The Rectory Mice, 1982; The Story of Daniel, 1986; *autobiography:* A Child of the War, 1987 (Angel Literary Award, 1987). *Recreation:* Japanese swords. *Address:* Moyne Park, Tuam, County Galway, Eire.

McBRATNEY, George, CEng, FIMechE; Principal, College of Technology, Belfast, 1984–89; *b* 5 May 1927; *s* of George McBratney and Sarah Jane McBratney; *m* 1949, Margaret Rose Patricia, (Trissie), *d* of late John Robinson, Melbourne, Australia; one *s*. *Educ:* Coll. of Technology, Belfast (BSc(Eng) 1948); Northampton Coll. of Advanced Technol.; QUB (Dip Ed 1976). CEng, FIMechE 1971. Apprentice fitter/draughtsman, Harland and Wolff, Belfast, 1943–47; Teacher, Comber Trades Prep. Sch., 1947–54; College of Technology, Belfast: successively Asst Lectr, Lectr and Sen. Lectr, 1954–67; Asst to Principal, 1967–69; Vice-Principal, 1969–84. Council Member: IMechE, 1984–86 (Chm., NI Br., 1984–86); NI Manpower Council, 1984–; Lambeg Industrial Res. Assoc.

(formerly Linen Industry Res. Assoc.), 1984–90; BTEC, 1986–89; Chm., Further Educn Adv. Cttee, Faculty of Educn, Univ. of Ulster, 1986–90. *Publications:* Mechanical Engineering Experiments, vols 1 and 2 (with W. R. Mitchell), 1962, vol. 3 (with T. G. J. Moag), 1964; (with T. G. J. Moag) Science for Mechanical Engineering Technicians, vol. 1, 1966. *Recreation:* gardening. *Address:* 16 Glencregagh Drive, Belfast BT6 0NL. *T:* Belfast (0232) 796123.

McBREARTY, Tony; Head of Policy, London Borough of Newham, since 1988; *b* 26 April 1946; *s* of Patrick and Mary McBrearty; *m* 1969, Heather McGowan, solicitor; one *s.* Councillor (Lab) London Borough of Haringey, 1975–86 (Chm. of Personnel Cttee, 1976–79; Chm. of Housing Cttee, 1979–82); Mem. (Lab) Enfield N, 1981–86, Chm., Housing Cttee, 1982–86, GLC. Contested (Lab) W Herts, 1987. Chm., Central Technical Unit, 1986–88. *Recreations:* politics, history. *Address:* 112 Inderwick Road, Hornsey, N8 9JY. *T:* 081–348 8159.

McBRIDE, Commandant (Sara) Vonla (Adair), CB 1979; Director, City of London Region, Lloyds Bank Ltd, 1980–91; a Chairman, Civil Service Commissioners' Interview Panel, 1985–91; *b* 20 Jan. 1921; *d* of late Andrew Stewart McBride and Agnes McBride. *Educ:* Ballymena Acad., NI; TCD (Moderatorship in Mod. Lit; BA Hons). CBIM. Teacher of English and French, Ballymena Acad., 1942–45; Housemistress, Gardenhurst Sch., Burnham-on-Sea, Somerset, 1945–49. Dir, WRNS, 1976–79 (joined 1949); Hon. ADC to the Queen, 1976–79. Vice Pres., Officers' Pension Soc., 1989–. Freeman, City of London, 1978. Liveryman, Shipwrights' Co., 1983–. *Publication:* Never at Sea (autobiog.), 1966. *Recreations:* golf, theatre entertaining, continental travel. *Address:* Flat 11, 8 The Paragon, Blackheath, SE3. *T:* 081–852 8673. *Club:* Naval.

McBRIDE, Vonla; *see* McBride, S. V. A.

McBRIDE, William Griffith, AO 1977; CBE 1969; MD, FRCOG; FRACOG; Consultant Obstetrician and Gynaecologist: The Women's Hospital, Sydney, 1966–83; Royal Hospital for Women, 1983–88; St George Hospital, Sydney, since 1957; *b* 25 May 1927; *s* of late John McBride, Sydney; *m* 1957, Patricia Mary, *d* of late Robert Louis Glover; two *s* two *d.* *Educ:* Canterbury High Sch., Sydney; Univ. of Sydney; Univ. of London. MB, BS Sydney 1950; MRCOG 1954; MD Sydney 1962; FRCOG 1968; FAGO 1972; FRACOG 1979. Resident: St George Hosp., Sydney, 1950; Launceston Hosp., 1951; Med. Supt, Women's Hosp., Sydney, 1955–57; Cons. Gynaecologist, Bankstown Hosp., Sydney, 1957–66. Lectr in Obstetrics and Gynaecology, Univ. of Sydney, 1957–; Examr in Obstetrics and Gynaecology, Univ. of Sydney, 1960–; Medical Dir, Foundation 41 for the study of congenital abnormalities and mental retardation, 1972–. Vis. Prof. of Gynaecology, Univ. of Bangkok, 1968. Mem., WHO Sub-Cttee on safety of oral contraceptives, 1971–. Pres. Sect. of Obstetrics and Gynæcology, AMA, 1966–73. Fellow, Senate of Univ. of Sydney, 1976–90; FRSM 1988. Member: Faculty of Medicine, Univ. of NSW; Amer. Coll. of Toxicology; Soc. of Reproductive Biology; Endocrine Soc.; Teratology Soc.; Soc. for Risk Analysis; NY Acad. of Scis, 1987–. Mem. Council, Royal Agricl Soc. of NSW, 1987–. Member: Bd of Dirs, Australian Opera, 1979–82; Australian Opera Council, 1982–. BP Prize of Institut de la Vie, 1971 (for discovery of the teratogenic effects of the drug Thalidomide; first person to alert the world to the dangers of this drug and possibly other drugs). *Publications:* Drugs, 1960–70; contrib. (on Teratogenic Effect of the Drug Thalidomide), Lancet 1961 (London); numerous papers in internat. med. jls and scientific jls. *Recreations:* tennis, swimming, riding, music, cattle breeding. *Address:* Foundation 41, 365 Crown Street, Sydney, NSW 2010, Australia. *T:* 221–3898. *Clubs:* Union, Australian Jockey, Palm Beach Surf, Royal Sydney Golf (all in Sydney).

McBURNEY, Air Vice-Marshal Ralph Edward, CBE 1945; CD; RCAF, retired; *b* Montreal, Quebec, 17 Aug. 1906; *s* of Irville Albert and Lilian McBurney, Saskatoon, Sask.; *m* 1931, Gertrude Elizabeth Bate, Saskatoon; two *s* one *d.* *Educ:* Univs of Saskatchewan and Manitoba. BSc (EE); Commenced flying training as a cadet in RCAF, 1924; Pilot Officer, 1926; employed on Forest Fire Patrols and photographic mapping; Course in RAF School of Army Co-operation and tour as Instructor in RCAF School of Army Co-operation, 1931; Course at RAF Wireless School, Cranwell, and tour as Signals Adviser at Air Force HQ, Ottawa, 1935–36; RAF Staff Coll., Andover, 1939; Dir of Signals, AFHQ, Ottawa, 1939–42; CO, RCAF Station, Trenton, Ont., 1943; CO, RCAF Station, Dishforth, Yorks, 1943; Air Cdre 1944; Base Comdr of 61 Training Base, and later, 64 Operational Base in No 6 (RCAF) Bomber Group of Bomber Comd; SASO of the Group, Dec. 1944; AOC RCAF Maintenance Comd, 1945–46; Senior Canadian Air Force Liaison Officer, London, 1946–48; AOC Air Materiel Comd, RCAF, Ottawa, 1948–52. Business Consultant, 1952–60; Chief, Technical Information Service, Nat. Research Council, Ottawa, 1960–72. Pres., Internat. Fedn for Documentation, 1968–72. *Address:* 2022 Sharon Avenue, Ottawa, Ontario K2A 1L8, Canada.

McBURNIE, Tony; Chairman: Marketing Quality Assurance Ltd; Reed QT Search, 1989–90; *b* 4 Aug. 1929; *s* of William McBurnie and Bessie McKenzie Harvey McBurnie; *m* 1954, René Keating; one *s* one *d.* *Educ:* Lanark Grammar Sch.; Glasgow Univ. (MA). FCIM (FInstM 1984). National Service, RAF (FO), 1951–53. Divisional Manager Mullard Ltd, 1958–65; Group Marketing Dir, United Glass Ltd, 1965–69; Chairman and Managing Director: Ravenhead Co. Ltd, 1970–79; United Glass Containers Ltd, 1979–82; Man. Dir, United Glass PT&D Gp, 1982–84; Dir, United Glass Holdings PLC, 1966–84; Dir Gen., Chartered Inst. of Marketing (formerly Inst. of Marketing), 1984–89; Managing Director: Coll. of Marketing Ltd, 1985–89; Marketing Training Ltd, 1984–89; Marketing House Publishers Ltd, 1985–89. Director: Reed Executive plc, 1987–90; Beard Dove Ltd, 1988–. Pres., Assoc. of Glass Container Manufacturers, 1981–83; Chm., NJIC for Glass Industry, 1982–83; Dir, European Glass Fedn, 1979–83. *Publications:* (with David Clutterbuck) The Marketing Edge, 1987; Marketing Plus, 1989. *Recreations:* golf, swimming, theatre, the arts. *Address:* Prince Consort Drive, Ascot, Berks SL5 8AW. *Club:* Wentworth.

MacCABE, Brian Farmer, MC and Bar, 1942; Honorary President, Foote, Cone & Belding Ltd (London) (Chairman, 1948–78, President, 1978–80); Director and Senior Vice-President, Foote, Cone & Belding Communications Inc. (New York), 1953–80; *b* 9 Jan. 1914; *s* of late James MacCabe and Katherine MacCabe (*née* Harwood); *m* 1940, Eileen Elizabeth Noel Hunter (*d* 1984); one *s.* *Educ:* Christ's Coll., Finchley. Executive, C. R. Casson Ltd, 1934–40. Major RTR (wounded 3 times, Sqdn Comd, Alamein), 1940–45. World-wide Advertising Manager, BOAC, 1945–47; Chm., FCB International Inc. (NY), 1967–74. Mem. Council: Inst. of Practitioners in Advertising, 1951–80 (Pres., 1963–65); Advertising Assoc., 1952–69; Internat. Marketing Programme, 1965–80. Mem., Reith Commn on Advertising, 1962–66; Dir, American Chamber of Commerce, 1971–80; Member: Promotion Cttee, BNEC, 1965–68; Marketing Cttee, Ashridge Management Coll., 1965–78; Advertising Standards Authority, 1969–72; Appeals Cttee, Olympic and Commonwealth Games, 1952–80; Management Cttee, British Sports Assoc. for the Disabled, 1962–65; Nat. Council, Brit. Polio Fellowship, 1959–65. Royal Humane Soc. Medal for saving life from drowning, 1934. *Recreations:* finalist: (800 metres) Olympic Games, Berlin, 1936; (880 yards) British Commonwealth Games, Sydney, 1938; golf, fishing. *Address:* Somerford, Penn Road, Beaconsfield, Bucks HP9 2LN. *T:* Beaconsfield (0494) 673365. *Clubs:* Boodle's; Wasps RFC; LAC (Vice-Pres.), Bucks AA (Vice-Pres.), Beaconsfield Golf, Denham Golf.

MacCABE, Prof. Colin Myles Joseph; Head of Research, British Film Institute, since 1989; Professor of English, University of Pittsburgh, since 1987; *b* 9 Feb. 1949; *s* of Myles Joseph MacCabe and Ruth Ward MacCabe; two *s* one *d.* *Educ:* Trinity College, Cambridge (BA English and Moral Scis 1971, MA 1974, PhD 1976); Ecole Normale Supérieure, 1972–73 (pensionnaire anglais). University of Cambridge: Research Fellow, Emmanuel College, 1974–76; Fellow, King's College, 1976–81; Asst Lectr, Faculty of English, 1976–81; Prof. of English Studies, 1981–85, Vis. Prof., 1985–, Strathclyde Univ.; Head of Production, BFI, 1985–89. Vis. Fellow, School of Humanities, Griffith Univ., 1981, 1984; Chm., John Logie Baird Centre for Research in Television and Film, 1985– (Dir, 1983–85); Mellon Vis. Prof., Univ. of Pittsburgh, 1985. Mem., Editl Bd, Screen, 1973–81; Editor, Critical Qly, 1990– (Critical Editor, 1987–90). *Publications:* James Joyce and the Revolution of the Word, 1979; Godard: Images, Sounds, Politics, 1980; (ed) The Talking Cure: essays in psychoanalysis and language, 1981; (ed) James Joyce: new perspectives, 1982; Theoretical Essays: film, linguistics, literature, 1985; (ed jtly) The BBC and Public Sector Broadcasting, 1986; (ed) High Theory/Low Culture: analysing popular television and film, 1986; (ed) Futures for English, 1987; (ed jtly) The Linguistics of Writing, 1987. *Recreations:* eating, drinking, talking. *Address:* British Film Institute Research Division, 21 Stephen Street, W1P 1PL. *T:* 071–255 1444.

McCABE, Eamonn Patrick; Picture Editor, The Guardian, since 1988; *b* 28 July 1948; *s* of James and Celia McCabe; *m* 1972, Ruth Calvert; one *s* one *d.* *Educ:* Challoner School, Finchley; San Francisco State Coll. FRPS 1990. Freelance photographer on local papers and with The Guardian for one year; staff photographer, The Observer, 1977–86 and 1987–88; official photographer for the Pope's visit to England, 1982; Picture Editor, Sportsweek, 1986–87. Fellow in Photography, Nat. Mus. of Photography and TV, Bradford, 1988. Sports photographer of the year, RPS and Sports Council, 1978, 1979, 1981, 1984; News photographer of the year, British Press Awards, 1985. *Publications:* Sports Photographer, 1981; Eamonn McCabe, Photographer, 1987. *Recreations:* playing tennis, squash, occasional jogging. *Address:* 58 The Mall, Southgate, N14 6LN. *T:* 081–886 5742. *Club:* Nine Elms Dynamos Soccer Team.

McCABE, John, CBE 1985; professional musician; composer and pianist; *b* 21 April 1939; *s* of Frank and Elisabeth McCabe; *m* 1974, Monica Christine Smith. *Educ:* Liverpool Institute High Sch. for Boys; Manchester Univ. (MusBac); Royal Manchester Coll. of Music (ARMCM); Hochschule für Musik, Munich. Pianist-in-residence, University Coll., Cardiff, 1965–68; freelance musical criticism, 1966–71; Director, London Coll. of Music, 1983–90. Career as composer and pianist: many broadcasts and recordings as well as concert appearances in various countries. Prizewinner in Gaudeamus Competition for Interpreters of Contemporary Music, Holland, 1969. Recordings incl. 16–record set of complete piano music by Haydn; complete piano music of Nielsen (2 records). Awarded Special Citation by Koussevitsky Internat. Recording Foundn of USA, for recording of Symph. No 2 and Notturni ed Alba, 1974; Special Award by Composers' Guild of Gt Brit. (services to Brit. music), 1975; Ivor Novello Award (TV theme tune, Sam), 1977. Pres., ISM, 1983–84; Chm., Assoc. of Professional Composers, 1984–85. Hon. FRMCM; Hon. FLCM 1983; Hon. FRCM 1984; Hon. RAM 1985; Hon. FTCL 1989. *Publications:* many compositions, incl. three symphonies, two operas, ballets, concerti, orchestral works incl. The Chagall Windows and Hartmann Variations, Notturni ed Alba, for soprano and orch., Fire at Durilgai for orch., Cloudcatcher Fells for brass band, chamber music, keyboard works, and vocal compositions. Rachmaninov (short biog.), 1974; Bartok's Orchestral Music (BBC Music Guide), 1974; Haydn Piano Sonatas (Ariel Music Guide), 1986. *Recreations:* cricket, snooker, books, films. *Address:* 49 Burns Avenue, Southall, Mddx UB1 2LR.

McCAFFREY, Sir Thos Daniel, (Sir Tom McCaffrey), Kt 1979; public affairs consultant; *b* 20 Feb. 1922; *s* of William P. and B. McCaffrey; *m* 1949, Agnes Campbell Douglas; two *s* four *d.* *Educ:* Hyndland Secondary Sch. and St Aloysius Coll., Glasgow. Served War, RAF, 1940–46. Scottish Office, 1948–61; Chief Information Officer, Home Office, 1966–71; Press Secretary, 10 Downing Street, 1971–72; Dir of Information Services, Home Office, 1972–74; Head of News Dept, FCO, 1974–76; Chief Press Sec. to Prime Minister, 1976–79; Chief of Staff to Rt Hon. James Callaghan, MP, 1979–80; Chief Asst to Rt Hon. Michael Foot, MP, 1980–83; Hd, Chief Executive's Office, BPCC, 1983–84; Dir, Public Affairs, and Special Advr to the Publisher, Mirror Gp Newspapers, 1984–85. *Address:* Balmaha, The Park, Great Bookham, Surrey KT23 3JL. *T:* Bookham (0372) 54171.

MacCAIG, Norman (Alexander), OBE 1979; MA; FRSL; FRSE; ARSA; *b* 14 Nov. 1910; *s* of Robert McCaig and Joan MacLeod; *m* 1940, Isabel Munro (*d* 1990); one *s* one *d.* *Educ:* Edinburgh University. MA Hons Classics. FRSL 1965; ARSA 1981; FRSE 1983. Schoolteacher, 1932–67 and 1969–70; Fellow in Creative Writing, Univ. of Edinburgh, 1967–69; Lectr in English Studies, Univ. of Stirling, 1970–72, Reader in Poetry, 1972–77. Travelling Scholarship, Soc. of Authors, 1964; RSL Award (Heinemann Bequest), 1967; Cholmondeley Award, 1975; Scottish Arts Council Awards, 1954, 1966–67, 1970, 1971, 1978, 1980, 1986; Royal Bank of Scotland Saltire Award, 1985; Queen's Gold Medal for Poetry, 1986. DUniv Stirling, 1981; Hon. DLitt Edinburgh, 1983; Hon. LLD Dundee, 1986. *Publications: poetry:* Far Cry, 1943; The Inward Eye, 1946; Riding Lights, 1955; The Sinai Sort, 1957; A Common Grace, 1960; A Round of Applause, 1962; Measures, 1965; Surroundings, 1966; Rings on a Tree, 1968; A Man in My Position, 1969; The White Bird, 1973; The World's Room, 1974; Tree of Strings, 1977; The Equal Skies, 1980; A World of Difference, 1983; Collected Poems, 1985; Voice-over, 1988; Collected Poems, a new edition, 1990; (ed anthology) Honour'd Shade, 1959; (with Alexander Scott, ed anthology) Contemporary Scottish Verse, 1970. *Recreations:* fishing, music. *Address:* 7 Leamington Terrace, Edinburgh EH10 4JW. *T:* 031–229 1809. *Club:* Scottish Arts (Edinburgh).

McCALL, Sir (Charles) Patrick (Home), Kt 1971; MBE 1944; TD 1946; solicitor; Clerk of the County Council, 1960–72, Clerk of the Peace, 1960–71, and Clerk of the Lieutenancy, Lancashire, 1960–74; *b* 22 Nov. 1910; *s* of late Charles and Dorothy McCall; *m* 1934, Anne, *d* of late Samuel Brown, Sedlescombe, Sussex; two *s* one *d.* *Educ:* St Edward's Sch., Oxford. Served 1939–45; Substantive Major TA. Hon. Lt-Col. Mem., Economic and Social Cttee, EEC, 1973–78. *Recreations:* travel, walking, swimming, gardening. *Address:* Auchenhay Lodge, Corsock, by Castle Douglas, Kirkcudbrightshire DG7 3HZ. *T:* Corsock (06444) 651.

See also R. H. McCall.

McCALL, Christopher Hugh; QC 1987; *b* 3 March 1944; *yr s* of Robin Home McCall, *qv*; *m* 1981, Henrietta Francesca Sharpe. *Educ:* Winchester (Scholar); Magdalen Coll., Oxford (Demy; BA Maths, 1964; Eldon Law Scholar, 1966). Called to the Bar, Lincoln's Inn, 1966. Second Jun. Counsel to the Inland Revenue in chancery matters, 1977–87; Jun. Counsel to Attorney Gen. in charity matters, 1981–87. Mem, Bar Council, 1973–76; Jt

Hon. Treas., Barristers Benevolent Assoc., 1981–86. *Recreations:* music, travel, Egyptomania. *Address:* 7 New Square, Lincoln's Inn, WC2A 3QS. *T:* 071–405 1266. *Clubs:* Royal Automobile; Leander (Henley-on-Thames); Climbers.

McCALL, David Slesser, CBE 1988; Director since 1970 and Chief Executive since 1976, Anglia Television Ltd; Chief Executive, Anglia Television Group PLC, since 1986; *b* 3 Dec. 1934; *s* of Patrick McCall and Florence Kate Mary Walker; *m* 1968, Lois Patricia Elder. *Educ:* Robert Gordon's Coll., Aberdeen. Mem., Inst. of Chartered Accountants of Scotland, 1958. National Service, 1959–61. Accountant, Grampian Television Ltd, 1961–68; Company Sec., Anglia Television Ltd, 1968–76. Chm., Oxford Scientific Films Ltd, 1982–89; Director: Anglia Television Group plc, 1970–; ITN, 1978–86; Ind. Television Publications Ltd, 1971–89; Ind. Television Cos Assoc. Ltd, 1976–; Sodastream Holdings Ltd, 1976–85; Norwich City Football Club, 1979–85; Channel Four Television Co., 1981–85; Radio Broadland, 1984–91; Super Channel Ltd, 1986–88; British Satellite Broadcasting, 1987–90; E Adv. Bd, National Westminster Bank, 1988–; Television Sales and Marketing Services, 1989–. Chm., ITCA, subseq. Ind. Television Assoc., 1986–88. Pres., Norfolk and Norwich Chamber of Commerce, 1988–90 (Dep. Pres., 1986–88). FRTS 1988. CBIM 1988. *Recreations:* sport, travel. *Address:* Woodland Hall, Redenhall, Harleston, Norfolk IP20 9QW. *T:* Harleston (0379) 4442.

McCALL, John Armstrong Grice, CMG 1964; *b* 7 Jan. 1913; 2nd *s* of Rev. Canon J. G. McCall; *m* 1951, Kathleen Mary Clarke; no *c. Educ:* Glasgow Academy; Trinity Coll., Glenalmond; St Andrews Univ.; St John's Coll., Cambridge. MA 1st class hons Hist. St Andrews, 1935. Colonial Administrative Service (HMOCS), Nigeria, 1935–67; Cadet, 1936; Class I, 1956; Staff Grade, 1958. Chm., Mid-Western Nigeria Development Corp., Benin City, 1966–67, retired 1967. Asst Chief Admin. Officer, East Kilbride Develt Corp., 1967–76. Scottish Rep., Executive Cttee, Nigerian-British Chamber of Commerce, 1977–88. Mem. 1969, Vice-Chm. 1971, S Lanarkshire Local Employment Cttee; Mem. Panel, Industrial Tribunals (Scotland), 1972–74; Gen. Sec., Scotland, Royal Over-Seas League, 1978–80. Sec., West Linton Community Council, 1980–83. *Recreations:* golf, walking. *Address:* Burnside, West Linton, Peeblesshire EH46 7EW. *T:* West Linton (0968) 60488. *Clubs:* Caledonian; Old Glenalmond (Chm., 1978–81); Royal and Ancient (St Andrews).

McCALL, John Donald; Director, Consolidated Gold Fields Ltd, 1959–81 (Chairman, 1969–76); *b* 1 Feb. 1911; *s* of late Gilbert Kerr McCall; *m* 1942, Vere Stewart Gardner; one *s* one *d. Educ:* Clifton Coll.; Edinburgh Univ. Gold Mining industry, S Africa, 1930–39. Served War of 1939–45: commissioned, Gordon Highlanders. Joined Consolidated Gold Fields Ltd, London, 1946 (Dir, 1959; Jt Dep. Chm., 1968). Dir, Ultramar plc, 1965–. *Address:* 64 Pont Street, SW1. *Club:* Caledonian.

McCALL, Sir Patrick; *see* McCall, Sir C. P. H.

McCALL, Robin Home, CBE 1976 (OBE 1969); retired 1976; *b* 21 March 1912; *s* of late Charles and Dorothy McCall; *m* 1937, Joan Elizabeth Kingdon (*d* 1989); two *s* one *d. Educ:* St Edward's Sch., Oxford. Solicitors Final (Hons), 1935. Served War, RAFVR Night Fighter Controller (Sqdn Ldr); D Day landing Normandy, in command of 15083 GCI, 1944. Asst Solicitor: Bexhill Corp., 1935–39; Hastings Corp., 1939–46; Bristol Corp., 1946–47; Dep. Town Clerk, Hastings, 1947–48; Town Clerk and Clerk of the Peace, Winchester, 1948–72; Sec., Assoc. of Municipal Corporations, later Assoc. of Metropolitan Authorities, 1973–76. Hon. Sec., Non-County Boroughs Cttee for England and Wales, 1958–69; Member: Reading Cttee (Highway Law Consolidation); Morris Cttee (Jury Service); Kennett Preservation Gp (Historic Towns Conservation); Exec. Cttee, European Architectural Heritage Year, 1972–; UK delegn to ECLA (Council of Europe); North Hampshire Hosp. Cttee, 1969–72. Governor, St Swithin's Sch., Winchester, 1978–87; Mem., Winchester Excavations Cttee, 1962–. Hon. Freeman, City of Winchester, 1973. *Publications:* contrib. Local Government, Halsbury's Laws, 4th edn, 1980; various articles and reviews on local govt. *Recreations:* gardening, mountains. *Address:* Bernina, St Giles Hill, Winchester SO23 8JW. *T:* Winchester (0962) 854101. *Club:* Alpine.
See also C. H. McCall, Sir C. P. H. McCall.

McCALL, William; General Secretary, Institution of Professional Civil Servants, 1963–89; *b* 6 July 1929; *s* of Alexander McCall and Jean Corbet Cunningham; *m* 1955, Olga Helen Brunton; one *s* one *d. Educ:* Dumfries Academy; Ruskin College, Oxford. Civil Service, 1946–52; Social Insurance Dept, TUC, 1954–58; Asst Sec., Instn of Professional Civil Servants, 1958–63; Mem., Civil Service Nat. Whitley Council (Staff Side), 1963–89, Chm. 1969–71, Vice-Chm. 1983. Hon. Treasurer, Parly and Scientific Cttee, 1976–80; Part-time Mem., Eastern Electricity Board, 1977–86; Member: Cttee of Inquiry into Engrg Profession, 1977–79; PO Arbitration Tribunal, 1980–; TUC Gen. Council, 1984–89; Pay and Employment Policy Cttee, CVCP, 1990–. Mem. Ct, Univ. of London, 1984–; Mem. Council, Goldsmiths' Coll., 1989–. *Address:* Foothills, Gravel Path, Berkhamsted, Herts HP4 2PF. *T:* Berkhamsted (0442) 864974.

McCALL, Rt. Rev. William David Hair; *see* Willochra, Bishop of.

McCALLUM, Archibald Duncan Dugald, TD 1950; MA; Headmaster, Strathallan School, 1970–75; *b* 26 Nov. 1914; *s* of late Dr A. D. McCallum and Mrs A. D. McCallum; *m* 1950, Rosemary Constance, *widow* of Sqdn Ldr John Rhind, RAF, and *d* of William C. Thorne, OBE, Edinburgh; two *s* (one step *s*). *Educ:* Fettes Coll., Edinburgh; St John's Coll., Cambridge (Classical Sizar). Asst Master and Housemaster, Fettes Coll., 1937–39, 1945–51. Served War of 1939–45 (despatches): Home Forces, India, and Burma. Second Master, Strathallan Sch., 1951–56; Headmaster: Christ Coll., Brecon, 1956–62; Epsom Coll., 1962–70. FRSA 1969–75. *Recreations:* golf, reading. *Address:* 1 Church Row Cottages, Burnham Market, King's Lynn, Norfolk PE31 8DH. *T:* Fakenham (0328) 738518.

McCALLUM, Sir Donald (Murdo), Kt 1988; CBE 1976; FEng 1982; FRSE; DL; General Manager, Scottish Group, Ferranti plc, 1968–85; Hon. President: Ferranti Defence Systems Ltd, 1987–90 (Chairman, 1984–87); Ferranti Industrial Electronics Ltd, 1987–90 (Chairman, 1984–87); Director, Ferranti plc, 1970–87; *b* 6 Aug. 1922; *s* of Roderick McCallum and Lillian (*née* McPhee); *m* 1st, 1949, Barbara Black (*d* 1971); one *d*; 2nd, 1974, Mrs Margaret Illingworth (*née* Broadbent). *Educ:* George Watson's Boys' Coll.; Edinburgh Univ. (BSc). FIEE; FRAeS; CBIM. Admiralty Signal Establishment, 1942–46; Standard Telecommunication Laboratories, 1946; Ferranti Ltd, 1947. Dir, Short Bros Ltd, 1981–89; Chm., Laser Ecosse Ltd, 1990–. Chairman: Scottish Tertiary Education Adv. Council, 1984–87; Scottish Council Develt & Industry, 1985–; Scottish Sub-Cttee, UGC, 1987–88; Mem., UFC, 1989–91 (Chm., Scottish Sub-Cttee, 1989–91). Mem. Court, Heriot-Watt Univ., 1979–85. Hon. Life Mem., Edinburgh Univ. Students' Assoc., 1984. Liveryman, Company of Engineers, 1984; Freeman, City of London. DL City of Edinburgh, 1984. Hon. Fellow, Paisley Coll. of Technol., 1987; Fellow, SCOTVEC, 1988. DUniv Stirling, 1985; Hon. DSc: Heriot-Watt, 1986; Napier Coll. of Commerce and Technology, Edinburgh, 1986; Hon. LLD: Strathclyde, 1987; Aberdeen, 1989. British Gold Medal, RAcS, 1985. *Recreations:* photography, fishing. *Address:* 46 Heriot Row, Edinburgh EH3 6EX. *T:* 031–225 9331. *Clubs:* Caledonian; New (Edinburgh).

McCALLUM, Googie; *see* Withers, Googie.

McCALLUM, Ian; *see* McCallum, John.

McCALLUM, Ian Stewart; Executive Sales Manager, Save & Prosper Sales Ltd, since 1989 (Sales Manager, 1985–87, Area Manager, 1987–89); *b* 24 Sept. 1936; *s* of late John Blair McCallum and Margaret Stewart McCallum; *m* 1st, 1957, Pamela Mary (*née* Shave) (marr. diss. 1984); one *s* two *d*; 2nd, 1984, Jean (*née* Lynch); two step *d. Educ:* Kingston Grammar Sch. Eagle Star Insurance Co. Ltd, 1953–54; National Service, Highland Light Infantry, 1954–56; Eagle Star Insce Co. Ltd, 1956–58; F. E. Wright and Co., Insurance Brokers, 1958–63; H. Clarkson (Home) Ltd, Insurance Brokers, 1963–68; Save & Prosper Group Ltd, 1968–. Leader, Woking Borough Council, 1972–76 and 1978–81, Dep. Leader, 1981–82; Mayor of Woking, 1976–77; Chm., Assoc. of Dist Councils, 1979–84 (Leader, 1974–79); Vice-Chairman: Standing Cttee on Local Authorities and Theatre, 1977–81; UK Steering Cttee on Local Authority Superannuation, 1974–84; Member: Local Authorities Conditions of Service Adv. Bd, 1973–84; Consultative Council on Local Govt Finance, 1975–84; Council for Business in the Community, 1981–84; Audit Commn, 1983–86; Health Promotion Res. Trust, 1983–. Vice-Chm., Sports Council, 1980–86. *Recreations:* swimming, jogging, walking, reading, badminton. *Address:* 5 Minters Orchard, Maidstone Road, St Marys Platt, near Sevenoaks, Kent TN15 8QJ. *T:* Borough Green (0732) 883653. *Club:* St Stephen's Constitutional.

McCALLUM, John, BSc, FEng, FRINA, FICE; consultant naval architect; Chief Ship Surveyor, Lloyd's Register of Shipping, 1970–81; *b* 13 Oct. 1920; *s* of Hugh McCallum and Agnes Falconer McCallum (*née* Walker); *m* 1948, Christine Peggy Sowden (*d* 1989); two *s. Educ:* Allan Glen's Sch., Glasgow; Glasgow Univ. (BSc (First Cl. Hons Naval Architecture) 1943). Apprenticed John Brown & Co., Clydebank, 1938–43; Jun. Lectr, Naval Architecture, Glasgow Univ., 1943–44; Ship Surveyor, Lloyd's Register of Shipping, Newcastle upon Tyne, 1944, Glasgow, 1949, London, 1953; Naval Architect, John Brown & Co., 1961 (Chief Ship Designer, QE2); Technical Dir, John Brown Shipbuilders, 1967, Upper Clyde Shipbuilders, 1969. FRINA (Mem. Council, 1970–; Chm., 1971–73; Vice-Pres., 1975–); FEng 1977; FICE 1978. Mem., IES, 1962– (past Mem. Council); Member: SNAME, 1970–81, Fellow, 1981–; Smeatonian Soc. of Civil Engrs, 1979–; CEI Cttee on Internat. Affairs, 1980–83; Lloyd's Register Technical Cttee, 1981–. Liveryman, Worshipful Co. of Shipwrights, 1975 (Mem. Educn Cttee, 1975–90). *Publications:* various technical papers to Royal Soc., RINA, NE Coast IES, Assoc. Tech. Maritime et Aéronautique (1978 Medal), and other Europ. learned socs. *Recreations:* golf, piano, pastel art. *Address:* Dala, Garvock Drive, Kippington, Sevenoaks, Kent TN13 2LT. *T:* Sevenoaks 455462. *Clubs:* Caledonian, Caledonian Westminster Business.

McCALLUM, John Neil, CBE 1971; Chairman and Executive Producer, Fauna Films, Australia, since 1967, and John McCallum Productions, since 1976; actor and producer; *b* 14 March 1918; *s* of John Neil McCallum and Lilian Elsie (*née* Dyson); *m* 1948, Georgette Lizette Withers (*see* Googie Withers); one *s* two *d. Educ:* Oatlands Prep. Sch., Harrogate; Knox Grammar Sch., Sydney; C of E Grammar Sch., Brisbane; RADA. Served War, 2/5 Field Regt, AIF, 1941–45. Actor, English rep. theatres, 1937–39; Stratford-on-Avon Festival Theatre, 1939; Old Vic Theatre, 1940; British films and theatre, 1946–58; films include: It Always Rains On Sunday; Valley of Eagles; Miranda; London stage plays include: Roar Like a Dove; Janus; Waiting for Gillian; J. C. Williamson Theatres Ltd, Australia: Asst Man. Dir, 1958; Jt. Man. Dir, 1959–65; Man. Dir, 1966. Appeared in: (with Ingrid Bergman) The Constant Wife, London, 1973–74; (with Googie Withers) The Circle, London, 1976–77, Australia, 1982–83; (with Googie Withers) The Kingfisher, Australia, 1978–79; The Skin Game, The Cherry Orchard, and Dandy Dick, theatrical tour, England, 1981; The School for Scandal, British Council European tour, 1984; (with Googie Withers, and dir.) Stardust, tours England, 1984, Australia, 1984–85; The Chalk Garden, Chichester Fest., 1986; Hay Fever, Chichester Fest., 1988; The Royal Baccarat Scandal, Chichester Fest., 1988, Haymarket, 1989; (with Googie Withers) The Cocktail Hour, Australian and UK tour, 1989–90. Author of play, As It's Played Today, produced Melbourne, 1974. Produced television series, 1967–: Boney; Barrier Reef; Skippy; Bailey's Bird. Prod., Attack Force Z (feature film), 1980; Exec. Prod., The Highest Honor (feature film), 1982. Pres., Aust. Film Council, 1971–72. *Publication:* Life with Googie, 1979. *Recreation:* golf. *Address:* 1740 Pittwater Road, Bayview, NSW 2104, Australia. *T:* Sydney 9976879. *Clubs:* Garrick, MCC; Melbourne (Melbourne); Australian, Elanora Country (Sydney).

McCALLUM, Prof. Robert Ian, CBE 1987; MD, DSc; FRCP, FRCPEd, FFOM; Hon. Consultant, Institute of Occupational Medicine, Edinburgh, since 1985; Emeritus Professor, University of Newcastle upon Tyne, since 1985; *b* 14 Sept. 1920; *s* of Charles Hunter McCallum and Janet Lyon Smith; *m* 1952, Jean Katherine Bundy Learmonth; two *s* two *d. Educ:* Dulwich Coll., London; Guy's Hosp., London Univ. (MD 1946; DSc 1971). FRCP 1970; FRCPEd 1985; FFOM 1979. Ho. phys., ho. surgeon, Guy's Hosp., 1943; ho. phys., Brompton Hosp., 1945. Rockefeller Travelling Fellowship in Medicine (MRC), USA, 1953–54. Reader in Industrial Health, 1962–81, Prof. of Occupational Health and Hygiene, 1981–85, Univ. of Newcastle upon Tyne. Hon. Physician, Industrial Medicine, Royal Victoria Infirmary, Newcastle upon Tyne, 1958–85; Hon. Consultant in Occ. Health to the Army, 1980–86. Mem., MRC Decompression Sickness Panel, 1962– (Chm., 1982–85); Chm., Health Adv. Cttee, CEGB, 1987–89. British Council: Vis. Consultant, USSR, 1977; Vis. Specialist, Istanbul, 1987; Vis. Lectr, Faculty of Medicine, Baghdad, 1987. Stanley Melville Meml Lectr, Coll. of Radiographers, 1983; Sydenham Lectr, Soc. of Apothecaries, London, 1983; Ernestine Henry Lectr, RCP, 1987. Dean, Faculty of Occ. Medicine, RCP, 1984–86; President: Sect. of Occ. Medicine, RSM, 1976–77; Soc. of Occ. Medicine, 1979–80; British Occ. Hygiene Soc., 1983–84; Mem., Adv. Cttee on Pesticides, 1975–87. Hon. Dir, North of England Industrial Health Service, 1975–84. Editor, British Jl of Industrial Medicine, 1973–79. *Publications:* papers on pneumoconiosis, decompression sickness, dysbaric bone necrosis, and antimony toxicology. *Recreations:* gardening, swimming, Scottish country dancing. *Address:* 4 Chessel's Court, Canongate, Edinburgh EH8 8AD. *T:* 031–556 7977. *Clubs:* Royal Society of Medicine; University of Edinburgh Staff (Edinburgh).

McCAMLEY, Sir Graham (Edward), KBE 1986 (MBE 1981); Owner, Cattle Properties; *b* 24 Aug. 1932; *s* of Edward William George and Ivy McCamley; *m* 1956, Shirley Clarice Tindale; one *s* two *d. Educ:* Rockhampton Boys Grammar Sch. President: Aust. Brahman Breeders, 1971–74; Central Coastal Graziers, 1974–75; Cattlemen's Union of Australia, 1976–78. Mem. Producer of Australian Meat and Livestock Co., 1982–84. *Recreations:* tennis, boating, flying. *Clubs:* Queensland (Brisbane); Rockhampton, Rockhampton and District Masonic.

MAC CANA, Prof. Proinsias; Senior Professor, School of Celtic Studies, Dublin Institute for Advanced Studies, since 1985; *b* 6 July 1926; *s* of George Mc Cann and Mary Catherine Mallon; *m* 1952, Réiltín (*née* Supple); one *s* one *d. Educ:* St Malachy's Coll., Belfast; The Queen's Univ., Belfast (BA, MA, PhD); Ecole des Hautes Etudes, Paris. Asst Lectr, Celtic Dept, QUB, 1951–54; University College Wales, Aberystwyth: Asst Lectr in Early Irish, 1955–57; Lectr, 1957–61; Prof., Sch. of Celtic Studies, Dublin Inst. for Advanced Studies, 1961–63; Prof. of Welsh, 1963–71, Prof. of Early (incl. Medieval) Irish, 1971–85, UC Dublin. Prof. of Celtic Langs and Lits (Fall semester), Harvard Univ.,

1987–. Co-editor, Ériu (RIA Jl of Irish Studies), 1973–; General editor, Medieval and Modern Welsh Series, Dublin Inst. for Advanced Studies, 1962–. Chm., Governing Bd, Sch. of Celtic Studies, Dublin Inst. for Advanced Studies, 1975–85. PRIA, 1979–82. Mem., Academia Europaea, 1989. For. Hon. Mem., Amer. Acad. Arts and Scis, 1989. Hon. LittD Dublin, 1985; Hon. DLitt Ulster, 1991. *Publications:* Scéalaíocht na Ríthe (collection of early Irish tales trans. into Modern Irish), 1956; Branwen Daughter of Llŷr: the second branch of the Mabinogi, 1958; Celtic Mythology, 1970; The Mabinogi, 1977; Regnum and Sacerdotium: notes on Irish Tradition (Rhŷs Meml Lecture, British Academy), 1979; The Learned Tales of Medieval Ireland, 1980; (ed jtly) Rencontres de Religions, 1986. *Address:* 9 Silchester Road, Glenageary, Co. Dublin. *T:* Dublin 805062. *Club:* Kildare Street and University (Dublin).

McCANCE, Robert Alexander, CBE 1953; FRS 1948; Professor of Experimental Medicine, Medical Research Council and University of Cambridge, 1945–66, now Emeritus; Director, MRC Infantile Malnutrition Research Unit, Mulago Hospital, Kampala, 1966–68; Fellow of Sidney Sussex College; *b* near Belfast, Northern Ireland, 9 Dec. 1898; *s* of Mary L. Bristow and J. S. F. McCance, linen merchant, Belfast; *m* 1922, Mary L. MacGregor (*d* 1965); one *s* one *d. Educ:* St Bees Sch., Cumberland; Sidney Sussex Coll., Cambridge. RN Air Service and RAF, 1917–18; BA (Cambridge), 1922; Biochemical Research, Cambridge, 1922–25; qualified in medicine King's Coll. Hosp., London, 1927; MD (Cambridge), 1929; Asst Physician i/c biochemical research, King's Coll. Hosp., London; FRCP 1935; Goulstonian Lectr, RCP, 1936; Humphrey Rolleston Lectr, RCP, 1953; Groningen Univ. Lectr, 1958; Leonard Parsons Lectr, Birmingham Univ., 1959; Lumleian Lectr, RCP, 1962. Reader in Medicine, Cambridge Univ., 1938; War of 1939–45, worked on medical problems of national importance; visited Spain and Portugal on behalf of British Council, 1943, South Africa, 1965; i/c Medical Research Council Unit, Germany, 1946–49. Hon. FRCOG; Hon. Member: Assoc. of American Physicians; American Pediatric Soc.; Swiss Nutrition Soc.; Brit. Pædiatric Assoc.; Nutrition Soc. Gold Medal, West London Medico-Chirurgical Soc., 1949. Conway Evans Prize, RCP and Royal Society, 1960; James Spence Medal, Brit. Pæd. Assoc., 1961. Hon. DSc Belfast, 1964. *Publications:* Medical Problems in Mineral Metabolism (Goulstonian Lectures), 1936; (jointly) The Chemical Composition of Foods; An Experimental Study of Rationing; (jointly) Breads White and Brown; numerous papers on the physiology of the newborn animal. *Recreations:* mountaineering, cycling, gardening. *Address:* 32 Havenfield, Arbury Road, Cambridge CB4 2JY.

McCANN, His Eminence Cardinal Owen, DD, PhD, BCom; Archbishop Emeritus of Cape Town; Cardinal since 1965 (Titular Church, St Praxedes); *b* 26 June 1907. *Educ:* St Joseph's Coll., Rondebosch, CP; Univ. of Cape Town; Collegium Urbanianum de Propaganda Fide, Rome. Priest, 1935. Editor, The Southern Cross, 1940–48 and 1986–; Administrator, St Mary's Cathedral, Cape Town, 1948–50; Archbishop of Cape Town, 1950–84. Hon. DLitt Univ. of Cape Town, 1968; Hon. Dr Hum. Lett. Coll. of St Joseph, Portland, Maine, USA, 1984. Freeman of City of Cape Town, 1984. *Address:* Oak Lodge, Fair Seat Lane, Wynberg, CP, South Africa; Chancery Office, Cathedral Place, 12 Bouquet Street, Cape Town. *Club:* City and Civil Service (Cape Town).

McCANN, Peter Toland McAree, CBE 1977; JP; DL; Lord Provost of the City of Glasgow and Lord-Lieutenant of the City of Glasgow, 1975–77; *b* 2 Aug. 1924; *s* of Peter McCann and Agnes (*née* Waddell); *m* 1958, Maura Eleanor (*née* Ferris); one *s. Educ:* St Mungo's Academy; Glasgow Univ. (BL). Solicitor and Notary Public. Pres., Glasgow Univ. Law Soc., 1946; Pres., St Thomas More Soc., 1959. Mem. Glasgow Corp., 1961. Chm., McCann Cttee (Secondary Educn for Physically Handicapped Children), 1971. DL Glasgow, 1978. OStJ 1977. Medal of King Faisal of Saudi Arabia, 1976. *Recreations:* music, history, model aeroplane making. *Address:* 31 Queen Mary Avenue, Glasgow G42 8DS.

McCARRAHER, David, VRD 1964; **His Honour Judge McCarraher;** a Circuit Judge, since 1984; *b* 6 Nov. 1922; *s* of Colin McCarraher and Vera Mabel McCarraher (*née* Hickley) *m* 1950, Betty Johnson (*née* Haywood) (*d* 1990); one *s* three *d. Educ:* King Edward VI Sch., Southampton; Magdalene Coll., Cambridge (MA Law). RN, 1941–45. Called to the Bar, Lincoln's Inn, 1948; practised Western Circuit until 1952, disbarred at own request to be articled; admitted solicitor, 1955; Sen. Partner in private practice, 1960–84; a Recorder, 1979–84. Mem. Panel, Dep. Circuit Judges, 1973–79. Founder Mem. and Past Pres., Southampton Junior Chamber of Commerce. Governor, King Edward VI Sch., Southampton, 1961–84 (Chm., 1983–84; Fellow, 1986). Sub-Lieut, RNVR, 1943–45, RNVSR, 1946–52; served to Captain RNR, 1969; CO Solent Div., RNR, 1969–72; ADC to the Queen, 1972–73; retired 1975. Hon. Sec., RNR Benevolent Fund, 1973–84. *Recreations:* family, golf, sailing. *Clubs:* Naval; Thames Rowing, Law Society's Yacht; Stoneham Golf (Southampton); Royal Naval Sailing Association (Portsmouth); Southampton Police (Hon. Mem.) (Southampton).

McCARTHY, family name of **Baron McCarthy.**

McCARTHY, Baron *cr* 1975 (Life Peer), of Headington; **William Edward John McCarthy,** DPhil; Fellow of Nuffield College and Associate Fellow of Templeton College, Oxford; University Lecturer in Industrial Relations; engaged in Industrial Arbitration and Chairman of Committees of Inquiry and Investigation, since 1968; *b* 30 July 1925; *s* of E. and H. McCarthy; *m* 1957, Margaret, *d* of Percival Godfrey. *Educ:* Holloway County; Ruskin Coll.; Merton Coll.; Nuffield Coll. MA (Oxon), DPhil (Oxon). Trade Union Scholarship to Ruskin Coll., 1953; Research Fellow of Nuffield Coll., 1959; Research Dir, Royal Commn on Trade Unions and Employers' Assocs, 1965–68; Sen. Economic Adviser, Dept of Employment, 1968–71. Chm., Railway Staff Nat. Tribunal, 1973–86; Special Advisor on Industrial Relations to Sec. of State for Social Services, 1975–77; Member: Houghton Cttee on Aid to Political Parties, 1975–76; TUC Independent Review Cttee, 1976; Pres., British Univ. Industrial Relations Assoc., 1975–78; Special Comr, Equal Opportunities Commn, 1977–80; Dep. Chm., Teachers' Nat. Conciliation Cttee, 1979–. Chairman: TUC Newspaper Feasibility Adv. Study Gp, 1981–83; Independent Inquiry into Rover Closure Proposals, 1989–90. Mem., H of L Select Cttee on Unemployment, 1980–82; Opposition front bench spokesman on employment, 1980–. Mem., All Party Motor Industry Gp, 1989–. *Publications:* The Closed Shop in Britain, 1964; The Role of Shop Stewards in British Industrial Relations, 1966; (with V. L. Munns) Employers' Associations, 1967; (with A. I. Marsh) Disputes Procedures in Britain, 1968; The Reform of Collective Bargaining at Plant and Company Level, 1971; (ed) Trade Unions, 1972, 2nd edn, 1985; (with A. I. Collier) Coming to Terms with Trade Unions, 1973; (with N. D. Ellis) Management by Agreement, 1973; (with J. F. O'Brien and V. E. Dowd) Wage Inflation and Wage Leadership, 1975; Making Whitley Work, 1977; (jtly) Change in Trade Unions, 1981; (jtly) Strikes in Post-War Britain, 1983; Freedom at Work 1985; The Future of Industrial Democracy, 1988; (with C. Jennings and R. Undy) Employee Relations Audits, 1989; articles in: Brit. Jl of Industrial Relns; Industrial Relns Jl. *Recreations:* gardening, theatre, ballet. *Address:* 4 William Orchard Close, Old Headington, Oxford OX3 9DR. *T:* Oxford (0865) 62016. *Club:* Reform.

McCARTHY, Adolf Charles; HM Diplomatic Service, retired; Hon. British Consul at Freiburg, since 1985; *b* 19 July 1922; *s* of Herbert Charles McCarthy and Anna Schnorf; *m* 1949, Ursula Vera Grimm; one *s* two *d. Educ:* London Univ. (BScEcon). Served War, RN, 1942–46. Min. of Agriculture, Fisheries and Food, 1939–64; Min. of Overseas Develt, 1964–66; HM Diplomatic Service, 1966; First Secretary: (Economic), Pretoria, 1968–70; (Commercial), Wellington, 1971–74; Asst Head of Western European Dept, FCO, 1974–77; Consul-Gen., Stuttgart, 1977–82. *Publication:* Robert Grimm: the Swiss revolutionary, 1990. *Recreations:* music, modern political history. *Address:* Buchenstrasse 4, 7803 Gundelfingen, Federal Republic of Germany. *Club:* Rotary (Freiburg i. Br.).

McCARTHY, Donal John, CMG 1969; HM Diplomatic Service, retired; *b* 31 March 1922; *s* of Daniel and Kathleen McCarthy. *Educ:* Holloway Sch.; London Univ. Served Royal Navy, 1942–46. Foreign Office, 1946; Middle East Centre for Arab Studies, 1947–48; 3rd and 2nd Sec., Brit. Embassy, Jedda, 1948–51; 2nd Sec., Political Div., Brit. Middle East Office, 1951–55; 1st Sec., FO, 1955–58; Asst Polit. Agent, Kuwait, 1958–60; Brit. High Commn, Ottawa, 1960–63; FO, 1963–64; Counsellor, Brit. High Commn, Aden, and Polit. Adviser to C-in-C Middle East, 1964–67; Head of Aden Dept, FO, 1967–68, of Arabian Dept, FCO, 1968–70; IDC, 1970–71; Minister (Economic and Social Affairs), UK Mission to UN, 1971–73; Ambassador to United Arab Emirates, 1973–77; FCO, 1978–79. *Recreations:* music, sailing, skiing. *Address:* Church Farmhouse, Sudbourne, Suffolk IP12 2BP. *T:* Orford (0394) 443. *Clubs:* Travellers', Royal Automobile, Ski Club of Great Britain.

McCARTHY, Eugene Joseph; writer, since 1971; *b* 29 March 1916; *s* of Michael J. and Anna Baden McCarthy; *m* 1945, Abigail Quigley McCarthy; one *s* three *d. Educ:* St John's Univ., Collegeville (BA); Univ. of Minnesota (MA). Teacher in public schools, 1935–40; Coll. Prof. of Econs and Sociology, and civilian techn. Asst in Mil. Intell. for War Dept, 1940–48; US Representative in Congress of 4th District, Minnesota, 1949–58; US Senator from Minnesota, 1959–70. Independent. Holds hon. degrees. *Publications:* Frontiers in American Democracy, 1960; Dictionary of American Politics, 1962; A Liberal Answer to the Conservative Challenge, 1964; The Limits of Power, 1967; The Year of the People, 1969; Other Things and the Aardvark (poetry), 1970; The Hard Years, 1975; Mr Raccoon and his Friends (children's stories), 1977; (with James Kilpatrick) A Political Bestiary, 1978; Ground Fog and Night (poetry), 1978; America Revisited: 150 years after Tocqueville, 1978; The Ultimate Tyranny: the majority over the majority, 1980; Gene McCarthy's Minnesota, 1982; Complexities and Contraries, 1982; The View from Rappahannock, 1984; Up 'Til Now, 1987; Required Reading, 1988; The View from Rappahannock II, 1989; contribs to Saturday Review, Commonweal, Harper's, New Republic, USA Today. *Address:* Box 22, Woodville, Va 22749, USA.

McCARTHY, Nicholas Melvyn, OBE 1983; HM Diplomatic Service; Deputy Head of Mission, Brussels, since 1990; *b* 4 April 1938; *s* of Daniel Alfred McCarthy and Florence Alice McCarthy; *m* 1961, Gillian Eileen Hill; three *s* one *d. Educ:* Queen Elizabeth's Sch., Faversham; London Univ. (BA Hons). Attaché, Saigon, 1961–64; Language Student, then Second Sec., Tokyo, 1964–69; FCO, 1969–73; First Sec., Brussels, 1973–78; FCO, 1978–80; Head of Chancery, Dakar, 1980–84; FCO, 1984–85; Consul-Gen., Osaka, 1985–90. *Recreations:* bridge, squash, windsurfing, tennis. *Address:* c/o Foreign and Commonwealth Office, King Charles Street, SW1A 2AH. *Club:* Sundridge Park Lawn Tennis.

McCARTHY, (Patrick) Peter; Regional Chairman, London North, Industrial Tribunals, 1987–90; Part-time Chairman, Industrial Tribunals, 1990–April 1992; *b* 10 July 1919; *er s* of late William McCarthy and Mary McCarthy; *m* 1945, Isabel Mary, *y d* of late Dr Joseph Unsworth, St Helens; two *s* three *d. Educ:* St Francis Xavier's Coll., Liverpool; Liverpool Univ. LLB 1940, LLM 1942. Admitted Solicitor, 1942; in private practice until 1974. Part-time Chm., 1972–74, full-time Chm., 1975–90, Regl Chm., Liverpool, 1977–87, Industrial Tribunals; part-time Chm., Rent Assessment Cttee, 1972–74. JP Liverpool, 1968–74. *Address:* Brook Cottage, Sham Castle Lane, Bathwick, Bath BA2 6JH.

McCARTHY, Rt. Hon. Sir Thaddeus (Pearcey), PC 1968; KBE 1974; Kt 1964; Judge of the Court of Appeal of New Zealand, 1963–76, President, 1973–76; Chairman, New Zealand Press Council, 1978–89; *b* 24 Aug. 1907; *s* of Walter McCarthy, Napier, merchant; *m* 1938, Joan Margaret Miller; one *s* two *d* (and one *d* decd). *Educ:* St Bede's Coll., Christchurch, New Zealand; Victoria Univ. Coll., Wellington. Master of Laws (1st Class Hons) 1931. Served War of 1939–45 in MEF with 22 Bn 2 NZEF, later as DJAG, 2 NZEF. Practised as Barrister and Solicitor until 1957 when appointed to Supreme Court. Chairman: Royal Commn on State Services, 1961–62; Winston Churchill Memorial Trust, 1966–76; Royal Commissions: on Salary and Wage Fixing Procedures in the State Services, 1968; on Social Security, 1969; on Horse Racing, Trotting and Dog Racing, 1969; on Salaries and Wages in the State Services, 1972; on Nuclear Power Generation, 1976–78; on Maori Land Courts, 1979–; Chm., Security Review Authority and Comr of Security Appeals, 1977–. Chm. Adv. Cttee, NZ Computer Centre, 1977–86. Vice-Pres., NZ Sect., Internat. Commn of Jurists. Chm., Queen Elizabeth II Nat. Trust, 1978–84. Fellow, NZ Inst. of Public Admin, 1984. Hon. Bencher, Middle Temple, 1974. Hon. LLD Victoria Univ. of Wellington, 1978. *Recreations:* golf (Captain, Wellington Golf Club, 1952, Pres., 1973–77), sailing. *Address:* Wharenui, 274 Oriental Parade, Wellington, New Zealand. *Club:* Wellington (Wellington, NZ) (Pres., 1976–78).

McCARTIE, Rt. Rev. (Patrick) Leo; see Northampton, Bishop of, (RC).

McCARTNEY, Gordon Arthur; consultant; Secretary, Association of District Councils, 1981–91; *b* 29 April 1937; *s* of Arthur and Hannah McCartney; *m* 1st, 1960, Ceris Ysobel Davies (marr. diss. 1987); two *d*; 2nd, 1988, Wendy Ann Vyvyan Titman. *Educ:* Grove Park Grammar Sch., Wrexham. Articled to Philip J. Walters, MBE (Town Clerk, Wrexham), 1954–59; admitted solicitor, 1959. Asst Solicitor, Birkenhead County Bor. Council, 1959–61; Asst Solicitor, 1961–63, Sen. Asst Solicitor, 1963–65, Bootle County Bor. Council; Dep. Clerk, Wrexham RDC, 1965–73; Clerk, Holywell RDC, 1973–74; Chief Exec., Delyn Bor. Council, 1974–81. Dir, Nat. Transport Tokens Ltd, 1984–. Secretary-General, British Section, IULA/CEMR, 1984–88; Co. Sec., Local Govt Internat. Bureau, 1988–. *Recreations:* gardening, football, cricket, music. *Address:* 33 Duck Street, Elton, Peterborough PE8 6RQ. *T:* Oundle (0832) 280659; 108 Frobisher House, Dolphin Square, SW1. *T:* 071–798 8777. *Clubs:* City and Counties (Peterborough); Middlesex CCC, Northants CCC.

McCARTNEY, Hugh; *b* 3 Jan. 1920; *s* of John McCartney and Mary Wilson; *m* 1949, Margaret; one *s* two *d. Educ:* Royal Technical Coll., Glasgow; John Street Senior Secondary School. Apprentice in textile industry, 1934–39; entered aircraft engrg industry, Coventry, 1939; joined Rolls Royce, Glasgow, 1941; joined RAF as aero-engine fitter, 1942 and resumed employment with Rolls Royce, 1947; representative with company (later one of GKN group) specialising in manufacture of safety footware, 1951. Joined Ind. Labour Party, 1934; joined Labour Party, 1936. Town Councillor, 1955–70 and Magistrate, 1965–70, Kirkintilloch; Mem., Dunbarton CC, 1965–70. MP (Lab): Dunbartonshire E, 1970–74; Dunbartonshire Central, 1974–83; Clydebank and Milngavie, 1983–87. Scottish Regional Whip, 1979–83; Mem., Speaker's Panel of Chairmen, 1984–87. Chm., TGWU Parly Group, 1986–87. Mem., Rent Assessment Panel for Scotland, 1968–70. *Recreation:* spectating at football matches and athletic meetings (political activities permitting). *Address:* 23 Merkland Drive, Kirkintilloch G66 3PG.

See also I. McCartney.

McCARTNEY, Ian; MP (Lab) Makerfield, since 1987; *b* 25 April 1951; *s* of Hugh McCartney, *qv*; *m* (marr. diss.); one *s* two *d*; *m* 1988, Ann Parkes (*née* Kevan). *Educ:* State primary, secondary schools; Tech. Colls. Led paper boy strike, 1965; joined Labour Party, 1966; joined trade union, 1966; seaman, local govt manual worker, chef, 1966–71; unemployed, 1971–73; Labour Party Organiser, 1973–87. Councillor, Wigan Borough, 1982–87. Hon. Parly Adviser: to Greater Manchester Fire and Civil Defence Authy, 1987– (Mem., 1986); to Nat. Assoc. for Safety in the Home, 1989–. Mem., Parly Select Cttee on Health and Social Security; Jt Sec., Parly Leasehold Reform Gp. All Party Chairman: Rugby League Gp; Home Safety Gp, 1988–; Child Abduction Gp, 1990–; Chm., T&GWU Parly Gp, 1989–. Sponsored by TGWU. *Recreations:* Wigan Rugby League fanatic; head of McCartney family, a family of proud working class stock. *Address:* 95 Victoria Road, Platt Bridge, Wigan WN2 5ND. *T:* Wigan (0942) 861502. *Club:* Platt Bridge Labour.

McCARTNEY, (James) Paul, MBE 1965; musician, composer; *b* Allerton, Liverpool, 18 June 1942; *s* of late James McCartney and Mary McCartney; *m* 1969, Linda Eastman; one *s* two *d*, and one step *d*. *Educ:* Liverpool Inst. Mem., skiffle group, The Quarry Men, 1957–59; toured Scotland with them and Stu Sutcliffe as the Silver Beetles; made 1st important appearance as the Beatles at Litherland Town Hall, nr Liverpool, Dec. 1960; appeared as mem. of Beatles: UK, Sweden, and Royal Variety perf., London, 1963; UK, Netherlands, Sweden, France, Denmark, Hong Kong, Australia, NZ, Canada, 1964; TV appearances, USA, and later, coast-to-coast tour, 1964; UK, France, Italy, Spain, USA, Canada, 1965; Beatles disbanded 1970; formed MPL group of cos, 1970, and own pop group, Wings, 1971; toured: UK, Europe, 1972–73; UK, Australia, 1975; Europe, USA, 1976; UK, 1979; Wings disbanded 1981; Europe, UK, Canada, USA, Brazil, 1989/90. *Songs* with John Lennon include: Love Me Do; Please Please Me; She Loves You; Can't Buy Me Love; I Want to Hold Your Hand; I Saw Her Standing There; Eight Days a Week; All My Loving; Help!; Ticket to Ride; I Feel Fine; I'm A Loser; A Hard Day's Night; No Reply; I'll Follow The Sun; Yesterday; Eleanor Rigby; Yellow Submarine; Penny Lane; All You Need Is Love; Lady Madonna; Hey Jude; From Me To You; We Can Work It Out; Day Tripper; Paperback Writer; Hello, Goodbye; Get Back; Let It Be; The Long and Winding Road; subseq. *songs* include: Maybe I'm Amazed; My Love; Let 'Em In; Silly Love Songs; Mull of Kintyre; Coming Up; No More Lonely Nights. *Albums* with the Beatles: Please Please Me, 1963; With The Beatles, 1963; A Hard Day's Night, 1964; Beatles for Sale, 1964; Help!, 1965; Rubber Soul, 1965; Revolver, 1966; Sgt Pepper's Lonely Hearts Club Band, 1967; Magical Mystery Tour, 1967; The Beatles (White Album), 1968; Yellow Submarine, 1969; Abbey Road, 1969; Let it Be, 1970; subseq. *albums* include: McCartney, 1970; Ram, 1971; Wildlife, 1971; Red Rose Speedway, 1973; Band on the Run, 1973; Venus and Mars, 1975; Wings at the Speed of Sound, 1976; Wings over America, 1976; London Town, 1978; Wings Greatest, 1978; Back to the Egg, 1979; McCartney II, 1980; Tug of War, 1982; Pipes of Peace, 1983; Give My Regards to Broad Street, 1984; Press to Play, 1986; All the Best!, 1987; CHOBA B CCCP, 1988; Flowers in the Dirt, 1989; Tripping the Live Fantastic, 1990. *Films* (with the Beatles): A Hard Day's Night, 1964; Help!, 1965; Yellow Submarine, 1968; Let It Be, 1970; (with Wings) Rockshow, 1981; (wrote, composed score, and acted in) Give My Regards To Broad Street, 1984; (wrote, composed score and produced) Rupert and the Frog Song, 1984 (BAFTA award, Best Animated Film). *Film scores:* The Family Way, 1967; Live and Let Die, 1973 (title song only); Twice In A Lifetime, 1984 (title song only); *TV score:* The Zoo Gang (series), 1973. Live Russian 'phone link-up, BBC Russian Service, 1989. Numerous Grammy Awards, Nat. Acad. of Recording Arts and Scis, USA, incl. Lifetime Achievement Award, 1990; Ivor Novello Award: for Internat. Achievement, 1980; for Internat. Hit of the Year (Ebony and Ivory), 1982; for Outstanding Contrib. to Music, 1989; PRS special award for unique achievement in popular music, 1990. Freeman, City of Liverpool, 1984. DUniv Sussex, 1988. *Address:* c/o MPL Communications Ltd, 1 Soho Square, W1V 6BQ.

McCAUGHEY, John Davis, AC 1987; Governor of Victoria, Australia, 1986–91; *b* 12 July 1914; *s* of John and Lizzie McCaughey; *m* 1940, Jean Middlemas Henderson; three *s* two *d*. *Educ:* Pembroke Coll., Cambridge (MA; Hon. Fellow, 1988); New Coll., Edinburgh; Presbyterian Coll., Belfast. Ordained in Presbyt. Ch. in Ireland, 1942; Study Sec., SCM, 1946–52; Prof. of NT Studies, Ormond Coll., Univ. of Melbourne, 1953–64, Master of the Coll. 1959–79; Dep. Chancellor, Univ. of Melbourne, 1978–79, 1982–85. Pres., Uniting Church in Australia, 1977–79. Hon. FRACP 1988. Hon. DD Edinburgh, 1966; Hon. LLD: Melbourne, 1982; QUB, 1987. *Publications:* Christian Obedience in the University, 1958; Diversity and Unity in the New Testament Picture of Christ, 1969; Piecing Together a Shared Vision (Boyer Lectures), 1988; articles in Colloquium, Aust. Biblical Rev., etc. *Recreations:* reading, listening, golf. *Address:* 82 Story Street, Parkville, Vic 3052, Australia. *Clubs:* Melbourne, Royal Melbourne Golf.

McCAUSLAND, Benedict Maurice Perronet T.; *see* Thompson-McCausland.

McCAVE, Prof. Ian Nicholas, FGS; Woodwardian Professor of Geology, since 1985, and Head of the Department of Earth Sciences, since 1988, University of Cambridge; Fellow, St John's College, Cambridge, since 1986; *b* 3 Feb. 1941; *s* of Thomas Theasby McCave and Gwendoline Marguerite McCave (*née* Langlois); *m* 1972, Susan Caroline Adams (*née* Bambridge); three *s* one *d*. *Educ:* Elizabeth Coll., Guernsey; Hertford Coll., Oxford (MA, DSc); Brown Univ., USA (PhD). FGS 1963. NATO Research Fellow, Netherlands Inst. for Sea Research, 1967–69; Lectr 1969–76, Reader 1976–84, UEA, Norwich. Vis. Prof., Oregon State Univ., 1974; Vis. Investigator, Woods Hole Oceanographic Instn, 1978–85. *Publications:* (ed) The Benthic Boundary Layer, 1976; over 80 papers in jls. *Recreations:* pottering about in the garden, rowing. *Address:* Marlborough House, 23 Victoria Street, Cambridge CB1 1JP.

McCAW, Hon. Sir Kenneth (Malcolm), Kt 1975; QC (Australia) 1972; Attorney-General of New South Wales, 1965–75, retired; *b* 8 Oct. 1907; *s* of Mark Malcolm and Jessie Alice McCaw; *m* 1968, Valma Marjorie Cherlin (*née* Stackpool); *s* one *d*. *Educ:* matriculated evening college. Left school, 1919; farm and saw-mill hand; clerk, commercial offices and law office, 1922–28; articled law clerk, 1928–33; admitted Solicitor and founded city law firm, 1933; Attorney, Solicitor and Proctor, NSW Supreme Court, until 1965; admitted to NSW Bar, 1965. Councillor, NSW Law Soc., 1945–48. MLA (Lib.) for Lane Cove, NSW, 1947–75, retired. *Publication:* People Versus Power, 1978. *Recreations:* swimming, walking, Braille reading, music, elocution. *Address:* Woodrow House, Charlish Lane, Lane Cove, NSW 2066, Australia. *T:* 427–1900. *Clubs:* Sydney, Lane Cove Businessmen's, (Charter Mem.) Lane Cove Lions (all Sydney/Metropolitan).

McCLEAN, Prof. (John) David; Professor of Law, since 1973, Pro-Vice-Chancellor, since 1991, Dean of Faculty of Law, 1978–81, Public Orator, 1988–91, University of Sheffield; *b* 4 July 1939; *s* of Major Harold McClean and Mrs Mabel McClean; *m* 1966, Pamela Ann Loader; one *s* one *d*. *Educ:* Queen Elizabeth's Grammar Sch., Blackburn; Magdalen Coll., Oxford (DCL, 1984). Called to the Bar, Gray's Inn, 1963. Asst Lectr 1961, Lectr 1963, Sen. Lectr 1968, Univ. of Sheffield. Vis. Lectr in Law, Monash Univ., Melbourne, 1968, Vis Prof., 1978. Vice-Chm., C of E Bd for Social Responsibility, 1978–80. Member: Gen. Synod of C of E, 1970– (Vice-Chm., House of Laity, 1979–85, Chm. 1985–); Crown Appts Commn, 1977–87. *Publications:* Criminal Justice and the Treatment of Offenders (jtly), 1969; (contrib.) Halsbury's Laws of England, 4th edn 1974; The Legal Context of Social Work, 1975, 2nd edn 1980; (jtly) Defendants in the Criminal Process, 1976; (ed jtly) Shawcross and Beaumont, Air Law, 4th edn 1977, reissue (new edn of one vol.) 1983; (jtly) Recognition and Enforcement of Judgments, etc, within the Commonwealth, 1977; (ed jtly) Dicey and Morris, Conflict of Laws, 10th edn 1980, 11th edn 1987; Recognition of Family Judgments in the Commonwealth, 1983. *Recreation:* detective fiction. *Address:* 6 Burnt Stones Close, Sheffield S10 5TS. *T:* Sheffield (0742) 305794. *Club:* Commonwealth Trust.

McCLEAN, Kathleen; *see* Hale, Kathleen.

McCLELLAN, Col Sir (Herbert) Gerard (Thomas), Kt 1986; CBE 1979 (OBE 1960); TD 1955; JP; DL; company director; *b* 24 Sept. 1913; *s* of late George McClellan and Lilian (*née* Fitzgerald); *m* 1939, Rebecca Ann (Nancy) Desforges (*d* 1982); one *s* three *d*. Served War of 1939–45, Loyal (N Lancs) Regt, RA, London Irish Rifles, in ME, N Africa and Italy (wounded; despatches). Commanded 626 HAA (Liverpool Irish) Regt and 470 LAA (3rd West Lancs) Regt, RA TA, 1955–60; County Comdt, W Lancs ACF, 1961–66; Member: W Lancs T&AVRA, 1955–66 (Vice-Chm., 1966–68); NW England and IoM T&AVRA, 1968–70 (Vice-Chm., 1970–75; Chm., 1975–79). Former Mem. (C) for Childwall, Liverpool City Council; Member: Liverpool Cons. Assoc., 1960– (Vice-Chm., 1966–75; Chm., 1975–85), NW Area Cons. Assoc., 1971–; Exec. Cttee, Nat. Union of Cons. and Unionist Assocs, 1982–87; Chairman: Wavertree Cons. Assoc., 1962–67 (Pres., 1967–76); Liverpool European Cons. Constituency Council, 1978–84; Merseyside W European Cons. Constit. Council, 1984–85 (Pres., 1985–); President: Garston Cons. Assoc., 1979–; Halewood Cons. Club, 1983–; Crosby Cons. Assoc., 1986–; Vice-Pres. Woolton Ward Cons. Assoc., 1981–. Vice-President: Merseyside Co. SSAFA, 1975–; Incorp. Liverpool Sch. of Tropical Medicine, 1987–. FIAM. DL Lancs later Merseyside, 1967; JP Liverpool, 1968; High Sheriff of Merseyside, 1980–81. *Address:* Westwood, Windermere Road, Hightown, Liverpool L38 3RJ. *T:* 051-929 2269. *Clubs:* Army and Navy; Athenæum (Liverpool).

McCLELLAN, John Forrest; Under Secretary, Industry Department for Scotland (formerly Scottish Economic Planning Department), 1980–85, retired; *b* 15 Aug. 1932; *s* of John McClellan and Hester (*née* Niven); *m* 1956, Eva Maria Pressel; three *s* one *d*. *Educ:* Ferryhill Primary Sch., Aberdeen; Aberdeen Grammar Sch.; Aberdeen Univ. (MA). Served Army, 2nd Lieut, Gordon Highlanders and Nigeria Regt, RWAFF, 1954–56. Entered Civil Service, 1956; Asst Principal, Scottish Educn Dept, 1956–59; Private Sec. to Perm. Under Sec. of State, Scottish Office, 1959–60; Principal, Scottish Educn Dept, 1960–68; Civil Service Fellow, Glasgow Univ., 1968–69; Asst Sec., Scottish Educn Dept, 1969–77; Asst Under Sec. of State, Scottish Office, 1977–80. Dir, Scottish Internat. Educn Trust, 1986–; Mem., Management Cttee, Hanover (Scotland) Housing Assoc., 1986–. Hon. Fellow, Dundee Inst. of Technology, 1988. *Publication:* Then a Soldier, 1991. *Recreations:* gardening, walking. *Address:* Grangeneuk, West Linton, Peeblesshire EH46 7HG. *T:* West Linton (0968) 60502. *Club:* Royal Scots (Edinburgh).

McCLELLAND, Hon. Douglas, AC 1987; High Commissioner for Australia in the United Kingdom, 1987–91; *s* of Alfred McClelland and Gertrude Amy Cooksley; *m* Lorna Belva McNeill; one *s* two *d*. Mem. NSW ALP Executive, 1956–62; Hon. Dir, St George Hosp., Sydney, 1957–68. Member, Australian Senate for NSW, 1962–87; Senate appointments: Minister for the Media, 1972–75; Manager, Govt Business, 1974–75; Special Minister of State, June–Nov. 1975; Opposition spokesman on Admin. Services, 1976–77; Manager, Opposition Business, 1976–77; Dep. Leader of Opposition, May–Dec. 1977; Dep. Pres. and Chm of Cttees, 1981–82; Pres. of the Australian Senate, 1983–87. *Recreations:* No 1 supporter, St George Rugby League FC; reading, making friends. *Address:* c/o Department of Foreign Affairs, Sydney, NSW, Australia. *Clubs:* City Tattersalls (Life Mem.); St George Rugby League Football.

McCLELLAND, George Ewart, CB 1986; Solicitor, Department of Employment, 1982–87; *b* 27 March 1927; *s* of George Ewart McClelland and Winifred (*née* Robinson); *m* 1956, Ann Penelope, *yr d* of late Judge Arthur Henry Armstrong; one *s* two *d*. *Educ:* Stonyhurst Coll.; Merton Coll., Oxford (Classical Scholar; MA). Called to the Bar, Middle Temple, 1952. Entered Solicitor's Dept, Min. of Labour, 1953; Asst Solicitor, 1969; Principal Asst Solicitor, 1978.

McCLELLAND, Prof. (William) Grigor, DL; MA; MBA; Chairman: Tyne Tees Telethon Trust, since 1987; Tyne and Wear Foundation, since 1988; *b* 2 Jan. 1922; *o c* of Arthur and Jean McClelland, Gosforth, Newcastle upon Tyne; *m* 1946, Diana Avery Close; two *s* two *d*. *Educ:* Leighton Park; Balliol Coll., Oxford. First Class PPE, 1948. Friends' Ambulance Unit, 1941–46. Man. Dir, Laws Stores Ltd, 1949–65, 1978–85 (Chm., 1966–85); Sen. Res. Fellow in Management Studies, Balliol Coll., 1962–65; Dir, Manchester Business Sch., 1965–77, and Prof. of Business Administration, 1967–77, Univ. of Manchester; Dep. Chm., Nat. Computing Centre, 1966–68; Chm., Washington Develt Corp., 1977–88. Chm., EDC for the Distributive Trades, 1980–84 (Mem., 1965–70); Member: The Consumer Council, 1963–66; Economic Planning Council, Northern Region, 1965–66; IRC, 1966–71; NEDC, 1969–71; SSRC, 1971–74; North Eastern Industrial Develt Bd, 1977–86. Vis. Prof., Durham Univ. Business Sch., 1977–. Trustee: Anglo-German Foundn for the Study of Industrial Soc., 1973–79; Employment Inst., 1985–; Governor: Nat. Inst. of Econ. and Social Research; Leighton Park Sch., 1952–60 and 1962–66; Trustee, 1956–, and Chm., 1965–78, Joseph Rowntree Charitable Trust. CBIM. Hon. DCL Dunelm, 1985. DL Tyne and Wear, 1988. *Publications:* Studies in Retailing, 1963; Costs and Competition in Retailing, 1966; And a New Earth, 1976; Washington: over and out, 1988; (ed) Quakers Visit China, 1957; Editor, Jl of Management Studies, 1963–65. *Recreations:* tennis, ski-ing, fell-walking. *Address:* 66 Elmfield Road, Gosforth, Newcastle upon Tyne NE3 4BD.

MACCLESFIELD, 8th Earl of *cr* 1721; **George Roger Alexander Thomas Parker;** Baron Parker, 1716; Viscount Parker, 1721; DL; *b* 6 May 1914; *e s* of 7th Earl of Macclesfield and Lilian Joanna Vere (*d* 1974), *d* of Major Charles Boyle; *S* father, 1975; *m* 1938, Hon. Valerie Mansfield, *o d* of 4th Baron Sandhurst, OBE; two *s*. DL Oxfordshire, 1965. *Heir: s* Viscount Parker, *qv*. *Address:* Shirburn, Watlington, Oxon.

MACCLESFIELD, Archdeacon of; *see* Gaisford, Ven. J. S.

McCLEVERTY, Prof. Jon Armistice; Professor of Inorganic Chemistry, University of Bristol, since 1990; *b* 11 Nov. 1937; *s* of John and Nessie McCleverty; *m* 1963, Dianne Barrack; two *d*. *Educ:* Univ. of Aberdeen (BSc 1960); Imperial College, London (DIC, PhD 1963); Massachusetts Inst. of Technology. Asst Lectr, part-time, Acton Coll. of Technology, 1962–63; Asst Lectr, then Lectr, Sen. Lectr, and Reader, Univ. of Sheffield,

1964–80; Prof. of Inorganic Chem., 1980–90, and Head of Dept of Chem., 1984–90, Univ. of Birmingham. Chairman: Cttee of Heads of Univ. Chem. Depts, 1989–91; Chemistry Cttee, SERC, 1990–; Mem., Science Bd, SERC, 1990–. Tilden Lectr, RSC, 1981. RSC Medal, for work on chem. and electrochem. of transition metals, 1985. Golden Order of Merit (Poland), 1990. *Publications:* numerous articles, principally in Jl of Chem. Soc. *Recreations:* gardening, DIY, travel, traditional jazz. *Address:* School of Chemistry, University of Bristol, Cantock's Close, Bristol BS8 1TS.

McCLINTOCK, Surg. Rear-Adm. Cyril Lawson Tait, CB 1974; OBE 1964; Medical Officer in Charge, Royal Naval Hospital, Haslar and Command Medical Adviser on staff of Commander-in-Chief Naval Home Command, 1972–75; retired 1975; *b* 2 Aug. 1916; *o* surv. *s* of late Lawson Tait McClintock, MB, ChB, Loddon, Norfolk; *m* 1966, Freda Margaret, *o d* of late Robert Jones, Caergwle, Denbighshire; two step *s. Educ:* St Michael's, Uckfield; Epsom; Guy's Hospital. MRCS, LRCP 1940; DLO 1955. Joined RN Medical Service, 1940; served War of 1939–45 in Western Approaches, N Africa, Eritrea, India and Singapore; Korea, 1950–51; ENT Specialist, RN Hosps, Port Edgar, Chatham, Hong Kong, Portland, Haslar, Malta and Russell Eve Building, Hamilton, Bermuda; MO i/c RN Hosp. Bighi, Malta, 1969; David Bruce RN Hosp. Mtarfa, Malta, 1970–71; Comd Med. Adviser to C-in-C Naval Forces Southern Europe, 1969–71. QHS 1971–75. FRSocMed 1948; MFCM 1974. CStJ 1973. *Recreations:* cricket, tennis, Rugby refereeing, history. *Address:* 5 Ambleside Court, Alverstoke, Hants PO12 2DJ. *Clubs:* Army and Navy, MCC.

McCLINTOCK, David, TD; writer, naturalist and plantsman; *b* 4 July 1913; *o s* of Rev. E. L. L. McClintock, Glendaragh, Crumlin, Co. Antrim, and Margaret McClintock, *d* of John Henry Buxton, Easneye, Ware, Herts; *m* Elizabeth Anne, *d* of Maj. V. J. Dawson, Miserden, Glos; two *s* two *d. Educ:* West Downs Sch., Winchester; Harrow Sch.; Trinity Coll., Cambridge. BA 1934, MA 1940. FCA 1938; FLS 1953. 2nd Lieut, Herts Yeomanry RA TA, 1938; HQ 54 Div., Captain, 1941; Intelligence Trng Centre, 1941–43; Major, 1942; Civil Affairs Trng Centre, 1943–44; Lt-Col, 1944; BAOR, 1944–45. K-H Newsletter, 1938–46; Commercial Manager, Air Contractors Ltd, 1946–47; Chief Accountant and Admin. Officer, Coal Utilisation Council, 1951–73. Member: Wild Flower Soc., 1934– (Chm., 1981–, Treasurer, 1978–82); Council, Botanical Soc. of British Isles, 1954–64 (Pres., 1971–73); Council, Kent Trust for Nature Conservation, 1958–62 (Vice-Pres., 1963–); Council, Ray Soc., 1968–72, 1976–80 (Vice-Pres., 1972–76; Pres., 1980–83; Hon. Vice-Pres., 1983–); Council, Linnean Soc., 1970–78 (Vice-Pres., 1971–74; Editl Sec., 1974–78); Plant Variety Rights Adv. Panel for heathers, 1973–; Royal Horticultural Society: Scientific Cttee, 1978– (Vice-Chm., 1983–), Publications Cttee, 1982–87; Council, Internat. Dendrology Soc., 1979– (Editor, 1979–83; Vice-Pres., 1990–); Council, Nat. Trust, 1980–84. President: Kent Field Club, 1978–80; Heather Soc., 1989– (Vice-Pres., 1960–89; Pres., 1989–). Internat. Registrar for heather cultivars, 1970–; holder of national collection of Sasa bamboos, 1986–. Membre d'Honneur, Soc. Guernesiaise, 1968–. Veitch Meml Medal in gold, 1981. *Publications:* Pocket Guide to Wild Flowers (with R. S. R. Fitter), 1956; Supplement to the Pocket Guide to Wild Flowers, 1957; (jtly) Natural History of the Garden of Buckingham Palace, 1964; Companion to Flowers, 1966; Guide to the Naming of Plants, 1969, 2nd edn 1980; Wild Flowers of Guernsey, 1975, Supplement, 1987; (with J. Bichard) Wild Flowers of the Channel Islands, 1975, Supplement, 1987; Joshua Gosselin of Guernsey, 1976; (with F. Perring and R. E. Randall) Picking Wild Flowers, 1977; (ed) H. J. van de Laar, The Heather Garden, 1978; Guernsey's Earliest Flora, 1982; contribs to several other books and numerous periodicals. *Recreations:* anything to do with wild life and gardening, music, formerly shooting, fishing, tennis etc. *Address:* Bracken Hill, Platt, Sevenoaks, Kent TN15 8JH. *T:* Borough Green (0732) 884102. *Clubs:* Horticultural, Linnean Dining.

See also Baron Hazlerigg, C. H. G. Kinahan.

McCLINTOCK, Sir Eric (Paul), Kt 1981; *b* 13 Sept. 1918; *s* of Robert and Ada McClintock; *m* 1942, Eva Lawrence; two *s* one *d. Educ:* De La Salle Coll., Armidale; Sydney Univ. (DPA). Supply Dept, Dept of the Navy, Australia, 1935–47; served successively in Depts of Commerce, Agriculture, and Trade, in Washington, New York, Melbourne and Canberra, 1947–61 (1st Asst Sec. on resignation); investment banking, 1962–. Chairman: Upper Hunter Newspapers Pty Ltd; Williams Bros Engineering Pty Ltd; McClintock Associates Ltd; Aust. Overseas Projects Corp., 1978–84; Woolworths Ltd, 1982–87; AFT Ltd, 1984–87; Dep. Chm., Development Finance Corp. Ltd, 1980–87; Director: Philips Industries Holdings Ltd, 1978–85; O'Connell Street Associates Pty Ltd, 1978–; Wormalds Internat. Holdings Ltd, 1986–87; Ashton Mining Ltd, 1986–; Plutonic Resources Ltd. Chm., Trade Develt Council, 1970–74. Pres., Royal Life Saving Soc. (NSW). Governor, Sydney Inst. *Recreations:* tennis, golf. *Address:* 16 O'Connell Street, Sydney, NSW 2000, Australia. *T:* 225 3244. *Clubs:* Australian (Sydney); Commonwealth (Canberra).

McCLINTOCK, Nicholas Cole, CBE 1979; Secretary-General of the Order of St John, 1968–81 (Deputy Secretary-General, 1963–68); Chairman, Aidis Trust, since 1988; *b* 10 Sept. 1916; *s* of late Col Robert Singleton McClintock, DSO (3rd *s* of Adm. Sir Leopold McClintock), and Mary Howard, *d* of Sir Howard Elphinstone, VC; *m* 1953, Pamela Sylvia, *d* of late Major Rhys Mansel, Smedmore, Dorset; two *s* two *d. Educ:* Stowe Sch.; Trinity Coll., Cambridge (MA; Capt., Univ. Fencing Team). Entered Colonial Admin. Service, N Nigeria, 1939 but went immediately on War Service with 18th and 28th Field Regts RA, Dunkirk 1940, India and Burma, 1942–45; commanded 1st Field Battery RA in final Burma campaign. Asst Principal, Appointments Dept, CO, Feb.-Oct. 1946; Asst Dist Officer, N Nigeria, 1946–49; Private Sec. to Governor (Sir John Macpherson), 1949–50; Clerk to Exec. Council and Clerk, Legislature, N Nigeria, 1951–53; Sen. Dist Officer and Actg Resident, Kano Province, 1955–59; Admin. Officer Grade 1 and Resident, Bornu Province, 1960–62, retd. KStJ 1968. *Publication:* Kingdoms in the Sand and Sun, 1991. *Address:* Lower Westport, Wareham, Dorset BH20 4PR. *T:* Wareham (0929) 553252. *Club:* Army and Navy.

McCLINTOCK-BUNBURY, family name of **Baron Rathdonnell.**

McCLOSKEY, Bernard Mary; Deputy Director of Public Prosecutions for Northern Ireland, 1972–84; *b* 7 Aug. 1924; *s* of Felix and Josephine McCloskey; *m* 1952, Rosalie Donaghy; three *s* two *d. Educ:* St Malachy's Coll., Belfast; Queen's Univ., Belfast (LLB (Hons)). Admitted solicitor (Northern Ireland), 1947; private practice, 1947–72. Joint Solicitor to Scarman Tribunal of Enquiry, 1969–71. *Recreations:* swimming, golf. *Address:* c/o Royal Courts of Justice, Chichester Street, Belfast, Northern Ireland BT1 3NX. *T:* Belfast (0232) 35111. *Club:* Fortwilliam Golf (Hon. Mem.).

McCLUNE, Rear-Adm. (William) James, CB 1978; *b* Londonderry, 20 Nov. 1921; *s* of James McClune, MBE, Carrickmacross, Co. Monaghan, and Matilda (*née* Burns); *m* 1953, Elizabeth, *yr d* of A. E. D. Prideaux, LDS, Weymouth; one *s* one *d. Educ:* Model Sch. and Foyle Coll., Derry; QUB (BSc 1st Cl. Hons Elec. Eng, 1941); RN Staff Coll., Greenwich (1961); Univ. of Birmingham (Ratcliff Prizeman, MSc 1970); RN War Coll. (1971). Bronze Medal, CGLI, 1940; Belfast Assoc. of Engrs' Prize, 1940, 1941. CEng, MIEE; CBIM. Radar Officer, RNVR, 1941–47; Eng Dept, GPO, 1947–49; RN, 1949–78; CSO (Engrg) to C-in-C Fleet, 1976–78; Chm. Trustees, Royal Sailors Rests; Mem., RNLI Management Cttee. Chm., Christian Alliance Housing Assoc.; Chm. of Governors, Monkton Combe Sch. *Recreation:* sailing. *Address:* Harlam Lodge, Lansdown, Bath; 7 Theed Street, SE1. *Clubs:* Commonwealth Trust; Royal Naval and Royal Albert Yacht (Portsmouth).

McCLUNEY, Ian, CMG 1990; HM Diplomatic Service; Deputy High Commissioner, Calcutta, since 1991; *b* 27 Feb. 1937; *e s* of John McCluney and Annie (*née* Currie); *m* 1962, Elizabeth Mary Walsh; two *s* one *d. Educ:* Orange Hill Grammar Sch.; Edinburgh Univ. (BSc). Served HM Forces, Lieut RASC, 1958–62. Joined FO, 1964; Commerical Attaché, Addis Ababa, 1964–67; Asst Private Sec. to Foreign and Commonwealth Sec., 1969–70; Head, British Interests Section, Baghdad, 1972–74; FCO, 1975–78; Head of Chancery, Kuwait, 1979–82; Consul-Gen., Alexandria, 1982–86; FCO, 1986–88; Ambassador to Somalia, 1989–90. *Recreation:* sailing. *Address:* c/o Foreign and Commonwealth Office, King Charles Street, SW1A 2AH. *Club:* Little Ship.

McCLURE, David, RSA 1971 (ARSA 1963); RSW 1965; RGI 1990; SSA 1951; painter and printmaker; *b* 20 Feb. 1926; *s* of Robert McClure, MM, and Margaret Helena McClure (*née* Evans); *m* 1950, Joyce Dixon Flanigan (*d* 1988); two *s* one *d. Educ:* Queen's Park Sch., Glasgow; Glasgow Univ., 1943–44; (coal-miner, 1944–47); Edinburgh Univ., 1947–49; Edinburgh Coll. of Art, 1947–52 (DA). Travelled in Spain and Italy, 1952–53; on staff of Edinburgh Coll. of Art, 1953–55; one year painting in Italy and Sicily, 1956–57; Duncan of Jordanstone Coll. of Art, Dundee: Lectr, 1957–71, Sen. Lectr, 1971–83; Head of Drawing and Painting, 1983–85. *One man exhibitions:* Palermo, 1957; Edinburgh, 1957, 1961, 1962, 1966, 1969; 14 Scottish Painters, London, 1964; Univ. of Birmingham, 1965; Thackeray Gall., London, 1978, 1986, 1991; retrospective exhibn, Dundee Art Galls, 1984; Forty Years of Painting, Fine Art Soc., Glasgow, Edinburgh, 1988. *Work in public and private collections:* UK, USA, Canada, Italy. *Publication:* John Maxwell (monograph), 1976. *Recreations:* collecting Victorian china, gardening, the pianoforte, cooking. *Address:* 16 Strawberry Bank, Dundee, Scotland. *T:* Dundee (0382) 66959.

McCLURE, Joseph Robert; JP; Councillor, Tyne and Wear County Council, 1974–81 (Chairman, 1977–78); *b* 23 Oct. 1923; *s* of Thomas Render McClure and Catherine Bridget McClure; *m* 1943, Evelyn Joice; one *d. Educ:* Prior Street Sch.; Oakwellgate Sch., Gateshead. Served War, Royal Marines, 1941–46. Elected Councillor, County Borough of Gateshead, 1964, Dep. Mayor, 1973–74. President, Gateshead Royal British Legion, 1976–. JP Gateshead and Blaydon 1979. *Recreation:* bowls. *Address:* 170 Rectory Road, Gateshead, Tyne and Wear. *T:* 091–477 0709.

McCLUSKEY, family name of **Baron McCluskey.**

McCLUSKEY, Baron *cr* 1976 (Life Peer), of Churchhill in the District of the City of Edinburgh; **John Herbert McCluskey,** a Senator of the College of Justice in Scotland, since 1984; *b* 12 June 1929; *s* of Francis John McCluskey, Solicitor, and Margaret McCluskey (*née* Doonan); *m* 1956, Ruth Friedland; two *s* one *d. Educ:* St Bede's Grammar Sch., Manchester; Holy Cross Acad., Edinburgh; Edinburgh Univ. Harry Dalgety Bursary, 1948; Vans Dunlop Schol., 1949; Muirhead Prize, 1949; MA 1950; LLB 1952. Sword of Honour, RAF Spitalgate, 1953. Admitted Faculty of Advocates, 1955; Standing Jun. Counsel to Min. of Power (Scotland), 1963; Advocate-Depute, 1964–71; QC (Scot.) 1967; Chm., Medical Appeal Tribunals for Scotland, 1972–74; Sheriff Principal of Dumfries and Galloway, 1973–74; Solicitor General for Scotland, 1974–79. Chm., Scottish Assoc. for Mental Health, 1985–. Independent Chairman: Scottish Football League's Compensation Tribunal, 1988–; Scottish Football Association's Appeals Tribunal, 1990–. Reith Lectr, BBC, 1986. Editor, Butterworth's Scottish Criminal Law and Practice series. Hon. LLD Dundee, 1989. *Publication:* Law, Justice and Democracy, 1987. *Recreations:* tennis, pianoforte. *Address:* Court of Session, Parliament House, Edinburgh EH1 1RF. *T:* 031–225 2595. *Clubs:* Royal Air Force; Edinburgh University Staff, Scottish Arts (Edinburgh).

McCLUSKIE, John Cameron; QC (Scot.) 1989; Legal Secretary to the Lord Advocate and First Scottish Parliamentary Counsel, since 1989; *b* 1 Feb. 1946; *s* of Thomas and Marjorie McCluskie; *m* 1970, Janis Mary Helen McArthur; one *s* one *d. Educ:* Hyndland Sch., Glasgow; Glasgow Univ. (LLB Hons 1967). Admitted Solicitor, Scotland, 1970; admitted Faculty of Advocates, 1974. Apprentice Solicitor, Boyds, Glasgow, 1967–69; Asst Town Clerk, Burgh of Cumbernauld, 1969–70; Legal Assistant: Macdonald, Jameson and Morris, Glasgow, 1970; SSEB, 1970–72; Asst, then Sen. Asst, Legal Sec. and Parly Draftsman, Lord Advocate's Dept, 1972–89. *Recreation:* growing vegetables. *Address:* Strathblane, Hearts Delight Road, Tunstall, Sittingbourne, Kent ME9 8JA. *T:* Sittingbourne (0795) 474453.

McCLUSKIE, Samuel Joseph; Executive Officer, Rail, Maritime and Transport Union, 1990–91; General Secretary, National Union of Seamen, 1986–90 (Assistant General Secretary, 1976–86); *b* 11 Aug. 1932; *s* of James and Agnes McCluskie; *m* 1961, Alice (*née* Potter); one *s* one *d. Educ:* St Mary Primary School, Leith; Holy Cross Academy, Edinburgh. Merchant Navy, 1955; Union Delegate, 1963; Mem., Labour Party Nat. Exec. Cttee, 1974–, Treasurer, 1984–; Chairman, Labour Party, 1983. *Recreations:* coursing, greyhounds, watching Glasgow Celtic. *Address:* 23/7 Ferryfield, Edinburgh EH5 2PR. *T:* 031–552 9791; (office) 071–622 5588.

McCOLL, family name of **Baron McColl of Dulwich.**

McCOLL OF DULWICH, Baron *cr* 1989 (Life Peer), of Bermondey in the London Borough of Southwark; **Ian McColl,** MS, FRCS, FACS, FRCSE; Professor of Surgery, University of London at the United Medical Schools of Guy's and St Thomas' Hospitals, since 1971; Director of Surgery, since 1985, and Consultant Surgeon, since 1971, Guy's Hospital; Consultant Surgeon: King's College Hospital, since 1971; Edenbridge District Memorial Hospital, since 1978; Lewisham Hospital, since 1983; *b* 6 Jan. 1933; *s* of late Frederick George McColl and Winifred E. McColl, Dulwich; *m* 1960, Dr Jean Lennox, 2nd *d* of Arthur James McNair, FRCS, FRCOG; one *s* two *d. Educ:* Hutchesons' Grammar Sch., Glasgow; St Paul's Sch., London; Guy's Hosp., London. MB, BS 1957; FRCS 1962; FRCSE 1962; MS 1966; FACS 1975. Junior staff appts at St Bartholomew's, Putney, St Mark's, St Peter's, Great Ormond Street, Barnet, St Olave's and Guy's Hosps, 1957–67; Research Fellow, Harvard Med. Sch., and Moynihan Fellowship, Assoc. of Surgeons, 1967; Reader in Surgery, St Bartholomew's Hosp. Med. Coll., 1967 (Sub Dean, 1969); Dir of Surgical Unit, Guy's Hosp., 1971–. Visiting Professor: Univ. of South Carolina, 1974; Johns Hopkins Hosp., 1976. Hon. Consultant in Surgery to the Army, 1982–. External examiner in Surgery to Univs of Newcastle upon Tyne and Cardiff, QUB, TCD and NUI. Royal College of Surgeons: Examr in Pathology, 1970–76; Regl Advr, SE Reg., 1975–80; Mem. Council, 1986–; Arris and Gale Lectr, 1964, 1965; Erasmus Wilson Lectr, 1972. Medical Advisor, BBC Television, 1976–. Member: Central Health Services Council, 1972–74; Standing Medical Adv. Cttee, 1972–82; Management Cttee, King Edward VII Hospital Fund (Chm., R&D Cttee), 1975–80; Council, Metrop. Hosp. Sunday Fund, 1986–91; Chairman: King's Fund Centre Cttee, 1976–86; Govt Wkg Pty on

Artificial Limb and Appliance Centres in England, 1984–86; Vice Chm., SHA for Disablement Services, 1987–91. Hon. Sec., British Soc. of Gastroenterology, 1970–74. Patron and Hon. Consultant, Nat. Assoc. for Limbless Disabled, 1989–; Vice-Pres., John Grooms Assoc. for Disabled People, 1990–; Pres., Soc. of Minimally Invasive Gen. Surgery, 1991–. Governor-at-Large for England, Bd of Governors, Amer. Coll. of Surgeons, 1982–88. Pres., Mildmay Mission Hosp., 1985–; Governor, Dulwich Coll. Prep. Sch., 1978–. *Publications:* (ed jtly) Intestinal Absorption in Man, 1975; Talking to Patients, 1982; NHS Data Book, 1984; med. articles, mainly on gastroenterology. *Recreation:* forestry. *Address:* Department of Surgery, Guy's Hospital, SE1 9RT. *Club:* Athenæum.

McCOLL, Sir Colin (Hugh Verel), KCMG 1990 (CMG 1983); Counsellor, Foreign and Commonwealth Office, since 1977; *b* 6 Sept. 1932; *s* of Dr Robert McColl and Julie McColl; *m* 1st, 1959, Shirley Curtis (*d* 1983); two *s* two *d*; 2nd, 1985, Sally Wyld. *Educ:* Shrewsbury School; The Queen's College, Oxford (BA). Foreign Office, 1956; Third Secretary, Bangkok, 1958, Vientiane, 1960; Second Secretary, FO, 1962; First Secretary, Warsaw, 1966; Consul and First Secretary (Disarmament), Geneva, 1973. *Recreations:* music, walks, cycling, tennis, classics. *Address:* c/o Foreign and Commonwealth Office, SW1. *Club:* Commonwealth Trust.

McCOLL, Ian, CBE 1983; Chairman, Scottish Express Newspapers Ltd, 1975–82; *b* 22 Feb. 1915; *e s* of late John and Morag McColl, Glasgow and Bunessan, Isle of Mull; *m* 1968, Brenda, *e d* of late Thomas and Mary McKean, Glasgow; one *d*. *Educ:* Hillhead High Sch., Glasgow. Served in RAF, 1940–46 (despatches, 1945): Air Crew, Coastal Comd 202 Sqdn. Joined Scottish Daily Express as cub reporter, 1933; held various editorial executive posts; Editor, Scottish Daily Express, 1961–71; Editor, Daily Express, 1971–74; Dir, Express Newspapers Ltd, 1971–82. Contested (L): Dumfriesshire, 1945; Greenock, 1950. Mem., Presbytery of Glasgow and Synod of Clydesdale, 1953–71; Mem., General Assembly Publications Cttee, until 1971; Session Clerk, Sandyford-Henderson Memorial Church of Scotland, Glasgow, 1953–71. Mem., Press Council, 1975–78; a Vice-Pres., Newspaper Press Fund, 1981–. Mem., Gen. Assembly Bd of Communication, 1983–86. Chm. Media Div., XIII Commonwealth Games, Scotland 1986, 1983–86. Mem., Saints and Sinners Club of Scotland, Chm., 1981–82. *Address:* 12 Newlands Road, Newlands, Glasgow G43 2JB.

McCOLLUM, Sir Liam; *see* McCollum, Sir W. P.

McCOLLUM, Sir William (Paschal), (Sir Liam), Kt 1988; **Hon. Mr Justice McCollum;** Judge of the High Court of Justice in Northern Ireland, since 1987; *b* 13 Jan. 1933; *s* of Patrick McCollum and Mary Ellen McCollum (*née* Strain); *m* 1958, Anne Bernadette Fitzpatrick; six *s* two *d*. *Educ:* Waterside School; St Columb's Coll., Derry; University College Dublin (BA 1953; LLB 1954). Called to the Bar of N Ireland, 1955; called to Irish Bar, 1963; QC 1971. *Address:* Royal Courts of Justice, Chichester Street, Belfast BT1 3JF.

McCOLOUGH, (Charles) Peter; Chairman, Executive Committee, Xerox Corporation, 1985–87; *b* 1 Aug. 1922; *s* of Reginald W. McColough and Barbara Martin McColough; *m* 1953, Mary Virginia White. *Educ:* Dalhousie Univ. (LLB); Harvard Grad. Sch. of Business Administration (MBA). Lehigh Coal & Navigation Co., Philadelphia, 1951–54; Xerox Corp.: Gen. Man., Reproduction Service Centers, 1954–56; Man. Marketing, 1957–59; Gen. Sales Man., 1959–60; Vice-Pres. Sales, 1960–63; Exec. Vice-Pres., Ops, 1963–66; Pres., 1966–68; Pres. and Chief Exec. Officer, 1968–71; Chm., 1971–85. Director: Knight Ridder Inc.; Citibank, NA; Citicorp; Fuji Xerox Co., Ltd; Union Carbide Corp.; Council on Foreign Relations; Trustee: Eisenhower Exchange Fellowship; Univ. of Rochester; Member: Corp. of Greenwich Hospital Assoc. Inc.; The Business Council; Adv. Council of Industrial Estates Ltd, Nova Scotia. *Address:* Xerox Corporation, PO Box 1600, Stamford, Conn 06904, USA. *Clubs:* Harvard, River (New York); Belle Haven, Greenwich Country (Connecticut).

McCOMB, Leonard William Joseph, RA 1991 (ARA 1987); artist; *b* 3 Aug. 1930; *s* of Archibald and Delia McComb, Glasgow; *m* 1st, 1955, Elizabeth Henstock (marr. diss. 1963); 2nd, 1966, Joan Allwork (*d* 1967); 3rd, 1975, Barbara Elenora. *Educ:* Manchester Art Sch.; Slade Sch. of Fine Art, Univ. of London (Dip. Fine Art, 1960). Teacher at art schools, Bristol, Oxford, RA schools, Slade, Goldsmiths', Sir John Cass, 1960–. *Exhibitions include:* Human Clay, Arts Council, 1976; British Painting 1952–77, RA, 1977; (one-man exhibn) Blossoms and Flowers, Coracle Press, 1979; Painters of the 80's, Venice, 1980; British Sculpture, Whitechapel, 1981; British Drawings and Watercolours, China, 1982; Arts Council Touring Exhibn, 1983; Hard Won Image, Tate, 1984; 50 Years of British Art, 1985; Representation Abroad, Washington, 1986; Large Watercolours and Drawings, Berlin, 1986; Museum of Modern Art, Brussels, 1987; Paintings from the South, London, 1989; School of London Drawings, London, 1989; (one-man exhibn) Recent Work, London, 1990; Twin Images, London, 1990; Recent Paintings, Pastels and Drawings, Rome, 1991; *work in public collections:* Arts Council; British Council; ICA; Cambridge Univ.; Tate; V&A; Art Galls of Birmingham, Manchester, Swindon, Worcester. Jubilee Prize, RA, 1977; Korn/Ferry Prize, RA, 1988. *Recreations:* travelling and walking in the countryside.

McCOMBE, Richard George Bramwell; QC 1989; *b* 23 Sept. 1952; *s* of Barbara Bramwell McCombe, MA, FCA; *m* 1st (marr. diss.); 2nd, 1986, Carolyn Sara Birrell; one *s* one *d*. *Educ:* Sedbergh Sch.; Downing Coll., Cambridge (MA). Called to the Bar, Lincoln's Inn, 1975. Second Jun. Counsel to Dir-Gen. of Fair Trading, 1982–87, First Jun. Counsel, 1987–89. Mem., Senate of Inns of Court and of Bar Council, 1981–86; Chm., Young Barristers' Cttee, Bar Council, 1983–84; Co-opted Mem., Bar Council Cttees, 1986–89. *Recreations:* cricket, Rugby (both as spectator), travel. *Address:* 13 Old Square, Lincoln's Inn, WC2A 3UA. *T:* 071–404 4800. *Clubs:* Royal Automobile, MCC; London Scottish Football, Harlequin Football; Lancs CC.

McCONNELL, Albert Joseph, MA, ScD, Hon. DSc: Belfast; Ulster; Hon. ScD Columbia; Hon. LLD NUI; Hon. Fellow of Oriel College, Oxford; Provost of Trinity College, Dublin, 1952–74; Member of Council of State, Ireland, since 1973; *b* 19 Nov. 1903; *s* of Joseph McConnell; *m* 1st, 1934, Hilda (*d* 1966), *d* of late Francis McGuire; 2nd, 1983, Jean (*d* 1985), *d* of late Robert Shekleton. *Educ:* Ballymena Acad.; Trinity Coll., Dublin (Scholar, First Math. Moderator and Univ. Student); Univ. of Rome. Dr of Univ. of Rome, 1928; ScD (Dublin), 1929; MRIA, 1929. Lectr in Maths, Trinity Coll., Dublin, 1927–30; Fellow of Trinity Coll., Dublin, 1930–52; Prof. of Natural Philosophy, Univ. of Dublin, 1930–57; Special Univ. Lectr, Univ. of London, 1949. Vis. Professor: Univ. of Alexandria, 1946–47; Univ. of Kuwait, 1970. Chm., Governing Bd, Sch of Theoretical Physics, 1970– (Mem., 1940–); Mem. Council, Dublin Inst. for Advanced Studies, 1970–. *Publications:* Applications of the Absolute Differential Calculus, 1931; (ed) The Mathematical Papers of Sir William Rowan Hamilton, vol. II, 1940; Applications of Tensor Analysis, 1957; papers on relativity, geometry and dynamics in various mathematical jls. *Address:* Seafield Lodge, Seafield Road, Killiney, Dublin. *Clubs:* Athenæum; Dublin University (Dublin).

McCONNELL, Prof. James Desmond Caldwell, FRS 1987; Professor of the Physics and Chemistry of Minerals, Department of Earth Sciences, University of Oxford, since 1986; Fellow of St Hugh's College, Oxford, since 1986; *b* 3 July 1930; *s* of Samuel D. and Cathleen McConnell; *m* 1956, Jean Elspeth Ironside; one *s* two *d*. *Educ.* Queen's Univ. of Belfast (BSc, MSc 1952); Univ. of Cambridge (MA 1955; PhD 1956); MA Oxon 1986. Univ. of Cambridge: Demonstrator, 1955; Lectr, 1960; Reader, 1972–82; Churchill College: Fellow, 1962–82; Extraordinary Fellow, 1983–88; Head of Dept of Rock Physics, 1983–86, Schlumberger Cambridge Research. *Publications:* Principles of Mineral Behaviour (with A. Putnis), 1980, Russian edn, 1983; papers in physics jls and mineralogical jls. *Recreations:* local history, hill walking, singing. *Address:* 8 The Croft, Old Headington, Oxford OX3 9BU. *T:* Oxford (0865) 69100.

McCONNELL, John, RDI 1987; FCSD; designer; Director: Pentagram Design, since 1974; Faber & Faber, since 1985; Clarks of England Inc., since 1987; *b* 14 May 1939; *s* of Donald McConnell and Enid McConnell (*née* Dimberline); *m* 1963, Moira Rose Macgregor; one *s* one *d*. *Educ:* Borough Green Secondary Modern School; Maidstone College of Art (NDD). FCSD (FSIAD 1980). Employed in advertising and design, 1959–62; Lectr, Colchester College of Art, 1962–63; freelance design practice, 1963–74; co-founder, Face Photosetting, 1968. Member: Alliance Graphique Internat., 1976; Post Office Stamp Adv. Cttee, 1984; Pres., D&AD, 1986 (President's Award, 1985); served on design competition juries, D&AD. Gold medallist at Biennale, Warsaw. *Publications:* (jtly) Living by Design, 1978; (jtly) Ideas on Design, 1986; Editor, Pentagram Papers. *Recreations:* house restoration, cooking. *Address:* 11 Needham Road, W11 2RP. *T:* 071–229 3477; 42 Bassett Road, W10 9JL. *T:* 081–969 2014. *Club:* Groucho.

McCONNELL, (Sir) Robert Shean, (4th Bt *cr* 1900); *S* father, 1987, but does not use the title. *Heir:* *b* James Angus McConnell.

McCONNELL, Rt. Hon. Robert William Brian, PC (N Ireland) 1964; Social Security (formerly National Insurance) Commissioner, Northern Ireland, 1968–87; *b* 25 Nov. 1922; *s* of late Alfred E. McConnell, Belfast; *m* 1951, Sylvia Elizabeth Joyce Agnew; two *s* one *d*. *Educ:* Sedbergh Sch.; Queen's Univ., Belfast (BA, LLB). Called to Bar of Northern Ireland, 1948. MP (U) for South Antrim, NI Parlt, 1951–68; Dep. Chm. of Ways and Means, NI Parlt, 1962; Parly Sec. to Min. of Health and Local Govt for N Ireland, 1963; Minister of Home Affairs for Northern Ireland, 1964–66; Minister of State, Min. of Develt, 1966–67; Leader of the House of Commons, NI, 1967–68. Pres., Industrial Court of NI, 1968–81. Vice-Chm., European Move in NI, 1987–. *Address:* 50 Glenavy Road, Knocknadona, Lisburn, Co. Antrim, Northern Ireland BT28 3UT. *T:* Lisburn (0846) 663432. *Club:* Ulster Reform (Belfast).

MacCONOCHIE, John Angus, MBE 1943; FCIT; Chairman: Furness Withy & Co. Ltd, 1968–72 (Director, 1964–73); Shaw Savill & Albion Co. Ltd, 1968–73 (Director, 1957–73); *b* 12 April 1908; *m* 1938, Peggy, *d* of late Robert Gunson Martindale, MA, Worthing, Sussex; one *s* one *d*. *Educ:* Royal Caledonian Schools, Bushey, Herts. Joined Shaw Savill Line, 1927. Seconded to Min. of War Transport, 1942; served on Staff of Resident Minister for W Africa, Accra; Min. of War Transport Rep. in Gold Coast (MBE); London, 1944; Min. HQ with 21 Army Group; subseq. Paris, Marseilles, Naples. Returned to Shaw Savill Line, 1945: New Zealand, 1949; subseq. Manager for Australia; Gen. Manager for New Zealand, 1953; returned to Britain, 1958; Dir, 1957. Chm., Royal Mail Lines, 1968–73; Director: Economic Insurance, 1967 (Chm. 1969–73); British Maritime Trust, 1966–73; Pacific Steam Navigation Co. Ltd, 1967–73; Pacific Maritime Services, 1967–73; Houlder Bros & Co. Ltd, 1967–73; Whitehall Insurance Co. Ltd, 1967–73; Manchester Liners Ltd, 1968–73; National Bank of New Zealand, 1970 (NZ Bd, 1973–78). Member: Council, Chamber of Shipping; Council of Management, Ocean Travel Development (past Chm.); Cttee, NZ Society (PP); British Ship Adoption Soc. (past Chm.); Pres., UK Chamber of Shipping, 1972–73 (Pres.-designate 1971). Patron, Auckland Maritime Soc. *Address:* 36 Barlow Place, Chatswood, Auckland 10, New Zealand. *Club:* Northern (Auckland).

McCONVILLE, Michael Anthony, MBE 1958; writer; *b* 3 Jan. 1925; *s* of late Lt-Col James McConville, MC and late Winifred (*née* Hanley); *m* 1952, Beryl Anne (*née* Jerrett); two *s* four *d*. *Educ:* Mayfield Coll.; Trinity Coll., Dublin. Royal Marines, 1943–46. Malayan Civil Service, 1950–61: served in Perak, Johore, Trengganu, Negri Sembilam, Pahang and Kedah; retd as Chm., Border War Exec. Cttee. CRO (later HM Diplomatic Service), 1961–77: Colombo, 1963–64; Kingston, Jamaica, 1966–67; Ottawa, 1967–71; Consul-Gen., Zagreb, 1974–77. Kesatria Mankgu Negara (Malaya), 1962. *Publications:* (as Anthony McCandless): Leap in the Dark, 1980; The Burke Foundation, 1985; (as Michael McConville) Ascendancy to Oblivion: the story of the Anglo-Irish, 1986; A Small War in the Balkans: the British in war time Yugoslavia, 1986; (as Miles Noonan): Tales from the Mess, 1983; (as Patrick Plum): articles and short stories in Blackwoods, etc. *Recreations:* walking, gardening, watching Rugby. *Club:* Kildare Street and University (Dublin).

McCORD, Brig. Mervyn Noel Samuel, CBE 1978 (OBE 1974); MC 1951; retired; *b* 25 Dec. 1929; *s* of Major G. McCord, MBE and Muriel King; *m* 1953, Annette Mary, *d* of C. R. W. Thomson; three *s*. *Educ:* Coleraine, NI; RMA Sandhurst. Commissioned Royal Ulster Rifles, 1949; Korea, 1950–51; School of Infantry, 1958–60; Staff Coll., Camberley, 1961–62; DAQMG, Eastern Command, Canada, 1963–65; BM, HQ 6 Infantry Brigade, 1967–69; JSSC, 1969; GSO1, HQNI, 1970–71; CO, 1st Bn The Royal Irish Rangers, 1971–74; Brig. 1975; Commander, Ulster Defence Regt, 1976–78; Dep. Comdr, Eastern Dist, 1978–81; Brig. King's Div., 1981–84. ADC, 1981–84. Col, The Royal Irish Rangers, 1985–90 (Dep. Col, 1976–81). Chairman: SHAA, 1986–; SHAA Retirement Homes plc, 1986–. FBIM (MBIM 1978). *Recreations:* cricket, athletics, country sports, gardening. *Address:* c/o Royal Bank of Scotland, Whitehall, SW1. *Club:* Army and Navy.

McCORKELL, Col Michael William, OBE 1964; TD 1954; JP; Lord-Lieutenant, County Londonderry, since 1975; *b* 3 May 1925; *s* of late Captain B. F. McCorkell, Templeard, Culmore, Co. Londonderry and of Mrs E. M. McCorkell; *m* 1950, Aileen Allen, OBE 1975, 2nd *d* of late Lt-Col E. B. Booth, DSO, Darver Castle, Dundalk, Co. Louth, Eire; three *s* one *d*. *Educ:* Aldenham. Served with 16/5 Lancers, 1943–47; Major (TA) North Irish Horse, 1951; Lt-Col 1961; comd North Irish Horse (TA); retd, 1964. T&AVR Col, NI, 1971–74; Brevet Col, 1974; Pres., T&AVR, NI, 1977–88; ADC to the Queen, 1972. Co. Londonderry: High Sheriff 1961; DL 1962; JP 1980. *Recreations:* fishing, shooting. *Address:* Ballyarnett, 50 Berah Hill Road, Londonderry, Northern Ireland BT48 8LY. *T:* Londonderry (0504) 351239. *Club:* Cavalry and Guards.

MacCORMAC, Richard Cornelius, PRIBA; Partner, MacCormac, Jamieson, Prichard, Architects, since 1972; President, Royal Institute of British Architects, since 1991; *b* 3 Sept. 1938; *s* of Henry MacCormac, CBE, MD, FRCP and Marion Maud, *d* of B. C. Broomhall, FRCS; *m* 1964, Susan Karin Landen; one *s* (and one *s* decd). *Educ:* Westminster Sch.; Trinity Coll., Cambridge (BA 1962); University College London (MA 1965). RIBA 1967. Served RN, 1957–59. Proj. Archt, London Bor. of Merton, 1967–69; estabd private practice, 1969; taught in Dept of Arch., Cambridge Univ., 1969–75 and 1979–81,

Univ. Lectr, 1976–79; Vis. Prof., Univ. of Edinburgh (Dept of Architecture), 1982–85. Dir, Spitalfields Workspace, 1981–. Chm., Good Design in Housing Awards, RIBA London Region, 1977; Mem., Royal Fine Art Commn, 1983–. FRSA 1982. *Publications:* articles in Architectural Review and Archts Jl. *Recreations:* sailing, music, reading. *Address:* 9 Heneage Street, E1 5LJ. *T:* 071–377 9262.

McCORMACK, Arthur Gerard; Director, Population and Development Office, Rome, 1973–86; Consultant to United Nations Fund for Population Activities, since 1975; *b* 16 Aug. 1911; *s* of Francis McCormack and Elizabeth Ranard. *Educ:* St Francis Xavier Coll., Liverpool; Durham Univ. (MA Hons History and Econs). Ordained, 1936. Mill Hill Missionary, Africa, 1940–48 (invalided home, 1948); after lengthy illness and convalescence, hosp. chaplain and subseq. teacher-chaplain in secondary modern sch., Widnes; Adviser to Superior Gen., Mill Hill Missionaries, 1963; attended II Vatican Council as expert on population and develt of developing countries, 1963–65; part Founder, Vatican Commn, Justice and Peace (mem. staff for 7 yrs). Special Adviser to Sec. Gen., World Population Conf., Bucharest, 1974. *Publications:* People, Space, Food, 1960; (ed) Christian Responsibility and World Poverty, 1963; World Poverty and the Christian, 1963; Poverty and Population, 1964; The Population Problem, 1970; The Population Explosion and Christian Concern, 1973; Multinational Investment: Boon or Burden for the Developing Countries, 1980; contrib. The Tablet, Population & Develt Rev., Populi, etc. *Recreations:* reading, driving scooter. *Address:* St Joseph's College, Lawrence Street, Mill Hill, NW7 4JX. *T:* 081–959 8493.

McCORMACK, Most Rev. John; Bishop of Meath (RC), 1968–90, now Emeritus; *b* 25 March 1921; *s* of Peter McCormack and Bridget Mulvany. *Educ:* St Finian's Coll., Mullingar; Maynooth Coll.; Lateran Univ., Rome. Priest, 1946. Ministered: Multyfarnham, 1950–52; St Loman's Hosp., 1952–58; Mullingar, 1958–68; Diocesan Sec., 1952–68. *Address:* Bishop's House, Dublin Road, Mullingar, Co. Westmeath, Ireland. *T:* Mullingar 48841/42038.

McCORMACK, John P(atrick); Vice President, in charge of Latin American and South African Operations, General Motors Corporation, 1983; *b* New York, 23 Nov. 1923; *s* of John McCormack and Margaret (*née* Bannon); *m* 1952, Mari Martha Luhrs; two *s*. *Educ:* St John's Univ., Jamaica, NY (Bachelor of Business Admin); NY Univ., NYC (LLB). Joined General Motors, 1949; Gen. Clerk, Accounting Dept, NY, 1949, Sen. Clerk 1950, Sen. Accountant 1952; Asst to Treas., Djakarta Br., 1953; Asst Treas., Karachi Br., 1956; Asst Treas., Gen. Motors South African (Pty) Ltd, Port Elizabeth, 1958, Treas. 1961; Asst Finance Man., Overseas Div., NY, 1966; Treas., subseq. Man. Dir, Gen. Motors Continental, Antwerp, 1968; Finance Man., Adam Opel, 1970, Man. Dir and Chm. Bd, 1974; Gen. Dir, European Ops, Gen. Motors Overseas Corp., 1976; Vice Pres. i/c joint ventures and African ops, 1980. *Recreations:* golf, photography. *Address:* c/o General Motors Corporation, General Motors Building, Detroit, Michigan 48202, USA.

McCORMACK, Mark Hume; Chairman and Chief Executive Officer, International Management Group; *b* 6 Nov. 1930; *s* of Ned Hume McCormack and Grace Wolfe McCormack; *m* 1st, 1954, Nancy Breckenridge McCormack; two *s* one *d*; 2nd, 1986, Betsy Nagelsen. *Educ:* Princeton Univ.; William and Mary Coll. (BA); Yale Univ. (LLB). Admitted to Ohio Bar, 1957; Associate in Arter, Hadden, Wykoff & Van Duzer, 1957–63; Partner, 1964–; started Internat. Management Gp, 1962. Commentator for televised golf, BBC. *Publications:* The World of Professional Golf, annually, 1967–; Arnie: the evolution of a legend, 1967; The Wonderful World of Professional Golf, 1973; What they don't teach you at Harvard Business School, 1984; The Terrible Truth about Lawyers, 1987; Success Secrets, 1989; monthly newsletters Success Secrets. *Recreations:* golf, tennis. *Address:* No 1300, One Erieview Plaza, Cleveland, Ohio 44114, USA. *T:* 216/522–1200. *Clubs:* Royal & Ancient Golf (St Andrews); Wentworth (Virginia Water); Sunningdale Golf (Berkshire, England); Old Prestwick (Prestwick); Royal Dornoch (Dornoch); Deepdale (NY); Pepper Pike, Country Club of Cleveland (Ohio); Isleworth, Bay Hill (Florida).

MacCORMICK, Prof. (Donald) Neil, FBA 1986; Regius Professor of Public Law, University of Edinburgh, since 1972; *b* 27 May 1941; *yr s* of J. M. MacCormick, MA, LLD (Glasgow) and Margaret I. Miller, MA, BSc (Glasgow); *m* 1965, Caroline Rona Barr (marr. diss. 1991), MA (Glasgow); three *d*. *Educ:* High School, Glasgow; Univ. of Glasgow (MA, 1st cl. Philos. and Eng. Lit.); Balliol Coll., Oxford (BA, 1st cl. Jurisprudence; MA); LLD Edinburgh, 1982. Pres., Oxford Union Soc., 1965. Called to the Bar, Inner Temple, 1971. Lecturer, St Andrew's Univ. (Queen's Coll., Dundee), 1965–67; Fellow and Tutor in Jurisprudence, Balliol Coll., Oxford, 1967–72, and CUF Lectr in Law, Oxford Univ., 1968–72; Pro-Proctor, Oxford Univ., 1971–72; Dean of Faculty of Law, Univ. of Edinburgh, 1973–76 and 1985–88. Corry Lectr, Queen's Univ., Kingston, Ont, 1981; Vis. Prof., Univ. of Sydney, 1981; Dewey Lectr, NY Univ., 1982; Higgins Visitor, NW Sch. of Law, Oregon, 1987; Or Emet Lectr, Osgoode Hall, 1988; Anne Green Vis. Prof., Univ. of Texas, 1990. Contested (SNP): Edinburgh North, 1979; Edinburgh, Pentlands, 1983, 1987; Prospective Parly Candidate (SNP), Argyll and Bute, 1990–. President: Assoc. for Legal and Social Philosophy, 1974–76; Soc. of Public Teachers of Law, 1983–84. Member: Houghton Cttee on Financial Aid to Political Parties, 1975–76; Broadcasting Council for Scotland, 1985–89. FRSE 1986. Hon. LLD Uppsala, 1986. *Publications:* (ed) The Scottish Debate: Essays on Scottish Nationalism, 1970; (ed) Lawyers in their Social Setting, 1976; Legal Reasoning and Legal Theory, 1978; H. L. A. Hart, 1981; Legal Right and Social Democracy: essays in legal and political philosophy, 1982; (with O. Weinberger) Grundlagen des Institutionalistischen Rechtspositivismus, 1985; An Institutional Theory of Law, 1986 (trans. Italian, 1991); (ed jtly) Enlightenment, Right and Revolution, 1989; contribs to various symposia, jls on law, philosophy and politics. *Recreations:* hill walking, bagpiping, sailing. *Address:* The Old College, Edinburgh EH8 9YL.

See also I. S. MacD. MacCormick.

MacCORMICK, Iain Somerled MacDonald; Director, First-In Ltd, since 1990; *b* 28 Sept. 1939; *er s* of John MacDonald MacCormick, MA, LLB, LLD and Margaret Isobel MacCormick, MA, BSc; *m* 1st, 1964, Micky Trefusis Elsom (marr. diss.); two *s* three *d*; 2nd, 1988, Carole Burnett (*née* Story). *Educ:* Glasgow High Sch.; Glasgow Univ. (MA). Queen's Own Lowland Yeomanry, 1957–67 (Captain). Major Account Manager, 1982, Dir Liaison Manager, 1984, BT plc. Contested (SNP) Argyll, 1970; MP (SNP) Argyll, Feb. 1974–1979; introduced, as private member's bill, Divorce (Scotland) Act, 1976. Founder Mem., SDP, 1981. Mem., Argyll and Bute District Council, 1979–80. *Recreations:* Rugby football, sailing, local history. *Club:* Brooks's.

See also Prof. D. N. MacCormick.

McCORMICK, Prof. James Stevenson, FRCPI, FRCGP; FFCM; Professor of Community Health, Trinity College Dublin, 1973–91 (Dean of School of Physic, 1974–79); *b* 9 May 1926; *s* of Victor Ormsby McCormick and Margaretta Tate (*née* Stevenson); *m* 1954, Elizabeth Ann Dimond; three *s* one *d*. *Educ:* The Leys Sch., Cambridge; Clare Coll., Cambridge (BA, MB); St Mary's Hospital, W2. Served RAMC, 1960–62; St Mary's Hosp., 1963; general practice, 1964–73. Chairman: Eastern Health Board, 1970–72; Nat. Health Council, 1984–86. Pres., Irish Coll. of General Practitioners, 1986–87. Hon. MCFP 1982. *Publications:* The Doctor—Father Figure or Plumber, 1979; (with P. Skrabanek) Follies and Fallacies in Medicine, 1989; papers, espec. on General Practice and Ischaemic Heart Disease. *Recreations:* open air, patients. *Address:* The Barn, Windgates, Bray, Co. Wicklow, Ireland. *T:* Dublin 874113.

McCORMICK, John; The Secretary of the BBC, since 1987; *b* 24 June 1944; *s* of Joseph and Roseann McCormick; *m* 1973, Jean Frances Gibbons; one *s* one *d*. *Educ:* St Michael's Acad., Irvine; Univ. of Glasgow (MA Modern History with Econ. History 1967; MEd 1970). Teacher, St Gregory's Secondary Sch., Glasgow, 1968–70; Education Officer, BBC School Broadcasting Council, 1970–75; Senior Education Officer, Scotland, 1975–82; Sec., and Head of Information, BBC Scotland, 1982–87. Member: Glasgow Children's Panel, 1972–77; Vis. Cttee, Glenochil Young Offenders' Instn, 1979–85; Vice-Chm., Youth-at-risk, (Scotland), 1985–. *Recreation:* newspapers. *Address:* Broadcasting House, Portland Place, W1A 1AA. *T:* 071–580 4468.

McCORMICK, John Ormsby, CMG 1965; MC 1943; HM Diplomatic Service, retired; *b* Dublin, 7 Feb. 1916; *s* of Albert Victor McCormick and Sarah Beatty de Courcy; *m* 1955, Francine Guieu (*née* Pâris); one *d*, one step *s*. *Educ:* The Leys Sch., Cambridge; New Coll., Oxford. BA Hon. Mods and Greats (Oxford), 1938. Passed Competitive Exam. for Consular Service, 1939, and appointed Asst Officer, Dept of Overseas Trade. Served War of 1939–45, in Royal Corps of Signals, Africa, Sicily, Germany, 1940–45. 2nd Sec. (Commercial), British Embassy, Athens, 1945–47; FO, London, 1948–50; 1st Sec., UK High Commn, Karachi, 1950–52; Consul, New York, 1952–54; transferred to Washington, 1954–55; NATO Defence Coll., 1955; Asst Head, SE Asia Dept, FO, 1956–59; Foreign Service Officer, Grade 6, 1959; Counsellor (Commercial), British Embassy, Djakarta, 1959–62; Corps of Inspectors, FO, 1962–64; Counsellor (Commercial), British Embassy, Ankara, 1965–67; Consul-General, Lyons, 1967–72. *Address:* Oldfort, Newcastle, Co. Wicklow, Ireland.

MacCORMICK, Neil; *see* MacCormick, D. N.

McCORQUODALE, Mrs Barbara; *see* Cartland, Barbara H.

McCOWAN, Rt. Hon. Sir Anthony (James Denys), Kt 1981; PC 1989; **Rt. Hon. Lord Justice McCowan;** a Lord Justice of Appeal, since 1989; Senior Presiding Judge of England and Wales, since 1991; *b* 12 Jan. 1928; *yr s* of John Haines Smith McCowan, MBE, and Marguerite McCowan, Georgetown, British Guiana; *m* 1961, Sue Hazel Anne, *d* of late Reginald Harvey and of Mrs Harvey, Braiseworth Hall, Tannington, Suffolk; two *s* one *d*. *Educ:* Epsom Coll.; (Open Hist. schol.) Brasenose Coll., Oxford (MA, BCL). Called to Bar, Gray's Inn, 1951, Atkin Scholar; Bencher, 1980. Dep. Chm., E Sussex QS, 1969–71; a Recorder of the Crown Court, 1972–81; QC 1972; a Judge of the High Court, QBD, 1981–89. Leader, 1978–81, Presiding Judge, 1986–89, SE Circuit. Member: Parole Bd, 1982–84; Crown Court Rule Cttee, 1982–88. *Recreations:* sport, history, travel. *Address:* c/o Royal Courts of Justice, Strand, WC2A 2LL.

See also J. M. Archer.

McCOWAN, Sir Hew Cargill, 3rd Bt, *cr* 1934; *b* 26 July 1930; *s* of Sir David James Cargill McCowan, 2nd Bt and Muriel Emma Annie, *d* of W. C. Willmott; *S* father, 1965. *Heir:* *b* David William Cargill McCowan, *b* 28 Feb. 1934.

McCOWEN, Alec, (Alexander Duncan McCowen), CBE 1986 (OBE 1972); actor; *b* 26 May 1925; *s* of late Duncan McCowen and Hon. Mrs McCowen. *Educ:* Skinners' Sch., Tunbridge Wells; RADA, 1941. Repertory: York, Birmingham, etc, 1943–50; Escapade, St James's, 1952; The Matchmaker, Haymarket, 1954; The Count of Clérambard, Garrick, 1955; The Caine Mutiny Court Martial, Hippodrome, 1956; Look Back in Anger, Royal Court, 1956; The Elder Statesman, Cambridge, 1958; Old Vic Seasons, 1959–61: Touchstone, Ford, Richard II, Mercutio, Oberon, Malvolio; Dauphin in St Joan; Algy in The Importance of Being Earnest; Royal Shakespeare Company, 1962–63: Antipholus of Syracuse in The Comedy of Errors; Fool, in King Lear; Father Fontana in The Representative, Aldwych, 1963; Thark, Garrick, 1965; The Cavern, Strand, 1965; After the Rain, Duchess, 1967, Golden Theatre, NY, 1967; Hadrian VII, Birmingham, 1967, Mermaid, 1968, New York, 1969; Hamlet, Birmingham, 1970; The Philanthropist, Royal Court, 1970, NY, 1971; Butley, Criterion, 1972; The Misanthrope, NT, 1973, 1975, NY 1975; Equus, NT, 1973; Pygmalion, Albery, 1974; The Family Dance, Criterion, 1976; Antony and Cleopatra, Prospect Co., 1977; solo performance of St Mark's Gospel, Riverside Studios, Mermaid and Comedy, 1978, Globe, 1981, UK tour, 1985, Half Moon, 1990; Tishoo, Wyndham's, 1979; The Browning Version, and A Harlequinade, NT, 1980; The Portage to San Cristobal of A. H., Mermaid, 1982; Kipling (solo performance), Mermaid, 1984; The Cocktail Party, Phoenix, 1986; Fathers and Sons, Waiting for Godot, NT, 1987; Shakespeare, Cole & Co. (solo performance), UK tour, 1988; The Heiress, Chichester, 1989; Exclusive, Strand, 1989; A Single Man, Greenwich, 1990; Dancing at Lughnasa, NT, 1990, transf. Phoenix, 1991. Dir, Definitely the Bahamas, Orange Tree, Richmond, 1987. Films include: Frenzy, 1971; Travels with My Aunt, 1972; Stevie, 1978; Never Say Never Again, 1983. TV series, Mr Palfrey of Westminster, 1984. Evening Standard (later Standard) Drama Award, 1968, 1973, 1982; Stage Actor of the Year, Variety Club, 1970. *Publications:* Young Gemini (autobiog.), 1979; Double Bill (autobiog.), 1980; Personal Mark, 1984. *Recreations:* music, gardening.

McCRAE, Alister Geddes, CBE 1973; Chairman: Clyde Port Authority, 1966–77; British Ports Association, 1972–74; *b* 7 Aug. 1909; *s* of Alexander McCrae; *m* 1st, 1938, Margaret Montgomery Reid (*d* 1977); one *s*; 2nd, 1978, Norah Crawford Orr. *Educ:* Kelvinside Academy; High School of Glasgow. Joined: P. Henderson & Co., Shipowners, Glasgow, 1927; Irrawaddy Flotilla Co. Ltd (in Burma), 1933; Served War: Middle East and Burma, 1941–45; Lt-Col, Royal Indian Engrs (despatches). Irrawaddy Flotilla Co. Ltd, 1946–48 (Dep. Gen. Manager, in Burma); re-joined P. Henderson & Co., as Partner, 1948; Sen. Partner and Man. Dir, British & Burmese Steam Navigation Co. Ltd, 1963; retd 1972. Member: Nat. Dock Labour Bd, 1953–57; UK Chamber of Shipping Council, 1954–65; Clyde Navigation Trust, 1962–65; British Transport Docks Bd, 1963–65; Nat. Ports Council, 1967–71; Scottish Economic Council, 1969–74; Aldington/Jones Commn on Docks, 1972; Chm., Clyde Estuary Develt Gp, 1968–71; Dir, Hunterston Develt Co. Ltd, 1970–74. Chm., Glasgow Old People's Welfare Assoc. (Age Concern), 1969–79. Freeman, City of London, 1959; Liveryman, Worshipful Co. of Shipwrights, 1959. FRSA. *Publications:* Irrawaddy Flotilla, 1978; (jtly) Tales of Burma, 1981; Pioneers in Burma, 1986, new edn as Scots in Burma, 1990. *Recreation:* country walking. *Address:* Belwood, Killearn, Stirlingshire G63 9LG.

McCRAITH, Col Patrick James Danvers, MC 1943; TD; DL; Solicitor and Notary Public; *b* 21 June 1916; *s* of late Sir Douglas McCraith; *m* 1946, Hon. Philippa Mary Ellis, *yr d* of 1st and last Baron Robins, KBE, DSO, of Rhodesia and Chelsea; one *s* one *d*. *Educ:* Harrow. 2nd Lieut, Sherwood Rangers Yeomanry, 1935; served War, 1939–45, N Africa and NW Europe (three times wounded); raised and commanded Yeomanry Patrol of Long Range Desert Group, 1940–41; commanded Sherwood Rangers Yeomanry, 1953–57; Bt Colonel, 1958. Hon. Col, B (Sherwood Rangers Yeomanry) Squadron, The

Royal Yeomanry, 1968–79. High Sheriff of Nottinghamshire, 1963; DL Notts, 1965. *Address:* Cranfield House, Southwell, Notts NG25 0HQ. *T:* Southwell (0636) 812129. *Clubs:* Special Forces; Nottingham and Notts United Services (Nottingham).

McCREA, Rev. Robert Thomas William; MP (DUP) Mid Ulster, since 1983 (resigned seat Dec. 1985 in protest against Anglo-Irish Agreement; re-elected Jan. 1986); Minister, Free Presbyterian Church of Ulster, since 1967; *b* 6 Aug. 1948; *s* of Robert T. and Sarah J. McCrea; *m* 1971, Anne Shirley McKnight; two *s* three *d*. *Educ:* Cookstown Grammar Sch.; Theol Coll., Free Presbyterian Church of Ulster. Civil servant, 1966; Free Presbyterian Minister of the Gospel, 1967–. Dist Councillor, Magherafelt, 1973–; Mem. (DUP) Mid Ulster, NI Assembly, 1982–86. Dir, Daybreak Recording Co., 1981–. Gospel singer and recording artist; Silver, Gold and Platinum Discs for record sales. Hon. DD Marietta Bible Coll., Ohio, 1989. *Publication:* In His Pathway—the story of the Reverend William McCrea, 1980. *Recreations:* music, horse riding. *Address:* 10 Highfield Road, Magherafelt, Co. Londonderry BT45 5JD. *T:* Magherafelt (0648) 32664.

McCREA, Sir William (Hunter), Kt 1985; FRS 1952; MA; PhD, ScD (Cambridge); BSc (London); FRSE, FRAS, MRIA; Research Professor of Theoretical Astronomy, University of Sussex, 1966–72, now Emeritus; *b* Dublin, 13 Dec. 1904; *er s* of late Robert Hunter McCrea; *m* 1933, Marian Nicol Core, 2nd *d* of late Thomas Webster, JP, Burdiehouse, Edinburgh; one *s* two *d*. *Educ:* Chesterfield Grammar Sch.; Trinity Coll., Cambridge (Scholar); University of Göttingen. Wrangler, Rayleigh Prizeman, Sheepshanks Exhibitioner, and Isaac Newton Student, of Cambridge Univ.; Rouse Ball Travelling Student, and Rouse Ball Senior Student, of Trinity Coll.; Comyns Berkeley Bye-Fellow, Gonville and Caius Coll., Cambridge, 1952–53. Lecturer in Mathematics, Univ. of Edinburgh, 1930–32; Reader in Mathematics, Univ. of London, and Assistant Prof., Imperial Coll. of Science, 1932–36; Prof. of Mathematics: Queen's Univ., Belfast, 1936–44; Royal Holloway Coll., Univ. of London, 1944–66 (Hon. Fellow, 1984). Visiting Prof. of Astronomy: Univ. of California, 1956; Case Inst. of Technology, 1964; Univ. of BC, Vancouver, 1975–76; Consulting Astronomer, Kitt Peak National Observatory, Arizona, 1965, 1975; Royal Society Exchange Visitor: to USSR, 1960, 1968; to Mexico, 1971; to Argentina, 1971, 1983; to India, 1976; to Egypt, 1981; For. Visiting Prof. of American Astronomical Soc. and Vis. Prof., Berkeley Astronomy Dept, 1967; first occupant, Chaire Georges Lemaître, Louvain Univ., 1969; Royal Soc. Leverhulme Vis. Prof. of Astronomy, Cairo Univ., 1973; Vis. Prof., Istanbul Univ., 1977, 1978; William Evans Vis. Prof., Otago Univ., 1979. Visiting Lecturer: Univ. of Liège, 1960; Technische Hochschule, Aachen, 1962; various universities in Greece and Turkey (British Council), 1971; York Univ., 1965; Lectures: Harland, Univ. of Exeter, 1970; Larmor, QUB, 1970; Halley, Oxford, 1975; Milne, Oxford, 1985; R. H. Fowler Meml, Cambridge, 1989. Temp. Prin. Experimental Officer, Admty, 1943–45; commnd RAFVR (Training Branch), 1941–45. Mem., Governing Board of School of Theoretical Physics, Dublin Institute for Advanced Studies, 1940–50; Governor: Royal Holloway Coll., 1946–49; Ottershaw Sch., 1947–52; Barclay Sch. for Partially Sighted Girls, 1949–66; Mem. Adv. Council, Chelsea Coll. of Aeronautical and Automobile Engineering, 1958–86. Secretary of Section A of British Assoc., 1935–39, Pres. 1966; Pres., Mathematical Assoc., 1973–74 (Hon. Mem., 1985). Joint Editor of The Observatory, 1935–37. Pres., Royal Astronomical Soc., 1961–63 (Sec., 1946–49; Foreign Correspondent, 1968–71; Treasurer, 1976–79). Fellow, Imperial Coll., 1967–; Leverhulme Emeritus Fellow, 1973–75. Mem., Akademie Leopoldina, 1972–; Foreign Mem., Turin Acad. of Scis, 1990–. Freeman, City of London, 1988. Keith Prize, RSE, 1939–41; Gold Medal, RAS, 1976. Hon. DSc: National Univ., Ireland, 1954; QUB, 1970; Sussex, 1978; Dr *hc* National Univ., Cordoba, Argentina, 1971; Hon. ScD Dublin, 1972. *Publications:* Relativity Physics, 1935; Analytical Geometry of Three Dimensions, 1942; Physics of the Sun and Stars, 1950; trans. A. Unsöld's The New Cosmos, 1969; Royal Greenwich Observatory, 1975; (jtly) History of the Royal Astronomical Society 1920–1980, 1987; various papers and reviews in mathematical and astronomical journals. *Address:* 87 Houndean Rise, Lewes, East Sussex BN7 1EJ. *Club:* Athenæum.

McCREERY, His Honour (Henry Edwin) Lewis, QC 1965; a Circuit Judge (formerly Judge of County Courts), 1971–90, retired; *b* 26 July 1920; *s* of late Rev. William John McCreery, BD, and late Anne Cullen McCreery; *m* 1945, Margaret Elizabeth Booth (*d* 1990); two *d*. *Educ:* St Andrew's Coll., Dublin; Trinity Coll., Dublin. RAF, 1942–47. Called: Irish Bar King's Inns, 1943; English Bar, Middle Temple, 1946 (Bencher, 1971). Dep. Chm., Quarter Sessions: Cornwall, 1966–71; Devon, 1967–71; Recorder of Salisbury, 1969–71. *Recreation:* gardening. *Address:* Drumbeg, Ellisfield, Basingstoke, Hants RG25 2QE. *Club:* Royal Air Force.

McCRICKARD, Donald Cecil; Chief Executive, TSB Group plc, since 1990; Chairman, Hill Samuel Bank, since 1991; *b* 25 Dec. 1936; *s* of late Peter McCrickard and Gladys Mary McCrickard; *m* 1960, Stella May, *d* of Walter Edward Buttle, RN retd; two *d*. *Educ:* Hove Grammar Sch.; LSE; Univ. of Malaya. Financial, marketing and gen. management appts to 1975; Chief Exec., American Express Co. UK, 1975, American Express Co. Asia, Pacific, Australia, 1980; Man. Dir, UDT Holdings, later TSB Commercial Holdings, 1983; Chairman: Swan National, 1983; UDT Bank, 1983; Dir, and Dep. Group Man. Dir, 1987, Chief Exec., Banking, 1988, TSB Group; Chief Exec., TSB Bank plc, 1989–91. *Recreations:* golf, photography, theatre, restaurants. *Address:* TSB Group plc, 25 Milk Street, EC2V 8LU. *T:* 071–606 7070. *Club:* Royal Automobile.

MacCRINDLE, Robert Alexander, QC 1963; commercial lawyer; Partner, Shearman and Sterling; *b* 27 Jan. 1928; *s* of F. R. MacCrindle; *m* 1959, Pauline Dilys, *d* of Mark S. Morgan; one *s* one *d*. *Educ:* Girvan High Sch.; King's Coll., London; Gonville and Caius Coll., Cambridge. LLB London, 1948. Served RAF, 1948–50, Flt-Lt. LLM Cantab, Chancellor's Medal, 1951. Called to Bar, Gray's Inn, 1952 (Bencher, 1969); Junior Counsel to Board of Trade (Export Credits), 1961–63; Mem., Hong Kong Bar, 1967. Mem., Royal Commn on Civil Liability and Compensation for Personal Injury, 1973–78. Honorary Fellow: American Coll. of Trial Lawyers, 1974; Conseil Juridique (France). *Publication:* McNair's Law of the Air, 1953. *Recreation:* golf. *Address:* 4 Essex Court, Temple, EC4. *T:* 071–583 9191; 88 avenue de Breteuil, 75015 Paris, France. *T:* (1) 45.67.11.93. *Club:* University (New York).

McCRINDLE, Sir Robert (Arthur), Kt 1990; MP (C) Brentwood and Ongar, since 1974 (Billericay, 1970–74); *b* 19 Sept. 1929; *o s* of Thomas Arthur and Isabella McCrindle; *m* 1953, Myra Anderson; two *s*. *Educ:* Allen Glen's Coll., Glasgow. Vice-Chm., Sausmarez, Carey & Harris, Financial Consultants, 1972–75; Director: Langham Life Assurance Co. Ltd, 1972–76; Worldmark Travel Ltd, 1978–82; Hogg Robinson PLC, 1987–; M & G Assurance Gp, 1988–; Chairman: Cometco Ltd, Commodity Brokers, 1972–78; Citybond Storage, 1975–. Consultant, British Caledonian Airways, 1984–88. Contested: Dundee (East), 1959; Thurrock, 1964. PPS to Minister of State, Home Office, 1974; Chm., All-Party Parly Aviation Cttee, 1980–; Mem., Transport Select Cttee, 1988–. Mem., UK Delegn to N Atlantic Assembly, 1977– (Chm., Economic Cttee, 1980–84). Parliamentary Consultant: British Transport Police Fedn; British Insurance and Investment Brokers' Assoc.; Guild of Business Travel Agents, 1975–78. Nat. Vice-Pres., Corp. of Mortgage Brokers, 1970–76. Fellow, Corp. of Insurance Brokers; ACII. *Address:* 26 Ashburnham Gardens, Upminster, Essex RM14 1XA. *T:* Upminster (04022) 27152.

McCRIRRICK, (Thomas) Bryce, CBE 1987; FEng, FIEE; Director of Engineering, BBC, 1978–87; *b* 19 July 1927; *s* of late Alexander McCrirrick and Janet McCrirrick (*née* Tweedie); *m* 1953, Margaret Phyllis Yates; three *s*. *Educ:* Galashiels Academy; Heriot Watt Coll., Edinburgh; Regent Street Polytechnic, London. BBC Radio, Studio Centres in Edinburgh, Glasgow and London, 1943–46; served RAF, 1946–49; BBC Television, 1949; Engineer-in-Charge Television Studios, 1963; Head of Engineering Television Recording, and of Studio Planning and Installation Dept, 1969; Chief Engineer, Radio Broadcasting, 1970; Asst Dir of Engrg, 1971; Dep. Dir of Engrg, 1976. Technical Assessor, Investigation into Clapham Junction Rly Accident, 1989. Pres., Soc. of Electronic and Radio Technicians, 1981–85 (Vice-Pres., 1979–80); Vice-Pres., IERE, 1985–88; Pres., IEE, 1988–89 (Dep. Pres., 1986–88, Vice-Pres., 1982–86); Mem. Council, Fellowship of Engrg, 1989–. Gov., Imperial Coll., 1985–. FRTS 1980; FBKSTS 1982; FSMPTE 1989. Hon. DSc Heriot Watt, 1987. *Recreations:* skiing, theatre. *Address:* Surrey Place, Coach House Gardens, Fleet, Hants GU13 8QX. *T:* Fleet (0252) 623422.

McCRONE, Robert Gavin Loudon, CB 1983; FRSE 1983; Secretary of the Scottish Office Environment Development (formerly Scottish Development Department), since 1987 and Chief Economic Adviser at the Scottish Office, since 1972; *b* 2 Feb. 1933; *s* of Robert Osborne Orr McCrone and Laura Margaret McCrone; *m* 1959, Alexandra Bruce Waddell; two *s* one *d*. *Educ:* Stowe Sch.; St Catharine's Coll., Cambridge (Economics Tripos; MA); University Coll. of Wales, Aberystwyth (Milk Marketing Bd Research Schol. in agricl economics; MSc 1959); Univ. of Glasgow (PhD 1964). Fisons Ltd, 1959–60; Lectr in Applied Economics, Glasgow Univ., 1960–65; Economic Consultant to UNESCO and Mem. Educnl Planning Mission to Libya, 1964; Fellow of Brasenose Coll., Oxford, 1965–72; Chm., Oxford Univ. Economics Subfaculty, 1968–70; Mem. NEDC Working Party on Agricl Policy, 1967–68; Economic Adviser to House of Commons Select Cttee on Scottish Affairs, 1969–70; Special Economic Adviser to Sec. of State for Local Govt and Regional Planning, 1970; Sen. Economic Adviser and Head of Economics and Statistics Unit, 1970–72, Under-Sec. for Regional Develt, 1972–80, Scottish Office; Sec., Industry Dept for Scotland (formerly Scottish Economic Planning Dept), 1980–87. Visiting Professor of Economics: Univ. of Strathclyde, 1983–86; Univ. of Glasgow, 1988–. Member Council: Royal Economic Soc., 1977–82; Scottish Economic Soc., 1982–; ESRC, 1986–89. Hon. LLD Glasgow 1986. *Publications:* The Economics of Subsidising Agriculture, 1962; Scotland's Economic Progress 1951–60, 1963; Agricultural Integration in Western Europe, 1963; Regional Policy in Britain, 1969; Scotland's Future, 1969; contribs to various economic jls. *Recreation:* walking. *Address:* St Andrews House, Edinburgh EH1 3DE. *T:* 031–224 4047. *Club:* United Oxford & Cambridge University.

McCRORIE, Linda Esther, (Mrs Peter McCrorie); *see* Gray, L. E.

McCRUM, Michael William, MA; Master of Corpus Christi College, Cambridge, since 1980; Chairman, Cathedrals Fabric Commission for England, since 1991; *b* 23 May 1924; 3rd *s* of late Captain C. R. McCrum, RN and Ivy Hilda Constance (*née* Nicholson); *m* 1952, Christine Mary Kathleen, *d* of Sir Arthur ffforde, GBE; three *s* one *d*. *Educ:* Horris Hill, Newbury; Sherborne Sch.; Corpus Christi Coll., Cambridge. Entrance Scholar to CCC, Dec. 1942. Served RN, 1943–45 (Sub-Lt RNVR, Dec. 1943). CCC, Cambridge, 1946–48; Part I, Class. Tripos, First Class, 1947; Part II, First Class, with distinction, 1948. Asst Master, Rugby School, Sept. 1948–July 1950 (Lower Bench Master, 1949–50); Fellow CCC, Cambridge, 1949; Second Tutor, 1950–51; Tutor, 1951–62; Headmaster, Tonbridge Sch. 1962–70; Head Master of Eton, 1970–80; Vice-Chancellor, Cambridge Univ., 1987–89. Lectures: Lansdowne, Univ. of Victoria, BC, 1985; Clayesmore, Blandford Forum, 1986; Lady Margaret's Preacher, Univ. of Cambridge, 1987. Member: Council of the Senate, University of Cambridge, 1955–58, 1981–89; General Board of Faculties, 1957–62, 1987–89; Financial Bd, 1985–89; Chairman: Faculty Bd of Educn, 1981–86, 1990–; Bd of Extra-Mural Studies, 1982–86, Cambridge. Chairman: HMC, 1974; Joint Educnl Trust, 1984–87; GBA, 1989– (Dep. Chm., 1982–89); Member: Oxford and Cambridge Schs Exam. Bd, 1960–62, 1966–87 (Chm., 1981–87); Governing Body, Schools Council, 1969–76 (also mem., various cttees); ISJC, 1982– (Dep. Chm., 1989–). Governor: Bradfield Coll., 1956–62; Eastbourne Coll., 1960–62; King's Sch., Canterbury, 1980–; Sherborne Sch., 1980–; Oakham Sch., 1981–85; United World Coll. of the Atlantic, 1981–; Rugby Sch., 1982–. Pres., Cambridge Soc., 1989–. Trustee: King George VI and Queen Elizabeth Foundn of St Catharine's, Cumberland Lodge, 1983–; Nat. Heritage Meml Fund, 1984–90; Cambridge Foundn, 1989–. Hon. Freeman, Skinners' Co., 1980. Hon. DEd Victoria, BC, 1989. Comendador de la Orden de Isabel la Católica (Spain), 1988. *Publications:* Select Documents of the Principates of the Flavian Emperors AD 68–96 (with A. G. Woodhead), 1961; Thomas Arnold, Head Master, 1989. *Address:* The Master's Lodge, Corpus Christi College, Cambridge CB2 1RH. *T:* Cambridge (0223) 338029. *Clubs:* Athenæum, United Oxford & Cambridge University, East India, Devonshire, Sports and Public Schools; Hawks (Cambridge).

McCUBBIN, Very Rev. David; Provost and Canon of Cumbrae Cathedral since 1987; *b* 2 Nov. 1929; *s* of late David McCubbin and late Annie Robertson Cram (*née* Young). *Educ:* Finnart School; Greenock Academy; King's Coll., London (AKC 1954); St Boniface Coll., Warminster. National service, RAF, 1948–50. Deacon 1955, priest 1956; Curate: Christ Church, Frome, 1955–57; Glastonbury Parish Church, 1957–60; Rector: Holy Trinity, Dunoon, 1960–63; St Peter's, Kirkcaldy, 1963–70; Wallsend (and Surrogate), 1970–79; St John's, Aberdeen, 1979–81; St Bride's, Kelvinside, 1981–87; St Andrew's, Millport, 1987; Canon of St John's Cathedral, Oban, 1987; Synod Clerk, Diocese of Argyll and The Isles, 1988–. Chm., Prayer Book Soc., Scotland, 1988–. *Recreations:* music, reading, walking. *Address:* The College, Millport, Isle of Cumbrae KA28 0HE. *T:* Millport (0475) 530353.

McCUBBIN, Henry Bell; Member (Lab) Scotland North East, European Parliament, since 1989; *b* 15 July 1942; *s* of Henry McCubbin and Agnes (*née* Rankine); *m* 1967, Katie M. Campbell; three *d*. *Educ:* Allan Glen's Sch., Glasgow. BA Hons Open Univ. Film Cameraman: BBC TV, 1960–77; Grampian TV, 1977–89. Dir, Dundee Reportory Th., 1983–. *Recreations:* theatre, hill walking, politics. *Address:* 58 Castle Street, Broughty Ferry, Dundee DD5 2EJ. *T:* Dundee (0382) 730773.

McCULLIN, Donald; freelance photojournalist; *b* 9 Oct. 1935; *m* 1959 (marr. diss. 1987); two *s* one *d*; and one *s* by Laraine Ashton. *Educ:* Tollington Park Secondary Sch., Morden; Hammersmith Jun. Art Sch. Started work at 15 yrs of age after death of father; National Service (RAF), 1954–56; first pictures published by The Observer, 1958; thereafter began photographic career; worked for The Sunday Times for 18 yrs, covering wars, revolutions and travel stories. Hon. FRPS 1977. *Publications:* Destruction Business, 1971; Is Anyone Taking Any Notice, 1971; The Palestinians, 1979; Homecoming, 1979; Hearts of Darkness, 1980; Battle Beirut, a City in Crisis, 1983; Perspectives, 1987; Skulduggery, 1987; Open Skies, 1989; (with Lewis Chester) Unreasonable Behaviour (autobiog.), 1990. *Recreation:* protecting the English countryside. *Address:* Holly Hill House, Batcombe, Shepton Mallet, Somerset BA4 6BL.

MacCULLOCH, Dr Malcolm John, MD; DPM; FRCPsych; Research Psychiatrist, Ashworth Hospital, Merseyside, since 1990; *b* 10 July 1936; *s* of William MacCulloch and Constance Martha MacCulloch; *m* 1962, Mary Louise Beton (marr. diss. 1975); one *s* one *d*; *m* 1975, Carolyn Mary Reid; two *d*. *Educ:* King Edward VII Sch., Macclesfield, Cheshire; Manchester Univ. (MB, ChB, DPM, MD). Consultant Child Psychiatrist, Cheshire Child Guidance Service, 1966–67; Director Univ. Dept, Child Psychiatry and Subnormality, Birmingham Univ., 1967–70; Sen. Lectr, Adult Psychiatry, Univ. of Liverpool, 1970–75; PMO, DHSS, 1975–78; SPMO, Mental Health Div., DHSS, 1979–80; Dir. Special Hosps Res. Unit, London, 1979–86; Med. Dir, Park Lane Hosp., Liverpool, 1979–89; Advr to Ontario Govt on Forensic Psychiatric Services, 1988–. Vis. Prof., Clarke Inst. of Psychiatry, Toronto, 1987–88. *Publications:* Homosexual Behaviour: therapy and assessment, 1971; Human Sexual Behaviour, 1980; numerous med. papers on aspects of psychiatry. *Recreations:* inventing, playing music. *Address:* Ashworth Hospital, Parkbourne, Merseyside L31 1HW. *T:* 051–520 2244.

McCULLOCH, Rt. Rev. Nigel Simeon; *see* Taunton, Bishop Suffragan of.

McCULLOUGH, Sir Charles; *see* McCullough, Sir I. C. R.

McCULLOUGH, Hon. Sir (Iain) Charles (Robert), Kt 1981; **Hon. Mr Justice McCullough;** a Judge of the High Court of Justice, Queen's Bench Division, since 1981; *b* 1931. National Service, 1950–52, commnd Royal Artillery; RA (TA), 1952–54. Called to Bar, Middle Temple, 1956 (Harmsworth Law Schol.); Bencher, 1980. Midland Circuit, 1957–71, Midland and Oxford Circuit, 1972–81; Dep. Chm., Notts QS, 1969–71; QC 1971; a Recorder of the Crown Court, 1972–81. Member: Criminal Law Revision Cttee, 1973–; Gen. Council of the Bar, 1966–70; Parole Bd, 1984–86. *Address:* Royal Courts of Justice, Strand, WC2A 2LL.

McCUNN, Peter Alexander, CBE 1980; Deputy Chairman, Cable and Wireless plc, 1978–82 (and Group Managing Director, 1978–81); *b* 11 Nov. 1922; *m* 1943, Margaret Prescott; two *s* (and one *s* decd). *Educ:* Mexborough Grammar Sch.; Edinburgh University. Commnd W Yorks Regt, 1942; served in Normandy, Malta, Italy; left Army, Nov. 1946 (Captain). Joined Cable & Wireless, 1947; Director: Cable & Wireless/Western Union International Inc. of Puerto Rico, 1968–70; Cable & Wireless, 1969– (Exec. Dep. Chm., 1977); Nigerian External Telecommunications Ltd, 1969–72; Sierra Leone External Telecommunications Ltd, 1969–72; Trinidad and Tobago External Telecommunications Ltd, 1972–77; Jamaica International Telecommunications Ltd, 1972–77; Cable and Wireless (Hong Kong) Ltd, 1981–84; Mercury Communications Ltd, 1981–84. *Recreations:* music, gardening, swimming, reading, crosswords. *Address:* Wychelms, 14 Lime Walk, Pinkneys Green, Maidenhead, Berks SL6 6QB. *T:* Maidenhead (0628) 24308. *Clubs:* Exiles (Twickenham); Phyllis Court (Henley).

McCURLEY, Anna Anderson; Head of Government Affairs, Corporate Communications Strategy, since 1990; *b* 18 Jan. 1943; *d* of George Gemmell and Mary (*née* Anderson); *m* (marr. diss.); one *d*. *Educ:* Glasgow High Sch. for Girls; Glasgow Univ. (MA); Jordanhill Coll. of Educn (Dip. in Secondary Educn); Strathclyde Univ. Secondary history teacher, 1966–72; College Methods Tutor, Jordanhill Coll. of Educn, 1972–74. Strathclyde Regional Councillor, Camphill/Pollokshaws Div., 1978–82. Sen. Exec., Dewe Rogerson, 1987–89. Contested (C) Renfrew W and Inverclyde, 1987. MP (C) Renfrew W and Inverclyde, 1983–87. Mem., Scottish Select Cttee, 1984–87. Mem., Horserace Betting Levy Bd, 1988–. *Recreations:* music, cookery, painting in oils. *Address:* Woodsley, 12 Shore Road, Skelmorlie PA17 5DY.

McCUSKER, Sir James (Alexander), Kt 1983; Founder, Town and Country Permanent Building Society, 1964, Foundation Chairman 1964–83; *b* Perth, WA, 2 Dec. 1913; *m* Mary Martindale McCusker; three *c*. *Educ:* Perth Modern Sch. Served War of 1939–45, 2½ years with 1st Armoured Div. (Sgt). 30 years with Commonwealth Bank of Aust.; resigned 1959, as Sen. Branch Manager in Perth. Chm., State Cttee of Inquiry into Rates and Taxes, 1980. Councillor: WA Permanent Building Socs Assoc., 1964–83 (former Pres.); Aust. Assoc. of Permanent Building Socs; Fellow, Aust. Inst. of Valuers; Member: Council of Rural and Allied Industries; WA Indicative Planning Cttee (Housing). Patron, Paraplegic Assoc. of WA. *Address:* 195 Brookdale Street, Floreat Park, Perth, WA 6014, Australia.

McCUTCHEON, Dr William Alan, FRGS, FSA, MRIA; author, lecturer and consultant; School Teacher (Geography Specialist), Ditcham Park School, Petersfield, since 1986; *b* 2 March 1934; *s* of late William John and Margaret Elizabeth McCutcheon; *m* 1956, Margaret Craig; three *s*. *Educ:* Royal Belfast Academical Instn; The Queen's University of Belfast (Hugh Wisnom Scholar, 1960; BA (Hons Geog.) 1955, MA 1958, PhD 1962). FRGS 1958; FSA 1970; MRIA 1983. School Teacher (Geography Specialist), Royal Belfast Academical Instn, 1956–62; Director, N Ireland Survey of Industrial Archaeology, 1962–68; Keeper of Technology and Local History, Ulster Museum, Belfast, 1968–77; Dir, Ulster Museum, 1977–82. Vis. Teacher, Glenalmond Coll., 1984, 1986. Chairman: Historic Monuments Council (NI), 1980–85; Jt Cttee on Industrial Archaeology (NI), 1981–85; Member: Malcolm Cttee on Regional Museums in Northern Ireland, 1977–78; Industrial Archaeol. Cttee, Council for British Archaeol., 1981–85. *Publications:* The Canals of the North of Ireland, 1965; Railway History in Pictures, Ireland: vol. 1 1970, vol. 2 1971; (contrib.) Travel and Transport in Ireland, 1973; (contrib.) Folk & Farm, 1976; Wheel and Spindle—Aspects of Irish Industrial History, 1977; The Industrial Archaeology of Northern Ireland, 1980 (Library Assoc. high commendation as an outstanding reference book); (contrib.) Some People and Places in Irish Science and Technology, 1985; (contrib.) An Economic and Social History of Ulster 1820–1939, 1985; numerous papers. *Recreations:* reading, classical music, photography, travel, gardening, swimming. *Address:* 3 Coxes Meadow, Petersfield, Hants GU32 2DU. *T:* Petersfield (0730) 65366.

McDERMID, Ven. Norman George Lloyd Roberts; Archdeacon of Richmond since 1983; *b* 5 March 1927; *s* of Lloyd Roberts McDermid and Annie McDermid; *m* 1953, Vera Wood; one *s* three *d*. *Educ:* St Peter's School, York; St Edmund Hall, Oxford (MA); Wells Theological Coll. Deacon 1951, priest 1952; Curate of Leeds, 1951–56, in charge of St Mary, Quarry Hill, Leeds, 1953–56; Vicar of Bramley, Leeds, 1956–64; Rector of Kirkby Overblow, 1964–80; Stewardship Adviser, Ripon Diocese, 1964–76, Bradford and Wakefield, 1973–76; Vicar of Knaresborough, 1980–83. Hon. Canon of Ripon Cathedral, 1972–; RD of Harrogate, 1977–83. Member: General Synod, 1970–; Church of England Pensions Bd, 1972–78; Redundant Churches Fund, 1977–89; Central Bd of Finance of C of E, 1985–. Church Commissioner, 1978–83. *Recreations:* investment, historic churches, pedigree cattle, gardening. *Address:* 62 Palace Road, Ripon, N Yorks HG4 1HA. *T:* Ripon (0765) 604342. *Club:* National Liberal.

See also Rev. Canon R. T. W. McDermid.

McDERMID, Rev. Canon Richard Thomas Wright; Vicar of Christ Church, Harrogate, since 1970; Chaplain to The Queen, since 1986; *b* 10 July 1929; *s* of Lloyd Roberts McDermid and Annie McDermid; *m* 1956, Joyce Margaret (*née* Pretty); one *s* four *d*. *Educ:* St Peter's Sch., York; Univ. of Durham, 1950–55 (MA, DipTh). Served Intelligence Corps, 1947–49. Deacon 1955, Priest 1956; Curate of Seacroft, Leeds, 1955–61; Vicar of St Mary's, Hawksworth Wood, Leeds, 1961–70. Hon. Canon of Ripon Cath., 1983–. *Publication:* Beverley Minster Fasti, 1991. *Recreations:* local history, brass rubbing, gardening. *Address:* Christ Church Vicarage, 11 St Hilda's Road, Harrogate, N Yorks HG2 8JX. *T:* Harrogate (0423) 883390.

MacDERMOT, Brian (Charles), CBE 1966; LVO 1961; HM Diplomatic Service, retired; *b* 29 Jan. 1914; *m* 1949, Mary Arden Hunter; seven *s* two *d*. Probationer Vice-Consul, Peking, China, 1936; served at: Hankow, China, 1939–40; Kobe, Japan, 1940–41; Kunming, South China, 1942; Vice-Consul, Shiraz, Persia, 1943; Paris, 1944, promoted Consul, 1945; Foreign Office, 1946; Consul, Beirut, 1948; First Secretary, Belgrade, 1950; First Secretary, Berne, 1951, acted as Charge d'Affaires, 1951, 1952, 1953; transferred to Foreign Office, 1954; transferred to Holy See, 1955, acted as Chargé d'Affaires, 1958, 1959, 1960 and 1961; HM Consul-General, Oporto, 1962–68; Ambassador and Consul-Gen., Paraguay, 1968–72. *Address:* Little Orchard, Wetherden, Stowmarket, Suffolk IP14 3LY.

MACDERMOT, Niall, CBE 1991 (OBE (mil.) 1944); QC 1963; barrister-at-law; Secretary-General, International Commission of Jurists, 1970–90; *b* 10 Sept. 1916; *s* of late Henry MacDermot, KC, Dublin; *m* 1940, Violet Denise Maxwell (marr. diss.); one *s*; *m* 1966, Ludmila Benvenuto. *Educ:* Rugby Sch.; Corpus Christi Coll., Cambridge; Balliol Coll., Oxford. Served in Intelligence Corps, 1939–46; GSO1 HQ 21 Army Group, 1944–45. MP (Lab) Lewisham North, Feb. 1957–59, Derby North, April 1962–1970; Mem. Exec., London Labour Party, 1958–62. Dep. Chm., Beds QS, 1961–64, 1969–72; Recorder of Newark-on-Trent, 1963–64; a Recorder of the Crown Court, 1972–74. Master of the Bench, Inner Temple, 1970–. Financial Sec., Treasury, 1964–67; Minister of State, Min. of Housing and Local Govt, 1967–68. Hon. Treasurer, Justice, 1968–70. Member: Council, Internat. Inst. of Human Rights, Strasbourg, 1972–; Adv. Council, Interights, 1984–; Bd, Internat. Alert, 1985–; Pres., Special NGO Cttee on Human Rights, Geneva, 1973–86, Vice-Pres., 1986–. Founding Mem., Groupe de Bellerive, 1977–. Trustee of Tate Gall., 1969–76. *Address:* 34 avenue Weber, 1208 Geneva, Switzerland. *T:* Geneva 35.40.86.

MacDERMOTT, Edmond Geoffrey; Metropolitan Stipendiary Magistrate, 1972–84. Called to Bar, Gray's Inn, 1935; Dept of Dir of Public Prosecutions, 1946–72; Asst Dir of Public Prosecutions, 1968–72.

McDERMOTT, Sir Emmet; *see* McDermott, Sir L. E.

MacDERMOTT, Rt. Hon. Sir John Clarke, Kt 1987; PC 1987; **Rt. Hon. Lord Justice MacDermott;** a Lord Justice of Appeal, Supreme Court of Judicature, Northern Ireland, since 1987; *b* 1927; *s* of Baron MacDermott, PC, PC (NI), MC, and of Louise Palmer, *o d* of Rev. J. C. Johnston, DD; *m* 1953, Margaret Helen, *d* of late Hugh Dales, Belfast; four *d*. *Educ:* Campbell Coll., Belfast; Trinity Hall, Cambridge (BA); QUB. Called to Bar, Inner Temple and Northern Ireland, 1949; QC (NI) 1964. Judge, High Court of NI, 1973–87. *Address:* Royal Courts of Justice, Belfast, Northern Ireland; 6 Tarawood, Holywood, Co. Down.

McDERMOTT, Sir (Lawrence) Emmet, KBE 1972; Lord Mayor of Sydney, 1969–72; Alderman, Sydney, 1962–77; Dental Surgeon; *b* 6 Sept. 1911; *s* of O. J. McDermott; *m* 1939, Arline Beatrice Olga (*d* 1987); one *s* one *d*. *Educ:* St Ignatius Coll., Sydney; Univ. of Sydney; Northwestern Univ., Chicago. MDS Sydney; DDS Northwestern; FICD, FRACDS, FACD; FAIM 1983. Hon. Consultant Dental Surgeon: Royal Prince Alfred Hosp., 1942–; Eastern Suburbs Hosp., 1945–; Pres., Bd of Control, United Dental Hosp., Sydney, 1967–79; Mem., NSW Dental Bd, 1967–79; Pres., Australian Dental Assoc. (NSW Br.), 1960–61; Councillor, Australian Dental Assoc., 1962–66. Mem., Liberal Party State Council, 1969; Councillor, Sydney County Council, 1973–80, Dep. Chm., 1975–77, Chm., 1977–78. Dir, City Mutual Life Assce Soc. Ltd, 1970–83, Dep. Chm., 1976–83; Member: Sydney Cove Redevelopment Authority, 1971–76; Convocation, Macquarie Univ., 1966–; Australia-Britain Soc. (NSW Br.), Vice-Pres., 1972–77. *Recreations:* golf, swimming (Sydney Univ. Blue), bowls. *Address:* T&G Tower, Hyde Park Square, Park & Elizabeth Streets, Sydney, NSW 2000, Australia. *T:* 264–3660; 20 Carnarvon Road, Roseville, NSW 2069. *T:* 46–2086. *Clubs:* Australian Jockey, Royal Sydney Golf, Elanora Country, Tattersall's, American National, Chatswood Bowling, City Bowling, Warrawee Bowling (all Sydney).

McDERMOTT, Patrick Anthony, MVO 1972; HM Diplomatic Service; Counsellor, Paris, since 1990; *b* 8 Sept. 1941; *e s* of Patrick McDermott and Eileen (*née* Lyons); *m* 1976, Christa, *d* of Emil and Anne-Marie Herminghaus, Krefeld, W Germany; four *s*. *Educ:* Clapham College, London. FO 1960; Mexico City, 1963; Attaché, UK Delegn to UN, NY, 1966; Vice-Consul, Belgrade, 1971; FCO, 1973; Second Sec., Bonn, 1973; First Sec., Paris, 1976; FCO, 1979; Consul-Gen., and Econ. and Financial Advr to British Military Government, W Berlin, 1984; FCO, 1988. Freeman, City of London, 1986. *Address:* c/o Foreign and Commonwealth Office, SW1A 2AH.

MacDONAGH, Prof. Oliver Ormond Gerard; W. K. Hancock Professor of History, Australian National University, 1973, now Emeritus; *b* 23 Aug. 1924; *s* of Michael A. MacDonagh and Loretto (*née* Oliver); *m* 1952, Mary Carmel Hamilton; three *s* four *d*. *Educ:* Clongowes Wood Coll., Co. Kildare; University Coll. Dublin (MA); King's Inns, Dublin (BL); Univ. of Cambridge (PhD). Fellow, St Catharine's Coll., Cambridge, 1952–64, Vis. Fellow, 1986, Hon. Fellow, 1987; Foundn Prof. of History, Flinders Univ., SA, 1964–68; Prof. of Modern History, UC, Cork, 1968–73. Vis. Prof., Yale Univ., 1970; Overseas Schol., St John's Coll., Cambridge, 1981. FASSA 1965; FAHA 1977; Corresp. FBA 1984. Hon. LittD: Flinders, 1982; Sydney, 1989; NUI, 1989. *Publications:* A Pattern of Government Growth, 1961; Ireland: the Union and its Aftermath, 1968, 2nd edn 1977; English Victorian Government, 1977; The Inspector-General, 1981; States of Mind, 1983, 2nd edn 1985; The Hereditary Bondsman: Daniel O'Connell 1775–1829, 1987; The Emancipist: Daniel O'Connell 1830–1847, 1989; Jane Austen: Real and Imagined Worlds, 1991. *Recreations:* bridge, Nineteenth Century novels. *Address:* 13 Landsborough Street, Griffith, ACT, Australia. *T:* Canberra 956263.

MACDONALD, family name of **Barons Macdonald** and **Macdonald of Gwaenysgor.**

MACDONALD, 8th Baron *cr* 1776; **Godfrey James Macdonald of Macdonald;** JP; DL; Chief of the Name and Arms of Macdonald; *b* 28 Nov. 1947; *s* of 7th Baron Macdonald, MBE, TD, and Anne (*d* 1988), *o d* of late Alfred Whitaker; *S* father, 1970; *m* 1969, Claire, *e d* of Captain T. N. Catlow, CBE, RN, Gabriel Cottage, Tunstall, Lancs; one *s* three *d*. JP Skye and Lochalsh, 1979; DL Ross and Cromarty, Skye and Lochalsh, 1986. *Heir:* *s* Hon. Godfrey Evan Hugo Thomas Macdonald of Macdonald, yr, *b* 24 Feb. 1982. *Address:* Kinloch Lodge, Isle of Skye. *Club:* New (Edinburgh).

McDONALD, Hon. Lord; Robert Howat McDonald, MC 1944; a Senator of the College of Justice in Scotland, 1973–89; *b* 15 May 1916; *s* of Robert Glassford McDonald, and Roberta May Howat, Paisley, Renfrewshire; *m* 1949, Barbara Mackenzie, *d* of John Mackenzie, Badcaul, Ross-shire; no *c*. *Educ:* John Neilson Institution, Paisley. MA

(Glasgow) 1935; LLB (Glasgow) 1937; admitted Faculty of Advocates, 1946; QC (Scot.) 1957. Served with KOSB, 1939–46 (despatches, 1945). Sheriff Principal of Ayr and Bute, 1966–71. Mem., Criminal Injuries Compensation Board, 1964–71; Pres., Industrial Tribunals for Scotland, 1972–73; Chm., Gen. Nursing Council for Scotland, 1970–73; Chm., Mental Welfare Commn for Scotland, 1965–83; Mem., Employment Appeal Tribunal, 1976–86. Chm., Queen's Nursing Inst., Scotland, 1981–. *Address:* 5 Doune Terrace, Edinburgh. *Club:* New (Edinburgh).

MACDONALD OF GWAENYSGOR, 2nd Baron *cr* 1949, of Gwaenysgor, Flint; **Gordon Ramsay Macdonald;** business consultant; *b* 16 Oct. 1915; *er s* of 1st Baron Macdonald of Gwaenysgor, PC, KCMG; *S* father, 1966; *m* 1941, Leslie Margaret Taylor; three *d. Educ:* Manchester Univ. MA, Economics and Commerce. Served War, 1940–46; Army, Major, Artillery; GSO2 Operations and Intelligence (despatches, Burma). Board of Trade, 1946–53: Principal, 1946–47; UK Trade Comr, Canberra, ACT, 1947–53. With Tube Investments Ltd, and Man. Dir TI (Export) Ltd, 1953–64; Chief Exec., Telecommunications Group, Plessey Co., 1964–67; Chm., Hayek Engrg (UK) Ltd, 1967–76; Chm. and Chief Exec., Ferro Metal and Chemical Comp., and Satra Consultants (UK) Ltd, 1977. *Recreations:* golf, chess. *Heir:* none. *Address:* c/o House of Lords, SW1.

MACDONALD of Sleat (Btcy); *see under* Bosville Macdonald.

MACDONALD, Alastair John Peter, CB 1989; Deputy Under Secretary of State, Ministry of Defence (Procurement Executive), since 1990; *b* 11 Aug. 1940; *s* of late Ewen Macdonald and Hettie Macdonald; *m* 1969, Jane, *d* of late T. R. Morris; one *s* two *d. Educ:* Wimbledon Coll.; Trinity Coll., Oxford. Editorial staff of Spectator, 1962; Financial Times, 1963–68: Washington DC, 1965–66; Features Editor, 1966–68; joined Home Civil Service as Asst Principal, DEA, 1968; Principal, DTI, 1971; Sec., Lord Devlin's Commn into Industrial and Commercial Representation, 1971–72; Asst Sec., DoI, 1975; RCDS, 1980; Under Sec., DTI, 1981. Dep. Sec., DTI, 1985–90. Non-exec. Dir, Rank Leisure Ltd (subsid. of Rank Organisation), 1981–85. *Address:* Ministry of Defence, Whitehall, SW1A 2HB.

McDONALD, Alex Gordon; Chief Scientific Officer, Department of Health and Social Security, 1975–82; *b* 29 Jan. 1921; *m* 1st, 1942, P. Thomas; 2nd, 1950, J. James; two *d. Educ:* Tiffin Sch., Kingston upon Thames; Royal Coll. of Science (BSc, ARCS). Served RNVR, Lieut (A), Fleet Air Arm, 1939–46. Home Office, 1949; Chief of Staffs, MoD, 1956; Police Research and Develt Br., 1963; DHSS, 1970. Sometime Lectr at: Inst. of Criminology, Inst. of Advanced Legal Study, London Hosp. Sch. of Forensic Pathology, London Sch. of Hygiene and Trop. Med., and Univ. of Warwick Sch. of Business Studies. Member, Bd of Studies in Community Med., London. Hon. Prof. in Industrial and Business Studies, and Dir, Res. Centre on Mathematical Modelling of Clinical Trials, Univ. of Warwick. *Publications:* contrib. learned jls on OR and Systems Analysis. *Recreations:* Basset Hounds, Blood Hounds, needlework, reading. *Address:* 40 Wolsey Road, East Molesey, Surrey KT8 9EN. *Club:* Kennel.

McDONALD, Alexander Gordon; *see* McDonald, Alex G.

McDONALD, Prof. Alexander John, MA (Cantab), LLB, WS; Professor of Conveyancing, University of Dundee (formerly Queen's College), 1955–82, now Emeritus (Dean of the Faculty of Law, 1958–62, 1965); Senior Partner, Thornton Oliver (formerly Thornton, Dickie & Brand), WS, Dundee, 1978–84, now Consultant; *b* 15 March 1919; *o s* of late John McDonald, and Agnes Mary Stewart McDonald; *m* 1951, Doreen Mary, *o d* of late Frank Cook, OBE; two *s* two *d. Educ:* Cargilfield Sch.; Fettes Coll. (open scholar); Christ's Coll., Cambridge (Classical Exhibn, BA 1942); Edinburgh Univ. (Thow Schol. and John Robertson Prize in Conveyancing; LLB with dist., 1949). Admitted as Solicitor and Writer to the Signet, 1950; Lectr in Conveyancing, Edinburgh Univ., 1952–55. *Publications:* Conveyancing Case Notes, 2nd edn 1984; Registration of Title Manual, 1986; Conveyancing Manual, 4th edn 1989. *Address:* 1 Regent Place, Broughty Ferry, Dundee DD5 1AT. *T:* Dundee (0382) 77301.

McDONALD, Alistair; Economic Development Officer, Wandsworth Borough Council, 1983–89; *b* 13 March 1925; *e s* of late John Bell McDonald and Mary McDonald; *m* 1954, Isabel Margaret Milne; two *d. Educ:* Fraserburgh Academy; Aberdeen Univ. (BSc 1st Cl. Hons Natural Philosophy). Served RAF and Fleet Air Arm, 1943–46. Malayan Meteorological Service, 1950–56; ICI, 1956–66; Min. of Technology, 1966–70; Dept of Trade and Industry, 1970–74; Dept of Industry, 1974–77; Director, British Shipbuilders (on secondment), 1977–79; Regional Dir, NW Region, Dept of Industry, 1979–83. *Recreation:* golf.

MacDONALD, Alistair Archibald, MA, LLB; DL; Sheriff of Grampian, Highland and Islands; at Lerwick and Kirkwall, since 1975; *b* 8 May 1927; *s* of James and Margaret MacDonald; *m* 1950, Jill Russell; one *s* one *d. Educ:* Broughton Sch.; Edinburgh Univ. Served in Army, 1945–48. Called to Scottish Bar, 1954. Formerly Sheriff Substitute, Caithness, Sutherland, Orkney and Zetland at Lerwick, 1961 and at Kirkwall, 1968. DL Shetland Islands, 1986. KHS 1988. *Address:* West Hall, Shetland Islands. *Club:* Royal Northern (Aberdeen).

MACDONALD, Alistair H.; Deputy Secretary, Equipment Leasing Association, 1971–87, retired; *b* 18 May 1925. *Educ:* Dulwich Coll.; Enfield Technical Coll.; Corpus Christi Coll., Cambridge. MP (Lab) Chislehurst, 1966–70. Councillor, Chislehurst and Sidcup UDC, 1958–62; Alderman, 1964–68, Councillor, 1971–90, London Borough of Bromley. *Address:* 1 Springbourne Court, The Avenue, Beckenham, Kent BR3 2ED. *T:* 081–658 6953.

McDONALD, Alistair Ian, CBE 1978; Director: Schroder Global Trust plc (formerly Trans Oceanic Trust), 1981–89; TR Trustees Corporation PLC, 1982–89; *b* 12 Sept. 1921; *s* of late Angus McDonald and Blanche Elizabeth McDonald; *m* 1947, Olwen (*née* Evans); one *d. Educ:* Greenwich Sch. Served War, RAF, 1940–46. Church Comrs, 1947–81: Dep. Investments Sec., 1966–68; Investments Sec., 1968–81. Director: Datastream Ltd, 1981–82; Trust Union Ltd, 1981–82; TR Industrial and Gen. Trust PLC, 1982–89; Chm., Cirkit Hldgs PLC, 1983–87. Royal Coll. of Nursing: Investment Adviser, 1967–90; Vice Pres., 1975–. Chm., Lampada Housing Assoc., 1975–. *Recreations:* grandsons, gardening, reading. *Club:* Caledonian.

McDONALD, Allan Stuart; Headmaster, George Heriot's School, Edinburgh, 1970–83; *b* 20 Aug. 1922; *s* of Allan McDonald and Clementina Peebles (*née* Stuart), both of Edinburgh; *m* 1948, Margaret Wilson, *d* of late James Adams, Paisley and Stranraer, and of Margaret Wilson (*née* Ferguson); one *s* two *d. Educ:* Royal High Sch., Edinburgh; Giffnock and Eastwood Schs, Renfrewshire; Glasgow Univ.; Sorbonne. MA Hons 1944; DipEd 1948. Commnd, Royal Corps of Signals (21st Army Group Signals), 1943–45. Asst Master: Johnstone High Sch., 1948–50; Eastwood Sch., 1950–54; Principal Teacher: Modern Languages, Fortrose Acad., 1954–59; German, George Heriot's Sch., 1959–70; Depute Headmaster, George Heriot's Sch., 1967–70. *Recreations:* formerly Rugby, cricket; now gardening, photography. *Address:* 1 The Grove, Maxwell Park, Dalbeattie DG5 4LY. *T:* Dalbeattie (0556) 611231.

MACDONALD, Angus Cameron; His Honour Judge Macdonald; a Circuit Judge, since 1979; *b* 26 Aug. 1931; *o s* of late Hugh Macdonald, OBE, and of Margaret Cameron Macdonald (*née* Westley); *m* 1956, Deborah Anne, *d* of late John Denny Inglis, DSO, MC, JP, and of Deborah Margery Meiklem Inglis (*née* Thomson); three *d. Educ:* Bedford Sch.; Trinity Hall, Cambridge (BA 1954, MA 1960). Nat. service, 1950–51, commissioned, TA, 1951–57. Called to Bar, Gray's Inn, 1955; Resident Magistrate, then Crown Counsel, Nyasaland Govt, 1957–65; Sen. State Counsel, Malawi Govt, 1965–67; practised, NE Circuit, 1967–79; a Recorder of the Crown Court, 1974–79. *Recreations:* singing, fishing, shooting. *Address:* 21 Lindisfarne Road, Newcastle upon Tyne NE2 2HE. *T:* 091–281 1695; Blaren, Kilninver, by Oban, Argyll PA34 4UX. *T:* Kilmelford (08522) 246. *Club:* Northern Counties (Newcastle upon Tyne).

MACDONALD, Angus John, (Gus); Managing Director, Scottish Television, since 1990 (Director of Programmes, 1986–90); Visiting Professor, Media and Film Studies, Stirling University, since 1985; *b* 20 Aug. 1940; *s* of Colin Macdonald and Jean (*née* Livingstone); *m* 1963, Alice Theresa McQuaid; two *d. Educ:* Scotland Street Sch., Glasgow; Allan Glen's Sch., Glasgow. Marine fitter, 1955–63; Circulation Manager, Tribune, 1963–65; feature writer, The Scotsman, 1965–66; Editor, Financial Scotsman, 1966–67; Granada Television: Editor/Exec. Producer, World in Action, 1969–75; successively Head of Current Affairs, Regl Progs. Features, 1975–82; presenter, variously, Camera, Devil's Advocate, Granada 500, Party conferences, What the Papers Say, World in Action, Union World; ombudsman, Right to Reply (viewers' complaints about independent television), Channel Four, 1982–88. Board Member: Scottish Television Film Enterprises, 1988–; Mac III Productions Inc., LA, 1987–. Chm., ITV Children's Programming Gp, 1988–90; Member: ITV Network Controllers', Finance and Film Purchase Gps, 1988–90; ITVA Council, 1990–; ITC Standing Consultative Cttee, 1990–. Chm. (Founder), Edinburgh Internat. Television Festival, 1976 and 1977; Dep. Chm., Edinburgh Internat. Film Festival, 1975–84. Gov. Nat. Film and Television Sch., 1986–. FRSA 1989; FInstD 1990; CBIM 1990. *Publications:* The Documentary Idea and Television Today, 1977; Camera: Victorian eyewitness, 1979. *Recreations:* pictures, moving and still; exploring Scotland past and present. *Address:* Scottish Television, Cowcaddens, Glasgow G2 3PR. *T:* 041–332 9999. *Clubs:* Reform, Royal Automobile.

MACDONALD, Angus Stewart, CBE 1985; DL; FRAgS; farmer; *b* 7 April 1935; *s* of Angus Macdonald and Mary Macdonald (*née* Anderson); *m* 1959, Janet Ann Somerville; three *s. Educ:* Conon Bridge School; Gordonstoun School. FRAgS 1982. Director: British Wool Marketing Board and Associated Cos; Scottish English Welsh Wool Growers; Grampian Television; Chairman: Reith & Anderson (Tain & Dingwall) Ltd; SCOTVEC, Sector Bd 1. Chairman: RHAS, 1978–79; Scottish Agricl Develt Council, 1980–86; Member: Highlands & Islands Develt Bd; Panel of Agricl Arbiters; The MacRobert Trust. Crown Estate Comr, 1990–. Dir, Animal Disease Res. Assoc. Mem. Queen's Body Guard for Scotland (Royal Co. of Archers), 1985–. Governor: Gordonstoun School (Chm., 1989–); Aberlour School. DL Ross and Cromarty, 1984. *Recreations:* field sports. *Address:* Torgorm, Conon Bridge, Dingwall, Ross-shire IV7 8DN. *T:* Dingwall (0349) 61365.

MacDONALD, Gen. Sir Arthur (Leslie), KBE 1978 (OBE 1953); CB 1969; *b* 30 Jan. 1919; *s* of late Arthur Leslie MacDonald, Yaamba, Queensland; *m* 1940, Joan Bevington, *d* of late Sidney Brady, Brisbane, Queensland; one *d. Educ:* The Southport School, Southport, Queensland; Royal Military College, Duntroon, ACT. Regtl and Staff appts, Aust., ME and New Guinea, 1940–44; Instructor, Staff Coll., Camberley, 1944–45; CO 3rd Bn, The Royal Australian Regt, Korea, 1953–54; Dir of Mil. Ops, AHQ, 1955–56; Senior Aust. Planner, SEATO, Bangkok, 1957–58; Commandant, Jungle Training Centre, Canungra, 1959–60; Dir of Staff Duties, AHQ, 1960–61; Imperial Defence Coll., 1962; Dep. Commander, 1st Div., 1963–64; Commander, Papua New Guinea Comd, 1965–66; Dep. Chief of the General Staff, 1966–67; Commander Australian Force, Viet Nam, 1968–69; Adjutant-Gen., 1969–70; GOC Northern Comd, 1970–73; Chief of Operations, 1973; Vice Chief of Gen. Staff, 1973–75; CGS, 1975–77; Chief of Defence Force Staff, 1977–79, retired. Col Comdt, Royal Aust. Regt, 1981–85. Director: Carricks Ltd and associated cos, 1980–86; Gas Corp. of Qld, 1983–91. *Address:* 7/32 Dunmore Terrace, Auchenflower, Qld 4066, Australia. *Club:* Queensland (Brisbane).

McDONALD, Air Marshal Sir Arthur (William Baynes), KCB 1958 (CB 1949); AFC 1938; CEng, FRAeS 1959; DL; retired; *b* 14 June 1903; *s* of late Dr Will McDonald, OBE, Antigua, BWI; *m* 1928, Mary Julia Gray, Hindhead, Surrey; two *s* two *d. Educ:* Antigua Grammar Sch.; Epsom Coll.; Peterhouse, Cambridge (MA). Joined RAF, 1924; served in Singapore, 1933–35; in Air Ministry, 1939–40; Fighter Command, 1941. Appointed Air Defence Commander, Ceylon, 1942; Air Officer Training, Air HQ, India, 1943–44; Air Officer Commanding No. 106 Group, 1945–46; Comdt RAF Staff Coll., Bulstrode and later Andover, 1947–48; Student Imperial Defence Coll., 1949; OC Aeroplane and Armament Experimental Establishment, under the Ministry of Supply, 1950–52; Director-General of Manning, Air Ministry, 1952–55; Commander-in-Chief, Royal Pakistan Air Force, 1955–57; AOC-in-C, RAF Technical Training Comd, 1958–59; Air Mem. for Personnel, Air Council, 1959–61, retired 1962. DL Hampshire, 1965. *Recreation:* sailing (rep. Great Britain in Olympic Games, 1948). *Clubs:* Royal Air Force; Royal Lymington Yacht; RAF Sailing Association (Adm.).

MACDONALD, Calum Alasdair; MP (Lab) Western Isles, since 1987; *b* 7 May 1956; *s* of Malcolm and Donella Macdonald. *Educ:* Bayble Sch.; The Nicolson Inst.; Edinburgh Univ.; Univ. of California at Los Angeles. Member: TGWU; Crofters Union. *Address:* 28 Francis Street, Stornoway, Isle of Lewis. *T:* Stornoway (0851) 4684.

McDONALD, David Arthur; Director of Information, Department of the Environment, since 1990; *b* 16 Jan. 1940; *s* of late Campbell McDonald and Ethel McDonald; *m* 1st, 1963, Barbara MacCallum (marr. diss.); one *d*; 2nd, 1971, Mavis Lowe (*see* Mavis McDonald); one *s. Educ:* Campbell College, Belfast; Trinity College, Dublin. BA (Moderatorship) Classics. Asst Master, Classics, Methodist College, Belfast, 1963–66; Press Sec. to Minister of Education, N Ireland, 1967–68; joined Min. of Housing and Local Govt, 1970; Asst Private Sec. to Sec. of State for the Envt, 1974–76; Asst Sec., Local Govt Finance Divs, 1977–82, Dir of Information, 1982–87, Under Sec., Construction Industry, and Sport and Recreation, Directorates, 1987–90, DoE. Pres., Civil Service Men's Hockey Club, London. *Recreations:* golf, watching rugby and cricket. *Clubs:* Reform; Wimbledon Park Golf.

MACDONALD, David Cameron; Senior UK Adviser to Credit Suisse First Boston, since 1983; Chairman, Pittard Garnar, since 1985 (Director, 1984); Director: Coutts and Co., since 1980; Sears, since 1981; Merivale Moore, since 1985; *b* 5 July 1936; *s* of James Fraser Macdonald, OBE, FRCS and Anne Sylvia Macdonald (*née* Hutcheson); *m* 1st, 1968, Melody Jane Coles (marr. diss. 1980); two *d*; 2nd, 1983, Mrs Sally Robertson; one *s* one *d. Educ:* St George's Sch., Harpenden; Newport Grammar Sch. Admitted a solicitor with Slaughter and May, 1962; joined Philip Hill Higginson Erlangers (now Hill Samuel & Co. Ltd), 1964: Dir, 1968; Dep. Chm., 1979–80; Dir, Hill Samuel Gp Ltd, 1979–80; Chief Exec., Antony Gibbs Holdings Ltd and Chm., Antony Gibbs & Sons, 1980–83;

Chairman: Bath and Portland Gp, 1982–85; Sound Diffusion, 1987–89. Dir Gen., Panel on Takeovers and Mergers, 1977–79. Adviser to Govt on Upper Clyde Shipbuilders crisis, 1971. Chm., Issuing Houses Assoc., 1975–77. Mem., BTA, 1971–82. Trustee, London City Ballet, 1983–87. *Recreations:* music, fishing. *Address:* 13A Bolton Gardens, SW5. *T:* 071–373 1296; Upton Noble House, Upton Noble, near Shepton Mallet, Somerset. *T:* Upton Noble (074985) 572.

McDONALD, David Wylie, CMG 1978; DA, RIBA, ARIAS, FHKIA; Secretary for Lands and Works, Hong Kong, 1981–83; MLC Hong Kong, 1974–83; *b* 9 Oct. 1927; *s* of William McDonald and Rebecca (*née* Wylie); *m* 1951, Eliza Roberts Steele; two *d.* *Educ:* Harris Acad., Dundee; School of Architecture, Dundee Coll. of Art (Lorimer Meml Prize, RIAS, 1950; City Coronation Design Prize, Corporation of Dundee, 1953; DA 1953). Architect with Gauldie, Hardie, Wright and Needham, Chartered Architects, Dundee, 1953–55; Public Works Department, Hong Kong: Architect, 1955; Sen. Architect, 1964; Chief Architect, 1967; Govt Architect, 1970; Principal Govt Architect, 1972; Dir of Building Develt, 1973; Dir of Public Works, 1974. Member: Finance Cttee, Legislative Council, 1974–83; Commonwealth Parly Assoc., 1974–. Director: Mass Transit Railway Corp., Hong Kong, 1975–83; Ocean Park Ltd, Hong Kong, 1976–83; Hong Kong Industrial Estate Corp., 1981–83; Mem., Hong Kong Housing Auth., 1982–83. Mem. Exec. Cttee: Girl Guides Assoc. (Hong Kong Br.), 1977–83; Hong Kong Red Cross, 1981–83. Mem. Cttee of Management, Margaret Blackwood Hsg Assoc., 1984–; Trustee, Scottish Trust for Physically Disabled, 1984–. Mem., Mensa, 1968–. JP Hong Kong, 1972–83. Silver Jubilee Medal, 1977. *Recreations:* swimming (Coach and Manager, Hong Kong Swimming Team at Commonwealth Games, Christchurch, NZ, 1974), drawing, painting and calligraphy. *Address:* Northbank, Backmuir of Liff, by Dundee DD2 5QT. *T:* Dundee (0382) 580483. *Clubs:* Hong Kong (Hong Kong) (Chairman, 1977); Royal Hong Kong Jockey (Hong Kong).

MACDONALD, Rev. Donald Farquhar Macleod, CBE 1979; Principal Clerk of General Assembly of the Church of Scotland, 1972–85; *b* 1 May 1915; *s* of John Murchison Macdonald and Margaret Macleod; *m* 1948, Anne Jane Vance Sinclair; one *s* two *d.* *Educ:* North Kelvinside Secondary Sch.; Glasgow Univ. (MA, LLB). Ordained to Glasford Parish, 1948; Clerk to Presbytery of Hamilton, 1952–72; Dep. Clerk of General Assembly, 1955–71. Hon. Fellow and Hon. DLit, Central Sch. of Religion, Worcester, 1985. *Publications:* (ed) Practice and Procedure in the Church of Scotland, 6th edn, 1977; (ed and comp.) Fasti Ecclesiae Scoticanae, vol. X, 1981. *Recreations:* chess, swimming, gardening. *Address:* 29 Auchingramont Road, Hamilton, Lanarkshire ML3 6JP. *T:* Hamilton (0698) 423667; 3 Chapmans Place, Elie, Fife. *Club:* Royal Scots (Edinburgh).

MACDONALD, Hon. Donald (Stovel), PC (Canada) 1968; lawyer; Counsel, McCarthy Tétrault, Toronto, since 1991; *b* 1 March 1932; *s* of Donald Angus Macdonald and Marjorie Stovel Macdonald; *m* 1st, 1961, Ruth Hutchison (*d* 1987), Ottawa; four *d*; 2nd, 1988, Adrian Lang; three step *s* four step *d.* *Educ:* Univ. of Toronto (BA 1951); Osgoode Hall Law Sch. (1955); Harvard Law Sch. (LLM 1956); Cambridge Univ. (Dip. in Internat. Law, 1957). Called to Ont Bar, 1955; Prize in Insurance Law, Law Soc. of Upper Canada, 1955; Rowell Fellow, Canadian Inst. of Internat. Affairs, 1956; McCarthy & McCarthy, law firm, Toronto, 1957–62, Partner, 1978–88; High Comr for Canada in UK, 1988–91. Special Lectr, Univ. of Toronto Law Sch., 1978–83, 1986–88. MP Rosedale, 1962–78; Parly Sec. to Ministers of Justice, Finance, Ext. Affairs, Industry, 1963–68; Minister without Portfolio, 1968; Pres., Queen's Privy Council, and Govt House Leader, 1968–70; Minister of National Defence, 1970–72; Minister of Energy, Mines and Resources, 1972–75; Minister of Finance, 1975–77. Director: McDonnell Douglas Corp., 1978–88; Du Pont Canada Inc., 1978–88; Bank of Nova Scotia, 1980–88; Alberta Energy Co. Ltd, 1981–88; MacMillan-Bloedel Ltd, 1986–88. Chm., Internat. Develt Res. Centre, Canada, 1981–84. Chm., Royal Commn on Econ. Union and Develt Prospects for Canada, 1982–85. Freeman, City of London, 1990; Liveryman, Distillers' Co. LLD (*hc*): St Lawrence Univ., 1974; Univ. of New Brunswick at Saint John, 1990; Hon. DEng Colorado Sch. of Mines, 1976. *Recreations:* fishing, cross-country skiing, tennis. *Address:* 27 Marlborough Avenue, Toronto, Ont M5R 1X5, Canada; McCarthy Tétrault Toronto Dominion Tower, PO Box 48, Toronto-Dominion Centre, Toronto, Ont M5K 1E6. *Clubs:* Reform; York, Toronto (Toronto).

McDONALD, Sir Duncan, Kt 1983; CBE 1976; BSc, FH-WC, FRSE, FEng, CBIM, SMIEEE; Chairman, Northern Engineering Industries plc, 1980–86 (Group Managing Director, 1977–80; Chief Executive, 1980–83); *b* 20 Sept. 1921; *s* of Robert McDonald and Helen Orrick; *m* 1955, Jane Anne Guckian; three *s* one *d.* *Educ:* Inverkeithing Public Sch.; Dunfermline High Sch.; Edinburgh Univ. (BSc). Grad. App., BTH, Rugby, 1942–45; Transformer Design, Research and Develt, BTH, 1945–54. Bruce Peebles Industries Ltd: Chief Transformer Designer, 1954–59; Chief Engr, 1959; Dir and Chief Engr, 1960; Managing Dir, 1962; Chm. and Chief Exec. (and of A. Reyrolle & Co. Ltd), 1974; Reyrolle Parsons Ltd: Dir, 1973–77; Chief Exec., 1976–77. Director: Barclays Bank (Newcastle), 1980–86; Nat. Nuclear Corp., 1982–86; General Accident, 1983–; Northern Rock (Scotland), 1986–; Adv. Dir, Barclays Bank (Scotland), 1986–91. Member: Scottish Council Develt and Industry, 1967– (Vice-Pres., 1984–90); Scottish Economic Council, 1975–87. Mem. Court, Heriot-Watt Univ., 1984–90. Pres. Watt Club, 1986–87. FH-WC 1962. Fellow, Scottish Council (Develt and Industry), 1987. FRSA. Hon. FIEE 1984. Hon. DSc Heriot-Watt, 1982; Hon. DEng Newcastle, 1984. *Publications:* various papers to learned socs, nat. and internat. *Recreations:* fishing, golf. *Address:* Duncliffe, Kinellan Road, Edinburgh EH12 6ES. *T:* 031–337 4814. *Club:* New (Edinburgh).

McDONALD, (Edward) Lawson, MA, MD Cantab; FRCP; FACC; Consultant Cardiologist, National Heart Hospital, since 1961; Cardiologist, to King Edward VII's Hospital for Officers, London, since 1968, to King Edward VII Hospital, Midhurst, since 1970; Senior Lecturer (formerly Lecturer) to the Institute of Cardiology, since 1961; Hon. Consultant Cardiologist, Canadian Red Cross Memorial Hospital, Taplow, since 1960; *b* 1918; *s* of late Charles Seaver McDonald and Mabel Deborah (*née* Osborne); *m* 1953, Ellen Greig Rattray (marr. diss. 1972); one *s.* *Educ:* Felsted Sch.; Clare Coll., Cambridge; Middlesex Hospital; Harvard Univ. House appointments Middlesex Hospital, 1942–43. Temp. Surgeon-Lt, RNVR, 1943–46; served War of 1939–45, in N Atlantic and Normandy Campaigns. RMO, Nat. Heart Hosp., 1946–47; Asst Registrar, Inst. of Cardiology, 1947–48; Med. Registrar, Middlesex Hosp., 1948–49; studied in Stockholm, 1949; Asst to Prof. of Medicine, Middlesex Hosp., 1949–52; Rockefeller Travelling Fellow in Medicine, 1952–53; Asst in Medicine, Med. Dept, Peter Bent Brigham Hosp., Boston, Mass. and Research Fellow in Medicine, Harvard Univ., 1952–53; Clinical and Research Asst, Dept of Cardiology, Middlesex Hosp., 1953–55; Asst Dir, Inst. of Cardiology and Hon. Asst Physician, Nat. Heart Hosp., 1955–61; Physician, and Physician to Cardiac Dept, London Hosp., 1960–78. Member: Bd of Governors, National Heart and Chest Hosps, 1975–82; Council, British Heart Foundn, 1975–83. Visiting Lecturer: American Coll. of Cardiology; American Heart Assoc.; Univ. of Toronto, Queen's Univ., Kingston, Ont; Univ. of Bombay; University of Barcelona, Eliseo Migoya Inst. of Cardiology, Bilbao, Spain; Istanbul Univ., Turkey; Univs of Chicago, Cincinnati and Kansas; Harvard Univ.; Mayo Foundation, USA; Univs of Belgrade, Ljubljana and Zagreb, Yugoslavia; Nat. Univ. of Cordoba, Argentine; Univ. of Chile, and Catholic Univ., Santiago; Nat. Univ. of Colombia; Nat. Inst. of Cardiology, Mexico; Nat. Univ. of Mexico; University of San Marcos and University of Cayetano Heredia, Peru; Nat. Univ. of Venezuela; Vis. Prof., Univ. of Oregon Med. Sch., since 1961, has addressed numerous heart societies in Europe, Africa, Australia, Canada, NZ, USA, People's Republic of China, USSR, and South America; St Cyres Lecturer, 1966; First Charles A. Berns Meml Lectr, Albert Einstein Coll. of Medicine, NY, 1973; Vth World Congress of Cardiology Souvenir Orator and Lectr's Gold Medallist, 1977. Advisor to the Malaysian Govt on Cardiac Services. Member: British Cardiac Soc.; Assoc. of Physicians of Great Britain and Ireland, and other societies; FACC; Corresp. Mem. or Hon. Mem. of various socs of Cardiology or Angiology in S America. Hon. Fellow, Turkish Med. Soc.; Internat. Fellow, Council on Clinical Cardiol., Amer. Heart Assoc.; Mem., Italian Soc. of Cardiology; Hon. Member: Pakistan Cardiac Soc,; Scientific Council, Revista Portuguesa de Cardiologia. Member, Most Honourable Order of the Crown of Johore, 1980. Editorial Bd, New Istanbul Contribution to Clinical Science. *Publications:* (ed) Pathogenesis and Treatment of Occlusive Arterial Disease, 1960; Medical and Surgical Cardiology, 1969; (ed) Very Early Recognition of Coronary Heart Disease, 1978; numerous contribs to learned jls; also papers and addresses. *Recreations:* art, ski-ing, mountain walking, sailing. *Address:* 9 Bentinck Mansions, Bentinck Street, W1M 5RJ. *T:* 071–935 0868/7101.

McDONALD, Elaine Maria, OBE 1983; Associate Artistic Director, Northern Ballet Theatre, since 1990; *b* 2 May 1943; *d* of Wilfrid Samuel and Ellen McDonald. *Educ:* Convent of the Ladies of Mary Grammar Sch., Scarborough; Royal Ballet Sch., London. Walter Gore's London Ballet, 1962–64; Western Theatre Ballet, 1964–69; Principal Dancer, 1969–89, Artistic Controller, 1988–89, Scottish Ballet; has also danced with London Fest. Ballet, Portuguese Nat. Ballet, Galina Samsova and Andre Prokovsky's New London Ballet, Cuban Nat. Ballet. Mem., Scottish Arts Council, 1986– (Mem., Dance and Mime Cttee, 1982–). Hon. LittD Strathclyde, 1990. *Relevant publication:* Elaine McDonald, ed J. S. Dixon, 1983. *Recreations:* physical therapy, theatre, travel, reading.

MacDONALD, Hon. Flora Isabel; Special Advisor to President, Commonwealth of Learning, since 1990; Presenter, North/South, weekly television programme, since 1990; *b* N Sydney, Nova Scotia, 3 June 1926. *Educ:* schools in North Sydney, Nova Scotia; Empire Business Coll., Canadian Nat. Defence Coll. With Nat. HQ, Progressive Cons. Party, 1957–66 (Exec. Dir, 1961–66); Nat. Sec., Progressive Cons. Assoc. of Canada, 1966–69; Administrative Officer and Tutor, Dept of Political Studies, Queen's Univ., Kingston, 1966–72; MP (Progressive C) Kingston, Ontario, 1972–88; Minister for External Affairs, Canada, 1979–80; Minister of Employment and Immigration, 1984–86; Minister for Communications, 1986–88. Vis. Scholar, Centre for Canadian Studies, Univ. of Edinburgh, 1989. Dir, C. T. Financial Services, 1989–; Director: The Urban Inst., Washington (formerly Mem. Adv. Council); Canadian Centre for Advanced Film Studies; Canadian Civil Liberties Assoc.; Inst. for Res. on Public Policy, 1989–. Chm., Commonwealth Human Rights Initiative. Member: Canadian Inst. of Internat. Affairs; Canadian Inst. of Public Affairs; Elizabeth Fry Soc., Kingston (former Pres.); Cttee for an Indep. Canada (former exec. dir); Canadian Political Science Assoc. (former dir). Hon. Chm., Nat. Ballet Sch., 1989–. FRSA. Hon. degrees from Univs throughout Canada and the US. *Publications:* papers on political subjects. *Recreations:* speedskating, mountain climbing. *Address:* #502, 350 Queen Elizabeth Driveway, Ottawa, Ont K1S 3N1, Canada.

McDONALD, (Francis) James; Chairman, Beaumont Hospital Foundation, since 1987; President and Chief Operating Officer, General Motors, 1981–87; *b* Saginaw, Mich, 3 Aug. 1922; *s* of Francis and Mary McDonald; *m* 1944, Betty Ann Dettenthaler; two *s* one *d.* *Educ:* General Motors Inst. Served USN, 1944–46 (Lieut). Joined Saginaw Malleable Iron Plant, 1946; Transmission Div., Detroit, 1956–65; Pontiac Motor Div., 1965–68; Dir, Manufacturing Operations, Chevrolet Motor Div., 1968–69; Vice-Pres., and Mem. Admin Cttee, Gen. Motors, 1969; General Manager: Pontiac Motor Div., 1969–72; Chevrolet Motor Div., 1972–74; Exec. Vice-Pres. and a Dir, 1974; Mem. Finance Cttee, 1979; Chm., Exec. and Admin Cttees, 1981. Holds hon. degrees from univs and colls in the US, incl. Michigan State Univ. and Notre Dame Univ.

MACDONALD, His Honour George Grant; a Circuit Judge, 1972–87; *b* 5 March 1921; *s* of late Patrick Macdonald, MA, Aberdeen, MB, ChB, Edinburgh, and Charlotte Primrose (*née* Rintoul); *m* 1967, Mary Dolores (*née* Gerrish), *widow* of G. G. Taylor; no *c.* *Educ:* Kelly Coll., Tavistock; Bristol Univ. (LLB (Hons)). Served War of 1939–45: in Royal Navy, Aug. 1941–July 1946, in Western Approaches, and Mine Sweeping, RNVR. Called to Bar, Gray's Inn, 1947; practised on Western Circuit, from Albion Chambers, Bristol; Dep.-Chm., Dorset QS, apptd 1969; Temp. Recorder of Barnstaple, Dec. 1971. *Recreations:* sailing, bridge, chess. *Address:* Flat 1, Minterne House, Minterne Magna, Dorchester, Dorset. *T:* Cerne Abbas (03003) 329. *Club:* Clifton (Bristol).

McDONALD, Graeme Patrick Daniel, OBE 1988; Managing Director, Anglia Films Ltd, since 1988; *b* 30 July 1930; *s* of Daniel McDonald and Eileen (*née* McLean); unmarried. *Educ:* St Paul's Sch.; Jesus Coll., Cambridge. Entered TV, 1960; Dir, Granada TV, 1960–65; BBC Television: Producer, 1966–76: prodns include Thirty Minute Theatre, 1966–67, Wednesday Play, 1967–70 and Play for Today, 1970–76; Head of Drama Series and Serials, 1977–81; Head of Drama Gp, 1981–83; Controller, BBC 2, 1983–87. *Address:* c/o Anglia Films, 48 Leicester Square, WC2H 7FB. *Club:* Savile.

MACDONALD, Gus; *see* Macdonald, A. J.

MACDONALD, Sir Herbert (George deLorme), KBE 1967 (OBE 1948); JP (Jamaica); retired government officer (Jamaica); company director; sportsman; President Organising Committee, IX Central American and Caribbean Games, 1962, and 8th British Empire and Commonwealth Games, 1966 (compiled and edited history); Chairman, National Sports Ltd (a Government body owning and operating National Stadium and Sports Centre), 1960–67, subsequently President (specially created post); Director: Prospect Beach Ltd; Macdonald Ltd; *b* Kingston, 23 May 1902; *s* of late Ronald Macdonald, JP, planter, and late Louise (*née* Alexander). *Educ:* Wolmer's Boys' Sch., Jamaica; Northeast High Sch., Philadelphia, USA. Clerical and planting activities, 1919–43. Published Sportsman Magazine (with late Sir Arthur Thelwell). Accompanied Jamaica's team to World Olympics, London, 1948, and (as Manager) to Helsinki, 1952, Melbourne, 1956; Chef de Mission, WI Olympic Team to Rome, 1960; Deleg., Tokyo, 1964. Chief Liaison Officer, BWI Central Lab. Org. (USA), 1943–55; Pres., Jamaica Olympic Assoc., 1940–44 and 1956–58; Pres., WI Olympic Assoc. (from inception), 1958–61 (when Polit. Fedn was broken up). Past Pres. etc, various Jamaican sporting assocs and boards; Mem. Exec. Cttee Pan American Sports Organisation which controls Pan American Games; Exec. Sec., Jamaica Tercentenary Celebrations Cttee, 1955. Mem. Bd of Trustees, Wolmer's Sch. Diploma of Merit, 1966 Internat. Olympic Cttee, 1968. Is an Anglican. *Recreations:* all sports; stamp collecting (athletic stamps); represented Jamaica in football and tennis *v* foreign teams, 1925–32. *Address:* 1 Liguanea Row, Kingston 6, Jamaica. *T:* 927–8213. *Clubs:* (Life Mem., past Hon. Sec.) Kingston Cricket (Kingston, Jamaica); Constant Spring Golf.

MACDONALD, Howard; see Macdonald, J. H.

MACDONALD, Prof. Hugh Ian, OC 1977; Professor, Department of Economics and Faculty of Administrative Studies, York University, Toronto, since 1974; President Emeritus and Director, York International, since 1984; b Toronto, 27 June 1929; s of Hugh and Winnifred Macdonald; m 1960, Dorothy Marion Vernon; two s three d. Educ: public schs, Toronto; Univ. of Toronto; Oxford Univ. BCom (Toronto), MA (Oxon), BPhil (Oxon). Univ. of Toronto: Lectr in Economics, 1955; Dean of Men, 1956; Asst Prof., Economics, 1962. Govt of Ontario: Chief Economist, 1965; Dep. Provincial Treas., 1967; Dep. Treas. and Dep. Minister of Economics, 1968; Dep. Treas. and Dep. Minister of Economics and Intergovernmental Affairs, 1972. Pres., York Univ., 1974–84. Director: General Electric Canada Inc.; the AGF Cos; CIBA-GEIGY Canada Ltd; Aetna Life Insce Co. of Canada; McGraw-Hill Ryerson Ltd; Member, Board of Directors: Theatre Plus; Council for Canadian Unity; World Encyclopaedia of Contemp. Theatre; North-South Inst.; Member, Bd of Governors, York-Finch Hosp.; Member: Adv. Council, Niagara Inst.; Council and Exec. Cttee, Interamerican Org. for Higher Educn (Vice-Pres., Canada); Past Chairman: Bd, Corp. to Promote Innovation Develt for Employment Advancement (Govt of Ontario); Commn on Financing of Elementary and Secondary Educn in Ontario; Ont. Municipal Trng and Educn Adv. Council; Inst. for Political Involvement; Pres., Canadian Rhodes Scholars Foundn. Chm., Hockey Canada; Member: Canadian Economics Assoc.; Amer. Economics Assoc.; Royal Economic Soc. (London); Canadian Assoc. for Club of Rome; Inst. of Public Admin of Canada; Lambda Alpha Fraternity (Land Economics); Amer. Soc. for Public Admin; Past President: Empire Club of Canada; Ticker Club; Couchiching Inst. Public Affairs; Past Chm., Toronto Men's Br. of CIIA; Past Member: Admin. Bd, Internat. Assoc. of Univs; Attorney General's Cttee on Securities Legislation; Economic Council of Canada. KLJ 1978; Citation of Merit, Court of Canadian Citizenship, 1980. Hon. LLD Toronto, 1974. Canada Centennial Medal, 1967; Silver Jubilee Medal, 1977. Recreations: hockey, tennis; public service in various organizations. Address: 7 Whitney Avenue, Toronto, Ont M4W 2A7, Canada. T: 921–2908; York University, 4700 Keele Street, N York, Ont M3J 1P3, Canada. T: 736–5177.

MACDONALD, Prof. Hugh John; Avis Blewett Professor of Music, Washington University, St Louis, since 1987; b 31 Jan. 1940; s of Stuart and Margaret Macdonald; m 1st, 1963, Naomi Butterworth; one s three d; 2nd, 1979, Elizabeth Babb; one s. Educ: Winchester College; Pembroke College, Cambridge (MA; PhD). FRCM 1987. Cambridge University: Asst Lectr, 1966–69; Lectr, 1969–71; Fellow, Pembroke Coll., 1963–71; Lectr, Oxford Univ., 1971–80, and Fellow, St John's Coll; Gardiner Prof. of Music, Glasgow Univ., 1980–87. Vis. Prof., Indiana Univ., 1979. Gen. Editor, New Berlioz Edition, 1966–. Szymanowski Medal, Poland, 1983. Publications: Berlioz Orchestral Music, 1969; Skryabin, 1978; Berlioz, 1981; articles in New Grove Dict. of Music and Musicians, Musical Times, Music and Letters, Revue de Musicologie. Recreations: bridges, typewriters. Address: Department of Music, Washington University, St Louis, Mo 63130, USA. T: (314) 889 5581.

MACDONALD, Iain Smith, CB 1988; MD; FRCPE, FFPHM; Chief Medical Officer, Scottish Home and Health Department, 1985–88, retired; b 14 July 1927; s of Angus Macdonald, MA and Jabina Urie Smith; m 1958, Sheila Foster; one s one d. Educ: Univ. of Glasgow (MD, DPH). Lectr, Univ. of Glasgow, 1955; Deputy Medical Officer of Health: Bury, 1957; Bolton, 1959; joined Scottish Home and Health Dept, 1964, Dep. Chief Med. Officer, 1974–85. Mem., MRC, 1985–88. QHP 1984–87. Address: 36 Dumyat Drive, Falkirk FK1 5PA. T: Falkirk (0324) 25100.

MacDONALD, Ian; see Mayfield, Hon. Lord.

MACDONALD, Ian Alexander; QC 1988; b 12 Jan. 1939; s of late Ian Wilson Macdonald and Helen Nicolson, MA; m 1st, 1968, Judith Roberts; two s; 2nd, 1978, Jennifer Hall; one s; 3rd, 1991, Jasmin Sharif. Educ: Glasgow Acad.; Cargilfield Sch., Edinburgh; Rugby Sch.; Clare Coll., Cambridge (MA, LLB). Called to the Bar, Middle Temple, 1963; Astbury Scholar, 1962–65; SE Circuit. Lectr in Law, Kingston Polytechnic, 1968–72; Senior Legal Writer and Research Consultant, Incomes Data Services Ltd, 1974–80 (monitoring develts in employment law). Chm., Indep. Inquiry into Racial Violence in Manchester Schs, 1987–88. Pres., Immigration Law Practitioners' Assoc., 1984–. Mem. Editl Adv. Bd, Immigration and Nationality Law and Practice. Publications: Resale Price Maintenance, 1964; (with D. P. Kerrigan) The Land Commission Act 1967, 1967; Race Relations and Immigration Law, 1969; Immigration Appeals Act 1969, 1969; Race Relations: the new law, 1977; (with N. Blake) The New Nationality Law, 1982; Immigration Law and Practice, 1983, 3rd edn 1991; (Consulting Editor) Encyclopaedia of Forms and Precedents: Nationality, 1985; Murder in the Playground: report of Macdonald Inquiry into Racial Violence in Manchester Schools, 1990; (contrib.) Family Guide to the Law, 1971, 1972; articles in professional jls. Recreations: swimming, squash, watching football, reading. Address: 2 Garden Court, Temple, EC4Y 9BL. T: 071–353 1633. Club: Cumberland Lawn Tennis.

MACDONALD, Prof. Ian Grant, FRS 1979; Professor of Pure Mathematics, Queen Mary and Westfield College (formerly Queen Mary College), University of London, 1976, now Emeritus; b 11 Oct. 1928; s of Douglas Grant Macdonald and Irene Alice Macdonald; m 1954, Margaretha Maria Lodewijk Van Goethem; two s three d. Educ: Winchester Coll.; Trinity Coll., Cambridge (MA). Asst Principal and Principal, Min. of Supply, 1952–57; Asst Lectr, Univ. of Manchester, 1957–60; Lectr, Univ. of Exeter, 1960–63; Fellow, Magdalen Coll., Oxford, 1963–72; Fielden Prof. of Pure Maths, Univ. of Manchester, 1972–76. Publications: Introduction to Commutative Algebra (with M. F. Atiyah), 1969; Algebraic Geometry, 1969; articles in math. jls. Address: 8 Blandford Avenue, Oxford OX2 8DY. T: Oxford (0865) 515373.

MacDONALD, Isabel Lillias, (Mrs J. G. MacDonald); see Sinclair, I. L.

McDONALD, Iverach; Associate Editor, The Times, 1967–73; Director, The Times Ltd, 1968–73; b 23 Oct. 1908; s of Benjamin McDonald, Strathcool, Caithness, and Janet Seel; m 1935, Gwendoline, o d of late Captain Thomas R. Brown; one s one d. Educ: Leeds Gram. Sch. Asst Editor, Yorkshire Post, 1933; sub-editor, The Times, 1935; correspondent in Berlin, 1937; diplomatic correspondent 1938; Asst Editor, 1948; Foreign Editor, 1952; Managing Editor, 1965. War of 1939–45: Capt., Gen. Staff, 1939–40; travelled extensively in Soviet Union, Far East and America; reported all allied conferences after the war, including San Francisco, 1945, Paris, 1946 and 1947, Moscow, 1947, Colombo, 1950, and Bermuda, 1953. Sen. Associate Mem., St Antony's Coll., Oxford, 1976–. Publications: A Man of the Times, 1976; The History of The Times, vol. V, 1939–1966, 1984; chapters in: Walter Lippmann and His Times, 1959; The Times History of our Times, 1971. Address: Whistlers, Beckley Common, Oxford OX3 9UR. T: Stanton St John (086735) 226.

McDONALD, James; see McDonald, F. J.

MACDONALD, Prof. James Alexander, BSc (Agric.), PhD (Edinburgh), DSc (St Andrews); Professor of Botany, University of St Andrews, 1961–77, now Emeritus; b 17 June 1908; s of late James Alexander Macdonald and Jessie Mary Simpson; m 1935, Constance Mary Simmie; one d. Educ: Inverness Royal Academy; Edinburgh Univ.; Steven Scholarship in Agriculture, 1930; DSc with Sykes Gold Medal, 1947. Asst Lecturer in Botany, East of Scot. Coll. of Agriculture, 1932–35; St Andrews University: Lecturer in Botany, 1935–52; Senior Lecturer, 1952–60; Dean, Faculty of Science, 1967–69. Pres., Botanical Soc. of Edinburgh, 1955–57; FRSE 1940 (Council Mem., 1956–59); Vice-Pres. RSE, 1961–64. Fellow, Inst. Biology. Silver Jubilee Medal, 1977. Publications: Introduction to Mycology, 1951; scientific papers in Trans Brit. Mycol. Soc., Annals Applied Biol., Mycologia, Proc. and Trans Bot. Soc. Edinburgh, Proc. and Trans Royal Soc. Edinburgh. Recreations: golf, fishing, philately. Address: 17 Hepburn Gardens, St Andrews, Fife KY16 9DF. Club: Royal and Ancient (St Andrews).

MACDONALD, John B(arfoot), DDS, MS, PhD; Chairman, Addiction Research Foundation, 1981–87 (President and Chief Executive Officer, 1976–81); Executive Director, Council of Ontario Universities, 1968–76; Professor of Higher Education, University of Toronto, 1968–76; b 23 Feb. 1918; s of Arthur A. Macdonald and Gladys L. Barfoot; m; two s one d; m 1967, Liba Kucera; two d. Educ: Univ. of Toronto, University of Illinois, Columbia Univ. DDS (with hons) Toronto, 1942; MS (Bact) Ill, 1948; PhD (Bact) Columbia, 1953. Lectr, Prev. Dentistry, University of Toronto, and private practice, 1942–44. Canadian Dental Corps, 1944–46 (Capt.) Instr, Bacteriol, University of Toronto, and private practice, 1946–47; Res. Asst, Univ. of Illinois, 1947–48; Kellogg Fellow and Canadian Dental Assoc. Res. Student, Columbia Univ., 1948–49; University of Toronto: Asst Prof. of Bacteriol., 1949–53; Assoc. Prof. of Bacteriol., 1953–56; Chm., Div. of Dental Res., 1953–56; Prof. of Bacteriol., 1956; Cons. in Dental Educn, University of BC, 1955–56; Dir, Forsyth Dental Infirmary, 1956–62 (Cons. in Bacteriol., 1962); Prof. of Microbiol., Harvard Sch., of Dental Med., 1956–62 (Dir of Postdoctoral Studies, 1960–62); President, Univ. of British Columbia, 1962–67. Consultant: Dental Med. Section of Corporate Research Div. of Colgate-Palmolive Co., 1958–62; Donwood Foundn, Toronto, 1967 (Chm. of Bd, 1972–75); Science Council of Canada, 1967–69; Addiction Research Foundn of Ontario, 1968–74 (Mem., 1974–76); Nat. Inst. of Health, 1968– (Mem., Dental Study Sect., 1961–65). Chm., Commn on Pharmaceutical Services of the Canadian Pharmaceutical Assoc., 1967; Mem. and Vice-Chm., Ontario Council of Health, 1981–84; Councillor-at-Large, Internat. Assoc. for Dental Research, 1963, Pres. 1968–69. Fellow, Mem. or Chm. of numerous assocs. etc, both Canadian and international. FACD 1955; Hon. FICD 1965. Hon. AM, Harvard Univ., 1956; Hon. LLD: Univ. of Manitoba, 1962; Simon Fraser Univ., 1965; Hon DSc Univ. of British Columbia, 1967; Hon. LLD: Wilfred Laurier Univ., 1976; Brock Univ., 1976; Univ. of W Ontario, 1977; Hon. DSc Univ. of Windsor, 1977. Publications: Higher Education in British Columbia and a Plan for the Future, 1962, etc.; numerous contribs to learned jls. Recreations: golf, fishing. Address: 1137 Royal York Road #1008, Etobicoke, Ont M9A 4A7, Canada. Clubs: University of BC Faculty, Vancouver (Vancouver); Canadian, Faculty, University of Toronto (Toronto).

MACDONALD, Air Commodore John Charles, CB 1964; CBE 1957; DFC 1940 (Bar 1942); AFC 1941; President, Abbeyfield (Weymouth) Society; b 25 Dec. 1910; s of late Robert Macdonald; m 1952, Gladys Joan, d of John Hine, Beaminster, Dorset; two s. Educ: Berkhamsted Sch.; RAF Cadet Coll., Cranwell. Commissioned RAF, 1930. Served War of 1939–45 in Bomber Command; POW Stalag Luft III, 1942–45, escaped April 1945. Commanded RAF Akrotiri during Suez campaign; UK National Military Representative, SHAPE, 1959–61; Comdr RAF East Africa, 1961–64; Min. of Defence, 1964; retd, 1964. Chevalier, Légion d'Honneur, 1958; Croix de Guerre, 1958. Recreations: golf, sailing, shooting. Address: Woodbine Cottage, Osmington, Dorset. T: Preston (0305) 833259.

McDONALD, Prof. John Corbett, MD; FRCP, FFCM, FFOM; Professor of Epidemiology, and Head of School of Occupational Health, McGill University, 1981–83, Professor Emeritus, since 1988; Professor of Occupational Health, London School of Hygiene and Tropical Medicine, London University, 1976–81, Professor Emeritus, since 1981; Head, Epidemiological Research Unit, National Heart and Lung Institute (London Chest Hospital), University of London, since 1990; b 20 April 1918; s of John Forbes McDonald and Sarah Mary McDonald; m 1942, Alison Dunstan Wells; one s three d. Educ: London Univ. (MD); Harvard Univ. (MS). DPH, DIH; FRCP (Canada) 1970; FRCP 1976; FFCM 1976; FFOM 1978. Served War, MO, RAMC, 1942–46. Epidemiologist, Public Health Lab. Service, 1951–64 (Dir, Epidemiol Res. Lab., 1960–64); Prof. and Head, Dept of Epidemiology and Health, McGill Univ., Montreal, 1964–76; Dir, TUC Centenary Inst. of Occupational Health, 1976–81; Chm., Dept of Clinical Epidemiology, Nat. Heart and Lung (formerly Cardiothoracic) Inst. (Brompton Hosp.), Univ. of London, 1986–90. Publications: (ed) Recent Advances in Occupational Health, 1981; papers on epidemiol subjects. Recreations: skiing, cycling. Address: 536 Pine Avenue West, Montreal, Quebec H2W 1S6, Canada; 4 Temple West Mews, West Square, SE11 4TJ. Club: Athenæum.

MacDONALD, Maj.-Gen. John Donald, CBE 1986 (OBE 1981); Director General of Transport and Movements, Ministry of Defence, since 1991; b 5 April 1938; s of Lt-Col John MacDonald, OBE; m 1964, Mary, d of Dr Graeme M. Warrack, CBE, DSO, TD; one s two d. Educ: George Watson's Coll., Edinburgh; RMA Sandhurst. Commnd, 1958; saw service with KOSB, RASC, RCT and Airborne Forces Berlin, UK, BAOR, N Africa, India (Defence Services Staff Coll.), 1958–71; NDC, 1976; Turkey NATO HQ Izmir, CO 4 Armoured Div, RTR, 1978–80; Instr Australian Comd and Staff Coll., 1980–82; Chief Instr and Comdt, RCT Officers' Sch., 1983; DCS 3 Armoured Div., 1983–86; Col Personnel Br. 8 Mil. Sec., 1987–88; Comdr Transport, 1st BR Corps and Garrison Comdr Bielefeld, 1988–91. Chm., Combined Services Rugby, 1991–. Freeman, City of London, 1991; Hon. Mem. Ct of Assts, Carmens' Co., 1991. Recreations: Rugby (played for Scotland, Barbarians, Combined Services and Army), ski-ing, golf, travel, moving house, collecting. Address: c/o Bank of Scotland, 141 Princes Street, Edinburgh. Clubs: Army and Navy, British Sportsman; London Scottish, Royal & Ancient (St Andrews), Honourable Co. of Edinburgh Golfers (Muirfield), Rugby Internationalists Golfing Society.

MacDONALD, John Grant, CBE 1989 (MBE 1962); HM Diplomatic Service; Ambassador to Panama, since 1989; b 26 Jan. 1932; er s of late John Nicol MacDonald and Margaret MacDonald (née Vasey); m 1955, Jean, o c of late J. K. K. Harrison; one s two d. Educ: George Heriot's School. Entered HM Foreign (later Diplomatic) Service, 1949; FO, 1949; served HM Forces, 1950–52; FO, 1952; Berne, 1954–59; Third Sec. and Vice Consul, Havana, 1960–62; FO, 1962; DSAO, 1965; Second, later First Sec. (Comm.), Lima, 1966–71; Nat. Defence Coll., Latimer, 1971–72; Parly Clerk of FCO, 1972–75; First Sec. (Comm.), Hd of Trade Promotion Sect., Washington, 1975–79; Hd of Chancery, Dhaka, 1980–81; Hd of Chancery and HM Consul, Bogotá, 1981–84; Counsellor, FCO, 1985–86; Ambassador, Paraguay, 1986–89. Recreations: travel, photography, swimming. Address: c/o Foreign and Commonwealth Office, SW1A 2AH. Clubs: Naval and Military, Royal Over-Seas League.

MACDONALD, (John) Howard, CA; FCT; Director: BOC Group plc; Weir Group plc; McDermott International Inc.; b 5 June 1928; s of John and Helen Macdonald; m

1961, Anne Hunter; three *d. Educ:* Hermitage, Helensburgh. CA 1954. Thomson McLintock & Co. (served articles), 1949–55; Walter Mitchell & Sons, 1955–58; Aircraft Marine Products, 1958; Finance Manager, Keir & Cawder Arrow Drilling, 1958–60; Royal Dutch Shell Group, 1960–83, Group Treasurer, 1978–83; Chairman and Chief Executive: Dome Petroleum, 1983–88; NatWest Investment Bank, 1989–91. Mem., Assoc. of Corporate Treasurers, 1979. *Recreations:* golf, theatre. *Address:* 18 Fairbourne, Cobham, Surrey KT11 2BP. *Club:* Caledonian.

MACDONALD, John Reginald, QC 1976; barrister-at-law; Commercial, Chancery and Administrative Lawyer; *b* 26 Sept. 1931; *s* of Ranald Macdonald and Marion Olive (*née* Kirkby); *m* 1958; one *s* one *d. Educ:* St Edward's Sch., Oxford; Queens' Coll., Cambridge. Called to Bar, Lincoln's Inn, 1955, Bencher, 1985; called to Bar of Eastern Caribbean, 1988. Represented: the people of Ocean Island, 1975; Yuri Orlov, the Soviet dissident, 1977–86; Canadian Indians, 1982; the Ilios, who were removed from Diego Garcia to make way for a US base, 1983; appeared for the people of Barbuda at the Antigua Indep. Conf. at Lancaster House in 1980; an observer in Namibia, pre-election period, 1989; led Internat. Commn of Jurists mission to investigate violence in Natal, 1990. Drafted written constitution for the UK published by Liberal Democrats, 1990. Contested: Wimbledon (L) 1966 and 1970; Folkestone and Hythe (L) 1983, (L/Alliance) 1987. Chm., Assoc. of Liberal Lawyers, 1973–78. *Recreation:* the theatre. *Address:* 12 New Square, Lincoln's Inn, WC2A 3SW. *T:* 071–405 3808. *Clubs:* National Liberal; MCC.

MACDONALD, Sir Kenneth (Carmichael), KCB 1990 (CB 1983); Second Permanent Under-Secretary of State, Ministry of Defence, 1988–90; *b* 25 July 1930; *s* of William Thomas and Janet Millar Macdonald; *m* 1960, Ann Elisabeth (*née* Pauer); one *s* two *d. Educ:* Hutchesons' Grammar Sch.; Glasgow Univ. MA (Hons Classics). RAF, 1952–54. Asst Principal, Air Ministry, 1954; Asst Private Sec. to Sec. of State, 1956–57; Private Sec. to Permanent Sec., 1958–61; HM Treasury, 1962–65; MoD, 1965; Asst Sec., 1968; Counsellor (Defence), UK Delegn to NATO, 1973–75; Asst Under-Sec. of State, 1975, Dep. Under-Sec. of State, 1980, MoD. *Recreation:* golf. *Address:* c/o Barclays Bank, 357–366 Strand, WC2R 0NX. *Club:* Royal Air Force.

McDONALD, Lawson; *see* McDonald, E. L.

MacDONALD, Margaret; *see* Casson, M. MacD, (Lady Casson).

MacDONALD, Margo, (Mrs James Sillars); television and radio presenter and reporter; *b* 19 April 1944; *d* of Robert and Jean Aitken; *m* 1st, 1965, Peter MacDonald (marr. diss. 1980); two *d*; 2nd, 1981, James Sillars, *qv. Educ:* Hamilton Academy; Dunfermline Coll. (Diploma of Physical Educn). Contested (SNP) Paisley, Gen. Elec., 1970; MP (SNP) Glasgow (Govan), Nov. 1973–Feb. 1974; contested (SNP): Glasgow (Govan), Gen. Elec., Feb. 1974 and Oct. 1974; Hamilton, by-election, May 1978. Vice-Chm., Scottish National Party, 1972–79 (Senior Vice-Chm., 1974–78); Mem., SNP Nat. Exec., 1980–81; Chm., SNP '79 Group, 1978–81. Director of Shelter (Scotland), 1978–81. *Recreations:* more work, music, swimming. *Address:* 15 Woodburn Terrace, Edinburgh EH10 4SJ.

McDONALD, Mavis; Under Secretary, Directorate of Personnel Management, Department of the Environment, since 1990; *b* 23 Oct. 1944; *d* of late Richard Henry and of Elizabeth Lowe; *m* 1971, David Arthur McDonald, *qv*; one *s. Educ:* Chadderton Grammar Sch. for Girls; London Sch. of Econs and Pol Science (BSc Econ). Joined Min. of Housing and Local Govt, 1966; Asst Private Sec. to Minister for Housing and Local Govt, 1969–70, to Sec. of State for the Environment, 1970–71; Private Sec. to Perm. Sec., DoE, 1973–75; Asst Sec., Central Policy Planning Unit, 1981–83; Head of Personnel Management (Envmnt) Div., DoE, 1983–86; Finance, Local Authority Grants, 1986; Dep. Dir, Local Govt Finance, 1987; Under Sec., Directorate of Admin. Resources, DoE, 1988–90. Non-exec. Dir, Tarmac Housing Div., 1988–. *Recreations:* piano, needlepoint, swimming.

MACDONALD, Morag, (Mrs Walter Simpson); Secretary of the Post Office, since 1985; *b* 8 Feb. 1947; *d* of Murdoch Macdonald Macdonald and Isobel Macdonald (*née* Black); *m* 1st, 1970, Adam Somerville; 2nd, 1983, Walter Simpson; one *d. Educ:* Bellahouston Academy, Glasgow; Univ. of Glasgow (LLB Hons); College of Law, London. Called to the Bar, Inner Temple, 1974. Joined Post Office as graduate trainee, 1968; posts in Telecommunications and Corporate HQ, 1969–79; PA to Managing Dir, Girobank, 1980; Dep. Sec., Post Office, 1983–85. FRSA 1990. *Recreations:* walking, embroidery, very indifferent piano playing. *Address:* The Post Office, 30 St James's Square, SW1Y 4PY. *T:* 071–389 8030.

McDONALD, Dr Oonagh; management consultant, financial services industry; *b* Stockton-on-Tees, Co. Durham; *d* of Dr H. D. McDonald. *Educ:* Roan Sch. for Girls, Greenwich; East Barnet Grammar Sch.; Univ. of London (BD Hons 1959; MTh 1962, PhD 1974, King's Coll.). Teacher, St Barnabas Sch., S Woodford, 1959–62; Lectr for Dip. in Sociology, Toynbee Hall, 1964–65; Teacher, Hornsey Grammar Sch. and Boreham Wood Sch., 1964–65; Lectr in Philosophy, Bristol Univ., 1965–76. Gwilym Gibbon Res. Fellow, Nuffield Coll., Oxford, 1988–89; Sen. Res. Fellow, Univ. of Warwick, 1990. Contested (Lab): S Glos, Feb. and Oct. 1974; Thurrock, 1987. MP (Lab) Thurrock, July 1976–87. PPS to Chief Sec. to Treasury, 1977–79; Opposition front bench spokesman on defence, 1981–83, on Treasury and economic affairs, 1983–87, on Civil Service, 1983–87. Member: Public Accounts Cttee, 1977–78; Select Cttee on Employment, 1981; Jobs and Industry Policy Cttee, 1985–87. Mem., USDAW, 1990–; Industrial Policy sub-cttee, Labour Party NEC, 1976–83 (Finance and Economic Affairs sub-cttee, 1978–83). Mem. Council, Consumers' Assoc., 1988–. Consultant, Unity Trust Bank plc, 1987–88. Gov., Birkbeck Coll., 1987–. Devised TV documentary, A Woman's Life. *Publications:* (jtly) The Economics of Prosperity, 1980; Own Your Own: social ownership examined, 1989; Parliament at Work, 1989; articles on taxation, child benefit, industrial strategy, etc. *T:* 081–940 5563.

MACDONALD OF CLANRANALD, Ranald Alexander; 24th Chief and Captain of Clanranald; Chairman and Managing Director, Tektura Ltd; *b* 27 March 1934; *s* of late Captain Kenneth Macdonald of Inchkenneth, DSO, and late Marjory Broad Smith, Basingstoke; *S* kinsman as Chief of Clanranald, 1944; *m* 1961, Jane Campbell-Davys, *d* of late I. E. Campbell-Davys, Llandovey, Carms; two *s* one *d. Educ:* Christ's Hospital. Founded: Fairfix Contracts Ltd, 1963; Tektura Wallcoverings, 1970. Chm., British Contract Furnishing Assoc., 1975–76. Lieut (TA) Cameron Highlanders, 1958–68. Mem., Standing Council of Scottish Chiefs, 1957–; Pres., Highland Soc. of London, 1988–91 (Dir, 1959–80); Vice Pres., Caledonian Catholic Assoc. of London. Chief Exec., Clan Donald Lands Trust, 1978–80; Chm., Museum of the Isles, 1981–90. Kt of Justice Constantinian Order of St George, 1982. *Recreations:* sailing, fishing. *Heir: s* Ranald Og Angus Macdonald, younger of Clanranald, *b* 17 Sept. 1963. *Address:* Wester Lix, by Killin, Perthshire FK21 8RD. *T:* (office) 071–837 8000. *Clubs:* White's, Turf, Beefsteak, Pratt's; New, Puffin's (Edinburgh).

McDONALD, Robert Howat; *see* McDonald, Hon. Lord.

MACDONALD, Vice-Adm. Sir Roderick (Douglas), KBE 1978 (CBE 1966); retired; artist, since 1979; *b* Java, 25 Feb. 1921; *s* of Douglas and Marjorie Macdonald; *m* 1st, 1943, Joan Willis (marr. diss. 1980); two *s* (and one *s* decd); 2nd, 1980, Mrs Pamela Bartosik. *Educ:* Fettes. Entered Royal Navy, 1939. Served War: Fleet and Convoy ops throughout 1939–45 (Atlantic, Norway, Mediterranean, Eastern Fleet, East Coast and Normandy). Commanded HMS Leeds Castle, 1953, also HMS Essington; Sen. Officer, 104th Mine-Sweeping Sqdn and HMS Walkerton, 1957 (despatches, Cyprus); Comdr Sea Trng, 1959; Comd HMS Falmouth, 1961; Comdr, Naval Forces and Jt Force Comdr, Borneo, 1965 (CBE); Comd HMS Galatea; Captain (D): Londonderry Sqdn, 1968; First Frigate Sqdn, Far East, 1969; Captain of the Fleet, 1970; Comd HMS Bristol, 1972; COS to C-in-C, Naval Home Command, 1973–76; ADC to the Queen, 1975; COS to Comdr, Allied Naval Forces Southern Europe, 1976–79. One-man exhibitions: Naples, 1978; Edinburgh, 1980, 1989; London, 1981, 1983, 1985, 1987, 1991. Younger Brother of Trinity House; Vice-Pres. 1976–85, and Fellow, Nautical Inst. President: Isle of Skye Highland Games; Isle of Skye Piping Soc.; Inverness Sea Cadets. Trustee, Clan Donald Lands Trust. *Recreation:* gardening. *Address:* Ollach, Braes, Isle of Skye IV51 9LJ. *Clubs:* Caledonian; Royal Scottish Pipers Society (Edinburgh); Royal Naval Sailing Assoc.

MACDONALD, Roderick Francis; QC (Scot.) 1988; Advocate-Depute, since 1987, Home Advocate-Depute, since 1990; *b* 1 Feb. 1951; *s* of Finlay Macdonald and Catherine Maclean. *Educ:* St Mungo's Acad., Glasgow; Glasgow Univ. (LLB Hons). Admitted advocate, 1975. *Recreation:* hill walking. *Address:* 6A Lennox Street, Edinburgh EH4 1QA. *T:* 031–332 7240.

MACDONALD, Maj.-Gen. Ronald Clarence, CB 1965; DSO 1944 and Bar, 1945; OBE 1953; Director, Griffin Farms Ltd, Norfolk; *b* 1 Aug. 1911; 2nd *s* of late Col C. R. Macdonald, CMG; *m* 1st, 1939, Jessie Ross Anderson (*d* 1986); one *s* one *d*; 2nd, 1986, Constance Margaret Davies. *Educ:* Rugby; RMC, Sandhurst. Royal Warwicks Regt: Commissioned, 1931; Comdr 2nd Bn, 1945–46; Comdr 1st Bn, 1953–55; Bn Comdr, France, Germany Campaign, 1944–45; Mil. Asst to CIGS, 1946–49; GSO1, HQ, West Africa Comd, 1950–53; Col Gen. Staff, SHAPE, 1955–56; Comdr 10th Inf. Bde Gp, 1956–59; DDI, War Office, 1959–60; Chief of Staff, HQ Middle East Comd, 1960–62; Dep. Chief of Staff, Headquarters, Allied Land Forces, Central Europe, 1962–65; retired, 1965. Col Royal Warwicks Fusiliers, 1963–68; Dep. Col (Warwicks), The Royal Regt of Fusiliers, 1968–74. *Recreation:* golf. *Address:* 6 The Beeches, Shaw, Melksham, Wilts.

MACDONALD, Ronald John, CEng, MIMechE; Director-General, Royal Ordnance Factories/Production, 1974–79, retired; *b* 2 Nov. 1919; *s* of Ronald Macdonald and Sarah Jane Macdonald; *m* 1944, Joan Margaret Crew; two *s. Educ:* Enfield Grammar Sch.; Enfield Technical Coll. Engrg apprenticeship at Royal Small Arms Factory, Enfield, 1936–40. Army service, REME, in India, China and Hong Kong, 1943–47 (Major). Established Civil Servant, Royal Small Arms Factory, 1948; Royal Ordnance Factory, Radway Green, 1949; ROF Headquarters, Mottingham, 1953; ROF, Blackburn, 1960; Director: ROF, Birtley, Co. Durham, 1964; Ordnance Factories/Ammunition, 1972. *Address:* 72 Lincoln Park, Amersham, Bucks HP7 9HF. *T:* Amersham (0494) 727402. *Club:* Army and Navy.

MacDONALD, Prof. Simon Gavin George, FRSE; Professor of Physics, University of Dundee, 1973–88, now Emeritus; *b* 5 Sept. 1923; *s* of Simon MacDonald and Jean H. Thomson; *m* 1948, Eva Leonie Austerlitz; one *s* one *d. Educ:* George Heriot's Sch., Edinburgh; Edinburgh Univ. (MA (1st Cl. Hons) Maths and Nat. Phil); PhD (St Andrews). FIP 1958, FRSE 1972. Jun. Scientific Officer, RAE, Farnborough, 1943–46; Lectr, Univ. of St Andrews, 1948–57; Senior Lecturer: University Coll. of the West Indies, 1957–62; Univ. of St Andrews, 1962–67; Visiting Prof., Ohio Univ., 1963; University of Dundee: Sen. Lectr, then Prof., 1967–88; Dean of Science, 1970–73; Vice-Principal, 1974–79. Convener, Scottish Univs Council on Entrance, 1977–83 (Dep. Convener, 1973–77); Chm., Stats Cttee, UCCA, 1989– (Mem. Exec. Cttee, 1977–; Chm., Technical Cttee, 1979–83; Dep. Chm., 1983–89). Chm., Bd of Dirs, Dundee Rep. Th., 1975–89; Chm., Fedn of Scottish Theatres, 1978–80. *Publications:* Problems and Solutions in General Physics, 1967; Physics for Biology and Premedical Students, 1970, 2nd edn 1975; Physics for the Life and Health Sciences, 1975; articles in physics jls. *Recreations:* bridge, golf, fiction writing. *Address:* 10 Westerton Avenue, Dundee DD5 3NJ. *T:* Dundee (0382) 78692. *Club:* Commonwealth Trust.

MACDONALD, Rt. Rev. Thomas Brian, OBE 1970; Coadjutor Bishop of Perth, Western Australia, 1964–79, retired; *b* 25 Jan. 1911; *s* of Thomas Joseph Macdonald, MD, and Alice Daisy Macdonald; *m* 1936, Audrey May Collins; three *d. Educ:* Mercers' Sch., Holborn, EC. Licentiate of Theology 1932, Aust. Coll. of Theol. Deacon 1934, priest 1935, Diocese of Ballarat, Vic.; Deacon in charge of All Saints, Ballarat, 1934; Priest in charge of Landsborough, 1935; Rector of Williams, Dio. of Bunbury, 1935–39; Rector of Manjimup, WA, 1939–40. Chaplain, Australian Imperial Forces, 1940–44 (despatches). Rector of Christ Church, Claremont, Dio. of Perth, 1944–50; Chaplain of Collegiate Sch. of St Peter, Adelaide, S Australia, 1950–58; Dean of Perth, Western Australia, 1959–61; Archdeacon of Perth, 1961–63. Administrator, Diocese of Perth during 1963 and 1969. *Address:* 33 Thomas Street, Nedlands, WA 6009, Australia. *Club:* Weld (Perth).

MACDONALD, Air Vice-Marshal Thomas Conchar, CB 1962; AFC 1942; MD (retired); *b* 6 Aug. 1909; *s* of John Macdonald, MA, BSc, and Mary Jane Conchar; *m* 1937, Katharine Cairns Frew. *Educ:* Hermitage Sch.; Glasgow High Sch.; University of Glasgow; MB, ChB 1932; MD 1940; DPH (London) 1949. Joined RAF Medical Br., 1933; served in Iraq, Egypt and England, before 1939. War service included RAF Inst. of Aviation Med., Farnborough, as Asst to Consultant in Applied Physiology, 1939–41; USA and Canada, 1941–42; DPMO (Flying) Fighter Command, 1942–45; Far East, 1945–46 (despatches, AFC). Post-war appts include: PMO 2nd TAF (Germany), 1951–53; Dir of Hygiene and Research, Air Min., 1953–56 (Chm. Aero-Medical Panel of Advisory Gp for Research and Develt (AGARD) of NATO); PMO, Bomber Command, 1956–58; PMO Middle East Air Force, 1958–61; PMO Technical Training Command, RAF, 1961–66. Air Vice-Marshal, 1961. QHP 1961–66; CStJ 1961. *Publications:* contributions to various med. jls. *Recreations:* sailing, fishing. *Address:* Wakeners Wood, Midhurst Road, Haslemere, Surrey GU27 2PT. *T:* Haslemere (0428) 3685. *Club:* Royal Air Force.

McDONALD, Sir Tom, Kt 1991; OBE 1983; Chairman: Education Assets Board, since 1988; Dale Electric International, since 1988; Director, S. Jerome & Sons (Holdings), since 1983; *b* 5 Aug. 1923; *s* of Robert and Edna McDonald; *m* 1951, Pamela Anne Glaisby; three *s* one *d. Educ:* Dewsbury Wheelwright Grammar Sch.; Leeds Univ. (BCom Hons). FCA. Armitage & Norton: Audit Manager, 1953–62; Partner, 1962–86; Chm., 1982–86. Chairman: Old Swan Hotel (Harrogate) Ltd, 1973–82; Yorkshire Chemicals, 1977–83; Yorks and Humberside and E Midlands Indust. Develt Bd, 1982–; W Yorks Residuary Body, 1986–91; W Midlands Residuary Body, 1990–91; Yorkshire Enterprise Ltd, 1990–; Consultant, KPMG Peat Marwick, 1987–. Dir, Opera North, 1982–. Pres., W Yorks Soc. of Chartered Accountants, 1986–87. *Recreations:* history, travel, music. *Address:* 10 Lime Crescent, Sandal, Wakefield, W Yorks WF2 6RY. *T:* Wakefield (0924) 258871. *Club:* Leeds (Leeds).

McDONALD, William, CA; JP; Chamberlain, 1962–89, and Secretary, 1971–89, Company of Merchants of City of Edinburgh; Bursar, Carnegie Trust for the Universities of Scotland, since 1990; *b* 9 Nov. 1929; *yr s* of late Joseph McDonald and Margaret Pringle (*née* Gibb); *m* 1956, Anne Kidd Laird Donald; one *s* one *d*. *Educ:* Perth Acad. Sec., South Mills and Grampian Investment, Dundee, 1957–62. Clerk and Treasurer, Incorp. of Guildry in Edinburgh, 1975–89; Jt Sec., Scottish Council of Independent Schs, 1978–89. Dep. Chief Comr of Scotland, Scout Assoc., 1977–79 (Hon. Treas., Scotland, 1989–); Chm., Scottish Environmental and Outdoor Centres Assoc. (formerly Scottish Nat. Camps Assoc.), 1986–; Mem., High Constables of Edinburgh (Colinton Ward), 1983–. Mem., Rotary Club of Edinburgh, 1989–. *Recreations:* Scout Association, bridge, golf. *Address:* 1/3 Wyvern Park, The Grange, Edinburgh EH9 2JY. *Club:* New (Edinburgh).

McDONALD, Very Rev. William James Gilmour; Moderator of the General Assembly of the Church of Scotland, 1989–90; Parish Minister of Mayfield, Edinburgh, since 1959; *b* 3 June 1924; *s* of Hugh Gilmour McDonald and Grace Kennedy Hunter; *m* 1952, Margaret Patricia Watson; one *s* two *d*. *Educ:* Daniel Stewart's College, Edinburgh; Univ. of Edinburgh (MA, BD); Univ. of Göttingen. Served Royal Artillery and Indian Artillery, 1943–46. Parish Minister, Limekilns, Fife, 1953–59. Convener, Cttee on Education for the Ministry, 1974–78; Convener, Assembly Council, 1984–87. Hon. DD Edinburgh, 1987. *Address:* 26 Seton Place, Edinburgh EH9 2JT. *T:* 031–667 1286.

McDONALD, Hon. Sir William (John Farquhar), Kt 1958; *b* 3 Oct. 1911; *s* of John Nicholson McDonald and Sarah McDonald (*née* McInnes); *m* 1935, Evelyn Margaret Koch; two *d*. *Educ:* Scotch Coll., Adelaide, South Australia. Served AIF, 1939–45, Capt. Councillor, Shire of Kowree, 1946–61. MLA, electorate of Dundas, Victoria, 1947–52, 1955–70; Speaker, Legislative Assembly, Victoria, 1955–67; Minister of Lands, Soldier Settlement, and for Conservation, 1967–70. Mem., Exec. Council, Victoria. Trustee, Shrine of Remembrance, 1955–70. Victoria State Pres., Poll Shorthorn Soc. of Aust., 1962–72; Trustee, Royal Agricultural Soc. of Victoria, 1968–. Trustee, Victoria Amateur Turf Club, 1969. *Address:* Brippick, 102 St Georges Road, Toorak, Vic. 3142, Australia. *T:* 241 5839. *Clubs:* Hamilton (Hamilton, Victoria); Australian, Naval and Military, Melbourne (Melbourne).

MACDONALD, Prof. William Weir, PhD, DSc; FIBiol; Selwyn Lloyd Professor of Medical Entomology, since 1980 and Dean, 1983–88, Liverpool School of Tropical Medicine; *b* 5 Dec. 1927; *s* of William Sutherland Macdonald and Ina Weir; *m* 1950, Margaret Lawrie; two *d*. *Educ:* Univ. of Glasgow (BSc 1948). MSc 1964, PhD 1965, Univ. of Liverpool; DSc 1973, Univ. of Glasgow; FIBiol 1966. Strang-Steel Scholar, Glasgow Univ., 1948; Colonial Office Res. Scholar, 1949–50; Entomologist, E African Fisheries Res. Org., Uganda, 1950–52; Res. Fellow, Inst. for Med. Res., Kuala Lumpur, 1953–60; Lectr, Sen. Lectr, and Reader, Liverpool Sch. of Trop. Medicine, 1960–76; Prof. of Med. Entomology, London Sch. of Hygiene and Trop. Medicine, 1977–80. Consultant: WHO; various overseas govts; Hon. Consultant on Entomology to the Army. Chalmers Medal, Royal Soc. of Trop. Medicine and Hygiene, 1972. *Publications:* papers on med. entomology in scientific jls. *Recreations:* golf, gardening. *Address:* 10 Headland Close, West Kirby, Merseyside L48 3JP. *T:* 051–625 7857. *Club:* Savage.

MacDONALD SCOTT, Mary, (Mrs Michael MacDonald Scott); *see* Lavin, Mary.

MACDONALD-SMITH, Maj.-Gen. Hugh, CB 1977; *b* 8 Jan. 1923; *s* of Alexander and Ada Macdonald-Smith; *m* 1947, Désirée Violet (*née* Williamson); one *s* one *d* (and one *d* decd). *Educ:* Llanelli Grammar Sch.; Llandovery Coll.; Birmingham Univ. BSc. CEng, FIMechE, FIEE. Commissioned REME, 1944; served: India, 1945–47; Singapore, 1956–58; BAOR, 1961–63; Technical Staff Course, 1949–51; Staff Coll., Camberley, 1953; Lt-Col, 1963; Asst Dir, Electrical and Mechanical Engineering, HQ Western Comd, 1963–65; Asst Mil. Sec., MoD, 1965–66; Comd REME, 1 (BR) Corps Troops, 1966–67; Technical Gp, REME, 1967–72; Col, 1967; Brig. 1970; Dep. Dir, Electrical and Mechanical Engineering (Eng. Pol.), (Army), 1972–75; Dir, later Dir Gen., Electrical and Mech. Engrg (Army), 1975–78; retired 1978. Col Comdt, REME, 1978–83; Rep. Col Comdt, REME, 1979–80. Dir, TEMA, 1981–87 (Sec. to Council, 1979–80). Mem., Cttee of Inquiry into Engrg Profession, 1977–79. Mem. Council, IMechE, 1975–76. *Recreations:* golf, gardening, photography. *Address:* c/o Lloyds Bank, Llanelli.

MACDONALD-SMITH, Sydney, CMG 1956; retired; *b* 9 July 1908; *s* of late John Alfred Macdonald-Smith, MB, ChB, FRCSE; *m* 1st, 1935, Joyce (*d* 1966), *d* of Austen Whetham, Bridport, Dorset; one *s* one *d*; 2nd, 1968, Winifred Mary Atkinson, JP, *widow* of Captain T. K. W. Atkinson, RN. *Educ:* Nottingham High Sch.; New Coll., Oxford. Entered Colonial Administrative Service, Nigeria, 1931; Controller of Imports, 1945; Director of Supplies, 1947; Under-Sec., Gold Coast, 1949; Permanent Sec. Ministry of Communications and Works, 1950; Chief Regional Officer, Northern Territories, 1954–57; retired Nov. 1957. *Recreation:* gardening. *Address:* Woodman's, Westbourne, Emsworth, Hants. *T:* Emsworth (0243) 372943.

McDONAUGH, James, CBE 1970 (OBE 1965); retired 1973; reappointed 1973–75, Director North Europe Department, British Council; *b* 26 July 1912; *s* of late Edward McDonaugh and late Christina, *d* of William Bissell; *m* 1944, Mary-Eithné Mitchell, *d* of James Vyvyan Mitchell; three *s* two *d*. *Educ:* Royal Grammar Sch., Worcester; St Edmund Hall, Oxford (Exhibitioner, MA). Asst Master, Ampleforth Coll., 1935–40; War Service, 1940–45; Lecturer, Graz and Innsbruck Univs, 1947–50; Asst Rep., British Council, Austria, 1950–54; Representative, Malta, 1954–58; Dep. Counsellor (Cultural), Bonn, 1958–59; Dep. Rep., Germany, 1958–61; Dir Specialist Tours Dept, 1961–65; Asst Controller, Education Div., 1965; Rep., Germany, 1966–73. *Address:* Old Rectory Cottage, Whitestaunton, Chard, Somerset TA20 3DL.

MacDONELL OF GLENGARRY, Air Cdre Aeneas Ranald Donald, CB 1964; DFC 1940; Hereditary 22nd Chief of Glengarry; *b* 15 Nov. 1913; *e s* of late Ranald MacDonell of Glengarry, CBE; *m* 1st, Diana Dorothy (*d* 1980), *yr d* of late Henry Keane, CBE; two *s* one *d*; 2nd, Lois Eirene Frances, *d* of Rev. Gerald Champion Streatfeild; one *s* one *d*. *Educ:* Hurstpierpoint Coll.; Royal Air Force Coll., Cranwell. No 54 Fighter Sqdn, 1934; Fleet Air Arm, 1935–37; Flying Instructor, 1938–39; Air Ministry, 1939–40; No 64 Fighter Sqdn, 1940–41; POW, 1941–45; Ministry of Defence, 1946–47; HQ Flying Training Command, 1947–49; Chief Flying Instructor, RAF Coll., Cranwell, 1949–51; Ministry of Defence, 1952–54; Senior RAF Instructor, Joint Services Staff Coll., 1954–56; Air Attaché, Moscow, 1956–58; Dir of Management and Work Study, Ministry of Defence, Air Force Dept, 1960–64, retd. Ops Res. Manager, CJB, 1964–67; Personnel Manager, CITB, 1967–73; Dept Head, Industrial Soc., 1973–76; Partner, John Courtis and Partners, 1976–80. MBIM. *Recreations:* ciné photography, art, travel. *Address:* Elonbank, 23 Castle Street, Fortrose, Ross-shire IV10 8TH. *T:* Fortrose (0381) 20121. *Club:* Royal Air Force.

McDONNELL, family name of **Earl of Antrim.**

McDONNELL, Christopher Thomas, CB 1991; Deputy Under-Secretary of State, Ministry of Defence, 1988–91; *b* 3 Sept. 1931; *s* of Christopher Patrick McDonnell and Jane McDonnell; *m* 1955, Patricia Anne (*née* Harvey) (*d* 1967); three *s* one *d*. *Educ:* St Francis Xavier's Coll., Liverpool; Corpus Christi Coll., Oxford (MA). WO, 1954; HM Treasury, 1966–68; RCDS, 1973; Asst Under-Sec. of State, MoD, 1976–88.

McDONNELL, David Croft; National Managing Partner, Grant Thornton, since 1989; *b* 9 July 1943; *s* of Leslie and Catherine McDonnell; *m* 1967, Marieke (*née* Bos); three *d*. *Educ:* Quarry Bank High School, Liverpool. FCA. Qualified Chartered Accountant, 1965; Partner, Thornton Baker, later Grant Thornton, 1972. *Recreations:* sailing, motor racing (spectating), mountain walking. *Address:* Grant Thornton, Grant Thornton House, Melton Street, NW1 2EP. *T:* 071–383 5100.

McDONNELL, His Honour Denis Lane, OBE 1945; a Circuit Judge (formerly a County Court Judge), 1967–86; *b* 2 March 1914; *o c* of late David McDonnell, LLD and Mary Nora (*née* Lane), Riversdale, Sundays Well, Cork and Fairy Hill, Monkstown, Co. Cork and *g s* of Denny Lane, poet and Young Irelander; *m* 1940, Florence Nina (Micky), *d* of late Lt-Col Hugh T. Ryan, DSO and Clare Emily (*née* Conry), Castle View, Ballincollig, Co. Cork; three *d* (and one *s* one *d* decd). *Educ:* Christian Brothers' Coll., Cork; Ampleforth Coll.; Sidney Sussex Coll., Cambridge (MA). Served in RAFVR, Equipment and Admin. and Special Duties Branches, 1940–45 in UK and with No. 84 Gp in NW Europe (Wing Comdr). Called to Bar, Middle Temple, 1936; Bencher, 1965. Practised at Bar, 1938–40 and 1946–67. Hon. Sec., Council of HM Circuit Judges, 1979–83 (Pres., 1985). FCIArb 1988. *Publications:* Kerr on Fraud and Mistake (7th edn, with J. G. Monroe), 1952; titles on carriage in Encyclopædias of Forms and Precedents and Court Forms and Precedents, and in Halsbury's Laws of England. *Recreations:* family life, listening to music, golf, gardening. *Clubs:* Piltdown Golf, Rye Golf, Woking Golf, Royal Cinque Ports Golf.

McDONNELL, John; Secretary, Association of London Authorities, since 1987; *b* 8 Sept. 1951; *s* of Robert and Elsie McDonnell; *m* 1971, Marilyn Jean Cooper (marr. diss. 1987); two *d*. *Educ:* Great Yarmouth Grammar Sch.; Burnley Technical Coll.; Brunel Univ. (BSc); Birkbeck Coll., Univ. of London (MSc Politics and Sociology). Prodn worker, 1968–72; Research Assistant: NUM, 1976–78; TUC, 1978–82; full-time GLC Councillor, Hillingdon, Hayes and Harlington, 1982–86; Dep. Leader, GLC, 1984–85; Chm., GLC F and GP Cttee, 1982–85; Prin. Policy Advr, Camden Bor. Council, 1985–87; Editor, Labour Herald, 1985–88. Contested (Lab) Hampstead and Highgate, 1983; Prospective Parly Cand. (Lab) Hayes and Harlington. Housefather (pt-time) of family unit, children's home, 1972–87. *Recreations:* gardening, reading, cycling; generally fermenting the overthrow of capitalism. *Address:* Association of London Authorities, 36 Old Queen Street, SW1H 9JF; 128 Fleet Road, NW3 2QX. *T:* 071–267 2466.

McDONNELL, John Beresford William; QC 1984; *b* 26 Dec. 1940; *s* of Beresford Conrad McDonnell and Charlotte Mary McDonnell (*née* Caldwell); *m* 1968, Susan Virginia, *d* of late Wing Comdr H. M. Styles, DSO and of Audrey (*née* Jorgensen, who *m* 2nd, 1947, Gen. Sir Charles Richardson, *qv*); two *s* one *d*. *Educ:* City of London School (Carpenter Scholar); Balliol College, Oxford (Domus Scholar; Hon. Mention, Craven Scholarship, 1958; 1st Cl. Hon. Mods 1960; 2nd LitHum 1962, 2nd Jurisp 1964; MA); Harvard Law Sch. (LLM 1965). Called to the Bar, Inner Temple, 1968. Pres., Oxford Union Soc. and Amer. Debating Tour, 1962; Harkness Fellowship, 1964–66; Amer. Political Science Assoc. Congressional Fellowship, 1965–66 (attached Rep. Frank Thompson Jr, NJ and Senator George McGovern, SDak); Cons. Research Dept, 1966–69; HM Diplomatic Service, 1969–71, First Sec., Asst Private Sec. to Sec. of State for Foreign and Commonwealth Affairs, 1970–71; practising at Chancery Bar, 1972–. Cllr, Lambeth Borough Council, 1968–69. London Rowing Club Grand VIII, Henley, 1958. *Recreation:* sculling. *Address:* 20 Brompton Square, SW3 2AD. *T:* 071–584 1498; 1 New Square, Lincoln's Inn, WC2A 3SA. *T:* 071–405 0884.

McDOUGALL, Hon. Barbara Jean; Secretary of State for External Affairs, Canada, since 1991; *b* Toronto, 12 Nov. 1937. *Educ:* Univ. of Toronto (BA Hons Econ. and Pol Sci. 1960). Chartered Financial Analyst, 1973. Worked in financial sector in Vancouver, Edmonton and Toronto; Exec. Dir, Canadian Council Financial Analysts, 1982–84; financial columnist, national magazines and on TV. Elected MP for St Paul's, Toronto, 1984; Minister of State: Finance, 1984–86; Privatisation, 1986–88; Minister Responsible for Status of Women, 1986–90 and for Regulatory Affairs; Minister, Employment and Immigration, 1988–91; Chairperson, Cabinet Cttee on Foreign Affairs and Defence Policy, 1991–; Member Cabinet Cttees: Planning and Priorities, 1991–; Canadian Unity and Constitutional Negotiations, 1991–. Active in community organisations, including Community Occupational Therapy Associates, Elizabeth Fry Soc. *Address:* 125 Sussex Drive, Lester B. Pearson Building, 10th Floor, MINA, Tower A, Ottawa, Ont K1A 0G2, Canada; House of Commons, Ottawa, Ontario K1A 0A6, Canada.

MacDOUGALL, Sir (George) Donald (Alastair), Kt 1953; CBE 1945 (OBE 1942); FBA 1966; economist; *b* 26 Oct. 1912; *s* of late Daniel Douglas MacDougall, Glasgow, and late Beatrice Amy Miller; *m* 1st, 1937, Bridget Christabel Bartrum (marr. diss. 1977); one *s* one *d*; 2nd, 1977, Margaret Hall (*see* L. M. MacDougall). *Educ:* Kelvinside Acad., Glasgow; Shrewsbury Sch.; Balliol Coll., Oxford. George Webb Medley Junior (1934) and Senior (1935) Scholarships in Political Economy; Asst Lecturer (later Lecturer) in Economics, University of Leeds, 1936–39; First Lord of the Admiralty's Statistical Branch, 1939–40; Prime Minister's Statistical Branch, 1940–45 (Chief Asst, 1942–45). Work on Reparations and German Industry, Moscow and Berlin, 1945; Mem. of Heavy Clothing Industry Working Party, 1946; Official Fellow of Wadham Coll., Oxford, 1945–50, Domestic Bursar, 1946–48, Hon. Fellow, 1964–; Econ. Dir, OEEC, Paris, 1948–49; Faculty Fellow, Nuffield Coll., 1947–50, Professorial Fellow, 1950–52, Official Fellow, 1952–64, First Bursar, 1958–64, Hon. Fellow, 1967–; Nuffield Reader in Internat. Economics, Oxford Univ., 1950–52; Chief Adviser, Prime Minister's Statistical Branch, 1951–53; Visiting Prof., Australian Nat. Univ., 1959; MIT Center for Internat. Studies, New Delhi, 1961; Dir, Investing in Success Equities, Ltd, 1959–62; Economic Dir, NEDO, 1962–64; Mem. Turnover Tax Cttee, 1963–64; Dir-Gen., Dept of Economic Affairs, 1964–68; Head of Govt Economic Service, and Chief Economic Adviser to the Treasury, 1969–73; Chief Economic Advr, CBI, 1973–84. Mem. Council, Royal Econ. Soc., 1950– (Hon. Sec., 1958–70; Vice-Pres., 1970–72, 1974–; Pres., 1972–74); Pres., Soc. for Strategic and Long Range Planning, 1977–85, Vice-Pres., 1968–77; Vice-Pres., Soc. of Business Economists, 1978–; Chm., Exec. Cttee NIESR, 1974–87; Mem., EEC Study Gp on Economic and Monetary Union, 1974–75; Chm., EEC Study Gp on Role of Public Finance in European Integration, 1975–77. Hon. LLD Strathclyde, 1968; Hon. LittD Leeds, 1971; Hon. DSc Aston, 1979. *Publications:* (part author) Measures for International Economic Stability, UN, 1951; The World Dollar Problem, 1957; (part author) The Fiscal System of Venezuela, 1959; The Dollar Problem: A Reappraisal, 1960; Studies in Political Economy (2 vols), 1975; Don and Mandarin: memoirs of an economist, 1987; contrib. to various economic and statistical jls. *Address:* 86A Denbigh Street, Westminster, SW1V 2EX. *T:* 071–821 1998. *Club:* Reform.

MacDOUGALL, Laura Margaret, (Lady MacDougall); Hon. Fellow of Somerville College, Oxford, since 1975; *d* of George E. Linfoot and Laura Edith Clayton; *m* 1932, Robert L. Hall (later Lord Roberthall, who *d* 1988) (marr. diss. 1968); two *d*; *m* 1977, Sir

Donald MacDougall, *qv*. *Educ:* Sheffield Girls' High Sch. and High Storrs Grammar Sch.; Somerville Coll., Oxford. Hon. Scholar, 1st Cl. Hons Philosophy, Politics and Economics; Jun. George Webb Medley Scholar. US Govt Office of Price Admin, 1941–44; UNNRA Planning Div., Washington, DC, Sydney and London, 1944–45; Lectr, Lincoln Coll., Oxford, 1946–47; Lectr, 1947–49, and Fellow and Tutor, 1949–75, Somerville Coll., Oxford; University Lectr in Economics, 1949–75. Consultant, NEDO, 1962–87; Economic Consultant, Distillers' Co. plc, 1978–84. Member: Treasury Purchase Tax Cttee, 1954; Interdeptal Cttee on Economic and Social Research, 1957–58; Gaitskell Indep. Co-operative Commn, 1958; Min. of Ag. Cttee on the Remuneration of Milk Distributors in the UK, 1962; Reith Indep. Commn on Advertising, 1964; Covent Garden Market Authority Adv. Cttee, 1972; Distributive Trades Industrial Trng Bd's Research Cttee, 1972; EDC for Distributive Trades, 1963–87; Monopolies and Mergers Commn, 1973–76; Past Member: Retail Furnishing and Allied Trades Wages Council; Retail Newsagency, Confectioner and Tobacconist Wages Council. Visiting Professor: MIT, USA, 1961–62; in Distributive Studies, Univ. of Stirling, 1984–87 (Hon. Prof., 1987–). Hon. LLD Nottingham, 1979. *Publications:* US Senate Cttee Print, Effect of War on British Retail Trade, 1943; Distributive Trading: an economic analysis, 1954; Distribution in Great Britain and North America (with Knapp and Winsten), 1961; contribs to: The British Economy, 1945–50, 1952; The British Economy in the 1950s, 1962; (Bolton Cttee, Research Report No 8) The Small Unit in Retail Trade, 1972; numerous contribs to various economic and statistical jls. *Address:* 86A Denbigh Street, Westminster, SW1V 2EX. *T:* 071–821 1998.

MACDOUGALL, Neil; Hon. Mr Justice Macdougall; Justice of Appeal of the Supreme Court of Hong Kong, since 1989; *b* 13 March 1932; *s* of Norman Macdougall and Gladys Clare Kennerly; *m* 1987, Helen Lui. *Educ:* Aquinas Coll., Perth, WA; Univ. of Western Australia (LLB 1954). Admitted Barrister and Solicitor of Supreme Court, WA, 1957, and of High Court of Australia, 1958; Solicitor of Supreme Court of England, 1976, and of Supreme Court of Hong Kong, 1977. Crown Counsel, Hong Kong, 1965; Director of Public Prosecutions, Hong Kong, 1978; a Judge of the High Court, Hong Kong, 1980. *Recreations:* classical music, study of natural history, photography. *Address:* 8B Severn Road, The Peak, Hong Kong. *T:* 8497077. *Clubs:* Hong Kong, Jockey (all in Hong Kong).

MACDOUGALL, Patrick Lorn, FCA; Chief Executive, since 1985, and Chairman, since 1989, Chartered WestLB Ltd (formerly Standard Chartered Merchant Bank Ltd); *b* 21 June 1939; *s* of late James Archibald Macdougall, WS, and of Valerie Jean Macdougall; *m* 1st, 1967, Alison Noel Offer (marr. diss. 1982); two *s*; 2nd, 1983, Bridget Margaret Young; three *d*. *Educ:* schools in Kenya; Millfield; University Coll., Oxford (MA Jurisprudence). FCA 1976. Called to the Bar, Inner Temple, 1962. Manager, N. M. Rothschild & Sons Ltd, 1967–70; Exec. Dir, Amex Bank (formerly Rothschild Intercontinental Bank Ltd), 1970–77, Chief Exec., 1977–78; Exec. Dir, Jardine Matheson Holdings Ltd, 1978–85; Gp Exec. Dir, Standard Chartered PLC, 1988–89. Mem., Internat. Adv. Bd, Creditanstalt–Bankverein, Vienna, 1982–85. FRSA 1988. *Recreations:* ski-ing, golf, opera, bridge. *Address:* 40 Stevenage Road, SW6 6ET. *T:* 071–736 3506. *Clubs:* Royal Automobile, Hurlingham; Hongkong, Shek O (Hong Kong).

McDOWALL, Brenda, (Mrs K. D. McDowall); *see* Dean, B.

MacDOWALL, Dr David William, MA, DPhil; FSA, FRAS; Chairman, Society for South Asian Studies (formerly Society for Afghan Studies), since 1982 (Hon. Secretary, 1972–82); *b* 2 April 1930; *o s* of late William MacDowall and late Lilian May MacDowall (*née* Clarkson); *m* 1962, Mione Beryl, *yr d* of late Ernest Harold Lashmar and Dora Lashmar; two *d*. *Educ:* Liverpool Inst.; Corpus Christi Coll., Oxford; British Sch. at Rome. Hugh Oldham Scholar 1947, Pelham Student in Roman History 1951; Barclay Head Prize for Ancient Numismatics, 1953 and 1956. 2nd Lieut Royal Signals, 1952. Asst Principal, Min. of Works, 1955; Asst Keeper, Dept of Coins and Medals, British Museum, 1956; Principal, Min. of Educn, 1960; Principal, Univ. Grants Cttee, 1965; Asst Sec. 1970; Master of Univ. Coll., Durham, 1973; Hon. Lectr in Classics and in Oriental Studies, Univ. of Durham, 1975; Dir, Polytechnic of N London, 1980–85. Hon. Treasurer: Royal Numismatic Soc., 1966–73; British Archaeol Assoc., 1989–. Member: Council, Royal Asiatic Soc., 1989–; Governing Body, SOAS, 1990–. Corresponding Mem., Istituto Italiano per il Medio ed Estremo Oriente, 1987. *Publications:* Coin Collections, their preservation, classification and presentation, 1978; The Western Coinages of Nero, 1979; (contrib.) Mithraic Studies, 1975; (contrib.) The Archaeology of Afghanistan, 1978; articles in Numismatic Chron., Jl Numismatic Soc. India, Schweizer Münzblätter, Acta Numismatica, S Asian Archaeology, Afghan Studies, S Asian Studies; etc. *Recreations:* travel, antiquities, photography, natural history, gardening, genealogy. *Address:* Admont, Dancers End, Tring, Herts HP23 6JY. *Club:* Athenæum.

McDOWALL, Keith Desmond, CBE 1988; independent consultant on public affairs and government relations, since 1988; Chairman, Kiss FM Radio, since 1990 (Chairman, steering committee, 1989–90); *b* 3 Oct. 1929; *s* of William Charteris McDowall and Edna Florence McDowall; *m* 1st, 1957, Shirley Margaret Russell Astbury (marr. diss. 1985); two *d*; 2nd, 1988, Brenda Dean, *qv*. *Educ:* Heath Clark Sch., Croydon, Surrey. Served RAF, National Service, 1947–49. South London Press, 1947–55; Daily Mail, 1955–67: Indust. Corresp., 1958; Indust. Editor, 1961–67; Man. Dir, Inca Construction (UK) Co. Ltd, 1967–69; Govt Information Service: successively Chief Inf. Officer, DEA, BoT, Min. of Housing and Local Govt, DoE, and Home Office, 1969–72; Dir of Inf., NI Office, 1972–74; Dir of Inf., Dept of Employment, 1974–78; Man. Dir Public Affairs, British Shipbuilders, 1978–80. Dir, Govan Shipbuilders Ltd, 1978–80. Dir of Information, 1981–86, Dep. Dir Gen., 1986–88, CBI. *Publications:* articles in newspapers and various pubns. *Recreations:* sailing, tennis, mingling. *Clubs:* Reform; Medway Yacht (Rochester).

McDOWALL, Stuart, CBE 1984; Senior Lecturer in Economics, University of St Andrews, since 1967; *b* 19 April 1926; *s* of Robert McDowall and Gertrude Mary Collister; *m* 1951, Margaret Burnside Woods Gyle; three *s*. *Educ:* Liverpool Institute; St Andrews University (MA hons 1950). Personnel Manager, Michael Nairn & Co., 1955–61; Lectr in Econs, St Andrews Univ., 1961–67; Master, United Coll. of St Salvator and St Leonard, 1976–80. Dep. Chm., Central Arbitration Cttee, 1976–; Local Govt Boundary Comr for Scotland, 1983–; Mem., Monopolies and Mergers Commn, 1985–89. Econ. Consultant to UN in Saudi Arabia, 1985–89. Sec., Scottish Economic Soc., 1970–76. *Publications:* (with P. R. Draper) Trade Adjustment and the British Jute Industry, 1978; (with H. M. Begg) Industrial Performance and Prospects in Areas Affected by Oil Developments, 1981; articles on industrial economics and regional economics. *Recreations:* golf, hill walking. *Address:* 10 Woodburn Terrace, St Andrews, Fife KY16 8BA. *T:* St Andrews (0334) 73247. *Clubs:* Commonwealth Trust; Royal and Ancient Golf (St Andrews).

McDOWELL, Prof. Coulter; *see* McDowell, Prof. M. R. C.

McDOWELL, Sir Eric (Wallace), Kt 1990; CBE 1982; FCA; Chairman, Industrial Development Board for Northern Ireland, since 1986 (Member, since 1982); *b* 7 June 1925; *s* of Martin Wallace McDowell and Edith Florence (*née* Hillock); *m* 1954, Helen Lilian (*née* Montgomery); one *s* two *d*. *Educ:* Royal Belfast Academical Instn. FCA 1957. Served War, 1943–46. Student Chartered Accountant, 1942, qualified 1948; Partner, Wilson Hennessey & Crawford, and (after merger in 1973) Deloitte, Haskins & Sells, 1952–85 (Sen. Partner, Belfast, 1980–85, retd). Director: NI Transport Holding Co., 1971–74; Spence Bryson Ltd, 1986–89; TSB Northern Ireland, 1986–. Member: Council, Inst. of Chartered Accountants in Ireland, 1968–77 (Pres., 1974–75); Industries Develt Adv. Cttee, 1971–82 (Chm., 1978–82); Adv. Cttee of NI Central Investment Fund for Charities, 1975– (Chm., 1980–); NI Econ. Council, 1977–83; Exec. Cttee, Relate: Marriage Guidance, NI, 1981–; Broadcasting Council for NI, 1983–86. Trustee, Presbyterian Church in Ireland, 1983–. Treas., Abbeyfield Belfast Soc., 1986–. Governor, Royal Belfast Academical Instn, 1959– (Chm. of Governors, 1977–86). Hon. DSc(Econ) QUB, 1989. *Recreations:* music, drama, foreign travel. *Address:* Beechcroft, 19 Beechlands, Belfast BT9 5HU. *T:* Belfast (0232) 668771. *Clubs:* Royal Over-Seas League; Ulster Reform (Belfast).

McDOWELL, George Roy Colquhoun, CBE 1988; CEng, FIEE; Chairman, British Standards Institution, 1985–88; *b* 1 Sept. 1922; *s* of Robert Henry McDowell and Jean McDowell; *m* 1948, Joan Annie Bryan; two *s*. *Educ:* Coleraine Academical Instn; Queen's Univ., Belfast (BSc Eng). Signals Officer, RAF, 1942–46. Works Manager, Distribn Transformer Div., subseq. Works Manager, Power Transformer Div., Ferranti Ltd, 1950–69; Dir, 1969–87, Man. Dir Designate, 1969–72, Chm. and Man. Dir, 1972–87, George H. Scholes. Director: WSK (Electrical), 1980–; Clipsal (UK), 1983–; L. T. Switchgear, 1984–; Peter Peregrinus, 1985–; Capstead Controls Ltd, 1986; Pentland Electronics Ltd, 1987; PDL-Wylex Sdn Bhd, Malaysia, 1980–; Clipsal Switchgear Pty, Australia, 1982–. Menvier-Swain Group, 1985–; Chairman: Electrical Installation Equipment Manufacturers' Assoc., 1977–80; British Electrotechnical Cttee, BSI; Electrotechnical Council, BSI, 1982–85; President: British Electrical and Allied Manufacturers' Assoc., 1981–82; Internat. Electrotechnical Commn, 1987–; IEEIE; Institution of Electrical Engineers: Chm., Power Bd; Chm., Finance Cttee; Mem. Council. Grand Decoration of Honour for Services to the Republic of Austria, 1978. *Recreations:* golf, Rugby, cricket. *Address:* 24 Oak Drive, Bramhall, Stockport, Cheshire SK7 2AD. *T:* 061–439 4552. *Club:* Army and Navy.

McDOWELL, Sir Henry (McLorinan), KBE 1964 (CBE 1959); retired; *b* Johannesburg, S Africa, 10 Dec. 1910; *s* of John McDowell and Margaret Elizabeth Bingham; *m* 1939, Norah, *d* of Walter Slade Douthwaite; one *s* one *d*. *Educ:* Witwatersrand Univ.; Queen's Coll., Oxford; Yale Univ. Served War of 1939–45, 1 Bn Northern Rhodesia Regt, East Africa and South-East Asia, 1940–44. Entered HM Colonial Service (Cadet, Northern Rhodesia), 1938; Clerk, Legislative and Executive Councils, 1945; Assistant Secretary, 1950; Deputy Financial Secretary, 1952. Imperial Defence Coll., 1948; seconded Colonial Office, 1949. Economic and Financial Working Party, in preparation for federation of Rhodesias and Nyasaland, 1953; Federal Treasury, 1954; Secretary, Ministry of Transport, 1955; Secretary, Federal Treasury, 1959–63. Chm., Zimbabwe Board, Barclays Bank Internat. Ltd, 1969–79; Chm. or Dir, other cos in Zimbabwe, 1964–79. Chancellor, Univ. of Rhodesia, 1971–81; Chm. or Mem., governing bodies, educational institutions, Zimbabwe, 1964–79. Hon. LLD Witwatersrand, 1971; Hon. DLitt Rhodesia, 1975. *Recreations:* walking, reading. *Address:* 2 Donne Court, Burbage Road, SE24. *Club:* Harare.

See also J. H. McDowell.

McDOWELL, Prof. John Henry, FBA 1983; University Professor of Philosophy, University of Pittsburgh, since 1988 (Professor of Philosophy, 1986–88); *b* 7 March 1942; *s* of Sir Henry McDowell, *qv*; *m* 1977, Andrea Lee Lehrke. *Educ:* St John's College, Johannesburg; University College of Rhodesia and Nyasaland; New College, Oxford. BA London; MA Oxon. Fellow and Praelector in Philosophy, UC, Oxford, 1966–86, Emeritus Fellow, 1988; Univ. Lectr (CUF), Oxford Univ., 1967–86. James C. Loeb Fellow in Classical Philosophy, Harvard Univ., 1969; Visiting Professor: Univ. of Michigan, 1975; Univ. of California, Los Angeles, 1977; Univ. of Minnesota, 1982; Jadavpur Univ., Calcutta, 1983; John Locke Lectr, Oxford Univ., 1991. Sen. Fellow, Council of Humanities, Princeton Univ., 1984. *Publications:* Plato, Theaetetus (trans. with notes), 1973; (ed with Gareth Evans) Truth and Meaning, 1976; (ed) Gareth Evans, The Varieties of Reference, 1982; (ed with Philip Pettit) Subject, Thought, and Context, 1986; articles in jls and anthologies. *Recreations:* reading, music, lawn tennis. *Address:* c/o Department of Philosophy, University of Pittsburgh, Pittsburgh, Pa 15260, USA. *T:* (412)–624–5792.

McDOWELL, Malcolm, (Malcolm Taylor); actor; *b* 13 June 1943; *m* 1980, Mary Steenburgen; one *s* one *d*. *Educ:* Leeds. *Stage:* RSC Stratford, 1965–66; Entertaining Mr Sloane, Royal Court, 1975; Look Back in Anger, NY, 1980; In Celebration, NY, 1984; Holiday, Old Vic, 1987; *films:* If, 1969; Figures in a Landscape, 1970; The Raging Moon, 1971; A Clockwork Orange, 1971; O Lucky Man, 1973; Royal Flash, 1975; Aces High, 1976; Voyage of the Damned, 1977; Caligula, 1977; The Passage, 1978; Time After Time, 1979; Cat People, 1981; Blue Thunder, 1983; Get Crazy, 1983; Britannia Hospital, 1984; Gulag, 1985; Cross Creek, 1985; Sunrise, 1988; Assassin of the Tsar, 1991. *Address:* c/o ICM, 388–396 Oxford Street, W1 9HE.

McDOWELL, Prof. (Martin Rastall) Coulter, JP; FRAS, FInstP; Professor of Applied Mathematics, 1969–86, now Emeritus, and Head of Department of Mathematics, 1982–86, Royal Holloway and Bedford New College (formerly at Royal Holloway College), University of London; *b* 30 Jan. 1932; *s* of late Richard Whiteside Coulter McDowell and Evelyn Jean McDowell; *m* 1956, Brenda Gordon Blair, *d* of late Robert Cooke Blair and of Mildred Martley Blair; two *s*. *Educ:* Methodist College, Belfast; Queen's University, Belfast (BSc 1953, PhD 1957); Columbia University, NY (MA 1954). Gassiot Research Fellow, QUB, 1956–57; Lectr in Mathematics, Royal Holloway Coll., 1957–64; apptd Teacher, Univ. of London, 1960; Vis. Scholar, Georgia Inst. of Tech., Atlanta, 1959–60; Reader in Appl. Maths, Univ. of Durham, 1964–69; Senior Research Associate, Goddard Space Flight Center, 1967–68; Dean of Science, 1972–75 and 1982–85, RHC, Univ. of London; Member: Council, RHC, 1973–76, 1984–85; Senate, Univ. of London, 1983–85. JP Surrey, 1981. *Publications:* (ed) Atomic Collision Processes, 1964; (ed with E. W. McDaniel) Case Studies in Atomic Collision Physics, Vol. 1 1969, Vol. 2 1972, Vol. 3 1974, Vol. 4 1975; (with J. P. Coleman) Theory of Ion-Atom Collisions, 1970; (with H. J. W. Kleinpoppen) Electron and Photon Interactions with Matter, 1976; (with A. Ferendici) Atomic Processes in Thermonuclear Plasmas, 1980; (with J. W. Humberston) Positrons in Gases, 1984; papers in learned jls. *Recreations:* Roman archaeology, drinking wine.

McDOWELL, Stanley; Town Clerk and Chief Executive, Belfast City Council, since 1989; *b* 14 June 1941; *s* of William McDowell and Annie Storey; *m* 1966, Charlotte Elizabeth Stockdale; three *d*. *Educ:* Royal Belfast Academical Instn; Queen's Univ. of Belfast (BSc Econ). FCIS. Belfast City and Dist Water Comrs, 1959–70; Antrim County Council, 1971–73; DoE (NI), 1973–79; Belfast City Council, 1979–. *Address:* 12 Slievedarragh Park, Belfast BT14 8JA. *T:* Belfast (0232) 716472.

MACDUFF, Earl of; David Charles Carnegie; *b* 3 March 1961; *s* and *heir* of 3rd Duke of Fife, *qv; m* 1987, Caroline, *d* of Martin Bunting, *qv;* two *s. Educ:* Eton; Pembroke College, Cambridge (BA Law 1982, MA 1986); Royal Agricultural College, Cirencester; Edinburgh Univ. (MBA 1990). Cazenove & Co., 1982–85; Bell Lawrie & Co., 1988–89. *Heir: s* Hon. Charles Duff Carnegie, *b* 1 July 1989.

MACE, Brian Anthony; Director, Savings and Investment Division, Board of Inland Revenue, since 1990; *b* 9 Sept. 1948; *s* of Edward Laurence Mace and Olive (*née* Bennett); *m* 1973, Anne Margaret Cornford. *Educ:* Maidstone Grammar Sch.; Gonville and Caius Coll., Cambridge (MA Mathematics). Admin trainee, Bd of Inland Revenue, 1971–73; seconded to Secretariat, Inflation Accounting Cttee, 1974–75; Inland Revenue: Principal, 1975–82; Asst Sec., 1982–90; Under Sec., 1990–. *Recreations:* opera, chamber music and song, theatre, cricket, historic buildings. *Address:* Board of Inland Revenue, Somerset House, Strand, WC2R 1LB. *T:* 071–438 6614.

MACE, Lt-Gen. Sir John (Airth), KBE 1990 (OBE 1974; MBE 1967); CB 1986; New Zealand Chief of Defence Force, since 1987; *b* 29 June 1932; *m* Margaret Theodocia; one *s* one *d. Educ:* Ashburton High Sch., NZ; Nelson Coll., NZ; RMC Duntroon, Australia. Commissioned NZ Army, 1953; NZ SAS, 1955–57; active service in Malayan Emergency; despatches, 1958; Comd SAS Sqdn, 1960–62 and 1965; Comd Co. of 1 RNZIR 1st Bn, Borneo, 1966; Vietnam, 1967; appts include: Dir of Infantry and NZ SAS; CO, 1st Bn RNZIR, Singapore; Dir, Officer Postings; Comdr, Army Logistics Support Gp; Comdr, 1st Inf. Bde Gp; Army Staff Coll., Camberley; JSSC, Canberra; Comdr, NZ Force SE Asia, 1979–80; RCDS 1981; Dep. Chief of Defence Staff, 1982–84; Chief of General Staff, 1984–87. *Recreations:* golf, walking, reading. *Address:* Headquarters, New Zealand Defence Force, Wellington, New Zealand. *Clubs:* Wellesley, Wellington, Wellington Golf (Wellington).

MacEACHEN, Hon. Allan Joseph, PC (Canada); Leader of Opposition in the Senate, since 1984; *b* Inverness, Nova Scotia, 6 July 1921; *s* of Angus and Annie MacEachen. *Educ:* St Francis Xavier Univ. (BA 1944); Univ. of Toronto (MA 1946); Univ. of Chicago; MIT. Prof. of Economics, St Francis Xavier Univ., 1946–48; Head of Dept of Economics and Social Sciences; MP (L) Cape Breton Highlands-Canso, Nova Scotia, 1953–84; Special Asst and Consultant on Econ. Affairs to Hon. Lester Pearson, 1958; Minister: of Labour, 1963–65; of Nat. Health and Welfare, 1965–68; of Manpower and Immigration, 1968–70; of External Affairs, 1974–76; of Finance, 1980–82; Sec. of State for External Affairs, 1982–84; Pres., Privy Council and Govt Leader in House of Commons, Canada, 1970–74 and 1976–79; Dep. Prime Minister, 1977–79 and 1980–84; Dep. Leader of the Opposition and Opposition House Leader, 1979–80; called to Senate, 1984, Leader of Govt in Senate, 1984. Hon. Degrees: St Francis Xavier Univ.; Acadia Univ.; Loyola Coll; St Mary's Univ.; Dalhousie Univ.; Wilfrid Laurier Univ. *Address:* The Senate, Ottawa K1A 0A4, Canada.

McEACHERN, Allan; Hon. Mr Justice McEachern; Chief Justice of British Columbia, since 1988; *b* 20 May 1926; *s* of John A. and I. B. McEachern; *m* 1953, Gloria L.; two *d. Educ:* Univ. of British Columbia (BA 1949; LLB 1950). Called to the Bar of British Columbia, 1951. Partner, Russell and DuMoulin, Barristers, 1950–79; Chief Justice, Supreme Court of BC, 1979–88. Hon. LLM Univ. of BC, 1990. *Recreation:* walking. *Address:* The Law Courts, 800 Smithe Street, Vancouver, BC V6Z 2E1, Canada. *T:* 604–660–2710.

McEACHRAN, Colin Neil, QC (Scot.) 1982; JD; *b* 14 Jan. 1940; *s* of Eric Robins McEachran and Nora Helen Bushe; *m* 1967, Katherine Charlotte Henderson; two *d. Educ:* Trinity Coll., Glenalmond; Merton Coll., Oxford (BA 1961); Univ. of Glasgow (LLB 1963); Univ. of Chicago (Commonwealth Fellow; JD 1965). Admitted Solicitor, 1966; admitted to Faculty of Advocates, 1968. Solicitor, Glasgow, 1966–67; Advocate Depute, 1975–78. Mem., Scottish Legal Aid Bd, 1990–. *Recreations:* target rifle shooting (Silver Medal, Commonwealth Games, NZ, 1974; Chm., Scottish Rifle Assoc.), hill walking. *Address:* 1 Saxe-Coburg Place, Edinburgh EH3 5BR. *T:* 031–332 6820.

MACEDO, Prof. Helder Malta, PhD; Camoens Professor of Portuguese, University of London at King's College, since 1982; *b* 30 Nov. 1935; *s* of Adelino José de Macedo and Aida Malta de Macedo; *m* 1960, Suzette Armanda (*née* de Aguiar). *Educ:* Faculty of Law, Univ. of Lisbon; King's Coll., Univ. of London (BA, PhD); FKC 1991. Lectr in Portuguese and Brazilian Studies, KCL, 1971–82; Sec. of State for Culture, Portuguese Govt, 1979. Vis. Prof., Harvard Univ., 1981. Fellow, Academia das Ciências de Lisboa, 1987. Editor, Portuguese Studies Jl, 1985–. *Publications:* Nós, Uma Leitura de Cesário Verde, 1975, 3rd edn 1986; Do Significado Oculto da 'Menina a Moça', 1977; Poesia 1957–77, 1978; Camões e a Viagem Iniciática, 1980; The Purpose of Praise: Past and Future in The Lusiads of Luís de Camões, 1983; Cesário Verde: O Romântico e o Feroz, 1988. *Address:* Department of Portuguese and Brazilian Studies, King's College London, Strand, WC2R 2LS. *T:* 071–836 5454.

McELHERAN, John; Principal Assistant Solicitor (Under Secretary), Ministry of Agriculture, Fisheries and Food, 1983–89; *b* 18 Aug. 1929; *s* of late Joseph Samuel McElheran and Hilda McElheran (*née* Veale); *m* 1956, Jean Patricia Durham; one *s* two *d. Educ:* Archbishop Holgate's Grammar Sch., York; St Edmund Hall, Oxford (BA English, DipEd). Solicitor. Short period of teaching; articled clerk, Thomson & Hetherton, York, 1954; Asst Solicitor 1959, Partner 1962, Leathes Prior & Son, Norwich; Senior Legal Asst, Land Commn, Newcastle upon Tyne, 1967; Sen. Legal Asst 1971, Asst Solicitor 1974, Dept of Trade and Industry and successor Depts. *Recreation:* photography. *Address:* 12 Bedern, York YO1 2LP. *T:* York (0904) 628987. *Club:* Civil Service.

McELROY, Roy Granville, CMG 1972; LLD, PhD; Pro-Chancellor of the University of Auckland, 1968–74; *b* 2 April 1907; *s* of H. T. G. McElroy and Frances C. Hampton; *m* Joan H., *d* of R. O. H. Biss; two *d. Educ:* Auckland Univ.; Clare Coll., Cambridge. LLM NZ 1929; PhD Cantab 1934; LLD NZ 1936. Barrister. Lectr in Law, Auckland Univ., 1936–37. Mem., Auckland City Council, 1938–53; Dep. Mayor of Auckland, 1953, Mayor, 1965–68; Chm., Auckland Metro Planning Cttee, 1953; Mem., Auckland Regional Planning Authority, 1954–66; Chairman: Auckland Old People's Welfare Cttee, 1950–65; NZ Welfare of Aged Persons Distribution Cttee, 1962–75; Sunset Home Inc., 1972–82; Member: Bd of Trustees, NZ Retirement Life Care, 1972–82; Council, Dr Barnardo's in NZ; Auckland Medico-Legal Soc. Consular Agent of France in Auckland, 1948–72; Dean, Auckland Consular Corps, 1965 and 1971. Chm., NZ Section Internat. Commn of Jurists, 1965–72. Chm. Legal Research Foundn, Auckland Univ., 1968–72; Mem., Auckland Univ. Council, 1939–54 and 1960–78; Chm., Auckland Br., NZ Inst. of Internat. Affairs, 1970. FRSA 1971. Hon. DLitt Auckland Univ., 1976. Chevalier de l'Ordre National de la Légion d'Honneur, 1954. *Publications:* Law Reform Act 1936 NZ, 1937; Impossibility of Performance of Contracts, 1942; articles in Modern Law Review, NZ Law Jl, NZ Financial Times. *Recreation:* reading. *Address:* Highpoint, 119 St Stephens Avenue, Parnell, Auckland, New Zealand. *T:* 30–645. *Club:* Northern (Auckland).

McENERY, John Hartnett; author, consultant and conceptual analyst, since 1981; *b* 5 Sept. 1925; *y s* of late Maurice Joseph and Elizabeth Margaret McEnery (*née* Maccabe); *m*

1977, Lilian Wendy, *yr d* of late Reginald Gibbons and Lilian Gibbons (*née* Cox). *Educ:* St Augustine's Sch., Coatbridge; St Aloysius Coll., Glasgow; Glasgow Univ. (MA(Hons)). Served War of 1939–45: RA, 1943–47; Staff Captain, Burma Command, 1946–47. Glasgow Univ., 1947–49. Asst Principal, Scottish Educn Dept, 1949; Principal, 1954; Cabinet Office, 1957; HM Treasury, 1959; Min. of Aviation, 1962; UK Delegn to NATO, 1964; Counsellor (Defence Supply), British Embassy, Bonn, 1966; Asst Sec., Min. of Technology, 1970; Dept of Trade and Industry, 1970–72; Under-Sec. and Regional Dir for Yorks and Humberside, DTI, 1972, Dept of Industry, 1974–76; Under Sec., Concorde and Nationalisation Compensation Div., Dept of Industry, 1977–81. *Publications:* Manufacturing Two Nations—the sociological trap created by the bias of British regional policy against service industry, 1981; Towards a New Concept of Conflict Evaluation, 1985; Epilogue in Burma 1945–48: the military dimension of British withdrawal, 1990; articles in Jl of Economic Affairs. *Recreations:* various games and sports, chess, travel. *Address:* 56 Lillian Road, SW13 9JF. *Club:* Hurlingham.

McENERY, Peter; actor; Associate Artist, Royal Shakespeare Co.; *b* 21 Feb. 1940; *s* of Charles and Mary McEnery; *m* 1978; one *d. Educ:* various state and private schs. First stage appearance, Brighton, 1956; first London appearance in Flowering Cherry, Haymarket, 1957; *stage:* rôles with RSC include, 1961–: Laertes, Tybalt, Johnny Hobnails in Afore Night Come, Bassanio, Lorenzaccio, Orlando, Sachs in The Jail Diary of Albie Sachs, Pericles, Brutus, Antipholus of Ephesus, Godber in A Dream of People; other rôles include: Rudge in Next Time I'll Sing to You, Criterion, 1963; Konstantin in The Seagull, Queen's, 1964; Harry Winter in The Collaborators, Duchess, 1973; Trigorin in The Seagull, Lyric, 1975; Edward Gover in Made in Bangkok, Aldwych, 1986; Fredrik in A Little Night Music, Chichester, transf. Piccadilly, 1989; directed: Richard III, Nottingham, 1971; The Wound, Young Vic, 1972. *Films* include: Tunes of Glory, 1961; Victim, 1961; The Moonspinners, 1963; Entertaining Mr Sloane, 1970; *television:* Clayhanger, 1976; The Aphrodite Inheritance, 1979; The Jail Diary of Albie Sachs, 1980; Japanese Style, 1982; Pictures, 1983; The Collectors, 1986; The Mistress, 1986. *Recreations:* steam railway preservation, ski-ing. *Address:* c/o Hutton Management, 200 Fulham Road, SW10.

McENTEE, Peter Donovan, CMG 1978; OBE 1963; HM Diplomatic Service, retired; Governor and Commander-in-Chief of Belize, 1976–80; *b* 27 June 1920; *s* of Ewen Brooke McEntee and Caroline Laura Clare (*née* Bayley); *m* 1945, Mary Elisabeth Sherwood; two *d. Educ:* Haileybury Coll., Herts. Served War, HM Forces, 1939–45, KAR (Major). HM Overseas Civil Service, 1946–63: Dist Commissioner; retired as Principal of Kenya Inst. of Administration; First Secretary: Commonwealth Relations Office, 1963; Lagos, 1964–67; Commonwealth Office (later Foreign and Commonwealth Office), 1967–72; Consul-Gen., Karachi, 1972–75. Dep. Chm., Royal Over-Seas League; Mem. Council and Exec., Royal Commonwealth Soc. for the Blind. *Recreations:* music, natural history. *Address:* Woodlands, Church Lane, Danehill, Sussex RH17 7EU. *Club:* Royal Over-Seas League.

MACER, Dr Richard Charles Franklin, MA, PhD; consultant, since 1985; *b* 21 Oct. 1928; *s* of Lionel William Macer and Adie Elizabeth Macer; *m* 1952, Vera Gwendoline Jeapes; three *d. Educ:* Worthing High Sch.; St John's Coll., Cambridge. Research, St John's Coll., Cambridge, 1949–55, Hutchinson Res. Student, 1952–53; Hd of Plant Pathology Section, Plant Breeding Inst., Cambridge, 1955–66; Dir and Dir of Res., Rothwell Plant Breeders Ltd, Lincs, 1966–72; Prof. of Crop Production, Univ. of Edinburgh, 1972–76; Dir, Scottish Plant Breeding Station, 1976–81; Gen. Manager, Plant Royalty Bureau Ltd, 1981–85. *Publications:* papers on fungal diseases of cereals. *Recreations:* hill walking, archaeology, reading. *Club:* Farmers'.

McEVOY, David Dand; QC 1983; barrister-at-law; a Recorder of the Crown Court, since 1979; *b* 25 June 1938; *s* of David Dand McEvoy and Ann Elizabeth McEvoy (*née* Breslin); *m* 1974, Belinda Anne Robertson; three *d. Educ:* Mount St Mary's Coll.; Lincoln Coll., Oxford. BA (PPE). 2nd Lieut The Black Watch, RHR, 1958–59. Called to the Bar, Inner Temple, 1964. *Recreations:* golf, fishing. *Address:* Chambers Court, Longdon, Tewkesbury, Glos GL20 6AS. *T:* Birtsmorton (068481) 626. *Clubs:* Caledonian; Blackwell Golf; Midland Flyfishers.

McEVOY, Air Chief Marshal Sir Theodore Newman, KCB 1956 (CB 1951); CBE 1945 (OBE 1941); *b* 21 Nov. 1904; *s* of late Rev. C. McEvoy, MA, Watford; *m* 1935, Marian, *d* of late W. A. E. Coxon, Cairo; one *s* one *d. Educ:* Haberdashers' School; RAF Coll., Cranwell. Served with Fighter Squadrons and in Iraq, 1925–36; psa 1937; Air Ministry, 1938–41; commanded Northolt, 1941; Group Captain Operations, HQ Fighter Command, 1942–43; SASO No 11 Group, 1943; SASO No 84 Group, 1944 (despatches); Air Ministry (DST), 1945–47; idc 1948; AOC No 61 Group, 1949–50; Assistant Chief of Air Staff (Training), 1950–53; RAF Instructor, Imperial Defence Coll., 1954–56; Chief of Staff, Allied Air Forces, Central Europe, 1956–59; Air Secretary, Air Ministry, 1959–62; Air ADC to the Queen, 1959–62; retired, 1962. Vice-President, British Gliding Assoc. Commander Order of Polonia Restituta (Poland), 1942. *Recreations:* gardening, glass engraving. *Address:* Hurstwood, West Drive, Aldwick Bay Estate, Bognor Regis PO21 4LZ. *Club:* Royal Air Force.

McEWAN, Geraldine, (Mrs Hugh Cruttwell); actress; *b* 9 May 1932; *d* of Donald and Norah McKeown; *m* 1953, Hugh Cruttwell, *qv;* one *s* one *d. Educ:* Windsor County Girls' School. Acted with Theatre Royal, Windsor, 1949–51; Who Goes There, 1951; Sweet Madness, 1952; For Better For Worse, 1953; Summertime, 1955; Love's Labour's Lost, Stratford-on-Avon, 1956; The Member of the Wedding, Royal Court Theatre, 1957; The Entertainer, Palace, 1957–58; Stratford-on-Avon, 1958: Pericles; Twelfth Night; Much Ado About Nothing; 1961: Much Ado About Nothing; Hamlet; Everything in the Garden, Arts and Duke of York's, 1962; School for Scandal, Haymarket, and USA, 1962; The Private Ear, and The Public Eye, USA, 1963; Loot, 1965; National Theatre, 1965–71: Armstrong's Last Goodnight; Love For Love; A Flea in Her Ear; The Dance of Death; Edward II; Home and Beauty; Rites; The Way of the World; The White Devil; Amphitryon 38; Dear Love, Comedy, 1973; Chez Nous, Globe, 1974; The Little Hut, Duke of York's, 1974; Oh Coward!, Criterion, 1975; On Approval, Haymarket, 1975; Look After Lulu, Chichester, and Haymarket, 1978; A Lie of the Mind, Royal Court, 1987; Lettice and Lovage, Globe, 1988; National Theatre: The Browning Version and Harlequinade, 1980; The Provok'd Wife, 1980; The Rivals, 1983; Two Inches of Ivory, 1983; You Can't Take It With You, 1983. Directed: As You Like It, Birmingham Rep., transf. Phoenix, 1988; Treats, Hampstead, 1989. *Television series:* The Prime of Miss Jean Brodie, 1978; The Barchester Chronicles, 1982; Mapp and Lucia, 1985, 1986; Oranges are not the only Fruit, 1990. *Films:* The Adventures of Tom Jones, 1975; Escape from the Dark, 1978; Foreign Body, 1986; Henry V, 1989; Robin Hood, Prince of Thieves, 1991. *Address:* c/o Marmont Management Ltd, Langham House, 302–308 Regent Street, W1R 5AL.

McEWAN, Ian Russell, FRSL 1982; author; *b* 21 June 1948; *s* of Major (retd) David McEwan and Rose Lilian Violet Moore; *m* 1982, Penny Allen; two *s* two *d. Educ:* Woolverstone Hall Sch.; Univ. of Sussex (BA Hons Eng. Lit.); Univ. of East Anglia (MA Eng. Lit.). Began writing, 1970. Hon. DLitt Sussex, 1989. *Films:* The Ploughman's Lunch,

1983; Last Day of Summer, 1984; Soursweet, 1988. *Publications:* First Love, Last Rites, 1975; In Between the Sheets, 1978; The Cement Garden, 1978; The Imitation Game, 1981; The Comfort of Strangers, 1981; Or Shall we Die? (oratorio; score by Michael Berkeley), 1982; The Ploughman's Lunch (film script), 1985; The Child in Time (novel), 1987 (Whitbread Award); Soursweet (film script), 1989; The Innocent (novel), 1990. *Recreations:* hiking, tennis. *Address:* c/o Jonathan Cape, 32 Bedford Square, WC1B 3EL.

McEWAN, Robin Gilmour, QC (Scot.) 1981; PhD; Sheriff of South Strathclyde, Dumfries and Galloway at Ayr, since 1988 (at Lanark, 1982–88); Temporary Judge, Court of Session and High Court of Justiciary, since 1991; *b* 12 Dec. 1943; *s* of late Ian G. McEwan and of Mary McEwan, Paisley, Renfrewshire; *m* 1973, Sheena, *d* of late Stewart F. McIntyre and of Lilian McIntyre, Aberdour; two *d*. *Educ:* Paisley Grammar Sch.; Glasgow Univ. (1st Cl. Hons LLB; PhD). Faulds Fellow in Law, Glasgow Univ., 1965–68; admitted to Faculty of Advocates, 1967. Standing Jun. Counsel to Dept of Energy, 1974–76; Advocate Depute, 1976–79. Chm., Industrial Tribunals, 1981–; Mem., Scottish Legal Aid Bd, 1989–. *Publications:* Pleading in Court, 1980; (with Ann Paton) A Casebook on Damages, 1983; contrib. Stair Memorial Encyclopaedia of the Laws of Scotland, 1987. *Recreation:* golf. *Address:* Sheriff's Chambers, Sheriff Court House, Wellington Square, Ayr KA7 1DR. *T:* Ayr (0292) 268474. *Clubs:* New (Edinburgh); Honourable Company of Edinburgh Golfers, Prestwick Golf.

MacEWEN, Ann Maitland, RIBA (DisTP), MRTPI; Planning Consultant; *b* 15 Aug. 1918; *d* of Dr Maitland Radford, MD, DPH, MOH St Pancras, and Dr Muriel Radford; *m* 1st, 1940, John Wheeler, ARIBA, AADip (Hons), Flt-Lt, RAF (killed on active service, 1945); two *d*; 2nd, 1947, Malcolm MacEwen, *qv*; one *d*. *Educ:* Howell's Sch., Denbigh, N Wales; Architectural Assoc. Sch. of Architecture (AA Dip., RIBA); Assoc. for Planning and Regional Reconstruction Sch. of Planning (SP Dip., MRTPI). Architectural Asst, 1945–46; Planning Asst, Hemel Hempstead New Town Master Plan, 1946–47; Architect-Planner with LCC, 1949–61; Mem., Colin Buchanan's Gp, Min. of Transport, which produced official report, Traffic in Towns, 1961–63; res. work, Transport Section, Civil Engineering Dept, Imperial Coll., 1963–64; Partner, Colin Buchanan and Partners, 1964–73. Senior Lectr, Bristol Univ. Sch. of Advanced Urban Studies, 1974–77; Hon. Res. Fellow, UCL, 1977–84. Mem., Noise Adv. Council, 1971–73. RIBA Distinction in Town Planning, 1967. *Publications:* National Parks—Cosmetics or Conservation? (with M. MacEwen), 1982; (with Joan Davidson) The Livable City, 1983; (with M. MacEwen) Greenprints for the Countryside? the story of Britain's National Parks, 1987. *Address:* Manor House, Wootton Courtenay, Minehead, Somerset. *T:* Timberscombe (0643) 841325.

M'EWEN, Ewen, CBE 1975; MScEng; FRSE; Consulting Engineer, since 1980; *b* 13 Jan. 1916; *e s* of Clement M'Ewen and Doris Margaret Pierce-Hope; *m* 1938, Barbara Dorrien, *d* of W. F. Medhurst; two *s* one *d*. *Educ:* Merchiston; University Coll., London. BSc (Eng) 1st class Hons, 1935; MSc (Eng) 1948; Head Memorial Medallist and Prizeman, 1935. CEng; FIMechE; FASME. Graduate Apprentice David Brown & Sons (Huddersfield) Ltd, 1935–37, Research Engineer, 1937–40, Asst Works Manager, 1940–42; Served War of 1939–45, 1942–46: Lt-Col 1943; Lt-Col (Hon. Col) REME (TA retd); Asst Dir, Dept of Tank Design, 1943–46; Asst Chief Engineer, Fighting Vehicles Design Dept, 1946–47. Prof. of Agricultural Engineering, King's Coll., Univ. of Durham, Newcastle upon Tyne, 1947–54, and Reader in Applied Mechanics, 1952–54; Dir Armament R and D Establishment, Fort Halstead, 1955–58; Dir of Engineering, Massey Ferguson Ltd, 1958–63; Dep. Man. Dir, 1963, Man. Dir, 1965–67, Hobourn Group Ltd; Vice-Chm. (Engrg), Joseph Lucas Ltd, 1967–80. Visiting Professor: Imperial Coll., London, 1971–78; UCL, 1978–. Commanded REME 50 (N) Infantry Div. (TA), 1949–52. Hon. Col Durham Univ. OTC, 1955–60. Member: Council, Instn of Mech. Engs, 1961–81 (Vice-Pres., 1970–76; Pres., 1976–77); Design Council, 1971–77; Armed Forces Pay Review Body, 1971–83; Chm., Metrology and Standards Requirements Bd, 1973–77. Chm., Lanchester Polytechnic, Coventry, 1970–73. Fellow, UCL, 1965; FRSE 1973. Hon. DSc: Heriot-Watt, 1976; Newcastle, 1977. Liveryman, Glaziers Company; Hammerman, Glasgow. *Publications:* papers and articles in Technical Press. *Recreation:* sailing. *Address:* 45 Pearce Avenue, Poole, Dorset BH14 8EG. *T:* Parkstone (0202) 742067. *Clubs:* Army and Navy; Royal Thames Yacht; Parkstone Yacht, Royal Motor Yacht.

McEWEN, Rev. Prof. James Stevenson, DD; Professor of Church History, University of Aberdeen, 1958–77; Master of Christ's College, Aberdeen, 1971–77; *b* 18 Feb. 1910; *s* of Rev. Thomas McEwen and Marjorie Bissett; *m* 1945, Martha M. Hunter, Auchendrane, Alexandria; two *s*. *Educ:* George Watson's Coll., Edinburgh Univ. Ordained Church of Scotland, 1940; held parishes at Rathen, Hawick and Invergowrie; Lecturer in Church History at University of Edinburgh, 1953. *Publication:* The Faith of John Knox, 1961. *Address:* 8 Westfield Terrace, Aberdeen AB2 4RU. *T:* Aberdeen (0224) 645413.

McEWEN, Sir John (Roderick Hugh), 5th Bt *cr* 1953; *b* 4 Nov. 1965; *s* of Sir Robert Lindley McEwen, 3rd Bt, of Marchmont and Bardrochat, and of Brigid Cecilia, *d* of late James Laver, CBE, and Veronica Turleigh; *S* brother, 1983. *Educ:* Ampleforth; University Coll. London. *Heir: cousin* Adam Hugo McEwen, *b* 9 Feb. 1965. *Address:* Polwarth Crofts, Polwarth, Duns, Berwickshire.

MacEWEN, Malcolm; journalist; *b* 24 Dec. 1911; *s* of late Sir Alexander MacEwen and of Lady (Mary Beatrice) MacEwen; *m* 1st, 1937, Barbara Mary Stebbing, BSc (*d* 1944); one *d*; 2nd, 1947, Mrs Ann Maitland Wheeler (*see* Ann Maitland MacEwen); one *d* (and two step *d*). *Educ:* Edinburgh Univ. (MA, LLB). Member (Lab) Ross and Cromarty CC, 1938–40; wrote for Daily Worker, mainly as Parliamentary Correspondent, 1943–56; Asst Editor, Architects' Jl, 1956–60; Editor, RIBA Jl, 1964–71; RIBA: Head of Information Services, 1960–66; Publishing Services, 1966–70; Dir, Public Affairs, 1971–72. Leverhulme Res. Fellow, 1972–73; Research Fellow: UCL, 1977–84; Birkbeck Coll., 1985–88. Mem., Exmoor Nat. Park Cttee, 1973–81. Hon. Fellow, RIBA, 1974. *Publications:* Crisis in Architecture, 1974; (ed) Future Landscapes, 1976; (with Mrs A. M. MacEwen) National Parks—Cosmetics or Conservation?, 1982; (with G. Sinclair) New Life for the Hills, 1983; (jtly) Countryside Conflicts, 1986; (with A. M. MacEwen) Greenprints for the Countryside? the story of Britain's National Parks, 1987; The Greening of a Red, 1991. *Address:* Manor House, Wootton Courtenay, Somerset. *T:* Timberscombe (0643) 841325.

MACEY, Rear-Adm. David Edward, CB 1984; Registrar and Secretary, Order of the Bath, since 1990; Receiver-General, Canterbury Cathedral, since 1984; *b* 15 June 1929; *s* of Frederick William Charles Macey and Florence May Macey; *m* 1st, 1958, Lorna Therese Verner (decd), *o d* of His Honour Judge Oliver William Verner; one *s* one *d*, and one step *s* two step *d*; 2nd, 1982, Fiona, *o d* of Vice-Adm. Sir William Beloe, KBE, CB, DSC; three step *s*. *Educ:* Sir Joseph Williamson's Mathematical Sch., Rochester; Royal Naval Coll., Dartmouth. Midshipman, 1948; Cruisers, Carriers, Destroyers, 1950–63; Comdr, 1963; Amer. Staff Coll., 1964; Comdr, RNC Dartmouth, 1970; Captain, 1972; Directorate Naval Plans, 1972–74; RCDS, 1975; Dir, RN Staff Coll., 1976–78; Dir, Naval Manpower, 1979–81; Rear-Adm., 1981; Dep. Asst Chief of Staff (Ops), SACEUR, 1981–84. ADC to HM the Queen, 1981. Gentleman Usher of the Scarlet Rod, Order of the Bath, 1985–90. *Recreations:* walking, cricket, cooking. *Address:* Petham Oast, Garlinge Green, Canterbury, Kent CT4 5RT. *Clubs:* Anglo-Belgian, MCC; Band of Brothers (Kent).

MACEY, Air Vice-Marshal Eric Harold, OBE, 1975; Director General of Training (Royal Air Force), 1989–91, retired; *b* 9 April 1936; *s* of Harold Fred and Katrina Emma Mary Macey; *m* 1957, Brenda Ann Bracher; one *s* one *d*. *Educ:* Shaftesbury Grammar School; Southampton Tech. Coll. Asst Sci. Officer, Min. of Supply, 1953–54; RAF, 1954; commissioned, 1955; Pilot's Wings, 1956; RAF Staff Coll., 1966; RCDS 1983; AOC and Comdt, RAF Coll., Cranwell, 1985–87; ACDS (Policy and Nuclear), 1987–89. *Recreations:* music, walking, DIY. *Address:* Ebblemead, Homington, Salisbury, Wilts SP5 4NL. *Club:* Royal Air Force.

McFADDEN, Jean Alexandra, JP, MA; Vice Lord Lieutenant of City of Glasgow, since 1980; *b* 26 Nov. 1941; *d* of John and Elma Hogg; *m* 1966, John McFadden (*d* 1991). *Educ:* Univ. of Glasgow (MA 1st Cl. Hons Classics); Univ. of Strathclyde (LLB 1st Cl. Hons). Principal Teacher of Classics, Strathclyde Schools, 1967–86. Entered Local Govt as Mem. of Glasgow Corp. for Cowcaddens Ward, 1971; Mem. for Scotstoun Ward, 1984– (due to boundary changes); Chm., Manpower Cttee, 1974–77; Leader of Labour Group, 1977–86; Leader, 1980–86, Treasurer, 1986–, Glasgow DC. Convener, Scottish Local Govt Information Unit, 1984–; Pres., Convention of Scottish Local Auths, 1990–; Bd. Mem., SDA, 1989–91. Chm., Mayfest (Glasgow Internat. Arts Fest.), 1983–. JP Glasgow, 1972; DL 1980. *Recreations:* cycling, theatre, walking, gliding, canoeing, golf. *Address:* 16 Lansdowne Crescent, Glasgow G20 6NQ. *T:* 041–334 3522. *Club:* Tron Theatre (Glasgow).

McFADYEAN, Colin William; Director of Coaching, Bristol Football Club (Rugby Union), since 1990; *b* 11 March 1943; *s* of Captain Angus John McFadyean, MC, 1st Bn London Scottish Regt (killed in action, 1944) and Joan Mary McFadyean (*née* Irish); *m* 1970, Jeanette Carol Payne; one *s*. *Educ:* Plymouth Coll.; Bristol Grammar Sch.; Loughborough Coll. of Education; Keele Univ. (DLC hons, Adv. DipEd). Phys. Educn teacher, Birmingham, 1965–67; Phys. Educn Lectr, 1967–72, Sen. Lectr, 1972–74, Cheshire; Dep. Dir, Nat. Sports Centre, Lilleshall, 1974–78; Chief Coach, Jubilee Sports Centre, Hong Kong, 1979–82; Sports Master and House Master, Dulwich Coll., 1983–85; Dir Gen., NPFA, 1985–87; with Croydon Educn Authy, 1988–90. Internat. Rugby career includes: 11 England caps, 1966–68; 4 Tests British Lions *v* NZ, 1966; (captain) *v* Ireland, 1968; (captain) *v* Wales, 1968; scored 5 tries, 1 dropped goal (in 15 Tests); other sport: coach to Hong Kong disabled team to Olympics, Arnhem, 1980; Adviser, Hong Kong table tennis team to World Championships, Yugoslavia, 1981. Broadcaster with Hong Kong TV and commercial radio. *Recreations:* tennis, golf, music. *Address:* c/o The Memorial Ground, Filton Avenue, Horfield, Bristol BS7 0AQ. *Clubs:* British Sportsman's; England Rugby International's; Rugby Internationals Golf, Chipping Sodbury Golf; Moseley Football (Vice-Pres.); Penguins Rugby Football (Vice-Pres).

MACFADYEN, Donald James Dobbie, QC (Scot.) 1983; *b* 8 Sept. 1945; *er s* of late Donald James Thomson Macfadyen and of Christina Dick Macfadyen; *m* 1971, Christine Balfour Gourlay Hunter; one *s* one *d*. *Educ:* Hutchesons' Boys' Grammar Sch., Glasgow; Glasgow Univ. (LLB 1967). Admitted to Faculty of Advocates, 1969; Advocate Depute, 1979–82. Standing Jun. Counsel to Dept of Agric. and Fisheries for Scotland, 1977–79, to SHHD, 1982–83. Part-time Chm., Med. Appeal Tribunals and Vaccine Damage Tribunals, 1989–. ACIArb 1990. *Address:* 66 Northumberland Street, Edinburgh EH3 6JE. *T:* 031–556 6043. *Club:* New (Edinburgh).

McFADZEAN, family name of **Barons McFadzean** and **McFadzean of Kelvinside.**

McFADZEAN, Baron, *cr* 1966 (Life Peer); **William Hunter McFadzean,** KT 1976; Kt 1960; Director, Midland Bank, 1959–81 (Deputy Chairman, 1968–77); Hon. President, BICC plc, 1973 (Managing Director, 1954–61; Chairman, 1954–73); *b* Stranraer, 17 Dec. 1903; *s* of late Henry and of Agnes McFadzean, Stranraer; *m* 1933, Eileen, *e d* of Arthur Gordon, Blundellsands, Lancs.; one *s* one *d*, one adopted *d*. *Educ:* Stranraer Academy and High Sch.; Glasgow Univ. Served articles with McLay, McAllister & McGibbon, Chartered Accountants, Glasgow, 1922–27; qualified as Chartered Accountant, 1927; with Chalmers Wade & Co., 1927–32; joined British Insulated Cables Ltd, as Accountant, 1932 (Financial Secretary, 1937; Exec. Manager, 1942); on amalgamation of British Insulated Cables Ltd and Callender's Cable & Construction Co. Ltd, in 1945, appointed to Board of British Insulated Callender's Cables Ltd as Exec. Director (Dep. Chairman, 1947; Chief Exec. Director, 1950), retd 1973; Chairman: Standard Broadcasting Corp. (UK) Ltd, 1972–79 (Hon. Pres., 1979–83); Home Oil (UK) Ltd, 1972–78; Scurry-Rainbow (UK) Ltd, 1974–78; Deputy Chairman: RTZ/BICC Aluminium Holdings Ltd, 1967–73; National Nuclear Corp., 1973–80; Canada Life Unit Trust Managers Ltd (Chm., 1971–82); Director: Anglesey Aluminium Ltd, 1968–73; Midland Bank Executor and Trustee Co., 1959–67; English Electric Co., 1966–68; Steel Co. of Wales Ltd, 1966–67; Canadian Imperial Bank of Commerce, 1967–74; Canada Life Assurance Co., 1969–79; Canada Life Assurance Co. of GB, 1971–84 (Dep. Chm., 1971–84); Home Oil Co. Ltd, 1972–77; Standard Broadcasting Corp. Ltd, 1976–79. Pres. FBI, 1959–61. Chairman: Council of Industrial Fedns of EFTA, 1960–63; (Founder) Export Council for Europe, 1960–64 (Hon. Pres. 1964–71); Commonwealth Export Council, 1964–66; British Nat. Export Council, 1964–66 (Pres. 1966–68); President: Brit. Electrical Power Convention, 1961–62; Brit. Nuclear Forum, 1964–66; Coal Trade Benevolent Assoc., 1967–68; Electrical and Electronics Industries Benevolent Assoc., 1968–69. Vice-President: Middle East Assoc., 1965; City of London Soc., 1965–72; British/Swedish Chamber of Commerce, 1963–74. Member: Inst. of Directors, 1954–76 (Council, 1954–74); Min. of Labour Adv. Bd on Resettlement of Ex-Regulars, 1957–60; Bd of Trade Adv. Council on ME Trade, 1958–60; MoT Shipping Adv. Panel, 1962–64; Ct of British Shippers' Council, 1964–74 (Pres., 1968–71); Council, Foreign Bondholders, 1968–74; Anglo-Danish Soc., 1965–75 (Chm., 1969–75; Hon. Pres., 1975); Adv. Cttee, Queen's Award for Industry, 1965–67 (Chm., Review Cttee, 1970). CompIEE 1956. JDipMA 1965. Commander Order of Dannebrog (Denmark), 1964, Grand Commander, 1974; Grande Oficial da Ordem do Infante Dom Henrique, Portugal, 1972. *Address:* 16 Lansdown Crescent, Bath, Avon BA1 5EX. *T:* Bath (0225) 335487. *Club:* Carlton.

McFADZEAN OF KELVINSIDE, Baron *cr* 1980 (Life Peer), of Kelvinside in the District of the City of Glasgow; **Francis Scott McFadzean;** Kt 1975; Former Director, Shell Transport and Trading Company Ltd; Director: Shell Petroleum Company Ltd, 1964–86; Beecham Group Ltd, 1974–86; Coats Patons Ltd, 1979–86; *b* 26 Nov. 1915; *m* 1st, 1938, Isabel McKenzie Beattie (*d* 1987); one *d*; 2nd, 1988, Sonja Khung. *Educ:* Glasgow Univ.; London Sch. of Economics (Hon. Fellow, 1974). MA. BoT, 1938; Treasury, 1939; War Service, 1940–45; Malayan Govt, 1945; Colonial Develt Corp., 1949; Shell Petroleum Co. Ltd, 1952; Man. Dir, Royal Dutch/Shell Group of Companies, 1964–76; Dir, 1964–, Man. Dir 1971, Chm., 1972–76, "Shell" Transport and Trading Co. Ltd; Chairman: Shell International Marine Ltd, 1966–76; Shell Canada Ltd, 1970–76; Shell Petroleum Co. Ltd, 1972–76; British Airways, 1976–79 (Dir, 1975); Rolls Royce

Ltd, 1980–83; Dir, Shell Oil Co., 1972–76. Chairman: Trade Policy Research Centre, 1971–82; Steering Bd, Strathclyde Div., Scottish Business Sch., 1970–76; Vis. Prof. of Economics, Strathclyde Univ., 1967–76. FRSE 1989. Hon. LLD Strathclyde, 1970. Comdr, Order of Oranje Nassau. *Publications*: Galbraith and the Planners, 1968; Energy in the Seventies, 1971; The Operation of a Multi-National Enterprise, 1971; (jtly) Towards an Open World Economy, 1972; The Economics of John Kenneth Galbraith: a study in fantasy, 1977; (jtly) Global Strategy for Growth: a report on North-South issues, 1981. *Address*: House of Lords, SW1A 0PW.

See also Baron Marsh.

McFALL, John; MP (Lab) Dumbarton, since 1987; *b* 4 Oct. 1944; *s* of John and Jean McFall; *m* 1969, Joan Ward; three *s* one *d*. *Educ*: St Patrick's Primary and Secondary Schools, Dumbarton; Paisley College (BSc Hons); Strathclyde Univ. (MBA); Open Univ. (BA). Schoolteacher, to Assistant Head Teacher, 1974–87. An Opposition Whip, 1989–. Member: House of Commons Select Cttee on Defence, 1988–; Exec. Cttee, Parly Gp for Energy Studies, 1988–. Vis. Prof., Strathclyde Business Sch., Univ. of Strathclyde. *Recreations*: running, golf, reading. *Address*: 14 Oxhill Road, Dumbarton G82 4DG. *T*: Dumbarton (0389) 31437.

McFALL, Richard Graham; Chairman, 1980–86, Director, 1976–86, Fleming Enterprise Investment Trust plc (formerly Crossfriars Trust plc); *b* 31 Jan. 1920; 3rd *s* of Henry Joseph Marshall and Sarah Gertrude McFall; *m* 1945, Clara Louise Debonnaire Mitford; one *s* one *d*. *Educ*: Holmwood Prep. Sch., Lancs; Clifton Coll., Bristol. Joined Pacol Ltd, 1938; Mil. Service, HAC, 1939–40; Colonial Office, 1941–45 (Asst Sec., then Sec., W African Produce Control Bd); Motor & Air Products Ltd, 1946–48; re-joined Pacol Ltd, 1949, Dir 1951; Chm., London Cocoa Terminal Market Assoc., 1954–55; Chm., Cocoa Assoc. of London, 1958–59; Dir 1962–82, Man. Dir 1965–74, Chm., 1970–76, Vice-Chm., 1976–78, Gill & Duffus Group PLC. *Recreation*: golf. *Address*: Springfold Cottage, Green Dene, East Horsley, Surrey KT24 5RG. *T*: East Horsley (04865) 3282. *Clubs*: Farmers'; Effingham Golf.

McFARLAND, Dr David John; Fellow, and Tutor in Psychology, Balliol College, Oxford, since 1966; University Reader in Animal Behaviour, University of Oxford, since 1974; *b* 31 Dec. 1938; *s* of John Cyril and Joan Elizabeth McFarland; *m* 1962, Frances Jill Tomlin; one *s* one *d*. *Educ*: Leighton Park Sch., Reading; Liverpool Univ. (BSc 1st Cl. Hons Zoology, 1961); Oxford Univ. (DPhil Psychology, 1965). Lecturer in Psychology: Durham Univ., 1964; Oxford Univ., 1966. Hofmeyer Fellow, Univ. of the Witwatersrand, 1974; Visiting Professor: Dalhousie Univ., 1968; Rutgers Univ., 1971; Univ. of Penn, 1977; SUNY, Stonybrook, 1978; Univ. of Oregon, 1978; Univ. of Münster, Germany, 1989. Pres., Internat. Ethological Conf., 1981. Editor, Animal Behaviour, 1969–74. *Publications*: (with J. McFarland) An Introduction to the Study of Behaviour, 1969; Feedback Mechanisms in Animal Behaviour, 1971; (ed) Motivational Control Systems Analysis, 1974; (ed) The Oxford Companion to Animal Behaviour, 1981; (with A. Houston) Quantitative Ethology: the state space approach, 1981; (ed) Functional Ontogeny, 1982; Animal Behaviour, 1985 (also USA); Problems of Animal Behaviour, 1989; Biologie des Verhaltens, (Germany) 1989; articles in scientific learned jls. *Recreations*: keeping animals, pottery. *Address*: Balliol College, Oxford OX1 3BJ. *T*: Oxford (0865) 277760.

McFARLAND, Sir John (Talbot), 3rd Bt *cr* 1914, of Aberfoyle, Londonderry; TD 1967; Chairman: Lanes (Business Equipment), since 1977; J. T. McFarland Holdings, since 1984; McFarland Farms Ltd, since 1980; Director, G. Kinnaird & Son Ltd, since 1984; *b* 3 Oct. 1927; *s* of Sir Basil Alexander Talbot McFarland, 2nd Bt, CBE, ERD, and Anne Kathleen (*d* 1952), *d* of late Andrew Henderson; *S* father, 1986; *m* 1957, Mary Scott, *d* of late Dr W. Scott Watson, Londonderry; two *s* two *d*. *Educ*: Marlborough College; Trinity Coll., Oxford. Captain RA (TA), retired 1967. Chairman: R. C. Malseed & Co. Ltd, 1957–90; Lanes (Derry) Ltd, 1977–84; Lanes (Fuel) Oils Ltd; Lanes Patent Fuels Ltd; Holmes Coal Ltd; Alexander Thompson & Co. Ltd; Nicholl Ballintyne Ltd; J. W. Corbett Ltd; Wattersons Ltd. Chm., Londonderry Lough Swilly Railway Co., 1978–81; Director: Londonderry Gaslight Co., 1958–89; Donegal Holdings Ltd, 1963–85. Member: Londonderry County Borough Council, 1955–69; NW HMC, 1960–73; Londonderry Port and Harbour Commrs, 1965–73. Jt Chm., Londonderry and Foyle Coll., 1971–76. High Sheriff, Co. Londonderry 1958, City of County of Londonderry 1965–67; DL Londonderry 1962, resigned 1982. *Recreations*: golf, shooting. *Heir*: *er s* Anthony Basil Scott McFarland [*b* 29 Nov. 1959; *m* 1988, Anne Margaret, *d* of T. K. Laidlaw, Gernonstown, Kells, Co. Meath. *Educ*: Marlborough Coll.; Trinity College, Dublin (BA). ACA]. *Address*: Dunmore House, Carrigans, Lifford, Co. Donegal. *T*: Letterkenny 40120. *Clubs*: Kildare Street and University (Dublin); Northern Counties (Londonderry).

MACFARLANE, family name of **Baron Macfarlane of Bearsden.**

MACFARLANE OF BEARSDEN, Baron *cr* 1991 (Life Peer), in the District of the City of Glasgow; **Norman Somerville Macfarlane,** Kt 1983; FRSE; Chairman: Macfarlane Group (Clansman) PLC, since 1973 (Managing Director, 1973–90); United Distillers PLC, since 1987; Joint Deputy Chairman, Guinness PLC, since 1989 (Chairman, 1987–89); *b* 5 March 1926; *s* of Daniel Robertson Macfarlane and Jessie Lindsay Somerville; *m* 1953, Marguerite Mary Campbell; one *s* four *d*. *Educ*: High Sch. of Glasgow. FRSE 1991. Commnd RA, 1945; served Palestine, 1945–47. Founded N. S. Macfarlane & Co. Ltd, 1949; became Macfarlane Group (Clansman) PLC, 1973. Underwriting Mem. of Lloyd's, 1978–; Chairman: The Fine Art Society PLC, 1976–; American Trust PLC, 1984– (Dir, 1980–); Director: Clydesdale Bank PLC, 1980–; General Accident Fire & Life Assce Corp. plc, 1984–; Edinburgh Fund Managers plc, 1980–. Dir, Glasgow Chamber of Commerce, 1976–79; Member: Council, CBI Scotland, 1975–81; Bd, Scottish Develt Agency, 1979–87. Chm., Glasgow Develt Agency (formerly Glasgow Action), 1985–. Vice Chm., Scottish Ballet, 1983–87 (Dir, 1975–); Dir, Scottish National Orch., 1977–82; Pres., Royal Glasgow Inst. of the Fine Arts, 1976–87; Mem., Royal Fine Art Commn for Scotland, 1980–82; Scottish Patron, National Art Collection Fund, 1978–; Governor, Glasgow Sch. of Art, 1976–87; Trustee: Nat. Heritage Meml Fund, 1984–; Nat. Galls of Scotland, 1986–. Dir, Third Eye Centre, 1978–81. Chm. Governors, High Sch. of Glasgow, 1979–; Mem. Court, Univ. of Glasgow, 1979–87. President: Stationers' Assoc. of GB and Ireland, 1965; Co. of Stationers of Glasgow, 1968–70; Glasgow High Sch. Club, 1970–72. HRSA 1987; HRGI 1987; Hon. FRIAS 1984. Hon. LLD: Strathclyde, 1986; Glasgow, 1988. *Recreations*: golf, cricket, theatre, art. *Address*: Macfarlane Group (Clansman) PLC, Sutcliffe Road, Glasgow G13 1AH; 50 Manse Road, Bearsden, Glasgow. *Clubs*: Art, Royal Scottish Automobile (Glasgow); Glasgow Golf.

McFARLANE OF LLANDAFF, Baroness *cr* 1979 (Life Peer), of Llandaff in the County of South Glamorgan; **Jean Kennedy McFarlane;** Professor and Head of Department of Nursing, University of Manchester, 1974–88, now Professor Emeritus; *b* 1 April 1926; *d* of late James and Elvina Alice McFarlane. *Educ*: Howell's Sch., Llandaff; Bedford and Birkbeck Colls, Univ. of London. MA, BSc(Soc); SRN, SCM, HV Tutor's Cert.; FRCN 1976; FCNA 1984. Staff Nurse, St Bartholomew's Hosp., 1950–51; Health Visitor, Cardiff CC, 1953–59; Royal Coll. of Nursing: Organising Tutor, Integrated Course, Educn Div., London, 1960–62; Educn Officer, Birmingham, 1962–66; Res. Project Ldr (DHSS sponsored), London, 1967–69; Dir of Educn, Inst. of Advanced Nursing Educn, London, 1969–71; Univ. of Manchester: Sen. Lectr in Nursing, Dept of Social and Preventive Medicine, 1971–73; Sen. Lectr and Head of Dept of Nursing, 1973–74. Member: Royal Commn on NHS, 1976–79; Commonwealth War Graves Commn, 1983–88. Chm., English Bd for Nursing, Midwifery and Health Visiting, 1980–83. Mem., Gen. Synod of C of E, 1990–. Hon. FRCP 1990. Hon. MSc Manchester, 1979; Hon. DSc Ulster, 1981; Hon. DEd CNAA, 1983; Hon. MD Liverpool, 1990. *Publications*: The Problems of Developing Criteria of Quality for Nursing Care (thesis), 1969; The Proper Study of the Nurse, 1970; (with G. Castledine) The Practice of Nursing using the Nursing Process, 1982. *Recreations*: music, walking, travelling, photography. *Address*: 5 Dovercourt Avenue, Heaton Mersey, Stockport SK4 3QB. *T*: 061–432 8367.

MACFARLANE, Prof. Alan Donald James, FRAI; FRHistS; FBA 1986; Professor of Anthropological Science, University of Cambridge, since 1991; *b* 20 Dec. 1941; *s* of Donald Kennedy Macfarlane and Iris Stirling Macfarlane; *m* 1st, 1966, Gillian Ions; one *d*; 2nd, 1981, Sarah Harrison. *Educ*: Sedbergh School; Worcester College, Oxford (MA, DPhil); LSE (MPhil); SOAS (PhD). University of Cambridge: Senior Research Fellow in History, King's College, 1971–74; Univ. Lectr in Social Anthropology, 1975–81; Reader in Historical Anthropology, 1981–91. Lectures: Frazer Meml, Liverpool Univ., 1974; Malinowski Meml, LSE, 1978. Rivers Meml Medal, RAI, 1984; William J. Goode Award, Amer. Sociol Assoc., 1987. *Publications*: Witchcraft in Tudor and Stuart England, 1970; The Family Life of Ralph Josselin, 1970; Resources and Population, 1976; (ed) The Diary of Ralph Josselin, 1976; Reconstructing Historical Communities, 1977; Origins of English Individualism, 1978; The Justice and the Mare's Ale, 1981; A Guide to English Historical Records, 1983; Marriage and Love in England, 1986; The Culture of Capitalism, 1987; The Cambridge Database System User Manual, 1990; The Nagas: hill peoples of North-east India, 1990. *Recreations*: walking, gardening, second-hand book hunting. *Address*: 25 Lode Road, Lode, near Cambridge CB5 9ER. *T*: Cambridge (0223) 811976.

MacFARLANE, Prof. Alistair George James, CBE 1987; FRS 1984; FEng 1981; FRSE; Principal and Vice-Chancellor of Heriot-Watt University, since 1989; *b* 9 May 1931; *s* of George R. MacFarlane; *m* 1954, Nora Williams; one *s*. *Educ*: Hamilton Academy; Univ. of Glasgow. BSc 1953, DSc 1969, Glasgow; PhD London 1964; MSc Manchester 1973; MA 1974, ScD 1979, Cantab. FIEE; FIEEE; FRSE 1990; CBIM 1991. Metropolitan-Vickers, Manchester, 1953–58; Lectr, Queen Mary Coll., Univ. of London, 1959–65, Reader 1965–66; Reader in Control Engrg, Univ. of Manchester Inst. of Sci. and Technology, 1966–69, Prof. 1969–74; Prof. of Engrg and Hd of Information Engrg Div., Univ. of Cambridge, 1974–88; Fellow, 1974–88, Vice-Master, 1980–88, Hon. Fellow, 1989–, Selwyn Coll., Cambridge. Chm., Cambridge Control Ltd, 1985–90; Non-Exec. Dir, Lothian and Edinburgh Enterprise Ltd, 1990–. Member: Council, SERC, 1981–85; Computer Board, 1983–88; Adv. Cttee for Safety of Nuclear Installations, 1987–90; Engineering Tech. Adv. Cttee, DTI, 1991–. *Publications*: Engineering Systems Analysis, 1964; Dynamical System Models, 1970; (with I. Postlethwaite) A Complex Variable Approach to the Analysis of Linear Multivariable Feedback Systems, 1979; (ed) Frequency-Response Methods in Control Systems, 1979; (ed) Complex Variable Methods for Linear Multivariable Feedback Systems, 1980; (with S. Hung) Multivariable Feedback: a quasi-classical approach, 1982; (with G. K. H. Pang) An Expert Systems Approach to Computer-Aided Design of Multivariable Systems, 1987. *Address*: Hermiston House, Hermiston, Edinburgh EH14 4AQ. *Club*: Caledonian.

MACFARLANE, Rev. Alwyn James Cecil; Parish Minister of Newlands (South), Church of Scotland, 1968–85; Chaplain to the Queen in Scotland, 1977; *b* 14 June 1922; *s* of James Waddell Macfarlane and Ada Cecilia Rankin; *m* 1953, Joan Cowell Harris; one *s* one *d*. *Educ*: Cargilfield Sch.; Rugby Sch.; Oxford Univ. (MA); Edinburgh Univ. Served War: N Africa, Italy, Greece; Liaison Officer in Black Watch with 12th Bde, 1942–46. Ordained, 1951; served in parishes in Ross-shire, Edinburgh, Glasgow, Australia. *Recreations*: photography, walking. *Address*: 4/9 Belhaven Place, Edinburgh EH10 5JN.

MACFARLANE, Anne Bridget; Master of the Court of Protection, since 1982; *b* 26 Jan. 1930; *d* of late Dr David Griffith and Dr Grace Griffith; *m* 1957, James Douglas Macfarlane; two *d*. *Educ*: nine schools; Bristol Univ. (LLB). Admitted Solicitor, 1954. HM Land Registry, 1966–75; Registrar, Bromley County Court, 1975–82. *Publication*: (contrib.) Atkin's Court Forms, 2nd edn 1983. *Recreation*: collecting Victorian tiles. *Address*: Stewart House, 24 Kingsway, WC2B 6JX. *T*: 071–269 7000. *Club*: Law Society.

MACFARLANE, Sir (David) Neil, Kt 1988; MP (C) Sutton and Cheam, since Feb. 1974; *b* 7 May 1936; *yr s* of late Robert and of Dulcie Macfarlane; *m* 1961, June Osmond King, Somerset; two *s* one *d*. *Educ*: St Aubyn's Prep. Sch.; Bancroft's, Woodford Green. Short Service Commission, Essex Regt, 1955–58; served TA, 265 LAA, RA, 1961–66. Joined Shell Mex and BP, 1959; contested (C): East Ham (North), 1970; Sutton and Cheam, by-election, 1972. Parly Under-Sec. of State, DoE, 1981–85 (with spec. responsibility for Sport, 1981–85, for Children's Play, 1983–85). Mem., All Party Select Cttee on Science and Technology, 1974–79; Parly Under Sec. of State (Dep. Minister for the Arts), DES, 1979–81. Chairman: Sports Aid Foundn, 1986–87; Golf Fund PLC; Vice-Pres. PGA, 1985–. Mem., National Trust, 1976–. *Publication*: Sport and Politics: a world divided, 1986. *Recreations*: golf, cricket-watching. *Address*: House of Commons, SW1A 0AA. *T*: 071–219 3404; 48 Benhill Avenue, Sutton, Surrey. *Clubs*: MCC, Lord's Taverners; Essex County Cricket; Royal & Ancient Golf; Huntercombe Golf; Sunningdale Golf; Wentworth Golf; Harlequins Rugby Football.

MACFARLANE, Sir George (Gray), Kt 1971; CB 1965; BSc; Dr Ing (Dresden); FEng; Member of the Board, British Telecommunications Corporation, 1981–84; Corporate Director, British Telecom plc, 1984–87; *b* 8 Jan. 1916; *s* of late John Macfarlane, Airdrie, Lanarks; *m* 1941, Barbara Grant, *d* of Thomas Thomson, Airdrie, Lanarks; one *s* one *d*. *Educ*: Airdrie Academy; Glasgow Univ.; Technische Hochschule, Dresden, Germany. FIMA; FPhysS. On scientific staff, Air Ministry Research Establishment, Dundee and Swanage, 1939–41; Telecommunications Research Establishment (TRE), Malvern, 1941–60; Deputy Chief Scientific Officer (Individual Merit Post), 1954–60; Deputy Director, National Physical Laboratory, 1960–62; Director, Royal Radar Establishment, 1962–67; Controller (Research), Min. of Technology and Min. of Aviation Supply, 1967–71; Controller, Research and Develt Establishments and Research, MoD, 1971–75. Member: PO Review Cttee, 1976–77; PO Bd, 1977–81; NEB, 1980–85 and NRDC, 1981–85 (now British Technology Gp). Mem., Bd of Trustees, Imperial War Museum, 1978–86. Deputy-Pres., IEE, 1976–78 (Vice-Pres., 1972–74), Hon. FIEE, 1988; Hunter Meml Lecturer, IEE, 1966; Council Mem., Fellowship of Engrg, 1982–87 (Vice-Pres. 1983–86). Hon. LLD Glasgow. Glazebrook Medal and Prize, Inst. of Physics, 1978. *Publications*: papers in IEE, Proc. Phys. Society, Phys. Review. *Recreations*: walking, gardening. *Address*: Red Tiles, 17 Orchard Way, Esher, Surrey KT10 9DY. *T*: Esher (0372) 463778. *Club*: Athenæum.

McFARLANE, Sir Ian, Kt 1984; Chairman and Managing Director: Southern Pacific Petroleum NL, since 1968; Central Pacific Minerals NL, since 1968; Chairman, Trans Pacific Consolidated Ltd, since 1964; *b* 25 Dec. 1923; *s* of Stuart Gordon McFarlane, CMG, MBE and Mary Grace McFarlane; *m* 1956, Ann, *d* of M. A. Shaw, Salt Lake City, USA; one *s* two *d. Educ:* Melbourne Grammar School; Harrow; Sydney Univ. (BSc, BE); MIT (MS). Served War of 1939–45, RANVR. Morgan Stanley & Co., 1949–59; Mem., Sydney Stock Exchange, 1959–64; Partner, Ord, Minnett, T. J. Thompson & Partners, 1959–64; Dep. Chm., Magellan Petroleum, 1964–70; Director: Trans City Discount Ltd, 1960–64; Consolidated Rutile Ltd, 1964–68; International Pacific Corp., 1967–73; Aust. Gen. Insurance Co., 1968–74; Mercantile Mutual Insurance Co., 1969–74; Concrete Construction, 1972–74; International Pacific Aust. Investments, 1972–73; Morgan Stanley Internat., NYC, 1976–80. Mem. Council, Imperial Soc. of Knights Bachelor, 1985–. Founder, Sir Ian McFarlane Travelling Professorship in Urology, 1980. Chm., Royal Brisbane Hosp. Foundn, 1985–. Life Governor, Royal Prince Alfred Hosp., Sydney, 1982; Founding Governor, St Luke's Hosp. Foundn, Sydney, 1982–. Fellow Commoner, Christ's Coll., Cambridge, 1987. Kentucky Col, 1984. *Address:* 40 Wentworth Road, Vaucluse, NSW 2030, Australia. *Clubs:* Australian (Sydney); Queensland (Brisbane); Commonwealth (Canberra); University (NY); Royal Sydney Golf; Royal Motor Yacht of NSW; Monaco Yacht.

McFARLANE, Prof. Ian Dalrymple, MBE 1946; FBA 1978; Professor of French Literature, University of Oxford, 1971–83, now Emeritus; Professorial Fellow, Wadham College, Oxford, 1971–83, now Emeritus Fellow; *b* 7 Nov. 1915; *s* of James Blair McFarlane and Valérie Edith Liston Dalrymple; *m* 1939, Marjory Nan Hamilton; one *s* one *d. Educ:* Lycée St-Charles, Marseilles; Tormore Sch., Upper Deal, Kent; Westminster Sch.; St Andrews Univ. MA 1st class Hons, 1938; Carnegie Research Scholar, 1938–39. Served 1st Bn Black Watch, RHR, 1940–45. Apptd Lectr in French, Cambridge Univ., 1945; Gonville and Caius College: elected Fellow, 1947 (Hon. Fellow, 1990); appointed Senior Tutor, 1956; Prof. of French Language and Literature, St Andrews, 1961–70. Zaharoff Lectr, Oxford, 1984; Hon. Faculty Prof., University Coll., Cardiff, 1984. Hon. Sen. Res. Fellow, Inst. of Romance Studies, Univ. of London. Member, Scottish Cert. of Educn Examination Board, 1964; Member Academic Planning Board, University of Stirling, 1964–67; Mem. Cttee on Research and Develt in Modern Languages, 1966. Pres., MHRA, 1986. Doctor of Univ. of Paris, 1950; Dr *hc*, Univ. of Tours, 1982; Hon. DLitt St Andrews, 1982. Officier des Palmes Académiques, 1971. *Publications:* critical edn of M. Scève's Délie, 1966; Renaissance France 1470–1589, 1974; Buchanan, 1981; The Entry of Henri II into Paris, 1549, 1982; various, in learned periodicals. *Recreations:* cricket, music. *Address:* Wadham College, Oxford OX1 3PN.

McFARLANE, James Sinclair, CBE 1986; CEng, FIM, CBIM; Director, Turriff Corporation plc, since 1988; Director General, Engineering Employers' Federation, 1982–89; *b* 8 Nov. 1925; *s* of John Mills McFarlane and Hannah McFarlane; *m* 1951, Ruth May Harden; three *d. Educ:* Manchester Grammar Sch.; Emmanuel Coll., Cambridge (MA, PhD). CEng, FIM 1961. ICI Ltd, 1949–53; Henry Wiggin & Co. Ltd, 1953–69; Chm. and Man. Dir, Smith-Clayton Forge Ltd (GKN Ltd), 1969–76; Man. Dir, Garringtons Ltd (GKN Ltd), 1976–77; Guest Keen & Nettlefolds Ltd: Gen. Man., Personnel, 1977–79; Exec. Dir, 1979–82. Mem., NEDC, 1982–89; a Civil Service Comr (pt-time), 1983–88. *Publications:* contrib. scientific and technical jls. *Recreation:* music. *Address:* 24 Broad Street, Ludlow, Shropshire SY8 1NJ. *T:* Ludlow (0584) 872495. *Clubs:* Caledonian, United Oxford & Cambridge University.

McFARLANE, Prof. James Walter; Professor of European Literature, University of East Anglia, 1964–82, now Emeritus; *b* 12 Dec. 1920; *s* of James and Florence McFarlane; *m* 1944, Lillie Kathleen Crouch; two *s* one *d. Educ:* Bede Grammar Sch., Sunderland; St Catherine's Society, Univ. of Oxford. MA, BLitt 1948. War service, Intell. Corps, 1941–46 (Major); Oxford Soccer blue, 1947; Lectr and Sen. Lectr, Dept of German and Scandinavian Studies, King's Coll., Univ. of Durham, later Univ. of Newcastle upon Tyne, 1947–63; University of East Anglia: Founding Dean of European Studies, 1964–68; Public Orator, 1964–68, 1974–75, 1978–79; Pro-Vice-Chancellor, 1968–71; Professorial Fellow, 1982–86. Vis. Prof., Univ. of Auckland, NZ, 1967; Herbert F. Johnson Vis. Res. Prof., Inst. for Res. in Humanities, Univ. of Wisconsin-Madison, 1983–84. Mem., BBC Gen. Adv. Council, 1970–75; Chm., East Anglia Regional Adv. Council, 1970–75; Chm., Hunworth Crafts Trust, 1973–77; Mem. Exec., Eastern Arts Assoc., 1977–82. Founder Trustee, Norwich Puppet Theatre, 1979; Chm., The Wells Centre, Norfolk, 1981–88. Editor, Scandinavica: an International Journal of Scandinavian Studies, 1975–; Man. Editor, Norvik Press, 1985–. Leverhulme Faculty Fellow in European Studies, 1971–72; Brit. Acad. Wolfson Fellow. Fellow, Det Norske Videnskaps-Akademie, Oslo, 1977; Corresp. Mem., Svenska Litteratursällskapet i Finland, Helsinki, 1977; Foreign Member: Royal Norwegian Soc. of Sciences and Letters, 1982; Royal Danish Acad. of Sciences and Letters, 1983. Hon. Mem., Phi Beta Kappa, 1984. Hon. DLitt Loughborough, 1990. Commander's Cross, Royal Norwegian Order of St Olav, 1975. *Publications:* Ibsen and the Temper of Norwegian Literature, 1960; Discussions of Ibsen, 1962; Henrik Ibsen, 1970; (with Malcolm Bradbury) Modernism: European Literature 1890–1930, 1976; Ibsen and Meaning, 1989; (editor and translator) The Oxford Ibsen, 1960–77: vol. 1, Early Plays, 1970; vol. 2, The Vikings at Helgeland, Love's Comedy, The Pretenders, 1962; vol. 3, Brand, Peer Gynt, 1972; vol. 4, The League of Youth, Emperor and Galilean, 1963; vol. 5, Pillars of Society, A Doll's House, Ghosts, 1961; vol. 6, An Enemy of the People, The Wild Duck, Rosmersholm, 1960; vol. 7, The Lady from the Sea, Hedda Gabler, The Master Builder, 1966; vol. 8, Little Eyolf, John Gabriel Borkman, When We Dead Awaken, 1977; (editor and translator with Janet Garton) Slaves of Love and other Norwegian short stories, 1982; *festschrift:* (ed J. Garton) Facets of European Modernism: essays in honour of James McFarlane, 1985; (ed with Harald Næss) Knut Hamsun's Letters, vol. 1, 1990; *translations:* Hamsun's Pan, 1955; Hamsun's Wayfarers, 1980; Obstfelder's A Priest's Diary, 1988. *Recreation:* domestic odd-jobbery. *Address:* The Croft, Stody, Melton Constable, Norfolk NR24 2EE. *T:* Melton Constable (0263) 860505.

MACFARLANE, Sir James (Wright), Kt 1973; PhD; FRSE; CEng, FIEE, FIMechE; JP; DL; Managing Director, Cathcart Investment Co. Ltd, since 1964; *b* 2 Oct. 1908; *s* of late James C. Macfarlane, OBE, MIEE, WhSch; *m* 1937, Claire Ross. *Educ:* Allan Glen's Sch.; Royal Technical Coll. (DRTC); Glasgow Univ. (PhD); London Univ. WhSch and WhSen.Sch. FIFire E. War of 1939–45: Home Guard (Major); Intell.; Lt-Col (TA) Comdg Renfrewshire Bn, Army Cadet Force. Apprentice, Engineer and Director, Macfarlane Engrg Co. Ltd, 1926–; Chm., Macfarlane Engrg Co. Ltd, Cathcart, 1967–69. Past Pres., Assoc. of County Councils in Scotland; Past Mem. various instns; Member: Royal Commn on the Police, 1960–62; Departmental Cttee on the Fire Service, 1968–70. JP 1940; entered local govt, 1944; DL 1962, Renfrewshire; Convener, County of Renfrew, 1967–73. Chm. of Governors, Paisley Coll. of Technology. *Publications:* numerous papers in IEE and IMechE Jls. *Recreations:* motor cycles and cars (vintage), sailing. *Address:* 2 Sandringham Court, Newton Mearns, Glasgow G77 5DT. *T:* 041–639 1842. *Clubs:* RNVR (Scotland); Royal Gourock Yacht (Gourock).

MACFARLANE, Sir Neil; *see* Macfarlane, Sir D. N.

MacFARLANE, Maj.-Gen. Robert Goudie, MBE 1952; FRCP; FRCPE; Deputy Secretary, Scottish Council for Postgraduate Medical Education, 1975–84; *b* 1 March 1917; *s* of late Archibald Forsyth MacFarlane and Jessie Robertson Goudie; *m* 1945, Mary Campbell Martin; three *s. Educ:* Hillhead High Sch., Glasgow; Glasgow Univ. MB, ChB, 1940; MD 1955; FRCPE 1964; MRCP 1970; FRCP 1979. Served War: commissioned RAMC, 1941; in Madagascar, India, Burma, 1941–45. Specialist in Medicine and Consultant Physician, 1948–; CO, British Mil. Hosp., Iserlohn, 1968–70; Prof. of Mil. Med., Royal Army Medical Coll., 1970–71; Consulting Physician, BAOR, 1971–73. Dir. of Army Medicine and Consulting Physician to the Army, 1973–74. QHP 1973. *Address:* 6 Redholm, Greenheads Road, North Berwick, East Lothian EH39 4RA.

MACFARLANE, Maj.-Gen. William Thomson, CB 1981; Consultant/Administrator, Sion College, since 1984; *b* Bath, 2 Dec. 1925; *s* of late James and Agnes Macfarlane; *m* 1955, Dr Helen D. Meredith; one *d.* Commissioned Royal Signals, 1947. Served Europe, Near East, ME, and Far East. Commanded 16th Parachute Bde Signal Squadron, 1961–63; Military Asst, Commander FARELF, 1964–66; Comd 1st Div. HQ and Signal Regt, BAOR, 1967–70; Services Mem., Cabinet Office Secretariat, 1970–72; Comd, Corps Royal Signals, 1972–73; Dir of Public Relations (Army), MoD, 1973–75; C of S, UKLF, 1976–78; Chief, Jt Services Liaison Organisation, Bonn, 1978–80. Exec. Dir, Hong Kong Resort Co. Ltd, 1981–84; Director: CITICARE (London) Ltd; Compton Manor Farms Ltd. Col Comdt, 1980–85, Rep. Col Comdt, 1985, Royal Corps of Signals. jssc; psc. FBIM. *Recreations:* golf, music. *Address:* Colts Paddock, Aveley Lane, Farnham, Surrey GU9 8PR. *Club:* Naval and Military.

MacFARQUHAR, Prof. Roderick Lemonde; Professor of Government, since 1984, Director of Fairbank Center for East Asian Research, since 1986, Leroy B. Williams Professor of History and Political Science, since 1990, Harvard University; *b* 2 Dec. 1930; *s* of Sir Alexander MacFarquhar, KBE, CIE, and of Berenice Whitburn; *m* 1964, Emily Jane Cohen; one *s* one *d. Educ:* Fettes Coll.; Oxford Univ. (BA.) Harvard Univ. (AM); LSE (PhD). Specialist on China, Daily Telegraph (and later Sunday Telegraph), 1955–61; Founding Editor, China Quarterly, 1959–68; Rockefeller Grantee, 1962; Reporter, BBC TV programme Panorama, 1963–64. Associate Fellow, St Antony's Coll., Oxford, 1965–68. Mem., Editorial Bd, New Statesman, 1965–69; Ford Foundation Grant, 1968; Senior Research Fellow, Columbia Univ., 1969; Senior Research Fellow, RIIA, 1971–74 (Mem. Council, 1978–83); Co-presenter, BBC Gen. Overseas Services 24 Hours prog., 1972–74, 1979–80. Governor, SOAS, 1978–83. Contested: (Lab) Ealing South, 1966; (Lab) Meriden, March 1968; (SDP) Derbys S, 1983. MP (Lab) Belper, Feb. 1974–1979; PPS to Minister of State, FCO, March 1974; resignation accepted, April 1975; reappointed June 1975; PPS to Sec. of State, DHSS, 1976–78. Member: N Atlantic Assembly, 1974–79; Select Cttee for Sci. and Technology, 1976–79; Trilateral Commn, 1976–(Mem. Exec. Cttee, 1976–84); Exec. Cttee, Fabian Soc., 1976–80. Leverhulme Res. Fellow, 1980–83; Fellow, Woodrow Wilson Center, Smithsonian Instn, 1980–81; Vis. Prof. of Govt, Harvard, 1982; Vis. Fellow, St Antony's Coll., Oxford, 1983; inaugurated Inchon Meml Lectureship, Korea Univ., 1987. *Publications:* The Hundred Flowers, 1960; The Sino-Soviet Dispute, 1961; Chinese Ambitions and British Policy (Fabian Pamphlet), 1966; (ed) China under Mao, 1966; Sino-American Relations, 1949–71, 1972; The Forbidden City, 1972; The Origins of the Cultural Revolution: Vol. 1, Contradictions among the People 1956–1957, 1974; Vol. 2, The Great Leap Forward 1958–1960, 1983; (ed jtly) Cambridge History of China, Vol. 14, 1987; (ed jtly) The Secret Speeches of Chairman Mao, 1989; articles in Foreign Affairs, The World Today, Atlantic Monthly, Pacific Affairs, Commentary, Newsweek, NY Review of Books, etc. *Recreations:* reading, listening to music, travel. *Address:* Fairbank Center, 1737 Cambridge Street, Cambridge, Mass 02138, USA.

McFEELY, Elizabeth Sarah Anne C.; *see* Craig McFeely.

McFETRICH, (Charles) Alan; Managing Partner, Coopers & Lybrand Deloitte, since 1990; *b* 15 Dec. 1940; *s* of late Cecil McFetrich, OBE, FCA and of Kathleen M. McFetrich (*née* Proom); *m* 1990, Janet Elizabeth Henkel (*née* Munro); two *s* one *d* from previous *m. Educ:* Oundle Sch.; Magdalene Coll., Cambridge. FCA. Trainee Accountant, Graham Proom & Smith, 1959–61 and 1964–66; Deloitte Haskins & Sells: Accountant, 1966–68; Consultant, 1968–73; Consultancy Partner, 1973–80; seconded to Dept of Industry, 1981–82; Nat. Operations Partner, 1983–85; Nat. Managing Partner, 1985–90. FRSA 1989. *Recreations:* gardening, theatre. *Address:* Coopers & Lybrand Deloitte, Plumtree Court, EC4A 4HT. *T:* 071–583 5000.

McGAHERN, John, FRSL; author; *b* 12 Nov. 1934; *s* of Francis McGahern and Susan McManus; *m* 1973, Madeline Green. Research Fellow, Univ. of Reading, 1968–71; O'Connor Prof., Colgate Univ., 1969, 1972, 1977, 1979 and 1983. Member: Aosdana Irish Acad of Letters. British Northern Arts Fellow, 1974–76. McCauley Fellowship, 1964; British Arts Council Award, 1967; Soc. of Authors Award, 1975; Amer. Irish Foundn Literary Award, 1985. *Publications:* The Barracks, 1962 (AE Meml Award, 1962); The Dark, 1965; Nightlines, 1970; The Leavetaking, 1975; Getting Through, 1978; The Pornographer, 1979; High Ground, 1985; The Rockingham Shoot, 1987; Amongst Women, 1990. *Address:* c/o Faber & Faber, 3 Queen Square, WC1N 3AU.

McGARRITY, J(ames) Forsyth, CB 1981; MA, MEd, BSc; HM Senior Chief Inspector of Schools (Scotland), 1973–81; *b* 16 April 1921; *s* of late James McGarrity and Margaret Davidson; *m* 1951, Violet S. G. Philp, MA; one *s* one *d. Educ:* Bathgate Academy; Glasgow Univ. Schoolmaster, 1949–57; HM Inspector of Schools, 1957–68; HM Chief Inspector of Schools, 1968–73. *Recreations:* golf, gardening. *Address:* 30 Oatlands Park, Linlithgow, Scotland EH49 6AS. *T:* Linlithgow (0506) 843258.

McGARRY, Ian; General Secretary, British Actors' Equity Association, since 1991; *b* 27 Feb. 1941; *s* of John and Jean McGarry; *m* 1964, Christine Smith (marr. diss. 1989); one *s. Educ:* Chichester High Sch.; Lewes County Grammar Sch. Labour Party Constituency Agent, Putney, 1964–76; Asst General Sec., Equity, 1976–91. *Recreations:* golf, football (spectator), horse racing. *Address:* 8 Harley Street, W1N 2AB. *T:* 071–637 9311.

McGARVEY, Alan; independent specialist, industrial development and investment, since 1990; Senior Consultant, Warwick Research Institute; *b* 22 June 1942; *s* of William Johnson McGarvey and Rosina McGarvey; *m* 1967, Eileen Cook. *Educ:* Wallsend Grammar Sch.; Coll. of Further Educn; Newcastle Univ. (BSc); Cranfield Sch. of Management (MBA). C. A. Parsons, 1958–64 (apprentice); RTZ, 1968–71; Decca Gp, 1972–76; MK Electric, 1976–78; Director, Small Company Div., NEB, 1978–82; Chief Exec., Greater London Enterprise Bd, 1982–86; management consultant, 1986–88; Man. Dir, Greater Manchester Econ. Develt Ltd, 1987–90. Labour Party, 1974–; Mem., Wandsworth Borough Council, 1981–86 (Dep. Opposition Leader, 1982–83); Chm., Battersea Constituency Labour Parties, 1978–82. Exec. Mem., Wandsworth CRC, 1973–82; Board Member: Battersea Arts Centre Trust, 1982–88; Northern Chamber Orch., 1988–. Member: Jt Governing Board, Centre for Development of Industry (EEC-ACP Lomé), 1981–90; Adv. Council, Cttee for Industrial Co-operation (EEC-ACP), 1990–. Governor, Polytech. of South Bank, 1985–87; Chm. Govs, Medlock Sch., Manchester, 1989–. *Recreations:* community affairs, home and garden, science fiction;

amateur sculptor. *Address:* 11 Old Hall Mews, Old Hall Lane, Bolton BL1 7PW. *T:* Bolton (0204) 40141, *Fax:* Bolton (0204) 40723.

McGEE, Prof. James O'Donnell; Professor of Morbid Anatomy, University of Oxford, Fellow of Linacre College, Oxford, since Oct. 1975; *b* 27 July 1939; *s* of Michael and Bridget McGee; *m* 1961, Anne Lee; one *s* two *d*. *Educ:* Univ. of Glasgow. MB, ChB, PhD, MD; MA (Oxon). FRCPath 1986; FRCPGlas 1989. Various appts in Univ. Dept of Pathology, Royal Infirmary, Glasgow, 1962–69; Roche Inst. of Molecular Biology, Nutley, NJ: MRC Fellow 1969–70; Vis. Scientist 1970–71; Distinguished Vis. Scientist, 1989; Dept of Pathology, Royal Infirmary, Glasgow: Lectr 1971–74; Sen. Lectr, 1974–75. Member: Scientific Cttee, Cancer Res. Campaign, 1978–; Cttee on Safety of Medicines, 1987–89 (Safety and Efficacy Sub Cttee, 1984–87); Kettle Meml Lectr, RCPath, 1980; Annual Guest Lecturer: Royal Coll. of Physicians, Ireland, 1986; Royal Acad. of Medicine (Ireland), 1985. Bellahouston Gold Medal, Glasgow Univ., 1973. *Publications:* Biopsy Pathology of Liver, 1980, 2nd edn 1988; In Situ Hybridisation: principles and practice, 1990; Oxford Textbook of Pathology, 1992; papers in scientific jls on liver disease and non-istopic methods of gene detection. *Recreations:* talking with my family, swimming. *Address:* Nuffield Department of Pathology and Bacteriology, Level 1, John Radcliffe Hospital, Headington, Oxford OX3 9DU.

McGEOCH, Vice-Adm. Sir Ian (Lachlan Mackay), KCB 1969 (CB 1966); DSO 1943; DSC 1943; Director, Midar Systems Ltd, since 1986; *b* 26 March 1914; 3rd *s* of L. A. McGeoch of Dalmuir; *m* 1937, Eleanor Somers, *d* of Rev. Canon Hugh Farrie; two *s* two *d*. *Educ:* Pangbourne Coll. Joined RN, 1932. Comd HM Submarine Splendid, 1942–43; Staff Officer (Ops) 4th Cruiser Sqdn, 1944–45; Comd: HMS Fernie, 1946–47; 4th Submarine Squadron, 1949–51; 3rd Submarine Squadron, 1956–57; Dir of Undersurface Warfare, Admiralty, 1959; IDC 1961; Comd HMS Lion 1962–64; Admiral Pres., RNC, Greenwich, 1964–65; Flag Officer Submarines, 1966–67; Flag Officer, Scotland and Northern Ireland, 1968–70. Trustee, Imperial War Mus., 1977–87. Mem., The Queen's Body Guard for Scotland, Royal Co. of Archers, 1969–. MPhil Edinburgh, 1975. FNI 1986. Editor, The Naval Review, 1972–80. *Publications:* (jtly) The Third World War: a future history, 1978; The Third World War: the untold story, 1982; An Affair of Chances, 1991. *Recreations:* sailing, music. *Address:* c/o Coutts & Co., 440 Strand, WC2R 0QS. *Clubs:* Army and Navy, Special Forces; Royal Yacht Squadron, Royal Naval Sailing Association (Cdre 1968–70), Royal Cruising.

McGEOUGH, Prof. Joseph Anthony, CEng, FIMechE, FIProdE, MIM; Regius Professor of Engineering and Head of Department of Mechanical Engineering at University of Edinburgh, since 1983; *b* 29 May 1940; *s* of late Patrick Joseph McGeough and Gertrude (*née* Darroch); *m* 1972, Brenda Nicholson; two *s* one *d*. *Educ:* St Michael's Coll., Irvine; Glasgow Univ. (BSc, PhD); Aberdeen Univ. (DSc). Vacation-apprentice, Malcolm & Allan Ltd, 1957–61; Research Demonstrator, Leicester Univ., 1966; Sen. Res. Fellow, Queensland Univ., 1967; Res. Metallurgist, International Research & Development Co. Ltd, Newcastle upon Tyne, 1968–69; Sen. Res. Fellow, Strathclyde Univ., 1969–72; Lectr 1972–77, Sen. Lectr 1977–80, Reader 1980–83, Dept of Engineering, Aberdeen Univ. Royal Society/SERC Industrial Fellow, 1987–89. Mem., Technical Adv. Cttee, Scottish Centre of Agricultural Engineering, 1987–; Chm., Edinburgh and SE Scotland Panel, IMechE, 1988– (Vice-Chm., Scottish Branch, 1991). Chm., Dyce Academy College Council, 1980–83; Hon. Vice-Pres., Aberdeen Univ. Athletic Assoc., 1981–91; Hon. Pres., Lichfield Sci. and Engrg Soc., 1988–89. Editor, Processing of Advanced Materials, 1991–. FRSE 1990. *Publications:* Principles of Electrochemical Machining, 1974; Advanced Methods of Machining, 1988; papers mainly in Journals of: Mech. Engrg Science, Inst. of Mathematics and its Applications, Applied Electrochemistry; contrib. Encyclopaedia Britannica; various patents. *Recreations:* gardening, golf, athletics. *Address:* 39 Dreghorn Loan, Colinton, Edinburgh EH13 0DF. *T:* 031–441 1302.

McGEOWN, Prof. Mary Graham, (Mrs J. M. Freeland), CBE 1985; FRCP, FRCPE, FRCPI; Professorial Fellow, Queen's University of Belfast, since 1988; *b* 19 July 1923; *d* of James Edward McGeown and Sarah Graham Quinn; *m* 1949, Joseph Maxwell Freeland (*d* 1982); three *s*. *Educ:* Lurgan College; Queen's University of Belfast (MB, BCh, BAO, with hons, 1946; MD, PhD). House Physician and Surgeon, Royal Victoria Hosp., Belfast, 1947–48; Sen. House Physician, Royal Belfast Hosp. for Sick Children, 1948; Asst Lectr in Pathology, 1948–50, in Biochemistry, 1950–53, QUB; res. grant, MRC, 1953–56; Res. Fellow, Royal Victoria Hosp., 1956–58; Belfast City Hospital: Sen. Hosp. MO, 1958–62; Consultant Nephrologist, 1962–88; Physician in Admin. Charge, Renal Unit, 1968–88. Hon. Reader in Nephrology, QUB, 1972–87. Chm., UK Transplant Management Cttee, 1983–91; Hon. Treas., Renal Assoc., 1986–89 (Pres., 1983–86); Pres., Ulster Med. Soc., 1985–86. Chm., Corrigan Club, 1987. Mem., Unrelated Living Transplants Regulatory Authority, 1990–; Hon. Member: British Transplantation Soc.; Renal Assoc.; European Dial. Transplant Assoc.; European Renal Assoc. Graves Lectr, Royal Acad. of Medicine, Ireland, 1963. Hon. DSc New Univ. of Ulster, 1983; Hon. MSc QUB, 1991. *Publications:* Clinical Management of Electrolyte Disorders, 1983; numerous papers and chapters in books on calcium metabolism, renal stones, phosphate metabolism, parathyroid function and disease, renal transplantation, kidney diseases. *Recreations:* gardening, antique collecting, genealogy. *Address:* 14 Osborne Gardens, Belfast BT9 6LE. *T:* Belfast (0232) 669918. *Club:* Commonwealth Trust.

McGHEE, George Crews, Legion of Merit; businessman; former diplomat; Director: Mobil Oil Co., 1969–82; Procter and Gamble Co., 1969–82; American Security & Trust Co., 1969–82; Trans World Airlines, 1976–82; *b* Waco, Texas, 10 March 1912; *s* of George Summers McGhee and Magnolia (*née* Spruce); *m* 1938, Cecilia Jeanne DeGolyer; two *s* four *d*. *Educ:* Southern Methodist Univ., Dallas; Univ. of Oklahoma; Oxford Univ. (Rhodes Schol.); Univ. of London. BS (Oklahoma) 1933; DPhil (Oxon) 1937. Served with US Navy, 1943–45 (Asiatic ribbon with three battle stars). Geologist and geophysicist, 1930–40; Oil producer, sole owner, McGhee Production Co., 1940–. Special Asst to Under-Sec of State for Economic Affairs, 1946; Coordinator for Aid to Greece and Turkey, 1947; Asst Sec. of State for Near Eastern, South Asian and African Affairs, 1949; US Ambassador to Turkey, 1951–53; Consultant, Nat. Security Council, 1958; Mem. President's Cttee to Study Mil. Asst Program, 1958; Counselor of Dept of State and Chm. of State Dept Policy Planning Council, 1961; Under-Sec. of State for Political Affairs, 1961; Bd, Panama Canal Co., 1962; US Ambassador to the Federal Republic of Germany, 1963–68; Ambassador-at-Large, 1968–69. Chairman: English Speaking Union of US, 1969–74; Business Council for Internat. Understanding, 1969–73; Vice-Chm., Inst. for Study of Diplomacy, 1978–; Member Board: Geo. C. Marshall Res. Foundn, 1972–85; Amer. Council on Germany, 1969–; Resources for Future, 1977–82; Asia Foundn, 1974–84; Atlantic Council, 1975–; Atlantic Inst. for Internat. Affairs, 1977–; Smithsonian Nat. Associates, 1971– (Chm., 1975–76); Population Crisis Cttee, 1969–82; Council of Amer. Ambassadors, 1983–; Amer. Inst. for Contemp. German Studies, 1983–. Member: Inst. of Turkish Studies, 1983–86; Sackler Gall. Vis. Cttee, Smithsonian Instn. Trustee: Duke Univ.; Cttee for Economic Develt, 1957–72; Aspen Inst. for Humanistic Studies, 1958–; Salzburg Seminar, 1969–71; Nat. Civil Service League, 1969–71; Folger Library Council, 1983–85. Chm., Saturday Review World, 1974–77. Hon. Fellow, Queen's Coll., Oxford, 1969. Distinguished Service Citation, Univ. of Oklahoma, 1952; Hon. DCL, Southern Methodist Univ., 1953; Hon. LLD: Tulane Univ., 1957; Univ. of Maryland, 1965; Hon. DSc, Univ. of Tampa, 1969. Ouissam Alaouite Cherifien, Govt Morocco, 1950; Hon. Citizen, Ankara, Turkey, 1954; Outstanding Citizen Award, Amer. Friends of Turkey, 1983. *Publications:* Envoy to the Middle World, 1983; (ed) Diplomacy for the Future, 1987; At the Creation of a New Germany, 1989; (ed) National Interest and Global Goals, 1989; The US-Turkish-NATO Middle East Connection, 1990; contribs to Foreign Affairs, Gewerkschaftliche Rundschau, Werk und Wir, Europa Archiv, Universitas, Ruperto-Carola Weltraumfahrt-Raketentechnik, Europa, Washington Post, New York Times, etc. *Recreations:* hunting, tennis, photography. *Address:* 2808 N Street, NW, Washington, DC 20007, USA; Farmer's Delight, Middleburg, Va, USA. *Clubs:* Bohemian (California); Metropolitan, Cosmos (Washington, DC); Century Association (New York); Colonnade (Univ. of Virginia); Mill Reef (Antigua).

McGHIE, James Ironside, CMG 1973; HM Diplomatic Service, retired; *b* 12 Oct. 1915; *s* of William I. McGhie and Annie E. Ratcliffe; *m* 1946, Ellen-Johanne Gran, *d* of Maj. T. Gran, MC, Norway, and Ingeborg Gran (*née* Meinich); two *s* one *d*. *Educ:* King Henry VIII Sch., Coventry. Journalist, 1933–39. Army, 1940–46, attached Royal Norwegian Army, 1943–46. Entered Foreign Service, 1946; served: Stockholm, Helsinki, FO, Tokyo, FO, Singapore; Dir, British Information Services, Saigon; Head of Chancery, Bucharest; Consul-General, Seattle; Counsellor, Commercial, Stockholm; Minister (Commercial and Econ.), Tokyo; retired, 1975. Special Advr on Japanese market to BOTB, 1975–77; Co-Chm., Japan Task Force, 1976–77. Order of the Rising Sun (Japan) 3rd class, 1975. *Recreations:* Scandinavian studies and translations. *Address:* Poplars, South Street, Faversham, Kent ME13 9NS. *T:* Canterbury (0227) 751424.

McGHIE, James Marshall; QC (Scot.) 1983; *b* 15 Oct. 1944; *s* of James Drummond McGhie and Jessie Eadie Bennie; *m* 1968, Ann Manuel Cockburn; one *s* one *d*. *Educ:* Perth Acad.; Edinburgh Univ. (LLB Hons). Called to the Scottish Bar, 1969; Advocate-depute, 1983–86. Pt-time Chm., Medical Appeal Tribunal, 1987–. *Recreations:* dining and Dunning. *Address:* 3 Lauder Road, Edinburgh EH9 2EW. *T:* 031–667 8325.

MacGIBBON, Dr Barbara Haig, (Mrs John Roberts), CB 1988; FRCPath; part-time Research Fellow (Toxicology), Robens Institute, Surrey University, since 1988; Assistant Director (Medical), National Radiological Protection Board, since 1988; *b* 7 Feb. 1928; *d* of Ronald Ross MacGibbon and Margaret Fraser; *m* 1954, John Roberts; one *s* one *d*. *Educ:* Lady Margaret Hall, Oxford; University College Hosp. Registrar, then Res. Assistant, Dept of Haematology, Royal Postgraduate Med. Sch., 1957–64; Sen. Registrar, Sen. Lectr/Hon. Consultant, then Sen. Res. Fellow, Dept of Haematology, St Thomas' Hosp. Med. Sch., 1969–79; SMO, then PMO, Toxicology and Environmental Health, DHSS, 1979; SPMO, DHSS, 1983–88. *Publications:* articles in various med. jls. *Address:* c/o National Radiological Protection Board, Chilton, Oxon OX11 0RQ.

McGILL, Angus, MBE 1990; journalist; *b* 26 Nov. 1927; *s* of Kenneth and Janet McGill. *Educ:* Warehousemen, Clerks' and Drapers' Schools, Addington, Surrey. Reporter, Shields Gazette, 1944; Army service; feature writer, Evening Chronicle, Newcastle, 1948; Londoner's Diary, Evening Standard, 1957; columnist, Evening Standard, 1961–. British Press Award, descriptive writer of the Year, 1968. *Publications:* Augusta, daily comic strip (drawn by Dominic Poelsma), 1968–; Yea Yea Yea (novel), 1969; (with Kenneth Thomson) Live Wires, 1982. *Address:* 83 Winchester Court, Vicarage Gate, W8 4AF. *T:* 071–937 2166; Ford Manor, Dormansland, Lingfield, Surrey. *T:* Lingfield (0342) 835047.

MacGILL, George Roy Buchanan, CBE 1965; General Manager, Cumbernauld Development Corporation, 1956–70; Deputy Chairman, Scottish Special Housing Association, 1971–76; *b* 20 Dec. 1905; *s* of George Buchanan MacGill; *m* 1934, Jean Ferguson Anderson; two *d*. *Educ:* Glasgow High Sch. Chartered Accountant, 1928. FIMTA 1938. Town Chamberlain, Airdrie, 1932; Burgh Chamberlain, Dunfermline, 1947. *Recreations:* golf, music. *Address:* 28 Roman Court, Bearsden, Glasgow.

McGILL, Maj.-Gen. Nigel Harry Duncan, CB 1966; Chief of Staff to Commandant-General, Royal Marines, 1967–68, retired, 1968; *b* 15 Oct. 1916; *s* of Lt-Col H. R. McGill; *m* 1944, Margaret Constance Killen; two *s* one *d*. *Educ:* Victoria Coll., Jersey. Commissioned 2nd Lt RM 1934; Maj.-Gen. 1964; Comdr, Portsmouth Group, RM, 1964–67. Representative Col Comdt RM, 1977–78. Exec., Rolls Royce Ltd, 1968–78. *Recreation:* cricket. *Address:* Alderwood, Manor Farm Road, Fordingbridge, Hants.

McGILL, Rt. Rev. Stephen; Bishop of Paisley, (RC), 1968–88, now Bishop Emeritus; *b* Glasgow, 4 Jan. 1912; *s* of Peter McGill and Charlotte Connolly. *Educ:* St Aloysius', Glasgow; Blairs College, Aberdeen; Coutances, France; Institut Catholique, Paris. Ordained Priest of St Sulpice, 1936. STL Paris. St Mary's College, Blairs, Aberdeen: Spiritual Director, 1940–51; Rector, 1951–60; Bishop of Argyll and the Isles, 1960–68. *Address:* 13 Newark Street, Greenock PA16 7UH.

McGILLIGAN, Denis Brian; Assistant Solicitor, Ministry of Agriculture, Fisheries and Food, 1973–83; *b* 26 June 1921; *s* of Michael McGilligan, SC, and Mary Georgina McGilligan (*née* Musgrave); *m* 1952, Hazel Patricia Pakenham Keady; one *s* two *d*. *Educ:* St Gerard's, Bray, Co. Wicklow; Trinity Coll., Dublin (BA). Practised at Irish Bar, 1945–52; Crown Counsel, Sarawak, and Dep. Legal Adviser, Brunei, 1952–58; Senior Magistrate, Sarawak, 1958–59; Acting Puisne Judge, Combined Judiciary, 1959–60; Senior Magistrate, Sarawak, 1960–63; Puisne Judge, Combined Judiciary of Sarawak, North Borneo and Brunei, March, 1963; Judge of the High Court in Borneo, Malaysia, 1963–66. Called to the Bar, Gray's Inn, 1966. *Recreations:* golf, swimming, walking, reading. *Address:* Wychbury, Ringmore Drive, Bigbury on Sea, Devon TQ7 4AU. *T:* Bigbury (0548) 810604.

MacGILLIVRAY, Barron Bruce, FRCP; Consultant in Clinical Neurophysiology and Neurology, Royal Free Hospital, since 1964 (Dean, School of Medicine, 1975–89); Consultant in Clinical Neurophysiology, National Hospital for Nervous Diseases, since 1971; *b* 21 Aug. 1927; *s* of late John MacGillivray and of Doreene (*née* Eastwood), S Africa; *m* 1955, Ruth Valentine; two *s* one *d*. *Educ:* King Edward VII Sch., Johannesburg; Univ. of Witwatersrand (BSc Hons 1949); Univ. of Manchester; Univ. of London (MB, BS 1962). FRCP 1973. House Surg., House Phys., Manchester Royal Infirm., 1955–56; RMO, Stockport and Stepping Hill Hosp., 1957–59; Registrar, subseq. Sen. Registrar, Nat. Hosp. for Nervous Diseases, Queen Sq., London, 1959–64; Res. Fellow, UCLA, 1964–65.Pro-Vice Chancellor, Medicine, Univ. of London, 1985–87. Member: Camden and Islington AHA(T), 1975–78; NE Thames RHA, 1979–84; CVCP, 1983–87; Senate, Collegiate Council, Univ. of London; Univ. rep., Council, Sch. of Pharmacy and British Postgraduate Med. Fedn; Examr and Teacher, Univ. of London. Pres., Electrophys. Technicians Assoc., 1976–82. FRSocMed; FRSA. *Publications:* papers in sci. jls on cerebral electrophysiol., epilepsy, computing and cerebral death. *Recreations:* flying, photography, D-I-Y. *Address:* Rosslyn Tower, 18 St John's Avenue, Putney, SW15 2AA. *T:* 081–788 5213.

MacGILLIVRAY, Prof. Ian, MD, FRCP; FRCOG; Regius Professor of Obstetrics and Gynæcology, University of Aberdeen, 1965–84 (Dean of Medical Faculty, 1976–79), now Emeritus Professor; *b* 25 Oct. 1920; *yr s* of W. and A. MacGillivray; *m* 1950, Edith Mary Margaret Cook; one *s* twin *d. Educ:* Vale of Leven Academy, Alexandria; University of Glasgow (MB, ChB 1944; MD 1953); MRCOG 1949, FRCOG 1959; FRCPGlas 1973. Gardiner Research Schol., 1949–51, Lectr in Midwifery, 1951–53, Univ. of Glasgow; Senior Lecturer: in Obstetrics and Gynæcology, Univ. of Bristol, 1953–55; in Midwifery and Gynæcology, Univ. of Aberdeen, 1955–61; Prof. of Obstetrics and Gynæcology, University of London, at St Mary's Hospital Medical Sch., 1961–65. Mem., GMC, 1979–84. Founder Pres., Internat. Soc. for Study of Hypertension in Pregnancy, 1976–80; Pres., Internat. Soc. for Twin Studies, 1980–83; Mem. Council, RCOG, 1974–80. *Publications:* Outline of Human Reproduction, 1963; Combined Textbook of Obstetrics and Gynaecology, 1976; Human Multiple Reproduction, 1976; Pre-eclampsia: the hypertensive disease of pregnancy, 1983; contrib. to: British Medical Journal, Lancet, Journal of Obstetrics and Gynæcology of the British Empire; Clinical Science. *Address:* Errogie, 35A Coombe Lane, Stoke Bishop, Bristol BS9 2BL. *T:* Bristol (0272) 686218.

McGILLIVRAY, Robert, CEng, FICE, FIWEM; Chief Engineer (Under Secretary), Scottish Development Department, 1987–91; *b* 11 May 1931; *o s* of late William Gilchrist McGillivray and of Janet Love Jamieson; *m* 1955, Pauline, *e d* of late Alexander Davie; one *s. Educ:* Boroughmuir Sch., Edinburgh; Univ. of Edinburgh (BSc CivEng.). National Service, 1949–51. Training with J. & A. Leslie & Reid, CE, 1955–57; Asst Engr, Midlothian CC, 1957–60; CE, Dept of Agric. & Fisheries for Scotland, 1960–72; Scottish Development Department: Prin. CE, 1972–75; Engrg Inspector, 1976–80; Asst Chief Engr, 1980–85; Dep. Chief Engr, 1985–87. *Publication:* A History of the Clan MacGillivray (with George B. Macgillivray), 1973. *Recreations:* music, genealogy, Highland history. *Club:* Commonwealth Trust.

McGILVRAY, Prof. James William; Professor of Economics, University of Strathclyde, since 1988; *b* 21 Feb. 1938; *m* 1966, Alison Ann Wingfield; one *s* one *d. Educ:* St Columba's Coll., Dublin; Univ. of Edinburgh (MA); Trinity Coll., Dublin (MLitt). Lectr in Econs, TCD, 1962–69; Res. Fellow, Harvard Univ., 1969–70; Sen. Lectr, Univ. of Stirling, 1970–75; Res. Prof., 1975–80, Dir, 1980–85, Fraser of Allander Inst., Univ. of Strathclyde; Dir of Econs, Dar Al-Handasah Consultants, 1985–88. *Publications:* Irish Economic Statistics, 1968, 2nd edn 1983; Use and Interpretation of Medical Statistics (with G. J. Bourke), 1969, 4th edn 1991; articles in Econometrica, Economic Jl, Rev. of Econs and Statistics, Jl of Reg. Sci., etc. *Recreations:* golf, gardening. *Address:* Gartinstarry Lodge, Buchlyvie, Stirling FK8 3PD. *Clubs:* National Liberal; Fitzwilliam (Dublin)

MacGINNIS, Francis Robert, CMG 1979; HM Diplomatic Service, retired; Minister and Deputy Commandant, British Military Government, Berlin, 1977–83; *b* 6 March 1924; *s* of late Dr Patrick MacGinnis, Murray House, Chesterfield; *m* 1955, Carolyn, *d* of late Col D. W. McEnery, USA; three *s* two *d. Educ:* Stonyhurst; Merton Coll., Oxford (MA). Served with Rifle Bde, 1942–47 (Temp. Captain). Joined HM Foreign (subseq. Diplomatic) Service, 1949; served in London, Washington, Paris and Warsaw; Dir-Gen., British Information Services, New York, 1968–72; Counsellor, Bonn, 1972–76; RCDS, 1976. *Address:* Boîte Postale 47, Fayence 83440, Var, France. *T:* 94-76-17-05. *Club:* Travellers'.

McGIRR, Prof. Edward McCombie, CBE 1978; BSc, MD Glasgow; FRCP, FRCPE, FRCPGlas; FACP (Hon.); FFCM; FRSE; Dean, 1974–81, Administrative Dean, 1978–81, and Professor of Administrative Medicine, 1978–81 now Professor Emeritus, Faculty of Medicine, University of Glasgow; Physician, Glasgow Royal Infirmary, 1952–81; Honorary Consultant Physician to the Army in Scotland, 1975–81; *b* 15 June 1916; *yr s* of William and Ann McGirr, Hamilton, Lanarkshire; *m* 1949, Diane Curzon, *y c* of Alexander Woods, MBE, TD, DL, and Edith E. C. Woods, Birmingham and London; one *s* three *d. Educ:* Hamilton Academy; Glasgow Univ. BSc 1937; MB, ChB (Hons) Glasgow, 1940; MD (Hons) and Bellahouston Medal, 1960. Served RAMC, 1941–46, in UK, India, Burma, Siam, Indo-China; Medical Specialist; demobilized with hon. rank of Major. Glasgow University: various appointments incl. Lectr and Sen. Lectr in Medicine, at Royal Infirmary, Glasgow, 1947–61; Muirhead Prof. of Medicine, 1961–78. Visitor, Royal Coll. of Physicians and Surgeons of Glasgow, 1968–70, President 1970–72. Member: Medical Appeals Tribunals, 1961–88; Nat. Radiological Protection Bd, 1976–83; Scottish Health Service Planning Council, 1977–84 (Chm., 1978–84); Nat. Med. Consultative Cttee, 1977–81; Med. Sub-Cttee, UGC, 1977–81; GNC for Scotland, 1978–83; Greater Glasgow Health Bd, 1979–85; Nat. Bd for Nursing, Midwifery and Health Visiting for Scotland, 1980–83; Cttee of ten, Tenovus-Scotland, 1981–89; BBC/IBA Scottish Appeals Adv. Cttee, 1982–86; Chairman: Scottish Council for Postgrad. Med. Educn, 1979–85; Scottish Council for Opportunities for Play Experience, 1985–87; Professional Adv. Panel, Prince and Princess of Wales Hospice, 1985–87; Working Party on Play in Scotland, 1986–87; Clyde Estuary Amenity Council, 1986–90. Member: Assoc. of Physicians of Gt Britain and Ireland, 1955– (mem. of editorial panel, Quarterly Journal of Medicine, 1968–76; Mem. Council, 1972–76; Hon. Mem., 1990–); Scottish Soc. of Physicians; Scottish Soc. for Experimental Med. (Treas., 1960–66); Pres., Harveian Soc. of Edin., 1979; Corresp. Member: Amer. Thyroid Assoc.; Medical Research Soc. (mem. of council, 1967–69); Royal Medico-Chirurgical Soc. of Glasgow (Pres., 1965–66). *Publications:* chiefly in relation to thyroid gland dysfunction, nuclear medicine, medical education and policy planning in the NHS. *Recreations:* family life, curling. *Address:* Anchorage House, Bothwell, by Glasgow G71 8NF. *T:* Bothwell (0698) 852194. *Club:* Royal Scottish Automobile.

McGIVERN, Eugene; Under Secretary, Board of Inland Revenue, since 1986; *b* 15 Sept. 1938; *s* of late James McGivern and of Eileen McGivern; *m* 1960, Teresa Doran; two *s* one *d. Educ:* St Mary's Grammar School, Belfast. Joined Inland Revenue, 1955; seconded to Welsh Office as Private Sec. to Minister of State, 1967–69; Inland Revenue, 1969–. *Address:* Board of Inland Revenue, Somerset House, Strand, WC2R 1LB. *T:* 071–438 6622.

McGLASHAN, John Reid Curtis, CBE 1974; HM Diplomatic Service, retired 1979; *b* 12 Dec. 1921; *s* of late John Adamson McGlashan and Emma Rose May McGlashan; *m* 1947, Dilys Bagnall (*née* Buxton Knight); one *s* two *d. Educ:* Fettes; Christ Church, Oxford (Rugger Blue, 1945). RAF (Bomber Command), 1940–45 (POW, 1941–45). Entered Foreign Service, 1953; Baghdad, 1955; Tripoli, 1963; Madrid, 1968; Counsellor, FCO, 1970–79. *Recreations:* gardening, reading. *Address:* Allendale, Selsey Bill, West Sussex PO20 9DB. *Club:* Vincent's (Oxford).

MacGLASHAN, Maureen Elizabeth; HM Diplomatic Service; Head, Western European Department, Foreign and Commonwealth Office, since 1991; *b* 7 Jan. 1938; *d* of Kenneth and Elizabeth MacGlashan. *Educ:* Luton High Sch.; Girton Coll., Cambridge (MA, LLM). Joined FO, 1961; 2nd Sec., Tel Aviv, 1964–67; FCO, 1967–72; Head of Chancery, East Berlin, 1973–75; UK Representation to EEC, 1975–77; seconded to Home Civil Service, 1977–82; Counsellor, Bucharest, 1982–86; Asst Dir, Res. Centre for Internat. Law, and bye-Fellow, Girton Coll., Cambridge Univ., 1986–90; Counsellor, Consul-Gen. and Dep. Head of Mission, Belgrade, 1990. Ed., Iran–US Claims Tribunal Reports, vols 8–22. *Publication:* (trans.) Weil, Maritime Delimitation, Consolidated Index to the International Law Reports, vols 36–80. *Address:* c/o Foreign and Commonwealth Office, SW1A 2AH. *Club:* University Women's.

McGLASHAN, Prof. Maxwell Len, FRSC; Professor of Chemistry and Head of the Department of Chemistry, University College London, 1974–89, now Professor Emeritus; Hon. Research Fellow, since 1989; *b* 1 April 1924; *s* of late Leonard Day McGlashan and late Margaret Cordelia McGlashan; *m* 1947, Susan Jane, *d* of late Col H. E. Crosse, MC, OBE, and late Mrs D. Crosse, Patoka Station, Hawkes Bay, NZ. *Educ:* Greymouth, NZ; Canterbury Univ. Coll., Christchurch, NZ; Univ. of Reading. MSc (NZ) 1946, PhD (Reading) 1951, DSc (Reading) 1962. Asst Lectr, 1946–48, Lectr, 1948–53, Sen. Lectr, 1953, in Chemistry, at Canterbury Univ. Coll., Christchurch, NZ. Sims Empire Scholar, 1949–52; Lectr in Chem., Univ. of Reading, 1954–61; Reader in Chem., Univ. of Reading, 1962–64; Prof. of Physical Chem., Univ. of Exeter, 1964–74 (Dean, Faculty of Science, 1973–74). Mem., 1963–65, Vice-Chm., 1965–67, Chm., 1967–71, Commn on Physicochemical Symbols, Terminology, and Units. Chm., Interdivl Cttee on Nomenclature and Symbols, Internat. Union of Pure and Applied Chem., 1971–76; Member: Royal Society Symbols Cttee, 1963–88; BSI's Tech. Cttee on physical quantities and units, 1963– (Chm., 1978–); Council, Faraday Soc., 1965–67; Metrication Bd, 1969–80; Comité Consultatif des Unités (Metre Convention), 1969–; Council, Chem. Soc., 1970–73; SRC Chem. Cttee, 1974–76; Data Compilation Cttee, 1974–77; Res. Cttee, British Gas Corp., 1979–90; Trustee, Ramsay Meml Fellowships Trust, 1982– (Chm. Adv. Council, 1975–89). Editor, Jl of Chemical Thermodynamics, 1969–. Hon. Fellow, UCL, 1991. *Publications:* Physicochemical Quantities and Units, 1968 (Royal Inst. of Chem.), 2nd edn, 1971; Chemical Thermodynamics, 1979; papers on chemical thermodynamics and statistical mechanics in Proc. Roy. Soc., Trans Faraday Soc., Jl Chem. Thermodynamics, etc. *Recreations:* climbing in the Alps, gardening, the theatre. *Address:* Patoka, Fairwarp, Uckfield, E Sussex TN22 3DT. *T:* Nutley (082571) 2172. *Club:* Athenæum.

McGONAGLE, Stephen; Senator, Seanad Éireann, Dublin, 1983–87; *b* 17 Nov. 1914; *m*; five *s* one *d. Educ:* Christian Brothers', Derry. Chairman, NI Cttee, Irish Congress of Trade Unions, 1959; Vice-Chm., Derry Develt Commn, 1969–71; Pres., Irish Congress of Trade Unions, 1972–73; Mem., NI Economic Council, Indust. Tribunal, Indust. Ct, until 1973; Dist Sec., Irish Transport and General Workers' Union, Dec. 1973; NI Parly Comr For Admin, and Comr for Complaints, 1974–79; Chm., NI Police Complaints Bd, 1977–83. *Recreations:* fishing, boating, reading. *Address:* 10 Kingsfort Park, Derry.

MACGOUGAN, John; Member, Central Arbitration Committee, 1977–83; *b* 21 Aug. 1913; *m* 1941, Lizzie Faulkner; three *s* one *d. Educ:* various Northern Ireland Schs; Technical Sch.; Correspondence courses. Accountancy profession, 1930–45. Irish Officer, NUTGW, in charge of all Irish affairs, 1945–69; Gen. Sec., NUTGW, 1969–79. Contested (Irish Labour) N Ireland Parly Elections, Oldpark 1938, Falls Div. 1951; Westminster Parly Election, South Down 1950; Member: Belfast Corporation, 1949–58; Executive, Irish TUC, 1950–69 (Pres. 1957–58 and 1963–64); TUC Gen. Council, 1970–79; MSC, 1977–79; Economic and Social Cttee, EEC, 1978–80. Irish and UK Rep., ILO, 1962–85. *Recreations:* proletarian pastimes. *Address:* 96 Whalley Drive, Bletchley, Milton Keynes, Bucks MK3 6HU. *T:* Milton Keynes (0908) 372174.

McGOUGH, Roger; poet; *b* 9 Nov. 1937; *s* of Roger Francis and Mary Agnes McGough; *m* 1st, 1970 (marr. diss. 1980); two *s*; 2nd, 1986, Hilary Clough; one *s* one *d. Educ:* St Mary's Coll., Crosby, Liverpool; Hull Univ. (BA, Grad. Cert. Ed.). Fellow of Poetry, Univ. of Loughborough, 1973–75. Mem. Exec. Council, Poetry Soc., 1989–. *Television:* Kurt, Mungo, BP and Me (BAFTA Award), 1984. Lyrics for Wind in the Willows, Broadway, 1985–86. *Publications:* Watchwords, 1969; After The Merrymaking, 1971; Out of Sequence, 1972; Gig, 1972; Sporting Relations, 1974; In The Glassroom, 1976; Summer with Monika, 1978; Holiday on Death Row, 1979; Unlucky For Some, 1981; Waving at Trains, 1982; Melting into the Foreground, 1986; Selected Poems 1967–1987, 1989; You at the Back, 1991; *children's books:* Mr Noselighter, 1977; The Great Smile Robbery, 1982; Sky in the Pie, 1983; The Stowaways, 1986; Noah's Ark, 1986; Nailing the Shadow, 1987; An Imaginary Menagerie, 1988; Helen Highwater, 1989; Counting by Numbers, 1989; Pillow Talk, 1990; The Lighthouse That Ran Away, 1991; contributed to: Penguin Modern Poets, No 10, Mersey Sound, 1967, rev. edn 1983; Oxford Book of 20th Century Verse, 1973; The Norton Anthology of Modern Poetry, 1973; edited: Strictly Private, 1981; Kingfisher Book of Comic Verse, 1986. *Address:* c/o Peters Fraser and Dunlop, 5th floor, The Chambers, Chelsea Harbour, Lots Road, SW10 0XF. *T:* 071–376 7676. *Club:* Chelsea Arts (Chm., 1984–86).

McGOVERN, George Stanley; United States Senator, 1963–81; *b* Avon, S Dakota, 19 July 1922; *s* of Rev. Joseph C. McGovern and Francis (*née* McLean); *m* 1943, Eleanor Faye Stegeberg; one *s* four *d. Educ:* Dakota Wesleyan Univ. (BA); Northwestern Univ. (MA, PhD). Served World War II, USAAF (DFC). Prof. of History and Govt, Dakota Wesleyan Univ., 1950–53. Exec. Sec., S Dakota Democratic Party, 1953–56; Mem., 1st Dist, S Dakota, US House of Reps, 1957–61; Dir, Food for Peace Programme, 1961–62; Senator from South Dakota, 1963–81. Democratic nominee for US President, 1972. Visiting Professor: Columbia Univ., 1977; Univ. of Pa, 1978; Northwestern Univ., 1981; Univ. of New Orleans, 1982; University Coll., Dublin, 1982; Duke Univ., 1985; Univ. of Munich, 1987. Mem., Amer. Hist. Assoc. *Publications:* The Colorado Coal Strike, 1913–14, 1953; War Against Want, 1964; Agricultural Thought in the Twentieth Century, 1967; A Time of War, A Time of Peace, 1968; (with Leonard F. Guttridge) The Great Coalfield War, 1972; An American Journey, 1974; Grassroots, an Autobiography, 1978. *Address:* PO Box 5591, Friendship Station, Washington, DC 20016, USA.

McGOWAN, family name of **Baron McGowan.**

McGOWAN, 3rd Baron, *cr* 1937; **Harry Duncan Cory McGowan;** Partner, Panmure, Gordon & Co., since 1971; *b* 20 July 1938; *e s* of Harry Wilson McGowan, 2nd Baron McGowan, and Carmen, *d* of Sir (James) Herbert Cory, 1st Bt; *S* father, 1966; *m* 1962, Lady Gillian Angela Pepys, *d* of 7th Earl of Cottenham; one *s* two *d. Educ:* Eton. *Heir: s* Hon. Harry John Charles McGowan, *b* 23 June 1971. *Address:* House of Lords, Westminster, SW1; Highway House, Lower Froyle, Alton, Hants. *T:* Bentley (0420) 22104; 12 Stanhope Mews East, SW7. *T:* 071–370 2346. *Club:* Boodle's.

McGOWAN, Alan Patrick, PhD; Archivist, Royal Naval College, Greenwich, since 1989; Callendar Curator, National Maritime Museum, since 1989 (Chief Curator, 1986–88); *b* 16 Nov. 1928; *s* of Hugh McGowan and Alice Chilton; *m* 1958, Betty Eileen, *e d* of Mr and Mrs F. L. MacDougall, Ontario; three *s. Educ:* Spring Grove Grammar Sch.; Borough Road Coll.; Univ. of Western Ontario (BA, MA); Univ. of London (PhD). Served RASC (Air Freight), 1947–49. Asst Master (History), 1953–63; Lectr, Univ. of Western Ont Summer Sch., 1964; Canada Council Fellow, 1964–66; Asst Keeper, 1967–71, Head, 1971–87, Dept of Ships, National Maritime Museum. Associate Prof. of History, Univ. of Western Ont Summer Sch., 1977. Member: Council, Navy Records Soc., 1968–; Adv. Council on Export of Works of Art, 1972–88; Victory Adv. Technical Cttee, 1974– (Chm., 1983–); Mary Rose Adv. Cttee, 1974–78; Ships Cttee, Maritime Trust, 1977–; Council, Soc. for Nautical Res., 1981–; Cttee, Falkland Islands

Foundn, 1981–83. Associate RINA, 1980–88. *Publications:* (ed) Jacobean Commissions of Enquiry, 1608 and 1618, vol. 113 of Navy Records Society, 1971; Royal Yachts, 1975; (with J. Fabb) The Victorian and Edwardian Navy in Photographs, 1976; (ed and prefaced) Steel's Naval Architecture, 1976; Sailor, 1977; (ed and prefaced) Steel's Rigging and Seamanship, 1978; The Century before Steam, 1980; Tiller and Whipstaff, 1981; articles in jls of history and in encyclopaedia. *Recreations:* golf, reading, music. *Address:* c/o National Maritime Museum, Greenwich, SE10 9NF.

McGOWAN, Bruce Henry, MA; FRSA; Headmaster, Haberdashers' Aske's School, Elstree, 1973–87; *b* 27 June 1924; *er s* of late Rt Rev. Henry McGowan, sometime Bishop of Wakefield, and Nora Heath McGowan (*née* Godwin); *m* 1947, Beryl McKenzie (*née* Liggitt); one *s* three *d. Educ:* King Edward's Sch., Birmingham; Jesus Coll., Cambridge. War service, Royal Artillery, 1943–46 (India and Burma). Asst Master, King's Sch., Rochester, 1949–53; Senior History Master, Wallasey Gram. Sch., 1953–57; Headmaster: De Aston Sch., Market Rasen, Lincs, 1957–64; Solihull Sch., 1964–73. Page Scholar of the English-Speaking Union, 1961. Member: Church Assembly, 1963–70; Public Schools Commn, 1968–70; Council, Church Schools Co., 1986– (Chm., 1987–); Chairman: Boarding Schools Assoc., 1967–69; Headmasters' Conference, 1985 (Chairman: London Div. 1977; Community Service Cttee, 1976–80; Political and Public Relations Cttee, 1981–84). *Recreations:* foreign travel, walking, music, the theatre. *Address:* 57 Oxford Street, Woodstock, Oxford OX7 1TJ. *Club:* East India.

McGOWAN, Ian Duncan; Librarian, National Library of Scotland, since 1990; *b* 19 Sept. 1945; *s* of Alexander McGowan and Dora (*née* Sharp); *m* 1971, Elizabeth Ann Weir; two *d. Educ:* Liverpool Inst.; Exeter Coll., Oxford (BA 1st Cl. Hons Russian Lang. and Lit., 1967); Sch. of Slavonic and E European Studies, Univ. of London. National Library of Scotland: Asst Keeper, 1971–78; Keeper (Catalogues and Automation), 1978–88; Sec. of the Library, 1988–90. *Recreations:* books, gardens. *Address:* 23 Blackford Road, Edinburgh EH9 2DT. *T:* 031–667 2432.

McGOWAN, Michael; Member (Lab) Leeds, European Parliament, since 1984; *b* 19 May 1940; *m;* two *s* one *d. Educ:* Leicester University. Formerly: lecturer; BBC journalist; cooperative employment development officer, Kirklees Council, to 1984. *Address:* 3 Grosvenor Terrace, Otley, West Yorks LS21 1HJ.

McGRADY, Edward Kevin; MP (SDLP) Down South, since 1987; Partner, M. B. McGrady & Co., chartered accountants and insurance brokers; *b* 3 June 1935; *y s* of late Michael McGrady and late Lilian Leatham; *m* 1959, Patricia, *d* of Wm Swail and Margaret Breen; two *s* one *d. Educ:* St Patrick's High Sch., Downpatrick. ACA 1957, FCA 1962. Councillor, Downpatrick UDC, 1961–89; Chm. of UDC, 1964–73; Vice-Chm., Down District Council, 1973, 1975–76, 1977, Chm. 1974, 1976, 1978, 1981, 1982. 1st Chm. of SDLP, 1971–73; 1st Chm. of SDLP Assembly Party. Mem. (SDLP) S Down: NI Assembly, 1973–75; NI Constitutional Convention, 1975–76; NI Assembly, 1982–86; Head of Office of Executive Planning and Co-ordination (Minister for Co-ordination, Jan.-May 1974); contested (SDLP) Down S, gen. elections, 1979, 1983 and 1986. *Recreations:* golf, badminton, choral work. *Address:* Cois Na Cille, Saul Brae, Downpatrick, Co. Down BT30 6NL. *T:* Downpatrick 612307/612882; House of Commons, SW1A 0AA. *T:* 071–219 4481.

McGRAIL, Prof. Sean Francis, FSA; Visiting Professor of Maritime Archaeology: University of Oxford, since 1986; University of Southampton, since 1991; Chief Archaeologist, National Maritime Museum, 1976–89; *b* 5 May 1928; *m* 1955, Ursula Anne Yates, BA; one *s* three *d. Educ:* Royal Navy (Master Mariner); Univ. of Bristol (BA); Univ. of London (PhD); MA 1988, DSc 1989, Oxon. FSA 1981. Served RN, 1946–68: Seaman Officer; awarded Wings (pilot), 1952; comd 849 Sqdn, FAA, 1962–63. Undergrad., Univ. of Bristol, 1968–71 (Harry Crook Scholar, 1969–71); Postgrad. Student, Inst. of Archaeology, London, 1972–73; Postgrad. Student (pt-time), UCL, 1973–78; National Maritime Museum, 1972–89; Hd of Archaeol Res. Centre, 1976–86. Mem., DoE Adv. Cttee on Historic Wrecks, 1975–. Vice-Chm., Trust for Preservation of Oxford Coll. Barges, 1987–. *Publications:* Building and Trials of a Replica of an Ancient Boat, 1974; Logboats of England and Wales, 1978; Rafts, Boats and Ships, 1981; Ancient Boats, 1983; Ancient Boats of North West Europe, 1987; Medieval Boat and Ship Timbers from Dublin, 1991; *edited:* Sources and Techniques in Boat Archaeology, 1977; Medieval Ships and Harbours, 1979; Paul Johnstone, Seacraft of Prehistory, 1980, 2nd edn 1988; Brigg 'raft' and her Prehistoric Environment, 1981; Woodworking Techniques before 1500, 1982; Aspects of Maritime Archaeology and Ethnography, 1984; (with J. Coates) Greek Trireme of 5th Century BC, 1984; (with E. Kentley) Sewn Plank Boats, 1985; Maritime Celts, Saxons and Frisians, 1990; articles in archaeological and maritime jls. *Recreations:* strategic gardening, real ale specialist. *Address:* Institute of Archaeology, 36 Beaumont Street, Oxford OX1 2PG. *T:* Oxford (0865) 278240.

McGRATH, Brian Henry, CVO 1988; Private Secretary, since 1982, and Treasurer, since 1984, to the Duke of Edinburgh (Assistant Private Secretary, 1982); *b* 27 Oct. 1925; *s* of William Henry and Hermione Gioja McGrath; *m* 1959, Elizabeth Joan Bruce (*née* Gregson-Ellis) (*d* 1977); two *s*, and one step *d. Educ:* Eton College. Served War of 1939–45, Irish Guards, 1943–46, Lieut. Cannon Brewery Co., 1946–48; Victoria Wine Co.: joined, 1948; Dir, 1949; Chm., 1960–82; Dir, 1960, Chm., 1975–82, Grants of St James's Ltd; Dir, Allied Breweries Ltd (subseq. Allied-Lyons plc), 1970–82; Chm., Broad Street Securities, 1983–. Master of Wine. *Recreations:* golf, tennis, shooting. *Address:* Flat 3, 9 Cheyne Gardens, SW3. *Clubs:* Boodle's, White's.

McGRATH, Prof. John Christie; Regius Professor of Physiology, University of Glasgow, since 1991; *b* 8 March 1949; *s* of John Christie McGrath and Margaret Gilmore Cochrane McGrath (*née* Murray); *m* 1970, Wilma Nicol; one *s* one *d. Educ:* Cross Arthurlie Primary Sch.; John Neilson Instn; Univ. of Glasgow (BSc 1st class Hons 1970; PhD 1974). Wellcome Interdisciplinary Research Fellowship, Dept of Pharmacology and Univ. Dept of Anaesthesia, Glasgow Royal Infirmary, Univ. of Glasgow, 1973–75; Institute of Physiology, University of Glasgow: Lectr, 1975; Wellcome Trust Research Leave Fellowship, 1982; Sen. Lectr, Reader, Titular Prof., 1983–91. Member: British Pharmacol Soc. 1975 (Sandoz Prize, 1980); Cttee, Physiolog. Soc., 1988– (Mem., 1978); Internat. Soc. for Heart Research, 1989. Mem., Labour Party. Member: Editl Bd, Pharmacological Reviews, 1990–; Editl Bd, British Jl of Pharmacology, 1985–91. 1st Pfizer Award for Biology, 1983. *Publications:* contribs to learned jls in fields of pharmacology and physiology. *Recreations:* running, politics. *Address:* Institute of Physiology, University of Glasgow, Glasgow G12 8QQ. *T:* 041–330 4483, *Fax:* 041–330 4100.

McGRATH, John Peter; writer and director, theatre, film and television; Director: Freeway Films, since 1983; Channel Four Television, since 1989; *b* 1 June 1935; *s* of John Francis McGrath and Margaret McGrath; *m* 1962, Elizabeth Maclennan; two *s* one *d. Educ:* Alun Grammar Sch., Mold; St John's Coll., Oxford. Theatre (playwright), 1958–61; BBC Television, 1960–65; film (screenwriting) and theatre (writing and directing), 1965–70; theatre, with regular forays into television and film, as writer and director, 1970–; founded 7:84 Theatre Co., 1971, Artistic Dir, 1971–88. Has produced or directed over 75 plays in the theatre, including: The Catch, 1982; Women in Power, 1983; The Albannach, (adaptation), 1984; The Baby and the Bathwater, 1984; All the Fun of the Fair, 1985; There is a Happy Land, 1986; Mairi Mhor, 1987; Border Warfare, 1989; John Brown's Body, 1990; many TV plays performed on BBC and ITV; cinema: Blood Red Roses, 1986 (screenplay/dir); The Dressmaker, 1988 (screenplay/exec. producer); wrote libretto for Alexander Goehr's opera, Behold the Sun; writes songs and poems. *Publications: plays:* Events While Guarding the Bofors Gun, 1966; Random Happenings in the Hebrides, 1972; Bakke's Night of Fame, 1973; The Cheviot, The Stag and The Black Black Oil, 1974, 2nd edn 1981; The Game's A Bogey, 1974; Fish in the Sea, 1977; Little Red Hen, 1977; Yobbo Nowt, 1978; Joe's Drum, 1979; Blood Red Roses (filmed for TV, 1986), and Swings and Roundabouts, 1981; *general:* A Good Night Out, 1981; The Bone Won't Break, 1990. *Address:* c/o Freeway Films, 67 George Street, Edinburgh EH2 2JG.

McGRATH, Dr Patrick Gerard, CB 1981; CBE 1971; Senior Consultant Psychiatrist and Physician Superintendent, Broadmoor Hospital, 1956–81, now Physician Superintendent Emeritus; *b* 10 June 1916; *s* of late Patrick McGrath and Mary (*née* Murray), Glasgow; *m* 1949, Helen Patricia O'Brien; three *s* one *d. Educ:* St Aloysius Coll., Glasgow; Glasgow and Edinburgh Univs. MB, ChB Glasgow 1939; DipPsych Edinburgh 1955; FRCPsych (Vice-Pres., 1978–80), Hon. FRCPsych 1981; FRSocMed. RAMC, 1939–46 (Hon. Lt-Col); various trng posts in psychiatry, Glasgow, London and Colchester, 1946–51; Psychiatrist, Ayrshire, 1951–56. Member: Parole Board, 1982–85; Adv. Council, Inst. of Criminology, Univ. of Cambridge, 1982–86. *Publications:* chapter in Psychopathic Disorder, 1966; Mentally Abnormal Offender, 1968; contrib. Jl of RSH, Cropwood publications, etc. *Recreation:* golf (purely social). *Address:* 18 Heathermount Drive, Crowthorne, Berks RG11 6HN. *T:* Crowthorne (0344) 774552. *Club:* East Berks Golf.

McGREGOR, family name of **Baron McGregor of Durris.**

McGREGOR OF DURRIS, Baron *cr* 1978 (Life Peer), of Hampstead; **Oliver Ross McGregor;** Chairman, Press Complaints Commission, since 1991; Professor of Social Institutions in the University of London, 1964–85; Head of Department of Sociology, at Bedford College, 1964–77; Joint Director, Rowntree Legal Research Unit, 1966–84; *b* 25 Aug. 1921; *s* of late William McGregor and late Anne Olivia Ross; *m* 1944, Nellie Weate; three *s. Educ:* Worksop Coll.; University of Aberdeen; London School of Economics (Hon. Fellow 1977). Temp. civil servant, War Office and Ministry of Agriculture, 1940–44. Asst Lecturer and Lecturer in Economic History, University of Hull, 1945–47; Lecturer, Bedford Coll., 1947–60, Reader in University of London, 1960–64; Simon Senior Research Fellow, University of Manchester, 1959–60. Fellow of Wolfson Coll., Oxford, 1972–75; Dir, Centre for Socio-Legal Studies, Univ. of Oxford, 1972–75. Member: Cttee on Enforcement of Judgment Debts, 1965; Cttee on Statutory Maintenance Limits, 1966; Cttee on Land Use (Recreation and Leisure), 1967; National Parks Commission, 1966–68; Independent Television Authority's General Advisory Council, 1967–73; Countryside Commission, 1968–80; Legal Aid Adv. Cttee, 1969–78; Cttee on One-Parent Families, 1969–74; Chairman: Royal Commn on Press, 1975–77 (Mem., 1974); Advertising Standards Authy, 1980–90; Forest Philharmonic Soc., 1975–. President: Nat. Council for One Parent Families, 1975–91; Nat. Assoc. of Citizens' Advice Bureaux, 1981–86. Chm., Reuters Founders Share Co., 1987– (Independent Trustee, 1984–). Lectures: Fawcett Meml, 1966; James Seth Meml, 1968; Hobhouse Meml, 1971; Maccabaean in Jurisprudence, 1973; Hamlyn, 1979; Eleanor Rathbone Meml, 1979; Ian Gulland, 1980. Hon. LLD Bristol, 1986. *Publications:* Divorce in England, 1957; (ed) Lord Ernle, English Farming Past and Present, 6th edn, 1960; (jtly) Separated Spouses, 1970; Social History and Law Reform, 1981; various papers in British Journal of Sociology and other journals. *Address:* Press Complaints Commission, 1 Salisbury Square, EC4Y 8AE. *T:* 071–353 1248; Far End, Wyldes Close, NW11 7JB. *T:* 081–458 2856. *Club:* Garrick.

McGREGOR, Rev. Alistair Gerald Crichton; QC (Scot.) 1982; WS; Minister, North Leith Parish Church, Edinburgh, since 1987; *b* 15 Oct. 1937; *s* of late James Reid McGregor, CB, CBE, MC, and Dorothy McGregor; *m* 1965, Margaret Lees or McGregor; two *s* one *d. Educ:* Charterhouse; Pembroke Coll., Oxford (BA (Hons) Jurisprudence); Edinburgh Univ. (LLB; BD). Intelligence Corps, 1956–58. Solicitor and WS, 1965–66; Advocate, 1967–82. Clerk to Court of Session Rules Council, 1972–75; Standing Junior Counsel to: SHHD, 1977–79; Scottish Develt Dept, 1979–82. Chm., Family Care (Scotland), 1983–88; Dir, Apex (Scotland), 1988–. Licensed, Church of Scotland, 1986. *Recreations:* squash, tennis. *Address:* 22 Primrose Bank Road, Edinburgh EH5 3JG. *T:* 031–551 2802. *Clubs:* University Staff, Sports (Edinburgh).

McGREGOR, Dr Angus; Regional Medical Officer, West Midlands Regional Health Authority, 1979–88; Visiting Professor, University of Keele, since 1988; *b* 26 Dec. 1926; *s* of Dr William Hector Scott McGregor and Dr Olwen May Richards; *m* 1951, May Burke, BA; one *d. Educ:* Solihull Sch.; St John's Coll., Cambridge. MA, MD; FRCP; FFCM; DPH. Junior hospital posts, 1950; Army service, RAMC, 1951–52; general practice, 1953; Asst MOH, Chester, 1954–56; Deputy Medical Officer of Health: Swindon, 1957–58; Hull, 1958–65; MOH and Port MO, Southampton, 1965–74; District Community Physician, East Dorset, 1974–79. Mem. Bd, FCM, RCP, 1982–88. FRSA 1986. *Publications:* (with T. Bunbury) Disciplining and Dismissing Doctors in the NHS, 1988; contrib. papers to medical journals. *Recreation:* piano. *Address:* (home) 4 Meon Close, Upper Quinton, Stratford-upon-Avon CV37 8SX. *T:* Stratford-upon-Avon (0789) 720149. *Club:* Royal Over-Seas League.

MACGREGOR, Sir Edwin (Robert), 7th Bt *cr* 1828; Deputy Minister, Ministry of Crown Lands, Province of British Columbia, Victoria, BC; *b* 4 Dec. 1931; *e s* of Sir Robert McConnell Macgregor, 6th Bt, and of Annie Mary Lane; *S* father, 1963; *m* 1st, 1952, (Margaret Alice) Jean Peake (marr. diss. 1981); one *s* two *d* (and one *s* decd); 2nd, 1982, Helen Linda Herriott; two step *d. Educ:* University of British Columbia. BASc 1955, MASc 1957, Metallurgical Engineering. Member: Assoc. of Professional Engrs, Province of British Columbia; Canadian Inst. of Mining and Metallurgy. *Publications:* contribs to Trans Amer. Inst. of Mining, Metallurgical and Petroleum Engrg, Jl Amer. Chem. Soc. *Recreations:* reading; participation in several outdoor sports such as golf, swimming, fishing, etc.; music. *Heir: s* Ian Grant Macgregor, *b* 22 Feb. 1959. *Address:* 6136 Kirby Road, RR3, Sooke, BC V0S 1N0, Canada.

MacGREGOR, Geddes; *see* MacGregor, J. G.

McGREGOR, Dr Gordon Peter; Principal, University College (formerly College) of Ripon and York St John, since 1980; *b* Aldershot, Hants, 13 June 1932; 2nd *s* of William A. K. McGregor and Mary A. McGregor (*née* O'Brien); *m* 1957, Jean Olga Lewis; three *d. Educ:* Bishop Road Jun. Sch., Bristol; St Brendan's Coll., Bristol; Univ. of Bristol (BA Hons); Univ. of East Africa (MEd); Univ. of Sussex (DPhil); Dip. Coll. of Teachers of the Blind. Educn Officer, RAF, 1953–56; Asst Master, Worcester Coll. for the Blind, 1956–59; Asst Master, King's Coll., Budo, Uganda, 1959–62; Lecturer in English Language, Makerere Univ. Coll., Uganda 1963–66; Univ. of Zambia: Sen Lecturer in Educn, 1966–68; Reader and Head of Dept of Education, 1968–70; Prof. of Educn, 1970; Principal, Bishop Otter Coll., Chichester, 1970–80. Danforth Fellow, Colorado Coll.,

USA, 1972; Commonwealth Educn Consultant, Sri Lanka, 1973; British Council ELT Consultant, Iraq, 1975. Chm., York Diocesan Educn Council, 1980–; Member: York DHA, 1982–86; UK Commn for UNESCO, 1984–86; Voluntary Sector Consultative Council, 1985–89; Bd of Nat. Adv. Body for Higher Educn, 1987–88. FRSA 1976. Hon. DLitt Ripon Coll., Wisconsin, 1986. *Publications:* King's College, Budo, The First Sixty Years, 1967; Educating the Handicapped, 1967; English for Education?, 1968; Teaching English as a Second Language (with J. A. Bright), 1970; English in Africa, (UNESCO), 1971; Bishop Otter College and Policy for Teacher Education 1839–1980, 1981; A Church College for the 21st Century?: the first 150 years of Ripon and York St John, 1991; contrib. Univs Qly, Times Higher Educn Supplement, PNEU Jl, Studies in Higher Educn. *Recreations:* music, literature, theatre, travel, swimming, walking, armchair rugby and cricket. *Address:* Principal's House, University College of Ripon and York St John, Lord Mayor's Walk, York. *T:* York (0904) 56771.

MacGREGOR OF MacGREGOR, Brig. Sir Gregor, 6th Bt, *cr* 1795; ADC 1979; 23rd Chief of Clan Gregor; *b* 22 Dec. 1925; *o s* of Capt. Sir Malcolm MacGregor of MacGregor, 5th Bt, CB, CMG, and Hon. Gylla Lady MacGregor of MacGregor, OBE (*d* 1980); *S* father 1958; *m* 1958, Fanny, *o d* of C. H. A. Butler, Shortgrove, Newport, Essex; two *s*. *Educ:* Eton. Commissioned Scots Guards, 1944; served War of 1939–45. Served in Palestine, 1947–48; Malaya, 1950–51; Borneo, 1965. Staff Coll. Course, 1960; Brigade Major, 16th Parachute Bde Gp, 1961–63; Joint Services Staff Coll., 1965; commanding 1st Bn Scots Guards, 1966–69; GSO1 (BLO) Fort Benning, USA, 1969–71; Col Recruiting, HQ Scotland, 1971; Lt-Col commanding Scots Guards, 1971–74; Defence and Mil. Attaché, British Embassy, Athens, 1975–78; Comdr, Lowlands, 1978–80. Grand Master Mason of Scotland, 1988–. Mem. of the Royal Company of Archers (Queen's Body Guard for Scotland), 1949–. *Heir: s* Captain Malcolm Gregor Charles MacGregor of MacGregor, Scots Guards [*b* 23 March 1959; *m* 1988, Cecilia, *er d* of Sir Ilay Campbell of Succoth, Bt, *qv*]. *Address:* Bannatyne, Newtyle, Blairgowrie, Perthshire. *T:* Newtyle (08285) 314; R-5 Buttonwood Bay, 96000 Overseas Highway, Key Largo, Florida 33037–2124, USA. *T:* 305–852–5740. *Clubs:* Pratt's; New (Edinburgh).

McGREGOR, Harvey, QC 1978; DCL; Fellow, since 1972, and Warden, since 1985, New College, Oxford; *b* 25 Feb. 1926; *s* of late William Guthrie Robertson McGregor and Agnes (*née* Reid). *Educ:* Inverurie Acad.; Scarborough Boys' High Sch.; Queen's Coll., Oxford (Hastings Scholar; BA 1951, BCL 1952, MA 1955, DCL 1983). Dr of Juridical Science, Harvard, 1962. Called to the Bar, Inner Temple, 1955, Bencher, 1985. Flying Officer, RAF, 1946–48. Bigelow Teaching Fellow, Univ. of Chicago, 1950–51; Vis. Prof., New York Univ. and Rutgers Univ., 1963–69 (various times). Consultant to Law Commn 1966–73. Pres., Harvard Law Sch. Assoc. of UK, 1981–. Dep. Independent Chm., London Theatre Council, 1971–; Trustee, Oxford Union Soc., 1977–. Fellow, Winchester Coll., 1985–. Mem. Editorial Cttee, 1967–86, Mem., Editorial Bd, 1986–, Modern Law Review. *Publications:* McGregor on Damages, 12th edn 1961– 15th edn 1988; (contrib.) International Encyclopedia of Comparative Law, 1972; articles in legal jls. *Recreations:* music, theatre, travel, sailing. *Address:* Warden's Lodgings, New College, Oxford OX1 3BN. *T:* Oxford (0865) 279501; (chambers) 4 Paper Buildings, Temple, EC4Y 7EX. *T:* 071–353 3366; (residence) Gray's Inn Chambers, Gray's Inn, WC1R 5JA. *T:* 071–242 4942. *Club:* Garrick.

McGREGOR, Sir Ian (Alexander), Kt 1982; CBE 1968 (OBE 1959); FRS 1981; FRSE; Visiting Professor (formerly Professorial Fellow), Department of Tropical Medicine, Liverpool School of Tropical Medicine, since 1981; *b* 26 Aug. 1922; *s* of John McGregor and Isabella (*née* Taylor), Cambuslang, Lanarks; *m* 1954, Nancy Joan, *d* of Frederick Small, Mapledurham, Oxon; one *s* one *d*. *Educ:* Rutherglen Academy; St Mungo Coll., Glasgow. LRCPE, LRCSE, LRFPS(G) 1945; DTM&H 1949; MRCP 1962; FRCP 1967; FFCM 1972; Hon. FRCPGlas 1984. Mil. Service, 1946–48 (despatches). Mem. Scientific Staff, Human Nutrition Research Unit, MRC, 1949–53; Dir, MRC Laboratories, The Gambia, 1954–74, 1978–80; Head of Laboratory of Trop. Community Studies, Nat. Inst. for Med. Research, Mill Hill, 1974–77; Mem., External Staff, MRC, 1981–84. Chm., WHO Expert Cttee on Malaria, 1985–89; Member: WHO Adv. Panel on Malaria, 1961–; Malaria Cttee, MRC, 1962–71; Cttee on Nutrition Surveys, Internat. Union of Nutrition Sciences, 1971–75; Tropical Medicine Res. Bd, MRC, 1974–77, 1981–83; Steering Cttee on Immunology of Malaria, WHO, 1978–89; Steering Cttee on Applied Field Res. in Malaria, WHO, 1984–90; Council, Royal Soc., 1985–87. Lectures: Heath Clark, London Sch. of Hygiene and Tropical Medicine, 1983–84; Fred Soper, Amer. Soc. of Trop. Medicine and Hygiene, 1983; Lord Cohen History of Medicine, Liverpool Univ., 1989. Pres., Royal Soc. of Trop. Medicine and Hygiene, 1983–85 (Vice-Pres., 1981–83). FRSE 1987. Hon. Fellow Liverpool Sch. of Trop. Medicine, 1980; Hon. Member: Amer. Soc. of Trop. Medicine and Hygiene, 1983; British Soc. for Parasitology, 1988. Hon. LLD Univ. of Aberdeen, 1983; Hon. DSc Glasgow, 1984. Chalmers Medal, Royal Soc. Trop. Med. and Hygiene, 1963; Stewart Prize, BMA, 1970; Darling Foundn Medal, WHO, 1974; Laveran Medal, Société de Pathologie Exotique de Paris, 1983; Glaxo Prize for Medical Writing, 1989. *Publications:* (ed with W. Wernsdorfer) Malaria: the principles and practice of malariology, 1988; scientific papers on infections, nutrition, immunity, child health and community medicine in tropical environments. *Recreations:* ornithology, golf, fishing. *Address:* The Glebe House, Greenlooms, Hargrave, Chester CH3 7RX.

McGREGOR, Ian Alexander, FRCS, FRCSGlas; Consulting Plastic Surgeon, Glasgow Royal Infirmary, since 1986; Director, West of Scotland Regional Plastic and Oral Surgery Unit, 1980–86; *b* 6 June 1921; *s* of late Walker McGregor and Mary Duncan (*née* Thompson); *m* 1st, 1950, Christeen Isabel Mackay (decd); three *s*; 2nd, 1970, Frances Mary Vint. *Educ:* North Kelvinside Secondary Sch.; Glasgow Univ. (MB, ChB 1944; ChM 1972). FRCS 1950, FRFPSG 1951, FRCSGlas 1962; Hon. FRACS 1977; Hon. FRCSI 1984; Hon. FRCSE 1985; Hon. FACS 1986. Served RAMC, 1945–48. Consultant Surgeon, Glasgow Royal Infirmary, 1957–59; Consultant Plastic Surgeon, Greater Glasgow Health Bd, 1959–80. Visitor, 1982–84, Pres., 1984–86, RCPSGlas. Hon. DSc Glasgow, 1986. *Publications:* Fundamental Techniques of Plastic Surgery, 1960, 8th edn 1989; (with W. H. Reid) Plastic Surgery for Nurses, 1966; (with Frances M. McGregor) Cancer of the Face and Mouth, 1986; scientific papers to surgical jls on reconstructive aspects of plastic surgery. *Recreations:* music, literature, golf. *Address:* 7 Ledcameroch Road, Bearsden, Glasgow G61 4AB. *T:* 041–942 3419.

MacGREGOR, Sir Ian (Kinloch), Kt 1986; Chairman: Clyde Cable Vision, since 1987; Trusthouse Forte Inc., USA, since 1988; HunterPrint, since 1990; Director: Scottish Heritable Trust, since 1987; Mountleigh, since 1987; *b* 21 Sept. 1912; *m* Sibyl Spencer; one *s* one *d*. *Educ:* George Watson's Coll., Edinburgh; Hillhead High Sch., Glasgow; Univ. of Glasgow. BSc (1st cl. Hons); Royal Coll. of Science and Technol. (now Univ. of Strathclyde) (Dip. with distinction). Pres. and Chief Exec., 1966, Chm., 1969–77, Amax Inc. (Hon. Chm., 1977–82); Deputy Chairman, BL Ltd, 1977–80; Chm. and Chief Exec., BSC, 1980–83; Chm., NCB, 1983–86. Chm., North Sea Assets, 1987–88; Non-exec. Dir, Lazard Brothers & Co., 1986–90. President of the International Chamber of Commerce, Paris, 1978. Hon. degrees from Univs. of Glasgow (LLD), Strathclyde (LLD), Denver (LLD), Montana State (DEng), Rochester (LLD), Colorado Sch. of Mines (DEng), Wyoming (LLD), and Tri-State Coll., Indiana (DSc). Jackling Medal, Amer. Inst. of Mining and Metallurgical Engrs; John Fritz Gold Medal, Amer. Inst. of Mining, Metallurgical and Petroleum Engrs, 1981; Bessemer Gold Medal, Metals Soc., London, 1983. Chevalier, Légion d'Honneur, 1972. *Publication:* The Enemies Within, 1986. *Address:* Castleton House, Lochgilphead, Argyll; 450 South Ocean Boulevard, Manalapan, Fla 33462, USA.

McGREGOR, James Stalker; Chairman, Honeywell Ltd, 1981–89; *b* 30 Oct. 1927; *s* of John McGregor and Jean McCabe; *m* 1953, Iris Millar Clark; one *s*. *Educ:* Dumfries Acad.; Royal Tech. Coll., Glasgow (ARTC); Glasgow Univ. BSc (Hons); CEng, MIMechE; CBIM. Production Engr, Rolls Royce Ltd, 1952–56; Sales Engr, Sandvik Swedish Steels, 1956–57; Honeywell Control Systems: Assembly Manager, later Production Control Manager and Admin Manager, 1957–65; Divl Dir, Temperature Controls Gp, 1965–71; Man. Dir, 1971–86. Hon. LLD Strathclyde, 1984. *Recreation:* golf. *Address:* 19 Burgess Wood Road, Beaconsfield, Bucks HP9 1EQ.

MacGREGOR, Prof. (John) Geddes, DèsL (Sorbonne), DPhil, DD Oxon, BD Edinburgh et Oxon, LLB Edinburgh; FRSL 1948; Distinguished Professor of Philosophy, University of Southern California, 1966–75, now Emeritus; Dean of Graduate School of Religion, 1960–66; first holder of Rufus Jones Chair of Philosophy and Religion, Bryn Mawr, USA, 1949–60; Canon Theologian of St Paul's Cathedral, Los Angeles, 1968–74; *b* 13 Nov. 1909; *o s* of late Thomas and Blanche Geddes MacGregor, Angus; *m* 1941, Elizabeth, *e d* of late Archibald McAllister, Edinburgh; one *s* one *d*. *Educ:* Universities of Edinburgh, Paris, Heidelberg; The Queen's Coll., Oxford. Senior Assistant to Dean of Chapel Royal in Scotland, at St Giles' Cathedral, Edinburgh, 1939–41; served in Civil Defence, War of 1939–45; Minister, Trinity Church, Glasgow, S1, 1941–49; Assistant to Prof. of Logic and Metaphysics, Edinburgh Univ., 1947–49; Examiner: Swarthmore Coll., USA, 1950, 1953, 1955–57; Hebrew Union Coll., USA, 1959, 1961; Occasional Lectr at many US and Canadian Univs (Birks, Montreal, 1976; Warren, Dubuque, 1979; Arnett, Kansas, 1982; Fairchild, Miss, 1982); Visiting Professor: Univ. of British Columbia, 1963, 1966, 1973; Hebrew Union Coll., 1964–65; Univ. of Santa Clara, 1968; World Campus Afloat (Orient, 1974; Mediterranean, 1975); McGill Univ., Montreal, 1976; Inst. for Shipboard Educn (round-the-world-voyage), 1977; Univ. of Iowa, 1979; Univ. of Saskatchewan, 1979; Vis. Fellow, Dept of Religious Studies, Yale Univ., 1967–68; Vis. Lectr, Rikkyo Univ., Tokyo, 1981; Vis. Fellow, Coll. of Preachers, Washington Nat. Cathedral, 1991. Dir, Amer. Friends of the Univ. of Edinburgh, 1983–86; Hon. Fellow, Emporia State Univ., Kansas, 1982. Diplomate, Internat. Soc. for Philosophical Enquiry, 1986. Special Preacher: St Paul's Cathedral, London, 1969; Westminster Abbey, 1970. Regent, American-Scottish Foundation, Inc., NY; Hon. Chaplain and Historian, St Andrew's Soc. of LA, 1981– (Pres., 1987–88); Hon. Canon of San Diego, California, 1987. Hon. LHD Hebrew Union, 1978. Hon. Phi Kappa Phi, 1972 (Distinguished Award, 1982). Hon. Assoc., Order of Agape and Reconciliation, 1988. California Literature Award (Gold Medal, non-fiction), 1964. Medallist, Nat. Soc. of the Sons of the American Revolution, 1989. *Publications:* Aesthetic Experience in Religion, 1947; Christian Doubt, 1951; Les Frontières de la Morale et de la Religion, 1952; From a Christian Ghetto, 1954; The Vatican Revolution, 1957; The Tichborne Impostor, 1957; The Thundering Scot, 1957; Corpus Christi, 1959; Introduction to Religious Philosophy, 1959; The Bible in the Making, 1959; The Coming Reformation, 1960; The Hemlock and the Cross, 1963; God Beyond Doubt, 1966; A Literary History of the Bible, 1968; The Sense of Absence, 1968; So Help Me God, 1970; Philosophical Issues in Religious Thought, 1973; The Rhythm of God, 1974; He Who Lets Us Be, 1975, rev. edn 1987; Reincarnation in Christianity, 1978 (trans. German as vol. I, Reinkarnation und Karma im Christentum, 1985); Gnosis, 1979; Scotland Forever Home, 1980, rev. edn 1984; The Nicene Creed, 1981; Reincarnation as a Christian Hope, 1982; The Gospels as a Mandala of Wisdom, 1982; The Christening of Karma, 1984 (trans. German as vol. II, Reinkarnation und Karma im Christentum, 1986); Apostles Extraordinary, 1986; (ed) Immortality and Human Destiny, 1986; Angels: ministers of grace, 1988; Dictionary of Religion and Philosophy, 1989; Scotland: an intimate portrait, 1990. *Recreations:* manual labour; now oftener reading, music. *Address:* 876 Victoria Avenue, Los Angeles, California 90005–3751, USA. *T:* 213–938–4826. *Clubs:* Athenæum, English-Speaking Union, Commonwealth Trust; Union Society (Oxford); Automobile (Los Angeles).

MACGREGOR, John Malcolm; HM Diplomatic Service; Head of Chancery, British Embassy, Paris, since 1990; *b* 3 Oct. 1946; *s* of late Dr D. F. Macgregor and K. A. Macgregor (*née* Adams); *m* 1982, Judith Anne Brown; three *s* one *d*. *Educ:* Kibworth Beauchamp Grammar Sch., Leics; Balliol Coll., Oxford (BA 1967). ARCO 1965. Taught at Cranleigh Sch., Surrey, 1969–73; joined HM Diplomatic Service, 1973; 1st Sec. (political), New Delhi, 1975; FCO, 1979; Pvte Sec. to Minister of State, FCO, 1981; Assistant, Soviet Dept, FCO, 1983; Dep. Head of Mission, Prague, 1986. *Recreations:* music, languages, travel. *Address:* c/o Foreign and Commonwealth Office, King Charles Street, SW1A 2AH. *T:* Paris 42 66 91 42. *Club:* Cercle Interallié (Paris).

MacGREGOR, Rt. Hon. John (Roddick Russell), OBE 1971; PC 1985; MP (C) South Norfolk, since Feb. 1974; Lord President of the Council and Leader of the House of Commons, since 1990; *b* 14 Feb. 1937; *s* of late Dr. N. S. R. MacGregor; *m* 1962, Jean Mary Elizabeth Dungey; one *s* two *d*. *Educ:* Merchiston Castle Sch., Edinburgh; St Andrews Univ. (MA, 1st cl. Hons); King's Coll., London (LLB; FKC 1988). Univ. Administrator, 1961–62; Editorial Staff, New Society, 1962–63; Special Asst to Prime Minister, Sir Alec Douglas-Home, 1963–64; Conservative Research Dept, 1964–65; Head of Private Office of Rt Hon. Edward Heath, Leader of Opposition, 1965–68; an Opposition Whip, 1977–79; a Lord Comr of HM Treasury, 1979–81; Parly Under-Sec. of State, DoI, 1981–83; Minister of State, MAFF, 1983–85; Chief Sec. to HM Treasury, 1985–87; Minister of Agriculture, Fisheries and Food, 1987–89; Sec. of State for Educn and Sci., 1989–90. Hill Samuel & Co. Ltd, 1968–79 (Dir, 1973–79). Chairman: Fedn of University Cons. and Unionist Assocs, 1959; Bow Group, 1963–64; 1st Pres., Conservative and Christian Democratic Youth Community, 1963–65; formerly Treasurer, Federal Trust for Educn and Research; formerly Trustee, European Educnl Research Trust. *Publications:* contrib. The Conservative Opportunity; also pamphlets. *Recreations:* music, reading, travelling, gardening, conjuring (Mem., Magic Circle, 1989). *Address:* House of Commons, SW1A 0AA.

MACGREGOR, His Honour John Roy; a Circuit Judge, 1974–87; Honorary Recorder of Margate, 1972–79; *b* Brooklyn, NY, 9 Sept. 1913; 4th *s* of Charles George McGregor, of Jamaica and New York. *Educ:* Bedford School. Called to the Bar, Gray's Inn, 1939; Inner Temple (*ad eundem*), 1968; Holker Sen. Scholar, Gray's Inn, 1947. Served in Royal Artillery, 1939–46; RA (TA) and Special Air Service (TA), 1950–61. Dep. Chm., Cambridgeshire and Isle of Ely QS, 1967–71; a Recorder, 1972–74. Legal Assessor to Gen. Optical Council, 1972–74. *Address:* Nether Gaulrig, Yardley Hastings, Northampton NN7 1HD. *T:* Yardley Hastings (060129) 861. *Club:* Special Forces.

MacGREGOR, Neil; *see* MacGregor, R. N.

McGREGOR, Peter, CEng, FIEE; Consultant, Export Group for the Constructional Industries, since 1991 (Director General, 1984–91); Associate Director, Corporate

Renewal Associates Ltd, since 1988; *b* 20 May 1926; *s* of Peter McGregor and Margaret Thomson McGregor (*née* McAuslan); *m* 1954, Marion, *d* of H. T. Downer; one *s* one *d*. *Educ:* Cardiff High Sch.; Univ. of Birmingham; London Sch. of Economics (BSc (Econs)); CompIProdE; MCIM; FBIM. National Service, RE, 1946–48. Various appointments, Ferranti Ltd, 1950–74, incl. Works Manager, Distribution Transformer Dept, Sales Manager, Transformer Div., Gen. Manager, Power Div.; Dir, Industrie Elettriche di Legnano (Italy), 1970–74; Dir, Oxford Univ. Business Summer Sch., 1972; first Sec. Gen., Anglo-German Foundn for Study of Industrial Soc., 1974–81; Industrial Dir (Dep. Sec.), NEDO, 1981–84. Chm., Textile Machinery EDC, 1982–86; Dir, Templeton Technol. Seminar, 1985. Member: N American Adv. Gp, BOTB, 1968–74; Europ. Trade Cttee, BOTB, 1981–83; Adv. Bd, Public Policy Centre, 1984–88; Cttee on Exchange Rate, Public Policy Centre, 1984–87. Industrial Advr to Liberal Party, 1960–73; an Industrial Advr to Social and Liberal Democrats, 1988–90; Chm., Hazel Grove Liberal Assoc., 1971–74; contested (L) Ilford South, 1964. Mem., Königswinter Conf. steering cttee, 1976–90. Hon. Treasurer, Anglo-German Assoc., 1983–91. FRSA. *Publications:* various articles and pamphlets especially on industrial relations, company structure, market economy. *Recreations:* sailing, walking, reading, listening to music, writing, conversation. *Address:* Kingsbury House, 15/17 King Street, SW1Y 6QU. *T:* 071–930 5377. *Clubs:* Athenæum, Caledonian.

MacGREGOR, (Robert) Neil; Director, National Gallery, since 1987; *b* 16 June 1946; *s* of Alexander Rankin MacGregor and Anna Fulton Scobie MacGregor (*née* Neil). *Educ:* Glasgow Acad.; New Coll., Oxford; Ecole Normale Supérieure, Paris; Univ. of Edinburgh; Courtauld Inst. of Art. Mem., Faculty of Advocates, Edinburgh, 1972. Lectr in History of Art and Architecture, Univ. of Reading, 1976; Editor, The Burlington Magazine, 1981–86. Trustee, Pilgrim Trust, 1990–. *Publications:* contribs to Apollo, The Burlington Magazine, Connoisseur, etc. *Address:* National Gallery, Trafalgar Square, WC2.

MacGREGOR, Susan Katriona, (Sue); Presenter, Today, BBC Radio Four, since 1984; *b* 30 Aug. 1941; *d* of Dr James MacGregor and Margaret MacGregor (*née* MacGregor). *Educ:* Herschel School, Cape, South Africa. Announcer/producer, South African Broadcasting Corp., 1962–67; BBC Radio reporter, World at One, World This Weekend, PM, 1967–72; Presenter: Woman's Hour, BBC Radio 4, 1972–87; Tuesday Call, 1973–86; Conversation Piece, 1978–; Around Westminster, BBC TV, 1990–. Dir, Hemming Publishing (formerly Municipal Journal) Ltd, 1980–. FRSA. *Recreations:* theatre, cinema, ski-ing. *Address:* c/o BBC, Portland Place, W1A 1AA. *T:* 071–927 5566.

McGRIGOR, Captain Sir Charles Edward, 5th Bt, *cr* 1831; DL; Rifle Brigade, retired; Member Royal Company of Archers (HM Body Guard for Scotland); *b* 5 Oct. 1922; *s* of Lieut-Colonel Sir Charles McGrigor, 4th Bt, OBE, and Lady McGrigor, *d* of Edward Lygon Somers Cocks, Bake, St Germans, Cornwall; *S* father, 1946; *m* 1948, Mary Bettine, *e d* of Sir Archibald Charles Edmonstone, 6th Bt; two *s* two *d*. *Educ:* Eton. War of 1939–45 (despatches); joined Army, 1941, from Eton; served with Rifle Bde, N. Africa, Italy, Austria. ADC to Duke of Gloucester, 1945–47, in Australia and England. Exon, Queen's Bodyguard, Yeoman of the Guard, 1970–85. Mem. Cttee of Management, a Dep. Chm. and a Vice-Pres., RNLI and Convenor, Scottish Lifeboat Council. DL Argyll and Bute, 1987. *Recreations:* fishing, gardening. *Heir:* *s* James Angus Rhoderick Neil McGrigor [*b* 19 Oct. 1949; *m* 1987, Caroline, *d* of late Jacques Roboh, Paris; two *d*]. *Address:* Upper Sonachan, Dalmally, Argyll PA33 1BJ. *Club:* New (Edinburgh).

McGROUTHER, Prof. (Duncan) Angus, MD; FRCSGlas, FRCS; Professor of Plastic and Reconstructive Surgery, University College London, since 1989 (first British chair in this subject); *b* 3 March 1946; *s* of Dr John Ingram McGrouther and Margot Christina Cooke Gray; *m* 1967, Sandra Elizabeth Jackson; one *s* one *d*. *Educ:* Glasgow High Sch.; Univ. of Glasgow (MB ChB 1969; MD Hons 1988); Univ. of Strathclyde (MSc Bioengineering 1975). Glasgow Royal Infirmary, 1969–74; Cruden Med. Res. Fellow, Bioengrg Unit, Univ. of Strathclyde, 1972–73; Registrar and Sen. Registrar in Plastic Surgery, Canniesburn Hosp., Glasgow, 1975–78; Assistentarzt, Klinikum Rechts der Isar, Munich, 1978; Consultant Plastic Surgeon: Shotley Bridge Gen. Hosp. and Sunderland Dist Gen. Hosp., 1979–80; Canniesburn Hosp., 1981–89. Christine Kleinert Vis. Prof., Univ. of Louisville, 1988. Kay-Kilner Prize, 1979; Pulvertaft Prize, 1981. *Publications:* papers on anatomy, biomechanics, plastic surgery, hand surgery and microsurgery. *Recreations:* mountains, sea, books, fundraising for Phoenix Appeal. *Address:* Department of Plastic and Reconstructive Surgery, University College London, Rayne Institute, University Street, WC1E 6JJ. *T:* 071–380 9867.

McGUFFIN, Prof. Peter, PhD; FRCP; FRCPsych; Professor of Psychological Medicine, University of Wales College of Medicine, since 1987; *b* 4 Feb. 1949; *s* of Captain W. B. McGuffin, RD, RNR and M. M. McGuffin; *m* 1972, Dr Anne E. Farmer; one *s* two *d*. *Educ:* Univ. of Leeds (MB ChB); Univ. of London (PhD). MRCP 1976, FRCP 1988; MRCPsych 1978, FRCPsych 1990. St James Univ. Hosp., Leeds, 1972–77; Registrar, Sen. Registrar, Maudsley Hosp., 1977–79; MRC Fellow, MRC Sen. Clinical Fellow, Inst. of Psychiatry, 1979–86; Hon. Consultant, Maudsley and King's Coll. Hosps, 1983–86. Vis. Fellow, Washington Univ., St Louis, 1981–82. *Publications:* Scientific Principles of Psychopathology, 1984; The New Genetics of Mental Illness, 1991; articles, research papers on psychiatry and genetics. *Recreations:* classical guitar, sailing, listening to Gardeners' Question Time. *Address:* 68 Heol-y-Delyn, Lisvane, Cardiff CF4 5SR.

MacGUIGAN, Hon. Mark Rudolph, PC (Can.) 1980; PhD, JSD; **Hon. Mr Justice MacGuigan;** Judge, Federal Court of Appeal, Canada, since 1984; *b* 17 Feb. 1931; *s* of Hon. Mark R. MacGuigan and Agnes V. Trainor; two *s* one *d*; *m* 1987, Judge Patricia Dougherty, Oklahoma Ct of Appeals. *Educ:* Queen Square Sch.; Prince of Wales (Jun.) Coll.; St Dunstan's Univ., Charlottetown (BA *summa cum laude*); Univ. of Toronto (MA, PhD); Osgoode Hall Law Sch. (LLB); Columbia Univ. (LLM, JSD). Admitted to Law Soc. of Upper Canada, 1958. Asst Prof. of Law, 1960–63, and Associate Prof. of Law, 1963–66, Univ. of Toronto; Prof. of Law, Osgoode Hall Law Sch., 1966–67; Dean, Faculty of Law, Univ. of Windsor, 1967–68. MP for Windsor–Walkerville, Ont, 1968–84; Parly Secretary: to Minister of Manpower and Immigration, 1972–74; to Minister of Labour, 1974–75; Opposition Critic of Solicitor Gen., 1979–80; Sec. of State for External Affairs, 1980–82; Minister of Justice, 1982–84. Chairman: House of Commons Special Cttee on Statutory Instruments, 1968–69; Standing Cttee on Justice and Legal Affairs, 1975–79; Sub-Cttee on Penitentiary System in Canada, 1976–77; Co-Chairman, Special Jt Cttee on Constitution of Canada, 1970–72 and 1978. Hon. LLD: Univ. of PEI, 1971; St Thomas Univ., 1981; Law Soc. of Upper Canada, 1983; Univ. of Windsor, Ont, 1983. *Publications:* Cases and Materials on Creditors' Rights, 2nd edn 1967; Jurisprudence: readings and cases, 2nd edn 1966. *Recreations:* running, tennis, skiing, swimming. *Address:* 23 Linden Terrace, Ottawa, Ont K1S 1Z1, Canada. *Clubs:* Rideau, Cercle universitaire (Ottawa).

McGUIGAN BURNS, Simon Hugh; *see* Burns.

McGUINNESS, Maj.-Gen. Brendan Peter, CB 1986; Director of Education and Training Liaison, Engineering Employers' West Midlands Association, since 1988 (Head of Educational Liaison, 1987–88); *b* 26 June 1931; *s* of Bernard and May McGuinness; *m* 1968, Ethne Patricia (*née* Kelly); one *s* one *d*. *Educ:* Mount St Mary's College. psc, rcds. Commissioned Royal Artillery, 1950; regimental duty, 1950–60; Staff, 1960–62; sc 1963; Adjutant, 1964–65; Staff, 1965–68 (despatches,Borneo, 1966); Battery Comdr, 1968–70; Staff Coll. Directing Staff, 1970–72; CO 45 Medium Regt, 1972–75; CRA 1st Armd Div., 1975–77; RCDS 1978; MoD Staff, 1979–81; Dep. Comdr, NE District, 1981–83; GOC W Dist, 1983–86. Hon. Col, Birmingham Univ. OTC, 1987–; Hon. Regtl Col, 45 Field Regt, 1985–. Project Dir, 1987–88, Governor, 1988–, The City Technol. Coll., Kingshurst. *Recreations:* tennis, hill walking, beagling. *Address:* The Old Rectory, 14 Whittington Road, Worcester WR5 2JU. *T:* Worcester (0905) 360102. *Club:* Army and Navy.

McGUINNESS, Rt. Rev. James Joseph; *see* Nottingham, Bishop of, (RC).

McGUIRE, Gerald, OBE 1974; Chairman, Countryside Link Group, 1982–86; *b* 12 July 1918; *s* of John Charles McGuire and Adelaide Maud McGuire (*née* Davies); *m* 1942, Eveline Mary Jenkins; one *s* one *d*. *Educ:* Trinity County Sch., Wood Green. Youth Hostels Association: Reg. Sec., N Yorks, 1944–64; National Countryside and Educn Officer, 1964–74; Dep. Nat. Sec., 1974–82; Pres., N England Region, 1989–. President: Ramblers Assoc., 1975–78 (Vice Pres., 1978–; Pres., Lake Dist Area, 1983–86; Pres., E Yorks and Derwent Area, 1987–90); Assoc. of National Park and Countryside Voluntary Wardens, 1978–80; Council for Nat. Parks, 1990– (Vice Pres., 1983–90; Vice Chm., 1981–83). Member: N York Moors Nat. Park Cttee, 1953–72, 1985–91; Exec. Cttee, CPRE, 1966–76, 1981–84; Gosling Cttee on Footpaths, 1967–68; Countryside Commn, 1976–79; Commn on Energy and the Environment, 1978–81; Recreation and Conservation Cttee, Yorks Water Authority, 1984–89; Yorks Regional Cttee, Nat. Trust, 1985–. Vice Pres., Open Spaces Soc., 1982– (Vice Chm. 1971–76); Vice Chairman: Standing Cttee on Nat. Parks, 1970–76; Council for Environmental Conservation, 1981–82; Trustee, Gatliff Trust, 1983–. Hon. Mem., Cyclists Touring Club, 1978–. Cert. of Merit, Internat. Youth Hostel Fedn, 1983; Richard Schirrmann (Founder's) Medal, German Youth Hostels Assoc., 1983; Nat. Blood Transfusion Service Award for 100 donations, 1983. *Recreations:* reading, music, walking in the countryside. *Address:* 24 Castle Howard Drive, Malton, North Yorks YO17 0BA. *T:* Malton (0653) 692521.

McGUIRE, Michael Thomas Francis; *b* 3 May 1926; *m* 1954, Marie T. Murphy; three *s* two *d*. *Educ:* Elementary Schools. Coal miner. Whole-time NUM Branch Secretary, 1957–64. Joined Lab. Party, 1951. MP (Lab): Ince, 1964–83; Makerfield, 1983–87. PPS to Minister of Sport, 1974–77. Member: Council of Europe, 1977–87; WEU, 1977–87. *Recreations:* most out-door sports, especially Rugby League football; traditional music, especially Irish traditional music. *Address:* 21 Haydock Park Gardens, Newton-le-Willows, Lancs WA12 0JF.

McGURK, Colin Thomas, OBE 1971 (MBE 1963); HM Diplomatic Service, retired; *b* 9 July 1922; *m* 1946, Ella Taylor; one *s*. *Educ:* St Mary's Coll., Middlesbrough. Served in Army, 1942–45. HM Foreign (subseq. Diplomatic) Service; served in British Embassies, Cairo, Addis Ababa, Ankara; 3rd Sec., HM Legation, Sofia, 1953–55; 2nd Sec. (Commercial), Athens, 1956–58; FO, 1958–62; HM Consul, Stanleyville, 1962; 1st Sec., Yaoundé, Brussels and Kuwait, 1962–70; Commercial Counsellor, Kuwait, 1971–72; Commercial Inspector, FCO, 1972–75; Counsellor (Economic and Commercial), New Delhi, 1975–77 and Canberra, 1977–81. *Recreations:* computer programming, painting, sailing. *Address:* 113 High Street, Burnham-on-Crouch, Essex CM0 8AH. *T:* Maldon (0621) 782467. *Club:* Royal Burnham Yacht.

McHALE, Keith Michael; His Honour Judge McHale; a Circuit Judge, since 1980; *b* 26 March 1928; *s* of late Cyril Michael McHale and Gladys McHale; *m* 1966, Rosemary Margaret Arthur; one *s* one *d*. Called to the Bar, Gray's Inn, 1951. *Address:* Oak Lodge, Albemarle Road, Beckenham, Kent BR3 2HS.

McHARDY, Prof. William Duff, CBE 1990; Regius Professor of Hebrew, Oxford University, and Student of Christ Church, 1960–78; *b* 26 May 1911; *o s* of late W. D. McHardy, Cullen, Banffshire; *m* 1941, Vera (*d* 1984), *y d* of late T. Kemp, York; one *d*. *Educ:* Fordyce Academy; Universities of Aberdeen, Edinburgh, and Oxford (St John's College). MA, BD (Aberdeen), MA (Edinburgh), DPhil (Oxford). Research Fellow in Syriac, Selly Oak Colleges, Birmingham, 1942; Lecturer in Aramaic and Syriac, University of Oxford, 1945; Samuel Davidson Professor of Old Testament Studies in the University of London, 1948–60. Examiner, Universities of Aberdeen, Cambridge, Durham, Edinburgh, Leeds, London, Oxford and University Colleges of the Gold Coast/Ghana and Ibadan. Hon. Curator of Mingana Collection of Oriental Manuscripts, 1947. Grinfield Lecturer on the Septuagint, Oxford, 1959–61. Dep. Dir, 1968, Jt Dir, 1971, New English Bible; Dir, Revised English Bible, 1973–90. Burgess, Royal Burgh of Cullen, 1975. Hon. DD Aberdeen, 1958. Hon. Fellow, Selly Oak Colleges, 1980. *Publications:* articles in journals. *Address:* 2 Ogilvie Park, Cullen, Banffshire AB5 2XZ. *T:* Cullen (0542) 41008.

McHENRY, Donald F.; University Research Professor of Diplomacy and International Affairs, Georgetown University, since 1981; *b* 13 Oct. 1936; *s* of Limas McHenry and Dora Lee Brooks; *m* Mary Williamson (marr. diss.); one *s* two *d*. *Educ:* Lincoln Senior High Sch., East St Louis, Ill; Illinois State Univ. (BS); Southern Illinois Univ. (MSc); Georgetown Univ. Taught at Howard Univ., Washington, 1959–62; joined Dept of State, 1963; Head of Dependent Areas Section, Office of UN Polit. Affairs, 1965–68; Asst to Sec. of State, US, 1969; Special Asst to Counsellor, Dept of State, 1969–71; Lectr, Sch. of Foreign Service, Georgetown Univ.; Guest Scholar, Brookings Inst., and Internat. Affairs Fellow, Council on Foreign Relations (on leave from State Dept), 1971–73; resigned from State Dept, 1973; Project Dir, Humanitarian Policy Studies, Carnegie Endowment for Internat. Peace, Washington, 1973–76; served in transition team of President Carter, 1976–77; Ambassador and Deputy Rep. of US to UN Security Council, 1977–79, Permanent Rep., 1979; US Ambassador to UN, 1979–81. Director: Internat. Paper Co.; First National Bank of Boston; Bank of Boston Corp.; Smith Kline Beecham Corp.; Coca-Cola; American Telephone and Telegraph; Inst. for Internat. Economics; American Ditchley Foundn; Nat. Inst. for Dispute Resolution. Chm., Bd of Dirs, Africare. Trustee: Mount Holyoke Coll.; Ford Foundn; Brookings Instn; Phelps-Stokes Fund. Member, Amer. Polit. Sci. Assoc. Hon. degrees: Dennison, Duke, Eastern Illinois, Georgetown, Harvard, Illinois State, Michigan, Princeton, Southern Illinois, Tufts, and Washington Univs; Amherst, Bates, Boston and Williams Colleges. Superior Honor Award, Dept of State, 1966. Chm. and Mem. Council on Foreign Relations and Editorial Bd, Foreign Policy Magazine. *Publication:* Micronesia: Trust Betrayed, 1975. *Address:* Georgetown University, 37th and O Streets, NW, Washington, DC 20057, USA.

MACHIN, Arnold, OBE 1965; RA 1956 (ARA 1947); sculptor, FRBS 1955; Master of Sculpture, Royal Academy School, 1958–67; Tutor, Royal College of Art, 1951–58; *b* 1911; *s* of William James Machin, Stoke-on-Trent; *m* 1949, Patricia, *d* of late Lt-Col Henry Newton; one *s*. *Educ:* Stoke School of Art; Derby School of Art; Royal College of Art. Silver Medal and Travelling Scholarship for Sculpture, 1940; two works in terracotta: St John the Baptist and The Annunciation, purchased by Tate Gallery, 1943; Spring terracotta purchased by President and Council of Royal Academy under terms of Chantrey

Bequest, 1947; designed: new coin effigy, 1964, 1967 (decimal coinage); definitive issue of postage stamp, 1967; Silver Wedding commemorative crown, 1972; commemorative Silver Jubilee crown, 1977. *Recreations:* music, garden design. *Address:* 4 Sydney Close, SW3; Garmelow Manor, near Eccleshall, Staffordshire.

MACHIN, David; Under Treasurer, Gray's Inn, since 1989; *b* 25 April 1934; *s* of late Noel and Joan Machin; *m* 1963, Sarah Mary, *yr d* of late Col W. A. Chester-Master; two *d. Educ:* Eton (Oppidan Scholar); Trinity Coll., Cambridge. National Service, 1952–54 (2nd Lieut Welsh Guards). Editor, William Heinemann Ltd, 1957–66; Literary Agent, Gregson & Wigan Ltd and London International, 1966–68; Partner, A. P. Watt & Son, 1968–70; Director: Jonathan Cape Ltd, 1970–78; Chatto, Bodley Head and Jonathan Cape Ltd, 1977–78, 1981–87; Jt Man. Dir, 1981, Man. Dir, 1982–87, The Bodley Head Ltd; Dir, Triad Paperbacks Ltd, 1983–86; Gen. Sec., The Society of Authors, 1978–81. Vice-Chm., Hammersmith Democrats, 1988–89. FRSA. *Publications:* (contrib.) Outlook, 1963; articles in The Author, The Bookseller. *Address:* 4 South Square, Gray's Inn, WC1R 5HP. *Club:* Garrick.

MACHIN, Edward Anthony, QC 1973; a Recorder of the Crown Court, 1976–90; a Judge of the Courts of Appeal of Jersey and Guernsey, since 1988; *b* 28 June 1925; *s* of Edward Arthur Machin and Olive Muriel Smith; *m* 1953, Jean Margaret McKanna; two *s* one *d. Educ:* Christ's Coll., Finchley; New Coll., Oxford. MA 1950; BCL 1950; Vinerian Law Scholar, 1950; Tancred Student, 1950; Cassel Scholar, 1951. Called to Bar, Lincoln's Inn, 1951; Bencher, 1980. *Publications:* Redgrave's Factories Acts, 1962, 1966, 1972; Redgrave's Offices and Shops, 1965 and 1973; Redgrave's Health and Safety in Factories, 1976, 1982; Health and Safety at Work, 1980; Health and Safety, 1990; (contrib.) Medical Negligence, 1990. *Recreations:* music, sailing, languages. *Address:* Strand End, Strand, Topsham, Exeter EX3 0BB. *T:* Topsham (0392) 877992; 26 Woodridge Way, Northwood, Mddx HA6 2BE. *T:* Northwood (09274) 29197. *Club:* Bar Yacht.

MACHIN, Kenneth Arthur; QC 1977; His Honour Judge Machin; a Circuit Judge, since 1984 (Deputy Circuit Judge, 1976–79); Chief Social Security Commissioner, since 1990; *b* 13 July 1936; *o s* of Thomas Arthur Machin and Edith May Machin; *m* 1983, Amaryllis Francesca (Member of Court of Common Council, Cripplegate Ward, City of London), *o d* of Dr Donald and Lucille Bigley. *Educ:* St Albans School. Called to the Bar, Middle Temple, 1960; South Eastern Circuit and Central Criminal Court; a Recorder of the Crown Court, 1979–84. Freeman, City of London. *Recreations:* painting, martello towers, Scalextric. *Address:* New Court, Temple, EC4. *T:* 071–353 7741; The Penthouse, 502 Ben Jonson House, Barbican, EC2.

McHUGH, James, CBE 1989; FEng 1986; Chairman, British Pipe Coaters Ltd, since 1991; *b* 4 May 1930; *s* of late Edward McHugh and Martha (*née* Smith); *m* 1953, Sheila (*née* Cape); two *d. Educ:* Carlisle Grammar Sch.; various colls. FIMechE, FIGasE, FInstPet; FIQA; CBIM. FRSA. Served Army, National Service. Entered Gas Industry, 1947; technical and managerial appts in Northern and E Midlands Gas Bds; Prodn Engr 1967, Dir of Engrg 1971, W Midlands Gas Bd; British Gas Corporation, subseq. British Gas plc: Dir of Ops, 1975; Mem., 1979; Man. Dir, Prodn and Supply, 1982; Man. Dir, 1986; Gp Exec. Mem., 1989–91. Dir, Lloyd's Register Quality Assurance Ltd, 1985–. Member: Meteorological Cttee, MoD, 1981–85; Engrg Council, 1989–; Pres., IGasE, 1986–87. Freeman, City of London. *Recreations:* mountaineering, dinghy sailing. *Address:* British Pipe Coaters Ltd, 152 Grosvenor Road, SW1V 3JL. *Clubs:* Royal Automobile, Anglo-Belgian.

McHUGH, Dr Mary Patricia; Coroner for Southern District of London, 1965–85; *b* 5 June 1915; *d* of J. C. McHugh, MB, BS, BAO, Royal Univ., Dublin, and Madeleine Jeffroy Leblan, Brittany, France; *m* 1943, E. G. Murphy, FRCS (marr. diss., 1952); one *s* two *d. Educ:* Nymphenburg, Munich, Bavaria; Notre Dame, Clapham; Birmingham Univ. MB, ChB, 1942; PhD Fac. of Laws, London 1976. Birmingham House Physician and Anæsthetist, St Chad's Hospital, Birmingham, 1942–43; General Practice, London, 1944–65. Called to the Bar, Inner Temple, 1959. Past Chm., Whole Time Coroner's Assoc.; Mem., British Academy of Forensic Sciences, 1963; Founder Mem., RCGP; Associate, Inst. of Linguists, 1981; Associate to Res. and Adv. Cttee, Cantab Gp of Toxicology and Biosciences, Cambridge, 1983–. Medico Legal Columnist, Pulse, 1981–. *Publication:* Treasure Trove and the Law (Med. Sci. Law vol. 16 no 2), 1976. *Recreations:* cooking, languages. *Address:* 8 Hitherwood Drive, College Road, Dulwich, SE19 1XB. *T:* 081–670 8400.

McILVENNA, Maj.-Gen. John Antony, CB 1980; Director of Army Legal Services, 1978–80, retired; *b* 10 Dec. 1919; *s* of Joseph Henry McIlvenna and Dorothy (*née* Brown); *m* Dr Hildegard Paula Gertrud Overlack; one *s* one *d. Educ:* Royal Grammar School, Newcastle upon Tyne; Hymers Coll., Hull; Durham Univ. LLB 1940. Private, KOYLI; 2nd Lieut, DLI, 1941; despatches 1945; admitted Solicitor, 1947; Captain, Army Legal Services, 1950; served in Hong Kong, Aden, Egypt, Libya and BAOR; Maj.-Gen. and Dir, newly formed Army Legal Corps, 1978. Chm. and Dir, United Services Catholic Assoc., 1979–81, Vice-Pres., 1981–. *Recreations:* swimming, music, history. *Address:* Westfield, Biddenden, Kent TN27 8BB. *Club:* Army and Navy.

McILWAIN, Alexander Edward, CBE 1985; WS; President, Law Society of Scotland, 1983–84; Senior Partner, Leonards, Solicitors, Hamilton, since 1984 (Partner, since 1963); *b* 4 July 1933; *s* of Edward Walker McIlwain and Gladys Edith Horne or McIlwain; *m* 1961, Moira Margaret Kinnaird; three *d. Educ:* Aberdeen Grammar Sch.; Aberdeen Univ. MA 1954; LLB 1956. Pres., Students Representative Council, Univ. of Aberdeen, 1956–57. Commnd RCS, 1957–59, Lieut. Admitted Solicitor in Scotland, 1957; SSC, 1966. Burgh Prosecutor, Hamilton, 1966–75; District Prosecutor, Hamilton, 1975–76; Dean, Soc. of Solicitors of Hamilton, 1981–83; Vice Pres., Law Soc. of Scotland, 1982–83; Hon. Sheriff, Sheriffdom of South Strathclyde, Dumfries and Galloway at Hamilton, 1982; Temp. Sheriff, 1984. WS 1985. Chm., Legal Aid Central Cttee, 1985–87 (Mem., 1980–83); Member: Lanarkshire Health Bd, 1981–; Central Adv. Cttee on Justices of the Peace, 1987–; Review Cttee, Scottish Legal Aid Bd, 1987–. Hon. Vice-Pres., Scottish Lawyers for Nuclear Disarmament, 1985– (Mem., 1984–). Chm., Lanarkshire Scout Area, 1981– (Mem. Council, Scout Assoc., 1987–). Hon. Mem., Amer. Bar Assoc., 1983. *Recreations:* work, gardening, listening to music. *Address:* Craigievar, Bothwell Road, Uddingston, Glasgow G71 7EY. *T:* Uddingston (0698) 813368. *Club:* New (Edinburgh).

McILWAIN, Prof. Henry, DSc, PhD; Professor of Biochemistry in the University of London at Institute of Psychiatry, British Postgraduate Medical Federation, 1954–80, now Emeritus; Hon. Senior Research Fellow, Department of Pharmacology, University of Birmingham, since 1987; *b* Newcastle upon Tyne, 20 Dec. 1912; *e s* of John McIlwain, Glasgow, and Louisa (*née* Widdowson), Old Whittington; *m* 1st, 1941, Valerie (*d* 1977), *d* of K. Durston, Bude, Cornwall; two *d*; 2nd, 1979, Marjorie Allan Crennell, *d* of E. A. Crennell, Newcastle upon Tyne. *Educ:* King's Coll., Newcastle upon Tyne (University of Durham); The Queen's Coll., Oxford. Leverhulme Research Fellow and later Mem. of Scientific Staff, Medical Research Council, in Council's Dept of Bacterial Chemistry (Middlesex Hosp., London) and Unit for Research in Cell Metabolism (Univ. of Sheffield), 1937–47; Lectr in Biochemistry, Univ. of Sheffield, 1944–47; Senior Lectr (later Reader) in Biochemistry, Inst. of Psychiatry (British Postgraduate Medical Fedn), Univ. of London, 1948–54. Vis. Prof., St Thomas's Hospital Med. Sch., 1980–87. Hon. Biochemist, Bethlem Royal Hosp. and Maudsley Hosp., 1948–80. Mem. Editorial Bd, Biochemical Jl, 1947–50; Historian, Internat. Soc. for Neurochemistry, 1984–. Research Associate, Univ. of Chicago, 1951; Visiting Lectr, Univ. of Otago, New Zealand, 1954; Lectr and Medallist, Univ. of Helsinki, 1973; Thudichum Lectr and Medallist, Biochemical Soc., 1975. Dr *hc* Univ. d'Aix-Marseille, 1974. *Publications:* Biochemistry and the Central Nervous System, 1955, 5th edn (with H. S. Bachelard), 1985; Chemotherapy and the Central Nervous System, 1957; (with R. Rodnight) Practical Neurochemistry, 1962; Chemical Exploration of the Brain, 1963; (ed) Practical Neurochemistry, 1975; 250 papers in the Biochemical Journal and other scientific and medical publications. *Address:* 68 Cartway, Bridgnorth, Shropshire WV16 4BG. *T:* Bridgnorth (0746) 761353.

McILWRAITH, Arthur Renwick; Sheriff of South Strathclyde, Dumfries and Galloway (formerly Lanark) at Airdrie, 1972–85, retired; *b* 8 April 1914; *s* of Nicholas Renwick McIlwraith and Adaline Gowans McIlwraith; *m* 1950, Thelma Preston or Sargent; one *s* one *d. Educ:* High Sch. of Glasgow; Univ. of Glasgow (MA, LLB). Grad. 1938. Served War: Highland Light Infantry, 1939–45. Solicitor, 1945–72. *Recreation:* fishing. *Address:* 29 Kelvin Court, Anniesland, Glasgow G12 0AB.

McINDOE, William Ian, CB 1978; Deputy Secretary, Department of the Environment, 1979–86; *b* 11 March 1929; *s* of John McIndoe, Leven, Fife and Agnes Scott; *m* 1st, 1954, Irene Armour Mudie (*d* 1966); one *s* two *d*; 2nd, 1971, Jamesanna Smart (*née* MacGregor). *Educ:* Sedbergh; Corpus Christi Coll., Oxford. 2nd Lieut 2 RHA, 1951–53; CRO, 1953–63, served in Canberra and Salisbury, 1956–62, Private Sec. to Sec. of State, 1962–63; Private Sec. to Sec. of Cabinet, later Asst Sec., Cabinet Office, 1963–66; Scottish Office, 1966–76, Under-Sec., 1971; Dep. Sec., Cabinet Office, 1976–79. Dep. Chm., Housing Corp., 1986–90. *Address:* Speedyburn House, Station Road, Gifford, E Lothian EH41 4QL. *T:* Gifford (062081) 363. *Club:* New (Edinburgh).

McINERNEY, Prof. John Peter; Glanely Professor of Agricultural Policy and Director of Agricultural Economics Unit, University of Exeter, since 1984; *b* 10 Jan. 1939; *s* of Peter McInerney and Eva McInerney; *m* 1961, Audrey M. Perry; one *s* one *d. Educ:* Colyton Grammar Sch., Colyford, Devon; Univ. of London (BScAgric Hons); Univ. of Oxford (DipAgricEcons); Iowa State Univ. (PhD). Lectr in Agricl Econs, Wye Coll., Univ. of London, 1964–66; Lectr and Sen. Lectr in Agricl Econs, Univ. of Manchester, 1967–78; Prof. of Agricl Econs and Management, Univ. of Reading, 1978–84. Research Economist and Cons., World Bank, Washington, DC, 1972–. Phi Kappa Phi 1964, Gamma Sigma Delta 1964. *Publications:* The Food Industry: economics and policy (jtly), 1983; Badgers and Bovine Tuberculosis (jtly), 1986; Disease in Farm Livestock: economics and policy (jtly), 1987; Diversification in the Use of Farm Resources, 1989; chapters in: Current Issues in Economic Policy, 1975, 2nd edn 1980; Resources Policy, 1982, etc; articles in Jl of Agricl Econs, Amer. Jl of Agricl Econs, Canadian Jl of Agricl Econs, Outlook on Agric. *Recreations:* doing it myself, tentative farming, introspection. *Address:* c/o Agricultural Economics Unit, University of Exeter, Exeter EX4 6TL. *T:* Exeter (0392) 263837. *Club:* Templeton Social.

MacINNES, Archibald, CVO 1977; Under Secretary, Property Services Agency, Department of the Environment, 1973; retired 1989; *b* 10 April 1919; *s* of Duncan and Catherine MacInnes; *m* 1950, Nancey Elisabeth Blyth (*d* 1976); one *s* two *d. Educ:* Kirkcudbright Academy; Royal Technical Coll., Glasgow. FIMechE. Scott's Shipbuilding and Engineering Co., Greenock, 1937–44; Colonial Service, Nigeria, 1945–59; War Office Works Organisation: Gibraltar, 1959–63; Southern Comd, Salisbury, Wilts, 1963–64; MPBW, Bristol, 1964–68; DoE, Germany, 1968–72; Dir, London Region, PSA, DoE, 1972–79; part-time Planning Inspector, DoE, 1980–89. FBIM. Coronation Medal. *Recreations:* golf, shooting, fishing. *Address:* Lower Road, Homington, Salisbury, Wilts SP5 4NG. *T:* Coombe Bissett (072277) 336.

MacINNES, Hamish, OBE 1979; BEM; Founder and Leader, Glencoe Mountain Rescue Team, since 1960; author and film consultant (safety and production), BBC and major movies; Director, Glencoe Productions Ltd, since 1989; Hon. Director, Leishman Memorial Research Centre, Glencoe, since 1975; *b* 7 July 1930. Dep. Leader, British Everest Expedition, 1975. Mountain Rescue Cttee for Scotland (Past Sec.). Founder and Hon. Pres., Search and Rescue Dog Assoc.; Past Pres., Alpine Climbing Group; Pres., Guide Dogs for the Blind Adventure Gp, 1986–. Designer of climbing equipment, incl. the first all metal ice axe, terrodactyl ice tools, the MacInnes stretchers, MacInnes Boxes for high altitude mountain camping. Hon. LLD Glasgow, 1983; Hon. DSc Aberdeen, 1988. *Publications:* Climbing, 1964; Scottish Climbs, 2 vols, 1971, 2nd edn (1 vol.) 1981; International Mountain Rescue Handbook, 1972, 2nd edn 1984 (also USA); Call-Out: mountain rescue, 1973, 4th edn 1986; Climb to the Lost World, 1974; Death Reel (novel), 1976; West Highland Walks, vols 1 and 2, 1979, Vol. 3, 1983, Vol. 4, 1988; Look Behind the Ranges, 1979; Scottish Winter Climbs, 1980; High Drama (stories), 1980; Beyond the Ranges, 1984; Sweep Search, 1985; The Price of Adventure, 1987; My Scotland, 1988; The Way Through the Glens, 1989; Land of Mountain and Mist, 1989; books have been translated into Russian, Japanese and German. *Address:* Achnacone, Glencoe, Argyll PA39 4LA.

McINNES, John Colin; QC (Scot.) 1990; Sheriff of Tayside Central and Fife, since 1974 (at Cupar and Perth); *b* 21 Nov. 1938; *s* of late Mr I. W. McInnes, WS, and of Mrs Lucy McInnes, Cupar, Fife; *m* 1966, Elisabeth Mabel Neilson; one *s* one *d. Educ:* Cargilfield Sch., Edinburgh; Merchiston Castle Sch., Edinburgh; Brasenose Coll., Oxford (BA); Edinburgh Univ. (LLB). 2nd Lieut 8th Royal Tank Regt, 1957–58; Lieut Fife and Forfar Yeomanry/Scottish Horse (TA), 1958–64. Advocate, 1963. In practice at Scottish Bar, 1963–73; Tutor, Faculty of Law, Edinburgh Univ., 1965–73; Sheriff of the Lothians and Peebles, 1973–74. Mem. and Vice-Pres., Security Service Tribunal, 1989–. Director: R. Mackness & Co. Ltd, 1963–70; Fios Group Ltd, 1970–72 (Chm., 1970–72). Chm., Fife Family Conciliation Service, 1988–90. Mem. Court, St Andrews Univ., 1983–91. Contested (C) Aberdeen North, 1964. *Publication:* Divorce Law and Practice in Scotland, 1990. *Recreations:* shooting, fishing, ski-ing, photography. *Address:* Parkneuk, Blebo Craigs, Cupar, Fife KY15 5UG. *T:* Strathkinness (033485) 366.

MacINNES, Keith Gordon, CMG 1984; HM Diplomatic Service; Ambassador to the Philippines, since 1987; *b* 17 July 1935; *s* of late Kenneth MacInnes and of Helen MacInnes (*née* Gordon); *m* 1st, 1966, Jennifer Anne Fennell (marr. diss. 1980); one *s* one *d*; 2nd, 1985, Hermione Pattinson. *Educ:* Rugby; Trinity Coll., Cambridge (MA); Pres., Cambridge Union Soc., 1957. HM Forces, 1953–55. FO, 1960; Third, later Second Secretary, Buenos Aires, 1961–64; FO, 1964 (First Sec., 1965); Private Sec. to Permanent Under-Sec., Commonwealth Office, 1965–68; First Sec. (Information), Madrid, 1968–70; FCO, 1970–74; Counsellor and Head of Chancery: Prague, 1974–77; Dep. Perm. Rep., UK Mission, Geneva, 1977–80; Head of Information Dept, FCO, 1980–83; Asst Under-Sec. of State and Principal Finance Officer, FCO, 1983–87. *Recreations:* golf, bridge. *Address:* c/o Foreign and Commonwealth Office, SW1A 2AH.

McINTOSH, family name of **Baron McIntosh of Haringey.**

McINTOSH OF HARINGEY, Baron *cr* 1982 (Life Peer), of Haringey in Greater London; **Andrew Robert McIntosh;** Chairman, SVP United Kingdom Ltd, since 1983; *b* 30 April 1933; *s* of Prof. A. W. McIntosh and late Jenny (*née* Britton); *m* 1962, Naomi Ellen Sargant; two *s. Educ:* Haberdashers' Aske's Hampstead Sch.; Royal Grammar Sch., High Wycombe; Jesus Coll., Oxford (MA); Ohio State Univ. (Fellow in Econs, 1956–57). Gallup Poll, 1957–61; Hoover Ltd, 1961–63; Market Res. Manager, Osram (GEC) Ltd, 1963–65; Man. Dir, 1965–81, Chm., 1981–88, Dep. Chm., 1988–, IFF Research Ltd. Member: Hornsey Bor. Council, 1963–65; Haringey Bor. Council, 1964–68 (Chm., Develt Control); Greater London Council: Member for Tottenham, 1973–83; Chm., NE Area Bd, 1973–74, W Area Bd, 1974–76, and Central Area Bd, 1976; Opposition Leader on Planning and Communications, 1977–80; Leader of the Opposition, 1980–81. Opposition spokesman on educn and science, 1985–87, on industry matters, 1983–87, on the environment, 1987–, House of Lords. Chairman: Market Res. Soc., 1972–73; Assoc. for Neighbourhood Councils, 1974–80; Computer Sub-Cttee, H of L Offices Cttee, 1984–; Mem., Metrop. Water Bd, 1967–68. Chm., Fabian Soc., 1985–86 (Mem., NEC, 1981–87). Principal, Working Men's Coll., NWI, 1988–; Governor, Drayton Sch., Tottenham, 1967–83. Editor, Jl of Market Res. Soc., 1963–67. *Publications:* Industry and Employment in the Inner City, 1979; (ed) Employment Policy in the UK and United States, 1980; Women and Work, 1981; jl articles on theory, practice and findings of survey research. *Recreations:* cooking, reading, music. *Address:* 27 Hurst Avenue, N6 5TX. *T:* 081–340 1496.

See also N. E. S. McIntosh.

McINTOSH, Prof. Angus, FRSE 1978; FBA 1989; consultant on linguistics problems; Hon. Consultant, Gayre Institute for Medieval English and Scottish Dialectology, University of Edinburgh, since 1986; *b* 10 Jan. 1914; *s* of late Kenneth and Mary McIntosh (*née* Thompson), Cleadon, Sunderland, Co. Durham; *m* 1st, 1939, Barbara (*d* 1988), *d* of late Dr William Seaman and Mrs Bainbridge (*née* June Wheeler), New York City; two *s* one *d*; 2nd, 1988, Karina Williamson (*née* Side), *widow* of Colin Williamson, Fellow of Jesus Coll., Oxford. *Educ:* Ryhope Grammar Sch., Co. Durham; Oriel Coll., Oxford (BA, 1st Class Hons, English Lang., and Lit., 1934); Merton Coll., Oxford (Harmsworth Scholar); (Dip. of Comparative Philology, University of Oxford, 1936); Harvard Univ. (Commonwealth Fund Fellow, AM, 1937). MA (Oxford) 1938. Lecturer, Dept of English, University College, Swansea, 1938–46. Served War of 1939–45, beginning as trooper in Tank Corps, finishing as Major in Intelligence Corps. University Lecturer in Mediæval English, Oxford, 1946–48; Lecturer in English, Christ Church, Oxford, 1946–47; Student of Christ Church, 1947–48; University of Edinburgh: Prof. of English Language and General Linguistics, 1948–64; Forbes Prof. of Eng. Lang., 1964–79; Dir, Middle English Dialect Atlas Project, 1979–86. Co-Chm., Hon. Adv. Bd, Encyclopedia of Lang. and Linguistics, 1988–. Rockefeller Foundation Fellowship, US, June-Sept. 1949; Leverhulme Emeritus Res. Fellow, 1984–86. Hon. Pres., Scottish Text Soc., 1989– (Pres., 1977–89). For. Mem., Finnish Acad. of Science and Letters, 1976. Hon. DPhil Poznan Univ., 1972; Hon. DLitt Durham, 1980. Sir Israel Gollancz Prize, British Acad., 1989. *Publications:* books, articles and reviews on subject of English language and related topics. *Recreations:* gardening, painting, music. *Address:* 32 Blacket Place, Edinburgh EH9 1RL. *T:* 031–667 5791.

McINTOSH, Anne Caroline Ballingall; Member (C) North-East Essex, European Parliament, since 1989; a Junior Whip, European Democratic Group, since 1989; *b* 20 Sept. 1954; *d* of Dr Alastair Ballingall McIntosh and Grethe-Lise McIntosh (*née* Thomsen). *Educ:* Harrogate Coll., Harrogate, Yorks; Univ. of Edinburgh (LLB Hons); Univ. of Aarhus, Denmark. Admitted to Faculty of Advocates, 1982. Unqualified legal advr in private EEC practice, Brussels, 1979–80; Bar apprentice with Simpson and Marwick, WS, and devilling at Scottish Bar, 1980–82; private legal practice, Brussels, specialising in EEC law, 1982–83; Secretariat Mem., responsible for transport, youth, culture, educn and tourism, and relations with Scandinavia, Austria, Switzerland and Yugoslavia, EDG, Europ. Parlt, 1983–89. Mem., Transport, Legal Affairs Cttees and EDG Spokesman on Rules Cttee, Europ. Parlt, 1989–; Norway Parly Delegn. *Recreations:* swimming, cinema, walking. *Address:* (constituency office) The Old Armoury, Museum Street, Saffron Walden, Essex CB10 1JN. *T:* Saffron Walden (0799) 23631; (European Parliament) 97 Rue Belliard, B-1040 Brussels. *T:* 322 284 5239.

MACINTOSH, Dr Farquhar, CBE 1982; Rector (Headmaster), The Royal High School, Edinburgh, 1972–89; *b* 27 Oct. 1923; *s* of John Macintosh and Kate Ann Macintosh (*née* MacKinnon); *m* 1959, Margaret Mary Inglis, Peebles; two *s* two *d. Educ:* Portree High Sch., Skye; Edinburgh Univ. (MA); Glasgow Univ. (DipEd). Served RN, 1943–46; commnd RNVR, 1944. Headmaster, Portree High Sch., 1962–66; Rector, Oban High Sch., 1967–72. Mem., Highlands and Islands Develt Consultative Council, 1965–82; Chairman: BBC Secondary Programme Cttee, 1972–80; School Broadcasting Council for Scotland, 1981–85; Scottish Examination Bd, 1977–90; Scottish Assoc. for Educnl Management and Admin, 1979–82. Chm. of Governors, Jordanhill Coll. of Educn, 1970–72; Mem. Court, Edinburgh Univ., 1975–. Elder, Church of Scotland. FEIS 1970. Hon. DLitt Heriot-Watt, 1980. *Publications:* regular contribs to TES Scotland; contrib. to European Jl of Educn. *Recreations:* hill-walking, occasional fishing, Gaelic. *Address:* 12 Rothesay Place, Edinburgh EH3 7SQ. *T:* 031–225 4404. *Clubs:* East India; Rotary of Murrayfield and Cramond (Edinburgh).

MacINTOSH, Prof. Frank Campbell; FRS 1954; FRSC 1956; J. M. Drake Professor of Physiology, McGill University, Montreal, Canada, 1949–78, Emeritus Professor since 1980; *b* 24 Dec. 1909; *s* of Rev. C. C. MacIntosh, DD, and Beenie MacIntosh (*née* Matheson); *m* 1938, Mary M. MacKay; two *s* three *d. Educ:* Dalhousie Univ., Halifax, NS (MA); McGill Univ. (PhD). Member of research staff, Medical Research Council of Great Britain, 1938. Hon. LLD: Alberta, 1964; Queen's, 1965; Dalhousie, 1976; St Francis Xavier, 1985; Hon. MD Ottawa, 1974; Hon. DSc McGill, 1980. *Publications:* papers in physiological journals. *Address:* Department of Physiology, McGill University, 3655 Drummond Street, Montreal H3G 1Y6, Canada; 145 Wolseley Avenue, Montreal West, H4X 1V8, Canada. *T:* 481–7939.

McINTOSH, Genista Mary; Executive Director, Royal National Theatre, since 1990; *b* 23 Sept. 1946; *d* of late Geoffrey Tandy and of Maire Tandy; *m* 1971, Neil Scott Wishart McIntosh, *qv* (marr. diss.); one *s* one *d. Educ:* Univ. of York (BA Philosophy and Sociology). Press Sec., York Festival of Arts, 1968–69; Royal Shakespeare Co.: Casting Dir, 1972–77; Planning Controller, 1977–84; Sen. Administrator, 1986–90; Associate Producer, 1990. Dir, Marmont Management Ltd, 1984–86. *Address:* Royal National Theatre, Upper Ground, SE1 9PX. *T:* 071–928 2033.

McINTOSH, Rev. Canon Hugh; Honorary Canon, St Mary's Cathedral, Glasgow, since 1983; *b* 5 June 1914; *s* of Hugh Burns McIntosh and Mary (*née* Winter); *m* 1951, Ruth Georgina, *er d* of late Rev. William Skinner Wilson and Enid (*née* Sanders); two *s* one *d. Educ:* Hatfield Coll., Durham (Exhibr); Edinburgh Theological Coll. (Luscombe Schol.). LTh, 1941; BA (dist.), 1942; MA 1945. Deacon and Priest, 1942. Precentor and Senior Chaplain, St Paul's Cathedral, Dundee, 1942–46; Senior Chaplain, St Mary's Cathedral, Edinburgh, 1946–49; Curate, St Salvador's, Edinburgh, 1949–51; Rector, St Adrian's,

Gullane, 1951–54; Rector, St John's, Dumfries, 1954–66; Canon of St Mary's Cathedral, Glasgow, and Synod Clerk of Glasgow and Galloway, 1959; Provost of St Mary's Cathedral, Glasgow, 1966–70; Rector, Christ Church, Lanark, 1970–83. *Recreations:* reading, writing, and (a little) arithmetic. *Address:* 2 Ridgepark Drive, Lanark ML11 7PG. *T:* Lanark (0555) 3458.

McINTOSH, Vice-Admiral Sir Ian (Stewart), KBE 1973 (MBE 1941); CB 1970; DSO 1944; DSC 1942; Management Selection Consultant, 1973–78; *b* 11 Oct. 1919; *s* of late A. J. McIntosh, Melbourne, Australia; *m* 1943, Elizabeth Rosemary Rasmussen; three *s* (one *d* decd). *Educ:* Geelong Grammar Sch. Entered RN, 1938; comd HM Submarine: H44, 1942; Sceptre, 1943–44; Alderney, 1946–48; Aeneas, 1950–51; Exec. Officer, HMS Ark Royal, 1956–58; comd 2nd Submarine Sqn, 1961–63; comd HMS Victorious, 1966–68; Dir-Gen., Weapons (Naval), 1968–70; Dep. Chief of Defence Staff (Op. Req.), 1971–73, retd 1973. Captain, 1959; Rear-Adm., 1968; Vice-Adm., 1971. Chairman: Sea Cadet Assoc., 1973–83; HMS Cavalier Trust, 1974–88. *Recreations:* friends, reading, music. *Address:* 19 The Crescent, Alverstoke, Hants. *T:* Gosport (0705) 580510. *Club:* Royal Over-Seas League.

MACINTOSH, Joan, (Mrs I. G. Macintosh), CBE 1978; Chairman, Scottish Child Law Centre, since 1989; Lay Observer for Scotland (Solicitors (Scotland) Act), 1981–89; *b* 23 Nov. 1919; *m* 1952, Ian Gillies Macintosh; one *s* two *d* (and one *s* decd). *Educ:* Amer. and English schs; Oxford Univ. (MA Modern History). BBC, 1941–42; Amer. Div., Min. of Inf., 1942–45; HM Foreign Service, 1945–52; retd on marriage. Voluntary work in India, 1953–69; CAB Organiser, Glasgow, 1972–75; Chm. Council, Insurance Ombudsman Bureau, 1981–85. Member: Royal Commn on Legal Services in Scotland, 1975–80; Chm., Scottish Consumer Council, 1975–80; Vice-Chm., National Consumer Council, 1976–84; Vice-Pres., Nat. Fedn of Consumer Gps, 1982–; Hon. Pres., Scottish Legal Action Group, 1990. Hon. LLD Dundee, 1982; DUniv Stirling, 1988. *Recreations:* tapestry, gardening. *Address:* Wynd End, Auchterarder, Perthshire PH3 1AD. *T:* Auchterarder (0764) 62499.

McINTOSH, Dr Malcolm Kenneth; Chief of Defence Procurement, Ministry of Defence, since 1991; *b* Melbourne, 14 Dec. 1945; *s* of Kenneth Stuart McIntosh and Valerie McIntosh (*née* MacKenzie); *m* 1971, Margaret Beatrice (*née* Stevens); three *s* one *d. Educ:* Telopea Park; Australian National Univ. (BSc Hons, PhD Physics). Research Scientist, Aust. Weapons Res. Estabt, 1970–72; Aust. Army, 1972–74 (Major); Aust. Economic Ministries, 1974–82; Australian Department of Defence, 1982–90: Chief of Defence Production, 1987; Dep. Sec., Acquisition and Logistics, 1988; Sec., Aust. Dept of Industry, Technology and Commerce, 1990. *Address:* Procurement Executive, Ministry of Defence, Whitehall, SW1A 2HB.

McINTOSH, Prof. Naomi Ellen Sargant, (Lady McIntosh of Haringey); writer and consultant; *b* 10 Dec. 1933; *d* of late Tom Sargant, OBE, and of Marie Cerny (*née* Hlouskova); *m* 1st, 1954, Peter Joseph Kelly; one *s*; 2nd, 1962, Andrew Robert McIntosh (now Baron McIntosh of Haringey, *qv*); two *s. Educ:* Friends' Sch., Saffron Walden, Essex; Bedford Coll., London (BA Hons Sociology). Social Surveys (Gallup Poll) Ltd, 1955–67; Sen. Lectr in Market Res., Enfield Coll., of Technol., 1967–69; Open University: Sen. Lectr in Res. Methods, 1970–75; Reader in Survey Research, 1975–78; Head, Survey Res. Dept, Inst. of Educnl Technol., 1972–81; Pro Vice-Chancellor (Student Affairs), 1974–78; Prof. of Applied Social Research, 1978–81; Sen. Commng Editor for Educnl Programming, Channel 4, 1981–89. Vis. Prof. in Higher Educn (part-time), Univ. of Mass, Amherst, 1974–75. Councillor, and Chm. Children's Cttee, London Bor. of Haringey, 1964–68; Vice-Chm., London Boroughs Trng Cttee (Social Services), 1966–68. Chm., National Gas Consumers' Council, 1977–80. Pres., Nat. Soc. for Clean Air, 1981–83. Member: Council and Exec. Cttee, Social Work Adv. Service, 1966–68; Local Govt Trng Bd, 1967–68; Energy Commn, 1978–79; Commn on Energy and the Environment, 1978–81; Nat. Consumer Council, 1978–81; Adv. Council for Adult and Continuing Educn, 1977–83; Council, Bedford Coll., Univ. of London, 1977–83; Council, Polytechnic of the South Bank, 1982–86; Exec. Cttee, Nat. Inst. of Adult and Continuing Educn, 1986–89; Gov., Haringey Coll., 1984–87; Vice-Chm., Poly. of E London HEC, 1989– (Gov., NE London Poly., 1987–89); Acting Chief Exec., Open Poly., 1990. Vice Chm., Film, TV and Video Panel, Arts Council of GB, 1986–90. Trustee, Nat. Extension Coll., 1975–. Mem. RTS, 1982–. Pres., Highgate Horticultural Soc., 1990. FRSA 1991. Hon. Fellow RCA, 1988. *Publications:* A Degree of Difference, 1976 (New York 1977); (with A. Woodley) The Door Stood Open, 1980; Learning and 'Leisure', 1991. *Recreation:* gardening. *Address:* 27 Hurst Avenue, N6 5TX. *T:* 081–340 1496.

McINTOSH, Neil Scott Wishart; Chief Executive, Centre for British Teachers, since 1990; *b* 24 July 1947; *s* of William Henderson McIntosh and Mary Catherine McIntosh; *m* 1971, Genista Mary Tandy (*see* G. M. McIntosh) (marr. diss. 1990); one *s* one *d; m* 1991, Melinda Jane Frances Letts; one *s. Educ:* Merchiston Castle Sch., Edinburgh; Univ. of York (BA Politics); London Sch. of Econs (MSc Industrial Relations). Res. Associate, PEP, 1969–73; Res. Dir, Southwark Community Develt Proj., 1973–76; Dir, Shelter, 1976–84; Dir, VSO, 1985–90. Councillor, London Bor. of Camden, 1971–77; Chm., Housing Cttee, 1974–76. Dir, Stonham Housing Assoc., 1982–. Vice Pres., BSA, 1985–91. Chm., Homeless Internat., 1988–; Treasurer, Campaign for Freedom of Information, 1984–; Mem., Independent Broadcasting Telethon Trust, 1987–. *Publication:* The Right to Manage?, 1971 (2nd edn 1976). *Recreations:* golf, hill walking, theatre. *Address:* 40 Kiver Road, N19 4PD. *Clubs:* Commonwealth Trust; Highgate Golf.

McINTOSH, Sir Ronald (Robert Duncan), KCB 1975 (CB 1968); Chairman, APV plc, 1982–89; Director: S. G. Warburg & Co. Ltd, 1978–90; Foseco plc, 1978–90; London & Manchester Group plc, 1978–90; *b* 26 Sept. 1919; *s* of late Thomas Steven McIntosh, MD, FRCP, MRCS, and late Christina Jane McIntosh; *m* 1951, Doreen Frances, *o d* of late Commander Andrew MacGinnity, Frinton-on-Sea. *Educ:* Charterhouse (Scholar); Balliol Coll., Oxford. Served in Merchant Navy, 1939–45; Second Mate, 1943–45. Assistant Principal, Board of Trade, 1947; General Manager, Dollar Exports Board, 1949–51; Commercial Counsellor, UK High Commn, New Delhi, 1957–61; Under-Secretary: BoT, 1961–64; DEA, 1964–66; Dep. Under-Sec. of State, Dept of Economic Affairs, 1966–68; Dep. Secretary, Cabinet Office, 1968–70; Dep. Under-Sec. of State, Dept of Employment, 1970–72; Dep. Sec., HM Treasury, 1972–73; Dir-Gen. Nat. Economic Development Office, and Mem. NEDC, 1973–77. Dir, Fisons Ltd, 1978–81. Chairman: British Food Consortium, 1989–; Danish–UK Chamber of Commerce, 1990–. Member: British Overseas Trade Adv. Cttee, 1975–77; Council, CBI, 1980–90; Co-Chm., British-Hungarian Round Table, 1980–84. Patron, British-Hungarian Soc., 1990–. Patron, Re-Action Trust, 1991. CBIM; FRSA. Hon. DSc Aston, 1977. *Recreations:* sailing, travel. *Address:* 24 Ponsonby Terrace, SW1P 4QA. *Club:* Royal Thames Yacht.

MacINTYRE, Prof. Alasdair Chalmers; McMahon/Hank Professor of Philosophy, University of Notre Dame, Indiana, since 1988; *b* 12 Jan. 1929; *o s* of Eneas John MacIntyre, MD (Glasgow), and Margaret Emily Chalmers, MB, ChB (Glasgow); *m* 1977, Lynn Sumida Joy; one *s* three *d* by previous marriages. *Educ:* Epsom Coll. and privately;

Queen Mary Coll., Univ. of London (Fellow, 1984); Manchester Univ. BA (London); MA (Manchester); MA (Oxon). Lectr in Philosophy of Religion, Manchester Univ., 1951–57; Lectr in Philosophy, Leeds Univ., 1957–61; Research Fellow, Nuffield Coll., Oxford, 1961–62; Sen. Fellow, Council of Humanities, Princeton Univ., 1962–63; Fellow and Preceptor in Philosophy, University Coll., Oxford, 1963–66; Prof. of Sociology, Univ. of Essex, 1966–70; Prof. of History of Ideas, Brandeis Univ., 1970–72; Univ. Prof. in Philos. and Political Sci., Boston Univ., 1972–80; Luce Prof., Wellesley Coll., 1980–82; W. Alton Jones Prof. of Philosophy, Vanderbilt Univ., 1982–88. Pres., Eastern Div., Amer. Phil Assoc., 1984. Fellow, Amer. Acad. of Arts and Scis, 1985. Hon. Mem., Phi Beta Kappa, 1973. Hon. DHL Swarthmore, 1983; Hon. DLit QUB, 1988. *Publications:* Marxism and Christianity, 1954 (revised, 1968); New Essays in Philosophical Theology (ed, with A. G. N. Flew), 1955; Metaphysical Beliefs (ed), 1956; The Unconscious: a conceptual analysis, 1958; A Short History of Ethics, 1965; Secularisation and Moral Change, 1967; Marcuse: an exposition and a polemic, 1970; Sociological Theory and Philosophical Analysis (ed with D. M. Emmet), 1971; Against the Self-Images of the Age, 1971; After Virtue, 1981; Whose Justice? Which Rationality?, 1988; Three Rival Versions of Moral Enquiry, 1990. *Address:* Department of Philosophy, University of Notre Dame, Notre Dame, Indiana 46556, USA.

McINTYRE, Prof. Alasdair Duncan, FRSE 1975; Emeritus Professor of Fisheries and Oceanography, Aberdeen University, since 1987; *b* 17 Nov. 1926; *s* of Alexander Walker McIntyre and Martha Jack McIntyre; *m* 1967, Catherine; one *d.* *Educ:* Hermitage Sch., Helensburgh; Glasgow Univ. BSc (1st class Hons Zoology) 1948; DSc 1973. Scottish Home Department (since 1960, DAFS) Marine Laboratory, Aberdeen: Develt Commn Grant-aided Student, 1948–49; Scientific Officer, 1950; Head, Lab. Environmental Gp, 1973; Dep. Dir, 1977; Dir, 1983. Dir of Fisheries Res. Services for Scotland, Dept of Agric. and Fisheries for Scotland, 1983–86. UK Co-ordinator, Fisheries Res. and Develt, 1986. Pres., Scottish Marine Biological Assoc., 1988–; Chairman: UN Gp of Experts on Scientific Aspects of Marine Pollution (GESAMP), 1981–84; Adv. Cttee on Marine Pollution, Internat. Council for the Exploration of the Sea, 1982–84; Marine Forum for Envmtl Issues, 1988–. Mem., NCC for Scotland, 1991. Hon. Res. Prof., Aberdeen Univ., 1983. Vice Chm., Trustees of Buckland Foundn, 1988–. Ed., Fisheries Research, 1988–. *Publications:* some 70 articles in scientific jls on marine ecology and pollution. *Recreations:* cooking, wine, walking. *Address:* 63 Hamilton Place, Aberdeen AB2 4BW. *T:* Aberdeen (0224) 645633.

MACINTYRE, Angus Donald, DPhil; Official Fellow and Tutor in Modern History, since 1963, Senior Fellow, since 1989, Magdalen College, Oxford; *b* 4 May 1935; *e s* of Major Francis Peter Macintyre, OBE, and Evelyn, *d* of Nicholas Synnott, JP, Furness, Naas, Co. Kildare, Eire; *m* 1958, Joanna Musgrave Harvey, *d* of Sir Richard Musgrave Harvey, 2nd Bt; two *s* one *d.* *Educ:* Wellington; Hertford Coll., Oxford (Baring Scholar); St Antony's Coll., Oxford (MA, DPhil). Coldstream Guards, 1953–55, 1956 (Lieut). Magdalen College, Oxford: Sen. Tutor, 1966–68; Vice-Pres., 1981–82; Actg Pres., Jan–July 1987. Governor: Magdalen Coll. Sch., Brackley, 1965–77; Wolverhampton Grammar Sch., 1987–; Magdalen Coll. Sch., Oxford, 1990– (Chm., 1987–90). Chm., Thomas Wall Trust, London, 1971–. Gen. Editor, Oxford Historical Monographs, 1971–79; Editor, English Historical Review, 1978–86. FRHistS 1972. *Publications:* The Liberator: Daniel O'Connell and the Irish Parliamentary Party 1830–47, 1965; (ed with Kenneth Garlick) The Diary of Joseph Farington 1793–1821, vols I-II, 1978; vols III-VI, 1979; (contrib.) Thank You Wodehouse by J. H. C. Morris, 1981; (contrib.) Daniel O'Connell: portrait of a Radical, ed Nowlan and O'Connell, 1984; (ed) General Index, English Historical Review, vols LXXI–C, 1956–85, 1986; (jtly) Magdalen College and the Crown, 1988; (contrib.) Pour Jean Malaurie, 1990. *Recreations:* cricket, bibliophily. *Address:* Magdalen College, Oxford OX1 4AU. *T:* Oxford (0865) 276000. *Club:* MCC.

McINTYRE, Donald Conroy, CBE 1985 (OBE 1977); opera singer, free-lance; *b* 22 Oct. 1934; *s* of George Douglas McIntyre and Mrs Hermyn McIntyre; *m*; three *d.* *Educ:* Mount Albert Grammar Sch.; Auckland Teachers' Trng Coll.; Guildhall Sch. of Music. Debut in Britain, Welsh National Opera, 1959; Sadler's Wells Opera, many roles, 1960–67; Royal Opera, Covent Garden, from 1967; also Vienna, Bayreuth, La Scala, Milan and Metropolitan, NY. *Principal roles:* Barak, in Die Frau Ohne Schatten, Strauss; Wotan and Wanderer, in The Ring, Wagner; Hollander, Wagner; Hans Sachs, in Die Meistersinger von Nurnberg, Wagner; Heyst, in Victory, Richard Rodney Bennett; Macbeth, Verdi; Scarpia, in Tosca, Puccini; Count, in Figaro, Mozart; Dr Schön, in Wozzeck, Berg; title role in Cardillac, Hindemith; Siegfried, Metropolitan, NY; Rocco, in Fidelio; Prospero, in Un Re in Ascolto, Berio; Bulstrode, in Peter Grimes, Britten; Bayreuth: Wotan, Wanderer, Hollander; Telramund, in Lohengrin; Klingsor, Amfortas and Gurnemanz in Parsifal; Bayreuth Centenary Ring, 1976–81. *Video and films include:* Der Fliegende Holländer, 1975; Electra, 1976; Die Meistersinger, 1984; Bayreuth Centenary Ring, 1976–81; recordings include Pelléas et Mélisande, Il Trovatore, The Messiah, Oedipus Rex, The Ring, Beethoven's 9th Symphony, Damnation of Faust, Bayreuth Centenary Ring. Fidelio Award, 1989. *Recreations:* gardening, swimming, tennis, farming. *Address:* Foxhill Farm, Jackass Lane, Keston, Bromley, Kent BR2 6AN. *T:* Farnborough (0252) 55368.

MacINTYRE, Rt. Hon. Duncan, PC (NZ) 1980; DSO 1945; OBE 1956; ED; Deputy Prime Minister of New Zealand, 1981–84; *b* 1915; *s* of A. MacIntyre; *m* Diana, *d* of Percy Hunter. Sheep farming, 1933–39 and 1946–. Served War, NZ Army, 1939–46; Territorial Force, 1949–60 (Brig. 1956); Col Comdt RNZAC, 1976. MP (National Party) Hastings, 1960–72, Bay of Plenty, 1975–78, East Cape, 1978–84; Minister: of Lands, of Forests, and i/c of Valuation Dept, 1966–72; of Maori Affairs and of Island Affairs, 1969–72; for the Environment, 1972; of Agriculture, of Fisheries, and i/c of Rural Banking and Finance Corp., 1975–84; of Maori Affairs, 1975–78. *Address:* Taikura, RD4, Waipukurau, New Zealand.

MacINTYRE, Prof. Iain; Emeritus Professor of Chemical Pathology, University of London, since 1989; Senior Research Fellow, Department of Medicine, Royal Postgraduate Medical School, since 1989; Hon. Consultant Chemical Pathologist: Hammersmith Hospital, since 1960; Queen Charlotte's Hospital; *b* 30 Aug. 1924; *s* of John MacIntyre, Tobermory, and Margaret Fraser Shaw, Stratherick, Inverness-shire; *m* 1947, Mabel Wilson Jamieson, MA, *y d* of George Jamieson and J. C. K. K. Bell, Largs, Ayrshire; one *d.* *Educ:* Jordanhill Coll. Sch., Glasgow; Univ. of Glasgow. MB, ChB Glasgow 1947; PhD London 1960; MRCPath 1963 (Founder Mem.), FRCPath 1971; FRCP 1977 (MRCP 1969); DSc London 1970. Asst Clinical Pathologist, United Sheffield Hosps, and Hon. Demonstrator in Biochem., Sheffield Univ., 1948–52; Royal Postgraduate Medical School: Registrar in Chemical Pathology, 1952–54; Sir Jack Drummond Meml Fellow, 1954–56; Asst Lectr in Chem. Path., 1956–59; Reader in Chem. Path., 1963–67; Dir, Endocrine Unit, 1967–89; Prof., Chem. Path., London Univ., 1967–89. Director: Dept of Chem. Path., Hammersmith Hosp., 1982–89; of Chem. Path., Hammersmith Hosp., Chelsea Hosp. for Women, Queen Charlotte's Hosp. for Women, 1986–89. Vis. Scientist, Nat. Insts of Health, Bethesda, 1960–61; Visiting Professor: San Francisco Medical Center, 1964; Melbourne Univ., 1979–80; St George's Hosp. Med. Sch., 1989–; Vis. Prof. and Associate Dir, William Harvey Res. Inst., St Bart's Hosp. Med. Coll., 1991–; Vis. Lectr, Insts of Molecular Biol. and Cytol., USSR Acad. of Scis, 1978. Mem., Hammersmith and Queen Charlotte's SHA, 1982–. Chm. Organizing Cttee, Hammersmith Internat. Symposium on Molecular Endocrinology, 1967–79; Member: Org Cttee, Hormone and Cell Regulation Symposia, 1976–79; Adv. Council, Workshop on Vitamin D, 1977–79. Pres., Bone and Tooth Soc., 1984–87; Member: Cttee, Soc. for Endocrinology, 1978–80; Biochem. Soc.; NIH Alumni Assoc; Amer. Endocrine Soc.; Amer. Soc. for Bone and Mineral Res.; European Calcified Tissue Soc.; Assoc. of Clin. Biochemists. Vice-Pres., English Chess Assoc., 1989–. Hon. MD Turin, 1985. Member Editorial Board: Clinical Endocrinology, 1975–79; Molecular and Cellular Endocrinology, 1975–80; Jl of Endocrinological Investigation; Jl of Mineral and Electrolyte Metabolism; Jl of Investigative and Cell Pathol.; Jl of Metabolic Bone Disease and Related Res. Gairdner Internat. Award, Toronto, 1967. *Publications:* articles in endocrinology. *Recreations:* tennis, squash, chess, music. *Address:* Great Broadhurst Farm, Broad Oak, Heathfield, East Sussex TN21 8UX. *T:* Burwash (0435) 883515. *Clubs:* Athenæum; Queen's, Hurlingham.

McINTYRE, Ian James; writer and broadcaster; *b* Banchory, Kincardineshire, 9 Dec. 1931; *y s* of late Hector Harold McIntyre, Inverness, and late Annie Mary Michie, Ballater; *m* 1954, Leik Sommerfelt, 2nd *d* of late Benjamin Vogt, Kragerø, Norway; two *s* two *d.* *Educ:* Prescot Grammar Sch.; St John's Coll., Cambridge (Scholar; Med. and Mod. Langs Tripos, Pts I and II; BA 1953; MA); Coll. of Europe, Bruges. Pres., Cambridge Union, 1953. Commnd, Intelligence Corps, 1955–57. Current affairs talks producer, BBC, 1957; Editor, At Home and Abroad, 1959; Man. Trng Organiser, BBC Staff Trng Dept, 1960; Programme Services Officer, ITA, 1961; staff of Chm., Cons. Party in Scotland, 1962; Dir of Inf. and Res., Scottish Cons. Central Office, 1965; contested (C) Roxburgh, Selkirk and Peebles, 1966; long-term contract, writer and broadcaster, BBC, 1970–76; presenter and interviewer, Analysis, and other programmes on politics, for. affairs and the arts; travelled widely in Europe, N America, Africa, Asia and ME; Controller: BBC Radio 4, 1976–78; BBC Radio 3, 1978–87. Associate Ed., The Times, 1989–90. *Publications:* The Proud Doers: Israel after twenty years, 1968; (ed and contrib.) Words: reflections on the uses of language, 1975; articles in The Listener, The Times, The Independent. *Recreation:* family life. *Address:* Spylaw House, Newlands Avenue, Radlett, Herts WD7 8EL. *T:* Radlett (0923) 853532. *Clubs:* Beefsteak; Union (Cambridge).

McINTYRE, Very Rev. Prof. John, CVO 1985; DD, DLitt; FRSE; Professor of Divinity, University of Edinburgh, 1956–86, now Emeritus; Dean of the Order of the Thistle, 1974–89; an Extra Chaplain to the Queen in Scotland, 1974–75 and since 1986 (Chaplain to the Queen in Scotland, 1975–86); Moderator of the General Assembly of the Church of Scotland, 1982; *b* 20 May 1916; *s* of late John C. McIntyre, Bathgate, Scotland, and Annie McIntyre; *m* 1945, Jessie B., *d* of late William Buick, Coupar Angus; two *s* one *d.* *Educ:* Bathgate Academy; University of Edinburgh; MA 1938; BD 1941; DLitt 1953. Ordained, 1941; Locum Tenens, Parish of Glenorchy and Inishail, 1941–43; Minister of Parish of Fenwick, Ayrshire, 1943–45; Hunter Baillie Prof. of Theology, St Andrew's Coll., University of Sydney, 1946–56; Principal of St Andrew's Coll., 1950–56; Principal Warden, Pollock Halls of Residence, Univ. of Edinburgh, 1960–71; actg Principal and Vice-Chancellor, Edinburgh Univ., 1973–74, 1979; Principal, New Coll., and Dean of Faculty of Divinity, 1968–74. FRSE 1977 (Vice-Pres., 1983–86). DD *hc* Glasgow, 1961; DHL *hc*, Coll. of Wooster, Ohio, 1983; Dr *hc* Edinburgh, 1987. *Publications:* St Anselm and His Critics, 1954; The Christian Doctrine of History, 1957; On the Love of God, 1962; The Shape of Christology, 1966; Faith, Theology and Imagination, 1987; articles and reviews in various learned jls of Theology. *Address:* 22/4 Minto Street, Edinburgh EH9 1RQ. *T:* 031–667 1203.

McINTYRE, Dr Michael Edgeworth, FRS 1990; Reader in Atmospheric Dynamics, Cambridge, since 1987; *b* 28 July 1941; *s* of Archibald Keverall McIntyre and Anne Hartwell McIntyre; *m* 1968, Ruth Hecht; one step *d* two step *s.* *Educ:* King's High School, Dunedin, NZ; Univ. of Otago, NZ; Trinity Coll., Cambridge. PhD Cantab 1967 (geophysical fluid dynamics); postdoctoral Fellow, Woods Hole Oceanographic Inst., 1967. Research Associate, Dept of Meteorology, MIT, 1967; Asst Dir of Research, 1969, Univ. Lectr, 1972, Reader in Atmospheric Dynamics, 1987, University of Cambridge. Member: Atmospheric Sci. Cttee, NERC, 1989–; Sci. Steering Gp, UK Univs Global Atmos. Modelling Project, 1990–. Member: Academia Europaea, 1989; Euro. Geophys. Soc., Amer. Geophys. Union, Catgut Acoust. Soc.; FRMetS; Fellow, Amer. Met. Soc., 1991 (Carl-Gustaf Rossby Res. Medal, 1987). *Publications:* numerous papers in professional jls. *Recreations:* music, gliding. *Address:* 98 Windsor Road, Cambridge CB4 3JN.

McINTYRE, Prof. Neil, FRCP; Professor of Medicine and Chairman, Department of Medicine, Royal Free Hospital School of Medicine, since 1978; Hon. Consultant Physician, Royal Free Hospital, since 1968; *b* 1 May 1934; *s* of John William McIntyre and Catherine (*née* Watkins); *m* 1966, Wendy Ann Kelsey; one *s* one *d.* *Educ:* Porth County School for Boys; King's Coll. London (BSc 1st Cl. Hons Physiol); King's Coll. Hosp. (MB BS (Hons), MD). House Officer: KCH, 1959; Hammersmith Hosp., 1960; RAF Med. Br. (Flt Lieut), 1960–63; MRC Res. Fellow, Registrar, Lectr in Medicine, Royal Free Hosp., 1963–66; MRC Travelling Fellowship, Harvard Med. Sch., 1966–68; Sen. Lectr 1968–73, Reader in Medicine 1973–78, Royal Free Hosp. Sch. of Medicine. Non-Exec. Dir, N Middlesex Hosp. NHS Trust, 1991–. MRSM 1968. Liveryman, Soc. of Apothecaries, 1971–. Sam E. Roberts Medal, Univ. of Kansas Med. Sch., 1980. *Publications:* Therapeutic Agents and the Liver, 1965; The Problem Orientated Medical Record, 1979; Lipids and Lipoproteins, 1990; Clinical Hepatology, 1991; papers on liver disease, lipoprotein metabolism, med. educn. *Recreations:* reading, photographing medical statues, poor golf. *Address:* Royal Free Hospital School of Medicine, Pond Street, Hampstead, NW3 2QG. *T:* 071–794 0500. *Club:* Athenæum.

McINTYRE, Robert Douglas, MB, ChB (Edinburgh), DPH (Glasgow); JP; Hon. Consultant, Stirling Royal Infirmary (Consultant Chest Physician, Stirlingshire and Clackmannan, 1951–79); Member, Stirling and Clackmannan Hospital Board, 1964–74; *b* Dec. 1913; 3rd *s* of Rev. John E. McIntyre and Catherine, *d* of Rev. William Morison, DD; *m* 1954, Letitia, *d* of Alexander Macleod; one *s.* *Educ:* Hamilton Acad.; Daniel Stewart's Coll.; University of Edinburgh. MP (Scottish Nationalist), Motherwell and Wishaw, April-July 1945. Contested (SNP): Motherwell, 1950; Perth and E Perthshire, 1951, 1955, 1959, 1964; W Stirlingshire, 1966, 1970; Stirling, Falkirk and Grangemouth, by-election 1971, Feb. and Oct. 1974. Chm., 1948–56, Pres., 1958–80, Scottish National Party; Mem., Stirling Town Council (Hon. Treas., 1958–64, Provost, 1967–75); Chancellor's Assessor, Stirling Univ. Court, 1979–. Fellow, Scottish Council, 1987. Freeman, Royal Burgh of Stirling, 1975. DUniv Stirling 1976. JP Co. Stirling. *Publications:* numerous articles on Scottish, political and medical subjects, including regular contribs to the Scots Independent. *Recreation:* yachting. *Address:* 8 Gladstone Place, Stirling FK8 2NN. *T:* Stirling (0786) 73456. *Clubs:* Scottish Arts (Edinburgh); Stirling and County.

MACINTYRE, William Ian; Under Secretary, Coal Division, Department of Energy, since 1991; *b* 20 July 1943; *s* of late Robert Miller Macintyre, CBE and of Florence Mary Macintyre; *m* 1967, Jennifer Mary Pitblado; one *s* two *d.* *Educ:* Merchiston Castle School, Edinburgh; St Andrews University. MA. British Petroleum Co. Ltd, 1965–72; ECGD,

1972–73; DTI, later Dept of Energy, 1973–77; seconded to ICFC, 1977–79; Asst Sec., Dept of Energy, Gas Div., 1979–83; Under-Sec. 1983, Dir-Gen., Energy Efficiency Office, 1983–87; Under Sec., Electricity Div., 1987–88, Electricity Div. B, 1988–91, Dept of Energy. Governor, East Sheen Primary Sch. *Address:* Department of Energy, 1 Palace Street, SW1E 5HE.

McINTYRE, William Ian Mackay, CBE 1990; PhD; FRCVS; Professor Emeritus of Veterinary Medicine, University of Glasgow, since 1991 (Senior Lecturer, 1951–61, Professor, 1961–83); *b* 7 July 1919; *s* of George John and Jane McIntyre; *m* 1948, Ruth Dick Galbraith; three *s*. *Educ:* Altnaharra Primary and Golspie Secondary Sch., Sutherland; Royal (Dick) Veterinary Coll. (MRCVS); University of Edinburgh (PhD). FRCVS 1983. Clinical Asst, Royal (Dick) Veterinary Coll., 1944–48; Lectr, Vet. Med., Royal (Dick) Vet. Coll., 1948–51. Seconded to University of East Africa, University Coll., Nairobi, as Dean, Faculty of Veterinary Science, and Prof., Clinical Studies, 1963–67. Dir, International Trypanotolerance Centre, The Gambia, 1984–89. Hon. DVM Justus Liebig Univ., Giessen, 1987. *Publications:* various, on canine nephritis, parasitic diseases and vaccines, clinical communications, and African Trypanosomiasis. *Address:* Stuckenduff, Shandon, Helensburgh G84 8NW. *T:* Rhu (0436) 820571.

McIVOR, Rt. Hon. Basil; *see* McIvor, Rt Hon. W. B.

McIVOR, Donald Kenneth; Director and Senior Vice-President, Exxon Corporation, New York, since 1985; *b* 12 April 1928; *s* of Kenneth MacIver McIvor and Nellie Beatrice McIvor (*née* Rutherford); *m* 1953, Avonia Isabel Forbes; four *s* one *d*. *Educ:* Univ. of Manitoba (BSc Hons in Geol.). Joined Imperial Oil, 1950; operational and res. assignments, Exploration Dept, 1950–58; gen. planning and res. management positions, 1958–68; Asst Manager and Manager, Corporate Planning, 1968–70; Exploration Manager, 1970–72; Nat. Defence Coll., 1972–73; Sen. Vice-Pres., 1973–75; Exec. Vice-Pres., 1975–77; Vice-Pres., oil and gas exploration and prodn, Exxon Corp., NY, 1977–81; Dep. Chm., Imperial Oil, 1981; Chm. and Chief Exec. Officer, Imperial Oil, 1982–85. *Address:* (office) 1251 Avenue of the Americas, New York, NY 10020, USA. *Club:* York (Toronto).

McIVOR, (Frances) Jill; Northern Ireland Parliamentary Commissioner for Administration, since 1991; Deputy Chairman, Radio Authority, since 1990; *b* 10 Aug. 1930; *d* of Cecil Reginald Johnston Anderson and Frances Ellen (*née* Henderson); *m* 1953, William Basil McIvor, *qv*; two *s* one *d*. *Educ:* Methodist Coll.; Lurgan Coll.; Queen's Univ. of Belfast (LLB Hons). Called to Bar of Northern Ireland, 1980. Asst Librarian (Law), QUB, 1954–55; Tutor in Legal Res., Law Faculty, QUB, 1965–74; editorial staff, NI Legal Qtly, 1966–76; Librarian, Dept of Dir of Public Prosecutions, 1977–79. NI Mem., IBA, 1980–86. Chm., Lagan Valley Regional Park Cttee, 1984–89 (Mem., 1975); Member: Ulster Countryside Cttee, 1984–89; Fair Employment Agency, 1984–89; Fair Employment Commn, 1990–91; Lay Panel, Juvenile Court, 1976–77; GDC, 1979–91; Exec., Belfast Voluntary Welfare Soc., 1981–88; Adv. Council, 1985–90, Bd, 1987–90, Co-operation North; Adv. Panel on Community Radio, 1985–86; NI Adv. Cttee, British Council, 1986–. Chairman: Ulster–NZ Trust, 1987–; Educnl Guidance Service for Adults, 1988–90. Mem. Bd of Visitors, QUB, 1988–. FRSA 1988. *Publications:* Irish Consultant (and contrib.), Manual of Law Librarianship, 1976; (ed) Elegentia Juris: selected writings of F. H. Newark, 1973; Chart of the English Reports (new edn), 1982. *Recreations:* gardening, bees. *Address:* Larkhill, 98 Spa Road, Ballynahinch, Co. Down. *T:* Ballynahinch (0238) 563534. *Clubs:* Commonwealth Trust, Royal Over-Seas League.

McIVOR, Rt. Hon. (William) Basil, OBE 1991; PC (NI) 1971; *b* 17 June 1928; 2nd *s* of Rev. Frederick McIvor, Methodist clergyman and Lilly McIvor; *m* 1953, Frances Jill Anderson (*see* F. J. McIvor); two *s* one *d*. *Educ:* Methodist Coll., Belfast; Queen's Univ., Belfast. LLB 1948. Called to NI Bar, 1950; Jun. Crown Counsel, Co. Down, Sept. 1974, Resident Magistrate, Dec. 1974. MP (UU) Larkfield, NI Parlt, 1969; Minister of Community Relations, NI, 1971–72; Member (UU) for S Belfast, NI Assembly, 1973–75; Minister of Education, NI, 1974. Founder Mem., 1976–, Chm., 1988–, Fold Housing Assoc. Chm., All Children Together (the pioneering movement for integrated educn by consent), 1990– (Mem., 1974–). Governor, Campbell Coll., 1975– (Chm., 1983–85); Chm. Bd of Governors, Lagan Coll., Belfast, 1981– (the first integrated RC and Protestant school in NI). *Recreations:* golf, music, gardening. *Address:* Larkhill, 98 Spa Road, Ballynahinch, Co. Down. *T:* Ballynahinch (0238) 563534. *Club:* Commonwealth Trust.

MACK, Prof. Alan Osborne, MDS; FDSRCS; Professor of Dental Prosthetics, Institute of Dental Surgery, University of London, 1967–80, now Emeritus; Consultant Dental Surgeon, Eastman Dental Hospital; Civilian Consultant in Dental Prosthetics to the Royal Air Force since 1976; *b* 24 July 1918; *s* of Arthur Joseph Mack, Glos, and Florence Emily Mack (*née* Norris); *m* 1943, Marjorie Elizabeth (*née* Westacott); two *s* one *d*. *Educ:* Westbourne Park Sch.; London Univ. LDS RCS 1942; MDS Durham, 1958; FDS RCS 1971. House Surgeon, Royal Dental Hosp., Sch. of Dental Surgery, University of London, 1942–43; served in RAF Dental Branch, 1943–47; Demonstrator, Prosthetics Dept Royal Dental Hosp., 1948; successively Asst Dir, Prosthetics Dept, and Senior Lecturer, London Univ., Royal Dental Hosp., 1949–56; Prof. of Dental Prosthetics, Univ. of Newcastle upon Tyne (formerly King's Coll., Univ. of Durham), 1956–67; Examiner in Dental Prosthetics, Royal Coll. of Surgeons of England, 1956; Examiner, University of Manchester, 1959, Leeds, 1961, Glasgow, 1961, Liverpool, 1965, London, 1965, Edinburgh, 1968, Lagos, 1970, Singapore, Khartoum, 1977; Benghazi, 1978; Examination Visitor, GDC; Advisor, Univ. of Malaya. Mem. Board of Faculty, Royal College of Surgeons, 1959. Pres. British Soc. for Study of Prosthetic Dentistry (BSSPD), 1963. Hon. Consultant, Stoke Mandeville Hosp., 1976; part-time Consultant, John Radcliffe Hosp., 1980–88. Visiting Professor: Univ. of Singapore, 1981; Univ. of Sci. and Technol., Irbid, Jordan, 1987. Hon. Mem., Amer. Acad. of Implant Dentures, 1966. *Publications:* Full Dentures, 1971; articles in British Dental Jls. *Recreations:* gardening, pottery, bowls. *Address:* Home Farm, London Road, Aston Clinton, Bucks HP22 5HG.

MACK, Brian John, DPhil; Keeper of Ethnography, British Museum, since 1991; *b* 10 July 1949; *m* 1975, Caroline Jenkins; one *s* one *d*. *Educ:* Campbell Coll., Belfast; Univ. of Sussex (MA); Merton Coll., Oxford (DPhil 1975). Res. Asst, 1976, Asst Keeper, 1977, Dept of Ethnograpy, BM. Member: Council, British Inst. in Eastern Africa, 1981–; Council, RAI, 1983–86; Council, African Studies Assoc., 1986–88. Mem. Editl Bd, Art History, 1982–91. Nat. Art Collections Fund Award for Images of Africa, BM, 1991. *Publications:* (with J. Picton) African Textiles (Craft Adv. Council Book of the Year), 1979, 2nd edn 1989; Zulus, 1980; (with P. T. Robertshaw) Culture History in the Southern Sudan, 1982; (with M. D. McLeod) Ethnic Sculpture, 1984; Madagascar, Island of the Ancestors, 1986; Ethnic Jewellery, 1988; Malagasy Textiles, 1989; Emil Torday and the Art of the Congo 1900–1909, 1990; articles and revs in learned jls. *Address:* 6 Burlington Gardens, W1X 2EX. *T:* 071–636 1555.

MACK, Keith Robert; Director-General, European Organisation for the Safety of Air Navigation (Eurocontrol), since 1989; *b* 2 March 1933; *s* of late David Stanley Mack and Dorothy Ivy Mack (*née* Bowes); *m* 1960, Eileen Mary Cuttell; two *s* four *d*. *Educ:* Edmonton County School. RAF Pilot, 1951–58; Civilian Air Traffic Control Officer, Scottish and Oceanic Air Traffic Control Centre, 1960–67; RAF Staff College, Bracknell, 1968; NATS HQ, 1969–71; ATC Watch Supervisor, Scottish ATCC, 1972–73; CAA Chief Officer, Cardiff Airport, 1974; NATS HQ, 1975–76; ATC Watch Supervisor, London ATCC, 1977; NATS Dep. Dir of Control (Airspace Policy), 1978–79; Supt, London ATCC, 1980–82; Dep. Controller, NATS, 1983–84; Mem. (full-time) and Gp Dir, CAA, and Controller, NATS, 1985–88. *Recreations:* music, walking, photography. *Address:* European Organisation for the Safety of Air Navigation, Rue de la Loi 72, 1040 Brussels, Belgium.

MACK SMITH, Denis, CBE 1990; FBA 1976; FRSL; Extraordinary Fellow, Wolfson College, Oxford, since 1987; Emeritus Fellow, All Souls Coll., Oxford, 1987; *b* 3 March 1920; *s* of Wilfrid Mack Smith and Altiora Gauntlett; *m* 1963, Catharine Stevenson; two *d*. *Educ:* St Paul's Cathedral Choir Sch.; Haileybury Coll.; Peterhouse, Cambridge Univ. (organ and history schols). MA Cantab, MA Oxon. Asst Master, Clifton Coll., 1941–42; Cabinet Offices, 1942–46; Fellow of Peterhouse, Cambridge, 1947–62 (Hon. Fellow, 1986); Tutor of Peterhouse, 1948–58; Univ. Lectr, Cambridge, 1952–62; Sen. Res. Fellow, 1962–87, Sub-Warden, 1984–86, All Souls Coll., Oxford. Chm., Assoc. for Study of Modern Italy, 1987–. Commendatore dell'Ordine al Merito della Repubblica Italiana. For. Hon. Mem., Amer. Acad. of Arts and Sciences. Oratore Ufficiale della Repubblica di San Marino, 1982. Awards: Thirlwall, 1949; Serena, 1960; Elba, 1972; Villa di Chiesa, 1973; Mondello, 1975; Nove Muse, 1976; Duff Cooper Meml., 1977; Wolfson Literary, 1977; Rhegium Julii, 1983; Polifemo d'Argento, 1988; Fregene, 1990. *Publications:* Cavour and Garibaldi 1860, 1954; Garibaldi, 1957; (jtly) British Interests in the Mediterranean and Middle East, 1958; Italy, a Modern History, 1959 (enlarged edn 1969); Medieval Sicily, 1968; Modern Sicily, 1968; Da Cavour a Mussolini, 1968; (ed) The Making of Italy 1796–1870, 1968; (ed) Garibaldi, 1969; (ed) E. Quinet, Le Rivoluzioni d'Italia, 1970; Victor Emanuel, Cavour and the Risorgimento, 1971; (ed) G. La Farina, Scritti Politici, 1972; Vittorio Emanuele II, 1972; Mussolini's Roman Empire, 1976; Un Monumento al Duce, 1976; Cento Anni di Vita Italiana attraverso il Corriere della Sera, 1978; L'Italia del Ventesimo Secolo, 1978; (ed) G. Bandi, I mille: da Genova a Capua, 1981; Mussolini, 1981; (ed) F. De Sanctis, Un Viaggio Elettorale, 1983; Cavour, 1985; (jtly) A History of Sicily, 1986; Italy and its Monarchy, 1989; Jt Editor, Nelson History of England, 1962–. *Address:* White Lodge, Osler Road, Headington, Oxford OX3 9BJ. *T:* Oxford (0865) 62878.

McKAIG, Adm. Sir (John) Rae, KCB 1973; CBE 1966; *b* 24 April 1922; *s* of late Sir John McKaig, KCB, DSO, and Lady (Annie Wright) McKaig (*née* Lee); *m* 1945, Barbara Dawn, *d* of Dr F. K. Marriott, MC, Yoxford, Suffolk; two *s* one *d*. *Educ:* Loretto Sch. Joined RN as Special Entry Cadet, 1939; served in cruisers and destroyers in Home and Mediterranean Waters, 1940–43; in Amphibious Force S at invasion of Normandy, 1944; in coastal forces until 1945; qual. in Communications, 1945; Commander, 1952; Captain, 1959; served as Dep. to Chief Polaris Exec., 1963–66; comd HM Signal Sch., 1966–68; Rear-Adm., 1968; Asst Chief of Naval Staff (Operational Requirements), 1968–70; Vice-Adm., 1970; Flag Officer, Plymouth, and Port Admiral, Devonport, 1970–73; Adm., 1973; UK Mil. Rep. to NATO, 1973–75. Chm. and Chief Exec., Gray Mackenzie & Co., 1983–86; Dir, Inchcape plc, 1981–86. Mem., Royal Patriotic Fund Corp., 1978–. Dir, ALVA, 1989–. *Recreations:* offshore sailing, shooting, fishing. *Clubs:* Army and Navy, Royal Ocean Racing.

McKANE, Prof. William, FRSE 1984; FBA 1980; Professor of Hebrew and Oriental Languages, University of St Andrews, 1968–90, now Emeritus; Principal of St Mary's College, St Andrews, 1982–86; *b* 18 Feb. 1921; *s* of Thomas McKane and Jemima Smith McKane; *m* 1952, Agnes Mathie Howie; three *s* two *d*. *Educ:* Univ. of St Andrews (MA 1949); Univ. of Glasgow (MA 1952, PhD 1956, DLitt 1980). RAF, 1941–45. University of Glasgow: Asst in Hebrew, 1953–56; Lectr in Hebrew, 1956–65; Sen. Lectr, 1965–68; Dean, Faculty of Divinity, St Andrews, 1973–77. Fellow, Nat. Humanities Center, NC, USA, 1987–88. Foreign Sec., Soc. for Old Testament Study, 1981–86 (Pres., 1978); Chm., Peshitta project (Old Testament in Syriac), Internat. Org. for Study of Old Testament. DD (*hc*) Edinburgh, 1984. Burkitt Medal, British Acad., 1985. *Publications:* Prophets and Wise Men, 1965; Proverbs: a new approach, 1970; Studies in the Patriarchal Narratives, 1979; Jeremiah 1–25 (International Critical Commentary series), 1986; Selected Christian Hebraists, 1989; articles and reviews in British and European learned jls. *Recreations:* St Andrews association football blue (1949), walking, including hill walking. *Address:* 51 Irvine Crescent, St Andrews, Fife KY16 8LG. *T:* St Andrews (0334) 73797. *Club:* Royal and Ancient Golf (St Andrews).

MACKANESS, George Bellamy, MB, BS, DPhil; FRS 1976; President, Squibb Institute for Medical Research and Development, 1976–87, retired; *b* Sydney, Australia, 20 Aug. 1922; *s* of James V. Mackaness and Eleanor F. Mackaness; *m* 1945, Gwynneth Patterson; one *s*. *Educ:* Sydney Univ. (MB, BS Hons 1945); London Univ. (DCP 1948); Univ. of Oxford (Hon. MA 1949, DPhil 1953). Resident MO, Sydney Hosp., 1945–46; Resident Pathologist, Kanematsu Inst. of Pathology, Sydney Hosp., 1946–47; Dept of Path., Brit. Postgrad. Med. Sch., London Univ., 1947–48 (DCP); ANU Trav. Scholarship, Univ. of Oxford, 1948–51; Demonstrator and Tutor in Path., Sir William Dunn Sch. of Path., Oxford, 1949–53; Dept of Experimental Pathology, Australian National University: Sen. Fellow, 1954–58; Associate Prof. of Exp. Path., 1958–60; Professorial Fellow, 1960–63; Vis. Investigator, Rockefeller Univ., NY, 1959–60; Prof. of Microbiology, Univ. of Adelaide, 1963–65; Dir, Trudeau Inst. for Med. Res., NY, 1965–76; Adjunct Prof. of Path., NY Univ. Med. Center, 1969–. Director: Josiah Macy Jr Foundn, 1982–86; Squibb Corp., 1984–87. Member: Allergy and Immunol. Study Sect., Nat. Insts of Health, 1967–71; Bd of Sci. Counsellors, Nat. Inst. of Allergy and Infect. Diseases, 1971–75; Armed Forces Epidemicol Bd, 1967–73; Bd of Governors, W. Alton Jones Cell Science Center, 1970–72; Council, Tissue Culture Assoc., 1973–; Bd of Sci. Consultants, Sloan-Kettering Inst. Member: Amer. Assoc. of Immunologists; Amer. Assoc. for Advancement of Science; Reticuloendothelial Soc.; Lung Assoc.; Internat. Union Against Tuberculosis; Amer. Soc. of Microbiologists. Fellow, Amer. Acad. of Arts and Scis, 1978. Paul Ehrlich-Ludwig Darmstaedter Prize, 1975. *Address:* 2783 Little Creek, Johns Island, SC 29455, USA. *T:* (803) 768–1620.

MACKAY, family name of **Earl of Inchcape, Lord Reay** and **Barons Mackay of Ardbrecknish, Mackay of Clashfern** and **Tanlaw.**

MACKAY OF ARDBRECKNISH, Baron *cr* 1991 (Life Peer), of Tayvallich in the District of Argyll and Bute; **John Jackson Mackay;** Chairman, Sea Fish Industry Authority, since 1990; *b* 15 Nov. 1938; *s* of Jackson and Jean Mackay; *m* 1961, Sheena Wagner; two *s* one *d*. *Educ:* Glasgow Univ. (BSc, DipEd). Formerly, Head of Maths Dept, Oban High Sch.; Chief Exec., Scottish Cons. Central Office, 1987–90. MP (C): Argyll, 1979–83; Argyll and Bute, 1983–87; Parly Under-Sec. of State, Scottish Office, 1982–87. *Recreations:* fishing, sailing. *Address:* Innishail, 51 Springkell Drive, Pollokshields, Glasgow G41 4EZ.

MACKAY OF CLASHFERN, Baron *cr* 1979 (Life Peer), of Eddrachillis in the District of Sutherland; **James Peter Hymers Mackay;** PC 1979; FRSE 1984; Lord High

Chancellor of Great Britain, since 1987; *b* 2 July 1927; *s* of James Mackay and Janet Hymers; *m* 1958, Elizabeth Gunn Hymers; one *s* two *d*. *Educ:* George Heriot's Sch., Edinburgh. MA Hons Maths and Nat. Philosophy, Edinburgh Univ., 1948; Lectr in Mathematics, Univ. of St Andrews, 1948–50; Major Schol., Trinity Coll., Cambridge, in Mathematics, 1947, taken up 1950; Senior Schol. 1951; BA (Cantab) 1952; LLB Edinburgh (with Distinction) 1955. Admitted to Faculty of Advocates, 1955; QC (Scot.) 1965; Standing Junior Counsel to: Queen's and Lord Treasurer's Remembrancer; Scottish Home and Health Dept; Commissioners of Inland Revenue in Scotland; Sheriff Principal, Renfrew and Argyll, 1972–74; Vice-Dean, Faculty of Advocates, 1973–76; Dean, 1976–79; Lord Advocate of Scotland, 1979–84; a Senator of Coll. of Justice in Scotland, 1984–85; a Lord of Appeal in Ordinary, 1985–87. Chancellor, Heriot-Watt Univ., 1991–. Part-time Mem., Scottish Law Commn, 1976–79. Hon. Master of the Bench, Inner Temple, 1979. Fellow: Internat. Acad. of Trial Lawyers, 1979; Inst. of Taxation, 1981. Dir, Stenhouse Holdings Ltd, 1976–77. Mem., Insurance Brokers' Registration Council, 1977–79. A Comr of Northern Lighthouses, 1975–84; Elder Brother of Trinity House, 1990. Hon. Mem., SPTL, 1986. Hon. Fellow: Trinity Coll., Cambridge, 1989; Girton Coll., Cambridge, 1990; Hon. FRCSE, 1989; Hon. FRCP 1990; Hon. FICE, 1988. Hon. LLD: Edinburgh, 1983; Dundee, 1983; Strathclyde, 1985; Aberdeen, 1987; St Andrews, 1989; Cambridge, 1989; Coll. of William and Mary, Va, 1989; Birmingham, 1990; Hon. DCL Newcastle, 1990. *Publication:* Armour on Valuation for Rating, 5th edn (Consultant Editor), 1985. *Recreation:* walking. *Address:* Lord Chancellor's Residence, House of Lords, SW1A 0PW. *Clubs:* Athenæum; New (Edinburgh).

MACKAY, Prof. Alan Lindsay, FRS 1988; Professor of Crystallography, Birkbeck College, University of London, since 1986; *b* 6 Sept. 1926; *s* of Robert Lindsay Mackay, OBE, MC, BSc, MD and Margaret Brown Mackay, OBE, MB ChB, JP; *m* 1951, Sheila Thorne Hague, MA; two *s* one *d*. *Educ:* Wolverhampton Grammar Sch.; Oundle Sch.; Trinity Coll., Cambridge (BA, MA); BSc, PhD, DSc London. Lectr, Reader, Prof., Dept of Crystallography, Birkbeck Coll., 1951–. Visiting Professor: Univ. of Tokyo, 1969; Univ. of Tsukuba, 1980; Korean Advanced Inst. of Sci. and Tech., 1987; Hon. Professor: Central China Univ; Sichuan Inst. of Sci. Studies; China Inst. for Sci. Studies; Univ. de Paris-Sud, 1989. Zaheer Lectr, New Delhi, 1977. *Publications:* The Harvest of a Quiet Eye, 1977; (with A. N. Barrett) Spatial Structure and the Microcomputer, 1987; papers in learned jls. *Recreation:* Asian studies. *Address:* 22 Lanchester Road, N6 4TA. *T:* 081–883 4810.

MACKAY, Alastair, CMG 1966; *b* 27 Sept. 1911; *s* of late Alexander Mackay; *m* 1st, 1939, Janetta Brown Ramsay (*d* 1973); one *s* one *d*; 2nd, 1975, Edith Whicher. *Educ:* George Heriot's Sch.; Edinburgh Univ.; Berlin Univ. Entered HM Treasury, 1940. Member UK Treasury and Supply Delegation, Washington, 1951–54; seconded to Foreign Service Inspectorate, 1957–59; Financial Adviser to the British High Commissioner in India, 1963–66; Under-Sec., HM Treasury, 1967–71; Financial and Development Sec., Gibraltar, 1971–75. *Recreations:* golf, gardening. *Address:* 3 Cloona House, 38 Carlisle Road, Eastbourne, E Sussex BN20 7TD. *T:* Eastbourne (0323) 22738.

McKAY, Prof. Alexander Gordon, OC 1988; FRSC 1965; Professor of Classics, McMaster University, 1957–90, now Emeritus; Adjunct Professor of Humanities and Classics, York University, since 1990; President, Royal Society of Canada, 1984–87; *b* 24 Dec. 1924; *s* of Alexander Lynn McKay and Marjory Maude Redfern Nicoll McKay; *m* 1964, Helen Jean Zulauf; two step *d*. *Educ:* Trinity Coll., Toronto (Hons BA Classics 1946); Yale Univ. (MA 1947); Princeton Univ. (AM 1948; PhD 1950). Classics faculty: Wells Coll., NY, 1949–50; Univ. of Pennsylvania, 1950–51; Univ. of Manitoba, 1951–52; Mount Allison Univ., 1952–53; Waterloo Coll., Ont., 1953–55; Univ. of Manitoba, 1955–57; McMaster Univ., 1957–90: Chm. of Dept, 1962–68, 1976–79; Founding Dean of Humanities, 1968–73; Senator, 1968–73, 1985–87. Dist. Vis. Prof., Univ. of Colorado, 1973; Prof. i/c, Intercollegiate Center for Classical Studies in Rome (Stanford Univ.), 1975; Mem. Inst. for Advanced Study, Princeton, 1979, 1981; Vis. Schol., Univ. of Texas, Austin, 1987; Vis. Fellow Commoner, Trinity Coll., Cambridge, 1988. Dir, Internat. Union of Academies, 1980–83, 1986–90 (Vice-Pres., 1983–86). Hon. LLD: Manitoba, 1986; Brock Univ., Ont, 1990; Queen's Univ., Kingston, 1991. KStJ 1986. Silver Jubilee Medal, 1977. *Publications:* Naples and Campania: texts and illustrations, 1962; Roman Lyric Poetry: Catullus and Horace, 1962; Vergil's Italy, 1970; Cumae and the Phlegraean Fields, 1972; Naples and Coastal Campania, 1972; Houses, Villas and Palaces in the Roman World, 1975, German edn 1980; Roman Satire, 1976; Vitruvius, Architect and Engineer, 1978; Roma Antiqua: Latium and Etruria, 1986; Selections from Vergil's Aeneid Books I, IV, VI: Dido and Aeneas, 1988; Housing for the Spirit, 1991. *Recreations:* pianoforte, travel. *Address:* 1 Turner Avenue, Hamilton, Ont L8P 3K4, Canada. *T:* 416 526 1331. *Clubs:* Princeton (NY); University (Pittsburgh); Tamahaac (Ancaster, Hamilton); Arts and Letters (Toronto); President's (McMaster Univ.); Canadian (Hamilton).

McKAY, Maj.-Gen. Alexander Matthew, CB 1975; FEng 1984; Secretary, Institution of Mechanical Engineers, 1976–87; *b* 14 Feb. 1921; *s* of Colin and Anne McKay; *m* 1949, Betty Margaret Lee; one *s* one *d* (and one *d* decd). *Educ:* Esplanade House Sch.; RN Dockyard Sch.; Portsmouth Polytechnic. FIEE, FIMechE; psc, sm; MASME. Served War of 1939–45 (despatches twice); 2nd Lieut, 1943; Lieut 1944; Captain 1944; Major 1947; Lt-Col 1960; Col 1966; Brigadier 1968; Maj.-Gen. 1972. Served with 6th Airborne Div.; Staff Coll., Quetta, 1954; staff appts include GS02, DAA&QMG, DAQMG, AQMG; Dir, Elect. and Mech. Engrg, Army, 1972–75; Col Comdt, REME, 1974–80. Gen. Sec., IChemE, 1975–76. Mem. Council, IEE, 1973–76. Chm., Stocklake Hldgs 1976–87; Vice-Chm., Mechanical Engrg Publications Ltd, 1976–87. Pres. and Chm., Winchester Div., SSAFA, 1988–. FRSE, 1985. Freeman, City of London, 1984; Liveryman, Engineers' Co., 1984–88. *Publications:* papers in Proceedings IMechE and REME Institution. *Recreations:* fly fishing, gardening, restoring antique furniture. *Address:* Church Cottage, Martyr Worthy, near Winchester, Hants SO21 1DY.

McKAY, Allan George; Regional Chairman, British Gas North Eastern, since 1989; *b* 5 Sept. 1935; *s* of George Allan McKay and Wilhelmina McKay; *m* 1962, Margaret Currie Baxter; one *s* two *d*. *Educ:* Royal High School, Edinburgh. FCCA, ACIS, CIGasE. Accountant, Scottish Gas Board, 1961; Dir of Finance, Scottish Gas, 1975; Deputy Chairman: British Gas East Midlands, 1982; British Gas North Thames, 1987. *Recreation:* golf. *Address:* British Gas, North Eastern, New York Road, Leeds LS2 7PE. *T:* Leeds (0532) 436291.

McKAY, Allen; JP; MP (Lab) Barnsley West and Penistone, since 1983 (Pensistone, July 1978–1983); *b* 5 Feb. 1927; *s* of Fred and Martha Anne McKay; *m* 1949, June Simpson; one *s*. *Educ:* Hoyland Kirk Balk Secondary Modern School; extramural studies, Univ. of Sheffield. Clerical work, Steel Works, 1941–45; general mineworker, 1945–47; Mining Electrical Engineer, 1947–65; NCB Industrial Relations Trainee, 1965–66; Asst Manpower Officer, Barnsley Area, NCB, 1966–78. Opposition Whip, 1981. JP Barnsley, 1971. *Recreation:* reading. *Address:* House of Commons, SW1; 24 Springwood Road, Hoyland, Barnsley, South Yorks S74 0AZ. *T:* Barnsley (0226) 743418.

MacKAY, Andrew James; MP (C) Berkshire East, since 1983; *b* 27 Aug. 1949; *s* of Robert James MacKay and Olive Margaret MacKay; *m* 1975, Diana Joy (*née* Kinchin) one *s* one *d*. *Educ:* Solihull. MP (C) Birmingham, Stechford, Mar. 1977–1979; PPS to Sec. of State for NI, 1986–89, to Sec. of State for Defence, 1989–. Mem., Environment Select Cttee, 1985–86; Sec., Cons. Parly For. Affairs Cttee, 1985–86. Mem., Conservative Party Nat. Exec., 1979–82. *Recreations:* golf, squash, good food. *Address:* House of Commons, SW1A 0AA. *T:* 071–219 4109. *Clubs:* Berkshire Golf; Aberdovey Golf (Wales).

McKAY, Archibald Charles; Sheriff of Glasgow and Strathkelvin, since 1979; *b* 18 Oct. 1929; *s* of Patrick McKay and Catherine (*née* McKinlay); *m* 1956, Ernestine Maria Tobia; one *s* three *d*. *Educ:* Knocknacarry, Co. Antrim; St Aloysius' Coll., Glasgow; Glasgow Univ. (MA, LLB 1954). National Service, 1955–56. Started practice in Glasgow as solicitor, 1957; estabd own firm of solicitors, 1961; apptd to the Bench, 1978. Pres., Glasgow Bar Assoc., 1967–68. *Recreations:* flying, motor cycling, amateur radio, tennis. *Address:* 96 Springkell Avenue, Pollokshields, Glasgow G41 4EL. *T:* 041–427 1525.

MACKAY, A(rthur) Stewart, ROI 1949; Teacher, Hammersmith College of Art, 1960–68, retired; *b* 25 Feb. 1909; British. *Educ:* Wilson's Grammar Sch.; Regent Street Polytechnic School of Art. Art Master, Regent Street Polytechnic School of Art, 1936, Assistant Lecturer, 1936–60. Served War of 1939–45: enlisted Army, Jan. 1942; released with rank of Captain, 1946. Exhibitor: RA (44 pictures exhibited); Paris Salon; ROI; RBA; Leicester Galleries; Imperial War Museum; Royal Scottish Academy; New York. *Publications:* How to Make Lino Cuts, 1935; articles for Artist and Kent Life, 1953, 1963. *Recreations:* reading, writing. *Address:* 4 Dog Kennel Hill, East Dulwich, SE22 8AA.

MACKAY, Charles, CB 1986; FIBiol; Chief Agricultural Officer, Department of Agriculture and Fisheries for Scotland, 1975–87; *b* 12 Jan. 1927; *s* of Hugh and Eliza Mackay; *m* 1956, Marie A. K. Mackay (*née* Mitchell); one *s* one *d*. *Educ:* Strathmore Sch., Sutherland; Lairg Higher Grade Sch., Sutherland; Univ. of Aberdeen (BScAgric); Univ. of Kentucky (MSc). Department of Agriculture and Fisheries for Scotland: Temporary Inspector, 1947–48; Asst Inspector, 1948–54; Inspector, 1954–64; Sen. Inspector, 1964–70; Technical Develt Officer, 1970–73; Dep. Chief Agricl Officer, 1973–75. Hon. Order of Kentucky Colonels, 1960. *Recreations:* fishing, golf. *Address:* 4/3 Craufurdland, Edinburgh EH4 6DL. *T:* Edinburgh 031–339 8770.

MACKAY, Colin Crichton; QC 1989; *b* 26 Sept. 1943; *s* of Sir James Mackerron Mackay, KBE, CB, and Katherine Millar Crichton Mackay (*née* Hamilton); *m* 1969, Rosamond Diana Elizabeth Collins; one *d* two *s*. *Educ:* Radley Coll.; Corpus Christi Coll., Oxford (Open Classical Schol; MA). Harmsworth Entrance Exhibnr, 1965, and Astbury Schol., 1967; called to the Bar, Middle Temple, 1967. *Recreations:* opera, sport, Scotland. *Address:* 39 Essex Street, WC2R 3AT. *T:* 071–583 1111. *Club:* Vincent's (Oxford).

MACKAY, Donald George; Under Secretary, Scottish Office, 1983–88; *b* 25 Nov. 1929; *s* of William Morton Mackay and Annie Tainsh Higgs; *m* 1965, Elizabeth Ailsa Barr; two *s* one *d*. *Educ:* Morgan Academy, Dundee; St Andrews Univ. (MA). Assistant Principal, Scottish Home Dept, 1953; Asst Sec., Royal Commission on the Police, 1960–62; Sec., Royal Commission on Local Govt in Scotland, 1966–69; Scottish Development Dept, 1969–79 and 1985–88; Dept of Agriculture and Fisheries for Scotland, 1980–85. *Recreations:* hill walking, photography, music. *Address:* 38 Cluny Drive, Edinburgh EH10 6DX. *T:* 031–447 1851.

MacKAY, Prof. Donald Iain; Chairman, PIEDA Ltd, since 1974; Consultant to Secretary of State for Scotland, since 1971; *b* 27 Feb. 1937; *s* of William and Rhona MacKay; *m* 1961, Diana Marjory (*née* Raffan); one *s* two *d*. *Educ:* Dollar Academy; Univ. of Aberdeen (MA). English Electric Co., 1959–62; Lectr in Political Economy, Univ. of Aberdeen, 1962–65; Lectr in Applied Economics, Univ. of Glasgow, 1965–68, Sen. Lectr, 1968–71; Prof. of Political Economy, Univ. of Aberdeen, 1971–76; Prof. of Economics, Heriot-Watt Univ., Edinburgh, 1976–82, Professorial Fellow 1982–. Lister Lectr, British Assoc. for the Advancement of Science, 1974. Director: Adam and Co., 1983–; Grampian Holdings, 1987–. Mem., Scottish Econ. Council, 1985. Gov., NIESR, 1981. *Publications:* Geographical Mobility and the Brain Drain, 1969; Local Labour Markets and Wage Structures, 1970; Labour Markets under Different Employment Conditions, 1971; The Political Economy of North Sea Oil, 1975; (ed) Scotland 1980: the economics of self-government, 1977; articles in Econ. Jl, Oxford Econ. Papers, Manch. Sch., Scottish Jl Polit. Econ., Jl Royal Stat. Soc. *Recreations:* tennis, golf, bridge. *Address:* Newfield, 14 Gamekeeper's Road, Edinburgh EH4 6LU.

MACKAY, Donald Sage; QC (Scot.) 1987; *b* 30 Jan. 1946; *s* of Rev. Donald George Mackintosh Mackay and Jean Margaret Mackay; *m* 1979, Lesley Ann Waugh; one *s* two *d*. *Educ:* George Watson's Boys' Coll., Edinburgh; Univ. of Edinburgh (LLB 1966, LLM 1968); Univ. of Virginia (LLM 1969). Law apprentice, 1969–71; Solicitor with Allan McDougall & Co., SSC, Edinburgh, 1971–76; called to the Scottish Bar, 1976; Advocate Depute, 1982–85. Mem., Criminal Injuries Compensation Bd, 1989–. *Recreations:* golf, gardening, Isle of Arran. *Address:* 39 Hermitage Gardens, Edinburgh EH10 6AZ. *T:* 031–447 1412; Kinneil Cottage, Lamlash, Isle of Arran KA27 8JT. *T:* Lamlash (07706) 646; Advocates' Library, Parliament House, Edinburgh EH1 1RF. *T:* 031–226 5071. *Club:* Western (Glasgow).

MACKAY, Eileen Alison, (Mrs A. Muir Russell); Under Secretary, Housing, Scottish Office Environment Department (formerly Scottish Development Department), since 1988; *b* 7 July 1943; *d* of Alexander William Mackay and Alison Jack Ross; *m* 1983, A(lastair) Muir Russell, *qv*. *Educ:* Dingwall Acad.; Edinburgh Univ. (MA Hons Geography). Dept of Employment, Scottish HQ, 1965–72; Scottish Office, 1972–78; HM Treasury, 1978–80; CPRS, Cabinet Office, 1980–83; Scottish Office, 1983–. Chm., Castlemilk Partnership, 1988–; Dir, Moray Firth Maltings, 1988–. *Address:* Scottish Office Environment Department, St Andrews House, Edinburgh EH1 3DE.

MACKAY, Eric Beattie; Editor of The Scotsman, 1972–85; *b* 31 Dec. 1922; *s* of Lewis Mackay and Agnes Johnstone; *m* 1954, Moya Margaret Myles Connolly (*d* 1981); three *s* one *d*. *Educ:* Aberdeen Grammar Sch.; Aberdeen Univ. (MA). Aberdeen Bon-Accord, 1948; Elgin Courant, 1949; The Scotsman, 1950; Daily Telegraph, 1952; The Scotsman, 1953: London Editor, 1957; Dep. Editor, 1961. *Recreations:* travel, golf, theatre. *Address:* 5 Strathearn Place, Edinburgh EH9 2AL. *T:* 031–447 7737.

MACKAY, Maj.-Gen. Eric MacLachlan, CBE 1971 (MBE 1944); *b* 26 Dec. 1921; *s* of Ian MacLachlan Mackay and Violet Aimée Scott-Smith; *m* 1954, Ruth Thérèse Roth (*d* 1985); one *s*. *Educ:* Fettes Coll., Edinburgh. Served War: enlisted Royal Scots Fusiliers, 1940; commissioned Oct. 1941, Royal Engineers; 2/Lieut-Major, 1st Parachute Sqdn, RE, 1941–45, N Africa, Sicily, Italy, Arnhem, PoW (escaped) Norway. OC, Field Company, 20 Indian Div., French Indo-China, 1945–46; 2 i/c 23 Indian Div. Engrs, Java, 1946; OC, 35 Indian Field Company, Malaya, 1947; Supplementary Engrg Course, SME, 1948; GSO 2 Intell., Jt Intell. Bureau, 1949–50; Staff Coll., 1951; GSO 2, Org. and Equipment, HQ, ALFCE, 1952–53; Sen. Instructor Tactics, SME, 1954–55; OC, 33 Field Sqdn, RE, Cyprus, Suez, 1956–58; GSO 2, Wpns, MoD, 1958–60; JSSC, 1960; 2 i/c 2 Div. Engrs, 1961–62; Chief Engr, Malaysian Army, Borneo/Malaya, 1963–65; GSO 1, Co-ord.,

Master-Gen. of the Ordnance, 1966–67; Col, GS, RSME, 1968–69; Chief Engr (Brig.): Army Strategic Command, 1970–71; UK Land Forces, 1972; Maj.-Gen. 1973; Chief Engr, BAOR, 1973–76, retired. Managing Director: Cementation Sico Oman Ltd, 1977; Galadari Cementation Pte Ltd, 1978–83; Forum Develt Pte Ltd, 1983–85; Regional Dir Iraq, Engineering Services Internat., 1981–82; Chm., Amorshield Security Products, 1986–90. CEng 1976; MICE 1976. DSC (USA), 1944; Pingat Peringatan Malaysia (PPM), 1965. *Recreations:* motoring, skiing, photography. *Address:* 32 Briarwood Road, SW4 9PX.

McKAY, Frederick; *see* McKay, J. F.

MACKAY, Sir (George Patrick) Gordon, Kt 1966; CBE 1962; Director, World Bank, 1975–78; Member, Board of Crown Agents, 1980–82; *b* 12 Nov. 1914; *s* of Rev. Adam Mackay and Katie Forrest (*née* Lawrence); *m* 1954, Margaret Esmé Martin; one *s* two *d*. *Educ:* Gordon Sch., Huntly; Aberdeen Univ. Joined Kenya and Uganda Railways and Harbours (later East African Railways and Harbours), 1938; Chief Asst to Gen. Manager, 1948; Chief Operating Supt, 1954; Dep. General Manager, 1960, General Manager, 1961–64; with World Bank, 1965–78. FCIT (MInstT 1961). OStJ 1964. *Recreation:* golf. *Address:* Well Cottage, Sandhills, Brook, Surrey GU8 5UP. *T:* Wormley (042879) 2549. *Club:* Nairobi (Kenya).

MACKAY, Sir Gordon; *see* Mackay, Sir G. P. G.

McKAY, Very Rev. (James) Frederick, CMG 1972; OBE 1964 (MBE 1953); retired; Associate Minister, St Stephen's Uniting (formerly Presbyterian) Church, Sydney, 1974–80; Chairman, Uniting Church Negotiators, NSW, 1976–80; recognised as a foundation minister of Uniting Church in Australia at time of Union, 1977; *b* 15 April 1907; father, Northern Ireland; mother, Australian; *m* 1938, Margaret Mary Robertson; one *s* three *d*. *Educ:* Thornburgh Coll., Charters Towers, Qld; Emmanuel Coll., Brisbane, Qld; University of Queensland. MA; BD. Ordained Minister, Presbyterian Church of Australia, 1935; Patrol Padre, Australian Inland Mission (working with Flynn of the Inland), 1935–41; Chaplain, RAAF, 1941–46; Command Chaplain, Middle East, 1943–45; Minister, Toowong Parish, Qld, 1946–50; Superintendent (succeeding Flynn of the Inland), Aust. Inland Mission, 1951–74, Archivist, 1974–75. Moderator, Presbyterian Church of NSW, 1965; Moderator-Gen., Presbyterian Church of Australia, 1970–73. Editor, Frontier News, 1951–74. Vocational Award, Sydney Rotary, 1972. *Address:* Hawkesbury Village, Chapel Street, Richmond, NSW 2753, Australia. *T:* (045) 78 4561. *Club:* Australian (Sydney).

McKAY, Sir James (Wilson), Kt 1971; JP; DL; former Lord Provost of Edinburgh, and Lord Lieutenant of the County of the City of Edinburgh, 1969–72; *b* 12 March 1912; *s* of John McKay; *m* 1942, Janette Urquhart; three *d*. *Educ:* Dunfermline High Sch.; Portobello Secondary Sch., Edinburgh. Insurance Broker; Man. Dir, John McKay (Insurance) Ltd, Edinburgh; Dir, George S. Murdoch & Partners Ltd, Aberdeen. Served with RN, 1941–46 (Lieut, RNVR). Hon. DLitt Heriot-Watt, 1972. JP Edinburgh, 1972; DL County and City of Edinburgh, 1972. Order of Cross of St Mark (Greek Orthodox Church), 1970; Knight, Order of Orange-Nassau, 1972. *Recreations:* walking, gardening, reading. *Address:* T'Windward, 11 Cammo Gardens, Edinburgh EH4 8EJ. *T:* 031–339 6755. *Clubs:* New (Edinburgh); RNVR (Glasgow); Caledonian (Hon. Mem.) (San Francisco).

MACKAY, John; Headmaster, Bristol Grammar School, 1960–75; *b* 23 June 1914; *s* of William Mackay, Nottingham, and Eliza Mackay; *m* 1952, Margaret Ogilvie; two *s* two *d*. *Educ:* Mundella Grammar Sch., Nottingham; University of Nottingham; Merton Coll., Oxford. BA London (External) 1st Class Hons (English), 1935; Cambridge Teacher's Certificate, 1936. On staff of SCM, 1936–38; English Lecturer, St John's Coll., York, 1938–40. Served War of 1939–45, in Royal Navy, 1940–46. Merton Coll., Oxford, 1946–48; DPhil (Oxon) 1953. English Master, Merchant Taylors' School, Crosby, Liverpool, 1948–54; Second Master, Cheltenham Coll., 1954–60. Chm., HMC, 1970, Treasurer, 1974–75. *Recreations:* literature, gardening, cricket, arguing, senile reminiscence. *Address:* The Old Post Office, Tormarton, Badminton, Avon GL9 1HU. *T:* Badminton (045421) 243. *Club:* East India, Devonshire, Sports and Public Schools.

McKAY, Sir John (Andrew), Kt 1972; CBE 1966; QPM 1968; HM Chief Inspector of Constabulary for England and Wales, 1970–72; *b* 28 Nov. 1912; *s* of late Denis McKay, Blantyre, Lanarkshire; *m* 1st, 1947, Gertrude Gillespie Deighan (*d* 1971); two *d*; 2nd, 1976, Mildred Grace Kilday, *d* of late Dr Emil Stern and Grace Mildred Pleasants, San Francisco. *Educ:* Glasgow Univ. MA Glasgow, 1934. Joined Metropolitan Police, 1935; seconded to Army for service with Military Govt in Italy and Austria, 1943–47 (Lt-Col); Asst Chief Constable, then Deputy Chief Constable, Birmingham, 1953–58; Chief Constable of Manchester, 1959–66; HM Inspector of Constabulary, 1966–70. Freeman of City of London, 1972. OStJ 1963. Hon. MA, Manchester, 1966; Hon. Fellow, Manchester Polytechnic, 1971. *Address:* 212 Mocking Bird Circe, Santa Rosa, Calif 95409, USA. *T:* 707–538–8285.

McKAY, Dr John Henderson, CBE 1987; JP; DL; Secretary and Treasurer, Royal Caledonian Horticultural Society, since 1988; *b* 12 May 1929; *s* of Thomas Johnstone McKay and Patricia Madeleine Henderson; *m* 1964, Catherine Watson Taylor; one *s* one *d*. *Educ:* West Calder High School. BA Hons, PhD, Open University. Labourer, clerk, Pumpherston Oil Co. Ltd, 1948–50; National Service, Royal Artillery, 1950–52; Officer and Surveyor, Customs and Excise, 1952–85. Mem., 1974–77 and 1978–88, Lord Provost and Lord Lieutenant, 1984–88, City of Edinburgh DC; Chm., Edinburgh Internat. Fest. Soc., 1984–88; Jt Chm., Edinburgh Mil. Tattoo Policy Cttee, 1984–88; Councillor, Royal Caledonian Horticultural Soc., 1974–78, 1980–81, 1984–88. JP 1984, DL 1988, Edinburgh. Dr *hc* Edinburgh, 1989. *Recreations:* gardening, listening to music. *Address:* 2 Buckstone Way, Edinburgh EH10 6PN. *T:* 031–445 2865. *Club:* Lothianburn Golf (Edinburgh).

MACKAY, Maj.-Gen. Kenneth, CB 1969; MBE 1943; idc, psc; GOC, Field Force Command Australia, Nov. 1973–Feb. 1974, retired; *b* 17 Feb. 1917; *m* 1943, Judith, *d* of F. Littler; two *s* one *d*. *Educ:* University High Sch., Melbourne; RMC Duntroon. Served War of 1939–45: Artillery, and Liaison Officer HQ 9th Australian Division, Middle East, 1940–41; ME Staff Sch., 1942; Bde Maj. 26 Bde, 1942–44; MO 12, War Office, 1944–45; Joint Sec., JCOSA, 1945–48; CO, 67 Inf. Bn, 1948; CO, 3 Bn Royal Aust. Regt, 1949; AHQ, 1949–52; Chief Instructor, Sch. of Tactics and Admin. 1952–55; Asst Aust. Defence Rep. UK, 1955–57; successively Dir of Maintenance, Personnel Admin., Quartering and Military Training, 1957–61; IDC, 1962; Dir Military Operations and Plans, Army HQ, Canberra, 1962–66; Comdr Aust. Force Vietnam, 1966; Commander 1st Division Australian Army, 1967–68; QMG AHQ, 1968–71; GOC Eastern Comd, 1971–73. *Recreations:* fishing, golf. *Address:* 65 Matthew Flinders Drive, Port Macquarie, NSW 2444, Australia. *Clubs:* Australian; Port Macquarie; New South Wales Golf.

McKAY, Mrs Margaret; Public Relations Consultant; *b* Jan. 1911. *Educ:* Elementary. Joined Labour Party 1932. Chief woman officer, TUC, 1951–62; Member of Co-operative Society, 1928–. Held administrative posts with Civil Service Clerical Association and Transport and General Workers' Union. MP (Lab) Clapham, 1964–70. Commander, Order of the Cedar of Lebanon. World Culture Award, Accademia Italia, 1984. *Publications:* Generation in Revolt (pen name Margaret McCarthy), 1953; Women in Trade Union History (TUC), 1954; Arab Voices from the Past; Electronic Arabia, 1974; The Chainless Mind, 1974; Timeless Arabia, 1978; Strangers in Palestine, 1982; Gulf Saga, 1982; Eve's Daring Daughters, 1985. *Address:* PO Box 668, Abu Dhabi, Union of Arab Emirates.

MacKAY, Prof. Norman, MD; FRCPG, FRCPE; Dean of Postgraduate Medicine and Professor of Postgraduate Medical Education, University of Glasgow, since 1989; *b* 15 Sept. 1936; *s* of Donald MacKay and Catherine MacLeod; *m* 1961, Grace Violet McCaffer; two *s* two *d*. *Educ:* Glasgow Univ. (MB ChB, MD). Junior posts, Glasgow hosps, 1959–66; Lectr in Medicine, Nairobi, 1966–67; Sen. Registrar, Victoria Infirmary, Glasgow, 1967–68; Acting Sen. Lectr, Materia Medica, Univ. of Glasgow, 1968–72; Acting Consultant Physician, Falkirk, 1972–73; Consultant Physician, Victoria Infirmary, 1973–89, Hon. Consultant, 1989–. Hon. Sec., RCPSG, 1973–83. *Publications:* articles in med. jls. *Recreations:* gardening, golf, soccer. *Address:* 4 Erskine Avenue, Dumbreck, Glasgow G41 5AL. *T:* 041–427 0900.

MACKAY, Peter; Secretary, Scottish Office Industry Department, since 1990; *b* Arbroath, 6 July 1940; *s* of John S. Mackay, FRCS, and Patricia M. Atkinson; *m* 1964, Sarah Holdich; one *s* two *d*. *Educ:* Glasgow High Sch.; St Andrews Univ. (MA Political Economy). Teacher, Kyogle High Sch., NSW, 1962–63; joined Scottish Office as Asst Principal, 1963; various posts, incl. Private Sec. to successive Ministers of State, 1966–68 and Secs of State, 1973–75; Nuffield Travelling Fellow, Canada, Australia and NZ, 1978–79; seconded: as Dir for Scotland, MSC, 1983–85; as Under Sec., Manpower Policy, Dept of Employment, London, 1985–86; Under Sec., Further and Higher Educn, Scottish Educn Dept, 1987–89; Principal Establishment Officer, Scottish Office, 1989–90. *Recreations:* high altitudes and latitudes, dinghy sailing, sea canoeing. *Address:* 6 Henderland Road, Edinburgh EH12 6BB. *T:* 031–337 2830. *Clubs:* Clyde Canoe, Scottish Arctic.

McKAY, Rev. Roy; Hon. Canon, Chichester Cathedral, since 1957; *b* 4 Nov. 1900; *s* of William McKay and Sarah Evelyn (*née* Littlewood); *m* 1927, Mary Oldham Fraser; one *s* one *d*. *Educ:* Marlborough Coll.; Magdalen Coll., Oxford. Curate, S Paul's, Kingston Hill, 1926; Curate-in-charge and Vicar of St Mark's Londonderry, Smethwick, 1928; Vicar of Mountfield, Sussex, 1932; Chaplain of Christ's Chapel of Alleyn's College of God's Gift, Dulwich, 1937; Vicar of Goring-by-Sea, Sussex, 1943; Chaplain of Canford Sch., 1948; Head of Religious Broadcasting, 1955–63; Preacher to Lincoln's Inn, 1958–59; Rector of St James, Garlickhythe, EC4, 1965–70. *Publications:* Tell John (with Bishop G. F. Allen), 1932; The Pillar of Fire, 1933; Take Care of the Sense, 1964; John Leonard Wilson: Confessor for the Faith, 1973. *Address:* 12 Torkington Gardens, West Street, Stamford, Lincs.

McKAY, William Robert; Clerk of the Journals, House of Commons, since 1987; *b* 18 April 1939; *s* of late William Wallace McKay and of Margaret H. A. Foster; *m* 1962, Margaret M., *d* of E. M. Fillmore, OBE; twin *d*. *Educ:* Trinity Academy, Leith; Edinburgh Univ. (MA Hons). Clerk in the House of Commons, 1961; Clerk of Financial Cttees, H of C, 1985–87; Secretary: to the House of Commons Commn, 1981–84; to the Public Accounts Commn, 1985–87. *Publications:* (ed) Erskine May's Private Journal 1883–86, 1984; Secretaries to Mr Speaker, 1986; Clerks in the House of Commons 1363–1989: a biographical list, 1989; (ed) Observations, Rules and Orders of the House of Commons: an early procedural collection, 1989; The Northern Whig, George Mackay third Lord Reay and the Jacobites, 1991. *Recreation:* dry-stone walling. *Address:* 26 Earl Street, Cambridge CB1 1JR.

MACKAY LEWIS, Maj.-Gen. Kenneth Frank; *see* Lewis.

McKEAN, Charles Alexander, FSAScot; FRSA; Secretary and Treasurer, Royal Incorporation of Architects in Scotland, since 1979; *b* 16 July 1946; *s* of John Laurie McKean and Nancy Burns Lendrum; *m* 1975, Margaret Elizabeth Yeo; two *s*. *Educ:* Fettes Coll., Edinburgh; Univ. of Bristol (BA Hons). Regional Secretary, RIBA, 1968–79; Architectural Correspondent: The Times, 1977–83; Scotland on Sunday, 1988–89; Trustee, Thirlestane Castle Trust, 1983–; Director, Workshops and Artists Studios Scotland (WASPS), 1980–85; Member: Scottish Arts Council Exhibitions Panel, 1980–83; Adv. Council for the Arts in Scotland, 1984–87. Bossom Lectr, RSA, 1986. Hon. Mem., Saltire Soc. Hon. FRIBA. General Editor, RIAS/Landmark Trust series to Scotland, 1982–. Architectural Journalist of the Year, 1979 and 1983; Building Journalist of the Year, 1983. *Publications:* (with David Atwell) Battle of Styles, 1974; Guide to Modern Buildings in London 1965–75, 1976; Fight Blight, 1977; Architectural Guide to Cambridge and East Anglia 1920–80, 1980; Edinburgh—an illustrated architectural guide, 1982, 3rd edn 1983; (with David Walker) Dundee—an illustrated introduction through its buildings, 1984, 2nd edn 1986; Stirling and the Trossacks, 1984; The Scottish Thirties, 1987; The District of Moray—an illustrated introduction, 1987; (jtly) Central Glasgow—an illustrated architectural guide, 1989; Banff and Buchan—an illustrated architectural guide, 1990; For a Wee Country, 1990. *Recreations:* gardening, topography, books and glass collecting. *Address:* 10 Hill Park Road, Edinburgh EH4 7AW. *T:* 031–336 2753. *Club:* Scottish Arts.

McKEAN, Douglas, CB 1977; *b* 2 April 1917; *s* of late Alexander McKean, Enfield, Mddx; *m* 1942, Anne, *d* of late Roger Clayton, Riding Mill, Northumberland; two *s*. *Educ:* Merchant Taylors' Sch.; St John's Coll., Oxford. War Office, 1940; transferred to HM Treasury, 1949; Asst Sec., 1956; Under-Sec., 1962; on loan to Dept of the Environment, 1970–72; retired as Under Sec., HM Treasury, 1977. Dir, Agric. Mortgage Corp., 1978–87. Dep. Sec., Central Bd of Finance, Church of England, 1978–83. Trustee, Irish Sailors and Soldiers Land Trust, 1980–; Governor, Whitelands Coll., 1984–89. *Publication:* Money Matters: a guide to the finances of the Church of England, 1987. *Recreation:* mountain walking. *Address:* The Dower House, Forty Hill, Enfield, Middlesex EN2 9EJ. *T:* 081–363 2365. *Club:* United Oxford & Cambridge University.

McKEARNEY, Philip, CMG 1983; HM Diplomatic Service, retired; *b* 15 Nov. 1926; *s* of Philip McKearney, OBE; *m* 1950, Jean Pamela Walker; two *s*. *Educ:* City of London Sch.; Hertford Coll., Oxford. 4/7th Dragoon Guards, 1946–53; joined HM Diplomatic Service, 1953; 3rd Sec., British Embassy, Damascus, 1955–56; 1st Sec., British Legation, Bucharest, 1959–62; British Political Agent, Qatar, 1962–65; Counsellor and Consul-Gen., Baghdad, 1968–70; Counsellor, Belgrade, 1970–74; Inspector, FCO, 1975–77; Consul-General: Zagreb, 1977–80; Boston, Mass, 1980–83; Amb. to Romania, 1983–86; Dir, Foreign Service Prog., Oxford Univ., 1987–88.

McKECHNIE, Sheila Marshall; Director of Shelter, National Campaign for the Homeless, since 1985; *b* Falkirk, 3 May 1948. *Educ:* Falkirk High School; Edinburgh Univ. (MA Politics and History); Warwick Univ. (MA Industrial Relations). Research Asst, Oxford Univ., 1971–72; Asst Gen. Sec., Wall Paper Workers Union Staff Section, 1972–74; WEA Tutor, Manchester, 1974–76; Health and Safety Officer, ASTMS, 1976–85. *Address:* Shelter, 88 Old Street, EC1V 9HU. *T:* 071–253 0202.

McKEE, Major Sir Cecil; see McKee, Major Sir William Cecil.

McKEE, Major Sir (William) Cecil, Kt 1959; ERD; JP; Estate Agent; b 13 April 1905; s of late W. B. McKee and M. G. B. Bulloch; m 1932, Florence Ethel Irene Gill; one d. Educ: Methodist Coll., Belfast; Queen's Univ., Belfast. Alderman, Belfast Corporation, 1934; High Sheriff, Belfast, 1946; Deputy Lord Mayor, 1947, Lord Mayor of Belfast, 1957–59. JP Belfast, 1957. Pres., NI Br., Inst. of Dirs, 1957–59. Served with Royal Artillery in War of 1939–45. KStJ. 1982. Hon. LLD Queen's Univ., Belfast, 1960. Recreation: golf. Address: 250 Malone Road, Belfast. T: Belfast (0232) 666979. Clubs: Ulster Reform (Belfast); Royal County Down Golf.

McKEE, Dr William James Ernest, MA, MD, FFCM; Regional Medical Officer and Advisor, Wessex Regional Health Authority, 1976–89; b 20 Feb. 1929; s of John Sloan McKee, MA, and Mrs Annie Emily McKee (née McKinley); m Josée Tucker; three d. Educ: Queen Elizabeth's, Wakefield; Trinity Coll., Cambridge; Queen's Coll., Oxford. MA, MD, BChir (Cantab); LRCP, MRCS, FFCM. Clinical trng and postgrad. clinical posts at Radcliffe Infirmary, Oxford, 1952–57; med. res., financed by Nuffield Provincial Hosps Trust, 1958–61; successive posts in community medicine with Metrop. Regional Hosp. Bds, 1961–69; Sen. Admin. Med. Officer, Liverpool Regional Hosp. Bd, 1970–74; Regional Med. Officer, Mersey RHA, 1974–76. Chairman: Regional Med. Officers' Gp, 1984–86; Wessex Regl Working Party to review policy for Mental Handicap Services, 1979; UK Head of Delegation, EEC Hosp. Cttee, 1986–89; Member: Council for Postgrad. Med. Educn in England and Wales, 1975–85; Hunter Working Party on Med. Admin, 1972–83; DHSS Adv. Cttee on Med. Manpower Planning, 1982–85; DHSS Jt Planning Adv. Cttee on Med. Manpower, 1985–89; Bd of Faculty of Medicine, Univ. of Southampton, 1976–89. QHP 1987–90. Publications: papers on tonsillectomy and adenoidectomy in learned jls. Recreations: fly-fishing, golf. Address: 22a Bereweeke Avenue, Winchester SO22 6BH. T: Winchester (0962) 861369.

MacKEIGAN, Hon. Ian Malcolm; Supernumerary Justice of Appeal Division of Supreme Court of Nova Scotia (Chief Justice of Nova Scotia and Chief Justice of Appeal Division of Supreme Court of Nova Scotia, 1973–85); b 11 April 1915; s of Rev. Dr J. A. MacKeigan and Mabel (née McAvity); m 1942, Jean Catherine Geddes; two s one d. Educ: Univs of Saskatchewan, Dalhousie and Toronto. BA (Great Distinction) 1934, MA 1935, LLB 1938, Dalhousie; MA Toronto 1939. Member of Nova Scotia and Prince Edward Island Bars; QC (Nova Scotia) 1954. Dep. Enforcement Administrator, Wartime Prices and Trade Bd, Ottawa, 1942–46; Dep. Comr, Combines Investigation Commn, Ottawa, 1946–50; Partner, MacKeigan, Cox, Downie & Mitchell and predecessor firms, Halifax, NS, 1950–73; Chm., Atlantic Develt Bd, 1963–69; Dir, Gulf Oil (Canada) Ltd, 1968–73; Dir, John Labatt Ltd, 1971–73. Hon. LLD Dalhousie, 1975. Centennial Medal, 1967; Jubilee Medal, 1977. Publications: articles in Can. Bar Review and Can. Jl Polit. Sci. and Econs. Recreations: fishing, golf. Address: 833 Marlborough Avenue, Halifax, NS B3H 3G7, Canada. T: 902–429–1043. Clubs: Halifax, Saraguay, Ashburn Golf (Halifax).

McKELLEN, Sir Ian (Murray), Kt 1991; CBE 1979; actor and director since 1961; b 25 May 1939; s of late Denis Murray McKellen and Margery (née Sutcliffe). Educ: Wigan Grammar Sch.; Bolton Sch.; St Catharine's Coll., Cambridge (BA; Hon. Fellow, 1982). Pres., Marlowe Soc., 1960–61. Elected to Council of Equity, 1971–72. 1st appearance (stage): Belgrade Theatre, Coventry, in A Man for all Seasons, Sept. 1961. Arts Theatre, Ipswich, 1962–63; Nottingham Playhouse, 1963–64. 1st London appearance: A Scent of Flowers, 1964 (Clarence Derwent Award). National Theatre Co., 1965, Old Vic and Chichester Festival; A Lily in Little India; Man of Destiny/O'Flaherty VC, Mermaid Theatre, EC4; Their Very Own and Golden City, Royal Court, 1966; The Promise, Fortune and Broadway, 1967; White Lies/Black Comedy; Richard II, Prospect Theatre Co., 1968; Recruiting Officer, Chips with Everything, Cambridge Theatre Co., 1968; revived Richard II with Edward II, Edinburgh Festival; British and European Tour; Mermaid and Piccadilly Theatres, 1969–70; Hamlet, British and European Tours and Cambridge Theatre, WC2, 1971. Founder Mem., Actors' Company: Ruling the Roost, 'Tis Pity She's a Whore, Edin. Fest., 1972; Knots, Wood-Demon, Edin. Fest., 1973, and with King Lear, Brooklyn Acad. of Music, Wimbledon Theatre season, 1974; Royal Shakespeare Co.: Dr Faustus, Edin. Fest., 1974; Marquis of Keith, Aldwych, 1974–75; King John, Aldwych, 1975; Too True to Be Good, Aldwych and Globe, 1975; Romeo and Juliet, The Winter's Tale, Macbeth (Plays and Players award, 1976), Stratford, 1976–77; Romeo and Juliet, Macbeth, Pillars of the Community (SWET Award, 1977), Days of the Commune, The Alchemist (SWET Award, 1978), Aldwych and RSC Warehouse, 1977–78; Iago, in Othello, The Other Place, Stratford, 1989, Young Vic, BBC TV (Evening Standard and London Critics' Award); RSC touring company (also artistic dir), 1978: Twelfth Night; Three Sisters; Is There Honey Still for Tea?; Ashes, Young Vic, 1975; solo recitals: Words, Words, Words, Edin. Fest. and Belfast Fest., 1976; repeated with Acting Shakespeare, Edin. and Belfast, 1977; Every Good Boy Deserves Favour, RFH, 1977 and Barbican Centre, 1982; Bent, Royal Court, Criterion, 1979 (SWET Award, 1979), NT, Garrick, 1990; Amadeus, Broadhurst, NY (Drama Desk, NY Drama League, Outer Critics' Circle, and Tony Awards), 1980–81; Acting Shakespeare tour, Israel, Norway, Denmark, Sweden, 1980, Spain, France, Cyprus, Israel, Poland and Romania, 1982, Los Angeles and Ritz, NYC (Drama Desk Award), 1983, revival, San Francisco, Washington DC, Los Angeles, Olney, Cleveland, San Diego, Boston (Elliot Norton Award), 1987, Playhouse, London, 1987–88; Short List, Hampstead, 1983; Cowardice, Ambassadors, 1983; Venice Preserv'd, Wild Honey (Laurence Olivier Award; Plays and Players Award; Los Angeles and NY, 1986–87), Coriolanus (London Standard Award), National, 1984–85; Henceforward, Vaudeville, 1988; as Associate Dir of NT, 1985–86, produced and acted in: The Duchess of Malfi, The Real Inspector Hound, The Critic, The Cherry Orchard (Paris and Chicago); Kent, in King Lear, and title rôle, Richard III, NT, 1990, world tour, 1990–91; Napoli Milionaria, 1991. Directed: Liverpool Playhouse, 1969; Watford and Leicester, 1972; A Private Matter, Vaudeville, 1973; The Clandestine Marriage, Savoy 1975; Associate Producer: King Lear (Kent); Richard III (UK, European and FE tour). Films, 1968–: A Touch of Love, The Promise, Alfred the Great, Priest of Love, Scarlet Pimpernel, Plenty, Zina, Scandal. Has appeared on television, 1966–, incl. Walter, 1982 (RTS Performance Award for 1982), Walter and June, 1983. Cameron Mackintosh Prof. of Contemporary Drama, Univ. of Oxford, 1991. Hon. DLitt Nottingham, 1989. Address: c/o James Sharkey, 15 Golden Square, W1R 3AG. T: 071–434 3801/6.

McKELVEY, Air Cdre John Wesley, CB 1969; MBE 1944; CEng, MRAeS; RAF, retired; b 25 June 1914; s of late Captain John Wesley McKelvey, Enfield, Mddx; m 1938, Eileen Amy Carter, d of John Charles Carter, Enfield; two s. Educ: George Spicer Sch., Enfield. RAF Aircraft Apprentice, 1929; commnd 1941 (Eng Branch); served 1939–45, Egypt, Syria, Iraq and Bomber Comd (despatches, 1943); Group Captain 1960; Dep. Dir Intelligence (Tech.), 1962–64; Dir of Aircraft and Asst Attaché, Defence Research and Development, British Embassy, Washington, 1964–66; Air Officer Wales and CO, RAF St Athan, 1966–69; retd Aug. 1969. RAF Benevolent Fund: Sec. (Appeals), 1971–77; Legacies and Trusts Officer, 1977–79. Recreations: bowls, gardening, photography. Address: 19 Greensome Drive, Ferndown, Dorset BH22 8BE. T: Ferndown (0202) 894464. Club: Royal Air Force.

McKELVEY, William; MP (Lab) Kilmarnock and Loudoun, since 1983 (Kilmarnock, 1979–83); b Dundee, July 1934; m; two s. Educ: Morgan Acad.; Dundee Coll. of Technology. Joined Labour Party, 1961; formerly Sec. Organiser, Lab. Party, and full-time union official. Mem., Dundee City Council. Address: House of Commons, SW1; 41 Main Street, Kilmaurs, Ayrshire.

McKELVIE, Peter, FRCS, FRCSE; Consultant Ear, Nose and Throat Surgeon: London Hospital, since 1971; Royal National Throat, Nose and Ear Hospital, London, since 1972; b 21 Dec. 1932; s of William Bryce McKelvie, MD, ChM, FRCSE, DLO, and Agnes E. McKelvie (née Winstanley), Headmistress; m Myra Chadwick, FRCP, Cons. Dermatologist; one d. Educ: Manchester Grammar Sch.; Rugby Sch.; Univ. of Manchester (MB ChB, MD, ChM). FRCS 1962, FRCSE 1989. House Surgeon: Manchester Royal Inf., 1957; Royal Nat. Throat, Nose and Ear Hosp., London, 1958; Lectr in Anatomy, KCL, 1959; Casualty Surg., St Mary's Hosp., London, 1960; Reader in Laryngology, UCL, 1968–70; Dean, Inst. of Laryngology and Otology, London, 1984–89. Examiner: London Univ.; Royal Colls of Surgeons of England, Edinburgh and Glasgow. MRSM, 1966. Publications: numerous, on head and neck cancer. Recreations: mirth, watching young surgeons develop, Mediterranean Basin. Address: Elmcroft, 9 Farm Way, Northwood, Mddx HA6 3EG. T: Northwood (09274) 23544.

McKENNA, David, CBE 1967 (OBE 1946; MBE 1943); FCIT; Member, British Railways Board, 1968–76 (part-time Member, 1976–78); b 16 Feb. 1911; s of late Rt Hon. Reginald McKenna and Pamela Margaret McKenna (née Jekyll); m 1934, Lady Cecilia Elizabeth Keppel, d of 9th Earl of Albemarle, MC; three d. Educ: Eton; Trinity Coll., Cambridge. London Passenger Transport Board, 1934–39, and 1946–55; Asst General Manager, Southern Region of BR, 1955–61; Chief Commercial Officer, HQ, BR, 1962; General Manager, Southern Region of BR, and Chairman Southern Railway Board, 1963–68; Chairman, British Transport Advertising, 1968–81. Mem., Dover Harbour Bd, 1969–80. Dir, Isles of Scilly Steamship Co. War Service with Transportation Service of Royal Engineers, 1939–45; Iraq, Turkey, India and Burma; Lieut-Colonel. Pres., Chartered Inst. of Transport, 1972. Chairman of Governors, Sadler's Wells, 1962–76. Vice-Pres., Royal College of Music; Chairman of Bach Choir, 1964–76. FRCM. Commandeur de l'Ordre National du Mérite, 1974. Publications: various papers on transport subjects. Recreations: music, sailing. Address: Rosteague, Portscatho, Truro, Cornwall TR2 5EF. Clubs: Brooks's; Royal Cornwall Yacht (Falmouth).

McKENNA, Hon. Francis Joseph, (Frank); PC (Can.) 1987; MLA (Liberal Party), Chatham, New Brunswick, since 1982; Premier of New Brunswick, since 1987; b 19 Jan. 1948; s of Durward and Olive McKenna; m Julie Friel; two s one d. Educ: Apohaqui Elementary Sch.; Sussex High Sch.; St Francis Xavier Univ. (BA); Queen's Univ.; Univ. of New Brunswick (LLB). Lawyer; Mem., NB and Canadian Bar Assocs; Founder and 1st Pres., Chatham Downtown Merchants' Assoc.; former Pres., Chatham Chamber of Commerce. Leader, NB Liberal Party, 1985–; Pres., Privy Council of Canada (Mem., Org. and Policy Cttees). Former Member: Standing Cttee, Law Amendments and Public Accounts; Select Cttee of Science and Technology. Hon. DSP Moncton, 1988; Hon. LLD New Brunswick, 1988. Vanier Award, 1988. Address: Office of the Premier, Fredericton, New Brunswick E3B 5H1, Canada.

MacKENNA, Robert Ogilvie, MA, ALA; University Librarian and Keeper of the Hunterian Books and MSS, Glasgow, 1951–78; b 21 March 1913; s of late Dr John G. MacKenna and Katherine Ogilvie; m 1942, Ray, o d of late Samuel Mullin, Glasgow. Educ: Paisley Grammar Sch.; Glasgow Univ. Assistant Librarian, Glasgow Univ., 1936; Sub-Librarian, Leeds Univ., 1946; Librarian, King's Coll., Newcastle upon Tyne (University of Durham), 1948–51. Served War as officer, RNVR, 1939–45. Trustee, National Library of Scotland, 1953–79. President, Scottish Library Association, 1966; Chairman, Standing Conference of National and University Libraries, 1967–69. President Scottish Cricket Union, 1968. Editor, The Philosophical Journal, 1976–77. Publication: Glasgow University Athletic Club: the story of the first hundred years, 1981. Recreations: watching and talking cricket, hill-walking. Address: 40 Kelvin Court, Glasgow G12 0AE. Club: College (Glasgow).

MACKENZIE, family name of **Earl of Cromartie**.

MACKENZIE of Gairloch; see under Inglis of Glencorse.

McKENZIE, Sir Alexander, KBE 1962; Past Dominion President, New Zealand National Party (1951–62); b Invercargill, New Zealand, 1896; m 1935, Constance Mary Howard; two s two d. Educ: Isla Bank Primary Sch.; Southland Technical Coll.; Southland Boys' High Sch. Chm. Ponsonby Electorate, NZ Nat. Party, 1938–41; Chm., Auckland Div., NZ Nat. Party, 1941–51. Overseas Rep. for NZ Forest Products Ltd, 1925–29; engaged in Stock and Share Broking, 1929–; Mem. Auckland Stock Exchange; Dir of companies covering finance, merchandising, manufacturing, etc. Mem. Anglican Church. Recreations: trout fishing, surfing, bowling, gardening. Address: 1/46 King Edward Parade, Devonport, Auckland, New Zealand. Club: Auckland (Auckland, NZ).

MACKENZIE, Sir Alexander Alwyne H. C. B. M.; see Muir Mackenzie.

MACKENZIE, Sir (Alexander George Anthony) Allan, 4th Bt, of Glen-Muick, cr 1890; CD 1957; retired; b 4 Jan. 1913; s of late Capt. Allan Keith Mackenzie (3rd s of 2nd Bt) and Hon. Louvima, o d of 1st Viscount Knollys (she m 2nd, 1922, Richard Henry Spencer Checkley); S uncle, 1944; m 1937, Marjorie McGuire, Vancouver, BC; four d. Educ: Stowe School. Page of Honour to King George V; Member Royal Canadian Mounted Police, 1932–37; served War of 1939–45, with Seaforth Highlanders of Canada (Captain), in Italy and in NW Europe. Subsequently Black Watch (RHR) of Canada (Regular Army). Canada Centennial Medal, 1967.

MACKENZIE, Sir Allan; see Mackenzie, Sir (Alexander George Anthony) Allan.

MACKENZIE, Archibald Robert Kerr, CBE 1967; HM Diplomatic Service, retired; b 22 Oct. 1915; s of James and Alexandrina Mackenzie; m 1963, Virginia Ruth Hutchison. Educ: Glasgow, Oxford, Chicago and Harvard Universities. Diplomatic Service, with duty at Washington, 1943–45; United Nations, 1946–49; Foreign Office, 1949–51; Bangkok, 1951–54; Cyprus, 1954; Foreign Office, 1955–57; OEEC, Paris, 1957–61; Commercial Counsellor, HM Embassy, Rangoon, 1961–65; Consul-General, Zagreb 1965–69; Ambassador, Tunisia, 1970–73; Minister (Econ. and Social Affairs), UK Mission to UN, 1973–75. Brandt Commission, 1978–80. Recreation: golf. Address: Strathcashel Cottage, Rowardennan, near Glasgow G63 0AW. T: Balmaha 262. Clubs: Commonwealth Trust; Royal Scottish Automobile (Glasgow).

MACKENZIE, Major Colin Dalzell, MBE 1945; MC 1940; Vice Lord-Lieutenant of Inverness, since 1986; b 23 March 1919; s of Lt-Col Douglas William Alexander Dalziel Mackenzie, CVO, DSO, DL; m 1947, Lady Anne FitzRoy, d of 10th Duke of Grafton; one s three d (and one s decd). Educ: Eton; RMC Sandhurst. Page of Honour to King George V, 1932–36; joined Seaforth Highlanders, 1939; ADC to Viceroy of India, 1945–46, Dep. Mil. Sec. to Viceroy, 1946–47; retired Seaforth Highlanders, 1949. Mem.,

Queen's Body Guard for Scotland, Royal Company of Archers, 1959–. Mem., Inverness-shire County Council, 1949–51. *Recreation:* fishing. *Address:* Farr House, Inverness IV1 2XB. *T:* Farr (08083) 202. *Clubs:* Turf, Pratt's; New (Edinburgh).

MACKENZIE, Colin Scott; Procurator Fiscal, Stornoway, since 1969; Vice Lord-Lieutenant, Western Isles, since 1984; *b* 7 July 1938; *s* of late Major Colin Scott Mackenzie, BL and of Mrs Margaret S. Mackenzie, MA; *m* 1966, Christeen Elizabeth Drysdale McLauchlan. *Educ:* Nicolson Inst., Stornoway; Fettes Coll., Edinburgh; Edinburgh Univ. (BL 1959). Admitted Solicitor and Notary Public, 1960. Clerk to the Lieutenancy, Stornoway, 1975. Dir, Harris Tweed Assoc. Ltd, 1979–; Trustee, Western Isles Kidney Machine Trust, 1977–. Council Mem for Western Isles, Orkney, Shetland etc, Law Soc. of Scotland, 1985–91. Presbytery of Lewis, Comr to Gen. Assembly, 1991. DL Islands Area of Western Isles, 1975. *Publication:* contrib. Stair Memorial Encyclopaedia of Laws of Scotland, 1987. *Recreations:* amateur radio, boating, fishing, local history, shooting, trying to grow trees. *Address:* Park House, 8 Matheson Road, Stornoway, Western Isles. *T:* Stornoway (0851) 702008. *Clubs:* New (Edinburgh); Royal Scottish Automobile (Glasgow).

McKENZIE, Dan Peter, PhD; FRS 1976; Professor of Earth Sciences, Department of Earth Sciences, Cambridge University, since 1984; Fellow of King's College, Cambridge, 1965–73 and since 1977; *b* 21 Feb. 1942; *s* of William Stewart McKenzie and Nancy Mary McKenzie; *m* 1971, Indira Margaret Misra; one *s*. *Educ:* Westminster Sch.; King's Coll., Cambridge (BA 1963, PhD 1966). Cambridge University: Sen. Asst in Res., 1969–75; Asst Dir of Res., 1975–79; Reader in Tectonics, 1979–84. Hon. MA Cambridge, 1966. (Jtly) Geology and Geophysics Prize, Internat. Balzan Foundn of Italy and Switzerland, 1981; (jtly) Japan Prize, Science and Technology Foundn of Japan, 1990. *Publications:* papers in learned jls. *Recreation:* gardening. *Address:* Bullard Laboratories, Madingley Road, Cambridge CB3 0EZ. *T:* Cambridge (0223) 337177.

MACKENZIE, David James Masterton, CMG 1957; OBE 1947 (MBE 1944); FRCP; Hon. Research Associate, Department of Medical Microbiology, Medical School, University of Cape Town, 1970–84; Visiting Scientist, Malaria Eradication Program, Communicable Disease Center, Atlanta, Georgia, 1965–69; Director of Medical and Health Services in Hong Kong, 1958–64; Colonial Medical Service, retired; *b* 23 July 1905; *s* of John Henderson Mackenzie and Agnes Masterton; *m* 1934, Patricia Eleanor Margaret Bailey; two *d*. *Educ:* Rutherford College School; Edinburgh Univ. MB, ChB, Edinburgh, 1929; DPH (Edinburgh), 1948; MRCPE 1956, FRCPE 1959. Edinburgh Royal Infirmary, 1930–31. Joined Colonial Medical Service, 1934; DDMS, 1944–46, DMS, 1946–49, Bechuanaland Protectorate; DMS Nyasaland, 1949–55; DMS Northern Nigeria, 1955–57. *Recreations:* golf, fishing. *Address:* 8 Avondrust Avenue, Bergvliet, 7945, S Africa. *T:* 72–4541. *Clubs:* Royal Hong Kong Golf; Zomba Gymkhana (Malaŵi).

MACKENZIE, Rear-Adm. David John, CB 1983; FNI; Royal Navy, retired 1983; Director, Atlantic Salmon Trust, since 1985; *b* 3 Oct. 1929; *s* of late David Mackenzie and of Alison Walker Lawrie; *m* 1965, Ursula Sybil Balfour; two *s* one *d*. *Educ:* Cargilfield Sch., Barnton, Edinburgh; Royal Naval Coll., Eaton Hall, Cheshire. Cadet to Comdr, 1943–72: served in East Indies, Germany, Far East, Home and Mediterranean Fleets, and commanded: HMML 6011, HM Ships: Brinkley, Barrington, Hardy, Lincoln, Hermione; Captain 1972; Senior Officers War Course, 1972; commanded HMS Phoenix (NBCD School), 1972–74; Captain F8 in HMS Ajax, 1974–76; Director of Naval Equipment, 1976–78; Captain: HMS Blake, 1979; HMS Hermes, 1980; Rear Admiral 1981; Flag Officer and Port Admiral, Gibraltar, Comdr Gibraltar Mediterranean, 1981–83. Younger Brother of Trinity House, 1971–. Member, Queen's Body Guard for Scotland (Royal Company of Archers), 1976–. Vice Pres., Nautical Inst., 1985–. *Recreations:* shooting and fishing. *Address:* c/o Atlantic Salmon Trust, Moulin, Pitlochry, Perthshire PH16 5JQ. *Club:* New (Edinburgh).

McKENZIE, Prof. Donald Francis, FBA 1986; Professor of Bibliography and Textual Criticism, since 1989, and Professorial Fellow, Pembroke College, since 1986, University of Oxford; *b* 5 June 1931. *Educ:* Victoria UC, Wellington, NZ (BA 1954; DipJourn 1955; MA 1957); Corpus Christi Coll., Cambridge (PhD 1961); MA, DPhil Oxford, 1986. Public servant, NZ PO, 1949–56; various teaching positions, Victoria UC and Victoria Univ. of Wellington, 1956–69; Prof. of Eng. Lang. and Lit., Victoria Univ. of Wellington, 1969–87, now Emeritus; Reader in Textual Criticism, Oxford Univ., 1986–89. Fellow, Corpus Christi Coll., Cambridge, 1960–66; Sandars Reader in Bibliography, Cambridge, 1975–76; Lyell Reader in Bibliography, Oxford Univ., 1987–88. Panizzi Lectr, British Liby, 1985. Founder-manager, Wai-te-ata Press, 1961–86. Pres., Bibliographical Soc., 1982–83 (Gold Medal, 1990); Hon. Member: Bibliographical Soc. of America, 1986; Cambridge Bibliographical Soc., 1988. Corresp. FBA 1980; Hon. Fellow, Australian Acad. of Humanities, 1988. Mark Fitch Gold Medal for Bibliography, 1988. *Publications:* (ed) Stationers' Company Apprentices 1605–1800, 3 vols, 1961–78; The Cambridge University Press 1696–1712: a bibliographical study, 1966; (ed with J. C. Ross) A Ledger of Charles Ackers, 1968; (ed) Robert Tailor, The Hogge hath lost his Pearl, 1972; Oral Culture, Literacy and Print in early New Zealand, 1985; Bibliography and the Sociology of Texts, 1986; contribs to bibliographical jls. *Address:* Pembroke College, Oxford OX1 1DW. *T:* Oxford (0865) 276406.

MacKENZIE, Gillian Rachel, (Mrs N. I. MacKenzie); *see* Ford, G. R.

MacKENZIE, Rt. Hon. Gregor; *see* MacKenzie, Rt Hon. J. G.

MacKENZIE, Hector Uisdean; General Secretary, Confederation of Health Service Employees, since 1987; *b* 25 Feb. 1940; *s* of George MacKenzie and Williamina Budge Sutherland; *m* 1961, Anna Morrison (marr. diss.); one *s* three *d*. *Educ:* Nicholson Inst., Stornaway, Isle of Lewis; Portree High Sch., Skye; Leverndale School of Nursing, Glasgow; West Cumberland School of Nursing, Whitehaven. RGN, RMN. Student Nurse, Leverndale Hosp., 1958–61; Asst Lighthouse Keeper, Clyde Lighthouses Trust, 1961–64; Student Nurse, 1964–66, Staff Nurse 1966–69, West Cumberland Hosp.; Confederation of Health Service Employees: Asst Regl Sec., 1969; Regl Sec., Yorks and E Midlands, 1970–74; Nat. Officer, 1974–83; Asst Gen. Sec., 1983–87. *Recreations:* work, reading, aviation. *Address:* Glen House, High Street, Banstead, Surrey SM7 2LH. *T:* Burgh Heath (0737) 353322.

MACKENZIE, Vice-Adm. Sir Hugh Stirling, KCB 1966 (CB 1963); DSO 1942 and Bar 1943; DSC 1945; *b* 3 July 1913; 3rd *s* of Dr and Mrs T. C. Mackenzie, Inverness; *m* 1946, Helen Maureen, *er d* of Major J. E. M. Bradish-Ellames; one *s* two *d*. *Educ:* Cargilfield Sch.; Royal Naval Coll., Dartmouth. Joined Royal Naval Coll., 1927; qualified in Submarines, 1935. Served throughout War of 1939–45 in Submarines, comdg HMS Thrasher, 1941–43; HMS Tantalus, 1943–45; Comdr 1946; Capt. 1951; Rear-Adm. 1961; Flag Officer, Submarines, 1961–63; Chief Polaris Executive, 1963–68; Vice-Adm. 1964; retired 1968. Chm., Navy League, 1969–74; Dir, Atlantic Salmon Research Trust Ltd, 1969–79 (renamed Atlantic Salmon Trust, 1979), Chm., 1979–83, Vice Pres., 1984–. Hon. Freeman, Borough of Shoreditch, 1942. CBIM. *Recreation:* the country. *Address:* Sylvan Lodge, Puttenham, near Guildford, Surrey GU3 1BB. *Club:* Naval and Military.

MACKENZIE, Ian Clayton, CBE 1962; HM Diplomatic Service, retired; Ambassador to Korea, 1967–69; *b* 13 Jan. 1909; *m* 1948, Anne Helena Tylor; one *s* one *d*. *Educ:* Bedford Sch.; King's Coll., Cambridge. China Consular Service, 1932–41; Consul, Brazzaville, 1942–45, Foreign Office, 1945; 1st Sec., Commercial, Shanghai, 1946–49; Santiago, 1949–53; Commercial Counsellor: Oslo, 1953–58; Caracas, 1958–63; Stockholm, 1963–66. *Address:* Koryo, Armstrong Road, Brockenhurst, Hants SO42 7TA. *T:* Lymington (0590) 23453.

MACKENZIE, James, BSc; CEng, FIM, FICeram; Director, Lloyds Register Quality Assurance Ltd; *b* 2 Nov. 1924; *s* of James Mackenzie and Isobel Mary Chalmers; *m* 1950, Elizabeth Mary Ruttle; one *s* one *d*. *Educ:* Queen's Park Sch., Glasgow; Royal Technical Coll., Glasgow (BSc). The United Steel Companies Ltd, Research and Develt Dept, 1944–67; British Steel Corporation, 1967–85, a Man. Dir, 1976–85; former Dir, Geo. Cohen Sons & Co. Ltd. President: Inst. of Ceramics, 1965–67; Metals Soc., 1983–85. *Address:* Westhaven, Beech Waye, Gerrards Cross, Bucks SL9 8BL. *T:* Gerrards Cross (0753) 886461.

MacKENZIE, James Alexander Mackintosh, CB 1988; FEng 1982; Chief Road Engineer, Scottish Development Department, 1976–88, retired; *b* Inverness, 6 May 1928; *m* 1970, Pamela Dorothy Nixon; one *s* one *d*. *Educ:* Inverness Royal Acad. FICE, FIHT. Miscellaneous local govt appts, 1950–63; Chief Resident Engr, Durham County Council, 1963–67; Dep. Dir, 1967–71, Dir, 1971–76, North Eastern Road Construction Unit, MoT, later DoE. *Recreations:* golf, fishing. *Address:* Pendor, 2 Dean Park, Longniddry, East Lothian EH32 0QR. *T:* Longniddry (0875) 52643.

MacKENZIE, Rt. Hon. (James) Gregor, PC 1977; *b* 15 Nov. 1927; *o s* of late James and Mary MacKenzie; *m* 1958, Joan Swan Provan; one *s* one *d*. *Educ:* Queen's Park Sch.; Glasgow Univ. (School of Social Studies). Joined Labour Party, 1944. Contested (Lab): East Aberdeenshire, 1950; Kinross and West Perthshire, 1959. Chm., Scottish Labour League of Youth, 1948; Mem. and Magistrate, Glasgow Corporation, 1952–55, 1956–64. MP (Lab): Rutherglen, May 1964–1983; Glasgow, Rutherglen, 1983–87. PPS to Rt Hon. James Callaghan, MP, 1965–70; Opposition spokesman on Posts and Telecommunications, 1970–74; Parly Under-Sec. of State for Industry, 1974–75, Minister of State for Industry, 1975–76; Minister of State, Scottish Office, 1976–79. JP Glasgow, 1962. *Address:* 30/1 Haggswood Avenue, Pollokshields, Glasgow G41 4RH. *T:* 041–427 0485. *Club:* Caledonian.

MacKENZIE, James Sargent Porteous, OBE 1963; *b* 18 June 1916; *s* of late Roderick and Daisy W. MacKenzie; *m* 1944, Flora Paterson; three *s*. *Educ:* Portree High Sch.; Edinburgh Univ. (MA Hons 1939); Glasgow Univ. (Dip. Social Studies 1947). War Service, 1939–45: Captain RA (Combined Ops, Burma and Normandy). Scottish HQ, Min. of Labour, 1947–56; Labour Advr, UK High Commn, New Delhi, 1956–62 (First Sec., 1956, Counsellor, 1959); Ministry of Labour: Asst Controller, Scottish HQ, 1962–65; Dep. Controller, Yorks and Humberside Regional Office, 1965–67; Principal Dep. Controller, Scottish HQ, Dept of Employment, 1967–72; Asst Sec., 1970; Counsellor (Labour) British Embassy, Bonn, 1972–77, retired 1977. Exec. Mem., Church of Scotland Cttee on Church and Nation, 1977–83. *Address:* 11 Baberton Park, Juniper Green, Edinburgh EH14 5DW.

MACKENZIE, Lt-Gen. Jeremy John George, OBE 1982; Commander 1st (British) Corps, since 1991; *b* 11 Feb. 1941; *s* of late Lt-Col John William Elliot Mackenzie, DSO, QPM and of Valerie (*née* Dawes); *m* 1969, Elizabeth Lyon (*née* Wertenbaker); one *s* one *d*. *Educ:* Duke of York Sch., Nairobi, Kenya. psc, HCSC. Commnd Queen's Own Highlanders, 1961; Canadian Forces Staff Coll., 1974; Bde Major, 24 Airportable Bde, 1975–76; CO 1 Queen's Own Highlanders, NI and Hong Kong, 1979–82; Instructor, Staff Coll., 1982–83; Col Army Staff Duties 2, 1983–84; Comdr 12th Armoured Bde, 1984–86; Service Fellowship, King's Coll., Univ. of London, 1987; Dep. Comdt, 1987–89, Comdt, 1989, Staff Coll; GOC 4th Armoured Div., BAOR, 1989–91. Col Comdt, WRAC, 1990–. Mem., Queen's Body Guard for Scotland, Royal Company of Archers, 1986–. *Publication:* The British Army and the Operational Level of War, 1989. *Recreations:* shooting, fishing, painting. *Address:* c/o Lloyds Bank, Cox & King's, F Section, 7 Pall Mall, SW1. *Clubs:* Commonwealth Trust, Royal Victoria League.

MACKENZIE, Brig. John Alexander, CBE 1955; DSO 1944 and Bar, 1944; MC 1940 and Bar, 1940; retired; *b* 9 March 1915; *s* of late Louis Robert Wilson Mackenzie; *m* 1952, Beryl Cathreen Culver; one *s*. *Educ:* Nautical Coll., Pangbourne; RMC, Sandhurst. 2nd Bn Gloucestershire Regt, 1935–43; Bn Comd, 2nd Bn Lancs Fusiliers, Tunisia, Sicily and Italy Campaigns, 1943–44 (despatches, 1944); Bde Comd: 11 Inf. Bde, Italy, 1944; 10 Inf. Bde, Greece, 1945–46; psc 1947; GSO1 HQ British Troops, Berlin, 1948–49; AAG (Organisation), HQ, BAOR, 1950; jssc 1951; GSO1 HQ Western Comd, 1951–54; Comd: Britcom Sub-area N, S Korea, 1955; Inf. Trng Team, HQ Jordan Arab Army, 1956; Jt Concealment Centre, 1957–58; Small Arms Sch., Hythe, 1958–59; idc 1960; Comd: 1 Bde, Nigeria, 1961–63; 3 Bde, Congo, 1962; Actg GOC, Royal Nigerian Army, 1963; BGS Army Trng, MoD, 1964–67; ADC to the Queen, 1967–70; Comdt and Inspector of Intelligence, 1967–70; retired 1970. *Recreation:* gardening. *Address:* Slaybrook Hall, Sandling Road, Saltwood, Hythe, Kent CT21 4HG.

McKENZIE, John Cormack, FEng 1984; FICE; Hon. Secretary, Overseas Affairs, Fellowship of Engineering; Vice-Chairman, Thomas Telford Ltd, 1982–90; Director, H. R. Wallingford plc; *b* 21 June 1927; *s* of William Joseph McKenzie and Elizabeth Frances Robinson; *m* 1954, Olga Caroline Cleland; three *s* one *d*. *Educ:* St Andrews Coll.; Trinity Coll., Dublin (MA, MAI); Queen's Univ., Belfast (MSc). FIPM, FIEI, FIE(Aust). McLaughlin & Harvey, and Sir Alexander Gibb & Partners, 1946–48; Asst Lectr, QUB, 1948–50; Edmund Nuttall Ltd, 1950–82, Dir, 1967–82; Chm., Nuttall Geotechnical Services Ltd, 1967–82; Dir, British Wastewater Ltd, 1978–82. Sec., ICE, 1982–90. Secretary General: Commonwealth Engineers' Council, 1983–; World Fedn of Engrg Orgs, 1987–. Mem., SEPSU Res. Cttee. Pres., Beaconsfield Adv. Centre, 1978–. *Publications:* papers: Research into some Aspects of Soil Cement, 1952; Engineers: Administrators or Technologists?, 1971; (contrib.) Civil Engineering Procedure, 3rd edn 1979. *Recreations:* philately, collecting ancient pottery, climbing. *Address:* Fellowship of Engineering, 2 Little Smith Street, SW1P 3DL. *T:* 071–222 2688, *Fax:* 071–233 0054. *Club:* Athenæum.

McKENZIE, Prof. John Crawford; Rector, The London Institute, since 1986; *b* 12 Nov. 1937; *s* of Donald Walter McKenzie and Emily Beatrice McKenzie; *m* 1960, Ann McKenzie (*née* Roberts); two *s*. *Educ:* London School of Economics and Political Science (BScEcon); Bedford Coll., London (MPhil). Lecturer, Queen Elizabeth Coll., Univ. of London, 1961; Dep. Director, Office of Health Econs, 1966; Market Inf. Manager, Allied Breweries Ltd, 1968; various posts, Kimpher Ltd, 1969, finally Chief Exec., Kimpher Marketing Services, 1973; Head of Dept, London Coll. of Printing, 1975; Principal: Ilkley Coll., 1978; Bolton Inst. of Higher Educn, 1982; Rector, Liverpool Poly., 1984. Visiting Professor: Queen Elizabeth Coll., 1976–80; Univ. of Newcastle, 1981–87. Director: Res. for Management Ltd; Food and Drink Res. Ltd; Antiquarian Pastimes Ltd; Developments at The London Inst. Ltd. Member: NAB/UGC Continuing Educn Cttee,

1985–88; NAB Good Management Practice Gp, 1985–87; Council for Industry and Higher Educn, 1985–90. MRSoc.Med. *Publications:* (ed jtly) Changing Food Habits, 1964; (ed jtly) Our Changing Fare, 1966; (ed jtly) The Food Consumer, 1987; many articles in Proc. Nutrition Soc., British Jl Nutrition, Nutrition Bull., etc. *Recreation:* collecting antiquarian books. *Address:* The London Institute, 388–396 Oxford Street, W1R 1FE. *Clubs:* Athenæum, Chelsea Arts.

McKENZIE, Rear-Adm. John Foster, CB 1977; CBE 1974 (OBE 1962); *b* Waiuku, 24 June 1923; *s* of Dr J. C. McKenzie; *m* 1945, Doreen Elizabeth, *d* of Dr E. T. and Dr G. M. McElligott; one *s* one *d*. *Educ:* Timaru Boys' High Sch.; St Andrews Coll., Christchurch, NZ. Served War of 1939–45: Royal Navy; transferred to Royal New Zealand Navy, 1947; Head, Defence Liaison Staff, London, 1966–68; Imperial Defence Coll., 1969; Asst Chief of Defence Staff (Policy), Defence HQ, NZ, 1970–71; Deputy Chief of Naval Staff, 1972; Commodore, Auckland, 1973–75; Chief of Naval Staff, and Mem. Defence Council, 1975–77, retired 1977. ADC 1972–75. *Recreations:* gardening, fishing. *Address:* 64 Lohia Street, Khandallah, Wellington 4, New Zealand.

MACKENZIE of Mornish, John Hugh Munro; Chairman: Tace plc, 1967–91; Scottish, English and European Textiles plc, since 1969; Goring Kerr plc, 1983–91; *b* 29 Aug. 1925; *s* of Lt-Col John Munro Mackenzie of Mornish, DSO, JP, Mil. Kt of Windsor, Henry VIII Gateway, Windsor Castle, and Mrs E. H. M. Mackenzie (*née* Taaffe); *m* 1951, Eileen Louise Agate, *d* of Alexander Shanks, OBE, MC, and Mrs Shanks; four *s* one *d* (and one *s* decd). *Educ:* Edinburgh Acad.; Loretto Sch.; Trinity Coll., Oxford (MA (Hons)); Hague Acad. of Internat. Law; Inns of Court Law Schs; McGill Univ., Montreal. Served Army, 1945–49: Captain, The Royal Scots (Royal Regt); war service, Europe; 1st KOSB, A Company, 9th Brigade, 3rd Inf. Div. (despatches, certs of gallantry) and Far East HQ Allied Land Forces SE Asia and HQ Ceylon Army Comd, Staff Captain, Mil. Sec's Branch; HM Guard of Honour, Balmoral, 1946; HQ 3rd Auto Aircraft Div., 1946–47, GSO III. Harmsworth Law Scholar, Middle Temple, 1950; called to the Bar, Middle Temple, 1950. United Dominions Trust Ltd, trainee, ICI Ltd, Legal Asst, Estates Dept, 1951; Hudson's Bay Scholar, 1952–53; ICI Ltd, Buyer Crop and misc. products, 1953–54; Trubenised (GB) Ltd and Associated Cos, Co. Sec. and Legal Advisor, 1955–56; Aspro-Nicholas Ltd, Gp Develt Officer, 1956–57; PA to Man. Dir, Knitmaster Holdings, 1957; formed: Grampian Holdings Ltd (Manager and Sec.), 1958, Man. Dir, 1960; London and Northern Gp Ltd (Dep. Chm. and Man. Dir), 1962, Chm., 1967–87; Tace plc, 1967 (Chm.); Scottish, English and European Textiles plc, 1969 (Chm.); Chm., Pauling plc, 1976–87. Eight Queen's Awards for Export won by Group Cos. FRSA, FBIM. *Recreations:* opera, bridge, shooting, fishing, all field sports. *Address:* Mortlake House, Vicarage Road, SW14 8RU; Scaliscro Lodge, Isle of Lewis, Outer Hebrides; Shellwood Manor, Leigh, Surrey RH2 8NX. *Clubs:* Royal Automobile; Royal Scots, New (Edinburgh).

McKENZIE, Julia Kathleen, (Mrs Jerry Harte); actress and singer; *b* 17 Feb. 1941; *d* of Albion McKenzie and Kathleen Rowe; *m* 1972, Jerry Harte. *Educ:* Guildhall School of Music and Drama. Hon. FGSM, 1988. *Stage:* Maggie May, 1965; Mame, 1969; Promises, Promises, 1970; Company, 1972; Cowardy Custard, 1973; Cole, 1974; Side by Side by Sondheim, 1977 (London and Broadway); Norman Conquests, 1978; Ten Times Table, 1979; On the 20th Century, 1981; Guys and Dolls, NT, 1982; Schweyk in 2nd World War, NT, 1982; Woman in Mind, Vaudeville, 1986; Follies, Shaftesbury, 1987; Into the Woods, Phoenix, 1990. directed: Stepping Out, London, 1984; Steel Magnolias, Lyric, 1989; Just So, Watermill, Bagnor, Berks, 1989; *film:* Shirley Valentine, 1989; *television films:* Those Glory Glory Days; Hotel Du Lac; *series:* Fame is the Spur; Blott on the Landscape; Maggie and Her; Fresh Fields; French Fields; Sharing Time; Dear Box No; Absent Friends; Julia and Company (TV special), 1986; numerous TV musicals. *Recreations:* cooking, gardening. *Address:* c/o April Young Ltd, The Clockhouse, 6 St Catherine's Mews, Milner Street, SW3 2PU. *T:* 071–584 1274.

MacKENZIE, Kelvin Calder; Editor of The Sun, since 1981; *b* 22 Oct. 1946; *m* 1969, Jacqueline Mary Holland; two *s* one *d*. *Educ:* Alleyn's Sch., Dulwich. *Address:* The Sun, Virginia Street, E1 9BH. *T:* 071–782 4000.

MACKENZIE, Kenneth Edward, CMG 1970; HM Diplomatic Service, retired; *b* 28 April 1910; *s* of late A. E. Mackenzie, Dundee, and late K. M. Mackenzie (*née* Foley); *m* 1935, Phyllis Edith Fawkes; one *s*. *Educ:* schools in India, Australia and in the UK; University Coll., London. Engineering industry, 1926–29; University Coll., London, 1929–32, BSc (Hons) in civil and mechanical engineering. Inst. of Civil Engineers, 1932–34; Dept of Overseas Trade, 1934–36; HM Embassy, Brussels, 1936–40; interned in Germany, 1940–41; HM Embassy, Tehran, 1942–45. Trade Commissioner: in India, 1945–48; in Malaya, 1949–54; Asst Sec., Bd of Trade, 1954–66; Counsellor (Commercial), HM Embassy, Stockholm, and Chargé d'Affaires *ad interim*, 1966–70; Counsellor (Investment), 1973; Counsellor (Investment), HM Embassy, Copenhagen, 1974–75. *Address:* 11 St James Close, Pangbourne, Berks RG8 7AP. *T:* Pangbourne (0734) 842228.

MacKENZIE, Kenneth John; Under Secretary, Scottish Office Home and Health Department, since 1988; *b* 1 May 1943; *s* of John Donald MacKenzie and Elizabeth Pennant Johnston Sutherland; *m* 1975, Irene Mary Hogarth; one *s* one *d*. *Educ:* Woodchurch Road Primary School, Birkenhead; Birkenhead School; Pembroke College, Oxford (Exbnr; MA Mod. Hist.); Stanford Univ., Calif (AM Hist.). Scottish Home and Health Dept, 1965; Private Sec. to Jt Parly Under Sec. of State, Scottish Office, 1969–70; Scottish Office Regional Develt Div., 1970–73; Scottish Educn Dept, 1973–76; Civil Service Fellow, Glasgow Univ., 1974–75; Principal Private Sec. to Sec. of State for Scotland, 1977–79; Asst Sec., Scottish Economic Planning Dept, 1979–83; Scottish Office Finance Div., 1983–85; Principal Finance Officer, Scottish Office, 1985–88. Hon. Pres., Edinburgh CS Dramatic Soc. *Address:* Scottish Office Home and Health Department, St Andrew's House, Edinburgh EH1 3DE. *Club:* National Liberal.

MacKENZIE, Kenneth William Stewart, CMG 1958; CVO 1975; FRAI; a Director of Studies, Royal Institute of Public Administration (Overseas Unit), 1976–90; *b* 30 July 1915; *s* of late W. S. MacKenzie and E. MacKenzie (*née* Johnson); *m* 1939, Kathleen Joyce Ingram; one *s* one *d*. *Educ:* Whitcliffe Mount Gram. Sch., Cleckheaton; Downing Coll., Cambridge. 1st Cl. Hist. Tripos, Part I, 1935; Class II, Div. I, 1936; 1st Cl. Arch. and Anthrop. Tripos, Section A, 1937, BA 1936, MA 1962. Cadet, Colonial Administrative Service, Basutoland, 1938; Asst Sec., Mauritius, 1944; Administrative Officer, Kenya, 1948; Asst Financial Sec., Kenya, 1950; seconded to HM Treasury, 1951–53; Dep. Sec., 1954 and Permanent Sec., 1955, Treasury, Kenya; Minister for Finance and Development and Financial Sec., Kenya, 1959–62. MLC Kenya, 1955–62; MLA East Africa, 1959–62. Retired, 1963 to facilitate constitutional change. Re-employed as Principal, Colonial Office, 1963; Principal, HM Treasury, 1966–70; Asst Sec., DoE, 1970–75. *Publication:* pamphlet, How Basutoland is Governed, 1944. *Recreations:* reading, gardening. *Address:* Beaumont, 28 Greenhurst Lane, Oxted, Surrey RH8 0LB. *T:* Oxted (0883) 3848. *Clubs:* Royal Over-Seas League; Achilles; Nairobi (Nairobi).

MACKENZIE, Maxwell Weir, OC 1972; CMG 1946; Director: Canadian Imperial Bank of Commerce, 1955–77, now Emeritus; Canron Ltd, 1961–77; International Multifoods Corp., 1964–77; Royal Trust, 1960–67; Imperial Life, 1962–75; *b* 30 June 1907; *s* of late Hugh Blair Mackenzie, Gen. Man., Bank of Montreal, Montreal, and Maude Marion Weir; *m* 1931, Jean Roger Fairbairn; two *s* two *d*. *Educ:* Lakefield Preparatory Sch., Lakefield, Ont.; Trinity Coll. School, Port Hope, Ont.; McGill Univ., Montreal (BCom 1928). Joined McDonald, Currie & Co., Chartered Accountants of Montreal, 1928; Mem. Soc. of Chartered Accountants of the Province of Quebec, 1929; Jr Partner, McDonald, Currie & Co., Montreal, 1935; on loan to Foreign Exchange Control Board, Ottawa, 1939–42; to Wartime Prices and Trade Board, Ottawa, 1942–44 (Dep. Chm. 1943–44); Mem., Royal Commission on Taxation of Annuities and Family Corporation, 1944; Dep. Minister of Trade and Commerce, 1945–51; Dep. Minister of Defence Production, Canada, 1951–52; Pres., Canadian Chemical & Cellulose Company, Ltd, 1954–59 (Exec. Vice-Pres., 1952–54). Mem., Economic Council of Canada, 1963–71. Dir, C. D. Howe Res. Inst., 1973–80. Chairman: Royal Commission on Security, 1966; Federal Inquiry into Beef Marketing, 1975. Hon. LLD McGill, 1973. *Recreation:* ski-ing. *Address:* 1245 Scollard Drive, Peterborough, Ontario K9H 7K8, Canada. *Club:* Rideau (Ottawa).

McKENZIE, Michael; QC 1991; Master of the Crown Office and Queen's Coroner and Attorney, Registrar of Criminal Appeals and of the Courts Martial Appeal Court, since 1988; *b* Hove, Sussex, 25 May 1943; *s* of Robert John McKenzie and Kitty Elizabeth McKenzie; *m* 1964, Peggy Dorothy, *d* of Thomas Edward William Russell and Dorothy Mabel Russell; three *s*. *Educ:* Varndean Grammar Sch., Brighton. Town Clerk's Dept, Brighton, 1961–63; Asst to Clerk of the Peace, Brighton Quarter Sessions, 1963–67; Sen. Clerk of the Court, 1967–70, Dep. Clerk of the Peace, 1970–71, Middlesex Quarter Sessions; Called to the Bar, Middle Temple, 1970; Deputy to Courts Administrator, Middlesex Crown Court, 1972–73; Courts Administrator (Newcastle), NE Circuit, 1974–79; Courts Administrator, Central Criminal Court, and Coordinator for Taxation of Crown Court Costs, S Eastern Circuit, 1979–84; Dep. Circuit Administrator, SE Circuit, 1984–86; Asst Registrar, Ct of Appeal Criminal Div., 1986–88. Freeman, City of London, 1979. FRSA 1990. Hon. Fellow, Kent Sch. of Law, Canterbury Univ. *Recreations:* Northumbrian stick dressing, fell walking. *Address:* Royal Courts of Justice, Strand, WC2A 2LL.

MACKENZIE, Michael Philip; Director-General, Food and Drink Federation, since 1986; *b* 26 June 1937; *s* of Brig. Maurice Mackenzie, DSO, and Mrs Vivienne Mackenzie; *m* 1966, Jill (*née* Beckley); one *s* one *d*. *Educ:* Downside Sch.; Lincoln Coll., Oxford (BA); Harvard Business Sch., USA. United Biscuits plc, 1966–86: Prodn Dir, various businesses within United Biscuits, 1974–83; Man. Dir, D. S. Crawford Bakeries, 1983–86. FRSA. *Recreations:* hill-walking, gardening, music, theatre. *Address:* Ebony Cottage, Reading Street, near Tenterden, Kent TN30 7HT. *Club:* Travellers'.

MACKENZIE, Sir Peter Douglas, 13th Bt *cr* 1673 (NS), of Coul, Ross-shire; *b* 1949; *s* of Henry Douglas Mackenzie (*d* 1965) and Irene Carter Freeman; *S* kinsman, 1990.

MACKENZIE, Sir Roderick McQuhae, 12th Bt *cr* 1703, of Scatwell; FRCP(C); medical practitioner; *b* 17 April 1942; *s* of Captain Sir Roderick Edward François McQuhae Mackenzie, 11th Bt, CBE, DSC, RN and of Marie Evelyn Campbell, *o c* of late William Ernest Parkinson; *S* father, 1986; *m* 1970, Nadezhda, (Nadine), Baroness von Rorbas, *d* of Georges Frederic Schlatter, Baron von Rorbas; one *s* one *d*. *Educ:* Sedbergh; King's College London. MB, BS; MRCP; DCH. *Heir: s* Gregory Roderick McQuhae Mackenzie, *b* 8 May 1971. *Address:* 2431 Udell Road NW, Calgary, Alberta T2N 4H9, Canada.

McKENZIE, Sir Roy (Allan), KBE 1989; Director: Rangatira Ltd, since 1946; James Cook Hotel Ltd, since 1970; *b* 7 Nov. 1922; *s* of John Robert McKenzie and Ann May McKenzie (*née* Wrigley); *m* 1949, Shirley Elizabeth Howard; two *s* one *d*. *Educ:* Timaru Boys' High Sch. ACA 1948. Executive, 1949–70, Exec. Dir, 1955, McKenzie NZ Ltd; Chairman: Rangatira Investment Co. Ltd, 1968–85; J. R. McKenzie Trust, 1970–87. Chairman and Founder: McKenzie Educn Foundation; Roy McKenzie Foundn; Chairman: Outward Bound Trust NZ, 1968; Te Omanga Hospice, 1979–. *Publication:* The Roydon Heritage, 1978. *Recrations:* tennis, ski-ing, tramping, breeding standardbreds (horses). *Address:* 21 Marine Drive, Lowry Bay, Eastbourne, New Zealand. *T:* 684 492.

MACKENZIE, Wallace John, OBE 1974; Director, Slough Estates plc, 1986–91 (Group Managing Director, 1975–86); *b* 2 July 1921; *s* of Wallace D. Mackenzie and Ethel F. Williamson; *m* 1951, Barbara D. Hopson; two *s* one *d*. *Educ:* Harrow Weald County Grammar Sch. Gen. Manager, Slough Estates Canada Ltd, 1952–72; Dep. Man. Dir, Slough Estates Ltd, 1972–75. Dir, Investors in Industry plc, 1982–86; Chm., Trust Parts Ltd, 1986– (Dir, 1985). Member: Commn for New Towns, 1978–; London Residuary Body, 1985–. *Recreations:* golf, bridge. *Address:* Manitou, Spring Coppice, Lane End, High Wycombe, Bucks. *T:* High Wycombe (0494) 881032.

MACKENZIE, Prof. William James Millar, CBE 1963; FBA 1968; Professor of Politics, Glasgow University, 1966–74, now Emeritus; *b* 8 April 1909; *s* of Laurence Millar Mackenzie, WS, Edinburgh; *m* 1943, Pamela Muriel Malyon; one *s* four *d*. *Educ:* Edinburgh Academy; Balliol Coll., Oxford (MA) (Ireland Schol. 1929); Edinburgh Univ. (LLB); Fellow of Magdalen Coll., Oxford, 1933–48, Emeritus Fellow, 1990; Temp. Civil Servant, Air Ministry, 1939–44; Official War Historian, SOE, 1945–48. Faculty Fellow, Nuffield Coll., 1948; Lecturer in Politics, Oxford Univ., 1948; Prof. of Government, Manchester Univ., 1949–66, Glasgow Univ., 1966–74; Special Comr, for Constitutional Development, Tanganyika, 1952; Co-opted Mem., Manchester City Educn Cttee, 1953–64; apptd Mem., British Wool Marketing Board, 1954–66; Mem. Royal Commn on Local Govt in Greater London, 1957; Constitutional Adviser, Kenya, 1959; Vice-Chm., Bridges Cttee on Training in Public Administration for Overseas Countries, 1962; Member: Maud Cttee on Management in Local Govt, 1964–66; Cttee on Remuneration of Ministers and Members of Parliament, 1963–64; North-West Regional Economic Planning Council, 1965–66; SSRC, 1965–69; Parry Cttee on University Libraries, 1964–67; Chm., Children's Panel Adv. Cttee, Glasgow City, 1973–75. Hon. LLD: Dundee, 1968; Lancaster, 1970; Manchester, 1975; Hon. DLitt Warwick, 1972; Hon. DSc (Econ) Hull, 1981; DUniv Open Univ., 1984. *Publications:* (in part) British Government since 1918, 1950; (jtly) Central Administration in Great Britain, 1957; Free Elections, 1958; (ed with Prof. K. Robinson) Five Elections in Africa, 1959; Politics and Social Science, 1967; (jtly) Social Work in Scotland, 1969; Power, Violence, Decision, 1975; Explorations in Government, 1975; Political Identity, 1977; Biological Ideas in Politics, 1978; Power and Responsibility in Health Care, 1979. *Address:* 12 Kirklee Circus, Glasgow G12 0TW.

MACKENZIE CROOKS, Air Vice-Marshal Lewis, CBE 1963 (OBE 1950); Consultant Adviser in Orthopaedic Surgery, RAF, 1966–70, retired; Locum Consultant in Orthopaedic Surgery, Cornwall, since 1970; *b* 20 Jan. 1909; *s* of David Mackenzie Crooks and Mary (*née* McKechnie); *m* 1936, Mildred, *d* of A. J. Gwyther; two *s* one *d*. *Educ:* Epworth Coll.; Liverpool Univ. MB, ChB 1931; FRCS 1937; ChM (Liverpool) 1945. House Surgeon: Northern Hosp., Liverpool, 1931–32; Shropshire Orthop. Hosp., Oswestry, 1932–33; Sen. House Surgeon: Selly Oak Hosp., Birmingham, 1933–34; All Saints Hosp., London, 1934–35; commnd RAF, 1935; surgical hosp. appts in RAF, 1936–52; overseas service: Palestine, 1937–39; Iraq, 1939–42 (despatches 1941); Egypt,

1950–51. Clinical Tutor, Edinburgh Royal Infirmary, 1947; Cons. in Orthop. Surgery, 1952; Sen. Cons. in Orthop. Surgery, 1955. QHS, 1966–70. *Publication:* article on chondromalaca patellae in Jl of Bone and Joint Surgery. *Recreations:* golf, gardening. *Address:* Trelawney, Harlyn Bay, Padstow, Cornwall PL28 8SF. *T:* Padstow (0841) 520631. *Clubs:* Royal Air Force; Trevose Golf, Country (Constantine Bay, Cornwall).

McKENZIE JOHNSTON, Henry Butler, CB 1981; Vice-Chairman, Commission for Local Administration in England, 1982–84 (Commissioner, 1981–84); *b* 10 July 1921; *er s* of late Colin McKenzie Johnston and late Bernardine (*née* Fawcett Butler); *m* 1949, Marian Allardyce Middleton, *e d* of late Brig. A. A. Middleton and late Winifred (*née* Salvesen); one *s* two *d*. *Educ:* Rugby. Served with Black Watch (RHR), 1940–46; Adjt 6th Bn, 1944–45; Temp. Major 1945. Staff of HM Embassy, Athens, 1946–47; entered Foreign (subseq. Diplomatic) Service, 1947; Paris, 1948–51; British High Commn, Germany, 1951–54; FO, 1954–56; 1st Sec. (Commercial), Montevideo, 1956–60; FO, 1960–63; Counsellor (Information), Mexico City, 1963–66; Dep. High Comr, Port of Spain, 1966–67; seconded to Min. of Overseas Develt, 1968–70; Consul-Gen., Munich, 1971–73; seconded to Office of Parly Comr, 1973–79, transferred permanently, 1979–81; Dep. Parly Comr for Admin, 1974–81. Mem., Broadcasting Complaints Commn, 1986–90. Mem., Social Security Appeal Tribunal, Kensington, subseq. Central London, 1985–88. Chm., British-Mexican Soc., 1977–80. *Address:* 6 Pembroke Gardens, W8 6HS. *Clubs:* Athenæum, Hurlingham.

McKENZIE SMITH, Ian, RSA 1987; PRSW (RSW 1981); FSAScot 1970; FMA 1987; City Arts Officer, City of Aberdeen, since 1989; *b* 3 Aug. 1935; *s* of James McKenzie Smith and Mary Benzie; *m* 1963, Mary Rodger Fotheringham; two *s* one *d*. *Educ:* Robert Gordon's Coll., Aberdeen; Gray's Sch. of Art, Aberdeen; Hospitalfield Coll. of Art, Arbroath. Teacher of art, 1960–63; Educn Officer, Council of Industrial Design, Scottish Cttee, 1963–68; Dir, Aberdeen Art Gall. and Museums, 1968–89. Work in permanent collections: Scottish Nat. Gall. of Modern Art; Scottish Arts Council; Arts Council of NI; Contemp. Art Soc.; Aberdeen Art Gall. and Museums; Glasgow Art Gall. and Museums; Abbot Hall Art Gall., Kendal; Hunterian Mus., Glasgow; Nuffield Foundn; Carnegie Trust; Strathclyde Educn Authority; RSA; DoE. Mem., Scottish Arts Council, 1970–77. Pres., RSW, 1988–; Treas., RSA, 1990– (Dep. Pres., 1990–91). Governor: Edinburgh Coll. of Art, 1976–88; Robert Gordon's Inst. of Technology, 1989–. FSS 1981; FRSA 1973. Hon. LLD Aberdeen, 1991. *Address:* 70 Hamilton Place, Aberdeen AB2 4BA. *T:* Aberdeen (0224) 644531. *Club:* Royal Northern (Aberdeen).

MACKENZIE SMITH, Peter; Director of Projects Division, British Council, since 1989; *b* 12 Jan. 1946; *s* of Antony and Isobel Mackenzie Smith; *m* 1973, Sandra Gay-French; three *d*. *Educ:* Downside; Jesus Coll., Cambridge (BA Classical Tripos). Teacher: British Inst., Oporto, 1967–68; Internat. House, London, 1969; British Council, 1969–: Asst Rep., Lagos, 1969–72; Asst Cultural Attaché, Cairo, 1972–77; Regl Dir, Southampton, 1977–80; Educnl Contracts Dept, 1980–83; Dep. Rep., Cairo, 1983–87; Dir, Educnl Contracts, 1987–89. *Address:* Cleve House, Cherville Street, Romsey, Hants SO51 8FB. *T:* Romsey (0794) 513467.

MACKENZIE STUART, family name of **Baron Mackenzie-Stuart.**

MACKENZIE-STUART, Baron *cr* 1988 (Life Peer), of Dean in the District of the City of Edinburgh; **Alexander John Mackenzie Stuart;** President of the Court of Justice, European Communities at Luxembourg, 1984–88 (Judge of the Court of Justice, 1972–84); a Senator of the College of Justice in Scotland, 1972; *b* 18 Nov. 1924; *s* of late Prof. A. Mackenzie Stuart, KC, and Amy Margaret Dean, Aberdeen; *m* 1952, Anne Burtholme Millar, *d* of late J. S. L. Millar, WS, Edinburgh; four *d*. *Educ:* Fettes Coll., Edinburgh (open Schol.); Sidney Sussex Coll., Cambridge (schol. 1949, 1st cl. Pt II Law Tripos, BA 1949, Hon. Fellow, 1977); Edinburgh Univ. (LLB (dist.) 1951). Royal Engineers (Temp. Capt. 1946), 1942–47. Admitted Faculty of Advocates, 1951; QC (Scot.) 1963; Keeper of the Advocates Library, 1970–72. Standing Junior Counsel: to Scottish Home Dept, 1956–57; to Inland Revenue in Scotland, 1957–63. Sheriff-Principal of Aberdeen, Kincardine and Banff, 1971–72. Governor, Fettes College, 1962–72. Hon. Bencher: Middle Temple, 1978; King's Inn, Dublin, 1984; Hon. Mem., SPTL, 1982. FRSE 1991. Hon. Prof., Collège d'Europe, Bruges, 1974–77. DUniv. Stirling, 1973; Hon. LLD: Exeter, 1978; Edinburgh, 1978; Glasgow, 1981; Aberdeen, 1983; Cambridge, 1987; Birmingham, 1988. Prix Bech for services to Europe, 1989. Grand Croix, Ordre Grand-Ducal de la Couronne de Chene de Luxembourg, 1988. *Publications:* Hamlyn Lectures: The European Communities and the Rule of Law, 1977; articles in legal publications. *Recreation:* collecting. *Address:* 7 Randolph Cliff, Edinburgh EH3 7TZ; Le Garidel, Gravières, 07140 Les Vans, Ardèche, France. *Clubs:* Athenæum; New (Edinburgh); Golf Club du Grand Guérin (Villefort).

McKEOWN, Prof. Patrick Arthur, OBE 1991; MSc; FEng 1986; FIProdE; FIQA; FIMechE; Professor of Precision Engineering since 1974, Director of Cranfield Unit for Precision Engineering since 1969, Cranfield Institute of Technology (Head of Department for Design of Machine Systems, 1975–85); Chairman and Chief Executive, Cranfield Precision Engineering Ltd, since 1987; *b* 16 Aug. 1930; *s* of Robert Matthew McKeown and Augusta (*née* White); *m* 1954, Mary Patricia Heath; three *s*. *Educ:* Cambridge County High Sch. for Boys; Bristol Grammar Sch.; Cranfield Inst. of Technol. (MSc). CEng, MIMechE 1969; FIProdE 1971; FIQA 1973. National Service, RE, 1949–51; Suez Campaign, 1956: Captain RE; port maintenance. Student apprentice, Bristol Aircraft Co. Ltd, Bristol, 1951–54 (HNC National State Scholarship); Cranfield Inst. of Technol., 1954–56; Société Genevoise, Newport Pagnell and Geneva, 1956–68 (Technical and Works Dir, 1965). Chairman: Cranfield Precision Systems Ltd, 1984–87; Cranfield Moulded Structures Ltd, 1984; non-executive Director: Control Techniques plc, 1990; AMTRI, 1990. Vice-Pres., Inst. of Qual. Assurance, 1976; Pres., CIRP (Internat. Instn for Prodn Engrg Research), 1988–89. Member: Evaluation Panel, National Bureau of Standards, Washington, USA; Metrology and Standards Requirements Bd, DTI, 1983–; Advanced Manufg Technol. Cttee, DTI, 1983–87; Vis. Cttee, RCA, 1984–87; ACARD working gp, 1987–88. Clayton Meml Lectr, IMechE, 1986. Charter Fellow, Soc. of Manufacturing Engineers, 1985. Fulbright Award (Vis. Prof. of Mechanical Engrg, Univ. of Wisconsin-Madison), 1982; F. W. Taylor Award, Soc. of Manufacturing Engrs, 1983; Thomas Hawksley Gold Medal, IMechE, 1987; Mensforth Gold Medal, IProdE, 1988. *Publications:* papers in CIRP Annals. *Recreations:* walking, travel, enjoyment of wine, good food, music, theatre. *Address:* 37 Church End, Biddenham, Bedford MK40 4AR. *T:* Bedford (0234) 267678.

MACKEOWN, Thomas Frederick William; Administrator and Secretary, University College Hospital, London, 1946–63; *b* 3 Jan. 1904; *s* of Rev. William Mackeown, Rushbrooke, Co. Cork; *m* 1936, Lorraine, *d* of Major R. Hayes, Sherburn-in-Elmet, Yorks; one *d*. *Educ:* Felsted; Worcester Coll., Oxford (MA). Qualified as Chartered Accountant, 1927. Hospital Administrator: Liverpool Stanley Hospital, 1934–37; Clayton Hospital, Wakefield, 1937–45; Royal Infirmary, Sunderland, 1945–46; Hill Homes, Highgate (actg), 1966; King Edward VII Memorial Hospital, Bermuda, 1967; Vice-Chm., Management Cttee, Harefield and Northwoods Hosps, 1960–74; undertook Hosp. Domestic Staff Survey under aegis of King Edward's Hosp. Fund for London, 1968. Lay FRSocMed, 1974. *Address:* 4 Westhill Court, Millfield Lane, N6. *T:* 081–348 1952.

McKERN, Leo, (Reginald McKern), AO 1983; actor; *b* 16 March 1920; *s* of Norman Walton McKern and Vera (*née* Martin); *m* 1946, Joan Alice Southa (Jane Holland); two *d*. *Educ:* Sydney Techn. High Sch. Engrg apprentice, 1935–37; artist, 1937–40; AIF (Corp., Engrs), 1940–42; actor, 1944; arrived England, 1946; CSEU tour, Germany; Arts Council tours, 1947; Old Vic, 1949–52; Shakespeare Meml Theatre, 1952–54; Old Vic last season, 1962–63; New Nottingham Playhouse, 1963–64; *stage:* Toad of Toad Hall, Princes, 1954; Queen of the Rebels, Haymarket, 1955; Cat on a Hot Tin Roof, Aldwych, 1958; Brouhaha, Aldwych, 1958; Rollo, Strand, 1959; A Man for all Seasons, Globe, 1960; The Thwarting of Baron Bolligrew, RSC, Aldwych, 1965; Volpone, Garrick, 1967; The Wolf, Apollo, 1973; The Housekeeper, Apollo, 1982; Number One, Queen's, 1984; Boswell for the Defence, Australia, later Playhouse, 1989, tour 1991; *films:* The French Lieutenant's Woman, 1983; Ladyhawke, 1984; The Chain, 1985; Travelling North, 1986; *television:* Rumpole of the Bailey (series), 1977–; Reilly—Ace of Spies, 1983; King Lear, 1983; Monsignor Quixote; Murder With Mirrors (film), 1985; The Master Builder, 1988. *Publication:* Just Resting (biographical memoir), 1983. *Recreations:* sailing, swimming, photography, painting, environment preservation. *Address:* c/o Richard Hatton Ltd, 29 Roehampton Gate, SW15 5JR.

MACKERRAS, Sir (Alan) Charles (MacLaurin), Kt 1979; CBE 1974; Hon. RAM 1969; FRCM 1987; Musical Director, Welsh National Opera, 1987–July 1992; Guest Conductor: Vienna State Opera; Paris and Zurich Opera; Royal Opera House Covent Garden; English National Opera; Metropolitan and San Francisco Opera; *b* Schenectady, USA, 17 Nov. 1925; *s* of late Alan Patrick and Catherine Mackerras, Sydney, Australia; *m* 1947, Helena Judith (*née* Wilkins); two *d*. *Educ:* Sydney Grammar Sch. Principal Oboist, Sydney Symphony Orchestra, 1943–46; Staff Conductor, Sadler's Wells Opera, 1949–53; Principal Conductor BBC Concert Orchestra, 1954–56; freelance conductor with most British and many continental orchestras; concert tours in USSR, S Africa, USA, 1957–66; First Conductor, Hamburg State Opera, 1966–69; Musical Dir, Sadler's Wells Opera, later ENO, 1970–77; Chief Guest Conductor, BBC SO, 1976–79; Chief Conductor, Sydney Symphony Orch., ABC, 1982–85; Principal Guest Conductor, Royal Liverpool Philharmonic Orch., 1986–88; frequent radio and TV broadcasts; many commercial recordings, notably Handel series for DGG and Janáček operas for Decca; appearances at many internat. festivals and opera houses. Hon. DMus Hull, 1990. Evening Standard Award for Opera, 1977; Janáček Medal, 1978; Gramophone Record of the Year, 1977, 1980; Gramophone Operatic Record of the Year Award, 1983, 1984; Gramophone Best Choral Record, 1986; Grammy Award for best opera recording, 1981. *Publications:* ballet arrangements of Pineapple Poll and of Lady and the Fool; Arthur Sullivan's lost Cello Concerto, 1986; contrib. 4 appendices to Charles Mackerras: a musicians' musician, by Nancy Phelan 1987; articles in Opera Magazine, Music and Musicians and other musical jls. *Recreations:* languages, yachting. *Address:* 10 Hamilton Terrace, NW8 9UG. *T:* 071–286 4047.

MACKESON, Sir Rupert (Henry), 2nd Bt *cr* 1954; *b* 16 Nov. 1941; *s* of Brig. Sir Harry Ripley Mackeson, 1st Bt, and Alethea, Lady Mackeson (*d* 1979), *d* of late Comdr R. Talbot, RN; *S* father, 1964. *Educ:* Harrow; Trinity Coll., Dublin (MA). Captain, Royal Horse Guards, 1967, retd 1968. *Recreations:* art, racing. *Heir:* none.

MACKESY, Dr Piers Gerald, FRHistS; FBA 1988; Fellow of Pembroke College, Oxford, 1954–87, now Emeritus; *b* 15 Sept. 1924; *s* of Maj.-Gen. Pierse Joseph Mackesy, CB, DSO, MC and Dorothy (*née* Cook), (Leonora Starr); *m* 1st, 1957, Sarah Davies; one *s* two *d*; 2nd, 1978, Patricia Timlin (*née* Gore). *Educ:* Wellington Coll.; Christ Church, Oxford (1st cl. Hons Modern Hist., 1950; DPhil 1953; DLitt 1978). FRHistS 1965. Lieut, The Royal Scots Greys (NW Europe, 1944–47). Robinson Schol., Oriel Coll., Oxford, 1951–53; Harkness Fellow, Harvard Univ., 1953–54; Vis. Fellow, Inst. for Advanced Study, Princeton, 1962–63; Vis. Prof., CIT, 1966; Huntingdon Liby, San Marino, Calif, 1967. Lectures: Lees-Knowles, Cambridge, 1972; American Bicentennial, at Williamsburg, Va, Clark Univ., Naval War Coll., US Mil. Acad., Nat. War Coll., Peabody Mus., N Eastern Univ., Capitol Historical Soc. Member, Council: Inst. for Early Amer. Hist. and Culture, 1970–73; Nat. Army Mus., 1983–; Soc. for Army Historical Res., 1985–. *Publications:* The War in the Mediterranean 1803–10, 1957; The War for America 1775–83, 1964; Statesmen at War: the Strategy of Overthrow 1798–99, 1974; The Coward of Minden: the affair of Lord George Sackville, 1979; War without Victory: the downfall of Pitt 1799–1802, 1984; contribs to various books and jls. *Recreations:* hunting, hill walking. *Address:* Leochel Cushnie House, Alford, Aberdeenshire AB33 8LJ. *T:* Muir of Fowlis (09755) 81379. *Club:* Army and Navy.

MACKEY, Prof. James Patrick; Thomas Chalmers Professor of Theology, since 1979, and Dean, Faculty of Divinity, 1984–88, University of Edinburgh; *b* 9 Feb. 1934; *e s* of Peter Mackey and Esther Mackey (*née* Morrissey); *m* 1973, Hanorah Noelle Quinlan; one *s* one *d*. *Educ:* Mount St Joseph Coll., Roscrea; Nat. Univ. of Ireland (BA); Pontifical Univ., Maynooth (LPh, BD, STL, DD); Queen's Univ. Belfast (PhD); postgraduate study at Univs of Oxford, London, Strasbourg. Lectr in Philosophy, QUB, 1960–66; Lectr in Theology, St John's Coll., Waterford, 1966–69; Associate Prof. and Prof. of Systematic and Philosophical Theol., Univ. of San Francisco, 1969–79. Visiting Professor: Univ. of California, Berkeley, 1974; Dartmouth Coll., NH, 1989; Mem., Centre for Hermeneutical Studies, Berkeley, 1974–79. *Television series:* The Hall of Mirrors, 1984; The Gods of War, 1986; Perspectives, 1986–87; radio programmes. Associate Editor: Herder Correspondence, 1966–69; Concilium (church history section), 1965–70; Horizons, 1973–79. *Publications:* The Modern Theology of Tradition, 1962; Life and Grace, 1966; Tradition and Change in the Church, 1968; Contemporary Philosophy of Religion, 1968; (ed) Morals, Law and Authority, 1969; The Church: its credibility today, 1970; The Problems of Religious Faith, 1972; Jesus: the man and the myth, 1979; The Christian Experience of God as Trinity, 1983; (ed) Religious Imagination, 1986; Modern Theology: a sense of direction, 1987; (with Prof. J. D. G. Dunn) New Testament Theology in Dialogue, 1987; (ed) Introduction to Celtic Christianity, 1989; contribs to theol. and philosoph. jls. *Recreations:* yachting; rediscovery of original Celtic culture of these islands. *Address:* 10 Randolph Crescent, Edinburgh EH3 7TT. *T:* 031–225 9408. *Clubs:* Edinburgh University; St Brendan Cruising (Dungarvan).

MACKEY, Most Rev. John, CBE 1983; Bishop of Auckland, NZ, (RC), 1974–83. *Educ:* Auckland Univ. (MA, DipEd); Notre Dame Univ., USA (PhD). Formerly Professor in Theological Faculty, National Seminary of Mosgiel, Dunedin. *Publications:* The Making of a State Education System, 1967; Reflections on Church History, 1975. *Address:* c/o Bishop's House, 36 New Street, Ponsonby, PO Box 47255, Auckland 1, New Zealand. *T:* 764–244.

MACKEY, William Gawen; Partner, 1952, Managing Partner UK Operations, 1981–86, Ernst & Whinney; retired 1986; *b* 22 Sept. 1924; *s* of William Gawen Mackey and Jane Mackey; *m* 1948, Margaret Reeves Vinycomb; two *s*. *Educ:* Dame Allan's Sch., Newcastle upon Tyne. Qualified Chartered Accountant, 1949. Served RN, 1942–45 (Sub-Lt). Joined

Ernst & Whinney, 1952, Newcastle; transf. London, 1973, with responsibility for corporate restructuring and insolvency services in UK. Receiver: Airfix; British Tanners; Laker; Stone-Platt. Chm., Insolvency Sub Cttee, CCAB, 1978–82; Dir, Inst. Corporate Insolvency Courses, 1974–80. *Publications:* articles and lectures on corporate management, restructuring and insolvency. *Recreations:* opera, gardening, France. *Address:* Eynesse, Ste Foy La Grande 33220, France. *T:* 57 41 00 42; 7 Radnor Mews, W2 2SA. *T:* 071–402 0198.

MACKIE; *see* John-Mackie.

MACKIE, family name of **Barons John-Mackie** and **Mackie of Benshie.**

MACKIE OF BENSHIE, Baron *cr* 1974 (Life Peer), of Kirriemuir; **George Yull Mackie,** CBE 1971; DSO 1944; DFC 1944; Chairman: Caithness Glass Ltd, 1966–85; Caithness Pottery Co. Ltd, 1975–84; The Benshie Cattle Co. Ltd; Land and Timber Services Ltd, since 1986; *b* 10 July 1919; *s* of late Maitland Mackie, OBE, Hon. LLD; *m* 1st, 1944, Lindsay Lyall Sharp (*d* 1985), *y d* of late Alexander and Isabella Sharp, OBE, Aberdeen; three *d* (one *s* decd); 2nd, 1988, Jacqueline, *widow* of Andrew Lane, and *d* of late Col. Marcel Rauch. *Educ:* Aberdeen Grammar Sch.; Aberdeen Univ. Served War of 1939–45, RAF; Bomber Command, (DSO, DFC); Air Staff, 1944. Farming at Ballinshoe, Kirriemuir, from 1945. Contested (L) South Angus, 1959; MP (L) Caithness and Sutherland, 1964–66; contested (L) Scotland NE, European Parliamentary election, 1979. Pres., Scottish Liberal Party, 1983–88 (Chm., 1965–70); Member: EEC Scrutiny Cttee (D), House of Lords; Liberal Shadow Admin; Exec., Inter-Parly Union; Governing Body, GB/East Europe Centre; Council of Europe, 1986–; WEU, 1986–; Liberal Spokesman, House of Lords: Devolution, Agriculture, Scotland, Industry. Chm., Cotswold Wine Co. (UK) Ltd, 1983–85. Dir, Scottish Ballet, 1986–. Rector, Dundee Univ., 1980–83. Hon. LLD Dundee, 1982. *Publication:* Policy for Scottish Agriculture, 1963. *Address:* Cortachy House, by Kirriemuir, Angus. *T:* Kirriemuir (0575) 4229. *Clubs:* Garrick, Farmers', Royal Air Force.
  See also Baron John-Mackie, Sir Maitland Mackie, I. L. Aitken, A. G. Sharp, Sir R. L. Sharp.

MACKIE, Air Cdre (Retd) Alastair Cavendish Lindsay, CBE 1966; DFC 1943 and Bar 1944; Director General, Health Education Council, 1972–82; Director, Ansador Ltd, since 1983; *b* 3 Aug. 1922; *s* of George Mackie, DSO, OBE, MD, Malvern, Worcs and May (*née* Cavendish); *m* 1944, Rachel Goodson; two *s*. *Educ:* Charterhouse. Royal Air Force, 1940–68; Under Treas., Middle Temple, 1968; Registrar, Architects' Registration Council, 1970; Sec., British Dental Assoc., 1971; Pres., Internat. Union for Health Educn, 1979–82. Vice-Pres., CND, 1990–. *Recreation:* allotmenteering. *Address:* 4 Warwick Drive, SW15 6LB. *T:* 081–789 4544. *Club:* Royal Air Force.

MACKIE, Prof. Andrew George; Professor of Applied Mathematics, 1968–88, Vice-Principal 1975–80, University of Edinburgh; *b* 7 March 1927; *s* of late Andrew Mackie and of Isobel Sigsworth Mackie (*née* Storey); *m* 1959, Elizabeth Maud Mackie (*née* Hebblethwaite); one *s* one *d*. *Educ:* Tain Royal Acad.; Univ. of Edinburgh (MA); Univ. of Cambridge (BA); Univ. of St Andrews (PhD). Lecturer, Univ. of Dundee, 1948–50; Bateman Res. Fellow and Instructor, CIT, 1953–55; Lecturer: Univ. of Strathclyde, 1955–56; Univ. of St Andrews, 1956–62; Prof. of Applied Maths, Victoria Univ. of Wellington, NZ, 1962–65; Res. Prof., Univ. of Maryland, 1966–68. Visiting Professor: CIT, 1984; Univ. of NSW, 1985. FRSE 1962. *Publications:* Boundary Value Problems, 1965, 2nd edn 1989; numerous contribs to mathematical and scientific jls. *Recreation:* golf. *Address:* 47 Cluny Drive, Edinburgh EH10 6DU. *T:* 031–447 2164.

MACKIE, Clive David Andrew, FCA, FSS; Secretary-General, Institute of Actuaries, since 1983; *b* 29 April 1929; *s* of David and Lilian Mackie; *m* 1953, Averil Ratcliff; one *s* three *d*. *Educ:* Tiffin Sch., Kingston-on-Thames. FCA 1956; FSS 1982. Director: cos in Grundy (Teddington) Group, 1959–67; D. Sebel & Co. Ltd, 1967–70; post in admin of higher educn, 1970–73; Dep. Sec., 1973–77 and Sec., 1977–83, Inst. of Actuaries. *Recreations:* music (post 1800), cricket, carpentry, walking. *Address:* Withermere, Burwash, East Sussex TN19 7HN. *T:* Burwash (0435) 882427. *Clubs:* Reform; Actuaries; Kent CC.

MACKIE, Eric Dermott, OBE 1987; Chairman and Managing Director, Govan Kvaerner Ltd (formerly Govan Shipbuilders Ltd), since 1979; *b* 4 Dec. 1924; *s* of James Girvan and Ellen Dorothy Mackie; *m* 1950, Mary Victoria Christie; one *s* one *d*. *Educ:* Coll. of Technology, Belfast. CEng; MIMechE, FIMarE, FRINA. 1st Class MoT Cert. (Steam and Diesel). Trained with James Mackie & Son (Textile Engrs), 1939–44; Design draughtsman, Harland & Wolff, Belfast, 1944–48; 2nd Engineer (sea-going) in both steam and diesel ships for Union Castle Mail Steamship Co., 1948–53; Harland & Wolff, Belfast, 1953–75: Test Engr; Manager, Shiprepair Dept; Gen. Manager i/c of Southampton branch; Gen. Manager i/c of ship prodn and shiprepair, Belfast; Man. Dir, James Brown Hamer, S Africa, 1975–79; Chief Exec. and Man. Dir of Shiprepair in UK, British Shipbuilders, 1979–81. Denny Gold Medal, IMarE, 1987. *Publications:* articles for marine engrg instns on various subjects pertaining to marine engrg and gen. engrg. *Recreations:* golf, swimming, reading. *Address:* Middle Barton, Whittingham, near Alnwick, Northumberland. *T:* Whittingham (066574) 648. *Clubs:* Durban, Rand (Johannesburg, SA).

MACKIE, George, DFC 1944; RSW 1968; RDI 1973; freelance graphic artist and painter; Head of Design, Gray's School of Art, Aberdeen, 1958–80 (retd); *b* 17 July 1920; *s* of late David Mackie and late Kathleen Grantham; *m* 1952, Barbara Balmer, ARSA, RSW; two *d*. Served Royal Air Force, 1940–46. Consultant in book design to Edinburgh University Press, 1960–87. Paintings in various private and public collections incl. HRH the Duke of Edinburgh's and Scottish Nat. Gall. of Modern Art. *Publication:* Lynton Lamb: Illustrator, 1979. *Address:* 32 Broad Street, Stamford, Lincs. *T:* Stamford (0780) 53296. *Club:* Double Crown.

MACKIE, Prof. George Owen, FRS 1991; DPhil; Professor of Biology, University of Victoria, since 1968; *b* 20 Oct. 1929; *s* of Frederick P. Mackie and Mary E. H. Mackie (*née* Owen); *m* 1956, Gillian V. Faulkner; three *s* two *d*. *Educ:* Oxford (BA 1954; MA 1956; DPhil 1956). FRSC 1982. Univ. of Alberta, 1957–68; Univ. of Victoria, 1968–; Chm., Biol. Dept, 1970–73. Editor, Canadian Jl of Zoology, 1980–89. Fry Medal, Canadian Soc. of Zoologists, 1989. *Publications:* (ed) Coelenterate Ecology and Behavior, 1976; numerous research articles in books and jls. *Recreations:* chamber music ('cello), earthenware pottery. *Address:* University of Victoria, Department of Biology, PO Box 1700, Victoria, BC V8W 2Y2, Canada. *T:* (604) 721–7146.

McKIE, Rt. Rev. John David; Assistant Bishop, Diocese of Coventry, 1960–80; Vicar of Great and Little Packington, 1966–80; *b* 14 May 1909; *s* of Rev. W. McKie, Melbourne, Vic; *m* 1952, Mary Lesley, *d* of late Brig. S. T. W. Goodwin, DSO and of Mrs Goodwin, Melbourne, Vic; four *d*. *Educ:* Melbourne Church of England Grammar Sch.; Trinity Coll., Melbourne Univ.; New Coll., Oxford. BA (Trinity Coll., Melbourne Univ.). 1931; MA (New Coll., Oxford), 1945; Deacon, 1932; Priest, 1934; Asst Chap. Melbourne Church of England Grammar Sch., 1932–33; Chap. and lecturer, Trinity Coll., Melbourne,

1936–39; served War of 1939–45 (despatches): AIF, 1939–44; Asst CG; Vicar Christ Church, South Yarra, 1944–46; Coadjutor, Bishop of Melbourne (with title of Bishop of Geelong) and Archdeacon of Melbourne, 1946–60, Chaplain and Sub-Prelate, Order of St John of Jerusalem, 1949. *Address:* 13 Morven Street, Mornington, Victoria 3931, Australia.

MACKIE, Lily Edna Minerva, (Mrs John Betts), OBE 1986; Head Mistress, City of London School for Girls, 1972–86; *b* 14 April 1926; *d* of late Robert Wood Mackie and late Lilian Amelia Mackie (*née* Dennis); *m* 1985, John Betts. *Educ:* Plaistow Grammar Sch.; University Coll., London (BA); Lycée de Jeunes Filles, Limoges; Université de Poitiers. Asst Mistress: Ilford County High Sch. for Girls, 1950–59; City of London Sch. for Girls, 1960–64; Head Mistress: Wimbledon County Sch., 1964–69; Ricards Lodge High Sch., Wimbledon, 1969–72. FRSA. *Recreations:* theatre, music, gardening, travel, boating. *Address:* Cotswold, 59–61 Upper Tooting Park, SW17 7SU.

MACKIE, Sir Maitland, Kt 1982; CBE 1965; JP; farmer since 1932; *b* 16 Feb. 1912; *s* of late Dr Maitland Mackie, OBE and Mary (*née* Yull); *m* 1st, 1935, Isobel Ross (*d* 1960); two *s* four *d*; 2nd, 1963, Martha Pauline Turner. *Educ:* Aberdeen Grammar Sch.; Aberdeen Univ. (BScAgric). FEIS 1972; FRAgSS 1974; FInstM. County Councillor, Aberdeenshire, 1951–75 (Convener 1967–75); Chm., NE Develt Authority, 1969–75; Chairman: Jt Adv. Cttee, Scottish Farm Bldgs Investigation Unit, 1963–; Aberdeen Milk Marketing Bd, 1965–82; Peterhead Bay Management Co., 1975–86; Hanover (Scotland) Housing Assoc., 1981–86. Member: Agric. Sub-Cttee, UGC, 1965–75; Bd, Scottish Council for Development and Industry, 1975– (Chm., Oil Policy Cttee, 1975–); Clayson Cttee on Drink Laws in Scotland. Chm., Aberdeen Cable Services, 1983–87; Director: Scottish Telecommunications, 1969–85; Aberdeen Petroleum plc, 1980–. Governor: N of Scotland Coll. of Agriculture, 1968–82 (Vice-Chm., 1974–78); Rowett Inst., 1973–82. Fellow, Scottish Council Develt and Industry, 1986. Burgess of Guild, Aberdeen, 1978. JP 1956; Lord-Lieut, Aberdeenshire, 1975–87. KStJ 1977. Hon. LLD Aberdeen, 1977. *Recreation:* travel. *Address:* High Trees, Inchmarlo Road, Banchory AB3 3RR. *T:* Banchory (03302) 4274. *Clubs:* Farmers'; Royal Northern (Aberdeen).
  See also Barons John-Mackie and Mackie of Benshie.

McKIERNAN, Most Rev. Francis J.; *see* Kilmore, Bishop of, (RC).

MACKILLIGIN, David Patrick Robert; HM Diplomatic Service; High Commissioner in Belize, since 1991; *b* 29 June 1939; *s* of R. S. Mackilligin, CMG, OBE, MC and Patricia (*née* Waldegrave); *m* 1976, Gillian Margaret Zuill Walker; two *d*. *Educ:* St Mary's Coll., Winchester; Pembroke Coll., Oxford (2nd Cl. Hons PPE). Asst Principal, CRO, 1961–62; Third, later Second Sec., Pakistan, 1962–66; Asst Private Sec. to Sec. of State for Commonwealth Relations, 1966–68; Private Sec. to Minister Without Portfolio, 1968–69; Dep. Comr, Anguilla, 1969–71 (Actg Comr, July-Aug. 1970); First Sec., Ghana, 1971–73; First Sec., Head of Chancery and Consul, Cambodia, 1973–75 (Chargé d'Affaires at various times); FCO, 1975–80 (Asst Head of W African Dept, 1978–80); Counsellor (Commercial and Aid), Indonesia, 1980–85; NATO Defence Coll., Rome, 1985–86; Counsellor (Economic and Commercial), and Dir of Trade Promotion, Canberra, 1986–90. *Recreations:* walking and swimming in remote places, ruins, second-hand bookshops, theatre, literature. *Address:* c/o Foreign and Commonwealth Office, King Charles Street, SW1A 2AH. *Clubs:* United Oxford & Cambridge University, Commonwealth Trust.

MacKINLAY, Sir Bruce, Kt 1978; CBE 1970; company director; *b* 4 Oct. 1912; *s* of Daniel Robertson MacKinlay and Alice Victoria Rice; *m* 1943, Erica Ruth Fleming; two *s*. *Educ:* Scotch Coll. Served War, AASC, 1940–45 (Lieut). Dir, J. Gadsden Australia Ltd, 1954–77. President: WA Chamber of Manufactures, 1958–61; Confedn of WA Industry, 1976–78; WA Employers' Fedn, 1974–75; Fremantle Rotary Club, 1956; Vice-Pres., Associated Chambers of Manufactures of Aust., 1960. Chairman: WA Inst. of Dirs, 1975–77; WA Div., National Packaging Assoc., 1967–69; WA Finance Cttee for the Duke of Edinburgh's Third Commonwealth Study Conf., 1967–68; Mem., Commonwealth Manufg Industries Adv. Council, 1962–70. Leader: Aust. Trade Mission, E Africa, 1968; WA Trade Mission, Italy, 1970; Employers' Rep., Internat. Labour Conf., 1977; Comr, State Electricity Commn, 1961–74. University of Western Australia: Mem. Senate, 1970–84; Chm., Master of Business Admin Appeal, 1973. Life Governor, Scotch Coll. Council (Chm., 1969–74); Chm. Nat. Council, Keep Australia Beautiful, 1984–86 (Mem. 1967–; Chm. 1981–86, WA Council); Councillor: Organising Council of Commonwealth and Empire Games, 1962; Aust. Council on Population and Ethnic Affairs, 1981–83. Pres., Most Excellent Order of the British Empire, WA Div., 1983–90. *Recreations:* swimming, gardening. *Address:* 9B Melville Street, Claremont, WA 6010, Australia. *T:* 3832220. *Clubs:* Weld, WACA, Claremont Football (WA).

McKINLEY, Air Vice-Marshal David Cecil, CB 1966; CBE 1957; DFC 1940; AFC 1944, Bar 1945; RAF; *b* 18 Sept. 1913; *s* of David McKinley, Civil Engineer, and May McKinley (*née* Ward); *m* 1940, Brenda Alice (*née* Ridgway); three *s*. *Educ:* Bishop Foy Sch., Waterford; Trinity Coll., Dublin. Radio Engineering, Ferranti Ltd, 1935. Entered (regular) Royal Air Force, 1935; served continuously since that date; AOC Malta and Dep. C-in-C (Air), Allied Forces, Mediterranean, 1963–65; SASO, Transport Command, 1966, Air Support Command, 1967–68; retired 1968. Freeman, The Guild of Air Pilots and Air Navigators, 1959. FIN 1949. *Recreations:* sailing, fishing, water ski-ing, gardening. *Address:* 4 Courtil Lubin, Alderney, Channel Islands. *T:* Alderney (04812) 2497; Midland Bank, Alderney, CI. *Club:* Royal Air Force.

McKINLEY, John Key; Chairman and Chief Executive Officer, Texaco Inc., 1980–86 (President, 1971–83), retired; *b* Tuscaloosa, Ala, 24 March 1920; *s* of Virgil Parks McKinley and Mary Emma (*née* Key); *m* 1946, Helen Grace Heare; two *s*. *Educ:* Univ. of Alabama (BS Chem. Engrg, 1940; MS Organic Chemistry, 1941); Harvard Univ. (Graduate, Advanced Management Program, 1962). Served War, AUS, Eur. Theatre of Ops, 1941–45 (Major; Bronze Star). Texaco Inc., 1941–86: Asst Dir of Res., Beacon, NY, 1957–59; Asst to the Vice-Pres., 1959–60; Manager of Commercial Develt Processes, 1960; Gen. Man., Worldwide Petrochemicals, NYC, 1960–67, Vice-Pres., Petrochem. Dept, 1967–71 (also Vice-Pres. i/c Supply and Distribution); Sen. Vice-Pres., Worldwide Refining, Petrochems, Supply and Distbn, 1971, Pres. and Dir, 1971–83; Director: Texaco Inc., 1971–; Merck & Co., Inc., 1982–90; Manufacturers Hanover Corp., 1980–90; Hanover Trust Co., 1980–90; Martin Marietta, 1985–90; Apollo Computer, 1987–89; Burlington Industries Inc., 1977–87; Federated Stores, Inc., 1990–. Hon. Dir, Amer. Petroleum Inst. Man. Dir, Met. Opera Assoc., 1980–; National Chm., Met. Opera Centennial Fund, 1980. Dir, Americas Soc. Member: Bd of Overseers, Meml Sloan-Kettering Cancer Center, 1981–; Brookings Council, 1986; Business Council. Fellow, Amer. Inst. of Chem. Engrs; Sesquicentennial Hon. Prof., Univ. of Alabama; Hon. LLD: Univ. of Alabama, 1972; Troy State Univ., 1974. *Address:* Tuscaloosa, Alabama, USA; Darien, Conn 06820; Buffalo, Wyoming. *Clubs:* Links, Brook (NYC); Wee Burn Country (Darien); Augusta (Ga); National Golf, Blind Brook Country (Port Chester, NY); Clove Valley Rod and Gun (LaGrangeville, NY).

McKINNEY, Mrs J. P.; *see* Wright, Judith.

McKINNEY, (Sheila Mary) Deirdre; Her Honour Judge McKinney; a Circuit Judge, since 1981; *b* 20 Oct. 1928; *d* of Patrick Peter McKinney and Mary Edith (*née* Conoley). *Educ:* Convent of the Cross, Boscombe, Bournemouth. Called to the Bar, Lincoln's Inn, 1951; a Recorder of the Crown Court, 1978–81.

McKINNON, Hon. Donald Charles; MP (Nat. Party) Albany, New Zealand, since 1978; Deputy Prime Minister, New Zealand, and Minister of External Relations and Trade, since 1990; *b* 27 Feb. 1939; *s* of Maj.-Gen. Walter Sneddon McKinnon, *qv*; *m* 1964, Patricia Maude Moore; three *s* one *d*. *Educ:* Lincoln Coll., New Zealand. AREINZ. Farm Manager, 1964–72; Farm Management Consultant, 1973–78; Real Estate Agent, 1974–78. Dep. Leader of the Opposition, 1987. *Recreations:* enthusiastic jogger and tennis player. *Address:* Parliament Building, Wellington, New Zealand. *T:* 0064 4 719 997.

MacKINNON, Prof. Donald MacKenzie, MA; FRSE 1984; FBA 1978; Norris-Hulse Professor of Divinity, Cambridge University, 1960–78; Fellow of Corpus Christi College, Cambridge, since 1960; *b* Oban, 27 Aug. 1913; *o s* of late D. M. MacKinnon, Procurator Fiscal, and late Grace Isabella Rhind; *m* 1939, Lois, *e d* of late Rev. Oliver Dryer; no *c*. *Educ:* Cargilfield Sch., Edinburgh; Winchester Coll. (scholar); New Coll., Oxford (scholar). Asst in Moral Philosophy (to late Prof. A. E. Taylor) at Edinburgh, 1936–37; Fellow and Tutor in Philosophy at Keble Coll., Oxford, 1937–47; Dir of Course for special courses in Philosophy for RN and RAF cadets at Oxford, 1942–45; Lectr in Philosophy at Balliol Coll., 1945–47; Wilde Lectr in Natural and Comparative Religion at Oxford, 1945–47; Regius Prof. of Moral Philosophy at Aberdeen, 1947–60. Lectures: Scott Holland, 1952; Hobhouse, 1953; Stanton, in the Philosophy of Religion, Cambridge, 1956–59; Gifford, Edinburgh, 1965–66; Prideaux, Exeter, 1966; Coffin, London, 1968; Riddell, Newcastle-upon-Tyne, 1970; D. Owen Evans, Aberystwyth, 1973; Drummond, Stirling, 1977; Martin Wight Meml, LSE, 1979; Boutwood, CCC Cambridge, 1981. President: Aristotelian Soc., 1976–77; Soc. for Study of Theol., 1981–82; Mem., Scottish Episcopal Church. Supporter, CND. Hon. DD: Aberdeen, 1961; Edinburgh, 1988; DUniv Stirling, 1989. *Publications:* (ed) Christian Faith and Communist Faith, 1953; The Notion of a Philosophy of History, 1954; A Study in Ethical Theory, 1957; (with Prof. G. W. H. Lampe) The Resurrection, 1966; Borderlands of Theology and other papers, 1968; The Stripping of the Altars, 1969; The Problem of Metaphysics, 1974; Explorations in Theology, 1979; Creon and Antigone, 1981; Themes in Theology: the threefold cord, 1987; articles, reviews, etc in periodicals and symposia in UK, France, Italy and Germany. *Recreations:* walking, cats, the cinema. *Address:* Dunbar Cottage, 10 Dunbar Street, Old Aberdeen AB2 1UE.

McKINNON, James, CA, FCMA; Director General, Office of Gas Supply, since 1986; *b* 1929. *Educ:* Camphill School. CA 1952, FCMA 1956. Company Secretary, Macfarlane Lang & Co. Ltd, Glasgow, 1955–65; Business Consultant, McLintock, Moores & Murray, Glasgow, 1965–67; Finance Director, Imperial Group plc, London, 1967–86. Pres., Inst. of Chartered Accountants of Scotland, 1985–86. *Publications:* papers to learned jls and articles in Accountants' magazine. *Recreation:* ski-ing. *Address:* Office of Gas Supply, Southside, 105 Victoria Street, SW1E 6QT.

McKINNON, Prof. Kenneth Richard, FACE; Vice-Chancellor, University of Wollongong, Australia, since 1981; President, Australian Vice-Chancellors' Committee, since 1991; *b* 23 Feb. 1931; *s* of Charles and Grace McKinnon; *m* 1st, 1956 (marr. diss.); one *s*; 2nd, 1981, Suzanne H., *d* of W. Milligan. *Educ:* Univ. of Adelaide (BA); Univ. of Queensland (BEd); Harvard Univ. (EdD). FACE 1972. Teacher, headmaster and administrator, 1957–65; Dir of Educn, Papua New Guinea, 1966–73; Chairman: Australian Schs Commn, 1973–81; Bd of Educn, Vic, 1982–85; Australian Nat. Commn for UNESCO, 1984–88. Mem., Australia Council, 1974–77 (Dep. Chm., 1976–77). Consultant in the Arts, Aust. Govt, 1981. *Publications:* Realistic Educational Planning, 1973; articles in jls and papers. *Recreations:* swimming, theatre, music, reading. *Address:* 2 Parrish Avenue, Mount Pleasant, Wollongong, NSW 2519, Australia. *T:* (042) 842–926. *Club:* Commonwealth (Canberra, Australia).

MACKINNON, Dame Patricia; *see* Mackinnon, Dame U. P.

McKINNON, Hon. Sir Stuart (Neil), Kt 1988; **Hon. Mr Justice McKinnon;** a Judge of the High Court of Justice, Queen's Bench Division, since 1988; *b* 14 Aug. 1938; *s* of His Honour Neil Nairn McKinnon, QC and late Janet, *d* of late Michael Lilley, Osterley; *m* 1966, Rev. Helena Jacoba Sara (*née* van Hoorn); two *d*. *Educ:* King's Coll. Sch., Wimbledon; Council of Legal Educn; Trinity Hall, Cambridge (BA, LLB 1963; MA 1967). Called to the Bar, Lincoln's Inn, 1960, Bencher, 1987; Junior at the Common Law Bar, 1964–80; QC 1980; a Recorder, 1985–88. Mem., Lord Chancellor's Mddx Adv. Cttee on JPs, 1990–. Pres., Cambridge Univ. Law Soc., 1962–63. *Recreation:* golf. *Address:* Royal Courts of Justice, Strand, WC2A 2LL. *Club:* Addington Golf.

MACKINNON, Dame (Una) Patricia, DBE 1977 (CBE 1972); *b* Brisbane, 24 July 1911; *d* of Ernest T. and Pauline Bell; *m* 1936, Alistair Scobie Mackinnon; one *s* one *d*. *Educ:* Glennie School and St Margaret's School, Queensland. Member Cttee of Management, Royal Children's Hospital, Melbourne, 1948–79; Vice-President, 1958; President, 1965–79; Chm., Research Bd, 1967–85. *Recreations:* gardening, reading history and biographies. *Address:* 5 Ross Street, Toorak, Vic 3142, Australia. *Club:* Alexandra (Melbourne).

McKINNON, Maj.-Gen. Walter Sneddon, CB 1966; CBE 1961 (OBE 1947); *b* 8 July 1910; *s* of Charles McKinnon and Janet Robertson McKinnon (*née* Sneddon); *m* 1937, Anna Bloomfield Plimmer; four *s* one *d*. *Educ:* Otago Boys High Sch., Dunedin, NZ; Otago Univ. (BSc); commissioned in NZ Army, 1935; various military courses, including Staff Coll., Camberley, England. Served War of 1939–45: Pacific, Italy (Lt-Col; despatches), Japan (occupation) (OBE); Brigadier, 1953; subsequent appointments: Comdr, Southern Mil. Dist (NZ), 1953; Head, NZ Joint Mil. Mission, Washington, DC, 1954–57; Comdr, Northern Military District, 1957–58; Adjutant-General, 1958–63; Quartermaster-General, 1963–65, Maj.-General, 1965; Chief of the General Staff, NZ Army, 1965–67; retired, 1967. Chm., NZ Broadcasting Corp., 1969–74. Member: Taupo Borough Council, 1977–80; Tongariro United Council, 1979–80. Pres., Taupo Regional Museum and Art Centre, 1975–79; Mem., Social Develt Council, New Zealand, 1976–79. *Recreations:* golf, fishing and gardening. *Address:* 43 Birch Street, Taupo, New Zealand. *Clubs:* Wellesley (Wellington); Taupo Golf.

See also Hon. D. C. McKinnon.

MACKINTOSH, family name of **Viscount Mackintosh of Halifax.**

MACKINTOSH OF HALIFAX, 3rd Viscount *cr* 1957; **John Clive Mackintosh;** Bt 1935; Baron 1948; *b* 9 Sept. 1958; *s* of 2nd Viscount Mackintosh of Halifax, OBE, BEM; *S* father, 1980; *m* 1982, Elizabeth, *o d* of late David G. Lakin; two *s*. *Educ:* The Leys School, Cambridge; Oriel College, Oxford (MA in PPE). President, Oxford Univ. Conservative Assoc., 1979. Chartered accountant. *Recreations:* cricket, bridge, golf. *Heir:* *s* Hon. Thomas Harold George Mackintosh, *b* 8 Feb. 1985. *Address:* House of Lords, SW1. *Clubs:* MCC, Carlton, Coningsby.

MACKINTOSH, Prof. Allan Roy, FRS 1991; Professor of Physics, University of Copenhagen, since 1970; *b* 22 Jan. 1936; *s* of Malcolm Roy Mackintosh and Alice Mackintosh (*née* Williams); *m* 1958, Jette Stannow; one *s* two *d*. *Educ:* Nottingham High Sch.; Peterhouse, Cambridge (scholar; BA, PhD). Associate Prof., Iowa State Univ., 1960–66; Res. Prof., Technical Univ. of Denmark, 1966–70; Dir, Risø Nat. Lab., Denmark, 1971–76; Dir, Nordic Inst. for Theoretical Physics, 1986–89. Alfred P. Sloan Res. Fellow, 1964–66; Lectures: D. K. C. MacDonald, Canada, 1975; F. H. Spedding, USA, 1983; Vis. Miller Prof., Univ. of California, Berkeley, 1989. Pres., European Phys. Soc., 1980–82. Mem., Royal Danish Acad. of Scis and Letters, 1977. Fil. Dr *hc* Uppsala, 1980. F. H. Spedding Award for Rare Earth Res., 1986. Kt of the Dannebrog (Denmark), 1984. *Publications:* Rare Earth Magnetism: Structures and Excitations (with Jens Jensen), 1991; articles on physics in learned jls. *Recreations:* sedate squash, listening to music, reading, walking. *Address:* Henrik Thomsenvej 4, DK-3460 Birkerød, Denmark. *T:* 45 42 815038; Physics Laboratory, H. C. Ørsted Institute, Universitetsparken 5, DK-2100 Copenhagen, Denmark. *T:* 45 31 353133.

MACKINTOSH, Cameron Anthony; producer of musicals; Chairman, Cameron Mackintosh, since 1981; *b* 17 Oct. 1946; *s* of Ian and Diana Mackintosh. *Educ:* Prior Park Coll., Bath. Hon. Fellow, St Catherine's Coll., Oxford, 1990. Decided to be producer of musical stage shows at age 8, after seeing Slade's Salad Days; spent brief period at Central Sch. of Speech and Drama; stage hand at Theatre Royal, Drury Lane; later Asst Stage Manager; worked with Emile Littler, 1966, with Robin Alexander, 1967; produced first musical, 1969. *London productions:* Little Women, 1967; Anything Goes, 1969; Trelawney, 1972; The Card, 1973; Winnie the Pooh, 1974; Owl and Pussycat Went to See, 1975; Godspell, 1975; Side by Side by Sondheim, 1976; Oliver!, 1977; Diary of a Madam, 1977; After Shave, 1977; Gingerbread Man, 1978; Out on a Limb, 1978; My Fair Lady, 1979; Oklahoma!, 1980; Tomfoolery, 1980; Jeeves Takes Charge, 1981; Cats, 1981; Song and Dance, 1982; Blondel, 1983; Little Shop of Horrors, 1983; Abbacadabra, 1983; The Boyfriend, 1984; Les Misérables, 1985; Café Puccini, 1985; Phantom of the Opera, 1986; Follies, 1987; Miss Saigon, 1989; Just So, 1990. *Recreations:* taking holidays, cooking. *Address:* Cameron Mackintosh Ltd, 1 Bedford Square, WC1B 3RA. *T:* 071–637 8866. *Club:* Groucho.

McKINTOSH, Ian; His Honour Judge McKintosh; a Circuit Judge, since 1988; *b* 23 April 1938; *s* of late Stanley and of Gertrude McKintosh; *m* 1967, Alison Rosemary, *e d* of Kenneth Blayney Large and Margaret Wharton Large; two *s* one *d*. *Educ:* Leeds Grammar Sch.; Exeter Coll., Oxford (MA). Admitted Solicitor of the Supreme Court, 1966. Served RAF, 1957–59. Articled to Town Clerk, Chester and to Laces & Co., Liverpool, 1962–66; Dept of Solicitor to Metropolitan Police, New Scotland Yard, 1966–69; Partner, Lemon & Co., Swindon, 1969–88; a Recorder, 1981–88. *Recreations:* cricket, sailing. *Address:* c/o The Crown Court, Edward Street, Truro, Cornwall TR1 2PB. *Clubs:* MCC, XL.

MACKINTOSH, (John) Malcolm, CMG 1975; HM Diplomatic Service, retired; *b* 25 Dec. 1921; *s* of late James Mackintosh, MD, LLD, FRCP, and Marjorie Mackintosh; *m* 1946, Elena Grafova; one *s* one *d* (and one *s* decd). *Educ:* Mill Hill; Edinburgh Academy; Glasgow Univ. MA (Hons) 1948. Served War, Middle East, Italy and Balkans, 1942–46; Allied Control Commn, Bulgaria, 1945–46. Glasgow Univ., 1946–48. Programme Organiser, BBC Overseas Service, 1948–60; Foreign Office, engaged on research, 1960–68; Asst Sec., Cabinet Office, 1968–87. Sen Fellow in Soviet Studies, IISS, 1989–; Hon. Sen. Res. Fellow, KCL, 1987–. *Publications:* Strategy and Tactics of Soviet Foreign Policy, 1962, 2nd edn 1963; Juggernaut: a history of the Soviet armed forces, 1967. *Recreations:* walking, climbing. *Address:* 21 Ravensdale Avenue, N12 9HP. *T:* 081–445 9714. *Club:* Garrick.

MACKINTOSH OF MACKINTOSH, Lt-Comdr Lachlan Ronald Duncan, OBE 1972; JP; 30th Chief of Clan Mackintosh; Lord-Lieutenant of Lochaber, Inverness, Badenoch and Strathspey, since 1985 (Vice-Lieutenant, 1971–85); Chairman, Highland Exhibitions Ltd, 1964–84; *b* 27 June 1928; *o s* of Vice-Adm. Lachlan Donald Mackintosh of Mackintosh, CB, DSO, DSC (*d* 1957); *m* 1962, Mabel Cecilia Helen (Celia), *yr d* of Captain Hon. John Bernard Bruce, RN; one *s* two *d* (and one *d* decd). *Educ:* Elstree; RNC Dartmouth. Flag Lieut to First Sea Lord, 1951; spec. communications, 1954; served in HM Yacht Britannia, 1957; retd 1963. Vice-Pres., Scottish Conservative and Unionist Assoc., 1969–71. DL 1965, CC 1970–75, Inverness-shire; Regional Cllr, Highland Region, 1974–; JP Inverness, 1982. *Heir:* *s* John Lachlan Mackintosh, younger of Mackintosh, *b* 2 Oct. 1969. *Address:* Moy Hall, Tomatin, Inverness IV13 7YQ. *T:* Tomatin (08082) 211. *Club:* Naval and Military.

MACKINTOSH, Malcolm; *see* Mackintosh, J. M.

MACKINTOSH, Prof. Nicholas John, DPhil; FRS 1987; Professor of Experimental Psychology, and Professorial Fellow of King's College, University of Cambridge, since 1981; *b* 9 July 1935; *s* of Dr Ian and Daphne Mackintosh; *m* 1st, 1960, Janet Ann Scott; one *s* one *d*; 2nd, 1978, Bundy Wilson; two *s*. *Educ:* Winchester; Magdalen Coll., Oxford. BA 1960, MA, DPhil 1963. Univ. Lectr, Univ. of Oxford, 1964–67; Res. Fellow, Lincoln Coll., Oxford, 1966–67; Res. Prof., Dalhousie Univ., 1967–73; Prof., Univ. of Sussex, 1973–81. Visiting Professor: Univ. of Pennsylvania, 1965–66; Univ. of Hawaii, 1972–73; Bryn Mawr Coll., 1977. Editor, Qly Jl of Experimental Psychology, 1977–84. *Publications:* (ed with W. K. Honig) Fundamental Issues in Associative Learning, 1969; (with N. S. Sutherland) Mechanisms of Animal Discrimination Learning, 1971; The Psychology of Animal Learning, 1974; Conditioning and Associative Learning, 1983; papers in psychological journals. *Address:* King's College, Cambridge CB2 1ST. *T:* Cambridge (0223) 351386.

McKISSOCK, Sir Wylie, Kt 1971; OBE 1946; MS (London), FRCS; Consulting Neurological Surgeon in London, 1936–71, now retired; Neurological Surgeon, National Hospital for Nervous Diseases, Queen Square and Metropolitan Ear, Nose and Throat Hospital; Neurological Surgeon, Hospital for Sick Children, Great Ormond Street; Neurological Surgeon, St Andrew's Hospital, Northampton; Visiting Neurological Surgeon, Graylingwell Hospital, Chichester, St James's Hospital, Portsmouth, Belmont Hospital, Sutton, and Park Prewett Hospital, Basingstoke; Associate Neurological Surgeon, Royal Marsden Hospital; Director of Institute of Neurology, Queen Square; Surgeon in Charge, Department of Neuro-Surgery, Atkinson Morley Hospital branch of St George's Hospital; Hon. Civil Consultant in Neuro-Surgery to RAF; Hon. Neurological Surgeon, Welsh Regional Hospital Board; Teacher of Surgery, St George's Hospital Medical School (University of London); Member, Panel of Consultants, Royal Navy, British European Airways, British Overseas Airways Corporation; *b* 27 Oct. 1906; *s* of late Alexander Cathie McKissock; *m* 1934, Rachel, *d* of Leonard Marcus Jones, Beckenham, Kent; one *s* two *d*. *Educ:* King's Coll. and St George's Hospital, University of London. Junior University Schol., St George's Hospital, 1928; Laking Memorial Prize, 1932–33 and 1933–34; Rockefeller Schol. in Neuro-Surgery, 1937–38; Casualty Officer, House Surgeon, House Physician, House Surgeon to Ear, Nose, Throat and Eye Depts, Assistant Curator of Museum, Surgical Registrar, Surgical Chief Asst, St George's Hosp.; Surgical

Registrar, Maida Vale Hosp. for Nervous Diseases, Hosp. for Sick Children, Great Ormond St, and Victoria Hospital for Children, Tite St. FRSM; Fellow, Society of British Neurological Surgeons (President, 1966); FRCR (Hon.) 1962; Corresponding Member, American Association of Neurological Surgeons, 1968. Hon. DSc, Newcastle upon Tyne, 1966. *Publications:* contributions to medical journals. *Recreations:* wine, food, gardening, ornithology, antagonism to Bureaucracy and the enjoyment of retirement. *Address:* Camus na Harry, Lechnaside, Gairloch, West Ross IV21 2AP. *T:* Badachro (044583) 224.

McKITTRICK, Neil Alastair; Stipendiary Magistrate, Middlesex, since 1989; *b* 1 Jan. 1948; *s* of late Ian James Arthur McKittrick and of Mary Patricia McKittrick (*née* Hobbs); *m* 1975, Jean Armstrong; one *s* one *d*. *Educ:* King's Sch., Ely; College of Law, Guildford. LLB London. Solicitor, 1972. Articled Clerk and Asst Solicitor, Cecil Godfrey & Son, Nottingham, 1967–73; Prosecuting Solicitor, Notts, 1973–77; Clerk to the Justices, 1977–89 (Darlington 1977, E Herts 1981, N Cambs 1986–89). Member: Council, Justices' Clerks' Soc., 1985–89 (Chm., Professional Purposes Cttee, 1987–89); President's Family Cttee, 1985–89; Justice Cttee on Witnesses, 1986; Domestic Courts Cttee, Magistrates' Assoc., 1988–91; Adv. Gp, Magistrates' Training Courses, 1989–; Middlesex Area Probation Cttee, 1990–. Editor, Justice of the Peace, 1985–89; Licensing Editor, Justice of the Peace Reports, 1983–; Editor, Jl of Criminal Law, 1990– (Mem., Editl Bd, 1985–). *Publications:* (ed jtly) Wilkinson's Road Traffic Offences, 14th edn, 1989; papers and articles in learned jls. *Recreations:* writing, walking, keeping the wolf from the door. *Address:* Magistrates' Courts Brent, Church End, 448 High Road, NW10 2DZ. *T:* 081–451 7111. *Club:* Reform.

MACKLEN, Victor Harry Burton, CB 1975; consultant to Ministry of Defence, since 1980; *b* 13 July 1919; *s* of H. Macklen and A. C. Macklen, Brighton, Sussex; *m* 1950, Ursula Irene Fellows; one *d*. *Educ:* Varndean Sch., Brighton; King's Coll., London. Air Defence Experimental Establishment, 1941; Operational Research Group, 1942; served Army, 1943–49; WO Scientific Staff, 1949–51; Head, Operational Research Section, BAOR, 1951–54; MoD Scientific Staff, 1954–60; Head, Technical Secretariat Reactor Group, UKAEA, 1960–64; Dep. Director, Technical Operations Reactor Group, UKAEA, 1966–67; Asst Chief Scientific Adviser (Studies and Nuclear), MoD, 1967–69; Dep. Chief Scientific Adviser (Projects and Nuclear), MoD, 1969–79; Personal Advr to Chm., British Telecom, 1980–87. Chm., Hartlip Parish Council, 1983–91. FRSA 1975. *Address:* Stepp House, Hartlip, near Sittingbourne, Kent ME9 7TH. *T:* Newington (0795) 842591. *Club:* Army and Navy.

MACKLEY, Ian Warren, CMG 1989; HM Diplomatic Service; Deputy High Commissioner, Canberra, since 1989; *b* 31 March 1942; *s* of late Harold William Mackley and of Marjorie Rosa Sprawson (*née* Warren); *m* 1st, 1968, Jill Marion (*née* Saunders) (marr. diss. 1988); three *s*; 2nd, 1989, Sarah Anne Churchley; one *s* one *d*. *Educ:* Ardingly College. FO, 1960; Saigon, 1963; Asst Private Sec. to Ministers of State, FCO, 1967; Wellington, 1969; First Sec., 1972; FCO 1973; Head of Inf. Services, New Delhi, 1976; Asst Head, UN Dept, FCO, 1979; seconded to ICI, 1982; Counsellor, Dep. Hd of UK Delegn to Conf. on Confidence- and Security-Building Measures and Disarmament in Europe, Stockholm, 1984–86; Chargé d'Affaires, Kabul, 1987–89. Pres., Kabul Golf and Country Club, Afghanistan, 1987–89. *Recreations:* golf, armchair sport. *Address:* c/o Foreign and Commonwealth Office, SW1A 2AH. *Clubs:* Travellers'; Commonwealth (Canberra).

MACKLIN, Sir Bruce (Roy), Kt 1981; OBE 1970; FCA; company director; Chairman: GRE Holdings Ltd, since 1986; Homestake Gold Australia Ltd, since 1987; Standard Chartered Bank Australia Ltd, since 1987; *b* 23 April 1917; *s* of Hubert Vivian Macklin and Lillian Mabel Macklin; *m* 1944, Dorothy Potts, Tynemouth, England; two *s* one *d*. *Educ:* St Peter's Coll., Adelaide; St Mark's Coll., Univ. of Adelaide (AUA Commerce). Served RAAF (Aircrew), 1941–45. Practising chartered accountant, 1947–69. Pres., Aust. Chamber of Commerce, 1967–69. Hon. Consul in S Aust. for Fed. Republic of Germany, 1968–; Leader, Aust. Govt Mission to Papua New Guinea, 1971. Mem. Council of Governors, St Peter's Coll., 1962–69; Mem. Council, Univ. of Adelaide, 1965–71. A Founder, Adelaide Festival of Arts, 1958, Chm. Bd of Governors, 1972–78; Dep. Nat. Chm., Queen Elizabeth II Silver Jubilee Trust for Young Australians. Silver Jubilee Medal 1977; Commander's Cross, Order of Merit of Fed. Republic of Germany, 1986. *Recreations:* tennis, gardening, music. *Address:* Rothe Road, Echunga, SA 5153, Australia. *T:* 388 8180. *Clubs:* Adelaide, Naval, Military and Air Force (South Australia).

MACKLIN, David Drury, CBE 1989; DL; Member, Boundary Commission for England, since 1989; *b* 1 Sept. 1928; *s* of Laurence Hilary Macklin and Alice Dumergue (*née* Tait); *m* 1955, Janet Smallwood; four *s*. *Educ:* Felsted Sch., Essex; St John's Coll., Cambridge. MA. Articled to Baileys Shaw & Gillett, Solicitors, 1951–54; Assistant Solicitor: Coward Chance & Co., 1954–56; Warwickshire CC, 1956–61; Devon CC, 1961–69; Dep. Clerk, Derbyshire CC, 1969–73; Chief Executive: Lincolnshire CC, 1973–79; Devon CC, 1979–88. Vice-Chm., Community Council of Devon, 1989–; Mem., Devon and Cornwall Housing Assoc., 1989–. DL Devon, 1991. *Recreations:* sailing, music, golf, theatre, walking. *Address:* Randolls, Victoria Road, Topsham, Exeter EX3 0EU. *T:* Topsham (0392) 873160.

MACKNIGHT, Dame Ella (Annie Noble), DBE 1969; Consultant Emeritus (Obstetrician and Gynaecologist), Queen Victoria Hospital, Melbourne, since 1964; *b* 7 Aug. 1904; 4th *d* of Dr Conway Macknight. *Educ:* Toorak Coll., Melbourne; Univ. of Melbourne, resident student, Janet Clarke Hall. MB, BS 1928; MD Melbourne 1931; DGO Melbourne 1936; MRCOG 1951; FRCOG 1958; FRACS 1971; FAGO 1973; FRACOG (FAustCOG 1978); Fellow AMA, 1976. Hon. Obstetrician and Gynaecologist, Queen Victoria Hosp., Melbourne, 1935–64; Pres., Queen Victoria Hosp., Melbourne, 1971–77 (Vice-Pres., 1965–71); Hon. Sec., 1963–67, Vice-Pres., 1967–70, Pres., 1970–72, Australian Council, RCOG. Hon. MD Monash, 1972. *Recreation:* golf. *Address:* 692 Toorak Road, Malvern, Victoria 3144, Australia. *Clubs:* Lyceum (Melbourne); Royal Melbourne Golf.

MACKSEY, Kenneth John, MC 1944; freelance author, since 1968, and publisher, since 1982; *b* 1 July 1923; *s* of Henry George Macksey and Alice Lilian (*née* Nightingall); *m* 1946, Catherine Angela Joan Little; one *s* one *d*. *Educ:* Goudhurst Sch.; Sandhurst; Army Staff Coll., Camberley. Served War, RAC: trooper, 1941–44; commnd 141st Regt RAC (The Buffs), 1944; Western Europe, 1944–45; Royal Tank Regt, 1946; served: India, 1947; Korea, 1950; Germany, 1957 and 1960–62; Singapore, 1958–60; retd, 1968. Dep. Editor, Purnell's History of the Second World War, and History of the First World War, 1968–70. Consultant to Canadian Armed Forces, 1981–. Town Councillor, 1972–83. *Publications:* To the Green Fields Beyond, 1965 (2nd edn 1977); The Shadow of Vimy Ridge, 1965; Armoured Crusader: the biography of Major-General Sir Percy Hobart, 1967; Afrika Korps, 1968 (4th edn 1976); Panzer Division, 1968 (4th edn 1976); Crucible of Power, 1969; Tank, 1970 (3rd edn 1975); Tank Force, 1970; Beda Fomm, 1971; Tank Warfare, 1971; Vimy Ridge, 1972; Guinness Book of Tank Facts and Feats, 1972 (3rd edn 1980); The Guinness History of Land Warfare, 1973 (2nd edn 1976); Battle, 1974; The Partisans of Europe, 1975; (jtly) The Guinness History of Sea Warfare, 1975; Guderian, Panzer General, 1975 (2nd edn 1976); (with Joan Macksey) The Guinness Guide to Feminine Achievements, 1975; (jtly) The Guinness History of Air Warfare, 1976; The Guinness Book of 1952, 1977; The Guinness Book of 1953, 1978; The Guinness Book of 1954, 1978; Kesselring: the making of the Luftwaffe, 1978; Rommel: battles and campaigns, 1979; The Tanks, vol. 3, 1979; Invasion: the German invasion of England July 1940, 1980 (2nd edn 1990); The Tank Pioneers, 1981; A History of the Royal Armoured Corps, 1914–1975, 1983; Commando Strike, 1985; First Clash, 1985; Technology in War, 1986; Godwin's Saga, 1987; Military Errors of World War II, 1987; Tank versus Tank, 1988; For Want of a Nail, 1989; (jtly) The Penguin Encyclopedia of Modern Warfare, 1991; contributor to DNB; articles and reviews in RUSI Jl, Army Qly, Brit. Army Rev., and The Tank. *Recreations:* umpiring ladies hockey, listening to music, living in Beaminster. *Address:* Whatley Mill, Beaminster, Dorset DT8 3EN. *T:* Beaminster (0308) 862321. *Club:* Social (Beaminster).

McKUEN, Rod; poet, composer, author, performer, columnist, classical composer; *b* Oakland, Calif, 29 April 1933. Has appeared in numerous films, TV, concerts, nightclubs, and with symphony orchestras. Composer: modern classical music; scores for motion pictures and TV. President: Stanyan Records; Discus Records; New Gramophone Soc.; Mr Kelly Prodns; Montcalm Prodns; Stanyan Books; Cheval Books; Biplane Books; Rod McKuen Enterprises; Vice-Pres., Tamarack Books; Dir, Animal Concern; Member, Advisory Board: Fund for Animals; Internat. Educn; Market Theatre, Johannesburg; Member, Board of Directors: National Ballet Theatre; Amer. Dance Ensemble; Amer. Guild of Authors and Composers; Exec. Pres., Amer. Guild of Variety Artists; Member: Amer. Soc. of Composers, Authors and Publishers; Writers' Guild; Amer. Fedn of TV and Radio Artists; Screen Actors' Guild; Equity; Modern Poetry Assoc.; Amer. Guild of Variety Artists; AGAC; Internat. Platform Assoc. Mem., Bd of Governors, National Acad. of Recording Arts and Sciences; Trustee: Univ. of Nebraska; Freedoms Foundn. Nat. spokesperson for Amer. Energy Awareness; Internat. spokesperson for Cttee for Prevention of Child Abuse (also Nat. Bd Mem.). Numerous awards, including: Grand Prix du Disc, Paris, 1966, 1974, 1975 and 1982; Golden Globe Award, 1969; Grammy for best spoken word album, Lonesome Cities, 1969; Entertainer of the Year, 1975; Man of the Year Award, Univ. of Detroit, 1978; awards from San Francisco, LA, Chattanooga, Topeka, Lincoln and Nebraska; Freedoms Foundn Patriot Medal, 1981; Salvation Army Man of the Year, 1982. Over 200 record albums; 41 Gold and Platinum records internationally; nominated Pulitzer Prize in classical music for The City, 1973. *Publications: poetry:* And Autumn Came, 1954; Stanyan Street and Other Sorrows, 1966; Listen to the Warm, 1967; Lonesome Cities, 1968; Twelve Years of Christmas, 1968; In Someone's Shadow, 1969; A Man Alone, 1969; With Love, 1970; Caught in the Quiet, 1970; New Ballads, 1970; Fields of Wonder, 1971; The Carols of Christmas, 1971; And to Each Season, 1972; Pastorale, 1972; Grand Tour, 1972; Come to Me in Silence, 1973; America: an Affirmation, 1974; Seasons in the Sun, 1974; Moment to Moment, 1974; Beyond the Boardwalk, 1975; The Rod McKuen Omnibus, 1975; Alone, 1975; Celebrations of the Heart, 1975; Finding my Father: one man's search for identity (prose), 1976; The Sea Around Me, 1977; Hand in Hand, 1977; Coming Close to the Earth, 1978; We Touch the Sky, 1979; Love's Been Good to Me, 1979; Looking for a Friend, 1980; An Outstretched Hand (prose), 1980; The Power Bright and Shining, 1980; Too Many Midnights, 1981; Rod McKuen's Book of Days, 1981; The Beautiful Strangers, 1981; The Works of Rod McKuen: Vol. 1, Poetry, 1950–82, 1982; Watch for the Wind . . ., 1982; Rod McKuen—1984 Book of Days, 1983; The Sound of Solitude, 1983; Suspension Bridge, 1984; Another Beautiful Day, 1984, vol. 2, 1985; Valentines, 1986; Intervals, 1987; *major classical works:* Symphony No One; Concerto for Guitar and Orchestra; Concerto for Four Harpsichords; Concerto for Cello and Orch.; Concerto for Bassoon and Orch.; Seascapes; Concerto for Piano and Orchestra; Adagio for Harp and Strings; Piano Variations; The Black Eagle (opera); Birch Trees (Concerto for Orch.); various other classical commns; numerous lyrics; *film and television scores:* Joanna, 1968; Travels with Charley, 1968; The Prime of Miss Jean Brodie (Academy Award Nomination), 1969; Me, Natalie, 1969; The Loner, 1969; A Boy Named Charlie Brown (Academy Award Nomination), 1970; Come to your Senses, 1971; Scandalous John, 1971; Wildflowers, 1971; The Borrowers, 1973; Lisa Bright and Dark, 1973; Hello Again, 1974; Emily, 1975; The Unknown War, 1979; Man to Himself, 1980; Portrait of Rod McKuen, 1982; The Beach, 1984. *Address:* PO Box G, Beverly Hills, Calif 90213, USA.

MACKWORTH, Commander Sir David Arthur Geoffrey, 9th Bt, *cr* 1776; RN retired; *b* 13 July 1912; *o s* of late Vice-Admiral Geoffrey Mackworth, CMG, DSO, and Noel Mabel, *d* of late William I. Langford; *S* uncle, 1952; *m* 1st, 1941, Mary Alice (marr. diss. 1972), *d* of Thomas Henry Grylls; one *s*; 2nd, 1973, Beryl Joan, formerly wife of late Ernest Henry Sparkes, and 3rd *d* of late Pembroke Henry Cockayn Cross and of Jeanie Cross. *Educ:* Farnborough Sch., Hants; RNC Dartmouth. Joined RN 1926; served HMS Eagle, HMS Suffolk, 1939–45; Commander, 1948; Naval Adviser to Director of Guided Weapon Research and Development, Ministry of Supply, 1945–49; retired, 1956. MRIN. *Recreations:* sailing, cruising. *Heir: s* Digby John Mackworth [*b* 2 Nov. 1945; *m* 1971, Antoinette Francesca, *d* of Henry James McKenna, Ilford, Essex; one *d*. *Educ:* Wellington Coll. Served Australian Army Aviation Corps, Malaysia and Vietnam (Lieut). With British Airways]. *Address:* 36 Wittering Road, Hayling Island, Hants. *Clubs:* Royal Ocean Racing; Royal Naval and Royal Albert Yacht (Portsmouth); Royal Naval Sailing Association; Royal Yacht Squadron (Cowes).

MACKWORTH-YOUNG, Sir Robert Christopher, (Sir Robin Mackworth-Young), GCVO 1985 (KCVO 1975; CVO 1968; MVO 1961); Librarian Emeritus to HM the Queen; *b* 12 Feb. 1920; *s* of late Gerard Mackworth-Young, CIE; *m* 1953, Rosemarie, *d* of W. C. R. Aue, Menton, France; one *s*. *Educ:* Eton (King's Schol.); King's Coll., Cambridge. Pres., Cambridge Union Soc., 1948. Served in RAF, 1939–46. HM Foreign Service, 1948–55; Deputy Librarian, Windsor Castle, 1955–58; Librarian, Windsor Castle, and Asst Keeper of the Queen's Archives, 1958–85. Mem. Bd, British Library, 1984–90. FSA; Hon. FLA. *Recreations:* music, electronics, ski-ing. *Address:* c/o Baring Brothers & Co. Ltd, 8 Bishopsgate, EC2N 4AE. *Club:* Roxburghe.

McLACHLAN, Dr Andrew David, FRS 1989; Scientific Staff, Medical Research Council Laboratory of Molecular Biology, Cambridge, since 1967; Fellow of Trinity College, Cambridge, since 1959; *b* 25 Jan. 1935; *s* of Donald Harvey McLachlan and Katherine (*née* Harman); *m* 1959, Jennifer Margaret Lief Kerr; three *s*. *Educ:* Winchester Coll. (Schol.); Trinity Coll., Cambridge (BA, MA, PhD, ScD). Res. Fellow, Trinity Coll., 1958; Harkness Fellow, USA, 1959–61; Lectr in Physics, Trinity Coll., 1961–87; Lectr in Chemistry, Cambridge Univ., 1965–67. Visiting Professor: CIT, 1964; Brandeis Univ., 1975; UCLA, 1989. *Publications:* (with A. Carrington) Introduction to Magnetic Resonance, 1967; papers in various jls, including Jl of Molecular Biology, Nature, and Proceedings of the Royal Soc. *Recreations:* walking, music, camping. *Address:* Medical Research Laboratory of Molecular Biology, Hills Road, Cambridge CB2 2QH. *T:* Cambridge (0223) 248011; Trinity College, Cambridge CB2 1TQ. *T:* Cambridge (0223) 338400.

McLACHLAN, Angus Henry; journalist; *b* 29 March 1908; *s* of James H. and Mabel McLachlan; unmarried. *Educ:* Scotch Coll., Melbourne; University of Melbourne.

Melbourne Herald, 1928–36; joined Sydney Morning Herald, 1936; News Editor, 1937–49; General Manager, John Fairfax & Sons Ltd (publishers of Sydney Morning Herald, Australian Financial Review), 1949–64, Dir, 1965–80 (Man. Dir, 1965–70). Jt Man. Dir, Australian Associated Press Pty Ltd, 1965–82 (Chairman, 1958–59, 1964–65, 1975–77); Director: Reuters Ltd, London, 1966–71 (Trustee, 1979–84, Chm. 1980–84); Amalgamated Television Services Pty Ltd, 1955–85; Macquarie Broadcasting Holdings Ltd, 1966–80; David Syme & Co. Ltd, Publishers of The Age, 1970–79; Federal Capital Press Ltd, Publishers of Canberra Times, 1970–79; Mem. Council, Library of NSW, 1966–75 (Dep. Pres., 1974–75); Mem., Library Council of NSW, 1975–78; Member, Sydney University Extension Board, 1960–75. *Address:* Box 5303, GPO, Sydney, NSW 2001, Australia. *Clubs:* Australian, Union (Sydney); Royal Sydney Yacht Squadron.

McLACHLAN, Gordon, CBE 1967; BCom; FCA; Secretary, Nuffield Provincial Hospitals Trust, 1956–86; *b* 12 June 1918; *s* of late Gordon McLachlan and Mary McLachlan (*née* Baird); *m* 1951, Monica Mary Griffin; two *d*. *Educ:* Leith Academy; Edinburgh Univ. Served with RNVR, 1939–46; Gunnery Specialist, 1943–46. Accountant, Edinburgh Corp., 1946–48; Dep. Treas., NW Met. Regional Hosps Bd, 1948–53; Accountant Nuffield Foundn, Nuffield Provincial Hosps Trust, Nat. Corp. for Care of Old People, 1953–56. Asst Dir, Nuffield Foundn, 1955–56. Henry Cohen Lectr, Univ. of Jerusalem, 1969; Parker B. Francis Foundn Distinguished Lectr, Amer. Coll. of Hosp. Admin, 1976; Rock Carling Fellow, 1989–90. Consultant, American Hospitals Assoc. and American Hospitals Research and Educational Trust, 1964–65; Member Council, American Hospitals Research and Educational Trust, 1965–74 (citation for meritorious service, AHA, 1976); Mem., Inst. of Medicine, Nat. Acad. of Sciences, Washington DC, 1974–. General Editor, Nuffield Provincial Hospitals Trust publications, 1956–86; Consulting Editor, Health Services Research Journal (US), 1966–74. Hon. FRCGP 1978. Hon. LLD Birmingham, 1977. *Publications:* What Price Quality?, 1990; editor of many publications on Nuffield Provincial Hospitals Trust list; contrib. to Lancet, Practitioner, Times, Twentieth Century, etc. *Recreations:* reading, watching ballet, theatre, Rugby football. *Address:* 95 Ravenscourt Road, W6. *T:* 081–748 8211. *Club:* Caledonian.

McLACHLAN, Air Vice-Marshal Ian Dougald, CB 1966; CBE 1954; DFC 1940; *b* Melbourne, 23 July 1911; *s* of Dugald McLachlan, author and teacher, and Bertha Frances (*née* Gilliam); *m* 1946, Margaret Helen Chrystal (marr. diss. 1968); one *d*. *Educ:* Melbourne High Sch.; Royal Military Coll., Duntroon. Imperial Defence Coll., 1954; Dir, Flying Trng, Air Min., London 1955–56; Dep. Chief of Air Staff, Australia, 1959–61; Australian Defence Adviser, Washington, 1962–63; Air Mem. for Supply and Equipment, Australian Air Bd, 1964–68. Consultant, Northrop Corp., 1968–87; Chairman: Mainline Corp., 1970–74; Pokolbin Winemakers, 1971–73; Information Electronics, 1984–87; Director: Capitol Motors, 1969–75; Reef Oil, 1969–75. *Recreations:* tennis, squash, golf. *Address:* 2 Eastbourne Road, Darling Point, NSW 2027, Australia. *T:* (02) 326–1860. *Clubs:* Australian (Sydney); Naval and Military (Melbourne); Melbourne Cricket, Royal Sydney Golf, Royal Canberra Golf.

McLACHLAN, Peter John, OBE 1983; Director: Bryson House, since 1980 (formerly General Secretary, Belfast Voluntary Welfare Society); North City Training Ltd; *b* 21 Aug. 1936; *s* of Herbert John McLachlan and Joan Dorothy McLachlan (*née* Hall); *m* 1965, Gillian Mavis Lowe; two *d*. *Educ:* Magdalen College Sch., Oxford; Queen's Coll., Oxford (schol.; BA Lit. Hum.; MA). Administrative trainee, Min. of Finance, NICS, 1959–62; Administrator, NYO of GB, 1962–65 and 1966–69; Personal Asst to Chm., IPC, 1965–66; Cons. Res. Dept, 1970–72; Exec. Dir, Watney & Powell Ltd, 1972–73; Mem. (Unionist) S Antrim, NI Assembly, 1973–75; Gen. Manager, S. H. Watterson Engineering, 1975–77; Jt Man. Dir, Ulster Metalspinners Ltd, 1976–77; Projects Manager, Peace By Peace Ltd, 1977–79; Sec., Peace People Charitable Trust, 1977–79; Chm., Community of The Peace People, 1978–80. Founder Chairman: NI Fedn of Housing Assocs, 1976–78; Belfast Improved Houses Ltd, 1975–81; Dismas House, 1983–87; Chm., NI Peace Forum, 1980–82; Vice-Chm., NI Hospice Ltd, 1981–; Member: The Corrymeela Community; Minister's Adv. Cttee on Community Work, NI, 1982–84; Central Personal Social Services Adv. Cttee, 1984–88; Administrative Council: Royal Jubilee Trusts, 1975–81; NI Projects Trust, 1977–88; Trustee: Children's Holiday Scheme NI, 1983–; Buttle Trust, 1987–; Cecil King Meml Foundn, 1991–. Hon. Sec., NI Fedn Victims Support Schemes, 1981–; Mem. Council, Victim Support UK, 1983– (Vice Chm., 1988–90). Mem., Bd of Visitors, HM Prison Maghaberry, 1986–. Dir, Belfast Community Radio, 1989–. Salzburg Seminar Alumnus, 1979; UK Eisenhower Fellow, 1986. *Recreations:* piano playing, mountain walking, gardening, mediation. *Address:* Larch View, 82 Moira Road, Hillsborough, Co. Down, Northern Ireland BT26 6DY. *T:* Hillsborough (0846) 683497. *Club:* Commonwealth Trust.

MACLAGAN, Michael, CVO 1988; FSA; FRHistS; Richmond Herald of Arms, 1980–89; *b* 14 April 1914; *s* of Sir Eric Robert Dalrymple Maclagan, KCVO, CBE, and Helen Elizabeth (*née* Lascelles); *m* 1st, 1939, Brenda Alexander (marr. diss. 1946); one *s*; 2nd, 1949, Jean Elizabeth Brooksbank Garnett, *d* of late Lt-Col W. B. Garnett, DSO; two *d* (one *s* decd). *Educ:* Winchester Coll.; Christ Church, Oxford (BA 1st Cl. Hons Modern History, MA). FSA 1948; FRHistS 1961; FSG 1970; FHS 1972. Lectr, Christ Church, Oxford, 1937–39; Fellow of Trinity Coll., 1939–81, Emeritus Fellow 1981, Sen. Proctor, 1954–55. 2/Lieut TA, 1938; served war, 1939–46: 16/5 Lancers; sc; Major, GSOII War Office. Slains Pursuivant, 1948–70; Portcullis Pursuivant, 1970–80. Vis. Professor, Univ. of S Carolina, 1974; Fellow of Winchester Coll., 1975–89; Sen. Librarian, Oxford Union, 1960–70; Trustee, Oxford Union, 1970. Councillor, Oxford CBC, 1946–74; Sheriff, 1964–65; Lord Mayor of Oxford, 1970–71. Chm., Oxford Dio. Adv. Cttee, 1961–85. Master of Scriveners' Co., 1988–89. OStJ 1952. *Publications:* (ed) Bede: Ecclesiastical History I and II, 1949; Trinity College, 1955, rev. edn 1963; (jtly) The Colour of Heraldry, 1958; (ed) Richard de Bury: Philobiblon, 1960; 'Clemency' Canning, 1962 (Wheatley Gold Medal); City of Constantinople, 1968; (with J. Louda) Lines of Succession, 1981 (trans. French, 1984); articles in DNB, VCH, etc. *Recreations:* real tennis, wine, walking, travel. *Address:* 20 Northmoor Road, Oxford OX2 6UR. *T:* Oxford (0865) 58536; Trinity College, Oxford OX1 3BH. *Clubs:* Cavalry and Guards, Pratt's; Oxford Union (Oxford).

McLAGGAN, Murray Adams; JP; Lord Lieutenant of Mid Glamorgan since 1990; *b* 29 Sept. 1929; *s* of Sir John Douglas McLaggan, KCVO, FRCS, FRCSE and Elsa Violet Lady McLaggan (*née* Adams), MD, DPH; *m* 1959, Jennifer Ann Nicholl; two *s* one *d*. *Educ:* Winchester College; New College, Oxford (MA 1st Cl. Hons). Called to the Bar, Lincoln's Inn, 1955; Student and Tutor in Law, Christ Church, Oxford, 1957–66. Mem., Parly Boundary Commn for Wales, 1980–; Chairman: Forestry Commn Regional Adv. Cttee (Wales); NRA Regl Flood Defence Cttee (Wales), 1990–; Dep. Chm., Nat. Trust Cttee for Wales, 1984–. High Sheriff Mid Glamorgan, 1978–79, DL 1982; JP Glamorgan, 1968. *Recreations:* bibliophily, dendrology, amateur operatics. *Address:* Merthyr Mawr House, Bridgend, Mid Glamorgan CF32 0LR. *T:* Bridgend (0656) 652038.

McLAREN, family name of **Baron Aberconway.**

McLAREN, Dr Anne Laura, FRS 1975; FRCOG; Director, Medical Research Council's Mammalian Development Unit, since 1974; *b* 26 April 1927; *d* of 2nd Baron Aberconway; *m* 1952, Donald Michie (marr. diss.); one *s* two *d*. *Educ:* Univ. of Oxford (MA, DPhil). FRCOG *ad eund* 1986. Post-doctoral research, UCL, 1952–55 and Royal Vet. Coll., London, 1955–59; joined staff of ARC Unit of Animal Genetics at Edinburgh Univ., 1959. Mem., ARC, 1978–83. Member: Cttee of Managers, Royal Instn, 1976–81; Council, Royal Soc., 1985–87. Scientific Medal, Zool Soc. London, 1967. *Publications:* Mammalian Chimaeras, 1976; Germ Cells and Soma, 1980; papers on reproductive biology, embryology, genetics and immunology in sci. jls. *Address:* 9 Steele's Road, NW3 4SG.

McLAREN, Clare, (Mrs Andrew McLaren); *see* Tritton, E. C.

McLAREN, Prof. Digby Johns, OC 1987; PhD; FRS 1979; FRSC 1968; President, Royal Society of Canada, 1987–90; *b* 11 Dec. 1919; *s* of James McLaren and Louie Kinsey; *m* 1942, Phyllis Matkin; two *s* one *d*. *Educ:* Sedbergh Sch.; Queens' Coll., Cambridge (BA, MA); Univ. of Michigan (PhD). Served RA (Gunner to Captain), ME and Italy, 1940–46. Field Geologist, Geological Survey of Canada, in Alberta and British Columbia Rocky Mountains, District of Mackenzie, Yukon Territory, Arctic Islands, 1948–80; first Dir, Inst. of Sedimentary and Petroleum Geology, Calgary, Alberta, 1967–73; Dir Gen., Geological Survey of Canada, 1973–80; Prof., Dept of Geology, Univ. of Ottawa, 1981–89; Sen. Science Adviser, Dept of Energy, Mines and Resources, Ottawa, 1981–84. Pres., Commn on Stratigraphy, IUGS, 1972–76; Chm. of Bd, Internat. Geol Correlation Programme, UNESCO-IUGS, 1976–80; IUGS Deleg. to People's Republic of China to advise on participation in international science, 1977. President: Paleontol Soc., 1969; Canadian Soc. Petroleum Geologists, 1971; Geol Soc. of America, 1981; Hon. Mem. and Leopold von Buch Medallist, Geol Soc. of Germany, 1982; Corresp. Mem., Geol Soc. of France, 1975; Foreign Associate, Nat. Acad. of Scis, USA, 1979. For. Hon. Fellow, European Union of Geoscis, 1983; Hon. FGS, 1989. Hon. DSc Ottawa, 1980. Gold Medal (for Pure and Applied Science), Professional Inst. of Public Service of Canada, 1979; Edward Coke Medal, Geol Soc. of London, 1985; Logan Medal, Geol Assoc. of Canada, 1987. *Publications:* (ed) Resources and World Development (proceedings of 2 Dahlem Workshops), 1987; memoirs, bulletins, papers, geological maps, and scientific contribs to journals on regional geology, paleontology, geological time, correlation, extinctions and global change and resource depletion. *Recreations:* skiing, swimming, gardening, music. *Address:* 248 Marilyn Avenue, Ottawa, Ont K1V 7E5, Canada. *T:* (613) 737–4360.

McLAREN, Sir Robin John Taylor, KCMG 1991 (CMG 1982); HM Diplomatic Service; Ambassador to People's Republic of China, since 1991; *b* 14 Aug. 1934; *s* of late Robert Taylor McLaren and of Marie Rose McLaren (*née* Simond); *m* 1964, Susan Ellen Hatherly; one *s* two *d*. *Educ:* Richmond and East Sheen County Grammar Sch. for Boys; Ardingly Coll.; St John's Coll., Cambridge (Schol.; MA). Royal Navy, 1953–55. Entered Foreign Service, 1958; language student, Hong Kong, 1959–60; Third Sec., Peking, 1960–61; FO, 1961–64; Asst Private Sec. to Lord Privy Seal (Mr Edward Heath), 1963–64; Second, later First Sec., Rome, 1964–68; seconded to Hong Kong Govt as Asst Political Adviser, 1968–69; First Sec., FCO, 1970–73; Dep. Head of Western Organisations Dept, 1974–75; Counsellor and Head of Chancery, Copenhagen, 1975–78; Head of Hong Kong and Gen. Dept, 1978–79, of Far Eastern Dept, 1979–81, FCO; Political Advr, Hong Kong, 1981–85; Ambassador to Philippines, 1985–87; Asst Under Sec. of State, FCO, 1987–90; Dep. Under Sec. of State, FCO, 1990–91. Sen. British Rep., Sino-British Jt Liaison Gp, 1987–89. *Recreations:* music, China, hill-walking. *Address:* c/o Foreign and Commonwealth Office, SW1A 2AH. *Clubs:* United Oxford & Cambridge University; Hong Kong (Hong Kong).

McLAREN-THROCKMORTON, Clare; *see* Tritton, E. C.

McLAUCHLAN, Madeline Margaret Nicholls; Head Mistress, North London Collegiate School, 1965–85; *b* 4 June 1922; *o c* of late Robert and Gertrude McLauchlan, Birmingham. *Educ:* King Edward VI Grammar Sch. for Girls, Camp Hill, Birmingham; Royal Holloway College, University of London. Asst Mistress: Shrewsbury High Sch., GPDST, 1944; Manchester High Sch., 1952. Senior Walter Hines Page Scholar, E-SU, 1955. Head Mistress, Henrietta Barnett Sch., 1958. Chm., Schoolboy and Schoolgirl Exchange Cttee, E-SU (Mem., Educn Cttee, 1966); Member: Exec. Cttee, Assoc. of Head Mistresses, 1966–76, Chm., 1974–76; Exec. Cttee, UCCA, 1968–85; Direct Grant Cttee, GBGSA, 1972–; Assisted Places Cttee, ISJC, 1980–85; Council, Westfield Coll., Univ. of London, 1975–78; Council, The Francis Holland Schools Trust, 1985–; Vice-Chm., Church Schs Co., 1988– (Mem. Council, 1985–). Governor: Imperial Coll., 1968–85; Bedford Coll., 1981–85; St Christopher's Sch., NW3, 1985–; Rougemont Sch., Newport, Gwent, 1988–; Llanbedr Village Sch., 1989–; NYO, 1985– (Mem. Council, 1975, Vice-Chm. Council, 1981). Freeman, Goldsmiths' Co., 1986. *Recreations:* music, mountain walking, housekeeping. *Address:* The Coach House, Moor Park, Llanbedr, Crickhowell, Powys NP8 1SS. *Club:* English-Speaking Union.

McLAUCHLAN, Thomas Joseph; Stipendiary Magistrate, 1966–82; *b* 15 May 1917; *s* of Alexander and Helen McLauchlan; *m* 1945, Rose Catherine Gray, MA. *Educ:* St Aloysius Coll., Glasgow; Univ. of Glasgow (BL). War service, Merchant Navy and RAF Y Section, Signals Intell., Wireless Officer, 1940–46. Legal Asst to Manager of large industrial insurance co., 1947–49; Clerk to Glasgow Police Courts, 1949–66. JP Scotland. *Recreations:* golf, bridge, travel. *Address:* 75 Clouston Street, Glasgow G20 8QW. *T:* 041–946 4222. *Club:* Centenary (Glasgow).

McLAUGHLAN, Rear-Adm. Ian David, CB 1970; DSC 1941 and Bar, 1953; Admiral Commanding Reserves and Director General, Naval Recruiting, 1970–72, retired; *b* 2 May 1919; *s* of Richard John and Margaret McLaughlan; *m* 1942, Charity Pomeroy Simonds; two *d*. *Educ:* St Paul's Sch. Entered Navy, 1937; served in destroyers, 1940–45 (despatches three times); comd HMS: Flint Castle, 1948–50; Concord, 1950–52; jssc 1952; Armed Forces Staff Coll., Norfolk, Va, 1953; HMS Jupiter, 1953–55; comd HMS: Chieftain, 1955; Chevron, 1955–56 (despatches); Staff of C-in-C, Portsmouth, 1957–59; Asst Dir of Plans, Admty, 1959–61; Capt. (F), 2nd Frigate Sqdn, 1961–62; idc 1963; Dir, Naval Ops and Trade, 1964–66; comd HMS Hampshire, 1966–67; Chief of Staff to Comdr Far East Fleet, 1967–70. Comdr 1951; Capt. 1958; Rear-Adm. 1968. Commendador d'Aviz, 1956. *Recreations:* gardening. *Address:* The Five Gables, Mayfield, East Sussex TN20 6TZ. *T:* Mayfield (0435) 872218.

McLAUGHLIN, Eleanor Thomson, JP; Lord Provost and Lord Lieutenant of Edinburgh, since 1988; *b* 3 March 1938; *d* of Alexander Craig and Helen Thomson; *m* 1959, Hugh McLaughlin; one *s* two *d*. *Educ:* Broughton School. Mem. (Lab), Edinburgh District Council, 1974–. Chairman: Edinburgh Festival Soc., 1988–; Edinburgh Military Tattoo Ltd, 1988–. JP Edinburgh, 1975. *Recreations:* Shetland lace knitting, gardening (Alpine plants). *Address:* 28 Oxgangs Green, Edinburgh EH13 9JS. *T:* 031–445 4052.

McLAUGHLIN, Mrs (Florence) Patricia (Alice), OBE 1975; *b* 23 June 1916; *o d* of late Canon F. B. Aldwell; *m* 1937, Henry, *o s* of late Major W. McLaughlin, of McLaughlin & Harvey Ltd, London, Belfast and Dublin; one *s* two *d*. *Educ:* Ashleigh House, Belfast; Trinity Coll., Dublin. MP (UU) Belfast West, 1955–64; Hon. Sec., Parly Home Safety Cttee, 1956–64; Deleg. to Council of Europe and WEU, 1959–64. Past Chm., Unionist

Soc.; Past Vice-Chm., Women's National Advisory Cttee of Cons. Party; Former Nat. Advisor on Women's Affairs to European Movement. Has been active in voluntary and consumer work for many years; Chairman: Steering Gp on Food Freshness, 1973–75; Housewife's Trust; Former Mem., Exec. Cttee, BSI. Vice-Pres., Royal Society for Prevention of Accidents, 1962–85. *Recreations:* talking and travelling. *Address:* 31 Headbourne Worthy House, Winchester, Hants SO23 7JG.

McLAUGHLIN, Mrs Patricia; *see* McLaughlin, Mrs F. P. A.

MacLAURIN, Sir Ian (Charter), Kt 1989; Chairman, Tesco PLC, since 1985 (Managing Director, 1973–85; Deputy Chairman, 1983–85; Director, 1970); non-executive Director: Guinness PLC, since 1986; National Westminster Bank plc, since 1990; *b* Blackheath, 30 March 1937; *s* of Arthur George and Evelina Florence MacLaurin; *m* 1961, Ann Margaret (*née* Collar); one *s* two *d*. *Educ:* Malvern Coll., Worcs. Served in RAF, 1956–58. Joined Tesco, 1959. Dir, Enterprise Oil, 1984–90. Chm., Food Policy Gp, Retail Consortium, 1980–84; Pres., Inst. of Grocery Distribution, 1989–. Governor and Mem. Council, Malvern Coll. Mem. Cttee, MCC, 1986–. FRSA 1986; FIM 1987. Liveryman, Carmen's Co., 1982–. DUniv Stirling, 1987. *Recreation:* golf. *Address:* Tesco PLC, Tesco House, Delamere Road, Cheshunt, Herts. *Clubs:* Institute of Directors, Royal Automobile; MCC, Lord's Taverners, XL, Band of Brothers.

MACLAY, family name of **Baron Maclay** and **Viscount Muirshiel.**

MACLAY, 3rd Baron *cr* 1922, of Glasgow; **Joseph Paton Maclay,** DL; Bt 1914; Director, Denholm Ship Management (Holdings) Ltd, since 1991; *b* 11 April 1942; *s* of 2nd Baron Maclay, KBE, and of Nancy Margaret, *d* of R. C. Greig, Hall of Caldwell, Uplawmoor, Renfrewshire; *S* father, 1969; *m* 1976, Elizabeth Anne, *o d* of G. M. Buchanan, Delamere, Pokataroo, NSW; two *s* one *d*. *Educ:* Winchester; Sorbonne Univ. Managing Director: Denholm Maclay Co. Ltd, 1970–83; Denholm Maclay (Offshore) Ltd, 1975–83; Triport Ferries (Management) Ltd, 1975–83; Dep. Man. Dir, Denholm Ship Management Ltd, 1982–83; Man. Dir, Milton Timber Services Ltd, 1984–90; Director: Milton Shipping Co. Ltd, 1970–83; Marine Shipping Mutual Insce Co., 1982–83; Pres., Hanover Shipping Inc., 1982–83. Director: British Steamship Short Trades Assoc, 1978–83; N of England Protection and Indemnity Assoc., 1976–83. Chm., Scottish Br., British Sailors Soc., 1979–81; Vice-Chm., Glasgow Shipowners & Shipbrokers Benevolent Assoc., 1982–83. DL Renfrewshire, 1986. *Heir:* *s* Hon. Joseph Paton Maclay, *b* 6 March 1977. *Address:* Duchal, Kilmacolm, Renfrewshire.

McLAY, Hon. James Kenneth, (Jim); Managing Director and Principal, J. K. McLay Ltd (international business consultants), since 1987; *s* of late Robert McLay and of Joyce McLay; *m* 1983, Marcy Farden. *Educ:* St Helier's Sch.; King's Sch.; King's Coll.; Auckland Univ. (LLB 1967); Pennsylvania State Univ. (EMP 1987). Solicitor in practice on own account, 1971; barrister 1974. MP (National Party) for Birkenhead, NZ, 1975–87; Attorney-Gen. and Minister of Justice, 1978–84; Government Spokesperson for Women, 1979–84; Dep. Prime Minister, 1984; Leader, National Party and Leader of the Opposition, 1984–86. Mem., Ministerial Wkg Party on Accident Compensation and Incapacity, 1990–91. *Recreation:* trout fishing. *Address:* PO Box 8885, Symonds Street Post Office, Auckland 1, New Zealand.

MacLEAN, Hon. Lord; Ranald Norman Munro MacLean; a Senator of the College of Justice in Scotland, since 1990; *b* 18 Dec. 1938; *s* of John Alexander MacLean, *qv*; *m* 1963, Pamela Ross; two *s* one *d* (and one *s* decd). *Educ:* Inverness Royal Acad.; Fettes Coll.; Clare Coll., Cambridge Univ. (BA); Edinburgh Univ. (LLB); Yale Univ., USA (LLM). Called to the Scottish Bar, 1964; QC (Scot.) 1977; Advocate Depute, 1972–75, 1979–82, Home Advocate Depute, 1979–82; Standing Jun. Counsel, Health and Safety Exec. (Scotland), 1975–77; Member Council on Tribunals, 1985–90 (Chm., Scottish Cttee, 1985–90); Scottish Legal Aid Bd, 1986–90. Mem., Stewart Cttee on Alternatives to Prosecution, 1977–82. Chm. of Council, Cockburn Assoc., 1988–. Governor, 1977–, Dep. Chm., 1986–, Fettes Coll. *Publication:* (ed jtly) Gloag and Henderson, Introduction to the Law of Scotland, 7th edn 1968, 8th edn 1980. *Recreations:* hill walking, Munro collecting, birdwatching. *Address:* 12 Chalmers Crescent, Edinburgh EH9 1TS. *T:* 031–667 6217. *Clubs:* Scottish Arts, New (Edinburgh).

MACLEAN of Dochgarroch, yr, Very Rev. Allan Murray; Provost of St John's Cathedral, Oban, since 1986; *b* 22 Oct. 1950; *o s* of Rev. Donald Maclean of Dochgarroch and Loraine Maclean of Dochgarroch (*née* Calvert); *m* 1990, Anne, *widow* of David Lindsay; one *s*. *Educ:* Dragon School, Oxford; Trinity College, Glenalmond; Univ. of Edinburgh (MA 1st cl. Hons Scottish History); Cuddesdon Coll. and Pusey House, Oxford. Deacon 1976, Priest 1977; Chaplain of St Mary's Cathedral, Edinburgh, 1976–81; Rector of Holy Trinity, Dunoon, 1981–86; Exam. Chaplain to Bishop of Argyll and the Isles, 1983–. Vice-Pres., Clan Maclean Assoc., 1982–. Editor: Clan Maclean, 1975–85; Argyll and the Isles, 1984–. *Publication:* Telford's Highland Churches, 1989. *Recreations:* topography, history, genealogy, architecture. *Address:* The Rectory, Oban, Argyll PA34 5DJ. *T:* Oban (0631) 62323; 3 Rutland Square, Edinburgh EH1 2AS. *T:* 031–228 6036. *Club:* New (Edinburgh).

McLEAN, Colin, CMG 1977; MBE 1964; HM Diplomatic Service, retired; UK Permanent Representative to the Council of Europe (with the personal rank of Ambassador), 1986–90; *b* 10 Aug. 1930; *s* of late Dr L. G. McLean and H. I. McLean; *m* 1953, Huguette Marie Suzette Leclerc; one *s* one *d*. *Educ:* Fettes; St Catharine's Coll., Cambridge (MA). 2RHA, 1953–54. District Officer, Kenya, 1955–63; Vice-Principal, Kenya Inst. of Administration, 1963–64; HM Diplomatic Service, 1964; served Wellington, Bogotá and FCO, 1964–77; Counsellor, Oslo, 1977–81; Head of Trade Relations and Export Dept, FCO, 1981–83; High Comr in Uganda, 1983–86. *Recreation:* sailing. *Address:* 28 The Heights, Foxgrove Road, Beckenham, Kent BR3 2BY. *T:* 081–650 9565.

MACLEAN, David John; MP (C) Penrith and the Border, since July 1983; Parliamentary Secretary, Ministry of Agriculture, Fisheries and Food, since 1989; *b* 16 May 1953; *s* of John and Catherine Jane Maclean; *m* 1977, Jayalaluna Dawn Gallacher. Asst Govt Whip, 1987–88; a Lord Comr of HM Treasury (Govt Whip), 1988–89. *Address:* House of Commons, SW1A 0AA.

McLEAN, Denis Bazeley Gordon, CMG 1989; Secretary of Defence, New Zealand, 1979–88; *b* Napier, NZ, 18 Aug. 1930; *s* of John Gordon McLean and Renée Maitland Smith; *m* 1958, Anne Davidson, Venado Tuerto, Argentina; two *s* one *d*. *Educ:* Nelson Coll., NZ; Victoria Univ. Coll., NZ (MSc); Rhodes Schol. 1954; University Coll., Oxford (MA). Jun. Lectr in Geology, Victoria UC, 1953–54; joined Dept of External Affairs of NZ Govt, London, 1957; served in: Wellington, 1958–60; Washington, 1960–63; Paris, 1963–66; Kuala Lumpur, 1966–68; Asst Sec. (Policy), MoD, Wellington, 1969–72; RCDS, 1972; Dep. High Comr, London, 1973–77; Dep. Sec. of Defence, NZ, 1977. Visiting Fellow: Strategic and Defence Studies Centre, ANU, Canberra, 1989; Wilson Center, Washington, 1990. *Publication:* The Long Pathway: Te Ara Roa, 1986. *Recreations:* walking, modest mountaineering, geology. *Address:* 11 Dekka Street, Wellington, New Zealand. *Clubs:* Travellers'; Wellington (NZ).

MACLEAN, Sir Donald (Og Grant), Kt 1985; optometrist, practising in Ayr, since 1965; *b* 13 Aug. 1930; *s* of Donald Og Maclean and Margaret Maclean (*née* Smith); *m* 1958, Muriel Giles (*d* 1984); one *s* one *d*. *Educ:* Morrison's Academy, Crieff; Heriot Watt Univ. FBOA; Fellow, British Coll. of Opticians. RAMC, 1952–54. Optical practice: Newcastle upon Tyne, 1954–57; Perth, 1957–65. Chm., Ayr Constituency Cons. Assoc., 1971–75; Scottish Conservative and Unionist Association: Vice-Pres., 1979–83; Pres., 1983–85; Chm., W of Scotland Area, 1977–79; Exec. Mem., Nat. Union, 1979–89; Scottish Conservative Party: Dep. Chm., 1985–89; Vice-Chm., 1989–91. Chm., Ayrshire and Arran Local Optical Cttee, 1986–88. Freeman: Spectacle Makers' Co., 1986 (Liveryman, 1989–); City of London, 1987. *Recreations:* coastal shipping, reading, photography, philately. *Address:* Dun Beag II, 22 Woodend Road, Alloway, Ayr KA7 4QR. *Club:* Royal Scottish Automobile (Glasgow).

MACLEAN, Rear-Adm. Euan, CB 1986; FRINA, FIMechE; Director General Fleet Support Policy and Services, 1983–86; *b* 7 July 1929; *s* of John Fraser Maclean and Dorothy Mary Maclean; *m* 1954, Renée Shaw; two *d*. *Educ:* BRNC Dartmouth; RNEC Keyham/Manadon. FRINA 1980; FIMechE 1980. Joined Exec. Br., RN, 1943; transf. to Engr Br., 1947; sea service in HMS Sirius, Illustrious, Gambia, Ocean, Indefatigable, Defender, Hermes, Eagle and Ark Royal, 1950–72; on loan to Royal Malaysian Navy, 1965–68; Prodn Dept, Portsmouth Dockyard, 1968–71; HMS Ark Royal, 1971–72; Exec. Officer, HMS Sultan, 1973; Dep. Prodn Man., Devonport Dockyard, 1974–77; Fleet Marine Engr Officer, 1977–79; student, RCDS, 1980; Prodn Man., Portsmouth Dockyard, 1981–83. ADC to the Queen, 1982. Comdr 1965, Captain 1974, Rear-Adm. 1983. *Recreation:* rough country.

MACLEAN of Dunconnel, Sir Fitzroy Hew, 1st Bt, *cr* 1957; CBE (mil.) 1944; 15th Hereditary Keeper and Captain of Dunconnel; *b* 11 March 1911; *s* of Major Charles Maclean, DSO; *m* 1946, Hon. Mrs Alan Phipps, 2nd *d* of 16th Baron Lovat, KT; two *s*. *Educ:* Eton; Cambridge. 3rd Sec., Foreign Office, 1933; transferred to Paris, 1934, and to Moscow, 1937; 2nd Sec., 1938; transferred to Foreign Office, 1939; resigned from Diplomatic Service, and enlisted as private in Cameron Highlanders; 2nd Lt Aug. 1941; joined 1st Special Air Service Regt Jan. 1942; Capt. Sept. 1942; Lt-Col 1943; Brig. Comdg British Military Mission to Jugoslav partisans, 1943–45. Lees Knowles Lecturer, Cambridge, 1953. MP (C) Lancaster, 1941–59, Bute and N Ayrshire, 1959–Feb. 1974; Parly Under-Sec. of State for War and Financial Sec. War Office, Oct. 1954–Jan. 1957. Member: UK Delegn to North Atlantic Assembly, 1962–74 (Chm., Mil. Cttee, 1964–74); Council of Europe and WEU, 1972–74. Hon. Col, 23rd SAS Regt, 1984–88. Hon. LLD: Glasgow 1969; Dalhousie 1971; Dundee, 1984; Hon. DLitt Acadia, 1970. French Croix de Guerre, 1943; Order of Kutusov, 1944; Partisan Star (First Class), 1945; Order of Merit, Yugoslavia, 1969; Order of the Yusoslav Star with Ribbon, 1981. *Publications:* Eastern Approaches, 1949; Disputed Barricade, 1957; A Person from England, 1958; Back to Bokhara, 1959; Jugoslavia, 1969; A Concise History of Scotland, 1970; The Battle of Neretva, 1970; To the Back of Beyond, 1974; To Caucasus, 1976; Take Nine Spies, 1978; Holy Russia, 1979; Tito, 1980; The Isles of the Sea, 1985; Portrait of the Soviet Union, 1988; Bonnie Prince Charlie, 1988. *Heir:* *s* Charles Maclean, yr of Dunconnel [*b* 31 Oct. 1946; *m* 1986, Deborah, *d* of Lawrence Young; two *d*]. *Address:* Strachur House, Argyll. *T:* Strachur (036986) 242. *Clubs:* White's, Pratt's; Puffin's, New (Edinburgh).

McLEAN, Sir Francis (Charles), Kt 1967; CBE 1953 (MBE 1945); *b* 6 Nov. 1904; *s* of Michael McLean; *m* 1930, Dorothy Mabel Blackstaffe; one *s* one *d*. *Educ:* University of Birmingham (BSc). Chief Engineer, Psychological Warfare Division, SHAEF, 1943–45. Dep. Chief Engineer, BBC, 1952–60; Dep. Dir of Engineering, BBC, 1960–63; Director, Engineering, BBC, 1963–68. Dir, Oxley Developments Ltd, 1961–. Chairman: BSI Telecommunications Industry Standards Cttee, 1960–77; Royal Commn on FM Broadcasting in Australia, 1974. Pres., Newbury Dist Field Club. FIEE. *Publications:* contrib. Journal of IEE. *Address:* Greenwood Copse, Tile Barn, Woolton Hill, Newbury, Berks. *T:* Newbury (0635) 253583.

McLEAN, Geoffrey Daniel, CBE 1988; QPM 1981; Assistant Commissioner (Territorial Operations), Metropolitan Police, 1984–91; *b* 4 March 1931; *s* of late William James McLean and Matilda Gladys (*née* Davies); *m* 1959, Patricia Edna Pope; two *s* two *d*. Following service in RA, joined Metropolitan Police, 1951; Chief Supt, 1969; Staff Officer to HMCIC, Home Office, 1970–72; Comdr, 1975; Graduate, RCDS, 1978; Dep. Asst Comr, 1979; Dep. Comdt, Police Staff Coll., 1981–83. *Recreations:* Met. Police Athletics Assoc. (Chm., 1984); Met. Police Football Club (Chm., 1984); Met. Police Race-Walking Club (Chm., 1978); riding. *Address:* c/o New Scotland Yard, Broadway, SW1H 0BG. *T:* 071–230 1212.

MacLEAN, Vice-Adm. Sir Hector Charles Donald, KBE 1962; CB 1960; DSC 1941; JP; DL; *b* 7 Aug. 1908; *s* of late Captain D. C. H. Maclean, DSO, The Royal Scots; *m* 1933, Opre, *d* of late Captain Geoffrey Vyvyan, Royal Welch Fusiliers; one *s* two *d*. *Educ:* Wellington. Special Entry into Navy, 1926; Captain 1948; idc 1951; Comd HMS Saintes and 3rd Destroyer Sqdn, 1952–53; Dir of Plans, Admiralty, 1953–56; Comd HMS Eagle, 1956–57; Chief of Staff, Home Fleet, 1958–59; Chief of Allied Staff, Mediterranean, 1959–62; Vice-Adm. 1960; retired 1962. JP Norfolk, 1963; DL Norfolk, 1977. *Address:* Deepdale Old Rectory, Brancaster Staithe, King's Lynn, Norfolk PE31 8DD. *T:* Brancaster (0485) 210281. *Club:* Norfolk (Norwich).

McLEAN, Hector John Finlayson; Archbishops' Appointments Secretary, since 1987; *b* 10 Feb. 1934; *s* of late Dr Murdoch McLean, MB ChB and Dr Edith Muriel Finlayson McLean (*née* McGill), MB ChB, DPH, DOMS; *m* 1959, Caroline Elizabeth Lithgow; one *s* two *d*. *Educ:* Dulwich Coll.; Pembroke Coll., Cambridge (BA Hons 1958); FIPM 1965; Harvard Business Sch., Switzerland (SMP6 1976). 2nd Lieut, KOSB, 1954–55. Imperial Chemical Industries, 1958–87: Central Staff Dept, 1958; various personnel and admin. posts in Dyestuffs and Organics Divs, 1959–72; Personnel Manager, Organics Div., 1972–74; Polyurethanes Business Area Manager, 1974–75; Dir, Agricl Div., 1975–86. Non-exec. Chairman: People & Potential Ltd, 1987–; Teesside Positive People, 1987–. Mem. Exec. Cttee, N of England Develt Council, 1978–83; Teesside Industrial Mission: Mem., Management Cttee, 1978–85; Chm., 1982–85; Dir, Cleveland Enterprise Agency, 1982–87. Mem., Northern Regl Council, CBI, 1981–85; Trustee: NE Civic Trust, 1976–88; Northern Heritage Trust, 1984–87. Mem., Chemical and Allied Products ITB, 1979–82. Gov. Teesside Polytechnic, 1978–84; Mem. Council, Newcastle Univ., 1985–87. *Recreations:* music (especially choral music), travel, gardening, walking. *Address:* College Farm House, Purton, near Swindon, Wilts SN5 9AE. *T:* Swindon (0793) 770525. *Club:* United Oxford & Cambridge University.

MACLEAN, Hector Ronald; Sheriff of Lothian and Borders, at Linlithgow, since 1988; *b* 6 Dec. 1931; *s* of Donald Beaton Maclean and Lucy McAlister; *m* 1967, Hilary Elizabeth Jenkins; three *d*. *Educ:* High Sch. of Glasgow; Glasgow Univ. Admitted to Faculty of Advocates, 1959. Sheriff of N Strathclyde (formerly Renfrew and Argyll), 1968–88. *Recreation:* golf. *Address:* Barrfield, Houston, Renfrewshire. *T:* Bridge of Weir (0505) 612449.

McLEAN, Ian Graeme; His Honour Judge McLean; a Circuit Judge since 1980; *b* Edinburgh, 7 Sept. 1928; *s* of Lt-Gen. Sir Kenneth McLean, KCB, KBE; *m* 1957, Eleonore Maria Gmeiner, Bregenz, Austria; two *d. Educ:* Aldenham Sch.; Christ's Coll., Cambridge. BA Hons Law 1950; MA 1955. Intell. Corps, 1946–48. Called to English Bar, Middle Temple, Nov. 1951; admitted Faculty of Advocates, Edinburgh, 1985; practised London and on Western Circuit, 1951–55; Crown Counsel, Northern Nigeria, 1955–59; Sen. Lectr and Head of Legal Dept of Inst. of Administration, Northern Nigeria, 1959–62; Native Courts Adviser, 1959–62; returned to English Bar, 1962; practised London and South Eastern Circuit, 1962–70; occasional Dep. Chm., Inner, NE, SW and Mddx Areas, London QS, 1968–70; occasional Dep. Recorder, Oxford, 1969–70; Adjudicator under Immigration Acts, 1969–70; Metropolitan Stipendiary Magistrate, 1970–80. *Publications:* Cumulative Index West African Court of Appeal Reports, 1958; (with Abubakar Sadiq) The Maliki Law of Homicide, 1959; (with Sir Lionel Brett) Criminal Law Procedure and Evidence of Lagos, Eastern and Western Nigeria, 1963; (with Cyprian Okonkwo) Cases on the Criminal Law, Procedure and Evidence of Nigeria, 1966; (with Peter Morrish) A Practical Guide to Appeals in Criminal Courts, 1970; (with Peter Morrish) The Crown Court, an index of common penalties, etc, 1972–90; (ed, with Peter Morrish) Harris's Criminal Law, 22nd edn, 1972; (with Peter Morrish) The Magistrates' Court, an index of common penalties, annually 1973–90; (with Peter Morrish) The Trial of Breathalyser Offences, 1975, 3rd edn 1990; A Practical Guide to Criminal Appeals, 1980; A Pattern of Sentencing, 1981; (with John Mulhern) The Industrial Tribunal: a practical guide to employment law and tribunal procedure, 1982; (with Sheriff Stone) Fact-Finding for Magistrates, 1990; contrib. Archbold's Criminal Pleadings, 38th edn, and Halsbury's Laws of England, 4th edn, title Criminal Law. *Recreations:* family, gardening, writing, languages.

MacLEAN, Dr John Alexander, CBE 1968; Chairman, Northern Regional Hospital Board (Scotland), 1971–74; *b* 12 Oct. 1903; *s* of Donald MacLean, Achiltibuie, Ross-shire; *m* 1935, Hilda M. L. Munro, BSc, Aberdeen; one *s* one *d. Educ:* Dingwall Academy; Aberdeen Univ. MA, LLB, PhD; FEIS. Aberdeen Educn Authority: Teacher, 1926–39; Asst Dir of Educn, 1939–43; Dir of Educn, Inverness-shire Educn Authority, 1943–68, retd. Member: Exec. Cttee, National Trust for Scotland, 1967–82; Scottish Council, Royal Over-Seas League, 1969–81; Scottish Arts Council, 1964–68; Sec. of State's Council for Care of Children; Council on School Broadcasting. *Publication:* Sources for History of the Highlands in the Seventeenth Century, 1939. *Recreation:* sport. *Address:* 12 Eriskay Road, Inverness IV2 3LX. *T:* Inverness (0463) 231566. *Club:* Royal Over-Seas House (Edinburgh).

See also Hon. Lord MacLean.

McLEAN, John Alexander Lowry, QC 1974; Principal Secretary to Lord Chief Justice (formerly Permanent Secretary, Supreme Court of Northern Ireland) and Clerk of the Crown for Northern Ireland, since 1966; *b* 21 Feb. 1921; *o s* of John McLean and Phoebe Jane (*née* Bowditch); *m* 1950, Diana Elisabeth Campbell (*d* 1986), *e d* of S. B. Boyd Campbell, MC, MD, FRCP, and Mary Isabella Ayre, St John's, Newfoundland; one *s* two *d. Educ:* Methodist Coll., Belfast; Queen's University Belfast. Served Intell. Corps, 1943–47. Called to Bar of Northern Ireland, 1949. Asst Sec., NI Supreme Court, and Private Sec. to Lord Chief Justice of NI 1956; Under Treas., Hon. Soc. of Inn of Court of NI, 1966; Clerk of Restrictive Practices Court in NI, 1957. Member: Jt Working Party on Enforcement of Judgments of NI Courts, 1963; Lord Chancellor's Cttee on NI Supreme Court, 1966; Lord Chancellor's Foreign Judgments Working Party, 1974. *Publications:* contrib. legal periodicals. *Recreations:* not golf. *Address:* 24 Marlborough Park South, Belfast BT9 6HR. *T:* Belfast (0232) 667330; Lifeboat Cottage, Cloughey, Co. Down BT22 1HS. *T:* Portavogie (02477) 71313. *Club:* Commonwealth Trust.

MacLEAN, Hon. (John) Angus, PC 1957; DFC, CD; Premier of Prince Edward Island, 1979–81; *b* 15 May 1914; *s* of late George A. MacLean; *m* 1952, Gwendolyn Esther M. Burwash; two *s* two *d. Educ:* Mount Allison Academy; Summerside High Sch.; Univ. of British Columbia; Mount Allison Univ. BSc. Served War of 1939–45, RCAF: commanded Test and Development Estabt, 1943–45; Missing and Enquiry Unit, Europe, 1945–47, Wing Comdr (despatches). First elected to House of Commons by by-election, June 1951, re-elected 1953, 1957, 1958, 1962, 1963, 1965, 1968, 1972, 1974; Minister of Fisheries in the Diefenbaker Cabinet, 1957–63; elected Leader of PC Party of PEI, 1976; first elected to PEI Legislature at by-election, 1976, re-elected 1978 and 1979. PEI's Comr to EXPO '86. Member: PEI Energy Commn, 1984–87; Sen. Adv. Bd, Maritime Provinces Educn Foundn, 1983–86; Nat. Mus. of Natural Scis, Nat. Museums of Canada, 1985–88. Mem. Royal Air Forces Escaping Soc. (Canadian Br.). Hon. LLD: Mount Allison Univ., 1958; Univ. of PEI, 1985. OStJ 1982. *Recreations:* genealogical research, bird watching. *Address:* Lewes, RR3, Belle River, Prince Edward Island COA 1B0, Canada. *T:* Murray River, PEI (902) 962–2235. *Clubs:* United Services, Charlottetown, RCAF Association, Masonic Lodge, AF and AM, Royal Canadian Legion, Charlottetown Chamber of Commerce, Canadian (PEI).

McLEAN, (John David) Ruari (McDowall Hardie), CBE 1973; DSC 1943; freelance typographer and author; *b* 10 June 1917; *s* of late John Thomson McLean and late Isabel Mary McLean (*née* Ireland); *m* 1945, Antonia Maxwell Carlisle; two *s* one *d. Educ:* Dragon Sch., Oxford; Eastbourne Coll. First studied printing under B. H. Newdigate at Shakespeare Head Press, Oxford, 1936. Industrial printing experience in Germany and England, 1936–38; with The Studio, 1938; Percy Lund Humphries, Bradford, 1939. Served Royal Navy, 1940–45. Penguin Books, 1945–46; Book Designer (freelance), 1946–53; Tutor in Typography, Royal College of Art, 1948–51; Typographic Adviser to Hulton Press, 1953; Founder Partner, Rainbird, McLean Ltd, 1951–58; Founder Editor, and Designer, Motif, 1958–67. Typographic Consultant to The Observer, 1960–64; Hon. Typographic Adviser to HM Stationery Office, 1966–80. Sandars Reader in Bibliography, Univ. of Cambridge, 1982–83; Alexander Stone Lectr in Bibliophily, Univ. of Glasgow, 1984. Member: Nat. Council for Diplomas in Art and Design, 1971; Vis. Cttee of RCA, 1977–83. Crown Trustee, Nat. Library of Scotland, 1981–. Croix de Guerre (French), 1942. *Publications:* George Cruikshank, 1948; Modern Book Design, 1958; Wood Engravings of Joan Hassall, 1960; Victorian Book Design, 1963, rev. edn 1972; Tschichold's Typographische Gestaltung (Trans.), 1967; (ed) The Reminiscences of Edmund Evans, 1967; Magazine Design, 1969; Victorian Publishers' Book-bindings in Cloth and Leather, 1973; Jan Tschichold, Typographer, 1975; Joseph Cundall, 1976; (ed) Edward Bawden: A Book of Cuts, 1979; Thames and Hudson Manual of Typography, 1980; Victorian Publishers' Book-Bindings in Paper, 1983; Benjamin Fawcett, Engraver and Colour Printer, 1988; (ed) Edward Bawden, War Artist, 1989; Nicolas Bentley drew the Pictures, 1990. *Recreations:* sailing, reading, acquiring books. *Address:* Pier Cottage, Carsaig, Pennyghael, Isle of Mull. *Clubs:* Double Crown; New (Edinburgh).

MacLEAN, Kenneth Smedley, MD, FRCP; Consultant Physician to Guy's Hospital, 1950–79, now Emeritus; *b* 22 Nov. 1914; *s* of Hugh MacLean and Ida Smedley; *m* 1939, Joan Hardaker; one *s* one *d* (and one *s* decd). *Educ:* Westminster; Clare Coll., Cambridge. MRCS, LRCP, 1939; House appts at Guy's, 1939; MB, BChir 1939. RNVR, 1939–46, Surg.-Lt and Surg.-Lt-Comdr. MRCP 1946; House Officer and Medical Registrar, Guy's Hosp., 1946–48; MD Cantab 1948; FRCP 1954; elected to Assoc. of Physicians of Great Britain and Ireland, 1956. Assistant Director, Dept of Medicine, Guy's Hospital Medical Sch., 1949, Director, 1961–63. Chm., University Hosps Assoc., 1975–78. Pres., Assurance Medical Soc., 1985–87. *Publication:* Medical Treatment, 1957. *Recreation:* golf. *Address:* 7 Icehouse Wood, Oxted, Surrey. *T:* Oxted (0883) 716652.

MACLEAN, Hon. Sir Lachlan Hector Charles, 12th Bt *cr* 1631 (NS), of Duart and Morvern; Major, Scots Guards, retired; 28th Chief of Clan Maclean; *b* 25 Aug. 1942; *s* of Baron Maclean, KT, GCVO, KBE, PC and of Elizabeth, *er d* of late Frank Mann; *S* to baronetcy of father, 1990; *m* 1966, Mary Helen, *e d* of W. G. Gordon; two *s* two *d* (and one *d* decd). *Educ:* Eton. *Heir: s* Malcolm Lachlan Charles Maclean, *b* 20 Oct. 1972. *Address:* Arngask House, Glenfarg, Perthshire PH2 9QA.

MacLEAN, Murdo; Private Secretary to the Government Chief Whip, since 1979; *b* 21 Oct. 1943; *s* of Murdo MacLean and Johanna (*née* Martin). *Educ:* Glasgow. Temp. Clerk, Min. of Labour Employment Exchange, Govan, Glasgow, 1963–64; BoT, 1964–67; Prime Minister's Office, 1967–72; Dept of Industry, 1972–78. FRSA 1990. *Address:* c/o 12 Downing Street, SW1. *T:* 071–219 3595/4400. *Club:* Garrick.

McLEAN, Peter Standley, CMG 1985; OBE 1965; Head of East Asia Department, Overseas Development Administration, 1985–87; *b* 18 Jan. 1927; *s* of late William and Alice McLean; *m* 1954, Margaret Ann Minns; two *s* two *d. Educ:* King Edward's Sch., Birmingham; Wadham Coll., Oxford (MA). Served Army, 1944–48; Lieut, 15/19th King's Royal Hussars. Colonial Service, Uganda, 1951–65, retired from HMOCS as Permanent Sec., Min. of Planning and Economic Develt; Ministry of Overseas Development: Principal, 1965; Private Sec. to Minister for Overseas Develt, 1973; Head of Eastern and Southern Africa Dept, 1975; Head of Bilateral Aid and Rural Develt Dept, 1979; Minister and UK Perm. Rep to FAO, 1980. *Recreations:* watching sport, DIY, painting. *Address:* 17 Woodfield Lane, Ashtead, Surrey KT21 2BQ. *T:* Ashtead (0372) 278146.

McLEAN, Philip Alexander; HM Diplomatic Service; HM Consul-General, Boston, since 1988; *b* 24 Oct. 1938; *s* of late Wm Alexander McLean and Doris McLean (*née* Campbell); *m* 1960, Dorothy Helen Kirkby; two *s* one *d. Educ:* King George V Sch., Southport; Keble Coll., Oxford (MA Hons). National Service, RAF, 1956–58. Industry, 1961–68; entered HM Diplomatic Service by Open Supplementary Competition, 1968; Second, later (1969) First, Secretary, FCO; La Paz, 1970–74: Head of Chancery, 1973; FCO, 1974–76; Dep. Director of British Trade Development Office and Head of Industrial Marketing, New York, 1976–80; Counsellor and Consul-Gen., Algiers, 1981–83; Diplomatic Service Inspector, 1983–85; Hd, S America Dept, FCO, 1985–87. *Recreation:* free time. *Address:* c/o Foreign and Commonwealth Office, SW1A 2AH. *Club:* United Oxford & Cambridge University.

MacLEAN, Ranald Norman Munro; *see* MacLean, Hon. Lord.

MACLEAN, Sir Robert (Alexander), KBE 1973; Kt 1955; DL; Honorary President, Stoddard Holdings Ltd; *b* 11 April 1908; *s* of Andrew Johnston Maclean, JP, Cambuslang, Lanarkshire, and Mary Jane Cameron; *m* 1938, Vivienne Neville Bourke, *d* of Captain Bertram Walter Bourke, JP, Heathfield, Co. Mayo; two *s* two *d. Educ:* High Sch. of Glasgow. JDipMA. President: Glasgow Chamber of Commerce, 1956–58; Association British Chambers of Commerce, 1966–68; Chairman: Council of Scottish Chambers of Commerce, 1960–62; Scottish Cttee, Council of Industrial Design, 1949–58 (Mem., CoID, 1948–58); Council of Management, Scottish Industries Exhibns, 1949, 1954 and 1959; Scottish Exports Cttee, 1966–70; Scottish Industrial Estates Corp., 1955–72 (Mem., 1946–72); Pres., British Industrial Exhibn, Moscow, 1966; Vice-Chm., Scottish Bd for Industry, 1952–60; Member: Pigs and Bacon Marketing Commn, 1955–56; BNEC, 1966–70; Scottish Aerodromes Bd, 1950–61; Export Council for Europe, 1960–64; BoT Trade Exhbns Adv. Cttee, 1961–65; Nat. Freight Corp., 1969–72; Regional Controller (Scotland): Board of Trade, 1944–46; Factory and Storage Premises, 1941–44. Director: Scottish Union & Nat. Insce Co., 1965–68; Scottish Adv. Bd, Norwich Union Insce Gp., 1965–81. Former Vice-Pres., Scottish Council (Develt and Industry), 1955–82. Trustee, Clyde Navigational Trust, 1956–58; Pres., Scottish Youth Clubs, 1959–68. DL Renfrewshire, 1970. CStJ 1975. FRSA; CBIM. Hon. LLD Glasgow, 1970. *Recreations:* golf, fishing. *Address:* South Branchal Farm, Bridge of Weir, Renfrewshire PA11 3SJ. *Clubs:* Carlton; Western (Glasgow).

McLEAN, Ruari; *see* McLean, J. D. R. McD. H.

McLEAN, Dr Thomas Pearson, CB 1990; FRSE; CPhys, FInstP; CEng, FIEE; Director, Atomic Weapons Establishment, Ministry of Defence, 1987–90; *b* Paisley, 21 Aug. 1930; *s* of Norman Stewart McLean and Margaret Pearson McLean (*née* Ferguson); *m* 1957, Grace Campbell Nokes; two *d. Educ:* John Neilson Instn, Paisley; Glasgow Univ. (BSc, PhD); Birmingham Univ. Royal Radar Estabt (becoming Royal Signals and Radar Estabt, 1976), 1955–80: Head of Physics Gp, 1973–77; Dep. Dir, 1977–80; Under Sec., Dir Gen. Air Weapons and Electronic Systems, MoD, 1980–83; Dir, RARDE, MoD, 1984–86; Dep. Controller, Aircraft, MoD, 1987. Member: Physics Cttee, SRC, 1968–73; Optoelectronics Cttee, Rank Prize Funds, 1972–81; Council, Inst. of Physics, 1980–84. Hon. Prof. of Physics, Birmingham Univ., 1977–80. Dep. Editor, Jl of Physics C, 1976–77. *Publications:* papers in Physical Rev., Jl of Physics, etc. *Recreations:* music, Scottish country dancing.

MacLEARY, Alistair Ronald; Member, Lands Tribunal for Scotland, since 1989; *b* 12 Jan. 1940; *s* of Donald Herbert MacLeary and Jean Spiers (*née* Leslie); *m* 1967, Mary-Claire Cecilia (*née* Leonard); one *s* one *d. Educ:* Inverness Royal Acad.; Coll. of Estate Management, London; Edinburgh Coll. of Art, Heriot-Watt Univ.; Strathclyde Univ. MSc, DipTP; FRICS, FRTPI. Gerald Eve & Co., 1963–65; Murrayfield Real Estate Co., 1965–67; Dept of Environment (on secondment), 1971–73; Wright, Partners, 1967–76; MacRobert Prof. of Land Economy, 1976–89, Dean, Faculty of Law, 1982–85, Aberdeen Univ. Univ. of Auckland Foundn Visitor and Fletcher Challenge Vis. Fellow, 1985; Memorialist, MacAuley Inst. for Soil Science, 1986–87. Mem., Cttee of Inquiry into Acquisition and Occupancy of Agricl Land, 1977–79; Chm., Watt Cttee, Energy Working Gp on Land Resources, 1977–79; Mem., Exec. Cttee, Commonwealth Assoc. of Surveying and Land Economy, 1980–85; Chm., Bd of Surveying Educn of CASLE, 1981–90; Member: Home Grown Timber Adv. Cttee, Forestry Commn, 1981–87; NERC, 1988–91 (Chm., Terrestrial and Freshwater Sci. Cttee, 1990–91). Mem., Gen. Council, RICS, 1983–87 (Pres., Planning and Develt Divl Council, 1984–85). FRSA, MBIM. Founder and Editor, Land Development Studies, 1983–90. *Publications:* (ed with N. Nanthakumeran) Property Investment Theory, 1988; National Taxation for Property Management and Valuation, 1990. *Recreations:* golf, hill walking, field sports, ski-ing. *Address:* St Helen's, Ceres, Fife KY15 5NQ. *T:* Ceres (033482) 8862. *Clubs:* Royal Northern and University (Aberdeen); Royal Aberdeen Golf.

See also D. W. MacLeary.

MacLEARY, Donald Whyte; principal male dancer with the Royal Ballet since 1959; Repetiteur to the Principal Artists, Royal Ballet, since 1981; *b* Glasgow, 22 Aug. 1937; *s* of Donald Herbert MacLeary, MPS, and Jean Spiers (*née* Leslie). *Educ:* Inverness Royal

Academy; The Royal Ballet School. Ballet Master, Royal Ballet, 1975–81. *Classical Ballets:* (full length) Swan Lake, Giselle, 1958; Sleeping Beauty, Cinderella, Sylvia, 1959; Ondine, La Fille Mal Gardée, 1960; (centre male rôle) in Ashton's Symphonic Variations, 1962; Sonnet Pas de Trois, 1964; Romeo and Juliet, 1965; Eugene Onegin, Stuttgart, 1966; Apollo, 1966; Nutcracker, 1968; Swan Lake with N. Makarova, 1972. *Creations:* (1954–74): Solitaire, The Burrow, Danse Concertante, Antigone, Diversions, Le Baiser de la Fée, Jabez and the Devil, Raymonda Pas de Deux (for Frederick Ashton), two episodes in Images of Love; Song of the Earth; Lilac Garden (revival); Jazz Calendar; Raymonda (for Nureyeff); The Man in Kenneth MacMillan's Checkpoint; leading role in Concerto no 2 (Balanchine's Ballet Imperial, renamed); Elite Syncopations, 1974; Kenneth MacMillan's Four Seasons Symphony; the Prince in Cinderella. Toured Brazil with Royal Ballet, Spring 1973. Guest dancer, Scottish Ballet, 1979. *Recreations:* reading, theatre, records (all types); riding, fox hunting, swimming. *Address:* Bunyans Cottage, Wainwood, Preston, Herts; Casa Svetlana, Quinta do Lazo, Algarve, Portugal. *Club:* Queen's.
    See also A. R. MacLeary.

MACLEAY, Very Rev. John Henry James; Dean of Argyll and The Isles, since 1987; Rector of St Andrew's, Fort William, since 1978; *b* 7 Dec. 1931; *s* of James and Isabella Macleay; *m* 1970, Jane Speirs Cuthbert; one *s* one *d*. *Educ:* St Edmund Hall, Oxford (MA); College of the Resurrection, Mirfield. Deacon 1957, priest 1958, Southwark; Curate: St John's, East Dulwich, 1957–60; St Michael's, Inverness, 1960–62, Rector 1962–70; Priest-in-charge, St Columba's, Grantown-on-Spey with St John the Baptist's, Rothiemurchus, 1970–78; Canon of St Andrew's Cathedral, Inverness, 1977–78; Canon of St John's Cathedral, Oban and Synod Clerk, Diocese of Argyll and the Isles, 1980–87. *Recreations:* fishing, reading, visiting cathedrals and churches. *Address:* St Andrew's Rectory, Parade Road, Fort William PH33 6BA. *T:* Fort William (0397) 702979.

MACLEHOSE, family name of **Baron MacLehose of Beoch.**

MACLEHOSE OF BEOCH, Baron *cr* 1982 (Life Peer), of Maybole in the District of Kyle and Carrick, and of Victoria in Hong Kong; **Crawford Murray MacLehose,** KT 1983; GBE 1976 (MBE 1946); KCMG 1971 (CMG 1964); KCVO 1975; DL; HM Diplomatic Service, retired; *b* 16 Oct. 1917; *s* of Hamish A. MacLehose and Margaret Bruce Black; *m* 1947, Margaret Noël Dunlop; two *d*. *Educ:* Rugby; Balliol Coll., Oxford. Served War of 1939–45, Lieut, RNVR. Joined Colonial Service, Malaya, 1939; joined Foreign Service, 1947; Acting Consul, 1947, Acting Consul-General, 1948, Hankow; promoted First Secretary, 1949; transferred to Foreign Office, 1950; First Secretary (Commercial), and Consul, Prague, 1951; seconded to Commonwealth Relations Office, for service at Wellington, 1954; returned to Foreign Office and transferred to Paris, 1956; promoted Counsellor, 1959; seconded to Colonial Office and transferred to Hong Kong as Political Adviser; Counsellor, Foreign Office, 1963; Principal Private Secretary to Secretary of State, 1965–67; Ambassador: to Vietnam, 1967–69; to Denmark, 1969–71; Governor and C-in-C, Hong Kong, 1971–82. Dir, Nat. Westminster Bank, 1982–88. Chairman: Scottish Trust for the Physically Disabled, 1982–90; Margaret Blackwood Housing Assoc., 1982–90. Chm. Govs, SOAS, Univ. of London, 1985–90. DL Ayr and Arran, 1983. Hon. LLD: York, 1983; Strathclyde, 1984. KStJ 1972. *Recreations:* sailing, fishing. *Address:* Beoch, Maybole, Ayrshire KA19 8EN. *Clubs:* Athenæum; New (Edinburgh).

McLEISH, Henry Baird; MP (Lab) Central Fife, since 1987; *b* 15 June 1948; *s* of Harry McLeish and late Mary McLeish; *m* 1968, Margaret Thomson Drysdale; one *s* one *d*. *Educ:* Heriot-Watt Univ. (BA Hons planning). Research Officer, Social Work Dept, Edinburgh, 1973–74; part time Lectr/Tutor, Heriot-Watt Univ., 1973–87. Planning Officer, Fife County Council, 1974–75; Planning Officer, Dunfermline DC, 1975–87. Part-time employment consultant, 1984–87. Member: Kirkcaldy DC (Chm., Planning Cttee, 1974–77); Fife Regl Council (Chm., Further Educn Cttee, 1978–82; Leader, Council, 1982–87). *Recreations:* reading, malt whisky (history and development of), history, life and works of Robert Burns, Highlands and Islands of Scotland. *Address:* 27 Braid Drive, Glenrothes, Fife KY7 4ES. *T:* Glenrothes (0592) 755330. *Clubs:* Denbeath Miners' Welfare; Glenrothes Football Recreation.

MacLELLAN, Maj.-Gen. (Andrew) Patrick (Withy), CB 1981; CVO 1989; MBE 1964; Resident Governor and Keeper of the Jewel House, HM Tower of London, 1984–89; *b* 29 Nov. 1925; *y s* of late Kenneth MacLellan and Rachel Madeline MacLellan (*née* Withy); *m* 1954, Kathleen Mary Bagnell; one *s* twin *d*. *Educ:* Uppingham. Commnd Coldstream Guards, 1944; served Palestine 1945–48, N Africa 1950–51, Egypt 1952–53, Germany 1955–56; psc 1957; DAA&QMG 4th Guards Brigade Group, 1958–59; Mil. Asst to Chief of Defence Staff, 1961–64; Instructor, Staff Coll., Camberley, 1964–66; GSO1 (Plans) Far East Comd, 1966–67; CO 1st Bn Coldstream Guards, 1968–70; Col GS Near East Land Forces, 1970–71; Comdr 8th Inf. Brigade, 1971–72; RCDS 1973; Dep. Comdr and COS, London District, 1974–77; Pres., Regular Commns Bd, 1978–80. Mem., Exec. and Finance Cttee, Officers' Assoc. Mem. Cttee, Royal Humane Soc.; Adv. Council, Women's Transport Corps (FANY). Mem. (Walbrook Ward), Court of Common Council, City of London, 1989–. Freeman: City of London, 1984; Co. of Watermen and Lightermen; Liveryman, Fletchers' Co., 1986–. Chevalier de la Légion d'Honneur, 1960. *Address:* c/o Bank of Scotland, London Chief Office, 38 Threadneedle Street, EC2P 2EH. *Clubs:* White's, Pratt's, City Livery.

McLELLAN, Prof. David; DPhil; Professor of Political Theory, University of Kent, since 1975; *b* 10 Feb. 1940; *s* of Robert Douglas McLellan and Olive May Bush; *m* 1967, Annie Brassart; two *d*. *Educ:* Merchant Taylors' Sch.; St John's Coll., Oxford (MA, DPhil). Lectr in Politics, Univ. of Kent, 1966–71; Vis. Prof., State Univ. of New York, 1969; Guest Fellow in Politics, Indian Inst. of Advanced Studies, Simla, 1970; Sen. Lectr in Politics, Univ. of Kent, 1972, Reader in Political Theory, 1973. *Publications:* The Young Hegelians and Karl Marx, 1969 (French, German, Italian, Spanish and Japanese edns); Marx before Marxism, 1970, 2nd edn 1972; Karl Marx: The Early Texts, 1971; Marx's Grundrisse, 1971, 2nd edn 1973; The Thought of Karl Marx, 1971 (Portuguese and Italian edns); Karl Marx: His Life and Thought, 1973, 22nd edn 1976 (German, Italian, Spanish, Japanese, Swedish and Dutch edns); Marx (Fontana Modern Masters), 1975; Engels, 1977; Marxism after Marx, 1979; (ed) Marx: the first hundred years, 1983; Karl Marx: the legacy, 1983; Ideology, 1986; Marxism and Religion, 1987; Simone Weil: Utopian pessimist, 1989; Christianity and Politics, 1990. *Recreations:* chess, Raymond Chandler, hill walking. *Address:* Eliot College, University of Kent, Canterbury, Kent CT2 7NS. *T:* Canterbury (0227) 764000.

McLELLAN, His Honour Eric Burns; a Circuit Judge (formerly County Court Judge), 1970–86; *b* 9 April 1918; *s* of late Stanley Morgan McLellan, Christchurch, Newport, Mon; *m* 1949, Elsa Sarah, *d* of late Gustave Mustaki, Alexandria; one *s* one *d*. *Educ:* Newport High Sch.; New Coll., Oxford. BA 1939; MA 1967. Served RAF, 1940–46, N Africa, Italy, Egypt, 205 Group; Flt-Lt. Called to Bar, Inner Temple, 1947. Dep. Chm., IoW QS, 1967–72. Official Principal, Archdeaconry of Hackney, 1967–72; Dep. Chm., Workmen's Compensation Supplementation Bd and Pneumoconiosis, Byssinosis and Miscellaneous Diseases Benefit Bd, 1969–70; Mem., Dept of Health and Social Security

Adv. Group on Use of Fetuses and Fetal Material for Research, 1970. Governor, Portsmouth Grammar Sch., 1980–87. *Publications:* (contrib.) The History of the Royal Air Force; contribs to medico-legal jls. *Recreations:* heraldry and genealogy. *Address:* Spinning Field, Hambledon, near Portsmouth, Hants PO7 6RU. *Clubs:* United Oxford & Cambridge University, Royal Air Force; Leander (Henley-on-Thames).

MacLELLAN, Prof. George Douglas Stephen, MA, PhD (Cantab); CEng; FIMechE, FIEE; Professor and Head of Department of Engineering, University of Leicester, 1965–88, now Emeritus Professor; *b* Glasgow, 1 Nov. 1922; *e s* of late Alexander Stephen MacLellan. *Educ:* Rugby Sch.; Pembroke Coll., Cambridge. Mech. Sci. Tripos, 1942. Dept of Colloid Science, Cambridge, and Callenders Cable and Construction Co. Ltd, 1942–44; Fellow, Pembroke Coll., 1944–59; Vickers-Armstrong Ltd, Newcastle upon Tyne, 1944–46; University Demonstrator and Lecturer in Engineering, Cambridge, 1947–59; Rankine Professor of Mechanical Engineering (Mechanics and Mechanism), University of Glasgow, 1959–65. Commonwealth Fund Fellow, MIT, 1948–49; Visiting Professor: Michigan State University, 1958; MIT, 1962; Nanyang Technological Inst., Singapore, 1986, 1989–90, 1990–91; Nat. Univ. of Singapore, 1988–89. Pres. of the Soc. of Instrument Technology, 1964–65. Member: CNAA, 1970–80; Engrg Bd, SRC, 1971–74; Vis. Cttee, RCA, 1973–82; Council, IMechE, 1974–76; Nominations Cttee, Engrg Council, 1984–; Council, Loughborough Univ. of Technology, 1979–; Chm., Engrg Professors' Conference, 1983–85. *Publications:* contribs to mech. and elec. jls. *Address:* 6 Southmeads Close, Leicester LE2 2LT. *T:* Leicester (0533) 715406. *Clubs:* Athenæum, Leander.

MacLELLAN, Maj.-Gen. Patrick; *see* MacLellan, A. P. W.

McLELLAND, Charles James; Director General, Association of British Travel Agents, 1987; *b* 19 Nov. 1930; *s* of Charles John McLelland and Jessie Steele Barbour; *m* 1961, Philippa Mary Murphy; one *s* three *d*. *Educ:* Kilmarnock Acad.; Glasgow Acad.; Glasgow Univ. (MA). Commissioned Royal Artillery, 1952–54. Sub-Editor, Leader Writer, Glasgow Herald, 1954–58; Scriptwriter, European Productions, BBC, 1958–61; Head of Programmes, Radio Sarawak, 1962–64; Indian Programme Organiser, BBC, 1964–67; Asst Head, Arabic Service, BBC, 1967–71; Head of Arabic Service, 1971–75; Controller, BBC Radio 2, 1976–80 (also Radio 1, 1976–78); Dep. Man. Dir and Dir of Progs, BBC Radio, 1980–86. Chm., EBU Radio Prog. Cttee, 1985–86; Pres., Overseas Broadcasters' Club, 1985–89, Hon. Vice-Pres., 1990–. Mem. Council, Officers' Assoc., 1989–. *Recreations:* gardening, reading, flying. *Address:* 79 Gayville Road, SW11 6JW. *Club:* Travellers'.

MacLENNAN, Maj.-Gen. Alastair, OBE 1945; Curator, Royal Army Medical Corps Historical Museum, Mytchett, Hants, 1969–Feb. 1977; *b* 16 Feb. 1912; *s* of Col. Farquhar MacLennan, DSO; *m* 1940, Constance Anne Cook; two *s* one *d*. *Educ:* Aberdeen Grammar Sch.; University of Aberdeen (MB, ChB). Commissioned Lieut, RAMC, 1934; Captain, 1935; Major, 1942; Lieut-Colonel, 1942; Colonel, 1952; Brigadier, 1964; Maj.-General, 1967; retired 1969. Appointments held include regimental, staff and Ministry of Defence in UK, Malta, NW Europe, India, Malaya, Korea, Egypt and Germany; ADGMS (Army), Min. of Defence, 1957–61; DDMS, HQ, BAOR, 1961–64; Inspector Army Medical Services, 1964–66; DDMS: 1 (Br) Corps, 1966–67; HQ Eastern Command, 1967–68; Dep. Dir-Gen., Army Med. Services, MoD, 1968–69; Col Comdt, RAMC, 1971–76. US Bronze Star Medal, 1952. OStJ, 1966. QHP, 1968–69. *Publications:* papers on history of military firearms and on Highland Regts in North America 1756–1783. *Recreations:* bird-watching, military history, collecting antique military firearms and swords, vintage motor-cars. *Address:* Gable House, Chequers Lane, North Crawley, Bucks MK16 9LJ. *T:* North Crawley (023065) 700.

MacLENNAN, David Ross; HM Diplomatic Service; Consul General, Jerusalem, since 1990; *b* 12 Feb. 1945; *s* of David Ross MacLennan and Agnes McConnell; *m* 1964, Margaret Lytollis; two *d*. *Educ:* West Calder High Sch. FO, 1963; ME Centre for Arab Studies, 1966–69; Third, later Second Sec., Aden, 1969–71; Second, later First Sec., FCO, 1972–75; First Sec., UK Delegn to OECD, Paris, 1975–79; First Sec., Hd of Chancery, Abu Dhabi, 1979–82; Asst Hd, N America Dept, FCO, 1982–84; EEC, Brussels, 1984–85; Counsellor, Kuwait, 1985–88; Dep. High Comr, Nicosia, 1989–90. *Recreations:* archaeology, natural history. *Address:* c/o Foreign and Commonwealth Office, SW1.

MACLENNAN, Prof. Duncan; Director, Centre for Housing Research and Professor of Land Economics and Finance, University of Glasgow, since 1990; Member of Board, Scottish Homes, since 1989; *b* 12 March 1949; *s* of James Dempster Maclennan and Mary Mackechnie (*née* Campbell); *m* (separated); one *s* one *d*. *Educ:* Allan Glen's Sch., Glasgow; Univ. of Glasgow (MA, MPhil). Aberdeen University: Lectr in Pol Econ., 1976–79; Lectr in Applied Econs, 1979–81; Sen. Lectr, 1981–84; Titular Prof., 1984–88; Prof. of Urban Studies, 1988–90. Susman Prof. of Real Estate Finance, Wharton Bus. Sch., 1988. Chairman: Care and Repair (Scotland), 1987–; Shelter (Scotland) Adv. Council, 1989–; Dir, Joseph Rowntree Res. Programme, 1988–. *Publications:* Regional Policy in Britain, 1979; Housing Economics, 1982; Paying for Britain's Housing, 1990; The Housing Authority of the Future, 1991; contribs to Urban Studies, Housing Studies, Economic Jl, Applied Econs. *Recreations:* gardening, cooking, Rugby, watching Glasgow get better. *Address:* 3 Glenburn Road, Bearsden, Glasgow G61 4PT. *T:* 041–942 1394.

McLENNAN, Gordon; General Secretary, Communist Party of Great Britain, 1975–89; *b* Glasgow, 12 May 1924; *s* of a shipyard worker; *m; four c*. *Educ:* Hamilton Crescent Sch., Partick, Glasgow. Engineering apprentice, Albion Motors Ltd, Scotstoun, 1939, later engineering draughtsman. Elected Glasgow Organiser, Communist Party, 1949; Sec., Communist Party in Scotland, 1957; Nat. Organiser, Communist Party of GB, 1966. *Recreations:* golf and other sports; cultural interests. *Address:* c/o Executive Committee of the Communist Party, 16 St John Street, EC1M 4AY.

MacLENNAN, Graeme Andrew Yule, CA; Director, Phillips & Drew Fund Management Ltd, since 1990; *b* 24 Aug. 1942; *s* of Finlay and Helen MacLennan; *m* 1st, 1973, Diane Marion Gibbon (*née* Fyfe) (marr. diss. 1989); two *s* two *d*; 2nd, 1989, Diana Rosemary Steven (*née* Urie). *Educ:* Kelvinside Academy, Glasgow. Asst Investment Manager, Leopold Joseph & Sons Ltd, London, 1964–68; Investment Man., Murray Johnstone & Co., Glasgow, 1969–70; Edinburgh Fund Managers: Investment Man., 1970; Dir, 1980, Jt Man. Dir, 1983–88; Investment Dir, Ivory & Sime plc, 1988–90. *Recreations:* hill walking, fishing. *Address:* (office) Triton Court, 14 Finsbury Square, EC2A 1PD. *Club:* Caledonian.

McLENNAN, Sir Ian (Munro), KCMG 1979; KBE 1963 (CBE 1956); President, Australian Academy of Technological Sciences, 1976–83, The Foundation President, since 1983; *b* 30 Nov. 1909; *s* of R. B. and C. O. McLennan; *m* 1937, Dora H., *d* of J. H. Robertson; two *s* two *d*. *Educ:* Scotch Coll., Melbourne; Melbourne Univ. Broken Hill Pty Co. Ltd: Cadet engineer, 1933; Asst Manager, Newcastle Steelworks of BHP Co. Ltd, 1943; Asst Gen. Man., BHP Co. Ltd, 1947; Gen. Man., 1950; Sen. Gen. Man., 1956; Chief Gen. Man., 1959; Man. Dir, 1967–71; Chm., 1971–77; Chairman: BHP-GKN Hldgs Ltd, 1970–78; Tubemakers of Australia Ltd, 1973–79; Australia and New Zealand Banking Group Ltd, and Australia and New Zealand Group Hldgs Ltd, 1977–82;

Interscan Australia Pty Ltd, 1978–84; Bank of Adelaide, 1979–80; Henry Jones IXL Ltd, 1981; Elders IXL Ltd, 1981–85; Dir, ICI Australia Ltd, 1976–79. Chairman: Defence (Industrial) Cttee, 1956–75; Ian Clunies Ross Meml Foundn; Australian Mineral Development Laboratories, 1959–67, Mem. Council, 1959–77; Dep. Chm., Immigration Planning Council, 1949–67. Former Dir, International Iron and Steel Inst.; Pres., Australia-Japan Business Co-operation Cttee, 1977–85; Member: Internat. Council, Morgan Guaranty Trust Co. of NY, 1973–79; Australian Mining Industry Council, 1967–77; Australasian Inst. of Mining and Metallurgy (Pres., 1951, 1957 and 1972); Australian Mineral Industries Research Assoc. Ltd, 1958–77; General Motors Australian Adv. Council, 1978–82; Adv. Council, CSIRO, 1979–82. Chm., Queen Elizabeth II Jubilee Trust for Young Australians, 1978–81. For. Associate, Nat. Acad. of Engrg (USA), 1978; For. Mem., Fellowship of Engrg, UK, 1986. FIAM 1978; FAA 1980. Hon. DEng: Melbourne, 1968; Newcastle, 1968; Hon. DSc Wollongong, 1978; Hon. LLD Melbourne, 1988. *Recreations:* golf, gardening. *Address:* Apt 3, 112–120 Walsh Street, South Yarra, Victoria 3141, Australia. *Clubs:* Melbourne, Athenæum, Australian (all Melbourne); Union (Sydney); Royal Melbourne Golf; Melbourne Cricket.

MACLENNAN, Robert Adam Ross; MP Caithness and Sutherland, since 1966 (Lab 1966–81, SDP 1981–88, Lib Dem since 1988); Leader, Social Democratic Party, 1987–88; Jt Leader, Social and Liberal Democrats, 1988; Barrister-at-Law; *b* 26 June 1936; *e s* of late Sir Hector MacLennan and Isabel Margaret Adam; *m* 1968, Mrs Helen Noyes, *d* of Judge Ammi Cutter, Cambridge, Mass, and *widow* of Paul H. Noyes; one *s* one *d*, and one step *s*. *Educ:* Glasgow Academy; Balliol Coll., Oxford; Trinity Coll., Cambridge; Columbia Univ., New York City. Called to the Bar, Gray's Inn, 1962. Parliamentary Private Secretary: to Secretary of State for Commonwealth Affairs, 1967–69; to Minister without Portfolio, 1969–70; an Opposition Spokesman: on Scottish Affairs, 1970–71; on Defence, 1971–72; Parly Under-Sec. of State, Dept of Prices and Consumer Protection, 1974–79; opposition spokesman on foreign affairs, 1980–81; SDP spokesman: on agriculture, fisheries and food; on home and legal affairs; Lib Dem convenor on home and legal affairs, 1988–; Member: House of Commons Estimates Cttee, 1967–69; House of Commons Select Cttee on Scottish Affairs, 1969–70; Public Accounts Cttee, 1979–. Mem., Latey Cttee on Age of Majority, 1968. *Recreations:* theatre, music, art, the 2,800 square miles of Caithness and Sutherland.

MACLEOD, family name of **Baroness Macleod of Borve.**

MACLEOD OF BORVE, Baroness *cr* 1971 (Life Peer), of Borve, Isle of Lewis; **Evelyn Hester Macleod,** JP; DL; *b* 19 Feb. 1915; *d* of Rev. Gervase Vanneck Blois (*d* 1961), and Hon. Hester Murray Pakington (*d* 1973), *y d* of 3rd Baron Hampton; *m* 1st, 1937, Mervyn Charles Mason (killed by enemy action, 1940); 2nd, 1941, Rt Hon. Iain Norman Macleod, MP (Minister of Health, 1952–55; Minister of Labour and Nat. Service, 1955–59; Secretary of State for the Colonies, 1959–61; Chancellor of the Duchy of Lancaster and Leader of the House of Commons, 1961–63; Chancellor of the Exchequer, June 1970) (*d* 1970), *e s* of late Norman A. Macleod, MD, Scaliscro, Isle of Lewis; one *s* one *d*. Chm., 1973–85, Pres., 1985–, Nat. Association of the Leagues of Hospital Friends; first Chm., Nat. Gas Consumers' Council, 1972–77; Member: IBA (formerly ITA), 1972–75; Energy Commn, 1977–78; Metrication Bd, 1978–80. Co-Founder, Crisis at Christmas, 1967; Pres., Nat. Assoc. of Widows, 1976–. Governor, Queenswood Sch., 1978–85. JP Middlesex, 1955; DL Greater London, 1977. *Recreation:* my family. *Address:* House of Lords, SW1; Luckings Farm, Coleshill, Amersham, Bucks.

MacLEOD, Aubrey Seymour H.; *see* Halford-MacLeod.

MacLEOD, Dr Calum Alexander, CBE 1991; Chairman, Britannia Life, since 1990; *b* 25 July 1935; *s* of Rev. Lachlan Macleod and Jessie Mary Morrison; *m* 1962, Elizabeth Margaret Davidson; two *s* one *d*. *Educ:* Nicolson Inst., Stornoway; Glenurquhart Sch.; Aberdeen Univ. Partner, Paull & Williamsons Advocates, Aberdeen, 1964–80; Chairman: Aberdeen Petroleum, 1982–; Harris Tweed Assoc., 1984–; North of Scotland, subseq. Abtrust Scotland, Investment Co., 1986–; Dep. Chairman: Grampian Television, 1982–; Scottish Eastern Investment Trust, 1988–; Dir, Aberdeen Bd, Bank of Scotland, 1980–. Member: White Fish Authy, 1973–80; N of Scotland Hydro-Electric Bd, 1976–84; Highlands and Islands Develt Bd, 1984–91; Chancellor's Assessor, Aberdeen Univ., 1979–90; Chm., Robert Gordon's Coll., 1981–; Chm., SATRO North Scotland, 1986–90; Vice-Chm., Scottish Council of Indep. Schs, 1988–. Hon LLD Aberdeen, 1986. *Recreations:* golf, motoring, hill-walking, reading, music. *Address:* 6 Westfield Terrace, Aberdeen AB2 4RU. *T:* Aberdeen (0224) 641614. *Clubs:* Royal Northern and University (Aberdeen); Royal Aberdeen Golf; Nairn Golf.

McLEOD, Sir Charles Henry, 3rd Bt, *cr* 1925; *b* 7 Nov. 1924; *o surv. s* of Sir Murdoch Campbell McLeod, 2nd Bt, and Annette Susan Mary (*d* 1964), *d* of Henry Whitehead, JP, 26 Pelham Crescent, SW7; *S* father 1950; *m* 1957, Gillian (*d* 1978), *d* of Henry Bowlby, London; one *s* two *d*. *Educ:* Winchester. Diploma Master Brewer, 1950. Member, London Stock Exchange, 1955–. Represented India, Squash Rackets Internat., 1956–58. *Heir: s* James Roderick Charles McLeod [*b* 26 Sept. 1960; *m* 1990, Helen M. Cooper, *d* of Captain George Cooper, OBE, RN].

MacLEOD, Donald Alexander; HM Diplomatic Service, retired; *b* 23 Jan. 1938; *er s* of late Col Colin S. MacLeod of Glendale, OBE, TD, and of Margaret Drysdale Robertson MacLeod; *m* 1963, Rosemary Lilian Abel (*née* Randle); two *s* two *d*. *Educ:* Edinburgh Academy; Pembroke Coll., Cambridge, 1958–61 (BA). National Service, Queen's Own Cameron Highlanders, 1956–58. HM Foreign Service, 1961; School of Oriental and African Studies, London, 1961–62; British Embassy, Rangoon, 1962–66; Private Sec. to Minister of State, Commonwealth Office, 1966–69; First Secretary, Ottawa, 1969–73; FCO, 1973–78; First Sec./Head of Chancery, Bucharest, 1978–80; Counsellor (Econ. and Commercial), Singapore, 1981–84. Dep. High Comr, Bridgetown, 1984–87; Hd of Protocol Dept, FCO, 1987–89. *Address:* Kinlochfollart, by Dunvegan, Isle of Skye IV55 8WQ.

MacLEOD, Air Vice-Marshal Donald Francis Graham, CB 1977; Director of Royal Air Force Dental Services, 1973–77, retired; *b* Stornoway, Isle of Lewis, Scotland, 26 Aug. 1917; *s* of Alexander MacLeod; both parents from Isle of Lewis; *m* 1941, Marjorie Eileen (*née* Gracie); one *s* one *d*. *Educ:* Nicolson Inst., Stornoway, Isle of Lewis; St Andrews Univ.; Royal Coll. of Surgeons, Edinburgh. LDS St And. 1940; FDS RCSEd 1955. Qualif. in Dental Surgery, 1940; two years in private practice. Joined Royal Air Force Dental Branch, 1942; served in various parts of the world, mainly in hospitals doing oral surgery. QHDS, 1972. Royal Humane Society Resuscitation Certificate for life saving from the sea in the Western Isles, 1937. *Recreations:* golf, gardening; Captain of Soccer, St Andrews Univ., 1938 (full blue), Captain of Badminton, 1939 (half blue). *Address:* 20 Witchford Road, Ely, Cambs CB6 3DP. *T:* Ely (0353) 663164. *Club:* Royal Worlington Golf.

MacLEOD, Sir (Hugh) Roderick, Kt 1989; Chairman, Lloyd's Register of Shipping, since 1983; *b* 20 Sept. 1929; *s* of Neil MacLeod and Ruth MacLeod (*née* Hill); *m* 1958, Josephine Seager Berry (marr. diss. 1985); two *s* one *d*. *Educ:* Bryanston Sch.; St John's Coll., Cambridge. Served 2nd Regt, RHA, 1948–50. Joined The Ben Line Steamers Limited, 1953, Jt Man. Dir, 1964–82; Partner, Wm Thomson & Co., 1959, Director, 1964; Chairman, Associated Container Transportation Ltd, 1975–78. Member: Leith Docks Commn, 1960–65; Forth Ports Authority, 1967–70; National Ports Council, 1977–80; pt-time Mem. Bd, BR, 1980–86. Chm., Scottish Bd, BR, 1980–82. *Recreations:* outdoor pursuits, music. *Address:* 14 Dawson Place, W2.

MacLEOD, Prof. Iain Alasdair, PhD; CEng, FICE, FIStructE; Professor of Structural Engineering, University of Strathclyde, since 1981; *b* 4 May 1939; *s* of Donald MacLeod and Barbara (*née* MacKenzie); *m* 1967, Barbara Jean Booth; one *s* one *d*. *Educ:* Lenzie Acad.; Univ. of Glasgow (BSc 1960, PhD 1966). CEng 1968; FIStructE 1982; FICE 1984. Asst Engr, Crouch & Hogg, Glasgow, 1960–62; Asst Lectr in Civil Engrg, Univ. of Glasgow, 1962–66; Structural Engineer: H. A. Simons Internat., Vancouver, Canada, 1966–67; Portland Cement Assoc., Skokie, USA, 1968–69; Lectr in Civil Engrg, Univ. of Glasgow, 1969–73; Prof. and Head of Dept of Civil Engrg, Paisley Coll. of Technol., 1973–81. Vice-Pres., IStructE, 1989–90; Mem., Standing Cttee on Structural Safety, 1990–. *Publications:* Analytical Modelling of Structural Systems, 1990; over 40 published papers. *Recreations:* sailing, hill walking, ski-ing. *Address:* Department of Civil Engineering, University of Strathclyde, Glasgow G4 0NG. *T:* 041–552 4400, ext. 3275.

MACLEOD, Ian Buchanan, FRCSE; Consultant Surgeon, Royal Infirmary, Edinburgh, and Hon. Senior Lecturer, Department of Clinical Surgery, University of Edinburgh, since 1969; Surgeon to the Queen in Scotland, since 1987; *b* 20 May 1933; *s* of Donald Macleod, MB, ChB, and Katie Ann Buchanan; *m* 1961, Kathleen Gillean Large; one *s* one *d*. *Educ:* Wigan Grammar Sch.; Univ. of Edinburgh (BSc Hons; MB ChB Hons). FRCSE 1962. Resident appts, Royal Inf., Edinburgh, 1957–59. National Service, MO RAMC, 1959–61. Res. Fellow, Lectr and Sen. Lectr, Univ. of Edinburgh, 1962–; Hon. and Cons. Surg., Royal Inf., Edinburgh, 1969–. Editor, Journal of Royal College of Surgeons of Edinburgh, 1982–87. *Publications:* Principles and Practice of Surgery (with A. P. M. Forrest and D. C. Carter), 1985; (contrib.) A Companion to Medical Studies, 1968, 3rd edn 1985; (contrib.) Farquharson's Textbook of Operative Surgery, 1986; papers in surgical jls. *Recreations:* golf, photography. *Address:* Derwent House, 32 Cramond Road North, Edinburgh EH4 6JE. *T:* 031–336 1541. *Clubs:* University Staff, Bruntsfield Links Golfing Society (Edinburgh).

See also N. R. B. Macleod.

McLEOD, Sir Ian (George), Kt 1984; JP; Managing Director, EDP Services Computer Bureau, since 1964; *b* 17 Oct. 1926; *s* of George Gunn McLeod; *m* 1950, Audrey Davis; two *d*. *Educ:* Kearsney College, Natal; Natal University; ACIS. Played for Rosslyn Park Rugby Team, 1951. Chm., London Transport Passengers Cttee, 1979–83; Board Mem., SE Electricity Board, 1983–89; Dir, Seeboard plc, 1990–. Chairman: Croydon Central Cons. Assoc., 1973–76; Greater London Area Conservatives, 1981–84; Cons. Policy Gp for London, 1984–87; Nat. Union of Cons. and Unionist Assocs, 1988–90 (Vice-Chm., 1985–87); Mem., Nat. Union Exec. Cttee, Cons. Party, 1974–; Chm., Brighton Cons. Conf., 1988. Mem., Croydon Borough Council, 1974–78; Dep. Mayor, 1976–77. Governor, Old Palace Girls' Sch., Croydon, 1974–87. JP SE London, 1977. *Recreations:* politics, reading history. *Address:* Pine Ridge, Pine Coombe, Shirley Hills, Croydon, Surrey. *T:* 081–654 4869. *Clubs:* Carlton, MCC.

McLEOD, Rev. John; Minister of Resolis and Urquhart, since 1986; Chaplain to the Queen in Scotland, since 1978; *b* 8 April 1926; *s* of Angus McLeod and Catherine McDougall; *m* 1958, Sheila McLeod; three *s* two *d*. *Educ:* Inverness Royal Academy; Edinburgh Univ. (MA); New Coll., Edinburgh. Farming until 1952; at university, 1952–58; ordained, Inverness, 1958. Missionary in India: Jalna, 1959–68; Poona, 1969–74; involved in rural development with special emphasis on development and conservation of water resource; also responsible for pastoral work in Church of N India, St Mary's, Poona, 1970–74; Church of Scotland Minister, Livingston Ecumenical Team Ministry, 1974; Warden of Nether Dechmont Farm Community Centre, 1977–81. *Recreations:* hill walking, gardening. *Address:* The Manse, Culbokie, Dingwall, Ross-shire IV7 8JM. *T.* Culbokie (034987) 452.

MacLEOD OF MacLEOD, John; 29th Chief of MacLeod; *b* 10 Aug. 1935; second *s* of late Captain Robert Wolrige-Gordon, MC, and Joan, *d* of Hubert Walter and Dame Flora MacLeod of MacLeod, DBE; officially recognised in name of MacLeod of MacLeod by decree of Lyon Court, 1951; *S* grandmother, 1976; *m* 1973, Melita Kolin; one *s* one *d*. *Educ:* Eton. *Heir: s* Hugh Magnus MacLeod, younger of MacLeod. *Address:* Dunvegan Castle, Isle of Skye. *T:* Dunvegan (047022) 206.

See also P. Wolrige-Gordon.

MacLEOD, Hon. Sir (John) Maxwell (Norman), 5th Bt *cr* 1924, of Fuinary, Morven, Co. Argyll; *b* 23 Feb. 1952; *s* of Baron MacLeod of Fuinary (Life Peer), MC and Lorna Helen Janet (*d* 1984), *er d* of late Rev. Donald Macleod; *S* to baronetcy of father, 1991. *Educ:* Gordonstoun. *Heir: b* Hon. Neil David MacLeod, *b* 25 Dec. 1959. *Address:* Fuinary Manse, Loch Aline, Morven, Argyll.

McLEOD, Keith Morrison, CBE 1975; Financial Controller, British Airports Authority, 1971–75; *b* 26 May 1920; *yr s* of John and Mary McLeod; *m* 1943, Patricia Carter; two *s* one *d*. *Educ:* Bancroft's School. Asst Auditor, Exchequer and Audit Dept, 1939; served RAF, 1941–46; Asst Principal, Min. of Supply, 1948; Principal, 1950; BJSM, Washington, 1955–57; Asst Sec., Min. of Supply, 1957; Cabinet Office, 1962; Finance Dir, British Airports Authority, 1966. *Address:* 161 Banstead Road, Banstead, Surrey. *T:* 081–393 9005.

McLEOD, Malcolm Donald; Director, Hunterian Museum and Art Gallery, Glasgow, since 1990; *b* 19 May 1941; *s* of Donald McLeod and Ellen (*née* Fairclough); *m* 1st, 1965, Jacqueline Wynborne (marr. diss. 1980); two *s* one *d*; 2nd, 1980, Iris Barry. *Educ:* Birkenhead Sch.; Hertford and Exeter Colls, Oxford. MA, BLitt. Lectr, Dept of Sociology, Univ. of Ghana, 1967–69; Asst Curator, Museum of Archaeology and Ethnology, Cambridge, 1969–74; Lectr, Girton Coll., Cambridge, 1969–74; Fellow, Magdalene Coll., Cambridge, 1972–74; Keeper of Ethnography, BM, 1974–90. Member: Hist. and Current Affairs Selection Cttee, Nat. Film Archive, 1978–84; Council, Museums Assoc., 1983–86; UK Unesco Cultural Adv. Cttee, 1980–85. Hon. Lectr, Anthropology Dept, UCL, 1976–81. Lectures: Marett, Exeter Coll., Oxford, 1982; Sydney Jones, Liverpool Univ., 1984; Arthur Batchelor, UEA, 1987. *Publications:* The Asante, 1980; Treasures of African Art, 1980; (with J. Mack) Ethnic Art, 1984; (with E. Bassani) Jacob Epstein: collector, 1987; An English-Kriolu, Kriolu-English Dictionary, 1990; articles and reviews in learned jls. *Address:* Mossfennan, Bowden, Roxburghshire TD6 0ST. *Club:* Athenæum.

MacLEOD, Hon. Sir Maxwell; *see* MacLeod, Hon. Sir J. M. N.

MACLEOD, Nathaniel William Hamish, JP; Financial Secretary, Hong Kong, since 1991; *b* 6 Jan. 1940; *s* of George Henry Torquil Macleod and Ruth Natalie Wade; *m* 1970, Fionna Mary Campbell; one *s* one *d*. *Educ:* Univ. of St Andrews (MA Soc. Sci. Hons); Univ. of Bristol (Dip. Soc. Sci. Sociology); Birmingham Coll. of Commerce. ACIS. Commercial trainee, Stewarts & Lloyds, Birmingham, 1958–62; Hong Kong Government: Admin. Officer, 1966; Dir of Trade and Chief Trade Negotiator, 1983–87;

Secretary for Trade and Industry, 1987–89; Sec. for the Treasury, 1989–91. JP Hong Kong, 1979. *Recreations:* competitive sailing, ski-ing, tennis, walking. *Address:* Government Secretariat, Lower Albert Road, Hong Kong. *T:* 810 2589, *Fax:* 840 0569. *Club:* Royal Hong Kong Yacht.

MACLEOD, Nigel Ronald Buchanan, QC 1979; a Recorder of the Crown Court, since 1981; *b* 7 Feb. 1936; *s* of Donald Macleod, MB, ChB, and Katherine Ann Macleod; *m* 1966, Susan Margaret (*née* Buckley); one *s* one *d. Educ:* Wigan Grammar Sch.; Christ Church, Oxford (MA, BCL). Served RAF, 1954–56. Called to the Bar, Gray's Inn, 1961, Inner Temple *ad eundem* 1984. Asst Comr, Boundary Commn for England, 1981–85. *Publications:* contribs to legal jls. *Recreations:* sailing, walking. *Address:* The Start, Start Lane, Whaley Bridge, Derbyshire SK12 7BP. *T:* Whaley Bridge (0663) 2732; Cascades, West Ferry Road, E14. *T:* 071–538 2859.

See also I. B. Macleod.

MacLEOD, Norman Donald; QC (Scot) 1986; MA, LLB; Advocate; Sheriff Principal of Glasgow and Strathkelvin, since 1986; *b* 6 March 1932; *s* of late Rev. John MacLeod, Edinburgh and Catherine MacRitchie; *m* 1957, Ursula Jane, *y d* of late George H. Bromley, Inveresk; two *s* two *d. Educ:* Mill Hill Sch.; George Watson's Boys' Coll., Edinburgh; Edinburgh Univ.; Hertford Coll., Oxford. Passed Advocate, 1956. Colonial Administrative Service, Tanganyika: Dist. Officer, 1957–59; Crown Counsel, 1959–64; practised at Scots Bar, 1964–67; Sheriff of Glasgow and Strathkelvin (formerly Lanarkshire at Glasgow), 1967–86. Vis. Prof., Law Sch., Univ. of Strathclyde, 1988–. *Recreations:* sailing, gardening. *Address:* Sheriffs' Library, Sheriff Court, PO Box 23, 1 Carlton Place, Glasgow. *T:* 041–429 8888.

MacLEOD, Sir Roderick; *see* MacLeod, Sir H. R.

MACLEOD-SMITH, Alastair Macleod, CMG 1956; retired; *b* 30 June 1916; *s* of late R. A. Smith, MIEE, and Mrs I. Macleod-Smith (*née* Kellner); *m* 1945, Ann (*née* Circuitt); one *s* one *d. Educ:* The Wells House, Malvern Wells, Worcs; Ellesmere Coll., Salop; The Queen's Coll., Oxford. BA Oxon 1938. Entered HM Oversea Service as administrative cadet, Nigeria, 1939; Asst Dist Officer, 1942, Dist Officer, Nigeria, 1949; seconded to Windward Islands as Financial and Economic Adviser, 1949–52; Financial Sec., Western Pacific High Commission, 1952–57; Financial Sec., Sierra Leone, 1957–61. Dir, Selection Trust Ltd, 1967–80; Consultant, National Westminster Bank, 1981–83. *Recreation:* golf. *Address:* Roughetts Lodge, Coldharbour Lane, Hildenborough, Kent TN11 9JX. *Clubs:* United Oxford & Cambridge University; Knole Park Golf.

McLINTOCK, (Charles) Alan, CA; Chairman: Woolwich Building Society, since 1984 (Deputy Chairman, 1980–84; Director, since 1970); Govett Atlantic Investment Trust (formerly Stockholders Investment Trust), since 1978; Govett Strategic Investment Trust (formerly Border and Southern Stockholders Investment Trust), since 1975; Ecclesiastical Insurance Group (formerly Ecclesiastical Insurance Office), since 1981 (Director, since 1972); AJ's Family Restaurants, since 1987; Director, M&G Group, since 1982; *b* 28 May 1925; *s* of late Charles Henry McLintock, OBE, and Alison McLintock; *m* 1955, Sylvia Mary Foster Taylor; one *s* three *d. Educ:* Rugby School. Served Royal Artillery, 1943–47; commnd 1945; Captain RHA 1946. With Thomson McLintock & Co., Chartered Accountants, 1948–87; qualified, 1952; Partner, 1954; Sen. Partner, KMG Thomson McLintock, 1982–87; Partner, Klynveld Main Goerdeler (KMG), 1979–87. Chm., Grange Trust, 1973–81 (Dir, 1958–81); Director: Trust Houses Ltd, 1967–71; Lake View Investment Trust, later Govett Oriental Investment Trust, 1971–90 (Chm., 1975–90); National Westminster Bank, 1979–90 (Adv. Bd, 1990–91); Acxiom UK (formerly Southwark Computer Services), 1988–90. Vice-Pres., Metropolitan Assoc. of Building Socs, 1985–90. Chairman of Governors: Rugby Sch., 1988– (Gov., 1973–); Westonbirt Sch., 1991– (Gov., 1977–); Vice-Pres., Clergy Orphan Corp. Cttee, 1984– (Mem., Cttee of Management, 1963–84); Member: Royal Alexandra and Albert Sch. Bd of Management, 1965–88; Court, London Univ., 1987–. *Recreations:* music, family pursuits. *Address:* Manor House, Westhall Hill, Burford, Oxon OX18 4BJ. *T:* Burford (099382) 2276. *Club:* Army and Navy.

McLINTOCK, Sir Michael (William), 4th Bt *cr* 1934, of Sanquhar, Co. Dumfries; *b* 13 Aug. 1958; *s* of Sir William Traven McLintock, 3rd Bt and André, *d* of Richard Lonsdale-Hands; *S* father, 1987. *Heir: b* Andrew Thomson McLintock, *b* 1960.

McLOUGHLIN, George Leeke, CB 1988; Deputy Director of Public Prosecutions for Northern Ireland, 1982–87; *b* 2 July 1921; *e s* of Charles M. and Rose W. McLoughlin; *m* 1953, Maureen Theresa McKaigney; two *s* six *d. Educ:* St Columb's College, Londonderry; Queen's Univ. Belfast (BA). Barrister, N Ireland, practised 1945–58; joined HMOCS 1958; Resident Magistrate, 1958, Crown Counsel, 1958–63, Northern Rhodesia; Parly Draftsman, Zambia, 1965; Solicitor General, Zambia, 1968–70, retired; Office of Law Reform, N Ireland, 1971–72; Sen. Asst Dir of Public Prosecutions, NI (Under Secretary, NI Civil Service), 1973–82. *Recreations:* gardening, photography, armchair sports following. *Address:* c/o Northern Bank, 12–13 Shaftesbury Square, Belfast, Northern Ireland.

McLOUGHLIN, Patrick Allen; MP (C) W Derbyshire, since May 1986; Parliamentary Under Secretary of State, Department of Transport, since 1989; *b* 30 Nov. 1957; *s* of Patrick and Gladys Victoria McLoughlin; *m* 1984, Lynne Newman; one *s* one *d. Educ:* Cardinal Griffin Roman Catholic Sch., Cannock. Mineworker, Littleton Colliery, 1979–85; Marketing Official, NCB, 1985–86. PPS to Sec. of State for Trade and Industry, 1988–89. *Address:* House of Commons, SW1A 0AA.

MACLURE, Sir John (Robert Spencer), 4th Bt *cr* 1898; Headmaster, Croftinloan School, Pitlochry, Perthshire, since 1978; *b* 25 March 1934; *s* of Sir John William Spencer Maclure, 3rd Bt, OBE, and Elspeth (*d* 1991), *er d* of late Alexander King Clark; *S* father, 1980; *m* 1964, Jane Monica, *d* of late Rt Rev. T. J. Savage, Bishop of Zululand and Swaziland; four *s. Educ:* Winchester College. IAPS Diploma. 2nd Lt, 2nd Bn KRRC, 1953–55, BAOR; Lt, Royal Hampshire Airborne Regt, TA. Assistant Master: Horris Hill, 1955–66 and 1974–78; St George's, Wanganui, NZ, 1967–68; Sacred Heart Coll., Auckland, NZ, 1969–70; St Edmund's, Hindhead, Surrey, 1971–74. *Heir: s* John Mark Maclure, *b* 27 Aug. 1965. *Address:* Croftinloan School, Pitlochry, Perthshire PH16 5JR. *T:* Pitlochry (0796) 2837; Wild Goose Cottage, Gooseham, Bude, N Cornwall EX23 9PG. *Clubs:* MCC; Royal and Ancient (St Andrews).

MACLURE, (John) Stuart, CBE 1982; Editor, Times Educational Supplement, 1969–89; *b* 8 Aug. 1926; *s* of Hugh and Bertha Maclure, Highgate, N6; *m* 1951, Constance Mary Butler; one *s* two *d. Educ:* Highgate Sch.; Christ's Coll., Cambridge. MA. Joined The Times, 1950; The Times Educational Supplement, 1951; Editor, Education, 1954–69. Hon. Prof. of Educn, Keele Univ., 1981–84; Dist. Vis. Fellow, PSI, 1989–90. President: Br. Sect., Comparative Educn Soc. in Europe, 1979; Educnl Sect., BAAS, 1983; Member: Educnl Adv. Council, IBA, 1979–84; Consultative Cttee, Assessment of Performance Unit, 1974–82. Regents' Lecturer, Univ. of California, Berkeley, 1980. Hon. Fellow, City of Sheffield Polytechnic, 1976; Hon. FCP 1985; Hon. Fellow, Westminster Coll., 1990. DUniv Open, 1991. *Publications:* Joint Editor (with T. E. Utley) Documents on Modern Political Thought, 1956; Editor, Educational Documents, 1816–1963, 1965; A Hundred Years of London Education, 1970; (with Tony Becher) The Politics of Curriculum Change, 1978; (ed with Tony Becher) Accountability in Education, 1979; Education and Youth Employment in Great Britain, 1979; Educational Development and School Building, 1945–1973, 1984; Education Re-formed, a guide to the Education Reform Act, 1988; A History of Education in London 1870–1990, 1990; Missing Links—The Challenge to Further Education, 1991. *Address:* 109 College Road, Dulwich, SE21. *Club:* MCC.

McLUSKEY, Very Rev. J(ames) Fraser, MC; MA, BD, DD; Minister at St Columba's Church of Scotland, Pont Street, London, 1960–86; Moderator of the General Assembly of the Church of Scotland, 1983–84; *b* 1914; *s* of James Fraser McLuskey and Margaret Keltie; *m* 1st, 1939, Irene (*d* 1959), *d* of Pastor Calaminus, Wuppertal; two *s*; 2nd, 1966, Ruth Quartermaine (*née* Hunter), *widow* of Lt-Col Keith Briant. *Educ:* Aberdeen Grammar Sch.; Edinburgh Univ. Ordained Minister of Church of Scotland, 1938; Chaplain to Univ. of Glasgow, 1939–47. Service as Army Chaplain, 1943–46 (1st Special Air Service Regt, 1944–46); Sub Warden Royal Army Chaplains' Training Centre, 1947–50; Minister at Broughty Ferry East, 1950–55; Minister at New Kilpatrick, Bearsden, 1955–60. *Publication:* Parachute Padre, 1951. *Recreations:* walking, music, reading. *Address:* 14 Buckingham Terrace, Edinburgh EH4 3AA. *T:* 031–332 0935. *Clubs:* Caledonian, Special Forces.

McMAHON, Andrew, (Andy); *b* 18 March 1920; *s* of Andrew and Margaret McMahon; *m* 1944; one *s* one *d. Educ:* District School, Govan. Boilermaker, Govan shipyards, 1936; unemployed, 1971–79. MP (Lab) Glasgow, Govan, 1979–83; first and only Boilermaker to enter House of Commons. Member, Glasgow Dist. Council, 1973–79. Chm., Scottish Arab Friendship Assoc., 1972–85; Sec. Gen., British-Iraqi Friendship Assoc., 1989– (Pres., 1986–89). *Recreations:* youth work, care and comfort for elderly. *Address:* 21 Morefield Road, Govan, Glasgow G51 4NG.

McMAHON, Sir Brian (Patrick), 8th Bt *cr* 1817; engineer; *b* 9 June 1942; *s* of Sir (William) Patrick McMahon, 7th Bt, and Ruth Stella (*d* 1982), *yr d* of late Percy Robert Kenyon-Slaney; *S* father, 1977; *m* 1981, Kathleen Joan, *d* of late William Hopwood. *Educ:* Wellington. BSc, AIM. Assoc. Mem., Inst of Welding. *Heir: brother* Shaun Desmond McMahon [*b* 29 Oct. 1945; *m* 1971, Antonia Noel Adie; *m* 1985, Jill Rosamund, *yr d* of Dr Jack Cherry; two *s*]. *Address:* 157B Wokingham Road, Reading, Berks RG6 1LP.

McMAHON, Sir Christopher William, (Sir Kit), Kt 1986; Director: Midland Bank, since 1986 (Chief Executive and Deputy Chairman, 1986–87; Chairman, 1987–91); Taylor Woodrow, since 1991; Pentos, since 1991; *b* Melbourne, 10 July 1927; *s* of late Dr John Joseph McMahon and late Margaret Kate (*née* Brown); *m* 1st, 1956, Marion Kelso; two *s*; 2nd, 1982, Alison Barbara Braimbridge, *d* of late Dr J. G. Cormie and late Mrs B. E. Cormie. *Educ:* Melbourne Grammar Sch.; Univ. of Melbourne (BA Hons Hist. and English, 1949); Magdalen Coll., Oxford. 1st cl. hons PPE, 1953. Tutor in English Lit., Univ. of Melbourne, 1950; Econ. Asst, HM Treasury, 1953–57; Econ. Adviser, British Embassy, Washington, 1957–60; Fellow and Tutor in Econs, Magdalen Coll., Oxford, 1960–64 (Hon. Fellow, 1986); Tutor in Econs, Treasury Centre for Admin. Studies, 1963–64; Mem., Plowden Cttee on Aircraft Industry, 1964–65; entered Bank of England as Adviser, 1964; Adviser to the Governors, 1966–70; Exec. Dir, 1970–80; Dep. Governor, 1980–85. Director: Eurotunnel, 1987–91; Hongkong and Shanghai Banking Corp., 1987–91; Royal Opera House, 1989–. Mem., Gp of Thirty, 1978–84; Chairman: Working Party 3, OECD, 1980–85; Young Enterprise, 1989–. Mem. Court, Univ. of London, 1984–86. Trustee: Whitechapel Art Gall., 1984–; Royal Opera House Trust, 1984–86. Hon. Fellow, UCNW, 1988. Chevalier, Légion d'Honneur (France), 1990. *Publications:* Sterling in the Sixties, 1964; (ed) Techniques of Economic Forecasting, 1965. *Recreations:* looking at pictures, buying books, going to the movies, gardening in good weather. *Address:* c/o Taylor Woodrow, 1 St Katherine's Way, E1 9TW. *Club:* Garrick.

MacMAHON, Gerald John, CB 1962; CMG 1955; *b* 26 Sept. 1909; 2nd *s* of late Jeremiah MacMahon and Kathleen MacMahon (*née* Dodd); unmarried. *Educ:* Clongowes Wood Coll., Co. Kildare, Ireland; Emmanuel Coll., Cambridge (BA). Entered Board of Trade, 1933; Asst Sec., 1942. Imperial Defence Coll., 1949. Senior UK Trade Commissioner in India, 1952–58; Under-Sec., Board of Trade 1958–62 and 1964–70; Admiralty, Nov. 1962–64. *Address:* 19 Lower Park, Putney Hill, SW15. *Club:* Reform.

McMAHON, Hugh Robertson; Member (Lab) Strathclyde West, European Parliament, since 1984; *b* 17 June 1938; *s* of Hugh McMahon and Margaret Fulton Robertson. *Educ:* Glasgow University (MA Hons); Jordanhill College. Assistant Teacher: Largs High School, 1962–63; Stevenston High School, 1963–64; Irvine Royal Academy, 1964–68; Principal Teacher of History, Mainholm Academy, Ayr, 1968–71; Principal Teacher of History and Modern Studies, 1971–72, Asst Head Teacher, 1972–84, Ravenspark Academy, Irvine. *Recreations:* golf, reading, walking, languages. *Address:* 6 Whitlees Court, Ardrossan, Ayrshire. *T:* Ardrossan (0294) 66692; (office) Abbey Mills Business Centre, Seedhill, Paisley PA1 1JN. *T:* 041–889 9990. *Clubs:* Saltcoats Labour; Ravenspark Golf; Irvine Bogside Golf.

McMAHON, Sir Kit; *see* McMahon, Sir C. W.

McMAHON, Rt. Rev. Thomas; *see* Brentwood, Bishop of, (RC).

McMANNERS, Rev. Prof. John, DLitt; FBA 1978; Fellow and Chaplain, All Souls College, Oxford, since 1984; *b* 25 Dec. 1916; *s* of Rev. Canon Joseph McManners and Mrs Ann McManners; *m* 1951, Sarah Carruthers Errington; two *s* two *d. Educ:* St Edmund Hall, Oxford (Hon. Fellow, 1983); Durham Univ. BA 1st cl. hons Mod. History Oxon, 1939; DipTheol Dunelm, 1947; DLitt Oxon 1980. Military Service, 1939–45 in Royal Northumberland Fusiliers (Major). Priest, 1948; St Edmund Hall, Oxford: Chaplain, 1948; Fellow, 1949; Dean, 1951; Prof., Univ. of Tasmania, 1956–59; Prof., Sydney Univ., 1959–66; Vis. Fellow, All Souls Coll., Oxford, 1965–66; Prof. of History, Univ. of Leicester, 1967–72; Canon of Christ Church and Regius Prof. of Ecclesiastical History, Oxford Univ., 1972–84. Birkbeck Lectr, Cambridge, 1976; John Coffin Meml Lectr, London Univ., 1982; Sir Owen Evans Lectr, Univ. of Wales, 1984; F. D. Maurice Lectr, King's Coll. London, 1985; Zaharoff Lectr, 1985, Hensley Henson Lectr, 1986, Oxford; Trevelyan Lectr, Cambridge, 1989. Dir d'études associé, Ecole Pratique des Hautes Etudes, sect. IV, Paris, 1980–81. Mem., Doctrinal Commn of C of E, 1978–82. Trustee, Nat. Portrait Gallery, 1970–78; Mem. Council, RHistS, 1971; Pres., Ecclesiastical Hist. Soc., 1977–78. FAHA 1970. Hon. DLitt Durham, 1984. Officer, Order of King George I of the Hellenes, 1945; Comdr, Ordre des Palmes académiques (France), 1991. *Publications:* French Ecclesiastical Society under the Ancien Régime: a study of Angers in the 18th Century, 1960; (ed) France, Government and Society, 1965, 2nd edn 1971; Lectures on European History 1789–1914: Men, Machines and Freedom, 1966; The French Revolution and the Church, 1969; Church and State in France 1870–1914, 1972; Death and the Enlightenment, 1981 (Wolfson Literary Award, 1982); (ed) The Oxford Illustrated History of Christianity, 1990; contrib.: New Cambridge Modern History vols

VI and VIII; Studies in Church History, vols XII, XV and XXII. *Recreation:* tennis. *Address:* All Souls College, Oxford. *T:* Oxford (0865) 279368.

McMANUS, Francis Joseph; solicitor; *b* 16 Aug. 1942; *s* of Patrick and Celia McManus; *m* 1971, Carmel V. Doherty, Lisnaskea, Co. Fermanagh; two *s* one *d.* *Educ:* St Michael's, Enniskillen; Queen's University, Belfast. BA 1965; Diploma in Education, 1966. Subsequently a Teacher. MP (Unity) Fermanagh and S Tyrone, 1970–Feb. 1974. Founder Mem. and Co-Chm., Irish Independence Party, 1977–. *Address:* Lissadell, Drumlin Heights, Enniskillen, Co. Fermanagh, N Ireland. *T:* Enniskillen (0365) 23401.

MacMANUS, His Honour John Leslie Edward, TD 1945; QC 1970; a Circuit Judge (formerly a Judge of County Courts), 1971–90, retired; *b* 7 April 1920; *o s* of E. H. MacManus and H. S. MacManus (*née* Colton); *m* 1942, Gertrude (Trudy) Mary Frances Koppenhagen; two *d.* *Educ:* Eastbourne College. Served 1939–45 with RA: Middle East, Italy, Crete, Yugoslavia; Captain 1942; Major 1945. Called to Bar, Middle Temple, 1947. Dep. Chm., East Sussex QS, 1964–71. *Recreations:* gardening, travel. *Address:* The Old Rectory, Twineham, Haywards Heath, West Sussex RH17 5NR. *T:* Bolney (0444) 881221. *Club:* Sussex Martlets.

McMASTER, Brian John, CBE 1987; Director, Edinburgh International Festival, since 1991; *b* 9 May 1943; *s* of Brian John McMaster and Mary Leila Hawkins. *Educ:* Wellington Coll.; Bristol Univ. LLB. International Artists' Dept, EMI Ltd, 1968–73; Controller of Opera Planning, ENO, 1973–76; Gen Administrator, subseq. Man. Dir, WNO, 1976–91; Artistic Dir, Vancouver Opera, 1984–89. *Address:* 1 Cowper Court, Wordsworth Avenue, Cardiff. *T:* Cardiff (0222) 497694; 71 Breton House, Barbican, EC2. *T:* 071–638 4365; Edinburgh International Festival, 21 Market Street, Edinburgh EH1 1BW. *T:* 031–226 4001.

McMASTER, Gordon James; MP (Lab) Paisley South since Nov. 1990; *b* 13 Feb. 1960; *s* of William McMaster, retired Parks Superintendant and Alison McMaster, (*née* Maxwell), clerkess. *Educ:* Cochrane Castle Primary Sch.; Johnstone High Sch.; Woodburn House FE Centre (City and Guilds in Horticulture); West of Scotland Agr. Coll. (OND Hort.); Jordanhill Coll. of Education (Cert. in Further Educn.) Apprentice gardner, Renfrew DC, 1976–77; full time student, 1977–78 and 1979–80; trainee hort. technician, Renfrew DC, 1978–79; Craftsman Gardener, Renfrew DC, 1980; Lectr in Hort., Langside Coll., 1980–86, Sen. Lectr, 1986–88; Co-ordinator, Growing Concern Initiative, Strathclyde, 1988–90. Member: Johnstone Community Council 1980–84 (Chm., 1982–84); Renfrew DC, 1984— (Dep. Leader, 1987–88; Leader, 1988–90). *Recreations:* reading, gardening, computers. *Address:* 36 Bevan Grove, Johnstone PA5 8TP. *T:* Johnstone (0505) 36529; House of Commons, SW1A 0AA. *T.* 071–219 5104. *Clubs:* United Services (Johnstone); Lilybank Bowling.

McMASTER, Hughan James Michael, RIBA; Chief Architect and Director of Works, Home Office, 1980–87, retired; *b* 27 July 1927; *s* of William James Michael and Emly McMaster; *m* 1950; one *s* two *d.* *Educ:* Christ's Coll., Finchley; Regent Street Polytechnic (DipArch). ARIBA 1951. Served RAF, India and Far East, 1946–48. Joined Civil Service, 1961; Navy Works, 1961–69; Whitehall Development Gp, Directorate of Home Estate Management and Directorate of Civil Accommodation, 1969–76; Defence Works (PE and Overseas), 1976–80. FRSA. *Recreations:* ski-ing, swimming, theatre, music.

McMASTER, Peter, CB 1991; FRICS; Director General, Ordnance Survey, 1985–91; Member, Lord Chancellor's Panel of Independent Inspectors, since 1991; *b* 22 Nov. 1931; *s* of Peter McMaster and Ada Nellie (*née* Williams); *m* 1955, Catherine Ann Rosborough; one *s* one *d.* *Educ:* Kelvinside Academy, Glasgow; RMA Sandhurst; RMCS Shrivenham. BScEng London. Called to the Bar, Middle Temple, 1969. Commissioned into Royal Engineers, 1952; served Middle and Far East; retired (major), 1970; joined Civil Service, 1970; W Midland Region, Ordnance Survey, 1970–72; Caribbean Region, Directorate of Overseas Survey, 1972–74; Headquarters, Ordnance Survey, 1974–91. Vis. Prof., Kingston Polytechnic, 1991–. Mem. Council, RGS, 1990–. FIIM 1990. *Recreations:* travel, walking, chess. *Address:* Hillhead, Stratton Road, Winchester, Hampshire SO23 8JQ. *T:* Winchester (0962) 862684.

McMASTER, Stanley Raymond; *b* 23 Sept. 1926; *o s* of F. R. McMaster, Marlborough Park, Belfast, N Ireland; *m* 1959, Verda Ruth Tynan, SRN, Comber, Co Down, Northern Ireland; two *s* two *d* (and one *d* decd). *Educ:* Campbell Coll., Belfast; Trinity Coll., Dublin (MA, BComm). Called to the Bar, Lincoln's Inn, 1953. Lectr in Company Law, Polytechnic, Regent Street, 1954–59. Parliamentary and Legal Sec., to Finance and Taxation Cttee, Association of British Chambers of Commerce, 1958–59. MP (UU) Belfast E, March 1959–Feb. 1974; contested (UU) Belfast S, Oct. 1974. *Publications:* various articles in legal and commercial journals. *Recreations:* golf, rowing and shooting. *Address:* 31 Embercourt Road, Thames Ditton, Surrey; 10 Marlborough Park North, Belfast. *Clubs:* Knock Golf, etc.

McMICHAEL, Prof. Andrew James, PhD; Medical Research Council Clinical Research Professor of Immunology, University of Oxford, since 1982; Fellow of Trinity College, Oxford, since 1983; *b* 8 Nov. 1943; *s* of Sir John McMichael, *qv* and Sybil McMichael; *m* 1968, Kathryn Elizabeth Cross; two *s* one *d.* *Educ:* St Paul's Sch., London; Gonville and Caius Coll., Cambridge (MA; BChir 1968; MB 1969); St Mary's Hosp. Med. Sch., London. PhD 1974; MRCP 1971; FRCP 1985. House Physician, St Mary's Hosp., Royal Northern Hosp., Hammersmith Hosp. and Brompton Hosp., 1968–71; MRC Jun. Res. Fellow, National Inst. for Med. Res., 1971–74; MRC Travelling Fellow, Stanford Univ. Med. Sch., 1974–76; Oxford University: Wellcome Sen. Clin. Fellow, Nuffield Depts of Medicine and Surgery, 1977–79; University Lectr in Medicine and Hon. Consultant Physician, 1979–82. Member: Adv. Bd. Beit Meml Trust, 1984–; MRC Systems Bd, 1987–91; MRC AIDS Steering Cttee, 1988–. *Publications:* (ed with J. W. Fabre) Monoclonal Antibodies in Clinical Medicine, 1982; articles on genetic control of human immune response and transplantation antigens. *Recreations:* reading, walking, sailing.

McMICHAEL, Sir John, Kt 1965; MD, FRCP, FRCPE; FRS 1957; Director, British Post-graduate Medical Federation, 1966–71; Emeritus Professor of Medicine, University of London; *b* 25 July 1904; *s* of James McMichael and Margaret Sproat; *m* 1942, Sybil E. Blake (*d* 1965); four *s*; *m* 1965, Sheila M. Howarth. *Educ:* Kirkcudbright Acad.; Edinburgh Univ. Ettles Scholar, 1927; Beit Memorial Fellow, 1930–34. MD (Gold Medal) Edinburgh 1933; MD Melbourne 1965; FRCPE 1940 (Hon. FRCPE 1981); FRCP 1946. Johnston and Lawrence Fellow, Royal Society, 1937–39; Univ. teaching appointments in Aberdeen, Edinburgh and London. Dir, Dept of Medicine, Post-grad. Med. Sch. of London, 1946–66; Mem. Medical Research Council, 1949–53. A Vice-Pres., Royal Soc., 1968–70. Pres., World Congress of Cardiology, 1970. Hon. Member: American Medical Association, 1947; Medical Soc., Copenhagen, 1953; Norwegian Medical Soc., 1954; Assoc. Amer. Physicians, 1959. For. Mem. Finnish Acad. of Science and Letters, 1963; Hon. For. Mem., Acad. Roy. de Med. Belgique, 1971; For. Associate, Nat. Acad. Sci., Washington, 1974. Thayer Lectr, Johns Hopkins Hosp., 1948; Oliver Sharpey Lectr, 1952; Croonian Lectr, 1961, RCP; Watson Smith Lectr RCPEd, 1958. Cullen Prize, RCPEd, 1953. Jacobs Award, Dallas, 1958; Morgan Prof., Nashville, Tenn, 1964. Fellow, Royal Postgrad. Med. Sch., 1972. Moxon Medal, RCP, 1960; Gairdner Award, Toronto, 1960; Wihuri Internat. Prize, Finland, 1968. Harveian Orator, RCP, 1975. Krug Award of Excellence, 1980. Trustee, Wellcome Trust, 1960–77. Hon. FRCPE; Hon. FACP; Hon. LLD Edin.; Hon. DSc: Newcastle; Sheffield; Birmingham; Ohio; McGill; Wales; Hon. ScD Dublin. *Publications:* Pharmacology of the Failing Human Heart, 1951. Numerous papers on: Splenic Anaemia, 1931–35; Cardiac Output in Health and Disease, 1938–47; Lung Capacity in Man, 1938–39; Liver Circulation and Liver Disease, 1932–43. *Recreation:* gardening. *Address:* 2 North Square, NW11 7AA. *T:* 081–455 8731.

See also A. J. McMichael.

MACMILLAN, family name of **Earl of Stockton.**

MACMILLAN OF OVENDEN, Viscount; Daniel Maurice Alan Macmillan; *b* 9 Oct. 1974; *s* and *heir* of Earl of Stockton, *qv.* *Address:* 8 The Little Boltons, SW10 9LP. *T:* 071–373 6379.

McMILLAN, Alan Austen, CB 1986; Solicitor to the Secretary of State for Scotland, 1984–87; *b* 19 Jan. 1926; *s* of Allan McMillan and Mabel (*née* Austin); *m* 1949, Margaret Moncur; two *s* two *d.* *Educ:* Ayr Acad.; Glasgow Univ. Served in Army, 1944–47. Qualified Solicitor in Scotland, 1949; Legal Assistant, Ayr Town Council, 1949–55; Scottish Office: Legal Assistant, 1955–62; Sen. Legal Assistant, 1962–68; Asst Solicitor, 1968–82, seconded to Cabinet Office Constitution Unit, 1977–78; Dep. Solicitor, 1982–84. *Recreations:* reading, music, theatre.

MACMILLAN, Sir (Alexander McGregor) Graham, Kt 1983; Director, Scottish Conservative Party, 1975–84; *b* 14 Sept. 1920; *s* of James Orr Macmillan and Sarah Dunsmore (*née* Graham); *m* 1947, Christina Brash Beveridge; two *s* two *d.* *Educ:* Hillhead High Sch., Glasgow. Served War, RA, 1939–46. Conservative Agent: W Lothian, 1947–50; Haltemprice, 1950–53; Bury St Edmunds, 1953–60; Dep. Central Office Agent, NW Area, 1960–61; Central Office Agent, Yorks Area, 1961–75. Chairman: Bury St Edmunds Round Table, 1959–60; Bury St Edmunds Br., Multiple Sclerosis Soc., 1987–; M & P Financial Services Ltd, 1986–87 (Dir, 1984–); Mid-Anglian Enterprise Agency Ltd, 1988–; Exec. Sec., YorCan Communications Ltd, 1989–; Mem., Transport Users' Consultative Cttee for E England, 1987–. Hon. Sec., Suffolk Assoc. of Boys' Clubs, 1986–88. Governor, Leeds Grammar Sch., 1968–75. *Recreations:* fishing, watching cricket and rugby. *Address:* 46 Crown Street, Bury St Edmunds, Suffolk IP33 1QX. *T:* Bury St Edmunds (0284) 704443. *Club:* St Stephen's Constitutional.

MACMILLAN, Alexander Ross, FIBScot, CBIM; Director, 1974–87, Chief General Manager, 1971–82, Clydesdale Bank PLC; *b* 25 March 1922; *s* of Donald and Johanna Macmillan; *m* 1961, Ursula Miriam Grayson; two *s* one *d.* *Educ:* Tain Royal Acad. FIBScot 1969; CBIM 1980. Served War, RAF, 1942–46 (despatches, King's Birthday Honours, 1945). Entered service of N of Scotland Bank Ltd, Tain, 1938; after War, returned to Tain, 1946; transf. to Supt's Dept, Aberdeen, and thereafter to Chief Accountant's Dept, Clydesdale Bank, Glasgow, 1950, on amalgamation with N of Scotland Bank; Chief London Office, 1952; Gen. Manager's Confidential Clerk, 1955; Manager, Piccadilly Circus Br., 1958; Supt of Branches, 1965; Gen. Manager's Asst, 1967; Asst Gen. Man., 1968. Director: Caledonian Applied Technology Ltd, 1982–87; Highland-North Sea Ltd, 1982– (Chm., 1982–); John Laing plc, 1982–86; Martin-Black PLC, 1982–85; Radio Clyde plc, 1982–; Scottish Develt Finance Ltd, 1982–; Kelvin Technology Develts Ltd, 1982–; The High Sch. of Glasgow Ltd, 1979–; Compugraphics Internat. Ltd, 1982–87; Highland Deephaven Ltd, 1983–; TEG Products Ltd, 1986–87; New Generation Housing Soc. Ltd, 1986–; Castle Wynd Housing Soc. Ltd, 1987–89; Wilsons Garage (Argyll) Ltd, 1987–; Wilsons Fuels Ltd, 1987–; EFT Gp (formerly Edinburgh Financial Trust) plc, 1987–; Balmoral Gp Ltd, 1988–; North of Scotland Radio Ltd, 1989–; Chm., First Northern Corporate Finance Ltd, 1983–87. Chm., Nat. House Bldg Council (Scotland), 1982–88. Mem. Court, Univ. of Glasgow, 1981–. Freeman, Royal Burgh of Tain, 1975. DUniv Glasgow, 1989. *Recreation:* golf. *Address:* St Winnins, 16 Ledcameroch Road, Bearsden G61 4AB. *T:* 041–942 6455. *Club:* Golf (Killermont).

MacMILLAN, Prof. Andrew, RSA 1990; RIBA; FRIAS; Professor of Architecture, Glasgow University, and Head, Mackintosh School of Architecture, since 1973; *b* 11 Dec. 1928; *s* of Andrew Harkness MacMillan of Murlaggan and Mary Jane McKelvie; *m* 1955, Angela Lillian McDowell; one *s* three *d.* *Educ:* Maryhill Public Sch.; North Kelvinside Sen. Secondary Sch., Glasgow; Glasgow Sch. of Architecture (MA). FRIAS 1973. Apprenticeship, Glasgow Corp. Housing Dept, 1945–52; Architectural Asst, East Kilbride New Town Develt Corp., 1952–54; Asst Architect, 1954–63, Partner, 1966–88, Gillespie Kidd & Coia; consultant architect in private practice, 1988–. Davenport Vis. Prof., Yale Univ., 1986. Mem., Scottish Arts Council, 1978–82; Vice-Pres. for Educn, RIBA, 1981–85; Vice President: Prince and Princess of Wales Hospice, 1981–; Charles Rennie Mackintosh Soc., 1984–; Patron, Arts Educn Trust, 1988–. Royal Scottish Acad. Gold Medal, 1975; RIBA Bronze Medal, 1985; RIBA Award for Arch., 1966, 1967, 1968 and 1982; Saltire awards and Civic Trust awards at various times. *Publications:* papers and articles mainly dealing with urban design, urban building, architectural educn, Glasgow arch. of 20th century, and Charles Rennie Mackintosh. *Recreations:* travel, sailing, watercolours. *Address:* Mackintosh School of Architecture, 177 Renfrew Street, Glasgow G3 6RQ; 1 Falcon Terrace, Glasgow G20 0AG. *T:* 041–946 4358.

McMILLAN, Col Donald, CB 1959; OBE 1945; Chairman, Cable & Wireless Ltd, and associated companies, 1967–72; *b* 22 Dec. 1906; *s* of Neil Munro McMillan and Isabella Jamieson; *m* 1946, Kathleen Ivy Bingham; one *s.* *Educ:* Sloane Sch., Chelsea; Battersea Polytechnic. Post Office Engineering Dept, 1925–54; Director External Telecommunications, Post Office External Telecommunications Executive, 1954–67. BSc Eng (London); FIEE. *Publications:* contribs to Institution Engineers Journal, Post Office Institution Engineers Journal. *Recreations:* golf and gardening. *Address:* 46 Gatehill Road, Northwood, Mddx. *T:* Northwood (09274) 22682. *Club:* Grim's Dyke Golf.

McMILLAN, Rt. Rev. Monsignor Donald Neil; Parish Priest, St Nicholas' Church, Winchcombe, since 1986; *b* 21 May 1925; *s* of Daniel McMillan and Mary Cameron McMillan (*née* Farrell). *Educ:* St Brendan's Coll., Bristol; Prior Park Coll., Bath; Oscott Coll., Sutton Coldfield. Ordained Priest, Dio. Clifton, 1948; Curate: Bath, 1948–49; Gloucester, 1949–51; Taunton, 1951. Commissioned Army Chaplain, 1951; Served: BAOR, 1961–63, 1966–68, 1975–77; Middle East, 1956–59, 1968–70; Far East, 1952–55; Principal RC Chaplain and Vicar Gen. (Army), 1977–81; Parish Priest: St Augustine's Church, Matson Lane, Gloucester, 1981–85; St Teresa's Church, Filton, Bristol, 1985–86. Apptd Prelate of Honour by Pope Paul VI, 1977. *Recreations:* reading, walking. *Address:* St Nicholas Presbytery, Chandos Street, Winchcombe, Glos GL54 5HX. *T:* Cheltenham (0242) 602412. *Clubs:* Army and Navy, Challoner.

McMILLAN, Prof. Duncan; John Orr Professor of French Language and Romance Linguistics, University of Edinburgh, 1955–80, now Emeritus; *b* London, 1914; *o s* of late Duncan McMillan and Martha (*née* Hastings); *m* 1945, Geneviève, *er d* of late M and Mme Robert Busse, Paris; one *s.* *Educ:* Holbeach Rd LCC; St Dunstan's Coll.; University

Coll., London (Troughton Schol., Rothschild Prizeman, Univ. Postgrad. Student); Sorbonne, Paris (Clothworkers Schol., British Inst. in Paris). BA, PhD (London); Diplôme de l'Ecole des Hautes Etudes, Paris. Army, 1940–46. Lecteur d'anglais, Univ. of Paris, 1938–40; Lectr in French and Romance Philology, Univ. of Aberdeen, 1946–50, Univ. of Edinburgh, 1950–55. Founder Mem., Société Rencesvals, 1955, Pres., British Sect., 1956–59; Member Council: Société des anciens textes français, 1963; Société de Linguistique romane, 1977–83. Chevalier de la Légion d'Honneur, 1958; Médaille d'Honneur, Univ. of Liège, 1962. *Publications:* La Chanson de Guillaume (Société des anciens textes français), 2 vols, 1949–50; (in collaboration with Madame G. McMillan) An Anthology of the Contemporary French Novel, 1950; Le Charroi de Nîmes, 1972, 2nd edn 1978. *Address:* 11 rue des Prés Hauts, 92290 Châtenay Malabry, France. *T:* (1) 4660 3713. *Club:* Scottish Arts (Edinburgh).

MACMILLAN, Very Rev. Gilleasbuig Iain; Minister of St Giles', The High Kirk of Edinburgh, since 1973; Chaplain to the Queen in Scotland, since 1979; Dean of the Order of the Thistle, since 1989; *b* 21 Dec. 1942; *s* of Rev. Kenneth M. Macmillan and Mrs Mary Macmillan; *m* 1965, Maureen Stewart Thomson; one *d. Educ:* Oban High School; Univ. of Edinburgh. MA, BD. Asst Minister, St Michael's Parish, Linlithgow, 1967–69; Minister of Portree Parish, Isle of Skye, 1969–73. Extra Chaplain to the Queen in Scotland, 1978–79. Hon. Chaplain: Royal Scottish Academy; Royal Coll. of Surgeons of Edinburgh; Soc. of High Constables of City of Edinburgh. *Address:* St Giles' Cathedral, Edinburgh EH1 1RE. *T:* 031–225 4363. *Club:* New (Edinburgh).

MACMILLAN, Sir Graham; see Macmillan, Sir A. M. G.

MACMILLAN, Iain Alexander, CBE 1978; LLD; Sheriff of South Strathclyde, Dumfries and Galloway at Hamilton, since 1981; *b* 14 Nov. 1923; *s* of John and Eva Macmillan; *m* 1954, Edith Janet (*née* MacAulay); two *s* one *d. Educ:* Oban High Sch.; Glasgow Univ. (BL). Served war, RAF, France, Germany, India, 1944–47. Glasgow Univ., 1947–50. Subseq. law practice; Sen. Partner, J. & J. Sturrock & Co., Kilmarnock, 1952–81. Law Society of Scotland: Mem. Council, 1964–79; Pres., 1976–77. Chm. Lanarkshire Br., Scottish Assoc. for Study of Delinquency, 1986–. Hon. LLD Aberdeen, 1975. *Recreation:* golf. *Address:* 2 Castle Drive, Kilmarnock KA3 1TN. *T:* Kilmarnock (0563) 25864.

MacMILLAN, Jake; see MacMillan, John.

McMILLAN, John, CBE 1969; *b* 29 Jan. 1915; *s* of late William McArthur McMillan, Sydney, NSW; *m* 1958, Lucy Mary, *d* of late Edward Moore, DSO; three *s* two *d. Educ:* Scots Coll., Sydney. Manager, Internat. Broadcasting Co. Ltd, London, 1936–38; Manager, EMI Ltd, developing the long-playing record, 1938–39. Served War: joined horsed cavalry as trooper, 1939; commissioned, S Wales Borderers, 1940; OC No 1 Field Broadcasting Unit, British Forces Network, and Telecommns Dir in interim NW German PO, 1945–46 (despatches). Asst, and later Chief Asst, to Controller, BBC Light Programme, 1946–53; USA television, 1954; Manager, Associated Broadcasting Develt Co., London, 1954–55; Controller of Programmes, later Gen. Man. and Dir Rediffusion Television Ltd, 1955–68; Director: Independent Television News Ltd, 1955–68; Global Television Services Ltd, 1960–68; Dir of Special Events and Sport, ITV, 1965–71; Sen. rep. of ITV cos at EBU (Geneva and Brussels), 1968–71. Member: ITA Programme Policy Cttee, 1960–68; Independent Television Standing Consultative Cttee, 1964–68; Independent Television Cos Assoc. (Chm., Finance and General Purposes Cttee), 1964–68; UK Consortium of Communications Satellite Cttee (INTELSAT), Washington DC, 1964–68. Dir, Theatre Royal Windsor Co., 1963–79; Man. Dir, Brompton Production Co. Ltd, 1971–77; Chm. and Man. Dir, Sportsdata Ltd, 1978–80; Chm., Vernons Viewdata Services Ltd, 1978–80. *Recreations:* swimming, gardening, study of 1919–39 European history. *Address:* c/o Lloyds Bank, 6 Pall Mall, SW1.

MacMILLAN, Prof. John, (Jake), PhD Glasgow; DSc Bristol; FRS 1978; CChem, ARIC; Alfred Capper Pass Professor of Organic Chemistry, 1985–89, and Head of Department of Organic Chemistry, 1983–89, University of Bristol, now Professor Emeritus; *b* 13 Sept. 1924; *s* of John MacMillan and Barbara Lindsay; *m* 1952, Anne Levy; one *s* two *d. Educ:* Lanark Grammar Sch.; Glasgow Univ. Res. Chemist, Akers Res. Labs, ICI Ltd, 1949; Associate Res. Manager, Pharmaceuticals Div., ICI Ltd, 1962; Lectr in Org. Chemistry, Bristol Univ., 1963, Reader 1968, Prof. 1978. Pres., Internat. Plant Growth Substance Assoc., 1973–76. *Publications:* research papers in learned jls on natural organic products, esp. plant growth hormones. *Recreations:* golf, gardening, theatre, music. *Address:* 1 Rylestone Grove, Bristol BS9 3UT. *T:* Bristol (0272) 620535.

MacMILLAN, Lt-Gen. Sir John Richard Alexander, KCB 1988; CBE 1978 (OBE 1973); GOC Scotland and Governor of Edinburgh Castle, 1988–91; *b* 8 Feb. 1932; *m* 1964, Belinda Lumley Webb; one *s* two *d. Educ:* Trinity Coll., Cambridge (BA 1953; MA 1958); rcds, psc. Commnd Argyll and Sutherland Highlanders, 2nd Lieut, 1952; GSO2 (Ops Int. Trng), Trucial Oman Scouts, 1963–64; BM, HQ 24 Inf. Bde, 1967–69; Chief Recruiting and Liaison Staff, Scotland, 1970; CO, 1st Bn The Gordon Highlanders, 1971–73; GSO1 (DS), Staff Coll., 1973–75; Col GS, Mil. Ops 4, 1975–76; Brig., 1976; Bde Comd, 39 Inf. Bde, 1977–78; RCDS 1979; COS, 1 (Br) Corps, 1980–82; Maj.-Gen., 1982; GOC Eastern Dist, 1982–84; ACGS, MoD, 1984–87; Lt-Gen., 1988. Col, The Gordon Highlanders, 1978–86; Col Comdt, Scottish Div., 1986–91; Hon. Col, Aberdeen Univ. OTC, 1987–. *Address:* c/o Northern Bank, 9 Donegall Square North, Belfast BT1 5GJ.

MacMILLAN, Sir Kenneth, Kt 1983; Principal Choreographer to the Royal Ballet, Covent Garden, since 1977; Artistic Associate, American Ballet Theatre, since 1984; *b* 11 Dec. 1929; *m* 1974, Deborah Williams. *Educ:* Great Yarmouth Gram. Sch. Started as Dancer, Royal Ballet; became Choreographer, 1953; Dir of Ballet, Deutsche Oper, Berlin, 1966–69; Resident Choreographer, and Dir, Royal Ballet, 1970–77. First professional ballet, Danses Concertantes (Stravinsky-Georgiades). Principal ballets: The Burrow; Solitaire; Agon; The Invitation; Romeo and Juliet; Diversions; La Création du Monde; Images of Love; The Song of the Earth; Concerto; Anastasia; Cain and Abel; Olympiad; Triad; Ballade; The Poltroon; Manon; Pavanne; Elite Syncopations; The Four Seasons; Rituals; Requiem; Mayerling; My Brother, My Sisters; La Fin du Jour; Gloria; Isadora; Valley of Shadows; Different Drummer; The Wild Boy; Requiem (Andrew Lloyd Webber); The Prince of the Pagodas; Winter Dreams. Has devised ballets for: Ballet Rambert, American Ballet, Royal Ballet Sch., theatre, television, cinema, musical shows. Directed: Ionesco's plays, The Chairs and The Lesson, New Inn, Ealing, 1982; The Dance of Death, Royal Exchange, Manchester, 1983; The Kingdom of Earth, Hampstead Theatre Club, 1984. Dr *hc* Edinburgh, 1976. Evening Standard Ballet Award, 1979; Ballet Award, SWET Managers, 1980 and 1983. *Recreation:* cinema. *Address:* c/o Royal Opera House, Covent Garden, WC2.

MACMILLAN, Matthew, CBE 1983 (OBE 1977); educational consultant, since 1990; *b* 14 July 1926; *s* of late David Craig Macmillan and Barbara Cruikshank Macmillan (*née* Gow); *m* 1949, Winifred (*née* Sagar); one *s* two *d. Educ:* Robert Gordon's Coll., Aberdeen; Aberdeen Univ. (MA Hons); Manchester Univ. (Teacher's Dip.) Served Royal Air Force, 1944–47. Schoolmaster, Chatham House Grammar Sch., Ramsgate, 1951–57; Sen. Lectr,

Univ. of Science and Technology, Kumasi, Ghana, 1958–62; Associate Prof., University Coll. of Cape Coast, Ghana, 1962–64; Prof. of English, Univ. of Khartoum, The Sudan, 1965–70; British Council, London: Director, English-Teaching Information Centre, 1970–72; Dep. Controller, English Teaching Div., 1972–74; Asst Educn Adviser (English Studies), British Council, India, 1974–78; Controller, English Lang. and Lit. Div., British Council, 1978–83; Prof. of English, 1983–89, Principal, 1986–89, University Coll., Univ. of E Asia, Macau; Prof., English Programmes, E Asia Open Inst., Hong Kong, 1989–90. *Publications:* articles on the teaching of English as a second/foreign language. *Recreations:* gardening, walking. *Address:* Manor House Cottage, The Row, Elham, Canterbury, Kent CT4 6UL. *T:* Elham (0303) 840427. *Club:* Commonwealth Trust.

MACMILLAN, Prof. Robert Hugh; Professor of Vehicle Design and Head of School of Automotive Studies, 1977–82, Dean of Engineering, 1980–82, Cranfield Institute of Technology; *b* Mussoorie, India, 27 June 1921; *s* of H. R. M. Macmillan and E. G. Macmillan (*née* Webb); *m* 1950, Anna Christina Roding, Amsterdam; one *s* two *d. Educ:* Felsted Sch.; Emmanuel Coll., Cambridge. Technical Branch, RAFVR, 1941; Dept of Engrg, Cambridge Univ., 1947; Asst Prof. MIT, 1950–51; Prof. of Mech. Engrg, Swansea, 1956; Dir, Motor Industry Res. Assoc., 1964–77; Associate Prof., Warwick Univ., 1965–77. 20th Leonardo Da Vinci Lectr, 1973. Mem. Council, Loughborough Univ., 1966–81, 1988–; Chm. Council, Automobile Div., IMechE, 1976–77; Member: Noise Adv. Council, 1970–77; Internat. Technical Commn, FIA, 1975–88; FISITA: Mem. Council, 1970–80; Chm., London Congress, 1972. Approved Lectr for NADFAS, 1985–; official guide, Winslow Hall, 1985–, Ascott, 1988–. Editor, The Netherlands Philatelist, 1984–88. FRSA; MIEE; FIMechE; FRPSL. Gold Medal, FISITA, 1970. *Publications:* Theory of Control, 1951; Automation, 1956; Geometric Symmetry, 1978; Dynamics of Vehicle Collisions, 1983. *Recreations:* music, philately, national heritage. *Address:* 43 Church Road, Woburn Sands, Bucks MK17 8TG. *T:* Milton Keynes (0908) 584011. *Clubs:* Royal Air Force, Royal Over-Seas League.

MACMILLAN, Wallace, CMG 1956; retired; *b* 16 Oct. 1913; *s* of late David Hutchen Macmillan and late Jean Wallace, Newburgh, Fife; *m* 1947, Betty Bryce, *d* of late G. R. Watson and Margaret Bryce; three *s. Educ:* Bell-Baxter Sch.; University of St Andrews; Kiel Univ.; Corpus Christi Coll., Oxford. Administrative Officer, Tanganyika, 1937; District Officer, 1947; Administrator of Grenada, BWI, 1951–57. Acted as Governor, Windward Is, periods 1955. Federal Establishment Sec. (subsequently Permanent Sec., Min. of Estabts and Service Matters), Federation of Nigeria, 1957–61. Dir, Management Selection Ltd, 1961–78. *Recreations:* bridge, chess, golf. *Address:* Flat 1, 6 Spylaw Road, Edinburgh EH10 5BL.

MACMILLAN, Rt. Rev. William Boyd Robertson; Moderator of the General Assembly of the Church of Scotland, May 1991–May 1992 (subseq. designation Very Rev.); Minister, Dundee Parish Church (St Mary's), since 1978; Chaplain to the Queen in Scotland, since 1988; *b* 3 July 1927; *s* of Robert and Annie Simpson Macmillan; *m* 1962, Mary Adams Bisset Murray. *Educ:* Royal High Sch., Edinburgh; Univ. of Aberdeen (MA, BD). Served RN, 1946–48. Minister: St Andrew's, Bo'ness, 1955–60; Fyvie, 1960–67; Bearsden, South, 1967–78. Convener, General Assembly, Church of Scotland: Bd of Practice and Procedure, 1985–88; Business Cttee, 1985–88. Hon. LLD Dundee, 1990; Hon. DD Aberdeen, 1991. *Recreations:* reading, golf, stamp collecting. *Address:* Manse of Dundee, 371 Blackness Road, Dundee DD2 1ST. *T:* Dundee (0382) 69406.

McMILLAN-SCOTT, Edward; Member (C) York, European Parliament, since 1984; *b* 15 Aug. 1949; *s* of Walter Theodore Robin McMillan-Scott, ARIBA and Elizabeth Maud Derrington Hudson; *m* 1972, Henrietta Elizabeth Rumney Hudson, solicitor; two *d. Educ:* Blackfriars School, Llanarth; Blackfriars School, Laxton; Exeter Technical College. Tour director in Europe, Scandinavia, Africa and USSR, 1968–75; PR exec., then parly consultant, 1976–84; political adviser to Falkland Islands Govt, London office 1983–84. European Parliament: Member: Political Affairs Cttee, 1989–; Transport Cttee, 1989–; Vice-Chm., 1979 Cttee (Cons. back-bench cttee), 1988–. Mem., Gen. Council, Cons. Gp for Europe. Vice-Pres., Yorks and Humberside Develt Assoc. Mem. Court, Univ. of York. *Publication:* Mulberry; the artificial harbours, 1979 (with Sir Bruce White). *Recreations:* music, reading. *Address:* European Parliament, 2 Queen Anne's Gate, SW1. *Club:* St Stephen's Constitutional.

McMINN, Prof. Robert Matthew Hay; Emeritus Professor of Anatomy, Royal College of Surgeons and University of London; *b* 20 Sept. 1923; *o s* of late Robert Martin McMinn, MB, ChB, Auchinleck and Brighton, and Elsie Selene Kent; *m* 1948, Margaret Grieve Kirkwood, MB, ChB, DA; one *s* one *d. Educ:* Brighton Coll. (Schol.); Univ. of Glasgow. MB, ChB 1947, MD (commendation) 1958, Glasgow; PhD Sheffield 1956; FRCS 1978. Hosp. posts and RAF Med. Service, 1947–50; Demonstrator in Anatomy, Glasgow Univ., 1950–52; Lectr in Anatomy, Sheffield Univ., 1952–60; Reader 1960–66, Prof. of Anatomy 1966–70, King's Coll., London Univ.; Sir William Collins Prof. of Human and Comparative Anatomy, RCS, Conservator, Hunterian Museum, RCS, and Prof. of Anatomy, Inst. of Basic Med. Scis, London Univ., 1970–82, prematurely retd. Examnr, RCP&S Glasgow; late Examnr to RCS and Univs of London, Cambridge, Edinburgh, Belfast, Singapore, Malaya and Makerere. Arris and Gale Lectr, RCS, 1960; Arnott Demonstrator, RCS, 1970. Former Treas., Anatomical Soc. of Gt Britain and Ireland; Foundn Sec., British Assoc. of Clinical Anatomists; FRSocMed; Member: Amer. Assoc. of Anatomists; Amer. Assoc. of Clinical Anatomists; British Soc. of Gastroenterology; BMA; Trustee, Skin Res. Foundn. *Publications:* Tissue Repair, 1969; The Digestive System, 1974; The Human Gut, 1974; (jtly) Colour Atlas of Human Anatomy, 1977, 2nd edn 1988; (jtly) Colour Atlas of Head and Neck Anatomy, 1981; (jtly) Colour Atlas of Foot and Ankle Anatomy, 1982; (jtly) Colour Atlas of Applied Anatomy, 1984; (jtly) Picture Tests in Human Anatomy, 1986; (jtly) The Human Skeleton, 1987; (ed) Last's Anatomy, 8th edn 1990; (jtly) Human Form and Function, 1991; articles in various med. and sci. jls. *Recreations:* motoring, photography, archaeology, short-wave radio. *Address:* Tavistone Lodge, Commonside, Great Bookham, Leatherhead, Surrey KT23 3LA. *T:* Leatherhead (0372) 459271.

McMINNIES, John Gordon, OBE 1965; HM Diplomatic Service, retired 1977; *b* 1 Oct. 1919; *s* of late William Gordon McMinnies and Joyce Millicent McMinnies; *m* 1947, Mary (*née* Jackson) (*d* 1978), novelist. *Educ:* Bilton Grange; Rugby Sch.; Austria (language trng). Reporter: Western Mail, 1938; Reuters, 1939. Served War, Army, 1940–46: comd R Troop, RHA; retd, Major. HM Diplomatic Service (Athens, Warsaw, Bologna, Malaysia, Cyprus, Nairobi, Lusaka, New Delhi), 1946–77; retd, Counsellor. *Recreations:* crazy paving, crosswords, cricketology, the sea. *Address:* 2 rue de la République, 34300 Agde, France. *T:* 67.21.44.38.

McMULLAN, Rt. Rev. Gordon; see Down and Dromore, Bishop of.

McMULLAN, Michael Brian; His Honour Judge McMullan; a Circuit Judge, since 1980; *b* 15 Nov. 1926; *s* of late Joseph Patrick McMullan and Frances McMullan (*née* Burton); *m* 1960, Rosemary Jane Margaret, *d* of late Stanley Halse deL. de Ville; one *s* two *d. Educ:* Manor Farm Road Sch.; Tauntons Sch., Southampton; The Queen's College, Oxford (MA). Called to the Bar, Gray's Inn, 1960. National Service, Army, 1946–48.

Colonial Administrative Service: Gold Coast and Ghana, Political Administration Ashanti, Min. of Finance, Accra, Agricl Development Corp., 1949–60. In practice as Barrister, SE Circuit, 1961–80; a Recorder of the Crown Court, 1979. *Club:* United Oxford & Cambridge University.
See also J. P. M. Stern.

McMULLEN, Prof. David Lawrence; Professor of Chinese, University of Cambridge, since 1989; Fellow of St John's College, Cambridge, since 1967; *b* 10 Aug. 1939; *m* 1983, Sarah Jane Clarice Croft; two *d. Educ:* Monkton Combe Sch., Bath; St John's Coll., Cambridge (BA, MA, PhD). National Service, RAF, 1957–59. Taiwan Min. of Educn Schol., 1963–64; Harkness Commonwealth Fellowship, 1965–67; Asst Lectr 1967, Lectr 1972, in Chinese Studies, Cambridge Univ. Pres., British Assoc. for Chinese Studies, 1985–87. *Publications:* Concordances and Indexes to Chinese Texts, 1975; State and Scholars in T'ang China, 1988; contribs to jls of E Asian studies. *Recreations:* collecting porcelain, rowing, gardening. *Address:* 50 Grantchester Road, Newnham, Cambridge CB3 9ED. *T:* Cambridge (0223) 62519.

McMULLIN, Rt. Hon. Sir Duncan (Wallace), Kt 1987; PC 1980; Judge of Court of Appeal, New Zealand, 1979–89; *b* 1 May 1927; *s* of Charles James McMullin and Kathleen Annie Shout; *m* 1955, Isobel Margaret, *d* of Robert Ronald Atkinson, ED; two *s* two *d. Educ:* Auckland Grammar Sch.; Univ. of Auckland (LLB). Judge of Supreme Court, 1970. Chm., Royal Commn on Contraception, Sterilisation and Abortion in NZ, 1975–77. Chm., Wanganui Computer Centre Policy Cttee. *Recreations:* forestry, farming. *Address:* 707 Remuera Road, Auckland, New Zealand. *T:* Auckland 5246583. *Club:* Wellington (Wellington, NZ).

McMURRAY, Dr Cecil Hugh, FRSC, FIFST; Chief Scientific Officer, Department of Agriculture for Northern Ireland, since 1988; *b* 19 Feb. 1942; *s* of Edwin McMurray and Margaret (*née* Smyth); *m* 1967, Ann Stuart; two *s* one *d. Educ:* Royal Belfast Academical Instn; Queen's University, Belfast (BSc 1965; BAgr 1966); PhD Bristol, 1970. FRSC 1981; FIFST 1987. Res. Fellow, Dept of Chem., Harvard Univ., 1970–72; Head of Biochem. Dept, Vet. Res. Lab., Dept of Agric. for NI, 1972–84; Prof. of Food and Agricl Chem., QUB, and concurrently DCSO, Dept of Agric. for NI, 1984–88. Expert Advr, WHO, 1983, 1986; Assessor to: AFRC, 1988–; Priorities Bd for R&D in Agric. and Food, 1988–; Technology Bd for NI, 1988–. Pres., Agricl Gp, BAAS, 1986–87. Mem. Cttee, Coronary Prevention Gp, 1985–89. Trustee, Agricl Inst. for NI, 1985–; Mem. Governing Body, Rowett Res. Inst., Aberdeen, 1986–89. Mem. Editl Bd, Fertiliser Res., 1985–. *Publications:* over 100 scientific publications in various jls incl. Biochemical Jl, Jl of Amer. Chemical Soc., Clin. Chem., CIBA Foundn Symposia, Jl of Chromatography, British Vet. Jl, Vet. Record, Jl Assoc. of Anal Chem., Trace Metals in Man and Domestic Animals, Biology of Total Envmt. *Recreations:* reading, photography, walking, gardening. *Address:* Department of Agriculture for Northern Ireland, Dundonald House, Upper Newtownards Road, Belfast BT4 3SB. *T:* Belfast (0232) 650111.

McMURRAY, David Bruce, MA; Headmaster, Oundle School, since 1984; *b* 15 Dec. 1937; *s* of late James McMurray, CBE, and of Kathleen McMurray (*née* Goodwin); *m* 1962, Antonia Murray; three *d. Educ:* Loretto Sch.; Pembroke Coll., Cambridge (BA, MA). National service, Royal Scots, 1956–58, 2nd Lieut. Pembroke Coll., Cambridge, 1958–61; Asst Master, Stowe Sch., 1961–64; Fettes College: Asst Master, 1964–72; Head of English, 1967–72; Housemaster, 1972–76; Headmaster, Loretto Sch., 1976–84. HM Comr, Queen Victoria Sch., Dunblane, 1977–87; Mem., Edinburgh Fest. Council, 1980–84. FRSA 1989. CCF Medal, 1976. *Recreations:* cricket, golf, sub-aqua diving, poetry. *Address:* Cobthorne, West Street, Oundle, Peterborough. *T:* Oundle (0832) 273536. *Clubs:* East India, Devonshire, Sports and Public Schools, MCC, Free Foresters.

MacMURRAY, Mary Bell McMillan, (Mrs Ian Mills), QC 1979; **Her Honour Judge MacMurray;** a Circuit Judge, since 1988; *d* of Samuel Bell MacMurray and Constance Mary MacMurray (*née* Goodman); *m* 1971, Ian Donald Mills. *Educ:* Queen Margaret's School, Escrick, York. Called to the Bar, Lincoln's Inn, 1954, Bencher, 1986. Barrister-at-Law, 1954–88; a Recorder of the Crown Court, 1978–88. Coronation Medal, 1953. *Recreation:* golf. *Address:* c/o Courts Administrator, Westgate House, Westgate Road, Newcastle upon Tyne NE1 1RR. *Clubs:* Durham County; Whitburn Golf; Boldon Golf.

McMURTRIE, Group Captain Richard Angus, DSO 1940; DFC 1940; Royal Air Force, retired; *b* 14 Feb. 1909; *s* of Radburn Angus and Ethel Maud McMurtrie; *m* 1st, 1931, Gwenyth Mary (*d* 1958), 3rd *d* of Rev. (Lt-Col) H. J. Philpott; no *c*; 2nd, 1963, Laura, 4th *d* of Wm H. Gerhardi. *Educ:* Royal Grammar Sch., Newcastle on Tyne. First commissioned in Territorial Army (72nd Brigade, RA), 1927; transferred to Royal Air Force, 1929, as Pilot Officer; served in No 2 (AC) Squadron, 1931–32, and Fleet Air Arm (442 Flight, and 822 Squadron in HMS *Furious*), 1932–33; Cranwell, 1934–35; Flt Lieut, 1935; Calshot and No. 201 (Flying Boat) Squadron, 1935–38; Squadron Leader, 1938, and commanded Recruits Sub-Depot, RAF, Linton-on-Ouse; served War of 1939–45 (despatches thrice, DFC, DSO); No 269 GR Squadron, 1939–41; Wing Commander, 1940; HQ No 18 Group RAF, 1941; Group Captain, commanding RAF Station, Sumburgh (Shetlands), 1942–43; HQ Coastal Command, 1943; RAF Staff Coll., Air Ministry, Whitehall, and HQ Transport Command, 1944; commanded RAF Station, Stoney Cross, Hants, 1945; and formed and commanded No. 61 Group (Reserve Command), 1946; Joint Services Mission, Washington, DC, 1946–49; commanded RAF Station, Cardington, 1949–52; HQ No 1 Group, RAF, 1952–54; Royal Naval College, Greenwich, 1954; HQ, Supreme Allied Commander, Atlantic (NATO), Norfolk, Virginia, USA, 1954–56; HQ, Coastal Command, RAF, Northwood, Mddx, 1957–59, now farming. *Recreations:* sailing, photography. *Address:* Rose in Vale Farm, Constantine, Falmouth, Cornwall TR11 5PU. *T:* Falmouth (0326) 40338. *Clubs:* RAF Yacht (Hon. Life Mem.), Royal Cornwall Yacht.

McMURTRY, (Roland) Roy; QC 1970; Member of law firm, Blaney, McMurtry, Stapells, since 1988; *b* 31 May 1932; *s* of Roland Roy McMurtry and Doris Elizabeth Belcher; *m* 1957, Ria Jean Macrae; three *s* three *d. Educ:* St Andrew's Coll., Aurora, Ont; Trinity Coll., Univ. of Toronto (BA Hons); Osgoode Hall Law Sch., Toronto (LLB). Called to the Bar of Ontario, 1958. Partner, Benson, McMurtry, Percival & Brown, Toronto, 1958–75. Elected to Ontario Legislature, 1975; re-elected, 1977 and 1981; Attorney General for Ontario, 1975–85; Solicitor General for Ontario, 1978–82. High Comr in UK, 1985–88. Freeman, City of London, 1986. Hon. LLD: Univ. of Ottawa, 1983; Law Soc. of Upper Canada, 1984; Univ. of Leeds, 1988. *Recreations:* painting, skiing, tennis. *Address:* 1400–20 Queen Street West, Toronto, Ont M5H 2V3, Canada. *T:* (416) 593–1221. *Clubs:* Albany, Badminton and Racket (Toronto).

MACNAB, Brigadier Sir Geoffrey (Alex Colin), KCMG 1962 (CMG 1955); CB 1951; retired; *b* 23 Dec. 1899; *s* of Brig.-General Colin Macnab, CMG; *m* 1930, Norah (*d* 1981), *d* of Captain H. A. Cramer-Roberts, Folkestone. *Educ:* Wellington Coll.; RMC Sandhurst. 1st Commission, 1919, Royal Sussex Regt; Instr, Small Arms Sch., Hythe, 1925–28; Captain, Argyll and Sutherland Highlanders, 1931; Staff Coll., Camberley, 1930–31; GSO 3, WO, 1933–35; BM 10 Infantry Bde, 1935–38; Military Attaché,

Prague and Bucharest, 1938–40; served War of 1939–45, campaigns Western Desert, Greece, Crete; Brigadier, 1944; Military Mission, Hungary, 1945; DMI, Middle East, 1945–47; Military Attaché, Rome, 1947–49; Military Attaché, Paris, 1949–54; retired 1954. Service in Ireland, Germany, Far East, India, Middle East. Secretary, Government Hospitality Fund, 1957–68. *Address:* Stanford House, Stanford, Ashford, Kent. *T:* Sellindge (030381) 2118. *Clubs:* Army and Navy, MCC.

MACNAB OF MACNAB, James Charles; The Macnab; 23rd Chief of Clan Macnab; Senior Consultant, Hill Samuel Investment Services Ltd, since 1982; *b* 14 April 1926; *e s* of late Lt-Col James Alexander Macnabb, OBE, TD (*de jure* 21st of Macnab), London, SW3, and Mrs G. H. Walford, Wokingham, Berks; *S* gt uncle Archibald Corrie Macnab, (*de facto*) 22nd Chief, 1970; *m* 1959, Hon. Diana Mary, *er d* of Baron Kilmany, PC, MC, and of Monica Helen, (Lady Kilmany), OBE, JP, *o c* of late Geoffrey Lambton, 2nd *s* of 4th Earl of Durham; two *s* two *d. Educ:* Cothill House; Radley Coll.; Ashbury Coll., Ottawa. Served in RAF and Scots Guards, 1944–45; Lieut, Seaforth Highldrs, 1945–48. Asst Supt, then Dep. Supt, Fedn of Malaya Police Force, 1948; retd, 1957. Mem., Western DC of Perthshire, 1961–64; CC, Perth and Kinross Jt County Council, 1964–75; Mem., Central Regional Council, 1978–82. Member, Royal Company of Archers, Queen's Body Guard in Scotland. JP Perthshire, 1968–75, Stirling, 1975–86. *Recreations:* shooting, travel. *Heir:* *s* James William Archibald Macnab, younger of Macnab, *b* 22 March 1963. *Address:* West Kilmany House, Kilmany, Cupar, Fife KY15 4QW. *T:* Gauldry (082624) 247 and 527. *Club:* New (Edinburgh).

McNAB, John Stanley; Chief Executive, Port of Tilbury (Port of London Authority), since 1987; *b* 23 Sept. 1937; *s* of Robert Stanley McNab and Alice Mary McNab; *m* 1st, 1961, Carol Field (marr. diss. 1978); two *d*; 2nd, 1980, Jacqueline Scammell. *Educ:* Gravesend Grammar Sch. FCCA. Nat. Service, Royal Engineers, Libya, 1956–58. Port of London Authority: joined 1954; Accountant, India and Millwall Docks, 1965, Upper Docks, 1970; Man. Dir, PLA (Thames) Stevedoring, 1973; Dir, Upper Docks, 1974; Exec. Dir (Manpower) and Group Board Mem., 1978; Dir, Tilbury, 1983. Freeman: City of London, 1988; Co. of Watermen and Lightermen of River Thames, 1988. MBIM. *Recreations:* walking the dogs, swimming, tennis, DIY, learning Spanish and Portuguese. *Address:* Port of Tilbury, Leslie Ford House, Tilbury Docks, Essex RM18 7EH. *T:* Tilbury (0375) 852427.

McNAB JONES, Robin Francis, FRCS; Surgeon: ENT Department, St Bartholomew's Hospital, 1961–87; Royal National Throat, Nose and Ear Hospital, 1962–83; *b* 22 Oct. 1922; *s* of E. C. H. Jones, CBE, and M. E. Jones, MBE; *m* 1950, Mary Garrett; one *s* three *d. Educ:* Manchester Grammar Sch.; Dulwich Coll.; Med. Coll., St Bartholomew's Hosp. (MB BS 1945). FRCS 1952. Ho. Surg., St Bart's, 1946–47; MO, RAF, 1947–50; Demonstrator of Anatomy, St Bart's, 1950–52; Registrar, Royal Nat. Throat, Nose and Ear Hosp., 1952–54; Sen. Registrar, ENT Dept, St Bart's, 1954–59; Lectr, Dept of Otolaryngology, Univ. of Manchester, 1959–61; Dean, Inst. of Laryngology and Otology, Univ. of London, 1971–76; Vice-Pres., St Bart's Hosp. Med. Coll., 1984–87. Mem., Court of Examiners, 1972–78, and Mem. Council (for Otolaryngology), 1982–87, RCS; External Examiner, RCSI, 1980–83, 1988–. Hon. Sec., Sect. of Otology, 1965–68, Pres., Sect. of Laryngology, 1981–82, RSocMed. *Publications:* various chapters in standard med. textbooks; contribs to med. jls. *Recreations:* tennis, ski-ing, golf, fishing, gardening. *Address:* The Consulting Suite, Fitzroy Nuffield Hospital, 10–12 Bryanston Square, W1H 8BB. *T:* 071–723 1288; 52 Oakwood Avenue, Beckenham, Kent BR3 2PJ. *T:* 081–650 0217.

MACNAGHTEN, Sir Patrick (Alexander), 11th Bt *cr* 1836; farmer; *b* 24 Jan. 1927; *s* of Sir Antony Macnaghten, 10th Bt, and of Magdalene, *e d* of late Edmund Fisher; *S* father, 1972; *m* 1955, Marianne, *yr d* of Dr Erich Schaefer and Alice Schaefer, Cambridge; three *s. Educ:* Eton; Trinity Coll., Cambridge (BA Mechanical Sciences). Army (RE), 1945–48. Project Engineer, Cadbury Bros (later Cadbury Schweppes), 1950–69; in General Management, Cadbury-Schweppes Ltd, 1969–84. *Recreations:* fishing, shooting. *Heir:* *s* Malcolm Francis Macnaghten, *b* 21 Sept. 1956. *Address:* Dundarave, Bushmills, Co. Antrim, Northern Ireland. *T:* Bushmills (02657) 31215.

MACNAGHTEN, Robin Donnelly, MA; Headmaster of Sherborne, 1974–88; *b* 3 Aug. 1927; 2nd *s* of late Sir Henry P. W. Macnaghten and of Lady Macnaghten; *m* 1961, Petronella, *er d* of late Lt-Col A. T. Card and Mrs Card; two *s* one *d. Educ:* Eton (Schol.); King's Coll., Cambridge (Schol.). 1st cl. Class. Tripos Pt I, 1947; 1st cl. with dist. Pt II, 1948; Browne Medallist; MA 1954. Travelled in Italy and Turkey, 1949. Asst, Mackinnon Mackenzie & Co., Bombay, 1949–54. Asst Master, Eton Coll., 1954, and Housemaster, 1965. Hon. Sec. and Treas., OEA, 1970–74; Pres., Old Shirburnian Soc., 1984–85. Governor: Forres Sch., 1974–88; Sandroyd Sch., 1986–; Dauntsey's Sch., 1988–; Chm. of Govs, Hall Sch., Wincanton, 1978–. *Publication:* trans. Vita Romana (by U. E. Paoli), 1963. *Recreations:* numismatics (FRNS), walking, gardening. *Address:* Prospect House, Tisbury, Wilts SP3 6QQ. *T:* Tisbury (0747) 870355. *Club:* Western India Turf (Bombay).

McNAIR, family name of **Baron McNair.**

McNAIR, 3rd Baron *cr* 1955, of Gleniffer; **Duncan James McNair;** *b* 26 June 1947; *s* of 2nd Baron McNair and Vera, *d* of Theodore James Faithfull; *S* father, 1989. *Educ:* Bryanston. *Heir:* *b* Hon. William Samuel Angus McNair, *b* 19 May 1958. *Address:* House of Lords, SW1.

McNAIR, Archie, (Archibald Alister Jourdan); Co-founder, 1955, and Chairman, 1955–88, Mary Quant Group of Companies; Founder, 1971, and Chairman, 1971–88, Thomas Jourdan plc; Director, City and Capital Hotels plc, since 1986; *b* 16 Dec. 1919; *s* of late Donald McNair and Janie (*née* Jourdan); *m* 1954, Catherine Alice Jane, *d* of late John and of Margaret Fleming; one *s* one *d. Educ:* Blundell's. Articled to Ford Simey & Ford, Solicitors, Exeter, 1938. Served War, 1939–45: River Thames Formation. Photographer, 1950–57. *Recreations:* growing fruit, carving wood, tennis, chess. *Address:* c/o Coutts & Co., 440 Strand, WC2N 5LJ. *Club:* Turf.

MACNAIR, Maurice John Peter; His Honour Judge Macnair; a Circuit Judge since 1972; *b* 27 Feb. 1919; *s* of late Brig. J. L. P. Macnair and Hon. Mrs Macnair (*née* Atkin); *m* 1952, Vickie Reynolds, *d* of Hugh Reynolds; one *s* two *d. Educ:* Bembridge Sch.; St Paul's Sch.; St Edmund Hall, Oxford. BA 1947. Served War of 1939–45, Western Desert, Sicily, Italy; wounded 1944; Captain, RA. Called to Bar, Gray's Inn, 1948. Dep. Chm., W Sussex QS, 1968–72. *Address:* Lambeth County Court, Cleaver Street, SE11.

McNAIR, Thomas Jaffrey, CBE 1988; MD; FRCSE, FRCS, FRCPE, FRCPGlas; Surgeon to the Queen in Scotland, 1977–87; Consultant Surgeon, Royal Infirmary of Edinburgh, 1961–87; *b* 1 March 1927; *s* of David McMillan McNair and Helen (*née* Rae); *m* 1951, Dr Sybil Monteith Dick Wood; one *s* one *d. Educ:* George Watson's Coll.; Univ. of Edinburgh (MB, ChB, MD). FRCSE 1955: FRCS 1956; FRCPE 1989; FRCPGlas 1989. Ho. Surg., Registrar, Clinical Tutor, Royal Infirmary of Edin., 1949–60; MO, Marlu, Gold Coast, 1950. Served as Flt Lt, RAF, 1950–52. Lectr in Clin. Surgery, Univ. of Edin., 1960; Instr in Surgery, Univ. of Illinois, USA, 1960; Consultant Surgeon: Eastern Gen. Hosp., 1961–64; Chalmers Hosp., 1964–81. Hon. Sen. Lectr in Clin. Surg., Univ. of Edin.,

1976–87. RCSEd: Pres., 1985–88; Examr, 1964–88. Hon. FRACS 1988. *Publications:* Emergency Surgery, 8th and 9th edns, 1967 and 1972; various, on surgical subjects. *Recreations:* golf, sailing. *Address:* Easter Carrick, Chapel Green, Earlsferry, Leven, Fife KY9 1AD. *Clubs:* New (Edinburgh); Golf House (Elie).

McNAIR-WILSON, Sir Michael; *see* McNair-Wilson, Sir R. M. C.

McNAIR-WILSON, Sir Patrick (Michael Ernest David), Kt 1989; MP (C) New Forest, since 1968 (Lewisham West, 1964–66); Consultant; *b* 28 May 1929; *s* of Dr Robert McNair-Wilson; *m* 1953, Diana Evelyn Kitty Campbell Methuen-Campbell, *d* of Hon. Laurence Methuen-Campbell; one *s* four *d*. *Educ:* Eton. Exec. in French Shipping Co., 1951–53; various appointments at Conservative Central Office, 1954–58; Staff of Conservative Political Centre, 1958–61; Director, London Municipal Society, 1961–63; Executive with The British Iron and Steel Federation, 1963–64. Opposition Front Bench Spokesman on fuel and power, 1965–66; Vice-Chm., Conservative Parly Power Cttee, 1969–70; PPS to Minister for Transport Industries, DoE, 1970–74; Opposition Front Bench Spokesman on Energy, 1974–76; Chm., Jt Lords and Commons Select Cttee on Private Bill Procedure, 1987–; Mem., Select Cttee on Members Interests, 1985–86. Editor of The Londoner, 1961–63. *Recreations:* sailing, pottery. *Address:* House of Commons, SW1A 0AA.

See also Sir R. M. C. McNair-Wilson.

McNAIR-WILSON, Sir (Robert) Michael (Conal), Kt 1988; MP (C) Newbury, since 1974 (Walthamstow East, 1969–74); *b* 12 Oct. 1930; *y s* of late Dr Robert McNair-Wilson and of Mrs Doris McNair-Wilson; *m* 1974, Mrs Deidre Granville; one *d*. *Educ:* Eton College. During national service, 1948–50, was commissioned in Royal Irish Fusiliers. Farmed in Hampshire, 1950–53. Journalist on various provincial newspapers, and did freelance work for BBC in Northern Ireland, 1953–55. Joined Sidney-Barton Ltd, internat. public relations consultants, Dir, 1961–79; consultant to Extel Advertising and Public Relations Ltd (when it acquired Sidney-Barton), 1979–86. Contested (C) Lincoln, Gen. Elec., 1964; PPS to Minister of Agriculture, 1979–83. Mem. Council, Bow Group, 1965–66; Jt Secretary: UN Parly Gp, 1969–70; Cons. Greater London Members Gp, 1970–72; Cons. Constitution Cttee, 1986; Sec., 1969–70, Vice-Chm., 1970–72, Chm., 1972–74, Cons. Aviation Cttee; Member Select Cttee on: Nationalised Industries, 1973–79; Members Interests, 1986–; Educn, Science and the Arts, 1986–; Dep. Chm., Air Safety Gp, 1979–. Member: Council, Air League, 1972–76; Watching Cttee, Friends of Ulster, 1985–. Mem. Ct, Reading Univ., 1979–. Pres., Nat. Fedn of Kidney Patients Assocs; Vice-Pres., Cons. Disability Gp; Mem., Unrelated Live Transplant Regulatory Authy. First MP on kidney dialysis, and first MP with a kidney transplant. *Publications:* Blackshirt, a biography of Mussolini (jointly), 1959; No Tame or Minor Role (Bow Group pamphlet on the Common Market) (jointly), 1963. *Recreations:* gardening, sailing, ski-ing, riding. *Address:* House of Commons, SW1.

See also Sir P. M. E. D. McNair-Wilson.

McNALLY, Tom; Head of Public Affairs, Hill and Knowlton, since 1987; *b* 20 Feb. 1943; *s* of John P. McNally and Elizabeth May (*née* McCarthy); *m* 1st, 1970, Eileen Powell (marr. diss. 1990); 2nd, 1990, Juliet Lamy Hutchinson. *Educ:* College of St Joseph, Blackpool; University Coll., London (BScEcon). President of Students' Union, UCL, 1965–66; Vice-Pres., Nat. Union of Students, 1966–67; Asst Gen. Sec. of Fabian Society, 1966–67; Labour Party researcher, 1967–68; Internat. Sec. of Labour Party, 1969–74; Political Adviser to: Foreign and Commonwealth Sec., 1974–76; Prime Minister, 1976–79. MP (Lab 1979–81, SDP 1981–83) Stockport S; SDP Parly spokesman on educn and sport, 1981–83. Mem., Select Cttee on Industry and Trade, 1979–83. Contested (SDP) Stockport, 1983. Public Affairs Adviser, GEC, 1983–84; Dir-Gen., Retail Consortium, and Dir, British Retailers Association, 1985–87. *Recreations:* playing and watching sport, reading political biographies. *Address:* Hill and Knowlton, International Public Relations Counsel, 5–11 Theobalds Road, WC1X 8SH.

McNAMARA, (Joseph) Kevin; MP (Lab) Hull North, since 1983 (Kingston-upon-Hull North, Jan. 1966–1974; Kingston-upon-Hull Central, 1974–83); *b* 5 Sept. 1934; *s* of late Patrick and Agnes McNamara; *m* 1960, Nora (*née* Jones), Warrington; four *s* one *d*. *Educ:* various primary schools; St Mary's Coll., Crosby; Hull Univ. (LLB). Head of Dept of History, St Mary's Grammar Sch., Hull, 1958–64; Lecturer in Law, Hull Coll. of Commerce, 1964–66. Opposition spokesman on defence, 1982–83, on defence and disarmament, 1983–85, dep. opposition spokesman on defence, 1985–87, opposition spokesman on Northern Ireland, 1987–. Member: Select Cttee on For. Affairs, until 1982 (former Chm., Overseas Develt Sub-Cttee); Parly Assembly, NATO, 1984–88; Vice-Chm., Economic Cttee, NATO, 1985–87; former Chairman: Select Cttee on Overseas Develt; PLP NI Gp; Sec., Parly Gp, TGWU. Former Mem., UK Delegn to Council of Europe. Commendatore, Order Al Merito della Repubblica Italiana, 1977. *Recreations:* family and outdoor activities. *Address:* House of Commons, SW1; 145 Newland Park, Hull HU5 2DX.

McNAMARA, Air Chief Marshal Sir Neville (Patrick), KBE 1981 (CBE 1972); AO 1976; AFC 1961; Royal Australian Air Force, retired 1984; *b* Toogoolawah, Qld, 17 April 1923; *s* of late P. F. McNamara; *m* 1950, Dorothy Joan Miller; two *d*. *Educ:* Christian Brothers Coll., Nudgee, Qld. Enlisted RAAF, 1941; commnd 1944; Fighter Pilot WWII with No 75 Sqdn, Halmaheras and Borneo; served with No 77 Sqdn in Japan on cessation of hostilities; Air Traffic Control duties, HQ NE Area, 1948; Flying Instructor, Central Flying Sch., 1951–53; operational tour with No 77 Sqdn in Korean War; Pilot Trng Officer, HQ Trng Comd, 1954–55; Staff Officer, Fighter Operations Dept Air, 1955–57; CO No 25 Sqdn W Australia, 1957–59; CO No 2 Operational Conversion Unit, 1959–61; CO and Sen. Air Staff Officer, RAAF Staff, London, 1961–63; Director of Personnel (Officers), Dept Air, 1964–66; OC RAAF Contingent, Thailand, 1966–67; Air Staff Officer, RAAF Richmond, 1967–69; Dir-Gen., Organisation Dept Air, 1969–71; Comdr RAAF Forces Vietnam, 1971–72; Aust. Air Attaché, Washington, 1972–75; Dep. Chief of Air Staff, 1975–79; Chief of Air Staff, 1979–82; Chief of Defence Force Staff, 1982–84. RAAF psc, pfc, jssc. *Recreations:* golf, fishing. *Address:* 19 Jukes Street, Hackett, Canberra, ACT 2602, Australia. *T:* 06–2498196. *Club:* Commonwealth (Canberra).

McNAMARA, Robert Strange; Medal of Freedom with Distinction; *b* San Francisco, 9 June 1916; *s* of Robert James McNamara and Clara Nell (*née* Strange); *m* 1940, Margaret McKinstry Craig (decd); one *s* two *d*. *Educ:* University of California (AB); Harvard Univ. (Master of Business Administration); Asst Professor of Business Administration, Harvard, 1940–43. Served in USAAF, England, India, China, Pacific, 1943–46 (Legion of Merit); released as Lieut-Colonel. Joined Ford Motor Co., 1946; Executive, 1946–61; Controller, 1949–53; Asst General Manager, Ford Div., 1953–55; Vice-President, and General Manager, Ford Div., 1955–57; Director, and Group Vice-President of Car Divisions, 1957–61, President, 1960–61; Secretary of Defense, United States of America, 1961–68; Pres., The World Bank, 1968–81; Director: Royal Dutch Petroleum, 1981–87; Bank of America, 1981–87; Corning, 1981–90; The Washington Post, 1981–89. Trustee: Urban Inst.; Trilateral Commn. Hon. degrees from: Harvard, Calif, Mich, Columbia, Ohio, Princeton, NY, Notre Dame, George Washington, Aberdeen, St Andrews, Fordham and Oxford Univs; Williams, Chatham and Amherst Colls. Phi Beta Kappa. Albert Pick Jr Award, Univ. of Chicago (first recipient), 1979; Albert Einstein Peace Prize, 1983; Franklin D. Roosevelt Freedom from Want Medal, 1983; Amer. Assembly Service to Democracy Award; Dag Hammarskjöld Hon. Medal; Extrepreneurial Excellence Medal, Yale Sch. of Organization and Management; Olive Branch Award for Outstanding Book on subject of World Peace, 1987; Sidney Hillman Foundn Award, 1987; Onassis Athinai Prize, 1988. *Publications:* The Essence of Security, 1968; One Hundred Countries, Two Billion People: the dimensions of development, 1975; The McNamara Years at the World Bank, 1981; Blundering into Disaster, 1987; Out of the Cold, 1990. *Address:* 1455 Pennsylvania Avenue NW, Washington, DC 20004, USA.

McNAUGHT, John Graeme; His Honour Judge McNaught; a Circuit Judge, since 1987; *b* 21 Feb. 1941; *s* of Charles William McNaught and Isabella Mary McNaught; *m* 1966, Barbara Mary Smith; two *s* one *d*. *Educ:* King Edward VII Sch., Sheffield; The Queen's Coll., Oxford (BA Jurisprudence, 1962). Bacon Scholar, Gray's Inn, 1962; called to the Bar, Gray's Inn, 1963; a Recorder, 1981–87. *Address:* The Swindon Combined Court Centre, Islington Street, Swindon SN1 2HG.

McNAUGHTON, Lt-Col Ian Kenneth Arnold; Chief Inspecting Officer of Railways, Department of Transport, 1974–82; *b* 30 June 1920; *er s* of late Brig. F. L. McNaughton, CBE, DSO and Betty, *d* of late Rev. Arnold Pinchard, OBE; *m* 1946, Arthea, *d* of late Carel Begeer, Voorschoten, Holland; two *d*. *Educ:* Loretto Sch.; RMA Woolwich; RMCS Shrivenham. BScEng, CEng, FIMechE, FCIT, FIRSE. 2nd Lieut RE, 1939; served War of 1939–45, NW Europe (Captain) (despatches); GHQ MELF, 1949 (Major); Cyprus, 1955; OC 8 Rly Sqdn, 1958; Port Comdt Southampton, 1959 (Lt-Col); SOI Transportation HQ BAOR, 1960; retd 1963. Inspecting Officer of Rlys, Min. of Transport, 1963. Chm., Rlys Industry Adv. Cttee, Health and Safety Commn, 1978–82. *Recreations:* gardening, foreign travel. *Address:* Chawton Glebe, Alton, Hants GU34 1SH. *T:* Alton (0420) 83395.

MACNAUGHTON, Prof. Sir Malcolm (Campbell), Kt 1986; MD; FRCPG; FRCOG; FRSE; Muirhead Professor of Obstetrics and Gynaecology, University of Glasgow, 1970–90; *b* 4 April 1925; *s* of James Hay and Mary Robieson Macnaughton; *m* 1955, Margaret-Ann Galt; two *s* three *d*. *Educ:* Glasgow Academy; Glasgow Univ. (MD). Lectr, Univ. of Aberdeen, 1957–61; Sen. Lectr, Univ. of St Andrews, 1961–66; Hon. Sen. Lectr, Univ. of Dundee, 1966–70. Pres., RCOG, 1984–87. Hon. FACOG; Hon. FSLCOG; Hon. FFARCS; Hon. FRACOG. Hon. LLD Dundee, 1988. *Publications:* Combined Textbook of Obstetrics and Gynaecology (ed jtly), 9th edn 1976; (ed and contrib.) Handbook of Medical Gynaecology, 1985; numerous papers in obstetric, gynaecological, endocrine and general medical jls. *Recreations:* fishing, walking, curling. *Address:* Beechwood, 15 Boclair Road, Bearsden, Glasgow G61 2AF. *T:* 041–942 1909. *Club:* Glasgow Academical (Glasgow).

McNEE, Sir David (Blackstock), Kt 1978; QPM 1975; Commissioner, Metropolitan Police, 1977–82; non-executive director and adviser to a number of public limited companies; *b* 23 March 1925; *s* of John McNee, Glasgow, Lanarkshire; *m* 1952, Isabella Clayton Hopkins; one *d*. *Educ:* Woodside Senior Secondary Sch., Glasgow. Joined City of Glasgow Police, 1946. Apptd Dep. Chief Constable, Dunbartonshire Constabulary, 1968; Chief Constable: City of Glasgow Police, 1971–75; Strathclyde Police, 1975–77. Lectures: Basil Henriques, Bristol Univ., 1978; London, in Contemporary Christianity, 1979; Dallas, Glasgow, 1980; Peter le Neve Foster Meml, RSA, 1981. President: Royal Life Saving Soc., 1982–90; National Bible Soc. of Scotland, 1983–; Glasgow City Cttee, Cancer Relief, 1987–; Glasgow Battalion, Boys' Brigade, 1984–87; Hon. Vice-Pres., Boys' Bde, 1980–; Vice-Pres., London Fedn of Boys Clubs, 1982–. Member: Lord's Taverners, 1981–; Saints and Sinners Club of Scotland, 1982–. Patron, Scottish Motor Neurone Assoc., 1982–. Hon. Col, 32 (Scottish) Signal Regt (V), TA, 1988–. Freeman of the City of London, 1977. FBIM 1977; FRSA 1981. KStJ 1991. *Publication:* McNee's Law, 1983. *Recreations:* fishing, golf, music. *Clubs:* Caledonian, Naval (Life Mem.).

McNEICE, Sir (Thomas) Percy (Fergus), Kt 1956; CMG 1953; OBE 1947; *b* 16 Aug. 1901; *s* of late Canon W. G. McNeice, MA, and Mary Masterson; *m* 1947, Yuen Peng Loke, *d* of late Dr Loke Yew, CMG, LLD; one *s* one *d*. *Educ:* Bradford Grammar Sch.; Keble Coll., Oxford (MA). Malayan Civil Service, 1925; Captain, Straits Settlements Volunteer Force (Prisoner of War, 1942–45). MLC, Singapore, 1949; MEC 1949; President of the City Council, Singapore, 1949–56, retired. FZS. *Recreations:* bird watching, walking and swimming. *Address:* 12 Jalan Sampurna, Singapore 1026. *Club:* Commonwealth Trust.

McNEIL, (David) John, CBE 1988; WS; NP; Partner, Morton Fraser & Milligan, since 1968; President, Law Society of Scotland, 1986–87; *b* 24 March 1937; *s* of Donald S. McNeil and Elizabeth (*neé* Campbell); *m* 1962, Georgina Avril Sargent; one *s* two *d*. *Educ:* Daniel Stewart's Coll., Edinburgh; Edinburgh Univ. (MA Hons, LLB). Apprenticed to Davidson & Syme, WS, Edinburgh, 1959–62; admitted Solicitor in Scotland, 1962; WS 1964; Partner, Fraser, Stodart and Ballingall, 1964–68. Mem. Council, Law Soc. of Scotland, 1972–. Mem., Warnock Inquiry into Aspects of Human Infertility and Embryology, 1982–84. *Recreations:* golf, snooker, music and opera, theatre. *Address:* St Catherine's Royal Terrace, Linlithgow, West Lothian EH49 6HQ. *T:* Linlithgow (0506) 843100. *Clubs:* New, Bruntsfield Golf (Edinburgh).

McNEIL, Ian Robert, JP; FCA; Partner, Moores Rowland, Chartered Accountants, since 1958; *b* 14 Dec. 1932; *s* of Robert and Doris May McNeil; *m* 1963, Ann Harries-Rees; two *d*. *Educ:* Brighton Coll. Qualified as CA, 1955. Partner, Nevill Hovey Gardner (later amalgamated into Moores Rowland), 1958. Institute of Chartered Accountants in England and Wales: Vice-Pres., 1989–90; Dep. Pres., 1990–91; Pres., 1991–June 1992. Member: Curriers' Co., 1959; Chartered Accountants' Co., 1989. JP Hove 1967 (Chm., Hove Bench, 1988–89); Mem. Council, Magistrates' Assoc., 1983–89. *Address:* Lancasters, West End Lane, Henfield, West Sussex BN5 9RB. *T:* Henfield (0273) 492606. *Club:* Athenæum.

MACNEIL OF BARRA, Prof. Ian Roderick; The Macneil of Barra; 46th Chief of Clan Macneil and of that Ilk; Baron of Barra; Wigmore Professor of Law, Northwestern University, since 1980; *b* 20 June 1929; *s* of Robert Lister Macneil of Barra and Kathleen, *d* of Orlando Paul Metcalf, NYC, USA; *m* 1952, Nancy, *e d* of James Tilton Wilson, Ottawa, Canada; two *s* one *d* (and one *s* decd). *Educ:* Univ. of Vermont (BA 1950); Harvard Univ. (LLB 1955). Lieut, Infty, Army of US, 1951–53 (US Army Reserve, 1950–69, discharged honorably, rank of Major). Clerk, US Court of Appeals, 1955–56; law practice, Concord, NH, USA, 1956–59. Cornell Univ., USA: Asst Prof. of Law, 1959–62; Associate Prof., 1962–63; Prof. of Law, 1962–72 and 1974–76; Ingersoll Prof. of Law, 1976–80; Prof. of Law, Univ. of Virginia, 1972–74. Visiting Professor of Law: Univ. of East Africa, Dar es Salaam, Tanzania, 1965–67; Harvard Univ., 1988–89; Guggenheim Fellow, 1978–79; Vis. Fellow, Wolfson Coll., Oxford, 1979. Hon. Vis. Fellow, Faculty of Law, Edinburgh Univ., 1979 and 1987. Member: American Law Inst.; Standing Council of Scottish Chiefs. FSAScot. *Publications:* Bankruptcy Law in East Africa, 1966; (with R. B. Schlesinger, *et al*) Formation of Contracts: A Study of the Common Core of Legal Systems, 1968; Contracts: Instruments of Social Co-operation-

East Africa, 1968; (with R. S. Morison) Students and Decision Making, 1970; Contracts: Exchange Transactions and Relations, 1971, 2nd edn 1978; The New Social Contract, 1980. *Heir*: *s* Roderick Wilson Macneil, Younger of Barra [*b* 22 Oct. 1954; *m* 1988, Sau Ming, *d* of Chun Kwan, Hong Kong]. *Address*: Kisimul Castle, Isle of Barra, Scotland. *T*: Castlebay (08714) 300. *Club*: New (Edinburgh).

McNEIL, John; *see* McNeil, D. J.

McNEIL, John Struthers, CBE 1967; Chief Road Engineer, Scottish Development Department, 1963–69; *b* 4 March 1907; *s* of R. H. McNeil, Troon; *m* 1931, Dorothea Yuille; two *s*. *Educ*: Ayr Academy; Glasgow Univ. BSc Hons, Civil Engineering, 1929; FICE 1955. Contracting and local government experience, 1929–35; joined Ministry of Transport as Asst Engineer, 1935; Divisional Road Engineer, NW Div. of England, 1952–55; Asst Chief Engineer, 1955–57; Dep. Chief Engineer, 1957–63. Telford Gold Medal, ICE. *Publications*: contribs. to technical journals. *Recreations*: fishing, gardening. *Address*: 306–250 Douglas Street, Victoria, BC V8V 2P4, Canada.

MacNEIL, Most Rev. Joseph Neil; *see* Edmonton (Alberta), Archbishop of, (RC).

McNEILL, (Gordon) Keith; Editor, Woman's Own, since 1990; *b* 6 Aug. 1953; *s* of Gordon Francis McNeill and Vera McNeill; *m* 1983, Ruth Brotherhood. *Educ*: Slough Grammar School. Features Editor, Chat Magazine, 1985; London Evening News, 1988; Deputy Editor, Woman's Own, 1988. *Recreations*: walking, AFC Bournemouth, modern art, historical architecture. *Address*: Woman's Own, King's Reach Tower, Stamford Street, SE1 9LS. *T*: 071–261 5500. *Clubs*: Porcupine, Ascot.

McNEILL, James Walker, QC (Scot) 1991; *b* 16 Feb. 1952; *s* of James McNeill and Edith Anna Howie Wardlaw; *m* 1986, Katherine Lawrence McDowall; two *s*. *Educ*: Dunoon Grammar Sch.; Cambridge Univ. (MA); Edinburgh Univ. (LLB). Advocate 1978; Standing Junior Counsel: to Dept of Transport in Scotland, 1984–88; to Inland Revenue in Scotland, 1988–91. *Recreations*: music, hill-walking, golf, sailing, travel. *Address*: 28 Kingsburgh Road, Edinburgh EH12 6DZ. *Club*: New (Edinburgh).

McNEILL, Prof. John, PhD; Director, Royal Ontario Museum, Toronto, since 1991; *b* 15 Sept. 1933; *s* of Thomas McNeill and Helen Lawrie Eagle; *m* 1st, 1961, Bridget Mariel Winterton (marr. diss. 1990); two *s*; 2nd, 1990, Marilyn Lois James. *Educ*: George Heriot's, Edinburgh; Univ. of Edinburgh (BSc Hons, PhD). Asst Lectr and Lectr, Dept of Agricl Botany, Univ. of Reading, 1957–61; Lectr, Dept of Botany, Univ. of Liverpool, 1961–69; Plant (later Biosystematics) Research Institute, Agriculture Canada, Ottawa: Res. Scientist, 1969–77, Chief, Vascular Plant Taxonomy Sect., 1969–72; Sen. Res. Scientist, 1977–81; Prof. and Chm., Dept of Biology, Univ. of Ottawa, 1981–87; Regius Keeper, Royal Botanic Garden, Edinburgh, 1987–89; Associate Dir Curatorial, Royal Ontario Mus., Toronto, 1989–90, Acting Dir, 1990–91. Hon. Professor: Univ. of Edinburgh, 1989; Univ. of Toronto, 1990–; Adjunct Prof., Univ. of Ottawa, 1987–91. *Publications*: Phenetic and phylogenetic classification (jt ed), 1964; (jtly) Grasses of Ontario, 1977; (jt ed) International Code of Botanical Nomenclature, 1983, new edn 1988; (jtly) Preliminary Inventory of Canadian Weeds, 1988; over 20 chapters or sections of sci. books and over 90 contribs to sci. res. jls. *Recreation*: botanical nomenclature. *Address*: Royal Ontario Museum, 100 Queen's Park, Toronto, Ont M5S 2C6, Canada.

McNEILL, Maj.-Gen. John Malcolm, CB 1963; CBE 1959 (MBE 1942); *b* 22 Feb. 1909; *s* of Brig.-General Angus McNeill, CB, CBE, DSO, TD, Seaforth Highlanders, and Lilian, *d* of Maj.-General Sir Harry Barron, KCVO; *m* 1939, Barbara, *d* of Colonel C. H. Marsh, DSO, Spilsby, Lincs; two *d*. *Educ*: Imperial Service Coll., Windsor; RMA, Woolwich. 2nd Lieut, RA, 1929. Served Western Desert, Sicily, Italy, N.W. Europe and Burma, 1939–45; Commanded 1st Regt RHA, 1948–51; Student Imperial Defence Coll., 1952; Dep. Secretary, Chiefs of Staff Cttee, Ministry of Defence, 1953–55; Comdr RA 2nd Div. 1955–58; Comdt School of Artillery, 1958–60; Commander, British Army Staff, and Military Attaché, Washington, DC, 1960–63; Col Comdt RA, 1964–74. Principal Staff Officer to Sec. of State for Commonwealth Relations, 1964–69. ADC to the Queen, 1958–60. *Address*: Hole's Barn, Pilton, Shepton Mallet, Som BA4 4DF. *T*: Pilton (074989) 212. *Clubs*: Army and Navy, English-Speaking Union.

McNEILL, Keith; *see* McNeill, G. K.

McNEILL, Peter Grant Brass, PhD; QC (Scot) 1988; Sheriff of Lothian and Borders at Edinburgh, since 1982; *b* Glasgow, 3 March 1929; *s* of late William Arnot McNeill and late Lillias Philips Scrimgeour; *m* 1959, Matilda Farquhar Rose, *d* of Mrs Christina Rose; one *s* three *d*. *Educ*: Hillhead High Sch., Glasgow; Morrison's Academy, Crieff; Glasgow Univ. MA (Hons Hist.) 1951; LLB 1954; Law apprentice, Biggart Lumsden & Co., Glasgow, 1952–55; Carnegie Fellowship, 1955; Faulds Fellowship, 1956–59; Scottish Bar, 1956; PhD, 1961. Hon. Sheriff Substitute of Lanarkshire, and of Stirling, Clackmannan and Dumbarton, 1962; Standing Junior Counsel to Scottish Development Dept (Highways), 1964; Advocate Depute, 1964; Sheriff of Lanarks, subseq. redesignated Glasgow and Strathkelvin, at Glasgow, 1965–82. Pres., Sheriffs' Assoc., 1982–85. Chm., Review Bd, Chinook Helicopter Accident, 1988. Mem., Scottish Records Adv. Council, 1989–. Chm. Council, Stair Soc., 1990. *Publications*: (ed) Balfour's Practicks (Stair Society), 1962–63; (ed jtly) An Historical Atlas of Scotland *c* 400–*c* 1600, 1975; Adoption of Children in Scotland, 1982, 2nd edn 1986; legal and historical articles in Encyclopaedia Britannica, Juridical Review, Scots Law Times, Glasgow Herald, etc. *Recreations*: legal history, gardening, bookbinding. *Address*: Sheriffs' Chambers, Sheriff Court House, Lawnmarket, Edinburgh EH1 2NS. *T*: 031–226 7181.

McNEISH, Prof. Alexander Stewart, FRCP; Professor of Paediatrics and Child Health, and Director of the Institute of Child Health, since 1980, and Dean, Faculty of Medicine and Dentistry, 1987–Aug. 1992, University of Birmingham; *b* 13 April 1938; *s* of Angus Stewart McNeish and Minnie Howieson (*née* Dickson); *m* 1963, Joan Ralston (*née* Hamilton); two *s* one *d*. *Educ*: Glasgow Acad.; Univ. of Glasgow (MB); Univ. of Birmingham (MSc). FRCP 1977; FRCPGlas 1985. Sen. Lectr in Paediatrics and Child Health, Univ. of Birmingham, 1970–76; Foundn Prof. of Child Health, Univ. of Leicester, 1976–80. Mem., GMC, 1984–. *Publications*: papers on paediatric gastroenterology in Lancet, BMJ and in Archives of Disease in Childhood. *Recreations*: golf, music. *Address*: 128 Westfield Road, Edgbaston, Birmingham B15 3JQ. *T*: 021–454 6081. *Clubs*: Athenæum; Blackwell Golf.

McNICOL, David Williamson, CBE 1966; Australian Diplomatic Service, retired; *b* 20 June 1913; *s* of late Donald McNicol, Adelaide; *m* 1947, Elsa Margaret, *d* of N. J. Hargrave, Adelaide; one *s*. *Educ*: Carey Grammar Sch., Melbourne; Kings Coll., Adelaide; Adelaide Univ. (BA). RAAF, 1940–45, Pilot, 201 and 230 Sqdns RAF, Atlantic, Madagascar, Italy and Dodecanese. Australian Minister to Cambodia, Laos and Vietnam, 1955–56; idc 1957; Australian Comr to Singapore, 1958–60; Asst Sec., Dept of External Affairs, Australia, 1960–62; Australian High Comr to Pakistan, 1962–65 and to New Zealand, 1965–68; Australian Ambassador to Thailand, 1968–69; Australian High Comr to Canada, 1969–73; Dep. High Comr for Australia in London, 1973–75; Ambassador to S Africa, and High Comr to Botswana, Lesotho and Swaziland, 1975–77. *Recreations*: golf, gardening. *Address*: 18 Fishburn Street, Red Hill, ACT 2603, Australia. *Clubs*: Naval and Military (Melbourne); Royal Canberra Golf.

McNICOL, Prof. Donald; Vice-Chancellor and Principal, University of Sydney, since 1990; *b* 18 April 1939; *s* of Ian Robertson McNicol and Sadie Isabelle Williams; *m* 1963, Kathleen Margaret Wells; one *s* two *d*. *Educ*: Unley High Sch.; Univ. of Adelaide (BA 1964); St John's Coll., Cambridge (PhD 1967). Fellow, Aust. Psych. Soc. Lectr in Psychology, Univ. of Adelaide, 1967–71; Research Fellow, St John's Coll., Cambridge, 1968–69; Sen. Lectr in Psych., Univ. of NSW, 1971–74; Associate Prof. in Psych., Univ. of NSW, 1975–81; Prof. of Psych., Univ. of Tasmania, 1981–86, now Emeritus Prof.; Comr for Univs and Chm., Univs Adv. Council, Commonwealth Tertiary Educn, 1986–88; Vice-Chancellor, Univ. of New England, NSW, 1988–90. FRSA. *Publication*: A Primer of Signal Detection Theory, 1972. *Recreations*: walking, music, reading. *Address*: University of Sydney, NSW 2006, Australia. *T*: (02) 6923058.

McNICOL, Prof. George Paul, FRSE 1984; Principal and Vice-Chancellor, University of Aberdeen, 1981–91; Member, Aberdeen Local Board, Bank of Scotland, since 1983; *b* 24 Sept. 1929; *s* of Martin and Elizabeth McNicol; *m* 1959, Susan Ritchie; one *s* two *d*. *Educ*: Hillhead High Sch., Glasgow; Univ. of Glasgow. MD, PhD, FRCP, FRCPG, FRCPE, FRCPath. House Surg., Western Infirmary, Glasgow, 1952; House Phys., Stobhill Gen. Hosp., Glasgow, 1953; Regimental MO, RAMC, 1953–55; Asst, Dept Materia Medica and Therapeutics, Registrar, Univ. Med. Unit, Stobhill Gen. Hosp., 1955–57; Univ. Dept of Medicine, Royal Infirmary, Glasgow: Registrar, 1957–59; Hon. Sen. Registrar, 1961–65; Lectr in Medicine, 1963–65; Hon. Cons. Phys., 1966–71; Sen. Lectr in Medicine, 1966–70; Reader in Medicine, 1970–71; Prof. of Medicine and Hon. Cons. Phys., Leeds Gen. Infirmary, 1971–81; Chm., Bd of Faculty of Medicine, Leeds Univ., 1978–81. Harkness Fellow, Commonwealth Fund, Dept of Internal Medicine, Washington Univ., 1959–61; Hon. Clinical Lectr and Hon. Cons. Phys., Makerere UC Med. Sch. Extension, Kenyatta Nat. Hosp., Nairobi (on secondment from Glasgow Univ.), 1965–66. Chm. Med. Adv. Cttee, Cttee of Vice-Chancellors and Principals, 1985–90; Member: British Council Cttee on Internat. Co-op. in Higher Educn, 1985–91; Council, ACU, 1988–91; Former Mem., Adv. Council on Misuse of Drugs. Chm., Part I Examining Bd, Royal Colls of Physicians (UK). Chm., Bd of Governors, Rowett Res. Inst., 1981–89; Mem., Bd of Governors, N of Scotland Coll. of Agriculture, 1981–91. Mem., Exec. Cttee, Scottish Council (Develt and Industry), 1989–. FRSA 1985. Hon. FACP. Foreign Corresp. Mem., Belgian Royal Acad. of Medicine, 1985. Hon. DSc Wabash Coll., Indiana, 1989. *Publications*: papers in sci. and med. jls on thrombosis and bleeding disorders. *Recreations*: sailing, skiing. *Address*: Chanonry Green, Kincurdie Drive, Rosemarkie, Ross-shire IV10 8SJ. *T*: Fortrose (0381) 21211.*Clubs*: Athenæum, Caledonian; Royal Northern & University (Aberdeen).

See also A. H. Smallwood.

McNISH, Althea Marjorie, (Althea McNish Weiss), CMT 1976; freelance textile designer, since 1957; *b* Trinidad; *d* of late J. Claude McNish, educnl reformer, and late Margaret (*née* Bourne); *m* 1969, John Weiss. *Educ*: Port-of-Spain, by her father and others; London Coll. of Printing; Central School of Art and Crafts; Royal Coll. of Art. NDD, DesRCA; FCSD (FSIA 1968, MSIA 1960). Painted throughout childhood; after design educn in London, freelance practice in textile and other design; commns from Ascher and Liberty's, 1957; new techniques for laminate murals, for SS Oriana and hosp. and coll. in Trinidad; Govt of Trinidad and Tobago travelling schol., 1962; interior design (for Govt of Trinidad and Tobago) in NY, Washington and London, 1962; Cotton Bd trav. schol. to report on export potential for British printed cotton goods in Europe, 1963; collection of dress fabric designs for ICI and Tootal Thomson for promotion of Terylene Toile, 1966; special features for Daily Mail Ideal Home Exhibn, 1966–78; (with John Weiss) etched silver dishes, 1973–; interior design for Sec.-Gen. of Commonwealth, 1975; bedlinen collection for Courtaulds, 1978; (with John Weiss) textile design develt for BRB, 1978–81; textile hangings for BRB Euston offices, 1979; banners for Design Centre, 1981; (with John Weiss) improvements to London office of High Comr for Trinidad and Tobago, 1981; advr on exhibn design for Govt of Trinidad and Tobago, Commonwealth Inst., 1982–84; fashion textile designs for Yugoslav textile printers, 1985–; furnishing textile designs for Fede Cheti, Milan, 1986–; murals and hangings for Royal Caribbean Cruise Line: MS Nordic Empress, 1990; MS Monarch of the Seas, 1991. Paintings and various work in exhibitions include: individual and gp exhibns, London, 1954–; paintings, Jamaica, 1975; hangings, Kilkenny, 1981; hangings, individual exhibn, Peoples Gall., 1982; hangings, Magazine Workspace, Leicester, 1983; textile designs in exhibitions: Inprint, Manchester and London, 1964–71; Design Council/BoT, USA and Sweden, 1969, London, 1970, London and USA, 1972; Design-In, Amsterdam, 1972–74; Design Council, 1975–80; The Way We Live Now, V&A Mus., 1978; Indigo, Lille, 1981–82; Commonwealth Fest. Art Exhibn, Brisbane, 1982; Designs for British Dress and Furnishing Fabrics, V&A Mus., 1986; Make or Break, Henry Moore Gall., 1986; Surtex, New York, 1987; Ascher, V&A Mus., 1987; work represented in permanent collection of V&A Mus. Research tours: Czechoslovakia, 1968; Yugoslavia, 1972; Tunisia, 1974; Caribbean and N America, 1976; Yugoslavia, 1985–. Vis. Lecturer: Central Sch. of Art and Crafts and other colls and polytechnics, 1960–; USA, 1972; Italy, W Germany and Yugoslavia, 1985–; Advisory Tutor in Furnishing and Surface Design, London Coll. of Furniture, 1972–90. External assessor for educnl and professional bodies, incl. CSD and NCDAD/CNAA, 1966–; Mem. jury for Leverhulme schols, 1968; Judge: Portuguese textile design comp., Lisbon, 1973; 'Living' Design Awards, 1974; Carnival selection panels, Arts Council, 1982 and 1983. Vice-Pres., SIAD, 1977–78; Design Council: Mem., selection panels for Design Awards and Design Index, 1968–80; Mem. Bd, 1974–81; Mem., Jubilee Souvenir Selection Panel, 1976; Mem., Royal Wedding Souvenir Selection Panel, 1981. Member: Fashion and Textiles Design Bd, CNAA, 1975–78; London Local Adv. Cttee, IBA, 1981–; Formation Cttee, London Inst., ILEA, 1985. Mem. Governing Body, Portsmouth Coll. of Art, 1972–81. *BBC-TV*: studio setting for Caribbean edn of Full House, 1973. Has appeared, with work, in films for COI and Gas Council. Chaconia Medal (Gold) (Trinidad and Tobago), 1976, for service to art and design. *Publications*: textile designs produced in many countries, 1957–; designs illustrated in: V. D. Mendes and F. M. Hinchcliffe, Ascher, 1987; Did Britain Make It?, ed P. Sparke, 1986; M. Schoeser, Fabrics and Wallpapers, 1986; published in Decorative Art, Designers in Britain and design jls. *Recreations*: ski-ing, travelling, music, gardening. *Address*: 142 West Green Road, N15 5AD. *T*: 081–800 1686. *Club*: Soroptimist.

McNULTY, (Robert William) Roy; Managing Director, and Chief Executive, Short Brothers PLC, since 1988; *b* 7 Nov. 1937; *s* of Jack and Nancy McNulty; *m* 1963, Ismay Ratcliffe Rome; one *s* two *d*. *Educ*: Portora Royal School, Enniskillen; Trinity College, Dublin (BA, BComm). Audit Manager, Peat Marwick Mitchell & Co., Glasgow, 1963–66; Accounting Methods Manager, Chrysler UK, Linwood, 1966–68; Harland & Wolff, Belfast: Management Accountant, 1968–72; Computer Services Manager, 1972–74; Management Services Manager, 1975–76; Sen. Management Consultant, Peat Marwick Mitchell & Co., Belfast, 1977–78; Short Brothers: Exec. Dir, Finance and Admin, 1978–85; Dep. Managing Dir, 1986–88. Mem., Council, SBAC, 1988. Mem., Regional Council, CBI, 1987; Council Mem., Co-operation North, 1989. Associate

Fellow, Dept of Engineering, Univ. of Warwick. CBIM. *Recreations:* jogging, golf, reading. *Address:* Short Brothers PLC, Airport Road, Belfast BT3 9DZ.

MACONCHY, Dame Elizabeth, (Dame Elizabeth LeFanu), DBE 1987 (CBE 1977); FRCM; Hon. RAM; composer of serious music; *b* 19 March 1907; of Irish parentage; *d* of Gerald E. C. Maconchy, Lawyer, and Violet M. Poë; *m* 1930, William Richard LeFanu (author of Betsy Sheridan's Journal, 1960, repr. 1986, Bibliography of Nehemiah Grew, 1990, etc); two *d. Educ:* privately; Royal College of Music, London. Held Blumenthal Scholarship and won Sullivan Prize, Foli and other exhibitions, at RCM; pupil of Vaughan-Williams; travelled with Octavia Scholarship, 1929–30. First public performance: Piano Concerto with Prague Philharmonic Orchestra, 1930. Sir Henry Wood introduced "The Land", Promenade Concerts, 1930. Has had works performed at 3 Festivals of International Society for Contemporary Music (Prague, 1935; Paris, 1937; Copenhagen, 1947). Largest output has been in Chamber Music; String Quartets played as a series in BBC Third Programme, 1955, 1975. Chairman: Composers Guild of Great Britain, 1960; Soc. for Promotion of New Music, 1972–75 (Pres., 1977–). Hon. Fellow, St Hilda's Coll., Oxford, 1978. *Compositions:* Suite for Orchestra, The Land; Nocturne; Overture, Proud Thames (LCC Coronation Prize, 1953); Dialogue for piano and orchestra; Serenata Concertante for violin and orchestra, 1963; Symphony for double string orchestra; Concertino for: bassoon and string orchestra; Piano and chamber orchestra; Concerto for oboe, bassoon and string orchestra; Variazioni Concertanti for oboe, clarinet, bassoon, horn and strings, 1965; Variations for String Orchestra; twelve String Quartets (No 5, Edwin Evans Prize; No 9, Radcliffe Award, 1969); Oboe Quintet (Daily Telegraph Prize); Violin Sonata; Cello Divertimento; Duo for 2 Violins; Duo for Violin and Cello; Variations for solo cello; Reflections, for oboe, clarinet, viola and harp (Gedok International Prize, 1961); Clarinet Quintet; Carol Cantata, A Christmas Morning; Samson and the Gates of Gaza for chorus and orchestra, 1964; 3 settings of Gerard Manley Hopkins for soprano and chamber orchestra; Sonatina for harpsichord and Notebook for harpsichord, 1965; Three Donne settings, 1965; Nocturnal for unaccompanied chorus, 1965; Music for brass and woodwind, 1966; An Essex Overture, 1966; 6 Miniatures for solo violin, 1966; Duo for piano duet, 1967; Extravaganza, The Birds, after Aristophanes, 1968; And Death shall have no Dominion for chorus and brass, 3 Choirs Festival, 1969; The Jesse Tree, masque for Dorchester Abbey, 1970; Music for double-bass and piano, 1971; Ariadne (C. Day Lewis), for soprano and orch., King's Lynn Festival, 1971; Faustus, scena for tenor and piano, 1971; Prayer Before Birth, for women's voices, 1971; 3 Bagatelles for oboe and harpsichord, 1972; oboe quartet, 1972; songs for voice and harp, 1974; The King of the Golden River, opera for children, 1975; Epyllion, for solo cello and strings, Cheltenham Festival, 1975; Sinfonietta, for Essex Youth Orch., 1976; Pied Beauty, and Heaven Haven (G. M. Hopkins), for choir and brass, Southern Cathedrals Fest., 1976; Morning, Noon and Night, for harp, Aldeburgh Fest., 1977; Sun, Moon and Stars (Traherne), song cycle for soprano and piano, 1977; Heloise and Abelard, for 3 soloists, chorus and orch., 1977–78; The Leaden Echo & the Golden Echo (Hopkins), for choir and 3 instruments, 1978; Contemplation, for cello and piano, 1978; Colloquy, for flute and piano, 1979; Romanza, for solo viola and 11 instruments, 1979; Creatures, for mixed voices, 1979; Fantasia, for clarinet and piano, 1980; Little Symphony, for Norfolk Youth Orch., 1980; 4 Miniatures for chorus, 1981; Trittico for 2 oboes, bassoon and harpsichord, 1981; Piccola Musica for string trio, 1981; My Dark Heart, for soprano and 6 instruments, for RCM cent., 1982; Wind Quintet, 1982; L'Horloge (Baudelaire), for soprano, clarinet and piano, 1982; Music for Strings, Proms, 1983; 5 Sketches for Solo Viola, 1983; O Time Turn Back, chorus with cello, 1983; Narration for solo cello, 1984; Still Falls the Rain for double choir, 1984; Excursion for solo bassoon, 1985; Life Story for string orchestra, 1985; Two songs by Auden in memory of W. B. Yeats, and It's No Go (MacNeice), 1985; songs, piano pieces, etc; Three One-Act Operas (The Sofa, The Three Strangers, The Departure). *Address:* Shottesbrook, Boreham, Chelmsford, Essex CM3 3EJ. *T:* Chelmsford (0245) 467286.

See also N. F. LeFanu.

MACOUN, Michael John, CMG 1964; OBE 1961; QPM 1954; Overseas Police Adviser, and Inspector-General of Police, Dependent Territories, Foreign and Commonwealth Office, 1967–79, retired; Police Training Adviser, Ministry of Overseas Development, 1967–79; *b* 27 Nov. 1914; *o s* of late John Horatio Macoun, Comr of Chinese Maritime Customs; *m* 1940, Geraldine Mabel, *o d* of late Brig.-Gen. G. C. Sladen, CB, CMG, DSO, MC; two *s. Educ:* Stowe Sch., Buckingham; Univ. of Oxford (MA); Munich Univ. (Diploma in German Language and Literature). At Metropolitan Police Coll., 1938; Tanganyika Police, 1939–42, 1945–58; War Service, 1943–44; Inspector-Gen. of Police, Uganda, 1959–64; Directing Staff, Police Coll., Bramshill, 1965; Commonwealth Office, 1966. Lecture tour: of USA, under auspices of British Information Services, 1964; of Eastern Canada, for Assoc. of Canadian Clubs, 1966; Vis. Lectr, Police Coll., Bramshill, 1980–86. Rep. of Sec. of State, Police Appointments Bd, Hong Kong Govt, 1980–86; non-exec. Dir, Control Risks Gp, 1983–86; research and information consultant. Colonial Police Medal, 1951; OStJ 1959. *Recreations:* travel, walking. *Address:* Furzedown, Rowledge, near Farnham, Surrey GU10 4EB. *T:* Frensham (025125) 3196. *Clubs:* Commonwealth Trust; County (Guildford).

McPARTLIN, Noel; Advocate, since 1976; Sheriff of Grampian, Highland and Islands at Elgin, since 1985; *b* 25 Dec. 1939; *s* of Michael Joseph McPartlin and Ann Dunn or McPartlin; *m* 1965, June Anderson Whitehead; three *s* three *d. Educ:* Galashiels Acad.; Edinburgh Univ. (MA, LLB). Solicitor in Glasgow, Linlithgow and Stirling, 1964–76. Sheriff of Grampian, Highland and Islands at Peterhead and Banff, 1983–85. *Recreation:* country life. *Address:* Rowan Lodge, Mayne Road, Elgin. *Club:* Elgin.

MacPHAIL, Bruce Dugald, FCA; Managing Director, Peninsular and Oriental Steam Navigation Co., since 1985; *b* 1 May 1939; *s* of late Dugald Ronald MacPhail and Winifred Marjorie MacPhail; *m* 1st, 1963, Susan Mary Gregory (*d* 1975); three *s*; 2nd, 1983, Caroline Ruth Grimston Curtis-Bennett (*née* Hubbard). *Educ:* Haileybury Coll.; Balliol Coll., Oxford (MA); Harvard Business Sch., Mass, USA (MBA 1967). FCA 1976. Articled, Price Waterhouse, 1961–65; Hill Samuel & Co. Ltd, 1967–69; Finance Director: Sterling Guarantee Trust Ltd, 1969–74; Town & City Properties Ltd, 1974–76; Man. Dir, Sterling Guarantee Trust, 1976–85. Gov., Royal Ballet Sch., 1982–; Mem. Council, Templeton Coll., Oxford, 1987–. *Recreations:* reading, wine, scuba diving. *Address:* Thorpe Lubenham Hall, Lubenham, Market Harborough, Leics LE16 9TR.

MACPHAIL, Iain Duncan; QC (Scot.) 1989; Member, Scottish Law Commission, since 1990; *b* 24 Jan. 1938; *o s* of late Malcolm John Macphail and Mary Corbett Duncan; *m* 1970, Rosslyn Graham Lillias, *o d* of E. J. C. Hewitt, MD, TD, Edinburgh; one *s* one *d. Educ:* George Watson's Coll.; Edinburgh and Glasgow Univs. MA Hons History Edinburgh 1959, LLB Glasgow 1962. Admitted to Faculty of Advocates, 1963; in practice at Scottish Bar, 1963–73; Faulds Fellow in Law, Glasgow Univ., 1963–65; Lectr in Evidence and Procedure, Strathclyde Univ., 1968–69 and Edinburgh Univ., 1969–72; Standing Jun. Counsel to Scottish Home and Health Dept and to Dept of Health and Social Security, 1971–73; Extra Advocate-Depute, 1973; Sheriff: of Lanarks, later Glasgow and Strathkelvin, 1973–81; of Tayside, Central and Fife, 1981–82; of Lothian and Borders, 1982–89. Examiner in legal subjects, Glasgow and Edinburgh Univs, 1979–. Chm., Scottish Assoc. for Study of Delinquency, 1978–81; Dir, Edinburgh Contemporary Arts Trust, 1990. *Publications:* Law of Evidence in Scotland (Scottish Law Commn), 1979; Evidence, 1987; Sheriff Court Practice, 1988; articles and reviews in legal jls. *Recreations:* music, theatre, reading and writing. *Address:* Scottish Law Commission, 140 Causewayside, Edinburgh EH9 1PR. *T:* 031–668 2131. *Club:* New (Edinburgh).

MACPHERSON, family name of **Barons Macpherson of Drumochter** and **Strathcarron.**

MACPHERSON OF DRUMOCHTER, 2nd Baron, *cr* 1951; **(James) Gordon Macpherson;** Chairman and Managing Director of Macpherson, Train & Co. Ltd, and Subsidiary and Associated Companies, since 1964; Chairman, A. J. Macpherson & Co. Ltd (Bankers), since 1973; founder Chairman, Castle Dairies (Caerphilly) Ltd; *b* 22 Jan. 1924; *s* of 1st Baron (*d* 1965) and Lucy Lady Macpherson of Drumochter (*d* 1984); *S* father, 1965; *m* 1st, 1947, Dorothy Ruth Coulter (*d* 1974); two *d* (one *s* decd); 2nd, 1975, Catherine, *d* of Dr C. D. MacCarthy; one *s* two *d. Educ:* Loretto; Wells House, Malvern. Served War of 1939–45, with RAF; 1939–45 Campaign medal, Burma Star, Pacific Star, Defence Medal, Victory Medal. Founder Chm. and Patron, British Importers Confedn, 1972–. Member: Council, London Chamber of Commerce, 1958–73; (Gen. Purposes Cttee, 1959–72); East European Trade Council, 1969–71; PLA, 1973–76; Exec. Cttee, W India Cttee, 1959–83 (Dep. Chm. and Treasurer, 1971, Chm. 1973–75). Freeman of City of London, 1969; Mem., Butchers' Co., 1969–. Governor, Brentwood Sch. JP Essex, 1961–76; Dep. Chm., Brentwood Bench, 1972–76; Mem. Essex Magistrates Court Cttee, 1974–76. Hon. Game Warden for Sudan, 1974; Chief of Scottish Clans Assoc. of London, 1972–74; Member: Macpherson Clan Assoc. (Chm., 1963–64); Sen. Golfers' Soc., 1981–. FRSA 1971; FRES 1940; FZS 1965. *Recreations:* shooting, fishing, golf. *Heir: s* Hon. James Anthony Macpherson, *b* 27 Feb. 1979. *Address:* Kyllachy, Tomatin, Inverness-shire IV13 7YA. *T:* Tomatin (08082) 212. *Clubs:* Boodle's, East India, Devonshire, Sports and Public Schools, Shikar; House of Lords Yacht; Royal and Ancient (St Andrews); Thorndon Park Golf (capt. 1962–63); Hartswood Golf (Founder Pres., 1970–74).

MACPHERSON, Sheriff Alexander Calderwood; a Sheriff of South Strathclyde, Dumfries and Galloway, at Hamilton, since 1978; *b* 14 June 1939; *s* of Alexander and Jean Macpherson; *m* 1963, Christine Isobel Hutchison (marr. diss. 1985); two *s*; *m* 1990, Marian Claire Hall. *Educ:* Glasgow Academy; Glasgow Univ. (MA 1959, LLB 1962). Qualified as solicitor, 1962; private practice, 1962–78; part-time Assistantship in Private Law at Glasgow Univ., 1962–69; Partner in West, Anderson & Co., Solicitors, Glasgow, 1968–78; Lectr in Evidence and Procedure at Strathclyde Univ., 1969–78. Chairman, Glasgow North and East Br., Multiple Sclerosis Soc., 1973–88. *Recreations:* piping (especially Piobaireachd), psychotherapy, reading. *Address:* Sheriff Court, Hamilton, Lanarks ML3 6AA. *Clubs:* Glasgow Highland, Glasgow Art, Royal Scottish Automobile (Glasgow); Royal Scottish Pipers' Society (Edinburgh).

McPHERSON, James Alexander Strachan, CBE 1982; JP; FSA (Scot.); Lord-Lieutenant of Grampian Region (Banffshire), since 1987; Solicitor, since 1954; *b* 20 Nov. 1927; *s* of Peter John McPherson and Jean Geddie Strachan; *m* 1960, Helen Marjorie Perks; one *s* one *d. Educ:* Banff Academy; Aberdeen Univ. MA, BL, LLB. National Service, 1952–54; commissioned RA. Solicitor; Partner, Alexander George & Co., Macduff, 1954–, Senior Partner, 1986–. Macduff Town Council: Mem., 1958–75; Treasurer, 1965–72; (last) Provost, 1972–75; Banff County Council: Mem., 1958–75; Chm., Educn Cttee, 1967–70; Chm., Management and Finance Cttee, 1970–75; (last) Convener, County Council, 1970–75; Mem., Assoc. of County Councils for Scotland, 1965–75; Mem., Grampian Regional Council, 1974–90 (Chm., Public Protection Cttee, 1974–86). Former Mem., numerous Scottish Cttees and Boards; Chm., Banff and Buchan JP Adv. Cttee, 1987–; Hon. Sheriff of Banffshire, 1972–. JP Banff and Buchan, 1974. *Recreations:* sailing, swimming and reading. *Address:* Dun Alastair, Macduff, Banffshire AB4 1XD. *T:* (home) Macduff (0261) 32377; (office) Macduff (0261) 32201. *Club:* Banff Town and County.

MACPHERSON, Sir Keith (Duncan), Kt 1981; company director; Consultant, The Herald and Weekly Times Ltd, Melbourne, since 1986; *b* 12 June 1920; *m* 1946, Ena Forester McNair; three *s* two *d. Educ:* Scotch Coll., Melbourne. Joined The Herald and Weekly Times Ltd, 1938; Sec., 1959–64; Asst Gen. Man., 1965–67; Gen. Man., 1968–70; Dir, 1974–86; Chief Exec., 1975–85; Chm., 1977–86; non-exec. Chm., 1985–86. Chairman: Australian Newsprint Mills Holdings Ltd, 1978–86 (Vice-Chm., 1976–78); West Australian Newspapers Ltd, 1981–86 (Dir, 1970; Man. Dir, 1970–75); South Pacific Post Pty Ltd (New Guinea Newspapers), 1965–70; Queensland Press Ltd, 1983–86 (Dep. Chm., 1981–83, Dir, 1978–86). Director: Tasman Pulp & Paper Co. Ltd, 1977–78; Davies Bros Ltd, 1975–86; New Nation Publishing Ltd, Singapore, 1974–81. Pres., Australian Newspapers Council, 1968–70; Chairman: Newspaper Proprietors' Assoc. of Melbourne, 1968–70; Media Council of Aust., 1969–70. *Recreations:* swimming, gardening. *Address:* Gleneagles, 24 Balwyn Road, Canterbury, Vic 3126, Australia. *T:* 836–8571. *Clubs:* Melbourne, Athenæum, Melbourne Cricket, Royal Automobile of Victoria, Victoria Racing, Victoria Amateur Turf, Moonee Valley Racing (Melbourne); American National (Sydney).

M'PHERSON, Prof. Philip Keith, CEng, FIEE; Managing Director, MacPherson Systems Ltd, since 1984; Visiting Professor: City University, since 1987; Royal College of Military Science, since 1990; *b* 10 March 1927; *s* of Ven. Kenneth M'Pherson and Dulce M'Pherson; *m* 1975, Rosalie Margaret, *d* of Richard and Mary Fowler. *Educ:* Marlborough Coll.; Royal Naval Engineering Coll.; Royal Naval Coll., Greenwich; Massachusetts Inst. of Technology (SM); MA Oxon. Engineer Officer, Royal Navy, 1948–59; research in Admiralty Gunnery Estabt, 1955–59, retired as Lt-Comdr, 1959. Head, Dynamics Gp, Atomic Energy Estabt, UKAEA, 1959–65, SPSO, 1963; Fellow of St John's Coll., Oxford, 1965–67; Prof. of Systems Sci., later Systems Engrg and Management, 1967–87, and Pro-Vice-Chancellor, 1982–87, City Univ. Vis. Scholar, Internat. Inst. of Applied Systems Analysis, Austria, 1976–77; Adjunct Prof., Xian Jiaotong Univ., China, 1980–84. Member: Executive Cttee, UK Automation Council, 1964–68; SRC Control Engrg Cttee, 1970–75; Chairman: IMechE Automatic Control Gp, 1967–69; IEE Systems Engrg Gp Cttee, 1966–69; IEE Control and Automation Div., 1967–69; IEE Systems Engrg Cttee, 1984–90; Soc. for General Systems Research (UK), 1973–76. Archbishops' Commn on Rural Areas, 1988–89. Freeman, City of London, 1985; Liveryman, Engineers' Co., 1986. *Publications:* many papers in the scientific literature. *Recreations:* walking, singing, making things. *Address:* The Wash, Dam Green, Kenninghall, Norfolk. *Club:* City Livery.

MACPHERSON, Roderick Ewen; Fellow, King's College, Cambridge, since 1942; Registrary, University of Cambridge, 1969–83; *b* 17 July 1916; *s* of Ewen Macpherson, Chief Charity Commissioner, and Dorothy Mildred Hensley; *m* 1941, Sheila Joan Hooper, *d* of H. P. Hooper; two *s* two *d. Educ:* Eton College; King's College, Cambridge. Math. Tripos, Part II, Wrangler; Math. Tripos, Part III, Distinction; Smith's Prizeman, 1940. Served RAFVR, 1940–46, Navigator (Radio). Fellow, King's Coll., Cambridge, 1942–; Third Bursar, King's College, 1947–50, Second Bursar, 1950–51, First Bursar,

1951–62; University Treasurer, Univ. of Cambridge, 1962–69; Member: Council of the Senate, 1957–62; Financial Board, 1955–62. Cambridge City Council, 1958–74, Hon. Councillor, 1974–. *Recreations:* gardening, hill-walking. *Address:* Orion, Coton Road, Grantchester, Cambridge CB3 9NX. *T:* Cambridge (0223) 840266.

MACPHERSON, Ronald Thomas Stewart, (Tommy), CBE (mil.) 1968; MC 1943, Bars 1944 and 1945; TD 1960; DL; Chairman: Boustead plc, since 1986; Cosmopolitan Textile Co. Ltd, since 1984; Employment Conditions Abroad Ltd, since 1984; Webb-Bowen International Ltd, since 1984; Allstate Reinsurance Ltd, since 1983; Owl Creek Investments plc, since 1989; *b* 4 Oct. 1920; 5th *s* of late Sir Thomas Stewart Macpherson, CIE, LLD, and Lady (Helen) Macpherson, (*née* Cameron); *m* 1953, Jean Henrietta, *d* of late David Butler Wilson; two *s* one *d. Educ:* Edinburgh Acad.; Cargilfield; Fettes Coll. (scholar); Trinity Coll., Oxford (1st open classical scholar; MA 1st Cl. Hons PPE). Athletics Blue and Scottish International; British Team World Student Games, Paris, 1947; represented Oxford in Rugby football and hockey, 1946–47. Reader Middle Temple. 2nd Lieut. Queen's Own Cameron Highlanders TA, 1939; Scottish Commando, 1940; POW, 1941–43, escaped 1943; Major 1943; served Special Forces with French and Italian Resistance, 1944–45. Consultant, Italo-Yugoslav Border Commn, 1946. Comd 1st Bn London Scottish TA, 1961–64; Col TA London Dist, 1964–67. Mem., Queen's Body Guard for Scotland (Royal Co. of Archers). Chm., 1961–79, Pres., 1979–, Achilles Club; Vice-Pres., Newtonmore Camanachd Club. Chairman: Mallinson-Denny Gp, 1981–82 (Man. Dir, 1967–81); Allstate Insurance Co., 1983–87; Birmid Qualcast, 1984–88; Exec. Dir, Brooke Bond Gp plc, 1981–82; Director: Transglobe Expedition Ltd, 1978–83; C. H. Industrials PLC, 1983–; Scottish Mutual Assurance Soc., 1982–; NCB, 1983–86; TSB Scotland, 1986–; New Scotland Insurance plc, 1987–; Fitzwilton (UK) plc, 1990–; UK Consultant, Sears Roebuck & Co., Chicago, 1984–; Consultant: Bain & Co. (USA), 1987–; Candover Investment plc, 1989–. Chairman: Nat. Employment Liaison Cttee for TA and Reserves, 1986–; ABCC, 1986–; Vice-Pres., London Chamber of Commerce, 1985– (Chm., Council, 1980–82). Member: Council, CBI (Chm., London and SE Reg., CBI, 1975–77); Scottish Council, London; Prices and Incomes Bd, 1968–69; Council, GBA, 1979–83; Council, Strathclyde Univ. Business Sch., 1982–86. Governor, Fettes Coll. Prime Warden, Co. of Dyers, 1985–86. FRSA, FBIM. DL 1977, High Sheriff, 1983–84, Greater London. Chevalier, Légion d'Honneur, and Croix de Guerre with 2 palms, France; Medaglia d'Argento and Resistance Medal, Italy; Kt of St Mary of Bethlehem. *Recreations:* shooting, outdoor sport, languages. *Address:* 27 Archery Close, W2 2BE. *T:* 071–262 8487; Balavil, Kingussie, Inverness-shire PH21 1LU. *T:* Kingussie (05402) 470. *Clubs:* Hurlingham, MCC.

MacPHERSON, Stewart Myles; Radio Commentator; Journalist; Variety Artist; Special Events Coordinator, Assiniboia Downs Racetrack, Winnipeg; *b* Winnipeg, Canada, 29 Oct. 1908; *m* 1937, Emily Comfort; one *s* one *d. Educ:* Canada. Started broadcasting, 1937, on ice hockey; War Correspondent. Commentator on national events and world championships. Question Master, Twenty Questions and Ignorance is Bliss. Compère, Royal Command Variety Performance, 1948; Dir of Programs, C-Jay Television, Winnipeg, 1960. *Publication:* The Mike and I, 1948; *relevant publication:* Highlights with Stewart MacPherson, by John Robertson, 1980. *Recreations:* golf, bridge, poker. *Address:* 709–3200 Portage Avenue, Winnipeg, Manitoba, Canada. *T:* (204) 889–0210.

MACPHERSON, Tommy; *see* Macpherson, R. T. S.

MACPHERSON OF CLUNY (and Blairgowrie), Hon. Sir William (Alan), Kt 1983; TD 1966; **Hon. Mr Justice Macpherson of Cluny;** Judge of the High Court of Justice, Queen's Bench Division, since 1983; Cluny Macpherson; 27th Chief of Clan Macpherson; *b* 1 April 1926; *s* of Brig. Alan David Macpherson, DSO, MC, RA (*d* 1969) and late Catherine Richardson Macpherson; *m* 1962, Sheila McDonald Brodie; two *s* one *d. Educ:* Wellington Coll., Berkshire; Trinity Coll., Oxford (MA). Called to Bar, Inner Temple, 1952; Bencher, 1978; QC 1971; a Recorder of the Crown Court, 1972–83; Presiding Judge, Northern Circuit, 1985–88; Pres., Interception of Communications Tribunal, 1990–. Mem., Bar Council and Senate, 1981–83; Hon. Mem., Northern Circuit, 1987. Served, 1944–47, in Scots Guards (Capt.). Commanded (Lt-Col) 21st Special Air Service Regt (TA), 1962–65, Hon. Col, 1983–91; Mem., Queen's Body Guard for Scotland, Royal Co. of Archers, 1977–, Brigadier 1989. Gov., Royal Scottish Corporation, 1972– (Vice-Pres., 1989–). *Recreations:* golf, fishing; Past Pres., London Scottish FC. *Heir: s* Alan Thomas Macpherson yr of Cluny and Blairgowrie. *Address:* Newton Castle, Blairgowrie, Perthshire; Royal Courts of Justice, Strand, WC2A 2LL. *Clubs:* Caledonian, Highland Society of London (Pres., 1991), Special Forces; Blairgowrie Golf; Denham Golf.

MACPHIE, Maj.-Gen. Duncan Love; Commander Medical, British Army of the Rhine, 1987–90, retired; *b* 15 Dec. 1930; *s* of Donald Macphie and Elizabeth Adam (*née* Gibson); *m* 1957, Isobel Mary Jenkins; one *s* two *d. Educ:* Hutchesons' Grammar Sch.; Glasgow Univ. MB ChB. Stonehouse and Hairmyres Hosps, 1957–58; commnd RAMC, 1958; RMO, 1st Bn The Royal Scots, 1958–61; GP, Glasgow, 1961–63; RMO, 3 RHA, 1963–67; CO, BMH Dharan, Nepal, 1970–72; CO, 24 Field Ambulance, 1972–75; CO, BMH Munster, 1976–78; ADMS, 4 Armd Div., 1978–80; Asst DGAMS, MoD, 1980–83; CO, Queen Elizabeth Mil. Hosp., Woolwich, 1983–85; Chief, Med. Plans Branch, SHAPE, 1985–87. QHS 1985–90. OStJ. *Recreations:* gardening, Rugby, cricket, classical music, reading.

McQUAID, James, PhD; CEng, FIMinE; Research Director, Health and Safety Executive, since 1985; *b* 5 Nov. 1939; *s* of late James and Brigid McQuaid; *m* 1968, Catherine Anne, *d* of late Dr James John Hargan and of Dr Mary Helen Hargan; two *s* one *d. Educ:* Christian Brothers' Sch., Dundalk; University Coll., Dublin (BEng); Jesus Coll., Cambridge (PhD); DSc NUI 1978. MIMechE 1972; FIMinE 1986. Graduate engrg apprentice, British Nylon Spinners, 1961–63; Sen. Res. Fellow 1966–68, Sen. Scientific Officer 1968–72, PSO 1972–78, Safety in Mines Res. Estabt; seconded as Safety Advr, Petrochemicals Div., ICI, 1976–77; Dep. Dir, Safety Engrg Lab., 1978–80; Dir, 1980–85. Chm., Electrical Equipment Certification Management Bd, 1985–; Member: Safety in Mines Res. Adv. Bd, 1985–; Council, Midland Inst. of Mining Engrs, 1987–; Council, IMinE, 1991–; Adv. Bd for Mech. Engrg, Univ. of Liverpool, 1987–; Court, Univ. of Sheffield, 1985–. Pres., Sheffield Trades Hist. Soc., 1989–. Mem., Council, S Yorks Trades Hist. Trust, 1989–. *Publications:* numerous papers in technical jls. *Recreations:* ornamental turning, model engineering, industrial archaeology. *Address:* 61 Pingle Road, Sheffield S7 2LL. *T:* Sheffield (0742) 365349. *Club:* Athenæum.

McQUAIL, Paul Christopher; Deputy Secretary, Department of the Environment, since 1988; *b* 22 April 1934; *s* of Christopher McQuail and Anne (*née* Mullan); *m* 1964, Susan Adler; one *s* one *d. Educ:* St Anselm's, Birkenhead; Sidney Sussex Coll., Cambridge. Min. of Housing and Local Govt, 1957; Principal, 1962; Asst Sec., 1969; DoE, 1970; Special Asst to Permanent Sec. and Sec. of State, 1972–73; Sec., Royal Commn on the Press, 1974–77; Under Sec., DoE, 1977–88; Chief Exec., Hounslow Bor. Council, 1983–85 (on secondment). Mem., Environment and Planning Cttee, ESRC, 1983–87. *Recreations:* alpinism and other harmless pleasures. *Address:* Department of the Environment, 2 Marsham Street, SW1P 3EB.

MACQUAKER, Donald Francis, CBE 1991; solicitor; Partner, T. C. Young & Son, Glasgow, since 1957; *b* 21 Sept. 1932; *s* of Thomas Mason Macquaker, MC, MA, BL and Caroline Bertha Floris Macquaker; *m* 1964, Susan Elizabeth, *d* of Mr and Mrs W. A. K. Finlayson, High Coodham, Symington, Ayrshire; one *s* one *d. Educ:* Winchester Coll.; Trinity Coll., Oxford (MA); Univ. of Glasgow (LLB). Admitted Solicitor, 1957. Mem. Bd of Management, Glasgow Royal Maternity Hosp. and associated hosps, 1965–74 (Vice-Chm., 1972–74); Greater Glasgow Health Board: Mem., 1973–87; Chm., 1983–87; Convener, F and GP Cttee, 1974–83; Chm., Common Services Agency for Scottish Health Service, 1987–91. Dir, Lithgows Ltd, 1987–. *Recreations:* shooting, fishing, travelling, gardening. *Address:* Blackbyres, by Ayr KA7 4TS. *T:* Alloway (0292) 41088. *Clubs:* The Western (Glasgow); Leander (Henley-on-Thames).

McQUARRIE, Sir Albert, Kt 1987; Chairman: A. McQuarrie & Son (Great Britain) Ltd, 1946–88; Sir Albert McQuarrie & Associates Ltd, since 1988; Haverstock plc, since 1990; *b* 1 Jan. 1918; *s* of Algernon Stewart McQuarrie and Alice Maud Sharman; *m* 1st, 1945, Roseleen McCaffery (*d* 1986); one *s*; 2nd, 1989, Rhoda Annie Gall. *Educ:* Highlanders Acad., Greenock; Greenock High Sch.; Royal Coll. of Science and Technology, Univ. of Strathclyde. MSE, PEng 1945. Served in HM Forces, 1939–45 (Officer in RE). Director: Westminster House plc, 1988–; Hunterston Develt Co., 1989–; Albert Abela (Scotland)), 1988–; Consultant, Bredero Projects Ltd, 1975–. Former Dean of Guild, Gourock Town Council; Chm., Fyvie/Rothienorman/Monquhitter Community Council, 1975–79. Contested (C): Banff and Buchan, 1987; Highlands and Islands, European Parly elecn, 1989. MP (C): Aberdeenshire E, 1979–83; Banff and Buchan, 1983–87. Chm., British/Gibraltar All Party Gp, 1979–87; Vice Chm., Conservative Fisheries Sub Cttee, 1979–87; Member: Select Cttees on Scottish Affairs, 1979–83, on Agriculture, 1983–85, on Private Bill Procedure, 1987; Speaker's Panel of Chairmen, 1986–87. Mem. Council, Soc. of Engineers, 1978–87. Hon. Pres., Banff and Buchan Cons. and Unionist Assoc., 1989–; Hon. Vice-Pres., Gourock Horticultural Soc., 1954–. FRSH 1952. Freeman, City of Gibraltar, 1982. *Recreations:* golf, bridge, music, soccer, swimming, horticulture. *Address:* Crimond, 11 Balcomie Crescent, Troon, Ayrshire KA10 7AR. *T:* Troon (0292) 316467. *Clubs:* Lansdowne, Challoner (Chm., 1982–); Western, Royal Scottish Automobile (Glasgow); Ayr; Marine Highland (Troon).

MACQUARRIE, Rev. Prof. John, TD 1962; FBA 1984; Lady Margaret Professor of Divinity, University of Oxford, and Canon of Christ Church, 1970–86; *b* 27 June 1919; *s* of John Macquarrie and Robina Macquarrie (*née* McInnes); *m* 1949, Jenny Fallow (*née* Welsh); two *s* one *d. Educ:* Paisley Grammar Sch.; Univ. of Glasgow. MA 1940; BD 1943; PhD 1954; DLitt 1964; DD Oxon 1981. Royal Army Chaplains Dept, 1945–48; St Ninian's Church, Brechin, 1948–53; Lecturer, Univ. of Glasgow, 1953–62; Prof. of Systematic Theology, Union Theological Seminary, NY, 1962–70. Consultant, Lambeth Conf., 1968 and 1978. Hon. degrees: STD: Univ. of the South, USA, 1967; General Theological Seminary, New York, 1968; DD: Univ. of Glasgow, 1969; Episcopal Seminary of SW, Austin, Texas, 1981; Virginia Theol Seminary, 1981; DCnL, Nashotah House, Wisconsin, 1986. *Publications:* An Existentialist Theology, 1955; The Scope of Demythologising, 1960; Twentieth Century Religious Thought, 1963; Studies in Christian Existentialism, 1965; Principles of Christian Theology, 1966; God-Talk, 1967; God and Secularity, 1967; Martin Heidegger, 1968; Three Issues in Ethics, 1970; Existentialism, 1972; Paths in Spirituality, 1972; The Faith of the People of God, 1972; The Concept of Peace, 1973; Thinking about God, 1975; Christian Unity and Christian Diversity, 1975; The Humility of God, 1978; Christian Hope, 1978; In Search of Humanity, 1982; In Search of Deity (Gifford Lectures), 1984; Theology, Church and Ministry, 1986; Jesus Christ in Modern Thought, 1990; Mary for All Christians, 1991. *Address:* 206 Headley Way, Headington, Oxford OX3 7TA. *T:* Oxford (0865) 61889.

MACQUEEN, Angus, CMG 1977; Director, The British Bank of the Middle East, 1970–79 (Chairman, 1975–78); Member, London Advisory Committee, The Hongkong and Shanghai Banking Corporation, 1975–78; Chairman, Incotes Ltd, 1975–85; *b* 7 April 1910; *s* of Donald Macqueen and Catherine Thomson; *m* 1st, 1940, Erica A. L. Sutherland (marr. diss.); one *d*; 2nd, 1950, Elizabeth Mary Barber; one *s* one *d. Educ:* Campbeltown Grammar Sch. Joined Union Bank of Scotland, 1927; Imperial Bank of Persia (now The British Bank of the Middle East), 1930; overseas service in Iraq, Iran, Kuwait, Aden, Lebanon, Morocco; Gen. Manager, 1965–70. Director: The British Bank of the Middle East (Morocco), 1961–70; The Bank of Iran and the Middle East, 1965–74; Bank of North Africa, 1965–70. Member: London Chamber of Commerce (Middle East Section), 1962–66; Council, Anglo-Arab Assoc., 1968–75; Corona (Overseas Students) Housing Assoc., 1969–81. AIB (Scot.). National Cedar Medal, Lebanon, 1960. *Recreations:* walking, foreign travel. *Address:* 18 Montagu Square, W1H 1RD. *T:* 071–935 9015. *Club:* Oriental.

MacQUEEN, Prof. John; Endowment Fellow, University of Edinburgh, since 1988; *b* 13 Feb. 1929; *s* of William L. and Grace P. MacQueen; *m* 1953, Winifred W. McWalter; three *s. Educ:* Hutchesons' Boys' Grammar Sch.; Glasgow Univ.; Cambridge Univ. MA English Lang. and Lit., Greek, Glasgow; BA, MA Archaeology and Anthropology, Section B, Cambridge. RAF, 1954–56 (Flying Officer). Asst Prof. of English, Washington Univ., Missouri, 1956–59; University of Edinburgh: Lectr in Medieval English and Scottish Literature, 1959–63; Masson Prof. of Medieval and Renaissance Literature, 1963–72; Prof. of Scottish Lit. and Oral Tradition, 1972–88, now Emeritus; Dir, Sch. of Scottish Studies, 1969–88. Barclay Acheson Vis. Prof. of Internat. Relations, Macalester Coll., Minnesota, 1967; Vis. Prof. in Medieval Studies, Australian Nat. Univ., 1971; Winegard Vis. Prof., Univ. of Guelph, Ont, 1981. Chairman: British Branch, Internat. Assoc. of Sound Archives, 1978–80; Exec. Cttee, Scottish Nat. Dictionary Assoc., 1978–87; Scottish Dictionary Jt Council, 1988–; Pres., Scottish Text Soc., 1989–; Mem., Scottish Film Council, 1981– (Chm., Archive Cttee, 1980–). Hon. DLitt NUI, 1985. Fletcher of Saltoun Award, 1990. *Publications:* St Nynia, 1961, rev. edn 1991; (with T. Scott) The Oxford Book of Scottish Verse, 1966; Robert Henryson, 1967; Ballattis of Luve, 1970; Allegory, 1970; (ed with Winifred MacQueen) A Choice of Scottish Verse, 1470–1570, 1972; Progress and Poetry, 1982; Numerology, 1985; The Rise of the Historical Novel, 1989; (ed with Winifred MacQueen) Scotichronicon, Bks III and IV, 1989; (ed) Humanism in Renaissance Scotland, 1990; articles and reviews in learned jls. *Recreations:* music, walking, archaeology. *Address:* 12 Orchard Toll, Edinburgh EH4 3JF. *T:* 031–332 1488; Slewdonan, Damnaglaur, Drummore, Stranraer DG9 9QN. *Clubs:* University Staff, Scottish Arts (Edinburgh).

McQUIGGAN, John, MBE 1955; independent consultant; Executive Director, United Kingdom-South Africa Trade Association Ltd, 1978–86; retired at own request from HM Diplomatic Service, 1977; *b* 24 Nov. 1922; *s* of John and Sarah Elizabeth McQuiggan; *m* 1950, Doris Elsie Hadler; three *s* one *d. Educ:* St Edwards Coll., Liverpool. Served War, in RAF, 1942–47 (W Africa, Europe and Malta). Joined Dominions Office, 1940; Administration Officer, British High Commission, Canberra, Australia, 1950–54; Second Sec., Pakistan, Lahore and Dacca, 1954–57; First Sec. (Inf.), Lahore, 1957–58; Dep. Dir,

UK Inf. Services, Australia (Canberra and Sydney), 1958–61; Dir, Brit. Inf. Services, Eastern Nigeria (Enugu), 1961–64; Dir, Brit. Inf. Services in Uganda, and concurrently First Sec., HM Embassy, Kigali, Rwanda, 1964–69; W African Dept, FCO, 1969–73; HM Consul, Chad, 1970–73 (London based); Dep. High Comr and Counsellor (Econ. and Commercial), Lusaka, Zambia, 1973–76. Dir-Gen., Brit. Industry Cttee on South Africa, 1986. Mem., Royal African Soc.; MIPR 1964; Mem., Internat. Public Relations Assoc., 1975. Fellow, Inst. of Dirs. *Publications:* pamphlets and contribs to trade and economic jls. *Recreations:* tennis, carpentry, craftwork. *Address:* 7 Meadowcroft, Bickley, Kent BR1 2JD. *T:* 081–467 0075. *Club:* Royal Over-Seas League.

McQUILLAN, William Rodger; HM Diplomatic Service, retired; *b* 18 March 1930; *s* of late Albert McQuillan and Isabella Glen McQuillan; *m* 1970, Sheriell May Fawcett; one *s* two *d*. *Educ:* Royal High Sch., Edinburgh; Edinburgh Univ.; Yale Univ. Served RAF, 1954–57. Asst Sec., Manchester Univ. Appointments Board, 1957–65; HM Diplomatic Service, 1965–83: First Sec., CRO, 1965; Lusaka, 1968, Head of Chancery, 1969; First Sec. (Commercial), Santiago, Chile, 1970; Counsellor and HM Consul, Guatemala City, 1974; Head of Inf. Policy Dept, FCO, 1978–81; Ambassador to Iceland, 1981–83. *Recreations:* hill walking, choral singing, reading.

MacQUITTY, James Lloyd, OBE 1983; QC (NI) 1960; Chairman, Ulster Television Ltd, 1977–83; *b* 2 Nov. 1912; *s* of James MacQuitty and Henrietta Jane (*née* Little); *m* 1941, Irene Frances McDowell. *Educ:* Campbell Coll. and Methodist Coll., Belfast; St Catherine's Coll., Oxford (MA); Trinity Hall, Cambridge (MA, LLM). Vice-Pres., Cambridge Univ. Conservative Assoc., 1936. HG Instructor, 1940–43; HAA, 1943–44. Called to English Bar, 1938, to NI Bar, 1941. Chairman: Compensation Appeals Tribunal; Compensation Tribunal for Loss of Employment through Civil Unrest; Wages Councils in NI, 1951–89; Arbitrator under the Industrial Courts Act 1919, 1958–78; Mem., Industrial Injuries Adv. Council, 1960–86. Before reorganisation in 1973 of Local Govt in NI, was Chm. of former Jt Adv. Bds for Local Authorities' Services, Municipal Clerks, Rural Dist Clerks and County Chief Educn Officers and County Surveyors. Vice-Chm., Management Cttee, Glenlola Collegiate Sch., 1964–75; Chm., Trustees of Ulster Folk and Transport Museum, 1976–85 (Vice-Chm., 1969–76). Hon. LLD QUB, 1987. Freeman, City of London, 1967. Chevalier de l'Ordre de St Lazare, 1962. *Recreations:* swimming, sailing. *Address:* 10 Braemar Park, Bangor, Co. Down, Northern Ireland BT20 5HZ. *T:* Bangor (0247) 454420. *Clubs:* Carlton; Royal Ulster Yacht.

MacRAE, (Alastair) Christopher (Donald Summerhayes), CMG 1987; HM Diplomatic Service; High Commissioner to Nigeria, and concurrently Ambassador (non resident) to Benin, since 1991; *b* 3 May 1937; *s* of Dr Alexander Murray MacRae and Dr Grace Maria Lynton Summerhayes MacRae; *m* 1963, Mette Willert; two *d*. *Educ:* Rugby; Lincoln Coll., Oxford (BA Hons English); Harvard (Henry Fellow in Internat. Relations). RN, 1956–58. CRO, 1962; 3rd, later 2nd Sec., Dar es Salaam, 1963–65; ME Centre for Arab Studies, Lebanon, 1965–67; 2nd Sec., Beirut, 1967–68; FCO, 1968–70; 1st Sec. and Head of Chancery: Baghdad, 1970–71; Brussels, 1972–76; attached Directorate-Gen. VIII, European Commn, Brussels, on secondment from FCO, 1976–78; Ambassador to Gabon, 1978–80, and to Sao Tomé and Principé (non-resident), 1979–80; Head of W Africa Dept, FCO, 1980–83, and Ambassador (non-resident) to Chad, 1982–83; Political Counsellor and Head of Chancery, Paris, 1983–86; Minister and Head of British Interests Section, Iran, 1987; Vis. Fellow, IISS, 1987–88; Support Services Scrutiny, FCO, 1988; Under Sec. (on secondment), Cabinet Office, 1988–91. *Recreation:* trying to keep fit. *Address:* c/o Foreign and Commonwealth Office, King Charles Street, SW1A 2AH. *Club:* Commonwealth Trust.

MacRAE, Prof. Donald Gunn; Martin White Professor of Sociology, University of London, 1978–87, now Emeritus; *b* 20 April 1921; *o s* of Donald MacRae and Elizabeth Maud Gunn; *m* 1st, 1948, Helen Grace McHardy; two *d*; 2nd, 1987, Mrs Jean Ridyard; one *s* one *d*. *Educ:* various schools in Scotland; Glasgow High Sch.; Glasgow Univ.; Balliol Coll., Oxford. MA Glasgow 1942; BA 1945, MA 1949, Oxon. Asst Lectr, LSE, 1945; Univ. Lectr in Sociology, Oxford, 1949; Reader in Sociology, London Univ., 1954; Prof. of Sociology: UC Gold Coast, 1956; Univ. of California, Berkeley, 1959; Univ. of London, 1961–87. Fellow, Center for Advanced Studies in Behavioral Sciences, Stanford, 1967. Vis. Prof., Univ. of the Witwatersrand, 1975; Senior Member, Keynes Coll., Darwin Coll., Univ. of Kent at Canterbury. Member: Council, CNAA (Chm. Cttee for Arts and Social Studies, to 1978); Archbp of Canterbury's Gp on Divorce Law, 1964–66; Gaitskell Commn of Inquiry into Advertising, 1962–66; Internat. Council on the Future of the University, 1973–82. Editor, British Jl of Sociology, from formation to 1965. *Publications:* Ideology and Society, 1960; (ed) The World of J. B. Priestley, 1967; (ed with intro.) The Man Versus the State, by Herbert Spencer, 1969; Ages and Stages, 1973; Max Weber, 1974. *Recreations:* talking, music, walking. *Address:* 90B Hornsey Lane, Highgate, N6 5LT. *T:* 071–281 0758; 38 Bowling Street, Sandwich, Kent CT13 9EY. *Club:* Athenæum.

McRAE, Frances Anne, (Mrs Hamish McRae); *see* Cairncross, F. A.

McRAE, Hamish Malcolm Donald; Business and City Editor, and an Assistant Editor, The Independent, since 1989; *b* 20 Oct. 1943; *s* of Donald and Barbara McRae (*née* Budd); *m* 1971, Frances Anne Cairncross, *qv*; two *d*. *Educ:* Fettes College; Trinity College, Dublin (BA Hons Economics and Political Science). Liverpool Post, 1966–67; The Banker, 1967–72 (Asst Editor, 1969, Dep. Editor, 1971); Editor, Euromoney, 1972–74; Financial Editor, The Guardian, 1975–89. Wincott Foundn financial journalist of the year, 1979. *Publications:* (with Frances Cairncross) Capital City: London as a financial centre, 1973, 5th edn 1991; (with Frances Cairncross) The Second Great Crash, 1975; Japan's role in the emerging global securities market, 1985. *Recreations:* walking, ski-ing, cooking. *Address:* 6 Canonbury Lane, N1 2AP.

MACRAE, John Esmond Campbell, CMG 1986; DPhil; HM Diplomatic Service; Ambassador to the Kingdom of Morocco, since 1990, and to Mauritania (non-resident), since 1986; *b* 8 Dec. 1932; *s* of Col Archibald Campbell Macrae, IMS, and Euretta Margaret Skelton; *m* 1962, Anne Catherine Sarah Strain; four *s*. *Educ:* Sheikh Bagh Sch., Kashmir; Fettes Coll., Edinburgh; Christ Church Oxford (Open Scholar); Princeton, USA. DPhil, MA; FRGS. Atomic Energy and Disarmament Dept, Foreign Office, 1959–60; 2nd Sec., British Embassy, Tel Aviv, 1961–64; 1st Secretary: Djakarta, 1964; Vientiane, 1964–66; FO, NE African Dept, 1966; Central Dept, 1967–69; Southern African Dept, 1970–72; UK Mission to the UN, New York (dealing with social affairs, population and outer space), 1972–75; Counsellor, Science and Technology, Paris, 1975–80; Head of Cultural Relns Dept, FCO, 1980–85; RCDS, 1985; Ambassador to Senegal, 1985–90. *Recreations:* music, travel, picnics in unusual places. *Address:* c/o Foreign and Commonwealth Office, Whitehall, SW1A 2AH. *Club:* Garrick.

MacRAE, Kenneth Charles; His Honour Judge MacRae; a Circuit Judge, since 1990; *b* 14 March 1944; *s* of William and Ann MacRae; *m* 1981, Hilary Vivien Williams; one *d*. *Educ:* Redruth County Grammar School; Cornwall Tech. Coll.; Fitzwilliam Coll., Cambridge (BA Hons). Called to the Bar, Lincoln's Inn, 1969; a Recorder of the Crown Court, 1985. *Recreations:* gardening, walking, music. *Address:* c/o Courts Administrator, 10 Sundial Court, Tolworth Rise South, Surbiton, Surrey KT5 9NN. *T:* 081–335 3090.

MACRAE, Col Sir Robert (Andrew Alexander Scarth), KCVO 1990; MBE 1953; JP; Lord-Lieutenant of Orkney, 1972–90 (Vice-Lieutenant, 1967–72); Farmer; *b* 14 April 1915; *s* of late Robert Scarth Farquhar Macrae, CIE, CBE, Grindelay House, Orphir, Orkney; *m* 1945, Violet Maud, *d* of late Walter Scott MacLellan; two *s*. *Educ:* Lancing; RMC Sandhurst. 2nd Lt Seaforth Highlanders, 1935; Col 1963; retd 1968. Active Service: NW Europe, 1940–45 (despatches, 1945); Korea, 1952–53; E Africa, 1953–54. Member: Orkney CC, 1970–74; Orkney Islands Council, 1974–78; Vice Chairman: Orkney Hospital Bd, 1971–74; Orkney Health Bd, 1974–79. Hon. Sheriff, Grampian, Highlands and Islands, 1972. DL, Co. of Orkney, 1946; JP Orkney, 1975. *Recreations:* sailing, fishing. *Address:* Grindelay House, Orkney KW17 2RD. *T:* Orphir (085681) 228. *Clubs:* Army and Navy; New, Puffin's (Edinburgh).

MACREADIE, John Lindsay; National Officer, since 1970 and Deputy General Secretary, since 1987, Civil and Public Services Association; *b* 19 Sept. 1946; *s* of John and Mary Macreadie; *m* 1967, Roisin Ann Boden; one *s* one *d*. *Educ:* Primary and Secondary State Schools, Glasgow. Civil Servant, 1964–70. Mem., TUC General Council, 1987–88. *Recreations:* politics, football, cinema. *Address:* 1 The Green, Morden, Surrey. *T:* 081–542 5880. *Club:* William Morris Labour (Wimbledon).

MACREADY, Sir Nevil (John Wilfrid), 3rd Bt *cr* 1923; CBE 1983; Managing Director, Mobil Oil Co. Ltd, 1975–85; Chairman, Horseracing Advisory Council, since 1986; *b* 7 Sept. 1921; *s* of Lt-Gen. Sir Gordon (Nevil) Macready, 2nd Bt, KBE, CB, CMG, DSO, MC, and Elisabeth (*d* 1969), *d* of Duc de Noailles; *S* father 1956; *m* 1949, Mary, *d* of late Sir Donald Fergusson, GCB; one *s* three *d*. *Educ:* Cheltenham; St John's Coll., Oxford. Served in RA (Field), 1942–47 (despatches); Staff Captain, 1945. BBC European Service, 1947–50. Vice-Pres. and Gen. Manager, Mobil Oil Française, 1972–75. Pres., Inst. of Petroleum, 1980–82. Chm., Crafts Council, 1984–91. Pres., Royal Warrant Holders' Assoc., 1979–80; Trustee V&A Museum, 1985–. *Recreations:* racing, fishing, theatre, music. *Heir:* *s* Charles Nevil Macready [*b* 19 May 1955; *m* 1981, Lorraine, *d* of Brian McAdam; one *s* one *d*]. *Address:* The White House, Odiham, Hants RG25 1LG. *T:* Odiham (0256) 702976. *Clubs:* Boodle's, Naval and Military; Jockey (Paris).

MacROBBIE, Prof. Enid Anne Campbell, FRS 1991; Professor of Plant Biophysics, University of Cambridge, since 1987; Fellow of Girton College, since 1958; *b* 5 Dec. 1931; *d* of late George MacRobbie and Agnes Kerr MacRobbie (*née* Campbell). *Educ:* Mary Erskine Sch., Edinburgh; Univ. of Edinburgh (BSc, PhD); MA, ScD Cantab. Res. Fellow, Univ. of Copenhagen, 1957–58; Cambridge University: Res. Fellow, Botany Sch., 1958–62; Demonstrator in Botany, 1962–66; Lectr in Botany, 1966–73; Reader in Plant Biophysics, 1973–87. *Publications:* papers in sci jls. *Address:* Girton College, Cambridge CB3 0JG. *T:* Cambridge (0223) 338999.

McROBERT, Rosemary Dawn Teresa, OBE 1985; Deputy Director, Consumers' Association, 1980–88; *b* Maymyo, Burma, 29 Aug. 1927; *e d* of late Lt-Col Ronald McRobert, MB, ChB, FRCOG, IMS, and Julie Rees. *Educ:* privately and at Gloucestershire College of Educn. Journalist and broadcaster on consumer subjects, 1957–63; Founder editor, Home Economics, 1954–63; Chief Information Officer, Consumer Council, 1965–70; Consumer Representation Officer, Consumers' Assoc., 1971–73; Adviser on consumer affairs in DTI and Dept of Prices and Consumer Protection, 1973–74; Dir, Retail Trading Standards Assoc., 1974–80. Member Council: Inst. of Consumer Ergonomics, 1974–81; Consumers' Assoc., 1974–79; Advertising Standards Authority, 1974–80; Member: Adv. Council on Energy Conservation, 1974–82; Design Council, 1975–84; Post Office Review Cttee, 1976; Policyholders' Protection Bd, 1976–; Nuffield Enquiry into Pharmacy Services, 1984–86; Council for Licensed Conveyancers, 1989–; British Hallmarking Council, 1989–. Chm., Management Cttee, Camden Consumer Aid Centres, 1977–80. Vice-Pres., Patients Assoc., 1988–. Dir, Investors Compensation Scheme, 1988–. Liveryman, Glovers' Co., 1979. *Address:* 57 Lawford Road, NW5 2LG. *Club:* Reform.

MACRORY, Sir Patrick (Arthur), Kt 1972; Director, Rothman Carreras Ltd, 1971–82; Barrister-at-Law; *b* 21 March 1911; *s* of late Lt-Col F. S. N. Macrory, DSO, DL, and Rosie, *d* of Gen. Brabazon Pottinger; *m* 1939, Elizabeth, *d* of late Rev. J. F. O. Lewis; three *s* (one *d* decd). *Educ:* Cheltenham Coll.; Trinity Coll., Oxford (MA). Called to the Bar, Middle Temple, 1937. Served War, 1939–45, Army. Unilever Ltd: joined 1947; Secretary, 1956; Director, 1968–71, retd. Dir, Bank of Ireland Gp, 1971–79; Chm., Merchant Ivory Productions, 1976–. Mem., Northern Ireland Development Council, 1956–64; Gen. Treasurer, British Assoc. for Advancement of Science, 1960–65; Chm., Review Body on Local Govt in N Ireland, 1970; Pres., Confedn of Ulster Socs, 1980–84 (Chm., 1974–79); Member: Commn of Inquiry into Industrial Representation, 1971–72; Cttee on the Preparation of Legislation, 1973. Mem. Council, Cheltenham Coll. (Dep. Pres., 1980–83). *Publications:* Borderline, 1937; Signal Catastrophe—the retreat from Kabul 1842, 1966, repr. as Kabul Catastrophe: the retreat of 1842, 1986; Lady Sale's Journal, 1969; The Siege of Derry, 1980; Days that are Gone, 1983. *Recreations:* golf, military history. *Address:* Amberdene, Walton-on-the-Hill, Tadworth, Surrey KT20 7UB. *T:* Tadworth (0737) 813086. *Clubs:* Athenæum; Walton Heath Golf; Castlerock Golf (Co Londonderry).

McSHARRY, Deirdre; Consultant, National Magazine Company, and Magazine Division, The Hearst Corporation, since 1990; *b* 4 April 1932; *d* of late Dr John McSharry and of Mrs Mary McSharry. *Educ:* Dominican Convent, Wicklow; Trinity Coll., Dublin. Woman's Editor, Daily Express, 1962–66; Fashion Editor, The Sun, 1966–72; Editor, Cosmopolitan, 1973–85; Editor-in-Chief, Country Living, 1986–89. Magazine Editor of the Year, PPA, 1981, 1987. *Recreations:* architecture, gardening, Ireland. *Address:* c/o National Magazine Company, 72 Broadwick Street, W1.

MacSHARRY, Raymond; Member, Commission of the European Communities, since 1989; *b* Sligo, April 1938; *m* Elaine Neilan; three *s* three *d*. *Educ:* St Vincent's Nat. Sch., Sligo; Ballincutranta Nat. Sch., Beltra, Co. Sligo; Marist Brothers Nat. Sch., Sligo; Summerhill Coll., Sligo. TD (FF) for Sligo Leitrim, 1969–88; opposition front bench spokesman on Office of Public Works, 1973–75; Mem., Cttee of Public Accts, 1969–77; Minister of State, Dept of Finance and the Public Service, 1977–79; Minister of Agriculture, 1979–81; opposition spokesman on Agric., 1981–82; Tánaiste and Minister for Finance, 1982; Minister for Finance and the Public Service, 1987–88. Formerly Member: New Ireland Forum; Nat. Exec., Fianna Fáil Party (later, also an Hon Treas.). Mem. for Connaught/Ulster, Europ. Parlt, 1984–87; Mem., Council of Ministers, 1984–87; Pres., Budget Council dealing with Europ. Parlt during Ireland's Presidency of EEC, 1979; Governor, Europ. Investment Bank, 1982. Councillor, Sligo CC, 1967–78; Chairman: Bd of Management, Sligo Reg. Tech. Coll., 1974 (Mem., 1970–78); Sligo Hosp. Exec. Cttee, 1972–78; NW Health Bd, 1974–75 (Mem., 1971–78); Member: Sligo Corp., 1967–78 (Alderman, 1974–78); Town of Sligo Vocational Educn Cttee, 1967–78; Bd of Management, Sligo-Leitrim Reg. Develt Org., 1973–78; Sligo Jun. Chamber,

1965– (PP). *Address:* Rue de la Loi 200, 1049 Brussels, Belgium; (home) Alacantra, Pearse Road, Sligo.

McSHINE, Hon. Sir Arthur Hugh, TC; Kt 1969; Chief Justice of Trinidad and Tobago, 1968–71; Acting Governor-General, Trinidad and Tobago, 1972; *b* 11 May 1906; *m* Dorothy Mary Vanier; one *s* one *d*. *Educ:* Queen's Royal Coll., Trinidad. Called to Bar, Middle Temple, 1931. Practised at Trinidad Bar for eleven years; Magistrate, 1942; Senior Magistrate, 1950; Puisne Judge, 1953; Justice of Appeal, 1962. Acting Governor-Gen., Trinidad and Tobago, 1970. *Recreations:* music and chess (Pres., Caribbean Chess Fedn and Trinidad Chess Assoc.); flying (holder of private pilot's licence). *Address:* 6 River Road, Maraval, Port-of-Spain, Trinidad. *Clubs:* Trinidad and Tobago Turf, Trinidad and Tobago Yacht.

MACTAGGART, Fiona; teacher, Lyndhurst School, Camberwell, since 1988; *b* 12 Sept. 1953; *d* of Ian Auld Mactaggart and Rosemary Belhaven. *Educ:* Cheltenham Ladies' Coll.; King's Coll., London (BA Hons). Gen. Sec., London Students' Organisation, 1977–78; Vice-Pres., 1978–80, Nat. Sec., 1980–81, NUS; Gen. Sec., Jt Council for Welfare of Immigrants, 1982–86. Mem. (Lab) Wandsworth BC, 1986–90 (Leader of the Opposition, 1988–90). *Address:* 61 Taybridge Road, SW11 5PX. *T:* 071–228 4468.

MACTAGGART, Sir John (Auld), 4th Bt *cr* 1938, of King's Park, City of Glasgow; FRICS; *b* 21 Jan. 1951; *s* of Sir Ian Auld Mactaggart, 3rd Bt and of Rosemary, *d* of Sir Herbert Williams, 1st Bt, MP; *S* father, 1987; *m* 1st, 1977, Patricia (marr. diss. 1990), *y d* of late Major Harry Alastair Gordon, MC; 2nd, 1991, Caroline, *y d* of Eric Williams. *Educ:* Shrewsbury; Trinity Coll., Cambridge (MA). Chairman: Central and City Holdings; Western Heritable Investment Co. Ltd; Dir, The Scottish Ballet. *Heir: b* Philip Auld Mactaggart, *b* 26 Feb. 1956. *Address:* 22 Tregunter Road, SW10 9LH.

MACTAGGART, William Alexander, CBE 1964; JP; Chairman, 1960–70, and Managing Director, 1945–68, Pringle of Scotland Ltd, Knitwear Manufacturers, Hawick; *b* 17 Aug. 1906; *o s* of late William Alexander and Margaret Mactaggart, Woodgate, Hawick; *m* 1932, Marjorie Laing Innes; two *s* one *d*. *Educ:* Sedbergh Sch., Yorks. Joined Robert Pringle & Son Ltd (later Pringle of Scotland Ltd), 1925; Dir, 1932; Joint Managing Dir, 1933. Served War of 1939–45: Captain, RASC, Holland, Belgium, France, 1942–45. Elder of Lilliesleaf Parish Church. *Address:* Bewlie House, Lilliesleaf, Melrose, Roxburghshire TD6 9ER. *T:* Lilliesleaf (08357) 267.

MacTAGGART, Air Vice-Marshal William Keith, CBE 1976 (MBE 1956); CEng, FIMechE; FRAeS; FBIM; Consultant: MPE Ltd, 1989–91 (Managing Director, 1984–89); Adwest plc, 1989–91; *b* 15 Jan. 1929; *s* of Duncan MacTaggart and Marion (*née* Keith); *m* 1st, 1949 Christina Carnegie Geddes (marr. diss. 1977); one *s* two *d*; 2nd, 1977, Barbara Smith Brown, *d* of Adm. Stirling P. Smith, late USN, and Mrs Smith; one step *d*. *Educ:* Aberdeen Grammar Sch.; Aberdeen Univ. (BScEng 1948). FIMechE 1973; FRAeS 1974; FBIM 1978. Commnd RAF, 1949; 1949–67: Engr Officer; Pilot; AWRE, Aldermaston (Montebello and Maralinga atomic trials); attended RAF Staff Coll., and Jt Services Staff Coll.; Def. Intell.; Systems Analyst, DOAE, West Byfleet, and MoD (Air); Head of Systems MDC, RAF Swanton Morley, 1968; OC RAF Newton, 1971 (Gp Captain); Dep. Comd Mech. Engr, HQ Strike Comd, 1973; Dir of Air Armament, MoD (PE), 1973 (Air Cdre); RCDS, 1977; Vice-Pres. (Air), Ordnance Bd, 1978 (Air Vice-Marshal), Pres., 1978–80. Dep. Chm., Tomash Holdings Ltd, 1980–84. *Recreations:* music, travel. *Address:* Croft Stones, Lothmore, Helmsdale, Sutherland KW8 6HP. *T:* Helmsdale (04312) 439. *Club:* Royal Air Force.

MacTHOMAS OF FINEGAND, Andrew Patrick Clayhills; 19th Chief of Clan MacThomas (Mac Thomaidh Mhor); *b* 28 Aug. 1942; *o s* of late Captain Patrick Watt MacThomas of Finegand and of Elizabeth, *d* of late Becket Clayhills-Henderson, Invergowrie, Angus; *S* father 1970; *m* 1985, Anneke Cornelia Susanna, *o d* of A. and S. Kruyning-Van Hout, Netherlands; one *s* one *d*. *Educ:* St Edward's, Oxford. Public Affairs, Barclays Bank, London. FSA (Scot.) 1973. Pres., Clan MacThomas Soc., 1970–; Hon. Vice-Pres., Clan Chattan Assoc., 1970–. *Recreations:* steeplechasing, travelling, promoting Scotland. *Heir: s* Thomas David Alexander MacThomas, Yr of Finegand, *b* 1 Jan. 1987. *Address:* c/o Clan MacThomas Society, 19 Warriston Avenue, Edinburgh EH3 5MD.

MacVICAR, Rev. Kenneth, MBE (mil.) 1968; DFC 1944; Chaplain in ordinary to the Queen in Scotland, since 1974; Minister of Kenmore and Lawers, Perthshire, since 1950; *b* 25 Aug. 1921; *s* of Rev. Angus John MacVicar, Southend, Kintyre; *m* 1946, Isobel Guild McKay; three *s* one *d*. *Educ:* Campbeltown Grammar Sch.; Edinburgh Univ.; St Andrews Univ. (MA); St Mary's Coll., St Andrews. Mem., Edinburgh Univ. Air Squadron, 1941; joined RAF, 1941: Pilot, 28 Sqdn, RAF, 1942–45, Flt Comdr, 1944–45 (despatches, 1945). Chaplain, Scottish Horse and Fife and Forfar Yeomanry/Scottish Horse, TA, 1953–65. Convener, Church of Scotland Cttee on Chaplains to HM Forces, 1968–73. Clerk to Presbytery of Dunkeld, 1955–. District Councillor, 1951–74. *Recreation:* golf. *Address:* Manse of Kenmore, Aberfeldy, Perthshire PH15 2HE. *T:* Kenmore (08873) 218.

MACVICAR, Neil, QC (Scotland) 1960; MA, LLB; Sheriff of Lothian and Borders (formerly the Lothians and Peebles), at Edinburgh, 1968–85; *b* 16 May 1920; *s* of late Neil Macvicar, WS; *m* 1949, Maria, *d* of Count Spiridon Bulgari, Corfu; one *s* two *d*. *Educ:* Loretto Sch.; Oriel Coll., Oxford; Edinburgh Univ. Served RA, 1940–45. Called to Scottish Bar, 1948. Chancellor, Dio. of Edinburgh, 1961–74. Chm. of Govs, Dean Orphanage and Cauvin's Trust, 1967–85. *Publication:* A Heart's Odyssey, 1991. *Address:* 25 Blackford Road, Edinburgh EH9 2DT. *T:* 031–667 2362; Kapoutsi, Gastouri, Corfu, Greece. *Clubs:* New (Edinburgh); Anagnostiki Etairia (Corfu).

McWATTERS, George Edward; Director of Corporate Affairs, HTV Group plc, 1989–91; Chairman: TVMM, 1988–91; HTV West, 1969–88; *b* India, 17 March 1922; *s* of Lt-Col George Alfred McWatters and Ellen Mary Christina McWatters (*née* Harvey); *m* 1st, 1946, Margery Robertson (*d* 1959); 2nd, 1960, Joy Anne Matthews; one *s*. *Educ:* Clifton Coll., Bristol. Vintners' Scholar, 1947. Served War of 1939–45: enlisted ranks Royal Scots, 1940; commissioned 14th Punjab Regt, Indian Army, 1941–46. John Harvey & Sons (family wine co.): joined, 1947; Dir, 1951; Chm., 1956–66; estab. a holding co. (Harveys of Bristol Ltd), 1962, but Showerings took over, 1966, and he remained Chm. until resignation, Aug. 1966; Chm., John White Footwear Holdings Ltd, later Ward White Gp Ltd, 1967–82; Actg Chm., HTV Group plc, 1985–86; Chm., HTV Ltd, 1986–88 (Vice-Chm., 1969–86). Chm., Bristol Avon Phoenix, 1987–90; Director: Bristol and West Bldg Soc., 1985– (Vice-Chm., 1988–); Martins Bank, 1960–70; Local Adv. Dir (Peterborough), Barclays Bank, 1970–82; Local Dir (Northampton), Commercial Union Assce Co., 1969–82; Dir, Bain Clarkson Ltd, 1982–. Mem., CBI Grand Council, 1970–82. Mem. Cttee, Automobile Assoc., 1962–. Chairman: Council, Order of St John, Avon, 1983–; Bishop of Bristol's Urban Fund, 1989–; Vice-Pres., Avon Wildlife Trust, 1989– (Chm., Appeal Cttee, 1982). Pres., Avon and Bristol Fedn of Boys Clubs, 1985–. Governor: Clifton Coll., 1958–; Kimbolton Sch., 1970–82. Master, Soc. of Merchant Venturers, 1986. City Councillor, Bristol, 1950–53. JP, Bristol, 1960–67; JP, Marylebone, 1969–71; High Sheriff, Cambridgeshire, 1979. *Recreations:* swimming, walking. *Address:* Burrington House, Burrington, Bristol BS18 7AD. *T:* Blagdon (0761) 62291. *Clubs:* Buck's, MCC.

McWATTERS, Stephen John; Headmaster, The Pilgrims' School, 1976–83, retired; *b* 24 April 1921; *er s* of late Sir Arthur Cecil McWatters, CIE; *m* 1957, Mary Gillian, *o d* of late D. C. Wilkinson and Mrs G. A. Wilkinson; one *s* two *d*. *Educ:* Eton (Scholar); Trinity Coll., Oxford (Scholar, MA). 1st Cl. Class. Mods, 1941. Served in The King's Royal Rifle Corps, 1941–45. Distinction in Philosophy section of Litterae Humaniores, Oxford, 1946. Asst Master, Eton Coll., 1947–63 (Master in Coll., 1949–57, Housemaster, 1961–63); Headmaster, Clifton Coll., 1963–75. *Recreations:* music, bird-watching. *Address:* 26 Edgar Road, Winchester SO23 9TN. *T:* Winchester (0962) 867523.

McWEENY, Prof. Roy; Professor of Theoretical Chemistry, University of Pisa, since 1982; *b* 19 May 1924; *o s* of late Maurice and Vera McWeeny; *m* 1947, Patricia M. Healey (marr. diss. 1979); one *s* one *d*. *Educ:* Univ. of Leeds; University Coll., Oxford. BSc (Physics) Leeds 1945; DPhil Oxon 1949. Lectr in Physical Chemistry, King's Coll., Univ. of Durham, 1948–57; Vis. Scientist, Physics Dept, MIT, USA, 1953–54; Lectr in Theoretical Chemistry, Univ. Coll. of N Staffs, 1957–62; Associate Dir, Quantum Chemistry Gp, Uppsala Univ., Sweden, 1960–61; Reader in Quantum Theory, 1962–64, Prof. of Theoretical Chemistry, 1964–66, Univ. of Keele; Prof. of Theoretical Chem., 1966–82, and Hd of Chemistry Dept, 1976–79, Sheffield Univ. Vis. Prof., America, Japan, Europe. Mem., Acad. Européenne des Scis, des Arts et des Lettres, 1988. *Publications:* Symmetry, an Introduction to Group Theory and its Applications, 1963; (with B. T. Sutcliffe) Methods of Molecular Quantum Mechanics, 1969, 2nd edn as sole author, 1989; Spins in Chemistry, 1970; Quantum Mechanics: principles and formalism, 1972; Quantum Mechanics: methods and basic applications, 1973; Coulson's Valence, 3rd rev. edn 1979; contrib. sections in other books and encyclopædias; many research papers on quantum theory of atomic and molecular structure in Proc. Royal Soc., Proc. Phys. Soc., Phys. Rev., Revs. Mod. Phys., Jl Chem. Phys., etc. *Recreations:* drawing, sculpture, travel. *Address:* Via Pietro Giordani 16, Gello, 56017 Pisa, Italy.

McWHIRTER, Norris Dewar, CBE 1980; author, publisher, broadcaster; Director, Guinness Publications Ltd (formerly Guinness Superlatives Ltd), since 1954 (Managing Director, 1954–76); *b* 12 Aug. 1925; *er (twin) s* of William Allan McWhirter, Managing Director of Associated Newspapers and Northcliffe Newspapers Group, and Margaret Williamson; *m* 1957, Carole (*d* 1987), *d* of George H. Eckert; one *s* one *d*; *m* 1991, Tessa Mary Dunsdon, *d* of late Joseph Dunsdon Pocock and Dorothy Pocock (*née* von Weichardt). *Educ:* Marlborough; Trinity Coll., Oxford. BA (Internat. Rel. and Econs), MA (Contract Law). Served RN, 1943–46: Sub-Lt RNVR, 2nd Escort Gp, Atlantic; minesweeping Pacific. Dir, McWhirter Twins Ltd, 1950–; Chm., Wm McWhirter & Sons, 1955–86; co-founder, Redwood Press (Chm., 1966–72); Dir, Gieves Group plc, 1972–. Founder Editor (with late Ross McWhirter till 1975) and compiler, Guinness Book of Records, 1954–86 (1st edn 1955), Adv. Editor, 1986–; by 1991, edns in 35 languages; over 65 million sales. Athletics Correspondent: Observer, 1951–67; Star, 1951–60; BBC TV Commentator, Olympic Games, 1960–72; What's In the Picture, 1957; The Record Breakers, 1972–. Guinness Hall of Fame, 1986–. Mem., Sports Council, 1970–73. Chm., Freedom Assoc., 1983– (Dep. Chm., 1975–83). Pres., Marlburian Club, 1983–84. Contested (C) Orpington, 1964, 1966. Trustee: Ross McWhirter Foundn; Police Convalescent and Rehabilitation Home. *Publications:* Get To Your Marks, 1951; (ed) Athletics World, 1952–56; Dunlop Book of Facts, 5 edns, 1964–73; Guinness Book of Answers, 1976, 7th edn 1989; Ross: story of a shared life, 1976; Guinness Book of Essential Facts, 1979 (US). *Recreations:* family tennis, ski-ing, watching athletics (Oxford 100 yds, Scotland 1950–52, GB in Norway 1951) and Rugby football (Mddx XV, 1950). *Address:* c/o 33 London Road, Enfield EN2 6DJ. *T:* 081–367 4567. *Clubs:* Caledonian; Vincent's (Oxford); Achilles.

McWHIRTER, Prof. Robert, CBE 1963; FRCSEd; FRCPEd; FRCR; FRSE; Professor of Medical Radiology, Edinburgh University, 1946–70; Director of Radiotherapy, Royal Infirmary, Edinburgh, 1935–70; President, Medical and Dental Defence Union of Scotland, 1959–90, now Hon. Fellow; *b* 8 Nov. 1904; *s* of Robert McWhirter and Janet Ramsay Gairdner; *m* 1937, Dr Susan Muir MacMurray; one *s*. *Educ:* Girvan Academy; Glasgow and Cambridge Universities. MB, ChB (High Commendn), Glasgow, 1927; FRCS Edinburgh 1932; DMRE Cambridge, 1933; FFR 1939. Formerly: Student, Mayo Clinic; British Empire Cancer Campaign Research Student, Holt Radium Institute, Manchester; Chief Assistant, X-Ray Dept, St Bartholomew's Hospital, London. Member, British Institute of Radiology; Pres., Sect. of Radiology, RSM, 1956; Fellow Royal College of Radiologists (Twining Memorial Medal, 1943; Skinner Memorial Lecturer, 1956; Warden, 1961–66; Knox Memorial Lecturer, 1963, Pres. 1966–69); Past Pres., Internat. Radio Therapists Visiting Club; Hon. Member, American Radium Society; Membre Corresp. Etranger, Société Française d'Electro-Radiologie Médicale, 1967; Membro d'onore, Società Italiana della Radiologia Medica e Medicine Nucleare, 1968; Hon. Member: Sociedade Brasileira de Patologia Mamária, 1969; Nippon Societas Radiologica, 1970; Groupe Européen des Radiotherapeutes, 1971. Caldwell Memorial Lecturer, American Roentgen Ray Society, 1963; Hon. Fellow: Australasian College of Radiologists, 1954; American College of Radiology, 1965; Faculty of Radiologists, RCSI, 1967. Gold Medal, Nat. Soc. for Cancer Relief, 1985. *Publications:* contribs to medical journals. *Recreation:* golf. *Address:* 2 Orchard Brae, Edinburgh EH4 1NY. *T:* 031–332 5800. *Club:* University (Edinburgh).

McWIGGAN, Thomas Johnstone, CBE 1976; aviation electronics consultant; Secretary General, European Organisation for Civil Aviation Electronics, 1979–87; *b* 26 May 1918; *s* of late Thomas and Esther McWiggan; *m* 1947, Eileen Joyce Moughton; two *d*. *Educ:* UC Nottingham. Pharmaceutical Chemist. FIEE, FRAeS, SMIEEE. Signals Officer (Radar), RAFVR, 1941–46. Civil Air Attaché (Telecommunications) Washington, 1962–65; Dir of Telecommunications (Plans), Min. of Aviation, 1965; Dir of Telecommunications (Air Traffic Services), BoT, 1967; Dir Gen. Telecommunications, Nat. Air Traffic Services, 1969–79 (CAA, 1972–79). *Publications:* various technical papers. *Recreations:* photography, cabinet-making, gardening. *Address:* The Squirrels, Liberty Rise, Addlestone, Weybridge, Surrey. *T:* Weybridge (0932) 843068.

MacWILLIAM, Very Rev. Alexander Gordon; Dean of St Davids Cathedral, 1984–90; *b* 22 Aug. 1923; *s* of Andrew George and Margaret MacWilliam; *m* 1951, Catherine Teresa (*née* Bogue); one *s*. *Educ:* Univ. of Wales (BA Hons Classics, 1943); Univ. of London (BD 2nd Cl. Hons, 1946, PhD 1952, DipEd 1962). Deacon 1946, priest 1947; Curate of Penygroes, Gwynedd, 1946–49; Minor Canon, Bangor Cathedral, 1949–55; Rector of Llanfaethlu, Gwynedd, 1955–58; Head of Dept of Theology, Trinity Coll., Carmarthen, Dyfed, 1958–74; Head of School of Society Studies, Trinity Coll. (Inst. of Higher Education, Univ. of Wales), 1974–84; Canon of St Davids Cathedral and Prebendary of Trefloden, 1978. Examining Chaplain to Bishop of St Davids, 1969. Vis. Prof. of Philosophy and Theology, Central Univ. of Iowa, USA, 1983. *Publications:* contribs to Learning for Living (Brit. Jl of Religious Education), UCW Jl of Educn. *Recreations:* travel to archaeological sites and art centres, classical music, food and wine. *Address:* Pen Parc, Smyrna Road, Llangain, Carmarthen, Dyfed SA33 5AD.

McWILLIAM, (Frederick) Edward, CBE 1966; RA 1989; Sculptor; *b* 30 April 1909; *yr s* of Dr William Nicholson McWilliam, Banbridge, County Down, Ireland; *m* 1932, Elizabeth Marion Crowther (*d* 1988); two *d*. *Educ:* Campbell Coll., Belfast; Slade School of Fine Art; Paris. Served War of 1939–45, RAF, UK and Far East. Member of Staff, Slade Sch. of Fine Art, London Univ., 1947–66. Mem. Art Panel, Arts Council, 1960–68. First one-man exhibn., sculpture, London Gall., 1939; subsequently Hanover Gallery, 1949, 1952, 1956; Waddington Galleries, 1961, 1963, 1966, 1968, 1971, 1973, 1976, 1979, 1984; Dawson Gallery, Dublin; Felix Landau Gallery, Los Angeles; exhibn to mark eightieth birthday, New Art Centre, 1989; Mayor Gall., 1990; retrospective exhibns: Belfast, Dublin, Londonderry, 1981; Warwick Arts Trust, 1982; Tate Gall., 1989. Has exhibited in International Open-Air Exhibitions, London, Antwerp, Arnheim, Paris. Work included in British Council touring exhibitions USA, Canada, Germany, South America. Fellow, UCL, 1972. Hon. DLit Belfast, 1964. *Relevant Publication:* McWilliam, Sculptor, by Roland Penrose, 1964. *Address:* 8A Holland Villas Road, W14 8BP.

McWILLIAM, John David; MP (Lab) Blaydon, since 1979; *b* 16 May 1941; *s* of Alexander and Josephine McWilliam; *m* 1965, Lesley Mary Catling; two *d*. *Educ:* Leith Academy; Heriot Watt Coll.; Napier College of Science and Technology. Post Office Engineer, 1957–79. Councillor, Edinburgh CC, 1970–75 (last Treasurer of City of Edinburgh and only Labour one, 1974–75); Commissioner for Local Authority Accounts in Scotland, 1974–78. Member: Scottish Council for Technical Educn, 1973–85; Select Cttee on Educn, Science and the Arts, 1980–83; Select Cttee on Procedure, 1984–87; Services Cttee (Chm., Computer sub-cttee, 1983–87); Select Cttee on Defence, 1987–; Speaker's Panel of Chairmen, 1988–. Dep. to the Shadow Leader of the House of Commons, 1983; Opposition Whip, 1984–87. Mem., Gen. Adv. Council, BBC, 1984–89. *Recreations:* reading, listening to music, angling. *Clubs:* Bleach Green Labour (Blaydon); Chopwell Social, Chopwell RAOB (Chopwell); Dunston Social, Dunston Mechanics Institute (Dunston); Ryton Social (Ryton); Blackhall Mill Social (Blackhall Mill); Greenside and District Social (Greenside); Winlaton West End (Winlaton). *Address:* House of Commons, SW1A 0AA.

McWILLIAM, Michael Douglas; Director, School of Oriental and African Studies, University of London, since 1989; *b* 21 June 1933; *s* of Douglas and Margaret McWilliam; *m* 1960, Ruth Arnstein; two *s*. *Educ:* Cheltenham Coll.; Oriel Coll., Oxford (MA); Nuffield Coll., Oxford (BLitt). Kenya Treasury, 1958; Samuel Montagu & Co., 1962; joined Standard Bank, subseq. Standard Chartered Bank, 1966; Gen. Manager, 1973; Gp Man. Dir, 1983–88. Mem. Bd, Commonwealth Development Corp., 1990–; Vice-Pres., Royal African Soc., 1991– (Mem. Council, 1979–). Pres. Council, Cheltenham Coll., 1988– (Mem., 1977–). *Address:* 24 Alleyn Road, Dulwich SE21 8AL. *Club:* Commonwealth Trust (Mem. Bd, 1989–).

McWILLIAMS, Francis; conciliator and arbitrator, since 1978; *b* 8 Feb. 1926; *s* of John J. and Mary Anne McWilliams; *m* 1950, Winifred (*née* Segger); two *s*. *Educ:* Holy Cross Acad., Edinburgh; Edinburgh Univ. (BSc Eng 1945); Inns of Court Sch. of Law. FICE; FCIArb; MIE (Malaysia). Engineer in local govt, 1945–54; Town Engineer, Petaling Jaya New Town, Malaysia, 1954–64; Consulting Civil and Struct. Engineer, Kuala Lumpur, 1964–76. Bar student, 1976–78; called to the Bar, Lincoln's Inn, 1978. Mem., Jt Consultative Cttee, London Court of Internat. Arbitration, 1979– (Chm., 1988–89). Mem., Common Council, City of London, 1978–80; Alderman, Ward of Aldersgate, 1980–; Sheriff, City of London, 1988–89. Master: Arbitrators' Co., 1985–86; Engineers' Co., 1990–91; Asst, Court, Loriners' Co.; Pres., Aldersgate Ward Club. Vice-Chm., St John's Ambulance City Br., 1987–. FRSA. PJK, Selangor, Malaysia, 1963; Dato Seri Selera, Selangor, 1973. Order of Merit (Senegal); Order of Independence (Cl. III) (UAE). *Recreations:* golf, ski-ing, gardening. *Address:* Prae Wood House, Hemel Hempstead Road, St Albans, Herts AL3 6AB. *T:* St Albans (0727) 42834. *Clubs:* City Livery; Hon. Company of Edinburgh Golfers, Muirfield, Verulam Golf; Royal Selangor Golf, Royal Alam Shah Golfing Society, Selangor, Lake (Kuala Lumpur).

MADARIAGA, Prof. Isabel Margaret de, FRHistS; FBA 1990; Professor of Russian Studies, University of London at School of Slavonic and East European Studies, 1981–85, now Professor Emerita; *b* 27 Aug. 1919; *d* of late Salvador de Madariaga and Constance Archibald, MA; *m* 1943, Leonard Bertram Schapiro, CBE, FBA (marr. diss 1976; he *d* 1983). *Educ:* Ecole Internationale, Geneva; Instituto Escuela, Madrid and fifteen other schools; Univ. of London (BA, PhD). FRHistS 1967. BBC Monitoring Service, 1940–43; Min. of Information (later COI), 1943–47; Economic Information Unit, HM Treasury, 1947–48; Editl Asst, Slavonic and East European Review, 1951–64; Asst Lectr and Lectr, LSE, intermittently, 1951–66; Lectr in Modern History, Univ. of Sussex, 1966–68; Sen. Lectr in Russian Hist., Univ. of Lancaster, 1968–71; Reader in Russian Studies, SSEES, Univ. of London, 1971–81. Member, Editorial Boards: Government and Opposition, 1965–; Slavonic and E European Review, 1971–86; European History Qly, 1971–. *Publications:* Britain, Russia and the Armed Neutrality, 1963; (with G. Ionescu) Opposition, 1968; Russia in the Age of Catherine the Great, 1981; Catherine the Great: a short history, 1990; articles in learned jls. *Recreation:* music. *Address:* 25 Southwood Lawn Road, Highgate, N6 5SD. *T:* 081–341 0862. *Club:* United Oxford & Cambridge University.

MADDEN, (Albert) Frederick (McCulloch), DPhil; Reader in Commonwealth Government, Oxford, 1957–84; Professorial Fellow of Nuffield College, 1958–84, Emeritus Fellow since 1984, Pro-Proctor, 1988–89; *b* 27 Feb. 1917; *e s* of A. E. and G. McC. Madden; *m* 1941, Margaret, *d* of Dr R. D. Gifford; one *s* one *d*. *Educ:* privately, by mother; Bishop Vesey's Grammar Sch.; Christ Church, Oxford. Boulter and Gladstone exhibns; BA 1938, BLitt 1939, DPhil 1950. Dep. Sup., Rhodes House Library, 1946–48; Beit Lectr, 1947–57; Sen. Tutor to Overseas Service Courses, 1950–; Co-Dir, Foreign Service Course, 1959–72; Dir, Inst. of Commonwealth Studies, 1961–68; Vice-Chm., History Bd, 1968–73. Canadian Vis. Fellow, 1970; Vis. Prof., Cape Town, 1973; Vis. Fellow, Res. Sch., ANU, 1974. Dir, Hong Kong admin. course, 1975–86. Dir, Prospect Theatre, 1963–66. FRHistS 1952. *Publications:* (with V. Harlow) British Colonial Developments, 1774–1834, 1953; (with K. Robinson) Essays in Imperial Government, 1963; chapter in Cambridge History of British Empire III, 1959; Imperial Constitutional Documents, 1765–1965, 1966; (with W. Morris-Jones) Australia and Britain, 1980; (with D. K. Fieldhouse) Oxford and the Idea of Commonwealth, 1982; Perspectives on Imperialism and Decolonisation (Festschrift), 1984; Select Documents on the Constitutional History of the British Empire: Vol. I, The Empire of the Bretaignes 1165–1688, 1985; Vol. II, The Classical Period of the First British Empire 1689–1783, 1986; Vol. III, Imperial Reconstruction 1763–1840, 1987; Vol. IV, Settler Self-government 1840–1900, 1989; Vol. V, The Dependencies and Ireland 1840–1900, 1991; reviews in English Historical Review, etc. *Recreations:* acting (Cranmer in Quatercentenary, St Mary's, Oxford, and 151 other parts); photographing islands and highlands, hill towns, country houses, churches; Renaissance art; writing music and listening. *Address:* Oak Apples, Shotover Hill, Oxford. *T:* Oxford (0865) 62972.

MADDEN, Admiral Sir Charles (Edward), 2nd Bt, *cr* 1919; GCB 1965 (KCB 1961; CB 1955); Vice Lord-Lieutenant of Greater London, 1969–81; *b* 15 June 1906; *s* of Admiral of the Fleet Sir Charles E. Madden, 1st Bart, GCB, OM, and Constance Winifred (*d* 1964), 3rd *d* of Sir Charles Cayzer, 1st Bart; *S* father, 1935; *m* 1942, Olive (*d* 1989), *d* of late G. W. Robins, Caldy, Cheshire; one *d*. *Educ:* Royal Naval Coll., Osborne. ADC to the Queen, 1955. Served War: Exec. Officer, HMS Warspite, 1940–42 (despatches); Captain, HMS Emperor, 1945 (despatches); Naval Asst to 1st Sea Lord, 1946–47. Captain, 1946; Rear-Admiral, 1955; Vice-Admiral, 1958; Admiral, 1961. Chief of Naval Staff, NZ, 1953–55; Dep. Chief of Naval Personnel, 1955–57; Flag Officer, Malta, 1957–59; Flag Officer, Flotillas, Home Fleet, 1959–60; C-in-C Plymouth, 1960–62; C-in-C Home Fleet and NATO C-in-C Eastern Atlantic Command, 1963–65; retired, 1965. Chairman, Royal National Mission to Deep Sea Fishermen, 1971–81 (Dep. Chm., 1966–71); Vice-Chairman, Sail Training Assoc., 1968–70. Trustee: National Maritime Museum, 1968– (Chm., 1972–77); Portsmouth Royal Naval Museum, 1973–77. Chm., Standing Council of the Baronetage, 1975–77. Dep. Warden, Christ Church, Victoria Rd, 1970–86. Grand Cross of Prince Henry the Navigator, Portugal, 1960. *Recreation:* painting. *Heir: nephew* Peter John Madden, *b* 10 Sept. 1942. *Address:* 21 Eldon Road, W8. *Club:* Arts.

MADDEN, Rear-Admiral Colin Duncan, CB 1966; CBE 1964; LVO 1954; DSC 1940 and Bar, 1944; Registrar and Secretary, Order of the Bath, 1979–85; *b* 19 Aug. 1915; *s* of late Archibald Maclean Madden, CMG, and Cecilia Catherine Moor; *m* 1943, Agnes Margaret, *d* of late H. K. Newcombe, OBE, Canada and London, and Eleanor Clare; two *d*. *Educ:* RN Coll., Dartmouth. During War of 1939–45, took part in blocking Ijmuiden harbour and Dutch evacuation; Navigating Officer of 7th Mine Sweeping Flotilla; HMS Arethusa; Assault Group J1 for invasion of Europe, and HMS Norfolk. Thence HMS Triumph. Commander, 1950; Comd HMS Crossbow, 1952; staff of Flag Officer Royal Yachts, SS Gothic and Comdr (N) HM Yacht Britannia, for Royal Commonwealth Tour, 1953–54; Captain, Naval Attaché, Rome; Captain D 7 in HMS Trafalgar; IDC. Comd HMS Albion, 1962; Rear-Admiral, 1965; Senior Naval Member Directing Staff, Imperial Defence Coll., 1965–67; retired, 1967. Dir, Nat. Trade Develt Assoc., 1967–69. Gentleman Usher of the Scarlet Rod to the Order of the Bath, 1968–79. Dir Gen., Brewers' Soc., 1969–80. *Recreations:* sailing, gardening, fishing, tapestry. *Clubs:* Army and Navy, Royal Cruising.

MADDEN, Frederick; *see* Madden, A. F. McC.

MADDEN, Max; MP (Lab) Bradford West, since 1983; *b* 29 Oct. 1941; *s* of late George Francis Leonard Madden and Rene Frances Madden; *m* 1972, Sheelagh Teresa Catherine Howard. *Educ:* Lascelles Secondary Modern Sch.; Pinner Grammar Sch. Journalist: East Essex Gazette; Tribune (political weekly); Sun, London; Scotsman, London; subseq. Press and Information Officer, British Gas Corp., London; Dir of Publicity, Labour Party, 1979–82. MP (Lab) Sowerby, Feb. 1974–1979. *Address:* House of Commons, SW1A 0AA.

MADDEN, Michael; Under Secretary, Ministry of Agriculture, Fisheries and Food, since 1985; *b* 12 Feb. 1936; *s* of late Harold Madden and Alice Elizabeth (*née* Grenville); *m* 1960 (marr. diss. 1977); two *s* one *d*. *Educ:* King Edward VII Sch., Sheffield. Exec. Officer, Min. of Transport and Civil Aviation, 1955; Ministry of Agriculture, Fisheries and Food: Asst Principal, 1963–67; Asst Private Sec. to Minister, 1966–67; Principal, 1967; Asst Sec. (as Head, Tropical Foods Div.), 1973; Under Sec., 1985; Head, Management Services Gp, 1985; Flood Defence, Plant Protection and Agricl Resources, 1990. *Recreations:* walking, eating and drinking with friends, music, planning expeditions. *Address:* Ministry of Agriculture, Fisheries and Food, 3 Whitehall Place, SW1A 2HH.

MADDISON, Vincent Albert, CMG 1961; TD 1953; *b* 10 Aug. 1915; *s* of late Vincent Maddison; *m* 1954, Jennifer Christian Bernard; two *s* one *d*. *Educ:* Wellingborough Sch.; Downing Coll., Cambridge (MA). Colonial Administrative Service, 1939. Served War of 1939–45: Ethiopian and Burma Campaigns. District Officer, Kenya, 1947; seconded to Secretariat, 1948; Director, Trade and Supplies, 1953; Secretary, 1954, Perm. Secretary, 1957–63, Min. of Commerce and Industry; retired from Kenya Government, 1963; Chairman: East African Power and Lighting Co. Ltd, 1965–70; Tana River Development Co. Ltd, 1965–70; The Kenya Power Co. Ltd 1965–70; Director: Nyali Ltd, 1966–70; Kisauni Ltd, 1966–70; East African Trust and Investment Co. Ltd, 1966–70; East African Engineering Consultants, 1966–70. *Recreations:* ski-ing, gardening, sailing. *Address:* 1 Shobdon Court Mews, Shobdon, Leominster, Herefordshire HR6 9LZ. *T:* Kingsland 688. *Club:* Muthaiga Country (Kenya).

MADDOCKS, Arthur Frederick, CMG 1974; HM Diplomatic Service, retired; Ambassador and UK Permanent Representative to OECD, Paris, 1977–82; *b* 20 May 1922; *s* of late Frederick William Maddocks and Celia Elizabeth Maddocks (*née* Beardwell); *m* 1945, Margaret Jean Crawford Holt; two *s* one *d*. *Educ:* Manchester Grammar Sch.; Corpus Christi Coll., Oxford. Army, 1942–46; Foreign (later Diplomatic) Service, 1946–: Washington, 1946–48; FO, 1949–51; Bonn, 1951–55; Bangkok, 1955–58; UK Delegn to OEEC, 1958–60; FO, 1960–64; UK Delegn to European Communities, Brussels, 1964–68; Political Adviser, Hong Kong, 1968–72; Dep. High Comr and Minister (Commercial), Ottawa, 1972–76. Mem., OECD Appeals Tribunal, 1984–89. *Address:* Lynton House, 83 High Street, Wheatley, Oxford OX9 1XP. *Club:* Hong Kong (Hong Kong).

MADDOCKS, Bertram Catterall; His Honour Judge Maddocks; a Circuit Judge, since 1990; *b* 7 July 1932; *s* of His Honour George Maddocks and of Mary Maddocks (*née* Day); *m* 1964, Angela Vergette Forster; two *s* one *d*. *Educ:* Malsis Hall, near Keighley; Rugby; Trinity Hall, Cambridge (schol.; MA; Law Tripos Part 2 1st Cl. 1955). Nat. Service, 2nd Lieut, RA, 1951; Duke of Lancaster's Own Yeomanry (TA), 1958–67. Called to the Bar, Middle Temple, 1956; Harmsworth Schol.; Mem., Lincoln's Inn; a Recorder, 1983–90. Pt-time Chm., VAT Tribunals, 1977–. *Recreations:* real tennis, lawn tennis, ski-ing, bridge. *Address:* Moor Hall Farm, Prescot Road, Aughton, Lancashire L39 6RT. *T:* Aughton Green (0695) 421601. *Clubs:* Queen's; Northern Counties (Newcastle); Manchester Tennis and Racquet.

MADDOCKS, Fiona Hamilton; Feature Writer, The Independent, since 1991; *b* 1 June 1955; *d* of William Hunter Maddocks and Dorothy Christina Hill; *m* 1989, Robert James Cooper; one *d*. *Educ:* Blackheath High Sch. (GPDST), London; Royal Coll. of Music; Newnham Coll., Cambridge (English Tripos; MA; Associate, 1985). Taught English Literature, Istituto Orsoline, Cortina d'Ampezzo, Italy, 1977–78; Medici Soc., London, 1978–79; News trainee, Producer and Sen. Producer, LBC, 1979–82; Founder Producer/Editor, Comment, 1982–85, Asst Commng Editor, Music, 1985–86, Channel 4; The Independent: Dep. Arts Editor, 1986–88, and writer; Music Editor and Associate Arts Editor, 1988–91. Launched Garden Venture, project with Royal Opera House, 1988–89. Mem. Exec. Cttee, SPNM, 1990–. BP Arts Journalism Press Award, 1991. *Recreations:* playing chamber music, Italy. *Address:* Corner Cottage, Chilson, near Charlbury, Chipping Norton, Oxon OX7 3HU.

MADDOCKS, Sir Kenneth (Phipson), KCMG 1958 (CMG 1956); KCVO 1963; *b* 8 Feb. 1907; *s* of Arthur P. Maddocks, Haywards Heath, Sussex; *m* 1st, 1951, Elnor Radcliffe, CStJ (*d* 1976), *d* of late Sir E. John Russell, OBE, FRS; no *c*; 2nd, 1980, Patricia

Josephine, *d* of Algernon and Irma Hare Duke and *widow* of Sir George Mooring, KCMG. *Educ:* Bromsgrove Sch.; Wadham Coll., Oxford. Colonial Administrative Service, Nigeria, 1929; Civil Secretary, Northern Region, Nigeria, 1955–57; Dep. Governor, 1957–58. Acting Governor, Northern Region, Nigeria, 1956 and 1957. Governor and Commander-in-Chief of Fiji, 1958–63; Dir and Secretary, E Africa and Mauritius Assoc., 1964–69. KStJ (Mem. Chapter-Gen., Order of St John, 1969–75). *Recreations:* fishing, gardening. *Address:* 11 Lee Road, Aldeburgh, Suffolk IP15 5HG. *T:* Aldeburgh (0725) 453443.

MADDOCKS, Rt. Rev. Morris Henry St John; Adviser on the Ministry of Health and Healing to Archbishops of Canterbury and York, since 1983; Hon. Assistant Bishop, Diocese of Chichester, since 1987; *b* 28 April 1928; *s* of late Rev. Canon Morris Arthur Maddocks and Gladys Mabel Sharpe; *m* 1955, Anne Miles; no *c*. *Educ:* St John's Sch., Leatherhead; Trinity Coll., Cambridge; Chichester Theological Coll. BA 1952, MA 1956, Cambridge. Ordained in St Paul's Cathedral, London, 1954. Curate: St Peter's, Ealing, 1954–55; St Andrews, Uxbridge, 1955–58; Vicar of: Weaverthorpe, Helperthorpe and Luttons Ambo, 1958–61; S Martin's on the Hill, Scarborough, 1961–71; Bishop Suffragan of Selby, 1972–83. Chm., Churches' Council for Health and Healing, 1982–85 (Co-Chm., 1975–82). FRSM 1988. *Publications:* The Christian Healing Ministry, 1981; The Christian Adventure, 1983; Journey to Wholeness, 1986; A Healing House of Prayer, 1987; Twenty Questions about Healing, 1988; The Vision of Dorothy Kerin, 1991. *Recreations:* music, walking, gardening. *Address:* Whitehill Chase, High Street, Bordon, Hants GU35 0AP. *T:* Bordon (0420) 478121. *Club:* Army and Navy.

MADDOCKS, William Henry, MBE 1975; General Secretary, National Union of Dyers, Bleachers and Textile Workers, 1979–82; *b* 18 Feb. 1921; *m* 1944, Mary Holdsworth; one *d*. *Educ:* Eastwood Elem. Sch.; Holycroft Council Sch., Keighley. W of England full-time Organiser for National Union of Dyers, Bleachers and Textile Workers, 1963. Mem., TUC Gen. Council, 1978–82. JP Gloucestershire, 1968. *Address:* 50 Waterside, Silsden, Keighley, W Yorks BD20 0LQ. *T:* Steeton (0535) 652893. *Clubs:* Yeadon Trades Hall (Yeadon, W Yorks); Keighley Cricket.

MADDOX, John (Royden); writer and broadcaster; Editor, Nature, 1966–73 and since 1980; *b* 27 Nov. 1925; *s* of A. J. and M. E. Maddox, Swansea; *m* 1st, 1949, Nancy Fanning (*d* 1960); one *s* one *d*; 2nd, 1960, Brenda Power Murphy; one *s* one *d*. *Educ:* Gowerton Boys' County Sch.; Christ Church, Oxford; King's Coll., London. Asst Lecturer, then Lecturer, Theoretical Physics, Manchester Univ., 1949–55; Science Correspondent, Guardian, 1955–64; Affiliate, Rockefeller Institute, New York, 1962–63; Asst Director, Nuffield Foundation, and Co-ordinator, Nuffield Foundation Science Teaching Project, 1964–66; Man. Dir, Macmillan Journals Ltd, 1970–72; Dir, Macmillan & Co. Ltd, 1968–73; Chm., Maddox Editorial Ltd, 1972–74; Dir, Nuffield Foundn, 1975–80. Member: Royal Commn on Environmental Pollution, 1976–81; Genetic Manipulation Adv. Gp, 1976–80; British Library Adv. Council, 1976–81; Council on Internat. Develt, 1977–79; Chm. Council, Queen Elizabeth Coll., 1980–85; Mem. Council, King's Coll. London, 1985–89. *Publications:* (with Leonard Beaton) The Spread of Nuclear Weapons, 1962; Revolution in Biology, 1964; The Doomsday Syndrome, 1972; Beyond the Energy Crisis, 1975. *Address:* Macmillan Magazines Ltd, 4 Little Essex Street, WC2; 9 Pitt Street, W8. *T:* (office) 071–836 6633; (home) 071–937 9750. *Club:* Athenæum.

MADDOX, Ronald, PRI 1989 (RI 1959); artist, illustrator and designer; *b* 5 Oct. 1930; *s* of Harold George and Winifred Maddox; *m* 1958, Camilla Farrin; two *s*. *Educ:* Hertfordshire College of Art and Design, St Albans; London College of Printing and Graphic Art. FCSD, FSAI; Hon. RWS 1990. Nat. Service, RAF, 1949–51, Air Min. Design Unit. Designer, illustrator, art director, London advertising agencies, 1951–61; private practice, 1962–; commissioned by nat. and multinat. cos and corps, govt depts, public authorities, TV; designer British postage stamps and philatelic material, 1972– (winner Prix de l'art Philatelique, 1987); exhibns, RA, RI, London and provincial galls; paintings in royal, govt and public bodies' collections. Vice-Pres., RI, 1979; Hon. Member: Soc. of Architect Artists; Fedn of Canadian Artists; United Soc. of Artists; Campine Assoc. of Watercolours, Belgium. FRSA. Winsor & Newton/RI Award, 1981, 1991. *Recreations:* compulsive drawing, walking, cycling, gardening. *Address:* Herons, 21 New Road, Digswell, Herts AL6 0AQ. *T:* Welwyn (043871) 4884.

MADDRELL, Geoffrey Keggen; Chief Executive, Tootal Group plc, 1987–91; *b* 18 July 1936; *s* of Captain Geoffrey Douglas Maddrell and Barbara Marie Kennaugh; *m* 1964, Winifred Mary Daniel Jones; two *s* one *d*. *Educ:* King William's Coll., Isle of Man; Corpus Christi Coll., Cambridge (MA Law and Econs); Columbia Univ., New York (MBA). Lieut, Parachute Regt, 1955–57. Shell Internat. Petroleum Co. Ltd, 1961–69; Boston Consulting Gp, Boston, USA, 1971–72; Bowater Corp., 1972–86, apptd to main bd, 1979; joined Tootal Gp as Man. Dir, 1986. Chm., Manchester TEC. Gov., UMIST. *Recreations:* running, golf, theatre. *Address:* 28 Sussex Street, SW1V 4RL. *T:* 071–834 3874.

MADDRELL, Dr Simon Hugh Piper, FRS 1981; Fellow of Gonville and Caius College, Cambridge, since 1964; Senior Principal Scientific Officer, Agricultural and Food Research Council Unit of Insect Neurophysiology and Pharmacology (formerly Unit of Invertebrate Chemistry and Physiology), Cambridge University, since 1968; *b* 11 Dec. 1937; *s* of Hugh Edmund Fisher Maddrell and Barbara Agnes Mary Maddrell; *m* 1961, Anna Myers; three *s* one *d*. *Educ:* Peter Symonds' Sch., Winchester; St Catharine's Coll., Cambridge. BA, MA, PhD 1964, ScD 1978. Res. Fellow, Dalhousie Univ., Canada, 1962–64; College Fellow and Lectr, Gonville and Caius Coll., Cambridge, 1968–. Financial Sec., Co. of Biologists Ltd, 1965–. Scientific Medal, Zool Soc. of London, 1976. *Publication:* Neurosecretion, 1979. *Recreations:* cycling, golf, gardening, wine-tasting, cinema. *Address:* Gonville and Caius College, Cambridge; Ballamaddrell, Ballabeg, Arbory, Isle of Man. *T:* Castletown (IOM) (0624) 822787.

MADEL, (William) David; MP (C) Bedfordshire South West, since 1983 (South Bedfordshire, 1970–83); *b* 6 Aug. 1938; *s* of late William R. Madel and of Eileen Madel (*née* Nicholls); *m* 1971, Susan Catherine, *d* of late Lt-Comdr Hon. Peter Carew; one *s* one *d*. *Educ:* Uppingham Sch.; Keble Coll., Oxford. MA Oxon 1965. Graduate Management Trainee, 1963–64; Advertising Exec., Thomson Organisation, 1964–70. Contested (C) Erith and Crayford Nov. 1965, 1966. PPS to Parly Under-Sec. of State for Defence, 1973–74, to Minister of State for Defence, 1974. Chm., Cons. Backbench Educn Cttee, 1983–85; Vice-Chm., Cons. Backbench Employment Cttee, 1974–81; Member: Select Cttee on Educn, Sci. and Arts, 1979–83; H of C European Legislation Cttee, 1983–. *Recreations:* cricket, tennis, reading. *Address:* 120 Pickford Road, Markyate, Herts. *Clubs:* Carlton, Coningsby; Mid-Cheshire Pitt (Chester).

MADELUNG, Prof. Wilferd Willy Ferdinand; Laudian Professor of Arabic, University of Oxford, since 1978; *b* 26 Dec. 1930; *s* of Georg Madelung and Elisabeth (*née* Messerschmitt); *m* 1963, A. Margaret (*née* Arent); one *s*. *Educ:* Eberhard Ludwig Gymnasium, Stuttgart; Univs of Georgetown, Cairo, Hamburg. PhD (Hamburg). Cultural Attaché, W German Embassy, Baghdad, 1958–60. Vis. Professor, Univ. of Texas, Austin, 1963; Privatdozent, Univ. of Hamburg, 1963–64; University of Chicago: Asst Prof., 1964; Associate Prof., 1966; Prof. of Islamic History, 1969. Guggenheim Fellowship, 1972–73. Decoration of Republic of Sudan (4th cl.), 1962. *Publications:* Der Imam al-Qāsim ibn Ibrāhīm und die Glaubenslehre der Zaiditen, 1965; Religious Schools and Sects in Medieval Islam, 1985; Religious Trends in Early Islamic Iran, 1988; articles in learned jls and Encyc. of Islam. *Recreation:* travel. *Address:* The Oriental Institute, Pusey Lane, Oxford OX1 2LE. *T:* Oxford (0865) 59272.

MADEN, Margaret; County Education Officer, Warwickshire County Council, since 1989; *b* 16 April 1940; *d* of Clifford and Frances Maden. *Educ:* Arnold High Sch. for Girls, Blackpool; Leeds Univ. (BA Hons); Univ. of London Inst of Educn (PGCE). Asst Teacher of Geography, Stockwell Manor Comprehensive Sch., SW9, 1962–66; Lectr, Sidney Webb Coll. of Educn, 1966–71; Dep. Head, Bicester Comprehensive Sch., Oxon, 1971–75; Headmistress, Islington Green Comprehensive Sch., 1975–82; Dir, Islington Sixth Form Centre, 1983–86; Principal Advr, Tertiary Develt, ILEA, 1986–87; Dep. County Educn Officer, Warwickshire CC, 1987–88. *Publications:* contributions to: Dear Lord James, 1971; Teachers for Tomorrow (ed Calthrop and Owens), 1971; Education 2000 (ed Wilby and Pluckrose), 1979; The School and the University, an International Perspective (ed Burton R. Clark), 1984. *Recreations:* European painting, writing and films; politics, opera.

MADGE, Charles Henry; *b* 10 Oct. 1912; *s* of Lieut-Colonel C. A. Madge and Barbara (*née* Hylton Foster); *m* 1st, Kathleen Raine (marr. diss.); one *s* one *d*; 2nd, Inez Pearn (*d* 1976); one *s* one *d*; 3rd, Evelyn Brown (*d* 1984). *Educ:* Winchester Coll. (Scholar); Magdalene Coll., Cambridge (Scholar). Reporter on Daily Mirror, 1935–36; founded Mass-Observation, 1937; directed survey of working-class saving and spending for National Institute of Economic and Social Research, 1940–42; Research staff of PEP, 1943; Director, Pilot Press, 1944; Social Development Officer, New Town of Stevenage, 1947; Prof. of Sociology, Univ. of Birmingham, 1950–70. Mission to Thailand on UN Technical Assistance, 1953–54. UNESCO Missions to India, 1957–58, to South-East Asia, 1959 and 1960 and Leader of Mission to Ghana for UN Economic Commission for Africa, 1963. *Publications:* The Disappearing Castle (poems), 1937; The Father Found (poems), 1941; part-author of Britain by Mass-Observation, 1938, and other books connected with this organisation; War-time Pattern of Saving and Spending, 1943; (ed) Pilot Papers: Social Essays and Documents, 1945–47; Society in the Mind, 1964; (with Barbara Weinberger) Art Students Observed, 1973; (with Peter Willmott) Inner City Poverty in Paris and London, 1981; (ed with Mary-Lou Jennings) Pandaemonium, by Humphrey Jennings, 1985; (with Tom Harrisson) Britain by Mass-Observation, 1986; (with Humphrey Jennings) May the Twelfth, 1987; Of Love, Time and Places (poems), 1991; contributions to Economic Journal, Town Planning Review, Human Relations, etc. *Address:* 28 Lynmouth Road, N2 9LS.

MADGE, James Richard, CB 1976; Deputy Secretary, Department of the Environment, on secondment as Chief Executive, Housing Corporation, 1973–84; *b* 18 June 1924; *s* of James Henry Madge and Elisabeth May Madge; *m* 1955, Alice June Annette (*d* 1975), *d* of late Major Horace Reid, Jamaica; two *d*. *Educ:* Bexhill Co. Sch.; New Coll., Oxford. Pilot in RAFVR, 1942–46. Joined Min. of Civil Aviation, 1947; Principal Private Secretary: to Paymaster-General, 1950–51; to Minister of Transport, 1960–61; Asst Secretary, Min. of Transport, 1961–66; Under-Sec., Road Safety Gp, 1966–69; Head of Policy Planning, 1969–70; Under-Sec., Housing Directorate, DoE, 1971–73. Churchwarden, St Mary Abbots, Kensington, 1987–. *Recreations:* lawn tennis, swimming, furniture-making. *Address:* 56 Gordon Place, Kensington, W8 4JF. *T:* 071–937 1927.

MADIGAN, Sir Russel (Tullie), Kt 1981; OBE 1970; Chairman, Remproc Ltd, since 1991; *b* 22 Nov. 1920; *s* of Dr Cecil T. Madigan and Wynnis K. Wollaston; *m* 1st, 1942, Margaret Symons (decd); four *s* one *d*; 2nd, 1981, Satsuko Tamura. *Educ:* Univ. of Adelaide (BScEng 1941, BE 1946, ME 1954, LLB 1960). FSASM 1941; FTS. Joined Zinc Corp., 1946; Gowrie Schol. in Canada and USA, 1947–49; Underground Manager, Zinc Corp., NBHC Ltd, 1956–59; CRA, Conzinc Rio Tinto of Australia Ltd: Gen. Manager, Gen. Mining Div., 1960–64; Dir, 1968–87; Dep. Chm., 1978–87; Hamersley Iron: Man. Dir, 1965–71; Chm., 1971–81. Chairman: Blair Athol Coal Pty, 1971–80; Interstate Oil, 1972–81; Hamersley Hldgs, 1971–81; APV Asia Pacific, 1983–87; Muswellbrook Energy & Minerals, 1987–90; Director: Nat. Commercial Union, 1969–; Rio Tinto Zinc Corp., 1971–85; APV Hldgs, 1983–87. Pres., Aust. Inst. of Internat. Affairs, 1984–89; Chairman: Aust.-Japan Foundn, 1977–81; Aust. Mineral Foundn, 1984–88; Aust. Pacific Econ. Co-operation Cttee, 1986–; Member: Export Develt Council, 1970–86; Consultative Cttee on Relations with Japan, 1977–82; Life Mem., Pacific Basin Econ. Council, 1982; Councillor: Australasian Inst. of Mining and Metallurgy, 1958–87 (Pres., 1980); Aust. Acad. of Technological Scis and Engrg, 1978–89 (Treas., 1985–89). *Recreations:* flying, farming. *Address:* 99 Spring Street, Melbourne, Vic 3000, Australia. *Clubs:* Athenæum, Melbourne, Royal Melbourne Golf.

MAEHLER, Prof. Herwig Gustav Theodor, FBA 1986; Professor of Papyrology, University College London, since 1981; *b* 29 April 1935; *s* of Ludwig and Lisa Maehler; *m* 1963, Margaret Anderson; two *d*. *Educ:* Katharineum Lübeck (Grammar Sch.); Univs of Hamburg (PhD Classics and Classical Archaeol.), Tübingen and Basel. British Council Schol., Oxford, 1961–62; Res. Assistant, Hamburg Univ., 1962–63, Hamburg Univ. Liby, 1963–64; Keeper of Greek Papyri, Egyptian Mus., W Berlin, 1964–79; Habilitation for Classics, 1975, Lectr in Classics, 1975–79, Free Univ. of W Berlin; Reader in Papyrology, UCL, 1979–81. Corresp. Mem., German Archaeol Inst., 1979. *Publications:* Die Auffassung des Dichterberufs im frühen Griechentum bis zur Zeit Pindars, 1963; Die Handschriften des S Jacobi-Kirche Hamburg, 1967; Urkunden römischer Zeit, (BGU XI), 1968; Papyri aus Hermupolis (BGU XII), 1974; Die Lieder des Bakchylides, 2 vols, 1982; (with G. Cavallo) Greek Bookhands of the Early Byzantine Period, 1987; editions of Bacchylides and Pindar, 1970, 1987, 1989; articles in learned jls. *Address:* Department of Greek, University College London, Gower Street, WC1E 6BT. *T:* 071-380 7490.

MAFFEY, family name of **Baron Rugby.**

MAGEE, Bryan; writer; Opera Critic, The Independent on Sunday, since 1991; Visiting Scholar in Philosophy, Wolfson College, Oxford, since 1991; Hon. Senior Research Fellow in History of Ideas, King's College London, since 1984; *b* 12 April 1930; *s* of Frederick Magee and Sheila (*née* Lynch); *m* 1954, Ingrid Söderlund (marr. diss.); one *d*. *Educ:* Christ's Hospital; Lycée Hôche, Versailles; Keble Coll., Oxford (Open Scholar). Pres., Oxford Union, 1953; MA 1956. Henry Fellow in Philosophy, Yale, 1955–56. Music criticism for many publications, 1959–; Theatre Critic, The Listener, 1966–67; regular columnist, The Times, 1974–76. Current Affairs Reporter on TV; Critic of the Arts on BBC Radio 3; own broadcast series include: Conversations with Philosophers, BBC Radio 3, 1970–71; Men of Ideas, BBC TV 2, 1978; The Great Philosophers, BBC TV 2, 1987. Silver Medal, RTS, 1978. Contested (Lab): Mid-Bedfordshire, Gen. Elec., 1959; By-Elec., 1960; MP (Lab 1974–82, SDP 1982–83) Leyton, Feb. 1974–1983; contested (SDP) Leyton, 1983. Elected to Critics' Circle, 1970, Pres., 1983–84. Judge: for Evening Standard annual Opera Award, 1973–84; for Laurence Olivier Annual Opera Award, 1990–91. Lectr in Philosophy, Balliol Coll., Oxford, 1970–71; Visiting Fellow of

All Souls Coll., Oxford, 1973–74; Vis. Schol. in Philos., Harvard, 1979, Sydney Univ., 1982; German Marshall Fund Fellow to USA, 1989; Vis. Scholar in Philos., Univ. of California, Santa Barbara, 1989 (Girvetz Meml Lectr). Charles Carter Lectr, Univ. of Lancaster, 1985; Bithell Meml Lectr, Univ. of London, 1989. Hon. Pres., Edinburgh Univ. Philosophy Soc., 1987–88. Governor, 1979–, Mem. Council, 1982–, Ditchley Foundn. Hon. Fellow, QMC, 1988; Fellow: Queen Mary and Westfield Coll., London, 1989; Royal Philharmonic Soc., 1990. *Publications:* Crucifixion and Other Poems, 1951; Go West Young Man, 1958; To Live in Danger, 1960; The New Radicalism, 1962; The Democratic Revolution, 1964; Towards 2000, 1965; One in Twenty, 1966; The Television Interviewer, 1966; Aspects of Wagner, 1968, rev. edn 1988; Modern British Philosophy, 1971; Popper, 1973; Facing Death, 1977; Men of Ideas, 1978; The Philosophy of Schopenhauer, 1983; The Great Philosophers, 1987. *Recreations:* music, theatre, travel. *Address:* 12 Falkland House, Marloes Road, W8 5LF. *T:* 071–937 1210. *Clubs:* Beefsteak, Brooks's, Garrick, Savile.

MAGGS, Air Vice-Marshal William Jack, CB 1967; OBE 1943; MA; Fellow and Domestic Bursar, Keble College, Oxford, 1969–77, Emeritus Fellow since 1981; *b* 2 Feb. 1914; *s* of late Frederick Wilfrid Maggs, Bristol; *m* 1940, Margaret Grace, *d* of late Thomas Liddell Hetherington, West Hartlepool; one *s* one *d.* *Educ:* Bristol Grammar Sch.; St John's Coll., Oxford (MA). Management Trainee, 1936–38. Joined RAF, 1939; Unit and Training duties, 1939–42; Student, Staff Coll., 1942; Planning Staffs, and participated in, Algerian, Sicilian and Italian landings, 1942–44; SESO Desert Air Force, 1944; Jt Admin. Plans Staff, Cabinet Offices, Whitehall, 1945–48; Instructor, RAF Coll., Cranwell, 1948–50; comd No 9 Maintenance Unit, 1950–52; exchange officer at HQ, USAF Washington, 1952–54; Student Jt Services Staff Coll., 1954–55; No 3 Maintenance Unit, 1955–57; Dep. Director of Equipment, Air Ministry, 1958–59; SESO, HQ, NEAF, Cyprus, 1959–61; Student, Imperial Defence Coll., 1962; Director of Mech. Transport and Marine Craft, Air Ministry, 1963–64; Director of Equipment, Ministry of Defence (Air), 1964–67; SASO, RAF Maintenance Comd, 1967–69. Group Captain, 1958; Air Commodore, 1963; Air Vice-Marshal, 1967. Governor, Bristol Grammar Sch., 1980–89. *Recreations:* golf, gardening. *Club:* Royal Air Force.

MAGILL, Air Vice-Marshal Graham Reese, CB 1966; CBE 1962 (OBE 1945); DFC 1941 and Bar, 1943; retired Jan. 1970; *b* 23 Jan. 1915; *s* of late Robert Wilson Magill and late Frances Elizabeth Magill, Te Aroha, NZ; *m* 1942, Blanche Marie Colson (*d* 1991); two *s.* *Educ:* Te Aroha High Sch.; Hamilton Technical Coll., NZ. Joined Royal Air Force, 1936. Served War of 1939–45, Sudan and Eritrea (despatches 1941), Egypt, UK, NW Europe; subsequently, UK, Egypt, France. Director of Operations (Bomber and Reconnaissance), Air Ministry, 1959–62; Commandant, RAF College of Air Warfare, Manby, Lincs, 1963–64; Director-General of Organisation (RAF), Ministry of Defence, 1964–67; AOC, 25 Group, RAF, 1967–68; AOC 22 Group, RAF, 1968–69. *Address:* c/o Holmhurst, The Southra, Dinas Powys, S Glamorgan CF6 4DL. *Club:* Royal Air Force.

MAGINNIS, John Edward, JP; *b* 7 March 1919; *s* of late Edward Maginnis and Mary E. Maginnis, Mandeville Hall, Mullahead, Tanderagee; *m* 1944, Dorothy, *d* of late R. J. Rusk, JP, of Cavanaleck, Fivemiletown, Co. Tyrone; one *s* four *d.* *Educ:* Moyallon Sch., Co. Down; Portadown Technical Coll. Served War of 1939–45, Royal Ulster Constabulary. MP (UU) Armagh, Oct. 1959–Feb. 1974. JP, Co. Armagh, 1956. Group Secretary, North Armagh Group, Ulster Farmers' Union, 1956–59; Member, Co. Armagh Agricultural Society. Hon. LLD, 1990. *Recreations:* football, hunting, shooting. *Address:* Mandeville Hall, 68 Mullahead Road, Tandragee, Craigavon, Co. Armagh, N Ireland BT62 2LB. *T:* Tandragee (0762) 840260.

MAGINNIS, Ken; MP (UU) Fermanagh and South Tyrone, since 1983 (resigned seat Dec. 1985 in protest against Anglo-Irish Agreement; re-elected Jan. 1986); *b* 21 Jan. 1938; *m* 1961, Joy Stewart; two *s* two *d.* *Educ:* Royal Sch., Dungannon; Stranmillis Coll., Belfast. Served UDR, 1970–81, commissioned 1972, Major. Party spokesman on internal security and defence. Mem., Dungannon District Council, 1981–; Mem. (UU) Fermanagh and S Tyrone, NI Assembly, 1982–86. Contested (UU) Fermanagh and S Tyrone, Aug. 1981. Mem., H of C Select Cttee on Defence, 1984–86. *Address:* House of Commons, SW1A 0AA; 1 Park Lane, Dungannon, Co. Tyrone.

MAGNIAC, Rear-Admiral Vernon St Clair Lane, CB 1961; *b* 21 Dec. 1908; *s* of late Major Francis Arthur Magniac and of Mrs Beatrice Caroline Magniac (*née* Davison); *m* 1947, Eileen Eleanor (*née* Witney); one *s* one *d* (and one *d* decd). *Educ:* Clifton Coll. Cadet, RN, 1926; Served in HM Ships Courageous, Effingham, Resolution and Diamond, 1931–37; RN Engineering Coll., 1937–39; HMS Renown, 1940–43; Combined Ops, India, 1943–45; HM Ships Fisgard, Gambia, and Nigeria, 1945–50; HM Dockyards Chatham, Malta and Devonport, 1950–62. *Recreations:* golf, fishing. *Address:* Marlborough, Down Park, Yelverton, Devon PL20 6BN.

MAGNUS, Sir Laurence (Henry Philip), 3rd Bt *cr* 1917, of Tangley Hill, Wonersh; Executive Director, Samuel Montagu & Co. Ltd, Merchant Bankers, since 1988; *b* 24 Sept. 1955; *s* of Hilary Barrow Magnus, QC (*d* 1987), and of Rosemary Vera Anne Magnus (*née* Masefield); *S* uncle, Sir Philip Magnus-Allcroft, 2nd Bt, CBE, 1988; *m* 1983, Jocelyn Mary, *d* of R. H. F. Stanton; two *s* one *d.* *Educ:* Eton College; Christ Church, Oxford (MA). Corporate Finance Executive, Samuel Montagu & Co. Ltd, 1977–84; Head of Corporate Finance, Samuel Montagu & Co. Ltd (Singapore Branch), 1984–87; Group Country Manager, Singapore Region, Midland Bank plc (Singapore), 1987–88. *Recreations:* reading, fishing, walking. *Heir:* *s* Thomas Henry Philip Magnus, *b* 30 Sept. 1985. *Address:* c/o Samuel Montagu & Co. Ltd, 10 Lower Thames Street, EC3R 6AE. *T:* 071–260 9440. *Club:* Millennium.

MAGNUS, Prof. Philip Douglas, FRS 1985; R. P. Doherty, Jr–Welch Regents Professor of Chemistry, University of Texas at Austin, since 1989; *b* 15 April 1943; *s* of Arthur Edwin and Lillian Edith Magnus; *m* 1963, Andrea Claire (*née* Parkinson); two *s.* *Educ:* Imperial College, Univ. of London (BSc, ARCS, PhD, DSc). Asst Lectr, 1967–70, Lectr, 1970–75, Imperial College; Associate Prof., Ohio State Univ., 1975–81; Prof. of Chemistry, 1981–87, Distinguished Prof., 1987–88, Indiana Univ. Corday Morgan Medal, RSC, 1978. *Publications:* papers in leading chemistry jls. *Recreations:* golf, chess. *Address:* 3111D Windsor Road, Austin, Texas 78703, USA. *T:* (512) 471–3966.

MAGNUS, Samuel Woolf; Justice of Appeal, Court of Appeal for Zambia, 1971; Commissioner, Foreign Compensation Commission, 1977–83; *b* 30 Sept. 1910; *s* of late Samuel Woolf Magnus; *m* 1938, Anna Gertrude, *o d* of Adolph Shane, Cardiff; one *d.* *Educ:* University Coll., London. BA Hons, 1931. Called to Bar, Gray's Inn, 1937. Served War of 1939–45, Army. Practised in London, 1937–59. Treas., Assoc. of Liberal Lawyers, Mem. Council, London Liberal Party and Pres., N Hendon Liberal Assoc., until 1959. Contested (L) Central Hackney, 1945. Partner in legal firm, Northern Rhodesia, 1959–63; subseq. legal consultant. QC 1964, MLC 1962, MP Jan.-Oct. 1964, Northern Rhodesia; MP, Zambia, 1964–68. Puisne Judge, High Court for Zambia, 1968. Chm., Law, Parly and Gen. Purposes Cttee, Bd of Deputies of British Jews, 1979–83. FCIArb 1987. *Publications:* (with M. Estrin) Companies Act 1947, 1947; (with M. Estrin) Companies: Law and Practice, 1948, 5th edn 1978, and Supplement, 1981; (with A. M. Lyons) Advertisement Control, 1949; Magnus on Leasehold Property (Temporary Provisions) Act 1951, 1951; Magnus on Landlord and Tenant Act 1954, 1954; Magnus on Housing Repairs and Rents Act 1954, 1954; Magnus on the Rent Act 1957, 1957; (with F. E. Price) Knight's Annotated Housing Acts, 1958; (with Tovell) Magnus on Housing Finance, 1960; (with M. Estrin) Companies Act 1967, 1967; Magnus on the Rent Act 1968, 1969; Magnus on Business Tenancies, 1970; Magnus on the Rent Act 1977, 1978; Butterworth's Company Forms Manual, 1987; contributor: Law Jl; Halsbury's Laws of England; Encycl. of Forms and Precedents; Atkin's Court Forms and Precedents. *Recreations:* writing, photography, enthusiastic spectator at all games, preferably on TV. *Address:* 33 Apsley House, Finchley Road, St John's Wood, NW8. *T:* 071–586 1679. *Clubs:* MCC, Middlesex CC.

MAGNUSSON, Magnus, Hon. KBE 1989; MA (Oxon); FRSE 1980; FRSA; writer and broadcaster; *b* 12 Oct. 1929; *s* of late Sigursteinn Magnusson, Icelandic Consul-Gen. for Scotland, and Ingibjorg Sigurdardottir; *m* 1954, Mamie Baird; one *s* three *d* (and one *s* decd). *Educ:* Edinburgh Academy; Jesus Coll., Oxford (MA; Hon. Fellow, 1990). Subseq. Asst Editor, Scottish Daily Express and Asst Editor, The Scotsman. Presenter, various television and radio programmes including: Chronicle; Mastermind; Pebble Mill at One; BC, The Archaeology of the Bible Lands; Tonight; Cause for Concern; All Things Considered; Living Legends; Vikings!; Birds For All Seasons; Scottish Television Personality of the Year, 1974. Editor: The Bodley Head Archaeologies; Popular Archaeology, 1979–80. Chairman: Ancient Monuments Bd for Scotland, 1981–89; NCC for Scotland, 1991–April 1992; Scottish Natural Heritage, April 1992–. Stewards, York Archaeol Trust; Scottish Churches Architectural Heritage Trust, 1978–85; Scottish Youth Theatre, 1976–78; Member: Bd of Trustees, Nat. Museums of Scotland, 1985–89; UK Cttee for European Year of the Environment, 1987; Pres., RSPB, 1985–90; Hon. Vice-President: Age Concern Scotland; RSSPCC. Rector, Edinburgh Univ., 1975–78. FSAScot 1974; FRSA 1983; Hon. FRIAS 1987; FSA 1991; FRSGS 1991. Dr *hc* Edinburgh, 1978; DUniv York, 1981. Iceland Media Award, 1985; Medlicott Medal, HA, 1989. Knight of the Order of the Falcon (Iceland), 1975, Knight Commander, 1986; Silver Jubilee Medal, 1977. *Publications:* Introducing Archaeology, 1972; Viking Expansion Westwards, 1973; The Clacken and the Slate (Edinburgh Academy, 1824–1974), 1974; Hammer of the North (Norse mythology), 1976, 2nd edn, Viking Hammer of the North, 1980; BC, The Archaeology of the Bible Lands, 1977; Landlord or Tenant? a view of Irish history, 1978; Iceland, 1979; Vikings!, 1980; Magnus on the Move, 1980; Treasures of Scotland, 1981; Lindisfarne: The Cradle Island, 1984; Iceland Saga, 1987; *translations* (all with Hermann Pálsson): Njal's Saga, 1960; The Vinland Sagas, 1965; King Harald's Saga, 1966; Laxdaela Saga, 1969; (all by Halldor Laxness): The Atom Station, 1961; Paradise Reclaimed, 1962; The Fish Can Sing, 1966; World Light, 1969; Christianity Under Glacier, 1973; (by Samivel) Golden Iceland, 1967; *contributor:* The Glorious Privilege, 1967; The Future of the Highlands, 1968; Strange Stories, Amazing Facts, 1975; Pass the Port, 1976; Book of Bricks, 1978; Chronicle, 1978; Discovery of Lost Worlds, 1979; Pass the Port Again, 1981; Second Book of Bricks, 1981; *introduced:* Ancient China, 1974; The National Trust for Scotland Guide, 1976; Karluk, 1976; More Lives Than One?, 1976; Atlas of World Geography, 1977; Face to Face with the Turin Shroud, 1978; Modern Bible Atlas, 1979; Living Legends, 1980; The Hammer and the Cross, 1980; Household Ghosts, 1981; Great Books for Today, 1981; The Voyage of Odin's Raven, 1982; Robert Burns: Bawdy Verse & Folksongs, 1982; Mastermind 4, 1982; Northern Voices, 1984; The Village, 1985; Secrets of the Bible Seas, 1985; Beowulf, 1987; Complete Book of British Birds, 1988; Trustlands, 1989; The Wealth of a Nation, 1989; The Return of Cultural Treasures, 1990; *edited:* Echoes in Stone, 1983; Readers Digest Book of Facts, 1985; Chambers Biographical Dictionary, 5th edn 1990; The Nature of Scotland, 1991. *Recreations:* digging and delving. *Address:* Blairskaith House, Balmore-Torrance, Glasgow G64 4AX. *T:* Balmore (0360) 20226.

MAGONET, Rabbi Dr Jonathan David; Principal, Leo Baeck College, since 1985; *b* 2 Aug. 1942; *s* of Alexander Philip and Esther Magonet; *m* 1974, Dorothea (*née* Foth); one *s* one *d.* *Educ:* Westminster Sch.; Middlesex Hosp. Med. Sch. (MB BS). Leo Baeck Coll.; Univ. of Heidelberg (PhD). Junior hosp. doctor, 1966–67; Leo Baeck College: Rabbinic studies, 1967–71; Head of Dept of Bible Studies, 1974–85. Vice-Pres., World Union for Progressive Judaism, 1988–. Member Editorial Board: European Judaism, 1978–; Christian-Jewish Relations, 1987–. *Publications:* Form and Meaning: studies in literary techniques in the Book of Jonah, 1976; (ed jtly) Forms of Prayer, vol. I, Daily and Sabbath Prayerbook, 1977, vol. III, Days of Awe Prayerbook, 1985; (ed jtly) The Guide to the Here and Hereafter, 1988; A Rabbi's Bible, 1991. *Address:* 18 Wellfield Avenue, N10 2EA. *T:* 081–444 3025.

MAGOR, Major (Edward) Walter (Moyle), CMG 1960; OBE 1956 (MBE 1947); DL; *b* 1 June 1911; *e s* of late Edward John Penberthy Magor, JP, Lamellen, St Tudy, Cornwall, and Gilian Sarah Magor, JP; *m* 1939, Daphne Davis (*d* 1972), *d* of late Hector Robert Lushington Graham, Summerhill, Thomastown, Co. Kilkenny; two *d.* *Educ:* Marlborough; Magdalen, Oxford; Magdalene, Cambridge. MA. Indian Army, 1934–47; RARO, 10th Hussars, 1949–61; Indian Political Service, 1937–39 and 1943–47; Colonial Administrative Service, 1947–61; Kenya: Asst Chief Secretary, 1953; Permanent Secretary, Ministry of Defence, 1954; Acting Minister for Defence, 1956; Secretary to the Cabinet, 1958. Home Civil Service, DTI, formerly BoT, 1961–71; Asst Secretary, 1964; retired 1971. Chm., St John Council for Cornwall, 1973–78. Editor, RHS Rhododendron and Camellia Yearbook, 1974–82; Chm., RHS Rhododendron and Camellia Gp, 1976–80. President: Cornwall Garden Soc., 1981–84; Royal Cornwall Agricl Assoc., 1983. DL Cornwall, 1974; High Sheriff of Cornwall, 1981. CStJ 1978 (OStJ 1975). Médaille de la Belgique Reconnaissante, 1961; Veitch Meml Medal, RHS, 1986. Lord of the Manor of Kellygreen. *Recreation:* gardening (Mem., Garden Soc.). *Address:* Lamellen, St Tudy, Cornwall PL30 3NR. *T:* Bodmin (0208) 850207.

MAGRUTSCH, Dr Walter; Commander's Cross, Austria, 1988; Austrian Ambassador to the Court of St James's, since 1987; *b* 16 July 1929; *s* of Hans and Magdalena Magrutsch; *m* 1955, Elisabeth Pihofsky; three *d.* *Educ:* Univ. of Vienna (Dr jur 1953); post-graduate studies in Paris. Practising law, Austrian courts, 1953–54; entered Austrian Diplomatic Service, 1954; Attaché, New Delhi, 1955–56; Secretary, Bonn, 1957–61; Counsellor, Prague, 1964–69; Envoy Extr. and Minister Plen., 1970; Head of Political Div. for Eastern Europe, China and Middle East, Min. of Foreign Affairs, 1970–74; Ambassador to Canada, 1974–78, to Brazil, 1978–81; Dir-Gen., Legal and Consular Affairs Section, MFA, 1982–87, concurrently Dep. Sec.-Gen. for Foreign Affairs, 1986–87. Decorations from FRG, Hungary, Indonesia, Brazil, France, Belgium. *Recreations:* mountaineering, tennis, piano playing. *Address:* Austrian Embassy, 18 Belgrave Square, SW1X 8HU. *T:* 071–235 7268. *Clubs:* Travellers', Queen's.

MAGUIRE, (Albert) Michael, MC 1945; MM 1943; QC 1967; *b* 30 Dec. 1922; *s* of late Richard Maguire and Ruth Maguire. *Educ:* Hutton Grammar Sch.; Trinity Hall, Cambridge (BA 1948). Served War of 1939–45, North Irish Horse (Captain), in Africa (MM) and Italy (MC). Inns of Court Regt, 1946. War Crimes Investigation Unit, 1946. Called to the Bar, Middle Temple, 1949 (Harmsworth Scholar); Bencher, 1973; Leader,

Northern Circuit, 1980–84. Last Recorder of Carlisle (1970–71). *Address*: Goldsmith Building, Temple, EC4Y 7BL; Chestnuts, 89 Lower Bank Road, Fulwood, Preston, Lancs. *T*: Preston (0772) 719291. *Club*: United Oxford & Cambridge University.

MAGUIRE, (Benjamin) Waldo, OBE 1973; *b* 31 May 1920; *s* of Benjamin Maguire and Elizabeth Ann Eldon; *m* 1944, Lilian Joan Martin; four *s*. *Educ*: Portadown Coll.; Trinity Coll., Dublin. BA 1st cl. hons Philosophy. Intell. Service, WO and FO, 1942–45; BBC Latin American Service, 1945; BBC Radio News, 1946–55; BBC TV News, 1955; Editor, BBC TV News, 1962–64; Controller, News and Public Affairs, NZ Broadcasting Corp., 1965–66; BBC Controller, NI, 1966–72; Head of Information Programmes, NZ TV2, 1975–76. *Recreations*: gardening, conversation, angling. *Address*: 116 Park Avenue, Ruislip, Mddx. *T*: Ruislip (0895) 635981.

MAGUIRE, Air Marshal Sir Harold John, KCB 1966 (CB 1958); DSO 1946; OBE 1949; Director, Commercial Union Assurance Co., 1975–82 (Political and Economic Adviser, 1972–79); *b* 12 April 1912; *s* of Michael Maguire, Maynooth, Ireland, and Harriett (*née* Warren), Kilkishen, Co. Clare, Ireland; *m* 1940, Mary Elisabeth Wild (*d* 1991), Dublin; one *s* one *d*. *Educ*: Wesley Coll., Dublin; Dublin Univ. Royal Air Force Commn, 1933; service in flying boats, 230 Sqdn, Egypt and Far East, 1935–38; commanded night fighter sqdn, UK, 1939–40 and day fighter sqdn, 1940; OC 266 (Fighter) Wing, Dutch E Indies, 1942; POW, Java, 1942; Staff Coll., 1947; Fighter Command Staff Duties, 1948–50; OC, RAF, Odiham, 1950–52; Senior Air Staff Officer, Malta, 1952–55; staff of CAS, Air Ministry, 1955–58; Senior Air Staff Officer, HQ No 11 Group, RAF, 1958–59; AOC No 13 Group, RAF, 1959–61; AOC No 11 Group, Fighter Command, 1961–62; SASO Far East Air Force, 1962–64; ACAS (Intelligence), 1964–65; Dep. Chief of Defence Staff (Intelligence), 1965–68; retired, 1968; Dir-Gen. of Intelligence, MoD, 1968–72. *Address*: c/o Lloyds Bank, 7 Pall Mall, SW1. *Club*: Royal Air Force.

MAGUIRE, Hugh, FRAM; violinist and conductor; Director of Strings, Britten-Pears School for Advanced Music Studies, since 1978; Professor of Violin, Royal Academy of Music, since 1957; *b* 2 Aug. 1926; *m* 1953, Suzanne Lewis, of International Ballet; two *s* three *d*. *Educ*: Belvedere Coll., SJ, Dublin; Royal Academy of Music, London (David Martin); Paris (Georges Enesco). Leader: Bournemouth Symphony Orchestra, 1952–56; London Symphony Orchestra, 1956–62; BBC Symphony Orchestra, 1962–67; Cremona String Quartet, 1966–68; Allegri String Quartet, 1968–76; Melos Ensemble, 1972–85; Orch. of Royal Opera House, Covent Garden, 1983–91. Artistic Dir, Irish Youth Orch. String coach, European Commn Youth Orch. Mem., Irish Arts Council. Hon. MMus Hull, 1975; Hon. DLitt Univ. of Ulster, 1986. Harriet Cohen Internat. Award; Councils Gold Medal (Ireland), 1963; Cobbett Medal, Musicians' Co., 1982. *Address*: Manor Farm, Benhall, Suffolk IP17 1HN. *T*: Saxmundham (0728) 603245.

MAGUIRE, Mairead C.; *see* Corrigan-Maguire.

MAGUIRE, Michael; *see* Maguire, A. M.

MAGUIRE, Rt. Rev. Robert Kenneth, MA, DD; Hon. Assisting Bishop: Diocese of Western New York, 1984–86; Diocese of Southeast Florida, 1984–89, retired; *b* 31 March 1923; *s* of late Robert Maguire and late Anne Crozier; unmarried. *Educ*: Trinity Coll., Dublin. BA 1945; Divinity Testimonium, 1947. Deacon, 1947; Priest, 1948. Curate of St Mark, Armagh, 1947–49; St James the Apostle, Montreal, 1949–52; Dean of Residence, Trinity Coll., Dublin, 1952–60; Curate-in-charge of St Andrew's, Dublin, 1954–57; Minor Canon of St Patrick's Cathedral, Dublin, 1955–58; Dean and Rector of Christ Church Cathedral, Montreal, 1961–62; Bishop of Montreal, 1963–75. Co-ordinator: Canadian Conf., Theology '76, 1975–76; North American Consultation on the Future of Ministry, 1979–80. Assistant to the Primate, Anglican Church of Canada, 1980–84. DD (*jure dig.*): Dublin Univ., 1963; Montreal Diocesan Theolog. Coll., 1963; DCL (*hc*), Bishop's Univ., Lennoxville, Qué., 1963. *Address*: 4875 Dundas Street West, Apt 304, Islington, Ontario M9A 1B3, Canada.

MAGUIRE, Waldo; *see* Maguire, B. W.

MAHATHIR bin MOHAMAD, Dato Seri Dr; MHR for Kubang Pasu, since 1974; Prime Minister of Malaysia, since 1981, and Minister of Home Affairs, since 1986; *b* 20 Dec. 1925. *Educ*: Sultan Abdul Hamid Coll.; College of Medicine, Singapore. Medical Officer, Kedah and Perlis, 1953–57; in private practice, 1957–64. MHR for Kota Star Selatan, 1964–69; Mem., Senate, 1972–74; Minister of Education, 1974–77; Trade and Industry, 1977–81; Dep. Prime Minister, 1976–81. President, United Malays Nat. Organisation, 1981– (Mem., Supreme Council, 1972–). *Publication*: The Malay Dilemma, 1969. *Address*: Office of the Prime Minister, Kuala Lumpur, Malaysia.

MAHER, Terence; Metropolitan Stipendiary Magistrate, since 1983; a Chairman, Inner London Juvenile Courts, since 1985; a Recorder, since 1989; *b* 20 Dec. 1941; *s* of late John Maher and of Bessie Maher; *m* 1965 (marr. diss. 1983); two *d*. *Educ*: Burnley Grammar Sch.; Univ. of Manchester. LLB (hons). Admitted Solicitor, 1966; articled to Town Clerk, Burnley; Asst Sol., City of Bradford, 1966–68; Prosecuting Sol., Birmingham Corp., 1968–70; Dep. Pros. Sol., Thames Valley Police, 1970–73; Asst Sol. and partner, Cole & Cole, Oxford, 1973–83. Gen. Sec., Univ. of Manchester Students' Union, 1962–63; Chm., Chipping Norton Round Table, 1975–76; Treasurer/Vice-Chm. and Chm., Oxford and District Solicitors' Assoc., 1980–83; Mem., Law Society Standing Cttee on Criminal Law, 1980–85. Mem. Editl Bd, Jl of Criminal Law. *Recreations*: walking, reading, anything to do with France and the French. *Address*: c/o Magistrates' Court, Horseferry Road, SW1. *Club*: Frewen (Oxford).

MAHER, Terence Anthony, FCCA; Founder, Chairman and Chief Executive, Pentos plc, since 1972; Chairman: Dillons Bookstores, since 1977; Athena International, since 1980; Ryman, since 1987; *b* 5 Dec. 1935; *s* of late Herbert and Lillian Maher; *m* 1960, Barbara (*née* Grunbaum); three *s*. *Educ*: Xaverian Coll., Manchester. ACCA 1960, FCCA 1970. Carborundum Co. Ltd, 1961–69; First National Finance Corp., 1969–72. Founder Trustee, Lib Dem, 1988. FRSA 1988. *Publications*: (jtly) Counterblast, 1965; Effective Politics, 1966. *Recreations*: reading, ski-ing, tennis, walking. *Address*: 33 Clarence Terrace, Regent's Park, NW1 4RD. *T*: 071–723 4254; The Old House, Whichford, near Shipston-on-Stour, Warwickshire CV36 5PG. *T*: Long Compton (060884) 614.

MAHER, Very Rev. William Francis, SJ; Provincial Superior of the English Province of the Society of Jesus, 1976–81; *b* 20 June 1916. *Educ*: St Ignatius' College, Stamford Hill; Heythrop College, Oxon. STL. Entered the Society of Jesus, 1935; ordained priest, 1948; Principal, Heythrop College, 1974–76. *Address*: St Bernard, 20A Southbourne Road, Holbury, Hants SO4 1NT.

MAHFOUZ, Naguib; Egyptian novelist; *b* 11 Dec. 1911; *m* Attiyah-Allah; *c*. *Educ*: King Fuad I Univ. (now Cairo Univ.). Sec., King Fuad I Univ.; Min. of Religious Affairs, 1939–54; screen writer (over 30 film scripts), 1945–; Dept of Arts, 1954; retired 1972. Nobel Prize for Literature, 1988. *Publications* include: trans. (into Arabic), James Baikie, Ancient Egypt, 1932; *novels*: 'Abath al-aqdar (Games of Fate), 1939; Radubis (Radobis),

1943; Kifah Tibah (The Struggle of Thebes), 1944; Al-Qahira al-jadida (New Cairo), 1946; Zuqaq al-middaq (Midaq Alley), 1947; Al-Sarab (The Mirage), 1949; Bidaya wa nihaya (The Beginning and the End), 1951; trilogy: Bayn al-qasrayn (Between the Two Palaces), vol. 1, 1956, Qasr al-shawq (The Palace of Desire), vol. 2, 1957, Al-Sukkariyya (The Sugar Bowl), vol. 3, 1957 (State Prize for Literature); trilogy: Awlad haritna (The Children of Our Lane), 1959; Al-Liss wa'l-kilab (The Thief and the Dogs), 1961; Al-Samman wa'l-kharif (Autumn Quail), 1962; Dunya'llah (God's World), 1964; Al-Shahhat (The Beggar), 1965; Tharthara fawq al-nil (Small-talk on the Nile), 1966; Miramar, 1967; Hadrat al-muhtaram (Respected Sir), 1975; Afrah al-qubba (Wedding Songs), 1981; *short stories and plays for reading*: Taht al-mizalla (Under the Awning), 1969; Al-Mar'aya (Mirrors), 1972; Al'Hubb taht al-matar (Love in the Rain), 1973. *Address*: c/o Cinema Organisation, TV Building, Maspero Street, Cairo, Egypt.

MAHLER, Dr Halfdan Theodor; Director-General, World Health Organization, 1973–88, now Emeritus; Secretary-General, International Planned Parenthood Federation, since 1989; *b* 21 April 1923; *m* 1957, Dr Ebba Fischer-Simonsen; two *s*. *Educ*: Univ. of Copenhagen (MD, EOPH). Planning Officer, Internat. Tuberculosis Campaign, Ecuador, 1950–51; Sen. WHO Med. Officer, Nat. TB Programme, India, 1951–61; Chief MO, Tuberculosis Unit, WHO/HQ, Geneva, 1961–69; Dir, Project Systems Analysis, WHO/HQ, Geneva, 1969–70; Asst Dir-Gen., WHO, 1970–73. Hon. FFPHM 1975; Hon. FRSM 1976; Hon. FRCGP 1986; Hon. Fellow: Indian Soc. for Malaria and other Communicable Diseases, Delhi; Faculty of Community Med., RCP, 1975; Hon. Professor: Univ. Nacional Mayor de San Marcos, Lima, Peru, 1980; Fac. of Medicine, Univ. of Chile, 1982; Beijing Med. Coll., China, 1983; Shanghai Med. Univ., 1986; Bartel World Affairs Fellow, Cornell, 1988; Hon. Fellow: LSHTM, 1979; Coll. of Physicians and Surgeons, Dacca, Bangladesh, 1980; Hon. Member: Soc. médicale de Genève; Union internat. contre la Tuberculose; Société Française d'Hygiène, de Médecine Sociale et Génie Sanitaire, 1977; Med. Assoc. of Argentina, 1985; Latin American Med. Assoc., 1985; Italian Soc. of Tropical Medicine, 1986; APHA, 1988; Swedish Soc. of Medicine, 1988; Hon. Foreign Corresp. Mem., BMA, 1990; Hon. Life Mem., Uganda Medical Assoc., 1976; Assoc. Mem., Belgian Soc. of Trop. Medicine; List of Honour, Internat. Dental Fedn, 1984. FRCP 1981. Hon. LLD: Nottingham, 1975; McMaster, 1989; Exeter, 1990; Toronto, 1990; Hon. MD: Karolinska Inst., 1977; Charles Univ., Prague, and Mahidol Univ., Bangkok, 1982; Aarhus, 1988; Copenhagen, 1988; Aga Khan, Pakistan, 1989; Newcastle upon Tyne, 1990; Hon. Dr de l'Univ. Toulouse (Sciences Sociales), 1977; Hon. Dr Public Health, Seoul Nat. Univ., 1979; Hon DSc: Lagos, 1979; Emory, Atlanta, 1989; SUNY, 1990; Hon. Dr Med. Warsaw Med. Acad., 1980; Hon. Dr Faculty of Medicine, Univ. of Ghent, Belgium, and Universidad Nacional Autonoma de Nicaragua, Managua, 1983; Hon. DHL CUNY, 1989; Dr *hc*: Universidad Nacional 'Federico Villarreal', Lima, Peru, 1980; Semmelweis Univ. of Medicine, Budapest, 1987. Jane Evangelisty Purkyne Medal, Prague, 1974; Comenius Univ. Gold Medal, Bratislava, 1974; Carlo Forlanini Gold Medal, 1975; Ernst Carlsens Foundn Prize, Copenhagen, 1980; Georg Barfred-Pedersen Prize, Copenhagen, 1982; Hagedorn Medal and Prize, Denmark, 1986; Freedom from Want Medal, Roosevelt Inst., 1988; Bourgeoisie d'Honneur, Geneva, 1989. Grand Officier: l'Ordre Nat. du Bénin, 1975; l'Ordre Nat. Voltaïque, 1978; l'Ordre du Mérite, République du Sénégal, 1982; Ordre National Malgache (Madagascar), 1987; Comdr (1st cl.), White Rose Order of Finland, 1983; Commandeur, l'Ordre National du Mali, 1982; Grand Cordon, Order of the Sacred Treasure (Japan), 1988; Storkors Af Dannebrogsordenen (Denmark), 1988; Grand Cross: Order of the Falcon (Iceland), 1988; Order of Merit (Luxembourg), 1990. *Publications*: papers etc on the epidemiology and control of tuberculosis, the political, social, economic and technological priority setting in the health sector, and the application of systems analysis to health care problems. *Recreations*: sailing, ski-ing. *Address*: 12 chemin du Pont-Ceard, 1290 Versoix, Switzerland.

MAHLER, Prof. Robert Frederick, FRCP, FRCPE; Editor, Journal of Royal College of Physicians, since 1987; Consultant Physician, Clinical Research Centre, Northwick Park Hospital, Harrow, 1979–90, retired; *b* 31 Oct. 1924; *s* of Felix Mahler and Olga Lowy; *m* 1951, Maureen Calvert; two *s*. *Educ*: Edinburgh Academy; Edinburgh Univ. BSc; MB, ChB. Research fellowships and univ. posts in medicine, biochemistry and clinical pharmacology at various med. schs and univs: in Gt Britain: Royal Postgrad. Med. Sch., Guy's Hosp., Manchester, Dundee, Cardiff; in USA: Harvard Univ., Univ. of Indiana; in Sweden: Karolinska Inst., Stockholm; Prof. of Med., Univ. of Wales, 1970–79. Member: MRC, 1977–81; Commonwealth Scholarship Commn, 1980–; Council, Imperial Cancer Res. Fund, 1984–; Res. Cttee, British Diabetic Assoc., 1984–87; Scientific Co-ord. Cttee, Arthritis and Rheumatism Council, 1986–91. *Publications*: contribs to British and Amer. med. and scientific jls. *Recreations*: opera, music, theatre. *Address*: 14 Manley Street, NW1. *Club*: Royal Society of Medicine.

MAHMUD HUSAIN, Syed Abul Basher; Chief Justice of Bangladesh, 1975–78; *b* 1 Feb. 1916; *s* of late Syed Abdul Mutakabbir Abul Hasan, eminent scholar; *m* 1936, Sufia Begum; three *s* five *d*. *Educ*: Shaistagonj High Sch.; M. C. Coll., Sylhet; Dacca Univ. (BA, BL). Pleader, Judge's Court, Dacca, 1940–42; Hon. Supt, Darul-Ulum Govt-aided Sen. Madrassa, Dacca, 1937–42; Additional Govt Pleader, Habiganj, 1943–48; Advocate, Dacca High Ct Bar, 1948–51; Attorney, Fed. Ct of Pakistan, 1951, Advocate, 1953, Sen. Advocate, Supreme Ct of Pakistan, 1958; Asst Govt Pleader, High Ct of E Pakistan, 1952–56; Sen. Govt Pleader, 1956–65; Actg Advocate-Gen., E Pakistan for some time; Judge: High Ct of E Pakistan, 1965; High Ct of Bangladesh, 1972; Appellate Div. of High Ct of Bangladesh, Aug. 1972; Appellate Div. of Supreme Ct of Bangladesh, Dec. 1972. Mem. Bar Council, High Ct, Dacca, 1958–66; Chm., Enrolment Cttee, E Pakistan Bar Council, 1966–69; played important role in Muslim League and Pakistan Movement. Member: Coll. Rover Crew, 1933–34; Dacca Univ. OTC, 1935–39; Local Bd, Habiganj, 1944–50; Councillor: Assam Provincial Muslim League, 1944–47; All India Muslim League, 1945–47; All Pakistan Muslim League, 1947–55; Member: Constituent Assembly of Pakistan, 1949–54; Commonwealth Parly Assoc., 1950–54; Inter-Parly Union, 1950–54; Pakistan Tea Bd, 1951–54; Exec. Council, Univ. of Dacca, 1952–54; Local Adv. Cttee, East Bengal Rlwy, 1952–54; Dir, Pakistan Refugees Rehabilitation Finance Corp., 1953–54. Leader of Hajj Delegn of Bangladesh, 1975; attended Internat. Islamic Conf., London, 1976 (Chm., Third Session). *Address*: 56/1, Shah Saheb Lane, Narinda, Dhaka, Bangladesh. *T*: 238986.

MAHON, Alice; MP (Lab) Halifax, since 1987; *b* 28 Sept. 1937; *m*; two *s*. Lectr, Bradford and Ilkeley Community Coll. Member: Calderdale Bor. Council; Calderdale DHA. *Address*: House of Commons, SW1A 0AA; 125 The Hough, Northowram, Halifax, W Yorks HX3 7DE.

MAHON, Charles Joseph; His Honour Judge Mahon; a Circuit Judge, since 1989; *b* 16 Aug. 1939; *s* of late Frank and Amy Agnes Mahon; *m* 1974, Lavinia Gough (*née* Breaks); one *d* and one step *s* two step *d*. *Educ*: Chetham's Hosp.; Gonville and Caius Coll., Cambridge (BA, LLB). Called to the Bar, Gray's Inn, 1962. Parachute Regt, TA, 1964–72. *Recreations*: music—playing and writing, books, militaria, walking.

MAHON, Sir Denis; *see* Mahon, Sir J. D.

MAHON, Rt. Rev. Gerald Thomas; Auxiliary Bishop of Westminster (Bishop in West London) (RC) and Titular Bishop of Eanach Duin since 1970; *b* 4 May 1922; *s* of George Elborne Mahon and Mary Elizabeth (*née* Dooley). *Educ:* Cardinal Vaughan Sch., Kensington; Christ's Coll., Cambridge. Priest, 1946. Teaching, St Peter's Coll., Freshfield, 1950–55; missionary work in Dio. of Kisumu, Kenya, 1955–63; Superior General of St Joseph's Missionary Society of Mill Hill, 1963–70. *Address:* 34 Whitehall Gardens, Acton, W3 9RD.

MAHON, Sir (John) Denis, Kt 1986; CBE 1967; MA Oxon; FBA 1964; Art Historian; Trustee of the National Gallery, 1957–64 and 1966–73; Member, Advisory Panel, National Art-Collections Fund, since 1975; *b* 8 Nov. 1910; *s* of late John FitzGerald Mahon (4th *s* of Sir W. Mahon, 4th Bt) and Lady Alice Evelyn Browne (*d* 1970), *d* of 5th Marquess of Sligo. *Educ:* Eton; Christ Church, Oxford. Has specialised in the study of 17th-Century painting in Italy and has formed a collection of pictures of the period; is a member of the Cttee of the Biennial Exhibitions at Bologna, Italy; was awarded, 1957, Medal for Benemeriti della Cultura by Pres. of Italy for services to criticism and history of Italian art; Archiginnasio d'Oro, City of Bologna, 1968; Serena Medal for Italian Studies, British Acad., 1972. Elected Accademico d'Onore, Clementine Acad., Bologna, 1964; Sen. Fellow, RCA, 1988; Corresp. Fellow: Accad. Raffaello, Urbino, 1968; Deputazione di Storia Patria per le provincie di Romagna, 1969. Ateneo Veneto, 1987. Hon. Citizen, Cento, 1982. Hon. DLitt, Newcastle, 1969. *Publications:* Studies in Seicento Art and Theory, 1947; Mostra dei Carracci, Catalogo critico dei Disegni, 1956 (1963); Poussiniana, 1962; Catalogues of the Mostra del Guercino (Dipinti, 1968; Disegni, 1969); (with Nicholas Turner) The Drawings of Guercino in the Collection of Her Majesty the Queen at Windsor Castle, 1989; contributed to: Actes of Colloque Poussin, 1960; Friedlaender Festschrift, 1965; Problemi Guardeschi, 1967; (consultant) Luigi Salerno, I Dipinti del Guercino, 1988; articles, including a number on Caravaggio and Poussin, in art-historical periodicals, *eg,* The Burlington Magazine, Apollo, The Art Bulletin, Journal of the Warburg and Courtauld Institutes, Bulletin of the Metropolitan Museum of New York, Gazette des Beaux-Arts, Art de France, Paragone, Commentari, Zeitschrift für Kunstwissenschaft; has collaborated in the compilation of catalogues raisonnés of exhibitions, *eg,* Artists in 17th Century Rome (London, 1955), Italian Art and Britain (Royal Academy, 1960), L'Ideale Classico del Seicento in Italia (Bologna, 1962), Omaggio al Guercino (Cento, 1967). *Address:* 33 Cadogan Square, SW1X 0HU. *T:* 071–235 7311, 071–235 2530.

MAHON, Peter, JP; *b* 4 May 1909; *s* of late Alderman Simon Mahon, OBE, JP, Bootle, Liverpool; *m* 1935, Margaret Mahon (*née* Hannon). *Educ:* St James Elementary Sch.; St Edward's Coll. (Irish Christian Brothers). One of the longest serving Local Govt representatives in GB (42 years); Bootle Borough Council, 1933–70 (Mayor, 1954–55); Liverpool City Council, 1970–75; Liverpool DC, 1973–80 (Mem. (L) Old Swan Ward); Chm. or Dep. Chm. numerous cttees; Mem. Nat. Cttee of TGWU. Prospective Parly Candidate (Lab) Blackburn, 1952–54, contested (Lab) Preston, 1962–64; MP (Lab) Preston South, 1964–70; contested Liverpool Scotland, April 1971, as first Against Abortion candidate in UK; expelled from Labour Party. Talked out first Abortion Bill, House of Commons, 1966. *Recreations:* football and swimming enthusiast; fond of music. *Address:* Seahaven, Burbo Bank Road, Blundellsands, Liverpool L23 8TA.

MAHON, Colonel Sir William (Walter), 7th Bt *cr* 1819 (UK), of Castlegar, Co. Galway; *b* 4 Dec. 1940; *s* of Sir George Edward John Mahon, 6th Bt and Audrey Evelyn (*née* Jagger) (*d* 1957); *S* father, 1987; *m* 1968, Rosemary Jane, *yr d* of Lt-Col M. E. Melvill, OBE, Symington, Lanarks; one *s* two *d*. *Educ:* Eton. *Recreations:* shooting, watercolours, collecting, military history. *Heir: s* James Willliam Mahon, *b* 29 Oct. 1976.

MAHONEY, Dennis Leonard; Chairman, Alexander Howden, since 1984; Joint Chairman, Alexander Howden Group, since 1984; *b* 20 Sept. 1950; *s* of late Frederick Mahoney; *m* 1st, Julia McLaughlin (marr. diss.); one *s* one *d*; 2nd, 1988, Jacqueline Fox; one *s* one *d*. *Educ:* West Hatch Technical High School. Broker; Managing Dir, Sedgwick Forbes N America, 1979; Dep. Chm., Sedgwick Forbes N America and Dir, Sedgwick Ltd, 1982. *Recreations:* ski-ing, shooting. *Address:* Alexander Howden Ltd, 8 Devonshire Square, EC2M 4QR.

MAHONEY, Rev. Prof. John Aloysius, (Jack), SJ; F. D. Maurice Professor of Moral and Social Theology, University of London at King's College, since 1986; Mercers' School Memorial Professor of Commerce, Gresham College London, since 1988; Founding Director, King's College Business Ethics Research Centre, since 1987; *b* Coatbridge, 14 Jan. 1931; *s* of Patrick Mahoney and Margaret Cecilia Mahoney (*née* Doris). *Educ:* Our Lady's High Sch., Motherwell; St Aloysius' Coll., Glasgow; Univ. of Glasgow (MA 1951). LicPhil 1956; LicTheol 1963; DTheol *summa cum laude,* Pontifical Gregorian Univ., Rome, 1967. Entered Society of Jesus, 1951; ordained priest, 1962; Jesuit Tertianship, NY, 1963–64. Lect in Moral and Pastoral Theology, Heythrop Coll., Oxon, 1967–70, and Heythrop Coll., London, 1970–86; Principal, Heythrop Coll., London, 1976–81; Dean, Faculty of Theol., London Univ., and Faculty of Theol. and Religious Studies, KCL, 1990–. Martin D'Arcy Meml Lectr, Campion Hall, Oxford, 1981–82. Mem., Internat. Theol. Commn, Rome, 1974–80; Sector Pres., Nat. Pastoral Congress, 1980; Mem., Internat. Study Gp on Bioethics, Internat. Fedn of Catholic Univs. 1984–. Pres., Catholic Theolog. Assoc., 1984–86. Chaplain to Tablet Table, 1983–; Domestic Chaplain to Lord Mayor of London, 1989–90. FRSA. Founding Editor, Business Ethics, A European Review, 1992–. *Publications:* Seeking the Spirit, 1981; Bioethics and Belief, 1984; The Making of Moral Theology, 1987; The Ways of Wisdom, 1987; Teaching Business Ethics in the UK, Europe and USA, 1990. *Recreations:* piano, sketching, unrequited golf. *Address:* Farm Street Church, 114 Mount Street, W1Y 6AH. *T:* 071–493 7811.

MAHONY, Francis Joseph, CB 1980; OBE 1972; President, Repatriation Review Tribunal, Australia, 1979–84; *b* 15 March 1915; *s* of Cornelius J. Mahony and Angela M. Heagney; *m* 1939, Mary K. Sexton; seven *s* one *d*. *Educ:* De La Salle Coll., Armidale; Sydney Univ. (LLB 1940). Served War, CMF and AIF, 1942–44. Called to the Bar, Supreme Court of NSW, 1940; Commonwealth Crown Solicitor's Office, 1941; admitted Practitioner, High Ct of Australia, 1950; admitted Solicitor, Supreme Ct of NSW, 1952; Dep. Commonwealth Crown Solicitor, NSW, 1963–70; Dep. Sec., Attorney-Gen.'s Dept, Canberra, 1970–79. Leader, Aust. Delegn to Diplomatic Conf. on Humanitarian Law Applicable in Armed Conflicts, 1974–77. Chairman: Criminology Res. Council, 1972–79; Bd of Management, Aust. Inst. of Criminology, 1973–79; Mem. UN Cttee, Crime Prevention and Control, 1980–83. *Recreation:* golf. *Address:* 92 Cliff Avenue, Northbridge, NSW 2063, Australia. *T:* (02) 958 7853. *Club:* Northbridge Golf.

MAHY, Brian Wilfred John, PhD, ScD; Director, Division of Viral and Rickettsial Diseases, Centers for Disease Control, Atlanta, since 1989; *b* 7 May 1937; *s* of Wilfred Mahy and Norah Dillingham; *m* 1st, 1959, Valerie Pouteaux (marr. diss. 1986); two *s* one *d*; 2nd, 1988, Penny Scott (*née* Cunningham). *Educ:* Elizabeth Coll., Guernsey; Univ. of Southampton (BSc, PhD); Univ. of Cambridge (MA, ScD). Res. Biologist, Dept of Cancer Res., London Hosp. Med. Coll., Univ. of London, 1962–65; Asst Dir, Res. Virology, Dept of Pathology, Cambridge Univ., 1965–79; Fellow and Tutor, University (Wolfson) Coll., 1967–75; Librarian, Wolfson Coll., 1975–80; Huddersfield Lectr in Special Path. (Virology), 1979–84; Head, Div. of Virology, Cambridge, 1979–84; Head, Pirbright Lab., AFRC Inst. for Animal Health (formerly Animal Virus Res. Inst. and AFRC Inst. for Animal Disease Res.), 1984–89. Vis. Prof., Univ. of Minnesota, 1968; Eleanor Roosevelt Internat. Cancer Fellow, Dept of Microbiol., Univ. of California, San Francisco, 1973–74; Vis. Prof., Inst. für Virologie, Univ. of Würzburg, 1980–81. Convener, Virus Group, 1980–84, Mem. Council, 1983–87, Soc. for General Microbiology; Vice-Chm., 1987–90, Chm., 1990–, Virology Div., Internat. Union of Microbiol Socs. FRSocMed 1985. *Publications:* (jtly) The Biology of Large RNA Viruses, 1970; Negative Strand Viruses, 1975; Negative Strand Virus and the Host Cell, 1978; Lactic Dehydrogenase Virus, 1975. A Dictionary of Virology, 1981; Virus Persistence, 1982; The Microbe 1984: pt 1, Viruses, 1984; Virology: a practical approach, 1985; The Biology of Negative Strand Viruses, 1987; Genetics and Pathogenicity of Negative Strand Viruses, 1989; numerous articles on animal virology in learned jls. *Recreations:* playing the violin in chamber and orchestral groups, gardening. *Address:* Division of Viral and Rickettsial Diseases (A30), Centers for Disease Control, 1600 Clifton Road, NE, Atlanta, Ga 30333, USA.

MAHY, Margaret May; writer; *b* 21 March 1936; *d* of Francis George Mahy and Helen May Penlington; two *d*. *Educ:* Whakatane Primary and High Schs; Univ. of NZ (BA). Asst Librarian, Petone Public Library, 1959; Asst Children's Librarian, Christchurch Public Library, 1960; Librarian i/c of school requests, Sch. Library Service (Christchurch Br.), 1967; Children's Librarian, Christchurch Public Library, 1977; full time writer, 1980–. Carnegie Medal, 1982, 1984; Esther Glen Medal. *Publications: picture books:* The Dragon of an Ordinary Family, 1969; A Lion in the Meadow, 1969; Mrs Discombobulous, 1969; Pillycock's Shop, 1969; The Procession, 1969; The Little Witch, 1970; Sailor Jack and the Twenty Orphans, 1970; The Princes and the Clown, 1971; The Boy with Two Shadows, 1971; The Man whose Mother was a Pirate, 1972; The Railway Engine and the Hairy Brigands, 1973; Rooms for Rent/Rooms to Let, 1974; The Witch in the Cherry Tree, 1974; The Rare Spotted Birthday Party, 1974; Stepmother, 1974; The Ultra-Violet Catastrophe, 1975; The Great Millionaire Kidnap, 1975; The Wind Between the Stars, 1976; David's Witch Doctor, 1976; The Boy who was Followed Home, 1977; Leaf Magic, 1976; Jam, 1985; *collections of stories:* three Margaret Mahy Story Books, 1972, 1973, 1975; Nonstop Nonsense, 1977; The Great Piratical Rumbustification and The Librarian and the Robbers, 1978; The Chewing-Gum Rescue, 1982; The Birthday Burglar and a Very Wicked Headmistress, 1984; Ups and Downs, 1984; Wibble Wobble, 1984; The Dragon's Birthday, 1984; The Spider in the Shower, 1984; The Downhill Crocodile Whizz, 1986; Mahy Magic, 1986; The Three Wishes, 1986; The Door in the Air, 1988; *junior novels:* Clancy's Cabin, 1974; The Bus Under the Leaves, 1975; The Pirate Uncle, 1977; Raging Robots and Unruly Uncles, 1981; The Pirates' Mixed-Up Voyage, 1983; The Blood and Thunder Adventure on Hurricane Peak, 1989; *novels for older readers:* The Haunting, 1982; The Changeover, 1984; The Catalogue of the Universe, 1985; Aliens in the Family, 1986; The Tricksters, 1986; Memory, 1987; *for schools:* The Crocodile's Christmas Jandals, 1982; The Bubbling Crocodile, 1983; Mrs Bubble's Baby, 1983; Shopping with a Crocodile, 1983; Going to the Beach, 1984; The Great Grumbler and the Wonder Tree, 1984; Fantail Fantail, 1984; A Crocodile in the Garden, 1985; The Crocodile's Christmas Thongs, 1985; Horrakapotchin, 1985; *for emergent readers:* The Adventures of a Kite, 1985; Sophie's Singing Mother, 1985; The Earthquake, 1985; The Cake, 1985; The Catten, 1985; Out in the Big Wild World, 1985; A Vary Happy Bathday, 1985; Clever Hamburger, 1985; Muppy's Ball, 1986; Baby's Breakfast, 1986; The Tree Doctor, 1986; The Garden Party, 1986; The Man who Enjoyed Grumbling, 1986; The Trouble with Heathrow, 1986; The Pop Group, 1986; Feeling Funny, 1986; A Pet to the Vet, 1986; The New House Villain, 1986; Tai Taylor is Born, 1986; The Terrible Topsy-Turvy Tissy-Tossy Tangle, 1986; Trouble on the Bus, 1986; Mr Rumfitt, 1986; My Wonderful Aunt, 1986; *verse:* Seventeen Kings and Forty-Two Elephants, 1972; *non-fiction:* Look Under 'V', 1977. *Recreations:* reading, gardening. *Address:* No 1 RD, Lyttelton, New Zealand. *T:* 03.299703.

MAIDEN, Colin James, ME, DPhil; Vice-Chancellor, University of Auckland, New Zealand, since 1971; *b* 5 May 1933; *s* of Henry A. Maiden; *m* 1957, Jenefor Mary Rowe; one *s* three *d*. *Educ:* Auckland Grammar Sch.; Univ. of Auckland, NZ; Oxford Univ. ME(NZ), DPhil (Oxon). Post-doctorate research, Oxford Univ., Oxford, Eng. (supported by AERE, Harwell), 1957–58; Head of Hypersonic Physics Section, Canadian Armament Research and Develt Estabt, Quebec City, Canada, 1958–60; Sen. Lectr in Mechanical Engrg, Univ. of Auckland, 1960–61; Head of Material Sciences Laboratory, Gen. Motors Corp., Defense Research Laboratories, Santa Barbara, Calif, USA, 1961–66; Manager of Process Engineering, Gen. Motors Corp., Technl Centre, Warren, Michigan, USA, 1966–70. Chairman: NZ Synthetic Fuels Corp. Ltd, 1980–90; National Insurance Co. of NZ Ltd, 1988–; Fisher & Paykel Ltd, 1978–; Director: Mason Industries Ltd, 1971–78; Farmers Trading Co. Ltd, 1973–86; Wilkins & Davies Co. Ltd, 1986–89; Winstone Ltd, 1978–88; NZ Steel Ltd, 1988–; Independent Newspapers Ltd, 1989–; ANZ Banking Gp (NZ) Ltd, 1990–. Chairman: NZ Energy R&D Cttee, 1974–81; Liquid Fuels Trust Bd, 1978–86; Chm., NZ Vice-Chancellors' Cttee, 1977–78; Hon. Treasurer, ACU, 1988–. Member: Spirit of Adventure Trust Bd, 1972–80; NZ Metric Adv. Bd, 1973–77. NZ Agent for Joint NZ/US Sci. and Technol Agreement, 1974–81. Thomson Medal, Royal Soc. NZ, 1986; Medal, Univ. of Bonn, 1983. *Publications:* numerous scientific and technical papers. *Recreation:* tennis. *Address:* 7 Chatfield Place, Remuera, Auckland, New Zealand. *T:* (09) 529 0380. *Clubs:* Vincent's (Oxford); Northern, Rotary (Auckland); Remuera Racquets, Eden Epsom Tennis, International Lawn Tennis of NZ, Auckland Golf.

MAIDEN, Robert Mitchell, FIB(Scot); Managing Director, Royal Bank of Scotland plc, and Executive Director, Royal Bank of Scotland Group plc, 1986–91; *b* 15 Sept. 1933; *s* of Harry and Georgina Maiden; *m* 1958, Margaret Mercer (*née* Nicolson). *Educ:* Montrose Acad., Tayside, Scotland. Royal Bank of Scotland: various appts, 1950–74; Supt of branches, 1974–76; Treasurer, 1976–77; Chief Accountant, 1977–81; Gen. Man. (Finance), 1981–82; Exec. Dir, 1982–86. FBIM. *Recreations:* music, golf, reading, hill walking. *Address:* Trinafour, 7 Bonaly Road, Edinburgh EH13 0EB. *Club:* New (Edinburgh).

MAIDMENT, Francis Edward, (Ted); Headmaster, Shrewsbury School, since 1988; *b* 23 Aug. 1942; *s* of Charles Edward and late Olive Mary Maidment. *Educ:* Pocklington Sch., York; Jesus Coll., Cambridge (Scholar). Asst Master, Lancing Coll., 1965–81 (Housemaster, 1975–81); Headmaster, Ellesmere Coll., Shropshire, 1982–88. *Recreations:* singing, medieval history, modest tennis. *Address:* Shrewsbury School, Shropshire SY3 9BA. *T:* Shrewsbury (0743) 4537.

MAIDMENT, Ted; *see* Maidment, F. E.

MAIDSTONE, Viscount; Daniel James Hatfield Finch Hatton; nurse in community for mentally handicapped adults; *b* 7 Oct. 1967; *s* and *heir* of 16th Earl of Winchilsea, *qv*.

Educ: Ansford Comprehensive School, Castle Cary, Som. *Recreations:* swimming, sport. *Address:* South Cadbury House, near Yeovil, Somerset.

MAIDSTONE, Bishop Suffragan of, since 1987; **Rt. Rev. David James Smith;** Bishop to the Forces, since 1990; *b* 14 July 1935; *s* of Stanley James and Gwendolen Emie Smith; *m* 1961, Mary Hunter Moult; one *s* one *d. Educ:* Hertford Grammar School; King's College, London (AKC). Assistant Curate: All Saints, Gosforth, 1959–62; St Francis, High Heaton, 1962–64; Long Benton, 1964–68; Vicar: Longhirst with Hebron, 1968–75; St Mary, Monkseaton, 1975–81; Felton, 1982–83; Archdeacon of Lindisfarne, 1981–87. *Recreations:* fell walking, reading science fiction. *Address:* Bishop's House, Pett Lane, Charing, Ashford, Kent TN27 0DL. *T:* Charing (023371) 2950.

MAIDSTONE, Archdeacon of; *see* Evans, Ven. P. A. S.

MAILER, Norman; *b* 31 Jan. 1923; *s* of Isaac Barnett Mailer and Fanny Schneider; *m* 1st, 1944, Beatrice Silverman (marr. diss., 1951); one *d*; 2nd, 1954, Adèle Morales (marr. diss., 1962); two *d*; 3rd, 1962, Lady Jeanne Campbell (marr. diss., 1963); one *d*; 4th, 1963, Beverly Bentley; two *s*; 5th, Carol Stevens; one *d*; 6th, Norris Church; one *s. Educ:* Harvard. Infantryman, US Army, 1944–46. Co-founder of Village Voice, 1955; an Editor of Dissent, 1953–63. Democratic Candidate, Mayoral Primaries, New York City, 1969. Directed films: Wild 90, 1967; Beyond the Law, 1967; Maidstone, 1968; Tough Guys Don't Dance, 1988. Pulitzer Prize for Fiction, 1980. *Publications:* The Naked and the Dead, 1948; Barbary Shore, 1951; The Deer Park, 1955 (dramatized, 1967); Advertisements for Myself, 1959; Deaths For The Ladies, 1962; The Presidential Papers, 1963; An American Dream, 1964; Cannibals and Christians, 1966; Why Are We In Vietnam?, 1967 (a novel); The Armies of the Night, 1968 (Pulitzer Prize, 1969); Miami and the Siege of Chicago, 1968 (National Book Award, 1969); Of a Fire on the Moon, 1970; The Prisoner of Sex, 1971; Existential Errands, 1972; St George and the Godfather, 1972; Marilyn, 1973; The Faith of Graffiti, 1974; The Fight, 1975; Some Honorable Men, 1975; Genius and Lust, 1976; A Transit to Narcissus, 1978; The Executioner's Song, 1979; Of a Small and Modest Malignancy, Wicked and Bristling with Dots, 1980; Of Women and Their Elegance, 1980; The Essential Mailer, 1982; Ancient Evenings, 1983; Tough Guys Don't Dance, 1984. *Address:* c/o Rembar, 19 W 44th Street, New York, NY 10036, USA.

MAILLART, Ella (Kini); traveller; *b* 20 Feb. 1903; Swiss father and Danish mother; unmarried. *Educ:* Geneva; and also while teaching French at two schools in England. Took to the seas at 20, cruising with 3 ton Perlette, 10 ton Bonita, 45 ton Atalante-all these manned by girls; then 120 ton Volunteer, 125 ton Insoumise; in Mediterranean, Biscay, Channel; sailed for Switzerland, Olympic Games, Paris, 1924, single-handed competition; hockey for Switzerland as captain in 1931; skied for Switzerland in the FIS races in 1931–34; went to Russia for 6 months, 1930; travelled in Russian Turkestan for 6 months 1932; went to Manchoukuo for Petit Parisien, 1934; returned overland accompanied by Peter Fleming, via Koko Nor; travelled overland to Iran and Afghanistan in 1937 and 1939, in South India, 1940–45, Nepal, 1951, Everest Base Camp, 1965. Fellow RGS, London; Member: Royal Soc. for Asian Affairs; Club des Explorateurs, Paris; Hon. Mem., GB-China Centre. Sir Percy Sykes Medal. *Publications:* Parmi la Jeunesse Russe, 1932; Des Monts Célestes aux Sables Rouges, 1934 (in English as Turkestan Solo, 1934, repr. 1985); Oasis Interdites, 1937 (in English as Forbidden Journey, 1937, repr. 1983); Gipsy Afloat, 1942; Cruises and Caravans, 1942; The Cruel Way, 1947, repr. 1986; Ti-Puss, 1952; The Land of the Sherpas, 1955. *Recreations:* ski-ing, gardening. *Address:* 10 Avenue G. Vallette, 1206 Geneva, Switzerland. *T:* Geneva 46.46.57; Atchala, Chandolin sur Sierre, Switzerland. *Clubs:* Kandahar, (hon.) Ski Club of Great Britain; (hon.) Alpine.

MAIN, Frank Fiddes, CB 1965; FRCPEd; Chief Medical Officer, Ministry of Health and Social Services, Northern Ireland, 1954–68, retired; *b* 9 June 1905; *s* of Frank and Mary Main, Edinburgh; *m* 1931, Minnie Roberta Paton; two *s* two *d. Educ:* Daniel Stewart's Coll., Edinburgh; Edinburgh Univ. MB, ChB 1927; DPH 1931; MRCPEd 1954; FRCPEd 1956. Medical Officer of Health, Perth, 1937–48; Senior Administrative Medical Officer, Eastern Regional Hosp. Bd (Scotland), 1948–54. Crown Mem., Gen. Med. Council, 1956–69. QHP 1956–59. *Recreation:* golf. *Address:* 8 Argyle Court, Argyle Street, St Andrews, Fife KY16 9BX. *T:* St Andrews (0334) 78527.

MAIN, John Roy, QC 1974; **His Honour Judge Main;** a Circuit Judge, since 1976; *b* 21 June 1930; *yr s* of late A. C. Main, MIMechE; *m* 1955, Angela de la Condamine Davies, *er d* of late R. W. H. Davies, ICS; two *s* one *d. Educ:* Portsmouth Grammar Sch.; Hotchkiss Sch., USA; Brasenose Coll., Oxford (MA). Called to Bar, Inner Temple, 1954; a Recorder of Crown Court, 1972–76. Mem. Special Panel, Transport Tribunal, 1970–76; Dep. Chm., IoW QS, 1971. Gov., Portsmouth Grammar Sch., 1988–. *Recreations:* walking, gardening, music. *Address:* 4 Queen Anne Drive, Claygate, Surrey KT10 0PP. *T:* Esher (0372) 466380.

MAIN, Sir Peter (Tester), Kt 1985; ERD 1964; Director, 1985–91, Vice-Chairman, 1990–91, W. A. Baxter and Sons Ltd; Member, Scottish Development Agency, 1986–91; *b* 21 March 1925; *s* of late Peter Tester Main and Esther Paterson (*née* Lawson); *m* 1st, 1952, Dr Margaret Fimister, MB, ChB (*née* Tweddle) (*d* 1984); two *s* one *d*; 2nd, 1986, May Hetherington Anderson (*née* McMillan). *Educ:* Robert Gordon's Coll., Aberdeen; Univ. of Aberdeen (MB, ChB 1948, MD 1963; Hon. LLD 1986). MRCPE 1981, FRCPE 1982. Captain, RAMC, 1949–51; MO with Field Ambulance attached to Commando Bde, Suez, 1956; Lt-Col RAMC (AER), retd 1964. House Surg., Aberdeen Royal Infirmary, 1948; House Physician, Woodend Hosp., Aberdeen, 1949; Demonstrator, Univ. of Durham, 1952; gen. practice, 1953–57; joined Res. Dept, Boots, 1957; Dir of Res., 1968; Man. Dir, Industrial Div., 1979–80; Dir, 1973–85, Vice-Chm., 1980–81, Chm., 1982–85, The Boots Company PLC. Chm., Inveresk Res. Internat., 1986–89; Dir, John Fleming and Co., 1985–89. Chm., Cttee of Inquiry into Teachers' Pay and Conditions, Scotland, 1986; Member: NEDC, 1984–85; Scottish Health Service Policy Board, 1985–88. Governor, Henley Management Coll., 1983–86; Chm., Grantown Heritage Trust, 1987–; Trustee, Univ. of Aberdeen Develt Trust, 1988–. CBIM (FBIM 1978). *Recreations:* fly fishing, Scottish music. *Address:* Lairig Ghru, Dulnain Bridge, Grantown-on-Spey, Moray PH26 3NT. *Clubs:* Naval and Military.

MAINES, James Dennis, CEng, FIEE; Director General, Guided Weapons and Electronics Systems, Ministry of Defence, since 1988; *b* 26 July 1937; *s* of Arthur Burtonwood Maines and Lilian Maines (*née* Carter); *m* 1960, Janet Enid Kemp; three *s. Educ:* Leigh Grammar School; City University (BSc). Joined RSRE (then RRE), Malvern, 1956 (Sandwich course in applied physics, 1956–60); Head of Guided Weapons Optics and Electronics Group, 1981; Head, Microwave and Electro-optics Group, 1983; Head, Sensors, Electronic Warfare and Guided Weapons, ARE, Portsdown, 1984–86; Dep. Dir (Mission Systems), RAE, 1986–88. Wolfe Award for outstanding MoD research (jtly), 1973. *Publications:* contrib. to Surface Wave Filters (ed Matthews), 1977; papers in learned jls. *Recreations:* sailing, cricket, squash, painting, non-labour intensive gardening. *Address:* Ministry of Defence, Fleetbank House, 2–6 Salisbury Square, EC4Y 8AT. *Club:* Civil Service Sailing.

MAINGARD de la VILLE ès OFFRANS, Sir (Louis Pierre) René, (Sir René Maingard), Kt 1982; CBE 1961; company chairman and director, Mauritius; Chairman, Colonial Steamships Co. Ltd, since 1948; *b* 9 July 1917; *s* of Joseph René Maingard de la Ville ès Offrans and Véronique Hugnin; *m* 1946, Marie Hélène Françoise Raffray; three *d. Educ:* St Joseph's Coll.; Royal Coll. of Mauritius; Business Training Corp., London. Clerk, Rogers & Co. Ltd, 1936, Man. Dir, 1948. Chairman: Rogers & Co. Ltd, 1956–82; Mauritius Steam Navigation Co. Ltd, 1964–; Mauritius Portland Cement Co. Ltd, 1960–; De Chazal du Mée Associates Ltd, 1982–. Director: Mauritius Commercial Bank Ltd, 1956–; New Mauritius Dock Co. Ltd, 1948–. Formerly, Consul for Finland in Mauritius. Chevalier 1st Cl., Order of the White Rose, Finland, 1973. *Recreations:* golf, fishing, boating. *Address:* Rogers & Co. Ltd, PO Box 60, Port Louis, Mauritius. *T:* 08 68 01. *Clubs:* Royal Air Force; Dodo, Mauritius Naval & Military Gymkhana (Mauritius).

MAINI, Sir Amar (Nath), Kt 1957; CBE 1953 (OBE 1948); *b* Nairobi, 31 July 1911; *e s* of late Nauhria Ram Maini, Nairobi, Kenya, and Ludhiana, Punjab, India; *m* 1935, Ram Saheli Mehra (*d* 1982), Ludhiana; two *s. Educ:* Govt Indian Sch., Nairobi; London Sch. of Economics (BCom, Hons 1932). Barrister-at-law, Middle Temple, London, 1933. Advocate of High Court of Kenya, and of High Court of Uganda. Sometime an actg MLC, Kenya, and Mem. Nairobi Municipal Council. From 1939 onwards, in Uganda; associated with family cotton business of Nauhria Ram & Sons (Uganda) Ltd. Formerly: Mem. Kampala Township Authority, Chm., Kampala Municipal Council, 1st Mayor of Kampala (1950–55); Dep. Chm., Uganda Electricity Board; Member: Uganda Development Corporation; Lint Marketing Board; Civil Defence Bd; Asian Manpower Cttee; Transport Bd; Supplies Bd; Immigration Advisory Bd; Advisory Bd of Health; Railway Advisory Council; Advisory Bd of Commerce; Rent Restriction Bd; Makerere Coll. Assembly, etc. Past Pres. Central Council of Indian Assocs in Uganda; Indian Assoc., Kampala; served on Cttees of Cotton Association. Formerly: Mem. Uganda Legislative and Exec. Councils; Development Council, Uganda; EA Legislative Assembly; EA Postal Advisory Bd; EA Transport Adv. Council; EA Air Adv Council, etc. Minister for Corporations and Regional Communications in the Government of Uganda, 1955–58; Minister of Commerce and Industry in Uganda, 1958–61; Speaker, E African Central Legislative Assembly, 1961–67; Mem., E African Common Market Tribunal, 1967–69. Dep. Chm. Kenya Broadcasting Corp., 1962–63. *Recreations:* walking, listening. *Address:* 55 Vicarage Road, East Sheen, SW14 8RY. *T:* 081–878 1497. *Clubs:* Reform; Nairobi.

MAINWARING, Captain Maurice K. C.; *see* Cavenagh-Mainwaring.

MAIR, Prof. Alexander; FRSE 1980; Professor of Community and Occupational Medicine (formerly of Public Health and Social Medicine), University of Dundee, 1954–82, now Emeritus; *m* 1945, Nancy Waddington; two *s* one *d. Educ:* Aberdeen Univ. MB, ChB, 1942, DPH, 1948, MD (Hons), 1952 (Aberdeen); DIH (London) 1955; FRCPE 1966; FFCM 1976; FFOM 1979. RAMC 1942–46. Lecturer, Univ. of Aberdeen, 1948–52; Senior Lecturer, Univ. of St Andrews, at Dundee, 1952–54. Formerly Founder and Dir, Scottish Occupational Health Laboratory Service, Ltd; Member: Steering Cttee, East of Scotland Occupational Health Service; Nat. Adv. Cttee for Employment of Disabled; Asbestos Adv. Cttee, 1976–; Adv. Cttee, Health and Safety Exec., 1976–82; Industrial Injuries Adv. Council, 1977–82; formerly Chm., Scottish Cttee for Welfare of Disabled and Sub-Cttee on Rehabilitation; Consultant, Occupational Health, to RN in Scotland. First Chm., British Soc. for Agriculture Labour Science. Occasional consultant to WHO, Geneva. Hon. FIOH 1989. *Publications:* Student Health Services in Great Britain and Northern Ireland, 1966; (jointly) Custom and Practice in Medical Care, 1968; Hospital and Community II, 1969; Sir James Mackenzie, MD, 1973 (Abercrombie Award); contrib.: Cerebral Palsy in Childhood and Adolescence, 1961; Further Studies in Hospital and Community, 1962; numerous publications on Researches into Occupational Diseases, especially Silicosis, Byssinosis, etc. *Address:* Tree Tops, Castle Roy, Broughty Ferry, Angus. *T:* Dundee (0382) 78727. *Club:* Caledonian.

MAIR, Alexander, MBE 1967; Chief Executive and Director, Grampian Television Ltd, 1970–87, retired; *b* 5 Nov. 1922; *s* of Charles Mair and Helen Dickie; *m* 1953, Margaret Isobel Gowans Rennie. *Educ:* Skene, Aberdeenshire; Webster's Business Coll., Aberdeen; Sch. of Accountancy, Glasgow. Associate, CIMA, 1953. Chief Accountant, Bydand Holdings Ltd, 1957–60; Company Sec., Grampian Television, 1961–70; apptd Dir, 1967; Director: ITN, 1980–87; Cablevision (Scotland) Ltd, 1983–88; TV Publication Ltd, 1970–87. Chairman: British Regional Television Assoc., 1973–75; ITCA Management Cttee, 1980–84; Robert Gordon Inst. of Technol. Offshore Survival Centre Ltd, 1989–. Pres., Aberdeen Junior Chamber of Commerce, 1960–61; Mem. Council, Aberdeen Chamber of Commerce, 1973– (Vice-Pres., 1987–89; Pres., 1989–91). Gov., Robert Gordon's Coll., Aberdeen, 1987–. FRSA 1973. FRTS 1987. *Recreations:* golf, ski-ing, gardening. *Address:* Ravenswood, 66 Rubislaw Den South, Aberdeen AB2 6AX. *T:* Aberdeen (0224) 317619. *Club:* Royal Northern (Aberdeen).

MAIR, John Magnus; Director of Social Work, Edinburgh, 1969–75; Lecturer in Social Medicine, University of Edinburgh, 1959–75; *b* 29 Dec. 1912; *s* of Joseph Alexander Mair and Jane Anderson; *m* 1940, Isobelle Margaret Williamson (*d* 1969); three *s. Educ:* Anderson Inst., Lerwick; Univs of Aberdeen (MB, ChB) and Edinburgh (DPH). MFCM. Asst GP, Highlands and Islands Medical Service, 1937–40; RAMC, 1940–45; Edinburgh Public Health Dept (latterly Sen. Depute Medical Officer of Health), 1945–69. *Recreation:* golf. *Address:* 46 Allington Road, Hendon, NW4 3DE. *T:* 081–202 4186. *Clubs:* Edinburgh University Staff; Grampian (Corby).

MAIR, Prof. William Austyn, CBE 1969; MA; FEng 1984; Francis Mond Professor of Aeronautical Engineering, University of Cambridge, 1952–83; Head of Engineering Department, 1973–83; Fellow of Downing College, Cambridge, 1953–83, Hon. Fellow, 1983; *b* 24 Feb. 1917; *s* of William Mair, MD; *m* 1944, Mary Woodhouse Crofts; two *s. Educ:* Highgate Sch.; Clare Coll., Cambridge. Aerodynamics Dept, Royal Aircraft Establishment, Farnborough, 1940–46; Dir, Fluid Motion Laboratory, Univ. of Manchester, 1946–52. Mem. various cttees, Aeronautical Research Council, 1946–80. Dir, Hovercraft Development Ltd, 1962–81. John Orr Meml Lectr, S Africa, 1983. Chm., Editorial Bd, Aeronautical Qly, 1975–81. FRAeS (Silver Medal 1975). Hon. DSc Cranfield Inst. of Technology, 1990. *Publications:* papers on aerodynamics. *Address:* 74 Barton Road, Cambridge CB3 9LH. *T:* Cambridge (0223) 350137. *Club:* United Oxford & Cambridge University.

MAIS, family name of **Baron Mais.**

MAIS, Baron, *cr* 1967 (Life Peer); **Alan Raymond Mais,** GBE 1973 (OBE (mil.) 1944); TD 1944; ERD 1958; FEng 1977; DL; JP; Colonel; Director, Royal Bank of Scotland, 1969–81; Chairman, Peachey Property Corporation, 1977–81; *b* July 1911; *s* of late Capt. E. Mais, Mornington Court, Kensington; *m* 1936, Lorna Aline, *d* of late Stanley Aspinall Boardman, Addiscombe, Surrey; two *s* one *d. Educ:* Banister Court, Hants; Coll. of Estate Management, London Univ. Commissioned RARO, Royal West Kent Regt, 1929; transf. RE 1931; Major 1939, Lt-Col 1941, Col 1944; served War of 1939–45; France, BEF 1939–40 (despatches); Special Forces, MEF, Iraq and Persia, 1941–43 (despatches); Normandy and NW Europe, 1944–46 (OBE, despatches), wounded; CRE 56 Armd Div.,

TA, 1947–50; CO 101 Field Engr Regt, 1947–50, Hon. Col, 1950–63; Comd Eng Gp, AER, 1951–54; DDES, AER, 1954–58. Worked for Richard Costain and other cos on Civil Engrg Works at home and abroad, 1931–38; Private Practice, A. R. Mais & Partners, Structural Engineers & Surveyors, 1938–39 and 1946–48. Dir Trollope & Colls Ltd, Bldg and Civil Engrg contractors and subsid. cos, 1948–68, Chm. and Man. Dir 1963–68; Chairman: City of London Insurance Co. Ltd, 1970–77; Hay-MSL Consultants, 1969–81; Director: Nat. Commercial Bank of Scotland, 1966–69; Slag Reduction Co. Ltd, 1962–85. Member: EDC Cttee for Constructional Industry, 1964–68; Marshall Aid Commemoration Commn, 1964–74. Treasurer: Royal Masonic Hosp., 1973–86; Fellowship of Engrg, 1977–81. City University: Mem., Court and Council, 1965–; Chancellor, 1972–73; Pro-Chancellor, 1979–84. Governor, The Hon. Irish Soc., 1978–80. Lieut, City of London, 1963–81; Alderman, Ward of Walbrook, 1963–81; Sheriff, 1969–70; Lord Mayor of London, 1972–73. JP London (City Bench), 1963–83; DL: Co. London (later Greater London), 1951–76; Kent, 1976–. Master: Cutlers' Co., 1968–69; Paviors' Co., 1975–76; Marketors' Co., 1983–84. FICE 1953 (Hon. FICE 1975); FIStructE, MSocCE (France), FIArb, FRICS. GCStJ 1987 (KStJ 1973). Hon. DSc: City, 1972; Ulster, 1981. Order of Patriotic War (1st class), USSR, 1942; Order of Aztec Eagle, Mexico, 1973; Order of Merit, Mexico, 1973. *Publications:* Yerbury Foundation Lecture, RIBA, 1960; Bossom Foundation Lecture, 1971. *Recreations:* family, Territorial Army. *Address:* Griffins, 43A Sundridge Avenue, Bromley, Kent. *Clubs:* City Livery, Army and Navy, London Welsh.

MAIS, Francis Thomas; Secretary, Royal Northern College of Music, 1982–90; *b* 27 June 1927; *s* of Charles Edward Mais and Emma (*née* McLoughlin); *m* 1st, Margaret Edythe Evans (*d* 1984); one *d*; 2nd, 1987, Joan Frost-Smith. *Educ:* Barnsley Grammar Sch.; Christ's Coll., Cambridge (MA). Northern Ireland Civil Service, 1951–82: Permanent Secretary: Dept of Commerce, 1979–81; Dept of Manpower Services, 1981–82. Governor, Associated Bd, Royal Schs of Music, 1985–. Hon. RNCM 1987. *Address:* The Old Smithy, Rosgill, Penrith, Cumbria CA10 2QX. *T:* Shap (09316) 413.

MAIS, Hon. Sir (Robert) Hugh, Kt 1971; Judge of the High Court of Justice, Queen's Bench Division, 1971–82; *b* 14 Sept. 1907; *s* of late Robert Stanley Oliver Mais, Chobham, Surrey; *m* 1938, Catherine (*d* 1987), *d* of J. P. Pattinson, *widow* of C. E. Kessler; one *s*, two step *s* (and one step *d* decd). *Educ:* Shrewsbury Sch.; Wadham Coll., Oxford (MA, 1948, Hon. Fellow, 1971). Called to the Bar, 1930, Bencher, Inner Temple, 1971; Mem. of Northern Circuit. Chancellor of the Diocese of: Manchester, 1948–71; Carlisle, 1950–71; Sheffield, 1950–71. Judge of County Courts: Circuit No 37 (West London), 1958–60; Circuit No 42 (Marylebone), 1960–71. Dep. Chm., Berkshire QS, 1964–71; Commissioner of Assize: SE Circuit, 1964, 1967; Oxford Circuit, 1968, 1969; NE Circuit, 1971. Mem., Winn Cttee on Personal Injuries Litigation. Served as Wing Comdr, RAF, 1940–44. *Recreations:* fishing, golf. *Address:* Ripton, Streatley-on-Thames, Berks RG8 9LE. *T:* Goring (0491) 872397.

MAISEY, Prof. Michael Norman, BSc, MD; FRCP; FRCR; Professor of Radiological Sciences, United Medical and Dental Schools of Guy's and St Thomas's Hospitals, since 1984; Consultant Physician in Endocrinology and Nuclear Medicine, Guy's Hospital, since 1973; *b* 10 June 1939; *s* of Harold Lionel Maisey and Kathleen Christine Maisey; *m* 1965, Irene Charlotte (*née* Askay); two *s*. *Educ:* Caterham Sch.; Guy's Hosp. Med. Sch. (BSc, MD). ABNM 1972; FRCP 1980. House appts, 1964–66; Registrar, Guy's Hosp., 1966–69; Fellow, Johns Hopkins Med. Instns, 1970–72; Sen. Registrar, Guy's Hosp., 1972–73. Hon. Consultant to the Army in Endocrinology and Nuclear Medicine, 1978–. *Publications:* Nuclear Medicine, 1980; Clinical Nuclear Medicine, 1982; books and papers on thyroid diseases and nuclear medicine. *Address:* Guy's Hospital, St Thomas Street, SE1 9RT. *T:* 071–955 9000.

MAISNER, Air Vice-Marshal Aleksander, CB 1977; CBE 1969; AFC 1955; *b* 26 July 1921; *s* of Henryk Maisner and Helene Anne (*née* Brosin); *m* 1946, Mary (*née* Coverley); one *s* one *d*. *Educ:* High Sch. and Lyceum, Czestochowa, Poland; Warsaw Univ. Labour Camps, USSR, 1940–41; Polish Artillery, 1941–42; Polish Air Force, 1943–46; joined RAF, 1946; Flying Trng Comd, 1946–49; No 70 Sqdn Suez Canal Zone, 1950–52; No 50 Sqdn RAF Binbrook, 1953–55; No 230 (Vulcan) OCU, RAF Waddington, 1955–59; psa 1960; OC Flying Wing, RNZAF Ohakea, 1961–62; Dirg Staff, RAF Staff Coll., Andover, 1963–65; DD Air Plans, MoD, 1965–68; CO, RAF Seletar, Singapore, 1969–71; Asst Comdt, RAF Coll., Cranwell, 1971–73; Dir, Personnel (Policy and Plans), MoD, 1973–75; Asst Air Sec., 1975; Dir-Gen. of Personnel Management, RAF, 1976. Personnel Exec., Reed Internat. Ltd, 1977–82; Dir, Industry and Parlt Trust, 1984–87. Governor, Shiplake Coll., 1978–. Pres., Polish Air Force Assoc., 1982–. Comdr's Cross with Star, Order of Polonia Restituta (Poland), 1990. *Recreations:* gardening, reading. *Address:* c/o Lloyds Bank, 1 Reading Road, Henley-on-Thames, Oxon RG9 1AE. *Club:* Royal Air Force.

MAISONROUGE, Jacques Gaston; management consultant; *b* Cachan, Seine, 20 Sept. 1924; *s* of Paul Maisonrouge and Suzanne (*née* Cazas); *m* 1948, Françoise Andrée Féron; one *s* four *d*. *Educ:* Lycée Voltaire and Saint Louis, Paris. Studied engineering; gained dip. of Ecole Centrale des Arts et Manufactures. Engineer, 1948; various subseq. appts in IBM Corp., France; Chm. and Chief Exec. Officer, IBM World Trade Europe/ME/Africa Corp., 1974–81; Pres., IBM Europe, 1974–81; Sen. Vice-Pres., 1972–84, and Mem. Bd of Dirs, 1983–84, IBM Corp.; Chm., IBM World Trade Corp., 1976–84; Vice Chm., Liquid Air Corp., 1984–86; Dir-Gen. of Industry, France, 1986–87; Chm. of Bd, French Centre for Foreign Trade, 1987–89. Chm., St Honoré Europe, 1989–; Director: L'Air Liquide, 1964–; Case Poclain, 1987–; IBM Europe/ME/Africa, 1987–. Chm., Bd of Trustees, Ecole Centrale des Arts et Manufactures, 1976–87; Chancellor, Internat. Acad. of Management, 1987–. Commander: Ordre de la Légion d'Honneur; Ordre National du Mérite; des Palmes Académiques; Order of Merit of the Italian Republic; Order of Saint Sylvester; Order of Star of North (Sweden); Grand Officer, Order of Malta. *Publication:* Inside IBM: a European's story, 1985. *Recreations:* interested in sport (tennis, riding). *Address:* 90 rue de la Faisanderie, 75116 Paris, France. *Club:* Automobile of France, Cercle Interallié.

MAITLAND, family name of **Earl of Lauderdale.**

MAITLAND, Viscount; Master of Lauderdale; **Ian Maitland;** Regional Manager, Middle East, National Westminster Bank, since 1975; *b* 4 Nov. 1937; *s* and *heir* of Earl of Lauderdale, *qv*; *m* 1963, Ann Paule, *d* of Geoffrey Clark; one *s* one *d*. *Educ:* Radley Coll., Abingdon; Brasenose Coll., Oxford (MA Modern History). Various appointments since 1960; with Hedderwick Borthwick & Co., 1970–74. Royal Naval Reserve (Lieutenant), 1963–73; Mem., Queen's Body Guard for Scotland, Royal Co. of Archers, 1986–. *Recreations:* photography, sailing. *Heir:* *s* Master of Maitland, *qv*. *Address:* 150 Tachbrook Street, SW1. *Clubs:* Overseas Bankers, Royal Ocean Racing; New (Edinburgh).

MAITLAND, Master of; Hon. John Douglas Maitland; *b* 29 May 1965; *s* and *heir* of Viscount Maitland, *qv*. *Educ:* Emanuel School; Radley College; Van Mildert College, Durham. *Recreations:* cycling, camping, sailing. *Address:* 150 Tachbrook Street, SW1.

MAITLAND, Alastair George, CBE 1966; Consul-General, Boston, 1971–75, retired; *b* 30 Jan. 1916; *s* of late Thomas Douglas Maitland, MBE, and Wilhelmina Sarah Dundas; *m* 1st, 1943, Betty Hamilton (*d* 1981); two *s* one *d*; 2nd, 1986, Hazel Margaret Porter. *Educ:* George Watson's Coll., Edinburgh; Universities of Edinburgh (MA First Class Hons), Grenoble and Paris, Ecole des Sciences Politiques. Vice-Consul: New York, 1938; Chicago, 1939; New York, 1939; Los Angeles, 1940; apptd to staff of UK High Commissioner at Ottawa, 1942; apptd to Foreign Office, 1945; Brit. Middle East Office, Cairo, 1948; Foreign Office, 1952; UK Delegation to OEEC, Paris, 1954; Consul-General: at New Orleans, 1958–62; at Jerusalem, 1962–64; at Cleveland, 1964–68; Dir-Gen., British Trade Develt Office, NY, 1968–71. Hon. LLD Lake Erie Coll., Ohio, 1971. CStJ. *Recreations:* music, golf, gardening, reading. *Address:* Box 31, Heath, Mass 01346, USA.

MAITLAND, David Henry, CVO 1988; non-executive director of companies; *b* 9 May 1922; *s* of George and Mary Annie Maitland; *m* 1955, Judeth Mary Gold; three *d*. *Educ:* Eton; King's College, Cambridge. FCA. Army, 1941–46, Captain, Oxf. & Bucks Light Inf. Articled Whinney Smith & Whinney, 1946; qualified ACA 1950; Mobil Oil Co., 1952–60; Save & Prosper Group: Comptroller, 1960; Managing Dir and Chief Exec., 1966; Chm., 1979; non-exec. Dir, 1981; retired 1987. Chm., Unit Trust Assoc., 1973–75; Member: City Capital Markets Cttee, 1975–84; Inflation Accounting Steering Group, 1976–80; Council, Duchy of Lancaster, 1977–87; Bethlem Royal Hosp. and Maudsley Hosp. SHA, 1982–90; Royal Commn for 1851 Exhibn, 1984–. Vice-Chm., Crafts Council, 1989–90 (Mem., 1984–90). Chairman: Cttee of Management, Inst. of Psychiatry, 1987–90; Gabbitas Truman & Thring Educnl Trust, 1986–89. *Recreations:* gardening, golf. *Address:* St Paul's House, Upper Froyle, near Alton, Hants GU34 4LB. *T:* Bentley (0420) 22183. *Clubs:* City of London (Chm., 1986–88); Woking Golf.

MAITLAND, Sir Donald (James Dundas), GCMG 1977 (CMG 1967); Kt 1973; OBE 1960; Chairman, Health Education Authority, since 1989; Director, Slough Estates, since 1983; *b* 16 Aug. 1922; *s* of Thomas Douglas Maitland and Wilhelmina Sarah Dundas; *m* 1950, Jean Marie Young, *d* of Gordon Young; one *s* one *d*. *Educ:* George Watson's Coll.; Edinburgh Univ. Served India, Middle East, and Burma, 1941–47 (Royal Scots; Rajputana Rifles). Joined Foreign Service, 1947; Consul, Amara, 1950; British Embassy, Baghdad, 1950–53; Private Sec. to Minister of State, Foreign Office, 1954–56; Director, Middle East Centre for Arab Studies, Lebanon, 1956–60; Foreign Office, 1960–63; Counsellor, British Embassy, Cairo, 1963–65; Head of News Dept, Foreign Office, 1965–67; Principal Private Sec. to Foreign and Commonwealth Secretary, 1967–69; Ambassador to Libya, 1969–70; Chief Press Sec., 10 Downing St, 1970–73; UK Permanent Rep. to UN, 1973–74; Dep. Under-Sec. of State, FCO, 1974–75; UK Mem., Commonwealth Group on Trade, Aid and Develt, 1975; Ambassador and UK Perm. Rep. to EEC, 1975–79; Dep. to Perm. Under-Sec. of State, FCO, Dec. 1979–June 1980; Perm. Under-Sec. of State, Dept of Energy, 1980–82. Chm., Independent Commn for World-Wide Telecommunications Develt, 1983–85. Govt Dir, Britoil, 1983–85; Dir, Northern Engrg Industries, 1986–89. Dep. Chm., IBA, 1986–89. Chairman: UK National Cttee for World Communications Year, 1983; Christians for Europe, 1984–. Mem., Commonwealth War Graves Commn, 1983–87. President: Bath Inst. for Rheumatic Diseases, 1986–; Federal Trust for Educn and Res., 1987–; Vice-Pres., Centre Européen de Prospective et de Synthèse, Paris, 1990–. *Recreations:* hill-walking, music. *Address:* Murhill Farm House, Limpley Stoke, Bath BA3 6HH. *T:* Limpley Stoke (0225) 723157.

MAITLAND, Sir Richard John, 9th Bt, *cr* 1818; farmer; *b* 24 Nov. 1952; *s* of Sir Alexander Keith Maitland, 8th Bt, and of Lavender Mary Jex, *y d* of late Francis William Jex Jackson, Kirkbuddo, Forfar; *S* father, 1963; *m* 1981, Carine, *er d* of J. St G. Coldwell, Somerton, Oxford; one *s* one *d*. *Educ:* Rugby; Exeter Univ. (BA Hons 1975); Edinburgh Sch. of Agriculture. Mem., Queen's Body Guard for Scotland, Royal Co. of Archers, 1987–. *Heir:* *s* Charles Alexander Maitland, *b* 3 June 1986. *Address:* Burnside, Forfar, Angus.

MAITLAND DAVIES, Keith Laurence; Metropolitan Stipendiary Magistrate, since 1984; *b* 3 Feb. 1938; *s* of Wyndham Matabele Davies, QC and Enid Maud Davies; *m* 1964, Angela Mary (*née* Fraser-Jenkins); two *d* one *s*. *Educ:* Winchester; Christ Church, Oxford (MA). Called to the Bar, Inner Temple, 1962; private practice, 1962–84. *Address:* c/o 1 Paper Buildings, Temple, EC4.

MAITLAND-MAKGILL-CRICHTON; *see* Crichton.

MAITLAND SMITH, Geoffrey; Chairman, Sears plc (formerly Sears Holdings plc), since 1985; chartered accountant; *b* 27 Feb. 1933; *s* of late Philip John Maitland Smith and of Kathleen (*née* Goff). *Educ:* University Coll. Sch., London. Partner, Thornton Baker & Co., Chartered Accountants, 1960–70; Sears Holdings plc: Dir, 1971–; Dep. Chm., 1978–85; Jt Chm., 1984; Chief Exec., 1978–88; Chairman: British Shoe Corp. Ltd, 1984–; Selfridges Ltd, 1985– (Dep. Chm., 1978–85); Director: Asprey plc, 1980–; Central Independent Television plc, 1983–85; Courtaulds plc, 1983–90; Imperial Group plc, 1984–86; Mallett plc, 1986–89; Midland Bank plc, 1986–. Mem. Bd, Financial Reporting Council, 1990–. Hon. Vice Pres., Inst. of Marketing, 1987–. Chm. Council, University Coll. Sch. Liveryman, Worshipful Co. of Gardeners. *Recreations:* opera, music. *Address:* (office) 40 Duke Street, W1A 2HP. *T:* 071–408 1180. *Club:* Cripplegate Ward.

MAITLIS, Prof. Peter Michael, FRS 1984; Professor of Chemistry, Sheffield University, since 1972; *b* 15 Jan. 1933; *s* of Jacob Maitlis and Judith Maitlis; *m* 1959, Marion (*née* Basco); three *d*. *Educ:* Univ. of Birmingham (BSc 1953); Univ. of London (PhD 1956, DSc 1971). Asst Lectr, London Univ., 1956–60; Fulbright Fellow and Res. Associate, Cornell Univ., 1960–61, Harvard Univ., 1961–62; Asst Prof, 1962–64, Associate Prof., 1964–67, Prof., 1967–72, McMaster Univ., Hamilton, Ont, Canada; Prof. of Inorganic Chemistry, Univ. of Sheffield, 1972–. Chm., Chemistry Cttee, SERC, 1985–88. Fellow, Alfred P. Sloan Foundn, USA, 1968–70; Tilden Lectr, RSC, London, 1979–80; Sir Edward Frankland Prize Lectr, RSC, 1985. Member: Royal Soc. of Chemistry (formerly Chem. Soc.), 1952– (Pres., Dalton Div., 1985–87); Amer. Chemical Soc., 1963–. E. W. R. Steacie Prize (Canada), 1971; Medallist, RSC (Noble Metals and their Compounds), 1981. *Publications:* The Organic Chemistry of Palladium, vols 1 and 2, 1971; many research papers in learned jls. *Recreations:* travel, music, reading, swimming. *Address:* Department of Chemistry, The University, Sheffield S3 7HF. *T:* Sheffield (0742) 768555, ext. 4480.

MAJITHIA, Dr Sir Surendra Singh, Kt 1946; Industrialist; *b* 4 March 1895; *s* of late Hon. Sardar Bahadur Dr Sir Sundar Singh Majithia, CIE, DOL; *m* 1921, Lady Balbir Kaur (*d* 1977), *d* of late General Hazura Singh, Patiala. *Educ:* Khalsa Collegiate High Sch.; Khalsa Coll., Amritsar. Chairman, Saraya Sugar Mills Ltd, Sardarnagar; Senior Managing Partner, Saraya Surkhi Mill, Sardarnagar; Dir, Punjab & Sind Bank Ltd, Amritsar. Member: Khalsa College Council, Amritsar; Akal College Council, Gursagar; UP Fruit Development Board, Lucknow. President, Chairman, etc., of many educational foundations and social activities. Past member, various Advisory and Consultative Cttees. Chairman, Lady Parsan Kaur Charitable Trust (Educnl Soc.), Sardarnagar; Patron: Wrestling Federation of India; UP Badminton Assoc.; Life Mem., Internal Soc. of Krishna Consciousness; Hon. Mem., Mark Twain Soc., USA; Member, Garden Advisory Cttee,

Gorakhpur. Hon. DLitt Gorakhpur, 1970. *Address:* PO Sardarnagar, Dist Gorakhpur, Uttar Pradesh, India. *Clubs:* Gorakhpur, Nepal (Gorakhpur).

MAJOR; *see* Henniker-Major, family name of Baron Henniker.

MAJOR, Rt. Hon. John, PC 1987; MP (C) Huntingdon, since 1983 (Huntingdonshire, 1979–83); Prime Minister and First Lord of the Treasury, since 1990; *b* 29 March 1943; *s* of late Thomas Major and Gwendolyn Minny Coates; *m* 1970, Norma Christina Elizabeth (*née* Johnson); one *s* one *d. Educ:* Rutlish. AIB. Banker, Standard Chartered Bank: various executive posts in UK and overseas, 1965–79. Contested (C) St Pancras North (Camden), Feb. 1974 and Oct. 1974; PPS to Ministers of State at the Home Office, 1981–83; an Asst Govt Whip, 1983–84; a Lord Comr of HM Treasury (a Govt Whip), 1984–85; Parly Under-Sec. of State for Social Security, DHSS, 1985–86; Minister of State for Social Security, DHSS, 1986–87; Chief Sec. to HM Treasury, 1987–89; Sec. of State for Foreign and Commonwealth Affairs, 1989; Chancellor of the Exchequer, 1989–90. Member, Lambeth Borough Council, 1968–71 (Chm. Housing Cttee, 1970–71). Jt Sec., Cons. Parly Party Environment Cttee, 1979–81; Parly Consultant, Guild of Glass Engravers, 1979–83. Mem. Bd, Warden Housing Assoc., 1975–83. Pres., Eastern Area Young Conservatives, 1983–85. *Recreations:* opera, cricket. *Address:* The Views, George Street, Huntingdon, Cambs. *Clubs:* Carlton, MCC.

MAJOR, John, FRICS; Land Agent to HM the Queen, Sandringham Estate, since 1991; *b* 16 June 1945; *s* of John Robert Major and Vera Major; *m* 1967, (Mary) Ruth Oddy; one *s* one *d. Educ:* Wellingborough Sch.; RAC, Cirencester. FRICS 1980. Partner, Osmond Tricks, Bristol, 1980–85; Land Agent, Castle Howard, N Yorks, 1986–91. *Recreation:* sailing. *Address:* Laycocks, Sandringham, King's Lynn, Norfolk PE35 6EB. *Club:* Farmers'.

MAJOR, Kathleen, FBA 1977; Professor (part-time) of History, University of Nottingham, 1966–71; Principal of St Hilda's College, Oxford, 1955–65; Hon. Fellow, St Hilda's College, 1965; *b* 10 April 1906; *er d* of late George Major and Gertrude Blow. *Educ:* various private schools; St Hilda's College, Oxford. Honour School of Modern History, 1928; BLitt 1931. Librarian, St Hilda's College, 1931. Archivist to the Bishop of Lincoln, 1936; Lecturer, 1945, subsequently Reader in Diplomatic in the University of Oxford, until July 1955. Hon. Secretary, Lincoln Record Society, 1935–56 and 1965–74, Hon. Gen. Editor, 1935–75. Member Academic Planning Board for the University of Lancaster, 1962, and of Academic Advisory Cttee, 1964–70. Trustee of the Oxford Preservation Trust, 1961–65; a Vice-Pres., RHistS, 1967–71, Hon. Vice-Pres., 1981–; Pres., Lincoln Civic Trust, 1980–84. Hon. DLitt Nottingham, 1961. *Publications:* (joint editor with late Canon Foster) Registrum Antiquissimum of the Cathedral Church of Lincoln, vol. IV, 1938, (sole editor) vols V-X, 1940–73; *Acta Stephani Langton,* 1950; The D'Oyrys of South Lincolnshire, Norfolk and Holderness, 1984; (with S. R. Jones and J. Varley) A Survey of Ancient Houses in Lincoln, Fascicule I, Minster Yard I, 1984, Fascicule II, Minster Yard II, 1987, Fascicule III, Minster Yard III, 1990; articles in English Hist. Review, Journal of Ecclesiastical Hist., etc. *Recreation:* reading. *Address:* 21 Queensway, Lincoln LN2 4AJ. *Club:* English-Speaking Union.

MAJURY, Maj.-Gen. James Herbert Samuel, CB 1974; MBE 1961; Senior Steward, National Greyhound Racing Club, 1976–88; *b* 26 June 1921; *s* of Rev. Dr M. Majury, BA, DD, and Florence (*née* Stuart), Antrim, N Ireland; *m* 1948, Jeanetta Ann (*née* Le Fleming); two *s. Educ:* Royal Academical Institution, Belfast; Trinity College, Dublin. Royal Ulster Rifles, 1940; attached 15 Punjab Regt, 1942; seconded South Waziristan Scouts, 1943–47; Korean War, 1950 (Royal Ulster Rifles); Prisoner of War, Korea, 1950–53 (despatches 1954); Parachute Regiment, 1957–61; Comd Royal Irish Fusiliers, 1961–62; Comd 2nd Infantry Bde, 1965–67; GOC West Midland District, 1970–73. idc 1968. Col. Comdt, The King's Division, 1971–75, Col The Royal Irish Rangers, 1972–77; Hon. Col, 2nd Bn Mercian Volunteers, 1975–79. President: SSAFA for E Sussex, 1986–; Indian Army Assoc., 1987–. *Recreations:* golf, racing. *Club:* Naval and Military.

MAKAROVA, Natalia; dancer and choreographer; *b* Leningrad, 21 Nov. 1940; *m* 1976, Edward Karkar; one *s. Educ:* Vaganova Ballet Sch.; Leningrad Choreographic Sch. Mem., Kirov Ballet, 1959–70; London début, as Giselle, Covent Garden, 1961; joined American Ballet Theatre, 1970; formed dance co., Makarova & Co., 1980; Guest Artist: Royal Ballet, Covent Garden, 1972; London Festival Ballet, 1984. Has danced many classical and contemporary rôles in UK, Europe and USA, 1970–; appearances include: La Bayadère (which she also staged, and choreographed in part), NY Met, 1980, Manchester, 1985; On Your Toes, London and NY, 1984–86; choreographed new prodn of Swan Lake for London Fest. Ballet, London and tour, 1988. Honoured Artist of RSFSR, 1970. *Publications:* A Dance Autobiography, 1979; On Your Toes, 1984. *Address:* c/o Herbert Breslin Inc., 119 W 57th Street, New York, NY 10019, USA.

MAKEPEACE, John, OBE 1988; FCSD; FBIM, FRSA; designer and furniture maker, since 1961; Founder and Director: The Parnham Trust and School for Craftsmen in Wood, 1977; Hooke Park College, 1989; *b* 6 July 1939; *m* 1st, 1964, Ann Sutton (marr. diss. 1979); *m* 2nd, 1983, Jennie Moores (*née* Brinsden). *Educ:* Denstone Coll., Staffs. Study tours: Scandinavia 1957; N America, 1961; Italy, 1968; W Africa, 1972; USA, 1974; Australia, 1979. Furniture in private collections and Templeton Coll. and Keble Coll., Oxford, Nuffield Foundn, Portals plc, Reed International, Royal Soc. of Arts, Royal Museum of Scotland, Post Office, Lambeth Palace. *Public Collections:* Cardiff Museum; Fitzwilliam Museum, Cambridge; Leeds Museum; Museum of Art, Chicago; Museum für Kunsthandwerk, Frankfurt; V & A Museum. *Exhibitions:* Herbert Art Gall., Coventry, 1963; New Art Centre, London, 1971; Fine Art Soc., London, 1977; Interior, Kortrijk, Belgium, 1978; Royal Show, Stoneleigh, 1981–87; Crafts Council Open, 1984; National Theatre, 1980, 1986; Wimborne, Dorset, 1988; Parnham at Smiths Gall., 1988–91; Sotheby's, London and Tokyo, 1988; New Art Forms Exposition, Chicago, 1989–91; NY Furniture Fair, 1990–91; British Design Exhibn, Japan, 1990. *Consultancies/Lectures:* Crafts Council, 1972–77; India Handicrafts Bd, 1975; Jammu and Kashmir Govt, 1977; Belgrade Univ., 1978; Artist in Context, V&A Mus., 1979; Chm., Wood Programme, World Crafts Conf., Kyoto, Japan, 1979; Loughborough Design Lecture, 1982; Oxford Farming Conf., 1990. Trustee, V & A Mus., 1987–91. Founder, American Friends of Parnham, 1991. *Television Films:* Made by Makepeace, 1975; History of English Furniture, 1978; Heritage in Danger, 1979; First Edition, 1980; Touch Wood, 1982; Tomorrow's World, 1986. Winner, Observer Kitchen Design, 1971; Parnham Trust Winner, UK Conservation Award, 1987; British Construction Industry Award, 1990. *Recreations:* tree pruning, collecting works by young artists. *Address:* Parnham House, Beaminster, Dorset DT8 3NA. *T:* Beaminster (0308) 862204.

MAKEPEACE-WARNE, Maj.-Gen. Antony, MBE 1972; Commandant, Joint Service Defence College, since 1990; *b* 3 Sept 1937; *e s* of late Keith Makepeace-Warne and Nora (*née* Kelstrup); *m* 1966, Jill Estelle Seath; two *d. Educ:* Taunton School. BA Open Univ., 1990. Commissioned KOYLI, 1960; served BAOR, Malaya, Aden, Berlin, MoD, to 1969; Staff College, 1970; 2nd Bn LI, 1971–72; 24 Airportable Bde, 1972–74; Instructor, Staff Coll., 1975–77; CO 1st Bn LI, 1977–80; Col ASD2, MoD, 1980–82; Comdr, Berlin Inf. Bde, 1982–84; RCDS 1985; ACOS HQ UKLF, 1986–88; GS Study of Indiv. Trg Orgn, 1988–89. Dep. Col, LI (Somerset and Cornwall), 1987–89; Colonel, The Light Infantry, 1990. *Recreations:* fishing, reading, music, theatre. *Address:* RHQ Light Infantry, Peninsula Barracks, Romsey Road, Winchester, Hants SO23 8TS. *Club:* Army and Navy.

MAKGILL, family name of **Viscount of Oxfuird.**

MAKGILL CRICHTON MAITLAND, Major John David; Lord-Lieutenant of Renfrewshire, since 1980; *b* 10 Sept. 1925; *e s* of late Col Mark Edward Makgill Crichton Maitland, CVO, DSO, DL, JP, The Island House, Wilton, Salisbury, Wilts, and late Patience Irene Fleetwood Makgill Crichton Maitland (*née* Fuller); *m* 1st, 1954, Jean Patricia (*d* 1985), *d* of late Maj.-Gen. Sir Michael Creagh, KBE, MC, Pigeon Hill, Homington, Salisbury; one *s* one *d*; 2nd, 1987, Mary Ann Vere, *o d* of late Major Charles Herbert Harberton Eales, MC, and *widow* of Capt. James Quintin Penn Curzon. *Educ:* Eton. Served War, 1944–45, Grenadier Guards. Continued serving until 1957 (temp. Major, 1952; retd 1957), rank Captain (Hon. Major). Renfrew CC, 1961–75. DL Renfrewshire 1962, Vice-Lieutenant 1972–80. *Address:* Houston House, Houston, by Johnstone, Renfrewshire PA6 7AR. *T:* Bridge of Weir (0505) 612545.

MAKHULU, Most Rev. Walter Paul Khotso; *see* Central Africa, Archbishop of.

MAKINS, family name of **Baron Sherfield.**

MAKINS, Nora; *see* Beloff, N.

MAKINS, Sir Paul (Vivian), 4th Bt *cr* 1903; Company Director, 1962–73; *b* 12 Nov. 1913; *yr s* of Sir Paul Makins, 2nd Bt, and Gladys Marie (*d* 1919), *d* of William Vivian, Queen's Gate, London; *S* brother, 1969; *m* 1945, Maisie (*d* 1986), *d* of Major Oswald Pedley and *widow* of Major C. L. J. Bowen, Irish Guards; no *c. Educ:* Eton Coll.; Trinity Coll. Cambridge (MA). Commissioned in Welsh Guards, 1935. Served War of 1939–45: France, 1940; Italy, 1944–45. Dir and Sec. Vitalba Co. Ltd (Gibraltar), 1962–73; Dir, Compañia Rentistica SA (Tangier), 1967–73. Kt of Magistral Grace, SMO Malta, 1955; JP Gibraltar, 1964–70. *Heir:* none. *Address:* Casas Cortijo 135, Sotogrande, Provincia de Cadiz, Spain. *Clubs:* Cavalry and Guards, Pratt's.
See also Archbishop of Southwark.

MAKINSON, William, CBE 1977; engineering management consultant; *b* 11 May 1915; *s* of Joshua Makinson and Martha (*née* Cunliffe); *m* 1952, Helen Elizabeth Parker; one *s* three *d. Educ:* Ashton-in-Makerfield Grammar Sch.; Manchester Univ. Asst Lecturer, Electronics, Manchester Univ., 1935–36; Education Officer, RAF Cranwell, 1936–39; RAE Farnborough, 1939–52; Hon. Squadron-Ldr, RAF, 1943–45; Superintendent, Blind Landing Experimental Unit, 1952–55; Defence Research Policy Staff, 1955–56; Managing Director, General Precision Systems Ltd, 1956–64; Group Jt Managing Director, Pullin, 1964–65; Mem., NRDC, 1967–80 (Man. Dir, 1974–80, Chief Exec., Engrg Dept, 1965–74). *Publications:* papers to Royal Aeronautical Society. *Recreation:* golf. *Address:* Ridings, Snows Paddock, Snows Ride, Windlesham, Surrey. *T:* Ascot (0344) 22431. *Club:* Directors.

MAKKAWI, Dr Khalil; Chevalier, Order of Cedar, Lebanon; Ambassador and Permanent Representative of Lebanon to the United Nations, New York, since 1990; *b* 15 Jan. 1930; *s* of Abdel Basset Makkawi and Rosa Makkawi; *m* 1958, Zahira Sibaei; one *s* one *d. Educ:* Amer. Univ. of Beirut (BA Polit. Science); Cairo Univ. (MA Polit. Science); Colombia Univ., NY, USA (PhD Internat. Relations). Joined Lebanese Min. of Foreign Affairs, 1957; UN Section at Min., 1957–59; Attaché to Perm. Mission of Lebanon to UN, New York, 1959, Dep. Perm. Rep., 1961–64; First Sec., Washington, 1964–66; Chief of Internat. Relations Dept, Min. of For. Affairs, Beirut, 1967–70; Counsellor, London, 1970–71; Minister Plenipotentiary, London, 1971–73; Ambassador to: German Democratic Republic, 1973–78; Court of St James's, and Republic of Ireland, 1979–83; Dir of Political Dept, Min. of Foreign Affairs, Beirut, 1983–85; Amb. to Italy, and Permanent Rep. to UNFAO, 1985–90. Mem., Lebanese Delegn to UN Gen. Assembly Meetings, 14th-39th Session; Chairman of Lebanese Delegations to: Confs and Councils, FAO, 1985–89; Governing Councils, IFAD, 1985–89; 16th Ministerial Meeting, Islamic conf. in Fès, 1986; 8th Summit Conf. of Non-Aligned Countries, Harare, 1986; Ministerial Meeting, Mediterranean Mems, Non-Aligned Countries, Brioni, Yugoslavia, 1987; IMO Conf., Rome, 1988. *Recreations:* sports, music. *Address:* Suite 531–33, 866 United Nations Plaza, New York, NY 10017, USA.

MAKLOUF, Raphael David; sculptor; painter; Chairman, Tower Mint, since 1975; *b* Jerusalem, 10 Dec. 1937; *m* 1968, Marillyn Christian Lewis, *d* of Gwilym Hugh Lewis, DFC; two *s* one *d. Educ:* studied art at Camberwell School of Art, under Karel Vogel, 1953–58. Official commissions: Tower of London, Carnegie Hall, NY, etc. New portrait effigy of the Queen on all UK and Commonwealth coinage from 1985, on Britannia gold coins, from 1989. Bronze portraits of the Queen, 1988, at Royal Nat. Theatre, Richmond Riverside Develt and Westminster Sch. Science Building, unveiled by the Queen. Sitters have included: HM Queen; HRH Prince Philip; Rt Hon Margaret Thatcher; Joan Collins; Michael Parkinson; Bobby Moore; David Bailey; Sir Ian Mactaggart; Gen. Sir John Mogg. FRSA 1985. *Address:* 3 St Helena Terrace, Richmond, Surrey TW9 1NR. *Clubs:* City Livery; St Helena Swimming (Richmond).

MAKUTA, Hon. Friday Lewis; Hon. Mr Justice Makuta; Chief Justice of Malaŵi, since 1985; *b* 25 Oct. 1936; *s* of late Lewis and Anne Makuta; *m* 1962; four *s* one *d. Educ:* Malamulo Mission; Dedza Secondary Sch. Called to the Bar, Middle Temple, 1967. Joined Civil Service, Malaŵi, 1967; State Advocate, 1967; Chief Legal Aid Advocate, 1970; Dir of Public Prosecutions, 1972; Judge of the High Court, 1975; Attorney Gen. and Sec. for Justice, 1976; SC 1979; Dep. Sec. to the Pres. and Cabinet, 1984. *Address:* High Court of Malaŵi, PO Box 30244, Chichiri, Blantyre 3, Malaŵi. *Club:* Civil Service (Lilongwe, Malaŵi).

MALAND, David; barrister; *b* 6 Oct. 1929; *s* of Rev. Gordon Albert Maland and Florence Maud Maland (*née* Bosence); *m* 1953, Edna Foulsham; two *s. Educ:* Kingswood Sch.; Wadham Coll., Oxford. BA 2nd class Mod. Hist., 1951; MA 1957; Robert Herbert Meml Prize Essay, 1959. Nat. service commn RAF, 1951–53. Asst Master, Brighton Grammar Sch., 1953–56; Senior History Master, Stamford Sch., 1957–66; Headmaster: Cardiff High Sch., 1966–68; Denstone Coll., 1969–78; High Master, Manchester Grammar Sch., 1978–85. Chm., Assisted Places Sub-Cttee of Headmasters' Conf., 1982–83. Called to the Bar, Gray's Inn, 1986. Gen. Gov., British Nutrition Foundn, 1987–. Governor: Stonyhurst Coll., 1973–80; Abingdon Sch., 1979–; GPDST, 1984–88. *Publications:* Europe in the Seventeenth Century, 1966; Culture and Society in Seventeenth Century France, 1970; Europe in the Sixteenth Century, 1973; Europe at War, 1600–1650, 1980; (trans.) La Guerre de Trente Ans, by Pagès, 1971; articles and reviews in History. *Address:* Windrush, Underhill Lane, Westmeston, Hassocks, East Sussex BN6 8XG; 1 Garden Court, Temple, EC4Y 9BJ. *Club:* Athenæum.

MALCOLM, Hon. David Kingsley; Hon. Mr Justice Malcolm; Chief Justice of Western Australia, since 1988, and Lieutenant-Governor, since 1990; *b* 6 May 1938; *s* of Colin Kingsley Malcolm and Jeanne (*née* Cowan); *m* 1965, Jennifer Birney; one *s. Educ:*

Guildford Grammar Sch.; Univ. of Western Australia (LLB 1st Cl. Hons); Oxford Univ. (Rhodes Schol.; BCL 1st Cl. Hons). Partner, Muir Williams Nicholson, 1964–67; Counsel, Asst Gen. Counsel, Dep. Gen. Counsel, Asian Development Bank, Manila, 1967–70; Partner, Muir Williams Nicholson & Co., 1970–79; Independent Bar, 1980–88. QC: WA, 1980; NSW, 1983. Member: Law Reform Commn of WA, 1966–67 and 1975–82 (Chm., 1976, 1979–82); Copyright Tribunal, 1978–86; Chm., Town Planning Appeal Tribunal, 1979–86. Mem., Council of Law Soc. of WA, 1966–67, 1985–88 (Vice-Pres., 1986–88); Pres., WA Bar Assoc., 1982–84; Vice Pres., Aust. Bar Assoc., 1984. Chm. Adv. Bd, Neuromuscular Res. Inst. of Aust., 1989–; Mem. Senate, Univ. of WA, 1988–. *Publications:* articles in various learned jls, incl. Aust. Law Jl, Aust. Bar Rev., Aust. Business Law Rev., Univ. of WA Law Rev., LAWASIA Jl. *Recreations:* Rugby Union, equestrian sports, windsurfing. *Address:* Chief Justice's Chambers, Supreme Court, Perth, WA 6000, Australia. *T:* (chambers) 09–4215337. *Clubs:* Weld (Perth, WA); Manila Polo (Manila).

MALCOLM, Sir David (Peter Michael), 11th Bt *cr* 1665; *b* 7 July 1919; *s* of Sir Michael Albert James Malcolm, 10th Bt, and Hon. Geraldine Margot (*d* 1965), *d* of 10th Baron Digby; *S* father, 1976; *m* 1959, Hermione, *d* of Sir David Home, Bt, *qv*; one *d*. *Educ:* Eton; Magdalene Coll., Cambridge (BA). Served with Scots Guards, 1939–46 (Major). Mem., Inst. of Chartered Accountants of Scotland, 1949. Member: Stock Exchange, 1956–80; Stock Exchange Council, 1971–80. Mem., Queen's Body Guard for Scotland, Royal Co. of Archers, 1952–. *Recreations:* shooting, golf. *Heir: cousin* James William Thomas Alexander Malcolm [*b* 15 May 1930; *m* 1955, Gillian Heather, *d* of Elton Humpherus; two *s* two *d*]. *Address:* Whiteholm, Gullane, East Lothian EH31 2BD. *Club:* New (Edinburgh).

MALCOLM, Derek Elliston Michael; film critic, The Guardian, since 1971; President, International Film Critics, since 1991 (Chairman, UK Section, since 1982); Governor, British Film Institute, since 1989; *b* 12 May 1932; *s* of J. Douglas Malcolm and Dorothy Taylor; *m* 1962, Barbara Ibbott (marr. diss. 1966); one *d*. *Educ:* Eton; Merton College, Oxford (BA Hons Hist.). Actor, amateur rider (National Hunt), 1953–56; Drama Critic, Gloucestershire Echo, 1956–62; Sub-Editor, The Guardian, 1962–69; Racing correspondent, The Guardian, 1969–71. Dir, London Internat. Film Fest., 1984–86. Pres., Critics' Circle of UK, 1980 (Chm., Film Section, 1978–81); Internat. Publishing Cos Critic of the Year, 1972. *Publication:* Robert Mitchum, 1984. *Recreations:* cricket, tennis, squash, music. *Address:* 28 Avenue Road, Highgate, N6. *T:* 081–348 2013.

MALCOLM, Dugald, CMG 1966; CVO 1964; TD 1945; HM Diplomatic Service, retired; Minister to the Holy See, 1975–77; *b* 22 Dec. 1917; 2nd *s* of late Maj.-Gen. Sir Neill Malcolm, KCB, DSO, and Lady (Angela) Malcolm; *m* 1st, 1957, Patricia Anne Gilbert-Lodge (*d* 1976), *widow* of Captain Peter Atkinson-Clark; one *d* one step *d*; 2nd, 1989, Margaret Roy Anderson, *d* of Rev. R. P. R. Anderson. *Educ:* Eton; New Coll., Oxford. Served Argyll and Sutherland Highlanders, 1939–45; discharged wounded. Appointed Foreign Office, Oct. 1945; Served Lima, Bonn, Seoul; HM Vice-Marshal of the Diplomatic Corps, 1957–65; Ambassador: to Luxembourg, 1966–70; to Panama, 1970–74. Member Queen's Body Guard for Scotland (Royal Company of Archers). *Address:* Flat 14, 55 Cornwall Gardens, SW7 4BE. *Clubs:* Travellers', Boodle's, Brooks's.

MALCOLM, Ellen, RSA 1976 (ARSA 1968); *b* 28 Sept. 1923; *d* of John and Ellen Malcolm; *m* 1962, Gordon Stewart Cameron, *qv*. *Educ:* Aberdeen Acad.; Gray's Sch. of Art, Aberdeen. DA (Aberdeen) 1944. Teacher of Art, Aberdeen Grammar Sch. and Aberdeen Acad., 1945–62. Paintings in public galleries in Southend, Aberdeen, Perth, Milngavie, Edinburgh, and in private collections in Scotland, England, Wales, America, Switzerland, Sweden and Australia. Chalmers-Jervise Prize, 1946; Guthrie Award, Royal Scottish Acad., 1952; David Cargill Award, Royal Glasgow Inst., 1973. *Recreation:* reading. *Address:* 7 Auburn Terrace, Invergowrie, Dundee DD2 5AB. *T:* Dundee (0382) 562318.

MALCOLM, George (John), CBE 1965; musician; *b* London, 28 Feb. 1917; *o s* of George Hope Malcolm, Edinburgh, and Johanna Malcolm. *Educ:* Wimbledon Coll.; Balliol Coll., Oxford (Scholar); Royal College of Music (Scholar). MA, BMus (Oxon). Served in RAFVR, 1940–46. Master of the Cathedral Music, Westminster Cathedral, 1947–59, training unique boys' choir for which Benjamin Britten wrote Missa Brevis, Op. 63. Now mainly known as harpsichordist, pianist and conductor (making frequent concert tours). Cobbett Medal, Worshipful Company of Musicians, 1960; Hon. RAM, 1961; Hon. Fellow, Balliol Coll., Oxford, 1966; FRCM 1974; Hon. FRCO 1987; Hon. DMus, Sheffield, 1978. Papal Knight of the Order of St Gregory the Great, 1970. *Address:* 99 Wimbledon Hill Road, SW19 7QT.

MALCOLM, Gerald; *see* Malcolm, W. G.

MALCOLM, Prof. John Laurence; Regius Professor of Physiology, University of Aberdeen, 1959–75, retired; *b* 28 Aug. 1913; *s* of late Professor J. Malcolm, Dunedin, New Zealand; *m* 1st, 1940, Sylvia Bramston (*d* 1958), *d* of late Basil B. Hooper, Auckland, New Zealand; one *s* one *d*; 2nd, 1961, Margaret Irvine Simpson (*d* 1967), *d* of late Colonel J. C. Simpson, Skene, Aberdeenshire. *Publications:* contributions to the Proceedings of Royal Society, Journal of Physiology, Journal of Neuro-physiology. *Address:* Heath Cottage, Crathie, Aberdeenshire AB3 5UP.

MALCOLM, Prof. Wilfred Gordon; Vice-Chancellor, University of Waikato, New Zealand, since 1985; *b* 1933; *s* of Norman and Doris Malcolm; *m* 1959, Edmée Ruth Prebensen; two *s* four *d*. *Educ:* Victoria Univ. of Wellington (MA, PhD); Emmanuel Coll., Cambridge (BA). Victoria University of Wellington: Lectr in Mathematics, 1960–62; Gen. Sec., Inter Varsity Fellowship of Evangelical Unions, 1963–66; Lectr/Reader in Mathematics, 1967–74; Prof. of Pure Mathematics, 1975–84. *Address:* University of Waikato, Private Bag 3105, Hamilton 2020, New Zealand. *T:* (071) 562 889.

MALCOLM, (William) Gerald, CB 1976; MBE 1943; Member, Planning Appeals Commission (NI), 1978–83; Permanent Secretary, Department of the Environment for Northern Ireland, 1974–76; *b* Stirling, 19 Dec. 1916; *s* of late John and Jane M. Malcolm; *m* 1949, Margaret Cashel. *Educ:* High Sch. of Stirling; Glasgow Univ. (MA) (Hons French and German, 1945); London Univ. (BA 1945). Served War, Army, 1939–46: RASC and Intelligence Corps; Major, 1944; Africa and Italy Stars, 1939–45. Min. of Home Affairs for NI, Asst Principal, 1948; Min. of Agriculture for NI: Principal, 1956; Asst Sec., 1962; Sen. Asst Sec., 1966; Dep. Sec., 1970. *Recreations:* angling, swimming, ornithology, nature.

MALCOLMSON, Kenneth Forbes, MA, BMus (Oxon), FRCO; Precentor and Director of Music, Eton College, 1956–71; *b* 29 April 1911; *m* 1972, Mrs B. Dunhill. Organ Scholar, Exeter Coll., Oxford, 1931–35; Commissioner, Royal School of Church Music, 1935–36; Temporary Organist, St Alban's Cathedral, 1936–37; Organist, Halifax Parish Church, 1937–38; Organist and Master of the Music, Newcastle Cathedral, 1938–55. *Recreations:* gardening, swimming, walking. *Address:* Dixton House, Dixton Road, Monmouth, Gwent NP5 3PR. *T:* Monmouth (0600) 714509.

MALDEN; *see* Scott-Malden.

MALDEN, Viscount; Frederick Paul de Vere Capell; Deputy Head Teacher, Skerton County Primary School, Lancaster, since 1990; *b* 29 May 1944; *s* and *heir* of 10th Earl of Essex, *qv*. *Educ:* Skerton Boys' School; Lancaster Royal Grammar School; Didsbury College of Education, Manchester; Northern School of Music. ACP, LLCM(TD). Assistant teacher, Marsh County Junior School, 1966–72; Deputy Head, 1972–75; Acting Head, 1975–77; Deputy Head Teacher, Marsh County Primary School, 1977–78; Head Teacher, Cockerham Parochial CE School, Cockerham, Lancaster, 1979–80; in charge of Pastoral Care, Curriculum Develt and Music, Skerton County Primary School, Lancaster, 1981–90. Patron, Morecambe Philharmonic Choir. FRSA. *Recreations:* music, hi-fi. *Address:* 35 Pinewood Avenue, Brookhouse, Lancaster LA2 9NU.

MALE, David Ronald, CBE 1991; FRICS; Consultant, Gardiner & Theobald, Chartered Quantity Surveyors, since 1992 (Senior Partner, 1979–91); a Church Commissioner, since 1989; *b* 12 Dec. 1929; *s* of Ronald Male and Gertrude Simpson; *m* 1959, Mary Louise Evans; one *s* two *d*. *Educ:* Aldenham Sch., Herts. Served RA, 2nd Lieut, 1948–49. With Gardiner & Theobald, 1950–. Mem., Gen. Council, RICS, 1976– (Pres., 1989–90); Pres., Quantity Surveyors Divl Council, 1977–78. Member: Bd of Dirs, Building Centre, 1970–80; Govt Construction Panel, 1973–74; EDC for Building, 1982–86; Chm., NEDC Commercial Bldg Steering Gp, 1984–88; Dir, London and Bristol Developments, 1985–91. Mem., Court of Benefactors, RSocMed, 1986–. Gov., Aldenham Sch., 1974–; Pres., Old Aldenhamian Soc., 1986–89. FRSA 1991. Master, Chartered Surveyors' Co., 1984–85; Liveryman, Painter-Stainers' Co., 1961–. *Recreations:* opera and ballet, lawn tennis, Real tennis, golf. *Address:* 6 Bowland Yard, Kinnerton Street, SW1X 8EE. *Clubs:* Boodle's, Garrick, MCC (Mem. Cttee, 1984–; Chm., Estates Sub-Cttee, 1984–).

MALE, Peter John Ellison, CMG 1967; MC 1945; HM Diplomatic Service, retired; Ambassador to Czechoslovakia, 1977–80; *b* 22 Aug. 1920; *s* of late H. J. G. Male and late Mrs E. A. Male; *m* 1947, Patricia Janet Payne; five *s* two *d*. *Educ:* Merchant Taylors' Sch.; Emmanuel Coll., Cambridge. HM Forces, 1940–45. HM Foreign Service (now HM Diplomatic Service), 1946; served in: Damascus, 1947–49; Wahnerheide, 1949–53; London, 1953–55; Guatemala City, 1955–57; Washington, 1957–60; London, 1960–62; Oslo, 1962–66; Bonn, 1966–70; New Delhi, 1970–74; Asst Under-Sec. of State, FCO, 1974–77. *Recreations:* gadgets, gardening. *Address:* Swinley Edge, Coronation Road, Ascot, Berks SL5 9LG. *Club:* United Oxford & Cambridge University.

MALECELA, Cigwiyemisi John Samwel; Prime Minister and First Vice President of the United Republic of Tanzania, since 1990; *b* 20 April 1934; *m*; four *c*. *Educ:* Alliance Secondary Sch., Dodoma; St Andrews Coll., Minaki, Dar es Salaam; Univ. of Bombay (BCom); post-grad. studies, Cambridge Univ. Appts for Tanganyikan Govt, 1962–64; for Tanzania: Ambassador to UN, 1964–68, to Ethiopia, 1968; Minister for East African Community affairs, 1969–71; Minister for Foreign Affairs, 1972–75, for Agriculture, 1975–80, for Minerals, 1980–82, for Transport, Communication and Works, 1983–85; Regional Comr, Iringa, 1987; High Comr for Tanzania in UK, 1989–90.

MALEK, Redha; Algerian Ambassador to the Court of St James's, 1982–84; *b* 21 Dec. 1931; *m* 1963, Rafida Cheriet; two *s* one *d*. *Educ:* Algiers; Paris. BA. Mem. Governing Bd, Gen. Union of Moslem Algerian Students, 1956; Dir and Editor in Chief, El Moudjahid, party newspaper of Front de la Libération Nationale, 1957–62; Ambassador to: Yugoslavia, 1963–65; France, 1965–70; USSR, 1970–77; Minister of Information and Culture, Algeria, 1977–79; Ambassador to USA, 1979–82 (negotiated release of the 52 American hostages in Iran, 1980–81). Mem. and spokesman, Algerian delegn to negotiations of Evian, 1961–62; Member, Drafting Committee: Programme of Tripoli, setting out FLN political programme, 1962; Nat. Charter, 1976. Mem., Central Cttee, FLN, 1979–. *Address:* 2 Rue Ahmed Bey, Algiers, Algeria.

MALET, Sir Harry (Douglas St Lo), 9th Bt *cr* 1791, of Wilbury, Wiltshire; JP; farmer, Australia and England; *b* 26 Oct. 1936; *o s* of Col Sir Edward William St Lo Malet, 8th Bt, OBE and Baroness Benedicta von Maasburg (*d* 1979); *S* father, 1990; *m* 1967, Julia Gresley, *d* of Charles Harper, Perth, WA; one *s*. *Educ:* Downside; Trinity Coll., Oxford (BA Eng. Lit.). Commnd QRIH, 1958–61. JP W Somerset, 1982. *Recreation:* equestrian sports. *Heir:* *s* Charles Edward St Lo Malet, *b* 30 Aug. 1970. *Address:* Wrestwood, RMB 184, Boyup Brook, WA 6244, Australia. *Club:* Weld (Perth).

MALIK, Bidhubhusan; *b* 11 Jan. 1895; *s* of Raibahadur Chandrasekhar Malik, Chief Judge, Benares State; *m* 1916, Leelabati, *d* of Saratkumar Mitra, Calcutta; two *s*. *Educ:* Central Hindu Coll., Benares (graduated, 1917); Ewing Christian Coll. (MA in Economics, 1919); Allahabad Univ. (LLB 1919); LLD (*hc*), Saugur Univ. Vakil, Allahabad High Court, 1919; started practice in the civil courts in Benares; left for England in Sept. 1922; called to Bar, Lincoln's Inn, 1923; joined Allahabad High Court Bar, 1924; Member of Judicial Cttee of Benares State, 1941; Special Counsel for Income Tax Dept, 1943; Judge, Allahabad High Court, 1944; Chief Justice, High Court, Allahabad, Dec. 1947; thereafter Chief Justice, UP, from 26 July 1948–55, excepting 3 March-1 May 1949, when acted as Governor, Uttar Pradesh. Commissioner for Linguistic Minorities in India, 1957–62. Member: Constitutional Commission for the Federation of Malaya, 1956–57; Air Transport Council of India, 1955–62; National Integration Commn, India. Constitutional Adviser to Mr Jomo Kenyatta and the Kenya African National Union, Lancaster House Conference, London, 1961–62; Constitutional Expert for Republic of Congo appointed by UNO, Aug.-Oct. 1962; Constitutional Adviser to Kenya Government, Kenya Independence Conference, Lancaster House, Sept.-Oct. 1963; Adviser, Mauritius Constitutional Conference, London, Sept.-Nov. 1965. Vice-Chancellor, Calcutta Univ., 1962–68 (Life-Mem. Senate); President: Jagat Taran Educn Soc., 1924–; Jagat Taran Degree Coll., 1924–; Jagat Taran Inter Coll., 1924–; Jagat Taran Golden Jubilee Eng. Med. Sch. and Hindi Med. Primary Sch., 1924–; Harijan Ashram Degree Coll., Allahabad, 1968–. Former Mem. Council, Ewing Christian Coll., Pres., Old Boys' Assoc., 1976–. Founder Mem., Lions Club, Allahabad, 1959–60; Rotary Club: Pres., Allahabad; Mem., Allahabad and Calcutta. Founder President: Golf Club, Allahabad, 1949–55; Allahabad Badminton Assoc., 1949–55. *Address:* 23 Muir Road, Allahabad, India.

MALIM, Rear-Adm. Nigel Hugh, CB 1971; LVO 1960; DL; FIMechE; *b* 5 April 1919; *s* of late John Malim, Pebmarsh, and Brenda Malim; *m* 1944, Moonyeen, *d* of late William and Winefride Maynard; two *s* one *d*. *Educ:* Weymouth Coll.; RNEC Keyham. Cadet, RN, 1936; HMS Manchester, 1940–41; HMS Norfolk, 1942; RNC Greenwich, 1943–45; HMS Jamaica, 1945–47; Staff of RNEC, 1948–50; Admty, 1951–54; HMS Triumph, 1954–56; Admty, 1956–58; HM Yacht Britannia, 1958–60; District Overseer, Scotland, 1960–62; Asst, and later Dep., Dir Marine Engrg, 1962–65; idc 1966; Captain, RNEC Manadon, 1967–69; Chief Staff Officer Technical to C-in-C, W Fleet, 1969–71, retd. Man. Dir, Humber Graving Dock & Engrg Co. Ltd, 1972–82. Chm., Fabric Council, Lincoln Cathedral, 1985. DL Lincoln, 1987. *Recreations:* offshore racing and cruising. *Address:* The Old Vicarage, Caistor, Lincoln LN7 6UG. *Clubs:* Royal Ocean Racing, Royal Naval Sailing Association.

MALIN, Prof. Stuart Robert Charles; Mathematics Teacher, Dulwich College, since 1989; Visiting Professor, Department of Physics and Astronomy, University College London, since 1983; *b* 28 Sept. 1936; *s* of Cecil Henry Malin and Eleanor Mary Malin (née Howe); *m* 1963, Irene Saunders; two *d. Educ:* Royal Grammar Sch., High Wycombe; King's College, London. BSc 1958, PhD 1972, DSc 1981; FInstP 1971; CPhys 1985; FRAS 1961 (Mem. Council, 1975–78). Royal Greenwich Observatory, Herstmonceux: Asst Exptl Officer, 1958; Scientific Officer, 1961; Sen. Scientific Officer, 1965; Institute of Geological Sciences, Herstmonceux and Edinburgh: PSO, 1970; SPSO (individual merit), 1976, and Hd of Geomagnetism Unit, 1981; Hd of Astronomy and Navigation, Nat. Maritime Museum, 1982. Cape Observer, Radcliffe Observatory, Pretoria, 1963–65; Vis. Scientist, Nat. Center for Atmospheric Res., Boulder, Colorado, 1969; Green Schol., Scripps Instn of Oceanography, La Jolla, 1981. Pres., Jun. Astronomical Soc., 1989–91. Associate Editor, Qly Jl, RAS, 1987–. *Publications:* (with Carole Stott) The Greenwich Meridian, 1984; Spaceworks, 1985; The Greenwich Guide to the Planets, 1987; The Greenwich Guide to Stars, Galaxies and Nebulae, 1989; The Story of the Earth, 1991; contribs to scientific jls. *Recreations:* croquet, clocks. *Address:* 30 Wemyss Road, Blackheath, SE3 0TG. *T:* 081–318 3712.

MALINS, Humfrey Jonathan; MP (C) North West Croydon, since 1983; *b* 31 July 1945; *s* of Rev. Peter Malins and late Lilian Joan Malins; *m* 1979, Lynda Ann; one *s* one *d. Educ:* St John's Sch., Leatherhead; Brasenose Coll., Oxford (MA Hons Law). College of Law, Guildford, 1967; joined Tuck and Mann, Solicitors, Dorking, 1967, qual. as solicitor, 1971; Partner, Tuck and Mann, 1973. Councillor, Mole Valley DC, Surrey, 1973–83 (Chm., Housing Cttee, 1980–81). Contested: Toxteth Division of Liverpool, Feb. and Oct. 1974; E Lewisham, 1979. PPS to Minister of State, Home Office, 1987–89, to Minister of State, DoH, 1989–. *Recreations:* Rugby football, golf, gardening. *Address:* Highbury, Westcott Street, Westcott, Dorking, Surrey RH4 3NU. *T:* Dorking (0306) 885554. *Clubs:* Coningsby; Vincent's (Oxford); Richmond Rugby Football; West Sussex Golf.

MALINS, Julian Henry; QC 1991; *b* 1 May 1950; *s* of Rev. Peter Malins and late (Lilian) Joan Malins (née Dingley); *m* 1972, Joanna Pearce; three *d. Educ:* St John's School, Leatherhead; Brasenose College, Oxford (MA). Called to the Bar, Middle Temple, 1972. Mem., General Council of the Bar, 1986–. Mem., Court of Common Council, City of London, 1981–. *Recreations:* fishing, chess, conversation. *Address:* Brick Court Chambers, 15/19 Devereux Court, WC2R 3JJ. *T:* 071–583 0777. *Club:* Carlton.

See also H. J. Malins.

MALINS, Penelope, (Mrs John Malins); *see* Hobhouse, P.

MALJERS, Floris Anton; Chairman, Unilever NV, and Vice Chairman, Unilever PLC, since 1984; *b* 12 Aug. 1933; *s* of A. C. J. Maljers and L. M. Maljers-Kole; *m* 1958, J. H. Maljers-de Jongh; two *s* (one *d* decd). *Educ:* Univ. of Amsterdam. Joined Unilever, 1959; various jobs in the Netherlands until 1965; Man. Dir., Unilever-Colombia, 1965–67; Man. Dir., Unilever-Turkey, 1967–70; Chairman, Van den Bergh & Jurgens, Netherlands, 1970–74; Co-ordinator of Man. Group, edible fats and dairy, and Dir of Unilever NV and Unilever PLC, 1974–. Member: Unilever's Special Committee, 1982–; Supervisory Bd, ABN Bank, Amsterdam, 1984–. Chm., Concertgebouw Foundn, 1987–. *Address:* Unilever PLC, Unilever House, Blackfriars, EC4P 4BQ. *T:* 071–822 5531.

MALLABY, Sir Christopher (Leslie George), KCMG 1988 (CMG 1982); HM Diplomatic Service; Ambassador to the Federal Republic of Germany, since 1988; *b* 7 July 1936; *s* of late Brig. A. W. S. Mallaby, CIE, OBE, and Margaret Catherine Mallaby (née Jones); *m* 1961, Pascale Françoise Thierry-Mieg; one *s* three *d. Educ:* Eton; King's Coll., Cambridge. British Delegn to UN Gen. Assembly, 1960; 3rd Sec., British Embassy, Moscow, 1961–63; 2nd Sec., FO, 1963–66; 1st Sec., Berlin, 1966–69; 1st Sec., FCO, 1969–71; Harvard Business Sch., 1971; Dep. Dir, British Trade Develt Office, NY, 1971–74; Counsellor and Head of Chancery, Moscow, 1975–77; Head of Arms Control and Disarmament Dept, FCO, 1977–79, Head of East European and Soviet Dept, 1979–80, Head of Planning Staff, 1980–82, FCO; Minister, Bonn, 1982–85; Dep. Sec., Cabinet Office, 1985–88. *Recreations:* fishing, reading, travel. *Address:* c/o Foreign and Commonwealth Office, SW1A 2AH. *Clubs:* Brooks's, Beefsteak.

MALLALIEU, Baroness *cr* 1991 (Life Peer), of Studdridge in the County of Buckinghamshire; **Ann Mallalieu;** QC 1988; a Recorder, since 1985; *b* 27 Nov. 1945; *d* of Sir (Joseph Percival) William Mallalieu and of Lady Mallalieu; *m* 1979, Timothy Felix Harold Cassel, *qv;* two *d. Educ:* Holton Park Girls' Grammar Sch., Wheatley, Oxon; Newnham Coll., Cambridge (MA, LLM). (First woman) Pres., Cambridge Union Soc., 1967. Called to the Bar, Inner Temple, 1970; Mem., Gen. Council of the Bar, 1973–75. *Recreations:* sheep, hunting, poetry, horseracing. *Address:* 6 King's Bench Walk, Temple, EC4Y 7DR. *T:* 071–583 0410.

MALLE, Louis; Film Director; *b* 30 Oct. 1932; *s* of Pierre Malle and Françoise Béghin; one *s; m* 1980, Candice Bergen; one *d. Educ:* Paris Univ.; Institut d'Etudes Politiques. Television, 1953; Asst to Comdt Cousteau on the Calypso, 1953–55. Films: Co-prod. Le Monde du Silence, 1955 (Palme d'Or, Cannes); Collab. techn of Robert Bresson for Un Condamné a mort s'est echappé, 1956; Author and Producer of: Ascenseur pour l'échafaud, 1957 (Prix Louis-Delluc, 1958); Les Amants, 1958 (Prix spécial du Jury du Festival de Venise, 1958); Zazie dans le métro, 1960; Vie privée, 1962; Le Feu Follet (again, Prix spécial, Venise, 1963); Viva Maria, 1965 (Grand Prix du Cinéma français); Le Voleur, 1966; Histoires extraordinaires (sketch), 1968; Calcutta, 1969 (prix de la Fraternité); Phantom India, 1969; Le Souffle au Coeur, 1971 (nominated Best Screenplay, US Acad. Awards, 1972); Humain, trop humain, 1972; Place de la République, 1973; Lacombe Lucien, 1974; Black Moon, 1975; Pretty Baby, 1977; films directed: Atlantic City, 1979 (Jt winner, Golden Lion, Venice Film Fest., 1980; Best Director, BAFTA awards, 1982; nominated Best Film and Best Director, US Acad. Awards, 1982); My Dinner With André, 1981; Crackers, 1984; Alamo Bay, 1985; (also cameraman) God's Country (for Public TV), 1985; And the Pursuit of Happiness, 1986; (also writer) Au Revoir Les Enfants, 1987 (Golden Lion, Venice Film Fest.; Best Film Director, BAFTA Award, 1988); Milou in May, 1990. *Address:* c/o NEF, 15 rue du Louvre, 75001 Paris, France.

MALLET, Sir Ivo; *see* Mallet, Sir W. I.

MALLET, John Valentine Granville, FSA; FRSA; Keeper, Department of Ceramics, Victoria and Albert Museum, 1976–89; *b* 15 Sept. 1930; *s* of late Sir Victor Mallet, GCMG, CVO, and Lady Mallet (née Andreae); *m* 1958, Felicity Ann Basset; one *s. Educ:* Winchester Coll.; Balliol Coll., Oxford (BA Modern History). Mil. service in Army: commnd; held temp. rank of full Lieut in Intell. Corps, 1949–50. Messrs Sotheby & Co., London, 1955–62; Victoria and Albert Museum: Asst Keeper, Dept of Ceramics, 1962; Sec. to Adv. Council, 1967–73. Indep. Mem., Design Selection Cttee, Design Council, 1981–89; Mem. Exec. Cttee, Nat. Art Collections Fund, 1989–. Mem., Court of Assistants, Fishmongers' Co., 1970–, Prime Warden, 1983–84. *Publications:* articles on ceramics in Burlington Magazine, Apollo, Trans English Ceramic Circle, and Faenza. *Recreation:* tennis. *Address:* 11 Pembroke Square, W8.

See also P. L. V. Mallet.

MALLET, Philip Louis Victor, CMG 1980; HM Diplomatic Service, retired; *b* 3 Feb. 1926; *e s* of late Sir Victor Mallet, GCMG, CVO and Christiana Jean, *d* of Herman A.

Andreae; *m* 1953, Mary Moyle Grenfell Borlase; three *s. Educ:* Winchester; Balliol Coll., Oxford. Army Service, 1944–47. Entered HM Foreign (subseq. Diplomatic) Service, 1949; served in: FO, 1949; Baghdad, 1950–53; FO, 1953–56; Cyprus, 1956–58; Aden, 1958; Bonn, 1958–62; FO, 1962–64; Tunis, 1964–66; FCO, 1967–69; Khartoum, 1969–73; Stockholm, 1973–76; Head of Republic of Ireland Dept, FCO, 1977–78; High Comr in Guyana and non-resident Ambassador to Suriname, 1978–82. *Address:* Wittersham House, Wittersham, Kent TN30 7ED. *Club:* Brooks's.

See also J. V. G. Mallet.

MALLET, Roger; Chairman, North Western Electricity Board, 1972–76, retired; *b* 7 June 1912; British; *m* 1942, Kathleen Els Walker; two *s* two *d. Educ:* Eastbourne Coll.; Trinity Hall, Cambridge. BA Mech. Sci. Tripos; CEng, FIEE. West Cambrian Power Co., S Wales, 1937–40; Buckrose Light & Power Co., Yorks, 1940–45; Shropshire, Worcestershire and Staffordshire Electric Power Co., 1945–47; Midlands Electricity Board, 1948–72. *Recreation:* golf.

MALLETT, Conrad Richard, FRICS; Member, Lands Tribunal, since 1980; *b* 11 May 1919; *s* of Captain Raymond Mallett, OBE, MN and Joyce Mallett (née Humble); *m* 1942, Elisabeth (Paulina) Williams; one *s* two *d. Educ:* Wellingborough Sch. Ordinary Airman to Lieut Comdr (A), RNVR, 1939–46 (despatches 1941). Partner, Montagu Evans and Son, Chartered Surveyors, London and Edinburgh, 1950–80. *Recreation:* cruising under sail. *Address:* 2 Hadley Hurst Cottages, Hadley Common, Barnet, Herts EN5 5QF. *T:* 081–449 5933. *Clubs:* Naval, Cruising Association.

MALLETT, Edmund Stansfield; Director of Applications Programmes, European Space Agency, Paris, 1981–85, retired; *b* 21 April 1923; *s* of Cecil Finer Mallett and Elsie Stansfield; *m* 1st, 1953, Nancy Campbell (*d* 1983); three *s;* 2nd, 1985, Jocelyn Maynard Ghent, BA, MA, PhD. *Educ:* Bradford Grammar Sch.; Leeds Univ. (BSc). CEng, MIEE; FBIS. Gramophone Co., 1944; Fairey Aviation Co., 1948; Royal Aircraft Establishment: joined 1950; Head, Data Transmission and Processing Div., 1961; Supt, Central Unit for Scientific Photography, 1966; Head, Instrumentation Div., 1968; Head of Instruments Br., Min. of Technol., 1969; Head of Instrumentation and Ranges Dept, RAE, 1971; Director Space, DoI, 1976; Under Sec., and Head of Res. and Technol. Requirements and Space Div., DoI, 1978; Dir, Nat. Maritime Inst., 1979. *Publications:* papers and articles on instrumentation and measurement. *Recreations:* music, art, genealogy, solving problems. *Address:* 580 Prospect Avenue, Rockcliffe Park, Ottawa, Ontario K1M 0X7, Canada. *T:* 748 7219.

MALLETT, Francis Anthony, CBE 1984; Chief Executive, South Yorkshire County Council, 1973–84; Clerk of the Lieutenancy, South Yorkshire, 1974–84; solicitor; *b* 13 March 1924; *s* of Francis Sidney and Marion Mallett; *m* 1956, Alison Shirley Melville, MA; two *s* one *d. Educ:* Mill Hill; London Univ. (LLB). Army, 1943–47: commissioned, Royal Hampshire Regt, 1944; served in Middle East, Italy and Germany. Second Dep. Clerk, Herts CC, 1966–69; Dep. Clerk, West Riding CC, 1969–74. Chairman: Assoc. of Local Authority Chief Execs, 1979–84; Crown Prosecution Service Staff Commn, 1985–87; Mem., W Yorks Residuary Body, 1985–91. *Recreations:* gardening, fishing, tennis. *Address:* Lurley Manor, Tiverton, Devon. *T:* Tiverton (0884) 255363. *Club:* Lansdowne.

MALLETT, Ven. Peter, CB 1978; AKC; Chaplain-General to the Forces, 1974–80; Managing Director, Inter-Church Travel, 1981–86; *b* 1925; *s* of Edwin and Beatrice Mallett; *m* 1958, Joan Margaret Bremer; one *s* two *d. Educ:* King's Coll., London; St Boniface Coll., Warminster, Wilts. Deacon, 1951, priest, 1952. Curate, St Oswald's, Norbury, S London, 1951–54. Joined Royal Army Chaplains' Dept (CF), 1954, and has served overseas in Far East, Aden, Germany (despatches, Malaya, 1957). Has been Senior Chaplain of Aden Brigade, and at RMA, Sandhurst; Dep. Asst Chaplain-General, Berlin, 1968, in N Ireland, 1972; Asst Chaplain-General, BAOR, 1973. QHC 1973. Canon, dio. of Europe, 1982. OStJ 1976. FRGS 1987. Hon. DLitt Geneva Theol Coll., 1976. *Address:* Hawthorne Cottage, Hampstead Lane, Yalding, Kent ME18 6HJ. *T:* Maidstone (0622) 812607. *Clubs:* Army and Navy, Naval and Military (Hon.).

MALLIN, Rev. Canon Stewart Adam Thomson, CSG; Minister, St Paul's, Strathnairn, since 1991; *b* 12 Aug. 1924; *s* of George Garner Mallin and Elizabeth Thomson. *Educ:* Lasswade Secondary School; Coates Hall Theological Coll., Edinburgh. Deacon 1961, priest 1962; Curate, St Andrew's Cathedral, Inverness, 1961–64; Itinerant Priest, Diocese of Moray, Ross and Caithness, 1964–68; Priest-in-Charge of St Peter and the Holy Rood, Thurso, and St John's, Wick, 1968–77; Rector, St James, Dingwall and St Anne's, Strathpeffer, 1977–91; Dean of Moray, Ross and Caithness, 1983–91. Member of CSG, 1968–; Canon of St Andrew's Cathedral, Inverness, 1974. Hon. Chaplain, British Legion. Associate, Order of the Holy Cross (USA). *Recreations:* amateur drama, amateur opera. *Address:* St Paul's Parsonage, Croachy, Strathnairn, Inverness IV1 2UB. *Club:* Rotary (Thurso, then Dingwall); Pres., Dingwall, 1985–86).

MALLINCKRODT, Georg Wilhelm von; *see* von Mallinckrodt.

MALLINSON, Anthony William; Senior Partner, Slaughter and May, 1984–86; *b* 1 Dec. 1923; *s* of Stanley Tucker Mallinson and Dora Selina Mallinson (née Burridge); *m* 1955, Heather Mary Gardiner. *Educ:* Cheam School; Marlborough College; Gonville and Caius College, Cambridge (Exbnr 1948, Tapp Post-Graduate Scholar, 1949, BA, LLM). Served RA, 1943–47, Major. Admitted solicitor, England and Wales, 1952, Hong Kong, 1978; Partner, Slaughter and May, 1957–86; Solicitor to Fishmongers' Co., 1964–86. Mem. London Bd, Bank of Scotland, 1985–; Director: Stratton Investment Trust, 1986–; Morgan Grenfell Asset Management Ltd, 1986–91. Mem., BoT Cttee examining British Patent System (Banks Cttee), 1967–70; Chm., Cinematograph Films Council, 1973–76. Hon. Legal Adviser to Accounting Standards Cttee, 1982–86; Member: Council, Section on Business Law, Internat. Bar Assoc., 1984–90; Financial Services Tribunal, 1988–; Financial Reporting Review Panel, 1991–; Exec. Cttee, Essex County Cricket Club, 1986–; Registration Cttee, TCCB, 1986–. *Recreations:* watching sport, particularly cricket, reading. *Address:* 15 Douro Place, W8 5PH. *T:* 071–937 2739. *Club:* MCC.

MALLINSON, Dennis Hainsworth; Director, National Engineering Laboratory, East Kilbride, Department of Industry, 1974–80; *b* 22 Aug. 1921; *s* of David and Anne Mallinson; *m* 1945, Rowena Mary Brooke; one *s* two *d. Educ:* Leeds Univ. (BSc). RAE, 1942, early jet engines; Power Jets (R&D) Ltd, later Nat. Gas Turbine Estabt, 1944–63; Min. of Aviation and successors: Asst Dir, 1963; Dir, 1964; Dir-Gen., Engines, Procurement Exec., MoD, 1972–74. Vis. Prof., Strathclyde Univ., 1976–82. Mem. Council, Instn Engrs and Shipbuilders in Scotland, 1977–80. *Address:* 19 Rossett Holt Close, Harrogate HG2 9AD.

MALLINSON, John Russell; General Manager, Corporation of Lloyd's, since 1989; *b* 29 June 1943; *s* of Wilfred and Joyce Helen Mallinson; *m* 1968, Susan Rebecca Jane Godfree; one *s* one *d. Educ:* Giggleswick Sch.; Balliol Coll., Oxford (Keasbey Schol. 1963; BA). Solicitor (Hons.), 1972. Asst Solicitor, Coward Chance, 1972–74; Sen. Legal Assistant, DTI, 1974–79; Assistant Solicitor: Law Officers' Dept, AG's Chambers, 1979–81; DTI,

1982–84; Under Sec. (Legal), DTI, 1985–89. *Recreations:* reading, conversation, music, looking at paintings. *Address:* 4 Nunappleton Way, Hurst Green, Surrey RH8 9AW. *T:* Oxted (0883) 714775.

MALLINSON, William Arthur, CBE 1978; FEng 1985; Vice Chairman, Smiths Industries PLC, 1978–85; *b* 12 June 1922; *s* of Arthur Mallinson and Nellie Jane Mallinson; *m* 1948, Muriel Ella Parker; two *d*. *Educ:* William Hulme's Grammar Sch., Manchester; Faculty of Technol., Manchester Univ. (BScTech 1st Cl. Hons). MIEE, MIMechE, MRAeS; FBIM 1976. Electrical Officer, Tech. Br., RAFVR, 1943–47; Elec. Designer, Electro-Hydraulics Ltd, 1947–51; Ferranti Ltd: Proj. Engr, GW Dept, 1951–55; Chief Engr, Aircraft Equipment Dept, 1955–68; Smiths Industries Ltd, 1968–85: Technical Dir, then Gen. Man., Aviation Div.; Divl Man. Dir; Main Bd Dir; Corporate Man. Dir. Member: Airworthiness Requirements Bd, CAA, 1981–85; Electronics and Avionics Requirements Bd, DTI, 1983–85 (Chm., Aviation Cttee, 1984–85). *Recreations:* music, horticulture. *Address:* Chestnut Cottage, Dukes Covert, Bagshot, Surrey GU19 5HU. *T:* Bagshot (0276) 72479.

MALLINSON, Sir William (John), 4th Bt *cr* 1935, of Walthamstow; *b* 8 Oct. 1942; *s* of Sir William Paul Mallinson, 3rd Bt, FRCP, FRCPsych and Eila Mary (*d* 1985), *d* of Roland Graeme Guy; *S* father, 1989; *m* 1968, Rosalind Angela (marr. diss. 1978), *o d* of Rollo Hoare; one *s* one *d*. *Educ:* Charterhouse. *Recreations:* sailing, tennis, ski-ing. *Heir: s* William James Mallinson, *b* 22 April 1970. *Address:* 1 Hollywood Mews, Chelsea, SW10 9HU. *T:* 071–352 3821. *Clubs:* Royal Thames Yacht, Bembridge Sailing.

MALLON, Rt. Rev. Mgr Joseph Laurence; Principal Roman Catholic Chaplain and Vicar General (Army), since 1989; *b* 8 Aug. 1942; *s* of John Mallon and Mary (*née* O'Neill). *Educ:* St Nathy's Coll., Ballaghadereen; St Kiernan's Coll., Kilkenny. Ordained priest, Dio. of Salford, 1966; Curate: St Joseph's, Bury, 1966–67; St Anne's, Stretford, 1967–73; commnd into RAChD, 1973; service in England, NI, Germany and Cyprus; Sen. RC Chaplain, BAOR, 1988. Prelate of Honour, 1989. *Recreations:* bridge, golf, recreational mathematics, The Times crossword. *Address:* Ministry of Defence, Bagshot Park, Bagshot, Surrey GU19 5PL. *T:* Bagshot (0276) 71717.

MALLON, Seamus; MP (SDLP) Newry and Armagh, since Jan. 1986; *b* 17 Aug. 1936; *s* of Francis P. Mallon and Jane O'Flaherty; *m* 1966, Gertrude Cush; one *d*. *Educ:* St Joseph's Coll. of Educn. Member: NI Assembly, 1973–74 and 1982; NI Convention, 1975–76; Irish Senate, 1981–82; New Ireland Forum, 1983–84; Armagh Dist Council, 1973–. Dep. Leader, SDLP, 1978–. Member: Select Cttee on Agric., 1987–; Anglo-Irish Inter-Parly Body, 1990–. Author of play, Adam's Children, prod. radio, 1968, and stage, 1969. *Recreations:* angling, gardening. *Address:* 5 Castleview, Markethill, Armagh BT60 1QP. *T:* Markethill (0861) 551555; House of Commons, SW1A 0AA; (office) 2 Mill Street, Newry, Co. Down; (office) 6 Seven Houses, Armagh, Co. Armagh.

MALLORIE, Air Vice-Marshal Paul Richard, CB 1979; AFC 1947; retired RAF, 1980; Military Command and Control Systems Consultant; *b* 8 March 1923; *s* of late Rev. W. T. Mallorie and Margaret Mallorie; *m* 1951, Ursula Joyce Greig; three *s* one *d*. *Educ:* King's Sch., Canterbury. Flying Instructor, 1945; India and Middle East, 1946–49; Air Ministry, 1951–53; Staff Coll., 1954; No 139 Sqdn, 1955–57; JSSC, 1960; UK Mil. Advisers' Rep., SEATO, Bangkok, 1963–66; OC RAF Wittering, 1967–68; IDC, 1969; Min. of Defence, 1974–76; Asst Chief of Staff (Info. Systems), SHAPE, 1976–79. Res. Fellow, NATO, 1981–82. *Recreations:* gardening, computers. *Address:* c/o Barclays Bank, Framlingham, Woodbridge, Suffolk. *Club:* Royal Air Force.

MALLOWS, Surg. Rear-Adm. Harry Russell; Senior Medical Officer, Shell Centre, 1977–85; *b* 1 July 1920; *s* of Harry Mallows and Amy Mallows (*née* Law); *m* 1942, Rhona Frances Wyndham-Smith; one *s* two *d*. *Educ:* Wrekin Coll.; Christ's Coll., Cambridge (MA, MD); UCH, London. FFPHM, FFOM, DPH, DIH. SMO, HM Dockyards at Hong Kong, Sheerness, Gibraltar and Singapore, 1951–67; Naval MO of Health, Scotland and NI Comd, and Far East Stn, 1964–68; Dir of Environmental Medicine, Inst. of Naval Medicine, 1970–73; Comd MO, Naval Home Comd, 1973–75; QHP, 1974–77; Surgeon Rear-Adm. (Ships and Estabts), 1975–77; retd 1977. CStJ 1976. *Publications:* articles in BMJ, Royal Naval Med. Service Jl, Proc. RSM. *Recreations:* music, travel. *Address:* 1 Shear Hill, Petersfield, Hants GU31 4BB. *T:* Petersfield (0730) 63116.

MALMESBURY, 6th Earl of *cr* 1800; **William James Harris;** TD 1944 (2 Clasps); JP; DL; Baron Malmesbury, 1788; Viscount FitzHarris, 1800; Official Verderer of the New Forest, 1966–74; Lord-Lieutenant and Custos Rotulorum of Hampshire, 1973–82; served Royal Hampshire Regiment, TA; *b* 18 Nov. 1907; *o s* of 5th Earl and Hon. Dorothy Gough-Calthorpe (*d* 1973), CBE (Lady of Grace, Order of St John of Jerusalem, Order of Mercy, with bar), *y d* of 6th Lord Calthorpe; *S* father 1950; *m* 1932, Hon. Diana Carleton (*d* 1990), *e d* of 6th Baron Dorchester, OBE; one *s* two *d*; *m* 1991, Margaret Fleetwood (*née* Campbell-Preston), *widow* of Raymond Baring. *Educ:* Eton; Trinity Coll., Cambridge (MA). Vice-Pres. of the Cambridge Univ. Conservative Association, 1929; Professional Associate of Surveyors Institution, 1937. Personal Liaison Officer to Min. of Agric., SE Region, 1958–64; Mem., Agric. and Forestry Cttee, RICS, 1953–69; Chm., Hants Agric. Exec. Cttee, 1959–67; Cttee which produced White Paper on the Growing Demand for Water, 1961. Dir, Mid-Southern Water Co., 1961–78. Pres., New Forest 9th Centenary Trust, 1987– (Chm., 1977–87). Chairman: Hants Br., Country Landowners Assoc., 1954–56; T&AFA, Hants and IoW, 1960–68; first Chm., Eastern Wessex TA&VRA, 1968–70 (Vice-Pres., 1973–78; Pres., 1978–80); Hon. Col, 65th (M) Signal Regt, R Sigs (TA), 1959–66; Hon. Col, 2nd Bn The Wessex Regt (V), 1970–73. Mem. Basingstoke RDC, 1946–52; County Councillor, Hants CC, 1952; Vice-Lt, Co. Southampton, 1960–73; DL Hants, 1955 and 1983. Master, Worshipful Co. of Skinners, 1952–53. KStJ 1973. Coronation Medal, 1937, 1953; Silver Jubilee Medal, 1977. *Heir: s* Viscount FitzHarris, *qv*. *Address:* The Coach House, Greywell Hill, Basingstoke, Hants RG25 1DB. *T:* Odiham (0256) 702033. *Club:* Royal Yacht Squadron (Vice-Cdre, 1971–77).

See also J. N. Maltby.

MALMESBURY, Bishop Suffragan of, since 1983; **Rt. Rev. Peter James Firth;** *b* 12 July 1929; *s* of Atkinson Vernon Firth and Edith Pepper; *m* 1955, Felicity Mary Wilding; two *s* two *d* (and one long-term foster *d*). *Educ:* Stockport Grammar School; Emmanuel Coll., Cambridge (Open Exhibnr, MA, DipEd); St Stephen's House Theol Coll., Oxford. Ordained, 1955; Assistant Curate, St Stephen's, Barbourne in Worcester, 1955–58; Priest-in-charge, Church of the Ascension, Parish of St Matthias, Malvern Link, Worcs, 1958–62; Rector of St George's, Abbey Hey, Gorton in Manchester, 1962–66; Religious Broadcasting Assistant, North Region, BBC, 1966–67; Religious Broadcasting Organiser and Senior Producer, Religious Programmes, BBC South and West, Bristol, 1967–83. Internat. Radio Festival winner, Seville, 1975. *Publication:* Lord of the Seasons, 1978. *Recreations:* theatre, photography, music, travel, Manchester United. *Address:* 7 Ivywell Road, Bristol BS9 1NX. *T:* Bristol (0272) 685931.

MALONE, Hon. Sir Denis (Eustace Gilbert), Kt 1977; **Hon. Mr Justice Malone;** Puisne Judge of the Commonwealth of the Bahamas, since 1979; *b* 24 Nov. 1922; *s* of Sir Clement Malone, OBE, QC, and Lady Malone; *m* 1963, Diana Malone (*née* Traynor). *Educ:* St Kitts-Nevis Grammar Sch.; Wycliffe Coll., Stonehouse, Glos; Lincoln Coll., Oxford (BA). Called to Bar, Middle Temple, 1950. Royal Air Force, Bomber Comd, 1942–46. Attorney General's Chambers, Barbados, WI, 1953–61, Solicitor-Gen., 1958–61; Puisne Judge: Belize, 1961–65; Trinidad and Tobago, 1966–74; Chief Justice of Belize, 1974–79. *Recreations:* tennis, swimming, walking, bridge, reading. *Address:* c/o The Supreme Court, PO Box N8167, Nassau, Bahamas.

MALONE, (Peter) Gerald; Editor, The Sunday Times Scotland, 1989–90, Editorial Consultant, since 1990; *b* 21 July 1950; *s* of P. A. and J. Malone; *m* 1981, Dr Anne S. Blyth; one *s* one *d*. *Educ:* St Aloysius Coll., Glasgow; Glasgow Univ. (MA, LLB). Admitted solicitor, 1972. MP (C) Aberdeen S, 1983–87. PPS to Parly Under Secs of State, Dept of Energy, 1985; an Asst Government Whip, 1986–87. Prospective Parly Candidate (C) Winchester, 1990–. Dir of European Affairs, Energy and Envmtl Policy Center, Harvard Univ., 1987–90; Presenter, Talk In Sunday, Radio Clyde, 1988–90. *Recreations:* opera, motoring. *Address:* Winchester Conservative Association, Eastgate House, Eastgate Street, Winchester, Hants SO23 8DZ. *Clubs:* Art (Glasgow); Royal Northern University, Aberdeen Conservative (Aberdeen).

MALONE, Rt. Rev. Vincent; an Auxiliary Bishop of Liverpool, (RC), and Titular Bishop of Abora, since 1989; *b* 11 Sept. 1931; *s* of Louis Malone and Elizabeth Malone (*née* McGrath). *Educ:* St Francis Xavier's Coll, Liverpool; St Joseph's Coll., Upholland; Liverpool Univ. (BSc 1959); Cambridge Univ. (CertEd 1960; DipEd 1964). FCP 1967. Chaplain to Notre Dame Training Coll., Liverpool, 1955–59; Curate, St Anne's, Liverpool, 1960–61; Asst Master, Cardinal Allen Grammar School, Liverpool, 1961–71; RC Chaplain to Liverpool Univ., 1971–79; Administrator, Liverpool Metropolitan Cathedral, 1979–89. *Address:* 17 West Oakhill Park, Liverpool L13 4BN. *T:* 051–228 7637.

MALONE-LEE, Michael Charles; Deputy Secretary (Director of Operations), Department of Health, since 1990; *b* 4 March 1941; *s* of Dr Gerard Brendan and Theresa Malone-Lee; *m* 1971, Claire Frances Cockin; two *s*. *Educ:* Stonyhurst College; Campion Hall, Oxford (MA). Ministry of Health, 1968; Principal Private Sec. to Sec. of State for Social Services, 1976–79; Asst Sec., 1977; Area Administrator, City and East London AHA, 1979–81; District Administrator, Bloomsbury Health Authy, 1982–84; Under Secretary, 1984, Dir, Personnel Management, 1984–87, DHSS; Prin. Fin. Officer, Home Office, 1987–90. Non-exec Dir, ICI (Agrochemicals), 1986–89. *Recreations:* natural history, marathon running. *Address:* c/o Department of Health, Whitehall, SW1.

MALONEY, Michael John, JP; MA; Principal, Moreton Hall, 1990–Aug. 1992; *b* 26 July 1932; *s* of John William Maloney and Olive Lois Maloney; *m* 1960, Jancis Ann (*née* Ewing); one *s* one *d*. *Educ:* St Alban's Sch.; Trinity Coll., Oxford (MA). Nat. Service, 2nd Lieut RA, served with RWAFF, 1955–57. May & Baker Ltd, 1957–58; Asst Master, Shrewsbury Sch., 1958–66; Sen. Science Master, Housemaster, Dep. Headmaster, Eastbourne Coll., 1966–72; Headmaster: Welbeck Coll., 1972–85; Kamazu Acad., Malaŵi, 1986–89. JP Worksop, 1975–86, Shrewsbury, 1991. *Publication:* (with D. E. P. Hughes) Advanced Theoretical Chemistry, 1964. *Recreations:* Rugby football, ornithology, cryptography. *Address:* Lower Lane Cottage, Chirbury, Montgomery, Powys SY15 6UD. *T:* Chirbury (093872) 303; (until Aug. 1992) Moreton Hall, Weston Rhyn, Oswestry, Salop SY11 3EW. *T:* Oswestry (0691) 773671.

MALOTT, Deane Waldo; President Cornell University, Ithaca, NY, 1951–63, President Emeritus, 1963; Consultant, Association of American Colleges, 1963–70; *b* 10 July 1898; *s* of Michael Harvey Malott and Edith Gray Johnson; *m* 1925, Eleanor Sisson Thrum; one *s* two *d*. *Educ:* Univ. of Kansas (AB); Harvard Univ. (MBA). Asst Dean, Harvard Business Sch., 1923–29; Assoc. Prof. of Business, 1933–39; Vice-Pres., Hawaiian Pineapple Co., Honolulu, 1929–33; Chancellor, Univ. of Kansas, 1939–51. Educational Advisor, Ops Analysis Div., US Army Air Corps, 1943–45; Mem., Business Council, Washington, DC, 1944–; Trustee: Corning Museum of Glass, 1952–73; Teagle Foundation, 1952–85; William Allen White Foundation, 1952–; Kansas Univ. Endowment Assoc., 1962–; Pacific Tropical Botanical Garden, 1964–; Mem. Bd, Univ. of Kansas Alumni Assoc., 1974–; Director: General Mills, Inc., 1948–70; Citizens Bank, Abilene, Kans, 1944–73; Pitney-Bowes, Inc., 1951–71; First Nat. Bank, Ithaca, NY, 1951–83; Owens-Corning Fiberglas Corp., 1951–72; Lane Bryant, Inc., 1963–77; Servomation Corp., 1963–74. Mem., Adv. Bd, Security Northstar Bank, 1983–. Hon. LLD: Washburn Univ., 1941; Bryant Coll., 1951; Hamilton Coll., 1951; Univ. of California 1954; Univ. of Liberia, 1962; Univ. of New Hampshire, 1963; Emory Univ., 1963; Juniata Coll., 1965; DCS, Univ. of Pittsburgh, 1957; Hon. DHL, Long Island Univ., 1967. Holds foreign Orders. *Publications:* Problems in Agricultural Marketing, 1938; (with Philip Cabot) Problems in Public Utility Management, 1927; (with J. C. Baker) Introduction to Corporate Finance, 1936; (with J. C. Baker and W. D. Kennedy) On Going into Business, 1936; (with B. F. Martin) The Agricultural Industries, 1939; Agriculture—the Great Dilemma (an essay in Business and Modern Society), 1951. *Address:* 322 Wait Avenue, Cornell University, Ithaca, NY 14850, USA. *Clubs:* University, Cornell (New York); Bohemian (San Francisco).

MALPAS, Prof. James Spencer, DPhil; FFPM; FRCR; FRCP; Consultant Physician, St Bartholomew's Hospital, since 1973; Professor of Medical Oncology, since 1979, and Director, Imperial Cancer Research Fund Medical Oncology Unit, since 1976, St Bartholomew's Hospital; *b* 15 Sept. 1931; *s* of Tom Spencer Malpas, BSc, MICE and Hilda Chalstrey; *m* 1957, Joyce May Cathcart; two *s*. *Educ:* Sutton County Grammar Sch.; St Bartholomew's Hosp., London Univ. Schol. in Sci., 1951; BSc Hons, 1952; MB BS, 1955; DPhil, 1965; FRCP 1971; FRCR 1983; FFPM 1989. Junior appts in medicine, St Bartholomew's Hosp. and Royal Post-Grad. Med. Sch.; Nat. Service in RAF, 1957–60; Aylwen Bursar, St Bartholomew's Hosp., 1961; Lectr in Medicine, Oxford Univ., 1962–65; St Bartholomew's Hospital: Sen. Registrar in Medicine, 1966–68; Sen. Lectr in Medicine, 1968–72; Dean, 1969–72, Treasurer, 1986–87, and Vice Pres., 1987–, of Med. Coll.; Dep. Dir (Clinical), ICRF, 1986–90. Cooper Res. Schol. in Med., 1966, 1967, 1968. Examiner in Medicine: Univ. of Oxford, 1974; Univ. of London, 1985, 1986. Asst Registrar, RCP, 1975–80; Treasurer, Postgrad. Med. Fellowship, 1984–87. Lockyer Lectr, RCP, 1978; Skinner Lectr, RCR, 1986; Subodh Mitra Meml Orator, New Delhi, 1991. *Publications:* contrib. many medical textbooks; papers in BMJ, Brit. Jl Haematology, Jl Clinical Pathology, etc. *Recreations:* travel, history, painting, ski-ing, sailing, wind surfing. *Address:* 36 Cleaver Square, SE11 4EA. *T:* 071–735 7566. *Club:* Little Ship.

MALPAS, Robert, CBE 1975; FEng 1978; FIMechE, FIChemE, FIMH; Chairman, Cookson Group, since 1991; *b* 9 Aug. 1927; *s* of late Cheshyre Malpas and of Louise Marie Marcelle Malpas; *m* 1956, Josephine Dickenson. *Educ:* Taunton Sch.; St George's Coll., Buenos Aires; Durham Univ. BScMechEng (1st Cl. Hons). Joined ICI Ltd, 1948; moved to Alcudia SA (48.5 per cent ICI), Spain, 1963; ICI Europa Ltd, Brussels, 1965; Chm., ICI Europa Ltd, 1973; ICI Main Board Dir, 1975–78; Pres., Halcon International Inc., 1978–82; a Man. Dir, BP, 1983–89; Chm., PowerGen, 1989–90; Director: BOC Group, 1981–; Eurotunnel, 1987–; Barings plc, 1989–; Repsol, Spain. Member: Engineering Council, 1983–88 (Vice-Chm., 1984–88); ACARD, 1983–86. Sen. Vice

Pres., Fellowship of Engrg, 1988– (Chm., LINK Steering Gp, 1987–). Hon. DTech Loughborough, 1983; DUniv Surrey, 1984; Hon. DEng Newcastle, 1991; Hon. DSc Bath, 1991. Order of Civil Merit, Spain, 1967. *Recreations:* sport, music. *Address:* 2 Belgrave Mews West, SW1X 8HT. *Clubs:* Royal Automobile; River (NY); Mill Reef (Antigua); Real Automóvil Club de España (Madrid).

MALPASS, Brian William, PhD; CChem; Chief Executive, De La Rue Co. plc, 1987–89; *b* 12 Sept. 1937; *s* of William and Florence Malpass; *m* 1960, Hazel Anne; two *d*. *Educ:* Univ. of Birmingham (Open Schol.; Frankland Prize 1960; BScChem 1st Cl. Hons, PhD). MRSC. Passfield Res. Laboratories, 1963–68; De La Rue Co., 1968–89; Finance Dir, 1980–84; Man. Dir, Thomas De La Rue Currency Div., 1984–87. *Publications:* numerous papers in scientific jls. *Recreations:* golf, cinema, writing. *Address:* 13 Spinfield Mount, Marlow, Bucks SL7 2JU. *Club:* Maidenhead Golf.

MALTA, Archbishop of, (RC), since 1977; **Most Rev. Joseph Mercieca,** STD, JUD; *b* Victoria, Gozo, 11 Nov. 1928. *Educ:* Gozo Seminary; Univ. of London (BA); Gregorian Univ., Rome (STD); Lateran Univ., Rome (JUD). Priest, 1952; Rector of Gozo Seminary in late 1960s; Permanent Judge at Sacred Roman Rota and Commissioner to Congregation for the Sacraments and Congregation for the Doctrine of the Faith, 1969; Auxiliary Bishop of Malta, and Vicar-General, 1974–77. *Address:* Archbishop's Curia, PO Box 29, Valletta, Malta. *T:* 23 43 17.

MALTBY, Antony John, JP; DL; MA; Headmaster of Trent College, 1968–88; *b* 15 May 1928; *s* of late G. C. Maltby and Mrs Maltby (*née* Kingsnorth); *m* 1959, Jillian Winifred (*née* Burt); four *d*. *Educ:* Clayesmore Sch., Dorset; St John's Coll., Cambridge. BA Hons (History) 1950; MA. Schoolmaster: Dover Coll., 1951–58; Pocklington Sch., 1958–68. JP Ilkeston, 1980; DL Derbyshire, 1984. *Recreations:* squash, travel. *Address:* Little Singleton Farm, Great Chart, Ashford, Kent. *T:* Ashford (0233) 629397. *Clubs:* East India, Devonshire, Sports and Public Schools; Hawks (Cambridge).

MALTBY, John Newcombe, CBE 1988; Chairman: United Kingdom Atomic Energy Authority, since 1990 (Member, since 1988); Dover Harbour Board, since 1989; Harrisons and Crosfield plc, since 1991; Deputy Chairman, British Ports Federation, since 1990; *b* 10 July 1928; *s* of Air Vice-Marshal Sir Paul Maltby, KCVO, KBE, CB, DSO, AFC, DL and Winifred Russell Paterson; *m* 1956, Lady Sylvia Veronica Anthea Harris, *d* of Earl of Malmesbury, *qv*; one *s* two *d*. *Educ:* Wellington Coll.; Clare Coll., Cambridge (MA Mech. Scis). Shell Internat. Petrolem, 1951–69; Founder and Man. Dir, Panocean Shipping & Terminals, 1969–75; Man. Dir, Panocean-Anco Ltd, 1975–79; The Burmah Oil plc: Dir, 1980–82; Dep. Chm., 1982–83; Gp Chief Exec., 1982–88; Chm., 1983–90. Director: J. Bibby and Sons plc, 1984–87; DRG plc, 1987–89. *Recreations:* history, gardening, sailing. *Address:* (office) 11 Charles II Street, SW1Y 4QP; (home) Broadford House, Stratfield Turgis, Basingstoke, Hants RG27 0AS. *Clubs:* Brooks's, Naval and Military.

MALTRAVERS, Lord; Henry Miles Fitzalan-Howard; *b* 3 Dec. 1987; *s* and *heir* of Earl of Arundel and Surrey, *qv*.

MALVERN, 3rd Viscount *cr* 1955, of Rhodesia and of Bexley, Kent; **Ashley Kevin Godfrey Huggins;** *b* 26 Oct. 1949; *s* of 2nd Viscount Malvern, and of Patricia Marjorie, *d* of Frank Renwick-Bower, Durban, S Africa; *S* father, 1978. *Heir: uncle* Hon. (Martin) James Huggins, *b* 13 Jan. 1928.

MAMALONI, Solomon; MP (People's Alliance Party), 1977; Prime Minister of Solomon Islands, 1981–85, and since 1989; *b* 1943. *Educ:* King George VI School; Te-Aute College, NZ. Exec. Officer, Civil Service, later Clerk to Legislative Council; MP Makira, 1970–76, West Makira, 1976–77; Chief Minister, British Solomon Islands, 1974–76; founder and leader, People's Progress Party (merged with Rural Alliance Party to form People's Alliance Party, 1979); Man. Dir, Patosha Co., 1977. *Address:* Office of the Prime Minister, Honiara, Guadalcanal, Solomon Islands.

MAMBA, George Mbikwakhe, Hon. GCVO 1987; High Commissioner for the Kingdom of Swaziland to UK, 1978–88, concurrently High Commissioner to Malta, Ambassador to Denmark, Sweden and Norway, and Permanent Delegate to UNESCO; Senior High Commissioner, 1984, and Doyen of the Diplomatic Corps, 1985–88; *b* 5 July 1932; *s* of Ndabazebelungu Mamba and Getrude Mthwalose Mamba, and *g s* of late Chief Bokweni Mamba; *m* 1960, Sophie Sidzandza Sibande; three *s* two *d*. *Educ:* Franson Christian High Sch.; Swazi National High Sch.; Morija Teacher Trng Coll.; Cambridge Inst. of Educn; Nairobi Univ. Head Teacher, Makhonza Mission Sch., 1956–60; Teacher, Kwaluseni Central Sch., 1961–65; Head Teacher, Enkamheni Central Sch., 1966–67; Inspector of Schs, Manzini Dist, 1969–70; Welfare/Aftercare Officer, Prison Dept, 1971–72; Counsellor, Swaziland High Commn, Nairobi, 1972–77. Vice-Pres., Swaziland NUT, 1966–67. Field Comr, Swaziland Boy Scouts Assoc., 1967–68, Chief Comr, 1971–72. *Publication:* Children's Play, 1966. *Recreations:* scouting, reading. *Address:* c/o Ministry of Foreign Affairs, PO Box 518, Mbabane, Swaziland.

MAMET, David Alan; writer; stage and film director; *b* 30 Nov. 1947; *s* of Bernard Morris Mamet and Lenore June Mamet (*née* Silver); *m* 1977, Lindsay Crouse. *Educ:* Goddard College, Plainfield, Vt (BA Eng. Lit. 1969); Neighbourhood Playhouse Sch., NY. Founding Mem. and first Artistic Dir, St Nicholas Theater Co., Chicago, 1974. *Plays written and produced include:* American Buffalo, 1976; A Life in the Theatre, 1976; The Water Engine, 1976; The Woods, 1977; Glen Garry Glen Ross, 1984; Speed the Plow, 1987; Bobby Gould in Hell, 1989; The Old Neighborhood, 1990; *written for films:* The Verdict, 1980; The Untouchables, 1986; House of Games, 1986; (with Shel Silverstein) Things Change, 1987; Hoffa, 1990; Homicide, 1991; *films directed:* House of Games, 1986; Things Change, 1988; Homicide, 1991. Pulitzer Prize for Drama, 1984. *Publications:* Writing in Restaurants, 1986; Some Freaks, 1989; The Hero Pony, 1990; On Directing Film, 1991. *Address:* c/o Howard Rosenstone, Rosenstone/Wender Agency, 3 East 48th Street, New York, NY 10017, USA.

MAMO, Sir Anthony (Joseph) Kt 1960; OBE 1955; Companion of Honour, National Order of Merit (Malta), 1990; *b* 9 Jan. 1909; *s* of late Joseph Mamo and late Carola (*née* Brincat); *m* 1939, Margaret Agius; one *s* two *d*. *Educ:* Royal Univ. of Malta. BA 1931; LLD 1934. Mem. Statute Law Revision Commn, 1936–42; Crown Counsel, 1942–51; Prof., Criminal Law, Malta Univ., 1943–57; Dep. Attorney-Gen., 1952–54, Attorney-Gen., 1955, Malta; Chief Justice and President, Court of Appeal, Malta, 1957–71; President, Constitutional Court, Malta, 1964–71; Governor-General, Malta, 1971–74; President, Republic of Malta, 1974–76. QC (Malta) 1957. Hon. DLitt Malta, 1969; Hon. LLD Libya, 1971. KStJ 1969. *Publications:* Lectures on Criminal Law and Criminal Procedure delivered at the University of Malta. *Address:* 49 Stella Maris Street, Sliema, Malta. *T:* 330708. *Club:* Casino (1852).

MAN, Archdeacon of; *see* Willoughby, Ven. D. A.

MANASSEH, Leonard Sulla, OBE 1982; RA 1979 (ARA 1976); PRWA; FRIBA; Partner, Leonard Manasseh Partnership (formerly Leonard Manasseh & Partners), since 1950; *b* 21 May 1916; *s* of late Alan Manasseh and Esther (*née* Elias); *m* 1st, 1947 (marr diss. 1956); two *s*; 2nd, 1957, Sarah Delaforce; two *s* (one *d* decd). *Educ:* Cheltenham College; The Architectural Assoc. Sch. of Architecture (AA Dip.). ARIBA 1941, FRIBA 1964; FCSD (FSIAD 1965); PRWA 1989 (RWA 1972). Asst Architect, CRE N London and Guy Morgan & Partners; teaching staff, AA and Kingston Sch. of Art, 1941–43; Fleet Air Arm, 1943–46; Asst Architect, Herts CC, 1946–48; Senior Architect, Stevenage New Town Develt Corp., 1948–50; won Festival of Britain restaurant competition, 1950; started private practice, 1950; teaching staff, AA Sch. of Architecture, 1951–59; opened office in Singapore and Malaysia with James Cubitt & Partners (Cubitt Manasseh & Partners), 1953–54. Member: Council, Architectural Assoc., 1959–66 (Pres., 1964–65); Council of Industrial Design, 1965–68; Council, RIBA 1968–70, 1976–82 (Hon. Sec., 1979–81); Council, National Trust, 1977–; Ancient Monuments Bd, 1978–84; Bd, Chatham Historic Dockyard Trust, 1984–. Pres., Franco-British Union of Architects, 1978–79. Governor: Alleyn's Sch., Dulwich, 1987–; Dulwich Coll., 1987–; Dulwich Picture Gallery, 1987–. FRSA 1967. *Work includes:* houses, housing and schools; industrial work; power stations; conservation plan for Beaulieu Estate; Nat. Motor Museum, Beaulieu; Wellington Country Park, Stratfield Saye; Pumping Station, Weymouth; British Museum refurbishment; (jtly) New Research Station, British Gas. *Publications:* Office Buildings (with 3rd Baron Cunliffe), 1962, Japanese edn 1964; Snowdon Summit Report (Countryside Commission), 1974; Eastbourne Harbour Study (Trustees, Chatsworth Settlement), 1976; (jtly) planning reports and studies. *Recreations:* photography, painting, being optimistic. *Address:* 6 Bacon's Lane, Highgate, N6 6BL. *T:* 081–340 5528. *Clubs:* Athenæum, Arts, Royal Automobile.

MANBY, Mervyn Colet, CMG 1964; QPM 1961; retired; *b* 20 Feb. 1915; *s* of late Harold B. and Mary Manby (*née* Mills), late of Petistree, Suffolk; *m* 1949, Peggy Aronson, Eastern Cape, South Africa; one *s* one *d*. *Educ:* Bedford Sch., Bedford; Pembroke Coll., Oxford (MA). Colonial Police Service, 1937; Malaya, 1938–47; Basutoland, 1947–54; Kenya, 1954–64. Dep. Inspector General, Kenya Police, 1961–64; retired, 1964. United Nations Technical Assistance Adviser to Government of Iran, 1965–70; UN Div. of Narcotic Drugs, 1971–75; special consultant, UN Fund for Drug Abuse Control, 1975. Mem. Council, Inst. for Study of Drug Dependence, 1975–78. *Address:* Old Well Cottage, Barham, Canterbury, Kent CT4 6PB. *T:* Canterbury (0227) 381369.

MANCE, Jonathan Hugh; QC 1982; a Recorder, since 1990; barrister; *b* 6 June 1943; *e s* of late Sir Henry Stenhouse Mance and of Lady (Joan Erica Robertson) Mance; *m* 1973, Mary Howarth Arden, *qv*; one *s* two *d*. *Educ:* Charterhouse; University Coll., Oxford (MA). Called to the Bar, Middle Temple, 1965. Worked in Germany, 1965. *Publications:* (asst editor) Chalmer's Sale of Goods, 1981; (ed jtly) Sale of Goods, Halsbury's Laws of England, 4th edn 1983. *Recreations:* tennis, languages, music. *Address:* 11 Frognal Lane, NW3 7DG. *T:* 071–794 8011. *Club:* Cumberland Lawn Tennis.

MANCE, Mary Howarth; *see* Arden, M. H.

MANCHAM, Sir James Richard Marie, KBE 1976; international trade consultant, since 1981; Chairman, Airominor Ltd, since 1987; Founder and Chairman, Crusade for the Restoration of Democracy in Seychelles, since 1990; President, Republic of the Seychelles, 1976–77; *b* 11 Aug. 1939; adopted British nationality, 1984; *e s* of late Richard Mancham and Evelyne Mancham, MBE (*née* Tirant); *m* 1963, Heather Jean Evans (marr. diss. 1974); one *s* one *d*; *m* 1985, Catherine Olsen; one *s*. *Educ:* Seychelles Coll.; Wilson Coll., London. Called to Bar, Middle Temple, 1961. Auditeur Libre à la Faculté de Droit ès Sciences Economiques, Univ. of Paris, 1962; Internat. Inst. of Labour Studies Study Course, Geneva, Spring 1968. Legal practice, Supreme Court of Seychelles. Seychelles Democratic Party (SDP), Pres. 1964; Mem. Seychelles Governing Council, 1967; Leader of Majority Party (SDP), 1967; Mem., Seychelles Legislative Assembly, 1970–76; Chief Minister, 1970–75; Prime Minister, 1975–76; led SDP to Seychelles Constitutional Conf., London, 1970 and 1976. Founder, Seychelles Weekly, 1962. Lecturer, 1981, on struggle for power in Indian Ocean, to US and Eur. univs and civic gps. Hon. Trustee, Cary Ann Lindblad Intrepid Foundn, 1986–. Hon. Citizen: Dade County, Florida, 1963; New Orleans, 1965. FRSA 1968. Cert. of Merit for Distinguished Contribn to Poetry, Internat. Who's Who in Poetry, 1974. Officier de la Légion d'Honneur, 1976; Grande Médaille de la Francophonie, 1976; Grande médaille vermeille, Paris, 1976; Quaid-i-Azam Medallion (Pakistan), 1976; Gold Medal for Tourism, Mexico, 1977; Gold Medal of Chamber of Commerce and Industries of France, 1977; Gold Medal des Excellences Européennes, 1977; Plaque of Appreciation, Rotary Club of Manila, Philippines, 1987. *Publications:* Reflections and Echoes from Seychelles, 1972 (poetry); L'Air des Seychelles, 1974; Island Splendour, 1980; Paradise Raped, 1983; Galloo—The undiscovered paradise, 1984; New York's Robin Island, 1985; Peace of Mind, 1989. *Recreations:* travel, water sports, tennis, writing. *Address:* c/o Lloyds Bank, 81 Edgware Road, W2 2HY. *Clubs:* Royal Automobile, Annabel's, Les Ambassadeurs, Wig and Pen; Intrepids (NY); Cercle Saint Germain des Prés (Paris).

MANCHESTER, 12th Duke of, *cr* 1719; **Angus Charles Drogo Montagu;** Baron Montagu, Viscount Mandeville, 1620; Earl of Manchester, 1626; *b* 9 Oct. 1938; *yr s* of 10th Duke of Manchester, OBE, and Nell Vere (*d* 1966), *d* of Sydney Vere Stead, Melbourne; *S* brother, 1985; *m* 1st, 1961, Mary Eveleen (marr. diss. 1970), *d* of Walter Gillespie McClure; two *s* one *d*; 2nd, 1971, Diane Pauline (marr. diss. 1985), *d* of Arthur Plimsaul; 3rd, 1989, Mrs Ann-Louise Bird. *Educ:* Gordonstoun. *Heir: s* Viscount Mandeville, *qv*. *Address:* c/o House of Lords, SW1A 0PW.

MANCHESTER, Bishop of, since 1979; **Rt. Rev. Stanley Eric Francis Booth-Clibborn;** *b* 20 Oct. 1924; *s* of late Eric and Lucille Booth-Clibborn; *m* 1958, Anne Roxburgh Forrester, *d* of late Rev. William Roxburgh Forrester, MC; two *s* two *d*. *Educ:* Highgate School; Oriel Coll., Oxford (MA); Westcott House, Cambridge. Served RA, 1942–45; Royal Indian Artillery, 1945–47, Temp. Captain. Curate, Heeley Parish Church, Sheffield, 1952–54, The Attercliffe Parishes, Sheffield, 1954–56; Training Sec., Christian Council of Kenya, 1956–63; Editor-in-Chief, East African Venture Newspapers, Nairobi, 1963–67; Leader, Lincoln City Centre Team Ministry, 1967–70; Vicar, St Mary the Great, University Church, Cambridge, 1970–79. Hon. Canon, Ely Cathedral, 1976–79. Member: Div. of Internat. Affairs, BCC, 1968–80; Standing Cttee, General Synod, 1981–90; BCC delegn to Namibia, 1981; Chm., Namibia Communications Centre, 1983–; Pres., St Ann's Hospice, 1979–. Moderator, Movement for Ordination of Women, 1979–82. Introduced to House of Lords, 1985. Hon. Fellow, Manchester Polytechnic, 1989. *Publication:* Taxes—Burden or Blessing?, 1991. *Recreations:* photography, tennis, listening to music. *Address:* Bishopscourt, Bury New Road, Manchester M7 0LE. *T:* 061–792 2096/1779. *Club:* Commonwealth Trust.

MANCHESTER, Dean of; *see* Waddington, Very Rev. R. M.

MANCHESTER, Archdeacon of; *see* Harris, Ven. R. B.

MANCHESTER, William; Purple Heart (US) 1945; author; Fellow, East College, 1968–86, writer in residence since 1974, and Adjunct Professor of History since 1979, Wesleyan University; *b* 1 April 1922; *s* of William Raymond Manchester and Sallie E. R.

(*née* Thompson); *m* 1948, Julia Brown Marshall; one *s* two *d*. *Educ:* Springfield Classical High School; Univ. of Massachusetts; Dartmouth Coll., NH; Univ. of Missouri. Served US Marine Corps, 1942–45. Reporter, Daily Oklahoman, 1945–46; Reporter, foreign corresp., war corresp., Baltimore Sun, 1947–55; Man. editor, Wesleyan Univ. Publications, 1955–65; Fellow, Center for Advanced Studies, 1959–60, Lectr in English, 1968–69, Wesleyan Univ. Trustee, Friends of Univ. of Massachusetts Library, 1970–76, Pres., 1970–72; Mem., Soc. of Amer. Historians. Guggenheim Fellow, 1959; Hon. Dr of Humane Letters: Univ. of Mass, 1965; Univ. of New Haven, 1979; Hon. LittD: Skidmore Coll., 1987; Univ. of Richmond, 1988. Dag Hammarskjold Internat. Prize in Literature, 1967; Overseas Press Club (New York) Award for Best Book of the Year on Foreign Affairs, 1968; Univ. of Missouri Medal, 1969; Connecticut Book Award, 1974; President's Cabinet Award, Detroit Univ., 1981; Frederick S. Troy Medal, 1981; McConaughy Award, 1981; Lincoln Literary Award, 1983; Distinguished Public Service Award, Conn Bar Assoc., 1985. *Publications:* Disturber of the Peace, 1951 (publ. UK as The Sage of Baltimore, 1952); The City of Anger, 1953; Shadow of the Monsoon, 1956; Beard the Lion, 1958; A Rockefeller Family Portrait, 1959; The Long Gainer, 1961; Portrait of a President, 1962; The Death of a President, 1967; The Arms of Krupp, 1968; The Glory and the Dream, 1974; Controversy and other Essays in Journalism, 1976; American Caesar, 1978; Goodbye, Darkness, 1980; One Brief Shining Moment, 1983; The Last Lion: vol. 1, Visions of Glory, 1983; vol. 2, Alone, 1987 (publ. UK as The Caged Lion, Winston Spencer Churchill 1932–1940, 1988); This is Our Time, 1989; contrib. to Encyclopedia Britannica and to periodicals. *Recreation:* photography. *Address:* Wesleyan University, Middletown, Conn 06457, USA. *T:* 203–347–9422, ext. 2388. *Clubs:* Century, Williams (New York), University (Hartford).

MANCHESTER, Sir William (Maxwell), KBE 1987 (CBE 1973); FRCS, FRACS, FACS; private plastic surgical practice, since 1979; *b* 31 Oct. 1913; *s* of James Manchester and Martha Browne; *m* 1945, Lois Yardley Cameron. *Educ:* Waimate Primary Sch.; Timaru Boys' High Sch.; Otago Univ. Med. Sch. MB ChB 1938. FRCS 1949; FRACS 1957; FACS 1973. NZ Medical Corps: joined as RMO, Feb. 1940; 2nd NZ Exped. Force, May 1940; seconded for training as plastic surgeon, Nov. 1940; served in UK, Egypt and NZ (mostly in plastic surgery) until 1946. Head of plastic surgical services, Auckland Hosp Bd, 1950–79; Prof. of Plastic and Reconstructive Surgery, Univ. of Auckland, 1977–79; Mem., Auckland Hosp. Bd, 1980–89. Mem., James IV Assoc. of Surgeons, 1969. *Publications:* chapters in: Operative Surgery, 1956, 3rd edn 1976; Long-term Results in Plastic and Reconstructive Surgery, 1980; The Artistry of Reconstructive Surgery, 1987; Management of Cleft Lip and Palate, ed J. Bardach and H. L. Morris, 1990; contribs to British and US med. jls. *Recreations:* classical music, gardening, cooking. *Address:* Watch Hill, Jeffs Road, RD1, Papatoetoe, Auckland, New Zealand. *T:* (09) 274–6702. *Club:* Northern (Auckland).

MANCROFT, family name of **Baron Mancroft.**

MANCROFT, 3rd Baron *cr* 1937, of Mancroft in the City of Norwich; **Benjamin Lloyd Stormont Mancroft;** Bt 1932; *b* 16 May 1957; *s* of 2nd Baron Mancroft, KBE, TD and of Diana Elizabeth, *d* of late Lt-Col Horace Lloyd, DSO; *S* father, 1987; *m* 1990, Emma Louisa, *e d* of Thomas Peart. *Educ:* Eton. MFH, Vale of White Horse Hunt, 1987–89. Hon. Sec., Promis Trust, 1986–90; Chm., Addiction Recovery Foundn, 1989–. Exec., Assoc. of Cons. Peers, 1990–. *Address:* House of Lords, SW1A 0PW.

MANDELA, Nelson Rolihlahia; South African politician and lawyer; President, African National Congress, since 1991 (National Organizer and Vice-President, 1989–91); *b* 1918; *s* of Chief of Tembu tribe; *m* Winnie Mandela. *Educ:* Univ. Coll., Fort Hare; Univ. of Witwatersrand. Legal practice, Johannesburg, 1952. On trial for treason, 1956–61 (acquitted); sentenced to five years' imprisonment, 1962; tried for further charges, 1963–64, and sentenced to life imprisonment; released, 1990. Jawaharlal Nehru Award, India, 1979; Simon Bolivar Prize, UNESCO, 1983; Sakharov Prize, 1988. *Publication:* No Easy Walk to Freedom, 1965. *Address:* Soweto, Transvaal, South Africa.

MANDELSON, Peter Benjamin; Industrial Consultant, SRU Group, since 1990; *b* 21 Oct. 1953; *s* of George Mandelson and Mary (*née* Morrison). *Educ:* Hendon County Grammar Sch.; St Catherine's Coll., Oxford (Hons degree, PPE). Econ. Dept, TUC, 1977–78; Chm., British Youth Council, 1978–80; producer, LWT, 1982–85; Dir of Campaigns and Communications, Labour Party, 1985–90. Prospective Parly Candidate (Lab) Hartlepool, 1990–. Mem. Council, London Bor. of Lambeth, 1979–82. *Publications:* Youth Unemployment: causes and cures, 1977; Broadcasting and Youth, 1980. *Recreations:* swimming, country walking. *Address:* 30 Hutton Avenue, Hartlepool, Cleveland TS26 9PN. *T:* Hartlepool (0429) 866173.

MANDELSTAM, Prof. Joel, FRS 1971; Emeritus Professor, University of Oxford, and Emeritus Fellow, Linacre College, since 1987; *b* S Africa, 13 Nov. 1919; *s* of Leo and Fanny Mandelstam; *m* 1954, Dorothy Hillier; one *s* one *d*; *m* 1975, Mary Maureen Dale. *Educ:* Jeppe High Sch., Johannesburg; University of Witwatersrand. Lecturer, Medical Sch., Johannesburg, 1942–47; Queen Elizabeth Coll., London, 1947–51; Scientific Staff, Nat. Institute for Med. Research, London, 1952–66; Iveagh Prof. of Microbiology, and Fellow of Linacre College, Univ. of Oxford, 1966–87; Deptl Demonstrator, Sir William Dunn Sch. of Pathology, Univ. of Oxford, 1987–90. Fulbright Fellow, US, 1958–59; Vis. Prof., Univ. of Adelaide, 1971. Mem., ARC, 1973–83. Leewenhoek Lectr, Royal Soc., 1975. Editorial Board, Biochemical Journal, 1960–66. *Publications:* Biochemistry of Bacterial Growth (with K. McQuillen and I. Dawes), 1968; articles in journals and books on microbial biochemistry. *Address:* 13 Cherwell Lodge, Water Eaton Road, Oxford OX2 7QH.

MANDELSTAM, Prof. Stanley, FRS 1962; Professor of Physics, University of California. *Educ:* University of the Witwatersrand, Johannesburg, Transvaal, South Africa (BSc); Trinity Coll., Cambridge (BA). PhD, Birmingham. Formerly Professor of Math. Physics, University of Birmingham; Prof. Associé, Univ. de Paris Sud, 1979–80 and 1984–85. *Publications:* (with W. Yourgrau) Variational Principles in Dynamics and Quantum Theory, 1955 (revised edn, 1956); papers in learned journals. *Address:* Department of Physics, University of California, Berkeley, California 94720, USA.

MANDER, Sir Charles (Marcus), 3rd Bt, *cr* 1911; Underwriting Member of Lloyd's; Director: Manders (Holdings) Ltd, 1951–58; Mander Brothers Ltd, 1948–58; Headstaple Ltd, since 1977; *b* 22 Sept. 1921; *o s* of Sir Charles Arthur Mander, 2nd Bart, and late Monica Claire Cotterill, *d* of G. H. Neame; *S* father, 1951; *m* 1945, Maria Dolores Beatrice, *d* of late Alfred Brodermann, Hamburg; two *s* one *d*. *Educ:* Eton Coll., Windsor; Trinity Coll., Cambridge. Commissioned Coldstream Guards, 1942; served War of 1939–45, Canal Zone, 1943; Italy, 1943, Germany, 1944; War Office (ADC to Lieut-General R. G. Stone, CB), 1945. Chairman: Arlington Securities Ltd, 1977–83; London & Cambridge Investments Ltd, 1983–91. High Sheriff of Staffordshire, 1962–63. *Recreations:* shooting, music. *Heir:* *s* Charles Nicholas Mander [*b* 23 March 1950; *m* 1972, Karin Margareta, *d* of Arne Norin; four *s* one *d*]. *Address:* Little Barrow, Moreton-in-Marsh, Glos GL56 0XU. *T:* Cotswold (0451) 30265; Greville House, Kinnerton Street, SW1. *T:* 071–235 1669. *Clubs:* Boodle's, Royal Thames Yacht.

MANDER, Prof. Lewis Norman, FRS 1990; Professor of Chemistry, Australian National University, since 1980; *b* 8 Sept. 1939; *s* of John Eric and Anne Frances Mander; *m* 1965, Stephanie Vautin; one *s* two *d*. *Educ:* Mount Albert Grammar Sch.; Univ. of Sydney (PhD 1965). FRACI 1980; FAA 1983. Postdoctoral Fellow, Univ. of Michigan, 1964–65; Postdoctoral Associate, Caltech, 1965–66; Lectr and Sen. Lectr in Organic Chem., Univ. of Adelaide, 1966–75; Sen. Fellow, 1975–80, Dean, 1981–86, Res. Sch. of Chem., ANU. Nuffield Commonwealth Fellow, Cambridge, 1972; Fulbright Sen. Schol., Caltech, 1977, Harvard, 1986. H. G. Smith Medal, RACI, 1981; Flintoff Medal and Prize, RSocChem, 1990. *Publications:* numerous articles in learned jls, mainly on synthesis of organic molecules. *Recreations:* bushwalking, speleology. *Address:* Research School of Chemistry, Australian National University, GPO Box 4, Canberra, ACT 2601, Australia. *T:* (06) 2493761, *Fax:* (06) 2495995.

MANDER, Michael Harold; His Honour Judge Mander; a Circuit Judge, since 1985; *b* 27 Oct. 1936; *e s* of late Harold and Ann Mander; *m* 1960, Jancis Mary Dodd, *er d* of late Revd Charles and Edna Dodd. *Educ:* Workington Grammar School; Queen's College, Oxford (MA, 2nd cl. hons Jurisp.; Rigg Exbnr). Nat. Service, RA (2nd Lieut) to 1957. Articled clerk; solicitor, 2nd cl. hons, 1963; called to the Bar, Inner Temple, 1972. Asst Recorder, 1982–85. Dep. Chm., Agricultural Lands Tribunal, 1983–85. *Recreation:* life under the Wrekin. *Address:* Garmston, Eaton Constantine, Shrewsbury SY5 6RL. *T:* Cressage (0952) 510288. *Club:* Wrekin Rotary (Hon. Mem.).

MANDER, Noel Percy, MBE 1979; FSA; Managing Director, N. P. Mander Ltd, since 1946; *b* 19 May 1912; *s* of late Percy Mander and Emily Pike, Hoxne, Suffolk; *m* 1948, Enid Watson; three *s* two *d*. *Educ:* Haberdashers Aske's Sch., Hatcham. Organ building from 1930, interrupted by war service with RA (Hampshire Bde) in N Africa, Italy and Syria, 1940–46. FSA 1974. Mem., Nat. Council of Christians and Jews (former Chm., N London Council). Governor, Sir John Cass Foundn. Liveryman, Musicians' Co.; Past Master, Parish Clerks' Co. of City of London; Mem., Art Workers' Guild. Churchill Life Fellow, Westminster Coll., Fulton, 1982; Hon. Dr Arts Westminster Coll., 1984. Builder of Winston Churchill Meml Organ, Fulton, Missouri, and organs in many parts of world; organ builder to St Paul's Cathedral London and Canterbury Cathedral, and to HM Sultan of Oman. *Publications:* St Lawrence Jewry, A History of the Organs from the Earliest Times to the Present Day, 1956; St Vedast, Foster Lane, A History of the Organs from Earliest Times to the Present Day, 1961; St Vedast Foster Lane, in the City of London: a history of the 13 United Parishes, 1973; (with C. M. Houghton) St Botolph Aldgate: a history of the organs from the Restoration to the Twentieth Century, 1973. *Recreations:* archaeology, horology, reading. *Address:* The Street, Earl Soham, Woodbridge, Suffolk. *T:* Earl Soham (072882) 312; The Lodge, St Peter's Organ Works, St Peter's Close, E2 7AF. *T:* 071–739 4746. *Club:* Savage.

MANDEVILLE, Viscount; Alexander Charles David Drogo Montagu; *b* 11 Dec. 1962; *s* and *heir* of 12th Duke of Manchester, *qv*.

MANDUCA, John Alfred; High Commissioner for Malta in London, 1987–90; (concurrently) Ambassador to Norway, Sweden and Denmark, 1988–90, and to Ireland, 1990; *b* 14 Aug. 1927; *s* of Captain Philip dei Conti Manduca and Emma (*née* Pullicino); *m* 1954, Sylvia Parnis; two *s* two *d*. *Educ:* St Edward's Coll., Malta. Joined Allied Malta Newspapers Ltd, 1945, Dep. Editor, 1953–62; Malta Correspondent, The Daily Telegraph and The Sunday Telegraph, 1946–62; joined Broadcasting Authority, Malta, 1962; BBC attachment, 1963; Chief Exec., Broadcasting Authority, Malta, 1963–68; Dir and Manager, Malta Television Service Ltd, 1968–71; Man. Dir, Rediffusion Gp of Cos in Malta, 1971–76; Chm., Tourist Projects Ltd, 1976–83; Dir. Gen., Confedn of Private Enterprises, 1983–87. Chairman: Malta Br., Inst. of Journalists, 1957, 1959 and 1961; Hotels and Catering Establishments Bd, 1970–71; Hon. Treas., Malta Br., Inst. of Dirs, 1975; Member: Tourist Bd, 1969–70; Broadcasting Authority, 1979–81; Bd of Governors, St Edward's Coll., 1966–75, 1991–. Served 11 HAA Regt, Royal Malta Artillery (T), 1952–55 (commnd 1953). *Publications:* Tourist Guide to Malta and Gozo, 1967, 7th edn 1980; Tourist Guide to Harbour Cruises, 1974, 3rd edn 1981; Connoisseur's Guide to City of Mdina, 1975, 3rd edn 1985; Gen. Ed., Malta Who's Who, 1987. *Recreations:* collecting Melitensia, current affairs, gardening. *Address:* Beaulieu, Bastion Square, Citta Vecchia (Mdina), Malta. *T:* 674009. *Club:* Casino Maltese (Malta).

MANDUCA, Paul Victor Sant; Chairman, Touche Remnant & Co., since 1989; *b* 15 Nov. 1951; *s* of Victor Manduca and Elizabeth Manduca (*née* Johnson); *m* 1982, Ursula Vogt; two *s*. *Educ:* Harrow Sch.; Hertford Coll., Oxford (Hons Mod. Langs). Colegrave & Co., 1973–75; Rowe & Pitman, 1976–79; Hill Samuel Inv. Management, 1979–83; Touche Remnant, 1983– (Dir 1986, Vice-Chm. 1987); Dir, TR Smaller Cos Investment Trust (formerly Trustees Group), 1986–; Man. Dir, TR Industrial & General, 1986–88; Chm., TR High Income, 1989–. Dir, Clydesdale IT, 1987–88. Chm., Assoc. of Investment Trust Cos, 1991– (Dep. Chm., 1989–91). *Recreations:* golf, squash. *Address:* 54 Brompton Square, SW3 2AG. *T:* 071–584 3987. *Clubs:* Lansdowne; Wentworth Golf.

MANDUELL, Sir John, Kt 1989; CBE 1982; FRAM, FRCM, FRNCM, FRSAMD; composer; Principal, Royal Northern College of Music, since 1971; *b* 2 March 1928; *s* of Matthewman Donald Manduell, MC, MA, and Theodora (*née* Tharp); *m* 1955, Renna Kellaway; three *s* one *d*. *Educ:* Haileybury Coll.; Jesus Coll., Cambridge; Univ. of Strasbourg; Royal Acad. of Music. FRAM 1964; FRNCM 1974; FRCM 1980; FRSAMD 1982; Hon. FTCL 1973; Hon. GSM 1986. BBC: music producer, 1956–61; Head of Music, Midlands and E Anglia, 1961–64; Chief Planner, The Music Programme, 1964–68; Univ. of Lancaster: Dir of Music, 1968–71; Mem. Court and Council, 1972–77, 1979–83. Prog. Dir, Cheltenham Festival, 1969–. Arts Council: Mem. Council, 1976–78, 1980–84; Mem. Music Panel, 1971–76, Dep. Chm., 1976–78, Chm., 1980–84; Mem. Touring Cttee, 1975–80, Chm., 1976–78; Mem. Trng Cttee, 1973–77. Mem. Music Adv. Cttee, British Council, 1963–72, Chm., 1973–80; Chm. Music Panel, North West Arts, 1973–79; Chairman: British Arts Fests Assoc., 1981–88 (Vice-Chm., 1977–81, Pres., 1988–); Manchester Olympic Fest., 1990; European Music Year (1985): Dep. Chm. UK Cttee, 1982–85; Member: Eur. Organising Cttee, 1982–86; Eur. Exec. Bureau, 1982–86; Internat. Prog. Cttee, 1982–84; Mem. Exec. Cttee, Composers' Guild of GB, 1984–87 (Vice Chm., 1987–89, Chm., 1989–); Gulbenkian Foundn Enquiry into Trng Musicians; Opera Bd, Royal Opera House, 1988–; Chm., Cttee of Heads of Music Colls, 1986–; Governor: Chetham's Sch., 1971–; National Youth Orch., 1964–73, 1978–; President: Lakeland Sinfonia, 1972–89; Jubilate Choir, 1979–; European Assoc. of Music Academies, 1988–; Director: London Opera Centre, 1971–79; Associated Bd of Royal Schools of Music, 1971–; Northern Ballet Theatre, 1973–86 (Chm., 1986–89); Manchester Palace Theatre Trust, 1978–84; London Orchestral Concert Bd, 1980–85; Lake Dist Summer Music, 1984–. Hon. Member: Roy. Soc. of Musicians, 1972; Chopin Soc. of Warsaw, 1973. Engagements and tours as composer, conductor and lectr in Canada, Europe, Hong Kong, S Africa and USA. Chairman: BBC TV Young Musicians of the Year, 1978, 1980; Munich Internat. Music Comp., 1982, 1984, 1985; Chm. or mem., national and internat. music competition juries. FRSA 1981; Fellow, Manchester Polytechnic, 1983. First Leslie Boosey Award, Royal Phil. Soc. and PRS, 1980. *Publications:* (contrib.) The Symphony, ed Simpson, 1966; *compositions:* Overture, Sunderland Point, 1969; Diversions for

Orchestra, 1970; String Quartet, 1976; Prayers from the Ark, 1981; Double Concerto, 1985. *Recreations:* cricket; travel; French life, language and literature. *Address:* Royal Northern College of Music, Oxford Road, Manchester M13 9RD. *T:* 061–273 6283.

MANGHAM, Maj.-Gen. William Desmond, CB 1978; Director, The Brewers' Society, 1980–90; *b* 29 Aug. 1924; *s* of late Lt-Col William Patrick Mangham and Margaret Mary Mangham (*née* Donnachie); *m* 1960, Susan, *d* of late Col Henry Brabazon Humfrey; two *s* two *d. Educ:* Ampleforth College. 2nd Lieut RA, 1943; served India, Malaya, 1945–48; BMRA 1st Div. Egypt, 1955; Staff, HQ Middle East, Cyprus, 1956–58; Instructor, Staff Coll., Camberley and Canada, 1962–65; OC 3rd Regt Royal Horse Artillery, 1966–68; Comdr RA 2nd Div., 1969–70; Royal Coll. of Defence Studies, 1971; Chief of Staff, 1st British Corps, 1972–74; GOC 2nd Div., 1974–75; VQMG, MoD, 1976–79. Colonel Commandant: RA, 1979–88; RHA, 1983–88. *Recreations:* shooting, golf. *Address:* Redwood House, Woolton Hill, Newbury, Berks RG15 9UZ. *Club:* Army and Navy.

MANGO, Prof. Cyril Alexander, FBA 1976; Bywater and Sotheby Professor of Byzantine and Modern Greek, Oxford University, since 1973; *b* 14 April 1928; *s* of Alexander A. Mango and Adelaide Damonov; *m* 1st, 1953, Mabel Grover; one *d*; 2nd, 1964, Susan A. Gerstel; one *d*; 3rd, 1976, Maria C. Mundell. *Educ:* Univ. of St Andrews (MA); Univ. of Paris (Dr Univ Paris). From Jun. Fellow to Lectr in Byzantine Archaeology, Dumbarton Oaks Byzantine Center, Harvard Univ., 1951–63; Lectr in Fine Arts, Harvard Univ., 1957–58; Visiting Associate Prof. of Byzantine History, Univ. of California, Berkeley, 1960–61; Koraës Prof. of Modern Greek and of Byzantine History, Language and Literature, King's Coll., Univ. of London, 1963–68; Prof. of Byzantine Archaeology, Dumbarton Oaks Byzantine Center, 1968–73. FSA. *Publications:* The Homilies of Photius, 1958; The Brazen House, 1959; The Mosaics of St Sophia at Istanbul, 1962; The Art of the Byzantine Empire, Sources and Documents, 1972; Architettura bizantina, 1974; Byzantium, 1980; Byzantium and its Image, 1984; Le Développement Urbain de Constantinople, 1985. *Address:* Exeter College, Oxford.

MANGOLD, Thomas Cornelius; Reporter, BBC TV Panorama, since 1976; *b* 20 Aug. 1934; *s* of Fritz Mangold and Dorothea Mangold; *m* 1972, Valerie Ann Hare (*née* Dean); three *d. Educ:* Dorking Grammar Sch. Reporter, Croydon Advertiser, 1952. Served RA, 1952–54. Reporter: Croydon Advertiser, 1955–59; Sunday Pictorial, 1959–62; Daily Express, 1962–64; BBC TV News, 1964–70; BBC TV 24 Hours, later Midweek, 1970–76. *Publications:* (jtly) The File on the Tsar, 1976; (jtly) The Tunnels of Cu Chi, 1985; Cold Warrior, 1991. *Recreations:* writing, playing Blues harp. *Address:* c/o BBC TV, Lime Grove, W12. *T:* 081–743 8000.

MANGWAZU, Timon Sam, MA Oxon; Malaŵi Ambassador to the United States and Permanent Representative to the United Nations, 1985–89; *b* 12 Oct. 1933; *s* of Sam Isaac Mangwazu, Farmer; *m* 1958, Nelly Kathewera; three *s* three *d. Educ:* Ruskin Coll., Oxford; Brasenose Coll., Oxford (BA; MA 1976). Teacher at Methodist Sch., Hartley, S Rhodesia, 1955; Clerical Officer, Government Print, Agricultural Dept and Accountant General's Dept, 1956–62; Asst Registrar of Trade Unions, Ministry of Labour, 1962–63; Malaŵi Ambassador, West Germany, Norway, Sweden, Denmark, Netherlands, Belgium, Switzerland and Austria, 1964–67; High Comr in London for Republic of Malaŵi, and Ambassador to Belgium, Portugal, Netherlands and Holy See, 1967–69; Brasenose Coll., Oxford, 1969–72; Malaŵi Ambassador to EEC, Belgium and the Netherlands, 1973–78; Malaŵi Ambassador to South Africa and High Comr to Lesotho, 1982–84. Press Group of Companies: Dep. Man. Dir, 1978–80; Man. Dir, 1980; Gp Man. Dir, 1980–81; Chm., Nat. Bank of Malaŵi, 1978–81. Ran own business (farming and trading etc), 1984–85. Mem. Council, Univ. of Malaŵi; Chm., Bd of Governors, Malaŵi Polytechnic, 1980–87. *Recreation:* fishing. *Address:* c/o Ministry of External Affairs, PO Box 30315, Lilongwe 3, Malaŵi.

MANKIEWICZ, Joseph Leo; American writer and film director; *b* 11 Feb. 1909; *s* of Frank Mankiewicz and Johanna (*née* Blumenau); *m* 1939, Rosa Stradner (*d* 1958); two *s* (and one *s* by previous marriage); *m* 1962, Rosemary Matthews; one *d. Educ:* Columbia Univ. (AB 1928). Has written, directed and produced for the screen, 1929–. President, Screen Directors' Guild of America, 1950. *Films include:* Manhattan Melodrama, Fury, Three Comrades, Philadelphia Story, Woman of the Year, Keys of the Kingdom, The Ghost and Mrs Muir, A Letter to Three Wives (Academy Awards for Best Screenplay and Best Direction), No Way Out, All About Eve (Academy Awards for Best Screenplay and Best Direction), People Will Talk, Five Fingers, Julius Caesar, The Barefoot Contessa, Guys and Dolls; The Quiet American; Suddenly Last Summer; The Honey Pot; There Was a Crooked Man; Sleuth. Directed La Bohème for Metropolitan Opera, 1952. Formed own company, Figaro Inc., 1953, dissolved 1961. Fellow, Yale Univ., 1979–. Work in progress on The Performing Woman (when and how women came to perform the roles of women on the stages of the Western theatre). Received Screen Directors' Guild Award, 1949 and 1950; Screen Writers' Guild Award for best American comedy, 1949 and 1950; Laurel Award, Writers Guild of America, 1963; D. W. Griffith Award, Directors Guild of America, for Lifetime Achievement, 1986. Erasmus Award, City of Rotterdam, 1984; Alexander Hamilton Medal, Columbia Coll., NYC, 1986; Leone D'Oro Award, for lifetime achievement, Venice Film Fest., 1987; Akira Kurosawa Award, for lifetime achievement, San Francisco Internat. Film Festival, 1989. Order of Merit (Italy), 1965; Hon. Citizen of Avignon (France), 1980; Chevalier de la Légion d'Honneur (France), 1988. *Address:* Guard Hill Road, Bedford, NY 10506, USA.

MANKOWITZ, Wolf; author; Honorary Consul to the Republic of Panama in Dublin, 1971; *b* 7 Nov. 1924; *s* of Solomon and Rebecca Mankowitz; *m* 1944, Ann Margaret Seligmann; four *s. Educ:* East Ham Grammar Sch.; Downing Coll., Cambridge (MA, English Tripos). University of New Mexico: Adjunct Prof. of English, 1982–86; Adjunct Prof., Theatre Arts, 1987–88. Exhibn, Recent Collages, Davis Gall., Dublin, 1990. *Plays include:* Belle (musical), 1961; Passion Flower Hotel (musical), 1965; Samson and Delilah, 1978 (published as The Samson Riddle); Casanova's Last Stand, 1980; *films:* Make Me an Offer, 1954; A Kid for Two Farthings, 1954; The Bespoke Overcoat, 1955; Expresso Bongo, 1960; The Millionairess, 1960; The Long and The Short and The Tall, 1961; The Day the Earth Caught Fire, 1961; The Waltz of the Toreadors, 1962; Where The Spies Are, 1965; Casino Royale, 1967; The Assassination Bureau, 1969; Bloomfield, 1970; Black Beauty, 1971; Treasure Island, 1972; The Hebrew Lesson (wrote and dir.), 1972; The Hireling, 1973; Almonds and Raisins (a treatment of Yiddish films, 1929–39), 1984; *television:* Dickens of London, 1976. *Publications: novels:* Make Me An Offer, 1952; A Kid for Two Farthings, 1953; Laugh Till You Cry, 1955 (USA); My Old Man's a Dustman, 1956; Cockatrice, 1963; The Biggest Pig in Barbados, 1965; Penguin Wolf Mankowitz, 1967; Raspberry Reich, 1979; ¡Abracadabra!, 1980; The Devil in Texas, 1984; Gioconda, 1987; The Magic Cabinet of Professor Smucker, 1988; Exquisite Cadaver, 1990; A Night with Casanova, 1991; *short stories:* The Mendelman Fire, 1957; The Blue Arabian Nights, 1973; The Day of the Women and The Night of the Men (fables), 1977; *histories:* Wedgwood, 1953, 3rd repr. 1980; The Portland Vase, 1953; An Encyclopaedia of English Pottery and Porcelain, 1957; *biography:* Dickens of London, 1976; The Extraordinary Mr Poe, 1978; Mazeppa, 1982; *poetry:* 12 Poems, 1971; *plays:* The Bespoke Overcoat and Other Plays, 1955; Expresso Bongo (musical), 1958–59; Make Me An Offer (musical), 1959; Pickwick, 1963 (musical); The Samson Riddle, 1972; Stand and Deliver! (musical), 1972; The Irish Hebrew Lesson, 1978; Iron Butterflies, 1986. *Recreations:* sleeping or making collage. *Address:* The Bridge House, Ahakista, Co. Cork. *Club:* Savile.

MANKTELOW, Rt. Rev. Michael Richard John; *see* Basingstoke, Bishop Suffragan of.

MANLEY, Ivor Thomas, CB 1984; Deputy Secretary, Department of Employment, 1987–91; *b* 4 March 1931; *s* of Frederick Stone and Louisa Manley; *m* 1952, Joan Waite; one *s* one *d. Educ:* Sutton High Sch., Plymouth. Entered Civil Service, 1951; Principal: Min. of Aviation, 1964–66; Min. of Technology, 1966–68; Private Secretary: to Rt Hon. Anthony Wedgwood Benn, 1968–70; to Rt Hon. Geoffrey Rippon, 1970; Principal Private Sec. to Rt Hon. John Davies, 1970–71; Asst Sec., DTI, 1971–74; Department of Energy: Under-Sec., Principal Estabt Officer, 1974–78, Under Sec., Atomic Energy Div., 1978–81; Dep. Sec., 1981–87. UK Governor, IAEA, 1978–81; Mem., UKAEA, 1981–86. Chm., Task Force on Tourism and the Envmt, 1990–91; Board Member: Business in the Community, 1988–89; BTA, 1991– (Chm., Marketing Cttee, 1991–). *Recreations:* walking, reading. *Address:* 28 Highfield Avenue, Aldershot, Hants GU11 3BZ. *T:* Aldershot (0252) 22707.

MANLEY, Rt. Hon. Michael Norman, PC 1989; Prime Minister of Jamaica, 1972–80, and since 1989; President, People's National Party, Jamaica, since 1969 (Member, Executive, since 1952); MP for Central Kingston, Jamaica, since 1967; President, National Workers Union, since 1984; *b* St Andrew, Jamaica, 10 Dec. 1924; *s* of late Rt Excellent Norman W. Manley, QC, and Edna Manley (*née* Swithenbank); *m* 1972, Beverly Anderson (marr. diss. 1990); one *s* one *d*; one *s* two *d* by previous marriages. *Educ:* Jamaica Coll.; London Sch. of Economics (BSc Econ Hons). Began as freelance journalist, working with BBC, 1950–51; returned to Jamaica, Dec. 1951, as Associate Editor of Public Opinion, 1952–53; Sugar Supervisor, Nat. Workers' Union, 1953–54; Island Supervisor and First Vice-Pres., 1955–72; Mem. Senate, 1962–67; Leader of the Opposition, 1969–72, and 1980–89. Has held various posts in Labour cttees and in Trade Union affairs; organised strike in sugar industry, 1959, which led to Goldenberg Commn of Inquiry. Vice-Pres., Socialist Internat., 1978. Hon. Doctor of Laws Morehouse Coll., Atlanta, 1973. UN Special Award for contrib. to struggle against apartheid, 1978; Joliot Curie Medal, World Peace Council, 1979. Order of the Liberator, Venezuela, 1973; Order of Mexican Eagle, 1975; Order of Jose Marti, Cuba, 1975. *Publications:* The Politics of Change, 1974; A Voice at the Workplace, 1976; The Search for Solutions, 1977; Jamaica: Struggle in the Periphery, 1982; A History of West Indies Cricket, 1988; The Poverty of Nations, 1991. *Recreations:* sports, music, gardening, reading. *Address:* 89 Old Hope Road, Kingston 6, Jamaica.

MANN; *see* Douglas-Mann.

MANN, Prof. (Colin) Nicholas (Jocelyn); Director, Warburg Institute, University of London, and Professor of the History of the Classical Tradition, since 1990; *b* 24 Oct. 1942; *s* of Colin Henry Mann and Marie Elise Mann (*née* Gosling); *m* 1964, Joëlle Bourcart; one *s* one *d. Educ:* Eton; King's Coll., Cambridge (MA, PhD). Res. Fellow, Clare Coll., Cambridge, 1965–67; Lectr, Univ. of Warwick, 1967–72; Vis. Fellow, All Souls Coll., Oxford, 1972; Fellow and Tutor, Pembroke Coll., Oxford, 1973–90. Mem. Council, Mus. of Modern Art, Oxford, 1984– (Chm., 1988–90). Romance Editor, Medium Ævum, 1982–90. *Publications:* Petrarch Manuscripts in the British Isles, 1975; Petrarch, 1984; A Concordance to Petrarch's Bucolicum Carmen, 1984; articles in learned jls. *Recreations:* yoga, sculpture. *Address:* Warburg Institute, Woburn Square, WC1H 0AB. *T:* 071–580 9663.

MANN, Eric John; Controller, Capital Taxes Office, 1978–81; *b* 18 Dec. 1921; *s* of Percival John Mann and Marguerite Mann; *m* 1960, Gwendolen Margaret Salter; one *s* one *d. Educ:* University Coll. Sch., Hampstead; Univ. of London (LLB). Entered Inland Revenue, 1946; Dep. Controller, Capital Taxes Office, 1974. *Publications:* (ed jtly) Green's Death Duties, 5th-7th edns, 1962–71. *Address:* Lawn Gate Cottage, Moccas, Herefordshire HR2 9LF.

MANN, Dr Felix Bernard; medical practitioner; *b* 10 April 1931; *s* of Leo and Caroline Mann; *m* 1986, Ruth Csorba von Borsai. *Educ:* Shrewsbury House; Malvern Coll.; Christ's Coll., Cambridge; Westminster Hosp. MB, BChir, LMCC. Practised medicine or studied acupuncture in England, Canada, Switzerland, France, Germany, Austria and China. Founder, Medical Acupuncture Soc., 1959. *Publications:* Acupuncture; the ancient Chinese art of healing, 1962, 2nd edn 1971; The Treatment of Disease by Acupuncture, 1963; The Meridians of Acupuncture, 1964; Atlas of Acupuncture, 1966; Acupuncture: cure of many diseases, 1971; Scientific Aspects of Acupuncture, 1977; Textbook of Acupuncture, 1987; also edns in Italian, Spanish, Dutch, Finnish, Portuguese, German, Japanese and Swedish; contrib. various jls on acupuncture. *Recreations:* walking in the country and mountains. *Address:* 15 Devonshire Place, W1N 1PB. *T:* 071–935 7575. *Club:* Royal Society of Medicine.

MANN, (Francis) George, CBE 1983; DSO 1942; MC 1941; Director, 1977–87, and non-executive Deputy Chairman, 1980–86, Extel Group; *b* 6 Sept. 1917; *s* of Frank Mann and Enid Mann (*née* Tilney); *m* 1949, Margaret Hildegarde (*née* Marshall Clark); three *s* one *d. Educ:* Eton; Cambridge Univ. BA. Served War of 1939–45, Scots Guards (DSO, MC). Director: Mann Crossman and Paulin, Watney Mann, Watney Mann and Truman Brewers, 1946–77. Middlesex County Cricket Club: first played, 1937; Captain, 1948–49; Pres., 1983–87; captained England in SA, 1948–49 and against NZ, 1949. Chairman: TCCB, 1978–83; Cricket Council, 1983. *Address:* West Woodhay, Newbury, Berks. *T:* Inkpen (04884) 243. *Club:* MCC (Pres., 1984–85; Hon. Life Vice-Pres., 1989).

MANN, George; *see* Mann, F. G.

MANN, Prof. Jill, (Gillian Lesley Mann), FBA 1990; Professor of Medieval and Renaissance English, and Professorial Fellow of Girton College, University of Cambridge, since 1988; *b* 7 April 1943; *d* of late Edward William Ditchburn and Kathleen Ditchburn (*née* Bellamy); *m* 1964, Michael Mann (marr. diss. 1976). *Educ:* Bede Grammar Sch., Sunderland; St Anne's Coll., Oxford (BA 1964); Clare Hall, Cambridge (MA; PhD 1971). Research Fellow, Clare Hall, 1968–71; Lectr, Univ. of Kent at Canterbury, 1971–72; Official Fellow, Girton Coll., Cambridge, 1972–88; Asst Lectr, 1974–78, Lectr, 1978–88, Cambridge Univ. British Academy Research Reader, 1985–87. Hon. Fellow, St Anne's Coll., Oxford, 1990. *Publications:* Chaucer and Medieval Estates Satire, 1973; Ysengrimus, 1987; (ed with Piero Boitani) The Cambridge Chaucer Companion, 1986; Geoffrey Chaucer, 1991; articles on Middle English and Medieval Latin. *Recreations:* riding (badly), walking, travel. *Address:* Girton College, Cambridge CB3 0JG. *T:* Cambridge (0223) 338999.

MANN, John Frederick; educational consultant; Secretary, Society of Education Consultants, since 1990; *b* 4 June 1930; *e s* of Frederick Mann and Hilda G. (*née* Johnson);

m 1966, Margaret (*née* Moore); one *s* one *d*. *Educ:* Poole and Tavistock Grammar Schs; Trinity Coll., Oxford (MA). Asst Master, Colchester Royal Grammar Sch., 1954–61; Admin. Asst, Leeds County Bor., 1962–65; Asst Educn Officer, Essex CC, 1965–67; Dep. Educn Officer, Sheffield County Bor., 1967–78; Sec., Schools Council for the Curriculum and Exams, 1978–83; Dir of Educn, London Bor. of Harrow, 1983–88. Member: Iron and Steel Industry Trng Bd, 1975–78; Exec., Soc. of Educn Officers, 1976–78; Sch. Broadcasting Council, 1979–83; Council, British Educn Management and Admin Soc., 1979–84. Governor, Welbeck Coll., 1975–84. Hon. Fellow, Sheffield Polytechnic, 1980; Hon. FCP, 1986. FBIM; FRSA. JP Sheffield, 1976–79. *Publications:* Education, 1979; contrib. to Victoria County History of Essex, Local Govt Studies, and Educn. *Recreations:* travel, books, theatre, gardening. *Address:* 109 Chatsworth Road, NW2 4BH. *T:* 081–459 5419.

MANN, Martin Edward; QC 1983; a Recorder, since 1990; *b* 12 Sept. 1943; *s* of S. E. Mann and M. L. F. Mann; *m* 1966, Jacqueline Harriette (*née* Le Maître); two *d*. *Educ:* Cranleigh Sch. Called to the Bar, Gray's Inn, 1968 (Lord Justice Holker Sen. Exhibn), Lincoln's Inn, 1973 (*ad eund*); Bencher, Lincoln's Inn, 1991. Mem., Senate of the Inns of Court and the Bar, 1979–82. *Publication:* (jtly) What Kind of Common Agricultural Policy for Europe, 1975. *Recreations:* ski-ing/mountaineering, farming, the arts. *Address:* 24 Old Buildings, Lincoln's Inn, WC2A 3UJ. *T:* 071–404 0946; Kingston St Mary, Somerset. *Clubs:* Royal Automobile; Exeter Centre Fire Pistol.

MANN, Rt. Hon. Sir Michael, Kt 1982; PC 1988; **Rt. Hon. Lord Justice Mann;** a Lord Justice of Appeal, since 1988; *b* 9 Dec. 1930; *s* of late Adrian Bernard Mann, CBE and of Mary Louise (*née* Keen); *m* 1st, 1957 (marr. diss. 1988); two *s*; 2nd, 1989, Audrey Edith Umpleby. *Educ:* Whitgift; King's Coll., London (LLB, PhD; FKC 1984). Called to Bar, Gray's Inn, 1953, Bencher 1980; practised, 1955–82; Junior Counsel to the Land Commn (Common Law), 1967–71; QC 1972; a Recorder of the Crown Court, 1979–82; a Judge of the High Court of Justice, QBD, 1982–88. Asst Lectr 1954–57, Lectr 1957–64, in Law, LSE; part-time Legal Asst, FO, 1954–56. Inspector, Vale of Belvoir Coal Inquiry, 1979–80. *Publications:* (ed jtly) Dicey, Conflict of Laws, 7th edn, 1957; Dicey and Morris, Conflict of Laws, 8th edn 1967 to 10th edn, 1980. *Address:* The Royal Courts of Justice, WC2A 2LL. *Club:* Athenæum.

MANN, Rt. Rev. Michael Ashley, KCVO 1989; Dean of Windsor, 1976–89; Chairman, St George's House, 1976–89; Register, Order of the Garter, 1976–89; Domestic Chaplain to the Queen, 1976–89; Prelate, Order of St John, since 1990; *b* 25 May 1924; *s* of late H. G. Mann and F. M. Mann, Harrow; *m* 1949, Jill Joan Jacques (*d* 1990); one *d* (and one *s* decd); *m* 1991, Elizabeth Pepys. *Educ:* Harrow Sch.; RMC Sandhurst; Wells Theological Coll.; Graduate School of Business Admin., Harvard Univ. Served War of 1939–45: RMC, Sandhurst, 1942–43; 1st King's Dragoon Guards, 1943–46 (Middle East, Italy, Palestine). Colonial Admin. Service, Nigeria, 1946–55. Wells Theological Coll., 1955–57; Asst Curate, Wolborough, Newton Abbot, 1957–59; Vicar: Sparkwell, Plymouth, 1959–62; Christ Church, Port Harcourt, Nigeria, 1962–67; Dean, Port Harcourt Social and Industrial Mission; Home Secretary, The Missions to Seamen, 1967–69; Residentiary Canon, 1969–74, Vice-Dean, 1972–74, Norwich Cathedral; Adviser to Bp of Norwich on Industry, 1969–74; Bishop Suffragan of Dudley, 1974–76. Church Comr, 1977–85; Comr, Royal Hospital Chelsea, 1985–91. Trustee: Imperial War Museum, 1980–; Army Museums Ogilby Trust, 1984–; British Library, 1990–. Chm., Soc. of Friends of Nat. Army Mus., 1989–. Governor: Harrow Sch., 1976–91 (Chm., 1980–88); Atlantic Coll., 1987–91. CBIM. KStJ 1990. *Publications:* A Windsor Correspondence, 1984; And They Rode On, 1984; A Particular Duty, 1986; China 1860, 1989; Some Windsor Sermons, 1989; Survival or Extinction, 1989. *Recreations:* military history, philately, ornithology. *Address:* The Cottage, Lower End Farm, Eastington, Northleach, Glos GL54 3PN. *T:* Cotswold (0451) 60767. *Club:* Cavalry and Guards.

MANN, Murray G.; *see* Gell-Mann.

MANN, Nicholas; *see* Mann, C. N. J.

MANN, Patricia Kathleen Randall, (Mrs Pierre Walker); Director of External Affairs, J. Walter Thompson Group, and Vice President International, JWT, since 1981; Editor, Consumer Affairs, since 1978; Member, Monopolies and Mergers Commission, since 1984; *b* 26 Sept. 1937; *d* of late Charles Mann and of Marjorie Mann (*née* Heath); *m* 1962, Pierre George Armand Walker; one *d*. *Educ:* Clifton High School, Bristol. FCAM, FIPA; CBIM. Joined J. Walter Thompson Co., 1959, Copywriter, 1959–77, Head of Public Affairs, 1978. Director: Yale and Valor plc, 1985–91; Woolwich (formerly Woolwich Equitable) Building Soc., 1983–. Member: Council, Inst. of Practitioners in Advertising, 1965– (Hon. Sec., 1979–83); Advertising Creative Circle, 1965–; Council, Nat. Advertising Benevolent Soc., 1973–77; Council, Advertising Standards Authy, 1973–86; Board, European Assoc. of Advertising Agencies, 1984–; Gas Consumers Council, 1981–90; Board, UK CEED, 1984–; Food Adv. Cttee, MAFF, 1986–; Kingman Cttee on English, DES, 1987. Governor: CAM Educn Foundn, 1971–77; Admin. Staff Coll., Henley, 1976–; Mem. Ct, Brunel Univ., 1976–. Mem., Awards Nomination Panel, RTS, 1974–78. Mackintosh Medal, Advertising Assoc., 1977. FRSA. *Publications:* 150 Careers in Advertising, 1971; Advertising, 1979; (ed) Advertising and Marketing to Children, 1980. *Recreations:* word games, watching showjumping. *Address:* c/o J. Walter Thompson, 40 Berkeley Square, W1X 6AD. *T:* 071–629 9496. *Clubs:* Reform, Women's Advertising, London Cornish Association.

MANN, Pauline, (Mrs R. D. Mann); *see* Vogelpoel, P.

MANN, Rt. Rev. Peter Woodley; Bishop of Dunedin, 1976–90; *b* 25 July 1924; *s* of Edgar Allen and Bessie May Mann; *m* 1955, Anne Victoria Norman; three *d*. *Educ:* Prince Alfred Coll., Adelaide; St John's Coll., Auckland (Fellow); Univ. of London (BD). Deacon, Dio. Waiapu, 1953; priest, 1954; Curate: Waiapu Cathedral, 1953–55; Rotorua, 1955–56; Vicar: Porangahau, 1956–61; Dannevirke, 1961–66; Vicar of Blenheim and Archdeacon of Marlborough, 1966–71; Vicar of St Mary's and Archdeacon of Timaru, 1971–75; Vicar of St James' Lower Hutt, 1975–76. *Recreations:* tennis, athletics. *Address:* 182 Maitland Street, Dunedin, New Zealand. *T:* (03) 4775245.

MANN, Sir Rupert (Edward), 3rd Bt *cr* 1905; *b* 11 Nov. 1946; *s* of Major Edward Charles Mann, DSO, MC (*g s* of 1st Bt) (*d* 1959), and of Pamela Margaret, *o d* of late Major Frank Haultain Hornsby; *S* great uncle, 1971; *m* 1974, Mary Rose, *d* of Geoffrey Butler, Stetchworth, Newmarket; two *s*. *Educ:* Malvern. *Heir:* *s* Alexander Rupert Mann, *b* 6 April 1978. *Address:* Billingford Hall, Diss, Norfolk IP21 4HN. *Clubs:* MCC; Norfolk.

MANN, Thaddeus Robert Rudolph, CBE 1962; FRS 1951; Biochemist; Professor of the Physiology of Reproduction, University of Cambridge, 1967–76, now Emeritus (Reader in Physiology of Animal Reproduction, 1953–67); Hon. Fellow of Trinity Hall, Cambridge, since 1979 (Fellow, 1961–79); Member of the Staff of Agricultural Research Council, 1944–76; *b* 1908; *s* of late William Mann and Emilia (*née* Quest); *m* 1934, Dr Cecilia Lutwak-Mann. *Educ:* Trin. Hall, Cambridge; MD Lwów 1935, PhD Cantab 1937, ScD Cantab 1950; Rockefeller Research Fellow, 1935–37; Beit Mem. Research Fellow, 1937–44. Dir, ARC Unit of Reproductive Physiology and Biochemistry, Cambridge, 1954–76. Awarded Amory Prize of Amer. Academy of Arts and Sciences, 1955; Senior Lalor Fellow at Woods Hole, 1960; Vis. Prof. in Biology at Florida State Univ., 1962; Vis. Prof. in Biological Structure and Zoology, Univ. of Washington, 1968; Vis. Scientist, Reproduction Res. Br., Nat. Insts of Health, USA, 1978–82. Gregory Pincus Meml Lectr, 1969; Albert Tyler Meml Lectr, 1970. For. Member: Royal Belgian Acad. of Medicine, 1970; Polish Acad. of Science, 1980. Hon. doctorate: of Veterinary Medicine, Ghent, 1970, Hanover, 1977; of Natural Scis, Cracow, 1973. Cavaliere Ufficiale, Order of Merit (Italy), 1966. *Publications:* The Biochemistry of Semen, 1954; The Biochemistry of Semen and of the Male Reproductive Tract, 1964; (with C. Lutwak-Mann) Male Reproductive Function and Semen—Themes and Trends in Physiology, Biochemistry and Investigative Andrology, 1981; Spermatophores—Development, Structure, Biochemical Attributes and Role in the Transfer of Spermatozoa, 1984; papers on Carbohydrate Metabolism of Muscle, Yeast and Moulds, on Metaloprotein Enzymes, and on Biochemistry of Reproduction. *Address:* 1 Courtney Way, Cambridge CB4 2EE.

MANN, William Neville, MD, FRCP; Consultant Physician Emeritus, Guy's Hospital, 1976; *b* 4 April 1911; *s* of William Frank Mann and Clara, *d* of John Chadwick; *m* Pamela, *yr d* of late H. E. Chasteney; two *s* four *d*. *Educ:* Alleyn's Sch.; Guy's Hospital. MB, BS (London), 1935; MRCP 1937; MD (London), 1937; FRCP, 1947. House Physician, Demonstrator of Pathology and Medical Registrar, Guy's Hospital, 1935–39. Served, 1940–45, in RAMC in Middle East and Indian Ocean (Temp. Lt-Col). Physician, Guy's Hosp., 1946–76. Hon. Visiting Physician to Johns Hopkins Hosp., Baltimore, USA. Physician: to HM Household, 1954–64; to HM the Queen, 1964–70; King Edward VII's Hosp. for Officers, 1965–76. Sen. Censor and Sen. Vice-Pres., RCP, 1969–70. Hon. DHL Johns Hopkins, 1986. *Publications:* Clinical Examination of Patients (jointly), 1950; The Medical Works of Hippocrates (jointly), 1950. Editor, Conybeare's Text-book of Medicine, 16th edn, 1975. *Address:* 90 Alleyn Road, SE21 8AH. T: 081–670 2451. *Club:* Garrick.

MANNERS, family name of **Baron Manners,** and **Duke of Rutland.**

MANNERS, 5th Baron *cr* 1807; **John Robert Cecil Manners;** DL; Consultant, Osborne, Clarke & Co., Solicitors, Bristol (Partner, 1952–84); *b* 13 Feb. 1923; *s* of 4th Baron Manners, MC, and of Mary Edith, *d* of late Rt Rev. Lord William Cecil; *S* father, 1972; *m* 1949, Jennifer Selena, *d* of Ian Fairbairn; one *s* two *d*. *Educ:* Eton; Trinity College, Oxford. Served as Flt-Lieut, RAFVR, 1941–46. Solicitor to the Supreme Court, 1949. Official Verderer of the New Forest, 1983–. DL Hampshire, 1987. *Recreations:* hunting and shooting. *Heir:* *s* Hon. John Hugh Robert Manners [*b* 5 May 1956; *m* 1983, Lanya Mary Jackson, *d* of late Dr H. E. Heitz and of Mrs Ian Jackson; one *d*]. *Address:* Sabines, Avon, Christchurch, Dorset. *Club:* Brooks's.

MANNERS, Elizabeth Maude, TD 1962; MA; Headmistress of Felixstowe College, Suffolk, 1967–79; Member, East Anglia Regional Health Authority, 1982–85; *b* 20 July 1917; *d* of William George Manners and Anne Mary Manners (*née* Sced). *Educ:* Stockton-on-Tees Sec. Sch.; St Hild's Coll., Durham Univ. BA (Dunelm) 1938; MA 1941. Teacher of French at: Marton Grove Sch., Middlesbrough, 1939–40; Ramsey Gram. Sch., IOM, 1940–42; Consett Sec. Sch., Durham, 1942–44; Yarm Gram. Sch., Yorks, 1944–54; Deputy Head, Mexborough Gram. Sch., Yorks, 1954–59; Head Mistress, Central Gram. Sch. for Girls, Manchester, 1959–67. Vice-President: Girl Guides Assoc., Co. Manchester, 1959–67; Suffolk Agric. Assoc., 1967–82. Member: Educn Cttee, Brit. Fedn of Univ. Women, 1966–68; Council, Bible Reading Fellowship, 1973–81; Cttee, E Br., RSA, 1974–90; Cttee, ISIS East, 1974–79. Mem., Suffolk CC, 1977–85 (Member: Educn Cttee, 1977–85; Staff Joint and Personnel Cttees, 1981–85; Vice-Chm., Secondary Educn Cttee, 1981–85); Mem., Suffolk War Pensions Cttee, 1980–90. Sponsor, the Responsible Society, 1982–90. Chm. Governors, Felixstowe Deben High Sch., 1985–88. Enlisted ATS (TA), 1947; commissioned, 1949. FRSA 1972. Coronation Medal, 1953. *Publications:* The Vulnerable Generation, 1971; The Story of Felixstowe College, 1980. *Recreations:* foreign travel, theatre, motoring, good food and wine. *Address:* 6 Graham Court, Hamilton Gardens, Felixstowe, Suffolk IP11 7ES.

MANNERS, Prof. Gerald; Professor of Geography, University College London, since 1980; Chairman, Sadler's Wells Foundation and Trust, since 1986 (Governor, since 1978, Vice-Chairman, 1982–86); *b* 7 Aug. 1932; *s* of George William Manners and Louisa Hannah Manners; *m* 1st, 1959, Anne (*née* Sawyer) (marr. diss. 1982); one *s* two *d*; 2nd, 1982, Joy Edith Roberta (*née* Turner); one *s*. *Educ:* Wallington County Grammar School; St Catharine's College, Cambridge (MA). Lectr in Geography, University Coll. Swansea, 1957–67; Reader in Geography, UCL, 1967–80. Vis. Schol., Resources for the Future, Inc., Washington DC, 1964–65; Vis. Associate, Jt Center for Urban Studies, Harvard and MIT, 1972–73; Vis. Fellow, ANU, 1990. Dir, Economic Associates Ltd, 1964–74. Member: Council, Inst. of British Geographers, 1967–70; LOB 1970–80; SE Economic Planning Council, 1971–79; Council, TCPA, 1980–; Subscriber, Centre for Environmental Studies Ltd, 1981–. Specialist Advr to H of C Select Cttee on Energy, 1980–; Advr to Assoc. for Conservation of Energy, 1981–; Chairman: Regl Studies Assoc., 1981–84; RSA Panel of Inquiry into regl problem in UK, 1982–83. Mem., Central Governing Body, City Parochial Foundn, 1977– (Chm., Estate Cttee, 1987–). Trustee, Chelsea Physic Garden, 1980–83. Mem. Court, City Univ., 1985–. *Publications:* Geography of Energy, 1964, 2nd edn 1971; South Wales in the Sixties, 1964; Changing World Market for Iron Ore 1950–1980, 1971 (ed) Spatial Policy Problems of the British Economy, 1971; Minerals and Man, 1974; Regional Development in Britain, 1974, 2nd edn 1980; Coal in Britain, 1981; Office Policy in Britain, 1986; contribs to edited volumes and learned jls. *Recreations:* music, dance, theatre, walking, undergardening. *Address:* 105 Barnsbury Street, N1 1EP. *T:* 071–607 7920.

MANNERS, Hon. Thomas (Jasper); Director, Lazard Brothers, since 1965 (Deputy Chairman, 1986–89); *b* 12 Dec. 1929; *y s* of 4th Baron Manners, MC, and of Mary Edith, *d* of late Rt Rev. Lord William Cecil; *m* 1955, Sarah, *d* of Brig. Roger Peake, DSO; three *s*. *Educ:* Eton. Lazard Brothers & Co. Ltd, 1955–; Director: Legal & General Gp, 1972–; Scapa Gp, 1970–; Davy Corp., 1985–. *Recreations:* shooting, fishing. *Address:* The Old Malt House, Ashford Hill, Newbury, Berks RG15 8BN. *T:* Tadley (07356) 4865; 9 Cadogan Square, SW1. *T:* 071–235 7367. *Clubs:* Pratt's, White's.

MANNING, Prof. Aubrey William George, DPhil, FRSE, FIBiol; Professor of Natural History, University of Edinburgh, since 1973; *b* 24 April 1930; *s* of William James Manning and Hilda Winifred (*née* Noble); *m* 1st, 1959, Margaret Bastock, DPhil (*d* 1982); two *s*; 2nd, 1985, Joan Herrmann, PhD; one *s*. *Educ:* Strode's School, Egham, Surrey; University Coll., London (BSc); Merton Coll., Oxford (DPhil). FRSE 1975; FIBiol 1980. Commnd RA, 1954–56. University of Edinburgh: Asst Lectr, 1956–59; Lectr, 1959–68; Reader, 1968–73. Sec. Gen., Internat. Ethological Cttee, 1971–79; Pres., Assoc. Study Animal Behaviour, 1983–86; Member: Scottish Cttee, NCC, 1982–88; NCC Adv. Cttee on Science, 1984–88; Chm. Council, Scottish Wildlife Trust, 1990–. Dr *hc* Univ. Paul Sabatier, Toulouse, 1981. *Publications:* An Introduction to Animal Behaviour, 1967, 4th edn (with Dr M. Dawkins) 1991; papers on animal behaviour in learned jls. *Recreations:* woodland regeneration, hill-walking, architecture, 19th century novels. *Address:* The Old Hall, Ormiston, East Lothian EH35 5NJ. *T:* Pencaitland (0875) 340536.

MANNING, Frederick Allan, CVO 1954; ISO 1971; JP; retired, 1970; Commissioner for Transport, Queensland, 1967–70, (Deputy Commissioner, 1960–67); *b* Gladstone, Qld, Australia, 27 Aug. 1904; British parentage; *m* 1934, Phyllis Maud Fullerton; no *c.* *Educ:* Central Boys' State Sch. and Boys' Gram. Sch., Rockhampton, Qld. Entered Qld State Public Service as Clerk in Petty Sessions Office, Rockhampton, 1920; Clerk of Petty Sessions and Mining Registrar, 1923; Stipendiary Magistrate and Mining Warden, 1934; Petty Sessions Office, Brisbane, 1926; Relieving Clerk of Petty Sessions and Mining Registrar, 1931 (all parts of State); seconded to Commonwealth Govt for service in Qld Directorate of Rationing Commission, 1942; Asst Dep. Dir of Rationing, 1943. Dep. Dir, 1944, for Qld; returned to Qld Public Service, 1947; Sec., Dept of Transport, 1947–60; JP, Qld, 1925–. Coronation Medal, 1953; State Dir, Royal Visit to Queensland, 1954 (CVO). Exec. Vice-Chm, Qld Road Safety Coun., and Qld Rep. Aust. Road Safety Coun., 1962. Mem., Greyhound Racing Control Bd of Queensland, 1971–77. *Recreation:* bowls. *Address:* 126 Indooroopilly Road, Taringa, Brisbane, Qld 4068, Australia. *T:* 370–1936. *Club:* Tattersalls (Brisbane).

MANNING, Dr Geoffrey, CBE 1986; FInstP; Chairman, Active Memory Technology Ltd, since 1986; Visiting Professor, Department of Physics and Astronomy, University College London, since 1987; *b* 31 Aug. 1929; *s* of Jack Manning and Ruby Frances Lambe; *m* 1951, Anita Jacqueline Davis; two *s* one *d.* *Educ:* Tottenham Grammar Sch.; Imperial Coll., London Univ. BSc, PhD; ARCS. Asst Lectr in Physics, Imperial Coll., 1953–55; Research worker: English Electric Co., 1955–56; Canadian Atomic Energy Co., 1956–58; Calif Inst. of Technol., 1958–59; AERE, 1960–65; Rutherford Laboratory, Science Research Council: Gp Leader, 1965–69; Dep. Dir, 1969–79; Head of High Energy Physics Div., 1969–75; Head of Atlas Div., 1975–79; Dir, Rutherford (Rutherford & Appleton Labs), 1979–81; Dir, Rutherford Appleton Lab., SERC, 1981–86. Mem., Visiting Cttee, Physics Dept, Imperial Coll., 1988–. Chm., Parallel and Novel Architectures Sub Cttee, DTI, 1988–; Mem., Systems Architecture Cttee, DTI, 1988–. Glazebrook Medal and Prize, Inst. of Physics, 1986. *Recreations:* golf, squash, ski-ing. *Address:* 38 Sunningwell Village, Abingdon, Oxon OX13 6RB. *T:* Oxford (0865) 736123.

MANNING, Jane Marian, OBE 1990; freelance concert and opera singer (soprano), since 1965; *b* 20 Sept. 1938; *d* of Gerald Manville Manning and Lily Manning (*née* Thompson); *m* 1966, Anthony Edward Payne, composer. *Educ:* Norwich High Sch.; Royal Academy of Music (LRAM 1958); Scuola di Canto, Cureglia, Switzerland. GRSM 1960, ARCM 1962. London début (Park Lane Group), 1964; first BBC broadcast, 1965; début Henry Wood Promenade Concerts, 1972; founded own ensemble, Jane's Minstrels, 1988; regular appearances in leading concert halls and festivals in UK and Europe, with leading orchestras and conductors; many broadcasts and gramophone recordings, lectures and master classes. Specialist in contemporary music (over 200 world premières given); Warsaw Autumn Fest., 1975–78 and 1987; Wexford Opera Fest., 1976; Scottish Opera, 1978; Brussels Opera, 1980. Canadian début, 1977; tour of Australia, 1990; tours: of Australia and New Zealand, 1978, 1980, 1982, 1984, 1986; of USA, 1981, 1983, 1985, 1986, 1987, 1988 and 1989. Milhaud Vis. Prof., Mills Coll. Oakland, 1983; Lucie Stern Vis. Prof., Mills Coll., Oakland, 1981 and 1986. Vice Pres., SPNM, 1984–. Member: Exec. Cttee, Musicians Benevolent Fund, 1989–; Arts Council Music Panel, 1990–; Internat. Jury, Gaudeamus Young Interpreters Competition, Holland, 1976, 1979, 1987; Jury, Eur. Youth Competition for Composers, Eur. Cultural Foundn, 1985. Hon. ARAM 1972, Hon. FRAM 1984. Hon. DMus York, 1988. Special award, Composers Guild of Gt Britain, 1973. *Publications:* (chapter in) How Music Works, 1981; New Vocal Repertory, 1986; articles in Composer, and Music and Musicians. *Recreations:* cooking, cinema, ornithology. *Address:* 2 Wilton Square, N1 3DL. *T:* 071–359 1593.

MANNING, Thomas Henry, OC 1974; zoologist; *b* 22 Dec. 1911; *s* of Thomas E. and Dorothy (*née* Randall) Manning, Shrublands, Dallington, Northampton; *m* 1938, Ella Wallace Jackson. *Educ:* Harrow; Cambridge. Winter journey across Lapland, 1932–33; Survey and Zoological work on Southampton Island, 1933–35; Leader, Brit. Canadian-Arctic Exped., 1936–41; Royal Canadian Navy, 1941–45; Geodetic Service of Canada, 1945–47; Leader Geographical Bureau Expedition to Prince Charles I. (Foxe Basin), 1949; Zoological and Geographical work in James Bay, 1950; Leader Defence Research Board Expeditions: Beaufort Sea, 1951; Banks Island, 1952, 1953; Nat. Mus. Canada Expedition; King William Island, Adelaide Peninsula, 1957, Prince of Wales Island, 1958. Hon. LLD McMaster, 1979. Bruce Medal (Royal Society of Edinburgh, RPS, RSGS), 1944; Patron's Gold Medal, RGS, 1948; Massey Medal, Royal Canadian Geographical Soc., 1977. Guggenheim Fellow, 1959. *Publications:* The Birds of North Western Ungava, 1949; Birds of the West James Bay and Southern Hudson Bay Coasts, 1952; Birds of Banks Island, 1956; Mammals of Banks Island, 1958; A Biological Investigation of Prince of Wales Island, 1961; articles in The Auk, Journal Mamm. and Geog. Journal, Canadian Geog. Jl, Canadian Field-Naturalist, Arctic, Nat. Mus. Can. Bull., Canadian Jl of Zool., Syllogeus. *Recreations:* shooting, book-binding, cabinet-making, gardening. *Address:* RR4, Merrickville, Ont K0G 1N0, Canada. *T:* 613–269–4940.

MANNINGHAM-BULLER, family name of **Viscount Dilhorne.**

MANS, Keith Douglas Rowland; MP (C) Wyre, since 1987; *b* 10 Feb. 1946; *s* of Maj.-Gen. R. S. N. Mans, *qv*; *m* 1972, Rosalie Mary McCann; one *s* two *d.* *Educ:* Berkhamsted School; RAF College Cranwell; Open Univ. (BA). Pilot, RAF, 1964–77 (Flight Lieut); Pilot, RAF Reserve, 1977–. Retail Manager, John Lewis Partnership, 1978–87. PPS to Minister of State, Dept of Health, 1990–. Mem., H of C Environment Select Cttee, 1987–91; Vice-Chm., Backbench Fisheries Cttee, 1987–; Secretary: Backbench Aviation Cttee, 1987–90; Backbench Envmt Cttee, 1990–91; All Party Aviation Gp, 1991–. *Recreation:* flying. *Address:* Underbank Cottage, Raikes Road, Thornton, Lancs FY5 5LS. *T:* Cleveleys (0253) 822502. *Clubs:* Army and Navy, Royal Air Force.

MANS, Maj.-Gen. Rowland Spencer Noel, CBE 1971 (OBE 1966, MBE 1956); Director, Military Assistance Office, 1973–76, retired; *b* 16 Jan. 1921; *s* of Thomas Frederick Mans and May Seigenberg; *m* 1945, Veeo Ellen Sutton; three *s.* *Educ:* Surbiton Grammar Sch.; RMC, Sandhurst; jssc, psc. Served War, Queen's Royal Regt and King's African Rifles, 1940–45. Regtl and Staff Duty, 1945–59; Instr, Staff Colleges, Camberley and Canada, 1959–63; Comd, 1st Tanganyika Rifles, 1963–64; Staff Duty, Far East and UK, 1964–68; Comd, Aldershot, 1969–72; DDPS (Army), 1972–73. Col, Queen's Regt, 1978–83 (Dep. Col (Surrey), 1973–77). Defence consultant and writer on defence and political affairs. Mem., Hampshire CC, 1984–89. *Publications:* Kenyatta's Middle Road in a Changing Africa, 1977; Canada's Constitutional Crisis, 1978. *Recreations:* writing, reading, gardening. *Address:* Ivy Bank Cottage, Vinegar Hill, Milford-on-Sea, Hants SO41 0RZ. *T:* Lymington (0590) 643982. *Clubs:* Army and Navy; Royal Lymington Yacht.
See also K. D. R. Mans.

MANSAGER, Felix Norman, KBE (Hon.) 1976 (Hon. CBE 1973); Honorary Director, Hoover Co. USA (President-Chairman, Hoover Co. and Hoover World-wide Corporation, 1966–75); Director, Hoover Ltd UK (Chairman, 1966–75); *b* 30 Jan. 1911; *s* of Hoff Mansager and Alice (*née* Qualseth); *m* Geraldine (*née* Larson); one *s* two *d.* *Educ:* South Dakota High Sch., Colton. Joined Hoover Co. as Salesman, 1929; Vice-Pres., Sales, 1959; Exec. Vice-Pres. and Dir, 1961. Dir, Belden and Blake Energy Co. Member: Council on Foreign Relations; Newcomen Soc. in N America; Trustee, Graduate Theological Union (Calif); The Pilgrims of the US; Assoc. of Ohio Commodores; Masonic Shrine (32nd degree Mason); Mem. and Governor, Ditchley Foundn; Member Board of Trustees: Ohio Foundn of Indep. Colls; Indep. Coll. Funds of America. Hon. Mem., World League of Norsemen. Marketing Award, British Inst. of Marketing, 1971. Executive Prof. of Business (Goodyear Chair), Univ. of Akron (Mem. Delta Sigma Pi; Hon. Mem., Beta Sigma Gamma). Hon. Fellow, UC Cardiff, 1973. Hon. Dr of Laws Capital Univ., 1967; Hon. LLD Strathclyde, 1970; Hon. DHL Malone Coll., Canton, Ohio, 1972; Hon. PhD Walsh Coll., Canton, 1974; Hon. Dr Humanities Wartburg Coll., Waverly, Iowa, 1976; Medal of Honor, Vassa Univ., Finland, 1973; Person of Year, Capital Univ. Chapter of Tau Pi Phi, 1981. Grand Officer, Dukes of Burgundy, 1968; Chevalier: Order of Leopold, 1969; Order of St Olav, Norway, 1971; Legion of Honour, France, 1973; Grande Officiale, Order Al Merito della Republica Italiana, 1975. *Recreation:* golf. *Address:* 3421 Lindel Court NW, Canton, Ohio 44718, USA. *Clubs:* Metropolitan (NYC); Congress Lake Country (Hartville, Ohio); Torske (Hon.) (Minneapolis).

MANSEL, Rev. Canon James Seymour Denis, KCVO 1979 (LVO 1972); Extra Chaplain to the Queen, since 1979; Priest Vicar, Westminster Abbey, 1983–88, now Emeritus; *b* 18 June 1907; *e s* of Edward Mansel, FRIBA, Leamington, and Muriel Louisa (*née* Denis Browne); *m* 1942, Ann Monica (*d* 1974), *e d* of Amyas Waterhouse, MD, Boars Hill, Oxford, and Ruth (*née* Gamlen); one *d.* *Educ:* Brighton Coll.; Exeter Coll., Oxford (MA); Westcott House. Asst Master, Dulwich Coll., 1934–39; Asst Master, Chaplain and House Master, Winchester Coll., 1939–65; Sub-Dean of HM Chapels Royal, Deputy Clerk of the Closet, Sub-Almoner and Domestic Chaplain to the Queen, 1965–79; Canon and Prebendary of Chichester Cathedral, 1971–81, Canon Emeritus, 1981; Asst Priest, St Margaret's, Westminster, 1980–88. Mem., Winchester City Coun., 1950–56. JP: City of Winchester, 1964; Inner London Commn, 1972. FSA. ChStJ. *Address:* 15 Sandringham Court, Maida Vale, W9 1UA. *Club:* Athenæum.
See also R. E. Jack.

MANSEL, Sir Philip, 15th Bt, *cr* 1621; FInstSM; Chairman and Managing Director of Eden-Vale Engineering Co. Ltd; *b* 3 March 1943; *s* of Sir John Mansel, 14th Bt and Hannah, *d* of Ben Rees; *S* father, 1947; *m* 1968, Margaret, *o d* of Arthur Docker; two *s* one *d.* *Heir:* *s* John Philip Mansel, *b* 19 April 1982. *Address:* 4 Redhill Drive, Fellside Park, Whickham, Newcastle upon Tyne NE16 5TY.

MANSEL-JONES, David; Chairman, Huntingdon Research Centre plc, 1978–86 (Vice-Chairman, 1974–78); *b* 8 Sept. 1926; *o s* of Rees Thomas Jones and Ceinwen Jones; *m* 1952, Mair Aeronwen Davies; one *s.* *Educ:* St Michael's Sch., Bryn; London Hospital. MB, BS 1950; MRCP 1973. Jun. Surgical Specialist, RAMC; Dep. Med. Dir, Wm R. Warner & Co. Ltd, 1957–59; Med. Dir, Richardson-Merrell Ltd, 1959–65; formerly PMO, SMO and MO, Cttee on Safety of Drugs; formerly Med. Assessor, Cttee on Safety of Medicines; Consultant to WHO, 1970–86; Senior PMO, Medicines Div., DHSS, 1971–74. Vis. Prof., Gulbenkian Science Inst., Portugal, 1981; Examiner, Dip. Pharm. Med., Royal Colls of Physicians, UK, 1980–87. *Publications:* papers related to safety of medicines. *Recreations:* music, painting. *Address:* 9 Aldeburgh Lodge Gardens, Aldeburgh, Suffolk IP15 5DP. *T:* Aldeburgh (0728) 453136.

MANSEL LEWIS, David Courtenay; Lord-Lieutenant of Dyfed, since 1979 (Lieutenant, 1974–79; HM Lieutenant for Carmarthenshire, 1973–74); JP; *b* 25 Oct. 1927; *s* of late Charlie Ronald Mansel Lewis and Lillian Georgina Warner, *d* of Col Sir Courtenay Warner, 1st Bt, CB; *m* 1953, Lady Mary Rosemary Marie-Gabrielle Montagu-Stuart-Wortley, OBE, JP, 4th *d* of 3rd Earl of Wharncliffe; one *s* two *d.* *Educ:* Eton; Keble Coll., Oxford (BA). Served in Welsh Guards, 1946–49; Lieut 1946, RARO. High Sheriff, Carmarthenshire, 1965; JP 1969; DL 1971. FRSA; KStJ. *Recreations:* music, sailing. *Address:* Stradey Castle, Llanelli, Dyfed SA15 4PL. *T:* Llanelli (0554) 774626. *Clubs:* Lansdowne; Royal Yacht Squadron (Cowes).

MANSELL, Gerard Evelyn Herbert, CBE 1977; Managing Director, External Broadcasting, BBC, 1972–81; Deputy Director-General, BBC, 1977–81; retired; *b* 16 Feb. 1921; 2nd *s* of late Herbert and Anne Mansell, Paris; *m* 1956, Diana Marion Sherar; two *s.* *Educ:* Lycée Hoche, Versailles; Lycée Buffon, Paris; Ecole des Sciences Politiques, Paris; Chelsea Sch. of Art. Joined HM Forces, 1940; served in Western Desert, Sicily and NW Europe, 1942–45 (despatches). Joined BBC European Service, 1951; Head, Overseas Talks and Features Dept, 1961; Controller, BBC Radio 4 (formerly Home Service), and Music Programme, 1965–69; Dir of Programmes, BBC, Radio, 1970. Chairman: British Cttee, Journalists in Europe, 1978–; Jt Adv. Cttee on Radio Journalism Trng, 1981–87; Sony Radio Awards Organising Cttee, 1983–87; Communications Adv. Cttee, UK Nat. Commn for UNESCO, 1983–85; Friends of UNESCO, 1986–88; Member: Communication and Cultural Studies Bd, CNAA, 1982–87; Exec. Cttee, GB–China Centre, 1986– (Vice-Chm., 1988–); Franco-British Council, 1990–. Governor, Falmouth Sch. of Art and Design, 1988–; Chm., New Hampstead Garden Suburb Trust, 1984–90. FRSA 1979. French Croix de Guerre, 1945. *Publications:* Tragedy in Algeria, 1961; Let Truth be Told, 1982. *Address:* 46 Southway, NW11 6SA.

MANSELL-JONES, Richard; Chairman, J. Bibby & Sons PLC, since 1988 (Director, since 1982); *b* 4 April 1940; *s* of Arnaud Milward Jones and Winifred Mabel (*née* Foot); *m* 1971, Penelope Marion, *y d* of Major Sir David Henry Hawley, 7th Bt. *Educ:* Queen Elizabeth's, Carmarthen; Worcester College, Oxford (MA). FCA. Articled to Price, Waterhouse & Co., 1963–68; with N. M. Rothschild & Sons, 1968–72; Brown, Shipley & Co., 1972–88, Dir, 1974–88; Director: Brown, Shipley Holdings, 1985–; Barr & Wallace Arnold Trust, 1984–; Barlow Rand Ltd, 1988–; Rand Mines Ltd, 1988–. *Address:* 19 Astell Street, SW3 3RT. *T:* 071–352 6789. *Clubs:* Oriental; City (Chester).

MANSER, John; *see* Manser, P. J.

MANSER, Michael John; architect in private practice, Manser Associates (formerly Michael Manser Associates), since 1961; President, Royal Institute of British Architects, 1983–85; *b* 23 March 1929; *s* of late Edmund George Manser and Augusta Madge Manser; *m* 1953, Dolores Josephine Bernini; one *s* one *d.* *Educ:* Sch. of Architecture, Polytechnic of Central London (DipArch). RIBA 1954. Intermittent architectural journalism, including: News Editor, Architectural Design, 1961–64; Architectural Correspondent, The Observer, 1963–65. Councillor: RIBA, 1977–80 and 1982; RSA, 1987– (Chm., Art for Architecture Award Scheme, 1990–); RIBA Rep., Council, Nat. Trust, 1991–. Hon. Fellow, Royal Architectural Inst. of Canada, 1985. Civic Trust Awards, 1967 and 1973; Award for Good Design in Housing, DoE, 1975; Heritage Year Award, 1975; Structural Steel Award, BSC, 1976; Commendation, RIBA Awards, 1977. *Publication:* (with José Manser) Planning Your Kitchen, 1976. *Recreations:* going home, architecture, music, books, boats, sketching, gardening (under supervision). *Address:* Morton House, Chiswick Mall, W4 2PS. *Club:* Brooks's.

MANSER, (Peter) John, FCA; Group Chief Executive, Robert Fleming Holdings Ltd, since 1990 (Director since 1972); Chairman, Robert Fleming & Co. Ltd, since 1990; Deputy Chairman, Robert Fleming Asset Management Ltd, since 1990 (Chief Executive, since 1988); a Director, Securities and Investments Board Ltd, since 1986; *b* 7 Dec. 1939; *s* of late Peter Robert Courtney Manser and Florence Delaplaine Manser; *m* 1969, Sarah Theresa Stuart (*née* Todd); two *d*. *Educ:* Marlborough Coll. Man. Dir, Jardine Fleming & Co. Ltd, 1975–79; Dep. Chm., FIMBRA, 1984–85; Chief Exec., Save & Prosper Gp Ltd, 1983–88. Dir, Cancer Research Campaign, 1985–. *Recreations:* gardening, walking, shooting. *Address:* 51 Hamilton Terrace, NW8 9RG. *T:* 071–286 7595. *Clubs:* Boodle's, City of London, MCC.

MANSFIELD, family name of **Baron Sandhurst.**

MANSFIELD AND MANSFIELD, 8th Earl of, *cr* 1776 and 1792 (GB); **William David Mungo James Murray;** JP, DL; Baron Scone, 1605; Viscount Stormont, 1621; Baron Balvaird, 1641; (Earl of Dunbar, Viscount Drumcairn, and Baron Halldykes in the Jacobite Peerage); Hereditary Keeper of Bruce's Castle of Lochmaben; First Crown Estate Commissioner, since 1985; *b* 7 July 1930; *o s* of 7th Earl of Mansfield and Mansfield, and of Dorothea Helena (*d* 1985), *y d* of late Rt Hon. Sir Lancelot Carnegie, GCVO, KCMG; *S* father, 1971; *m* 1955, Pamela Joan, *o d* of W. N. Foster, CBE; two *s* one *d*. *Educ:* Eton; Christ Church, Oxford. Served as Lieut with Scots Guards, Malayan campaign, 1949–50. Called to Bar, Inner Temple, 1958; Barrister, 1958–71. Mem., British Delegn to European Parlt, 1973–75; an opposition spokesman in the House of Lords, 1975–79; Minister of State: Scottish Office, 1979–83; NI Office, 1983–84. Mem., Tay Salmon Fisheries Bd, 1971–79. Director: General Accident, Fire and Life Assurance Corp. Ltd, 1972–79, 1985–; American Trust, 1985–; Pinneys of Scotland, 1985–89; Ross Breeders Ltd, 1989–. Ordinary Dir, Royal Highland and Agricl Soc., 1976–79. President: Fédn des Assocs de Chasse de l'Europe, 1977–79; Scottish Assoc. for Care and Resettlement of Offenders, 1974–79; Scottish Assoc. of Boys Clubs, 1976–79; Royal Scottish Country Dance Soc., 1977–; Chm., Scottish Branch, Historic Houses Assoc., 1976–79. Mem., Perth CC, 1971–75; Hon. Sheriff for Perthshire, 1974–; JP 1975, DL 1980, Perth and Kinross. *Heir:* *s* Viscount Stormont, *qv*. *Address:* Scone Palace, Perthshire PH2 6BE; 16 Thorburn House, Kinnerton Street, SW1. *Clubs:* White's, Pratt's, Turf, Beefsteak.

MANSFIELD, Rear-Adm. David Parks, CB 1964; *b* 26 July 1912; *s* of Comdr D. Mansfield, RD, RNR; *m* 1939, Jean Craig Alexander (*d* 1984); one *s* one *d*. *Educ:* RN Coll., Dartmouth; RN Engineering Coll., Keyham. Lt (E) 1934; HMS Nelson, 1934–36; Staff of C-in-C Med., 1936–39; HMS Mauritius, 1939–42; Lt-Comdr (E) 1942; HMS Kelvin, 1942–43; Chatham Dockyard, 1943–46; Comdr (E) 1945; Admty (Aircraft Maintenance Dept), 1946–49; Staff of FO Air (Home), 1949–51; HMS Kenya, 1951–53; RN Engrg Coll., 1953–55; Captain 1954; RNAS Anthorn (in command), 1955–57; RN Aircraft Yard, Fleetlands (Supt.), 1957–60; Admty Dir of Fleet Maintenance, 1960–62; Rear-Adm. 1963; Rear-Adm. Aircraft, on Staff of Flag Officer Naval Air Command, 1963–65. *Recreation:* family affairs. *Address:* The Outlook, Salisbury Road, St Margaret's Bay, Dover, Kent CT15 6DL. *T:* Dover (0304) 852237. *Club:* Army and Navy.

MANSFIELD, Vice-Adm. Sir (Edward) Gerard (Napier), KBE 1974; CVO 1981; retired 1975; *b* 13 July 1921; *s* of late Vice-Adm. Sir John Mansfield, KCB, DSO, DSC, and Alice Talbot Mansfield; *m* 1943, Joan Worship Byron, *d* of late Comdr John Byron, DSC and Bar, and late Frances Byron; two *d*. *Educ:* RNC, Dartmouth. Entered Royal Navy, 1935. Served War of 1939–45 in destroyers and Combined Ops (despatches), taking part in landings in N Africa and Sicily. Comdr, 1953; comd HMS Mounts Bay, 1956–58; Captain 1959; SHAPE, 1960–62; Captain (F) 20th Frigate Sqdn, 1963–64; Dir of Defence Plans (Navy), 1965–67; Cdre Amphibious Forces, 1967–68; Senior Naval Member, Directing Staff, IDC, 1969–70; Flag Officer Sea Training, 1971–72; Dep. Supreme Allied Comdr, Atlantic, 1973–75. Chm., Assoc. of RN Officers, 1975–86; Chm. Council, Operation Raleigh, 1984–89. Chm., Crondall Parish Council, 1977–81. Mem. Admin. Council, Royal Jubilee Trusts, 1978–81. *Recreations:* golf, gardening. *Address:* White Gate House, Heath Lane, Ewshot, Farnham, Surrey GU10 5AH. *T:* Aldershot (0252) 850325. *Club:* Army and Navy.

MANSFIELD, Dr Eric Harold, FRS 1971; FEng 1976; Visiting Professor, Department of Mechanical Engineering, University of Surrey, 1984–90; *b* 24 May 1923; *s* of Harold Goldsmith Mansfield and Grace Phundt; *m* 1st, 1947, Mary Ola Purves Douglas (marr. diss. 1973); two *s* one *d*; 2nd, 1974, Eunice Lily Kathleen Shuttleworth-Parker. *Educ:* St Lawrence Coll., Ramsgate; Trinity Hall, Cambridge. MA, ScD; FRAeS, FIMA. Research in Structures Department, Royal Aircraft Establishment, Farnborough, Hants, 1943–83, CSO (individual merit), 1980–83. Member: British Nat. Cttee for Theoretical and Applied Mechanics, 1973–79; Gen. Assembly of IUTAM, 1976–80; Council, Royal Soc., 1977–78. UK winner (with I. T. Minhinnick), World Par Bridge Olympiad, 1951. Member, Editorial Advisory Boards: Internat. Jl of Non-linear Mechanics, 1965–; Internat Jl of Mechanical Scis, 1977–84. *Publications:* The Bending and Stretching of Plates, 1964, 2nd edn 1989; Bridge: The Ultimate Limits, 1986; contribs to: Proc. Roy. Soc., Phil. Trans., Quarterly Jl Mech. Applied Math., Aero Quarterly, Aero Research Coun. reports and memos, and to technical press. *Recreations:* duplicate bridge, palaeontology, snorkling. *Address:* Manatoba, Dene Close, Lower Bourne, Farnham, Surrey GU10 3PP. *T:* Farnham (0252) 713558.

MANSFIELD, Sir Gerard; *see* Mansfield, Sir E. G. N.

MANSFIELD, Michael; QC 1989; *b* 12 Oct. 1941; *s* of Frank Le Voir Mansfield and Marjorie Mansfield; *m* 1967, Melian Mansfield (*née* Bordes) (separated); three *s* two *d*; lives with Yvette Vanson; one *s*. *Educ:* Highgate Sch.; Keele Univ. (BA Hons). Called to the Bar, Gray's Inn, 1967. Estabd set of chambers of which head, 1984. *Recreations:* my children's interests. *Address:* 14 Tooks Court, Cursitor Street, EC4. *T:* 071–405 8828.

MANSFIELD, Prof. Peter, FRS 1987; Professor of Physics, University of Nottingham, since 1979; *b* 9 Oct. 1933; *s* of late Rose Lilian Mansfield (*née* Turner) and late Sidney George Mansfield; *m* 1962, Jean Margaret Kibble; two *d*. *Educ:* William Penn Sch., Peckham; Queen Mary Coll., London (BSc 1959, PhD 1962; Fellow, 1985). Research Associate, Dept of Physics, Univ. of Illinois, 1962–64; Lectr, Univ. of Nottingham, 1964, Sen. Lectr, 1968, Reader, 1970–79; Sen. Visitor, Max Planck Inst. für Medizinische Forschung, Heidelberg, 1972–73. Society of Magnetic Resonance in Medicine: Gold Medal, 1983; President, 1987–88. Sylvanus Thompson Lectr and Medal, British Inst. of Radiology, 1988; Gold Medal, Royal Soc. Wellcome Foundn, 1984; Duddell Medal and Prize, Inst. of Physics, 1988; Silvanus Thompson Medal, British Inst. of Radiology, 1988; Antoine Béclère Medal, Internat. Radiol Soc. and Antoine Béclère Inst., 1989; Mullard Medal and Award, Royal Soc., 1990. *Publications:* NMR Imaging in Biomedicine (with P. G. Morris), 1982; papers in learned jls on nuclear magnetic resonance. *Recreations:* languages, reading, travel. *Address:* Department of Physics, University of Nottingham, Nottingham NG7 2RD. *T:* (office) Nottingham (0602) 484848, ext. 2830.

MANSFIELD, Sir Philip (Robert Aked), KCMG 1984 (CMG 1973); HM Diplomatic Service, retired; Ambassador to the Netherlands, 1981–84; *b* 9 May 1926; *s* of Philip Theodore Mansfield, CSI, CIE and Helen Rosamond Asked; *m* 1953, Elinor Russell MacHatton; two *s*. *Educ:* Winchester; Pembroke Coll., Cambridge. Grenadier Guards, 1944–47. Sudan Political Service, 1950–55. Entered HM Diplomatic Service, 1955; served in: Addis Ababa, Singapore, Paris, Buenos Aires; Counsellor and Head of Rhodesia Dept, FCO, 1969–72; RCDS, 1973; Counsellor and Head of Chancery, 1974–75, Dep. High Comr, 1976, Nairobi; Asst Under Sec. of State, FCO, 1976–79; Ambassador and Dep. Perm. Representative to UN, 1979–81. Consultant to: Rank Xerox, 1987–; BPB Industries, 1987–. *Recreations:* walking, tree planting, cooking. *Address:* Gill Mill, Stanton Harcourt, Oxford OX8 1AN. *T:* Witney (0993) 702554. *Clubs:* Commonwealth Trust; Aberdare Country (Kenya).

MANSFIELD, Prof. Terence Arthur, FRS 1987; FIBiol; Professor of Plant Physiology, since 1977, and Director, Institute of Environmental and Biological Sciences, since 1988, University of Lancaster; *b* 18 Jan. 1937; *s* of Sydney Walter Mansfield and Rose (*née* Sinfield); *m* 1963, Margaret Mary James; two *s*. *Educ:* Univ. of Nottingham (BSc); Univ. of Reading (PhD). FIBiol 1984. Lectr, then Reader, Univ. of Lancaster, 1965–77. Mem., AFRC, 1989–. *Publications:* Physiology of Stomata, 1968; Effects of Air Pollutants on Plants, 1976; Stomatal Physiology, 1981; many contribs to books and jls in plant physiology. *Recreations:* cricket, hill walking, classical music. *Address:* 25 Wallace Lane, Forton, Lancs PR3 0BA. *T:* Forton (0524) 791338.

MANSFIELD, Terence Gordon; Managing Director, National Magazine Co., since 1982; Chairman, COMAG, since 1984; *b* 3 Nov. 1938; *s* of Archer James Mansfield and Elizabeth Mansfield; *m* 1965, Helen Leonora Russell; two *d*. *Educ:* Maynard Road Jun. Sch., Essex; SW Essex Technical Sch. MInstM 1969; MInstD 1976. D. H. Brocklesby, Advertising Agents, 1954; S. H. Benson, Advertising Agents, 1956; served RAF, Christmas Island, 1957–59; Conde Nast Publications, 1960–66; Queen Magazine, 1966; National Magazine Co.: Advertisement Man., Harpers and Queen, 1969; Publisher, Harpers and Queen, 1975; Dep. Man. Dir, National Magazine Co., 1980; Representative of Hearst Corp. for GB, 1986–. Member: Advertising Assoc.; Marketing Soc. 1975–; British Fashion Council, 1988–; Action Res. for Crippled Child, 1989–; Adv. Bd for Victim Support, 1990–. Friend of Epping Forest. *Recreations:* family, running, windsurfing, walking dogs. *Address:* 5 Grosvenor Gardens Mews North, SW1W 0JP. *T:* 071–730 7740. *Clubs:* Mark's, Harry's Bar, Solus.

MANSFIELD COOPER, Prof. Sir William, Kt 1963; LLM; Professor of Industrial Law, University of Manchester, 1949–70, now Professor Emeritus; Vice-Chancellor of the University, 1956–70; *b* Newton Heath, Manchester, 20 Feb. 1903; *s* of William and Georgina C. Cooper; *m* 1936, Edna Mabel, *o c* of Herbert and Elizabeth Baker; one *s*. *Educ:* Elementary Sch.; Ruskin Coll., 1931–33; Manchester Univ., 1933–36 (LLB, Dauntesey Jun. Law Schol., Dauntesey Special Prizeman in International Law). Grad. Res. Schol., 1936–37; Lecturer WEA (LLM 1938). University of Manchester: Asst Lecturer, 1938; Lecturer, 1942; Asst to Vice-Chancellor, 1944; Registrar and Senior Lecturer in Law, 1945; Professor of Industrial and Commercial Law, 1949, continuing as Joint Registrar until 1952; Acting Vice-Chancellor, Nov. 1953–May 1954 and July 1954–Oct. 1954. Called to the Bar (Gray's Inn), 1940. Chairman John Rylands Library, 1956–70; Chairman Cttee of Vice-Chancellors and Principals, 1961–64; President, Council of Europe Cttee on Higher Education and Research, 1966–67; Vice-President, Standing Conference of European Rectors and Vice-Chancellors, 1964–69. Dep. Chm., Cttee of Inquiry into London Univ., 1970–72. Hon. Mem., Manchester Royal Coll. Music, 1971. Hon. LLD: Manitoba, 1964; Liverpool, 1970; Manchester, 1970; Hon. DLitt Keele, 1967; Hon. DSc Kharkov, 1970; Hon. DHL Rochester, 1970. Hon. Fellow, Manchester Inst. Science and Technology, 1972. *Publications:* Outlines of Industrial Law, 1947, 6th edn by John C. Wood, 1972; papers and reviews in learned journals. *Recreation:* reading. *Address:* Flat 32, The Chestnuts, West Street, Godmanchester, Huntingdon PE18 8HH. *Club:* Athenæum.

MANSON, Ian Stuart; Chief Crown Prosecutor, West Midlands Area, Crown Prosecution Service, 1986–89; *b* 15 March 1929; *s* of late David Alexander Manson and Elsie May (*née* Newton); *m* 1957, Pamela Horrocks-Taylor; three *s*. *Educ:* Heath Grammar Sch., Halifax; Clare Coll., Cambridge (Open Exhibnr; BA Hons). Admitted Solicitor, 1956. Asst Prosecuting Solicitor, Bradford, 1956–57; Prosecuting Solicitor: Southampton, 1957–58; Portsmouth, 1958–60; Asst Prosecuting Solicitor, Birmingham, 1960–66; Prosecuting Solicitor, W Midlands Police Authority, 1966–74; Chief Prosecuting Solicitor, W Midlands CC, 1974–86. *Recreations:* reading, music, gardening.

MANT, Prof. (Arthur) Keith, MD; FRCP; FRCPath; Emeritus Professor of Forensic Medicine, University of London, since 1984; *b* 11 Sept. 1919; *s* of George Arthur Mant and Elsie Muriel (*née* Slark); *m* 1947, Heather Smith, BA; two *s* one *d*. *Educ:* Denstone Coll., Staffs; St Mary's Hosp., Paddington. MB BS 1949, MD 1950; MRCS, LRCP 1943; FRCPath 1967; MRCP 1977; FRCP 1982. Dept Obst. and Gynæc., St Mary's Hosp., 1943; RAMC, i/c Path. Section, War Crimes Gp, 1945–48 (Major); Registrar (ex-service), Med. Unit, St Mary's Hosp., 1948–49; Dept of Forensic Medicine, Guy's Hospital, Univ. of London: Research Fellow, 1949–55; Lectr, 1955–66; Reader in Forensic Med., 1966–74; Prof. of Forensic Med., 1974–84; Head of Dept, 1972–84. Sen. Lectr in Forensic Med., 1965, Hon. Consultant in Forensic Med., 1967–84, KCH. WHO Consultant, Sri Lanka, 1982, 1984 and 1987. Visiting Lectr in Med. Jurisprudence and Toxicology, St Mary's Hosp., 1955–84; British Council Lectr, India, 1979; Visiting Professor: Univ. of Jordan, 1985; Nihon Univ., Japan, 1985. Lectures: Niels Dungal Meml, Reykjavic, 1979; J. B. Firth Meml, London, 1981; W. D. L. Fernando Meml, Sri Lanka, 1982; Douglas Kerr Meml, London, 1985. Examiner in Forensic Medicine: NUI, 1960; St Andrews Univ., 1967; Dundee Univ., 1968; RCPath, 1971; Soc. of Apothecaries, 1971; Univ. of Riyadh, Saudi Arabia, 1976; Univ. of Garyounis-Libya, 1976; Univ. of Tripoli, 1979. A. D. Williams Distinguished Scholar Fellowship, Univ. Med. Coll. of Virginia, 1963 and 1968. President: Internat. Assoc. in Accident and Traffic Med., 1972–83 (now Pres. Emeritus); British Acad. of Forensic Sci., 1975–76; President: Forensic Sci. Soc., 1963–65; British Assoc. in Forensic Med., 1970–71; Vice-Pres., Medico-Legal Soc. Nat. correspondent for GB, Internat. Acad. of Legal and Social Med.; Mem., Amer. Acad. of Forensic Sci.; Corresp. For. Mem., Soc. de Méd. Légale; Hon. Member: Brazilian Assoc. for Traffic Med.; Soc. de Méd. Légale, Belgium. Member, Editorial Board: Internat. Reference Org. in Forensic Med. (INFORM), 1971–; Amer. Jl of Forensic Medicine and Pathology, 1980–; Hon. Editor, Jl of Traffic Medicine, 1989–; formerly English Editor, Zeitschrift für Rechtsmedizin; Internat. Editorial Bd, Excerpta Medica (Forensic Sci. abstracts). Fellow: Indian Acad. of Forensic Sci.; Indian Assoc. in Forensic Medicine; Swedish Soc. of Med. Scis. Hon. DMJ(Path) Soc. of Apothecaries, 1979. *Publications:* Forensic Medicine: observation and interpretation, 1960; Modern Trends in Forensic Medicine, Series 3, 1973; (ed) Taylor's Principles and Practice of Medical Jurisprudence, 13th edn, 1984; contribs to med. and sci. literature. *Recreations:* fishing, orchid culture. *Address:* 29 Ashley Drive, Walton-on-Thames, Surrey KT12 1JT. *T:* Walton-on-Thames (0932) 225005.

MANT, Keith; *see* Mant, A. K.

MANTELL, Hon. Sir Charles (Barrie Knight), Kt 1990; **Hon. Mr Justice Mantell;** Judge of the High Court of Justice, Queen's Bench Division, since 1990; *b* 30 Jan. 1937; *s* of Francis Christopher Knight Mantell and Elsie Mantell; *m* 1960, Anne Shirley Mantell; two *d*. *Educ:* Manchester Grammar Sch.; Manchester Univ. (LLM). Called to the Bar, Gray's Inn, 1960, Bencher, 1990. Flying Officer, RAF, 1958–61. In practice at Bar, London and Manchester, 1961–82; a Recorder of the Crown Court, 1978–82; QC 1979; Judge of Supreme Court, Hong Kong, 1982–85; a Circuit Judge, 1985–90. *Recreations:* golf, reading, watching cricket. *Address:* Royal Courts of Justice, Strand, WC2A 2LL. *Clubs:* Lansdowne; Big Four (Manchester); Hong Kong (Hong Kong); Royal Western Yacht (Plymouth).

MANTHORP, Rev. Brian Robert, MA; FCollP; Headmaster, Worcester College for the Blind, since 1980; *b* 28 July 1934; *s* of Alan Roy Manthorp and Stella Manthorp; *m* 1955, Jennifer Mary Caradine; three *s* one *d*. *Educ:* Framlingham Coll.; Pembroke Coll., Oxford (MA Hons English); Westcott House, Cambridge. Instructor Lieut, RN, 1955–58. Ordained priest, Guildford, 1961. Assistant Master, Charterhouse, 1958–65; Head of English: Lawrence Coll., Pakistan, 1965–67; Aitchison Coll., Pakistan, 1968–70; Oakbank Sch., Keighley, 1970–73; Headmaster, Holy Trinity Senior Sch., Halifax, 1973–80. *Publication:* Fifty Poems for Pakistan, 1971. *Recreations:* sport, sketching. *Address:* The Headmaster's House, Worcester College for the Blind, Whittington Road, Worcester WR5 2JU. *T:* Worcester (0905) 356599; The Brew House, High Street, Chipping Campden, Glos. *Club:* East India.

MANTHORPE, John Jeremy; Chief Executive, since 1985, and Chief Land Registrar, since 1990, HM Land Registry; *b* 16 June 1936; *s* of Margaret Dora Manthorpe; *m* 1967, Kathleen Mary Ryan; three *s* one *d*. *Educ:* Beckenham and Penge Grammar School. HM Land Registry: Plans Branch, 1952; Principal Survey and Plans Officer, 1974; Controller (Registration), 1981–85. *Recreations:* walking and watching the Ashdown Forest. *Address:* Beurles, Fairwarp, Uckfield, East Sussex. *T:* Nutley (082571) 2795.

MANTON, 3rd Baron, *cr* 1922, of Compton Verney; **Joseph Rupert Eric Robert Watson;** DL; Landowner and Farmer; *b* 22 Jan. 1924; *s* of 2nd Baron Manton and Alethea (*d* 1979), 2nd *d* of late Colonel Philip Langdale, OBE; *S* father, 1968; *m* 1951, Mary Elizabeth, twin *d* of Major T. D. Hallinan, Ashbourne, Glounthaune, Co. Cork; two *s* three *d* (of whom two *s* one *d* are triplets). *Educ:* Eton. Joined Army, 1942; commissioned Life Guards, 1943; Captain, 1946; retired, 1947; rejoined 7th (QO) Hussars, 1951–56. DL Humberside, 1980. *Recreations:* hunting, shooting, racing. *Heir: s* Major the Hon. Miles Ronald Marcus Watson, Life Guards [*b* 7 May 1958; *m* 1984, Elizabeth, *e d* of J. R. Story; two *s*]. *Address:* Houghton Hall, Sancton, York. *T:* Market Weighton (0696) 873234. *Clubs:* White's, Jockey.
See also Baron Hesketh.

MANWARING, Randle (Gilbert), MA; FSS, FPMI; poet and author; retired company director; *b* 3 May 1912; *s* of late George Ernest and Lilian Manwaring; *m* 1941, Betty Violet, *d* of H. P. Rout, Norwich; three *s* one *d*. *Educ:* private schools. MA Keele, 1982. Joined Clerical, Medical and Gen. Life Assce Soc., 1929. War service, RAF, 1940–46, W/Cdr; comd RAF Regt in Burma, 1945. Clerical, Medical & Gen. Pensions Rep., 1950; joined C. E. Heath & Co. Ltd, 1956: Asst Dir, 1960, Dir, 1964, Man. Dir. 1969; Founder Dir (Man.), C. E. Heath Urquhart (Life and Pensions), 1966–71, and a Founder Dir, Excess Life Assce Co., 1967–75; Dir, Excess Insurance Group, 1975–78; Insurance Adviser, Midland Bank, 1971; first Man. Dir, Midland Bank Ins. Services, 1972–74, Vice-Chm., 1974–77, Dir, 1977–78. Chm., Life Soc., Corp. of Insce Brokers, 1965–66; Dep. Chm., Corp. of Insce Brokers, 1970–71; Pres., Soc. of Pensions Consultants, 1968–70. Chairman of Governors: Luckley-Oakfield Sch., 1972–83; Northease Manor Sch., 1972–84. Diocesan Reader (Chichester), 1968–; Mem., Diocesan Synod, 1985–; Churchwarden, St Peter-upon-Cornhill, London, 1985–90. Chm., Vine Books Ltd; Dir, Crusaders Union Ltd, 1960– (Vice-Pres., 1983–). Chm. of Trustees, Careforce, 1980–87. Chm., Probus Club, Uckfield, 1989–90. *Publications:* The Heart of this People, 1954; A Christian Guide to Daily Work, 1963; Thornhill Guide to Insurance, 1976; The Run of the Downs, 1984; From Controversy to Co-existence, 1985; The Good Fight, 1990; A Study of Hymnwriting and Hymnsinging in the Christian Church, 1991; *poems:* Posies Once Mine, 1951; Satires and Salvation, 1960; Under the Magnolia Tree, 1965; Slave to No Sect, 1966; Crossroads of the Year, 1975; From the Four Winds, 1976; In a Time of Unbelief, 1977; Poem Prayers for Growing People, 1980; The Swifts of Maggiore, 1981; In a Time of Change, 1983; Collected Poems, 1986; contrib. poems and articles to learned jls in GB and Canada. *Recreations:* music, reading, following cricket. *Address:* Marbles Barn, Newick, Lewes, East Sussex BN8 4LG. *T:* Newick (082572) 3845. *Clubs:* Royal Air Force, MCC; Sussex County Cricket.

MANZIE, Sir (Andrew) Gordon, KCB 1987 (CB 1983); Chairman, Anglo Japanese Construction Ltd, since 1990; Director: Motherwell Bridge Holdings, since 1990; Altnacraig Shipping, since 1990; *b* 3 April 1930; *s* of late John Mair and Catherine Manzie; *m* 1955, Rosalind Clay; one *s* one *d*. *Educ:* Royal High Sch. of Edinburgh; London Sch. of Economics and Political Science (BScEcon). Joined Civil Service as Clerical Officer, Scottish Home Dept, 1947. National Service, RAF, 1949. Min. of Supply: Exec. Officer (Higher Exec. Officer, 1957). Private Sec. to Perm. Sec., Min. of Aviation, 1962; Sen. Exec. Officer, 1963; Principal, 1964; Sec. to Cttee of Inquiry into Civil Air Transport (Edwards Cttee), 1967; Asst Sec., Dept of Trade and Industry, on loan to Min. of Posts and Telecommunications, 1971; Dept of Industry, 1974; Under-Sec., Dir, Office for Scotland, Depts of Trade and Industry, 1975; Under Sec., Scottish Economic Planning Dept, 1975–79; Dir, Industrial Develt Unit, 1980–81, Dep. Sec., 1980–84, Dept of Industry (Dept of Trade and Industry, 1983–84); Second Perm. Sec. and Chief Exec., PSA, DoE, 1984–90, retd. CBIM 1987; Hon. FCIOB 1990. *Recreations:* golf, reading. *Club:* Caledonian.

MANZINI, Raimondo; Gran Croce, Ordine Merito Repubblica, 1968; GCVO (Hon.) 1969; Italian Ambassador to the Court of St James's, 1968–75; *b* Bologna, 25 Nov. 1913. *Educ:* Univ. of California (Berkeley); Clark Univ., Mass. (MA); Dr of Law, Bologna Univ. Entered Diplomatic Service, 1940; served San Francisco, 1940–41; Lisbon, 1941–43; Min. of Foreign Affairs in Brindisi, Salerno, Rome, 1943–44; London, 1944–47; Consul General for Congo, Nigeria and Gold Coast, 1947–50; Consul General, Baden Baden, 1951–52; Head of Information Service, CED, Paris, 1952–53; Ministry of Foreign Affairs, 1953–55; Adviser to the Minister of Foreign Trade, 1955–58; Chef de Cabinet of Minister for Foreign Affairs, 1958; Diplomatic Adviser to the Prime Minister, 1958–59; Advr to Minister of Industry, 1960–64; Perm. Rep. to OECD, Paris, 1965–68; Sec.-Gen., Min. of Foreign Affairs, 1975–78. Commandeur, Légion d'Honneur (France), 1976. *Address:* Villa Bellochio, 83 Boulevard de Garavan, Menton, France.

MAPLE, Graham John; District Judge, Principal Registry of Family Division, High Court of Justice, since 1991; *b* 18 Dec. 1947; *s* of Sydney George and Thelma Olive Maple; *m* 1974, Heather Anderson; two *s*. *Educ:* Shirley Secondary Modern Sch.; John Ruskin Grammar Sch., Croydon; Bedford Coll., London (LLB 1973). Lord Chancellor's Dept, 1968; Sec., Principal Registry of Family Div., 1989. *Publications:* (Co-Editor) Rayden and Jackson on Divorce, 12th–15th edns, 16th edn, 1991; (ed) Holloway's Probate Handbook, 8th edn, 1987. *Recreations:* steam and model railways. *Address:* Principal Registry, Family Division, High Court of Justice, Somerset House, WC2R 1LP.

MAPLES, Ven. Jeffrey Stanley; Archdeacon of Swindon and Hon. Canon Diocesan, Bristol Cathedral, 1974–82, Archdeacon Emeritus, 1982; *b* 8 Aug. 1916; *o s* of Arthur Stanley and Henrietta Georgina Maples; *m* 1945, Isobel Eileen Mabel Wren; four *s* (and one *s* decd). *Educ:* Downing Coll., Cambridge; Chichester Theological Coll. Asst Curate St James, Milton, Portsmouth, 1940–46; Asst Curate, Watlington, Diocese of Oxford, 1946–48. Vicar of Swinderby, Dio. Lincoln, and Diocesan Youth Chaplain, 1948–50; Vicar of St Michael-on-the-Mount, Lincoln, and Director of Religious Education: for Lincoln Dio., 1950–56; for Salisbury Dio., 1956–63; Canon of Lincoln, 1954–56; Chancellor of Salisbury Cathedral, 1960–67; Director of the Bible Reading Fellowship, 1963–67; Proctor in Convocation for Salisbury Diocese, 1957–70; Canon Emeritus of Salisbury Cathedral, 1967–; Vicar of St James, Milton, Portsmouth, 1967–74; Rural Dean of Portsmouth, 1968–73; Hon. Canon, Portsmouth Cathedral, 1972–74. *Address:* 88 Exeter Street, Salisbury, Wilts SP1 2SE. *T:* Salisbury (0722) 323848.

MAPLES, John Cradock; MP (C) West Lewisham, since 1983; Economic Secretary to HM Treasury, since 1990; *b* 22 April 1943; *s* of late Thomas Cradock Maples and Hazel Mary Maples; *m* 1986, Jane Corbin. *Educ:* Marlborough Coll., Wiltshire; Downing Coll., Cambridge; Harvard Business Sch., USA. PPS to Financial Sec. to HM Treasury, 1987–90. *Recreations:* sailing, skiing. *Address:* House of Commons, SW1.

MAPLES EARLE, Ven. E. E.; *see* Earle.

MAR, Countess of (*suo jure*, 31st in line from Ruadri, 1st Earl of Mar, 1115); Premier Earldom of Scotland by descent; Lady Garioch, *c* 1320; **Margaret of Mar;** *b* 19 Sept. 1940; *er d* of 30th Earl of Mar, and Millicent Mary Salton; *S* father, 1975; recognised in surname "of Mar" by warrant of Court of Lord Lyon, 1967, when she abandoned her second forename; *m* 1st, 1959, Edwin Noel Artiss (marr. diss. 1976); one *d*; 2nd, 1976, (cousin) John Salton (marr. diss. 1981); 3rd, 1982, J. H. Jenkin, MA (Cantab), FRCO, LRAM, ARCM. Lay Mem., Immigration Appeal Tribunal, 1985–. Patron, Dispensing Doctors' Assoc., 1985–. Governor, King's Sch., Gloucester, 1984–87. *Heir: d* Mistress of Mar, *qv*. *Address:* St Michael's Farm, Great Witley, Worcester WR6 6JB. *T:* Great Witley (0299) 896608.

MAR, Mistress of; Lady Susan Helen of Mar; Secretary to Rt Hon. Edward Heath, MBE, MP; *b* 31 May 1963; *d* and *heiress* of Countess of Mar, *qv*; *m* 1989, Bruce Alexander Wyllie. *Educ:* King Charles I School, Kidderminster; Christie College, Cheltenham. *Address:* 5 Vine Cottages, Grove Footpath, Faversham, Surrey KT5 8AT.

MAR, 13th Earl of, *cr* 1565, **and KELLIE,** 15th Earl of, *cr* 1619; **John Francis Hervey Erskine;** Baron Erskine, 1429; Viscount Fentoun, 1606; Baron Dirleton, 1603; Premier Viscount of Scotland; Hereditary Keeper of Stirling Castle; Representative Peer for Scotland, 1959–63; Major Scots Guards; retired 1954; Major, Argyll and Sutherland Highlanders (TA) retired 1959; Lord Lieutenant of Clackmannan, since 1966; *b* 15 Feb. 1921; *e s* of late Lord Erskine (John Francis Ashley Erskine), GCSI, GCIE; *S* grandfather, 1955; *m* 1948, Pansy Constance (OBE, 1984; Pres., UK Cttee for UNICEF, 1979–84; Chm., Youth at Risk Adv. Gp; Chm. and Vice-Chm., Scottish Standing Conf., Voluntary Youth Orgns, 1967–81. Elder of Church of Scotland. JP 1971; CStJ 1983), *y d* of late General Sir Andrew Thorne, KCB; three *s* one *d*. *Educ:* Eton; Trinity Coll., Cambridge. 2nd Lieut, Scots Guards, 1941; served in Egypt, N. Africa, Italy and Germany with 2nd Bn Scots Guards and HQ 201 Guards' Brigade, 1942–45 (wounded, despatches). Staff Coll., Camberley, 1950; DAAG, HQ, 3rd Infantry Div., 1951–52. DL Clackmannanshire, 1954, Vice-Lieutenant, 1957, JP 1962; County Councillor for Clackmannanshire, 1955–75 (Vice-Convener, 1961–64); Chairman: Forth Conservancy Board, 1957–68; Clackmannanshire T&AFA, 1961–68. An Elder of the Church of Scotland. Member of the Queen's Body Guard for Scotland (Royal Company of Archers). KStJ 1966. *Heir: s* Lord Erskine, *qv*. *Address:* Claremont House, Alloa, Clackmannanshire FK10 2JF. *T:* Alloa (0259) 212020. *Club:* New (Edinburgh).

MARA, Rt. Hon. Ratu Sir Kamisese Kapaiwai Tuimacilai, GCMG 1983; KBE 1969 (OBE 1961); PC 1973; Tui Nayau; Tui Lau; Prime Minister of the Republic of Fiji, since 1987 (of Fiji, 1970–87); Hereditary High Chief of the Lau Islands; *b* 13 May 1920; *s* of late Ratu Tevita Uluilakeba, Tui Nayau; *m* 1951, Adi Lady Lala Mara (Roko Tui Dreketi); three *s* five *d*. *Educ:* Fiji; Sacred Heart Coll., NZ; Otago Univ., NZ; Wadham Coll., Oxford (MA), Hon. Fellow, 1971; London Sch. of Economics (Dip. Econ. & Social Admin.), Hon. Fellow, 1985. Administrative Officer, Colonial Service, Fiji, Oct. 1950; Fijian MLC, 1953–89, and MEC, 1959–61 (elected MLC and MEC, 1959). Member for Natural Resources and Leader of Govt Business; Alliance Party, 1964–66 (Founder of Party); Chief Minister and Mem., Council of Ministers, Fiji, 1967; Minister for Foreign Affairs and Civil Aviation, 1986–87. Hon. Dr of Laws: Univ. of Guam, 1969; Univ. of Papua New Guinea, 1982; Hon. LLD: Univ. of Otago, 1973; New Delhi, 1975; Hon. DPolSc Korea, 1978; Hon. Dr Tokai Univ., 1980; DU Univ. of South Pacific, 1980. Man of the Pacific Award, 1984. Grand Cross, Order of Lion, Senegal, 1975; Order of Diplomatic Service Merit, Korea, 1978. *Recreations:* athletics, cricket, Rugby football, golf, fishing. *Address:* 6 Berkley Crescent, Domain, Suva, Fiji; Villa 1429, Pacific Harbour, Deuba. *Clubs:* United Oxford & Cambridge University, Achilles (London); Defence (Suva, Fiji).
See also Ratu E. Nailatikau.

MARAJ, Dr James Ajodhya; Permanent Secretary, Prime Minister's Office, Ministry of Foreign Affairs and Civil Aviation, Fiji, 1986; High Commissioner for Fiji to India, 1986; Vice-Chancellor, University of the South Pacific, 1975–82 (Hon. Professor of Education, since 1978); *b* 28 Sept. 1930; *s* of Ramgoolam Maraj and Popo Maraj; *m* 1951, Etress (*née* Ouditt); two *s* two *d*. *Educ:* St Mary's Coll. and Govt Teachers' Coll., Trinidad; Univ. of Birmingham (BA, PhD). FRICS 1981. Teacher, Lectr, 1947–60; Sen. Lectr, Univ. of West Indies, 1965–70; Head, Inst. of Educn, UWI, 1968–70; Dir, Educn Div., Commonwealth Secretariat, 1970–72; Commonwealth Asst Sec.-Gen., 1973–75; Sen. Evaluation Officer, The World Bank, 1982–84; High Comr for Fiji in Australia, Malaysia and Singapore, 1985–86. External Examr, Educn Adviser and Consultant to several countries; Chm. or Sec. nat. or internat. commns. Hon. DLitt Loughborough, 1980; DU Univ. of South Pacific, 1983. Gold Medal of Merit, Trinidad and Tobago, 1974; Pacific Person of the Year, Fiji Times, 1978; Dist. Scholar's Award, British Council, 1979. Chevalier de la Légion d'Honneur, France, 1982. *Publications:* miscellaneous research papers. *Recreations:* sport: cricket, squash, horse-racing; poetry, music. *Address:* c/o Ministry of Foreign Affairs, Government Buildings, Suva, Fiji. *Clubs:* Athenæum, Commonwealth Trust, Royal Over-Seas League.

MARCEAU, Marcel; Officier de la Légion d'Honneur; Officier de l'Ordre National du Mérite; Commandeur des Arts et Lettres de la République Française; mime; Founder and Director, Compagnie de Mime Marcel Marceau, since 1949; Director, International School of Mime of Paris Marcel Marceau; *b* Strasbourg, 22 March 1923; *s* of Charles and

Anne Mangel; two *s* two *d*. *Educ:* Ecole des Beaux Arts; Arts Décoratifs, Limoges; Ecole Etienne Decroux; Ecole Charles Dullin. First stage appearance, in Paris, 1946; with Barrault/Renaud Co., 1946–49; founded his company, 1949; since then has toured constantly, playing in 65 countries. Created about 100 pantomimes (most famous are The Creation of the World, The Cage, The Maskmaker, The Tree, Bip Liontamer, Bip hunts Butterfly, Bip plays David and Goliath, Bip at a Society Party, Bip in the Modern and Future Life, Bip Soldier, etc), and 26 mimodrames, and in particular the character 'Bip' (1947); *Mimodrames:* Bip et la fille des rues, 1947; Bip et L'Oiseau, 1948; Death Before Dawn, 1948; The Fair, 1949; The Flute Player, 1949; The Overcoat, 1951; Moriana and Galvan, Pierrot of Montmartre, 1952; Les Trois Perruques, 1953; Un Soir aux Funambules, 1953; La Parade en bleu et noir, 1956; le 14 juillet, 1956; Le Mont de Piété, 1956; Le Loup de Tsu Ku Mi, 1956; Le Petit Cirque, 1958; Les Matadors, 1959; Paris qui rit, Paris qui pleure, 1959; Don Juan, 1964; Candide, 1970, with Ballet de l'Opéra de Hambourg; *films:* The Overcoat, 1951; Barbarella, 1967; Scrooge (BBC London), 1973; Shanks, US, 1973; Silent Movie, 1976. Has made frequent TV appearances and many short films for TV, incl. Pantomimes, 1954, A Public Garden, 1955, Le mime Marcel Marceau, 1965, The World of Marcel Marceau, 1966, 12 short films with Enc. Brit., NY, 1974. Member: Acad. of Arts and Letters (DDR); Akad. der schönen Künste, Munich; Acad. des Beaux Arts, Paris. Emmy Awards (US), 1955, 1968. Hon. Dr, Univ. of Oregon; Dr *hc* Univ. of Princeton, 1981. Gold Medal of Czechoslovak Republic (for contribution to cultural relations). *Publications:* Les 7 Péchés Capitaux (lithographs); Les Rêveries de Bip (lithographs); La Ballade de Paris et du Monde (text, lithographs, water-colours, drawings in ink and pencil); Alphabet Book; Counting Book; L'Histoire de Bip (text and lithographs); The Third Eye (lithoprint); Pimporello. *Recreations:* painting, poetry, fencing. *Address:* Compagnie de Mime Marcel Marceau, 21 rue Jean-Mermoz, 75008 Paris, France. *T:* 42.25.06.05 and 42.56.32.76.

MARCH AND KINRARA, Earl of; Charles Henry Gordon-Lennox; *b* 8 Jan. 1955; *s* and *heir* of Duke of Richmond and Gordon, *qv; m* 1976, Sally (marr. diss. 1989), *d* of late Maurice Clayton and of Mrs Denis Irwin; one *d*. *Educ:* Eton. *Address:* Goodwood House, Chichester, West Sussex.

MARCH, Sir Derek (Maxwell), KBE 1988 (CBE 1982; OBE 1973); HM Diplomatic Service, retired; High Commissioner in Kampala, 1986–90; *b* 9 Dec. 1930; *s* of Frank March and Vera (*née* Ward); *m* 1955, Sally Annetta Riggs; one *s* two *d*. *Educ:* Devonport High Sch.; Birkbeck Coll., London. National Service, RAF, 1949–51. Joined HM Diplomatic Service, 1949; FO, 1951; Bonn, 1955; Vice Consul, Hanover, 1957; Asst Trade Comr, Salisbury, 1959; Consul, Dakar, 1962; First Secretary: FO, 1964; Rawalpindi, 1968; Peking, 1971; FCO, 1974; Counsellor, seconded to Dept of Trade, 1975; Senior British Trade Comr, Hong Kong, 1977–82; Counsellor, seconded to DTI, 1982–86. *Recreations:* golf, cricket, Rugby Union. *Address:* Soke House, The Soke, Alresford, Hants SO24 9DB. *T:* Alresford (0962) 732588. *Clubs:* MCC, East India, Devonshire, Sports and Public Schools; Hong Kong (Hong Kong); Alresford Golf.

MARCH, Lionel John, ScD; FRSA; Professor and Head of Architecture/Urban Design Program, Graduate School of Architecture and Urban Planning, University of California, Los Angeles, since 1984; *b* 26 Jan. 1934; *o s* of Leonard James March and Rose (*née* Edwards); *m* 1st, 1960, Lindsey Miller (marr. diss. 1984); one *s* two *d*; 2nd, 1984, Maureen Vidler; one step *s* two step *d*. *Educ:* Hove Grammar Sch. for Boys; Magdalene Coll., Cambridge (MA, ScD). FIMA, FRSA. Nat. Service: Sub-Lt, RNVR, 1953–55. Harkness Fellow, Commonwealth Fund, Harvard Univ. and MIT, 1962–64; Asst to Sir Leslie Martin, 1964–66; Lectr in Architecture, Univ. of Cambridge, 1966–69; Dir, Centre for Land Use and Built Form Studies, Univ. of Cambridge, 1969–73; Prof., Dept of Systems Design, Univ. of Waterloo, Ontario, 1974–76; Prof. of Design, Faculty of Technology, Open Univ., 1976–81; Rector and Vice-Provost, RCA, 1981–84. Chm., Applied Res. of Cambridge Ltd, 1969–73. Mem., Governing Body, Imperial Coll. of Science and Technology, 1981–84. General Editor (with Leslie Martin), Cambridge Urban and Architectural Studies, 1970–; Editor, Environment and Planning B, Planning and Design, 1974–. *Publications:* (with Philip Steadman) The Geometry of Environment, 1971; (ed with Leslie Martin) Urban Space and Structures, 1972; (ed) The Architecture of Form, 1976. *Address:* The How House, 2422 Silver Ridge Avenue, Silver Lake, Los Angeles, Calif 90039, USA. *T:* (213) 661–7907.

MARCH, Prof. Norman Henry; Coulson Professor of Theoretical Chemistry, University of Oxford, since 1977; Fellow of University College, Oxford, since 1977; *b* 9 July 1927; *s* of William and Elsie March; *m* 1949, Margaret Joan Hoyle; two *s*. *Educ:* King's Coll., London Univ. University of Sheffield: Lecturer in Physics, 1953–57; Reader in Theoretical Physics, 1957–61; Prof. of Physics, 1961–72; Prof. of Theoretical Solid State Physics, Imperial Coll., Univ. of London, 1973–77. Hon. DTech Chalmers, Gothenburg, 1980. *Publications:* The Many-Body Problem in Quantum Mechanics (with W. H. Young and S. Sampanthar), 1967; Liquid Metals, 1968; (with W. Jones) Theoretical Solid State Physics, 1973; Self-Consistent Fields in Atoms, 1974; Orbital Theories of Molecules and Solids, 1974; (with M. P. Tosi) Atomic Dynamics in Liquids, 1976; (with M. Parrinello) Collective Effects in Solids and Liquids, 1983; (with S. Lundqvist) The Theory of the Inhomogeneous Electron Gas, 1983; (with M. P. Tosi) Coulomb Liquids, 1984; (with M. P. Tosi) Polymers, Liquid Crystals and Low-Dimensional Solids, 1984; (with R. A. Street and M. P. Tosi) Amorphous Solids and the Liquid State, 1985; Chemical Bonds outside Metal Surfaces, 1986; (with P. N. Butcher and M. P. Tosi) Crystalline Semiconducting Materials and Devices, 1986; (with B. M. Deb) The Single Particle Density in Physics and Chemistry, 1987; (with S. Lundqvist and M. P. Tosi) Order and Chaos in Nonlinear Physical Systems, 1988; (with J. A. Alonso) Electrons in Metals and Alloys, 1989; Liquid Metals, 1990; Chemical Physics of Liquids, 1990; Electron Density Theory of Atoms and Molecules; many scientific papers on quantum mechanics and statistical mechanics in Proceedings Royal Society, Phil. Magazine, Phys. Res., Jl of Chem. Phys, etc. *Recreations:* music, chess, cricket. *Address:* Elmstead, 6 Northcroft Road, Englefield Green, Egham, Surrey. *T:* Egham (0784) 433078.

MARCH, Valerie, (Mrs Andrew March); *see* Masterson, V.

MARCHAMLEY, 3rd Baron, *cr* 1908, of Hawkstone; **John William Tattersall Whiteley;** late Lieutenant, Royal Armoured Corps; *b* 24 April 1922; *s* of 2nd Baron and Margaret Clara (*d* 1974), *d* of Thomas Scott Johnstone of Glenmark, Waipara, New Zealand; *S* father, 1949; *m* 1967, Sonia Kathleen Pedrick; one *s*. Served War of 1939–45, Captain, 19th King George V Own Lancers. *Heir: s* Hon. William Francis Whiteley, *b* 27 July 1968. *Address:* Whetcombe, North Huish, South Brent, Devon TQ10 9NG.

MARCHANT, Catherine; *see* Cookson, C.

MARCHANT, Edgar Vernon; retired; *b* 7 Dec. 1915; *s* of E. C. Marchant; *m* 1945, Joyce Allen Storey; one *s* two *d*. *Educ:* Marlborough Coll.; Lincoln Coll., Oxford. Engr, Bahrain Petroleum Co., 1938; various technical and scientific posts in Min. of Aircraft Production, Min. of Supply and RAE, 1940–51; Principal, Min. of Supply, 1951; Principal, BoT, 1955; Asst Sec., BoT, 1959; Asst Registrar of Restrictive Trading Agreements, 1964; Asst Sec., Dept of Economic Affairs, 1966; Nat. Board for Prices and Incomes: Asst Sec., 1967–68; Under-Sec., 1968–71; Under-Sec., DTI, 1971–75. Dir, Paddington Building Soc., 1977–87. Mem., CS Appeal Bd, 1976–84. *Recreations:* gardening, messing about in boats. *Address:* 87 New Forest Drive, Brockenhurst, Hants SO42 7QT. *Club:* Royal Southampton Yacht.

MARCHANT, Ven. George John Charles; Archdeacon Emeritus and Canon Emeritus of Durham, since 1983; *b* 3 Jan. 1916; *s* of late T. Marchant, Little Stanmore, Mddx; *m* 1944, Eileen Lillian Kathleen, *d* of late F. J. Smith, FCIS; one *s* three *d*. *Educ:* St John's Coll., Durham (MA, BD); Tyndale Hall, Bristol. Deacon 1939, priest 1940, London; Curate of St Andrew's, Whitehall Park, N19, 1939–41; Licence to officiate, London dio., 1941–44 (in charge of Young Churchmen's Movement); Curate of St Andrew-the-Less, Cambridge (in charge of St Stephen's), 1944–48; Vicar of Holy Trinity, Skirbeck, Boston, 1948–54; Vicar of St Nicholas, Durham, 1954–74; Rural Dean of Durham, 1964–74; Hon. Canon of Durham Cathedral, 1972–74; Archdeacon of Auckland and Canon Residentiary, Durham Cathedral, 1974–83. Pre-Retirement Advr, Dio. Norwich Clergy, 1990–. Member of General Synod, 1970–80 (Proctor in Convocation for Dio. Durham). Chm. Editorial Bd, Anvil, 1983–91. *Publications:* contributed to: Baker's Dictionary of Theology, 1960; Bishops in the Church, 1966; articles in Evangelical Qly, Churchman, and Anvil; book reviews. *Recreations:* record-music, bird watching, gardening. *Address:* 28 Greenways, Eaton, Norwich NR4 6PE. *T:* Norwich (0603) 58295.

MARCHANT, Graham Leslie; Head of Site Improvement, South Bank Centre, since 1989; *b* 2 Feb. 1945; *s* of Leslie and Dorothy Marchant. *Educ:* King's School, Worcester; Selwyn College, Cambridge (MA). Administrator, Actors' Company, 1973–75; General Manager, English Music Theatre, 1975–78; Gen. Administrator, Opera North, 1978–82; Administrator, Tricycle Theatre, 1983–84; Chief Exec., Riverside Studios, 1984; Managing Dir, Playhouse Theatre Co., 1985–86; Dir, Arts Co-ordination, Arts Council, 1986–89. *Recreations:* reading, gardening, walking. *Address:* 142 Elsley Road, SW11 5LH. *T:* 071–223 1151.

MARCHWOOD, 3rd Viscount *cr* 1945, of Penang and of Marchwood, Southampton; **David George Staveley Penny;** Bt 1933; Baron 1937; Managing Director, Moët & Chandon (London) Ltd, since 1987; *b* 22 May 1936; *s* of 2nd Viscount Marchwood, MBE and Pamela (*d* 1979), *o d* of John Staveley Colton-Fox; *S* father, 1979; *m* 1964, Tessa Jane, *d* of W. F. Norris; three *s*. *Educ:* Winchester College. 2nd Lt, Royal Horse Guards (The Blues), 1955–57. Joined Schweppes Ltd, 1958, and held various positions in the Cadbury Schweppes group before joining his present company. *Recreations:* cricket, shooting, racing. *Heir: s* Hon. Peter George Worsley Penny, *b* 8 Oct. 1965. *Address:* Filberts, Aston Tirrold, near Didcot, Oxon. *T:* Blewbury (0235) 850386. *Clubs:* White's, MCC.

MARCUS, Frank Ulrich; playwright; Television Critic for Plays International Magazine, since 1984; *b* Breslau, Germany, 30 June 1928; *s* of late Frederick and Gertie Marcus; *m* 1951, Jacqueline (*née* Sylvester); one *s* two *d*. *Educ:* Bunce Court Sch., Kent (evac. to Shropshire during war); St Martin's Sch. of Art, London. Actor, Dir, Scenic Designer, Unity Theatre, Kensington (later Internat. Theatre Gp). Theatre Critic, Sunday Telegraph, 1968–78. *Stage plays:* Minuet for Stuffed Birds, 1950; The Man Who Bought a Battlefield, 1963; The Formation Dancers, 1964; The Killing of Sister George, 1965 (3 'Best Play of the Year' Awards: Evening Standard, Plays and Players, Variety); Cleo, 1965; Studies of the Nude, 1967; Mrs Mouse, Are You Within?, 1968; The Window, 1969; Notes on a Love Affair, 1972; Blank Pages, 1972; Carol's Christmas, 1973; Beauty and the Beast, 1975; Portrait of the Artist (mime scenario), 1977; Blind Date, 1977; The Ballad of Wilfred the Second, 1978; The Merman of Orford (mime scenario), 1978; *television plays:* A Temporary Typist, 1966; The Glove Puppet, 1968; *radio plays:* The Hospital Visitor, 1980; The Beverley Brooch, 1981; The Row over La Ronde, 1982; *translations:* Schnitzler's Reigen, 1952 (as La Ronde, TV, 1982); Liebelei (TV), 1954; Anatol, 1976; Molnar's The Guardsman, 1978 (first perf., 1969); Kaiser's From Morning Till Midnight, 1979; Hauptmann's The Weavers, 1980. *Publications:* The Formation Dancers, 1964; The Killing of Sister George, 1965; The Window, 1968; Mrs Mouse, Are You Within?, 1969; Notes on a Love Affair, 1972; Blank Pages, 1973; Beauty and the Beast, 1977; Blind Date, 1977; *translations:* Molnar, The Guardsman, 1978; Hauptmann, The Weavers, 1980; Schnitzler, La Ronde, and Anatol, 1982; contribs to: Behind the Scenes, 1972; Those Germans, 1973; On Theater, 1974 (US), etc, also to London Magazine, Plays and Players, Dramatists' Quarterly (US), New York Times, etc. *Recreation:* observing. *Address:* 8 Kirlegate, Meare, Glastonbury, Somerset BA6 9TA. *T:* Meare Heath (04586) 398; c/o Margaret Ramsay Ltd, 14a Goodwin's Court, St Martin's Lane, WC2.

MARDELL, Peggy Joyce, CBE 1982; Regional Nursing Officer, North West Thames Regional Health Authority, 1974–82; *b* 8 July 1927; *d* of Alfred Edward and Edith Mary Mardell. *Educ:* George Spicer Sch., Enfield; Highlands Hosp., London (RFN); E Suffolk Hosp., Ipswich (Medallist, SRN); Queen Charlotte's Hosp. Battersea Coll. of Further Educn (Hons Dip., RNT). Queens Inst. of District Nursing, Guildford, 1951–52 (SCM); Ward Sister, Night Sister, Bethnal Green Hosp., 1953–55; Sister Tutor, Royal Surrey County Hosp., 1957–64; Asst Regional Nursing Officer, NE Metrop. Regional Hosp. Bd, 1964–70; Chief Regional Nursing Officer, NW Metrop. Regional Hosp. Bd, 1970–74. Lectr, British Red Cross, 1958–60; Examr, Gen. Nursing Council, 1962–70; Nurse Mem., Surrey AHA, 1977–82; Member: Royal Coll. of Nursing; Regional Nurse Trng Cttee, 1970–82; Assessor for Nat. Nursing Staff Cttee, 1970–82. *Recreations:* renovating old furniture, gardening, reading. *Address:* 3 Corvill Court, Shelley Road, Worthing, W Sussex BN11 4DF. *T:* Worthing (0903) 211876.

MARDEN, John Louis, CBE 1976; JP; Former Chairman, Wheelock, Marden and Co. Ltd; *b* Woodford, Essex, 12 Feb. 1919; *s* of late George Ernest Marden; *m* 1947, Anne Harris; one *s* three *d*. *Educ:* Gresham Sch., Norfolk; Trinity Hall, Cambridge (MA). Served War, as Captain 4th Regt RHA, in N Africa, France and Germany, 1940–46. Joined Wheelock, Marden & Co. Ltd, as trainee (secretarial and shipping, then insurance side of business), 1946; Dir of company, 1952, Chm., 1959. Chm., Hong Kong Shipowners' Assoc., 1978–. JP Hong Kong, 1964. *Recreations:* golf, water ski-ing, ski-ing. *Address:* 14 Shek O, Hong Kong.

MARDER, Bernard Arthur; QC 1977; **His Honour Judge Marder;** a Circuit Judge, since 1983; *b* 25 Sept. 1928; *er s* of late Samuel and Marie Marder; *m* 1953, Sylvia Levy, MBE; one *s* one *d*. *Educ:* Bury Grammar Sch.; Manchester Univ. (LLB 1951). Called to the Bar, Gray's Inn, 1952. A Recorder of the Crown Court, 1979–83. Formerly Asst Comr, Local Govt and Parly Boundary Commns; Chairman: Panel of Inquiry into W Yorks Structure Plan, 1979; Mental Health Review Tribunals, 1987–89; Mem., Lands Tribunal, 1989–. Mem. Bd, Orange Tree Theatre, 1986–; Trustee, Richmond Parish Lands Charity, 1987–. *Recreations:* music, theatre, wine, walking. *Address:* 4/5 Gray's Inn Square, Gray's Inn, WC1R 5AY.

MARDON, Lt-Col (John) Kenric La Touche, DSO 1945; TD 1943; DL; MA; JP; Vice Lord-Lieutenant, Avon, 1974–80; Chairman, Mardon, Son & Hall, Ltd, Bristol, 1962–69; Director, Bristol & West Building Society, 1969–82; *b* 29 June 1905; *e s* of late Evelyn John Mardon, Halsway Manor, Crowcombe and late Maud Mary (*née* Rothwell);

m 1933, Dulcie Joan, 3rd *d* of late Maj.-Gen. K. M. Body, CB, CMG, OBE; two *s* one *d*. *Educ:* Clifton; Christ's Coll., Cambridge. Commissioned in Royal Devon Yeomanry, 1925; Major, 1938; Lieut-Colonel, RA, 1942; served War of 1939–45, in N.W. Europe, 1944–45 (despatches). JP Somerset, 1948; High Sheriff of Somerset, 1956–57; DL 1962. Master, Society of Merchant Venturers, Bristol, 1959–60; Governor, Clifton Coll., 1957. Pres., Bristol YMCA, 1969–79. *Recreations:* shooting, lawn tennis, squash rackets (rep. Cambridge v. Oxford, 1925). *Address:* 4 Rivers Street, Bath BA1 2PZ. *T:* Bath (0225) 337725. *Club:* Bath and County (Bath).

MAREK, John, PhD; MP (Lab) Wrexham, since 1983; *b* 24 Dec. 1940; *m* 1964, Anne. *Educ:* Univ. of London (BSc (Hons), PhD). Lecturer in Applied Mathematics, University College of Wales, Aberystwyth, 1966–83. Opposition frontbench spokesman: on health, 1985–87; on treasury and economic affairs, and on the Civil Service, 1987–. *Publications:* various research papers. *Address:* House of Commons, SW1A 0AA. *T:* 071–219 4149.

MARGADALE, 1st Baron, *cr* 1964, of Islay, Co. Argyll; **John Granville Morrison,** TD; JP; DL; Lord-Lieutenant of Wiltshire, 1969–81; Member Royal Company of Archers (Queen's Body Guard for Scotland); *b* 16 Dec. 1906; *s* of late Hugh Morrison; *m* 1928, Hon. Margaret Esther Lucie Smith (*d* 1980), 2nd *d* of 2nd Viscount Hambleden; three *s* one *d*. *Educ:* Eton; Magdalene Coll., Cambridge. Served 1939–45 with Royal Wilts Yeomanry; in MEF, 1939–42. MP (C) Salisbury Division of Wilts, 1942–64; Chairman, Conservative Members' (1922) Cttee, 1955–64. Yeomanry Comdt and Chm., Yeomanry Assoc., 1965–71; Hon. Col, The Royal Wiltshire Yeomanry Sqdn, 1965–71; Hon. Col, The Royal Yeomanry, 1965–71; Dep. Hon. Col, The Wessex Yeomanry, 1971–. JP 1936, High Sheriff, 1938, DL 1950, Wilts. MFH S and W Wilts Foxhounds, 1932–65. KStJ 1972. *Heir: s* Hon. James Ian Morrison, *qv*. *Address:* Fonthill House, Tisbury, Salisbury, Wilts SP3 5SA. *T:* Tisbury (0747) 870202; Eallabus, Bridgend, Islay, Argyll. *T:* Bowmore (049681) 223. *Clubs:* Turf, Jockey, White's.

See also Hon. Sir C. A. Morrison, Hon. M. A. Morrison, Rt Hon. Sir P. H. Morrison.

MARGÁIN, Hugo B.; GCVO; Ambassador of Mexico to the United States, 1965–70 and 1977–82; *b* 13 Feb. 1913; *s* of Cesar R. Margáin and Maria Teresa Gleason de Margáin; *m* 1941, Margarita Charles de Margáin; two *s* three *d* (and one *s* decd). *Educ:* National Univ. of Mexico (UNAM); National Sch. of Jurisprudence (LLB). Prof. of Constitutional Law, 1947, of Constitutional Writs, 1951–56, and of Fiscal Law, 1952–56, Univ. of Mexico. Govt posts include: Dir-Gen., Mercantile Transactions Tax, 1951–52, and Dir-Gen., Income Tax, 1952–59, Min. for Finance. Official Mayor, Min. for Industry and Commerce, 1959–61; Dep. Minister of Finance, Sept. 1961–Dec. 1964; Sec. of Finance, Aug. 1970–May 1973; Ambassador to the UK, 1973–77. Chm., Nat. Commn on Corporate Profit-Sharing (ie labour participation), 1963–64; Govt Rep. on Bd of Nat. Inst. for Scientific Res., 1962–63 (Chm. of Bd, 1963–64). Holds hon. degrees from univs in USA. Hon. GCVO 1975. *Publications:* Avoidance of Double Taxation Based on the Theory of the Source of Taxable Income, 1956; Preliminary Study on Tax Codification, 1957; (with H. L. Gumpel) Taxation in Mexico, 1957; Civil Rights and the Writ of Amparo in Administrative Law, 1958; The Role of Fiscal Law in Economic Development, 1960; Profit Sharing Plan, 1964; Housing Projects for Workers (Infonavit), 1971. *Recreations:* riding, swimming. *Address:* Fujiyama No 745, Col. Las Aguilas, Del. Alvaro Obregón, México 01710 DF, México.

MARGASON, Geoffrey, CEng, FICE, FIHE; FBIM; Director, Transport and Road Research Laboratory, Crowthorne, 1984–88, retired (Deputy Director, 1980–84); *b* 19 Sept. 1933; *s* of Henry and Edna Margason; *m* 1958, Bernice Thompson; one *s* two *d*. *Educ:* Humberston Foundation Sch., Cleethorpes; Loughborough College of Advanced Technology (DLCEng). With British Transport Commission and Mouchel Associates, Consulting Engineers, until 1960; Transport and Road Research Laboratory: Researcher in Geotechnics, 1960–69; Research Manager in Construction Planning, Scottish Br. and Transport Planning, 1969–75; Sen. Research Manager in Transport Operations, 1975–78; Head of Research and Science Policy Unit, Depts of Environment and Transport, 1978–80. *Publications:* papers in jls of various professional instns and to nat. and internat. confs on range of topics in highway transportation; reports of TRRL. *Recreations:* pétanque, caravanning. *Address:* Franche Cottage, Pankridge Street, Crondall, Farnham, Surrey GU10 5QZ. *T:* Aldershot (0252) 850399. *Club:* Frensham Pond (Farnham).

MARGERISON, Thomas Alan; author, journalist and broadcaster on scientific subjects; Consultant, British Nuclear Forum, since 1989; *b* 13 Nov. 1923; *s* of late Ernest Alan Margerison and Isabel McKenzie; *m* 1950, Pamela Alice Tilbrook; two *s*. *Educ:* Huntingdon Grammar Sch.; Hymers Coll., Hull; King's Sch., Macclesfield; Sheffield University. Research Physicist, 1949; film script writer, Film Producers Guild, 1950; Scientific Editor, Butterworths sci. pubns, Ed. Research, 1951–56; Man. Editor, Heywood Pubns and National Trade Press, 1956. First Scientific Editor, The New Scientist, 1956–61; Science Corresp., Sunday Times, 1961; Dep. Editor, Sunday Times Magazine, 1962; Man. Dir, Thomson Technical Developments Ltd, 1964; Dep. Man. Dir, 1967–69, Chief Exec., 1969–71, London Weekend Television; Dir, 1966, Chm., 1971–75, Computer Technology Ltd. Formerly Dir, Nuclear Electricity Information Gp. Chm., Communications Cttee, UK Nat. Commn for UNESCO. Worked for many years with Tonight team on BBC. Responsible for applying computers to evening newspapers in Reading and Hemel Hempstead. *Publications:* articles and television scripts, indifferent scientific papers; (ed) popular science books. *Recreation:* sailing. *Club:* Savile.

MARGESSON, family name of **Viscount Margesson.**

MARGESSON, 2nd Viscount *cr* 1942, of Rugby; **Francis Vere Hampden Margesson;** *b* 17 April 1922; *o s* of 1st Viscount Margesson, PC, MC, and Frances H. Leggett (*d* 1977), New York; *S* father, 1965; *m* 1958, Helena, *d* of late Heikki Backstrom, Finland; one *s* three *d*. *Educ:* Eton; Trinity Coll., Oxford. Served War of 1939–45, as Sub-Lt, RNVR. A Director of Thames & Hudson Publications, Inc., New York, 1949–53. ADC to Governor of the Bahamas, 1956; Information Officer, British Consulate-General, NY, 1964–70. *Heir: s* Captain the Hon. Richard Francis David Margesson, Coldstream Guards [*b* 25 Dec. 1960; *m* 1990, Wendy Maree, *d* of James Hazelton]. *Address:* Ridgely Manor, Box 245, Stone Ridge, New York, NY 12484, USA.

MARGETSON, Sir John (William Denys), KCMG 1986 (CMG 1979); HM Diplomatic Service, retired; *b* 9 Oct. 1927; *yr s* of Very Rev. W. J. Margetson and Marion Jenoure; *m* 1963, Miranda, *d* of Sir William Menzies Coldstream, CBE and Mrs Nancy Spender; one *s* one *d*. *Educ:* Blundell's; St John's Coll., Cambridge. Lieut, Life Guards, 1947–49. Colonial Service, District Officer, Tanganyika, 1951–60 (Private Sec. to Governor, Sir Edward Twining, subseq. Lord Twining, 1956–57); entered Foreign (subseq. Diplomatic) Service, 1960; The Hague, 1962–64; speech writer to Foreign Sec., Rt Hon. George Brown, MP, subseq. Lord George-Brown, 1966–68; Head of Chancery, Saigon, 1968–70; Counsellor 1971, seconded to Cabinet Secretariat, 1971–74; Head of Chancery, UK Delegn to NATO, 1974–78; Ambassador to Vietnam, 1978–80; seconded to MoD as Senior Civilian Instructor, RCDS, 1981–82; Ambassador and Dep. Perm. Rep. to UN, NY, and Pres., UN Trusteeship Council, 1983–84; Ambassador to the Netherlands, 1984–87. Dir, John S. Cohen Foundn, 1988–. Chm., Foster Parents Plan (UK), 1988–90. Chairman: RSCM, 1988–; Jt Cttee, London Royal Schs of Music, 1991–; Governor, Yehudi Menuhin Sch., 1989– (Chm., 1990–); Trustee, Fitzwilliam Museum Trust, 1990–. FRSA. *Recreation:* music. *Address:* c/o National Westminster Bank, 62 Victoria Street, SW1E 6QE. *Club:* Brooks's.

MARGRIE, Victor Robert, CBE 1984; FCSD; studio potter; *b* 29 Dec. 1929; *s* of Robert and Emily Miriam Margrie; *m* 1955, Janet Smithers (separated); three *d*. *Educ:* Southgate County Grammar Sch.; Hornsey Sch. of Art (now Mddx Polytechnic) (NDD, ATD 1952). FSIAD 1975. Part-time teaching at various London art colls, 1952–56; own workshop, making stoneware and latterly porcelain, 1954–71; Head of Ceramics Dept, Harrow Sch. of Art, 1956–71 (founded Studio Pottery Course, 1963); Sec., Crafts Adv. Cttee, 1971–77; Dir, Crafts Council, 1977–84; Professorial appt, RCA, 1984–85; own studio, Bristol, 1985. One-man exhibns, British Craft Centre (formerly Crafts Centre of GB), 1964, 1966 and 1968; represented in V&A Museum and other collections. Vice-Chm., Crafts Centre of GB, 1965; Member: Cttee for Art and Design, DATEC, 1979–84; Cttee for Art and Design, CNAA, 1981–84; Design Bursaries Bd, RSA, 1980–84; Working Party, Gulbenkian Craft Initiative, 1985–; Fine Art Adv. Cttee, British Council, 1983–86; UK National Commn for UNESCO, 1984–85 (also Mem., Culture Adv. Cttee); Adv. Council, V&A Mus., 1979–84; Craftsmen Potters Assoc., 1960–89; Internat. Acad. of Ceramics, 1972–. Ext. Examiner, Royal Coll. of Art: Dept of Ceramics and Glass, 1977; Dept of Silversmithing and Jewellery, 1978–80; Ext. Advisor, Dept of Ceramics, Bristol Polytechnic, 1987–; Mem., Bd of Studies in Fine Art, Univ. of London, 1989–. Governor: Herts Coll. of Art and Design, 1977–79; Camberwell Sch. of Art and Crafts, 1975–84; W Surrey Coll. of Art and Design, 1978–87; Loughborough Coll. of Art and Design, 1984–89, 1990–. *Publications:* contributed to: Oxford Dictionary of Decorative Arts, 1975; Europaischt Keramik Seit 1950, 1979; Lucie Rie, 1981; contrib. specialist pubns and museum catalogues. *Address:* Bowlders, Doccombe, Moretonhampstead, Devon TQ13 8SS. *T:* Moretonhampstead (0647) 40264.

MARIN, Manuel; Grand Cross of Isabel la Católica; a Vice President, Commission of the European Communities, since 1986; *b* 21 Oct. 1949; *m*; *c*. *Educ:* Univ. of Madrid; Centre d'études européennes, Univ. of Nancy; Collège d'Europe, Bruges. MP for Ciudad Real, La Mancha, 1977–82; Sec. of State for relations with EEC, 1982–85. Mem., Spanish Socialist Party, 1974–. *Address:* 200 rue de la Loi, 1049 Brussels, Belgium.

MARIO, Dr Ernest; Chief Executive, Glaxo Holdings plc, since 1989; *b* 12 June 1938; *s* of Jerry and Edith Mario; *m* 1961, Mildred Martha Daume; three *s*. *Educ:* Rutgers College of Pharmacy, New Brunswick, NJ (BSc Pharmacy); Univ. of Rhode Island (MS; PhD). Vice Pres., Manufacturing Operation, Smith Kline, 1974; E. R. Squibb & Sons: Vice Pres., Manufacturing for US Pharmaceutical Div., 1977; Vice Pres. and Gen. Man., Chemical Div., 1979; Pres., Chemical Engrg Div. and Sen. Vice Pres. of company, 1981; Pres. and Chief Exec. Officer, Squibb Medical Product, 1983; elected to Bd, 1984; joined Glaxo Inc. as Pres. and Chief Exec. Officer, 1986; apptd to Bd of Glaxo Holdings, 1988. Chairman: Nat. Foundn for Infectious Diseases, Washington, 1989–; American Foundn for Pharmaceutical Educn, NY, 1991–. *Recreations:* golf, swimming. *Address:* Glaxo Holdings plc, Lansdowne House, Berkeley Square, W1X 6BP. *T:* 071–493 4060.

MARJORIBANKS, (Edyth) Leslia, JP; MA; Headmistress, The Henrietta Barnett School, London, 1973–89; *b* 17 Feb. 1927; *d* of late Stewart Dudley Marjoribanks and late Nancye (*née* Lee) *Educ:* Cheltenham Ladies' Coll.; Girton Coll., Cambridge (BA Hons Hist. 1951, MA 1955); Hughes Hall, Cambridge (Certif. Educn 1952). Talbot Heath, Bournemouth: Asst History Mistress, 1952–57; Head of History Dept, 1957–68; Headmistress, Holly Lodge High Sch., Liverpool, 1969–73. Mem. Governing Council, Examinations Cttee and Curriculum Sub-Cttee of North-West Sec. Schs Exam. Board, 1969–73. JP City of Liverpool, 1971–73, Inner London, 1976. *Recreations:* gardening, cookery. *Address:* 29 Park Farm Close, N2 0PU. *T:* 081–883 6609.

MARJORIBANKS, Sir James Alexander Milne, KCMG 1965 (CMG 1954); Chairman, Scotland in Europe, 1979–90; *b* 29 May 1911; *y s* of Rev. Thomas Marjoribanks of that Ilk, DD, and Mary Ord, *d* of William Logan, Madras CS; *m* 1936, Sonya Patricia (*d* 1981), *d* of David Stanley-Alder, Alderford Grange, Sible Hedingham, Essex, and Sylvia Marie Stanley; one *d*. *Educ:* Merchiston; Edinburgh Academy; Edinburgh Univ. (MA, 1st class hons). Entered Foreign Service, Nov. 1934; HM Embassy, Peking, 1935–38; Consulate-General, Hankow, 1938; Marseilles, 1939–40; Consul, Jacksonville, 1940–42; Vice-Consul, New York, 1942–44; Asst to UK Political Rep., Bucharest, 1944–45; Foreign Office, 1945–49; Dep. to Secretary of State for Foreign Affairs in Austrian Treaty negotiations, 1947–49; Official Secretary, UK High Commn, Canberra, 1950–52; Dep. Head of UK Delegation to High Authority of European Coal and Steel Community, 1952–55; Cabinet Office, 1955–57; HM Minister (Economic), Bonn, 1957–62; Asst Under-Secretary of State, Foreign Office, 1962–65; Ambassador and Head of UK Delegn to European Economic Community, European Atomic Energy Community and ECSC, 1965–71. Director: Scottish Council (Develt and Industry), 1971–81 (Vice-Pres., 1981–83); The Distillers Co. Ltd, 1971–76; Governing Mem., Inveresk Research International, 1978–90. Gen. Council Assessor, Edinburgh Univ. Ct, 1975–79. *Recreations:* hill walking, croquet. *Address:* 13 Regent Terrace, Edinburgh EH7 5BN; Lintonrig, Kirk Yetholm, Roxburghshire TD5 8PH. *Club:* New (Edinburgh).

MARJORIBANKS, Kevin McLeod, PhD; FSS; FASSA; FACE; Vice-Chancellor, University of Adelaide, since 1987; *b* 25 July 1940; *s* of Hugh and Irene Marjoribanks; *m* 1962, Janice Humphreys; one *s* one *d*. *Educ:* Universities of: New South Wales (BSc); New England (BA); Harvard (MA); Toronto (PhD). FSS 1977; FASSA 1982; FACE 1983. Asst Prof., Univ. of Toronto, 1969; Lectr, Univ. of Oxford, 1970–74; University of Adelaide: Prof. of Educn, 1975–86; Pro Vice-Chancellor, 1986. Visiting Professor: Stanford Univ., 1979; Haifa Univ., 1983. *Publications:* Environments for Learning, 1974; Families and their Learning Environments, 1979; Ethnic Families and Children's Achievements, 1980; The Foundations of Children's Learning, 1989. *Recreations:* writing, music listening, walking. *Address:* 81 Molesworth Street, North Adelaide, SA 5006, Australia. *Clubs:* Adelaide; Harvard of Australia.

MARJORIBANKS, Leslia; *see* Marjoribanks, E. L.

MARK, James, MBE 1943; Under-Secretary, Ministry of Overseas Development, 1965–74, retired; *b* 12 June 1914; *s* of late John Mark and Louisa Mary (*née* Hobson); *m* 1941, Mary Trewent Rowland; three *s* two *d*. *Educ:* William Hulme's Grammar Sch., Manchester; Trinity Coll., Cambridge; Universities of Munich and Münster. MA 1939. PhD 1939, Cambridge. Intelligence Corps, 1940–46. Principal, Control Office for Germany and Austria, 1946–48; HM Treasury, 1948–64; Asst Secretary, 1950; Economic Counsellor, Washington, 1951–53. Jt Editor, Theology, 1976–83. *Publications:* The Question of Christian Stewardship, 1964; articles and reviews on theological and related subjects. *Recreations:* reading, music, theatre. *Address:* 6 Manorbrook, SE3. *T:* 081–852 9289.

See also Sir Robert Mark.

MARK, Sir Robert, GBE 1977; Kt 1973; QPM 1965; Commissioner, Metropolitan Police, 1972–77 (Deputy Commissioner, 1968–72); Chairman, Forest Mere Ltd, since 1978; *b* Manchester, 13 March 1917; *y s* of late John Mark and Louisa Mark (*née* Hobson); *m* 1941, Kathleen Mary Leahy; one *s* one *d*. *Educ:* William Hulme's Grammar Sch., Manchester. Constable to Chief Superintendent, Manchester City Police, 1937–42, 1947–56; Chief Constable of Leicester, 1957–67; Assistant Commissioner, Metropolitan Police, 1967–68. Vis. Fellow, Nuffield Coll., Oxford, 1970–78 (MA Oxon 1971). Member: Standing Advisory Council of Penal System, 1966; Adv. Cttee on Police in Northern Ireland, 1969; Assessor to Lord Mountbatten during his Inquiry into Prison Security, 1966. Royal Armoured Corps, 1942–47: Lieut, Phantom (GHQ Liaison Regt), North-West Europe, 1944–45; Major, Control Commission for Germany, 1945–47. Lecture tour of N America for World Affairs Council and FCO, Oct. 1971; Edwin Stevens Lecture to the Laity, RCM, 1972; Dimbleby Meml Lecture (BBC TV), 1973. Director: Phoenix Assurance Co. Ltd, 1977–85; Control Risks Ltd, 1982–87. Mem. Cttee, AA, 1977–87; Governor and Mem. Admin. Bd, Corps of Commissionaires, 1977–86; Hon. Freeman, City of Westminster, 1977. Hon. LLM Leicester Univ., 1967; Hon. DLitt Loughborough, 1976; Hon. LLD: Manchester, 1978; Liverpool, 1978. KStJ 1977. *Publications:* Policing a Perplexed Society, 1977; In the Office of Constable, 1978. *Address:* Esher, Surrey KT10 8LU.

See also James Mark.

MARKALL, Most Rev. Francis, SJ; *b* 24 Sept. 1905; *e s* of late Walter James Markall and Alice Mary Gray, London. *Educ:* St Ignatius' College, London. Entered Society of Jesus, 1924; continued classical and philosophical studies, 1926–31; Assistant Master, Stonyhurst College, 1931–34; theological studies, 1934–38; Missionary in Rhodesia, 1939–56; Titular Archbishop of Cotieo and Coadjutor with right of succession to Archbishop of Salisbury, April 1956; Archbishop of Salisbury and Metropolitan of Province of Rhodesia, Nov. 1956; retired, 1976. *Address:* Nazareth House, PO Box HG295, PO Highlands, Harare, Zimbabwe. *T:* Harare 45144.

MARKESINIS, Prof. Basil Spyridonos, PhD, LLD; Denning Professor of Comparative Law, University of London, at Queen Mary and Westfield (formerly Queen Mary) College, since 1986; Professor of Anglo-American Private Law, University of Leiden, since 1986; *b* 10 July 1944; *s* of Spyros B. Markesinis (former Prime Minister of Greece) and Ieta Markesinis; *m* 1970, Eugenie (*née* Trypanis); one *s* one *d*. *Educ:* Univ. of Athens (LLB, DIur); MA, PhD, LLD Cambridge. Asst Prof., Law Faculty, Univ. of Athens, 1965–68; Gulbenkian Res. Fellow, Churchill Coll., Cambridge, 1970–74; called to the Bar, Gray's Inn, 1973; Fellow of Trinity Coll., Cambridge, and Univ. Lectr in Law, 1975–86; Dep. Dir, Centre for Commercial Law Studies, Univ. of London, 1986–; Founder and Dir, Leiden Inst. of Anglo-American Law, 1987–. Advocate to Greek Supreme Court, 1976–86. Visiting Professor: Univs of Paris I and II; Siena; Cornell; Michigan (Ann Arbor); Texas (Austin); Francqui Vis. Prof., Univ. of Gent, 1989–90. Associate Fellow, Internat. Acad. of Comp. Law; Mem., Amer. Law Inst., 1989. *Publications:* The Mother's right to Guardianship according to the Greek Civil Code, 1968; The Theory and Practice of Dissolution of Parliament, 1972 (Yorke Prize); The English Law of Torts, 1976; (jtly) An Outline of the Law of Agency, 1979, 2nd edn 1986; Richterliche Rechtspolitik im Haftungsrecht, 1981; (jtly) Tortious Liability for unintentional harm in the Common Law and the Civil Law, 2 vols, 1982; (jtly) Tort Law, 1984, 2nd edn 1989; The German Law of Torts, 1986, 2nd edn 1990; many articles in learned jls in Belgium, Canada, England, France, Greece, Italy and USA. *Recreations:* painting, music, chess. *Address:* Queen Mary and Westfield College, 339 Mile End Road, E1 4NS; 27 Barrow Road, Cambridge CB2 2AP.

MARKHAM, Sir Charles (John), 3rd Bt, *cr* 1911; *b* 2 July 1924; *s* of Sir Charles Markham, 2nd Bt, and Gwladys, *e d* of late Hon. Rupert Beckett; *S* father 1952; *m* 1949, Valerie, *o d* of Lt-Col E. Barry-Johnston, Makuyu, Kenya; two *s* one *d*. *Educ:* Eton. Served War of 1939–45, Lieut in 11th Hussars (despatches). Vice-Chm., Nairobi Co. Council, 1953–55; MLC Kenya, 1955–60. Pres., Royal Agricultural Soc., Kenya, 1958. KStJ 1973. *Heir: s* Arthur David Markham [*b* 6 Dec. 1950; *m* 1977, Carolyn, *yr d* of Captain Mungo Park; two *d*]. *Address:* PO Box 42263, Nairobi, Kenya, East Africa. *Club:* Cavalry and Guards.

MARKING, Sir Henry (Ernest), KCVO 1978; CBE 1969; MC 1944; CompRAeS 1953; FCIT; Deputy Chairman and Managing Director, British Airways, 1972–77; *b* 11 March 1920; *s* of late Isaac and Hilda Jane Marking. *Educ:* Saffron Walden Gram. Sch.; University Coll., London. Served War of 1939–45: 2nd Bn The Sherwood Foresters, 1941–45; North Africa, Italy and Middle East; Adjutant, 1944–45. Middle East Centre of Arab Studies, Jerusalem, 1945–46. Admitted solicitor, 1948. Asst Solicitor, Cripps, Harries, Hall & Co., Tunbridge Wells, 1948–49; Asst Solicitor, 1949, Sec., 1950, Chief Exec., 1964–72, Chm., 1971–72, BEA; Mem. Bd, BOAC, 1971–72; Mem., British Airways Board, 1971–80. Chm., Rothmans UK, 1979–86; Director: Rothmans International, 1979–86; Barclays International, 1977–86. Mem., 1969–77, Chm., 1977–84, British Tourist Authority. Trustee, 1962–, Chm. Internat. Cttee, 1970–, Leonard Cheshire Foundn. FBIM 1971. *Club:* Reform.

MARKOVA, Dame Alicia, DBE 1963 (CBE 1958); **(Dame Lilian Alicia Marks);** Prima Ballerina Assoluta; Professor of Ballet and Performing Arts, College-Conservatory of Music, University of Cincinnati, since 1970; President, London Festival Ballet, since 1986; *b* London 1910; *d* of Arthur Tristman Marks and Eileen Barry. With Diaghilev's Russian Ballet Co., 1925–29; Rambert Ballet Club, 1931–33; Vic-Wells Ballet Co., 1933–35; Markova-Dolin Ballet Co., 1935–37; Ballet Russe de Monte Carlo, 1938–41; Ballet Theatre, USA, 1941–46. Appeared with Anton Dolin, guest and concert performances, 1948–50. Co-Founder and Prima Ballerina, Festival Ballet, 1950–51; Guest Prima Ballerina: Buenos Aires, 1952; Royal Ballet, 1953 and 1957; Royal Danish Ballet, 1955; Scala, Milan, 1956; Teatro Municipal, Rio de Janeiro, 1956; Festival Ballet, 1958 and 1959; Guest appearances at Metropolitan Opera House, New York, 1952, 1953–54, 1955, 1957, 1958; Dir, Metropolitan Opera Ballet, 1963–69; produced Les Sylphides for Festival Ballet and Aust. Ballet, 1976, for Royal Ballet School and Northern Ballet Theatre, 1978, for Royal Winnipeg Ballet, Canada, 1979. Guest Professor: Royal Ballet Sch., 1973–; Paris Opera Ballet, 1975; Australian Ballet Sch., 1976; Yorkshire Ballet Seminars, 1975–; Pres., All England Dance Competition, 1983–. Vice-Pres., Royal Acad. of Dancing, 1958–; Governor, Royal Ballet, 1973–; President: London Ballet Circle, 1981–; Trust of the Arts Educational Schs, 1984–; Pavlova Meml Museum, 1988–. Concert, television and guest appearances (general), 1952–61. BBC series, Markova's Ballet Call, 1960; Masterclass, BBC2, 1980. Queen Elizabeth II Coronation Award, Royal Acad. of Dancing, 1963. Hon. DMus: Leicester, 1966; East Anglia, 1982. *Publications:* Giselle and I, 1960; Markova Remembers, 1986. *Address:* c/o Barclays Bank, 137 Brompton Road, SW3 1QF.

MARKOWITZ, Prof. Harry M., PhD; Professor of Finance and Economics, Baruch College, City University of New York, since 1982; *b* 24 Aug. 1927; *s* of Morris Markowitz and Mildred (*née* Gruber); *m* Barbara Gay. *Educ:* Univ. of Chicago (PhB Liberal Arts 1947; MA 1950, PhD 1954 Econs). Res. Associate, Rand Corp., 1952–60 and 1961–63; Consultant, Gen. Electric Corp., 1960–61; Chm., Bd and Technical Dir, Consolidated Analysis Centres Inc., 1963–68; Prof. of Finance, UCLA, 1968–69; Pres., Arbitrage Management Co., 1969–72, Consultant, 1972–74; Vis. Prof. of Finance, Wharton Bus. Sch., 1972–74; Res. Staff Mem., T. J. Watson Res. Center, IBM, 1974–83; Adj. Prof. of Finance, Rutgers Univ., 1980–82; Consultant, Daiwa Securities, 1990–. Director: Amer. Finance Assoc.; TIMS. Fellow: Econometric Soc.; Amer. Acad. Arts and Sciences, 1987. Von Neumann Theory Prize, ORSA/TIMS, 1989; Nobel Prize for Economics, 1990. *Publications:* Portfolio Selection: efficient diversification of investments, 1959, 3rd edn 1991; Simscript: a simulation programming language, 1963; (jtly) Studies in Process Analysis: economy-wide production capabilities, 1963 (trans. Russian 1967); (jtly) The Simscript II Programming Language, 1969; (jtly) The EAS-E Programming Language, 1981; (jtly) Adverse Deviation, 1981; Mean-Variance Analysis in Portfolio Choice and Capital Markets, 1987; contrib. chapters to numerous books and papers in professional jls, incl. Jl of Finance, Management Science, Jl of Portfolio Management. *Recreations:* music, canoeing, snorkeling. *Address:* Department of Economics and Finance, Baruch College, 17 Lexington Avenue, New York, NY 10010, USA. *T:* 212–447–3151.

MARKS, family name of **Baron Marks of Broughton.**

MARKS OF BROUGHTON, 2nd Baron, *cr* 1961; **Michael Marks;** *b* 27 Aug. 1920; *o s* of 1st Baron and Miriam (*d* 1971), *d* of Ephraim Sieff; *S* father 1964; *m* (marr. diss.); one *s* two *d*. *Heir:* son.

MARKS, Bernard Montague, OBE 1984; Life President, Alfred Marks Bureau Group of Companies, 1985 (Managing Director, 1946–81 and Chairman, 1946–84); *b* 11 Oct. 1923; *s* of Alfred and Elizabeth Marks; *m* 1956, Norma Renton (*d* 1990); two *s*. *Educ:* Highgate Public Sch.; Royal Coll. of Science. Served Somerset LI, seconded to RWAFF (Staff Capt.), 1944–46. Chm. or Vice-Chm., Fedn of Personnel Services of GB, 1965–79, 1983–84. Mem., Equal Opportunities Commn, 1984–86. *Publication:* Once Upon A Typewriter, 1974. *Recreations:* bridge, golf, ski-ing. *Address:* Leyfield House, Onslow Road, Burwood Park, Walton-on-Thames, Surrey. *Club:* St George's Hill Golf.

MARKS, John Emile, CBE 1970; Chairman, Peckerbond Ltd; *m* 1975, Averil May Hannah (*née* Davies); two *s* two *d* by former marriage. *Educ:* Eton College. Served War of 1939–45 (despatches 1944). *Recreations:* tennis, golf. *Address:* Shaldon, Devon.

MARKS, John Henry, MD; FRCGP; General Practitioner, Boreham Wood, 1954–90; Chairman of Council, British Medical Association, 1984–90; *b* 30 May 1925; *s* of Lewis and Rose Marks; *m* 1954, Shirley Evelyn, *d* of Alic Nathan, OBE; one *s* two *d*. *Educ:* Tottenham County Sch.; Edinburgh Univ. MD; FRCGP; D(Obst)RCOG. Served RAMC, 1949–51. Chairman: Herts LMC, 1966–71; Herts Exec. Council, 1971–74; Member: NHS Management Study Steering Cttee, 1971–72; Standing Med. Adv. Cttee, 1984–90; Council for Postgrad. Med. Educn, 1984–90. British Medical Association: Fellow, 1976; Member: Gen. Med. Services Cttee, 1968–90 (Dep. Chm., 1974–79); Council, 1973–; GMC, 1979–84, 1990–; Chairman: Representative Body, 1981–84; Foundn for AIDS. Mem. Council, ASH, 1991–. *Publications:* The Conference of Local Medical Committees and its Executive: an historical view, 1979; papers on the NHS and general medical practice. *Recreations:* philately, walking, gardening. *Address:* Brown Gables, Barnet Lane, Elstree, Herts WD6 3RQ. *T:* 081–953 7687.

MARKS, Richard Charles, PhD; FSA; Director, Royal Pavilion, Art Gallery and Museums in Brighton, since 1985; *b* 2 July 1945; *s* of William Henry Marks and Jeannie Eileen Marks (*née* Pigott); *m* 1970, Rita Spratley. *Educ:* Berkhamsted Sch.; Queen Mary Coll., Univ. of London (BA (Hons) History); Courtauld Inst. of Art, Univ. of London (MA, PhD, History of European Art). Research Asst for British Acad. *Corpus Vitrearum Medii Aevi* Cttee, 1970–73; Asst Keeper, Dept of Medieval and Later Antiquities, British Mus., 1973–79; Keeper of Burrell Collection and Asst Dir, Glasgow Museums and Art Galls, 1979–85. Chm., Group of Directors of Museums, 1989–; Mem., Corpus Vitrearum Medii Aevi Cttee, British Acad., 1985–; Trustee, Stained Glass Museum Trust, 1990–. Liveryman, Glaziers' Co., 1990. FSA 1977. *Publications:* (jtly) British Heraldry from its origins to *c* 1800, 1978; (jtly) The Golden Age of English Manuscript Painting, 1980; Burrell Portrait of a Collector, 1983, 2nd edn 1988; The Glazing of the Collegiate Church of the Holy Trinity, Tattershall, Lincs, 1984; (jtly) Sussex Churches and Chapels, 1989; articles and reviews in learned jls. *Recreations:* opera, cricket, rowing, parish churches, travelling in the Levant. *Address:* 14 Hampton Place, Brighton, East Sussex BN1 3DD; 38 High Street, Wing, near Leighton Buzzard, Beds LU7 0NR. *Clubs:* MCC; Clydesdale Amateur Rowing (Glasgow); Bedford Rowing; North British Rowing (the Borders).

MARKS, Prof. Shula Eta; Director, since 1983, and Professor of Commonwealth History, since 1984, Institute of Commonwealth Studies, University of London; *b* Cape Town, S Africa, 14 Oct. 1936; *d* of Chaim and Frieda Winokur; *m* 1957, Isaac M. Marks; one *s* one *d*. *Educ:* Univ. of Cape Town (Argus Scholar, 1958–59; BA 1959). PhD London, 1967. Came to London, 1960; Lectr in the History of Southern Africa, SOAS and Inst. of Commonwealth Studies, 1963–76, Reader, 1976–83; Vice-Chancellor's Visitor to NZ, 1978. Dir, Ford Foundn Grant to Univ. of London on S African History, 1975–78; Pres., African Studies Assoc. of UK, 1978. Mem., Adv. Council on Public Records, 1989–. Editor, Jl of African History, 1971–77; Mem. Council, Jl of Southern African Studies, 1974– (Founding Mem., 1974). *Publications:* Reluctant Rebellion: an assessment of the 1906–8 disturbances in Natal, 1970; (ed with A. Atmore) Economy and Society in Pre-industrial South Africa, 1980; (ed with R. Rathbone) Industrialization and Social Change in South Africa, 1870–1930, 1982; (ed with P. Richardson) International Labour Migration: historical perspectives, 1983; The Ambiguities of Dependence in Southern Africa: class, nationalism and the state in twentieth-century Natal, 1986; (ed) Not either an experimental doll: the separate worlds of three South African women, 1987; (ed with Stanley Trapido) The Politics of Race, Class & Nationalism in Twentieth Century South Africa, 1987; chapters in Cambridge Hist. of Africa, vols 3, 4 and 6; contrib. Jl of African Hist. and Jl of Southern African Studies. *Address:* Institute of Commonwealth Studies, 27–28 Russell Square, WC1B 5DS. *T:* 071–580 5876.

MARKUS, Rika, (Rixi), MBE 1975 (for services to Bridge); Bridge journalist and author; *b* 27 June 1910; *d* of Michael and Louise Scharfstein; *m* 1929, Salomon Markus (marr. diss. 1947); one *d* decd. *Educ:* Vienna and Dresden. Turned to bridge after a severe illness; arrived in London, March 1938 (3 days after Hitler occupied Austria; parents lived already in London). Bridge correspondent of: The Guardian and Weekly Guardian, 1955– (organizer of Eastern Bridge Guardian Tournament); Harpers & Queen (organizer of Championship for Women); formerly of the Evening Standard; writes for Express Syndication Gp; commentator and contributor to Daily Bulletin on major European and world championships. Organises annual bridge match between House of Lords and House of Commons (Challenge Cup donated by The Guardian); matches held with parliamentarians and players in other countries, *eg* France, Holland, Dubai, USA, Sweden and Morocco; player in Master Bridge, Channel Four TV series, 1983. Acclaimed as best woman player in the world; European Bridge Champion, 1935 and 1936; World Champion, 1937; 1st Woman Grand Master, 1974; Charles Goren Award for the player of the year, 1976; 5 World titles (incl. 4 gold Olympic medals), 1937, 1962, 1964 and

1974; 3 silver Olympic medals, 1970, 1976; 10 Eur. Championships; first European Grand Master, 1987; many national and internat. titles. *Publications:* Bid Boldly, Play Safe, 1965; Common-Sense Bridge, 1972; Aces and Places, 1972; Bridge around the World, 1977; Improve Your Bridge, 1977; Play Better Bridge with Rixi Markus, 1978; Table Tales by Rixi Markus, 1979; Bridge with Rixi, 1983; More Deadly than the Male, 1984; Best Bridge Hands, 1985; The Rixi Markus Book of Bridge, 1985; A Vulnerable Game (memoirs), 1988; Better Bridge for Club Players, 1989. *Recreations:* music, cooking, watching all sports, theatre. *Address:* 22 Lowndes Lodge, Cadogan Place, SW1X 9RZ. *T:* 071–235 7377. *Club:* St James Bridge.

MARKUS, Prof. Robert Austin, FBA 1985; Professor of Medieval History, Nottingham University, 1974–82, now Emeritus; *b* 8 Oct. 1924; *s* of Victor Markus and Lily Markus (*née* Elek); *m* 1955, Margaret Catherine Bullen; two *s* one *d. Educ:* Univ. of Manchester (BSc 1944; MA 1948; PhD 1950). Mem., Dominican Order, 1950–54; Asst Librarian, Univ. of Birmingham, 1954–55; Liverpool University: Sub-Librarian, 1955–59; Lectr, Sen. Lectr, Reader in Medieval Hist., 1959–74. Mem., Inst. for Advanced Study, Princeton, 1986–87; Distinguished Prof. of Early Christian Studies, Catholic Univ. of America, Washington, 1988–89. Pres., Ecclesiastical Hist. Soc., 1978–79. *Publications:* Christian Faith and Greek Philosophy (with A. H. Armstrong), 1964; Saeculum: history and society in the theology of St Augustine, 1970; Christianity in the Roman world, 1974; From Augustine to Gregory the Great, 1983; The End of Ancient Christianity, 1990; contribs to Jl of Ecclesiastical Hist., Jl of Theol Studies, Byzantion, Studies in Church Hist., etc. *Recreation:* music. *Address:* 100 Park Road, Chilwell, Beeston, Nottingham NG9 4DE. *T:* Nottingham (0602) 255965.

MARLAND, Michael, CBE 1977; Headmaster, North Westminster Community School, since 1980; *b* 28 Dec. 1934; *m* 1st, 1955, Eileen (*d* 1968); four *s* one *d*; 2nd, 1971, Rose (marr. diss. 1977); *m* 1989, Linda. *Educ:* Christ's Hospital Sch.; Sidney Sussex Coll., Cambridge (MA). Head of English, Abbey Wood Sch., 1961–64; Head of English and subseq. Dir of Studies, Crown Woods Sch., 1964–71; Headmaster, Woodberry Down Sch., 1971–79. Hon. Prof., Dept of Educn, Univ. of Warwick, 1980–. Member: many educn cttees, incl. Bullock Cttee, 1972–75; Commonwealth Inst. Educn Cttee, 1982–; Arts Council of GB Educn Cttee, 1988–; Educn and Human Develt Cttee, ESRC (formerly SSRC), 1983–88; Nat. Assoc. for Educn in the Arts, 1986–; Nat. Book League Council, 1984; Finniston Cttee on Technol. in Educn, 1985–; Video Adv. Cttee, British Bd of Film Censors, 1989–; Chairman: Schools Council English Cttee, 1978–81; Books in Curriculum Res. Project, 1982–; Royal Ballet Educn Adv. Council, 1983–; Nat. Assoc. for Pastoral Care in Educn, 1982–86; Royal Opera House Educnl Adv. Council, 1984–; Nat. Textbook Ref. Library Steering Cttee, 1984–. Mem., Paddington and N Kensington DHA, 1982–84. *Publications:* Towards The New Fifth, 1969; The Practice of English Teaching, 1970; Peter Grimes, 1971; Head of Department, 1971; Pastoral Care, 1974; The Craft of the Classroom, 1975; Language Across the Curriculum, 1977; Education for the Inner City, 1980; Departmental Management, 1981; Sex Differentiation and Schooling, 1983; Short Stories for Today, 1984; Meetings and Partings, 1984; School Management Skills, 1985; The Tutor and the Tutor Group, 1990; General Editor of: Blackie's Student Drama Series; Longman Imprint Books; The Times Authors; Heinemann Organisation in Schools Series; Longman Tutorial Resources; contrib. Times Educnl Supplement. *Recreations:* music, literature. *Address:* 22 Compton Terrace, N1 2UN. *T:* 01–226 0648; The Green Farmhouse, Cranmer Green, Walsham-le-Willows, Bury St Edmunds, Suffolk. *T:* Walsham-le-Willows (0359) 259483.

MARLAND, Paul; MP (C) Gloucestershire West, since 1979; *b* 19 March 1940; *s* of Alexander G. Marland and Elsa May Lindsey Marland; *m* 1st, 1965, Penelope Anne Barlow (marr. diss. 1982); one *s* two *d*; 2nd, 1984, Caroline Ann Rushton. *Educ:* Gordonstoun Sch., Elgin; Trinity Coll., Dublin (BA, BComm). Hopes Metal Windows, 1964; London Press Exchange, 1965–66; farmer, 1967–. Jt PPS to Financial Sec. to the Treasury and Economic Sec., 1981–83, to Minister of Agriculture, Fisheries and Food, 1983–86. Chm., back-bench Agric. Cttee, 1989–. *Recreations:* skiing, shooting, riding, fishing. *Address:* Ford Hill Farm, Temple Guiting, Cheltenham, Glos. *Club:* Boodle's.

MARLAR, Robin Geoffrey; Management Consultant, since 1968; cricket correspondent, Sunday Times, since 1970; *b* 2 Jan. 1931; *o s* of late Edward Alfred Geoffrey Marlar and Winifred Marlar (*née* Stevens); *m* 1st, 1955, Wendy Ann Dumeresque; two *s* four *d*; 2nd, 1980, Gill Taylor. *Educ:* King Edward's Sch., Lichfield; Harrow; Magdalene Coll., Cambridge (BA). Asst Master, Eton Coll., 1953–54; Librarian, Arundel Castle, 1954–59; Captain, Sussex CCC, 1955–59; sportswriter, Daily Telegraph, 1954–60; Asst Training Officer, Training Officer, Group Personnel and Public Relations Officer, De La Rue Co. and Marketing Services Manager, Thomas Potterton, 1960–68; Consultant and Partner, Spencer-Stuart and Associates, 1968–71; Founder, Marlar International and Marlar Group of Consultancies, 1971. Sunday Times Sports Staff, 1961. Contested (C): Bolsover, 1959; Leicester NE, 1962 by-election. *Publications:* The Story of Cricket, 1978; (ed) The English Cricketers Trip to USA and Canada 1859, 1979; Decision Against England, 1983. *Recreations:* gardening, sport. *Address:* Branting's Hay, Sampleoak Lane, Chilworth. *Clubs:* Garrick, MCC; Sussex CCC.

MARLBOROUGH, 11th Duke of, *cr* 1702; **John George Vanderbilt Henry Spencer-Churchill;** DL; Baron Spencer, 1603; Earl of Sunderland, 1643; Baron Churchill, 1685; Earl of Marlborough, 1689; Marquis of Blandford, 1702; Prince of the Holy Roman Empire; Prince of Mindelheim in Suabia; late Captain Life Guards; *b* 13 April 1926; *s* of 10th Duke of Marlborough and Hon. Alexandra Mary Hilda Cadogan, CBE (*d* 1961), *d* of late Henry Arthur, Viscount Chelsea; *S* father, 1972; *m* 1st, 1951, Susan Mary (marr. diss., 1960; she *m* 1962, Alan Cyril Heber-Percy), *d* of Michael Hornby, *qv*; one *s* one *d* (and one *s* decd); 2nd, 1961, Mrs Athina Livanos (marr. diss. 1971; she *d* 1974), *d* of late Stavros G. Livanos, Paris; 3rd, 1972, Rosita Douglas; one *s* one *d* (and one *s* decd). *Educ:* Eton. Lieut Life Guards, 1946; Captain, 1953; resigned commission, 1953. Chairman: Martini & Rossi, 1979–; London Paperweights Ltd, 1974–. President: Thames and Chilterns Tourist Board, 1974–; Oxfordshire Branch, CLA, 1978–; Oxfordshire Assoc. of Boys' Clubs, 1972–; Oxford Br., SSAFA, 1977–; Sports Aid Foundn (Southern), 1981–; Oxford United Football Club, 1964–; Dep. Pres., Nat. Assoc. of Boys' Clubs, 1987–; Mem. Council, Winston Churchill Meml Trust, 1966–; Patron, Oxfordshire Br., BRCS. CC 1961–64, Oxfordshire; JP 1962; DL 1974. *Heir: s* Marquis of Blandford, *qv*. *Address:* Blenheim Palace, Woodstock, Oxon. *Clubs:* Portland, White's.

MARLER, David Steele, OBE 1984; Director, Asia, Pacific and Americas Division, British Council, since 1990; *b* 19 March 1941; *s* of Steele Edward and Dorothy Marler; *m* 1963, Belinda Mary Handisyde; two *s. Educ:* Brighton, Hove and Sussex Grammar Sch.; Merton Coll., Oxford (Postmaster; BA, MA). British Council, 1962–: seconded SOAS, 1962–63; Asst Rep., Bombay, 1963; Regional Officer, India, 1967; Dep. Rep., Ethiopia, 1970; Rep., Ibadan, Nigeria, 1974; Dir, Policy Res., 1977; Rep., Cyprus, 1980; seconded SOAS, 1984; National Univ., Singapore, 1985; Rep., Peking, 1987–90. *Recreations:* sailing, travel, reading, walking. *Address:* 53 The Hall, Foxes Dale, Blackheath, SE3 9BG. *T:* 081–318 5874. *Club:* Changi Sailing (Singapore).

MARLER, Dennis Ralph Greville, FRICS; Chairman, Falcon Property Trust, since 1988; *b* 15 June 1927; *s* of late Greville Sidney Marler, JP, FRICS and Ivy Victoria (*née* Boyle); *m* 1952, Angela (*née* Boundy); one *s* one *d. Educ:* Marlborough. Served Royal Lincolnshire Regt, Palestine, 1946–48; articled pupil, Knight, Frank & Rutley, 1948–50; Partner, Marler & Marler, 1950–83; Jt Man. Dir, 1966–76, Man. Dir, 1976–85, Chm., 1985–90, Capital & Counties plc; Chairman: Knightsbridge Green Hotel Ltd, 1966–; Pension Fund Property Unit Trust, 1987–89. Member: NEDO Working Party for Wood Report (Public Client and Construction Industry), 1974–75; Adv. Bd, Dept of Construction Management, Univ. of Reading, 1981–88; DHSS Nat. Property Adv. Gp, 1984–; FCO *ad hoc* Adv. Panel on Diplomatic Estate, 1985–. A Vice-Pres., TCPA, 1983–; Pres., British Property Fedn, 1983–84. Mem. Ct of Assistants, Merchant Taylors' Co., 1984–. CBIM, FRSA. *Recreations:* reading, golf, travel. *Address:* 13 Whaddon House, William Mews, SW1X 9HG. *T:* 071–245 6139; 13 Slipway Cottages, Rock, Cornwall. *T:* Trebetherick (0208) 862141. *Clubs:* Royal Thames Yacht, St Stephen's Constitutional, Roehampton; St Enodoc Golf.

MARLESFORD, Baron *cr* 1991 (Life Peer), of Marlesford in the County of Suffolk; **Mark Shuldham Schreiber;** political consultant, farmer and journalist; *b* 11 Sept. 1931; *s* of late John Shuldham Schreiber, DL, Marlesford Hall, Suffolk and Maureen Schreiber (*née* Dent); *m* 1969, Gabriella Federica, *d* of Conte Teodoro Veglio di Castelletto d'Uzzone; two *d. Educ:* Eton; Trinity Coll., Cambridge. Nat. Service in Coldstream Guards, 1950–51. Fisons Ltd, 1957–63; Conservative Research Dept, 1963–67; Dir, Conservative Party Public Sector Research Unit, 1967–70; Special Advr to the Govt, 1970–74; Special Adviser to Leader of the Opposition, 1974–75; Editorial Consultant, 1974–91, lobby correspondent, 1976–91, The Economist. Director: Royal Ordnance Factories, 1972–74; British Railways (Anglia), 1988–; Eastern Electricity plc, 1990–; Financial Insurance Gp Ltd, 1990–. Member: Govt Computer Agency Council, 1973–74; Countryside Commn, 1980–; Rural Development Commn, 1985–. Mem., East Suffolk CC, 1968–70. *Recreation:* fighting history. *Address:* Marlesford Hall, Woodbridge, Suffolk; 5 Kersley Street, SW11. *Club:* Pratt's.

MARLING, Sir Charles (William Somerset), 5th Bt *cr* 1882; *b* 2 June 1951; *s* of Sir John Stanley Vincent Marling, 4th Bt, OBE, and Georgina Brenda (Betty) (*d* 1961), *o d* of late Henry Edward FitzRoy Somerset; *S* father, 1977; *m* 1979, Judi P. Futrille; three *d. Address:* The Barn, The Street, Eversley, Hants RG27 0PJ.

MARLOW, Antony Rivers; MP (C) Northampton North, since 1979; *b* 17 June 1940; *s* of late Major Thomas Keith Rivers Marlow, MBE, RE retd, and Beatrice Nora (*née* Hall); *m* 1962, Catherine Louise Howel (*née* Jones); three *s* two *d. Educ:* Wellington Coll.; RMA Sandhurst; St Catharine's Coll., Cambridge (2nd Cl. Hons (1) Mech. Sciences, MA). Served Army, 1958–69; retd, Captain RE; management consultant and industrial/commercial manager, 1969–79. *Recreations:* livestock farming, Rugby spectator, opera, ballet. *Address:* House of Commons, SW1A 0AA.

MARLOW, David Ellis; Chief Executive, 3i Group, since 1988; *b* 29 March 1935; *m* 1959, Margaret Anne Smith; one *d* (one *s* decd). Chartered Accountant. Investors in Industry, subseq. 3i, 1960–. *Recreations:* playing tennis, the piano and organ; scrambling in the Alps. *Address:* The Platt, Elsted, Midhurst GU29 0LA. *T:* Harting (0730) 825261.

MARLOWE, Hugh; see Patterson, Harry.

MARMION, Prof. Barrie P.; Visiting Professor, Department of Pathology, University of Adelaide (Adelaide Medical School), since 1985; *b* 19 May 1920; *s* of J. P. and M. H. Marmion, Alverstoke, Hants; *m* 1953, Diana Ray Newling, *d* of Dr P. Ray Newling, Adelaide, SA; one *d. Educ:* University Coll. and University Coll. Hosp., London. MD London 1947, DSc London 1963; FRCPath 1962, FRCPA 1964, FRCPE 1970, FRACP 1984; FRSE 1976. House Surg., UCH, 1942; Bacteriologist, Public Health Laboratory Service, 1943–62; Rockefeller Trav. Fellow, at Walter and Eliza Hall Inst., Melbourne, 1951–52; Foundation Prof., Microbiology, Monash Univ., Melbourne, Australia, 1962–68; Prof. of Bacteriology, Univ. of Edinburgh, 1968–78; Dir, Div. of Virology, Inst. of Med. and Vet. Science, Adelaide, 1978–85, retd. DUniv Adelaide, 1990. Distinguished Fellow Award (Gold Medal), RCPath Australia, 1986. *Publications:* (ed) Mackie and McCartney's Medical Microbiology, 13th edn 1978; numerous papers on bacteriology and virology. *Recreations:* swimming, music. *Address:* Department of Pathology, University of Adelaide, North Terrace, Adelaide, SA 5000, Australia.

MARNOCH, Hon. Lord; Michael Stewart Rae Bruce; Senator of the College of Justice in Scotland, since 1990; *b* 26 July 1938; *s* of late Alexander Eric Bruce, Advocate in Aberdeen, and late Mary Gordon Bruce (*née* Walker); *m* 1963, Alison Mary Monfries Stewart; two *d. Educ:* Loretto Sch.; Aberdeen Univ. (MA, LLB). Admitted Faculty of Advocates, 1963; QC Scot. 1975; Standing Counsel: to Dept of Agriculture and Fisheries for Scotland, 1973; to Highlands and Islands Develt Bd, 1973; Advocate Depute, 1983–86. Mem., Criminal Injuries Compensation Bd, 1986–90. *Recreations:* fishing, golf. *Clubs:* New (Edinburgh); Honourable Company of Edinburgh Golfers.

MAROWITZ, Charles; West Coast critic, Theatre Week magazine, since 1990; Artistic Director, Malibu Stage Company, since 1990; *b* 26 Jan. 1934; Austrian mother, Russian father; *m* 1982, Jane Elizabeth Allsop. *Educ:* Seward Park High Sch.; University Coll. London. Dir, In-Stage Experimental Theatre, 1958; Asst Dir, Royal Shakespeare Co., 1963–65; Artistic Director: Traverse Theatre, 1963–64; Open Space Theatre London, 1968–81; Open Space Theatre of Los Angeles, 1982; Associate Dir, LA Theater Center, 1984–89. Drama Critic: Encore Magazine, 1956–63; Plays and Players, 1958–74; The Village Voice, 1955–; The NY Times, 1966–. *West End* Director: Loot, Criterion, 1967; The Bellow Plays, Fortune, 1966; Fortune and Men's Eyes, Comedy, 1969; productions *abroad:* Woyzeck, 1965, The Shrew, 1979, Nat. Theatre, Bergen; Hedda, 1978, Enemy of the People, 1979, Nat. Theatre, Oslo; Measure for Measure, Oslo New Theatre, 1981; The Father, Trondheim, 1981; A Midsummer Night's Dream, Odense, Denmark; Tartuffe, Molde, Norway; Ah Sweet Mystery of Life, Seattle, 1981; productions in *Los Angeles:* Artaud at Rodez, 1982; Sherlock's Last Case, 1984; The Petrified Forest, 1985; The Fair Penitent, 1986; The Shrew, 1986; Importance of Being Earnest, 1987; What the Butler Saw, 1988; Wilde West, 1989; Variations on Measure for Measure, 1990; A MacBeth, 1991. Order of the Purple Sash, 1969. *Publications:* The Method as Means, 1960; The Marowitz Hamlet, 1967; A Macbeth, 1970; Confessions of a Counterfeit Critic, 1973; Open Space Plays, 1974; Measure for Measure, 1975; The Shrew, 1975; Artaud at Rodez, 1976; Variations on The Merchant of Venice; The Act of Being, 1977; The Marowitz Shakespeare, 1978; New Theatre Voices of the 50s and 60s, 1981; Sex Wars, 1982; Prospero's Staff, 1986; Potboilers (collection of plays), 1986; Recycling Shakespeare, 1991; Burnt Bridges, 1991. *Recreation:* balling. *Address:* 3058 Sequit Drive, Malibu, Calif 90265, USA.

MARPLES, Brian John; Emeritus Professor of Zoology, University of Otago, NZ; *b* 31 March 1907; 2nd *s* of George and Anne Marples; *m* 1931, Mary Joyce Ransford; two *s. Educ:* St Bees Sch.; Exeter Coll., Oxford. Lecturer in Zoology, Univ. of Manchester, 1929–35; Lecturer in Zoology, Univ. of Bristol, 1935–37; Prof. of Zoology, Univ. of

Otago, NZ, 1937–67. *Publications:* Freshwater Life in New Zealand, 1962; various technical zoological and archaeological papers. *Address:* 1 Vanbrugh Close, Old Woodstock, Oxon OX7 1YB.

MARQUAND, Prof. David (Ian), FRHistS; Professor of Politics, University of Sheffield, since 1991; Joint Editor, The Political Quarterly, since 1987; *b* 20 Sept. 1934; *s* of Rt Hon. Hilary Marquand, PC; *m* 1959, Judith Mary (*née* Reed); one *s* one *d*. *Educ:* Emanuel Sch.; Magdalen Coll., Oxford; St Antony's Coll., Oxford (Sen. Schol.). 1st cl. hons Mod. Hist., 1957. FRHistS 1986. Teaching Asst, Univ. of Calif., 1958–59; Leader Writer, The Guardian, 1959–62; Research Fellow, St Antony's Coll., Oxford, 1962–64; Lectr in Politics, Univ. of Sussex, 1964–66. Contested: (Lab) Barry, 1964; (SDP) High Peak, 1983; MP (Lab) Ashfield, 1966–77; PPS to Minister of Overseas Develt, 1967–69; Jun. Opposition Front-Bench Spokesman on econ. affairs, 1971–72; Member: Select Cttee on Estimates, 1966–68; Select Cttee on Procedure, 1968–73; Select Cttee on Corp. Tax, 1971; British Deleg. to Council of Europe, 1970–73. Chief Advr, Secretariat-Gen., European Commission, 1977–78; Prof. of Contemporary History and Politics, Salford Univ., 1978–91. Vis. Scholar, Hoover Instn, Stanford, USA, 1985–86. Member: Nat. Steering Cttee, SDP, 1981–88; Policy Cttee, Soc & Lib Dem, 1988–. Member Board: Aspen Inst., Berlin, 1982–; Public Policy Centre (formerly Social Scis Res. Trust), 1983–; Mem. Adv. Council, Inst. of Contemporary British History, 1987–. Thomas Jefferson Meml Lectr, Univ. of Calif at Berkeley, 1981. George Orwell Meml Prize (jtly), 1980. *Publications:* Ramsay MacDonald, 1977; Parliament for Europe, 1979; The Politics of Nostalgia, 1980; Taming Leviathan, 1980; (with David Butler) European Elections and British Politics, 1981; (ed) John Mackintosh on Politics, 1982; The Unprincipled Society, 1988; The Progressive Dilemma, 1991; contrib. to: The Age of Austerity, 1964; A Radical Future, 1967; Coalitions in British Politics, 1978; Britain in Europe, 1980; The Political Economy of Tolerable Survival, 1980; The Rebirth of Britain, 1982; European Monetary Union Progress and Prospects, 1982; Social Theory and Political Practice, 1982; The Changing Constitution, 1985; Thatcherism, 1987; The Radical Challenge, 1987; The Ruling Performance, 1987; articles and reviews in The Guardian, The Times, The Sunday Times, New Statesman, Encounter, Commentary, etc. *Recreation:* walking. *Address:* Department of Politics, Sheffield University, Sheffield S10 2TN.

MÁRQUEZ, Gabriel García; Colombian novelist; *b* 1928; *m* Mercedes García Márquez; two *s*. *Educ:* Univ. of Bogotá; Univ. of Cartagena. Corresp., El Espectador, Rome and Paris; formed Cuban Press Agency, Bogotá; worked for Prensa Latina, Cuba, later as Dep. Head, NY office, 1961; lived in Venezuela, Cuba, USA, Spain, Mexico; returned to Colombia, 1982; divides time between Mexico and Columbia. Rómulo Gallegos Prize, 1972; Nobel Prize for Literature, 1982. *Publications:* La hojarasca, 1955 (Leaf Storm, 1973); El coronel no tiene quien la escriba, 1961 (No One Writes to the Colonel, 1971); La mala hora, 1962 (In Evil Hour, 1980); Los funerales de la Mamá Grande, 1962; Cien años de soledad, 1967 (One Hundred Years of Solitude, 1970); La increíble y triste historia de la cándida Eréndira, 1972 (Innocent Erendira and other stories, 1979); El otoño del patriarca, 1975 (The Autumn of the Patriarch, 1977); Crónica de una muerte anunciada, 1981 (Chronicle of a Death Foretold, 1982; filmed, 1987); (with P. Mendoza) El olor de la Guayaba, 1982 (Fragrance of Guava, ed T. Nairn, 1983); El amor en los tiempos del cólera, 1984 (Love in the Time of Cholera, 1988); Relato de un naufrago (The Story of a Shipwrecked Sailor, 1986); Clandestine in Chile: adventures of Miguel Littín, 1986; Amores Difíciles, 1989; El General en su Laberinto, 1989 (The General in his Labyrinth, 1991). *Address:* c/o Agencia Literaria Carmen Balcelos, Diagonal 580, Barcelona, Spain.

MARQUIS, family name of **Earl of Woolton.**

MARQUIS, James Douglas, DFC 1945; Managing Director, Irvine Development Corporation, 1972–81; *b* 16 Oct. 1921; *s* of James Charles Marquis and Jessica Amy (*née* Huggett); *m* 1945, Brenda Eleanor, *d* of Robert Reyner Davey; two *s*. *Educ:* Shooters Hill Sch., Woolwich. Local Govt, 1938–41. Served War: RAF: 1941–46 (RAF 1st cl. Air Navigation Warrant, 1945), Navigation Officer, 177 Sqdn, 224 Gp, and AHQ Malaya (Sqdn Ldr 1945). Local Govt, 1946–56; Harlow Develt Corp., 1957–68; Irvine Develt Corp.: Chief Finance Officer, 1968–72; Dir of Finance and Admin., 1972. Pres., Ayrshire Chamber of Industries, 1979–80. Mem., Scottish Bonsai Assoc. FRMetS 1945; IPFA 1950; FCIS 1953. *Publication:* An Ayrshire Sketchbook, 1979. *Recreations:* sketching and painting (five one-man exhibns, incl. one in Sweden; works in collections: Japan, Sweden, Norway, Denmark, Australia, USA, Canada); gardening, bonsai. *Address:* 3 Knoll Park, Ayr KA7 4RH. *T:* Alloway (0292) 42212.

MARR, (Sir) Leslie Lynn, (2nd Bt, *cr* 1919, but does not use the title); MA Cambridge; painter and draughtsman; late Flight Lieutenant RAF; *b* 14 Aug. 1922; *o s* of late Col John Lynn Marr, OBE, TD, (and *g s* of 1st Bt,) and Amelia Rachel, *d* of late Robert Thompson, Overdinsdale Hall, Darlington; *S* grandfather 1932; *m* 1st, 1948, Dinora Delores Mendelson (marr. diss. 1956); one *d*; 2nd, 1962, Lynn Heneage; two *d*. *Educ:* Shrewsbury; Pembroke Coll., Cambridge. Has exhibited at Ben Uri, Drian, Woodstock, Wildenstein, Whitechapel, Campbell and Franks Galls, London; also in Norwich, Belfast, Birmingham, Newcastle upon Tyne, Bristol and Paris. *Publication:* From My Point of View, 1979. *Heir:* *cousin* James Allan Marr [*b* 17 May 1939; *m* 1965, Jennifer, *yr d* of late J. W. E. Gill; two *s* one *d*].

MARR-JOHNSON, Frederick James Maugham; His Honour Judge Marr-Johnson; a Circuit Judge, since 1991; *b* 17 Sept. 1936; *s* of late Kenneth Marr-Johnson and Hon. Diana Marr-Johnson; *m* 1966, Susan Eyre; one *s* one *d*. *Educ:* Winchester Coll.; Trinity Hall, Cambridge (MA). Called to the Bar, Lincoln's Inn, 1962; practised on SE Circuit, 1963–91. *Recreations:* sailing, ski-ing. *Address:* 59 Perrymead Street, SW6 3SN. *T:* 071–731 0412. *Club:* Island Cruising (Salcombe).

MARRACK, Rear-Adm. Philip Reginald, CB 1979; CEng, FIMechE, FIMarE; *b* 16 Nov. 1922; *s* of Captain Philip Marrack, RN and Annie Kathleen Marrack (*née* Proud); *m* 1954, Pauline Mary (*née* Haag); two *d*. *Educ:* Eltham Coll.; Plymouth Coll.; RNC Dartmouth; RN Engineering Coll., Manadon. War service at sea, HM Ships Orion and Argus, 1944–45; Advanced Engineering Course, RNC Greenwich, 1945–47; HM Submarines Templar and Token, 1947–50; served in Frigate Torquay, Aircraft Carriers Glory and Hermes, and MoD; Captain 1965; Commanded Admiralty Reactor Test Estab., Dounreay, 1967–70; CSO (Mat.) on Staff of Flag Officer Submarines, and Asst Dir (Nuclear), Dockyard Dept, 1970–74; Rear-Adm. 1974; Dir, Naval Ship Production, 1974–77; Dir, Dockyard Production and Support, 1977–81, retd. *Recreations:* fly fishing, gardening, viticulture, wine making. *Address:* c/o Barclays Bank, Princess Street, Plymouth PL1 2HA.

MARRE, Romola Mary, (Lady Marre), CBE 1979; Vice Chairman, City Parochial Foundation, since 1989 (Trustee, 1975–89); *b* 25 April 1920; *d* of late Aubrey John Gilling and Romola Marjorie Angier; *m* 1943, Sir Alan Samuel Marre, KCB (*d* 1990); one *s* one *d*. *Educ:* Chelmsford County High Sch. for Girls; Bedford Coll., Univ. of London. BA Hons Philosophy. Asst Principal (Temp.), Min. of Health, 1941–42; Sgt, subseq. Jun. Comdr, ATS Officer Selection Bd, 1942–45. Organiser, West Hampstead Citizen's Advice Bureau, 1962–65; Dep. Gen. Sec., Camden Council of Social Service, 1965–73; Adviser on Community Health Councils to DHSS, 1974–75; Chairman: London Voluntary Service Council (formerly London Council of Social Service), 1974–84; Cttee on the Future of the Legal Profession, 1986–88; Panel of Four Commn of Enquiry into Human Aids to Communication, 1990–91; Member: Lord Chancellor's Adv. Cttee on Legal Aid, 1975–80; Milk Marketing Bd, 1973–82; BBC and IBA Central Appeals Adv. Cttee, 1980–87 (Chm., 1984–87); Council of Management, Charity Projects, 1987–90; Dep. Chm., Royal Jubilee Trusts, 1981–88; Chairman: Volunteer Centre, 1973–78; Adv. Gp on Hospital Services for children with cancer in North Western Region, Jan.-June 1979; Prince of Wales' Adv. Gp on Disability, 1982–84; Founder Pres., Barnet Voluntary Service Council, 1979–; Chm., COPE UK, 1981–87. *Recreations:* cooking, gardening, walking, talking. *Address:* 44 The Vale, NW11 8SG. *T:* 081–458 1787.

MARRINER, Sir Neville, Kt 1985; CBE 1979; conductor; Founder and Director, Academy of St Martin in the Fields, since 1956; *b* 15 April 1924; *s* of Herbert Henry Marriner and Ethel May Roberts; *m* 1955, Elizabeth Mary Sims; one *s* one *d*. *Educ:* Lincoln Sch.; Royal College of Music (ARCM). Taught music at Eton Coll., 1948; Prof., Royal Coll. of Music, 1950. Martin String Quartet, 1949; Jacobean Ensemble, 1951; London Symphony Orchestra, 1954; Music Director: Los Angeles Chamber Orchestra, 1968–77; Minnesota Orchestra, 1979–86; Stuttgart Radio Symphony Orch., 1984–89. Artistic Director: South Bank Summer Music, 1975–77; Meadow Brook Festival, Detroit Symphony Orchestra, 1979–83; Barbican Summer Festival, 1985–87. Hon. ARAM; Hon. FRCM 1983. *Club:* Garrick.

MARRIOTT, Bryant Hayes; Controller, Special Duties, Radio BBC, 1990–91; *b* 9 Sept. 1936; *s* of Rev. Horace Marriott and Barbara Marriott; *m* 1963, Alison Mary Eyles; one *s* two *d*. *Educ:* Tormore Sch., Upper Deal, Kent; Marlborough Coll., Wilts; New Coll., Oxford (MA). Joined BBC, 1961–: Studio Manager, 1961; Producer, 1963; Staff Training Attachments Officer, 1973; Chief Asst to Controller Radio 1 and 2, 1976; Head of Recording Services, 1979; Controller, Radio Two, 1983. *Recreations:* gardening, sailing, drumming. *Address:* 95 Queens Road, Richmond, Surrey TW10 6HF. *Club:* Brancaster Staithe Sailing.

MARRIOTT, Sir Hugh Cavendish S.; *see* Smith-Marriott.

MARRIOTT, John Brook, CVO 1991 (LVO 1978); Keeper of the Royal Philatelic Collection, since 1969; *b* 27 July 1922; *er s* of late John Morley Marriott and Maud Marriott (*née* Brook); *m* 1952, Mary Eleanor Norcliffe Thompson; two *s*. *Educ:* Merchant Taylors' Sch., Northwood; St John's Coll., Cambridge (Wrangler Math. Tripos; MA). Army Op. Res. Gp., Min. of Supply, 1943; Foreign Office, Bletchley, 1944. Asst Master, Charterhouse, 1945–82, Housemaster 1960–75. Mem., Nat. Postal Mus. Bd, 1989; Royal Philatelic Society: London Fellow, 1958; Council Mem., 1969; Vice-Pres., 1979–83; Pres., 1983–86; London Medal, 1987. Corresp. Mem., l'Académie de Philatelie, Paris. Liveryman, Merchant Taylors' Co., 1950. Gov., St Edmund's Sch., Hindhead, 1979–87. Tilleard Medal, 1968; Tapling Medal, 1976; numerous other awards. *Publications:* Philatelic History of Trinidad to 1862, 1963; contribs to London Philatelist. *Recreations:* cricket, football, philately. *Clubs:* Arts, Army and Navy, MCC: Hawks (Cambridge).

MARRIOTT, John Miles; Non-Executive Director, Phillips & Drew Fund Management Ltd, since 1986; *b* 11 Oct. 1935; *s* of Arthur James Marriott and May Lavinia (*née* Goodband); *m* 1967, Josephine Anne (*née* Shepherd). *Educ:* High Pavement Grammar Sch., Nottingham. CIPFA 1962; MBCS 1970. E Midlands Electricity Bd, Nottingham (incl. 2 yrs National Service in RAF), 1952–60; Morley Bor. Council, 1960–62; Wolverhampton County Bor. Council, 1962–67; Asst Bor. Treasurer, Torbay Co. Bor. Council, 1967–70; Dep. Bor. Treas., 1970–72, and Bor. Treas., 1972–73, Ipswich Co. Bor. Council; Dir of Finance, Bolton Metrop. Bor. Council, 1973–78; County Treasurer, Greater Manchester Council, 1978–86; Principal, Grant Thornton, Chartered Accountants, 1986–90. *Publications:* papers in prof. jls. *Recreations:* golf, reading, bird watching, motoring. *Address:* 12 Martinsclough, Lostock, Bolton BL6 4PF. *T:* Bolton (0204) 47444.

MARRIOTT, Martin Marriott; Headmaster, Canford School, 1976–Aug. 1992; *b* 28 Feb. 1932; *s* of late Rt Rev. Philip Selwyn Abraham, Bishop of Newfoundland, and Elizabeth Dorothy Cicely, *d* of late Sir John Marriott; *m* 1956, Judith Caroline Guerney Lubbock; one *s* two *d*. *Educ:* Lancing College; New College, Oxford. MA, DipEd. RAF Educn Branch, 1956–59. Asst Master, Heversham Grammar Sch., 1959–66; Asst Master, Housemaster, Second Master, Acting Master, Haileybury College, 1966–76. Chm., HMC, 1989. *Recreations:* Royal tennis, golf, sailing, gardening. *Address:* Headmaster's House, Canford School, Wimborne, Dorset BH21 3AD. *T:* Wimborne (0202) 883031. *Club:* East India.

MARRIS, James Hugh Spencer; Regional Chairman, British Gas, Northern, since 1988; *b* 30 July 1937; *s* of Harry V. Marris and Agnes E. Hutchinson; *m* 1963, Susan Mary Husband; one *s* one *d*. *Educ:* King William's College, Isle of Man; Royal Technical College, Salford. ARTCS, CEng, FIGasE. Dir of Engineering, E Midlands Gas, 1978–82; Regional Dep. Chm., Eastern Gas, 1982–83; HQ Dir (Ops), British Gas, 1983–87. *Publications:* contribs to IGasE Jl. *Recreations:* golf, gardening. *Address:* 3 Apple Tree Rise, Corbridge, Northumberland NE45 5HD. *T:* 091–216 3000.

MARRIS, Prof. Robin Lapthorn; Professor of Economics, 1981–86, and Head of Department of Economics, 1983–86, Birkbeck College, University of London, now Professor Emeritus; *b* 31 March 1924; *s* of Eric Denyer Marris, CB, and late Phyllis, *d* of T. H. F. Lapthorn, JP; *m* 1st, 1949, Marion Ellinger; 2nd, 1954, Jane Evelina Burney Ayres; one *s* two *d*; 3rd, 1972, Anne Fairclough Mansfield; one *d*. *Educ:* Bedales Sch.; King's Coll., Cambridge. BA 1946, ScD 1968, Cantab. Asst Principal, HM Treasury, 1947–50; UN, Geneva, 1950–52; Fellow of King's Coll., Cambridge, 1951–76; Lectr, 1951–72, Reader, 1972–76, in Econs, Univ. of Cambridge; Prof. 1976–81 and Chm., 1976–79, Dept of Economics, Univ. of Maryland. Visiting Professor: Univ. of California, Berkeley, 1961; Harvard, 1967; Trento Univ., Italy, 1989–91. Dir, World Economy Div., Min. of Overseas Develt, 1964–66. Mem., Vis. Cttee, Open Univ., 1982–. *Publications:* Economic Arithmetic, 1958; The Economic Theory of Managerial Capitalism, 1964; The Economics of Capital Utilisation, 1964; (with Adrian Wood) The Corporate Economy, 1971; The Corporate Society, 1974; The Theory and Future of the Corporate Economy and Society, 1979; The Higher Education Crisis, 1987; Reconstructing Keynsian Economics with Imperfect Competitions, 1991; contrib. Econ. Jl, Rev. Econ. Studies, Economica, Jl Manchester Stat. Soc., Jl Royal Stat. Soc., Amer. Econ. Rev., Qly Jl of Econs, Economie Appliquée, etc. *Recreations:* cooking, horticulture, ski-ing, sailing. *Address:* Lingard House, Chiswick Mall, W4 2PJ.
See also S. N. Marris.

MARRIS, Stephen Nicholson; economic consultant; *b* 7 Jan. 1930; *s* of Eric Denyer Marris, CB, and Phyllis May Marris (*née* Lapthorn); *m* 1955, Margaret Swindells; two *s* one *d*. *Educ:* Bryanston School; King's College, Cambridge. MA, PhD. Nat. Inst. of Economic and Social Research, 1953–54; economist and international civil servant; with

Org. for European Economic Co-operation, later Org. for Economic Co-operation and Development (OECD), 1956–83: Dir, Economics Branch, 1970; Economic Advr to Sec.-Gen., 1975; Sen. Fellow, Inst. for Internat. Econs, Washington, 1983–88. Vis. Res. Prof. of Internat. Economics, Brookings Instn, Washington DC, 1969–70; Vis. Prof., Institut d'Etudes Politiques, Paris, 1986. Hon. Dr Stockholm Univ., 1978. *Publication:* Deficits and the Dollar: the World Economy at Risk, 1985. *Recreation:* sailing. *Address:* 8 Sentier des Pierres Blanches, 92190 Meudon, France. *T:* (1) 46.26.98.12.

See also R. L. Marris.

MARRISON, Dr Geoffrey Edward; Associate, Centre for South-East Asian Studies, University of Hull, since 1989; *b* 11 Jan. 1923; *s* of John and Rose Marrison; *m* 1958, Margaret Marian Millburn; one *s* three *d. Educ:* SOAS, Univ. of London; Bishops' Coll. Cheshunt; Kirchliche Hochschule, Berlin. BA Malay 1948, PhD Linguistics 1967, London. Indian Army, 1942–46. SOAS, 1941–42 and 1946–49; ordained Priest, Singapore, 1952; in Malaya with USPG, 1952–56; Vicar of St Timothy, Crookes, Sheffield, 1958–61; Linguistics Adviser British and Foreign Bible Soc., 1962–67, incl. service in Assam, 1962–64; Asst Keeper, British Museum, 1967–71, Dep. Keeper 1971–74; Dir and Keeper, Dept of Oriental Manuscripts and Printed Books, British Library, 1974–83; Tutor, Carlisle Diocesan Training Inst., 1984–90. Mem., Koninklijk Instituut voor Taal-, Land- en Volkenkunde, The Netherlands, 1983–. Hon. Canon of All Saints Pro-Cathedral, Shillong, 1963. FRAS. *Publications:* The Christian Approach to the Muslim, 1958; articles in Jl Malayan Branch Royal Asiatic Soc., Bible Translator. *Recreations:* ethno-linguistics of South and South East Asia, Christian and oriental art. *Address:* 1 Ainsworth Street, Ulverston, Cumbria LA12 7EU. *T:* Ulverston (0229) 56874.

MARS-JONES, Adam; Film Critic, The Independent, since 1986; *b* 26 Oct. 1954; *s* of Hon. Sir William Mars-Jones, *qv. Educ:* Westminster School; Cambridge Univ. (BA 1976). *Publications:* Lantern Lecture, 1981 (Somerset Maugham Award 1982); (with Edmund White) The Darker Proof, 1987, 2nd edn 1988; Venus Envy, 1990. *Address:* 42B Calabria Road, Highbury, N5 1HU. *T:* 071–226 2890.

MARS-JONES, Hon. Sir William (Lloyd), Kt 1969; MBE 1945; a Judge of the High Court of Justice, Queen's Bench Division, 1969–90; *b* 4 Sept. 1915; *s* of Henry and Jane Mars Jones, Llansannan, Denbighshire; *m* 1947, Sheila Mary Felicity Cobon; three *s. Educ:* Denbigh County Sch.; UCW, Aberystwyth (LLB Hons); St John's Coll., Cambridge (BA). Entrance Schol., Gray's Inn, 1936; Pres. Students' Rep. Counc. and Central Students' Rep. Counc., UCW, 1936–37; MacMahon Studentship, 1939; Barrister-at-Law, 1941, QC 1957. War of 1939–45, RNVR (MBE); Lt-Comdr RNVR 1945. Contested W Denbigh Parly Div., 1945. Joined Wales and Chester Circuit, 1947, Presiding Judge, 1971–75. Recorder of: Birkenhead, 1959–65; Swansea, 1965–68; Cardiff, 1968–69; Dep. Chm., Denbighshire Quarter Sessions, 1962–68. Bencher, Gray's Inn, 1964, Treasurer, 1982. Comr of Assize, Denbigh and Mold Summer Assize, 1965. Member: Bar Council, 1962; Home Office Inquiry into allegations against Metropolitan Police Officers, 1964; Home Secretary's Adv. Council on Penal System, 1966–68. President: N Wales Arts Assoc., 1976–; UCNW, Bangor, 1983–; UCW Old Students' Assoc., 1987–88; London Welsh Trust, 1989–. Hon. LLD UCW, Aberystwyth, 1973. *Recreations:* singing, acting, guitar. *Club:* Garrick.

See also A. Mars-Jones.

MARSDEN, Arthur Whitcombe, MSc, DIC, ARCS; formerly Education Officer/Technical Editor, Animal Production and Health Division, FAO, Rome, 1964–73; *b* Buxton, Derbyshire, 14 June 1911; *o s* of late Hubert Marsden and Margaret Augusta Bidwell; *m* 1940, Ailsa Anderson, *yr d* of late William Anderson McKellar, physician, and Jessie Reid Macfarlane, of Glasgow and Chester-le-Street, Co. Durham; one *s* two *d. Educ:* St Paul's; Imperial Coll. (Royal College of Science), London. BSc Special and ARCS, 1933; research in agricultural chemistry at Imperial Coll., 1933–36; research asst, 1936; demonstrator, 1937; asst lecturer, 1939; MSc and DIC, 1940. Temp. Instr Lieut RN, 1942; HMS Diomede, 1943; HMS King Alfred, 1944; RN Coll., Greenwich, and HMS Superb, 1945. Lecturer, Imperial Coll., London, 1946; Dept Head, Seale-Hayne Agricultural Coll., Newton Abbot, 1946–48; dir of research to grain companies in Aberdeen, 1948–49. Dir of Commonwealth Bureau of Dairy Science and Technology, Shinfield, Reading, 1950–57; Organising Secretary: 15th International Dairy Congress, London, 1957–60; 2nd World Congress of Man-made Fibres, 1960–63. Hon. Sec., Agriculture Group, Soc. of Chem. Industry, 1947–52, Chm., 1954–56; Organising Cttee of 2nd International Congress of Crop Protection, London, 1949; delegate on OEEC Technical Assistance Mission in USA and Canada, 1951; toured research centres in Pakistan, India, Australia, NZ and USA, Oct. 1954–Feb. 1955. *Publications:* papers in scientific journals. *Recreations:* gardening, music, philately, making model ships. *Address:* 109 Willingdon Road, Eastbourne, East Sussex BN21 1TX. *T:* Eastbourne (0323) 33602.

MARSDEN, Prof. (Charles) David, DSc; FRCP; FRS 1983; Professor of Clinical Neurology, since 1987, Director, MRC Human Movement and Balance Unit, Institute of Neurology and National Hospitals for Nervous Diseases, Queen Square, since 1988; *b* 15 April 1938; *s* of Charles Moustaka Marsden, CBE and Una Maud Marsden; *m* 1961, Jill Slaney Bullock; two *s* three *d*; *m* 1979, Jennifer Sandom. *Educ:* Cheltenham Coll.; St Thomas's Hosp. Med. Sch. (MSc 1960; MB, BS 1963). FRCP 1975 (MRCP 1965); MRCPsych 1978. Sen. House Physician, National Hosp. for Nervous Diseases, 1968–70; Institute of Psychiatry and King's College Hospital, London: Sen. Lectr in Neurol., 1970–72; Prof. of Neurol., 1972–87. Mem., MRC, 1988–. *Publications:* papers on human movement disorders, motor physiology, and basal ganglia pharmacology. *Recreation:* the human brain. *Address:* Institute of Neurology and National Hospitals for Nervous Diseases, Queen Square, WC1. *Club:* Athenæum.

MARSDEN, Edmund Murray; Director of Corporate Affairs, British Council, since 1990; *b* 22 Sept. 1946; *s* of Christopher Marsden and Ruth Marsden (*née* Kershaw); *m* 1981, Megan McIntyre; one *s. Educ:* Winchester College; Trinity College, Cambridge. Partner, Compton Press, Salisbury, 1968–70; Nuffield Foundn Publications Unit, 1970–71; British Council: Ghana, 1971; Belgium, 1973; Algeria, 1975; Management Accountant, 1977; Syria, 1980; Dir, Educn Contracts, 1982; Turkey, 1987–90. *Address:* British Council, 10 Spring Gardens, SW1A 2BN. *T:* 071–389 4892.

MARSDEN, Frank; JP; *b* Everton, Liverpool, 15 Oct. 1923; *s* of Sidney Marsden and Harriet Marsden (*née* Needham); *m* 1943, Muriel Lightfoot; three *s. Educ:* Abbotsford Road Sec. Mod. Sch., Liverpool. Served War, with RAF Bomber Command, 115 Sqdn (Warrant Officer), 1941–46. Joined Lab. Party and Co-op. Movement, 1948. MP (Lab) Liverpool, Scotland, Apr. 1971–Feb. 1974. Local Councillor: Liverpool St Domingo Ward, May 1964–67; Liverpool Vauxhall Ward, 1969–71; Knowsley DC, 1976–. Chm. Liverpool Markets, 1965–67; Past Mem. Exec. Cttee: Liverpool Trades Council; Liverpool Lab. Party. JP (City of Liverpool), 1969. *Recreations:* jazz music, gardening. *Address:* 2 Thunderbolt Cottage, 6 Alder Lane, Knowsley, Prescot, Merseyside L34 9EQ. *T:* 051–546 1959.

MARSDEN, Dr John Christopher; Executive Secretary, Linnean Society, since 1989; *b* 4 March 1937; *s* of Ewart and May Marsden; *m* 1962, Jessany Margaret Hazel Macdonald; two *s. Educ:* Bristol Grammar Sch.; Keble Coll., Oxford (MA, DPhil). FRSC; FIBiol. Lectr in Biology, Univ. of York, 1965–71; Sen. Res. Fellow, Inst. of Child Health, 1971–72; Reader in Cell Physiology, City of London Polytechnic, 1972–74; Polytechnic of Central London: Head of Life Scis, 1974–86; Dean, Faculty of Engrg and Sci., 1986–88, retired. *Publications:* Enzymes and Equilibria (with C. F. Stoneman), 1974; numerous contribs to biol. jls. *Recreations:* book collecting, cookery. *Address:* 7 Surrey Close, Tunbridge Wells, Kent TN2 5RF. *T:* Tunbridge Wells (0892) 33784.

MARSDEN, Sir Nigel (John Denton), 3rd Bt *cr* 1924, of Grimsby; gardener since 1983; *b* 26 May 1940; *s* of Sir John Denton Marsden, 2nd Bt and of Hope, *yr d* of late G. E. Llewelyn; *S* father, 1985; *m* 1961, Diana Jean, *d* of Air Marshal Sir Patrick Hunter Dunn, *qv*; three *d. Educ:* Ampleforth College, York. Vice-Chairman and Managing Director of family business, Consolidated Fisheries Ltd, of Grimsby, 1973 until 1982, when Company ceased trading and was sold. *Recreations:* walking, shooting, family. *Heir: b* Simon Neville Llewelyn Marsden [*b* 1 Dec. 1948; *m* 1970, Catherine Thérèse (marr. diss.), *d* of late Brig. James Charles Windsor-Lewis, DSO, MC; *m* 1984, Caroline, *y d* of John Stanton, Houghton St Giles, Norfolk; one *d*]. *Address:* The Homestead, 1 Grimsby Road, Waltham, Grimsby, South Humberside DN37 0PS. *T:* Grimsby (0472) 822166.

MARSDEN, Rear-Adm. Peter Nicholas; Executive Director, 21st Century Trust, since 1989; *b* 29 June 1932; *s* of Dr James Pickford Marsden and Evelyn (*née* Holman); *m* 1956, Jean Elizabeth Mather; two *s* one *d. Educ:* Felsted Sch., Essex. Joined RN, 1950; Commander, 1968; Captain, 1976; Commodore, Admiralty Interview Bd, 1983–84; Sen. Naval Mem., DS, RCDS, 1985–88. *Recreations:* golf, beagling, gardening. *Address:* c/o National Westminster Bank, Standishgate, Wigan, Lancs.

MARSDEN, Susan; Part-time Chairman, Social Security Appeal Tribunals (Leeds), since 1987; Chair, EYE on the Aire, since 1988; *b* 6 Dec. 1931; *d* of late John Marsden-Smedley and Agatha (*née* Bethell). *Educ:* Downe House Sch.; Girton Coll., Cambridge (MA). Called to the Bar, Middle Temple, 1957. Worked in consumer organisations in Britain and US, 1957–65; Senior Research Officer, Consumer Council, 1966–70; Legal Officer, Nuffield Foundation Legal Advice Research Unit, 1970–72; Exec. Dir, 1972–78, and Course Dir, 1978–81, Legal Action Gp (Editor, LAG Bulletin, 1972–78); Sec., Public Sector Liaison, RIBA, 1981–84; Asst Dir, Nat. Assoc. of CAB, 1985–86. Chm., Greater London CAB Service, 1979–85; Member: Council, National Assoc. of CAB, 1980–84; Royal Commn on Legal Services, 1976–79; Yorks Regional Rivers Adv. Cttee, Nat. Rivers Authority, 1989–; Council, Leeds Civic Trust, 1989–. *Publication:* Justice Out of Reach, a case for Small Claims Courts, 1969. *Recreations:* conservation along the River Aire, tree planting and preservation, gardening, looking at modern buildings. *Address:* Flat 5, 28 Newlay Lane, Horsforth, Leeds LS18 4LE. *T:* Leeds (0532) 580936.

MARSDEN, William, CMG 1991; HM Diplomatic Service; Ambassador to Costa Rica, and concurrently Ambassador (non-resident) to Nicaragua, since 1988; *b* 15 Sept. 1940; *s* of Christopher Marsden and Ruth (*née* Kershaw); *m* 1964, Kaia Collingham; one *s* one *d. Educ:* Winchester Coll.; Lawrenceville Sch., USA; Trinity Coll., Cambridge (MA); London Univ. (BSc Econs). FO, 1962–64; UK Delegn to NATO, 1964–66; Rome, 1966–69; seconded as Asst to Gen. Manager, Joseph Lucas Ltd, 1970; First Sec., FCO, 1971–76; First Sec. and Cultural Attaché, Moscow, 1976–79; Asst Head, European Community Dept, FCO, 1979–81; Counsellor, UK Representation to EEC, 1981–85; Head, E Africa Dept, FCO, and Comr, British Indian Ocean Territory, 1985–88. Chairman: Diplomatic Service Assoc., 1987–88; Twickenham Town Cttee, 1981–88. MBIM. *Address:* c/o Foreign and Commonwealth Office, SW1A 2AH.

MARSH, family name of **Baron Marsh.**

MARSH, Baron *cr* 1981 (Life Peer), of Mannington in the County of Wiltshire; **Richard William Marsh;** PC 1966; Kt 1976; FCIT; Chairman, Mannington Management Services, since 1989; Chairman and Chief Executive, Laurentian Holding Co., since 1989 (Director, since 1986); *b* 14 March 1928; *s* of William Marsh, Belvedere, Kent; *m* 1st, 1950, Evelyn Mary (marr. diss. 1973), *d* of Frederick Andrews, Southampton; two *s*; 2nd, 1973, Caroline Dutton (*d* 1975); 3rd, 1979, Felicity, *d* of Baron McFadzean of Kelvinside, *qv. Educ:* Jennings Sch., Swindon; Woolwich Polytechnic; Ruskin Coll., Oxford. Health Services Officer, National Union of Public Employees, 1951–59; Mem., Clerical and Administrative Whitley Council for Health Service, 1953–59; MP (Lab) Greenwich, Oct. 1959–April 1971; promoted Offices Act 1961; Member: Select Cttee Estimates, 1961; Chm. Interdepartmental Cttee to Co-ordinate Govt Policy on Industrial Training, 1964; Parly Sec., Min. of Labour, 1964–65; Joint Parly Sec., Min. of Technology, 1965–66; Minister of Power, 1966–68; Minister of Transport, 1968–69. Chairman: British Railways Bd, 1971–76; Newspaper Publishers' Assoc., 1976–90; British Iron and Steel Consumers' Council, 1977–82; Allied Investments Ltd, 1977–81; Member: NEDC, 1971–; Freight Integration Council, 1971–; Council, CBI, 1970–. Chairman: Michael Saunders Management Services, 1970–71; Allied Medical Group, 1977–81; Vivat Hldgs PLC, 1982–88; TV-am, 1983–84 (Dep. Chm., 1980–83); China & Eastern Investments, 1990– (Dir, 1987–); Deputy Chairman: United Medical Enterprises Ltd, 1978–81; Lopex PLC, 1986– (Dir, 1985–); Director: National Carbonising Co. Ltd (Chm., NCC Plant and Transport), 1970–71; Concord Rotoflex International Ltd, 1970–71; Imperial Life of Canada UK, 1983–; Imperial Life Assurance Co. of Canada, 1984–90; Charles Church Developments, 1987–; BAII Hldgs, 1987–; Thameside Developments Corp., 1987–; Laurentian Group Corp. (Montreal), 1990–; Advisor: Nissan Motor Co., 1981–; Fujitec, 1982–. Pres., Council ECSC, 1968. Governor: British Transport Staff Coll. (Chm.); London Business Sch. FBIM; FInstD; FInstM. *Publication:* Off the Rails (autobiog.), 1978. *Address:* Laurentian House, Barnwood, Gloucester GL4 7RZ. *T:* Gloucester (0452) 371371. *Clubs:* Reform, Buck's.

MARSH, Ven. Bazil Roland, BA; Archdeacon of Northampton, Non-Residentiary Canon of Peterborough, and Rector of St Peter's, Northampton, 1964–91; *b* Three Hills, Alta, Canada, 11 Aug. 1921; *s* of late Ven. Wilfred Carter Marsh and late Mary Jean (*née* Stott), Devil's Lake, North Dakota, USA; *m* 1946, Audrey Joan, *d* of late Owen George Oyler, farmer, of Brookmans Park, Hatfield, and Alma Lillian Oyler; three *s* one *d. Educ:* State schs in USA and Swindon, Wilts; Leeds Univ.; Coll. of the Resurrection, Mirfield, Yorks. Curate of: St Mary the Virgin, Cheshunt, Herts, 1944–46; St John Baptist, Coventry, 1946–47; St Giles-in-Reading, Berks, 1947–51; Rector of St Peter's, Townsville, Qld, Australia, 1951–56; Vicar of St Mary the Virgin, Far Cotton, Northampton, 1956–64. MLitt Lambeth, 1990. *Address:* 12 Parkway, Northampton NN3 3BS. *T:* Northampton (0604) 406644. *Club:* Commonwealth Trust.

MARSH, Rt. Rev. Edward Frank; *see* Newfoundland, Central, Bishop of.

MARSH, Rear-Adm. Geoffrey Gordon Ward, CB 1985; OBE 1969; jssc; Project Manager, NATO Frigate 90, Hamburg, 1988–90, retired; *m*; one *s* one *d. Educ:* St Albans Sch.; Queens' Coll., Cambridge. Britannia Royal Naval Coll., 1947; served on HM Ships: Indefatigable; Victorious; Carron; Norfolk; Girdle Ness; Bristol; involved in develt of

Sea Dart missile; Hd of Propulsion Machinery Control, Ship Dept; Asst Dir (Surface Warfare), Naval Op. Req.; Dir, Weapons Co-ordination and Acceptance (Naval), MoD, 1978–80; i/c HMS Thunderer, 1980–82; ACNS (Op. Req.), 1982–84; Dep. Controller, Warships Equipment, MoD (Navy), 1984–87; Chief Naval Engr Officer, 1985–87. *Address:* c/o The Naval Secretary, Ministry of Defence, Old Admiralty Building, Whitehall, SW1.

MARSH, Gordon Victor, MA; FHSM; Member, Police Complaints Authority, since 1989; *b* 14 May 1929; *s* of late Ven. Wilfred Carter Marsh, Devil's Lake, North Dakota, USA and Rosalie (*née* Holliday); *m* Millicent, *e d* of late Christopher Thomas and Edith Rowsell; one *s* one *d. Educ:* Grammar Schs, Swindon; Keble Coll., Oxford (MA); Inst. of Health Service Administrators (FHA 1964); Sloan Business Sch., Cornell Univ., USA. NHS admin. posts, England and Wales, 1952–72; Administrator and Sec., Bd of Governors, UCH, 1972–74; Area Administrator, Lambeth, Southwark and Lewisham AHA(T), 1974–82; Dep. Health Service Comr, 1982–89, retd. Vice-Chm., Assoc. of Chief Administrators of Health Authorities, 1980–82; Member: Council, National Assoc. of Health Authorities, 1979–82; Adv. Bd, Coll. of Occupational Therapists, 1974–. Chm., Trelawn Cttee of Richmond Fellowship, 1970–83; Hon. Sec. to Congregational Meeting and Wandsman, St Paul's Cathedral, 1980–. *Publications:* articles in professional jls. *Recreations:* music, gardening. *Address:* Springwater, St Lucian's Lane, Wallingford, Oxon OX10 9ER. *T:* Wallingford (0491) 36660. *Club:* United Oxford & Cambridge University.

MARSH, Rt. Rev. Henry Hooper, MA, DD; *b* 6 Oct. 1898; *s* of Rev. Canon Charles H. Marsh, DD; *m* Margaret D. Heakes; one *s* one *d. Educ:* University College, Toronto, BA 1921; Wycliffe College, Toronto, 1924, MA 1925; DD 1962. Deacon, 1924; Priest, 1925; Curate of St Anne, Toronto, 1924–25; Curate of St Paul, Toronto, 1925–30; Priest-in-charge of St Timothy's Mission, City and Diocese of Toronto, 1930–36; Rector, Church of St Timothy, 1936–62; Canon of Toronto, 1956–62; Bishop of Yukon, 1962–67. Canadian Centennial Medal, 1967. *Recreation:* bird watching. *Address:* Hedgerows, RR6, Cobourg, Ont K9A 4J9, Canada.

MARSH, (Henry) John, CBE 1967; international management consultant, writer and lecturer; director of companies; *b* 17 Aug. 1913; *s* of late Jasper W. P. Marsh and Gladys M. Carruthers; *m* 1950, Mary Costerton; two *s* two *d. Educ:* Chefoo Sch., China; Queen Elizabeth's Grammar Sch., Wimborne. Commerce, China, 1930–32; Shanghai Volunteer Force, 1930–32; engineering apprenticeship and apprentice supervisor, Austin Motor Co., 1932–39. Served War of 1939–45, Royal Army Service Corps TA, 48th and 56th Divisions; Singapore Fortress; BEF France, 1940; Malaya, 1941–42 (despatches twice); Prisoner of War, 1942–45; released with rank of Major, 1946. Personnel Officer, BOAC, 1946–47; Dir of Personnel Advisory Services, Institute of Personnel Management, 1947–49; Dir, Industrial (Welfare) Soc., 1950–61; British Institute of Management: Dir, later Dir-Gen., 1961–73; Asst Chm. and Counsellor, 1973–75. Mem., Nat. Coal Board, 1968–74. Hon. Administrator, Duke of Edinburgh's Study Conference, 1954–56; Chairman:. Brit. Nat. Conference on Social Work, 1957–60; VSO, 1957–60; Member: Youth Service Cttee, 1958–59; BBC General Advisory Council, 1959–64; Advisory Cttee on Employment of Prisoners, 1960–63; Council for Technical Educn and Training for Overseas Countries, 1961–74; UK Advisory Council on Education for Management, 1962–66; Russell Cttee on Adult Educn, 1969–72; Court, Univ. of Cranfield, 1962–69; Court, Univ. of Surrey, 1969–79; Food Manufacturing EDC, 1967–69; Adv. Council, Civil Service College, 1970–77; UK Mem., Commonwealth Team of Industrial Specialists, 1976–78. Governor, King's Coll. Hosp., 1971–74. British Information Service Lectures: Ardeshir Dalal Meml, India, 1953; Clarke Hall, Lincoln's Inn, 1957; E. W. Hancock, IProdE, 1960; MacLaren Meml, Birmingham, 1962; Tullis Russell, Glasgow, 1967; Allerdale-Wyld, Galashiels, 1972; RSA, 1973; Geden Foster, RSA, 1977; Chester, Sheffield Cathedral, 1978; Stantonbury, Milton Keynes, 1981; lecture tours: India and Pakistan, 1959 and 1963; Nigeria, 1964; Malaysia, 1965; Australia, 1967; Latin America, 1971, 1973; Malaysia, NZ, 1974. FIAM 1969; Hon. Fellow, Canadian Inst. of Management, 1973; CBIM (FBIM 1967); FIMC 1980. Hon. CIPM 1985. Hon. DSc Bradford, 1968. Verulam Medal, 1976. *Publications:* Introduction to Human Relations at Work, 1952; People at Work, 1957; Partners in Work Relations, 1960; Work and Leisure Digest, 1961; Pursuit of God, 1968; Ethics in Business, 1970; Organisations of the Future, 1980; Late Glimpses (verse), 1984; Management of Change, 1989. *Recreations:* writing, music, counselling, idling. *Address:* 13 Frank Dixon Way, Dulwich, SE21 7ET.

MARSH, Jean Lyndsey Torren; actress; Artistic Director, Adelphi University Theatre, Long Island, New York, 1981–83; *b* 1 July 1934; *d* of Henry Charles and Emmeline Susannah Marsh; *m* 1955, Jon Devon Roland Pertwee (marr. diss. 1960). Began as child actress and dancer; *films:* Return to Oz; Willow; danced in Tales of Hoffmann, Where's Charley?, etc; acted in repertory companies: Huddersfield, Nottingham, etc; Broadway debut in Much Ado About Nothing, 1959; West End debut, Bird of Time, 1961; *stage:* Habeas Corpus, The Importance of Being Earnest, Too True to be Good, Twelfth Night, Blithe Spirit, Whose Life is it Anyway?, Uncle Vanya, On the Rocks, Pygmalion, Hamlet; *television:* co-created and co-starred (Rose) in series Upstairs Downstairs; series, Nine to Five. Hon. DH Maryland Coll., NY, 1980. *Publications:* The Illuminated Language of Flowers, 1978; articles for Sunday Times, Washington Post and New York Times. *Recreations:* cross-country skiing, reading, cooking, eating. *Address:* Hamstead Farm Cottage, Drift Lane, Chidham, W Sussex.

MARSH, Prof. the Rev. John, CBE 1964; MA (Edinburgh et Oxon), DPhil (Oxon); DD (Hon.) Edinburgh and Nottingham; Moderator, Free Church Federal Council, 1970–71; Principal, Mansfield College, Oxford, 1953–70; *b* 5 Nov. 1904; *s* of George Maurice and Florence Elizabeth Ann Marsh, East Grinstead, Sussex; *m* 1934, Gladys Walker, *y d* of George Benson and Mary Walker, Cockermouth, Cumberland; two *s* one *d. Educ:* The Skinners Company Sch., Tunbridge Wells; Yorkshire United Coll., Bradford; Edinburgh Univ.; Mansfield Coll. and St Catherine's Soc., Oxford; Marburg Univ. Lecturer, Westhill Training Coll., 1932; Minister, Congregational Church, Otley, Yorks, 1934; Tutor and Chaplain, Mansfield Coll., Oxford, 1938; Prof. of Christian Theology, The University, Nottingham, 1949–53. Gray Lectr, Duke Univ., NC; Reinecke Lectr, Prot. Episc. Semin., Alexandria, Va, 1958. Delegate: First Assembly, World Council of Churches, Amsterdam, 1948; Second Assembly, Evanston, Ill., 1954; Third Assembly, New Delhi, 1961; Fourth Assembly, Uppsala, 1968. Sec. World Conference on Faith and Order's Commn on "Intercommunion"; Chm., Section 2 of British Council of Churches Commn on Broadcasting, 1949; Mem., Working Cttee, Faith and Order Dept, World Council of Churches, 1953; Sec., European Commission on Christ and the Church, World Council of Churches, 1955; Mem. Central Religious Advisory Cttee to BBC, 1955–60; Mem. Sub-Cttee of CRAC acting as Religious Advisory Panel to ITA, 1955–65; Chm. British Council of Churches Commn of Faith and Order, 1960–62. Mem. Central Cttee, World Council of Churches, 1961–68; Chm. Division of Studies, World Council of Churches, 1961–68; Select Preacher, University of Oxford, 1962; Chm. Congregational Union of England and Wales, 1962–63; Chairman: Inter-Church Relationships Cttee, Congregational Church in England and Wales, 1964–67; Board of Faculty of Theology, Oxford Univ., 1966–68; Exec. Cttee, Congregational Church in England and Wales, 1966–72; Joint Chm. Joint Cttee for Conversations between Congregationalists and Presbyterians, 1965–72; Lay Vice-Chm., Derwent Deanery Synod, 1979–82. Vice-Pres., Philosophical Soc. of England, 1986–. Chm., Buttermere Parish Council, 1973–80. Governor, Westminster Coll., Oxford, 1967–70. *Publications:* The Living God, 1942; Congregationalism Today, 1943; (jtly) A Book of Congregational Worship, 1948; (Jt Ed.) Intercommunion, 1952; contrib. Biblical Authority Today, 1951; and Ways of Worship, 1951; The Fulness of Time, 1952; The Significance of Evanston, 1954; trans. Stauffer, Theology of the New Testament, 1955; A Year with the Bible, 1957; contributed to Essays in Christology for Karl Barth, 1957; Amos and Micah, 1959; trans. Bultmann, The History of the Synoptic Tradition, 1963; Pelican Commentary on St John's Gospel, 1968; Jesus in his Lifetime, 1981. *Recreations:* water colour painting, wood turning. *Address:* 5 Diamond Court, Moreton Road, Oxford OX2 7AA. *T:* Oxford (0865) 57479.

MARSH, John; *see* Marsh, H. J.

MARSH, Prof. Leonard George, MEd; DPhil; Principal, Bishop Grosseteste College, since 1974; *b* 23 Oct. 1930; third *c* of late Ernest Arthur Marsh and Anne Eliza (*née* Bean); *m* 1953, Ann Margaret Gilbert; one *s* one *d. Educ:* Ashford (Kent) Grammar Sch.; Borough Road Coll., London Inst. of Educn (London Univ. Teachers' Certif. and Academic Dip.); Leicester Univ. (MEd); DPhil York, 1988. Lectr in Educn and Mathematics, St Paul's Coll., Cheltenham, 1959–61; Lectr, 1961–63, Sen. Lectr, 1963–65, Principal Lectr and Head of Postgraduate Primary Educn Dept, 1965–74, Goldsmiths' Coll., London. Hon. Prof., Hull Univ., 1987–. Visiting Lectr, Bank Street Coll., New York, and Virginia Commonwealth Univ.; former Consultant, OECD, Portugal; Educnl Consultant, Teacher Trng Proj., Botswana, 1981; Specialist tour to India for British Council. Member: Gen. Adv. Council, IBA, 1977–82; N Lincolnshire AHA, 1984–; Chm., Nat. Assoc. for Primary Educn, 1981–83. FRSA; FCP 1989 .*Publications:* Let's Explore Mathematics, Books 1–4, 1964–67; Children Explore Mathematics, 1967, 3rd edn 1969; Exploring Shapes and Numbers, 1968, 2nd edn 1970; Exploring the Metric System, 1969, 2nd edn 1969; Exploring the Metric World, 1970; Approach to Mathematics, 1970; Alongside the Child in the Primary School, 1970; Let's Discover Mathematics, Books 1–5, 1971–72; Being A Teacher, 1973; Helping your Child with Maths—a parents' guide, 1980; The Guinness Mathematics Book, 1980; The Guinness Book for Young Scientists, 1982. *Recreations:* photography, theatre, walking, films. *Address:* The Principal's House, Bishop Grosseteste College, Lincoln LN1 3DY. *T:* Lincoln (0522) 28241.

MARSH, Nevill Francis, CBE 1969; Director-General, St John Ambulance, 1972–76; *b* 13 Aug. 1907; *m* 1st, 1935, Betty Hide (decd); one *s* one *d*; 2nd, 1989, Gillian Hodnett. *Educ:* Oundle Sch., Northants; Clare Coll., Cambridge (MA). Traction Motor Design Staff, Metropolitan-Vickers Electrical Co. Ltd, 1930–32; Mid-Lincolnshire Electric Supply Co. Ltd: Dist Engineer, 1932–38; Engineer and Manager, 1938–48; Chief Commercial Officer, E Midlands Electricity Board, 1948–55; Dep.-Chm., N Eastern Electricity Board, 1955–57; Dep.-Chm., E Midlands Electricity Board, 1957–59; Chm., East Midlands Electricity Board, 1959–61; a Dep. Chm., Electricity Council, 1962–71; Chm., British Electrotechnical Cttee, 1970–72. Dir for Gtr London, St John Ambulance Assoc., 1971–72. Also formerly: Dir, Altrincham Electric Supply Ltd, and Public Utilities (Elec.) Ltd, and Supervising Engineer, Campbeltown & Mid-Argyll Elec. Supply Co. Ltd, and Thurso & District Elec. Supply Co. Ltd. FIEE; Pres. of Assoc. of Supervising Electrical Engineers, 1966–68. KStJ 1973. *Publications:* jt contrib. Jl Inst. Electrical Engineers, 1955. *Address:* 66 Elmtree Avenue, Frinton-on-Sea, Essex CO13 0AS. *T:* Frinton (0255) 672995. *Club:* Royal Air Force.

MARSH, Norman Stayner, CBE 1977; QC 1967; Law Commissioner, 1965–78; Member, Royal Commission on Civil Liability and Compensation for Personal Injury, 1973–78; *b* 26 July 1913; 2nd *s* of Horace Henry and Lucy Ann Marsh, Bath, Som; *m* 1939, Christiane Christinnecke, 2nd *d* of Professor Johannes and Käthe Christinnecke, Magdeburg, Germany; two *s* two *d. Educ:* Monkton Combe Sch.; Pembroke Coll., Oxford (2nd Class Hons, Final Honour Sch. of Jurisprudence, 1935; 1st Cl. Hons BCL; Hon. Fellow, 1978). Vinerian Scholar of Oxford Univ., Harmsworth Scholar of Middle Temple, called to Bar, 1937; practice in London and on Western Circuit, 1937–39; Lieut-Col Intelligence Corps and Control Commission for Germany, 1939–46. Stowell Civil Law Fellow, University Coll., Oxford, 1946–60; University Lecturer in Law, 1947–60; Estates Bursar, University Coll., 1948–56; Secretary-General, International Commission of Jurists, The Hague, Netherlands, 1956–58. Member: Bureau of Conference of Non-Governmental Organisations with Consultative Status with the United Nations, 1957–58; Internat. Cttee of Legal Science (Unesco), 1960–63. Dir of British Institute of International and Comparative Law, 1960–65. Mem., Younger Cttee on Privacy, 1970–72. Hon. Vis. Prof. in Law, KCL, 1972–77. Vice-Chm., Age Concern, England, 1979–86. General editor, International and Comparative Law Quarterly, 1961–65; Mem., Editorial Board, 1965–. *Publications:* The Rule of Law as a supra-national concept, in Oxford Essays in Jurisprudence, 1960; The Rule of Law in a Free Society, 1960; Interpretation in a National and International Context, 1974; (editor and part-author) Public Access to Government-held Information, 1987; articles on common law and comparative law in English, American, French and German law jls. *Address:* Wren House, 13 North Side, Clapham Common, SW4. *T:* 071–622 2865.

See also B. K. Cherry.

MARSH, Prof. Paul Rodney; Professor of Management and Finance, London Business School, since 1985; *b* 19 Aug. 1947; *s* of Harold Marsh and Constance (*née* Miller); *m* 1971, Stephanie Beatrice (*née* Simonow). *Educ:* Poole Grammar Sch.; London School of Economics (BScEcon, 1st Cl. Hons); London Business Sch. (PhD). Systems Analyst, Esso Petroleum, 1968–69; Scicon, 1970–71; London Business School, 1974–: Bank of England Res. Fellow, 1974–85; Dir, Sloan Fellowship Prog., 1980–83; Non-exec. Dir, Centre for Management Develt, 1984–; Mem. Govg Body, 1986–; Faculty Dean, 1987–90; Dep. Principal, 1989–90. Member: CBI Task Force on City-Industry Relationships, 1986–88; Exec. Cttee, British Acad. of Management, 1986–88. Non-exec. Dir, M&G Investment Management Ltd, 1989–; Dir, Hoare Govett Indices Ltd. *Publications:* Cases in Corporate Finance, 1988; Managing Strategic Investment Decisions, 1988; Accounting for Brands, 1989; Short-termism on Trial, 1990; The HGSC Smaller Companies Index, 1991; numerous articles in Jl of Financial Econs, Jl of Finance, Harvard Business Review, Jl of Inst. of Actuaries, Managerial Finance, Res. in Marketing, Mergers and Acquisitions, Investment Analyst, Long Range Planning, Investment Management Rev., etc. *Recreations:* gardening, investment. *Address:* London Business School, Sussex Place, Regent's Park, NW1 4SA. *T:* 071–262 5050.

MARSHALL, family name of **Baron Marshall of Goring.**

MARSHALL OF GORING, Baron *cr* 1985 (Life Peer), of South Stoke in the County of Oxfordshire; **Walter Charles Marshall;** Kt 1982; CBE 1973; FRS 1971; Chairman, World Association of Nuclear Operators, since 1989; *b* 5 March 1932; *s* of late Frank Marshall and Amy (*née* Pearson); *m* 1955, Ann Vivienne Sheppard; one *s* one *d. Educ:*

Birmingham Univ. Scientific Officer, AERE, Harwell, 1954–57; Research Physicist: University of California, 1957–58; Harvard Univ., 1958–59; AERE, Harwell: Group Leader, Solid State Theory, 1959–60; Head of Theoretical Physics Div., 1960–66; Dep. Dir, 1966–68; Dir, 1966–75; Chief Scientist, Dept of Energy, 1974–77; United Kingdom Atomic Energy Authority: Dir, Research Gp, 1969–75; Mem., 1972–82; Dep. Chm., 1975–81; Chm., 1981–82; Chm., CEGB, 1982–89. Member: NRDC, 1969–75; NEDC, 1984–86; Chairman: Adv. Council on R&D for Fuel and Power, 1974–77; Offshore Energy Technology Bd, 1975–77. Pres., Assoc. of Science Educn, 1987. Editor, Oxford Internat. Series of Monographs on Physics, 1966–. Freeman, City of London, 1984. Fellow, Royal Swedish Acad. of Engrg Scis, 1977; For. Associate, Nat. Acad. of Engineering, USA. Hon. FWeldI, 1987; Hon. Fellow, St Hugh's Coll., Oxford, 1983; Hon. DSc Salford, 1977. Maxwell Medal, 1964; Glazebrook Medal, 1975. Henry DeWolf Smyth Nuclear Statesman Award, USA, 1985. *Publications:* Thermal Neutron Scattering, 1971; Nuclear Power Technology, 1984; research papers on magnetism, neutron scattering and solid state theory. *Recreations:* gardening, origami, physics. *Address:* (office) World Association of Nuclear Operators, 262A Fulham Road, SW10 9EL. *T:* 071-351 3249.

MARSHALL, Mrs Alan R.; *see* Marshall, V. M.

MARSHALL, Alan Ralph; education consultant; *s* of Ralph Marshall and Mabel Mills; *m* 1958, Caterina Gattico; one *s* one *d*. *Educ:* Shoreditch College (Teacher's Cert. 1953); London Univ. (Dip Ed 1959; MPhil 1965); Eastern Washington State Univ. (MEd 1964); Stanford Univ. (MA 1969). Teacher, schools in UK and USA, 1954–62; Lectr, Shoreditch Coll., 1962–68; Vis. Prof., Eastern Washington State Univ., 1964–65; Field Dir, Project Technology, Schools Council, 1970–72; Editor, Nat. Centre for School Technology, 1972–73; Course Team Chm., Open Univ., 1973–76; HM Inspector, DES, 1976–91, HM Chief Inspector of Schools, 1985–91. FRSA. DEd CNAA, 1990. *Publications:* (ed) School Technology in Action, 1974; (with G. T. Page and J. B. Thomas) International Dictionary of Education, 1977; Giving Substance to a Vision, 1990; articles in jls. *Recreations:* travel, reading, various crafts. *Address:* 98 Wheathampstead Road, Harpenden, Herts AL5 1JB.

MARSHALL, Alexander Badenoch, (Sandy); Chairman: The Maersk Co. Ltd, since 1987 (Director, since 1980; Vice-Chairman, 1983–87); Royal Bank of Canada Holdings UK Ltd, since 1988; Director: Royal Bank of Canada, since 1985; Maersk Air Ltd, since 1988; *b* 31 Dec. 1924; *m* 1961, Mona Kurina Douglas Kirk, South Africa; two *s* one *d*. *Educ:* Trinity Coll., Glenalmond; Worcester Coll., Oxford (MA). Served War, Sub-Lieut RNVR, 1943–46. P&O Group of Companies: Mackinnon Mackenzie & Co., Calcutta, 1947–59; Gen. Manager, British India Steam Navigation Co., 1959–62; Man. Dir, Trident Tankers Ltd, 1962–68; Dir, 1968–72, Man. Dir, 1972–79, Peninsular and Oriental Steam Navigation Co.; Chairman: Bestobell Plc, 1979–85; Commercial Union Assurance Co. plc, 1983–90 (Dir, 1970–90); Vice-Chm., The Boots Co. Plc, 1985–91 (Dir, 1981–91). Co-Chm., British-N American Cttee, 1984–90. *Recreations:* family, gardening. *Address:* Crest House, Woldingham, Surrey CR3 7DH. *T:* Woldingham (0883) 65229. *Clubs:* Oriental; Tollygunge (Calcutta).

MARSHALL, Arthur C.; *see* Calder-Marshall.

MARSHALL, Sir Arthur Gregory George, Kt 1974; OBE 1948; DL; Life President, Marshall of Cambridge (Holdings), 1990; *b* 4 Dec. 1903; *s* of David Gregory Marshall, MBE, and Maude Edmunds Wing; *m* 1931, Rosemary Wynford Dimsdale (*d* 1988), *d* of Marcus Southwell Dimsdale; two *s* one *d*. *Educ:* Tonbridge Sch.; Jesus Coll., Cambridge (Hon. Fellow, 1990). Engrg, MA. Joined Garage Company of Marshall (Cambridge) Ltd, 1926, which resulted in estabt of Aircraft Company, now Marshall of Cambridge (Engineering) Ltd, 1929, Chm. and Jt Man. Dir, 1942–89. Chm., Aerodrome Owners Assoc., 1964–65; Member: Air Cadet Council, 1951–59 and 1965–76; Adv. Council on Technology, 1967–70. Hon. Old Cranwellian, 1979; CRAeS 1980. DL 1968, High Sheriff of Cambridgeshire and Isle of Ely, 1969–70. Order of El Istiqlal, First Class (Jordan), 1990. *Recreations:* Cambridge Athletics Blue, Olympic Team Reserve, 1924; flying. *Address:* Horseheath Lodge, Linton, Cambridge CB1 6PT. *T:* Cambridge (0223) 891318. *Clubs:* Royal Air Force; Hawks (Cambridge).

MARSHALL, Arthur Hedley, CBE 1956; MA; BSc (Econ); PhD; City Treasurer, Coventry, 1944–64, retired; Senior Research Fellow in Public Administration, Birmingham University, 1964–74; Visiting Lecturer, City University, 1977–83; *b* 6 July 1904; *s* of Rev. Arthur Marshall; *m* 1933, Margaret L. Longhurst (*d* 1987); one *s*. *Educ:* Wolverhampton Grammar Sch.; London Sch. of Economics. Incorporated Accountant (Hons), 1934; Fellow Institute Municipal Treasurers and Accountants and Collins gold medal, 1930 (Pres. 1953–54); DPA (London) 1932. Chm. Royal Institute of Public Administration, 1952–53; Adviser in Local Govt to Sudan Govt, 1948–49; and to Govt of British Guiana, 1955. Chm., Cttee on Highway Maintenance, 1967–70; Member: Colonial Office Local Government Advisory Panel, 1950–; Central Housing Adv. Cttee, 1957–65; Cttee for Training Public Administration in Overseas Countries, 1961–62; Arts Council Drama Panel, 1965–76; Arts Council, 1973–76; Uganda Commission, 1961; Kenya Commission, 1962; Royal Commission on Local Government in England, 1966–69. Hon. LLD Nottingham, 1972. *Publications:* Local Authorities: Internal Financial Control, 1936; Consolidated Loans Funds of Local Authorities (with J. M. Drummond), 1936; Report on Local Government in the Sudan, 1949, and on British Guiana, 1955; Financial Administration in Local Government, 1960; Financial Management in Local Government, 1974; Local Authorities and the Arts, 1974; various contribs to learned jls on Local Government, Accountancy, and administration of the arts. *Recreation:* music. *Address:* 39 Armorial Road, Coventry CV3 6GH. *T:* Coventry (0203) 414652.
See also N. H. Marshall.

MARSHALL, Arthur Stirling-Maxwell, CBE 1986 (OBE 1979); HM Diplomatic Service, retired; *b* 29 Jan. 1929; *s* of Victor Stirling-Maxwell Marshall and Jeannie Theodora Hunter; *m* 1st, 1955, Eleni Kapralou, Athens (*d* 1969); one *s* two *d*; 2nd, 1985, Cheryl Mary Hookens, Madras; one *d*. *Educ:* Daniel Stewart's Coll., Edinburgh. Served Royal Navy, 1947–59. Foreign Office, 1959; Middle East Centre for Arab Studies, Lebanon, 1959–61; Political Officer, British Political Agency, Bahrain and Registrar for HBM Court of Bahrain, 1961–64; Attaché, Athens, 1964–67; Information Officer, Rabat, Morocco, 1967–69; Commercial Secretary: Nicosia, Cyprus, 1970–75; Kuwait, 1975–79; Deputy High Commissioner, Madras, 1980–83; Counsellor, Kuwait, 1983–85; Ambassador to People's Democratic Republic of Yemen, 1986–89. *Recreations:* music, nature. *Address:* 147 Highbury Grove, N5 1HP. *Clubs:* Oriental; Madras (Madras).

MARSHALL, Hon. (Cedric) Russell; Chairman, New Zealand Commission for UNESCO, since 1990; *b* 15 Feb. 1936; *s* of Cedric Thomas Marshall and Gladys Margaret Marshall; *m* 1961, Barbara May Watson; two *s* one *d*. *Educ:* Nelson Coll.; Christchurch Teachers Coll.; Auckland Univ. (DipTeaching). Primary teacher, Nelson, 1955–56; Trinity Methodist Theol Coll., 1958–60; Methodist Minister: Christchurch, Spreydon, 1960–66; Masterton, 1967–71; teacher, Wanganui High Sch., 1972. MP (Lab) Wanganui, 1972–90; Opposition education spokesman, 1976–84; Chief Opposition Whip, 1978–79; Minister of Education, 1984–87, for the Environment, 1984–86, of Conservation, 1986–87, of Disarmament and Arms Control, 1987–89, of Foreign Affairs, 1987–90, for Pacific Island Affairs, 1988–90. Hon. PhD Univ. of Khon Kaen, Thailand, 1989. *Recreations:* reading, listening to music, archaeology. *Address:* 26 Mana Esplanade, Paremata, Wellington, New Zealand. *T:* (04) 339178.

MARSHALL, Sir Colin (Marsh), Kt 1987; Chief Executive, since 1983, and Deputy Chairman, since 1989, British Airways; *b* 16 Nov. 1933; *s* of Marsh Edward Leslie and Florence Mary Marshall; *m* 1958, Janet Winifred (*née* Cracknell); one *d*. *Educ:* University College Sch., Hampstead. Progressively, cadet purser to Dep. Purser, OSNC, 1951–58; Hertz Corp., 1958–64: management trainee, Chicago and Toronto, 1958–59; Gen. Man., Mexico, Mexico City, 1959–60; Asst to Pres., New York, 1960; Gen. Manager: UK London, 1961–62; UK Netherlands and Belgium, London, 1962–64; Avis Inc., 1964–79: Reg. Man./Vice-Pres., Europe, London, 1964–66; Vice-Pres. and Gen. Man., Europe and ME, London, 1966–69; Vice-Pres. and Gen. Man., International, London, 1969–71; Exec. Vice-Pres. and Chief Operating Officer, New York, 1971–75; Pres. and Chief Operating Officer, New York, 1975–76; Pres. and Chief Exec. Officer, New York, 1976–79; Norton Simon Inc., New York, 1979–81: Exec. Vice-Pres. and Sector Exec.; Mem., Office of the Chm.; co-Chm. of Avis Inc.; Sears Holdings plc, 1981–83: Dir and Dep. Chief Exec. Director: Grand Metropolitan PLC, 1988–; Midland Group, 1989–; Mem. Bd, IBM UK Ltd, 1990–. Mem., British Tourist Authority Bd, 1986–. *Recreations:* tennis, skiing. *Address:* c/o British Airways Head Office, PO Box 10, Heathrow Airport London, Hounslow, Mddx TW6 2JA. *T:* 081–562 5474. *Club:* Queen's.

MARSHALL, David; MP (Lab) Glasgow, Shettleston, since 1979 (sponsored by TGWU); former transport worker; *b* May 1941; *m*; two *s* one *d*. *Educ:* Larbert, Denny and Falkirk High Schs; Woodside Sen. Secondary Sch., Glasgow. Joined Labour Party, 1962; former Lab. Party Organiser for Glasgow; Member: TGWU; Select Cttee, Scottish Affairs; Hon. Sec., Scottish Gp of Labour MPs; Private Member's Bill, The Solvent Abuse (Scotland) Act, May 1983. Member: Glasgow Corp., 1972–75; Strathclyde Reg. Council, 1974–79 (Chm., Manpower Cttee); Chm., Manpower Cttee, Convention of Scottish Local Authorities; Mem., Local Authorities Conditions of Service Adv. Bd. *Address:* House of Commons, SW1; 32 Enterkin Street, Glasgow G32 7BA.

MARSHALL, Sir Denis (Alfred), Kt 1982; solicitor; with Barlow Lyde & Gilbert, 1937–83, now a consultant; *b* 1 June 1916; *s* of Frederick Herbert Marshall and Winifred Mary Marshall; *m* 1st, 1949, Joan Edith Straker (*d* 1974); one *s*; 2nd, 1975, Jane Lygo. *Educ:* Dulwich Coll. Served War: HAC, 1939; XX Lancs Fusiliers (Temp. Major), 1940–46. Articled to Barlow Lyde & Gilbert, Solicitors, 1932–37; admitted Solicitor, 1937. Mem. Council, Law Soc., 1966–86, Vice-Pres., 1980–81, Pres., 1981–82. Member: Insurance Brokers Registration Council, 1979–; Criminal Injuries Compensation Bd, 1982–90; Council, FIMBRA, 1986–90. *Recreations:* sailing, gardening. *Address:* Redways, Warfleet Road, Dartmouth, S Devon TQ6 9BZ. *Clubs:* Naval and Military; Royal Dart Yacht.

MARSHALL, Dr Edmund Ian; Lecturer in Management Science, University of Bradford, since 1984; *b* 31 May 1940; *s* of Harry and Koorali Marshall; *m* 1969, Margaret Pamela, *d* of John and Maud Antill, New Southgate, N11; one *d*. *Educ:* Magdalen Coll., Oxford (Mackinnon Schol.). Double 1st cl. hons Maths, and Junior Mathematical Prize, Oxon, 1961; PhD Liverpool, 1965. Various univ. appts in Pure Maths, 1962–66; mathematician in industry, 1967–71. Mem., Wallasey County Borough Council, 1963–65. Contested (L) Louth Div. of Lincs, 1964 and 1966; joined Labour Party, 1967. MP (Lab) Goole, May 1971–1983; PPS to Sec. of State for NI, 1974–76, to Home Sec., 1976–79; Chm., Trade and Industry sub-cttee of House of Commons Expenditure Cttee, 1976–79; Mem., Chairmen's Panel in House of Commons, 1981–82; Opposition Whip, 1982–83; joined SDP, 1985. Contested (SDP/Alliance) Bridlington, 1987. Non-Exec. Dir, Wakefield FHSA, 1990–. Member: British Methodist Conf., 1969–72, 1980 and 1985–91 (Vice-Pres., 1992); World Methodist Conf., 1971; British Council of Churches, 1972–78. Governor: Woodhouse Grove Sch., Bradford, 1986–; Wakefield Grammar Schools Foundn, 1989–. *Publications:* (jtly) Europe: What Next? (Fabian pamphlet), 1969; Parliament and the Public, 1982; various papers in mathematical and other jls. *Recreations:* word games, music. *Address:* 14 Belgravia Road, Wakefield, West Yorks WF1 3JP. *Club:* Yorks County Cricket.

MARSHALL, Dr Frank Graham, FIEE; Group Research and Development Director, Colt Group Ltd, since 1990; *b* 28 March 1942; *s* of Frank and Vera Marshall; *m* 1965, Patricia Anne (*née* Bestwick); two *s* one *d*. *Educ:* Birmingham Univ. (BSc Physics); Nottingham Univ. (PhD Physics). FIEE 1984. Joined Royal Signals and Radar Estabt (MoD) (Physics and Electronic Device Res.), 1966; Sen. Principal Scientific Officer, 1975–80; seconded to HM Diplomatic Service as Science and Technology Counsellor, Tokyo, 1980–82. Man. Dir, Plessey Electronic Systems Res., later Plessey Res. Roke Manor, 1983–87; Technical Dir, Plessey Naval Systems, 1987–90. (Jtly) IEEE Best Paper award, 1973; (jtly) Wolfe Award, 1973. *Publications:* numerous papers on electronic signal processing devices in various jls. *Recreations:* country life, electronics. *Address:* Colt Group Ltd, New Lane, Havant, Hants PO9 2LY.

MARSHALL, Fredda, (Mrs Herbert Marshall); *see* Brilliant, F.

MARSHALL, Geoffrey, MA, PhD; FBA 1971; Fellow and Tutor in Politics, The Queen's College, Oxford, since 1957; *b* 22 April 1929; *s* of Leonard William and Kate Marshall; *m* 1957, Patricia Ann Christine Woodcock; two *s*. *Educ:* Arnold Sch., Blackpool, Lancs; Manchester Univ. MA Manchester, MA Oxon, PhD Glasgow. Research Fellow, Nuffield Coll., 1955–57. Andrew Dixon White Vis. Prof., Cornell Univ., Ithaca, NY, 1985–. Mem. Oxford City Council, 1965–74; Sheriff of Oxford, 1970–71. *Publications:* Parliamentary Sovereignty and the Commonwealth, 1957; Some Problems of the Constitution (with G. C. Moodie), 1959; Police and Government, 1965; Constitutional Theory, 1971; Constitutional Conventions, 1984; Ministerial Responsibility, 1989. *Recreation:* middle-aged squash. *Address:* The Queen's College, Oxford. *T:* Oxford (0865) 279176.

MARSHALL, Hazel Eleanor, (Mrs H. C. J. Marshall); *see* Williamson, H. E.

MARSHALL, Howard Wright; retired; Under Secretary, Department of Transport, 1978–82; *b* 11 June 1923; *s* of Philip Marshall, MBE, and Mary Marshall; *m* 1st (marr. diss.); two *s*; 2nd, 1963, Carol Yvonne (*née* Oddy); one *d*. *Educ:* Prudhoe West Elementary, Northumberland; Queen Elizabeth Grammar Sch., Hexham. Served War, RAF, 1941–46; POW, 1943–45. Min. of Health, Newcastle upon Tyne, 1940; Regional Offices, Ministries of Health, Local Govt and Planning, Housing and Local Govt, 1948–55; HQ, Min. of Housing and Local Govt, 1955–59; National Parks Commn, 1959–62; Min. of Housing and Local Govt, later DoE, 1962; Asst Sec., 1968; Under Sec., 1976; Regional Dir, Eastern Region, Depts of Environment and Transport, 1976–78; Chm., East Anglia Regional Economic Planning Bd, 1976–78. *Recreations:* gardening, sport. *Address:* Brackenwood, Farthing Green Lane, Stoke Poges, Bucks SL2 4JH. *T:* Fulmer (0753) 662974. *Clubs:* Caterpillar; Wexham Park Golf and Leisure.

MARSHALL, Rev. Canon Hugh Phillips; Chief Secretary, General Synod of Church of England's Advisory Board of Ministry, since 1990; *b* 13 July 1934; *s* of Dr Leslie Phillips Marshall and Dr (Catherine) Mary Marshall; *m* 1962, Diana Elizabeth Gosling; one *s* three *d. Educ:* Marlborough Coll.; Sidney Sussex Coll., Cambridge (BA, MA); Bishop's Hostel, Lincoln. RN, 1952–54. Ordained deacon 1959, priest 1960, Dio. London; Curate, St Stephen with St John, Westminster, 1959–65; Vicar of St Paul, Tupsley, Hereford, 1965–74; Vicar and Team Rector of Wimbledon, 1974–87; Rural Dean of Merton, 1979–85; Vicar of Mitcham, Surrey, 1987–90; Hon. Canon of Southwark Cathedral, 1989, Hon. Canon Emeritus, 1990. *Recreations:* broadcasting, DIY, cooking, travel. *Address:* 30 Woodville Road, Morden, Surrey SM4 5AF. *T:* 081–542 3962.

MARSHALL, James; MP (Lab) Leicester South, Oct. 1974–1983, and since 1987; *b* 13 March 1941; *m* 1962, Shirley (marr. diss.), *d* of W. Ellis, Sheffield; one *s* one *d; m* 1986, Susan, *d* of G. Carter, Leicester. *Educ:* City Grammar Sch., Sheffield; Leeds Univ. BSc, PhD. Joined Lab Party, 1960. Mem., Leeds City Council, 1965–68; Leicester City Council: Mem., 1971–76; Chm., Finance Cttee, 1972–74; Leader, 1974. Contested (Lab): Harborough, 1970; Leicester South, Feb. 1974, 1983. An Asst Govt Whip, 1977–79. *Address:* Flat 15, The Woodlands, 31 Knighton Road, Leicester. *T:* Leicester (0533) 708237.

MARSHALL, Jeremy; *see* Marshall, John J. S.

MARSHALL, John; *see* Sessions, J.

MARSHALL, John, MA; JP; Headmaster, Robert Gordon's College, Aberdeen, 1960–77; *b* 1 July 1915; *s* of Alexander Marshall and Margaret Nimmo Carmichael; *m* 1940, May Robinson Williamson; two *d. Educ:* Airdrie Acad.; Glasgow Univ. MA (1st cl. hons Classics), 1935; Medley Memorial Prizeman, History 1934; John Clark Schol., Classics, 1935. Asst Master: Bluevale Sch., 1937–39; Coatbridge Sec. Sch., 1939–41; Principal Teacher of Classics, North Berwick High Sch., 1941–50; Rector, North Berwick High Sch., 1950–60. Mem., Adv. Coun. on Educn for Scotland, 1955–57; Trustee, Scottish Sec. Schools Travel Trust, 1960–78 (Chm., 1971–78; Sec., 1978–80); Pres., Headmasters' Assoc. of Scotland, 1962–64; Member: Gen. Teaching Coun. for Scotland, 1966–70; Exec. Cttee, UCCA, 1970–78; Co-ordinator, Scottish Scheme of Oxford Colls' Admissions, 1978–84. Trustee, Gordon Cook Foundn, 1974–. JP City of Aberdeen, 1967. *Publications:* Off the Beaten Track in Switzerland, 1989; The Visitor's Guide to Switzerland, 1990; The Visitor's Guide to The Rhine and Mosel, 1992; numerous articles on educational and travel subjects. *Recreations:* photography, writing, language studies. *Address:* 11 Hazledene Road, Aberdeen AB1 8LB. *T:* Aberdeen (0224) 318003. *Club:* Royal Northern and University (Aberdeen).

MARSHALL, Prof. John, CBE 1990; FRCP, FRCPE; Professor of Clinical Neurology in the University of London, 1971–87, now Emeritus; *b* 16 April 1922; *s* of James Herbert and Bertha Marshall; *m* 1946, Margaret Eileen Hughes; two *s* three *d. Educ:* Univ. of Manchester (MB ChB 1946, MD 1951, DSc 1981). FRCPE 1957, FRCP 1966; DPM 1952. Sen. Registrar, Manchester Royal Infirmary, 1947–49; Lt-Col RAMC, 1949–51; MRC research worker, 1951–53; Sen. Lectr in Neurology, Univ. of Edinburgh, 1954–56; Reader in Clinical Neurology, Univ. of London, 1956–71. Chm., Attendance Allowance Bd, 1982–. Knight of the Order of St Sylvester (Holy See), 1962, KCSG 1986 (KSG 1964). Auenbrugger Medal, Univ. of Graz, 1983. *Publications:* The Management of Cerebrovascular Disease, 1965, 3rd edn 1976; The Infertile Period, Principles and Practice, 1963, 2nd rev. edn 1969. *Recreations:* gardening, walking. *Address:* 203 Robin Hood Way, SW20 0AA. *T:* 081–942 5509.

MARSHALL, John Alexander, CB 1982; Deputy Secretary, Northern Ireland Office, 1979–82; *b* 2 Sept. 1922; *s* of James Alexander Marshall and Mena Dorothy Marshall; *m* 1947, Pauline Mary (*née* Taylor); six *s. Educ:* LCC elem. sch.; Hackney Downs School. Paymaster General's Office, 1939; FO, 1943; HM Treasury, 1947: Principal, 1953; Asst Sec., 1963; Under-Sec., 1972; Cabinet Office, 1974–77; Northern Ireland Office, 1977–82. Gen. Sec., Distressed Gentlefolk's Aid Assoc., 1982–89. *Recreations:* literature, music. *Address:* 48 Long Lane, Ickenham, Mddx UB10 8TA. *T:* Ruislip (0895) 672020.

MARSHALL, (John) Jeremy (Seymour); Chief Executive, De La Rue Co. plc, since 1989; *b* 18 April 1938; *s* of late Edward Pope Marshall and of Nita Helen Marshall (*née* Seymour); *m* 1962, Juliette Butterley; one *s* two *d. Educ:* Sherborne Sch.; New Coll., Oxford (MA Chem.). Nat. Service, Royal Signals, 1956–58. Wiggins Teape, 1962–64; Riker Labs, 1964–67; CIBA Agrochemicals, 1967–71; Hanson Trust: Managing Director: Dufaylite Developments, 1971–76; SLD Olding, 1976–79; Chief Executive: Lindustries, 1979–86; Imperial Foods, 1986–87; BAA plc, 1987–89. FBIM 1980; FCIT 1989. *Recreations:* squash, lawn tennis, music. *Address:* Willow House, Bourn, Cambridge CB3 7SQ. *T:* Caxton (0954) 719435. *Clubs:* Army and Navy, Royal Automobile.

MARSHALL, John Leslie; MP (C) Hendon South, since 1987; Consultant, Carr, Kitcat & Aitken, since 1991; *b* 19 Aug. 1940; *s* of late Prof. William Marshall and Margaret Marshall; *m* 1978, Susan Elizabeth, *d* of David Mount, Petham, Kent; two *s. Educ:* Glasgow Academy; St Andrews Univ. (MA). ACIS. Asst Lecturer in Economics, Glasgow Univ., 1962–66; Lectr in Economics, Aberdeen Univ., 1966–70; Mem., Internat. Stock Exchange; Carr Sebag & Co., 1979–82; Partner, 1983–86, Dir, 1986–90, Kitcat & Aitken. Contested (C): Dundee East, 1964 and 1966; Lewisham East, Feb. 1974. MEP (C) London N, 1979–89; Asst Whip, EDG, Eur. Parlt, 1986–89. PPS to Minister for the Disabled, Dept of Social Security, 1989–90, to Sec. of State for Social Security, 1990–. Member: Aberdeen Town Council, 1968–70; Ealing Borough Council, 1971–86 (Chm., Finance Bd, 1978–82; Chm., Local Services Cttee, 1982–84). Dir, Beta Global Emerging Markets Investment Trust plc, 1990–. *Publications:* articles on economics in several professional jls; pamphlets on economic questions for Aims. *Recreations:* watching cricket, football and Rugby; gardening, bridge, theatre. *Address:* c/o House of Commons, SW1A 0AA. *Clubs:* Carlton; Middlesex County Cricket.

MARSHALL, John Roger; Joint Managing Director, John Mowlem and Co. PLC, since 1989; *b* 20 April 1944; *s* of John Henry Marshall and Betty Alaine Rosetta Marshall; *m* 1968, Marilyn Anne Archer; one *s* two *d. Educ:* Rendcomb College; Bristol Univ. (BSc Hons Civil Eng.). MICE, CEng, FIHT. Balfour Beatty Consultants, W. C. French and R. McGregor & Sons, 1966–70; Mears Construction, 1970–78; Henry Boot, 1978–83; Man. Dir, Mowlem Management, 1983–87; Dir, John Mowlem & Co., 1987–. *Recreations:* arts (visual, dramatic and operatic), exercise. *Address:* Redland, Bristol.

MARSHALL, Margaret Anne; concert and opera singer; soprano; *b* 4 Jan. 1949; *d* of Robert and Margaret Marshall; *m* 1970, Dr Graeme Griffiths King Davidson; two *d. Educ:* High School, Stirling; Royal Scottish Academy of Music and Drama (DRSAMD). Performances in Festival Hall, Barbican, Covent Garden; concerts and opera in major European events; numerous recordings. First Prize, Munich International Competition, 1974. *Recreations:* squash, golf. *Address:* Woodside, Main Street, Gargunnock, Stirling FK8 3BP. *Club:* Gleneagles Country.

MARSHALL, Mark Anthony, CMG 1991; HM Diplomatic Service; Ambassador to the Republic of Yemen (formerly Yemen Arab Republic) and the Republic of Djibouti, since 1987; *b* 8 Oct. 1937; *s* of late Thomas Humphrey Marshall, CMG and of Nadine, *d* of late Mark Hambourg; *m* 1970, Penelope Lesley Seymour; two *d. Educ:* Westminster Sch.; Trinity Coll., Cambridge (BA). MECAS, 1958; Third Sec., Amman, 1960; FO, 1962; Commercial Officer, Dubai, 1964; FO, 1965; Aden, 1967; First Sec., 1968; Asst Dir of Treasury Centre for Admin. Studies, 1968; UK Delegn to Brussels Conf., 1970; First Sec./Head of Chancery, Rabat, 1972; First Sec., FCO, 1976; Counsellor: Tripoli, 1979–80; Damascus, 1980–83; Head of Finance Dept, FCO, 1984–87. *Recreations:* swimming, golf, fell walking. *Address:* c/o Foreign and Commonwealth Office, King Charles Street, SW1.

MARSHALL, Martin John, CMG 1967; HM Diplomatic Service, retired; *b* 21 March 1914; *s* of late Harry Edmund Marshall and late Kate Ann (*née* Bishop); *m* 1938, Olive Emily Alice, *d* of Thomas and Olive King; two *d. Educ:* Westminster City Sch.; London Sch. of Economics, University of London. Customs and Excise Officer, 1935–39; Technical Officer, Min. of Aircraft Prod., 1940–46; Principal, Min. of Supply, 1947–50. Called to Bar, Gray's Inn, 1947. Trade Commissioner: Montreal, 1950–52; Atlantic Provinces, 1953; Alberta, 1954–57; Principal Trade Commissioner: Montreal, 1957–60; Calcutta (for Eastern India), 1961–63; Dep. High Comr, Sydney, 1963–67; Consul-General, Cleveland, Ohio, 1968–71; Dep. High Comr, Bombay, 1971–74. Dir, Finance/Administration, Royal Assoc. for Disability and Rehabilitation, 1977–79. *Recreation:* golf. *Address:* 8 Sunnyside Place, SW19 4SJ. *T:* 081–946 5570. *Club:* Royal Wimbledon Golf.

MARSHALL, Sir Michael; *see* Marshall, Sir R. M.

MARSHALL, Rt. Rev. Michael Eric, MA; Founding Episcopal Director, Anglican Institute, St Louis, Missouri, since 1984; an Assistant Bishop, Diocese of London, since 1984; *b* Lincoln, 14 April 1936. *Educ:* Lincoln Sch.; Christ's Coll., Cambridge (Tancred Scholar, Upper II: Hist. Pt 1 and Theol Pt 1a, MA); Cuddesdon Theological Coll. Deacon, 1960; Curate, St Peter's, Spring Hill, Birmingham, 1960–62; Tutor, Ely Theological Coll. and Minor Canon of Ely Cath., 1962–64; Chaplain in London Univ., 1964–69; Vicar of All Saints', Margaret Street, W1, 1969–75; Bishop Suffragan of Woolwich, 1975–84. Preb. of Wightring in Chichester Cathedral and Wightring Theol Lectr, 1990–. Dir of Evangelism, Chichester Theol Coll., 1991–. Founder and Director: Inst. of Christian Studies, 1970; Internat. Inst. for Anglican Studies, 1982; Member: Gen. Synod, 1970, also Diocesan and Deanery Synods; Liturgical Commn; Anglican/Methodist Liaison Commn until 1974; SPCK Governing Body; USPG Governing Body; Exam. Chap. to Bp of London, 1974. Has frequently broadcast on BBC and commercial radio; also lectured, preached and broadcast in Canada and USA. *Publications:* A Pattern of Faith, 1966 (co-author); Glory under Your Feet, 1978; Pilgrimage and Promise, 1981; Renewal in Worship, 1982; The Anglican Church, Today and Tomorrow, 1984; Christian Orthodoxy Revisited, USA 1985; The Gospel Conspiracy in the Episcopal Church, 1986; The Restless Heart, USA 1987; Founder and co-editor, Christian Quarterly. *Recreations:* music, cooking. *Address:* The Anglican Institute, 6330 Ellenwood Avenue, PO Box 11887, St Louis, Missouri 63105, USA; 18 Andrewes House, The Barbican, EC2. *Club:* University (St Louis, Mo, USA).

MARSHALL, Noël Hedley, CMG 1986; HM Diplomatic Service; UK Permanent Representative to the Council of Europe (with the personal rank of Ambassador), since 1990; *b* 26 Nov. 1934; *s* of Arthur Hedley Marshall, *qv. Educ:* Leighton Park Sch.; Lawrenceville Sch., NJ (E-SU Exchange Scholar, 1953–54); St John's Coll., Cambridge (BA 1957; Sir Joseph Larmor Award, 1957). Pres., Cambridge Union Soc., 1957. Entered Foreign (later Diplomatic) Service; FO, 1957–59; Third Sec., Prague, 1959–61; FO, 1961–63; Second (later First) Sec., Moscow, 1963–65; CRO, 1965–66; First Sec. (Economic): Karachi, 1966–67; Rawalpindi, 1967–70; Chargé d'affaires ai, Ulan Bator, 1967; FCO, 1970–74; First Sec. (later Counsellor) Press, Office of UK Permanent Rep. to European Communities, Brussels, 1974–77; NATO Defence Coll., Rome, 1977–78; Counsellor, UK Delegn to Cttee on Disarmament, Geneva, 1978–81; Head of N America Dept, FCO, 1982–85; Overseas Inspector, 1985–86; Minister, Moscow, 1986–89; Co-ordinator, British Days in the USSR, Kiev, 1990. *Recreations:* sailing, the theatre. *Address:* c/o Foreign and Commonwealth Office, SW1A 2AH. *Clubs:* Royal Ocean Racing; Europe House.

MARSHALL, Norman Bertram, MA, ScD; FRS 1970; Professor and Head of Department of Zoology and Comparative Physiology, Queen Mary College, University of London, 1972–77, now Professor Emeritus; *b* 5 Feb. 1915; *s* of Arthur Harold and Ruby Eva Marshall; *m* 1944, Olga Stonehouse; one *s* three *d. Educ:* Cambridgeshire High Sch.; Downing Coll., Cambridge. Plankton Biologist, Dept of Oceanography, UC Hull, 1937–41; Army (mostly involved in operational research), 1941–44; seconded from Army for Service in Operation Tabarin to Antarctic, 1944–46; British Museum (Natural History): Marine fishes, 1947–72; Sen. Principal Scientific Officer, 1962–72. In charge of Manihine Expedns to Red Sea, 1948–50; Senior Biologist, Te Vega Expedn, 1966–67. Polar Medal (Silver), 1948; Rosenstiel Gold Medal for distinguished services to marine science; Senior Queen's Fellow in Marine Science, Aust., 1982. *Publications:* Aspects of Deep Sea Biology, 1954; The Life of Fishes, 1965; Explorations in the Life of Fishes, 1970; Ocean Life, 1971; Developments in Deep Sea Biology, 1979; various papers in learned jls. *Recreations:* music, fishing, golf. *Address:* 6 Park Lane, Saffron Walden, Essex. *T:* Saffron Walden (0799) 22528.

MARSHALL, Prof. Sir (Oshley) Roy, Kt 1974; CBE 1968; High Commissioner for Barbados in the United Kingdom, 1989–91; Vice-Chancellor, Hull University, 1979–85, Emeritus Professor since 1985; *b* 21 Oct. 1920; *s* of Fitz Roy and Corene Carmelita Marshall; *m* 1945, Eirwen Lloyd; one *s* three *d. Educ:* Harrison Coll., Barbados, WI; Pembroke Coll., Cambridge; University Coll., London (Fellow, 1985). Barbados Scholar, 1938; BA 1945, MA 1948 Cantab; PhD London 1948. Barrister-at-Law, Inner Temple, 1947. University Coll., London: Asst Lecturer, 1946–48; Lecturer, 1948–56; Sub-Dean, Faculty of Law, 1949–56; Prof. of Law and Head of Dept of Law, Univ. of Sheffield, 1956–69, Vis. Prof. in Faculty of Law, 1969–80; on secondment to University of Ife, Ibadan, Nigeria, as Prof. of Law and Dean of the Faculty of Law, 1963–65; Vice-Chancellor, Univ. of West Indies, 1969–74; Sec.-Gen., Cttee of Vice-Chancellors and Principals, 1974–79. Chairman: Commonwealth Educn Liaison Cttee, 1974–81; Cttee on Commonwealth Legal Co-operation, 1975; Commonwealth Standing Cttee on Student Mobility, 1982–; Council for Educn in the Commonwealth, 1985–91; Review Cttee on Cave Hill Campus, Univ. of WI, 1986; Constitutional Commn on the Turks and Caicos Islands, 1986; Member: Police Complaints Bd, 1977–81; Council, RPMS, 1976–83; Council, ACU, 1979–85; Management Cttee, Universities Superannuation Scheme Ltd, 1980–85; UGC for Univ. of S Pacific, 1987; Chm., Bd of Governors, Hymers Coll., Hull, 1985–89; Vice-Chm., Governing Body of Commonwealth Inst., 1980–81; Mem., Bd of Governors, Commonwealth of Learning, 1988–91; Trustee, Commonwealth Foundn, 1981. Hon. LLD: Sheffield, 1972; West Indies, 1976; Hull, 1986. *Publications:* The Assignment of Choses in Action, 1950; A Casebook on Trusts (with J. A. Nathan), 1967; Theobald on Wills, 12th edn, 1963. *Recreations:* racing and cricket. *Address:* Kirk House, Kirk Croft, Cottingham, North Humberside HU16 4AU. *Club:* Commonwealth Trust.

MARSHALL, Percy Edwin Alan J.; *see* Johnson-Marshall.

MARSHALL, Peter, QPM 1979; Commissioner of Police for the City of London, 1978–85; *b* 21 June 1930; *s* of late Christopher George Marshall and Sylvia Marshall; *m* 1954, Bridget Frances Humphreys; three *s* one *d.* *Educ:* St Clement Danes Holborn Estate Grammar Sch. Trooper, 8th Royal Tank Regt, 1948–50. Police Officer, Metropolitan Police, 1950–78. *Recreations:* reading, gardening. *Address:* The Cottage, Cock Lane, Elham, Canterbury, Kent CT4 6TL.

MARSHALL, Sir Peter (Harold Reginald), KCMG 1983 (CMG 1974); Chairman: Commonwealth Trust, since 1988; Royal Commonwealth Society, since 1988; President, Queen Elizabeth House, Oxford, since 1990; *b* 30 July 1924; 3rd *s* of late R. H. Marshall; *m* 1st, 1957, Patricia Rendell Stoddart (*d* 1981); one *s* one *d*; 2nd, 1989, Judith, *widow* of E. W. F. Tomlin. *Educ:* Tonbridge; Corpus Christi Coll., Cambridge (Hon. Fellow 1989). RAFVR, 1943–46. HM Foreign (later Diplomatic) Service, 1949–83: FO, 1949–52; 2nd Sec. and Private Sec. to Ambassador, Washington, 1952–56; FO, 1956–60; on staff of Civil Service Selection Board, 1960; 1st Sec. and Head of Chancery, Baghdad, 1961, and Bangkok, 1962–64; Asst Dir of Treasury Centre for Administrative Studies, 1965–66; Counsellor, UK Mission, Geneva, 1966–69, Counsellor and Head of Chancery, Paris, 1969–71; Head of Financial Policy and Aid Dept, FCO, 1971–73; Asst Under-Sec. of State, FCO, 1973–75; UK Rep. on Econ. and Social Council of UN, 1975–79; Ambassador and UK Perm. Rep. to Office of UN and Other Internat. Organisations at Geneva, 1979–83; Commonwealth Dep. Sec. Gen. (Econ.), 1983–88. Vice Pres., Council for Educn in World Citizenship, 1985–; Governor, E-SU of the Commonwealth, 1984–90; Trustee, King George VI and Queen Elizabeth Foundn of St Catharine's, 1987–. Vis. Lectr, Diplomatic Acad. of London, 1989–. *Publications:* The Dynamics of Diplomacy, 1990; Chapter in The United Kingdom—The United Nations, 1990. *Recreations:* music, golf. *Address:* c/o Commonwealth Trust, 18 Northumberland Avenue, WC2N 5BJ. *T:* 071–930 6733.

MARSHALL, Peter Izod; Chairman, Ocean Group (formerly Ocean Transport and Trading), since 1987; *b* 16 April 1927; *s* of Charles and Gwendoline Marshall; *m* 1955, Davina Mary (*née* Hart); one *s* one *d.* *Educ:* Buxton College. FCA; LRAM. Commercial Dir, EMI Electronics, 1962–67; Dir of Finance, Norcros, 1967–77; Dep. Chief Exec., Plessey Co., 1977–87. *Recreations:* music, swimming, golf. *Address:* Moyns, Christchurch Road, Virginia Water, Surrey GU25 4PJ. *T:* Wentworth (09904) 2118. *Clubs:* Les Ambassadeurs; Wentworth.

MARSHALL, Prof. Peter James, DPhil; Rhodes Professor of Imperial History, King's College, London, since 1980; *b* 28 Oct. 1933; *s* of Edward Hannaford Marshall and Madeleine (*née* Shuttleworth). *Educ:* Wellington College; Wadham Coll., Oxford (BA 1957, MA, DPhil 1962). Military service, King's African Rifles, Kenya, 1953–54. Assistant Lecturer, Lecturer, Reader, Professor, History Dept, King's Coll., London, 1959–80. Mem., History Wkg Gp, National Curriculum, 1989–90. Vice-Pres., RHistS, 1987–. Editor, Journal of Imperial and Commonwealth History, 1975–81; Associate Editor, Writings and Speeches of Edmund Burke, 1976–. *Publications:* Impeachment of Warren Hastings, 1965; Problems of Empire: Britain and India 1757–1813, 1968; (ed, with J. A. Woods) Correspondence of Edmund Burke, vol. VII, 1968; The British Discovery of Hinduism, 1972; East India Fortunes, 1976; (ed) Writings and Speeches of Edmund Burke, vol. V, 1981, vol. VI, 1991; (with Glyndwr Williams) The Great Map of Mankind, 1982; Bengal: the British bridgehead (New Cambridge History of India, Vol. II, 2), 1988; articles in Economic History Rev., History, Modern Asian Studies, etc. *Address:* 7 Malting Lane, Braughing, Ware, Herts SG11 2QZ. *T:* Ware (0920) 822232.

MARSHALL, Air Cdre Philippa Frances, CB 1971; OBE 1956; Director of the Women's Royal Air Force, 1969–73; *b* 4 Nov. 1920; *d* of late Horace Plant Marshall, Stoke-on-Trent. *Educ:* St Dominic's High Sch., Stoke-on-Trent. Joined WAAF, 1941; Comd WRAF Admin. Officer, Strike Comd, 1968–69, Air Cdre 1969; ADC, 1969–73. *Recreations:* music, cookery. *Club:* Royal Air Force.

MARSHALL, Sir Robert (Braithwaite), KCB 1971 (CB 1968); MBE 1945; Chairman, National Water Council, 1978–82; *b* 10 Jan. 1920; *s* of Alexander Halford Marshall and Edith Mary Marshall (*née* Lockyer); *m* 1945, Diana Elizabeth Westlake; one *s* three *d.* *Educ:* Sherborne Sch.; Corpus Christi Coll., Cambridge. Mod. Langs, Pt I, 1938–39; Economics Pts I and II, 1945–47. BA Cambridge. Foreign Office temp. appointment, 1939–45. Entered Home Civil Service, 1947; Ministry of Works, 1947–50; Private Sec. to Sec., Cabinet Office, 1950–53; Min. of Works, 1953–62; Min. of Aviation, 1962–66; Min. of Power, 1966–69; Min. of Technology, 1969–70; Under-Sec., 1964; Dep. Sec. 1966; Second Perm. Sec., 1970; Secretary (Industry), DTI, 1970–73; Second Permanent Sec., DoE, 1973–78. Chm., Cair Ltd, 1985–86. Trustee, Wateraid and other trusts. Mem. and Vice Chm. Council, Surrey Univ., 1975–87; Chm. Governors, W Surrey Coll. of Art, 1985–89. Coronation Medal, 1953. *Recreations:* travel, gardening, music and arts. *Address:* 1 Shatcombe, Uploders, Bridport, Dorset DT6 4NR. *T:* Powerstock (030885) 348.

MARSHALL, Robert Leckie, OBE 1945; Principal, Co-operative College, and Chief Education Officer, Co-operative Union Ltd, 1946–77; *b* 27 Aug. 1913; *s* of Robert Marshall and Mary Marshall; *m* 1944, Beryl Broad; one *s.* *Educ:* Univ. of St Andrews (MA Mediaeval and Modern History; MA 1st Cl. Hons English Lit.); Commonwealth Fellow, Yale Univ. (MA Polit. Theory and Govt). Scottish Office, 1937–39. Served War, 1939–46: RASC and AEC; finally Comdt, Army Sch. of Educn. Pres., Co-op. Congress, 1976. Missions on Co-op. develt to Tanganyika, Nigeria, India, Kenya, S Yemen and Thailand. Member: Gen. Adv. Council and Complaints Rev. Bd, IBA, 1973–77; Monopolies and Mergers Commn, 1976–82; Distributive Studies Bd, Business Educn Council, 1976–79; Chm., Quest House, Loughborough, 1980–86; Vice-Chm., Charnwood Community Council, 1980–90. Mem. Court, Loughborough Univ. of Technol., 1981–. Hon. MA Open Univ., 1977; Hon. DLitt Loughborough Univ. of Technol., 1977. Editor, Jl of Soc. for Co-operative Studies, 1967–. *Publications:* Lippen on Angus—a celebration of North Angus Co-operative Society, 1983; contribs to educnl and co-op jls. *Recreations:* walking, reading, swimming, golf. *Address:* Holly Cottage, 15 Beacon Road, Woodhouse Eaves, Loughborough, Leics LE12 8RN. *T:* Woodhouse Eaves (0509) 890612.

MARSHALL, Sir (Robert) Michael, Kt 1990; MP (C) Arundel since Feb. 1974; *b* 21 June 1930; *s* of late Robert Ernest and Margaret Mary Marshall, Brookside Cottages, Hathersage; *m* 1972, Caroline Victoria Oliphant, *d* of late Alexander Hutchison of Strathairly; two step *d.* *Educ:* Bradfield Coll.; Harvard and Stanford Univs. MBA Harvard 1960. Joined United Steel Cos Ltd, 1951; Branch Man., Calcutta, 1954–58; Man. Dir, Bombay, 1960–64; Commercial Dir, Workington, 1964–66; Man. Dir, Head Wrightson Export Co. Ltd, 1967–69; Management Consultant, Urwick Orr & Partners Ltd, 1969–74. Parly Under-Sec. of State, DoI, 1979–81. Chairman: Parly Space Cttee, 1982–; IPU, 1987–90 (Vice Chm., 1985–87); Parly IT Cttee, 1986– (Vice-Chm., 1982–86); Vice-Chairman: Cons. Party Parly Industry Cttee, 1976–79; All Party Parly Cttee on Management, 1974–79; Mem., Select Cttee on Defence, 1982–87; Parly Adviser: British Aerospace, 1982–; Cable and Wireless, 1982–; SWET, 1984–; Williams Hldgs, 1988–. Member: Equity; BAFTA. Hon. DL New England Coll., 1982. FRSA. *Publications:* Top Hat and Tails: the story of Jack Buchanan, 1978; (ed) The Stanley Holloway Monologues, 1979; More Monologues and Songs, 1980; The Book of Comic and Dramatic Monologues, 1981; The Timetable of Technology, 1982; No End of Jobs, 1984; Gentlemen and Players, 1987; (contrib.) A Celebration of Lords and Commons Cricket, 1989; My Lord's, 1990. *Recreations:* writing books and for radio and TV, cricket commentating, golf. *Address:* Old Inn House, Slindon, Arundel, W Sussex BN18 0RB. *Clubs:* Garrick, MCC, Lord's Taverners; Sussex; Royal & Ancient Golf (St Andrews), Goodwood Golf.

MARSHALL, Maj.-Gen. Roger Sydenham, CB 1974; TD 1948; Director of Army Legal Services, Ministry of Defence, 1971–73, retired; *b* 15 July 1913; 2nd *s* of Robert Sydenham Cole Marshall and Enid Edith Langton Cole; *m* 1940, Beryl Marie, *d* of William Vaughan Rayner; one *d.* Solicitor, Supreme Court, 1938. Commnd N Staffs Regt, TA, 1933; mobilised TA, 1939; comd 365 Batt. 65th Searchlight Regt, RA, 1942–44; Trans. Army Legal Services, 1948; DADALS: HQ MELF, 1948–49; HQ E Africa, 1949–52; GHQ MELF, 1952–53; WO, 1953–55; ADALS: WO, 1955–56; HQ BAOR, 1956–58; WO, 1960–61; HQ E Africa Comd, 1961–62; DDALS, GHQ FARELF, 1962–63; Col Legal Staff, WO, 1964–69; Brig. Legal Staff, 1969–71; Maj.-Gen. 1971. *Recreations:* golf, reading history. *Address:* Aynho Park, Aynho, near Banbury, Oxon.

MARSHALL, Sir Roy; *see* Marshall, Sir O. R.

MARSHALL, Hon. Russell; *see* Marshall, Hon. C. R.

MARSHALL, Thomas Daniel; Member, Newcastle City Council, since 1986; *b* 6 Nov. 1929; *s* of James William and Leonora Mary Marshall; *m* 1953, Eileen James; one *s.* *Educ:* St George's RC Elementary Sch., Bell's Close, Newcastle upon Tyne; Ruskin Coll.; Open Univ. Post Office, then Nat. Assistance Board, 1960; DHSS, 1966. Councillor, Newburn UDC, 1967; Mem., Tyne and Wear CC, 1974–86 (Chm., 1978–79). Chairman: Northern Region IT Inst.; NE Region IT Enterprise Agency; Tyne and Wear Enterprise Trust; Throckley Community Hall Ltd; Newburn Riverside Recreation Assoc. Ltd; Director: Tyne and Wear Innovation Centre and Development Co.; Bowes Railway Co.; Tyneside Stables Project Ltd; MARI Advanced Microelectronics Ltd; Tyne Theatre and Opera House; Trustee: Industrial Monuments Trust; Building Preservation Trust Ltd; Grange Welfare Assoc. *Recreation:* reading. *Address:* 7 Hallow Drive, Throckley, Newcastle upon Tyne NE15 9AQ. *T:* 091–267 0956. *Clubs:* Grange Welfare; Newburn Memorial (Newcastle).

MARSHALL, Thurgood; Associate Justice of US Supreme Court, 1967–91; *b* 2 July 1908; *s* of William C. and Norma A. Marshall; *m* 1st, 1929, Vivian Burey (*d* 1955); 2nd, 1955, Cecilia A. Suyat; two *s.* *Educ:* Lincoln Univ. (AB 1930); Howard Univ. Law Sch. Admitted Maryland Bar, 1933. Special Counsel, NAACP, 1938–50 (Asst, 1936–38); Dir, NAACP Legal Defense and Educ. Fund, 1940–61. Judge, 2nd Circuit Court of Appeals, 1961–65; Solicitor-Gen. of USA, 1965–67. Holds hon. doctorates at many US Univs. Spingarn Medal, 1946.

MARSHALL, Valerie Margaret, (Mrs A. R. Marshall); Head of Business Enterprise, Scottish Development Agency, 1988–90 (Investment Executive, 1980–84; Investment Manager, 1984–88); *b* 30 March 1945; *d* of Ernest Knagg and Marion Knagg; *m* 1972, Alan Roger Marshall; two *s* one *d.* *Educ:* Brighton and Hove High Sch.; Girton Coll., Cambridge (MA); London Graduate Sch. of Business Studies (MSc). LRAM. Financial Controller, ICFC, 1969–80. Director: Renfrew Development Co. Ltd, 1988–; Scottish Food Fund. Member: Scottish Cttee, Design Council, 1975–77; Monopolies and Mergers Commn, 1976–81. Chm., Scottish Music Inf Centre, 1986–. *Recreations:* music, ballet, collecting antiquarian books, walking, entertaining. *Address:* Auchenbrae, 35 Newark Drive, Pollokshields, Glasgow G41 4QA.

MARSHALL, William; Assistant Under-Secretary of State, Ministry of Defence (Navy), 1968–72, retired; *b* 30 Sept. 1912; *e s* of late Allan and Julia Marshall, Whitecraigs, Renfrewshire; *m* 1st, 1940, Jessie Gardner Miller (*d* 1962); one *s*; 2nd, 1963, Doreen Margaret Read. *Educ:* Allan Glen's Sch., Glasgow; Glasgow Univ. MA Glasgow 1932, LLB (*cum laude*) Glasgow 1935. War of 1939–45: Temp. Asst Principal, Air Ministry, 1940; Service with Royal Navy (Ord. Seaman), and Admin. Staff, Admty, 1941. Private Sec. to Permanent Sec. of Admty (Sir J. G. Lang), 1947–48; Principal Private Sec. to successive First Lords of Admty (Lord Hall, Lord Packenham and Rt Hon. J. P. L. Thomas, later Lord Cilcennin), 1951–54; Asst Sec. in Admty, 1954; on loan to HM Treasury, 1958–61; returned to Admiralty, 1961. Chm., cttee to review submarine escape trng, 1974. *Recreations:* golf, travel, gardening. *Address:* 37 West Drive, Cheam, Surrey. *T:* 081–642 3399. *Club:* Banstead Downs Golf.

MARSHALL-ANDREWS, Robert Graham; QC 1987; a Recorder of the Crown Court, since 1982; *b* 10 April 1944; *s* of Robin and Eileen Nora Marshall; *m* 1968, Gillian Diana Elliott; one *s* one *d.* *Educ:* Mill Hill Sch.; Univ. of Bristol (LLB). Called to the Bar, Gray's Inn, 1967; Recorder, Oxford and Midland Circuit, 1982–. Trustee: George Adamson Trust; Geffrye Museum. *Publication:* The Palace of Wisdom (novel), 1989. *Recreations:* theatre, reading, Rugby (watching), sailing, travelling about. *Address:* 4 Paper Buildings, Temple, EC4. *T:* 071–353 3366. *Club:* Druidston (Pembrokeshire).

MARSHALL EVANS, David; *see* Evans.

MARSHAM, family name of **Earl of Romney.**

MARSLAND, Prof. Edward Abson, BDS, PhD; FDSRCS, FRCPath; Vice-Chancellor and Principal, University of Birmingham, 1981–86; Professor of Oral Pathology, University of Birmingham, 1964–81, Emeritus since 1986; *b* Coventry, 18 May 1923; *s* of T. Marsland; *m* 1957, Jose, *d* of J. H. Evans; one *s* two *d.* *Educ:* King Edward's Sch. and Univ. of Birmingham. House Surgeon, Gen. and Dental Hosps, Birmingham, 1946; Birmingham University: Research Fellow, 1948–50; Lectr in Dental Pathology, 1950–58; Sen. Lectr, 1958–64; Pro-Vice-Chancellor, 1977–79; Vice-Principal, 1979–81; Dir, Birmingham Dental Sch., 1969–74. Chairman: Co-ord. Cttee for Welfare of Handicapped, Birmingham, 1972–81; W Midlands Council for Disabled People, 1977–83 (Pres., 1985–); Midlands Council for Preparatory Trng of Disabled, 1987–89 (Vice-Chm., 1976–87); Regional Council, Sense in the Midlands, 1990–; Member: W Midlands RHA, 1984–87 (Chm., Rehabilitation Cttee, 1987–); Disablement Services Authority, 1987–91. Pres., Blue Coat Sch., Birmingham, 1984–; Hon. Vice-Pres., Ironbridge Museum Trust, 1986; Chairman: Council, Edgbaston C of E Coll. for Girls, 1988– (Mem. Council, 1984–88); Council of Management, St Mary's Hospice, 1990– (Mem. Council, 1987–90). Trustee: Selly Oak Colls, 1987– (Hon. Fellow, 1986); Sense in the Midlands Foundn, 1987–. Hon. LLD Birmingham, 1987; DUniv Open, 1987. Gold Medal, Birmingham

Civic Soc., 1988. *Publications:* An Atlas of Dental Histology, 1957; A Colour Atlas of Oral Histopathology, 1975; scientific papers in various jls; articles on disability. *Recreations:* work for disabled people, gardening, motoring, photography. *Address:* 9 Bryony Road, Selly Oak, Birmingham B29 4BY. *T:* 021–475 4365.

MARTELL, Vice-Adm. Sir Hugh (Colenso), KBE 1966 (CBE 1957); CB 1963; *b* 6 May 1912; *s* of late Engineer Capt. A. A. G. Martell, DSO, RN (Retd) and late Mrs S. Martell; *m* Margaret, *d* of late Major A. R. Glover. *Educ:* Edinburgh Academy; RNC Dartmouth. Royal Navy, 1926–67, retired; served War, 1940–45 (despatches): Gunnery Officer in HMS Berwick and HMS Illustrious. Naval Adviser to Dir Air Armament Research and Development, Min. of Supply, 1952–54; Capt. (F) 7 and in Comd HMS Bigbury Bay, 1954–55; Overall Operational Comdr, Nuclear Tests, in Monte Bello Is as Cdre, 1956; IDC, 1957; Capt., HMS Excellent, 1958; ADC, 1958; Dir of Tactical and Weapons Policy, Admiralty and Naval Mem. Defence Research Policy Staff, Min. of Defence, 1959–62; Admiral Commanding Reserves and Dir-Gen. of Naval Recruiting (as Rear-Adm.), 1962–65; Chief of Allied Staff, Mediterranean, Aegean and Black Sea (as Vice-Adm.), 1965–67. Mem., RNSA. *Recreation:* sailing. *Clubs:* Naval; Royal Dorset Yacht (Weymouth).

MARTEN, Francis William, CMG 1967; MC 1943; formerly Counsellor, Foreign and Commonwealth Office; *b* 8 Nov. 1916; *er s* of late Vice-Adm. Sir Francis Arthur Marten and late Lady Marten (*née* Phyllis Raby Morgan); *m* 1940, Hon. Avice Irene Vernon (*d* 1964); one *s* one *d*; 2nd, 1967, Miss Anne Tan; one *s*. *Educ:* Winchester Coll.; Christ Church, Oxford. Served HM Forces, 1939–46. Entered HM Foreign Service, 1946; served FO, 1946–48; Washington, 1948–52; FO, 1952–54; Teheran, 1954–57; NATO Defence Coll., Paris, 1957–58; Bonn, 1958–62; Leopoldville, 1962–64; Imperial Defence Coll., 1964–65; Dep. High Comr, Eastern Malaysia, 1965–67; ODM, 1967–69. *Recreation:* gardening. *Address:* 113 Pepys Road, SE14 5SE. *T:* 071–639 1060.

MARTIN; *see* Holland-Martin.

MARTIN, Sir Andrew; *see* Martin, Sir R. A. St G.

MARTIN, Archer John Porter, CBE 1960; FRS 1950; MA, PhD; *b* 1 March 1910; *s* of Dr W. A. P. and Mrs L. K. Martin; *m* 1943, Judith Bagenal; two *s* three *d*. *Educ:* Bedford Sch.; Peterhouse, Cambridge, Hon. Fellow, 1974. Nutritional Lab., Cambridge, 1933–38; Chemist, Wool Industries Research Assoc., Leeds, 1938–46; Research Dept, Boots Pure Drug Co., Nottingham, 1946–48; staff, Medical Research Council, 1948–52; Head of Phys. Chem. Div., National Inst. of Medical Research, 1952–56; Chemical Consultant, 1956–59; Director, Abbotsbury Laboratories Ltd, 1959–70; Consultant to Wellcome Research Laboratories, 1970–73. Extraordinary Prof., Technological Univ. of Eindhoven, 1965–73; Professorial Fellow, Univ. of Sussex, 1973–78; Robert A. Welch Prof. of Chemistry, Univ. of Houston, Texas, 1974–79; Invited Prof. of Chemistry, Ecole Polytechnique Fédérale de Lausanne, 1980–84. Berzelius Gold Medal, Swedish Medical Soc., 1951; (jointly with R. L. M. Synge) Nobel Prize for Chemistry, 1952; John Scott Award, 1958; John Price Wetherill Medal, 1959; Franklin Institute Medal, 1959; Leverhulme Medal, Royal Society, 1963; Koltoff Medal, Acad. of Pharmaceutical Science, 1969; Callendar Medal, Inst. of Measurement and Control, 1971; Fritz-Pregl Medal, Austrian Soc. of Microchem. and Analytical Chem., 1985. Hon. DSc Leeds, 1968; Hon. LLD Glasgow, 1973. *Address:* 47 Roseford Road, Cambridge CB4 2HA.

MARTIN, Arthur Bryan, CB 1987; Member of Health and Safety Executive, 1985–88, and Director, Resources and Planning Division, 1977–88; Head of UK Delegation, and Alternate Chairman, Channel Tunnel Safety Authority, since 1989; *b* 16 July 1928; *s* of Frederick Arthur Martin and Edith Maud Martin; *m* 1953, Dyllis Naomi Eirne Johnstone-Hogg; two *s*. *Educ:* Bristol Grammar Sch.; Royal Mil. Coll. of Science (BSc). Joined Army, REME, 1948; commnd, 1948; Lt-Col, 1967–69; served in UK, Germany, Malaya, Cyprus and Aden; joined Civil Service (Dept of Employment), 1969, as direct entrant principal; Asst Sec., Factory Inspectorate, 1973; Under Sec., HSE, 1977. *Address:* Ashford Old Farm, Ilton, near Ilchester, Som TA19 9ED.

MARTIN, Bruce; *see* Martin, R. B.

MARTIN, Charles Edmund, MA; Headmaster, Bristol Grammar School, since 1986; *b* 19 Sept. 1939; *s* of late Flight Lieut Charles Stuart Martin and of Sheila Martin; *m* 1966, Emily Mary Bozman; one *s* one *d*. *Educ:* Lancing College; Selwyn College, Cambridge (Hons English; MA); Bristol University (PGCE). VSO, Sarawak, 1958–59; Asst Master, Leighton Park School, Reading, 1964–68; Day Housemaster and Sixth Form Master, Sevenoaks School, 1968–71; Head of English Dept and Dep. Headmaster, Pocklington School, 1971–80; Headmaster, King Edward VI Camp Hill Boys' School, Birmingham, 1980–86. *Recreations:* travel, hill walking, theatre, ornithology, bee keeping. *Address:* The Grammar School, University Road, Bristol BS8 1SR. *Club:* East India.

MARTIN, Charlie; *see* Martin, J. C.

MARTIN, Christopher George; Director of Personnel, British Broadcasting Corporation, 1981–89, retired; *b* 29 May 1938; *s* of George and Lizbette Martin; *m* 1st, 1960, Moira Hughes (marr. diss. 1975); one *s* one *d*; 2nd, 1981, Elizabeth Buchanan Keith; one *s* decd. *Educ:* Beckenham Sch., Kent. Royal Marines, 1956–62. Group Personnel Manager: Viyella Internat., 1964–70; Great Universal Stores, 1970–74; Personnel Dir, Reed Paper & Board, 1974–76; UK Personnel Dir, Air Products Ltd, 1976–78; Gp Personnel Controller, Rank Organisation Ltd, 1978–81. CBIM 1984; FIPM 1984. *Publication:* contrib. Jl of Textile Inst. *Recreations:* music, sailing. *Address:* c/o Long Acre, Tanyard Lane, North Wooton, Shepton Mallet, Somerset. *Clubs:* Brook's.

MARTIN, Christopher Sanford; Headmaster, Millfield School, since 1990; *b* 23 Aug. 1938; *s* of Geoffrey Richard Rex Martin and Hazel Matthews; *m* 1968, Mary Julia Parry-Evans; one *s* one *d*. *Educ:* St Andrews Univ. (MA Mod. Langs; PGCE). Commissioned 2/10 Gurkha Rifles, 1957. Taught at Westminster Sch., 1963–78, at Philips, Exeter Acad., USA, 1966; Head Master, Bristol Cathedral Sch., 1979–90. Mem., Privy Council Educnl Panel, 1986–; Chairman: SW Div., HMC, 1987; Choir Schools' Assoc., 1987–89; HMC/SHA Working Party on teacher shortage, 1987–90; Nat. Rep., HMC Cttee, 1987–89; Mem., Engineering Council Educn Cttee, 1988–; founded Textbooks for Africa scheme (ODA), 1988. *Recreations:* walking, sailing, ski-ing, rebuilding a farmhouse in SW France. *Address:* Millfield School, Street, Somerset BA16 0YD. *T:* Street (0458) 42291.

MARTIN, Prof. David Alfred, PhD; Senior Professorial Fellow, Institute for the Study of Economic Culture, Boston University, 1990–92; Professor of Sociology, London School of Economics and Political Science, London University, 1971–88, now Emeritus; *b* 30 June 1929; *s* of late Frederick Martin and late Rhoda Miriam Martin; *m* 1st, 1953, Daphne Sylvia Treherne (*d* 1975); one *s*; 2nd, 1962, Bernice Thompson; two *s* one *d*. *Educ:* Richmond and East Sheen Grammar Sch.; Westminster Coll. (DipEd 1952); Westcott House, Cambridge. BSc (Ext.) 1st Cl. Hons, London Univ., 1959; PhD 1964. School teaching, 1952–59; postgrad. scholar, LSE, 1959–61; Asst Lectr, Sheffield Univ., 1961–62; Lectr, LSE, 1962–67, Reader, 1967–71. JSPS Scholar, Japan, 1978–79; Scurlock Prof. of Human Values, Southern Methodist Univ., Dallas, Texas, 1986–90. Lectures: Cadbury, Birmingham Univ., 1973; Ferguson, Manchester Univ., 1977; Gore, Westminster Abbey, 1977; Firth, Nottingham Univ., 1980; Forwood, Liverpool Univ., 1982; Prideaux, Exeter Univ., 1984; F. D. Maurice, KCL, 1991; Select Preacher, Cambridge Univ., 1979. Pres., Internat. Conf. of Sociology of Religion, 1975–83. Ordained Deacon, 1983, Priest 1984. *Publications:* Pacifism, 1965; A Sociology of English Religion, 1967; The Religious and the Secular, 1969; Tracts against the Times, 1973; A General Theory of Secularisation, 1978; Dilemmas of Contemporary Religion, 1978; (ed) Crisis for Cranmer and King James, 1979; The Breaking of the Image, 1980; (ed jtly) Theology and Sociology, 1980; (ed jtly) No Alternative, 1981; (ed jtly) Unholy Warfare, 1983; Tongues of Fire, 1989; Divinity in a Grain of Bread, 1989; contrib. Encounter, TLS, THES, Daedalus, TES. *Recreation:* piano accompaniment. *Address:* Cripplegate Cottage, 174 St John's Road, Woking, Surrey GU22 9NP. *T:* Woking (0483) 762134.

MARTIN, David John Pattison; MP (C) Portsmouth South, since 1987; *b* 5 Feb. 1945; *s* of late John Besley Martin, CBE and Muriel Martin; *m* 1977, Basia Dowmunt; one *s* three *d* (and one *d* decd). *Educ:* Norwood Sch., Exeter; Kelly College; Fitzwilliam College, Cambridge (BA Hons 1967). Governor, Dummer Academy, USA, 1963–64; called to the Bar, Inner Temple, 1969; practised until 1976; formerly Dir, family caravan and holiday business. Teignbridge District Councillor (C), 1979–83. Contested Yeovil, 1983. *Recreations:* music, golf, chief arbitrator of children's squabbles. *Address:* House of Commons, SW1. *T:* 071–219 6912. *Club:* Hawks (Cambridge).

MARTIN, David Weir; Member (Lab) Lothians, European Parliament, since 1984; a Vice President of the European Parliament, since 1989; *b* 26 Aug. 1954; *s* of William Martin and Marion Weir; *m* 1979, Margaret Mary Cook; one *s* one *d*. *Educ:* Liberton High School; Heriot Watt University (BA Econs). Stockbroker's clerk, 1970–74; animal rights campaigner, 1975–78. Lothian Regional Councillor, 1982–84. Leader, British Lab Gp, European Parliament, 1987–88. Vice-Pres., National Playbus Assoc., 1985–. Vice-Pres., Internat. Inst. for Democracy; Mem. Cttee, Advocates for Animals (formerly Scottish Soc. for Prevention of Vivisection), 1985–. Mem. Bd of Govs, Road Industry Training Bd, Livingston Multi Occupational Trng Educn Centre, 1985–. Dir, St Andrew Animal Fund, 1986–. *Publications:* Fabian pamphlet on the Common Market; Wheatley pamphlet on European Union. *Recreations:* soccer, reading. *Address:* (office) Ruskin House, 15 Windsor Street, Edinburgh EH7 5LA. *T:* 031–557 0936; (home) 7 Mortonhall Park Gardens, Edinburgh EH17 8SL. *T:* 031–664 9178.

MARTIN, Prof. Derek H.; Professor of Physics, Queen Mary and Westfield College (formerly Queen Mary College), University of London, since 1967; *b* 18 May 1929; *s* of Alec Gooch Martin and Winifred Martin; *m* 1951, Joyce Sheila Leaper; one *s* one *d*. *Educ:* Hitchin Grammar Sch.; Eastbourne Grammar Sch.; Univ. of Nottingham. BSc; PhD. Queen Mary College, London: Lectr, 1954–58, 1962–63; Reader in Experimental Physics, 1963–67; Dean, Faculty of Science, 1968–70; Head of Dept of Physics, 1970–75. DSIR Res. Fellow, 1959–62; Vis. Prof., Univ. of Calif, Berkeley, 1965–66. Member: Astronomy, Space and Radio Bd, SRC, 1975–78; Bd, Athlone Press, 1973–79; Royal Greenwich Observatory Cttee, 1977–80; Senate, Univ. of London, 1981–86; Court, Univ. of Essex, 1986–. Fellow, Inst. of Physics (Hon. Sec., 1984–); Mem., Internat. Astronomical Union. NPL Metrology Award, 1983. Editor, Advances in Physics, 1974–84. *Publications:* Magnetism in Solids, 1967; Spectroscopic Techniques, 1967; numerous articles and papers in Proc. Royal Soc., Jl of Physics, etc. *Address:* Hermanus, Hillwood Grove, Brentwood, Essex. *T:* Brentwood (0277) 210546. *Club:* Athenæum.

MARTIN, Evelyn Fairfax; Co-Chair, Women's National Commission, since 1991; *b* 12 Aug. 1926; *d* of late Kenneth Gordon Robinson and Beatrice Robinson (*née* Monro); *m* 1949, Dennis William Martin; three *d* (and one *d* decd). *Educ:* Belvedere Girls' Sch., Liverpool; Huyton Coll. for Girls, Liverpool; Mrs Hoster's Secretarial Coll. Foster parent, 1960–71. Chairman: Battered Wives Hostel, Calderdale, 1980–82; Calderdale Well Woman Centre, 1982–86; Calderdale CHC, 1982–84; Women's Health and Screening Delegn, 1985–91; Nat. Pres., Nat. Council of Women of GB, 1986–88. *Recreations:* gardening, foreign travel, animals. *Address:* 32 Clifton Road, Halifax HX3 0BT. *T:* Halifax (0422) 360438. *Club:* University Women's.

MARTIN, (Francis) Troy K.; *see* Kennedy Martin.

MARTIN, Frank Vernon, MA (Oxon); graphic artist; printmaker; engraver; illustrator; *b* Dulwich, 14 Jan. 1921; *er s* of late Thomas Martin; *m* 1942, Mary Irene Goodwin; three *d*. *Educ:* Uppingham Sch.; Hertford Coll., Oxford (History Schol.); St Martin's Sch. of Art. Army, 1941–46. Studied wood engraving with Gertrude Hermes and etching with John Buckland Wright. In free-lance professional practice as wood engraver and book illustrator, 1948–. Teacher of etching and engraving, Camberwell Sch. of Art, 1953–80 (Hd of Dept of Graphic Arts, 1976–80). Printmaker, 1966–; etchings, drypoints, woodcuts in colour. Fifteen one-man exhibitions in UK, Europe and USA, 1956–; works in various public and private collections in UK and abroad. RE 1955–74; MSIA 1955–71; Mem., Soc. of Wood Engravers; Hon. Academician, Accademia delle Arti del Disegno, Florence, 1962. *Address:* Studio L, Chelsea Studios, 416 Fulham Road, SW6.

MARTIN, Frederick Royal, BSc, CEng, FICE, FIStructE; Under-Secretary, Department of the Environment and Director, Defence Services II, Property Services Agency, 1975–79, retired; *b* 10 Oct. 1919; *e s* of late Frederick Martin and Lois Martin (*née* Royal); *m* 1946, Elsie Winifred Parkes (*d* 1984); one *s* three *d*. *Educ:* Dudley Grammar Sch.; Univ. of Birmingham (BSc (Hons)). Asst Engr, Birmingham, Tame and Rea Dist Drainage Bd, 1940; entered Air Min. Directorate-Gen. of Works, as Engrg Asst, 1941; Asst Civil Engr: Heathrow, Cardington, London, 1944–48; Civil Engr: Cambridge, Iraq, Jordan, Persian Gulf, London, 1948–54; Sqdn Leader, RAF, 1949–52; Sen. CE, London, 1954–58; Suptg CE, London, also Chief Engr, Aden, Aden Protectorate, Persian Gulf and E Africa, 1958–62; Suptg CE, Exeter, 1962–64; Min. of Public Bdg and Works, Area Officer, Bournemouth, 1964–66; Suptg CE, Directorate of Civil Engrg Develt, 1966–70; Asst Dir, 1970–72; Dir of Directorate of Social and Research Services, Property Services Agency, 1972; Chief Engineer, Maplin Develt Authority, 1973–74. Crampton Prize, ICE, 1946. *Publications:* various papers and articles to Instn Civil Engrs, etc, on airfield pavements. *Recreations:* looking at medieval building, reading, gardening. *Address:* 25 East Avenue, Bournemouth, Dorset BH3 7BS. *T:* Bournemouth (0202) 555858.

MARTIN, Geoffrey; *see* Martin, T. G.

MARTIN, Geoffrey Haward, CBE 1986; DPhil; FSA, FRHistS; Senior Research Fellow, Merton College, Oxford, since 1990; Research Professor of History, University of Essex, since 1990; *b* 27 Sept. 1928; *s* of late Ernest Leslie Martin and Mary H. Martin (*née* Haward); *m* 1953, Janet, *d* of late Douglas Hamer, MC and Enid Hamer; three *s* one *d*. *Educ:* Colchester Royal Grammar Sch.; Merton Coll., Oxford (MA, DPhil); Univ. of Manchester. FSA 1975; FRHistS 1958; FRSA 1987. University of Leicester (formerly University Coll. of Leicester): Lectr in Econ. History, 1952–65; Reader in History, 1966–73; Prof. of History, 1973–82; Public Orator, 1971–74; Dean, Faculty of Arts, 1972–75; Pro-Vice-Chancellor, 1979–82; Hon. Archivist, 1989–. Keeper of Public

Records, 1982–88. Vis. Prof. of Medieval History, Carleton Univ., Ottawa, 1958–59 and 1967–68; Vis. Res. Fellow, Merton Coll., Oxford, 1971; Sen. Res. Fellow, Loughborough Univ. of Technol., 1987–; Hon. Res. Fellow, Dept of Library and Archive Studies, UCL, 1987–; Dist. Vis. Prof. of History, Univ. of Toronto, 1989; Emeritus Fellow, Leverhulme Trust, 1989–91. Chairman: Board of Leicester University Press, 1975–82; Selection Cttee, Miners' Welfare National Educn Fund, 1978–84; British Records Assoc., 1982–; Commonwealth Archivists' Assoc., 1984–88; Arts and Humanities Res. Degrees Sub-Cttee, CNAA, 1986–; Mem., RCHM, 1987–. Vice-Pres., RHistS, 1984–88; Council, Soc. of Antiquaries, 1989–91. Gov., Museum of London, 1989–. Hon. Gen. Editor, Suffolk Record Soc., 1956–. Dist. Mem., Sistema Nacional de Archivos, Mexico, 1988. DUniv Essex, 1989. Besterman Medal, Library Assoc., 1972. *Publications:* The Town: a visual history, 1961; Royal Charters of Grantham, 1963; (with Sylvia McIntyre) Bibliography of British and Irish Municipal History, vol. 1, 1972; Ipswich Recognizance Rolls: a calendar, 1973; contribs to various learned jls. *Recreations:* fell-walking, adjusting phrases, gardening. *Address:* 27 Woodside House, Woodside, Wimbledon, SW19 7QN. *T:* 081–946 2570. *Clubs:* Commonwealth Trust, United Oxford & Cambridge University.

MARTIN, George Henry, CBE 1988; Chairman, Air Group of companies, since 1965; Director, Chrysalis Group, since 1978; *b* 3 Jan. 1926; *s* of Henry and Bertha Beatrice Martin; *m* 1st, 1948, Sheena Rose Chisholm; one *s* one *d*; 2nd, 1966, Judy Lockhart Smith; one *s* one *d*. *Educ:* St Ignatius Coll., Stamford Hill, London; Bromley County Sch., Kent; Guildhall Sch. of Music and Drama. Sub-Lieut, FAA, RNVR, 1944–47. BBC, July 1950; EMI Records Ltd, Nov. 1950–1965; formed Air Gp of cos, 1965; built Air Studios, 1969; built Air Studios, Montserrat, 1979; company merged with Chrysalis Gp, 1974; produced innumerable records, including all those featuring The Beatles; scored the music for fifteen films; nominated for Oscar for A Hard Day's Night, 1964; Grammy Awards, USA, 1964, 1967 (two), 1973; Ivor Novello Awards, 1963, 1979. Hon. DMus Berklee Coll. of Music, Boston, Mass, 1989. *Publications:* All You Need Is Ears, 1979; Making Music, 1983. *Recreations:* boats, sculpture, tennis, snooker. *Clubs:* Oriental; Alderney Sailing.

MARTIN, Lt-Gen. Henry James, CBE 1943; DFC; Chief of Defence Staff, South African Defence Force, retired; *b* 10 June 1910; *s* of Stanley Charles Martin and Susan C. Fourie; *m* 1940, Renée Viljoen; one *s* two *d*. *Educ:* Grey Coll. Sch., Bloemfontein; Grey Univ. Coll., Bloemfontein. Joined S African Air Force, 1936, and played important rôle in British Empire Training Scheme in South Africa; commanded No 12 Sqdn in Western Desert (DFC, Croix Militaire de première classe Belgique); commanded No 3 Wing (a unit of Desert Air Force) and campaigned from El Alamein to Tunis; returned to Union, 1943. *Recreation:* rugger (represented Orange Free State, 1931–34, Transvaal, 1935–37, South Africa, 1937). *Address:* 169 Pennys Way, Lynnwood Glen, Pretoria 0081, S Africa.

MARTIN, Ian; Secretary General, Amnesty International, since 1986 (Head of Asia Research Department, 1985–86); *b* 10 Aug. 1946; *s* of Collin and Betty Martin; *m* 1977, Vivien Stern. *Educ:* Brentwood Sch.; Emmanuel Coll., Cambridge; Harvard Univ. Ford Foundn Representative's Staff, India, 1969–70, Pakistan, 1970–71, Bangladesh, 1972; Community Relations Officer, Redbridge Community Relations Council, 1973–75; Gen. Sec., Jt Council for the Welfare of Immigrants, 1977–82 (Dep. Gen. Sec., 1976–77; Exec. Cttee Mem., 1982–86); Gen. Sec., The Fabian Soc., 1982–85. Member: Exec. Cttee, NCCL, 1983–85; Redbridge and Waltham Forest AHA, 1977–82; Redbridge HA, 1982–83. Councillor, London Borough of Redbridge, 1978–82. *Publications:* Immigration Law and Practice (with Larry Grant), 1982; *contributed to:* Labour and Equality, Fabian Essays, 1980; Civil Liberties, Cobden Trust Essays, 1984; Public Interest Law (ed J. Cooper and R. Dhavan), 1986. *Address:* 1 Easton Street, WC1X 8DJ. *T:* 071–413 5500.

MARTIN, Ian Alexander; Group Managing Director, Grand Metropolitan plc, since 1991 (Director, since 1985); *b* 28 Feb. 1935; *s* of Alexander Martin and Eva (*née* Gillman); *m* 1963, Phyllis Mitchell-Bey; one *s* two *d*. *Educ:* Univ. of St Andrews (MA). Mem., Inst. of Chartered Accountants, Scotland. Dir, Mine Safety Appliances Co. Ltd, 1969–72; Div. Dir, ITT Europe, 1977–79; Chairman: Intercontinental Hotels, 1968–88; Burger King Corp., 1989–; Pres. and Chief Exec. Officer, Pillsbury Co., 1989–; Dir, St Paul Companies Inc., 1989–. Member of Board: Univ. of Minnesota Sch. of Mgmt, 1985–; Nat. Commn on Children, USA, 1990–. Chm., United Negro Coll. Drive, 1991. Freeman, City of London, 1982. BIM, 1986. *Recreations:* angling, golf, music. *Address:* 20 St James's Square, SW1Y 4RR. *T:* 071–321 6000. *Clubs:* Minneapolis (Minnesota); Frenchmans Creek Yacht and Country (Florida).

MARTIN, James Arthur, CMG 1970; FASA; company director; *b* 25 July 1903; *s* of late Arthur Higgins Martin and Gertrude, *d* of George Tippins. *Educ:* Stawell and Essendon High Schools, Victoria; Melbourne Univ. FASA 1924. Joined The Myer Emporium Ltd, Melbourne, 1918; The Myer Emporium (SA) Ltd, Adelaide, 1928, Man. Dir 1936, Chm. and Man. Dir, 1956–68, retd; Dir, Myer (Melbourne) Ltd, department store, 1936–68, retd. *Recreations:* gardening, walking, motoring. *Address:* 17 Hawkers Road, Medindie, SA 5081, Australia. *T:* Adelaide 442535. *Clubs:* South Australian Cricket, South Australian Jockey (Adelaide).

MARTIN, James Brown; General Secretary, Educational Institute of Scotland, since 1988; *b* 6 Dec. 1953; *s* of James and Annie Martin; *m* 1975, Anne McNaughton; one *s* one *d*. *Educ:* Larbert Village and High Schs; Heriot-Watt Univ. (BAEcon); Moray House College of Educn. Teacher, Falkirk High Sch., 1975–79; Field Officer 1979–83, Asst Sec. 1983–88, EIS. *Recreations:* Hibernian FC, watching football. *Address:* 46 Moray Place, Edinburgh EH3 6BH. *T:* 031–225 6244.

MARTIN, Janet, (Mrs K. P. Martin); Relief Warden (Assisted Independence), Test Valley Housing, since 1991; *b* Dorchester, Dorset, 8 Sept. 1927; *d* of James Wilkinson and Florence Steer; *m* 1951, Peter Martin (retired Southampton HA, Senior Consultant AT and T (ISTEL) Ltd); one *s* one *d*. *Educ:* Dorchester Grammar Sch., Dorset; Weymouth Tech. Coll.; occupational training courses. PA to Group Sec., Herrison HMC, 1949; admin./clerical work, NHS and other, 1956; social research fieldwork, mainly NHS (Wessex mental health care evaluation team), and Social Services (Hants CC and Nat. Inst. for Social Work), 1967–76; residential social worker (children with special needs), Southampton, 1976–78; Social Services Officer, Test Valley, 1978–86; Senior Residential Care Officer (Elderly), Test Valley Social Services, 1986–87; Housing Warden (Elderly), 1988–91. Interviewer, MRC 'National' Survey, 1970–85; Psychosexual Counsellor, Aldermoor Clinic, 1981–84. Mem., Press Council, 1973–78. *Recreations:* buildings, books. *Address:* Hunter's Lodge, Linden Avenue, Dorchester, Dorset DT1 1EJ. *T:* Dorchester (0305) 269839.

MARTIN, John Christopher, (Charlie), CBE 1989; Deputy Chief Scientific Officer (Special Merit), United Kingdom Atomic Energy Authority, 1974–86; *b* 21 Sept. 1926; *s* of late Percy Martin and Marjorie Etta Caselton. *Educ:* Edward Alleyn's Sch.; King's Coll., London (BSc (Hons Physics) 1946). MoS, Fort Halstead, Sept. 1947; Woolwich Arsenal, 1950; UKAEA/MoD, AWRE, Aldermaston, Nov. 1952–89. EMP Fellow, 1988. USA Defense Nuclear Agency Exceptional Public Service Gold Medal, 1977; (first) Erwin Marx Award in Pulse Power Technology, 3rd Internat. Meeting on Pulsed Power, 1981. *Publications:* contribs to learned jls. *Recreations:* friends, food, snorkling, science fiction and fact (not always distinguishable). *Address:* Boundary Hall, Tadley, Basingstoke, Hants RG26 6QD.

MARTIN, Brig. John Douglas K.; *see* King-Martin.

MARTIN, Vice-Adm. Sir John (Edward Ludgate), KCB 1972 (CB 1968); DSC 1943; FNI; retired; Lieutenant-Governor and Commander-in-Chief of Guernsey, 1974–80; *b* 10 May 1918; *s* of late Surgeon Rear-Admiral W. L. Martin, OBE, FRCS and Elsie Mary Martin (*née* Catford); *m* 1942, Rosemary Ann Deck; two *s* two *d*. *Educ:* RNC, Dartmouth. Sub Lt and Lt, HMS Pelican, 1938–41; 1st Lt, HMS Antelope, 1942; navigation course, 1942; Navigation Officer, 13th Minesweeping Flotilla, Mediterranean, 1943–44, including invasions N Africa, Sicily, Pantelleria, Salerno; RNAS Yeovilton, 1944; Navigation Officer: HMS Manxman and HMS Bermuda, 1944–46; HMS Nelson, 1947; HMS Victorious, 1948; Staff Coll., 1949; Navigation Officer, HMS Devonshire, 1950–51; Dirg Staff, Staff Coll., 1952–54; Jt Services Planning Staff, Far East, 1954–55; Exec. Off., HMS Superb, 1956–57; Jt Services Staff Coll., 1958; Dep. Dir Manpower Planning and Complementing Div., Admty, 1959–61; Sen. Naval Off., W Indies, 1961–62; Comdr Brit. Forces Caribbean Area, 1962–63; Capt. Britannia Royal Naval Coll., Dartmouth, 1963–66; Flag Officer, Middle East, 1966–67; Comdr, British Forces Gulf, 1967–68 (despatches); Dir-Gen., Naval Personal Services and Training, 1968–70; Dep. Supreme Allied Comdr, Atlantic, 1970–72. Comdr 1951; Captain 1957; Rear-Adm. 1966; Vice-Adm. 1970. Pres., Nautical Inst., 1975–78. *Recreations:* fishing, shooting, beagling (Jt Master Britannia Beagles, 1963–66), sailing. *Clubs:* Army and Navy; Royal Naval Sailing Association; Royal Yacht Squadron.

MARTIN, John Francis Ryde; HM Diplomatic Service; Counsellor (Economic and Social), UK Mission to the United Nations, since 1988; *b* 8 Feb. 1943; *s* of Frank George Martin and Phyllis Mary Wixcey; *m* 1st, 1966, Hélène Raymonde Henriette Pyronnet (marr. diss. 1984); two *s*; 2nd, 1985, Kathleen Marie White; one *s*. *Educ:* Bedford School; Brasenose College, Oxford (MA); Bologna Center, Johns Hopkins Univ. FCO, 1966; Buenos Aires, 1968–70; Athens, 1970–74; Private Sec. to Minister of State, FCO, 1976–78; Nicosia, 1978–81; Asst Sec., Internat. Telecommunications, DTI, 1983–84; Counsellor, Lagos, 1984–88. *Recreations:* travel, collecting, bibliomania. *Address:* c/o Foreign and Commonwealth Office, SW1. *Club:* Travellers'.

MARTIN, Sir (John) Leslie, Kt 1957; RA 1986; MA, PhD Manchester; MA Cantab; MA Oxon; Hon. LLD Leicester, Hull, Manchester; DUniv Essex; Hon. FRSAMD; FRIBA; Professor of Architecture, University of Cambridge, 1956–72; Emeritus Professor, 1973; Fellow, Jesus College, Cambridge, 1956–73, Hon. Fellow 1973, Emeritus Fellow, 1976; *b* 17 Aug. 1908; *s* of late Robert Martin, FRIBA; *m*, Sadie Speight, MA, ARIBA; one *s* one *d*. *Educ:* Manchester Univ. Sch. of Architecture. Asst Lectr, Manchester Univ. Sch. of Architecture, 1930–34; Head of Sch. of Architecture, Hull, 1934–39; Principal Asst Architect, LMS Railway, 1939–48; Dep. Architect, LCC, 1948–53; Architect to the LCC, 1953–56. Slade Prof. of Fine Art, Oxford, 1965–66; Ferens Prof. of Fine Art, Hull, 1967–68; William Henry Bishop Vis. Prof. of Architecture, Univ. of Yale, 1973–74; Lethaby Prof., RCA, 1981. Lectures: Gropius, Harvard, 1966; Cordingley, Manchester, 1968; Kenneth Kassler, Princeton, 1974; annual, Soc. Arch. Historians, 1976; Townsend, UCL, 1976; Convocation, Leicester, 1978. Consultant to Gulbenkian Foundn, Lisbon, 1959–69. Buildings include: work in Cambridge and for Univs of Cambridge, Oxford, Leicester and Hull; RSAMD, Glasgow; Gall. of Modern Art, Gulbenkian Foundn, Lisbon; scheme design, Royal Concert Hall, Glasgow. Mem. Council, RIBA, 1952–58 (Vice-Pres., 1955–57); Mem. Royal Fine Art Commn, 1958–72. RIBA Recognised Schs Silver Medallist, 1929; Soane Medallist, 1930; London Architecture Bronze Medallist, 1954; RIBA Distinction in Town Planning, 1956; Civic Trust Award, Oxford, 1967; Commend. Cambridge, 1972; Concrete Soc. Award, Oxford, 1972; Royal Gold Medal for Architecture, RIBA, 1973. Hon. Mem. Assoc. of Finnish Architects, Accademico corrispondente National Acad. of S Luca, Rome. Comdr, Order of Santiago da Espada, Portugal. *Publications:* Jt Editor, Circle, 1937, repr. 1971; The Flat Book, 1939 (in collab. with wife); Whitehall: a Plan for a National and Government Centre, 1965; The Framework of Planning (Inaugural Lecture) Hull, 1967; Jt Editor, Cambridge Urban and Architectural Studies, Vol. I: Urban Space and Structure, 1972; Building and Ideas (1933–83) from the Studio of Leslie Martin, 1983; contrib. various jls; papers include: An Architect's Approach to Architecture; Education Without Walls; Education Around Architecture; Notes on a Developing Architecture. *Address:* The Barns, Church Street, Great Shelford, Cambridge CB2 5EL. *T:* Cambridge (0223) 842399. *Club:* Athenæum.

MARTIN, Prof. John Powell; Research Professor, University of Southampton, since 1989; *b* 22 Dec. 1925; *s* of Bernard and Grace Martin; *m* 1st, 1951, Sheila Feather (marr. diss. 1981); three *s*; 2nd, 1983, Joan Higgins. *Educ:* Leighton Park Sch., Reading; Univ. of Reading (BA); London Sch. of Economics and Political Science (Certif. in Social Admin., PhD); Univ. of Cambridge (MA). Lectr, London Sch. of Economics, 1953–59; Asst Dir of Research, Inst. of Criminology, Univ. of Cambridge, 1960–66; Fellow, King's Coll., Cambridge, 1964–67; Prof. of Sociology and Social Admin, later of Social Policy, Univ. of Southampton, 1967–89. Hill Foundn Vis. Prof., Univ. of Minnesota, 1973; Vis. Fellow, Yale Law Sch., 1974. Mem., Jellicoe Cttee on Boards of Visitors of Penal Instns, 1974–75. *Publications:* Social Aspects of Prescribing, 1957; Offenders as Employees, 1962; The Police: a study in manpower (with Gail Wilson), 1969; The Social Consequences of Conviction (with Douglas Webster), 1971; (ed) Violence and the Family, 1978; (jtly) The Future of the Prison System, 1980; Hospitals in Trouble, 1984; (with J. B. Coker) Licensed to Live, 1985; articles in: Lancet, British Jl of Criminology, British Jl of Sociology, International Review of Criminal Policy, etc. *Recreations:* sailing, photography, do-it-yourself. *Address:* Department of Sociology and Social Policy, The University, Southampton SO9 5NH. *T:* Southampton (0703) 595000. *Club:* Lymington Town Sailing.

MARTIN, John Sinclair, CBE 1977; farmer; *b* 18 Sept. 1931; *s* of Joseph and Claire Martin, Littleport, Ely; *m* 1960, Katharine Elisabeth Barclay, MB, BS; three *s* one *d*. *Educ:* The Leys Sch., Cambridge; St John's Coll., Cambridge (MA, Dip. in Agriculture). Chairman: Littleport and Downham IDB, 1971–88; JCO Arable Crops and Forage Bd, 1973–76; Eastern Regional Panel, MAFF, 1981–86 (Mem., 1972–78); Great Ouse Local Land Drainage Cttee, AWA, 1983–88; Anglian Drainage Cttee, 1988–89; Anglian Regional Flood Defence Cttee, National Rivers Authority, 1989–; Member: Eastern Counties Farmers' Management Cttee, 1960–70; ARC, 1968–78; Great Ouse River Authority, 1970–74; Lawes Agricl Trust Cttee, 1982–84; MAFF Priorities Bd, 1984–88; Anglian Water Authority, 1988–89; Vice-Pres., Assoc. of Drainage Authorities, 1986–. Chairman: Ely Br., NFU, 1963; Cambs NFU, 1979. High Sheriff, Cambs, 1985–86. *Address:* Denny Abbey, Waterbeach, Cambridge CB5 9PQ. *T:* Cambridge (0223) 860282. *Club:* Farmers'.

MARTIN, John William Prior; HM Diplomatic Service; Counsellor, Foreign and Commonwealth Office, since 1985; *b* 23 July 1934; *er s* of Stanley Gordon Martin and Frances Heather (*née* Moore); *m* 1960, Jean Fleming; three *s* one *d*. *Educ:* CIM Sch.,

Chefoo and Kuling; Bristol Grammar Sch.; St John's Coll., Oxford (MA). National Service, 1953–55 (2nd Lieut Royal Signals). Joined FO, 1959; Beirut, 1960; Saigon, 1963; Language Student, Hong Kong, 1965–67; Dar es Salaam, 1968; FCO, 1971; Singapore, 1974; FCO, 1978; Kuala Lumpur, 1982. *Recreations:* reading, travel, ornithology. *Address:* c/o Foreign and Commonwealth Office, SW1A 2AH.

MARTIN, Jonathan Arthur; Head of Sport and Events, BBC Television, since 1987 (Head of Sport, 1981–87); *b* 18 June 1942; *s* of Arthur Martin and Mabel Gladys Martin (*née* Bishop); *m* 1967, Joy Elizabeth Fulker; two *s. Educ:* Gravesend Grammar School; St Edmund Hall, Oxford (BA 1964, English). Joined BBC as general trainee, 1964; producer, Sportsnight 1969; producer, Match of the Day, 1970; editor, Sportsnight and Match of the Day, 1974; exec. producer, BBC TV Wimbledon tennis coverage, 1979–81; producer, Ski Sunday and Grand Prix, 1978–80; managing editor, Sport, 1980. Vice-Pres., EBU Sports Gp, 1984–. *Recreations:* skiing, golf, watching sport, watching television. *Address:* Arkle, Valentine Way, Chalfont St Giles, Bucks HP8 4JB; BBC, Kensington House, W14. *T:* 081–743 1272. *Club:* Harewood Downs Golf.

MARTIN, Mrs Kenneth Peter; *see* Martin, Janet.

MARTIN, Prof. Laurence Woodward; DL; Director, Royal Institute of International Affairs, since 1991; *b* 30 July 1928; *s* of Leonard and Florence Mary Martin; *m* 1951, Betty Parnall; one *s* one *d. Educ:* St Austell Grammar Sch.; Christ's Coll., Cambridge (MA); Yale Univ. (MA, PhD). Flying Officer, RAF, 1948–50; Instr, Yale Univ., 1955–56; Asst Prof., MIT, 1956–61; Rockefeller Fellow for Advanced Study, 1958–59; Associate Prof., Sch. of Advanced Internat. Studies, The Johns Hopkins Univ., 1961–64; Wilson Prof. of Internat. Politics, Univ. of Wales, 1964–68; Prof. of War Studies, King's Coll., Univ. of London, 1968–77, Fellow 1983–; Vice-Chancellor, Univ. of Newcastle upon Tyne, 1978–90, Emeritus Prof., 1991. Research Associate, Washington Center of Foreign Policy Research, 1964–76, 1979–; Vis. Prof., Univ. of Wales, 1985–. Lees-Knowles Lectr, Cambridge, 1981; BBC Reith Lectr, 1981. Dir, Tyne Tees Television. Member: SSRC, 1969–76 (Chm. Res. Grants Bd); Res. Council, Georgetown Center of Strategic Studies, 1969–77, 1979–; Council, IISS, 1975–83. Consultant, Sandia Labs. DL Tyne and Wear, 1986. Hon. DCL Newcastle, 1991. *Publications:* The Anglo-American Tradition in Foreign Affairs (with Arnold Wolfers), 1956; Peace without Victory, 1958; Neutralism and Non-Alignment, 1962; The Sea in Modern Strategy, 1967; (jtly) America in World Affairs, 1970; Arms and Strategy, 1973; (jtly) Retreat from Empire?, 1973; (jtly) Strategic Thought in the Nuclear Age, 1979; The Two-Edged Sword, 1982; Before the Day After, 1985; The Changing Face of Nuclear Warfare, 1987. *Address:* Royal Institute of International Affairs, Chatham House, 10 St James's Square, SW1Y 4LE.

MARTIN, Sir Leslie; *see* Martin, Sir J. L.

MARTIN, Leslie Vaughan; Hon. Research Fellow, Exeter University; *b* 20 March 1919; *s* of late Hubert Charles Martin and late Rose Martin (*née* Skelton) *m* 1949, Winifred Dorothy Hopkins; one *s* one *d. Educ:* Price's Sch., Fareham. FIA 1947. Served with RAMC and REME, 1940–46. Deptl Clerical Officer, Customs and Excise, 1936–38; joined Govt Actuary's Dept, 1938; Asst Actuary, 1949; Actuary, 1954; Principal Actuary, 1962; Directing Actuary (Superann. and Research), 1974–79. Mem. Council, Inst. of Actuaries, 1971–76; Vice-Chm., CS Medical Aid Assoc., 1976–79. Churchwarden, St Barnabas, Dulwich, 1965–70, 1977–79, Vice-Chm. of PCC, 1970–79; Treasurer: Morchard Bishop Parochial Church Council, 1980–83; Cadbury Deanery Synod, 1981–88; Chulmleigh Deanery Synod, 1989–. *Recreations:* crosswords, chess, scrabble. *Address:* Pickwick House, Down St Mary, Crediton, Devon EX17 6EQ. *T:* Copplestone (0363) 84581.

MARTIN, Michael John; MP (Lab) Springburn Division of Glasgow, since 1979; *b* 3 July 1945; *s* of Michael and Mary Martin; *m* 1965, Mary McLay; one *s* one *d. Educ:* St Patrick's Boys' Sch., Glasgow. Sheet metal worker; AUEW Shop Steward, Rolls Royce, Hillington, 1970–74; Trade Union Organiser, 1976–79; Mem., and sponsored by, Nat. Union of Sheet Metal Workers, Coppersmiths and Heating and Domestic Engineers; PPS to Rt Hon. Denis Healey, MP, 1981–83; Member: Select Cttee for Trade and Industry, 1983–; Speaker's Panel of Chairmen, 1987–; Chm., Scottish Grand Cttee. Councillor: for Fairfield Ward, Glasgow Corp., 1973–74; for Balornock Ward, Glasgow DC, 1974–79. *Recreations:* hill walking, local history. *Address:* 144 Broomfield Road, Balornock, Glasgow G21 3UE.

MARTIN, Oliver Samuel, QC 1970; **His Honour Judge Martin;** a Circuit Judge, since 1975; *b* 26 Nov. 1919; *s* of Sidney Edward Martin and Nita Martin; *m* 1st, 1954, Marion Eve (marr. diss. 1982); two *s*; 2nd, 1982, Gloria Audrey. *Educ:* King's College Sch., Wimbledon; London University. Served RNVR, 1939–46. Called to Bar, Gray's Inn, 1951. Dep. Chm. E Sussex QS, 1970–71; a Recorder of the Crown Court, 1972–75. *Recreations:* golf, music, reading, writing, holidays. *Address:* c/o Bloomsbury County Court, Marylebone Road, NW1.

MARTIN, Patrick William, TD; JP; MA; Headmaster of Warwick School, 1962–77; *b* 20 June 1916; *e s* of Alan Pattinson Martin, Bowness-on-Windermere, Westmorland; *m* 1st, 1939, Gwendoline Elsie Helme (*d* 1987), MA, St Hilda's Coll., Oxford; two *d*; 2nd, 1989, Eileen Muriel Beattie, JP. *Educ:* Windermere Grammar Sch.; Balliol Coll., Oxford. 2nd cl. hons in Modern History, Balliol Coll., 1937. Asst Master, Abingdon Sch., Berks, 1938–40. Commissioned in TA, 1938; served War of 1939–45, on active service with Royal Artillery; Staff College, Quetta; GSO 2, and 1 HQRA 14th Army in Burma (despatches); British Mil. Mission to Belgium, 1946. Schoolmaster, 1946–49; Asst Dir of Educn, Brighton, 1950–52; Headmaster: Chipping Norton Grammar Sch., 1952–57; Lincoln Sch., 1958–62. Chm., Midland Div., Headmasters' Conf., 1972–; Pres., Headmasters' Assoc., 1976; Treasurer, Warwick Univ., 1983–89. CC Warwickshire, 1977–85 (Leader, 1981–83). JP Warwicks 1966, Dep. Chm., Warwick Petty Sessions. *Publications:* History of Heart of England Building Society, 1981; articles in educational and other periodicals. *Recreations:* books, music, foreign countries and people; being alone in the countryside. *Address:* 80 High Street, Kenilworth, Warwicks. *T:* Kenilworth (0926) 54140.

MARTIN, Hon. Paul Joseph James, PC (Canada) 1945; CC (Canada) 1976; QC (Canada); High Commissioner for Canada in the United Kingdom, 1974–79; *b* Ottawa, 23 June 1903; *s* of Philip Ernest Martin and Lumina Marie Chouinard; *m* 1937, Alice Eleanor Adams; one *s* one *d. Educ:* Pembroke Separate Schs; St Alexandre Coll.; St Michael's Coll.; University of Toronto (MA); Osgoode Hall Law Sch., Toronto; Harvard Univ. (LLM); Trinity Coll., Cambridge; Geneva Sch. of Internat. Studies. Wilder Fellow, 1928; Alfred Zimmern Schol., 1930; Barrister-at-Law; Partner, Martin, Laird & Cowan, Windsor, Ont, 1934–63; QC 1937. Lectr, Assumption Coll., 1931–34. Can. Govt Deleg., 19th Ass. League of Nations, Geneva, 1938; Parl. Asst to Minister of Labour, 1943; Deleg. to ILO Confs, Phila, 1944, London, 1945. Apptd Sec. of State, 1945. Deleg. to 1st, 4th, 7th, 9th, 10th General Assembly, UN (Chm. Can. Del., 9th, 18th, 19th, 20th, 21st). Deleg. 1st, 3rd, 5th sessions, Economic and Social Council, 1946–47. Minister of National Health and Welfare, Dec. 1946–June 1957; Sec. of State for External Affairs, 1963–68; Pres., N Atlantic Council, 1965–66; Govt Leader in Senate, Canada, 1968–74. First elected to Canadian House of Commons, Gen. Elec., 1935; Rep. Essex East until 1968; apptd to Senate, 1968. Chancellor, Wilfrid Laurier Univ., 1972–. Holds several hon. doctorates. Hon. Life Mem., Canadian Legion. Christian Culture Award, 1956. Freedom, City of London, 1977. Hon. LLD Cambridge, 1980. *Publications:* A Very Public Life (autobiog.), vol. I 1983, vol. II 1986; London Diaries 1975–1979, 1988. *Address:* 2021 Ontario Street, Windsor, Ontario N8Y 1N3, Canada. *Clubs:* Rideau (Ottawa); Beach Grove Golf and Country (Windsor, Ont).

MARTIN, Peter; *see* Martin, R. P.

MARTIN, Peter Anthony; County Treasurer, Kent County Council, since 1986 (Deputy County Treasurer, 1981–86); *b* 8 Dec. 1946; *s* of Frank and Renie Martin; *m* 1970, Jennifer Margaret (*née* Shaw); one *s* three *d. Educ:* Nottingham High Sch.; St John's Coll., Oxford (BA Hons); Univ. of Kent at Canterbury (MA Management). CIPFA 1973. Accountant, Derbyshire CC, 1969–76; Asst County Treasurer, W Sussex CC, 1976–81. *Recreations:* cricket, reading, family. *Address:* 64 Maidstone Road, Rochester, Kent ME1 3BS.

MARTIN, Maj.-Gen. Peter Lawrence de Carteret, CBE 1968 (OBE 1964); President, Lady Grover's Hospital Fund for Officers' Families, since 1989 (Chairman, 1975–85; Vice President, 1985–89); Member: National Executive Committee, Forces Help Society, since 1975; Ex-Services Mental Welfare Society, since 1977; *b* 15 Feb. 1920; *s* of late Col Charles de Carteret Martin, MD, ChD, IMS and of Helen Margaret Hardinge Grover; *m* 1st, 1949, Elizabeth Felicia (marr. diss. 1967), *d* of late Col C. M. Keble; one *s* one *d*; 2nd, 1973, Mrs Valerie Singer. *Educ:* Wellington Coll.; RMC Sandhurst. FBIM 1979 (MBIM 1970). Commnd Cheshire Regt, 1939; BEF (Dunkirk), 1940; Middle East, 1941; N Africa 8th Army, 1942–43 (despatches); invasion of Sicily, 1943; Normandy landings and NW Europe, 1944 (despatches); Palestine, 1945–47; GSO2 (Int.), HQ British Troops Egypt, 1947; Instructor, RMA Sandhurst, 1948–50; psc 1951; Bde Major 126 Inf. Bde (TA), 1952–53; Chief Instructor MMG Div. Support Weapons Wing, Sch. of Infantry, 1954–56; Malayan Ops, 1957–58 (despatches); DAAG GHQ FARELF, 1958–60; CO 1 Cheshire, N Ireland and BAOR, 1961–63; AA&QMG Cyprus District, 1963–65; comd 48 Gurkha Inf. Bde, Hong Kong, 1966–68; Brig. AQ HQ Army Strategic Comd, 1968–71; Dir, Personal Services (Army), 1971–74. Col The 22nd (Cheshire) Regt, 1971–78; Col Comdt, Mil. Provost Staff Corps, 1972–74. Services Advr, Variety Club of GB, 1976–86. *Recreations:* golf, ski-ing. *Address:* 17 Station Street, Lymington, Hants. *T:* Lymington (0590) 672620. *Club:* Army and Navy.

MARTIN, Peter Lewis, CBE 1980; building services engineer, retired; *b* 22 Sept. 1918; *s* of George Lewis and Madeleine Mary Martin; *m* 1949, Elizabeth Grace, *d* of John David Melling; two *d. Educ:* Wyggeston Boys Sch., Leicester; Kibworth Beauchamp Grammar Sch.; Leicester Coll. of Art and Technology; Borough Polytechnic. CEng; MConsE. Apprenticed to engrg contractor, 1934–39. Served War, 1940–46, RAF Engrg Branch. Joined consulting engrg practice of Dr Oscar Faber, 1947; Partner, 1961–83; Consultant, 1983–85. Pres., IHVE, 1971–72; Chairman: Heating and Ventilating Res. Assoc., 1967–69; Assoc. of Consulting Engrs, 1983–84; Member: Cttee for Application of Computers to the Construction Industry, 1970–72; Technical Data on Fuel Cttee, World Energy Conf., 1971–77; Construction and Housing Res. Adv. Council, 1975–77; Building Services Bd, CNAA, 1975–80; Engrg Council, 1982–86. Vis. Prof., Univ. of Strathclyde, 1974–85; Hon. DSc Strathclyde, 1985. Governor, Herts Coll. of Building, 1970–74. Master, Plumbers' Co., 1979–80; Liveryman: Fanmakers' Co., 1971–; Engineers' Co., 1983–. Silver Medal, 1956, Bronze Medal, 1968, Gold Medal, 1976, IHVE. *Publications:* (jtly) Heating and Air Conditioning of Buildings, by Faber and Kell, 5th edn 1971 to 7th edn 1989; contribs to engrg jls and confs. *Recreation:* avoiding gardening. *Address:* Quietways, Lower Bodham, Holt, Norfolk NR25 6PS. *T:* Holt (0263) 712591. *Club:* Lansdowne.

MARTIN, Prof. Raymond Leslie, AO 1987; MSc, PhD, ScD, DSc; FRACI, FRSC, FTS, FAA; Professor of Chemistry, Monash University, Melbourne, since 1987 (Vice-Chancellor, 1977–87); Chairman, Australian Science and Technology Council, since 1988; *b* 3 Feb. 1926; *s* of Sir Leslie Harold Martin, CBE, FRS, FAA and late Gladys Maude Elaine, *d* of H. J. Bull; *m* 1954, Rena Lillian Laman; three *s* one *d. Educ:* Scotch Coll., Melbourne; Univ. of Melb. (BSc, MSc); Sidney Sussex Coll., Cambridge (PhD, ScD). FRACI 1956; FRSC (FRIC 1974); FTS 1989; FAA 1971. Resident Tutor in Chemistry, Queen's Coll., Melb., 1947–49 (Fellow, 1979); Sidney Sussex Coll., Cambridge: 1851 Exhibn Overseas Scholar, 1949–51; Sen. Scholar, 1952–54; Res. Fellow, 1951–54; Sen. Lectr, Univ. of NSW, 1954–59; Section Leader, 1959–60, and Associate Res. Manager, 1960–62, ICIANZ; Prof. of Inorganic Chem., 1962–72, and Dean of Faculty of Science, 1971, Univ. of Melb.; Australian National University, Canberra: Prof. of Inorganic Chem., Inst. of Advanced Studies, 1972–77, Prof. Emeritus 1977; Dean, Res. Sch. of Chem., 1976–77; DSc. Vis. Scientist: Technische Hochschule, Stuttgart, 1953–54; Bell Telephone Labs, NJ, 1967; Vis. Prof., Columbia Univ., NY, 1972. Royal Aust. Chemical Institute: Smith Medal, 1968; Olle Prize, 1974; Inorganic Medal, 1978; Leighton Medal, 1989; Fed. Pres., 1968–69. Chm., Internat. Commn on Atomic Weights and Isotopic Abundances, 1983–87; Mem., Prime Minister's Science Council, 1989–. Director: Circadian Technologies Ltd, 1986–; Heide Park and Art Gall., 1988–; Winston Churchill Meml Trust (and Chm., Vic Regional Cttee), 1983–; Trustee, Selby Scientific Foundn, 1990–. Council Mem., Victorian Coll. of the Arts, 1984– (Dep. Pres., 1991–). *Publications:* papers and revs on physical and inorganic chem. mainly in jls of London, Amer. and Aust. Chem. Socs. *Recreations:* golf; lawn tennis (Cambridge Univ. team *v* Oxford, Full Blue; Cambs County Colours). *Address:* Department of Chemistry, Monash University, Clayton, Vic 3168, Australia. *Clubs:* Melbourne (Melbourne); Hawks (Cambridge); Frankston Golf (Victoria).

MARTIN, Richard Graham; Vice-Chairman, 1988–Oct. 1992, and Chief Executive, 1989–Oct. 1992, Allied-Lyons; Chairman and Chief Executive, Hiram Walker-Allied Vintners, since 1991 (Director, since 1989); *b* 4 Oct. 1932; *s* of Horace Frederick Martin, MC and Phyllis Jeanette Martin; *m* 1958, Elizabeth Savage; two *s* one *d. Educ:* Sherborne School. Joined Friary Holroyd & Healy's Brewery, 1955, Dir, 1959; Dir, Friary Meux, 1963–66; Managing Dir, Ind Coope (East Anglia), 1966–69; Director: Joshua Tetley & Son, 1969–72; Allied Breweries, 1972–; Chief Exec., Joshua Tetley & Son, 1972–78; Vice-Chm., Joshua Tetley & Son and Tetley Walker, 1978–79; Chm., Ind Coope, 1979–85; Dir, Allied Lyons, 1981–; Man. Dir, 1985–86, Chm. and Chief Exec., 1986–88, Allied Breweries; Chm., J. Lyons & Co. Ltd, 1989–91. Chm., Brewers' Soc., 1991– (Vice-Chm., 1989–91). Pres., Shire Horse Soc., 1981–82. *Recreations:* travel, music, food. *Address:* Allied-Lyons PLC, 24 Portland Place, W1N 4BB. *T:* 071–323 9000.

MARTIN, Col Sir (Robert) Andrew (St George), KCVO 1988; OBE 1959 (MBE 1949); JP; Lord-Lieutenant and Custos Rotulorum of Leicestershire, 1965–89; *b* 23 April 1914; *o s* of late Major W. F. Martin, Leics Yeo., and late Violet Anne Philippa (*née* Wynter); *m* 1950, Margaret Grace (JP Leics 1967), *e d* of late J. V. Buchanan, MB, ChB and late Waiata Buchanan (*née* Godsal); one *s. Educ:* Eton Coll.; RMC Sandhurst. Commissioned Oxf. and Bucks Lt Inf., 1934; ADC to Gov.-Gen. of S Africa, 1938–40;

war service 4 Oxf. and Bucks, 1940–42; 2/7 R Warwick Regt, 1942–44; 5 DCLI, 1944–45 in NW Europe (despatches); Staff Coll., Camberley, 1945; DAMS, HQ ALFSEA, 1946; Mil. Asst to C of S, GHQ, SEALF, 1946–49 (MBE); Chief Instr, School of Mil. Admin., 1949–50; 1 Som. LI, 1950–52; AMS, HQ BAOR, 1952–54; 1 Oxf. and Bucks, 1954–55; Military Sec. to Gov.-Gen. of Australia, 1955–57; Comd 1 Oxf. and Bucks Lt Inf. and 1 Green Jackets, 1957–59; Bde Col Green Jackets Bde, 1959–62; Comd Recruiting and Liaison Staff, HQ Western Command, 1962–65. Pres., E Midlands TA&VRA, 1968–86. Hon. LLD Leicester, 1984; Hon. DTech Loughborough, 1988. JP Leics, 1965. KStJ 1966 (Pres., Council, Leics, 1966–). Order of Orange Nassau, 1950. *Recreations:* hunting, shooting, gardening. *Address:* The Brand, Woodhouse Eaves, Loughborough, Leics LE12 8SS. *T:* Woodhouse Eaves (0509) 890269. *Clubs:* Army and Navy, MCC.

MARTIN, (Robert) Bruce, QC 1977; Chairman, North Western Regional Health Authority, since 1988; *b* 2 Nov. 1938; *s* of late Robert Martin and Fay Martin; *m* 1967, Elizabeth Georgina (*née* Kiddie); one *s* one *d. Educ:* Shrewsbury Sch.; Liverpool Univ. (LLB Hons 1959). Called to the Bar, Middle Temple, 1960; a Recorder of the Crown Court, 1978–86. Chm., The Bob Martin Co., 1980–. Vice-Chm., Mersey RHA, 1986–88 (Mem., 1983–88). *Recreations:* music, golf, fishing. *Address:* 4 Montpelier Terrace, SW7. *T:* 071–584 0649. *Club:* Royal Birkdale Golf.

MARTIN, Robert Logan; QC (Scot.) 1988; *b* 31 July 1950; *s* of Robert Martin and Dr Janet Johnstone Logan or Martin; *m* 1984, Fiona Frances Neil; one *s* one *d. Educ:* Paisley Grammar Sch.; Univ. of Glasgow (LLB). Solicitor, 1973–76; admitted to Faculty of Advocates, 1976; Mem., Sheriff Court Rules Council, 1981–84; Standing Junior Counsel to Dept of Employment in Scotland, 1983–84; Advocate-Depute, 1984–87; called to the Bar, Lincoln's Inn, 1990. Admitted to Bar of NSW, 1987. Chm., Industrial Tribunals, 1991–. *Recreations:* shooting, ski-ing. *Address:* Hardengreen House, by Eskbank, Midlothian EH22 3LF. *Club:* New (Edinburgh).

MARTIN, Robin Geoffrey; Director, Hewetson plc, since 1980 (Chairman, 1980–88); *b* 9 March 1921; *s* of Cecil Martin and Isabel Katherine Martin (*née* Hickman); *m* 1946, Margery Chester Yates; two *s* one *d. Educ:* Cheltenham Coll.; Jesus Coll., Cambridge (MA). FIQ. Tarmac Ltd: Dir 1955; Gp Man. Dir 1963; Dep. Chm. 1967; Chm. and Chief Exec., 1971–79; Dir, Serck Ltd, 1971, Dep. Chm., 1974, Chm., 1976–81; Director: Burmah Oil Co,. 1975–85; Ductile Steels Ltd, 1977–82. Mem., Midlands Adv. Bd, Legal and General Assurance Soc. Ltd, 1977–84. Chm., Ironbridge Gorge Develt Trust, 1976–78. Life Governor, Birmingham Univ., 1970–85. *Recreations:* gardening, bridge. *Club:* East India.

MARTIN, Roger John Adam; formerly HM Diplomatic Service; Director, Somerset Trust for Nature Conservation, since 1988; *b* 21 Jan. 1941; *s* of late Geoffrey (Richard Rex) Martin and of Hazel (*née* Matthews); *m* 1972, Ann Cornwell (*née* Sharp); one *s. Educ:* Westminster School; Brasenose College, Oxford (BA). VSO, Northern Rhodesia, 1959–60; Commonwealth Office, 1964–66; Second Sec., Djakarta, 1967, Saigon, 1968–70; First Sec., FCO, 1971–74, Geneva, 1975–79; seconded to Dept of Trade, as Head of Middle East/North Africa Br., 1981–83; Dep. High Comr, Harare, 1983–86; resigned. Vis. Fellow, Univ. of Bath. Mem., Nat. Exec., VSO, 1988–91. *Publication:* Southern Africa: the price of apartheid, 1988. *Recreations:* walking, ski-ing, archaeology, music. *Address:* Coxley House, Coxley, near Wells, Somerset BA5 1QS. *T:* Wells (0749) 72180.

MARTIN, Ronald, MBE 1945; *b* 7 Nov. 1919; *o s* of late Albert and Clara Martin; *m* 1943, Bettina, *o d* of late H. E. M. Billing; one *d. Educ:* St Olave's Grammar Sch. Asst Traffic Superintendent, GPO, 1939. Served War of 1939–45, Royal Signals, NW Europe. GPO: Asst Princ., 1948; Princ., 1950; Treasury, 1954; Princ. Private Sec. to PMG, 1955; Staff Controller, GPO, London, 1956; Asst Sec., 1957; Dir Establishments and Organisation, GPO, 1966; Dir Telecommunications Personnel, 1967; Dir of Marketing, Telecommunications HQ, 1968–75; Sen. Dir, Customer Services, 1975–79. *Recreations:* music, motoring, horology. *Address:* 23 Birch Close, Send, Woking, Surrey GU23 7BZ.

MARTIN, (Roy) Peter, MBE 1970; author; *b* 5 Jan. 1931; *s* of Walter Martin and Annie Mabel Martin; *m* 1st, 1951, Marjorie Peacock (marr. diss. 1960); 2nd, Joan Drumwright (marr. diss. 1977); two *s*; 3rd, 1978, Catherine Sydee. *Educ:* Highbury Grammar Sch.; Univ. of London (BA 1953, MA 1956); Univ. of Tübingen. Nat. Service (RAF Educn Branch), 1949–51. Worked as local govt officer, schoolteacher and tutor in adult educn; then as British Council officer, 1960–83; service in Indonesia, Hungary (Cultural Attaché) and Japan (Cultural Counsellor). *Publications:* (with Joan Martin) Japanese Cooking, 1970; (as James Melville): The Wages of Zen, 1979; The Chrysanthemum Chain, 1980; A Sort of Samurai, 1981; The Ninth Netsuke, 1982; Sayonara, Sweet Amaryllis, 1983; Death of a Daimyo, 1984; The Death Ceremony, 1985; Go Gently Gaijin, 1986; The Imperial Way, 1986; Kimono For A Corpse, 1987; The Reluctant Ronin, 1988; A Haiku for Hanae, 1989; A Tarnished Phoenix, 1990; The Bogus Buddha, 1990. *Recreations:* music, books. *Address:* c/o Curtis Brown, 162–168 Regent Street, W1R 5TB. *Clubs:* Travellers', Detection.

MARTIN, Samuel Frederick Radcliffe, CB 1979; First Legislative Draftsman, 1973–79; *b* 2 May 1918; 2nd *s* of late William and Margaret Martin; *m* 1947, Sarah, *y d* of late Rev. Joseph and Margaret McKane; three *s. Educ:* Royal Belfast Academical Instn; Queen's Univ., Belfast (LLB). Called to Bar, Gray's Inn, 1950. Examr, Estate Duty Office, NI, 1939; Professional Asst, Office of Parly Draftsmen, 1956. Legal Adviser to Examiner of Statutory Rules, NI, 1979–81; Asst Comr, Local Govt Boundaries' Commn, 1983–84. Northern Ireland Editor, Current Law. *Publications:* articles in NI Legal Qly and Gazette of Incorp. Law Soc. *Recreation:* golf. *Address:* Brynburn, 196 Upper Road, Greenisland, Carrickfergus, Co. Antrim BT38 8RW. *T:* Whiteabbey (0232) 862417.

MARTIN, Sir Sidney (Launcelot), Kt 1979; FRSC; Pro Vice-Chancellor, University of the West Indies, and Principal, Cave Hill Campus, 1964–83, retired; *b* 27 Sept. 1918; *s* of Sidney A. Martin and late Miriam A. Martin (*née* McIntosh); *m* 1944, Olga Brett (*née* Dolphin); three *s. Educ:* Wolmers Boys' Sch., Jamaica (Jamaica schol. 1937); Royal College of Science, Imperial Coll. London, 1938–42 (BScChem, ARCS, DIC; Fellow, 1981); MSc London. FRIC 1949 (ARIC 1940). Materials Research Laboratory, Phillips Electrical Ltd, Surrey, 1942; Head. Phys. Chem. Div., 1946–49; University College of the West Indies, later University of the West Indies: Lectr, 1949–52, Sen. Lectr, 1952–63, in Phys. Chem.; Warden, Taylor Hall, 1954–64; Acting Registrar, on secondment, 1961–63; Registrar, 1963–66; Principal, Cave Hill, and Pro Vice-Chancellor on secondment, 1964–66, substantively, 1966–83; Hon. LLD Univ. of West Indies, 1984. Chairman: Sci. Res. Council of Jamaica, 1961–64; Barbados Nat. Council for Sci. and Technology, 1977–84; Member: Bd of Management, Coll. of Arts, Sci. and Technology, Jamaica, 1958–64; Educnl Adv. Cttee, Jamaica, 1960–64; Public Services Commn of Barbados, 1964–69; Bd of Management, Codrington Coll., Barbados, 1969–84. Member: Faraday Soc., London, 1943–68; Chemical Soc., London, 1942–; RSA, 1972–. Queen's Silver Jubilee Medal, 1977. *Publications:* articles in various chemical and physical jls. *Recreations:* bridge, reading. *Address:* c/o University of the West Indies, Cave Hill Campus, PO Box 64, Barbados. *T:* 425–1310; 2 Balmoral Apartments, Balmoral Gap, Hastings, Christchurch, GPO 28, Barbados. *T:* 429–5288.

MARTIN, Stanley William Frederick, LVO 1981; HM Diplomatic Service; First Assistant Marshal of the Diplomatic Corps, since 1981 and Associate Head of Protocol Department, Foreign and Commonwealth Office, since 1986; *b* 9 Dec. 1934; *s* of Stanley and Winifred Martin; *m* 1960, Hanni Aud Hansen, Copenhagen; one *s* one *d. Educ:* Bromley Grammar Sch.; University Coll., Oxford (MA Jurisprudence); Inner Temple (student Scholar). Nat. Service, 2nd Lieut RASC, 1953–55. Entered CRO, 1958; Asst Private Sec. to Sec. of State, 1959–62; First Secretary: Canberra, 1962–64; Kuala Lumpur, 1964–67; FCO (Planning Staff and Personnel Dept), 1967–70; seconded to CSD (CSSB), 1970–71; Asst Marshal of the Diplomatic Corps, 1972–81. Vis. Prof., Diplomatic Acad., Polytechnic of Central London, 1987–. Mem., Central Council, Royal Over-Seas League, 1982–. FRSA. Freeman of the City of London, 1988. *Publications:* contribs to Jl of Orders and Medals Res. Soc. *Recreations:* collecting books and manuscripts, historical research and writing, walking. *Address:* c/o Protocol Department, Foreign and Commonwealth Office, SW1A 2AF. *Club:* Royal Over-Seas League.

MARTIN, Thomas Ballantyne; *b* 1901; *s* of late Angus Martin, FRCSE, Forest Hall, and Robina, *d* of Thomas Pringle, Middleton Hall, Wooler, Northumberland; *m* 1953, Jean Elisabeth, *e d* of Lt-Col O. D. Bennett and Audrey, *d* of Sir Hamilton Grant, 12th Bt of Dalvey; two *d. Educ:* Cambridge Univ. (MA). MP (C) Blaydon Div. of Co. Durham, 1931–35. Political Correspondent of Daily Telegraph, 1936–40. RAFVR; Squadron Leader, Middle East Intelligence Centre, 1940–43; Adviser on Public Relations to UK High Comr in Australia, 1943–45; Sec. of United Europe Movement, 1947–48; Sec. to British all-party delegn to Congress of Europe at The Hague. Mem., London Stock Exchange, 1949–74, retired. *Address:* Noad's House, Tilshead, Salisbury, Wilts SP3 4RY. *T:* Shrewton (0980) 620258. *Clubs:* Army and Navy, Pratt's.

MARTIN, (Thomas) Geoffrey; Head of External Relations, Commission of the European Communities Office, London, since 1987; *b* 26 July 1940; *s* of Thomas Martin and Saidee Adelaide (*née* Day); *m* 1968, Gay (Madeleine Annesley) Brownrigg; one *s* three *d. Educ:* Queen's Univ., Belfast (BSc Hons). President, National Union of Students of England, Wales and Northern Ireland, 1966–68; City of London: Banking, Shipping, 1968–73; Director, Shelter, 1973–74; Diplomatic Staff, Commonwealth Secretariat, 1974–79; Head of EC Office, NI, 1979–85; Head of EC Press and Inf. Services, SE Asia, 1985–87. *Address:* Commission of the European Communities, 8 Storey's Gate, SW1P 3AT. *Club:* Travellers'.

MARTIN, Victor Cecil, OBE; HM Diplomatic Service, retired; *b* 12 Oct. 1915; *s* of late Cecil Martin and Isabel Katherine Martin (*née* Hickman). *Educ:* Cheltenham Coll.; Jesus Coll., Cambridge (Scholar; Classical Tripos Parts 1 and 2; MA). Asst Principal, Board of Education, 1939. Served Intelligence Corps, 1940–45; Major 1944, Persia and Iraq Force. Principal, Min. of Education, 1946; transferred to CRO, 1948; British High Commn, New Delhi, 1951–54, 1956–60; Asst Sec., CRO, 1962; Head of West Africa Dept, 1961–64; Head of S Asia Dept, 1964–66; Head of Cultural Relations Dept, 1966–68; Dep. High Comr, Madras, 1968–71; Special Adviser to High Comr, British High Commn, New Delhi, 1972–75. *Recreations:* ornithology, music. *Address:* 76 Swan Court, Flood Street, SW3. *Clubs:* United Oxford & Cambridge University, Commonwealth Trust, Royal Over-Seas League.

MARTIN, William McChesney, Jun.; Chairman, Board of Governors, Federal Reserve System, 1951–70; *b* St Louis, Mo, 17 Dec. 1906; *s* of William McChesney Martin and Rebecca (*née* Woods); *m* 1942, Cynthia Davis; one *s* two *d. Educ:* Yale Univ. (BA 1928); Benton Coll. of Law, St Louis, 1931. Graduate student (part time), Columbia Univ., 1931–37. Served in bank examination dept of Federal Reserve Bank of St Louis, 1928–29; Head of statistics dept, A. G. Edwards & Sons, St Louis, 1929–31; partner, May 1931–July 1938. Mem., New York Stock Exch., June 1931–July 1938; Gov., 1935–38; Chm. Cttee on Constitution, 1937–38; Sec. Conway Cttee to reorganize the Exchange, 1937–38; Chm. Bd and Pres. pro. tem. May-June 1938; Pres. July 1938–April 1941. Asst Exec. President's Soviet Protocol Cttee and Munitions Assignments Board, Wash., DC, 1942; appointed Mem. Export-Import Bank, Nov. 1945; Chm. and Pres., 1946–49 (as Chm. of Federal Reserve Board, served on National Advisory Council on Internat. Monetary and Financial Problems). Asst Sec. of the Treasury, Feb. 1949–April 1951; US Exec. Dir, IBRD, 1949–52. Dir of several corporations. Trustee: Berry Schs, Atlanta, Ga; Johns Hopkins Univ., Baltimore; Nat. Geographic Soc. Holds numerous Hon. Degrees from Univs in USA and Canada. Drafted, Selective Service Act, private, US Army, 1941, Sergeant, GHQ Army War Coll., 1941; Commnd 1st Lt, Inf., Feb. 1942; Captain Aug. 1942; Major, 1943; Lt-Col 1944; Col 1945. Legion of Merit, 1945. *Recreations:* tennis, squash. *Address:* 2861 Woodland Drive, NW, Washington, DC 20008, USA. *Clubs:* West Side Tennis, Yale; Metropolitan, Jefferson Island, Alibi (Washington); Chevy Chase (Md).

MARTIN-BATES, James Patrick, MA; JP; FCIS; CBIM; Director: Atkins Holdings Ltd, 1986–90 (Chairman, 1987–89); W. S. Atkins Ltd, since 1986; W. S. Atkins Group Ltd, 1970–86; *b* 17 April 1912; *er s* of late R. Martin-Bates, JP, Perth, Scotland; *m* 1939, Clare, *d* of late Prof. James Miller, MD, DSc; one *s* two *d. Educ:* Perth Academy; Glenalmond; Worcester Coll., Oxford. BA 1933; MA 1944. Lamson Industries, 1933–36; Dorman Long & Co. Ltd, 1936–38; PE Group, 1938–61: Man. Dir, Production Engineering Ltd, 1953–59; Vice-Chm., PE Holdings, 1959–61; Director: Hutchinson Ltd, 1958–78; Avery's Ltd, 1970–77; Charringtons Industrial Holdings Ltd, 1972–77. Principal, Administrative Staff Coll., Henley-on-Thames, 1961–72. Chm., Management Consultants Association, 1960; Member: Council, British Institute of Management, 1961–66; UK Advisory Council on Education for Management, 1961–66; Council, Glenalmond, 1963–82; Bd of Visitors, HM Borstal, Huntercombe, 1964–67; The Council for Technical Education and Training for Overseas Countries, 1962–73; Council, University Coll., Nairobi, 1965–68; Council, Chartered Institute of Secretaries, 1965–74; EDC for Rubber Industry, 1965–69; Council, Univ. of Buckingham (formerly University Coll. at Buckingham), 1977–87. Governor, Aylesbury Grammar Sch., 1983–89. UN Consultant in Iran, 1972–78. High Sheriff of Buckinghamshire, 1974; Chm., Marlow Bench, 1978–82. FCIS 1961; FBIM 1960; Fellow Internat. Acad. of Management, 1964. DUniv Buckingham, 1986. Burnham Medal, BIM, 1974. *Publications:* various articles in Management Journals. *Recreations:* golf, fishing. *Address:* Ivy Cottage, Fingest, near Henley-on-Thames, Oxon RG9 6QD. *T:* Turville Heath (049163) 202. *Clubs:* Caledonian; Royal and Ancient (St Andrews).

MARTIN-BIRD, Col Sir Richard Dawnay, Kt 1975; CBE 1971 (OBE (mil.) 1953); TD 1950; DL; President, Yates Brothers Wine Lodges PLC, Manchester; *b* 19 July 1910; *s* of late Richard Martin Bird and Mildred, 2nd *d* of late Peter Peel Yates; *m* 1935, Katharine Blanche, *d* of Sir Arthur Selborne Jelf, CMG; one *s* three *d* (and one *s* decd). *Educ:* Charterhouse. Served with 8th (Ardwick) Bn, The Manchester Regt (TA), 1936–53; war service 1939–45; Lt-Col comdg, 1947–53; Hon. Col, 1953–67; Hon. Col, The Manchester Regt (Ardwick and Ashton) Territorials, 1967–71; Dep. Comdr, 127 Inf. Bde (TA), 1953–57 and 1959–63; Regtl Councillor, The King's Regt, 1967–; ADC (TA) to the Queen, 1961–65; Chairman: E Lancs T&AFA, 1963–68; TA&VRA for Lancs, Cheshire and IoM, later TA&VRA for NW England and IoM, 1968–75; Vice-Chm., Council, TA&AVR Assocs, 1973–75; Mem., TAVR Adv. Cttee, 1973–75. Pres., Wine and Spirit Assoc. of GB, 1978–79. DL Lancs 1964–74, Cheshire 1974; High Sheriff Greater Manchester, 1976–82. *Address:* Stockinwood, Chelford, Cheshire SK11 9BE. *T:* Chelford (0625) 861523. *Clubs:* Army and Navy; St James's (Manchester); Winckley (Preston).

MARTIN-JENKINS, Christopher Dennis Alexander; cricket correspondent, Daily Telegraph, since 1991; BBC cricket commentator, since 1973; *b* 20 Jan. 1945; *s* of Dennis Frederick Martin-Jenkins, *qv*; *m* 1971, Judith Oswald Hayman; two *s* one *d*. *Educ:* Marlborough; Fitzwilliam Coll., Cambridge (BA (Modern Hist.); MA). Dep. Editor, The Cricketer, 1967–70; sports broadcaster, 1970–73, Cricket Correspondent, 1973–80, 1984–91, BBC; Editor, 1981–88, Editl Dir, 1988–91, The Cricketer International. *Publications:* Testing Time, 1974; Assault on the Ashes, 1975; MCC in India, 1977; The Jubilee Tests and the Packer Revolution, 1977; In Defence of the Ashes, 1979; Cricket Contest, 1980; The Complete Who's Who of Test Cricketers, 1980; The Wisden Book of County Cricket, 1981; Bedside Cricket, 1981; Twenty Years On: Cricket's years of change, 1984; Cricket: a way of life, 1984; (ed) Cricketer Book of Cricket Eccentrics, 1985; (ed) Seasons Past, 1986; (ed jtly) Quick Singles, 1986; Grand Slam, 1987; Cricket Characters, 1987; Sketches of a Season, 1989. *Recreations:* cricket, Rugby fives, tennis, golf, gardening, walking. *Address:* Daily Telegraph, South Quay, 185 Marsh Wall, E14 9SR. *Clubs:* MCC; I Zingari, Free Foresters, Arabs, Marlborough Blues, Cranleigh Cricket, Albury Cricket, Rudgwick Cricket, Horsham Cricket, Surrey Cricket.

MARTIN-JENKINS, Dennis Frederick, TD 1945; Chairman, Ellerman Lines Ltd, 1967–81 (Managing Director, 1967–76); formerly chairman or director of many other companies; retired; *b* 7 Jan. 1911; 2nd *s* of late Frederick Martin-Jenkins, CA and late Martha Magdalene Martin-Jenkins (*née* Almeida); *m* 1937, Rosemary Clare Walker, MRCS, LRCP; three *s*. *Educ:* St Bede's Sch., Eastbourne; Marlborough College. FCIT. Served RA, 1939–45 (Lt-Col). Insce, 1930–35; joined Montgomerie & Workman Ltd, 1935; transf. City Line Ltd, 1938; transf. Hall Line Ltd, 1947 (Dir 1949); Dir, Ellerman Lines Ltd and associated cos, 1950. Chamber of Shipping of UK: Mem. 1956 (Hon. Mem., 1975); Vice-Pres. 1964; Pres. 1965; Chm., Deep Sea Liner Section, 1969–76; Chairman: Gen. Council of British Shipping for UK, 1963; Internat. Chamber of Shipping, 1971–77; Past Chm., London Gen. Shipowners' Soc.; formerly Member: Mersey Docks and Harbour Bd; Bd of PLA; Nat. Dock Labour Bd; Exec. Cttee, Nat. Assoc. of Port Employers; Mem., British Transport Docks Bd, 1968–81. Chm. and Trustee, Moorgate Trust Fund; Trustee, New Moorgate Trust Fund. *Recreations:* golf, gardening. *Address:* Maytree House, Woodcote, Guildford Road, Cranleigh, Surrey GU6 8NZ. *T:* Cranleigh (0483) 276278. *Clubs:* United Oxford & Cambridge University; Woking Golf, Thurlestone Golf.
See also C. D. A. Martin-Jenkins.

MARTINDALE, Air Vice-Marshal Alan Rawes, CB 1984; Royal Air Force, retired; *b* 20 Jan. 1930; *s* of late Norman Martindale and Edith (*née* Rawes); *m* 1952, Eileen Alma Wrenn; three *d*. *Educ:* Kendal Grammar Sch.; University Coll., Leicester (BA History, London Univ., 1950). Commissioned RAF, 1951; served, 1951–71: RAF Driffield, Oakington, Eindhoven, Stafford, Wickenby, Faldingworth and Marham; Instructor, RAF Coll., Cranwell; Staff AHQ Malta; RAF Staff Coll., Bracknell, MoD, Jt Services Staff Coll. (student and Directing Staff), and HQ Maintenance Comd; Dep. Dir of Supply Management, MoD, Harrogate, 1971–72; Comd Supply Officer, RAF Germany, 1972–74; Dir of Supply Management, MoD, Harrogate, 1974–75; RCDS, 1976; Air Cdre Supply and Movements, RAF Support Comd, 1977; Dep. Gen. Man., NAMMA, 1978–81; Dir of Supply Policy (RAF), MoD, 1981–82; Dir Gen. of Supply (RAF), 1982–84; retd 1985. Dist Gen. Manager, Hastings HA, 1985–90; Census Area Manager, S Kent and Hastings, 1990–91. *Recreations:* golf, gardening. *Address:* Taylors Cottage, Mountfield, Robertsbridge, East Sussex TN32 5JZ. *Club:* Royal Air Force.

MARTINEAU, Charles Herman; Chairman, Electricity Consultative Council for South of Scotland, 1972–76; *b* 3 Sept. 1908; *s* of Prof. Charles E. Martineau, Birmingham; *m* 1939, Margaret Shirley Dolphin; two *s* one *d*. *Educ:* King Edward's Sch., Birmingham. Jas Williamson & Son Ltd, Lancaster and Nairn-Williamson Ltd, Kirkcaldy: Man. Dir, 1952–66. Part-time Mem., S of Scotland Electricity Bd, 1971–76. Mem., Fife CC, 1967 (Vice-Convener, 1970–73); Mem., Fife Regional Council, 1978–82. *Recreations:* chess, golf. *Address:* Gladsmuir, Hepburn Gardens, St Andrews, Fife. *T:* St Andrews (0334) 73069. *Club:* Royal and Ancient (St Andrews).
See also Rt Rev. R. A. S. Martineau.

MARTINEAU, Rt. Rev. Robert Arnold Schürhoff, MA; *b* 22 Aug. 1913; *s* of late Prof. C. E. Martineau, MA, MCom, FCA, and Mrs Martineau, Birmingham; *m* 1941, Elinor Gertrude Ap-Thomas; one *s* two *d*. *Educ:* King Edward's Sch., Birmingham; Trinity Hall, Cambridge; Westcott House, Cambridge. Tyson Medal for Astronomy, 1935. Deacon 1938, priest 1939; Curate, Melksham, 1938–41. Chaplain: RAFVR, 1941–46; RAuxAF, 1947–52. Vicar: Ovenden, Halifax, 1946–52; Allerton, Liverpool, 1952–66; St Christopher, San Lorenzo, Calif, 1961–62. Hon. Canon of Liverpool, 1961–66; Rural Dean of Childwall, 1964–66. Proctor in Convocation, 1964–66. Bishop Suffragan of Huntingdon, 1966–72; Residentiary Canon of Ely, 1966–72; Bishop of Blackburn, 1972–81. First Jt Chm., C of E Bd of Educn and Nat. Soc. for Promoting Religious Educn, 1973–79. Chm., Central Readers Bd, C of E, 1971–76. *Publications:* The Church in Germany in Prayer (ed jtly), 1937; Rhodesian Wild Flowers, 1953; The Office and Work of a Reader, 1970; The Office and Work of a Priest, 1972; Moments that Matter, 1976; Preaching through the Christian Year; Truths that Endure, 1977; Travelling with Christ, 1981. *Recreations:* gardening, swimming. *Address:* Gwenallt, Park Street, Denbigh, Clwyd LL16 3DB.
See also C. H. Martineau.

MARTINEAU-WALKER, Roger Antony; *see* Walker.

MARTINEZ ZUVIRIA, Gen. Gustavo; historian; Argentine Ambassador to the Court of St James's, 1970–74; *b* 28 Dec. 1915; *s* of Dr Gustavo Martinez Zuviria and Matilde de Iriondo de Martinez Zuviria; *m* 1940, Maria Eugenia Ferrer Deheza; five *s* four *d* (and one *s* decd). *Educ:* Col. El Salvador, Buenos Aires; Mount St Mary's Coll. (Nr Sheffield); San Martin Mil. Academy. Promoted to 2nd Lt, 1938; Capt. 1951. He participated in attempt to overthrow the Peron regime; imprisoned, but when Peron was overthrown, he continued career in Army; among other posts he served in: Cavalry Regt No 12, 1940; Granaderos a Caballo, 1944; Cavalry Regt No 7, 1945; Military Sch.: Instr of cadets, 1944; Asst Dir and Dir of Sch., 1958. Mil. Attaché to Peru, 1955; Chief of 3rd Regt of Cavalry, 1957; Chief of Staff, Argentine Cav. Corps, 1961; Dir, in Superior War Staff Coll., 1962; Dir, Sch. of Cav. and Cav. Inspector, 1963; Comdr, 2nd Cav. Div., 1964; 2nd Comdr, 3rd Army Corps, 1965; Comdr, 1st Army Corps, 1966; Comdr, Southern Joint Forces, 1969; retd from Army and was designated Sec. of State in Intelligence (Secretario de Informaciones de Estado), in 1970. Presidente dela Comisión de Caballería, 1974–76. Member: Genealogical Studies Centre, 1962; Nat. Sanmartinian Historical Academy, 1966; Nat. Acad. of History, 1978. Lectured in Paris and Brussels, Feb. 1978, on bicentenary of birth of Gen. San Martín. Holds several foreign orders. *Publications:* numerous (related to professional and historical subjects); notably Los tiempos de Mariano Necochea, 1961 (2nd edn, 1969) (1st award mil. lit. and award Fundación Eguiguren); Retreta del Desierto, 1956 (14 edns); José Pidsudski; San Martin y O'Brien, 1963; Historia de Angel Pacheco, 1969. *Recreations:* riding, shooting. *Address:* Avenida del Libertador 15249, 1640 Acassuso, Buenos Aires, Argentina. *Clubs:* Naval and Military, Travellers', Hurlingham, Turf (all in London); Cowdray Park Polo (Sussex); Circulo Militar, Jockey (Buenos Aires); Club Social de Paraná (Entre Rios).

MARTINI, His Eminence Cardinal Carlo Maria, SJ; Archbishop of Milan, since 1980; *b* 15 Feb. 1927; *s* of Leonardo and Olga Maggia. *Educ:* Pontifical Gregorian Univ. (DTheol); Pontifical Biblical Inst. (Doctorate in holy scripture). Ordained priest, 1952; Rector, Pontifical Biblical Inst., 1969–78; Rector, Gregorian Univ., 1978–79. Cardinal 1983. Pres., Consilium Conferentiarum Episcopalium Europae, 1987–. *Address:* Piazza Fontana 2, 20122 Milano, Italy. *T:* 2.85561.

MARTLEW, Eric Anthony; MP (Lab) Carlisle, since 1987; *b* 3 Jan. 1949; *m* 1970, Elsie Barbara Duggan. *Educ:* Harraby Secondary School, Carlisle; Carlisle Tech. Coll. Nestlé Co. Ltd, 1966–87: joined as lab. technician; later Personnel Manager, Dalston Factory, Carlisle. Member: Carlisle County Borough Council, 1972–74; Cumbria CC, 1973–88 (Chm., 1983–85). Mem., Cumbria Health Authy, later E Cumbria HA, 1977–87 (Chm., 1977–79). *Recreations:* photography, fell walking, horse racing. *Address:* 42 Beaumont Road, Carlisle. *T:* Carlisle (0228) 20077.

MARTONMERE, 2nd Baron *cr* 1964; **John Stephen Robinson;** *b* 10 July 1963; *s* of Hon. Richard Anthony Gasque Robinson (*d* 1979) and of Wendy Patricia (who *m* subseq. Ronald De Mara), *d* of late James Cecil Blagden; *S* grandfather, 1989. *Educ:* Lakefield College School; Senaca College. *Heir:* *b* David Alan Robinson, *b* 15 Sept. 1965. *Address:* 99 Parklea Drive, Toronto, Ontario M4G 2J9, Canada. *T:* 416–696–0077.

MARTY, Cardinal François, Officier de la Légion d'honneur; *b* Pachins, Aveyron, 18 May 1904; *s* of François Marty, cultivateur, and Zoé (*née* Gineste). *Educ:* Collège de Graves et Villefranche-de-Rouergue; Séminaire de Rodez; Institut Catholique de Toulouse (Dr en Th.). Priest, 1930. Vicaire: Villefranche-de-Rouergue, 1932; Rodez, 1933; Parish Priest: Bournazel, 1940; Rieupeyroux, 1943; Archpriest, Millau, 1949; Vicar-General, Rodez, 1951; Bishop of Saint Flour, 1952; Coadjutor Archbishop, 1959, and Archbishop of Reims, 1960; Archbishop of Paris, 1968–81. Cardinal, 1969. Pres., Comité Episcopal of Mission de France, 1965; Mem. Bureau, then Vice-Pres., Perm. Council of French Episcopate, 1966, and Pres., French Episcopal Conf., 1969–75, responsable des Catholiques orientaux. Member: Rome Commission for Revision of Canon Law; Congregations: Divine Worship; Clergy; Eastern Church. *Publications:* Dieu est tenace, 1973; Evangile au présent, 1974; Prophètes de la joie, 1978; l'Evêque dans la ville, 1979; Cardinal Marty: chronique vécue de l'église de France, 1980. *Address:* Monteils, 12200 Villefranche de Rouergue, France.

MARTYN, Charles Roger Nicholas; Master of the Supreme Court, since 1973; *b* 10 Dec. 1925; *s* of Rev. Charles Martyn; *m* 1960, Helen, *d* of Frank Everson; two *s* one *d*. *Educ:* Charterhouse, 1939–44; Merton Coll., Oxford, 1947–49. MA (Hons) Mod. Hist. Joined Regular Army, 1944; commissioned 60th Rifles (KRRC), 1945; CMF, 1946–47; special release, 1947. Articles, 1950–52, and admitted as solicitor, 1952. Sherwood & Co., Parly Agents (Partner), 1952–59; Lee, Bolton & Lee, Westminster (Partner), 1961–73; Notary Public, 1969. Mem. and Dep. Chm., No 14 Legal Aid Area Cttee, 1967–73; Hon. Legal Adviser to The Samaritans (Inc), 1955–73. Chm., Family Welfare Assoc., 1973–78; Member: Gtr London Citizens' Advice Bureaux Management Cttee, 1974–79; Council, St Gabriel's Coll. (Further Education), Camberwell, 1973–77 (Vice-Chm.); Council, Goldsmiths' Coll., Univ. of London, 1988– (Mem., Delegacy, 1977–88). *Recreations:* walking, sailing (Vice-Cdre, Thames Barge Sailing Club, 1962–65), observing people, do-it-yourself, nigrology. *Address:* 29 St Albans Road, NW5 1RG. *T:* 071–267 1076.

MARTYN-HEMPHILL, family name of **Baron Hemphill.**

MARWICK, Prof. Arthur John Brereton, FRHistS; Professor of History, The Open University, since 1969; *b* 29 Feb. 1936; *s* of William Hutton Marwick and Maeve Cluna Brereton; unmarried; one *d*. *Educ:* George Heriot's School, Edinburgh; Edinburgh Univ. (MA, DLitt); Balliol Coll., Oxford (BLitt). Asst Lectr in History, Univ. of Aberdeen, 1959–60; Lectr in History, Univ. of Edinburgh, 1960–69; Dean and Dir of Studies in Arts, Open Univ., 1978–84. Vis. Prof. in History, State Univ. of NY at Buffalo, 1966–67; Vis. Scholar, Hoover Instn and Vis. Prof., Stanford Univ., 1984–85; Directeur d'études invité, l'Ecole des Hautes Etudes en Sciences Sociales, Paris, 1985; Visiting Professor: Rhodes Coll., Memphis, 1991; Univ. of Perugia, 1991. *Publications:* The Explosion of British Society, 1963; Clifford Allen, 1964; The Deluge, 1965, new edn 1991; Britain in the Century of Total War, 1968; The Nature of History, 1970, 3rd edn 1989; War and Social Change in the Twentieth Century, 1974; The Home Front, 1976; Women at War 1914–1918, 1977; Class: image and reality in Britain, France and USA since 1930, 1980, rev. edn 1990; (ed) Illustrated Dictionary of British History, 1980; British Society since 1945, 1982, rev. edn 1990; Britain in Our Century, 1984; (ed) Class in the Twentieth Century, 1986; Beauty in History: society, politics and personal appearance c 1500 to the present, 1988; (ed) Total War and Social Change, 1988; (ed) The Arts, Literature and Society, 1990; Culture in Britain since 1945, 1991; contribs to English Hist. Review, Amer. Hist. Review, Jl of Contemporary Hist. *Recreations:* wine, women, football. *Address:* 67 Fitzjohns Avenue, Hampstead, NW3 6PE. *T:* 071–794 4534. *Clubs:* Open University Football, Open University Tennis.

MARWICK, Sir Brian (Allan), KBE 1963 (CBE 1954; OBE 1946); CMG 1958; *b* 18 June 1908; *s* of James Walter Marwick and Elizabeth Jane Flett; *m* 1934, Riva Lee (*d* 1988), *d* of Major H. C. Cooper; two *d*. *Educ:* University of Cape Town; CCC, Cambridge. Administrative Officer: Swaziland, 1925–36; Nigeria, 1937–40; Swaziland, 1941–46; First Asst Sec.: Swaziland, 1947–48; Basutoland, 1949–52; Dep. Resident Comr and Govt Sec., Basutoland, 1952–55; Administrative Sec. to High Comr for Basutoland, the Bechuanaland Protectorate and Swaziland, 1956; Resident Comr, Swaziland, 1957–63; HM Comr, Swaziland, 1963–64; Permanent Secretary: Min. of Works and Town Planning Dept, Nassau, Bahamas, 1965–68; Min. of Educn, Bahamas, 1968–71. *Publication:* The Swazi, 1940. *Recreation:* golf.

MARWICK, Ewan; Secretary and Chief Executive, Glasgow Chamber of Commerce, since 1983; *b* 23 April 1952; *s* of Kenneth and Valerie Marwick, Edinburgh; *m* 1980, Helen Daw, MA, PhD; four *s* one *d*. *Educ:* Daniel Stewart's Coll.; Edinburgh Univ. (MA Jt Hons Econs and Econ. Hist. 1974). Post-grad. res. and consultancy work on econ. implications of devolution, 1978; Asst Sec., RICS, 1979–80; Dep. Sec., Glasgow Chamber of Commerce, 1980–83. Sec., Assoc. of Scottish Chambers of Commerce, 1982–. Chm., Certification and Internat. Trade Formalities Cttee, 1991–. Non-Exec. Dir, Edinburgh Financial and General Holdings Ltd. Contested (C) Paisley North, Nov. 1990. *Publications:*

occasional articles on current affairs. *Recreations:* fishing, shooting. *Address:* Chamber of Commerce, 30 George Square, Glasgow G2 1EQ. *T:* 041–204 2121. *Club:* Glasgow Nomads.

MARX, Enid Crystal Dorothy, RDI 1944; Painter and Designer; *b* London, 20 Oct. 1902; *y d* of Robert J. Marx. *Educ:* Roedean Sch.; Central Sch. of Arts and Crafts; Royal College of Art Painting Sch. Designing and printing handblock printed textiles, 1925–39. Exhibited in USA and Europe; various works purchased by Victoria and Albert Museum, Musée des Arts Décoratifs, Boston Museum, Scottish Arts Council, Sheffield Art Gall., etc. Mem. Society of Wood Engravers. Wood engraving and autolithography pattern papers, book jackets, book illustration and decorations, trademarks, etc; designed moquettes and posters for LPTB. Industrial designing for printed and woven furnishing fabrics, wallpapers, ceramics, plastics. Fellow, 1982, Senior Fellow, 1987, RCA; FRSA, FSIAD; original mem. National Register of Industrial Designers of Central Institute of Art and Design. Mem. of Bd of Trade design panel on utility furniture. Designed postage stamps: ½d-2d for first issue Elizabeth II; Christmas 1976 issue. Lectures on textiles and folk art. *Publications:* (jointly) English Popular and Traditional Art, 1947; (with Margaret Lambert) English Popular Art, 1951, 2nd edn 1988; articles and broadcasts on aspects of industrial design in various countries; author and illustrator of twelve books for children. *Recreations:* study of popular art in different countries; gardening. *Address:* The Studio, 39 Thornhill Road, Barnsbury Square, N1. *T:* 071–607 2286.

MARY LEO, Sister; *see* Leo, Dame Sister Mary.

MARYCHURCH, Sir Peter (Harvey), KCMG 1985; Director, Government Communications Headquarters, 1983–89; *b* 13 June 1927; *s* of Eric William Alfred and Dorothy Margaret Marychurch; *m* 1965, June Daphne Ottaway (*née* Pareezer). *Educ:* Lower School of John Lyon, Harrow. Served RAF, 1945–48. Joined GCHQ, 1948; Asst Sec. 1975; Under Sec. 1979; Dep. Sec. 1983. *Recreations:* theatre, music (especially opera), gardening. *Address:* Midland Bank, 2 The Promenade, Cheltenham, Glos GL50 1LS. *Club:* Naval and Military.

MARYON DAVIS, Dr Alan Roger, FFPHM; Consultant in Public Health Medicine, West Lambeth Health Authority, since 1988; Senior Lecturer in Public Health, United Medical and Dental Schools (St Thomas's Campus), since 1988; *b* 21 Jan. 1943; *s* of Cyril Edward Maryon Davis and Hilda May Maryon Davis; one *s*; *m* 1981, Glynis Anne Davies; two *d*. *Educ:* St Paul's Sch.; St John's Coll., Cambridge (MA 1968; MB BChir 1970); St Thomas's Hosp. Med. Sch.; London Sch. of Hygiene and Tropical Medicine. MSc (Social Med.) London 1978; MRCP 1972; FFPHM (FFCM 1986); FRIPHH 1989. Early med. career in gen. medicine and rheumatology, later in community medicine; MO, 1977–84, CMO, 1984–87, Health Educn Council; Sen. Med. Adviser, Health Educn Authority, 1987–88; Hon. Consultant, Paddington and N Kensington HA, 1985–87; Hon. Sen. Lectr in Community Medicine, St Mary's Hosp. Med. Sch., 1985–88. Mem. Council, RIPH&H, 1989–. Trustee, Health Information Trust, 1987–; Patron, Healthcare Foundn, 1987–. Regular broadcaster on health matters, 1975–; BBC radio series: Action Makes the Heart Grow Stronger (Med. Journalist's Assoc. Radio Award), 1983; Back in 25 Minutes, 1985; Not Another Diet Programme, 1986; Cancer Check, 1987; Spring Into Summer, 1989; *television series:* Your Mind in Their Hands, 1982; Consider Yourself, 1983; Body Matters, 1985–89; Save a Life, 1986; The BBC Diet Programme, 1988; Go For It!, 1989; Healthwatch, 1990. Editor-in-Chief, Health Education Jl, 1984–88; Med. Advice Columnist, Woman magazine, 1988–. *Publications:* Family Health and Fitness, 1981; Body Facts, 1984; (with J. Thomas) Diet 2000, 1984; (with J. Rogers) How to Save a Life, 1987; PSSST—a Really Useful Guide to Alcohol, 1989; Reduce Your Cholesterol Now, 1991. *Recreations:* eating well, drinking well, singing (not so well) with the humorous group Instant Sunshine. *Address:* 4 Sibella Road, Clapham, SW4 6HX. *T:* 071-720 5659.

MASCALL, Rev. Canon Eric Lionel, DD Oxon, DD Cantab, BSc London; FBA 1974; an Hon. Canon of Truro Cathedral, with duties of Canon Theologian, 1973–84, now Canon Emeritus; Professor of Historical Theology, London University, at King's College, 1962–73, now Professor Emeritus; Dean, Faculty of Theology, London University, 1968–72; *b* 12 Dec. 1905; *s* of John R. S. Mascall and S. Lilian Mascall, *née* Grundy; unmarried. *Educ:* Latymer Upper Sch., Hammersmith; Pembroke Coll., Cambridge (Scholar); Theological Coll., Ely. BSc (London) 1926; BA (Wrangler) 1927, MA 1931, BD 1943, DD 1958 Cantab; DD Oxon, 1948. Sen. Maths Master, Bablake Sch., Coventry, 1928–31; ordained, 1932; Mem., Oratory of the Good Shepherd, 1938–; Asst Curate, St Andrew's, Stockwell Green, 1932–35; St Matthew's, Westminster, 1935–37; Sub-warden, Scholae Cancellarii, Lincoln, 1937–45; Lecturer in Theology, Christ Ch., Oxford, 1945–46; Student and Tutor of Christ Ch., Oxford, 1946–62, Emeritus Student, 1962–; University Lectr in Philosophy of Religion, 1947–62; Chaplain at Oxford to Bishop of Derby, 1947–48; Commissary to Archbishop of Cape Town, 1964–73; Examining Chaplain to: Bishop of Willesden, 1970–73; Bishop of Truro, 1973–81; Bishop of London, 1981–. Visiting Professor: Gregorian Univ., Rome, 1976; Pontifical Coll. Josephinum, Columbus, Ohio, 1977; Lectures: Bampton, Oxford, 1956; Bampton, Columbia, 1958; Boyle, 1965–66; Charles A. Hart Memorial, Cath. Univ. of America, Washington, DC, 1968; Gifford, Univ. of Edinburgh, 1970–71. FKC, 1968–. Hon. DD St Andrews, 1967. *Publications:* Death or Dogma, 1937; A Guide to Mount Carmel, 1939; Man, his Origin and Destiny, 1940; The God-Man, 1940; He Who Is, 1943, rev. edn 1966; Christ, the Christian and the Church, 1946; Existence and Analogy, 1949; Corpus Christi, 1953, rev. edn 1965; Christian Theology and Natural Science, 1956; Via Media, 1956; Words and Images, 1957; The Recovery of Unity, 1958; The Importance of Being Human, 1958; Pi in the High, 1959; Grace and Glory, 1961; Theology and History (Inaugural Lecture), 1962; Theology and Images, 1963; Up and Down in Adria, 1963; The Secularisation of Christianity, 1965; The Christian Universe, 1966; Theology and The Future, 1968; (jt author) Growing into Union, 1970; The Openness of Being, 1971; Nature and Supernature, 1976; Theology and the Gospel of Christ, 1977, rev. edn 1984; Whatever Happened to the Human Mind, 1980; Jesus: who he is and how we know him, 1985; Compliments of the Season, 1985; The Triune God, 1986; Editor: The Church of God, 1934; The Mother of God, 1949; The Angels of Light and the Powers of Darkness, 1954; The Blessed Virgin Mary, 1963; contribs to: Man, Woman and Priesthood, 1978; When Will Ye Be Wise?, 1983. *Address:* St Mary's House, Kingsmead, Belgrave Road, Seaford, East Sussex BN25 2ET.

MASCHLER, Fay; restaurant critic, Evening Standard, since 1972; *b* 15 July 1945; *d* of Mary and Arthur Frederick Coventry; *m* 1970, Thomas Michael Maschler, *qv* (marr. diss. 1987); one *s* two *d*. *Educ:* Convent of the Sacred Heart, Greenwich, Conn. Copywriter, J. Walter Thompson, 1964; journalist, Radio Times, 1969. *Publications:* Cooking is a Game You Can Eat, 1975; A Child's Book of Manners, 1979; Miserable Aunt Bertha, 1980; Fay Maschler's Guide to Eating Out in London, 1986; Eating In, 1987; Howard & Maschler on Food, 1987; Teach Your Child to Cook, 1988. *Address:* Epworth, Antrim Road, NW3 4XN. *T:* 071–722 1376. *Clubs:* Groucho, Car Clamp.

MASCHLER, Thomas Michael; Publisher, Jonathan Cape Children's Books, since 1991; Director, Jonathan Cape Ltd, since 1960 (Chairman, 1970–91); *b* 16 Aug. 1933; *s* of Kurt Leo Maschler and of Rita Masseron (*née* Lechner); *m* 1970, Fay Coventry (*see* Fay Maschler) (marr. diss. 1987); one *s* two *d*; *m* 1988, Regina Kulinicz. *Educ:* Leighton Park School. Production Asst, Andre Deutsch, 1955; Editor, MacGibbon & Kee, 1956–58; Fiction Editor, Penguin Books, 1958–60; Jonathan Cape: Editorial Dir, 1960; Man. Dir, 1966. Associate Producer, The French Lieutenant's Woman (film), 1981. *Publications:* (ed) Declarations, 1957; (ed) New English Dramatists Series, 1959–63. *Address:* 20 Vauxhall Bridge Road, SW1V 2SA.

MASEFIELD, John Thorold, CMG 1986; HM Diplomatic Service; High Commissioner to Tanzania, since 1989; *b* 1 Oct. 1939; *e s* of Dr Geoffrey Bussell Masefield, DSc and Mildred Joy Thorold Masefield (*née* Rogers); *m* 1962, Jennifer Mary, *d* of late Rev. Dr H. C. Trowell, OBE and late K. M. Trowell, MBE; two *s* one *d* (and one *d* decd). *Educ:* Dragon Sch., Oxford; Repton Sch.; St John's Coll., Cambridge (Scholar) (MA). Joined CRO, 1962; Private Sec. to Permanent Under Sec., 1963–64; Second Secretary: Kuala Lumpur, 1964–65; Warsaw, 1966–67; FCO, 1967–69; First Sec., UK Delegn to Disarmament Conf., 1970–74; Dep. Head, Planning Staff, FCO, 1974–77; Far Eastern Dept, FCO, 1977–79; Counsellor, Head of Chancery and Consul Gen., Islamabad, 1979–82; Head of Personnel Services Dept, FCO, 1982–85; Head, Far Eastern Dept, FCO, 1985–87; Fellow, Center for Internat. Affairs, Harvard Univ., 1987–88; seconded to CSSB, 1988–89. *Publication:* article in International Affairs. *Recreations:* fruit and vegetables. *Address:* c/o Foreign and Commonwealth Office, SW1A 2AH. *Clubs:* Commonwealth Trust; Gymkhana, Yacht (Dar es Salaam).

MASEFIELD, Sir Peter (Gordon), Kt 1972; MA Cantab; CEng; Hon. FRAeS; FCIT; Chairman, Brooklands Museum Trust, since 1987; Director, London Transport International, since 1981; *b* Trentham, Staffs, 19 March 1914; *e s* of late Dr W. Gordon Masefield, CBE, MRCS, and Marian A. Masefield (*née* Lloyd-Owen); *m* 1936, Patricia Doreen, 3rd *d* of late Percy H. Rooney, Wallington, Surrey; three *s* one *d*. *Educ:* Westminster Sch.; Chillon Coll., Switzerland; Jesus Coll., Cambridge (BA (Eng) 1935). On Design Staff, The Fairey Aviation Co. Ltd, 1935–37; Pilot's licence, 1937–70; joined The Aeroplane newspaper, 1937, Technical Editor, 1939–43; Air Correspondent Sunday Times, 1940–43; War Corresp. with RAF and US Army Eighth Air Force on active service, 1939–43; Editor, The Aeroplane Spotter, 1941–43; Chm. Editorial Cttee, The Inter-Services Journal on Aircraft Recognition, MAP, 1942–45; Personal Adviser to the Lord Privy Seal (Lord Beaverbrook) and Sec. of War Cabinet Cttee on Post War Civil Air Transport, 1943–45; first British Civil Air Attaché, British Embassy, Washington, DC, 1945–46 (Signator to Anglo-American Bermuda Air Agreement, 1946); Dir-Gen. of Long Term Planning and Projects, Ministry of Civil Aviation, 1946–48; Chief Executive and Mem. of Board of BEA, 1949–55; Managing Dir, Bristol Aircraft Ltd, 1956–60; Man. Dir, Beagle Aircraft Ltd, 1960–67, Chm., 1968–70; Dir, Beagle Aviation Finance Ltd, 1962–71. Chm., British Airports Authority, 1965–71. Chm., Nat. Jt Council for Civil Air Transport, 1950–51; Member: Cairns Cttee on Aircraft Accident Investigation, 1960; Min. of Aviation Advisory Cttees on Civil Aircraft Control and on Private and Club Flying and Gliding; Aeronautical Research Council, 1958–61; Board, LTE, 1973–82 (Chm. and Chief Exec., London Transport, 1980–82). Mem., Cambridge Univ. Appointments Bd, 1956–69. Director: Pressed Steel Co. Ltd, 1960–68; Worldwide Estates Ltd, 1972–88; Nationwide Building Soc., 1973–86; British Caledonian Aviation Gp Plc, 1975–88 (Dep. Chm., 1978–87); Chm., Project Management Ltd, 1972–88. RAeS: Chm., Graduates and Students Sect., 1937–39; Mem. Council, 1945–65; Pres., 1959–60; British Commonwealth and Empire Lectr, 1948; RAeS/AFITA Bleriot Meml Lectr, 1966; Pres., Inst. Transport, 1955–56 (Brancker Meml Lectr, 1951, 1967); President: Inst. of Travel Managers, 1967–70; Duxford Aviation Soc., 1970–; Assoc. of British Aviation Consultants, 1979–; Chairman: Bd of Trustees, Imperial War Museum, 1977–78; Industry Year, 1986; Littlewood Meml Lectr, Soc. of Automotive Engrs (USA), 1971. Mem. Council, Royal Aero Club (Chm., Aviation Cttee, 1960–65; Chm., 1968–70). Mem., HMS Belfast Trust; Chm., Bd of Governors, Reigate Grammar Sch., 1979–; Governor, Ashridge Management Coll., 1981–. Pres., IRTE, 1979–81. FRSA (Chm. Council, 1977–79; Vice-Pres., 1979–); CBIM. Hon. FAIAA; Hon. FCASI; Hon. DSc Cranfield, 1977; Hon. DTech Loughborough, 1977. Liveryman, Guild of Air Pilots and Air Navigators; Freeman, City of London. *Publications:* To Ride the Storm, 1982; articles on aviation, transport, management, and First World War. *Recreations:* reading, writing, gardening. *Address:* Rosehill, Doods Way, Reigate, Surrey RH2 0JT. *T:* Reigate (0737) 42396. *Clubs:* Athenæum, Royal Aero; National Aviation (Washington).

MASERI, Attilio, MD; FRCP; FACC; Professor of Cardiology, and Director of Institute of Cardiology, Catholic University of Rome, Italy, since 1991; *b* 12 Nov. 1935; *s* of Adriano and Antonietta Albini, Italian nobles; *m* 1960, Countess Francesca Maseri Florio di Santo Stefano; one *s*. *Educ:* Classic Lycée Cividale, Italy; Padua Univ. Med. Sch. Special bds in Cardiology, 1963, in Nuclear Medicine, 1965, Italy. Research fellow: Univ. of Pisa, 1960–65; Columbia Univ., NY, 1965–66; Johns Hopkins Univ., Baltimore, 1966–67; University of Pisa: Asst Prof., 1967–70; Prof. of Internal Medicine, 1970; Prof. of Cardiovascular Pathophysiology, 1972–79; Prof. of Medicine (Locum), 1977–79; Sir John McMichael Prof. of Cardiovascular Medicine, RPMS, Univ. of London, 1979–91. Chevalier d'honneur et devotion, SMO Malta. *Publications:* Myocardial Blood Flow in Man, 1972; Primary and Secondary Angina, 1977; Perspectives on Coronary Care, 1979; articles in major internat. cardiological and med. jls. *Recreations:* skiing, tennis, sailing. *Address:* Via Zandonai 9–11, Rome, Italy. *Club:* Queen's.

MASHAM OF ILTON, Baroness *cr* 1970 (Life Peer); **Susan Lilian Primrose Cunliffe-Lister, (Countess of Swinton);** DL; *b* 14 April 1935; *d* of Sir Ronald Sinclair, 8th Bt and Reba Blair (who *m* 2nd, 1957, Lt-Col H. R. Hildreth, MBE; she *d* 1985), *d* of Anthony Inglis, MD; *m* 1959, Lord Masham (now Earl of Swinton, *qv*); one *s* one *d* (both adopted). *Educ:* Heathfield School, Ascot; London Polytechnic. Has made career in voluntary social work. Mem., Peterlee and Newton Aycliffe New Town Corp., 1973–85. Vice-Chairman: All-Party Parly Drug Misuse Cttee, 1984–; Parly All-Party AIDS Cttee; Member: Parly All-Party Disabled Cttee, 1970–; Parly All-Party Penal Affairs Cttee, 1975–; All-Party Children's Gp. President: N Yorks Red Cross, 1963–88 (Patron, 1989–); Yorks Assoc. for the Disabled, 1963–; Spinal Injuries Assoc., 1982–; Chartered Soc. of Physiotherapy, 1975–82; Papworth and Enham Village Settlements; Vice-President: CSP; British Paraplegic Sports Soc.; British Sports Assoc. for the Disabled; Disabled Drivers Assoc.; Disabled Drivers Motor Club; Assoc. of Occupnl Therapists; Action for Dysphasic Adults; Hosp. Saving Assoc.; Chairman: Bd of Dirs, Phoenix House (Drug Rehabilitation), 1986–; Home Office Working Gp on Young People and Alcohol, 1987; Member: Yorks RHA, 1982–90; N Yorks FHSA, 1990–; Bd of Visitors, Wetherby Young Offenders Instn (formerly Wetherby Youth Custody Centre), 1963–; Winston Churchill Meml Trust, 1980–; Trustee, Spinal Res. Trust; Patron: Disablement Income Gp; Yorks Faculty of GPs; Mem. and Governor, Ditchley Foundn, 1980–; former Mem., Volunteer Centre. Freedom, Borough of Harrogate, 1989. DL North Yorks, 1991. Hon. FRCGP, 1981; Hon. Fellow, Bradford and Ilkley Community Coll., 1988. Hon. MA Open, 1981; DUniv York, 1985; Hon. LLD Leeds, 1988; Hon. DSc Ulster, 1990. *Publication:* The World Walks By, 1986. *Recreations:* breeding highland ponies, swimming, table tennis, fishing, flower decoration, gardening. *Address:* Dykes Hill House, Masham, near Ripon,

N Yorks HG4 4NS. *T:* Ripon (0765) 89241; 46 Westminster Gardens, Marsham Street, SW1P 4JG. *T:* 071–834 0700.
See also Sir J. R. N. B. Sinclair, Bt.

MASIRE, Quett Ketumile Joni; Naledi ya Botswana; MP; President of Botswana, since 1980; *b* 23 July 1925; *m* 1957, Gladys Olebile; three *s* three *d*. *Educ:* Kanye; Tiger Kloof. Founded Seepapitso Secondary School, 1950; reporter, later Dir, African Echo, 1958; Mem., Bangwaketse Tribal Council, Legislative Council (former Mem., Exec. Council); founder Mem., Botswana Democratic Party (Editor, Therisanyo, 1962–67); Member, Legislative Assembly (later National Assembly): Kanye S, 1966–69; Ngwaketse-Kgalagadi, 1974–79; Dep. Prime Minister, 1965–66; Vice-Pres. and Minister of Finance and Development Planning, 1966–80. *Address:* State House, Private Bag 001, Gaborone, Botswana. *T:* 350850; PO Box 70, Gaborone, Botswana. *T:* 353391.

MASLIN, David Michael E.; *see* Eckersley-Maslin.

MASON, family name of **Baron Mason of Barnsley.**

MASON OF BARNSLEY, Baron *cr* 1987 (Life Peer), of Barnsley in South Yorkshire; **Roy Mason,** PC 1968; *b* 18 April 1924; *s* of Joseph and Mary Mason; *m* 1945, Marjorie, *d* of Ernest Sowden; two *d*. *Educ:* Carlton Junior Sch.; Royston Senior Sch.; London Sch. of Economics (TUC Scholarship). Went underground at 14 years of age, 1938–53; NUM branch official, 1947–53; mem. Yorks Miners' Council, 1949. MP (Lab): Barnsley, March 1953–1983; Barnsley Central, 1983–87. Labour party spokesman on Defence and Post Office affairs, 1960–64; Minister of State (Shipping), Bd of Trade, 1964–67; Minister of Defence (Equipment), 1967–April 1968; Postmaster-Gen., April-June 1968; Minister of Power, 1968–69; President, Bd of Trade, 1969–70; Labour party spokesman on Civil Aviation, Shipping, Tourism, Films and Trade matters, 1970–74; Secretary of State for: Defence, 1974–76; Northern Ireland, 1976–79; opposition spokesman on agriculture, fisheries and food, 1979–81. Mem., Council of Europe and WEU, 1973. Chm., Yorkshire Gp of Labour MPs, 1972–74; Chm., Miners Gp of MPs, 1974, Vice-Chm., 1980. Consultant: Amalgamated Distilled Products, 1971–74; H. P. Bulmer, 1971–74; Imperial Tobacco, 1984–. *Recreation:* work, provided one stays on top of it. *Address:* 12 Victoria Avenue, Barnsley, S Yorks S70 2BH.

MASON, Alastair Michael Stuart; Regional Medical Officer, South Western Regional Health Authority, since 1988; *b* 4 March 1944; *s* of Adair Stuart and Rosemary Mason; *m* 1967, Kay Marion; two *s* two *d*. *Educ:* Downside Sch.; London Hosp., London Univ. MB BS. MRCP, MRCS, FFPHM. Hosp. junior appts, 1967–73; Sen. Medical Officer, Dept of Health, 1974–84; Sen. Manager, Arthur Andersen & Co., 1984–88. *Publications:* (ed) Walk don't run, 1985; Information for Action, 1988. *Recreations:* walking, reading, theatre. *Address:* 29 Forester Road, Bathwick, Bath BA2 6QE.

MASON, Hon. Sir Anthony (Frank), AC 1988; KBE 1972 (CBE 1969); **Hon. Justice Mason;** Chief Justice, High Court of Australia, since 1987; *b* Sydney, 21 April 1925; *s* of F. M. Mason; *m* 1950, Patricia Mary, *d* of Dr E. N. McQueen; two *s*. *Educ:* Sydney Grammar Sch.; Univ. of Sydney. BA, LLB. RAAF Flying Officer, 1944–45. Admitted to NSW Bar, 1951; QC 1964. Commonwealth Solicitor-General, 1964–69; Judge, Court of Appeal, Supreme Court of NSW, 1969–72; Justice, High Court of Australia, 1972–87. Vice-Chm., UN Commn on Internat. Trade Law, 1968. Member: Management Cttee, British Inst. of Internat. and Comparative Law, 1987–; Council, ANU, 1969–72; Pro-Chancellor, ANU, 1972–75; Hon. LLD: ANU, 1980; Sydney, 1988. FASSA 1989. Hon. Bencher, Lincoln's Inn, 1987. *Recreations:* gardening, tennis, swimming. *Address:* Chief Justice's Chambers, High Court of Australia, PO Box E435, Canberra, ACT 2600, Australia.

MASON, Arthur Malcolm; Director, Reckitt & Colman Ltd, 1958–79 (Chairman, 1970–77); *b* 19 Dec. 1915; British parents; *m* 1938, Mary Hall (*d* 1981); one *s* (one *d* decd). *Educ:* Linton House, London; Blundells School. Trainee, Unilever Ltd, 1934–38; Chiswick Products Ltd: Asst Sales Man., 1938; Sales and Advertising Man., 1939; Dir, 1943; Chm., 1957; Reckitt & Colman Holdings Ltd: Assoc. Dir, 1957; Dir, 1958; Vice-Chm., 1965–70. FInstD. OStJ 1975. *Recreations:* sailing, sea fishing, gardening. *Address:* Cambisgate, Pier Road, Seaview, Isle of Wight. *T:* Isle of Wight (0983) 613389. *Clubs:* Seaview Yacht, Brading Haven Yacht.

MASON, Sir (Basil) John, Kt 1979; CB 1973; FRS 1965; DSc (London); Director-General of the Meteorological Office, 1965–83; President, University of Manchester Institute of Science and Technology, since 1986; *b* 18 Aug. 1923; *s* of late John Robert and Olive Mason, Docking, Norfolk; *m* 1948, Doreen Sheila Jones; two *s*. *Educ:* Fakenham Grammar Sch.; University Coll., Nottingham. Commissioned, Radar Branch RAF, 1944–46. BSc 1st Cl. Hons Physics (London), 1947, MSc 1948; DSc (London) 1956. Shirley Res. Fellow, Univ. of Nottingham, 1947; Asst Lectr in Meteorology, 1948, Lectr, 1949, Imperial Coll.; Warren Res. Fellow, Royal Society, 1957; Vis. Prof. of Meteorology, Univ. of Calif, 1959–60; Prof. of Cloud Physics, Imperial Coll. of Science and Technology (Univ. of London), 1961–65. Dir, Royal Soc. prog. on Acidification of Surface Waters, 1983–90; Sen . Advr, Global Envt Res. Centre, Imperial Coll., 1990–; Chairman: WMO/ICSU Scientific Cttee, World Climate Res. Prog., 1984–88; Co-ordinating Cttee, Marine Science and Technol., 1988–91. Hon. Gen. Sec. British Assoc., 1965–70; President: Physics Section, British Assoc., 1965; Inst. of Physics, 1976–78; BAAS, 1982–83; Nat. Soc. for Clean Air, 1989–; Pres., 1968–70, Hon. Mem., 1985, Royal Meteorol. Soc.; Sen. Vice-Pres., 1976–86, and Treasurer, 1976–86, Royal Soc. UK Perm. Rep., World Meteorological Orgn, 1965–83 (Mem. Exec. Cttee, 1966–75 and 1977–83). Member: ABRC, 1983–87; Astronomy, Space Radio Bd, SERC, 1981–85. Chm. Council, 1970–75, Pro-Chancellor, 1979–85, Surrey Univ. Lectures: James Forrest, ICE, 1967; Kelvin, IEE, 1968; Dalton, RIC, 1968; Bakerian, Royal Soc., 1971; Hugh MacMillan, IES, 1975; Symons, Royal Meteorol. Soc., 1976; Halley, Oxford, 1977; Rutherford, Royal Soc., 1990. Mem., Academia Europaea, 1989; Hon. Mem., Amer. Meteorol Soc., 1988. Hon. Fellow: Imperial Coll. of Science and Technology, 1974; UMIST, 1979. Hon. DSc: Nottingham, 1966; Durham, 1970; Strathclyde, 1975; City, 1980; Sussex, 1983; Plymouth Polytechnic, 1990; Heriot-Watt Univ., 1991; Hon. ScD East Anglia, 1988. Hugh Robert Mill Medal, Royal Meteorol. Soc., 1959; Charles Chree Medal and Prize, Inst. Physics and Phys. Soc., 1965; Rumford Medal, Royal Soc., 1972; Glazebrook Medal, Inst. Physics, 1974; Symons Meml Gold Medal, Royal Meteorol. Soc., 1975. *Publications:* The Physics of Clouds, 1957, 2nd edn 1971; Clouds, Rain and Rain-Making, 1962, 2nd edn 1975; The Surface Waters Acidification Programme, 1990; papers in physics and meteorological journals. *Recreations:* foreign travel, music. *Address:* 64 Christchurch Road, East Sheen, SW14 7AW.

MASON, Catherine Emily, (Mrs R. K. Mason); *see* Lampert, C. E.

MASON, David Arthur; Director of Social Services, Liverpool City Council, since 1987; *b* 13 May 1946; *s* of Arthur J. Mason and Vera M. Mason. *Educ:* Birmingham Polytechnic (Cert. Social Work, 1970); Univ. of Aston in Birmingham (MSc Public Sector Management, 1981). Social worker, 1966–70; Sen. Social worker, Hounslow, 1970–72; Unit Organiser, Birmingham Family Service Unit, 1972–75; Area Man., Birmingham, 1975–81; Divl Dir of Social Services, Warwickshire, 1981–84; Dir of Social Services, Knowsley, 1985–87. *Address:* Liverpool Social Services Department, 26 Hatton Garden, Liverpool L3 2AW. *T:* 051–225 3800.

MASON, Prof. David Kean, CBE 1987; BDS, MD; FRCSGlas, FDSRCPS Glas, FDSRCSE, FRCPath; Professor of Oral Medicine and Head of the Department of Oral Medicine and Pathology, University of Glasgow Dental School, since 1967; Dean of Dental Education, University of Glasgow, since 1980; *b* 5 Nov. 1928; *s* of George Hunter Mason and Margaret Kean; *m* 1967, Judith Anne Armstrong; two *s* one *d*. *Educ:* Paisley Grammar Sch.; Glasgow Acad.; St Andrews Univ. (LDS 1951, BDS 1952); Glasgow Univ. (MB, ChB 1962, MD (Commendation) 1967). FDSRCSE 1957; FDSRCPS Glas 1967; FRCSGlas 1973; FRCPath 1976 (MRCPath 1967); Hon. FFDRCSI 1988; Hon. FDSRCPS Glas 1990. Served RAF, Dental Br., 1952–54. Registrar in Oral Surgery, Dundee, 1954–56; gen. dental practice, 1956–62; Vis. Dental Surgeon, Glasgow Dental Hosp., 1956–62, Sen. Registrar 1962–64; Sen. Lectr in Dental Surgery and Pathology, Univ. of Glasgow, 1964–67; Hon. Consultant Dental Surgeon, Glasgow, 1964–67. Chm., National Dental Consultative Cttee, 1976–80 and 1983–; Member: Medicines Commn, 1976–80; Dental Cttee, MRC, 1973–; Physiol Systems Bd, MRC, 1976–80; Jt MRC/Health Depts/SERC Dental Cttee, 1984–87; GDC, 1976– (Mem., Disciplinary Cttee, 1980–85; Health Cttee, 1985–; Pres., 1989–); Dental Cttee, UGC, 1977–87 (Chm., 1983–87); Supervised Trng Gp, UGC, 1984–86; Dental Rev. Wkg Party, UGC, 1986–87; Jt Cttee for Higher Trng in Dentistry, 1977–84; Dental Strategy Rev. Gp, 1980–81; Scientific Prog. Cttee, FDI, 1980–; Consultant to Commn on Dental Res., FDI, 1973–80. President: W of Scotland Br., BDA, 1983–84; British Soc. for Dental Res., 1984–86; British Soc. for Oral Medicine, 1984–86; GDC, 1989–; Convener, Dental Council, RCPGlas, 1977–80. Lectures: Charles Tomes, RCS, 1975; Holme, UCH, London, 1977; Caldwell Meml, Univ. of Glasgow, 1983; Evelyn Sprawson, London Hosp. Med. Coll., 1984. Dr *hc* Wales, 1991. John Tomes Prize, RCS, 1979. *Publications:* (jtly) Salivary Glands in Health and Disease, 1975; (jtly) Introduction to Oral Medicine, 1978; (jtly) Self Assessment: Manual I, Oral Surgery, 1978; Manual II, Oral Medicine, 1978; (ed jtly) Oral Manifestations of Systemic Disease, 1980, rev. edn 1990. *Recreations:* golf, tennis, gardening, enjoying the pleasures of the countryside. *Address:* Greystones, Houston Road, Kilmacolm, Renfrewshire PA13 4NY. *Clubs:* Royal Scottish Automobile (Glasgow); Royal & Ancient Golf, Elie Golf House, Kilmacolm Golf.

MASON, Vice-Adm. Dennis Howard, CB 1967; CVO 1978; *b* 7 Feb. 1916; *s* of Wilfred Howard Mason, Broadwater, Ipswich, and Gladys (Mouse) Mason (*née* Teague), Trevenson, Cornwall; *m* 1940, Patricia D. M. (*née* Hood); three *d*. *Educ:* Royal Naval Coll., Dartmouth. Served War of 1939–45, Coastal Forces, Frigates and Destroyers; Comdr 1951; Captain 1956; Senior Naval Officer, Northern Ireland, 1961–63; Dir RN Tactical Sch., 1964–65; Rear-Adm. 1965; Chief of Staff to Commander, Far East Fleet, 1965–67; Vice-Adm. 1968; Comdt, Jt Services Staff Coll., 1968–70, retired 1970. ADC 1964. With Paper and Paper Products Industry Training Bd, 1971–72; Warden, St George's House, Windsor Castle, 1972–77. Mem., East Hants DC, 1979–87. *Recreations:* fishing, gardening. *Address:* Church Cottage, East Meon, Hants GU32 1NJ. *T:* East Meon (073087) 466.
See also Vice-Adm. Hon. Sir N. J. Hill-Norton.

MASON, Frances Jane, (Mrs A. S. Mason); *see* Gumley, F. J.

MASON, Sir Frederick (Cecil), KCVO 1968; CMG 1960; HM Diplomatic Service, retired; *b* 15 May 1913; *s* of late Ernest Mason and Sophia Charlotte Mason (*née* Dodson); *m* 1941, Karen Rørholm; two *s* one *d* (and two *d* decd). *Educ:* City of London Sch.; St Catharine's Coll., Cambridge. Vice-Consul: Antwerp, 1935–36; Paris, 1936–37; Leopoldville, 1937–39; Elisabethville, 1939–40; Consul at Thorshavn during British occupation of Faroes, 1940–42; Consul, Colon, Panama, 1943–45; First Sec., British Embassy, Santiago, Chile, 1946–48; First Sec. (Information), Oslo, 1948–50; Asst Labour Adviser, FO, 1950–53; First Sec. (Commercial), UK Control Commission, Bonn, 1954–55; Counsellor (Commercial), HM Embassy, Athens, 1955–56; Counsellor (Economic), HM Embassy, Tehran, 1957–60; Head of Economic Relations Dept, Foreign Office, 1960–64; Under-Sec., Ministry of Overseas Development, 1965, and CRO, 1966; Ambassador to Chile, 1966–70; Under-Sec. of State, FCO, Oct. 1970–Apr. 1971; Ambassador and Perm. UK Rep. to UN and other Internat. Orgns, Geneva, 1971–73. Dir, New Court Natural Resources, 1973–83. British Mem., Internat. Narcotics Control Bd, Geneva, 1974–77. Chm., Anglo-Chilean Soc., 1978–82. Grand Cross, Chilean Order of Merit, 1968. *Recreations:* ball games, walking, painting. *Address:* The Forge, Ropley, Hants SO24 0DS. *T:* Ropley (09627) 2285. *Club:* Canning.

MASON, His Honour (George Frederick) Peter; QC 1963; FCIArb 1986; a Circuit Judge, 1970–87; *b* 11 Dec. 1921; *s* of George Samuel and Florence May Mason, Keighley, Yorks; *m* 1st, 1950 (marr. diss. 1977); two *s* two *d* (and one *d* decd); 2nd, 1981, Sara, *er d* of Sir Robert Ricketts, Bt, *qv*. *Educ:* Lancaster Royal Grammar Sch.; St Catharine's Coll., Cambridge. Open Exhibnr St Catharine's Coll., 1940. Served with 78th Medium Regt RA (Duke of Lancaster's Own Yeo.) in Middle East and Italy, 1941–45, latterly as Staff Capt. RA, HQ 13 Corps. History Tripos Pt 1, 1st cl. hons with distinction, 1946; called to Bar, Lincoln's Inn, 1947; MA 1948; Cholmeley Schol., 1949. Asst Recorder of Huddersfield, 1961; Dep. Chairman: Agricultural Land Tribunal, W Yorks and Lancs, 1962; West Riding of Yorks Quarter Sessions, 1965–67; Recorder of York, 1965–67; Dep. Chm., Inner London QS, 1970; Dep. Chm., NE London QS, 1970–71; Senior Judge: Snaresbrook Crown Ct, 1974–81; Inner London Crown Court, 1983–87. Member: Council, Assoc. of Futures Brokers and Dealers, 1987–91; Bd, Securities and Futures Authy, 1991–. Freeman, City of London, 1977. Liveryman, Wax Chandlers' Co., 1980–. *Recreations:* music, golf, cycling, carpentry. *Address:* Lane Cottage, Amberley, Glos GL5 5AB. *T:* Amberley (0453) 872412. *Clubs:* Athenæum; Hawks.

MASON, James Stephen, CB 1988; Parliamentary Counsel, since 1980; *b* 6 Feb. 1935; *s* of Albert Wesley Mason and Mabel (*née* Topham); *m* 1961, Tania Jane Moeran; one *s* two *d*. *Educ:* Windsor County Grammar Sch.; Univ. of Oxford (MA, BCL). Called to the Bar, Middle Temple, 1958; in practice, 1961–67; Office of Parly Counsel, 1967–. *Recreations:* being an indulgent father, reading, walking and playing the piano. *Club:* United Oxford & Cambridge University.

MASON, Sir John; *see* Mason, Sir B. J.

MASON, Sir John (Charles Moir), KCMG 1980 (CMG 1976); Chairman: Thorn-EMI (Australia) Ltd, since 1985; Vickers Shipbuilders (Australia) Ltd, since 1985; Multicon Ltd, since 1987; Prudential Corporation Australia Ltd (formerly Prudential (Australia and New Zealand) Ltd), since 1987; Prudential Assets Management Ltd, since 1987; Prudential Funds Management Ltd, since 1987; Board of Advice, Spencer Stuart and Associates, Sydney, since 1985; *b* 13 May 1927; *o s* of late Charles Moir Mason, CBE and late Madeline Mason; *m* 1954, Margaret Newton; one *s* one *d*. *Educ:* Manchester Grammar Sch.; Peterhouse, Cambridge. Lieut, XX Lancs Fusiliers, 1946–48; BA 1950, MA 1955, Cantab; Captain, Royal Ulster Rifles, 1950–51 (Korea); HM Foreign Service, 1952; 3rd Sec., FO, 1952–54; 2nd Sec. and Private Sec. to Ambassador, British Embassy, Rome,

1954–56; 2nd Sec., Warsaw, 1956–59; 1st Sec., FO, 1959–61; 1st Sec. (Commercial), Damascus, 1961–65; 1st Sec. and Asst Head of Dept, FO, 1965–68; Dir of Trade Develt and Dep. Consul-Gen., NY, 1968–71; Head of European Integration Dept, FCO, 1971–72; seconded as Under-Sec., ECGD, 1972–75; Asst Under-Sec. of State (Economic), FCO, 1975–76; Ambassador to Israel, 1976–80; High Commissioner to Australia, 1980–84. Chairman: Lloyd's Bank (NZA), Sydney, 1985–90; Lloyds International Ltd, 1985–90; Director: Nat. Bank of NZ, 1984–90; Wellcome (Australia) Ltd, 1985–90; Fluor Daniel (Australia) Ltd, 1985–; Pirelli Cables, Australia, 1987–. Chm., North Shore Heart Foundn, Sydney, 1986–; Dir, Churchill Meml Trust, Aust., 1985–. *Address:* 147 Dover Road, Dover Heights, NSW 2030, Australia; c/o Lloyds Bank, 7 Pall Mall, SW1. *Clubs:* Athenæum; Melbourne (Melbourne); Union (Sydney).

MASON, Prof. John Kenyon French, CBE 1973; Regius Professor of Forensic Medicine, University of Edinburgh, 1973–85, now Emeritus; *b* 19 Dec. 1919; *s* of late Air Cdre J. M. Mason, CBE, DSC, DFC and late Alma French; *m* 1943, Elizabeth Latham (decd); two *s*. *Educ:* Downside Sch.; Cambridge Univ.; St Bartholomew's Hosp. MD, FRCPath, DMJ, DTM&H; LLD Edinburgh 1987. Joined RAF, 1943; Dir of RAF Dept of Aviation and Forensic Pathology, 1956; retd as Group Captain, Consultant in Pathology, 1973. Pres., British Assoc. in Forensic Medicine, 1981–83. L. G. Groves Prize for Aircraft Safety, 1957; R. F. Linton Meml Prize, 1958; James Martin Award for Flight Safety, 1972; Douglas Weightman Safety Award, 1973; Swiney Prize for Jurisprudence, 1978; Lederer Award for Aircraft Safety, 1985. *Publications:* Aviation Accident Pathology, 1962; (ed) Aerospace Pathology, 1973; Forensic Medicine for Lawyers, 1978, 2nd edn 1983; (ed) The Pathology of Violent Injury, 1978; Law and Medical Ethics, 1983, 3rd edn 1991; Butterworth's Medico-Legal Encyclopaedia, 1987; Human Life and Medical Practice, 1989; Medico-legal Aspects of Reproduction, 1990; The Courts and the Doctor, 1990; papers in medical jls. *Address:* 66 Craiglea Drive, Edinburgh EH10 5PF. *Club:* Royal Air Force.

MASON, Rt. Rev. Kenneth Bruce, AM 1984; Chairman, Australian Board of Missions, General Synod of the Anglican Church of Australia, since 1983; *b* 4 Sept. 1928; *s* of Eric Leslie Mason and Gertrude Irene (*née* Pearce); unmarried. *Educ:* Bathurst High Sch.; Sydney Teachers' Coll.; St John's Theological Coll., Morpeth; Univ. of Queensland. Deacon, 1953; Priest, 1954. Primary Teacher, 1948–51; St John's Theological Coll., Morpeth, 1952–53 (ThL); Member, Brotherhood of the Good Shepherd, 1954; Parish of: Gilgandra, NSW, 1954–58; Darwin, NT, 1959–61; Alice Springs, NT, 1962; University of Queensland, 1963–64 (BA, Dip Div); resigned from Brotherhood, 1965; Trinity Coll., Melbourne Univ.: Asst Chaplain, 1965; Dean, 1966–67; Bishop of the Northern Territory, 1968–83. Member, Oratory of the Good Shepherd, 1962, Superior, 1981–87. *Recreations:* listening to music, railways. *Address:* ABM House, 91 Bathurst Street, Sydney, NSW 2000, Australia. *T:* 02–264–1021.

MASON, Rev. Canon Kenneth Staveley; Principal, Edinburgh Theological College, Scottish Episcopal Church, and Canon of St Mary's Cathedral, Edinburgh, since 1989; *b* 1 Nov. 1931; *s* of Rev. William Peter Mason and Anna Hester (*née* Pildrem); *m* 1958, Barbara Thomson; one *s* one *d*. *Educ:* Imperial College of Science, London (BSc, ARCS); BD (ext.) London; Wells Theological Coll. Assistant Curate: St Martin, Kingston upon Hull, 1958; Pocklington, 1961; Vicar of Thornton with Allerthorpe and Melbourne, 1963; Sub-Warden and Librarian, KCL, at St Augustine's Coll., Canterbury, 1969; Dir, Canterbury Sch. of Ministry, 1977, Principal, 1981. Examining Chaplain to Archbp of Canterbury, 1979–; Six Preacher in Canterbury Cath., 1979–84; Hon. Canon of Canterbury, 1984–89. *Publications:* George Herbert, Priest and Poet, 1980; Anglicanism, a Canterbury essay, 1987. *Recreation:* bird-watching. *Address:* The Theological College, Rosebery Crescent, Edinburgh EH12 5JT. *T:* 031–337 3838.

MASON, Monica; Principal Répétiteur, since 1984, Assistant Director, since 1989, Royal Ballet; *b* 6 Sept. 1941; *d* of Richard Mason and Mrs E. Fabian; *m* 1968, Austin Bennett. *Educ:* Johannesburg, SA; Royal Ballet Sch., London. Joined Royal Ballet in Corps de Ballet, 1958; Sen. Principal until 1989; created role of Chosen Maiden in Rite of Spring, 1962; also created roles in: Diversions, Elite Syncopations, Electra, Manon, Romeo and Juliet, Rituals, Adieu, Isadora, The Four Seasons, The Ropes of Time. Assistant to the Principal Choreographer, Royal Ballet, 1980–84. *Address:* Royal Opera House, Covent Garden, WC2.

MASON, Dr Pamela Georgina Walsh, FRCPsych; Vice-Chairman, Taunton and Somerset NHS Trust, since 1991; Senior Principal Medical Officer (Under Secretary), Department of Health and Social Security, 1979–86, retired; re-employed as Senior Medical Officer, Department of Health, 1986–90; *d* of late Captain George Mason and Marie Louise Walsh; god-daughter and ward of late Captain William Gregory, Hon. Co. of Master Mariners; *m* 1st, 1949, David Paltenghi (*d* 1961); two *s*; 2nd, 1965, Jan Darnley-Smith. *Educ:* Christ's Hosp. Sch.; Univ. of London, Royal Free Hosp. Sch. of Medicine (MRCS, LRCP, 1949; MB, BS 1950). DPM 1957; MRCPsych 1971. Various appointments at: Royal Free Hosp., 1951–53; Maudsley Hosp. and Bethlem Royal Hosp., 1954–58; Guy's Hosp., 1958–60; Home Office, 1961–71; DHSS, later DoH, 1971–90. Vis. Psychiatrist, Holloway Prison, 1962–67; Adviser: C of E Children's Soc., 1962–; Royal Philanthropic Soc., 1962–; WRAF Health Educn Scheme, 1962–67. Chairman: WHO Working Gp on Youth Advisory Services, 1976; WHO Meeting of Nat. Mental Health Advrs, 1979. Member: Council of Europe Select Cttee of Experts on Alcoholism, 1976–77; Cttee of Experts on Legal Problems in the Medical Field, 1979–80. FRSocMed. QHP 1984–87. *Publications:* contribs to various professional jls and Govt pubns. *Recreations:* antiquities, humanities, ballet, films, tennis, seafaring and expeditions. *Address:* Blindwell House, Nether Stowey, Bridgwater, Som. *T:* Nether Stowey (0278) 732707.

MASON, Peter; *see* Mason, G. F. P.

MASON, Peter Geoffrey, MBE 1946; High Master, Manchester Grammar School, 1962–78; *b* 22 Feb. 1914; *o s* of Harry Mason, Handsworth, Birmingham; *m* 1st, 1939, Mary Evelyn Davison (marr. diss.); three *d*; 2nd, 1978, Elizabeth June Bissell (*d* 1983); 3rd, 1985, Marjorie Payne. *Educ:* King Edward's Sch., Birmingham; Christ's Coll., Cambridge (Scholar). Goldsmith Exhibitioner, 1935; Porson Scholar, 1936; 1st Class, Classical Tripos, Pts 1 and 2, 1935, 1936. Sixth Form Classical Master, Cheltenham Coll., 1936–40, Rugby Sch., 1946–49; Headmaster, Aldenham Sch., 1949–61. War Service, 1940–46: commissioned into Intelligence Corps, 1940; various staff appointments including HQ 21 Army Group; later attached to a dept of the Foreign Office. Member: Advisory Cttee on Education in the Colonies, 1956; ITA Educnl Adv. Council, 1964–69; Council, University of Salford, 1969–87; Council, British Volunteer Programme (Chm., 1966–74); Chairman: Council of Educn for World Citizenship, 1966–83; Reg. Conf. on IVS, 1972–82; (first), Eur. Council of Nat. Assocs of Indep. Schs, 1988–; Hon. Dir of Research, ISIS, 1981–. *Publications:* Private Education in the EEC, 1983; Private Education in the USA and Canada, 1985; Private Education in Australia and New Zealand, 1987; Independent Education in Southern Africa, 1990; articles and reviews in classical and educational journals. *Recreations:* travel, fly-fishing, walking. *Address:* Leeward, Longborough, Moreton-in-Marsh, Glos GL56 0QR. *T:* Cotswold (0451) 30147. *Club:* Athenæum.

MASON, Philip, CIE 1946; OBE 1942; writer; *b* 19 March 1906; *s* of Dr H. A. Mason, Duffield, Derbs; *m* 1935, Eileen Mary, *d* of Courtenay Hayes, Charmouth, Dorset; two *s* two *d*. *Educ:* Sedbergh; Balliol. 1st Cl. Hons Philosophy, Politics and Economics, Oxford, 1927; MA 1952; DLitt 1972. ICS: Asst Magistrate United Provinces, 1928–33; Under-Sec., Government of India, War Dept, 1933–36; Dep. Commissioner Garhwal, 1936–39; Dep. Sec. Govt of India, Defence Co-ordination and War Depts, 1939–42; Sec. Chiefs of Staff Cttee, India, and Head of Conf. Secretariat, SE Asia Command, 1942–44; represented War Dept in Central Assembly, 1946; Joint Sec. to Government of India, War Dept, 1944–47; Tutor and Governor to the Princes, Hyderabad, 1947; retd from ICS, 1947. Mem. Commn of Enquiry to examine problems of Minorities in Nigeria, 1957. Dir of Studies in Race Relations, Chatham House, 1952–58; Dir, Inst. of Race Relations, 1958–69. Chairman: National Cttee for Commonwealth Immigrants, 1964–65; Exec. Cttee, UK Council for Overseas Student Affairs, 1969–75; Trustees, S African Church Develt Trust, 1976–83 (Pres., 1983–88). Hon. Fellow, Sch. of Oriental and African Studies, 1970; Hon. DSc Bristol, 1971. Received into Catholic Church, 1978. *Publications:* (as Philip Woodruff): Call the Next Witness, 1945; The Wild Sweet Witch, 1947; Whatever Dies, 1948; The Sword of Northumbria, 1948; The Island of Chamba, 1950; Hernshaw Castle, 1950; Colonel of Dragoons, 1951; The Founders, 1953; The Guardians, 1954; (as Philip Mason): Racial Tension, 1954; Christianity and Race, 1956; The Birth of a Dilemma, 1958; Year of Decision, 1960; (ed) Man, Race and Darwin, 1960; Common Sense about Race, 1961; Prospero's Magic, 1962; (ed) India and Ceylon: Unity and Diversity, 1967; Patterns of Dominance, 1970; Race Relations, 1970; How People Differ, 1971; A Matter of Honour, 1974; Kipling: The Glass The Shadow and The Fire, 1975; The Dove in Harness, 1976; A Shaft of Sunlight, 1978; Skinner of Skinner's Horse, 1979; The English Gentleman, 1982; A Thread of Silk, 1984; The Men who Ruled India (abridged from The Founders, and The Guardians), 1985. *Recreation:* living. *Address:* 4 Mulberry House, Church Street, Fordingbridge, Hants SP6 1BE. *T:* Fordingbridge (0425) 54495. *Club:* Travellers'.

MASON, Richard; author; *b* 16 May 1919. *Educ:* Bryanston School. *Publications: novels:* The Wind Cannot Read, 1947; The Shadow and the Peak, 1949; The World of Suzie Wong, 1957; The Fever Tree, 1962. *Address:* c/o A. M. Heath & Co. Ltd, 79 St Martin's Lane, WC2N 4AA.

MASON, Air Vice-Marshal Richard Anthony, CB 1988; CBE 1981; Leverhulme Airpower Research Director, Foundation for International Security, since 1989; *b* 22 Oct. 1932; *s* of William and Maud Mason; *m* 1956, Margaret Stewart; one *d*. *Educ:* Bradford Grammar Sch.; St Andrews Univ. (MA); London Univ. (MA). Commissioned RAF, 1956; Director of Defence Studies, 1977; Director of Personnel (Ground), 1982; Deputy Air Secretary, 1984; Air Sec., 1985–89. *Publications:* Air Power in the Next Generation (ed), 1978; Readings in Air Power, 1979; (with M. J. Armitage) Air Power in the Nuclear Age, 1981; The RAF Today and Tomorrow, 1982; British Air Power in the 1980s, 1984; The Soviet Air Forces, 1986; War in the Third Dimension, 1986; Air Power and Technology, 1986; To Inherit the Skies, 1990; articles in internat. jls on defence policy and strategy. *Recreations:* Rugby, writing, gardening. *Address:* c/o Lloyds Bank, Montpelier Walk, Cheltenham GL50 1SH. *Club:* Royal Air Force.

MASON, Ven. Richard John; Archdeacon of Tonbridge, since 1977; Minister of St Luke's, Sevenoaks, since 1983; *b* 26 April 1929; *s* of Vice-Adm. Sir Frank Mason, KCB. *Educ:* Shrewsbury School. Newspaper journalist, 1949–55; Lincoln Theological College, 1955–58; Asst Curate, Bishop's Hatfield, Herts, 1958–64; Domestic Chaplain to Bishop of London, 1964–69; Vicar of Riverhead with Dunton Green, Kent, 1969–73; Vicar of Edenbridge, 1973–83, also Priest in Charge of Crockham Hill, 1981–83. *Address:* St Luke's House, 30 Eardley Road, Sevenoaks, Kent TN13 1XT. *T:* Sevenoaks (0732) 452462.

MASON, Prof. Sir Ronald, KCB 1980; FRS 1975; Professor of Chemistry, University of Sussex, 1971–88 (Pro-Vice-Chancellor, 1977); Chairman, British Ceramic Research Ltd, since 1990; *b* 22 July 1930; *o s* of David John Mason and Olwen Mason (*née* James); *m* 1952, E. Pauline Pattinson; three *d*; *m* 1979, Elizabeth Rosemary Grey-Edwards. *Educ:* Univs of Wales and London (Fellow, University College Cardiff, 1981). Research Assoc., British Empire Cancer Campaign, 1953–61; Lectr, Imperial Coll., 1961–63; Prof. of Inorganic Chemistry, Univ. of Sheffield, 1963–71; Chief Scientific Advr, MoD, 1977–83. Vis. Prof., Univs in Australia, Canada, France, Israel, NZ and US, inc. A. D. Little Prof., MIT, 1970; Univ. of California, Berkeley, 1975; Ohio State Univ., 1976; North Western Univ., 1977; Prof. associé, Univ. de Strasbourg, 1976; Erskine Vis. Prof., Christchurch, NZ, 1977; Prof., Texas, 1982; Vis. Prof. of Internat. Relns, UCW, 1985–. Schmidt Meml Lectr, Israel, 1977. SRC: Mem., 1971–75; Chm. Chemistry Cttee, 1969–72; Chm. Science Bd, 1972–75; Data Cttee, 1975; Member: Chief Scientist's Requirement Bd, DTI later Dept of Industry, 1973; BBC Adv. Group, 1975–79; Consultant and Council Mem., RUSI, 1984–88; UK Mem., UN Commn of Disarmament Studies, 1984–; Chm., Council for Arms Control, 1986–90; Pres., BHRA, 1986– (Chm., BHR Gp, 1990–); Mem., ABRC, 1977–83. Chm., Hunting Engineering Ltd, 1987 (Dep. Chm., 1985–87). Hon. DSc Wales, 1986. Corday-Morgan Medallist, 1965, and Tilden Lectr, 1970, Chemical Society; Medal and Prize for Structural Chem., Chem. Soc., 1973. *Publications:* (ed) Advances in Radiation Biology, 1964 (3rd edn 1969); (ed) Advances in Structure Analysis by Diffraction Methods, 1968 (6th edn 1978); (ed) Physical Processes in Radiation Biology, 1964; many papers in Jl Chem. Soc., Proc. Royal Soc., etc, and on defence issues. *Address:* Chestnuts Farm, Weedon, Bucks HP22 4NH. *Club:* Athenæum.

MASON, Prof. Stephen Finney, FRS 1982; FRSC; Emeritus Professor of Chemistry, University of London; *b* 6 July 1923; *s* of Leonard Stephen Mason and Christine Harriet Mason; *m* 1955, Joan Banus; three *s*. *Educ:* Wyggeston Sch., Leicester; Wadham Coll., Oxford. MA, DPhil, DSc. Demonstrator, Mus. of Hist. of Sci., Oxford Univ., 1947–53; Research Fellow in Med. Chemistry, ANU, 1953–56; Reader in Chemical Spectroscopy, Univ. of Exeter, 1956–64; Professor of Chemistry: Univ. of East Anglia, 1964–70; KCL, 1970–87. Fellow, Wolfson Coll., Cambridge, 1988–. *Publications:* A History of the Sciences: main currents of scientific thought, 1953; Molecular Optical Activity and the Chiral Discriminations, 1982; Chemical Evolution: origin of the elements, molecules and living systems, 1991; articles in Jl Chem. Soc., 1945–. *Recreations:* history and philosophy of science. *Address:* Department of Chemistry, King's College, Strand, WC2R 2LS. *T:* 01–836 5454; 12 Hills Avenue, Cambridge CB1 4XA. *T:* Cambridge (0223) 247827.

MASON, Sydney, FSVA; Chairman, The Hammerson Property Investment and Development Corporation plc, since 1958 (Director since 1949; Joint Managing Director, 1958–88); *b* 30 Sept. 1920; *s* of Jacob Mason and Annie (*née* Foreman); *m* 1945, Rosalind Victor. FSVA 1962. Manager, Land Securities plc, 1943–49. Mem., Gen. Council, British Property Fedn, 1974– (Hon. Life Mem., 1985). Chm. Exec., Lewis W. Hammerson Meml Home for the Elderly, 1959–80; Mem. Exec., Norwood Orphanage, 1958–76 (Chm., 1968–76). Liveryman, Worshipful Co. of Masons, 1971. *Recreation:* painting in oils and

MASSEY, William Edmund Devereux, CBE 1961; OStJ; retired from HM Diplomatic Service; *b* 1901; *m* 1942, Ingrid Glad-Block, Oslo; one *d*. Entered Foreign Office, 1922; served in diplomatic and consular posts in Poland, France, Japan, Brazil, Roumania, Sweden, Luxembourg (Chargé d'Affaires), Germany; Ambassador and Consul-General to Nicaragua, 1959–61. Hon. Consul for Nicaragua in London, 1969–79. Freeman of City of London. Chm., UK Permanent Cttee on Geographical Names for Official Use, 1965–81; UK Deleg., 2nd UN Conf. on Geographical Names, 1972. FRGS. OStJ 1945. Grand Ducal Commemorative Medal, Luxembourg, 1953.

MASSIE, Allan Johnstone, FRSL 1982; author and journalist; *b* 19 Oct. 1938; *s* of Alexander Johnstone Massie and Evelyn Jane Wilson Massie (*née* Forbes); *m* 1973, Alison Agnes Graham Langlands; two *s* one *d*. *Educ:* Drumtochty Castle Sch.; Trinity College, Glenalmond; Trinity College, Cambridge (BA). Schoolmaster, Drumtochty Castle Sch., 1960–71; TEFL, Rome, 1972–75; fiction reviewer, The Scotsman, 1976–; Creative Writing Fellow: Edinburgh Univ., 1982–84; Glasgow and Strathclyde Univs, 1985–86; columnist: Glasgow Herald, 1985–88; Sunday Times Scotland, 1987–; Daily Telegraph, 1991–. Mem., Scottish Arts Council, 1989–. *Publications: fiction:* Change and Decay In All Around I See, 1978; The Last Peacock, 1980; The Death of Men, 1981; One Night in Winter, 1984; Augustus, 1986; A Question of Loyalties, 1989; The Hanging Tree, 1990; Tiberius, 1991; The Sins of the Fathers, 1991; *non-fiction:* Muriel Spark, 1979; Ill-Met by Gaslight, 1980; The Caesars, 1983; A Portrait of Scottish Rugby, 1984; Colette, 1986; 101 Great Scots, 1987; Byron's Travels, 1988; Glasgow, 1989; The Novel Today, 1990; *plays:* Quintet in October; The Minstrel and the Shirra; contribs to Spectator, Sunday Telegraph. *Recreations:* reading, lunching; watching cricket, Rugby, horse-racing, and my daughter competing in Pony Club events; walking the dogs. *Address:* Thirladean House, Selkirk TD7 5LU. *T:* Selkirk (0750) 20393. *Clubs:* Academy; Selkirk RFC.

MASSINGHAM, John Dudley, CMG 1986; HM Diplomatic Service, retired; Consul General and Director of Trade Promotion, Johannesburg, 1987–90; *b* 1 Feb. 1930; *yr s* of Percy Massingham and Amy (*née* Sanders); *m* 1952, Jean Elizabeth Beech; two *s* two *d*. *Educ:* Dulwich Coll.; Magdalene Coll., Cambridge (MA); Magdalen Coll., Oxford. HM Overseas Civil Service, N Nigeria, 1954–59; BBC, 1959–64; HM Diplomatic Service, 1964–: First Secretary, CRO, 1964–66; Dep. High Comr and Head of Chancery, Freetown, 1966–70; FCO, 1970–71; seconded to Pearce Commn, Jan.-May 1972; First Sec. (Information), later Aid (Kuala Lumpur), 1972–75; First Sec. and Head of Chancery, Kinshasa, 1976–77; Chief Sec., Falkland Islands Govt, 1977–79; Consul-General, Durban, June-Dec. 1979; Counsellor (Economic and Commercial), Nairobi, 1980–81; Governor and C-in-C, St Helena, 1981–84; High Comr to Guyana and non-resident Ambassador to Suriname, 1985–87. *Recreations:* bird watching, avoiding physical exercise. *Address:* 24 Cherry Orchard, Pershore, Worcs WR10 1EL.

MASSY, family name of **Baron Massy.**

MASSY, 9th Baron *cr* 1776 (Ire.); **Hugh Hamon John Somerset Massy;** *b* 11 June 1921; *o s* of 8th Baron, and Margaret, 2nd *d* of late Richard Leonard, Meadsbrook, Ashbourne, Co. Limerick, and *widow* of Dr Moran, Tara, Co. Meath; *S* father 1958; *m* 1943, Margaret, *d* of late John Flower, Barry, Co. Meath; four *s* one *d*. *Educ:* Clongowes Wood Coll.; Clayesmore Sch. Served War, 1940–45, Private, RAOC. *Heir:* *s* Hon. David Hamon Somerset Massy, *b* 4 March 1947.

MASSY-GREENE, Sir (John) Brian, AC 1989; Kt 1972; Chairman, Hazelton Air Services Holdings Ltd, since 1984; *b* Tenterfield, NSW, 20 April 1916; *s* of late Sir Walter Massy-Greene, KCMG, and Lula May Lomax; *m* 1942, Margaret Elizabeth Ritchie Sharp, *d* of late Dr Walter Alexander Ramsay Sharp, OBE; two *s* two *d*. *Educ:* Sydney C of E Grammar Sch.; Geelong Grammar Sch.; Clare Coll., Cambridge (MA). Served War 1939–45: New Guinea, AIF, as Lieut, 1942–45. Joined Metal Manufacturers Ltd, as Staff Cadet, 1939; later transferred to their wholly-owned subsid. Austral Bronze Co. Pty Ltd; Gen. Manager, 1953–62. Managing Dir, 1962–76, and Chm., 1966–77, Consolidated Gold Fields Australia Ltd; Chairman: The Bellambi Coal Co. Ltd, 1964–72; Goldsworthy Mining Ltd, 1965–76; The Mount Lyell Mining & Railway Co. Ltd, 1964–76; Lawrenson Alumasc Holdings Ltd, 1964–73 (Dir, 1962–73); Pacific Dunlop (formerly Dunlop Olympic) Ltd, 1979–86 (Dir, 1968–86; Vice-Chm., 1977–79); Santos Ltd, 1984–88 (Dir, 1984); Commonwealth Banking Corp., 1985–88 (Dep. Chm., 1975–85; Dir, 1968–88); Director: Associated Minerals Consolidated Ltd, 1962–76; Commonwealth Mining Investments (Australia) Ltd, 1962–72 and 1978–85; Consolidated Gold Fields Ltd, London, 1963–76; Dalgety Australia Ltd, 1967–78 (Dep. Chm., 1975–78); Zip Holdings Ltd, 1964–73; Australian European Finance Corp., 1975–89 (Chm., 1987–88); Nat. Mutual Life Assoc. Ltd, 1977–85. Member: Exec. Cttee, Australian Mining Industry Council, 1967–78 (Pres. 1971); Manuf. Industries Adv. Council, 1968–77; NSW Adv. Cttee, CSIRO, 1968–75. Mem., Aust. Inst. Mining and Metallurgy. FAIM; FIEAust. *Recreations:* farming, fishing, flying. *Address:* Nandillyar Heights, Molone, NSW 2866, Australia. *T:* (063) 66–8028. *Club:* Australian.

MASTEL, Royston John, CVO 1977; CBE 1969; Assistant Commissioner (Administration and Operations), Metropolitan Police, 1972–76; *b* 30 May 1917; *s* of late John Mastel and late Rose Mastel (*née* Gorton); *m* 1940, Anne Kathleen Johnson; two *s*. *Educ:* Tottenham Grammar School. Joined Metropolitan Police as Constable, 1937; Pilot, RAF, 1941–45; Metro. Police: Sergeant 1946; Inspector 1951; Supt 1955; Comdr, No 2 District, 1966; subseq. Dep. Asst Comr, Head of Management Services Dept and D Dept (Personnel); Asst Comr (Personnel and Training), 1972. OStJ 1976. *Recreations:* Rugby football, golf. *Address:* The Retreat, Nottage, Porthcawl CF36 3RU.

MASTER, Simon Harcourt; Group Deputy Chairman, Random Century Group, since 1989 (Group Managing Director, 1989–90); Chairman and Chief Executive, Arrow, since 1990; *b* 10 April 1944; *s* of Humphrey Ronald Master and Rachel Blanche Forshaw (*née*Plumbly); *m* 1969, Georgina Mary Cook Batsford, *d* of Sir Brian Batsford; two *s*. *Educ:* Ardingly Coll.; Univ. de La Rochelle. Hatchards Booksellers, 1963; Pan Books Ltd, 1964, Sen. Editor, 1967; Sen. Editor, B. T. Batsford Ltd, 1969; Pan Books Ltd: Editorial Dir, 1971; Publishing Dir, 1973; Man. Dir, 1980–87; Chief Exec., Random House UK Ltd, 1987–89; Vice Pres., Internat. Random House Inc., 1987–90. Non-Exec. Dir, HMSO, 1990–. Mem. Council, Publishers Assoc., 1989–. *Recreations:* gardening, scuba diving, golf, old cars. *Address:* 13 Patten Road, SW18 3RH. *T:* 081–874 2204. *Clubs:* Groucho; Sherborne Golf.

MASTERS, Rt. Rev. Brian John; *see* Edmonton, Area Bishop of.

MASTERS, Dr Christopher; Chief Executive, Christian Salvesen, since 1989; *b* 2 May 1947; *s* of Wilfred and Mary Ann Masters; *m* 1971, Gillian Mary (*née* Hodson); two *d*. *Educ:* Richmond Sch.; King's Coll. London (BSc, AKC); Leeds Univ. (PhD). Research Chemist, Shell Research, Amsterdam, 1971–77; Corporate Planner, Shell Chemicals UK, 1977–79; Business Develt Manager, Christian Salvesen, 1979–81; Dir of Planning, Merchants Refrigerating Co., NY, 1981–82; Managing Director: Christian Salvesen Seafoods, 1983–86; Christian Salvesen Industrial Services, 1984–89. *Publications:* Homogeneous Transition—Metal Catalysis, 1981, Russian edn 1983; numerous research papers and patents. *Recreations:* antique clocks, wine. *Address:* Christian Salvesen, 50 East Fettes Avenue, Edinburgh EH4 1EQ. *T:* 031–552 7101.

MASTERS, Sheila Valerie, (Mrs C. B. Noakes); Director of Finance, NHS Management Executive, Department of Health, since 1988; *d* of Albert Frederick Masters and Iris Sheila Masters (*née* Ratcliffe); *m* 1985, Colin Barry Noakes. *Educ:* Eltham Hill Grammar Sch.; Univ. of Bristol (LLB). FCA; Associate, Inst. of Taxation. Joined Peat Marwick Mitchell & Co., 1970, Partner, 1983; seconded to Dept of Health, 1988–. *Recreations:* ski-ing, horse racing, opera, early classical music. *Address:* 1 Puddle Dock, Blackfriars, EC4V 3PD. *T:* 071–236 8000. *Club:* Farmers'.

MASTERSON, Valerie, (Mrs Andrew March), CBE 1988; opera and concert singer; *d* of Edward Masterson and Rita McGrath; *m* 1965, Andrew March; one *s* one *d*. *Educ:* Holt Hill Convent; studied in London and Milan on scholarship, and with Edwardo Asquez. Début, Landestheater Salzburg; appearances with: D'Oyly Carte Opera, Glyndebourne Festival Opera, ENO, Royal Opera, Covent Garden, etc; appears in principal opera houses in Paris, Aix-en-Provence, Toulouse, Munich, Geneva, Barcelona, Milan, San Francisco, Chile, etc; leading roles in: La Traviata, Le Nozze di Figaro, Manon, Faust, Alcina, Die Entführung aus dem Serail, Così fan tutte, La Bohème, Semele (SWET award, 1983), Die Zauberflöte, Julius Caesar, Rigoletto, Romeo and Juliet, Carmen, Count Ory, Mireille, Louise, Idomeneo, Les Dialogues des Carmélites, The Merry Widow, Xerxes, Orlando, Lucia di Lammermoor. Recordings include: La Traviata; Elisabetta, Regina d'Inghilterra; Der Ring des Nibelungen; The Merry Widow; Julius Caesar; Scipione; several Gilbert and Sullivan operas. Broadcasts regularly on radio and TV. *Recreations:* tennis, swimming, ice skating. *Address:* c/o Music International, 13 Ardilaun Road, Highbury, N5 2QR.

MATACA, Most Rev. Petero; *see* Suva, Archbishop of, (RC).

MATANE, Sir Paulias (Nguna), Kt 1986; CMG 1980; OBE 1975; Chairman: Triad Pacific (PNG) Pty Ltd, since 1987; Ocean Trading Co. Pty, since 1990 (Director, since 1987); *b* 5 July 1932; *s* of Ilias Maila Matane and Elsa Toto; *m* 1957, Kaludia Peril Matane; two *s* two *d*. *Educ:* Teacher's College (Dip. Teaching and Education). Asst Teacher, Tauran Sch., PNG, 1957, Headmaster, 1958–61; School Inspector, 1962–66; Dist Sch. Inspector and Dist Educn Officer, 1967–68; Supt, Teacher Educn, 1969; Foundn Mem., Public Schs Bd, 1969–70; Sec., Dept of Business Develt, 1971–74; Ambassador to USA, Mexico and UN, and High Comr to Canada, 1975–80; Sec., Foreign Affairs, PNG, 1980–85. Director: Inter Pacific Finance Co., 1988–; Newton Pacific (PNG) Pty Ltd, 1990–; Pacific New Guinea Lines, 1991–. Chairman: Review Cttee on Philosophy of Educn, 1986; Cocoa Industry Investigating Cttee, 1987; PNG Censorship Bd, 1990–; Advance PNG, 1991–. Hon. DTech Univ. of Technol., Lae, 1985; Hon. PhD Univ. of PNG, 1986. UN 40th Anniv. Medal, 1985. *Publications:* Kum Tumun of Minj, 1966; A New Guinean Travels through Africa, 1971; My Childhood in New Guinea, 1972; What Good is Business?, 1972; Two New Guineans Travel through SE Asia, 1974; Aimbe the Challenger, 1974; Aimbe the School Dropout, 1974; Aimbe the Magician, 1976; Aimbe the Pastor, 1979; Two Papua New Guineans Discover the Bible Lands, 1987; To Serve with Love, 1989; Chit-Chat, 1991; East to West—the longest train trip in the world, 1991. *Recreations:* reading, gardening, squash, fishing, writing. *Address:* PO Box 680, Rabaul, Papua New Guinea. *Clubs:* Tamukavar, Tauran Ex Student and Citizens', Cathay (Papua New Guinea).

MATE, Rt. Rev. Martin; *see* Newfoundland, Eastern, and Labrador, Bishop of.

MATES, Lt-Col Michael John; MP (C) East Hampshire, since 1983 (Petersfield, Oct. 1974–1983); *b* 9 June 1934; *s* of Claude John Mates; *m* 1959, Mary Rosamund Paton (marr. diss. 1980); two *s* two *d*; *m* 1982, Rosellen, *d* of Mr and Mrs W. T. Bett; one *d*. *Educ:* Salisbury Cathedral Sch.; Blundell's Sch.; King's Coll., Cambridge (choral schol.). Joined Army, 1954; 2nd Lieut, RUR, 1955; Queen's Dragoon Guards, RAC, 1961; Major, 1967; Lt-Col, 1973; resigned commn 1974. Vice-Chairman: Cons. NI Cttee, 1979–81 (Sec., 1974–79); Chairman: All-Party Anglo-Irish Gp, 1979–; Select Cttee on Defence, 1987– (Mem., 1979–); Cons. Home Affairs Cttee, 1987–88 (Vice-Chm., 1979–87); Sec., 1922 Cttee, 1987–88; introduced: Farriers Registration Act, 1975; Rent Amendment Act, 1985. Farriers' Co.: Liveryman, 1975–; Asst, 1981; Master, 1986–87. *Address:* House of Commons, SW1A 0AA.

MATHER, Sir Carol; *see* Mather, Sir D. C. MacD.

MATHER, Sir (David) Carol (Macdonell), Kt 1987; MC 1944; *b* 3 Jan. 1919; *s* of late Loris Emerson Mather, CBE; *m* 1951, Hon. Philippa Selina Bewicke-Copley, *o d* of 5th Baron Cromwell, DSO; one *s* three *d*. *Educ:* Harrow; Trinity Coll., Cambridge. War of 1939–45: commissioned Welsh Guards, 1940; served in Western Desert Campaigns, 1941–42; PoW, 1942; escaped, 1943; NW Europe, 1944–45 (despatches); wounded, 1945; Palestine Campaign, 1946–48. Asst Mil. Attaché, British Embassy, Athens, 1953–56; GSO 1, MI Directorate, War Office, 1957–61; Mil. Sec. to GOC-in-C, Eastern Command, 1961–62; retd as Lt-Col, 1962. Conservative Research Dept, 1962–70; contested (C) Leicester (NW), 1966. MP (C) Esher, 1970–87. An Opposition Whip, 1975–79; a Lord Comr of HM Treasury, 1979–81; Vice-Chamberlain of HM Household, 1981–83; Comptroller of HM Household, 1983–86. FRGS. *Club:* Brooks's.

See also Sir W. L. Mather.

MATHER, Graham Christopher Spencer; General Director, Institute of Economic Affairs, since 1987; solicitor; *b* 23 Oct. 1954; *er s* of Thomas and Doreen Mather; *m* 1981, Fiona Marion McMillan, *e d* of Sir Ronald McMillan Bell, QC, MP and of Lady Bell; two *s*. *Educ:* Hutton Grammar School; New College, Oxford (Burnet Law Scholar); MA Jurisp. Institute of Directors: Asst to Dir Gen., 1980; Head of Policy Unit, 1983; Dep. Dir, IEA, 1987. Member: HM Treasury Working Party on Freeports, 1982; Council, Small Business Research Trust; Consultant, Cameron Markby Hewitt, law firm. Mem., Monopolies and Mergers Commission, 1989–. Mem., Westminster City Council, 1982–86; contested (C) Blackburn, 1983. Radio and television broadcaster. *Publications:* lectures, papers and contribs to jls; contribs to The Times. *Address:* (office) 2 Lord North Street, SW1P 3LB. *T:* 071-799 3745. *Club:* United Oxford & Cambridge University.

MATHER, John Douglas, FCIT, FILDM; CBIM; Chief Executive, National Freight Consortium plc, since 1984; *b* 27 Jan. 1936; *s* of John Dollandson and Emma May Mather; *m* 1958, Hilda Patricia (*née* Kirkwood); one *s* (one *d* decd). *Educ:* Manchester Univ. (BACom, MAEcon). MIPM. Personnel Management: Philips Electrical, 1959–66; Convoys Ltd, 1966–67; Personnel Management, Transport Management, National Freight Company, 1967–. Mem., Worshipful Co. of Carmen. *Recreations:* golf, gardening, travel. *Address:* Roundhale, Love Lane, Kings Langley, Hertfordshire WD4 9HW. *T:* Kings Langley (09277) 63063. *Clubs:* Royal Automobile; Woburn Golf and Country.

MATHER, Sir William (Loris), Kt 1968; CVO 1986; OBE 1957; MC 1945; TD and 2 clasps 1949; MA, CEng; Vice Lord-Lieutenant of Cheshire, 1975–90; *b* 17 Aug. 1913; *s* of Loris Emerson Mather, CBE; *m* 1937, Eleanor, *d* of Prof. R. H. George, Providence, RI, USA; two *s* two *d*. *Educ:* Oundle; Trinity Coll., Cambridge (MA Engrg and Law, 1939).

acrylics. *Address:* Bolney Court, Lower Shiplake, Henley-on-Thames, Oxon RG9 3NR. *T:* Wargrave (0734) 402095; (office) 071–629 9494. *Clubs:* Naval, City Livery, Royal Thames Yacht.

MASON, Timothy Ian Godson; Chief Executive, London Arts Board, since 1991; *b* 11 March 1945; *s* of Ian Godson Mason and Muriel (*née* Vaile); *m* 1975, Marilyn Ailsa Williams; one *d* one *s*. *Educ:* St Alban's Sch., Washington, DC; Bradfield Coll., Berkshire; Christ Church, Oxford (MA). Assistant Manager, Oxford Playhouse, 1966–67; Assistant to Peter Daubeny, World Theatre Season, London, 1967–69; Administrator: Ballet Rambert, 1970–75; Royal Exchange Theatre, Manchester, 1975–77; Director: Western Australian Arts Council, 1977–80; Scottish Arts Council, 1980–90; Consultant on implementation of changes in structure of arts funding, Arts Council of GB, 1990–91. Mem., Gen. Adv. Council, BBC, 1990–. *Recreations:* the arts, family. *Address:* 30 Chatsworth Way, SE27 9HN.

MASON, Walter W.; *see* Wynne Mason.

MASON, William Ernest, CB 1983; Deputy Secretary (Fisheries and Food), Ministry of Agriculture, Fisheries and Food, 1982–89, retired; Director, Allied-Lyons PLC, since 1989; consultant on food and drink industry; *b* 12 Jan. 1929; *s* of Ernest George and Agnes Margaret Mason; *m* 1959, Jean (*née* Bossley); one *s* one *d*. *Educ:* Brockley Grammar Sch.; London Sch. of Economics (BScEcon). RAF, 1947–49; Min. of Food, 1949–54; MAFF, 1954; Principal 1963; Asst Sec. 1970; Under Sec., 1975; Fisheries Sec., 1980. Member: Econ. Develt Cttee for Distrib. Trades, 1975–80; Econ. Develt Cttee for Food and Drink Manufg Inds, 1976–80. FRSA 1989; FIGD 1989; Hon. FIFST 1989. Hon. Keeper of the Quaiche, 1989–. *Recreations:* music, reading, modern British painting. *Address:* 82 Beckenham Place Park, Beckenham, Kent BR3 2BT. *T:* 081–650 8241. *Club:* Reform.

MASRI, Taher Nashat; Order of Al-Kawkab, Jordan, 1974; Hon. GBE; MP; Prime Minister and Minister of Defence, Jordan, since 1991; *b* 5 March 1942; *s* of Nashat Masri and Hadiyah Solh; *m* 1968, Samar Bitar; one *s* one *d*. *Educ:* North Texas State Univ. (BBA 1965). Central Bank of Jordan, 1965–73; MP Nablus Dist, 1973–75 and 1984–88; Minister of State for Occupied Territories Affairs, 1973–74; Ambassador to: Spain, 1975–78; France, 1978–83; Belgium (non-resident), 1978–80; Britain, 1983–84; Perm. Delegate to UNESCO, 1978–83; Foreign Minister, 1984–89 and 1991; Dep. Prime Minister and Minister of State for Economic Affairs, April–Aug. 1989; Chm., Foreign Relations Cttee, 1989–91; Minister for Econ. Affairs, 1989–91. Grand Cross, Order of Civil Merit, Spain, 1977; Order of Isabel the Catholic, Spain, 1978; Commander, Legion of Honour, France, 1981. *Address:* PO Box 5550, Amman, Jordan. *T:* 810600.

MASSE, Hon. Marcel; MP (Progressive C) Frontenac, Québec, since 1984; Minister of National Defence, Canada, since 1991; *b* 27 May 1936; *s* of Rosaire Masse and Angeline Masse (*née* Clermont); *m* 1960, Cécile, *d* of René and Clementine Martin; one *s* one *d*. *Educ:* École Normale Jacques-Cartier, Montréal; Univ. de Montréal; Inst. of Pol Sci., Paris; Sorbonne, Paris; City of London Coll.; Inst. Européen d'Admin. des Affaires, Fontainebleau. History teacher, Joliette, Québec, 1962–66; Mem., Québec Nat. Assembly, 1966–73 (Minister, 1966–70); Dir, Lavalin Inc., Montréal, 1974–84; Minister of Communications, Canada, 1984–86, 1989–91; Minister of Energy, Mines and Resources, 1986–89. *Recreations:* reading, music, fishing, ski-ing. *Address:* House of Commons, Ottawa, Ontario K1A 0E4, Canada. *Clubs:* Rideau (Ottawa); Albany.

MASSEREENE, 13th Viscount, *cr* 1660, **AND FERRARD,** 6th Viscount, *cr* 1797; **John Clotworthy Talbot Foster Whyte-Melville Skeffington;** Baron of Loughneagh, 1660; Baron Oriel, 1790; Baron Oriel (UK), 1821; DL; *b* 23 Oct. 1914; *s* of 12th Viscount (*d* 1956) and Jean Barbara (*d* 1937), *e d* of Sir John Stirling Ainsworth, MP, JP, 1st Bt, of Ardanaiseig, Argyllshire; *S* father 1956; *m* 1939, Annabelle Kathleen, *er d* of late Mr and Mrs Henry D. Lewis, Combwell Priory, Hawkhurst, Kent; one *s* one *d*. *Educ:* Eton. Lt, Black Watch SR, 1933–36, re-employed, 1939–40 (invalided); retired; served in Small Vessels Pool, Royal Navy, 1944. Mem. IPU Delegation to Spain, 1960; Whip, Conservative Peers Cttee (IUP), House of Lords, 1958–65, Jt Dep. Chm., 1965–70; introduced in House of Lords: Deer Act, 1963; Riding Establishments Act, 1964; Export of Animals for Research Bill, 1968; Riding Establishments Act, 1970; Valerie Mary Hill and Alan Monk (Marriage Enabling) Act, 1984; Industrial Training Act, 1986; Protection of Animals (Penalties) Bill, 1987; Southern Water Authority Bill, 1988; moved debates on Overseas Information Services and other matters. Pres., Monday Club, 1981–; Member: CPA delegn to Malawi, 1976; Select Cttee on Anglian Water Authority Bill, 1976; Nat. Cttee, 900th Anniversary of Doomesday, 1987. Posts in Cons. Constituency organisations incl. Pres., Brighton, Kemp Town Div., Vice-Pres. and former Treasurer, Ashford Div. Chm. and Dir of companies; Chm., Sunset and Vine plc. Driver of leading British car, Le Mans Grand Prix, 1937. One of original pioneers in commercial develt of Cape Canaveral, Florida; promoted first scheduled air service Glasgow-Oban-Isle of Mull, 1968; presented operetta Countess Maritza at Palace Theatre, London. Comr, Hunterston Ore Terminal Hearing, Glasgow, 1973. Pres., of Charitable and other organisations incl.: Ponies of Britain, 1970–86; Kent Hotels and Restaurants Assoc., 1975–85. Pres., Canterbury Br., RNLI. Former Mem., Senechal Council, Canterbury Cathedral. Chief, Scottish Clans Assoc. of London, 1974–76. Chm. Kent Branch Victoria League, 1962–87. Treas., Kent Assoc. of Boys' Clubs, 1963–86. Master, Ashford Valley Foxhounds, 1953–54; Vice-Pres., Animal Welfare Year, 1976–77. Commodore, House of Lords Yacht Club, 1972–85. Freeman, City of London, and Mem. Worshipful Company of Shipwrights. Gold Staff Officer, Coronation, 1953. FZS. DL Co. Antrim, 1957–. Cross of Comdr, Order of Merit, SMO Malta, 1978. *Publications:* The Lords, 1973; contributes articles to newspapers, chiefly sporting and natural history. *Recreations:* all field sports; farming; forestry; racing. *Heir:* *s* Hon. John David Clotworthy Whyte-Melville Foster Skeffington [*b* 3 June 1940; *m* 1970, Ann Denise, *er d* of late Norman Rowlandson; two *s* one *d*]. *Address:* Knock, Isle of Mull, Argyll. *T:* Aros (06803) 356; (Seat) Chilham Castle, Kent. *T:* Canterbury (0227) 730319. *Clubs:* Carlton, Turf, Pratt's, Royal Yacht Squadron.

MASSEVITCH, Prof. Alla; Chief Scientist of the Astronomical Council of the USSR Academy of Sciences since 1988 (Vice-President, 1952–88); Professor of Astrophysics, Moscow University, since 1946; Vice-President, USSR Peace Committee, 1977; *b* Tbilisi, Georgia, USSR, 9 Oct. 1918; *m* 1942; one *d*. *Educ:* Moscow Univ. Lectured at the Royal Festival Hall, London, and at the Free Trade Hall, Manchester, etc., on The Conquest of Space, 1960; she is in charge of network of stations for tracking Sputniks, in Russia. Pres. Working Group 1 (Tracking and Telemetring) of COSPAR (Internat. Cttee for Space Research) 1961–66. Pres., Commission 35 (Internal Structure of Stars) of the Internat. Astronom. Union, 1967–70; Dep. Sec. Gen., UNISPACE 82 (UN Conf. on Exploration and Peaceful Uses of Outer Space), Vienna, 1981–83. Chm., Space Science Studies Cttee, Internat. Acad. of Astronautics, 1983–86; Associate Editor, Astrophysics and Space Science, 1987–; Mem. Editorial Bd, Astrophysics (Russian), 1985–. Foreign Member: Royal Astronomical Soc., 1963; Indian Nat. Acad. of Sciences, 1979; Austrian Acad. Scis, 1985; Internat. Acad. Astronautics, 1964. Vice-Pres., Inst. for Soviet-American Relations, 1967; Mem. Board, Soviet Peace Cttee, and Internat. Peace Cttee, 1965. Internat. Award for Astronautics (Prix Galabert), 1963; Govtl decorations, USSR, Sign of Honour, 1963, Red Banner, 1975; USSR State Prize, 1975. Hon. Scientist Emeritus, 1978. *Publications:* Use of Satellite Tracking Data for Geodesy (monograph), 1980; Physics and Evolution of Stars (monograph), 1989; 131 scientific papers on the internal structure of the stars, stellar evolution, and optical tracking of artificial satellites, in Russian and foreign astronomical and geophysical journals. *Address:* 48 Pjatnitskaja Street, Moscow 109017, USSR. *T:* 2313980; Khmeleva Street 6, Apt 4, Moscow 103045. *Club:* Club for Scientists (Moscow).

MASSEY, Anna (Raymond); actress; *b* 11 Aug. 1937; *d* of late Raymond Massey and of Adrianne Allen; *m* 1st, 1958, Jeremy Huggins (marr. diss., 1963); one *s*; 2nd, 1988, Uri Andres. *Educ:* London; New York; Switzerland; Paris; Rome. *Plays:* The Reluctant Debutante, 1955; Dear Delinquent, 1957; The Elder Statesman, 1958; Double Yolk, 1959; The Last Joke, 1960; The Miracle Worker, 1961; The School for Scandal, 1962; The Doctor's Dilemma, 1963; The Right Honourable Gentleman, 1964; The Glass Menagerie, 1965; The Prime of Miss Jean Brodie, 1966; The Flip Side, 1967; First Day of a New Season, 1967; This Space is Mine, 1969; Hamlet, 1970; Spoiled, 1971; Slag, 1971; Jingo, 1975; Play, Royal Court, 1976; The Seagull, Royal Court, 1981; *at National Theatre:* Heartbreak House, 1975; Close of Play, 1979; Summer; The Importance of Being Earnest; A Kind of Alaska, and Family Voices, in Harold Pinter trio Other Places, 1982; King Lear, 1986. *Films:* Gideon's Day, 1957; Peeping Tom, 1960; Bunny Lake is Missing, 1965; The Looking Glass War, 1969; David Copperfield, 1969; De Sade, 1971; Frenzy, 1972; A Doll's House, 1973; Sweet William, 1979; The Corn is Green, 1979; Five Days One Summer, 1982; Another Country, 1984; The Chain, 1985; Le Couleur du Vent, 1988; The Tall Guy, 1989. *Films for television:* Journey into the Shadows, Sakharov, 1984; Sacred Hearts, 1985; Hotel du Lac, 1986; The Christmas Tree, 1987; Sunchild, 1988; A Tale of Two Cities, 1989; Man From the Pru, 1990; Broadway Bound, 1991; numerous appearances in TV plays, including Shalom, Joan Collins, 1990. *Address:* c/o Jeremy Conway Ltd, 18–21 Jermyn Street, SW1Y 6HP.
See also D. R. Massey.

MASSEY, Daniel (Raymond); actor; *b* London, 10 Oct. 1933; *s* of late Raymond Massey and of Adrianne Allen; *m* 1st, Adrienne Corri (marr. diss.); 2nd, Penelope Alice Wilton (marr. diss.); one *d*. *Educ:* Eton; King's Coll., Cambridge. Connaught Theatre, Worthing, 1956–57. *Plays:* The Happiest Millionaire, Cambridge, 1957; Living for Pleasure, Garrick, 1958; Make Me an Offer (musical), New, 1959; The School for Scandal, Haymarket, 1962; The Three Musketeers, and A Subject of Scandal and Concern, Nottingham, 1962; She Loves Me (musical), NY, 1963; Julius Caesar, Royal Court, 1964; A Month in the Country, and Samson Agonistes, Guildford, 1965; Barefoot in the Park, Piccadilly, 1965; The Rivals, Haymarket, 1966; The Importance of Being Earnest, Haymarket, 1967; Spoiled, Glasgow, 1970; Abelard and Heloise, Wyndham's, 1970; Three Sisters, and Trelawny of The Wells, 1971; Becket, Guildford, 1972; Popkiss, Globe, 1972; Gigi, NY, 1973; Bloomsbury, Phoenix, 1974; The Gay Lord Quex, Albery, 1975; Othello, Nottingham, 1976; Rosmersholm, Haymarket, 1977; Don Juan comes back from the War, Betrayal, Nat. Theatre, 1978; The Philanderer, Nat. Theatre, 1979; Appearances, May Fair, 1980; Man and Superman, The Mayor of Zalamea, The Hypochondriac, Nat. Theatre, 1981; The Time of Your Life, Twelfth Night, Measure for Measure, RSC, 1983; Breaking the Silence, Waste, RSC, 1984; Follies, Shaftesbury, 1987; The Doll's House, Haymarket, Leicester, 1989. *Films:* include: Girls at Sea, 1957; Upstairs and Downstairs; The Entertainer; The Queen's Guard, 1960; Go to Blazes, 1962; Moll Flanders, 1966; Star, 1968 (Best Supporting Actor, Hollywood Golden Globe Award, 1968); The Incredible Sarah, 1977; The Cat and the Canary, 1978; Escape to Victory, 1981. *TV: serials:* Roads to Freedom, 1970; The Golden Bowl, 1972; Good Behaviour, 1982; Intimate Contact, 1987; numerous plays. Best Supporting Actor, Hollywood Golden Globe Award, 1968; Actor of the Year, SWET Award, 1981. *Recreations:* golf, classical music, reading. *Address:* c/o Julian Belfrage Associates, 68 St James's Street, SW1.

MASSEY, Doreen Elizabeth; Director, Family Planning Association, since 1989; *b* 5 Sept. 1938; *d* of Mary Ann Hall (*née* Sharrock) and Jack Hall; *m* 1966, Dr Leslie Massey; two *s* one *d*. *Educ:* Darwen Grammar Sch., Lancs; Birmingham Univ. (BA Hons French 1961); DipEd 1962; Inst. of Educn, London Univ. (MA 1985). Graduate service overseas, Gabon, 1962–63; teacher: S Hackney Sch., 1964–67; Springside Sch., Philadelphia, 1967–69; Pre-School Play Group Association, 1973–77; teacher, Walsingham Sch., London, 1977–83 (co-ordinator Health Educn, Head of Year, senior teacher); advisory teacher for personal, social and health educn, ILEA, 1983–85; Manager, Young People's Programme, Health Educn Council, 1985–87; Dir of Educn, FPA, 1987–89. Member: Bd, Teachers' Adv. Council for Alcohol and Drug Educn; Nat. Council of Women; Women's Nat. Cancer Control Campaign; Pre-School Playgroup Assoc.; Nat. Trust; school governor. *Publications:* Sex Education: Why, What and How?, 1988; Sex Education Factpack, 1988; Sex Education: theory and practice, 1991; (jtly) Sex Education Training Manual, 1991; articles on sex educn, family planning, health educn. *Recreations:* reading, cinema, theatre, opera, art and design, health and fitness, vegetarian cookery, travel. *Address:* Family Planning Association, 27 Mortimer Street, W1. *T:* 071–636 7866.

MASSEY, Roy Cyril; Organist and Master of the Choristers, Hereford Cathedral, since 1974; *b* 9 May 1934; *s* of late Cyril Charles Massey and Beatrice May Massey; *m* 1975, Ruth Carol Craddock Grove. *Educ:* Univ. of Birmingham (BMus); privately with David Willcocks. FRCO (CHM); ADCM; ARCM; FRSCM (for distinguished services to church music) 1972. Organist: St Alban's, Conybere Street, Birmingham, 1953–60; St Augustine's, Edgbaston, 1960–65; Croydon Parish Church, 1965–68; Warden, RSCM, 1965–68; Conductor, Croydon Bach Soc., 1966–68; Special Comr of RSCM, 1964–; Organist to City of Birmingham Choir, 1954–; Organist and Master of Choristers, Birmingham Cath., 1968–74; Dir of Music, King Edward's Sch., Birmingham, 1968–74. Conductor, Hereford Choral Soc., 1974–; Conductor-in-Chief, alternate years Associate Conductor, Three Choirs Festival, 1975–; Advisor on organs to dioceses of Birmingham and Hereford, 1974–. Mem. Council and Examiner, RCO, 1970–; Mem., Adv. Council, 1976–78, Council, 1984–, RSCM. President: Birmingham Organists' Assoc., 1970–75; Cathedral Organists' Assoc., 1982–84; IAO, 1991. Fellow, St Michael's Coll., Tenbury, 1976–85. DMus Lambeth, 1990. *Recreations:* motoring, old buildings, climbing the Malvern Hills. *Address:* 14 College Cloisters, Hereford HR1 2NG. *T:* Hereford (0432) 272011. *Club:* Conservative (Hereford).

MASSEY, Prof. Vincent, PhD; FRS 1977; Professor of Biological Chemistry, University of Michigan, since 1963; *b* 28 Nov. 1926; *s* of Walter Massey and Mary Ann Massey; *m* 1950, Margot Eva Ruth Grünewald; one *s* two *d*. *Educ:* Univ. of Sydney (BSc Hons 1947); Univ. of Cambridge (PhD 1953). Scientific Officer, CSIRO, Australia, 1947–50; Ian McMaster Scholar, Cambridge, 1950–53, ICI Fellow, 1953–55; Researcher, Henry Ford Hosp., Detroit, 1955–57; Lectr, then Sen. Lectr, Univ. of Sheffield, 1957–63. Visiting Professor: Univ. of Ill, 1960; Univ. of Konstanz, Germany, 1973–74 (Permanent Guest Prof., 1975–); Inst. of Applied Biochem., Mitake, Japan, 1985; Guest Prof., Yokohama City Univ., Japan, 1988. *Publications:* Flavins and Flavoproteins (ed jtly), 1982; over 300 articles in scholarly jls and books. *Recreations:* walking, sailing, gardening. *Address:* Department of Biological Chemistry, University of Michigan, Ann Arbor, Mich 48109, USA. *T:* (313) 7647196, *Fax:* (313) 7634581.

Commissioned Cheshire Yeomanry, 1935; served War of 1939–45: Palestine, Syria, Iraq, Iran, Western Desert, Italy, Belgium, Holland, Germany (wounded twice, MC); Instructor, Staff Coll., Camberley, and GSO1, 1944–45. Chm., Mather & Platt Ltd, 1960–78; Divisional Dir, BSC, 1968–73; Chairman: CompAir Ltd, 1978–83 (Dir, 1973–83); Neolith Chemicals Ltd, 1983–88; Advanced Manufacturing Technology Group, 1985–88. Director: District Bank, 1960–84; National Westminster Bank, 1970–84 (Chm., Northern Bd, 1972–84); Manchester Ship Canal Co. Ltd, 1970–84; Wormold Internat. Ltd, 1975–78; Imperial Continental Gas Assoc. Ltd, 1980–84. Chairman: NW Regional Economic Planning Council, 1968–75; Inst. of Directors, 1979–82 (Manchester Inst. of Dirs, 1967–72); British Pump Manufrs Assoc., 1970–73; President: Manchester Chamber of Commerce, 1964–66 (Emeritus Dir, 1978–89); Manchester Guardian Soc. for Protection of Trade, 1971–85; British Mech. Engrg Confedn, 1975–78; Civic Trust for the NW, 1979– (Chm., 1961–78); Vice Pres., Assoc. of British Chambers of Commerce, 1979–85; Pres., Mech. Engrg Council, 1978–80; Member: Council of Industrial Design, 1960–71; Engineering Industries Council, 1976–80; Council, Duchy of Lancaster, 1977–85. Member Court: Manchester Univ., 1956–; Salford Univ., 1968–86; Royal College of Art, 1967–85; Mem. Council, Manchester Business Sch., 1964–85; Governor: Manchester University Inst. of Science and Technology (Pres., 1976–85; Hon. Fellow, 1986); Manchester Grammar Sch., 1965–80; Feoffee, Chetham's Hosp. Sch., 1961–; Pres., Manchester YMCA, 1982– (Chm., 1953–82). Hon. Fellow, Manchester Coll. of Art and Design, 1967; Hon. DEng Liverpool, 1980; Hon. LLD Manchester, 1983. Comdr, Cheshire Yeomanry, 1954–57; Col and Dep. Comdr, 23 Armoured Bde, TA, 1957–60; ADC to the Queen, 1961–66. CBIM; FRSA. DL City and County of Chester, 1963; High Sheriff of Cheshire, 1969–70. KLJ 1988. *Recreations:* field sports, golf, swimming. *Address:* Whirley Hall, Macclesfield, Cheshire SK10 4RN. *T:* Macclesfield (0625) 22077. *Clubs:* Naval and Military, Leander.

See also Sir D. C. M. Mather.

MATHERS, Sir Robert (William), Kt 1981; Director: National Mutual Life Association of Australasia Ltd, since 1988; Kidston Gold Mines Ltd, since 1988; Buderim Ginger Ltd, since 1989; *b* 2 Aug. 1928; *s* of William Mathers and Olive Ida (*née* Wohlsen); *m* 1957, Betty Estelle Greasley; three *d*. *Educ:* Church of England Grammar Sch., E Brisbane. FAIM; FRMIA 1982. Chm. and Man. Dir, Mathers Enterprises Ltd, 1973–88; Chm., Kinney Shoes (Australia) Ltd, 1988–90; Dep. Chm., Bligh Coal Ltd, 1981–88. Life Mem., Retailers Assoc. of Qld, 1990 (Mem. Council, 1952–90); Pres., Footwear Retailers Assoc., 1960–63. Member: Council, Australian Bicentennial Authority, 1980–89; Finance Adv. Cttee for XII Commonwealth Games, 1979; Australiana Fund, 1980–; Brisbane Adv. Bd, Salvation Army, 1990–; Adv. Bd, Bond Univ. Sch. of Business, 1991–; Councillor: Griffith Univ., 1978–88; Enterprise Australia, 1983–; Deputy Chairman: Nat. Finance Cttee, Australian Stockman's Hall of Fame and Outback Heritage Centre, 1984–89; Organising Cttee, Brisbane Bid for 1992 Olympics, 1985–88. Trustee: WWF, Australia, 1981–87; Queensland Art Gall., 1983–87 (Founding Cttee Mem., Qld Art Gall. Foundn, 1979). Hon. FAMI 1984; FRSA 1989. Cavaliere, Order of Merit (Italy), 1983. *Recreations:* golf, tennis, swimming. *Address:* 1 Wybelenna Street, Kenmore, Queensland 4069, Australia. *T:* (07) 378 5503. *Clubs:* Brisbane, Rotary, Royal Queensland Yacht Squadron, Tattersalls, Brisbane Polo, Milton Tennis, Queensland Rugby Union, Indooroopilly Golf (Brisbane).

MATHESON, Duncan, MA, LLM; QC 1989; a Recorder of the Crown Court, since 1985. *Address:* 1 Crown Office Row, Temple, EC4Y 7HH.

MATHESON, Sir (James Adam) Louis, KBE 1976 (MBE 1944); CMG 1972; FTS; FEng; Vice-Chancellor, Monash University, Melbourne, 1959–76; Chancellor, Papua New Guinea University of Technology, 1973–75; Chairman, Australian Science and Technology Council, 1975–76; *b* 11 Feb. 1912; *s* of William and Lily Edith Matheson; *m* 1937, Audrey Elizabeth Wood; three *s*. *Educ:* Bootham Sch., York; Manchester Univ. (MSc 1933). Lectr, Birmingham Univ., 1938–46 (PhD 1946); Prof. of Civil Engineering, Univ. of Melbourne, Australia, 1946–50; Beyer Prof. of Engineering, Univ. of Manchester, 1951–59. Hon. FICE (Mem. Council, 1965); Hon. FIEAust (Mem. Council, 1961–81, Vice-Pres., 1970–74, Pres., 1975–76); Fellow, Aust. Acad. of Technological Scis and Engrg, 1976; Fellow, Fellowship of Engrg, 1980. Member: Mission on Technical Educn in W Indies, 1957; Royal Commn into failure of King's Bridge, 1963; Ramsay Cttee on Tertiary Educn in Victoria, 1961–63; CSIRO Adv. Council, 1962–67; Exec., Aust. Council for Educational Research, 1964–69; Interim Council, Univ. of Papua New Guinea, 1965–68; Enquiry into Post-Secondary Educn in Victoria, 1976–78; Chairman: Council, Papua New Guinea Inst. of Technology, 1966–73; Aust. Vice-Chancellors' Cttee, 1967–68; Assoc. of Commonwealth Univs, 1967–69; Newport Power Stn Review Panel, 1977; Schools Commn Buildings Cttee, 1977–81; Victorian Planning and Finance Cttee, Commonwealth Schools Commn, 1979–83; Sorrento Harbour Inquiries, 1984 and 1987; St Kilda Harbour Inquiry, 1986. Trustee, Inst. of Applied Science (later Science Mus. of Victoria), 1963–83 (Pres., 1969–73). Dir, Nauru Phosphate Corp., 1977–79. Hon. DSc Hong Kong, 1969; Hon. LLD: Manchester, 1972; Monash, 1975; Melbourne, 1975. Kernot Meml Medal, 1972; Peter Nicol Russell Medal, 1976. *Publications:* Hyperstatic Structures: Vol. 1, 1959; Vol. 2, 1960; Still Learning, 1980; various articles on engineering and education. *Recreations:* music, woodcraft. *Address:* 26/166 West Toorak Road, South Yarra, Victoria 3141, Australia. *Club:* Melbourne.

MATHESON, Very Rev. James Gunn; Moderator of General Assembly of Church of Scotland, May 1975–76; *b* 1 March 1912; *s* of Norman Matheson and Henrietta Gunn; *m* 1937, Janet Elizabeth Clarkson; three *s* one *d* (and one *d* decd). *Educ:* Inverness Royal Academy; Edinburgh Univ. (MA, BD). Free Church of Olrig, Caithness, 1936–39; Chaplain to HM Forces, 1939–45 (POW Italy, 1941–43); St Columba's Church, Blackhall, Edinburgh, 1946–51; Knox Church, Dunedin, NZ, 1951–61; Sec. of Stewardship and Budget Cttee of Church of Scotland, 1961–73; Parish Minister, Portree, Isle of Skye, 1973–79; retired 1979. Hon. DD Edinburgh, 1975. *Publications:* Do You Believe This?, 1960; Saints and Sinners, 1975; contrib. theol jls. *Recreations:* gardening, fishing. *Address:* Husabost, Totaig, Dunvegan, Isle of Skye IV55 8ZU. *Club:* New (Edinburgh).

MATHESON, Maj.-Gen. John Mackenzie, OBE 1950; TD 1969; retired; *b* Gibraltar, 6 Aug. 1912; *s* of late John Matheson and late Nina Short, Cape Town; *m* 1942, Agnes, *d* of Henderson Purves, Dunfermline; one *d*. *Educ:* George Watson's Coll., Edinburgh; Edinburgh Univ. (Vans Dunlop Schol.). MB, ChB 1936; MRCP 1939; MD 1945; FRCSEd 1946; FRCS 1962; FRCP 1972. Royal Victoria Hosp. Tuberculosis Trust Research Fellow, 1936–37; Lieut, RAMC (TA), 1936. Served War of 1939–45: Middle East, N Africa and Italy; Regular RAMC Commn, 1944 (despatches). Clinical Tutor, Surgical Professorial Unit, Edinburgh Univ., 1947–48; Med. Liaison Officer to Surgeon-Gen. US Army, Washington, DC, 1948–50; Asst Chief, Section Gen. Surgery, Walter Reed Army Hosp., Washington, DC, 1950–51; Cons. Surgeon: MELF, 1963–64; BAOR, 1967; Far East, 1967–69; Jt Prof. Mil. Surg., RAM Coll. and RCS of Eng., 1964–67; Brig. 1967; Comdt and Dir of Studies, Royal Army Med. Coll., 1969–71; Postgrad. Dean, Faculty of Medicine, Univ. of Edinburgh, 1971–80. QHS 1969–71. Hon. Col, 205 (Scottish) Gen. Hosp., T&AVR, 1978–80. Alexander Medal, 1961; Simpson-Smith Memorial Lectr, 1967; Gordon-Watson Lectr, RCS of Eng., 1967; Mitchiner Meml Lectr, RAM Coll., Millbank, 1988. Senior Fellow, Assoc. of Surgeons of GB and Ireland; British Medical Association: Mem., Armed Forces Cttee, 1983–88; Mem., Bd of Educn and Science, 1985–88; Pres., Lothian Div., 1978–80. President: Scottish Br., Royal Soc. of Tropical Medicine and Hygiene, 1978–80; Military Surgical Soc., 1984–86; Edinburgh Univ. Graduates Assoc., 1987–89 (Vice-Pres., 1985–86); Chm. Council, Edinburgh Royal Infirmary Samaritan Soc., 1983–. FRSocMed. *Publications:* (contrib.) Military Medicine, in Dictionary of Medical Ethics, 1977; papers (on gun-shot wounds, gas-gangrene and sterilisation) to medical jls. *Recreation:* travel. *Address:* 2 Orchard Brae, Edinburgh EH4 1NY.

MATHESON, Sir Louis; *see* Matheson, Sir J. A. L.

MATHESON, Stephen Charles Taylor; Deputy Secretary and Director General (Management), Inland Revenue, since 1989; *b* 27 June 1939; *s* of Robert Matheson and Olive Lovick; *m* 1960, Marna Rutherford Burnett; two *s*. *Educ:* Aberdeen Grammar Sch.; Aberdeen Univ. (MA hons English Lang. and Lit., 1961). HM Inspector of Taxes, 1961–70; Principal, Bd of Inland Revenue, 1970–75; Private Sec. to Paymaster General, 1975–76, to Chancellor of the Exchequer, 1976–77; Board of Inland Revenue, 1977–; Project Manager, Computerisation of Pay As You Earn Project; Under Sec., 1984; Dir of IT, 1984; Comr, 1989. MBCS (Dep. Pres., 1990–91); Associate Mem., PITCOM. *Publication:* Maurice Walsh, Storyteller, 1985. *Recreations:* Scottish and Irish literature, book collecting, cooking, music. *Address:* Somerset House, WC2R 1LB. *T:* 071–438 6789.

MATHESON OF MATHESON, Sir Torquhil (Alexander), 6th Bt *cr* 1882, of Lochalsh; Chief of Clan Matheson; DL; FSAScot; one of HM Body Guard of the Honourable Corps of Gentlemen at Arms, since 1977, Clerk of the Cheque and Adjutant, since 1990; *b* 15 Aug. 1925; *s* of General Sir Torquhil George Matheson, 5th Bt, KCB, CMG; *S* father, 1963, *S* kinsman as Chief of Clan Matheson, 1975; *m* 1954, Serena Mary Francesca, *o d* of late Lt-Col Sir Michael Peto, 2nd Bt of Barnstaple; two *d*. *Educ:* Eton. FSAScot 1989. Served War of 1939–45; joined Coldstream Guards, July 1943; commnd, March 1944; 5th Bn Coldstream Guards, NW Europe, Dec. 1944–May 1945 (wounded). Served with 3rd Bn Coldstream Guards: Palestine, 1945–48 (despatches); Tripoli and Egypt, 1950–53; seconded King's African Rifles, 1961–64. Captain, 1952; Major, 1959; retd 1964. 4th Bn, Wilts Regt, TA, 1965–67; Royal Wilts Territorials (T&AVR III), 1967–69. DL Somerset, 1987. *Heir* (to Baronetcy and Chiefship): *b* Major Fergus John Matheson, late Coldstream Guards [*b* 22 Feb. 1927; *m* 1952, Hon. Jean Elizabeth Mary Willoughby, *yr d* of 11th Baron Middleton, KG, MC, TD; one *s* two *d*. One of HM Body Guard of the Honourable Corps of Gentlemen at Arms, 1979–]. *Address:* Standerwick Court, Frome, Som. *Clubs:* Army and Navy; Leander (Henley-on-Thames).

MATHEW, John Charles, QC 1977; *b* 3 May 1927; *s* of late Sir Theobald Mathew, KBE, MC, and Lady Mathew; *m* 1952, Jennifer Jane Mathew (*née* Lagden); two *d*. *Educ:* Beaumont Coll. Served, Royal Navy, 1945–47. Called to Bar, Lincoln's Inn, 1949; apptd Junior Prosecuting Counsel to the Crown, 1959; First Sen. Prosecuting Counsel to the Crown, 1974–77. Elected a Bencher of Lincoln's Inn, 1970. *Recreations:* golf, backgammon, cinema. *Address:* 47 Abingdon Villas, W8. *T:* 071–937 7535. *Club:* Garrick.

MATHEW, Theobald David; Windsor Herald of Arms, since 1978; *b* 7 April 1942; *s* of Robert Mathew, Porchester Terrace, London, and West Mersea Hall, Essex, solicitor, and Joan Alison, *d* of Sir George Young, Bt, MVO, of Formosa. *Educ:* Downside; Balliol Coll., Oxford (MA). Green Staff Officer at Investiture of HRH the Prince of Wales, 1969; Rouge Dragon Pursuivant of Arms, 1970; Dep. Treasurer, Coll. of Arms, 1978–. OStJ 1986. *Recreations:* cricket and sailing. *Address:* 76 Clifton Hill, NW8. *T:* 071–624 8448; College of Arms, EC4V 4BT. *T:* 071–248 0893. *Clubs:* Athenæum, MCC, Middlesex CCC; Royal Harwich Yacht.

MATHEWS, Rev. Arthur Kenneth, OBE 1942; DSC 1944; Vicar of Thursley, 1968–76; Rural Dean of Godalming, 1969–74; *b* 11 May 1906; *s* of late Reverend Canon A. A. and Mrs Mathews; *m* 1st, 1936, Elisabeth (*d* 1981), *d* of late E. M. Butler and Mrs Butler; no *c*; 2nd, 1987, Diana, *d* of late Maj.-Gen. A. A. Goschen, CB, DSO. *Educ:* Monkton Combe Sch.; Balliol Coll., Oxford (Exhibitioner); Cuddesdon Theol. Coll. Deacon 1932, priest 1933, at Wakefield; Asst Curate of Penistone; Padre of the Tanker Fleet of the Anglo-Saxon Petroleum Co. Ltd; licensed to officiate, Diocese of Wakefield, 1935–38; Vicar of Forest Row, 1938–44; Temp. Chaplain, RNVR, 1939–44 (Chaplain HMS Norfolk, 1940–44); on staff of Christian Frontier Council, 1944–46; Vicar of Rogate and Sequestrator of Terwick, 1946–54; Rural Dean of Midhurst, 1950–54; Hon. Chaplain to Bishop of Portsmouth, 1950–55; Commissary to: Bishop of Singapore, 1949–64; Bishop of Wellington, 1962–72; Student of Central Coll. of Anglican Communion at St Augustine's Coll., Canterbury, 1954–55; Dean and Rector of St Albans, 1955–63; Rector of St Peter's, Peebles, 1963–68. Hon. Chaplain to Bishop of Norwich, 1969–71. Member: Council, Marlborough Coll., 1953–74; Governing Body, Monkton Combe Sch., 1959–77. *Recreations:* walking and gardening. *Address:* The Tallat, Westwell, near Burford, Oxon OX8 4JT.

See also Baroness Brooke of Ystradfellte.

MATHEWS, Hon. Jeremy Fell, CMG 1989; Attorney General of Hong Kong, since 1988; *b* 14 Dec. 1941; *s* of George James and Ivy Priscilla Mathews; *m* 1968, Sophie Lee; two *d*. *Educ:* Palmer's Grammar Sch., England. Qualified as solicitor, London, 1963; private practice, London, 1963–65; Dep. Dist Registrar in the High Court of Australia, Sydney, 1966–67; Hong Kong Government: Crown Counsel, 1968; Dep. Law Draftsman, 1978; Dep. Crown Solicitor, 1981; Crown Solicitor, 1982. *Recreations:* reading, trekking, music. *Address:* Attorney General's Chambers, Queensway Government Offices, 66 Queensway, Hong Kong. *T:* 8672001. *Clubs:* Hong Kong; Hong Kong Football.

MATHEWS, Marina Sarah Dewe, (Mrs John Dewe Mathews); *see* Warner, M. S.

MATHEWSON, George Ross, CBE 1985; BSc, PhD, MBA; FRSE; CEng, MIEE; Deputy Group Chief Executive, Royal Bank of Scotland Group, since 1990; Director: Royal Bank of Scotland, since 1987; Royal Bank of Scotland Group, since 1987; *b* 14 May 1940; *s* of George Mathewson and Charlotte Gordon (*née* Ross); *m* 1966, Sheila Alexandra Graham (*née* Bennett); two *s*. *Educ:* Perth Academy; St Andrews Univ. (BSc, PhD); Canisius Coll., Buffalo, NY (MBA). Assistant Lecturer, St Andrews Univ., 1964–67; various posts in Research & Development, Avionics Engineering, Bell Aerospace, Buffalo, NY, 1967–72; joined Industrial & Commercial Finance Corp., Edinburgh, 1972; Area Manager, Aberdeen, 1974, and Asst General Manager and Director, 1979; Chief Exec. and Mem., Scottish Devel Agency, 1981–87; Dir of Strategic Planning and Devel, Royal Bank of Scotland Group, 1987–90; Dir, Royal Bank Group Services Ltd, 1987–. Director: Scottish Investment Trust Ltd, 1981–; EftPos UK Ltd, 1988–; Scottish Financial Enterprise, 1988–; Citizens Financial Gp, Inc., 1989–; Royal Scottish Assurance plc, 1989–; Royal Santander Financial Services SA, 1989–; Direct Line Insurance plc, 1990–. Vis. Prof., Strathclyde Business Sch., 1984–89. CBIM 1985; FRSE 1988. Hon. LLD Dundee, 1983.

Publications: various articles on engineering/finance. *Recreations:* geriatric Rugby, tennis, business. *Address:* 29 Saxe Coburg Place, Edinburgh EH3 5BP. *Club:* New (Edinburgh).

MATHIAS, Surg. Rear-Adm. (D) Frank Russell Bentley; retired 1985; Director, Naval Dental Services, 1983–85, and Deputy Director of Defence Dental Services (Organisation), Ministry of Defence, 1985; *b* 27 Dec. 1927; *s* of Thomas Bentley Mathias and Phebe Ann Mathias; *m* 1954, Margaret Joyce (*née* Daniels); one *s* one *d*. *Educ:* Narberth Grammar Sch.; Guy's Hosp., London. LDSRCS Eng. 1952. House Surgeon, Sussex County Hosp., Brighton, 1952–53; joined RN, 1953; principal appointments: Staff Dental Surgeon, Flag Officer Malta, 1972; Flotilla Dental Surgeon, Flag Officer Submarines, 1972–74; Comd Dental Surgeon, Flag Officer Naval Air Comd, 1974–76; Dep. Dir, Naval Dental Services, 1976–80; Comd Dental Surgeon to C-in-C Naval Home Comd, 1980–83. QHDS 1982–85. OStJ 1981.

MATHIAS, Lionel Armine, CMG 1953; apple grower, 1962–84, retired; *b* 23 Jan. 1907; *s* of Hugh Henry Mathias and Amy Duncan Mathias (*née* Mathias); *m* 1935, Rebecca Gordon Rogers (*d* 1984); two *d* (and one *d* decd). *Educ:* Christs Coll., New Zealand; St Paul's Sch.; Keble Coll., Oxford. Appointed Asst District Commissioner, Uganda, 1929; Labour Commissioner, 1949–53; Member: Uganda Exec. Council, 1948, Legislative Council, 1949–53; Kampala Municipal Council, 1952–53; Uganda Students Adviser, 1953–62; Chm., Uganda Britain Soc., 1964–65. *Address:* Little Copt Farm, Shoreham, Sevenoaks, Kent. *T:* Otford (09592) 2040.

MATHIAS, Pauline Mary; Headmistress, More House School, 1974–89; Member, Independent Television Commission, since 1991; *b* 4 Oct. 1928; *d* of Francis and Hilda Donovan; *m* 1954, Prof. Anthony Peter Mathias; two *s*. *Educ:* La Retraite High School; Bedford College, London (BA Hons; DipEd). Head of English Dept, London Oratory Sch., 1954–64; Sen. Lectr in English and Admissions Tutor, Coloma Coll. of Education, 1964–74. Pres., Girls' Schs Assoc., 1982–83; Vice-Pres., Women's Careers Foundn, 1985–89. Chm., ISIS, 1984–86. Governor: Westminster Cathedral Choir Sch., 1978–; ESU, 1986–; St Felix Sch., Southwold, 1986– (Chm. Governors, 1990–); New Hall Sch., Chelmsford. *Recreations:* embroidery, golf, birdwatching, bicycling in France. *Address:* 18 Lee Road, Aldeburgh, Suffolk IP15 5HG.

MATHIAS, Dr Peter, CBE 1984; MA, DLitt; FBA 1977; Master of Downing College, Cambridge, since 1987; *b* 10 Jan. 1928; *o c* of John Samuel and Marion Helen Mathias; *m* 1958, Elizabeth Ann, *d* of Robert Blackmore, JP, Bath; two *s* one *d*. *Educ:* Colston's Sch., Bristol; Jesus Coll., Cambridge (Schol.; Hon. Fellow, 1987). 1st cl. (dist) Hist. Tripos, 1950, 1951; DLitt: Oxon, 1985; Cantab, 1987. Research Fellow, Jesus Coll., Cambridge, 1952–55; Asst Lectr and Lectr, Faculty of History, Cambridge, 1955–68; Dir of Studies in History and Fellow, Queens' Coll., Cambridge, 1955–68 (Hon. Fellow, 1987); Tutor, 1957–68; Senior Proctor, Cambridge Univ., 1965–66; Chichele Prof. of Economic History, Oxford Univ., and Fellow of All Souls Coll., Oxford, 1969–87. Vis. Professor: Univ. of Toronto, 1961; School of Economics, Delhi, 1967; Univ. of California, Berkeley, 1967; Univ. of Pa, 1972; Virginia Gildersleeve, Barnard Coll., Columbia Univ., 1972; Johns Hopkins Univ., 1979; ANU, Canberra, 1981; Geneva, 1986; Leuven, 1990. Chairman: Business Archives Council, 1968–72 (Vice-Pres., 1980–84; Pres., 1984–); Econ. and Social History Cttee, SSRC, 1975–77 (Mem., 1970–77); Acad. Adv. Council, University Coll., Buckingham, 1979–84 (Mem., 1984–); Wellcome Trust Adv. Panel for History of Medicine, 1981–88; Friends of Kettle's Yard, 1989–; Fitzwilliam Mus. Enterprises Ltd, 1990–; Syndic of Fitzwilliam Mus., 1987–; Member: ABRC, 1983–89; Round Table, Council of Industry and Higher Educn, 1989–; Adv. Cttee (Humanities and Social Scis), British Library, 1990–. Treasurer, Econ. Hist. Soc., 1968–88 (Pres., 1989–); Hon. Treasurer, British Acad., 1980–89; International Economic History Association: Sec., 1959–62; Pres., 1974–78; Hon. Pres., 1978–; Vice Pres., Internat. Inst. of Economic History Francesco Datini, Prato, 1987– (Mem. Exec. Cttee, 1972–); Jerusalem Cttee, 1978–; Mem., Academia Europaea, 1989. Foreign Member: Royal Danish Acad., 1982; Royal Belgian Acad., 1988. Curator, Bodleian Library, 1972–87. FRHistS 1972 (Vice-Pres., 1976–80). Hon. DLitt: Buckingham, 1985; Birmingham, 1988. Asst Editor, Econ. Hist. Rev., 1955–57; Gen. Editor, Debates in Economic History, 1967–86. *Publications:* The Brewing Industry in England 1700–1830, 1959; English Trade Tokens, 1962; Retailing Revolution, 1967; The First Industrial Nation, 1969, rev. edn 1983; (ed) Science and Society 1600–1900, 1972; The Transformation of England, 1979; General Editor, Cambridge Economic History of Europe, 1968–. *Recreation:* travel. *Address:* Downing College, Cambridge. *T:* Cambridge (0223) 334800.

MATHIAS, Prof. William (James), CBE 1985; DMus, FRAM; composer, conductor, pianist; Professor and Head of the Department of Music, University College of North Wales, Bangor, 1970–88, Research Professor, 1989; *b* 1 Nov. 1934; *s* of James Hughes Mathias and Marian (*née* Evans); *m* 1959, Margaret Yvonne Collins; one *d*. *Educ:* University Coll. of Wales, Aberystwyth (Robert Bryan Schol.; Fellow, 1990); Royal Academy of Music (Lyell-Taylor Schol.). DMus Wales, 1966; FRAM 1965 (LRAM 1958). Lectr in Music, UC of N Wales, Bangor, 1959–68; Sen. Lectr in Music, Univ. of Edinburgh, 1968–69. Member: Welsh Arts Council, 1974–81 (Chm., Music Cttee, 1982–88); Music Adv. Cttee, British Council, 1974–83; ISCM (British Section), 1976–80; BBC Central Music Adv. Cttee, 1979–86; Welsh Adv. Cttee, British Council, 1979–90; Council, Composers' Guild of GB, 1982–; Bd of Governors, Nat. Museum of Wales, 1973–78; Artistic Dir, N Wales Music Festival, 1972–; Vice-President: British Arts Fests Assoc., 1988– (Vice-Chm., 1983–88); RCO, 1985; Pres., ISM, 1989–90. Governor, NYO of GB, 1985–. Hon. DMus Westminster Choir Coll., Princeton, 1987. Arnold Bax Society Prize, 1968; John Edwards Meml Award, 1982. *Publications include:* Piano Concerto No 2, 1964; Piano Concerto No 3, 1970; Harpsichord Concerto, 1971; Harp Concerto, 1973; Clarinet Concerto, 1976; Horn Concerto, 1984; Organ Concerto, 1984; Oboe Concerto, 1990; Violin Concerto, 1992; *orchestral compositions:* Divertimento for string orch., 1961; Serenade for small orch., 1963; Prelude, Aria and Finale, 1966; Symphony No 1, 1969; Festival Overture, 1973; Celtic Dances, 1974; Vistas, 1977; Laudi, 1978; Vivat Regina (for brass band), 1978; Helios, 1978; Requiescat, 1979; Dance Variations, 1979; Investiture Anniversary Fanfare, 1979; Reflections on a theme by Tomkins, 1981; Symphony No 2: Summer Music (commnd by Royal Liverpool Philharmonic Soc.), 1983; Ceremonial Fanfare (for 2 trumpets), 1983; Anniversary Dances (for centenary of Univ. Coll. Bangor), 1985; Carnival of Wales, 1987; Threnos, for string orch., 1990; Symphony No 3, 1991; *chamber compositions:* Sonata for violin and piano, 1963; Piano Sonata, 1965; Divertimento for flute, oboe and piano, 1966; String Quartet, 1970; Capriccio for flute and piano, 1971; Wind Quintet, 1976; Concertino, 1977; Zodiac Trio, 1977; Clarinet Sonatina, 1978; String Quartet No 2, 1981; Piano Sonata No 2, 1984; Violin Sonata No 2, 1984; Piano Trio, 1986; Flute Sonatina, 1986; String Quartet No 3, 1986; Soundings for Brass Quintet, 1988; Little Suite for piano, 1989; Santa Fe Suite for harp, 1989; Summer Dances, for Brass Quintet, 1990; *choral and vocal compositions:* Wassail Carol, 1965; Three Medieval Lyrics, 1966; St Teilo, 1970; Ave Rex, 1970; Sir Christemas, 1970; Culhwch and Olwen, 1971; A Babe is born, 1971; A Vision of Time and Eternity (for contralto and piano), 1974; Ceremony after a fire raid, 1975; This Worlde's Joie, 1975; Carmen Paschale, 1976; Elegy for a Prince (for baritone and orch.), 1976; The Fields of Praise (for tenor and piano), 1977; A Royal Garland, 1978; Nativity Carol, 1978; A May Magnificat, 1980; Shakespeare Songs, 1980; Songs of William Blake (for mezzo-soprano and orch.), 1980; Rex Gloriae (four Latin motets), 1981; Te Deum, for soli, chorus and orchestra (commnd for centenary of the Chapel at Haddo House), 1981; Lux Aeterna, for soli, chorus and orchestra (commnd for Three Choirs Fest.), 1982; Salvator Mundi: a carol sequence, 1983; Angelus, 1983; Four Welsh Folk Songs, 1984; The Echoing Green, 1985; O Aula Nobilis (for opening of Orangery at Westonbirt Sch. by TRH Prince and Princess of Wales), 1985; Veni Sancte Spiritus (Hereford Three Choirs Fest.), 1985; Gogoneddawg Arglwydd (for Nat. Youth Choir of Wales), 1985; Riddles, 1987; Jonah (a musical morality), 1988; Sweet was the Song, 1988; Learsongs, 1989; World's Fire (poems of Gerard Manley Hopkins) for soprano and baritone soli, SATB chorus and orchestra, 1989; Bell Carol, 1989; Yr Arglwydd yw fy Mugail (male voices and piano), 1989; *organ compositions:* Variations on a Hymn Tune, 1963; Partita, 1963; Postlude, 1964; Processional, 1965; Chorale, 1967; Toccata giocosa, 1968; Jubilate, 1975; Fantasy, 1978; Canzonetta, 1978; Antiphonies, 1982; Organ Concerto, 1984; Berceuse, 1985; Recessional, 1986; A Mathias Organ Album, 1986; Fanfare for organ, 1987; Fenestra, 1989; Carillon, 1989; *anthems and church music:* O Sing unto the Lord, 1965; Make a joyful noise, 1965; Festival Te Deum, 1965; Communion Service in C, 1968; Psalm 150, 1969; Lift up your heads, 1970; O Salutaris Hostia, 1972; Gloria, 1972; Magnificat and Nunc Dimittis, 1973; Alleluya Psallat, 1974; Missa Brevis, 1974; Communion Service (Series III), 1976; Arise, shine, 1978; Let the people praise thee, O God (anthem composed for the wedding of the Prince and Princess of Wales), 1981; Praise ye the Lord, 1982; All Wisdom is from the Lord, 1982; Except the Lord build the House, 1983; A Grace, 1983; Jubilate Deo, 1983; O how amiable, 1983; Tantum ergo, 1984; Let us now praise famous men, 1984; Alleluia! Christ is risen, 1984; Missa Aedis Christi—in memoriam William Walton, 1984; Salve Regina, 1986; O clap your hands, 1986; Let all the world in every corner sing, 1987; Rejoice in the Lord, 1987; I will lift up mine eyes unto the hills, 1987; Cantate Domino, 1987; Thus saith God the Lord—An Orkney anthem, 1987; O Lord our Lord, 1987; As truly as God is our Father, 1987; The Heavens Declare, 1988; I Will Celebrate, 1989; Praise is due to you, O God, 1989; The Doctrine of Wisdom, 1989; Lord, Thou hast been our dwelling place, 1990; In the Time appointed, 1990; Hodie Christus natus est, 1990; *opera:* The Servants (libretto by Iris Murdoch), 1980. *Address:* Y Graigwen, Cadnant Road, Menai Bridge, Anglesey, Gwynedd LL59 5NG. *T:* Menai Bridge (0248) 712392. *Club:* Athenæum.

MATHIESON, Janet Hilary; *see* Smith, J. H.

MATHIESON, William Allan Cunningham, CB 1970; CMG 1955; MBE 1945; consultant to international organisations; *b* 22 Feb. 1916; *e s* of Rev. William Miller Mathieson, BD, and Elizabeth Cunningham Mathieson (*née* Reid); *m* 1946, Elizabeth Frances, *y d* of late Henry Marvell Carr, RA; two *s*. *Educ:* High Sch. of Dundee; Edinburgh and Cambridge Univs. Joined Colonial Office, 1939; served War, 1940–45; Royal Artillery in UK, France and Germany (Major, despatches). Rejoined Colonial Office, 1945; Middle East Dept, 1945–48; Private Sec. to Minister of State, 1948–49; Asst Sec., Colonial Office, 1949; Counsellor (Colonial Affairs) UK Delegn to UN, New York, 1951–54; Head of East African Department, CO, 1955–58; Minister of Education, Labour and Lands, Kenya, 1958–60; Under-Sec., Dept of Technical Co-operation, 1963–64; Under-Sec., 1964–68, Dep. Sec., 1968–75, Min. of Overseas Development; Consultant, UN Develt Prog., 1976–81. Chm., Executive Council, Commonwealth Agricultural Bureaux, 1963; Member: Exec. Bd, Unesco, 1968–74; Bd of Trustees, Internat. Centre for Maize and Wheat Improvement (Mexico), 1976–86; Council, ODI, 1977–90; Council, Commonwealth Soc. for the Deaf, 1979–; Bd of Management, LSHTM, 1981–84; Bd of Governors, Internat. Centre for Insect Physiol. and Ecol., Nairobi, 1985–90; Chm., Bd of Trustees, Internat. Service for Nat. Agr. Res., 1980–84. Hon. Fellow: Queen Elizabeth House, Oxford, 1973; African Acad. of Scis, 1989. FRSA. *Recreations:* photography, travel. *Address:* 13 Sydney House, Woodstock Road, W4 1DP.

MATLHABAPHIRI, Hon. Gaotlhaetse Utlwang Sankoloba; MP, Botswana; General Secretary, Youth Wing, Botswana Democratic Party; *b* 6 Nov. 1949; *s* of late Sankoloba and Khumo Matlhabaphiri; two *d*. *Educ:* Diamond Corporation Training Sch.; London; Friederick Ebert Foundn, Gaborone (Labour Economics). Clerk, Standard Chartered Bank, 1971–72; teacher, also part-time Dep. Head Master, Capital Continuation Classes, Gaborone, 1971–72; diamond sorter valuator, 1973–79; Gen. Sec., Botswana Democratic Party Youth Wing, 1977–85; MP Botswana, 1979–80; Asst Minister of Agriculture, 1979–85; Mem., Central Cttee, Botswana Democratic Party, 1982–85; Ambassador of Botswana to Nordic countries, 1985–86; High Comr for Botswana in UK, 1986–88 (concurrently Ambassador (non-resident) to Romania and Yugoslavia). Asst Gen. Sec., Bank Employees Union, 1972; Gen. Sec., Botswana Diamond Sorters Valuators Union, 1976–79; Chm., Botswana Fedn of Trade Unions, 1979; Mem., CPA. Conductor/Dir, Botswana Democratic Party Internat. Choir. Governor, IFAD, 1980–84. *Recreations:* footballer, athlete; choral music. *Address:* c/o PO Box 28, Gaborone, Botswana. *Clubs:* Royal Over-Seas League, Commonwealth Trust; Gaborone Township Rollers.

MATLOCK, Jack Foust; American Career Diplomat; Ambassador to Soviet Union, 1987–91; *b* 1 Oct. 1929; *s* of late Jack F. Matlock and of Nellie Matlock (*née* McSwain); *m* 1949, Rebecca Burrum; four *s* one *d*. *Educ:* Duke Univ. (BA 1950); Columbia Univ. (MA 1952). Editor and translator on Current Digest of the Soviet Press, 1952–53; Russian language and literature Instructor, Dartmouth Coll., 1953–56; joined US Foreign Service, 1956; served in Moscow, Austria, Ghana, Zanzibar, Tanzania; Vis. Prof. of Political Science, Vanderbilt Univ., 1978–79; Dep. Dir, Foreign Service Inst., 1979–80; Chargé d'Affaires, Moscow, 1981; Ambassador to Czechoslovakia, 1981; Special Asst to President for Nat. Security Affairs and Sen. Dir, European and Soviet Affairs on Nat. Security Council Staff, 1983–86. Masaryk Award, 1983; Superior Honor Award, Dept of State, 1981; Presidential Meritorious Service Award, 1984, 1987. *Publications:* Handbook to Russian edn of Stalin's Works, 1972; articles on US-Soviet relations. *Club:* International (Washington DC).

MATOKA, Hon. Peter Wilfred; High Commissioner for Zambia in Zimbabwe, 1984–89; Senior Regional Advisor, Economic Commission for Africa, United Nations, Addis Ababa, 1979–83; *b* 8 April 1930; *m* 1957, Grace Joyce; two *s* one *d*. *Educ:* Mwinilunga Sch.; Munali Secondary Sch.; University Coll. of Fort Hare (BA Rhodes); American Univ., Washington (Dipl. Internat. Relations); Univ. of Zambia (MA). Minister: of Information and Postal Services, 1964–65; of Health, 1965–66; of Works, 1967; of Power, Transport and Works, 1968; of Luapula Province, 1969; High Comr for Zambia in UK and Ambassador to the Holy See, 1970–71; Minister of Health, 1971–72; Minister of Local Govt and Housing, 1972–77; Minister of Economic and Technical Co-operation, 1977–79; MP for Mwinilunga in Parlt of Zambia. Mem. Central Cttee, United National Independence Party, 1971–. Pres., AA of Zambia, 1969–70. Kt of St Gregory the Great, 1964; Mem., Knightly Assoc. of St George the Martyr, 1986–. *Recreations:* fishing, shooting, discussion, photography. *Address:* (office) Freedom House, PO Box 30302, Lusaka, Zambia; 1806 Kasangula Road, Roma Township, Lusaka, Zambia.

MATOLENGWE, Rt. Rev. Patrick Monwabisi; a Bishop Suffragan of Cape Town, 1976–88, retired; Dean and Bishop in Residence, All Saints' Cathedral, Diocese of

Milwaukee, since 1990; *b* 12 May 1937; *s* of David and Emma Matolengwe; *m* 1967, Crecentia Nompumelelo (*née* Nxele); three *s* two *d*. *Educ:* Healdtown Institution, Fort Beaufort (matric.); Lovedale Teacher Training Coll., Alice; Bishop Gray Coll., Cape Town; Federal Theol Sem., Alice (Cert. Theol.). Teaching, 1959–60; Court Interpreter, 1960–61; theological studies, 1962–65; Curacy at Herschel, Dio. Grahamstown, 1965–68; Rector of Nyanga, Dio. Cape Town, 1968–76, of St Luke's Church, Whitewater, Dio. of Milwaukee, 1988–89. *Recreations:* scouting, singing, music, reading, tennis. *Address:* 818 E Juneau Avenue, Milwaukee, Wis 53202, USA.

MATTHEW, Chessor Lillie, FRIBA, FRIAS, MRTPI; JP; Principal, Duncan of Jordanstone College of Art, Dundee, 1964–78, retired; *b* 22 Jan. 1913; *s* of William Matthew and Helen Chessor Matthew (*née* Milne); *m* 1939, Margarita Ellis; one *s*. *Educ:* Gray's School of Art; Robert Gordon's Coll., Aberdeen. Diploma in Architecture. Lectr, Welsh Sch. of Architecture, Cardiff, 1936–40. Served RAF, 1940–46, Flt-Lt. Sen. Lectr, Welsh Sch. of Architecture, Cardiff, 1946–57; Head of Sch. of Architecture, Duncan of Jordanstone Coll. of Art, Dundee, 1958–64. *Recreations:* hill walking, foreign travel. *Address:* Craigmhor, 36 Albany Road, West Ferry, Dundee DD5 1NW. *T:* Dundee (0382) 78364.

MATTHEW, (Henry) Colin Gray, DPhil; FBA 1991; Fellow and Tutor in Modern History, St Hugh's College, Oxford, since 1978; Lecturer in Gladstone Studies, Christ Church, Oxford, since 1970; *b* 15 Jan. 1941; *s* of Henry Johnston Scott and Joyce Mary Matthew; *m* 1966, Sue Ann (*née* Curry); two *s* one *d*. *Educ:* Sedbergh Sch.; Christ Church, Oxford (MA, DPhil); Makerere Coll., Univ. of E Africa (DipEd). Education Officer, Grade IIA, Tanzanian Civil Service, 1963–66; Student of Christ Church, Oxford, 1976–78. Literary Dir, RHistS, 1985–89. Editor, The Gladstone Diaries, 1972–. *Publications:* The Liberal Imperialists, 1973; (ed) The Gladstone Diaries: vols 3 and 4 (with M. R. D. Foot), 1974; vols 5 and 6, 1978; vols 7 and 8, 1982; vol. 9, 1986; vols 10 and 11, 1990; Gladstone 1809–1874, 1986; contributor to: Studies in Church History, vol. xv, Oxford Illustrated History of Britain, 1984, and learned jls. *Recreations:* fishing, bag-pipe playing, second-hand book buying. *Address:* 107 Southmoor Road, Oxford OX2 6RE. *T:* Oxford (0865) 274900 or 57959.

MATTHEWMAN, Keith; QC 1979; **His Honour Judge Matthewman;** a Circuit Judge, since 1983; *b* 8 Jan. 1936; *e s* of late Lieut Frank Matthewman and Elizabeth Matthewman; *m* 1962, Jane (*née* Maxwell); one *s*. *Educ:* Long Eaton Grammar Sch.; University College London (LLB). Called to the Bar, Middle Temple, 1960. Commercial Assistant, Internat. Div., Rolls-Royce Ltd, 1961–62; practice at the Bar, 1962–83, Midland Circuit, later Midland and Oxford Circuit; a Recorder of the Crown Court, 1979–83. Mem. Cttee, Council of HM's Circuit Judges, 1984–89. Mem., Notts Probation Cttee, 1986–. Mem., Heanor UDC, 1960–63. *Recreation:* gardening. *Address:* c/o Crown Court, Nottingham NG1 7EJ. *Club:* Beeston Fields Golf (Bramcote).

MATTHEWS, family name of Baron Matthews.

MATTHEWS, Baron *cr* 1980 (Life Peer), of Southgate in the London Borough of Enfield; **Victor Collin Matthews,** FRSA, CBIM; Trafalgar House plc: Deputy Chairman, 1973–85; Group Managing Director, 1968–77; Group Chief Executive, 1977–83; *b* 5 Dec. 1919; *s* of A. and J. Matthews; *m* 1942, Joyce Geraldine (*née* Pilbeam); one *s*. *Educ:* Highbury. Served RNVR, 1939–45. Chairman: Trafalgar House Develt Hldgs, 1970–83; Cunard Steam-Ship Co., 1971–83; Ritz Hotel (London), 1976–83; Trafalgar House Construction Hldgs, 1977–83; Express Newspapers plc, 1977–85 (Chief Exec., 1977–82); Cunard Cruise Ships, 1978–83; Cunard Line, 1978–83; Evening Standard Co. Ltd, 1980–85; Fleet Publishing Internat. Hldgs Ltd, 1978–82; Fleet Hldgs, 1982–85; (non-exec.) Ellerman Hldgs, 1983–86; Director: Associated Container Transportation (Australia) Ltd, 1972–83; Cunard Crusader World Travel Ltd, 1974–85; Racecourse Holdings Trust Ltd, 1977–85; Associated Communications Corp. plc, 1977–82; Goldquill Ltd, 1979–83; Darchart Ltd, 1980–83; Garmaine Ltd, 1980–83. *Recreations:* racehorse breeder/owner, cricket, golf. *Address:* Waverley Farm, Mont Arthur, St Brelades, Jersey, Channel Islands. *Clubs:* MCC, Royal Automobile; Royal & Ancient Golf.

MATTHEWS, Colin, DPhil; composer; *b* 13 Feb. 1946; *s* of Herbert and Elsie Matthews; *m* 1977, Belinda Lloyd; one *s* two *d*. *Educ:* Univ. of Nottingham (BA Classics, MPhil Composition); Univ. of Sussex (DPhil). Studied composition with Arnold Whittall and Nicholas Maw, 1967–70; collaborated with Deryck Cooke on performing version of Mahler's Tenth Symphony, 1964–74; asst to Benjamin Britten, 1971–76; worked with Imogen Holst, 1972–84; taught at Univ. of Sussex, 1971–72, 1976–77. Associate Composer, LSO, 1990–. Dir, Holst Estate and Holst Foundn, 1973–; Trustee, Britten-Pears Foundn, and Dir, Britten Estate, 1983–; Mem. Council and Exec. Cttee, SPNM, 1981–; Exec. Mem. Council, Aldeburgh Foundn, 1984–. Patron, Musicians against Nuclear Arms, 1985–. *Principal works:* Fourth Sonata, 1974; Night Music, 1976; Sonata no 5 'Landscape', 1977–81; String Quartet no 1, 1979; Oboe Quartet, 1981; The Great Journey, 1981–88; Divertimento for Double String Quartet, 1982; Toccata Meccanica, 1984; Night's Mask, 1984; Cello Concerto, 1984; Suns Dance, 1985; Five Duos, 1985; Three Enigmas, 1985; String Quartet no 2, 1985; Pursuit (ballet), 1986; Monody, 1986–87; Eleven Studies in Velocity, 1987; Two Part Invention, 1987; Cortège, 1988; Hidden Variables, 1989; Quatrain, 1989; Second Oboe Quartet, 1990; Five Concertinos, 1990; Chiaroscuro, 1990; Machines and Dreams, 1990. Scottish National Orch. Ian Whyte Award, 1975; Park Lane Group Composer Award, 1983. *Publications:* contribs to Musical Times, Tempo, TLS, etc. *Recreations:* wine, very amateur astrophysics. *Address:* c/o Faber Music Ltd, 3 Queen Square, WC1N 3AU. *T:* 071–278 6881. *Club:* Leyton Orient Supporters'.

MATTHEWS, David John; composer; *b* 9 March 1943; *s* of Herbert and Elsie Matthews. *Educ:* Bancroft's Sch., Woodford; Univ. of Nottingham (BA Classics). Studied composition with Anthony Milner, 1967–69; Asst to Benjamin Britten, 1966–70. Musical Dir, Deal Fest., 1989–. Collaborated with Deryck Cooke on performing version of Mahler's Tenth Symphony, 1964–74. *Compositions include:* 3 songs for soprano and orchestra, 1968; String Quartet No 1, 1970; Symphony No 1, 1975; String Quartet No 2, 1976; Symphony No 2, 1977; String Quartet No 3, 1977; September Music, for small orch., 1979; Ehmals und Jetzt, 6 songs for soprano and piano, 1979; The Company of Lovers, 5 choral songs, 1980; String Quartet No 4, 1981; Serenade, for chamber orch., 1982; Violin Concerto, 1982; The Golden Kingdom, 9 songs for high voice and piano, 1983; Piano Trio, 1983; Clarinet Quartet, 1984; Symphony No 3, 1985; In the Dark Time, for orch., 1985; Variations for strings, 1986; Concertino, for oboe and string quartet, 1987; Chaconne, for orch., 1987; Cantiga, for soprano and chamber orch., 1988; The Ship of Death, for chorus, 1989; Piano Sonata, 1989; String Trio, 1989; Romanza, for 'cello and small orch., 1990; The Music of Dawn, for orch., 1990; Symphony No 4, 1990; Capriccio, for 2 horns and strings, 1991; String Quartet No 6, 1991. *Publications:* Michael Tippett, 1980; contribs to Tempo, TLS. *Recreations:* walking, sketching. *Address:* c/o Faber Music Ltd, 3 Queen Square, WC1N 3AU.
See also Colin Matthews.

MATTHEWS, David Napier, CBE 1976 (OBE 1945); MA, MD, MCh (Cambridge); FRCS; Hon. FDSRCS; retired; Consulting Plastic Surgeon, University College Hospital and Hospital for Sick Children; Civilian Consultant in Plastic Surgery to the Royal Navy since 1954; *b* 7 July 1911; *m* 1940, Betty Eileen Bailey Davies; two *s* one *d*. *Educ:* Leys Sch., Cambridge; Queens' Coll., Cambridge; Charing Cross Hosp. Qualified as doctor, 1935. Surgical Registrar, Westminster Hospital, until 1940; Surgeon Plastic Unit, East Grinstead, 1939–41; Surgical Specialist, RAFVR, 1941–46; Plastic Surgeon: UCH and Hosp. for Sick Children, 1946–76; Royal Nat. Orthopædic Hosp., 1947–54; King Edward's Hosp. for Officers, 1972–80. Adviser in Plastic Surgery, DHSS, 1962–77. Consulting Practice as Surgeon 1946–80; Hunterian Professor, RCS, 1941, 1944, 1976; President: British Assoc. of Plastic Surgeons, 1954 and 1971; Plastic Section, RSM, 1970–71; Sec., Harveian Soc. of London, 1951, Vice-Pres., 1954, Pres., 1962; Gen. Sec. Internat. Confederation for Plastic Surgery, 1959; Pres., Chelsea Clinical Soc., 1962. *Publications:* Surgery of Repair, 1943, 2nd edn, 1946; (Ed.) Recent Advances in the Surgery of Trauma, 1963; chapters in surgical books; contrib. to Lancet, BMJ and Post Graduate Jl etc. *Recreation:* fishing. *Address:* River Walk, Shooters Hill, Pangbourne, Reading RG8 7DU. *T:* Pangbourne (0734) 844476.

MATTHEWS, Douglas, BA; FLA; Librarian, The London Library, since 1980; *b* 23 Aug. 1927; *s* of Benjamin Matthews and Mary (*née* Pearson); *m* 1968, Sarah Maria Williams (marr. diss. 1991); two *d*. *Educ:* Acklam Hall Sch., Middlesbrough; Durham Univ. Assistant: India Office Library, 1952–62; Kungl. Biblioteket, Stockholm, 1956–57; Librarian, Home Office, 1962–64; Dep. Librarian, London Library, 1965–80. *Address:* 1 Priory Terrace, Mountfield Road, Lewes, Sussex BN7 2UT. *T:* Lewes (0273) 475635. *Club:* Garrick.

MATTHEWS, Dr Drummond Hoyle, VRD 1967; FRS 1974; Senior Research Associate, Scientific Director, British Institutions Reflection Profiling Syndicate, at the University of Cambridge, 1982–90; Fellow, Wolfson College, Cambridge, 1980–90; *b* 5 Feb. 1931; *s* of late Captain C. B. and late Mrs E. M. Matthews; *m* 1st, 1963, Elizabeth Rachel McMullen (marr. diss. 1980); one *s* one *d*; 2nd, 1987, Sandie Adam. *Educ:* Bryanston Sch.; King's Coll., Cambridge. BA 1954, MA 1959, PhD 1962. RNVR, 1949–51, retd 1967. Geologist, Falkland Islands Dependencies Survey, 1955–57; returned to Cambridge (BP student), 1958; Research Fellow, King's Coll., 1960; Sen. Asst in Research, Dept of Geophysics, 1960; Asst Dir of Research, 1966; Reader in Marine Geology, 1971. Balzan Prize (jtly), 1982. *Publications:* papers on marine geophysics in jls and books. *Recreations:* walking, sailing. *Address:* Orchard Cottage, Sparkhayes Lane, Porlock, Som TA24 8NE. *Clubs:* Antarctic, Cruising Association.

MATTHEWS, Edwin James Thomas, TD 1946; Chief Taxing Master of the Supreme Court, 1979–83 (Master, 1965–78); *b* 2 May 1915; *s* of Edwin Martin Matthews (killed in action, 1917); *m* 1939, Katherine Mary Hirst, BA (Oxon.), Dip. Soc. Sc. (Leeds); two *d*. *Educ:* Sedbergh Sch., Yorks. Admitted as Solicitor of Supreme Court, 1938; practice on own account in Middlesbrough, 1938–39. Served in Royal Artillery, 1939–46, UK, France and Belgium (Dunkirk 1940); released with rank of Major. Partner, Chadwick Son & Nicholson, Solicitors, Dewsbury, Yorks, 1946–50; Area Sec., No. 6 (W Midland) Legal Aid Area Cttee of Law Soc., 1950–56; Sec. of Law Soc. for Contentious Business (including responsibility for administration of Legal Aid and Advice Schemes), 1956–65. Toured Legal Aid Offices in USA for Ford Foundation and visited Toronto to advise Govt of Ontario, 1963. Mem., Council, British Academy of Forensic Sciences, 1965–68. Special Consultant to NBPI on Solicitors' Costs, 1967–68; General Consultant, Law Soc., 1983–84. Member: Lord Chancellor's Adv. Cttee on Legal Aid, 1972–77; Working Party on Legal Aid Legislation, 1974–76; Working Party on the Criminal Trial, 1980–83; Supreme Ct Procedure Cttee, 1982–83. Lectr, mainly on costs and remuneration for solicitors and counsel, for Coll. of Law, Legal Studies and Services Ltd and to various provincial Law Socs, 1983–89. *Publications:* contrib. Halsbury's Laws of England, 1961 and Atkins Encyclopaedia of Forms and Precedents, 1962; (with Master Graham-Green) Costs in Criminal Cases and Legal Aid, 1965; (jointly) Legal Aid and Advice Under the Legal Aid and Advice Acts, 1949 to 1964, 1971; (ed jtly) Supreme Court Practice; contribs to legal journals. *Recreations:* trout fishing, theatre, gardening, French wines. *Address:* 2 Downside Road, Winchester, Hants SO22 5LU. *T:* Winchester (0962) 862478.

MATTHEWS, Prof. Ernest, DDS, PhD, MSc, ARCS, DIC, FDSRCS; Director of Prosthetics, University of Manchester, 1935–70, now Professor Emeritus; *b* 14 Dec. 1904; *s* of James Alfred Matthews, Portsmouth; *m* 1928, Doris Pipe (decd); one *d* (two *s* decd). *Educ:* Imperial Coll., London; Cambridge; Guy's Hospital, London. Demonstrator and Lecturer, Guy's Hospital Medical and Dental Schs, 1926–34; Prosthetic Dental Surgeon, Manchester Royal Infirmary, 1937; Dean and Dir, Turner Dental Sch., 1966–69; Cons. Dental Surgeon, Christie Hosp., 1945; Hon. Adviser in Dental Surgery to Manchester Regional Hospital Board, 1951. Silver Jubilee Medal, 1977. *Recreation:* gardening. *Address:* 16 The Spain, Petersfield, Hants GU32 3LA.

MATTHEWS, Prof. Geoffrey, MA, PhD; FIMA; Shell Professor of Mathematics Education, Centre for Science and Mathematics Education, Chelsea College, University of London, 1968–77, now Emeritus; *b* 1 Feb. 1917; *s* of Humphrey and Gladys Matthews; *m* 1st, 1941, Patricia Mary Jackson; one *s* one *d*; 2nd, 1972, Julia Comber. *Educ:* Marlborough; Jesus Coll., Cambridge (MA); PhD (London). Wiltshire Regt, Intelligence Officer 43rd (Wessex) Div., 1939–45, Captain (dispatches, 1945; US Bronze Star, 1945). Teacher: Haberdashers' Aske's Sch., 1945–50; St Dunstan's Coll., 1950–64, Dep. Head and head of mathematics dept; Organiser, Nuffield Mathematics Teaching Project, 1964–72; Co-director (with Julia Matthews), Schools Council Early Mathematical Experiences project, 1974–79; Co-dir (with Prof. K. W. Keohane) SSRC funded prog. Concepts in Secondary Sch. Maths and Sci., 1974–79. Presenter of BBC TV programmes in series Tuesday Term, Middle School Mathematics, and Children and Mathematics; consultant to BBC series Maths in a Box and You and Me, and to ATV series Towards Mathematics. Consultant to maths teaching projects in Italy, Greece, Portugal, Sri Lanka and Thailand; has lectured extensively abroad. Pres., Mathematical Assoc., 1977–78 (Hon. Mem., 1990); Founder Mem., Commonwealth Assoc. of Sci. and Maths Educators, 1964; Member: Internat. Cttee, 3rd Congress, ICME, 1976; Council, Inst. of Maths and its Applications, 1978–81; Cttee, Soc. of Free Painters and Sculptors, 1978–89. One man shows, Loggia Gall., 1986, 1989. *Publications:* Calculus, 1964; Matrices I & II, 1964; Mathematics through School, 1972; Mainly on the Bright Side, 1989; papers in Proc. Kon. Akad. Wetensch. (Amsterdam); numerous articles in Math. Gaz., etc. *Recreations:* sculpture, travel. *Address:* 50 Sydney Road, Bexleyheath, Kent DA6 8HG. *T:* 081–303 4301.

MATTHEWS, Geoffrey Vernon Townsend, OBE 1986; Director of Research and Conservation, 1955–88, and Deputy Director, 1973–88, Wildfowl Trust, Slimbridge; *b* 16 June 1923; *s* of Geoffrey Tom Matthews and Muriel Ivy Townsend; *m* 1st, 1946, Josephine (marr. diss. 1961), *d* of Col Alured Charles Lowther O'Shea Bilderdeck; one *s* one *d*; 2nd, 1964, Janet (marr. diss. 1978), *d* of Harold Kear; 3rd, 1980, Mary Elizabeth, *d* of William Evans; one *s* one *d*. *Educ:* Bedford Sch.; Christ's Coll., Cambridge (MA, PhD). RAF Operational Res., Bomber and SE Asia Comds (Sci. Officer/Flt Lieut), 1943–46. Post-doctoral res., Cambridge Univ., 1950–55; Special Lectr, Bristol Univ., 1965–88; Hon.

Lectr 1966–69, Professorial Fellow 1970–90, UC, Cardiff. Dir, Internat. Waterfowl Res. Bureau, 1969–89, Counsellor of Honour, 1989–. Served on numerous non-govtl and govtl cttees; travelled widely. Pres., Assoc. for the Study of Animal Behaviour, 1971–74; Vice-Pres., British Ornithologists' Union, 1972–75, Union Medal, 1980. FIBiol, 1974; Corresp. Fellow, Amer. Ornithologists Union, 1969–. RSPB Medal, 1990. Officer, Dutch Order of Golden Ark, 1987. *Publications:* Bird Navigation, 1955, 2nd edn 1968; chapters contributed to several multi-authored books; more than 90 papers in sci. and conservation jls. *Recreations:* fossil hunting, collecting zoological stamps, reading, household maintenance. *Address:* 32 Tetbury Street, Minchinhampton, Glos GL6 9JH. *T:* Brimscombe (0453) 884769. *Club:* Victory.

MATTHEWS, George Lloyd; Archivist, Communist Party of Great Britain; *b* 24 Jan. 1917; *s* of James and Ethel Matthews, Sandy, Beds; *m* 1940, Elisabeth Lynette Summers; no *c*. *Educ:* Bedford Modern Sch.; Reading Univ. Pres., Reading Univ. Students Union, 1938–39; Vice-Pres., Nat. Union of Students, 1939–40; Vice-Pres., University Labour Fedn, 1938–39. County Chm., Nat. Union of Agricultural Workers, 1945–49; Mem. Exec. Cttee, Communist Party, 1943–79; Asst Gen. Sec., Communist Party, 1949–57; Asst Editor, 1957–59, Editor, 1959–74, Daily Worker, later Morning Star; Head of Press and Publicity Dept, Communist Party of GB, 1974–79. *Publication:* (ed with F. King) About Turn, 1990. *Recreation:* music. *Address:* c/o Communist Party, 6 Cynthia Street, N1 9JF. *T:* 071–278 4443.

MATTHEWS, Gordon (Richards), CBE 1974; FCA; *b* 12 Dec. 1908; *m* 1st, 1934, Ruth Hillyard Brooks, *d* of Sir David Brooks, GBE (*d* 1980); one *s* one *d* (and one *d* decd); 2nd, 1982, Freda E. Evans (*née* Ledger). *Educ:* Repton Sch. Chartered Accountant, 1932. Contested (U) General Election, Deritend, Birmingham, 1945, and Yardley, Birmingham, 1950; MP (C) Meriden Division of Warwicks, 1959–64; PPS to the Postmaster-General, 1960–64. Hon. Treas., Deritend Unionist Assoc., 1937–45; Hon. Sec., Birmingham Unionist Association, 1948–53. Pres. City of Birmingham Friendly Soc., 1957–64; Mem. Board of Management, Linen and Woollen Drapers Institution and Cottage Homes, 1950–65 (Pres. of Appeal, 1954–55); Chm. of Exec. Cttee, Birmingham Area of YMCA, 1951–59; Mem., Nat. Council and Nat. Exec. Cttee, YMCA, 1968–71; Chm., Finance Cttee, YWCA, Birmingham Area, 1965–72. Chm., Oxfordshire Br., CPRE, 1978–81. Pres., West Midlands Cons. Council, 1983–85 (Dep. Chm., 1967–70; Chm., 1970–73). FRSA 1986. *Recreations:* fly-fishing and foreign travel. *Address:* 12 Cherry Orchard Close, Chipping Campden, Glos GL55 6DH. *T:* Evesham (0386) 840626.

MATTHEWS, Henry Melvin; Managing Director, Texaco Ltd, 1982–88; *b* 26 Feb. 1926; *s* of Phillip Lawrence and Agnes K. Matthews; *m* 1947, Margaret Goodridge; one *s* two *d*. *Educ:* Columbia University; Tufts Univ. (BSNS, BSME). Commnd Ensign, 1945, USNR; retired 1986. General Manager, Texaco Europe, USA, 1976; Vice Pres. Manufacture and Marketing, Texaco Europe, USA, 1980. Mem., US Navy League, London. *Recreations:* tennis, golf, swimming, gardening, music (choir), YMCA, Congregational Church. *Address:* (winter) 6756 Pacific Drive, Stuart, Fla 34997, USA; (summer) 9 Danvers Lane, New Canaan, Conn 06840. *Club:* Field (New Canaan, USA); Mariner Sands CC (Stuart, Fla).

MATTHEWS, Horatio Keith, CMG 1963; MBE 1946; JP; HM Diplomatic Service, 1948–74; *b* 4 April 1917; *s* of late Horatio Matthews, MD and of Ruth Matthews (*née* McCurry); *m* 1940, Jean Andrée Batten; two *d*. *Educ:* Epsom Coll.; Gonville and Caius Coll., Cambridge. Entered Indian Civil Service, 1940, and served in Madras Presidency until 1947; appointed to Foreign Service, 1948; Lisbon, 1949; Bucharest, 1951; Foreign Office, 1953; Imperial Defence Coll., 1955; Political Office with Middle East Forces, Cyprus, 1956; Counsellor, UK High Commission, Canberra, 1959; Political Adviser to GOC Berlin, 1961; Corps of Inspectors, Diplomatic Service, 1964; Minister, Moscow, 1966–67; High Commissioner in Ghana, 1968–70; UN Under-Sec.-Gen. for Admin and Management, 1971–72; Asst Under-Sec. of State, MoD (on secondment), 1973–74. Mem., Bd of Visitors, HM Prison, Albany, 1976–82. JP IoW 1975. *Address:* Elm House, Bembridge, IoW PO35 5UA. *T:* Isle of Wight (0983) 872327.

MATTHEWS, Jeffery Edward, FCSD; freelance graphic designer and consultant, since 1952; *b* 3 April 1928; *s* of Henry Edward Matthews and Sybil Frances (*née* Cooke); *m* 1953, (Sylvia Lilian) Christine (*née* Hoar); one *s* one *d*. *Educ:* Alleyn's; Brixton Sch. of Building (Interior Design; NDD). AIBD 1951; FCSD (FSIAD 1978). Graphic designer with J. Edward Sander, 1949–52; part-time tutor, 1952–55. Lettering and calligraphy assessor for SIAD, 1970–. Designs for Post Office: decimal to pay labels, 1971; fount of numerals for definitive stamps, 1981; stamps: United Nations, 1965; British bridges, 1968; definitives for Scotland, Wales, NI and IOM, 1971; Royal Silver Wedding, 1972; 25th Anniversary of the Coronation, 1978; London, 1980; 80th birthday of the Queen Mother, 1980; Christmas, 1980; Wedding of Prince Charles and Lady Diana Spencer, 1981; Quincentenary of College of Arms, 1984; 60th birthday of the Queen, 1986; Wedding of Prince Andrew and Sarah Ferguson, 1986; Order of the Thistle Tercentenary of Revival, 1987; 150th Anniversary of the Penny Black, 1990; also first-day covers, postmarks, presentation packs, souvenir books and posters; one of three stamp designers featured in PO film, Picture to Post, 1969. Other design work includes: title banner lettering and coat of arms, Sunday Times, 1968; cover design and lettering for official prog., Royal Wedding, 1981; The Royal Mint, commemorative medal, Order of the Thistle, 1987; official heraldry and symbols, HMSO; hand-drawn lettering, COI; stamp designs, first-day covers, calligraphy, packaging, promotion and bookbinding designs, logotypes, brand images and hand-drawn lettering, for various firms including Unicover Corp., USA, Harrison & Sons Ltd, Metal Box Co., DRG, Reader's Digest Assoc. Ltd, Encyc. Britannica Internat. Ltd, ICI and H. R. Higgins (Coffee-man) Ltd. Work exhibited in A History of Bookplates in Britain, V&A Mus., 1979. Citizen and Goldsmith of London (Freedom by Patrimony), 1949. FRSA 1987. *Publications:* (contrib.) Designers in Britain, 1964, 1971; (contrib.) 45 Wood-engravers, 1982; (contrib.) Royal Mail Year Book, 1984, 1986, 1987. *Recreations:* furniture restoration, playing the guitar, gardening, DIY. *Address:* 46 Kings Hall Road, Beckenham, Kent BR3 1LS.

MATTHEWS, John, CBE 1990; FRAgS; Director, Institute of Engineering Research, Agricultural and Food Research Council (formerly National Institute of Agricultural Engineering), 1984–90; *b* 4 July 1930; *s* of John Frederick Matthews and Catherine Edith Matthews (*née* Terry); *m* 1982, Edna Agnes Luckhurst; two *d*. *Educ:* Royal Latin School, Buckingham. BSc (Physics) London. CPhys, FInstP; CEng. Scientist, GEC Res. Labs, 1951–59; National Institute of Agricultural Engineering: joined 1959; Head of Tractor Performance Dept, 1967–73; Head of Tractor and Cultivation Div., 1973–83; Asst Dir, 1983–84; Dir, 1984–90. Vis. Prof., Cranfield Inst. of Technology, 1987–. Mem., Bd of Management, AFRC, 1986–90. Formerly Chm., Technical Cttees, Internat. Standards Orgn and OECD; Pres., Inst. of Agricl Engineers, 1986–88. Chm., Governing Body, Luton Coll. of Higher Educn, 1989–. Fellow, Ergonomics Soc. Research Medal, RASE, 1983. *Publications:* (contrib.) Fream's Elements of Agriculture, 1984; contribs to other books and jls on agricultural engineering and ergonomics. *Recreations:* farming, gardening, Lions International club, travel. *Address:* Church Cottage, Tilsworth, Leighton Buzzard, Beds. *T:* Leighton Buzzard (0525) 210204.

MATTHEWS, Prof. John Burr Lumley, (Jack), FRSE; Director, Dunstaffnage Marine Laboratory, Natural Environment Research Council, since 1988; Director and Secretary, Scottish Marine Biological Association, since 1988; *b* 23 April 1935; *s* of Dr John Lumley Matthews and Susan Agnes Matthews; *m* 1962, Jane Rosemary Goldsmith; one *s* two *d*. *Educ:* Warwick Sch.; St John's Coll., Oxford (MA, DPhil). FRSE 1988. Res. Scientist, Oceanographic Lab., Edinburgh, 1961–67; University of Bergen: Lectr, Sen. Lectr, Marine Biology, 1967–78; Prof., Marine Biology, 1978–84; Dep. Dir, Scottish Marine Biol Assoc., 1984–88. Vis. Prof., Oceanography, Univ. of British Columbia, 1977–78; Hon. Prof., Biology, Univ. of Stirling, 1984–. Mem., Cttee for Scotland, Nature Conservancy Council, 1989–. FRSA 1989. *Publications:* (ed jtly) Freshwater on the Sea, 1976; contribs to marine sci. jls. *Recreations:* country wines, pethau Cymraeg. *Address:* Grianaig, Rockfield Road, Oban, Argyll PA34 5DH. *T:* Oban (0631) 62734.

MATTHEWS, Dr John Duncan, CVO 1989; FRCPE; retired; Consultant Physician, Royal Infirmary, Edinburgh, 1955–86; Hon. Senior Lecturer, University of Edinburgh, 1976–86; *b* 19 Sept. 1921; *s* of Joseph Keith Matthews and Ethel Chambers; *m* 1945, Constance Margaret Moffat; two *s*. *Educ:* Shrewsbury; Univ. of Cambridge (BA); Univ. of Edinburgh (MB, ChB). FRCPE 1958. Surgeon, High Constables and Guard of Honour, Holyroodhouse, 1961–87, Moderator, 1987–89. Hon. Consultant in Medicine to the Army in Scotland, 1974–86; Examr in Medicine, Edinburgh and Cambridge Univs and Royal Colleges of Physicians. Vice-Pres., RCPE, 1982–85; Mem./Chm., various local and national NHS and coll. cttees. Sec., Edinburgh Medical Angling Club, 1963–86. *Publications:* occasional articles in med. jls on diabetes and heart disease. *Recreations:* cricket (Free Foresters, Grange, and Scotland), fishing, golf, gardening. *Address:* 3 Succoth Gardens, Edinburgh EH12 6BR.

MATTHEWS, John Frederick, DPhil; FRHistS; FBA 1990; Reader in the Middle and Late Roman Empire, Oxford University, since 1990; Fellow, and Praelector in Ancient History, Queen's College, Oxford, since 1976; *b* 15 Feb. 1940; *s* of Jack and Mary Matthews; *m* 1965, Elaine Jackson; two *d*. *Educ:* Wyggeston Boys' Sch., Leicester; Queen's Coll., Oxford (MA 1965; DPhil 1970). FRHistS 1986. Oxford University: Dyson Jun. Res. Fellow in Greek Culture, Balliol Coll., 1965–69; Conington Prize, 1971; Univ. Lectr in Middle and Late Roman Empire, 1969–90; Official Fellow, Corpus Christi Coll., 1969–76. Inst. for Advanced Study, Princeton, 1980–81; British Acad. Reader in Humanities, 1988–90; Chm. of Govs, Cheney Sch., Oxford, 1986–91. *Publications:* Western Aristocracies and Imperial Court AD 364–425, 1975; (with T. J. Cornell) Atlas of the Roman World, 1982; Political Life and Culture in late Roman Society, 1985; The Roman World of Ammianus, 1989; (with Peter Heather) The Goths in the Fourth Century, 1991. *Recreations:* playing the piano, listening to music, suburban gardening. *Address:* Queen's College, Oxford OX1 4AW. *T:* Oxford (0865) 279132.

MATTHEWS, Maj.-Gen. Michael, CB 1984; DL; Engineer in Chief (Army), 1983–85; Secretary, Council of TAVR Associations, since 1986; *b* 22 April 1930; *s* of late W. Matthews and of M. H. Matthews; *m* 1955, Elspeth Rosemary, *d* of late Lt-Col Sir John Maclure, 3rd Bt, OBE, and Lady Maclure; two *s* two *d*. *Educ:* King's Coll., Taunton, Somerset. CompICE, 1984; FBIM. rcds, psc. Commissioned, Royal Engineers, 1951; served overseas, Egypt, Cyprus, Jordan, Kenya, Aden and BAOR; DAA and QMG HQ 24 Inf. Bde, Kenya, 1962–65; OC, Indep. Para Sqn RE, UK and Aden, 1965–67; GSO1 (DS) Staff College, Camberley, 1968–70; CO 35 Engr Regt, BAOR, 1970–72; Col GS Ops, Exercise Planning Staff and Trg, HQ BAOR, 1972–74; CCRE, HQ1 (BR) Corps, BAOR, 1974–76; RCDS 1977; DQMG HQ BAOR, 1978–80; Dir of Personal Services (Army), 1980–83. Col Comdt, RE, 1985–; Hon. Colonel: Southampton Univ. OTC, 1985–; 131 Indep. Commando Sqn RE (V), 1985–. DL Hants, 1991. *Recreations:* Rugby, cricket, hockey, hang gliding. *Address:* c/o Lloyds Bank, Chagford, Newton Abbot, Devon. *Clubs:* Army and Navy, MCC; British Sportsman's.

MATTHEWS, Michael Gough; Director, Royal College of Music, since 1985; *b* 12 July 1931; *s* of late Cecil Gough Matthews and Amelia Eleanor Mary Matthews. *Educ:* Chigwell School; Royal College of Music (Open Scholarship, 1947; Hopkinson Gold Medal, 1953; ARCM, FRCM 1972); ARCO; Diploma del Corso di Perfezionamento St Cecilia, Rome. Diploma of Honour and Prize, Chopin Internat. Piano Competition, 1955; Italian Govt Scholarship, 1956; Chopin Fellowship, Warsaw, 1959. Pianist; recitals, broadcasts, concerts, UK, Europe and Far East. Supervisor Junior Studies, RSAMD, 1964–71; Royal College of Music: Dir, Junior Dept, and Prof. of Piano, 1972–75; Registrar, 1975; Vice-Dir, 1978–84. Member: Governing Cttee, Royal Choral Soc., 1985–; NYO GB; Royal Philharmonic Soc., 1985– (Member: Hon. Council of Management, 1987–; Awards Sub-Cttee, 1987–); Bd of Management, London Internat. String Quartet Competition, 1988–; Music Study Gp, EEC, 1989–; Comité d'Honneur, Presence de l'Art, Paris, 1990–. Vice-President: RCO, 1985–; Nat. Youth Choir, 1986–; Herbert Howells Soc., 1987–. Hon. FLCM 1976; Hon. RAM 1979; FRSAMD 1986; FRSA; Hon. GSM 1987. *Publications:* various musical entertainments; arranger of educational music. *Recreation:* gardening. *Address:* Royal College of Music, Prince Consort Road, SW7 2BS. *T:* 071–589 3643. *Club:* Athenæum.

MATTHEWS, Mrs Pamela Winifred, (Mrs Peter Matthews), BSc (Econ.); Principal, Westfield College (University of London), 1962–65; *b* 4 Dec. 1914; *d* of Lt-Col C. C. Saunders-O'Mahony; *m* 1938, H. P. S. Matthews (*d* 1958); one *s* one *d*. *Educ:* St Paul's Girls' Sch.; London Sch. of Economics. Royal Institute of International Affairs, 1938–39; Foreign Office, 1939–40; The Economist Newspaper, 1940–43; Foreign Office, 1943–45; Reuters, 1945–61; Nat. Inst. for Social Work Trg, 1961–62. Independent Mem., Advertising Standards Authority, 1964–65; Industrial Tribunal rep. for CAB, 1974–89. Mem., RIIA, 1990. Governor: Northwood Coll., Middlesex, 1962–89; Cardinal Manning Boys' RC School, 1980–91. *Publications:* diplomatic correspondence for Reuters. *Recreations:* travel, theatre. *Address:* 1 Edwardes Place, Kensington High Street, W8 6LR. *T:* 071–603 8458.

MATTHEWS, Percy; *b* 24 July 1921; *s* of Samuel and Minnie Matthews; *m* 1946, Audrey Rosenthal; one *s* two *d*. *Educ:* Parmiters Sch., London. Overseas Associate, J. O. Hambro & Co. Hon. Fellow, St Peter's Coll., Oxford. Freeman, City of London. *Recreations:* painting, golf.

MATTHEWS, Mrs Peter; *see* Matthews, Mrs Pamela W.

MATTHEWS, Sir Peter (Alec), Kt 1975; AO 1980; Chairman, Pegler-Hattersley plc, 1979–87 (Director, 1977–87); Director: Lloyds Bank, since 1974 (Chairman, Central London Regional Board, since 1978); Cookson Group (formerly Lead Industries Group), since 1980; Hamilton Oil Great Britain, since 1981; *b* 21 Sept. 1922; *s* of Major Alec Bryan Matthews and Elsie Lazarus Barlow; *m* 1946, Sheila Dorothy Bunting; four *s* one *d*. *Educ:* Shawnigan Lake Sch., Vancouver Island; Oundle Sch. Served Royal Engineers (retired as Major), 1940–46. Joined Stewarts and Lloyds Ltd, 1946; Director of Research and Technical Development, 1962; Member for R&D, BSC, 1968–70, Dep. Chm., 1973–76; Vickers PLC: Man. Dir, 1970–79; Chm., 1980–84; Director: British Electric Traction Plc, 1976–87; Sun Alliance and London Insurance, 1979–89; Lloyds & Scottish, 1983–86. Chm., Armed Forces Pay Review Body, 1984–89; Mem., Top Salaries Review

Body, 1984–89. Member: BOTB, 1973–77; Export Guarantees Adv. Council, 1973–78; Status Review Cttee, ECGD, 1983–84; Pres., Sino-British Trade Council, 1983–85. Member: NRDC, 1974–80; Engineering Industries Council, 1976– (Chm., 1980–); Adv. Council for Applied R&D, 1976–80. Pres., Engineering Employers Fedn, 1982–84; Chm., Council, University Coll., London, 1980–89 (Hon. Fellow, 1982). CBIM, FRSA. *Recreations:* sailing, gardening. *Address:* Chalkwell, Nether Wallop, Stockbridge, Hants SO20 8HE. *T:* Andover (0264) 782136. *Club:* Royal Yacht Squadron (Cowes).

MATTHEWS, Prof. Peter Bryan Conrad, FRS 1973; MD, DSc; Professor of Sensorimotor Physiology, since 1987 and Student of Christ Church since 1958, University of Oxford; *b* 23 Dec. 1928; *s* of Prof. Sir Bryan Matthews, CBE, FRS; *m* 1956, Margaret Rosemary Blears; one *s* one *d.* *Educ:* Marlborough Coll.; King's Coll., Cambridge; Oxford Univ. Clinical School. Oxford University: Univ. Lectr in Physiology, 1961–77; Reader, 1978–86; Tutor, Christ Church, 1958–86. Sir Lionel Whitby Medal, Cambridge Univ., 1959; Robert Bing Prize, Swiss Acad. of Med. Science, 1971. *Publications:* Mammalian Muscle Receptors and their Central Actions, 1972; papers on neurophysiology in various scientific jls. *Address:* University Laboratory of Physiology, Parks Road, Oxford OX1 3PT. *T:* Oxford (0865) 272500.

MATTHEWS, Prof. Peter Hugoe, LittD; FBA 1985; Professor and Head of Department of Linguistics, and Fellow of St John's College, University of Cambridge, since 1980; *b* 10 March 1934; *s* of John Hugo and Cecily Eileen Emsley Matthews; *m* 1984, Lucienne Marie Jeanne Schleich; one step *s* one step *d.* *Educ:* Montpellier Sch., Paignton; Clifton Coll.; St John's Coll., Cambridge (MA 1960; LittD). Lectr in Linguistics, UCNW, 1961–65 (on leave Indiana Univ., Bloomington, 1963–64); University of Reading: Lectr in Linguistic Science, 1965–69; Reader, 1969–75; Prof., 1975–80 (on leave as Fellow, King's Coll., Cambridge, 1970–71, and as Fellow, Netherlands Inst. of Advanced Study, Wassenaar, 1977–78). An Editor, Jl of Linguistics, 1970–79. *Publications:* Inflectional Morphology, 1972; Morphology, 1974; Generative Grammar and Linguistic Competence, 1979; Syntax, 1981; articles esp. in Jl of Linguistics. *Recreations:* cycling, bird-watching. *Address:* 10 Fendon Close, Cambridge CB1 4RU. *T:* Cambridge (0223) 247553; 22 Rue Nina et Julien Lefevre, L-1952 Luxembourg. *T:* (010 352) 24146.

MATTHEWS, Sir Peter (Jack), Kt 1981; CVO 1978; OBE 1974; QPM 1970; DL; Chief Constable of Surrey, 1968–82; *b* 25 Dec. 1917; *s* of Thomas Francis Matthews and Agnes Jack; *m* 1944, Margaret, *er d* of Cecil Levett, London; one *s.* *Educ:* Blackridge Public Sch., West Lothian. Joined Metropolitan Police, 1937; Flt-Lt (pilot) RAF, 1942–46; Metropolitan Police, 1946–65; seconded Cyprus, 1955; Chief Supt P Div. 1963–65; Chief Constable: of East Suffolk, 1965–67; of Suffolk, 1967–68. President: British Section, Internat. Police Assoc., 1964–70 (Internat. Pres. 1966–70); Assoc. of Chief Police Officers of England, Wales and NI, 1976–77 (Chm., Sub-Cttee on Terrorism and Allied Matters, 1976–82; Rep. at Interpol, 1977–80); Chief Constables' Club, 1980–81; Vice-Chm., Home Office Standing Adv. Cttee on Police Dogs, 1982– (Chm., 1978–82; Chm., Training Sub-Cttee, 1972–82); led British Police Study Team to advise Singapore Police, 1982; specialist advr to Parly Select Cttee on Defence, 1984; Mem., MoD Police Review Cttee, 1985. Lecture tour of Canada and USA, 1979; Lectr, Airline Training Associates Ltd, 1984–; Lectr to International Military Services Ltd, 1987–. CBIM 1978. DL Surrey, 1981. Final Reader, HM The Queen's Police Gold Medal Essay Competition, 1983–. *Club:* Royal Air Force.

MATTHEWS, Richard Bonnar, CBE 1971; QPM 1965; Chief Constable, Warwickshire, 1964–76 (Warwickshire and Coventry, 1969–74); *b* 18 Dec. 1915; *er s* of late Charles Richard Matthews, Worthing; *m* 1943, Joan, *d* of late Basil Worsley, Henstridge, Som; two *d.* *Educ:* Stowe School. Served War of 1939–45, Lieut, RNVR. Joined Metropolitan Police, 1936; Asst Chief Constable, E Sussex, 1954–56; Chief Constable of Cornwall and Isles of Scilly, 1956–64. Chm., Traffic Cttee, Assoc. of Chief Police Officers, 1973–76. Mem., Williams Cttee on Obscenity and Film Censorship, 1977–79; Chm., CS selection bds, 1979–85. Founder, Adv. Cttee on Beach Life Saving for Cornwall, 1959. *Recreations:* ski-ing, fishing, gardening. *Address:* Smoke Acre, Great Bedwyn, Marlborough, Wilts SN8 3LP. *T:* Marlborough (0672) 870584. *Club:* Naval.

MATTHEWS, Prof. Richard Ellis Ford, ONZ 1988; ScD; FRS 1974; FRSNZ; FNZIC; Professor of Microbiology, Department of Cell Biology, University of Auckland, New Zealand, 1962–86, now Emeritus; *b* Hamilton, NZ, 20 Nov. 1921; *s* of Gerald Wilfrid Matthews and Ruby Miriam (*née* Crawford); *m* 1950, Lois Ann Bayley; three *s* one *d.* *Educ:* Mt Albert Grammar Sch.; Auckland University Coll.; Univ. of Cambridge. MSc (NZ), PhD, ScD (Cantab). Postdoctoral Research Fellow, Univ. of Wisconsin, 1949. Plant Diseases Div., DSIR, Auckland, NZ: Mycologist, 1950–53; Sen. Mycologist, 1954–55; (on leave from DSIR as a visiting worker at ARC Virus Research Unit, Molteno Inst., Cambridge, 1952–56); Sen. Principal Scientific Officer, DSIR, 1956–61; Head of Dept of Cell Biology, Univ. of Auckland, 1962–77, 1983–85. Pres., Internat. Cttee for Taxonomy of Viruses, 1975–81. *Publications:* Plant Virus Serology, 1957; Plant Virology, 1970, 3rd edn 1991; over 130 original papers in scientific jls. *Recreations:* gardening, sea fishing, bee keeping. *Address:* 1019 Beach Road, Torbay, Auckland 10, New Zealand. *T:* Auckland 4737709; (summer residence) RD4 Hikurangi. *T:* (09) 4037403.

MATTHEWS, Prof. Robert Charles Oliver, CBE 1975; FBA 1968; Master of Clare College, Cambridge, since 1975; *b* 16 June 1927; *s* of Oliver Harwood Matthews, WS, and Ida Finlay; *m* 1948, Joyce Hilda Lloyds; one *d.* *Educ:* Edinburgh Academy; Corpus Christi Coll., Oxford (Hon. Fellow, 1976). Student, Nuffield Coll., Oxford, 1947–48; Lectr, Merton Coll., Oxford, 1948–49; University Asst Lectr in Economics, Cambridge, 1949–51, and Univ. Lectr, 1951–65; Fellow of St John's Coll., Cambridge, 1950–65; Drummond Prof. of Political Economy, Oxford, and Fellow of All Souls Coll., 1965–75; Prof. of Pol Economy, Cambridge Univ., 1980–91. Vis. Prof., Univ. of California, Berkeley, 1961–62. Chm., SSRC, 1972–75. A Managing Trustee, Nuffield Foundn, 1975–; Trustee, Urwick Orr and Partners Ltd, 1978–86. Pres., Royal Econ. Soc., 1984–86; Mem., OECD Expert Group on Non-inflationary Growth, 1975–77. Chm., Bank of England Panel of Academic Consultants, 1977–. FIDE Internat. Master of chess composition, 1965. For. Hon. Mem., Amer. Acad. of Arts and Scis, 1985. Hon. DLitt Warwick, 1980. *Publications:* A Study in Trade Cycle History, 1954; The Trade Cycle, 1958; (with F. H. Hahn) Théorie de la Croissance Economique, 1972; (ed) Economic Growth: trends and factors, 1981; (with C. H. Feinstein and J. C. Odling-Smee) British Economic Growth 1856–1973, 1982; (ed with G. B. Stafford) The Grants Economy and Collective Consumption, 1982; (ed) Slower Growth in the Western World, 1982; (ed with J. R. Sargent) Contemporary Problems of Economic Policy: essays from the CLARE Group, 1983; articles in learned journals. (With M. Lipton and J. M. Rice) Chess Problems: Introduction to an Art, 1963. *Address:* The Master's Lodge, Clare College, Cambridge CB2 1TL. *Club:* Reform.

MATTHEWS, Ronald Sydney, CB 1978; Deputy Secretary, Department of Health and Social Security, 1976–81; *b* 26 July 1922; *s* of George and Louisa Matthews; *m* 1945, Eleanor Bronwen Shaw (*d* 1989); one *s* one *d.* *Educ:* Kingsbury County School. RAF, 1940–46. Clerical Officer, Min. of Health, 1939; Principal 1959; Private Sec. to Minister of Health, 1967–68; Private Sec. to Sec. of State for Social Services, 1968–69; Asst Sec. 1968; Under-Sec., DHSS, 1973–76. *Recreations:* walking, gardening, reading. *Address:* 4 Saxon Rise, Winterborne Stickland, Blandford Forum, Dorset DT11 0PQ.

MATTHEWS, Sir Stanley, Kt 1965; CBE 1957; professional footballer; *b* Hanley, Stoke-on-Trent, 1 Feb. 1915; *s* of late Jack Matthews, Seymour Street, Hanley; *m* 1st, 1935, Elizabeth Hall Vallance (marr. diss. 1975); one *s* one *d;* 2nd, 1975, Gertrud (Mila) Winterova. *Educ:* Wellington Sch., Hanley. Played in first Football League match, 1931; first played for England, 1934, and fifty-five times subsequently; Blackpool FC, 1947–61 (FA Cup, 1953); Stoke City FC, 1961–65. Freedom of Stoke-on-Trent, 1963. *Publication:* The Stanley Matthews Story, 1960. *Recreations:* golf, tennis. *Club:* National Sporting.

MATTHEWS, Rt. Rev. Timothy John; BA, DCL; LST, STh; Chaplain Emeritus, Bishop's College School; *b* 8 July 1907; *m* 1933, Mary Eileen, *d* of Dr T. E. Montgomery; four *s* one *d.* *Educ:* Bishop's Univ., Lennoxville. Deacon 1932, priest 1933, Edmonton; Vicar of Viking, 1933–37; Incumbent of Edson, 1937–40; Rector of Coaticook, 1940–44; Lake St John, 1944–52; Rector and Archdeacon of Gaspé, 1952–57; Rector of Lennoxville, 1957–71; Archdeacon of St Francis, 1957–71; Bishop of Quebec, 1971–77. Hon. Visitor, Bishops Univ. *Address:* 23 High Street, Lennoxville, PQ J1M 1E6, Canada. *Clubs:* St George's (Sherbrooke); Hole-in-One, Lennoxville Golf, Milby Golf; Lennoxville Curling.

MATTHEWS, Prof. Walter Bryan; Professor of Clinical Neurology, University of Oxford, 1970–87, now Emeritus; Fellow of St Edmund Hall, Oxford, 1970–87, now Emeritus; *b* 7 April 1920; *s* of Very Rev. Dr Walter Robert Matthews; *m* 1943, Margaret Forster; one *s* one *d.* *Educ:* Marlborough Coll.; University Coll., Oxford. MA, DM, FRCP. RAMC, 1943–46. Senior Registrar, Oxford, 1948; Chief Asst, Dept of Neurology, Manchester Royal Infirmary, 1949–52; Senior Registrar, King's College Hosp., 1952–54; Consultant Neurologist, Derbyshire Royal Infirmary, 1954–68; Consultant Neurologist, Manchester Royal Infirmary and Crumpsall Hosp., 1968–70. President: Section of Neurology, RSM, 1981; Assoc. of British Neurologists, 1982; Second Vice-Pres., RCP, 1986–87. Osler Orator, RCP, 1981. Editor-in-Chief, Jl of Neurological Scis, 1977–83. *Publications:* Practical Neurology, 1963, 3rd edn 1975; (with H. G. Miller) Diseases of the Nervous System, 1972, 3rd edn 1979; (ed) Recent Advances in Clinical Neurology I, 1975, II, 1978, IV, 1984; Multiple Sclerosis: the facts, 1978; (ed) McAlpine's Multiple Sclerosis, 1985, 2nd edn 1991; papers in Brain, Quarterly Jl of Medicine, etc. *Recreation:* walking. *Address:* Sandford House, Sandford-on-Thames, Oxford OX4 4YN.

MATTHÖFER, Hans; Member of the Bundestag (Social Democrat), 1961–87; *b* Bochum, 25 Sept. 1925; *m* Traute Matthöfer (*née* Mecklenburg). *Educ:* primary sch.; studied economics and social sciences in Frankfurt/Main and Madison, Wis, USA, 1948–53 (grad. Economics). Employed as manual and clerical worker, 1940–42; Reich Labour Service, 1942; conscripted into German Army, 1943 (Armoured Inf.), final rank NCO. Joined SPD (Social Democratic Party of Germany), 1950; employed in Economics Dept, Bd of Management, IG Metall (Metalworkers' Union) and specialized in problems arising in connection with automation and mechanization, 1953 (Head of Trng and Educn Dept, 1961). Member, OEEC Mission in Washington and Paris, 1957–61; Vice-Pres., Gp of Parliamentarians on Latin American Affairs (Editor of periodical Esprés Español until end of 1972); Mem., Patronage Cttee of German Section of Amnesty Internat.; Pres., Bd of Trustees, German Foundn for Developing Countries, 1971–73; Parly State Sec. in Federal Min. for Economic Co-operation, 1972; Federal Minister for Research and Technology, 1974, for Finance, 1978–82, for Posts and Telecommunications, 1982. Mem. of Presidency and Treasurer, SPD, 1985–87. Chm., Exec. Bd, Beteiligungsges. für Gemeinwirtschaft AG, trade union holding, 1987–92. Publisher, Vorwärts, 1985–. *Publications:* Der Unterschied zwischen den Tariflöhnen und den Effektivverdiensten in der Metallindustrie der Bundesrepublik, 1956; Technological Change in the Metal Industries (in two parts), 1961–62; Der Beitrag politischer Bildung zur Emanzipation der Arbeitnehmer—Materialien zur Frage des Bildungsurlaubs, 1970; Streiks und streikähnliche Formen des Kampfes der Arbeitnehmer im Kapitalismus, 1971; Für eine menschliche Zukunft—Sozialdemokratische Forschungs—und Technologiepolitik, 1976; Humanisierung der Arbeit und Produktivität in der Industriegesellschaft, 1977, 1978, 1980; numerous articles on questions of trade union, development, research and finance policies. *Address:* Schreyerstrasse 38, 6242 Kronberg im Taunus, Germany.

MATTINGLY, Alan; Director (formerly Secretary), Ramblers' Association, since 1974; *b* 19 May 1949; *s* of Alexander and Patricia Mattingly; *m* 1980, Wendy Mallard. *Educ:* The Latymer Sch., Edmonton; St John's Coll., Cambridge (BA). Chm., Council for Nat. Parks, 1979–83, 1990–; Vice-Pres., Countrywide Holidays Assoc., 1980–. Mem., (Lab) Newham Borough Council, 1980–86, Dep. Leader, 1983–85. *Publications:* Tackle Rambling, 1981; Walking in the National Parks, 1982. *Recreations:* walking, orienteering. *Address:* 45 Tonbridge Crescent, Kenton, Middlesex HA3 9LE.

MATTINGLY, Dr Stephen, TD 1964; FRCP; Consultant Physician, Middlesex Hospital, 1958–81, now Emeritus; Consultant Physician, 1956–82 and Medical Director, 1972–82, Garston Manor Rehabilitation Centre; Hon. Consultant in Rheumatology and Rehabilitation to the Army, 1976–81; *b* 1 March 1922; *s* of Harold Mattingly, CBE and Marion Grahame Meikleham; *m* 1945, Brenda Mary Pike; one *s.* *Educ:* Leighton Park Sch.; UCH (MB, BS); Dip. in Physical Med., 1953. FRCP 1970. House-surg., UCH, 1947; Regtl MO, 2/10 Gurkha Rifles, RAMC Far East, 1947–49; House-surg. and Registrar, UCH, 1950–55; Sen. Registrar, Mddx Hosp., 1955–56. Reg. Med. Consultant for London, S-Eastern, Eastern and Southern Regions, Dept of Employment, 1960–74. Mem., Attendance Allowance Bd, 1978–83. Lt-Col RAMC TA, 1952–67. *Publications:* (contrib.) Progress in Clinical Rheumatology, 1965; (contrib.) Textbook of Rheumatic Diseases, ed Copeman, 1969; (contrib.) Fractures and Joint Injuries, ed Watson Jones, 5th edn 1976, 6th edn 1982; (ed) Rehabilitation Today, 1977, 2nd edn 1981. *Recreation:* gardening. *Address:* Highfield House, Little Brington, Northants NN7 4HN. *T:* Northampton (0604) 770271.

MATUTES JUAN, Abel; Spanish Member, Commission of the European Communities, since 1986; *b* 31 Oct. 1941; *s* of Antonio Matutes and Carmen Juan; *m* Nieves Prats Prats; one *s* three *d.* *Educ:* University of Barcelona (Law and Economic Sciences). Prof., Barcelona Univ., 1963; Vice-Pres., Employers Organization for Tourism, Ibiza-Formentera, 1964–79; Mayor of Ibiza, 1970–71; Senator, Ibiza and Formentera in Alianza Popular (opposition party), 1977–79; Vice-Pres., Partido Popular (formerly Alianza Popular), 1979– (Pres., Economy Cttee); Pres., Nat. Electoral Cttee; Spokesman for Economy and Finance, Grupo Popular in Congress (Parlt). *Recreation:* tennis. *Address:* POB 416, Ibiza; c/o Commission of the European Communities, 200 Rue de La Loi, 1049 Brussels, Belgium. *Clubs:* Golf Rocalliza (Ibiza); de Campo Tennis (Ibiza).

MAUCERI, John Francis; Music Director, Scottish Opera, since 1987; Consultant for Music Theatre, Kennedy Center for Performing Arts, Washington, DC, since 1982; Chief Conductor, Los Angeles Philharmonic Hollywood Bowl Orchestra, since 1991; *b* 12 Sept. 1945; *s* of Gene B. Mauceri and Mary Elizabeth (*née* Marino); *m* 1968, Betty Ann Weiss; one *s.* *Educ:* Yale Univ. (BA, MPhil). Music Dir, Yale Symphony Orch., 1968–74; Associate Prof., Yale Univ., 1974–84; Music Director: Washington Opera, 1979–82;

Orchestras, Kennedy Center, 1979–; Amer. Symphony Orch., NYC, 1985–87; Leonard Bernstein Fest., LSO, 1986; Conductor, Amer. Nat. Tour, Boston Pops Orch., 1987; co-Producer, musical play, On Your Toes, 1983; Musical Supervisor, Song and Dance, Broadway, 1985. Dir, Charles Ives Soc., 1986– (Mem., 1986–); Mem., Adv. Bd, Amer. Inst. for Verdi Studies, 1986–; Trustee, Nat. Inst. for Music Theater, 1986–. Numerous recordings. Antoinette Perry Award, League of NY Theatres and Producers, 1983; Drama Desk Award, 1983; Outer Critics Circle Award, 1983; Arts award, Yale Univ., 1985; Grammy award for Candide recording, 1987; Olivier award for Best Musical for Candide, adaptation for Scottish Opera/Old Vic prodn, 1988; Wavenden All Music Award for Conductor of the Year, 1989. Publications: (contrib.) Sennets and Tuckets: a Bernstein celebration (ed Ledbetter), 1988; various articles for Scottish Opera programmes and newspapers. Address: Scottish Opera, 39 Elmbank Crescent, Glasgow G2 4PT. T: 041–248 4567.

MAUCHLINE, Lord; Michael Edward Abney-Hastings; ranger with New South Wales Pastures Protection Board; b 22 July 1942; s and heir of Countess of Loudoun (13th in line), qv, and s of Captain Walter Strickland Lord (whose marriage to the Countess of Loudoun was dissolved, 1945; his son assumed, by deed poll, 1946, the surname of Abney-Hastings in lieu of his patronymic); m 1969, Noelene Margaret McCormick, 2nd d of Mr and Mrs W. J. McCormick, Barham, NSW; two s three d (of whom one s one d are twins). Educ: Ampleforth. Address: 74 Coreen Street, Jerilderie, NSW 2716, Australia.

MAUD, Hon. Humphrey John Hamilton, CMG 1982; HM Diplomatic Service; Ambassador to Argentina Republic, since 1990; b 17 April 1934; s of Baron Redcliffe-Maud, GCB, CBE and of Jean, yr d of late J. B. Hamilton, Melrose; m 1963, Maria Eugenia Gazitua; three s. Educ: Eton; King's Coll., Cambridge (Scholar; Classics and History); MA. Mem., NYO, 1949–52. Instructor in Classics, Univ. of Minnesota, 1958–59; entered Foreign Service, 1959; FO, 1960–61; Madrid, 1961–63; Havana, 1963–65; FO, 1966–67; Cabinet Office, 1968–69; Paris, 1970–74; Nuffield Coll., Oxford (Econs), 1974–75; Head of Financial Relations Dept, FCO, 1975–79; Minister, Madrid, 1979–82; Ambassador, Luxembourg, 1982–85; Asst Under Sec. of State, FCO, 1985–88; High Comr, Cyprus, 1988–90. Member, Executive Committee: British Diabetic Assoc., 1986–; RCM, 1987–. Recreations: golf, tennis, music ('cellist), bird-watching. Address: c/o Foreign and Commonwealth Office, King Charles Street, SW1A 2AH. Club: United Oxford & Cambridge University.

MAUDE, family name of **Viscount Hawarden** and **Baron Maude of Stratford-upon-Avon.**

MAUDE OF STRATFORD-UPON-AVON, Baron cr 1983 (Life Peer), of Stratford-upon-Avon in the county of Warwickshire; **Angus Edmund Upton Maude;** Kt 1981; TD; PC 1979; author and journalist; b 8 Sept. 1912; o c of late Col Alan Hamer Maude, CMG, DSO, TD, and late Dorothy Maude (née Upton); m 1946, Barbara Elizabeth Earnshaw, o d of late John Earnshaw Sutcliffe, Bushey; two s two d. Educ: Rugby Sch. (Scholar); Oriel Coll., Oxford (MA). Financial journalist, 1933–39: The Times, 1933–34; Daily Mail, 1935–39. Commissioned in RASC (TA), May 1939; served in RASC 1939–45, at home and in North Africa (PoW, Jan. 1942–May 1945); Major 56th (London) Armd Divl Column RASC (TA), 1947–51. Dep. Dir of PEP, 1948–50; Dir, Cons. Political Centre, 1951–55; Editor, Sydney Morning Herald, 1958–61. MP (C) Ealing (South), 1950–57, (Ind. C), 1957–58, (C) Stratford-upon-Avon, Aug. 1963–1983; a Dep. Chm., Cons. Party, 1975–79 (Chm. Res. Dept, 1975–79); Paymaster Gen., 1979–81. Contested S Dorset, by-election, Nov. 1962. Publications: (with Roy Lewis) The English Middle Classes, 1949; Professional People, 1952; (with Enoch Powell) Biography of a Nation, 1955; Good Learning, 1964; South Asia, 1966; The Common Problem, 1969. Address: Old Farm, South Newington, near Banbury, Oxon. Club: Carlton.

See also P. D. G. Hayter, Hon. F. A. A. Maude.

MAUDE, Hon. Francis Anthony Aylmer; MP (C) Warwickshire North, since 1983; Financial Secretary to HM Treasury, since 1990; b 4 July 1953; s of Baron Maude of Stratford-upon-Avon, qv; m 1984, Christina Jane, yr d of late Peter Hadfield, Shrewsbury; one s two d. Educ: Abingdon Sch.; Corpus Christi Coll., Cambridge (MA (Hons) History; Avory Studentship; Halse Prize). Called to Bar, Inner Temple, 1977 (scholar; Forster Boulton Prize). Councillor, Westminster CC, 1978–84. PPS to Minister of State for Employment, 1984–85; an Asst Government Whip, 1985–87; Parly Under Sec. of State, DTI, 1987–89; Minister of State, FCO, 1989–90. Recreations: skiing, cricket, reading, music. Address: House of Commons, SW1A 0AA. T: 071–219 3438.

MAUGHAN, Air Vice-Marshal Charles Gilbert, CB 1976; CBE 1970; AFC; an Independent Panel Inspector, Department of the Environment, since 1983; b 3 March 1923. Educ: Sir George Monoux Grammar Sch.; Harrow County Sch. Served War, Fleet Air Arm (flying Swordfishes and Seafires), 1942–46. Joined RAF, 1949, serving with Meteor, Vampire and Venom sqdns in Britain and Germany; comd No 65 (Hunter) Sqdn, Duxford, Cambridgeshire (won Daily Mail Arch-to-Arc race, 1959). Subseq. comd: No 9 (Vulcan) Sqdn; flying bases of Honington (Suffolk) and Waddington (Lincs); held a staff post at former Bomber Comd, Air Staff (Ops), Strike Command, 1968–70; Air Attaché, Bonn, 1970–73; AOA Strike Command, 1974–75; SASO RAF Strike Command, 1975–77. Gen. Sec., Royal British Legion, 1978–83. Address: Whitestones, Tresham, Wotton-under-Edge, Glos GL12 7RW.

MAULEVERER, (Peter) Bruce; QC 1985; a Recorder, since 1985; b 22 Nov. 1946; s of late Algernon Arthur Mauleverer and Hazel Mary Mauleverer; m 1971, Sara (née Hudson-Evans); two s two d. Educ: Sherborne School; University College, Univ. of Durham (BA 1968). Called to the Bar, Inner Temple, 1969. Hon. Sec.-Gen., Internat. Law Assoc., 1986–. Recreations: sailing, skiing, travel. Address: Eliot Vale House, Eliot Vale, Blackheath, SE3 0UW. T: 081–852 2070.

MAUND, Rt. Rev. John Arthur Arrowsmith, CBE 1975; MC 1946; Chaplain to the Beauchamp Community, Malvern, since 1983; Hon. Assistant Bishop, Worcester; b 1909; s of late Arthur Arrowsmith and Dorothy Jane Maund, Worcester, England; m 1948, Catherine Mary Maurice, Bromley, Kent; no c. Educ: Worcester Cathedral King's Sch.; Leeds Univ.; Mirfield Theological Coll. BA Leeds 1931; Asst Priest, All Saints and St Laurence, Evesham, Worcs, 1933–36; Asst Priest, All Saints, Blackheath, London, 1936–38; Asst Priest, Pretoria Native Mission, Pretoria, South Africa, 1938–40; CF 1940–46 (despatches, 1942); Asst Priest, Pretoria Native Mission, in charge Lady Selborne, Pretoria, 1946–50; Bishop of Lesotho, 1950–76 (diocese known as Basutoland, 1950–66). Fellow Royal Commonwealth Society. Recreations: horse riding, gardening, bridge. Address: Flat 1, Warden's Lodge, The Quadrangle, Newland, Malvern, Worcs WR13 5AX. T: Malvern (06845) 68072.

MAUNDER, Prof. Leonard, OBE 1977; BSc; PhD; ScD; FEng; FIMechE; Professor of Mechanical Engineering, since 1967 (Professor of Applied Mechanics, 1961), Dean of the Faculty of Applied Science, 1973–78, University of Newcastle upon Tyne; b 10 May 1927; s of Thomas G. and Elizabeth A. Maunder; m 1958, Moira Anne Hudson; one s one d. Educ: Bishop Gore Grammar Sch., Swansea; University Coll. of Swansea (BSc;

Hon. Fellow, 1989); Edinburgh Univ. (PhD); Massachusetts Institute of Technology (ScD). Instructor, 1950–53, and Asst Prof., 1953–54, in Dept of Mech. Engrg, MIT; Aeronautical Research Lab., Wright Air Development Center, US Air Force, 1954–56; Lecturer in Post-Graduate Sch. of Applied Dynamics, Edinburgh Univ., 1956–61. Christmas Lectr, Royal Instn, 1983. Member: NRDC, 1976–; SRC Engrg Bd, 1976–80; Adv. Council on R&D for Fuel and Power, Dept of Energy, 1981–; British Technology Gp, 1981–; ACOST, 1987–; Dep. Chm., Newcastle Hospitals Management Cttee, 1971–73. President: Internat. Fedn Theory of Machines and Mechanisms, 1976–79; Engrg, BAAS, 1980. Vice-Pres., IMechE, 1975–80. Hon. Foreign Mem., Polish Soc. Theoretical and Applied Mechanics, 1984. Publications: (with R. N. Arnold) Gyrodynamics and Its Engineering Applications, 1961; Machines in Motion, 1986; numerous papers in the field of applied mechanics. Address: Stephenson Building, The University, Newcastle upon Tyne NE1 7RU.

MAUNDRELL, Rev. Canon Wolseley David; Priest-in-charge (NSM), Stonegate, since 1989; Canon and Prebendary of Chichester Cathedral, 1981–89; b 2 Sept. 1920; s of late Rev. William Herbert Maundrell, RN, and Evelyn Helen Maundrell; m 1950, Barbara Katharine Simmons (d 1985); one s one d. Educ: Radley Coll.; New Coll., Oxford. Deacon, 1943; Priest, 1944; Curate of Haslemere, 1943; Resident Chaplain to Bishop of Chichester, 1949; Vicar of Sparsholt and Lainston, Winchester, 1950; Rector of Weeke, Winchester, 1956; Residentiary Canon of Winchester Cathedral, 1961–70 (Treasurer, 1961–70; Vice-Dean, 1966–70); Examining Chaplain to Bishop of Winchester, 1962–70; Asst Chaplain of Holy Trinity Church, Brussels, 1970–71; Vicar of Icklesham, E Sussex, 1972–82; Rural Dean of Rye, 1978–84; Rector of Rye, 1982–89. Address: The Vicarage, Stonegate, Wadhurst, East Sussex TN5 7EJ. T: Ticehurst (0580) 200515.

MAUNSELL, Susan Pamela; Under Secretary, Policy Division A, Department of Social Security, since 1989; b 30 Jan. 1942; d of George Cruickshank Smith and Alice Monica Smith (née Davies); m 1965, Michael Brooke Maunsell (marr. diss. 1986). Educ: Nottingham High Sch. for Girls (GPDST); Girton Coll., Cambridge (schol.; BA classics; MA). Ministry of Health: Asst Principal, 1964; Private Sec. to Perm. Sec., 1967, to Parly Sec., 1968; Department of Health and Social Security: Principal, 1969; Asst Sec., 1976; Regl Controller, London S Social Security Reg., 1981–85. Recreations: travel, books, theatre, cinema, riding, food, wine, joint owner of French cottage. Address: 27 Longton Avenue, SE26 6RE. T: 081–778 5605.

MAURICE, Dr Rita Joy; Director of Statistics, Home Office, 1977–89; b 10 May 1929; d of A. N. Maurice and F. A. Maurice (née Dean). Educ: East Grinstead County Sch.; University Coll., London. BSc (Econ) 1951; PhD 1958. Asst Lectr, subseq. Lectr in Economic Statistics, University Coll., London, 1951–58; Statistician, Min. of Health, 1959–62; Statistician, subseq. Chief Statistician, Central Statistical Office, 1962–72; Head of Economics and Statistics Div. 6, Depts of Industry, Trade and Prices and Consumer Protection, 1972–77. Mem. Council, Royal Statistical Soc., 1978–82. Publications: (ed) National Accounts Statistics: sources and methods, 1968; articles in statistical jls. Address: 10 Fairfax Place, Swiss Cottage, NW6 4EH.

MAUROY, Pierre; Mayor of Lille, since 1973; Deputy, Nord, since 1986; b 5 July 1928; s of Henri Mauroy and Adrienne Mauroy (née Bronne) m 1951, Gilberte Deboudt; one s. Educ: Lycée de Cambrai; Ecole normale nationale d'apprentissage de Cachan. Joined Young Socialists at age of 16 (Nat. Sec., 1950–58); teacher of technical educn, Colombes, 1952; Sec.-Gen., Syndicat des collèges d'enseignement technique de la Fédération de l'Education nationale, 1955–59; Sec., Fedn of Socialist Parties of Nord, 1961; Mem., Political Bureau, 1963, Dep. Gen. Sec., 1966, Socialist Party; Mem. Exec. Cttee, Fédération de la gauche démocratique et socialiste, 1965–68; First Sec., Fedn of Socialist Parties of Nord and Nat. Co-ordination Sec., Socialist Party, 1971–79; First Sec., Socialist Party, 1988–. Member, from Le Cateau, and Vice-Pres., Conseil Gen. du Nord, 1967–73; Town Councillor and Deputy Mayor of Lille, 1971, Vice-Pres., Town Corp., 1971–81; Deputy, Nord, 1973–81; Prime Minister of France, 1981–84. Pres., Regional Council, Nord-Pas-de-Calais, 1974–81; Socialist Rep. and Vice-Pres., Political Commn, EEC, 1979–81. Political Dir, Action Socialiste Hebdo, 1979–; President: Communauté Urbaine de Lille, 1989–; Fédération nationale Léo Lagrange; Fédération Nationale des Elus Socialistes et Républicains, 1987–90. Publications: Héritiers de l'avenir, 1977; C'est ici le chemin, 1982; A gauche, 1985. Address: 17–19 rue Voltaire, 59800 Lille, France.

MAVOR, Prof. John, CPhys, CEng; Professor of Electrical Engineering since 1986, and Dean of Faculty of Science and Engineering, since 1989, Edinburgh University; b 18 July 1942; s of Gordon Hattersley Mavor and Wilhelmina Baillie McAllister; m 1968, Susan Christina Colton; two d. Educ: City Univ., London; London Univ. (BSc, PhD, DSc(Eng)). FRSE; FInstP; FIEEE; FIEE. AEI Res. Labs, London, 1964–65; Texas Instruments Ltd, Bedford, 1968–70; Emihus Microcomponents, Glenrothes, 1970–71; University of Edinburgh: Lectr, 1971; Reader, 1979; Lothian Chair of Microelectronics, 1980; Head of Dept of Electrical Engrg, 1984–89. Publications: MOST Integrated Circuit Engineering, 1973; Introduction to MOS LSI Design, 1983; over 100 technical papers in professional electronics jls. Recreations: gardening, walking. Address: 8 Esslemont Road, Edinburgh EH16 5PX.

MAVOR, Air Marshal Sir Leslie (Deane), KCB 1970 (CB 1964); AFC 1942; DL; FRAeS; b 18 Jan. 1916; s of William David Mavor, Edinburgh; m 1947, June Lilian Blackburn; four s. Educ: Aberdeen Grammar Sch. Commissioned RAF 1937. Dir of Air Staff Briefing, Air Ministry, 1961–64; AOC, No 38 Group, 1964–66; Asst CAS (Policy), 1966–69; AOC-in-C, RAF Training Comd, 1969–72; retd Jan. 1973. Principal, Home Office Home Defence Coll., 1973–80; Co-ordinator of Voluntary Effort in Civil Defence, 1981–84. DL N Yorks, 1976. Recreations: golf, fishing, shooting, gliding. Address: Barlaston House, Alne, York YO6 2HR. Clubs: Royal Air Force; Yorkshire.

MAVOR, Michael Barclay, CVO 1983; MA; Head Master, Rugby School, since 1990; b 29 Jan. 1947; s of William Ferrier Mavor and Sheena Watson Mavor (née Barclay); m 1970, Jane Elizabeth Sucksmith; one s one d. Educ: Loretto School; St John's Coll., Cambridge (Exhibn and Trevelyan Schol.). MA (English); CertEd. Woodrow Wilson Teaching Fellow, Northwestern Univ., Evanston, Ill, 1969–72; Asst Master, Tonbridge Sch., 1972–78; Course Tutor (Drama), Open Univ., 1977–78; Headmaster, Gordonstoun Sch., 1979–90. Recreations: theatre, writing, golf, fishing, cricket. Address: Rugby School, Rugby, Warwicks CV22 5EH. T: Rugby (0788) 543465. Club: Hawks (Cambridge).

MAVOR, Ronald Henry Moray, CBE 1972; author; b 13 May 1925; s of late Dr O. H. Mavor, CBE (James Bridie) and Rona Bremner; m 1959, Sigrid Bruhn (marr. diss. 1989); one s one d (and one d decd). Educ: Merchiston Castle Sch.; Glasgow Univ. MB, ChB 1948; MRCPGlas 1955, FRCPGlas 1989. In medical practice until 1957, incl. periods in RAMC, at American Hosp., Paris, and Deeside Sanatoria. Drama Critic, The Scotsman, 1957–65; Dir, Scottish Arts Council, 1965–71. Prof., Dept of Drama, Univ. of Saskatchewan, 1981 (Vis. Prof., 1977–78, 1979–81); Prof. Emeritus; Head, Dept of Drama, 1984–90. Vice-Chm., Edinburgh Festival Council, 1975–81 (Mem., 1965–81); Mem. Gen. Adv. Council, BBC, 1971–76; Mem. Drama Panel, British Council, 1973–79. Vis. Lectr on Drama, Guelph, Ontario, and Minneapolis, 1976. FRSA 1991. Plays: The

Keys of Paradise, 1959; Aurelie, 1960; Muir of Huntershill, 1962; The Partridge Dance, 1963; A Private Matter (originally A Life of the General), 1973; The Quartet, 1974; The Doctors, 1974; Gordon, 1978; A House on Temperance, 1980; The Grand Inquisitor, 1990. *Publications*: Art the Hard Way, in, Scotland, 1972; A Private Matter (play), 1974; Dr Mavor and Mr Bridie, 1988. *Address*: 19 Falkland Street, Glasgow G12 9PY. *T*: 041–339 3149.

MAW, (John) Nicholas; composer; *b* 5 Nov. 1935; *s* of Clarence Frederick Maw and Hilda Ellen (*née* Chambers); *m* 1960, Karen Graham; one *s* one *d*. *Educ*: Wennington Sch., Wetherby, Yorks; Royal Academy of Music. Studied in Paris with Nadia Boulanger and Max Deutsch, 1958–59. Fellow Commoner in Creative Arts, Trinity Coll., Cambridge, 1966–70; Visiting Professor of Composition: Yale Music Sch., 1984–85, 1989; Boston Univ., 1986; Prof. of Music, Milton Avery Grad. Sch. of Arts, Bard Coll., NY, 1990–. Midsummer Prize, Corp. of London, 1980. Compositions include: *operas*: One-Man Show, 1964; The Rising of The Moon, 1970; *for orchestra*: Sinfonia, 1966; Sonata for Strings and Two Horns, 1967; Serenade, for small orchestra, 1973, 1977; Life Studies, for 15 solo strings, 1973; Odyssey, 1974–86; Summer Dances, 1981; Spring Music, 1983; The World in the Evening, 1988; *for instrumental soloist and orchestra*: Sonata Notturna, for cello and string orchestra, 1985; Little Concert, for oboe and chamber orchestra, 1987; *for voice and orchestra*: Nocturne, 1958; Scenes and Arias, 1962; *for wind band*: American Games, 1991; *chamber music*: String Quartet, 1965; Chamber Music for wind and piano quintet, 1962; Flute Quartet, 1981; String Quartet no 2, 1983; Ghost Dances, for chamber ensemble, 1988; Piano Trio, 1991; *instrumental music*: Sonatina for flute and piano, 1957; Essay for organ, 1961; *Personae* for piano, nos I-III, 1973, IV–VI, 1985; Music of Memory, for solo guitar, 1989; *vocal music*: The Voice of Love, for mezzo soprano and piano, 1966; Six Interiors, for high voice and guitar, 1966; La Vita Nuova, for soprano and chamber ensemble, 1979; Five American Folksongs, for high voice and piano, 1988; Roman Canticle, for mezzo soprano, flute, viola and harp, 1989; *choral music*: Five Epigrams, for chorus, 1960; Round, for chorus and piano, 1963; Five Irish Songs, for mixed chorus, 1973; Reverdie, five songs for male voices, 1975; Te Deum, for treble and tenor soli, chorus, congregation and organ, 1975; Nonsense Rhymes; songs and rounds for children, 1975–76; The Ruin, for double choir and solo horn, 1980; Three Hymns, for mixed choir and organ, 1989. *Address*: c/o Faber Music Ltd, 3 Queen Square, WC1N 3AU.

MAWBY, Colin (John Beverley); Choral Director, Radio Telefis Eireann, since 1981; *b* 9 May 1936; *e s* of Bernard Mawby and Enid Mawby (*née* Vaux); *m* 1987, Beverley Courtney; two *s*. *Educ*: St Swithun's Primary Sch., Portsmouth; Westminster Cathedral Choir Sch.; Royal Coll. of Music. Organist and Choirmaster of Our Lady's Church, Warwick St, W1, 1953; Choirmaster of Plymouth Cath., 1955; Organist and Choirmaster of St Anne's, Vauxhall, 1957; Asst Master of Music, Westminster Cath., 1959; Master of Music, 1961–75; Dir of Music, Sacred Heart, Wimbledon, 1978–81. Conductor: Westminster Chamber Choir, 1971–78; Westminster Cathedral String Orchestra, 1971–78; New Westminster Chorus, 1972–80; Horniman Singers, 1979–80; Culwick Choral Soc., 1981–85. Prof. of Harmony, Trinity Coll. of Music, 1975–81. Director (Catholic) Publisher, L. J. Cary & Co., 1963; Vice-Pres., Brit. Fedn of *Pueri Cantores*, 1966; Member: Council, Latin Liturgical Assoc., 1969; Adv. Panel, Royal Sch. of Church Music, 1974; Music Sub-Cttee, Westminster Arts Council, 1974. Hon. FGCM 1988. Broadcaster and recording artist; free lance journalism. *Publications*: Church music including sixteen Masses, Anthems, Motets and Holy Week music. *Recreations*: gardening, wine drinking. *Address*: Gerrardstown, Garlow Cross, Navan, Co. Meath, Ireland.*T*: Navan (46) 29394.

MAWER, Philip John Courtney; Secretary-General, General Synod of the Church of England, since 1990; *b* 30 July 1947; *s* of Eric Douglas and Thora Constance Mawer; *m* 1972, Mary Ann Moxon; one *s* two *d*. *Educ*: Hull Grammar Sch.; Edinburgh Univ. (MA Hons Politics 1971); DPA (London Univ. External) 1973. Senior Pres., Student Representative Council, 1969–70. Home Office, 1971; Private Sec. to Minister of State, 1974–76; Nuffield and Leverhulme Travelling Fellowship, 1978–79; Sec., Lord Scarman's Inquiry into Brixton disturbances, 1981; Asst Sec., Head of Industrial Relations, Prison Dept, 1984–87; Principal Private Sec. to Home Sec. (Rt Hon. Douglas Hurd), 1987–89; Under-Secretary, Cabinet Office, 1989–90. *Recreations*: family and friends. *Address*: Church House, Great Smith Street, SW1P 3NZ. *T*: 071–222 9011.

MAWER, Ronald K.; *see* Knox-Mawer.

MAWHINNEY, Brian Stanley; MP (C) Peterborough, since 1979; Minister of State, Northern Ireland Office, since 1990; *b* 26 July 1940; *s* of Frederick Stanley Arnot Mawhinney and Coralie Jean Mawhinney; *m* 1965, Betty Louise Oja; two *s* one *d*. *Educ*: Royal Belfast Academical Instn; Queen's Univ., Belfast (BSc); Univ. of Michigan, USA (MSc); Univ. of London (PhD). Asst Prof. of Radiation Research, Univ. of Iowa, USA, 1968–70; Lectr, subsequently Sen. Lectr, Royal Free Hospital School of Medicine, 1970–84. Mem., MRC, 1980–83. Mem., Gen. Synod of C of E, 1985–90. PPS to Ministers in HM Treasury, Employment and NI, 1982–86; Under Sec. of State for NI, 1986–90. Pres., Cons. Trade Unionists, 1987–90 (Vice-Pres., 1984–87); Mem., AUT. Contested (C) Stockton on Tees, Oct. 1974. *Publication*: (jtly) Conflict and Christianity in Northern Ireland, 1976. *Recreations*: sport, reading. *Address*: House of Commons, SW1A 0AA.

MAWREY, Richard Brooks; QC 1986; a Recorder of the Crown Court, since 1986; *b* 20 Aug. 1942; *s* of Philip Stephen Mawrey and Alice Brooks Mawrey; *m* 1965, Gillian Margaret Butt, *d* of Francis Butt and Alice Margaret Butt; one *d*. *Educ*: Rossall School; Magdalen College, Oxford (BA, 1st class Hons Law, 1963; Eldon Law Scholar, 1964; MA 1967). Albion Richardson Scholar, Gray's Inn, 1964; called to the Bar, Gray's Inn, 1964; Lectr in Law, Magdalen College, Oxford, 1964–65, Trinity College, Oxford, 1965–69. *Publications*: (specialist editor) Consumer Credit Legislation, 1983; Butterworth's County Court Precedents, 1985; Computers and the Law, 1988. *Recreations*: history, opera, cooking. *Address*: 2 Harcourt Buildings, Temple, EC4Y 9DB. *T*: 071–583 9020.

MAWSON, David, OBE 1990; JP; DL; RIBA; FSA; Partner, Feilden and Mawson, Architects, Norwich, 1957–90, Consultant, since 1990; *b* 30 May 1924; *s* of John William Mawson and Evelyn Mary Mawson (*née* Bond); *m* 1951, Margaret Kathlyn Norton; one *s* one *d*. *Educ*: Merchant Taylors' Sch., Sandy Lodge; Wellington Coll., NZ; Auckland Univ., NZ; Kingston-upon-Thames Coll. of Art. Royal Navy, 1945–47. Chartered Architect, 1952–. Architect, Norwich Cathedral, 1977–90. Chairman: Norfolk Soc. (CPRE), 1971–76 (Vice Pres. 1976–); 54 Gp, 1982–; Friends of Norwich Museums, 1985–; Founder and Chm., British Assoc. of Friends of Museums, 1973–89 (Vice-Pres., 1989–); Founder Pres., World Fedn of Friends of Museums, 1975–81, Past Pres., 1981–. Mem., Cttee of Nat. Heritage, 1973–; Trustee, Norfolk Historic Bldgs Trust, 1975–90 (Dir, 1990–); Founder and Chm., Norfolk Gardens Trust, 1988–. Mem., Norfolk Assoc. of Architects, 1952– (Pres., 1979–81); Hon. Treas., Heritage Co-ordination Gp, 1981–87. Pres., Norfolk Club, 1986–87 (Vice-Pres., 1985–86). JP Norwich, 1972; DL Norfolk, 1986. FRSA 1982; FSA 1983. *Publication*: paper on British Museum Friends Socs in Proc. of First Internat. Congress of Friends of Museums, Barcelona, 1972; contrib. Jl of Royal

Soc. of Arts. *Recreations*: tennis, yachting. *Address*: Gonville Hall, Wymondham, Norfolk NR18 9JG. *T*: Wymondham (0953) 602166. *Club*: Norfolk (Norwich).

MAWSON, Stuart Radcliffe; Consultant Surgeon, Ear Nose and Throat Department, King's College Hospital, London, 1951–79, Head of Department, 1973–79, now Hon. Consultant; *b* 4 March 1918; *s* of late Alec Robert Mawson, Chief Officer, Parks Dept, LCC, and Ena (*née* Grossmith), *d* of George Grossmith Jr, Actor Manager; *m* 1948, June Irene, *d* of George Percival; two *s* two *d*. *Educ*: Canford Sch.; Trinity Coll., Cambridge; St Thomas's Hosp., London. BA Cantab 1940, MA 1976; MRCS, LRCP 1943; MB, BChir Cantab 1946; FRCS 1947; DLO 1948. House Surg., St Thomas's Hosp., 1943; RMO XIth Para. Bn, 1st Airborne Div., Arnhem, POW, 1943–44; Chief Asst, ENT Dept, St Thomas's Hosp., 1950; Consultant ENT Surgeon: King's Coll. Hosp., 1951; Belgrave Hosp. for Children, 1951; Recog. Teacher of Oto-Rhino-Laryngology, Univ. of London, 1958. Chm., KCH Med. Cttee and Dist Management Team, 1977–79. FRSocMed (Pres. Section of Otology, 1974–75); Liveryman, Apothecaries' Soc.; former Mem. Council, Brit. Assoc. of Otolaryngologists. *Publications*: Diseases of the Ear, 1963, 5th edn 1988; (jtly) Essentials of Otolaryngology, 1967; (contrib.) Scott-Brown's Diseases of the Ear, Nose and Throat, 4th edn 1979; (contrib.) Modern Trends in Diseases of the Ear, Nose and Throat, 1972; Arnhem Doctor, 1981; numerous papers in sci. jls. *Address*: Whinbeck, Knodishall, Saxmundham, Suffolk IP17 1UF. *Clubs*: Aldeburgh Golf, Aldeburgh Yacht.

MAXEY, Peter Malcolm, CMG 1982; HM Diplomatic Service, retired 1986; Senior Editor, Hilfe Ltd, since 1990; *b* 26 Dec. 1930; *m* 1st, 1955, Joyce Diane Marshall; two *s* two *d*; 2nd, Christine Irene Spooner. *Educ*: Bedford Sch.; Corpus Christi Coll., Cambridge. Served HM Forces, 1949–50. Entered Foreign Office, 1953; Third Sec., Moscow, 1955; Second Sec., 1956; First Sec., Helsinki, 1962; Moscow, 1965; First Sec. and Head of Chancery, Colombo, 1968; seconded to Lazard Bros, 1971; Inspector, 1972; Deputy Head UK Delegation to CSCE, Geneva, 1973; Head of UN Dept, FCO, 1974; NATO Defence Coll., Rome, 1977; Dublin, 1977; on secondment as Under Sec., Cabinet Office, 1978–81; Ambassador, GDR, 1981–84; Ambassador and Dep. Perm. Rep. to UN, NY, 1984–86. Editorial Dir, Global Analysis Systems, 1986–88. *Address*: 163 Verulam Road, St Albans, Herts AL3 4DW.

MAXTON, John Alston; MP (Lab) Glasgow, Cathcart, since 1979; *b* Oxford, 5 May 1936; *s* of John Maxton, agr. economist, and Jenny Maxton; *m* Christine Maxton; three *s*. *Educ*: Lord Williams' Grammar Sch., Thame; Oxford Univ. Lectr in Social Studies, Hamilton Coll. Chm., Assoc. of Lectrs in Colls of Educn, Scotland; Member: Educnl Inst. of Scotland; Socialist Educnl Assoc. Joined Lab. Party, 1970. Opposition spokesman on health, local govt, and housing in Scotland, 1985–87, on Scotland, 1987–; Scottish and Treasury Whip, 1984–85. Member: Scottish Select Cttee, 1981–83; Public Accounts Cttee, 1983–84. Mem., ASTMS. *Recreations*: family, listening to jazz, running. *Address*: House of Commons, SW1.

MAXWELL, family name of **Barons de Ros** and **Farnham**.

MAXWELL, Hon. Lord; Peter Maxwell; a Senator of the College of Justice in Scotland, 1973–88; *b* 21 May 1919; *s* of late Comdr and late Mrs Herries Maxwell, Munches, Dalbeattie, Kirkcudbrightshire; *m* 1941, Alison Susan Readman; one *s* two *d* (and one *s* decd). *Educ*: Wellington Coll.; Balliol Coll., Oxford; Edinburgh Univ. Served Argyll and Sutherland Highlanders, and late RA, 1939–46. Called to Scottish Bar, 1951; QC (Scotland) 1961; Sheriff-Principal of Dumfries and Galloway, 1970–73. Mem., Royal Commn on Legal Services in Scotland, 1976–80; Chm., Scottish Law Commn, 1981–88. *Address*: 19 Oswald Road, Edinburgh EH9 2HE. *T*: 031–667 7444.

MAXWELL, David Campbell F.; *see* Finlay-Maxwell.

MAXWELL of Ardwell, Col Frederick Gordon, CBE 1967; TD; FCIT; *b* 2 May 1905; *s* of late Lt-Col Alexander Gordon Maxwell, OBE, Hon. Corps of Gentlemen-at-Arms; *m* 1st, 1935, Barbara Margaret (decd), *d* of late Edward Williams Hedley, MBE, MD, Thursley, Surrey; two *s* (one *d* decd); 2nd, 1965, True Hamilton Exley, *d* of Francis George Hamilton, Old Blundells Cottage, Tiverton, Devon. *Educ*: Eton. OC 2nd Bn The London Scottish, 1939–42; GSO1, 52nd (Lowland) Div., 1943–44, served in Holland and Germany (despatches); GSO1, Allied Land Forces SE Asia, 1945; OC 1st Bn The London Scottish, 1947–50. Joined London Transport, 1924; Operating Manager (Railways), London Transport, 1947–70, retired 1971; Protocol and Conference Dept, FCO, 1971–88. Mem., Co. of London T&AFA, 1947–68; Lt-Col RE (T&AVR, IV), 1956–70; Regimental Col, The London Scottish, 1969–73. DL, Co. of London, 1962; DL Greater London, 1966–81. OStJ 1969. *Address*: 41 Cheyne Court, Cheyne Place, SW3 5TS. *T*: 071–352 9801. *Clubs*: Naval and Military, Highland Brigade.

MAXWELL, (Ian) Robert; MC 1945; Chairman, Mirror Group Newspapers Ltd (publisher of Daily Mirror, Daily Record, Sunday Mail, Sunday Mirror, The People, Sporting Life, Sporting Life Weekender, since 1984); Publisher and Editor in Chief, The European, since 1990; Founder and Publisher, Pergamon Press, Oxford, New York and Paris, 1949–91; Publisher: Magyar Hirlap; Moscow News (English edition), since 1988; Chairman and Chief Executive: Maxwell Communication Corporation plc (formerly The British Printing & Communication Corporation plc), since 1981; Macmillan Inc., since 1988; Chairman: Mirror Colour Print Ltd (formerly British Newspaper Printing Corporation plc), since 1983; British Cable Services Ltd (Rediffusion Cablevision), since 1984; Pergamon Media Trust plc, since 1986; Maxwell Pergamon Publishing Corporation plc (formerly Pergamon BPCC Publishing Corporation plc), since 1986; MTV Europe, since 1987; Maxwell Communication Corporation Inc., NY, since 1987; Macmillan Foundation, since 1988; Pergamon AGB plc (formerly Hollis plc), since 1988 (Director, since 1982); Maxwell Macmillan Pergamon International Publishing; Berlitz International Inc., since 1988; Scitex Corporation Ltd, Israel, since 1988; Thomas Cook Travel Inc., since 1989; Official Airline Guides Inc., since 1989; President, State of Israel Bonds (UK), since 1988; *b* 10 June 1923; *s* of Michael and Ann Hoch; *m* 1945, Elisabeth (*née* Meynard); three *s* four *d* (and one *s* one *d* decd). *Educ*: self-educated. Served War of 1939–45 (MC). In German Sect. of Foreign Office (Head of Press Sect., Berlin), 1945–47. Chm., Robert Maxwell & Co. Ltd, 1948–86; Director: SelecTV, 1982–; Central Television plc, 1983–; The Solicitors' Law Stationery Soc. plc, 1985–; Mirrorvision, 1985–; Clyde Cablevision Ltd, 1985–; Philip Hill Investment Trust, 1986–; Reuters Holdings plc, 1986–; TF1, 1987–; Maxwell Media, Paris, 1987–; Maxwell Business Communications Gp Ltd, 1989–; Maxwell Consumer Publishing & Communications Ltd, 1989–. Chm., Commonwealth Games (Scotland 1986) Ltd, 1986. Mem. Council, Newspaper Publishers' Assoc., 1984–. MP (Lab) Buckingham, 1964–70. Chm., Labour Nat. Fund Raising Foundn, 1960–69; Chm., Labour Working Party on Science, Govt and Industry, 1963–64; Mem., Council of Europe (Vice-Chm., Cttee on Science and Technology), 1968. Contested (Lab) Buckingham, Feb. and Oct. 1974. Treasurer, The Round House Trust Ltd (formerly Centre 42), 1965–83; Chairman: GB-Sasakawa Foundn, 1985–; Nat. AIDS Trust fundraising gp, 1987–; Trustee, Internat. Centre for Child Studies. Chairman: Oxford Utd FC plc, 1982–87; Derby County FC, 1987–. Kennedy Fellow, Harvard Univ., 1971. Hon. Mem., Acad. of Astronautics, 1974; Member: Club of Rome, 1979– (Exec. Dir,

British Gp); Senate, Leeds Univ., 1986–; Bd of Trustees, Polytech. Univ. of NY, 1987–. FIC 1988. Co-produced films: Mozart's Don Giovanni, Salzburg Festival, 1954; Bolshoi Ballet, 1957; Swan Lake, 1968; Producer, DODO the Kid from Outer Space (children's TV series), 1968. Hon. DSc Moscow State Univ., 1983; Hon. Dr of Science, Polytech. Univ. of NY, 1985; Hon. LLD Aberdeen 1988; Dr *hc*: Adama Mickiewicza Univ., 1989; Univ. du Québec à Trois-Rivières, 1989; Hon. Dr of Laws, Temple Univ., Pa, 1989; Hon. Dr, Bar-Ilan, Israel, 1989; Hon. DLitt Plymouth, 1989. Prism Award, NY Univ. Centre for Graphic Arts Management and Technology, 1989; World of Difference Award, Anti-Defamation League, NY, 1989. Royal Swedish Order of Polar Star (Officer 1st class), 1983; Bulgarian People's Republic Order Stara Planina (1st class), 1983; Comdr, Order of Merit with Star, Polish People's Republic, 1986; Order of the White Rose (1st class) (Finland), 1988; Officier de l'Ordre des Arts et des Lettres (France), 1989. Gen. Editor, Leaders of the World series, 1980–. *Publications:* The Economics of Nuclear Power, 1965; Public Sector Purchasing, 1968; (jt author) Man Alive, 1968. *Recreations:* chess, football. *Address:* Holborn Circus, EC1A 1DQ. *T:* 071–353 0246; Headington Hill Hall, Oxford OX3 0BB. *T:* Oxford (0865) 64881; 866 Third Avenue, New York, NY 10022, USA. *T:* 212–702 2000.

See also I. R. C. Maxwell, K. F. H. Maxwell.

MAXWELL, Ian Robert Charles; Joint Managing Director, Maxwell Communication Corporation plc, since 1988; *b* 15 June 1956; *s* of (Ian) Robert Maxwell, *qv*. *Educ:* Marlborough; Balliol Coll., Oxford (BA, MA). Various sen. management positions, France, Germany and USA, Pergamon Press, 1978–83; Prince's Charitable Trust, 1983–84; British Printing & Communication Corporation, later Maxwell Communication Corporation, 1985–; Sales Develt Dir, 1985–86; Chief Exec., Maxwell Pergamon Publishing Corp., 1988–89; Chairman: Agence Central de Presse, 1986–89; Maxwell Media, Paris, 1986–; Dir, Mirror Group Newspapers, 1987–; Exec. Dir, Pergamon AGB, 1989–. Mem., Nat. Theatre Develt Council, 1986–; Pres., Club d'Investissement Media, 1988–. Vice Chm., Derby County Football Club, 1987– (Chm., 1984–87). *Recreations:* music, ski-ing, water-skiing, football. *Address:* Headington Hill Hall, Oxford OX3 0BB. *T:* Oxford (0865) 64881.

MAXWELL, Kevin Francis Herbert; Chief Executive, Maxwell Communication Corporation plc, since 1991 (Director, since 1986); Vice Chairman, Macmillan Inc., since 1988; *b* 20 Feb. 1959; *s* of (Ian) Robert Maxwell, *qv*; *m* 1984, Pandora Deborah Karen Warnford-Davis; one *s* three *d*. *Educ:* Marlborough Coll.; Balliol Coll., Oxford (MA Hons). Dir, Guinness Mahon Hldgs, 1989–. Chm., Oxford United FC, 1987–. Trustee, New Sch. for Social Research, NYC, 1989. *Recreations:* water colour painting, football. *Address:* Headington Hill Hall, Oxford OX3 0BW.

MAXWELL, Sir Michael (Eustace George), 9th Bt *cr* 1681 (NS), of Monreith, Wigtownshire; ARICS; *b* 28 Aug. 1943; *s* of Major Eustace Maxwell (*d* 1971) and of Dorothy Vivien, *d* of Captain George Bellville; *S* uncle, 1987. *Educ:* Eton; College of Estate Management. *Recreations:* microlights, curling, tennis, ski-ing. *Address:* Laundry House, Farming Woods, Brigstock, Northants; 56 Queensmill Road, SW6. *Clubs:* Stranraer Rugby; Port William Tennis.

MAXWELL, Sir Nigel Mellor H.; *see* Heron-Maxwell.

MAXWELL, Patrick; Solicitor; *b* 12 March 1909; *e s* of late Alderman Patrick Maxwell, Solicitor, Londonderry; *m* 1st, 1935 (wife *d* 1962); two *d*; 2nd, 1969. *Educ:* Convent of Mercy, Artillery Street, Londonderry; Christian Brothers Sch., Brow-of-the-Hill, Londonderry; St Columb's Coll., Londonderry. Solicitor, 1932; entered Londonderry Corporation as Councillor, 1934; resigned as protest against re-destribution scheme, 1937; Leader of Anti-Partition Party in Londonderry Corporation from 1938; did not seek re-election, 1946; first Chairman of Irish Union Association, 1936; Chairman of Derry Catholic Registration Association, 1934–52. MP (Nat) Foyle Division of Londonderry City, Northern Ireland Parliament, 1937–53. Resident Magistrate, 1968–80. President: Law Society of Northern Ireland, 1967–68 (Vice-Pres., 1966–67); Londonderry Rotary Club, 1958–59; Chm. Rotary in Ireland, 1963–64; Mem., Council, International Bar Association, 1968.

MAXWELL, Peter; *see* Maxwell, Hon. Lord.

MAXWELL, Richard; QC 1988; *b* 21 Dec. 1943; *s* of Thomas and Kathleen Marjorie Maxwell; *m* 1966, Judith Ann Maxwell; two *s* two *d*. *Educ:* Nottingham High Sch.; Hertford College, Oxford (MA). Lectr in Law, 1966–68; called to the Bar, Inner Temple, 1968. *Recreations:* squash (daily), running (weekly), half marathon (annually), fly fishing (in season), windsurfing, wine. *Address:* 5 Castle Grove, The Park, Nottingham. *T:* Nottingham (0602) 418063. *Clubs:* Nottingham and Notts United Services; Nottingham Squash Rackets; Darley Dale Flyfishers'.

MAXWELL, Robert; *see* Maxwell, I. R.

MAXWELL, Sir Robert (Hugh), KBE 1961 (OBE 1942); *b* 2 Jan. 1906; *s* of William Robert and Nancy Dockett Maxwell; *m* 1935, Mary Courtney Jewell; two *s*. Comdr of Order of George I of Greece, 1961; Order of Merit of Syria. *Address:* Court Hay, Charlton Adam, Som TA11 7AS.

MAXWELL, Robert James; JP; Secretary and Chief Executive, The King's Fund, since 1980; *b* 26 June 1934; *s* of Dr George B. Maxwell and Cathleen Maxwell; *m* 1960, Jane FitzGibbon; three *s* two *d*. *Educ:* Leighton Park Sch.; New Coll., Oxford (BA 1st Cl. Hons, MA); Univ. of Pennsylvania (MA); LSE (PhD). FCMA. 2nd Lieut, Cameronians (Scottish Rifles), 1952–54. Union Corp., 1958–66; McKinsey & Co., 1966–75; Administrator to Special Trustees, St Thomas' Hosp., 1975–80. Pres., European Healthcare Management Assoc., 1985–87; Pres., Open Section, RSocMed, 1986–88. Chm., Court, LSHTM, 1985–; Gov., UMDS, 1989–; Dir, Guy's and Lewisham Trust, 1990–; Chm., Leighton Park Sch., 1981–. JP Inner London and Juvenile Court (Chm.), 1971–. *Publications:* Health Care: the growing dilemma, 1974; Health and Wealth, 1981; Reshaping the National Health Service, 1988; Spotlight on the Cities, 1989. *Recreations:* poetry, walking, stained glass, not being the other Robert Maxwell. *Address:* Pitt Court Manor, North Nibley, Dursley, Glos GL11 6EL; 14 Palace Court, W2 4HT. *Clubs:* Brooks's, Royal Society of Medicine.

MAXWELL, Rear-Adm. Thomas Heron, CB 1967; DSC 1942; idc, jssc, psc; Director-General of Naval Training, Ministry of Defence, 1965–67; retired, 1967; *b* 10 April 1912; *s* of late H. G. Maxwell; *m* 1947, Maeve McKinley; two *s* two *d*. *Educ:* Campbell Coll., Belfast; Royal Naval Engineering Coll. Cadet, 1930; Commander, 1946; Captain, 1956; Rear-Adm., 1965. *Address:* Tokenbury, Shaft Road, Bath, Avon BA2 7HP.

MAXWELL-HYSLOP, Robert John, (Robin); MP (C) Tiverton Division of Devon since Nov. 1960; *b* 6 June 1931; 2nd *s* of late Capt. A. H. Maxwell-Hyslop, GC, RN, and late Mrs Maxwell-Hyslop; *m* 1968, Joanna Margaret, *er d* of Thomas McCosh; two *d*. *Educ:* Stowe; Christ Church, Oxford (MA). Hons Degree in PPE Oxon, 1954. Joined Rolls-Royce Ltd Aero Engine Div., as graduate apprentice, Sept. 1954; served 2 years as such, then joined Export Sales Dept; PA to Sir David Huddie, Dir and GM (Sales and Service), 1958; left Rolls-Royce, 1960. Contested (C) Derby (North), 1959. Chm., Anglo-Brazilian Parly Gp. Member: Trade and Industry Select Cttee, 1971–; Standing Orders Cttee, 1977–; Procedure Select Cttee, 1978–. Politician of the Year Award (first recipient), Nat. Fedn of Self-employed and Small Businesses, 1989. *Recreations:* motoring, South American history. *Address:* 4 Tiverton Road, Silverton, Exeter, Devon.

MAXWELL SCOTT, Sir Dominic James, 14th Bt *cr* 1642, of Haggerston, Northumberland; *b* 22 July 1968; *s* of Sir Michael Fergus Maxwell Scott, 13th Bt and of Deirdre Moira, *d* of late Alexander McKechnie; *S* father, 1989. *Educ:* Eton; Sussex Univ. *Heir: b* Matthew Joseph Maxwell Scott, *b* 27 Aug. 1976. *Address:* c/o 130 Ritherdon Road, SW17 8QQ.

MAXWELL-SCOTT, Dame Jean (Mary Monica), DCVO 1984 (CVO 1969); Lady in Waiting to HRH Princess Alice, Duchess of Gloucester, since 1959; *b* 8 June 1923; *d* of Maj.-Gen. Sir Walter Maxwell-Scott of Abbotsford, Bt, CB, DSO, DL and Mairi MacDougall of Lunga. *Educ:* Couvent des Oiseaux, Westgate-on-Sea. VAD Red Cross Nurse, 1941–46. *Recreations:* gardening, reading, horses. *Address:* Abbotsford, Melrose, Roxburghshire TD6 9BQ. *T:* Galashiels (0896) 2043. *Club:* New Cavendish.

MAY, family name of **Baron May.**

MAY, 3rd Baron, *cr* 1935, of Weybridge; **Michael St John May;** 3rd Bt, *cr* 1931; late Lieut, Royal Corps of Signals; *b* 26 Sept. 1931; *o s* of 2nd Baron May and *d* of George Ricardo Thomas; *S* father 1950; *m* 1st, 1958, Dorothea Catherine Ann (marr. diss. 1963), *d* of Charles McCarthy, Boston, USA; 2nd, 1963, Jillian Mary, *d* of Albert Edward Shipton, Beggars Barn, Shutford, Oxon; one *s* one *d*. *Educ:* Wycliffe Coll., Stonehouse, Glos; Magdalene Coll., Cambridge. 2nd Lieut, Royal Signals, 1950. *Recreations:* sailing, travel. *Heir: s* Hon. Jasper Bertram St John May, *b* 24 Oct. 1965. *Address:* Gautherns Barn, Sibford Gower, Oxon OX15 5RY.

MAY, Hon. Sir Anthony (Tristram Kenneth), Kt 1991; **Hon. Mr Justice May;** a Judge of the High Court of Justice, Queen's Bench Division, since 1991; *b* 9 Sept. 1940; *s* of late Kenneth Sibley May and Joan Marguérite (*née* Oldaker); *m* 1968, Stella Gay Pattisson; one *s* two *d*. *Educ:* Bradfield Coll.; Worcester Coll., Oxford (Trevelyan Scholar 1960, Hon. Scholar 1962; MA). Inner Temple Scholar, 1965; called to the Bar, 1967, Bencher, 1985; QC 1979; a Recorder, 1985–91. Jun. Counsel to DoE for Land Commn Act Matters, 1972; Chm., Commn of Inquiry, Savings and Investment Bank Ltd, IoM, 1990. Vice-Chm., Official Referees Bar Assoc., 1987–91. Chm., Guildford Choral Soc. *Publication:* 5th edn, Keating on Building Contracts, 1991. *Recreations:* gardening, music, books, bonfires. *Address:* Royal Courts of Justice, Strand, WC2A 2LL.

MAY, Prof. Brian Albert, FEng 1990; Professor of Agricultural Engineering, since 1982, and Head, Cranfield Rural Institute, since 1989, Cranfield Institute of Technology; *b* 2 June 1936; *s* of Albert Robert and Eileen May; *m* 1961, Brenda Ann Smith; three *s*. *Educ:* Faversham Grammar Sch.; Aston Univ., Birmingham. FRAgS. Design Engineer, Massey Ferguson, 1958–63; National College of Agricultural Engineering: Lectr, 1963–68; Sen. Lectr, 1968–72; Principal Lectr, 1972–75; Head of Environmental Control and Processing Dept, 1972–75; Cranfield Institute of Technology: Prof. of Environmental Control and Processing, 1975–82; Head, Nat. Coll. of Agricl Engrg, later Silsoe Coll., 1976–89; Dean, Faculty of Agricl Engrg, Food Prodn and Rural Land Use, 1977–86. Dir, British Agricl Export Council, 1985–88. Member: Res. Requirements Bd on Plants and Soils, AFRC, 1980–86; Engrg Adv. Cttee, AFRC, 1984–88; Standing Cttee on University Entrance Requirements, 1984–; Agric. and Vet. Cttee, British Council, 1985–; Overseas Affairs Cttee, Fellowship of Engrg, 1991–. Pres., IAgrE, 1984–86; Mem. Council, Royal Agricl Soc. of England, 1984–. Governor, British Soc. for Res. in Agricl Engrg, 1979–90. *Publications:* Power on the Land, 1974; papers in agricl and engrg jls. *Recreations:* cricket, gardening, reading. *Address:* Fairfield Greenway, Campton Shefford, Beds SG17 5BN. *T:* Hitchin (0462) 813451. *Club:* Farmers'.

MAY, Charles Alan Maynard, FEng, FIEE; lately Senior Director, Development and Technology, British Telecom; retired 1984; *b* 14 April 1924; *s* of late Cyril P. May and Katharine M. May; *m* 1947, Daphne, *o d* of late Bertram Carpenter; one *s* two *d*. *Educ:* The Grammar Sch., Ulverston, Cumbria; Christ's Coll., Cambridge (Mech. Sciences tripos 1944, MA). CEng, FIEE 1967. Served REME and Indian Army, 1944–47. Entered Post Office Engrg Dept, 1948; Head of Electronic Switching Gp, 1956; Staff Engr, Computer Engrg Br., 1966; Dep. Dir (Engrg), 1970; Dir of Research, Post Office, later British Telecom, 1975–83. Dir, SIRA Ltd, 1982–89. Chm., IEE Electronics Divl Bd, 1977–78; Member: Council, IEE, 1970–72 and 1976–80; BBC Engrg Adv. Cttee, 1978–84; Adv. Cttee on Calibration and Measurement, 1978–83; Adv. Cttee, Dept of Electronic and Electrical Engrg, Sheffield Univ., 1979–82; Communications Systems Adv. Panel, Council of Educnl Technology, 1980–83; Ind. Adv. Bd, Sch. of Eng. and Applied Scis, Sussex Univ., 1981–84; Council, ERA Technology, 1983–88. Graham Young Lectr, Glasgow Univ., 1979. Vis. Examr, Imperial Coll., Univ. of London, 1980–82; External Examnr, NE London Polytechnic, 1982–86. Governor, Suffolk Coll. of Higher and Further Educn, 1980–83. FRSA 1985. *Publications:* contribs on telecommunications to learned jls. *Recreations:* gardening, travelling. *Address:* Sherbourne, Glendene Avenue, East Horsley, Leatherhead, Surrey KT24 5AY. *T:* East Horsley (04865) 2521.

MAY, Douglas James; QC (Scot) 1989; *b* 7 May 1946; *s* of Thomas May and Violet Mary Brough Boyd or May. *Educ:* George Heriot's Sch., Edinburgh; Edinburgh Univ. Advocate 1971. Temporary Sheriff, 1990–. Contested (C): Edinburgh E, Feb. 1974; Glasgow Cathcart, 1983. *Recreations:* golf, photography, travel, concert going. *Address:* Advocates' Library, Parliament House, Edinburgh. *T:* 031–226 5071. *Clubs:* Edinburgh University Staff; Merchants of Edinburgh Golf, Bruntsfield Links Golfing Society.

MAY, Geoffrey Crampton, CEng; Secretary, Royal Aeronautical Society, 1985–88; *b* 26 April 1930; *s* of late Thomas May and of Doris May; *m* 1954, Margaret (*née* Unwin); two *s* one *d*. *Educ:* Tupton Hall Grammar Sch.; Chesterfield College of Technology. MIProdE, MRAeS. Apprentice draughtsman, Plowright Bros, Chesterfield, 1946–52; Designer, Aerofall Mills, Toronto, 1952–54; Standards and Methods Engr, Avro Aircraft, Toronto, 1954–59; Technical Officer, BSI, London, 1959–66; Exec. Officer, CEGB, 1966–68; Sec., Inst. of British Foundrymen, 1968–76; Gen. Sec., Soc. for Underwater Technology, 1976–84; Gen. Man. Operations, RAeS, 1984–85. *Recreations:* gardening, music. *Clubs:* Royal Air Force, Les Ambassadeurs.

MAY, Gordon Leslie, OBE 1982; retired solicitor; *b* 19 Nov. 1921; *s* of A. Carveth May and Isobella May; *m* 1945, Nina Cheek; one *s* two *d*. *Educ:* Worcester College for the Blind; Manchester Univ. War service, 1939–45. Admitted Solicitor, 1947; South Eastern Gas Board: Solicitor, 1956; Secretary, 1961; Executive Board Member, 1968; British Gas Corporation: Dep. Chairman, SW Region, 1974; Sec., 1977–84; Mem. Executive, 1982–84. Consultant, Keene Marsland, solicitors, 1984–87. Mem. Exec. Council, RNIB, 1975–89. Chm. Bd of Governors, Worcester Coll. for the Blind, 1980–87. Liveryman, Solicitors' Co., 1963. *Recreation:* sailing. *Address:* Walsall House, High Street, Upnor,

Rochester, Kent ME2 4XG. *T:* Medway (0634) 716163. *Clubs:* Royal Automobile; Medway Yacht (Upnor); Alderney Sailing.

MAY, Graham; retired from Civil Service, 1981; *b* 15 Dec. 1923; *s* of Augustus May; *m* 1952, Marguerite Lucy Griffin; four *s. Educ:* Gravesend County Sch. for Boys; Balliol Coll., Oxford (BA). War Service, Royal Artillery, 1942–46. Asst Principal, Min. of Works, 1948, Principal 1952; seconded to Treasury, 1961–63; Asst Sec., MPBW, 1963; Under Sec., DoE, 1972–81. *Address:* 2 West Cross, Tenterden, Kent TN30 6JL.

MAY, John; Councillor, Tyne and Wear County Council, 1974–86 (Vice-Chairman, 1978–79, Chairman, 1979–80); *b* 24 May 1912; *s* of William and Sara May; *m* 1939, Mary Peacock (*d* 1980); two *s. Educ:* Holystone Council Sch., Newcastle upon Tyne. Councillor: Seaton Valley UDC, 1949–74 (Chm., 1963–64 and 1972–73); Northumberland CC, 1970–74; Tyne and Wear County Council: Chairman, Transport Cttee, 1980–86 (Vice-Chm., 1977–80). *Address:* 12 Cheviot View, Cheviot View Sheltered Home, West Street, West Allotments, North Tyneside.

MAY, Rt. Hon. Sir John (Douglas), Kt 1972; PC 1982; a Lord Justice of Appeal, 1982–89; *b* 28 June 1923; *s* of late Mr and Mrs E. A. G. May, of Shanghai and Chelsea; *m* 1958, Mary, *er d* of Sir Owen Morshead, GCVO, KCB, DSO, MC, and Paquita, *d* of J. G. Hagemeyer; two *s* one *d. Educ:* Clifton Coll. (Scholar); Balliol Coll., Oxford (Schol.). Lieut (SpSc) RNVR, 1944–46. Barrister-at-Law, Inner Temple, 1947 (Schol.), Master of the Bench, 1972; QC 1965; Recorder of Maidstone, 1971; Leader, SE Circuit, 1971; Presiding Judge, Midland and Oxford Circuit, 1973–77; a Judge of the High Ct, Queen's Bench Division, 1972–82; a Judge of the Employment Appeal Tribunal, 1978–82. Member: Parole Bd, 1977–80 (Vice-Chm., 1980); Royal Commn on Criminal Justice, 1991–; Chairman: Inquiry into UK Prison Services, 1978–79; University Comrs, 1989–; Guildford and Woolwich Inquiry, 1989–. Clifton College: Mem. Council, 1980–; Pres., 1987–. *Address:* Lindens, Sturminster Newton, Dorset DT10 1BU. *T:* Sturminster Newton (0258) 73321. *Club:* Vincent's (Oxford).

MAY, John Otto, CBE 1962 (OBE 1949); HM Diplomatic Service; retired; *b* 21 April 1913; *s* of late Otto May, FRCP, MD; *m* 1939, Maureen McNally; one *d. Educ:* Sherborne; St John's Coll., Cambridge. Apptd to Dept of Overseas Trade, 1937. Private Sec. to Comptroller-General, 1939; Asst Commercial Secretary: Copenhagen, 1939; Helsinki, 1940; Ministry of Economic Warfare (Representative in Caracas), 1942–44; First Sec. (Commercial): Rome, 1945, Bucharest, 1948; Foreign Office, 1950–53; First Sec., Helsinki, 1954. Acted as Chargé d'Affaires in 1954, 1955, and 1956; Counsellor (Commercial) and Consul-General, HM Embassy, Athens, 1957–60; Consul-General: Genoa, 1960–65; Rotterdam, 1965–68; Gothenburg, 1968–72. Coronation Medal, 1953. *Recreations:* travel, photography, walking, philately. *Address:* 6 Millhedge Close, Cobham, Surrey KT11 3BE. *T:* Cobham (0932) 864645. *Club:* United Oxford & Cambridge University.

MAY, Sir Kenneth Spencer, Kt 1980; CBE 1976; Director: Advertiser Newspapers Ltd, Adelaide, since 1988; The News Corporation Ltd, 1979–89; *b* 10 Dec. 1914; *s* of late N. May; *m* 1943, Betty C. Scott; one *s* one *d. Educ:* Woodville High School. Editorial staff, News, 1930; political writer, 1946–59; Asst Manager, News, Adelaide, 1959–64, Manager, 1964–69; Dir, News Ltd, 1969–86; Man. Dir, News Ltd, Aust., 1977–80; Chm., Mirror Newspapers Ltd and Nationwide News Pty Ltd, 1969–80; Director: Independent Newspapers Ltd, Wellington, NZ, 1971–84; Santos Ltd, 1980–83. *Address:* 26 Waterfall Terrace, Burnside, SA 5066, Australia.

MAY, Paul, CBE 1970; retired 1970; *b* 12 July 1907; *s* of William Charles May and Katharine Edith May; *m* 1st, 1933, Dorothy Ida Makower (*d* 1961); two *s* one *d*; 2nd, 1969, Frances Maud Douglas (*née* Tarver); two step *s. Educ:* Westminster; Christ Church, Oxford (MA). United Africa Co. Ltd, 1930–32; John Lewis Partnership, 1932–40; Min. of Aircraft Production, 1940–45; John Lewis Partnership, 1945–70 (Dep. Chm., 1955–70). Mem. Exec. Cttee, Land Settlement Assoc. Ltd, 1962–71. *Recreations:* walking, reading, etc. *Address:* Chesterford, Whittingham, Northumberland NE66 4UP. *T:* Whittingham (066574) 642.

MAY, Peter Barker Howard, CBE 1981; Lloyd's Insurance Broker since 1953; Underwriting Member of Lloyd's, 1962; Executive Director, Willis Wrightson Ltd, since 1987; *b* 31 Dec. 1929; *m* 1959, Virginia, *er d* of A. H. H. Gilligan; four *d. Educ:* Charterhouse; Pembroke Coll., Cambridge (MA). Cambridge cricket and football XIs v. Oxford, 1950, 1951 and 1952; Surrey County Cricket Cap, 1950; played cricket for England v S Africa 1951, v India 1952, v Australia 1953, v W Indies 1953, v Pakistan, Australia and New Zealand 1954; captained England 41 times, incl. v S Africa, 1955, v Australia 1956, v S Africa 1956–57, v W Indies, 1957, v New Zealand 1958, v Australia, 1958–59, v India, 1959, v West Indies, 1959–60, v Australia, 1961. Chm., England Cricket Selection Cttee, 1982–88. *Publications:* Peter May's Book of Cricket, 1956; A Game Enjoyed, 1985. *Recreations:* golf, eventing. *Address:* Hatch House, Liphook, Hants GU30 7EL. *Clubs:* MCC (Pres., 1980–81), Surrey County Cricket.

MAY, Sir Richard George, Kt 1991; **His Honour Judge May;** a Circuit Judge, since 1987; *b* 12 Nov. 1938; *s* of George William May, MB, and late Phyllis May; *m* 1974, Radmila Monica, *er d* of late J. D. A. Barnicot, OBE, and Elizabeth Barnicot; one *s* two *d. Educ:* Haileybury; Selwyn Coll., Cambridge. National Service, 2nd Lieut, DLI, 1958–60. Called to the Bar, Inner Temple, 1965; Midland and Oxford Circuit; a Recorder, 1985–87. Contested (Lab): Dorset South, 1970; Finchley, 1979. Councillor, Westminster CC, 1971–78 (Leader of the Opposition, 1974–77). *Publications:* (ed jtly) Phipson on Evidence, 12th edn 1976, 13th edn 1982; Criminal Evidence, 1986, 2nd edn 1990. *Address:* Devereux Chambers, Devereux Court, WC2R 3JJ. *T:* 071–353 7534. *Club:* Savile.

MAY, Prof. Robert McCredie, FRS 1979; Royal Society Research Professor, Department of Zoology, Oxford University, and Imperial College, London, since 1988; Fellow of Merton College, Oxford, since 1988; *b* 8 Jan. 1936; *s* of Henry W. May and Kathleen M. May; *m* 1962, Judith (*née* Feiner); one *d. Educ:* Sydney Boys' High Sch.; Sydney Univ. BSc 1956, PhD (Theoretical Physics) 1959. Gordon Mackay Lectr in Applied Maths, Harvard Univ., 1959–61; Sydney Univ.: Sen. Lectr in Theoretical Physics, 1962–64; Reader, 1964–69; Personal Chair, 1969–73; Princeton University: Prof. of Biology, 1973–88; Class of 1877 Prof. of Zoology, 1975–88; Chm., Univ. Res. Bd, 1977–88. Vis. Prof., Imperial Coll., 1975–88; visiting appointments at: Harvard, 1966; California Inst. of Technology, 1967; UKAEA Culham Lab., 1971; Magdalen Coll., Oxford, 1971; Inst. for Advanced Study, Princeton, 1972; King's Coll., Cambridge, 1976. Pres., British Ecol Soc., 1992–; Trustee: BM (Natural History), 1989–; WWF (UK), 1990–. Mem., Smithsonian Council, USA, 1988–. Linnean Medal, 1991. *Publications:* Stability and Complexity in Model Ecosystems, 1973, 2nd edn 1974; Theoretical Ecology: Principles and Applications, 1976, 2nd edn 1981; Population Biology of Infectious Diseases, 1982; Exploitation of Marine Communities, 1984; Perspectives in Ecological Theory, 1989; Infectious Diseases of Humans: dynamics and control, 1991; articles in mathematical, biol and physics jls. *Recreations:* tennis, running, bridge. *Address:* Department of Zoology, South Parks Road, Oxford OX1 3PS. *Club:* Athenæum.

MAY, Stuart; *see* May, W. H. S.

MAY, Valentine Gilbert Delabere, CBE 1969; Director, Yvonne Arnaud Theatre, Guildford, since 1975; *b* 1 July 1927; *s* of Claude Jocelyn Delabere May and Olive Gilbert; *m* 1st, 1955, Penelope Sutton; one *d*; 2nd, 1980, Petra Schroeder; one *d. Educ:* Cranleigh Sch.; Peterhouse Coll., Cambridge. Trained at Old Vic Theatre Sch. Director: Ipswich Theatre, 1953–57; Nottingham Playhouse, 1957–61; Bristol Old Vic Company, 1961–75. Plays directed for Bristol Old Vic which subseq. transf. to London incl.: War and Peace, 1962; A Severed Head, 1963; Love's Labour's Lost, 1964 (which also went on a British Council European tour); Portrait of a Queen, 1965; The Killing of Sister George, 1965; The Italian Girl, 1968; Mrs Mouse, Are You Within, 1968; Conduct Unbecoming, 1969; It's a Two-Foot-Six Inches Above the Ground World, 1970; Poor Horace, 1970; Trelawny, 1972; The Card, 1973. Directed at Old Vic: Richard II, 1959; Mourning Becomes Electra, 1961; Tribute to the Lady, 1974–75. Plays directed for Arnaud Theatre transferred to London: Baggage, 1976; Banana Ridge, 1976; The Dark Horse, 1978; House Guest, 1981. Directed: Little Me, Prince of Wales, 1984; Royal Baccarat Scandal, Chichester Fest., 1988, London, 1989; Henry IV (by Pirandello), London, 1990. Overseas prodns include: Romeo and Juliet, and Hamlet (NY and USA tour); The Taming of the Shrew (Hong Kong Fest. and Latin America tour); Broadway prodns: A Severed Head; Portrait of a Queen; The Killing of Sister George; Conduct Unbecoming; Murder Among Friends; Pygmalion. Hon. MA Bristol, 1975. *Recreations:* reading, architecture, music, astronomy. *Address:* Yvonne Arnaud Theatre, Millbrook, Guildford, Surrey GU1 3UX. *T:* Guildford (0483) 64571.

MAY, (William Herbert) Stuart; Senior Partner, Theodore Goddard, Solicitors, since 1989; *b* 5 April 1937; *s* of Arthur Douglas May and Jean Reid; *m* 1966, Sarah Margaret (*née* Maples); four *s. Educ:* Taunton School; Wadham College, Oxford (MA). Qualified Solicitor, 1965, with Theodore Goddard, Partner 1970, Sen. Partner, 1989. *Recreations:* gardening, theatre, spectator sport. *Address:* (office) 150 Aldersgate Street, EC1A 4EJ; Lower Farm, Hadstock, Cambridge CB1 6PF.

MAYALL, Sir (Alexander) Lees, KCVO 1972 (CVO 1965); CMG 1964; HM Diplomatic Service, retired; Ambassador to Venezuela, 1972–75; *b* 14 Sept. 1915; *s* of late Alexander Mayall, Bealings End, Woodbridge, Suffolk, and Isobel, *d* of F. J. R. Hendy; *m* 1st, 1940, Renée Eileen Burn (marr. diss., 1947); one *d*; 2nd, 1947, Hon. Mary Hermione Ormsby Gore, *e d* of 4th Baron Harlech, KG, PC, GCMG; one *s* two *d. Educ:* Eton; Trinity Coll., Oxford (MA). Entered HM Diplomatic Service, 1939; served with armed forces, 1940; transferred to HM Legation, Berne, 1940–44; First Secretary: HM Embassy, Cairo, 1947–49, Paris, 1952–54; Counsellor, HM Embassy: Tokyo, 1958–61; Lisbon, 1961–64; Addis Ababa, 1964–65; Vice-Marshal of the Diplomatic Corps and Head of Protocol and Conference Dept, FCO, 1965–72. President: West Wilts Conservative Assoc., 1984–; Bath Preservation Trust, 1986–. *Publication:* Fireflies in Amber, 1989. *Recreations:* travelling, reading. *Address:* Sturford Mead, Warminster, Wilts BA12 7QT. *T:* Westbury (0373) 832219. *Clubs:* Travellers', Beefsteak.

MAYER, Prof. Colin Peter; Price Waterhouse Professor of Corporate Finance, City University Business School, since 1987; *b* 12 May 1953; *s* of Harold Charles Mayer and Anne Louise Mayer; *m* 1979, Annette Patricia Haynes; two *d. Educ:* St Paul's Sch.; Oriel College, Oxford; Wolfson College, Oxford (MA, MPhil, DPhil); Harvard Univ. HM Treasury, 1976–78; Harkness Fellow, Harvard, 1979–80; Fellow in Economics, St Anne's College, Oxford, 1980–86. *Publications:* (with J. Kay and J. Edwards) Economic Analysis of Accounting Profitability, 1986; (with J. Franks) Risk, Regulation and Investor Protection, 1989; articles in economic jls. *Recreations:* piano, jogging, reading philosophy and science. *Address:* City University Business School, Frobisher Crescent, Barbican Centre, EC2Y 8HB. *T:* 071–920 0111.

MAYER, Thomas, CBE 1985; FEng 1987; Chairman, Eldonray Ltd, since 1990; *b* 17 Dec. 1928; *s* of Hans and Jeanette Mayer; *m* 1st, 1956 (marr. diss. 1975); one *s* one *d*; 2nd, 1975, Jean Patricia Burrows. *Educ:* King's Sch., Harrow; Regent Street Polytechnic (BScEng). FIEE 1964; FRTS 1968. Broadcasting Div., Marconi Co. Ltd, 1948–68; Man. Dir, Marconi Elliott Micro-Electronics Ltd, 1968–69; Man. Dir, Marconi Communication Systems Ltd, 1969–81; Man. Dir, 1981–86, Chm., 1981–90, THORN EMI Electronics Ltd; Chief Exec., THORN EMI Technology Gp, 1986–88; Exec. Dir, THORN EMI plc, 1987–90. Chairman: THORN EMI Varian Ltd, 1981–89; Holmes Protection Gp, 1990–; Director: Thorn Ericsson, 1981–88; Systron Donner Corp., 1983–90; Inmos Corp., 1985–88; Babcock Thorn Ltd, 1985–90; THORN EMI Australia, 1987–88; non-executive Director: Devonport Management Ltd, 1990–; Electron House plc, 1991–. Member: Council, IEE, 1971–74; Council, Electronic Engrg Assoc., 1974–75, 1981–87 (Pres., 1982–83); Nat. Electronics Council, 1983–; SBAC, 1984–90 (Pres., 1987–88). FRSA 1988. Liveryman, Worshipful Co. of Engineers. *Recreations:* golf, swimming. *Address:* 1590 A.D., Burton Lane, Monks Risborough, Bucks HP17 9JF. *T:* Princes Risborough (08444) 4194. *Clubs:* Royal Automobile; Whiteleaf Golf (Whiteleaf).

MAYER BROWN, Prof. Howard; *see* Brown, Prof. H. M.

MAYES, Maj.-Gen. Frederick Brian, FRCS; QHS 1991; Commander Medical, HQ BAOR, since 1990; *b* 24 Aug. 1934; *s* of late Harry Frederick and Constance Enid Mayes; *m* 1962, Mary Anna Georgina Roche; one *s* two *d* (and one *s* decd). *Educ:* Wyggeston Grammar Sch., Leicester; St Mary's Hosp. Med. Sch. (MB BS London 1958). Commissioned Lieut RAMC, 1960; served Aden, E Africa, BAOR, UK; Consultant in Surgery, 1972; CO, BMH Hannover, 1984–87; CO, Cambridge Mil. Hosp., Aldershot, 1987–88; Consultant Surgeon, HQ BAOR, 1988–90. *Recreations:* off-shore sailing, bridge, mountaineering. *Address:* Mornington, 9 Searle Road, Farnham, Surrey. *T:* Farnham (0252) 715453.

MAYFIELD, Hon. Lord; Ian MacDonald, MC 1945; a Senator of the College of Justice in Scotland, since 1981; *b* 26 May 1921; *s* of H. J. and J. M. MacDonald; *m* 1946, Elizabeth de Vessey Lawson; one *s* one *d. Educ:* Colston's Sch., Bristol; Edinburgh Univ. (MA, LLB). Served 1939–46: Royal Tank Regt (Capt.). TA Lothians and Border Horse, later Queen's Own Lowland Yeomanry, 1948–62. Called to Bar, 1952; QC (Scot.) 1964. Mem., Criminal Injuries Compensation Board, 1972–74. Sheriff Principal of Dumfries and Galloway, Feb.-Dec. 1973; Pres., Industrial Tribunals for Scotland, 1973–81. *Recreation:* sport. *Address:* 16 Mayfield Terrace, Edinburgh EH9 1SA. *T:* 031–667 5542. *Clubs:* Royal Scottish Automobile (Glasgow); Hon. Company of Edinburgh Golfers.

MAYFIELD, Rt. Rev. Christopher John; *see* Wolverhampton, Bishop Suffragan of.

MAYHEW, family name of **Baron Mayhew.**

MAYHEW, Baron *cr* 1981 (Life Peer), of Wimbledon in Greater London; **Christopher Paget Mayhew;** *b* 12 June 1915; *e s* of late Sir Basil Mayhew, KBE; *m* 1949, Cicely Elizabeth Ludlam; two *s* two *d. Educ:* Haileybury Coll. (Scholar); Christ Church, Oxford

(Open Exhibitioner, MA). Junior George Webb-Medley Scholar (Economics), 1937; Pres., Union Soc., 1937. Gunner Surrey Yeomanry RA; BEF Sept. 1939–May 1940; served with BNAF and CMF; BLA 1944 (despatches); Major, 1944. MP (Lab) S Norfolk, 1945–50; MP (Lab) Woolwich East, later Greenwich, Woolwich East, June 1951–July 1974; PPS to Lord Pres. of the Council, 1945–46; Parly Under-Sec. of State for Foreign Affairs, 1946–50; Minister of Defence (RN), 1964, resigned 1966; left Lab. Party, joined Lib. Party, 1974; MP (L) Greenwich, Woolwich East, July-Sept. 1974; contested (L): Bath, Oct. 1974 and 1979; Surrey, for European Parlt, 1979; London SW, for European Parlt, Sept. 1979; Liberal Party Spokesman on Defence, 1980; Pres., Alliance Action Gp for Electoral Reform. Pres., Middle East International (Publishers) Ltd; Chm., ANAF Foundn; former Chm., MIND (Nat. Assoc. for Mental Health). *Publications:* Planned Investment—The Case for a National Investment Board, 1939; Socialist Economic Policy, 1946; "Those in Favour . . ." (television play), 1951; Dear Viewer . . ., 1953; Men Seeking God, 1955; Commercial Television: What is to be done?, 1959; Coexistence Plus, 1962; Britain's Role Tomorrow, 1967; Party Games, 1969; (jtly) Europe: the case for going in, 1971; (jtly) Publish It Not . . .: the Middle East cover-up, 1975; The Disillusioned Voter's Guide to Electoral Reform, 1976; Time To Explain: an autobiography, 1987. *Recreations:* music, golf. *Address:* 39 Wool Road, Wimbledon, SW20 0HN. *Club:* National Liberal.

MAYHEW, Kenneth; Fellow and Tutor in Economics, Pembroke College, Oxford, since 1976; *b* 1 Sept. 1947; *s* of late Albert Chadwick Mayhew and of Alice Mayhew (*née* Leigh); *m* 1973, Margaret Humphreys (marr. diss. 1982); one *d*; *m* 1990, Gillian Alexandra McGrattan. *Educ:* Manchester Grammar Sch.; Worcester Coll., Oxford (MA); London School of Economics (MScEcon). Economic Asst, HM Treasury, 1970–72; Res. Officer, Queen Elizabeth House, Oxford, 1972; Asst Res. Officer, then Res. Officer, Inst. of Economics and Statistics, Oxford, 1972–81; Economic Dir, NEDO, 1989–91. Vis. Associate Prof., Cornell Univ., 1981. Advr, CBI, 1983. Editor, Oxford Bull. of Econs and Stats, 1976–88; Associate Editor, Oxford Review of Economic Policy, 1984–. *Publications:* Trade Unions and the Labour Market, 1983; (ed with D. Robinson) Pay Policies for the Future, 1983; (ed with A. Bowen) Improving Incentives for the Low Paid, 1990; numerous articles on labour econs and industrial relns in learned jls. *Recreations:* travel, literature. *Address:* 49 Hamilton Road, Oxford OX2 7PY. *T:* Oxford (0865) 510977. *Club:* Reform.

MAYHEW, Rt. Hon. Sir Patrick (Barnabas Burke), Kt 1983; PC 1986; QC 1972; MP (C) Tunbridge Wells, since 1983 (Royal Tunbridge Wells, Feb. 1974–1983); Attorney General, since 1987; *b* 11 Sept. 1929; *o surv. s* of late A. G. H. Mayhew, MC; *m* 1963, Jean Elizabeth Gurney, MA (Cantab), BD, AKC, *d* of John Gurney; four *s*. *Educ:* Tonbridge; Balliol Coll., Oxford (MA). President, Oxford Union Society, 1952. Commnd 4th/7th Royal Dragoon Guards, national service and AER, captain. Called to Bar, Middle Temple, 1955, Bencher 1980. Contested (C) Camberwell and Dulwich, in Gen. Election, 1970. Parly Under Sec. of State, Dept of Employment, 1979–81; Minister of State, Home Office, 1981–83; Solicitor General, 1983–87. Mem. Exec., 1922 Cttee, 1976–79; Vice Chm., Cons. Home Affairs Cttee, 1976–79. *Address:* House of Commons, SW1. *Clubs:* Garrick, Pratt's, Beefsteak.

MAYHEW-SANDERS, Sir John (Reynolds), Kt 1982; MA; FCA; business and management consultant; *b* 25 Oct. 1931; *e s* of Jack Mayhew-Sanders, FCA; *m* 1958, Sylvia Mary, *d* of George S. Colling; three *s* one *d*. *Educ:* Epsom Coll.; RNC, Dartmouth; Jesus Coll., Cambridge (MA Engrg). FCA 1958. RN, 1949–55. Mayhew-Sanders & Co., Chartered Accountants, 1955–58; P-E Consulting Gp Ltd, 1958–72 (Dir, 1968–72); Chief Exec., 1975–83, and Chm., 1978–83, John Brown PLC (Dir, 1972–83); Director: Dowty Gp, 1982–85; Rover Gp (formerly BL plc), 1980–89; Chm., Heidrick and Struggles UK, 1985–87; Chief Exec., Samuelson Gp, 1987. Member: Management Bd, Engineering Employers' Fedn, 1977–81; BOTB, 1980–83; BBC Consultative Gp on Industrial and Business Affairs, 1981–83; Chm., Overseas Projects Bd, 1980–83; Pres., British-Soviet Chamber of Commerce, 1982–88; Vice-Pres., Inst. of Export, 1982–. Governor, Sadler's Wells Foundn, 1983–89. CBIM 1980; FRSA 1983. *Recreations:* fishing, shooting, astronomy, gardening, music. *Address:* Earlstone House, Burghclere, Hants RG15 9HN. *T:* Burghclere (063527) 288.

MAYLAND, Rev. Canon Ralph, VRD 1962 and bar 1972; Canon and Treasurer of York Minster, since 1982; *b* 31 March 1927; *s* of James Henry and Lucy Mayland; *m* 1959, Jean Mary Goldstraw; one *d* and one adopted *d*. *Educ:* Cockburn High Sch., Leeds; Leeds City Training Coll.; Westminster Coll., London Univ.; Ripon Hall, Oxford. Schoolteacher, 1945–46; RN, 1946–51; perm. commn, RNR, 1952, Chaplain, 1961–82; 3rd yr student, 1951–52; schoolteacher, 1952–57; theol student, 1957–59. Curate of Lambeth, 1959–62; Priest-in-charge, St Paul's, Manton, Worksop, 1962–67; Vicar, St Margaret's, Brightside, 1968–72; Chaplain, Sheffield Industrial Mission, 1968–75; Vicar, St Mary's, Ecclesfield, 1972–82; Chaplain to Master Cutler, 1979–80. Life Mem., Royal Naval Assoc. *Recreations:* collecting Victorian children's literature, goat-keeping and rearing. *Address:* 3 Minster Court, York YO1 2JJ. *T:* York (0904) 625599.

MAYNARD, Brian Alfred, CBE 1982; Partner, Coopers & Lybrand, Chartered Accountants, 1950–81; *b* 27 Sept. 1917; *s* of late Alfred A. Maynard and Clarissa L. (*née* Shawe); *m* 1946, Rosemary Graham, *y d* of late Col E. C. Boutflower; two *s*. *Educ:* Leighton Park Sch.; Cambridge Univ. (MA). RNVR Commission, 1939–46, served Middle East and Europe. Member: Oxford Univ. Appts Cttee, 1959–81; Cttee of Duke of Edinburgh's Award Scheme, 1961–67; Council, Industry for Management Educn, 1968–81; Cttee of Enquiry into the Financial Control of Catering in the Services, 1973; Cttee of Enquiry into Problems facing the Nat. Theatre, 1978; Council for the Securities Industry, 1978; City Panel of Takeovers and Mergers, 1978; Chm., Adv. Cttee on Local Govt Audit, 1979–82. Mem. Council, Inst. of Chartered Accountants in England and Wales, 1968–81 (Pres., 1977–78); Chairman: London Soc. of Chartered Accountants, 1966–67; Management Consultants Assoc., 1970; Pres., Inst. of Management Consultants, 1974; Vice-Pres., European Fedn of Management Consultants Assoc., 1972–75; Pres., OECD Mission to USA, on Computers, 1960. *Recreations:* racing, shooting, farming. *Address:* Cowick Farm, Hilmarton, Calne, Wilts SN11 8RZ. *T:* Hilmarton (024976) 397; 5 Redanchor Close, Chelsea, SW3 5DW. *T:* 071–352 6777.

MAYNARD, Edwin Francis George; Overseas Business Consultant; Member, Export Council Advisory Panel; HM Diplomatic Service, retired; Deputy High Commissioner, Calcutta, 1976–80; *b* 23 Feb. 1921; *s* of late Edwin Maynard, MD, FRCS, DPH, and late Nancy Frances Tully; *m* 1945, Patricia Baker; one *s* one *d*; *m* 1963, Anna McGettrick; two *s*. *Educ:* Westminster. Served with Indian Army (4/8th Punjab Regt and General Staff) (Major, GSO II), Middle East and Burma, 1939–46. BBC French Service, 1947; Foreign Office, 1949; Consul and Second Sec., Jedda, 1950; Second, later First, Sec., Benghazi, 1952; FO 1954; Bogota, 1956; Khartoum, 1959; FO, 1960; Baghdad, 1962; Founder Dir, Diplomatic Service Language Centre, 1966; Counsellor, Aden, 1967; Counsellor, New Delhi, 1968–72; Minister (Commercial), 1972–76, Chargé d'Affaires, 1974–75, Buenos Aires. *Recreations:* shooting, fishing, languages, gardening. *Address:* Littlebourne Court, Littlebourne, Canterbury, Kent. *Club:* Brooks's.

MAYNARD, Prof. Geoffrey Walter; Economic Consultant, Investcorp International Ltd, since 1986; Director of Economics, Europe and Middle East, Chase Manhattan Bank, 1977–86 (Economic consultant, 1974); Director, Chase Manhattan Ltd, 1977–86; *b* 27 Oct. 1921; *s* of Walter F. Maynard and Maisie Maynard (*née* Bristow); *m* 1949, Marie Lilian Wright; two *d*. *Educ:* London School of Economics. BSc(Econ); PhD. Lectr and Sen. Lectr, UC of S Wales, Cardiff, 1951–62; Economic Consultant, HM Treasury 1962–64; Economic Advr, Harvard Univ. Develt Adv. Gp in Argentina, 1964–65; University of Reading: Reader, 1966–68; Prof. of Economics, 1968–76; Vis. Prof. of Economics, 1976–. Editor, Bankers' Magazine, 1968–72; Under-Sec. (Econs), HM Treasury, 1972–74 (on leave of absence); Dep. Chief Economic Advr, HM Treasury, 1976–77; occasional consultant, IBRD, Overseas Develt Administration of FCO. Mem., Econ. Affairs Cttee, ESRC, 1982–85. Mem. Governing Body, Inst. of Develt Studies, Sussex, 1984–; Mem. Council, Inst. of Fiscal Studies, 1988–. *Publications:* Economic Development and the Price Level, 1962; (jtly) International Monetary Reform and Latin America, 1966; (jtly) A World of Inflation, 1976; The Economy under Mrs Thatcher, 1988; chapters in: Development Policy: theory and practice, ed G. Papanek, 1968; Commonwealth Policy in a Global Context, ed Streeten and Corbet, 1971; Economic Analysis and the Multinational Enterprise, ed J. Dunning, 1974; Special Drawing Rights and Development Aid (paper), 1972; articles in Economic Jl, Oxford Economic Papers, Jl of Development Studies, World Development, etc. *Address:* Flat 219, Queens Quay, 58 Upper Thames Street, EC4. *Club:* Reform.

MAYNARD, Joan; *see* Maynard, V. J.

MAYNARD, Air Chief Marshal Sir Nigel (Martin), KCB 1973 (CB 1971); CBE 1963; DFC 1942; AFC 1946; *b* 28 Aug. 1921; *s* of late Air Vice-Marshal F. H. M. Maynard, CB, AFC, and of Irene (*née* Pim); *m* 1946, Daphne, *d* of late G R. P. Llewellyn, Baglan Hall, Abergavenny; one *s* one *d*. *Educ:* Aldenham; RAF Coll., Cranwell. Coastal Comd, UK, Mediterranean, W Africa, 1940–43; Flt-Lieut 1942; Sqdn-Ldr 1944; Mediterranean and Middle East, 1944; Transport Comd, 1945–49; comd 242 Sqdn on Berlin Air Lift; Air Staff, Air Min., 1949–51; Wing Comdr 1952; psa 1952; Staff Officer to Inspector Gen., 1953–54; Bomber Comd, 1954–57; jssc 1957; Gp Capt. 1957; SASO 25 Gp, 1958–59; CO, RAF Changi, 1960–62; Gp Capt. Ops, Transport Comd, 1963–64; Air Cdre 1965; Dir of Defence Plans (Air), 1965; Dir of Defence Plans and Chm. Defence Planning Staff, 1966; idc 1967; Air Vice-Marshal, 1968; Commandant, RAF Staff College, Bracknell, 1968–70; Commander, Far East Air Force, 1970–71; Air Marshal, 1972; Dep. C-in-C, Strike Command, 1972–73; C-in-C RAF Germany, and Comdr, 2nd Allied Tactical Air Force, 1973–76; Air Chief Marshal 1976; C-in-C, RAF Strike Command, and C-in-C, UK Air Forces, 1976–77. ADC to the Queen, 1961–65. *Address:* Manor House, Piddington, Bicester, Oxon OX6 0QB. *T:* Brill (0844) 238270. *Clubs:* Naval and Military, Royal Air Force; MCC.

MAYNARD, Roger Paul; Director, Investor Relations and Marketplace Performance, British Airways, since 1989; *b* 10 Feb. 1943; *s* of Leonard John Maynard and May Gertrude Blake; *m* 1966, Ruth Elizabeth Wakeling; three *s* (including twin *s*). *Educ:* Purley Grammar Sch., Surrey; Queens' Coll., Cambridge (MA Hons Economics). Asst Principal, Bd of Trade, 1965; Second Secretary, UK Mission to UN and Internat. Organisations, Geneva, 1968; Principal: Dept of Industry, Shipbuilding Division, 1972; Dept of Trade, Airports Policy, 1975; Asst Sec., Dept of Industry, Air Division, 1978; Counsellor, Aviation and Shipping, British Embassy, Washington, 1982; Vice Pres., Commercial Affairs, N America, 1987, Exec. Vice Pres., N America, 1989, British Airways. *Recreations:* cricket, golf, music. *Address:* Tylers, Manor Close, Penn, Bucks HP10 8HZ. *T:* (office) 081–562 5216.

MAYNARD, (Vera) Joan; JP; *b* 1921. Mem. Labour Party Nat. Exec. Cttee, 1972–82, 1983–87; Sec., Yorks Area, Agricl and Allied Workers National Trade Group TGWU (formerly Nat. Union of Agricl and Allied Workers), 1956–78 (Nat. Vice Chm., 1966–72, sponsored as MP by the Union). MP (Lab) Sheffield, Brightside, Oct. 1974–1987. Mem., Parly Select Cttee on Agriculture, 1975–87; Vice-Chm., Labour Party, 1980–81. Chair, Campaign Gp of Lab. MPs, 1979–87. Former Parish Rural Dist and County Councillor, N Yorks. JP Thirsk, 1950. *Address:* Lansbury House, 76 Front Street, Sowerby, Thirsk, N Yorks YO7 1JF. *T:* Thirsk (0845) 522355.

MAYNARD SMITH, Prof. John, FRS 1977; Professor of Biology, University of Sussex, 1965–85, now Emeritus; *b* 6 Jan. 1920; *s* of Sidney Maynard Smith and Isobel Mary (*née* Pitman); *m* 1941; two *s* one *d*. *Educ:* Eton Coll.; Trinity Coll., Cambridge (BA Engrg, 1941); UCL (BSc Zool., 1951; Fellow, 1979). Aircraft stressman, 1942–47; Lectr in Zool., UCL, 1952–65; first Dean of Biol Sciences, Univ. of Sussex, 1965–72. For. Associate, US Nat. Acad. of Scis, 1982. Hon. DSc: Kent, 1983; Oxon, 1987; Sussex, 1988; Chicago, 1988. *Publications:* The Theory of Evolution, 1958, 3rd edn 1975; Mathematical Ideas in Biology, 1968; On Evolution, 1972; Models in Ecology, 1974; The Evolution of Sex, 1978; Evolution and the Theory of Games, 1982; The Problems of Biology, 1985; Evolutionary Genetics, 1989. *Recreations:* gardening, fishing, talking. *Address:* The White House, Kingston Ridge, Lewes, East Sussex. *T:* Lewes (0273) 474659.

MAYNE, Prof. David Quinn, FRS 1985; FEng 1987; Professor of Electrical Engineering and Computer Science, University of California, Davis, since 1989; *b* 23 April 1930; *s* of Leslie Harper Mayne and Jane Theresa Quin; *m* 1954, Josephine Mary Hess; three *d*. *Educ:* Univ. of the Witwatersrand, Johannesburg (BSc (Eng), MSc); DIC, PhD, DSc London. FIEE, FIEEE. Lectr, Univ. of Witwatersrand, 1950–54, 1956–59; R&D Engineer, British Thomson Houston Co., Rugby, 1955–56; Imperial College: Lectr, 1959–67, Reader, 1967–71; Prof. of Control Theory, 1971–89; Sen. Sci. Res. Fellow, 1979–80; Hd of Dept of Electrical Engrg, 1984–88. Research Consultant, at Univs of California (Berkeley), Lund, Newcastle NSW, 1974–. Res. Fellow, Harvard Univ., 1970; Vis. Prof., Academia Sinica, Beijing, Shanghai and Guanzhou, 1981. Corresp. Mem., Nacional Acad. de Ingenieria, Mexico, 1983. *Publications:* Differential Dynamic Programming, vol. 24 in Modern Analytic and Computational Methods in Science and Mathematics (with D. H. Jacobson, ed R. Bellman), 1970; Geometric Methods in System Theory, proc. NATO Advanced Study Inst., (ed. with R. W. Brockett), 1973; contribs to learned jls. *Recreation:* walking. *Address:* 648 Lake Terrace Circle, Davis, Calif 95616, USA.

MAYNE, Eric; Under Secretary, General Functions Group, Department of Economic Development, Northern Ireland, 1986–87, retired; *b* 2 Sept. 1928; *s* of Robert P. Mayne and Margaret Mayne; *m* 1954, Sarah Boyd (*née* Gray); three *s* two *d*. *Educ:* Bangor Grammar Sch. Univ. of Reading (BSc); Michigan State Univ. (MS). Horticultural Advisor, Min. of Agriculture, NI, 1949–56; Kellogg Foundation Fellow, 1956–57; Horticultural Advisor, HQ Min. of Agriculture, NI, 1957–64; Principal Officer, 1964–67; Gen. Manager, NI Agric. Trust, 1967–74; Sen. Asst Secretary, Dept of Agriculture, NI, 1974–79; Dep. Sec., Dept of Manpower Services, NI, 1979–82; Under Sec., Dept of Econ. Develt, NI, 1982–87. *Recreations:* gardening, winemaking.

MAYNE, John Fraser, CB 1986; management consultant; *b* 14 Sept. 1932; *s* of late John Leonard Mayne and Martha Laura (*née* Griffiths); *m* 1958, Gillian Mary (*née* Key); one *s* one *d*. *Educ:* Dulwich Coll.; Worcester Coll., Oxford. National Service, Royal Tank Regt,

1951–53. Air Min., 1956–64; HM Treasury, 1964–67; MoD, 1967–70; Asst Private Sec. to Sec. of State for Defence, 1968–70; Cabinet Office and Central Policy Rev. Staff, 1970–73; MoD, 1973–78; Private Sec. to Sec. of State for Def., 1975–76; Asst Under-Sec. of State (Air Staff), 1976–78; Principal Establishments and Finance Officer, NI Office, 1979–81; Dir Gen. of Management Audit, MoD, 1981–83; Dep. Sec., Cabinet Office (MPO), 1984–86; Principal Estab. and Finance Officer, DHSS, later Dept of Health, 1986–90. Associate, PA Consulting Group, 1990–. Mem. Council, RUSI, 1986–89. Freeman, City of London, 1983. FBIM 1981; FIPM 1984. *Recreations:* music, fell-walking, cooking, work. *Club:* United Oxford & Cambridge University.

MAYNE, Very Rev. Michael Clement Otway; Dean of Westminster, since 1986; Dean of the Order of the Bath, since 1986; *b* 10 Sept. 1929; *s* of Rev. Michael Ashton Otway Mayne and Sylvia Clementina Lumley Ellis; *m* 1965, Alison Geraldine McKie; one *s* one *d. Educ:* King's Sch., Canterbury; Corpus Christi Coll., Cambridge (MA); Cuddesdon Coll., Oxford. Curate, St John the Baptist, Harpenden, 1957–59; Domestic Chaplain to the Bishop of Southwark, 1959–65; Vicar of Norton, Letchworth, 1965–72; Head of Religious Progs, BBC Radio, 1972–79; Vicar of Great St Mary's, Cambridge (the University Church), 1979–86. Select Preacher: Univ. of Cambridge, 1988; Univ. of Oxford, 1989. Mem. Council, St Christopher's Hospice, 1988. Chm. Governors, Westminster Sch., 1986–. *Publications:* Prayers for Pastoral Occasions, 1982; (ed) Encounters, 1985; A Year Lost and Found, 1987. *Recreations:* theatre, bird-watching, reading poetry and novels. *Address:* The Deanery, Westminster, SW1P 3PA. *T:* 071–222 2953.

MAYNE, Richard (John); writer; broadcaster; *b* 2 April 1926; *s* of John William Mayne and Kate Hilda (*née* Angus); *m* 1st, Margot Ellingworth Lyon; 2nd, Jocelyn Mudie Ferguson; two *d. Educ:* St Paul's Sch., London; Trinity Coll., Cambridge (1st Cl. Hons Pts I and II, Hist. Tripos; MA and PhD). War service, Royal Signals, 1944–47. Styring, Sen., and Res. Scholar, and Earl of Derby Student, Trinity Coll., Cambridge, 1947–53; Leverhulme European Scholar, Rome, and Rome Corresp., New Statesman, 1953–54; Asst Tutor, Cambridge Inst. of Educn, 1954–56; Official: ECSC, Luxembourg, 1956–58; EEC, Brussels, 1958–63; Dir of Documentation Centre, Action Cttee for United States of Europe, and Personal Asst to Jean Monnet, Paris, 1963–66; Paris Corresp., Encounter, 1966–71, Co-Editor, 1985–91, Contributing Editor, 1990–91. Vis. Prof., Univ. of Chicago, 1971; Dir of Federal Trust for Educn and Res., 1971–73; Head of UK Offices, 1973–79, Special Advr, 1979–80, EEC. Hon. Professorial Fellow, UCW, Aberystwyth, 1986–89. Film critic: Sunday Telegraph, 1987–89; The European, 1990–. *Publications:* The Community of Europe, 1962; The Institutions of the European Community, 1968; The Recovery of Europe, 1970 (rev. edn 1973); The Europeans, 1972; (ed) Europe Tomorrow, 1972; (ed) The New Atlantic Challenge, 1975; (trans.) The Memoirs of Jean Monnet, 1978 (Scott-Moncrieff Prize, 1979); Postwar: the dawn of today's Europe, 1983; (ed) Western Europe: a handbook, 1986; Federal Union: the pioneers, 1990; (trans.) Europe: a history of its peoples, 1990. *Recreations:* travel, sailing, fell-walking. *Address:* Albany Cottage, 24 Park Village East, Regent's Park, NW1 7PZ. *T:* 081–387 6654. *Clubs:* Groucho; Les Misérables (Paris).

MAYNE, Mrs Roger; *see* Jellicoe, P. A.

MAYNE, William; writer; *b* 16 March 1928; *s* of William and Dorothy Mayne. *Educ:* Cathedral Choir Sch., Canterbury, 1937–42 (then irregularly). Has pursued a career as novelist and has had published a large number of stories for children and young people—about 80 altogether, beginning in 1953 and going on into the foreseeable future. Lectr in Creative Writing, Deakin Univ., Geelong, Vic, Aust., academic years, 1976 and 1977; Fellow in Creative Writing, Rolle Coll., Exmouth, 1979–80. Library Assoc.'s Carnegie Medal for best children's book of the year (1956), 1957. *Address:* c/o David Higham Associates, 5–8 Lower John Street, Golden Square, W1R 4HA.

MAYO, 10th Earl of, *cr* 1785; **Terence Patrick Bourke;** Baron Naas, 1766; Viscount Mayo, 1781; Lieut RN (retired); Managing Director, Irish Marble Ltd, Merlin Park, Galway; *b* 26 Aug. 1929; *s* of Hon. Bryan Longley Bourke (*d* 1961) and Violet Wilmot Heathcote Bourke (*d* 1950); *S* uncle, 1962; *m* 1952, Margaret Jane Robinson Harrison; three *s. Educ:* St Aubyns, Rottingdean; RNC Dartmouth. Lieut, RN, 1952; Fleet Air Arm, 1952; Suez, 1956; Solo Aerobatic Displays, Farnborough, 1957; invalided, 1959. Mem., Gosport Borough Council, 1961–64; Pres., Gosport Chamber of Trade, 1962; Gov., Gosport Secondary Schs, 1963–64. Mem., Liberal Party, 1963–65; contested (L) Dorset South, 1964. *Recreations:* sailing, riding, shooting, fishing. *Heir: s* Lord Naas, *qv. Address:* Doon House, Maam, Co. Galway, Eire. *Club:* County Galway.

MAYO, Col (Edward) John, OBE 1976; Director General, Help the Aged, since 1983; *b* 24 May 1931; *s* of late Rev. Thomas Edward Mayo, JP, and Constance Muriel Mayo; *m* 1961, Jacqueline Margaret Anne Armstrong, MBE 1985, Lieut WRAC, *d* of late Brig. C. D. Armstrong, CBE, DSO, MC; one *s. Educ:* King's Coll., Taunton. Commissioned into Royal Regt of Artillery, 1951; served Malta and N Africa 36 HAA Regt, 1951–55; ADC to Governor of Malta, 1953–54; 2nd Regt RHA, BAOR, 1955–58; ADC to C-in-C BAOR/Comdr Northern Army Gp, 1958–60; 20 Field Regt, RA UK, 1960–61; Adjt 20 Field Regt, RA Malaya, 1961–63; Adjt 254 (City of London) Regt RA(TA), 1963–64; Instr RMA, Sandhurst, 1964–66; GS03 Mil. Operations, MoD, 1966–68; Second in Comd 20 Heavy Regt, RA BAOR, 1968–70; GS02 Instr Staff Coll., 1970–72; commanded 17 Trng Regt and Depot RA, 1972–74, and The Depot Regt RA, 1974–75; GS01 Public Relations MoD, 1976–79; Col GS; Public Information BAOR, 1979–83; retired 1983. Trustee: HelpAge India; HelpAge Kenya; Bd Mem., HelpAge Sri Lanka. *Publications:* miscellaneous articles on military matters. MIPR 1981. FRSA 1987. *Recreations:* fishing, gardening, sailing, riding, travelling, collecting and restoring antiques. *Address:* Help the Aged, St James's Walk, EC1R 0BE. *T:* 01–253 0253; Sehore House, 24 Tekels Avenue, Camberley, Surrey. *T:* Camberley (0276) 29653. *Clubs:* Army and Navy, Special Forces, MCC.

MAYO, Eileen; artist, author, printmaker and painter; *b* Norwich, 11 Sept. 1906. *Educ:* Clifton High School; Slade School of Art. Exhibited Royal Academy, London Group, United Society of Artists, Festival of Britain, etc; works acquired by British Council, British Museum, Victoria and Albert Museum, Contemporary Art Society, and public galleries in UK, USA, Australia and NZ. Designer of Australian mammals series of postage stamps, 1959–62, and Barrier Reef series, 1966; four Cook Bicentenary stamps, NZ, 1969, and other NZ stamps, 1970–78, and three for Christmas 1985. *Publications:* The Story of Living Things; Shells and How they Live; Animals on the Farm, etc. *Recreations:* printmaking, gardening.

MAYO, Col John; *see* Mayo, Col E. J.

MAYO, Rear-Adm. Robert William, CB 1965; CBE 1962; *b* 9 Feb. 1909; *s* of late Frank Mayo, Charminster; *m* 1st, 1942, Sheila (*d* 1974), *d* of late John Colvill, JP, of Campbeltown; one *s*; 2nd, 1980, Mrs Betty Washbrook. *Educ:* Weymouth Coll.; HMS Conway. Royal Naval Reserve and officer with Royal Mail Steam Packet Co., 1926–37; Master's Certificate; transferred to Royal Navy, 1937. Served War, 1939–45; Korea, 1952; Capt., 1953; Rear-Adm., 1964; retired, 1966. Sheriff Substitute of Renfrew and Argyll at Campbeltown. *Recreations:* gardening, fishing, yachting. *Address:* Bellgrove, Campbeltown, Argyll. *T:* Campbeltown (0586) 52101. *Club:* Royal Scottish Automobile.

MAYO, Simon Herbert; Hon. Mr Justice Mayo; a Judge of the High Court of Hong Kong, since 1980; *b* 15 Nov. 1937; *s* of late Herbert and Marjorie Mayo; *m* 1966, Catherine Yin Ying Young; one *s* one *d. Educ:* Harrow Sch. Admitted a solicitor, England and Wales, 1961, Hong Kong, 1963; called as barrister and solicitor, W Australia, 1967. Asst Legal Advr, GEC, 1961; Asst Solicitor, Deacons, Solicitors, Hong Kong, 1963; in private practice, WA, 1967; Asst Registrar, 1968, Registrar, 1976, Supreme Court of Hong Kong. *Recreations:* golf, music, literature, walking. *Address:* Supreme Court, Hong Kong. *T:* 8254417. *Clubs:* Hong Kong, Sheko Country (Hong Kong).

MAYOH, Raymond Blanchflower; Under Secretary, Department of Health and Social Security, 1979–83, retired; *b* 11 Nov. 1925; *s* of Charles and Isabella Mayoh; *m* 1956, Daphne Yvonne Bayliss; one *s* one *d* (and one *s* decd). *Educ:* Colwyn Bay County Sch.; University College of North Wales. Assistant Principal, Ministry of Pensions, 1950; Principal, Ministry of Health, 1955; Assistant Secretary, 1965. *Recreations:* gardening, bird watching. *Address:* 20 Willingale Way, Thorpe Bay, Southend-on-Sea, Essex SS1 3SL. *T:* Southend (0702) 586650.

MAYOR, Hugh Robert; QC 1986; barrister; a Recorder of the Crown Court, since 1982; *b* 12 Oct. 1941; *s* of George and Grace Mayor; *m* 1970, Carolyn Ann Stubbs; one *s* one *d. Educ:* Kirkham Grammar Sch.; St John's Coll., Oxford (MA). Lectr, Univ. of Leicester, 1964 (MA). Called to the Bar, Gray's Inn, 1968. *Recreations:* sailing, tennis. *Address:* The Grange, Slawston, Leics LE16 7UF. *T:* Hallaton (085889) 200. *Club:* United Oxford & Cambridge University.

MAYOR ZARAGOZA, Federico; Director-General of UNESCO, since 1987; *b* Barcelona, 27 Jan. 1934; *s* of Federico Mayor and Juana Zaragoza; *m* 1956, Maria Angeles Menéndez; two *s* one *d. Educ:* Madrid Complutense Univ. Granada University: Prof. of Biochemistry, 1963–73; Rector, 1968–72; Prof. of Biochemistry, Univ. Autónoma, Madrid, 1973. Chm., Molecular Biology Centre, Higher Council for Scientific Research, 1974–78. Under-Sec., Min. for Educn and Science, 1974–75; Pres., Commn for Study of Special Set of Rules for the four Catalan Provinces, 1976; Mem., Cortes (Parliament) for Granada, 1977–78; Dep. Dir-Gen., UNESCO, 1978–81; Minister for Educn and Science, Spain, 1981–82; Special Advr to Dir-Gen., UNESCO, 1982; Chm., Inst. of Sciences of Man, Madrid, 1983–87. Mem., European Parlt, 1987. *Address:* UNESCO, 7 place de Fontenoy, 75700 Paris Cedex, France.

MAYS, Colin Garth, CMG 1988; HM Diplomatic Service, retired; Bursar, Yehudi Menuhin School, since 1991; *b* 16 June 1931; *s* of William Albert Mays and Sophia May Mays (*née* Pattinson); *m* 1956, Margaret Patricia, *d* of Philemon Robert Lloyd and Gladys Irene (*née* Myers); one *s. Educ:* Acklam Hall Sch.; St John's Coll., Oxford (Heath Harrison Scholar). Served in Army, 1949–51; entered HM Foreign (subseq. Diplomatic) Service, 1955; FO, 1955–56; Sofia, 1956–58; Baghdad, 1958–60; FO, 1960; UK Delegn to Conf. of 18 Nation Cttee on Disarmament, Geneva, 1960; Bonn, 1960–65; FO, 1965–69; Prague, 1969–72; FCO, 1972–77; Head of Information Administration Dept, 1974–77; Counsellor (Commercial), Bucharest, 1977–80; seconded to PA Management Consultants, 1980–81; Diplomatic Service Overseas Inspector, 1981–83; High Commissioner: Seychelles, 1983–86; Bahamas, 1986–91. Liveryman, Painter-Stainers' Co., 1981. *Recreations:* sailing, swimming, travel. *Address:* Yehudi Menuhin School, Stoke d'Abernon, Cobham, Surrey KT11 3QQ. *Club:* Travellers'.

MAZANKOWSKI, Hon. Donald Frank; PC (Can.) 1979; Deputy Prime Minister of Canada, since 1986; Minister of Finance, since 1991; MP (Progressive Conservative), Vegreville, since 1968; *b* 27 July 1935; *s* of late Frank Mazankowski and Dora (*née* Lonowski); *m* 1958, Lorraine Poleschuk; three *s. Educ:* High Sch., Viking, Alberta. Minister for Transport and Minister responsible for Canadian Wheat Bd, 1979–80; Minister of Transport, 1984–86; Pres. of Queen's Privy Council for Canada, 1986–91; Minister of Agriculture, 1986–91; Minister responsible for Privatization, 1988. Govt House Leader, 1986–89. *Address:* Office of the Deputy Prime Minister, Room 203–5, Centre Block, House of Commons, Ottawa, Ont K1A 0A6, Canada.

MAZRUI, Prof. Ali A., DPhil; Albert Schweitzer Professor in the Humanities, State University of New York, Binghamton, since 1989; Andrew D. White Professor-at-Large, Cornell University, 1986–July 1992; Professor of Political Science and of Afroamerican and African Studies, University of Michigan, since 1974; *b* Kenya, 24 Feb. 1933; *s* of Al'Amin Ali Mazrui, Judge of Islamic Law, and Safia Suleiman Mazrui; marr. diss.; three *s. Educ:* Univ. of Manchester (BA with distinction 1960); Columbia Univ. (MA 1961); Oxford Univ. (DPhil 1966). Makerere University, Kampala, Uganda: Lectr, 1963–65; Prof. and Head of Dept of Political Science, 1965–73; Dean, Faculty of Social Sciences, 1967–69; Res. Prof., Univ. of Jos, Nigeria, 1981–86. Vis. Prof., Univs of London, Manchester, Sussex, Leeds, Harvard, Calif (LA), Northwestern, Stanford, Colgate, Ohio State, Bridgewater State Coll., Mass, Denver, Pennsylvania State, McGill, Canada, Nairobi, Cairo, Baghdad, Singapore and Australian National, 1965– Expert Adviser: World Bank, 1988–; UN Commn on Transnational Corps, 1987–. Member: Adv. Cttee, Trans-Africa Run for Wildlife Foundn, Inc., 1987–; Adv. Bd of Dirs, Detroit Chapter, AFRICARE, 1987–; Pan-African Adv. Council to UNICEF, 1988–. Pres., African Studies Assoc. of USA, 1978–79; Vice-President: Internat. Congress of African Studies, 1978–; Internat. African Inst., 1987–; World Congress of Black Intellectuals, 1988–. BBC Reith Lectr, 1979; Presenter, The Africans (BBC TV series), 1986. Editor, vol. VIII, UNESCO Gen. History of Africa, 1973–. *Publications:* Towards a Pax Africana, 1967; The Anglo-African Commonwealth, 1967; On Heroes and Uhuru-Worship, 1967; Violence and Thought, 1969; (with R. I. Rotberg) Protest and Power in Black Africa, 1970; The Trial of Christopher Okigbo (novel), 1971; Cultural Engineering and Nation-Building in East Africa, 1971; (with Hasu Patel) Africa in World Affairs: the next thirty years, 1973; World Culture and the Black Experience, 1974; Soldiers and Kinsmen in Uganda, 1975; Who are the Afrosaxons?: the political sociology of the English language, 1975; A World Federation of Cultures: an African perspective, 1976; Africa's International Relations, 1977; The Warrior Tradition in Modern Africa, 1978; Political Values and the Educated Class in Africa, 1978; The African Condition (The Reith Lectures), 1980; (with Michael Tidy) Nationalism and New States of Africa, 1984; The Africans: a triple heritage, 1986; Cultural Forces in World Politics, 1990. *Address:* Apartment 3E, 38–42 Front Street, Binghamton, NY 13905, USA. *T:* (607) 777–4494.

MBEKEANI, Nyemba W.; Chief Executive, Mkulumadzi Farm Bakeries Ltd, since 1981; Chairman: Spearhead Holdings Ltd, since 1987; Impala Farming Co. Ltd, since 1987; *b* 15 June 1929; Malawi parentage; *m* 1950, Lois Moses (*née* Chikankheni); two *s* three *d. Educ:* Henry Henderson Institute, Blantyre; London Sch. of Economics (Economic and Social Administration, 1963). Local Government Officer, 1945–58; political detention in Malawi and Southern Rhodesia, 1959–60; Business Executive, 1960–61; Local Govt Officer, 1963–64; Foreign Service, 1964; High Commissioner for Malawi in London, 1964–67; Ambassador to USA and Permanent Rep. at the UN, 1967–72; Ambassador to

Ethiopia, 1972–73; Gen. Manager, Malaŵi Housing Corp., 1973–81. Farmer, company director, tea broker, baker, confectioner. Chairman: Employers Consultative Assoc. of Malaŵi, 1983–; Petroleum Control Commn, 1987–; Board Member: Lingadzi Farming Co., 1987–; Kawalazi Farming Co., 1987–; Sable Farming Co., 1987–; Member, Executive Board: Grain and Milling Co., 1983–; Malaŵi Chamber of Commerce and Industry, 1984–; Malaŵi Railways, 1988–; African Businessmen Assoc. of Malaŵi, 1986–; Mem., Exec. Bd of Trustees, Small Enterprise Develt Orgn of Malaŵi, 1989–. Trustee, Small Farmers Fertilizer Revolving Fund, 1988–. Counsellor, Malaŵi Univ. Council, 1984–; Chm., Malaŵi Polytechnic Bd of Govs, 1988–. *Recreation:* flower gardening. *Address:* PO Box 2095, Blantyre, Malaŵi. *T:* 640633; *Telex:* 44847 Lumadzi MI.

M'BOW, Amadou-Mahtar; Director-General of Unesco, 1974–87; *b* 20 March 1921; *s* of Fara-N'Diaye M'Bow and N'Goné Casset, Senegal; *m* 1951, Raymonde Sylvain; one *s* two *d*. *Educ:* Univ. of Paris. Teacher, Rosso Coll., Mauritania, 1951–53; Dir, Service of Fundamental and Community Educn, Senegal, 1953–57; Min. of Education and Culture, 1957–58; Teacher at Lycée Faidherbe, St-Louis, Senegal, 1958–64; Prof., Ecole Normale Supérieure, Dakar, 1964–66; Minister of Educn, 1966–68; Mem. Nat. Assembly, Senegal, 1968–70; Minister of Culture, Youth and Sports 1968–70; Asst Dir-Gen. for Educn, UNESCO, 1970–74. Member: Acad. des Sciences d'Outre-Mer, 1977; Acad. of Kingdom of Morocco, 1981; Hon. Mem., Royal Acad. Fine Arts, San Temo, Spain, 1977; For. Mem., Acad. of Athens, 1983. Hon. Professor: Ecole normale supérieure, Dakar, 1979; Indep. Univ. of Santo Domingo, 1978; Nat. Indep. Univ. of Mexico, 1979. Hon. Dr: Buenos Aires, 1974; Granada (Lit. and Phil.), Sherbrooke (Educn), West Indies (Laws), 1975; Open, Kliment Okhridski, Sofia, Nairobi (Lit.), 1976; Malaya (Lit.), Philippines (Laws); Venice (Geog.), Uppsala (Soc. Scis), Moscow (Soc. Scis), Paris I, 1977; Andes (Philos.), Peru (Educn Scis), Haiti, Tribhunvan Univ., Nepal (Lit.), State Univ., Mongolia, Khartoum (Law), Sri Lanka, 1978; Charles Univ., Prague (Phil.), Tashkent, Québec, 1979; Nat. Univ. of Zaïre, Madras, Belgrade, Ivory Coast, Sierra Leone, 1980; Univ. Gama Filho, Brazil, 1981; Nat. Univ. of Lesotho, 1981; Univ. of Benin, 1981; Technical Univ. of Middle East, Ankara, 1981; Univ. of Ankara, 1981, Univ. of Gand, Belgium, 1982; Nat. Univ. of Seoul, 1982; State Univ. of Kiev, 1982; Laval Univ., Quebec, 1982; Quaid-i-Azam Univ., Islamabad, 1983; Jawaharlal Nehru Univ., New Delhi, 1983; Aix-Marseilles Univ., 1983; Beijing Univ., China, 1983; Kim Il Sung Univ., PDR of Korea (Pedagogy), 1983; Lucknow Univ., India (Lit.), 1983; Chulalongkorn Univ., Thailand (Pedagogy), 1983; Sokoto Univ., Nigeria (Lit.), 1984; Malta Univ., 1986; Polytechnic Univ. of Catalonia, Cauca Univ. Popayan (Colombia), Univ. of Mayor, Real y Pontificia de San Francisco Xavier de Chuquisara, Sucre (Bolivia), 1987; Grand Tribute, Univ. Candido Mendes, Brazil, 1981. Order of Merit, Senegal; Grand Cross: Order of the Liberator, Order of Andres Bello and Order of Francisco de Miranda, Venezuela; Order of Merit and Juan Montalvo National Order of Merit (Educn), Ecuador; Order of Miguel Antonio Caro y Rufino José Cuervo, Colombia; Order of Stara Planina, Bulgaria; Order of the Sun, Peru; Order of Merit of Duarte, Sanchez and Mella, Dominican Republic; National Order of the Lion, Senegal; Order of Alphonso X the Sabio, Spain; Order of the Southern Cross and Order of Merit of Guararapes, Brazil; Order of Distinguished Diplomatic Service Merit, Republic of Korea; Order of Sikatuna, Philippines; Order of Merit, Indonesia; Order of Merit, Syrian Arab Republic; Order of Merit, Jordan; Order of the Arab Republic of Egypt; Order of Felix Varela, Cuba; Grand Cross: Order of Nat. Flag (PDR of Korea); Order of Meritorious Action (Libya); Nat. Order of Andean Condor (Bolivia); Grand Order of Education (Bolivia); Grand Officer: National Order of Ivory Coast; National Order of Guinea; Order of Merit, Cameroon; National Order of Merit, Mauritania; Order of Independence, Tunisia; Commander: Order of Academic Palms; National Order of Upper Volta; Order of the Gabonese Merit; Order of Arts and Letters, France; Grand Medal, Order of the Inconfidência, State of Minas Gerais, Brazil; Medal: Order of Merit of Caetés, Olinda, Brazil; Order of Manual José Hurtado, Panama; Superior Decoration for Education, Jordan. Man and his World Peace Prize, Canada, 1978; Gold Medal of Olympic Order, 1981; Gold Medal of ALECSO (Arab Educnl, Cultural and Scientific Orgn), 1981; Internat. Dimitrov Prize, 1982; Gold Medal: Champion of Africa, 1986, of Andalucia, 1987. *Publications:* Le temps des peuples, ed R. Laffont, 1982; Where the Future Begins, 1982; Hope for the Future, 1984; Unesco: universality and international intellectual co-operation, 1985; numerous monographs, articles in educnl jls, textbooks, etc. *Address:* BP 5276, Dakar-Fann, Senegal; BP 434, R.P. Rabat, Morocco. *T:* Rabat (212) 756871.

MEACHER, Michael Hugh; MP (Lab) Oldham (West) since 1970; *b* 4 Nov. 1939; *s* of George Hubert and Doris May Meacher; *m* 1st, 1962, Molly Christine (*née* Reid) (marr. diss. 1987); two *s* two *d*; 2nd, 1988, Mrs Lucianne Sawyer. *Educ:* Berkhamsted Sch., Herts; New College, Oxford. Greats, Class 1. Sec. to Danilo Dolci Trust, 1964; Research Fellow in Social Gerontology, Univ. of Essex, 1965–66; Lecturer in Social Administration: Univ. of York, 1967–69; London Sch. of Economics, 1970. Parly Under-Secretary of State: DoI, 1974–75; DHSS, 1975–76; Dept of Trade, 1976–79; Mem., Shadow Cabinet, 1983–; chief opposition spokesman on health and social security, 1983–87, on employment, 1987–89, on social security, 1989–. Mem., Treasury Select Cttee, 1980–83 (a Chm. of its sub-cttee). Chm., Labour Co-ordinating Cttee, 1978–83; Member: Nat. Exec.'s Campaign for Press Freedom; Labour Party NEC, 1983–88. Vis. Prof., Univ. of Surrey, Dept of Sociology, 1980–87. *Publications:* Taken for a Ride: Special Residential Homes for the Elderly Mentally Infirm, a study of separatism in social policy, 1972; Fabian pamphlets, The Care of the Old, 1969; Wealth: Labour's Achilles Heel, in Labour and Equality, ed P. Townsend and N. Bosanquet, 1972; Socialism with a Human Face, 1981; numerous articles. *Recreations:* music, sport, reading. *Address:* 5 Cottenham Park Road, SW20.

MEAD, Prof. William Richard; Professor and Head of Department of Geography, University College, London, 1966–81, now Emeritus Professor; *b* 29 July 1915; *s* of William Mead and Catharine Sarah Stevens; unmarried. *Educ:* Aylesbury Gram. Sch. (Foundation Governor, 1981–); London Sch. of Economics (Hon. Fellow 1979). DSc(Econ) London, 1968. Asst Lectr and Lectr, University of Liverpool, 1947–49; Rockefeller Fellowship, held in Finland, 1949–50; Lectr, 1950, Reader, 1953, University Coll., London. Chm. Council, Sch. of Slavonic and E European Studies, 1978–80. Chm., Anglo-Finnish Soc., 1966–; President: Inst. of British Geographers, 1971 (Hon. Mem., 1989); Geog. Assoc., 1981–82; Hon. Sec., Royal Geographical Society, 1967–77 (Vice Pres., 1977–81, Hon. Vice-Pres., 1981–). Brown Meml Lectr, Univ. of Minnesota, 1983. Hon. Member: Finnish Geog. Soc.; Fenno-Ugrian Soc.; Porthan Soc.; Sydsvenska geografiska sällskapet; Det norske Videnskaps. Akademi, 1976; Det Norske Geografiske Selskab; Foreign Mem., Finnish Acad. of Science and Letters. Gill Memorial Award, 1951, Founder's Medal, 1980, RGS; Wahlberg Gold Medal, Swedish Geographical Soc., 1983; Fennia Medal, Finnish Geographical Soc., 1988; Res. Medal, RSGS, 1988. Dr *hc* University of Uppsala, 1966; DPhil *hc* Univ. of Helsinki, 1969; PhD *hc* Lund, 1987. Chevalier, Swedish Order of Vasa, 1962; Comdr, Orders of: Lion of Finland, 1963 (Chevalier, 1953); White Rose of Finland, 1976; Polar Star of Sweden, 1977. *Publications:* Farming in Finland, 1953; Economic Geography of Scandinavian States and Finland, 1958; (with Helmer Smeds) Winter in Finland, 1967; Finland (Modern Nations of the World Series), 1968; (with Wendy Hall) Scandinavia, 1972; The Scandinavian Northlands, 1973; (with Stig Jaatinen) The Åland Islands, 1974; An Historical Geography of Scandinavia, 1981; other books on Norway, Sweden, Canada and USA. *Recreations:* riding, music. *Address:* 6 Lower Icknield Way, Aston Clinton, near Aylesbury, Bucks HP22 5JS.

MEADE, family name of **Earl of Clanwilliam.**

MEADE, Eric Cubitt, FCA; Senior Partner, Deloitte Haskins & Sells, Chartered Accountants, 1982–85; *b* 12 April 1923; *s* of William Charles Abbott Meade and Vera Alicia Maria Meade; *m* 1960, Margaret Arnott McCallum; two *s* one *d*. *Educ:* Ratcliffe College. FCA 1947. Served War, Hampshire Regt, 1942–46; N Africa, Italy, prisoner of war, 1944–45; Captain. Chartered Accountant, 1947. Mem. Council, Inst. of Chartered Accountants in England and Wales, 1969–79 (Chm., Parly and Law Cttee, 1974–76; Chm., Investigation Cttee, 1976–77); Chm., Consultative Cttee., Accountancy Bodies Ethics Cttee, 1977–83; Mem. Council, FIMBRA, 1986–87; Lay Mem., Solicitors Complaints Bureau, 1986–89; Mem., Audit Commn, 1986–89. *Recreations:* tennis, bowls. *Address:* 56 Hurlingham Court, Ranelagh Gardens, Fulham, SW6 3UP. *T:* 071–736 5382. *Club:* Hurlingham.

MEADE, Sir Geoffrey; *see* Meade, Sir R. G. A.

MEADE, James Edward, CB 1947; FBA 1951; MA Oxon, MA Cantab; Hon. Dr, Universities of Basel, Bath, Essex, Glasgow, Hull and Oxford; Hon. Fellow: London School of Economics; Oriel College, Oxford; Hertford College, Oxford; Christ's College, Cambridge; Trinity College, Cambridge; *b* 23 June 1907; *s* of Charles Hippisley Meade and Kathleen Cotton-Stapleton; *m* 1933, Elizabeth Margaret, *d* of Alexander Cowan Wilson; one *s* three *d*. *Educ:* Malvern Coll.; Oriel Coll., Oxford; Trinity Coll., Cambridge. 1st Class Hon. Mods 1928; 1st Class Philosophy, Politics, and Economics, 1930. Fellow and Lecturer in Economics, 1930–37, and Bursar, 1934–37, Hertford Coll., Oxford; Mem. Economic Section of League of Nations, Geneva, 1938–40. Economic Asst (1940–45), and Dir (1946–47), Economic Section Cabinet Offices. Prof. of Commerce, with special reference to International Trade, London Sch. of Economics, 1947–57; Prof. of Political Economy, Cambridge, 1957–68; Nuffield Res. Fellow, 1969–74, and Fellow, Christ's Coll., Cambridge, 1957–74. Member: Coun. of Royal Economic Society, 1945–62 (Pres., 1964–66, Vice-Pres., 1966–); Council of Eugenics Soc., 1962–68 (Treasurer 1963–67). Visiting Prof., Australian National Univ., 1956. Pres. Section F, British Assoc. for the Advancement of Science, 1957; Chm. Economic Survey Mission, Mauritius, 1960. Trustee of Urwick, Orr and Partners Ltd, 1958–76. Governor: Nat. Inst. of Economic and Social Research, 1947–; LSE, 1960–74; Malvern Coll., 1972–. Chm., Cttee of Inst. for Fiscal Studies, 1975–77 (producing report on The Structure and Reform of Direct Taxation, 1978). Hon. Mem., Amer. Economic Assoc., 1962; For. Hon. Member: Soc. Royale d'Econ. Politique de Belgique, 1958; Amer. Acad. of Arts and Sciences, 1966; For. Associate, Nat. Acad. of Sciences, USA, 1981. (Jtly) Nobel Prize for Economics, 1977. *Publications:* Public Works in their International Aspect, 1933; The Rate of Interest in a Progressive State, 1933; Economic Analysis and Policy, 1936; Consumers' Credits and Unemployment, 1937; League of Nations' World Economic Surveys for 1937–38 and 1938–39; The Economic Basis of a Durable Peace, 1940; (with Richard Stone) National Income and Expenditure, 1944; Planning and the Price Mechanism, 1948; The Theory of International Economic Policy, Vol. I, 1951, Vol. II, 1955; A Geometry of International Trade, 1952; Problems of Economic Union, 1953; The Theory of Customs Unions, 1955; The Control of Inflation, 1958; A Neo-Classical Theory of Economic Growth, 1960; Three Case Studies in European Economic Union, 1962 (Joint Author); Efficiency, Equality, and the Ownership of Property, 1964; Principles of Political Economy, Vol. 1, The Stationary Economy, 1965, Vol. 2, The Growing Economy, 1968, Vol. 3, The Controlled Economy, 1972, Vol. 4, The Just Economy, 1976; The Theory of Indicative Planning, 1970; The Theory of Externalities, 1973; The Intelligent Radical's Guide to Economic Policy, 1975; Stagflation, vol. 1, Wage Fixing, 1982, vol. 2, (jtly) Demand Management, 1983; Alternative Systems of Business Organisation and of Workers' Remuneration, 1986; Collected Papers, vols 1, 2, 3, 1988, vol. 4, 1989; (jtly) Macroeconomic Policy: inflation, wealth and the exchange rate, 1989; Agathotopia: the economics of partnership, 1989. *Address:* 40 High Street, Little Shelford, Cambridge CB2 5ES. *T:* Cambridge (0223) 842491.

See also Prof. P. S. Dasgupta, T. W. Meade, Sir Geoffrey Wilson.

MEADE, Patrick John, OBE 1944; consultant in meteorology to various international organisations; Director of Services, and Deputy Director-General, Meteorological Office, 1966–73; *b* 23 Feb. 1913; *s* of late John Meade, Caterham, Surrey; *m* 1937, Winifred Jessie, *d* of Bertram Kent, Fawley, Hants; one *s* one *d* (and one *s* decd). *Educ:* Sir Joseph Williamson's Math. Sch., Rochester; Imperial Coll. of Science and Technology (Royal College of Science). ARCSc, BSc; Lubbock Mem. Prize in Maths, London Univ., 1933. Entered Met. Office, 1936; Southampton, 1937; Flt Lt RAFVR, Fr., 1939–40; Sqdn Leader, Sen. Met. Off., GHQ Home Forces, 1940–42; Wing Comdr (Gp Capt. 1944), Chief Met. Off., MAAF, 1943–45; Chief Met. Off., ACSEA, 1945–46; Head of Met. Office Trng Sch., 1948–52; London Airport, 1952–55; Research, 1955–60; idc 1958; Dep. Dir for Outstations Services, 1960–65. Hon. Sec., Royal Meteorological Society, 1956–61, Vice-Pres., 1961–63. *Publications:* papers in jls on aviation meteorology and on meteorological aspects of air pollution, atmospheric radioactivity and hydrology. *Recreations:* music, gardening. *Address:* Luccombe, Coronation Road, South Ascot, Berks SL5 9LP. *T:* Ascot (0344) 23206.

MEADE, Sir (Richard) Geoffrey (Austin), KBE 1963; CMG 1953; CVO 1961; *b* 8 March 1902; *s* of late Austin Meade, MA; *m* 1929, Elizabeth Ord, MA Oxon, 2nd *d* of late G. J. Scott, JP; three *d*. *Educ:* Ecole Alsacienne, Paris; Balliol Coll., Oxford. BA 1925. Entered Consular Service, 1925; served at Tangier, 1927, Salonica, 1929, Aleppo, 1930, Athens, 1931, Salonica, 1933, Tangier, 1935, Valencia, 1939, Crete, 1940, FO, 1941, Dakar, 1943, Tetuan, 1943, Cassablanca, 1945; Istanbul, 1947; idc, 1950; Marseilles, 1951; Tangier, 1956; Düsseldorf, 1957; Milan, 1958–62. Retired, 1962. *Address:* Baker's Close, 104 Lower Radley, Abingdon, Oxon OX14 3BA. *T:* Abingdon (0235) 521327.

MEADE, Richard John Hannay, OBE 1974; President, British Equestrian Federation, since 1989; *b* 4 Dec. 1938; *s* of John Graham O'Mahony Meade and Phyllis Brenda Meade; *m* 1977, Angela Dorothy Farquhar; two *s* one *d* (and one *s* decd). *Educ:* Lancing College; Magdalene College, Cambridge (Engineering Degree). Competed for GB in 3-day equestrian events, 1963–82; won 3 Olympic gold medals: team gold, 1968; team and individual gold, Munich, 1972; World Championships team medals include: gold, Punchestown, 1970; gold, Luhmühlen, 1982; European Championships team medals include: gold, Punchestown, 1967; gold, Burghley, 1971; gold, Horsens, 1981; won Burghley 1964 and Badminton 1970 and 1982. Mem., 3-day Event Cttee, 1977–80, Bureau Mem., 1990–, Internat. Equestrian Fedn. *Publication:* Fit for Riding, 1984. *Address:* Church Farm, West Littleton, Chippenham, Wilts SN14 8JB. *T:* Bath (0225) 891226.

MEADE, Thomas Wilson, DM; FRCP, FFPHM; Director, Medical Research Council Epidemiology and Medical Care Unit, Northwick Park Hospital, Harrow, since 1970; Hon. consultant in epidemiology, Northwick Park Hospital; Hon. Director, Cardiovascular Epidemiology Research Group, British Heart Foundation, since 1982; *b*

21 Jan. 1936; *s* of James Edward Meade, *qv; m* 1962, Helen Elizabeth Perks; one *s* two *d*. *Educ:* Westminster Sch.; Christ Church, Oxford; St Bartholomew's Hosp. Sen. Lectr, Dept of Public Health, London Sch. of Hygiene and Tropical Medicine (on secondment to Schieffelin Leprosy Research Sanatorium, S India, 1969–70), 1968–70. Member: MRC Physiological Systems and Disorders Bd, 1974–78; MRC Health Services Res. Panel and Cttee, 1981–90; Wellcome Trust Physiology and Pharmacology Panel, 1990–; Chm., Adv. Panel (to CSM) on Collection of data relating to Adverse Reactions to Pertussis Vaccine, 1977–81. *Publications:* papers on thrombosis, chronic disability, leprosy. *Recreations:* oboe, growing vegetables. *Address:* 28 Cholmeley Crescent, N6 5HA. *T:* 081–340 6260. *Club:* Leander (Henley-on-Thames).

MEADE-KING, Charles Martin, MA; Headmaster, Plymouth College, 1955–73, retired; *b* 17 Aug. 1913; *s* of late G. C. Meade-King, solicitor, Bristol; *m* 1948, Mary (*née* Frazer); one *s* one *d*. *Educ:* Clifton Coll.; Exeter Coll., Oxford (Stapeldon Scholar). Asst Master, King's Sch., Worcester, 1935–38; Asst Master, Mill Hill Sch., 1938–40. Intelligence Corps, 1940–45. Housemaster, Mill Hill Sch., 1945–55. *Recreations:* history, arts, games. *Address:* Whistledown, Yelverton, near Plymouth PL20 6HX. *T:* Yelverton (0822) 852237.

MEADOW, Prof. (Samuel) Roy, FRCP; Head of Department of Paediatrics and Child Health, St James's University Hospital, Leeds, since 1980; *b* 9 June 1933; *m* 1st, 1962, Gillian Margaret Maclennan; one *s* one *d*; 2nd, 1978, Marianne Jane Harvey. *Educ:* Wigan Grammar Sch.; Bromsgrove Sch.; Worcester Coll., Oxford (BA Hons Physiol. 1957; MA, BM BCh 1960). DRCOG 1962; DCH 1963; MRCP 1964, FRCP 1974. Partner GP, Banbury, 1962–64; junior appts at Guy's Hosp., Evelina Children's Hosp., Hosp. for Sick Children, London and Royal Alexandra Hosp., Brighton, 1964–67; MRC Sen. Res. Fellow, Birmingham Univ., 1967–68; Sen. Lectr and Consultant Paediatrician, Leeds Univ., 1970–80. Blackwell Vis. Prof., NZ, BPA, 1989; Kildorrory Lectr, Irish Paed. Assoc., 1987. Chairman: Assoc. for Child Psychology and Psychiatry, 1983–84; Academic Bd, BPA, 1990–. Editor, Archives of Diseases in Childhood, 1979–87. *Publications:* Lecture Notes on Paediatrics, 1973, 6th edn 1991; Bladder Control and Enuresis, 1973; The Child and His Symptoms, 1978; ABC of Child Abuse, 1989; Paediatric Kidney Disease, 1991; reports and papers on teratogenicity of anticonvulsant drugs, Munchausen Syndrome by proxy child abuse, childhood urinary tract disorders and child abuse. *Recreation:* gardening. *Address:* Weeton Grange, Weeton, Leeds LS17 0AP. *T:* Harrogate (0423) 734234.

MEADOWCROFT, Michael James; writer and journalist; *b* 6 March 1942; marr. diss.; one *s* one *d*; *m* 2nd, 1987, Elizabeth Bee. *Educ:* King George V Sch., Southport; Bradford Univ. (MPhil 1978). Chm., Merseyside Regl Young Liberal Orgn, 1961; Liberal Party Local Govt Officer, 1962–67; Sec., Yorks Liberal Fedn, 1967–70; Asst Sec., Joseph Rowntree Social Service Trust, 1970–78; Gen. Sec., Bradford Metropolitan Council for Voluntary Service, 1978–83. Senior Vis. Fellow, PSI, 1989. Member: Leeds City Council, 1968–83; W Yorks MCC, 1973–76, 1981–83. Dir, Leeds Grand Theatre and Opera House, 1971–83. Chm., Liberal Party Assembly Cttee, 1977–81; Pres. Elect, Liberal Party, 1987–88. Contested (L) Leeds W, Feb. and Oct. 1974, 1987. MP (L) Leeds W, 1983–87. Chm., Electoral Reform Soc. *Publications:* Liberal Party Local Government Handbook (with Pratap Chitnis), 1963; Success in Local Government, 1971; Liberals and a Popular Front, 1974; Local Government Finance, 1975; A Manifesto for Local Government, 1975; The Bluffer's Guide to Politics, 1976; Liberal Values for a New Decade, 1980; Social Democracy—Barrier or Bridge?, 1981; Liberalism and the Left, 1982; Liberalism and the Right, 1983; Liberalism Today and Tomorrow, 1989; The Politics of STV, 1991; Diversity in Danger, 1991. *Recreations:* music (including jazz), cricket. *Address:* Waterloo Lodge, 72 Waterloo Lane, Bramley, Leeds LS13 2JF. *T:* Leeds (0532) 576232. *Clubs:* National Liberal; Armley Liberal, Bramley Liberal, Burley Liberal, Kirkstall Liberal, New Wortley Liberal, Upper and Lower Wortley Liberal (Leeds).

MEADOWS, Prof. Arthur Jack, FInstP; FLA; FIInfSc; Professor of Library and Information Studies, since 1986, and Dean of Education and Humanities, since 1991, Loughborough University; *b* 24 Jan. 1934; *s* of Arthur Harold Meadows and Alice Elson; *m* 1958, Isobel Jane Tanner Bryant; one *s* two *d*. *Educ:* New Coll., Oxford (MA Physics; DPhil Astronomy); University Coll. London (MSc History and Philosophy of Science). Fulbright Schol., Vis. Fellow, Mt Wilson and Palomar Observatories, Asst Prof., Univ. of Illinois, 1959–61; Lectr, Univ. of St Andrews, 1961–63; Asst Keeper, British Mus., 1963–65; University of Leicester: Hd of Dept and Prof., Astronomy and History of Science Depts, 1965–86; Hd of Primary Communications Res. Centre, 1975–86; Hd of Office for Humanities Communication, 1982–86. *Publications:* Stellar Evolution, 1967; The High Firmament: a survey of astronomy in English literature, 1969; Early Solar Physics, 1970; Science and Controversy, 1972; Communication in Science, 1974; Greenwich Observatory: recent history (1836–1975), 1975; The Scientific Journal, 1979; (jtly) Dictionary of New Information Technology, 1982; (jtly) The Lamp of Learning: Taylor & Francis and the development of science publishing, 1984; (jtly) Maxwell's Equations and their Applications, 1985; Space Garbage, 1985; (jtly) Dictionary of Computing and Information Technology, 1987; The Origins of Information Science, 1987; (jtly) Principles and Practice of Journal Publishing, 1987; (jtly) The History of Scientific Discovery, 1987; Infotechnology, 1989; about 150 articles. *Recreation:* sleeping in meetings. *Address:* 47 Swan Street, Seagrave, Leics LE12 7NL. *T:* Sileby (050981) 2557.

MEADOWS, Bernard William; sculptor; Professor of Sculpture, Royal College of Art, 1960–80; *b* Norwich, 19 Feb. 1915; *s* of W. A. F. and E. M. Meadows; *m* 1939, Marjorie Winifred Payne; two *d*. *Educ:* City of Norwich Sch. Studied at Norwich Sch. of Art, 1934–36; worked as Asst to Henry Moore, 1936–40; studied at Royal College of Art, 1938–40 and 1946–48. Served with RAF, 1941–46. Commissioned by Arts Council to produce a work for Festival of Britain, 1951. Rep. (Brit. Pavilion) in Exhib. of Recent Sculpture, Venice Biennale, 1952; in Exhib., Kassel, Germany, 1959, etc. Exhibited in International Exhibitions of Sculpture (Open Air): Battersea Park, 1951, 1960; Musée Rodin, Paris, 1956; Holland Park, 1957; in 4th International Biennial, São Paulo, Brazil, 1957; also in Exhibns (Open Air) in Belgium and Holland, 1953–. *One man exhibitions:* Gimpel Fils, London, 1957, 1959, 1963, 1965, 1967; Paul Rosenberg, New York, 1959, 1962, 1967; Taranman, London, 1979. *Works in Collections:* Tate Gallery; Victoria and Albert Museum; Arts Council; British Council; Museum of Modern Art, New York; also in public collections in N and S America, Israel, Australia, and in Europe. Mem., Royal Fine Art Commn, 1971–76. Awarded Italian State Scholarship, 1956. *Publication:* 34 etchings and box (for Molloy by Samuel Beckett), 1967. *Address:* 34 Belsize Grove, NW3. *T:* 071–722 0772.

MEADOWS, Graham David; Director, Regional Policy, Commission of European Communities, since 1989; *b* 17 Dec. 1941; *s* of late Albert Edward Meadows and Jessica Maude Titmus; two *d*. *Educ:* Edinburgh Univ. MA Hons Political Economy. Journalist, 1958–69, specialising latterly in agric. affairs; European corresp., Farmers' Weekly (based in Brussels), 1973–75; EC 1975– (Mem., agric. policy unit); adviser on agricl, fisheries and envt policy, Office of Pres. of EEC (Gaston E. Thorn), 1981–84; Chef de Cabinet of Stanley Clinton Davis, Mem. of EEC responsible for transport, envmt and nuclear safety, 1985–89. *Recreations:* mountain walking, reading in the history of economic thought. *Address:* Commission of the European Communities, 200 rue de la Loi, 1049 Brussels, Belgium. *T:* (2) 235.61.81.

MEADOWS, Robert; company director, motor trade; Lord Mayor of Liverpool, 1972–73; *b* 28 June 1902; *m* 1st, 1926, Ivy L. Jenkinson (*d* 1963); three *s*; 2nd, 1967, Nora E. Bullen. *Educ:* locally and Bootle Technical Coll. Engineering, 1917–21. Liverpool: City Councillor, Fairfield Ward, 1945; City Alderman, Princes Park Ward, 1961–74. Pres., Exec. Cttee, Broadgreen Conservative Assoc. *Recreations:* motor vehicle development, property improvement, landscape gardening.

MEADOWS, Swithin Pinder, MD, BSc, FRCP; Consulting Physician: Westminster Hospital; National Hospital, Queen Square; Moorfields Eye Hospital; *b* 18 April 1902; *er s* of late Thomas and late Sophia Florence Meadows; *m* 1934, Doris Steward Noble; two *s* two *d*. *Educ:* Wigan Grammar Sch.; University of Liverpool; St Thomas' Hosp. Kanthack Medal in Pathology; Owen T. Williams Prize; House Physician and House Surgeon, Liverpool Royal Infirmary; House Physician, Royal Liverpool Children's Hospital; Medical Registrar and Tutor, St Thomas' Hosp.; RMO National Hosp., Queen Square; Medical First Asst, London Hosp.; Examiner in Neurology and Medicine, University of London; Hosp. Visitor, King Edward's Hosp. Fund for London; Mem., Assoc. of British Neurologists; Hon. Mem., Aust. Assoc. of Neurologists; Hunterian Prof., Royal College of Surgeons, 1952; Pres., Section of Neurology, Royal Society of Medicine, 1965–66; Visiting Prof., University of California, San Francisco, 1954; Doyne Meml Lectr, Oxford Ophthalmological Congress, 1969. Neurologist, British European Airways; Vice-Pres., Newspaper Press Fund. *Publications:* contributions to medical literature. *Recreations:* walking, music, country life. *Address:* 45 Lanchester Road, Highgate N6 4SX.

MEADWAY, (Richard) John, PhD; Head of Overseas Trade Division 2, Department of Trade and Industry, since 1989; *b* 30 Dec. 1944; *s* of late Norman Pardey Meadway and of Constance Meadway; *m* 1968, Jeanette Valerie Partis; two *d*. *Educ:* Collyer's Sch., Horsham; Peterhouse, Cambridge (MA NatScis); Edinburgh Univ. (PhD); Oxford Univ. (MA). Asst Principal, Min. of Technology, 1970; Private Secretary: to Minister for Trade and Consumer Affairs, 1973; to Sec. of State for Prices and Consumer Protection, 1974; to the Prime Minister, 1976–78; Asst Sec., 1979, Under Sec., 1989, Dept of Trade, later DTI. *Publications:* papers on the amino-acid sequences of proteins. *Recreations:* reading, travel. *Address:* c/o Department of Trade and Industry, 123 Victoria Street, SW1E 6RB. *Club:* Reform.

MEAGER, Michael Anthony, ARIBA; Director, Isle of Jura Mill Co. Ltd, since 1991; *b* 15 Feb. 1931; *s* of late Arthur Pattison Meager and Dora Edith Meager (*née* Greeves); *m* 1954, Val Cranmer Benson, *d* of late H. C. Benson; two *s* one *d*. *Educ:* Royal Naval Coll., Dartmouth; Clacton County High Sch.; Architectural Assoc. Sch. of Architecture. ARIBA 1955; AADip 1956. Architectural Asst, Moiret & Wood, 1954–55. National Service, RE, 1955–57: commnd 1956, served Cyprus, 1956–57. Architect, Hammett & Norton, 1957–58; HMOCS, Kenya, 1958–63: Dist Officer, Central Province, 1958–61; Asst Sec., Min. of Lands, Surveys and Town Planning, Nairobi, 1961–63; Architect: James Ralph, 1963–64; Tripe & Wakeham, 1964–66; Department of Health (formerly MoH and DHSS), 1966–91: Main Grade Architect, 1966–67; Prin. Arch., 1967–70; Suptg Arch., 1970–72; Asst Chief Arch., 1972–86; Chief Arch., 1986–88; Dir of Health Building, 1988–89; Dir of Estates, 1989–91, retd. *Recreations:* boats, walking, listening to music.

MEAKIN, Wilfred, CB 1982; CEng, FIMechE; defence systems consultant (W. M. Associates); Executive Director, Royal Ordnance plc, 1986; Chairman, Royal Ordnance Inc., 1986; *b* 1925. *Educ:* engineering apprenticeship in industry. Served War of 1939–45, RN. Technical Asst, ROF, Maltby, 1951; posts in ROF and former Inspectorate of Armaments; Asst Dir, ROF, Blackburn, 1966–72; Dir, ROF, Birtley, 1972–75; Dir, ROF Leeds, during 1975; Dir-Gen., Ordnance Factories (Weapons and Fighting Vehicles), 1975–79; Chief Exec. and Dep. Chm., Bd of ROF, later Royal Ordnance plc, 1979–86. Hon. CGIA.

MEALE, (Joseph) Alan; MP (Lab) Mansfield, since 1987; *b* 31 July 1949; *s* of Albert Henry and Elizabeth Meale; *m* 1983, Diana Gilhespy; one *s* one *d*. *Educ:* St Joseph's RC School; Ruskin College, Oxford. Seaman, British Merchant Navy, 1964–68; engineering worker, 1968–75; Nat. Employment Develt Officer, NACRO, 1977–80; Asst (Personal Research) to Gen. Sec., ASLEF, 1980–83; Parly and Political Advisor to Michael Meacher, MP, 1983–87. Mem., Select Cttee on European Legislation, 1987–89, on Home Affairs, 1989–; Treas., Parly All Party Football Gp, 1989; Sec., Parly All Party Myalgic Encephmyolitis Gp. Vice Chair, PLP Employment Gp, 1987–. Mem., MSF Parly Cttee. *Recreations:* reading, writing. *Address:* 2 Westhill Way, Mansfield, Notts NG18 1TS. *T:* Mansfield (0623) 660531; House of Commons, SW1A 0AA. *T:* 071–219 4159. *Clubs:* Labour, Woodhouse Working Men's, Bellamy Road Working Men's (Mansfield).

MEANEY, Sir Patrick (Michael), Kt 1981; Chairman: The Rank Organisation Plc, since 1983 (Director since 1979); A. Kershaw and Sons PLC, since 1983; Mecca Leisure Group, since 1990; Deputy Chairman: Midland Bank, since 1984 (Director, since 1979); Horserace Betting Levy Board, since 1985; *b* 6 May 1925; *m* Mary June Kearney; one *s*. *Educ:* Wimbledon College; Northern Polytechnic. HM Forces, 1941–47. Joined Thomas Tilling Ltd, 1951; Dir 1961, Man. Dir and Chief Exec. 1973–83. Director: Cable and Wireless PLC, 1978–84; ICI PLC, 1981–; Metropolitan and Country Racecourse Mgt Hldgs Ltd, 1985–; Racecourse Technical Services Ltd, 1985–; MEPC PLC, 1986–; Tarmac PLC, 1990–; Member, Internat. Adv. Board: WEF Foundn, 1979–; CRH PLC (formerly Cement Roadstone), 1985–. Member Council: British North American Cttee and Res. Assoc., 1979–90; CBI, 1979–; London Chamber of Commerce and Industry, 1977–82; RSA, 1987–; BESO, 1987–; Stock Exchange Listed Cos Adv. Cttee, 1987–; President's Cttee, Advertising Assoc., 1987–; Pres., Chartered Inst. of Marketing (formerly Inst. of Marketing), 1981–; Chm., Govt Review Cttee on Harland & Wolff, 1980; Mem., Conference Bd, 1982–87. CBIM 1976; FCIM (FInstM 1981; Pres., 1981–); FRSA 1976. *Recreations:* sport, music, education. *Address:* Harefield House, Sandridge, Herts AL4 9EG. *T:* (office) 071–706 1111. *Clubs:* Harlequins, British Sportsman's.

MEARS, Dr Adrian Leonard; Director (C), Electronics Division, Defence Research Agency, since 1991; *b* 27 May 1944; *s* of Leonard Mears and Marjorie (*née* Isaac); *m* 1969, Barbara Bayne; two *s*. *Educ:* Highgate Sch.; Christ Church, Oxford (DPhil, MA). Res. Associate, Univ. of Md, USA, 1969–71; joined RRE (later Royal Signals and Radar Establishment), 1971: worked on display technology, optoelectronics and lasers, 1971–81; Hd, Signals Processing, 1981–86; Dir of Science (Comd, Control, Communications and Inf. Systems), MoD, 1987–89; Dep. Dir, RSRE, 1990–91. *Recreations:* walking, DIY, music. *Address:* DRA Electronics Division, RSRE, St Andrew's Road, Malvern, Worcs WR14 3PS. *T:* Malvern (0684) 894468.

MEARS, Rt. Rev. John Cledan; *see* Bangor, Bishop of.

MEATH, 14th Earl of, *cr* 1627; **Anthony Windham Normand Brabazon;** Baron Ardee, Ireland, 1616; Baron Chaworth, of Eaton Hall, Co. Hereford, UK, 1831; late Major Grenadier Guards; *b* 3 Nov. 1910; *o s* of 13th Earl of Meath, CB, CBE and Lady Aileen Wyndham-Quin (*d* 1962), *d* of 4th Earl of Dunraven; *S* father 1949; *m* 1940, Elizabeth Mary, *d* of late Capt. Geoffrey Bowlby, Royal Horse Guards, and Hon. Mrs Geoffrey Bowlby, CVO; two *s* two *d*. *Educ:* Eton; RMC Sandhurst. Joined Grenadier Guards, 1930. ADC to Governor of Bengal, 1936; Capt., 1938; served War of 1939–45, Grenadier Guards (wounded, Italy, 1943); Major, 1941; retired, 1946. *Heir: s* Lord Ardee, *qv*. *Address:* Killruddery, Bray, Co. Wicklow, Ireland.

MEATH, Bishop of, (RC), since 1990; **Most Rev. Michael Smith;** *b* 6 June 1940; *s* of John Smith and Bridget Fagan. *Educ:* Gilson Endowed Sch., Oldcastle; St Finian's Coll., Mullingar; Lateran Univ., Rome (DCL 1966). Ordained priest, 1963; Curate, Clonmellon, 1967–68; Chaplain: St Loman's Hosp., 1968–74; Sacred Heart Hosp., 1975–84; Auxiliary Bp of Meath, 1984–88; Coadjutor Bp of Meath, 1988–90. Diocesan Sec., dio. of Meath, 1968–84; Sec., Irish Bishops' Conf., 1984– (Asst Sec., 1970–84). *Recreations:* golf, walking. *Address:* Bishop's House, Dublin Road, Mullingar, Co. Westmeath, Ireland. *T:* Mullingar (044) 48841, 42038, *Fax:* Mullingar (044) 43020.

MEATH AND KILDARE, Bishop of, since 1985; **Most Rev. Walton Newcombe Francis Empey;** *b* 26 Oct. 1934; *m* 1960, Louise E. Hall; three *s* one *d*. *Educ:* Portora Royal School and Trinity College, Dublin. Curate Assistant, Glenageary, Dublin, 1958–60; Parish Priest, Grand Falls, NB, Canada, 1960–63; Parish Priest, Edmundston, NB, 1963–66; Incumbent, Stradbally, Co. Laois, Ireland, 1966–71; Dean of St Mary's Cathedral and Rector, Limerick City Parish, 1971–81; Bishop of Limerick and Killaloe, 1981–85. *Recreations:* reading, fishing and walking. *Address:* Moyglare, Maynooth, Co. Kildare, Ireland.

MEDAWAR, Nicholas Antoine Macbeth; QC 1984; **His Honour Judge Medawar;** a Circuit Judge, since 1987; *b* 25 April 1933; *e s* of Antoine Medawar and Innes (*née* Macbeth); *m* 1st, 1962, Joyce Catherine (*née* Crosland-Boyle) (marr. diss.); one *s* (one *d* decd); 2nd, 1977, Caroline Mary, *d* of Harry Samuel Collins, of Nottingham and Buckley. *Educ:* Keswick School; Trinity College, Dublin. BA Mod., LLB. Called to the Bar, Gray's Inn, 1957. Nat. Service, RASC, 1957–59, 2nd Lieut. A Recorder of the Crown Court, 1985–87. A Legal Assessor, Gen. Optical Council, 1984–87. *Recreations:* skittles, walking, mathematical diversions. *Address:* 2/11 Wedderburn Road, Hampstead, NW3 5QS. *T:* 01–794 0876; 4 Paper Buildings, Temple, EC4Y 7EX.

MEDD, Patrick William, OBE 1962; QC 1973; **His Honour Judge Medd;** a Circuit Judge, since 1981; President, Value Added Tax Tribunals, since 1988; *b* 26 May 1919; *s* of E. N. Medd; *m* 1st, 1945, Jeananne Spence Powell (marr. diss.); three *d*; 2nd, 1971, Elizabeth Spinks D'Albuquerque. *Educ:* Uppingham Sch.; Selwyn Coll., Cambridge. Served in Army, 1940–46, S Staffs Regt and E African Artillery, Major. Called to Bar, Middle Temple, 1947, Bencher 1969; Mem. Gen. Council of the Bar, 1965–67. Dep. Chm., Shropshire QS, 1967–71; Jun. Counsel to Comrs of Inland Revenue, 1968–73; Recorder of Abingdon, 1964–71 (Hon. Recorder, 1972–); a Recorder of the Crown Court, 1972–81. Chm., Bd of Referees, and Finance Act 1960 Tribunal, 1978–; UK rep., panel of arbitrators, Internat. Centre for Settlement of Investment Disputes, 1979–87; Co-Pres., Nat. Reference Tribunal for Coalmining Ind., 1985–; Special Comr of Income Tax, 1986– (Presiding Special Comr, 1990–). *Publications:* (jtly) The Rule of Law, 1955; (jtly) Murder, 1956; (jtly) A Giant's Strength, 1958; Romilly, 1968. *Recreation:* gardening. *Address:* c/o The Crown Court, Oxford.

MEDHURST, Brian; Managing Director (International Division), Prudential Corporation plc, since 1985; *b* 18 March 1935; *s* of late Eric Gilbert Medhurst and Bertha May (*née* Kinggett); *m* 1960, Patricia Anne Beer; two *s* one *d*. *Educ:* Godalming Grammar Sch.; Trinity Coll., Cambridge (MA). FIA 1962 (Mem. Council, 1982–87). Joined Prudential Assurance Co. Ltd, 1958; Deputy Investment Manager, 1972; Investment Manager, 1975; Jt Chief Investment Manager, 1981; Gen. Manager, 1982. *Recreations:* squash, golf, piano duets, tree felling. *Address:* Longacre, Fitzroy Road, Fleet, Hants GU13 8JJ. *T:* Fleet (0252) 614159. *Clubs:* North Hants Golf; Royal Aldershot Officers'.

MEDLEY, (Charles) Robert (Owen), CBE 1982; RA 1986; Painter and Theatrical Designer; Chairman, Faculty of Painting, British School at Rome, 1966–77; *b* 19 Dec. 1905; *s* of late C. D. Medley, and A. G. Owen. *Educ:* Gresham's Sch., Holt. Studied art in London and Paris; Art Dir of the Group Theatre and designed the settings and costumes for plays by T. S. Eliot, W. H. Auden, Christopher Isherwood, Louis Macneice, and Verdi's Othello, Sadler's Wells Theatre, Coppelia, Sadler's Wells Theatre Ballet; exhibited in London and New York World's Fair; pictures bought by: Tate Gallery; V. & A. (collection of drawings); Walker Art Gallery, Liverpool; City Art Gallery, Birmingham, and other provincial galleries; National Gallery of Canada, Ontario; Contemporary Art Society; Arts Council for Festival of Britain, 1951. Official War Artist, 1940. Retrospective Exhibitions: Whitechapel Art Gallery, 1963; Mus. of Modern Art, Oxford, then touring, 1984. Diocletian in Sebastiane (film), 1976. *Publications:* (illustr.) Milton's Samson Agonistes, 1981; Drawn from the Life, a memoir (autobiog.), 1983. *Address:* Charterhouse, Charterhouse Square, EC1M 6AN.

MEDLEY, George Julius, OBE 1989; Director, World Wide Fund for Nature (formerly World Wildlife Fund) (UK), since 1978; *b* 2 Aug. 1930; *s* of late Brig. Edgar Julius Medley, DSO, OBE, MC and Norah Medley (*née* Templer); *m* 1952, Vera Frances Brand; one *s* one *d*. *Educ:* Winchester College; Wye College, Univ. of London. BSc (Hort.). Fruit farmer, 1952–56; Manager, Chemical Dept, Harrisons & Crosfield, Colombo, 1957–63; Dir, Fisons (Ceylon), 1960–63; Tech. Develt Manager, Tata Fison, Bangalore, 1963–64; Gen. Manager Pesticides Div., Tata Fison Industries, Bombay, 1964–68; Sales Manager, Western Hemisphere, Agrochemicals, Fisons Internat. Div., 1968–69; Overseas Manager, Fisons Agrochemical Div., 1970–71; Dep. Managing Dir, Glaxo Labs, India, 1972–73, Managing Dir, 1973–77. Vice-Pres., Organisation of Pharmaceutical Producers of India, 1974–77; Founder Mem. and Vice-Chm., Inst. of Charity Fundraising Managers, 1983 (Chm., 1984–85); Trustee: Farming and Wildlife Trust, 1984–; Falkland Islands Foundn, 1985–. FBIM; FICFM 1988; FRSA 1989. *Publications:* contrib. to Strategic Planning Soc. Jl. *Recreations:* gardening, DIY. *Address:* Hoddinotts House, Tisbury, Wilts SP3 6QQ. *T:* Tisbury (0747) 870677.

MEDLICOTT, Michael Geoffrey; Chief Executive, British Tourist Authority, since 1986; *b* 2 June 1943; *s* of Geoffrey Henry Medlicott and Beryl Ann Medlicott (*née* Burchell); *m* 1973, Diana Grace Fallaw; one *s* three *d*. *Educ:* Downside School; Lincoln College, Oxford (Scholar; MA). Management Trainee, P&O-Orient Lines, 1965–66; Shipping Asst, Mackinnon, Mackenzie & Co., Bombay, 1966–68, Tokyo, 1968–69; Asst to Management, P&O-Orient Lines, 1969–71; P&O Cruises: Develt Analyst, 1971–73; Asst Fleet Manager, 1973–75; Gen. Manager, Fleet, 1975–80; Gen. Manager, Europe, 1980–83; Dir, Europe, 1983–86; Man. Dir, Swan Hellenic, 1983–86; Man. Dir, P&O Air Holidays, 1980–86; Dir, P&O Travel, 1980–84. Member Council of Management: Passenger Shipping Assoc., 1983–86; Heritage of London Trust, 1987–; Mem. of Council and of Policy Adv. Bd, Tidy Britain Gp, 1988–. Memer: Adv. Panel, Languages Lead Body, Dept of Employment, 1990–; Adv. Council, Univ. of Surrey Tourist Dept, 1991–. Trustee, British Travel & Educnl Trust, 1986–. FRSA 1986. *Publications:* contribs to British West Indies Study Circle Bulletin, 1970–. *Recreations:* philately, theatre, gardening, tennis. *Address:* British Tourist Authority, Thames Tower, Blacks Road, W6 9EL. *T:* 081-846 9000.

MEDLYCOTT, Sir Mervyn (Tregonwell), 9th Bt *cr* 1808, of Ven House, Somerset; *b* 20 Feb. 1947; *s* of Thomas Anthony Hutchings Medlycott (*d* 1970) (2nd *s* of 7th Bt) and of Mrs Cecilia Mary Medlycott, Cowleaze, Edmondsham, Dorset, *d* of late Major Cecil Harold Eden; *S* uncle, 1986. Genealogist; FSG 1990; Member: AGRA; HHA; Pres., Somerset and Dorset Family History Soc., 1986– (Founder and Hon. Sec., 1975–77; Chm., 1977–84; Vice-Pres., 1984–86). *Heir:* none. *Address:* The Manor House, Sandford Orcas, Sherborne, Dorset DT9 4SB. *T:* Corton Denham (096322) 206.

MEDWAY, Lord; John Jason Gathorne-Hardy; student; *b* 26 Oct. 1968; *s* and *heir* of 5th Earl of Cranbrook, *qv*. *Educ:* Woodbridge Sch., Suffolk; Pembroke Coll., Oxford. *Recreations:* natural history, drawing, photography. *Address:* 7 Woodfall Street, Chelsea, SW3 4DJ.

MEDWIN, Robert Joseph G.; *see* Gardner-Medwin.

MEECHIE, Brig. Helen Guild, CBE 1986; Deputy Director General, Personal Services, Ministry of Defence, 1990–91, retired; *b* 19 Jan. 1938; *d* of John Strachan and Robina Guild Meechie. *Educ:* Morgan Academy, Dundee; St Andrew's University (MA). Commissioned 1960; served in UK, Cyprus and Hong Kong, 1961–76, in UK and Germany, 1977–82; Dir, WRAC, 1982–86; Mem., RCDS, 1987; Dir, Army Service Conditions, MoD, 1988–90. Hon. ADC to the Queen, 1982–86; ADC to the Queen, 1986. Hon. Col, Tayforth Univs OTC, 1986–. Mem. Council, Union Jack Club, 1989–. Gov., Royal Soldiers' Daughters' Sch., 1984–. Freeman, City of London, 1983. CBIM 1986. Hon. LLD Dundee, 1986. *Recreations:* golf, gardening, travel. *Address:* c/o Clydesdale Bank, 31 St James's Street, SW1A 1HW.

MEEK, Brian Alexander, OBE 1982; JP; Deputy Chairman, Livingston Development Corporation, since 1986; Director, Capital Publicity Ltd, since 1987; *b* 8 Feb. 1939; *s* of Walter Harold Meek and Elsbeth Dearden Meek; *m* 1st, 1962, Glenda (*née* Smith) (marr. diss. 1983); one *s* one *d*; 2nd, 1983, Frances (*née* Horsburgh). *Educ:* Royal High Sch. of Edinburgh; Edinburgh Commercial Coll. Sub-editor, The Scotsman and Edinburgh Evening Dispatch, 1958–63; Features and Leader Writer, Scottish Daily Express, 1963–74; Rugby Football Correspondent, Scottish Daily Express and Sunday Express, 1974–86; Political Columnist, Glasgow Herald, 1986–. Councillor: Edinburgh Corp., 1969–74; Edinburgh Dist Council, 1974–82 (Chm., Recreation Cttee, 1974–77); Lothian Regional Council, 1974– (Leader, Conservative Opposition, 1974–82, 1986–90; Convener and Leader of the Admin, 1982–86). Vice-Pres., Scottish Cons. and Unionist Assoc., 1989–. Magistrate, Edinburgh, 1971, JP 1974. *Recreations:* golf, theatre, cinema, travel. *Address:* Lothian Regional Chambers, Parliament Square, Edinburgh EH1 1TT. *T:* 031–229 9292. *Club:* Caledonian (Edinburgh).

MEEK, Charles Innes, CMG 1961; Chief Executive, 1962–81, Chairman, 1973–81, White Fish Authority, retired; *b* 27 June 1920; *er s* of late Dr C. K. Meek; *m* 1947, Nona Corry Hurford; two *s* one *d*. *Educ:* King's Sch., Canterbury; Magdalen Coll., Oxford (MA). Demyship, Magdalen Coll., Oxford, 1939. Served in Army, 1940–41; District Officer, Tanganyika, 1941; Principal Asst Sec., Tanganyika, 1958; Permanent Sec., Chief Secretary's Office, 1959; Permanent Sec. to Prime Minister, Sec. to Cabinet, 1960; Government Dir, Williamson Diamonds; Head of the Civil Service, Tanganyika, 1961–62, retd. FRSA 1969. *Publications:* occasional articles in Journal of African Administration, etc. *Recreations:* travel, Spectator crossword. *Address:* Mariteau Cottage, German Street, Winchelsea, E Sussex TN36 4ES. *T:* Rye (0797) 226408. *Club:* Royal Over-Seas League.

MEEK, Prof. John Millar, CBE 1975; DEng; FEng 1976; FInstP; FIEE; David Jardine Professor of Electrical Engineering, University of Liverpool, 1946–78; Public Orator, 1973–76, and Pro-Vice-Chancellor, 1974–77, University of Liverpool; *b* Wallasey, 21 Dec. 1912; *s* of Alexander Meek and Edith Montgomery; *m* 1942, Marjorie, *d* of Bernard Ingleby; two *d*. *Educ:* Monkton Combe Sch.; University of Liverpool. College Apprentice, Metropolitan-Vickers Electrical Co. Ltd, 1934–36; Research Engineer, Metropolitan-Vickers Electrical Co. Ltd, 1936–38, 1940–46. Commonwealth Fund Research Fellow, Physics Dept, University of California, Berkeley, 1938–40. Mem. of Council, IEE, 1945–48, 1960–63 (Vice-Pres. 1964–68, Pres., 1968–69), Faraday Medal, 1975. Mem., IBA (formerly ITA), 1969–74. Hon. DSc Salford, 1971. *Publications:* The Mechanism of the Electric Spark (with L. B. Loeb), 1941; Electrical Breakdown of Gases (with J. D. Craggs), 1953, new edn 1978; High Voltage Laboratory Technique (with J. D. Craggs), 1954; papers in various scientific journals concerning research on electrical discharges in gases. *Recreations:* golf, gardening, theatre. *Address:* 4 The Kirklands, West Kirby, Merseyside L48 7HW. *T:* 051–625 5850.

MEEK, Marshall, CBE 1989; RDI 1986; FEng 1990; FRINA; FIMarE; President, Royal Institution of Naval Architects, since 1990 (Vice President, 1979–90); Consultant, British Maritime Technology, 1988–89 (Deputy Chairman, 1985–86; Director, 1986–88); *b* 22 April 1925; *s* of Marshall Meek and Grace R. Smith; *m* 1957, Elfrida M. Cox; three *d*. *Educ:* Bell Baxter School, Cupar; Glasgow University (BSc). Caledon Shipbuilding Co., 1942–49; Asst Naval Architect, BSRA, 1949–53; Naval Architect, Ocean Fleets, 1953–79 (Dir, 1964–79); Head of Ship Technology, British Shipbuilders, 1979–84; Managing Dir, National Maritime Inst., 1984–85. Visiting Professor in Naval Architecture: Strathclyde Univ., 1972–83; UCL, 1983–86. Mem., Lloyds Register of Shipping Technical Cttee, 1979–. Chm., Defence Scientific Adv. Council, Marine Technology Bd, 1984–88. Pres., NE Coast Inst. of Engrs and Shipbuilders, 1984–86. Chm., Northumberland Br., Gideons International in UK. JP City of Liverpool, 1977–79. FRSA. *Publications:* numerous papers to RINA and other marine jls. *Recreations:* gardening, reading. *Address:* Redstacks, Tranwell Woods, Morpeth, Northumberland NE61 6AG. *Club:* Caledonian.

MEERES, Norman Victor, CB 1963; Under-Secretary, Ministry of Defence, 1971–73, retired; *b* 1 Feb. 1913; *m* 1938, Elizabeth Powys Fowler; two *s* one *d*. *Educ:* Sloane Sch., Chelsea; Magdalene Coll., Cambridge. Asst Principal, Air Ministry, 1935; Principal, 1940, Asst Sec., 1944, Ministry of Aircraft Prod.; Asst Sec., Min. of Supply, 1946; Under Secretary: Min. of Supply, 1956; Min. of Aviation, 1959–67; seconded to Dipl. Service in Australia, with title Minister (Defence Research and Civil Aviation), 1965–68; Under-Sec., Min. of Technology, 1969–70. ARCM (piano teaching), 1974. *Recreations:* music, lawn tennis. *Address:* 89 Grove Way, Esher, Surrey KT10 8HF. *T:* 081–398 1639.

MEESE, Edwin, III; lawyer; Distinguished Fellow, Heritage Foundation, Washington, since 1988; Distinguished Visiting Fellow, Hoover Institution, Stanford University, Calif, since 1988; *b* Oakland, Calif, 1931; *s* of Edwin Meese Jr and Leone Meese; *m* 1958, Ursula Herrick; one *s* one *d* (and one *s* decd). *Educ:* Oakland High Sch.; Yale Univ. (BA 1953); Univ. of Calif at Berkeley (JD 1958). Dep. Dist Attorney, Alameda County, 1959–67; Sec. of Legal Affairs to Gov. of Calif, Ronald Reagan, 1967–69; Exec. Assistant and C of S to Gov. of Calif, 1969–75; Vice-Pres., Rohr Industries, 1975–76; Attorney at Law, 1976–80; Dir, Center for Criminal Justice Policy and Management, Univ. of San Diego, 1977–81; Prof. of Law, Univ. of San Diego Law Sch., 1978–81; Counsellor to Pres. of USA, 1981–85; Attorney Gen. of USA, 1985–88. Hon. LLD: Delaware Law Sch.; Widener Univ.; Univ. of San Diego; Valparaiso Univ.; California Lutheran Coll.; Universidad Francisco Marroquin, Guatemala. *Publications*: contribs to professional jls. *Address*: The Heritage Foundation, 214 Massachusetts Avenue, NE, Washington, DC 20002, USA.

MEGAHEY, Leslie; writer, director, television producer; *b* 22 Dec. 1944; *s* of Rev. Thomas and Beatrice Megahey. *Educ*: King Edward VI Grammar Sch., Lichfield; Pembroke Coll., Oxford. BBC general trainee, 1965; radio drama, script editor, producer, 1967; director, producer, TV arts series, 1968–; Exec. Producer, Arena, 1978–79; Editor, Omnibus, 1979–81, Co-Editor, 1985–87; Head of Music and Arts, BBC TV, 1988–91; other *television*: The RKO Story; Artists and Models; The Orson Welles Story; numerous drama-documentaries; *films*: Schalcken the Painter, 1979; Cariani and the Courtesans, 1987; Duke Bluebeard's Castle (filmed opera), 1988. Mem., Arts Council Adv. Panel, Film and TV, 1985–89. Awards: BAFTA, 1980; Prague, 1975; Asolo, 1985; NY, 1987; Banff, 1987; Royal Philharmonic, 1989; Prix Italia, 1989. *Address*: 3 Holly Villas, Wellesley Avenue, W6.

MEGAHY, Thomas; Member (Lab) SW Yorkshire, European Parliament, since 1979; *b* 16 July 1929; *s* of Samuel and Mary Megahy; *m* 1954, Jean (*née* Renshaw); three *s. Educ*: Wishaw High Sch.; Ruskin Coll., Oxford, 1953–55; College of Educn (Technical), Huddersfield, 1955–56 and 1968–69; London Univ. (external student), 1959–63. BScEcon London; DipEcon and PolSci Oxon; DipFE Leeds. Left school at 14 to work on railway; National Service, RN, 1947–49; railway signalman, 1950–53. Lecturer: Rotherham Coll. of Technology, 1956–59; Huddersfield Technical Coll., 1960–65; Park Lane Coll., Leeds, 1965–79. European Parliament: Vice Pres., 1987–89; Dep. Leader, British Labour Group of MEPs, 1985–87; Member: Social Affairs Cttee, 1984–. Active member of Labour Party, 1950–; Chm., Scottish Labour League of Youth; Executive Mem., Dewsbury CLP, 1962–. Councillor, Mirfield UDC, 1963–74; Leader, Kirklees Metropolitan Borough Council, 1973–76; Opposition Leader, 1976–78. Member, Yorks and Humberside REPC, 1974–77; Vice-President: AMA, 1979–; Yorks and Humberside Develt Assoc., 1981–. *Address*: 6 Lady Heton Grove, Mirfield, West Yorks WF14 9DY. *T*: Mirfield (0924) 492680.

MEGARRY, Rt. Hon. Sir Robert (Edgar), Kt 1967; PC 1978; FBA 1970; a Judge of the Chancery Division of the High Court of Justice, 1967–76; the Vice-Chancellor: of that Division, 1976–81; of the Supreme Court, 1982–85; *b* 1 June 1910; *e s* of late Robert Lindsay Megarry, OBE, MA, LLB, Belfast, and of late Irene, *d* of Maj.-Gen. E. G. Clark; *m* 1936, Iris, *e d* of late Elias Davies, Neath, Glam; three *d. Educ*: Lancing Coll.; Trinity Hall, Cambridge (Hon. Fellow, 1973). MA, LLD (Cantab); Music Critic, Varsity, 1930–32; Solicitor, 1935–41; taught for Bar and Solicitors' exams, 1935–39; Mem., Faculty of Law, Cambridge Univ., 1939–40; Certificate of Honour, and called to Bar, Lincoln's Inn, 1944, in practice, 1946–67; QC 1956–67; Bencher, Lincoln's Inn, 1962, Treasurer 1981. Principal, 1940–44, and Asst Sec., 1944–46, Min. of Supply; Book Review Editor and Asst Ed., Law Quarterly Review, 1944–67; Dir of Law Society's Refresher Courses, 1944–47; Sub-Lector, Trinity Coll., Cambridge, 1945–46; Asst Reader, 1946–51, Reader, 1951–67, Hon. Reader, 1967–71 in Equity in the Inns of Court (Council of Legal Educn); Member: Gen. Council of the Bar, 1948–52; Lord Chancellor's Law Reform Cttee, 1952–73; Senate of Inns of Court and Bar, 1966–70, 1980–82; Adv. Council on Public Records, 1980–85; Consultant to BBC for Law in Action series, 1953–66; Chairman: Notting Hill Housing Trust, 1967–68; Bd of Studies, and Vice-Chm., Council of Legal Educn, 1969–71; Friends of Lancing Chapel, 1969–; Incorporated Council of Law Reporting, 1972–87; Comparative Law Sect., British Inst. of Internat. and Comp. Law, 1977–89; President: Soc. of Public Teachers of Law, 1965–66; Lancing Club, 1974–; Selden Soc., 1976–79. Visiting Professor: New York Univ. Sch. of Law, 1960–61; Osgoode Hall Law Sch., Toronto, 1964; Regents' Prof., UCLA, 1983; Lectures: John F. Sonnett, Fordham Univ., 1982; Tyrrell Williams, Washington Univ., St Louis, 1983; Leon Ladner, Univ. of British Columbia, 1984. Visitor: Essex Univ., 1983–90; Clare Hall, Cambridge, 1984–89. Hon. LLD: Hull, 1963; Nottingham, 1979; Law Soc. of Upper Canada (Osgoode Hall), 1982; London, 1988; DU Essex, 1991. Hon. Life Member: Canadian Bar Assoc., 1971; Amer. Law Inst., 1985. *Publications*: The Rent Acts, 1939, 11th edn, Vols 1 and 2, 1988, Vol. 3, 1989; A Manual of the Law of Real Property, 1946, 6th edn (ed D. J. Hayton), 1982; Lectures on the Town and Country Planning Act, 1947, 1949; Miscellany-at-Law, 1955; (with Prof. H. W. R. Wade QC) The Law of Real Property, 1957, 5th edn 1984; Lawyer and Litigant in England (Hamlyn Lectures, 1962); Arabinesque-at-Law, 1969; Inns Ancient and Modern, 1972; A Second Miscellany-at-Law, 1973; Editor, Snell's Equity, 23rd edn 1947, 27th edn (with P. V. Baker, QC), 1973; contrib. to legal periodicals. *Recreations*: heterogeneous. *Address*: The Institute of Advanced Legal Studies, 17 Russell Square, WC1B 5DR. *T*: 071–637 1731; 5 Stone Buildings, Lincoln's Inn, WC2A 3XT. *T*: 071–242 8607.

MEGAW, Arthur Hubert Stanley, CBE 1951; MA Cantab; FSA; *b* Dublin, 1910; *s* of late Arthur Stanley Megaw; *m* 1937, Elene Elektra, *d* of late Helias Mangoletsi, Koritsa, Albania; no *c. Educ*: Campbell Coll., Belfast; Peterhouse, Cambridge. Walston Student (University of Cambridge), 1931. Macmillan Student, British School of Archæology at Athens, 1932–33, Asst Dir, 1935–36; Dir of Antiquities, Cyprus, 1936–60; Field Dir, Byzantine Institute, Istanbul, 1961–62; Dir, British Sch. of Archæology, Athens, 1962–68. CStJ 1967. *Publications*: (with A. J. B. Wace) Hermopolis Magna-Ashmunein, Alexandria, 1959; (with E. J. W. Hawkins) The Church of the Panagia Kanakariá in Cyprus, its Mosaics and Frescoes, 1977; various papers in archæological journals. *Recreation*: armchair travel. *Address*: 27 Perrin's Walk, NW3; PO Box 132, Paphos, Cyprus.

MEGAW, Rt. Hon. Sir John, PC 1969; Kt 1961; CBE 1956; TD 1951; a Lord Justice of Appeal, 1969–80; *b* 16 Sept. 1909; 2nd *s* of late Hon. Mr Justice Megaw, Belfast; *m* 1938, Eleanor Grace Chapman; one *s* two *d. Educ*: Royal Academical Institution, Belfast; St John's Coll., Cambridge Univ. (open schol. in classics; Hon. Fellow, 1967); Harvard Univ. Law Sch. (Choate Fellowship). Served War, 1939–45; Col, RA. Barrister-at-Law, Gray's Inn, 1934 (Certificate of Honour, Bar Final exam.); Bencher, 1958; Treasurer, 1976; QC 1953; QC (N Ire.) 1954; Recorder of Middlesbrough, 1957–61; Judge of the High Court of Justice, Queen's Bench Div., 1961–69; Pres., Restrictive Practices Court, 1962–68. Chm., Cttee of Inquiry into Civil Service Pay, 1981–82. Visitor: New Univ. of Ulster, 1976; Univ. of Ulster, 1984–89. Hon. LLD Queen's Univ., Belfast, 1968; Hon. DSc Ulster, 1990. Legion of Merit (US), 1946. Played Rugby football for Ireland, 1934, 1938.

MEGGESON, Michael; Solicitor and Notary Public; Senior Partner, Warner, Goodman & Streat; a Recorder of the Crown Court, since 1981; *b* 6 Aug. 1930; *s* of Richard Ronald Hornsey Meggeson and Marjorie Meggeson; *m* 1975, Alison Margaret (*née* Wood). *Educ*: Sherborne; Gonville and Caius Coll., Cambridge. BA 1953; MA 1963. Nat. Service, RA, 1949–50; 5th Bn Royal Hampshire Regt, TA, 1950–63. Admitted a Solicitor, 1957; Asst

Solicitor, 1957–59, Partner, 1959–, Warner & Sons, subseq. Warner Goodman & Co., and Warner, Goodman & Streat; Dep. Circuit Judge, 1978–81. Mem. Cttee, Solicitors Staff Pension Fund, 1980– (Chm., Cttee of Management, 1988–); Pres., Hampshire Incorp. Law Soc., 1981–82. *Recreations*: sailing, golf, gardening, music. *Address*: Church Farm, Langrish, near Petersfield, Hants GU32 1RQ. *T*: Petersfield (0730) 4470. *Clubs*: Royal Ocean Racing; Royal Southern Yacht (Hamble); Hayling Island Golf.

MEHAFFEY, Rt. Rev. James; see Derry and Raphoe, Bishop of.

MEHEW, Peter; Assistant Under Secretary of State (Civilian Management) (C), Ministry of Defence, 1983–86, retired; *b* 22 Jan. 1931; *er s* of Oliver Mehew and Elsie (*née* Cox); *m* 1956, Gwyneth Sellors (*d* 1982); one *s* one *d. Educ*: Bishop Wordsworth's Sch.; St Catharine's Coll., Cambridge (BA 1954). Asst Principal, Admiralty, 1954, Principal 1959; Assistant Secretary: CSD, 1970–73; MoD, 1973–80; Dep. Head, UK Delegn to Negotiations on Mutual and Balanced Force Reductions, 1975–77; Asst Under Sec. of State (Sales Admin), MoD, 1981–83. Fellow Commoner, CCC Cambridge, 1980. *Address*: 6 Anderson Road, Salisbury SP1 3DX. *T*: Salisbury (0722) 326364.

MEHROTRA, Prakash Chandra; High Commissioner for India in London, 1984; *b* 26 Feb. 1925; *s* of F. Gopalji Mehrotra and M. Raj Dulari; *m* 1978, Priti Mehrotra; one *s* four *d. Educ*: Allahabad University; arts graduate; Sec., Univ. Union, 1945–46. Business, 1947–76; Mem. Parliament (Rajya Sabha), 1976–81; Sec., Congress (I) Parly Party, 1980–81; Governor, Assam and Meghalaya, 1981–84. *Recreations*: music, sports, gardening. *Club*: India International Centre (New Delhi).

MEHROTRA, Prof. Ram Charan, MSc, DPhil, PhD, DSc; Director, Special Assistance Programme, University of Rajasthan, Jaipur, since 1979 (Professor of Chemistry, 1979–83, now Emeritus); *b* 16 Feb. 1922; *s* of late R. B. Mehrotra; *m* 1944, Suman; one *s* two *d. Educ*: Allahabad Univ. (MSc 1943, DPhil 1948); London Univ. (PhD 1952, DSc 1964). Research Chemist, Vigyan Kala Bhawan, Meerut, 1943–44; Lectr, Allahabad Univ., 1944–54; Reader, Lucknow Univ., 1954–58; Prof., 1958–62, Dean, Faculty of Science, 1959–62, Gorakhpur Univ.; Prof., 1962–74, Dean, Faculty of Science, 1962–65, Chief Rector, 1965–67, Vice-Chancellor, 1968–69 and 1972–73, Rajasthan Univ., Jaipur; Vice-Chancellor, Univ. of Delhi, 1974–79. Mem., UGC, 1982–. President: Chemistry Section, Indian Sci. Congress, 1967; Indian Chemical Soc., 1976–77; Indian Science Congress, 1978–79; Vice-Pres., Indian Nat. Science Acad., 1977–78; Member: Inorganic Chem. Div., IUPAC, 1977–81; Inorganic Nomenclature Commn, 1981–; Convener, Internat. Symposium, Nanjing, 1987. Fedn of Asian Chem. Socs Lecture, Seoul, 1987. Sir S. S. Bhatnagar award, 1965; Fedn of Indian Chambers of Commerce and Industry award, 1975; Prof. T. R. Seshadri's Birthday Commem. Medal, 1976; P. C. Ray Meml Medal, 1981; Golden Jubilee Medal, Inst. of Science, Bombay, 1983; Popularization of Science Award (by the Prime Minister), 1985; J. C. Ghosh Medal, Indian Chem. Soc., 1986; Achievement Award, Inst. of Oriental Phil., 1987; Platinum Jubilee Distinguished Service Award, Indian Science Congress, 1988; Atma Ram Award, for popularization of science, 1989; Dhar Meml Award, Diamond Jubilee Nat. Acad. of Science, 1991; Chatterjee Award, Indian Science Congress Assoc., 1991. Hon. DSc Meerut, 1976. *Publications*: (contrib.) Sol-Gel Science and Technology, 1989; Organometallic Chemistry, 1991; (contrib.) Chemistry, Spectroscopy and Applications of Sol-Gel Glasses, 1991; (contrib.) Chemistry of Silicon and Tin, 1991; treatises on: Metal Alkoxides and Metal β-Diketonates and Allied Derivatives, 1978; Metal Carboxylates, 1983; numerous research papers in nat. and internat. jls of chemistry; continuous references in the chemistry progress reports of Chem. Soc. London. *Recreation*: photography. *Address*: P4, University Campus, Jaipur 302004, India. *T*: (office) 510306; (home) 511476.

MEHTA, Ved (Parkash); writer and journalist; *b* Lahore, 21 March 1934; 2nd *s* of late Dr Amolak Ram Mehta, former Dep. Director General of Health Services, Govt of India, and of Shanti Devi Mehta (*née* Mehra); naturalized citizen of USA, 1975; *m* 1983, Linn Fenimore Cooper, *d* of late William L. Cary; two *d. Educ*: Arkansas Sch. for the Blind; Pomona Coll.; Balliol Coll., Oxford; Harvard Univ. BA Pomona, 1956; BA Hons Mod. Hist. Oxon, 1959, MA 1962; MA Harvard, 1961. Phi Beta Kappa, 1955. Hazen Fellow, 1956–59; Harvard Prize Fellow, 1959–60; Guggenheim Fellow, 1971–72, 1977–78; Ford Foundn Travel and Study Grantee, 1971–76, Public Policy Grantee, 1979–82; MacArthur Prize Fellow, 1982–87; Vis. Schol., Case Western Reserve, 1974; Beatty Lectr, McGill Univ., 1979; Vis. Prof. of Literature, Bard Coll., 1985, 1986; Noble Foundn Vis. Prof. of Art and Cultural History, Sarah Lawrence Coll., 1988; Vis. Fellow (Literature), Balliol Coll., 1988–89; Vis. Prof. of English, NY Univ., 1989–90; Rosenkranz Writer in Residence, Lectr in History, Yale Coll., and Residential Fellow, Berkeley Coll., Yale Univ., 1990–. Staff writer, New Yorker, 1961–. Mem. Council on Foreign Relations, 1979. Mem. Usage Panel, Amer. Heritage Dictionary, 1982. Fellow, NY Inst. for Humanities, 1988–. Hon. DLitt: Pomona, 1972; Bard, 1982; Williams, 1986; DUniv Stirling, 1988. Assoc. of Indians in America Award, 1978; Distinguished Service Award, Asian/Pacific Americans Liby Assoc., 1986; NYC Mayor's Liberty Medal, 1986; Centenary Barrows Award, Pomona Coll., 1987; NY Public Liby Lion Medal, 1990. *Publications*: Face to Face, 1957 (Secondary Educn Annual Book Award, 1958; BBC dramatization on Home prog., serial reading on Light prog., 1958; reissued 1967, 1978; Excerpts, 1981); Walking the Indian Streets, 1960 (rev. edn 1971); Fly and the Fly-Bottle, 1963, 2nd edn 1983 introd. Jasper Griffin; The New Theologian, 1966; Delinquent Chacha (fiction), 1967; Portrait of India, 1970; John Is Easy to Please, 1971; Mahatma Gandhi and His Apostles, 1977; The New India, 1978; Photographs of Chachaji, 1980; A Family Affair: India under three Prime Ministers, 1982; Three Stories of the Raj (fiction), 1986; Continents of Exile (autobiography): Daddyji, 1972; Mamaji, 1979; Vedi, 1982; The Ledge Between the Streams, 1984; Sound-Shadows of the New World, 1986; The Stolen Light, 1989; numerous translations; articles and stories in Amer., British and Indian newspapers and magazines from 1957, inc. Ved Mehta: a bibliography, in Bulletin of Bibliography, March 1985. Writer and commentator of TV documentary film Chachaji: My Poor Relation, PBS, 1978, BBC, 1980 (DuPont Columbia Award for Excellence in Broadcast Journalism, 1977–78). *Recreation*: listening to Indian and Western music. *Address*: c/o The New Yorker, 20 West 43rd Street, New York, NY 10036, USA. *T*: 212–536–5662; (home) 139 East 79th Street, New York, NY 10021, USA; (country) Dark Harbor, Me 04848, USA. *Club*: Century Association (NY) (Trustee, 1973–75).

MEHTA, Zubin; Music Director for life, Israel Philharmonic Orchestra (Musical Adviser, 1962–78); Artistic Director, Maggio Musicale Fiorentino, since 1986; *b* 29 April 1936; *s* of Mehli Mehta; *m* 1st, 1958, Carmen Lasky (marr. diss. 1964); one *s* one *d*; 2nd, 1969, Nancy Kovack. *Educ*: St Xavier's Coll., Bombay; Musikakademie, Vienna. First Concert, Vienna, 1958; first prize internat. comp., Liverpool, 1958; US debut, Philadelphia Orch., 1960; debut with Israel and Vienna Philharmonic Orchs, 1961; apptd Music Director, Montreal Symphony Orch., 1961; European tour with this orch., 1962; guest conducting, major European Orchs, 1962; Music Director: Los Angeles Philharmonic Orch., 1962–78; New York Philharmonic, 1978–91. Opera debut, Montreal, Tosca, 1964; debut Metropolitan Opera, Aida, 1965; operas at Metropolitan incl.: Tosca, Turandot, Otello, Carmen, Mourning becomes Elektra (world première), Trovatore, etc. Tours regularly with New York Philharmonic and Israel Philharmonic Orchs and occasionally with

Vienna Phil. Orch.; regular guest conducting with Vienna Phil., Berlin Phil., Orch. de Paris. Hon. Doctorates: Colgate Univ.; Brooklyn Coll.; Westminster Coll.; Occidental Coll.; Sir George Williams Univ., Canada; Weizmann Inst. of Science, Israel; Tel-Aviv Univ. Holds numerous awards; Padma Bhushan (India), 1967; Commendatore of Italy; Médaille d'Or Verneil, City of Paris, 1984. *Address:* c/o Toni Ceceri, PO Box 353, Ramsey, NJ 07446, USA. *T:* (201) 818 8811.

MEIER, David Benjamin; Metropolitan Stipendiary Magistrate, since 1985; *b* 8 Oct. 1938; *s* of Arnold Meier, PhD and Irma Meier; *m* 1964, Kathleen Lesly Wilton; one *d.* *Educ:* Bury Grammar Sch.; King's College London (LLB). Admitted Law Society, 1964; Solicitor; Assistant Recorder, 1988. Pres., Mental Health Tribunals, 1988; Chm., Juvenile Court, 1988; Chm., Family Panel, 1991. Pres., N Middx Law Soc., 1984–85. *Recreations:* riding, cricket, golf. *Address:* c/o Old Street Magistrates' Court, Old Street, EC1. *T:* 071-739 2373.

MEINERTZHAGEN, Sir Peter, Kt 1980; CMG 1966; General Manager, Commonwealth Development Corporation, 1973–85; Director, Booker Tate Ltd, since 1989; *b* 24 March 1920; *y s* of late Louis Ernest Meinertzhagen, Theberton House, Leiston, Suffolk and Gwynnedd, *d* of Sir William Llewellyn, PRA; *m* 1949, Dido Pretty; one *s* one *d.* *Educ:* Eton. Served Royal Fusiliers, 1940–46 (Croix de Guerre, France, 1944). Alfred Booth & Co., 1946–57; Commonwealth Development Corporation, 1958–85. Member: Council, London Chamber of Commerce, 1968–69; Council, Overseas Develt Inst., 1979–85. *Address:* Mead House, Ramsbury, Wilts SN8 2QP. *T:* Marlborough (0672) 20715. *Club:* Muthaiga Country (Nairobi).

MEINERTZHAGEN, Peter Richard; Chairman, Hoare Govett, since 1991; *s* of late Daniel Meinertzhagen and of Marguerite Meinertzhagen (*née* Leonard); *m* 1967, Nikki Phillips; five *d.* *Educ:* Eton College; Sorbonne. Hoare & Co.: joined 1965; Partner, 1973; Dir, Institutional Sales, 1973–90; Chm., Hoare Govett Corporate Finance, 1990–. *Recreations:* golf, tennis, horse-racing, music. *Address:* 20 Tite Street, SW3 4HZ. *T:* 071–352 6806. *Club:* White's.

MEIRION-JONES, Prof. Gwyn Idris, FSA 1981; author and consultant on historic buildings; *b* 24 Dec. 1933; *e s* of late Maelgwyn Meirion-Jones and Enid Roberts, Manchester; *m* 1961, Monica, *e d* of late George and Marion Havard, Winchester. *Educ:* North Manchester Grammar School; King's College London (BSc, MPhil, PhD). National Service, RAF, 1954–56. Schoolmaster, 1959–68; Lectr in Geography, Kingston Coll. of Technology, 1968; Sir John Cass Coll., later City of London Polytechnic: Sen. Lectr i/c Geography, 1969; Principal Lectr i/c, 1970; Head of Geography, 1970–89; Personal Chair, 1983–89, now Prof. Emeritus; Hon. Research Fellow, 1989–. Leverhulme Research Fellow, 1985–87. British Assoc. for the Advancement of Science: Sec., 1973–78, Recorder, 1978–83, Pres., Sept. 1992–, Section H (Anthropology); Mem. Council, 1977–80; Mem. Gen. Cttee, 1977–83; Ancient Monuments Society: Mem. Council, 1974–79 and 1983–; Hon. Sec., 1976–79; Vice-Pres., 1979–; Editor, 1985–. Mem., Royal Commn on Historical Monuments of England, 1985–; Hon. Pres., Domestic Buildings Res. Gp (Surrey), 1991– (Pres., 1986–91); Mem., Comité Scientifique des Musées du Finistère, 1984–. Editor, Medieval Village Res. Gp, 1978–86. Hon. Corresp. Mem., Soc. Jersiaise, 1980–90 and 1990–; Corresp. Mem., Compagnie des Architectes en Chef des Monuments Historiques, 1989–. Exhibitions: vernacular architecture of Brittany, on tour 1982–89; Architecture vernaculaire en Bretagne (15e–20e siècles), Rennes and tour, 1984–89. *Publications:* La Maison traditionnelle (bibliog.), 1978; The Vernacular Architecture of Brittany, 1982; (with Michael Jones) Aimer les Châteaux de Bretagne, 1991 (trans. English and German); papers in sci., archaeol and ethnol jls. *Recreations:* food, wine, music, walking, swimming. *Address:* City of London Polytechnic, Old Castle Street, E1 7NT. *T:* 071–283 1030; 11 Avondale Road, Fleet, Hants GU13 9BH. *T:* and *Fax:* Fleet (0252) 614300. *Club:* Athenæum.

MEIXNER, Helen Ann Elizabeth, (Mrs J. E. C. Thornton); JP; Director of Libraries, Books and Information Division, British Council, since 1991; *b* 26 May 1941; *d* of Henry Gerard and Valerie Meixner; *m* Jack Edward Clive Thornton, *qv.* *Educ:* Sydney C of E Grammar Sch. for Girls, Darlinghurst; Univ. of Queensland (BA 1961). Teacher, Abbotsleigh Girls' Sch., Wahroonga, 1962; Educn Asst, ABC, 1963–64; joined British Council, 1966; Recruitment Unit, Zagreb Office, Exchanges, Courses, Staff Recruitment, Dir-Gen's and Personnel Depts; Head, Design, Production and Publishing Dept, 1984–86; Dep. Dir, Personnel and Head, Personnel Dept, 1986–91. JP Inner London, 1988. *Recreations:* music, reading, walking, entertaining, travel. *Address:* 131 Dalling Road, W6 0ET. *T:* 081–748 7692.

MELANESIA, Archbishop of, since 1988; **Most Rev. Amos Stanley Waiaru;** Bishop of Central Melanesia, since 1988; *b* 19 April 1944; *s* of late Stanley Qagora and Emma Kaifo; *m* 1976, Mary Marjorie Waiaru (*née* Mwele); one *s* three *d.* *Educ:* Bishop Patteson Theol Coll., Kohimarama, Solomon Is; Pacific Theol Coll., Suva, Fiji Is (DipTh). Tutor, Torgil Training Centre, Vanuatu, 1976; Chaplain, Vureas High School, Vanuatu, 1977–78, Head Master 1979–80; Bishop of Temotu, Solomon Is, 1981–87. Chm., S Pacific Anglican Council, 1991–. *Recreations:* gardening, fishing. *Address:* Bishop's House, PO Box 19, Honiara, Solomon Islands. *T:* (office) 21892, 23630, (home) 22339.

MELANESIA, CENTRAL, Bishop of; *see* Melanesia, Archbishop of.

MELBOURNE, Archbishop of, and Metropolitan of the Province of Victoria, since 1990; **Most Rev. Keith Rayner,** AO 1987; Acting Primate of Australia, since 1989; *b* 22 Nov. 1929; *s* of Sidney and Gladys Rayner, Brisbane; *m* 1963, Audrey Fletcher; one *s* two *d.* *Educ:* C of E Grammar Sch., Brisbane; Univ. of Queensland (BA 1951; PhD 1964). Deacon, 1953; Priest, 1953. Chaplain, St Francis' Theol Coll., Brisbane, 1954; Mem., Brotherhood of St John, Dalby, 1955–58; Vice-Warden, St John's Coll., Brisbane, 1958; Rotary Foundn Fellow, Harvard Univ., 1958–59; Vicar, St Barnabas', Sunnybank, 1959–63; Rector, St Peter's, Wynnum, 1963–69; Bishop of Wangaratta, 1969–75; Archbishop of Adelaide and Metropolitan of South Australia, 1975–90. Pres., Christian Conference of Asia, 1977–81; Chm., International Anglican Theological and Doctrinal Commission, 1980–88. Hon. ThD Aust. Coll. of Theology, 1987. *Recreation:* tennis. *Address:* Bishopscourt, 120 Clarendon Street, East Melbourne, Vic 3002, Australia.

MELBOURNE, Archbishop of, (RC), since 1974; **Most Rev. Thomas Francis Little,** KBE 1977; DD, STD; *b* 30 Nov. 1925; *s* of Gerald Thompson Little and Kathleen McCormack. *Educ:* St Patrick's Coll., Ballarat; Corpus Christi Coll., Werribee; Pontifical Urban Coll., Rome. STD Rome, 1953. Priest 1950; Asst Priest, Carlton, 1953–55; Secretary, Apostolic Deleg. to Aust., NZ and Oceania, 1955–59; Asst Priest, St Patrick's Cathedral, Melbourne, 1959–65; Dean, 1965–70; Episcopal Vicar for Lay Apostolate, 1969; Pastor, St Ambrose, Brunswick, 1971–73; Auxiliary Bishop, Archdiocese of Melbourne, 1972; Bishop, 1973. *Address:* St Patrick's Cathedral, Melbourne, Vic. 3002, Australia. *T:* 667 0377.

MELBOURNE, Assistant Bishops of; *see* Bayton, Rt Rev. J.; Butterss, Rt Rev. R. L.; Grant, Rt Rev. J. A.; Stewart, Rt Rev. J. C.; Wilson, Rt Rev. J. W.

MELCHETT, 4th Baron *cr* 1928; **Peter Robert Henry Mond;** Bt 1910; Executive Director, Greenpeace UK, since 1989 (Chairman, 1986–89); *b* 24 Feb. 1948; *s* of 3rd Baron Melchett and of Sonia Elizabeth (who *m* 2nd, 1984, A. A. Sinclair, *qv*), *er d* of Lt-Col R. H. Graham; *S* father, 1973. *Educ:* Eton; Pembroke Coll., Cambridge (BA); Keele Univ. (MA). Res. Worker, LSE and Addiction Res. Unit, 1973–74. A Lord in Waiting (Govt Whip), 1974–75; Parly Under-Sec. of State, DoI, 1975–76; Minister of State, NI Office, 1976–79. Chm., working party on pop festivals, 1975–76; Chm., Community Industry, 1979–85. Chm., Wildlife Link, 1979–87; Vice-Pres., Ramblers' Assoc., 1984– (Pres., 1981–84). *Address:* House of Lords, SW1.

MELCHIOR-BONNET, Christian; author; Director and founder, since 1946, Historia, Journal de la France; *b* Marseille, 10 April 1904; *s* of Daniel-Joseph Melchior-Bonnet and Geneviève (*née* de Luxer); *m* 1930, Bernardine Paul-Dubois-Taine (*g d* of the historian Taine, herself a historian, author of several historical works, recipient of Grand Prix Gobert of Académie Française); two *s* one *d.* *Educ:* St Jean de Béthune, Versailles; Ecole du Louvre, Faculté de droit de Paris. Secretary to Pierre de Nolhac, de l'Académie française, historian, at Jacquemart-André museum, 1927–36; formerly, Editor-in-Chief, Petit Journal, 1936–45 and Flambeau; Dir, historical and religious series of Editions Flammarion, 1932–46; Literary Dir, Fayard editions, 1946–67; Director of the reviews: Oeuvres Libres, 1946–64; Historia, 1946–; A la Page, 1964–69; Co-dir, Jardin des Arts; Literary Adviser to Nouvelles Littéraires, 1946–70. Privy Chamberlain to every Pope since 1946, incl. Pope John Paul II. Membre du jury: Prix Historia; Prix de la Fondation de France; Prix des Ambassadeurs. Officier de la Légion d'honneur; Commandeur de l'Ordre national du Mérite; Officier des Arts et des Lettres, et décorations étrangères. Prix du Rayonnement, Académie française, 1963. *Publications:* Scènes et portraits historiques de Chateaubriand, 1928; Les Mémoires du Comte Alexandre de Tilly, ancien page de la reine Marie-Antoinette, 1929; Les Mémoires du Cardinal de Retz, 1929; Principes d'action de Salazar, 1956; Le Napoléon de Chateaubriand, 1969; et nombreuses éditions de mémoires historiques. *Address:* 17 Boulevard de Beauséjour, 75016 Paris, France.

MELDRUM, Andrew, CBE 1962 (OBE 1956); KPM; Chief Inspector of Constabulary for Scotland, 1966–69, retired; *b* 22 April 1909; *s* of late Andrew Meldrum, Burntisland, Fife; *m* 1st, 1937, Janet H. (*d* 1987), *d* of late Robert Crooks, Grangemouth; one *s* one *d;* 2nd, 1990, Diana Cicely Meldrum, *d* of late Ernest Cecil Meldrum, Mayfield, Sussex. *Educ:* Burntisland, Fife. Joined Stirlingshire Police, 1927; Deputy Chief Constable, Inverness Burgh, 1943, Chief Constable, 1946; Chief Constable, County of Angus, 1949; Chief Constable of Fife, 1955; Inspector of Constabulary for Scotland, 1965–66. King's Police Medal, 1952. *Recreation:* golf. *Clubs:* Royal Burgess Golfing Society of Edinburgh; Royal Guernsey Golf; Royal Channel Islands Yacht (Guernsey).

MELDRUM, Maj.-Gen. Bruce, CB 1991; OBE 1986; Chief of New Zealand General Staff, since 1989; *b* 15 March 1938; *s* of late Ian Maitland Meldrum and of Vivienne Meldrum; *m* 1960, Janet Louise Boyling; one *s* one *d.* *Educ:* Feilding Agricl High Sch., NZ; RMC Duntroon. Lieut, RNZAC, 1959; Troop Comdr, Queen Alexandra's Regt, 1960–62; RAC Sch. of Tank Technol., UK, 1962–63; Sen. Instructor, then Chief Instructor, Sch. of Armour, Waiouru, 1963–66; OC 1 Armoured Sqdn, 1966–68; with US 11th Armoured Cavalry Regt, S Vietnam, Nov.–Dec. 1966; Staff Officer: Trng Directorate, Army HQ, 1968–69; HQ NZ Force Far East, Singapore, 1969–71; HQ NZ V Force, Saigon, 1971–72; Australian Comd and Staff Coll., 1972; Bde Maj., HQ 1 Inf. Bde, 1972–74; Lt-Col 1974; Staff Officer, HQ Field Force Comd, 1974–76; Dir, Ops and Plans, Army Gen. Staff, 1976–78; Australian JSSC, 1978; Special Projects Officer, 1978–80; Col 1980; Defence Advr, NZ High Commn, Kuala Lumpur, 1980–83; Comdr, Army Trng Gp, 1983–85; rcds, 1985–86; DCGS, 1986–89; Brig. 1987; Maj.-Gen. 1989. *Recreations:* golf, walking, reading. *Address:* 16/32 Hobson Street, Thorndon, Wellington, New Zealand. *T:* (04) 4991915. *Clubs:* Wellington, Wellesley (Wellington, NZ).

MELDRUM, Keith Cameron; Chief Veterinary Officer, Ministry of Agriculture, Fisheries and Food, since 1988; *b* 19 April 1937; *s* of Dr Walter James Meldrum and Mrs Eileen Lydia Meldrum; *m* 1st, 1962, Rosemary Ann (*née* Crawford) (marr. diss. 1980); two *s* one *d;* 2nd, 1982, Vivien Mary (*née* Fisher). *Educ:* Uppingham; Edinburgh Univ. Qualified as veterinary surgeon, 1961; general practice, Scunthorpe, 1961–63; joined MAFF, Oxford, 1963; Divl Vet. Officer, Tolworth, 1972, Leamington Spa, 1975; Dep. Regional Vet. Officer, Nottingham, 1978; Regional Vet. Officer, Tolworth, 1980; Asst Chief Vet. Officer, Tolworth, 1983; Dir of Vet. Field Service, 1986. *Recreations:* competitive target rifle shooting, outdoor activities. *Address:* Ministry of Agriculture, Fisheries and Food, Hook Rise South, Tolworth, Surbiton, Surrey KT6 7NF. *T:* 081–330 8050. *Clubs:* Farmers'; North London Rifle (Bisley).

MELGUND, Viscount; Gilbert Timothy George Lariston Elliot-Murray-Kynynmound; *b* 1 Dec. 1953; *s* and *heir* of 6th Earl of Minto, *qv;* *m* 1983, Diana, *yr d* of Brian Trafford; two *s* (and one *s* decd). *Educ:* Eton; North East London Polytechnic (BSc Hons 1983). ARICS. Lieut, Scots Guards, 1972–76. Mem., Royal Co. of Archers, Queen's Body Guard for Scotland, 1983–. *Heir:* *s* Hon. Gilbert Francis Elliot-Murray-Kynynmound, *b* 15 Aug. 1984. *Club:* White's.

MELHUISH, Michael Ramsay, CMG 1982; HM Diplomatic Service; Ambassador to Thailand, since 1989; *b* 17 March 1932; *s* of late Henry Whitfield Melhuish and Jeanette Ramsay Pender Melhuish; *m* 1961, Stella Phillips; two *s* two *d.* *Educ:* Royal Masonic Sch., Bushey; St John's Coll., Oxford (BA). FO, 1955; MECAS, 1956; Third Sec., Bahrain, 1957; FO, 1959; Second Sec., Singapore, 1961; First Sec. (Commercial) and Consul, Prague, 1963; First Sec. and Head of Chancery, Bahrain, 1966; DSAO (later FCO), 1968; First Sec., Washington, 1970; Counsellor, Amman, 1973; Head of N America Dept, FCO, 1976; Counsellor (Commercial), Warsaw, 1979–82; Ambassador, Kuwait, 1982–85; High Comr, Zimbabwe, 1985–89. *Recreations:* tennis, golf. *Address:* c/o Foreign and Commonwealth Office, SW1A 2AH. *Club:* United Oxford & Cambridge University.

MELIA, Dr Terence Patrick; Chief Inspector, Higher Education, HM Inspectorate of Schools, since 1986; *b* 17 Dec. 1934; *s* of John and Kathleen Melia (*née* Traynor); *m* 1976, Madeline (*née* Carney); one *d.* *Educ:* Sir John Deane's Grammar Sch., Northwich; Leeds Univ. (PhD). CChem, FRSC. Technical Officer, ICI, 1961–64; Lectr, then Sen. Lectr, Salford Univ., 1964–70; Principal, North Lindsey Coll. of Technology, 1970–74; HM Inspector of Schools, 1974–; Regional Staff Inspector, 1982–84; Chief Inspector, Further and Higher Educn, 1985–86. *Publications:* Masers and Lasers, 1967; papers on thermodynamics of polymerisation, thermal properties of polymers, effects of ionizing radiation, chemical thermodynamics, nucleation kinetics, thermal properties of transition metal compounds and gas kinetics. *Recreations:* golf, gardening. *Address:* Department of Education and Science, Sanctuary Buildings, Great Smith Street, SW1P 3BT.

MELINSKY, Rev. Canon (Michael Arthur) Hugh; Principal, Northern Ordination Course, 1978–88; *b* 25 Jan. 1924; *s* of late M. M. Melinsky and Mrs D. M. Melinsky; *m* 1949, Renate (*née* Ruhemann); three *d.* *Educ:* Whitgift Sch., Croydon; Christ's Coll., Cambridge (BA 1947, MA 1949); London Univ. Inst. of Education (TDip 1949); Ripon Hall, Oxford. Asst Master: Normanton Grammar Sch., 1949–52; Lancaster Royal Grammar Sch., 1952–57. Curate: Wimborne Minster, 1957–59; Wareham, 1959–61;

Vicar of St Stephen's, Norwich, 1961–68; Chaplain of Norfolk and Norwich Hosp., 1961–68; Hon. Canon and Canon Missioner of Norwich, 1968–73; Chief Sec., ACCM, 1973–77. Chairman: C of E Commn on Euthanasia, 1972–75; Inst. of Religion and Medicine, 1973–77; Mem., Social Policy Cttee, C of E Bd for Social Responsibilty, 1982–; Mem. Cttee for Theological Educn, ACCM, 1985–88. Hon. Res. Fellow, Dept of Theol Studies, Manchester Univ., 1984. *Publications:* The Modern Reader's Guide to Matthew, 1963; the Modern Reader's Guide to Luke, 1963; Healing Miracles, 1967; (ed) Religion and Medicine, 1970; (ed) Religion and Medicine 2, 1973; Patterns of Ministry, 1974; (ed) On Dying Well, 1975; Foreword to Marriage, 1984. *Address:* 15 Parson's Mead, Norwich, Norfolk NR4 6PG. *T:* Norwich (0603) 55042.

MELLAART, James, FSA; FBA 1980; Lecturer in Anatolian Archaeology, Institute of Archaeology, University of London, since 1964; *b* 14 Nov. 1925; *s* of J. H. J. Mellaart and A. D. Van Der Beek; *m* 1954, Arlette Meryem Cenani; one *s. Educ:* University College, London. BA Hons (Ancient Hist. and Egyptology) 1951. Archaeol field surveys in Anatolia as Scholar and Fellow of British Inst. of Archaeol. at Ankara, 1951–56; excavations at Hacilar, 1957–60; Asst Dir, British Inst. of Archaeol. at Ankara, 1959–61; excavations at Çatal Hüyük, Turkey, 1961–63 and 1965; Foreign Specialist, Lectr at Istanbul Univ., 1961–63. Corresp. Mem., German Archaeol Inst., 1961. *Publications:* Earliest Civilisations of the Near East, 1965; The Chalcolithic and Early Bronze Ages in the Near East and Anatolia, 1966; Çatal Hüyük, a Neolithic Town in Anatolia, 1967; Excavations at Hacilar, 1970; The Neolithic of the Near East, 1975; The Archaeology of Ancient Turkey, 1978; Çatal Hüyük and Anatolian Kilims, 1989; chapters in Cambridge Ancient History; numerous articles in Anatolian Studies, etc. *Recreations:* geology, Turkish ceramics, clan history, Gaelic and classical music, Seljuk art. *Address:* 13 Lichen Court, 79 Queen's Drive, N4 2BH. *T:* 081–802 6984.

MELLANBY, Kenneth, CBE 1954 (OBE 1945); ScD Cantab; ecological consultant and editor; *b* 26 March 1908; *s* of late Emeritus-Professor A. L. Mellanby; *m* 1933, Helen Neilson Dow, MD (marr. diss.); one *d; m* 1948, Jean Copeland, MA, JP; one *s. Educ:* Barnard Castle Sch.; King's Coll., Cambridge (Exhibitioner). Research Worker, London Sch. of Hygiene and Trop. Med., 1930–36 and 1953–55; Wandsworth Fellow, 1933; Sorby Research Fellow of Royal Society of London, 1936; Hon. Lecturer, University of Sheffield; CO (Sqdn Ldr RAFVR) Sheffield Univ. Air Sqdn. Dir Sorby Research Institute, 1941; first Principal, University Coll., Ibadan, Nigeria, 1947–53; Major, RAMC (Specialist in Biological Research), overseas service in N Africa, SE Asia, etc.; Dep. Dir, Scrub Typhus Research Laboratory, SEAC; Reader in Medical Entomology, University of London, 1945–47; Head of Dept of Entomology, Rothamsted Experimental Station, Harpenden, Herts, 1955–61; first Dir, Monks Wood Experimental Station, Huntingdon, 1961–74. Vice-Pres. and Mem. Council, Royal Entomological Soc. of London, 1953–56; Pres. Assoc. for Study of Animal Behaviour, 1957–60; Member: Inter-university Council for Higher Education Overseas, 1960–75; ARC Research Cttee on Toxic Chemicals; Council, and Chm., Tropical Group, Brit. Ecological Soc.; Nat. Exec., Cambs Br., CPRE (also Pres.); Council for Science and Technology Insts, 1976–77 (Chm.); Council for Environmental Science and Engrg, 1976– (Chm., 1981–); Pres., Sect. D (Zoology), 1972, and Sect. X (General), 1973, British Assoc.; Vice-Pres. of the Institute of Biology, 1967, Pres., 1972–73; Vice-Pres., Parly and Scientific Cttee; first Hon. Life Mem., Assoc. for Protection of Rural Australia; Pres., British Isles Bee Breeders' Assoc., 1978–. Hon. Professorial Fellow, University Coll. of S Wales; Hon. Prof. of Biology, Univ. of Leicester. Essex Hall Lectr, 1971. Fellow, NERC. Mem. Editorial Bd, New Naturalist series. Hon. Life Prof., Central London Polytechnic, 1980; DUniv Essex, 1980. Hon. DSc: Ibadan, 1963; Bradford, 1970; Leicester, 1972; Sheffield, 1983. First Charter Award, Inst. of Biology, 1981. *Publications:* Scabies, 1943, new edn 1973; Human Guinea Pigs, 1945, new edn 1973; The Birth of Nigeria's University, 1958, new edn 1975; Pesticides and Pollution, 1967; The Mole, 1971; The Biology of Pollution, 1972; Can Britain Feed Itself?, 1975; Talpa, the story of a mole, 1976; Farming and Wildlife, 1981; (ed) Air Pollution, Acid Rain and the Environment, 1988; Waste and Pollution, 1991; DDT in Perspective, 1990; many scientific papers on insect physiology, ecology, medical and agricultural entomology; ed, Monographs on Biological Subjects; British Editor of Entomologia Experimentalis et Applicata; Chm., Editorial Bd, Environmental Pollution. *Recreation:* austere living. *Address:* 38 Warkworth Street, Cambridge CB1 1ER. *T:* Cambridge (0223) 328733. *Club:* Athenæum.

MELLARS, Paul Anthony, ScD; FBA 1990; Fellow of Corpus Christi College, Cambridge, since 1981; University Reader in Archaeology, Cambridge University, since 1991 (University Lecturer, 1981–91); *b* 29 Oct. 1939; *s* of Herbert and Elaine Mellars; *m* 1969, Anny Chanut. *Educ:* Woodhouse Grammar Sch., Sheffield; Fitzwilliam Coll., Cambridge (Exhibnr; BA 1st Cl. Hons Archaeol. and Anthropol. 1962; MA 1965; PhD 1967; ScD 1988). FSA 1977. Sir James Knott Res. Fellow, Univ. of Newcastle upon Tyne, 1968–70; University of Sheffield: Lectr in Prehistory and Archaeol., 1970–75; Sen. Lectr, 1975–80; Reader, 1980–81. British Academy: Res. Reader, 1989–91; Reckitt Archaeol. Lectr, 1991; Vis. Prof., SUNY (Binghamton), 1974; Vis. Fellow, ANU, 1981; Danish Res. Council Vis. Lectr, Copenhagen and Aarhus Univs, 1985. Pres., Hunter Archaeol. Soc., 1975–80; Chm., Archaeol. Sci. Cttee, Council for British Archaeol., 1980–87. *Publications:* (ed) The Early Postglacial Settlement of Northern Europe, 1976; Excavations of Oronsay, 1987; (ed) Research Priorities of Archaeological Science, 1987; (ed) The Human Revolution, 1989; (ed) The Emergence of Modern Humans, 1990; (ed) Middle Palaeolithic Adaptations in Eurasia, 1991; articles in archaeol. jls. *Recreations:* music, foreign travel. *Address:* 15 Brook Street, Elsworth, Cambs CB3 8HX. *T:* Elsworth (09547) 275; Department of Archaeology, Downing Street, Cambridge CB2 3DZ. *T:* Cambridge (0223) 333520.

MELLERS, Prof. Wilfrid Howard, OBE 1982; DMus; Composer; Professor of Music, University of York, 1964–81, now Emeritus; *b* 26 April 1914; *s* of Percy Wilfrid Mellers and Hilda Maria (*née* Lawrence); *m* 1st, 1940, Vera Muriel (*née* Hobbs) (marr. diss.); 2nd, 1950, Peggy Pauline (*née* Lewis) (marr. diss. 1975); two *d;* 3rd, 1987, Robin Hildyard. *Educ:* Leamington Coll.; Downing Coll., Cambridge. BA Cantab 1939; MA Cantab 1945; DMus Birmingham 1962. FGSM 1982. Supervisor in English and College Lecturer in Music, Downing Coll., Cambridge, 1945–48; Staff Tutor in Music, Extra Mural Dept, University of Birmingham, 1949–60; Visiting Mellon Prof. of Music, University of Pittsburgh, USA, 1960–62; Vis. Prof., City Univ., 1984–. Hon. DPhil City, 1981. *Publications:* Music and Society, 1946; Studies in Contemporary Music, 1948; François Couperin and the French Classical Tradition, 1950, 2nd edn 1987; Music in the Making, 1951; Man and his Music, 1957; Harmonious Meeting, 1964; Music in a New Found Land, 1964; Caliban Reborn: renewal in 20th-century music, 1967 (US), 1968 (GB); Twilight of the Gods: the Beatles in retrospect, 1973; Bach and the Dance of God, 1981; Beethoven and the Voice of God, 1983; A Darker Shade of Pale: a backdrop to Bob Dylan, 1984; Angels of the Night: popular female singers of our time, 1986; The Masks of Orpheus, 1987; Vaughan Williams and the Vision of Albion, 1989; Le Jardin Parfumé: homage to Frederic Mompou, 1990; The Music of Percy Grainger, 1992; *compositions* include: Canticum Incarnations, 1960; Alba in 9 Metamorphoses, 1962; Rose of May, 1964; Life-Cycle, 1967; Yeibichai, 1968; Canticum Resurrectionis, 1968; Natalis Invicti

Solis, 1969; The Word Unborn, 1970; The Ancient Wound, 1970; De Vegetabilis et Animalibus, 1971; Venery for Six Plus, 1971; Sun-flower: the Quaternity of William Blake, 1972–73; The Key of the Kingdom, 1976; Rosae Hermeticae, 1977; Shaman Songs, 1980; The Wellspring of Loves, 1981; Hortus Rosarium, 1986. *Address:* Oliver Sheldon House, 17 Aldwark, York YO1 2BX. *T:* York (0904) 638686.

MELLERSH, Air Vice-Marshal Francis Richard Lee, CB 1977; DFC 1943 and Bar 1944; Air Officer Flying and Officer Training, HQ Training Command, 1974–77; *b* 30 July 1922; *s* of Air Vice-Marshal Sir Francis Mellersh, KBE, AFC; *m* 1967, Elisabeth Nathalie Komaroff; two *s* one *d. Educ:* Winchester House Sch.; Imperial Service College. Joined RAFVR, 1940; Nos 29, 600 and 96 Sqdns, 1941–45; various staff and flying appts, 1946–57; Dirg Staff, RAF Staff Coll., 1957–59; Staff of Chief of Defence Staff, 1959–61; Dep. Dir Ops (F), 1961–63; OC RAF West Raynham, 1965–67; Chief Current Plans, SHAPE, 1967–68; RCDS 1969; SASO, RAF Germany, 1970–72; ACDS (Ops), 1972–74. *Address:* Rother Lea, Lossenham Lane, Newenden, Kent. *Club:* Royal Air Force.

MELLING, Cecil Thomas, CBE 1955; MScTech, CEng, Hon. FIEE, FIMechE, Sen. FInstE, CBIM; *b* Wigan, 12 Dec. 1899; *s* of William and Emma Melling; *m* 1929, Ursula Thorburn Thorburn; two *s* one *d* (and one *s* and one *d* decd). *Educ:* Manchester Central High Sch.; College of Technology, University of Manchester. 2nd Lieut RE 1918. Metropolitan Vickers Electrical Co. Ltd, 1920–34; Yorkshire Electric Power Co., 1934–35; Edmundson's Electricity Corporation Ltd, 1935–43. Borough Electrical Engineer, Luton, 1943–48. Chm., Eastern Electricity Board, 1948–57; Member: British Electricity Authority, 1952–53 and 1957; Electricity Council, 1957–61 (a Dep. Chm., 1961–65); Clean Air Council, 1961–64; Adv. Cttee on R&D, 1961–64. Chm. Utilization Sect., Institution of Electrical Engineers, 1949–50, Vice-Pres., IEE, 1957–62, Pres., 1962–63; Chm. of Council, British Electrical Development Association, 1951–52; Founder-Chm. 1945, and Pres. 1947, Luton Electrical Soc.; Pres. Ipswich & District Electrical Assoc., 1948–57; Chm. of Council, British Electrical and Allied Industries Research Assoc., 1953–55; Pres. Assoc. of Supervising Electrical Engineers, 1952–54; Chm., British Nat. Cttee for Electro-Heat, 1958–68; Mem. Council, BIM, 1961–78; Vice-Pres. Internat. Union for Electro-Heat, 1964–68, Pres., 1968–72; Pres., Manchester Technol. Assoc., 1967; Pres., British Electrotechnical Approvals Bd, 1974–84 (Chm., 1964–73); Chm., Electricity Supply Industry Trg Bd, 1965–68; Vice-Pres., Union of Internat. Engineering Organisations, 1969–75; Pres., Soc. of Retired Chartered Engrs in SE Kent, 1988– (Founder Chm., 1982–84). *Publications:* Light in the East, 1987; contribs to Proc. Engineering Instns and Confs. *Address:* Durham Suite, The Grand, Folkestone CT20 2LR. *Club:* Athenæum.

MELLISH, family name of **Baron Mellish.**

MELLISH, Baron *cr* 1985 (Life Peer), of Bermondsey in Greater London; **Robert Joseph Mellish;** PC 1967; *b* 1913; *m* 1938, Anne Elizabeth, *d* of George Warner; five *s.* Served War of 1939–45, Captain RE, SEAC. Official, TGWU, 1938–46. MP (Lab 1946–82, Ind. 1982) Bermondsey, Rotherhithe 1946–50, Bermondsey 1950–74, Southwark, Bermondsey 1974–82. PPS to Minister of Pensions, 1951 (to Minister of Supply, 1950–51); Jt Parly Sec., Min. of Housing, 1964–67; Minister of Public Building and Works, 1967–69; Parly Sec. to Treasury and Govt Chief Whip, 1969–70 and 1974–76; Opposition Chief Whip, 1970–74. Chm., London Regional Lab. Party, 1956–77. Dep. Chm., LDDC, 1981–85. *Address:* House of Lords, SW1A 0PW.

MELLITT, Prof. Brian, FEng 1990; Engineering Director, London Underground Ltd, since 1989; Director, Metro Power, since 1990; *b* 29 May 1940; *s* of John and Nellie Mellitt; *m* 1961, Lyn Waring; one *s* one *d. Educ:* Loughborough Univ.; Imperial College, London Univ. (BTechEng, DIC). FIEE, FIMechE, FIRSE. Student apprentice, 1956, Junior Engineer, 1962, R&D Engineer, 1964, English Electric Co.; Lectr and Sen. Lectr, Huddersfield Polytechnic, 1966–67; Research Dept, British Rlys Bd, 1968–70; University of Birmingham: Lectr, 1971; Sen. Lectr, 1979; Prof., 1982; Head of Dept of Electronic and Electrical Engrg 1986; Dean, Faculty of Engrng, 1987–88; Hon. Prof. of Electronic Engrg, 1989. Consultant Engineer, railway related organisations, 1972–88. Editor, IEE Procs (B), 1978–. Hon. DTech Loughborough, 1991. Leonardo da Vinci Award, Italian Assoc. for Industrial Design, 1989. *Publications:* contribs on electric railway topics to learned jls. *Recreation:* bridge. *Address:* The Priory, 36 Church Street, Stilton, Cambs PE7 3RF. *T:* Peterborough (0733) 240573.

MELLON, Sir James, KCMG 1988 (CMG 1979); HM Diplomatic Service, retired; Chairman, Scottish Homes, since 1989; *b* 25 Jan. 1929; *m* 1st, 1956, Frances Murray (*d* 1976); one *s* three *d;* 2nd, 1979, Mrs Philippa Shuttleworth (*née* Hartley). *Educ:* Glasgow Univ. (MA). Dept of Agriculture for Scotland, 1953–60; Agricultural Attaché, Copenhagen and The Hague, 1960–63; FO, 1963–64; Head of Chancery, Dakar, 1964–66; UK Delegn to European Communities, 1967–72; Counsellor, 1970; Hd of Sci. and Technol. Dept, FCO, 1973–75; Commercial Counsellor, East Berlin, 1975–76; Head of Trade Relations and Export Dept, FCO, 1976–78; High Comr in Ghana and Ambassador to Togo, 1978–83; Ambassador to Denmark, 1983–86; Dir-Gen. for Trade and Investment, USA, and Consul-Gen., New York, 1986–88. *Publication:* A Danish Gospel, 1986. *Address:* Scottish Homes, Rosebery House, 9 Haymarket Terrace, Edinburgh EH12 5YA. *Clubs:* Travellers'; New (Edinburgh).

MELLON, Paul, Hon. KBE 1974; Hon. RA 1978; Hon. Trustee, National Gallery of Art, Washington, DC, since 1985 (Trustee, 1945–85; President, 1963–79; Chairman of Trustees, 1979–85); *b* 11 June 1907; *s* of late Andrew William Mellon and late Nora McMullen Mellon; *m* 1st, 1935, Mary Conover (decd); one *s* one *d;* 2nd, 1948, Rachel Lambert. *Educ:* Choate Sch., Wallingford, Conn; Yale Univ.; Univ. of Cambridge (BA 1931; MA 1938; Hon. LLD 1983). Trustee: Andrew W. Mellon Foundn (successor to merged Old Dominion and Avalon Foundns), 1969–; Virginia Mus. of Fine Arts, Richmond, Va, 1938–68, 1969–79. Member: Amer. Philosophical Soc., Philadelphia, 1971; Grolier Soc.; Soc. of Dilettanti; Roxburghe Club. Hon. Citizen, University of Vienna, 1965. Yale Medal, 1953; Horace Marden Albright Scenic Preservation Medal, 1957; Distinguished Service to Arts Award, Nat. Inst. Arts and Letters, 1962; Benjamin Franklin Medal, Royal Society of Arts, 1965, Benjamin Franklin Fellow, 1969; Alumni Seal Prize Award, Choate Sch., 1966; Skowhegan Gertrude Vanderbilt Whitney Award, 1972; Nat. Medal of Arts, USA, 1985; Medal in Architecture, Thomas Jefferson Meml Foundn, 1989; Hadrian Award, World Monuments Fund, 1989; Benjamin Franklin Award, Amer. Philosphical Soc., 1989. Hon. FRIBA 1978. Hon. DLitt, Oxford Univ., 1961; Hon. LLD, Carnegie Inst. of Tech., 1967; Hon. DHL, Yale, 1967. *Recreations:* fox-hunting, thoroughbred breeding and racing, sailing, swimming. *Address:* (office) 1729 H Street NW, Washington, DC 20006, USA; (home) Oak Spring, Upperville, Va 22176. *Clubs:* Buck's; Travellers' (Paris); Jockey, Knickerbocker, Links, Racquet and Tennis, River, Yale (New York); Metropolitan, 1925 F Street (Washington).

MELLOR, David, OBE 1981; DesRCA; RDI 1962; FCSD; designer, manufacturer and retailer; Chairman, Crafts Council, 1982–84; *b* 5 Oct. 1930; *s* of Colin Mellor; *m* 1966, Fiona MacCarthy; one *s* one *d. Educ:* Sheffield College of Art; Royal College of Art (DesRCA and Silver Medal, 1953, Hon. Fellow 1966); British School at Rome. Set up silver-smithing workshop, Sheffield, 1954; designer and maker of silver for Worshipful Co. of Goldsmiths, Cutlers' Co., Southwell Minster, Essex Univ., Darwin Coll., Cambridge, among others, and range of silver tableware for use in British embassies; designer of fountain in bronze for Botanic Gdns, Cambridge, 1970; concurrently opened industrial design office. Consultancies, 1954–, include: Walker & Hall, Abacus Municipal, Glacier Metal, ITT, Post Office, British Rail, James Neill Tools; Cons. to DoE on design of traffic signals, 1965–70, and on design of automatic half-barrier crossing, as result of Gibbens report, 1969; Chm., Design Council Cttee of Inquiry into standards of design in consumer goods in Britain, 1982–84; Mem., Art and Design Working Gp, Nat. Adv. Body for Local Auth. Higher Educn, 1982–84. Trustee, V & A Museum, 1984–88. *Work in collections:* Goldsmiths' Co., V&A, Sheffield City Mus., Mus. of Modern Art, NY. *Awards:* Design Centre: 1957, 1959, 1962, 1965, 1966; Design Council: 1974, 1977; RSA Presidential Award for Design Management, 1981. Liveryman, Goldsmiths' Co., 1980; Freeman, Cutlers' Co. of Hallamshire, 1981. FCSD (FSIAD 1964; CSD Medal 1988). Hon. Fellow, Sheffield City Polytechnic, 1979; Hon. DLitt Sheffield Univ., 1986. *Address:* The Round Building, Hathersage, Sheffield S30 1BA. *T:* Hope Valley (0433) 50220.

MELLOR, Prof. David Hugh, FBA 1983; Professor of Philosophy, University of Cambridge, since 1986; Fellow, Darwin College, Cambridge, since 1971 (Vice-Master, 1983–87); *b* 10 July 1938; *s* of Sydney David Mellor and Ethel Naomi Mellor (*née* Hughes). *Educ:* Manchester Grammar School; Pembroke College, Cambridge (BA Nat. Scis and Chem. Eng, 1960; MA; PhD 1968; ScD 1990); Univ. of Minnesota (Harkness Fellowship; MSc Chem. Eng, 1962). Technical Officer, ICI Central Instruments Lab., 1962–63; Cambridge University: Research Student in Philosophy, Pembroke Coll., 1963–68; Fellow, Pembroke Coll., 1965–70; Univ. Asst Lectr in Philosophy, 1965–70; Univ. Lectr in Philosophy, 1970–83; Univ. Reader in Metaphysics, 1983–85. Vis. Fellow in Philosophy, ANU, 1975; Radcliffe Trust Fellow in Philosophy, 1978–80. Hon. Prof. of Philosophy, Univ. of Keele, 1989–92. Pres., British Soc. for the Philos. of Science, 1985–87. Editor: British Journal for the Philosophy of Science, 1968–70; Cambridge Studies in Philosophy, 1978–82. *Publications:* The Matter of Chance, 1971; Real Time, 1981; Matters of Metaphysics, 1991; articles in Mind, Analysis, Philosophy of Science, Philosophy, Philosophical Review, Ratio, Isis, British Jl for Philosophy of Science. *Recreation:* theatre. *Address:* 25 Orchard Street, Cambridge CB1 1JS. *T:* Cambridge (0223) 460332.

MELLOR, Rt. Hon. David John, PC 1990; QC 1987; MP (C) Putney, since 1979; Chief Secretary to the Treasury, since 1990; *b* 12 March 1949; *s* of Mr and Mrs Douglas H. Mellor; *m* 1974, Judith Mary Hall; two *s*. *Educ:* Swanage Grammar Sch.; Christ's Coll., Cambridge (BA Hons 1970). FZS 1981. Called to the Bar, Inner Temple, 1972; in practice thereafter. Chm., Cambridge Univ. Conservative Assoc., 1970; contested West Bromwich E, Oct. 1974. PPS to Leader of Commons and Chancellor of the Duchy of Lancaster, 1981; Parly Under-Sec. of State, Dept of Energy, 1981–83, Home Office, 1983–86; Minister of State: Home Office, 1986–87; Foreign and Commonwealth Office, 1987–88; Dept of Health, 1988–89; Home Office, 1989–90; Privy Council Office (Minister for the Arts), 1990. Sec., Cons. Parly Legal Cttee, 1979–81; Vice-Chm., Greater London Cons. Members Cttee, 1980–81. Special Trustee, Westminster Hosp., 1980–87; Vice-Chm., Trustees, LPO, 1989–; Mem. Council, NYO, 1981–86. Hon. Associate, BVA, 1986. *Recreations:* classical music, reading, football. *Address:* House of Commons, SW1. *T:* 071–219 5481.

MELLOR, David John; His Honour Judge David Mellor; a Circuit Judge, since 1989; *b* 12 Oct. 1940; *s* of John Robert Mellor and Muriel Mary (*née* Field); *m* 1966, Carol Mary Clement, LLB, BA, AKC, Barrister, *o d* of David Morris Clement, *qv*; two *d*. *Educ:* Plumtree Sch., S Rhodesia; King's Coll., London (LLB). Called to the Bar, Inner Temple, 1964; a Recorder, 1986–89; Principal Judge in Civil Matters for counties of Cambridge, Norfolk and Suffolk, 1991–. *Address:* Old Hall, Mulbarton, Norwich NR14 8JS. *T:* Mulbarton (0508) 70241. *Club:* Norfolk (Norwich).

MELLOR, Derrick, CBE 1984; HM Diplomatic Service; retired; re-employed at Foreign and Commonwealth Office, since 1984; Occasional Lecturer, School of Oriental and African Studies, since 1987; *b* 11 Jan. 1926; *s* of William Mellor and Alice (*née* Hurst); *m* 1954, Kathleen (*née* Hodgson); two *s* one *d*. Served Army, 1945–49. Board of Trade, 1950–57; Trade Commission Service, 1958–64: served Kuala Lumpur and Sydney; HM Diplomatic Service, 1964–: served Copenhagen, Caracas, Asuncion (Ambassador, 1979–84) and London. *Recreations:* tennis, golf, skiing. *Address:* Summerford Farmhouse, Withyham, E Sussex TN7 4DA. *T:* Hartfield (089277) 886. *Clubs:* Commonwealth Trust, Travellers'.

MELLOR, Hugh Wright; Secretary and Director, National Corporation for Care of Old People (now Centre for Policy on Ageing), 1973–80; *b* 11 Aug. 1920; *s* of late William Algernon and Katherine Mildred Mellor; *m* 1944, Winifred Joyce Yates. *Educ:* Leys Sch., Cambridge; London Univ. (BScEcon). Friends Relief Service, 1940–45; Sec., St Albans Council of Social Service, 1945–48; Community Develt Officer, Hemel Hempstead Develt Corp., 1948–50; Asst Sec., Nat. Corp. for Care of Old People, 1951–73. Chm., Hanover Housing Assoc., 1980–85. *Publication:* The Role of Voluntary Organisations in Social Welfare, 1985. *Recreations:* walking, reading, music. *Address:* Lark Rise, Risborough Road, Great Kimble, Aylesbury, Bucks HP17 0XS. *Club:* Commonwealth Trust.

MELLOR, Brig. James Frederick McLean, CBE 1964 (OBE 1945); Norfolk County Commandant, Army Cadet Force, 1969–72; *b* 6 June 1912; *s* of late Col A. J. Mellor, RM, Kingsland, Hereford; *m* 1942, Margaret Ashley, *d* of Major F. A. Phillips, DSO, Holmer, Hereford; one *s* one *d*. *Educ:* Radley Coll.; Faraday House. C. A. Parsons, 1933; Yorkshire Electric Power, 1935. Commnd in Regular Army as Ordnance Mechanical Engr, 1936; France, Belgium, Dunkirk, 1940; Burma, Malaya, HQ, SEAC, 1944–47 (despatches, 1945); Brig. A/Q Northern Comd, 1961–64; Dir of Technical Trng and Inspector of Boys' Trng (Army), MoD, 1966–69; ADC to the Queen, 1963–69. Various appts in engineering and technical educn. Chm., IMechE Eastern Branch, 1971–72. DFH, FIMechE, FIEE. *Address:* Pinewood, Saxlingham Road, Blakeney, Holt, Norfolk NR25 7PB. *T:* Cley (0263) 740990. *Clubs:* Naval and Military, Royal Automobile; Norfolk (Norwich).

MELLOR, John Walter; a Recorder of the Crown Court, 1972–74 and 1978–82; *b* 24 Sept. 1927; *s* of William Mellor and Ruth (*née* Tolson); *m* 1957, Freda Mary (*née* Appleyard); one *s* three *d*. *Educ:* Grammar Sch., Batley; Leeds Univ. (LLB). Called to Bar, Gray's Inn, 1953. *Recreations:* golf, sailing, visiting West Cork. *Address:* 171 Scotchman Lane, Morley, Leeds, W Yorks. *T:* Morley (0532) 534093. *Clubs:* Morley Rugby Union; Crookhaven Yacht.

MELLOR, Kenneth Wilson, QC 1975; **His Honour Judge Mellor;** a Circuit Judge, since 1984; *m* 1957, Sheila Gale; one *s* three *d*. *Educ:* King's College Cambridge (MA, LLB). RNVR (Sub Lieut). Called to the Bar, Lincoln's Inn, 1950. Dep. Chm., Hereford QS, 1969–71; a Recorder, 1972–84. Chm., Agricultural Land Tribunal (West Midlands). *Address:* 5 Fountain Court, Steelhouse Lane, Birmingham B4 6DR; 1 Paper Buildings, Temple, EC4.

MELLOR, Ronald William, CBE 1984; FEng; FIMechE; Secretary, Institution of Mechanical Engineers, since 1987; *b* 8 Dec. 1930; *s* of William and Helen Edna Mellor; *m* 1956, Jean Sephton; one *s* one *d*. *Educ:* Highgate School; King's College London (BSc Eng). Ford Motor Co.: Manager Cortina Product Planning, 1964; Manager Truck Product Planning, 1965; Chief Research Engineer, 1969; Chief Engine Engineer, 1970; Chief Body Engineer, Ford Werke AG, W Germany, 1974; Vice Pres. Car Engineering, Ford of Europe Inc., 1975; Dir, Ford Motor Co. Ltd, 1983–87. Thomas Hawksley Lectr, IMechE, 1983. *Recreation:* yachting. *Address:* Institution of Mechanical Engineers, 1 Birdcage Walk, Westminster, SW1H 9JJ. *T:* 071–222 7899.

MELLOWS, Prof. Anthony Roger, TD 1969; PhD, LLD; Solicitor of the Supreme Court, since 1960; Professor of the Law of Property in the University of London, 1974–90, now Emeritus; Chancellor, Order of St John, since 1991; *b* 30 July 1936; *s* of L. B. and M. P. Mellows; *m* 1973, Elizabeth, *d* of Ven. B. G. B. Fox, MC, TD, and of Hon. Margaret Joan Fox, *d* of 1st Viscount Davidson, PC, GCVO, CH, CB. *Educ:* King's Coll., London. LLB 1957; LLM 1959; PhD 1962; BD 1968; LLD 1973; Fellow 1980. Commissioned Intelligence Corps (TA), 1959, Captain 1964; served Intell. Corps (TA) and (T&AVR) and on the Staff, 1959–71; RARO, 1971–. Admitted a solicitor, 1960; private practice, 1960–; Sen. Partner, Messrs Alexanders. Asst Lectr in Law, King's Coll., London, 1962, Lectr, 1964, Reader, 1971; Dir of Conveyancing Studies, 1969; Dean, Fac. of Laws, Univ. of London, 1981–84, and of Fac. of Laws, KCL, 1981–85; Hd of Dept of Laws, KCL, 1984–87; Mem. Council, KCL, 1972–80. Trustee: Kincardine Foundn, 1972–84; Nineveh Trust, 1985–; London Law Trust, 1968– (Chm. Trustees); Order of St John and British Red Cross Soc. Jt Cttee, 1987–. AKC, London, 1957; FRSA 1959. GCStJ 1991 (KStJ 1988; CStJ 1985; OStJ 1981; Mem. Council, 1981–88; Registrar, 1988–91). Freeman of the City of London, 1963. *Publications:* Local Searches and Enquiries, 1964, 2nd edn 1967; Conveyancing Searches, 1964, 2nd edn 1975; Land Charges, 1966; The Preservation and Felling of Trees, 1964; The Trustee's Handbook, 1965, 3rd edn 1975; Taxation for Executors and Trustees, 1967, 6th edn 1984; (jtly) The Modern Law of Trusts, 1966, 5th edn 1983; The Law of Succession, 1970, 4th edn 1983; Taxation of Land Transactions, 1973, 3rd edn 1982. *Address:* 22 Devereux Court, Temple Bar, WC2R 3JJ. *Club:* Athenæum.

MELLY, (Alan) George (Heywood); professional jazz singer; with John Chilton's Feetwarmers, since 1974; *b* 17 Aug. 1926; *s* of Francis Heywood and Edith Maud Melly; *m* 1955, Victoria Vaughan (marr. diss. 1962); one *d*; *m* 1963, Diana Margaret Campion Dawson; one *s* and one step *d*. *Educ:* Stowe School. Able Seaman, RN, 1944–47. Art Gallery Asst, London Gallery, 1948–50; sang with Mick Mulligan's Jazz Band, 1949–61. Wrote Flook strip cartoon balloons (drawn by Trog (Wally Fawkes)), 1956–71. Critic, The Observer: pop music, 1965–67; TV, 1967–71; films, 1971–73. Film scriptwriter: Smashing Time, 1968; Take a Girl Like You, 1970. Pres., British Humanist Assoc., 1972–74. Critic of the Year, IPC Nat. Press Awards, 1970. *Publications:* I Flook, 1962; Owning Up, 1965; Revolt into Style, 1970; Flook by Trog, 1970; Rum Bum and Concertina, 1977; (with Barry Fantoni) The Media Mob, 1980; Tribe of One: Great Naive and Primitive Painters of the British Isles, 1981; (with Walter Dorin) Great Lovers, 1981; Mellymobile, 1982; (ed) Edward James, Swans Reflecting Elephants: my early years, 1982; Scouse Mouse, 1984; It's All Writ Out for You: the life and work of Scottie Wilson, 1986; (with Michael Woods) Paris and the Surrealists, 1991. *Recreations:* trout fishing, singing and listening to blues of 1920s, collecting modern paintings. *Address:* 33 St Lawrence Terrace, W10 5SR. *Clubs:* Colony Room, Chelsea Arts.

MELMOTH, Christopher George Frederick Frampton, CMG 1959; South Asia Department, International Bank for Reconstruction and Development, 1962–75, retired; *b* 25 Sept. 1912; *s* of late George Melmoth and Florence Melmoth; *m* 1946, Maureen Joan (*née* Brennan); three *d*. *Educ:* Sandringham Sch., Forest Gate. Accountant Officer, Co-ordination of Supplies Fund, Malta, 1942–45; Administrative Officer, Hong Kong, 1946–55; Minister of Finance, Uganda, 1956–62. *Recreations:* tennis, golf, walking. *Address:* Hoptons Field, Kemerton, Tewkesbury, Glos GL20 7JE.

MELROSE, Prof. Denis Graham; Professor of Surgical Science, Royal Postgraduate Medical School, 1968–83, Emeritus since 1983; *b* 20 June 1921; *s* of late Thomas Robert Gray Melrose, FRCS and Floray Collings; *m* 1945, Ann, *d* of late Kathleen Tatham Warter; two *s*. *Educ:* Sedbergh Sch.; University Coll., Oxford; UCH London. MA, BM, BCh, MRCP, FRCS. Junior appts at Hammersmith Hosp. and Redhill County Hosp., Edgware, 1945; RNVR, 1946–48; subseq. Lectr, later Reader, Royal Postgrad. Med. Sch.; Nuffield Travelling Fellow, USA, 1956; Fulbright Fellow, 1957; Associate in Surgery, Stanford Univ. Med. Sch., 1958. *Publications:* numerous papers in learned jls and chapters in books, particularly on heart surgery, heart lung machine and med. engrg. *Recreations:* sailing, ski-ing. *Address:* Can Serreta, Apartado 19, 07820 San Antonio Abad, Ibiza, Baleares, Spain. *T:* 71 343364. *Club:* Royal Naval Sailing Association.

MELVILL JONES, Prof. Geoffrey, FRS 1979; FRSC 1979; FCASI; FRAeS; Hosmer Research Professor of Physiology, McGill University, Montreal, since 1978 (Associate Professor, 1961–68, Full Professor, since 1968); *b* 14 Jan. 1923; *s* of Sir Bennett Melvill Jones, CBE, AFC, FRS and Dorothy Laxton Jotham; *m* 1953, Jenny Marigold Burnaby; two *s* two *d*. *Educ:* King's Choir Sch.; Dauntsey's Sch.; Cambridge Univ. (BA, MA, MB, BCh). Appointments in UK, 1950–61: House Surgeon, Middlesex Hosp., 1950; Sen. Ho. Surg., Otolaryngology, Addenbrooke's Hosp., Cambridge, 1950–51; MO, RAF, 1951; Scientific MO, RAF Inst. of Aviation Medicine, Farnborough, Hants, 1951–55; Scientific Officer (external staff), Medical Research Council of Gt Britain, 1955–61. Dir, Aerospace (formerly Aviation), Med. Res. Unit, McGill Univ., 1961–88. Fellow, Aerospace Medical Assoc., 1969; FCASI 1965; FRAeS 1981. First recipient, Dohlman Medal for research in the field of orientation and postural control, 1986; Robert Bárány Jubilee Gold Medal for most significant research on vestibular function during past 5 years; Ashton Graybiel Lectureship Award, US Navy, 1989; Stewart Meml Lectureship Award, RAeS, 1989; Buchanan-Barbour Award, RAeS, 1990; McLaughlan Medal, RSCan, 1991. *Publications:* Mammalian Vestibular Physiology, 1979 (NY); Adaptive Mechanisms in Gaze Control, 1985; research papers in physiological jls. *Recreations:* outdoor activities, music. *Address:* Aerospace Medical Research Unit, McGill University, Room 1223, McIntyre Building, 3655 Drummond Street, Montreal, Quebec H3G 1Y6, Canada. *T:* (514) 398–6022.

MELVILLE; *see* Leslie Melville, family name of Earl of Leven and Melville.

MELVILLE, 9th Viscount *cr* 1802; **Robert David Ross Dundas;** Baron Duneira 1802; *b* 28 May 1937; *s* of Hon. Robert Maldred St John Melville Dundas (2nd *s* of 7th Viscount) (killed in action, 1940), and of Margaret Connell (who *m* 2nd, 1946, Gerald Bristowe Sanderson), *d* of late Percy Cruden Ross; *S* uncle, 1971; *m* 1982, Fiona Margaret Stilgoe, *d* of late Roger and of Mrs Stilgoe, Stogumber, Som; two *s*. *Educ:* Wellington College. District Councillor, Lasswade, Midlothian; Mem., Midlothian CC, 1964–67. Pres., Lasswade Civic Soc. Lieutenant, Ayrshire Yeomanry; Captain (Reserve), Scots Guards. *Recreations:* fishing, shooting, golf, chess. *Heir:* *s* Hon. Robert Henry Kirkpatrick

Dundas, *b* 23 April 1984. *Address:* Solomon's Court, Chalford, near Stroud, Glos. *T:* Brimscombe (0453) 883351; 3 Roland Way, Fulham, SW7. *T:* 071–370 3553. *Clubs:* Cavalry and Guards; House of Lords Motor; Midlothian County; Bonnyrigg and Lasswade District Ex-Servicemen's.

MELVILLE, Anthony Edwin; Headmaster, The Perse School, Cambridge, 1969–87; *b* 28 April 1929; *yr s* of Sir Leslie Melville, *qv*; *m* 1964, Pauline Marianne Surtees Simpson, *d* of Major A. F. Simpson, Indian Army; two *d. Educ:* Sydney Church of England Grammar Sch.; Univ. of Sydney (BA); King's Coll., Cambridge (MA). Sydney Univ. Medal in English, 1950; Pt II History Tripos, 1st cl. with dist., 1952; Lightfoot Schol. in Eccles. History, 1954. Asst Master, Haileybury Coll., 1953. *Recreations:* reading, gardening, music. *Address:* 4 Field Way, Cambridge CB1 4RW. *Club:* East India.

MELVILLE, Sir Harry (Work), KCB 1958; FRS 1941; FRSC; PhD Edinburgh and Cantab; DSc Edinburgh; MSc Birmingham; Principal, Queen Mary College, University of London, 1967–76; *b* 27 April 1908; *s* of Thomas and Esther Burnett Melville; *m* 1942, Janet Marian, *d* of late Hugh Porteous and Sarah Cameron; two *d. Educ:* George Heriot's Sch., Edinburgh; Edinburgh Univ. (Carnegie Res. Scholar); Trinity Coll., Cambridge (1851 Exhibitioner). Fellow of Trinity College, Cambridge, 1933–44. Meldola Medal, Inst. of Chemistry, 1936; Davy Medal, Royal Society, 1955; Colwyn Medal, Instn of the Rubber Industry. Asst Dir, Colloid Science Laboratory, Cambridge, 1938–40; Prof. of Chemistry, Univ. of Aberdeen, 1940–48; Scientific Adviser to Chief Superintendent Chemical Defence, Min. of Supply, 1940–43; Superintendent, Radar Res. Station, 1943–45; Mason Prof. of Chemistry, Univ. of Birmingham, 1948–56. Chief Scientific Adviser for Civil Defence, Midlands Region, 1952–56; Bakerian Lecture, Royal Society, 1956. Member: Min. of Aviation Scientific Adv. Council, 1949–51; Adv. Council, Dept of Scientific and Industrial Res., 1946–51; Res. Council, British Electricity Authority, 1949–56; Royal Commn on Univ. Educn in Dundee, 1951–52; Res. Council, DSIR, 1961–65; Chm., Adv. Council on Research and Devel, DTI, 1970–74; Member: Nuclear Safety Adv. Cttee, DTI, 1972–; Cttee of Managers, Royal Institution, 1976–; Sec. to Cttee of the Privy Council for Scientific and Industrial Research, 1956–65; Chm., SRC, 1965–67. Mem., London Electricity Bd, 1968–75. Mem., Parly and Scientific Cttee, 1971–75; Pres., Plastics Inst., 1970–75. Hon. LLD Aberdeen; Hon. DCL Kent; Hon. DSc: Exeter; Birmingham; Liverpool; Leeds; Heriot-Watt; Essex; Hon. DTech Bradford. *Publications:* papers in Proceedings of Royal Society, etc. *Address:* Norwood, Dodds Lane, Chalfont St Giles, Bucks HP8 4EL. *T:* Chalfont St Giles (02407) 2222.

MELVILLE, James; *see* Martin, R. P.

MELVILLE, Sir Leslie Galfreid, KBE 1957 (CBE 1953); Member of the Board of the Reserve Bank, Australia, 1959–63, and 1965–74; Member, Commonwealth Grants Commission, 1979–82 (Chairman, 1966–74); *b* 26 March 1902; *s* of Richard Ernest Melville and Lilian Evelyn Thatcher; *m* 1925, Mary Maud Scales; two *s. Educ:* Sydney Church of England Grammar Sch. Bachelor of Economics, University of Sydney, 1925; Public Actuary of South Australia, 1924–28; Prof. of Economics, University of Adelaide, 1929–31; Economic Adviser to Commonwealth Bank of Australia, 1931–49; Asst Gov. (Central Banking) Commonwealth Bank of Australia, 1949–53; Mem. of Commonwealth Bank Bd, 1951–53; Exec. Dir of International Monetary Fund and International Bank for Reconstruction and Development, 1950–53. Mem. of Cttees on Australian Finances and Unemployment, 1931 and 1932; Financial Adviser to Australian Delegates at Imperial Economic Conference, 1932; Financial Adviser to Australian Delegate at World Economic Conference, 1933; Mem. of Financial and Economic Advisory Cttee, 1939; Chm. of Australian Delegation to United Nations Monetary Conf. at Bretton Woods, 1944; Mem. of Advisory Council of Commonwealth Bank, 1945–51; Chm. UN Sub-Commn on Employment and Economic Stability, 1947–50; Member: Immigration Planning Council, 1956–61; Develt Adv. Service of Internat. Bank, 1963–65; Chm. of Tariff Bd, Australia, 1960–62; Chm., Tariff Adv. Cttee of Papua and New Guinea, 1969–71. Vice-Chancellor Australian National Univ., Canberra, ACT, 1953–60. Hon. LLD: Toronto, 1958; ANU, 1978; Hon. DSc Econ Sydney, 1980. *Address:* 71 Stonehaven Crescent, Canberra, ACT 2600, Australia. *Club:* Commonwealth.
See also A. E. Melville.

MELVILLE, Sir Ronald (Henry), KCB 1964 (CB 1952); *b* 9 March 1912; *e s* of Henry Edward Melville; *m* 1940, Enid Dorcas Margaret, *d* of late Harold G. Kenyon, Ware; two *s* one *d. Educ:* Charterhouse; Magdalene Coll., Cambridge. 1st Class Classical Tripos, Pts I and II, Charles Oldham Scholarship. Entered Air Ministry, 1934; Private Sec. to Chief of Air Staff, 1936, to Sec. of State, 1940; Asst Under-Sec., 1946; Dep. Under-Sec., 1958; Dep. Under-Sec., War Office, 1960–63; Second Permanent Under-Sec. of State, Ministry of Defence, 1963–66; Permanent Sec., Ministry of Aviation, 1966; Permanent Sec., attached Civil Service Dept, 1971–72; Director: Electronic Components Industry Fedn, 1972–81; Westland Aircraft, 1974–83. Chairman: Nat. Rifle Assoc., 1972–84 (Captain, GB Rifle Team, touring USA and Canada, 1976, and for Kolapore match in UK, 1977); Jt Shooting Cttee for GB, 1985–89; Pres., Herts Rifle Assoc., 1960–; has represented Cambridge Univ., TA and Scotland (40 times) at rifle shooting. Member Council: Herts TAA, 1960–80; Herts Soc., 1963–; ACFA, 1972–84. *Recreations:* painting, gardening. *Address:* The Old Rose and Crown, Braughing, Ware, Herts SG11 2QA. *Club:* Brooks's.

MELVILLE-ROSS, Timothy David; Director and Chief Executive, Nationwide (formerly Nationwide Anglia) Building Society, since 1987; *b* 3 Oct. 1944; *s* of Antony Stuart Melville-Ross and Anne Barclay Fane; *m* 1967, Camilla Mary Harlackenden; two *s* one *d. Educ:* Uppingham School; Portsmouth College of Technology (Dip Business Studies, 2nd cl. hons). FCIS; CBIM. British Petroleum, 1963–73; Rowe, Swann & Co., stockbrokers, 1973–74; joined Nationwide Building Soc., 1974, Dir and Chief Gen. Man., 1985–87. Member Council: Industrial Soc., 1986–; PSI, 1987–. Trustee, Uppingham Sch., 1988–. FRSA. *Recreations:* music, reading, bridge, tennis, the countryside.

MELVIN, John Turcan, TD and star; MA Cantab; *b* 19 March 1916; *m* 1951, Elizabeth Ann Parry-Jones; one *s* three *d. Educ:* Stowe Sch.; Trinity Coll., Cambridge; Berlin Univ. (Schol.). Asst Master, Sherborne Sch., 1938. Served with Dorset Regt, 1939–46. Housemaster, Sherborne Sch., 1950; Headmaster, Kelly Coll., 1959–72; Hd of German Dept, Foster's Sch., 1972–75; Sixth Form Tutor, Sherborne Sch., 1975–82. Governor: Hall Sch. Trust, Wincanton; St Francis Sch., Hook. *Recreations:* walking, reading, tennis, dramatics. *Address:* Culverhayes Lodge, Sherborne, Dorset DT9 3BY. *Club:* English-Speaking Union.

MELVYN HOWE, Prof. George; *see* Howe, Prof. G. M.

MENDE, Dr Erich; Member of the Bundestag, German Federal Republic, 1949–80; *b* 28 Oct. 1916; *m* 1948, Margot (*née* Hattje); three *s* one *d. Educ:* Humane Coll., Gross-Strehlitz; Universities of Cologne and Bonn (Dr jur). Military service in Infantry Regt 84, Gleiwitz. Served War of 1939–45, Comdr of a Regt (wounded twice, prisoner of war); Major, 1944. Co-founder of FDP (Free Democratic Party), 1945; Mem. Exec. Cttee, British Zone, FDP, 1947; Parliamentary Group of FDP: Whip, and Mem. Exec. Cttee, 1950–53; Dep. Chm., 1953; Chm., 1957; Chm. of FDP, 1960–68; joined CDU, 1970. Vice-Chancellor and Minister for All-German Affairs, Federal Republic of Germany, 1963–66. Mem., CDU Hessen, 1970. *Publications:* autobiography: Das verdammte Gewissen 1921–1945, 1982; Die neue Freiheit 1945–1961, 1984; Von Wende zu Wende 1962–1982, 1986. *Address:* Am Stadtwald 62, D5300 Bonn 2, Germany.

MENDIS, Vernon Lorraine Benjamin; Chairman, Sri Lanka Telecommunications Board, Colombo, since 1985; *b* 5 Dec. 1925; *m* 1953, Padma Rajapathirana; one *s. Educ:* Univ. of Ceylon (BA Hons History, 1948). Post Grad. Master of Philosophy, Sch. of Oriental and African Studies, Univ. of London, 1966; PhD Colombo Univ., 1986. High Commissioner for Sri Lanka: in Canada, 1974–75; in UK, 1975–77; Ambassador for Republic of Sri Lanka in France, 1978–80; UNESCO Rep. in Egypt and Sudan, 1980–85. *Publications:* The Advent of the British to Ceylon 1760–1815, 1971; Currents of Asian History, 1981; Foreign Relations of Sri Lanka, earliest times to 1965, 1982; British Governors and Colonial Policy in Sri Lanka, 1984. *Recreations:* hiking, bird watching. *Address:* Office of the Chairman, Sri Lanka Telecommunications Board, Bandaranaike Memorial International Conference Hall, Suite 4–101, PO Box 1571, Bauddhaloka Mawatha, Colombo 7, Sri Lanka. *Telex:* 22600 Laktel CE. *Club:* Travellers'.

MENDL, James Henry Embleton; His Honour Judge Mendl; a Circuit Judge since 1974; *b* 23 Oct. 1927; *s* of late R. W. S. Mendl, barrister and author, and of Dorothy Williams Mendl (*née* Burnett), and *g s* of late Sir S. F. Mendl, KBE; *m* 1971, Helena Augusta Maria Schrama, *d* of late J. H. and H. H. Schrama-Jekat, The Netherlands. *Educ:* Harrow; University Coll., Oxford (MA). Called to Bar, Inner Temple, 1953; South Eastern Circuit. Commissioned, Worcestershire Regt, 1947; served: Egypt, with 2nd N Staffs, 1947–48; with Royal Signals (TA), 1952–54, and Queen's Royal Regt (TA) (Captain, 1955), 1954–56. Councillor, Royal Borough of Kensington and Chelsea, 1964–74 (Vice-Chm., Town Planning Cttee, 1969; Chm. (Vice-Chm. 1970), Libraries Cttee, 1971). Contested (C) Gateshead East, 1966. *Recreations:* music, skiing.

MENDOZA, June Yvonne, AO 1989; RP; ROI; artist; *d* of John Morton and Dot (*née* Mendoza), musicians; *m* Keith Ashley V. Mackrell; one *s* three *d. Educ:* Lauriston Girls' Sch., Melbourne; St Martin's Sch. of Art. Member: RP 1970; ROI 1968. Portraits for govt, regts, industry and commerce, academia, medicine, theatre, sport (*eg* Chris Evert for Wimbledon Mus.), and in public and private collections internationally. These include: Queen Elizabeth II; Queen Elizabeth the Queen Mother; Prince and Princess of Wales; Margaret Thatcher; Prime Minister of Australia, Sir John Gorton; Prime Minister of Fiji, Ratu Sir Kamisese Mara; Pres. of Iceland, Vigdis Finnbogadottir; Pres. of Philippines, Corazón Aquino; large group paintings include: The House of Commons in Session, 1986; House of Representatives, for new Parliament building in Canberra; private series of musicians include: Sir Yehudi Menuhin; Sir Georg Solti; Dame Joan Sutherland; Paul Tortelier; Sir Michael Tippett. Occasional lectures for television and radio. Hon. DLitt Bath, 1986. *Address:* 34 Inner Park Road, SW19 6DD.

MENDOZA, Maurice, CVO 1982; MSM 1946; heritage consultant; Under Secretary, Ancient Monuments and Historic Buildings, Department of the Environment, 1978–81; *b* 1 May 1921; *e s* of Daniel and Rachel Mendoza; *m* 1949, Phyllis Kriger. *Educ:* Sir Henry Raine's Foundation. Dip. Sociology London. Clerical Officer, HM Office of Works, 1938; served Royal Signals and Cheshire Yeo., 1941–46 (Sgt); Mil. Mission to Belgium, 1944–46; Organisation Officer, Treasury, 1956–61; Principal, MPBW, 1963; Asst Sec. 1968; DoE, 1970; Under-Sec., 1973; Dir of Manpower and Management Services, DoE and later, also Dept of Transport, 1974–78. Chairman: Friends of the Ridgeway, 1982–; Common Land Forum, 1984–86; Sec., British Architectural Library Review Gp, 1987–88. Hon. Mem., 10th Battalion Transportation Corps, US Army, 1977. *Recreations:* theatre, walking, photography. *Address:* 45 Grange Grove, Canonbury, N1 2NP. *Clubs:* Athenæum, Civil Service.

MENDOZA, Vivian P.; *see* Pereira-Mendoza.

MENDOZA-ACOSTA, Vice-Adm. Felix; Venezuelan Ambassador to the Court of St James's, 1979–82; *b* 21 Feb. 1929; *s* of José Mendoza and Virginia Mendoza (*née* Acosta); *m* 1954, Patricia Hill; one *s* two *d. Educ:* Naval Academy, Venezuela; Naval Coll., USA. Professor, Naval Academy, Venezuela, 1957–59; held high appointments at High Court of Admiralty, Min. of Defence, 1960–72; Director, Naval Academy, 1973; Chief of Operations, Headquarters, High Court of Admiralty, 1974, Commander in Chief, 1976; Chief of General Staff, 1977; Inspector General of Armed Forces, 1978; in charge, Min. of Defence, on several occasions, 1978–79. Orden: del Libertador Simón Bolívar; Francisco de Miranda; Gen. Urdaneta; Andrés Bello; Diego de Lozada; naval decorations: Spain, Italy, Colombia, Argentina, Bolivia, Peru, Venezuela; Cross, 1st Cl.: Land Forces of Venezuela, Air Force of Venezuela, Naval Merit, National Guard. *Recreations:* walking, reading, music, conversation with family. *Address:* c/o Ministry of Foreign Affairs, Casa Amarilla, esq. de Principal, Carácas, Venezuela. *Clubs:* Les Ambassadeurs, Hurlingham, Annabel's, Belfry, White Elephant, Casanova; Officers' (Carácas).

MENEMENCIOGLU, Turgut; *b* Istanbul, 8 Oct. 1914; *s* of Muvatfak and Kadriye Menemencioğlu; *m* 1944, Nermin Moran; two *s. Educ:* Robert Coll., Istanbul; Geneva Univ. Joined Turkish Min. of Foreign Affairs, 1939; Permanent Delegate, European Office, UN Geneva, 1950–52; Counsellor, Turkish Embassy, Washington, 1952; Dir-Gen., Econ. Affairs, Min. of Foreign Affairs, 1952–54; Dep. Permanent Rep. to UN, 1954–60; Ambassador to Canada, 1960; Permanent Rep. to UN, 1960–62; Ambassador to USA, 1962–67; High Polit. Adviser, Mem., High Polit. Planning Bd, Min. of Foreign Affairs, 1967–68; Sec.-Gen., CENTO, 1968–72; Adviser, Min. of Foreign Affairs, 1972; Ambassador of Turkey to the Court of St James's, 1972–78; Sen. Polit. Adviser, Min. of Foreign Affairs, 1978–80. Turkish Representative, Turkish-Greek Cultural Relations Cttee, 1982. *Address:* Inünü Cad 31/12, Taksim, Istanbul, Turkey.

MENEVIA, Bishop of, (RC), since 1987; **Rt. Rev. Daniel Joseph Mullins;** *b* 10 July 1929; *s* of Timothy Mullins. *Educ:* Mount Melleray; St Mary's, Aberystwyth; Oscott Coll.; UC of S Wales and Mon, Cardiff (Fellow, University Coll., Cardiff). Hon. Fellow, St David's University Coll., Lampeter. Priest, 1953. Curate at: Barry, 1953–56; Newbridge, 1956; Bargoed, 1956–57; Maesteg, 1957–60; Asst Chaplain to UC Cardiff, 1960–64; Sec. to Archbp of Cardiff, 1964–68; Vicar General of Archdiocese of Cardiff, 1968; Titular Bishop of Stowe and Auxiliary Bishop in Swansea, 1970–87. Pres., Catholic Record Soc.; Chm., Cttee for Catechesis. Member of Court, UC Cardiff; Governor, Digby Stuart Coll. *Recreations:* golf, walking. *Address:* Bryn Rhos, 79 Walter Road, Swansea, West Glamorgan SA1 4PS.

MENHENNET, Dr David, CB 1991; Librarian of the House of Commons, 1976–91; Visiting Research Fellow, Goldsmiths' College, London University, since 1990; *b* 4 Dec. 1928; *s* of William and Everill Menhennet, Redruth, Cornwall; *m* 1954, Audrey, *o d* of William and Alice Holmes, Accrington, Lancs; two *s. Educ:* Truro Sch., Cornwall; Oriel Coll., Oxford (BA 1st Cl. Hons 1952); Queen's Coll., Oxford. Open Scholarship in Mod. Langs, Oriel Coll., Oxford, 1946; Heath Harrison Trav. Scholarship, 1951; Bishop Fraser Res. Scholar, Oriel Coll., 1952–53; Laming Fellow, Queen's Coll., Oxford, 1953–54; Zaharoff Trav. Scholarship, 1953–54. MA 1956, DPhil 1960, Oxon. Library Clerk,

House of Commons Library, 1954; Asst Librarian i/c Res. Div., 1964–67; Dep. Librarian, 1967–76. Mem., Study of Parliament Gp, 1964–90; Chm. Adv. Cttee, Bibliographic Services, British Library, 1986– (Mem., 1975–86); Mem. Exec. Cttee, Friends of Nat. Libraries, 1991–. Associate, Inst. of Cornish Studies, 1974–. FRSA 1966. Liveryman, Stationers' Co., 1990. Gen. Editor, House of Commons Library Documents series, 1972–90. *Publications:* (with J. Palmer) Parliament in Perspective, 1967; The Journal of the House of Commons: a bibliographical and historical guide, 1971; (ed with D. C. L. Holland) Erskine May's Private Journal, 1857–1882, 1972; (contrib.) The House of Commons in the Twentieth Century, ed S. A. Walkland, 1979; (contrib.) The House of Commons: Services and Facilities 1972–1982, ed M. Rush, 1983; The House of Commons Library: a history, 1991; articles in Lib. Assoc. Record, Parliamentarian, Parly Affairs, Polit. Qly, New Scientist, Contemp. Rev., Jl of Librarianship, Jl of Documentation, Book Collector. *Recreations:* walking, gardening, visiting old churches, French literature. *Address:* 50 Kelsey Lane, Beckenham, Kent BR3 3NE. *T:* 081–650 7787. *Club:* Athenæum.

MENIN, Rt. Rev. Malcolm James; *see* Knaresborough, Bishop Suffragan of.

MENKES, Suzy Peta, (Mrs D. G. Spanier); Fashion Editor, International Herald Tribune, since 1988; *b* 24 Dec. 1943; *d* of Edouard Gerald Lionel Menkès and Betty Curtis Lightfoot; *m* 1969, David Graham Spanier; three *s* (one *d* decd). *Educ:* Univ. of Cambridge (MA). Editor, Varsity newspaper, Cambridge, 1966; Jun. Reporter, The Times, 1966–69; Fashion Editor, Evening Standard, 1969–77; Women's Editor, Daily Express, 1977–80; Fashion Editor: The Times, 1980–87; The Independent, 1987–88. Freeman: City of Milan, 1986; City of London, 1987. British Press Awards Commendations, 1983 and 1984. *Publications:* The Knitwear Revolution, 1983; The Royal Jewels, 1985, 3rd edn 1988; The Windsor Style, 1987. *Recreations:* reading, opera, family life. *Address:* c/o International Herald Tribune, 181 avenue Charles de Gaulle, 92521 Neuilly Cedex, Paris, France. *T:* 46.37.93.00.

MENNEER, Stephen Snow, CB 1967; retired, 1970, as Assistant Under-Secretary of State, Department of Health and Social Security; *b* 6 March 1910; *s* of Sydney Charles Menneer, LLD, and Minnie Elizabeth Menneer; *m* 1935, Margaret Longstaff Smith (*d* 1976); one *s* one *d*. *Educ:* Rugby Sch.; Oriel Coll., Oxford. Min. of Information, 1939; Min. of National Insurance, 1948; Under-Sec., Min. of Pensions and Nat. Insurance, then Min. of Social Security, 1961. *Address:* Wester Ground, Chittlehamholt, Umberleigh, N Devon.

MENON, Prof. Mambillikalathil Govind Kumar, MSc, PhD; FRS 1970; MP; President, International Council of Scientific Unions, since 1988; *b* 28 Aug. 1928; *s* of Kizhekepat Sankara Menon and Mambillikalathil Narayaniamma; *m* 1955, Indumati Patel; one *s* one *d*. *Educ:* Jaswant Coll., Jodhpur; Royal Inst. of Science, Bombay (MSc); Univ. of Bristol (PhD). Tata Inst. of Fundamental Research: Reader, 1955–58; Associate Prof., 1958–60; Prof. of Physics and Dean of Physics Faculty, 1960–64; Senior Prof. and Dep. Dir (Physics), 1964–66, Dir, 1966–75. Chm., Electronics Commn, and Sec., Dept of Electronics, Govt of India, 1971–78; Scientific Advr to Minister of Defence, Dir-Gen. of Defence Res. and Develt Orgn, and Sec. in the Ministry of Defence for Defence Res., 1974–78; Dir-Gen., Council of Scientific and Industrial Res., 1978–81; Sec. to Govt of India, Dept of Science and Technology, 1978–82; Chm., Commn for Addtnl Sources of Energy, 1981–82; Mem., Planning Commn, 1982–89; Chm., Science Adv. Cttee to the Cabinet, 1982–85; Scientific Advr to the Prime Minister, 1986–89; Minister of State for Sci. and Technology, India, 1989–90. Pres., India Internat. Centre, 1983–88; Mem., UN Sec.-Gen.'s Adv. Cttee on Application of Sci. and Technol. to Develt, 1972–79 (Chm. for 2 yrs). Fellow: Indian Acad. of Sciences (Pres., 1974–76); Indian Nat. Science Acad. (Pres., 1981–82); Founding Fellow, Third World Acad. of Sciences; Pres., Indian Sci. Congress Assoc., 1981–82; Hon. Fellow: Nat. Acad. of Sciences, India (Pres., 1987–88); Indian Inst. of Sciences, Bangalore; Mem., Internat. Fedn of Insts for Advanced Study, Stockholm; For. Hon. Member: Amer. Acad. of Arts and Scis; USSR Acad. of Scis; Mem., Pontifical Acad. of Scis, Vatican; Hon. Pres., Asia Electronics Union; Hon. Mem., Instn of Electrical & Electronics Engrs Inc., USA. Member: Bd of Governors, Internat. Develt Res. Centre, 1986–90; Governing Council, UN Univ., 1986–. Hon. DSc: Jodhpur Univ., 1970; Delhi Univ., 1973; Sardar Patel Univ., 1973; Allahabad Univ., 1977; Roorkee Univ., 1979; Banaras Hindu Univ., 1981; Jadavpur Univ., 1981; Sri Venkateswara Univ., 1982; Indian Inst. of Tech. Madras, 1982; Andhra Univ., 1984; Utkal Univ., 1984; Aligarh Muslim Univ., 1986; Bristol Univ., 1990; N Bengal Univ., Indian Inst. of Technology, Kharagpur, 1990; Hon. Dr Engrg Stevens Inst. of Tech., USA, 1984. Royal Commn for Exhibn of 1851 Senior Award, 1953–55; Shanti Swarup Bhatnagar Award for Physical Sciences, Council of Scientific and Industrial Research, 1960; Khaitan Medal, RAS, 1973; Pandit Jawaharlal Nehru Award for Sciences, Madhya Pradesh Govt, 1983; G. P. Chatterjee Award, 1984; Om Prakash Bhasin Award for Science and Technol., 1985; C. V. Raman Medal, INSA, 1985; J. C. Bose Triennial Gold Medal, Bose Inst., 1983; National Awards: Padma Shri, 1961; Padma Bhushan, 1968; Padma Vibhushan, 1985. *Publications:* 128, on cosmic rays and elementary particle physics. *Recreations:* photography, bird-watching. *Address:* 77 Lodi Estate, New Delhi 110003, India. *T:* 11 4620062. *Clubs:* National Liberal; United Services (Bombay); India International Centre (New Delhi).

MENOTTI, Gian Carlo; composer; Founder and President, Spoleto Festivals, Italy and Charleston, USA; *b* Cadegliano, Italy, 7 July 1911. *Educ:* The Curtis Institute of Music, Philadelphia, Pa. Has been resident in the United States since 1928. Teacher of Composition at Curtis Inst. of Music, 1948–55. First performances of works include: Amelia Goes to the Ball (opera), 1936; The Old Maid and the Thief (radio opera), 1939 (later staged); The Island God, 1942; Sebastian (Ballet), 1943; Piano Concerto in F, 1945; The Medium (opera), 1946 (later filmed); The Telephone (opera), 1947; Errand into the Maze (ballet), 1947; The Consul (opera), 1950 (Pulitzer Prize); Apocalypse (orchestral), 1951; Amahl and the Night Visitors (television opera), 1951; Violin Concerto in A Minor, 1952; The Saint of Bleeker Street (opera), 1954 (Pulitzer Prize); The Unicorn, The Gorgon, and the Manticore, 1956; Maria Golovin (television opera), 1958; The Last Savage (opera), 1963; The Death of the Bishop of Brindisi (oratorio), 1963; Martin's Lie (opera), 1964; Canti della Lontananza (song cycle), 1967; Help, Help, the Globolinks (opera), 1968; The Leper (drama), 1970; Triplo Concerto a Tre (symphonic piece), 1970; The Most Important Man (opera), 1971; Fantasia for 'cello and orch., 1971; Tamu-Tamu (opera), 1973; The Egg (opera), 1976; The Trial of the Gypsy (opera), 1976; Landscapes & Remembrances, for chorus and orch., 1976; Symphony no 1, 1976; Chip & his Dog (opera), 1978; Juana la Loca (opera), 1979; Mass, O Pulchritudo, 1979; Song of Hope (cantata), 1980; A Bride from Pluto (opera), 1982; St Teresa (cantata), 1982; The Boy Who Grew Too Fast (opera), 1982; Goya (opera), 1986; Giorno di Nozze (opera), 1988; wrote libretto for Vanessa (opera, by Samuel Barber), 1958. Internationally recognised as a producer; has worked at the greatest opera houses, including La Scala, Metropolitan, Paris Opéra, Vienna Staatsoper. Guggenheim Award, 1946, 1947; Kennedy Centre Award, 1984; NYC Mayor's Liberty Award; Hon. Association, Nat. Inst. of Arts and Letters. *Publications:* his major works have been published, also some minor ones; he is the author of all his libretti, most of which have been written in English. *Address:* c/o Thea Dispeker, 59 East 54th Street, New York, NY 10022, USA; Yester House, Gifford, Haddington, East Lothian EH41 4JF.

MENSFORTH, Sir Eric, Kt 1962; CBE 1945; DL; MA Cantab; FEng; FIMechE; FRAeS; Hon. FIProdE; Vice Lord-Lieutenant, South Yorkshire, 1974–81; President, Westland Aircraft Ltd, 1979–85; (Director, 1968–83; Managing Director 1938–45; Vice-Chairman, 1945–53, 1968–71; Chairman, 1953–68); Director, John Brown & Co. Ltd, 1948–83 (Deputy Chairman, 1959–78); *b* 17 May 1906; 2nd *s* of late Sir Holberry Mensforth, KCB, CBE; *m* 1934, Betty, *d* of late Rev. Picton W. Francis; three *d*. *Educ:* Altrincham County High Sch.; University Coll. Sch.; King's Coll., Cambridge (Price Exhibn) (1st class mechanical sciences tripos). Engineering work at Woolwich Arsenal, Mather & Platt Ltd, Bolckow Vaughan Ltd, Kloecknerwerke A. G., Dorman Long Ltd, English Electric Ltd, Markham & Co. Ltd, T. Firth & John Brown Ltd, Firth Brown Tools Ltd, Wickman Ltd, Boddy Industries Ltd, Rhodesian Alloys Ltd, Normalair Ltd; Chief Production Adviser to: Chief Executive, Ministry of Aircraft Production, 1943–45; 100 KW Orkney Windmill, 1951; London Battersea Heliport, 1959. Master Cutler, Sheffield, 1965–66. Chairman: EDC for Electronics Industry, 1968–70; Cttee on Quality Assurance, 1968–70; Council of Engineering Instns, 1969–72; Governing Body, Sheffield Polytechnic, 1969–75; Member: British Productivity Council, 1964–69; Royal Ordnance Factories Bd, 1968–72; Council, RGS, 1968–70; Smeatonian Soc. of Civil Engrs, 1966–77; Treasurer, BAAS, 1970–75; Pres., IProdE, 1967–69; a founder Vice-Pres., Fellowship of Engineering, 1977. President: Helicopter Assoc. of GB, 1953–55; S Yorks Scouts' Assoc., 1969–76; CPRE (Sheffield and Peak District Branch), 1975–86. Hon. Fellow, Sheffield City Polytech. Hon. DEng Sheffield, 1967; Hon. DSc Southampton, 1970. DL S (formerly WR) Yorks, 1971. *Publications:* Air Frame Production, 1947 (Instn Prize, IMechE); Future of the Aeroplane (Cantor Lectures), 1959; Production of Helicopters and Hovercraft (Lord Sempill Lecture, IProdE), 1964; Future of Rotorcraft and Hovercraft (Cierva Meml Lecture, RAeS), 1967; Extracts from the Records of the Cutlers' Company, 1972; Family Engineers, 1981. *Address:* 42 Oakmead Green, Woodcote Side, Surrey KT18 7JS. *T:* Epsom (0372) 742313. *Clubs:* Alpine, Royal Automobile.

MENTER, Sir James (Woodham), Kt 1973; MA, PhD, ScD Cantab; FRS 1966; CPhys; FInstP; Principal, 1976–86, Fellow, 1986, Queen Mary College, London University; *b* 22 Aug. 1921; *s* of late Horace Menter and late Jane Anne Lackenby; *m* 1947, Marjorie Jean, *d* of late Thomas Stodart Whyte-Smith, WS; two *s* one *d*. *Educ:* Dover Grammar Sch.; Peterhouse, Cambridge. PhD 1949, ScD 1960. Experimental Officer, Admty, 1942–45; Research, Cambridge Univ., 1946–54 (ICI Fellow, 1951–54; Sir George Beilby Mem. Award, 1954); Tube Investments Research Laboratories, Hinxton Hall, 1954–68; Dir of Research and Develt, Tube Investments Ltd, 1965–76. Director: Tube Investments Res. Labs, 1961–68; Tube Investments Ltd, 1965–86; Round Oak Steelworks Ltd, 1967–76; British Petroleum Co., 1976–87; Steetley Co., 1981–85. Member: SRC, 1967–72; Cttee of Inquiry into Engrg Profession, 1977–79; a Vice-Pres., Royal Society, 1971–76, Treasurer, 1972–76; Royal Institution: a Manager, 1982–84; a Vice-Pres., 1983–85; Chm. Council, 1984–85. Fellow, Churchill Coll., Cambridge, 1966–88. President: Inst. of Physics, 1970–72; Metals Soc., 1976; Dep. Chm., Adv. Council Applied R&D, 1976–79. Mem. (part-time), BSC, 1976–79. Member: Bd of Govs, London Hosp. Med. Coll., 1976–86; Ct of Governors, City of London Polytechnic, 1982–85; Court, Stirling Univ., 1988–. Hon. DTech Brunel, 1974. Bessemer Medal, Iron and Steel Inst., 1973; Glazebrook Medal and Prize, Inst. of Physics, 1977. *Publications:* scientific papers in Proc. Royal Society, Advances in Physics, Jl Iron and Steel Inst., etc. *Recreation:* fishing. *Address:* Carie, Kinloch Rannoch, by Pitlochry, Perthshire PH17 2QJ. *T:* Kinloch Rannoch (08822) 341.

MENTETH, Sir James (Wallace) Stuart-, 6th Bt, *cr* 1838; *b* 13 Nov. 1922; *e s* of 5th Bt and Winifred Melville (*d* 1968), *d* of Daniel Francis and *widow* of Capt. Rupert G. Raw, DSO; *S* father, 1952; *m* 1949, Dorothy Patricia, *d* of late Frank Greaves Warburton; two *s*. *Educ:* Fettes; St Andrews Univ.; Trinity Coll., Oxford (MA). Served War of 1939–45, with Scots Guards, 1942–44; on active service in North Africa and Italy (Anzio) (severely wounded). *Recreations:* gardening, ornithology. *Heir:* *s* Charles Greaves Stuart-Menteth [*b* 25 Nov. 1950; *m* 1976, Nicola St Lawrence; three *d* (one *s* decd)].

MENTZ, Donald; Director General, CAB International (formerly Commonwealth Agricultural Bureaux), since 1985; *b* 20 Oct. 1933; *s* of Stanley Mentz and Marie Agnes (*née* Bryant); *m* 1959, Mary Josephine (*née* Goldsworthy); one *s* two *d*. *Educ:* Hampton High School, Victoria; Dookie Agricultural College, Victoria (DDA); Melbourne Univ. (BAgSci); Australian Nat. Univ. (BEcon). Dept of External Territories, Australia, 1969–73; Aust. Develt Assistance Bureau, Dept of Foreign Affairs, 1973–77; Dept of Business and Consumer Affairs, 1977–78; Dir of Operations, Asian Develt Bank, Philippines, 1979–81; Dep. Sec., Dept of Business and Consumer Affairs, Aust., 1981–82; Dep. Sec., Dept of Territories and Local Govt., 1983–84. *Recreations:* ski-ing, gardening. *Address:* Flat 1, 25 Longridge Road, Earls Court, SW5 9SB. *T:* 071–835 1208. *Clubs:* Athenæum; Commonwealth (Canberra).

MENUHIN, Sir Yehudi, OM 1987; KBE 1965; violinist, conductor; *b* New York, 22 April 1916; adopted British nationality, 1985; *s* of Moshe and Marutha Menuhin; *m* 1938, Nola Ruby, *d* of George Nicholas, Melbourne, Australia; one *s* one *d*; *m* 1947, Diana Rosamond, *d* of late G. L. E. Gould and late Lady Harcourt (Evelyn Suart); two *s*. *Educ:* private tutors; studied music under Sigmund Anker and Louis Persinger, in San Francisco; Georges Enesco, Rumania and Paris; Adolph Busch, Switzerland. Made début with orchestra, San Francisco, aged 7, Paris, aged 10, New York, 11, Berlin, 13; since then has played with most of world's orchestras and conductors; has introduced among contemp. works Sonata for Violin alone, by Béla Bartók (composed for Sir Yehudi Menuhin), as well as works by William Walton, Ben-Haim, Georges Enesco, Pizzetti, Ernest Bloch, etc. During War of 1939–45 devoted larger part of his time to concerts for US and Allied armed forces and benefit concerts for Red Cross, etc (500 concerts). Series of concerts in Moscow (by invitation), 1945; seven visits to Israel, 1950–; first tour of Japan, 1951; first tour of India (invitation of Prime Minister), 1952. Largely responsible for cultural exchange programme between US and Russia, 1955, and for bringing Indian music and musicians to West. Initiated his own annual music festival in Gstaad, Switzerland, 1957, and in Bath, 1959–68; Jt Artistic Dir, Windsor Festival, 1969–72. Founder, Live Music Now, 1977. Founded Yehudi Menuhin Sch. of Music, Stoke d'Abernon, Surrey, 1963; Founder/Pres., Internat. Menuhin Music Acad., Gstaad, 1976; Pres., Trinity Coll. of Music, 1971. Pres., Young Musicians' Symphony Orch., 1989–; Associate Conductor and Pres., Royal Philharmonic Orch., 1982–; Principal Guest Conductor: English String Orch., 1988–; Warsaw Sinfonia, 1982–. Mem., Comité d'Honneur Service Européen d'Information Ministerielle et Parlementaire, 1987; Hon. Fellow: St Catharine's Coll., Cambridge, 1970; Fitzwilliam Coll., Cambridge, 1991; Hon. DMus: Oxford, 1962; Cambridge, 1970; Sorbonne, 1976; Toronto, 1984; Virginia Commonwealth Univ., 1987; Hartford, Conn, 1987; Santa Clara, Calif, 1988; Hon. Dr Gakushuin, Tokyo, 1988, and 10 other degrees from Brit. Univs. Freedom of the City of Edinburgh, 1965; City of Bath, 1966. He records for several companies, both as soloist and as Conductor of Menuhin Festival Orch., with which has toured USA, Australia, NZ and Europe; appears regularly on American and British Television. Gold Medal, Royal Philharmonic Soc., 1962; Jawaharlal Nehru Award for International Understanding, 1970; Sonning Music Prize, Denmark, 1972; Handel Medal, NY; City of Jerusalem Medal; Peace Prize, Börsenverein des Deutschen Buchhandels, 1979; Albert Medal, RSA, 1981; Una Vita Nella Musica, Omaggio a Venezia, 1983; Grande Plaque du Bimillenaire de Paris, 1984; Ernst von Siemens Prize, 1984; Moses-Mendelssohn-Preis des Landes Berlin; Internat. Soc. of Performing Arts Administrators Award, 1987; Brahms Medal, City of Hamburg, 1987; Preis der Stiftung für Freiheit und Menschenrechte, Bern, 1987; Golden Viotti Prize, Vercelli, Italy, 1987; Diploma Magistrale, Italy, 1987; Buber-Rosenzweig Medal, Ges. für Christlich-Jüdische Zusammenarbeit, 1989; Epée d'Academicien, Académie des Beaux Arts, 1988; Wolf Foundn Prize, 1991. Decorations include: Grand Officier de la Légion d'Honneur, 1986; Commander: Order of Arts and Letters (France); Order of Leopold (Belgium); Grand Officer, Order of Merit of the Republic (Italy), 1987; Officer, Ordre de la Couronne (Belgium); Kt Comdr Order of Merit (Fed. Rep. of Germany); Royal Order of the Phœnix (Greece); Comdr, Order of Orange-Nassau (Netherlands); Grand Cross, Order of Merit (FRG); Hon. Citizen of Switzerland, 1970. *Publications:* The Violin: six lessons by Yehudi Menuhin, 1971; Theme and Variations, 1972; Violin and Viola, 1976; Sir Edward Elgar: My Musical Grandfather (essay), 1976; (autobiography) Unfinished Journey, 1977; The Music of Man, 1980; (with Christopher Hope) The King, the Cat and the Fiddle, (children's book), 1983; Life Class, 1986; *Relevant Publication:* Yehudi Menuhin, The Story of the Man and the Musician, by Robert Magidoff, 1956 (USA); Conversations with Menuhin, by Robin Daniels, 1979. *Films:* Stage Door Canteen; Magic Bow; The Way of Light (biog.). *Television series:* The Music of Man. *Address:* Anglo-Swiss Artists' Management, 4 and 5 Primrose Mews, 1A Sharpleshall Street, NW1 8YW. *Clubs:* Athenæum, Garrick.

MENZIES, John Maxwell; Chairman, John Menzies, since 1952; *b* 13 Oct. 1926; *s* of late John Francis Menzies, and of Cynthia Mary Graham; *m* 1953, Patricia Eleanor, *d* of late Comdr Sir Hugh Dawson, Bt, CBE and Lady Dawson; four *d*. *Educ:* Eton. Lieut Grenadier Guards. Berwickshire CC, 1954–57. Director: Scottish American Mortgage Co., 1959–63; Standard Life Assurance Co., 1960–63; Vidal Sassoon Inc., 1969–80; Gordon & Gotch plc, 1970–85; Atlantic Assets Trust, 1973–88 (Chm., 1983–88); Independent Investment Co. plc, 1973– (Chm., 1983–); Fairhaven International (formerly Nimslo International), 1980–88; Rocky Mountains Oil & Gas, 1980–85; Ivory & Sime plc, 1980–83; Personal Assets PLC, 1981–; Bank of Scotland, 1984–; Guardian Royal Exchange, 1985–; Malcolm Innes & Partners Ltd, 1989–. Trustee, Newsvendors' Benevolent Instn, 1974– (Pres., 1968–74). Mem., Royal Co. of Archers, HM's Body Guard for Scotland. *Recreations:* farming, shooting, reading, travel. *Address:* Kames, Duns, Berwickshire. *T:* Leitholm (089084) 202. *Clubs:* Turf, Boodle's; New (Edinburgh).

MENZIES, Dame Pattie (Maie), GBE 1954; *b* 2 March 1899; *d* of late Senator J. W. Leckie; *m* 1920, Robert Gordon Menzies (Rt Hon. Sir Robert Menzies, KT, AK, CH, QC, FRS; Prime Minister of the Commonwealth of Australia, 1939–41 and 1949–66) (*d* 1978); one *s* one *d* (and one *s* decd). *Educ:* Fintona Girls' Sch., Melbourne; Presbyterian Ladies' Coll., Melbourne. *Address:* 7 Monaro Close, Kooyong, Vic 3144, Australia. *Club:* Alexandra (Melbourne).

MENZIES, Sir Peter (Thomson), Kt 1972; Director: National Westminster Bank Ltd, 1968–82; Commercial Union Assurance Co. Ltd, 1962–82; *b* 15 April 1912; *s* of late John C. Menzies and late Helen S. Aikman; *m* 1938, Mary McPherson Alexander, *d* of late John T. Menzies and late Agnes Anderson; one *s* one *d*. *Educ:* Musselburgh Grammar Sch.; University of Edinburgh. MA, 1st Class Hons Math. and Natural Philosophy, 1934. Inland Revenue Dept, 1933–39; Treasurer's Dept, Imperial Chemical Industries Ltd, 1939–56 (Asst Treas. 1947, Dep. Treas. 1952); Director: Imperial Chemical Industries Ltd, 1956–72 (Dep. Chm., 1967–72); Imperial Metal Industries Ltd, 1962–72 (Chm., 1964–72). Part-time Mem., CEGB, 1960–72; Mem., Review Body on Doctors' and Dentists' Remuneration, 1971–83; Chairman: Electricity Council, 1972–77; London Exec. Cttee, Scottish Council (Develt and Industry), 1977–82. A Vice-Pres., Siol na Meinnrich; Pres., UNIPEDE, 1973–76; Vice-Pres. and Gen. Treas., BAAS, 1982–86. FInstP; CompIEE. *Address:* Kit's Corner, Harmer Green, Welwyn, Herts AL6 0ER. *T:* Welwyn (043871) 4386. *Club:* Caledonian.

MENZIES-WILSON, William Napier, CBE 1985; Chairman: Edinburgh Tankers plc, since 1986; Forth Tankers plc, since 1991; Director, National Freight Consortium, since 1986; *b* 4 Dec. 1926; *s* of James Robert Menzies-Wilson and Jacobine Napier Williamson-Napier; *m* 1953, Mary Elizabeth Darnell Juckes; two *s* one *d*. *Educ:* Winchester; New Coll., Oxford (MA); North Western Univ., Chicago. Joined Stewarts & Lloyds Ltd, 1950; Managing Director, Stewarts & Lloyds of South Africa Ltd, 1954–61, Chairman, 1961; Director, Stewarts & Lloyds Ltd, 1964; Dir, Supplies & Transport, British Steel Corporation, 1967–73; Chairman: Wm Cory & Son Ltd, 1973–77; Ocean Transport & Trading plc, Liverpool, 1980–86 (Dir, 1973–88); Viking Resources Trust, 1986–89; Director: Overseas Containers Holdings, 1979–86; Dunlop Holdings, 1982–84. Pres., Gen. Council of British Shipping, 1984–85; Mem. Exec. Bd, Lloyd's Register of Shipping, 1984–87. Chm., Bd of Trustees, Help the Aged, 1988–. *Recreations:* shooting, golf, gardening. *Address:* Last House, Old, Northampton NN6 9RJ. *T:* Northampton (0604) 781346. *Clubs:* Brooks's; Hon. Co. of Edinburgh Golfers.

MERCER, Prof. Alan; Professor of Operational Research, University of Lancaster, since 1968; *b* 22 Aug. 1931; *s* of Harold Mercer and Alice Ellen (*née* Catterall); *m* 1954, Lillian Iris (*née* Pigott); two *s*. *Educ:* Penistone Grammar Sch.; Cambridge Univ. (MA; DipMathStat); London Univ. (PhD). NCB, 1954–56; UKAEA, 1956–62; Armour & Co. Ltd, 1962–64; Univ. of Lancaster, 1964–: Chm., Sch. of Management and Organisational Scis, 1982–85. Mem., Central Lancashire Develt Corp., 1971–85; Mem., 1985–89, Chm., 1986–89, Warrington and Runcorn Develt Corp. Chm., Employers' Side of Whitley Council for New Towns Staff, 1979–89 (Mem., 1971–89); Mem., Management and Industrial Relns Cttee, SSRC, 1972–76, 1980–82; Chm., Industry and Employment Cttee, ESRC, 1984–87 (Vice Chm., 1982–84); Mem., NW Econ. Planning Council, 1973–79. Jt Editor, European Journal of Operational Research, 1977–. *Publications:* Operational Distribution Research (jtly), 1978; Innovative Marketing Research, 1991; numerous papers in learned jls. *Recreations:* travel, bridge, sport. *Address:* 11 The Buoymasters, St George's Quay, Lancaster LA1 1HL. *T:* Lancaster (0524) 37244.

MERCER, Rt. Rev. Eric Arthur John; *b* 6 Dec. 1917; *s* of Ambrose John Mercer, Kent; *m* 1951, Rosemary Wilma, *d* of John William Denby, Lincs; one *s* one *d*. *Educ:* Dover Gram. Sch.; Kelham Theol. Coll. Enlisted Sherwood Foresters, 1940; Capt. and Adjt, 14th Foresters, 1943; served Italy (despatches), 1944; Staff Coll., Haifa, 1944; DAA&QMG, 66 Inf. Bde, Palestine, 1945; GSO2 (SD), HQ, MEF, 1945. Returned Kelham Theol. Coll., 1946–47. Ordained, Chester; Curate, Coppenhall, Crewe, 1947–51; Priest in charge, Heald Green, 1951–53; Rector, St Thomas', Stockport, 1953–59; Chester Diocesan Missioner, 1959–65; Rector, Chester St Bridget, 1959–65; Hon. Canon of Chester Cathedral, 1964; Bishop Suffragan of Birkenhead, 1965–73; Bishop of Exeter, 1973–85. Church Commissioners: Dep. Chm., Pastoral Cttee, 1976–85; Mem., Bd of Governors, 1980–85. Nat. Chm., CEMS, 1974–78. *Publication:* (contrib.) Worship in a Changing Church, 1965. *Address:* Frickers House, Chilmark, Salisbury SP3 5AJ. *T:* Teffont (072276) 400.

MERCER, Ian Dews; Chief Executive, Countryside Council for Wales, since 1990; *b* 25 Jan. 1933; *s* of Eric Baden Royds Mercer and Nellie Irene Mercer; *m* 1st, 1957, Valerie Jean Hodgson; four *s*; 2nd, 1976, Pamela Margaret Gillies (*née* Clarkson). *Educ:* King Edward VI Sch., Stourbridge; Univ. of Birmingham (BA Hons). Sub-Lieut RNR, 1954–56. Field Centre appts, Preston Montford, 1956–57, Juniper Hall, 1957–59, Slapton Ley, 1959–68; Lectr, St Luke's Coll., Exeter, 1968–70; Warden, Malham Tarn Field Centre, 1970–71; County Conservation Officer, Devon CC; 1971–73; National Park Officer, Dartmoor, 1973–90. *Publications:* Nature Guide to the West Country, 1981; chapters in books on conservation matters. *Recreations:* painting, teaching adults birds and landscape, watching sons play Rugby. *Address:* Countryside Council for Wales, Plas Penrhos, Ffordd Penrhos, Bangor LL57 2LQ. *T:* Bangor (0248) 370444.

MERCER, John Charles Kenneth; a Recorder of the Crown Court, 1975–82; *b* 17 Sept. 1917; *s* of late Charles Wilfred Mercer and Cecil Maud Mercer; *m* 1944, Barbara Joan, *d* of late Arnold Sydney Whitehead, CB, CBE, and Maud Ethel Whitehead; one *s* one *d*. *Educ:* Ellesmere Coll.; Law Sch., Swansea University Coll. (LLB). Solicitor. War Service, 1940–45, Captain RA. Partner, Douglas-Jones & Mercer, 1946–88, now Consultant. Mem., Royal Commn on Criminal Procedure, 1978–81; Mem., SW Wales River Authority, 1960–74. *Recreations:* fishing, shooting, golf, watching sport. *Address:* 334 Gower Road, Killay, Swansea, West Glamorgan SA2 7AE. *T:* Swansea (0792) 202931. *Clubs:* City and County, Clyne Golf (Swansea).

MERCER, Dr Robert Giles Graham; Headmaster, Stonyhurst College, since 1985; *b* 30 May 1949; *s* of late Leonard and Florence Elizabeth Mercer; *m* 1974, Caroline Mary Brougham; one *s*. *Educ:* Austin Friars School, Carlisle; Churchill College, Cambridge (Scholar; 1st cl. Hist. Tripos, Pts I and II; MA); St John's College, Oxford (Sen. Schol., DPhil). Head of History, Charterhouse, 1974–76; Asst Principal, MoD, 1976–78; Dir of Studies and Head of History, Sherborne School, 1979–85. FRSA. *Publication:* The Teaching of Gasparino Barzizza, 1979. *Recreations:* art, music, travel, swimming. *Address:* St Philip's, Stonyhurst, Lancs BB6 9PT. *T:* Stonyhurst (025486) 247. *Clubs:* Athenæum, East India.

MERCER, Rt. Rev. Robert William Stanley, CR; Diocesan Bishop, Anglican Catholic Church of Canada, since 1989 (Assistant Bishop, 1988–89); *b* 10 Jan. 1935; *s* of Harold Windrum Mercer and Kathleen Frampton. *Educ:* Grey School, Port Elizabeth, S Africa; St Paul's Theological Coll., Grahamstown, SA (LTh). Deacon 1959, priest 1960, Matabeleland; Asst Curate, Hillside, Bulawayo, 1959–63; Novice, CR, 1963; professed, 1965; at Mirfield, 1963–66; at St Teilo's Priory, Cardiff, 1966–68; Prior and Rector of Stellenbosch, S Africa, 1968–70; deported from SA, 1970; Chaplain, St Augustine's School, Penhalonga, Rhodesia, 1971–72; Rector of Borrowdale, Salisbury, Rhodesia, 1972–77; Bishop of Matabeleland, 1977–87. Sub-Prelate, Order of St John of Jerusalem, 1981. *Address:* 225 First Avenue, Ottawa, Ontario K1S 2G5, Canada.

MERCER, Roger James, FSA, FSAScot; Secretary, Royal Commission on the Ancient and Historical Monuments of Scotland, since 1990; *b* 12 Sept. 1944; *o s* of Alan Mercer and Patricia (*née* Hicks); *m* 1970, Susan Jane Fowlie; one *s* one *d*. *Educ:* Harrow County Grammar Sch.; Edinburgh Univ. (MA). MIFA. Inspector of Ancient Monuments, DoE, 1969–74; Lectr and Reader, Dept of Archaeology, Univ. of Edinburgh, 1974–89. Mem., Ancient Monuments Bd for Scotland, 1988–; Vice President: Soc. of Antiquaries of Scotland, 1988–91; Prehistoric Soc., 1989–92. British Acad. Readership, 1989. *Publications:* Beaker Studies in Europe (ed), 1979; Hambledon Hill—a Neolithic Landscape, 1980; Grimes Graves—Excavations 1971–72, 1981; Carn Brea—a Neolithic Defensive Complex, 1981; (ed) Farming Practice in British Prehistory, 1981; Causewayed Enclosures, 1990; articles and reviews in learned jls. *Recreations:* music, books, good food. *Address:* 103 Morningside Drive, Edinburgh EH10 5NN. *T:* 031–447 4812.

MERCER NAIRNE PETTY-FITZMAURICE, family name of **Marquess of Lansdowne.**

MERCHANT, Ismail; film producer, since 1960; Partner, Merchant Ivory Productions, since formation, 1961; *b* 25 Dec. 1936; *s* of Noormohamed Haji Abdul Rehman and Hazra Memon. *Educ:* St Xavier's Coll., Bombay (BA); New York Univ. (MBA). Collaborator with Ruth Prawer Jhabvala and James Ivory on most of the following: *feature films:* The Householder, 1963; Shakespeare Wallah, 1965 (won Best Actress award, Berlin Film Fest., 1965); The Guru, 1969; Bombay Talkie, 1970; Savages, 1972; The Wild Party, 1975; Roseland, 1977; The Europeans, 1979 (official Brit. entry, Cannes Film Fest.); Quartet, 1981; Heat and Dust, 1982 (Brit. entry, Cannes Film Fest.); The Bostonians, 1984 (feature, Cannes Film Fest.); A Room with a View, 1986; Maurice, 1987 (Silver Lions for Best Picture, Best Actor and Best Composer); Slaves of New York, 1989; Mr and Mrs Bridge, 1990; *shorts:* The Creation of Woman, 1960 (Academy award nomination); Helen, Queen of the Nautch Girls, 1973; (directed) Mahatma and the Mad Boy, 1973; Sweet Sounds, 1976; *television:* Adventures of a Brown Man in Search of Civilization, 1971 (BBC); Autobiography of a Princess, 1975 (TV special, NY); Hullabaloo over Georgie and Bonnie's Pictures, 1978 (feature, LWT); Jane Austen in Manhattan, 1980 (feature, LWT and Polytel); (directed for Channel 4) The Courtesans of Bombay, 1983; The Curry Connection, 1990 (series, Channel 4). *Publications:* Ismail Merchant's Indian Cuisine, 1986; Hullabaloo In Old Jaypoore, 1988. *Recreations:* squash, bicycling, cooking. *Address:* 400 East 52nd Street, New York, NY 10022, USA. *T:* 212 759 3694; 32 Motlabai Street, Bombay, India. *T:* 378–376.

MERCHANT, John Richard; Secretary and Director, Council Policy and Administration, Science and Engineering Research Council, since 1988; *b* 4 June 1945; *s* of William Henry Merchant and Eileen Merchant; *m* 1966, Eileen McGill, two *s*. *Educ:* Gravesend Grammar Sch.; Sheffield Univ. (BSc); Cranfield Inst. of Technol. (MSc). FIS. Lyons Bakery Ltd, 1966–69; Lectr, Cranfield Inst. of Technol., 1969–75; Statistician, MoD, 1975–79; Chief Statistician, CS Coll., 1979–82; Asst Sec., Cabinet Office (MPO), 1982–84; Principal Finance and Estabt Officer, DPP, 1984–86, Crown Prosecution Service, 1986–88; Under Sec., 1985. *Recreations:* Nigerian postal history, fishing. *Address:* (office) Polaris House, North Star Avenue, Swindon, Wilts SN2 1ET. *T:* Swindon (0793) 411438.

MERCHANT, Piers Rolf Garfield; Director of Public Affairs, The Advertising Association, since 1990; *b* 2 Jan. 1951; *s* of Garfield Frederick Merchant and Audrey Mary Rolfe-Martin; *m* 1977, Helen Joan Burrluck; one *d*. *Educ:* Nottingham High School; Univ. of Durham. BA (Hons) Law and Politics, MA Political Philosophy. Reporter, Municipal Correspondent, Chief Reporter, Dep. News Editor, The Journal, 1973–80; News Editor, The Journal, 1980–82; Editor, Conservative Newsline, 1982–84. Dir of Corporate Publicity, NEI plc, 1987–90. Contested (C) Newcastle upon Tyne Central, 1979. MP (C) Newcastle upon Tyne Central, 1983–87; Prospective Parly Candidate (C), Beckenham, 1991–. Co-Chm., Freeflow of Information Cttee, Internat. Parly Gp, 1986–87; Vice-Chm., All-Party Parly Cttee on AIDS, 1987. Mem., Senior Common Room, University Coll., Durham. *Publications:* newspaper articles and features. *Recreations:* swimming, walking, genealogy, electronics, computers. *Address:* 176 Bromley Road, Beckenham, Kent BR2 3PG. *T:* 081–663 6854.

MERCHANT, Rev. Prof. William Moelwyn, FRSL; writer and sculptor; *b* 5 June 1913; *s* of late William Selwyn and Elizabeth Ann Merchant, Port Talbot, Glamorgan; *m* 1938, Maria Eluned Hughes, Llanelly; one *s* one *d*. *Educ:* Port Talbot Grammar Sch.; (Exhibnr) University Coll., Cardiff. BA, 1st Cl. English hons 1933; 2nd Cl. 1st div. Hist., 1934; MA 1950; DLitt 1960; Hon. Fellow, University Coll., Cardiff, 1981. Hist. Master, Carmarthen Grammar Sch., 1935; English Master, Newport High Sch., 1936; English Lectr, Caerleon Trg Coll., 1937; University Coll. Cardiff: Lectr in Eng. Lang. and Lit., 1939; Sen. Lectr, 1950; Reader, 1961; Prof. of English, Univ. of Exeter, 1961–74; Vicar of Llanddewi Brefi, dio. St Davids, 1974–78; Hon. Lectr, All Saints Church, Leamington Spa, 1979. Fellow, Folger Shakespeare Library, Washington, DC, and Fulbright Fellow, 1957; Woodward Lectr, Yale Univ., 1957; Dupont Lectr, Sewanee Univ., Tenn, 1963; Willett Prof. of English and Theology, Univ. of Chicago, 1971. Founded Rougemont Press, 1970 (with Ted Hughes, Eric Cleave and Paul Merchant). Welsh Cttee of Arts Council of Gt Brit., 1960 and 1975–; Council, Llandaff Festival, 1958–61. Consultant and script-writer on film, The Bible, Rome, 1960–64. Ordained to Anglican Orders, 1940; Examining Chaplain to the Bishop of Salisbury; Canon of Salisbury Cathedral, 1967–73, Canon Emeritus, 1973 (Chancellor, 1967–71); Mem., Archbishops' Commn on Faculty Jurisdiction, 1979–. Founded Llanddewi Brefi Arts Fest., 1975. Mem., Welsh Acad., 1991. FRSL 1976; Hon. Fellow, University Coll. of Wales, Aberystwyth, 1975. Hon. Prof. of Drama, UC Aberystwyth, 1985–87; Lyttelton Lectr, Eton Coll., 1983; Hon. Mem., Old Etonian Assoc., 1990. Hon HLD Wittenberg Univ., Ohio, 1973. *Publications:* Wordsworth's Guide to the Lakes (illus. John Piper), 1952 (US 1953); Reynard Library Wordsworth, 1955 (US 1955); Shakespeare and the Artist, 1959; Creed and Drama, 1965; (ed) Merchant of Venice, 1967; (ed) Marlowe's Edward the Second, 1967; Comedy, 1972; Tree of Life (libretto, music by Alun Hoddinott), 1972; Breaking the Code (poems), 1975; (ed) Essays and Studies, 1977; No Dark Glass (poems), 1979; R. S. Thomas, a critical evaluation, 1979 (US 1990); Confrontation of Angels (poems), 1986; Jeshua (novel), 1987 (US 1991); Fire from the Heights (novel), 1989 (US 1991); A Bundle of Papyrus (novel), 1989; Fragments of a Life (autobiog.), 1990 (Welsh Arts Council Literary Award, 1991); Inherit the Land (short stories), 1992; articles in Times Literary Supplement, Warburg Jl, Shakespeare Survey, Shakespeare Quarterly, Shakespeare Jahrbuch, Encyc. Britannica, etc. *Recreations:* theatre, typography, sculpting (thirty one-man exhibns at Exeter, Cardiff, Swansea, Plymouth, Southampton, Aberystwyth, Glasgow, Stirling, Birmingham, London, 1971–89). *Address:* 32A Willes Road, Leamington Spa, Warwicks. *T:* Leamington (0926) 314253.

MERCIECA, Most Rev. Joseph; *see* Malta, Archbishop of, (RC).

MEREDITH, Most Rev. Bevan; *see* Papua New Guinea, Archbishop of.

MEREDITH, John Michael; barrister-at-law; Magistrate, Hong Kong, since 1988; *b* 23 Oct. 1934; *s* of late John Stanley Meredith and of Lily Meredith; *m*; one *s* three *d*; *m* 1988, Linda (*née* Crossland). *Educ:* Crossley and Porter Schs, Halifax, Yorks; Leeds Univ. (LLB Hons 1956). Called to the Bar, Gray's Inn, 1958; Junior, NE Circuit, 1964; a Recorder, 1976–88. *Recreations:* shooting, sailing. *Address:* A1 Elm Tree Towers, 26th Floor, 8 Chun Tai Road, Tai Hang, Hong Kong. *T:* 576–9657. *Clubs:* Pwllheli Sailing (N Wales); Royal Hong Kong Yacht.

MEREDITH, Richard Alban Creed, MA; Church Missionary Society Area Secretary, dioceses of Derby, Leicester and Southwell, since 1990; *b* 1 Feb. 1935; *s* of late Canon R. Creed Meredith; *m* 1968, Hazel Eveline Mercia Parry; one *s* one *d*. *Educ:* Stowe Sch.; Jesus Coll., Cambridge. Asst Master (Modern Langs), 1957–70, Housemaster, 1962–70, King's Sch., Canterbury; Headmaster, Giggleswick Sch., 1970–78; Head Master, Monkton Combe Sch., 1978–90. *Recreations:* walking, foreign travel, music, gardening. *Address:* Beacon Knoll, 334 Beacon Road, Loughborough LE11 2RD. *T:* Loughborough (0509) 212008.

MEREDITH DAVIES, (James) Brian; *see* Davies.

MERIFIELD, Anthony James; Head of Senior and Public Appointments Group, Cabinet Office, since 1991; *b* 5 March 1934; *s* of late Francis Bertram Merifield and Richardina (*née* Parker); *m* 1980, Pamela Pratt. *Educ:* Chesterfield Sch.; Shrewsbury Sch.; Wadham Coll., Oxford (MA). National Service, 1952–54, Royal Tank Regt. HM Overseas Civil Service, Kenya, 1958–65; Department of Health and Social Security: Principal, 1965–71; Asst Sec., 1971–77; Under Secretary, 1978–82; Under Sec., NI Office, 1982–85; Dir of Regl Liaison, NHS Management Bd, DHSS, subseq. NHS Management Exec., DoH, 1986–91. *Address:* Office of Minister for Civil Service, Cabinet Office, Horse Guards Road, SW1P 3AL. *T:* 071–270 6220. *Club:* Commonwealth Trust.

MERLE, Robert; Croix du Combattant, 1945; Officier de l'Instruction publique, 1953; Professor of English Literature, University of Paris X, Nanterre, since 1965; Titular Professor: University of Rennes, Brittany, since 1944 (on leave, 1950–51); University of Toulouse, since 1957; University of Caen-Rouen, since 1960; University of Algiers, since 1963; *b* 29 Aug. 1908; father an officer; *m* 1st; one *d*; *m* 2nd, 1949; three *s* one *d*; 3rd, 1965; one *s*. *Educ:* Lycée Michelet, Paris; Sorbonne, Paris. Professor, 1944. Mobilised, 1939; Liaison agent with BEF (prisoner, 1940–43). *Publications:* Oscar Wilde, 1948; Week-end à Zuydcoote, 1949 (awarded Prix Goncourt); La Mort est mon métier, 1953; L'Ile, 1962 (awarded Prix de la Fraternité) (translated, as The Island, 1964); Un Animal doué de raison, 1967 (translated, as The Day of the Dolphin, 1969); Derrière la vitre, 1970; Malevil, 1972 (Campbell Award, USA); Les hommes protégés, 1974 (translated, as The Virility Factor, 1977); Madrapour, 1976; Fortune de France, 1978; En nos vertes années, 1979; Paris ma bonne ville, 1980; Le Prince que voilà, 1982; La violente amour, 1983; La Pique du jour, 1985; Le Jour ne se lève pas pour nous, 1986; L'Idole, 1987 (translated, as The Idol, 1989); Le Propre de l'Homme, 1989; La Volte des Vestugadins, 1991; *plays:* Flamineo (inspired by Webster's White Devil), 1953; Nouveau Sisyphe; *historical essays:* Moncada, 1965; Ben Bella, 1965; translations, articles. *Recreations:* swimming, tennis, yachting. *Address:* La Malmaison, Grosrouvre, 78490 Montfort L'Amaury, France.

MERLO, David, CEng; Director of Research, British Telecommunications plc, 1983–89; *b* 16 June 1931; *s* of Carlo G. Merlo and Catherine E. Merlo (*née* Stringer); *m* 1952, Patricia Victoria Jackson; two *s*. *Educ:* Kilburn Grammar Sch., London; London Univ. (BScEng 1st Cl. Hons 1954); W. B. Esson schol. of IEE, 1953, and IEE Electronics Premium, 1966. CEng 1967, FIEE 1973. Post Office Research Br., 1948; Executive Engineer, 1955; Sen. Scientific Officer, 1959; Principal Sci. Officer, 1967; Head of Division, 1974; Dep. Director of Research, 1977. Visiting Lecturer: Northampton Polytechnic, 1955–61; Regent Street Polytechnic, 1960–69; Governor, Suffolk College of Higher and Further Education, 1984–89. Served on numerous technical committees in telecommunications field. FRSA 1988. Patent award, 1970. *Publications:* miscellaneous contribs to learned jls. *Recreations:* reading, photography, wine. *Address:* Heather Lodge, Levington, Ipswich IP10 0NA. *T:* Nacton (0473) 659508.

MERMAGEN, Air Commodore Herbert Waldemar, CB 1960; CBE 1945 (OBE 1941); AFC 1940; retired, 1960; Director, Sharps, Pixley Ltd (Bullion Brokers), 1962–77; *b* 1 Feb. 1912; *s* of late L. W. R. Mermagen, Southsea; *m* 1937, Rosemary, *d* of late Maj. Mainwaring Williams, DSO and late Mrs Tristram Fox, Cheltenham; two *s*. *Educ:* Brighton Coll., Sussex. Joined RAF, 1930; 43(F) Sqdn, 1931–34; Instructor CFS, 1936–38; Squadron Leader, 1938; served War of 1939–45 in Fighter Command, UK, Middle East, France and Germany (SHAEF); AOC British Air Command, Berlin, 1945–46; Sen. RAF Liaison Officer, UK Services Liaison Staff, Australia, 1948–50; AOC, RAF Ceylon, 1955–57; Air Officer i/c Administration, Headquarters, RAF Transport Command, 1958–60. Air Commodore, 1955. Comdr Legion of Merit (USA), 1946; Medal for Distinguished Services (USSR), 1945; Chevalier, Légion d'Honneur (France) 1951. *Recreations:* rugby (RAF (colours), Sussex, Richmond), golf, gardening. *Address:* Allandale, Vicarage Street, Painswick, Glos. *Club:* Royal Air Force.

MERRETT, Charles Edwin, CBE 1979; Area Organiser, Union of Shop, Distributive and Allied Workers, 1948–83, retired; *b* 26 Jan. 1923; *s* of Charles and Eva Merrett; *m* 1950, Mildred Merrett; two *s*. *Educ:* Palfrey Senior Boys' Sch., Walsall. Bristol City Council: Councillor, 1957–, Leader, 1974–78; Lord Mayor of Bristol, 1978–79, Dep. Lord Mayor, 1979–80. Member: Policy Cttee, Assoc. of District Councils, 1974–78; Jt Consultative Cttee on Local Govt Finance, 1975–78; Chm., Adv. Council, BBC Radio Bristol, 1979–83. *Recreations:* watching sport, music, theatre. *Address:* 13 Gainsborough Square, Lockleaze, Bristol BS7 9XA. *T:* Bristol (0272) 515195.

MERRICKS, Walter Hugh; Assistant Secretary-General (Communications), Law Society, since 1987; *b* 4 June 1945; 2nd *s* of Dick and late Phoebe Merricks, Icklesham, Sussex; *m* 1982, Olivia Montuschi; one *s* one *d*, and one step *s*. *Educ:* Bradfield College, Berks; Trinity College, Oxford. MA Hons (Jurisp). Articled Clerk with Batt, Holden, 1968–70; admitted Solicitor, 1970; Hubbard Travelling Scholar, Montreal, 1971; Dir, Camden Community Law Centre, 1972–76; Lectr in Law, Brunel Univ., 1976–81; legal affairs writer, New Law Journal, 1982–85; Sec., Professional and Public Relations, Law Soc., 1985–87. Member: Royal Commn on Criminal Procedure, 1978–81; Fraud Trials (Roskill) Cttee, 1984–86. *Address:* 32 Cholmeley Crescent, N6 5HA. *T:* 081–341 0406; c/o The Law Society, 113 Chancery Lane, WC2A 1PL. *T:* 071–242 1222.

MERRIFIELD, Prof. Robert Bruce; Professor, since 1966, John D. Rockefeller Jr Professor, since 1984, Rockefeller University; *b* 15 July 1921; *s* of George and Lorene Merrifield; *m* 1949, Elizabeth L. Furlong; one *s* five *d*. *Educ:* Univ. of California, Los Angeles (BA 1943, Chemistry; PhD 1949, Biochemistry). Chemist, Philip R. Park Research Foundn, 1943–44; Research Asst, UCLA Med. Sch., 1948–49; Asst to Associate Prof., Rockefeller Inst. for Med. Research, 1949–66. Nobel Guest Prof., Uppsala, 1968. Member: Amer. Chem. Soc.; Amer. Soc of Biological Chemists; Amer. Inst. of Chemists; Nat. Acad. of Sciences. Associate Editor, Internat. Jl of Peptide and Protein Research; Mem. Editl Bd of Analytical Biochemistry. Numerous hon. degrees from Amer. univs and colls. Lasker Award for Basic Med. Research, 1969; Gairdner Award, 1970; Intra-Science Award, 1970; Amer. Chem. Soc. Award for Creative Work in Synthetic Organic Chemistry, 1972; Nichols Medal, 1973; Instrument Specialties Co. Award, Univ. of Nebraska, 1977; Alan E. Pierce Award, 1979; Nobel Prize in Chemistry, 1984; Hirschmann Award in Peptide Chem., ACS, 1990; Josef Rudinger Award, 1990. Order of San Carlos (Columbia), 1984. *Publications:* numerous papers in sci. jls, esp. on peptide chemistry, solid phase peptide synthesis. *Address:* The Rockefeller University, 1230 York Avenue, New York, NY 10021, USA. *T:* (212) 570–8244.

MERRIMAN, Air Vice-Marshal Alan; *see* Merriman, H. A.

MERRIMAN, Dr Basil Mandeville; FRAS, FRAI, FRGS; *b* 28 March 1911; *s* of Thomas Henry Merriman and Ida, *d* of Mandeville Blackwood Phillips; *m* 1938, Yvonne Flavelle (*d* 1974); one *s*. *Educ:* Colet Court Prep. Sch.; St Paul's School; St Bartholomew's Hospital Med. Coll.; MRCS, LRCP 1934. House Appointments, St Bartholomew's Hosp., 1934–36; post graduate studies, Berlin, Vienna, Prague, 1936–38; Medical Adviser, British Drug Houses, 1938; Med. Dir, Carter Foundn, 1956; Consultant, Home Office Prison Department, 1963. FRAS 1972; Fellow, Royal Soc. for Asian Affairs, 1973; FRAI 1974; FRGS 1976. *Publications:* contribs to medical and social jls on drug action and drug addiction and their relationship to crime, also various related aspects of social anthropology. *Recreation:* travel of all forms, particularly Asiatic (journeys mainly in Arab Asia, Central Asiatic region, and Japan). *Address:* 85 Holland Park, W11 3RZ. *T:* 071–727 8228.

MERRIMAN, Air Vice-Marshal (Henry) Alan, CB 1985; CBE 1973; AFC 1957, and Bar 1961; defence and aerospace consultant; *b* 17 May 1929; *s* of Henry Victor Merriman and Winifred Ellen Merriman; *m* 1965, Mary Brenda Stephenson; three *d*. *Educ:* Hertford Grammar Sch.; RAF Coll., Cranwell. Graduate, Empire Test Pilots Sch. FRAeS 1977. Commnd, 1951; Qual. Flying Instr, 263 F Sqdn, Empire Test Pilots Sch., Fighter Test Sqdn, A&AEE, Central Fighter Estabt, and RAF Staff Coll., 1952–63; Personal Air Sec. to Minister of Defence for RAF, 1964–66; Jt Services Staff Coll., 1966; OC Fighter Test Sqdn, A&AEE, 1966–69; HQ 38 Gp, 1969–70; Stn Comdr, RAF Wittering, 1970–72; RCDS, 1973; CO Empire Test Pilots Sch., 1974–75; Comdt, A&AEE, 1975–77; Dir, Operational Requirements (1), 1977–81; Mil. Dep. to Head of Defence Sales, 1981–84. Dir, Electronic Machine Co., 1987–89. Queen's Commendation for Valuable Services in the Air, 1956. *Recreations:* sailing, gardening. *Address:* 52 Chagford Street, NW1 6EE. *Club:* Royal Air Force.

MERRIMAN, James Henry Herbert, CB 1969; OBE 1961; MSc, MInstP, FEng, FIEE, FIEEIE; Chairman, National Computing Centre, 1977–83; Member for Technology, Post Office Corporation, 1969–76; *b* 1 Jan. 1915; *s* of Thomas P. Merriman, AMINA and A. Margaretta Jenkins; *m* 1942, Joan B. Frost; twin *s* one *d*. *Educ:* King's Coll. Sch., Wimbledon; King's Coll., University of London. BSc (Hons) 1935; MSc (Thesis) 1936. Entered GPO Engrg Dept (Research), 1936; Officer i/c Castleton Radio Stn, 1940; Asst Staff Engr, Radio Br., 1951; Imp. Def. Coll., 1954; Dep. Dir, Organisation and Methods, HM Treasury, 1956; GPO: Dep. Engr-in-Chief, 1965; Sen. Dir Engrg, 1967. Chairman: NEDO Sector Working Party on Office Machinery, 1979–83; NEDO Information Technology Cttee, 1980–83 (Mem. NEDO Electronics EDC, 1980–83); SERC/DoI/Industry Project Universe Steering Cttee, 1981–83; Home Office Radio Spectrum Review Cttee, 1982–83. Vis. Prof. of Electronic Science and Telecommunications, Strathclyde Univ., 1969–79. Governor, Imperial College, Univ. of London, 1971–83; Chm., Inspec, 1975–79; Dir, Infoline, 1976–80; Member: Nat. Electronics Council, 1969–76; Computer Bd for Univ. and Res. Councils, 1976–81; Exec. Bd, BSI, 1981–85 (Chm. Council for Inf. Systems); Science Museum Adv. Council, 1976–81; Council, Spurgeon's Coll., 1972–87. Mem. Council, IEE, 1965–80 (Chm. Electronics Div. Bd, 1968; Vice-Pres., 1969–72, Dep. Pres., 1972; Pres., 1974–75; Hon. FIEE 1981; Faraday Lectr, 1969–70); Royal Instn Discourse, 1971. FKC 1972. Mem., Hon. Soc. of Cymmrodorion, 1979–. Hon. DSc Strathclyde, 1974. *Publications:* contribs to scientific and professional jls on tele-communications and inf. technology subjects. *Recreations:* walking, music, cactus growing.

MERRITT, Prof. John Edward; Emeritus Professor, The Open University, since 1987; educational research in association with Charlotte Mason College, Ambleside, and Community Education Development Centre, Coventry, since 1985; *b* 13 June 1926; *s* of

Leonard Merritt and Janet (*née* Hartford); *m* 1948, Denise Edmondson; two *s*. *Educ:* Univ. of Durham (BA); Univ. of London (DipEdPsychol). ABPsS; FRSA. Sandhurst, 1945–46; Trng Officer, Border Regt, 1946–48. Educnl Psychologist, Lancs LEA, 1957–59; Sen. Educnl Psychologist, Hull LEA, 1959–63; Lectr, Inst. of Educn, Univ. of Durham, 1964–71; Prof. of Teacher Educn, Open Univ., 1971–85, retd. Emeritus Fellow, Leverhulme Trust, 1986–88. Pres., UK Reading Assoc., 1969–70; Chm., 5th World Congress on Reading, Vienna, 1974; Mem., Nat. Cttee of Inquiry into Reading and Use of English (Bullock Cttee), 1973–75. FRSA. *Publications:* Reading and the Curriculum (ed), 1971; A Framework for Curriculum Design, 1972; (ed jtly) Reading Today and Tomorrow, 1972; (ed jtly) The Reading Curriculum, 1972; Perspectives on Reading, 1973; What Shall We Teach, 1974; numerous papers in educnl jls. *Recreations:* fell walking, climbing, ski-ing, theatre. *Address:* Wetherlam, 20 Fisherbeck Park, Ambleside, Cumbria LA22 0AJ. *T:* Ambleside (05394) 32259.

MERRIVALE, 3rd Baron, *cr* 1925, of Walkhampton, Co. Devon; **Jack Henry Edmond Duke;** *b* 27 Jan. 1917; *o s* of 2nd Baron Merrivale, OBE, and Odette, *d* of Edmond Roger, Paris; *S* father 1951; *m* 1st, 1939, Colette (marr. diss. 1974), *d* of John Douglas Wise, Bordeaux, France; one *s* one *d*; 2nd, 1975, Betty, *widow* of Paul Baron. *Educ:* Dulwich; Ecole des Sciences Politiques, Paris. Served War of 1939–45, RAF, 1940; Flight-Lieut, 1944 (despatches). Formerly Chm., Scotia Investments Plc; Chm., Grecian Investments (Gibraltar) Ltd (formerly Leisure Investments (Gibraltar) Ltd), 1990–; Pres., Inst. of Traffic Administration, 1953–70; Chairman: Anglo-Malagasy Soc., 1961; British Cttee for Furthering of Relations with French-speaking Africa, 1973; GB–Senegal Friendship Assoc., 1990. Founder Mem., Club de Dakar, 1974. Freeman, City of London, 1979. FRSA 1964. Chevalier, Nat. Order of Malagasy, 1968. *Recreations:* sailing, riding, photography. *Heir: s* Hon. Derek John Philip Duke, *b* 16 March 1948. *Address:* 16 Brompton Lodge, SW7 2JA. *T:* 071–581 5678.

MERSEY, 4th Viscount *cr* 1916, of Toxteth; **Richard Maurice Clive Bigham;** Baron 1910; Master of Nairne; film director; *b* 8 July 1934; *e s* of 3rd Viscount Mersey, and of 12th Lady Nairne, *qv*; *S* father, 1979; *m* 1961, Joanna, *d* of John A. R. G. Murray, *qv*; one *s*. *Educ:* Eton and Balliol. Irish Guards, 1952–54 (final rank Lt). Films incl. documentaries for Shell, LEPRA and Government. Pres., SIESO and Combined Heat and Power Assoc., 1989–. Various awards in London and Venice. FRGS. *Publication:* The Hills of Cork and Kerry, 1987. *Heir: s* Hon. Edward John Hallam Bigham, *b* 23 May 1966. *Address:* 1 Rosmead Road, W11 2JG. *T:* 071–727 5057.

MERTENS DE WILMARS, Baron Josse (Marie Honoré Charles); Grand Croix de l'Ordre de la Couronne; Chevalier de l'Ordre de Léopold; Judge, 1967–80, and President, 1980–84, Court of Justice of the European Communities; Emeritus Professor, Faculty of Law, Catholic University of Leuven, since 1971; Member of the University Curatorium; Chief editor, Revue Internationale Droit Economique; *b* 12 June 1912; *s* of (Marie Antoine Joseph) Albert Mertens de Wilmars and Jeanne Eugénie Marie Anne Meert; *m* 1939, Elisabeth Simonne M. Hubertine van Ormelingen; three *s* five *d*. *Educ:* Abdijschool, Zevenkerke, Bruges; Catholic Univ. of Leuven (Dr in Law, Dr in Pol. and Diplomatic Science). Hon. Assessor, Legislative Dept of Council of State (Conseil d'Etat) (Assessor, 1950–52). Member: Chambre des Représentants de Belgique (Lower House of Parlt), 1952–62; former Mem., Bar Council. Hon. Mem., Bar of Antwerp. CStJ. Groot kruis von de Orde van Orange Nassau (Neth.); Grand Croix de l'Ordre de la Couronne de Chêne (Lux.); Gross Kreus des Verdienstordens der Bundesrepublik Deutschland. *Publications:* several works on Belgian and European Law. *Address:* 192 Jan Van Rijswijcklaan, B-2020 Antwerpen, Belgium. *T:* 03/238–07–68.

MERTHYR, Barony of (*cr* 1911); title disclaimed by 4th Baron; *see under* Lewis, Trevor Oswin.

MERTON, Viscount; Simon John Horatio Nelson; *b* 21 Sept. 1971; *s* and *heir* of 9th Earl Nelson, *qv*.

MERTON, John Ralph, MBE 1942; painter; *b* 7 May 1913; *s* of late Sir Thomas Merton, KBE, FRS; *m* 1939, Viola Penelope von Bernd; two *d* (and one *d* decd). *Educ:* Eton; Balliol Coll., Oxford. Served War of 1939–45 (MBE); Air Photo reconnaissance research, Lieut-Col 1944. Works include: Mrs Daphne Wall, 1948; The Artist's daughter, Sarah, 1949; Altar piece, 1952; The Countess of Dalkeith, at Drumlanrig, 1958; A myth of Delos, 1959; Clarissa, 1960; Mrs Julian Sheffield, 1970; Sir Charles Evans, 1973; Iona Colquhoun Duchess of Argyll, 1982; Triple Portrait of Sir David Piper, 1984 (in Nat. Portrait Gall.); James Meade, 1987; Triple Portrait of HRH The Princess of Wales (for Cardiff City Hall), 1987; HM The Queen (at Windsor Castle), 1989. Legion of Merit (USA), 1945. *Recreations:* music, making things, underwater photography. *Address:* Pound House, Oare, near Marlborough, Wilts SN8 4JA. *T:* Marlborough (0672) 63539. *Club:* Garrick.

See also Hon. Sir R. A. Morritt.

MERTON, Patrick Anthony, MD; FRCP; FRS 1979; Professor of Human Physiology, University of Cambridge, 1984–88; Fellow of Trinity College, Cambridge, since 1962; Hon. Consultant in Clinical Neurophysiology to the National Hospital, Queen Square, London, since 1979; *b* 8 Oct. 1920; *s* of late Gerald Merton, MC, PhD, FRAS; *m* 1951, Anna Gabriel Howe; one *s* three *d*. *Educ:* The Leys; Beaumont; Trinity Coll., Cambridge (MB 1946; MD 1982); St Thomas's Hosp. On staff of MRC's Neurol. Res. Unit, National Hosp., Queen Sq., 1946–57; Nobel Inst. for Neurophysiology, Stockholm, 1952–54; Lectr, 1957–77, Reader, 1977–84, Univ. of Cambridge; Hon. Sen. Res. Fellow, Royal Postgrad. Med. Sch., 1981–82. *Publications:* scientific papers. *Address:* Trinity College, Cambridge CB2 1TQ.

MERVYN DAVIES, David Herbert; *see* Davies, D. H. M.

MESSEL, Prof. Harry, CBE 1979; BA, BSc, PhD (NUI) 1951; Professor and Head of the School of Physics, and Director of Science Foundation for Physics, University of Sydney, Australia, 1952–87, now Emeritus Professor; *b* 3 March 1922. *Educ:* Rivers Public High Sch., Rivers, Manitoba. Entered RMC of Canada, 1940, grad. with Governor-General's Silver Medal, 1942. Served War of 1939–45: Canadian Armed Forces, Lieut, Canada and overseas, 1942–45. Queen's Univ., Kingston, Ont., 1945–48; BA 1st Cl. Hons in Mathematics, 1948, BSc Hons in Engineering Physics, 1948; St Andrews Univ., Scotland, 1948–49; Institute for Advanced Studies, Dublin, Eire, 1949–51; Sen. Lectr in Mathematical Physics, University of Adelaide, Australia, 1951–52. Mem., Aust. Atomic Energy Commn, 1974–81; Sen. Vice-Chm., Species Survival Commn, IUCN, 1978– (Chm., Crocodile Specialist Gp, 1989–). *Publications:* Chap. 4, Progress in Cosmic Ray Physics, vol. 2, (North Holland Publishing Company), 1953; co-author and editor of: A Modern Introduction to Physics (Horwitz-Grahame, Vols I, II, III, 1959, 1960, 1962); Selected Lectures in Modern Physics, 1958; Space and the Atom, 1961; A Journey through Space and the Atom, 1962; The Universe of Time and Space, 1963; Light and Life in the Universe, 1964; Science for High School Students, 1964; Time, 1965; Senior Science for High School Students, 1966; (jt) Electron-Photon Shower Distribution Function, 1970; (jt) Multistrand Senior Science for High School Students, 1975; Australian Animals and their Environment, 1977; Time and Man, 1978; Tidal Rivers in Northern Australia and their Crocodile Populations (20 monographs), 1979–87; The Study of Populations, 1985; editor of: From Nucleus to Universe, 1960; Atoms to Andromeda, 1966; Apollo and the Universe, 1967; Man in Inner and Outer Space, 1968; Nuclear Energy Today and Tomorrow, 1969; Pioneering in Outer Space, 1970; Molecules to Man, 1971; Brain Mechanisms and the Control of Behaviour, 1972; Focus on the Stars, 1973; Solar Energy, 1974; Our Earth, 1975; Energy for Survival, 1979; The Biological Manipulation of Life, 1981; Science Update, 1983; The Study of Population, 1985; Highlights in Science, 1987; numerous papers published in: Proc. Physical Soc., London; Philosophical Magazine, London; Physical Review of America. *Recreations:* conservation, water ski-ing, hunting, fishing and photography. *Address:* School of Physics, University of Sydney, Sydney, NSW 2006, Australia. *T:* 692 2537, 692 3383, *Fax:* 660 2903.

MESSER, Cholmeley Joseph; Chairman, Save & Prosper Group, 1981–89; *b* 20 March 1929; *s* of late Col Arthur Albert Messer, DSO. CBE, FRIBA, and Lilian Hope Messer (*née* Dowling); *m* 1956, Ann Mary Power; two *d*. *Educ:* Wellington Coll. Solicitor. Served KRRC, 2nd Lieut, 1948–49. Articled Lawrance Messer & Co., Solicitors, London 1949–54; Partner, 1957–66; Save & Prosper Group: Exec. Dir, 1967–72; Dep. Man. Dir, 1973–80; Man. Dir, 1980–84. Chm., Code of Advertising Practice Cttee, Advertising Standards Authority, 1977–78; Vice-Chm., Internat. Bar Assoc. Cttee on Investment Cos Funds and Trusts, 1978–81; Chm., Unit Trust Assoc., 1981–83; Mem., London Pension Funds Authority, 1989–. Chm., British Bobsleigh Assoc., 1989–. *Recreations:* armchair sport, gardening, golf, railways. *Address:* The Manor House, Normandy, Guildford, Surrey GU3 2AP. *T:* Guildford (0483) 810910. *Club:* City of London.

MESSERVY, Sir (Roney) Godfrey (Collumbell), Kt 1986; Chairman, Strathclyde Institute Ltd, since 1990; Director, ASDA (formerly ASDA—MFI) Group PLC, since 1986 (Chairman, 1991); *b* 17 Nov. 1924; *s* of late Roney Forshaw Messervy and Bertha Crosby (*née* Collumbell); *m* 1952, Susan Patricia Gertrude, *d* of late Reginald Arthur Nunn, DSO, DSC, RNVR, and Adeline Frances Nunn; one *s* two *d*. *Educ:* Oundle; Cambridge Univ. Served War, RE, 1943–47: Parachute Sqdn (Captain). CAV (Mem. of Lucas Group): joined as trainee, 1949; Dir of Equipment Sales, 1963; Dir and Gen. Man., 1966 (also dir of various Lucas subsids at home and abroad); Dir, 1972, Man. Dir, 1974–79, Joseph Lucas (Industries) Ltd; Chm. and Chief Exec., Lucas Industries plc, 1980–87; Chm., Costain Group, 1987–90 (Dir, 1978–90). Member: Council, Birmingham Chamber of Industry and Commerce, 1979– (Pres., 1982–83); Council, SMMT, 1980– (Mem. Exec. Cttee, 1980–; Vice-Pres., 1984–87; Pres., 1987–88; Dep. Pres., 1988–90); Engrg Industries Council, 1980–87; Nat. Defence Industries Council, 1980–87; Council, CBI, 1982–88; BOTB, 1984–88; Vice-Pres., EEF, 1982–87. Freeman, Worshipful Co. of Ironmongers, 1977, Liveryman, 1979. Hon. DSc: Aston in Birmingham, 1982; City, 1986. *Recreations:* farming, field sports, photography. *Address:* 26 Radnor Mews, W2 2SA.

MESSIAEN, Olivier; Grand Croix de la Légion d'Honneur; Grand Croix de l'Ordre national du Mérite; Commandeur des Arts et des Lettres; Member, Institut de France; composer and organist; *b* Avignon, 10 Dec. 1908; *s* of Pierre Messiaen and Cécile Sauvage; *m* 1st, Claire Delbos (*d* 1959); one *s*; 2nd, 1961, Yvonne Loriod (pianist). *Educ:* Lycée de Grenoble; Conservatoire Nat. supérieur de musique, Paris (7 1st prizes). Organist, Trinité, Paris, 1930; co-founder Jeune-France Movement, 1936. Professor: Ecole Normale and Schola Cantorum, 1936–39; of Harmony, Paris Conservatoire, 1941–47; of Analysis, Aesthetics and Rhythm, 1947–; of Composition, 1966–. Mem. Council, Order of Arts and Letters, 1975–. Member: Royal Academy; Acads of Brussels, Madrid, Stockholm. Hon. FRCO 1988. Erasmus Prize, 1971; Sibelius Prize, 1971; Von Siemens Prize, 1975; Léonie Sonning Prize, 1977; Bach-Hamburg Prize, 1979; Liebermann Prize, 1983; Wolf Foundn (Israel) Prize, 1983; Académie Berlin Prize, 1984; Inamori of Kyoto Prize, 1985; Paul VI Prize, 1989. *Works for organ include:* Le Banquet Céleste, 1928; Le Diptyque, 1929; L'Ascension, 1933; La Nativité du Seigneur, 1935; Les Corps Glorieux, 1939; Messe de la Pentecôte, 1949; Livre d'Orgue, 1951; Méditations sur le Mystère de la Sainte Trinité, 1969; Le Livre du Saint Sacrement, 1984; *other works include:* Préludes, 1929; Poèmes pour Mi, 1936; Chants de Terre et de Ciel, 1938; Quatuor pour la Fin du Temps, 1941; Visions de l'Amen, 1943; Vingt Regards sur l'Enfant Jésus, 1944; Trois Petites Liturgies de la Présence Divine, 1944; Harawi, 1945; Turangalila–Symphonie, 1946–48; Cinq Rechants, 1949; Etudes de Rythme, 1949; Réveil des Oiseaux, 1953; Oiseaux exotiques, 1955; Catalogue d'Oiseaux, 1956–58; Chronochromie, 1959; Sept Haïkaï, 1963; Couleurs de la Cité Céleste, 1964; Et Exspecto Resurrectionem Mortuorum, 1965; La Transfiguration de Notre Seigneur, Jésus-Christ, 1969; La Fauvette des Jardins (for piano), 1970; Des Canyons aux Etoiles, 1970–74; Saint François d'Assise (opera), 1975–83; Petites Esquisses d'oiseaux (for piano), 1985–; Un vitrail et des oiseaux (piano and small orch.), 1986; La Ville d'En-Haut (piano and orch.), 1987–; Eclairs sur l'Au-delà (large orch.), 1988–90; Un Sourire (orch.)., 1989–.

MESSITER, Air Commodore Herbert Lindsell, CB 1954; 2nd *s* of late Col Charles Bayard Messiter, DSO, OBE, Barwick Park, Yeovil, Som, and Alice Lindsell; *m* 1933, Lucy Brenda Short (decd); one *d*. *Educ:* Bedford Sch. Served War of 1939–45 (despatches 4 times): Egypt, N Africa, Belgium, Germany. Command Engineer Officer, Far East Air Force, 1950–52; Senior Technical Staff Officer, Bomber Command, RAF, 1952–56; Senior Technical Staff Officer, Middle East Air Force, 1956–59, retired. *Address:* Apartado 46, San Pedro de Alcantara, Málaga, Spain. *Club:* Royal Air Force.

MESSMER, Pierre Auguste Joseph; Grand Officier de la Légion d'Honneur; Compagnon de la Libération; Croix de Guerre, 1939–45; Médaille de la Résistance; Député (RPR) from Moselle, since 1968; *b* Vincennes (Seine), 20 March 1916; *s* of Joseph Messmer, industrialist, and of Marthe (*née* Farcy); *m* 1947, Gilberte Duprez. *Educ:* Lycées Charlemagne and Louis-le Grand; Faculty of Law, Paris; Ecole Nationale de la France d'Outre-Mer. Pupil Administrator of Colonies, 1938. Served War of 1939–45: Free French Forces, 1940; African Campaigns (Bir-Hakeim), France, Germany; parachuted Tonkin; PoW of Vietminh, 1945. Sec.-Gen., Interministerial Cttee of Indochina, 1946; Dir of Cabinet of E. Bollaert (High Commissioner, Indochina), 1947–48; Administrator-in-Chief of France Overseas, 1950; Governor: of Mauritania, 1952, of Ivory Coast, 1954–56; Dir of Cabinet of G. Defferre (Minister, France Overseas), Jan.-April 1956; High Commissioner: Republic of Cameroon, 1956–58; French Equatorial Africa, 1958; French West Africa, July 1958–Dec. 1959; Minister of Armed Forces: (Cabinets: M. Debré, 5 Feb. 1958–14 April 1962; G. Pompidou, April-Nov. 1962, 6 Dec. 1962–7 Jan. 1966, 8 Jan. 1966–1 April 1967, 7 April 1967–10 July 1968; M. Couve de Murville, 12 July 1968–20 June 1969); Minister of State in charge of Depts and Territories Overseas, Feb. 1971–72; Prime Minister, 1972–74; Mem. European Parliament, 1979–80. Pres., RPR Federal Cttee, Moselle, 1969–. Mayor of Sarrebourg, 1971–89. Mem., l'Institut (Académie des Sciences Morales et Politiques), 1988. Officer, American Legion. *Publication:* (jtly) Les écrits militaires de Charles de Gaulle: essai d'analyse thématique, 1986. *Recreations:* tennis, sailing. *Address:* 1 rue du Général Delanne, 92 Neuilly-sur-Seine, France.

MESTEL, Prof. Leon, PhD; FRS 1977; Professor of Astronomy, University of Sussex, since 1973; *b* 5 Aug. 1927; *s* of late Rabbi Solomon Mestel and Rachel (*née* Brodetsky); *m*

1951, Sylvia Louise Cole; two *s* two *d*. *Educ:* West Ham Secondary Sch., London; Trinity Coll., Cambridge (BA 1948, PhD 1952). ICI Res. Fellow, Dept of Maths, Univ. of Leeds, 1951–54; Commonwealth Fund Fellow, Princeton Univ. Observatory, 1954–55; University of Cambridge: Univ. Asst Lectr in Maths, 1955–58; Univ. Lectr in Maths, 1958–66; Fellow of St John's Coll., 1957–66; Vis. Mem., Inst. for Advanced Study, Princeton, 1961–62; J. F. Kennedy Fellow, Weizmann Inst. of Science, Israel, 1966–67; Prof. of Applied Maths, Manchester Univ., 1967–73. *Publications:* Magnetohydrodynamics (with N. O. Weiss), 1974 (Geneva Observatory); papers, revs and conf. reports on different branches of theoretical astrophysics. *Recreations:* reading, music. *Address:* 13 Prince Edward's Road, Lewes, E Sussex BN7 1BJ. *T:* Lewes (0273) 472731.

MESTON, family name of **Baron Meston.**

MESTON, 3rd Baron *cr* 1919, of Agra and Dunottar; **James Meston;** *b* 10 Feb. 1950; *s* of 2nd Baron Meston and of Diana Mary Came, *d* of Capt. O. S. Doll; *S* father, 1984; *m* 1974, Jean Rebecca Anne, *d* of John Carder; one *s* two *d*. *Educ:* Wellington College; St Catharine's Coll., Cambridge (MA). Barrister, Middle Temple, 1973. Pres., British Soc. of Commerce, 1984–. *Heir: s* Hon. Thomas James Dougall Meston, *b* 21 Oct. 1977. *Address:* Queen Elizabeth Building, Temple, EC4. *T:* 071–583 7837. *Club:* Hawks (Cambridge).

METCALF, David Michael, DPhil, DLitt; Keeper of Heberden Coin Room, Ashmolean Museum, Oxford, since 1982; Fellow of Wolfson College, Oxford, since 1982; *b* 8 May 1933; *s* of Rev. Thomas Metcalf and Gladys Metcalf; *m* 1958, Dorothy Evelyn (*née* Uren); two *s* one *d*. *Educ:* St John's College, Cambridge. MA, DPhil, DLitt; FSA. Asst Keeper, Ashmolean Museum, 1963. Sec., Royal Numismatic Soc., and Editor, Numismatic Chronicle, 1974–84. *Publications:* Coinage in South-eastern Europe 820–1396, 1979; Coinage of the Crusades and the Latin East, 1983; (ed with D. H. Hill) Sceattas in England and on the Continent, 1984; Coinage in Ninth-century Northumbria, 1987; articles on numismatics in various jls. *Address:* 40 St Margaret's Road, Oxford OX2 6LD; Ashmolean Museum, Oxford OX1 2PH.

METCALF, Prof. Donald, AO 1976; FRS 1983, FRACP, FRCPA, FAA; Head of Cancer Research Unit, Walter and Eliza Hall Institute of Medical Research, Melbourne, since 1965; Research Professor of Cancer Biology, University of Melbourne, since 1986; *b* 26 Feb. 1929; *s* of Donald Davidson Metcalf and Enid Victoria Metcalf (*née* Thomas); *m* 1954, Josephine Emily Lentaigne; four *d*. *Educ:* Sydney University. MD, BSc (med). Resident MO, Royal Prince Alfred Hosp., Sydney, 1953–54; Surgeon-Lieut, RANR, 1953–58; Carden Fellow in Cancer Res., 1954–65, Asst Director and Head of Cancer Res. Unit, 1965–, Walter and Eliza Hall Inst. Vis. Fellow, Harvard Med. Sch., 1956–58; Visiting Scientist: Roswell Park Meml Inst., Buffalo, 1966–67; Swiss Inst. for Experimental Cancer Res., Lausanne, 1974–75; Radiobiological Res. Inst., Rijswijk, 1980–81; Royal Soc. Guest Res. Fellow, Cambridge Univ., 1981. *Publications:* The Thymus, 1966; (with M. A. S. Moore) Haemopoietic Cells, 1971; Hemopoietic Colonies, 1977; Hemopoietic Colony Stimulating Factors, 1984; numerous scientific papers on cancer and leukaemia. *Recreations:* music, tennis. *Address:* 268 Union Road, Balwyn, Victoria 3103, Australia. *T:* (03) 836–1343.

METCALF, Malcolm, MC 1944; DL; Chairman, Surrey County Council, 1978–81; *b* 1 Dec. 1917; *s* of Charles Almond Metcalf and Martha Fatherly Atkins Metcalf; *m* 1945, Charis Thomas; two *s*. *Educ:* Merchant Taylors' Sch., Crosby. ACIS. Army service, 1939–46. Contested (C) Barrow-in-Furness, 1959; Mem., Surrey CC, 1965–89 (Leader, 1973–77; Vice-Chm., 1977–78); Member: Metrop. Water Board, 1965–74 (Vice-Chm. 1971–72); Thames Conservancy, 1970–74; Thames Water Authority, 1973–78, 1981–87. Mem., Assoc. of County Councils, 1975–88. DL Surrey, 1979. *Address:* 1 The Lodge, Watts Road, Thames Ditton KT7 0DE. *T:* 081–398 3057. *Clubs:* MCC, Burhill Golf (Walton-on-Thames).

METCALFE, Adrian Peter; Director of Programmes, Tyne Tees Television Ltd, since 1991; Director, Tyne Tees Television Holdings PLC, since 1991; *b* 2 March 1942; *s* of Hylton and Cora Metcalfe; *m* 1966, Anne Summerton; one *s* one *d*. *Educ:* Roundhay Sch., Leeds; Magdalen Coll., Oxford. Reporter, Sunday Express, 1964; Dep. Editor, World of Sport, ABC TV, 1965; Producer, Sports Arena, LWT, 1968; Vice Pres., Marvin H. Sugarman, 1972; Presenter, CBS Sports Spectacular, 1972–76; Man. Dir, AMO Productions, 1976; Sen. Commissioning Editor, Sport and Features, Channel 4 TV, 1981; Commentator, ITV, 1966–87; Dir of Programmes, Eurosport, Satellite TV, 1989–91. GB Record, 400m, 45·7, ranked No 1 in the world at 400m, 1961; Silver Medal, 4 × 400m, European and Commonwealth Games, 1962; Gold Medal, 400m and 4 × 400m, World Student Games, 1963; Silver Medal, 4 × 400m, Tokyo Olympics, 1964; 9 victories, Oxford *v* Cambridge, 1961–64; 7 British Records, 4 European Records, 1961–64. Pres., OUAC, 1962–63. Hon. Vice-Pres. and Trustee, Sports Aid Foundn, 1990–. Governor, Bracknell Coll., 1990–. *Recreations:* choral music, theatre, menus, wine lists, horses, forlorn jogging. *Address:* The Tally House, Winkfield Plain, near Windsor, Berks SL4 4QU. *T:* Winkfield Row (0344) 882859.

METCALFE, Prof. David Henry Harold, OBE 1989; Professor of General Practice, University of Manchester School of Medicine, since 1978; Director, DHSS Urban Primary care research unit, since 1978; *b* 3 Jan. 1930; *s* of Henry R. Metcalfe and Mary Metcalfe (*née* Evans); *m* 1957, Anne (*née* Page); three *s*. *Educ:* Leys School, Cambridge; Cambridge Univ. (clinical course at Liverpool) (MA, MB, BChir); MSc Manchester. FRCGP; FFPHM. United Liverpool Hosps, 1956–58; Principal in gen. practice, Hessle, E Yorks, 1960–70; Asst Prof. in Family Medicine, Univ. of Rochester, NY, 1970–72; Sen. Lectr (GP), Dept of Community Health, Nottingham Univ. Med. Sch., 1972–78. Vice-Chm., RCGP, 1983–84. *Publications:* papers on medical information handling, doctor-patient communication, patterns of general practice, and medical educn. *Recreations:* photography, sailing, hill walking. *Address:* 8 Netherwood Road, Manchester M22 4BQ. *T:* 061–998 1974.

METCALFE, Hugh, OBE 1969; FEng; FRAeS; Director: Hunting Engineering, since 1988; Ricardo International (formerly SAC International), since 1989; *b* 26 June 1928; *s* of Clifford and late Florence Ellen Metcalfe; *m* 1952, Pearl Allison Carter; three *s*. *Educ:* Harrow County Grammar School; Imperial College, Univ. of London. BSc, ARCS. RAF, 1946–48; joined Bristol Aeroplane Co., 1951; Divisional Dir, 1974; British Aerospace Dynamics Group: Group Dir, Naval Weapons, 1978; Man. Dir, Bristol Div., 1980; Man. Dir, Hatfield Div., 1981; Chief Exec., 1982; Dir, 1982–88, and Dep. Chief Exec. (Ops), 1986–88, BAe. Pres., RAeS, 1989–90. Hon. DSc Hatfield Polytechnic, 1988. RAeS gold medal, 1984. *Recreation:* choral music. *Address:* Amberley, 28 Druid Stoke Avenue, Stoke Bishop, Bristol BS9 1DD. *Clubs:* Athenæum; Leander; Savage's (Bristol).

METCALFE, Air Commodore Joan, CB 1981; RRC 1976; Director of RAF Nursing Services, and Matron in Chief, Princess Mary's Royal Air Force Nursing Service, 1978–81; *b* 8 Jan. 1923; *d* of late W. and S. H. Metcalfe. *Educ:* West Leeds High Sch. for Girls; Leeds Coll. of Commerce. St James's Hosp., Leeds, 1943–47 (SRN); St James's Hosp. and Redcourt Hostel, Leeds, 1947–48 (SCM), PMRAFNS 1948. Served in RAF Hospitals in Egypt, Iraq, Libya, Cyprus, Germany, Singapore, and UK. Sen. Matron, 1970; Principal Matron, 1973. QHNS 1978–81. OStJ 1977. *Recreations:* classical music, theatre, needlework, gardening, non-fiction literature. *Address:* 10 Amport Close, Harestock, Winchester, Hants SO22 6LP. *T:* Winchester (0962) 880260. *Club:* Royal Air Force.

METCALFE, Stanley Gordon; Chairman, Ranks Hovis McDougall PLC, since 1989 (Managing Director, 1981–89, Chief Executive, 1984–89, and Deputy Chairman, 1987–89); *b* 20 June 1932; *s* of Stanley Hudson Metcalfe and Jane Metcalfe; *m* 1968, Sarah Harter; two *d*. *Educ:* Leeds Grammar Sch.; Pembroke Coll., Oxford (MA). Commnd Duke of Wellington's Regt, 1952. Trainee, Ranks, Hovis McDougall, 1956–59; Director, Stokes & Dalton, Leeds, 1963–66; Managing Director, McDougalls, 1966–69; Director, Cerebos Ltd, 1969–70; Managing Director: RHM Overseas Ltd, 1970–73; RHM Cereals Ltd, 1973–79; Director, Ranks Hovis McDougall Ltd, 1979. Member: Exec. Cttee, FDF, 1987– (Pres., 1990–91); Priorities Bd for R&D in Agriculture and Food, 1987–; CBI President's Cttee, 1990–; Council, Business in the Community, 1990–. Chm., Adv. Bd, Inst. of Food Research, 1988–. President, Nat. Assoc. of British and Irish Millers, 1978. *Recreations:* cricket, golf, theatre. *Address:* The Oast House, Lower Froyle, Alton, Hants GU34 4LX. *T:* Bentley (0420) 22310. *Clubs:* MCC, IZ, Arabs.

METFORD, Prof. John Callan James; Professor of Spanish, 1960–81, now Emeritus Professor, Head of Department of Hispanic and Latin American Studies, 1973–81, University of Bristol; *b* 29 Jan. 1916; *s* of Oliver Metford and Florence Stowe Thomas; *m* 1944, Edith Donald; one *d*. *Educ:* Porth Grammar Sch.; Universities of Liverpool, Yale and California. Commonwealth Fund Fellow, 1939–41; British Council Lecturer in Brazil, 1942–44; Regional Officer, Latin American Department of the British Council, 1944–46; Lectr in Latin American Studies, Univ. of Glasgow, 1946–55; Bristol University: Head of Dept of Spanish and Portuguese, 1955–73; Prof., 1960–81; Dean of Faculty of Arts, 1973–76; Chm., Sch. of Modern Langs, 1976–79. Vis. Prof., Lehigh Univ., USA, 1968–69. Chm., Council of Westonbirt Sch., 1976–83; Mem., Central Cttee of Allied Schs, 1970–83; Governor, Coll. of St Matthias, Bristol, 1960–79; Mem., St Matthias Trust; Professorial Mem., Council of Univ. of Bristol, 1972–74. Mem., Diocesan Adv. Cttee, Bristol, 1984–. *Publications:* British Contributions to Spanish and Spanish American Studies, 1950; San Martín the Liberator, 1950, 2nd edn 1970; Modern Latin America, 1964; The Golden Age of Spanish Drama, 1969; Falklands or Malvinas?, rev. edn of J. Goebel: The Struggle for the Falkland Islands, 1982; Dictionary of Christian Lore and Legend, 1983; The Christian Year, 1991; articles in Bull. of Spanish Studies, Bull. of Hispanic Studies, Liverpool Studies in Spanish, International Affairs, Contemporary Review, etc. *Recreations:* opera, iconography. *Address:* 2 Parry's Close, Bristol BS9 1AW. *T:* Bristol (0272) 682284.

METGE, Dame (Alice) Joan, DBE 1987; research anthropologist and writer; *b* 21 Feb. 1930; *d* of Cedric Leslie Metge and Alice Mary (*née* Rigg). *Educ:* Auckland Univ. (MA); London School of Economics (PhD). Jun. Lectr, Geography Dept, Auckland Univ., 1952; research and doctoral study, 1953–61; Lectr, Univ. Extension, Auckland Univ., 1961–64; University of Wellington: Sen. Lectr, Anthropology Dept, 1965–67, Associate Prof., 1968–88. Fifth Captain James Cook Res. Fellow, 1981–83. Hutchinson Medal, LSE, 1958; Elsdon Best Meml Medal, Polynesian Soc., 1987. *Publications:* A New Maori Migration, 1964; The Maoris of New Zealand, 1967, rev. edn 1976; (with Patricia Kinloch) Talking Past Each Other, 1978; In and Out of Touch, 1986; Te Kohao o Te Ngira, 1990. *Recreations:* theatre, music, reading, gardening. *Address:* 8 Paisley Terrace, Karori, Wellington 6005, New Zealand. *T:* 766–980.

METHUEN, family name of **Baron Methuen.**

METHUEN, 6th Baron *cr* 1838; **Anthony John Methuen,** ARICS; *b* 26 Oct. 1925; *s* of 5th Baron Methuen and Grace (*d* 1972), *d* of Sir Richard Holt, 1st Bt; *S* father, 1975. *Educ:* Winchester; Royal Agricultural Coll., Cirencester. Served Scots Guards and Royal Signals, 1943–47. Lands Officer, Air Ministry, 1951–62; QALAS 1954. *Recreation:* shooting. *Heir: b* Hon. Robert Alexander Holt Methuen [*b* 22 July 1931; *m* 1958, Mary Catharine Jane, *d* of Ven. C. G. Hooper, *qv*; two *d*.] *Address:* Corsham Court, Corsham, Wilts. *Club:* Lansdowne.

METTERS, Dr Jeremy Stanley, FRCOG; Deputy Chief Medical Officer, Department of Health, since 1989; *b* 6 June 1939; *s* of late Thomas Lee Metters and Henrietta Currey; *m* 1962, Margaret Howell; two *s* one *d*. *Educ:* Eton; Magdalene College, Cambridge; St Thomas' Hosp. (MB BChir 1963, MA 1965). MRCOG 1970, FRCOG 1982. House officer posts, St Thomas' Hosp. and Reading, 1963–66; Lectr in Obst. and Gyn., St Thomas' Hosp., 1968–70; Registrar in Radiotherapy, 1970–72; DHSS 1972; SPMO (Under Sec.), 1984; Dep. Chief Scientist, DHSS, later Dept of Health, 1986–89. Member: Council of Europe Cttee on Bioethics (formerly Ethical and Legal Problems relating to Human Genetics), 1983–89; ESRC, 1986–88. *Publications:* papers in med. and sci. jls. *Recreations:* touring and travel, DIY, preserved steam railways.

METZGER, Rev. Prof. Bruce Manning; George L. Collord Professor of New Testament Language and Literature, Princeton Theological Seminary, 1964–84, now Emeritus; *b* Middletown, Pa, 9 Feb. 1914; *o s* of late Maurice R. Metzger and Anna Manning Metzger; *m* 1944, Isobel Elizabeth, *e d* of late Rev. John Alexander Mackay, DD; two *s*. *Educ:* Lebanon Valley Coll. (BA 1935); Princeton Theol Seminary (ThB 1938, ThM 1939); Princeton Univ. (MA 1940, PhD 1942, Classics). Ordained, United Presbyterian Church, USA, 1939; Princeton Theological Seminary: Teaching Fellow in NT Greek, 1938–40; Instr. in NT, 1940–44; Asst Prof., 1944–48; Associate Prof., 1948–54; Prof., 1954–64. Vis. Lectr, Sem. Theol. Presbyt. do Sul, Campinas, Brazil, 1952; Schol. in Residence, Tyndale Hse, Cambridge, 1969; Dist. Vis. Prof., Fuller Theol Sem., 1970; Vis. Fellow: Clare Hall, Cambridge, 1974; Wolfson Coll., Oxford, 1979; Vis. Prof., Gordon-Conwell Theol Sem., 1978; Lectr, New Coll. for Advanced Christian Studies, Berkeley, 1978; Vis Prof., Caribbean Grad. Sch. of Theol., Jamaica, 1990; many lectures to some 100 other academic instns on 5 continents. Chairman, Amer. Cttee on Versions, Internat. Greek NT Project, 1950–; Secretary: Panel of Translators, Rev. Standard Version of Apocrypha, 1952–57; Amer. Textual Criticism Seminar, 1954–56; Member: Kurat. of Vetus Latina Inst., Beuron, 1959–; Adv. Cttee, Inst. of NT Textual Res., Münster, Germany, 1961–; Inst. for Advanced Study, Princeton, 1964 and 1974; Chairman: Cttee on Trans., Amer. Bible Soc., 1964–70; Amer. Exec. Cttee, Internat. Greek NT Project, 1970–88; Cttee of Translators, New RSV of the Bible, 1977–90. President: Soc. of Biblical Lit., 1971; Stud. Novi Test. Soc., 1971–72; N Amer. Patristic Soc., 1972; Corresp. Fellow Brit. Acad., 1978; Hon. Fellow and Corresp. Mem., Higher Inst. of Coptic Studies, Cairo, 1955; Mem., Amer. Philosophical Soc., 1986–. Hon. DD: Lebanon Valley Coll., 1951 (also Dist. Alumnus award of Alumni Assoc. 1961); St Andrews, 1964; Hon. DTheol Münster, 1971; Hon. LHD Findlay Coll., 1962; Hon. DLitt Potchefstroom, 1985. *Publications:* The Saturday and Sunday Lessons from Luke in the Greek Gospel Lectionary, 1944; Lexical Aids for Students of New Testament Greek, 1946, enlarged edn 1955 (trans. Malagasy, Korean); A Guide to the Preparation of a Thesis, 1950, 2nd edn 1961; Index of Articles on the New Testament and the Early Church Published in Festschriften, 1951, Supplement 1955; Annotated Bibliography of the Textual Criticism of the New Testament, 1955;

(jtly) The Text, Canon, and Principal Versions of the Bible, 1956; An Introduction to the Apocrypha, 1957 (trans. Korean); Index to Periodical Literature on the Apostle Paul, 1960, 2nd edn 1970; Lists of Words Occurring Frequently in the Coptic New Testament (Sahidic Dialect), 1961; (jtly) The Oxford Concise Concordance to the Revised Standard Version of the Holy Bible, 1962; (jtly) The Oxford Annotated Bible, 1962; Chapters in the History of New Testament Textual Criticism, 1963; The Text of the New Testament, its Transmission, Corruption, and Restoration, 1964 (trans. German, Japanese, Korean, Chinese); The Oxford Annotated Apocrypha, 1965; The New Testament, its Background, Growth, and Content, 1965 (trans. Chinese, Korean); Index to Periodical Literature on Christ and the Gospels, 1966; Historical and Literary Studies, Pagan, Jewish, and Christian, 1968; A Textual Commentary on the Greek New Testament, 1971; The New Oxford Annotated Bible with the Apocrypha, expanded edn 1977; The Early Versions of the New Testament, their Origin, Transmission, and Limitations, 1977; New Testament Studies, Philological, Versional, and Patristic, 1980; Manuscripts of the Greek Bible, an Introduction to Greek Palaeography, 1981 (trans. Japanese); The Canon of the New Testament, its Origin, Development, and Significance, 1987; (general editor) Reader's Digest Condensed Bible, 1982 (trans. Italian, Korean); ed, New Testament Tools and Studies, fourteen vols, 1960–91; co-ed, The Greek New Testament, 1966, 3rd edn 1975; numerous articles in learned jls and encycs. *Recreations:* reading, woodworking. *Address:* 20 Cleveland Lane, Princeton, New Jersey 08540, USA. *T:* (609) 924–4060. *Club:* Nassau (Princeton, New Jersey).

MEXBOROUGH, 8th Earl of, *cr* 1766; **John Christopher George Savile;** Baron Pollington, 1753; Viscount Pollington, 1766; *b* 16 May 1931; *s* of 7th Earl of Mexborough, and of Josephine Bertha Emily, *d* of late Captain Andrew Mansel Talbot Fletcher; *S* father, 1980; *m* 1st, 1958, Lady Elizabeth Hariot (marr. diss. 1972; she *d* 1987), *d* of 6th Earl of Verulam; one *s* one *d*; 2nd, 1972, Mrs Catherine Joyce Vivian, *d* of late J. K. Hope, CBE; one *s* one *d*. *Heir: s* Viscount Pollington, *qv*. *Address:* Arden Hall, Hawnby, York. *T:* Bilsdale (04396) 348; 13 Ovington Mews, SW3. *T:* 071–589 3669. *Clubs:* All England Lawn Tennis and Croquet; Air Squadron.

MEYER, Sir Anthony John Charles, 3rd Bt, *cr* 1910; MP (C) Clwyd North West, since 1983 (West Flint, 1970–83); *b* 27 Oct. 1920; *o s* of Sir Frank Meyer, MP, 2nd Bt, Ayot House, Ayot St Lawrence, Herts; *S* father, 1935; *m* 1941, Barbadee Violet, *o c* of late A. Charles Knight, JP, and of Mrs Charles Knight, Herne Place, Sunningdale; one *s* three *d*. *Educ:* Eton (Capt. of Oppidans); New Coll., Oxford. Served Scots Guards, 1941–45 (wounded); HM Treasury, 1945–46; entered HM Foreign Service, 1946; HM Embassy, Paris, 1951; 1st Sec., 1953; transferred to HM Embassy, Moscow, 1956; London, 1958. MP (C) Eton and Slough, 1964–66. Cons. Research Dept, 1968. PPS to Chief Sec., Treasury, 1970–72; PPS to Sec. of State for Employment, 1972–74. Chm., Franco-British Parly Relations Cttee, 1979–; Vice-Chm., Cons. European Affairs Cttee, 1979–89; Mem., Panel of Chairmen, House of Commons, 1985–. Vice-Chm., Franco-British Council, 1986–; Mem. Bd, British Council of European Movement, 1990–. Trustee of Shakespeare National Memorial Theatre. Founder and Dir of political jl, Solon, 1969. Officier, Légion d'Honneur, France, 1983. *Publications:* A European Technological Community, 1966; Stand Up and Be Counted, 1990. *Recreations:* music, travel, skiing, cooking. *Heir: s* Anthony Ashley Frank Meyer [*b* 23 Aug. 1944; *m* 1966, Susan Mathilda (marr. diss. 1980), *d* of John Freestone; one *d*]. *Address:* Cottage Place, Brompton Square, SW3. *T:* 071–589 7416; Rhewl House, Llanasa, Clwyd. *Club:* Beefsteak.

MEYER, Christopher John Rome, CMG 1988; HM Diplomatic Service; Minister (Commercial), Washington, since 1989; *b* 22 Feb. 1944; *s* of Flight Lieut R. H. R. Meyer (killed in action 1944) and Mrs E. P. L. Meyer (now Mrs S. Landells); *m* 1976, Françoise Elizabeth Hedges, *d* of Air Cdre Sir Archibald Winskill, *qv*; two *s* one step *s*. *Educ:* Lancing College; Peterhouse, Cambridge (MA History); Johns Hopkins Sch. of Advanced Internat. Studies, Bologna. Third Sec., FO, 1966–67; Army Sch. of Education, 1967–68; Third, later Second, Sec., Moscow, 1968–70; Second Sec., Madrid, 1970–73; First Sec., FCO, 1973–78; First Sec., UK Perm. Rep. to European Communities, 1978–82; Counsellor and Hd of Chancery, Moscow, 1982–84; Head of News Dept, FCO, 1984–88; Fellow, Center for Internat. Affairs, Harvard, 1988–89. *Address:* c/o Foreign and Commonwealth Office, King Charles Street, SW1A 2AH.

MEYER, Rt. Rev. Conrad John Eustace; *b* 2 July 1922; *s* of William Eustace and Marcia Meyer; *m* 1960, Mary Wiltshire; no *c*. *Educ:* Clifton Coll.; Pembroke Coll., Cambridge; Westcott House. BA 1946, MA 1948. Served War of 1939–45: Royal Navy (commissioned from lower deck), 1942–46. Lieut (S) RNVR, post war, until apptd Chaplain, RNVR, 1950–54. Deacon, 1948; Priest, 1949; Asst Curate: St Francis, Ashton Gate, Bristol, 1948–51; Kenwyn, Truro, 1951; Falmouth Parish Church, 1954; Vicar of Devoran, Truro, 1956–65; Diocesan Youth Chaplain, 1956; Asst Dir of Religious Educn, 1958; Diocesan Sec. for Educn, 1960–69; Archdeacon of Bodmin, 1969–79; Hon. Canon of Truro, 1966–79; Examining Chaplain to Bishop of Truro, 1973–79; Bishop Suffragan of Dorchester, 1979–87 (Area Bishop, 1985–87). Hon. Asst Bishop, dio. of Truro, 1990–. Hon. Diocesan Sec., Nat. Soc., 1960–69. Society for Promoting Christian Knowledge: Mem. Governing Body, 1972–90; Chairman: Projects Cttee, 1973–87; Appeals Cttee, 1987–90; Vice Chm., 1988–90; Vice-Pres., 1990–. Chairman: Federation of Catholic Priests, 1976–79; Church Union Exec. Cttee, 1979–84; The Churches' Group on Funerals at Cemeteries and Crematoria, 1980–89. Fellow, Woodard Corp. of Schools, 1967; Provost, Western Div., Woodard Corp., 1970–; Hon. FICD. *Recreations:* swimming, walking, military history, civil defence, archaeology. *Address:* Hawk's Cliff, 38 Praze Road, Newquay, Cornwall TR7 3AF. *Club:* Commonwealth Trust.

MEYER, Michael Leverson; free-lance writer since 1950; *b* London, 11 June 1921; 3rd and *y s* of Percy Barrington Meyer and Eleanor Rachel Meyer (*née* Benjamin); unmarried; one *d*. *Educ:* Wellington Coll.; Christ Church, Oxford (MA). Operational Res. Section, Bomber Comd HQ, 1942–45; Lectr in English Lit., Uppsala Univ., 1947–50. Visiting Professor of Drama: Dartmouth Coll., USA, 1978; Univ. of Colorado, 1986; Colorado Coll., 1988; Hofstra Univ., 1989; UCLA 1991. Mem. Editorial Adv. Bd, Good Food Guide, 1958–72. FRSL. Gold Medal, Swedish Academy, 1964. Knight Commander, Polar Star (1st class), Sweden, 1977. *Publications:* (ed, with Sidney Keyes, and contrib.) Eight Oxford Poets, 1941; (ed) Collected Poems of Sidney Keyes, 1945, rev. edn 1989; (ed) The Minos of Crete, by Sidney Keyes, 1948; The End of the Corridor (novel), 1951; The Ortolan (play), 1967; Henrik Ibsen: The Making of a Dramatist, 1967; Henrik Ibsen: The Farewell to Poetry, 1971; Henrik Ibsen: The Top of a Cold Mountain, 1971 (Whitbread Biography Prize, 1971); Lunatic and Lover (play), 1981; (ed) Summer Days, 1981; Ibsen on File, 1985; Strindberg: a biography, 1985; File on Strindberg, 1986; Not Prince Hamlet (memoirs; US edn as Words through a Window Pane), 1989; *translated:* The Long Ships, by Frans G. Bengtsson, 1954; Ibsen: Brand, The Lady from the Sea, John Gabriel Borkman, When We Dead Awaken, 1960; The Master Builder, Little Eyolf, 1961; Ghosts, The Wild Duck, Hedda Gabler, 1962; Peer Gynt, An Enemy of the People, The Pillars of Society, 1963; The Pretenders, 1964; A Doll's House, 1965; Rosmersholm, 1966; Emperor and Galilean, 1986; Strindberg: The Father, Miss Julie, Creditors, The Stronger, Playing with Fire, Erik the Fourteenth, Storm, The Ghost Sonata, 1964; A Dream Play, 1973; To Damascus, Easter, The Dance of Death, The Virgin Bride, 1975; Master Olof, 1991; Fragments of a Life, by Hedi Fried, 1990. *Recreations:* real tennis, eating, sleeping. *Address:* 4 Montagu Square, W1H 1RA. *T:* 071–486 2573. *Clubs:* Savile, Garrick, MCC.

MEYER, Michael Siegfried; Chairman and Chief Executive, EMESS plc, since 1983; *b* 2 May 1950; *s* of Ernest Meyer and Gretta Gillis; *m* 1984, Jill Benedict (marr. diss. 1990). *Educ:* South African College School, Cape Town. FCIS. Company Secretary, Heenan Beddow International, 1973–75; Director, 1976–79, Chief Exec., 1980–82, EMESS; Director: Royal Sovereign Group, 1986–90; TR Smaller Cos Investment Trust, 1990–; Walker Greenbank, 1991–. *Recreations:* cricket, Rugby, theatre. *Address:* EMESS, 20 St James's Street, SW1A 1HA. *T:* 071–321 0127. *Clubs:* MCC, Royal Automobile; Wanderers (Johannesburg).

MEYJES, Sir Richard (Anthony), Kt 1972; DL; Deputy Chairman, Foseco plc (formerly Foseco Minsep), 1986–89 (Director, 1976–89); Director, Coates Bros plc, 1976–83 (Chairman, 1978–83); *b* 30 June 1918; *s* of late Anthony Charles Dorian Meyjes and Norah Isobel Meyjes; *m* 1939, Margaret Doreen Morris; three *s*. *Educ:* University College School, Hampstead. War Service, RASC, Sept. 1939–Jan. 1946 (temp. Captain). Qualified as Solicitor, June 1946; Legal Dept, Anglo-Saxon Petroleum Co., 1946–56; Manager, Thailand and Vietnam Division, Shell International Petroleum Co., 1956–58; Marketing Manager, Shell Co. of Philippines, Ltd, Manila, 1958–61; President, 1961–64; Head of Regional Marketing Div., Shell International Petroleum Co., London, 1964–66; Marketing Coordinator, 1966–70. Seconded to HM Govt (Mr Heath's Admin) as Head of Business Team, 1970–72; Dir and Group Personnel Co-ordinator, Shell International Petroleum Co. Ltd, 1972–76; Dir, Portals Hldgs, 1976–88. Vice-Pres., Assoc. of Optometrists, 1988–. Chm. Council, Univ. of Surrey, 1980–85. DL, 1983, High Sheriff, 1984, Surrey. Master, Worshipful Co. of Spectacle Makers, 1985–87. CBIM; FInstD; FRSA. DUniv Surrey, 1988. Officer of Philippine Legion of Honour, 1964. *Recreations:* gardening, walking. *Address:* Long Hill House, The Sands, near Farnham, Surrey GU10 1NQ. *T:* Runfold (02518) 2601. *Clubs:* Royal Over-Seas League, City Livery, Institute of Directors.

MEYNELL, Dame Alix (Hester Marie), (Lady Meynell), DBE 1949; *b* 2 Feb. 1903; *d* of late Surgeon Commander L. Kilroy, RN, and late Hester Kilroy; *m* 1946, Sir Francis Meynell, RDI (*d* 1975); no *c*. *Educ:* Malvern Girls' Coll.; Somerville Coll., Oxford. Joined civil service, Board of Trade, 1925. Seconded to the Monopolies and Restrictive Practices Commission as Sec., 1949–52; Under-Sec., Board of Trade, 1946–55; resigned from the Civil Service, 1955. Called to the Bar, 1956. Man. Dir, Nonesuch Press Ltd, 1976–86. Member: SE Gas Board, 1956–69 (Chm. Cons. Council, 1956–63); Harlow New Town Corpn, 1956–65; Performing Right Tribunal, 1956–65; Cttees of Investigation for England, Scotland and Great Britain under Agricultural Marketing Acts, 1956–65; Monopolies Commn, 1965–68; Cosford RDC, 1970–74. *Publication:* Public Servant, Private Woman (autobiog.), 1988. *Recreations:* family bridge, entertaining my friends and being entertained. *Address:* The Grey House, Lavenham, Sudbury, Suffolk CO10 9RB. *T:* Lavenham (0787) 247526.

MEYNELL, Benedict William; Hon. Director-General, Commission of the European Communities, since 1981; *b* 17 Feb. 1930; *s* of late Sir Francis Meynell, RDI, and of Lady (Vera) Meynell, MA; *m* 1st, 1950, Hildamarie (*née* Hendricks); two *d*; 2nd, 1967, Diana (*née* Himbury). *Educ:* Beltane Sch.; Geneva Univ. (Licencié-ès-sciences politiques); Magdalen Coll., Oxford (Doncaster schol.; MA). Asst Principal, Bd of Inland Revenue, 1954–56; Asst Principal, BoT, 1957–59, Principal, 1959–68; Principal British Trade Commissioner, Kenya, 1962–64; Board of Trade: Principal Private Sec. to Pres., 1967–68; Asst Sec., 1968–70; Commercial Counsellor, Brit. Embassy, Washington, DC, 1970–73; a Dir, EEC, responsible for relations with Far East, and for commercial safeguards and textiles negotiations, 1973–77, for relations with N America, Japan and Australasia, 1977–81. *Publications:* (paper) International Regulation of Aircraft Noise, 1971; contribs: Japan and Western Europe, ed Tsoukalis and White, 1982; A Survey of External Relations, in Yearbook of European Law 1982; Servir l'Etat, 1987 (Cahiers de l'Homme series). *Address:* 49 rue Père Eudore Devroye, 1040 Bruxelles, Belgium. *T:* (02) 736 4916.

MEYRICK, Sir David (John Charlton), 4th Bt *cr* 1880; *b* 2 Dec. 1926; *s* of Colonel Sir Thomas Frederick Meyrick, 3rd Bt, TD, DL, JP, and Ivy Frances (*d* 1947), *d* of Lt-Col F. C. Pilkington, DSO; *S* father, 1983; *m* 1962, Penelope Anne, *d* of late Comdr John Bertram Aubrey Marsden-Smedley, RN; three *s*. *Educ:* Eton; Trinity Hall, Cambridge (MA). FRICS. *Heir: s* Timothy Thomas Charlton Meyrick, [*b* 5 Nov. 1963. *Educ:* Eton; Bristol Univ.]. *Address:* Bush House, Gumfreston, Tenby, Dyfed SA70 8RA.

MEYRICK, Sir George (Christopher Cadafael Tapps Gervis), 7th Bt *cr* 1791, of Hinton Admiral; *b* 10 March 1941; *s* of Sir George David Eliott Tapps Gervis Meyrick, 6th Bt, MC and of Ann, *d* of late Clive Miller; *S* father, 1988; *m* 1968, Jean Louise, *d* of late Lord William Montagu Douglas Scott and of Lady William Montagu Douglas Scott; two *s* one *d*. *Educ:* Eton; Trinity College, Cambridge (MA). FRICS. *Heir: s* George William Owen Tapps Gervis Meyrick, *b* 3 April 1970. *Address:* Hinton Admiral, Christchurch, Dorset; Bodorgan, Isle of Anglesey. *Club:* Boodle's.

MEYSEY-THOMPSON, Sir (Humphrey) Simon, 4th Bt *cr* 1874; *b* 31 March 1935; *s* of Guy Herbert Meysey-Thompson (*d* 1961), and Miriam Beryl Meysey-Thompson (*d* 1985); *S* kinsman, Sir Algar de Clifford Charles Meysey-Thompson, 1967. *Address:* 10 Church Street, Woodbridge, Suffolk.

MIAKWE, Hon. Sir Akepa, KBE 1989 (OBE 1982); Chairman, Eastern Highlands Development Corporation, Papua New Guinea, since 1982; *b* 1934; *s* of Umakue Miakwe and Obio Opae; *m* Kora Maho; seven *s* five *d*. *Educ:* Grade 3, Kabiufa Primary Sch. Local Govt Councillor, 1960–77 (Pres., 1962–64, Sen. Vice-Pres., 1965–72); MP Goroka, 1972–76, Unggai/Bena, 1977–82; Minister for Correctional Services and Liquor Licensing under Nat. Party. Mem. Bd Dirs, Eastern Highlands Capital Authority, 1989–. *Address:* Eastern Highlands Development Corporation Pty Ltd, PO Box 971, Goroka, Papua New Guinea. *T:* 722443.

MIALL, (Rowland) Leonard, OBE 1961; Research Historian; *b* 6 Nov. 1914; *e s* of late Rowland Miall and S. Grace Miall; *m* 1st, 1941, Lorna (*d* 1974), *o d* of late G. John Rackham; three *s* one *d*; 2nd, 1975, Sally Bicknell, *e d* of late Gordon Leith. *Educ:* Bootham Sch., York (Scholar); Freiburg Univ.; St John's Coll., Cambridge (Sizar), MA. Pres. Cambridge Union, 1936; Ed. Cambridge Review, 1936. Lectured in US, 1937; Sec. British-American Associates, 1937–39; joined BBC; inaugurated talks broadcast to Europe, 1939; BBC German Talks and Features Editor, 1940–42. Mem. British Political Warfare Mission to US, 1942–44 (Dir of News, San Francisco, 1943; Head of New York Office, 1944); Personal Asst to Dep. Dir-Gen., Political Warfare Exec., London, 1944; attached to Psychological Warfare Division of SHAEF, Luxembourg, 1945. Rejoined BBC: Special Correspondent, Czechoslovakia, 1945; Actg Diplomatic Corresp., 1945; Chief Corresp. in US, 1945–53; Head of Television Talks, 1954; Asst Controller, Current Affairs and Talks, Television, 1961; Special Asst to Dir of Television, planning start of

BBC-2, 1962; Asst Controller, Programme Services, Television, BBC, 1963–66; BBC Rep. in US, 1966–70; Controller, Overseas and Foreign Relations, BBC, 1971–74; Research Historian, BBC, 1975–84. Inaugurated BBC Lunchtime Lectures, 1962; Advisor, Cttee on Broadcasting, New Delhi, 1965; Delegate to Commonwealth Broadcasting Confs, Jamaica, 1970, Kenya, 1972, Malta, 1974. Dir, Visnews Ltd (Dep. Chm., 1984–85); Overseas Dir, BAFTA, 1974–; Mem. Council, RTS, 1984–. FRTS 1986; FRSA. Cert. of Appreciation, NY City, 1970. *Publications:* Richard Dimbleby, Broadcaster, 1966; contribs to DNB and various jls. *Recreations:* writing, gardening, doing it oneself. *Address:* Maryfield Cottage, Taplow, Maidenhead, Berks SL6 0EX. *T:* Burnham (0628) 604195. *Clubs:* Garrick; Union (Cambridge).

MICHAEL, Alun Edward; JP; MP (Lab) Cardiff South and Penarth, since 1987; *b* 22 Aug. 1943; *m*; five *c*. *Educ:* Keele Univ. (BA). Journalist, South Wales Echo, 1966–71; Youth and Community Worker, Cardiff, 1972–84; Area Community Education Officer, Grangetown and Butetown, 1984–87. Mem., Cardiff City Council, 1973– (Chm., Econ. Devclt Cttee; formerly Chm., Finance and Planning Cttees). An Opposition Whip, 1987–88. JP Cardiff, 1972 (Chm., Cardiff Juvenile Bench, 1986–87). *Recreations:* long-distance running, walking, squash, music. *Address:* House of Commons, SW1A 0AA. *T:* 071–219 3441; (office) Cardiff (0222) 223533. *Clubs:* Penarth Labour; Grange Stars.

MICHAEL, Dr Duncan, FEng 1984; Director, Ove Arup and Partners, since 1977; *b* 26 May 1937; *s* of Donald Michael and Lydia Cameron MacKenzie; *m* 1960, Joan Clay; two *s* one *d*. *Educ:* Beauly Public School; Inverness Royal Academy. BSc Edinburgh; PhD Leeds. FICE; FIStructE; FHKIE. Lectr, Leeds Univ., 1961; Engineer, Ove Arup Partnership, 1962. Member: Council, IStructE, 1977–80, 1983–; SE Asia Trade Adv. Group, BOTB, 1982–85; Civil Engineering Cttee, SERC, 1980–83. Fellowship of Engrg Vis. Prof., Aberdeen Univ., 1989–; Vis. Prof., Leeds Univ., 1990–. *Publications:* Skyscrapers, 1987; lectures and engineering papers in technical jls. *Recreations:* garden, Scottish archaeology, opera. *Address:* 21 Marryat Road, SW19. *Club:* Caledonian.

MICHAEL, Prof. Ian David Lewis; King Alfonso XIII Professor of Spanish Studies, University of Oxford, since 1982; Fellow, Exeter College, Oxford, since 1982; *b* 26 May 1936; *o s* of late Cyril George Michael and of Glenys Morwen (*née* Lewis). *Educ:* Neath Grammar Sch.; King's Coll., London (BA First Class Hons Spanish 1957); PhD Manchester 1967. University of Manchester: Asst Lectr in Spanish, 1957–60; Lectr in Spanish, 1960–69; Sen. Lectr in Spanish, 1969–70; University of Southampton: Prof. of Spanish and Hd of Spanish Dept, 1971–82; Dep. Dean, Faculty of Arts, 1975–77, 1980–82; Sen. Curator and Chm., Univ. Library Cttee, 1980–82. Leverhulme Faculty Fellow in European Studies (at Madrid), 1977–78. Mem., Gp of Three for Spain (Humanities research review), Eur. Science Foundn, 1987. Pres., Assoc. of Hispanists of GB and Ire., 1990–March 1992. Comdr, Order of Isabel la Católica (Spain), 1986. *Publications:* The Treatment of Classical Material in the Libro de Alexandre, 1970; Spanish Literature and Learning to 1474, in, Spain: a Companion to Spanish studies, 1973, 3rd edn 1977; The Poem of the Cid, 1975, new edn 1984; Poema de Mio Cid, 1976, 2nd edn 1979; Gwyn Thomas, 1977; chapter on Poem of My Cid in New Pelican Guide to English Literature. I ii, 1983; articles in various learned jls and Festschriften; *as David Serafín:* Saturday of Glory, 1979 (John Creasey Meml Award, CWA, 1980); Madrid Underground, 1982; Christmas Rising, 1982; The Body in Cadiz Bay, 1985; Port of Light, 1987; The Angel of Torremolinos, 1988. *Recreations:* horticulture; collecting Art Nouveau and Art Déco, particularly ceramics; writing pseudonymous fiction; opera. *Address:* Exeter College, Oxford OX1 3DP. *T:* Oxford (0865) 270484. *Clubs:* Reform, Organon.

MICHAEL, Ian (Lockie), CBE 1972; Deputy Director, Institute of Education, University of London, 1973–78; *b* 30 Nov. 1915; 4th *c* of late Reginald Warburton Michael and Margaret Campbell Kerr; *m* 1942, Mary Harborne Bayley, *e c* of late Rev. William Henry Bayley; one *s* one *d*. *Educ:* St Bees Sch.; private study. BA (London) 1938; PhD (Bristol) 1963. Schoolmaster: St Faith's Sch., Cambridge, 1935–40; Junior Sch., Leighton Park, 1941–45, Headmaster, 1946–49; Lectr in Educn, Bristol Univ., 1950–63; Prof. of Educn, Khartoum Univ., 1963–64; Vice-Chancellor, Univ. of Malaŵi, 1964–73. Leverhulme Emeritus Fellowship, 1978–79, 1979–80; Vis. Prof. of Educn, Univ. of Cape Town, 1981. Hon. DLitt Malaŵi, 1974. *Publications:* English Grammatical Categories and the Tradition to 1800, 1970; The Teaching of English from the Sixteenth Century to 1870, 1987. *Address:* 9 Cornwallis House, Cornwallis Grove, Bristol BS8 4PG. *T:* Bristol (0272) 735977.

MICHAEL, Sir Peter (Colin), Kt 1989; CBE 1983; CBIM; Chairman, Cray Electronics, since 1989; *b* 17 June 1938; *s* of Albert and Enid Michael; *m* 1962, Margaret Baldwin; two *s*. *Educ:* Whitgift Sch., Croydon; Queen Mary Coll., Univ. of London (BSc Elec. Engrg; Fellow, 1983); CBIM 1982. Chairman: Micro Consultants Group, 1969–85; Quantel Ltd, 1974–89; Databasix Ltd, 1986–88; UEI plc: Dep. Chm., 1981–85; Chm., 1986–89. Member: Adv. Council for Applied R&D, 1982–85; NCB, 1983–86; ACARD Sub-Gp on Annual Review of Govt Funded R&D, 1985–86; Technol. Requirements Bd, DTI, 1986–88. Paper on City financing of electronics companies to PITCOM, 1988. Lectures: Humphrey Davies, QMC, 1984; IEE Electronics, 1984. Freeman, Goldsmiths' Co., 1984. Freeman, City of London, 1984; Liveryman, Goldsmiths' Co., 1988. FRSA 1984. Hon. FBKSTS 1981. The Guardian Young Businessman of the Year, 1982. *Recreations:* squash, tennis, opera. *Address:* 2 West Mills, Newbury, Berks RG14 5HG. *T:* Newbury (0635) 521321.

MICHAELS, Prof. Leslie, MD; FRCPath, FRCP(C); Professor of Pathology, Institute of Laryngology and Otology, 1973–90 (Dean, 1976–81); Emeritus Professor, Department of Histopathology, University College and Middlesex School of Medicine, London University, since 1990; *b* 24 July 1925; *s* of Henry and Minnie Michaels; *m* Edith (*née* Waldstein); two *d*. *Educ:* Parmiter Sch., London; King's Coll., London; Westminster Med. Sch., London (MB, BS; MD). FRCPath 1963, FRCP(C) 1962. Asst Lectr in Pathology, Univ. of Manchester, 1955–57; Lectr in Path., St Mary's Hosp. Med. Sch., London, 1957–59; Asst Prof. of Path., Albert Einstein Coll. of Medicine, New York, 1959–61; Hosp. Pathologist, Northern Ont, Canada, 1961–70; Sen. Lectr, Inst. of Laryn. and Otol., 1970–73. *Publications:* Pathology of the Larynx, 1984; Ear, Nose and Throat Histopathology, 1987; scientific articles in jls of medicine, pathology and otolaryngology. *Recreations:* reading, music, walking. *Address:* Romany Ridge, Hillbrow Road, Bromley, Kent BR1 4JL.

MICHAELS, Michael Israel, CB 1960; *b* 22 Dec. 1908; *m* 1932, Rosina, *e d* of late Joseph Sturges; one *s* one *d*. *Educ:* City of London College; London Sch. of Economics (Social Science Research Scholar, 1931). Asst Sec., New Survey London Life and Labour, 1932–34. Deputy Director, Programmes and Statistics, Ministry of Supply, 1940–45. Asst Sec., Ministry of Health, 1946–54; Under-Sec., Atomic Energy Office, 1955–59; Office of the Minister for Science (Atomic Energy Division), 1959–64; Under-Sec., Min. of Technology, 1964–71, retired. British Mem., Bd of Governors, Internat. Atomic Energy Agency, 1957–71. *Recreations:* music, gardening, history. *Address:* Tower House, Kelsale, Saxmundham, Suffolk. *T:* Saxmundham (0728) 3142.

MICHALOWSKI, Jerzy; Polish diplomat; *b* 26 May 1909; *s* of Andrzej and Maria Michalowski; *m* 1947, Mira Krystyna; two *s*. *Educ:* University of Warsaw. Asst In Polish Inst. of Social Affairs, 1933–36; Dir of Polish Workers Housing Organisation, 1936–39; Chief of Housing Dept of Warsaw City Council, 1945; Counsellor of Polish Embassy in London, 1945–46; Deputy Deleg. of Poland to UN, March-Nov. 1946; Ambassador of Republic of Poland to the Court of St James's 1946–53; Head of a department, Ministry of Foreign Affairs, Warsaw, 1953–54; Under Sec. of State for Educ., 1954–55; Deleg. of Poland to the Internat. Commn in Vietnam, 1955–56; Permanent Representative of Poland to UN, 1956–60; Dir-Gen., in Ministry of Foreign Affairs, Warsaw, 1960–67; Ambassador to USA, 1967–71. Pres. of ECOSOC, UN, 1962. *Publications:* Unemployment of Polish Peasants, 1934; Housing Problems in Poland (publ. by League of Nations), 1935; The Big Game for the White House, 1972. *Recreations:* tennis and winter sports. *Address:* Al. I Armii WP 16/20, Warsaw, Poland.

MICHEL, Prof. Dr Hartmut; Director, Max-Planck-Institut of Biophysics, Frankfurt am Main, since 1987; *b* Ludwigsburg, W Germany, 18 July 1948; *s* of Karl Michel and Frieda Michel; *m* 1979, Ilona Leger-Michel; one *s* one *d*. *Educ:* Universities of: Tübingen (Dip. in biochem.); Würzburg (PhD); Munich (habilitation for biochemistry, 1986). Res. associate with D. Oesterhelt, Univ. of Würzburg, 1977–79; group leader in D. Oesterhelt's dept, Max-Planck-Inst. of Biochemistry, Martinsried, until 1987. Various prizes, including: Biophysics Prize of Amer. Phys. Soc., 1986; Otto Klung Prize for Chemistry, 1986; (jtly) Otto Bayer Prize, 1988; (jtly) Nobel Prize for Chemistry, 1988. *Publication:* (ed) Crystallization of Membrane Proteins, 1990. *Recreations:* family life, wild life, physical exercise, readings on history and travel. *Address:* Max-Planck-Institut für Biophysik, Heinrich-Hoffmann-Strasse 7, W-6000 Frankfurt am Main 71, Germany. *T:* (69) 6704401.

MICHELIN, Reginald Townend, CMG 1957; CVO 1953; OBE 1952; General Manager: Agualta Vale Estates, Jamaica, 1958–64; Jamaica Tourist Board, 1964–73; *b* 31 Dec. 1903; *s* of V. A. Michelin, Planter, Jamaica; *m* 1940, Nina Gladys Faulkner, Iffley, Oxford; one *s* one *d*. *Educ:* Exeter Sch., England. Sub-Inspector, Police, Jamaica, 1924; Inspector, Police, Leeward Islands, 1928; Asst Commissioner of Police, Nigeria, 1930; Comr of Police, Barbados, 1949; Commissioner of Police, Jamaica, 1953–58, retd. *Address:* Western Mews, Winslow, Bucks.

MICHELL, Keith; actor since 1948; *b* Adelaide; *s* of Joseph Michell and Alice Maud (*née* Aslat); *m* 1957, Jeannette Sterke; one *s* one *d*. *Educ:* Port Pirie High Sch.; Adelaide Teachers' Coll.; Sch. of Arts and Crafts; Adelaide Univ.; Old Vic Theatre School. Formerly taught art. *Stage:* First appearance, Playbox, Adelaide, 1947; Young Vic Theatre Co., 1950–51; first London appearance, And So To Bed, 1951; Shakespeare Meml. Theatre Co., 1952–56, inc. Australian tour, 1952–53 (Henry IV Part 1, As You Like It, Midsummer Night's Dream, Troilus and Cressida, Romeo and Juliet, Taming of the Shrew, All's Well That Ends Well, Macbeth, Merry Wives of Windsor); Don Juan, Royal Court, 1956; Old Vic Co., 1956 (Antony and Cleopatra, Much Ado about Nothing, Two Gentlemen of Verona, Titus Andronicus); Irma La Douce, Lyric, 1958, Washington, DC, 1960 and Broadway, 1960–61; The Chances, Chichester Festival, 1962; The Rehearsal, NY, 1963; The First Four Hundred Years, Australia and NZ, 1964; Robert and Elizabeth, Lyric, 1964; The King's Mare, 1966; Man of La Mancha, 1968–69, NY, 1970; Abelard and Heloise, 1970, Los Angeles and NY, 1971; Hamlet, Globe, 1972; Dear Love, Comedy, 1973; The Crucifer of Blood, Haymarket, 1979; On the Twentieth Century (musical), Her Majesty's, 1980; Pete McGynty and the Dreamtime (own adap. of Peer Gynt), Melbourne Theatre Co., 1981; Captain Beaky Christmas Show, Lyric, Shaftesbury Ave., 1981–82; The Tempest, Brisbane, 1982; opened Keith Michell Theatre, Port Pirie, with one-man show, 1982; Amadeus (UK tour), 1983; La Cage Aux Folles, San Francisco and NY, 1984, Sydney and Melbourne, 1985; Portraits, Malvern Fest., 1987; *Chichester Festival Theatre:* Artistic Director, 1974–77; Tonight We Improvise, Oedipus Tyrannus, 1974; Cyrano de Bergerac, Othello, 1975; (dir and designed) Twelfth Night, 1976; Monsieur Perrichon's Travel, 1976; The Apple Cart, 1977; (dir and designed) In Order of Appearance, 1977; Murder in the Cathedral (Chichester Cathedral), 1977; Henry VIII, 1991; toured Australia with Chichester Co., 1978 (Othello, The Apple Cart); acted in: On the Rocks, 1982; Jane Eyre, 1986; The Royal Baccarat Scandal, 1988, transf. Theatre Royal Haymarket, 1989. *Films include:* Dangerous Exile; The Hell Fire Club; Seven Seas to Calais; The Executioner; House of Cards; Prudence and the Pill; Henry VIII and his Six Wives; Moments, The Deceivers. *Television includes:* Henry VIII in the Six Wives of Henry VIII (series), 1972; Keith Michell at Chichester, 1974; My Brother Tom, 1986; Captain James Cook, 1987. Many recordings. First exhibn of paintings, 1959; subseq. exhibns at John Whibley Gall., London and Wright Hepburn and Webster Gall., NY, Century Gall., Henley, Wylma Wayne Gall., London, Vincent Gall., Adelaide. Many awards. *Publications:* ed and illus. (lithographs), Twelve Shakespeare Sonnets, 1981; illus. and recorded Captain Beaky series, 1975–; (also illus.) Practically Macrobiotic, 1987. *Recreations:* painting, photography, swimming, cooking. *Address:* c/o London Management and Representation Ltd, 235 Regent Street, W1.

MICHELL, Michael John; Head of Radiocommunications Agency (formerly of Radio Division), Department of Trade and Industry, since 1988; *b* 12 Dec. 1942; *s* of John Martin Michell and Pamela Mary Michell; *m* 1st, 1965, Pamela Marianne Tombs (marr. diss. 1978); two *s* (one *d* decd); 2nd, 1978, Alison Mary Macfarlane; two *s*. *Educ:* Marlborough College; Corpus Christi College, Cambridge (BA 1964). Min. of Aviation, 1964; Private Sec. to Sir Ronald Melville, 1968–69; Concorde Div., 1969–73; Sec. to Sandilands Cttee on inflation accounting, 1973–75; Private Sec. to Sec. of State for Industry, 1975–77; HM Treasury, 1977–80; Industrial Policy Div., Dept. of Industry, 1980–82; RCDS 1983; Head, Air Div., DTI, 1984–88. *Recreations:* tapestry, glass collecting, reading, gardening. *Address:* Department of Trade and Industry, Waterloo Bridge House, SE1 8UA. *T:* 071–215 2000.

MICHELL, Prof. Robert Hall, FRS 1986; Royal Society Research Professor at the University of Birmingham, since 1987; *b* 16 April 1941; *s* of Rowland Charles Michell and Elsie Lorna Michell; one *s* one *d*. *Educ:* Crewkerne School, Somerset; Univ. of Birmingham (BSc Med. Biochem. and Pharmacol. 1962; PhD Med. Biochem. 1965; DSc 1978). Research Fellow, Birmingham, 1965–66, 1968–70, Harvard Med. Sch., 1966–68; Birmingham University: Lectr in Biochemistry, 1970–81; Sen. Lectr, 1981–84; Reader, 1984–86; Prof. of Biochemistry, 1986–87. Mem., Physiol. Systems and Disorders Bd, 1985–90, Chm., Grants Cttee B, 1988–90, MRC; Mem., EMBO, 1991–. Member, Editorial Boards: Jl Neurochem., 1975–80; Cell Calcium, 1979–; Biochem. Jl, 1983–88; Current Opinion in Cell Biology, 1988–; Procs Roy. Soc. B, 1989–. CIBA Medal, Biochemical Soc., 1988. *Publications:* (with J. B. Finean and R. Coleman) Membranes and their Cellular Functions, 1974, 3rd edn 1984; (ed with J. B. Finean) Membrane Structure, vol. 1 of New Comprehensive Biochemistry, 1981; (ed with J. W. Putney, Jr) Inositol Lipids in Cellular Signalling, 1987; (ed with M. J. Berridge) Inositol Lipids and Transmembrane Signalling, 1988; (ed jtly) Inositol Lipids and Cellular Signalling, 1989; contribs to Nature, Biochem. Jl and sci. jls. *Recreations:* birdwatching, wilderness. *Address:* 59 Weoley Park Road, Birmingham B29 6QZ. *T:* 021–472 1356.

MICHELMORE, Clifford Arthur, CBE 1969; Television Broadcaster and Producer; Managing Director: Michelmore Enterprises Ltd, since 1969; Communications Consultants Ltd, since 1969; Director, CP Video, since 1988; *b* 11 Dec. 1919; *s* of late Herbert Michelmore and Ellen Alford; *m* 1950, Jean Metcalfe (Broadcaster); one *s* one *d. Educ:* Cowes Senior Sch., Isle of Wight. Entered RAF, 1935; commnd 1940; left RAF 1947. Head, Outside Broadcasts and Variety, BFN, 1948; Dep. Station Dir, BFN, also returned to freelance as Commentator and Producer, 1949. Entered Television, 1950. Man. Dir, RM/EMI Visual Programmes, 1971–81. Has taken part in numerous radio and television programmes in Britain, Europe and the USA. Introduced: "Tonight" series, 1957–65; 24 Hours series, 1965–68; General Election Results programmes, 1964, 1966, 1970; So You Think . . . ., 1966–; Our World, 1967; With Michelmore (interviews); Talkback; Apollo Space Programmes, 1960–70; Holiday, 1969–86; Chance to Meet, 1970–73; Wheelbase, 1972; Getaway, 1975; Globetrotter, 1975; Opinions Unlimited, 1977–79; Presenter: Day by Day (Southern TV), 1980; Sudden Change (HTV), 1982; Cliff Michelmore Show (BBC Radio), 1982–83; Home on Sunday (BBC TV), 1983–; Waterlines (BBC Radio Four), 1984–; Lifeline (BBC TV), 1986–; Coastline (BBC Radio Four), 1991. Made films: Shaping of a Writer, 1977; Hong Kong: the challenge, 1978. FRSA, 1975. Television Society Silver Medal, 1957; Guild of TV Producers Award, Personality of the Year, 1958; TV Review Critics Award, 1959; Variety Club Award, 1961. *Publications:* (ed) The Businessman's Book of Golf, 1981; Cliff Michelmore's Holidays By Rail, 1986; (with Jean Metcalfe) Two-Way Story (autobiog.), 1986; Some of These Days, 1987; contribs to Highlife, Financial Weekly; various articles on television, broadcasting and travel. *Recreations:* golf, reading and doing nothing. *Address:* White House, Reigate, Surrey; Brookfield, Bembridge, Isle of Wight. *T:* Reigate (0737) 245014. *Clubs:* Garrick, Royal Air Force.

MICHENER, James Albert; author; *b* New York City, 3 Feb. 1907; *s* of Edwin Michener and Mabel (*née* Haddock); *m* 1st, 1935, Patti Koon (marr. diss. 1948); 2nd, 1948, Vange Nord (marr. diss., 1955); 3rd, 1955, Mari Yoriko Sabusawa; no *c. Educ:* Swarthmore Coll., Pennsylvania; St Andrews Univ., Scotland; Harvard Coll., Mass. Teacher, George Sch., Pa, 1933–36; Prof., Colorado State Coll. of Educn, 1936–41; Visiting Prof., Harvard, 1940–41; Associate Editor, Macmillan Co., 1941–49. Member: Adv. Cttee on the arts, US State Dept, 1957; Adv. Cttee, US Information Agency, 1970–76; Cttee to reorganise USIS, 1976. Served with USNR on active duty in South Pacific, 1944–45. Sec., Pennsylvania Constitutional Convention, 1968. Hon. DHL, LLD, LittD, DSci and DHum, from numerous univs. US Medal of Freedom, 1977. *Publications:* Unit in the Social Studies, 1940; (ed) Future of Social Studies, for NEA, 1940; Tales of the South Pacific (Pulitzer prize for fiction), 1947; The Fires of Spring, 1949; Return to Paradise, 1951; The Voice of Asia, 1951; The Bridges at Toko-ri, 1953; Sayonara, 1954; Floating World, 1955; The Bridge at Andau, 1957; (with A. Grove Day) Rascals in Paradise, 1957; Selected Writings, 1957; The Hokusai Sketchbook, 1958; Japanese Prints, 1959; Hawaii, 1959; Caravans, 1964; The Source, 1965; Iberia, 1968; Presidential Lottery, 1969; The Quality of Life, 1970; Kent State, 1971; The Drifters, 1971; Centennial, 1974; Michener on Sport, 1977; Chesapeake, 1978; The Covenant, 1980; (with A. Grove Day) Rascals in Paradise, 1980; United States of America, 1982; Space, 1982 (televised, 1987); Poland, 1983; Texas, 1985; Legacy, 1987; Alaska, 1988; Journey, 1989. *Recreations:* photography, philately, tennis.

MICHIE, Prof. David Alan Redpath, RSA 1972 (ARSA 1964); RGI 1984; Head, 1982–90 and Professor (personal chair), since 1988, School of Drawing and Painting, Edinburgh College of Art; *b* 30 Nov. 1928; *s* of late James Michie and late Anne Redpath, OBE, ARA, RSA; *m* 1951, Eileen Anderson Michie; two *d. Educ:* Edinburgh Coll. of Art (DA). National Service, 1947–49; Edinburgh Coll. of Art, 1949–53 (studied painting); travelling scholarship, Italy, 1953–54; Lectr in Painting, Gray's Sch. of Art, Aberdeen, 1958–62; Lectr in Painting, Edinburgh Coll. of Art, 1962–82. Vice-Principal, 1974–77. Vis. Prof. of Painting, Acad. of Fine Art, Belgrade, 1979. Member: Gen. Teaching Council for Scotland, 1976–80; Edinburgh Festival Soc., 1976–. Pres., Soc. of Scottish Artists, 1961–63. One Man Exhibitions: Mercury Gallery, London, 1967, 1969, 1971, 1974, 1980, 1983; Mercury Gall., Edinburgh, 1986; Lothian Region Chambers, 1977; Scottish Gall., Edinburgh, 1980. FRSA 1990. *Recreation:* fishing. *Address:* 17 Gilmour Road, Edinburgh EH16 5NS. *T:* 031–667 2684.

MICHIE, Prof. Donald, DPhil (Oxon), DSc (Oxon); Chief Scientist, Turing Institute, Glasgow, since 1986 (Director of Research, 1984–86); Professor, University of Strathclyde, since 1984; Technical Director, Intelligent Terminals Ltd (Knowledgelink), since 1984; *b* 11 Nov. 1923; *s* of late James Kilgour Michie and late Marjorie Crain Michie; *m* 1st, 1949, Zena Margaret Davies (marr. diss.); one *s*; 2nd, 1952, Anne McLaren (marr. diss.); one *s* two *d*; 3rd, 1971, Jean Elizabeth Hayes (*née* Crouch). *Educ:* Rugby Sch.; Balliol Coll., Oxford (Schol., MA). Sci. Fellow Zool Soc. of London, 1953; Fellow Royal Soc. Edinburgh 1969; Fellow Brit. Computer Soc., 1971. War Service in FO, Bletchley, 1942–45; Res. Associate, Univ. of London, 1952–58; Univ. of Edinburgh: Sen. Lectr, Surg. Science, 1958; Reader in Surg. Science, 1962; Dir of Expermtl Programming Unit, 1965; Chm. of Dept of Machine Intelligence and Perception, 1966; Prof. of Machine Intelligence, 1967–84; Prof. Emeritus, 1984–; Dir, Machine Intelligence Res. Unit, 1974–84. Royal Soc. Lectr in USSR, 1965; Wm Withering Lectr, Univ. of Birmingham, 1972; Vis. Lectr, USSR Acad. Sci., 1973, 1985; Geo. A. Miller Lectr, Univ. of Illinois, 1974, 1984; Herbert Spencer Lectr, Univ. of Oxford, 1976; Samuel Wilks Meml Lectr, Princeton Univ., 1978; S. L. A. Marshall Lectr, US Army Res. Inst. for the Behavioural and Soc. Scis, 1990; Vis. Fellow, St Cross Coll., Oxford, 1970; Visiting Professor: Stanford Univ., 1962, 1978, 1991; Syracuse Univ., USA, 1970, 1971; Virginia Polytechnic Inst. and State Univ., 1974; Univ. of California at Santa Cruz, 1975; Dartmouth Coll., USA, 1975; Illinois Univ., 1976, 1979–81; Carnegie Mellon Univ., 1977; Case Western Reserve Univ., 1978; McGill Univ., 1979; Univ. of NSW, 1991. Chief Editor, Machine Intelligence series, 1967–. Chm., A. M. Turing Trust, 1975–86. Hon. DSc CNAA, 1991. (With A. McLaren) Pioneer Award, Internat. Embryo Transfer Soc., 1988. *Publications:* (jtly) An Introduction to Molecular Biology, 1964; On Machine Intelligence, 1974, 2nd edn 1986; Machine Intelligence and Related Topics, 1982; (jtly) The Creative Computer, 1984; papers in tech. and sci. jls. *Recreations:* chess, travel. *Address:* 6 Inveralmond Grove, Cramond, Edinburgh EH4 6RA. *Clubs:* Athenæum; New (Edinburgh).

MICHIE, (Janet) Ray; MP Argyll and Bute, since 1987 (L 1987–88, Lib Dem, since 1988); *b* 4 Feb. 1934; *d* of Baron Bannerman of Kildonan, OBE; *m* 1957, Dr Iain Michie, MB, FRCP; three *d. Educ:* Aberdeen High Sch. for Girls; Lansdowne House Sch., Edinburgh; Edinburgh Coll. of Speech Therapy. LCST, MCST. Area Speech Therapist, Argyll and Clyde Health Board, 1977–87. Chm., Argyll Lib. Assoc., 1973–76; Vice-Chm., Scottish Lib. Party, 1977–79. Lib dem spokesman on Scotland and on women's issues, 1988–. Member: Scottish NFU; Scottish Crofters' Union; Rural Forum; An Comunn Gaidhealach. Contested (L): Argyll, 1979; Argyll and Bute, 1983. *Recreations:* golf, swimming, gardening. *Club:* National Liberal.

MICHIE, William, (Bill); MP (Lab) Sheffield Heeley, since 1983; *b* 24 Nov. 1935; *m*; two *s. Educ:* Abbeydale Secondary Sch., Sheffield. Nat. Service, RAF, 1957–59. Formerly

apprentice electrician; maintenance electrician; Lab. Technician, Computer Applications; unemployed, 1981–83. Joined Labour Party, 1965; Co-op. Party, 1966. Mem., AEU (formerly AUEW), 1952– (Br. Trustee; former Standing Orders Cttee Deleg., Lab. Party Yorks Regl Conf.; AEU sponsored MP, 1984–). Member: Sheffield City Council, 1970–84 (Chairman: Planning, 1974–81; Employment, 1981–83; Gp Sec./Chief Whip, 1974–83); South Yorks CC, 1974–86 (Area Planning Chm., 1974–81). *Recreations:* pub darts, gardening. *Address:* House of Commons, SW1. *T:* 071–219 4023; 54 Pinstone Street, Sheffield S1 2HN. *T:* Sheffield (0742) 701881.

MICKLETHWAIT, Sir Robert (Gore), Kt 1964; QC 1956; Chief National Insurance Commissioner, 1966–75 (Deputy Commissioner, 1959; National Insurance Commissioner and Industrial Injuries Commissioner, 1961); *b* 7 Nov. 1902; 2nd *s* of late St J. G. Micklethwait, KC and Annie Elizabeth Micklethwait (*née* Aldrich-Blake); *m* 1936, Philippa J., 2nd *d* of late Sir Ronald Bosanquet, QC; three *s* one *d. Educ:* Clifton Coll.; Trinity Coll., Oxford (2nd Class Lit. Hum., MA). Called to Bar, Middle Temple, 1925, Bencher, 1951; Autumn Reader, 1964; Dep. Treasurer, 1970, Treasurer, 1971. Oxford Circuit; Gen. Coun. of the Bar, 1939–40 and 1952–56; Supreme Court Rule Cttee, 1952–56. Royal Observer Corps, 1938–40; Civil Asst, WO, 1940–45; Recorder of Worcester, 1946–59. Deputy Chm., Court of Quarter Sessions for County of Stafford, 1956–59. Hon. LLD Newcastle upon Tyne, 1975. Hon. Knight, Hon. Soc. of Knights of the Round Table, 1972. *Publication:* The National Insurance Commissioners (Hamlyn Lectures), 1976. *Address:* 71 Harvest Road, Englefield Green, Surrey TW20 0QR. *T:* Egham (0784) 432521.

MIDDLEMAS, Prof. Robert Keith; Professor of History, University of Sussex, since 1986; *b* 26 May 1935; *s* of Robert James Middlemas, Solicitor and Eleanor Mary (*née* Crane), Howick, Northumberland; *m* 1958, Susan Mary, *d* of Laurence Edward Paul Tremlett and Marjorie Isobel Derrington Bell; one *s* three *d. Educ:* Stowe Sch.; Pembroke Coll., Cambridge (Exhibnr, scholar, BA 1st cl. History 1958); DPhil 1972, DLitt 1982, Sussex. 2nd Lieut, Northumberland Fusiliers, 1954–55 (served in Kenya); Clerk, House of Commons, 1958–66; Lectr in History, Univ. of Sussex, 1966–76, Reader, 1976–86. Visiting Professor: Stanford Univ. and Hoover Instn, Stanford, 1984; Univ. of Beijing, 1989. Member: UK Nat. Cttee, Unesco, 1980–86; Council, Inst. of Contemporary British History; Academic Bd, Hughenden Foundn. FRSA. Co-Founder and Editor, Catalyst: a jl of public debate, 1985–87. *Publications:* The Master Builders, 1963; The Clydesiders, 1965; (with John Barnes) Baldwin, 1969; Diplomacy of Illusion, 1972; (ed) Thomas Jones: Whitehall Diary, vols I and II, 1969–70, vol. III, 1972; Politics in Industrial Society, 1979; Cabora Bassa, 1975; Power and the Party, 1980; Industry, Unions and Government, 1984; Power, Competition and the State, vol. I, Britain in Search of Balance 1940–61, 1986, vol. 2, Threats to the Post-War Settlement: Britain 1961–74, 1990; vol. 3, The End of the Post-War Era: Britain since 1974, 1991; articles and reviews in learned jls. *Recreations:* sports, sailing, fishing, landscape gardening; Member, UK Nat. Rifle Team, Canadian tour, 1958. *Address:* West Burton House, West Burton, Pulborough, West Sussex RH20 1HD. *T:* Bury (0798) 831516. *Clubs:* Flyfishers'; North London Rifle (Bisley).

MIDDLESBROUGH, Bishop of, (RC), since 1978; **Rt. Rev. Augustine Harris;** *b* 27 Oct. 1917; *s* of Augustine Harris and Louisa Beatrice (*née* Rycroft). *Educ:* St Francis Xavier's Coll., Liverpool; Upholland Coll., Lancs. Ordained, 1942; Curate at: St Oswald's, Liverpool, 1942–43; St Elizabeth's, Litherland, Lancs, 1943–52; Prison Chaplain, HM Prison, Liverpool, 1952–65; Sen. RC Priest, Prison Dept, 1957–66; English Rep. to Internat. Coun. of Sen. Prison Chaplains (RC), 1957–66; Titular Bishop of Socia and Auxiliary Bishop of Liverpool, 1965–78. Mem. Vatican Delegn to UN Quinquennial Congress on Crime, London, 1960 and Stockholm, 1965; Liaison between English and Welsh Hierarchy (RC) and Home Office, 1966–; Episcopal Moderator to Fédération Internationale des Associations Médicales Catholiques, 1967–76; Episcopal Pres., Commn for Social Welfare (England and Wales), 1972–83; Chm., Dept for Social Responsibility, Bishops Conf. of Eng. and Wales, 1984–. Mem. Central Religious Advisory Council to BBC and IBA, 1974–78. *Publications:* articles for criminological works. *Address:* Bishop's House, 16 Cambridge Road, Middlesbrough, Cleveland TS5 5NN.

MIDDLESBROUGH, Auxiliary Bishop of, (RC); *see* O'Brien, Rt Rev. T. K.

MIDDLESEX, Archdeacon of; *see* Raphael, Ven. T. J.

MIDDLETON, 12th Baron *cr* 1711; **Digby Michael Godfrey John Willoughby,** MC 1945; DL; Bt 1677; *b* 1 May 1921; *er s* of 11th Baron Middleton, KG, MC, TD, and Angela Florence Alfreda (*d* 1978), *er d* of Charles Hall, Eddlethorpe Hall, Malton, Yorks; S father, 1970; *m* 1947, Janet, *o d* of General Sir James Marshall-Cornwall, KCB, CBE, DSO, MC; three *s. Educ:* Eton; Trinity Coll., Cambridge. BA 1950; MA 1958. Served War of 1939–45: Coldstream Guards, 1940–46; NW Europe, 1944–45 (despatches, MC, Croix de Guerre); Hon. Col, 2nd Bn Yorkshire Volunteers, TAVR, 1976–88. Mem., H of L Select Cttee on Europ. Communities, 1985–. Chm., Legal and Parly Cttee, CLA, 1973–79; Pres., CLA, 1981–83; Member: Yorks and Humberside Econ. Planning Council, 1968–79; Nature Conservancy Council, 1986–89. DL 1963, JP 1958, CC 1964–74, ER of Yorks; CC N Yorks, 1974–77. *Heir: s* Hon. Michael Charles James Willoughby [*b* 14 July 1948; *m* 1974, Hon. Lucy Sidney, *y d* of 1st Viscount De L'Isle, VC, KG, GCMG, GCVO, PC; two *s* three *d*]. *Address:* Birdsall House, Malton, N Yorks YO17 9NR. *T:* North Grimston (09446) 202. *Club:* Boodle's.

MIDDLETON, Bishop Suffragan of, since 1982; **Rt. Rev. Donald Alexander Tytler;** *b* 2 May 1925; *s* of Alexander and Cicely Tytler; *m* 1948, Jane Evelyn Hodgson (*d* 1990); two *d. Educ:* Eastbourne College; Christ's College, Cambridge (MA); Ridley Hall, Cambridge. Asst Curate of Yardley, Birmingham, 1949; SCM Chaplain, Univ. of Birmingham, 1952; Precentor, Birmingham Cathedral, 1955; Diocesan Director of Education, Birmingham, 1957; Vicar of St Mark, Londonderry and Rural Dean of Warley, dio. Birmingham, 1963; Canon Residentiary of Birmingham Cathedral, 1972; Archdeacon of Aston, 1977–82. *Publications:* Operation Think, 1963; (contrib.) Stirrings (essays), 1976. *Recreations:* music, gardening. *Address:* The Hollies, Manchester Road, Rochdale, Lancs OL11 3QY. *T:* Rochdale (0706) 358550.

MIDDLETON, Donald King, CBE 1981; HM Diplomatic Service, retired; British High Commissioner, Papua New Guinea, 1977–82; Member, Council, Voluntary Service Overseas, since 1983; *b* 24 Feb. 1922; *s* of late Harold Ernest Middleton and Ellen Middleton; *m* 1945, Marion Elizabeth Ryder (*d* 1988); one *d. Educ:* King Edward's Sch., Birmingham; Saltley College. Min. of Health, 1958–61; joined Commonwealth Relations Office, 1961; First Sec., British High Commn, Lagos, 1961–65; Head of Chancery, British Embassy, Saigon, 1970–72; British Dep. High Commissioner, Ibadan, 1973–75; HM Chargé d'Affaires, Phnom Penh, 1975; seconded to NI Office, Belfast, 1975–77. *Address:* Stone House, Ledgemoor, near Weobley, Herefordshire HR4 8RN. *Club:* Commonwealth Trust.

MIDDLETON, Edward Bernard; Partner, Pannell Kerr Forster, Chartered Accountants; *b* 5 July 1948; *s* of Bernard and Bettie Middleton; *m* 1971, Rosemary Spence Brown;

three *s*. *Educ:* Aldenham Sch., Elstree; Chartered Accountant, 1970. Joined London office of Pannell Kerr Forster, 1971; Nairobi office, 1973; Audit Manager, London office, 1975; Partner, 1979; seconded to DTI as Dir, Industrial Develt Unit, 1984–86. Mem. sub-cttee, Consultative Cttee of Accountancy Bodies, 1980–84. *Recreations:* sailing, photography. *Address:* Barrans, Bury Green, Little Hadham, Ware, Herts SG11 2ES. *T:* Bishops Stortford (0279) 658684. *Club:* Salcombe Yacht.

MIDDLETON, Francis; Advocate; Sheriff of Glasgow and Strathkelvin (formerly of Lanarkshire) at Glasgow, 1956–78, retired; Temporary Sheriff, 1979; *b* 21 Nov. 1913; Scottish; *m* 1942, Edith Muir; two *s* one *d*. *Educ:* Rutherglen Academy; Glasgow Univ. MA, LLB 1937. Practising as Solicitor, 1937–39; volunteered Sept. 1939; Cameronian Scottish Rifles; commissioned to 6th Battn 11th Sikh Regt, Indian Army, 1940; Captain 1940; Major 1942, injured; Interpreter 1st Class in Hindustani, 1943; posted to Judge Advocate's Branch, 1944; released Dec. 1945. Admitted Faculty of Advocates in Scotland, 1946. Sheriff Substitute of Inverness, Moray, Nairn and Ross and Cromarty, 1949–52, Fife and Kinross, 1952–56. Dir, YMCA, Glasgow. Chairman: Scottish Assoc. of Dowsers; Child and Family Trust. Mem., Rotary Club. *Recreations:* reading, gardening. *Address:* 20 Queens Court, Helensburgh G84 7AH. *T:* Helensburgh (0436) 78965.

MIDDLETON, Sir George (Humphrey), KCMG 1958 (CMG 1950); HM Diplomatic Service, retired; Chairman, Mondial Expatriate Services Ltd, since 1988; *b* 21 Jan. 1910; *e s* of George Close Middleton and Susan Sophie (*née* Harley, subsequently Elphinstone); *m* Marie Elisabeth Camille Françoise Sarthou, Bordeaux; one *s*; one step *s* one step *d*. *Educ:* St Lawrence Coll., Ramsgate; Magdalen Coll., Oxford. Entered Consular Service, 1933, Vice-Consul, Buenos Aires; transferred to Asuncion, 1934, with local rank of 3rd Sec. in Diplomatic Service; in charge of Legation, 1935; transferred to New York, 1936; to Lemberg (Lwow), 1939; local rank of Consul; in charge of Vice-Consulate at Cluj, 1939–40; appointed to Genoa, 1940, to Madeira, 1940, to Foreign Office, 1943; 2nd Sec. at Washington, 1944; 1st Sec. 1945; transferred to FO, 1947; Counsellor, 1949; Counsellor, British Embassy, Tehran, Jan. 1951; acted as Chargé d'Affaires, 1951 and 1952 (when diplomatic relations severed); Dep. High Comr for UK, in Delhi, 1953–56; British Ambassador at Beirut, 1956–58; Political Resident in the Persian Gulf, 1958–61; British Ambassador to: Argentina, 1961–64; United Arab Republic, 1964–66. Mem. *Ad hoc* Cttee for UN Finances, 1966. Consultant, Industrial Reorganisation Corporation, 1967–68; Director: Overseas Medical Supplies Ltd; Britarge Ltd; Decor France Ltd; Chm., Exec. Cttee, British Road Fedn, 1972; Chief Executive, British Industry Roads Campaign, 1969–76. Chairman: Bahrain Soc.; Anglo-Peruvian Soc.; British Moroccan Soc. FRSA. Comdr, Order of Merit, Peru. *Recreations:* fishing, gardening, talking. *Address:* 1 Carlyle Square, SW3 6EX. *T:* 071–352 2962. *Clubs:* Travellers', Pratt's.

MIDDLETON, Rear-Adm. John Patrick Windsor; Chief Staff Officer (Engineering) to C-in-C Fleet, since 1989; *b* 15 March 1938; *s* of late Comdr John Henry Dudley Middleton, RN and Norna Mary Tessimond (*née* Hitchings); *m* 1962, Jane Rodwell Gibbs; one *s* one *d*. *Educ:* Cheltenham College; BRNC Dartmouth; RNEC Manadon. CEng, MIMechE, MIMarE. Entered Royal Navy 1954; CSO(E) to Flag Officer Submarines, 1981; CSO(E) Falkland Islands, 1983; Captain Naval Drafting, 1984; Dir, In Service Submarines, 1987. Liveryman, Co. of Armourers and Brasiers. *Recreations:* sailing, walking. *Address:* Greenhill House, Sutton Veny, Warminster, Wilts BA12 7BR. *T:* Warminster (0985) 40658. *Club:* Royal Naval Sailing Association (Portsmouth).

MIDDLETON, Kenneth William Bruce; formerly Sheriff of Lothian and Borders at Edinburgh and Haddington; *b* Strathpeffer, Ross-shire, 1 Oct. 1905; 2nd *s* of W. R. T. Middleton; *m* 1st, 1938, Ruth Beverly (marr. diss. 1972), *d* of W. H. Mill; one *s* one *d*; 2nd, 1984, Simona Vere, *d* of T. C. Pakenham, *widow* of N. Iliff. *Educ:* Rossall Sch.; Merton Coll., Oxford; Edinburgh Univ. BA Oxford, LLB Edinburgh; called to Scottish Bar, 1931; Vans Dunlop Scholar in International Law and Constitutional Law and History, Edinburgh Univ.; Richard Brown Research Scholar in Law, Edinburgh Univ.; served War of 1939–45 with Royal Scots and Seaforth Highlanders; attached to Military Dept, Judge Advocate-Gen.'s Office, 1941–45. Sheriff-Substitute, subseq. Sheriff: Perth and Angus at Forfar, 1946–50; Lothians and Peebles, later Lothian and Borders, at Edinburgh and Haddington, 1950–86. *Publication:* Britain and Russia, 1947. *Address:* Cobblers Cottage, Ledwell, Middle Barton, Oxon.

MIDDLETON, Lawrence John, CMG 1985; PhD; HM Diplomatic Service; Ambassador to the Republic of Korea, 1986–90, retired; *b* 27 March 1930; *s* of John James Middleton and Mary (*née* Horgan); *m* 1963, Sheila Elizabeth Hoey; two *s* one *d*. *Educ:* Finchley Catholic Grammar Sch.; King's Coll., London (BSc 1951, PhD 1954). Scientific Officer, ARC, 1954–60 and 1962–63; Cons. to FAO and to UN Cttee on Effects of Atomic Radiation, 1960–62; CENTO Inst. of Nuclear Science, 1963–65; Principal, Min. of Agriculture, 1966–68; First Sec., FO, 1968; Washington, 1969–71; Kuala Lumpur, 1971–74; Counsellor (Commercial), Belgrade, 1974–78; Dir of Research, FCO, 1978–80; Cabinet Office, 1980–82; Counsellor, UK Delegn to Conf. on Disarmament, Geneva, 1982–84; Sen. DS, RCDS, 1984–86. *Publications:* articles on plant physiology and nuclear science in biology, 1954–63. *Address:* 12 Polstead Road, Oxford OX2 6TN.

MIDDLETON, Rear Adm. Linley Eric, CB 1986; DSO; FRAeS; FBIM; Managing Director, British International Helicopters, since 1987; Director: Maxwell Aviation International Group, since 1991; International Helicopters, since 1991; Maxwell Aviation Management, since 1987; *m* 1965, Pamela Mannerings (*née* Lewis); three *s*. *Educ:* Dale Coll., Kingwilliamstown. Qualified as FAA pilot, 1952; served HMS Centaur, HMS Eagle, HMS Mounts Bay, HMS Victorious and HMS Ark Royal, 1954–63; BRNC Dartmouth, 1964–65; CO, 809 Naval Air Squadron in HMS Hermes, 1966–67; Naval Staff, MoD, 1968–69; CO, HMS Whitby, 1970–71; Staff of Flag Officer, Naval Air Comd, 1971–73; Capt. 2nd Frigate Sqn and CO, HMS Undaunted, 1973–74, and CO, HMS Apollo, 1974–75; Chief Staff Officer to Flag Officer Carriers & Amphibious Ships, 1975–77; Dir, Naval Air Warfare, 1978–79; CO, HMS Hermes, 1980–82; Asst Chief of Naval Staff (Ops), 1983–84; Flag Officer, Naval Air Comd, 1984–87, retired. Liveryman, Coach Makers' and Coach Harness Makers' Co.; Upper Freeman, GAPAN. Pres., St George's Day Club.

MIDDLETON, Michael Humfrey, CBE 1975; Director, Civic Trust, 1969–86; *b* 1 Dec. 1917; *s* of Humfrey Middleton and Lilian Irene (*née* Tillard); *m* 1954, Julie Margaret Harrison; one *s* two *d*. *Educ:* King's Sch., Canterbury. Art Critic, The Spectator, 1946–56; Art Editor and Asst Editor, Picture Post, 1949–53; Exec. Editor, Lilliput, 1953–54; Editor, House and Garden, 1955–57; Sec. and Dep. Dir, Civic Trust, 1957–69; Mem. Council, Soc. of Industrial Artists and Designers, 1953–55, 1968–70; UK Sec.-Gen., European Architectural Heritage Year, 1972–75. Member: Adv. Cttee on Trunk Road Assessment, 1977–80; UK Commn for UNESCO, 1976–80. FCSD; Hon. Fellow: RIBA, 1974; Landscape Inst., 1986. Film scripts include A Future for the Past, 1972. Council of Europe Pro Merito Medal, 1976. *Publications:* Soldiers of Lead, 1948; Group Practice in Design, 1967; Man Made the Town, 1987; Cities in Transition, 1991; contributor to many conferences and jls, at home and abroad, on art, design and environmental matters. *Recreation:* looking. *Address:* 84 Sirdar Road, W11 4EG. *T:* 071–727 9136.

MIDDLETON, Sir Peter (Edward), GCB 1989 (KCB 1984); a Deputy Chairman and Director, and Chairman of Markets and Investment Banking Division, Barclays Bank, since 1991; *b* 2 April 1934; *m* 1st, 1964, Valerie Ann Lindup (*d* 1987); one *d* (one *s* decd); 2nd, 1990, Mrs Constance Owen. *Educ:* Sheffield City Grammar Sch.; Sheffield Univ. (BA; Hon. DLitt 1984); Bristol Univ. Served RAPC, 1958–60. HM Treasury: Senior Information Officer, 1962; Principal, 1964; Asst Director, Centre for Administrative Studies, 1967–69; Private Sec. to Chancellor of the Exchequer, 1969–72; Treasury Press Secretary, 1972–75; Head of Monetary Policy Div., 1975; Under Secretary, 1976; Dep. Sec., 1980–83; Permanent Sec., 1983–91. Vis. Fellow, Nuffield Coll., Oxford, 1981–89. Mem. Council, Manchester Business Sch., 1985–; Governor: London Business Sch., 1984–90; Ditchley Foundn, 1985–. Cdre, Civil Service Sailing Assoc., 1984–. *Address:* Barclays Bank plc, Johnson Smirke Building, 4 Royal Mint Court, EC3N 4HJ. *Club:* Reform.

MIDDLETON, Ronald George, DSC 1945; solicitor; *b* 31 July 1913; *o s* of late Sir George Middleton; *m* 1959, Sybil Summerscale (*d* 1976); no *c*. *Educ:* Whitgift Middle Sch.; University Coll., London. Solicitor, 1936. RNVR, 1939–47 (Lt-Comdr); Radar Officer HMS Queen Elizabeth, 1944–45; Fleet Radar Officer, Indian Ocean, 1945. Partner, Coward, Chance & Co., 1949, Senior Partner, 1972–80. Part-time Mem., NBPI, 1965–68. *Recreation:* sailing. *Address:* Flat 18, 76 Jermyn Street, SW1Y 6NP. *T:* 071–839 7993. *Clubs:* Reform, Garrick, Royal Ocean Racing.

MIDDLETON, Stanley; novelist; *b* Bulwell, Nottingham, 1 Aug. 1919; *y s* of Thomas and Elizabeth Ann Middleton; *m* 1951, Margaret Shirley, *y d* of Herbert and Winifred Vera Welch; two *d*. *Educ:* High Pavement Sch.; University Coll., Nottingham (later Univ. of Nottingham); Hon. MA Nottingham, 1975. Served Army (RA and AEC), 1940–46. Head of English Dept, High Pavement Coll., Nottingham, 1958–81. Judith E. Wilson Vis. Fellow, Emmanuel Coll., Cambridge, 1982–83. *Publications:* novels: A Short Answer, 1958; Harris's Requiem, 1960; A Serious Woman, 1961; The Just Exchange, 1962; Two's Company, 1963; Him They Compelled, 1964; Terms of Reference, 1966; The Golden Evening, 1968; Wages of Virtue, 1969; Apple of the Eye, 1970; Brazen Prison, 1971; Cold Gradations, 1972; A Man Made of Smoke, 1973; Holiday (jtly, Booker Prize 1974), 1974; Distractions, 1975; Still Waters, 1976; Ends and Means, 1977; Two Brothers, 1978; In A Strange Land, 1979; The Other Side, 1980; Blind Understanding, 1982; Entry into Jerusalem, 1983; The Daysman, 1984; Valley of Decision, 1985; An After Dinner's Sleep, 1986; After a Fashion, 1987; Recovery, 1988; Vacant Places, 1989; Changes and Chances, 1990; Beginning to End, 1991. *Recreations:* music, walking, listening, argument. *Address:* 42 Caledon Road, Sherwood, Nottingham NG5 2NG. *T:* Nottingham (0602) 623085. *Club:* PEN.

MIDDLETON, Sir Stephen Hugh, 9th Bt, *cr* 1662; *b* 1909; *s* of Lt Hugh Jeffery Middleton, RN, 3rd *s* of Sir Arthur Middleton, 7th Bt; *S* uncle 1942; *m* 1962, Mary (*d* 1972), *d* of late Richard Robinson. *Educ:* Eton; Magdalene Coll., Cambridge. *Heir: b* Lawrence Monck Middleton [*b* 23 Oct. 1912; *m* 1984, Primrose Westcombe]. *Address:* Belsay Castle, Northumberland.

MIDGLEY, Eric Atkinson, CMG 1965; MBE 1945; HM Diplomatic Service, retired; *b* 25 March 1913; *s* of Charles Ewart Midgley, Keighley, Yorks; *m* 1937, Catherine Gaminara; two *d*. *Educ:* Christ's Hosp.; Merton Coll., Oxford. Indian Civil Service, 1937; Trade Commissioner at Delhi, 1947; Board of Trade, 1957; Commercial Counsellor at The Hague, 1960; Minister (Economic) in India, 1963–67; Minister (Commercial), Washington, 1967–70; Ambassador to Switzerland, 1970–73. *Recreation:* sailing. *Address:* 2 Wellington Place, Captains Row, Lymington, Hants SO41 9RS. *Club:* Royal Lymington Yacht.

MIDLETON, 12th Viscount *cr* 1717 (Ire.); **Alan Henry Brodrick;** Baron Brodrick of Midleton, Co. Cork 1715; Baron Brodrick of Peper Harow 1796; Keeper of Horology, John Gershom Parkington Collection of Time Measurement Instruments, Bury St Edmunds, since 1986; *b* 4 Aug. 1949; *s* of Alan Rupert Brodrick (*d* 1972) (*g g s* of 7th Viscount) and of Alice Elizabeth, *d* of G. R. Roberts; *S* uncle, 1989; *m* 1978, Julia Helen, *d* of Michael Pitt; two *s* one *d*. *Educ:* St Edmund's School, Canterbury. FBHI. *Recreations:* conservation of turret clocks, bicycling, medieval and Renaissance music. *Heir: s* Hon. Ashley Rupert Brodrick, *b* 25 Nov. 1980. *Address:* 2 Burrells Orchard, Westley, Bury St Edmunds, Suffolk IP33 3TH. *Club:* Athenæum.

MIDWINTER, Eric Clare, MA, DPhil; Director, Centre for Policy on Ageing, 1980–91; *b* 11 Feb. 1932; *m*; two *s* one *d*. *Educ:* St Catharine's Coll., Cambridge (BA Hons History); Univs of Liverpool (MA Educn) and York (DPhil). Educational posts, incl. Dir of Liverpool Educn Priority Area Project, 1955–75; Head, Public Affairs Unit, Nat. Consumer Council, 1975–80. Chairman: Council, Adv. Centre for Educn, 1976–84; London Transport Users Consultative Cttee, 1977–84; London Regional Passengers' Cttee, 1984–. DUniv. Open, 1989. *Publications:* Victorian Social Reform, 1968; Law and Order in Victorian Lancashire, 1968; Social Administration in Lancashire, 1969; Nineteenth Century Education, 1970; Old Liverpool, 1971; Projections: an education priority project at work, 1972; Social Environment and the Urban School, 1972; Priority Education, 1972; Patterns of Community Education, 1973; ed, Teaching in the Urban Community School, 1973; ed, Pre-School Priorities, 1974; Education and the Community, 1975; Education for Sale, 1977; Make 'Em Laugh: famous comedians and their world, 1978; Schools and Society, 1980; W. G. Grace: his life and times, 1981; Age is Opportunity: education and older people, 1982; (ed) Mutual Aid Universities, 1984; The Wage of Retirement: the case for a new pensions policy, 1985; Fair Game: myth and reality in sport, 1986; Caring for Cash: the issue of private domiciliary care, 1986; Redefining Old Age, 1987; The Lost Seasons: wartime cricket 1939–1945, 1987; (ed) Retired Leisure, 1987; Polls Apart? Older Voters and the 1987 General Election, 1987; New Design for Old, Function, Style and Older People, 1988; Red Roses Crest the Caps: a history of Lancashire cricket, 1989; Creating Chances: arts by older people, 1990; Old Order: crime and older people, 1990; Out of Focus: old age, the press and broadcasting, 1991; Brylcreem summer: the 1947 cricket season, 1991. *Recreations:* sport, comedy. *Address:* London Regional Passengers' Committee, Golden Cross House, 8 Duncannon Street, WC2N 4JF. *Clubs:* Savage, MCC; Lancashire CCC.

MIDWINTER, Prof. John Edwin, OBE 1984; PhD; FRS 1985; FEng 1984; Pender Professor of Electronic Engineering, since 1991, and Head of Department of Electronic Engineering, since 1987, University College London; *b* 8 March 1938; *s* of Henry C. and Vera J. Midwinter; *m* 1961, Maureen Anne Holt; two *s* two *d*. *Educ:* St Bartholomew's Grammar Sch., Newbury, Berks; King's Coll., Univ. of London (BSc Physics, 1961; AKC 1961). PhD Physics, London (ext.), 1968. MInstP 1973; FIEE 1980; FIEEE 1983. Joined RRE, Malvern, as Scientific Officer, 1961 (research on lasers and non-linear optics); Sen. Scientific Officer, 1964–68; Perkin Elmer Corp., Norwalk, Conn, USA, 1968–70; Res. Center, Materials Research Center, Allied Chemical Corp., Morristown, NJ, USA, 1970–71; Head of Optical Fibre Develt, PO Res. Centre, Martlesham, 1971–77; Head, Optical Communications Technol., British Telecom Res. Labs, 1977–84; BT Prof. of Optoelectronics, UCL, 1984–91. Visiting Professor: Queen Mary Coll., London, 1979–84;

Southampton Univ., 1979–84. Chm., Project 208, Cttee of Science and Technology, EEC, 1977–85. Member: Cttee, IEE Electronics Div. Bd, 1979–82; IEEE COMSOC Internat. Activities Council, 1982–; Optoelectronics Adv. Cttee, Rank Prize Fund, 1983–. Lectures: Bruce Preller, RSE, 1983; Clifford Patterson, Royal Soc.,1983; Cantor, RSA, 1984. Electronics Div. Premium, 1976, J. J. Thompson Medal, 1987, IEE. Editor, Optical and Quantum Electronics, 1972–; Associate Editor, Jl of Lightwave Technology, IEEE, 1983–. *Publications:* Applied Non-Linear Optics, 1972; Optical Fibers for Transmission, 1979 (Best Book in Technol. Award, Amer. Publishers' Assoc., 1980); over 70 papers on lasers, non-linear optics and optical communications. *Recreations:* country and mountain walking, ski-ing, bird-watching, cycling, micro-computing. *Address:* Department of Electronic Engineering, University College London, Torrington Place, WC1E 7JE. *T:* 071–388 0427, 071–387 7050.

MIDWINTER, Stanley Walter, CB 1982; RIBA, FRTPI; architect and planning consultant; Chief Planning Inspector (Director of Planning Inspectorate), Departments of the Environment and Transport, 1978–84; *b* 8 Dec. 1922; *s* of late Lewis Midwinter and Beatrice (*née* Webb); *m* 1954, Audrey Mary Pepper (*d* 1988); one *d*. *Educ:* Regent Street Polytechnic Sch.; Sch. of Architecture (DipArch, ARIBA 1948); Sch. of Planning and Res. for Regional Develt (AMTPI 1952, FRTPI 1965); Dip. in Sociol., Univ. of London, 1976. Served War, RE, 1942–46: N Africa, Italy, Greece. Planning Officer, LCC, 1949–54; Bor. Architect and Planning Officer, Larne, NI, 1955–60; joined Housing and Planning Inspectorate, 1960; Dep. Chief Inspector, 1976. Assessor at Belvoir Coalfield Inquiry, 1979. Town Planning Institute: Exam. Prize, 1952; Thomas Adams Prize, 1955; President's Prize, 1958. *Publications:* articles in TPI Jl. *Address:* 14 Collett Way, Frome, Somerset.

MIERS, Sir (Henry) David (Alastair Capel), KBE 1985; CMG 1979; HM Diplomatic Service; Ambassador to Greece, since 1989; *b* 10 Jan. 1937; *s* of Col R. D. M. C. Miers, DSO, QO Cameron Highlanders, and Honor (*née* Bucknill); *m* 1966, Imelda Maria Emilia, *d* of Jean-Baptiste Wouters, Huizingen, Belgium; two *s* one *d*. *Educ:* Winchester; University Coll., Oxford. Tokyo, 1963; Vientiane, 1966; Private Sec. to Minister of State, FO, 1968; Paris, 1972; Counsellor, Tehran, 1977–79; Hd, Middle Eastern Dept, FCO, 1980–83; Ambassador to Lebanon, 1983–85; Asst Under-Sec. of State, FCO, 1986–89. *Address:* c/o Foreign and Commonwealth Office, SW1.

MIFSUD BONNICI, Dr Carmelo, BA, LLD; MP; Prime Minister of Malta, 1984–87; Leader of the Labour Party, since 1984; *b* 17 July 1933; *s* of Dr Lorenzo Mifsud Bonnici, and Catherine (*née* Buttigieg). *Educ:* Govt sch. and Lyceum, Malta; Univ. of Malta (BA, LLD); Univ. Coll. London. Lectr in Industrial and Fiscal Law, Univ. of Malta, 1969–. Legal Consultant, General Workers' Union, 1969–83; Dep. Leader, Labour Party, responsible for Party affairs, 1980–82; Designate Leader of the Labour Movement, 1982; co-opted to Parlt, 1983, Minister of Labour and Social Services, 1983; Sen. Dep. Prime Minister, 1983–84; Minister of Education, 1983–87, and of the Interior, 1984–87. *Recreation:* reading. *Address:* House of Representatives, Valletta, Malta.

MIKARDO, Ian; *b* 9 July 1908; *m* 1932, Mary Rosette; two *d*. *Educ:* Portsmouth. MP (Lab): Reading, 1945–50, South Div. of Reading, 1950–55, again Reading, 1955–Sept. 1959; Poplar, 1964–74; Tower Hamlets, Bethnal Green and Bow, 1974–83; Bow and Poplar, 1983–87. Member: Nat. Exec. Cttee of Labour Party, 1950–59, and 1960–78 (Chm., 1970–71); Internat Cttee of Labour Party (Chm., 1973–78); Chm., Parly Labour Party, March-Nov. 1974; Chm., Select Cttee on Nationalized Industries, 1966–70. Pres., ASTMS, 1968–73; Vice-Pres., Socialist International, 1978–83 (Hon. Pres. 1983–). *Publications:* Centralised Control of Industry, 1944; Frontiers in the Air, 1946; (with others) Keep Left, 1947; The Second Five Years, 1948; The Problems of Nationalisation, 1948; (jtly) Keeping Left, 1950; The Labour Case, 1950; It's a Mug's Game, 1951; Socialism or Slump, 1959; Back-Bencher (autobiog.), 1988. *Address:* 89 Grove Hall Court, NW8 9NS. *T:* 071–286 5961.

MILAN, Archbishop of; *see* Martini, His Eminence Cardinal C. M.

MILBANK, Sir Anthony (Frederick), 5th Bt *cr* 1882; farmer and landowner since 1977; Chairman, Moorland Association, since 1986; *b* 16 Aug. 1939; *s* of Sir Mark Vane Milbank, 4th Bt, KCVO, MC, and of Hon. Verena Aileen, Lady Milbank, *yr d* of 11th Baron Farnham, DSO; *S* father, 1984; *m* 1970, Belinda Beatrice, *yr d* of Brig. Adrian Gore, DSO; two *s* one *d*. *Educ:* Eton College. Brown, Shipley & Co. Ltd, 1961–66; M&G Securities Ltd, 1966–77. Member: NCC Cttee for England, 1989–91; CLA Exec. Cttee, 1989–. High Sheriff of Durham, 1991–92. *Recreations:* outdoor sports. *Heir:* *s* Edward Mark Somerset Milbank, *b* 9 April 1973. *Address:* Barningham Park, Richmond, N Yorks DL11 7DW.

MILBORNE-SWINNERTON-PILKINGTON, Sir T. H.; *see* Pilkington.

MILBOURN, Dr Graham Maurice; Director, National Institute of Agricultural Botany, 1981–90, retired; *b* 4 Sept. 1930; *s* of late Frank McLaren Milbourn, BSc and Winifred May Milbourn; *m* 1956, Louise Lawson; three *s*. *Educ:* Reading Univ. (BSc, MSc, PhD). Asst Lectr, Reading Univ., 1953–56; Radiobiological Lab., ARC, 1956–61; Sen. Lectr, Crop Production, Wye Coll., London Univ., 1961–77; Prof. of Crop Production, Sch. of Agric., Edinburgh Univ., 1977–81. Pres., Assoc. Applied Biologists, 1991. *Publications:* papers on physiology of cereals and vegetables, uptake of radio-nucleides by crops. *Recreation:* sailing. *Address:* Elmwood, Cuckoo Lane, Lolworth, Cambridge CB3 8HF. *T:* Elsworth (0954) 780815.

MILBURN, Sir Anthony (Rupert), 5th Bt *cr* 1905; landowner; *b* 17 April 1947; *s* of Major Rupert Leonard Eversley Milburn (*yr s* of 3rd Bt) (*d* 1974) and of Anne Mary, *d* of late Major Austin Scott Murray, MC; *S* uncle, 1985; *m* 1977, Olivia Shirley, *y d* of Captain Thomas Noel Catlow, CBE, DL, RN; two *s* one *d*. *Educ:* Hawtreys, Savernake Forest; Eton College; Cirencester Agricultural Coll. ARICS. Company Director. *Recreations:* sporting and rural pursuits. *Heir:* *s* Patrick Thomas Milburn, *b* 4 Dec. 1980. *Address:* Guyzance Hall, Acklington, Morpeth, Northumberland NE65 9AJ. *T:* Alnwick (0665) 711247. *Club:* New (Edinburgh).

MILBURN, Donald B.; *see* Booker-Milburn.

MILBURN, Very Rev. Robert Leslie Pollington, MA; FSA; *b* 28 July 1907; *er s* of late George Leslie and Elizabeth Esther Milburn; *m* 1944, Margery Kathleen Mary, *d* of Rev. Francis Graham Harvie; one *d* (one *s* decd). *Educ:* Oundle; Sidney Sussex Coll., Cambridge; New Coll., Oxford. Asst Master, Eton Coll., 1930–32; Select Preacher, University of Oxford, 1942–44; Fellow and Chaplain of Worcester Coll., Oxford, 1934–57, Tutor, 1945–57, Estates Bursar, 1946–57 (Junior Bursar, 1936–46), Hon. Fellow, 1978. University Lectr in Church History, 1947–57; Bampton Lectr, 1952. Examining Chaplain to Bishop of St Edmundsbury and Ipswich, 1941–53, to Bishop of Southwark, 1950–57, to Bishop of Oxford, 1952–57; Dean of Worcester, 1957–68, now Emeritus; Master of the Temple, 1968–80. Mem. of Oxford City Council, 1941–47. A Trustee, Wallace Collection, 1970–76. Grand Chaplain, United Grand Lodge of England, 1969. *Publications:* Saints and their Emblems in English Churches, 1949; Early Christian Interpretations of History, 1954; Early Christian Art and Architecture, 1988; articles in Journal of Theological Studies and Church Quarterly Review. *Address:* 5 St Barnabas, Newland, Malvern, Worcs WR13 5AX.

MILCHSACK, Dame Lilo, Hon. DCMG 1972 (Hon. CMG 1968); Hon. CBE 1958; Initiator, 1949, and Hon. Chairman, since 1982, Deutsch-Englische Gesellschaft eV (Hon. Secretary, 1949–77; Chairman, 1977–82); *b* Frankfurt/Main; *d* of Prof. Dr Paul Duden and Johanna Bertha (*née* Nebe); *m* Hans Milchsack; (*d* 1984); two *d*. *Educ:* Univs of Frankfurt, Geneva and Amsterdam. Awarded Grosses Bundesverdienstkreuz, 1959, with Stern, 1985. *Recreations:* gardening, reading. *Address:* An der Kalvey 11, D-4000 Düsseldorf 31–Wittlaer, Germany. *T:* Düsseldorf 40 13 87.

MILDON, Arthur Leonard, QC 1971; **His Honour Judge Mildon;** a Circuit Judge, since 1986; *b* 3 June 1923; *er s* of late Rev. Dr W. H. Mildon, Barnstaple; *m* 1950, Iva, *er d* of late G. H. C. Wallis, Plymouth; one *s* one *d*. *Educ:* Kingswood Sch., Bath; Wadham Coll., Oxford (MA). Pres., Oxford Univ. Liberal Club, 1948. Army Service, 1942–46: Lieut, 138th (City of London) Field Regt, RA; Captain, 1st Army Group, RA. Called to Bar, Middle Temple, 1950, Bencher, 1979; Member of Western Circuit; Dep. Chm., Isle of Wight QS, 1967–71; a Recorder, 1972–85. Mem., Bar Council, 1973–74. *Recreation:* sailing. *Address:* c/o 2 Crown Office Row, Temple, EC4. *T:* 071–583 8155. *Clubs:* Ski Club of Great Britain; Royal Solent Yacht.

MILEDI, Prof. Ricardo, MD; FRS 1970; Distinguished Professor, University of California, Irvine, since 1984; *b* Mexico City, 15 Sept. 1927; *m* 1955, Ana Carmen (Mela) Garces; one *s*. *Educ:* Univ. Nacional Autónoma, Mexico City. BSc 1948; MD 1954. Research at Nat. Inst. of Cardiology, Mexico, 1952–55; Rockefeller Travelling Fellowship at ANU, 1956–58; research at Dept of Biophysics, UCL, 1958–84. Fellow, Amer. Acad. of Arts and Scis, 1986; Hon. Mem., Hungarian Acad. of Scis, 1988; For. Mem., Nat. Acad. of Scis, 1989. Luigi Galvani Award, 1987; Internat. Prize for Science, King Faisal Foundn, 1988. *Address:* Laboratory of Cellular and Molecular Neurobiology, Department of Psychobiology, University of California, Irvine, Calif 92717, USA. *T:* (714) 856–5693; 9 Gibbs Court, Irvine, Calif 92717, USA. *T:* (714) 856–2677.

MILES, Prof. Albert Edward William, LRCP; MRCS; FDS; DSc; Professor of Dental Pathology at The London Hospital Medical College, 1950–76, retired; Hon. Curator, Odontological Collection, Royal College of Surgeons of England, 1955–89; *b* 15 July 1912; *m* 1st, 1939, Sylvia Stuart; one *s* decd; 2nd, 1979, Diana Cross. *Educ:* Stationers' Company Sch.; Charing Cross and Royal Dental Hosps. John Tomes Prize, RCS, 1954–56. Part-time Lectr, Anatomy Dept, London Hosp. Med. Coll., 1977–85. Charles Tomes Lecturer, RCS, 1957; Evelyn Sprawson Lectr, London Hosp. Med. Coll., 1977. Hunterian Trustee, 1978–. Hon. FRSM 1988. Howard Mummery Meml Prize, 1976; Colyer Gold Medal, RCS, 1978; Sir Arthur Keith Medal, 1990. Exec. Editor, Archives of Oral Biology, 1969–88. *Publications:* contrib. to scientific literature. *Address:* 1 Cleaver Square, Kennington, SE11 4DW. *T:* 071–735 5350. *Clubs:* Tetrapods, Zoo.

MILES, Anthony John; Executive Publisher, Globe Communications Corporation, Florida, USA, 1985–90; *b* 18 July 1930; *s* of Paul and Mollie Miles; *m* 1975, Anne Hardman. *Educ:* High Wycombe Royal Grammar Sch. On staff of (successively): Middlesex Advertiser; Nottingham Guardian; Brighton Evening Argus. Daily Mirror: Feature writer, 1954–66; Asst Editor, 1967–68; Associate Editor, 1968–71; Editor, 1971–74; Mirror Group Newspapers: Editorial Dir, 1975–84; Dep. Chm., 1977–79 and 1984; Chm., 1980–83. Dir, Reuters Ltd, 1978–84. Member: Press Council, 1975–78; British Exec. Cttee, IPI, 1976–84; Council, CPU, 1983–84; Appeal Chm. 1982–83, Vice-Pres., 1983–, Newspaper Press Fund. *Address:* 23331 Drayton Drive, Boca Raton, Florida 33433, USA. *Clubs:* Reform; Boca Raton.

MILES, Lieut-Comdr Brian, RD 1970; FNI; RNR (retired); Director, Royal National Lifeboat Institution, since 1988; *b* 23 Feb. 1937; *s* of Terence Clifford Miles and Muriel Irene Terry; *m* 1964, Elizabeth Anne Scott; one *s* two *d*. *Educ:* Reed's School, Cobham; HMS Conway; Merchant Navy Cadet School. Master Mariner (Foreign Going) Cert. P&O Orient Lines: Cadet, 1954–57; Deck Officer, 1958–64; RNLI: Divl Inspector, 1964–73; Asst to Director, 1974–79; Ops Staff Officer, 1979–81; Dep. Dir, 1982–87. FNI 1989. *Address:* 8 Longfield Drive, West Parley, Ferndown, Dorset BH22 8TY. *T:* Bournemouth (0202) 571739.

MILES, Mrs Caroline Mary; Chairman, Oxfordshire Health Authority, since 1984; Director, Ian Ramsey Centre, and Ian Ramsey Fellow, St Cross College, Oxford, since 1988; *b* 30 April 1929; *d* of Brig. A. J. R. M. Leslie, OBE. *Educ:* numerous schools; Somerville Coll., Oxford. HM Treasury, 1953–54; NIESR, 1954–56 and 1964–67; attached to UN Secretariat, NY, 1956–63. Associate Mem., Nuffield Coll., Oxford, 1972–74. Market Develt Consultant, Harwell Res. Lab., 1981–86. Member: Textile Council, 1968–71; Inflation Accounting Cttee (Sandilands Cttee), 1974–75; Monopolies and Mergers Commn, 1975–84; NEB, 1976–79; Nuffield Council on Bioethics, 1991–. Trustee, The Tablet, 1982–; Governor: Ditchley Foundn, 1983–; Oxford Polytechnic, 1988–. *Publications:* Lancashire Textiles, A Case Study of Industrial Change, 1968; numerous papers and articles. *Recreations:* music, picnics, poohsticks. *Address:* Millbrook, Brookend, Chadlington, Oxford OX7 3NF. *T:* Chadlington (060876) 309.

MILES, Prof. Charles William Noel, CBE 1980; Head of Department of Land Management and Development, 1968–81, Dean of Faculty of Urban and Regional Studies, 1972–75, and Professor Emeritus 1981, University of Reading; Chairman, Agricultural Wages Board for England and Wales, 1972–81; *b* 3 Nov. 1915; 2nd *s* of late Lt-Col Sir Charles W. Miles, 5th Bt; *m* 1940, Jacqueline (Dickie) Cross; one *d* (one *s* decd). *Educ:* Stowe Sch.; Jesus Coll., Cambridge (MA). FRICS. Army Service, 1939–46; Univ. Demonstrator and Univ. Lectr, Dept of Estate Management, Cambridge, 1946–54; Chief Agent to Meyrick Estates in Hants and Anglesey, 1954–68; Agent to Bisterne Estate, 1957–68. Pres., Chartered Land Agents Soc., 1965–66; Mem., Cambs AEC, 1953–54; Mem., SE Region Adv. Cttee of Land Commn, 1967–70. Mem., Yates Cttee on Recreation Management Trng, 1977–82. Leverhulme Trust Emeritus Fellowship, 1982–84. *Publications:* Estate Finance and Business Management, 1953, 4th edn 1981; Estate Accounts, 1960; Recreational Land Management, 1977; (co-ed) Walmesley's Rural Estate Management, 6th edn, 1978; Running an Open house, 1986. *Recreations:* walking, gardening, theatre. *Address:* Wheelers, Vicarage Lane, Mattingley, Basingstoke, Hants RG27 8LE. *T:* Heckfield (0734) 326357. *Club:* Farmers'.

See also Sir W. N. M. Miles, Bt.

MILES, Prof. Christopher John; Professor of Film and Television, Royal College of Art, since 1989; film director and producer; *b* 19 April 1939; *s* of late John Miles, MC and Clarice Baskerville (*née* Remnant); *m* 1967, Susan Helen Howard; one *d*. *Educ:* Winchester Coll.; Institut des Hautes Etudes Cinématographiques, Paris. Dir, Milesian Film Productions, 1962–; *films* include: Six Sided Triangle, 1963; The Virgin and the Gypsy, 1970 (Best Film Award, US and UK Critics, 1970); Time for Loving, 1972; The Maids, 1974; Alternative Three, 1976; Priest of Love: life of D. H. Lawrence, 1981; Lord Elgin and some stones of no value, 1985; *theatre:* Skin of our Teeth, Chicago, 1973. Lecture tours: India, for British Council, 1985; USA, 1986. *Publications:* Alternative Three, 1977 (trans. 5 langs); (contrib.) H of C Report on Film, 1982; contrib. Image et Son, D. H. Lawrence Soc. Jl. *Recreations:* film-making, long walks and sketching in Arcadia. *Address:* 10 Selwood Place, SW7 3QQ; Aghios Leos, Methoni, Greece. *Clubs:* Garrick, Hurlingham.

MILES, Dillwyn, FRGS 1946; The Herald Bard, since 1967; Director, Dyfed Rural Council, 1975–81; Chairman, National Association of Local Councils, 1977–87, Vice-President, since 1987; *b* 25 May 1916; *s* of Joshua Miles and Anne Mariah (*née* Lewis), Newport, Pembrokeshire; *m* 1944, Joyce Eileen (*d* 1976), *d* of Lewis Craven Ord, Montreal and London; one *s* one *d*. *Educ:* Fishguard County Sch.; University College of Wales, Aberystwyth. Served War of 1939–45, Middle East, Army Captain. National Organiser Palestine House, London, 1945–48; Extra-mural Lectr, Univ. of Wales, 1948–51; Community Centres Officer, Wales, 1951–54; Gen. Sec., Pembrokeshire Community Council, 1954–75. Founder: Jerusalem Welsh Soc., 1940; W Wales Tourist Assoc., 1962; Assoc. of Trusts for Nature Conservation in Wales, 1973; Hon. Sec., W Wales Naturalists Trust, 1958–75 (Vice-Pres., 1975–). Grand Sword Bearer, Gorsedd of Bards of Isle of Britain, 1959–67 (Mem. Bd, 1945–). Member: Pembrokeshire CC, 1947–63; Cemaes RDC, 1947–52; Newport Parish Council, 1946–52; Haverfordwest Bor. Council, 1957–63; Pembrokeshire Coast Nat. Park Cttee, 1952–75; Exec. Cttee, Council for Protection of Rural Wales, 1946–64; Nature Conservancy's Cttee for Wales, 1966–73; Council, Soc. for Promotion of Nature Reserves, 1961–73; Countryside in 1970 Cttee for Wales, 1969–70; Sports Council for Wales, 1965–69; Mental Health Rev. Tribunal for Wales, 1959–71; Rent Trib. for Wales, 1966–87; Court of Govs, Nat. Libr. for Wales, 1963–64; Court of Govs, Univ. of Wales, 1957–66; Pembroke TA Assoc., 1956–59; Council for Small Industries in Wales, 1968–72; Age Concern Wales, 1972–77; Exec. Cttee, Nat. Council for Social Service, 1978–81; Exec. Cttee, NPFA, 1977–81; Council, Royal Nat. Eisteddfod of Wales, 1967–; Prince of Wales Cttee, 1971–80 (former Chm., Dyfed Projects Gp); Welsh Environment Foundn, 1971–80; Heraldry Soc., 1974–; Rural Voice, 1980–87. Former Chairman: Further Educn and Libraries and Museums Cttees, Pembs CC; Pembs Cttee, Arthritis and Rheumatism Council; Pembs Jun. Ch. of Commerce; Pembs Community Health Council; Policy and Welsh Cttees, Nat. Assoc. of Local Councils. Chairman: Wales Playing Fields Assoc., 1965–81; Pembs PO and Telecom Adv. Cttee, 1984– (Vice-Chm., 1971–84); Pembs Wildlife Appeal, 1988–. Editor: The Pembrokeshire Historian, 1955–81; Nature in Wales, 1970–80. Mayor of Newport, Pembs, 1950, 1966, 1967, 1979, and Sen. Alderman. Mayor and Adm. of the Port, Haverfordwest, 1961, Sheriff 1963, Burgess Warden 1974–. Broadcaster, TV and radio, 1936–. *Publications:* ed, Pembrokeshire Coast National Park, 1973; (jtly) Writers of the West, 1974; The Sheriffs of the County of Pembroke, 1975; The Royal National Eisteddfod of Wales, 1978; A Pembrokeshire Anthology, 1982; The Castles of Pembrokeshire, 1979, 3rd edn 1988; Portrait of Pembrokeshire, 1984; The Pembrokeshire Coast National Park, 1987. *Recreations:* natural history, local history, books, food and wine. *Address:* 9 St Anthony's Way, Haverfordwest, Dyfed, Wales SA61 1EL. *T:* Haverfordwest (0437) 765275. *Clubs:* Savile, Wig and Pen.

MILES, (Frank) Stephen, CMG 1964; HM Diplomatic Service, retired; *b* 7 Jan. 1920; *s* of Harry and Mary Miles; *m* 1953, Margaret Joy (*née* Theaker); three *d*. *Educ:* John Watson's Sch., Edinburgh; Daniel Stewart's Coll., Edinburgh; St Andrews Univ. (MA); Harvard Univ. (Commonwealth Fellowship; MPA). Served with Fleet Air Arm, 1942–46 (Lt (A) RNVR). Scottish Home Dept, 1948; FCO (previously CRO), 1948–80; served in: New Zealand, 1949–52; E and W Pakistan, 1954–57; Ghana, 1959–62; Uganda, 1962–63; British Dep. High Commissioner, Tanzania, 1963–65 (Acting High Commissioner, 1963–64); Acting High Commissioner in Ghana, March-April 1966; Consul-Gen., St Louis, 1967–70; Dep. High Comr, Calcutta, 1970–74; High Comr, Zambia, 1974–78; High Comr, Bangladesh, 1978–79. A Dir of Studies, Overseas Services Unit, RIPA, 1980–83. Councillor: Tandridge DC, Surrey, 1982–90; Limpsfield Parish Council, 1983– (Chm., 1987–89). *Recreations:* cricket, tennis, golf. *Address:* Maytrees, 71 Park Road, Limpsfield, Oxted, Surrey RH8 0AN. *T:* Oxted (0883) 713132. *Clubs:* Commonwealth Trust, MCC; Tandridge Golf.

MILES, Geoffrey, OBE 1970; HM Diplomatic Service, retired; Consul-General, Perth, Western Australia, 1980–82; *b* 25 Oct. 1922; *s* of late Donald Frank Miles and Honorine Miles (*née* Lambert); *m* 1946, Mary Rozel Cottle (*d* 1989); one *s* one *d*. *Educ:* Eltham College. Joined Home Civil Service (Min. of Shipping), 1939; War service as pilot in RAF, 1941–46 (commnd 1945); Min. of Transport, 1946–50; British Embassy, Washington 1951; Sec., Copper-Zinc-Lead Cttee, Internat. Materials Conf., Washington 1952–53; BoT, 1953–55; Asst Trade Comr, Perth, 1955–59; Second Sec., Ottawa, 1960–63; First Sec., Salisbury, 1963–66, Dublin, 1967–71; Trade Comr (later Consul) and Head of Post, Edmonton, 1971–75, Consul-Gen., 1976–78; Consul-Gen., Philadelphia, 1979–80. *Recreations:* music, golf, amateur radio. *Address:* Farthings, Appledram Lane, Chichester, W Sussex PO20 7PE. *Clubs:* Royal Air Force; British Officers (Philadelphia); Goodwood Golf.

MILES, Prof. Hamish Alexander Drummond, OBE 1987; Barber Professor of Fine Arts and Director of the Barber Institute, University of Birmingham, 1970–90, Emeritus Director, and Professor at Large, 1990–91; *b* 19 Nov. 1925; *s* of J. E. (Hamish) Miles and Sheila Barbara Robertson; *m* 1957, Jean Marie, *d* of T. R. Smits, New York; two *s* two *d*. *Educ:* Douai Sch.; Univ. of Edinburgh (MA); Balliol Coll., Oxford. Served War: Army, 1944–47. Asst Curator, Glasgow Art Gallery, 1953–54; Asst Lectr, then Lectr in the History of Art, Univ. of Glasgow, 1954–66; Vis. Lectr, Smith Coll., Mass, 1960–61; Prof. of the History of Art, Univ. of Leicester, 1966–70. Trustee, National Galleries of Scotland, 1967–87; Mem., Museums and Galleries Commn, 1983–87. *Publications:* (jtly) The Paintings of James McNeill Whistler, 2 vols, 1980; sundry articles and catalogues. *Recreations:* beekeeping and woodland management. *Address:* 37 Carpenter Road, Birmingham B15 2JJ; Burnside, Kirkmichael, Blairgowrie, Perthshire PH10 7NA.

MILES, (Henry) Michael (Pearson), OBE 1989; Executive Director, John Swire & Sons Ltd, since 1988; *b* 19 April 1936; *s* of late Brig. H. G. P. Miles and Margaret Miles; *m* 1967, Carol Jane Berg; two *s* one *d*. *Educ:* Wellington Coll. National Service, Duke of Wellington's Regt, 1955–57. Joined John Swire & Sons,1958; Managing Director: John Swire & Sons (Japan) Ltd, 1973–76; Cathay Pacific Airways Ltd, 1978–84 (Chm., 1984–88); Chairman: Swire Pacific, 1984–88; John Swire & Sons (HK), 1984–88; Director: Thomas Cook Gp, 1988–; Sedgwick Lloyd's Underwriting Agents, 1989–; NAAFI, 1989–; Baring Brothers, 1989–; Johnson Matthey, 1990–; Portals Holdings, 1990–. Chm., Hong Kong Tourist Assoc., 1984–88. Gov., Wellington Coll., 1988–. *Recreations:* golf, tennis. *Address:* Shalbourne House, Shalbourne, near Marlborough, Wilts SN8 3QH. *Clubs:* Army and Navy, Royal and Ancient Golf; Berkshire Golf.

MILES, John Edwin Alfred, CBE 1979 (OBE 1961; MBE 1952); HM Diplomatic Service, retired; *b* 14 Aug. 1919; *s* of late John Miles and late Rose Miles (*née* Newlyn); *m* 1952, Barbara Fergus Ferguson; two *s* one *d*. *Educ:* Hornsey County Sch. Apptd to Dominions Office, 1937. Served War: joined Queen's Royal West Surrey Regt, 1940; commissioned in N Staffordshire Regt, 1941; attached Royal Indian Army Service Corps, 1942 (Maj. 1943); released, Sept. 1946, and returned to Dominions Office. Served in: Wellington, NZ, 1948–51; Calcutta, 1953–56; CRO, 1957–61; Trinidad (on staff of Governor-Gen.), 1961; Jamaica (Adviser to Governor, and later First Sec. in British High Commission), 1961–64; Wellington, NZ, 1964–68; Counsellor, 1968; Accra, Ghana, 1968–71; Dep. High Comr, Madras, India, 1971–75; High Comr to Swaziland, 1975–79. *Address:* Cartref, Ladyegate Road, Dorking, Surrey RH5 4AR. *T:* Dorking (0306) 884346.

MILES, John Seeley, FCSD, FSTD; typographer and partner in design group, Banks and Miles; *b* 11 Feb. 1931; *s* of Thomas William Miles and Winifred (*née* Seeley); *m* 1955, Louise Wilson; one *s* two *d*. *Educ:* Beckenham and Penge Grammar Sch.; Beckenham School of Art. FCSD (FSIAD 1973); FSTD 1974. UN travelling schol. to Netherlands to practise typography and punch cutting under Jan van Krimpen and S. L. Hartz, 1954–55; Assistant to Hans Schmoller at Penguin Books, 1955–58; joined Colin Banks, *qv*, to form design partnership, Banks and Miles, 1958. Consultant to: Zoological Soc., Regent's Park and Whipsnade, 1958–82; Expanded Metal Co., 1960–83; Consumers' Assoc., 1964–; British Council, 1968–83; The Post Office, 1972–83; E Midlands Arts Assoc., 1974–79; Curwen Press, 1970–72; Basilisk Press, 1976–79; Enschedé en Zn, Netherlands, 1980–; British Telecom, 1980–89; British Airports Auth., 1983–87; typographic advisor, HMSO, 1985–; design advisor: Agricl Inf. Workshop, Udaipur, India, 1973; Monotype Corp., 1985–; hon. design advr, UEA, 1990–. Designed banknote series Netherlands Antilles, 1987. Member, PO Design Adv. Cttee, 1972–76; American Heritage Lectr, New York, 1960; held seminar, Graphic Inst., Stockholm, 1977 and 1986. Chairman: Wynkyn de Worde Soc., 1973–74; Arbitration Cttee, Assoc. Typographique Internationale, 1984–; Mem., Soc. Roy. des Bibliophiles et Iconophiles de Belgique, 1991–. Governor, Central School of Arts and Crafts, 1978–85; External examiner: London Coll. of Printing, 1984–88; Technische Hoogschool Delft, 1986–87; Reading Univ., 1990–. Mem. CGLI, 1986. Exhibitions: London, 1971, 1978; Amsterdam and Brussels, 1977. FRSA 1988. (With Colin Banks) Green Product Award, 1989; BBC Envmtl Award, 1990. *Publications:* Design for Desktop Publishing, 1987; articles and reviews in professional jls. *Recreations:* gardening, painting, reading aloud. *Address:* 24 Collins Street, Blackheath, SE3 0GU. *T:* 081–318 4739. *Clubs:* Arts, Double Crown.

MILES, Dame Margaret, DBE 1970; BA; Headmistress, Mayfield School, Putney, 1952–73; *b* 11 July 1911; 2nd *d* of Rev. E. G. Miles and Annie Miles (*née* Jones). *Educ:* Ipswich High Sch., GPDST; Bedford Coll., Univ. of London (Hon. Fellow, 1983). History teacher: Westcliff High Sch., 1935–39; Badminton Sch., 1939–44; Lectr, Dept of Educn, University of Bristol, 1944–46; Headmistress, Pate's Grammar Sch., Cheltenham, 1946–52. Member: Schools Broadcasting Council, 1958–68; Educ. Adv. Council, ITA, 1962–67; Nat. Adv. Council on Trng and Supply of Teachers, 1962–65; BBC Gen. Adv. Council, 1964–73; Campaign for Comprehensive Educn, 1966– (Chm., 1972; Pres., 1979–); RSA Council, 1972–77; British Assoc., 1974–79; Council, Chelsea Coll., Univ. of London, 1965–82; former Mem., Council, Bedford Coll., Univ. of London (Vice-Chm.); Chairman: Adv. Cttee on Develt Educn, ODM, 1977–79; Central Bureau for Educl Visits and Exchanges, 1978–82; Vice-Chm., Educ. Adv. Cttee, UK Nat. Commn for Unesco, 1985. Chm., Meirionnydd Br., Council for Protection of Rural Wales, 1982–91; Pres., British Assoc. for Counselling, 1980–86. Hon. Fellow, Chelsea Coll., London, 1985. Hon. DCL, Univ. of Kent at Canterbury, 1973. *Publications:* And Gladly Teach, 1965; Comprehensive Schooling, Problems and Perspectives, 1968. *Recreations:* opera, films, reading, gardening, golf, walking, travel when possible. *Address:* Tanycraig, Pennal, Machynlleth SY20 9LB. *Clubs:* University Women's; Aberdovey Golf.

MILES, Michael; *see* Miles, H. M. P.

MILES, Oliver; *see* Miles, R. O.

MILES, Peter Charles H.; *see* Hubbard-Miles.

MILES, Sir Peter (Tremayne), KCVO 1986; an Extra Equerry to HM the Queen, since 1988; *b* 26 June 1924; *er s* of late Lt-Col E. W. T. Miles, MC; *m* 1956, Philippa Helen Tremlett; two *s* one *d*. *Educ:* Eton Coll.; RMC, Sandhurst. First The Royal Dragoons, 1944–49; J. F. Thomasson & Co., 1949–59; Gerrard & National Discount Co. Ltd, 1959–80 (Managing Director, 1964–80). Director: P. Murray-Jones Ltd, 1966–75; Astley & Pearce Holdings Ltd, 1975–80 (Chm., 1978–80). Keeper of the Privy Purse and Treas. to the Queen, 1981–87; Receiver-Gen., Duchy of Lancaster, 1981–87; Mem., Prince of Wales' Council, 1981–87. *Address:* 4 Kylestrome House, Cundy Street, SW1W 9JT. *T:* 071–730 5666; Mill House, Southrop, Lechlade, Gloucestershire GL7 3NU. *T:* Southrop (036785) 287. *Clubs:* Cavalry and Guards, Pratt's, White's; Swinley Forest Golf.

MILES, (Richard) Oliver, CMG 1984; HM Diplomatic Service; Head of Joint Directorate, Overseas Trade Services, Foreign and Commonwealth Office/Department of Trade and Industry, since 1991; *b* 6 March 1936; *s* of George Miles and Olive (*née* Clapham); *m* 1968, Julia, *d* of late Prof. J. S. Weiner; three *s* one *d*. *Educ:* Ampleforth Coll.; Merton Coll., Oxford (Oriental Studies). Entered Diplomatic Service, 1960; served in Abu Dhabi, Amman, Aden, Mukalla, Nicosia, Jedda; Counsellor, Athens, 1977–80; Head of Near East and N Africa Dept, FCO, 1980–83; Ambassador to: Libya, 1984; Luxembourg, 1985–88; Under-Sec., NI Office, Belfast (on secondment), 1988–90; Asst Under Sec. of State (Economic), FCO, 1990–91. Non-exec. Dir, Vickers Defence Systems, 1990–. *Recreations:* bird-watching, playing the flute. *Address:* c/o Foreign and Commonwealth Office, SW1A 2AH. *Club:* Travellers'.

MILES, Roger Steele, PhD, DSc; Head, Department of Public Services, The Natural History Museum (formerly British Museum (Natural History)), since 1975; *b* 31 Aug. 1937; *s* of John Edward Miles and Dorothy Mildred (*née* Steele); *m* 1960, Ann Blake; one *s* one *d*. *Educ:* Malet Lambert High Sch., Hull; King's Coll., Univ. of Durham (BSc, PhD, DSc). Sen. Res. Award, DSIR, 1962–64; Sen. Res. Fellow, Royal Scottish Museum, 1964–66, Sen. Scientific Officer, 1966–68; Sen. Sci. Officer, BM (Nat. Hist.), 1968–71, Principal Sci. Officer, 1971–74. Hon. Fellow, Columbia Pacific Univ., 1983. *Publications:* 2nd edn, Palaeozoic Fishes, 1971 (1st edn, J. A. Moy-Thomas, 1939); (ed, with P. H. Greenwood and C. Patterson) Interrelationships of Fishes, 1973; (ed, with S. M. Andrews and A. D. Walker) Problems in Vertebrate Evolution, 1977; (with others) The Design of Educational Exhibits, 1982, 2nd edn 1988; papers and monographs on anatomy and palaeontology of fishes, articles on museums, in jls. *Recreations:* music, twentieth century art and architecture. *Address:* 3 Eagle Lane, Snaresbrook, E11 1PF. *T:* 081–989 5684.

MILES, Stephen; *see* Miles, F. S.

MILES, Wendy Ann; *see* Henry, W. A.

MILES, William; Chief Executive, West Yorkshire County Council, and Clerk to the Lieutenancy, West Yorkshire, 1984–86; *b* 26 Sept. 1933; *s* of William and Gladys Miles; *m* 1961, Jillian Anne Wilson; three *s*. *Educ:* Wyggeston School, Leicester; Trinity Hall, Cambridge (MA, LLM). Solicitor. Asst Solicitor, Leicester, Doncaster and Exeter County Boroughs, 1960–66; Asst Town Clerk, Leicester Co. Borough, 1966–69; Dep. Town Clerk, Blackpool Co. Borough, 1969–73; City Legal Adviser, Newcastle upon Tyne, 1973–74; Chief Exec., Gateshead Borough Council, 1974–84. *Recreations:* bridge, hill walking, sport. *Address:* 23 Moor Crescent, Gosforth, Newcastle upon Tyne NE3 4AP. *T:* 091-285 1996.

MILES, Sir William (Napier Maurice), 6th Bt *cr* 1859; retired architect; *b* 19 Oct. 1913; *s* of Sir Charles William Miles, 5th Bt, OBE; *S* father, 1966; *m* 1946, Pamela, *d* of late Capt. Michael Dillon; one *s* two *d. Educ:* Stowe; University of Cambridge (BA). Architectural Assoc. Diploma, 1939. *Recreation:* surviving. *Heir: s* Philip John Miles, *b* 10 Aug. 1953. *Address:* Old Rectory House, Walton-in-Gordano, near Clevedon, Avon. *T:* Clevedon (0272) 873365. *Club:* Royal Western Yacht.
See also Prof. C. W. N. Miles.

MILFORD, 2nd Baron *cr* 1939; **Wogan Philipps;** Bt 1919; farmer and painter; *b* 25 Feb. 1902; *e s* of 1st Baron Milford; *S* father, 1962; *m* 1st, 1928, Rosamond Nina Lehmann, CBE; one *s* (one *d* decd); 2nd, 1944, Cristina, Countess of Huntingdon (*d* 1953); 3rd, 1954, Tamara Rust. *Educ:* Eton; Magdalen Coll., Oxford. Member of International Brigade, Spanish Civil War. Former Member of Henley on Thames RDC; Communist Councillor, Cirencester RDC, 1946–49; has taken active part in building up Nat. Union of Agric. Workers in Gloucestershire and served on its county cttee. Prospective Parly cand. (Lab), Henley on Thames, 1938–39; contested (Com) Cirencester and Tewkesbury, 1950. Has held one-man exhibitions of paintings in London, Milan and Cheltenham and shown in many mixed exhibns. *Heir: s* Hon. Hugo John Laurence Philipps [*b* 27 Aug. 1929; *m* 1st, 1951 (marr. diss., 1958); one *d*; 2nd, 1959, Mary (marr. diss. 1984), *e d* of Baron Sherfield, *qv*; three *s* one *d*; 3rd, 1989, Mrs Felicity Leach]. *Address:* Flat 2, 8 Lyndhurst Road, Hampstead, NW3 5PX.
See also Hon. R. H. Philipps.

MILFORD, John Tillman; QC 1989; a Recorder, since 1985; *b* 4 Feb. 1946; *s* of late Dr Roy Douglas Milford and Jessie Milford (*née* Rhind); *m* 1975, Mary Alice, *d* of late Dr E. A. Spriggs of Wylam, Northumberland; three *d. Educ:* The Cathedral School, Salisbury; Hurstpierpoint; Exeter Univ. (LLB). Called to the Bar, Inner Temple, 1969; in practice on NE Circuit, 1970–. *Recreations:* fishing, shooting, gardening. *Address:* (chambers) 12 Trinity Chare, Newcastle upon Tyne. *T:* 091–232 1927; Hill House, Haydon Bridge, Hexham, Northumberland. *T:* Hexham (0434) 684234. *Club:* Northern Counties (Newcastle upon Tyne).

MILFORD HAVEN, 4th Marquess of, *cr* 1917; **George Ivar Louis Mountbatten;** Earl of Medina, 1917; Viscount Alderney, 1917; *b* 6 June 1961; *s* of 3rd Marquess of Milford Haven, OBE, DSC, and of Janet Mercedes, *d* of late Major Francis Bryce, OBE; *S* father, 1970; *m* 1989, Sarah Georgina, *d* of George A. Walker, *qv*; one *d. Heir: b* Lord Ivar Alexander Michael Mountbatten, *b* 9 March 1963. *Address:* Moyns Park, Birdbrook, near Halstead, Essex CO9 4BP.

MILINGO, Most Rev. Emanuel; Former Archbishop of Lusaka (Archbishop, 1969–83); Special Delegate to the Pontifical Commission for Tourism and Immigration, since 1983; *b* 13 June 1930; *s* of Yakobe Milingo Chilumbu and Tomaide Lumbiwe Miti. *Educ:* Kachebere Seminary, Malawi; Pastoral Inst., Rome; University Coll., Dublin. Curate: Minga Parish, Chipata Dio., 1958–60; St Mary's Parish, 1960–61; Chipata Cathedral, 1963–64; Parish Priest, Chipata Cathedral, 1964–65; Sec. for Communications at Catholic Secretariat, Lusaka, 1966–69. Founder, The Daughters of the Redeemer, Congregation for young ladies, 1971. *Publications:* Amake-Joni, 1972; To Die to Give Life, 1975; Summer Lectures for the Daughters of the Redeemer, 1976; The Way to Daughterhood; My God is a Living God, 1981; Lord Jesus, My Lord and Saviour, 1982; Demarcations, 1982; The Flower Garden of Jesus the Redeemer; My Prayers Are Not Heard; Precautions in the Ministry of Deliverance. *Recreation:* music. *Address:* Pontificia Commissione per la Pastorale delle Migrazioni e del Turismo, Palazzo San Calisto, Vatican City.

MILKINA, Nina, (Mrs A. R. M. Sedgwick); Hon. RAM; concert pianist; *b* Moscow, 27 Jan. 1919; *d* of Jacques and Sophie Milkine; *m* 1943, Alastair Robert Masson Sedgwick, Dir Nielsen Sedgwick International; one *s* one *d. Educ:* privately. Musical studies with the late Leon Conus of the Moscow Conservatoire and at the Paris Conservatoire, also with Profs Harold Craxton and Tobias Matthay, London. First public appearance at age of 11 with Lamoureux Orchestra, Paris; has since been broadcasting, televising, and touring in Great Britain and abroad. Was commissioned by BBC to broadcast series of all Mozart's piano sonatas; invited to give Mozart recital for bicentenary celebration of Mozart's birth, Edinburgh Festival. Major works recorded: Mozart piano concertos K271 and K467; Mozart recitals; complete Chopin Mazurkas; Scarlatti Sonatas; Mozart and Haydn Sonatas; works by Rachmaninov, Prokofiev, Scriabin. Widely noted for interpretation of Mozart's piano works. *Publications:* works for piano. *Recreations:* swimming, chess, fly fishing. *Address:* London and Sardinia.

MILKOMANE, G. A. M.; *see* Sava, George.

MILL, Robert Duguid Forrest P.; *see* Pring-Mill.

MILLAIS, Sir Ralph (Regnault), 5th Bt *cr* 1885; *b* 4 March 1905; *s* of Sir Geoffroy William Millais, 4th Bt, and Madeleine Campbell (*d* 1963), *d* of C. H. Grace; *S* father, 1941; *m* 1st, 1939, Felicity Caroline Mary Ward Robinson (marr. diss.), *d* of late Brig.-Gen. W. W. Warner, CMG; one *s* one *d*; 2nd, 1947, Irene Jessie (marr. diss. 1971; she *d* 1985), *er d* of E. A. Stone, FSI; 3rd, 1975, Babette Sefton-Smith, *yr d* of Maj.-Gen. H. F. Salt, CB, CMG, DSO. *Educ:* Marlborough; Trinity Coll., Cambridge. Business career. Joined RAFVR at outbreak of war, 1939, Wing Comdr. *Recreations:* fishing, travel and the restoration of famous Vintage and Historic cars. *Heir: s* Geoffroy Richard Everett Millais, *b* 27 Dec. 1941. *Address:* Gate Cottage, Winchelsea, East Sussex.

MILLAN, Rt. Hon. Bruce, PC 1975; Member, Commission of the European Communities, since 1989; *b* 5 Oct. 1927; *s* of David Millan; *m* 1953, Gwendoline May Fairey; one *s* one *d. Educ:* Harris Academy, Dundee. Chartered Accountant, 1950–59. Chm. Scottish Labour Youth Council, 1949–50. Contested: West Renfrewshire, 1951, Craigton Div. of Glasgow, 1955. MP (Lab): Glasgow, Craigton, 1959–83; Glasgow, Govan, 1983–88; Parly Under-Sec. of State: for Defence, (RAF), 1964–66; for Scotland, 1966–70; Minister of State, Scottish Office, 1974–76; Sec. of State for Scotland, 1976–79; opposition spokesman on Scotland, 1979–83. *Address:* Commission of the European Communities, Rue de la Loi 200, 1049 Brussels, Belgium.

MILLAR, family name of **Baron Inchyra.**

MILLAR, Anthony Bruce; Executive Chairman, Albert Fisher Group PLC, since 1982; *b* 5 Oct. 1941; *s* of late James Desmond Millar and of Josephine Georgina Millar (*née* Brice); *m* 1964, Judith Anne (*née* Jester); two *d. Educ:* Haileybury; Imperial Service College. FCA. Asst to Group Management Accountant and Group Treasurer, Viyella Internat. Fedn, 1964–67; United Transport Overseas, Nairobi, and London (Dep. Group Financial Controller), 1967–72; Finance Dir, Fairfield Property Co., 1972–75; Consultant, 1975–77; Managing Dir, Provincial Laundries Ltd, 1977–81; Dep. Chm., Hawley Group, 1981–82. CBIM. *Recreations:* swimming, walking, bridge, racehorse owner. *Address:* Albert Fisher Group PLC, Fisher House, 61 Thames Street, Windsor, Berks SL4 1QW. *Club:* Mark's.

MILLAR, Betty Phyllis Joy; Regional Nursing Officer, South Western Regional Health Authority, 1973–84; *b* 19 March 1929; *o d* of late Sidney Hildersly Millar and May Phyllis Halliday. *Educ:* Ursuline High Sch. for Girls; Dumbarton Academy; Glasgow Royal Infirm.; Glasgow Royal Maternity Hosp.; Royal Coll. of Nursing, London. RGN 1950; SCM 1953; NA (Hosp.) Cert. 1961. Theatre Sister, Glasgow Royal Infirm., 1953–54; Ward and Theatre Sister, Henry Brock Meml Hosp., 1954–55; Nursing Sister, Iraq Petroleum Co., 1955–57; Clinical Instructor, Exper. Scheme of Nurse Trng, Glasgow, 1957–60; Admin. Student, Royal Coll. of Nursing, 1960–61; 2nd Asst Matron, Glasgow Royal Infirm., 1961–62; Asst Nursing Officer, Wessex Regional Hosp. Bd, 1962–67; Matron, Glasgow Royal Infirm., 1967–69; Chief Regional Nursing Officer, SW Regional Hosp. Bd, 1969–73. WHO Fellowship to study nursing services in Scandinavia, 1967. Mem. Jt Bd of Clinical Nursing Studies, 1970–82. *Address:* Pinedrift, 45 Stoneyfields, Easton-in-Gordano, Bristol BS20 0LL. *T:* Pill (0275) 372709.

MILLAR, Prof. Fergus Graham Burtholme, DPhil; DLitt; FSA; FBA 1976; Camden Professor of Ancient History, and Fellow of Brasenose College, Oxford University, since 1984; *b* 5 July 1935; *s* of late J. S. L. Millar and of Jean Burtholme (*née* Taylor); *m* 1959, Susanna Friedmann; two *s* one *d. Educ:* Edinburgh Acad.; Loretto Sch.; Trinity Coll., Oxford (1st Cl. Lit. Hum.); DPhil 1962, DLitt 1988, Oxon. Fellow: All Souls Coll., Oxford, 1958–64; Queen's Coll., Oxford, 1964–76; Prof. of Ancient History, UCL, 1976–84. Conington Prize, 1963. Pres., Soc. for the Promotion of Roman Studies, 1989– (Vice-Pres., 1977–89). FSA 1978. Corresp. Member: German Archaeolog. Inst., 1978; Bavarian Acad., 1987; Finnish Acad., 1989. Editor, Jl of Roman Studies, 1975–79. *Publications:* A Study of Cassius Dio, 1964; The Roman Empire and its Neighbours, 1967; (ed with G. Vermes) E. Schürer, history of the Jewish people in the age of Jesus Christ (175 BC-AD 135), Vol. I, 1973, Vol. II, 1979, Vol. III, parts 1 and 2 (ed with G. Vermes and M. D. Goodman), 1986–87; The Emperor in the Roman World (31 BC-AD 337), 1977; (ed with E. Segal) Caesar Augustus: seven aspects, 1984. *Address:* Brasenose College, Oxford OX1 4AJ; 80 Harpes Road, Oxford OX2 7QL. *T:* Oxford (0865) 515782.

MILLAR, George Reid, DSO 1944; MC; farmer and writer; *b* 19 Sept. 1910; 2nd *s* of Thomas Andrew Millar, architect, and Mary Reid Morton; *m* 1945, Isabel Beatriz (*d* 1990), *d* of Montague Paske-Smith, CMG, CBE; no *c. Educ:* Loretto; St John's, Cambridge. Architect, 1930–32; journalist, with Daily Telegraph and Daily Express, 1934–39; Paris correspondent Daily Express, 1939; served War of 1939–45, The Rifle Bde; escaped from German POW camp to England, then served as agent in France; Chevalier de la Légion d'Honneur; Croix de Guerre avec Palmes. Tenant farmer, 400 acres, 1962; increased to 1000 acres, 1966; reduced to 600 acres, 1982. *Publications:* Maquis, 1945; Horned Pigeon, 1946; My Past was an Evil River, 1946; Isabel and the Sea, 1948; Through the Unicorn Gates, 1950; A White Boat from England, 1951; Siesta, 1952; Orellana, 1954; Oyster River, 1963; Horseman, 1970; The Bruneval Raid, 1974; Road to Resistance, 1979. *Recreation:* sailing. *Address:* Sydling St Nicholas, Dorset. *T:* Cerne Abbas (03003) 205. *Clubs:* Royal Cruising; Royal Yacht Squadron (Cowes).

MILLAR, Ian Alastair D.; *see* Duncan Millar.

MILLAR, John Stanley, CBE 1979; County Planning Officer, Greater Manchester Council, 1973–83; *b* 1925; *s* of late Nicholas William Stanley Millar and late Elsie Baxter Millar (*née* Flinn); *m* 1961, Patricia Mary (*née* Land); one *d. Educ:* Liverpool Coll.; Univ. of Liverpool. BArch, DipCD, PPRTPI, RIBA. Planning Asst, then Sen. Asst Architect, City of Liverpool, 1948–51; Sectional Planning Officer, then Dep. Asst County Planning Officer, Lancs CC 1951–61; Chief Asst Planning Officer, then Asst City Planning Officer, City of Manchester, 1961–64; City Planning Officer, Manchester, 1964–73. *Publications:* papers in professional and technical jls. *Recreations:* walking, listening to music, travel, the sea. *Address:* 55 Stanneylands Drive, Wilmslow, Cheshire SK9 4EU. *T:* Wilmslow (0625) 523616.

MILLAR, Sir Oliver Nicholas, GCVO 1988 (KCVO 1973; CVO 1963; MVO 1953); FBA 1970; Director of the Royal Collection, 1987–88; Surveyor of the Queen's Pictures, 1972–88, Surveyor Emeritus, since 1988; *b* 26 April 1923; *er s* of late Gerald Millar, MC and late Ruth Millar; *m* 1954, Delia Mary, 2nd *d* of late Lt-Col Cuthbert Dawnay, MC; one *s* three *d. Educ:* Rugby; Courtauld Institute of Art, University of London (Academic Diploma in History of Art). Unable, for medical reasons, to serve in War of 1939–45. Asst Surveyor of the King's Pictures, 1947–49, Dep. Surveyor 1949–72. Trustee, Nat. Portrait Gallery, 1972–. Member: Reviewing Cttee on Export of Works of Art, 1975–87; Exec. Cttee, Nat. Art Collections Fund, 1986–; Management Cttee, Courtauld Inst., 1986–. Visitor, Ashmolean Mus., 1987–. Trustee, Nat. Heritage Meml Fund, 1988–. A Dir, Friends of the Tate Gall., 1989–; Chm., Patrons of British Art, 1989–. FSA. Corresponding Fellow: Ateneo Veneto, Venice; Koninklijke Academie voor Wetenschappen, Letteren en Schone Kunsten, Belgium. *Publications:* Gainsborough, 1949; William Dobson, Tate Gallery Exhibition, 1951; English Art, 1625–1714 (with Dr M. D. Whinney), 1957; Rubens's Whitehall Ceiling, 1958; Abraham van der Doort's Catalogue, 1960; Tudor, Stuart and Early Georgian Pictures in the Collection of HM the Queen, 1963; Zoffany and his Tribuna, 1967; Later Georgian Pictures in the Collection of HM the Queen, 1969; Inventories and Valuations of the King's Goods, 1972; The Age of Charles I (Tate Gallery Exhibn), 1972; The Queen's Pictures, 1977; Sir Peter Lely (Nat. Portrait Gall. Exhibn), 1978; Van Dyck in England (Nat. Portrait Gall. Exhibn), 1982; articles in the Burlington Magazine, etc; numerous catalogues, principally for The Queen's Gallery. *Recreations:* drawing, gardening, reading, listening to music. *Address:* The Cottage, Ray's Lane, Penn, Bucks HP10 8LH. *T:* Penn (049481) 2124. *Club:* Brooks's.

MILLAR, Peter Carmichael, OBE 1978; Deputy Keeper of HM Signet, 1983–91; Partner in law firm, Aitken Nairn, WS, since 1987; *b* 19 Feb. 1927; *s* of late Rev. Peter Carmichael Millar, OBE, DD and of Ailsa Ross Brown Campbell or Millar; *m* 1953, Kirsteen Lindsay Carnegie, *d* of late Col David Carnegie, CB, OBE, TD, DL, Dep. Gen. Manager, Clydesdale Bank; two *s* two *d. Educ:* Aberdeen Grammar Sch.; Glasgow Univ.; St Andrews Univ.; Edinburgh Univ. MA, LLB; WS. Served RN, 1944–47. Partner in law firms, Messrs W. & T. P. Manuel, WS, 1954–62; Aitken, Kinnear & Co., WS, 1963–87. Clerk to Soc. of Writers to HM Signet, 1964–83. Chairman: Church of Scotland Gen. Trustees, 1973–85; Mental Welfare Commn for Scotland, 1983–91; (part-time) Medical Appeal Tribunals, 1991–. *Recreations:* golf, hill-walking, music. *Address:* 25 Cramond Road North, Edinburgh EH4 6LY. *T:* 031-336 2069. *Clubs:* New (Edinburgh); Hon. Co. of Edinburgh Golfers, Bruntsfield Links Golfing Society.

MILLAR, Sir Ronald (Graeme), Kt 1980; playwright, screenwriter and political writer; Deputy Chairman, Theatre Royal Haymarket, since 1977; *b* 12 Nov. 1919; *s* of late Ronald Hugh Millar and Dorothy Ethel Dacre Millar (*née* Hill). *Educ:* Charterhouse; King's Coll., Cambridge. Served as Sub-Lt, RNVR, 1940–43 (invalided out). Began in the Theatre as an actor. First stage appearance, London, Swinging the Gate, Ambassadors', 1940, subseq. in Mr Bolfry, The Sacred Flame, Murder on the Nile, Jenny Jones, (own play) Zero Hour, 1944. Ealing Studios, 1946–48, worked on Frieda, Train of Events, etc;

screenwriter, Hollywood, 1948–54: So Evil My Love, The Miniver Story, Scaramouche, Rose-Marie, The Unknown Man, Never Let Me Go, Betrayed. Plays produced in London: Frieda, 1946; Champagne for Delilah, 1948, Waiting for Gillian, 1954; The Bride and the Bachelor, 1956; The More the Merrier, 1960; The Bride Comes Back, 1960; The Affair (from C. P. Snow novel), 1961, The New Men (from C. P. Snow), 1962; The Masters (from C. P. Snow), 1963; (book and lyrics) Robert and Elizabeth (musical), 1964; Number 10, 1967; Abelard and Heloise, 1970; The Case in Question (from C. P. Snow), 1975; A Coat of Varnish (from C. P. Snow), 1982. *Publication:* A View from the Wings (autobiog.), 1992. *Recreations:* all kinds of music, all kinds of people. *Address:* 7 Sheffield Terrace, W8 7NG. *T:* 071–727 8361. *Clubs:* Brooks's, Dramatists'.

MILLAR, Prof. William Malcolm, CBE 1971; MD; Crombie-Ross Professor of Mental Health, University of Aberdeen, 1949–77; *b* 20 April 1913; *s* of Rev. Gavin Millar, BD, Logiealmond, Perthshire, and Margaret Malcolm, Stanley, Perthshire; *m* 1st, 1941, Catherine McAuslin Rankin; two *s* four *d*; 2nd, 1981, Maria Helen Ramsay. *Educ:* George Heriot's Sch., Edinburgh; Edinburgh Univ. MB, ChB (Edinburgh) 1936; MD (Edinburgh) 1939; Dip. Psych. (Edinburgh) 1939; MRCPE 1958; FRCPE 1962. Asst Physician, Royal Edinburgh Hospital for Mental Disorders, 1937–39. Served 1939–46 (Lieut, Captain, Major), Specialist in Psychiatry, RAMC. Senior Lecturer, Dept of Mental Health, Aberdeen Univ., 1946–49. Dean, Faculty of Medicine, 1965–68. Member: MRC, 1960–64; Mental Welfare Commn for Scotland, 1964–78. FBPsS 1946. *Publications:* contributions to various learned journals. *Recreations:* golf, chess, gardening. *Address:* 35 Beechgrove Avenue, Aberdeen AB2 4HE.

MILLARD, Sir Guy (Elwin), KCMG 1972 (CMG 1957); CVO 1961; HM Diplomatic Service, retired; *b* 22 Jan. 1917; *s* of Col Baldwin Salter Millard, and Phyllis Mary Tetley; *m* 1st, 1946, Anne, *d* of late Gordon Mackenzie; one *s* one *d*; 2nd, 1964, Mary Judy, *d* of late James Dugdale and of Pamela, Countess of Aylesford; two *s*. *Educ:* Charterhouse; Pembroke Coll., Cambridge. Entered Foreign Office, 1939. Served Royal Navy, 1940–41. Asst Private Sec., to Foreign Sec., 1941–45; British Embassy, Paris, 1945–49, Ankara, 1949–52; Imperial Defence Coll., 1953; Foreign Office, 1954, Counsellor, 1955; Private Sec. to Prime Minister, 1955–56; British Embassy, Tehran, 1959–62; Foreign Office, 1962–64; Minister, UK Delegation to NATO, 1964–67; Ambassador to Hungary, 1967–69; Minister, Washington, 1970–71; Ambassador to Sweden, 1971–74; Ambassador to Italy, 1974–76. Chm., British-Italian Soc., 1977–83. Grand Officer, Order of Merit, Italy, 1981. *Address:* Fyfield Manor, Southrop, Glos. *T:* Southrop (036785) 234. *Club:* Boodle's.

MILLARD, Raymond Spencer, CMG 1967; PhD; FICE; FIHT; consulting engineer; *b* 5 June 1920; *s* of Arthur and Ellen Millard, Ashbourne, Derbs; *m* 1st, 1945, Irene Guy (marr. diss.); one *s* one *d*; 2nd, 1977, Sheila Taylor (*née* Akerman). *Educ:* Queen Elizabeth Grammar Sch., Ashbourne; University Coll., London (BSc (Eng)). RE and civil engineering contracting, 1941–44. Road Research Laboratory, 1944–74: Hd of Tropical Section, 1955–65; Dep. Dir, 1965–74; Partner, Peter Fraenkel & Partners, Asia, 1974–76; Highway Engrg Advisor, World Bank, 1976–82; Dir of Technical Affairs, British Aggregate Construction Inds, 1983–87. *Publications:* scientific and technical papers on road planning and construction. *Recreations:* bonsai culture, painting. *Address:* Drapers Cottage, 93 High Street, Odiham, Basingstoke, Hants RG25 1LB.

MILLEN, Brig. Anthony Tristram Patrick; Defence Advisor to British High Commissioner, Ottawa, Canada, 1980–83, retired; *b* 15 Dec. 1928; *s* of Charles Reginald Millen and Annie Mary Martin; *m* 1954, Mary Alice Featherston Johnston; three *s* two *d* (and two *s* decd). *Educ:* Mount St Mary's Coll. 5th Royal Inniskilling Dragoon Guards, 1948; served in Germany, Korea, Cyprus, N Ireland, Hong Kong, USA. *Publications:* articles in US military jls. *Recreation:* sailing. *Address:* The Manor House, Hutton Sessay, near Thirsk, N Yorks YO7 3BA. *T:* Thirsk (0845) 401444.

MILLER, (Alan) Cameron; MA; LLB; FCIT; advocate; Tutor at Fettes College, since 1974; Temporary Sheriff, 1979–82; *b* 10 Jan. 1913; *o s* of late Arthur Miller, Edinburgh; *m* 1945, Audrey Main; one *s* one *d*. *Educ:* Fettes Coll.; Edinburgh Univ. MA 1934; LLB 1936; Advocate, 1938; served War of 1939–45, RN; Interim Sheriff-Substitute at Dundee, 1946; Sheriff-Substitute of Inverness, Moray, Nairn, Ross and Cromarty, at Fort William, 1946–52; Legal Adviser (Scotland): British Transport Commn, 1952–62; BR Board, 1962–73. Chm., Inst. of Transport (Scotland), 1971–72. *Recreations:* golf and music. *Address:* 42 Great King Street, Edinburgh, Scotland.

MILLER, Alan John McCulloch, DSC 1941, VRD 1950; Chairman, Miller Insulation Ltd, 1975–86; *b* 21 April 1914; *s* of late Louis M. Miller and Mary McCulloch; *m* 1940, Kirsteen Ross Orr; three *s* one *d*. *Educ:* Kelvinside Academy; Strathclyde Univ. CEng, MRINA, MIESS, FBIM, FRSA. Family engrg business, 1933–39. Commnd RNVR (Clyde Div.), 1938; served RN, 1939–45: Far East, Indian Ocean, S Atlantic, HMS Dorsetshire, then destroyers; in comd, HMS Fitzroy, Wolverine, Holderness, St Nazaire, Dieppe raids, Russian convoys, 1943–44; psc 1944. Rejoined family business, 1945, until sold to Bestobell Ltd, 1951; Dir, Bestobell Ltd, 1951–73, Chm. and Man. Dir, 1965–73; Chm. and Man. Dir, Wm Simons & Co. Ltd, Shipbuilders, 1956–60; Dir, Truckline Ferries Ltd, 1972–88; Chairman: Antigua Slipway Ltd, 1966–86; Dev West Ltd, 1973–76; Low & Bonar, 1977–82. Chm., BNEC Southern Africa Cttee, 1970, until abolished. Member: Sports Council, 1973–80; Central Council of Physical Recreation. *Recreations:* sailing, golf, ski-ing, shooting. *Address:* Dollerie Lodge, by Crieff, Perthshire PH7 3NX. *T:* Crieff (0764) 2299. *Clubs:* Army and Navy, Royal Thames Yacht, Royal Ocean Racing, Royal Cruising; Royal and Ancient (St Andrews); Sunningdale Golf.

MILLER, Alastair Cheape, MBE 1948; TD; Prison Governor, retired 1972; *b* 13 March 1912 (twin-brother); *s* of John Charles Miller, Banker, Glasgow, and Jessie Amelia Miller; *m* 1943, Elizabeth S. Hubbard (marr. diss. 1967); one *s* one *d*. *Educ:* Melville Coll., Edinburgh; Bedford Sch., Bedford. Territorial Army, 1930–51; War Service (Gibraltar and Italy); 5th Bedfs and Herts Regt, 1st Herts Regt and 4th KOYLI, 1948–51. Barclays Bank Ltd; Junior Clerk to Cashier, 1929–45. Housemaster, Approved Sch., April-Nov. 1946. Prison Service: Asst Governor, Wakefield, Dec. 1946–Jan. 1953; Governor: Dover, 1953–59; Winchester, 1959–62; Hindley Borstal, 1962–65; Parkhurst Prison, 1966–70; Pentonville, 1970–72. Associated with St Mungo Community Trust i/c Old Charing Cross Hosp. project for homeless people, 1974–75. Freeman, City of London, 1980. *Publication:* Inside Outside, 1976. *Recreations:* golf, sailing. *Address:* 5 Cardigan Street, SE11 5PE. *Clubs:* Hampstead Golf; Seaford Golf (Seaford); Newport Golf (Pembs); Cowes Corinthian Yacht (Cowes); Newport Boat (Pembroke).

MILLER, Alexander Ronald, CBE 1970; President, Motherwell Bridge Holdings Ltd, since 1989 (Managing Director, 1958–85; Chairman, 1958–88); *b* 7 Nov. 1915; *s* of Thomas Ronald Miller and Elise Hay. *Educ:* Craigflower; Malvern Coll.; Royal Coll. of Science and Technology. Royal Engineers (Major) and Royal Bombay Sappers and Miners, 1940–46. Member: Scottish Council, CBI (formerly FBI), 1955–82 (Chm., 1963–65); Council, CBI, 1982–; Design Council (formerly CoID), 1965–71 (Chm. Scottish Cttee, 1965–67); Scottish Economic Planning Council, 1965–71 (Chm., Industrial Cttee, 1967–71); British Railways (Scottish) Board, 1966–70; British Rail Design Panel, 1966–82; Gen. Convocation, Univ. of Strathclyde, 1967–; Steering Cttee, W Central Scotland Plan, 1970–75; Lanarkshire Area Health Bd, 1973–85 (Chm., 1973–77); Oil Develt Council for Scotland, 1973–78; Instn of Royal Engineers; BIM Adv. Bd for Scotland, 1974–89; Coll. Council, Bell Coll. of Technology, Hamilton, 1976–89; Lloyd's Register of Shipping Scottish Cttee, 1977–89, Gen. Cttee, 1982–; Lloyd's Register Quality Assce Ltd, 1984–89; Incorporation of Hammermen, Merchants' House of Glasgow. Chm., Management Cttee, Scottish Health Servs Common Servs Agency, 1977–83. Pres., Lanarkshire (formerly Hamilton and Other Districts) Br., Forces Help Soc. and Lord Roberts Workshops, 1979–90. A Burgess of the City of Glasgow. DUniv Stirling, 1986. FRSA; AIMechE; CBIM. *Address:* Lairfad, Auldhouse, by East Kilbride, Lanarks. *T:* East Kilbride (03552) 63275. *Clubs:* Directors; Royal Scottish Automobile (Glasgow), Western (Glasgow).

MILLER, Amelia, (Mrs Michael Miller); *see* Freedman, A.

MILLER, Arjay; Dean, and Professor of Management, Graduate School of Business, Stanford University, 1969–79, now Dean Emeritus; Vice-Chairman, Ford Motor Company, 1968–69 (President, 1963–68); *b* 4 March 1916; *s* of Rawley John Miller and Mary Gertrude Schade; *m* 1940, Frances Marion Fearing; one *s* one *d*. *Educ:* University of California at Los Angeles (BS with highest hons, 1937). Graduate Student and Teaching Asst, University of California at Berkeley, 1938–40; Research Technician, Calif. State Planning Bd, 1941; Economist, Federal Reserve Bank of San Francisco, 1941–43. Captain, US Air Force, 1943–46. Asst Treas, Ford Motor Co., 1947–53; Controller, 1953–57; Vice-Pres. and Controller, 1957–61; Vice-Pres. of Finance, 1961–62; Vice-Pres., Staff Group, 1962–63. Trustee: Brookings Instn, Washington; Internat. Exec. Service Corps; Andrew W. Mellon Foundn; Urban Inst. Member, Board of Directors: SRI International; William and Flora Hewlett Foundn; Chronicle Publishing Co. Councillor, The Conference Board. Fellow, Amer. Acad. of Arts and Scis. Hon. LLD: Univ. of California (LA), 1964; Whitman Coll., 1965; Univ. of Nebraska, 1965; Ripon Coll., 1980; Washington Univ., St Louis, 1982. *Address:* 225 Mountain Home Road, Woodside, Calif 94062, USA. *Clubs:* Bohemian, Pacific Union (San Francisco).

MILLER, Arthur; playwright; *b* 17 Oct. 1915; *s* of Isadore Miller and Augusta Barnett; *m* 1940, Mary Grace Slattery (marr. diss.); one *s* one *d*; *m* 1956, Marilyn Monroe (marr. diss. 1961; she *d* 1962); *m* 1962, Ingeborg Morath; one *d*. *Educ:* University of Michigan, USA (AB). Pres. of PEN Club, 1965–69. *Publications:* Honors at Dawn, 1936; No Villains (They Too Arise), 1937; The Pussycat and the Expert Plumber who was a Man, 1941; William Ireland's Confession, 1941; The Man who had all the Luck, 1944; That They May Win, 1944; Situation Normal (reportage), 1944; Focus (novel), 1945; Grandpa and the Statue, 1945; The Story of Gus, 1947; All My Sons (play) (New York Drama Critics Award, 1948), 1947; Death of A Salesman (play) (New York Drama Critics Award, 1949, Pulitzer Prize, 1949), 1949, filmed, 1985; The Crucible (play), 1953; A View from the Bridge (play), 1955, filmed, 1962; A Memory of Two Mondays (play), 1955; Collected Plays, 1958; The Misfits (motion picture play), 1960; Jane's Blanket, 1963; After the Fall (play), 1963; Incident at Vichy (play), 1964; I Don't Need You Anymore (collected stories), 1967; The Price (play), 1968, and 1990; (jt author) In Russia, 1969; Fame, and the Reason Why, 1970; The Portable Arthur Miller, 1971; The Creation of the World and Other Business (play), 1972, musical version, Up From Paradise, 1974; (with Inge Morath) In the Country, 1977; (ed Robert Martin) The Theater Essays of Arthur Miller, 1978; (with Inge Morath) Chinese Encounters, 1979; The American Clock (play), 1980; Playing for Time (play) (Peabody Award, CBS-TV, 1981); Salesman in Beijing, 1984; Two Way Mirror, 1985; Danger: Memory! (plays), 1986; Timebends (autobiog.), 1987; contrib. stories and essays to Esquire, Colliers, Atlantic Monthly, etc. *Address:* c/o Kay Brown, ICM, 40 W 57th Street, New York, NY 10019, USA.

MILLER, Barry; Director General of Defence Quality Assurance, Ministry of Defence, Procurement Executive, since 1986; *b* 11 May 1942; *s* of Lt-Col Howard Alan Miller and Margaret Yvonne Richardson; *m* 1968, Katrina Elizabeth Chandler; one *s* one *d*. *Educ:* Lancaster Royal Grammar Sch. Exec. Officer, RAE Farnborough, 1961; Asst Principal, MoD, London, 1965; Principal: Defence Policy Staff, 1969; Naval Personnel Div., 1969; Equipment Secretariat (Army), 1972; Defence Secretariat, 1973; CSD, 1975; Asst Secretary: Civilian Management, 1977; Defence Secretariat, 1980; RCDS 1984; Asst Sec., Management Services (Organisation), 1985. *Address:* Ministry of Defence, Royal Arsenal West, Woolwich, SE18 6ST.

MILLER, Sir Bernard; *see* Miller, Sir O. B.

MILLER, Bruce; *see* Miller, John D. B.

MILLER, Cameron; *see* Miller, A. C.

MILLER, Maj.-Gen. David Edwin, CB 1986; CBE 1980 (OBE 1973); MC 1967; JP; Chief of Staff Live Oak, SHAPE, 1984–86, retired; *b* 17 Aug. 1931; *s* of late Leonard and Beatrice Miller; *m* 1958, Mary Lamley Fisher; two *s*. *Educ:* Loughton Sch., Essex; Royal Military Academy, Sandhurst. psc, jssc, ndc. Commissioned, Border Regt, 1951; Comd 1st Bn King's Own Royal Border Regt, 1971–73; Instructor, National Defence Coll., 1973–76; Colonel GS MoD, 1976–78; Comd Ulster Defence Regt, 1978–80; Dep. Chief of Staff Headquarters BAOR, 1980–83. Colonel, King's Own Royal Border Regt, 1981–88. JP Barnstaple, 1989. *Recreations:* wine, clocks, forestry. *Address:* c/o Barclays Bank PLC, 210 Fore Street, N18 2QF. *Club:* Army and Navy.

MILLER, David Quentin; His Honour Judge Miller; a Circuit Judge, since 1987; *b* 22 Oct. 1936; *s* of Alfred Bowen Badger and Mair Angharad Evans. *Educ:* Ellesmere Coll., Shropshire; London Sch. of Econs and Pol. Science, London Univ. (LLB Hons 1956). Called to the Bar, Middle Temple, 1958; admitted Barrister and Solicitor of the Supreme Court of NZ, 1959. In practice, SE Circuit, 1960–82; Metropolitan Stipendiary Magistrate, 1982–87; a Recorder, 1986–87. *Recreations:* history, walking, gardening, art, music, Trollope Society. *Address:* 31 Edinburgh Gardens, Windsor, Berks SL4 2AN. *T:* Windsor (0753) 866597.

MILLER, Donald C.; *see* Crichton-Miller.

MILLER, Sir Donald (John), Kt 1990; FEng; FRSE; Chairman, ScottishPower (formerly South of Scotland Electricity Board), since 1982; *b* 1927; *s* of John Miller and Maud (*née* White); *m* 1973, Fay Glendinning Herriot; one *s* two *d*. *Educ:* Banchory Academy; Univ. of Aberdeen. BSc(Eng); FEng 1981; FIMechE, FIEE. Metropolitan Vickers, 1947–53; British Electricity Authority, 1953–55; Preece, Cardew and Rider (Consulting Engrs), 1955–66; Chief Engr, North of Scotland Hydro-Electric Bd, 1966–74; Dir of Engrg, then Dep. Chm., SSEB, 1974–82. *Publications:* papers to IEE. *Recreations:* gardening, hill walking, sailing.

MILLER, Sir Douglas; *see* Miller, Sir I. D.

MILLER, Sir Douglas (Sinclair), KCVO 1972; CBE 1956 (OBE 1948); HM Overseas Colonial Service, retired; *b* 30 July 1906; British parentage; m 1933, Valerie Madeleine Carter; one *d*. *Educ:* Westminster Sch.; Merton Coll., Oxford. HM Overseas Colonial

Service, 1930–61: Supt of Native Educn, N Rhodesia, 1930–45; Director of Education: Basutoland, 1945–48; Nyasaland, 1948–52; Uganda, 1952–58; Kenya, 1958–59; Dir of Educn and Permanent Sec., Min. of Educn, Kenya, 1959–60; Temp. Minister of Educn, Kenya, 1960–61; Sec., King George's Jubilee Trust, 1961–71; Develt Adviser, Duke of Edinburgh's Award Scheme, 1971–85. *Address:* The Lodge, 70 Grand Avenue, Worthing, Sussex. *T:* Worthing (0903) 501195. *Clubs:* Commonwealth Trust; Kampala (Uganda).

MILLER, Edward, FBA 1981; Master, Fitzwilliam College, Cambridge, 1971–81, Hon. Fellow, 1981; *b* Acklington, Northumberland, 16 July 1915; *e s* of Edward and Mary Lee Miller; *m* 1941, Fanny Zara Salingar; one *s*. *Educ:* King Edward VI's Grammar Sch., Morpeth; St John's Coll., Cambridge (Exhibnr, Schol.). BA 1937; MA 1945; Strathcona Res. Student, 1937–39, Fellow, 1939–65, and Hon. Fellow, 1974, St John's Coll., Cambridge. Nat. Service, 1940–45 in Durham Light Inf., RAC and Control Commn for Germany; Major. Dir of Studies in History, 1946–55 and Tutor, 1951–57, St John's Coll., Cambridge; Asst Lectr in History, 1946–50 and Lectr, 1950–65, University of Cambridge; Warden of Madingley Hall, Cambridge, 1961–65; Prof. of Medieval Hist., Sheffield Univ., 1965–71. FRHistS; Chm., Victoria Co. Histories Cttee of Inst. Hist. Research, 1972–79; Dep. Chm., Cttee to review Local Hist., 1978–79; Mem., St Albans Res. Cttee. Chm., Editorial Bd, History of Parliament Trust, 1975–89. Hon. LittD Sheffield, 1972. *Publications:* The Abbey and Bishopric of Ely, 1951; Portrait of a College, 1961; (Jt Ed.) Cambridge Economic History of Europe, vol. iii, 1963, vol. ii, 2nd edn, 1987; Historical Studies of the English Parliament, 2 vols, 1970; (jtly) Medieval England: rural society and economic change, 1978; (ed) Agrarian History of England and Wales, vol. iii, 1991; articles in Victoria County Histories of Cambridgeshire and York, Agrarian History of England and Wales, vol. ii, English Hist. Rev., Econ. History Rev., Trans Royal Historical Society, Past and Present, etc. *Recreations:* with advancing years watching any form of sport, especially Rugby and cricket. *Address:* 36 Almoners Avenue, Cambridge CB1 4PA. *T:* Cambridge (0223) 246794.

MILLER, Edward, CBE 1988; Director of Education, Strathclyde, 1974–88; *b* 30 March 1930; *s* of Andrew and Elizabeth Miller; *m* 1955; two *s*. *Educ:* Eastbank Academy; Glasgow Univ. (MA, MEd). Taught at Wishaw High Sch., 1955–57 and Whitehill Secondary Sch., 1957–59; Depute Dir of Educn, West Lothian, 1959–63; Sen. Asst Dir of Educn, Stirlingshire, 1963–66; Depute, later Sen. Depute Dir of Educn, Glasgow, 1966–74. Hon. MLitt Glasgow Coll., 1985. *Recreations:* golf, reading, sailing. *Address:* 58 Heather Avenue, Bearsden, Glasgow G61 3JG.

MILLER, Air Chief Marshal Frank Robert, CC (Canada) 1972; CBE 1946; CD; retired from military service, 1966; Director, United Aircraft of Canada Ltd, 1967–76; *b* Kamloops, BC, April 1908; *m* Dorothy Virginia Minor, Galveston, Texas. *Educ:* Alberta Univ. (BSc, Civil Engrg). Joined RCAF, 1931. Served War of 1939–45: commanded Air Navigation Schs at Rivers, Man., and Penfield Ridge, NB, and Gen. Reconnaisance Sch., Summerside, PEI; subseq. Dir of Trng Plans and Requirements and Dir of Trng, Air Force HQ; service overseas with Can. Bomber Gp as Station Comdr, later Base Comdr, 1944; Tiger Force, 1945 (despatches); Chief SO (later AOC), Air Material Comd, 1945; US Nat. War Coll., 1948; Air Mem. Ops and Trng, Air Force HQ, 1949; Vice Chief of Air Staff, 1951; Vice Air Deputy, SHAPE HQ, Paris, 1954; Dep. Minister, Dept of Nat. Defence, 1955; Chm., Chiefs of Staff, 1960; first Pres., NATO Mil. Cttee, 1963–64; Chief of Defence Staff, Canada, 1964–66. Air Chief Marshal, 1961. Hon. LLD Alta, 1965; Hon. DScMil, RMC Canada, 1968. *Recreations:* golf, fishing. *Address:* 1654 Brandywine Drive, Charlottesville, Va 22901, USA.

MILLER, G(eorge) William; Chairman: G. William Miller & Co., Inc., Merchant Banking, since 1983; Federated Stores, Inc., since 1990; *b* Oklahoma, USA, 9 March 1925; *s* of James Dick Miller and Hazle Deane Miller (*née* Orrick); *m* 1946, Ariadna Rogojarsky. *Educ:* Borger High Sch.; Amarillo Junior Coll.; US Coast Guard Acad. (BS); School of Law, Univ. of California, Berkeley (JD). Served as US Coast Guard Officer, Pacific Area, 1945–49, stationed (one year) in China. Admitted to Bar of California, 1952, New York Bar 1953; law practice with Cravath, Swaine & Moore, NYC, 1952–56. Joined Textron Inc., Providence, RI, 1956; Vice-Pres. 1957; Treas. 1958; Pres. 1960; Chief Exec. 1968–78, also Chm., 1974–78; Chm., Bd of Governors of Federal Reserve System of US, 1978–79; Sec. of the Treasury, USA, 1979–81. Director: Repligen Corp.; Kleinwort Benson Aust. Income Fund, Inc.; Ralphs Grocery Co.; Chm., Supervising Cttee, Schroder Venture Trust. Chairman: The Conference Board, 1977–78; National Alliance of Business, 1978; US Industrial Payroll Savings Cttee, 1977. Mem., State Bar, California. Phi Delta Phi. *Recreations:* music, golf. *Address:* 1215 19th Street NW, Washington, DC 20036, USA. *T:* 202–429 1780. *Clubs:* Chevy Chase (Maryland); The Brook (NY); Burning Tree (Bethesda, Md); Lyford Cay (Bahamas).

MILLER, Sir Hilary Duppa, (Sir Hal Miller), Kt 1988; MP (C) Bromsgrove, since 1983 (Bromsgrove and Redditch, Feb. 1974–1983); *b* 6 March 1929; *s* of Lt-Comdr John Bryan Peter Duppa-Miller, *qv*; *m* 1st, 1956, Fiona Margaret McDermid; two *s* two *d*; 2nd, 1976, Jacqueline Roe, *d* of T. C. W. Roe and of Lady Londesborough; one *s* one *d*. *Educ:* Eton; Merton Coll., Oxford; London Univ. MA (Oxon) 1956; BSc (Estate Management) (London), 1962. With Colonial Service, Hong Kong, 1955–68. Company Director. Contested: (C), Barrow-in-Furness, 1970; Bromsgrove by-elec. May 1971. PPS to Sec. of State for Defence, 1979–81, to Chancellor of the Duchy of Lancaster, 1981, resigned; Vice-Chm., Conservative Party Orgn, and PPS to the Chm., 1984–87; Mem., UK delegn to Council of Europe, 1974–76. Jt Chm., All Party Motor Industry Gp, 1978. Fellow, Econ. Develt Inst. of World Bank, Washington. *Recreations:* sailing, fell walking, cricket, Rugby refereeing. *Address:* House of Commons, SW1A 0AA. *Clubs:* St Stephen's; Vincent's (Oxford); Aston Fields Royal British Legion (Bromsgrove); Eton Ramblers, Free Foresters, Blackheath Football.

See also Michael Miller.

MILLER, Sir Holmes; *see* Miller, Sir J. H.

MILLER, Mrs Horrie; *see* Durack, Dame M.

MILLER, Sir (Ian) Douglas, Kt 1961; FRCS; Hon. Consulting Neurosurgeon, since 1960 (Hon. Neurosurgeon, 1948), St Vincent's Hospital, Sydney, and Repatriation General Hospital; Chairman of Board, St Vincent's Hospital, 1966–76; Dean of Clinical School, St Vincent's Hospital, Sydney, 1931–64; *b* Melbourne, 20 July 1900; *m* 1939, Phyllis Laidley Mort; three *s* two *d*. *Educ:* Xavier Coll., Melbourne; University of Sydney. MB, ChM Sydney 1924; FRCS 1928. Hon. Asst Surgeon, St Vincent's Hosp., Sydney, 1929; Lectr in Surgical Anat., Univ. Sydney, 1930; Hon. Surg., Mater. Hosp. Sydney, 1934; Hon. Surg., St Vincent's Hosp., 1939; Major AIF, Surgical Specialist, 1940; Lt-Col (Surgical CO), 102 AGH, 1942; o/c Neurosurgical Centre, AIF. Chairman: Community Systems Foundn of Aust., 1965–72; Foundn of Forensic Scis, Aust. President: RACS, 1957–59 (Mem. Ct of Examrs, 1946; Mem. Council, 1947); Asian Australasian Soc. of Neurological Surgeons, 1964–67. Chairman: Editorial Cttee, ANZ Jl of Surgery, 1958–73; Editorial Bd, Modern Medicine in Australia, 1970–. Hon. FRCSE 1980. Hon. AM 1964, Hon. LittD 1974, Singapore; Hon. MD Sydney, 1979. *Publications:* A Surgeon's Story, 1985; Earlier Days, 1970; contrib. Med. Jl of Aust., 1956, 1960. *Recreation:* agriculture. *Address:* 170 Kurraba Road, Sydney, NSW 2089, Australia. *T:* 9092415. *Club:* Australian (Sydney).

MILLER, Dr Jacques Francis Albert Pierre, AO 1981; FRS 1970; FAA 1970; Head of Experimental Pathology Unit, Walter and Eliza Hall Institute of Medical Research, since 1966; *b* 2 April 1931; French parents; *m* 1956, Margaret Denise Houen. *Educ:* St Aloysius' Coll., Sydney. BSc (Med.) 1953, MB, BS 1955, Sydney; PhD 1960, DSc 1965, London. Sen. Scientist, Chester Beatty Res. Inst., London, 1960–66; Reader, Exper. Pathology, Univ. of London, 1965–66. For. Mem., Académie Royale de Médicine de Belgique, 1969; For. Associate, US Nat. Acad. Scis, 1982. Hon. MD Sydney, 1986. Langer-Teplitz Cancer Research Award (USA), 1965; Gairdner Foundn Award (Canada), 1966; Encyclopaedia Britannica (Australia) Award, 1966; Scientific Medal of Zoological Soc. of London, 1966; Burnet Medal, Austr. Acad. of Scis, 1971; Paul Ehrlich Award, Germany, 1974; Rabbi Shai Shacknai Meml Prize, Hadassah Med. Sch., Jerusalem, 1978; Saint-Vincent Internat. Prize for Med. Res., Italy, 1983; first Sandoz Immunology Prize, 1990; first Medawar Prize, Transplantation Soc., 1990. *Publications:* over 320 papers in scientific jls and several chapters in books, mainly dealing with thymus and immunity. *Recreations:* music, photography, art, literature. *Address:* Walter and Eliza Hall Institute of Medical Research, Royal Melbourne Hospital PO, Parkville, Victoria 3050, Australia. *T:* 345–2555.

MILLER, James, CBE 1986; Chairman and Managing Director, Miller Group Ltd (formerly James Miller & Partners), since 1970; *b* 1 Sept. 1934; *s* of Sir James Miller, GBE, and of Lady Ella Jane Miller; *m* 1st, 1959, Kathleen Dewar; one *s* two *d*; 2nd, 1969, Iris Lloyd-Webb; one *d*. *Educ:* Edinburgh Acad.; Harrow Sch.; Balliol Coll., Oxford (MA Engrg Sci.). Joined James Miller & Partners, 1958; Board Mem., 1960; Chm., British Linen Fund Managers, 1986–89; Director: Life Assoc. of Scotland, 1981–; British Linen Bank, 1983–; Britoil, 1988–90; British Petroleum, 1990–. Pres., FCEC, 1990– (Chm., 1985–86). Chm,. Court, Heriot-Watt Univ., 1990–. *Recreation:* shooting. *Address:* Miller Group Ltd, Miller House, 18 South Groathill Avenue, Edinburgh EH4 2LW. *T:* 031–332 2585. *Club:* City Livery.

MILLER, Lt-Comdr John Bryan Peter Duppa-, GC and King's Commendation 1941; *b* 22 May 1903; *er s* of Brian Stothert Miller, JP, Posbury, Devon, and Mary (*née* Sadler); *m* 1st, 1926, Barbara, *d* of Stanley Owen, 1st Viscount Buckmaster, GCVO; three *s*; 2nd, 1944, Clare, *d* of Francis Egerton Harding, JP, Old Springs, Market Drayton; 3rd, 1977, Greta, *d* of B. K. G. Landby, Royal Vasa Order, Gothenburg, Sweden. *Educ:* Rugby Sch.; Hertford Coll., Oxford. Dep. County Educn Officer, Hants, 1930–35; Asst Sec., Northants Educn Cttee, 1936–39; Torpedo and Mining Dept, Admty, 1940–45; a Dep. Dir-Gen., Trade and Econs Div., Control Commn for Germany, 1945; Inspector-Gen., Min. of Educn, Addis Ababa, 1945–47; Educn Dept, Kenya, 1947–57; Chm. of European Civil Servants' Assoc., and formation Chm. Staff Side, Central Whitley Coun. for Civil Service; Sec. to Kenya Coffee Marketing Bd, 1960–61; Sec. to Tanganyika Coffee Bd, 1961–62; Asst Sec. and Marketing Officer, Min. of Lands and Settlement, Kenya, 1963–65. *Publication:* Saints and Parachutes, 1951. *Recreations:* yachting, economics. *Address:* Box 222, Somerset West, 7130, South Africa.

See also Sir H. D. Miller, Michael Miller.

MILLER, Prof. J(ohn) D(onald) Bruce; Executive Director, Academy of the Social Sciences in Australia, 1989–91; Professor of International Relations, Research School of Pacific Studies, Australian National University, 1962–87, now Emeritus; *b* 30 Aug. 1922; *s* of Donald and Marion Miller, Sydney, Australia; *m* 1st, 1943, Enid Huthnance; one *s*; 2nd, 1957, Margaret Martin; one *s*; 3rd, 1990, Judith Bennet. *Educ:* Sydney High Sch.; University of Sydney. BEc, 1944; MEc 1951; MA Cantab 1978. Announcer and Talks Officer, Australian Broadcasting Commission, Sydney and Canberra, 1939–46; Staff Tutor, Department of Tutorial Classes, University of Sydney, 1946–52; Asst Lecturer in Political Science and International Relations, London Sch. of Economics, 1953–55; Lecturer in Politics, University Coll., Leicester, 1955–57; Prof. of Politics, University of Leicester, 1957–62; Dean of Social Sciences, 1960–62; Public Orator, 1961–62. Res. Associate, Chatham House, 1965, 1969, 1973. Visiting Professor: Indian Sch. of International Studies, 1959; Columbia Univ., New York, 1962, 1966, 1981; Yale, 1977; Princeton, 1984, 1986; Overseas Vis. Fellow, St John's Coll., and Smuts Vis. Fellow, Cambridge Univ., 1977–78; Macrossan Lectr, University of Queensland, 1966. Member: Aust. Population and Immigration Council, 1975–81; Aust. Res. Grants Cttee, 1975–81. Joint Editor, Journal of Commonwealth Political Studies, 1961–62; Editor, Australian Outlook, 1963–69; Chm., Editorial Adv. Bd for Austr. documents on foreign relations, 1971–77; Austr. Nat. Commn for UNESCO, 1982–84, 1990–. FASSA 1967 (Treas., 1979–83). *Publications:* Australian Government and Politics, 1954, 4th edn with B. Jinks 1970; Richard Jebb and the Problem of Empire, 1956; Politicians (inaugural), 1958; The Commonwealth in the World, 1958; The Nature of Politics, 1962; The Shape of Diplomacy (inaugural), 1963; Australia and Foreign Policy (Boyer Lectures), 1963; (ed with T. H. Rigby) The Disintegrating Monolith, 1965; Britain and the Old Dominions, 1966; Australia, 1966; The Politics of the Third World, 1966; (ed) India, Japan, Australia: Partners in Asia?, 1968; Survey of Commonwealth Affairs: problems of expansion and attrition 1953–1969, 1974; (ed) Australia's Economic Relations, 1975; The EEC and Australia, 1976; The World of States, 1981; Ideology and Foreign Policy, 1982; Norman Angell and the Futility of War, 1986; (ed) Australians and British, 1987; (ed with L. J. Evans) Policy and Practice, 1987; (ed with R. J. Vincent) Order and Violence, 1990. *Recreations:* books, garden. *Address:* 1 Mountbatten Park, Yarralumla, ACT 2600, Australia. *T:* Canberra 2825599. *Clubs:* National Press, Commonwealth (Canberra).

MILLER, Sir John Francis C.; *see* Compton Miller.

MILLER, John Harmsworth; architect in private practice; *b* 18 Aug. 1930; *s* of Charles Miller and Brenda Borrett; *m* 1st, 1957, Patricia Rhodes (marr. diss. 1975); two *d*; 2nd, 1985, Su Rogers. *Educ:* Charterhouse; Architectural Assoc. Sch. of Architecture (AA Dip. Hons 1957). ARIBA 1959. Private practice, Colquhoun and Miller, 1961–90, John Miller and Partners, since 1990; works include: Forest Gate High Sch., West Ham (Newham), 1965; Chemistry Labs, Royal Holloway Coll., London Univ., 1970; Melrose Activity Centre, Milton Keynes Develt Corp. (Commendation, Steel Awards, 1975); Pillwood House, Feock, Cornwall (RIBA Regional Award, 1975); Housing, Caversham Road/Gaisford Street, Camden, 1978; single person flats, Hornsey Lane, Haringey, 1980; Oldbrook, Milton Keynes (Silver Medal, Architectural Design; Highly Commended, Housing Design and Civic Trust Awards); Whitechapel Art Gall. extension, 1985; Gulbenkian Gall. for RCA, 1989. Exhibition Designs for Arts Council: Dada and Surrealism Reviewed, 1978; Ten Modern Houses, 1980; Picasso's Picassos, 1981; Adolf Loos, 1985. Tutor: RCA and AA, 1961–73; Cambridge Sch. of Arch., 1969–70; Prof. of Environmental Design, RCA, 1975–85, Fellow 1976, Hon. Fellow, 1985. FRSA 1985. Vis. Prof., Sch. of Arch., UC Dublin, 1985. Vis. Critic: Cornell Univ. Sch. of Arch., Ithaca, 1966, 1968 and 1971; Princeton Univ. Sch. of Arch., NJ, 1970; Dublin Univ. Sch. of Arch., 1972–73; Univ. of Toronto, 1985. RIBA Regl Award, 1988; Civic Trust Award, 1987; European Prize for Architecture, 1988. *Publications:* contribs to architect. jls. *Address:* 23 Regent's Park Road, NW1 7TL. *T:* 071–267 5800.

MILLER, Sir John Holmes, 11th Bt *cr* 1705, of Chichester, Sussex; *b* 1925; *er s* of 10th Bt and of Netta Mahalah Bennett; *S* father 1960; *m* 1950, Jocelyn Robson Edwards, Wairoa, NZ; two *d*. *Heir: b* Harry Holmes Miller [*b* 1927; *m* 1954, Gwynedd Margaret Sheriff; one *s* two *d*].

MILLER, John Ireland; Vice-President, Methodist Conference of Great Britain, 1973–74; *b* 20 June 1912; *s* of John William Miller and Emma Miller (*née* Minkley); *m* 1943, Vida Bertha Bracher; one *s* one *d*. *Educ:* Hardye's School, Dorchester; Taunton School, Taunton. Admitted Solicitor and Member of Law Society, 1933. HM Coroner: Poole Borough, 1972–74 (Deputy Coroner, 1939–72); East Dorset, 1974–85. *Address:* 25 Merriefield Drive, Broadstone, Dorset BH18 8BW. *T:* Broadstone (0202) 694057.

MILLER, Air Vice-Marshal John Joseph, CB 1981; Director of Studies, St George's House, Windsor Castle, since 1989; *b* 27 April 1928; *s* of Frederick George Miller and Freda Ruth Miller; *m* 1950, Adele Mary Colleypriest; one *s* two *d*. *Educ:* Portsmouth Grammar School. Commissioned RAF, 1947; called to the Bar, Gray's Inn, 1958; CO RAF Support Unit Fontainbleau, 1965; Directing Staff, RAF Staff Coll., 1967; DGPS (RAF) Staff, MoD, 1970; Group Captain Admin., RAF Halton, 1971; Comd Accountant, HQ Strike Comd, 1973; RCDS 1975; Dir, Personnel Management (Policy and Plans) RAF, MoD, 1976; Asst Chief of Defence Staff (Personnel and Logistics), 1978–81; Head of Administrative Branch, RAF, 1979–83; Dir Gen., Personal Services, RAF, 1982–83. Dir, Inst. of Personnel Management, 1983–89. Pres., Eur. Assoc. for Personnel Management, 1987–89. *Recreations:* walking, swimming, theatre, music, collecting (especially antiquarian books). *Address:* 35 Huntsmans Meadow, Ascot, Berks SL5 7PF. *T:* Ascot (0344) 20413. *Club:* Royal Air Force.

MILLER, Lt-Col Sir John (Mansel), GCVO 1987 (KCVO 1974; CVO 1966); DSO 1944; MC 1944; Crown Equerry, 1961–87, an Extra Equerry since 1987; *b* 4 Feb. 1919; 3rd *s* of Brig.-Gen. Alfred Douglas Miller, CBE, DSO, DL, JP, Royal Scots Greys, and of Ella Geraldine Fletcher, Saltoun, E Lothian. *Educ:* Eton; RMA, Sandhurst. 2nd Lieut Welsh Guards, 1939; Adjt 1942–44; ADC to F-M Lord Wilson, Washington, DC, 1945–47; Regtl Adjt, 1953–56; Brigade Major 1st Guards Brigade, 1956–58; comd 1st Bn Welsh Guards, 1958–61. President: Coaching Club, 1975–82; Nat. Light Horse Breeding Soc. (HIS), 1982; British Driving Soc., 1982–; Royal Windsor Horse Show Club, 1985–; Horse Rangers Assoc., 1985–; Cleveland Bay Horse Soc., 1986–; BSJA, 1988–; Vice-Pres., Irish Draught Horse Soc., GB, 1990–. Patron: Side Saddle Assoc., 1984–; Coloured Horse and Pony Soc., 1988. President: Wheatley Br, RNLI, 1982–; Wheatley Scouts, 1982–. *Recreations:* hunting, shooting, polo, driving. *Address:* Shotover House, Wheatley, Oxon. *T:* Wheatley (08677) 2450. *Clubs:* Pratt's, White's.

MILLER, Dr Jonathan Wolfe, CBE 1983; Research Fellow in Neuro-psychology, University of Sussex; *b* 21 July 1934; *s* of late Emanuel Miller, DPM, FRCP; *m* 1956, Helen Rachel Collet; two *s* one *d*. *Educ:* St Paul's Sch.; St John's Coll., Cambridge (MB, BCh 1959; Hon. Fellow 1982). Res. Fellow in Hist. of Med., UCL, 1970–73. Associate Director, Nat. Theatre, 1973–75; Artistic Dir, Old Vic, 1988–90. Mem., Arts Council, 1975–76. Vis. Prof. in Drama, Westfield Coll., London, 1977–; Fellow, UCL, 1981–. Co-author and appeared in Beyond the Fringe, 1961–64; stage directing in London and NY, 1965–67; *television:* Editor, BBC Monitor, 1965; directed films for BBC TV (incl. Alice in Wonderland), 1966; The Body in Question, BBC series, 1978; Exec. Producer, BBC Shakespeare series, 1979–81; *stage:* School for Scandal, 1968, The Seagull, 1969, The Malcontent, 1973, Nottingham Playhouse; King Lear, The Merchant of Venice, Old Vic, 1970; The Tempest, Mermaid, 1970; Hamlet, Arts Theatre, Cambridge, 1970; Danton's Death, 1971, School for Scandal, 1972, Measure for Measure, 1974, Marriage of Figaro, 1974, The Freeway, 1974, Nat. Theatre; The Taming of the Shrew, 1972, The Seagull, 1973, Chichester; Family Romances, 1974, The Importance of Being Earnest, 1975, All's Well, 1975, Greenwich; Three Sisters, Cambridge, 1976; She Would If She Could, Greenwich, 1979; Long Day's Journey Into Night, Haymarket, 1986; The Taming of the Shrew, RSC, Stratford, 1987, Barbican, 1988; (jtly adapted and directed) The Emperor, Royal Court, 1987 (televised, 1988); Andromache, One Way Pendulum, Bussy D'Ambois, The Tempest, Candide, Old Vic, 1988; King Lear, The Liar, Old Vic, 1989; *film:* Take a Girl Like You, 1970; *operas:* Arden Must Die, Sadler's Wells Theatre, 1974; The Cunning Little Vixen, Glyndebourne, 1975 and 1977; English National Opera: The Marriage of Figaro, 1978; The Turn of the Screw, 1979, 1991; Arabella, 1980; Otello, 1981; Rigoletto, 1982, 1985; Don Giovanni, 1985; The Magic Flute, 1986; Tosca, 1986; The Mikado, 1986, 1988; The Barber of Seville, 1987; Kent Opera: Cosi Fan Tutte, 1975; Rigoletto, 1975; Orfeo, 1976; Eugene Onegin, 1977; La Traviata, 1979; Falstaff, 1980, 1981; Fidelio, 1982, 1983, 1988; La Fanciulla del West, La Scala, 1991; Katya Kabanova, New York, 1991; Marriage of Figaro, Vienna State Opera, 1991. Hon. Fellow, RA, 1991; Hon. DLitt Leicester, 1981. Silver Medal, Royal TV Soc., 1981; Albert Medal, RSA, 1990. *Publications:* McLuhan, 1971; (ed) Freud: the man, his world, his influence, 1972; The Body in Question, 1978; Subsequent Performances, 1986; (ed) The Don Giovanni Book: myths of seduction and betrayal, 1990. *Recreation:* deep sleep. *Address:* c/o IMG Artists (Europe), Media House, 3 Burlington Lane, W4 2TH.

MILLER, Sir (Joseph) Holmes, Kt 1979; OBE 1958; Surveyor, New Zealand; Partner, Spencer, Holmes Miller and Jackson, Wellington, NZ; *b* Waimate, NZ, 12 Feb. 1919; *s* of Samuel Miller; *m* 1947, Marjorie, *d* of Harold Tomlinson; one *s* one *d*. *Educ:* Willowbridge Sch.; Waimate High Sch.; Victoria Univ., Wellington, NZ (BA). DSc 1979. Served War, 2 NZEF, 1940–44; NZ Artillery (wounded, Tunisia, 1943). Surveyor, Lands and Survey Dept, on rehabilitation farms, geodetic survey; consulting surveyor, Masterton, 1952–55; Wellington, 1959–. Fulton Medallion Exploratory Surveys, Fiordland, 1949; Expedition, Antipodes and Bounty Is, 1950; Dep. Leader, NZ Trans-Antarctic Expedn, 1955–58; Leader, NZ Expedn, Oates Land, Antarctica, 1963–64. Member: NZ Antarctic Soc. (Pres. 1960–63); NZ Inst. Surveyors, 1960–68 (Pres. 1969–71); NZ Survey Bd, 1962–71; NZ Geographic Bd, 1966–; Nature Conservation Council, 1972–. NZ Delegate to SCAR, Paris, 1964, Wyoming, 1974. *Publications:* numerous, on Antarctic and surveying literature. *Address:* 95 Amritsar Street, Khandallah, Wellington, New Zealand.

MILLER, Judith Henderson; Managing Director, MJM Publishing Projects, since 1985; *b* 16 Sept. 1951; *d* of Andrew and Bertha Cairns; *m* 1978, Martin John Miller, *qv*; two *d*. *Educ:* Galashiels Acad.; Edinburgh Univ. (MA Hons English, 1973). Copywriter, WHT Advertising, Auckland, NZ, 1973–74; Editor, Lyle Publications, Galashiels, 1974–75; Occupational Guidance Officer, Dept of Employment, 1975–79; Man. Dir and Editor, Miller Publications, 1979–; with Martin Miller opened Chilston Park Hotel, 1985; Co-Founder, Miller's Magazine, 1991. *Publications: with Martin Miller:* Miller's Antiques Price Guide, annually 1979–; The Antiques Directory—Furniture, 1985; Period Details, 1987; Miller's Antique Pocket Fact File, 1988; Period Style, 1989; Understanding Antiques, 1989; Miller's Collectables Price Guide, annually 1989–; Country Style, 1990; Miller's Collectors Cars Price Guide, annually 1991–; Miller's Art Deco Checklist, 1991; Furniture Checklist, 1991. *Recreations:* antiques!, bridge. *Address:* (office) Sissinghurst Court, Sissinghurst, Cranbrook, Kent TN17 2JA. *T:* Cranbrook (0580) 715101; Eldon Lodge, 52 Victoria Road, Kensington, W8. *Club:* Groucho.

MILLER, Prof. Karl Fergus Connor; Lord Northcliffe Professor of Modern English Literature, University College London, 1974–Sept. 1992; Editor, since 1979, and Co-Editor, since 1989, London Review of Books; *b* 2 Aug. 1931; *s* of William and Marion Miller; *m* 1956, Jane Elisabeth Collet; two *s* one *d*. *Educ:* Royal High School, Edinburgh; Downing Coll., Cambridge. Asst Prin., HM Treasury, 1956–57; BBC TV Producer, 1957–58; Literary Editor, Spectator, 1958–61; Literary Editor, New Statesman, 1961–67; Editor, Listener, 1967–73. *Publications:* (ed) Poetry from Cambridge, 1952–54, 1955; (ed, with introd.) Writing in England Today: The Last Fifteen Years, 1968; (ed) Memoirs of a Modern Scotland, 1970; (ed) A Listener Anthology, August 1967–June 1970, 1970; (ed) A Second Listener Anthology, 1973; (ed) Henry Cockburn, Memorials of his Time, 1974; Cockburn's Millennium, 1975; (ed, with introd.) Robert Burns, 1981; Doubles: studies in literary history, 1985; Authors, 1989. *Recreation:* football. *Address:* 26 Limerston Street, SW10.

MILLER, Dr Kenneth Allan Glen, CBE 1988; FEng; FIMechE; CBIM; Director-General, The Engineering Council, 1982–88; Deputy Chairman: ECCTIS 2000 Ltd, since 1990; Standing Conference on Schools' Science and Technology, since 1991; *b* 27 July 1926; *s* of Dr Allan Frederick Miller and Margaret Hutchison (*née* Glen); *m* 1954, Dorothy Elaine Brown; three *s*. *Educ:* Upper Canada Coll., Toronto; Trinity Hall, Cambridge (BA 1946; MA 1950); PhD Wales, 1949. Res. Asst to Prof. of Physics, Aberystwyth, 1946; joined ICI, Billingham, 1949; various posts on production and design, 1949–59; seconded to BTC, 1959–60; Asst Tech. Manager, 1960, Engrg Manager, 1963, Engrg Dir, 1965, HOC Div., ICI; Engrg Advr, ICI, 1971; Managing Director: APV Co., 1974; APV Holdings, 1977–82. Member: Cttee for Industrial Technol., 1972–76; UGC, 1981–83; Chm., Steering Cttee for Manufrg Adv. Service, 1977–82. Member Council: Fellowship of Engrg, 1982–85; CRAC, 1987–. *Recreations:* gardening, photography. *Address:* 4 Montrose Gardens, Oxshott, Surrey KT22 0UU. *T:* Oxshott (0372) 842093. *Club:* Leander.

MILLER, Prof. Marcus Hay, PhD; Professor of Economics, since 1978, Director, Parliamentary Policy Unit, since 1985, University of Warwick; *b* 9 Sept. 1941; *s* of J. Irvine Miller and Rose H. (*née* Moir); *m* 1967, Margaret Ellen Hummel (marr. diss.); two *d*. *Educ:* Price's Sch., Fareham, Hants; University Coll., Oxford (BA 1st Cl. PPE); Yale Univ. (Henry Fellowship, MA, PhD Econ). Lecturer, London School of Economics, 1967–76; Prof. of Economics, Univ. of Manchester, 1976–78. Economist, 1972–73, Houblon-Norman Fellow, 1981–82, Bank of England; Vis. Associate Prof. of Internat. Finance, Univ. of Chicago, 1976; Vis. Prof. of Public and Internat. Affairs, Princeton Univ., 1983. Member, Academic Panel, HM Treasury, 1976– (Chm., 1979–80); Adviser, House of Commons Select Cttee on the Treasury and Civil Service, 1980–81. Mem. Management Cttee, NIESR, 1980–. Mem., Economic Policy Gp, SDP, 1981–. *Publications:* joint editor: Monetary Policy and Economic Activity in West Germany, 1977; Essays on Fiscal and Monetary Policy, 1981; papers on macro and monetary economics, incl. effects of UK entry into EEC, reform of UK monetary system, inflation, exchange rates and liquidity preference, in Amer. Economic Rev., Economica, Nat. Inst. Economic Rev., Oxford Economic Papers, Rev. of Economic Studies. *Recreations:* swimming, orienteering. *Address:* Department of Economics, University of Warwick, Coventry CV4 7AL. *T:* Coventry (0203) 24011, ext. 2484.

MILLER, Martin John; Co-Founder and Managing Director, Milroy Estates Ltd, since 1983; Co-Founder and Publisher, Miller's Magazine, since 1991; Joint Proprietor, Chilston Park Hotel; *b* 24 Nov. 1946; *s* of Marcus and Phyllis Miller; *m* 1st, 1966, Elaine (marr. diss. 1975); three *d*; 2nd, 1978, Judith Henderson Cairns (*see* J. H. Miller); two *d*. *Educ:* West Tarring Secondary Modern Sch., Worthing. Freelance photographer, 1965–68; Co-Founder, Lyle Publications, 1968–74; semi-retirement, 1974–79; Co-Founder, MJM Publications, 1979; with Judith Miller opened Chilston Park Hotel, 1985. *Publications: with Judith Miller:* Miller's Antiques Price Guide, annually, 1979–; The Antiques Directory—Furniture, 1985; Period Details, 1987; Miller's Antique Pocket Fact File, 1988; Period Style, 1989; Understanding Antiques, 1989; Miller's Collectables Price Guide, annually 1989–; Country Style, 1990; Miller's Collectors Cars Price Guide, annually 1991–; Miller's Art Deco Checklist, 1991; Furniture Checklist, 1991. *Recreations:* shooting, indulging in fine wines and gourmet food. *Address:* (office) Sissinghurst Court, Sissinghurst, Cranbrook, Kent TN17 2JA; Eldon Lodge, 52 Victoria Road, Kensington, W8. *Club:* Groucho.

MILLER, Dame Mary Elizabeth H.; *see* Hedley-Miller.

MILLER, Maurice Solomon, MB; *b* 16 Aug. 1920; *s* of David Miller; *m* 1944, Renée, *d* of Joseph Modlin, Glasgow; two *s* two *d*. *Educ:* Shawlands Academy, Glasgow; Glasgow University. MB, ChB 1944. Elected Mem. of Glasgow Corporation, 1950; Bailie of Glasgow, 1954–57; JP Glasgow, 1957. MP (Lab): Glasgow Kelvingrove, 1964–74; E Kilbride, 1974–87. Asst Govt Whip, 1968–69. Visited Russia as mem. of medical delegation, 1955. *Publication:* Window on Russia, 1956.

MILLER, Michael, RD 1966; QC 1974; Barrister since 1958; *b* 28 June 1933; 2nd *s* of John Bryan Peter Duppa-Miller, *qv*; *m* 1958, Mary Elizabeth, *e d* of Donald Spiers Monteagle Barlow, *qv*; two *s* two *d*; *m* 1991, Dr Barbara Goodwin. *Educ:* Dragon Sch., Oxford; Westminster Sch. (King's Scholar); Christ Church, Oxford (Westminster Scholar). BA Lit. Hum. 1955; MA 1958. Ord. Seaman, RNVR, 1950; Sub-Lt 1956; qual. submarines, 1956; Lt-Comdr RNR. Called to Bar, Lincoln's Inn, 1958, Bencher 1984; practice at Chancery Bar from 1958; Mem. Bar Council, 1972–74 and 1988–; Mem. Senate of Inns of Court and Bar, 1974–76. Author and editor of computer programs incl. expert systems; founder of Clarendon Software. *Recreations:* sailing, music, chess, football. *Address:* 8 Stone Buildings, Lincoln's Inn, WC2A 3TA.

See also Sir H. D. Miller.

MILLER, Michael A.; *see* Ashley-Miller.

MILLER, Sir (Oswald) Bernard, Kt 1967; *b* 25 March 1904; *s* of late Arthur Miller and Margaret Jane Miller; *m* 1931, Jessica Rose Marie ffoulkes (*d* 1985); three *s*. *Educ:* Sloane Sch.; Jesus Coll., Oxford (Hon. Fellow, 1968); Stanhope Prize, 1925; BA 1927; MA 1930. Joined John Lewis Partnership, 1927; Dir, 1935; Chm., 1955–72. Chm., Retail Distributors Assoc., 1953; Member: Council of Industrial Design, 1957–66; Monopolies Commission, 1961–69; EDC for Distributive Trades, 1964–71. Chm. Southern Region, RSA, 1974–80; Mem. Council, RSA, 1977–82. Treasurer, Southampton Univ., 1974–82, Chm. Council, 1982–87, Pro-Chancellor, 1983–90. Hon. LLD Southampton, 1981. *Publication:* Biography of Robert Harley, Earl of Oxford, 1927. *Recreations:* fishing, gardening, opera and theatre. *Address:* 3 Sutton Manor Mews, Sutton Scotney, Hants SO21 3JX. *T:* Winchester (0962) 760997.

MILLER, Rev. Canon Paul William; Canon Residentiary of Derby Cathedral, 1966–83, Canon Emeritus since 1983; Chaplain to the Queen, 1981–88; *b* 8 Oct. 1918; *s* of F. W. Miller, Barnet. *Educ:* Haileybury; Birmingham Univ. (Dip. Theology). Served in ranks with Sherwood Foresters, 1939–45; POW of Japanese, 1942–45; despatches 1946. Deacon, 1949; Curate: of Staveley, Derbyshire, 1949–52; of Matlock, Derbyshire, 1952–55; Vicar of Codnor, Derbyshire, 1955–61; Novice, Community of the Resurrection, Mirfield, 1961–63; Priest-in-charge, Buxton, 1963–64; Chaplain, Derby Cathedral, 1964–66. *Recreations:* painting, travel. *Address:* 15 Forester Street, Derby DE1 1PP. *T:* Derby (0332) 44773.

MILLER, Peter Francis Nigel, RIBA, FCSD; Surveyor to the Fabric of Ely Cathedral, since 1974; *b* 8 May 1924; *s* of Francis Gerald Miller and Dorothy Emily (*née* Leftwich); *m* 1950, Sheila Gillian Branthwayt, ARCA FCSD, (*née* Stratton); one *s* two *d*. *Educ:* King's Sch., Canterbury; Sch. of Architecture, Coll. of Art, Canterbury. ARIBA 1952; FRIBA 1968; MSIA 1956; FSIA 1968. Served army, 1942–47, NW Europe, Austria, Italy and India; commnd Duke of Cornwall's LI, 1943. Private practice: Peter Miller and Sheila Stratton, 1954; Miller and Tritton, 1956; Purcell Miller and Tritton, 1965; Sen. Partner, Purcell Miller Tritton and Partners, Architects, Surveyors and Design Consultants, 1973, Consultant, 1988. Vice-Pres., SIAD, 1976. *Recreations:* deer stalking, shooting, wildfowling, fishing. *Address:* Thornage Watermill, Holt, Norfolk. *T:* Holt (0263) 711339; The Chapter House, The College, Ely, Cambs. *T:* Ely (0353) 667735. *Club:* Norfolk (Norwich).

MILLER, Sir Peter (North), Kt 1988; Chairman, Lloyd's, 1984–87; Chairman, Thos R. Miller & Son (Holdings), 1971–83 and since 1988; *b* 28 Sept. 1930; *s* of Cyril Thomas Gibson Risch Miller, CBE and Dorothy Alice North Miller, JP; *m* 1991, Jane Herbertson; two *s* one *d* by previous marriage. *Educ:* Rugby; Lincoln Coll., Oxford (MA Hons); City Univ (DEc). National Service, Intelligence Corps, 1949–50. Joined Lloyd's, 1953; qualified as barrister, 1954; Partner, Thos. R. Miller & Son (Insurance), 1959, Sen. Partner, 1971–; Dir, Thos R. Miller & Son (Underwriting Agents) Ltd, 1983–. Dep. Chm., Lloyd's Insurance Brokers' Asoc., 1974–75, Chm. 1976–77; Mem., Cttee of Lloyd's, 1977–80 and 1982– (Mem. Council of Lloyd's, 1983–); in charge of team responsible for passage of Lloyd's Bill (Fisher), 1980–82. Member: Baltic Exchange, 1966–; Insurance Brokers' Registration Council, 1977–81; Vice-Pres., British Insce Brokers' Assoc., 1978; Chm., British Cttee of Bureau Veritas, 1980–. One of HM's Lieutenants for the City of London, 1987–. FRSA 1986. Commendatore, Ordine al Merito della Repubblica Italiana, 1989. Hon. DSc City, 1987. *Recreations:* all sport (except cricket), including tennis, running, sailing; wine, music, old churches, gardening. *Address:* Dawson House, 5 Jewry Street, EC3N 2EX. *Clubs:* Brooks's, City of London; Vincent's (Oxford); Thames Hare and Hounds.

MILLER, Richard King; QC (Scot) 1988; *b* 19 Aug. 1949; *s* of late James Cyril King Miller, WS and of Ella Elizabeth Walker or Miller; *m* 1975, Lesley Joan Rist or Miller; two *s*. *Educ:* Edinburgh Acad,; Magdalene Coll., Cambridge (BA Hons); Edinburgh Univ. (LLB Hons). Called to the Scottish Bar, 1975. Temp. Sheriff of all Sheriffdoms of Scotland, 1988–. *Recreations:* shooting, fishing, tennis, reading and collecting good literature, good wine. *Address:* Leahurst, 16 Gillespie Road, Colinton, Edinburgh EH13 0LL. *T:* 031–441 3737.

MILLER, Richard Morgan; Chief Executive and Director, Willis Corroon plc, since 1990; *b* Nashville, Tenn, 1931; *m* 1953, Betty Ruth Randolph; one *s* two *d*. *Educ:* Montgomery Bell Acad., Nashville; Vanderbilt Univ., Nashville (BA 1953); Wharton Sch., Univ. of Pennsylvania. Served Korean War, 1953–55, Lt US Marine Corps; retired from US Marine Corps Reserve, 1960, Capt. Salesman, Dominion Insce Agency, 1955–58; established Richard M. Miller & Co., 1958, Pres., 1958–70; merger with Synercon Corp., 1970: Founder, Dir, Pres. and Chief Exec. Officer, 1970–76 (also Pres. and Chief Exec. Officer subsid. cos); Synercon Corp. merged into Corroon & Black Corp., 1976: Exec. Vice-Pres., Chief Operating Officer and Dir, 1976–78; Pres., Chief Operating Officer and Dir, 1978–88; Chief Exec. Officer, Pres. and Dir, 1988–89; Chm. Bd, Chief Exec. Officer and Dir, 1990–; Corroon & Black Corp. merged into Willis Faber plc, 1990. Member, National Associations of: Casualty and Surety Agents; Insurance Brokers; Surety Bond Producers; Mem., Nat. Fedn of Independent Business; Director: Consumer Benefit Life Insce Co.; Meridian Insce Co. (Bermuda); Third Nat. Bank, 1983–; Third Nat. Corp. Trustee and Member Executive Committee: Insce Inst. of America; Amer. Inst. for Property and Liability Underwriters. *Recreation:* golf. *Address:* Willis Corroon plc, 10 Trinity Square, EC3P 3AX. *Clubs:* City Midday, New York Athletic (New York); Belle Meade Country, Cumberland, Nashville City, Tennessee (Nashville, Tennessee); John's Island (Florida); Mid Ocean (Bermuda).

MILLER, Robert Alexander Gavin D.; *see* Douglas Miller.

MILLER, Robin Anthony; a Recorder of the Crown Court, since 1978; *b* 15 Sept. 1937; *s* of William Alexander Miller, CBE, BEM, and Winifred Miller; *m* 1962, Irene Joanna Kennedy; two *s* one *d*. *Educ:* Devonport High Sch., Plymouth; Wadham Coll., Oxford (MA). Called to the Bar, Middle Temple, 1960. *Address:* St Michael's Lodge, 192 Devonport Road, Stoke, Plymouth, Devon PL1 5RD. *T:* Plymouth (0752) 564943.

MILLER, Ronald Andrew Baird, CBE 1985; CA; Chairman and Chief Executive, Dawson International PLC, since 1982; *b* 13 May 1937; *m* 1965, Elizabeth Ann Gordon; one *s* one *d*. *Educ:* Daniel Stewart's Coll.; Univ. of Edinburgh (BSc). Joined Dawson International, 1968. Director: Securities Trust of Scotland, 1983–; Christian Salvesen, 1987–; Scottish Amicable Life Assce Soc., 1987–. *Address:* 9 Charlotte Square, Edinburgh EH2 4DR. *T:* 031–220 1919.

MILLER, Ronald Kinsman, CB 1989; Solicitor of Inland Revenue, 1986–90, retired; part-time Chairman, VAT Tribunals, since 1991; *b* 12 Nov. 1929; *s* of William Miller and Elsie May Kinsman; *m* 1952, Doris Alice Dew; one *s* one *d*. *Educ:* Colchester Royal Grammar Sch. Served RN, 1948–50. Called to the Bar, Gray's Inn, 1953. Joined Inland Revenue, 1950; Asst Solicitor, 1971; Law Officers' Dept, 1977–79; Principal Asst Solicitor, 1981–86. *Recreations:* gardening, reading, music. *Address:* 4 Liskeard Close, Chislehurst, Kent BR7 6RT. *T:* 081–467 8041. *Club:* Athenæum.

MILLER, Comdr Ronald S.; *see* Scott-Miller.

MILLER, Dr Roy Frank; Vice-Principal, Royal Holloway and Bedford New College, University of London, since 1985; *b* 20 Sept. 1935; *s* of Thomas R. Miller and Margaret Ann Tattum; *m* 1961, Ruth Naomi Kenchington; one *s*. *Educ:* Wembley County Grammar Sch.; University Coll. SW England, Exeter; Royal Holloway Coll. BSc, PhD; CPhys, FInstP. Teacher, Halbutt Secondary Modern Sch., 1957; Royal Holloway College: Demonstrator, 1957, Asst Lectr, 1960, Lectr, 1963, Sen. Lectr, 1973, Physics Dept; Vice-Principal, 1978–81; Acting Principal, 1981–82; Principal, 1982–85. Research Associate and Teaching Fellow, Case Western Reserve Univ., Ohio, USA, 1967–68. Mem. Senate, Univ. of London, 1981–85; Chm., Bd, Inst. of Classical Studies, Univ. of London, 1983–; Trustee and Governor, Strode's Foundn, Strode's Coll., Egham, 1982–. MRI; FRSA. *Publications:* articles in Jl Phys C, Phil. Mag., Vacuum. *Recreations:* mountaineering, squash, music. *Address:* Royal Holloway and Bedford New College, University of London, Egham Hill, Egham, Surrey TW20 0EX. *T:* Egham (0784) 434455. *Club:* Athenæum.

MILLER, Sidney James, MA; Higher Executive Officer, Department of Education and Science, since 1989; *b* 25 Jan. 1943; *s* of Sidney Tomsett Miller and Mary Ada Miller (*née* Marshall); *m* 1971, Judith Branney (*née* Passingham); three *s* one *d*. *Educ:* Clifton Coll., Bristol; Jesus Coll., Cambridge (MA); Harvard Univ. VIth Form Classical Master and House Tutor, Clifton Coll., Bristol, 1965–68; Asst Master and Classical Tutor, Eton Coll., 1968–73, Head of Classical Dept, 1971–73; Dep. Headmaster (Organisation), Bridgewater Hall, Stantonbury Campus, Milton Keynes, 1974–77; Headmaster, Kingston Grammar Sch., Kingston upon Thames, 1977–86; Head Master, Bedford Sch., 1986–88: Professional Officer, Sch. Exams and Assessment Council, 1988–89. *Publications:* (ed jtly) Greek Unprepared Translation, 1968; (ed jtly) Inscriptions of the Roman Empire AD14–117, 1971; article in Didaskalos, 1972. *Recreations:* watching sports, running, choral singing. *Address:* 43 Waterloo Road, Bedford MK40 3PG. *T:* (office) 071–934 0732. *Clubs:* MCC; Achilles.

MILLER, Sir Stephen (James Hamilton), KCVO 1979; MD, FRCS; Consulting Ophthalmic Surgeon, retired 1986; Hospitaller, St John Ophthalmic Hospital, Jerusalem, 1980–90; Surgeon-Oculist: to the Queen, 1974–80; to HM Household, 1965–74; Ophthalmic Surgeon: St George's Hospital, 1951–80; National Hospital, Queen Square, 1955–78; King Edward VII Hospital for Officers, 1965–80; Surgeon, Moorfields Eye Hospital, 1954–80; Recognised Teacher in Ophthalmology, St George's Medical School and Institute of Ophthalmology, University of London, retired; *b* 19 July 1915; *e s* of late Stephen Charles Miller and Isobel Hamilton; *m* 1949, Heather P. Motion; three *s*. *Educ:* Arbroath High Sch.; Aberdeen Univ. House Physician and Surgeon, Royal Infirmary, Hull, 1937–39. Surgeon Lieut-Comdr RNVR, 1939–46 (Naval Ophthalmic Specialist, RN Aux. Hosp., Kilmacolm and RN Hosp., Malta). Resident Surgical Officer, Glasgow Eye Infirmary, 1946; Registrar and Chief Clinical Asst, Moorfields Eye Hosp., 1947–50; Registrar St George's Hosp., 1949–51; Research Associate, Institute of Ophthalmology, 1949–80. Ophthalmic Surgeon, Royal Scottish Corp.; Advr in Ophthalmol., BUPA; Civilian Consultant in Ophthalmol. to RN and MoD, 1971–80. Member: Med. Commn for Accident Prevention. FRSocMed (Hon. Mem., Sect. of Ophthalmol.); Fellow Faculty of Ophthalmology; Editor, British Journal of Ophthalmology, 1973–83; Mem. Editorial Bd, Ophthalmic Literature; Ophthalmological Soc. of UK; Oxford Ophthalmological Congress (Master, 1969–70); Examiner in Ophthalmology: for Royal Colls and Brit. Orthoptic Bd; RCS and RCSE. Mem. Exec. Cttee, London Clinic, 1975–85; Governor, Moorfields Eye Hosp., 1961–67 and 1974–77. Trustee: Frost Foundn Charity; Guide Dogs for the Blind. Hon. FCOphth. Hon. Mem., Amer. Acad. of Ophthalmology. Freeman, City of London; Liveryman, Soc. of Apothecaries. Doyne Medal, 1972; Montgomery Medal, 1974. GCStJ 1987 (KStJ 1978). *Publications:* Modern Trends in Ophthalmology, 1973; Operative Surgery, 1976; Parsons' Diseases of the Eye, 1984, 18th edn 1990; Clinical Ophthalmology for the Post-Graduate, 1987; articles in BMJ, Brit. Jl of Ophthalmology, Ophthalmic Literature. *Recreations:* golf, fishing. *Address:* Sherma Cottage, Pond Road, Woking GU22 0JT. *T:* Woking (0483) 762287. *Clubs:* Caledonian; Woking and Muirfield Golf.

MILLER of Glenlee, Sir Stephen (William Macdonald), 8th Bt *cr* 1788, of Glenlee, Kirkcudbrightshire; FRCS; General Practitioner, since 1986; *b* 20 June 1953; *s* of Sir Macdonald Miller of Glenlee, 7th Bt and of Marion Jane Audrey Pettit, (Audrey, Lady Miller of Glenlee); *S* father, 1991; *m* 1st, 1978, Mary (*d* 1989), *d* of G. B. Owens; one *s* one *d*; 2nd, 1990, Caroline Clark (*née* Chasemore); one step *s* one step *d*. *Educ:* Rugby Sch.; St Bartholomew's Hosp. MB; FRCS 1981; MRCGP 1986. Surgical Registrar, Sheffield, 1979–81; Orthopaedic Registrar, Newcastle, 1982–84. *Publications:* various papers in med. jls. *Recreations:* gardening, fishing. *Heir:* *s* James Stephen Macdonald Miller, *b* 25 July 1981. *Address:* The Lawn, Shebbear, Beaworthy, Devon EX21 5RU.

MILLER, Terence George, TD 1960; MA Cantab; Director, Polytechnic of North London, 1971–80; *b* 16 Jan. 1918; *o s* of late George Frederick Miller, Cambridge, and late Marion Johnston, Port William, Wigtownshire; *m* 1944, Inga Catriona, 3rd *d* of Austin Priestman, MD, Folkestone, Kent; one *s* three *d*. *Educ:* Perse (foundn schol.); Jesus Coll., Cambridge (schol.). Wiltshire Prizeman, 1939. Served War of 1939–45: RA, Special Forces, Glider Pilot Regt; TA, 1947–67 (Lt-Col. 1964). Harkness Scholar, 1948; Research Fellow, Jesus Coll., 1949–54. University Demonstrator, 1948; Lectr in Geology, Univ. of Keele, 1953; Sen. Lectr, 1963, Prof. of Geography, Univ. of Reading, 1965–67; Principal, University Coll. of Rhodesia, 1967–69; Vis. Prof., Reading Univ., 1969–71. *Publications:* Geology, 1950; Geology and Scenery in Britain, 1953; scientific papers in various jls. *Recreations:* military history, dinghy sailing, beachcombing, listening. *Address:* 9 Shute Hill, Mawnan Smith, Falmouth, Cornwall. *T:* Falmouth (0326) 250691.

MILLER, Walter George, IPFA; FCCA; Chief Executive, Bristol City Council, 1990–91 (Acting Chief Executive, 1987–90); *b* 2 March 1932; *s* of Bert and Rosina Miller; *m* 1956, Sheila Mary Daw; one *s* two *d*. *Educ:* Howardian High Sch., Cardiff. Clerk, City Treasurer's Dept, Cardiff, 1948–50. Served RA, Hong Kong and Korea, 1950–52. Audit Asst, City Treasurer's Dept, Cardiff, 1952–55; Accountant, Treasurer's Dept: Nairobi, 1955–58; Cardiff, 1958–60; Caerphilly, 1960–63; Ilford, 1963–65; Redbridge, 1965; Bromley, 1965–68; Asst Borough Treasurer, Bromley, 1968–72; Bristol: Asst City Treasurer, 1972–73; Dep. City Treasurer, 1973–80; City Treasurer, 1980–90. Governor, St Joseph's Sch., Portishead, 1986–. *Publications:* contrib. local government and accountancy press. *Recreations:* writing and lecturing on local government and allied topics; writing, gardening. *Address:* 4 Nore Road, Portishead, Bristol BS20 9HN. *T:* Bristol (0272) 848559.

MILLER, William; *see* Miller, George William.

MILLER JONES, Hon. Mrs; *see* Askwith, Hon. B. E.

MILLER PARKER, Agnes; *see* Parker, A. M.

MILLES-LADE, family name of **Earl Sondes.**

MILLETT, Anthea Christine; Chief Inspector, HM Inspectorate of Schools, since 1987; *b* 2 Nov. 1941; *d* of Rupert Millett and Lucy Millett. *Educ:* Erdington Grammar School for Girls, Birmingham; Bedford Coll., Univ. of London (BA Hons). Teacher: Channing School, Highgate, 1963–65; Bournville Grammar Tech. Sch., Birmingham, 1965–67; Solihull High Sch., 1967–71 (Head of Dept); Dep. Head, Tile Hill Comprehensive Sch., Coventry, 1972–77; HM Inspectorate of Schools, 1978–. Mem., Cttee of Enquiry, Management and Government of Schools, 1975–76. *Recreations:* travel, walking, gardening, DIY. *Address:* Department of Education and Science, Sanctuary Buildings, Great Smith Street, SW1.

MILLETT, Hon. Sir Peter (Julian), Kt 1986; **Hon. Mr Justice Millett;** a Judge of the High Court of Justice, Chancery Division, since 1986; *b* 23 June 1932; *s* of late Denis Millett and Adele Millett; *m* 1959, Ann Mireille, *d* of late David Harris; two *s* (and one *s* decd). *Educ:* Harrow; Trinity Hall, Cambridge (Schol.; MA). Nat. Service, RAF, 1955–57 (Flying Officer). Called to Bar, Middle Temple, 1955, *ad eundem* Lincoln's Inn, 1959 (Bencher, 1980), Singapore, 1976, Hong Kong, 1979; at Chancery Bar, 1958–86; QC 1973. Examnr and Lectr in Practical Conveyancing, Council of Legal Educn, 1962–76. Junior Counsel to Dept of Trade and Industry in Chancery matters, 1967–73. Mem., General Council of the Bar, 1971–75. Outside Mem., Law Commn on working party on co-ownership of matrimonial home, 1972–73; Mem., Dept of Trade Insolvency Law Review Cttee, 1977–82. *Publications:* contrib. to Halsbury's Laws of England, Encycl. of Forms and Precedents; articles in legal jls. *Recreations:* philately, bridge, The Times crossword. *Address:* Royal Courts of Justice, Strand, WC2; 18 Portman Close, W1H 9HJ. *T:* 071–935 1152; St Andrews, Kewhurst Avenue, Cooden, Sussex.

MILLGATE, Prof. Michael Henry, PhD; FRSC; FRSL; Professor of English, Toronto University, since 1967; *b* 19 July 1929; *s* of Stanley Millgate and Marjorie Louisa (*née* Norris); *m* 1960, Jane, *d* of Maurice and Marie Barr. *Educ:* St Catharine's Coll., Cambridge (MA); Michigan Univ.; Leeds Univ. (PhD). FRSC 1982. Tutor-Organizer, WEA, E Lindsey, 1953–56; Lectr in English Lit., Leeds Univ., 1958–64; Prof. of English and Chm. of the Dept, York Univ., Ont, 1964–67. Killam Sen. Res. Schol., 1974–75, Killam Res. Fellow, 1986–88; John Simon Guggenheim Meml Fellow, 1977–78. FRSL 1984. *Publications:* William Faulkner, 1961; (ed) Tennyson: Selected Poems, 1963; American Social Fiction, 1964; (ed jtly) Transatlantic Dialogue, 1966; The Achievement of William Faulkner, 1966; (ed jtly) Lion in the Garden, 1968; Thomas Hardy: his career as a novelist, 1971; (ed with R. L. Purdy) The Collected Letters of Thomas Hardy, vols I-VII, 1978–88; Thomas Hardy: a biography, 1982; (ed) The Life and Work of Thomas Hardy, 1985; (ed) William Faulkner Manuscripts 20, 21, 22 and 23, 1987; (ed) New Essays on Light in August, 1987; (ed) Thomas Hardy: selected letters, 1990. *Address:* 75 Highland Avenue, Toronto, Ont M4W 2A4, Canada. *T:* (416) 920 3717.

MILLICHIP, Sir Frederick Albert, (Sir Bert), Kt 1991; Chairman, The Football Association, since 1981 (Member of Council, since 1970; Life Vice President, since 1990); *b* 5 Aug. 1914; *s* of late Hugh Bowater Millichip; *m* 1950, Joan Barbara Brown; one *s* one *d*. *Educ:* Solihull Sch., Warwicks. Qualified as Solicitor, 1950; Sen. Partner, 1959–88, Consultant, 1988–, Tyndelwood & Millichip (formerly Sharpe & Millichip). Served War, 1939–45, in England, N Africa, Sicily and Italy; joined S Staffs Regt as private, commnd RA (Captain). Member: UEFA Organising Cttee for European Championship, 1981–; FIFA Organising Cttee for World Cup, 1983–; Exec. Cttee, UEFA, 1988–; Chm., FA Disciplinary Cttee, 1978–81; Chm., Cttee for Five-a-Side Football, UEFA, 1988–. West Bromwich Albion Football Club: Dir, 1964–84; Chm., 1976–83; Pres., 1984–. *Recreation:* golf. *Address:* Fairlight, 52 Twatling Road, Barnt Green, Birmingham B45 8HU. *T:* 021–445 4688. *Club:* Blackwell Golf (Blackwell, Worcs).

MILLIGAN, Hon. Lord; James George Milligan; a Senator of the College of Justice in Scotland, since 1988; *b* 10 May 1934; *s* of Rt Hon. Lord Milligan; *m* 1st, 1961, Elizabeth Carnegie Thomson (*d* 1982), *e d* of late Hon. Lord Migdale and Louise (*née* Carnegie; later Mrs Thomson); two *s* three *d*; 2nd, 1985, Elizabeth Cynthia Rae Ashworth, *widow* of Rupert S. H. Ashworth, and *y d* of late P. Rae Shepherd. *Educ:* St Mary's Sch., Melrose; Rugby Sch.; Oxford Univ. (BA); Edinburgh Univ. (LLB). Admitted to Faculty of Advocates, 1959; Standing Junior Counsel to the Scottish Home and Health Dept and Dept of Health and Social Security in Scotland; Advocate-Depute, 1971–78; QC (Scot.) 1972; Chm., Med. Appeal Tribunal (Scotland), 1979–88. Chm., RSSPCC Edinburgh, 1978–. *Publication:* (contrib. small part of) Armour on Valuation for Rating, 3rd edn, 1961. *Recreations:* gardening, golf. *Address:* Parliament House, Edinburgh EH1 1RQ. *Club:* New (Edinburgh).

MILLIGAN, Iain Anstruther; QC 1991; *b* 21 April 1950; *s* of Wyndham Macbeth Moir Milligan, *qv*; *m* 1979, Zara Ann Louise Spearman; one *s* two *d*. *Educ:* Eton; Magdalene College, Cambridge (MA); College of Law. Called to the Bar, Inner Temple, 1973. *Recreations:* forestry, walking. *Address:* 3 Essex Court, Temple, EC4Y 9AL. *T:* 071–583 9294; Dunesslin, Dunscore, Dumfries DG2 0UR. *T:* Dunscore (038782) 345.

MILLIGAN, James George; *see* Milligan, Hon. Lord.

MILLIGAN, Terence Alan, (Spike Milligan); actor; author; *b* 16 April 1918; *s* of late Captain L. A. Milligan, MSM, RA retd, and Florence Winifred Milligan; *m* (wife *d* 1978); one *s* three *d*; *m* 1983, Shelagh Sinclair. *Educ:* Convent of Jesus and Mary, Poona; Brothers de La Salle, Rangoon; SE London Polytechnic, Lewisham. Appearances (comedy) as Spike Milligan: *stage:* The Bed-Sitting Room; Son of Oblomov; Ben Gunn, in Treasure Island, Mermaid, 1973, 1974; One man shows, 1979, 1980; writer, Ubu Roi, 1980; Spike Milligan and Friends, Lyric, 1982; *radio:* Goon Show (inc. special performance, 1972, to mark 50th Anniversary of BBC); Best British Radio Features Script, 1972; The Milligan Papers, 1987; *TV:* Show called Fred, ITV; World of Beachcomber, BBC; Q5, BBC; Oh in Colour, BBC; A Milligan for All Seasons, BBC, 1972–73; Marty Feldman's Comedy Machine, ITV (writing and appearing; awarded Golden Rose and special comedy award, Montreux, 1972); The Melting Pot, BBC, 1975; Q7, BBC series, 1977; Q8, 1978; Q9, 1979; TV Writer of the Year Award, 1956; *films:* The Magic Christian, 1971; The Devils, 1971; The Cherry Picker, 1972; Digby the Biggest Dog in the World, 1972; Alice's Adventures in Wonderland, 1972; The Three Musketeers, 1973; The Great McGonagall, 1975; The Last Remake of Beau Geste, 1977; The Hound of the Baskervilles, 1978; Monty Python Life of Brian, 1978; History of the World, Part 1, 1980; Yellowbeard, 1983. *Publications:* Dustbin of Milligan, 1961; Silly Verse for Kids, 1963; Puckoon, 1963; The Little Pot Boiler, 1965; A Book of Bits, 1965; Milliganimals, 1968; The Bedside Milligan, 1968; The Bed-Sitting Room (play), 1969; The Bald Twit Lion, 1970; Adolf Hitler, My Part in his Downfall, 1971 (filmed 1973; on record, 1980); Milligan's Ark, 1971; Small Dreams of a Scorpion, 1972; The Goon Show Scripts, 1972; Rommel: Gunner Who?, 1973; (for children) Badjelly the Witch, 1973; (with J. Hobbs) The Great McGonagall Scrapbook, 1975; The Milligan Book of Records, Games, Cartoons and Commercials, 1975; Dip the Puppy, 1975; Transports of Delight, 1975; William McGonagal, the truth at last, 1976; Monty, His Part in my Victory, 1976; Goblins (with Heath Robinson illus), 1978; Mussolini, His Part in my Downfall, 1978; Open Heart University, 1978; Spike Milligan's Q Annual, 1979; Get in the Q Annual, 1980; Unspun Socks from a Chicken's Laundry, 1981; Indefinite Articles and Scunthorpe, 1981; The 101 Best and Only Limericks of Spike Milligan, 1982; (for children) Sir Nobonk and the Terrible, Awful, Dreadful, Naughty, Nasty Dragon (illus. by Carol Barker), 1982; The Goon Cartoons, 1982; More Goon Cartoons, 1983; There's A Lot Of It About, 1983; The Melting Pot, 1983; Spike Milligan's Further Transports of Delight, 1985; Where have all the Bullets Gone? (autobiog.), 1985; Floored Masterpieces with Worse Verse (illus. by Tracey Boyd), 1985; Goodbye Soldier, 1986; The Looney: an Irish fantasy, 1987; The Mirror Running (poetry), 1987; Startling Verse for all the Family (children's poetry), 1987; The Lost Goon Shows, 1987; Milligan's War, 1988; McGonagall Meets George Gershwin, 1988; It Ends With Magic, 1990; Dear Robert, Dear Spike, 1991. *Recreations:* restoration of antiques, oil painting, water colours, gardening, eating, drinking, talking, wine, jazz. *Address:* 9 Orme Court, W2. *T:* 071–727 1544.

MILLIGAN, Veronica Jean Kathleen; Senior Partner, Civlec Advisory Industrial Development Services, industrial consultants, since 1966; *b* 11 March 1926; *d* of Gilbert John O'Neill and Jennie Kathleen Robertson; *m* 1945, Francis Sutherland Milligan; one *s* (and one *s* decd). *Educ:* Pontypridd Intermediate Grammar Sch.; University Coll., Cardiff (BA Wales, DipEd); (evenings) Polytechnic of Wales (HNC Elect. and Endorsements, Dip. Management Studies). CEng, MIEE; MBIM. Sch. teacher, Glam Educn Authority, 1948–51; Grad. Trainee/Senior Elec. Engr, Electricity Supply Industry, 1952–65. Manpower Adviser/Consultant to Manpower and Productivity Services, Dept of Employment (on secondment), 1969–73; Chm. and Dir, RTR Engineering Ltd, 1982–86; Dir, Vantage Engrg & Maintenance Ltd, 1985–87. Pres., Women's Engrg Soc., 1977–79; Chm., E Wales Area, IEE, 1976–77 and Mem. Council, 1976–78. Member: Gwent AHA, 1976–88; Gwent FPC, 1985–; National Water Council, 1977–80; Industrial Tribunals Panel, 1977–83; Commn on Energy and Environment, 1978–; Management Adv. Panel for Craftsmen, DHSS, 1979–88; Nat. Staff Cttee for Works Staff, DHSS, 1981–82; Rent Assessment Panel, 1981–; Monitoring Cttee, Nat. Financial Incentive Scheme for NHS Maintenance Depts, 1982–88. *Publications:* short papers in learned jls. *Recreations:* industrial careers advice to schools, industrial history, landscaping, walking. *Address:* Park Cottage, Rhiwderin, Newport, Gwent NP1 9RP. *T:* Newport (0633) 893557, Pontypool (0495) 762311.

MILLIGAN, Wyndham Macbeth Moir, MBE 1945; TD 1947; Principal of Wolsey Hall, Oxford, 1968–80, retired; *b* 21 Dec. 1907; *s* of Dr W. Anstruther Milligan, MD, London, W1; *m* 1941, Helen Penelope Eirene Cassavetti, London, W1; three *s* two *d*. *Educ:* Sherborne; Caius Coll., Cambridge (Christopher James Student, 1931; 1st Cl. Classical Tripos, Parts 1 and 2). Asst Master, Eton Coll., 1932–, House Master, Eton Coll., 1946; Warden, Radley Coll., 1954–68. Served 1939–45, with Scots Guards, in NW Europe (Major). Former Chm., N Berks Area Youth Cttee. Governor: St Mary's, Wantage (Chm.); Reed's Sch., Cobham; Lay Chm., Vale of White Horse Deanery Synod; Mem., Administrative Council, King George's Jubilee Trust. FRSA 1968. *Recreations:* gardening, sketching. *Address:* Church Hill House, Stalbridge, Sturminster Newton, Dorset DT10 2LR. *T:* Stalbridge (0963) 62815.

See also I. A. Milligan.

MILLING; *see* Crowley-Milling.

MILLING, Peter Francis, MB, BChir, FRCS; formerly: Surgeon, Ear, Nose and Throat Department, University College Hospital; Surgeon in charge, Throat and Ear Department, Brompton Hospital; Consultant Ear, Nose and Throat Surgeon: Epsom District Hospital; Oxted and Limpsfield Cottage Hospital; Visiting Laryngologist Benenden Chest Hospital. *Educ:* Cambridge University. BA Hons, 1937; MRCS, LRCP, 1940; MA, MB, BChir, 1941; FRCS, 1946. Formerly Chief Assistant, Ear, Nose and Throat Department, St Thomas' Hospital; Chief Clinical Assistant and Registrar, Ear, Nose and Throat Department, Guy's Hosp.; Surgical Registrar, Ear, Nose and Throat Dept, Royal Cancer Hospital. Member British Association of Otolaryngologists. *Publications:* contributions to medical text-books and journals. *Address:* 3 Homefield Park, Ballasalla, Isle of Man. *T:* Douglas (0624) 823072.

MILLINGTON, Anthony Nigel Raymond; President, Rolls-Royce (Far East) Ltd, since 1990; *b* 29 Jan. 1945; *s* of Raymond and Nancy Millington; *m* 1969, Susan Carolyn (*née* Steilberg); two *s*. *Educ:* Ipswich School; Univ. of Grenoble; Trinity College, Cambridge (BA); Univ. of Chicago. Joined FCO, 1968; Tokyo, 1969–76; FCO, 1976–80; Paris, 1980–84; Japanese National Defence College, 1984–85; Head of Chancery, Tokyo, 1985–88; Head of Far Eastern Dept, FCO, 1989–90; joined Rolls-Royce PLC, 1990. *Recreations:* squash, tennis, walking in the countryside. *Address:* c/o Rolls-Royce (Far East) Ltd, Room 3204, Kasumigaseki Building, 2-5 Kasumigaseki 3-chome, Tokyo 100, Japan. *T:* Tokyo 592–0966. *Club:* Royal Automobile.

MILLINGTON, Wing Comdr Ernest Rogers, DFC 1945; advisor on training, Youth Training Scheme, 1980–90; Teacher in charge of Teachers' Centre, London Borough of Newham, 1967–80, retired; Founder, and Editor, Project, 1967–80; *b* 15 Feb. 1916; *s* of Edmund Rogers Millington and Emily Craggs; *m* 1st, 1937 (marr. diss. 1974); four *d*; 2nd, 1975, Ivy Mary Robinson. *Educ:* Chigwell Sch., Essex; College of S Mark and S John, Chelsea; Birkbeck Coll., London Univ. Clerk; Accountant; Company Sec.; served War of 1939–45, soldier, gunner officer, pilot RAF, instructor and heavy bomber, CO of a Lancaster Sqdn. MP (Commonwealth) for Chelmsford, 1945–50. Re-joined Royal Air Force, 1954–57. Head of Social Educn, Shoreditch Comprehensive Sch., London, 1965–67. *Publications:* (edited): A Study of Film, 1972; The Royal Group of Docks, 1977; A Geography of London, 1979; National Parks, 1980. *Recreations:* Francophilia, travel, writing. *Address:* Villa Martine, Couze St Front, 24150 Lalinde, France. *T:* 53 24 94 31.

MILLNER, Ralph; QC 1965; Visiting Lecturer in Italian, University of Leicester, since 1980; *b* 25 Jan. 1912; *o s* of Ralph Millner, Merchant, Manchester; *m* 1st, 1935, Bruna, *d* of Arturo Rosa, Este, Italy (marr. diss. 1949); one *d* decd; 2nd, 1949, Monica, *d* of Prof. P. W. Robertson, Wellington, NZ; one *s* two *d*. *Educ:* William Hulme's Grammar Sch., Manchester; Clare Coll., Cambridge (MA); Bedford Coll., London (BA, Italian). Called to English Bar, Inner Temple, 1934; Ghana Bar (Gold Coast), 1950; Sierra Leone Bar, 1957; Nigerian Bar and S Cameroons Bar, 1959; Guyana Bar (formerly British Guiana), 1961; has also appeared in courts of Aden and Kenya. Lectr in Italian, QUB, 1972–77. Member: Soc. for Italian Studies; Haldane Soc. *Address:* 69 Anson Road, N7 0AS.

MILLS, family name of **Viscount Mills.**

MILLS, 3rd Viscount *cr* 1962; **Christopher Philip Roger Mills;** Bt 1953; Baron 1957; Fisheries Biologist, National Rivers Authority, since 1989; *b* 20 May 1956; *s* of 2nd Viscount Mills and of Joan Dorothy, *d* of James Shirreff; *S* father, 1988; *m* 1980, Lesley Alison, *er d* of Alan Bailey. *Educ:* Oundle School; Univ. of London (BSc Hons Biolog. Sciences; MSc Applied Fish Biology); Plymouth Polytechnic. Biologist at Salmon Research Trust of Ireland, 1980–89. *Publications:* papers in Aquaculture, Aquaculture and Fisheries Management. *Recreations:* flyfishing, fine wines. *Address:* House of Lords, SW1.

MILLS, Maj.-Gen. Alan Oswald Gawler; Director-General of Artillery, Ministry of Defence (Army), 1967–69, retired; *b* 11 March 1914; *o s* of John Gawler Mills; *m* 1941, Beata Elizabeth de Courcy Morgan Richards; one *s* one *d*. *Educ:* Marlborough Coll.; RMA, Woolwich. Commissioned RA, 1934; Hong Kong, 1938–45; Br. Jt Services Mission, USA, 1951–53; Techn SO Grade I, Min. of Supply, 1955–57; Mil. Dir of Studies, RMCS, 1957–61; Sen. Mil. Officer, Royal Armament Research and Develt Estabt, 1961–62; BGS, WO, 1962–65; Dir, Guided Weapons Trials, Min. of Aviation, 1966. *Recreations:* sailing, ski-ing. *Address:* 9 Redburn Street, Chelsea, SW3 4DA. *T:* 071–351 4272. *Club:* Seaview Yacht.

MILLS, Major Anthony David; *b* 14 Dec. 1918; *y s* of late Maj.-Gen. Sir Arthur Mills, CB, DSO; *m* 1948, Anne (*née* Livingstone); two *d*. *Educ:* Wellington Coll.; RMC, Sandhurst. Commnd Indian Army, 1939, 9th Gurkha Rifles; served War of 1939–45, NW Frontier and Burma, regimental duty and various staff appts; seconded Indian Para. Regt, 1944; retd from Army 1948. Apptd Asst Sec., All England Lawn Tennis Club and Wimbledon Championships, 1948, Sec. Treasurer, and Sec.-Gen., 1963–79. *Recreations:* golf, dog walking, consulting Who's Who. *Address:* c/o All England Lawn Tennis Club, Church Road, Wimbledon, SW19 5AE. *Clubs:* Naval and Military, Queen's (Hon.); All England Lawn Tennis; Royal Wimbledon Golf.

MILLS, Barbara Jean Lyon; QC 1986; Director of the Serious Fraud Office, since 1990; a Recorder of the Crown Court, since 1982; *b* 10 Aug. 1940; *d* of John and Kitty Warnock; *m* 1962, John Angus Donald Mills; four *c*. *Educ:* St Helen's Sch., Northwood; Lady Margaret Hall, Oxford (Gibbs Scholar, 1961; MA). Called to the Bar, Middle Temple, 1963, Bencher, 1990. Jun. Treasury Counsel, Central Criminal Court, 1981–86. Member: Criminal Injuries Compensation Bd, 1988–90; Parole Bd, 1990; Legal Assessor to GMC and GDC, 1988–90. *Recreation:* my family. *Address:* Serious Fraud Office, Elm House, 10–16 Elm Street, WC1X 0BJ. *T:* 071–239 7272.

MILLS, Prof. Bernard Yarnton, AC 1976; FRS 1963; FAA 1959; DSc Eng; Professor of Physics (Astrophysics), University of Sydney, 1965–85, Emeritus Professor 1986; *b* 8 Aug. 1920; *s* of Ellice Yarnton Mills and Sylphide Mills. *Educ:* King's Sch., New South Wales; University of Sydney. BSc 1940, DSc Eng 1959 (Sydney). Joined the then Council for Scientific and Industrial Research and worked on Develt of mil. radar systems; after working for many years on radioastronomy he joined Sydney Univ. to form a radioastronomy group in Sch. of Physics, 1960; Reader in Physics, 1960–65; responsible for Mills Cross radio-telescope, near Hoskinstown, NSW. Lyle Medal of Australian Academy of Science, 1957. *Publications:* (jtly) A Textbook of Radar, 1946; many contribs to sci. jls in Australia, England and America, mainly on subjects of radioastronomy and astrophysics. *Address:* 52 Victoria Street, Roseville, NSW 2069, Australia.

MILLS, Vice-Adm. Sir Charles (Piercy), KCB 1968 (CB 1964); CBE 1957; DSC 1953; *b* 4 Oct. 1914; *s* of late Capt. Thomas Piercy Mills, Woking, Surrey; *m* 1944, Anne Cumberlege; two *d*. *Educ:* RN College, Dartmouth. Joined Navy, 1928; Comdr 1947; Capt. 1953; Rear-Adm. 1963; Vice-Adm. 1966. Served War of 1939–45, Home Waters, Mediterranean and Far East; Korea, 1951–52; Flag Officer, Second in Command, Far East Fleet, 1966–67; C-in-C Plymouth, 1967–69; Lieut-Governor and C-in-C Guernsey, 1969–74. US Legion of Merit, 1955. KStJ 1969. *Recreations:* golf, yachting. *Address:* Park Lodge, Aldeburgh, Suffolk. *T:* Aldeburgh (0728) 452115.

MILLS, Edward (David), CBE 1959; FRIBA; Architect and Design Consultant in private practice since 1937; Senior Partner, Edward D. Mills & Partners, Architects, London, since 1956; *b* 19 March 1915; *s* of Edward Ernest Mills; *m* 1939, Elsie May Bryant; one *s* one *d*. *Educ:* Ensham Sch.; Polytechnic Sch. of Architecture. ARIBA 1937, FRIBA 1946. Mem. of RIBA Council, 1954–62 and 1964–69; Chm. RIBA Bd of Architectural Education, 1960–62 (Vice-Chm., 1958–60). RIBA Alfred Bossom Research Fellow, 1953; Churchill Fellow, 1969. FCSD (FSIAD 1975); Mem., Uganda Soc. of Architects. Chm., Faculty Architecture, British School at Rome; Patron, Soc. of Architectural Illustrators. Architect for British Industries Pavilion, Brussels Internat. Exhibn, 1958; works include: St Andrews Cathedral, Mbale, Uganda; Nat. Exhibn Centre, Birmingham; Birmingham Internat. Arena; churches, schools, industrial buildings, research centres, flats and houses in Great Britain and overseas. *Publications:* The Modern Factory, 1951; The New Architecture in Great Britain, 1953; The Modern Church, 1956; Architects Details, Vols 1–6, 1952–61; Factory Building, 1967; The Changing Workplace, 1971; Planning, 5 vols, 9th edn 1972, 10th edn (combined Golden Jubilee vol.), 1985; The National Exhibition Centre, 1976; Building Maintenance and Preservation, 1980, 2nd edn 1992; Design for Holidays and Tourism, 1983; contribs to RIBA journal, Architectural Review, etc. *Recreations:* photography, foreign travel. *Address:* The Studio, Gate House Farm, Newchapel, Lingfield, Surrey RH7 6LF. *T:* Lingfield (0342) 832241.

MILLS, Eric Robertson, CBE 1981; Registrar of the Privy Council, 1966–83; *b* 27 July 1918; *s* of late Thomas Piercy Mills, Woking, Surrey; *m* 1950, Shirley Manger; two *d*. *Educ:* Charterhouse; Trinity Coll., Cambridge (BA). Served Royal Artillery, 1939–46; Major 1944. Called to Bar, Inner Temple, 1947; Mem. of Western Circuit. Dep. Judge Advocate, 1955; Chief Clerk, Judicial Cttee of Privy Council, 1963. *Publications:* contribs to legal text books. *Address:* Lamber Green, St Catherines Drive, Guildford, Surrey GU2 5HE. *T:* Guildford (0483) 37218.

MILLS, Prof. Eric William, AM 1986; CChem, FRSC; FRACI; Director, South Australian Institute of Technology, 1978–85, retired; *b* 22 April 1920; *s* of William and Lucy Margaret Mills; *m* 1945, Inge Julia Königsberger; three *d*. *Educ:* Liverpool Institute; Univ. of Liverpool (BSc, PhD). Chemist, British Insulated Cables, 1941–45; Research Chemist, British Oxygen Co., 1948–49; Sen. Lectr, Birmingham College of Advanced Technology, 1949–52; Head of Dept, Rutherford Coll. of Technology, 1952–57; Principal: Carlisle Technical Coll., 1959–60; Chesterfield Coll. of Technology, 1960–63; Asst Dir, SA Inst. of Technology, 1964–77. *Address:* 3 Pam Street, Beaumont, SA 5066, Australia. *T:* 61–8–79–6674.

MILLS, Sir Frank, KCVO 1983; CMG 1971; HM Diplomatic Service, retired; Chairman of Council, Royal Commonwealth Society for the Blind (Sight Savers), since 1985; *b* 3 Dec. 1923; *s* of Joseph Francis Mills and Louisa Mills; *m* 1953, Trilby Foster; one *s* two *d*. *Educ:* King Edward VI Sch., Nuneaton; Emmanuel Coll., Cambridge. RAFVR, 1942–45. CRO, 1948; served in: Pakistan, 1949–51; S Africa, 1955–58; Malaysia, 1962–63; Singapore, 1964–66; India, 1972–75; High Comr, Ghana, 1975–78; Private Sec. to Sec. of State, 1960–62; RCDS, 1971; Dir of Communications, FCO, 1978–81; High Comr, Bangladesh, 1981–83. Chm., Camberwell HA, 1984–89. *Recreations:* golf, water colours. *Address:* 14 Sherborne Road, Chichester, W Sussex PO19 3AA. *Clubs:* Commonwealth Trust; Goodwood Golf.

MILLS, (George) Ian, FCA, FIMC; Senior Partner, Business Development Europe, Price Waterhouse, since 1989; *b* 19 Nov. 1935; *s* of George Haxton Mills and Evelyn Mary (*née* Owen); *m* 1968, Margaret Elizabeth Dunstan; one *s* one *d* (and one *s* decd). *Educ:* Taunton's Grammar Sch., Southampton. FCA 1960; FIMC 1964; LHSM 1985. Articled to Beal, Young & Booth, Southampton, 1954–60; Price Waterhouse, London, 1960–65; seconded to World Bank team assisting Govt of Pakistan Treasury, 1962; Chief Accountant, Univ. of Ibadan, Nigeria, 1965–68; rejoined Price Waterhouse, 1968; London Office, 1968–70; Newcastle upon Tyne Office, as Manager i/c Northern and Scottish Management Consultancy Ops, 1970–73; Partner, 1973; London Office, 1973–85: i/c Africa Management Consultancy Services, 1975–83; Nat. Dir, Central Govt Services, 1983–85; Nation Health Service Management Board, 1985–89: Dir of Financial Management, 1985–88; Dir of Resource Management, 1988–89; rejoined Price Waterhouse, 1989. *Publications:* articles in financial, educnl and med. jls. *Recreations:* classical music, photography, travel. *Address:* 60 Belmont Hill, SE13 5DN. *T:* 081–852 2457. *Club:* Commonwealth Trust.

MILLS, Maj.-Gen. Giles Hallam, CB 1977; CVO 1984; OBE 1964; retired; *b* 1 April 1922; 2nd *s* of late Col Sir John Digby Mills, TD, Bisterne Manor, Ringwood, Hampshire, and of Lady Mills; *m* 1947, Emily Snowden Hallam, 2nd *d* of late Captain W. H. Tuck, Perrywood, Maryland, USA, and of Mrs Tuck; two *s* one *d*. *Educ:* Eton Coll. Served War: 2nd Lieut, KRRC, 1941; 1st Bn, KRRC, N Africa, Italy (Adjt, despatches), 1943–47. Staff Coll., 1951; Armed Forces Staff Coll. (US), 1959; Mil. Asst to CIGS, 1961–63; CO, 2 Green Jackets, KRRC, 1963–65; Admin. Staff Coll., Henley, 1965; Regtl Col, Royal Green Jackets, 1966–67; Comd, 8 Infty Bde, 1968–69; IDC 1970; Comd, British Army Staff and Mil. Attaché, Washington, 1971–73; Divl Brig., The Light Div., 1973–74; Dir of Manning (Army), 1974–77, retd. Major and Resident Governor, HM Tower of London, and Keeper of the Jewel House, 1979–84. *Publications:* Annals of The King's Royal Rifle Corps, vol. VI (with Roger Nixon), 1971, vol. VII, 1979. *Recreations:* gardening, bird-watching, fishing, shooting, history. *Address:* Leeland House, Twyford, Winchester, Hants SO21 1NP. *Club:* Army and Navy.

MILLS, Maj.-Gen. Graham; *see* Mills, Maj.-Gen. W. G. S.

MILLS, Harold Hernshaw; Principal Finance Officer, Scottish Office, since 1988; *b* 2 March 1938; *s* of late Harold and of Margaret Mills; *m* 1973, Marion Elizabeth Beattie, MA. *Educ:* Greenock High Sch.; Univ. of Glasgow (BSc, PhD). Cancer Research Scientist, Roswell Park Memorial Inst., Buffalo, NY, 1962–64; Lectr, Glasgow Univ., 1964–69; Principal, Scottish Home and Health Dept, 1970–76; Asst Secretary: Scottish Office, 1976–81; Privy Council Office, 1981–83; Scottish Development Dept, 1983–84; Under Sec., Scottish Develt Dept, 1984–88. *Publications:* scientific papers in jls of learned socs on the crystal structure of chemical compounds. *Address:* Scottish Office, New St Andrew's House, Edinburgh.

MILLS, Iain Campbell; MP (C) Meriden, since 1979; *b* 21 April 1940; *s* of John Steel Mills and Margaret Leitch; *m* 1971, Gaynor Lynne Jeffries. *Educ:* Prince Edward Sch., Salisbury, Rhodesia. Dunlop Rhodesia Ltd, 1961–64; Dunlop Ltd, UK, 1964–79 (latterly Marketing Planning Manager). Parly Private Secretary: to Minister of State for Industry, 1981–82; to Sec. of State for Employment, 1982–83; to Sec. of State for Trade and Industry, 1983–85; to Chancellor of Duchy of Lancaster, 1985–87. Mem., Select Cttee on Employment, 1989–. Chm., Community Trade Mark Cttee, 1984–; Vice-Chm., Transport Safety Cttee, 1984–. *Address:* House of Commons, SW1A 0AA.

MILLS, Ian; *see* Mills, George I.

MILLS, Ivor; writer and broadcaster; corporate affairs and media consultant; *b* 7 Dec. 1929; *e s* of John Mills and Matilda (*née* Breen); *m* 1956, Muriel (marr. diss. 1987), *o d* of Wilson and Muriel Hay; one *s* one *d*. *Educ:* High sch.; Stranmillis Coll.; Queen's Univ., Belfast. Radio and television journalist, and freelance writer, Ulster TV, 1959, and Southern TV, 1963; freelance writer/editor/producer/presenter, contrib. to BBC World Service and Home Radio Networks, and ITV Regions, 1964; joined ITN as Reporter, 1965; newscaster, 1967–78; Head of Public Affairs, Post Office, 1978–81; Head of Public Affairs and Dep. Dir, Corporate Relns, British Telecommunications plc, 1981–88. Media consultant. Mem. Bd, Acad. of Ancient Music, 1989–. *Recreations:* art, music, theatre, tennis, food, wine. *Address:* 46B Glenhurst Avenue, Parliament Hill NW5 1PS.

MILLS, Ivor Henry, FRCP; Professor of Medicine in the University of Cambridge, 1963–88, now Emeritus; Fellow, Churchill College, Cambridge, 1963–88; Hon. Consultant to United Cambridge Hospitals since 1963; *b* 13 June 1921; 3rd *s* of late J. H. W. Mills and late Priscilla Mills; *m* 1947, Sydney Elizabeth Puleston (*née* Roberts); one *s* one *d*. *Educ:* Selhurst Grammar Sch., Croydon; Queen Mary Coll., London; Trinity Coll., Cambridge. BSc (London) 1942; PhD (London) 1946; BA (Cantab) 1948; MB, BChir Cantab 1951; MRCP 1953; MD Cantab 1956; MA Cantab 1963; FRCP 1964. Pres. Cambridge Univ. Medical Soc., 1947–48; Sen. Schol., Trinity Coll., Cambridge, 1948; MRC (Eli Lilly) Trav. Fellow, 1956; Vis. Scientist, Nat. Inst. of Health, 1957; Lectr in Medicine and Chem. Path., St Thomas's Hosp. Medical Sch., 1954; Reader in Medicine, St Thomas's Hosp. Medical Sch., London, 1962. Vis. Prof. in Physiology and Medicine, N Carolina Med. Sch., USA, 1972. Mem., Hunter Working Party on Medical Administrators, 1970–72. Sec., Soc. for Endocrinology, 1963–71; Mem. Council, RCP, 1971–74. Pro-Censor, RCP, 1974–75, Censor, 1975–76; Chm., Scientific Adv. Cttee, Mason Med. Res. Foundation, 1982–88. Hon. FACP. *Publications:* Clinical Aspects of Adrenal Function, 1964; contrib. Lancet, Science Jl of Endocr., Clin. Science, etc. *Recreation:* gardening. *Address:* 6 Spinney Drive, Great Shelford, Cambridge CB2 5LY.

MILLS, John; *see* Mills, Laurence J.

MILLS, John F. F. P.; *see* Platts-Mills.

MILLS, Sir John (Lewis Ernest Watts), Kt 1976; CBE 1960; Actor, Producer, Director; *b* 22 Feb. 1908; *m* 1941, Mary Hayley Bell, playwright; one *s* two *d*. *Educ:* Norwich. 1st appearance, stage, 1929. *Plays:* Cavalcade, London Wall, Words and Music, Five O'clock Girl, Give Me a Ring, Jill Darling, Floodlight, Red Night, We at the Cross Roads, Of Mice and Men, Men in Shadow, Duet for Two Hands, etc.; Old Vic Season, 1938; Top of the Ladder; Figure of Fun, Aldwych; Ross, New York, 1961; Power of Persuasion, Garrick, 1963; Veterans, Royal Court, 1972; At the End of the Day, Savoy, 1973; The Good Companions, Her Majesty's, 1974; Separate Tables, Apollo, 1977; Goodbye, Mr Chips, Chichester Fest., 1982; Little Lies, Wyndham's, 1983; The Petition, NT, (transf. Wyndham's) 1986; Pygmalion, Guildford and NY, 1987; When the Wind Blows (TV play), 1987. *Films:* The Midshipmaid, Britannia of Billingsgate, Brown on Resolution, OHMS, Cottage To Let, The Young Mr Pitt, We Dive at Dawn, In Which We Serve, The Way to the Stars, Great Expectations, So Well Remembered, The October Man, Scott of the Antarctic, The History of Mr Polly, The Rocking Horse Winner, Morning Departure, Mr Denning Drives North, Gentle Gunman, The Long Memory, Hobson's Choice, The Colditz Story, The End of the Affair, Above Us the Waves, Town on Trial, Escapade, Its Great to be Young, The Baby and the Battleship, War and Peace, Around the World in Eighty Days, Dunkirk, Ice Cold in Alex, I Was Monty's Double, Summer of the Seventeenth Doll, Tiger Bay, Swiss Family Robinson, The Singer not the Song, Tunes of Glory, Flame in the Streets, The Valiant, Tiara Tahiti, The Chalk Garden, The Truth about Spring, King Rat, Operation X Bow, Red Waggon, Sky West and Crooked (directed), The Wrong Box, The Family Way, Chuka, Showdown, Oh! What a Lovely War, The Return of the Boomerang, Ryan's Daughter (Best Supporting Actor Award, Oscar Award, 1971), Run Wild, Run Free, Emma Hamilton, Dulcima, Lamb, Young Winston, Oklahoma Crude, Trial by Combat, The Devil's Advocate, Great Expectations, The Big Sleep, Zulu Dawn, The 39 Steps, The Human Factor, Gandhi, Masks of Death, Murder with Mirrors, Who's That Girl?. Tribute to Her Majesty (film documentary), 1986. *TV and TV series:* The Zoo Gang, 1974; Quatermass, 1979; Tales of the Unexpected, 1979, 1980, 1981; Young at Heart, 1980, 1981, 1982; The True Story of Spit MacPhee; A Tale of Two Cities; Ending Up; A Woman of Substance. Member: SFTA (Vice-Pres.); RADA Council, 1965–; Chm., Stars Organization for Spastics, 1975–79. Pres., Mountview Theatre Sch., 1983–. Patron Life Mem., Variety Club. *Publications:* Up in the Clouds, Gentlemen Please (autobiog.), 1980; Book of Famous Firsts, 1984. *Recreations:* ski-ing, golf, painting. *Address:* c/o ICM, 388 Oxford Street, W1. *Clubs:* Garrick, St James's.

MILLS, John Robert, BSc; CEng, FIEE; CPhys, MInstP; Under Secretary and Deputy Director (Systems) Royal Signals and Radar Establishment, Ministry of Defence, 1976–77, retired; *b* 12 Nov. 1916; *s* of Robert Edward Mills and Constance H. Mills; *m* 1950, Pauline Phelps; two *s*. *Educ:* Kingston Grammar Sch., Kingston-upon-Thames; King's Coll., London (BSc 1939); MInstP; FIEE, 1971. Air Ministry Research Estab., Dundee, 1939; RAE Farnborough, 1940–42; TRE, later RRE, Malvern, 1942–60; Supt (Offensive), Airborne Radar, RRE, 1954–60; Asst Dir, Electronics R and D (Civil Aviation), Min. of Aviation, 1960–61; Head of Radio Dept, RAE Farnborough, 1961–65; Electronics Div.,

Min. of Technology, 1965–67; Dir, Signals R&D Establishment, Christchurch, 1967–76. *Publications:* (jointly) Radar article in Encyclopædia Britannica; various papers in journals. *Address:* Meadowbank, Holly Green, Upton-upon-Severn, Worcester WR8 0PG.

MILLS, John William, OBE 1945; QC 1962; *b* 24 Oct. 1914; *s* of late John William Mills, OBE and Jessie Mills; *m* 1942, Phyllis Mary, *yr d* of late Arthur Gibson Pears; no *c*. *Educ:* Clifton; Corpus Christi Coll., Cambridge (MA). Called to Bar, Middle Temple, 1938; Bencher, 1968; Treas., 1985; retired 1987. Lt-Col, Royal Signals, 1944; Comdr, Royal Signals, 46 Div., 1944; Hon. Lt-Col 1946. Member: Bar Council, 1961–64; Clifton Coll. Council, 1967–80. *Publication:* (editor/author) Wurtzburg, Law Relating to Building Societies, subseq. Wurtzburg and Mills, Building Society Law, 10th edn 1952 to 14th edn 1988, Ed. Emeritus of 15th edn 1989. *Recreations:* sailing, golf. *Address:* 38 Adam and Eve Mews, W8 6UJ. *T:* 071–937 1259; Greenleas, Highleigh, Chichester, Sussex PO20 7NP. *T:* Sidlesham (0243) 641396.

MILLS, (Laurence) John, CBE 1978; FEng 1978; Chairman: Osprey Belt Company Ltd, since 1986; Specialist Training and Technical Services Ltd, since 1989; Member, 1974–82, a Deputy Chairman, 1982–84, National Coal Board; *b* 1 Oct. 1920; *s* of late Archibald John and Annie Ellen Mills; *m* 1944, Barbara May (*née* Warner); two *s*. *Educ:* Portsmouth Grammar Sch.; Birmingham Univ. BSc (Hons); Hon. FIMinE, CIMEMME; CBIM. Mining Student, Houghton Main Colliery Co. Ltd, 1939; Corps of Royal Engrs, 1942–46, Major 1946; various mining appts, Nat. Coal Bd, 1947–67; Chief Mining Engr, HQ NCB, 1968; Area Dir, N Yorks Area, 1970; Area Dir, Doncaster Area, 1973. Chm., British Mining Consultants Ltd, 1983–85; Director: Coal Develts (Queensland) Ltd, 1980–84; Capricorn Coal Management Pty Ltd, 1981–84; Coal Develts (German Creek) Pty Ltd, 1980–84; German Creek Pty Ltd, 1981–84; Burnett and Hallamshire Holdings plc, 1986–88. Member: Mining Qualifications Bd, 1975–83; Safety in Mines Res. Adv. Bd, 1975–83; Adv. Council on Res. Develt for Fuel and Power, 1981–83. Pres., IMinE, 1975. Silver Medal, Midland Counties Instn of Engrs, 1959 and 1962; Douglas Hay Medal, IMinE, 1977; Clerk Maxwell Medal, Assoc. of Mining, Electrical and Mech. Engrs (now IMEMME), 1979; Robens Coal Science Lecture Gold Medal, 1981; Institution Medal, IMinE, 1982. *Publications:* techn. papers in Trans IMinE. *Recreation:* coastal and inland waterway cruising. *Address:* Unit 4, Bowers Parade, Harpenden, Herts AL5 2SH.

MILLS, Lawrence William Robert; Chief Executive, Dubai Commerce and Tourism Promotion Board, since 1989; *b* London, 7 May 1934; *s* of William H. Mills and late Ellaline May Mills; *m* 1964, Amy Kwai Lan (*née* Poon), Shanghai and Hong Kong; two *d*. *Educ:* Reigate Grammar Sch., Surrey. National Service: RN, 1953; Intell. Corps, 1954. Formerly, Jun. Exec., K. F. Mayer Ltd, London. Hong Kong Govt (Mem. of HMOCS): Exec. Officer, Cl. II, 1958; Asst Trade Officer, 1960; Trade Officer, 1964; Sen. Trade Officer, 1968; Principal Trade Officer, 1969; Asst Dir of Commerce and Industry, 1971; Chief Trade Negotiator, 1974–75, 1977–79, 1981–83; Counsellor (Hong Kong Affairs), UK Mission, Geneva, 1976–77; Director of Trade, Hong Kong, 1977–79, 1981–83; Comr of Industry, 1979–81; Regional Sec., Hong Kong and Kowloon, 1983; Official MLC, Hong Kong, 1983; retired from Hong Kong Govt Service, 1983. Chief Exec., Laws Fashion Knitters Ltd, Hong Kong and Sri Lanka, 1983–85. Dir Gen., Fedn of Hong Kong Industries, 1985–89. *Recreation:* music (classical jazz). *Address:* Dubai Commerce and Tourism Promotion Board, PO Box 594, Dubai, United Arab Emirates. *Clubs:* Naval and Military; Hong Kong, Hong Kong Country, Clearwater Bay Golf and Country (Hong Kong); Emirates Golf (Dubai).

MILLS, Leif Anthony; General Secretary, Banking, Insurance and Finance Union (formerly National Union of Bank Employees), since 1972; Member, Monopolies and Mergers Commission, since 1982; *b* 25 March 1936; *s* of English father and Norwegian mother; *m* 1958, Gillian Margaret Smith; two *s* two *d*. *Educ:* Balliol Coll., Oxford. BA Hons PPE. Commnd in Royal Military Police, 1957–59. Trade Union Official, Nat. Union of Bank Employees, 1960–: Research Officer, 1960; Asst Gen. Sec., 1962; Dep. Gen. Sec., 1968. Mem. various arbitration tribunals; Member: TUC Non-Manual Workers Adv. Cttee, 1967–72; TUC Gen. Council, 1983–; Office of Manpower Economics Adv. Cttee on Equal Pay, 1971; Chairman: TUC Financial Services Cttee, 1983–; TUC Educn and Training Cttee, 1989–. Member: Cttee to Review the Functioning of Financial Institutions, 1977–80; CS Pay Res. Unit Bd, 1978–81; BBC Consultative Gp on Social Effects of Television, 1978–80; Armed Forces Pay Review Body, 1980–87. Contested (Lab) Salisbury, 1964, 1965 (by-elecn). Mem. Governing Body, London Business Sch., 1988–. Trustee, Civic Trust, 1988–. *Publications:* biography (unpublished), Cook: A History of the Life and Explorations of Dr Frederick Albert Cook, SPRI ms 883, Cambridge, 1970. *Recreations:* rowing, chess. *Address:* 31 Station Road, West Byfleet, Surrey. *T:* Byfleet (09323) 42829. *Clubs:* United Oxford & Cambridge University; Oxford University Boat, Weybridge Rowing.

MILLS, Leonard Sidney, CB 1970; Deputy Director General (2), Highways, Department of the Environment, 1970–74; *b* 20 Aug. 1914; *s* of late Albert Edward Mills; *m* 1940, Kathleen Joyce Cannicott; two *s*. *Educ:* Devonport High Sch.; London Sch. of Economics; Birkbeck Coll., University of London. Entered Exchequer and Audit Dept, 1933; transferred to Min. of Civil Aviation, 1946; Asst Sec., 1950; Min. of Transport: Under-Sec., 1959; Chief of Highway Administration, 1968–70. Commonwealth Fund Fellow, 1953–54. *Recreations:* walking, croquet, photography, gardening. *Address:* Pine Rise, 7A Bedlands Lane, Budleigh Salterton, Devon EX9 6QH.

MILLS, Mary Bell McMillan, (Mrs Ian Mills); *see* MacMurray, M. B. McM.

MILLS, Neil McLay; Chairman, Sedgwick Group plc, 1979–84; *b* 29 July 1923; *yr s* of late L. H. Mills; *m* 1950, Rosamund Mary Kimpton, *d* of Col and Hon. Mrs A. C. W. Kimpton; two *s* two *d*. *Educ:* Epsom Coll.; University Coll. London. Served War, 1940–46: commnd RN; Lieut RNVR; Coastal Forces (mentioned in despatches, 1944). Joined Bland Welch & Co. Ltd, 1948; Exec. Dir, 1955; Chm., 1965–74; Chm., Bland Payne Holdings Ltd, 1974–79. Underwriting Mem. of Lloyd's, 1955–91. Director: Montagu Trust Ltd, 1966–74; Midland Bank Ltd, 1974–79; Wadlow Grosvenor International Ltd, 1984–88; Threadneedle Publishing Co. (formerly AVI Ltd), 1987–. Vice-President: Insurance Inst. of London, 1971–84; British Insurance Brokers Assoc., 1978–84 (Mem., Internat. Insurance Brokers Cttee); Mem. Cttee, Lloyd's Insurance Brokers Assoc., 1974–77. Member: Church Army Board, 1957–64 (Vice-Chm., 1959–64); Council, Oak Hill Theol Coll., 1958–62. Trustee and Governor, Lord Mayor Treloar Trust, 1975–81. *Recreations:* farming, mowing. *Address:* 15 Markham Square, SW3 4UY. *T:* 071–584 3995; The Dower House, Upton Grey, near Basingstoke, Hants. *T:* Basingstoke (0256) 862435.
See also Sir Peter (McLay) Mills.

MILLS, Air Marshal Sir Nigel (Holroyd), KBE 1991; FRCGP; FRCP; QHP 1988; Surgeon General, since 1990, and Director General Medical Services (Royal Air Force), since 1987; *b* 12 Nov. 1932; *s* of Air Chief Marshal Sir George (Holroyd) Mills, GCB, DFC, and Mary Austen Mills (*née* Smith); *m* 1956, Pamela (*née* Jones); three *d*. *Educ:* Berkhamsted Sch.; Middlesex Hosp. Med. Sch. (MB, BS). FFOM; DipAvMed; FRCGP 1991; FRCP 1991. OC RAF Inst. of Occupational and Community Medicine, 1979–82; OC RAF Med. Rehabilitation Unit, Headley Court, 1982–83; Dep. PMO, HQ RAF Strike Comd, 1983–84; PMO, RAF Germany, 1984–86; RCDS 1987; Dep. Surg. Gen. (Res. and Training, later Health Services), 1987–90. FRSM 1988. CStJ 1987. *Recreations:* sailing/windsurfing, computing. *Address:* c/o Lloyds Bank, Cox's and King's Branch, PO Box 1190, 7 Pall Mall, SW1Y 5NA. *Club:* Royal Air Force.

MILLS, Sir Peter (Frederick Leighton), 3rd Bt, *cr* 1921; *b* 9 July 1924; *s* of Major Sir Frederick Leighton Victor Mills, 2nd Bt, MC, RA, MICE, and Doris (*née* Armitage); *S* father 1955; *m* 1954, Pauline Mary, *d* of L. R. Allen, Calverton, Notts; one *s* (one adopted *d* decd). *Educ:* Eastbourne Coll.; Cedara Coll. of Agriculture, University of Natal (BSc Agric.). Served HM Forces, 1943–47. CS, Fedn Rhodesia and Nyasaland, 1953; with Rhodesia Min. of Agric., 1964, Zimbabwe Min. of Agric., 1980–90. *Heir: s* Michael Victor Leighton Mills, *b* 30 Aug. 1957. *Address:* PO Box A474, Avondale, Harare, Zimbabwe.

MILLS, Sir Peter (McLay), Kt 1982; *b* 22 Sept. 1921; *m* 1948, Joan Weatherley; one *s* one *d*. *Educ:* Epsom; Wye Coll. MP (C): Torrington, 1964–74; Devon W, 1974–83; Torridge and W Devon, 1983–87. Parly Sec., MAFF, 1972; Parly Under-Sec. of State, NI Office, 1972–74. Member: European Legislation Cttee, EEC, 1974–79; Select Cttee on Foreign Affairs, 1980–82; Dep. Chm., CPA, 1982–85; Chairman: Cons. Agriculture Cttee, 1979–87; Houses of Parlt Christian Fellowship, 1970–87; Minister of Agric. Panel for SW England, 1988–. Dir, Torridge Trng Ltd, 1987–; Chm., Devon Cable Vision Ltd, 1984–; Regl Chm., Portman Bldg Soc. (formerly Regency and W of England Bldg Soc.), 1988– *Recreations:* work and staying at home for a short time. *Address:* Priestcombe, Crediton, Devon EX17 5BT.

MILLS, Peter William; QC (Can.) 1985; Senior Vice President since 1988, General Counsel since 1980 and Director since 1982, The Woodbridge Company Limited (Vice President, 1980–87); Director: Hudson's Bay Company, since 1985; Markborough Properties Inc., since 1986; *b* 22 July 1942; *s* of Joseph Roger Mills and Jane Eveyln (*née* Roscoe); *m* 1967, Eveline Jane (*née* Black); two *s*. *Educ:* Dalhousie Univ. Law Sch. (LLB); Dalhousie Univ. (BComm). Barrister and solicitor, Ont, Canada; with McInnes, Cooper and Robertson, Halifax, 1967; Solicitor, Canadian Pacific Ltd, Montreal and Toronto, 1967–71; Dir, Cammell Laird Shipbuilders Ltd, 1971–76; Mem. Org. Cttee for British Shipbuilders, 1976–77; Manager, Currie, Coopers & Lybrand Ltd, Toronto, 1977–79; Dir, Corporate Develt, FP Publications Ltd, 1979–80. *Recreations:* golf, sailing, travel, reading. *Address:* The Woodbridge Company Limited, 65 Queen Street West, Toronto, Ont M5H 2M8, Canada. *Fax:* (416) 367–3549; 390 Glencairn Avenue, Toronto, Ont M5N 1V1. *Clubs:* Board of Trade, York Downs Golf and Country (Toronto); Royal Liverpool Golf (Hoylake).

MILLS, Richard Michael; Chairman, since 1979, and Chief Executive, since 1970, Bernard Delfont Ltd; *b* 26 June 1931; *s* of Richard Henry Mills and Catherine Keeley; *m* 1st, 1960, Lynda Taylor (marr. diss. 1967); one *d*; 2nd, 1983, Sheila White; two *s*. Commenced working in the theatre as an Assistant Stage Manager in 1948, and worked in every capacity, including acting and stage management. Joined Bernard Delfont Ltd, 1962; Dir, 1967; Dep. Chm. and Chief Exec., 1970; Chm. and Chief Exec., 1979; Managing Director: Prince of Wales Theatre, 1970–; Prince Edward Theatre, 1978–. Member: Nat. Theatre Bd, 1976–; Finance and Gen. Purposes Cttee, NT, 1976–; Drama Panel, Arts Council of GB, 1976–77; English Tourist Bd, 1982–85. Shows worked on in the West End, 1948–62, include: I Remember Mama, Tuppence Coloured, Medea, Adventure Story, Anne Veronica, The Devil's General, I Capture the Castle, No Escape, Three Times a Day, The Sun of York, To my Love, Be my Guest, Hunter's Moon, The Iceman Cometh, Brouhaha, Detour after Dark, The Ginger Man, Sound of Murder, Will You Walk a Little Faster, Pool's Paradise, Belle, Come Blow your Horn. Whilst Gen. Manager and Dir with Bernard Delfont Ltd: Never Too Late, Pickwick, 1962; Caligula, Maggie May, Little Me, Our Man Crichton, 1963; The Roar of the Greasepaint (NY), Pickwick (NY), Twang, Barefoot in the Park, 1964; The Owl and the Pussycat, The Matchgirls, Funny Girl, Joey Joey, The Odd Couple, 1965; Queenie, Sweet Charity, The Four Musketeers, 1966; Golden Boy, Look Back in Anger (rivival), 1967; Mame, Cat Among the Pigeons, 1968; Carol Channing, Danny La Rue at the Palace, 1969; Kean, Lulu, 1970; Applause, The Unknown Soldier and his Wife, 1971. With Lord Delfont has presented in the West End: The Good Old Bad Old Days, Mardi Gras, Brief Lives, Queen Daniella, Cinderella, Henry IV, Harvey, Sammy Cahn's Songbook, Streetcar Named Desire, Good Companions, It's All Right if I Do It, Charley's Aunt, An Evening with Tommy Steele, Gomes, The Wolf, Danny La Rue Show, Beyond the Rainbow, Dad's Army, Plumber's Progress, Paul Daniels Magic Show, Underneath the Arches, Little Me, and over 100 pantomimes and summer season shows. *Recreations:* golf, poker. *Address:* Prince of Wales Theatre, Coventry Street, W1V 8AS. *T:* 071–930 9901. *Clubs:* Royal Automobile; Wentworth Golf, Royal Mid-Surrey Golf.

MILLS, Robert Ferris; Under Secretary, Department of Finance and Personnel, Northern Ireland, since 1990; *b* 21 Sept. 1939; *s* of Robert and Rachel Mills; *m* 1st, 1968, Irene Sandra Miskelly (marr. diss. 1978); one *s* one *d*; 2nd, 1984, Frances Elizabeth Gillies; two step *d*. *Educ:* Sullivan Upper School, Holywood, Co. Down; Queen's Univ., Belfast (BA Hons). Inland Revenue, 1961–64; Min. of Commerce, NI, 1964–68; Dept of Housing and Local Govt, 1968–71; Dept of the Environment, NI, 1971–75; Asst Sec., 1975–83, Under Sec., 1983–90, Dept of Health and Social Services, NI. *Recreations:* golf, tennis. *Address:* Parliament Buildings, Belfast.

MILLS, Air Cdre Stanley Edwin Druce, CB 1968; CBE 1959; Royal Air Force, retired; *b* 1913; *s* of Edwin J. Mills; *m* 1938, Joan Mary, *d* of Robert Ralph James; one *s* one *d*. *Educ:* Collegiate Sch., Bournemouth, RAF Staff Coll. Entered RAF 1939; served RAF Middle East and Italy, 1942–45; Station Comdr, RAF Innsworth, 1957–60; Comd Accountant, RAF Germany, 1960–63; Dir of Personnel (Policy) (Air), MoD, 1963–65; Dir of Personal Services (Air), MoD, 1966–68. Bursar, Roedean Sch., 1968–73. FCA. *Recreation:* travel. *Address:* Maryland, Lullington Close, Seaford, E Sussex BN25 4JH. *T:* Seaford (0323) 895468. *Club:* Royal Air Force.

MILLS, Stratton; *see* Mills, W. S.

MILLS, Wilbur Daigh; lawyer and politician, USA; tax consultant, Shea & Gould (Mirabelli & Gould), since 1977; *b* Kensett, Ark, 24 May 1909; *s* of Ardra Pickens Mills and Abbie Lois Daigh; *m* 1934, Clarine Billingsley; two *d*. *Educ:* Hendrix Coll.; Harvard Law Sch. Admitted to State Bar of Arkansas, 1933; in private legal practice, Searcy; County and Probate Judge, White County, 1934–38; Cashier, Bank of Kensett, 1934–35. Mem., US House of Representatives, 1939–76 (Chm., Ways and Means Cttee, 1958–76). Democrat. *Address:* (office) 1775 Pennsylvania Avenue, Washington, DC 20006, USA; Kensett, Arkansas 72082, USA.

MILLS, Maj.-Gen. (William) Graham (Stead), CBE 1963; *b* 23 June 1917; *s* of William Stead Mills and Margaret Kennedy Mills; *m* 8 July 1941, Joyce Evelyn (*née* Ransom) (*d* 1981); three *s*. *Educ:* Merchiston Castle Sch., Edinburgh. Regtl duty, Royal Berks Regt, in India, 1938–43; Staff Coll., India, 1944; GSO2 and GSO1, Ops HQ 14th Army, Burma,

1944–45; despatches, 1945; WO and Washington, USA, 1946–50; Regtl duty with Parachute Regt, comdg 17th Bn, The Parachute Regt, 1958–60; GSO1, 2 Div. BAOR, 1956–58; Regtl Col The Parachute Regt, 1960–62; Comdg TA Brigade, Winchester, 1963–64; Brig. GS, HQ Middle East Comd, Aden, 1965–66; Imperial Defence Coll., Student, 1967; GOC West Midland District, 1968–70. Head of Home, Le Court Cheshire Home, 1972–77; Mem. Management Cttee, Park House Sandringham (Cheshire Foundn Country House Hotel for Disabled People), 1983–88. *Recreations:* normal. *Address:* Inglenook, Field Dalling, Holt, Norfolk. *T:* Binham (032875) 388.

MILLS, (William) Stratton; Partner in Mills, Selig & Bailie, Solicitors, Belfast; Company Director; *b* 1 July 1932; *o s* of late Dr J. V. S. Mills, CBE, Resident Magistrate for City of Belfast, and Margaret Florence (*née* Byford); *m* 1959, Merriel E. R. Whitla, *o d* of late Mr and Mrs R. J. Whitla, Belfast; three *s*. *Educ:* Campbell Coll., Belfast; Queen's Univ., Belfast (LLB). Vice-Chm., Federation of University Conservative and Unionist Assocs, 1952–53 and 1954–55; admitted a Solicitor, 1958. MP (UU) Belfast N, Oct. 1959–Dec. 1972; MP (Alliance) Belfast N, Apr. 1973–Feb. 1974; PPS to Parly Sec., Ministry of Transport, 1961–64; Member: Estimates Cttee, 1964–70; Exec. Cttee, 1922 Cttee, 1967–70, 1973; Hon. Sec. Conservative Broadcasting Cttee, 1963–70, Chm., 1970–73; Mem., Mr Speaker's Conference on Electoral Law, 1967. Mem., One Nation Gp, 1972–73. Chm., Ulster Orchestra Soc. Ltd, 1980–90. Mem. Council, Winston Churchill Meml Trust, 1990–. *Address:* (office) 20 Callender Street, Belfast BT1 5BQ. *T:* Belfast 243878; (home) 17 Malone Park, Belfast BT9 6NJ. *T:* Belfast (0232) 665210. *Clubs:* Carlton; Reform (Belfast).

MILLSON, John Albert; Assistant Under-Secretary of State, Ministry of Defence, 1972–78; *b* 4 Oct. 1918; *s* of late George Charles Millson and Annie Millson, London; *m* 1953, Megan Laura Woodiss; one *s* one *d*. *Educ:* St Olave's. Entered Air Min., 1936; Private Sec. to Parly Under-Sec. of State for Air, 1947–50; Principal, Air Min., 1955; Asst Sec., MoD, 1961; Asst Under-Sec. of State, 1972. Chm. of Governors, Homefield Prep. Sch., Sutton, 1975. *Recreations:* walking, listening to music. *Address:* 9 The Highway, Sutton, Surrey SM2 5QT. *T:* 081–642 3967.

MILLWARD, William, CB 1969; CBE 1954; with Government Communications Headquarters, 1946–74, retired (Superintending Director, 1958–69); *b* 27 Jan. 1909; *s* of William John and Alice Millward; *m* 1937, Nora Florella Harper; one *s* one *d*. *Educ:* Solihull Sch.; St Catherine's Society, Oxford. Asst Master, Dulwich Coll., 1930–41; RAF, 1941–46. *Recreations:* music, reading, walking. *Address:* 37 Pegasus Court, St Stephen's Road, Cheltenham. *T:* Cheltenham (0242) 525732.

MILMAN, Andrée, (Mrs David Milman); *see* Grenfell, A.

MILMAN, Lt-Col Sir Derek, 9th Bt *cr* 1800, of Levaton-in-Woodland, Devonshire; MC 1941; *b* 23 June 1918; *s* of Brig.-Gen. Sir Lionel Charles Patrick Milman, 7th Bt, CMG and Marjorie Aletta (*d* 1980), *d* of Col A. H. Clark-Kennedy; *S* brother, 1990; *m* 1942, Margaret Christine Whitehouse; two *s*. *Educ:* Bedford School; Sandhurst. Commnd Unattached List IA, 1938; joined 3/2nd Punjab Regt, 1939; served War of 1939–45, Eritrea (MC, despatches), N Africa, Burma; with Pakistan Army, 1947–50; joined 1st Bn Beds and Herts Regt, 1950; Instructor, RMA Sandhurst, 1957; comd 5th Beds TA, 1959–61; retired, 1963. Instructor, Civil Defence Staff Coll., 1963–68; London Business School, 1970–83. *Recreation:* bird watching. *Heir:* *s* David Patrick Milman [*b* 24 Aug. 1945; *m* 1969, Christina Hunt; one *s* one *d*]. *Address:* Forge Cottage, Wilby Road, Stradbroke, Eye, Suffolk IP21 5JN. *T:* Stradbroke (0379) 384225.

MILMINE, Rt. Rev. Douglas, CBE 1983; *b* 3 May 1921; *s* of Alexander Douglas Milmine and Rose Gertrude Milmine (*née* Moore); *m* 1945, Margaret Rosalind, *d* of Edward and Gladys Whitley, Kilmorie, Meadfoot, Torquay; three *s* one *d*. *Educ:* Sutton Valence School; St Peter's Hall, Oxford (MA 1946); Clifton Theological Coll. Deacon 1947, priest 1948; Curate: SS Philip and James, Ilfracombe, 1947–50; St Paul's, Slough, 1950–53; missionary with South American Missionary Society: Maquehue, Chile, 1954; Temuco, 1955–60; Santiago, 1961–68; Archdeacon of N Chile, Bolivia and Peru, 1964–68; Hon. Canon of Chile, 1969–72; Midland Area Sec. of SAMS, 1969–72; Bishop in Paraguay, 1973–85; retired 1986. *Recreations:* study of current affairs, walking. *Address:* 1c Clive Court, 24 Grand Parade, Eastbourne, East Sussex BN21 3DD. *T:* Eastbourne (0323) 34159.

MILMO, John Boyle Martin; QC 1984; a Recorder of the Crown Court, since 1982; *b* 19 Jan. 1943; *s* of Dermod Hubert Francis Milmo, MB BCh and Eileen Clare Milmo (*née* White). *Educ:* Downside Sch.; Trinity Coll., Dublin. MA, LLB. Called to the Bar, Lincoln's Inn, 1966. *Recreations:* opera, discography. *Address:* 1 High Pavement, Nottingham NG1 1HF. *T:* Nottingham (0602) 418218. *Club:* United Services (Nottingham).

MILMO, Patrick Helenus; QC 1985; *b* 11 May 1938; *s* of Sir Helenus Milmo; *m* 1968, Marina, *d* of late Alexis Schiray and of Xenia Schiray, rue Jules Simon, Paris; one *s* one *d*. *Educ:* Downside; Trinity Coll., Cambridge (BA 1961). Harmsworth Scholar; called to the Bar, Middle Temple, 1962. *Recreations:* wine, horse-racing, cinema. *Address:* 10 South Square, Gray's Inn, WC1; 7 Baalbec Road, N5. *Club:* Lansdowne.

MILNE, family name of **Baron Milne.**

MILNE, 2nd Baron, *cr* 1933, of Salonika and of Rubislaw, Co. Aberdeen; **George Douglass Milne,** TD; *b* 10 Feb. 1909; *s* of 1st Baron Milne, GCB, GCMG, DSO, Field Marshal from 1928, and Claire Marjoribanks, MBE, DGStJ (*d* 1970), *d* of Sir John N. Maitland, 5th Bt; *S* father, 1948; *m* 1940, Cicely, 3rd *d* of late Ronald Leslie; two *s* one *d*. *Educ:* Winchester; New Coll., Oxford. Mem., Inst. of Chartered Accountants of Scotland. Partner, Arthur Young McClelland Moores Co., 1954–73; Dir, London & Northern Group Ltd, 1973–87 (Dep. Chm., 1981). Master of the Grocers' Company, 1961–62, Sen. Court Mem., 1984–90. Served War of 1939–45, Royal Artillery (TA); prisoner of war, 1941; NWEF and MEF (wounded, despatches). *Recreation:* art: has exhibited RA, ROI, RP. *Heir:* *s* Hon. George Alexander Milne, *b* 1 April 1941. *Address:* 33 Lonsdale Road, Barnes, SW13 9JP. *T:* 081–748 6421.

MILNE, Alasdair David Gordon; Director, ABU Television Ltd, since 1988; Director-General, BBC, 1982–87; *b* 8 Oct. 1930; *s* of late Charles Gordon Shaw Milne and of Edith Reid Clark; *m* 1954, Sheila Kirsten Graucob; two *s* one *d*. *Educ:* Winchester Coll.; New Coll., Oxford (Hon. Fellow, 1985). Commnd into 1st Bn Gordon Highlanders, 1949. Hon. Mods Oxon 1952; BA Oxon Mod. Langs, 1954. Joined BBC, 1954; Dep. Editor, 1957–61, Editor, 1961–62, of Tonight Programme; Head of Tonight Productions, 1963–65; Partner, Jay, Baverstock, Milne & Co., 1965–67; rejoined BBC, Oct. 1967; Controller, BBC Scotland, 1968–72; Dir of Programmes, 1973–77, Man. Dir, 1977–82, BBC TV; Dep. Dir-Gen., BBC, 1980–82. Chm., Darrell Waters Ltd, 1988–90. Vis. Prof., Univ. of Miami, 1989. Vice-Pres., RTS, 1986–87. DUniv Stirling, 1983. Cyril Bennett Award, RTS, 1987. *Publication:* DG: the memoirs of a British broadcaster, 1988. *Recreations:* piping, salmon fishing, golf, tennis. *Address:* 30 Holland Park Avenue, W11 3QU. *Club:* Travellers'.

MILNE, (Alexander) Berkeley, OBE 1968; HM Diplomatic Service, retired; *b* 12 Feb. 1924; *s* of George and Mary Milne; *m* 1952, Patricia Mary (*née* Holderness); one *s* two *d*. *Educ:* Keith Grammar and Buckie High Schs, Banffshire, Scotland; Univ. of Aberdeen (MA (Hons Mental Phil.) 1943); University Coll., Oxford (BA (Hons Persian and Arabic) 1949). 3/2nd Punjab Regt, Indian Army: service in India and Java, 1943–46. Scarborough Schol., Tehran Univ., 1950–51; Lectr in Persian, Edinburgh Univ., 1951–52. Foreign Office, 1952–53; BMEO, Cyprus, 1953–54; Third, later Second Sec., Tehran, 1954–57; FO, 1958–61; Second, later First Sec., Brussels, 1961–64; FO (later FCO), 1964–65; First Sec., British Residual Mission, Salisbury, Rhodesia, 1966–67; First Sec., Jedda, Saudi Arabia, 1968–70; FCO, 1971–74; Counsellor, Tehran, 1974–77; GCHQ, 1978–83. Consultant, Oman Govt, 1983–86. *Recreations:* gardening, reading; playing chamber music, preferably second violin in string quartets. *Address:* 3 Paragon Terrace, Cheltenham, Glos GL53 7LA. *T:* Cheltenham (0242) 234849.

MILNE, Alexander Taylor; Fellow of University College London; Secretary and Librarian, Institute of Historical Research, University of London, 1946–71; *b* 22 Jan. 1906; *s* of late Alexander Milne and Shanny (*née* Taylor); *m* 1960, Joyce Frederica Taylor, Dulwich. *Educ:* Christ's Coll., Finchley; University Coll., London. BA History Hons 1927; Diploma in Education, 1928; MA (London), 1930; FRHistS, 1938; Vice-Pres., Historical Assoc., 1956–70, Pres., 1970–73; Asst Officer and Librarian, Royal Historical Society, 1935–40; Hon. Librarian, 1965–70. Fellow, Huntington Library, Calif, 1975. Served War of 1939–45: Buffs and Maritime Artillery, 1940–42; Army Bureau of Current Affairs, 1942–44; Research Dept, FO, 1944–46. Director, History Today, 1962–79. *Publications:* History of Broadwindsor, Dorset, 1935; Catalogue of the Manuscripts of Jeremy Bentham in the Library of University College, London, 1937, 2nd edn 1961; Writings on British History, 1934–45: a Bibliography (8 vols), 1937–60; Centenary Guide to Pubns of Royal Historical Society, 1968; (part-author) Historical Study in the West, 1968; (ed) Librarianship and Literature, essays in honour of Jack Pafford, 1970; (ed) Correspondence of Jeremy Bentham, vols. IV and V, 1788–1797, 1981; contribs to Cambridge History of the British Empire, Encyclopædia Britannica and learned journals. *Recreation:* golf. *Address:* 9 Frank Dixon Close, Dulwich, SE21 7BD. *T:* 081–693 6942. *Clubs:* Athenæum, Dulwich (1772).

MILNE, Andrew McNicoll, MA; Director, Eastern Arts Association; *b* 9 March 1937; *s* of late John McNicoll Milne and Daviona K. Coutts; *m* 1963, Nicola Charlotte, 2nd *d* of Ian B. Anderson and Sylvia Spencer; two *d*. *Educ:* Bishop Wordsworth's Sch., Salisbury; Worcester Coll., Oxford (MA 1961). Oundle: apptd, 1961; Head of History Dept, 1966–70; Housemaster, 1968–75; Second Master, 1975–79; Headmaster, The King's Sch., Worcester, 1979–83; Editor, Conference and Common Room (HMC magazine), 1983–86; Eastern Arts Assoc., 1984–. *Publications:* Metternich, 1975; contrib. to Practical Approaches to the New History. *Recreations:* music (classical and jazz), reading, writing. *Address:* 3 Radwinter Road, Saffron Walden, Essex CB11 3HU. *T:* Saffron Walden (0799) 28148.

MILNE, Berkeley; *see* Milne, A. B.

MILNE, David Calder; QC 1987; FCA; *b* 22 Sept. 1945; *s* of Ernest and Helena Milne; *m* 1978, Rosemary (*née* Bond); one *d*. *Educ:* Harrow Sch.; Oxford Univ. (MA). ACA 1969; FCA 1974. Articled to Whinney Murray & Co., chartered accountants, 1966–69; called to Bar, Lincoln's Inn, 1970. Treas., London Common Law and Commercial Bar Assoc., 1975–88; Mem., Taxation and Retirement Benefit Cttee, Bar Council, 1978–. *Recreations:* natural history, music, golf, Rugby. *Address:* (chambers) 4 Pump Court, Temple, EC4. *T:* 071–583 9770; (home) 14a Castelnau, Barnes, SW13. *T:* 081–748 6415. *Clubs:* Garrick, Hurlingham, Gnomes; Walton Heath Golf.

MILNE, Denys Gordon, (Tiny), CBE 1982; Chairman: Occupational and Environmental Health Span Ltd, since 1986; Stag Petroleum Co. Ltd, since 1986; *b* 12 Jan. 1926; *s* of late Dr George Gordon Milne and of Margaret (*née* Campbell); *m* 1951, Pamela Mary Senior; two *s* one *d*. *Educ:* Epsom Coll.; Brasenose Coll., Oxford (MA Hons Mod. History). Pilot Officer, RAF Regt, RAFVR, 1944–47. Colonial Admin. Service, Northern Nigeria, 1951–55; British Petroleum Company, 1955–81, retired as Man. Dir and Chief Exec., BP Oil Ltd; Dir, Business in the Community, 1981–84. Director: Silkolene Lubricants Plc, 1981–; Fluor Daniel Ltd (formerly Fluor (GB)), 1981–90; The Weir Group Plc, 1983–; Aviva Petroleum Inc., 1989–; Concertainer Ltd, 1990–. Member: Scottish Economic Council, 1978–81; Adv. Cttee on Energy Conservation, 1980–81. President: UK Petroleum Industry Assoc., 1980–81; Inst. of Petroleum, 1978–80. Chm., Horder Centre for Arthritics, 1983–. Trustee, Nat. Motor Mus., 1979–89. Chm. Council, Epsom Coll., 1990–. Mem., Court of Assistants, Tallow Chandlers' Co., 1986–. *Recreations:* gardening, cruising. *Address:* Westbury, Old Lane, St Johns, Crowborough, East Sussex. *T:* Crowborough (0892) 652634. *Clubs:* Caledonian, Royal Air Force; Inanda (Johannesburg).

MILNE, Maj.-Gen. Douglas Graeme; retired; Civilian Medical Officer, Ministry of Defence, 1979–84; Deputy Director General Army Medical Services, 1975–78; *b* 19 May 1919; *s* of George Milne and Mary Panton; *m* 1944, Jean Millicent Gove; one *d*. *Educ:* Robert Gordon's Coll.; Aberdeen Univ. MB, ChB, FFCM, DPH. Commnd into RAMC, 1943; service in W Africa, Malta, Egypt, BAOR, Singapore; Dir of Army Health and Research, 1973–75. QHS 1974–78. Col Comdt, RAMC, 1979–84. OStJ 1976. *Recreations:* gardening, reading. *Address:* 17 Stonehill Road, SW14 8RR.

MILNE, Ian Innes, CMG 1965; OBE 1946; a Senior Clerk, House of Commons, 1969–76; *b* 16 June 1912; *e s* of Kenneth John Milne, CBE, and Maud Innes; *m* 1939, Marie Mange (*d* 1989); one *d*. *Educ:* Westminster Sch.; Christ Church, Oxford. Advertising, 1935–40; RE, 1940–46 (Lieut-Col). FO, 1946–68; 2nd Sec., Teheran, 1948–51; 1st Sec., Berne, 1955–56; 1st Sec., Tokyo, 1960–63; retired 1968. US Legion of Merit (Off.), 1946. *Recreations:* gardening, music. *Address:* Red Willows, Urgashay, Yeovil, Somerset BA22 8HH.

MILNE, James L.; *see* Lees-Milne.

MILNE, Sir John (Drummond), Kt 1986; Director: Royal Insurance PLC, since 1982; Witan Investment Co., since 1988; Avon Rubber plc, since 1989; Solvay & Cie SA, since 1990; *b* 13 Aug. 1924; *s* of Frederick John and Minnie Elizabeth Milne; *m* 1948, Joan Akroyd; two *s* two *d*. *Educ:* Stowe Sch.; Trinity Coll., Cambridge. Served Coldstream Guards, 1943–47. APCM (now Blue Circle Industries): management trainee, 1948; Asst to Director i/c Overseas Investments, 1953; President, Ocean Cement, Vancouver, 1957; Director, APCM, 1964, Man. Dir and Chief Exec., 1975; Blue Circle Industries: Chm. and Managing Director, 1983; Chm., 1983–90 (non-exec., 1987–90); DRG plc (formerly The Dickinson Robinson Group): Dir, 1973–89; Chm., 1987–89. *Recreations:* golf, shooting, ski-ing. *Address:* Chilton House, Chilton Candover, Hants SO24 9TX. *Clubs:* Boodle's, MCC; Berkshire Golf.

MILNE, Kenneth Lancelot, CBE 1971; chartered accountant; *b* 16 Aug. 1915; *s* of F. K. Milne, Adelaide; *m* 1st, 1941, Mary (*d* 1980), *d* of E. B. Hughes; two *s* one *d*; 2nd, 1982, Joan Constance Lee, *d* of Claude W. J. Lee. *Educ:* St Peter's Coll., Adelaide. Entered Public

Practice as a Chartered Acct, 1946; Elected to State Council, 1951, Chm. 1958–60, Mem. Gen. Council, 1956–60. Served with RAAF, 1940–45, attaining rank of Flt Lieut. Municipality of Walkerville: Councillor, 1960; Mayor, 1961–63; Municipal Assoc. 1961 (Pres. 1964–65); Pres. SA Br Aust. Inst. of Internat. Affairs, 1958–60; Mem. Faculty of Economics, University of Adelaide, 1963–65; Agent Gen. and Trade Comr for S Aust. in UK, 1966–71. MLC (Australian Democrat) SA, 1979–85 (Parlt Leader, 1983–85). President: SA Branch, Royal Overseas League, 1975–; Royal Life Saving Soc. of SA, 1977–. Chm., State Govt Insce Commn, 1971–79; Member: Commn on Advanced Educn, 1973–77; Universities Commn, 1977–. Chm., Stirling Dist Bicentennary Cttee, SA, 1987–89. Freeman, City of London, 1970. *Publications:* Ostrich Heads, 1937; Forgotten Freedom, 1952; The Accountant in Public Practice, 1959. *Recreations:* rowing, tennis, conchology. *Address:* 50 Birch Road, Stirling, SA 5152, Australia. *T:* 08339 3674. *Clubs:* Naval, Military and Air Force (Adelaide); Adelaide Rowing (Pres., 1986–) (SA).

MILNE, Maurice, CB 1976; FEng 1980; Deputy Director General of Highways, Department of the Environment, 1970–76; retired; *b* 22 July 1916; *s* of James Daniel Milne, stone mason, and Isabella Robertson Milne; *m* 1947, Margaret Elizabeth Stewart Monro; one *d* decd. *Educ:* Robert Gordon's Coll., Aberdeen; Aberdeen University. BScEng (1st cl. Hons). FICE, FIStructE, FIHT, FRTPI. Chief Asst, D. A. Donald & Wishart, Cons. Engrs, Glasgow, 1947–48; Sen. Engr and Chief Engr, Crawley Develt Corp., 1948–59; Engr, Weir Wood Water Board, 1953–57; County Engr and Surveyor, W Sussex CC, 1960–68; Dir, S Eastern Road Construction Unit, MoT, 1968–70. Chairman: Downland Housing Soc. Ltd, 1978–83; London and SE Region Anchor Housing Assoc., 1982–88. Trustee: Humane Research Trust, 1983–; Rees Jeffreys Road Fund, 1976–. (Chm., 1990–). Hon. Sec., County Surveyors' Soc., 1963–67; Pres., Instn Highway Engineers, 1974–75; Mem. Council, ICE, 1967–71 and 1972–75; Pres., Perm. Internat. Assoc. of Road Congresses, 1977–84 (Hon. Pres., 1988–). *Publications:* contributions to Jl Instn of Civil, Municipal and Highway Engrs. *Recreations:* gardening, camping, photography. *Address:* Struan, Walton Lane, Bosham, Chichester, West Sussex. *T:* Bosham (0243) 573304.

MILNE, Norman; Sheriff of North Strathclyde at Campbeltown and Oban, 1975–81, retired; *b* 31 Dec. 1915; *s* of William Milne and Jessie Ferguson; *m* 1947, Phyllis Christina Philip Rollo; no *c*. *Educ:* Logie Central Sch., Dundee. Solicitor, 1939. Army, 1939–46: active service in Madagascar, Sicily, Italy, and Germany (despatches). Procurator Fiscal Depute: Perth, 1946–51; Edinburgh, 1951–55; Senior Depute Fiscal, Glasgow, 1955–58; Procurator Fiscal: Banff, 1959–64; Kirkcaldy, 1964–65; Paisley, 1965–71; Edinburgh, 1971–75. *Recreation:* music. *Address:* The Anchorage, Machrihanish, Argyll PA28 6PT.

MILNE, Peter Alexander, PhD; CEng, FIMechE, FIMarE, FNECInst; Managing Director, BMT Cortec, since 1990; *b* 23 April 1935; *s* of late Alexander Ogston Milne and of Lilian Winifred Milne (*née* Murray); *m* 1961, Beatrice Taylor Reid; two *d*. *Educ:* Tynemouth Sch.; Harwell Reactor Sch. BSc Marine Engrg Univ. of Durham 1957; PhD Applied Sci. Univ. of Newcastle 1960. Practical experience with apprenticeship at Wallsend Slipway & Engineering and at sea with Union Castle Mail Steamship; Trainee Manager, Swan Hunter Gp, 1961; Technical Dir, Swan Hunter Shipbuilders, 1970–74, Man. Dir, 1974–77; British Shipbuilders HQ at formation of Corp., 1977; Man. Dir, Shipbuilding Ops, 1978–80, Mem. Bd, 1981–90 (Bd Mem. for Engrg, 1981–83, for Merchant Ship and Enginebuilding, 1985–90), Man. Dir, Merchant and Composite Div., 1984, British Shipbuilders. Dir, Vosper Thornycroft, 1978–80. Bd Mem., SMRTB, 1971–75; Chm., BSI Ind. Cttee, 1972–76; Dir, Lloyds Register of Shipping, 1984–; Chm., Northern Engrg Centre, 1990–. Vis. Lectr in Marine Engrg, Newcastle Univ., 1970–75. Pres., NECInst, 1986–88. Liveryman, Shipwrights' Co., 1984–. *Publications:* papers related to science and industry. *Recreations:* squash, cricket. *Address:* 104 Holywell Avenue, Whitley Bay, Tyne and Wear NE26 3AF. *T:* 091–252 2708.

MILNE HOME, Captain Archibald John Fitzwilliam, DL; RN, retired; Member of Queen's Body Guard for Scotland (Royal Company of Archers) since 1963; *b* 4 May 1909; *e s* of late Sir John Milne Home; *m* 1936, Evelyn Elizabeth, *d* of late Comdr A. T. Darley, RN; three *s* one *d*. *Educ:* RNC Dartmouth. Joined RN, 1923: Comdr 1946; Captain 1952; retd 1962; ADC to the Queen, 1961–62. Chm., Whitbread (Scotland), 1968–73. Chm., SE Region, Scottish Woodland Owners Assoc., 1966–78. DL Selkirkshire, 1970. Cross of Merit, SMO Malta, 1963. *Recreations:* shooting, fishing. *Address:* Horsemill House, Bemersyde, Melrose, Roxburghshire TD6 9DP.

See also J. G. Milne Home.

MILNE HOME, John Gavin, TD; FRICS; Lord-Lieutenant of Dumfries and Galloway, 1988–91 (Vice-Lord-Lieutenant, 1983–88); *b* 20 Oct. 1916; *s* of Sir John Hepburn Milne Home and Lady (Mary Adelaide) Milne Home; *m* 1942, Rosemary Elwes; two *s* one *d*. *Educ:* Wellington College; Trinity College, Cambridge. BA Estate Management. Served with King's Own Scottish Borderers (4th Bn), 1939–45 (TA 1938–49); Factor for Buccleuch Estates Ltd and Duke of Buccleuch on part of Scottish estates, 1949–74; Mem., Dumfries County Council, 1949–75; DL Dumfries 1970. *Recreations:* fishing and shooting. *Address:* Kirkside of Middlebie, Lockerbie, Dumfriesshire. *T:* Ecclefechan (05763) 204.

See also Captain A. J. F. Milne Home.

MILNE-WATSON, Sir Michael, 3rd Bt *cr* 1937; Kt 1969; CBE 1953; MA; *b* 16 Feb. 1910; *yr s* of Sir David Milne-Watson, 1st Bt, and Olga Cecily (*d* 1952), *d* of Rev. George Herbert; *S* brother, 1982; *m* 1940, Mary Lisette, *d* of late H. C. Bagnall, Auckland, New Zealand; one *s*. *Educ:* Eton; Balliol Coll., Oxford. Served War of 1939–45. RNVR, 1943–45. Joined Gas Light & Coke Co., 1933; Managing Dir, 1945; Governor, 1946–49; Chairman: North Thames Gas Board, 1949–64; Richard Thomas & Baldwins Ltd, 1964–67; The William Press Group of Companies, 1969–74; a Dep. Chm., BSC, 1967–69 (Mem. Organizing Cttee, 1966–67); Mem., Iron and Steel Adv. Cttee, 1967–69. Director: Industrial and Commercial Finance Corp. Ltd, 1963–80; Commercial Union Assurance Co. Ltd, 1968–81; Finance for Industry Ltd, 1974–80; Finance Corp. for Industry Ltd, 1974–80; Rose Thomson Young (Underwriting) Ltd, 1982–87. President: Soc. of British Gas Industries Guild, 1970–71; Pipeline Industries Guild, 1971–72. Vice-Pres., BUPA, 1981– (Chm., 1976–81). Liveryman, Grocers' Co., 1947. Governor: Council, Reading Univ., 1971–82 (Pres., 1975–80); *Heir: s* Andrew Michael Milne-Watson [*b* 10 Nov. 1944; *m* 1st, 1970, Beverley Jane Gabrielle (marr. diss. 1981), *e d* of Philip Cotton, Majorca; one *s* one *d*; 2nd, 1983, Gisella Tisdall; one *s*]. *Address:* 39 Cadogan Place, SW1X 9RX; Oakfield, Mortimer, Berks. *T:* Burghfield Common (0734) 832200. *Clubs:* Athenæum, MCC; Leander.

MILNER, family name of **Baron Milner of Leeds.**

MILNER OF LEEDS, 2nd Baron, *cr* 1951; **Arthur James Michael Milner,** AE 1952; Consultant, Gregory, Rowcliffe & Milners (formerly Milners, Curry & Gaskell), Solicitors, London, since 1988 (Partner, 1953–88); *b* 12 Sept. 1923; *o s* of 1st Baron Milner of Leeds, PC, MC, TD and Lois Tinsdale (*d* 1982), *d* of Thomas Brown, Leeds; *S* father, 1967; *m* 1951, Sheila Margaret, *d* of Gerald Hartley, Leeds; one *s* two *d*. *Educ:* Oundle; Trinity Hall, Cambridge (MA). Served: RAFVR, 1942–46, Flt Lt; 609 (W Riding) Sqn, RAuxAF, 1947–52, Flt Lt. Admitted Solicitor, 1951. Opposition Whip, House of Lords, 1971–74. Member: Clothworkers' Co.; Pilgrims; Hon. Treas, Soc. of Yorkshiremen in London, 1967–70. *Heir: s* Hon. Richard James Milner [*b* 16 May 1959; *m* 1988, Margaret, *y d* of G. F. Voisin; one *d*]. *Address:* 2 The Inner Court, Old Church Street, SW3 5BY. *Club:* Royal Air Force.

MILNER, Prof. Arthur John Robin Gorell, FRS 1988; Professor of Computation Theory, University of Edinburgh, since 1984; *b* 13 Jan. 1934; *s* of John Theodore Milner and Muriel Emily (*née* Barnes-Gorell); *m* 1963, Lucy Petronella Moor; two *s* one *d*. *Educ:* Eton Coll.; King's Coll., Cambridge (BA Maths, 1957). Maths teacher, Marylebone Grammar Sch., 1959–60; Ferranti Ltd, London, 1960–63; Lectr in Maths and Computing, City Univ., London, 1963–68; Research Fellow: University Coll., Swansea, 1968–70; Artificial Intelligence Lab., Stanford Univ., Calif, 1970–72; Edinburgh University: Lectr, 1973–75; Sen. Lectr, 1975–78; Reader, 1978–84. Founder Mem., Academia Europaea, 1988. Hon. DSc(Eng) Chalmers Univ., Gothenburg, Sweden, 1988. *Publications:* Calculus for Communication and Concurrency, 1989; The Definition of Standard ML, 1990; Commentary on Standard ML, 1990; contribs to Computer Science on mechanised logic of computation and on calculus of communicating systems. *Recreations:* music, carpentry, walking. *Address:* 2 Garscube Terrace, Edinburgh EH12 6BQ. *T:* 031–337 4823.

MILNER, Prof. Brenda (Atkinson), OC 1984; OQ 1985; FRS 1979, FRSC 1976; Professor of Psychology, Department of Neurology and Neurosurgery, McGill University, and Head of Neuropsychology Research Unit, Montreal Neurological Institute, since 1970; *b* 15 July 1918; *d* of Samuel Langford and Clarice Frances Leslie (*née* Doig). *Educ:* Univ. of Cambridge (BA, MA, ScD); McGill Univ. (PhD). Experimental Officer, Min. of Supply, 1941–44; Professeur Agrégé, Inst. de Psychologie, Univ. de Montréal, 1944–52; Res. Associate, Psychology Dept, McGill Univ., 1952–53; Lectr, 1953–60, Asst Prof., 1960–64, Associate Prof., 1964–70, Dept of Neurology and Neurosurgery, McGill Univ. Hon. LLD Queen's Univ., Kingston, Ont, 1980; Hon. DSc: Manitoba, 1982; Lethbridge, 1986; Mount Holyoke, 1986; Toronto, 1987; Hon. DScSoc Laval, 1987; Hon. Dr Montreal, 1988. Izaak Walton Killam Prize, Canada Council, 1983; Hermann von Helmholtz Prize, Inst. for Cognitive Neuroscience, USA, 1984; Ralph W. Gerard Prize, Soc. for Neuroscience, 1987. Grand Dame of Merit, Order of Malta, 1985. *Publications:* mainly articles in neurological and psychological jls. *Address:* Montreal Neurological Institute, 3801 University Street, Montreal, Quebec H3A 2B4, Canada. *T:* (514) 398–8503, *Fax:* (514) 398–8540.

MILNER, Sir (George Edward) Mordaunt, 9th Bt *cr* 1716; *b* 7 Feb. 1911; *er s* of Brig.-Gen. G. F. Milner, CMG, DSO; *S* cousin (Sir William Frederick Victor Mordaunt Milner, 8th Bt) 1960; *m* 1st, 1935, Barbara Audrey (*d* 1951), *d* of Henry Noel Belsham, Hunstanton, Norfolk; two *s* one *d*; 2nd, 1953, Katherine Moodie Bisset, *d* of D. H. Hoey, Dunfermline. *Educ:* Oundle. Served War of 1939–45, Royal Artillery. Stipendiary Steward, Jockey Club of South Africa, 1954–59; Steward, Cape Turf Club, 1959–75; Steward, Jockey Club of SA, 1977–80. Mem. Council, Thoroughbred Breeders Assoc., 1975–82. *Publications:* Thoroughbred Breeding: notes and comments, 1987; Sons of the Desert, 1987; The Godolphin Arabian, 1989; *novels:* Inspired Information, 1959; Vaulting Ambition, 1962; The Last Furlong, 1965. *Heir: s* Timothy William Lycett Milner, *b* 11 Oct. 1936. *Address:* Natte Valleij, Klapmuts, Cape, S Africa. *T:* 02211–5171. *Clubs:* Rand (Johannesburg); Jockey Club of SA.

MILNER, Joseph, CBE 1975; QFSM 1962; Chief Officer of the London Fire Brigade, 1970–76; *b* 5 Oct. 1922; *e s* of Joseph and Ann Milner; *m* 1943, Bella Grice (*d* 1976), *e d* of Frederick George Flinton; one *s* one *d*; *m* 1976, Anne Cunningham, *e d* of J. Cunningham. *Educ:* Ladybarn Sch., Manchester. Served King's Regt (Liverpool), 1940–46: India/Burma, 1943–46 (Wingate's Chindits). Nat. Fire Service, 1946–48; North Riding Fire Bde, 1948–50; Manchester Fire Bde, 1950–51; Hong Kong Fire Bde, 1951–60; Dep. Dir, Hong Kong Fire Services, 1961–65; Dir, Hong Kong Fire Services, and Unit Controller, Auxiliary Fire Service, 1965–70. Mem., Hong Kong Council, Order of St John, 1965–70; JP Hong Kong, 1965–70. Regional Fire Commander (designate), London, 1970–76. Mem. Bd, Fire Service College, 1970–76; Mem., Central Fire Brigades Adv. Council, 1970–76; Adviser, Nat. Jt Council for Local Authority Fire Brigades, 1970–76; Chm., London Fire Liaison Panel, 1970–76; Mem., London Local Adv. Cttee, IBA, 1974–78; Fire Adviser, Assoc. of Metrop. Authorities, 1970–76. Vice-President: Fire Services Nat. Benevolent Fund (Chm., 1975–77); GLC Br., Royal British Legion, 1977–. Mem., Caston Parish Council, 1980–; Community Controller, Civil Defence, 1981–; Fellow, Instn of Fire Engineers, 1971; Associate Mem., Inst. of British Engineers, 1953; Associate, LCSP, 1987. OStJ 1971. *Recreations:* walking, poetry, hacking, horse management, remedial therapies. *Address:* Lam Low, Caston, Attleborough, Norfolk NR17 1DD. *T:* Caston (095383) 697. *Club:* Hong Kong (Hong Kong).

MILNER, Sir Mordaunt; *see* Milner, Sir G. E. M.

MILNER, Ralph; *see* Millner, Ralph.

MILNER, Rt. Rev. Ronald James; *see* Burnley, Bishop Suffragan of.

MILNER-BARRY, Sir (Philip) Stuart, KCVO 1975; CB 1962; OBE 1946; Ceremonial Officer, Civil Service Department (formerly Treasury), 1966–77; *b* 20 Sept. 1906; *s* of late Prof. E. L. Milner-Barry; *m* 1947, Thelma Tennant Wells; one *s* two *d*. *Educ:* Cheltenham Coll.; Trinity Coll., Cambridge (Major Schol.). 1st Class Hons, Classical Tripos (Pt I), Moral Science Tripos (Pt II). With L. Powell Sons & Co., Stockbrokers, 1929–38; Chess Correspondent, The Times, 1938–45; temporary civil servant, a Dept of the Foreign Office, 1940–45; Principal, HM Treasury, 1945; Asst Sec., 1947; Dir of Organisation and Methods, Treasury, 1954–58; Dir of Establishments and Organisation, Min. of Health, 1958–60; Under-Sec., Treasury, 1954–66. *Recreations:* Chess: British Boy Champion, 1923; British Championship Second, 1953; mem. British Internat. teams, 1937–61; Pres. British Chess Fedn, 1970–73; walking. *Address:* 12 Camden Row, SE3 0QA. *T:* 081–852 5808. *Club:* Brooks's.

MILNES, Rodney; *see* Blumer, Rodney Milnes.

MILNES COATES, Sir Anthony (Robert), 4th Bt *cr* 1911; BSc, MB BS, MD, MRCS, MRCP; Professor of Medical Microbiology, St George's Hospital Medical School, since 1990; *b* 8 Dec. 1948; *s* of Sir Robert Edward James Clive Milnes Coates, 3rd Bt, DSO, and of Lady Patricia Ethel, *d* of 4th Earl of Listowel; *S* father, 1982; *m* 1978, Harriet Ann Burton; one *s* two *d*. *Educ:* Eton; St Thomas's Hospital, London University. BSc; MRCS 1973; MB BS 1973; MRCP (UK) 1978; MD 1984. MRC Trng Res. Fellow, Dept of Bacteriology, RPMS, 1979–82; Sen. Registrar in Bacteriology, RPMS, 1982–84; Sen. Lectr (Hon. Consultant), Dept of Medical Microbiology, London Hosp. Medical Coll., 1984–90. *Heir: s* Thomas Anthony Milnes Coates, *b* 19 Nov. 1986. *Address:* Hereford Cottage, 135 Gloucester Road, SW7 4TH. *Club:* Brooks's.

MILOSLAVSKY, Dimitry T.; *see* Tolstoy, Dimitry.

MILOSZ, Czeslaw; poet, author; Professor of Slavic Languages and Literatures, University of California, Berkeley, 1961–78, now Emeritus; *b* Lithuania, 30 June 1911; naturalised US citizen, 1970; *s* of Aleksander and Weronika Milosz. *Educ:* High Sch., Wilno; Univ. of Wilno. MJuris 1934. Programmer, Polish Nat. Radio, 1935–39; Mem., Polish diplomatic service, Washington, Paris, 1945–50. Vis. Lectr, Univ. of Calif, Berkeley, 1960–61. Guggenheim Fellow, 1976. Member: Polish Inst. Letters and Scis in America; Amer. Acad. of Arts and Scis; PEN Club in Exile; Amer. Inst. of Arts and Letters. Hon. LittD Michigan, 1977; Hon. doctorates: Catholic Univ. of Lublin, 1981; Harvard Univ., 1989; Jagiellonian Univ., Krakow, 1989. Prix Littéraire Européen, Les Guildes du Livre, Geneva, 1953; Neustadt Internat. Prize for Literature, Univ. of Oklahama, 1978; citation, Univ. of Calif, Berkeley, 1978; Nobel Prize for Literature, 1980. *Publications:* Poemat o czasie zastyglym (Poem on Time Frozen), 1933; Trzy zimy (Three Winters), 1936; Ocalenie (Rescue), 1945; Zniewolony umysl (The Captive Mind), 1953; Zdobycie wladzy, 1953, trans. as The Usurpers (in US as Seizure of Power), 1955; Dolina Issy, 1955, trans. as The Issa Valley, 1981; Swiatlo dzienne (Daylight), 1955; Traktat poetycki (Poetic Treatise), 1957; Rodzinna Europa, 1958, trans. as Native Realm, 1968; Postwar Polish Poetry, 1965; Widzenia nad Zatoka San Francisco (Views from San Francisco Bay), 1969; The History of Polish Literature, 1970; Prywatne obowiazki (Private Obligations), 1972; Selected Poems, 1973, rev. edn 1981; Ziemia Ulro (The Land of Ulro), 1977; Emperor of the Earth, 1977; Bells in Winter, 1978; Hymn o perle, 1982; Visions from San Francisco Bay, 1983; The Witness of Poetry, 1983; Separate Notebooks, 1984; The Land of Ulro, 1985; Unattainable Earth, 1986; Collected Poems, 1988. *Address:* Department of Slavic Languages and Literatures, 5416 Dwinelle Hall, University of California, Berkeley, Calif 94720, USA.

MILROY, Rev. Dominic Liston, OSB; MA; Headmaster, Ampleforth College, since 1980; *b* 18 April 1932; *s* of Adam Liston Milroy and Clarita Burns. *Educ:* Ampleforth Coll.; St Benet's Hall, Oxford (1st Cl. Mod. Langs, MA). Entered Ampleforth Abbey, 1950; teaching staff, Ampleforth Coll., 1957–74; Head of Mod. Langs, 1963–74; Housemaster, 1964–74; Prior of Internat. Benedictine Coll. of S Anselmo, Rome, 1974–79. Chm., HMC, 1992; Chm. elect, Conf. of Catholic Secondary Schs and Colls. *Address:* Ampleforth College, York YO6 4ER. *T:* Ampleforth (04393) 224.

MILSOM, Stroud Francis Charles; QC 1985; FBA 1967; Professor of Law, Cambridge University, 1976–90; Fellow of St John's College, Cambridge, since 1976; *b* 2 May 1923; *yr s* of late Harry Lincoln Milsom and Isobel Vida Collins; *m* 1955, Irène, *d* of late Witold Szereszewski, Wola Krysztoporska, Poland. *Educ:* Charterhouse; Trinity Coll., Cambridge. Admiralty, 1944–45. Called to the Bar, Lincoln's Inn, 1947, Hon. Bencher, 1970; Commonwealth Fund Fellow, Univ. of Pennsylvania, 1947–48; Yorke Prize, Univ. of Cambridge, 1948; Prize Fellow, Fellow and Lectr, Trinity Coll., Cambridge, 1948–55; Fellow, Tutor and Dean, New Coll., Oxford, 1956–64; Prof. of Legal History, London Univ., 1964–76. Selden Society: Literary Dir, 1964–80; Pres., 1985–88. Mem., Royal Commn on Historical Manuscripts, 1975–. Vis. Lectr, New York Univ. Law Sch., several times, 1958–70; Visiting Professor: Yale Law Sch., several times, 1968–; Harvard Law Sch. and Dept of History, 1973; Associate Fellow, Trumbull Coll., Yale Univ., 1974–; Charles Inglis Thomson Prof., Colorado Univ. Law Sch., 1977. Maitland Meml Lectr, Cambridge, 1972; Addison Harris Meml Lectr, Indiana Univ. Law Sch., 1974; Vis. Prof. and Wilfred Fullagar Lectr, Monash Univ., 1981; Ford's Lectr, Oxford, 1986. Foreign Mem., Amer. Phil Soc., 1984. Hon. LLD: Glasgow, 1981; Chicago, 1985. Ames Prize, Harvard, 1972; Swiney Prize, RSA/RCP, 1974. *Publications:* Novae Narrationes (introd., trans. and notes), 1963; introd. reissue Pollock and Maitland, History of English Law, 1968; Historical Foundations of the Common Law, 1969, 2nd edn 1981; The Legal Framework of English Feudalism, 1976; Studies in the History of the Common Law (collected papers), 1985. *Address:* St John's College, Cambridge CB2 1TP; 113 Grantchester Meadows, Cambridge CB3 9JN. *T:* Cambridge (0223) 354100. *Club:* Athenæum.

MILSTEIN, César, PhD; FRS 1975; Scientific Staff of Medical Research Council, since 1963; Fellow, Darwin College, University of Cambridge, since 1981; Head, Division of Protein and Nucleic Acid Chemistry, MRC Laboratory of Molecular Biology, since 1983; *b* 8 Oct. 1927; *s* of Lázaro and Máxima Milstein; *m* 1953, Celia Prilleltensky. *Educ:* Colegio Nacional de Bahia Blanca; Univ. Nacional de Buenos Aires; Fitzwilliam Coll., Cambridge (Hon. Fellow 1982). Licenciado en Ciencias Quimicas 1952; Doctor en Quimica 1957; PhD Cantab 1960. British Council Fellow, 1958–60; Staff of Instituto Nacional de Microbiologia, Buenos Aires, 1957–63; Head of Div. de Biologia Molecular, 1961–63; Staff of MRC Laboratory of Molecular Biology, 1963–: Mem. Governing Bd, 1975–79; Head of Sub-div. of Protein Chemistry, 1969–83. For. Associate, Nat. Acad. of Scis, USA, 1981. Hon. FRCP, 1983. Biochem. Soc. Ciba Medal, 1978; Rosenstiel Medal, 1979; Avery-Landsteiner Preis, 1979; Rosenberg Prize, 1979; Mattia Award, 1979; Gross Horwitz Prize, 1980; Koch Preis, 1980; Wolf Prize in Med., 1980; Wellcome Foundn Medal, 1980; Gimenez Diaz Medal, 1981; William Bate Hardy Prize, Camb. Philos. Soc., 1981; Sloan Prize, General Motors Cancer Res. Foundn, 1981; Gairdner Award, Gairdner Foundn, 1981; Royal Medal, Royal Soc., 1982; Nobel Prize for Physiology or Medicine (with Prof. N. Jerne and Dr G. Koehler), 1984. Silver Jubilee Medal, 1977. *Publications:* original papers and review articles on structure, evolution and genetics of immunoglobulins and phosphoenzimes. *Recreations:* open air activities, cooking. *Address:* Medical Research Council Laboratory of Molecular Biology, Hills Road, Cambridge CB2 2QH. *Club:* Sefe (Cambridge).

MILSTEIN, Nathan; violinist; *b* Odessa, Russia, 31 Dec. 1904; *s* of Miron and Maria Milstein; *m* 1945, Thérèse Weldon; one *d*. *Educ:* with Prof. Stoliarsky, in Odessa; with Leopold Auer, at Royal Conservatory, St Petersburg; studied with Eugène Isaye, Le Zoot, Belgium. Many tours in Russia, 1920–26; left Russia, 1926; annual tours throughout Europe, also in North, Central and South America, from 1920, except for war years. Hon. Mem., Acad. of St Cecilia, Rome, 1963. Commandeur, Légion d'Honneur, 1983 (Officier, 1967); Ehrenkreuz, Austria, 1963. *Address:* c/o Shaw Concerts Inc., 1995 Broadway, New York, NY 10023, USA; 17 Chester Square, SW1W 9HS.

MILTON, Derek Francis, CMG 1990; HM Diplomatic Service; High Commissioner, Kingston, Jamaica, since 1989, and concurrently non-resident Ambassador to Haiti; *b* 11 Nov. 1935; *s* of Francis Henry Milton and Florence Elizabeth Maud Kirby; *m* 1st, 1960, Helge Kahle; two *s*; 2nd, 1977, Catherine Walmsley. *Educ:* Preston Manor County Grammar Sch., Wembley; Manchester Univ. (BA Hons Politics and Modern History, 1959). RAF, 1954–56. Colonial Office, 1959–63; Asst Private Sec. to Commonwealth and Colonial Sec., 1962–64; Commonwealth Prime Ministers' Meeting Secretariat, 1964; First Secretary: CRO (later FO), 1964–67; UK Mission to UN, New York, 1967–71; Rome, 1972–75; FCO, 1975–77; Counsellor: Civil Service Res. Fellow, Glasgow Univ., 1977–78; Caracas, 1978–79; Dept of Trade, 1980–82; Overseas Inspectorate, 1982–84; Minister-Counsellor, Mexico City, 1984–87; RCDS, 1988. *Recreations:* QPR Football Club, Poland, The Guardian, travel, languages. *Address:* c/o Foreign and Commonwealth Office, King Charles Street, SW1A 2AH.

MILTON-THOMPSON, Surg. Vice-Adm. Sir Godfrey (James), KBE 1988; FRCP; Chairman, Cornwall Community Healthcare Trust, since 1991; Medical Director General (Naval), 1985–90; Surgeon General, Ministry of Defence, 1988–90; *b* 25 April 1930; *s* of Rev. James Milton-Thompson and May LeMare (*née* Hoare); *m* 1952, Noreen Helena Frances, *d* of Lt-Col Sir Desmond Fitzmaurice, *qv*; three *d*. *Educ:* Eastbourne Coll.; Queens' Coll., Cambridge (MA); St Thomas' Hosp. (MB BChir); FRCP 1974 (MRCP 1961); DCH 1963. Joined Royal Navy, 1955; after general service and hosp. appts at home and abroad, Cons. Phys., RN Hosp., Plymouth, 1967–70 and 1972–75; Hon. Research Fellow, St Mark's Hosp., London, 1969–71; Prof. of Naval Medicine, 1975–80; RCDS 1981; Dep. Medical Director General (Naval), 1982–84; Surg. Rear-Adm. (Operational Med. Services), 1984–85; Dep. Surg. Gen. (Research and Trng), MoD, 1985–87. QHP, 1982–90. Member: Medical Research Soc., 1971–; British Soc. of Gastroenterology, 1972–. Hon. Col, 211 (Wessex) Field Hosp., RAMC(V), 1990–. Errol-Eldridge Prize, 1974; Gilbert Blane Medal, 1976. KStJ 1989 (Mem., Chapter Gen., 1988–; Hospitaller, 1991–). *Publications:* on clinical pharmacology of the gastro-intestinal tract and therapy of peptic ulcer, etc, in med. jls. *Recreations:* fishing, paintings and painting, literature. *Address:* c/o Lloyds Bank PLC, The Parade, Liskeard, Cornwall PL14 6AW. *Club:* Naval and Military.

MILVERTON, 2nd Baron *cr* 1947, of Lagos and of Clifton; **Rev. Fraser Arthur Richard Richards;** Rector of Christian Malford with Sutton Benger and Tytherton Kellaways, since 1967; *b* 21 July 1930; *s* of 1st Baron Milverton, GCMG, and Noelle Benda, *d* of Charles Basil Whitehead; *S* father, 1978; *m* 1957, Mary Dorothy, BD, *d* of late Leslie Fly, ARCM, Corsham, Wilts; two *d*. *Educ:* De Carteret Prep. Sch., Jamaica; Ridley Coll., Ontario; Clifton Coll.; Egerton Agric. Coll., Kenya; Bishop's Coll., Cheshunt. Royal Signals, 1949–50; Kenya Police, 1952–53. Deacon 1957, priest 1958, dio. Rochester; Curate: Beckenham, 1957–59; St John Baptist, Sevenoaks, 1959–60; Great Bookham, 1960–63; Vicar of Okewood with Forest Green, 1963–67. *Recreations:* family, reading, current affairs and history; enjoys music and walking; interested in tennis, swimming, cricket and Rugby Union. *Heir:* *b* Hon. Michael Hugh Richards [*b* 1 Aug. 1936; *m* 1960, Edna Leonie, *y d* of Col Leo Steveni, OBE, MC; one *s*]. *Address:* House of Lords, Westminster, SW1A 0PW.

MILWARD, Prof. Alan Steele, FBA 1987; Professor of Economic History, University of London, since 1986; External Professor of History, European University Institute, since 1986; *b* 19 Jan. 1935; *s* of Joseph Thomas Milward and Dorothy Milward (*née* Steele); *m* 1963, Claudine Jeanne Amélie (*née* Lemaître); one *d*. *Educ:* University College London (BA 1956); LSE (PhD 1960); MA Manchester 1981. Asst Lectr in Indian Archaeology, Univ. of London, 1959; Lectr in Economic History, Univ. of Edinburgh, 1960; Sen. Lectr in Social Studies, Univ. of East Anglia, 1965; Associate Prof. of Economics, Stanford Univ., 1969; Prof. of European Studies, UMIST, 1971; Prof. of Contemp. Hist., European Univ. Inst., 1983. Visiting Professor: Stanford Univ., 1966; Ecole Pratique des Hautes Etudes, 1977, 1990; Univ. of Illinois, 1978; Univ.-Gesamthochschule, Siegen, 1980; Oslo Univ., 1990. *Publications:* The German Economy at War, 1965; The Social and Economic Effects of the Two World Wars on Britain, 1971, 2nd edn 1984; The New Order and the French Economy, 1972; The Fascist Economy in Norway, 1972; (with S. B. Saul) The Economic Development of Continental Europe 1780–1870, 1973; (with S. B. Saul) The Development of the Economies of Continental Europe 1870–1914, 1977; War, Economy and Society, 1977; The Reconstruction of Western Europe 1945–1951, 1984, 2nd edn 1987; (with B. Martin) Landwirtschaft und Ernährung im Zweiten Weltkrieg, 1984. *Recreations:* theatre, cricket, reading timetables. *Address:* Department of Economic History, London School of Economics, Houghton Street, WC2A 2AE. *T:* 071–955 7077.

MIMS, Prof. Cedric Arthur, MD, FRCPath; Professor of Microbiology, Guy's Hospital Medical School, London, 1972–90; *b* 9 Dec. 1924; *s* of A. H. and Irene Mims; *m* 1952, Valerie Vickery; two *s* two *d*. *Educ:* Mill Hill Sch.; University Coll. London (BSc (Zool)); Middlesex Hosp. Med. Sch. (MB, BS, BSc, MD). Medical Research Officer, East African Virus Research Inst., Entebbe, Uganda, 1953–56; Research Fellow and Professorial Fellow, John Curtin Sch. of Med. Research, Australian Nat. Univ., Canberra, 1957–72; Rockefeller Foundn Fellow, Children's Hosp. Med. Centre, Boston, USA, 1963–64; Visiting Fellow, Wistar Inst., Philadelphia, USA, 1969–70. *Publications:* The Biology of Animal Viruses (jtly), 1974; The Pathogenesis of Infectious Disease, 1976, rev. edn 1987; (with D. O. White) Viral Pathogenesis and Immunology, 1984; numerous papers on the pathogenesis of virus infections. *Address:* Sheriff House, Hammingden Lane, Ardingly, Sussex RH17 6SR. *T:* Ardingly (0444) 892243.

MINCHINTON, Prof. Walter Edward; Professor of Economic History, University of Exeter, 1964–86 (Head of Department, 1964–84), now Emeritus; *b* 29 April 1921; *s* of late Walter Edward and Annie Border Minchinton; *m* 1945, Marjorie Sargood; two *s* two *d*. *Educ:* Queen Elizabeth's Hosp., Bristol; LSE, Univ. of London. 1st cl. hons BSc (Econ). FRHistS. War Service, RAOC, REME, Royal Signals (Lieut), 1942–45. UC Swansea: Asst Lectr, 1948–50; Lectr, 1950–59; Sen. Lectr, 1959–64. Rockefeller Research Fellow, 1959–60. Visiting Professor: Fourah Bay Coll., Sierra Leone, 1965; La Trobe Univ., Australia, 1981–82. Chairman: Confedn for Advancement of State Educn, 1964–67; Devon History Soc., 1967–86; Exeter Industrial Arch. Gp, 1967–; SW Maritime History Soc., 1984–87 (Pres., 1987–); British Agricultural History Soc., 1968–71 (Mem. Council, 1952–86); Export Research Group, 1971–72; Exeter Educn Cttee, 1972; Devon Historic Buildings Trust, 1980–86 (Mem. Council, 1967–). Vice-President: Assoc. for the History of the Northern Seas, 1989– (Pres., 1982–89); Internat. Commn for Maritime History, 1968–80 (Mem. Council, 1985–90; Mem. Council, British Cttee, 1974–); Council Member: Economic History Soc., 1955–66; Soc. for Nautical Research, 1969–72, 1978–81. Alexander Prize, RHistS, 1953. General Editor: Exeter Papers in Economic History, 1964–86; British Records Relating to America in Microform, 1962–89. *Publications:* The British Tinplate Industry: a history, 1957; (ed) The Trade of Bristol in the Eighteenth Century, 1957; (ed) Politics and the Port of Bristol in the Eighteenth Century, 1963; Industrial Archaeology in Devon, 1968; (ed) Essays in Agrarian History, 1968; (ed) Industrial South Wales 1750–1914, essays in Welsh economic history, 1969; (ed) Mercantilism, System or Expediency?, 1969; The Growth of English Overseas Trade in the Seventeenth and Eighteenth Centuries, 1969; Wage Regulation in Pre-industrial England, 1972; Devon at Work, 1974; Windmills of Devon, 1977; (with Peter Harper) American Papers in the House of Lords Record Office: a guide, 1983; A Limekiln Miscellany: the South-West and South Wales, 1984; (with Celia King and Peter Waite) Virginia Slave-Trade Statistics 1698–1775, 1984; A Guide to Industrial Archaeological Sites in Britain, 1984; Devon's Industrial Past: a guide, 1986; Life to the City: an illustrated history of Exeter's water supply from the Romans to the present day, 1987; (ed) Britain and the Northern Seas: some essays, 1988; (ed) The Northern Seas: politics, economics and culture: eight essays, 1989; articles in Econ. History Review, Explorations in Entrepreneurial History, Mariner's Mirror, Trans RHistS, etc. *Recreations:* walking, music, industrial archaeology, squash. *Address:* 53 Homefield Road, Exeter EX1 2QX. *T:* Exeter (0392) 77602.

MINFORD, Prof. (Anthony) Patrick (Leslie); Edward Gonner Professor of Applied Economics, University of Liverpool, since 1976; *b* 17 May 1943; *s* of Leslie Mackay Minford and Patricia Mary (*née* Sale); *m* 1970, Rosemary Irene Allcorn; two *s* one *d*. *Educ:* Horris Hill; Winchester Coll. (scholar); Balliol Coll., Oxford (schol.; BA); London

Sch. of Economics (grad. studies; MScEcon, PhD). Economic Asst, Min. of Overseas Development, London, 1966; Economist, Min. of Finance, Malawi, 1967–69; Economic Adviser: Director's Staff, Courtaulds Ltd, 1970–71; HM Treasury, 1971–73, and HM Treasury Delegn in Washington DC, 1973–74. Visiting Hallsworth Fellow, Manchester Univ., 1974–75. Dir, Merseyside Develt Corp., 1988–89. Mem., Monopolies and Mergers Commn, 1990–. Editor: NIESR Review, 1975–76; Liverpool Quarterly Economic Bulletin, 1980–. *Publications:* Substitution Effects, Speculation and Exchange Rate Stability, 1978; (jtly) Unemployment—Cause and Cure, 1983, 2nd edn 1985; (jtly) Rational Expectations and the New Macroeconomics, 1983; (jtly) The Housing Morass, 1987; The Supply Side Revolution in Britain, 1991; articles in learned jls on monetary and international economics. *Address:* Department of Economics and Accounting, University of Liverpool, PO Box 147, Liverpool L69 3BX.

MINGAY, (Frederick) Ray; Consul-General, Chicago, since 1988; *b* 7 July 1938; *s* of Cecil Stanley and Madge Elizabeth Mingay; *m* 1963, Joan Heather Roberts; three *s* one *d*. *Educ:* Tottenham Grammar Sch.; St Catharine's Coll., Cambridge (BA); London Univ. (Postgrad. Pub. Admin.). Nat. Service (2nd Lt RAEC) 1959–61. Administration, St Thomas' Hosp., 1961; Min. of Transport, 1962–64; BoT, 1964; Chrysler (UK) Ltd, 1968–70; Consul (Commercial), Milan, 1970–73; Asst Sec., Dept of Trade, 1973–78; Counsellor (Commercial), Washington, 1978–83; Under Secretary: Mechanical and Electrical Engrg Div., DTI, 1983–86; Investment and Develt Div., DTI, 1986–88. FBIM; FRSA. *Address:* c/o Foreign and Commonwealth Office, King Charles Street, SW1A 2AH.

MINHINNICK, Sir Gordon (Edward George), KBE 1976 (OBE 1950); Cartoonist, New Zealand Herald, 1930–76, retired; *b* 13 June 1902; *s* of Captain P. C. Minhinnick, RN, and Anne Sealy; *m* 1928, Vernor Helmore; one *s* (one *d* decd). *Educ:* Kelly Coll., Tavistock, Devon. Came to NZ, 1921; studied architecture for 4 years; Cartoonist: NZ Free Lance, 1926; Sun, Christchurch, and Sun, Auckland, 1927. *Address:* Apartment 219, Northbridge, Akoranga Drive, Northcote, Auckland, New Zealand.

MINNITT, Robert John, CMG 1955; *b* 2 April 1913; *s* of Charles Frederick Minnitt and Winifred May Minnitt (*née* Buddle); *m* 1st, 1943, Peggy Christine Sharp (*d* 1973); one *s* two *d*; 2nd, 1975, Hon. Primrose Keighley Muncaster, *widow* of Claude Muncaster. *Educ:* Marlborough Coll.; Trinity Coll., Cambridge. Appointed to Colonial Administrative Service, Hong Kong, 1935; Chief Sec., Western Pacific High Commission, 1952–58, retired. Furniture designer and craftsman, 1960–66; temp. Civil Servant, CO, 1966; FCO, 1968–69. *Address:* Whitelocks, Sutton, Pulborough, W Sussex RH20 1PS. *T:* Sutton (07987) 216.

MINOGUE, Prof. Kenneth Robert; Professor of Political Science, London School of Economics and Political Science, University of London, since 1984; *b* 11 Sept. 1930; *s* of Denis Francis Minogue and Eunice Pearl Minogue (*née* Porter); *m* 1954, Valerie Pearson Hallett; one *s* one *d*. *Educ:* Sydney Boys' High Sch.; Sydney Univ. (BA); London School of Economics (BScEcon). Asst Lectr, Univ. of Exeter, 1955–56; London School of Economics: Asst Lectr, 1956; Sen. Lectr, 1964; Reader, 1971. *Publications:* The Liberal Mind, 1961; Nationalism, 1967; The Concept of a University, 1974; Alien Powers: the pure theory of ideology, 1984; numerous contribs to learned jls. *Recreations:* opera, tennis, walking. *Address:* 16 Buckland Crescent, NW3 5DX. *T:* 071–722 1474.

MINOGUE, Maj.-Gen. Patrick John O'Brien; retired; *b* 28 July 1922; *s* of Col M. J. Minogue, DSO, MC, late East Surrey Regt, and Mrs M. V. E. Minogue; *m* 1950, June Elizabeth (*née* Morris); one *s* two *d*. *Educ:* Brighton Coll.; RMCS. CBIM, FBCS, FIWSP, FIMH; jssc, psc, ato. Indian Army, 1942–46; East Surrey Regt, 1947; RAOC, 1951; served UK, BAOR, USA, Cyprus; Col, 1969; Brig., 1971; Insp. RAOC, 1971–73; Comdt, Central Ord. Depot, Bicester, 1973–75; Maj.-Gen. 1975; Comdr, Base Orgn, RAOC, 1975–78. Hon. Col, RAOC (TAVR), 1975–78; Col Comdt, RAOC, 1980–87. Group Systems Controller, Lansing Bagnall Ltd, 1978–81; Chm., LT Electronics, 1979–81. Mem., Spanish Golf Fedn, 1982–; Pres., Cabrera Lawn Bowling Club, 1987–. *Recreations:* cricket, sailing (Cdre Wayfarer Class, UK, 1975), golf, shooting, gun-dogs, athletics, lawn bowling. *Address:* La Casa Rosada, Apartado 4, Cortijo Grande, Turre, Almeria, Spain. *Clubs:* Army and Navy, MCC; Army Sailing Association; Milocarian Athletic; Staff College (Camberley); Cortijo Grande Golf.

MINTO, 6th Earl of, *cr* 1813; **Gilbert Edward George Lariston Elliot-Murray-Kynynmound,** OBE 1986 (MBE (mil.) 1955); JP; DL; Bt 1700; Baron Minto, 1797; Viscount Melgund, 1813; late Captain Scots Guards; *b* 19 June 1928; *er s* of 5th Earl of Minto and Marion, OBE (*d* 1974), *d* of G. W. Cook, Montreal; *S* father, 1975; *m* 1st, 1952, Lady Caroline Child-Villiers (from whom he obtained a divorce, 1965), *d* of 9th Earl of Jersey; one *s* one *d*; 2nd, 1965, Mary Elizabeth (*b* 29 Dec. 1936; *d* 24 Jan. 1983), *d* of late Peter Ballantine and of Mrs Ballantine, Gladstone, New Jersey, USA; *m* 1991, Mrs Caroline Larlham. *Educ:* Eton; RMA, Sandhurst. Served Malaya, 1949–51; ADC to C-in-C FARELF, 1951, to CIGS, 1953–55, to HE Governor and C-in-C Cyprus, 1955; transferred to RARO, 1956. Brigadier, Queen's Body Guard for Scotland (Royal Company of Archers). Director, Noel Penny Turbines Ltd, 1971–. Regional Councillor (Hermitage Div.), Borders Region, 1974–80, 1986–; Convenor, Borders Regional Council, 1990–; Mem. Exec., COSLA, 1990–. Pres., Scottish Council on Alcohol, 1987– (Chm., 1973–87); Dep. Traffic Comr for Scotland, 1975–81; Pres., S of Scotland Chamber of Commerce, 1980–82 (Exec. Vice-Pres., 1978–80). JP Roxburghshire, 1961–; DL Borders Region, Roxburgh, Ettrick and Lauderdale, 1983–. *Heir:* *s* Viscount Melgund, *qv*. *Address:* Minto, Hawick, Scotland. *T:* Denholm (045087) 321. *Club:* Puffin's (Edinburgh).

MINTO, Dr Alfred, FRCPsych; Consultant Psychiatrist (Rehabilitation), Southern Derbyshire Health Authority, 1988–90; *b* 23 Sept. 1928; *s* of Alfred Minto and Marjorie Mavor Goudie Leask; *m* 1949, Frances Oliver Bradbrook; two *s* two *d*. *Educ:* Aberdeen Central Sch.; Aberdeen Univ. (MB ChB 1951); DPM RCS&P London 1961; MRCPsych 1972, FRCPsych 1974. House Physician, Huddersfield Royal Inf., 1952; Sen. House Officer/Jun. Hosp. Med. Officer, Fairmile Hosp., Wallingford, 1952–56; Sen. Registrar, St Luke's Hosp., Middlesbrough, 1956–59; Sen. Hosp. Med. Officer, 1959–63, Conslt Psychiatrist, 1963, Mapperley Hosp., Nottingham; Conslt Psychiatrist i/c, Alcoholism and Drug Addiction Service, Sheffield RHB, 1963–68; Conslt Psychiatrist, St Ann's and Mapperley Hosps, 1968–81; Med. Dir, Rampton Hosp., 1981–85; Associate Prof. of Psychiatry, Univ. of Calgary, and Clinical Dir of Forensic Psychiatry, Calgary Gen. Hosp., Alberta, 1986–87. Clinical Teacher, Nottingham Univ. Med. Sch., 1971–85; Special Lectr in Forensic Psych., Nottingham Univ., 1982–85. Conslt Psychiatrist, CS Comrs, 1964–85. *Publications:* Key Issues in Mental Health, 1982; papers on alcoholism, community care, toxoplasmosis. *Recreations:* books, people. *Address:* 76 Walsingham Road, Nottingham, NG5 4NR.

MINTOFF, Hon. Dominic, (Dom), BSc, BE&A, MA, A&CE; MP; MLA (Malta Labour Party), since 1947; Prime Minister of Malta, 1971–84; Leader of Labour Party, 1949–84; *b* Cospicua, 6 Aug. 1916; *s* of Lawrence Mintoff and late Concetta (*née* Farrugia); *m* 1947, Moyra de Vere Bentick; two *d*. *Educ:* Govt Elem. Sch., Seminary and Lyceum, Malta; Univ. of Malta (BSc 1937; BE&A, A&CE 1939); Hertford Coll., Oxford (Govt Travelling Scholar; Rhodes Scholar; MA Engrg Science). Practised as civil engineer in Britain, 1941–43, and as architect in Malta, 1943–. Gen. Sec. Malta Labour Party, 1936–37; Mem., Council of Govt and Exec. Council, 1945; Dep. Prime Minister and Minister for Works and Reconstruction, 1947–49 (resigned); Prime Minister and Minister of Finance, 1955–58; resigned office in 1958 to lead the Maltese Liberation Movement; Leader of Opposition, 1962–71; Minister of Foreign Affairs, 1971–81; Minister of the Interior, 1976–81 and 1983–84. Mem., Labour delegns to UK, 1945, 1947, 1948 and 1949. Negotiated removal of British Military base, 1971 and other foreign mil. bases by 1979. Dr *hc* Univ. of Pol. Studies, Ponterios, Greece, 1976. Order of the Republic, Libya, 1971; Grand Cordon: Order of the Republic, Tunisia, 1973; Order of Oissam Alaouite, 1978. *Publications:* scientific, literary and artistic works. *Recreations:* horse-riding, swimming, water skiing, bocċi. *Address:* The Olives, Tarxien, Malta.

MINTON, Yvonne Fay, CBE 1980; mezzo-soprano; *er d* of R. T. Minton, Sydney; *m* 1965, William Barclay; one *s* one *d*. *Educ:* Sydney Conservatorium of Music. Elsa Stralia Scholar, Sydney, 1957–60; won Canberra Operatic Aria Competition, 1960; won Kathleen Ferrier Prize at s'Hertogenbosch Vocal Competition, 1961. Joined Royal Opera House as a Principal Mezzo-Soprano, 1965. Major roles include: Octavian in Der Rosenkavalier; Dorabella in Cosi Fan Tutte; Marina in Boris Godounov; Helen in King Priam; Cherubino in Marriage of Figaro; Orfeo in Gluck's Orfeo; Sextus in La clemenza di Tito; Dido in The Trojans at Carthage; Kundry in Parsifal; Charlotte in Werther; Countess Geschwitz in Lulu. Recordings include Octavian in Der Rosenkavalier, Mozart Requiem, Elgar's The Kingdom, etc. Guest Artist with Cologne Opera Company, Oct. 1969–. Hon. RAM 1975. *Recreations:* reading, gardening. *Address:* c/o Ingpen and Williams, 14 Kensington Court, W8. *T:* 071–937 5158.

MIQUEL, Raymond Clive, CBE 1981; Chairman, Scottish Sports Council, since 1987; Member, Sports Council, since 1988; *b* 28 May 1931; *m* 1958; one *s* two *d*. *Educ:* Allan Glen's Sch., Glasgow; Glasgow Technical Coll. Joined Arthur Bell & Sons Ltd as Works Study Engineer, 1956; Production Controller, 1958; Production Director, 1962; Dep. Managing Director, 1965; Man. Dir, 1968–85; Dep. Chairman, 1972; Chm., 1973–85. Chairman: Towmaster Transport Co. Ltd, 1974–86; Canning Town Glass Ltd, 1974–86; Wellington Importers Ltd, 1984–86; Gleneagles Hotels PLC, 1984–86; Chm. and Chief Exec., Belhaven plc, 1986–88. Dir, Golf Fund Plc, 1989–. Vis. Prof. in Business Develt, Glasgow Univ., 1985–. Member: British Internat. Sports Cttee, 1987–; CCPR. Governor, Sports Aid Foundn, 1979–. CBIM. *Address:* Whitedene, Caledonian Crescent, Gleneagles, Perthshire, Scotland. *T:* Auchterarder (0764) 2642.

MIRMAN, Sophie, (Mrs R. P. Ross); Joint Managing Director, Trotters Childrenswear and Accessories, since 1990; *b* 28 Oct. 1956; *d* of Simone and Serge Mirman; *m* 1984, Richard Philip Ross; one *s* one *d*. *Educ:* French Lycée, London. Marks & Spencer, 1974–81; Man. Dir, Tie Rack, 1981–83; Co-Founder, Sock Shop International, 1983; Chm. and Joint Man. Dir, Sock Shop International plc, 1983–90. *Recreations:* family, sport. *Address:* 34 King's Road, SW3 4UD. *T:* 071–259 9622.

MIRON, Wilfrid Lyonel, CBE 1969 (OBE 1945; MBE 1944); TD 1950; JP; DL; Regional Chairman (Midlands), National Coal Board, 1967–76 and Regional Chairman (South Wales), 1969–76; National Coal Board Member (with Regional responsibilities), 1971–76; *b* 27 Jan. 1913; *s* of late Solman Miron and late Minnie Pearl Miron; *m* 1958, Doreen (*née* Hill); no *c*. *Educ:* Llanelli Gram. Sch. Admitted Solicitor, 1934; private practice and Legal Adviser to Shipley Collieries and associated companies. TA Commn, Sherwood Foresters, 1939; served War of 1939–45: Home Forces, 1939; France and Dunkirk, 1940; IO 139 Inf. Bde, 1940–41; GSO3 Aldershot Dist, 1941–42; Staff Coll., Quetta, 1942 (SC); DAAG 17 Ind. Div., 1943–44, and AA&QMG 17 Ind. Div., 1944–45, Chin Hills, Imphal, Burma (despatches, 1944). E Midlands Div. NCB: Sec. and Legal Adviser, 1946–51; Dep. Chm., 1951–60; Chm., 1960–67. Pres., Midland Dist Miners' Fatal Accident Relief Soc.; Chairman: E Mids Regional Planning Council, 1976–79 (Mem., 1965–76); (part-time), Industrial Tribunals, 1976–85. Freeman (by redemption) City of London; Master, Pattenmakers' Company, 1979–80. Hon. Lieut-Col. JP Notts, 1964 (Chairman: Nottingham PSD, 1982–83; Notts Magistrates' Cts Cttee, 1981–83); DL Notts, 1970. FRSA 1965–86. OStJ 1961. Hon. Fellow, Trent Polytechnic, 1980. *Publications:* Bitter Sweet Seventeen, 1946; articles and papers in mining and other jls. *Recreations:* cricket, music, reading, crosswords. *Address:* Briar Croft, School Lane, Halam, Newark, Notts NG22 8AD. *T:* Southwell (0636) 812446. *Clubs:* Army and Navy, MCC; XL; Nottingham and Notts United Services (Nottingham).

MIRRLEES, Prof. James Alexander, FBA 1984; Edgeworth Professor of Economics, University of Oxford, and Fellow of Nuffield College, since 1968; *b* 5 July 1936; *s* of late George B. M. Mirrlees; *m* 1961, Gillian Marjorie Hughes; two *d*. *Educ:* Douglas-Ewart High Sch., Newton Stewart; Edinburgh Univ.; Trinity Coll., Cambridge. MA Edinburgh Maths, 1957; BA Cantab Maths, 1959; PhD Cantab Econs, 1963. Adviser, MIT Center for Internat. Studies, New Delhi, 1962–63; Cambridge Univ. Asst Lectr in Econs and Fellow of Trinity Coll., 1963, University Lectr, 1965; Adviser to Govt of Swaziland, 1963; Res. Assoc., Pakistan Inst. of Develt Econs, Karachi, 1966–67. Vis. Prof., MIT, 1968, 1970, 1976, 1987, Univ. of California, Berkeley, 1986. Mem., Treasury Cttee on Policy Optimisation, 1976–78. Econometric Society: Fellow, 1970; Vice-Pres., 1980, Pres., 1982; Chm., Assoc. of Univ. Teachers of Econs, 1983–87; Pres., Royal Economic Soc., 1989–. For. Hon. Mem., Amer. Acad. of Arts and Scis, 1981; Hon. Mem., Amer. Economic Assoc., 1982. Hon. DLitt Warwick, 1982. *Publications:* (joint author) Manual of Industrial Project Analysis in Developing Countries, 1969; (ed jtly) Models of Economic Growth, 1973; (jt author) Project Appraisal and Planning, 1974; articles in economic jls. *Recreations:* reading detective stories and other forms of mathematics, playing the piano, travelling, listening. *Address:* Nuffield College, Oxford; 11 Field House Drive, Oxford OX2 7NT. *T:* Oxford (0865) 52436.

MIRRLEES, Robin Ian Evelyn Stuart de la Lanne-; Richmond Herald of Arms, 1962–67; *b* Paris, 13 Jan. 1925; grandson of Ambassador La Lanne; godson of 11th Duke of Argyll; one *s*. *Educ:* Merton Coll., Oxford (MA). Several language diplomas. Served India, 1942–46; Captain RA, 1944; Gen. Staff, New Delhi, 1946; Embassy Attaché, Tokyo, 1947; Rouge Dragon Pursuivant of Arms, 1952–62 (and as such attended Coronation). Co-editor, Annuaire de France, 1966–. ADC to HM the King of Yugoslavia, 1963–70. Has raised substantial funds for humanitarian organisations; undertook restoration of Inchdrewer Castle, Scotland, and others; Laird of Island of Bernera, pop. 350. Freeman of City of London, 1960. Patrician of San Marino, 1964. Succeeded to the title of Comte de Lalanne (France), 1962 and titular Prince of Coronata. Various foreign orders of knighthood. *Recreations:* foxhunting, piloting, travelling, painting, sculpture, mystic philosophy. *Address:* Bernera Lodge, Great Bernera Island, by Stornoway, Outer Hebrides, Scotland; 115 Rue de la Pompe, Paris 16me; Inchdrewer Castle, Banff, Scotland; Villa Lambins-Lalanne, Le Touquet, France; Schloss Ratzenegg, Carinthia, Austria. *Clubs:* Buck's; Puffin's (Edinburgh); Travellers' (Paris).

MIRVISH, Edwin, OC; CBE 1989; *b* 24 July 1914; *s* of David and Anna Mirvish; *m* 1941, Anne Maklin; one *s*. *Educ:* Toronto. Proprietor: Ed Mirvish Enterprises and other cos; several restaurants; Royal Alexandra Theatre, Toronto; Old Vic Theatre, 1982–. Hon. LLD: Trent Univ., 1967; Univ. of Waterloo, 1969; Fellow, Ryerson Technical Inst., 1981. Freeman, City of London, 1984. Award of Merit, City of Toronto. *Recreation*: ballroom dancing. *Address*: 581 Bloor Street West, Toronto, Ontario M6G 1K3, Canada. *T*: 416–537–2111. *Clubs*: Empire, Canadian, Arts and Letters, Variety (Toronto).

MISCAMPBELL, Norman Alexander, QC 1974; MP (C) Blackpool North since 1962; barrister; a Recorder of the Crown Court, since 1977; *b* 20 Feb. 1925; *s* of late Alexander and Eileen Miscampbell; *m* 1961, Margaret Kendall; two *s* two *d*. *Educ*: St Edward's Sch., Oxford; Trinity Coll., Oxford. Called to Bar, Inner Temple, 1952, Bencher 1983; N Circuit. Mem., Hoylake UDC, 1955–61. Contested (C) Newton, 1955, 1959. *Address*: House of Commons, SW1; 7 Abbey Road, West Kirby, Wirral, Merseyside.

MISCHLER, Norman Martin; Chairman: Hoechst UK Ltd, 1975–84; Hoechst Ireland Ltd, 1976–84; Berger Jenson & Nicholson Ltd, 1979–84; *b* 9 Oct. 1920; *s* of late Martin Mischler and Martha Sarah (*née* Lambert); *m* 1949, Helen Dora Sinclair; one *s* one *d*. *Educ*: St Paul's Sch., London; St Catharine's Coll., Cambridge (MA). Cricket Blue, 1946. Indian Army, 1940; served in Burma Campaign; released, rank of Major, 1946. Joined Burt, Boulton & Haywood, 1947, Vice-Chm. 1963; Dep. Man. Dir, Hoechst UK Ltd, 1966; Chairman: Harlow Chemical Co. Ltd, 1972–74; Kalle Infotec Ltd, 1972–74; Director: Berger, Jenson & Nicholson Ltd, 1975–84; Ringsdorff Carbon Co. Ltd, 1968–84; Vice-Chm., German Chamber of Industry and Commerce in London, 1974–84; Mem. Council, Chemical Industries Assoc. Ltd, 1975–84. Freeman, City of London. Officer's Cross, German Order of Merit, 1985. *Recreations*: cricket, opera, and theatre. *Address*: Scott House, Earsham Street, Bungay, Suffolk NR35 1AF. *Club*: Hawks (Cambridge).

MISHCON, family name of **Baron Mishcon.**

MISHCON, Baron *cr* 1978 (Life Peer), of Lambeth in Greater London; **Victor Mishcon;** DL; Solicitor; Senior Partner, Mishcon de Reya (formerly Victor Mishcon & Co.); Opposition spokesman on legal affairs, House of Lords, since 1983; *b* 14 Aug. 1915; *s* of Rabbi Arnold and Mrs Queenie Mishcon; *m* 1976, Joan Estelle Conrad; two *s* one *d* by previous marr. *Educ*: City of London Sch. Mem. Lambeth Borough Coun., 1945–49 (Chm. Finance Cttee, 1947–49); Mem. London CC for Brixton, 1946–65 (Chairman: Public Control Cttee, 1947–52; Gen. Purposes Cttee, 1952–54; Council, April 1954–55; Supplies Cttee, 1956–57; Fire Brigade Cttee, 1958–65); Mem. GLC for Lambeth, 1964–67 (Chm., Gen. Purposes Cttee, 1964–67); Mem., ILEA, 1964–67. Member: Jt Cttee with House of Commons on Consolidation of Bills, 1983–85; Law Sub-Cttee, House of Lords European Communities Cttee, 1978–86; House of Lords Select Cttee on Procedure, 1981–83; Opposition spokesman on home affairs, House of Lords, 1983–90. Vice Chm., Lords and Commons Solicitors Gp, 1983–. Chm. Governors, Cormont and Loughborough Secondary Schools, 1947–60; Governor: Stockwell Manor Sch., 1960–78 (Chm. of Governors, 1960–67, 1970–78); JFS Comprehensive Sch., 1970–85; Philippa Fawcett Coll. of Educn, 1970–80. Member: Standing Joint Cttee, Co. of London Sessions, 1950–65 (Vice-Chm. 1959–61); Nat. Theatre Board, 1965–67, 1968–90 (Mem., Finance and General Purposes Cttee); South Bank Theatre Board, 1977–82; London Orchestra Bd, 1966–67; Exec. Cttee, London Tourist Board, 1965–67; Government Cttee of Enquiry into London Transport, 1953–54; Departmental Cttee on Homosexual Offences and Prostitution, 1954–57. Vice-Chm., Council of Christians and Jews, 1976–77; Vice-Pres., Bd of Deputies of British Jews, 1967–73; Chm., Inst. of Jewish Studies, UCL; Hon. President, Brit. Technion Soc.; Vice-Pres. (Past Pres.) Assoc. of Jewish Youth; Pres., British Council of the Shaare Zedek Hosp., Jerusalem. Contested (Lab) NW Leeds, 1950, Bath, 1951, Gravesend, 1955, 1959. DL Greater London. Hon. LLD Birmingham, 1991. Comdr Royal Swedish Order of North Star, 1954; Star of Ethiopia, 1954. *Address*: House of Lords, SW1.

MISKIN, His Honour Sir James (William), Kt 1983; QC 1967; Recorder of London, 1975–90; *b* 11 March 1925; *s* of late Geoffrey Miskin and Joyce Miskin; *m* 1st, 1951, Mollie Joan Milne; two *s* two *d*; 2nd, 1980, Sheila Joan Collett, widow. *Educ*: Haileybury; Brasenose Coll., Oxford (MA). Sub-Lt, RNVR, 1943–46. Oxford, 1946–49 (Sen. Heath Harrison Exhibnr). Called to Bar, Inner Temple, 1951; Bencher, 1976; Mem. of Bar Council, 1964–67, 1970–73. Dep. Chm., Herts QS, 1968–71; a Recorder of the Crown Court, 1972–75; Leader of SE Circuit, 1974–75. City of London Magistrate, 1976. Chm., Bd of Discipline, LSE, 1972–75. Appeals Steward, British Boxing Bd of Control, 1972–75; Chm., Inner London Probation After Care Cttee, 1979–88. One of HM Lieutenants, City of London, 1976–. Liveryman, Worshipful Co. of Curriers; Hon. Liveryman, Worshipful Co. of Cutlers. *Recreation*: golf. *Clubs*: Vincent's (Oxford); All England Lawn Tennis.

MISKIN, Raymond John, CEng, FIMechE, FIMfgE, MRAeS, FIQA; Chief Executive, Certification Authority for Dental Laboratories and Suppliers, since 1989; *b* 4 July 1928; *s* of late Sydney George Miskin and Hilda (*née* Holdsworth); *m* 1951 (marr. diss. 1981); one *d* (one *s* decd). *Educ*: Woking Grammar Sch.; Southall Technical Coll. The Fairey Aviation Co. Ltd: apprentice, 1945–49; develt engr, 1949–59; Dep. Chief Inspector, 1959–63; Quality Control Manager and Chief Inspector, Graviner Ltd, 1963–69; Sec., Inst. of Qual. Assurance, 1969–73; Dep. Sec., 1973–76, Sec., 1976–87, IProdE; Dir, IPRODE Ltd, 1976–87. Mem. Council and Hon. Treasurer, Inst. of Qual. Assurance, 1963–69; Mem., Bd, Nat. Council for Qual. and Reliability, 1969–81 (Chm., 1975–77); Hon. Mem., Amer. Inst. of Industrial Engrs, 1985. FRSA. Hon. FIIPE 1979. Freeman, City of London, 1985. Internat. Industrial Management Award, San Fernando Valley Engineers Council, USA, 1978; Internat. Achievement Award, Los Angeles Council of Engrs, 1981; GTE (Hungary) Technical Achievement Medal, 1984. *Publications*: articles in technical pubns. *Recreation*: golf. *Address*: 36 Hayes Drive, Mosborough, Sheffield S19 5TR. *Club*: Renishaw Park Golf.

MISSELBROOK, (Bertram) Desmond, CBE 1972; FRSE 1978; Chairman, Livingston Development Corporation, 1972–78; *b* 28 May 1913; *s* of late C. J. and E. P. Misselbrook; *m* 1949, Anne, *er d* of late F. O. Goodman; two *s*. *Educ*: Chatham House, Ramsgate; Bristol Univ. Admiralty Psychologist, 1942–45. Lectr in Psychology and Dir, Unit of Applied Psychology, Edinburgh Univ., 1945–49; Senr Res. Fellow in Business Studies, 1970–71, Hon. Fellow, 1971. Personnel Adviser, 1949, Dir. 1955, Dep. Chm. 1963–70, British-American Tobacco Co. Ltd; Chm., Evershed and Vignoles Ltd, 1961–65; Chm., Mardon Packaging International Ltd, 1962–70; Dir, 1963, Dep. Chm. 1966–69, Wiggins Teape Ltd; Dir, Charterhouse Gp Ltd, 1969–72; Deputy Chairman: Standard Life Assurance Co., 1977–80 (Dir, 1970–84); Anderson Mavor Ltd, 1971–74; Chairman: Anderson Strathclyde Ltd, 1974–77; Seaforth Maritime Ltd, 1977–78. Mem. Council, British Inst. of Management, 1967–72 (a Vice-Chm., 1969); Chairman: Bd of Governors, Oversea Service, 1963–70; Construction Ind. Trng Bd, 1970–73; Council, Scottish Business Sch., 1972–77; Economic Development Cttees for Building and Civil Engineering Industries, 1969–72; Member: Adv. Council on Social Work (Scotland), 1970–74; Economic Consultant, Scottish Office, 1970–72. Hon. DSc Edinburgh, 1977. *Recreations*: fishing, gardening, walking. *Address*: Auchenfranco, Lochfoot, Dumfries DG2 8NZ. *T*: Dumfries (0387) 73208.

MISTRY, Dhruva, RA 1991; sculptor; *b* 1 Jan. 1957; *s* of Pramodray and Kantaben Mistry. *Educ*: Maharaja Sayajirao Univ. of Baroda (MA 1981); RCA (British Council schol.; MA 1983). Artist-in-residence, Kettle's Yard, and Fellow of Churchill Coll., Cambridge, 1984–85. Rep. Britain at 3rd Rodin Grand Prize Exhibn, Japan, 1990. *Recreations*: photography, reading, walking. *Address*: The Cottage, Dodds Farm, Ingatestone, Essex CM4 0NW.

MITCHAM, Heather; a Metropolitan Stipendiary Magistrate, since 1986; *b* 19 Dec. 1941; *d* of Louis George Pike and Dorothy Evelyn (*née* Milverton); *m* 1964, Anthony John Mitcham; one *s* one *d*. *Educ*: The King's Sch., Ottery St Mary. Called to the Bar, Gray's Inn, 1964. Examiner, Estate Duty Office, 1960–67; Dep. Chief Clerk, Inner London Magistrates' Court Service, 1967–78; Chief Clerk, Inner London Juvenile Courts, 1978–85; Senior Chief Clerk: Thames Magistrates' Court, 1985; S Western Magistrates' Court, 1986. *Recreations*: riding, horses, gardening. *Address*: c/o Camberwell Green Magistrates' Court, D'Eynsford Road, SE5.

MITCHELL, Adrian; writer; *b* 24 Oct. 1932; *s* of James Mitchell and Kathleen Fabian. *Educ*: Greenways Sch.; Dauntsey's Sch.; Christ Church, Oxford. Worked as reporter on Oxford Mail, Evening Standard, 1955–63; subseq. free-lance journalist for Daily Mail, Sun, Sunday Times, New Statesman; Granada Fellow, Univ. of Lancaster, 1968–69; Fellow, Center for Humanities, Wesleyan Univ., 1972; Resident Writer, Sherman Theatre, Cardiff, 1974–75; Vis. writer, Billericay Comp. Sch., 1978–80; Judith E. Wilson Fellow, Cambridge Univ., 1980–81; Resident writer, Unicorn Theatre for Children, 1982–83. FRSL 1987. *Plays*: Marat/Sade (stage adaptation), RSC, 1964; Man Friday, 7:84 Theatre Co., 1973 (TV 1972, Screenplay 1975); Mind Your Head, Liverpool Everyman, 1973; Daft as a Brush (TV), 1975; A Seventh Man, Hampstead, 1976; White Suit Blues, Nottingham, Edinburgh and Old Vic, 1977; Houdini, Amsterdam, 1977; Glad Day (TV), 1978; Uppendown Mooney, Welfare State Theatre Co., 1978; The White Deer, Unicorn Theatre, 1978; Hoagy, Bix and Wolfgang Beethoven Bunkhaus, King's Head Theatre, 1979; In the Unlikely Event of an Emergency, Bath, 1979; Peer Gynt (adaptation), Oxford Playhouse, 1980; You Must Believe All This (TV), 1981; The Tragedy of King Real, Welfare State Theatre Co., 1982; Mowgli's Jungle, Contact Theatre, Manchester, 1982; A Child's Christmas in Wales (with Jeremy Brooks), Great Lakes Fest., 1983; The Wild Animal Song Contest, Unicorn Theatre, 1983; Life's a Dream (adaptation with John Barton), RSC Stratford, 1983, Barbican, 1984; C'Mon Everybody, Tricycle Theatre, 1984; The Great Theatre of the World (adaptation), Mediaeval Players, 1984; Satie Day/Night, Lyric Studio, Hammersmith, 1986; Mirandolina (adaptation), Bristol Old Vic, 1987; The Last Wild Wood in Sector 88, Rugby Music Centre, 1987; Anna on Anna, Th. Workshop, Edin., 1988; Woman Overboard, The Patchwork Girl of Oz, Palace Th., Watford, 1988; The Snow Queen, NY, 1990; Vasilisa The Fair (adaptation), NY, 1991; Pieces of Peace (TV), 1991; National Theatre: Tyger, 1971; The Mayor of Zalamea (adaptation), 1981; Animal Farm (lyrics), 1984; The Government Inspector, 1985; The Pied Piper, 1986; Love Songs of World War Three, 1987; Fuente Ovejuna (adaptation), 1989; Triple Threat, 1989. *Publications*: novels: If You See Me Comin', 1962; The Bodyguard, 1970; Wartime, 1973; poetry: Poems, 1964; Out Loud, 1968; Ride the Nightmare, 1971; The Apeman Cometh, 1975; For Beauty Douglas, (Collected Poems 1953–1979), 1982; On the Beach at Cambridge, 1984; Nothingmas Day, 1984; Love Songs of World War Three, 1988; All My Own Stuff, 1991; *for children*: The Baron Rides Out, 1985; The Baron on the Island of Cheese, 1986; The Baron All At Sea, 1987; Leonardo the Lion from Nowhere, 1987; Our Mammoth, 1987; Our Mammoth Goes to School, 1987; Our Mammoth in the Snow, 1988; The Pied Piper, 1988; Strawberry Drums, 1989; also plays. *Address*: c/o Peters, Fraser and Dunlop, 5th Floor, The Chambers, Chelsea Harbour, Lots Road, SW10 0XF. *Clubs*: Chelsea Arts; Royal Free Hospital Recreation.

MITCHELL, Alec Burton, MA; CEng, MIMechE, FRINA; Director, Admiralty Marine Technology Establishment, 1977–84, retired; Scientific Adviser to Director General Ships, Ministry of Defence, 1981–84; *b* 27 Aug. 1924; *er s* of Ronald Johnson Mitchell and Millicent Annie Mitchell; *m* 1952, Barbara, *d* of Arthur Edward and Katie Florence Jane Archer; three *s*. *Educ*: Purley County Sch.; St. John's Coll., Cambridge (MA). Mechanical Sciences Tripos, Cambridge, 1944. Aeronautical Engineer with Rolls Royce Ltd, Hucknall, 1944–46; Grad. apprentice and gas turbine design engr with English Electric Co Ltd, Rugby, 1946–48. Joined RN Scientific Service, 1948; Dep. Head of Hydrodynamic Research Div., Admty Research Lab., 1961; promoted Dep. CSO, 1966; Dep. Dir, Admty Research Laboratory, 1973, Dir, 1974–77. *Publications*: numerous scientific papers on hydrodynamics and under-water propulsion systems. *Recreations*: golf, photography, wood-work. *Address*: 32 Ormond Crescent, Hampton, Mddx TW12 2TH.

MITCHELL, Alexander Graham, CBE 1973; DFM 1945; Governor, Turks and Caicos Islands, 1973–75 (Administrator, 1971–73); *b* 2 Nov. 1923; *s* of Alexander Mitchell and Evelyn Mitchell (*née* Green); *m* 1954, Pamela Ann Borman; three *d*. *Educ*: Dulwich College; Downing Coll., Cambridge (Exhibnr; MA). Served RAF, 1942–45. Sudan Government Civil Service, 1951–55; HM Overseas Civil Service, 1955; Western Pacific High Commission: various posts in British Solomon Islands Protectorate and British Residency, New Hebrides, 1955–71; Sec., Financial Affairs, British Residency, 1968–71; sabbatical, 1975–76, retired June 1977. Clerk to Governors, Dame Allan's Schools, Newcastle, 1977–88. *Recreations*: ancient and military history. *Address*: The Dene, Stocksfield, Northumberland NE43 7PB. *Club*: Royal Over-Seas League.

MITCHELL, Andrew John Bower; MP (C) Gedling, since 1987; *b* 23 March 1956; *s* of Sir David Bower Mitchell, *qv*; *m* 1985, Sharon Denise (*née* Bennett); two *d*. *Educ*: Rugby; Jesus Coll., Cambridge (MA History Hons). 1st RTR (Short Service (Limited) Commission), 1975; served with UNFICYP. Pres., Cambridge Union, 1978; Chm., Cambridge Univ. Conservatives; rep. GB in E-SU American debating tour, 1978. Internat. and Corp. business, Lazard Brothers & Co., 1979–87, Consultant, 1987–. Mem., Islington Health Authy, 1985–87. Contested (C) Sunderland South, 1983. PPS to Minister of State, FCO, 1988–90, to Sec. of State for Energy, 1990–; Chm., Finance Bill Cttee, 1988–91. Chairman: Coningsby Club, 1983; Islington North Conservatives, 1983–85; Conservative Collegiate Forum, 1991–. *Recreations*: ski-ing, music, travel. *Address*: 30 Gibson Square, N1. *T*: 071–226 5519; Dovecote Farmhouse, Tithby, Notts. *T*: Bingham (0949) 39587. *Clubs*: Cambridge Union Society; Carlton and District Constitutional.

MITCHELL, Angus; *see* Mitchell, J. A. M.

MITCHELL, Air Cdre Sir (Arthur) Dennis, KBE 1977; CVO 1961; DFC 1944, and Bar, 1945; AFC 1943; Founder and Managing Director, Aero Systems SA; an Extra Equerry to the Queen since 1962; *b* 26 May 1918; 2nd *s* of Col A. Mitchell, DSO, Carrickfergus, Belfast, N Ireland; *m* 1949, Comtesse Mireille Caroline Cornet de Ways Ruart; one *s*. *Educ*: Nautical Coll., Pangbourne; RAF Coll., Cranwell; Army Staff Coll., Camberley; RAF Flying Coll., Manby. Joined RAF, 1936. Served 1938–45, India, Burma, UK and NW Europe; RAF Delegn, Belgium, 1948–49; US Air Force, 1951–53; HQ Allied Air Forces Central Europe, NATO, Fontainebleau, 1953–56; o/c RAF Cottesmore Bomber Comd, 1959–62; Dep. Captain and Captain of the Queen's Flight, 1956–59 and

1962–64; ADC to the Queen, 1958–62. Founder: Brussels Airways; Aero Distributors SA. French Croix de Guerre, 1945. *Recreation:* golf. *Address:* 10 chemin des Chasseurs, 1380 Ohain, Belgium. *T:* 653.13.01; (office) (2)653.00.33. *Clubs:* Royal Air Force, Naval and Military.

MITCHELL, Austin Vernon, DPhil; MP (Lab) Great Grimsby, since 1983 (Grimsby, Apr. 1977–1983); *b* 19 Sept. 1934; *s* of Richard Vernon Mitchell and Ethel Mary Mitchell; *m* 1st, Patricia Dorothea Jackson (marr. diss.); two *d*; 2nd, Linda Mary McDougall; one *s* one *d*. *Educ:* Woodbottom Council Sch.; Bingley Grammar Sch.; Manchester Univ. (BA, MA); Nuffield Coll., Oxford (DPhil). Lectr in History, Univ. of Otago, Dunedin, NZ, 1959–63; Sen. Lectr in Politics, Univ. of Canterbury, Christchurch, NZ, 1963–67; Official Fellow, Nuffield Coll., Oxford, 1967–69; Journalist, Yorkshire Television, 1969–71; Presenter, BBC Current Affairs Gp, 1972–73; Journalist, Yorkshire TV, 1973–77; Co- presenter, Target, Sky TV, 1989–. Opposition frontbench spokesman on trade and industry, 1987–89. *Publications:* New Zealand Politics In Action, 1962; Government By Party, 1966; The Whigs in Opposition 1815–1830, 1969; Politics and People in New Zealand, 1970; Yorkshire Jokes, 1971; The Half-Gallon Quarter-Acre Pavlova Paradise, 1974; Can Labour Win Again, 1979; Westminster Man, 1982; The Case for Labour, 1983; Four Years in the Death of the Labour Party, 1983; Yorkshire Jokes, 1988; Teach Thissen Tyke, 1988; Britain: beyond the blue horizon, 1989; Competitive Socialism, 1989. *Recreation:* worriting (*sic*). *Address:* 15 New Cartergate, Grimsby, South Humberside DN31 1RB. *T:* Grimsby (0472) 342145; House of Commons, SW1A 0AA. *T:* 071–219 4559.

MITCHELL, Prof. Basil George, DD; FBA 1983; Nolloth Professor of the Philosophy of the Christian Religion, Oxford University, 1968–84; Fellow of Oriel College, 1968–84, now Emeritus; *b* 9 April 1917; *s* of George William Mitchell and Mary Mitchell (*née* Loxston); *m* 1950, Margaret Eleanor Collin; one *s* three *d*. *Educ:* King Edward VI Sch., Southampton; Queen's Coll., Oxford (Southampton Exhibitioner. 1st cl. Lit Hum 1939). Served Royal Navy, 1940–46; Lt RNVR 1942, Instructor Lt RN 1945. Lectr, Christ Church, Oxford, 1946–47; Fellow and Tutor in Philosophy, Keble Coll., Oxford, 1947–67, Emeritus Fellow, 1981; Sen. Proctor, 1956–57; Hebdomadal Council, 1959–65. Visiting Professor: Princeton Univ., 1963; Colgate Univ., 1976. Lectures: Stanton, in Philosophy of Religion, Cambridge Univ., 1959–62; Edward Cadbury, University of Birmingham, 1966–67; Gifford, Glasgow Univ., 1974–76; Nathaniel Taylor, Yale, 1986; Martin, Univ. of Hong Kong, 1987; Norton, Southern Baptist Theol Seminary, Louisville, 1989. Member: C of E Working Parties on Ethical Questions, 1964–78; Doctrine Commn, 1978–84. Chm., Ian Ramsey Centre, 1985–89. Hon. DD Glasgow, 1977; Hon. DLitHum Union Coll., Schenectady, 1979. *Publications:* (ed) Faith and Logic, 1957; Law, Morality and Religion in a Secular Society, 1967; Neutrality and Commitment, 1968; (ed) The Philosophy of Religion, 1971; The Justification of Religious Belief, 1973; Morality: Religious and Secular, 1980; How to Play Theological Ping Pong, 1990; articles in philosophical and theological periodicals. *Address:* Bridge House, Wootton, Woodstock, Oxford OX7 1DL. *T:* Woodstock (0993) 811265.

MITCHELL, Bob; *see* Mitchell, R. C.

MITCHELL, Charles Julian Humphrey; *see* Mitchell, Julian.

MITCHELL, Lt-Col Colin Campbell; former soldier and politician; Director, The HALO Trust, since 1987; *b* 17 Nov. 1925; *o s* of Colin Mitchell, MC, and Janet Bowie Gilmour; *m* 1956, Jean Hamilton Susan Phillips; two *s* one *d*. *Educ:* Whitgift Sch. British Army, 1943; commissioned Argyll and Sutherland Highlanders, 1944, serving in Italy (wounded); Palestine, 1945–48 (wounded); Korea, 1950–51; Cyprus, 1958–59; Borneo, 1964 (brevet Lt-Col); Aden, 1967 (despatches). Staff appts as ADC to GOC-in-C Scottish Command; Directorate of Mil. Ops (MO4), WO; Qualified Camberley Staff Coll., 1955; subsequently: GSO2, 51st Highland Div. (TA); Bde Major, King's African Rifles, and GSO1 Staff of Chief of Defence Staff at MoD. Retired at own request, 1968; subseq. Special Correspondent, Vietnam. MP (C) W Aberdeenshire, 1970–Feb. 1974 (not seeking re-election); PPS to Sec. of State for Scotland, 1972–73. Mem., Select Cttee on Armed Services, 1970–71. Specialist Consultant: Rhodesia, 1975–79; Mexico, 1980; Afghanistan, 1983; Nicaragua, 1985; Pakistan NWFP, 1986; Eritrea, 1987; Cambodia, 1990. Freedom of City of London, 1979. *Publication:* Having Been A Soldier, 1969. *Recreations:* reading, travel. *Address:* The Old Farmhouse, Hill Farm, Gressenhall, Dereham, Norfolk NR19 2NR. *T:* Dereham (0362) 695305. *Clubs:* Garrick; Puffin's (Edinburgh).

MITCHELL, Sir David (Bower), Kt 1988; MP (C) Hampshire North West, since 1983 (Basingstoke, 1964–83); *b* June 1928; *er s* of James Mitchell, Naval Architect; *m* 1954, Pamela Elaine Haward (separated); two *s* one *d*. *Educ:* Aldenham. Farming, 1945–50; businessman, wine merchant, 1951–79. An Opposition Whip, 1965–67; PPS to Sec. of State for Social Services, 1970–74; Parly Under Sec. of State, DoI, 1979–81, NI Office, 1981–83, Dept of Transport, 1983–85; Minister of State for Transport, 1986–88. Chm., Cons. Smaller Business Cttee, 1974–79; Founder, 1976, Trustee Mem., 1989–, Small Business Bureau. *Recreations:* gardening, walking, wine-tasting. *Address:* House of Commons, SW1A 0AA. *Club:* Carlton.
See also A. J. B. Mitchell.

MITCHELL, David William, CBE 1983; Chairman, Cumbernauld New Town Development Corporation, since 1987 (Member since 1985); *b* 4 Jan. 1933; *m* 1965, Lynda Katherine Marion Guy; one *d*. *Educ:* Merchiston Castle School, Edinburgh. Western RHB, 1968–75; Director: Mallinson, Denny (Scotland), 1975–89; Hunter Timber (Scotland), 1989–. Member: Exec. Cttee, Scottish Council Develt and Industry, 1979–; Scottish Council, CBI, 1980–85; Scottish Exec. Cttee, Inst. of Directors, 1984–. President: Timber Trade Benevolent Soc., 1974; Scottish Timber Trade Assoc., 1984. Pres., Scottish Cons. and Unionist Assoc., 1980– 82; Treasurer, Scottish Cons. Party, 1990–. *Recreations:* golf, shooting, fishing. *Address:* Dunmullen House, Blanefield, Stirlingshire G63 9AJ. *T:* Blanefield (0360) 70885. *Clubs:* Western (Glasgow); Royal and Ancient Golf, Prestwick Golf.

MITCHELL, Sir Dennis; *see* Mitchell, Sir A. D.

MITCHELL, Sir Derek (Jack), KCB 1974 (CB 1967); CVO 1966; Director, Bowater Inc., since 1984; Independent Director, The Observer Ltd, since 1981; Member, Royal National Theatre Board, since 1977; *b* 5 March 1922; *s* of late Sidney Mitchell, Schoolmaster, and Gladys Mitchell; *m* 1944, Miriam, *d* of late F. E. Jackson; one *s* two *d*. *Educ:* St Paul's Sch.; Christ Church, Oxford. Served War of 1939–45: Royal Armoured Corps and HQ London District, 1942–45. Asst Principal HM Treasury, 1947; Private Sec. to Economic Sec., 1948–49; Private Sec. to Permanent Sec. and Official Head of Civil Service (Sir Edward Bridges), 1954–56; Principal Private Sec. to: Chancellor of Exchequer (Mr Reginald Maudling), 1962–63; The Prime Minister (Mr Harold Wilson, previously Sir Alec Douglas-Home), 1964–66; Under-Sec., 1964; Dep. Under-Sec. of State, Dept of Economic Affairs, 1966–67; Dep. Sec., Min. of Agriculture, Fisheries and Food, 1967–69; Economic Minister and Head of UK Treasury and Supply Delegn, Washington, (also UK Executive Director for IMF and IBRD), 1969–72; Second Permanent Sec. (Overseas Finance), HM Treasury, 1973–77. Director: Guinness Mahon & Co., 1977–78; Bowater Corp., 1979–84; Bowater Industries, 1984–89; Standard Chartered, 1979–89; Sen. Advr, Shearson Lehman Brothers Internat., 1979–88. Mem., PLA, 1979–82. Dir, Peter Hall Production Co. Ltd, 1989–90; Chm., Royal Nat. Theatre Foundn, 1989– (Treas., 1982–89). Mem. Council, University Coll. London, 1978–82; Governing Trustee, Nuffield Provincial Hospitals Trust, 1978–; Trustee, Royal Nat. Theatre Endowment Fund, 1990–; Chm., Betty Rhodes Fund, 1989–. *Recreations:* opera, theatre, music, travel, motoring on minor roads. *Address:* 9 Holmbush Road, Putney, SW15 3LE. *T:* 081–788 6581. *Club:* Garrick.

MITCHELL, Douglas Svärd; Controller of Personnel and Administrative Services, Greater London Council, 1972–78; *b* 21 Aug. 1918; *er s* of late James Livingstone Mitchell and Hilma Josefine (*née* Svärd); *m* 1943, Winifred Thornton Paterson, *d* of late William and Ellen Paterson; one *s* two *d*. *Educ:* Morgan Academy, Dundee. Royal Ordnance Factories, 1937–51; Principal, Min. of Supply, 1951–55; Dir of Personnel and Admin., in Industrial, Production and Engineering Groups, UKAEA, 1955–63; Authority Personnel Officer for UKAEA, 1963–64; Dir of Establishments, GLC, 1964–72. *Address:* The Manor House, Horncastle, Lincolnshire LN9 5HF. *T:* Horncastle (0507) 523553.

MITCHELL, Sir (Edgar) William (John), Kt 1990; CBE 1976; FRS 1986; Fellow of Wadham College, Oxford, since 1978; *b* Kingsbridge, S Devon, 25 Sept. 1925; *s* of late Edgar and Caroline Mitchell; *m* 1985, Prof. Margaret Davies (*née* Brown); one *s* by previous *m*. *Educ:* Univs of Sheffield (BSc, MSc) and Bristol (PhD). FInstP. Metropolitan Vickers Research Dept, 1946–48, 1950–51; Univ. of Bristol, 1948–50; University of Reading, 1951–78: Prof. of Physics, 1961–78; Dean, Faculty of Science, 1966–69; Dep. Vice-Chancellor, 1976–78; University of Oxford: Dr Lee's Prof. of Experimental Philosophy, 1978–88; Prof of Physics, 1988–89. Science and Engineering Research Council (formerly Science Research Council): Mem., 1970–74, 1982–85; Chm., 1985–90; Mem., 1965–70, Chm., 1967–70, Physics Cttee; Chm., Neutron Beam Res. Cttee, 1966–74; Mem., Sci. Planning Gp for Spallation Neutron Source, 1978–85; Mem., Sci. Bd (formerly Univ. Sci. and Tech. Bd), 1967–70; Mem., Nuclear Physics Bd, 1980–85. Mem., Management Bd, British National Space Centre, 1986–90; devised scheme for extensive University use of nuclear res. reactors for condensed matter res. Acting Jt Dir, 1973, Mem., 1973–80, Sci. Council of Inst. Laue-Langevin, Grenoble; Member: Comité de Direction, Solid State Physics Lab., Ecole Normale and Univ. of Paris VI, 1975–79; Exec. Cttee, Univ. Council for Non-Academic Staff, 1979–82; UGC Phys. Sci. Cttee, 1982–85; Council, Inst. of Physics, 1982–86; ABRC, 1985–90; Council, Foundn of Sci. and Technol., 1985–90; Innovation Adv. Bd, DTI, 1988–90; Scientific Adv. Cttee for Nat. Gall., 1988–; Chm., SE Reg. Computing Cttee, 1974–76; Vice-Pres., European Sci. Foundn, 1989–; Mem. Council, CERN, 1985– (Vice-Pres., 1990; Pres., 1991–). Mem., Academia Europaea, 1989. Hon. DSc: Reading, 1987; Kent, 1988; Budapest, 1988; Birmingham, 1990. Officer Cross, Order of Merit (Germany), 1990. *Publications:* numerous papers on solid state physics. *Recreations:* good food, opera, motoring, physics. *Address:* Wadham College, Oxford.

MITCHELL, Mrs Eric; *see* Shacklock, Constance.

MITCHELL, Ewan; *see* Janner, Hon. G. E.

MITCHELL, Frank; *see* Mitchell, G. F.

MITCHELL, Rear-Adm. Geoffrey Charles, CB 1973; retired 1975; Director, The Old Granary Art and Craft Centre, Bishop's Waltham, Hants, 1975–86; *b* 21 July 1921; *s* of William C. Mitchell; *m* 1955, Jocelyn Rainger (*d* 1987), Auckland, NZ; one *s* two *d*; *m* 1990, Dr Hilary Gardiner. *Educ:* Marlborough College. Joined RN 1940; Captain 1961; Director Officer Recruiting, 1961–63; Captain (F), 2nd Frigate Sqdn, 1963–65; Director Naval Ops and Trade, 1965–67; Comdr, NATO Standing Naval Force Atlantic, 1968–69; Director Strategic Policy, to Supreme Allied Comdr Atlantic, 1969–71; Rear Adm. 1971; Dep. Asst Chief of Staff (Ops), SHAPE, 1971–74; Chm., RNR and Naval Cadet Forces Review Bd, 1974–75. *Recreations:* golf, painting, music, languages, sailing. *Address:* Crabwood Farm House, Sarum Road, Winchester SO22 5QS. *T:* Winchester (0962) 853340.

MITCHELL, Prof. George Archibald Grant, OBE 1945; TD 1950; Professor of Anatomy and Director of Anatomical Laboratories, Manchester University, 1946–74, now Professor Emeritus; late Dean of Medical School and Pro-Vice-Chancellor; *b* 11 Nov. 1906; *s* of George and Agnes Mitchell; *m* 1933, Mary Cumming; one *s* two *d*. *Educ:* Fordyce Academy; Aberdeen Central Sch.; Aberdeen Univ. MB, ChB (1st Cl. Hons), 1929; ChM 1933; MSc (Manchester); DSc (Aberdeen) 1950; FRCS 1968. Lecturer in Anatomy, 1930–33, in Surgery, 1933–34, Aberdeen Univ.; Surgical Specialist, Co. Caithness, 1934–37; Sen. Lecturer in Anatomy, Aberdeen Univ., 1937–39. Chm., Internat. Anatomical Nomenclature Commn, 1970–75. Pres., 3rd European Anatomical Congress; Pres., S Lancs and E Cheshire BMA Br. Council, 1972–73; Mem. Ct of Examnrs, RCS, 1950–68; Mem. Bd of Governors, United Manchester Hosps, 1955–74; Past President: Anatomical Soc. of GB and Ireland; Manchester Med. Soc. Served War, 1939–45: Surgical Specialist, Officer i/c No. 1 Orthopædic Centre, MEF; Officer i/c Surgical Divs, Adviser in Penicillin and Chemotherapy, 21 Army Gp. Hon. Alumnus, Univ. of Louvain, 1944; Hon. Member: Société Med. Chir. du Centre; Assoc. des Anatomistes; Amer. Assoc. Anat.; British Assoc. Clin. Anat. Chevalier First Class Order of the Dannebrog. *Publications:* The Anatomy of the Autonomic Nervous System, 1952; Basic Anatomy (with E. L. Patterson), 1954; Cardiovascular Innervation, 1956; ed Symposium, Penicillin Therapy and Control in 21 Army Group, 1945. Sections in: Penicillin (by Sir A. Fleming), 1946; Medical Disorders of the Locomotor System (by E. Fletcher), 1947; British Surgical Practice (by Sir Rock Carling and Sir J. Patterson Ross), 1951; Peripheral Vascular Disorders (by Martin, Lynn, Dible and Aird), 1956; Essentials of Neuroanatomy, 1966; Encyclopaedia Britannica, 15th edn; Editor, Nomina Anatomica, 1956–70. Numerous articles in Jl Anatomy, British Jl Surg., Jl Bone and Joint Surg., Brit. Jl Radiol., BMJ, Lancet, Acta Anat., Nature, Brit. Jl Urol., Edinburgh Medical Jl, Jl Hist. Med., Aberdeen Univ. Rev., Ann. Méd. Chir. du Centre, etc. *Recreations:* music, studying archaeology.

MITCHELL, George Francis (Frank), FRS 1973; MRIA; environmental historian; *b* 15 Oct. 1912; *s* of late David William Mitchell and late Frances Elizabeth Kirby; *m* 1940, Lucy Margaret Gwynn (*d* 1987); two *d*. *Educ:* High Sch., Dublin; Trinity Coll., Dublin (MA, MSc); FTCD 1945. Joined staff of Trinity Coll., Dublin, 1934; Professor of Quaternary Studies, 1965–79. Pro-Chancellor, Univ. of Dublin, 1985–88. Pres., Internat. Union for Quaternary Research, 1969–73. MRIA 1939, PRIA 1976–79. HRHA 1981; Hon. Life Mem., RDS, 1981; Hon. Member: Prehistoric Soc., 1983; Quaternary Res. Assoc., 1983; Hon. FRSE 1984. DSc (*hc*): Queen's Univ., Belfast, 1976; NUI, 1977; fil.D (*hc*) Uppsala, 1977. *Publications:* The Irish Landscape, 1976; Treasures of Early Irish Art, 1977; Shell Guide to Reading the Irish Landscape, 1986; Archaeology and Environment in Early Dublin, 1987; Man and Environment on Valencia Island, Co. Kerry, 1989; The Way that I Followed, 1990. *Address:* Gardener's Cottage, Townley Hall, Drogheda, Co. Louth, Republic of Ireland. *T:* Drogheda 34615.

MITCHELL, Harry; QC 1987; Company Secretary, The Wellcome Foundation Ltd, since 1976, and Wellcome plc, since 1985; *b* 27 Oct. 1930; *s* of Harry and Lily Mitchell; *m* 1960, Mrs Megan Knill (*née* Watkins); one step *s* one step *d. Educ:* Bolton School; Corpus Christi College, Cambridge (BA). FCIS. Called to the Bar, Gray's Inn, 1968. Asst District Comr, Colonial Service, Sierra Leone, 1954–59; Company Sec., Asbestos Cement, Bombay, 1960–64; Asst Company Sec., British Aluminium Co., 1964–66; Legal Manager/Exec. Dir Legal, Hawker Siddeley Aviation, 1966–76. Chm., Bar Assoc. for Commerce, Finance and Industry, 1984–85 (Vice-Pres., 1986–); Mem. Senate of Inns of Court and Bar and Bar Council, 1978–81, 1983–84. Mem., CBI London Regional Council, 1990–. *Publications:* articles in New Law Jl and Business Law Review. *Recreations:* playing piano, opera, reading, travel. *Address:* 13 Garrick Gardens, East Molesey, Surrey KT8 9SL. *T:* (home) 081–979 7154; (office) 071–387 4477.

MITCHELL, Helen Josephine; *see* Watts, H. J.

MITCHELL, Ian Edward; Manager, CKS Products Ltd, since 1982; *b* 24 Dec. 1932; *s* of George Thomas Mitchell and Lorna May Mitchell. *Educ:* Queensland, Australia. Town Clerk's Dept, Brisbane City Council, 1953–65; Gen. Sec., British Film Producers Assoc. Ltd, 1966–81; Co. Sec. and Dir, Central Casting Ltd, 1970–81; Administrator, Fedn of Specialised Film Producers Assocs, 1970–80. Manager, Vicars Saunderson and Partners, 1981–82. *Recreations:* amateur theatricals, opera, swimming, tennis.

MITCHELL, James; writer these many years; *b* South Shields, 12 March 1926; *s* of James Mitchell and Wilhelmina Mitchell; *m* 1968, Delia, *d* of Major and Mrs K. J. McCoy; two *s. Educ:* South Shields Grammar Sch.; St Edmund Hall, Oxford (BA 1948, MA 1950); King's Coll., Newcastle upon Tyne, Univ. of Durham (DipEd 1950). Worked in rep. theatre, 1948, then in shipyard, travel agency and Civil Service; taught for some fifteen years in almost every kind of instn from secondary modern sch. to coll. of art. Free-lance writer: novels; more than a hundred television scripts; several screenplays and a theatre play. *Publications:* Here's a Villain, 1957; A Way Back, 1959; Steady Boys, Steady, 1960; Among Arabian Sands, 1963; The Man Who Sold Death, 1964; Die Rich, Die Happy, 1965; The Money that Money can't Buy, 1967; The Innocent Bystanders, 1969; Ilion like a Mist, 1969; A Magnum for Schneider, 1969; The Winners, 1970; Russian Roulette, 1973; Death and Bright Water, 1974; Smear Job, 1975; When the Boat Comes In, 1976; The Hungry Years, 1976; Upwards and Onwards, 1977; The Evil Ones, 1982; Sometimes You Could Die, 1985; Dead Ernest, 1986; Dying Day, 1988; A Woman To Be Loved, 1990. *Recreations:* travel, military history, aristology. *Address:* 41 Baron's Keep, Gliddon Road, W14 9AU. *Club:* Lansdowne.

MITCHELL, James; Social Security Commissioner, since 1980; *b* 11 June 1926; *s* of James Hill Mitchell and Marjorie Kate Mitchell (*née* Williams); *m* 1957, Diane Iris Mackintosh; two *d. Educ:* Merchiston Castle Sch., Edinburgh; Brasenose Coll., Oxford, 1944–45 and 1948–51 (Open Exhibnr, BCL, MA). Served RAFVR, 1945–48. Assistant Master, Edge Grove Preparatory Sch., Herts, 1952–55; called to the Bar, Middle Temple, 1954; private practice as barrister/solicitor, Gold Coast/Ghana, 1956–58; practice as barrister, London, 1958–80. Most Hon. Order of Crown of Brunei, 3rd Cl. 1959, 2nd Cl. 1972. *Recreations:* sailing, walking, railways, the Jacobites. *Address:* (office) Harp House, 83/86 Farringdon Street, EC4A 4BL. *T:* 071–353 5145.

MITCHELL, Dr James Clyde, FBA 1990; Emeritus Fellow, Nuffield College, Oxford, 1985 (Official Fellow, 1973–85); *b* 21 June 1918; *s* of George Shellard Mitchell and Rosina Kate Jones; *m* 1st, 1942, Edna Masken (*d* 1962); three *s* one *d*, 2nd, 1964, Hilary Flegg (*d* 1976); one step *d*; 3rd, 1987, Jean Edwards. *Educ:* Univ. of Natal (BA(Soc. Sci)); Univ. of Oxford (MA, DPhil 1950); Univ. of Manchester (MA). Served War, Air Navigator, SAAF, 1942–45. Rhodes-Livingstone Institute, Northern Rhodesia: Asst Anthropologist, 1945–50; Sen. Sociologist, 1950–52; Dir, 1952–55; Prof. of African Studies and Sociology, UC of Rhodesia and Nyasaland, 1955–65; Prof. of Urban Studies, Univ. of Manchester, 1966–73. Rivers Meml Medal, for distinguished fieldwork, RAI, 1964. *Publications:* The Yao Village, 1956, 3rd edn 1971; The Kalela Dance, 1957; (ed) Social Networks in Urban Situations, 1969, 2nd edn 1971; (ed with J. Boissevain) Network Analysis: studies in interaction, 1973; (ed) Numerical Techniques in Social Anthropology, 1980; Cities, Society and Social Perception, 1987; contrib. sociol. and anthropol. jls. *Recreations:* bird-watching, gardening. *Address:* 25 Staunton Road, Headington, Oxford OX3 7TJ. *T:* Oxford (0865) 62539.

MITCHELL, Rt. Hon. James Fitzallen; PC 1985; MP for the Grenadines, since 1966; Prime Minister of St Vincent and the Grenadines, and Minister of Finance, since 1984; *b* 15 May 1931; *s* of Reginald and Lois Mitchell; *m* (marr. diss.); four *d. Educ:* Imperial College of Tropical Agriculture (DICTA); University of British Columbia (BSA). Agronomist, 1958–65; owner, Hotel Frangipani, Bequia, 1966–, and other cos; Minister of Trade, Agriculture and Tourism, 1967–72; Premier, 1972–74. Founder and Pres., New Democratic Party, 1975–. Alumni Award of Distinction, Univ. of BC, 1988. Order of the Liberator, Venezuela, 1972. *Publications:* World Fungicide Usage, 1967; Caribbean Crusade, 1989. *Recreations:* farming, yachting, windsurfing. *Address:* Bequia, St Vincent, West Indies. *T:* 809–458–3263. *Clubs:* St Vincent Nat. Trust; Bequia Sailing.

MITCHELL, (James Lachlan) Martin, RD 1969; Sheriff of Lothian and Borders (formerly Lothians and Peebles), since 1974 (as a floating Sheriff, 1974–78, and at Edinburgh, 1978); *b* 13 June 1929; *o s* of late Dr L. M. V. Mitchell, OBE, MB, ChB and Harriet Doris Riggall. *Educ:* Cargilfield; Sedbergh; Univ. of Edinburgh. MA 1951, LLB 1953. Admitted Mem. Faculty of Advocates, 1957; Standing Junior Counsel in Scotland to Admty Bd, 1963–74. Nat. Service, RN, 1954–55; Sub-Lt (S) RNVR 1954; Perm. Reserve, 1956; Comdr RNR 1966, retd 1974. *Recreations:* fishing, photography, gramophone. *Address:* 3 Great Stuart Street, Edinburgh EH3 6AP. *T:* 031–225 3384. *Clubs:* New (Edinburgh); Highland (Inverness).

MITCHELL, Jeremy George Swale Hamilton; consumer policy adviser; *b* 25 May 1929; *s* of late George Oswald Mitchell and late Agnes Josephine Mitchell; *m* 1st, 1956, Margaret Mary Ayres (marr. diss. 1988); three *s* one *d*; 2nd, 1989, Janet Rosemary Powney. *Educ:* Ampleforth; Brasenose and Nuffield Colls, Oxford (MA). Dep. Research Dir, then Dir of Information, Consumers' Assoc. (Which?), 1958–65; Asst Sec., Nat. Econ. Develt Office, 1965–66; Scientific Sec., then Sec., SSRC, 1966–74; Under Sec., and Dir of Consumer Affairs, Office of Fair Trading, 1974–77; Under Sec. and Dir, Nat. Consumer Council, 1977–86. Member: Economic Develt Cttee for the Distributive Trades, 1981–86; Independent Cttee for Supervision of Telephone Information Services, 1989–; Direct Mail Services Standards Bd, 1990–; Vice-Chm., Nat. Council on Gambling, 1981–. *Publications:* (ed) SSRC Reviews of Research, series, 1968–73; (ed jtly) Social Science Research and Industry, 1971; Betting, 1972; (ed) Marketing and the Consumer Movement, 1978; (ed jtly) The Information Society, 1985; (ed) Money and the Consumer, 1988; Electronic Banking and the Consumer, 1988; The Consumer and Financial Services, 1990; The Single European Market for Financial Services, 1991. *Recreation:* Swinburne. *Address:* 214 Evering Road, E5 8AJ. *Club:* Savile.

MITCHELL, Prof. Joan Eileen, (Mrs James Cattermole); Professor of Political Economy, University of Nottingham, 1978–85; *b* 15 March 1920; *d* of late Albert Henry Mitchell, Paper Merchant, and Eva Mitchell; *m* 1956, James Cattermole; one *s* one *d. Educ:* Southend-on-Sea High Sch.; St Hilda's Coll., Oxford. Economist, Min. of Fuel and Power, 1942; Tutor, St Anne's Coll., Oxford, 1945; Economist, BoT, 1947; Research Officer, Labour Party, 1950; Lectr in Econs, Nottingham Univ., 1952, Reader in Econs, 1962. Mem., NBPI, 1965–68; personal economic adviser to Sec. of State for Prices and Consumer Protection, 1974–76. Member: Cttee to Review the Functioning of Financial Institutions, 1977–80 (Chm. Res. Panel); Standing Commn on Pay Comparability, 1979–81. *Publications:* Britain in Crisis 1951, 1963; Groundwork to Economic Planning, 1966; The National Board for Prices and Incomes, 1972; Price Determination and Prices Policy, 1978. *Recreations:* gardening, cooking. *Address:* 15 Ranmoor Road, Gedling, Nottingham NG4 3FW.

MITCHELL, (John) Angus (Macbeth), CB 1979; CVO 1961; MC 1946; Secretary, Scottish Education Department, 1976–84; *b* 25 Aug. 1924; *s* of late John Fowler Mitchell, CIE and of Sheila Macbeth, MBE; *m* 1948, Ann Katharine Williamson, MA, MPhil, author; two *s* two *d. Educ:* Marlborough Coll.; Brasenose Coll., Oxford (Junior Hulme Scholar); BA Modern Hist., 1948. Served Royal Armoured Corps, 1943–46: Lieut, Inns of Court Regt, NW Europe, 1944–45; Captain East African Military Records, 1946. Entered Scottish Education Dept, 1949; Private Sec. to Sec. of State for Scotland, 1958–59; Asst Sec., Scottish Educn Dept, 1959–65; Dept of Agriculture and Fisheries for Scotland, 1965–68; Scottish Development Dept, 1968; Asst Under-Secretary of State, Scottish Office, 1968–69; Under Sec., Social Work Services Gp, Scottish Educn Dept, 1969–75; Under Sec., SHHD, 1975–76. Chairman: Scottish Marriage Guidance Council, 1965–69; Working Party on Social Work Services in NHS, 1976; Working Party on Relationships between Health Bds and Local Authorities, 1976; Consultative Cttee on the Curriculum, 1976–80; Stirling Univ. Court, 1984–; Scottish Action on Dementia, 1985–; Vice-Convenor, Scottish Council for Voluntary Orgs, 1986–91; Member: Commn for Local Authority Accounts in Scotland, 1985–89; Historic Buildings Council for Scotland, 1988–. Hon. Fellow, Edinburgh Univ. Dept of Politics, 1984–88. Hon. LLD Dundee, 1983. Kt, Order of Oranje-Nassau (Netherlands), 1946. *Publication:* Procedures for the Reorganisation of Schools in England (report), 1987. *Recreations:* old Penguins; gravestones. *Address:* 20 Regent Terrace, Edinburgh EH7 5BS. *T:* 031–556 7671. *Club:* New (Edinburgh).

MITCHELL, John Gall, QC (Scot.) 1970; a Social Security (formerly National Insurance) Commissioner, since 1979; *b* 5 May 1931; *s* of late Rev. William G. Mitchell, MA; *m* 1st, 1959, Anne Bertram Jardine (*d* 1986); three *s* one *d*; 2nd, 1988, Margaret, *d* of J. W. Galbraith. *Educ:* Royal High Sch., Edinburgh; Edinburgh Univ. (MA, LLB). Advocate 1957. Standing Junior Counsel, Customs and Excise, Scotland, 1964–70; Chairman: Industrial Tribunals, Scotland, 1966–80; Legal Aid Supreme Court Cttee, Scotland, 1974–79; Pensions Appeals Tribunal, Scotland, 1974–80. Hon. Sheriff of Lanarkshire, 1970–74. *Address:* Rosemount, Park Road, Eskbank, Dalkeith, Midlothian.

MITCHELL, John Logan, QC (Scot) 1987; *b* 23 June 1947; *s* of Robert Mitchell and Dorothy Mitchell; *m* 1973, Christine Brownlee Thomson; one *s* one *d. Educ:* Royal High School, Edinburgh; Edinburgh Univ. (LLB Hons). Called to the Bar, 1974; Standing Junior Counsel: to Dept of Agriculture and Fisheries for Scotland, 1979; Forestry Commission for Scotland, 1979; Advocate Depute, 1981–85. *Recreation:* golf. *Address:* 17 Braid Farm Road, Edinburgh. *T:* 031–447 8099. *Club:* Mortonhall Golf.

MITCHELL, John Matthew, CBE 1976; PhD; Assistant Director-General, 1981–84, Senior Research Fellow, 1984–85, British Council; retired; *b* 22 March 1925; *s* of Clifford George Arthur Mitchell and Grace Maud Jamson; *m* 1952, Eva Maria von Rupprecht; three *s* one *d. Educ:* Ilford County High Sch.; Worcester Coll., Oxford; Queens' Coll., Cambridge (MA). PhD Vienna. Served War, RN, 1944–46. British Council: Lectr, Austria, 1949–52 and Egypt, 1952–56; Scotland, 1957–60; Dep. Rep., Japan, 1960–63; Reg. Dir, Zagreb, 1963–66; Reg. Rep., Dacca, 1966–69; Dep. Controller, Home Div., 1969–72; Rep., Federal Republic of Germany, 1973–77; Controller, Educn, Medicine and Sci. Div., 1977–81. Vis. Fellow, Wolfson Coll., Cambridge, 1972–73; former Lectr, univs of Vienna, Cairo and Tokyo. Fellow, Inst. of Linguists (Chm., Translating Div.). *Publications:* International Cultural Relations, 1986; verse, short stories and trans. from German. *Recreations:* ski-ing, theatre, cinema, opera. *Address:* The Cottage, Pains Hill Corner, Pains Hill, Limpsfield, Surrey RH8 0RB. *T:* Oxted (0883) 723354. *Clubs:* National Liberal; Tandridge Golf.

MITCHELL, John Wesley, FRS 1956; PhD, DSc; Senior Research Fellow and Emeritus Professor, University of Virginia, since 1979; *b* 3 Dec. 1913; *s* of late John Wesley Mitchell and late Lucy Ruth Mitchell; *m* 1976, Virginia Hill; one step *d* of former marriage. *Educ:* Canterbury University Coll., Christchurch, NZ; Univ. of Oxford. BSc 1934. MSc 1935, NZ; PhD 1938, DSc 1960, Oxford. Reader in Experimental Physics in the Univ. of Bristol, 1945–59; Prof. of Physics, Univ. of Virginia, 1959–63; Dir of the National Chemical Laboratory, Oct. 1963–Aug. 1964; William Barton Rogers Prof. of Physics, Univ. of Virginia, 1964–79. *Publications:* various on photographic sensitivity and on plastic deformation of crystals in scientific journals. *Recreations:* mountaineering, colour photography. *Address:* Department of Physics, University of Virginia, Charlottesville, Virginia 22901, USA. *Clubs:* Athenæum; Cosmos (Washington, DC).

MITCHELL, Joseph Rodney; Director General of Defence Accounts, Ministry of Defence, 1973, retired; *b* 11 March 1914; *s* of late Joseph William and Martha Mitchell, Sheffield; *m* 1936, Marian Richardson; two *s* three *d. Educ:* Sheffield Central Secondary School. FCCA, ACMA, ACIS. Works Recorder and Junior Costs Clerk, United Steel Cos Ltd, Sheffield, 1930–35; Senior Accounts Clerk, Cargo Fleet Iron Co. Ltd, Middlesbrough, 1936–39; Royal Ordnance Factories, 1940–55: Chief Exec. Officer, 1951–55; Min. of Supply/Aviation/Technology, 1956–71: Dir of Accounts, 1967–71; Dep. Dir Gen. of Defence Accounts, MoD, 1971–72. *Recreation:* hill-walking. *Address:* 4 Orchard Court, Hathersage Road, Grindleford, Sheffield S30 1JH.

MITCHELL, Julian; writer; *b* 1 May 1935; *s* of late William Moncur Mitchell and of Christine Mary (*née* Browne). *Educ:* Winchester; Wadham Coll. Oxford. Nat. Service in Submarines, 1953–55; Temp. Acting Sub-Lieut, RNVR. Member: Literature Panel, Arts Council, 1966–69; Welsh Arts Council, 1988– (Chm. Drama Cttee, 1989–). John Llewellyn Rhys Prize, 1965; Somerset Maugham Award, 1966. Television plays include: Shadow in the Sun; A Question of Degree; Rust; Abide With Me (Internat. Critics Prize, Monte Carlo, 1977); Survival of the Fittest; adaptations of: Persuasion; The Alien Corn; Staying On; The Good Soldier; The Mysterious Stranger; The Weather in the Streets; Inspector Morse; series, Jennie, Lady Randolph Churchill, 1974; television documentary: All the Waters of Wye, 1990. Films: Arabesque, 1965; Vincent and Theo, 1990. Theatre: Adelina Patti, 1987. *Publications:* novels: Imaginary Toys, 1961; A Disturbing Influence, 1962; As Far As You Can Go, 1963; The White Father, 1964; A Circle of Friends, 1966; The Undiscovered Country, 1968; *biography:* (with Peregrine Churchill) Jennie: Lady Randolph Churchill, 1974; *translation:* Henry IV (Pirandello), 1979 (John Florio Prize,

1980); *plays:* Half-Life, 1977; The Enemy Within, 1980; Another Country, 1981 (SWET play of the year, 1982; filmed, 1984); Francis, 1983; After Aida (or Verdi's Messiah), 1986; (adapted from Ivy Compton-Burnett): A Heritage and Its History, 1965; A Family and a Fortune, 1975; contribs to: Welsh History Review, The Monmouthshire Antiquary. *Recreations:* local history, fishing. *Address:* c/o Peters, Fraser & Dunlop, The Chambers, Chelsea Harbour, SW10 0XF. *Club:* Garrick.

MITCHELL, Keith Kirkman, OBE; Lecturer in Physical Education, University of Leeds, 1955–90; *b* 25 May 1927; *s* of John Stanley Mitchell and Annie Mitchell; *m* 1950, Hannah Forrest; two *s*. *Educ:* Loughborough Coll. (Hons Dip. in Physical Educn). Phys. Educn Master, Wisbech Grammar Sch., 1950–52; Dir of Phys. Recreation, Manchester YMCA, 1952–55. Chm. Exec. Cttee, CCPR, 1981–87; Mem., Sports Council, 1976–87. Dir, 1953–84, Pres., 1985–, English Basketball Assoc. *Recreations:* basketball, photography, gardening, golf. *Address:* 7 Park Crescent, Guiseley, West Yorks LS20 8EL. *T:* Guiseley (0943) 875248.

MITCHELL, Martin; *see* Mitchell, J. L. M.

MITCHELL, Very Rev. Patrick Reynolds; Dean of Windsor, since 1989; Register, Order of the Garter, since 1989; Domestic Chaplain to the Queen, since 1989; *b* 17 March 1930; *s* of late Lt-Col Percy Reynolds Mitchell, DSO; *m* 1st, 1959, Mary Evelyn (*née* Phillips) (*d* 1986); three *s* one *d*; 2nd, 1988, Pamela, *d* of late A. G. Le Marchant and *widow* of Henry Douglas-Pennant; three step *s* one step *d*. *Educ:* Eton Coll.; Merton Coll., Oxford (MA Theol); Wells Theol Coll. Officer in Welsh Guards (National Service), 1948–49. Deacon, 1954; priest, 1955; Curate at St Mark's, Mansfield, 1954–57; Priest-Vicar of Wells Cathedral and Chaplain of Wells Theological Coll., 1957–60; Vicar of St James', Milton, Portsmouth, 1961–67; Vicar of Frome Selwood, Somerset, 1967–73; Dean of Wells, 1973–89; Director of Ordination Candidates for Bath and Wells, 1971–74. Res. Fellow, Merton Coll., Oxford, 1984. Member: Adv. Bd for Redundant Churches, 1978–; Cathedrals Adv. Commn for England, 1981–91. Hon. Freeman, City of Wells, 1986. FSA 1981. *Address:* The Deanery, Windsor Castle, Berks SL4 1NJ. *T:* Windsor (0753) 865561.

MITCHELL, Dr Peter Dennis, FRS 1974; Chairman and Hon. Director, Glynn Research Foundation, since 1987; *b* 29 Sept. 1920; *s* of Christopher Gibbs Mitchell, Mitcham, Surrey; *m* 1958, Helen, *d* of Lt-Col Raymond P. T. ffrench, late Indian Army; three *s* one *d*. *Educ:* Queens Coll., Taunton; Jesus Coll., Cambridge; BA 1943; PhD 1950; Hon. Fellow, 1980. Dept of Biochem., Univ. of Cambridge, 1943–55, Demonstrator 1950–55; Dir of Chem. Biol. Unit, Dept of Zoology, Univ. of Edinburgh, 1955–63, Sen. Lectr 1961–62, Reader 1962–63; Founder and Dir of Res., Glynn Res. Labs, later Glynn Res. Inst., 1964–86. Vis. Prof., KCL, 1987–89. Sir Hans Krebs Lect. and Medal, Fed. European Biochem. Socs, 1978; Fritz Lipmann Lectr, Gesellschaft für Biol. Chem., 1978; Humphry Davy Meml Lectr, RIC and Chilterns and Mddx Sect. of Chem. Soc., at Royal Instn of London, 1980; James Rennie Bequest Lectr, Univ. of Edinburgh, 1980; Croonian Lecture, Royal Soc., 1987. For. Associate, Nat. Acad. of Scis, USA, 1977; Associé Etranger de l'Acad. des Sciences, France, 1989; Foreign Mem., Acad. of Creators, USSR, 1989; Hon. Member: Soc. for Gen. Microbiology, 1984; Japanese Biochem. Soc., 1984; Biochemical Soc. of the USSR, 1991; Hon. Fellow, UMIST, 1990. Hon. Dr rer. nat. Tech. Univ., Berlin, 1976; Hon. DSc: Exeter, 1977; Chicago, 1978; Liverpool, 1979; Bristol, 1980; Edinburgh, 1980; Hull, 1980; Aberdeen, 1990; Hon. ScD: East Anglia, 1981; Cambridge, 1985; DUniv York, 1982. CIBA Medal and Prize, Biochem. Soc., for outstanding research, 1973; (jtly) Warren Trienniel Prize, Trustees of Mass Gen. Hosp., Boston, 1974; Louis and Bert Freedman Foundn Award, NY Acad. of Scis, 1974; Wilhelm Feldberg Foundn Prize, 1976; Lewis S. Rosenstiel Award, Brandeis Univ., 1977; Nobel Prize for Chemistry, 1978; Copley Medal, Royal Society, 1981; Medal of Honour, Athens Municipal Council, 1982. *Publications:* Chemiosmotic Coupling in Oxidative and Photosynthetic Phosphorylation, 1966; Chemiosmotic Coupling and Energy Transduction, 1968; papers in scientific jls. *Recreations:* enjoyment of family life, home-building and creation of wealth and amenity, restoration of buildings of architectural and historical interest, music, thinking, understanding, inventing, making, sailing. *Address:* Glynn House, Bodmin, Cornwall PL30 4AU. *T:* Cardinham (020882) 540. *Club:* Athenæum.

MITCHELL, Richard Charles, (Bob); Lecturer in Business Studies, Eastleigh College of Further Education, since 1984; *b* 22 Aug. 1927; *s* of Charles and Elizabeth Mitchell; *m* 1950, Doreen Lilian Gregory; one *s* one *d*. *Educ:* Taunton's Sch., Southampton; Godalming County Gram. Sch.; Southampton Univ. BSc(Econ) Hons 1951. Bartley County Sec. Sch.: Senior Master and Head of Maths and Science Dept, 1957–65; Dep. Headmaster, 1965–66. MP (Lab) Southampton Test, 1966–70; MP (Lab 1971–81, SDP 1981–83) Southampton, Itchen, May 1971–1983. Contested Southampton, Itchen (SDP) 1983, (SDP/Alliance) 1987. Mem., European Parlt, 1975–79. Member: Bureau of European Socialist Gp, 1976–79; Chairman's Panel, House of Commons, 1979–83. *Recreation:* postal chess (rep. Brit. Correspondence Chess Assoc. against other countries). *Address:* 49 Devonshire Road, Polygon, Southampton. *T:* Southampton (0703) 221781.

MITCHELL, Robert, OBE 1984; Chairman, R. Mitchell & Co. (Eng) Ltd, 1959–81; Councillor, Greater London Council, 1964–86; *b* 14 Dec. 1913; *s* of Robert Mitchell and Lizzie Mitchell (*née* Snowdon); *m* 1946, Reinholda Thoretta L. C. Kettlitz; two *s* one step *s*. *Educ:* West Ham Secondary Sch.; St John's Coll., Cambridge (MA Hons NatSci). Councillor, Wanstead and Woodford Council, 1958–65, Dep. Mayor, 1960–61. Chairman: GLC, 1971–72; Fire Brigade and Ambulance Cttees, 1967–71; Nat. Jt Negotiating Cttee for Local Authority Fire Brigades, 1970–71; Covent Gdn Jt Develt Cttee, 1972–73; Professional and Gen. Services Cttee, 1977–79; Greater London Jt Supply Bd, 1977–79. Member: CBI Cttee on State Intervention in Private Industry, 1976–78; London and SE Reg. Council, 1969–79; Smaller Firms Council, 1977–79; Policy Cttee, AMA, 1978–79. Wanstead and Woodford Conservative Association: Vice-Chm., 1961–65; Chm., 1965–68; Vice-Pres., 1968–; contested (C) West Ham South, 1964 and 1966 gen. elecs. Represented: Cambridge Univ., swimming and water polo, 1932–35 (Captain, 1935); England and Gt Britain, water polo, 1934–48, incl. Olympic Games, 1936 and 1948; Gt Britain, swimming and water polo, World Univ. Games, 1933, 1935; Rest of World *v* Champions, water polo, Univ. Games, 1935; Captain, 1946–49, Pres., 1955–56, Plaistow United Swimming Club; London Rep., Cambridge Univ. Swimming Club, 1953–75. Mem. Cttee, Crystal Palace Nat. Sports Centre, 1965–88. Chm., London Ecology Centre Ltd, 1986–88; Gov., London Ecology Centre Trust, 1985–88; Verderer, Epping Forest, 1976–; Mem., Lea Valley Regl Park Auth., 1982–85. Liveryman, Worshipful Co. of Gardeners, 1975. Governor, Chigwell Sch., 1966– (Vice-Chm., 1968–88). Grand Officer, Order of Orange Nassau (Holland), 1972; Order of Star (Afghanistan), 1971; Order of Rising Sun (Japan), 1971. *Publications:* newspaper and magazine articles mainly on countryside and political subjects. *Recreation:* planting trees, then sitting watching them grow. *Address:* Hatchwood House, Nursery Road, Loughton, Essex IG10 4EF. *T:* 081–508 9135; Little Brigg, Bessingham, Norfolk NR11 7JR. *Clubs:* Carlton, City Livery; Hawks (Cambridge).

MITCHELL, Maj.-Gen. Robert Imrie, OBE 1958 (MBE 1945); retired; *b* 25 Jan. 1916; *s* of James I. Mitchell; *m* 1947, Marion Lyell. *Educ:* Glasgow Academy; Glasgow Univ. BSc 1936, MB, ChB 1939. FFCM. 2/Lt 1937, Lieut 1938 (TA Gen. List); Lieut, RAMC, 1939; served war 1939–45 (despatches 1945); Captain 1940; Major 1947; Lt-Col 1958; Col 1962; Brig. 1968; DDMS, I (British) Corps, BAOR, 1968–69; Maj.-Gen. 1969; DDMS, Army Strategic Command, 1969–71; DMS, BAOR, 1971–73. QHP 1970–73. Hon. Colonel, Glasgow and Strathclyde Univs. OTC TA, 1977–82. OStJ 1966. *Recreations:* fishing, golf. *Address:* Hallam, Gargunnock, Stirlingshire FK8 3BQ. *T:* Gargunnock (078686) 600. *Clubs:* Naval and Military; Royal Scottish Automobile (Glasgow).

MITCHELL, Hon. Dame Roma (Flinders), AC 1991; DBE 1982 (CBE 1971); Governor of South Australia, since 1991; Senior Puisne Judge, Supreme Court of South Australia, 1979–83 (Judge of Supreme Court, 1965–83); *b* 2 Oct. 1913; *d* of Harold Flinders Mitchell and Maude Imelda Victoria (*née* Wickham). *Educ:* St Aloysius Coll., Adelaide; Univ. of Adelaide (LLB 1934). Admitted as Practitioner, Supreme Court of SA, 1934; QC 1962 (first woman QC in Australia). Sen. Dep. Chancellor, 1972–83, Chancellor, 1983–90, Univ. of Adelaide. Chairman: Parole Bd of SA, 1974–81; Criminal Law Reform Cttee of SA, 1971–81; Human Rights Commn of Australia, 1981–86; State Heritage Cttee of SA, 1978–81; SA Council on Child Protection, 1988–90; National President: Winston Churchill Meml Trust, 1988–91 (Dep. Chm., 1975–84; Nat. Chm., 1984–88); Australian Assoc. of Ryder-Cheshire Foundn, 1979–91. Member: Council for Order of Australia, 1980–90; Bd of Governors, Adelaide Festival of Arts, 1981–84. Boyer Lectr, ABC, 1975. DUniv Adelaide, 1985. *Recreations:* theatre, music, art, swimming, walking. *Address:* Government House, Adelaide, SA 5000, Australia. *Clubs:* Queen Adelaide, Lyceum (Adelaide).

MITCHELL, Prof. Ross Galbraith, MD, FRCPE, DCH; Professor of Child Health, University of Dundee and Pædiatrician, Ninewells Hospital, Dundee, 1973–85, now Emeritus; *b* 18 Nov. 1920; *s* of late Richard Galbraith Mitchell, OBE and Ishobel, *d* of late James Ross, Broadford, Skye; *m* 1950, June Phylis Butcher; one *s* three *d*. *Educ:* Kelvinside Acad.; University of Edinburgh. MB, ChB Edinburgh, 1944. Surg-Lt, RNVR, 1944–47; Jun. hosp. posts, Liverpool, London, Edinburgh, 1947–52; Rockefeller Res. Fellow, Mayo Clinic, USA, 1952–53; Lectr in Child Health, Univ. of St Andrews, 1952–55; Cons. Pædiatrician, Dundee Teaching Hosps, 1955–63; Prof. of Child Health, Univ. of Aberdeen, Pædiatrician, Royal Aberdeen Children's and Aberdeen Maternity Hosps, 1963–72; Univ. of Dundee: Dean, Faculty of Medicine and Dentistry, 1978–81; Mem. Court, 1982–85. Chairman: Scottish Adv. Council on Child Care, 1966–69; Specialist Adv. Cttee on Pædiatrics, 1975–79; Academic Bd, British Pædiatric Assoc., 1975–78; Spastics Internat. Med. Pubns, 1981–85; Mac Keith Press, London, 1986–; Mem., GMC, 1983–86. President: Harveian Soc., Edinburgh, 1982–83; Scottish Paediatric Soc., 1982–84. For. Corresp. Mem., Amer. Acad. of Cerebral Palsy and Developmental Medicine, 1965–. Jt Editor, Developmental Medicine and Child Neurology, 1968–80. *Publications:* Disease in Infancy and Childhood, (7th edn) 1973; Child Life and Health (5th edn), 1970; Child Health in the Community (2nd edn), 1980; contribs to textbooks of paediatrics, medicine and obstetrics and articles in scientific and medical jls. *Recreations:* Celtic language and literature, fishing. *Address:* Craigard, Abertay Gardens, Barnhill, Dundee DD5 2SQ.

MITCHELL, Stephen George; QC 1986; **His Honour Judge Mitchell;** a Circuit Judge, since 1989; *b* 19 Sept. 1941; *s* of Sydney Mitchell and Joan Mitchell (*née* Dick); *m* 1978, Alison Clare (*née* Roseveare); two *d*. *Educ:* Bedford Sch.; Hertford Coll., Oxford (MA). Called to the Bar, Middle Temple, 1964; Second Prosecuting Counsel to the Crown, Inner London Crown Court, 1975; Central Criminal Court: a Junior Prosecuting Counsel to the Crown, 1977; a Senior Prosecuting Counsel to the Crown, 1981–86; a Recorder, 1985–89. Mem., Judicial Studies Bd, 1991–.*Publications:* (ed) Phipson on Evidence, 11th edn, 1970; (ed) Archbold's Criminal Pleading Evidence and Practice, 1971–88.

MITCHELL, Terence Croft; Keeper of Western Asiatic Antiquities, British Museum, 1985–89; *b* 17 June 1929; *s* of late Arthur Croft Mitchell and Evelyn Violet Mitchell (*née* Ware). *Educ:* Holderness School, New Hampshire, USA; Bradfield Coll., Berks; St Catharine's Coll., Cambridge (MA 1956). REME Craftsman, 1947–49. Asst Master, St Catherine's Sch., Almondsbury, 1954–56; Resident Study, Tyndale House, Cambridge, 1956–58; European Rep., Aust. Inst. of Archaeology, 1958–59; Dept of Western, later Western Asiatic, Antiquities, British Museum, 1959, Dep. Keeper, 1974, Acting Keeper, 1983–85. Vice Chm., British Inst. at Amman for Archaeology and History, 1990–. Editor, Palestine Exploration Fund Monograph Series, 1990–. *Publications:* Sumerian Art at Ur and Al-'Ubaid, 1969; (ed) Sir Leonard Woolley, Ur Excavations VIII, The Kassite Period and the Period of the Assyrian Kings, 1965; VII, The Old Babylonian Period, 1976; (ed) Music and Civilization, 1980; chapters on Israel and Judah in Cambridge Ancient History, rev. edn III, 1982; The Bible in the British Museum: interpreting the evidence, 1988; articles and reviews. *Recreations:* music, reading, landscape gardening. *Address:* 32 Mallord Street, Chelsea, SW3 6DU. *T:* 071–352 3962. *Club:* Athenæum.

MITCHELL, Warren; *b* 14 Jan. 1926; *s* of Montague and Annie Misell, later Mitchell; *m* 1952, Constance Wake; three *s*. *Educ:* Southgate Co. Sch.; University Coll., Oxford; RADA. Demobbed RAF, 1946. First professional appearance, Finsbury Park Open Air Theatre, 1950; Theophile in Can-Can, Coliseum, 1954; Crookfinger Jake in The Threepenny Opera, Royal Court and Aldwych, 1956; Mr Godboy in Dutch Uncle, Aldwych, 1969; Satan in Council of Love, Criterion, 1970; Herbert in Jump, Queen's, 1971; Ion Will in The Great Caper, Royal Court, 1974; The Thoughts of Chairman Alf, Stratford E, 1976; Willie Loman in Death of a Salesman, Nat. Theatre, 1979; Ducking Out, Duke of York's, 1983; Harpagon in The Miser, Birmingham Rep, 1986; Max in The Homecoming, 1991; *films include:* Diamonds Before Breakfast; Assassination Bureau; Best House in London; Till Death Us Do Part; Moon Zero Two; Whatever Happened to Charlie Farthing; Jabberwocky; Stand Up Virgin Soldiers; Meetings with Remarkable Men; Norman Loves Rose; The Chain; *television:* Alf Garnett in Till Death Us Do Part, BBC, 1966–78, and In Sickness and in Health, BBC, 1985, 1986; Shylock in Merchant of Venice, BBC, 1981; Till Death, ITV, 1981; The Caretaker, BBC, 1981. TV Actor of the Year Award, Guild of Film and TV Producers, 1966; Actor of Year Award: Evening Standard, 1979; Soc. of West End Theatres, 1979; Plays and Players, 1979. *Recreations:* sailing, tennis, playing clarinet. *Address:* c/o ICM, 388/396 Oxford Street, W1N 9HE.

MITCHELL, Sir William; *see* Mitchell, Sir E. W. J.

MITCHELL, Rt. Rev. Mgr. William Joseph; Vicar General, Diocese of Clifton, since 1987; *b* 4 Jan. 1936; *s* of William Ernest and Catherine Mitchell. *Educ:* St Brendan's Coll., Bristol; Corpus Christi Coll., Oxford (MA); Séminaire S Sulpice, Paris; Gregorian Univ., Rome (LCL). Ordained Priest, Pro-Cathedral, Bristol, 1961; Curate, Pro-Cathedral, Bristol, 1963–64; Secretary to Bishop of Clifton, 1964–75; Parish Priest, St Bernadette, Bristol, 1975–78; Rector, Pontifical Beda Coll., Rome, 1978–87; Parish Priest, St John's, Bath, 1988–90. Prelate of Honour, 1978. *Address:* St Anthony's Presbytery, Satchfield Crescent, Henbury, Brostol BS10 7BE. *T:* Bristol (0272) 502509.

MITCHELL COTTS, Sir R. C.; *see* Cotts.

MITCHELL-THOMSON, family name of **Baron Selsdon.**

MITCHENSON, Francis Joseph Blackett, (Joe Mitchenson); Joint Founder and Director, The Raymond Mander and Joe Mitchenson Theatre Collection, since 1939 (Theatre Collection Trust, since 1977); *b* 4 Oct.; *s* of Francis William Mitchenson and Sarah Roddam. *Educ:* privately; Fay Compton Studio of Dramatic Art. First appeared on stage professionally in Libel, Playhouse, London, 1934; acted in repertory, on tour and in London, until 1948. With Raymond Mander, founded Theatre Collection, 1939; War Service with Royal Horse Artillery, invalided out, 1943; returned to stage, and collab. with Raymond Mander on many BBC progs. Collection subject of an Aquarius programme, 1971; many theatrical exhbns, incl. 50 Years of British Stage Design, for British Council, USSR, 1979. Archivist to: Sadler's Wells; Old Vic. Mem., Soc. of West End Theatre Awards Panel, 1976–78. Several TV appearances, 1987–88. *Publications:* with Raymond Mander: Hamlet Through the Ages, 1952 (2nd rev. edn 1955); Theatrical Companion to Shaw, 1954; Theatrical Companion to Maugham, 1955; The Artist and the Theatre, 1955; Theatrical Companion to Coward, 1957; A Picture History of British Theatre, 1957; (with J. C. Trewin) The Gay Twenties, 1958; (with Philip Hope-Wallace) A Picture History of Opera, 1959; (with J. C. Trewin) The Turbulent Thirties, 1960; The Theatres of London, 1961, illus. by Timothy Birdsall (2nd rev. edn, paperback, 1963; 3rd rev. edn 1975); A Picture History of Gilbert and Sullivan, 1962; British Music Hall: A Story in Pictures, 1965 (rev. and enlarged edn 1974); Lost Theatres of London, 1968 (2nd edn, rev. and enlarged, 1976); Musical Comedy: A Story in Pictures, 1969; Revue: A Story in Pictures, 1971; Pantomime: A Story in Pictures, 1973; The Wagner Companion, 1977; Victorian and Edwardian Entertainment from Old Photographs, 1978; Introd. to Plays, by Noël Coward (4 vols), 1979; Guide to the W. Somerset Maugham Theatrical Paintings, 1980; contribs to and revs in Encyc. Britannica, Theatre Notebook, and Books and Bookmen. *Recreations:* collecting anything and everything theatrical, sun bathing. *Address:* The Mansion, Beckenham Place, Kent BR3 2BP. *T:* 081–650 9322; (office) 081–658 7725.

MITCHISON, Avrion; *see* Mitchison, N. A.

MITCHISON, Dr Denis Anthony, CMG 1984; Professor of Bacteriology, Royal Postgraduate Medical School, 1971–84; Director, Medical Research Council's Unit for Laboratory Studies of Tuberculosis, 1956–84; retired; *b* 6 Sept. 1919; *e s* of Baron Mitchison, CBE, QC, and of Naomi Margaret Mitchison, *qv*; *m* 1940, Ruth Sylvia, *d* of Hubert Gill; two *s* two *d*. *Educ:* Abbotsholme Sch.; Trinity Coll., Cambridge; University Coll. Hosp., London (MB, ChB). House Physician Addenbrooke's Hosp., Royal Berkshire Hosp.; Asst to Pathologist, Brompton Hosp.; Prof. of Bacteriology (Infectious Diseases), RPGMS, 1968–71. FRCP; FRCPath. *Publications:* numerous papers on bacteriology and chemotherapy of tuberculosis. *Recreation:* computer programming. *Address:* 14 Marlborough Road, Richmond, Surrey TW10 6JR. *T:* 081–940 4751.

See also J. M. Mitchison, N. A. Mitchison.

MITCHISON, Prof. John Murdoch, ScD; FRS 1978; FRSE 1966; Professor of Zoology, University of Edinburgh, 1963–88, now Professor Emeritus and University Fellow; *b* 11 June 1922; *s* of Lord Mitchison, CBE, QC, and of N. Haldane (*see* Naomi M. Mitchison); *m* 1947, Rosalind Mary Wrong; one *s* three *d*. *Educ:* Winchester Coll.; Trinity Coll., Cambridge. Army Operational Research, 1941–46; Sen. and Research Scholar, Trinity Coll., Cambridge, 1946–50; Fellow, Trinity Coll., Cambridge, 1950–54; Edinburgh University: Lectr in Zoology, 1953–59; Reader in Zoology, 1959–62; Dean, Faculty of Science, 1984–85; Mem. of Court, 1971–74, 1985–88. J. W. Jenkinson Memorial Lectr, Oxford, 1971–72. Member: Council, Scottish Marine Biol. Assoc., 1961–67; Exec. Cttee, Internat. Soc. for Cell Biology, 1964–72; Biol Cttee, SRC, 1972–75; Royal Commn on Environmental Pollution, 1974–79; Science Bd, SRC, 1976–79; Working Gp on Biol Manpower, DES, 1968–71; Adv. Cttee on Safety of Nuclear Installations, Health and Safety Exec., 1981–84. Pres., British Soc. for Cell Biology, 1974–77. Mem., Academia Europaea, 1989. FInstBiol 1963. *Publications:* The Biology of the Cell Cycle, 1971; papers in scientific jls. *Address:* Great Yew, Ormiston, East Lothian EH35 5NJ. *T:* Pencaitland (0875) 340530.

See also D. A. Mitchison, N. A. Mitchison.

MITCHISON, Naomi Margaret, CBE 1985; **(Lady Mitchison** since 1964, but she still wishes to be called Naomi Mitchison); *b* Edinburgh, 1 Nov. 1897; *d* of late John Scott Haldane, CH, FRS, and Kathleen Trotter; *m* 1916, G. R. Mitchison (*d* 1970), CBE, QC, created a Baron (Life Peer), 1964; three *s* two *d*. *Educ:* Dragon Sch., Oxford; home student, Oxford. Officier d'Académie Française, 1924; Argyll CC, 1945–65, on and off; Highland and Island Advisory Panel, 1947–65; Highlands and Islands Develt Consult. Council, 1966–76; Tribal Mother to Bakgatla, Botswana, 1963–. DUniv.: Stirling, 1976; Dundee, 1985; DLitt Strathclyde, 1983. Hon. Fellow: St Anne's Coll., Oxford, 1980; Wolfson Coll., Oxford, 1983. *Publications:* The Conquered, 1923; When the Bough Breaks, 1924; Cloud Cuckoo Land, 1925; The Laburnum Branch, 1926; Black Sparta, 1928; Anna Comnena, 1928; Nix-Nought-Nothing, 1928; Barbarian Stories, 1929; The Hostages, 1930; Comments on Birth Control, 1930; The Corn King and the Spring Queen, 1931; The Price of Freedom (with L. E. Gielgud), 1931; Boys and Girls and Gods, 1931; The Powers of Light, 1932; (ed) An Outline for Boys and Girls, 1932; The Delicate Fire, 1933; Vienna Diary, 1934; The Home, 1934; We Have Been Warned, 1935; Beyond this Limit, 1935; The Fourth Pig, 1936; Socrates (with R. H. S. Crossman), 1937; An End and a Beginning, 1937; The Moral Basis of Politics, 1938; The Kingdom of Heaven, 1939; As It was in the Beginning (with L. E. Gielgud), 1939; The Blood of the Martyrs, 1939; (ed) Re-educating Scotland, 1944; The Bull Calves, 1947; Men and Herring (with D. Macintosh), 1949; The Big House, 1950; Spindrift (*play:* with D. Macintosh), Citizens' Theatre, Glasgow, 1951; Lobsters on the Agenda, 1952; Travel Light, 1952; The Swan's Road, 1954; Graeme and the Dragon, 1954; The Land the Ravens Found, 1955; To the Chapel Perilous, 1955; Little Boxes, 1956; Behold your King, 1957; The Far Harbour, 1957; Five Men and a Swan, 1958; Other People's Worlds, 1958; Judy and Lakshmi, 1959; The Rib of the Green Umbrella, 1960; The Young Alexander, 1960; Karensgaard, 1961; The Young Alfred the Great, 1962; Memoirs of a Space Woman, 1962; (ed) What the Human Race is Up To, 1962; The Fairy who Couldn't Tell a Lie, 1963; When we Become Men, 1965; Ketse and the Chief, 1965; Return to the Fairy Hill, 1966; Friends and Enemies, 1966; The Big Surprise, 1967; African Heroes, 1968; Don't Look Back, 1969; The Family at Ditlabeng, 1969; The Africans: a history, 1970; Sun and Moon, 1970; Cleopatra's People, 1972; A Danish Teapot, 1973; Sunrise Tomorrow, 1973; Small Talk: memoirs of an Edwardian childhood (autobiog.), 1973; A Life for Africa, 1973; Oil for the Highlands?, 1974; All Change Here (autobiog.), 1975; Solution Three, 1975; Snake!, 1976; The Two Magicians, 1979; The Cleansing of the Knife, 1979; You May Well Ask (autobiog.), 1979; Images of Africa, 1980; The Vegetable War, 1980; Mucking Around, 1980; What Do You Think Yourself, Scottish Stories, 1982; Not By Bread Alone, 1983; Among You Taking Notes, 1985; Beyond this Limit (short stories), 1986; Early in Orcadia, 1987; A Girl Must Live, 1990; Sea-Green Ribbons, 1991; The Oathtakers, 1991. *Recreation:* surviving so far. *Address:* Carradale House, Carradale, Campbeltown, Scotland.

See also D. A. Mitchison, J. M. Mitchison, N. A. Mitchison.

MITCHISON, Prof. (Nicholas) Avrion, FRS 1967; Jodrell Professor of Zoology and Comparative Anatomy, University College, London, since 1970; *b* 5 May 1928; 3rd *s* of Baron Mitchison, CBE, QC, and of Naomi Margaret Mitchison, *qv*; *m* 1957, Lorna Margaret, *d* of Maj.-Gen. J. S. S. Martin, CSI; two *s* three *d*. *Educ:* Leighton Park Sch.; New Coll., Oxford (MA 1949). Fellow of Magdalen College, 1950–52; Commonwealth Fund Fellow, 1952–54; Lecturer, Edinburgh Univ., 1954–61; Reader, Edinburgh Univ., 1961–62; Head of Div. of Experimental Biology, Nat. Inst. for Med. Research, 1962–71. Hon. MD Edinburgh, 1977. *Publications:* articles in scientific journals. *Address:* 14 Belitha Villas, N1.

See also D. A. Mitchison, J. M. Mitchison.

MITDANK, Joachim, Dr rer.pol.; Patriotic OM in Bronze, 1973; Banner of Labour, grade I, 1976 (grade II, 1974); Ambassador of the German Democratic Republic to the Court of St James's, 1989–90; *b* Leipzig, 27 June 1931; *s* of Herbert and Erika Mitdank; *m* 1954, Magdalena Keller; one *d*. *Educ:* Inst. of Internat. Relations, Babelsberg (DipPolSci); Acad. for Political and Legal Sciences (Dr rer.pol. 1968). Clerk, 1945–50; joined Min. of Foreign Affairs, 1956; Attaché, 1959; Dir, FRG Div., 1960–62; Counsellor, GDR Trade Mission, Helsinki, 1962–64; Advr, Exec. Bureau of Council of Ministers of GDR, 1965–68; Dir, W Berlin Div., Min. of For. Affairs, 1968–78; Amb. to Finland, 1978–82; Dir, N Europe/GB Div., 1983–89. Various state distinctions. *Recreations:* football, other ball games, literature (particularly classical German literature), theatre.

MITFORD, family name of **Baron Redesdale.**

MITFORD, Jessica Lucy, (Mrs Jessica Treuhaft); author; *b* 11 Sept. 1917; *d* of 2nd Baron Redesdale; *m* 1st, Esmond Marcus David Romilly (*d* 1941); one *d*; 2nd, 1943, Robert Edward Treuhaft; one *s*. Distinguished Prof., San José State Univ., Calif, 1973–74. *Publications:* (as Jessica Mitford): Hons and Rebels, 1960; The American Way of Death, 1963; The Trial of Dr Spock, 1969; Kind and Usual Punishment, 1974; The American Prison Business, 1975; A Fine Old Conflict, 1977; The Making of a Muckraker, 1979; Faces of Philip: a memoir of Philip Toynbee, 1984; Grace had an English Heart: the story of Grace Darling, heroine and Victorian superstar, 1988. *Address:* 6411 Regent Street, Oakland, Calif 94618, USA.

MITFORD, Rupert Leo Scott B.; *see* Bruce-Mitford.

MITFORD-SLADE, Patrick Buxton; Partner, Cazenove & Co., since 1972; Managing Director, Cazenove Money Brokers, since 1986; *b* 7 Sept. 1936; *s* of late Col Cecil Townley Mitford-Slade and Phyllis, *d* of E. G. Buxton; *m* 1964, Anne Catharine Stanton, *d* of Major Arthur Holbrow Stanton, MBE; one *s* two *d*. *Educ:* Eton Coll.; RMA Sandhurst. Commissioned 60th Rifles, 1955, Captain; served Libya, NI, Berlin and British Guyana; Adjt, 1st Bn The Royal Green Jackets, 1962–65; Instructor, RMA Sandhurst, 1965–67. Stockbroker, Cazenove & Co., 1968–. Asst Sec., Panel on Takeovers and Mergers, 1970–72; Mem., Stock Exchange, 1972–86, Internat. Stock Exchange, 1986– (Mem. Council, 1976–; Dep. Chm., 1982–85); Chairman: City Telecommunications Cttee, 1983–; Securities Industry Steering Cttee on Taurus, 1988–90. Chm., Officers' Assoc., 1985–. *Recreations:* shooting, fishing. *Address:* Damales House, Hartley Wintney, Basingstoke, Hants RG27 8JA. *Club:* City of London.

MITHEN, Dallas Alfred, CB 1983; Chairman, Forestry Training Council, since 1984; Commissioner for Harvesting and Marketing, Forestry Commission, 1977–83; *b* 5 Nov. 1923; *m* 1st, 1947, Peggy (*née* Clarke) (decd); one *s* one *d*; 2nd, 1969, Avril Teresa Dodd (*née* Stein). *Educ:* Maidstone Grammar Sch.; UC of N Wales, Bangor. BSc (Forestry). Fleet Air Arm, 1942–46. Joined Forestry Commission as District Officer, 1950; Dep. Surveyor, New Forest and Conservator SE (England), 1968–71; Senior Officer (Scotland), 1971–75; Head of Forest Management Div., Edinburgh, 1975–76. Pres., Inst. of Chartered Foresters, 1984–86; Pres., Forestry Section, BAAS, 1985. Trustee, Central Scotland Woodland Trust, 1985–. *Recreations:* gardening, swimming, walking. *Address:* Kings Knot, Bonnington Road, Peebles EH45 9HF. *T:* Peebles (0721) 20738.

MITRA, Dr Ashesh Prosad, FRS 1988; FNA; Secretary to the Government of India, Department of Industrial & Scientific Research, and Director-General, Council of Scientific and Industrial Research, since 1986; *b* 21 Feb. 1927; *s* of late A. C. Mitra and Subarna Prova Mitra; *m* 1956, Sunanda Mitra; two *d*. *Educ:* University of Calcutta (DPhil 1955). FNA 1963. Res. Assistant, Calcutta Univ., 1949–51; Colombo Plan Fellow, CSIRO, Sydney, 1951; Vis. Asst Prof. of Engrg Res., 1952–53, Vis. Prof., 1953–54, Penn. State Univ.; National Physical Laboratory, New Delhi: Sec., Radio Res. Cttee, 1954–56; Head, Radio Propagation Unit, later Radio Sci. Div., 1956–86; Director-level Scientist, 1974–82; Dir., 1982–86. Mem., Indian Acad. of Astronautics, 1974–; Fellow, Third World Acad. of Scis, Trieste, 1988. Hon. DSc Manipur, 1988. *Publications:* (ed) Proceedings of the International Geophysical Year Symposium, vols 1 & 2, 1962; The Chemistry of the Ionosphere, 1970; Advances in Space Exploration, vol. 6, 1979; 50 Years of Radio Science in India, 1984; (ed jtly) Handbook on Radio Propagation for Tropical and Subtropical Countries, 1987. *Recreation:* music. *Address:* Council of Scientific and Industrial Research, Rafi Marg, New Delhi–110001, India. *T:* 3710472. *Club:* Delhi Gymkhana (New Delhi).

MITSAKIS, Prof. Kariofilis; Professor of Modern Greek Literature, University of Athens, 1978–91; *b* 12 May 1932; *s* of Christos and Crystalli Mitsakis; *m* 1966, Anthoula Chalkia; two *s*. *Educ:* Univs of Thessaloniki (BA, PhD), Oxford (MA, DPhil) and Munich. Scientific Collaborator, National Research Foundn of Greece, 1959–62; Associate Prof. of Byzantine and Modern Greek Literature, Univ. of Maryland, 1966–68; Chm. of Dept of Comparative Literature, Univ. of Maryland, 1967–68; Sotheby and Bywater Prof. of Byzantine and Modern Greek Language and Literature, Univ. of Oxford, 1968–72; Prof. of Modern Greek Lit., Univ. of Thessaloniki, 1972–75; Dir, Inst. for Balkan Studies, Thessaloniki, 1972–80. *Publications:* Problems Concerning the Text, the Sources and the Dating of the Achilleid, 1962 (in Greek); The Greek Sonnet, 1962 (in Greek); The Language of Romanos the Melodist, 1967 (in English); The Byzantine Alexanderromance from the Cod. Vindob. theol. gr. 244, 1967 (in German); Byzantine Hymnography, 1971 (in Greek); Petrarchism in Greece, 1973 (in Greek); Introduction to Modern Greek Literature, 1973 (in Greek); Homer in Modern Greek Literature, 1976 (in Greek); George Viziynos, 1977 (in Greek); Modern Greek Prose: the Generation of the '30s, 1978 (in Greek); Modern Greek Music and Poetry, 1979 (in Greek and English); March Through the Time, 1982; The Living Water, 1983; Points of Reference, 1987 (in Greek); The Cycles with their trails that rise and fall, 1991 (in Greek); contribs to Balkan Studies, Byzantinisch-Neugriechische Jahrbücher, Byzantinische Zeitschrift, Comparative Literature Studies, Diptycha, Études Byzantines-Byzantine Studies, Glotta, Hellenika, Jahrbuch der Oesterreichischen Byzantinischen Gesellschaft, Nea Hestia, etc. *Recreations:* music, travelling. *Address:* 25 Troados Street, 15342 Agia Paraskevi, Athens, Greece.

MITTERRAND, François Maurice Marie; Grand Croix de l'Ordre National de la Légion d'Honneur; Grand Croix de l'Ordre National du Mérite; Croix de Guerre (1939–45); President of the French Republic, since 1981; advocate; *b* Jarnac, Charente, 26 Oct. 1916; *s* of Joseph Mitterrand and Yvonne (*née* Lorrain); *m* 1944, Danielle Gouze; two *s*. *Educ:* Coll. Saint-Paul, Angoulême; Facultés de droit et des lettres, Univ. of Paris.

Licencié en droit, Lic. ès lettres; Dip. d'études supérieures de droit public. Served War, 1939–40 (prisoner, escaped; Rosette de la Résistance). Missions to London and to Algiers, 1943; Sec.-Gen., Organisation for Prisoners of War, War Victims and Refugees, 1944–46. Deputy from Nièvre, 1946–58 and 1962–81; Minister for Ex-Servicemen, 1947–48; Sec. of State for Information, attached Prime Minister's Office, 1948–49; Minister for Overseas Territories, 1950–51; Chm., UDSR, 1951–52; Minister of State, Jan.-Feb. 1952 and March 1952–July 1953; Deleg. to Council of Europe, July-Sept. 1953; Minister of the Interior, June 1954–Feb. 1955; Minister of State, 1956–57; Senator, 1959–62; Candidate for Presidency of France, 1965, 1974; Pres., Fedn of Democratic and Socialist Left, 1965–68; First Sec., Socialist Party, 1971–81. Vice-Pres., Socialist International, 1972–. Pres., Conseil général de la Nièvre, 1964–. *Publications:* Aux frontières de l'Union française, 1953; Présence française et abandon, 1957; La Chine au défi, 1961; Le Coup d'Etat permanent, 1964; Ma part de vérité, 1969; Un socialisme du possible, 1970; La rose au poing, 1973; La paille et le grain, 1975; Politique 1, 1977; L'Abeille et l'architecte, 1978; Ici et maintenant, 1980; Politique 2, 1981; Reflexions sur la politique extérieure de la France, 1986; numerous contribs to the Press. *Recreation:* golf. *Address:* Palais de l'Elysée, 75008 Paris, France; (private) 22 rue de Bièvre, 75005 Paris, France.

MITTING, John Edward; QC 1987; a Recorder, since 1988; *b* 8 Oct. 1947; *s* of Alison Kennard Mitting and Eleanor Mary Mitting; *m* 1977, Judith Clare (*née* Hampson); three *s*. *Educ:* Downside Sch.; Trinity Hall, Cambridge (BA, LLB). Called to the Bar, Gray's Inn, 1970. *Recreations:* wine, food, bridge. *Address:* Hollow Dene, Coton, Gnosall, near Stafford ST20 0EQ. *T:* Stafford (0785) 822395. *Club:* Birmingham (Birmingham).

MITTLER, Prof. Peter Joseph, CBE 1981; MA, PhD, MEd; CPsychol; FBPsS; Professor of Special Education, since 1973, Director, Centre for Educational Guidance and Special Needs, Department of Education, since 1977, Deputy Director, School of Education, since 1989, University of Manchester; *b* 2 April 1930; *s* of Dr Gustav Mittler and Gertrude Mittler; *m* 1955, Helle Katscher; three *s*. *Educ:* Merchant Taylors' Sch., Crosby; Pembroke Coll., Cambridge (MA); PhD London; MEd Manchester. Clinical Psychologist, Warneford and Park Hosps, Oxford, 1954–58; Principal Psychologist, Reading Area Psychiatric Services, 1958–63; Lectr in Psychology, Birkbeck Coll., Univ. of London, 1963–68; Dir, Hester Adrian Res. Centre, Manchester Univ., 1968–82. Chm., Nat Develt Gp for Mentally Handicapped, 1975–80; Mem., Schs Assessment and Exam. Council, 1988–90. Pres., Internat. League of Socs for Persons with Mental Handicap, 1982–86 (Vice-Pres., 1978–82); Mem., Prince of Wales Adv. Gp on Disability, 1984–90; Advr on disability to UNESCO, WHO, ILO. *Publications:* ed, Psychological Assessment of Mental and Physical Handicaps, 1970; The Study of Twins, 1971; ed, Assessment for Learning in the Mentally Handicapped, 1973; ed, Research to Practice in Mental Retardation (3 vols), 1977; People not Patients, 1979; (jtly) Teaching Language and Communication to the Mentally Handicapped, (Schools Council), 1979; (ed jtly) Advances in Mental Handicap Research, 1980; (ed) Frontiers of Knowledge in Mental Retardation (2 vols), 1981; (ed jtly) Approaches to Partnership: professionals and parents of mentally handicapped people, 1983; (ed jtly) Aspects of Competence in Mentally Handicapped People, 1983; (ed jtly) Staff Training in Mental Handicap, 1987; (jtly) Inset and Special Educational Needs: running short, school-focused inservice courses, 1988; papers in psychol and educnl jls. *Recreations:* music, travel. *Address:* 10 Park Road, Cheadle Hulme, Cheshire SK8 7DA. *T:* 061–485 6491.

MITTON, Rev. Dr Charles Leslie, BA; MTh; PhD; Principal of Handsworth College, Birmingham, 1955–70 (Tutor, 1951–55); *b* 13 Feb. 1907; *s* of Rev. Charles W. Mitton, Bradford, Yorks; *m* 1937, Margaret J. Ramage; one *s* one *d*. *Educ:* Kingswood Sch., Bath; Manchester Univ.; Didsbury Coll., Manchester. Asst Tutor at Wesley Coll., Headingley, 1930–33; Minister in Methodist Church at: Dunbar, 1933–36; Keighley, 1936–39; Scunthorpe, 1939–45; Nottingham, 1945–51; Tutor in New Testament Studies at Handsworth Coll., Birmingham, 1951–70. Editor of Expository Times, 1965–76. Hon. DD, Aberdeen Univ., 1964. *Publications:* The Epistle to the Ephesians: Authorship, Origin and Purpose, 1951; Pauline Corpus of Letters, 1954; Preachers' Commentary on St Mark's Gospel, 1956; The Good News, 1961; The Epistle of James, 1966; Jesus: the fact behind the faith, 1974; The Epistle to the Ephesians: a commentary, 1976; Your Kingdom Come, 1978. *Recreations:* Rugby football, Association football, cricket, tennis. *Address:* 14 Cranbrook Road, Handsworth, Birmingham B21 8PJ. *T:* 021–554 7892.

MKONA, Callisto Matekenya, DSM (Malaŵi) 1966; Hon. GCVO 1985; High Commissioner for Malaŵi in Nairobi, since 1988, concurrently accredited to Egypt, Israel and Uganda, since 1988; *b* 4 June 1930; *s* of late Benedicto Mkona and of Martha Matekenya Mkona; *m* 1971, Helen Victoria (*née* Sazuze); two *s* two *d*. *Educ:* Zomba, Malaŵi; Urbanian Univ., Rome (DCL, Dip. Soc. Scis). Secondary School teacher, 1962–64; Mission Educn Liaison Officer, 1964–67; Educn Attaché (First Sec.), Washington and London, 1967–71; Ambassador to Ethiopia, 1971–72; Minister, Washington, 1972–73; High Comr in Zambia, 1973–75; Ambassador in Bonn, 1975–78; Dep. Principal Sec., Min. of External Affairs, 1978–79; Principal Sec., Office of the President and Cabinet, 1979–81; High Comr in London, also concurrently accredited to Denmark, France, Norway, Portugal, Sweden and Switzerland, 1981–87; Chm., Malaŵi Public Service Commn, 1987–88; CS retd, 1988. Permanent Representative to: UN Centre for Human Settlements (HABITAT), 1988–; UNEP, 1988–. *Recreations:* reading, walking, tennis, golf. *Address:* Malaŵi High Commission, Standard Street, PO Box 30453, Nairobi, Kenya.

MLINARIC, David; interior decorator and designer, since 1964; founded David Mlinaric Ltd, 1964; *b* 12 March 1939; *s* of Franjo and Mabel Mlinaric; *m* 1969, Martha Laycock; one *s* two *d*. *Educ:* Downside Sch.; Bartlett Sch. of Architecture; University Coll. London. Private and commercial interior decorating, often in historic bldgs. Recent work includes: rooms in Nat. Gall., London, 1986–; Spencer House, London, 1990.Hon. Fellow, RCA, 1987. *Recreations:* gardening, sightseeing. *Address:* 38 Bourne Street, SW1W 8JA. *T:* 071–730 9072.

MO, Timothy Peter; writer; *b* 30 Dec. 1950; *s* of Peter Mo Wan Lung and Barbara Helena Falkingham. *Educ:* Convent of the Precious Blood, Hong Kong; Mill Hill School; St John's Coll., Oxford (BA; Gibbs Prize 1971). *Publications:* The Monkey King, 1978 (Geoffrey Faber Meml Prize, 1979); Sour Sweet, 1982 (Hawthornden Prize, 1983; filmed, 1989); An Insular Possession, 1986; The Redundancy of Courage, 1991. *Recreations:* scuba diving, weight training, gourmandising.

MOATE, Roger Denis; MP (C) Faversham since 1970; Insurance Broker; *b* 12 May 1938; *m* 1st; one *s* one *d*; 2nd, Auriol (*née* Cran); one *d*. *Educ:* Latymer Upper Sch., Hammersmith. Joined Young Conservative Movement, in Brentford and Chiswick, 1954: Vice-Chm., Greater London Area Young Conservatives, 1964; contested (C) Faversham, Gen. Elec., 1966. *Recreation:* skiing. *Address:* House of Commons, SW1; The Old Vicarage, Knatchbull Road, SE5.

MOBBS, Sir (Gerald) Nigel, Kt 1986; DL; Chairman and Chief Executive, Slough Estates plc, since 1976 and Director of principal subsidiaries; Director, Barclays Bank PLC, since 1979; *b* 22 Sept. 1937; *s* of Gerald Aubrey Mobbs and Elizabeth (*née* Lanchester); *m* 1961, Hon. Pamela Jane Marguerite Berry, 2nd *d* of 2nd Viscount Kemsley, *qv*; one *s* twin *d*. *Educ:* Marlborough Coll.; Christ Church, Oxford. Joined Slough Estates plc, 1961; Director, 1963, Man. Dir, 1971. Director: Barclays Bank Trust Co. Ltd, 1973–86 (Chm., 1985–86); Charterhouse Gp, 1974–84 (Chm., 1977–83); Kingfisher plc (formerly Woolworth Holdings), 1982– (Dep. Chm., 1990–); Cookson Gp plc, 1985–; Howard de Walden Estates Ltd, 1989–; Chm., Groundwork Foundn, 1990–. Chairman: Corporate Health,1976–; Slough Social Fund, 1975–; Property Services Agency Adv. Bd, 1980–86; Aims of Industry, 1985–; Adv. Panel on Deregulation, DTI, 1988–. Pres., Slough & Dist Chamber of Commerce, 1969–72; Vice-Pres., Assoc. of British Chambers of Commerce, 1976– (Chm. 1974–76); Pres., British Property Fedn, 1979–81. Mem., Commonwealth War Graves Commn, 1988–. President: Bucks Assoc. of Boys' Clubs, 1984–; British Council for Officers, 1990–. Chm., Council, Univ. of Buckingham, 1987–. CBIM. Master, Spectacle Makers' Co., 1989. Hon. Fellow, Coll. of Estate Management, 1978; Hon. Mem., RICS, 1990. Hon. DSc City, 1988. High Sheriff, 1982, DL, 1985, Bucks. OStJ. *Recreations:* riding, hunting, ski-ing, golf, travel. *Address:* Widmer Lodge, Lacey Green, Aylesbury, Bucks HP17 0RJ. *T:* High Wycombe (0494) 488265. *Clubs:* Brooks's; Toronto, York (Toronto).

MOBERLY, Sir John (Campbell), KBE 1984; CMG 1976; HM Diplomatic Service, retired; Consultant, Middle East Programme, Royal Institute of International Affairs, since 1986; Chairman, Middle East Consultants Ltd, since 1986; *b* 27 May 1925; *s* of Sir Walter Moberly, GBE, KCB, DSO; *m* 1959, Patience, *d* of Major Sir Richard George Proby, 1st Bt, MC; two *s* one *d*. *Educ:* Winchester College; Magdalen College, Oxford. War Service in Royal Navy, 1943–47 (despatches). Entered HM Foreign (now Diplomatic) Service, 1950; Political Officer, Kuwait, 1954–56; Political Agent, Doha, 1959–62; First Secretary, Athens, 1962–66; Counsellor, Washington, 1969–73; Dir, Middle East Centre for Arab Studies, 1973–75; Ambassador, Jordan, 1975–79; Asst Under-Sec. of State, FCO, 1979–82; Ambassador, Iraq, 1982–85. CStJ 1979. *Recreations:* mountain walking and climbing, skiing, swimming. *Address:* 35 Pymers Mead, West Dulwich, SE21 8NH. *T:* 081–670 2680; The Cedars, Temple Sowerby, Penrith, Cumbria CA10 1RZ. *T:* Kirkby Thore (07683) 61437. *Clubs:* Royal Automobile; Leander (Henley-on-Thames).

MOBERLY, Sir Patrick (Hamilton), KCMG 1986 (CMG 1978); HM Diplomatic Service, retired; Ambassador to South Africa, 1984–87; *b* 2 Sept. 1928; *yr s* of G. H. Moberly; *m* 1955, Mary Penfold; two *s* one *d*. *Educ:* Winchester; Trinity Coll., Oxford (MA). HM Diplomatic Service, 1951–; diplomatic posts in: Baghdad, 1953; Prague, 1957; Foreign Office, 1959; Dakar, 1962; Min. of Defence, 1965; Commonwealth Office, 1967; Canada, 1969; Israel, 1970; FCO, 1974; Asst Under-Sec. of State, 1976–81; Ambassador to Israel, 1981–84. *Recreations:* tennis, opera. *Address:* 38 Lingfield Road, SW19 4PZ. *Club:* United Oxford & Cambridge University.

MOBERLY, Maj.-Gen. Richard James, CB 1957; OBE 1944; retired, 1960, and became Director, Communications Electronic Equipment, War Office, until 1964; *b* 2 July 1906; *o s* of late J. E. Moberly; *m* 1st, 1935, Mary Joyce Shelmerdine (*d* 1964); three *d*; 2nd, 1971, Mrs Vivien Mary Cameron (*d* 1981), *d* of Victor Bayley, CIE, CBE. *Educ:* Haileybury; Royal Military Academy, Woolwich. Commissioned Royal Signals, 1926; India, 1928–35; comd 1st Airborne Div. Signal Regt, 1942–43; CSO 1st Airborne Corps, 1943–45; Comdt Indian Signal Trng Centre, 1946–47; Dep. Comdt, Sch. of Signals, 1949–52; Dep. Dir of Signals, WO, 1952–54; CSO, Northern Army Gp, 1954–57; Signal Officer-in-Chief, WO, 1957–60. Col Comdt, Royal Signals, 1960–66. Comr for Dorset, St John Ambulance, 1968–76. KStJ 1986. *Address:* Steeple Cottage, Westport Road, Wareham, Dorset BH20 4PR. *T:* Wareham (0929) 552697.

MODIGLIANI, Prof. Franco; Institute Professor Emeritus, Massachusetts Institute of Technology, since 1988 (Professor of Economics and Finance, 1962–70; Institute Professor, 1970–88); *b* Rome, 1918; *s* of Enrico Modigliani and Olga (*née* Flaschel); *m* 1939, Serena Calabi; two *s*. *Educ:* Univ. of Rome (DJur 1939); DSocSci New Sch. for Social Research, New York, 1944. Instr in Economics and Statistics, New Jersey Coll. for Women, 1942; Instr, Associate in Economics and Statistics, Bard Coll. of Columbia Univ., 1942–44; Lectr, 1943–44, Asst Prof. of Math. Econ. and Econometrics, 1946–48, New Sch. for Social Research; Res. Associate and Chief Statistician, Inst. of World Affairs, NY, 1945–48; Res. Consultant, Cowles Commn for Res. in Economics, Univ. of Chicago, 1949–54; Associate Prof., 1949, Prof. of Economics, 1950–52, Univ. of Illinois; Prof. of Econ. and Indust. Admin, Carnegie Inst. of Technology, 1952–60; Prof. of Economics, Northwestern Univ., 1960–62. Social Science Research Council: Mem., Bd of Dirs, 1963–68; Mem., Cttee on Econ. Stability and Growth, 1970–; Jt Chm., Adv. Sub-Cttee on MIT-Pennsylvania SSRC Model, 1970–81; Mem., Sub-Cttee on Monetary Res., 1970–77. Academic Consultant, Bd of Governors, Federal Reserve System, 1966–; Sen. Adviser, Brookings Panel on Econ. Activity, 1971–; Consultant, Bank of Italy, Rome; Mem., Consiglio Italiano per le Scienze Sociali, 1974–; Perm. Mem., Conf. on Income and Wealth, Nat. Bureau of Econ. Res. Mem., Adv. Bd, Jl of Money, Credit and Banking, 1969–. Mem., Nat. Acad. of Scis, 1973–; Fellow, Econometric Soc., 1949; Fellow, 1960–, Council Mem., 1978–80, Amer. Acad. of Arts and Scis. Numerous hon. degrees. Nobel Prize in Economic Science, 1985. Kt Grand Cross, Italy, 1985. *Publications:* National Incomes and International Trade (with Hans Neisser), 1953; (jtly) Planning Production, Inventories and Work Forces, 1960; (with Kalman J. Cohen) The Role of Anticipations and Plans in Economic Behavior and their Use in Economic Analysis and Forecasting, 1961; (with Ezio Tarantelli) Mercato del Lavoro, Distribuzione del Reddito e Consumi Privati, 1975; (ed with Donald Lessard) New Mortgage Designs for Stable Housing in an Inflationary Environment, 1975; The Collected Papers of Franco Modigliani, vols 1, 2, 3, 1980, vols 4, 5, 1989 (trans. Hungarian, 1988); Il caso Italia, 1986; Reddito, Interesse, Inflazione, 1987; contribs to Corriere Della Sera, periodicals and learned jls. *Address:* Massachusetts Institute of Technology, Sloan School of Management, Cambridge, Mass 02139, USA.

MOERAN, Edward Warner; *b* 27 Nov. 1903; *s* of E. J. Moeran. *Educ:* Christ's Coll., Finchley; University of London. Solicitor. MP (Lab) South Beds, 1950–51. Pres., W London Law Soc., 1971–72. Chm., Solicitors' Ecology Gp, 1972–74. *Publications:* Practical Conveyancing, 1949; Invitation to Conveyancing, 1962; Practical Legal Aid, 1970; (jtly) Social Welfare Law, 1977; Legal Aid Summary, 1978; Introduction to Conveyancing, 1979. *Address:* 6 Frognal Gardens, Hampstead, NW3 6UX.

MOFFAT, Lt-Gen. Sir (William) Cameron, KBE 1985 (OBE 1975); FRCS; Chief Medical Adviser, British Red Cross Society, since 1988; *b* 8 Sept. 1929; *s* of William Weir Moffat and Margaret Garrett; *m* 1953, Audrey Watson; one *s*. *Educ:* King's Park Sch., Glasgow; Univ. of Glasgow, Western Infirmary (MB ChB). DTM&H. House Surgeon, Western Inf., Glasgow, 1952; Ship's Surg., Anchor Line, 1953; MO Seaforth Highlanders, 1954; SMO Edinburgh, 1956–57; Hammersmith Hosp., 1962; Birmingham Accident Hosp., 1964; Surg., RAAF Hosp. Malaya, 1965–67; Cons. Surg., BMH Rinteln, 1968–70; Prof. Military Surgery, RAM Coll. and RCS, 1970–75; CO BMH Rinteln, 1978–80; Comd MED HQ 1 (Br) Corps, 1980–83; PMO, UKLF, 1983–84; Surg. Gen./Dir Gen. Army Med. Servs, MoD, 1985–87, retired. QHS 1984–88. Hon. DSc Glasgow, 1991.

CStJ 1985. *Publications:* contribs to surgical text books and jls on missile wounds and their management. *Recreations:* golf, travel, bird-watching. *Address:* Kippax, Pound Green, Freshwater, Isle of Wight PO40 9HH.

MOFFATT, Prof. Henry Keith, ScD; FRS 1986; FRSE; Professor of Mathematical Physics, University of Cambridge, since 1980, (Head of Department of Applied Mathematics and Theoretical Physics, 1983–91); Fellow, Trinity College, Cambridge, 1961–76, and since 1980; *b* 12 April 1935; *s* of late Frederick Henry Moffatt and of Emmeline Marchant Fleming; *m* 1960, Katharine, (Linty), Stiven, *d* of late Rev. D. S. Stiven, MC, DD; one *s* two *d* (and one *s* decd). *Educ:* George Watson's Coll., Edinburgh; Edinburgh Univ. (BSc); Cambridge Univ. (BA, PhD, ScD). Lecturer in Mathematics, Cambridge Univ., and Director of Studies in Mathematics, Trinity Coll., 1961–76; Tutor, 1971–75; Sen. Tutor, 1975; Professor of Applied Mathematics, Bristol Univ., 1977–80. Visiting appts, Stanford Univ. and Johns Hopkins Univ., 1965, Univ. of Paris VI, 1975–76, Institut de Mécanique, Grenoble, 1986, Univ. of California, San Diego, 1987. Co-editor, Journal of Fluid Mechanics, 1966–83. FRSE 1988. *Dhc* Inst. Nat Polytechnique de Grenoble, 1987; Hon. DSc SUNY, 1990. *Publications:* Magnetic Field Generation in Electrically Conducting Fluids, 1978; (jt ed) Topological Fluid Mechanics, 1990; papers in fluid mechanics and dynamo theory in Jl Fluid Mech. and other jls. *Recreation:* allotmenteering. *Address:* 6 Banham's Close, Cambridge CB4 1HX. *T:* Cambridge (0223) 63338.

MOFFATT, John, MA, DPhil; Provost, The Queen's College, Oxford, since 1987; *b* 12 Oct. 1922; *s* of Jacob and Ethel Moffatt; *m* 1949, Una Lamorna Morris; one *d*. *Educ:* Keighley Boys' Grammar Sch.; Magdalen Coll., Oxford (MA, DPhil). Radar research with British Thomson-Houston Co. Ltd, Rugby, 1942–46; Oxford University: Sen. Res. Officer, Clarendon Lab., 1950; Lectr, Dept of Nuclear Physics, 1965; The Queen's College: Fellow and Praelector in Physics, 1950; Sen. Tutor, 1972–76. *Publications:* articles on physics in various scientific jls. *Address:* The Queen's College, Oxford OX1 4AW. *T:* Oxford (0865) 279120.

MOGG; *see* Rees-Mogg, family name of Baron Rees-Mogg.

MOGG, Gen. Sir John, GCB 1972 (KCB 1966; CB 1964); CBE 1960; DSO 1944; Bar, 1944; Deputy Supreme Allied Commander, Europe, 1973–76; *b* 17 Feb. 1913; *s* of late Capt. H. B. Mogg, MC and late Alice Mary (*née* Ballard); *m* 1939, Cecilia Margaret Molesworth; three *s*. *Educ:* Malvern Coll.; RMC Sandhurst. Coldstream Guards, 1933–35; RMC Sandhurst (Sword of Honour) 1935–37; commissioned Oxfordshire and Buckinghamshire Light Infantry, 1937. Served War of 1939–45 (despatches twice, 1944); comd 9 DLI (NW Europe), 1944–45; Instructor, Staff Coll., 1948–50; Commander 10th Parachute Bn, 1950–52; Chief Instructor, School of Infantry, Warminster, 1952–54; Instructor (GSO1), Imperial Defence Coll., 1954–56; Comdr, Commonwealth Brigade Gp, Malaya, 1958–60; Meritorious Medal (Perak, Malaya); Dir of Combat Development, War Office, 1961–62; Comdt, Royal Military Academy, Sandhurst, 1963–66; Comdr 1st (British) Corps, 1966–68; GOC-in-C Southern Comd, 1968; GOC-in-C Army Strategic Comd, 1968–70; Adjutant-Gen., MoD (Army), 1970–73. ADC Gen. to the Queen, 1971–74. Col Comdt: Army Air Corps, 1963–74; The Royal Green Jackets, 1965–73; Hon. Col, 10th Parachute Bn, TA, 1973–78. Kermit Roosevelt Lectr, 1969. President: Army Cricket Assoc.; Army Saddle Club, 1969; Army Boxing Assoc., 1970; Army Parachute Assoc., 1971; BHS, 1972; Ex Services Mental Welfare Soc.; Army Benevolent Fund, 1980– (Chm., 1976); Normandy Veterans Assoc., 1982–; Chairman: Army Free Fall Parachute Assoc., 1970; Army Football Assoc., 1960–63; Royal Soldiers' Daughters Sch., 1976; Operation Drake for Young Explorers, 1978–; Operation Drake Fellowship, 1980–83; Royal Internat. Horse Show, 1979; Vice-Pres., Operation Raleigh. Pres., Council Services Kinema Corp., 1970. Dir, Lloyds Bank S Midland Regional Bd, 1976. Member Council: Wessex TA&VRA, 1976; British Atlantic Cttee, 1977; Fairbridge Drake Soc., 1987. Comr, Royal Hospital Chelsea, 1976. Governor: Malvern College, 1967; Bradfield College, 1977; Chm. of Governors, Icknield Sch., 1981–. Hon. Liveryman, Fruiterers' Co. DL Oxfordshire, 1979, Vice Lord-Lieut, 1979–89. *Recreations:* cricket, most field sports, helicopter pilot. *Address:* Church Close, Watlington, Oxon. *Clubs:* Army and Navy, Flyfishers', MCC, Cavalry and Guards, Pitt.

MOGG, John Frederick; Deputy Director General, DGIII, European Commission, since 1990; *b* 5 Oct. 1943; *s* of Thomas W. Mogg and Cora M. Mogg; *m* 1967, Anne Smith; one *d* one *s*. *Educ:* Bishop Vesey's Grammar Sch., Sutton Coldfield; Birmingham Univ. (BA Hons). Rediffusion Ltd, 1965–74; Principal: Office of Fair Trading, 1974–76; Dept of Trade (Insurance Div.), 1976–79; First Sec., UK Perm. Representation, Brussels, 1979–82; Department of Trade and Industry: Asst Sec., Minerals and Metals Div., 1982–85; PPS to Sec. of State for Trade and Industry, 1985–86; Under Secretary: European Policy Div., 1986–87; Industrial Materials Market Div., 1987–89; Dep. Hd, European Secretariat, Cabinet Office, 1989–90. *Address:* Commission of the European Communities, DGIII, Rue de la loi 200, Bruxelles.

MOGGRIDGE, Harry Traherne, (Hal), OBE 1986; PPLI; RIBA; FIHort; Senior Partner, Colvin and Moggridge, Landscape Consultants (established 1922), since 1981 (Partner, since 1969); Member, Royal Fine Art Commission, since 1988; *b* London, 2 Feb. 1936; *s* of late Lt-Col Harry Weston Moggridge, CMG, and Helen Mary Ferrier Taylor; *m* 1963, Catherine Greville Herbert; two *s* one *d*. *Educ:* Tonbridge Sch.; Architectural Assoc.; evening lectures in landscape design under Prof. P. Youngman. Notts CC, 1960; Asst to Geoffrey Jellicoe, 1961–63; Site architect for Sir Wm Halcrow & Ptrs, Tema Harbour, Ghana, 1964–65; Landscape asst, GLC, 1966–67; own practice; entered into partnership with late Brenda Colvin, CBE, PPILA, 1969, continuing in partnership with Christopher Carter, ALI, and staff of nine. Prof. of Landscape Architecture, Univ. of Sheffield, 1984–86. Mem. Council, Landscape Inst., 1970–83 (Hon. Sec., Vice Pres., Pres. 1979–81) and 1987– (Deleg. to Internat. Fedn of Landscape Architects, 1980–; Chm., Internat. Cttee, 1986–); Bd Mem., Landscape Res. Gp, 1983–88; Mem., Nat. Trust Architectural Panel, 1991–. Landscape works include: Brenig Reservoir, Clwyd; White Horse Hill, a new car park and restoration of grass downland; Gale Common Hill, Yorkshire, woods and fields over 100 million cubic metres of waste ash and shale built over 60 years; quarries; countryside studies; reclamation; public and private gardens, incl. Fulham Palace, London, and Stevens Close, Jesus Coll., Oxford; Aldermaston Ct, near Reading, grounds for a new co. headquarters; current projects incl. some 5000 hectares of parkland, both restoration of historic parks (eg Blenheim, Knole) and creation of new parks. FRSA. *Publications:* numerous articles and chapters of books describing works or technical subjects. *Recreations:* looking at pictures, gardens, buildings, towns, landscapes and people in these places; walking, scene painting, dry stone walling, theatre. *Address:* Filkins, Lechlade, Glos GL7 3JQ. *T:* Filkins (0367) 860225. *Clubs:* Farmers.

MOHAMED ALI, Ibrahim; Ambassador of Sudan to the Court of St James's, 1985–89; *b* 13 Sept. 1932; *s* of Mohamed Ali Ibrahim and Batul Ali El Hag; *m* 1962, Alawia Ramzi Hussein; three *s* one *d*. *Educ:* Univ. of Cairo (BA; Dip. Inst. Pol. Sci.). Joined Min. of Foreign Affairs as Third Sec., 1957; served with Sudan Embassies in Athens, Belgrade, Dar es Salaam, Jeddah, Moscow; Diplomatic course at LSE, 1965; Ambassador to: Kuwait, 1972–74; Ivory Coast, 1974–76; Chief of State Protocol, 1976–78; Ambassador to: Canada, 1978–80; Spain, 1980–83; Under Sec., Min. of For. Affairs, 1984–85. Grand Cross, Order of Isobel la Católica (Spain), 1983; Officer of Legion of Honour (France). *Recreations:* fishing, sports (football, table tennis), photography. *Address:* c/o Ministry of Foreign Affairs, Khartoum, Sudan.

MOHYEDDIN, Zia; actor; producer and director, Central TV, since 1980; *b* 20 June 1931; *m* 1974, Nahid Siddiqui; three *s*. *Educ:* Punjab University (BA Hons). Freelance directing for Aust. broadcasting, 1951–52; RADA, 1953–54; Pakistan stage appearances, 1956–59; UK stage, 1959–71; Dir Gen., Pakistan Nat. Performing Ensemble, to 1977; *stage:* appearances include: A Passage to India, 1960; The Alchemist, 1964; The Merchant of Venice, 1966; Volpone, 1967; The Guide, 1968; On The Rocks, 1969; Measure for Measure, 1981; Film, Film, Film, 1986; *films:* Lawrence of Arabia, 1961; Sammy Going South, 1963; The Sailor from Gibraltar; Khartoum, 1965; Ashanti, 1982; Assam Garden, 1985; *television series:* The Hidden Truth, 1964; Gangsters, 1979; Jewel in the Crown, 1983; King of the Ghetto, 1986; Mountbatten, 1988; Shalom Salaam, 1989. *Recreations:* reading, bridge, watching cricket. *Address:* c/o Plunkett Greene Ltd, 4 Ovington Gardens, SW13 1LS. *Club:* Savile.

MOI, Hon. Daniel arap, EGH, EBS; President of Kenya, since 1978; Minister of Defence, since 1979; *b* Rift Valley Province, 1924. *Educ:* African Inland Mission Sch., Kabartonjo; Govt African Sch., Kapsabet. Teacher, 1946–56. MLC, 1957; Mem. for Baringo, House of Representatives, 1963–78; Minister for Educn, 1961; Minister for Local Govt, 1962–64; Minister for Home Affairs, 1964–67; Vice-Pres. of Kenya, 1967–78. Chm., Kenya African Democratic Union (KADU), 1960; Pres., Kenya African Nat. Union (KANU) for Rift Valley Province, 1966; Pres. of KANU, 1978–. Chm., Rift Valley Provincial Council. Former Member: Rift Valley Educn Bd; Kalenjin Language Cttee; Commonwealth Higher Educn Cttee; Kenya Meat Commn; Bd of Governors, African Girls' High Sch., Kikuyu. *Address:* Office of the President, PO Box 30510, Nairobi, Kenya; State House, PO Box 40530, Nairobi, Kenya.

MOIR, Sir Ernest Ian Royds, 3rd Bt, *cr* 1916; *b* 9 June 1925; *o s* of Sir Arrol Moir, 2nd Bt, and Dorothy Blanche, *d* of Admiral Sir Percy Royds, CB, CMG; *S* father, 1957; *m* 1954, Margaret Hanham Carter; three *s*. *Educ:* Rugby; Cambridge Univ. (BA). Served War of 1939–45 in Royal Engineers. *Heir: s* Christopher Ernest Moir [*b* 22 May 1955; *m* 1983, Mrs Vanessa Kirtikar, *yr d* of V. A. Crosby; twin *s* one *d*]. *Address:* Three Gates, 174 Coombe Lane West, Kingston, Surrey KT2 7DE. *T:* 081–942 7394. *Club:* Royal Automobile.

MOIR, (George) Guthrie, MA; retired; *b* 30 Oct. 1917; *s* of James William and May Flora Moir; *m* 1951, Sheila Maureen Ryan, SRN; one *s* two *d*. *Educ:* Berkhamsted; Peterhouse, Cambridge. Officer, 5th Suffolk Regt, 1940–46, POW Singapore, 1942. Chief Officer (with Countess (Edwina) Mountbatten of Burma), St John Ambulance Bde Cadets, 1947–50; Dir, European Youth Campaign, 1950–52; Chm., later Pres., World Assembly of Youth, 1952–56; Education Adviser, Hollerith Tab. Machine Co., 1957; adopted Bradenham Manor (Disraeli's) as a training centre; Asst Controller and Exec. Producer, Rediffusion TV, 1958–68; Controller of Educn and Religious Programmes, Thames TV, 1968–76. Serious damage under train in Sept. 1974. Member: Gen. Synod (formerly House of Laity, Church Assembly), 1956–75; Bd of Church Army, 1973–; Mem. Council, Reading Univ. Mem. Cttee Athenæum, 1974–. Contested (L) Aylesbury Div., 1950. CC Bucks, 1949–75; President: Old Berkhamstedians Assoc., 1974; Ivinghoe Beacon Villages, 1973; started Green Park in adjoining delicious Rothschild country (Chm., Youth Centre). Vice Pres., St John, Bucks. Papal Bene Merenti Medal 1970, for services to religious and educational broadcasting. FRSA 1980. OStJ. *Publications:* (ed) Why I Believe, 1964; (ed) Life's Work, 1965; (ed) Teaching and Television: ETV Explained, 1967; The Suffolk Regiment, 1969; Into Television, 1969; (ed) Beyond Hatred, 1969; contribs to Times, Times Ed. Supplement, Church Times, Contemporary Review, Frontier, etc. Many TV series, including This Week; Dialogue with Doubt; Royalist and Roundhead; Best Sellers; Treasures of the British Museum; (with Nat. Trust) A Place in the Country; A Place in History; A Place in Europe. *Recreations:* golf, poetry, churches, mountains. *Address:* The Old Rectory, Aston Clinton, Aylesbury, Bucks. *T:* Aylesbury (0296) 630393. *Club:* Nikaean.

MOIR, James William Charles; Head of Light Entertainment Group, BBC Television, since 1987; *b* 5 Nov. 1941; *s* of William Charles Moir and Mary Margaret Moir (*née* Daly); *m* 1966, Julia (*née* Smalley); two *s* one *d*. *Educ:* Gunnersbury Catholic Grammar School; Univ. of Nottingham (BA). Joined BBC TV Light Entertainment Group, 1963; Producer, Light Entertainment, 1970, Exec. Producer, 1979; Head of Variety, 1982–87. Hon. Mem. Council, NSPCC, 1990–. Mem., Vice Chancellor's Adv. Bd, Univ. of Nottingham, 1990. FRTS 1990. *Address:* The Lawn, Elm Park Road, Pinner, Middx HA5 3LE. *Clubs:* Savage, Reform.

MOIR CAREY, D. M.; *see* Carey.

MOISEIWITSCH, Prof. Benjamin Lawrence; Professor of Applied Mathematics, Queen's University of Belfast, since 1968; *b* London, 6 Dec. 1927; *s* of Jacob Moiseiwitsch and Chana Kotlerman; *m* 1953, Sheelagh M. McKeon; two *s* two *d*. *Educ:* Royal Liberty Sch., Romford; University Coll., London (BSc, 1949, PhD 1952). Sir George Jessel Studentship in Maths, UCL, 1949; Queen's University, Belfast: Lectr and Reader in Applied Maths, 1952–68; Dean, Faculty of Science, 1972–75; Hd, Dept of Applied Maths and Theoretical Physics, 1977–89. MRIA 1969. *Publications:* Variational Principles, 1966; Integral Equations, 1977; articles on theoretical atomic physics in scientific jls. *Address:* 21 Knocktern Gardens, Belfast, Northern Ireland BT4 3LZ. *T:* Belfast (0232) 658332.

MOISEIWITSCH, Tanya, (Mrs Felix Krish), CBE 1976; designer for the theatre; *b* 3 Dec. 1914; *d* of late Benno Moiseiwitsch, CBE, and 1st wife, Daisy Kennedy; *m* 1942, Felix Krish (decd). *Educ:* various private schs; Central School of Arts and Crafts, London; Scenic painting student at Old Vic, London. Abbey Theatre, Dublin, 1935–39; Q. Theatre, 1940; 1st West End prod. Golden Cuckoo, Duchess, 1940; Weekly Repertory, Oxford Playhouse, 1941–44. Stage designs include: Bless the Bride, Adelphi, 1947; Peter Grimes, Covent Garden, 1947; Beggar's Opera, English Opera Group, Aldeburgh Festival, 1948; Treasure Hunt, Apollo, 1949; Home at Seven, Wyndham's, 1950; The Holly and the Ivy, Lyric (Hammersmith) and Duchess, 1950; Captain Carvallo, St James's, 1950; Figure of Fun, Aldwych, 1951. Has designed for Old Vic Company since 1944; at Playhouse, Liverpool, 1944–45; at Theatre Royal, Bristol, 1945–46; productions for Old Vic Company include: (at New Theatre): Uncle Vanya, The Critic, Cyrano de Bergerac, 1945–46, The Cherry Orchard, 1948, A Month in the Country, 1949; (at Old Vic): Midsummer Night's Dream, 1951, Timon of Athens, 1952, Henry VIII, 1953; Two Gentlemen of Verona, 1957. Has designed for Royal Shakespeare Theatre, Stratford upon Avon: Henry VIII, 1950; The History Cycle (assisted by Alix Stone), 1951; Othello, 1954; Measure for Measure, 1956; Much Ado about Nothing (scenery), 1958; All's Well that Ends Well, 1959; also for 1st, and subsequent seasons, Shakespearean Festival, Stratford, Ont, incl. Cymbeline, 1970; The Imaginary Invalid, 1974; All's Well that Ends

Well, 1977; Mary Stuart (costumes), 1982; Tartuffe, 1983; (with Polly Scranton Bohdanetzky) The Government Inspector, Stratford, Ont, 1985; for The Matchmaker, Edinburgh Festival, 1954, and New York, 1955; for Cherry Orchard, Piccolo Teatro, Milan, 1955; for Merchant of Venice, Habimah Theatre, Israel, 1959; Tyrone Guthrie Theatre, Minneapolis, USA: 1963: Hamlet, The Miser, Three Sisters; 1964: St Joan, Volpone; 1965: The Way of the World; Cherry Orchard; 1966: As You Like It; Skin of our Teeth (with Carolyn Parker); 1967: The House of Atreus; 1973: (with J. Jensen) The Government Inspector (costumes); Metropolitan Opera, New York: Peter Grimes, 1967; Rigoletto, 1977; La Traviata, 1981; National Theatre: Volpone, 1968; The Misanthrope, 1973; Phaedra Britannica, 1975; The Double Dealer, 1978; Macook's Corner, Ulster Players, Belfast, 1969; Caucasian Chalk Circle, Sheffield Playhouse, 1969; Swift, Abbey Theatre, Dublin, 1969; Uncle Vanya, Minneapolis, 1969; The Barber of Seville, Brighton Festival, 1971; Australian Tour for Elizabethan Theatre Trust, 1974; The Misanthrope, St James' Theater, NY, 1975; The Voyage of Edgar Allan Poe (world première), Minnesota Opera Co., USA, 1976; Œdipus the King and Œdipus at Colonus (costumes and masks), Adelaide Fest., 1978; Red Roses for Me, Abbey Theatre, Dublin, 1980; The Clandestine Marriage, Compass Theatre Co. tour and Albery, 1984. Cons. designer, Crucible Theatre, Sheffield, 1971–73. For Granada TV, King Lear (costumes), 1983. Diplôme d'Honneur, Canadian Conference of the Arts; Hon. Fellow, Ontario Coll. of Art, 1979. Hon. DLitt: Birmingham, 1964; Waterloo, Ont, 1977; Hon. LLD Toronto, 1988. *Address:* 17B St Alban's Studios, St Alban's Grove, W8 5BT.

MOKAMA, Hon. Moleleki Didwell, BA, LLM (Harvard), LLM (London); Barrister-at-Law; Advocate of the Supreme Court of Botswana; Attorney-General of Botswana, since 1969; Member of Parliament *ex officio* and Member of the Cabinet *ex officio*; *b* 2 Feb. 1933; *e s* of Mokama Moleleki and Baipoledi Moleleki, Maunatlala, Botswana; *m* 1962, Kgopodiso Vivien Robi; one *s*. *Educ:* Moeng; Fort Hare; London Univ.; Inner Temple. Crown Counsel to Botswana Govt, 1963–66; High Comr for Botswana in London, 1966–69; Botswana Ambassador Extraordinary and Plenipotentiary: to France, 1967–69; to Germany, 1967–69; to Sweden, 1968–69; to Denmark, 1968–69. Hon. Mem., American Soc. of International Law, 1965. *Recreations:* swimming, shooting, hunting, photography. *Address:* Attorney-General's Chambers, Private Bag 009, Gaborone, Botswana.

MOLAPO, Mooki Motsarapane; High Commissioner for Lesotho in the United Kingdom, 1979–82; *b* 28 April 1928; *s* of Motsarapane and Mathebe Molapo; *m* 1958, Emily Mamanasse Thamae; three *s* one *d*. *Educ:* Lesotho (then Basutoland) High School. Government Service, 1950–83, retired. *Recreations:* football fan, walking, movies, theatre. *Address:* PO Box 1574, Maseru 100, Lesotho.

MOLE, David Richard Penton; QC 1990; *b* 1 April 1943; *s* of Rev. Arthur Penton Mole and Margaret Isobel Mole; *m* 1969, Anu-Reet (*née* Nigol); three *s* one *d*. *Educ:* St John's School, Leatherhead; Trinity College, Dublin (MA); LSE (LLM). City of London College, 1967–74 (Sen. Lectr, 1971); called to the Bar, Inner Temple, 1970; Standing Junior Counsel to Inland Revenue in rating valuation matters, 1984. Part-time cartoonist, 1979–83. *Publications:* contribs to Jl of Planning Law. *Recreations:* sailing, walking, ski-ing, drawing, painting. *Address:* 4-5 Gray's Inn Square, Gray's Inn, WC1R 5AY. *T:* 071–404 5252.

MOLESWORTH, family name of **Viscount Molesworth.**

MOLESWORTH, 11th Viscount, *cr* 1716 (Ireland); **Richard Gosset Molesworth;** Baron Philipstown, 1716; secretarial work since 1959; *b* 31 Oct. 1907; *s* of 10th Viscount and Elizabeth Gladys Langworthy (*d* 1974); *S* father, 1961; *m* 1958, Anne Florence Womersley, MA (*d* 1983); two *s*. *Educ:* Lancing Coll.; private tutors. Farmed for many years. Freeman, City of London, 1978. Served War, in RAF, 1941–44 (Middle East, 1941–43). *Recreations:* foreign travel, music. *Heir:* *s* Hon. Robert Bysse Kelham Molesworth [*b* 4 June 1959. *Educ:* Sussex Univ. (BA Hons)]. *Address:* Garden Flat, 2 Bishopswood Road, Highgate, N6. *T:* 081–348 1366.

MOLESWORTH, Allen Henry Neville; mangement consultant; *b* 20 Aug. 1931; *s* of late Roger Bevil Molesworth (Colonel RA), and of Iris Alice Molesworth (*née* Kennion); *m* 1970, Gail Cheng Kwai Chan. *Educ:* Wellington Coll., Berks; Trinity Coll., Cambridge (MA). FCA, FCMA, MIMC. 2nd Lt, 4th Queen's Own Hussars, Malaya, 1950. Project Accounts, John Laing & Sons (Canada) Ltd, 1954–58; Singleton Fabian & Co., Chartered Accountants, 1959–63; Consultant: Standard Telephones & Cables Ltd, 1963–67; Coopers & Lybrand Associates Ltd, 1967–76: India, 1970; Kuwait, 1971; France, 1972; New Hebrides, 1972; Laos, 1974; Tonga, 1975; Financial and Admin. Controller, Crown Agents, 1976–84; Chief Accountant, British Telecom Property, 1984–90. *Recreations:* shooting, skiing, music, restoring antiques. *Address:* c/o Lloyds Bank, Cox's & King's Branch, 7 Pall Mall, SW1. *Clubs:* 1900, Coningsby.

MOLESWORTH-ST AUBYN, Lt-Col Sir (John) Arscott, 15th Bt *cr* 1689, of Pencarrow; MBE 1963; DL; JP; *b* 15 Dec. 1926; *s* of Sir John Molesworth-St Aubyn, 14th Bt, CBE, and Celia Marjorie (*d* 1965), *d* of Lt-Col Valentine Vivian, CMG, DSO, MVO; *S* father, 1985; *m* 1957, Iona Audrey Armatrude, *d* of late Adm. Sir Francis Loftus Tottenham, KCB, CBE; two *s* one *d*. *Educ:* Eton. 2nd Lieut KRRC 1946; Captain 1954; psc 1959; Major 1961; jssc 1964; served Malaya and Borneo, 1961–63 and 1965; Royal Green Jackets, 1966; Lt-Col 1967; retd 1969. County Comr, Scouts, Cornwall, 1969–79. Mem., Cornwall River Authority, 1969–74; Chairman: West Local Land Drainage Cttee, SW Water Authority, 1974–89; West Local Flood Alleviation Cttee, Nat. Rivers Authority, SW Region, 1989–; Devon Exec. Cttee, 1975–77, and Cornwall Exec. Cttee, 1987–89, CLA. Wessex Region, Historic Houses Assoc., 1981–83. Pres., Royal Cornwall Agricl Assoc., 1976; Mem. Council, Devon County Agricl Assoc., 1979–82; JP Devon, 1971; DL Cornwall, 1971; High Sheriff Cornwall, 1975. *Recreations:* shooting, ornithology. *Heir:* *s* William Molesworth-St Aubyn [*b* 23 Nov. 1958; *m* 1988, Carolyn, *er d* of William Tozier]. *Address:* Pencarrow, Bodmin, Cornwall. *T:* St Mabyn (020884) 449; Tetcott Manor, Holsworthy, Devon. *T:* North Tamerton (040927) 220. *Clubs:* Army and Navy; Cornish 1768.

MOLITOR, Edouard, Hon. KCMG 1976; Grand Officier, Ordre du Mérite (Luxembourg), 1990; Commandeur, Ordre de la Couronne de Chêne, 1985; Officier, Ordre Civil et Militaire d'Adolphe de Nassau, 1977; Ambassador of Luxembourg to the Court of St James's, since 1989, and concurrently to Ireland and Iceland; *b* Luxembourg City, 14 Feb. 1931; *s* of Joseph Molitor and Lucie Michels; *m* 1960, Constance Scholtes; three *s*. *Educ:* Univs of Grenoble, Nancy and Paris. Dr en droit. Barrister, Luxembourg, 1955–60; joined Diplomatic Service, 1960 (Political Affairs); First Sec. and Rep. to UNESCO, Paris, 1964–69; Counsellor and Consul-Gen., Brussels, 1969–73; Dir of Protocol and Juridical Affairs, Min. of Foreign Affairs, 1973–78; Mem., Commn de Contrôle, EC, 1973–77; Ambassador to Austria, 1978–89; Perm. Rep. to UNIDO, IAEA, 1978–89 and to Council of WEU 1989–; Head of Luxembourg Delegn, MBFR Conf., 1978–89 and at CSCE Conf., Vienna, 1986–89. Foreign Decorations from: Norway, 1964; Italy, W Germany, Belgium, 1973; Greece, 1975; Denmark, Tunisia, Senegal, Netherlands, France, 1978; Vatican, Austria, 1989; Iceland, 1990. *Recreations:* swimming, hiking, ski-ing, shooting, hunting, music, literature. *Address:* Luxembourg Embassy, 27 Wilton Crescent, SW1X 8SD. *T:* 071–235 6961. *Clubs:* Travellers', Rotary, Anglo-Belgian.

MOLLISON, Prof. Patrick Loudon, CBE 1979; MD; FRCP; FRCPath; FRCOG; FRS 1968; Professor of Hæmatology, St Mary's Hospital Medical School, London University, 1962–79, now Emeritus Professor; Hon. Consultant Immunohaematologist, North London Blood Transfusion Centre, since 1983; *b* 17 March 1914; *s* of William Mayhew Mollison, Cons. Surgeon (ENT), Guy's Hospital; *m* 1st, 1940, Dr Margaret D. Peirce (marr. diss., 1964); three *s*; 2nd, 1973, Dr Jennifer Jones. *Educ:* Rugby Sch.; Clare Coll., Cambridge; St Thomas' Hosp., London. MD Cantab 1944; FRCP 1959; FRCPath 1963; FRCOG *ad eund*, 1980. House Phys., Medical Unit, St Thomas' Hosp., 1939; Medical Officer, S London Blood Supply Depot, 1939–43; RAMC, 1943–46; Dir, MRC Blood Transfusion Res. Unit, Hammersmith Hosp., 1946–60; part-time Dir, MRC Experimental Hæmatology Unit, 1960–79; Hon. Lectr, then Sen. Lectr, Dept of Medicine, Post-grad. Medical Sch., 1948; Consultant Hæmatologist: Hammersmith Hosp., 1947–60; St Mary's Hosp., 1960–79. Hon. FRSM 1979; Landsteiner Meml Award, USA, 1960; P. Levine Award, USA, 1973; Oehlecker Medal, Germany, 1974. *Publications:* Blood Transfusion in Clinical Medicine, 1951, 8th edn (jtly) 1987; papers on red cell survival and blood group antibodies. *Recreations:* music, gardening. *Address:* 60 King Henry's Road, NW3 3RR. *T:* 071–722 1947.

MOLLO, Joseph Molelekoa Kaibe; Managing Director, Trading Corporation of Lesotho; *b* 7 May 1944; *s* of Kaibe and Cyrian Mollo; *m* 1972, Makaibe; two *s* two *d*. *Educ:* Univ. of Botswana, Lesotho and Swaziland (BA Admin); Univ. of Saskatchewan (MCEd); Carleton Univ. (working on a Master's degree in Political Science since 1978). Asst Sec., Min. of Finance, 1971; Comr of Co-operatives, 1973; Dep. Perm. Sec., Finance, 1975; High Comr, Canada, 1976; Perm. Sec., Finance, 1980; High Comr in London, 1982–83; Ambassador to Denmark (also accredited to Sweden, Norway, Finland, Iceland, GDR and Poland), 1983–86. Unpublished thesis: Profit versus Co-operation: the struggle of the Western Co-operative College. *Recreations:* jogging, dancing, music, soccer. *Address:* TCL, P/Bag, A120, Maseru, Lesotho.

MOLLOY, family name of **Baron Molloy.**

MOLLOY, Baron *cr* 1981 (Life Peer), of Ealing in Greater London; **William John Molloy,** FRGS; *b* 26 Oct. 1918; *m* Eva Lewis; one *d*. *Educ:* elementary sch., Swansea; University Coll., Swansea (Political Economy, extra-mural). Served TA, 1938, Field Co., RE, 1939–46. Member: TGWU 1936–46; Civil Service Union, 1946–52; Co-op and USDAW, 1952; Parliamentary Adviser: COHSE, 1974–; Civil Service Union, 1974–79. Editor, Civil Service Review, 1947–52; Chm., Staff-Side Whitley Council, Germany and Austria Sections, FO, 1948–52, and Staff-Side Lectr, 1946–52. Member: Fulham Borough Council, 1954–62 (Leader, 1959–62); Fulham and Hammersmith Council, 1962–66. MP (Lab) Ealing N, 1964–79; former Vice-Chm., Parly Labour Party Gp for Common Market and European Affairs; Chm., PLP Social Services Gp, 1974; Parly Adviser, London Trades Council Transport Cttee, 1968–79; Mem., House of Commons Estimates Cttee, 1968–70; PPS to Minister of Posts and Telecom., 1969–70. Chm., British Tunisia Soc., 1987–; Vice-Chm., All Party British/Tunisian Parly Gp, 1987–. Member: CPA, 1964; IPU, 1964 (Mem. Exec., 1984–); Assemblies, Council of Europe and WEU, 1969–73; European Parlt, 1976–79. Mem., Parly and Scientific Cttee, 1982–; EC Mem., CAABU. Political Consultant: Confedn of Health Service Employees, 1979–; British Library Assoc., 1984–; Consultant and Adviser to Arab League, 1982–88. Vice-Pres., and a Trustee, Health Visitors Assoc., 1987–. Pres., Metropolitan Area, Royal British Legion, 1984–. Hon. Life Pres., London Univ. Debating Soc., 1970; Hon. Pres., London Univ. Union, 1983–; Hon. Patron, Stirling Univ. Debating Soc., 1991–; Mem. Court, Reading Univ., 1968–; Mem. Exec. Council, RGS, 1976–. Fellow, World Assoc. of Arts and Sciences, 1982. Hon. Fellow, UC of Swansea, Wales, 1987; Hon. Associate, BVA, 1988. *Recreations:* horse-riding, music, collecting dictionaries. *Address:* 2a Uneeda Drive, Greenford, Mddx UB6 8QB. *T:* (office) 071–219 6710; (home) 081–578 7736.

MOLLOY, Michael John; writer; *b* 22 Dec. 1940; *s* of John George and Margaret Ellen Molloy; *m* 1964, Sandra June Foley; three *d*. *Educ:* Ealing School of Art. Sunday Pictorial, 1956; Daily Sketch, 1960; Daily Mirror, 1962–85: Editor, Mirror Magazine, 1969; Asst Editor, 1970; Dep. Editor, 1975; Editor, Dec. 1975–1985; Editor, Sunday Mirror, 1986–88; Mirror Group Newspapers: Director, 1976–90; Editor in Chief, 1985–90. *Publications:* The Black Dwarf, 1985; The Kid from Riga, 1987; The Harlot of Jericho, 1989; The Century, 1990; The Gallery, 1991. *Recreations:* reading, writing. *Address:* 62 Culmington Road, W13. *Clubs:* Reform, Savile.

MOLONY, Thomas Desmond, 3rd Bt. Does not use the title, and his name is not on the Official Roll of Baronets.

MOLSON, family name of **Baron Molson.**

MOLSON, Baron, *cr* 1961, of High Peak (Life Peer); **(Arthur) Hugh (Elsdale) Molson,** PC 1956; President, Council for Protection of Rural England, 1971–80 (Chairman, 1968–71); *b* 29 June 1903; *o* surv. *s* of late Major J. E. Molson, MP, Gainsborough, and Mary, *d* of late A. E. Leeson, MD; *m* 1949, Nancy, *d* of late W. H. Astington, Bramhall, Cheshire. *Educ:* Royal Naval Colleges, Osborne and Dartmouth; Lancing; New Coll., Oxford. Pres. of Oxford Union, 1925; 1st Class Hons Jurisprudence. Served 36 Searchlight Regt, 1939–41. Staff Captain 11 AA, Div., 1941–42. Barrister-at-Law, Inner Temple, 1931; Political Sec., Associated Chambers of Commerce of India, 1926–29; Contested Aberdare Div. of Merthyr Tydfil, 1929; MP (U) Doncaster, 1931–35. MP (U) The High Peak Div. of Derbyshire, 1939–61. Parly Sec., Min. of Works, 1951–53; Joint Parly Sec., Min. of Transport and Civil Aviation, Nov. 1953–Jan. 1957; Minister of Works, 1957–Oct. 1959. Mem., Monckton Commission on Rhodesia and Nyasaland, 1960; Chm., Commn of Privy Counsellors on the dispute between Buganda and Bunyoro, 1962. Pres., TCPA, 1963–70. *Publications:* articles in various reviews on political and other subjects. *Address:* 20 Marsham Court, Marsham Street, SW1P 4JY. *T:* 071–828 2008. *Clubs:* Athenæum, Carlton.

MOLYNEAUX, Rt. Hon. James Henry; PC 1983; MP (UU) Lagan Valley, since 1983 (Antrim South, 1970–83); Leader, Ulster Unionist Party, since 1979; *b* 27 Aug. 1920; *s* of late William Molyneaux, Seacash, Killead, Co. Antrim; unmarried. *Educ:* Aldergrove Sch., Co. Antrim. RAF, 1941–46. Vice-Chm., Eastern Special Care Hosp. Man. Cttee, 1966–73; Chm. Antrim Br., NI Assoc. for Mental Health, 1967–70; Hon. Sec., S Antrim Unionist Assoc., 1964–70; Vice-Pres., Ulster Unionist Council, 1974. Mem. (UU) S Antrim, NI Assembly, 1982–86. Leader, UU Party, House of Commons, 1974–. Dep. Grand Master of Orange Order and Hon. PGM of Canada; Sovereign Grand Master, Commonwealth Royal Black Instn, 1971. JP Antrim, 1957–87; CC Antrim, 1964–73. *Recreations:* gardening, music. *Address:* Aldergrove, Crumlin, Co. Antrim, N Ireland BT29 4AR. *T:* Crumlin (08494) 22545.

MOLYNEUX, James Robert M.; *see* More-Molyneux.

MOLYNEUX, Wilfrid, FCA; *b* 26 July 1910; *s* of Charles Molyneux and Mary (*née* Vose); *m* 1937, Kathleen Eleanor Young; one *s* one *d*. *Educ:* Douai Sch. With Cooper Brothers & Co., 1934–67; Finance Mem., BSC, 1967–71. *Address:* 105 Park Road, Brentwood, Essex CM14 4TT.

MONAGHAN, Rt. Rev. James; Titular Bishop of Cell Ausaille, Archdiocese of St Andrews and Edinburgh since 1970; Parish Priest of Holy Cross, Edinburgh, since 1959; *b* Bathgate, 11 July 1914; *s* of Edward and Elizabeth Monaghan. *Educ:* St Aloysius' Coll., Glasgow; Blairs Coll., Aberdeen; Scots Coll., Valladolid; St Kieran's Coll., Kilkenny, Ireland. Priest, 1940; Secretary, 1953; Vicar-Gen. for Archdio. St Andrews and Edinburgh, 1958, Bp Auxiliary, 1970–89. *Address:* 252 Ferry Road, Edinburgh EH5 3AN. *T:* 031–552 3957.

MONCADA, Dr Salvador Enrique, FRS 1988; Director of Research, Wellcome Foundation Ltd, since 1986; *b* 3 Dec. 1944; *s* of Dr Salvador Eduardo Moncada and Jenny Seidner; *m* 1966, Dorys Lemus Valiente; one *d*. *Educ:* Univ. of El Salvador (DMS 1970); London Univ. (DPhil 1973; DSc 1983). GP, Social Service of El Salvador, 1969; Associate Prof. of Pharmacol. and Physiol., Univ. of Honduras, 1974–75; Wellcome Research Laboratories, 1971–73 and 1975–: Sen. Scientist, 1975–77; Hd of Dept of Prostaglandin Res., 1977–85; Dir, Therapeutic Res. Div., 1984–86. Vis. Prof., KCL, 1988. Consultant, Pan Amer. Health Orgn, 1972–. Mem., British Pharmacol Soc., 1974. Corresp. Mem., Cuba Soc. of Cardiol., 1984; Hon. Member: Colombian Soc. of Internal Medicine, 1982; Peruvian Pharmacol Soc., 1983; Associate Fellow, Third World Acad. of Sciences, 1988. Dr *hc*: Univ. of Complutense de Madrid, 1986; Univ. of Honduras, 1987; Univ. of Cantabria, 1988. Peter Debeye Prize (jtly), Limburg Univ., 1980; Nat. Sci. Prize, Republic of Honduras, 1985; Prince of Asturias Prize for Science and Technology, 1990. Sect. Ed., 1975, Consulting Ed., 1980, Prostaglandins; Member, Editorial Board: British Jl of Pharmacol., 1980–85; Atherosclerosis (Jl of Amer. Heart Assoc.), 1980–; European Jl of Clin. Investigation, 1986–; Thrombosis Research, 1989–. *Publications:* (Scientific Ed.) British Medical Bulletin, 39 pt 3: Prostacyclin, Thromboxane and Leukotrienes, 1983; Nitric oxide from L-arginine: a bioregulatory system, 1990. over 400 contribs to learned jls. *Recreations:* music, literature, theatre. *Address:* 25 Hitherwood Drive, SE19 1XA. *T:* 081–670 0298.

MONCEL, Lt-Gen. Robert William, OC 1968; DSO 1944; OBE 1944; CD 1944; retired 1966; *b* 9 April 1917; *s* of René Moncel and Edith Brady; *m* 1939, Nancy Allison, *d* of Ralph P. Bell; one *d*. *Educ:* Selwyn House Sch.; Bishop's Coll. Sch. Royal Canadian Regt, 1939; Staff Coll., 1940; Bde Major 1st Armd Bde, 1941; comd 18th Manitoba Dragoons, 1942; GSO1, HQ 2 Cdn Corps, 1943; comd 4th Armd Bde, 1944; Dir Canadian Armd Corps, 1946; Nat. War Coll., 1949; Canadian Jt Staff, London, 1949–54; Comdr 3 Inf. Bde, 1957; QMG, 1960; GOC Eastern Comd, 1963; Comptroller Gen., 1964; Vice-Chief of the Defence Staff, Canada, 1965–66. Col, 8th Canadian Hussars. Chm., Fishermen's Memorial Hosp., 1980–84; Dir, Nova Scotia Rehabilitation Center, 1986–. Mem. Bd of Regents, Mount Allison Univ., 1983–. Croix de Guerre, France, 1944; Légion d'Honneur, France, 1944. Hon. LLD Mount Allison Univ., 1968. *Recreations:* fishing, sailing, golf. *Address:* High Head, Murder Point, Nova Scotia B0J 2E0, Canada; Summer Gardens, 1470 Summer Street, Halifax, NS B3H 3A3, Canada. *Clubs:* Royal Ottawa Golf; Royal St Lawrence Yacht; Royal Nova Scotia Yacht.

MONCK, family name of **Viscount Monck.**

MONCK, 7th Viscount *cr* 1801; **Charles Stanley Monck;** *S* father, 1982 but does not use the title. *Heir:* *b* Hon. George Stanley Monck.

MONCK, Nicholas Jeremy, CB 1988; Second Permanent Secretary (Public Expenditure), HM Treasury, since 1990; *b* 9 March 1935; *s* of Bosworth Monck and Stella Mary (*née* Cock); *m* 1960, Elizabeth Mary Kirwan; three *s*. *Educ:* Eton; King's Coll., Cambridge; Univ. of Pennsylvania. Asst Principal, Min. of Power, 1959–62; NEDO, 1962–65; NBPI, 1965–66; Senior Economist, Min. of Agriculture, Tanzania, 1966–69; HM Treasury, 1969–: Asst Sec., 1971; Principal Private Sec. to Chancellor of the Exchequer, 1976–77; Under Sec., 1977–84; Dep. Sec. (Industry), 1984–90. Mem., BSC, 1978–80. *Address:* c/o HM Treasury, Parliament Street, SW1P 3AG.

MONCKTON, family name of **Viscount Galway** and **Viscount Monckton of Brenchley.**

MONCKTON OF BRENCHLEY, 2nd Viscount *cr* 1957; **Maj.-Gen. Gilbert Walter Riversdale Monckton,** CB 1966; OBE 1956; MC 1940; DL; FSA; retired, 1967; *b* 3 Nov. 1915; *o s* of 1st Viscount Monckton of Brenchley, PC, GCVO, KCMG, MC, QC, and Mary A. S. (*d* 1964), *d* of Sir Thomas Colyer-Fergusson, 3rd Bt; *S* father, 1965; *m* 1950, Marianna Laetitia (Dame of Honour and Devotion, SMO Malta (also Cross of Merit), OStJ, Pres., St John's Ambulance, Kent, 1975–80, High Sheriff of Kent, 1981–82), 3rd *d* of late Comdr Robert T. Bower; four *s* one *d*. *Educ:* Harrow; Trinity Coll., Cambridge. BA 1939, MA 1942. 2/Lt 5th Royal Inniskilling Dragoon Guards, SR 1938; Reg. 1939; France and Belgium, 1939–40; Staff Coll., 1941; Bde Major Armd Bde, 1942; Comd and Gen. Staff Sch., USA, 1943; Sqdn Ldr, 3rd King's Own Hussars, 1944, Italy and Syria; Sqdn Ldr, 5th Royal Inniskilling Dragoon Gds, 1945. RAF Staff Coll., 1949; GSO2, 7th Armd Div., 1949; Sqdn Ldr and 2 i/c 5th Royal Inniskilling Dragoon Gds, Korea and Egypt, 1951–52; GSO1, Mil. Ops, WO, 1954–56; Mil. Adv., Brit. Delegn, Geneva Confs on Indo-China and Korea, 1954; transf. 12th Royal Lancers and comd, 1956–58; Comdr Royal Armd Corps, 3rd Div., 1958–60; psc, idc 1961; Dep. Dir, Personnel Admin., WO, 1962; Dir of Public Relations, WO (subseq. MoD), 1963–65; Chief of Staff, HQ BAOR, 1965–67; Col 9th/12th Royal Lancers (Prince of Wales's), 1967–73; Hon. Col, Kent and Sharpshooters Yeomanry Sqdn, 1974–79. President: Kent Assoc. of Boys' Clubs, 1965–78; Inst. of Heraldic and Genealogical Studies, 1965; Kent Archæological Soc., 1968–75; Medway Productivity Assoc., 1968–72; Kent Co. Rifle Assoc., 1970–75; Anglo-Belgian Union, 1973–83; Chm., Thurnham Parish Council, 1968–70. FSA 1987. DL Kent, 1970. Liveryman Broderers' Co., Master 1978; KStJ; Chm., Council of Order of St John for Kent, 1969–75; SMO Malta: Bailiff, Grand Cross of Obedience (Chancellor of the British Assoc., 1963–68, Vice-Pres., 1968–74, Pres., 1974–83); Grand Cross of Merit, 1980; Comdr, Order of Crown (Belgium), 1965; Bailiff, Grand Cross of Justice, Constantinian Order of St George, 1975; Grand Officer, Order of Leopold II (Belgium), 1978. *Recreation:* archaeology. *Heir:* *s* Hon. Christopher Walter Monckton, *qv*. *Address:* Runhams Farm, Runham Lane, Harrietsham, Maidstone, Kent ME17 1NJ. *T:* Maidstone (0622) 850313. *Clubs:* Brooks's, MCC; Casino Maltese (Valetta).

MONCKTON, Hon. Christopher Walter; DL; Consulting Editor, Evening Standard, since 1987; *b* 14 Feb. 1952; *s* and *heir* of Viscount Monckton of Brenchley, *qv*; *m* 1990, Juliet Mary Anne, *y d* of Jørgen Malherbe Jensen. *Educ:* Harrow; Churchill Coll., Cambridge; University Coll., Cardiff. BA 1973, MA 1977 (Cantab); Dip. Journalism Studies (Wales), 1974. Standing Cttee, Cambridge Union Soc., 1973; Treas., Cambridge Univ. Conservative Assoc., 1973. Reporter, Yorkshire Post, 1974–75, Leader-Writer, 1975–77; Press Officer, Conservative Central Office, 1977–78; Editor-designate, The Universe, 1978, Editor, 1979–81; Managing Editor, Telegraph Sunday Magazine, 1981–82; Leader-Writer, The Standard, 1982; Special Advr to Prime Minister's Policy Unit (Home Affairs), 1982–86; Asst Editor, Today, 1986–87. Freeman, City of London, and Liveryman, Worshipful Co. of Broderers, 1973–. Member: Internat. MENSA Ltd, 1975–; St John Amb. Brigade (Wetherby Div.), 1976–77; Hon. Soc. of the Middle Temple, 1979–; RC Mass Media Commn, 1979–; Secretary: Economic Acctg Study Gp, 1980–81, Forward Strategy Gp, 1981, Health Study Gp, 1981, Employment Study Gp, 1982, Centre For Policy Studies. Vis. Lectr in Business Studies, Columbia Univ., NY, 1980. Editor, Not the Church Times, 1982. Kt SMO, Malta, 1973; OStJ 1973. DL Greater London, 1988. *Publications:* The Laker Story (with Ivan Fallon), 1982; Anglican Orders: null and void?, 1986; The Aids Report, 1987. *Recreations:* walking, talking, stalking. *Address:* 71 Albert Road, Richmond, Surrey. *T:* 081–940 6528. *Clubs:* Brooks's, Beefsteak, Pratt's.

MONCKTON-ARUNDELL, family name of **Viscount Galway.**

MONCREIFF, family name of **Baron Moncreiff.**

MONCREIFF, 5th Baron *cr* 1873; **Harry Robert Wellwood Moncreiff;** Bt, Nova Scotia 1626, UK 1871; Lt-Col (Hon.) RASC, retired; *b* 4 Feb. 1915; *s* of 4th Baron; *S* father, 1942; *m* 1952, Enid Marion Watson (*d* 1985), *o d* of Major H. W. Locke, Belmont, Dollar; one *s*. *Educ:* Fettes Coll., Edinburgh. Served War of 1939–45 (despatches). Retired, 1958. *Recreations:* Rugby football, tennis, shooting. *Heir:* *s* Hon. Rhoderick Harry Wellwood Moncreiff [*b* 22 March 1954; *m* 1982, Alison Elizabeth Anne, *d* of late James Duncan Alastair Ross; two *s*]. *Address:* Tulliebole Castle, Fossoway, Kinross-shire. *T:* Fossoway (05774) 236.

MONCRIEFF, William S.; *see* Scott-Moncrieff.

MONCTON, Archbishop of, (RC), since 1972; **Most Rev. Donat Chiasson;** *b* Paquetville, NB, 2 Jan. 1930; *s* of Louis Chiasson and Anna Chiasson (*née* Godin). *Educ:* St Joseph's Univ., NB; Holy Heart Seminary, Halifax, NS; Theological and Catechetical studies, Rome and Lumen Vitae, Belgium. *Address:* PO Box 248, Chartersville, Moncton, NB, Canada. *T:* 389.9531.

MOND, family name of **Baron Melchett.**

MONDALE, Walter Frederick; Vice-President of the United States of America, 1977–81; Partner with Dorsey & Whitney, since 1987; *b* Ceylon, Minnesota, 5 Jan. 1928; *s* of Rev. Theodore Sigvaard Mondale and Claribel Hope (*née* Cowan); *m* 1955, Joan Adams; two *s* one *d*. *Educ:* public schs, Minnesota; Macalester Coll., Univ. of Minnesota (BA *cum laude*); Univ. of Minnesota Law Sch. (LLB). Served with Army, 1951–53. Admitted to Minn. Bar, 1956; private law practice, Minneapolis, 1956–60; Attorney-Gen., Minnesota, 1960–64; Senator from Minnesota, 1964–76; Counsel with Winston & Strawn, 1981–87. Democratic Candidate for Vice-Pres., USA, 1976, 1980; Democratic Candidate for Pres., USA, 1984. Chm., Nat. Democratic Inst. for Internat. Affairs, 1987–. Mem., Democratic Farm Labor Party. *Publication:* The Accountability of Power. *Address:* c/o Dorsey & Whitney, 2200 First Bank Place East, Minneapolis, Minn 55402, USA.

MONDAY, Horace Reginald, CBE 1967 (OBE 1958); JP; *b* 26 Nov. 1907; *s* of late James Thomas Monday, Gambia Civil Servant, and late Rachel Ruth Davis; *m* 1932, Wilhelmina Roberta Juanita, *d* of late William Robertson Job Roberts, a Gambian businessman; one *s*. *Educ:* Methodist Mission Schools, in Banjul, The Gambia; correspondence course with (the then) London Sch. of Accountancy. Clerk, 1925–48; Asst Acct, Treasury, 1948–52; Acct and Storekeeper, Marine Dept, 1953–54; Acct-Gen., The Gambia Govt, 1954–65; Chm., Gambia Public Service Commn, 1965–68; High Comr for The Gambia in the UK and NI, 1968–71. MP Banjul Central, 1977–82. Chairman: Management Cttee, Banjul City Council, 1971–79; Gambia Utilities Corp., 1972–76. Dir, Gambia Currency Bd, 1964–68; Governor, Gambia High Sch., 1964–68; Pres., Gambia Red Cross Soc., 1967–68. JP 1944. Comdr, National Order of Republic of Senegal, 1968. *Address:* Rachelville, 24 Clarkson Street, Banjul, The Gambia. *T:* Banjul 511.

MONE, Rt. Rev. John Aloysius; *see* Paisley, Bishop of, (RC).

MONERAWELA, Chandra; High Commissioner in London for Sri Lanka, 1984–90; *b* 8 Sept. 1937; *m* 1965, Rupa Devi De Silva; one *s* two *d*. *Educ:* Trinity College, Kandy; University of Ceylon, Peradeniya. BA Hons Econ. Dept. of Fisheries, 1960; Sri Lanka Overseas Service, 1961; served Peking, and Washington DC; Chargé d'affaires of Sri Lanka in Thailand, and Perm. Rep. to ESCAP, 1974–80; Chief of Protocol, 1971–74, Dir, Economic Affairs, 1980–83, Ministry of Foreign Affairs; High Comr for Sri Lanka in Singapore, 1984; represented Sri Lanka at meetings, conferences and commissions in Asia, Australia, Europe, Pacific and USA. *Recreations:* athletics, cricket, rugby football, golf. *Address:* c/o Ministry of Foreign Affairs, Republic Building, Colombo 1, Sri Lanka.

MONEY, Ernle (David Drummond); Barrister-at-Law; *b* 17 Feb. 1931; *s* of late Lt-Col E. F. D. Money, DSO, late 4th Gurkha Rifles, and of Sidney, *o d* of D. E. Anderson, Forfar; *m* 1960, Susan Barbara, *d* of Lt-Col D. S. Lister, MC, The Buffs; two *s* two *d*. *Educ:* Marlborough Coll.; Oriel Coll., Oxford (open scholar). Served in Suffolk Regt, 1949–51, and 4th Bn, Suffolks Regt (TA), 1951–56; MA Hons degree (2nd cl.) in mod. hist., 1954. Tutor and lecturer, Swinton Conservative Coll., 1956. Called to Bar, Lincoln's Inn (Cholmeley Scholar), 1958. Mem., Bar Council, 1962–66. MP (C) Ipswich, 1970–Sept. 1974; Opposition Front Bench Spokesman on the Arts, 1974; Sec., Parly Cons. Arts and Amenities Cttee, 1970–73, Vice-Chm., 1974; Vice-Pres., Ipswich Cons. Assoc., 1979–. Regular columnist, East Anglian Daily Times. Governor, Woolverstone Hall Sch., 1967–70; co-opted Mem., GLC Arts Cttee, 1972–73; Mem., GLC Arts Bd, 1974–76; Mem., Cttee of Gainsborough's Birthplace, Sudbury. Fine Arts Correspondent, Contemporary Review, 1968–. Pres., Ipswich Town Football Club Supporters, 1974–; Vice-Pres., E Suffolk and Ipswich Branch, RSPCA, 1974–. *Publications:* (with Peter Johnson) The Nasmyth Family of Painters, 1970; Margaret Thatcher, First Lady of the House, 1975; regular contrib. various periodicals and newspapers on antiques and the arts. *Recreations:* music, pictures and antiques, watching Association football. *Address:* Bell Yard Chambers, 16 Bell Yard, WC2A 2JR. *T:* 071–306 9292. *Clubs:* Carlton; Ipswich and Suffolk (Ipswich).

MONEY, Hon. George Gilbert, CHB 1986; FCIB; Director, Barclays Bank International Ltd, 1955–81 (Vice-Chairman, 1965–73); *b* 17 Nov. 1914; 2nd *s* of late Maj.-Gen. Sir A. W. Money, KCB, KBE, CSI and late Lady Money (*née* Drummond). *Educ:* Charterhouse Sch. Clerk, L. Behrens & Soehne, Bankers, Hamburg, 1931–32; Clerk, Barclays Bank Ltd, 1932–35, Dir 1972–73; joined Barclays Bank DCO (now Barclays Bank PLC), London, 1935; served in Egypt, Palestine, Cyprus, Ethiopia, Cyrenaica, E Africa, 1936–52; Local Dir, W Indies, 1952; Director: Barclays Bank of California, 1965–75; Bermuda Provident Bank Ltd, 1969–89; Barclays Bank of the Netherlands, Antilles NV, 1970–86; Republic Finance Corp. Ltd, 1972–88; Republic Bank Ltd, 1972–88; Barclays Bank of Jamaica Ltd, 1972–77; Barclays Australia Ltd, 1972–75; New Zealand United Corp., 1972–75;

Chairman: Bahamas Internat. Trust Co. Ltd, 1970–72; Cayman Internat. Trust Co. Ltd, 1970–72; Mem., Caribbean Bd, Barclays Bank PLC, 1952–88. *Publication*: Nine Lives of a Bush Banker, 1990. *Recreations*: water ski-ing, fishing, bridge. *Address*: Saltram, St Joseph, Barbados.

MONEY-COUTTS, family name of **Baron Latymer.**

MONEY-COUTTS, Sir David Burdett, KCVO 1991; Chairman, Coutts & Co., since 1976 (Managing Director, 1970–86); *b* 19 July 1931; *s* of Hon. Alexander B. Money-Coutts (2nd *s* of 6th Baron Latymer, TD), and late Mary E., *er d* of Sir Reginald Hobhouse, 5th Bt; *m* 1958, Penelope Utten Todd; one *s* two *d*. *Educ*: Eton; New Coll., Oxford (MA). National Service, 1st Royal Dragoons, 1950–51; Royal Glos Hussars, TA, 1951–67. Joined Coutts & Co., 1954; Dir, 1958. Director: National Discount Co., 1964–69; Gerrard & National, 1969– (Dep. Chm. 1969–89); United States & General Trust Corp., 1964–73; Charities Investment Managers (Charifund), 1964– (Chm., 1984–); Dun & Bradstreet, 1973–87; Phoenix Assurance, 1978–85 (Dep. Chm., 1984–85); Sun Alliance & London Insurance, 1984–90; M & G Group, 1987–(Chm., 1990–). Mem. UK Adv. Bd, National Westminster Bank, 1990– (Regl Dir, 1969–88, Chm., SE Reg., 1986–88; Dir, 1976–90; Chm., S Adv. Bd, 1988–). Member: Kensington and Chelsea and Westminster AHA, 1974–82 (Vice-Chm., 1978–82); Bloomsbury HA, 1982–90 (Vice-Chm., 1982–88); Health Educn Council, 1973–77. Middlesex Hospital: Governor, 1962–74 (Dep. Chm. Governors, 1973–74); Chm., Finance Cttee, 1965–74; Mem., Med. Sch. Council, 1963–88 (Chm., 1974–88). Mem., Council, UCL, 1987–. Trustee, Multiple Sclerosis Soc., 1967–. Hon. Treas., Nat. Assoc. of Almshouses, 1960–; Hon. Sec., Old Etonian Trust, 1969–76, Chm. Council, 1976–; Trustee, Mansfield Coll., Oxford, 1988–. *Recreations*: odd jobs, living in the country. *Address*: Magpie House, Peppard Common, Henley-on-Thames, Oxon RG9 5JG. *T*: Rotherfield Greys (04917) 497. *Club*: Leander (Henley-on-Thames).

MONGER, George William; Head of Industry, Agriculture and Employment Group, HM Treasury, since 1990; *b* 1 April 1937; *s* of George Thomas Monger and Agnes Mary (*née* Bates). *Educ*: Holloway Sch.; Jesus Coll., Cambridge (PhD 1962). Entered Home Civil Service (Admin. Class), 1961: Min. of Power, Min. of Technol., DTI, and Dept of Energy; Principal, 1965; Asst Sec., 1972; Under-Secretary: Electricity Div., 1976, Coal Div., 1979, Dept of Energy; Social Services Gp, 1981, Fiscal Policy Gp, 1983, HM Treasury; Cabinet Office, 1987. Alexander Prize, RHistS, 1962. *Publication*: The End of Isolation: British Foreign Policy, 1900–1907, 1963. *Address*: c/o HM Treasury, Whitehall, SW1. *Club*: United Oxford & Cambridge University.

MONIBA, Harry Fumba, PhD; Vice-President, Republic of Liberia, since 1984; *b* 22 Oct. 1937; *s* of Mr Moniba and Mrs Janga Sando Moniba; *m* 1969, Minita Kollie; three *s* two *d*. *Educ*: Cuttington Univ. Coll., Liberia (all-round student award; BSEd, *cum laude*); State University of New York, New Paltz (MSc); New York Univ., NY (post grad. studies); Michigan State Univ., USA (PhD African Hist. and Internat. Relations). Teacher and Registrar, also Vice Principal, Holy Cross Bolahun Mission Schs, 1968–70; Special Asst and Dir of Research, Min. of Educn, 1975–76; First Secretary and Consul, Liberian Embassy: Washington DC, 1976–80; Ottawa, Canada, 1978–80; Asst Minister of Foreign Affairs for European Affairs, Min. of Foreign Affairs, 1980–81; Ambassador to London, 1981–84, and (non-resident) to the Holy See, 1983–84. *Recreations*: reading, soccer, fishing, hunting, dancing. *Address*: c/o Capitol Building, Capitol Hill, Monrovia, Liberia, West Africa.

MONIER-WILLIAMS, Evelyn Faithfull; His Honour Judge Monier-Williams; a Circuit Judge since 1972; *b* 29 April 1920; *o s* of late R. T. Monier-Williams, OBE, Barrister-at-Law, and Mrs G. M. Monier-Williams; *m* 1948, Maria-Angela Oswald (*d* 1983); one *s* one *d*. *Educ*: Charterhouse; University Coll., Oxford (MA). Admitted to Inner Temple, 1940; served Royal Artillery, 1940–46 in UK, Egypt, Libya, Tunisia, Sicily (8th Army), France, Low Countries and Germany; called to Bar, Inner Temple, 1948; South Eastern Circuit; Master of the Bench, Inner Temple, 1967, Reader, 1987, Treas., 1988; Mem. Senate of Four Inns of Court, 1969–73; Mem. Council, Selden Soc., 1970 (Vice Pres., 1990); Mem., Council of Legal Educn, 1971–87, Vice Chm., 1974–87; Mem., Adv. Cttee on Legal Educn, 1979–87; Mem., Council of the Inns of Court, 1987–88. Livery, Glaziers' Company, 1974. *Recreation*: collecting old books. *Address*: Inner Temple, EC4.

MONK, Alec; *see* Monk, D. A. G.

MONK, Rear-Adm. Anthony John, CBE 1973; Appeals Organizer, The Royal Marsden Hospital Cancer Fund, 1984–87; *b* 14 Nov. 1923; *s* of Frank Leonard and Barbara Monk; *m* 1951, Elizabeth Ann Samson; four *s* one *d*. *Educ*: Whitgift Sch.; RNC Dartmouth; RNEC Keyham. MSc, BScEng, FIMarE, FRAeS, FIMechE. Engr Cadet, 1941; served War of 1939–45, Pacific Fleet; flying trng, Long Air Engrg Course, Cranfield, 1946; RN Air Stn Ford; RNEC Manadon, 1950; Prodn Controller and Man., RN Aircraft Yard, Belfast, 1953–56; Mem. Dockyard Work Measurement Team, subseq. Engr Officer HMS Apollo, Techn. Asst to Dir-Gen. Aircraft, Sqdn Engr Officer to Flag Officer Aircraft Carriers, 1963–65; Asst Dir of Marine Engrg, 1965–68; Dir of Aircraft Engrg, 1968; Comd Engrg Officer to Flag Officer Naval Air Comd; Naval Liaison Officer for NI and Supt RN Aircraft Yard, Belfast, 1970; Port Admiral, Rosyth, 1974–76; Rear-Adm. Engineering to Flag Officer Naval Air Comd, 1976–78. Comdr 1956; Captain 1964; Rear-Adm. 1974. Dir Gen., Brick Develt Assoc., 1979–84. *Recreation*: swimming (ASA teacher). *Address*: Morning Glory, Kingsdown, Deal, Kent CT14 8AT.

MONK, Arthur James; Director, Components, Valves and Devices, Ministry of Defence, 1981–84, retired; *b* 15 Jan. 1924; *s* of late Rev. Arthur S. Monk, AKC, and late Lydia E. Monk; *m* 1953, Murial V. Peacock; one *s* two *d*. *Educ*: Latymer Upper School, Hammersmith; London Univ. BSc Hons Physics 1953; FIEE 1964. Served RAF, 1943–48. Services Electronic Research Labs, 1949–63; Asst Director (Co-ord. Valve Development), MoD, 1963–68; Student, Imperial Defence Coll., 1969; idc 1970; Admiralty Underwater Weapons Establishment, 1970–73; Dep. Director, Underwater Weapons Projects (S/M), MoD, 1973–76; Counsellor, Def. Equipment Staff, Washington, 1977–81. *Publications*: papers on electronics in jls of learned societies. *Recreations*: caravan touring, photography, family history and genealogy. *Address*: 63 Wyke Road, Weymouth, Dorset DT4 9QN. *T*: Weymouth (0305) 782338.

MONK, (David) Alec (George); Chief Executive Officer, Tri-Delta Corporation Ltd, since 1990; *b* 13 Dec. 1942; *s* of Philip Aylmer and Elizabeth Jane Monk; *m* 1965, Jean Ann Searle; two *s* two *d*. *Educ*: Jesus College, Oxford. MA (PPE). Research Staff, Corporate Finance and Taxation, Sheffield Univ., 1966 and London Business Sch., 1967; Senior Financial Asst, Treasurer's Dept, Esso Petroleum Co., 1968; various positions with The Rio Tinto-Zinc Corp., 1968–77, Dir, 1974–77; Vice-Pres. and Dir, AEA Investors Inc., 1977–81; Chm. and Chief Exec., The Gateway Corp. (formerly Dee Corp.) PLC, 1981–89. Director: Scottish Eastern Investment Trust, 1985–; Charles Wells Ltd, 1989–. Mem., NEDC, 1986–90. Pres., Inst. of Grocery Distribution, 1987–89. Vis. Indust. Fellow, Manchester Business Sch., 1984. Hon. Fellow, St Hugh's Coll., Oxford, 1985. Hon. LLD Sheffield, 1988. *Publication*: (with A. J. Merrett) Inflation, Taxation and Executive Remuneration, 1967. *Recreations*: sports, reading.

MONK BRETTON, 3rd Baron *cr* 1884; **John Charles Dodson,** DL; *b* 17 July 1924; *o s* of 2nd Baron and Ruth (*d* 1967), 2nd *d* of late Hon. Charles Brand; *S* father, 1933; *m* 1958, Zoë Diana Scott; two *s*. *Educ*: Westminster Sch.; New Coll., Oxford (MA). DL E Sussex, 1983. *Recreations*: hunting, farming. *Heir*: *s* Hon. Christopher Mark Dodson [*b* 2 Aug. 1958; *m* 1988, Karen, *o d* of B. J. McKelvain, Fairfield, Conn; one *s*]. *Address*: Shelley's Folly, Cooksbridge, near Lewes, East Sussex. *T*: Barcombe (0273) 231. *Club*: Brooks's.

MONKS, John Stephen; Deputy General Secretary, Trades Union Congress, since 1987; *b* 5 Aug. 1945; *s* of Charles Edward Monks and Bessie Evelyn Monks; *m* 1970, Francine Jacqueline Schenk; two *s* one *d*. *Educ*: Ducie Technical High Sch., Manchester; Nottingham Univ. (BA Econ). Joined TUC, 1969; Hd of Orgn and Industrial Relns Dept, 1977–87. Mem. Council, ACAS, 1979–. Trustee, Nat. Museum of Labour History, 1988–. Governor: Sedgehill Sch.; LSE. *Recreations*: squash, gardening, music. *Address*: Congress House, Great Russell Street, WC1 3LS. *T*: 071–636 4030.

MONKSWELL, 5th Baron *cr* 1885; **Gerard Collier;** Parliamentary consultant, since 1990; *b* 28 Jan. 1947; *s* of William Adrian Larry Collier and Helen (*née* Dunbar); *S* to disclaimed barony of father, 1984; *m* 1974, Ann Valerie Collins; two *s* one *d*. *Educ*: Portsmouth Polytechnic (BSc Mech. Eng, 1971); Slough Polytechnic (Cert. in Works Management 1972). Massey Ferguson Manfg Co. Ltd: Product Quality Engineer, 1972; Service Administration Manager, 1984. *Recreations*: politics, swimming, movies. *Heir*: *s* Hon. James Adrian Collier, *b* 29 March 1977. *Address*: 513 Barlow Moor Road, Chorlton, Manchester M21 2AQ. *T*: 061–881 3887.

MONMOUTH, Bishop of, since 1986; **Rt. Rev. Royston Clifford Wright;** *b* 4 July 1922; *s* of James and Ellen Wright; *m* 1945, Barbara Joyce Nowell; one *s* one *d*. *Educ*: Univ. of Wales, Cardiff (BA 1942); St Stephen's House, Oxford. Deacon 1945, priest 1946; Curate: Bedwas, 1945–47; St John Baptist, Newport, 1947–49; Walton-on-the-Hill, Liverpool, 1949–51; Chaplain RNVR, 1950; Chaplain RN, 1951–68; Vicar of Blaenavon, Gwent, 1968–74; RD of Pontypool, 1973–74; Canon of Monmouth, 1974–77; Rector of Ebbw Vale, Gwent, 1974–77; Archdeacon of Monmouth, 1977; Archdeacon of Newport, 1977–86. *Recreations*: four grandchildren; listening to Baroque music. *Address*: Bishopstow, Newport, Gwent NP9 4EA. *T*: Newport (Gwent) (0633) 263510.

MONMOUTH, Dean of; *see* Lewis, Very Rev. D. G.

MONOD, Prof. Théodore, DèsSc; Commandeur de la Légion d'Honneur, 1989 (Officier, 1958); Professor Emeritus at National Museum of Natural History, Paris (Assistant 1922, Professor, 1942–73); *b* 9 April 1902; *s* of Rev. Wilfred Monod and Dorina Monod; *m* 1930, Olga Pickova; two *s* one *d*. *Educ*: Sorbonne (Paris). Docteur èssciences, 1926. Sec.-Gen. (later Dir) of l'Institut Français d'Afrique Noire, 1938; Prof., Univ. of Dakar, 1957–59; Doyen, Science Faculty, Dakar, 1957–58. Mem., Academy of Sciences; Member: Acad. des Sciences d'Outre-Mer; Académie de Marine; Corresp. Mem., Académie des Sciences de Lisbonne and Académie Royale des Sciences d'Outre-Mer. Dr *hc* Köln, 1965, Neuchâtel, 1968. Gold Medallist, Royal Geographical Soc., 1960; Gold Medallist, Amer. Geographical Soc., 1961; Haile Sellassie Award for African Research, 1967. Comdr, Ordre du Christ, 1953; Commandeur, Mérite Saharien, 1962; Officier de l'Ordre des Palmes Académiques, 1966, etc. *Publications*: Méharées, Explorations au vrai Sahara, 1937, 3rd edn 1989; L'Hippopotame et le philosophe, 1942; Bathyfolages, 1954; (ed) Pastoralism in Tropical Africa, 1976; L'Emeraude des Garamantes, Souvenirs d'un Saharien, 1984; Sahara, désert magique, 1986; Déserts, 1988; Mémoires d'un Naturaliste Voyageur, 1990; many scientific papers in learned jls. *Address*: 14 quai d'Orléans, 75004 Paris, France. *T*: 43 26 79 50; Muséum national d'Histoire naturelle, 57 rue Cuvier, 75005 Paris, France. *T*: 43 31 40 10.

MONRO, (Andrew) Hugh; Headmaster, Clifton College, since 1990; *b* 2 March 1950; *s* of Andrew Killey Monro, FRCS and Diana Louise Rhys; *m* 1974, Elizabeth Clare Rust; one *s* one *d*. *Educ*: Rugby School; Pembroke College, Cambridge (MA; PGCE). Graduate trainee, Metal Box, 1973; Haileybury College, 1974–79; Noble & Greenough School, Boston, Mass, 1977–78; Loretto School, 1979–86; Headmaster, Worksop College, 1986–90. *Recreations*: running, golf, American literature. *Address*: Clifton College, Clifton, Bristol BS8 3JH. *T*: Bristol (0272) 735945. *Club*: Hawks (Cambridge).

MONRO, Sir Hector (Seymour Peter), Kt 1981; AE; JP; DL; MP (C) Dumfries since 1964; *b* 4 Oct. 1922; *s* of late Capt. Alastair Monro, Cameron Highlanders, and Mrs Monro, Craigcleuch, Langholm, Scotland; *m* 1949, Elizabeth Anne Welch, Longstone Hall, Derbs; two *s*. *Educ*: Canford Sch.; King's Coll., Cambridge. RAF, 1941–46, Flight Lt; RAuxAF, 1946–53 (AE 1953). Mem. of Queen's Body Guard for Scotland, Royal Company of Archers. Dumfries CC, 1952–67 (Chm. Planning Cttee, and Police Cttee). Chm. Dumfriesshire Unionist Assoc., 1958–63; Scottish Cons. Whip, 1967–70; a Lord Comr of HM Treasury, 1970–71; Parly Under-Sec. of State, Scottish Office, 1971–74; Opposition Spokesman on: Scottish Affairs, 1974–75; Sport, 1974–79; Parly Under-Sec. of State (with special responsibility for sport), DoE, 1979–81; Member, Select Committee: on Scottish Affairs, 1983–86; on Defence, 1987. Chairman: Scottish Cons. Members Cttee, 1983–; Cons. Parly Cttee on Sport, 1984–85. Vice Chm., Cons. Members Agricl Cttee, 1983–87. Mem. Dumfries T&AFA, 1959–67; Hon. Air Cdre, No 2622 RAuxAF Regt Sqdn, 1982–; Hon. Insp. Gen., RAuxAF, 1990–. Member: Area Executive Cttee, Nat. Farmers' Union of Scotland; Nature Conservancy Council, 1982–; Council, Nat. Trust for Scotland 1983–88. President: Auto-cycle Union, 1983–; NSRA, 1987–. JP 1963, DL 1973, Dumfries. *Recreations*: Rugby football (Mem. Scottish Rugby Union, 1958–77, Vice-Pres., 1975, Pres., 1976–77); golf, flying, country sports, vintage sports cars. *Address*: Williamwood, Kirtlebridge, Dumfriesshire. *T*: Kirtlebridge (04615) 213. *Clubs*: Royal Air Force, MCC; Royal Scottish Automobile (Glasgow).

MONRO, Hugh; *see* Monro, A. H.

MONRO DAVIES, William Llewellyn, QC 1974; **His Honour Judge Monro Davies;** a Circuit Judge, since 1976; *b* 12 Feb. 1927; *s* of Thomas Llewellyn Davies and Emily Constance Davies; *m* 1956, Jean, *d* of late E. G. Innes; one *s* one *d*. *Educ*: Christ Coll., Brecon; Trinity Coll., Oxford (MA, LitHum). Served in RNVR, 1945–48 (Sub-Lt). Called to the Bar, Inner Temple, 1954. Mem., Gen. Council of the Bar, 1971–75. A Recorder of the Crown Court, 1972–76. *Recreations*: the theatre and cinema; watching Rugby football. *Address*: Farrar's Buildings, Temple, EC4Y 7BD. *T*: 071–583 9241. *Club*: Garrick.

MONSELL, 2nd Viscount *cr* 1935, of Evesham; **Henry Bolton Graham Eyres Monsell;** *b* 21 Nov. 1905; *s* of 1st Viscount Monsell, PC, GBE, and Caroline Mary Sybil, CBE (*d* 1959), *d* of late H. W. Eyres, Dumbleton Hall, Evesham; *S* father, 1969. *Educ*: Eton. Served N Africa and Italy, 1942–45 (despatches); Lt-Col Intelligence Corps. US Medal of Freedom with bronze palm, 1946. *Recreation*: music. *Address*: The Mill House, Dumbleton,

Evesham, Worcs WR11 6TR. *Club:* Travellers'.
See also P. M. Leigh Fermor.

MONSON, family name of **Baron Monson.**

MONSON, 11th Baron *cr* 1728; **John Monson;** Bt *cr* 1611; *b* 3 May 1932; *e s* of 10th Baron and of Bettie Northrup (who *m* 1962, Capt. James Arnold Phillips), *d* of late E. Alexander Powell; *S* father, 1958; *m* 1955, Emma, *o d* of late Anthony Devas, ARA, RP; three *s*. *Educ:* Eton; Trinity Coll., Cambridge (BA). Pres., Soc. for Individual Freedom. *Heir: s* Hon. Nicholas John Monson [*b* 19 Oct. 1955; *m* 1981, Hilary, *o d* of Kenneth Martin, Nairobi and Diani Beach; one *s* one *d*]. *Address:* Manor House, South Carlton, Lincoln. *T:* 730263.

MONSON, Sir (William Bonnar) Leslie, KCMG 1965 (CMG 1950); CB 1964; HM Diplomatic Service, retired; *b* 28 May 1912; *o s* of late J. W. Monson and Selina L. Monson; *m* 1948, Helen Isobel Browne. *Educ:* Edinburgh Acad.; Hertford Coll., Oxford. Entered Civil Service (Dominions Office) 1935; transferred to Colonial Office, 1939; Asst Sec., 1944; seconded as Chief Sec. to West African Council, 1947–51; Asst Under-Sec. of State, Colonial Office, 1951–64; British High Commissioner in the Republic of Zambia, 1964–66; Dep. Under-Sec. of State, Commonwealth Office, later FCO, 1967–72. Dir, Overseas Relations Branch, St John Ambulance, 1975–81. KStJ 1975. *Address:* Golf House, Goffers Road, Blackheath, SE3 0UA. *Club:* United Oxford & Cambridge University.

MONTAGNIER, Prof. Luc; Head of Viral Oncology Unit, since 1972, and Professor, since 1985, Pasteur Institute, Paris; Director of Research, Centre national de la recherche scientifique, since 1974; *b* 18 Aug. 1932; *s* of Antoine Montagnier and Marianne (*née* Rousselet); *m* 1961, Dorothea Ackermann; one *s* two *d*. *Educ:* Collège de Châtellerault; Univ. de Poitiers; Univ. de Paris. Asst, 1955–60, Attaché, 1960, Head, 1963, Head of Research, 1967, Faculty of Science, Paris; Head of Lab., Inst. of Radium, 1965–71. Officier, Légion d'honneur; Commandeur, Ordre national du Mérite. *Publications:* Vaincre le Sida, 1986; scientific papers on research into AIDS virus, molecular biology, virolgy, etc. *Address:* Pasteur Institute, 28 rue du Docteur-Roux, 75724 Paris Cedex 15, France.

MONTAGU; *see* Douglas-Scott-Montagu.

MONTAGU, family name of **Duke of Manchester, Earldom of Sandwich,** and **Baron Swaythling.**

MONTAGU OF BEAULIEU, 3rd Baron *cr* 1885; **Edward John Barrington Douglas-Scott-Montagu;** Chairman, Historic Buildings and Monuments Commission, 1983–March 1992; *b* 20 Oct. 1926; *o s* of 2nd Baron and Pearl (who *m* 2nd, 1936, Captain Hon. Edward Pleydell-Bouverie, RN, MVO, *s* of 6th Earl of Radnor), *d* of late Major E. B. Crake, Rifle Brigade, and Mrs Barrington Crake; *S* father, 1929; *m* 1st, 1959, Elizabeth Belinda (marr. diss. 1974), *o d* of late Capt. the Hon. John de Bathe Crossley, and late Hon. Mrs Crossley; one *s* one *d*; 2nd, 1974, Fiona Herbert; one *s*. *Educ:* St Peter's Court, Broadstairs; Ridley Coll., St Catharines, Ont; Eton Coll.; New Coll., Oxford. Late Lt Grenadier Guards; released Army, 1948. Founded Montagu Motor Car Museum, 1952 and World's first Motor Cycle Museum, 1956; created Nat. Motor Museum Trust, 1970, to administer new Nat. Motor Museum at Beaulieu, opened 1972. Mem., Develt Commn, 1980–84. President: Museums Assoc., 1982–84; Historic Houses Assoc., 1973–78; Union of European Historic Houses, 1978–81; Fédération Internationale des Voitures Anciennes, 1980–83; Southern Tourist Bd; Assoc. of Brit. Transport Museums; English Vineyards Assoc.; Fedn of British Historic Vehicle Clubs, 1989–; Vice-Pres., Inst. of Motor Industry; Chancellor, Wine Guild of UK; Patron, Assoc. of Independent Museums. FRSA. Hon. FMA. Commodore: Nelson Boat Owners' Club; Beaulieu River Sailing Club; Vice Cdre, H of L Yacht Club. Founder and Editor, Veteran and Vintage Magazine, 1956–79. *Publications:* The Motoring Montagus, 1959; Lost Causes of Motoring, 1960; Jaguar, A Biography, 1961, rev. edn, 1986; The Gordon Bennett Races, 1963; Rolls of Rolls-Royce, 1966; The Gilt and the Gingerbread, 1967; Lost Causes of Motoring: Europe, vol. i, 1969, vol. ii, 1971; More Equal than Others, 1970; History of the Steam Car, 1971; The Horseless Carriage, 1975; Early Days on the Road, 1976; Behind the Wheel, 1977; Royalty on the Road, 1980; Home James, 1982; The British Motorist, 1987; English Heritage, 1987. *Heir: s* Hon. Ralph Douglas-Scott-Montagu, *b* 13 March 1961. *Address:* Palace House, Beaulieu, Hants SO42 7ZN. *T:* Beaulieu (0590) 612345; Flat 11, 24 Bryanston Square, W1. *T:* 071–262 2603. *Clubs:* Historical Commercial Vehicle (Pres.), Disabled Drivers Motor (Pres.), Steam Boat Assoc. of Gt Britain (Vice-Pres.), and mem. of many historic vehicle clubs.
See also Sir E. John Chichester, Bt, Earl of Lindsay.

MONTAGU, (Alexander) Victor (Edward Paulet); *b* 22 May 1906; *S* father, 1962, as 10th Earl of Sandwich, but disclaimed his peerages for life, 24 July 1964; *m* 1st, 1934, Rosemary, *d* of late Major Ralph Harding Peto; two *s* four *d*; 2nd, 1962, Anne, MBE (*d* 1981), *y d* of Victor, 9th Duke of Devonshire, KG, PC. *Educ:* Eton; Trinity Coll., Cambridge. MA (Nat. Sciences). Lt 5th (Hunts) Bn The Northamptonshire Regt, TA, 1926; served France, 1940, and afterwards on Gen. Staff, Home Forces. Private Sec. to Rt Hon. Stanley Baldwin, MP, 1932–34; Treasurer, Junior Imperial League, 1934–35; Chm., Tory Reform Cttee, 1943–44. MP (C) South Dorset Div. (C 1941, Ind. C 1957, C 1958–62); contested (C) Accrington Div. Lancs, Gen. Elec., 1964. *Publications:* Essays in Tory Reform, 1944; The Conservative Dilemma, 1970; articles in Quarterly Review, 1946–47. *Heir:* (*to disclaimed peerages*): *s* John Edward Hollister Montagu, *qv*. *Address:* Mapperton, Beaminster, Dorset DT8 3NR.

MONTAGU, Prof. Ashley; *b* 28 June 1905; *o c* of Charles and Mary Ehrenberg; *m* 1931, Helen Marjorie Peakes; one *s* two *d*. *Educ:* Central Foundation Sch., London; Univ. of London; Univ. of Florence; Columbia Univ. (PhD 1937). Research Worker, Brit. Mus. (Natural Hist.), 1926; Curator, Physical Anthropology, Wellcome Hist. Mus., London, 1929; Asst-Prof. of Anatomy, NY Univ., 1931–38; Dir, Div. of Child Growth and Develt, NY Univ., 1931–34; Assoc.-Prof. of Anat., Hahnemann Med. Coll. and Hosp., Phila, 1938–49; Prof. and Head of Dept of Anthropology, Rutgers Univ., 1949–55; Dir of Research, NJ Cttee on Growth and Develt, 1951–55. Chm., Anisfield-Wolf Award Cttee on Race Relations, 1950–91 (drafted Statement on Race, for Unesco, 1950). Vis. Lectr, Harvard Univ., 1945; Regent's Prof., Univ. of Calif, Santa Barbara, 1961; Lectr, Princeton Univ., 1978–83, and Dir, Inst. Natural Philosophy, 1979–85. Fellow, Stevenson Hall, Princeton Univ. Produced, directed and financed film, One World or None, 1946. DSc Grinnell Coll., Iowa, 1967; DLitt Ursinus Coll., Pa, 1972; DSc Univ. N Carolina, 1987. Distinguished Service Award, Amer. Anthropological Assoc., 1984; Phi Beta Kappa Distinguished Service Award, 1985; Distinguished Service Award, Nat. Assoc. of Parents and Professionals for Safe Alternatives in Childbirth, 1986. *Publications:* Coming Into Being Among the Australian Aborigines, 1937, 2nd edn 1974; Man's Most Dangerous Myth: The Fallacy of Race, 1942, 5th edn 1974; Edward Tyson, MD, FRS (1650–1708): And the Rise of Human and Comparative Anatomy in England, 1943; Introduction to Physical Anthropology, 1945, 3rd edn 1960; Adolescent Sterility, 1946; On Being Human, 1950, 2nd edn 1970; Statement on Race, 1951, 3rd edn 1972; On Being Intelligent, 1951, 3rd edn 1972; Darwin, Competition, and Cooperation, 1952; The Natural Superiority of Women, 1953, 3rd edn 1974; Immortality, 1955; The Direction of Human Development, 1955, 2nd edn 1970; The Biosocial Nature of Man, 1956; Education and Human Relations, 1958; Anthropology and Human Nature, 1957; Man: His First Million Years, 1957, 2nd edn 1969; The Reproductive Development of the Female, 1957, 3rd edn 1979; The Cultured Man, 1958; Human Heredity, 1959, 2nd edn 1963; Anatomy and Physiology (with E. B. Steen), 2 vols, 1959, 2nd edn 1984; A Handbook of Anthropometry, 1960; Man in Process, 1961; The Humanization of Man, 1962; Prenatal Influences, 1962; Race, Science and Humanity, 1963; The Dolphin in History (with John Lilly), 1963; The Science of Man, 1964; Life Before Birth, 1964, 2nd edn 1978; The Human Revolution, 1965; The Idea of Race, 1965; Man's Evolution (with C. Loring Brace), 1965; Up the Ivy, 1966; The American Way of Life, 1967; The Anatomy of Swearing, 1967; The Prevalence of Nonsense (with E. Darling), 1967; The Human Dialogue (with Floyd Matson), 1967; Man Observed, 1968; Man: His First Two Million Years, 1969; Sex, Man and Society, 1969; The Ignorance of Certainty (with E. Darling), 1970; Textbook of Human Genetics (with M. Levitan), 1971, 2nd edn 1977; Immortality, Religion and Morals, 1971; Touching: the human significance of the skin, 1971, 3rd edn 1986; The Elephant Man, 1971, 2nd edn 1979; Man and the Computer (with S. S. Snyder), 1972; (ed) The Endangered Environment, 1973; (ed) Frontiers of Anthropology, 1974; (ed) Culture and Human Development, 1974; (ed) The Practice of Love, 1974; (ed) Race and IQ, 1975; The Nature of Human Aggression, 1976; Human Evolution (with C. L. Brace), 1977; The Human Connection (with F. Matson), 1979; Growing Young, 1981, 2nd edn 1989; The Dehumanization of Man (with F. Matson), 1983; Humanity Speaking to Humankind, 1986; Living and Loving, 1986; The Peace of the World, 1987; The World of Humanity, 1988; Coming into Being, 1988; Editor: Studies and Essays in the History of Science and Learning; The Meaning of Love, 1953; Toynbee and History, 1956; Genetic Mechanisms in Human Disease, 1961; Atlas of Human Anatomy, 1961; Culture and the Evolution of Man, 1962; International Pictorial Treasury of Knowledge, 6 vols, 1962–63; The Concept of Race, 1964; The Concept of the Primitive, 1967; Culture: Man's Adaptive Dimension, 1968; Man and Aggression, 1968; The Origin and Evolution of Man, 1973; Learning Non-Aggression, 1978; Sociobiology Examined, 1980; Science and Creationism, 1983. *Recreations:* book collecting, gardening. *Address:* 321 Cherry Hill Road, Princeton, NJ 08540, USA. *T:* 609 924–3756.

MONTAGU, Jennifer Iris Rachel, PhD; FBA 1986; Curator of the Photograph Collection, Warburg Institute, since 1971; *b* 20 March 1931; *d* of late Hon. Ewen Edward Samuel Montagu, CBE, QC. *Educ:* Brearley Sch., New York; Benenden Sch., Kent; Lady Margaret Hall, Oxford (BA; Hon. Fellow 1985); Warburg Inst., London (PhD). Assistant Regional Director, Arts Council of Gt Britain, North West Region, 1953–54; Lecturer in the History of Art, Reading Univ., 1958–64; Asst Curator of the Photograph Collection, Warburg Inst., 1964–71. Slade Prof., Cambridge, and Fellow Jesus Coll., Cambridge, 1980–81. Member: Academic Awards Cttee, British Fedn of University Women, 1963–; Executive Cttee, National Art-Collections Fund, 1973–; Consultative Cttee, Burlington Magazine, 1975–; Cttee, The Jewish Museum, 1983–. Trustee, Wallace Collection, 1989–. *Publications:* Bronzes, 1963; (with Jacques Thuillier) Catalogue of exhibn Charles Le Brun, 1963; Alessandro Algardi, 1985 (special Mitchell Prize); Roman Baroque Sculpture: the industry of art, 1989; articles in learned periodicals. *Address:* 10 Roland Way, SW7 3RE. *T:* 071–373 6691; Warburg Institute, Woburn Square, WC1H 0AB.

MONTAGU, John Edward Hollister; (Viscount Hinchingbrooke, but does not use the title); freelance journalist and researcher; *b* 11 April 1943; *er s* of Victor Montagu, *qv*, and *heir* to disclaimed Earldom of Sandwich; *m* 1968, Caroline, *o d* of Canon P. E. C. Hayman, Cocking, W Sussex; two *s* one *d*. *Educ:* Eton; Trinity College, Cambridge. Inf. Officer, 1974–85, Res. Officer, 1985–86, Christian Aid; Editor, Save the Children Fund, 1987–; Consultant, CARE Britain, 1987–. Trustee, TSW Telethon Trust, 1987–; Managing Trustee, St Francis Sch., Dorset, 1987–. *Address:* 69 Albert Bridge Road, SW11 4QE.

MONTAGU, Montague Francis Ashley; *see* Montagu, A.

MONTAGU, Nicholas Lionel John; Deputy Secretary, Department of Social Security, since 1990; *b* 12 March 1944; *s* of late John Eric Montagu and Barbara Joyce Montagu, OBE; *m* 1974, Jennian Ford Geddes, *o d* of Ford Irvine Geddes, *qv*; two *d*. *Educ:* Rugby Sch.; New Coll., Oxford (MA). Asst Lectr 1966–69, Lectr 1969–74, in Philosophy, Univ. of Reading; Department of Social Security (formerly Department of Health and Social Security): Principal, 1974–81 (seconded to Cabinet Office, 1978–80); Asst Sec., 1981–86; Under Sec, 1986–90. *Publication:* Brought to Account (report of Rayner Scrutiny on National Insurance Contributions), 1981. *Recreations:* cooking, wild flowers, fishing. *Address:* Department of Social Security, Richmond House, 79 Whitehall, SW1A 2NS. *T:* 071–210 5470.

MONTAGU, Victor; *see* Montagu, A. V. E. P.

MONTAGU DOUGLAS SCOTT, family name of **Duke of Buccleuch.**

MONTAGU-POLLOCK, Sir Giles Hampden; *see* Pollock.

MONTAGU-POLLOCK, Sir William H., KCMG 1957 (CMG 1946); *b* 12 July 1903; *s* of Sir M. F. Montagu-Pollock, 3rd Bt; *m* 1st, 1933, Frances Elizabeth Prudence (marr. diss. 1945), *d* of late Sir John Fischer Williams, CBE, KC; one *s* one *d*; 2nd, 1948, Barbara, *d* of late P. H. Jowett, CBE, FRCA, RWS; one *s*. *Educ:* Marlborough Coll.; Trinity Coll., Cambridge. Served in Diplomatic Service at Rome, Belgrade, Prague, Vienna, Stockholm, Brussels, and at Foreign Office; British Ambassador, Damascus, 1952–53 (Minister, 1950–52); British Ambassador: to Peru, 1953–58; to Switzerland, 1958–60; to Denmark, 1960–62. Retired from HM Foreign Service, 1962. Governor, European Cultural Foundation; Chm., British Inst. of Recorded Sound, 1970–73; Vice-Pres., Soc. for Promotion of New Music. *Recreation:* washing up. *Address:* Flat 181, Coleherne Court, SW5 0DU. *T:* 071–373 3685.

MONTAGU-STUART-WORTLEY, family name of **Earl of Wharncliffe.**

MONTAGUE, family name of **Baron Amwell.**

MONTAGUE, Michael Jacob, CBE 1970; Director, Williams Holdings plc, since 1991; *b* 10 March 1932; *s* of David Elias Montague and Eleanor Stagg. *Educ:* High Wycombe Royal Grammar Sch.; Magdalen Coll. Sch., Oxford. Founded Gatehill Beco Ltd, 1958 (sold to Valor Co., 1962); Man. Dir, 1963, Chm., 1965–91, Yale and Valor plc. Chairman: English Tourist Bd, 1979–84; Nat. Consumer Council, 1984–87; Member: BTA, 1979–84; Ordnance Survey Advisory Bd, 1983–85. Pres., BAIE, 1983–85; Chairman: Asia Cttee, BNEC, 1968–71; Industrial Res. Soc. Non-exec. Director: Pleasurama PLC, 1985–88; Jarvis Hotels Ltd; Chm., Montague Multinational Ltd. Mem. Council, Royal Albert Hall, 1985–. *Address:* 17 Stratford Road, W8 6RB. *Club:* Oriental.

MONTAGUE, Air Cdre Ruth Mary Bryceson; Director, Women's Royal Air Force, since 1989; *b* 1 June 1939; *d* of Griffith John Griffiths and late Nancy Bryceson Griffiths (*née* Wrigley); *m* 1966, Roland Arthur Montague. *Educ:* Cavendish Grammar Sch. for

Girls, Buxton; Bedford Coll., Univ. of London (BSc). Commissioned RAF, 1962; UK and Far East, 1962–66; UK, 1966–80; HQ Strike Command, 1980–83; RAF Staff Coll., 1983–86; Dep. Dir, WRAF, 1986–89. ADC to the Queen, 1989–. *Recreations:* cookery, tapestry, gardening, swimming, clay pigeon shooting, world travel. *Address:* Ministry of Defence, Adastral House, Theobalds Road, WC1X 8RU. *T:* 071–430 7141. *Club:* Royal Air Force.

MONTAGUE BROWNE, Anthony Arthur Duncan, CBE 1965 (OBE 1955); DFC 1945; Deputy Chairman, Automobiles of Distinction PLC, since 1989; Director, Guaranty Trust Bank Ltd (Nassau), since 1988 (Deputy Chairman, 1983–86); Director of private companies; *b* 8 May 1923; *s* of late Lt-Col A. D. Montague Browne, DSO, OBE, Bivia House, Goodrich, Ross-on-Wye, and Violet Evelyn (*née* Downes); *m* 1st, 1950, Noel Evelyn Arnold-Wallinger (marr. diss. 1970); one *d*; 2nd, 1970, Shelagh Macklin (*née* Mulligan). *Educ:* Stowe; Magdalen Coll., Oxford; abroad. Pilot RAF, 1941–45. Entered Foreign (now Diplomatic) Service, 1946; Foreign Office, 1946–49; Second Sec., British Embassy, Paris, 1949–52; seconded as Private Sec. to Prime Minister, 1952–55; seconded as Private Sec. to Rt Hon. Sir Winston Churchill, 1955–65; Counsellor, Diplomatic Service, 1964; seconded to HM Household, 1965–67. Dir, 1967–74, a Man. Dir, 1974–83, Gerrard and National PLC. Chm., LandLeisure PLC, 1987–88; Dep. Chm., Highland Participants PLC, 1987–89. Trustee and Chm. of Council, Winston Churchill Memorial Trust; Vice-Pres., Univs Fedn for Animal Welfare, 1987– (Mem., Council, 1985–); Chm., Internat. Certificate of Deposit Market Assoc., 1980–82. Freeman, City of London, 1987. Hon. LLD Westminster Coll., Fulton, Missouri, 1988. *Address:* c/o R3 Section, Lloyds Bank, Cox's & King's Branch, 7 Pall Mall, SW1. *Clubs:* Boodle's, Pratt's.

MONTAGUE-JONES, Brigadier (retd) Ronald, CBE 1944 (MBE 1941); jssc; psc; *b* 10 Dec. 1909; *yr s* of late Edgar Montague Jones, until 1931 Headmaster of St Albans Sch., Herts, and of late Emmeline Mary Yates; *m* 1937, Denise Marguerite (marr. diss.), *y d* of late General Sir Hubert Gough, GCB, GCMG, KCVO; one *s*; *m* 1955, Pamela, *d* of late Lieut-Col Hastings Roy Harington, 8th Gurkha Rifles, and late Hon. Mrs Harington; one *s*. *Educ:* St Albans; RMA, Woolwich; St John's Coll., Cambridge (BA 1933, MA 1937). 2nd Lieut RE 1930; Temp. Brig. 1943; Bt Lt-Col 1952; Brig. 1958. Egypt, 1935; Palestine, 1936–39 (despatches twice); War of 1939–45 (MBE, CBE, US Bronze Star, Africa Star, 1939–45 Star, Italy Star, Burma Star, General Service Medal with Clasps Palestine, SE Asia and Malaya). CC Dorset, for Swanage, 1964–85. *Address:* 10 Battlemead, Swanage, Dorset BH19 1PH. *T:* Swanage (0929) 423186.

MONTEAGLE OF BRANDON, 6th Baron *cr* 1839; **Gerald Spring Rice;** late Captain, Irish Guards; one of HM Body Guard, Hon. Corps of Gentlemen-at-Arms, since 1978; *b* 5 July 1926; *s* of 5th Baron and Emilie de Kosenko (*d* 1981), *d* of Mrs Edward Brooks, Philadelphia, USA; *S* father 1946; *m* 1949, Anne, *d* of late Col G. J. Brownlow, Ballywhite, Portaferry, Co. Down; one *s* three *d* (of whom two are twins). *Educ:* Harrow. Member: London Stock Exchange, 1958–76; Lloyd's, 1978–. *Heir: s* Hon. Charles James Spring Rice [*b* 24 Feb. 1953; *m* 1987, Mary Teresa Glover; two *d*]. *Address:* 242A Fulham Road, SW10. *Clubs:* Cavalry and Guards, Pratt's; Kildare Street and University (Dublin).

MONTEFIORE, Harold Henry S.; *see* Sebag-Montefiore.

MONTEFIORE, Rt. Rev. Hugh William, MA, BD; Assistant Bishop, Diocese of Southwark, since 1987; *b* 12 May 1920; *s* of late Charles Sebag-Montefiore, OBE, and Muriel Alice Ruth Sebag-Montefiore; *m* 1945, Elisabeth Mary Macdonald Paton, *d* of late Rev. William Paton, DD, and Mrs Grace Paton; three *d*. *Educ:* Rugby Sch.; St John's Coll., Oxford (Hon. Fellow, 1981). Served during war, 1940–45; Capt. RA (Royal Bucks Yeo). Deacon 1949, priest 1950. Curate, St George's, Jesmond, Newcastle, 1949–51; Chaplain and Tutor, Westcott House, Cambridge, 1951–53; Vice-Principal, 1953–54; Examining Chaplain: to Bishop of Newcastle, 1953–70; to Bishop of Worcester, 1957–60; to Bishop of Coventry, 1957–70; to Bishop of Blackburn, 1966–70; Fellow and Dean of Gonville and Caius Coll., 1954–63; Lectr in New Testament, Univ. of Cambridge, 1959–63; Vicar of Great Saint Mary's, Cambridge, 1963–70; Canon Theologian of Coventry, 1959–70; Hon. Canon of Ely, 1969–70; Bishop Suffragen of Kingston-upon-Thames, 1970–78; Bishop of Birmingham, 1978–87. Mem., Archbishops' Commn on Christian Doctrine, 1967–76; Chm., General Synod Bd for Social Responsibility, 1983–87. Chairman: Indep. Commn on Transport, 1973; Transport 2000, 1987–. Hon. DD: Aberdeen, 1976; Birmingham, 1985. *Publications:* (contrib.) The Historic Episcopate and the Fullness of the Church, 1954; To Help You To Pray, 1957; (contrib.) Soundings, 1962; Josephus and the New Testament, 1962; (with H. E. W. Turner) Thomas and the Evangelists, 1962; Beyond Reasonable Doubt, 1963; (contrib.) God, Sex and War, 1963; Awkward Questions on Christian Love, 1964; A Commentary on the Epistle to the Hebrews, 1964; Truth to Tell, 1966; (ed) We Must Love One Another Or Die, 1966; (contrib.) The Responsible Church, 1966; Remarriage and Mixed Marriage, 1967; (contrib.) Journeys in Belief, 1968; (ed) Sermons From Great St Mary's, 1968; My Confirmation Notebook, 1968; The Question Mark, 1969; Can Man Survive, 1970; (ed) More Sermons From Great St Mary's, 1971; Doom or Deliverance?, 1972; (ed) Changing Directions, 1974; (ed) Man and Nature, 1976; Apocalypse, 1976; (ed) Nuclear Crisis, 1977; (ed) Yes to Women Priests, 1978; Taking our Past into our Future, 1978; Paul the Apostle, 1981; Jesus Across the Centuries, 1983; The Probability of God, 1985; So Near And Yet So Far, 1986; Communicating the Gospel in a Scientific Age, 1988; God, Sex and Love, 1989; Christianity and Politics, 1990; Reclaiming the High Ground, 1990; contribs to New Testament and Theological jls. *Address:* White Lodge, 23 Bellevue Road, Wandsworth Common, SW17 7EB. *Club:* Commonwealth Trust.

See also Rev. Canon D. M. Paton, Ven. M. J. M. Paton, Prof. Sir W. D. M. Paton.

MONTEITH, Charles Montgomery; Fellow of All Souls College, Oxford, 1948–88, now Emeritus; *b* 9 Feb. 1921; *s* of late James Monteith and Marian Monteith (*née* Montgomery). *Educ:* Royal Belfast Academical Instn; Magdalen Coll., Oxford (Demy 1939, Sen. Demy 1948, MA 1948, BCL 1949). Sub-Warden, All Souls Coll., Oxford, 1967–69. Served War, Royal Inniskilling Fusiliers, India and Burma (Major), 1940–45. Called to the Bar, Gray's Inn, 1949; joined Faber & Faber, 1953, Dir, 1954, Vice-Chm., 1974–76, Chm., 1977–80, Senior Editorial Consultant, 1981–86. Dir, Poetry Book Soc., 1966–81; Member: Literature Panel, Arts Council of GB, 1974–78; Library Adv. Council for England, 1979–81. Hon. DLitt: Ulster, 1980; Kent, 1982. *Address:* c/o Faber & Faber Ltd, 3 Queen Square, WC1. *T:* 071–465 0045. *Clubs:* Beefsteak, Garrick.

MONTEITH, Rt. Rev. George Rae, BA; *b* 14 Feb. 1904; *s* of John Hodge Monteith and Ellen (*née* Hall); *m* 1st, 1931, Kathleen Methven Mules; two *s* one *d*; 2nd, 1982, Hilary Llewellyn Etherington. *Educ:* St John's Coll., Auckland; Univ. of New Zealand. BA 1927. Deacon, 1928; priest, 1929; Curate: St Matthew's, Auckland, 1928–30; Stoke-on-Trent, 1931–33; Vicar of: Dargaville, NZ, 1934–37; Mt Eden, Auckland, NZ, 1937–49; St Mary's Cathedral Parish, Auckland, 1949–69; Dean of Auckland, 1949–69; Vicar-General, 1963–76; Asst Bishop of Auckland, NZ, 1965–76. *Address:* 7 Cathedral Place, Auckland 1, NZ. *T:* 734.449.

MONTEITH, Prof. John Lennox, FRS 1971; FRSE 1972; Emeritus Professor of Environmental Physics, University of Nottingham, 1989; Adjunct Professor, Departments of Agricultural Engineering and Agronomy, University of Florida, since 1991; *b* 3 Sept. 1929; *s* of Rev. John and Margaret Monteith; *m* 1955, Elsa Marion Wotherspoon; four *s* one *d*. *Educ:* George Heriot's Sch.; Univ. of Edinburgh (Hon. DSc 1989); Imperial Coll., London. BSc, DIC, PhD; FInstP, FIBiol. Mem. Physics Dept Staff, Rothamsted Experimental Station, 1954–67; Prof. of Environmental Physics, 1967–86, Dean of Faculty of Agricl Sci., 1985–86, Nottingham Univ; Dir, Resource Management Programme, Internat. Crops Res. Inst. for the Semi-Arid Tropics, 1987–91 (Vis. Scientist, 1984). Governor, Grassland Res. Inst., 1976–83. Vice Pres., British Ecological Soc., 1977–79; Pres., Royal Meteorol Soc., 1978–80. Member: NERC, 1980–84; British Nat. Cttee for the World Climate Programme, 1980–86; Lawes Agricl Trust Cttee, 1983–86. Nat. Res. Council Senior Res. Associate, Goddard Space Flight Center, Md, USA, 1985; Clive Behrens Lectr, Leeds Univ., 1986; York Distinguished Lectr, Univ. of Florida, 1991. Buchan Prize, RMetS, 1962; Solco Tromp Award, Internat. Soc. of Biometeorology, 1983; Rank Fund Nutrition Prize, 1989. *Publications:* Instruments for Micrometeorology (ed), 1972; Principles of Environmental Physics, 1973, 2nd edn (with M. H. Unsworth), 1990; (ed with L. E. Mount) Heat Loss from Animals and Man, 1974; (ed) Vegetation and the Atmosphere, 1975; (ed with C. Webb) Soil Water and Nitrogen, 1981; papers on Micrometeorology and Crop Science in: Quarterly Jl of RMetSoc.; Jl Applied Ecology, etc. *Recreations:* music, photography. *Address:* 21 St Alban's Road, Edinburgh EH9 2LT.

MONTEITH, Lt-Col Robert Charles Michael, OBE 1981; MC 1943; TD 1945; JP; Vice Lord-Lieutenant of Lanarkshire since 1964; Land-owner and Farmer since 1950; *b* 25 May 1914; *s* of late Major J. B. L. Monteith, CBE, and late Dorothy, *d* of Sir Charles Nicholson, 1st Bt; *m* 1950, Mira Elizabeth, *e d* of late John Fanshawe, Sidmount, Moffat; one *s*. *Educ:* Ampleforth Coll., York. CA (Edinburgh), 1939. Served with Lanarkshire Yeomanry, 1939–45: Paiforce, 1942–43; MEF, 1943–44; BLA, 1944–45. Contested (U) Hamilton Division of Lanarkshire, 1950 and 1951. Member: Mental Welfare Commn for Scotland, 1962–84; E Kilbride Develt Corp., 1972–76. DL 1955, JP 1955, CC 1949–64, 1967–74, Lanarkshire; Chm., Lanark DC, later Clydesdale DC, 1974–. Mem. Queen's Body Guard for Scotland, Royal Company of Archers. Mem. SMO of Knights of Malta; OStJ 1973. *Recreations:* shooting, curling. *Address:* Cranley, Cleghorn, Lanark ML11 7SN. *T:* Carstairs (0555) 870330. *Clubs:* New, Puffin's (Edinburgh).

MONTGOMERIE, family name of **Earl of Eglinton.**

MONTGOMERIE, Lord; Hugh Archibald William Montgomerie; Royal Naval officer, since 1988; *b* 24 July 1966; *s* and *heir* of 18th Earl of Eglinton and Winton, *qv*. *Address:* 61 Pinehurst Court, Colville Gardens, W11.

MONTGOMERY, family name of **Viscount Montgomery of Alamein.**

MONTGOMERY OF ALAMEIN, 2nd Viscount *cr* 1946, of Hindhead; **David Bernard Montgomery,** CBE 1975; Managing Director, Terimar Services (Overseas Trade Consultancy), since 1974; Director, Korn/Ferry International, since 1977; *b* 18 Aug. 1928; *s* of 1st Viscount Montgomery of Alamein, KG, GCB, DSO, and Elizabeth (*d* 1937), *d* of late Robert Thompson Hobart, ICS; *S* father, 1976; *m* 1st, 1953, Mary Connell (marr. diss. 1967); one *s* one *d*; 2nd, 1970, Tessa, *d* of late Gen. Sir Frederick Browning, GCVO, KBE, CB, DSO, and Lady Browning, DBE (Dame Daphne du Maurier). *Educ:* Winchester; Trinity Coll., Cambridge (MA). Shell International, 1951–62; Yardley International (Director), 1963–74; Chm., Antofagasta (Chile) and Bolivia Railway Co., 1980–82; Dir, NEI, 1981–87. Editorial Adviser, Vision Interamericana, 1974–. Chm., Economic Affairs Cttee, Canning House, 1973–75; Pres., British Industrial Exhibition, Sao Paulo, 1974. Councillor, Royal Borough of Kensington and Chelsea, 1974–78. Hon. Consul, Republic of El Salvador, 1973–77. Pres., Anglo-Argentine Soc., 1977–87; Chairman: Hispanic and Luso Brazilian Council, 1978–80 (Pres., 1987–); Brazilian Chamber of Commerce in GB, 1980–82; Baring Puma Fund, 1991–. Patron: D-Day and Normandy Fellowship, 1980–; 8th Army Veterans Assoc., 1985–. President: Redgrave Theatre, Farnham, 1977–89; Restaurateurs Assoc. of GB, 1982–90 (Patron, 1991–); Centre for International Briefing, Farnham Castle, 1985–. Governor, Amesbury Sch., 1976–. *Heir: s* Hon. Henry David Montgomery [*b* 2 April 1954; *m* 1980, Caroline, *e d* of Richard Odey, Hotham Hall, York; three *d*]. *Address:* 54 Cadogan Square, SW1X 0JW. *T:* 071–589 8747. *Clubs:* Garrick, Canning; Royal Fowey Yacht.

MONTGOMERY, Alan Everard, PhD; HM Diplomatic Service; Head of Migration and Visa Department, Foreign and Commonwealth Office, since 1989; *b* 11 March 1938; *s* of Philip Napier Montgomery and Honor Violet Coleman (*née* Price); *m* 1960, Janet Barton; one *s* one *d*. *Educ:* Royal Grammar Sch., Guildford; County of Stafford Training Coll. (Cert. of Educn); Birkbeck Coll., London (BA Hons, PhD). Served Mddx Regt, 1957–59. Teacher, Staffs and ILEA, 1961–65; Lectr, Univ. of Birmingham, 1969–72; entered FCO, 1972; 1st Secretary: FCO, 1972–75; Dhaka, 1975–77; Ottawa, 1977–80; FCO, 1980–83; Counsellor GATT/UNCTAD, UKMIS Geneva, 1983–87; Counsellor, Consul-Gen. and Hd of Chancery, Jakarta, 1987–89. *Publications:* (contrib.) Lloyd George: 12 essays, ed A. J. P. Taylor, 1971; contrib. Cambridge Hist. Jl. *Recreations:* historic buildings, jazz, swimming, camping, theatre. *Address:* c/o Foreign and Commonwealth Office, King Charles Street, SW1A 2AH.

MONTGOMERY, Sir (Basil Henry) David, 9th Bt, *cr* 1801, of Stanhope; JP; DL; landowner; Chairman, Forestry Commission, 1979–89; *b* 20 March 1931; *s* of late Lt-Col H. K. Purvis-Montgomery, OBE, and of Mrs C. L. W. Purvis-Russell-Montgomery (*née* Maconochie Welwood); *S* uncle, 1964; *m* 1956, Delia, *o d* of Adm. Sir (John) Peter (Lorne) Reid, GCB, CVO; one *s* four *d* (and one *s* decd). *Educ:* Eton. National Service, Black Watch, 1949–51. Member: Nature Conservancy Council, 1973–79; Tayside Regional Authority, 1974–79. Comr, Mental Welfare Commn for Scotland, 1990–. Trustee, Municipal Mutual Insurance Ltd, 1980–. Hon. LLD Dundee, 1977. DL Kinross-shire, 1960, Vice-Lieutenant 1966–74; JP 1966; DL Perth and Kinross, 1975. *Heir: s* James David Keith Montgomery [*b* 13 June 1957; *m* 1983, Elizabeth, *e d* of E. Lyndon Evans, Pentyrch, Mid-Glamorgan; one *s* one *d*. Served The Black Watch, RHR, 1976–86]. *Address:* Kinross House, Kinross KY13 7ET. *T:* Kinross (0577) 63416.

MONTGOMERY, (Charles) John, CBE 1977; Director: Lloyds Bank Plc, 1972–84 (a Vice-Chairman, 1978–84); Lloyds Bank International, 1978–84; Yorkshire Bank, 1980–84; *b* 18 Feb. 1917; *s* of late Rev. Charles James Montgomery; *m* 1950, Gwenneth Mary McKendrick; two *d*. *Educ:* Colwyn Bay Grammar School. Served with RN, 1940–46. Entered Lloyds Bank, 1935; Jt Gen. Man. 1968; Asst Chief Gen. Man. 1970; Dep. Chief Gen. Man. 1973; Chief Gen. Man., 1973–78. Pres., Inst. of Bankers, 1976–77, Vice Pres., 1977–. Chm., Chief Exec. Officers' Cttee, Cttee of London Clearing Bankers, 1976–78. *Recreations:* walking, photography. *Address:* High Cedar, 6 Cedar Copse, Bickley, Kent. *T:* 081–467 2410. *Clubs:* Naval, Overseas Bankers.

MONTGOMERY, Sir David; *see* Montgomery, Sir B. H. D.

MONTGOMERY, David, CMG 1984; OBE 1972; Foreign and Commonwealth Office, since 1987; *b* 29 July 1927; *s* of late David Montgomery and of Mary (*née* Walker Cunningham); *m* 1955, Margaret Newman; one *s* one *d*. Royal Navy, 1945–48. Foreign Office, 1949–52; Bucharest, 1952–53; FO, 1953–55; Bonn, 1955–58; Düsseldorf,

1958–61; Rangoon, 1961–63; Ottawa, 1963–64; Regina, Saskatchewan, 1964–65; FCO, 1966–68; Bangkok, 1968–72; Zagreb, 1973–76; FCO, 1976–79; Dep. High Comr to Barbados, 1980–84, also (non-resident) to Antigua and Barbuda, Dominica, Grenada, St Kitts and Nevis, St Lucia, St Vincent and the Grenadines, 1980–84; FCO, 1984–85. Governor, Southmead Sch., Wimbledon Park, 1990–. *Recreations:* golf, music (light and opera). *Address:* 8 Ross Court, Putney Hill, SW15 3NY. *Club:* Royal Over-Seas League.

MONTGOMERY, David John; Chief Executive, London Live Television, since 1991; *b* 6 Nov. 1948; *s* of William John and Margaret Jean Montgomery; *m* 1st, 1971, Susan Frances Buchanan Russell (marr. diss. 1987); 2nd, 1989, Heidi Kingstone, *d* of Prof. Edward Kingstone, McMaster Univ., Ont. *Educ:* Queen's University, Belfast (BA Politics/History). Sub-Editor, Daily Mirror, London/Manchester, 1973–78; Assistant Chief Sub-Editor, Daily Mirror, 1978–80; Chief Sub-Editor, The Sun, 1980; Asst Editor, Sunday People, 1982; Asst Editor, 1984, Editor, 1985–87, News of the World; Editor, Today, 1987–91 (Newspaper of the Year, 1988); Man. Dir, News UK, 1987–91. Director: Satellite Television PLC, 1986–91; News Group Newspapers, 1986–91. *Address:* 13 Warrington Crescent, W9.

MONTGOMERY, Prof. Desmond Alan Dill, CBE 1981 (MBE 1943); MD; FRCP, FRCPI; Chairman, Northern Ireland Council for Postgraduate Medical Education, 1979–87; *b* 6 June 1916; 3rd *s* of late Dr and Mrs J. Howard Montgomery, China and Belfast; *m* 1941, Dr Susan Holland, 2nd *d* of late Mr and Mrs F. J. Holland, Belfast; one *s* one *d*. *Educ:* Inchmarlo Prep. Sch.; Campbell Coll.; Queen's Univ., Belfast (3rd, 4th and final yr scholarships; MB, BCh, BAO 1st Cl. Hons 1940; MD (Gold Medal) 1946). Sinclair Medal in Surgery, Butterworth Prize in Medicine, Prize in Mental Disease, QUB. MRCP 1948, FRCP 1964; FRCPI 1975; FRCOG (*ae*) 1981. Served War, RAMC, 1941–46: Temp. Major India Comd; DADMS GHQ India, 1943–45. House Physician and Surgeon, Royal Victoria Hosp., Belfast, 1940–41, Registrar, 1946; Registrar, Royal Postgrad. Med. Sch. and Hammersmith Hosp., and National Heart Hosp., London, 1946–48; Royal Victoria Hosp., Belfast: Sen. Registrar, 1948–51; Consultant Physician, 1951–79, Hon. Consultant 1980–; Physician i/c Sir George E. Clark Metabolic Unit, 1958–79; Endocrinologist, Royal Maternity Hosp., Belfast, 1958–79; Hon. Reader in Endocrinol., Dept of Medicine, QUB, 1969–75, Hon. Prof., 1975–. Hon. Secretary: Royal Victoria Med. Staff Cttee, 1964–66 (Chm., 1975–77); Ulster Med. Soc., 1954–58 (Pres., 1975–76). Member: NI Council for Health and Personal Social Services, 1974–83 (Chm., Central Med. Adv. Cttee, 1974–83, Mem. 1983–87); NI Med. Manpower Adv. Cttee, 1974–83; Distinction and Meritorious Awards Cttee, 1975–87 (Chm., 1982–87); Faculty of Medicine, QUB, 1969–87 (Chm., Ethical Cttee, 1975–81); Senate, QUB, 1979–; GMC, 1979–84; Pres., QUB Assoc., 1988–89. Member: BMA; Assoc. of Physicians of GB and NI; Eur. Thyroid Assoc.; Corrigan Club (Chm., 1969); Irish Endocrine Soc. (1st Chm., Founder Mem.); Internat. Soc. for Internal Medicine; formerly Mem., Eur. Soc. for Study of Diabetes; Hon. Mem., British Dietetic Assoc. Lectured in USA, India, Greece, Australia and Nigeria; visited Russia on behalf of British Council, 1975. Pres., Belfast City Mission, 1973; Mem., Bd of Trustees, Presbyterian Church in Ireland. DSc (*hc*) NUI, 1980. Jt Editor, Ulster Med. Jl, 1974–84. *Publications:* (contrib.) Whitla's Dictionary of Treatment, 1957; (contrib.) Good Health and Diabetes, 1961, 3rd edn 1976; (contrib.) R. Smith, Progress in Clinical Surgery, 1961; (with R. B. Welbourn) Clinical Endocrinology for Surgeons, 1963; (contrib.) Progress in Neurosurgery, 1964; (with R. B. Welbourn) Medical and Surgical Endocrinology, 1975; (contrib.) M. D. Vickers, Medicine for Anaesthetists, 1977; articles in med. jls on endocrinology, diabetes mellitus and related subjects. *Recreations:* travel, photography, music, gardening, philately. *Address:* 59 Church Road, Newtownbreda, Belfast BT8 4AN. *T:* Belfast (0232) 648326; 15 Carrickmore Road, Ballycastle BT54 6QS. *T:* Ballycastle (02657) 62361.

MONTGOMERY, Sir Fergus; *see* Montgomery, Sir (William) Fergus.

MONTGOMERY, Prof. George Lightbody, CBE 1960; TD 1942; MD, PhD, FRCPE, FRCPGlas, FRCPath, FRCSE; FRSE; Professor of Pathology, University of Edinburgh, 1954–71, now Emeritus; *b* 3 Nov. 1905; *o s* of late John Montgomery and Jeanie Lightbody; *m* 1933, Margaret Sutherland, 3rd *d* of late A. Henry Forbes, Oban; one *s* one *d*. *Educ:* Hillhead High Sch., Glasgow; Glasgow Univ. MB, ChB, 1928; Commendation and RAMC Memorial Prize; PhD (St Andrews), 1937; MD Hons and Bellahouston Gold Medal (Glasgow), 1946. House Physician, House Surgeon, Glasgow Royal Infirmary, 1928–29; Lecturer in Clinical Pathology, Univ. of St Andrews, 1931–37; Lecturer in Pathology of Disease in Infancy and Childhood, Univ. of Glasgow, 1937–48; Asst Pathologist, Glasgow Royal Infirmary, 1929–31; Asst Pathologist, Dundee Royal Infirmary, 1931–37; Pathologist, Royal Hospital for Sick Children, Glasgow, 1937–48; Professor of Pathology (St Mungo-Notman Chair), Univ. of Glasgow, 1948–54. Chm. Scottish Health Services Council, 1954–59. Hon. Member: Pathological Soc. Gt Britain and Ireland; BMA. Col (Hon.) Army Medical Service. *Publications:* numerous contribs to medical and scientific journals. *Recreation:* music. *Address:* 2 Cumin Place, Edinburgh EH9 2JX. *T:* 031–667 6792.

MONTGOMERY, Group Captain George Rodgers, CBE 1946; DL; RAF (Retired); Secretary, Norfolk Naturalists' Trust, 1963–75; Hon. Appeal Secretary, and Member of the Court, University of East Anglia, since Nov. 1966; *b* 31 May 1910; *s* of late John Montgomery, Belfast; *m* 1st, 1932, Margaret McHarry Heslip (*d* 1981), *d* of late William J. Heslip, Belfast; two *s*; 2nd, 1982, Margaret Stephanie (*née* Reynolds), *widow* of Colin Vanner Hedworth Foulkes. *Educ:* Royal Academy, Belfast. Commnd in RAF, 1928; retd 1958. Served in UK and ME, 1928–38. War of 1939–45: Bomber Comd, NI, Air Min. and ME. Served UK, Japan and W Europe, 1946–58: Comdr RAF Wilmslow, 1946–47; Air Adviser to UK Polit. Rep. in Japan, and Civil Air Attaché, Tokyo, 1948–49; Chief Instr RAF Officers' Advanced Trg Sch., 1950; Comdt RAF Sch. of Admin, Bircham Newton, 1951–52; Comdr RAF Hednesford, 1953–54; DDO (Estabts) Air Min. and Chm. RAF Western European Estabts Cttee, Germany, 1955–57. On retirement, Organising Sec. Friends of Norwich Cathedral, 1959–62; Appeal Sec., Univ. of East Anglia, 1961–66; Hon. Vice-President: Norfolk Naturalists' Trust, 1979–; Broads Soc., 1983–; Mem., Great Bustard Trust Council, 1972–. DL Norfolk, 1979. *Recreations:* river cruising, gardening. *Address:* 24 Cathedral Close, Norwich, Norfolk NR1 4DZ. *T:* Norwich (0603) 628024. *Clubs:* Royal Air Force; Norfolk (Norwich).

MONTGOMERY, Hugh Bryan Greville; Chairman, Andry Montgomery group of companies (organisers, managers and consultants in exhibitions), since 1988 (Managing Director, 1952–88); *b* 26 March 1929; *s* of Hugh Roger Greville Montgomery, MC, and Molly Audrey Montgomery, OBE (*née* Neele). *Educ:* Repton; Lincoln Coll., Oxford (MA PPE). Founder member, Oxford Univ. Wine and Food Soc. Consultant and adviser on trade fairs and developing countries for UN; Consultant, Internat. Garden Festival, Liverpool, 1984. Chairman: Brit. Assoc. of Exhibn Organisers, 1970; Internat. Cttee, Amer. Nat. Assoc. of Exposition Managers, 1980–82 and 1990–; British Exhibn Promotion Council, 1982–83; Vice Pres., Union des Foires Internat., 1987–. Member: Adv. Bd, Hotel Inst. for Management, Montreux, 1986–; London Regl Cttee, CBI, 1987–90; BOTB, 1991–. Mem. Council, Design and Industries Assoc., 1983–85. Chm. of Trustees of ECHO (Supply of Equipment to Charity Hosps Overseas), 1978–89; Chairman: The Building Museum, 1988–; British Architectural Library Trust, 1989–; Vice-Chm., Bldg Conservation Trust, 1979– (Chm. Interbuild Fund, 1972–); Trustee: The Cubitt Trust, 1982–; Music for the World, 1990–; Hon. Treas., Contemporary Art Soc., 1980–82; Councillor, Acad. of St Martin-in-the-Fields Concert Soc., 1988–. Member Executive Committee: CGLI, 1974–; Nat. Fund for Research into Crippling Diseases, 1970–. Liveryman, 1952, Master, 1980–81, Worshipful Co. of Tylers and Bricklayers (Trustee, Charitable and Pension Trusts, 1981–). Silver Jubilee Medal, 1977. *Publications:* Industrial Fairs and Developing Countries (UNIDO), 1975; Going into Trade Fairs (UNCTAD/GATT), 1982; Exhibition Planning and Design, 1989; contrib. to Internat. Trade Forum (ITC, Geneva). *Recreations:* collecting contemporary art, theatre, wine tasting. *Address:* 11 Manchester Square, W1M 5AB. *T:* 071–486 1951; Snells Farm, Amersham Common, Bucks HP7 9QN. *Clubs:* United Oxford & Cambridge University, City Livery.

MONTGOMERY, John; *see* Montgomery, C. J.

MONTGOMERY, John Duncan; JP; Member, Monopolies and Mergers Commission, since 1989; *b* 12 Nov. 1928; *s* of Lionel Eric Montgomery and Katherine Mary Montgomery (*née* Ambler); *m* 1956, Pauline Mary Sutherland; two *d*. *Educ:* King's College Sch., Wimbledon; LSE (LLB, LLM). Admitted Solicitor 1951; Treasury Solicitor's Dept, 1960–68; Legal Adviser, Beecham Products, 1974–75; Head, Legal Div., Shell UK, 1975–88 and Company Sec., Shell UK, 1979–88. Former Chm., Youth Orgns, Merton. Freeman, City of London, 1987; Mem., Loriners' Co., 1988. JP SW London, 1985. *Recreations:* dinghy sailing, photography. *Address:* Monopolies and Mergers Commission, New Court, 48 Carey Street, WC2A 2JT. *T:* 071–324 1467. *Clubs:* MCC, City Livery.

MONTGOMERY, John Matthew; Clerk of the Salters' Company, since 1975; *b* 22 May 1930; *s* of Prof. George Allison Montgomery, QC, and Isobel A. (*née* Morison); *m* 1956, Gertrude Gillian Richards; two *s* one *d*. *Educ:* Rugby Sch.; Trinity Hall, Cambridge (MA). Various commercial appointments with Mobil Oil Corporation and First National City Bank, 1953–74. Mem. Exec. Cttee, Nat. Assoc. of Almshouses, 1980–; Chm., Age Concern, Gtr London, 1988–. Member: Council, Surrey Trust for Nature Conservation Ltd, 1965–89 (Chm., 1973–83; Vice-Pres., 1983–); Council, Royal Soc. for Nature Conservation, 1980–89. Founder Mem., London Wildlife Trust, 1981–. *Recreations:* various natural history interests. *Address:* Dunedin, Red Lane, Claygate, Esher, Surrey KT10 0ES. *T:* Esher (0372) 64780.

MONTGOMERY, Col John Rupert Patrick, OBE 1979; MC 1943; *b* 25 July 1913; *s* of George Howard and Mabella Montgomery; *m* 1st, 1940, Alice Vyvyan Patricia Mitchell (*d* 1976); one *s* two *d*; 2nd, 1981, Marguerite Beatrice Chambers (*née* Montgomery). *Educ:* Wellington Coll.; RMC, Sandhurst. Commissioned, Oxfordshire and Buckinghamshire LI, 1933; Regimental Service in India, 1935–40 and 1946–47. Served War in Middle East, N Africa and Italy, 1942–45. Commanded 17 Bn Parachute Regt (9 DLI), 1953–56; SHAPE Mission to Portugal, 1956–59; retired, 1962. Sec., Anti-Slavery Soc., 1963–80. Silver Medal, RSA, 1973. *Address:* The Oast House, Buxted, Sussex TN22 4PP. *Club:* Army and Navy.

MONTGOMERY, Sir (William) Fergus, Kt 1985; MP (C) Altrincham and Sale, since Oct. 1974; *b* 25 Nov. 1927; *s* of late William Montgomery and Winifred Montgomery; *m* Joyce, *d* of George Riddle. *Educ:* Jarrow Grammar Sch.; Bede Coll., Durham. Served in Royal Navy, 1946–48; Schoolmaster, 1950–59. Nat. Vice-Chm. Young Conservative Organisation, 1954–57, National Chm., 1957–58; contested (C) Consett Division, 1955; MP (C): Newcastle upon Tyne East, 1959–64; Brierley Hill, Apr. 1967–Feb. 1974; contested Dudley W, Feb. 1974; PPS to Sec. of State for Educn and Science, 1973–74, to Leader of the Opposition, 1975–76. Mem. Executive, CPA, 1983–. Councillor, Hebburn UDC, 1950–58. Has lectured extensively in the USA. *Recreations:* bridge, reading, going to theatre. *Address:* 181 Ashley Gardens, Emery Hill Street, SW1. *T:* 071–834 7905; 6 Groby Place, Altrincham, Cheshire. *T:* 061–928 1983.

MONTGOMERY CUNINGHAME, Sir John Christopher Foggo, 12th Bt *cr* 1672, of Corsehill, Ayrshire and Kirktonholm, Lanarkshire; Chairman: Ronald A. Lee PLC, since 1986; Euromax Electronics Ltd, since 1985; Director: Artemis Energy Co., since 1981 (Partner); Inertia Dynamics Corp., since 1980; Purolite International Ltd, since 1984, and other companies; *b* 24 July 1935; 2nd *s* of Col Sir Thomas Montgomery-Cuninghame, 10th Bt, DSO (*d* 1945), and of Nancy Macaulay (his 2nd wife), *d* of late W. Stewart Foggo, Aberdeen (she *m* 2nd, 1946, Johan Frederik Christian Killander); *b* of Sir Andrew Montgomery-Cuninghame, 11th Bt; *S* brother, 1959; *m* 1964, Laura Violet, *d* of Sir Godfrey Nicholson, 1st Bt; three *d*. *Educ:* Fettes; Worcester Coll., Oxford (MA). 2nd Lieut, Rifle Brigade (NS), 1955–56; Lieut, London Rifle Brigade, TA, 1956–59. *Recreation:* fishing. *Heir:* none. *Address:* The Old Rectory, Brightwalton, Newbury, Berks.

MONTGOMERY WATT, Prof. William; *see* Watt.

MONTLAKE, Henry Joseph; solicitor; Senior Partner, H. Montlake & Co., since 1954; a Recorder of the Crown Court, since 1983; *b* 22 Aug. 1930; *s* of Alfred and Hetty Montlake; *m* 1952, Ruth Rochelle Allen; four *s*. *Educ:* Ludlow Grammar Sch., Ludlow; London Univ. (LLB 1951). Law Soc.'s final exam., 1951; admitted Solicitor, 1952. National Service, commnd RASC, 1953. Dep. Registrar of County Courts, 1970–78; Dep. Circuit Judge and Asst Recorder, 1978–83. Pres., West Essex Law Soc., 1977–78. Chm., Ilford Round Table, 1962–63; Pres., Assoc. of Jewish Golf Clubs and Socs, 1984– (Sec., 1977–84). *Recreations:* golf, The Times crossword, people, travel. *Address:* Chelston, 5 St Mary's Avenue, Wanstead, E11 2NR. *T:* 081–989 7228. *Clubs:* Wig and Pen; Dyrham Park Golf; Abridge Golf (Chm. 1964, Captain 1965).

MONTMORENCY, Sir Arnold Geoffroy de; *see* de Montmorency.

MONTREAL, Bishop of, since 1991; **Rt. Rev. Andrew S. Hutchison;** *b* 19 Sept. 1938; *s* of Ralph Burton Hutchison and Kathleen Marian (*née* Van Nostrand); *m* 1960, Lois Arlene Knight; one *s*. *Educ:* Lakefield Coll. Sch.; Upper Canada Coll.; Trinity Coll. Toronto (LTh). Ordained deacon, 1969, priest, 1970; served fifteen years in the dio. of Toronto; Dean of Montreal, 1984–90. Pres., Montreal Diocesan Theol Coll., 1990–; Visitor, Bishops Univ., Lennoxville, 1990–; Chaplain: Canadian Grenadier Guards, 1986–; 6087 and 22 CAR, 1986–; Order of St John of Jerusalem, Quebec, 1987–; Last Post Fund, Quebec, 1986–. OStJ. *Address:* Bishopscourt, 3630 Mountain Street, Montreal, Quebec. *T:* (514) 849 4089. *Clubs:* United Services, Montreal Faculty, McGill University (Montreal).

MONTROSE, 7th Duke of, *cr* 1707; **James Angus Graham;** *cr* Baron Graham before 1451; Earl of Montrose, 1505; Bt of Nova Scotia, 1625; Marquis of Montrose, 1645; Duke of Montrose, Marquis of Graham and Buchanan, Earl of Kincardine, Viscount Dundaff, Baron Aberuthven, Mugdock, and Fintrie, 1707; Earl and Baron Graham (Peerage of England), 1722; Hereditary Sheriff of Dunbartonshire; *b* 2 May 1907; *e s* of 6th Duke of Montrose, KT, CB, CVO, VD, and Lady Mary Douglas-Hamilton, OBE (*d* 1957), *d* of 12th Duke of Hamilton; *S* father, 1954; *m* 1st, 1930, Isobel Veronica (marr. diss. 1950; she *d* 1990), *yr d* of late Lt-Col T. B. Sellar, CMG, DSO; one *s* one *d*; 2nd, 1952,

Susan Mary Jocelyn, *widow* of Michael Raleigh Gibbs and *d* of late Dr J. M. Semple; two *s* two *d*. *Educ:* Eton; Christ Church, Oxford. Lt-Comdr RNVR. MP for Hartley-Gatooma in Federal Assembly of Federation of Rhodesia and Nyasaland, 1958–62; Minister of Agriculture, Lands, and Natural Resources, S Rhodesia, 1962–63; Minister of Agric., Rhodesia, 1964–65; (apptd in Rhodesia) Minister of External Affairs and Defence, 1966–68. *Heir:* *s* Marquis of Graham, *qv*. *Address:* Nether Tillyrie, Milnathort, Kinross KY13 7RW; (seat) Auchmar, Drymen, Glasgow.

MOODY, Helen Wills; *see* Roark, H. W.

MOODY, John Percivale, OBE 1961; Counsellor to the Board, Welsh National Opera Co.; *b* 6 April 1906; *s* of Percivale Sadleir Moody; *m* 1937, Helen Pomfret Burra; one *s* decd. *Educ:* Bromsgrove; Royal Academy Schools. In publishing in the City, 1924–26; Painting; Academy Schs, 1927–28, various London Exhibitions; taught at Wimbledon Art Sch., 1928–29. Studied opera Webber Douglas Sch. Derby Day under Sir Nigel Playfair, Lyric, Hammersmith, 1931. West End plays include: The Brontës, Royalty, 1932; Hervey House, His Majesty's, 1935; After October, Criterion, 1936; played in Old Vic seasons 1934, 1937; Ascent of F6, Dog Beneath the Skin, Group Theatre, 1935; Dir Old Vic Sch., 1940–42. AFS Clerkenwell, 1940 (wounded and discharged). Producer Old Vic Co., Liverpool, 1942–44; Birmingham Repertory Theatre, 1944–45; Carl Rosa Opera Co., 1945; Sadler's Wells Opera Co., 1945–49; Drama Dir, Arts Council of Great Britain, 1949–54; Dir, Bristol Old Vic Co., 1954–59; Dir of Productions, 1960, and Jt Artistic Dir, 1970, Welsh Nat. Opera. First productions in England of Verdi's Simone Boccanegra, 1948, Nabucco, 1952, and The Battle of Legnano, 1960; Rimsky's May Night, 1960; also for Welsh Nat. Opera: Rossini's William Tell, 1961; Macbeth, 1963; Moses, 1965; Carmen, 1967; Boris Godunov, 1968; Simone Boccanegra, 1970; Rigoletto, 1972; The Pearl Fishers, 1973; What the Old Man Does is Always Right, Fishguard Festival, 1977. With wife, new translations of Carmen, Simone Boccanegra, Macbeth, La Traviata, The Pearl Fishers, Prince Igor, May Night, Battle of Legnano, William Tell, Moses and Fidelio. *Publications:* (with Helen Moody) translations of: The Pearl Fishers, 1979; Carmen, 1982; Moses, 1986; Songs of Massenet (2 vols), 1988. *Recreations:* swimming, gardening, painting. *Address:* 2 Richmond Park Road, Bristol BS8 3AT. *T:* Bristol (0272) 734436.

MOODY, Leslie Howard; General Secretary, Civil Service Union, 1977–82; *b* 18 Aug. 1922; *s* of George Henry and Edith Jessie Moody; *m* 1944, Betty Doreen Walton; two *s*. *Educ:* Eltham College. Telephone Engineer, General Post Office, 1940–53. Served Royal Signals, Far East, 1944–47. Asst Sec., Civil Service Union, 1953, Dep. Gen. Sec., 1963. *Recreations:* walking, music, theatre, educating management. *Address:* 9 Lock Chase, Blackheath, SE3 9HB. *T:* 081–318 1040. *Club:* Civil Service.

MOODY, Peter Edward, CBE 1981; Director: Prudential Corporation, 1981–91 (Deputy Chairman, 1984–88); The Laird Group, since 1981; *b* 26 Aug. 1918; *s* of late Edward Thomas Moody and Gladys (*née* Flint); *m* 1945, Peggy Elizabeth *d* of Edward Henry Causer and Elizabeth Theodora (*née* Finke); one *s* one *d*. *Educ:* Christ's Coll., Finchley. FIA. Prudential Assurance Co. Ltd: Dep. Investment Manager, 1960; Jt Sec. and Chief Investment Manager, 1973–80; Jt Sec. and Group Chief Investment Manager, Prudential Corp., 1979–80; Director: Triton Petroleum Ltd, 1971–89; United Dominions Trust, 1972–81; British American and General Trust, 1981–85; Inmos International, 1981–84; 3i Group plc (formerly FFI, then Investors in Industry), 1981–89; Equity Trustee Ltd, 1985–90. Mem., PO Bd, 1981–85. Trustee, Thalidomide Trust, 1984–. Institute of Actuaries: Hon. Sec., 1968–70; Vice-Pres., 1972–75; Pres., 1978–80; Master, Worshipful Co. of Actuaries, 1988–89. *Publications:* contrib. Jl of Inst. of Actuaries. *Recreation:* golf. *Address:* 46 Brookmans Avenue, Brookmans Park, Herts AL9 7QJ.

MOOKERJEE, Sir Birendra Nath, Kt 1942; MA Cantab, MIE (India); Partner of Martin & Co. and Burn & Co., Managing Director, Martin Burn Ltd, Engineers, Contractors, Merchants, Shipbuilders, etc; Chairman Steel Corporation of Bengal Ltd; President Calcutta Local Board of Imperial Bank of India; Director Darjeeling Himalayan Railway Co. Ltd and many other companies; *b* 14 Feb. 1899; *s* of late Sir Rajendra Nath Mookerjee, KCIE, KCVO, MIE (India), FASB, DSc (Eng); *m* 1925, Ranu Priti Adhikari, *d* of Phani Bhusan Adhikari, late Professor Benares Hindu Univ.; one *s* two *d*. *Educ:* Bishop's Collegiate Sch., Hastings House, Calcutta; Bengal Engineering Coll.; Trinity Coll., Cambridge. Mem., Viceroy's Nat. Defence Council; Adviser, Roger Mission; Mem., Munitions Production Adv. Cttee. Fellow Calcutta Univ.; Sheriff of Calcutta 1941. *Address:* Martin Burn Ltd, Martin Burn House, 12 Mission Row, Calcutta 1, India; 7 Harington Street, Calcutta 16. *Clubs:* National Liberal; Calcutta, Calcutta Polo, Royal Calcutta Turf, Calcutta South, Cricket Club of India (Calcutta), etc.

MOOLLAN, Sir (Abdool) Hamid (Adam), Kt 1986; QC (Mauritius) 1976; *b* 10 April 1933; *s* of Adam Sulliman Moollan and Khatija Moollan; *m* 1966, Sara Sidiot; three *s*. *Educ:* Soonee Surtee Musalman Society Aided School; Royal College School; King's College London (LLB); Faculté de Droit, Univ. de Paris. Called to the Bar, Middle Temple, 1956; joined Mauritian Bar, 1960. *Recreations:* tennis, horse racing, hunting, fishing. *Address:* (home) Railway Road, Phoenix, Mauritius. *T:* 6864983; (chambers) 43 Sir William Newton Street, Port-Louis, Mauritius. *T:* 208.3881. *Clubs:* Royal Over-Seas League; Mauritius Gymkhana, Mauritius Turf.

MOOLLAN, Sir Cassam (Ismael), Kt 1982; Chief Justice, Supreme Court of Mauritius, 1982–88, retired; Acting Governor-General, several occasions in 1984, 1985, 1986, 1987, 1988; Commander-in-Chief of Mauritius, 1984; *b* 26 Feb. 1927; *s* of Ismael Mahomed Moollan and Fatimah Nazroo; *m* 1954, Rassoulbibie Adam Moollan; one *s* two *d*. *Educ:* Royal Coll., Port Louis and Curepipe; London Sch. of Econs and Pol. Science (LLB 1950). Called to the Bar, Lincoln's Inn, 1951. Private practice, 1951–55; Dist Magistrate, 1955–58; Crown Counsel, 1958–64; Sen. Crown Counsel, 1964–66; Solicitor Gen., 1966–70; QC (Mauritius) 1969; Puisne Judge, Supreme Court, 1970; Sen. Puisne Judge, 1978. Editor, Mauritius Law Reports, 1982–84. Chevalier, Légion d'Honneur (France), 1986. *Recreations:* table tennis, tennis, bridge, Indian classical and semi-classical music. *Address:* Chambers, 43 Sir William Newton Street, Port Louis, Mauritius. *T:* 2120794, 083881; 22 Hitchcock Avenue, Quatre Bornes, Mauritius. *T:* 4546949. *Club:* Gymkhana (Port Louis).

MOON, Brenda Elizabeth, FLA; University Librarian, University of Edinburgh, since 1980; *b* 11 April 1931; *d* of Clement Alfred Moon and Mabel (*née* Berks). *Educ:* King Edward's Grammar Sch. for Girls, Camp Hill, Birmingham; St Hilda's Coll., Oxford (MA). MPhil Leeds; FLA 1958. Asst Librarian, Univ. of Sheffield, 1955–62; Sub-Librarian, 1962–67, Dep. Librarian, 1967–79, Univ. of Hull. *Publications:* Mycenaean Civilisation: publications since 1935, 1957; Mycenaean Civilisation: publications 1956–1960, 1961; Periodicals for South-East Asian Studies: a union catalogue of holdings in British and selected European libraries, 1979; articles in prof. jls. *Recreations:* walking, gardening, cruising on canals. *Address:* 4 Cobden Road, Edinburgh EH9 2BJ. *T:* 031–667 0071.

See also M. M. Moon.

MOON, Mary Marjorie; Head Mistress, Manchester High School for Girls, since 1983; *b* 28 Sept. 1932; *d* of Clement Alfred Moon and Mable Moon (*née* Berks). *Educ:* King Edward's Grammar Sch. for Girls, Birmingham; Univ. of Manchester (BA Hons, MEd); Univ. of London Inst. of Education (PGCE). Asst English Teacher, 1955–59, Head of English Dept, 1959–63, Orme Girls' Sch., Newcastle-under-Lyme; Head of English, Bolton Sch. (Girls' Div.), 1963–71; Head Mistress, Pate's Grammar Sch. for Girls, Cheltenham, 1971–83. *Recreations:* photography, sketching, travel. *Address:* 18 South Parade, Bramhall, Stockport, Cheshire SK7 3BH; Manchester High School for Girls, Grangethorpe Road, Manchester M14 6HS. *T:* 061–224 0447.

See also B. E. Moon.

MOON, Sir Peter Wilfred Giles Graham-, 5th Bt, *cr* 1855; Chairman, Trans Continental Corporation, since 1990; *b* 24 Oct. 1942; *s* of Sir (Arthur) Wilfred Graham-Moon, 4th Bt, and 2nd wife, Doris Patricia, *yr d* of Thomas Baron Jobson, Dublin; *S* father, 1954; *m* 1967, Sarah Gillian Chater (formerly *m* Major Antony Chater; marr. diss. 1966), *e d* of late Lt-Col Michael Lyndon Smith, MC, MB, BS, and Mrs Michael Smith; two *s*. *Recreations:* shooting, golf. *Heir:* *s* Rupert Francis Wilfred Graham-Moon, *b* 29 April 1968. *Address:* Battens Farm House, Lambourn Woodlands, Newbury, Berks RG16 7TN. *Clubs:* Cricketers; Royal Cork Yacht.

MOON, Philip Burton, FRS 1947; Poynting Professor of Physics in the University of Birmingham, 1950–74, now Emeritus; Dean of the Faculty of Science and Engineering, 1969–72; *b* 17 May 1907; *o s* of late F. D. Moon; *m* 1st, 1937, Winifred F. Barber (*d* 1971); one *s* one *d*; 2nd, 1974, Lorna M. Aldridge. *Educ:* Leyton County High Sch.; Sidney Sussex Coll., Cambridge. Hon. DSc Aston, 1970. *Publications:* Artificial Radioactivity, 1949; papers (1929–1989) on physics and molecular-beam chemistry. *Address:* 8 Oaks Road, Church Stretton, Shropshire SY6 7AX. *T:* Church Stretton (0694) 722497.

MOON, Sir Roger, 6th Bt *cr* 1887, of Copsewood, Stoke, Co. Warwick; retired; *b* 17 Nov. 1914; *s* of Jasper Moon (*d* 1975) (*g g s* of 1st Bt) and Isabel (*née* Logan); *S* brother, 1988; *m* 1950, Meg, *d* of late Arthur Mainwaring Maxwell, DSO, MC; three *d*. *Educ:* Sedbergh. Coffee planter, Kenya, 1933–35; Rubber planter, Malaya, 1939–41 and 1946–63; Oil palms planter, Malaya, 1963–67. *Recreations:* shooting, golf, gardening. *Heir:* *b* Humphrey Moon [*b* 9 Oct. 1919; *m* 1st, 1955, Diana Hobson (marr. diss. 1964); two *d*; 2nd, 1964, Elizabeth Anne, *d* of late George Archibald Drummond Angus and *widow* of H. J. Butler; one *d*]. *Address:* Mill House, Ruyton-XI-Towns, Shropshire. *T:* Baschurch (0939) 260354.

MOONEY, Bel; writer and broadcaster; *b* 8 Oct. 1946; *d* of Edward and Gladys Mooney; *m* 1968, Jonathan Dimbleby, *qv*; one *s* one *d*. *Educ:* Trowbridge Girls' High School; University College London (1st cl. Hons, Eng. Lang. and Lit.). Freelance journalist, 1970–79; columnist: Daily Mirror, 1979–80; Sunday Times, 1982–83; The Listener, 1984–86; contributor to The Times, 1970–; *television:* interview series: Mothers By Daughters, 1983; The Light of Experience Revisited, 1984; Fathers By Sons, 1985; various series for BBC Radio 4 and films for BBC TV. Governor, Bristol Polytechnic, 1989–91. *Publications:* The Year of the Child, 1979; Liza's Yellow Boat, 1980; The Windsurf Boy, 1983; Differences of Opinion (collected journalism), 1984; I Don't Want To!, 1985; The Anderson Question, 1985; (with Gerald Scarfe) Father Kissmass and Mother Claws, 1985; The Stove Haunting, 1986; The Fourth of July, 1988; Bel Mooney's Somerset, 1989; It's Not Fair!, 1989; From This Day Forward (anthol.), 1989; A Flower of Jet, 1990; But You Promised!, 1990; Why Not?, 1990; I Know!, 1991. *Recreations:* reading, music, art, friends. *Address:* c/o David Higham Associates, 5 Lower John Street, W1. *T:* 071–437 7888. *Club:* Groucho.

MOONIE, Lewis George; MP (Lab) Kirkcaldy, since 1987; *b* 25 Feb. 1947; *m*; two *c*. *Educ:* Grove Acad., Dundee; St Andrews Univ. (MB ChB 1970); Edinburgh Univ. (MSc 1981). MRCPsych 1979; MFCM 1984. Psychiatrist, Ciba-Geigy, Switzerland, and Organon Internat., Netherlands; Sen. Registrar (Community Medicine), subseq. Community Medicine Specialist, Fife Health Bd. Mem., Fife Regl Council, 1982–86. Mem., Social Services Select Cttee; opposition front-bench spokesman on technology, 1990–. *Address:* House of Commons, SW1A 0AA; 85 Sauchenbush Road, Kirkcaldy, Fife KY2 5RN.

MOONMAN, Eric, OBE 1991; Director, Natural History Museum Development Trust, since 1990; *b* 29 April 1929; *s* of Borach and Leah Moonman; *m* 1962, Jane; two *s* one *d*. *Educ:* Rathbone Sch., Liverpool; Christ Church, Southport; Univs of Liverpool and Manchester. Dipl. in Social Science, Liverpool, 1955. Human Relations Adviser, British Inst. of Management, 1956–62; Sen. Lectr in Industrial Relations, SW Essex Technical Coll., 1962–64; Sen. Research Fellow in Management Sciences, Univ. of Manchester, 1964–66. MSc Manchester Univ., 1967. MP (Lab) Billericay, 1966–70, Basildon, Feb. 1974–1979; PPS to Minister without Portfolio and Sec. of State for Educn, 1967–68. Chairman: All-Party Parly Mental Health Cttee, 1967–70 and 1974–79; New Towns and Urban Affairs Cttee, Parly Labour Party, 1974–79. Dir, Centre for Contemporary Studies, 1979–90. Chm., Zionist Fedn, 1975–80; Sen. Vice-Pres., Bd of Deputies, 1985–. Member: Stepney Council, 1961–65 (Leader, 1964–65); Tower Hamlets Council, 1964–67. Chm., Islington HA, 1981–. Mem., Council, Toynbee Hall Univ. Settlement (Chm., Finance Cttee); Governor, BFI, 1974–80. FRSA. *Publications:* The Manager and the Organization, 1961; Employee Security, 1962; European Science and Technology, 1968; Communication in an Expanding Organization, 1970; Reluctant Partnership, 1970; Alternative Government, 1984; (ed) The Violent Society, 1987. *Recreations:* football, theatre, cinema. *Address:* 1 Beacon Hill, N7 9LY.

MOORBATH, Dr Stephen Erwin, FRS 1977; Reader in Geology, Oxford University, since 1978; Professorial Fellow of Linacre College, since 1990 (Fellow, 1970); *b* 9 May 1929; *s* of Heinz Moosbach and Else Moosbach; *m* 1962, Pauline Tessier-Varlêt; one *s* one *d*. *Educ:* Lincoln Coll., Oxford Univ. (MA 1957, DPhil 1959). DSc Oxon 1969. Asst Experimental Officer, AERE, Harwell, 1948–51; Undergrad., Oxford Univ., 1951–54; Scientific Officer, AERE, Harwell, 1954–56; Research Fellow: Oxford Univ., 1956–61; MIT, 1961–62; Sen. Res. Officer, Oxford Univ., 1962–78. Wollaston Fund, Geol Soc. of London, 1968; Liverpool Geol Soc. Medal, 1968; Murchison Medal, Geol Soc. of London, 1978; Steno Medal, Geol Soc. of Denmark, 1979. *Publications:* contribs to scientific jls and books. *Recreations:* music, philately, travel, linguistics. *Address:* 53 Bagley Wood Road, Kennington, Oxford OX1 5LY. *T:* Oxford (0865) 739507.

MOORCRAFT, Dennis Harry; Under-Secretary, Inland Revenue, 1975–81; *b* 14 Aug. 1921; *s* of late Harry Moorcraft and Dorothy Moorcraft (*née* Simmons); *m* 1945, Ingeborg Utne, Bergen, Norway; one *s* one *d*. *Educ:* Gillingham County Grammar Sch. Tax Officer, Inland Revenue, 1938. RNVR, 1940–46. Inspector of Taxes, 1948; Sen. Inspector of Taxes, 1956; Principal Inspector of Taxes, 1963. *Recreations:* gardening, garden construction, croquet.

MOORE, family name of **Earl of Drogheda** and **Baron Moore of Wolvercote.**

MOORE, Viscount; Benjamin Garrett Henderson Moore; *b* 21 March 1983; *s* and *heir* of Earl of Drogheda, *qv*.

MOORE OF WOLVERCOTE, Baron *cr* 1986 (Life Peer), of Wolvercote in the City of Oxford; **Philip Brian Cecil Moore,** GCB 1985 (KCB 1980; CB 1973); GCVO 1983 (KCVO 1976); CMG 1966; QSO 1986; PC 1977; Private Secretary to the Queen and Keeper of the Queen's Archives, 1977–86; a Permanent Lord-in-Waiting to the Queen, since 1990; *b* 6 April 1921; *s* of late Cecil Moore, Indian Civil Service; *m* 1945, Joan Ursula Greenop; two *d*. *Educ:* Dragon Sch.; Cheltenham Coll. (Scholar); Oxford Univ. Classical Exhibitioner, Brasenose Coll., Oxford, 1940. RAF Bomber Command, 1940–42 (prisoner of war, 1942–45). Brasenose Coll., Oxford, 1945–46 (Hon. Fellow 1981). Asst Private Sec. to First Lord of Admiralty, 1950–51; Principal Private Sec. to First Lord of Admiralty, 1957–58; Dep. UK Commissioner, Singapore, 1961–63; British Dep. High Comr in Singapore, 1963–65; Chief of Public Relations, MoD, 1965–66; Asst Private Secretary to the Queen, 1966–72, Dep. Private Secretary, 1972–77. Dir, General Accident, Fire and Life Assurance Corp., 1986–91. Chm., King George VI and Queen Elizabeth Foundn of St Catharine's, Cumberland Lodge, 1986–. Vice-Pres., SPCK. *Recreations:* golf, Rugby football (Oxford Blue, 1945–46; International, England, 1951), hockey (Oxford Blue, 1946), cricket (Oxfordshire). *Address:* Hampton Court Palace, East Molesey, Surrey. *Clubs:* Athenæum, MCC.

MOORE, Alan Edward, CBE 1980; Director of Corporate Banking and Treasury, Lloyds Bank, since 1988; Director, Lloyds Bank, since 1989; *b* 5 June 1936; *s* of late Charles Edward and Ethel Florence Moore; *m* 1961, Margaret Patricia Beckley; one *s* one *d*. *Educ:* Berkhamsted Sch. AIB, ACIS, FCT. Glyn Mills & Co., then Williams & Glyn's Bank, London, 1953–74; Dir Gen., Bahrain Monetary Agency, 1974–79; Dir and Treas., Lloyds Bank Internat., 1980–84; Dir of Treasury, Lloyds Bank, 1985–88. MInstD 1988. *Recreations:* industrial archaeology, photography, steam railways. *Address:* Lloyds Bank, Faryners House, PO Box 545, 25 Monument Street, EC3R 8BQ. *T:* 071–283 1000.

MOORE, Alexander Wyndham Hume S.; *see* Stewart-Moore.

MOORE, Antony Ross, CMG 1965; *b* 30 May 1918; *o s* of late Arthur Moore and late Eileen Maillet; *m* 1st, 1941, Philippa Weigall (marr. diss.); two *d*; 2nd, 1963, Georgina Mary Galbraith (*see* G. M. Moore); one *s*. *Educ:* Rugby; King's Coll., Cambridge. Served in Friends Ambulance Unit, 1939–40; HM Forces, 1940–46. Apptd Mem. Foreign (subseq. Diplomatic) Service, Nov. 1946; transf. to Rome, 1947; FO, Nov. 1949; 1st Sec., 1950; transf. to Tel Aviv, 1952; acted as Chargé d'Affaires, 1953, 1954; apptd Consul, Sept. 1953; FO, 1955; UK Perm. Delegn to UN, NY, 1957; Counsellor and transf. to IDC, 1961; FO, 1962–64; Internat. Fellow, Center for Internat. Affairs, Harvard Univ., 1964–65; Regional Information Officer, Middle East, British Embassy, Beirut, 1965–67; Head of Eastern Dept, FO, 1967; retd from HM Diplomatic Service, Dec. 1968. Dir, Iranian Selection Trust, 1969–72. *Address:* Touchbridge, Boarstall, Aylesbury, Bucks. *T:* Brill (0844) 238247.

MOORE, Bobby; *see* Moore, Robert.

MOORE, Brian; novelist; *b* 25 Aug. 1921; *s* of James Bernard Moore, FRCS, Northern Ireland, and Eileen McFadden; *m* Jean Denney. Guggenheim Fellowship (USA), 1959; Canada Council Senior Fellowship (Canada), 1960; Scottish Arts Council Internat. Fellowship, 1983. National Institute of Arts and Letters (USA) Fiction Award 1960. *Publications: novels:* The Lonely Passion of Judith Hearne, 1955 (filmed, 1989); The Feast of Lupercal, 1956; The Luck of Ginger Coffey (Governor-Gen. of Canada's Award for Fiction), 1960 (filmed, 1963); An Answer from Limbo, 1962; The Emperor of Ice-Cream, 1965; I am Mary Dunne, 1968; Fergus, 1970; Catholics, 1972 (W. H. Smith Literary Award, 1973); The Great Victorian Collection (James Tait Black Meml Award; Governor Gen. of Canada's Award for Fiction), 1975; The Doctor's Wife, 1976; The Mangan Inheritance, 1979; The Temptation of Eileen Hughes, 1981; Cold Heaven, 1983 (filmed, 1990); Black Robe, 1985 (Heinemann Award, RSL, 1986); The Colour of Blood (Sunday Express Book of the Year Award), 1987; Lies of Silence, 1990 (filmed, 1991); *non-fiction:* Canada (with Editors of Life), 1964; The Revolution Script, 1972. *Address:* c/o Curtis Brown Ltd, 10 Astor Place, New York, NY 10003, USA.

MOORE, Brian Baden; Football Commentator/Presenter: London Weekend Television, since 1968; The Match, Independent Television, since 1988; *b* 28 Feb. 1932; *m* 1955, Betty (*née* Cole); two *s*. *Educ:* Cranbrook Sch., Kent. Sports Sub-Editor, World Sports, 1954–56; journalist: Exchange Telegraph, 1956–58; The Times, 1958–61; Football Commentator/Presenter: BBC Radio, 1961–68; Mid-Week Sports Special, Thames TV, 1978–86; Presenter, Brian Moore Meets (TV documentary series), 1979–. *Publication:* The Big Matches 1970–1980, 1980. *Recreations:* being at home, animal care, golf. *Address:* c/o London Weekend Television, South Bank Television Centre, Kent House, Upper Ground, SE1 9LT. *T:* 071–261 3434.

MOORE, Charles Hilary; Deputy Editor, The Daily Telegraph, since 1990; *b* 31 Oct. 1956; *s* of Richard and Ann Moore; *m* 1981, Caroline Mary Baxter; twin *s* and *d*. *Educ:* Eton Coll.; Trinity Coll., Cambridge (BA Hons History). Joined editorial staff of Daily Telegraph, 1979, leader writer, 1981–83; Assistant Editor and political columnist, 1983–84, Editor, 1984–90, The Spectator; weekly columnist, Daily Express, 1987–90. Trustee, Prayer Book Soc., 1989–. *Publications:* (ed with C. Hawtree) 1936, 1986; (with A. N. Wilson and G. Stamp) The Church in Crisis, 1986; (ed with Simon Heffer) A Tory Seer: the selected journalism of T. E. Utley, 1989. *Address:* 60 Ripplevale Grove, N1. *T:* 071–607 8872. *Club:* Beefsteak.

MOORE, Air Vice-Marshal Charles Stuart, CB 1962; OBE 1945; *b* London, 27 Feb. 1910; *s* of late E. A. Moore and E. B. Moore (*née* Druce); *m* 1st, 1937, Anne (*d* 1957), *d* of Alfred Rogers; 2nd, 1961, Jean Mary, *d* of John Cameron Wilson; one *d*. *Educ:* Sutton Valence Sch.; RAF Coll., Cranwell. Commissioned in General Duties Branch, Dec. 1930; served in Egypt, 1932–34 and 1936–41; Sqdn Ldr 1938; Sudan, 1941–42; Wing Comdr 1940; 11 Group, 1943–44; Gp Capt. 1943; OC, OTU, 1944–45; Gp Capt. Org., HQFC, 1945–46; Staff Coll., Bracknell, 1946–47; Dep. Dir Plans, Air Ministry, London, 1947–49; Student, US National War Coll., Washington, 1949–50; Staff of USAF Air War Coll., Alabama, 1950–53; Air Commodore, 1953; AOC 66 Group, 1953–55; Dir of Intelligence, Air Ministry, London, 1955–58; AOA, NEAF, 1958–62; Actg Air Vice-Marshal, 1960; retired, 1962. Joined HM Foreign Service, Oct. 1962; posted to British Embassy, Tehran, Iran; left HM Diplomatic Service, March 1969. *Recreations:* music, photography and travelling. *Address:* Ferndene, The Avenue, Crowthorne, Berks RG11 6PB. *T:* Crowthorne (0344) 772300. *Club:* Royal Air Force.

MOORE, Cicely Frances (Mrs H. D. Moore); *see* Berry, C. F.

MOORE, David James Ladd; Under Secretary, HM Treasury, since 1985; *b* 6 June 1937; *s* of James and Eilonwy Moore; *m* 1968, Kay Harrison; two *s*. *Educ:* King Edward VI Sch., Nuneaton; Brasenose Coll., Oxford (BA). PO, 1961–67 (Asst Principal 1961, Principal 1966); Cabinet Office, 1967–69; HM Treasury, 1969–80 (Asst Sec. 1973); Under Secretary: Cabinet Office, 1980–82; HM Treasury, 1982–83; Inland Revenue (Principal Finance Officer), 1983–85. *Recreations:* reading, theatre, tennis. *Address:* HM Treasury, 1 Parliament Street, SW1.

MOORE, Prof. Derek William, FRS 1990; Professor of Applied Mathematics, Imperial College, London, since 1973; *b* 19 April 1931; *s* of William McPherson Moore and Elsie Marjorie Moore (*née* Patterson). *Educ:* Jesus Coll., Cambridge (MA, PhD). Asst Lectr and Lectr in Maths, Bristol, 1958–64; Sen. Postdoctoral Res. Fellow, Nat. Acad. of Scis, USA, 1964; Imperial College London: Sen. Lectr, Dept of Maths, 1967; Reader in Theoretical Fluid Mechanics, 1968. Sherman Fairchild Dist. Scholar, CIT, 1986. Foreign Hon. Mem., Amer. Acad of Arts and Scis, 1985. *Recreation:* jazz tenor saxophone. *Address:* 71 Boileau Road, W5 3AP. *T:* 081–998 8572.

MOORE, Derry; *see* Drogheda, Earl of.

MOORE, Dudley Stuart John; actor (stage, films, TV and radio); composer (film music and incidental music for plays, etc); *b* 19 April 1935; *s* of late Ada Francis and John Moore; *m* 1st, 1958, Suzy Kendall (marr. diss.); 2nd, 1975, Tuesday Weld (marr. diss.); one *s*; 3rd, 1988, Brogan Lane. *Educ:* County High Sch., Dagenham, Essex; Guildhall Sch.; Magdalen Coll., Oxford (BA, BMus). *Stage:* Beyond the Fringe, 1960–62 (London), 1962–64 (Broadway, New York); Behind the Fridge, 1971–72; Good Evening, NY, 1974; Mikardo (Los Angeles, UK/LA Fest.), 1988; Vic Lewis, John Dankworth Jazz Bands, 1959–60; composed incidental music, Royal Court Theatre (various plays), 1958–60; Play it again Sam, Woody Allen, Globe Theatre, 1970; Behind the Fridge, Cambridge Theatre, 1972–73; Good Evening, Broadway, New York, 1973–74; tour of USA, 1975. *BBC TV:* own series with Peter Cook: Not only . . . but also, 1964, 1966, 1970; *series:* It's Lulu, not to mention Dudley Moore, 1973; in the sixties, *ITV:* Goodbye again; Royal Command Performance; *series:* Orchestra! (co-presenter with Sir Georg Solti), 1991. Various TV and radio guest spots with Jazz piano trio. *Films:* The Wrong Box, 1966; 30 is a Dangerous Age Cynthia, 1967; Bedazzled, 1968; Monte Carlo or Bust, The Bed-sitting room, 1969; Alice in Wonderland, 1972; The Hound of the Baskervilles, 1977; Foul Play, "10", 1979; Wholly Moses, 1980; Arthur, 1981; Lovesick, Romantic Comedy, 1982; Unfaithfully Yours, Best Defense, 1983; Mickey & Maude, 1984; Santa Claus—The Movie, 1985; Like Father Like Son, 1987; Arthur 2—On The Rocks, 1988; Crazy People, 1990. *Film music* composed for: Bedazzled, 30 is a dangerous age Cynthia, The Staircase, Inadmissable Evidence, Six Weeks, and various TV films. *Publications:* Dud and Pete: The Dagenham Dialogues, 1971, new edn 1988; Musical Bumps, 1986; The Complete Beyond the Fringe, 1987. *Recreations:* films, theatre, music. *Address:* c/o Louis Pitt, ICM, 8899 Beverly Boulevard, Los Angeles, Calif 90048, USA. *Club:* St James's.

MOORE, Rt. Rev. Edward Francis Butler, DD; *b* 1906; *s* of Rev. W. R. R. Moore; *m* 1932, Frances Olivia Scott; two *s* two *d*. *Educ:* Trinity Coll., Dublin (MA, PhD, DD). Deacon, 1930; Priest, 1931; Curate, Bray, 1930–32; Hon. Clerical Vicar, Christ Church Cathedral, Dublin, 1931–35; Curate, Clontarf, 1932–34; Incumbent, Castledermot with Kinneagh, 1934–40; Greystones, Diocese of Glendalough, 1940–49; Chaplain to Duke of Leinster, 1934–40; Rural Dean, Delgany 1950–59; Canon of Christ Church, Dublin, 1951–57; Archdeacon of Glendalough, 1957–59; Bishop of Kilmore and Elphin and Ardagh, 1959–81. *Recreations:* tennis, golf, fishing. *Address:* Drumlona, Sea Road, Kilcoole, Co. Wicklow, Ireland. *Club:* Royal Dublin Society (Dublin).

MOORE, Sir Edward Stanton, 2nd Bt *cr* 1923; OBE 1970; *b* 1910; *s* of Major E. C. H. Moore (killed, Vimy Ridge, 1917) and Kathleen Margaret (*d* 1970), *d* of H. S. Oliver, Sudbury, Suffolk; *S* grandfather, 1923; *m* 1946, Margaret, *er d* of T. J. Scott-Cotterell. *Educ:* Mill Hill Sch.; Cambridge. RAF 1940–46; Wing Cdr Special Duties; Managing Director, Spain and Western Mediterranean, BEA, 1965–72. Pres., British Chamber of Commerce in Spain, 1969–71; Dir, European British Chambers of Commerce, 1970–72. FCIT 1960. *Heir:* none. *Address:* Church House, Sidlesham, Sussex PO20 7RE. *T:* Sidlesham (024356) 369. *Clubs:* Special Forces; Chichester Yacht.

MOORE, Maj.-Gen. (retired) Frederick David, CB 1955; CBE 1954; *b* 27 Nov. 1902; *s* of Sir Frederick W. Moore; *m* 1932, Anna Morrell Hamilton (*d* 1974), *d* of Col T. H. M. Clarke, CMG, DSO; one *s*. *Educ:* Wellington Coll.; RMA Woolwich. Commnd in RFA, 1923. Served War of 1939–45: BEF 1940, 5th Regt RHA; BLA, 1944–45, CO 5th Regt RHA and CRA 53rd (W) Div.; GOC 5th AA Group, 1953–55; retd, 1956. DL Beds, 1958, Vice-Lieutenant, 1964–70. Officer Order of Crown (Belgian); Croix de Guerre (Belgian), 1940, with palm, 1945. *Recreations:* country pursuits. *Address:* Riverview, Bunclody, Co. Wexford, Ireland. *T:* Enniscorthy 77184. *Club:* Army and Navy.

MOORE, Geoffrey Herbert; Professor of American Literature and Head of the Department of American Studies, University of Hull, 1962–82, now Professor Emeritus; *b* 10 June 1920; *e s* of late Herbert Jonathan Moore, Norwich; *m* 1947, Pamela Marguerite (marr. diss. 1962), *d* of Bertram Munn, Twickenham; one *s* one *d*. *Educ:* Mitcham Grammar Sch.; Emmanuel Coll., Cambridge; Univ. of Paris. 1st Cl. English Tripos, Cambridge, 1946; MA 1951. War Service (Air Ministry and RAF), 1939–43. Instr in English, Univ. of Wisconsin, 1947–49; Vis. Prof. of English, Univs of Kansas City and New Mexico, 1948, 1949; Asst Prof. of English, Tulane Univ., 1949–51; Vis. Prof. of English, Univ. of Southern California and Claremont Coll., 1950; Extra Mural Lectr, London and Cambridge Univs, 1951–52; Editor and Producer, BBC Television Talks, 1952–54; Rose Morgan Prof., Univ. of Kansas, 1954–55; Lectr in Amer. Lit., Manchester Univ., 1955–59; Vis. Lectr, Univs of Mainz, Göttingen and Frankfurt, 1959; Rockefeller Fellow, Harvard Univ., 1959–60; Sen. Lectr in Amer. Lit., Manchester Univ., 1960–62; Dean, Faculty of Arts, Univ. of Hull, 1967–69. Visiting Professor: Univs of Montpellier, Aix-en-Provence and Nice, 1967, 1971; Univs of Frankfurt, Heidelberg, Mainz, Saarbrücken, Tübingen, 1967, 1968; Univs of Perpignan, Turin, Florence, Pisa, Rome, New Delhi, Hyderabad, Madras, Bombay, Calcutta, 1971; York Univ., Toronto, 1969–70; Univ. of Tunis, Spring 1970, 1971; Harvard, 1971; Univs of Düsseldorf, Heidelberg, Freiburg, Mainz, 1972; Univs of Teheran, Shiraz, Isfahan, Mashad, 1978; Univs of Berlin, Bremen, Osnabrück, 1981; Univs of Münster, Duisburg, Bonn, Düsseldorf, Aachen, 1982; Univ. of Göttingen, 1983; Tällberg, Sweden, 1984; Univs of Madrid, Bilbao, Barcelona, 1985; Fellow, Sch. of Letters, Indiana Univ., Summer 1970; Research Fellow: Univ. of California at San Diego, 1974; Rockefeller Centre, Bellagio, 1979. Mem. Cttee, British Assoc. for Amer. Studies, 1957–60. Sen. Scholar Award, Amer. Coun. of Learned Socs, 1965. Editor and Founder, The Bridge (Cambridge lit. mag.), 1946; reviewer, Financial Times, 1976–; Gen. Editor of Henry James for Penguin Classics, 1981–. *Publications:* Voyage to Chivalry (under pseud.), 1947; Poetry from Cambridge in Wartime, 1947; The Penguin Book of Modern American Verse, 1954; (ed) 58 Short Stories by O. Henry, 1956; Poetry Today, 1958; American Literature and the American Imagination, 1964; American Literature, 1964; The Penguin Book of American Verse, 1977, 2nd edn 1983; *edited:* Portrait of a Lady, 1984; Roderick Hudson, 1986; Daisy Miller, 1986; Selected Poems of Emily Dickinson, 1986; Selected Poems of Robert Frost, 1986; Selected Poems of Walt Whitman, 1987; Selected Poems of Edgar Allan Poe, 1988; Selected Poems of Longfellow, 1989; Selected Poems of Thomas Hardy, 1990; Selected Poems of John Keats, 1991; articles in TLS, Amer. Mercury, BBC Quarterly, Kenyon

Review, Review of English Lit., The Year's Work in English Studies, Jl of American Studies, Studi Americani and other scholarly and literary jls. *Recreations:* swimming, driving. *Club:* Savile.

MOORE, George; Chairman, Grayne Marketing Co. Ltd, since 1978; *b* 7 Oct. 1923; *s of* George Moore and Agnes Bryce Moore; *m* 1946, Marjorie Pamela Davies (*d* 1986); three *s. Educ:* University Coll. and Royal Technical Coll., Cardiff (Jt Engineering Diploma); Hull Univ. (Post Graduate Diploma in Economics). Graduate Engineer, Electricity Authority, 1948–50; Development Engineer, Anglo-Iranian Oil Co., Abadan, 1950–52; Chief Electrical Engineer, Distillers' Solvents Div., 1952–58; Management Consultant, Urwick, Orr & Partners, 1958–64; Executive Dir, Burton Group, 1964–66; Group Managing Dir, Spear & Jackson International Ltd and Chm., USA Subsidiary, 1966–75; Dir of cos in Sweden, France, India, Australia, Canada, S Africa, 1966–75; Under Sec. and Regional Industrial Dir, NW Regional Office, DoI, 1976–78; Dir, Cordel Corporate Develt Ltd, 1978–. FBIM; FInstD; MIMC. *Recreations:* golf, sailing. *Address:* Leasgill House, Leasgill, near Milnthorpe, Cumbria LA7 7ET. *Club:* Reform.

MOORE, George; Member, South Yorkshire County Council, 1974–86 (Chairman, 1978–79); *b* 29 Jan. 1913; *s of* Charles Edward Moore and Edith Alice Moore; *m* 1943, Hannah Kenworthy; two *d. Educ:* Woodhouse, Sheffield. Started work in pit at 14 yrs of age, 1927; worked in hotel business, 1930; publican in own right for several yrs, after which went into fruit and vegetable business, first as retailer and eventually as wholesaler and partner in small co. Served in RAF for short period during war. Elected to Barnsley Bor. Council, 1961: served as Vice Chm., Health and Housing Cttee, and Vice Chm., Fire and Licensing Dept; Chairman: Barnsley and Dist Refuse Disposal Cttee, 1959–64; Sanitary Cttee, Barnsley, 1963–73; first Chm., Fire Service Cttee, S Yorks CC, 1974–78. Chm., Barnsley Community Health Council, 1974–. *Recreation:* aviculture. *Address:* 34 Derwent Road, Athersley South, Barnsley, S Yorks S71 3QT. *T:* Barnsley (0226) 6644.

MOORE, His Honour George Edgar; HM First Deemster and Clerk of the Rolls, Isle of Man, 1969–74; *b* 13 July 1907; *er s of* Ramsey Bignall Moore, OBE, formerly HM Attorney-General for Isle of Man, and Agnes Cannell Moore; *m* 1937, Joan Mary Kissack; one *s one d. Educ:* Rydal School. Served in RAF, 1940–45 (Sqdn Ldr). Admitted to Manx Bar, 1930; Attorney-General for Isle of Man, 1957–63; HM Second Deemster, 1963–69; MLC; Chairman: IoM Criminal Injuries Compensation Tribunal, 1967–69; IoM Income Tax Appeal Comrs, 1969–74; Tynwald Common Market Select Cttee, 1970–74; Mem., Exec. Council Manx Museum and Nat. Trust, 1970–74; Chm. of Directors: Commercial Bank of Wales (IoM) Ltd, 1975–84; Securicor (IoM) Ltd, 1975–83; Trustee, Manx Blind Welfare Soc.; Pres., Isle of Man Badminton Assoc., 1953–72; Chm., Manx War Work Trust; Hon. County Representative of Royal Air Force Benevolent Assoc., 1948–72. *Address:* Brookdale, 8 Cronkbourne Road, Douglas, Isle of Man. *Club:* Ellan Vannin (IoM).

MOORE, George Herbert, MSc; FRPharmS; FRSC; *b* 1 June 1903; *s of* late R. Herbert Moore and Mabel Moore, Bath; *m* 1931, Dora, *d of* Frederick and Emily Blackmore, Bath; one *d. Educ:* King Edward's Sch., Bath; Bath Coll. of Chemistry and Pharmacy. FRPharmS (FPS 1928), FRSC (FRIC 1943); MSc Bristol 1953. Merchant Venturers' Technical Coll., Bristol; Lectr in Pharmaceutical Chemistry, 1929–38; Head of Science Dept, 1938–50; Vice-Principal, Bristol Coll. of Technology, 1950–54; Principal, Bristol Coll. of Science and Technology, 1954–66; Vice-Chancellor, Bath Univ., 1966–69. Vice-Pres. Royal Inst. of Chemistry, 1955–57. Hon. LLD Bath, 1968. *Publication:* University of Bath: the formative years 1949–69, 1982. *Recreations:* music, photography. *Address:* Hilcot, Horsecombe Vale, Combe Down, Bath BA2 5QR. *T:* Bath (0225) 837417.

MOORE, Mrs (Georgina) Mary, MA; Principal, St Hilda's College, Oxford, 1980–90, Hon. Fellow, 1990; *b* 8 April 1930; *yr d of* late Prof. V. H. Galbraith, FBA, and late Georgina Rosalie Galbraith (*née* Cole-Baker); *m* 1963, Antony Ross Moore, *qv;* one *s. Educ:* The Mount Sch., York; Lady Margaret Hall, Oxford (BA Modern History 1951; MA; Hon. Fellow, 1981). Joined HM Foreign (later Diplomatic) Service, 1951; posted to Budapest, 1954; UK Permanent Delegn to United Nations, New York, 1956; FO, 1959; First Secretary, 1961; resigned on marriage. Mem., Council for Industry and Higher Educn, 1986–90. A Trustee: British Museum, 1982–; Rhodes Trust, 1984–; Pilgrim Trust, 1991–. JP Bucks 1977–82. Under the name Helena Osborne has written plays for television and radio, including: The Trial of Madame Fahmy, Granada TV, 1980; for BBC Radio 4: An Early Lunch, 1980; An Arranged Marriage, 1982; Testimonies, 1990. *Publications:* (also as Helena Osborne): novels: The Arcadian Affair, 1969; Pay-Day, 1972; White Poppy, 1977; The Joker, 1979. *Address:* Touchbridge, Boarstall, Aylesbury, Bucks HP18 9UJ. *T:* Brill (0844) 238247. *Club:* University Women's.

See also J. H. Galbraith.

MOORE, Gordon Charles; Chief Executive, City of Bradford Metropolitan Council, 1974–86, retired; *b* 23 July 1928; *s of* John Edward and Jessie Hamilton Moore; *m* 1956, Ursula Rawle; one *s two d. Educ:* Uppingham; St Catharine's Coll., Cambridge (MA, LLM). Solicitor. CBIM. Legal Asst, Cambs CC, 1955–56; Asst Solicitor: Worcester CB, 1956–58; Bath CB, 1958–60; Sen. Asst Solicitor: Bath CB, 1960–63; Croydon CB, 1963–65; Asst Town Clerk, Croydon LB, 1965; Dep. Town Clerk, Bradford CB, 1965–68, Town Clerk, 1968–74. FRSA. Hon. DLitt Bradford, 1986. Silver Jubilee Medal, 1977. *Recreations:* music, railways, supporting Yorkshire County Cricket. *Address:* 22 Fern Hill Road, Shipley, W Yorks BD18 4SL. *T:* Bradford (0274) 585606.

MOORE, Sir Harry, (Henry Roderick), Kt 1978; CBE 1971; *b* 19 Aug. 1915; *er s of* late Roderick Edward Moore; *m* 1944, Beatrice Margaret, *d of* late Major J. W. Seigne; one *s one d. Educ:* Malvern Coll.; Pembroke Coll., Cambridge. Qualified as mem. of Institute of Chartered Accountants, 1939. Served War of 1939–45: North Africa, Italy, Europe; 2nd Lt Royal Fusiliers, 1939; Lt-Col, 1944. Director: Hill Samuel Group Ltd, 1949–80; Estates House Investment Trust Ltd, 1975–76; Chairman: Associated Engineering Ltd, 1955–75; Staveley Industries, 1970–79; Molins plc, 1978–86; Vice-Chm., Philip Hill Investment Trust plc, 1949–86. Chm., Bd of Governors, The London Hospital, 1960–74; Mem. Council, British Heart Foundn; Dep. Chm., Adv. Panel on Institutional Finance in New Towns, 1970–81; Chm., North East Thames RHA, 1974–84. High Sheriff of Bucks, 1966. *Address:* Huntingate Farm, Thornborough, near Buckingham MK18 2DE. *T:* Buckingham (0280) 812241; 70 Chesterfield House, Chesterfield Gardens, W1Y 5TD. *T:* 071–491 0666. *Clubs:* White's, Pratt's; Leander; Rand (Johannesburg).

MOORE, Sir Henry Roderick; *see* Moore, Sir Harry.

MOORE, Rt. Rev. Henry Wylie; General Secretary, Church Missionary Society, 1986–90; Hon. Assistant Bishop, Durham, since 1990; *b* 2 Nov. 1923; *m* 1951, Betty Rose Basnett; two *s three d. Educ:* Univ. of Liverpool (BCom 1950); Wycliffe Hall, Oxford. MA (Organization Studies) Leeds, 1972. LMS Railway Clerk, 1940–42. Served War with King's Regt (Liverpool), 1942–43; Rajputana Rifles, 1943–46. Curate: Farnworth, Widnes, 1952–54; Middleton, 1954–56; CMS, Khuzistan, 1956–59; Rector: St Margaret, Burnage, 1960–63; Middleton, 1963–74; Home Sec. and later Executive

Sec., CMS, 1974–83; Bishop in Cyprus and the Gulf, 1983–86. *Recreation:* family life. *Address:* Grosvenor House, Farnley Mount, Durham DH1 4DZ.

MOORE, Maj.-Gen. Sir Jeremy; *see* Moore, Maj.-Gen. Sir John J.

MOORE, Hon. Sir John (Cochrane), AC 1986; Kt 1976; President, Australian Conciliation and Arbitration Commission, 1973–85; *b* 5 Nov. 1915; *s of* E. W. Moore and L. G. Moore; *m* 1st, 1946, Julia Fay (*d* 1986), *d of* Brig. G. Drake-Brockman; two *s two d*; 2nd, 1988, Freda Beryl. *Educ:* N Sydney Boys' High Sch.; Univ. of Sydney (BA, LLB). Private, AIF, 1940; R of O Hon. Captain 1945. Admitted NSW Bar, 1940; Dept of External Affairs, 1945; 2nd Sec., Aust. Mission to UN, 1946; practice, NSW Bar, 1947–59; Dep. Pres., Commonwealth Conciliation and Arbitration Commn, 1959–72, Actg Pres. 1972–73. Chm. (Pres.), Aust. Council of Nat. Trusts, 1969–82; President: Nat. Trust of Aust. (NSW), 1966–69; Ind. Relations Soc. of NSW, 1972–73; Ind. Relations Soc. of Aust., 1973–74. Pres., NSW Br., Scout Assoc. of Aust., 1978–82. Hon. Vis. Prof., Univ. of NSW, 1987; Hon. Res. Associate, Univ. of Sydney, 1987. *Recreations:* swimming, reading. *Address:* 117 The Grange, McAuley Place, Waitara, NSW 2077, Australia. *T:* 4898961.

MOORE, Rt. Hon. John (Edward Michael), PC 1986; MP (C) Croydon Central since Feb. 1974; *b* 26 Nov. 1937; *s of* Edward O. Moore; *m* 1962, Sheila Sarah Tillotson; two *s one d. Educ:* London Sch. of Economics (BSc Econ). Nat. Service, Royal Sussex Regt, Korea, 1955–57 (commnd). Chm. Conservative Soc., LSE, 1958–59; Pres. Students' Union, LSE, 1959–60. Took part in expedn from N Greece to India overland tracing Alexander's route, 1960. In Banking and Stockbroking instns, Chicago, 1961–65; Democratic Precinct Captain, Evanston, Ill, USA, 1962; Democratic Ward Chm. Evanston, Illinois, 1964; Dir, 1968–79, Chm., 1975–79, Dean Witter Internat. Ltd. An Underwriting Mem. of Lloyds, 1978–. Conservative Councillor, London Borough of Merton, 1971–74; Chm., Stepney Green Conservative Assoc., 1968; a Vice-Chm., Conservative Party, 1975–79. Parly Under-Sec. of State, Dept. of Energy, 1979–83; HM Treasury: Economic Sec., June–Oct. 1983; Financial Sec., 1983–86; Secretary of State: for Transport, 1986–87; for Social Services, 1987–88; for Social Security, 1988–89. Director: Monitor Inc., 1990–. (Chm., Monitor European Exec. Cttee, 1990–.); Gartmore Investment Management, 1990–; Member: Internat. Adv. Bd. Marvin & Palmer Associates Inc., 1989–; Adv. Bd, Sir Alexander Gibb & Partners, 1990–. Mem. Council, Inst. of Dirs, 1991–. Mem. Ct of Governors, LSE, 1977–. *Address:* House of Commons, SW1A 0AA.

MOORE, Captain John Evelyn, RN; Editor: Jane's Fighting Ships, 1972–87; Jane's Naval Review, 1982–87; *b* Sant Ilario, Italy, 1 Nov. 1921; *s of* William John Moore and Evelyn Elizabeth (*née* Hooper); *m* 1st, 1945, Joan Pardoe; one *s two d*; 2nd, Barbara (*née* Kerry). *Educ:* Sherborne Sch., Dorset. Served War: entered Royal Navy, 1939; specialised in hydrographic surveying, then submarines, in 1943. Commanded HM Submarines: Totem, Alaric, Tradewind, Tactician, Telemachus. RN Staff course, 1950–51; Comdr, 1957; attached to Turkish Naval Staff, 1958–60; subseq. Plans Div., Admty; 1st Submarine Sqdn, then 7th Submarine Sqdn in comd; Captain, 1967; served as: Chief of Staff, C-in-C Naval Home Command; Capt. DI3 (Navy), Defence Intell. Staff; retired list at own request, 1972. FRGS 1942. Hon. Prof., Aberdeen Univ., 1987–. *Publications:* Jane's Major Warships, 1973; The Soviet Navy Today, 1975; Submarine Development, 1976; (jtly) Soviet War Machine, 1976; (jtly) Encyclopaedia of World's Warships, 1978; (jtly) World War 3, 1978; Seapower and Politics, 1979; Warships of the Royal Navy, 1979; Warships of the Soviet Navy, 1981; (jtly) Submarine Warfare: today and tomorrow, 1986. *Recreations:* gardening, swimming, archaeology. *Address:* Elmhurst, Rickney, Hailsham, Sussex BN27 1SF. *T:* Eastbourne (0323) 763294, 765862. *Clubs:* Naval, Anchorites.

MOORE, Maj.-Gen. Sir (John) Jeremy, KCB 1982 (CB 1982); OBE (mil.) 1973; MC 1952, Bar 1962; defence consultant; *b* 5 July 1928; *s of* Lt-Col Charles Percival Moore, MC, and Alice Hylda Mary (*née* Bibby); *m* 1966, Veryan Julia Margaret Acworth; one *s two d. Educ:* Brambletye Sch.; Cheltenham Coll. Joined RM as Probationary 2/Lt, 1947; training until 1950 (HMS Sirius, 1948); Troop subaltern, 40 Commando RM, 1950–53 (MC Malayan Emergency 1952); Housemaster, RM School of Music, 1954; ADC to MGRM Plymouth Gp, 1954–55; Instructor, NCO's Sch., RM, 1955–57; Adjt, 45 Cdo RM, 1957–59; Instr, RMA Sandhurst, 1959–62; Adjt and Company Comdr, 42 Cdo RM, 1962–63 (Bar to MC Brunei Revolt 1962); Australian Staff Coll., 1963–64; GSO2 Operations, HQ 17 Gurkha Div., 1965; Asst Sec., Chiefs of Staff Secretariat, MoD, 1966–68; HMS Bulwark, 1968–69; Officer Comdg, Officers Wing Commando Trng Centre RM, 1969–71; CO 42 Cdo RM, 1972–73 (OBE operational, NI 1973); Comdt RM School of Music (Purveyor of Music to the Royal Navy), 1973–75; RCDS 1976; Comdr 3rd Cdo Bde RM, 1977–79; Maj. Gen. Commando Forces, RM, 1979–82; Comdr, Land Forces, Falkland Islands, May-July 1982; MoD, 1982–83, retired. Col Comdt, RM, 1990–. Hon. Col, Wilts ACF, 1991–. Director-General: Food Manufacturers' Fedn, 1984–85; Food and Drink Fedn, 1984–85. Mem. Council, Cheltenham Coll.; Governor, Knighton House Sch., Blandford. Trustee, Suzy Lamplugh Trust. *Recreations:* music (no performing ability except on a gramophone), painting, sailing, hill walking. *Address:* c/o Lloyds Bank, Cox's and King's Branch, 7 Pall Mall, SW1. *Club:* Edward Bear (RMA Sandhurst).

MOORE, Sir John (Michael), KCVO 1983; CB 1974; DSC 1944; Second Crown Estate Commissioner, 1978–83; *b* 2 April 1921; *m* 1986, Jacqueline Cingel, MBE. *Educ:* Whitgift Middle Sch.; Selwyn Coll., Cambridge. Royal Navy, 1940–46. Royal Humane Society Bronze Medal, 1942. Ministry of Transport, 1946; Joint Principal Private Sec. to Minister (Rt Hon. Harold (later Lord) Watkinson), 1956–59; Asst Sec., 1959; Under-Sec. (Principal Estabt Officer), 1966; Under-Sec., DoE, 1970–72; Dep. Sec., CSD, 1972–78. Dep. Chm., Lymington Harbour Commn, 1990–. *Recreations:* sailing, walking hills and mountains. *Address:* 38 Daniells Walk, Lymington, Hants SO41 9PN. *T:* Lymington (0590) 679963. *Club:* Royal Lymington Yacht.

MOORE, Dr John Michael; JP; Headmaster, The King's School, Worcester, since 1983; *b* 12 Dec. 1935; *s of* Roy Moore, *qv; m* 1960, Jill Mary Maycock; one *s. Educ:* Rugby Sch.; Clare Coll., Cambridge (John Stewart of Rannoch Scholar, 1956; George Charles Winter Warr Scholar, 1957; 1st Cl. Hons Classical Tripos; MA; PhD 1960). Asst Master: Winchester Coll., 1960–64; Radley Coll., 1964–83; Jun. Fellow, Center for Hellenic Studies, Washington, DC, 1970–71. Hon. Fellow, Inst. for Advanced Res. in the Humanities, Birmingham Univ., 1986. JP Worcester City, 1986. Silver Jubilee Medal, 1977. *Publications:* The Manuscript Tradition of Polybius, 1965; (ed with P. A. Brunt) Res Gestae Divi Augusti, 1967, repr. with corrections 1973; (with J. J. Evans) Variorum, 1969; Timecharts, 1969; Aristotle and Xenophon on Democracy and Oligarchy, 1975, 2nd edn 1983; articles and reviews in Gnomon, Jl Soc. for Promotion of Hellenic Studies, Classical Qly, Greek, Roman and Byzantine Studies. *Recreations:* painting, gardening, travel. *Address:* 9 College Green, Worcester WR1 2LH.

MOORE, John Royston, CBE 1983; BSc, CChem, FRSC; Chairman, Bradford Health Authority, 1982–88; *b* 2 May 1921; *s of* late Henry Roland and Jane Elizabeth Moore; *m* 1947, Dorothy Mackay Hick, *d of* late Charles and Edith Mackay Hick; two *s. Educ:* Manchester Central Grammar Sch.; Univ. of Manchester (BSc Hons). War service, research and manufacture of explosives. Lecturer in schools and college, Manchester; Principal, Bradford Technical Coll., 1959–75; Sen. Vice Principal and Dir of Planning and Resources, Bradford Coll., 1975–80, retired. Chm., Wool, Jute and Flax ITB, 1981–83. Leader, Baildon Urban DC, 1965–68; Councillor, West Riding CC, until 1973; West Yorkshire MCC: Member, 1973–86; Leader, 1978–81; Leader of the Opposition, 1981–86. Dir, Yorkshire Enterprise Ltd, 1981–90. President, Yorks Conservative Adv. Cttee on Educn, 1975–89; past Chm., Conservative Nat. Adv. Cttee on Educn. Hon. Mem., and Councillor, City and Guilds of London Inst., 1977–. Hon. MA Bradford, 1986. *Recreations:* music, history, bridge. *Address:* Bicknor, 33 Station Road, Baildon, Shipley, West Yorkshire BD17 6HS. *T:* Bradford (0274) 581777.

MOORE, Jonathan Guy J.; *see* James-Moore.

MOORE, Julian Keith; Head of the Office of Civil Service Commissioners, since 1991; *b* 18 Aug. 1945; *s* of late George H. D. Moore and Amy (*née* Ashwell); *m* 1970, Susan (*née* Dand); one *s* one *d*. *Educ:* St Paul's School; New College, Oxford (Open Scholar, MA). HM Treasury, 1968; Civil Service Dept, 1969–72; Private Sec. to Minister of State, N Ireland Office, 1972–73; Civil Service Dept, 1973–77; Private Sec. to Lord Privy Seal and Leader of House of Lords, 1977–79; Assistant Secretary: CSD, 1979–82; Home Office, 1982–85; Cabinet Office (MPO), 1985–87; Civil Service Comr and Dir, CSSB, 1987–91. *Publications:* articles and reviews, Times Literary Supplement. *Recreations:* historical cryptography, walking. *Address:* Civil Service Commission, 24 Whitehall, SW1A 2ED. *T:* 071–210 3000. *Club:* Athenæum.

MOORE, Prof. Leslie Rowsell, BSc, PhD, DSc, CEng, FIMinE, FGS; Consultant Geologist; Professor of Geology, University of Sheffield, 1949–77, now Emeritus Professor; *b* 23 June 1912; *m* 1946, Margaret Wilson MacRae (*d* 1985); one *s*. *Educ:* Midsomer Norton Grammar Sch.; Bristol Univ. Univ. of Bristol, 1930–37; Lecturer and Senior Lecturer, Cardiff, 1939–46; Research Dir, Univ. of Glasgow, 1946–48; Reader in Geology, Univ. of Bristol, 1948–49. *Publications:* contributions to: Quarterly Journal Geol. Soc., London; Geological Magazine; S Wales Inst. Engineers. *Recreations:* soccer, cricket, golf. *Address:* 39 Packenham Village, Packenham Road, Edgbaston, Birmingham B15 2NE. *T:* 021–440 1692.

MOORE, Mary; *see* Moore, G. M.

MOORE, Rear Adm. Michael Antony Claës, LVO 1981; Deputy Assistant Chief of Staff (Operations) to Supreme Allied Commander Europe, since 1990; *b* 6 Jan. 1942; *s* of Lieut A. D. W. Moore, RN (killed HMS Audacity, 1941 and Agneta Moore (*née* Wachtmeister); *m* 1969, Penelope Jane, JP, *d* of Rear-Adm. F. C. W. Lawson, *qv*; one *s* three *d*. *Educ:* Wellington Coll.; RNC Dartmouth. Swedish Naval Interpreter. Joined RN, 1960; served HM Ships Gurkha, Britannia and Ashton, 1963–67; Flag Lieut to Comdr FEF, Singapore, 1967–68; i/c HMS Beachampton, 1969; qualified as Navigator, 1970; HM Ships Tenby, Brighton, Plymouth and Tartar (i/c), 1970–77; Naval Ops, MoD, 1977–79; HMY Britannia, 1979–81; Captain, 1981; Naval Asst to Chief of Fleet Support, MoD, 1981–82; i/c HMS Andromeda, and Capt. 8th Frigate Sqn, 1983–84; i/c Ops, Northwood MHQ, 1985–87; Dir, Naval Warfare, MoD, 1988–90; Rear Adm., 1990. Younger Brother, Trinity House, 1988. *Recreations:* classical music, organ, piano, windsurfing. *Address:* c/o Naval Secretary, Ministry of Defence, SW1.

MOORE, Prof. Michael Arthur, DPhil; FRS 1989; Professor of Theoretical Physics, University of Manchester, since 1976; *b* 8 Oct. 1943; *s* of John Moore and Barbara Atkinson; *m* 1967, Susan Eadington; three *s* one *d*. *Educ:* Huddersfield New Coll.; Oriel Coll., Oxford (BA 1964; DPhil 1967). Prize Fellow, Magdalen Coll., Oxford, 1967–71; Res. Associate, Univ. of Illinois, USA, 1967–69; Lectr in Physics, Univ. of Sussex, 1971–76. *Publications:* papers in scientific jls. *Recreation:* tennis. *Address:* The Schuster Laboratory, The University, Manchester M13 9PL.

MOORE, Rt. Hon. Michael Kenneth; PC 1990; MP (Lab) Christchurch North, New Zealand; Leader of the Opposition, since 1990; *b* 28 Jan. 1949; *m* 1975, Yvonne (*née* Dereany). *Educ:* Dilworth Sch.; Bay of Islands College (only Minister in Labour Govt without a degree). Worked as social worker, builder's labourer, meat freezing worker and printer; MP (Lab) Eden 1972–75 (youngest NZ MP ever elected); MP (Lab) Papanui, later named Christchurch North, 1978–; spokesperson on housing, regional, small town and community development, the environment, tourism, recreation and sport, overseas trade and marketing, external relations and trade, finance; Minister of Foreign Affairs and Trade, 1990; trade missions led incl. Japan, Europe, Soviet Union, Pakistan, Turkey; Prime Minister of NZ, Sept.–Oct. 1990. *Publications:* On Balance, 1980; Beyond Today, 1981; A Pacific Parliament, 1982; The Added Value Economy, 1984; Hard Labour, 1987. *Address:* Parliament Buildings, Wellington, New Zealand.

MOORE, Michael S.; *see* Stuart-Moore

MOORE, Michael Rodney Newton; Chairman, National Society for the Prevention of Cruelty to Children, since 1988; Chairman, Tomkins, since 1984; Managing Director, Coast Management, since 1982; *b* 15 March 1936; *s* of Gen. Sir Rodney Moore, GCVO, KCB, CBE, DSO, PMN and Olive Marion, *d* of Sir Thomas Bilbe Robinson, GBE, KCMG; *m* 1986, Jan, *d* of Paul and Lilian Adorian; one *s*. *Educ:* Eton; Magdalen College, Oxford (MA); Harvard Business Sch. (MBA). Nat. Service Commission, Grenadier Guards, 1957–59, serving in Cyprus, Lebanon (as ski instructor to Lebanese Army), UK. Called to the Bar, Gray's Inn, 1961; practised until 1964; joined Hill Samuel & Co., 1966 (Dir, 1970–71); subseq. Chm./Dir, various UK, USA & Swedish cos. Mem., Central Exec. Cttee, NSPCC, 1977– (Vice-Chm., 1981–87). *Recreations:* visiting ruins, opera, tennis. *Address:* 8 Carlos Place, W1Y 5AE. *T:* 071–491 7707. *Clubs:* Pratt's, Boodle's.

MOORE, Noel Ernest Ackroyd; Under-Secretary, Management and Personnel Office (formerly Civil Service Department), 1975–86, and Principal of Civil Service College, 1981–86, retired; Official Side Member, Civil Service Appeal Board, since 1987; *b* 25 Nov. 1928; *s* of late Rowland H. Moore and Hilda Moore (*née* Ackroyd); *m* 1954, Mary Elizabeth Thorpe; two *s*. *Educ:* Penistone Grammar Sch., Yorks; Gonville and Caius Coll., Cambridge (MA; Half-Blue for chess). Asst Principal, Post Office, 1952; Asst Private Sec. to Postmaster General, 1955–56; Private Sec. to Asst PMG, 1956–57; Principal, 1957; Sec., Cttee of Inquiry on Decimal Currency, 1961–63; Treasury, 1966; Asst Sec., 1967; Sec., Decimal Currency Bd, 1966–72; Civil Service Dept, 1972. Chm., Internat. Services Bd, 1988–, Council Mem., 1988–, RIPA. FIPM 1985; FITD 1985. *Publication:* The Decimalisation of Britain's Currency (HMSO), 1973.

MOORE, (Sir) Norman Winfrid (3rd Bt *cr* 1919; has established his claim but does not use the title); Senior Principal Scientific Officer, Nature Conservancy Council, 1965–83 (Principal Scientific Officer, 1958–65); Visiting Professor of Environmental Studies, Wye College, University of London, 1979–83; *b* 24 Feb. 1923; *s* of Sir Alan Hilary Moore, 2nd Bt; *S* father 1959; *m* 1950, Janet, *o d* of late Mrs Phyllis Singer; one *s* two *d*. *Educ:* Eton; Trinity Coll., Cambridge (MA); Univ. of Bristol (PhD). Served War, 1942–45, Germany and Holland (wounded, POW). *Publication:* The Bird of Time, 1987. *Heir:* *s* Peter Alan Cutlack Moore [*b* 21 Sept. 1951; *m* 1989, Pamela Edwards. *Educ:* Eton; Trinity Coll., Cambridge (MA); DPhil Oxon]. *Address:* The Farm House, Swavesey, Cambridge.

MOORE, Patrick Alfred Caldwell-, CBE 1988 (OBE 1968); free-lance author since 1968; *b* 4 March 1923; *s* of late Capt. Charles Caldwell-Moore, MC, and of Mrs Gertrude Lilian Moore. *Educ:* privately (due to illness). Served with RAF, 1940–45: Navigator, Bomber Command. Concerned in running of a school, 1945–52; free-lance author, 1952–65; Dir of Armagh Planetarium, 1965–68. TV Series, BBC, The Sky at Night, 1957–; radio broadcaster. Composed and performed in Perseus and Andromeda (opera), 1975, and Theseus, 1982. Pres., British Astronomical Assoc., 1982–84. Honorary Member: Astronomic-Geodetic Soc. of USSR, 1971; Royal Astronomical Soc. of New Zealand, 1983. Editor, Year Book of Astronomy, 1962–. Lorimer Gold Medal, 1962; Goodacre Gold Medal, 1968; Arturo Gold Medal (Italian Astronomical Socs), 1969; Jackson-Gwilt Medal, RAS, 1977; Roberts-Klumpke Medal, Astronom. Soc. of Pacific, 1979. Hon. DSc: Lancaster, 1974; Hatfield Polytechnic, 1989; Birmingham, 1990. *Publications:* More than 60 books, mainly astronomical, including The Amateur Astronomer, 1970, rev. edn 1990; Atlas of the Universe, 1970, rev. edn 1981; Guide to the Planets, 1976; Guide to the Moon, 1976; Can You Speak Venusian?, 1977; Guide to the Stars, 1977; Guide to Mars, 1977; (jtly) Out of the Darkness: the Planet Pluto, 1980; The Unfolding Universe, 1982; Travellers in Space and Time, 1983; (jtly) The Return of Halley's Comet, 1984; Stargazing, 1985; Exploring the Night Sky with Binoculars, 1986; The A–Z of Astronomy, 1986; TV Astronomer, 1987; Astronomy for the Under-Tens, 1987; Astronomers' Stars, 1987; (jtly) The Planet Uranus, 1988; The Planet Neptune, 1989; Space Travel for the Under Tens, 1989; Mission to the Planets, 1990; A Passion for Astronomy, 1991. *Recreations:* cricket, chess, tennis, music, xylophone playing (composer of music in records The Ever Ready Band Plays Music by Patrick Moore, 1979 and The Music of Patrick Moore, 1986). *Address:* Farthings, 39 West Street, Selsey, West Sussex. *Clubs:* Lord's Taverners; Sussex County Cricket.

MOORE, Very Rev. Peter Clement; Dean of St Albans, since 1973; *b* 4 June 1924; *s* of Rev. G. G. Moore and Vera (*née* Mylrea); *m* 1965, Mary Claire, *o d* of P. A. M. Malcolm and Celia (*née* Oldham); one *s* one *d*. *Educ:* Cheltenham Coll.; Christ Church, Oxford (MA, DPhil); Cuddesdon Coll., Oxford. FSA. Minor Canon of Canterbury Cathedral and Asst Master, Cathedral Choir School, 1947–49; Curate of Bladon with Woodstock, 1949–51; Chaplain, New Coll., Oxford, 1949–51; Vicar of Alfrick with Lulsley, 1952–59; Hurd Librarian to Bishop of Worcester, 1953–62; Vicar of Pershore with Pinvin and Wick, 1959–67; Rural Dean of Pershore, 1965–67; Canon Residentiary of Ely Cathedral, 1967–73; Vice-Dean, 1971–73. Select Preacher, Oxford Univ., 1986–87. Member: Archbishops' Liturgical Commission, 1968–76; General Synod, 1978–85; Governing Body, SPCK. Past Master, Worshipful Co. of Glaziers and Painters of Glass. Mem., Woodard Corp. Trustee, Historic Churches Preservation Trust. OStJ 1987. FRSA. *Publications:* Tomorrow is Too Late, 1970; Man, Woman and Priesthood, 1978; Footholds in the Faith, 1980; Crown in Glory, 1982; Bishops: but what kind?, 1982; In Vitro Veritas, 1985; The Synod of Westminster, 1985; Sharing the Glory, 1990. *Recreations:* gardening, music, fishing, barrel organs. *Address:* The Deanery, St Albans, Herts AL1 1BY. *T:* St Albans (0727) 52120; Thruxton House, Thruxton, Hereford. *T:* Wormbridge (098121) 376. *Club:* United Oxford & Cambridge University.

MOORE, Prof. Peter Gerald, TD 1963; PhD; FIA; Professor of Decision Science (formerly Professor of Statistics and Operational Research), London Business School, since 1965 (Deputy Principal, 1972–84; Principal, 1984–89); *b* Richmond, Surrey, 5 April 1928; *s* of Leonard Moore and late Ruby Moore; *m* 1958, Sonja Enevoldson Thomas, Dulwich; two *s* one *d*. *Educ:* King's College Sch., Wimbledon; University Coll. London (BSc (1st Cl. Hons Statistics), PhD; Rosa Morison Meml Medal 1949; Fellow, 1988). Served with 3rd Regt RHA, 1949–51, TA, 1951–65, Major 1963. Lectr, UCL, 1951–57; Commonwealth Fund (Harkness) Fellow, Princeton, NJ, 1953–54; Asst to Economic Adviser, NCB, 1957–59; Head of Statistical Services, Reed Paper Gp, 1959–65. Director: Shell UK, 1969–72; Copeman Paterson Ltd, 1978–87; Martin Paterson Associates, 1984–88; Elf Aquitaine UK (Hldgs) plc, 1989–; Partner, Duncan C. Fraser, 1974–77. Member: Review Body on Doctors' and Dentists' Pay, 1971–89; Cttee on 1971 Census Security, 1971–73; UGC, 1979–84 (Vice-Chm., 1980–83); Cons. to Wilson Cttee on Financial Instns, 1977–80. Pres., Royal Statistical Soc., 1989–91 (Mem. Council, 1966–78, Hon. Sec., 1968–74, Guy Medal, 1970); Pres., Inst. of Actuaries, 1984–86 (Mem. Council, 1966–; Vice-Pres., 1973–76); Member: Internat. Stat. Inst., 1972– (Council, 1985–); Council, Internat. Actuarial Assoc, 1984–87; Industry and Employment Cttee, ESRC, 1983–88; Jarratt Cttee on Univ. Efficiency, 1984–85; Council, Hong Kong Univ. of Science and Technology, 1986–91; Acad. Council, China Europe Management Inst., Beijing, 1986–; Univ. of London Senate, 1988–; Council, UCL, 1989–; Court, Cranfield Inst. of Technology, 1989–; Court, City Univ., 1990–; Chm., Council of Univ. Management Schs, 1974–76; a Governor: London Business Sch., 1968–89; NIESR, 1985–; Sevenoaks Sch., 1984–. Mem., Court of Assts, Tallow Chandlers' Co., 1987–. CBIM 1986. Hon. DSc Heriot-Watt, 1985. J. D. Scaife Medal, Instn of Prodn Engrs, 1964. *Publications include:* Principles of Statistical Techniques, 1958, 2nd edn 1969; (with D. E. Edwards) Standard Statistical Calculations, 1965; Statistics and the Manager, 1966; Basic Operational Research, 1968, 3rd edn 1986; Risk and Business Decisions, 1972; (jtly) Case Studies in Decision Analysis, 1975; (with H. Thomas) Anatomy of Decisions, 1976, 2nd rev. edn 1988; Reason by Numbers, 1980; The Business of Risk, 1983; articles in professional jls. *Recreations:* golf, walking, travel (particularly by train). *Address:* London Business School, Sussex Place, Regent's Park, NW1 4SA. *T:* 071–262 5050. *Clubs:* Athenæum; Knole Park Golf.

MOORE, Philip John, BMus; FRCO; Organist and Master of the Music, York Minster, since 1983; *b* 30 Sept. 1943; *s* of Cecil and Marjorie Moore; one *s* two *d*. *Educ:* Maidstone Grammar Sch.; Royal Coll. of Music (ARCM, GRSM). BMus Dunelm; FRCO 1965. Asst Music Master, Eton Coll., 1965–68; Asst Organist, Canterbury Cathedral, 1968–74; Organist and Master of the Choristers, Guildford Cathedral, 1974–83. *Publications:* anthems, services, cantatas, organ music, song cycles, chamber music. *Recreations:* flying kites, collecting old fountain pens, motor cars, gardening. *Address:* 1 Minster Court, York YO1 2JJ.

MOORE, Richard Valentine, GC 1940; CBE 1963; BSc (Eng); FIMechE; FIEE; retired; Managing Director (Reactor Group), UK Atomic Energy Authority, 1961–76; Member, 1971–76; *b* 14 Feb. 1916; *s* of Randall and Ellen Moore; *m* 1944, Ruby Edith Fair; three *s*. *Educ:* Strand Sch., London; London Univ. County of London Electric Supply Co., 1936–39. RNVR, 1939–46; HMS Effingham, 1939–40; HMS President, 1940–41; HMS Dido, 1942–44; British Admiralty Delegn, Washington, DC, 1944–46; Lieut-Comdr 1944. AERE Harwell, 1946–53; Dept of Atomic Energy, Risley, 1953; Design and Construction of Calder Hall, 1953–57; Chief Design Engineer, 1955; UKAEA, 1955; Dir of Reactor Design, 1958–61. Faraday Lectr, 1966. Hon. DTech Bradford, 1970. *Publications:* various papers to technical institutions. *Recreations:* golf, gardening. *Address:* Culleen House, Cann Lane, Appleton, Ches. *T:* Warrington (0925) 61023. *Club:* Naval.

MOORE, Robert, (Bobby Moore), OBE 1967; formerly professional footballer; Sports Editor, Sunday Sport, since 1986; *b* 12 April 1941; *m* 1962, Christina Elizabeth Dean (marr. diss. 1986); one *s* one *d.* Captained: England Youth, at 17 years old (18 caps); England Under 23 (8 caps); made 108 appearances for England (record number for England until 1989, and a world record until 1978), 90 as Captain (equalling Billy Wright's record). League debut for West Ham against Manchester United, Sept. 1958; England debut against Peru, 1962; played in World Cup, in Chile, 1962; Captained England for first time, against Czechoslovakia, 1963. Footballer of the Year, 1963–64; Holder of: FA Cup Winners' medal, 1964; European Cup Winners' medal, 1965; named Player of Players in World Cup (England the Winner), 1966; transferred to Fulham Football Club, 1974–77; played 1,000 matches at senior level. Manager, Oxford City Football Club, 1979–81; Coach: Eastern Ath. FC, Hong Kong, 1982–83; Carolina Lightnin, N Carolina, 1983; Manager and Dir, Southend United FC, 1983–86. Sports Editor, Sunday Sport, 1986–. *Publication:* Bobby Moore (autobiog.), 1976.

MOORE, Robert, CBE 1973; Commissioner for Local Administration in Scotland, 1975–78; *b* 2 Nov. 1915; *m* 1940, Jean Laird Dick; two *s.* *Educ:* Dalziel High Sch., Motherwell; Glasgow Univ. (BL). Admitted solicitor, 1939. Town Clerk, Port Glasgow, 1943–48; Secretary, Eastern Regional Hosp. Bd, 1948–60; Principal Officer: Scottish Hosp. Administrative Staffs Cttee, 1960–74; Manpower Div., Scottish Health Service, 1974–75. Lectr in Administrative Law, St Andrews Univ., 1960–65; External Examr in Administrative Law, Glasgow Univ., 1967–71. Mem., Scottish Cttee, Council on Tribunals, 1964–82. *Address:* (home) 93 Greenbank Crescent, Edinburgh EH10 5TB. *T:* 031–447 5493.

MOORE, Roger; actor; *b* London, 14 Oct. 1927; *m* 1st, Doorn van Steyn (marr. diss. 1953); 2nd, 1953, Dorothy Squires (marr. diss. 1969); 3rd, Luisa Mattioli; two *s* one *d.* *Educ:* RADA. Golden Globe World Film Favourite Award, 1980. Stage début, Androcles and the Lion. *TV series include:* Ivanhoe, 1958; The Alaskans, 1960–61; Maverick, 1961; The Saint, 1962–69 (dir some episodes); The Persuaders, 1972–73; *films include:* The Last Time I Saw Paris, 1954; The Interrupted Melody, 1955; The King's Thief, 1955; Diane, 1956; The Miracle, 1959; Rachel Cade, 1961; Gold of the Seven Saints, 1961; The Rape of the Sabine Women, 1961; No Man's Land, 1961; Crossplot, 1969; The Man Who Haunted Himself, 1970; Live and Let Die, 1973; The Man With The Golden Gun, 1974; Gold, 1974; That Lucky Touch, 1975; Street People, 1975; Shout at the Devil, 1975; Sherlock Holmes in New York, 1976; The Spy Who Loved Me, 1976; The Wild Geese, 1977; Escape to Athena, 1978; Moonraker, 1978; North Sea Hijack, 1979; The Sea Wolves, 1980; Sunday Lovers, 1980; For Your Eyes Only, 1980; The Cannonball Run, 1981; Octopussy, 1983; The Naked Face, 1983; A View to a Kill, 1985; Bed and Breakfast, 1989; Bullseye!, 1989; Fire, Ice and Dynamite, 1990. *Publication:* James Bond Diary, 1973. *Address:* c/o ICM Ltd, 388–396 Oxford Street, W1N 9HE.

MOORE, Roy, CBE 1962; *b* 10 Jan. 1908; *s* of Harry Moore and Ellen Harriet Post; *m* 1st, 1934, Muriel Edith (*d* 1959), *d* of late C. E. E. Shill; two *s*; 2nd, 1963, Lydia Elizabeth Newell Park, (*d* 1990), *widow* of David Park, Berkeley, Calif. *Educ:* Judd Sch., Tonbridge; King's Coll., London. 2nd Cl. Hons English, 1928; AKC 1928; MA 1931; Carter Prize for English Verse. Chief English Master, Mercers' Sch., London, 1931–40. Served War of 1939–45, Squadron Leader RAF Bomber Command, 1941–45. Head Master: Lawrence Sheriff Sch., Rugby, 1945–51; Mill Hill Sch., 1951–67. Fellow King's Coll., London, 1956. *Address:* 138 Santo Tomas Lane, Santa Barbara, Calif 93108, USA. *Club:* Athenæum.
See also J. M. Moore.

MOORE, Terence; Group Managing Director and Chief Executive Officer, Conoco Ltd, since 1987; *b* 24 Dec. 1931; *s* of Arthur Doncaster Moore and Dorothy Irene Gladys (*née* Godwin); *m* 1955, Tessa Catherine (*née* Wynne); two *s* one *d.* *Educ:* Strand Sch., London. BScEcon, Univ. of London; ACII 1958; AICS 1959. Shell Internat. Petroleum Co., 1948–64; Locana Corp. Ltd (investment bank), 1964–65; Conoco Ltd, 1965–: Dep. Man. Dir, Marketing and Operations, 1975; Man. Dir, Supply and Trading, Europe, 1979. FRSA. *Publications:* articles in industry jls. *Recreations:* music (Very catholic), reading (mainly biography, politics, poetry), jogging, badminton, family and friends. *Address:* 4 Oaklands Road, Groombridge, near Tunbridge Wells, Kent TN3 9SB. *T:* Langton Green (0892) 864568; 5 Gun Wharf, 130 Wapping High Street, E1 9NH. *T:* 071–481 0853.

MOORE, Thomas William, JP; Chairman (since inception) of Trojan Metals Ltd, Carseview Holdings Ltd, Dundee Timber Market Ltd, Inverlaw Property Co. Ltd; *b* 9 Aug. 1925; Scottish; *m* 1945, Mary Kathleen Thompson; four *s* two *d.* *Educ:* Stobswell Secondary Sch.; Leicester Coll. of Art and Technology. MBIM. Contested (Lab), Perth and East Perthshire, 1959. Lord Provost of Dundee, and Lord Lieutenant of County of City of Dundee, 1973–75; Chairman: Tay Road Bridge Jt Cttee, 1973; Tayside Steering Cttee. FInstD. *Recreations:* golf, reading. *Address:* 85 Blackness Avenue, Dundee. *Club:* Royal Automobile.

MOORE, Sir William (Roger Clotworthy), 3rd Bt *cr* 1932; TD 1962; DL; *b* 17 May 1927; *s* of Sir William Samson Moore, 2nd Bt, and Ethel Cockburn Gordon (*d* 1973); *S* father, 1978; *m* 1954, Gillian, *d* of John Brown, Co. Antrim; one *s* one *d.* *Educ:* Marlborough; RMC, Sandhurst. Lieut Royal Inniskilling Fusiliers, 1945; Major North Irish Horse, 1956. High Sheriff, Co. Antrim, 1964; DL Co. Antrim. *Heir:* *s* Richard William Moore [*b* 8 May 1955. *Educ:* Portora; RMA. Lieut Royal Scots, 1974]. *Address:* Moore Lodge, Ballymoney, Co. Antrim, Northern Ireland. *Club:* Army and Navy.

MOORE-BICK, Martin James; QC 1986; a Recorder, since 1990; *b* 6 Dec. 1946; *s* of John Ninian Moore-Bick and Kathleen Margaret Moore-Bick (*née* Beall); *m* 1974, Tessa Penelope Gee; two *s* two *d.* *Educ:* The Skinners' Sch., Tunbridge Wells; Christ's Coll., Cambridge (MA). Called to the Bar, Inner Temple, 1969. *Recreations:* early music, gardening, reading. *Address:* (chambers) 3 Essex Court, Temple, EC4Y 9AL. *T:* 071–583 9294; Little Bines, Witherenden Hill, Burwash, E Sussex TN19 7JE. *T:* Burwash (0435) 883284.

MOORE-BRABAZON, family name of **Baron Brabazon of Tara.**

MOORER, Admiral Thomas Hinman; Defense Distinguished Service Medals, 1973 and 1974; Navy DSM 1965, 1967, 1968, 1970; Army DSM 1974; Air Force DSM 1974; Silver Star 1942; Legion of Merit, 1945; DFC 1942; Purple Heart, 1942; Presidential Unit Citation, 1942; Board Member: Blount Inc.; Fairchild Industries; USLICO; CACI; *b* Mount Willing, Alabama, 9 Feb. 1912; *s* of Dr R. R. Moorer and Hulda Hill Hinson, Eufaula, Ala; *m* 1935, Carrie Ellen Foy Moorer; three *s* one *d.* *Educ:* Cloverdale High Sch., Montgomery, Ala; USN Acad.; Naval Aviation Trg Sch.; Naval War Coll. First ship, 1933; serving at Pearl Harbour in Fleet Air Wing, Dec. 1941; Pacific and East Indies areas, 1942; Mining Observer, C-in-C, US Fleet in UK, 1943; Strategic Bombing Survey in Japan, 1945; Naval Aide to Asst Sec. of Navy (Air), 1956; CO, USS Salisbury Sound, 1957; Special Asst to CNO, 1959; Comdr, Carrier Div. Six, 1960; Dir, Long Range Objectives Group, CNO, 1962; Comdr Seventh Fleet, 1964; C-in-C: US Pacific Fleet, 1965; Atlantic and Atlantic Fleet, and Supreme Allied Commander, Atlantic, 1965–67; Chief of Naval Operations, 1967–70; Chm., Jt Chiefs of Staff, USA, 1970–74, retired US Navy 1974. Captain 1952; Rear-Adm. 1958; Vice-Adm. 1962; Adm. 1964. Enshrined in Nat. Aviation Hall of Fame, 1987; introduced into Naval Aviation Hall of Honor, 1988. Gold Medal, Nat. Football Hall of Fame. Holds seventeen foreign decorations. Hon. LLD Auburn, 1968; Hon. DH Samford, 1970; Hon. Dr Mil. Science, The Citadel, 1983. *Recreations:* golfing, fishing, hunting. *Address:* 6901 Lupine Lane, McLean, Va 22101, USA. *Clubs:* Brook (New York); International, Army-Navy Town (Washington, DC); US Naval Inst. (Annapolis, Md); Chevy Chase (Chevy Chase, Md).

MOORES, Mrs Brian; *see* Moores, Yvonne.

MOORES, Hon. Frank Duff; Chairman, Executive Committee, Government Consultants International; Chairman and Chief Executive Officer, SSF (Holdings) Inc.; Premier of the Province of Newfoundland, 1972–79; *b* 18 Feb. 1933; *s* of Silas Wilmot Moores and Dorothy Duff Moores; *m* 1982, Beth Champion; two *s* six *d* by former marriages. *Educ:* United Church Academy, Carbonear; St Andrew's Coll., Aurora, Ont. MP, Canada, for Bonavista-Trinity-Conception, 1968–71; MHA for Humber W, Newfoundland, 1971; Pres., Progressive Conservative Party in Canada, 1969; Leader, Progressive Conservative Party, Newfoundland, 1970–79. Mem., Royal Commn on Economic Prospects of Newfoundland. Director: Council for Canadian Unity; Atlantic Salmon Fedn (Canada). Gov., Olympia Trust. Is a Freemason. Hon. LLD Meml Univ. of Newfoundland, 1975. *Recreations:* tennis, salmon fishing, golf. *Address:* Westmount, Quebec, Canada. *Clubs:* Rideau (Ottawa); Forest and Stream (Montreal); Mid Ocean (Bermuda); Hobe Sound Golf (Florida).

MOORES, Sir John, Kt 1980; CBE 1972; Founder of the Littlewoods Organisation, 1924, Chairman, 1924–77 and 1980–82, Life President, 1982; *b* Eccles, Lancs, 25 Jan. 1896; *s* of John William Moores and Louisa (*née* Fethney); *m* 1923 Ruby Knowles; two *s* two *d.* *Educ:* Higher Elementary Sch. Founded: Littlewoods Pools, 1924; Littlewoods Mail Order Stores, 1932; Littlewoods Stores, 1936. Hon. Freeman, City of Liverpool, 1970; Hon. LLB Liverpool, 1973; first winner of Liverpool Gold Medal for Achievement, 1978. *Recreations:* painting, languages, sport, travel. *Address:* c/o The Littlewoods Organisation PLC, JM Centre, Old Hall Street, Liverpool L70 1AB. *T:* 051–235 2222.
See also Baron Grantchester, Peter Moores.

MOORES, Peter, CBE 1991; Director: The Littlewoods Organization, since 1965 (Chairman, 1977–80); Singer & Friedlander, since 1978; *b* 9 April 1932; *s* of Sir John Moores, *qv*; *m* 1960, Luciana Pinto (marr. diss. 1984); one *s* one *d.* *Educ:* Eton; Christ Church, Oxford; Wiener Akademie der Musik und darstellenden Kunst. Worked in opera prodn at Glyndebourne and Vienna State Opera; sponsor of complete recordings in English of: Der Ring des Nibelungen, La Traviata, Otello, Rigoletto, Mary Stuart and Julius Caesar by ENO; Destiny (Osud) by WNO; The Cunning Little Vixen, Royal Opera; Maria Padilla, Emilia di Liverpool, L'Assedio di Calais and Il Crociato in Egitto with Opera Rara. Trustee, Tate Gall., 1978–85; Governor of the BBC, 1981–83. Hon. RNCM, 1985. Hon. MA Christ Church, 1975. Gold Medal of the Italian Republic, 1974. *Recreations:* wind-surfing, shooting, fishing. *Address:* Parbold Hall, Parbold, near Wigan, Lancs. *Club:* Boodle's.

MOORES, Yvonne, (Mrs Brian Moores); Chief Nursing Officer, The Scottish Office Home and Health Department, since 1988; *b* 14 June 1941; *d* of Tom Abraham Quick and of late Phyllis Quick (*née* Jeremiah); *m* 1st, 1969, Bruce Holmes Ramsden; 2nd, 1975, Brian Moores. *Educ:* Itchen Grammar Sch., Southampton; Royal South Hampshire Hosp. (RGN); Southampton Gen. Hosp. (RM). Ward Sister, Whittington Hosp. and Royal Hampshire County Hosp., 1964–70; Principal Nursing Officer: N London HMC, 1971–72; W Manchester, 1973–74; Dist Nursing Officer, N Manchester, 1974–76; Area Nursing Officer, Manchester AHA, 1976–81; Chief Nursing Officer, Welsh Office, 1982–88. Vice-Chm., NHS Supply Council, 1979–82; Pres., Infection Control Nurses Assoc., 1987–90. FRSH. *Recreations:* golf, bridge. *Address:* Grenelefe, Lawhill Road, Law, Lanarkshire ML8 5EZ. *T:* Lanark (0555) 72960.

MOOREY, Adrian Edward; Head of Public Relations Branch, Home Office, since 1990; *b* 4 May 1946; *s* of Edward Alfred Moorey and Lily Elizabeth Moorey; *m* 1st, 1969, Sandra Ann Jeffrey (marr. diss.); one *s*; 2nd, 1987, Lesley Nicola Hancock. *Educ:* Sir Joseph Williamson's Mathematical Sch., Rochester. Advertising and Marketing Asst, Lonsdale-Hands Orgn, 1964–67; Asst Information Officer, 1967–69, Inf. Officer, 1969–72, Home Office; Press Officer, PM's Office, 1973; Department of Employment: Sen. Press Officer, 1974–75; Chief Press Officer, 1976–81; Head of Inf., 1982–86; Dir of Inf., DTI, 1987–90. *Recreations:* cricket, golf. *Address:* The Pines, 16 Kent Road, East Molesey, Surrey KT8 9JZ. *T:* 081–979 0096.

MOOREY, (Peter) Roger (Stuart), DPhil; FBA 1977; FSA; Keeper, Department of Antiquities, Ashmolean Museum, Oxford, since 1983; Fellow of Wolfson College, since 1976; *b* 30 May 1937; *s* of late Stuart Moorey and Freda (*née* Harris). *Educ:* Mill Hill Sch.; Corpus Christi Coll., Oxford (MA, DPhil). FSA 1967. Nat. Service, 1956–58, Intelligence Corps. Asst Keeper, 1961–73, Sen. Asst Keeper, 1973–82, Ashmolean Museum, Oxford. Editor of Levant, 1968–86. Pres., British Sch. of Archaeology in Jerusalem, 1990–. *Publications:* Catalogue of the Ancient Persian Bronzes in the Ashmolean Museum, 1971; Ancient Persian Bronzes in the Adam Collection, 1974; Biblical Lands, 1975; Kish Excavations 1923–1933, 1978; Cemeteries of the First Millennium BC at Deve Hüyük, 1980; Excavation in Palestine, 1981; (ed) C. L. Woolley, Ur of the Chaldees, revd edn 1982; (with B. Buchanan) Catalogue of Ancient Near Eastern Seals in the Ashmolean Museum, II, 1984, III, 1988; Materials and Manufacture in Ancient Mesopotamia: the evidence of archaeology and art, 1985; museum booklets and articles in learned jls. *Recreations:* travel, walking. *Address:* Ashmolean Museum, Oxford. *T:* Oxford (0865) 278019, 278020.

MOORHOUSE, (Cecil) James (Olaf); Member (C) London South and Surrey East, European Parliament, since 1984 (London South, 1979–84); Vice-President, External Economic Relations Committee and co-ordinator on external economic relations for European Democratic Group, since 1989; *b* 1 Jan. 1924; *s* of late Captain Sidney James Humphrey Moorhouse and Anna Sophie Hedvig de Løvenskiold; *m* 1958, Elizabeth Clive Huxtable, Sydney, Aust.; one *s* one *d.* *Educ:* St Paul's School; King's Coll. and Imperial Coll., Univ. of London. BSc (Eng); DIC (Advanced Aeronautics); CEng. Designer with de Havilland Aircraft Co., 1946–48; Project Engr, BOAC, 1948–53; Technical Advr 1953–68, and Environmental Conservation Advr 1968–72, Shell International Petroleum; Environmental Advr, Shell Group of Companies in UK, 1972–73; Group Environmental Affairs Advr, Rio-Tinto Zinc Corp., 1973–80, Consultant, 1980–84. Dir, Project Development International, 1985–90. Contested (C) St Pancras North, 1966 and 1970. European Parliament: spokesman, 1979–84, co-ordinator, 1987–89, on transport for EDG; spokesman on external economic relations for EDG, 1984–87; Chm., delegn to N Europe and Nordic Council, 1979–84; First Vice-Chm, delegn to EFTA Parliamentarians, 1984–86. *Publications:* (with Anthony Teasdale) Righting the Balance: a new agenda for Euro-Japanese trade, 1987; numerous articles and papers on aviation. *Recreations:* walking, reading, travelling, watching cricket. *Address:* 34 Buckingham Palace Road, SW1W 0RE. *Clubs:* Royal Automobile; Croydon Conservative.

MOORHOUSE, Geoffrey, FRSL; writer; *b* Bolton, Lancs, 29 Nov. 1931; *s* of William Heald and Gladys Heald (*née* Hoyle, subseq. Moorhouse) and step *s* of Richard Moorhouse; *m* 1st, 1956, Janet Marion Murray; two *s* one *d* (and one *d* decd); 2nd, 1974, Barbara Jane Woodward (marr. diss. 1978); 3rd, 1983, Marilyn Isobel Edwards. *Educ:* Bury Grammar School. Royal Navy, 1950–52; editorial staff: Bolton Evening News, 1952–54; Grey River Argus (NZ), Auckland Star (NZ), Christchurch Star-Sun (NZ), 1954–56; News Chronicle, 1957; (Manchester) Guardian, 1958–70 (Chief Features Writer, 1963–70). FRGS 1972; FRSL 1982. *Publications:* in numerous editions and translations: The Other England, 1964; The Press, 1964; Against All Reason, 1969; Calcutta, 1971; The Missionaries, 1973; The Fearful Void, 1974; The Diplomats, 1977; The Boat and The Town, 1979; The Best-Loved Game, 1979 (Cricket Soc. Award); India Britannica, 1983; Lord's, 1983; To the Frontier, 1984 (Thomas Cook Award, 1984); Imperial City: the rise and rise of New York, 1988; At the George (essays), 1989; Apples in the Snow, 1990. *Recreations:* music, hill-walking, looking at buildings, watching cricket and both codes of Rugby football. *Address:* Park House, Gayle, near Hawes, North Yorkshire DL8 3RT. *T:* Wensleydale (0969) 667456. *Club:* Lancashire County Cricket.

MOORHOUSE, James; *see* Moorhouse, C. J. O.

MOORHOUSE, (Kathleen) Tessa; a District Judge (formerly Registrar), Family Division of the High Court of Justice, since 1982; *b* 14 Sept. 1938; *d* of late Charles Elijah Hall, MRCVS and of Helen Barbara Hall; *m* 1959, Rodney Moorhouse. *Educ:* Presentation Convent, Derbyshire; Leeds Univ.; King's Coll., London. Called to the Bar, Inner Temple, 1971. Asst, Jardine's Bookshop, Manchester, 1953–56; student, Leeds Univ., 1956–59; teacher of educationally subnormal, 1959–61; student, King's Coll., London, 1961–62; Classifier, Remand Home, 1962–64; Lectr in Law, 1964–71; barrister in practice, 1971–82. *Address:* Somerset House, Strand, WC2R 1LP. *T:* 071–405 7641; 4 Brick Court, Temple, EC4Y 9AD. *T:* 071–353 5392.

MOORMAN, Mrs Mary Caroline; *b* 19 Feb. 1905; *d* of George Macaulay Trevelyan, OM, CBE, FRS, FBA, and Janet Penrose Ward, CH; *m* 1930, Rt Rev. J. R. H. Moorman (*d* 1989). *Educ:* Berkhamsted Sch. for Girls; Somerville Coll., Oxford. BA 1926; MA 1950. Chm., Trustees of Dove Cottage, 1974–77. Hon. Lectr, Sch. of English, Leeds Univ., 1970–, and Dept of English, Durham Univ., 1980–. Hon. LittD: Leeds, 1967; Durham, 1968. *Publications:* William III and the Defence of Holland, 1672–73, 1930; William Wordsworth, A Biography: vol. 1, The Early Years, 1957, vol. 2, The Later Years, 1965 (James Tait Black Meml Prize, 1965); (ed) Letters of William and Dorothy Wordsworth, vol. II, The Middle Years: Part 1, 1806–1811, 2nd edn (rev. and ed), 1969; vol. III, The Middle Years: Part 2, 1812–1820, 2nd edn (rev. and ed with A. G. Hill), 1970; (ed) The Journals of Dorothy Wordsworth, 1971; George Macaulay Trevelyan, a Memoir, 1980. *Recreations:* country walking, bird-watching. *Address:* 22 Springwell Road, Durham DH1 4LR. *T:* Durham (091) 3863503.

MOORTHY, Arambamoorthy Thedchana; Sri Lanka Foreign Service, retired; private academic research and writing, since 1984; *b* 10 Aug. 1928; *s* of late Mr Arambamoorthy and Mrs Nesamma Arambamoorthy; *m* 1959, Suseela T. Moorthy, *d* of Justice P. Sri Skanda Rajah; one *s* two *d*. *Educ:* BAEcon Hons (Sri Lanka). Called to Bar, Gray's Inn, 1965. Entered Foreign Service of Sri Lanka, 1953; Second Secretary: Indonesia, 1955–57; China, 1957–59; First Secretary: London, 1961–63; Federal Republic of Germany, 1964–66; Chargé d'Affaires, *ai*, Thailand, and Permanent Representative of Sri Lanka to Economic Commn for Asia and Far East, 1969; Chargé d'Affaires, *ai*, Iraq, 1970; Ambassador in Pakistan, 1978–Dec. 1980, and concurrently, Jan-Dec. 1980, Ambassador to Iran with residence in Islamabad; High Comr in London, 1981–84. *Address:* 19 Caverleigh Way, Worcester Park, Surrey KT4 8DH. *T:* 081–337 2792.

MOOSONEE, Bishop of, since 1980; **Rt. Rev. Caleb James Lawrence;** *b* 26 May 1941; *s* of James Otis Lawrence and Mildred Viola Burton; *m* 1966, Maureen Patricia Cuddy; one *s* two *d*. *Educ:* Univ. of King's College. BA (Dalhousie Univ.) 1962; BST 1964. Deacon 1963, priest 1965; Missionary at Anglican Mission, Great Whale River, Quebec, 1965–75; Rector of St Edmund's Parish, Great Whale River, 1975–79; Canon of St Jude's Cathedral, Frobisher Bay, Diocese of The Arctic, 1974; Archdeacon of Arctic Quebec, 1975–79; Bishop Coadjutor, Diocese of Moosonee, Jan.-Nov. 1980. Hon. DD, Univ. of King's Coll., Halifax, NS, 1980. *Recreations:* reading, photography. *Address:* The Diocese of Moosonee, Synod Office, Box 841, Schumacher, Ontario P0N 1G0, Canada. *T:* 705–267–1129.

MOOTHAM, Sir Orby Howell, Kt 1962; *b* 17 Feb. 1901; *s* of Delmé George Mootham, ARIBA; *m* 1st, 1931, Maria Augusta Elisabeth Niemöller (*d* 1973); one *s* one *d*; 2nd, 1977, Mrs Beatrix Douglas Ward (*d* 1990), *widow* of Basil Ward, FRIBA. *Educ:* Leinster House Sch., Putney; London Univ. MSc (Econ). Called to Bar, Inner Temple, 1926 (Yarborough-Anderson Schol., 1924; Hon. Bencher, 1958). An Advocate of Rangoon High Court, 1927–40; DJAG, Army in Burma, 1940–41, thereafter service in Dept of JAG in India and as Chief Judicial Officer, Brit. Mil. Admin., Burma (despatches). Actg Judge, Rangoon High Court, 1945–46; Judge, Allahabad High Court, 1946–55; Chief Justice, 1955–61. Chm., Allahabad Univ. Enquiry Cttee, 1953–54; Legal Adviser's Dept, CRO, 1961–63. Deputy-Chairman of QS: Essex, 1964–71; Kent, 1965–71; Surrey, 1970–71; a Recorder of the Crown Court, 1972. Chm., Med. Appeals Tribunal, 1963–73; Mem. Governing Body, Froebel Educational Inst., 1965–79. *Publications:* Burmese Buddhist Law, 1939; The East India Company's Sadar Courts 1801–34, 1983; articles in Brit. Year Book of Internat. Law and other legal jls. *Address:* 25 Claremont Road, Teddington, Middlesex TW11 8DH. *T:* 081–977 1665. *Club:* Athenæum.

MORAES, Dom; Indian poet and author; *b* 1938; *s* of Frank Moraes (Editor of the Indian Express and biographer of Nehru); *m* 1970, Leela Naidu. *Educ:* Jesus Coll., Oxford. Read English, 1956–59. Took up residence in England at age of 16, after world-wide travel and a 2–yr stay in Ceylon. On loan to Govt of India from UNFPA, for a period. *Publications:* A Beginning (poems), 1957 (Hawthornden Prize, 1958); Gone Away (Travel), 1960; Poems, 1960; John Nobody (poems), 1965; The Brass Serpent (trans. from Hebrew poetry), 1964; Poems 1955–65 (collected poems), 1966; My Son's Father (autobiography), 1968; The People Time Forgot, 1972; The Tempest Within, 1972; A Matter of People, 1974; (ed) Voices for Life (essays), 1975; Mrs Gandhi, 1980; Bombay, 1980. *Recreation:* thinking. *Address:* c/o Praeger Publishers Inc., 521 Fifth Avenue, 12th floor, New York, NY 10017, USA.

MORAHAN, Christopher Thomas; television, film and theatre director; *b* 9 July 1929; *s* of Thomas Hugo Morahan and Nancy Charlotte Morahan (*née* Barker); *m* 1st, 1954, Joan (*née* Murray) (decd); two *s* (one *d* decd); 2nd, 1973, Anna (*née* Wilkinson, acting name Anna Carteret); two *d*. *Educ:* Highgate; Old Vic Theatre School. Directing for ATV, 1957–61; freelance director in TV for BBC and ITV, 1961–71; Head of Plays, BBC TV, 1972–76; National Theatre, 1977–88 (Dep. to Director, 1979–80); Director, Greenpoint Films, 1983–. *Stage:* Little Murders, RSC, Aldwych, 1967; This Story of Yours, Royal Court, 1968; Flint, Criterion, 1970; The Caretaker, Mermaid, 1972; Melon, Th. Royal, Haymarket, 1987; Major Barbara, Chichester Fest., 1988; for National Theatre: State of Revolution, Brand, Strife, The Philanderer, Richard III, The Wild Duck, Sisterly Feelings, Man and Superman, Wild Honey (London Standard, Olivier, British Theatre Assoc. and Plays and Players Awards for Best Dir of the Year, 1984); *films:* Clockwise, 1986; Paper Mask, 1990; *television: films:* The Gorge, 1967; In the Secret State, 1985; After Pilkington, 1987 (Special Jury Prize, San Francisco Film Fest., 1987, Prix Italia, 1987); Troubles, 1988; The Heat of the Day, 1989; Old Flames, 1990; Can You Hear Me Thinking?, 1990; *series:* Emergency Ward 10; The Orwell Trilogy; Talking to a Stranger; Fathers and Families; Jewel in the Crown (Internat. Emmy Award, BAFTA Best Series Dir Award, BAFTA Desmond Davis Award, 1984; Peabody Award, 1985; Golden Globe Award, Primetime Emmy Award, 1985); Ashenden, 1991. Best Play direction award, SFTA, 1969. *Recreations:* photography, bird watching. *Address:* c/o Michael Whitehall Ltd, 125 Gloucester Road, SW7 4TE. *T:* 071–244 8466. *Clubs:* Garrick, Chelsea Arts.

MORAN, 2nd Baron *cr* 1943; **Richard John McMoran Wilson,** KCMG 1981 (CMG 1970); *b* 22 Sept. 1924; *er s* of 1st Baron Moran, MC, MD, FRCP, and Dorothy (*d* 1983), MBE, *d* of late Samuel Felix Dufton, DSc; *S* father, 1977; *m* 1948, Shirley Rowntree Harris; two *s* one *d*. *Educ:* Eton; King's Coll., Cambridge. Served War of 1939–45; Ord. Seaman in HMS Belfast, 1943; Sub-Lt RNVR in Motor Torpedo Boats and HM Destroyer Oribi, 1944–45. Foreign Office, 1945; Third Sec., Ankara, 1948; Tel-Aviv, 1950; Second Sec., Rio de Janeiro, 1953; First Sec., FO, 1956; Washington, 1959; FO 1961; Counsellor, British Embassy in S Africa, 1965; Head of W African Dept, FCO, 1968–73, concurrently Ambassador to Chad (non-resident), 1970–73; Ambassador to Hungary, 1973–76, to Portugal, 1976–81; High Comr in Canada, 1981–84. Cross Bencher, H of L, 1984–; Mem., Envmt sub cttee, EC Cttee, 1986–; Vice-Chm., All Party Parly Conservation Gp, 1989–. Vice-Chm., Atlantic Salmon Trust, 1988– (Mem. Management Cttee, 1984–); Chm., Fisheries Adv. Cttee for Welsh Region, Nat. Rivers Authy, 1989–; Mem., Regl Fisheries Adv. Cttee, Welsh Water Authority, 1987–89; Pres., Welsh Salmon and Trout Angling Assoc., 1988–. Mem., Council, RSPB, 1989–. Grand Cross, Order of the Infante (Portugal), 1978. *Publications:* (as John Wilson): C. B.: a life of Sir Henry Campbell-Bannerman, 1973 (Whitbread Award, 1973); Fairfax, 1985. *Recreations:* fishing, fly-tying, bird-watching. *Heir:* *s* Hon. James McMoran Wilson [*b* 6 Aug. 1952; *m* 1980, Hon. Jane Hepburne-Scott, *y d* of Lord Polwarth, *qv*; one *s*]. *Address:* House of Lords, SW1A 0PW. *Clubs:* Beefsteak, Flyfishers' (Pres., 1987–88).

See also Baron Mountevans, Hon. G. H. Wilson.

MORAN, Rt. Rev. Monsignor John, CBE 1985; Principal RC Chaplain and Vicar General (Army), 1981–85; *b* 3 Dec. 1929; *s* of Thomas Moran and Gertrude May (*née* Sheer). *Educ:* De La Salle Coll., Sheffield; Ushaw Coll., Durham. Ordained Priest, Leeds Diocese, 1956; Curate, Dewsbury, 1956–60; Prison Chaplain, Armley, 1960–61; commissioned Army Chaplain, 1961; service in BAOR, Singapore, Malaya, Hong Kong, UK; Chaplain, RMA Sandhurst, 1968–70, Staff Chaplain, 1970–71; Senior Chaplain, HQ BAOR, 1977–79, and HQ UKLF, 1979–80. *Recreations:* music, rivers, clocks. *Address:* St Aidan's, Baildon Road, Baildon, West Yorks BD17 6AQ. *T:* Bradford (0274) 583032.

MORAN, Air Vice-Marshal Manus Francis; Senior Consultant, Royal Air Force, 1990–91; *b* 18 April 1927; *s* of John Thomas Moran and Katherine Mary (*née* Coyle); *m* 1955, Maureen Elizabeth Martin, *o d* of Martin Dilks; one *s* three *d* (and one *s* decd). *Educ:* Mount St Joseph Abbey, Roscrea; University College Dublin (MB ChB, BAO 1952; MCh 1964); DLO, RCP and RCS, 1963. St Vincent's Hosp., Dublin, 1952; GP, Lutterworth, 1953–54; joined RAF 1954; Department of Otorhinolaryngology: served London, 1955–56; Wroughton, 1956–58; Weeton, 1958–59; Akrotiri, 1959–61; Halton, 1963–65; Consultant in ORL, RAF, 1965; served Changi, Singapore, 1965–68; Vis. Consultant, Johore Bahru Gen. Hosp., 1966–68; Nocton Hall, 1968–75; Wegberg, 1975–78; Wroughton, 1978–83; Consultant Adviser in ORL (RAF), 1983–88; Dean of Air Force Medicine, 1988–90. QHP, 1988–91. Lectr in ORL, IAM Farnborough, for Dip. in Aviation medicine, RCP, 1983–88. Chm., Gen. Cttee, 8th British Acad. Conf. in ORL, 1987–91. Member: Irish Otological Soc.; Midland Inst. of Otology (Vice-Pres., 1971, 1975); Otology Section, RSM (Vice-Pres., Section of Laryngology, 1988–91, Pres., 1991–92); Council, British Assoc. of Otolaryngologists, 1983–88; Joseph Soc., BMA; BS Cttee on Auditory Alarms in med. monitoring equipment, 1983–88. Chm., Marston Meysey Charitable Trust, 1989– (Vice-Chm., 1987–89). Hon. FRCSI 1991. Liveryman, Apothecaries' Soc.; Freeman, City of London. CStJ 1990. Med. Soc. (UCD) Gold Medal, 1951; Lady Cade Medal, RCS, 1980. *Publications:* Upper Respiratory Problems in Yellow Nail Syndrome (jtly), 1976; contribs to learned jls on ORL applied to aviation medicine, ureamic rhinitis, vestibular dysfunction, acoustic trauma and hearing conservation. *Recreations:* preservation of rural amenities, walking, poetry, theology, power boating. *Address:* The Old Forge House, Marston Meysey, Cricklade, Wilts SN6 6LQ. *T:* Cirencester (0285) 810511. *Club:* Royal Air Force.

MORAUTA, Sir Mekere, Kt 1991; Managing Director, Papua New Guinea Banking Corporation, since 1983; *b* 12 June 1946; *s* of Morauta Hasu and Morikoai Elavo; *m* Roslyn; two *s*. *Educ:* Univ. of Papua New Guinea (BEcon); Flinders Univ., SA. Res. Officer (Manpower Planning), Dept of Labour, 1971; Economist, Office of the Economic Advr, 1972; Sec. for Finance, Govt of PNG, 1973–82. Director: PNG Banking Corp.; Nambawan Finance; Nat. Airline Commn; Highlands Gold (PNG); Metals Refining Operation; PNG Associated Industries; Thomas Nationwide Transport (PNG); James Barnes PNG; Resources Investment Finance; Angco; former Dir, numerous public and commercial bodies. Mem. Fund Raising Cttees, Salvation Army and Red Cross. Hon. DTech Univ. of Technology, PNG, 1987. *Publications:* numerous papers on economic and allied subjects. *Address:* PNG Banking Corporation, PO Box 78, Port Moresby NCD, Papua New Guinea. *T:* 229720.

MORAY, 20th Earl of, *cr* 1562; **Douglas John Moray Stuart;** Lord Abernethy and Strathearn, 1562; Lord Doune, 1581; Baron of St Colme, 1611; Baron Stuart (GB), 1796; *b* 13 Feb. 1928; *e s* of 19th Earl of Moray and Mabel Helen Maud Wilson (*d* 1968); *S* father, 1974; *m* 1964, Lady Malvina Murray, *er d* of 7th Earl of Mansfield and Mansfield; one *s* one *d*. *Educ:* Trinity Coll., Cambridge (BA), FLAS 1958. *Heir:* *s* Lord Doune, *qv*. *Address:* Doune Park, Doune, Perthshire. *T:* Doune (0786) 841333; Darnaway Castle, Forres, Moray, Scotland FK16 6HA. *Club:* New (Edinburgh).

MORAY, ROSS AND CAITHNESS, Bishop of, since 1970; **Rt. Rev. George Minshull Sessford;** *b* Aintree, Lancs, 7 Nov. 1928; *o s* of Charles Walter Sessford and Eliza Annie (*née* Minshull); *m* 1st, 1952, Norah (*d* 1985), *y d* of David Henry Hughes and Ellen (*née* Whitely); three *d*; 2nd, 1987, Joan Gwendoline Myra Black, *widow* of Rev. C. W. Black. *Educ:* Warbreck Primary Sch.; Oulton High and Liverpool Collegiate Schs; St Andrews Univ. (MA). Curate, St Mary's Cathedral, Glasgow, 1953; Chaplain, Glasgow Univ., 1955; Priest-in-Charge, Cumbernauld New Town, 1958; Rector, Forres, Moray, 1966. *Recreations:* Lanchester motor cars, donkey breeding, sailing. *Address:* Spynie House, 96 Fairfield Road, Inverness, Scotland IV3 5LL. *T:* Inverness (0463) 231059.

MORAY, ROSS AND CAITHNESS, Dean of; *see* Paul, Very Rev. J. D.

MORAY, Edward Bruce D.; *see* Dawson-Moray.

MORCOM, Rev. Canon Anthony John; *b* 24 July 1916; *s* of late Dr Alfred Farr Morcom and Sylvia Millicent Morcom (*née* Birchenough); *m* 1st, 1955, Pamela Cappel Bain (*d* 1963); 2nd, 1965, Richenda, *widow* of Frederick Williams. *Educ:* Repton; Clare Coll., Cambridge; Cuddesdon Coll. Curate: St Mary Magdalene, Paddington, 1939–42; St Mary the Virgin, Pimlico, 1942–47; Domestic Chaplain to the Bishop of London, 1947–55; Archdeacon of Middx, 1953–66; Vicar of St Cyprian's, Clarence Gate, 1955–66; Vicar of St Mary the Less, Cambridge, 1966–73; Rural Dean of Cambridge, 1971–73; Residentiary Canon, Ely Cathedral, 1974–84; Vice-Dean, 1981–84. *Recreation:* travel. *Address:* 33 Porson Road, Cambridge CB2 2ET. *T:* Cambridge (0223) 62352. *Clubs:* United Oxford & Cambridge University, MCC.

MORCOM, Christopher, QC 1991; *b* 4 Feb. 1939; *s* of Dr Rupert and Mary Carslake Morcom; *m* 1966, Diane, *d* of late Jose Antonio Toledo and Winifred Anne (*née* Wardlaw); one *s* two *d*. *Educ:* Sherborne Sch.; Trinity Coll., Cambridge (BA Hons 1961; MA 1964). Called to the Bar, Middle Temple, 1963 (Cert. Honour, Astbury Scholar); Barrister, Mauritius, 1979–. Mem. Senate, Law Soc. Jt Wking Party on Intellectual Property Law, 1976–. Chm., Competition Law Assoc., 1985–. *Publications:* Service Marks: a guide to the new law, 1987; legal articles in Law Soc. Gazette, Counsel, European Intellectual Property Rev. *Recreations:* music, walking. *Address:* 1 Essex Court, Temple, EC4Y 9AR. *T:* 071–936 3030. *Club:* Athenæum.

MORCOM, John Brian; a Social Security Commissioner, since 1981; *b* 31 May 1925; *s* of Albert John Morcom and Alice Maud Morcom (*née* Jones), Carmarthen; *m* 1st, 1958, Valerie Lostie de Kerhor Rivington (*d* 1960); one *s*; 2nd, 1965, Sheila Myfanwy Adams-Lewis (*d* 1986); one *d*. *Educ:* Queen Elizabeth Grammar Sch., Carmarthen; Balliol Coll., Oxford (State schol., 1943; MA). Bevin Ballottee, Oakdale Colliery, 1944; Medical Orderly, RAMC, Talgarth Mil. Mental Hosp. and BMH Suez, 1944–47. Called to the Bar, Inner Temple, 1952, Lincoln's Inn, 1955; Wales and Chester Circuit, 1954–81. *Publications:* Estate Duty Saving, 1959, 5th edn 1972; (jtly) Capital Transfer Tax, 1976, 2nd edn 1978. *Recreations:* Welsh genealogy, forestry. *Address:* Social Security Commission, Harp House, 83–86 Farringdon Street, EC4A 4DH. *Clubs:* Commonwealth Trust, London Welsh Association.

MORCOS-ASAAD, Prof. Fikry Naguib; Professor of Architecture, Department of Architecture and Building Science, University of Strathclyde, 1970–85, Professor Emeritus since 1986; *b* 27 Sept. 1930; *s* of Naguib and Marie A. Morcos-Asaad; *m* 1958, Sarah Ann (*née* Gribben); three *s*. *Educ:* Cairo Univ. (BArch); Georgia Inst. of Techn. (MArch); MIT (SM); IIT (PhD). FRIAS. Lectr in Architecture, Fac. of Engrg, Cairo Univ., 1952–54 and 1958–63; Dir of Structural Studies, Sch. of Arch., Univ. of Liverpool, 1963–70; Design Critic and Vis. Prof. in Arch. Engrg, Calif State Polytechnic Univ., 1969, 1970 and 1973; Vis. Prof. of Architecture, Assuit Univ., Egypt, 1980; Vis. Prof. of Architecture, 1985, of Architecture and Res., 1986–89, Univ. of Jordan, Amman. Research into: culture and arch.; housing design in hot, dry climates; prefabricated multi-storey housing in developing countries. Comr, Royal Fine Art Commn for Scotland, 1972–86; formerly Mem. Educn Cttee, Architects Registration Council of UK; former Member Council: Glasgow Inst. of Architects; Royal Incorp. of Architects in Scotland; Mem. Council, Glasgow Coll. of Building and Printing. Mem., Rotary International. *Publications:* Circular Forms in Architecture, 1955; High Density Concretes for Radiation Shielding, 1956; Structural Parameters in Multi-Storey Buildings under Dynamic Loading, 1956; The Egyptian Village, 1956; Architectural Construction, vol. 1 1960, vol. 2 1961; Plastic Design in Steel, 1975; Large-span Structures, 1976; Brickwork: some pertinent points, 1978; Design and Building for a Tropical Environment, 1978; Structural Systems in Architectural Configuration, 1987; Understanding Architectural Structure, 1988; various papers on structural form in architecture and on socio-cultural considerations in urban design. *Recreations:* renovation of antique clocks, gardening, reading, travelling. *Address:* Staneacre House, Townhead Street, Hamilton ML3 7BP. *T:* Hamilton (0698) 420644. *Clubs:* Rotary, Burns, Hamilton Civic Society (Hamilton).

MORDA EVANS, Raymond John; *see* Evans.

MORDAUNT, Sir Richard (Nigel Charles), 14th Bt *cr* 1611; (does not use the title at present); *b* 12 May 1940; *s* of Lt-Col Sir Nigel John Mordaunt, 13th Bt, MBE, and Anne (*d* 1980), *d* of late Arthur F. Tritton; *S* father, 1979; *m* 1964, Myriam Atchia; one *s* one *d*. *Educ:* Wellington. *Heir: s* Kim John Mordaunt, *b* 11 June 1966.

MORDUE, Richard Eric; Director of Economics and Statistics, Ministry of Agriculture, Fisheries and Food, since 1989; *b* 14 June 1941; *s* of Ralph Yielder Mordue and Helen Mary Mordue; *m* 1979, Christine Phillips; one *s* one *d*. *Educ:* Royal Grammar Sch., Newcastle upon Tyne; King's Coll., Univ. of Durham (BSc); Michigan State Univ. (MS). Joined MAFF as Asst Economist, 1964; Sen. Economic Advr, 1978; Head of Horticulture Div., 1982. *Recreations:* golf, bridge. *Address:* Ministry of Agriculture, Fisheries and Food, 3 Whitehall Place, SW1A 2HH. *T:* 071–270 8539.

MORE, Norman, FRICS; Consultant Chartered Surveyor, 1985–91; *b* 20 Dec. 1921; *s* of Herbert and Anna More; *m* 1952, Kathleen Mary Chrystal; two *s* one *d*. *Educ:* Royal High Sch., Edinburgh; Edinburgh Univ. FRICS 1970 (ARICS 1951). Served in Royal Engineers, Middle East, N Africa, Italy, Greece and Germany, Major, 1941–48. Surveyor, Directorate of Lands and Accommodation, Min. of Works, 1948–58; Sen. Valuer, City Assessor's Office, Glasgow Corporation, 1958–63; Valuation and Estates Officer, East Kilbride Development Corp., 1963–65; Redditch Development Corporation: Chief Estates Officer, 1965–79; Man. Dir, 1979–85. Consultant to Grimley J. R. Eve, London and Birmingham, 1985–90. Mem., W Midlands Regl Bd, TSB Gp, 1984–89. Chairman, West Midlands Br., Royal Instn of Chartered Surveyors, 1974–75. *Publications:* press articles and contribs to jls. *Recreations:* music, sport. *Address:* Mead Cottage, 192 Loxley Road, Stratford-upon-Avon, Warwickshire CV37 7DU. *T:* Stratford-upon-Avon (0789) 293763. *Club:* East India, Devonshire, Sports and Public Schools.

MORE-MOLYNEUX, James Robert, OBE 1983; Vice Lord Lieutenant of Surrey, since 1983; Chairman, Loseley Co-Partnership & Loseley Park Farms; *b* 17 June 1920; *s* of Brig. Gen. Francis Cecil More-Molyneux-Longbourne, CMG, DSO and Gwendoline Carew More-Molyneux; *m* 1948, Susan Bellinger; one *s*. *Educ:* Eton; Trinity Hall, Cambridge. War service in 4/7th Royal Dragoon Guards and 14th PWO The Scinde Horse, 1941–46; Founder Chm., Guildway Ltd, 1947–85 (introduced first manufactured timber frame houses with brick cladding to UK, 1960); founded Loseley Co-Partnership, 1950; opened Loseley House to public, 1950–; founded Loseley Dairy Products, 1967; part-time Dir, Seeboard, 1975–84. Founder: Loseley & Guildway Charitable Trust, 1973; Loseley Christian Trust, 1983. Mem. Exec. Cttee, Industrial Participation Assoc., 1952–77; Patron, Surrey Assoc. of Youth Clubs. Lay Pastoral Asst, 1986–. High Sheriff of Surrey, 1974; DL Surrey 1976. Bledisloe Gold Medal for Landowners, RASE, 1984. *Recreations:* countryside, riding, Christian Healing Ministry. *Address:* Loseley Park, Guildford, Surrey GU3 1HS. *T:* Guildford (0483) 304440. *Club:* Farmers'.

MOREAU, Jeanne; Officier, Ordre National du Mérite, 1988 (Chevalier, 1970); Chevalier de la Légion d'Honneur, 1975; actress; *b* 23 Jan. 1928; *d* of Anatole-Désiré Moreau and Kathleen Moreau (*née* Buckley); *m* 1949, Jean-Louis Richard (marr. diss.); one *s*; *m* 1977, William Friedkin (marr. diss.). *Educ:* Collège Edgar-Quinet; Conservatoire national d'art dramatique. *Theatre:* Comédie Française, 1948–52; Théâtre National Populaire, 1953; Le Récit de la Servante Zerline, 1986–89; La Celestine, 1989. Over 60 *films* including: Les amants, 1958; Les liaisons dangereuses, 1959; Le dialogue des Carmelites, 1959; Moderato cantabile, 1960; Jules et Jim, 1961; La Baie des Anges, 1962; Journal d'une femme de chambre, 1963; Viva Maria, 1965; Mademoiselle, 1965; The Sailor from Gibraltar, 1965; The Immortal Story, 1966; Great Catherine, 1967; The Bride wore Black, 1967; Monte Walsh, 1969; Chère Louise, 1971; Nathalie Granger, 1972; La Race des Seigneurs, 1974; Mr Klein, 1976; Lumière (also Dir), 1976; Le Petit Théâtre de Jean Renoir, 1976; Madame Rosa, 1978; L'Intoxe, 1980; Querelle, La Truite, 1982; L'Arbre, 1983; Sauve-toi Lola, Le Paltoquet, Le Miracule, 1986; La Nuit de l'Ocean, 1987; Ennemonde, 1988; Jour après Jour, 1988; Nikita, 1989; La Comédie d'un Jour, 1989; Anna Karamazoff, 1989; *television* plays and series: Huis Clos, BBC, 1984; The Last Seance, Granada, 1984; Le Tiroir Secret, 1985. Commandeur des Arts et des Lettres, 1985 (Chevalier, 1966). *Recreation:* reading. *Address:* c/o Agents Associés Georges Beaume, 4 rue de Ponthieu, 75008 Paris, France.

MORELAND, Robert John; management consultant; Member, Economic and Social Committee, European Community, since 1986; Chairman, Regional Policy and Town and Country Planning Section, since 1990; *b* 21 Aug. 1941; *s* of Samuel John Moreland and late Norah Mary, (Molly) (*née* Haines). *Educ:* Glasgow Acad.; Dean Close Sch., Cheltenham; Univ. of Nottingham (BA Econs); Inst. of World Affairs, Conn, and Warwick Univ. (postgrad. work). Civil Servant, Govt of NS, Canada, 1966–67, Govt of NB, 1967–72; Sen. Economist, W Central Scotland Planning Study, 1972–74; Management Consultant, Touche Ross and Co., London, 1974–; Consultant: Westminster and City Conferences Ltd, 1985–; Strategy Network Internat., 1988–. Mem. for Knightsbridge, Westminster City Council, 1990–. Contested (C) Pontypool, Oct. 1974; Mem. (C) Staffs, European Parlt, 1979–84, contested same seat, 1984; Chm., Eur. Cttee, Bow Gp, 1977–78; Vice-Chm., Conservative Gp for Europe, 1985–88. *Publications:* contrib. to Crossbow. *Recreations:* tennis, skiing, watching cricket and Rugby, golf. *Address:* 7 Vauxhall Walk, SE11 5JT. *T:* 071–582 2613. *Clubs:* Carlton, Royal Automobile.

MORETON, family name of **Earl of Ducie.**

MORETON, Lord; David Leslie Moreton; *b* 20 Sept. 1951; *s* and *heir* of 6th Earl of Ducie, *qv*; *m* 1975, Helen, *er d* of M. L. Duchesne; one *s* one *d*. *Educ:* Cheltenham College; Wye Coll., London Univ. (BSc 1973). *Heir: s* Hon. James Berkeley Moreton, *b* 6 May 1981. *Address:* Talbots End Farm, Cromhall, Glos.

MORETON, Sir John (Oscar), KCMG 1978 (CMG 1966); KCVO 1976; MC 1944; HM Diplomatic Service, retired; Gentleman Usher of the Blue Rod, Order of St Michael and St George, since 1979; *b* 28 Dec. 1917; *s* of Rev. C. O. Moreton; *m* 1945, Margaret Katherine, *d* of late Sir John Fryer, KBE, FRS; three *d*. *Educ:* St Edward's Sch., Oxford; Trinity Coll., Oxford (MA). War Service with 99th (Royal Bucks Yeomanry) Field Regt RA, 1939–46: France, Belgium, 1940; India, Burma, 1942–45. Colonial Office, 1946; Private Sec. to Perm. Under-Sec. of State, 1949–50; seconded to Govt of Kenya, 1953–55; Private Sec. to Sec. of State for Colonies (Rt Hon. Alan Lennox-Boyd), 1955–59; transf. to CRO, 1960; Counsellor, British High Commn, Lagos, 1961–64; IDC 1965; Asst Under-Sec. of State, CRO, 1965–66, CO 1966–68, FCO 1968–69; Ambassador to Vietnam, 1969–71; High Comr, Malta, 1972–74; Dep. Perm. Representative, with personal rank of Ambassador, UK Mission to UN, NY, 1974–75; Minister, British Embassy, Washington, 1975–77. Dir, Wates Foundn, 1978–87. Governor, St Edward's Sch., Oxford, 1980–. Hon. DL Hanover Coll., Indiana, 1976. *Recreations:* most outdoor activities, formerly athletics (Oxford Blue and International, 880 yds, 1939). *Address:* Woodside House, Woodside Road, Cobham, Surrey KT11 2QR. *Club:* Army and Navy.

MOREY, Anthony Bernard Nicholas; HM Diplomatic Service; Ambassador to Mongolia, since 1991; *b* 6 Dec. 1936; *s* of late Bernard Rowland Morey and Madeleine Morey; *m* 1961, Agni Campbell Kerr; two *s* one *d*. *Educ:* Wimbledon Coll. Nat. service, 1955–57. FO, 1957–60; Kuwait, 1960–62; FO, 1962–65; Madras, 1965–66; FO, 1966; Tehran, 1967; Kabul, 1968–71; FCO, 1971–72; Washington, 1972–76; Zagreb, 1976–80; Lagos, 1980–83; seconded to Guinness Mahon, 1983–85; Counsellor and Consul General, Moscow, 1985–88; Dep. High Comr, Madras, 1989–91. *Recreations:* gardening, music, cats. *Address:* c/o Foreign and Commonwealth Office, SW1A 2AH; The Coach House, Nutcombe Lane, Hindhead, Surrey. *Club:* Commonwealth Trust.

MORGAN; *see* Elystan-Morgan.

MORGAN; *see* Vaughan-Morgan, family name of Baron Reigate.

MORGAN, Rt. Rev. Alan Wyndham; *see* Sherwood, Bishop Suffragan of.

MORGAN, Anthony Hugh, CMG 1990; HM Diplomatic Service, retired; Consul-General, Zürich, Director of British Export Promotion in Switzerland and Consul-General, Liechtenstein, 1988–91; *b* 27 March 1931; *s* of late Cyril Egbert Morgan and Muriel Dorothea (*née* Nash); *m* 1957, Cicely Alice Voysey; two *s* one *d*. *Educ:* King's Norton Grammar Sch.; Birmingham Univ. (BA 1952). Served HM Forces (RAF Educn Br.), 1952–55. Joined HM Foreign (later Diplomatic) Service, 1956; Cairo, then Cyprus, 1956; Khartoum, 1957; FO, 1959; Saigon, 1962; Second Sec., 1963; UK Delegn to NATO, 1965; First Sec., 1968; FCO, 1969; First Sec. and Head of Chancery, Calcutta, 1973; FCO, 1976; Dep. Head of Inf. Policy Dept, 1977; Counsellor: (Information), Brussels, 1977–79; (Commercial), Copenhagen, 1979–82; Vienna, 1982–88. Comdr, Order of Dannebrog, Denmark, 1979. *Recreations:* listening to music, looking at pictures. *Club:* Royal Air Force.

MORGAN, Arthur William Crawford, (Tony Morgan); Non-executive Director, Alexander Corporation, since 1990; *b* 24 Aug. 1931; *s* of Arthur James and Violet Morgan; *m* 1955, Valerie Anne Williams; three *s*. *Educ:* Hereford High Sch.; Westcliff High Sch. Governor, BBC, 1972–77. Sailed Olympic Games, Tokyo; Silver Medal, Flying Dutchman, 1964; Jt Yachtsman of the Year, 1965; Member: British Olympic Yachting Appeal, 1970; Royal Yachting Assoc. Council, 1968–72. Chm., Hunger Project Trust, 1984–89. FRSA. *Publications:* various technical papers. *Recreations:* squash, skiing, sailing. *Address:* Bovingdon, Marlow Common, Bucks SL7 2QR. *T:* Marlow (0628) 890654; 16 Upper Wimpole Street, W1. *T:* 071–486 0674/2597; Haus Arbgrat, Zermatt, Switzerland. *T:* 672395. *Club:* Royal Thames Yacht.

MORGAN, Bill; *see* Morgan, J. W. H.

MORGAN, Rear-Adm. Brinley John, CB 1972; *b* 3 April 1916; *s* of Thomas Edward Morgan and Mary Morgan (*née* Parkhouse); *m* 1945, Margaret Mary Whittles; three *s*. *Educ:* Abersychan Grammar Sch.; University Coll., Cardiff (BSc 1937). Entered Royal Navy as Instr Lt, 1939. Served War of 1939–45: Cruisers Emerald and Newcastle, 1939–41; Aircraft Carrier Formidable, 1941–43; Naval Weather Service (Admty

Forecast Section), 1943–45. Staff of C-in-C Medit., 1945–48; HQ, Naval Weather Service, 1948–50; Staff of Flag Officer Trg Sqdn in HM Ships Vanguard, Indefatigable and Implacable, 1950–52; Instr Comdr, 1951; Lectr, RN Coll., Greenwich, 1952–54; Headmaster, RN Schools, Malta, 1954–59; Instr Captain, 1960; Staff of Dir, Naval Educn Service, 1959–61 and 1963–64; Sen. Officers' War Course, 1961; HMS Ganges, 1961–63; Dean, RN Engineering Coll., Manadon, 1964–69; Instr Rear-Adm., 1970; Dir, Naval Educn Service, 1970–75, retired. *Address:* 11 Selwyn House, Manor Fields, Putney Hill, SW15. *T:* 081–789 3269.

MORGAN, Bruce; Stipendiary Magistrate for West Midlands, since 1989; *b* 30 March 1945; *s* of Francis William Morgan, DFC, and Phyllis Marie Morgan; *m* 1988, Sandra Joy Beresford; twin *d. Educ:* Oswestry School. Solicitor of Supreme Court. Articled Clerk, Stourbridge, Worcs, 1964–69; Asst Solicitor, London, SE10, 1969–72; Partner with Lickfolds Wiley & Powles, 1973–86. Member: London Criminal Courts Solicitors Assoc. Cttee, 1971–73; Criminal Law Cttee, Westminster Law Soc., 1981–86; No 14 Area Regl Duty Solicitors Cttee, 1986–87; Metropolitan Stipendiary Magistrate, 1987–89. Member: British Acad. of Forensic Sci., 1970; Legal Medico Soc., 1970–. Chm., Greenwich Round Table, 1983–84. *Publications:* various articles in legal journals. *Recreations:* tennis, cricket, gardening, sheep husbandry, attending auctions, study of British birds and butterflies. *Address:* c/o Birmingham Magistrates' Court, Steelhouse Lane, Birmingham B6 6QJ.

MORGAN, Rev. Chandos Clifford Hastings Mansel, CB 1973; MA; Rector, St Margaret Lothbury, City of London, 1983–89; retired; *b* 12 Aug. 1920; *s* of Llewelyn Morgan, Anglesey; *m* 1946, Dorothy Mary (*née* Oliver); one *s. Educ:* Stowe; Jesus Coll., Cambridge (MA); Ridley Hall, Cambridge. Curate of Holy Trinity, Tunbridge Wells, 1944–51; staff of Children's Special Service Mission, 1947–51; Chaplain, RN, 1951; served in HM Ships: Pembroke, 1951; Vengeance and Ceylon, 1952; Drake, 1954; Theseus, 1956; Ocean, 1957; Caledonia, 1958; Adamant, 1960; Jufair, 1961; Heron, 1963; Ark Royal, 1965; Collingwood, 1967; Royal Arthur, 1969; Chaplain of the Fleet and Archdeacon of the Royal Navy, 1972–75; QHC 1972–75; Chaplain, Dean Close Sch., Cheltenham, 1976–83. *Recreations:* riding, shooting, sailing, gardening, etc. *Address:* Westwood Farmhouse, West Lydford, Somerton, Somerset TA11 7DL. *T:* Wheathill (096324) 301.

MORGAN, Rear-Adm. Charles Christopher; Naval Secretary, since 1990; *b* 11 March 1939; *s* of late Captain Horace Leslie Morgan, GMG, DSO, RN and Kathleen Hilda Morgan; *m* 1970, Susan Caroline Goodbody; three *d. Educ:* Clifton College; BRNC Dartmouth. MRIN 1989. Joined RN, 1957; served Brunei, 1962–66; HMS Greatford in Comd, 1966; Specialist Navigation Course, 1967; HMS Eskimo in Comd, 1976; NDC 1978; Comdr Sea Training, 1979; MoD, 1981–83; RCDS, 1984; Captain 5th Destroyer Sqdn (HMS Southampton), 1985–87; Staff, Jt Service Defence Coll., 1987–89. Younger Brother of Trinity House, 1977. FBIM. *Recreations:* golf, tennis, wine, gardening. *Address:* c/o Lloyds Bank, 75 Cheap Street, Sherborne, Dorset. *Clubs:* Army and Navy, Lansdowne; Royal North Devon Golf, Sherborne Golf.

MORGAN, Clifford Isaac, CVO 1986; OBE 1977; Head of Outside Broadcasts Group, BBC Television, 1975–87; *b* 7 April 1930; *m* 1955, Nuala Martin; one *s* one *d. Educ:* Tonyrefail Grammar School, South Wales. Played International Rugby Union for Wales, British Lions and Barbarians. Joined BBC, 1958, as Sports Organiser, Wales; Editor, Sportsview and Grandstand, 1961–64; Producer, This Week, 1964–66; freelance writer and broadcaster, 1966–72; Editor, Sport Radio, 1972–74; Head of Outside Broadcasts, Radio, 1974–75. President: London Glamorgan Soc., 1974–; Welsh Sports Assoc. for Mental Handicap, 1988–; Welsh Pres., Cystic Fibrosis Res. Trust, 1987–; Vice-President: Sequal, 1976–; Nat. Children's Home, 1987–. Chm., Saints and Sinners Club, 1984–85. Hon. Fellow, Polytechnic of Wales, 1989. Hon. MA Wales, 1988; DUniv Keele, 1989. *Recreation:* music. *Address:* 34 Kensington Mansions, Trebovir Road, SW5.

MORGAN, Cyril Dion, OBE 1970; TD 1945; FCIS; Secretary, Institution of Structural Engineers, 1961–82; *b* 30 Aug. 1917; *y s* of late Robert Dymant Morgan and of Nell (*née* Barrett); *m* 1948, Anthea Grace Brown; two *d. Educ:* Sloane Sch., Chelsea; City of London Coll. Served War, North Africa, Italy, 1939–46. Secretary: Inst. of Road Transport Engineers, 1948–53; British Road Fedn, 1953–61. Hon. Fellow, IStructE, 1983. FRSA. *Publications:* articles/reports in Proc. Instn of Structural Engrs. *Recreation:* thinking about gardening. *Address:* 12 Bartholomew Way, Westminster Park, Chester CH4 7RJ. *T:* Chester (0244) 675260.

MORGAN, (David) Dudley; retired from Theodore Goddard & Co., Solicitors, 1983; *b* 23 Oct. 1914; *y s* of Thomas Dudley Morgan; *m* 1948, Margaret Helene, *o d* of late David MacNaughton Duncan, Loanhead, Midlothian; two *d. Educ:* Swansea Grammar Sch.; Jesus Coll., Cambridge (MA, LLM). War Service with RAF in Intell. Br., UK, 1940–42 and Legal Br., India, 1942–46; Wing Comdr 1945. Admitted Solicitor, 1939, with Theodore Goddard & Co.; Partner 1948; Senior Partner, 1974–80; Consultant, 1980–83. An Underwriting Member of Lloyd's. *Recreation:* gardening. *Address:* St Leonard's House, St Leonard's Road, Nazeing, Waltham Abbey, Essex EN9 2HG. *T:* Nazeing (099289) 2124. *Club:* Carlton.

MORGAN, David Gethin; County Treasurer, Avon County Council, since 1973; *b* 30 June 1929; *s* of Edgar and Ethel Morgan; *m* 1955, Marion Brook. *Educ:* Jesus Coll., Oxford (MA Hons English). IPFA, FInstAM(Dip). Graduate Accountancy Asst, Staffordshire CC, 1952–58; Computer Systems Officer, Sen. O&M Officer, Cheshire CC, 1958–62; County Management Services Officer, Durham CC, 1962–65; Leicestershire CC: Asst County Treasurer, 1965–68; Dep. County Treasurer, 1968–73. Chm., Local Govt Finance Exec., CIPFA, 1987–; Pres., Soc. of County Treasurers in England and Wales, 1988–89. Hon. Freeman, City of London, 1989. *Publication:* Vol. XV Financial Information Service (IPFA). *Recreations:* local history, church architecture, tai chi. *Address:* 6 Wyecliffe Road, Henleaze, Bristol, Avon BS9 4NH. *T:* Bristol (0272) 629640.

MORGAN, David Glyn; His Honour Judge Glyn Morgan; a Circuit Judge, since 1984; *b* 31 March 1933; *s* of late Dr Richard Glyn Morgan, MC, and Nancy Morgan; *m* 1959, Ailsa Murray Strang; three *d. Educ:* Mill Hill Sch.; Merton Coll., Oxford (MA). Called to Bar, Middle Temple, 1958; practised Oxford Circuit, 1958–70; Wales and Chester Circuit, 1970–84. A Recorder of the Crown Court, 1974–84. 2nd Lieut, The Queen's Bays, 1955; Dep. Col, 1st The Queen's Dragoon Guards, 1976. An Hon. Pres., Royal Nat. Eisteddfod of Wales, Casnewydd, 1988. *Recreations:* fishing, Rugby football, gardening. *Address:* 2 Harcourt Buildings, Temple, EC4Y 9DB. *T:* 071–353 8549; 30 Park Place, Cardiff. *T:* Cardiff (0222) 398421. *Clubs:* Cavalry and Guards; Cardiff and County (Cardiff); Newport and County (Newport).

MORGAN, Sir David John H.; *see* Hughes-Morgan.

MORGAN, David Thomas; Chief Executive, Black Country Development Corporation, since 1987; *b* 22 Jan. 1946; *s* of Janet Catherine and Noel David Morgan; *m* 1968, Quita Valentine; two *d. Educ:* Alleyne's Grammar School, Stevenage; Univ. of Newcastle upon Tyne (BA Hons Land Use Studies 1968). MRTPI 1971. Somerset CC, 1968–70; Worcs CC, 1970–71; Peterborough Develt Corp., 1971–81; Housing Develt Manager, 1981–85, Dir, Planning Services, 1985–87, LDDC. *Recreations:* Rugby football, drama. *Address:* 3 Riverside Court, Caunsall, near Kidderminster, Worcs. *T:* Kidderminster (0562) 851688.

MORGAN, Rev. Dewi, (David Lewis); Rector, St Bride's Church, Fleet Street, EC4, 1962–84; a Prebendary of St Paul's Cathedral, 1976–84, now Prebendary Emeritus; *b* 5 Feb. 1916; *s* of David and Anne Morgan; *m* 1942, Doris, *d* of Samuel and Ann Povey; two *d. Educ:* Lewis Sch., Pengam; University Coll. Cardiff (BA); St Michael's Coll., Llandaff. Curate: St Andrew's, Cardiff, 1939–43; Aberdare, 1943–46; Aberavon, 1946–50. Soc. for the Propagation of the Gospel: Press Officer, 1950–52, Editorial and Press Sec., 1952–62; Editor, St Martin's Review, 1953–55; Associate Editor: Church Illustrated, 1955–67; Anglican World, 1960–67; Priest-in-charge, St Dunstan-in-the-West, 1978–80. Hon. FIPR 1984. Publicity Club of London Cup for services to advertising, 1984. Freeman of City of London, 1963. *Publications:* Expanding Frontiers, 1957; The Bishops Come to Lambeth, 1957; Lambeth Speaks, 1958; The Undying Fire, 1959; (ed) They Became Anglicans, 1959; 1662 And All That, 1961; But God Comes First, 1962; Agenda for Anglicans, 1963; Seeds of Peace, 1965; Arising From the Psalms, 1965; (ed) They Became Christians, 1966; God and Sons, 1967; The Church in Transition, 1970; The Phoenix of Fleet Street, 1973; Where Belonging Begins, 1988. *Recreation:* sleeping. *Address:* 217 Rosendale Road, West Dulwich, SE21 8LW. *T:* 081–670 1308. *Club:* Athenæum.

MORGAN, Douglas; IPFA; County Treasurer, Lancashire County Council, since 1985; *b* 5 June 1936; *s* of late Douglas Morgan and of Margaret Gardner Morgan; *m* 1960, Julia (*née* Bywater); two *s. Educ:* High Pavement Grammar Sch., Nottingham. IPFA 1963 (4th place in final exam. and G. A. Johnston (Dundee) Prize). Nat. Service, RAF, 1954–56. Nottingham CBC, 1952–61; Herefordshire CC, 1961–64; Berkshire CC, 1964–67; Asst Co. Treas., W Suffolk CC, 1967–70; Asst, later Dep., Co. Treas., Lindsey CC, 1970–73; Dep. Co. Treas., Lancashire CC, 1973–85. Chm., NW & N Wales Region, CIPFA, 1985–86; Pres., NW & N Wales Region, Students' Soc., CIPFA, 1989–90. Treas., Lancs Cttee, Royal Jubilee & Prince's Trust, 1985–; Hon. Treasurer: Lancs Playing Fields Assoc., 1985–; NW Region Library System and NW Sound Archive, 1986–. FRSA. *Publications:* articles for Public Finance & Accountancy and other local govt jls. *Recreations:* golf and "collecting" golf courses, jazz, playing "gypsy" in a motor caravan. *Address:* 8 Croyde Road, St Annes-on-Sea, Lancs FY8 1EX. *T:* (home) St Annes (0253) 725808; (office) Preston (0772) 264701. *Club:* Fairhaven Golf.

MORGAN, Dudley; *see* Morgan, David D.

MORGAN, Prof. Edwin (George), OBE 1982; Titular Professor of English, University of Glasgow, 1975–80, now Emeritus; *b* 27 April 1920; *s* of Stanley Lawrence Morgan and Margaret McKillop Arnott. *Educ:* Rutherglen Academy; High Sch. of Glasgow; Univ. of Glasgow. MA 1st Cl. Hons, Eng. Lang. and Lit., 1947. Served War, RAMC, 1940–46. University of Glasgow: Asst, 1947, Lectr, 1950, Sen. Lectr, 1965, Reader, 1971, in English. Vis. Prof., Strathclyde Univ., 1987–90; Hon. Prof., UCW, 1991–. Cholmondeley Award for Poets, 1968; Hungarian PEN Meml Medal, 1972; Scottish Arts Council Book Awards, 1968, 1973, 1975, 1977, 1978, 1983 and 1985; Soros Translation Award, NY, 1985. Visual/concrete poems in many internat. exhibns, 1965–. Opera librettos (unpublished): The Charcoal-Burner, 1969; Valentine, 1976; Columba, 1976; Spell, 1979. Hon. DLitt: Loughborough, 1981; Glasgow, 1990; Edinburgh, 1991; DUniv Stirling, 1989. *Publications: poetry:* The Vision of Cathkin Braes, 1952; Beowulf, 1952; The Cape of Good Hope, 1955; Poems from Eugenio Montale, 1959; Sovpoems, 1961; (ed) Collins Albatross Book of Longer Poems, 1963; Starryveldt, 1965; Emergent Poems, 1967; Gnomes, 1968; The Second Life, 1968; Proverbfolder, 1969; Penguin Modern Poets 15, 1969; Twelve Songs, 1970; The Horseman's Word, 1970; (co-ed) Scottish Poetry 1–6, 1966–72; Glasgow Sonnets, 1972; Wi the Haill Voice, 1972; Instamatic Poems, 1972; The Whittrick, 1973; From Glasgow to Saturn, 1973; Fifty Renascence Love-Poems, 1975; Rites of Passage, 1976; The New Divan, 1977; Colour Poems, 1978; Platen: selected poems, 1978; Star Gate, 1979; (ed) Scottish Satirical Verse, 1980; Poems of Thirty Years, 1982; Grafts/Takes, 1983; Master Peter Pathelin, 1983; Sonnets From Scotland, 1984; Selected Poems, 1985; From the Video Box, 1986; Newspoems, 1987; Themes on a Variation, 1988; Tales from Limerick Zoo, 1988; Collected Poems, 1990; Hold Hands Among the Atoms, 1991; *prose:* Essays, 1974; East European Poets, 1976; Hugh MacDiarmid, 1976; Twentieth Century Scottish Classics, 1987; Nothing Not Giving Messages (interviews), 1990; Crossing the Border: essays in Scottish Literature, 1990. *Recreations:* photography, scrapbooks, walking in cities. *Address:* 19 Whittingehame Court, Glasgow G12 0BG. *T:* 041–339 6260.

MORGAN, Edwin John; Director, Civil Service Selection Board, 1981–87, retired; *b* 10 Jan. 1927; *s* of Thomas Grosvenor Morgan and Florence (*née* Binmore); *m* 1954, Joyce Beryl, *o d* of Reginald and Gladys Ashurst, Bebington, Wirral; two *s* one *d. Educ:* Dauntsey's Sch.; St Edmund Hall, Oxford (Sen. Scholar, BA 1st Cl. Hons 1951). Served Army, Intell. Corps, Palestine and Cyprus, 1944–48. Lecteur d'anglais, Ecole normale supérieure, Paris, 1952; Asst, Dept of French Studies, Glasgow Univ., 1953; Asst Principal, Air Min., 1957, Principal, 1960; MoD, 1965; Registrar, RMCS, 1968; Asst Sec., 1970; CSD, 1971; CS Commn, 1975; Under Sec., 1980; CS Comr, 1980–87. Chm., CS Retirement Fellowship, 1987–July 1992. FIPM 1985. *Recreations:* reading, walking, music, swimming, domesticity. *Address:* Ashurst, 6 Links Drive, Robin Lane, High Bentham, Lancaster LA2 7BJ. *T:* Bentham (05242) 61406. *Club:* Civil Service.

MORGAN, Ellis, CMG 1961; HM Diplomatic Service, retired; *b* 26 Dec. 1916; *s* of late Ben Morgan and of Mary Morgan, The Grove, Three Crosses, Gower, S Wales; *m* 1st, 1948, Molly Darby (marr. diss.); three *d*; 2nd, 1975, Mary, *d* of late Slade Baker Stallard-Penoyre; one *s* twin *d* (one decd). *Educ:* Swansea Grammar Sch. (Bishop Gore Sch.). Dep. Librarian, County Borough of Swansea, 1937–39. Commissioned Royal Artillery, 1941; served War of 1939–45, in India, Burma, Malaya, 1943–47. Entered Foreign (subseq. Diplomatic) Service, 1948; 3rd Sec., 1948–50, 2nd Sec., 1951–53, subseq. 1st Sec., British Embassy, Rangoon; 1st Sec., British Embassy, Bangkok, 1954–55; 1st Sec., Office of Commissioner-Gen., Singapore, 1957–60; Student at Imperial Defence Coll., 1961; Counsellor: UK High Commission, New Delhi, 1964; FO, later FCO, 1966–73; Political and Economic Adviser, Commercial Union Assurance, 1973–79. *Club:* Farmers'.

MORGAN, Sir Ernest (Dunstan), ORSL; KBE 1971 (OBE 1951; MBE 1940); DCL; JP; *b* 17 Nov. 1896; *s* of Thomas William Morgan and Susan Barnett; *m* 1st, 1918, Elizabeth Mary Agnes Collier; one *d*; 2nd, 1972, Monica Fredericka Davies; one *s* three *d. Educ:* Zion Day School, Freetown; Methodist Boys' High School, Freetown. Government Dispenser, 1914–20; Druggist, 1917–. MHR Sierra Leone, 1956–61; Member: Freetown City Council, 1938–44; Fourah Bay Coll. Council, 1950–54; Chairman: Blind Welfare Soc., 1946–52; Public Service Commn, 1948–52. JP Sierra Leone, 1952. *Recreation:* tennis. *Address:* 15 Syke Street, Freetown, Sierra Leone. *T:* Freetown 23155 and 22366. *Club:* Freetown Dinner.

MORGAN, (Frank) Leslie, CBE 1988 (MBE 1973); Chairman, Morgan Bros (Mid Wales) Ltd, since 1959; Chairman, Development Board for Rural Wales (Mid Wales Development), 1981–89 (Member, 1977–81); *b* 7 Nov. 1926; *s* of Edward Arthur

Morgan and Beatrice Morgan; *m* 1962, Victoria Stoker (*née* Jeffery); one *s* two *d*. *Educ:* Llanfair Primary Sch.; Llanfair Grammar Sch.; University College of Wales (BA Econ Hons). Post graduate trainee and parts executive in motor industry, 1950–56. Chairman and President, Montgomery Conservative Assoc., 1964–81; Member, Welsh Council, 1970–79; Dep. Chm., Mid Wales New Town Development Corp., 1973–77; Director: Develt Corp. for Wales, 1981–83; Wales Adv. Bd, Abbey National (formerly Abbey National Bldg Soc.), 1982–90; Member: Welsh Development Agency, 1981–89; Wales Tourist Bd, 1982–89; Infrastructure Cttee, BTA, 1982–89; Design Council Welsh Cttee, 1981–85. Pres., Montgomeryshire Agricl Soc., 1986. Pres., Montgomery Cons. Assoc., 1989–. *Recreations:* reading, travel, jogging, swimming, cycling. *Address:* Wentworth House, Llangyniew, Welshpool, Powys SY21 9EL. *T:* Llanfair-Caereinion (0938) 810462.

MORGAN, Col Frank Stanley, CBE 1940; ERD 1954; DL; JP; *b* 10 Jan. 1893; *s* of F. A. Morgan, Commissioner Imperial Chinese Customs; *m* 1918, Gladys Joan (*d* 1953), *d* of Lt-Col H. M. Warde, CBE, DL Kent; no *c*; *m* 1956, Minnie Helen Pine, MBE, TD, DL, Lt-Col WRAC, The Manor House, Great Barrow, Cheshire. *Educ:* Marlborough; Christ Church, Oxford. Served European War, 1914–18; public work in Wales; Territorial and Reserve Service, 1919–39; Air Formation Signals, France, North Africa, Italy, Middle East, 1939–45; DL, Glamorgan, 1946; JP 1951; Hon. Col 50 and 81 AF Signal Regts, 1952–60. *Address:* Herbert's Lodge, Bishopston, Swansea. *T:* Bishopston (044128) 4222.

MORGAN, Gemmell; *see* Morgan, H. G.

MORGAN, Geoffrey Thomas, CB 1991; Under Secretary, Cabinet Office (Office of the Minister for the Civil Service), Director of Public Appointments Unit, 1985–91; *b* 12 April 1931; *s* of late Thomas Evan Morgan and Nora (*née* Flynn); *m* 1960, Heather, *d* of late William Henry Trick and of Margery Murrell Wells; two *d*. *Educ:* Roundhay Sch. National Service, Royal Signals, 1950–52; joined Civil Service, 1952; served in Mins of Supply and Aviation, 1952–65; HM Treasury, 1965–68 and 1981–83; CSD, 1968–81; seconded to Arthur Guinness Son & Co., 1970–72; Adviser to World Bank in Washington, 1977–78; Cabinet Office, 1983–91; Adviser to: UN in NY, 1987–; People's Republic of China in Beijing, 1988–; Govt of Hungary in Budapest, 1990–. Chm., Public Admin Cttee, WEU, 1990–91. *Recreation:* preserving the mulberry for posterity and the silkworm.

MORGAN, George Lewis Bush; Chief Registrar, Bank of England, 1978–83; *b* 1 Sept. 1925; *s* of late William James Charles Morgan and Eva Averill Morgan (*née* Bush); *m* 1949, Mary Rose (*née* Vine); three *s*. *Educ:* Cranbr Sch., Kent. Captain, Royal Sussex Regt, 1943–47. Entered Bank of England, 1947; Asst Chief Accountant, 1966; Asst Sec., 1969; Dep. Sec., 1973. Mem. Bd of Govs, Holmewood House Prep. Sch., Tunbridge Wells, 1983– (Chm., 1986–). *Recreations:* tennis, golf, gardening. *Address:* Hill Top House, Five Ashes, Mayfield, East Sussex TN20 6HT.

MORGAN, Geraint; *see* Morgan, W. G. O.

MORGAN, Gwyn; *see* Morgan, J. G.

MORGAN, Prof. (Henry) Gemmell; Professor of Pathological Biochemistry, University of Glasgow, 1965–88, now Professor Emeritus, and Hon. Senior Research Fellow, since 1988; *b* 25 Dec. 1922; *s* of John McIntosh Morgan, MC, MD, FRCPE, and Florence Ballantyne; *m* 1949, Margaret Duncan, BSc, MB, ChB; one *d*. *Educ:* Dundee High Sch.; Merchiston Castle Sch., Edinburgh; Univ. of St Andrews at University Coll., Dundee. BSc 1943; MB, ChB (distinction), 1946; FRCPE 1962; FRCPGlas 1968; FRCPath 1970; FRSE 1971. Hon. Consultant, Royal Infirmary, Glasgow, 1966–88. Chm., Med. Cttee, Royal Infirmary, Glasgow, 1984–87. Hon. Life Mem., Assoc. of Clinical Biochemists (UK), 1990 (Chm., 1982–85; Pres., 1985–87). Ext. Examnr, Final in Pathology, Charing Cross and Westminster Med. Sch., 1985–88, and UMDS of Guy's and St Thomas' Hosps, London; Examnr in primary FRCS, RCPGlas, 1970–. Chm., Scottish Br., Nutrition Soc., 1967–68. Adviser to Greater Glasgow Health Ed, SHHD. MInstD. *Publications:* chapters; papers in medical jls on calcium, and lipoproteins. *Recreations:* golf, foreign travel, history. *Address:* Firwood House, 8 Eaglesham Road, Newton Mearns, Glasgow G77 5BG. *T:* 041–639 4404. *Club:* Athenæum.

MORGAN, (Hywel) Rhodri; MP (Lab) Cardiff West, since 1987; *b* 29 Sept. 1939; *s* of Thomas John and Huana Morgan; *m* 1967, Julie Edwards; one *s* two *d*. *Educ:* St John's College, Oxford (Hons cl. 2, PPE 1961); Harvard Univ. (Masters in Govt 1963). Tutor Organiser, WEA, S Wales Area, 1963–65; Research Officer, Cardiff City Council, Welsh Office and DoE, 1965–71; Economic Adviser, DTI, 1972–74; Indust. Develt Officer, S Glamorgan County Council, 1974–80; Head of Bureau for Press and Inf., European Commn Office for Wales, 1980–87. Opposition spokesman on Energy, Electricity and the Environment, 1988–. *Recreations:* long-distance running, wood carving, marine wildlife. *Address:* Lower House, Michaelston-le-Pit, Dinas Powys, South Glamorgan CF6 4HE. *T:* (home) Cardiff (0222) 514262; (office) Cardiff (0222) 223207.

MORGAN, Janet; writer and consultant; *b* 5 Dec. 1945; *e d* of Frank Morgan and Shiela Sadler. *Educ:* Newbury Co. Girls Grammar Sch.; St Hugh's Coll., Oxford. MA, DPhil Oxon, MA Sussex. Kennedy Meml Scholar, Harvard Univ., 1968–69; Student, Nuffield Coll., Oxford, 1969–71; Res. Fellow, Wolfson Coll., Oxford and Res. Officer, Univ. of Essex, 1971–72; Res. Fellow, Nuffield Coll., Oxford, 1972–74; Lectr in Politics, Exeter Coll., Oxford, 1974–76; Dir of Studies, St Hugh's Coll., Oxford, 1975–76 and Lectr in Politics, 1976–78; Mem., Central Policy Rev. Staff, Cabinet Office, 1978–81. Mem. Bd, British Council, 1989–. Vis. Fellow, All Souls Coll., Oxford, 1983. Dir, Satellite Television PLC, 1981–83; Special Advr to Dir-Gen., BBC, 1983–86; Advr to Bd, Granada Gp, 1986–89; Mem., London Adv. Bd, Nat. and Provincial Bldg Soc., 1988–89; non-executive Director: Cable and Wireless, 1988–; W. H. Smith, 1989–; Midlands Electricity, 1990–; Pitney Bowes, 1991–. Vice-Pres., Videotext Industries Assoc., 1985–91; Dir, Hulton Deutsch Collection, 1988–90. Trustee: Amer. Sch. in London, 1985–88; Fairground Heritage Trust, 1987–; Cyclotron Trust, 1988–90. Member: Lord Chancellor's Adv. Council on Public Records, 1982–86; Ancient Monuments Bd for Scotland, 1990–. Mem., Editorial Bd, Political Quarterly, 1980–90. *Publications:* The House of Lords and the Labour Government 1964–70, 1975; Reinforcing Parliament, 1976; (ed) The Diaries of a Cabinet Minister 1964–70 by Richard Crossman, 3 vols 1975, 1976, 1977; (ed) Backbench Diaries 1951–63 by Richard Crossman, 1980; (ed with Richard Hoggart) The Future of Broadcasting, 1982; Agatha Christie: a biography, 1984; Edwina Mountbatten: a life of her own, 1991. *Recreations:* music of Handel, sea-bathing, gardens. *Address:* c/o David Higham Associates Ltd, 5–8 Lower John Street, Golden Square, W1R 4HA. *T:* 071–437 7888.

MORGAN, Sir John (Albert Leigh), KCMG 1989 (CMG 1982); HM Diplomatic Service, retired; President, International Federation of the Phonographic Industry, since 1990; *b* 21 June 1929; *s* of late John Edward Rowland Morgan, Bridge, Kent; *m* 1st, 1961, Hon. Fionn Frances Bride O'Neill (marr. diss. 1975), *d* of 3rd Baron O'Neill, Shane's Castle, Antrim; one *s* two *d*; 2nd, 1976, Angela Mary Eleanor, *e d* of Patrick Warre Rathbone, MBE (mil.), Woolton, Liverpool; one *s* one *d*. *Educ:* London School of Economics (BSc(Econ) Hons Econs and Law; Hon. Fellow, 1984). Served in Army, 1947–49: commnd 1948; interpreter with French Army, 1949. Entered Foreign Service, 1951; FO, 1951–53; 3rd Sec. and Private Sec. to HM Ambassador, Moscow, 1953–56; 2nd Sec., Peking, 1956–58; FO, 1958–63 (attended Geneva Conf. of Foreign Ministers on Berlin, 1959, and on Laos (interpreter in Russian and Chinese), 1961; interpreter for Mr Khrushchev's visits to UK, 1956, for Mr Macmillan's visit to Soviet Union, 1959, and for Summit Conf. in Paris, 1960); 1st Sec., 1960; Head of Chancery, Rio de Janeiro, 1963–64; FO, 1964–65; Chargé d'Affaires, Ulan Bator, 1965; Moscow, 1965–67; Dep. Hd, Econ. Relns Dept, subseq. Export Promotion Dept, FO, 1968; Head of Far Eastern Dept, FCO, 1970–72; Head of Cultural Relations Dept, FCO, 1972–80 (Member: Reviewing Cttee on Export of Works of Art; Fulbright Scholarship Commn; Selection Cttee, US Bicenternnial Scholarships Prog.); Ambassador and Consul Gen. to Republic of Korea, 1980–83; Ambassador to Poland, 1983–86; Ambassador to Mexico, 1986–89. Man. Dir (Internat. Relations), Maxwell Communications Corp., 1989–90; Dir, The European, 1990–. Served on Earl Marshal's Staff for State Funeral of Sir Winston Churchill, 1965, and for Investiture of Prince of Wales, 1969. Trustee, BM, 1991–. Governor, LSE, 1971–. Chm., Anglo-Korean Soc., 1990–; Mem., Internat. Council, United World Colleges, 1990–. FRSA; Fellow, Royal Asiatic Soc.; Hon. Life Member: Royal Philharmonic Orch.; GB-China Centre. Hon. DSc (Politics) Korea Univ., 1983; Hon. LLD Mexico Acad. of Internat. Law, 1987. *Publications:* (under a pseudonym): various works of French and Chinese literary criticism. *Recreations:* ornithology, oriental art, tennis. *Address:* 41 Hugh Street, SW1V 1QJ. *T:* 071–821 1037. *Club:* Travellers'.

MORGAN, John Alfred; Chief Executive, Investment Management Regulatory Organisation Ltd, since 1986; *b* 16 Sept. 1931; *s* of late Alfred Morgan and of Lydia Amelia Morgan; *m* 1959, Janet Mary Sclater-Jones; one *d*. *Educ:* Rugeley Grammar Sch.; Peterhouse, Cambridge (BA). Investment Research, Cambridge, 1953–59; Investment Manager, S. G. Warburg & Co. Ltd, 1959–67; Director: Glyn, Mills & Co., 1967–70; Finance and Investment, Williams & Glyn's Bank Ltd, 1970–76; Rothschild Asset Management, 1976–78; Central Trustee Savings Bank Ltd, 1982–86; Zurich Life Assce Co. Ltd, 1970–87; Sealink UK Ltd, 1983–85. Gen. Manager, British Railways Pension Funds, 1978–86. Chm., Post Office Users' Nat. Council, 1978–82. *Recreations:* music, contemporary art, fell walking. *Address:* 5 Grange Road, Highgate, N6 4AR. *Club:* Reform.

MORGAN, John Ambrose; His Honour Judge John Morgan; a Circuit Judge, since 1990; *b* 22 Sept. 1934; *s* of Joseph Michael Morgan and Monica Morgan; *m* 1970, Rosalie Mary Tyson; two *s*. *Educ:* St Edward's Coll., Liverpool; Univ. of Liverpool (Emmott Meml Scholar 1953; Alsopp Prizewinner 1953; LLB 1955). Law Soc. Finals 1957 (Local Govt Prize). Nat. Service, RAF, 1958–60. Admitted Solicitor, 1958; practised in local govt and private practice, 1960–70; called to the Bar, Gray's Inn, 1970; N Circuit, 1970–90; Dep. Stipendiary Magistrate, 1982; Asst Recorder, 1983; Recorder, 1988. *Recreations:* Rugby Union football (writing and broadcasting; Pres., Liverpool RFU, 1980–82), golf, cricket, music, amateur operatics. *Address:* Tarnbrick, 80 Beech Lane, Liverpool L18 3ER. *T:* 051–724 3232. *Clubs:* Lyceum (Liverpool); Liverpool St Helen's RFC, Woolton Golf, Sefton Cricket.

MORGAN, (John) Gwyn(fryn); Head, Delegation of the Commission of the European Community to Israel, since 1987; *b* 16 Feb. 1934; *s* of Arthur G. Morgan, coal miner, and Mary Walters; *m* 1st, 1960, Joan Margaret Taylor (marr. diss. 1974); one *d*; 2nd, 1979, Colette Anne Rumball (marr. diss. 1989); two *s* one *d*; 3rd, 1990, Margery Sue Greenfeld. *Educ:* Aberdare Boys' Grammar Sch.; UCW Aberystwyth. MA Classics 1957; Dip. Educn 1958. Senior Classics Master, The Regis Sch., Tettenhall, Staffs, 1958–60; Pres., National Union of Students, 1960–62; Sec.-Gen., Internat. Student Conf. (ISC), 1962–65; Head of Overseas Dept, British Labour Party, 1965–69; Asst Gen. Secretary, British Labour Party, 1969–72; Chef de Cabinet to Mr George Thomson, 1973–75; Head of Welsh Inf. Office, EEC, 1975–79; a Dir, Development Corp. for Wales, 1976–81, Hon. Consultant in Canada 1981–83; Head of EEC Press and Inf. Office for Canada, 1979–83; EEC Rep. in Turkey, 1983–86. Mem., Hansard Commn on Electoral Reform, 1975–76. Adjunct Prof., Univ. of Guelph, 1980–. *Publications:* contribs to numerous British and foreign political jls. *Recreations:* cricket, Rugby football, crosswords, wine-tasting. *Address:* 79 Hazorea Street, Kfar Shmaryahu, Tel Aviv, Israel. *Clubs:* Commonwealth Trust, Reform; Cardiff and County; Cercle Universitaire (Ottawa); Mount Stephens (Montreal).

MORGAN, John Lewis, OBE 1981; Member (C) Test Valley Borough Council, since 1974; *b* 12 May 1919; *s* of Charles Lewis Morgan and Elsie Winifred (*née* Smith); *m* 1943, Grace Barnes; one *s* three *d*. *Educ:* St Paul's Sch. Member: Wherwell Parish Council, 1947– (Chm., 1962–); Andover RDC, 1950–74 (Vice-Chm., 1960–72; Chm., 1972–74; Chm. of Finance, 1956–74); Hampshire CC, 1956–66; Mayor of Test Valley, 1977–78 and 1978–79. Mem., Assoc. of Dist Councils, 1974– (Chm., 1984–87, Vice-Chm., 1983–84; Chm. of Housing and Environmental Health, 1979–83); President: IULA/CEMR (British Sections), 1984– (Chm., 1980–84); CLRAE, Strasbourg, 1987–90 (Mem., 1975–; Vice-Pres., 1984–87; Pres., 1987–90; 1st Vice-Pres., 1990–; Chm., Environment and Town Planning Cttee, 1983–85); Chm., Eur. Affairs Cttee, IULA, The Hague, 1981–86; Vice-Chm., CEMR Paris, 1981–87; Chm., Consultative Cttee, CEMR/IULA, Brussels, 1986–. Church lay reader. *Recreations:* keen supporter of Southampton Football Club; avid gardener. *Address:* Dancing Ledge, Wherwell, Andover, Hants SP11 7JS. *T:* Andover (0264) 860296.

MORGAN, John William Harold, (Bill), FEng 1978; Chairman, Trafford Park Urban Development Corporation, since 1990; Director: AMEC plc, since 1983 (Chairman, 1984–88); Hill Samuel & Co., 1983–89; *b* 13 Dec. 1927; *s* of John Henry and Florence Morgan; *m* 1952, Barbara (*née* Harrison); two *d*. *Educ:* Wednesbury Boys' High Sch.; Univ. of Birmingham (BScEng, 1st Cl. Hons). FIMechE, MIEE. National Service commn with RAF, 1949–51. Joined English Electric Co., Stafford, as design engr, subseq. Chief Development Engr (Machines), 1953; Chief Develt Engr (Mechanical), 1957; Chief Engr (DC Machines), 1960; Product Div. Manager, 1962; Gen. Man., Electrical Machines Gp, 1965; Managing Director, English Electric-AEI Machines Gp (following merger with GEC/AEI), 1968; Asst Man. Dir and main board director, GEC plc, 1973–83. Chm., Staffordshire Cable, 1989–; Dep. Chm., Petbow Holdings, 1983–86; Director: Simon Engineering, 1983–88; Pitney Bowes, 1989–; Tekdata, 1989–; UMIST Ventures, 1989–. Mem. Council, Fellowship of Engrg, 1987–. FRSA. Royal Society's S. G. Brown award for an outstanding contrib. to promotion and development of mechanical inventions, 1968. *Recreations:* craft activities, particularly woodworking. *Address:* Mullion, Whitmore Heath, near Newcastle, Staffs ST5 5HF. *T:* Newcastle (Staffs) (0782) 680462.

MORGAN, Keith John, DPhil; FRACI, FRSC; FAIM; Vice-Chancellor, University of Newcastle, New South Wales, since 1987; *b* 14 Dec. 1929; *s* of C. F. J. Morgan and Winifred Burman (formerly Morgan, *née* Allen); *m* 1957, Hilary Chapman; one *d*. *Educ:* Manchester Grammar Sch.; Brasenose Coll., Oxford (MA, BSc, DPhil). Senior Research Fellow, Min. of Supply, 1955–57; ICI Res. Fellow, 1957–58; Lectr, Univ. of Birmingham, 1958–64; AEC Fellow, Purdue Univ., 1960–61; Lectr, Sen. Lectr, Prof., Dept. of Chemistry, Univ. of Lancaster, 1964–86 (Pro-Vice-Chancellor, 1973–78; Sen. Pro-Vice-Chancellor, 1978–86). Deputy Chairman: Hunter Technol. Develt Centre, 1987–; Hunter

Econ. Develt Council, 1989–. Chm., Regl Council, AIM, 1989–. Member: UCNS, 1980–86; Council, Lancashire Polytechnic, 1985–86. Mem., NSW Envmtl Res. Trust, 1990–. *Publications:* scientific papers in Jl Chm. Soc. and other jls. *Recreations:* mountains, Mozart, cricket. *Address:* University of Newcastle, NSW 2308, Australia. *T:* 049–215101. *Clubs:* Commonwealth Trust; Newcastle (NSW).

MORGAN, Kenneth, OBE 1978; Director, Press Complaints Commission, since 1991; *b* 3 Nov. 1928; *s* of Albert E. and Lily M. Morgan; *m* 1950, Margaret Cynthia, *d* of Roland E. Wilson; three *d. Educ:* Stockport Grammar School. Reporter, Stockport Express, 1944; Army, 1946, commissioned, 1947 (served Palestine, Egypt, GHQ MELF); journalism, 1949; Central London Sec., NUJ, 1962; Nat. Organiser, NUJ, 1966; Gen. Sec., NUJ, 1970–77, Mem. of Honour, 1978. Press Council: Consultative Mem., 1970–77; Jt Sec., 1977–78; Dep. Dir and Conciliator, 1978–79; Dir, 1980–90. Director: Journalists in Europe Ltd, 1982–; Reuters Founder's Share Co., 1984–. Mem. Exec. Cttee: Printing and Kindred Trades Fedn, 1970–73; Nat. Fedn of Professional Workers, 1970–77; Fedn of Broadcasting Unions, 1970–77; Confedn of Entertainment Unions, 1970–77; Bureau, Internat. Fedn of Journalists, 1970–78. Member: NEDC for Printing and Publishing Industry, 1970; Printing Industries Cttee, TUC, 1974–77; Printing and Publishing Industries Trng Bd, 1975–77; Jt Standing Cttee, Nat. Newspaper Industry, 1976–77; British Cttee, Journalists in Europe, 1977–; C of E General Synod Cttee for Communications Press Panel, 1981–90; CRE Media Gp, 1981–85; Internat. Ombudsman Inst., 1983–; Trustee, Reuters, 1984–. Associate Mem. IPI, 1980; FRSA 1980. Methodist Recorder Lectr, 1989. *Publications:* Press Conduct in the Sutcliffe Case, 1983; (with David Christie) New Connexions: the power to inform, 1989; *contributed to:* El Poder Judicial en le Conjunto de los Poderes del Estado y de la Sociedad, 1989; Media Freedom and Accountability, 1989; The Independence of the Journalist, Is de Klant of de Krant Koning, 1990; Beyond the Courtroom: alternatives for resolving press disputes, 1991. *Recreations:* theatre, military history, inland waterways. *Address:* (office) 1 Salisbury Square, EC4Y 8AE. *T:* 071–353 1248; 151 Overhill Road, Dulwich, SE22 0PT. *T:* 081–693 6585. *Club:* Press.

MORGAN, Prof. Kenneth Owen, FBA 1983, FRHistS 1964; Principal, University College of Wales, Aberystwyth, Pro-Vice-Chancellor and Professor in the University of Wales, since 1989; *b* 16 May 1934; *s* of David James Morgan and Margaret Morgan (*née* Owen); *m* 1973, Jane Keeler; one *s* one *d. Educ:* University College School, London; Oriel College, Oxford. MA, DPhil 1958, DLitt 1985. University College, Swansea: Lectr in History Dept, 1958–66 (Sen. Lectr, 1965–66); Hon. Fellow, 1985; Fellow and Praelector, Modern Hist. and Politics, Queen's Coll., Oxford, 1966–89. Supernumerary Fellow, Jesus Coll., Oxford, 1991–Sept. 1992. Amer. Council of Learned Socs Fellow, Columbia Univ., 1962–63; Vis. Prof., Columbia Univ., 1965. Member: Council, RHistS, 1983–86; Bd of Celtic Studies, 1972–; Council, Nat. Library of Wales, 1991–; Council, University Coll. of Wales, Aberystwyth, 1972–84. Editor, Welsh History Review, 1961–. *Publications:* Wales in British Politics, 1963, 3rd edn 1980; David Lloyd George: Welsh radical as world statesman, 1963, 2nd edn 1982; Freedom or Sacrilege?, 1966; Keir Hardie, 1967; The Age of Lloyd George, 1971, 3rd edn 1978; (ed) Lloyd George: Family Letters, 1973; Lloyd George, 1974; Keir Hardie: radical and socialist, 1975, 2nd edn 1984 (Arts Council prize, 1976); Consensus and Disunity, 1979, 2nd edn 1986; (with Jane Morgan) Portrait of a Progressive, 1980; Rebirth of a Nation: Wales 1880–1980, 1981, 2nd edn 1982 (Arts Council prize, 1982); David Lloyd George, 1981; Labour in Power 1945–1951, 1984, 2nd edn 1985; (ed jtly) Welsh Society and Nationhood, 1984; (ed) The Oxford Illustrated History of Britain, 1984; (ed) The Sphere Illustrated History of Britain, 1985; Labour People, 1987; (ed) The Oxford History of Britain, 1988; The Red Dragon and the Red Flag, 1989; The People's Peace: British History 1945–1989, 1990; many articles, reviews etc. *Recreations:* music, architecture, sport, travel. *Address:* Plas Penglais, Aberystwyth, Dyfed SY23 3DF. *T:* Aberystwyth 623853. *Club:* Athenæum.

MORGAN, Kenneth Smith; Editor of the Official Report (Hansard), House of Commons, 1979–89; *b* 6 Aug. 1925; *er s* of Edward and Florence Morgan; *m* 1952, Patricia Hunt; one *s* one *d. Educ:* Battersea and Dartford Grammar Schools. Commissioned Royal West Kent Regt, 1944; Burma, 1944–46. Weekly newspapers, 1947–51; Derby Evening Telegraph, 1951–52; Reuters Parliamentary Staff, 1952–54; joined Official Report, 1954; Dep. Asst Editor, 1972, Dep. Editor, 1978. Founded Commonwealth Hansard Editors Assoc., 1984. *Publication:* The Falklands Campaign: a digest of parliamentary debates on the Falklands, 1982. *Recreations:* Napoleonic warfare history, model soldiers, cricket, bridge. *Address:* 3 Highfield Road, Bexleyheath, Kent DA6 7HX.

MORGAN, Leslie; *see* Morgan, F. L.

MORGAN, Marilynne Ann; Under Secretary and Principal Assistant Solicitor, Department of the Environment, since 1991; *b* 22 June 1946; *d* of late J. Emlyn Williams and of Roma Elizabeth Williams (*née* Ellis); *m* 1970, Nicholas Alan, *e s* of Rear-Adm. Sir Patrick Morgan, KCVO, CB, DSC. *Educ:* Gads Hill Place, Higham-by-Rochester; Bedford Coll., Univ. of London (BA Hons History). Called to the Bar, Middle Temple, 1972. Res. Asst, Special Historical Sect., FCO, 1967–71; Department of Health and Social Security: Legal Asst, 1973; Sen. Legal Asst, 1978; Asst Solicitor, 1982; Under Sec. and Principal Asst Solicitor, 1985–91, DSS, 1988–91. Vice-Chm. 1983–84, Chm. 1984–86, Legal Sect. of Assoc. of First Div. Civil Servants. Mem., General Council of the Bar, 1987–. *Publications:* contributor, Halsbury's Laws of England, 1982, 1986; articles in learned jls. *Recreations:* homely pursuits. *Address:* Department of the Environment, 2 Marsham Street, SW1P 3EB. *Club:* University Women's.

MORGAN, Michael David; Chief Executive and General Manager, Telford Development Corporation, since 1986; *b* 19 Jan. 1942; *s* of Edward Arthur and Winifred Maud Morgan; *m* 1980, Ljiljana Radojcic; three *d. Educ:* Royal Liberty Sch., Romford; Prince Rupert Sch., Wilhemshaven, FRG; Coll. of Estate Management, London Univ. (BSc Est. Man.). FRICS. Sheffield City Council, 1964–67; Derby Borough Council, 1967–70; Telford Develt Corp., 1970–. *Recreations:* cricket, jogging, swimming, gardening. *Address:* 42 London Road, Shrewsbury SY2 6NX. *T:* Shrewsbury (0743) 352800.

MORGAN, Michael Hugh, CMG 1978; HM Diplomatic Service, retired; Director, Swansea Overseas Trust, since 1988; *b* 18 April 1925; *s* of late H. P. Morgan; *m* 1957, Julian Bamfield; two *s. Educ:* Shrewsbury Sch.; Downing College, Cambridge; School of Oriental and African Studies, London Univ. Army Service 1943–46. HMOCS Malaya, 1946–56. Foreign Office, 1956–57; First Secretary, Peking, 1957–60; Belgrade 1960–64; attached to Industry, 1964; First Secretary, FCO, 1964–68; Counsellor and Head of Chancery, Cape Town/Pretoria, 1968–72; Counsellor, Peking, 1972–75; Inspector, FCO, 1975–77; High Comr, Sierra Leone, 1977–81; Ambassador to the Philippines, 1981–85. Consultant, British Rail Engrg, 1986–88. *Address:* Strefford House, Strefford, Craven Arms, Shropshire SY7 8DE.

MORGAN, His Honour Peter Trevor Hopkin; QC 1972; a Deputy Judge, since 1987; a Circuit Judge, 1972–87; Liaison Judge to Gwent Magistrates, and Justice of the Peace, 1973–87; a Judge of the Provincial Court of the Church in Wales, since 1987; *b* 5 Feb. 1919; *o s* of Cyril Richard Morgan and Muriel Arceta (*née* Hole); *m* 1942, Josephine Mouncey, *d* of Ben Travers, CBE, AFC; one *s* three *d. Educ:* Mill Hill Sch.; Magdalen Coll., Oxford (BA). Called to Bar, Middle Temple, 1949; Wales and Chester Circuit; Lectr in Law, Univ. of Wales (Cardiff and Swansea), 1950–55. Liveryman, Fishmongers' Company. *Recreations:* inland waterways, viniculture, wine making. *Address:* 26 Westmead Lane, Chippenham, Wilts SN15 3HZ. *Club:* Garrick.

MORGAN, Peter William Lloyd; Director-General, Institute of Directors, since 1989; *b* 9 May 1936; *s* of late Matthew Morgan and of Margaret Gwynneth (*née* Lloyd); *m* 1964, Elisabeth Susanne Davis; three *d. Educ:* Llandovery Coll.; Trinity Hall, Cambridge (MA). Royal Signals, 1954–56 (2nd Lieut). Joined IBM UK Ltd, 1959; Dir, IBM UK Rentals Ltd, 1973–75 and 1980–83; Gp Dir of Marketing, IBM Europe, Paris, 1975–80; Director: IBM UK Ltd, 1983–87; IBM UK Holdings Ltd, 1987–89; IBM UK Trust Ltd, 1987–89. Director: NCC, 1981–89; South Wales Electricity PLC, 1989–; Director Publications Ltd, 1989–; National Provident Instn, 1990–. Member: Management Cttee, Action Resource Centre, 1987–; Council, British Executive Service Overseas, 1989–; Council for Charitable Support, 1990–; Council Nat. Forum for Management Educn and Develt, 1990–. Mem., Co. of Inf. Technologists, 1988–. Trustee, Llandovery Coll., 1990–. *Recreations:* music, history, gardening, ski-ing, exercising my dogs. *Address:* Institute of Directors, 116 Pall Mall, SW1Y 5ED. *T:* 071–839 1233. *Club:* United Oxford & Cambridge University.

MORGAN, Rev. Philip; Minister, St Andrew's United Reformed Church, Frognal, London, since 1990; *b* 22 June 1930; *s* of David Lewis and Pamela Morgan; *m* 1954, Greta Mary Hanson; one *s* one *d. Educ:* Overdale Coll.; Selly Oaks Colls; Univ. of Birmingham (BA Hons Theology). Ordained 1952; Ministries: Aberfan, Godreaman, Griffithstown, Merthyr Tydfil and Treharris, 1952–58; Eltham, London, 1958–62; Leicester and South Wigston, 1962–67; General Secretary, Churches of Christ in GB and Ireland, 1967–80; Gen. Sec., BCC, 1980–90. Moderator, URC, 1984–85. Hon. DD Christian Theological Seminary, USA, 1980. *Recreations:* hill walking, Celtic history, steam railways. *Address:* St Andrew's Manse, 33 Crediton Hill, West Hampstead, NW6 1H5.

MORGAN, Rhodri; *see* Morgan, H. R.

MORGAN, Richard Martin, MA; Warden, Radley College, since 1991; *b* 25 June 1940; *s* of His Honour Trevor Morgan, MC, QC, and late Leslie Morgan; *m* 1968, Margaret Kathryn, *d* of late Anthony Agutter and of Mrs Launcelot Fleming; three *d. Educ:* Sherborne Sch.; Caius Coll., Cambridge (MA, DipEd); York Univ. Assistant Master, Radley Coll., 1963; Housemaster, 1969; Headmaster, Cheltenham College, 1978–90. Member, Adv. Council, Understanding British Industry, 1977–79. JP Glos, 1978–90. *Recreations:* reading, music, games. *Address:* Spring Farmhouse, Hanwell, Banbury, Oxon OX17 1HN. *T:* Banbury (0295) 738122; Radley College, Abingdon, Oxon OX14 2HR. *T:* Abingdon (0235) 520294. *Clubs:* Free Foresters', Jesters'.

MORGAN, Robin Milne; Principal: Daniel Stewart's and Melville College, Edinburgh, 1977–89; The Mary Erskine School, 1979–89; *b* 2 Oct. 1930; *o s* of Robert Milne Morgan and Aida Forsyth Morgan; *m* 1955, Fiona Bruce MacLeod Douglas; three *s* one *d. Educ:* Mackie Academy, Stonehaven; Aberdeen Univ. (MA); London Univ. (BA, External). Nat. Service, 2nd Lieut The Gordon Highlanders, 1952–54; Asst Master: Arden House Prep. Sch., 1955–60; George Watson's Coll., 1960–71; Headmaster, Campbell Coll., Belfast, 1971–76. *Recreations:* music, archaeology, fishing, climbing.

MORGAN, Robin Richard; Editor, Sunday Express, 1989–91; *b* 16 Sept. 1953; *s* of Raymond Morgan and Jean Edith Bennett; *m* 1977, Ruth Winefride Mary O'Shea; two *s* one *d. Educ:* King Edward VI Grammar Sch., Stourbridge, W Midlands. County Express, Stourbridge, 1971–73; Evening Echo, Hemel Hempstead, 1973–79; Sunday Times, London, 1979–89: Reporter, 1979–83; Dep. News Editor, 1983–85; Insight Editor, 1985–87; Features Editor, 1987–89. Campaigning Journalist of the Year: (commended) 1982; (winner) 1983. *Publications:* (jtly) The Falklands War, 1982; (jtly) Rainbow Warrior, 1986; (jtly) Bullion, 1988; (ed) Manpower, 1988; (jtly) Ambush, 1989. *Recreations:* riding, reading, travel.

MORGAN, Roger Hugh Vaughan Charles, CBE 1991; Librarian, House of Lords, 1977–91; *b* 8 July 1926; *s* of late Charles Langbridge Morgan, and Hilda Vaughan, both novelists and playwrights; *m* 1st, 1951, Harriet Waterfield (marr. diss. 1965), *d* of Gordon Waterfield; one *s* one *d* (and one *s* decd); 2nd, 1965, Susan Vogel Marrian, *d* of Hugo Vogel, Milwaukee, USA; one *s. Educ:* Downs Sch., Colwall; Phillips Acad., Andover, USA; Eton Coll.; Brasenose Coll., Oxford. MA. Grenadier Guards, 1944–47 (Captain, 1946). House of Commons Library, 1951–63; House of Lords Library, 1963–91. FRSA. *Recreations:* painting, photography, cooking. *Address:* 30 St Peter's Square, W6 9UH. *T:* 081–741 0267; Cliff Cottage, Laugharne, Dyfed. *T:* Laugharne (0994) 427398. *Clubs:* Garrick, Beefsteak.

See also Marchioness of Anglesey.

MORGAN, Prof. Roger Pearce; Professor of Political Science, European University Institute, since 1988; *b* 3 March 1932; *s* of Donald Emlyn Morgan and Esther Mary Morgan (*née* Pearce); *m* 1st, 1957, Annie-Françoise, (Annette) Combes (marr. diss. 1988); three *s* one *d*; 2nd, 1988, Mrs Catherine Howell. *Educ:* Wolverton Grammar Sch.; Leighton Park Sch.; Downing Coll., Cambridge (MA 1957; PhD 1959); Univs of Paris and Hamburg. Staff Tutor, Dept of Extra-Mural Studies, London Univ., 1957–59; Asst Lectr and Lectr in Internat. Politics, UCW, Aberystwyth, 1959–63; Lectr in Hist. and Internat. Relations, Sussex Univ., 1963–67; Asst, then Dep. Dir of Studies, RIIA, 1968–74; Prof. of European Politics, 1974–78, and Dean, Sch. of Human and Environmental Studies, 1976–78, Loughborough Univ.; Head of European Centre for Political Studies, PSI, 1978–86; Vis. Fellow, Centre for Internat. Studies, LSE, 1987–88. Visiting Professor: Columbia Univ., 1965; Johns Hopkins Univ., 1969–70, 1988; Cornell Univ., 1972; Surrey Univ., 1980–84; Res. Associate, Center for Internat. Affairs, Harvard, 1965–66; Visiting Lecturer: Cambridge Univ., 1967; LSE, 1974, 1980–88; Associate Mem., Nuffield Coll., Oxford, 1980–83; Hon. Professorial Fellow, UCW, Aberystwyth, 1980–84, Hon. Prof., 1985–. Lectr at RCDS, CS Coll., RNC, etc. Member: Council, RIIA, 1976–85, 1986–; Academic Council, Wilton Park, 1982–83. Trustee, Gilbert Murray Trust, 1973–88. *Publications:* The German Social Democrats and the First International 1864–72, 1965; Modern Germany, 1966; (ed jtly) Britain and West Germany: changing societies and the future of foreign policy, 1971 (German edn, 1970); West European Politics since 1945, 1972; (ed) The Study of International Affairs, 1972; High Politics, Low Politics: toward a foreign policy for Western Europe, 1973; The United States and West Germany 1945–1973: a study in alliance politics, 1974 (German edn 1975); West Germany's Foreign Policy Agenda, 1978; (ed jtly) Moderates and Conservatives in Western Europe, 1982 (Italian edn 1983); (ed jtly) Partners and Rivals in Western Europe: Britain, France and Germany, 1986; (ed) Regionalism in European Politics, 1986; contribs to symposia and jls. *Recreations:* music, travel, watching cricket. *Address:* European University Institute, Badia Fiesolana, I-50016 San Domenico di Fiesole (FI), Italy. *T:* 055–50921; 32 Cruden Street, N1 8NH. *T:* 071–359 0526. *Clubs:* Reform, PEN; Middlesex County Cricket, Surrey County Cricket.

MORGAN, Rt. Rev. Thomas Oliver; *see* Saskatchewan, Bishop of.

MORGAN, Tom, CBE 1982; DL; JP; Lord Provost of the City of Edinburgh and Lord Lieutenant of the City and County of Edinburgh, 1980–84; *b* 24 Feb. 1914; *s* of Thomas Morgan; *m* 1940, Mary Montgomery (*d* 1991), *d* of Stephen McLauchlan; two *s*. *Educ:* Longside Public Sch., Aberdeenshire; Aberdeen Univ.; W of Scotland Coll. of Agriculture. Unigate Ltd for 36 yrs (Regional Dir for Scotland). Member, Edinburgh Corp., 1954–71 and Edinburgh DC, 1977–84. Chairman: Edinburgh Festival Soc., 1980–84; Edinburgh Mil. Tattoo Policy Cttee, 1980–84. Formerly: Magistrate; City Treasurer; Curator of Patronage, Univ. of Edinburgh; Governor, George Heriot's Trust; Governor, Edinburgh and E of Scotland Coll. of Agric.; Dir, Edinburgh Chamber of Commerce and Manufactures; Pres., Edinburgh City Business Club; Gen. Comr of Income Tax; Chm., Edinburgh Abbeyfield Soc. DL Edinburgh, 1984. OStJ. *Recreations:* golf, gardening. *Address:* 400 Lanark Road, Edinburgh EH13 0LX. *T:* 031–441 3245.

MORGAN, Tony; *see* Morgan, A. W. C.

MORGAN, Rt. Rev. Mgr. Vaughan Frederick John, CBE 1982; Chaplain, The Oratory School, since 1984; *b* Upper Hutt, New Zealand, 21 March 1931; *o s* of late Godfrey Frederick Vaughan Morgan and Violet (Doreen) Vaughan Morgan. *Educ:* The Oratory Sch., S Oxon; Innsbruck Univ. Ordained, 1957; Archdiocese of St Andrews and Edinburgh, 1959–62; entered Royal Navy as Chaplain, 1962; Prin. RC Chaplain (Naval), and Vicar Gen. for RN, 1979–84. Prelate of Honour to HH Pope John Paul II, 1979. *Publications:* contribs to journals. *Recreations:* music, swimming, painting, heraldry. *Address:* The Oratory School, Woodcote, Reading RG8 0PJ. *T:* Checkendon (0491) 680207. *Club:* Army and Navy.

MORGAN, Walter Thomas James, CBE 1959; FRS 1949; Director, Lister Institute of Preventive Medicine, London, 1972–75 (Deputy Director, 1952–68); *b* London, 5 Oct. 1900; *s* of Walter and Annie E. Morgan; *m* 1930, Dorothy Irene Price; one *s* two *d*. *Educ:* Univ. of London. Grocers' Company Scholar, 1925–27; Beit Memorial Med. Res. Fellow, 1927–28; First Asst and Biochemist, Lister Institute Serum Dept (Elstree), 1928–37; Rockefeller Research Fellow (Eidgenössiche Tech. Hochschule, Zürich), 1937. Reader, 1938–51, Lister Inst.; Prof. of Biochemistry, Univ. of London, 1951–68, now Prof. Emeritus. PhD 1927, DSc 1937, London Univ.; DrSc (Tech.) Zürich, 1938; FRIC 1929. Hon. Secretary: Biochemical Soc., 1940–45; Biological Council, 1944–47. Chm. Bd of Studies, Biochem., Univ. of London, 1954–57; Member: Scientific Advisory Council, 1956–60; MRC, 1966–70. Mem., Lawes Agricl Trust Cttee, 1964–76. Guest Lecturer, 100th meeting of Gesellschaft Deutscher Naturforscher und Ärzte, Germany, 1959; Royal Society: Croonian Lectr, 1959; Vice-Pres., 1961–64; Royal Medal, 1968. Vis. Prof., Japan Soc. for Promotion of Science, 1979. Hon. Member: Biochem. Soc., 1969; Internat. Soc. Blood Transfusion, 1980; British Soc. Blood Transfusion, 1984; Internat. Endotoxic Soc., 1987; Hon. FRCP 1982. MD *hc* Basel, 1964; DSc *hc* Michigan, 1969. Conway Evans Prize (Royal College of Physicians, London), 1964; (jointly) Landsteiner Memorial Award (USA), 1967; (jointly) Paul Ehrlich and Ludwig Darmstädter Prizes (Germany), 1968; Philip Levine Medal, Amer. Soc. of Clinical Pathologists, 1990. *Publications:* papers on biochemistry, immunology and pathology. *Address:* 57 Woodbury Drive, Sutton, Surrey SM2 5RA. *T:* 081–642 2319. *Club:* Athenæum.

MORGAN, Prof. William Basil; Professor of Geography, 1971–Sept. 1992, Professor Emeritus, since 1988, and Head of Geography Department, 1982–87, King's College London; *b* 22 Jan. 1927; *s* of William George Morgan and Eunice Mary (*née* Heys); *m* 1954, Joy Gardner; one *s* one *d*. *Educ:* King Edward's Sch., Birmingham; Jesus Coll., Oxford (MA); PhD Glasgow. Assistant, Glasgow Univ., 1948; Lecturer: University Coll., Ibadan, Nigeria, 1953; Univ. of Birmingham, 1959; Reader in Geography, KCL, 1967. *Publications:* West Africa (with J. C. Pugh), 1969; (with R. J. C. Munton) Agricultural Geography, 1971; Agriculture in the Third World: a spatial analysis, 1978; (with R. P. Moss) Fuelwood and rural energy production and supply in the humid tropics, 1981; contribs to geographical and other learned jls and to various conf. collections. *Recreation:* Polish agriculture. *Address:* 57 St Augustine's Avenue, South Croydon, Surrey CR2 6JQ. *T:* 081–688 5687.

MORGAN, (William) Geraint (Oliver), QC 1971; a Recorder of the Crown Court, since 1972; *b* Nov. 1920; *m* 1957, J. S. M. Maxwell; two *s* two *d*. *Educ:* University Coll. of Wales, Aberystwyth; Trinity Hall, Cambridge (Squire Law Schol.); London Univ.; BA, LLB. Served War of 1939–45 with Royal Marines; demobilised with Rank of Major, 1946. Called to the Bar, Gray's Inn, 1947 (Holt Scholar); Northern Circuit. Formerly FCIArb. MP (C) Denbigh, Oct. 1959–1983; Chm., Welsh Party Party, 1967; resigned from Cons. Party, 1983. Member: Lord Chancellor's Cttee (Payne Cttee) on Recovery of Judgment Debts, 1965–69; Investiture Cttee of HRH The Prince of Wales, 1968–69. Mem., Gorsedd of Bards of Royal Nat. Eisteddfod of Wales, 1969–. *Address:* 13 Owen Road, Prescot, Merseyside L35 0PJ.

MORGAN, Air Vice-Marshal William Gwyn, CB 1968; CBE 1960 (OBE 1945); RAF, retired 1969; *b* 13 Aug. 1914; *s* of T. S. Morgan; *m* 1962, Joan Russell. *Educ:* Pagefield Coll., Swansea. Joined Royal Air Force, 1939; Group Capt., 1958; Command Acct, HQ, FEAF, 1962; Air Commodore, 1965; DPS (2), RAF, 1965–66; AOA Technical Training Comd, 1966–68, Training Comd, 1968–69. Air Vice-Marshal, 1967; jssc; psc; FCCA; ACMA. *Recreation:* fell walking. *Address:* c/o Lloyds Bank, 6 Pall Mall, SW1. *Club:* Royal Air Force.

MORGAN, Rt. Hon. William James, PC (Northern Ireland) 1961; JP; Member (UUUC), for North Belfast, Northern Ireland Constitutional Convention, 1975–76; *b* 1914; *m* 1942; two *s* one *d*. Retired company director. MP, Oldpark Div. of Belfast, 1949–58, Clifton Div. of Belfast, 1959–69, NI Parlt; Minister: of Health and Local Government, Northern Ireland, 1961–64; of Labour and National Insurance, 1964; of Health and Social Services, 1965–69; Mem. (U), N Belfast, NI Assembly, 1973–75. *Address:* 6 Demesne Grove, Holywood, Co. Down, N Ireland. *T:* Holywood (02317) 3925.

MORGAN-GILES, Rear-Adm. Sir Morgan (Charles), Kt 1985; DSO 1944; OBE 1943 (MBE 1942); GM 1941; DL; *b* 19 June 1914; *e s* of late F. C. Morgan-Giles, OBE, MINA, Teignmouth, Devon; *m* 1946, Pamela (*d* 1966), *d* of late Philip Bushell, Sydney, New South Wales; two *s* four *d*; *m* 1968, Marigold, *d* of late Percy Lowe. *Educ:* Clifton Coll. Entered Royal Navy, 1932; served on China Station, and in destroyers. War Service: Atlantic convoys and Mediterranean; Tobruk garrison and Western Desert, 1941; with RAF, 1942; Sen. Naval Officer, Vis. (Dalmatia) and liaison with Commandos and Marshal Tito's Partisan Forces, 1943–44. Captain 1953; Chief of Naval Intelligence, Far East, 1955–56; Captain (D) Dartmouth Training Sqdn, 1957–58; HMS Belfast, in command, 1961–62; Rear-Adm. 1962; Adm. Pres., Royal Naval Coll., Greenwich, 1962–64; retd 1964. MP (C) Winchester, May 1964–79. Vice-Chm., Conservative Defence Cttee, 1965–75. Chm., HMS Belfast Trust, 1971–78; Life Vice-Pres., RNLI, 1989. Prime Warden, Shipwrights' Company, 1987–88. DL Hants, 1983. *Recreations:* sailing, country pursuits. *Address:* Frenchmoor Farm, West Tytherley, Salisbury SP5 1NU. *T:* Lockerley (0794) 41045. *Clubs:* Carlton; Royal Yacht Squadron; Australian (Sydney).
See also Baron Killearn.

MORGAN HUGHES, David; *see* Hughes, David M.

MORGAN-OWEN, John Gethin, CB 1984; MBE 1945; QC 1981; Judge Advocate General, 1979–84; *b* 22 Aug. 1914; *o s* of late Maj.-Gen. L. I. G. Morgan-Owen, CB, CMG, CBE, DSO, West Dene, Beech, Alton; *m* 1950, Mary, *d* of late F. J. Rimington, MBE, Master Mariner; two *s* one *d*. *Educ:* Shrewsbury; Trinity Coll., Oxford (BA). Called to Bar, Inner Temple, 1938; Wales and Chester Circuit, 1939; practised at Cardiff, 1939–52. 2nd Lieut Suppl. Reserve, S Wales Borderers, 1939; served 2nd Bn SWB, 1939–44: N Norway, 1940; NW Europe, 1944–45; DAA&QMG, 146 Inf. Bde, 1944–45; Hon. Major. Dep. Judge Advocate, 1952: Germany, 1953–56; Hong Kong, 1958–60; Cyprus, 1963–66; AJAG, 1966; DJAG, Germany, 1970–72; Vice JAG, 1972–79. Jt Chm., Disciplinary Appeals Cttee, ICA, 1985–87. *Recreations:* bad tennis, inland waterways, beagling. *Address:* St Nicholas House, Kingsley, Bordon, Hants GU35 9NW. *T:* Bordon (0420) 472040. *Club:* Army and Navy.

MORI, Haruki; Adviser to Japanese Foreign Office, since 1975; *b* 1911; *m* 1940, Tsutako Masaki; four *s*. *Educ:* Univ. of Tokyo. Ministry of Foreign Affairs, served USA and Philippines, 1935–41; Head of Economic Section, Dept of Political Affairs, 1950–53; Counsellor, Italy, 1953–55, Asian Affairs Bureau, 1955–56; Private Sec. to Prime Minister, 1956–57; Dep. Dir-Gen., Economic Affairs Bureau, 1957; Dir-Gen., American Affairs Bureau, 1957–60; Minister Plenipotentiary to UK, 1960–63, to France, 1963–64; Ambassador to OECD, 1964–67; Dep. Vice-Minister for Foreign Affairs, 1967–70; Vice-Minister for Foreign Affairs, 1970–72; Japanese Ambassador to the Court of St James's, 1972–75. *Recreation:* golf. *Address:* c/o Ministry of Foreign Affairs, Tokyo, Japan.

MORIARTY, Gerald Evelyn, QC 1974; a Recorder of the Crown Court, since 1976; *b* 23 Aug. 1928; *er s* of late Lt-Col G. R. O'N. Moriarty and Eileen Moriarty (*née* Moloney); *m* 1961, Judith Mary, *er d* of Hon. William Robert Atkin; four *s*. *Educ:* Downside Sch.; St John's Coll., Oxford (MA). Called to the Bar, Lincoln's Inn, 1951, Bencher, 1983. *Address:* 3 Stone Buildings, Lincoln's Inn, WC2A 3XL. *T:* 071–430 2318. *Club:* Reform.

MORIARTY, Brig. Joan Olivia Elsie, CB 1979; RRC 1977; Matron-in-Chief and Director of Army Nursing Services, 1976–80; *b* 11 May 1923; *d* of late Lt-Col Oliver Nash Moriarty, DSO, RA, and Mrs Georgina Elsie Moriarty (*née* Moore). *Educ:* Royal Sch., Bath; St Thomas' Hosp. (nursing); Queen Charlotte's Hosp. (midwifery). SRN. VAD, Somerset, 1941–42; joined QAIMNS (R), 1947; Reg. QAIMNS (later QARANC), 1948, retired Jan. 1981; appts incl.: Staff Captain, WO; Instr, Corps Trng Centre; Liaison Officer, MoD; served in UK, Gibraltar, BAOR, Singapore, Malaya, Cyprus; Matron, Mil. Hosp., Catterick, 1973–76; Comdt, QARANC Trng Centre, Aldershot, 1976. Major 1960; Lt-Col 1971; Col 1973; Brig. 1977. QHNS, 1977–80. OStJ 1977. *Recreation:* country pursuits. *Club:* Naval and Military.

MORIARTY, Michael John, CB 1988; Deputy Under-Secretary of State and Principal Establishment Officer, Home Office, 1984–90; *b* 3 July 1930; *er s* of Edward William Patrick Moriarty, OBE, and late May Lilian Moriarty; *m* 1960, Rachel Milward, *d* of J. S. Thompson and late Isobel F. Thompson; one *s* two *d*. *Educ:* Reading Sch., Reading; St John's Coll., Oxford (Sir Thomas White schol.; MA Lit. Hum.). Entered Home Office as Asst Principal, 1954; Private Sec. to Parliamentary Under-Secretaries of State, 1957–59; Principal, 1959; Civil Service Selection Bd, 1962–63; Cabinet Office, 1965–67; Asst Sec., 1967; Private Sec. to Home Sec., 1968; Head of Crime Policy Planning Unit, 1974–75; Asst Under-Sec. of State, 1975–84; seconded to NI Office, 1979–81; Broadcasting Dept, 1981–84. UK Representative, 1976–79, and Chm., 1978–79, Council of Europe Cttee on Crime Problems. Mem., Radio Authority, 1991–. Sub-Treas., Chichester Cathedral. *Recreations:* music, walking, local interests. *Address:* 22 Westgate, Chichester, West Sussex PO19 3EU. *T:* Chichester (0243) 789985.

MORICE, Prof. Peter Beaumont, DSc, PhD; FEng 1989; FICE, FIStructE; Professor of Civil Engineering, University of Southampton, since 1958; *b* 15 May 1926; *o s* of Charles and Stephanie Morice; *m* 1st, 1952, Margaret Ransom (marr. diss. 1986); one *s* two *d*; 2nd, 1986, Rita Corless (*née* Dunk). *Educ:* Barfield Sch.; Farnham Grammar Sch.; University of Bristol; University of London. Surrey County Council, 1947–48; Research Div., Cement and Concrete Assoc., 1948–57. Vis. Prof., Ecole Nat. des Ponts et Chaussées, Paris; Mem. Foundn Cttee, Sultan Qaboos Univ., Oman, 1980–86. Compagnon du Beaujolais, 1987. Order of Sultan Qaboos (Oman), 1986. *Publications:* Linear Structural Analysis, 1958; Prestressed Concrete, 1958; papers on structural theory in various learned journals. *Recreations:* sailing, reading, listening to music. *Address:* 12 Abbotts Way, Highfield, Southampton SO2 1QT. *T:* Southampton (0703) 557641. *Club:* Island Sailing (Cowes).

MORINI, Erica; concert violinist; *b* Vienna, 5 Jan. 1910; *m* 1938, Felice Siracusano; no *c*. *Educ:* at age of 4 years under father, Prof. Oscar Morini, and then under Prof. Ottocar Sevcik, masterclass of Viennese Conservatory, at age of 8. Debut under Arthur Nikisch, at age of 9, in Leipzig Gewandhaus (Beethoven Festival); from there on Concert-tours to: Australia, Asia, Africa, Europe; to USA, 1920. Hon. Mem., Sigma Alpha Beta. Hon. MusD: Smith Coll., Mass, 1955; New England Conservatory of Music, Mass, 1963. Gold Medal, City of NY, 1976. *Recreations:* mountain climbing and chamber music. *Address:* 1200 Fifth Avenue, New York, NY 10029, USA.

MORISHIMA, Prof. Michio, FBA 1981; Sir John Hicks Professor of Economics, London School of Economics and Political Science, 1984–88 (Professor of Economics, 1970–84); Emeritus Professor, University of London, 1988; *b* 18 July 1923; *s* of Kameji and Tatsuo Morishima; *m* 1953, Yoko; two *s* one *d*. Assistant Professor: Kyoto Univ., 1950–51; Osaka Univ., 1951–63; Prof., Osaka Univ., 1963–69. *Publications:* Equilibrium, Stability and Growth, 1964; Theory of Economic Growth, 1969; The Working of Econometric Models, 1972; Marx's Economics, 1973; Theory of Demand: real and monetary, 1973; The Economic Theory of Modern Society, 1976; Walras' Economics, 1977; Value, Exploitation and Growth, 1978; Why Has Japan 'Succeeded'?, 1982; The Economics of Industrial Society, 1985; Ricardo's Economics, 1989. *Address:* Ker, Greenway, Hutton Mount, Brentwood, Essex CM13 2NP. *T:* Brentwood (0277) 219595.

MORISON, Hon. Lord; Alastair Malcolm Morison; a Senator of the College of Justice, Scotland, since 1985; *b* 12 Feb. 1931; 2nd *s* of Sir Ronald Peter Morison, QC (Scotland); *m* 1st, 1957, Lindsay Balfour Oatts (marr. diss. 1977); one *s* one *d*; 2nd, 1980, Birgitte Hendil. *Educ:* Cargilfield; Winchester Coll.; Edinburgh Univ. Admitted to Faculty of Advocates, 1956; QC (Scotland) 1968. Chairman: Medical Appeals Tribunal, 1972–85; Performing Right Tribunal, 1984–85. *Recreations:* golf, fishing. *Address:* 6 Carlton Terrace, Edinburgh EH7 5DD. *T:* 031–556 6766. *Club:* New (Edinburgh).

MORISON, Hugh; Under Secretary, Scottish Office Industry Department (formerly Industry Department for Scotland), since 1988; Director, The Weir Group PLC, since 1989; *b* 22 Nov. 1943; *s* of Archibald Ian Morison and Enid Rose Morison (*née* Mawer); *m* 1971, Marion Smithers; two *d*. *Educ:* Chichester High School for Boys; St Catherine's

Coll., Oxford (MA English Language and Literature; DipEd). Asst Principal, SHHD, 1966–69; Private Sec. to Minister of State, Scottish Office, 1969–70; Principal: Scottish Educn Dept, 1971–73; Scottish Economic Planning Dept, 1973–74; Offshore Supplies Office, Dept of Energy, 1974–75; Scottish Economic Planning Dept, 1975–82, Asst Sec., 1979; Gwilym Gibbon Res, Fellow, Nuffield Coll., Oxford, 1982–83; Scottish Development Dept, 1983–84; Under Sec., SHHD, 1984–88. *Publications:* The Regeneration of Local Economies, 1987; (with Ilona Bellos) Dauphiné, 1991. *Recreations:* hill walking, cycling, sailing, music, looking at ruins. *Address:* c/o Scottish Office Industry Department, Alhambra House, 45 Waterloo Street, Glasgow G2 6AT. *T:* 041–248 2855. *Club:* Commonwealth Trust.

MORISON, Air Vice-Marshal Richard Trevor, CBE 1969 (MBE 1944); RAF retired; President, Ordnance Board, 1971–72; *s* of late Oscar Colin Morison and Margaret Valerie (*née* Cleaver); *m* 1964, Rosemary June Brett; one *s* one *d*. *Educ:* Perse Sch., Cambridge; De Havilland Sch. of Aeronautical Engineering. Commnd in RAF, 1940; RAF Staff Coll., 1952; Sen. Techn. Officer, RAF Gaydon, 1955–57; HQ Bomber Comd, 1958–60; STSO HQ 224 Group, Singapore, 1960–61; Dir of Techn. Services, Royal NZ Air Force, 1961–63; Comd Engrg Officer, HQ Bomber Comd, 1963–65; Air Officer i/c Engrg, HQ Flying Training Comd, 1966–68; Air Officer i/c Engrg, HQ Training Comd RAF, 1968–69; Vice-Pres. (Air) Ordnance Bd, 1969–70. *Recreation:* cabinet making. *Address:* Meadow House, Chedgrave, Loddon, Norfolk.

MORISON, Thomas Richard Atkin, QC 1979; barrister-at-law, since 1960; a Recorder, since 1987; *b* 15 Jan. 1939; *s* of Harold Thomas Brash Morison and Hon. Nancy Morison; *m* 1963, Judith Rachel Walton Morris; one *s* one *d*. *Educ:* Winchester Coll.; Worcester Coll., Oxford, 1959–62 (MA). Passed final Bar examinations, 1959; called to the Bar, Gray's Inn, 1960, Bencher, 1987; pupil in Chambers, 1962–63; started practice, 1963. *Recreations:* reading, sailing, cooking. *Address:* Fountain Court, Temple, EC4. *T:* 071–353 7356. *Club:* Oriental.

MORITA, Akio; Chairman and Chief Executive Officer, Sony Corporation, since 1976; *b* Nagoya, Japan, 26 Jan. 1921; *m* 1950, Yoshiko Kamei; two *s* one *d*. *Educ:* Osaka Imperial Univ. (BSc Physics). Sony Corporation, Tokyo (formerly Tokyo Tsushin Kogyo K. K.): co-founder, 1946; Man. Dir, 1947–55; Sen. Man. Dir, 1955–56; Exec. Vice-Pres., 1959–71; Pres., 1971–76; Sony Corporation of America: Pres., 1960–66, Chm., 1966–72; Chm. Finance Cttee, 1972–74; Chm. Exec. Cttee, 1974–77; Chm. Finance Cttee, 1977–81; Chm., Exec. Cttee, 1981–. Dir, IBM World Trade Americas/Far East Corp., 1972–77; Mem., Internat. Council, Morgan Guaranty Trust Co. Chm., Cttee on Internat. Industrial Co-operation, Keidanren (Japan Fedn of Economic Organizations), 1981–; Vice-Chm., Keidanren, 1986–. Albert Medal, RSA, 1982. Officier de la Légion d'Honneur, France, 1984; Commander's Cross, Order of Merit, FRG. *Publications:* Gakureki Muyooron (Never Mind Education Records), 1966; Shin Jitsuryoku Shugi (A New Merit System), 1969; Made in Japan: Akio Morita and the Sony Corporation, 1987; (jtly) A Japan That Can Say No, 1989. *Recreations:* music, golf, tennis. *Address:* Sony Corporation, 6–7–35 Kitashinagawa, Shinagawa-ku, Tokyo 141, Japan. *T:* 03–448–2600.

MORLAND, Martin Robert, CMG 1985; HM Diplomatic Service; Ambassador and UK Permanent Representative to the Office of the United Nations and other international organizations, Geneva, since 1990; *b* 23 Sept. 1933; *e s* of Sir Oscar Morland, GBE, KCMG and of Alice, *d* of Rt Hon. Sir F. O. Lindley, PC, GCMG; *m* 1964, Jennifer Avril Mary Hanbury-Tracy; two *s* one *d*. *Educ:* Ampleforth; King's Coll., Cambridge (BA). Nat. Service, Grenadier Guards, 1954–56; British Embassy, Rangoon, 1957–60; News Dept, FO, 1961; UK Delegn to Common Market negotiations, Brussels, 1962–63; FO, 1963–65; UK Disarmament Delegn, Geneva, 1965–67; Private Sec. to Lord Chalfont, 1967–68; European Integration Dept, FCO, 1968–73; Counsellor, 1973–77, Rome (seconded temporarily to Cabinet Office to head EEC Referendum Information Unit, 1975); Hd of Maritime Aviation and Environment Dept, FCO, 1977–79; Counsellor and Head of Chancery, Washington, 1979–82; seconded to Hardcastle & Co. Ltd, 1982–84; Under-Sec., Cabinet Office, 1984–86; Ambassador to Burma, 1986–90. *Address:* c/o Foreign and Commonwealth Office, SW1. *Club:* Garrick.

MORLAND, Hon. Sir Michael, Kt 1989; **Hon. Mr Justice Morland;** a Judge of the High Court of Justice, Queen's Bench Division, since 1989; Presiding Judge, Northern Circuit, since 1991; *b* 16 July 1929; *e s* of Edward Morland, Liverpool, and Jane Morland (*née* Beckett); *m* 1961, Lillian Jensen, Copenhagen; one *s* one *d*. *Educ:* Stowe; Christ Church, Oxford (MA). 2nd Lieut, Grenadier Guards, 1948–49; served in Malaya. Called to Bar, Inner Temple, 1953, Bencher 1979; Northern Circuit; QC 1972; a Recorder, 1972–89. Mem., Criminal Injuries Compensation Bd, 1980–89. *Address:* Royal Courts of Justice, Strand, WC2.

MORLAND, Sir Robert (Kenelm), Kt 1990; General Manager, Exports: Tate & Lyle Sugars, since 1987; Tate & Lyle International, since 1987; Director, Tate & Lyle Norway A/S, since 1987; *b* 7 April 1935; *s* of late Kenelm and Sybil Morland; *m* 1st, 1960, Eve Charters (marr. diss. 1965); one *s*; 2nd, 1972, Angela Fraser; one *s*. *Educ:* Birkenhead Sch.; Rydal Sch., Colwyn Bay. Joined Tate & Lyle, 1953; held various managerial positions. Member: Cheshire Riverboard Authy, 1962–65; Birkenhead Nat. Assistance Bd, Adv. Cttee, 1962–65. Member: Birkenhead CBC, 1959–65; Richmond upon Thames BC, 1968–71. Contested (C) Birkenhead, 1964. Chairman: Birkenhead Young Conservatives, 1955–58; Kew Conservatives, 1971–74; Richmond and Barnes Cons. Assoc., 1975–79 (Dep. Pres., 1985–); Cons. Docklands Action Cttee, 1990–; Vice-Pres., Gtr London Conservatives, 1990– (Dep. Chm., 1978–81; Jt Hon. Treas., 1981–87; Chm., 1987–90); Vice-Pres., Newham S Cons. Assoc., 1989–; Member: Cons. Nat. Union Exec. Cttee, 1978–; Cons. Bd of Finance, 1981–87. *Recreations:* theatre, travel, horseriding. *Club:* Carlton.

MORLEY; *see* Hope-Morley, family name of Baron Hollenden.

MORLEY, 6th Earl of, *cr* 1815; **John St Aubyn Parker,** JP; Lt-Col, Royal Fusiliers; Lord-Lieutenant of Devon, since 1982; Chairman, Plymouth Sound Ltd, since 1974; *b* 29 May 1923; *e s* of Hon. John Holford Parker (*y s* of 3rd Earl), Pound House, Yelverton, Devon; *S* uncle, 1962; *m* 1955, Johanna Katherine, *d* of Sir John Molesworth-St Aubyn, 14th Bt, CBE; one *s* one *d*. *Educ:* Eton. 2nd Lt, KRRC, 1942; served NW Europe, 1944–45; Palestine and Egypt, 1945–48; transferred to Royal Fusiliers, 1947; served Korea, 1952–53; Middle East, 1953–55 and 1956; Staff Coll., Camberley, 1957; Comd, 1st Bn Royal Fusiliers, 1965–67. Director: Lloyds Bank Ltd, 1974–78; Lloyds Bank UK Management Ltd, 1979–86; Chm., SW Region, Lloyds Bank, 1989–91 (Chm., Devon and Cornwall Regl Bd, 1974–89). Mem., Devon and Co. Cttee, Nat. Trust, 1969–84; President: Plymouth Incorporated Chamber of Trade and Commerce, 1970–; Cornwall Fedn of Chambers of Commerce and Trader Assocs, 1972–79; West Country Tourist Bd, 1971–89. Governor: Seale-Hayne Agric. Coll., 1973; Plymouth Polytechnic, 1975–82 (Chm., 1977–82). Pres., Council of Order of St John for Devon, 1979. DL 1973, Vice Lord-Lieutenant, 1978–82, Devon. JP Plymouth, 1972. *Heir:* *s* Viscount Boringdon, *qv*. *Address:* Pound House, Yelverton, Devon. *T:* Yelverton (0822) 853162.

MORLEY, Cecil Denis, CBE 1967; Secretary General, The Stock Exchange, London, 1965–71; retired; *b* 20 May 1911; *s* of Cornelius Cecil Morley and Mildred Irene Hutchinson; *m* 1936, Lily Florence Younge; one *s*. *Educ:* Clifton; Trinity Coll., Cambridge. Solicitor. Asst Sec., Share & Loan Dept, Stock Exchange, 1936; Sec. to Coun. of Stock Exchange, 1949. Served War of 1939–45, Major RA (TA). *Recreations:* travel, gardening. *Address:* Bearsward, Coastal Road, Kingston Gorse, West Sussex BN16 1SJ. *T:* Rustington (0903) 782837.

MORLEY, Elliot Anthony; MP (Lab) Glanford and Scunthorpe, since 1987; *b* 6 July 1952; *m* 1975; one *s* one *d*. *Educ:* St Margaret's C of E High Sch., Liverpool. Remedial teacher, comprehensive sch., Hull; head of individual learning centre, until 1987. Mem., Kingston upon Hull City Council, 1979–86; Chair, Hull City Transport Cttee, 1981–85. Contested (Lab) Beverley, 1983. Mem., Select Cttee for Agriculture, to 1990; Dep. Chair, PLP Educn Cttee. *Recreations:* ornithology, the environment. *Address:* House of Commons, SW1A 0AA; 9 West Street, Winterton, Scunthorpe, S Humberside DN15 9QG.

MORLEY, Eric Douglas; Chairman, Miss World Ltd; joined Mecca Ltd, 1946, Chairman on leaving, 1978; Director, Grand Metropolitan Group, 1970–78; orphaned age 11; *m* Julia Evelyn; four *s* (one *d* decd). *Educ:* grammar sch.; Army. Training ship, Exmouth, 1930–34; Royal Fusiliers Band Boy, 1934; left Army, 1945 (Captain). Creator: Come Dancing, 1949 (world's longest-running TV series); Miss World, 1951 (world's greatest beauty pageant with 84 countries entering in 1988); introduced commercial bingo to UK, 1961. President: Outward Bound Trust; Variety Clubs Internat., 1977–79 (world's greatest children's charity); with wife, Julia, has raised over £50 million for charity worldwide. Trustee, KCH. Freeman and Liveryman, City of London. Contested (C) Dulwich, Oct. 1974 and 1979 (reduced majority of the then Attorney-Gen. from 7,500 to 122). Liveryman, Marketors' Co. *Publication:* Miss World Story, 1967. *Recreations:* London Marathon for charity, French horn. *Club:* MCC.

MORLEY, Herbert, CBE 1974; Deputy Chairman and Director, Ellison Circlips Group Ltd, since 1990; Director, Ellison-Morlock, since 1985; *b* 19 March 1919; *s* of George Edward and Beatrice Morley; *m* 1942, Gladys Hardy (*d* 1991); one *s* one *d*. *Educ:* Almondbury Grammar Sch., Huddersfield; Sheffield Univ. (Assoc. Metallurgy); Univ. of Cincinnati (Post-Grad. Studies in Business Admin). Dir and Gen. Works Man., Samuel Fox & Co. Ltd, 1959–65; Dir and Gen. Man., Steel Peech Tozer, 1965–68; Dir, United Steel Cos, 1966–70; British Steel Corporation: Dir, Northern Tubes Gp, 1968–70; Man. Dir, Gen. Steel Div., 1970–73; Man. Dir, Planning and Capital Develt, 1973–76. Chm., Templeborough Rolling Mills Ltd, 1977–82; Dir, Bridon Ltd, 1973–85. *Recreations:* music, cricket lover, weekend golfer. *Address:* Honeysuckle Cottage, Firbeck, near Worksop, Notts S81 8JY. *T:* Rotherham (0709) 815710.

MORLEY, John; actor and playwright; Pantomime Writer for Triumph Productions Ltd, 1973–87; *b* 24 Dec. 1924; *s* of Austin Morley and Patricia (*née* Bray). *Educ:* Uppingham; St John's Coll., Cambridge; RADA. Served War: commnd Coldstream Guards, 1943. Wrote Coldstream Guards pantomime, Dick Whittington and his kit, 1944; performed in and wrote two revues and pantomime, St John's Coll., Cambridge, 1947–48; perf. in and co-author of Cambridge Footlights Revue, 1948; performed in: Private View, Fortune, 1948; Birmingham Rep., 1949; Bob's Your Uncle, Theatre Royal, Stratford, and Music at Midnight, Her Majesty's, 1950; Victorian Music Hall, Players, 1951; Fancy Free, Prince of Wales, 1951–53; Northampton Rep., 1953; Call Me Madam tour, 1953–54; After the Ball, Globe, 1954; Jubilee Girl, Victoria Palace, 1956; The Crystal Heart, Saville, and Love à la Carte, Richmond, 1958; Marigold, Savoy, 1959; Follow that Girl, Vaudeville, 1960; performer and writer, Café de Paris, 1955–60; pantomime writer for Howerd and Wyndham, 1964–73; author of: songs for The Art of Living, Criterion, 1960–61; (jtly) Puss in Boots, London Palladium, 1963; (jtly) Houdini, Man of Magic, Piccadilly, 1966; (jtly) The Littlest Clown, Round House, 1972; Aladdin, BBC Radio, 1980; Big Night Out (Thames Television variety series), 1963–66 (incl. The Beatles Night Out, Blackpool Night Out, Boxing Night Out); BBC Television pantomimes: Babes in the Wood, 1972; The Basil Brush Pantomime, 1980; Aladdin and the Forty Thieves, 1983; BBC Children's Television series: Crazy Bus, 1972; Captain Bonny the pirate, 1973–74; Children's Television Revue, 1975; Basil Brush, 1979–81; has written 153 pantomimes. *Publications:* (jtly) The Magic of Houdini, 1978; (jtly) The Performing Arts, 1980; Pinocchio (children's musical), 1983; The Wind in the Willows (children's musical), 1984; pantomimes: Aladdin; Jack and the Beanstalk; Sinbad the Sailor; Goldilocks and the Three Bears; Robinson Crusoe; Dick Whittington; Cinderella; Mother Goose; Babes in the Wood; The Sleeping Beauty. *Recreations:* architecture, furniture, travel, New York, Wagnerian opera, history of pantomime, British folklore, the Industrial Revolution. *Address:* 4 Stafford Terrace, W8 4SN. *T:* 071–937 5575.

MORLEY, John Harwood, FMA; writer and consultant (buildings and interiors); Keeper of Furniture and Interior Design, Victoria and Albert Museum, 1985–89; *b* 5 Dec. 1933; *s* of George Frederick Morley and Doris Simpson Morley; *m* 1960, Jacqueline Morgan; three *d*. *Educ:* Henry Mellish Grammar Sch.; Exeter Coll., Oxford (MA). FMA 1965. Archivist, Ipswich Corp., 1958–59; Art Asst, Herbert Art Gall., Coventry, 1959–61; Keeper of Art, Leicester Museums, 1961–65; Director: Bradford City Museums, 1965–68; Royal Pavilion, Art Gall. and Museums, Brighton, 1968–85. Mem. Council, Nat. Trust, 1985–89; Chairman (and Founder Member): Decorative Arts Soc. 1890–1940, 1975– (Pres., 1989–); The Brighton Soc., 1973–75; Sec. (and Founder Mem.), Friends of the Royal Pavilion, 1972–85; Trustee: Edward James Foundn, 1976–82; Geffrye Mus., 1990–; Patron, Thirties Soc.; Mem. Council, Attingham Summer Sch. Trust, 1983–87. *Publications:* Death, Heaven and the Victorians, 1971; Designs and Drawings: The Making of the Royal Pavilion, 1984; Regency Style: gardens, architecture and interiors, vol. 1, 1991, vol. 2, 1992; articles and reviews in Apollo, The Connoisseur, and Decorative Arts Soc. Bull. *Recreations:* music, gardening, reading, museums and houses. *Address:* 11 Vine Place, Brighton, East Sussex BN1 3HE.

MORLEY, Malcolm A.; artist; *b* 1931. *Educ:* Camberwell Sch. of Arts and Crafts; Royal Coll. of Art (ARCA 1957). *One Man Exhibitions:* Kornblee Gall., NY, 1957, 1964, 1967, 1969; Galerie Gerald Piltzer, Paris, 1973; Stefanotty Gall., NY, 1973, 1974; Clocktower Gall., Inst. for Art & Urban Resources, 1976; Galerie Jurka, Amsterdam, 1977; Galerie Jollenbeck, Cologne, 1977; Nancy Hoffman Gall., NY, 1979; Suzanne Hilberry Gall., Birmingham, Mich, 1979; Xavier Fourcade, NY, 1981, 1982, 1984; Galerie Nicholine Pon, Zurich, 1984; Fabian Carlsson Gall., London, 1985; Pace Gall., NY, 1988; *major exhibitions:* Wadsworth Atheneum, Hartford, Conn, 1980; Akron Art Mus., 1982; retrospective, Whitechapel Art Gall., also shown in Europe and USA, 1983–84; *work in collections:* Met. Mus. of Art, NY; Detroit Inst. of Art; Hirshhorn Mus. and Sculpture Gdn, Washington; Lousiana Mus., Humlebaek, Denmark; Neue Galerie der Stadt Aachen; Utrecht Mus.; Mus. of Contemp. Art, Chicago; Munson-Williams-Proctor Inst., Utica, NY; Mus. of Modern Art, NY; Mus. Moderner Kunst, Vienna. First Turner Prize, Tate Gall., 1984. *Address:* c/o The Pace Gallery, 32 East 57th Street, New York, NY 10022, USA.

MORLEY, Robert, CBE 1957; Actor-Dramatist; *b* Semley, Wilts, 26 May 1908; *s* of Major Robert Morley and Gertrude Emily Fass; *m* 1940, Joan North Buckmaster, *d* of

Dame Gladys Cooper, DBE; two *s* one *d*. *Educ:* Wellington Coll. Originally intended for diplomatic career; studied for stage at RADA. First appearance in Treasure Island, Strand Theatre, 1929; appeared in provinces; established repertory (with Peter Bull) at Perranporth, Cornwall; parts include: Oscar Wilde in play of that name, Gate, 1936, and Fulton (first New York appearance), 1938; Alexandre Dumas in The Great Romancer, Strand, 1937; Higgins in Pygmalion, Old Vic, 1937; Sheridan Whiteside in The Man Who Came to Dinner, Savoy, 1941; Prince Regent in The First Gentleman, New, 1945, and Savoy; Arnold Holt in Edward My Son, His Majesty's and Lyric, 1947, Martin Beck Theatre, New York, 1948; toured Australia, 1949–50; The Little Hut, Lyric, 1950; Hippo Dancing, Lyric, 1954; A Likely Tale, Globe, 1956; Fanny, Drury Lane, 1957; Hook, Line and Sinker, Piccadilly, 1958; A Majority of One, Phœnix, 1960; A Time to Laugh, Piccadilly, 1962; Halfway Up The Tree, Queen's, 1968; How the Other Half Loves, Lyric, 1970; A Ghost on Tiptoe, Savoy, 1974; Banana Ridge, Savoy, 1976. Directed: The Tunnel of Love, Her Majesty's Theatre, 1957; Once More, with Feeling, New Theatre, 1959. Entered films, 1937; *films:* Marie Antoinette; Major Barbara; Young Mr Pitt; Outcast of the Islands; The African Queen; Curtain Up; Mr Gilbert and Mr Sullivan; The Final Test; Beat the Devil; The Rainbow Jacket; Beau Brummell; The Good Die Young; Quentin Durward; Loser Takes All; Law and Disorder; The Journey; The Doctor's Dilemma; Libel; The Battle of the Sexes; Oscar Wilde; Go to Blazes; The Young Ones; The Boys; The Road to Hong Kong; Nine Hours to Rama; The Old Dark House; Murder at the Gallop; Take her, She's Mine; Hot Enough for June; Sold in Egypt; Topkapi; Of Human Bondage; Those Magnificent Men in Their Flying Machines; Ghengis Khan; ABC Murders; The Loved One; Life at the Top; A Study in Terror; Way Way Out; Finders Keepers; Hotel Paradiso; Le Tendre Voyou; Hot Millions; Sinful Davey; Song of Norway; Oliver Cromwell; When Eight Bells Toll; Doctor in Trouble; Theatre of Blood; Too Many Cooks; The Human Factor; Little Dorrit; The Wind. Hon. DLitt Reading, 1980. *Publications:* Short Story, 1935; Goodness How Sad, 1937; Staff Dance, 1944; (with Noel Langley) Edward My Son, 1948; (with Ronald Gow) The Full Treatment, 1953; Hippo Dancing, 1953; (with Dundas Hamilton) Six Months Grace, 1957; (with Sewell Stokes) Responsible Gentleman (autobiography), 1966; A Musing Morley, 1974; Morley Marvels, 1976; (ed) Robert Morley's Book of Bricks, 1978; (ed) Robert Morley's Book of Worries, 1979; Morley Matters, 1980; The Best of Morley, 1981; The Second Book of Bricks, 1981; The Pleasures of Age, 1988. *Recreations:* conversation, horse racing. *Address:* Fairmans, Wargrave, Berks.

See also S. R. Morley.

MORLEY, Sheridan Robert; author, journalist and broadcaster; London Drama Critic, International Herald Tribune, since 1979; *b* Ascot, Berks, 5 Dec. 1941; *s* of Robert Morley, *qv* and Joan Buckmaster; *m* 1965, Margaret Gudejko; one *s* two *d*. *Educ:* Sizewell Hall, Suffolk; Merton Coll., Oxford (MA (Hons) 1964). Newscaster, reporter and scriptwriter, ITN, 1964–67; interviewer, Late Night Line Up, BBC2, 1967–71; Presenter, Film Night, BBC2, 1972; Dep. Features Editor, The Times, 1973–75; Arts Editor, 1975–88, Drama Critic, 1975–89, Punch; Arts Diarist and TV Critic, The Times, 1989–90; Regular presenter: Kaleidoscope, BBC Radio 4; Meridian, BBC World Service; frequent radio and TV broadcasts on the performing arts, incl. Broadway Babes, Song by Song by Sondheim, and the Arts programme (Radio 2) and Sheridan Morley Meets (BBC1). Mem., Drama Panel, British Council, 1982–. Narrator: Side by Side by Sondheim, Guildford and Norwich, 1981–82; (also devised), Noël and Gertie (Coward anthology), King's Head, London, 1983, Sonning, 1985, Warehouse, London, 1986, Sydney, 1988, Comedy, London, 1989. BP Arts Journalist of the Year, 1989. *Publications:* A Talent to Amuse: the life of Noël Coward, 1969; Review Copies, 1975; Oscar Wilde, 1976; Sybil Thorndike, 1977; Marlene Dietrich, 1977; Gladys Cooper, 1979; (with Cole Lesley and Graham Payn) Noël Coward and his Friends, 1979; The Stephen Sondheim Songbook, 1979; Gertrude Lawrence, 1981; (ed, with Graham Payn) The Noël Coward Diaries, 1982; Tales from the Hollywood Raj, 1983; Shooting Stars, 1983; The Theatregoers' Quiz Book, 1983; Katharine Hepburn, 1984; The Other Side of the Moon, 1985; (ed) Bull's Eyes, 1985; Ingrid Bergman, 1985; The Great Stage Stars, 1986; Spread a Little Happiness, 1986; Out in the Midday Sun, 1988; Elizabeth Taylor, 1988; Odd Man Out: the life of James Mason, 1989; Our Theatres in the Eighties, 1990; ed, series of theatre annuals and film and theatre studies, incl. Punch at the Theatre, 1980; contribs to The Times, Sunday Telegraph, Evening Standard, Radio Times, Mail on Sunday, Playbill (NY), High Life, The Field and The Australian. *Recreations:* talking, swimming, eating, narrating Side by Side by Sondheim and Noël and Gertie. *Address:* 19 Carlyle Court, Chelsea Harbour, SW10 0XD. *Club:* Garrick.

MORLEY, Very Rev. William Fenton, CBE 1980; Dean Emeritus of Salisbury, since 1977; *b* 5 May 1912; *s* of Arthur Fenton and Margaret Morley; *m* 1937, Marjorie Rosa, *d* of Joseph Temple Robinson, Frinton; one *s* one *d*. *Educ:* St David's, Lampeter; Oriel Coll., Oxford; Wycliffe Hall, Oxford; University of London. Ordained, 1935; Curate of: Ely, Cardiff, 1935–38; Porthcawl, S Wales, 1938–43; Officiating Chaplain to the Forces, 1941–43; Vicar of Penrhiwceiber, 1943–46; Rector of Haseley, Oxon, 1946–50; Director of Music and Lecturer in Hebrew at Cuddesdon Coll., Oxon, 1946–50; Examiner in Hebrew and New Testament Greek, 1947–59 and External Lecturer in Biblical and Religious Studies, 1950–61, Univ. of London; Chaplain and Lecturer of St Gabriel's Training Coll., 1956–61; Education Sec. to Overseas Council of Church Assembly, 1950–56; Warburton Lectr, Lincoln's Inn, 1963–65; Chairman: Church of England Deployment and Payment Commission, 1965–68; Church of England Pensions Bd, 1974–80; Bath and Wells Diocesan Education Council, 1978–82. Public Preacher to Diocese of Rochester, 1950–56; Canon Residentiary and Precentor of Southwark Cathedral, 1956–61; Vicar of Leeds, Rural Dean of Leeds and Hon. Canon of Ripon, 1961–71; Dean of Salisbury, 1971–77. Editor, East and West Review, 1953–64. Chaplain to HM's Household, 1965–71; Church Comr, 1968–77. *Publications:* One Church, One Faith, One Lord, 1953; The Church to Which You Belong, 1955; The Call of God, 1959; Preaching through the Christian Year: Year 4, 1974, Year 6, 1977. *Recreations:* music, writing. *Address:* 7 Cavendish Place, Bath, Avon BA1 2UB. *T:* Bath (0225) 312598. *Club:* Commonwealth Trust.

MORLEY-JOHN, Michael, CBE 1979; RD 1970; Judge of the Supreme Court of Hong Kong, 1973–78; *b* 22 May 1923; *s* of late Clifford Morley-John and Norah (*née* Thompson); *m* 1951, Sheila Christine Majendie; one *s* one *d*. *Educ:* Wycliffe Coll.; Univ. of Bristol (LLB). Called to the Bar, Gray's Inn, 1950. Hong Kong: Crown Counsel, 1951; Dir of Public Prosecutions, 1961; Acting Solicitor Gen., 1966–67; Dist Judge, 1967; Judicial Comr, State of Brunei, 1974. Acting Comdr, RNR, 1973. *Recreations:* tennis, stamp collecting, sailing. *Address:* The Coach House, Woodland Way, Milford-on-Sea, Hants SO41 0NB. *T:* Lymington (0590) 44824. *Clubs:* Milford and South Hants (Milford-on-Sea); Royal Ocean Racing; Bar Yacht; Hong Kong, Hong Kong Kennel (former Pres.) (Hong Kong).

MORLING, Col Leonard Francis, DSO 1940; OBE 1946; TD 1942; Architect; *b* 2 Nov. 1904, British; 2nd *s* of late Ernest Charles Morling and Frances Ruth Baldwin; unmarried. *Educ:* Brighton Hove and Sussex Grammar Sch. Architect, 1927–36; Mem. of firm, C. Morling Ltd, Builders and Contractors, Seaford, 1936–39; social work, in London, 1948–50, Malaya, 1950–55; Personnel and Welfare Work, London, 1956–59, Australia, 1960–63, London, 1964. Comnd, Territorial Army, 1924; Capt. 1930; Major, 1934; Lt-Col, 1943; Col 1946; served France and Flanders (despatches, DSO); Persia, Iraq and India. *Publication:* Sussex Sappers, 1972. *Address:* c/o Lloyds Bank, Seaford, East Sussex.

MORLING, Norton Arthur; Member, Civil Aviation Authority, 1972–75; *b* 13 Feb. 1909; *o s* of Norton and Edith Morling, Hunsdon, Herts; *m* 1942, Rachel Paterson, *d* of James and Elizabeth Chapman, Johannesburg, SA; one *s* one *d*. *Educ:* Hertford Grammar Sch.; Cambridge Univ. (MA); Birmingham Univ. (MCom). Joined Turner & Newall Ltd as Management Trainee, 1931. War Service, N Africa and Italy, 1942–45 (despatches); Lt-Col 1944; ADS&T, AFHQ, 1944–45. Dir, and in some cases Chm., of various subsid. and associated companies, UK and overseas, 1946–64, including Turner Brothers Asbestos Co. Ltd and Ferodo Ltd: Gp Dir, 1957–67; Financial Dir, 1964–67; seconded as Industrial Advr to Nat. Economic Develt Office, 1967–70; Mem., Air Transport Licensing Bd, 1971–72. *Recreation:* gardening. *Address:* Little Brook House, Over Wallop, Stockbridge, Hants SO20 8HT. *T:* Andover (0264) 781296.

MORNINGTON, Earl of; Arthur Gerald Wellesley; *b* 31 Jan. 1978; *s* and *heir* of Marquess of Douro, *qv*.

MORO, Peter, CBE 1977; FRIBA, FCSD; Architect; *b* 27 May 1911; *s* of Prof. Ernst Moro and Grete Hönigswald; *m* 1940, Anne Vanneck (marr. diss. 1984); three *d*. *Educ:* Stuttgart, Berlin and Zürich. Swiss Dip. Architecture, 1936; FRIBA 1948; FSIA 1957. Practice with Tecton, 1937–39; Mem. Exec. Cttee, Mars Gp, 1938; Lectr, Sch. of Arch., Regent Street Polytechnic, 1941–47; LCC Associated Architect, Royal Festival Hall (now listed), 1948–51; Peter Moro Partnership, 1952–86; Tutor, Architectural Assoc., 1954–55. External Examiner: Strathclyde Univ., 1973, 1975; Manchester Univ., 1977, 1981; Visiting Critic: Thames Polytechnic; Bath Univ.; Oxford Polytechnic; Sheffield Univ.; QUB. Architect: Fairlawn Sch., LCC, 1957; own house, 1957 (listed 1988); Nottingham Playhouse, 1964; alterations, Royal Opera House, Covent Garden, 1964; Birstall Sch., Leics, 1964; housing schemes, GLC and Southwark, 1967–80; theatre, Hull Univ., the Gulbenkian Centre, 1970; additions and alterations, Bristol Old Vic, 1972; theatre, New Univ. of Ulster, 1976; Plymouth Theatre Royal, 1982; Taliesin Theatre, UC Swansea, 1984; theatre planning consultants, Hong Kong Acad. for Performing Arts, 1983–85. Sen. Pres., Assoc. of British Theatre Technicians (Founder Mem.); Member: Council, RIBA, 1967–73; Housing the Arts Cttee, Arts Council of GB, 1975–78. Governor, Ravensbourne Coll. of Art and Design, 1976–87. Lectures in UK, Finland, Norway, Germany and Holland. Bronze Medal, RIBA, 1964; 4 Civic Trust Awards and Commendations; Heritage Award, 1975; Concrete Award, 1983. *Publications:* contribs to technical jls in UK, Germany, France, Italy, Portugal and Japan. *Address:* 20 Blackheath Park, SE3 9RP. *T:* 081–852 0250.

MORPETH, Viscount; George William Beaumont Howard; Master of Ruthven; *b* 15 Feb. 1949; *s* and *heir* of 12th Earl of Carlisle, *qv*. *Educ:* Eton Coll.; Balliol Coll., Oxford. 9th/12th Royal Lancers, 1967–87; Lieut 1970, Captain 1974, Major 1981. Contested: (L/Alliance) Easington, 1987; (Lib Dem) Northumbria, European parly elecn, 1989. *Recreations:* reading, travel. *Address:* 8 Mill Terrace, Easington, Co. Durham. *Clubs:* Beefsteak, Brooks's.

MORPETH, Sir Douglas (Spottiswoode), Kt 1981; TD 1959; FCA; Chairman, Clerical Medical and General Life Assurance Society, since 1978; *b* 6 June 1924; *s* of late Robert Spottiswoode Morpeth and Louise Rankine Morpeth (*née* Dobson); *m* 1951, Anne Rutherford, *yr d* of Ian C. Bell, OBE, MC, Edinburgh; two *s* two *d*. *Educ:* George Watson's Coll., Edinburgh; Edinburgh Univ. (BCom). Commissioned RA; served 1943–47, India, Burma, Malaya. Mem., Inst. of Chartered Accountants in England and Wales, 1952, Fellow, 1957, Pres., 1972. Partner, 1958–85, Sen. Partner, 1977–85, Touche Ross & Co. Chairman: (of Trustees), British Telecom Staff Superannuation Scheme, 1983–; British Borneo Petroleum Syndicate, 1985–; Deputy Chairman: Brixton Estate plc, 1983–; Leslie Langton Hldgs, 1987–; Dir, Allied-Irish Banks, 1986–. Mem., Investment Grants Advisory Cttee, 1968–71; Chm., Inflation Accounting Steering Gp, 1976–80; Vice-Chm., Accounting Standards Cttee, 1970–82. Chm., Taxation Cttee, CBI, 1973–76. Honourable Artillery Company: Member, 1949–; Lt-Col, comdg 1st Regt HAC (RHA), 1964–66; Master Gunner within the Tower of London, 1966–69. Master, Co. of Chartered Accountants in England and Wales, 1977–78. FRCM (Hon. Treasurer, RCM, 1983–). *Recreations:* golf, tennis, gardening. *Address:* Summerden House, Shamley Green, near Guildford, Surrey GU5 0UD. *Clubs:* Athenæum, City Livery, Royal Automobile.

MORPHET, David Ian; Director of Planning and Development, Balfour Beatty Ltd, since 1989; *b* 24 Jan. 1940; *s* of late A. Morphet and of Sarah Elizabeth Morphet; *m* 1968, Sarah Gillian Sedgwick; two *s* one *d*. *Educ:* King James's Grammar Sch., Almondbury, Yorks; St John's Coll., Cambridge (History Schol.; English Tripos, class I, Pts I and II). Foreign Office, 1961; Vice Consul, Taiz, 1963; Doha, 1963–64; Arabian Dept, FO, 1964–66; Asst Private Sec. to Foreign Secretary, 1966–68; First Sec., Madrid, 1969–72; Diplomatic Service Observer, CS Selection Board, 1972–74; transf. to Dept of Energy, 1974; Asst Sec., 1975; Dep. Chm., Midlands Electricity Board (on secondment), 1978–79; Under-Secretary: Electricity Div., 1979–83; Energy Policy Div., 1983–85; Atomic Energy Div., 1985–89; UK Gov., IAEA, 1985–89. Dir, BICC Cables Ltd, 1981–89. FRSA. *Recreations:* music, theatre, walking. *Address:* 11 Daisy Lane, SW6. *Club:* Athenæum.

MORPHET, Richard Edward; Keeper, Modern Collection, Tate Gallery, since 1986; *b* 2 Oct. 1938; *s* of Horace Taylor Morphet and Eleanor Morphet (*née* Shaw); *m* 1965, Sally Richmond; two *d*. *Educ:* Bootham Sch., York; London Sch. of Economics (BA Hons History). Fine Arts Dept, British Council, 1963–66; Tate Gallery: Asst Keeper, 1966–73; Dep. Keeper, Modern Collection, 1973–86. *Publications:* numerous exhibition catalogues, magazine articles. *Address:* Tate Gallery, Millbank, SW1P 4RG. *T:* 071–821 1313.

MORPURGO, Jack Eric; Professor of American Literature, University of Leeds, 1969–83, now Emeritus; author; *b* 26 April 1918; *s* of late Mark Morpurgo, Islington; *m* 1946, Catherine Noel Kippe, *d* of late Prof. Emile Cammaerts; three *s* one *d*. *Educ:* Christ's Hosp.; Univ. of New Brunswick; Coll. of William and Mary, USA (BA); Durham Univ. Enlisted RA, 1939; served as regimental and staff officer in India, Middle East, Greece and Italy; GSO 2, Public Relations Directorate, War Office. Editorial Staff, Penguin Books, 1946–49; Editor Penguin Parade; General Editor, Pelican Histories, 1949–67; Asst Dir, Nuffield Foundation, 1950–54; Dir-Gen., Nat. Book League, 1955–69, Dep. Chm., 1969–71, Vice-Pres., 1971–87; Prof. of American Studies, Univ. of Geneva, 1968–70; Visiting Professor: Michigan State Univ., 1950; Free Univ., Berlin, 1958; George Washington Univ., 1970; Vanderbilt Univ., 1981; Scholar-in-residence: Rockefeller Res. Center, Italy, 1974; Coll. of Idaho, 1986; Vis. Fellow, ANU, 1975, 1977; has lectured in USA, Canada, Germany, India, Burma, etc. Dir of Unesco Seminar on Production of Reading Materials, Rangoon, 1957, Madras, 1959. Almoner, Christ's Hospital (Dep. Chm., 1980–84); Chm. Working Pty on Medical Libraries; Dir, William and Mary Historical Project, 1970–76. Director: Sexton Press Ltd, 1984–; P. and M. Youngman Carter Ltd,

1985–. Phi Beta Kappa, 1948; Hon. Fellow, Coll. of William and Mary, 1949. Hon. LitD Maine, 1961; Hon. DLitt Elmira, 1966; Hon. DHL William and Mary, 1970; Hon. DH Idaho, 1984. Yorkshire Post Special Literary Award, 1980. *Publications:* American Excursion, 1949; Charles Lamb and Elia, 1949; The Road to Athens, 1963; Barnes Wallis, 1972; Treason at West Point, 1975; Their Majesties Royall Colledge, 1976; Allen Lane: King Penguin, 1979; Verses Humorous and Post-Humorous, 1981; Master of None: an autobiography, 1990; Christ's Hospital: an introductory history, 1991; contributor to: The Impact of America, 1951; joint author of: History of The United States (with Russel B. Nye), 1955; Venice (with Martin Hürlimann), 1964; (with G. A. T. Allar) Christ's Hospital, 1984; edited: Leigh Hunt: Autobiography, 1949; E. J. Trelawny: Last Days of Shelley and Byron, 1952; Poems of John Keats, 1953; Rugby Football: An Anthology (with Kenneth Pelmear), 1958; Cobbett: a year's residence in USA, 1964; Cooper: The Spy, 1968; Cobbett's America, 1985; Margery Allingham: The Return of Mr Campion, 1989. *Recreations:* watching Rugby football, music. *Address:* 12 Laurence Mews, W12 9AT. *Clubs:* Army and Navy, Pilgrims.

MORPURGO DAVIES, Anna Elbina; *see* Davies, A. E.

MORRELL, Prof. David Cameron, OBE 1982; FRCP; FRCGP; Wolfson Professor of General Practice, United Medical and Dental Schools of Guy's and St Thomas' Hospitals, since 1974; *b* 6 Nov. 1929; *s* of William and Violet Morrell; *m* 1953, Alison Joyce Morrell; three *s* two *d.* *Educ:* Wimbledon Coll.; St Mary's Hosp. Med. Sch. (MB BS). DObstRCOG; FFPHM. Phys., RAF Med. Br., 1954–57; Principal in Gen. Practice, Hoddesdon, Herts, 1957–63; Lectr in Gen. Practice, Univ. of Edinburgh, 1963–67; Sen. Lectr, then Reader, in Gen. Practice, St Thomas's Hosp. Med. Sch., 1967–74. KSG 1982. *Publications:* The Art of General Practice, 1966, 4th edn 1991; An Introduction to Primary Medical Care, 1976, 2nd edn 1981; (with J. Cormack and M. Marinker) Practice: a handbook of general practice, 1976, 2nd edn 1987. *Recreations:* gardening, walking. *Address:* 14 Higher Green, Ewell KT17 3BA. *T:* 081–393 0886.

MORRELL, Frances Maine; Senior Research Fellow, Queen Mary and Westfield College, since 1991; *b* 28 Dec. 1937; *d* of Frank and Beatrice Galleway; *m* 1964, Brian Morrell; one *d.* *Educ:* Queen Anne Grammar Sch., York; Hull Univ. BA (Hons) English Lang. and Lit. Secondary Sch. Teacher, 1960–69; Press Officer, Fabian Soc. and NUS, 1970–72; Research into MPs' constituency role, 1973; Special Adviser to Tony Benn, as Sec. of State for Industry, then as Sec. of State for Energy, 1974–79. Dep. Leader, 1981–83, Leader, 1983–87, ILEA; Mem. for Islington S and Finsbury, GLC, 1981–86; Sec., Speaker's Commn on Citizenship, 1988–91. Member: Oakes Cttee, Enquiry into Payment and Collection Methods for Gas and Electricity Bills (report publ. 1976); Exec., Campaign for Labour Party Democracy, 1979–; Co Founder: Labour Co-ordinating Cttee, 1978; Women's Action Cttee, 1980–. Contested (Lab) Chelmsford, Feb. 1974. Mem. Bd of Dirs, Sadler's Wells Theatre, 1982–88. *Publications:* (with Tony Benn and Francis Cripps) A Ten Year Industrial Strategy for Britain, 1975; (with Francis Cripps) The Case for a Planned Energy Policy, 1976; From the Electors of Bristol: the record of a year's correspondence between constituents and their Member of Parliament, 1977; (jtly) Manifesto—a radical strategy for Britain's future, 1981; Children of the Future: the battle for Britain's schools, 1989. *Recreations:* reading, cooking, gardening. *Address:* Queen Mary and Westfield College, Mile End Road, E1 4NS. *T:* 071–975 5003.

MORRELL, Col (Herbert) William (James), OBE 1954; MC 1944; TD; MA Oxon; DL; JP; *b* 1 Aug. 1915; *er s* of James Herbert Morrell, MA, Headington Hill, Oxford; *m* 1947, Pamela Vivien Eleanor, *d* of Richard Stubbs, Willaston, Cheshire; one *s* two *d.* *Educ:* Eton; Magdalen Coll., Oxford. 2nd Lt RA, 1936; served War of 1939–45 (France, Madagascar, Burma); retired 1948. DL 1961, JP 1959, High Sheriff 1960, Oxon. *Recreations:* hunting, sailing. *Address:* Caphill, Sandford St Martin, Oxon OX5 4AL. *T:* Great Tew (060883) 291.

MORRELL, James George; Founder Director, Henley Centre for Forecasting, 1974–79; author and business forecaster; *b* 1923; *s* of late Frederick Morrell and Violet (*née* Smart); *m* 1st, 1944, Elizabeth Bristow (marr. diss. 1970); one *s* two *d*; 2nd, 1972, Margaret Helen Nickolls. *Educ:* Christ's Hospital; Ruskin and Wadham Colls, Oxford. MA Oxon 1953. Served RAF, 1941–46. Ford Motor Co., 1955; Phillips & Drew, 1957; Charterhouse Group, 1964; founded James Morrell & Associates, 1967. Consultant to OECD, 1985–87. Visiting Professor, Univ. of Bradford, 1970–73; Associate Fellow, Oxford Centre for Management Studies, 1981–84. *Publications:* Business Forecasting for Finance and Industry, 1969; Business Decisions and the Role of Forecasting, 1972; Inflation and Business Management, 1974; 2002: Britain plus 25, 1977; The Regeneration of British Industry, 1979; Britain through the 1980s, 1980; The Future of the Dollar and the World Reserve System, 1981; Employment in Tourism, 1982, 2nd edn 1985; Business Forecasts for the Housing Market, annually 1985–; The Impact of Tourism on London, 1985; Business Forecasts for the Motor Trades, annually 1986–; The Productivity Performance Index, 1989. *Recreations:* canals, Samuel Pepys, stock market. *Address:* 81 Speed House, Barbican, EC2Y 8AU.

MORRELL, Rt. Rev. James Herbert Lloyd; Canon and Prebend of Heathfield in Chichester Cathedral, 1959–82, Canon Emeritus since 1982; Provost of Lancing (Southern Division Woodard Schools), 1961–82; *b* 12 Aug. 1907; *s* of George Henry and Helen Adela Morrell. *Educ:* Dulwich Coll.; King's Coll., London; Ely Theological Coll. Deacon, 1931; Priest, 1932; Curate of St Alphage, Hendon, 1931–35; Curate of St Michael and All Angels, Brighton, 1935–39; Bishop of Chichester's Chaplain for men, 1939–41; Lecturer for The Church of England Moral Welfare Council, 1941–44; Vicar of Roffey, 1944–46; Archdeacon of Lewes, 1946–59; Bishop Suffragan of Lewes, 1959–77; Asst Bishop, Diocese of Chichester, 1978–85. Fellow of King's Coll., London, 1960. *Publications:* Four Words (broadcast talks to the Forces), 1941; The Heart of a Priest, 1958; A Priest's Notebook of Prayer, 1961; The Catholic Faith Today, 1964. *Recreations:* walking, photography. *Address:* 83 Davigdor Road, Hove BN3 1RA. *T:* Brighton (0273) 733971.

MORRELL, Leslie James, OBE 1986; JP; Chairman, Northern Ireland Water Council, since 1982; *b* 26 Dec. 1931; *s* of James Morrell; *m* 1958, Anne Wallace, BSc; two *s* one *d.* *Educ:* Portora Royal Sch., Enniskillen; Queen's Univ., Belfast. BAgric 1955. Member: Londonderry CC, 1969–73; Coleraine Bor. Council, 1973–77; Mem. (U) for Londonderry, NI Assembly, 1973–75; Minister of Agriculture, NI Exec., 1973–74; Dep. Leader, Unionist Party of NI, 1974–80. Mem., BBC Gen. Adv. Cttee, 1980–86; Chm., BBC NI Agricl Adv. Cttee, 1986–91. Chm., NI Fedn of Housing Assocs, 1978–80; Hon. Secretary: James Butcher Housing Assoc. (NI), 1981– (Chm., 1976–81); James Butcher Retirement Homes Ltd, 1985–. Mem. Exec., Assoc. of Governing Bodies of Voluntary Grammar Schs, 1978–84; Chm., Virus Tested Stem Cutting Potato Growers Assoc., 1977–88. JP Londonderry, 1966. *Address:* Dunboe House, Castlerock, Coleraine BT51 4UB. *T:* Castlerock (0265) 848352.

MORRELL, Col William; *see* Morrell, Col H. W. J.

MORRICE, Norman; choreographer; Director: the Royal Ballet, 1977–86; Choreographic Studies, Royal Ballet School, since 1987; Royal Ballet Choreographic Group, since 1987; *b* Mexico, of British parents. *Educ:* Rambert School of Ballet. Joined the Ballet Rambert in early 1950s as a dancer; notably danced Dr Coppélius, in Coppélia, and subseq. also choreographer; first considerable success with his ballet, Two Brothers, in America, and at first London perf., Sept. 1958; première of his 2nd ballet, Hazaña, Sadler's Wells Theatre, 1958; the New Ballet Rambert Company was formed in 1966 and he was Co-Director with Marie Rambert, to create new works by unknown and established choreographers; his ballet, Hazard, was danced at Bath Festival, 1967; he composed 10 new ballets by 1968 and had taken his place with leading choreographers; *ballets include:* 1–2–3, Them and Us and Pastorale Variée, which were staged at the Jeanetta Cochrane Theatre, 1968–69; Ladies, Ladies!, perf. by Ballet Rambert at Young Vic, 1972; Spindrift, at Round House, 1974, etc. Has danced frequently overseas.

MORRICE, Philip; HM Diplomatic Service; Minister-Counsellor, Consul-General and Director of Trade Promotion, Brasilia, since 1988; *b* 31 Dec. 1943; *s* of late William Hunter Morrice and Catherine Jane Cowie; *m* 1988, Margaret Clare Bower; one *s* one *d.* *Educ:* Robert Gordon's College, Aberdeen. Entered HM Diplomatic Service, 1963; served Kuala Lumpur, 1964–67; CO, later FCO, 1967–69; Caracas, 1969–72; First Sec., UK Delegn to OECD, Paris, 1973–75; First Sec. (Energy), UK Perm. Rep. to EC, Brussels, 1975–78; FCO, 1978–81; First Sec. (Commercial), later Counsellor (Comm.), Rome, 1981–85; Counsellor (Econ. and Comm.), Lagos, 1986–88. *Publications:* The Schweppes Guide to Scotch, 1983; The Whisky Distilleries of Scotland and Ireland, 1987; numerous articles. *Recreations:* travel, tennis, golf. *Address:* c/o Foreign and Commonwealth Office, SW1A 2AH. *Clubs:* Royal Over-Seas League, Royal Automobile.

MORRIS, family name of **Barons Killanin, Morris, Morris of Castle Morris** and **Morris of Kenwood.**

MORRIS, 3rd Baron *cr* 1918; **Michael David Morris;** *b* 9 Dec. 1937; *s* of 2nd Baron Morris and of Jean Beatrice (now Lady Salmon), *d* of late Lt-Col D. Maitland-Makgill-Crichton; *S* father, 1975; *m* 1st, 1959, Denise Eleanor (marr. diss. 1962), *o d* of Morley Richards; 2nd, 1962, Jennifer (marr. diss. 1969), *o d* of Squadron Leader Tristram Gilbert; two *d*; *m* 1980, Juliet, twin *d* of Anthony Buckingham; two *s* one *d.* *Educ:* Downside. FCA. *Heir:* *s* Hon. Thomas Anthony Salmon Morris, *b* 2 July 1982. *Address:* House of Lords, SW1A 0PW.

MORRIS OF CASTLE MORRIS, Baron *cr* 1990 (Life Peer), of St Dogmaels in the County of Dyfed; **Brian Robert Morris,** MA, DPhil; Principal, St David's University College, Lampeter, 1980–91; *b* 4 Dec. 1930; *o s* of William Robert Morris and Ellen Elizabeth Morris (*née* Shelley); *m* 1955, Sandra Mary James, JP; one *s* one *d.* *Educ:* Cardiff High School; Worcester Coll., Oxford (MA, DPhil). National service with Welch Regt, 1949–51. Fellow of Shakespeare Inst., Univ. of Birmingham, 1956–58; Asst Lectr 1958–60, Lectr 1960–65, Univ. of Reading; Lectr 1965–67, Sen. Lectr 1967–71, Univ. of York; Prof. of English Literature, Univ. of Sheffield, 1971–80. Gen. Editor: New Mermaid Dramatists, 1964–86; New Arden Shakespeare, 1974–82. Member: Council, Yorkshire Arts Assoc., 1973–81 (Chm. Literature Panel, 1973–77); Welsh Arts Council, 1983–86 (Mem. Lit. Cttee, 1978–86); Archbishops' Council on Evangelism, 1971–75; Yr Academi Gymreig, 1979–; British Library Bd, 1980–91; Council, Poetry Soc., 1980–90 (Vice-Pres., 1990–); Council, Nat. Library of Wales, 1981–91; Chm., Museums and Galls Commn, 1985–90 (Mem., 1975– (formerly Standing Commn on Museums and Galls)). Pres., Welsh Historic Gdns Trust, 1990–; Vice President: Council for Nat. Parks, 1985–; Museums Assoc., 1985–; Prayer Book Soc., 1990–. Trustee: Nat. Portrait Gall., 1977–; Nat. Heritage Meml Fund, 1980–; Welsh Adv. Cttee, British Council, 1983–; Anthony Panizzi Foundn, 1987–; Museum of Empire and Commonwealth, 1991–; Campaign for the Protection of Rural Wales, 1991–. Broadcaster, scriptwriter and presenter of television programmes. Hon. LittD Sheffield, 1991. *Publications:* John Cleveland: a Bibliography of his Poems, 1967; (with Eleanor Withington) The Poems of John Cleveland, 1967; (ed) New Mermaid Critical Commentaries I-III, 1969–72; Mary Quant's London, 1973; (ed) Ritual Murder, 1980; *edited plays:* Ford's The Broken Heart, 1965, and 'Tis Pity She's a Whore, 1968; (with Roma Gill) Tourneur's The Atheist's Tragedy, 1976; Shakespeare's The Taming of the Shrew, 1981; *poetry:* Tide Race, 1976; Stones in the Brook, 1978; Dear Tokens, 1987; contribs to journals. *Recreations:* music, mountains, and museums. *Address:* The Old Hall, Foolow, Eyam, Sheffield S30 1QR. *T:* Hope Valley (0433) 31186. *Clubs:* Athenæum, Beefsteak.

MORRIS OF KENWOOD, 2nd Baron *cr* 1950, of Kenwood; **Philip Geoffrey Morris,** JP; Company Director, retired 1990; *b* 18 June 1928; *s* of 1st Baron Morris of Kenwood, and Florence (*d* 1982), *d* of Henry Isaacs, Leeds; *S* father, 1954; *m* 1958, Ruth, *o d* of late Baron Janner and of Lady Janner, *qv*; one *s* three *d.* *Educ:* Loughborough Coll., Leics. Served RAF, Nov. 1946–Feb. 1949, July 1951–Oct. 1955. JP Inner London, 1967. *Recreations:* tennis, golf, ski-ing. *Heir:* *s* Hon. Jonathan David Morris, *b* 5 Aug. 1968. *Address:* Lawn Cottage, Orchard Rise, Kingston, Surrey KT2 7EY. *T:* 081–942 6321.

MORRIS, Air Marshal Sir Alec, KBE 1982; CB 1979; FEng 1989; Executive, British Aerospace Plc, since 1983; *b* 11 March 1926; *s* of late Harry Morris; *m* 1946, Moyna Patricia, *d* of late Norman Boyle; one *s* one *d* (twins). *Educ:* King Edward VI Sch., East Retford; King's Coll., Univ. of London; Univ. of Southampton. Commnd RAF, 1945; radar duties, No 90 (Signals) Gp, 1945–50; Guided Weapons Dept, RAE, 1953–56; exchange duty, HQ USAF, 1958–60; space res., Min. of Supply, 1960–63; DS, RAF Staff Coll., 1963–65; OC Eng, No 2 Flying Trng Sch., Syerston, 1966–68; Asst Dir, Guided Weapons R&D, Min. of Tech., 1968–70; OC RAF Central Servicing Devel Estabt, Swanton Morley, 1970–72; SASO, HQ No 90 (Signals) Gp, 1972–74; RCDS, 1974; Dir of Signals (Air), MoD, 1975–76; Dir Gen. Strategic Electronic Systems, MoD (PE), 1976–79; Air Officer Engineering, RAF Strike Command, 1979–81; Chief Engineer, RAF, 1981–83, retired. *Recreations:* tennis, gardening. *Address:* 6 Liverpool Road, Kingston-upon-Thames, Surrey KT2 7SZ. *Club:* Royal Air Force.

MORRIS, Rt. Hon. Alfred; PC 1979; QSO 1989; MP (Lab and Co-op) Manchester (Wythenshawe) since 1964; Opposition Front Bench Spokesman on Social Services, specialising in the problems of disabled people, 1970–74 and since 1979; *b* 23 March 1928; *s* of late George Henry Morris and Jessie Morris (*née* Murphy); *m* 1950, Irene (*née* Jones); two *s* two *d.* *Educ:* elem. and evening schs, Manchester; Ruskin Coll., Oxford; St Catherine's, Univ. of Oxford (MA); Univ. of Manchester (Postgrad. certif. in Educn). Employed in office of a Manchester brewing firm from age 14 (HM Forces, 1946–48); Teacher and Lectr, Manchester, 1954–56; Industrial Relations Officer, The Electricity Coun., London, 1956–64. Nat. Chm., Labour League of Youth, 1950–52; contested Liverpool (Garston), Gen. Elec. 1951; Observer, Coun. of Europe, 1952–53; PPS to Minister of Agric., Fisheries and Food, 1964–67, and to Lord President of the Council and Leader of House of Commons, 1968–70; Parly Under-Sec. of State, DHSS, as Britain's first-ever Minister for the Disabled, 1974–79. Treasurer, British Gp, IPU, 1971–74; Mem., UK Parly Delegn to UN Gen. Assembly, 1966; Chm., Food and Agriculture Gp of Parly Lab. Party, 1971–74; Representative of Privy Council on Council of RCVS, 1969–74; promoted Chronically Sick and Disabled Persons Act, 1970, Food and Drugs (Milk) Act, 1970, Police Act, 1972, as a Private Member; Parly Adviser to the Police

Fedn, 1971–74; Chairman: Co-operative Parly Group, 1971–72 and 1983–85; Parly and Scientific Cttee, 1988–; Vice-Chm., All-Party Parly Retail Trade Gp, 1972–74; Chairman: Managing Trustees, Parly Pensions Fund, 1983– (Man. Trustee, 1980–83); Managing Trustees, H of C Members' Fund, 1983–; Anzac Gp of MPs and Peers, 1982–; Jt Treasurer, British-Amer. Parly Gp, 1983–. Mem., Gen. Adv. Council, BBC, 1968–74, 1983–; Patron: Disablement Income Group, 1970–; Motability, 1978–; Mem., Exec. Cttee, Nat. Fund for Research into Crippling Diseases, 1970–74. Chm., World Cttee apptd to draft "Charter for the 1980's" for disabled people worldwide, 1980–81; Pres., N of England Regional Assoc. for the Deaf, 1980–; Trustee, Crisis at Christmas, 1982–. Hon. Fellow, Manchester Poly., 1990. Field Marshal Lord Harding Award, 1971, for services to the disabled; Grimshaw Meml Award of Nat. Fedn of the Blind, 1971. Hon. AO 1991. *Publications:* Value Added Tax: a tax on the consumer, 1970; The Growth of Parliamentary Scrutiny by Committee, 1970; (with A. Butler) No Feet to Drag, 1972; Ed. lectures (Human Relations in Industry), 1958; Ed. Jl (Jt Consultation) publ. Nat. Jt Adv. Coun. Elec. Supply Ind., 1959–61. *Recreations:* gardening, tennis, snooker, chess. *Address:* House of Commons, SW1A 0AA.

MORRIS, Alfred Cosier; Director, Bristol Polytechnic, since 1986; *b* 12 Nov. 1941; *s* of late Stanley Bernard Morris, Anlaby, E Yorks, and Jennie Fletcher; *m* 1970, Annette, *er d* of Eamonn and May Donovan, Cork, Eire; one *d.* *Educ:* Hymers Coll., Hull (E Riding Scholar); Univ. of Lancaster (MA Financial Control 1970). FCA; FSS. Articled clerk to Oliver Mackrill & Co., 1958–63; Company Sec., Financial Controller and Dir, several cos, 1963–71; Sen. Leverhulme Res. Fellow in Univ. Planning and Orgn, Univ. of Sussex, 1971–74; Vis. Lectr in Financial Management, Univ. of Warwick, 1973; Group Management Accountant, Arthur Guinness Ltd, 1974–76; Management Consultant, Deloitte Haskins & Sells, 1976–77; Financial Adviser, subsids of Arthur Guinness, 1977–80; Dep. Dir, Polytechnic of the South Bank, 1980–85, Acting Dir, 1985–86. Adviser to H of C Select Cttee on Educn, Sci. and Arts, 1979–83. Chm., PCFC Cttee on Performance Indicators in Higher Educn, 1989–90; Mem., CNAA, 1988–. Trustee, Bristol Cathedral Trust, 1988–. FRSA. *Publications:* (ed jtly and contrib.) Resources and Higher Education, 1982; articles and contribs to jls on higher educn. *Recreations:* sailing, wind-surfing. *Address:* Park Court, Sodbury Common, Old Sodbury, Avon BS17 6PX. *T:* Chipping Sodbury (0454) 319900. *Clubs:* Athenæum, Little Ship.

MORRIS, Anthony Paul; QC 1991; a Recorder of the Crown Court, since 1988; *b* 6 March 1948; *s* of late Isaac Morris Morris and Margaret Miriam Morris; *m* 1975, Jennie Foley; two *s.* *Educ:* Manchester Grammar Sch.; Keble Coll., Oxford (MA). Called to the Bar, Gray's Inn, 1970; practising on Northern Circuit, 1970–. *Recreations:* sport, film, music, family. *Address:* 2 Old Bank Street, Manchester M2 7PF. *T:* 061–832 3791. *Clubs:* Dunham Forest Golf, Bowdon Lawn Tennis (Cheshire).

MORRIS, Air Marshal Sir (Arnold) Alec; *see* Morris, Air Marshal Sir Alec.

MORRIS, Rt. Hon. Charles Richard; PC 1978; DL; *b* 14 Dec. 1926; *s* of George Henry Morris, Newton Heath, Manchester; *m* 1950, Pauline, *d* of Albert Dunn, Manchester; two *d.* *Educ:* Brookdale Park Sch., Manchester. Served with Royal Engineers, 1945–48. Pres., Clayton Labour Party, 1950–52. Mem. of Manchester Corporation, 1954–64: Chm. of Transport Cttee, 1959–62; Dep. Chm. of Establishment Cttee, 1963–64. Mem., Post Office Workers Union (Mem. Nat. Exec. Council, 1959–63). Contested (Lab) Cheadle Div. of Cheshire, 1959. MP (Lab) Manchester, Openshaw, Dec. 1963–1983; PPS to the Postmaster-General, 1964; Govt Asst Whip, 1966–67; Vice-Chamberlain, HM Household, 1967–69; Treasurer, HM Household (Deputy Chief Whip), 1969–70; PPS to Rt Hon. H. Wilson, MP, 1970–74; Minister of State: DoE, March-Oct. 1974; CSD, 1974–79; Dep. Shadow Leader of the House, 1980–83. Sec., NW Gp of Labour MPs, 1979–83. Dep. Chm., Ponti Gp, 1987–. Chm., Oldham–Rochdale Groundwork Trust, 1984–; Chm., Covent Garden Tenants' Adv. Gp, 1990–. DL Greater Manchester, 1985. *Address:* 24 Buxton Road West, Disley, Stockport, Cheshire. *T:* Disley (0663) 2450.

MORRIS, Christopher; National Director, Corporate Special Services, Touche Ross & Co., since 1980; *s* of Richard Archibald Sutton Morris and Josephine Fanny Mary Morris (*née* Galliano); *m* 1968, Isabel Claire Ramsden Knowles (marr. diss.); two *s.* *Educ:* privately. Chartered Accountant, 1967; Partner, Touche Ross & Co., 1970. Major insolvency assignments: Banco Ambrosiano; Laker Airways; Rush & Tomkins; Polly Peck. *Recreations:* music, travel, food and wine, countryside. *Address:* 55 High Holborn, WC1V 6DX. *T:* 071–405 8799. *Clubs:* Turf, Royal Automobile.

MORRIS, Rev. Dr Colin; broadcaster and writer; Controller, BBC Northern Ireland, 1987–90; *b* 13 Jan. 1929; *o s* of Daniel Manley Morris and Mary Alice Morris, Bolton, Lancs. *Educ:* Bolton County Grammar Sch.; Univs of Oxford and Manchester. Served RM, 1947–49. Student, Nuffield Coll., Oxford, 1953–56; Missionary, Northern Rhodesia, 1956–60; President: United Church of Central Africa, 1960–64; United Church of Zambia, 1965–68; Minister of Wesley's Chapel, London, 1969–73; Gen. Sec., Overseas Div., Methodist Church, 1973–78; Pres. of the Methodist Conference, 1976–77; Hd of Religious Programmes, BBC TV, 1978–84; Dep. Hd, 1978–79, Hd, 1979–87, Religious Broadcasting, BBC; Special Adviser to Dir-Gen., BBC, 1986–87. Chm., Community and Race Relations Unit, BCC, 1974–76; Mem., Lord Chancellor's Adv. Cttee on Legal Educn and Conduct, 1991–. Lectures: Willson, Univ. of Nebraska, 1968; Cousland, Univ. of Toronto, 1972; Voigt, S Illinois Conf. United Methodist Church, 1973; Hickman, Duke University, North Carolina, 1974; Palmer, Pacific NW Univ., 1976; Heslington, Univ. of York, 1983; Hibbert, BBC Radio 4, 1986; William Barclay Meml, Glasgow, 1986; Univ. of Ulster Convocation, 1988; St Cuthbert's, Edinburgh, 1990; Select Preacher, Univ. of Cambridge, 1975, Oxford, 1976. Holds several hon. degrees. Officer-Companion, Order of Freedom (Zambia), 1966. *Publications:* Black Government (with President K. D. Kaunda), 1960; Hour After Midnight, 1961; Out of Africa's Crucible, 1961; End of the Missionary, 1961; Church and Challenge in a New Africa, 1965; Humanist in Africa (with President K. D. Kaunda), 1966; Include Me Out, 1968; Unyoung, Uncoloured, Unpoor, 1969; What the Papers Didn't Say, 1971; Mankind My Church, 1971; The Hammer of the Lord, 1973; Epistles to the Apostle, 1974; The Word and the Words, 1975; Bugles in the Afternoon, 1977; Get Through Till Nightfall, 1979; (ed) Kaunda on Violence, 1980; God-in-a-Box: Christian strategy in the TV age, 1984; A Week in the Life of God, 1986; Raising the Dead: a preacher's notebook, 1987; Drawing the Line: taste and standards in BBC programmes, 1987; Starting from Scratch, 1990; Let God be God: TV sermons, 1990; Wrestling with an Angel, 1990; *relevant publication:* Spark in the Stubble, by T. L. Charlton, 1969. *Recreations:* writing, walking, music. *Address:* Tile Cottage, 8 Houndean Rise, Lewes, E Sussex BN7 1EG. *T:* Brighton (0273) 476969.

MORRIS, David; *see* Morris, W. D.

MORRIS, David Elwyn; a District Judge (formerly Registrar) of the Principal Registry of the Family Division of the High Court of Justice, 1976–91; *b* 22 May 1920; *s* of Rev. S. M. Morris and K. W. Morris; *m* 1st, 1947, Joyce Hellyer (*d* 1977); one *s* one *d*; 2nd, 1978, Gwendolen Pearce (*d* 1988), *widow* of Dr John Pearce; 3rd, 1990, Mrs C. M. Tudor. *Educ:* Mill Hill Sch.; Brasenose Coll., Oxford (Hulme Exhibnr; MA). With Friends' Ambulance Unit in China, 1942–44; served British Army in India, 1944–46. Called to Bar, Inner Temple, 1949; admitted Solicitor of the Supreme Court, 1955; Mem., Matrimonial Causes Rule Cttee, 1967–75. Partner, Jaques & Co. until 1975. Adv. Editor, Atkin's Encyclopaedia of Court Forms in Civil Proceedings, 1982–88. *Publications:* China Changed My Mind, 1948; The End of Marriage, 1971; contrib. Marriage For and Against, 1972; Pilgrim through this Barren Land, 1974. *Recreation:* reading. *Address:* 42 Frenchay Road, Oxford OX2 6TG. *T:* Oxford (0865) 58390. *Club:* United Oxford & Cambridge University.

MORRIS, David Griffiths; barrister; a Recorder, since 1984; *b* 10 March 1940; *s* of Thomas Griffiths Morris and Margaret Eileen Morris; *m* 1971, Carolyn Mary (*née* Miller); one *s* one *d.* *Educ:* Abingdon Sch.; King's Coll., Univ. of London (LLB Hons). Called to the Bar, Lincoln's Inn, 1965. Pupillage in London (Temple and Lincoln's Inn), 1965–67; Tenant in London Chambers (Temple), 1967–72; Tenant in Cardiff Chambers, 1972–; Asst Recorder, 1979–84; Local Junior for Cardiff Bar, 1981–87; Head of Chambers, June 1984. Founder Member: Llantwit Major Round Table and 41 Clubs; Llantwit Major Rotary Club (Pres., 1984–85); Llanmaes Community Council, 1982–84. *Recreations:* Rugby Union football, cricket, swimming, theatre, reading, gardening, family. *Address:* 30 Park Place, Cardiff CF1 3BA. *T:* Cardiff (0222) 398421. *Clubs:* Cardiff and County, United Services Mess (Cardiff).

MORRIS, Rev. David Richard; Member (Lab) Mid and West Wales, European Parliament, since 1984; *b* Llanelli, 28 Jan. 1930. *Educ:* Stebonheath Central Sch., Llanelli; Ruskin Coll., Oxford; University Coll., Swansea; Theological Coll., Aberystwyth. Former foundry labourer; Minister, Mid-Wales and Newport, Presbyterian Church of Wales, 1958–62; former district and county councillor; Educnl Advisor, Gwent CC, 1974–84. Contested (Lab) Brecon and Radnor, 1983. Member, European Parliament Committees: Agriculture, Fisheries and Food (Sen. Vice-Pres., Fisheries sub-cttee); Development; Full Mem., ACP/EEC Assembly. Contributor, Low Pay Unit. Member: TGWU; Socialist Educnl Assoc.; Tribune Gp; EPLP; CND; Socialist Health Assoc. *Address:* 39 St James Crescent, Swansea SA1 6DR.

MORRIS, David Richard, CEng, FIMechE; Chairman, Northern Electric plc, since 1989; *b* 25 July 1934; *s* of Frederick George Morris and Marjorie Amy (*née* Brown); *m* 1961, (Ann) Carole Birch; two *s* one *d.* *Educ:* Imperial College (BSc(Eng)). ACGI. Graduate Engrg apprenticeship, D. Napier & Son, Divl Chief Develt Engr and Gen. Manager, 1956–69, English Electric; Divl Gen. Manager and Divl Dir, General Electric Co., 1969–75; Subsid. Co. Man. Dir, Sears Holdings plc, 1975–80; Delta Group plc: Divl Man. Dir, 1980–84; Gp Exec. Dir, 1984–88. *Recreations:* sailing, golf. *Address:* Northern Electric plc, Carliol House, Market Street, Newcastle upon Tyne NE1 6NE. *Club:* Northern Counties (Newcastle upon Tyne).

MORRIS, Prof. David William, PhD; FRAgS; dairy and sheep farmer, since 1983; agricultural consultant, since 1986; *b* 7 Dec. 1937; *s* of late David William Morris and Mary Olwen Ann Lewis; *m* 1966, Cynthia Cooper; one *s* one *d.* *Educ:* Ardwyn Grammar Sch.; UC of Wales (BSc Agric.); Univ. of Newcastle upon Tyne (PhD). FRAgS 1974. Develt Officer, Agric. Div., ICI, 1963–64; Asst Dir, Cockle Park Exptl Farm, Newcastle upon Tyne Univ., 1964–68; Farms Manager for Marquis of Lansdowne, Bowood, Wilts, 1968–70; Principal, Welsh Agric. Coll., Aberystwyth, 1970–83; Prof. of Agric., UC Wales, Aberystwyth, 1979–83. Churchill Fellowship, 1973. *Publications:* Practical Milk Production, 1976, 3rd edn 1977; (with M. M. Cooper) Grass Farming, 5th edn 1984. *Recreation:* farming. *Address:* Wern Berni Farm, Llanboidy, Whitland, Dyfed. *T:* Whitland (0994) 448214. *Club:* Farmers'.

MORRIS, Denis Edward, OBE 1958; Head, and ultimately Controller of Light Programme, BBC, 1960–67; *b* 29 June 1907; *s* of Philip and Edith Morris; *m* 1st, 1931, Angela Moore (marr. diss., 1942); one *s*; 2nd, 1943, Catharine Garrett (*née* Anderton); one *s.* *Educ:* Tonbridge Sch. BBC Talks Producer, 1936; BBC Midland Public Relations Officer, 1938; BBC Empire Public Relations Officer, 1939; MOI Dir, Midland Region, 1940–42; BBC Midland Regional Programme Dir, 1943–48; Head of Midland Regional Programmes, 1948–60. Wine Correspondent, Daily Telegraph, 1967–87. Leicester City Council, 1933–36; Chm., Findon Parish Council, 1971–74; Chm., Lord Mayor of Birmingham's War Relief Fund Publicity and Appeals Cttee, 1942–48; Pres., Shoreham Cons. Assoc., 1976–79 and 1983–86 (Chm., 1971–75); Member: Hosp. Management Cttee, St Francis Hosp. and Lady Chichester Hosp., 1966–71; Exec. Cttee, Nat. Cricket Assoc., 1969–74 (Chm., Public Relations Standing Cttee, 1969–72); Dep. Chm., Lord's Taverners' Council, 1963–65 (Mem., 1962–67); Public Relations Advisor to MCC and the Counties, 1967–68; Mem., Public Relations and Promotion Sub-Cttee, TCCB, 1968–75. *Publications:* Poultry-Keeping for Profit, 1949; The French Vineyards, 1958; A Guide to the Pleasures of Wine-Drinking, 1972; ABC of Wine, 1977. *Recreations:* bridge, drinking wine. *Clubs:* MCC; Incogniti CC; Sussex Martlets CC; Gentlemen of Leicestershire CC; Blackheath Rugby Football; Sussex Rugby Football.
See also T. D. Morris.

MORRIS, Derek James, MA, DPhil; Fellow and Tutor, Oriel College, Oxford; *b* 23 Dec. 1945; *s* of Denis William and Olive Margaret Morris; *m* 1975, Susan Mary Whittles; two *s.* *Educ:* Harrow County Grammar Sch.; St Edmund Hall, Oxford; Nuffield Coll., Oxford. MA (Oxon); DPhil. Research Fellow, Centre for Business and Industrial Studies, Warwick Univ., 1969–70; Fellow and Tutor in Economics, Oriel Coll., Oxford, 1970–; Tutor and Sen. Tutor, Oxford University Business Summer Sch., 1970–78; Visiting Fellow, Oxford Centre for Management Studies, 1977–; Economic Dir, Nat. Economic Develt Office, 1981–84; Sir John Hicks Res. Fellow, Oxford Univ., 1991–92. Vis. Lectr, Univ. of Calif, Irvine, 1986–87. Chm., Oxford Economic Forecasting, 1984–; Editorial Board: Oxford Economic Papers, 1984–; Annual Register of World Events, 1985–; Asst Editor, Jl of Industrial Economics, 1984–87; Associate Editor, Oxford Review of Economic Policy, 1985–. *Publications:* (ed) The Economic System in the UK, 1977, 3rd edn 1985; (with D. Hay) Industrial Economics, Theory and Evidence, 1979, 2nd edn 1990; (with D. Hay) Unquoted Companies, 1984; (ed jtly) Strategic Behaviour and Industrial Competition, 1987; articles on unemployment, trade policy and performance, productivity growth, industrial policy, the Chinese economy, exchange rates and profitability. *Recreations:* skiing, badminton, Rugby, reading history. *Club:* Reform.

MORRIS, Desmond John, DPhil; writer on animal and human behaviour; *b* 24 Jan. 1928; *s* of Capt. Harry Howe Morris and Dorothy Marjorie Fuller Morris (*née* Hunt); *m* 1952, Ramona Baulch; one *s.* *Educ:* Dauntsey's Sch.; Birmingham Univ. (BSc); Magdalen Coll., Oxford (DPhil). Postdoctoral research in Animal Behaviour, Dept of Zoology, Oxford Univ., 1954–56; Head of Granada TV and Film Unit at Zool. Soc. of London, 1956–59; Curator of Mammals, Zool. Soc. of London, 1959–67; Dir, Inst. of Contemp. Arts, London, 1967–68; Research Fellow, Wolfson Coll., Oxford, 1973–81. Chm. of TV programmes: Zootime (weekly), 1956–67; Life (fortnightly), 1965–68; TV series: The Human Race, 1982; The Animals Roadshow, 1987–89; The Animal Contract, 1990. *Publications:* (Jt Ed.) International Zoo Yearbook, 1959–62; The Biology of Art, 1962; The Mammals: A Guide to the Living Species, 1965; (with Ramona Morris) Men and

Snakes, 1965; (with Ramona Morris) Men and Apes, 1966; (with Ramona Morris) Men and Pandas, 1966; The Naked Ape, 1967; (ed) Primate Ethology, 1967; The Human Zoo, 1969; Patterns of Reproductive Behaviour, 1970; Intimate Behaviour, 1971; Manwatching: a field guide to human behaviour, 1977; (jtly) Gestures: their origins and distribution, 1979; Animal Days (autobiog.), 1979; The Giant Panda, 1981; The Soccer Tribe, 1981; Inrock (novel), 1983; The Book of Ages, 1983; The Art of Ancient Cyprus, 1985; Bodywatching: a field guide to the human species, 1985; The Illustrated Naked Ape, 1986; Catwatching, 1986; Dogwatching, 1986; The Secret Surrealist, 1987; Catlore, 1987; The Human Nest-builders, 1988; The Animals Roadshow, 1988; Horsewatching, 1988; The Animal Contract, 1990; Animal-Watching, 1990; numerous papers in zoological jls. *Recreations:* painting, archæology. *Address:* c/o Jonathan Cape, Random Century House, 20 Vauxhall Bridge Road, SW1V 2SA.

MORRIS, Desmond Victor; HM Diplomatic Service, retired; *b* 26 June 1926; *s* of late John Walter Morris and Bessie (*née* Mason); *m* 1st, 1951, Peggy Iris Mumford; two *d* 2nd, 1961, Patricia Irene Ward, *d* of Charles Daniel and Emma Camwell; one *d*. *Educ:* Portsmouth Southern Secondary Sch. for Boys; Durham Univ. Served RAF, 1945–48 (Actg Corporal). Joined HM Diplomatic Service, 1948; served at Seattle, Budapest, Saigon, Addis Ababa, Berne, Ankara and Pretoria; Dep. High Comr, Georgetown, 1973–78; Dep. Head of Accommodation and Services Dept, FCO, 1979–82; Consul-Gen. and Counsellor (Administration), Washington, 1982–86. *Recreations:* gardening and the other fine arts. *Address:* Grayshott, Green Lane, Axminster, Devon EX13 5TD.

MORRIS, Edward Allan, CMG 1967; OBE 1961; *b* 8 Sept. 1910; *s* of late John Morris, Twickenham; *m* 1937, Phyllis, *d* of late Francis Guise, Twickenham; one *d* (one *s* decd). *Educ:* Hampton Grammar Sch.; Univ. of London (BCom). Entered Crown Agents' Office, 1928. RAFVR, 1942–46; Sqdn Leader (King's Commendation, 1946). Crown Agents' Office: Asst Head of Dept, 1956; Head of Dept, 1958; Asst Crown Agent, 1964; Crown Agent for Oversea Governments and Administrations, 1968–71. *Recreations:* cricket, Rugby Union football, church bells and change-ringing, preserving the riverside area of Twickenham. *Address:* 56 Lebanon Park, Twickenham, Mddx TW1 3DQ. *T:* 081–892 5856. *Clubs:* Royal Air Force, MCC, Corona (Hon. Treas.); Harlequin Football.

MORRIS, Air Commodore Edward James, CB 1966; CBE 1959; DSO 1942; DFC 1944; RAF, retired 1968; *b* 6 April 1915; *s* of late D. G. Morris, and late Mrs E. Morris, Bulawayo, Southern Rhodesia; *m* 1945, Alison Joan, *d* of Sir Charles Henderson, KBE; two *s*. *Educ:* Michaelhouse, Natal, S Africa. Commnd, 1937; Fighter Comd, 1938–41; Desert Air Force, 1941–45; Staff Coll., 1945–46; BAFO Germany, 1946–49; Old Sarum, 1949–52; Caledonian Sector, Fighter Command, 1952–53; RAF Flying Coll., 1953–54; Exchange Posting with USAF, Florida, 1954–56; SASO HQ 12 Group, 1956–58; OC Wattisham, 1958–59; HQ Fighter Command, 1959–60; Air Ministry, 1960–64; Chief of Staff, Headquarters Middle East Command, 1964–66; AOC Air Cadets, and Comdt Air Training Corps, 1966–68. American DFC 1945. *Recreations:* golf, fishing. *Address:* PO Box 133, Himeville, Natal 4585, South Africa.

MORRIS, Gareth; *see* Morris, J. G.

MORRIS, Gareth (Charles Walter); flautist; Professor of the Flute, Royal Academy of Music, 1945–85; *b* Clevedon, Som, 13 May 1920, *e s* of late Walter and Enid Morris; *m* 1954; one *d*; *m* 1975, Patricia Mary, *y d* of Neil and Sheila Murray, Romsey, Hampshire; one *s* two *d*. *Educ:* Bristol Cathedral Sch.; Royal Academy of Music, London. First studied the flute at age of twelve under Robert Murchie and later won a scholarship to RAM. Career since then has been as soloist, chamber music and symphonic player, teacher and lecturer; Principal Flautist, 1949–72, Chm., 1966–72, Philharmonia Orch. Has been mem. Arts Council Music Panel, and Warden of Incorporated Soc. of Musicians Soloists Section; Adjudicator, International Flute playing Competitions, Geneva, 1973, 1978, Munich, 1974, Leeds, 1977, 1980, Ancona, 1978, 1979, 1984. Played at Her Majesty's Coronation in Westminster Abbey in 1953. Gov., RSM; Trustee, Loan Fund for Musical Instruments. ARAM 1945; FRAM 1950; FRSA 1967 (Mem. Council, 1977–83; Chm., Music Cttee, 1981–83). *Publication:* Flute Technique, 1991. *Recreations:* reading and collecting books, astronomy, antiquarian horology. *Address:* 4 West Mall, Clifton, Bristol BS8 4BH. *T:* Bristol (0272) 734966. *Club:* Royal Over-Seas League.

MORRIS, Prof. Howard Redfern, FRS 1988; Professor of Biological Chemistry, Imperial College, University of London, since 1980; *b* 4 Aug. 1946; *s* of Marion Elizabeth and Herbert Morris, Bolton, Lancs; *m* 1st, 1969, Lene Verny Jensen (marr. diss.); two *d*; 2nd, 1988, Maria Panico; one *s* one *d*. *Educ:* Univ. of Leeds (BSc 1967; PhD 1970). SRC Fellow, Cambridge, 1970–72; Scientific Staff, MRC Lab. of Molecular Biol., Cambridge, 1972–75; Imperial College: Lectr, Dept of Biochem, 1975–78; Reader in Protein Chem., 1978–80; Hd, Dept of Biochem., 1985–88; Chm., Div. of Life Sciences, 1985–88. Founder Chm., M-Scan Ltd, analytical chem. consultants, 1979–. Visiting Professor: Univ. of Virginia, 1978; Soviet Acad. of Scis, 1982; Univ. of Naples, 1983; Life Scis Div., E. I. Dupont, USA, 1984–85; Dow Lectr in Analytical Chem., Univ. of British Columbia, 1989–90. Mem., EMBO, 1979–. BDH Gold Medal and Prize for analytical biochem., Biochem. Soc., 1978; Medal and Prize for macromolecules and polymers, RSC, 1982; Gold Medal for contribs to biopolymer sequencing and mass spectroscopy, Univ. of Naples/CNR Italy, 1989. *Publications:* (ed) Soft Ionisation Biological Mass Spectrometry, 1981; numerous contribs to learned jls, on enkephalin, SRS-A leukotrienes, interleukin, calcitonin gene related peptide, mass spectrometry, protein and glycoprotein structure elucidation. *Recreations:* fell walking, gardening, guitar. *Address:* Department of Biochemistry, Imperial College, Exhibition Road, SW7 2AZ. *T:* 071–589 5111.

MORRIS, Ivor Gray, CMG 1974; Former Chairman and Managing Director, Morris Woollen Mills (Ipswich) Pty Ltd; Chairman Queensland Export Advisory Committee; *b* 28 March 1911; *s* of John and Annie Morris, Talybont, Cards, and Ipswich, Qld; *m* 1944, Jessie Josephine Halley; two *d*. *Educ:* Scotch Coll., Melbourne; Scots Coll., Warwick, Qld; Ipswich Grammar Sch., Qld; Leeds Univ. Founded Morris Woollen Mills (Ipswich) Pty Ltd, 1934. Former Mem. Exec., Wool Textile Manufrs Assoc. of Australia; Life Mem., Nuclear Physics Foundn; Former Mem., Trade Devellt Council, Canberra. Former Chm. of Trustees, Ipswich Grammar Sch.; Vice-Pres., Qld Museum Trust, 1970–; Patron, St David's Welsh Soc.; Foundn Mem. and District Governor, Ipswich Apex Club (1st Apex Club formed in Austr.), 1938. *Recreations:* music, reading. *Address:* River Road, Redbank, Queensland 4301, Australia. *T:* 88–29–35. *Clubs:* Tattersall's (Brisbane); Ipswich, Ipswich North Rotary (Ipswich, Qld).

MORRIS, James; *see* Morris, Jan.

MORRIS, Air Vice-Marshal James, CBE 1984 (OBE 1977); Chief Executive, Scottish Society for the Prevention of Cruelty to Animals, since 1991; *b* 8 July 1936; *s* of late James and Davina Swann Morris; *m* 1959, Anna Wann Provan; three *s*. *Educ:* Kirkcaldy High Sch.; Edinburgh Univ. (BSc). Commnd RAF, 1957; Flying/Staff Duties, RAF, USN, RN, 1960–72; Flt Comdr 206 Sqdn, 1973–74; Sqdn Comdr 201 Sqdn, 1975–77; sc, 1977–78, psc; Central Tactics and Trials Organisation, 1978–81; Station Comdr RAF Kinloss, 1981–84; Staff HQ 18 Gp, 1984–86; Dir Operational Requirements (Air), MoD, 1986–89; AO Scotland and NI, 1989–91. *Recreations:* sailing, golf. *Address:* c/o Lloyds Bank, George Street, Edinburgh EH2 4TF. *Club:* Royal Air Force.

MORRIS, (James) Peter; public affairs analyst; *b* 17 Sept. 1926; *s* of Frank Morris and Annie (*née* Collindridge); *m* 1st, Peggy Giles (marr. diss.); 2nd, Margaret Law. *Educ:* Barnsley Grammar Sch.; Manchester Univ. (BA, Teaching Dip.). CAM Dip, 1976. MIPR 1965, FIPR 1990; AMInstR 1980; Fellow, Soc. of Assoc. Execs, 1985 (Sen. Vice-Pres., 1991–). Served RAF, 1945–48; Research Dept, Labour Party, 1952–59; Govt Information Services, 1960–73; Dir of Information, GLC, 1973–77; Sec. Gen., Nat. Cold Storage Fedn, 1977–90. Sen. Treas. and Mem. Travel Bd, NUS, 1952–56; Borough Councillor, Hackney, 1956–59; Member: Nat. Exec., IPCS, 1964–73; Council for Social Democracy, 1984–90; Council, CBI, 1989–90. *Publication:* Road Safety: a Study of Cost Benefit in Public Service Advertising, 1972. *Recreations:* painting, writing, cricket. *Address:* 88 Ridgmount Gardens, WC1E 7AY. *T:* 071–637 2141. *Clubs:* MCC, Reform.

MORRIS, (James) Richard (Samuel), CBE 1985; FEng; Chairman and Managing Director, 1980–90, Non-Executive Chairman, since 1990, Brown and Root (UK) Ltd; *b* 20 Nov. 1925; *o s* of James John Morris and Kathleen Mary Morris (*née* McNaughton); *m* 1958, Marion Reid Sinclair; two *s* two *d*. *Educ:* Ardingly Coll.; Birmingham Univ. BSc, 1st cl. hons Chem. Engrg; Vice-Chancellor's Prize, 1955; FEng, FIChemE. Captain Welsh Guards, 1944–48. Courtaulds Ltd, 1950–78: Man. Dir, National Plastics Ltd, 1959–64; Dep. Chm., British Cellophane Ltd, 1967–70; Chm., British Celanese Ltd, 1970–72; Chm., Northgate Gp Ltd, 1971–76; Chm., Meridian Ltd, 1972–76; Dir, 1967–78, Gp Technical Dir, 1976–78, Courtaulds Ltd. Chairman: Devonport Management Ltd, 1987–; Devonport Royal Dockyard plc, 1987–; UK Nirex, 1989–; Dir, British Nuclear Fuels Ltd, 1971–85. Vis. Prof. of Chem. Engrg, Univ. of Strathclyde, 1979–88; Pro-Chancellor, 1982–86, Sen. Pro-Chancellor and Chm. of Council, 1986–, Loughborough Univ. Member: Nuclear Power Adv. Bd, 1973; Adv. Council for Energy Conservation, 1974–80; Adv. Bd for Res. Councils, 1981–90, Dep. Chm., 1988–90; Dep. Chm., NEB, 1978–79; Industrial Adviser to Barclays Bank, 1980–85. Mem. Council, 1974, Vice-Pres., 1976, Pres., 1977, IChemE; Vice-Pres., Soc. of Chem. Industry, 1978–81; Hon. Sec., 1979–82, Hon. Sec. for Educn and Training, 1984–91, Vice Pres., 1987–, Fellowship of Engineering; President: Pipeline Industries Guild, 1983–85; Engrg Sect., BAAS, 1989; Assoc. of Science Educn, 1990. Chm. British Cttee, Det Norske Veritas. Gov., Repton Sch., 1987–. FRSA 1986. Hon. DSc: Leeds, 1981; Bath, 1981; Birmingham, 1985; Loughborough, 1991. *Recreations:* sheep farming, gardening, music. *Address:* Breadsall Manor, Derby DE7 6AL. *T:* Derby (0332) 831368. *Club:* Athenæum.

MORRIS, James Shepherd, RSA 1989 (ARSA 1975); RIBA, FRIAS; ALI; Partner, Morris & Steedman, Architects and Landscape Architects; *b* 22 Aug. 1931; *s* of Thomas Shepherd Morris and Johanna Sime Malcolm; *m* 1959, Eleanor Kenner Smith; two *s* one *d*. *Educ:* Daniel Stewart's Coll.; Edinburgh Sch. of Architecture (DipArch); Univ. of Pennsylvania (MLA). *Architectural works:* Edinburgh Univ., Strathclyde Univ., Princess Margaret Rose Hosp., Countryside Commn for Scotland. Member, Arts Council of Gt Britain, 1973–80; Vice-Chm., Scottish Arts Council, 1976–80 (Chm., Art Cttee, 1976–80; Mem., Enquiry into Community Arts, 1974); Mem., Council, RSA, 1991–; Past Member: Council, RIAS and Edinburgh AA, 1969–71; Council of Cockburn Assoc., Edinburgh; Cttee of Management, Traverse Theatre, Edinburgh. Convenor, Fellowship Cttee, RIAS, 1985–87. Trustee, Nat. Mus. of Antiquities, 1980–86. RIBA Award, 1974; 9 Civic Trust Awards, 1962–75; British Steel Award, 1971; European Architectural Heritage Award, 1975; European Heritage Business & Industry Award, 1975. *Publications:* contribs to RIBA Jl. *Recreations:* golf, tennis, skiing, painting. *Address:* (office) 38 Young Street North Lane, Edinburgh EH2 4JD. *T:* (office) 031–226 6563. *Clubs:* New (Edinburgh); Philadelphia Cricket (Philadelphia).

MORRIS, Jan, MA Oxon; FRSL; writer; *b* 2 Oct. 1926. Commonwealth Fellow, USA, 1953; Editorial Staff, The Times, 1951–56; Editorial Staff, The Guardian, 1957–62. Mem., Yr Academi Gymreig. *Publications* (as James Morris until 1973, subseq. as Jan Morris): Coast to Coast, 1956, rev. edn 1962; Sultan in Oman, 1957, rev. edn 1983; The Market of Seleukia, 1957; Coronation Everest, 1958; South African Winter, 1958; The Hashemite Kings, 1959; Venice, 1960, 2nd rev. edn, 1983; The Upstairs Donkey, 1962 (for children); The World Bank, 1963; Cities, 1963; The Presence of Spain, 1964, rev. edns (as Spain), 1979, 1982, 1988; Oxford, 1965, 2nd edn 1986; Pax Britannica, 1968; The Great Port, 1970, rev. edn 1985; Places, 1972; Heaven's Command, 1973; Conundrum, 1974; Travels, 1976; Farewell the Trumpets, 1978; The Oxford Book of Oxford, 1978; Destinations, 1980; My Favourite Stories of Wales, 1980; The Venetian Empire, 1980, 2nd edn 1988; The Small Oxford Book of Wales, 1982; A Venetian Bestiary, 1982; The Spectacle of Empire, 1982; (with Paul Wakefield) Wales, The First Place, 1982; (with Simon Winchester) Stones of Empire, 1983; The Matter of Wales, 1984; Journeys, 1984; Among the Cities, 1985; Last Letters from Hav, 1985; (with Paul Wakefield) Scotland, The Place of Visions, 1986; Manhattan '45, 1987; Hong Kong, 1988; Pleasures of a Tangled Life, 1989; (with Paul Wakefield) Ireland, Your Only Place, 1990; City to City (Canada), 1990; Sydney, 1992. *Address:* Trefan Morys, Llanystumdwy, Cricieth, Gwynedd LL52 0LP. *T:* Cricieth (0766) 522222, *Fax:* Cricieth 522426.

MORRIS, Prof. Jeremy Noah, CBE 1972; FRCP; Professor of Public Health, University of London, at London School of Hygiene and Tropical Medicine, 1967–78; *b* 6 May 1910; *s* of Nathan and Annie Morris; *m* 1939, Galina Schuchalter; one *s* one *d*. *Educ:* Hutcheson's Grammar Sch., Glasgow; Univ. of Glasgow; University Coll. Hosp., London; London School of Hygiene and Tropical Medicine (Hon. Fellow 1979). MA, DSc, DPH. Qual., 1934; hosp. residencies, 1934–37; general practice, 1937–38; Asst MOH, Hendon and Harrow, 1939–41; Med. Spec., RAMC, 1941–46 (Lt-Col 1944–46); Rockefeller Fellow, Prev. Med., 1946–47; Dir, MRC Social Med. Unit, 1948–75; Prof., Social Med., London Hosp., 1959–67. Visiting Professor: Yale, 1957; Berkeley, 1963; Jerusalem, 1968, 1980; Adelaide, 1983. Consultant, Cardiology, WHO, 1960–. Lectures: Ernestine Henry, RCP London; Chadwick Trust; Gibson, RCP Edinburgh; Fleming, RCPS Glasgow; Carey Coombs, Univ. of Bristol; Brontë Stewart, Univ. of Glasgow; St Cyres, Nat. Heart Hosp.; Alumnus, Yale; Delamar, Johns Hopkins Univ.; Wade Hampton Frost, APHA; George Clarke, Univ. of Nottingham. Member: Royal Commission on Penal Reform; Cttee, Personal Social Services, Working Party Med. Admin, 1964–72; Health Educn Council, 1978–80; Chairman: Nat. Adv. Cttee on Nutrition Educn, 1979–83; Fitness and Health Adv. Gp, Sports Council, and Health Educn Authority (formerly Health Educn Council), 1980–. Hon. Member: Amer. Epid. Soc., 1976; Soc. for Social Medicine, 1978; British Cardiac Soc., 1982; Swedish Soc. for Sports Medicine, 1984. JP Middx, 1956–66. Hon. FFCM, 1977. Hon. MD Edinburgh, 1974; Hon. DSc Hull, 1982. Bisset Hawkins Medal, RCP, 1980; Honor Award, Amer. Coll. of Sports Medicine, 1985; Jenner Medal, RSM, 1987. *Publications:* Uses of Epidemiology, 1957, 3rd edn 1975 (trans. Japanese, Spanish); papers on coronary disease and exercise, and on health and prevention. *Recreations:* walking, swimming, piano music. *Address:* 3 Briardale Gardens, NW3 7PN. *T:* 071–435 5024.

MORRIS, Rt. Hon. John, PC 1970; QC 1973; MP (Lab) Aberavon Division of Glamorgan since Oct. 1959; a Recorder of the Crown Court, since 1982; Opposition

Spokesman on Legal Affairs and Shadow Attorney General, since 1983; *b* Nov. 1931; *s* of late D. W. Morris, Penywern, Talybont, Cardiganshire; *m* 1959, Margaret M. Morris, JP, *d* of late Edward Lewis, OBE, JP, of Llandysul; three *d*. *Educ:* Ardwyn, Aberystwyth; University Coll. of Wales, Aberystwyth; Gonville and Caius Coll., Cambridge (LLM); Academy of International Law, The Hague; Holker Senior Exhibitioner, Gray's Inn. Commissioned Royal Welch Fusiliers and Welch Regt. Called to the Bar, Gray's Inn, 1954, Bencher, 1985. Parly Sec., Min. of Power, 1964–66; Jt Parly Sec., Min. of Transport, 1966–68; Minister of Defence (Equipment), 1968–70; Sec. of State for Wales, 1974–79. Dep. Gen. Sec. and Legal Adviser, Farmers' Union of Wales, 1956–58. Member: UK Delegn Consultative Assembly Council of Europe and Western European Union, 1963–64, 1982–83; N Atlantic Assembly, 1970–74. Chairman: Nat. Pneumoconiosis Jt Cttee, 1964–66; Joint Review of Finances and Management, British Railways, 1966–67; Nat. Road Safety Advisory Council, 1967; Mem. Courts of University Colls, Aberystwyth, Swansea and Cardiff. Hon. LLD Wales, 1983. *Address:* House of Commons, SW1.

MORRIS, John Evan A.; *see* Artro Morris.

MORRIS, Prof. (John) Gareth, FRS 1988; FIBiol; Professor of Microbiology, University College of Wales, Aberystwyth, since 1971; *b* 25 Nov. 1932; *s* of Edwin Morris and Evelyn Amanda Morris (*née* Griffiths); *m* 1962, Âine Mary Kehoe; one *s* one *d Educ:* Bridgend Grammar Sch.; Univ. of Leeds; Trinity Coll., Oxford. DPhil; FIBiol 1971. Guinness Res. Fellow, Univ. of Oxford, 1957–61; Rockefeller Fellow, Univ. of Calif at Berkeley, 1959–60; Tutor in Biochem., Balliol Coll., Oxford, 1960–61; Lectr, subseq. Sen. Lectr, Univ. of Leicester, 1961–71. Vis. Associate Prof., Purdue Univ., USA, 1965. Member: UGC, 1981–86; Royal Commn on Environmental Pollution, 1991–. *Publications:* A Biologist's Physical Chemistry, 1968, 2nd edn 1974; contribs on microbial biochemistry and physiology. *Recreations:* gardening, walking. *Address:* Cilgwyn, 16 Lôn Tyllwyd, Llanfarian, Aberystwyth, Dyfed SY23 4UH. *T:* Aberystwyth (0970) 612502.

MORRIS, Keith Elliot Hedley, CMG 1988; HM Diplomatic Service; Ambassador to Colombia, since 1990; *b* 24 Oct. 1934; *m* Maria del Carmen Carratala; two *s* two *d*. Entered Foreign Office, 1959; served Dakar, Algiers, Paris, Bogota; First Sec., FCO, 1971–76; Counsellor (Commercial), Warsaw, 1976–79; Minister-Counsellor, Mexico City, 1979–84; Head of Personnel Policy Dept, FCO, 1984–85; rcds, 1986; Minister (Commercial) and Consul-Gen., Milan, 1987–90. *Address:* c/o Foreign and Commonwealth Office, SW1.

MORRIS, Max; educational propagandist and reformer; pioneer of the Comprehensive School; Headmaster, Willesden High School, 1967–78, retired; *s* of Nathan and Annie Morris; *m* 1961, Margaret Saunders (*née* Howard), historian. *Educ:* Hutcheson's, Glasgow; Kilburn Grammar Sch., Mddx; University Coll., Univ. of London (BA 1st cl. Hons History); Inst. of Education, Univ. of London (DipEd); LSE. Began teaching, 1936, in Willesden. Served War, 1941–46, demobilised as Captain RASC. Sen. Lectr, Colls of Education, 1946–50; Dep. Head, Tottenham, 1960, after nine years of political discrimination in Middlesex; Headmaster, Chamberlayne Wood Secondary Sch., Willesden, 1962–67. NUT: Mem. Exec., 1966–79; Pres., 1973–74; Chm. Action Cttee, 1976–79. Chairman: Mddx Regional Examining Bd, 1975–79; London Regional Examining Bd, 1979–90; Vice-Chairman: Centre for Information and Advice on Educnl Disadvantage, 1975–80; London and E Anglian Gp, GCSE; Member: Schools Council Cttees, 1967–84; Burnham Cttee, 1970–79; Board of NFER, 1970–80; CLEA/School Teachers Cttee, 1972–79; Schools Broadcasting Council, 1972–80; Nat. Adv. Cttee on Supply and Trng of Teachers, 1973–78; Sub-Cttee on Educn, Labour Party NEC, 1978–83; Council, Inst. of Educn; Jt Council, GCE and CSE Boards. Mem. (Lab) Haringey Borough Council, 1984–86. *Publications:* The People's Schools, 1939; From Cobbett to the Chartists, 1948; Your Children's Future, 1953; (with Jack Jones) An A to Z of Trade Unionism and Industrial Relations, 1982, 2nd edn 1986; (ed jtly) Education: the wasted years 1973–1986?, 1988; contribs on educnl and historical subjects in newspapers, weeklies and jls. *Recreations:* baiting the Dept of Education and Science; ridiculing Trotskyists and trendies; tasting malt whisky. *Address:* 44 Coolhurst Road, N8. *T:* 081–348 3980.

MORRIS, Michael Sachs; Director-General, British Insurance Brokers' Association, 1980–85; *b* 12 June 1924; *s* of late Prof. Noah Morris, MD, DSc, and Hattie Michaelis; *m* 1952, Vera Leonie, *er d* of late Paul and Lona Heller; one *s* one *d*. *Educ:* Glasgow Acad.; St Catharine's Coll., Cambridge. Wrangler, 1948. Scientific Officer, Admty Signals Estabt, 1943–46; Asst Principal, BoT, 1948; idc 1970; Under Secretary: Insurance Div., DoT, 1973; Shipping Policy Div., DoT, 1978–80. Chm., Consultative Shipping Gp, 1979–80. Mem., Barnet Health Authy, 1985–90. *Recreation:* sitting in the sun. *Address:* 5 Sunrise View, The Rise, Mill Hill, NW7 2LL. *T:* 081–959 0837. *Club:* United Oxford & Cambridge University.

MORRIS, Michael Wolfgang Laurence; MP (C) Northampton South since Feb. 1974; Proprietor, A. M. International, communication consultancy, since 1980; *b* 25 Nov. 1936; *m* 1960, Dr Ann Appleby (Dr Ann Morris, MB, BS, MRCS, MRCP); two *s* one *d*. *Educ:* Bedford Sch.; St Catharine's Coll., Cambridge (MA). BA Hons Econs, MIPA, MInstM. Management Trainee to Marketing Manager, UK, India and Ceylon, Reckitt & Colman Gp, 1960–63; Service Advertising Ltd, 1964–68; Marketing Exec. to Account Supervisor, Horniblow Cox-Freeman Ltd, 1968–71, Dir 1969–71; Dir, Benton & Bowles Ltd, 1971–81. Contested (C) Islington North, 1966. Islington Council: Councillor, 1968–70; Alderman, 1970–74; Chm. of Housing, 1968; Leader, 1969–71. PPS to Minister of State, NI Office, 1979–81; Member: Public Accounts Cttee, 1979–; Select Cttee on Energy, 1982–85; Chairman's Panel, 1984–; Mem. Council, Europe and Western European Union, 1983–; Chairman: British Sri Lanka Cttee, 1979–; British Singapore Cttee, 1985–; British Malaysia Cttee, 1987–; British Burma Cttee, 1989–; Vice-Chm., British Indonesia Cttee; Treas., British Asean and Thai Cttees; Secretary: British Venezuela Cttee; Cons. Housing and Local Govt Cttee, 1974–76; Cons Trade Cttee, 1974–76; Cons. Environment Cttee, 1977–79; Vice-Chm., Cons. Energy Cttee, 1981–; Founder, Parly Food and Health Forum. Captain, Parly Golf Soc., 1988–91. Chm., Govs, Bedford Sch., 1989– (Governor, 1982–). *Publications:* (jtly) Helping the Exporter, 1967; (contrib.) Marketing below the Line: Studies in Management, 1972; The Disaster of Direct Labour, 1978. *Recreations:* restoration work, cricket, tennis, golf, budgerigars, forestry. *Address:* Caesar's Camp, Sandy, Beds. *T:* Sandy (0767) 80388. *Clubs:* Carlton; George Row, Conservative, Whitworth, Billing Road, St George's (Northampton); John O'Gaunt Golf.

MORRIS, Nigel Godfrey, CMG 1955; LVO 1966; QPM 1954; *b* 11 Nov. 1908; 2nd *s* of late Lt-Col G. M. Morris, 2/8th Gurkha Rifles and late Mrs Morris; *m* 1st, 1941, Mrs G. E. Baughan, *widow* (*d* 1982), *e d* of late J. C. Sidebottom; one *d* and one step *d;* 2nd, 1984, Mrs M. C. Berkeley-Owen (*née* Mullally). *Educ:* Wellington Coll. Asst Superintendent SS Police, 1928; Chinese language course, Amoy, China, 1929; Asst Supt of Police, Singapore CID 1931; Special Branch, 1935; Asst Supt of Police, Town Penang, 1939; interned by Japanese, 1942; repatriated to UK, 1945; Asst Dir, Malayan Security Service, 1946; Dir, Special Branch, Singapore, 1948; Dep. Commissioner, CID, Singapore, 1950, Comr, 1952; Deputy Inspector-General of Colonial Police, Colonial Office, 1957–63; Commissioner of Police, Bahamas, 1963–68, retired. Colonial Police Medal, 1949. *Recreation:* golf. *Address:* 118 Cranmer Court, SW3 3HE. *T:* 071–584 9875. *Club:* Phyllis Court (Henley).

MORRIS, Norma Frances; Administrative Secretary, Medical Research Council, since 1989; *b* 17 April 1935; *d* of Henry Albert Bevis and Lilian Eliza Bevis (*née* Flexon); *m* 1960, Samuel Francis Morris; one *s* two *d*. *Educ:* Ilford County High Sch. for Girls; University College London (BA, MA). Assistante Anglaise, Paris, 1956–57; Asst Lectr, Univ. of Hull, 1959–60; MRC, 1960–. *Recreations:* opera, edible fungi. *Address:* Medical Research Council, 20 Park Crescent, W1N 4AL. *T:* 071–637 6016.

MORRIS, Prof. Norman Frederick, MD, FRCOG; Medical Director, In Vitro Fertilisation Unit, Cromwell Hospital, since 1986; Professor of Obstetrics and Gynæcology, University of London, Charing Cross and Westminster Medical School (formerly Charing Cross Hospital Medical School), 1958–85, now Emeritus; Dean, Faculty of Medicine, University of London, 1971–76; Deputy Vice-Chancellor, University of London, 1976–80; *b* Luton, 26 Feb. 1920; *s* of F. W. Morris, Luton; *m* 1944, Lucia Xenia Rivlin; two *s* two *d*. *Educ:* Dunstable Sch., Dunstable; St Mary's Hospital Medical Sch. MRCS, LRCP 1943; MRCOG 1949; MB, BS (London) 1943; MD (London) 1949; FRCOG 1959. House appts St Mary's Hosp., Paddington and Amersham, 1944–46; Res. Obstetrician and Surg. Officer, East Ham Memorial Hosp., E6; Surg. Specialist RAF (Sqdn Ldr), 1946–48; Registrar, St Mary's Hosp., W2, and East End Maternity Hosp., E1, 1948–50; Sen. Registrar (Obst. and Gynæcol.), Hammersmith Hosp., 1950–52; First Asst, Obstetric Unit, Univ. Coll. Hosp., WC1, 1953–56; Reader, Univ. of London in Obst. and Gynæcol., Inst. of Obstetrics and Gynæcology, 1956–58. Dep. Chm., NW Thames RHA, 1974–80; Chm., NW Thames Reg. Res. Cttee, 1981–86. External Examiner, Univs of Sheffield, Leeds, Dundee and Liverpool. President: (founder) Internat. Soc. of Psychosomatic Obstetrics and Gynaecology, 1972–80; Section of Obstetrics and Gynaecology, RSocMed, 1978–79. Chairman: Assoc. of Profs of Obstets and Gynaecol. of UK, 1981–86; British Soc. of Psychosomatic Obstets, Gynaecol. and Andrology, 1988–. Mem., Academic Forum, DHSS, 1981–84; Chm., Steering Gp, Commonwealth Health Develt Prog., Commonwealth Secretariat, 1990–. Mem., Hammersmith and Fulham HA, 1983–84. Mem. Ct and Senate, Univ. of London, 1972–80; Governor: Wye Coll., 1973–80; St Paul's Sch., 1976–. Fellow, Soc. Gyn. et Obst., Italy, 1970–. Formerly Chm., Assoc. of University Clinical Academic Staff. Editor, Midwife and Health Visitor Jl. *Publications:* Sterilisation, 1976; Contemporary Attitudes to Care in Labour (The Psychosomatic Approach), 1986; Factors Influencing Population Control, 1986; articles in medical jls related to obstetric and gynaecological problems, 1952–. *Recreations:* travelling, collecting glass, music. *Address:* 16 Provost Road, NW3 4ST. *T:* 071–722 4244. *Clubs:* Athenæum, 1942.

MORRIS, Owen Humphrey, CB 1977; CMG 1967; Deputy Under-Secretary of State, Welsh Office, 1974–81, retired; *b* 15 June 1921; *o c* of late David Humphreys Morris, Ton Pentre, Rhondda, Glam., and Mrs Amy Ann Morris (*née* Jones); *m* 1972, Mair Annetta Evans, *d* of late Capt. Daniel Evans, DSC, Tynllys, Morfa Nefyn. *Educ:* Public Elem. Schs; King's Coll. Sch., Wimbledon (Schol.); Balliol Coll., Oxford (Schol.; MA). Served War of 1939–45: The Welch Regt and King's African Rifles, 1941–45 (Capt.). Asst Princ., Colonial Office, 1946; seconded Sierra Leone Administration, 1952–53; Asst Sec., 1955; Dept of Techn. Cooperation, 1962; Min. of Overseas Development, 1964; Min. of Housing and Local Govt, 1966; Welsh Office, 1969; Asst Under-Sec., 1970; Dep. Sec., 1974. Chm., Gwynedd Archaeol Trust, 1984–87. *Address:* Taltreuddyn Fawr, Dyffryn Ardudwy, Gwynedd LL44 2RQ.

MORRIS, Peter; *see* Morris, J. P.

MORRIS, Peter Christopher West; company director; *b* 24 Dec. 1937; *s* of C. T. R. and L. B. Morris; *m* 1st, 1959, Joy (marr. diss.); two *s* one *d*; 2nd, 1987, Terese; one step *s* two step *d*. *Educ:* Seaford Coll.; Christ's Coll., Cambridge, 1958–61 (MA, LLB). Hockey Blue, 1959, 1960, 1961; Hockey for Wales, 1962–65. National Service, 1956–58. Admitted Solicitor, 1965; Partner with Wild Hewitson & Shaw, 1967; a Recorder of the Crown Court, 1980–84; voluntary removal from Roll of Solicitors, 1982; called to the Bar, Middle Temple, 1982–84. *Recreations:* golf, cricket, squash, photography. *Address:* 1 Horse Pastures, Little Hawkwell Farm, Maidstone Road, Pembury, Tunbridge Wells, Kent TN2 4AQ. *Clubs:* Hawks (Cambridge); Cambridge University Hockey (Pres.).

MORRIS, Prof. Peter John; Nuffield Professor of Surgery, Oxford University, since 1974; Fellow of Balliol College, since 1974; *b* 17 April 1934; *s* of Stanley Henry and Mary Lois Morris; *m* 1960, Mary Jocelyn Gorman; three *s* two *d*. *Educ:* Xavier Coll., Melbourne; Univ. of Melbourne (MB, BS, PhD). FRCS, FRACS, FACS. Jun. surg. appts at St Vincent's Hosp., Melbourne, Postgrad. Med. Sch., London, Southampton Gen. Hosp. and MGH Boston, 1958–64; Research Fellow, Harvard Med. Sch., 1965–66; Asst Prof. in Surgery, Med. Coll. of Virginia, 1967; 2nd Asst in Surgery, Univ. of Melbourne, 1968–69, 1st Asst 1970–71; Reader in Surgery, Univ. of Melbourne, 1972–74. WHO Consultant, 1970–84; Cons. to Walter and Eliza Hall Inst. of Med. Res., 1969–74. Pres., Transplantation Soc., 1984–86; Chm., Nat. Kidney Res. Fund, 1987–90; Member: MRC, 1983–87; Oxford RHA, 1988–90. Hunterian Prof., RCS, 1972. USA Nat. Kidney Foundn Prof., 1986. Hon. Fellow, Amer. Surgical Assoc., 1982; Hon. FACS 1986. Selwyn Smith Prize, Univ. of Melbourne, 1971; Cecil Joll Prize, RCS, 1988. *Publications:* Kidney Transplantation: principles and practice, 1979, 3rd edn 1988; Tissue Transplantation, 1982; Transient Ischaemic Attacks, 1982; Progress in Transplantation, Vol. 1 1984, Vol. 2 1985, Vol. 3 1986; Transplantation Reviews, Vol. 1 1987, Vol. 2 1988, Vol. 3 1989; numerous sci. articles and chapters in books concerned mainly with transplantation and surgery. *Recreations:* golf, tennis, cricket. *Address:* 19 Lucerne Road, Oxford OX2 7QB. *Clubs:* United Oxford & Cambridge University, MCC; Frilford Heath Golf (Oxford); St Cyprien Golf (France); Melbourne Cricket (Melbourne).

MORRIS, Peter T.; *see* Temple-Morris.

MORRIS, Richard; *see* Morris, J. R. S.

MORRIS, Sir Robert (Byng), 10th Bt *cr* 1806, of Clasemont, Glamorganshire; *b* 25 Feb. 1913; *s* of Percy Byng Morris (*d* 1957) (*g s* of 2nd Bt), and Ethel Maud (*d* 1923), *d* of William Morley Glascott, Melbourne; *S* cousin, 1982; *m* 1947, Christina Kathleen, *d* of Archibald Field, Toddington, Glos; one *s* three *d*. *Heir: s* Allan Lindsay Morris [*b* 27 Nov. 1961; *m* 1986, Cheronne, *e d* of Dale Whitford, Par, Cornwall]. *Address:* Norton Creek Stables (RR5), St Chrysostome, Quebec, Canada.

MORRIS, Robert Matthew; Assistant Under Secretary of State, Home Office, since 1983; Registrar of the Baronetage, since 1991; *b* 11 Oct. 1937; *s* of late William Alexander Morris and of Mary Morris (*née* Bryant); *m* 1965, Janet Elizabeth Gillingham; two *s* one *d*. *Educ:* Handsworth Grammar Sch.; Christ's Coll., Cambridge. Joined Home Office, 1961; Asst Private Sec. to Home Sec., 1964–66; CSD, 1969–71; Principal Private Sec. to Home Sec., 1976–78; Sec. to UK Prison Services Inquiry (May Cttee), 1978–79; Head of Crime Policy Planning Unit, 1979–81. *Address:* c/o Home Office, 50 Queen Anne's Gate, SW1H 9AP.

MORRIS, Rear-Adm. Roger Oliver, CB 1990; FRGS; FRIN; Hydrographer of the Navy, 1985–90; *b* 1 Sept. 1932; *s* of Dr Oliver N. Morris and H. S. (Mollie) Morris (*née* Hudson). *Educ:* Mount House School, Tavistock; Royal Naval College, Dartmouth. Entered Royal Navy, 1946, commissioned 1952; specialized in Hydrographic Surveying, 1956; commanded HM Ships Medusa, Beagle, Hydra, Fawn, Hecla, Hydra, 1964–80; RCDS 1978; Director of Hydrographic Plans and Surveys, 1980–81; Asst Hydrographer, 1982–84. *Recreations:* heraldry, opera, bird watching. *Address:* c/o Lloyds Bank plc, Taunton, Somerset. *Club:* Commonwealth Trust.

MORRIS, Air Vice-Marshal Ronald James Arthur, CB 1974; retired; *b* 27 Nov. 1915; *s* of late Dr James Arthur Morris, Ladybank, Fife; *m* 1945, Mary Kerr Mitchell; one *s* two *d. Educ:* Madras Coll., St Andrews; St Andrews Univ. MB, ChB 1939; DPH Edinburgh, 1953; MFCM 1972. Commnd RAF, 1939; served on Fighter Comd Stns, 1940–41; India and Burma Campaign, 1941–45; HQ Techn. Trng Comd, 1946–48; SMO, HQ Air Forces Western Europe, 1948–50; Sen. Trng Officer and Comdt Med. Trng Estabt, 1950–52; Exchange Officer, Sch. of Aviation Medicine (USAF), 1955–56; Dept MA7, Air Min., 1956–60; OC RAF Chessington, 1960–61; OC RAF Hosp. Wroughton, 1961–63; PMO, Signals Comd, 1963–65; Dep. PMO, Far East Air Forces, 1965–69; PMO, Maintenance Comd, 1969–70; DDGMS (RAF), 1971–73; PMO, RAF Strike Comd, 1974–75. QHS, 1971–75. CStJ 1974. *Recreations:* golf, fishing. *Address:* 2 Cairnsden Gardens, St Andrews, Fife KY16 8SQ. *T:* St Andrews (0334) 75326.

MORRIS, Simon C.; *see* Conway Morris.

MORRIS, Prof. Terence Patrick, JP; Professor of Social Institutions, University of London, since 1981; *b* 8 June 1931; *s* of Albert and Norah Avis Morris; *m* 1954, Pauline Jeannette Peake (*née* Morris) (marr. diss. 1973); one *d*; *m* 1973, Penelope Jane, *y d* of Stanley and Alexandra Tomlinson. *Educ:* John Ruskin Grammar Sch., Croydon; LSE, Univ. of London (Leverhulme Schol.). BSc (Soc) 1953, PhD (Econ) 1955. Lectr in Sociology, LSE, 1955–63; Reader, 1963–69, Prof., 1969–81, Sociology (with special ref. to Criminology), London Univ. Vis. Prof. of Criminology, Univ. of California, 1964–65. Mem., Adv. Mission on Treatment of Offenders (Western Pacific, British Honduras, Bahamas), 1966. Vice-Pres., Howard League for Penal Reform, 1986–; Mem., Magistrates' Assoc. Treatment of Offenders Cttee (co-opted), 1969–77; Founder Mem., Inst. for Study of Drug Dependence. Man. Editor, British Jl of Sociology, 1965–74. JP Inner London, 1967. *Publications:* The Criminal Area, 1957; (with Pauline Morris) Pentonville: a sociological study of an English prison, 1963; (with L. J. Blom-Cooper) A Calendar of Murder, 1964; Deviance and Control: the secular heresy, 1976; Crime and Criminal Justice since 1945, 1989; contribs to Brit. Jl Criminology, Brit. Jl Sociology, Encycl. Britannica. *Recreations:* cycling, photography. *Address:* c/o London School of Economics, Houghton Street, WC2A 2AE. *Club:* Cyclists' Touring.

MORRIS, Most Rev. Thomas, DD; Archbishop of Cashel and Emly, (RC), 1960–88, now Emeritus; *b* Killenaule, Co. Tipperary, 16 Oct. 1914; *s* of James Morris and Johanna (*née* Carrigan). *Educ:* Christian Brothers Schs, Thurles; Maynooth Coll. Ordained priest, Maynooth, 1939; studied, Dunboyne Institute, 1939–41. (DD). Professor of Theology, St Patrick's Coll., Thurles, 1942–Dec. 1959, Vice-Pres., 1957–60; appointed Archbishop, 1959; consecrated, 1960; retired, 1988. *Recreation:* reading. *Address:* Holy Cross, Thurles, Co. Tipperary, Ireland.

MORRIS, Timothy Denis, DL; Director, Yattendon Investment Trust Ltd, since 1985; Chairman: Packet Newspapers (Cornwall) Ltd, since 1986; Herts & Essex Newspapers Ltd, since 1989; West of England Newspapers Ltd, since 1990; *b* 15 Feb. 1935; *s* of D. E. Morris, OBE, *qv*, and Mrs P. H. Skey; *m* 1959, Caroline Wynn; one *s* one *d. Educ:* Tonbridge Sch.; Pembroke Coll., Cambridge (MA). Dir, The Birmingham Post & Mail Ltd, 1967–90 (Chm., 1982–90); Man. Dir, Coventry Newspapers Ltd, 1970–77 (Dir, 1985–; Chm., 1988–90); Director: Cambridge Newspapers Ltd, 1970–77, 1985–; Press Association Ltd, 1980–87 (Chm., 1985–86); Burton Daily Mail Ltd, 1983–; South Hams Newspapers Ltd, 1985– (Chm., 1985–86); Reuters Founders Share Co. Ltd, 1987–; Midland Newspapers Ltd, 1988–90. Dir, W Midlands RHA, 1990–. Chairman: Birmingham Civic Soc., 1979–83; Birmingham Hippodrome Theatre Trust, 1990– (Dir, 1980–); Dir, Royal Opera House Ballet Bd, 1990–; President: W Midlands Newspaper Soc., 1975–76; Newspaper Soc., 1984–85; Coventry Chamber of Commerce, 1976–77. County Comr, Warwickshire Scouts, 1974–77. DL West Midlands, 1975. *Recreations:* golf, philately. *Address:* c/o Yattendon Investment Trust Ltd, 28 Colmore Circus, Queensway, Birmingham B4 6AX. *Club:* Naval.

MORRIS, Trefor Alfred, QPM 1985; HM Inspector of Constabulary, since 1990; *b* 22 Dec. 1934; *s* of late Kenneth Alfred Morris and of Amy Ursula (*née* Burgess); *m* 1958, Martha Margaret (*née* Wroe); two *d. Educ:* Ducie Technical High School, Manchester; Manchester University (Dip. Criminology); Nat. Exec. Inst., USA. Constable to Chief Superintendent, Manchester City Police, Manchester and Salford Police, Greater Manchester Police, 1955–76; Asst Chief Constable, Greater Manchester Police, 1976–79; Dep. Chief Constable, 1979–84, Chief Constable, 1984–90, Herts. CBIM 1986. OStJ. *Recreations:* squash, golf, wine, walking, gardening. *Address:* HM Inspectorate of Constabulary, Block B2, The Westbrook Centre, Milton Road, Cambridge CB4 1YQ. *Club:* Royal Over-Seas League.

MORRIS, Prof. Trevor Raymond, FIBiol; Professor of Animal Production and Head of Department of Agriculture, University of Reading, since 1984; *b* 11 April 1930; *s* of Ivor Raymond Morris and Dorothy May Morris; *m* 1954, Elisabeth Jean (*née* Warren); three *s* two *d. Educ:* Rendcomb Coll., Glos; Reading Univ. (BSc, PhD, DSc). University of Reading: Asst Lectr, 1952–54, 1956–57; Lectr in Agric., 1957–69; Reader in Agric., 1969–81; Prof. of Agriculture, 1981–84. *Publications:* over 100 articles in sci. jls. *Recreations:* music, gardening. *Address:* 36 Shinfield Road, Reading RG2 7BW. *T:* Reading (0734) 872529.

MORRIS, Walter Frederick; LLB London; ACII; FBIM; HM Diplomatic Service, retired; Consultant, Morris, Scott & Co., Solicitors, Highcliffe, Christchurch, Dorset; *b* 15 Oct. 1914; *s* of late Captain Frederick James Morris and Elsie Eleanor (*née* Williams); *m* 1945, Marjorie Vaughan, *o d* of late Thomas Vaughan Phillips and Eleanor Mirren (*née* Jones); one *s* one *d. Educ:* Cardiff High Sch.; University Coll., Cardiff (Law Prizeman). Admitted Solicitor, 1936; Legal practice, 1936–39. Served RA (TA), 1939–45: GHQ Home Forces (Intelligence); WO Sch. of Military Administration; Certificate of Merit, Western Comd; GSO1 (Lt-Col), HQ 21st Army Gp, BLA (later BAOR); commanded Legal Aid Organisation, which provided legal assistance to all British Army and RAF personnel in Europe; legal practice (and Hon. District Army Welfare Officer), 1945–47; entered Administrative Home Civil Service, 1947; Min. of Social Security, 1947–68 (Prin. Dep. Chief Insce Off., Asst Sec.); Admin. Staff Coll., Henley, 1953; on loan to Export Credits Guarantee Dept, 1955–57; Manchester Business Sch., 1968; trans. to HM Diplomatic Service, 1968; HM Consul-Gen., Cairo, 1968–70; ME Centre for Arab Studies, Shemlan, Lebanon, 1969; Head of Claims Dept, FCO, 1970–72; Dep. High Comr, later Consul-Gen., Lahore, 1972–73; retired from HM Diplomatic Service and re-entered legal practice, 1973. Mem., Law Soc. Liveryman, City of London Solicitor's Co.

Recreations: golf, travel. *Address:* 19463 Ravines Court, Pine Lakes Country Club, North Fort Myers, Fla 33903, USA. *T:* 813–731–2262. *Clubs:* Civil Service; Pine Lakes Golf (Florida); Punjab (Lahore).

MORRIS, William; Deputy General Secretary, Transport and General Workers Union, 1986–March 1992, General Secretary, from March 1992; *b* 19 Oct. 1938; *s* of William and Una Morris; *m* 1957, Minetta (*d* 1990); two *s. Educ:* Jamaica. TGWU: Dist Officer, Nottingham, 1973; Dist Sec., Northampton, 1976; Nat. Sec., Passenger Services, 1979–85. Mem., TUC Gen. Council, 1988–. Member: Commn for Racial Equality, 1977–87; IBA Gen. Adv. Council, 1981–86; BBC General Adv. Council, 1987–88; Employment Appeals Tribunal, 1988–. *Recreations:* walking, gardening, watching sports. *Address:* 156 St Agnells Lane, Grove Hill, Hemel Hempstead, Herts HP2 6EG. *T:* Hemel Hempstead (0442) 63110.

MORRIS, Prof. (William) David, PhD; Professor and Head of Department of Mechanical Engineering, University of Wales, Swansea, since 1985; *b* 14 March 1936; *s* of late William Daniel and Elizabeth Jane Morris; *m* 1959, Pamela Eira Evans; two *s* one *d. Educ:* Queen Mary College, London (1st Cl. Hons BSc Eng); Univ. Coll. of Swansea, Wales (PhD). CEng, FIMechE, FIProdE. Bristol Siddeley Engine Co., 1958–60; James Clayton Res. Fellow, Univ. of Wales, Swansea, 1960–63; Lectr, Dept of Mech. Engrg, Univ. of Liverpool, 1963–67; Lectr, 1967–72, Reader, 1972–79, Sch. of Engrg, Univ. of Sussex; J. H. Fenner Prof. of Mech. Engrg and Head, Dept of Engrg Design, Univ. of Hull, 1979–85. *Publications:* Differential Equations for Engineers and Applied Scientists, 1979; Heat Transfer and Fluid Flow in Rotating Coolant Channels, 1981. *Recreations:* oil painting, DIY, walking. *Address:* Department of Mechanical Engineering, University College of Swansea, Singleton Park, Swansea SA2 8PP. *T:* Swansea (0792) 295534.

MORRIS, Prof. William Ian Clinch; Professor of Obstetrics and Gynaecology, University of Manchester, 1949–72, Professor Emeritus since 1972; *b* 10 May 1907; *s* of Dr J. M. Morris, Neath; *m* 1938, Mary Farquharson (*d* 1976); one *d. Educ:* Royal High Sch., Edinburgh; Edinburgh Univ. Obstetrician to Ayr County Council, 1937–46; Sen. Lectr in Obstetrics and Gynaecology, Univ. of Edinburgh, 1946–49. RAMC (TA) 1935; war service, 1939–43. *Publications:* (jointly) A Combined Text-book of Obstetrics and Gynaecology, 1950; contribs to Jl of Obstetrics and Gynaecology of British Commonwealth, Lancet, Edinburgh Med. Jl, etc. *Address:* Edenfield House, Springfield, by Cupar, Fife KY15 5RT. *T:* Cupar (0334) 56222.

MORRIS, Very Rev. William James, JP; Minister of Glasgow Cathedral, since 1967; a Chaplain to the Queen in Scotland, since 1969; Dean of the Chapel Royal in Scotland, since 1991; *b* Cardiff, 22 Aug. 1925; *o s* of William John Morris and Eliza Cecilia Cameron Johnson; *m* 1952, Jean Daveena Ogilvy Howie, MBE, *o c* of Rev. David Porter Howie and Veena Christie, Kilmarnock; one *s. Educ:* Cardiff High Sch.; Univ. of Wales; Edinburgh Univ. BA 1946, BD 1949, Wales; PhD Edinburgh, 1954. Ordained, 1951. Asst, Canongate Kirk, Edinburgh, 1949–51; Minister, Presbyterian Church of Wales, Cadoxton and Barry Is, 1951–53; Buckhaven (Fife): St David's, 1953–57; Peterhead Old Parish, 1957–67; Chaplain to the Lord High Comr to the General Assembly of the Church of Scotland, 1975–76; Chaplain: Peterhead Prison, 1963–67; Glasgow DC, 1967–; Trades House of Glasgow, 1967–; W of Scotland Engrs Assoc., 1967–; The High Sch. of Glasgow, 1974–76, 1983–; Glasgow Acad., 1976–; Strathclyde Police, 1977–; Hon. Chaplain, The Royal Scottish Automobile Club; Moderator, Presbytery of Deer, 1965–66; Convener Adv. Bd, Church of Scotland, 1977–80; Vice-Chm., Bd of Nomination to Church Chairs, Church of Scotland, 1978–81. Mem. IBA, 1979–84 (Chm. Scottish Adv. Cttee). President: Rotary Club of Peterhead, 1965–66; Peterhead and Dist Professional and Business Club, 1967; Chairman: Iona Cath. Trust, 1976– (Trustee, 1967); Council, Soc. of Friends of Glasgow Cath., 1967; Club Service Cttee, Dist 101, RIBI, 1964–66; Prison Chaplaincies Bd (Church of Scotland Home Bd), 1969–83; Vice-Pres., St Andrew's Soc., Glasgow, 1967–82; Member: Scottish Cttee, British Sailors' Soc., 1967–83; Bd of Management, W of Scotland Convalescent Home, 1967–; Gen. Convocation, Strathclyde Univ., 1967–; Council of Management, Quarriers' Homes, 1968–88; Bd of Management, Glasgow YMCA, 1973–88; Scottish Council on Crime, 1974–76; Church of Scotland Bd of Practice and Procedure, 1981–85; Bd of Governors, Jordanhill Coll. of Educn, Glasgow, 1983–91; Hon. Pres., Glasgow Soc. of Social Services Inc., 1984–. Hon. Mem., Scottish Ambulance Assoc., 1981. JP: Co. of Aberdeen, 1963–71; Co. of City of Glasgow, 1971. ChStJ1991. Hon. LLD Strathclyde, 1974; Hon. DD Glasgow, 1979; FRCPS(Hon.) 1983. *Publication:* A Walk Around Glasgow Cathedral, 1986. *Recreations:* fishing, gardening. *Address:* 94 St Andrews Drive, Glasgow G41 4RX. *T:* 041–427 2757. *Clubs:* New (Edinburgh); RNVR (Scotland) (Hon.); University of Strathclyde Staff (Hon.); Rotary of Dennistoun (Hon.); Rotary of Glasgow (Hon.).

MORRIS, Wyn, FRAM; conductor; *b* 14 Feb. 1929; *s* of late Haydn Morris and Sarah Eluned Phillips; *m* 1962, Ruth Marie McDowell; one *s* one *d. Educ:* Llanelli Grammar Sch.; Royal Academy of Music; Mozarteum, Salzburg. August Mann's Prize, 1950; Apprentice Conductor, Yorkshire Symph. Orch., 1950–51; Musical Dir, 17th Trg Regt, RA Band, 1951–53; Founder and Conductor of Welsh Symph. Orch., 1954–57; Koussevitsky Memorial Prize, Boston Symph. Orch., 1957; (on invitation George Szell) Observer, Cleveland Symph. Orch., 1957–60; Conductor: Ohio Bell Chorus, Cleveland Orpheus Choir and Cleveland Chamber Orch., 1958–60; Choir of Royal National Eisteddfod of Wales, 1960–62; London debut, Royal Festival Hall, with Royal Philharmonic Orch., 1963; Conductor: Royal Choral Society, 1968–70; Huddersfield Choral Soc., 1969–74; Ceremony for Investiture of Prince Charles as Prince of Wales, 1969; Royal Choral Soc. tour of USA, 1969; former Chief Conductor and Musical Dir, Symphonica of London. FRAM 1964. Specialises in conducting of Mahler; has recorded Des Knaben Wunderhorn (with Dame Janet Baker and Sir Geraint Evans), Das Klagende Lied, Symphonies 1, 2, 5, 8 and 10 in Deryck Cooke's final performing version. Mahler Memorial Medal (of Bruckner and Mahler Soc. of Amer.), 1968. *Recreations:* chess, Rugby football, climbing, cynghanedd and telling Welsh stories.

MORRIS-JONES, Ifor Henry, QC 1969; **His Honour Judge Morris-Jones;** a Circuit Judge, since 1977; *b* 5 March 1922; *s* of late Rev. Prof. and Mrs D. Morris-Jones; *m* 1950, Anne Diana, *d* of late S. E. Ferris, OBE, Blundellsands; one *s* two *d. Educ:* Taunton Sch.; Sidney Sussex Coll., Cambridge. Called to the Bar, Lincoln's Inn, 1947. Joined Northern Circuit, 1947; Assistant Recorder, Carlisle, 1962; Dep. Chm., Cumberland Sessions, 1969–72; a Recorder, 1972–76. Mem., Bar Council, 1972. *Recreation:* golf. *Address:* 3 Paddock Close, Blundellsands, Liverpool L23 8UX. *T:* 051–924 4848. *Club:* Artists' (Liverpool).

MORRIS-JONES, Prof. Wyndraeth Humphreys; Emeritus Professor of University of London; *b* 1 Aug. 1918; *s* of late William James Jones, Carmarthen, and Annie Mary Jones (*née* Morris); *m* 1953, Graziella Bianca Genre; one *s* two *d. Educ:* University Coll. Sch., Hampstead; London Sch. of Economics (BSc(Econ.) First Class, 1938; Leverhulme Research Grant, 1939; Hon. Fellow, 1980); Christ's Coll., Cambridge Research Schol., 1940. Indian Army, 1941–46 (Lt-Col, Public Relations Directorate, 1944); Constitutional

Adviser to Viceroy of India, 1947; Lecturer in Political Science, London Sch. of Economics, 1946–55; Prof. of Political Theory and Instns, Univ. of Durham, 1955–65; Prof. of Commonwealth Affairs and Dir, Inst. of Commonwealth Studies, Univ. of London, 1966–83. Leverhulme Emeritus Fellow, 1984–87. Rockefeller Travel Grants, 1954, 1960 and 1967. Vis. Prof. of Commonwealth Hist. and Instns, Indian Sch. of Internat. Studies, New Delhi, 1960; Visiting Professor: Univ. of Chicago, 1962; Univ. of California, Berkeley, 1964–65. Editor, Jl of Commonwealth and Comparative Politics (formerly Commonwealth Polit. Studies), 1964–80. *Publications:* Parliament in India, 1957; Government and Politics of India, 1964, 4th edn 1987; (with Biplab Dasgupta) Patterns and Trends in Indian Politics, 1976; Politics Mainly Indian, 1978; articles in Polit. Studies, Asian Survey, Modern Asian Studies, etc. *Address:* 95 Ridgway, SW19 4SX.

MORRIS WILLIAMS, Christine Margaret; *see* Puxon, C. M.

MORRISH, John Edwin, (Jack); School Governor and education consultant; *b* 23 Sept. 1915; *s* of Henry Edwin Morrish and Ada Minnie (*née* Tapping); *m* 1st, 1937, Norah Lake (marr. diss.); one *d*; 2nd, 1944, Violet Saunders (marr. diss.); one *s* one *d*; 3rd, 1984, Betty Lupton (*née* Wear) (*d* 1990). *Educ:* Fleet Road, Hampstead, Elem. Sch.; University Coll. Sch.; Northampton Polytechnic, London; various work-faces; MA Leicester, 1991. Post Office Techn. Officer, 1932–54; coalminer, 1944–45. Trade Union Official: Civil Service Union, 1954–72; Soc. of Civil and Public Servants, 1972–76 (Gen. Sec., Customs and Excise Gp). Administrator, Northants Rural Community Council, 1979. Census Officer, 1980–81, 1990–91. Mem. (Lab), Dep. Leader, and Chm., Educn Cttee, Northants CC, 1981–85; Mem. (Lab), Hounslow BC, 1986–90 (Vice-Chm., Educn Cttee). Vice-Chm., E Midlands Further Educn Council, 1982–85; Member: Adv. Cttee, Supply and Educn of Teachers; Assoc. of County Councils, 1981–85; Burnham Cttee on Teachers' Pay, 1983–84, 1986–87; AMA, 1986–90. Hon. Chm., Northants Child Poverty Action Gp, 1980–84. Hon. Treas., UK Reading Assoc. (World Congress Local Arrangements Cttee), 1985–86. Chm., Nene Coll. Governors, 1981–85. *Publications:* The Future of Forestry, 1971; contrib. Trade Union jls. *Recreations:* thinking, pursuit of justice, music, talking. *Address:* The Old Bakehouse, 1 Church Street, Broughton, Kettering, Northants NN14 1LU. *T:* Kettering (0536) 790914. *Club:* Civil Service.

MORRISON, family name of **Viscount Dunrossil** and of **Barons Margadale** and **Morrison.**

MORRISON, 2nd Baron *cr* 1945, of Tottenham; **Dennis Morrison;** Manufacturing Executive with The Metal Box Co. Ltd, 1957–72, retired; *b* 21 June 1914; *e* and *o* surv. *s* of 1st Baron Morrison, PC, and Grace, *d* of late Thomas Glossop; *S* father 1953; *m* 1940, Florence Alice Helena (marr. diss. 1958), *d* of late Augustus Hennes, Tottenham; *m* 1959, Joan (marr. diss. 1975), *d* of late W. R. Meech. *Educ:* Tottenham County Sch. Employed by The Metal Box Co. Ltd on research work, 1937–51; Quality Controller, 1952–57. Lord Lieutenant's Representative for Tottenham, 1955–. FSS 1953–57. Vice-Pres., Acton Chamber of Commerce, 1972 (Mem., Exec. Cttee, 1962). Hon. President: Robert Browning Settlement, 1967–; 5th Acton Scout Group, 1969. *Recreation:* gardening. *Heir:* none. *Address:* 7 Ullswater Avenue, Felixstowe, Suffolk. *T:* Felixstowe (0394) 77405.

MORRISON, Alexander John Henderson; His Honour Judge Morrison; a Circuit Judge, since 1980; *b* 16 Nov. 1927; *yr s* of late Dr Alexander Morrison and Mrs A. Morrison; *m* 1978, Hon. Philippa, *y d* of 1st Baron Hives. *Educ:* Derby Sch.; Emmanuel Coll., Cambridge. MA, LLB. Called to the Bar, Gray's Inn, 1951. Mem. of Midland Circuit; Dep. Chm., Derbyshire QS, 1964–71; Regional Chm. of Industrial Tribunals, Sheffield, 1971–80; a Recorder of the Crown Court, 1971–80. A Pres., Mental Health Review Tribunals, 1983–. Pres., Derbys Union of Golf Clubs, 1977–79. *Recreations:* golf, music. *Address:* Derby Combined Court, Mortledge, Derby. *T:* Derby (0332) 31841.

MORRISON, Blake; *see* Morrison, P. B.

MORRISON, Hon. Sir Charles (Andrew), Kt 1988; MP (C) Devizes since May 1964; *b* 25 June 1932; 2nd *s* of 1st Baron Margadale, *qv*; *m* 1st, 1954, Hon. Sara Long (*see* Hon. Sara Morrison) (marr. diss. 1984); one *s* one *d*; 2nd, 1984, Mrs Rosalind Ward. *Educ:* Eton. Nat. Service in The Life Guards, 1950–52; Royal Wilts Yeo. (TA), 1952–66. County Councillor, Wilts, 1958–65 (Chm., Educn Cttee, 1963–64). Chm., Nat. Cttee for Electoral Reform, 1985–; Mem. Bd of Dirs, Global Cttee of Parliamentarians on Population and Develt, 1984–. Chairman: South West Regional Sports Council, 1966–68; Young Volunteer Force Foundn, 1971–74; British Trust for Conservation Volunteers, 1973–78; Game Conservancy, 1987–; Mem., Council, Salmon and Trout Assoc. A Vice-Chm., 1922 Cttee, 1974–83 (Mem. Exec., 1972–). Prime Warden, Fishmongers' Co., 1986–87. *Recreations:* gardening, shooting, fishing. *Address:* House of Commons, SW1A 0AA; Brook House, Luckington, Chippenham, Wilts. *T:* Malmesbury (0666) 840371. *Clubs:* White's, Pratt's.

See also Hon. J. I. Morrison, Hon. M. A. Morrison, Rt Hon. Sir P. H. Morrison.

MORRISON, Dennis John; Regional Director, Departments of the Environment and Transport, East Midlands Region, Nottingham, since 1989; *b* 20 May 1942; *s* of Leonard Tait Morrison and Alice Morrison; *m* 1967, Frances Joan Pollard; one *s* one *d*. *Educ:* Ashton-upon-Mersey Boys' School; Lymm Grammar School; Manchester Univ. (BA, DipT&CP). MRTPI. Planning appointments: Lancs CC, 1966–70; Welsh Office, Cardiff, 1970–75; NW Region, DoE, Manchester, 1975–81; Regional Controller, NW Enterprise Unit, DoE, 1981–84; Regional Controller (Urban and Economic Affairs), Merseyside Task Force, Liverpool, 1984–89. FRGS. *Recreations:* antiquarian horologist, antiquarian book collector, hill walking, gardening. *Address:* Cranbrook House, Cranbrook Street, Nottingham NG1 1EY. *T:* Nottingham (0602) 476121.

MORRISON, Donald Alexander Campbell; Assistant Under-Secretary of State, Home Office, 1972–76; *b* 30 Nov. 1916; *s* of late George Alexander Morrison, sometime MP for Scottish Univs. and late Rachel Brown Morrison (*née* Campbell); *m* 1st, 1951, Elma Margaret Craig (*d* 1970); one *s* one *d* (and one *s* decd); 2nd, 1973, Jane Margaret Montgomery; one step *s*. *Educ:* Fettes Coll.; Christ Church, Oxford (BA). Home Office, 1939; Asst Sec., 1955. A Senior Clerk (acting), House of Commons, 1976–81. War Service, 1940–45: 79th (Scottish Horse) Medium Regt, RA, 1942–45. *Publications:* Haps and Such (poems), 1986; *children's operas:* The Granite and the Heather, 1989 (perf. Aboynt, 1990); Little Jenny Nobody (perf. Aboynt), 1991. *Recreation:* music. *Address:* 27 High Street, Wingham, near Canterbury, Kent CT3 1AW. *T:* Canterbury (0227) 720774. *Club:* Royal Over-Seas League.

MORRISON, Sir Howard (Leslie), Kt 1990; OBE 1976; entertainer, self-employed, since 1957; Youth Development Director for Maori Affairs, since 1978; *b* 18 Aug. 1935; *s* of late Temuera Leslie Morrison and Gertrude Harete Morrison (*née* Davidson); *m* 1957, Rangiwhata Anne (*née* Manahi); two *s* one *d*. *Educ:* Huiarau Primary Sch.; Rotorua Primary Sch.; Rotorua High Sch.; Te Aute College. Surveyor's Asst, 1954–59; performer with Maori concert party groups since childhood; formed Howard Morrison Quartet, 1957 (part-time, later full-time); numerous recordings, TV, national tours; quartet disbanded 1965; solo entertainer, 1965–; tours in NZ, S Pacific, SE Asia; TV and films. *Recreations:* golf, swimming. *Address:* Korokai Street, Ohinemutu Village, Rotorua, New Zealand. *T:* (073) 485–735, *Fax:* (073) 480–910. *Club:* Carbine (Auckland, NZ).

MORRISON, Air Vice-Marshal Ian Gordon, CB 1965; CBE 1957 (OBE 1946); RNZAF (retired); *b* 16 March 1914; *s* of W. G. Morrison; *m* 1938, Dorothy, *d* of W. H. Franks; one *s* two *d*. *Educ:* Christchurch Boys' High Sch., NZ. RAF 1935; RNZAF 1939; No 75 Sqdn, UK, 1939; Comd RNZAF, Omaka, 1941; Comd RNZAF, Gisborne, 1942; SASO, Islands Gp, 1943; Comd No 3 BR Sqdn Pacific, 1944–45; jssc, UK, 1950; Comd RNZAF, Ohakea, 1952; Air Mem. for Supply, 1954; idc, 1958; AOC, RNZAF, HQ London, 1959–60; Air Mem. for Personnel, 1961–62; Chief of the Air Staff, Royal New Zealand Air Force, 1962–66. Develt Dir, A. S. Cornish Gp, 1970–80; Dep. Chm., Wm Scollay & Co., 1980–85. Nat. Pres., Scout Assoc. of NZ, 1967–79. *Recreations:* golf and angling. *Address:* 2 Taungata Road, York Bay, Eastbourne, New Zealand. *T:* Wellington 683367. *Clubs:* Wellington (Pres., 1978–82), Wellington Golf (both in NZ).

MORRISON, Hon. James Ian, TD, DL; director of companies; farmer; *b* 17 July 1930; *e s* and *heir* of Baron Margadale, *qv*; *m* 1952, Clare Barclay; two *s* one *d*. *Educ:* Eton Coll.; Royal Agricultural Coll., Cirencester. 2nd Lieut, Life Guards, 1949–50; Major, Royal Wilts Yeo., 1960–68; Hon. Colonel: A (RWY) Sqn Royal Yeomanry RAC TA, and B (RWY) Sqn Royal Wessex Yeomanry, 1982–89; Royal Wessex Yeomanry RAC TA, 1984–89. Member, Queen's Body Guard for Scotland, 1960–. County Councillor, Wilts, 1955 and 1973–77, County Alderman, 1969; Chairman, W Wilts Conservative Assoc., 1967–71, Pres., 1972–84; Chm., Wilts CLA, 1978–81. Chm., Tattersalls Cttee, 1969–80. DL 1977–, High Sheriff 1971, Wiltshire. *Recreations:* racing, shooting, hunting. *Address:* Hawking Down, Hindon, Salisbury, Wilts SP3 6DN; Islay Estate Office, Bridgend, Islay, Argyll PA44 7PA. *Clubs:* White's, Jockey.

See also Hon. Sir C. A. Morrison, Hon. M. A. Morrison, Rt Hon. Sir P. H. Morrison, Viscount Trenchard.

MORRISON, Ven. John Anthony; Archdeacon of Buckingham, since 1990; *b* 11 March 1938; *s* of Major Leslie Claude Morrison and Mary Sharland Morrison (*née* Newson-Smith); *m* 1968, Angela, *d* of late Major Jonathan Eric Bush; two *s* one *d*. *Educ:* Haileybury; Jesus Coll., Cambridge (BA 1960; MA 1964); Lincoln Coll., Oxford (MA 1968); Chichester Theol Coll. Deacon 1964, priest 1965; Curate: St Peter, Birmingham, 1964–68; St Michael-at-the-Northgate, Oxford, 1968–74; Chaplain, Lincoln Coll., Oxford, 1968–74; Vicar, Basildon, Berks, 1974–82; RD Bradfield, 1978–82; Vicar, Aylesbury, Bucks, 1982–89, Team Rector, 1989–90; RD Aylesbury, 1985–89. Mem., Gen. Synod, 1980–90. Exam. Chaplain to Bishop of Oxford, 1973–. *Address:* 60 Wendover Road, Aylesbury, Bucks HP21 9LW. *T:* Aylesbury (0296) 23269. *Clubs:* Leander (Henley-on-Thames); Vincent's (Oxford).

MORRISON, John Lamb Murray, CBE 1957; DSc; FEng; FIMechE; Formerly Professor of Mechanical Engineering, University of Bristol, Emeritus 1971; *b* 22 May 1906; *s* of late Latto A. Morrison, Biggar, Lanarkshire; *m* 1936, Olga, *d* of late M. Nierenstein, DSc; two *s*. *Educ:* Biggar High Sch.; Univ. of Glasgow (DSc 1939). Lecturer in Mechanical Engineering; Reader in Mechanical Engineering, Univ. of Bristol. Pres., IMechE, 1970–71. Hon. DSc Salford, 1972. *Publications:* An Introduction to the Mechanics of Machines, 1964; various papers on strength of materials and design of machines. *Recreations:* gardening, golf. *Address:* Dreva, Rayleigh Road, Bristol BS9 2AU. *T:* Bristol (0272) 681193.

MORRISON, John Sinclair, CBE 1991; President, Wolfson College (formerly University College), Cambridge, 1966–80; *b* 15 June 1913; *s* of Sinclair Morrison (and *g s* of William Morrison, NY and Stagbury, Chipstead, Surrey) and Maria Elsie, *d* of William Lamaison, Salmons, Kenley, Surrey; *m* 1942, Elizabeth Helen, *d* of S. W. Sulman, Bexhill, Sussex; three *s* two *d*. *Educ:* Charterhouse; Trinity Coll., Cambridge. Fellow Trinity College, Cambridge, 1937–45; Asst Lecturer Manchester University, 1937–39; Editor of Cambridge Review, 1939–40. Ordinary Seaman (Volunteer), 1940–41. In service of British Council, Cairo, Zagazig, Baghdad, 1941–42; British Council Rep. in Palestine and Transjordan, 1942–45; Pres. Jerusalem Rotary Club, 1945; Prof. of Greek and Head of Dept of Classics and Ancient History at the Durham Colls of Univ. of Durham, 1945–50; Fellow Tutor and Senior Tutor of Trinity Coll., Cambridge, 1950–60; Vice-Master and Sen. Tutor of Churchill Coll., Cambridge, 1960–65, now Hon. Fellow. Leverhulme Fellow, 1965. Mellon Prof., 1976–77, Kenan Prof., 1981–82, Reed Coll., Oregon, USA; Leverhulme Emeritus Fellow, 1984–85. Member: Sierra Leone Educn Commission, 1954; Annan Cttee on Teaching of Russian, 1961; Hale Cttee on University Teaching Methods, 1961; Schools Council, 1965–67; Jt Working Party on 6th Form Curriculum and Examinations, 1968–72; Governing Bodies Assoc., 1965; Governor: Bradfield Coll., 1963–83; Wellington Coll., 1963–83; Charterhouse Sch., 1970–. Jt Editor, Classical Review, 1968–75. Trustee, National Maritime Museum, 1975–82; Chm., Trireme Trust, 1984–. Hon. FBA 1988. Hon. DLitt Davidson Coll., N Carolina, 1987. Caird Medal, Nat. Maritime Mus., 1991. *Publications:* (with R. T. Williams) Greek Oared Ships, 1968; Long Ships and Round Ships, 1980; (with J. F. Coates) The Athenian Trireme, 1986. *Address:* Granhams, Granhams Road, Great Shelford, Cambridge CB2 5JX. *T:* Cambridge (0223) 843158.

MORRISON, Margaret, OBE 1991; BEM 1972; Co-Chairman, Women's National Commission, 1989–91; *b* 20 March 1924; *d* of William and May Campbell; *m* 1943, Thomas Morrison; one *d*. *Educ:* Royal Jubilee Juniors, Newcastle; Sandyford Secondary Modern, Newcastle. Civil Service Union: Nat. Exec. Cttee, 1968–78; Vice-Pres., 1978–79; Pres., 1980–87; Dep. Pres., Nat. Union of Civil and Public Servants, 1987–89; Vice-Chm., Northern Regional TUC, 1980– (Chm., Women's Adv. Gp, 1980–); Mem., TUC Women's Cttee, 1979–89; Director: Northern Development Co., 1984–89; Entrust, 1984–; Mem., European Women's TUC and Steering Cttee, 1982–. Mem., Civil Service Appeal Bd, 1991–. TUC Gold Badge, Woman Trade Unionist of the Year, 1973. *Publication:* (jtly) Homelessness Amongst Women, report, 1983. *Recreations:* music, reading, swimming, conversation. *Address:* Women's National Commission, Goverment Offices, Horse Guards Road, SW1P 3AL. *T:* 071–270 5903. *Club:* Victory.

MORRISON, Hon. Mary Anne, DCVO 1982 (CVO 1970); Woman of the Bedchamber to the Queen since 1960; *b* 17 May 1937; *o d* of Baron Margadale, *qv*. *Educ:* Heathfield School. *Address:* Fonthill House, Tisbury, Wilts. *T:* Tisbury (0747) 870202; Eallabus, Bridgend, Isle of Islay, Argyllshire. *T:* Bowmore (049681) 223.

See also Hon. Sir C. A. Morrison, Hon. J. I. Morrison, Rt Hon. Sir P. H. Morrison.

MORRISON, Nigel Murray Paton; QC (Scot.) 1988; *b* 18 March 1948; *o s* of late David Paton Morrison, FRICS, FLAS and Dilys Trenholm Pritchard or Morrison. *Educ:* Rannoch School. Called to the Bar, Inner Temple, 1972; admitted Scottish Bar, 1975; Asst Editor, Session Cases, 1976–82; Asst Clerk, Rules Council, 1978–84; Clerk of Faculty, Faculty of Advocates, 1979–87; Standing Junior Counsel to Scottish Develt Dept (Planning), 1982–86; Temporary Sheriff, 1982–; Second (formerly Junior) Counsel to Lord President of Court of Session, 1984–89; First Counsel to Lord President, 1989–; Counsel to Sec. of State under Private Legislation Procedure (Scotland) Act 1936, 1986–. Chm., Social Security Appeal Tribunals, 1982–. Trustee, Nat. Library of Scotland, 1989.

Publications: contribs to Stair Memorial Encyclopaedia of the Laws of Scotland. *Recreations*: music, riding, walking. *Address*: 9 India Street, Edinburgh. *T*: 031–225 2807. *Club*: New (Edinburgh).

MORRISON, Rt. Hon. Sir Peter (Hugh), Kt 1990; PC 1988; MP (C) City of Chester since Feb. 1974; *b* 2 June 1944; 3rd *s* of 1st Baron Margadale, *qv*. *Educ*: Eton; Keble Coll., Oxford (Hons Law; Hon. Fellow, 1989). Personal Asst to Rt Hon. Peter Walker, MP, 1966–67; Investment Manager, 1968–70; independent business, 1970–74. Sec., NW Cons. Members' Gp, 1974–76; Jt Sec., Cons. Smaller Businesses Cttee, 1974–76. An Opposition Whip, 1976–79; a Lord Comr of HM Treasury, and Govt Pairing Whip, 1979–81; Parly Under-Sec. of State, 1981–83, Minister of State, 1983–85, Dept of Employment; Minister of State, DTI, 1985–86, Dept of Energy, 1987–90; PPS to the Prime Minister, 1990. Dep. Chm., Cons. Party, 1986–89. Chairman: Cons. Collegiate Forum, 1987–89; One Nation Forum, 1987–89. Pres., Assoc. of Cons. Clubs, 1986–87; Vice-Pres., Nat. YCs, 1990–. FRSA. *Address*: House of Commons, SW1A 0AA. *Clubs*: White's, Pratt's.

See also Hon. Sir C. A. Morrison, Hon. J. I. Morrison, Hon. M. A. Morrison.

MORRISON, (Philip) Blake, FRSL; Literary Editor, The Independent on Sunday, since 1990; *b* 8 Oct. 1950; *s* of Arthur Blakemore Morrison and Agnes O'Shea; *m* 1976, Katherine Ann Drake; two *s* one *d*. *Educ*: Ermysteds Grammar Sch., Skipton; Nottingham Univ. (BA); McMaster Univ. (MA); University College London (PhD). FRSL 1988. Poetry and fiction editor, TLS, 1978–81; Dep. Literary Editor, 1981–86, Literary Editor, 1987–89, Observer. Eric Gregory Award, 1980; Somerset Maugham Award, 1984; Dylan Thomas Meml Prize, 1985; E. M. Forster Award, 1988. *Publications*: The Movement: English poetry and fiction of the 1950s, 1980; (ed jtly) The Penguin Book of Contemporary British Poetry, 1982; Seamus Heaney, 1982; Dark Glasses, 1984; The Ballad of the Yorkshire Ripper, 1987; The Yellow House, 1987. *Recreations*: football, tennis. *Address*: The Independent on Sunday, 40 City Road, EC1. *T*: 071–253 1222.

MORRISON, Maj.-Gen. Reginald Joseph Gordon, CB 1969; CBE 1959; MD, FRCP; retired; Physician, The Royal Hospital, Chelsea, 1969–79; Director of Medicine, Ministry of Defence (Army), and Consulting Physician to the Army, 1965–68; *b* 29 March 1909; *s* of R. Morrison; *m* 1947, Norma Jacqueline Nicholson; two *s*. *Educ*: Dulwich Coll.; St Joseph's Coll., SE19; St Bartholomew's Hosp. House Phys., St Bart's Hosp., 1934; Res. MO, Hove Gen. Hosp. Commnd RAMC, 1936; served as Med. Specialist, RAMC. Adviser in Medicine, EA Command, 1947–50; OC, Med. Div., QA Mil. Hosp., 1950–56; Cons. Phys., Far East, 1956–59; Prof. of Trop. Med., Royal Army Medical College, 1959–65. QHP 1963–68. *Publications*: (with W. H. Hargreaves) The Practice of Tropical Medicine, 1965; chapter in: Exploration Medicine, 1965; Medicine in the Tropics, 1974; various articles in Lancet, BMJ, Proc. RSM, etc. *Recreations*: rose growing, golf. *Address*: 1 Hollingdon Court, High Street, Chislehurst, Kent BR7 5AJ.

MORRISON, Hon. Sara Antoinette Sibell Frances, (Hon. Mrs Sara Morrison); *b* 9 Aug. 1934; *d* of 2nd Viscount Long and of Laura, Duchess of Marlborough; *m* 1954, Hon. Charles Andrew Morrison (*see* Hon. Sir C. A. Morrison) (marr. diss. 1984); one *s* one *d*. *Educ*: in England and France. Gen. Electric Co., 1975– (Dir 1980–); Director: Abbey National plc (formerly Abbey Nat. Building Soc.), 1979–86, 1987–; Imperial Group Ltd, 1981–86. Chairman: Nat. Council for Voluntary Orgns (formerly Nat. Council of Social Service), 1977–81; Nat. Adv. Council on Employment of Disabled People, 1981–84. County Councillor, then Alderman, Wilts, 1961–71; Chairman: Wilts Assoc. of Youth Clubs, 1958–63; Wilts Community Council, 1965–70; Vice-Chairman: Nat. Assoc. Youth Clubs, 1969–71; Conservative Party Organisation, 1971–75; Member: Governing Bd, Volunteer Centre, 1972–77; Annan Cttee of Enquiry into Broadcasting, 1974–77; Nat. Consumer Council, 1975–77; Bd, Fourth Channel TV Co., 1980–85; Video Appeals Cttee (Video Recordings Act, 1984), 1985–; Governing Council, Family Policy Studies Centre, 1983–; Nat. Radiological Protection Bd, 1989–; Council, PSI, 1980–; Governing Body, Imperial Coll., London, 1986–; Council, Surrey Univ. CBIM. FRSA. *Address*: Wyndham's Farm, Wedhampton, Devizes, Wilts SN10 3QE. *T*: Chirton (038084) 221; 16 Groom Place, SW1X 7BA. *T*: 071–245 6553.

MORRISON, Stephen Roger; Director of Programmes, Granada Television, since 1987; *b* 3 March 1947; *s* of Hyman Michael Morrison and Rebecca (*née* Zolkwer); *m* 1979, Gayle Valerie Broughall; three *d*. *Educ*: High Sch., Glasgow; Edinburgh Univ. (MA Hons); Nat. Film Sch., Beaconsfield (ANFS). BBC Scotland (Radio and TV), 1970; Granada Television: Producer/Dir, Northern Documentary Unit, 1974; Ed., Granada Regl Progs, 1977; Hd of Arts and Features, 1981; Feature Films Producer: The Magic Toyshop, 1986; The Fruit Machine, 1988; (Exec. Producer) My Left Foot, 1989; (Exec. Producer) The Field, 1990. *Recreations*: tennis, reading, films and theatre, talking and dining, touring delicatessens. *Address*: Granada Television, Manchester M60 9EA. *T*: 061–832 7211. *Club*: Garrick.

MORRISON, Dr Stuart Love; Professor of Community Medicine, University of Edinburgh, 1964–75, retired; *b* 25 Nov. 1922; *o s* of late William James Morrison, Ironfounder, Glasgow and late Isabella Murdoch, Edinburgh; *m* 1947, Dr Audrey Butler Lornie, *yr d* of late Lt-Col W. S. Lornie, MC, TD, MRCVS, Perth; one *d*. *Educ*: Glasgow Acad.; Dundee High Sch.; St Andrews and London Univs. MB, ChB (St Andrews) 1951; DPH (London) 1954; MRCP Edinburgh, 1966; FRCP Edinburgh, 1968; FFCM 1975. Served in RAF, 1939–46; Hosp. and gen. practice, 1951–53; Public Health appts, 1954–56; Mem., Scientific Staff, MRC Social Medicine Research Unit, 1956–62; Vis. Fellow, Epidemiology and Statistics, Univ. of N Carolina, 1961–62; Sen. Lectr in Social Med., Univ. of Edinburgh, 1962–64; Professorial Fellow in Community Medicine, 1976–82 and Dir of Centre for Med. Res., 1979–82, Univ. of Sussex; Vis. Prof. of Community Medicine, LSHTM, 1982–84; Prof. of Community Medicine, Univ. of Malta, 1984–86. *Publications*: (jtly) The Image and the Reality, 1978; contribs to med. jls on epidemiology, organisation of medical care and medical administration. *Recreation*: book collecting. *Address*: 4 Roselands, Sidmouth, Devon EX10 8PB.

MORRISON, William Charles Carnegie, CA; Deputy Senior Partner, Peat Marwick McLintock, since 1987; Visiting Professor in Accountancy, University of Strathclyde, since 1983; *b* 10 Feb. 1938; *s* of late William and Grace Morrison; *m* 1st; two *d*; 2nd, 1977, Joceline Mary (*née* Saint). *Educ*: Kelvinside Acad., Lathallan; Merchiston Castle Sch. Thomson McLintock & Co., subseq. KMG Thomson McLintock: qual. CA (with distinction), 1961; Partner, 1966; Jt Sen. Partner, Glasgow and Edinburgh, 1974–80; UK managing partner, 1980–87. Director: Thomas Cook & Son Ltd, 1971–72; Scottish Amicable Life Assurance Soc., 1973–87; Securities Trust of Scotland, 1976–80; Brownlee & Co., 1978–80. Pres., Inst. of Chartered Accountants of Scotland, 1984–85 (Vice-Pres., 1982–84). Vice Pres., Scottish Council (Develt and Industry), 1982– (mem. various cttees); Member: Scottish Telecommunications Bd, 1978–80; Scottish Cttee, Design Council, 1978–81. Governor, Kelvinside Acad., 1967–80 (Chm. of Governors, 1975–80); Hon. Treasurer, Transport Trust, 1982–88. *Publications*: occasional professional papers. *Recreations*: vintage transport, model railways. *Address*: 87 Campden Hill Court, Holland Street, W8 7HW. *T*: 071–937 2972. *Clubs*: Caledonian; Royal Scottish Automobile (Glasgow).

MORRISON, William Garth, DL; Chief Scout, since 1988; *b* 8 April 1943; *s* of Walter Courtenay Morrison and Audrey Elizabeth Morrison (*née* Gilbert); *m* 1970, Gillian Cheetham; two *s* one *d*. *Educ*: Pangbourne Coll.; Pembroke Coll., Cambridge (BA 1966). CEng, MIEE 1973. Service in RN, retiring as Lieut, 1961–73; farming in family partnership, 1973–. Scouting: Area Comr, E Lothian, 1973–81; Chief Comr of Scotland, 1981–88. Member: Lothian Region Children's Panel, 1976–83; Scottish Community Educn Council, 1988–. DL E Lothian, 1984. Argentine Gold Medal, 1962. *Publication*: chapter in The Scottish Juvenile Justice System, 1982. *Recreations*: golf, sailing, scouting. *Address*: West Fenton, North Berwick, East Lothian EH39 5AL. *T*: North Berwick (0620) 842154. *Clubs*: Naval; Hawks (Cambridge).

MORRISON-BELL, Sir William (Hollin Dayrell), 4th Bt *cr* 1905; solicitor; *b* 21 June 1956; *s* of Sir Charles Reginald Francis Morrison-Bell, 3rd Bt and of Prudence Caroline, *d* of late Lt-Col W. D. Davies, 60th Rifles (she *m* 2nd, Peter Gillbanks); *S* father, 1967; *m* 1984, Cynthia Hélène Marie White; one *s*. *Educ*: Eton; St Edmund Hall, Oxford. *Heir*: *s* Thomas Charles Edward Morrison-Bell, *b* 13 Feb. 1985. *Address*: Highgreen, Tarset, Hexham, Northumberland. *T*: Bellingham (0434) 240223; 106 Bishops Road, SW6. *T*: 071–736 4940.

MORRISON-LOW, Sir James; *see* Low.

MORRISON-SCOTT, Sir Terence Charles Stuart, Kt 1965; DSC 1944; DSc; DL; Director, British Museum (Natural History), 1960–68 (Director, Science Museum, 1956–60); *b* Paris, 24 Oct. 1908; *o s* of late R. C. S. Morrison-Scott, DSO, and Douairière Jhr. R. Quarles van Ufford; *m* 1935, Rita, 4th *d* of late E. J. Layton. *Educ*: Eton; Christ Church (MA of the House, 1947), Oxford; Royal College of Science (1st Class Hons Zoology, BSc, ARCS 1935, MSc 1939); FLS 1937; DSc London, 1952. Asst Master, Eton, 1935; Scientific Staff, Brit. Museum (Natural Hist.) in charge of Mammal Room, 1936–39, 1945–55 and part of 1956. Served War of 1939–45, with Royal Navy (DSC). Lt-Comdr RNVR. Treas., Zoological Soc. of London, 1950–76; Treas., XVth Internat. Congress of Zoology, 1958. Trustee, Imp. War Museum, 1956–60; Dir, Arundel Castle Trustees Ltd, 1976–86. Governor, Imperial Coll. of Science and Technology, 1956–76 (Fellow, 1963); Mem., Standing Commn on Museums and Galleries, 1973–76; National Trust: Mem., Properties Cttee, 1968–83; Chm., Nature Cons. Panel, 1970–81; Chm., Architectural Panel, 1973–82. Goodwood Flying Sch. (solo), 1975. DL West Sussex, 1982. *Publications*: Palaearctic and Indian Mammals (with J. R. E.), 1951; Southern African Mammals (with J. R. E. and R. W. H.), 1953; papers in scientific jls on taxonomy of mammals. *Address*: Upperfold House, Fernhurst, Haslemere, Surrey GU27 3JH. *Clubs*: Athenæum, Brooks's; Vincent's (Oxford); Leander.

MORRITT, Hon. Sir (Robert) Andrew, Kt 1988; CVO 1989; **Hon. Mr Justice Morritt**; a Judge of the High Court of Justice, Chancery Division, since 1988; *b* 5 Feb. 1938; *s* of Robert Augustus Morritt and Margaret Mary Morritt (*née* Tyldesley Jones); *m* 1962, Sarah Simonetta Merton, *d* of John Ralph Merton, *qv*; two *s*. *Educ*: Eton Coll.; Magdalene Coll., Cambridge (BA 1961). 2nd Lieut Scots Guards, 1956–58. Called to the Bar, Lincoln's Inn, 1962, Bencher, 1984; QC 1977. Junior Counsel: to Sec. of State for Trade in Chancery Matters, 1970–77; to Attorney-Gen. in Charity Matters, 1972–77; Attorney General to HRH The Prince of Wales, 1978–88. Member: Gen. Council of the Bar, 1969–73; Adv. Cttee on Legal Educn, 1972–76; Top Salaries Review Body, 1982–87. *Recreations*: fishing, shooting. *Address*: Royal Courts of Justice, Strand, WC2A 2LL. *Club*: Garrick.

MORROCCO, Alberto, RSA 1963 (ARSA 1952); RSW 1965; RP 1977; RGI; Head of School of Painting, Duncan of Jordanstone College of Art, Dundee, 1950–82; *b* 14 Dec. 1917; *m* 1941, Vera Cockburn Mercer; two *s* one *d*. *Educ*: Gray's Sch. of Art, Aberdeen. Carnegie Schol., 1937; Brough Schol., 1938. In the Army, 1940–46. Guthrie Award, 1943; San Vito Prize, Rome, 1959. Pictures in: Scottish Modern Arts Coll.; Contemporary Arts Soc.; Scottish Arts Council Coll.; Hull, Aberdeen, Glasgow, Perth, Dundee and Edinburgh City Art Galleries and Scottish Gall. of Modern Art. Mem., Royal Fine Art Commn for Scotland, 1978–88. Mem. Cttee, Saltire Soc. Hon. LLD Dundee, 1980; DUniv Stirling, 1987. *Recreations*: travel, swimming, eating. *Address*: Binrock, 456 Perth Road, Dundee. *T*: Dundee (0382) 69319. *Club*: Scottish Arts.

MORROGH, Henton, CBE 1969; FRS 1964; FEng 1979; Director, BCIRA (formerly British Cast Iron Research Association), 1959–85; *b* 29 Sept. 1917; *s* of Clifford and Amy Morrogh; *m* 1949, Olive Joyce Ramsay; one *d*. Distinguished for his work on the microstructure and solidification of cast iron and for the development of ductile cast iron. Visiting Prof., Dept of Industrial Engineering and Management Univ. of Technology, Loughborough, 1967–72. President: Instn of Metallurgists, 1967–68; Inst. of British Foundrymen, 1972–73; Internat. Cttee of Foundry Technical Assocs, 1978. Hon. Member: Japanese Foundrymen's Soc., 1984; Inst. of British Foundrymen, 1986. DSc (*hc*), Univ. of Birmingham, 1965; Iron and Steel Inst. Andrew Carnegie Gold Medal, 1946; E. J. Fox Medal Inst. of Brit. Foundrymen, 1951; McFadden Gold Medal, Amer. Foundrymen's Soc., 1952; Robert Hadfield Medal, Iron & Steel Inst., 1956; Gold Medal, Amer. Gray Iron Founders' Soc., 1961; Bessemer Gold Medal, Metals Soc., 1977. *Address*: Cedarwood, Penn Lane, Tanworth-in-Arden, Warwicks B94 5HH. *T*: Tanworth-in-Arden (05644) 2414.

MORROW, Sir Ian (Thomas), Kt 1973; CA; FCMA, JDipMA, FBIM; CompIEE; Chairman: MAI (formerly Mills and Allen International) plc, since 1974 (Director, since 1974); Additional Underwriting Agencies (No 3) Ltd, since 1985; Scotia Pharmaceuticals Ltd, since 1986; Efamol Holdings plc, since 1986; Insport Consultants Ltd, since 1988; Beale Dobie & Co. Ltd, since 1989; *b* 8 June 1912; *er s* of late Thomas George Morrow and Jamesina Hunter, Pilmour Links, St Andrews; *m* 1940, Elizabeth Mary Thackray (marr. diss. 1967); one *s* one *d*; *m* 1967, Sylvia Jane Taylor; one *d*. *Educ*: Dollar Academy, Dollar. Chartered Accountant 1936; FCMA 1945; Asst Accountant, Brocklehurst-Whiston Amalgamated Ltd, 1937–40; Partner, Robson, Morrow & Co., 1942–51; Financial Dir, 1951–52, Dep. Man. Dir, 1952–56, Joint Man. Dir, 1956–57, Man. Dir, 1957–58, The Brush Electrical Engineering Co. Ltd (now The Brush Group Ltd); Jt Man. Dir, H. Clarkson & Co. Ltd, 1961–72; Chairman: UKO International plc (formerly UK Optical & Industrial Holdings Ltd), 1959–86 (former Man. Dir and Chm. of subsidiary cos); Associated Fire Alarms Ltd, 1965–70; Rowe Bros & Co. (Holdings) Ltd, 1960–70; Kenwood Manufacturing Co. Ltd, 1961–68; Crane Fruehauf Trailers Ltd, 1969–71; Collett, Dickenson, Pearce Internat. Ltd, 1979–83; Scotia DAF Trucks Ltd, 1979–83; Agricultural Holdings Co. Ltd, 1981–84; W. M. Still & Sons Ltd, 1964–86; Martin-Black PLC, 1977–86; Pearl & Dean Ltd (Hong Kong), 1978–86; Hugh Paul Holdings Ltd, 1979–85; Harlow Meyer Savage, subseq. Harlow Ueda Savage (Eurodollars), 1980–88 (Dir, 1985–88); Strong & Fisher (Hldgs), 1981–90 (Dir, 1981–90); Argunex Ltd, 1985–89; Walbrook Insce Co., 1990–; Brightstone Estates, 1990–; Deputy Chairman, Rolls Royce Ltd, 1970–71, Rolls Royce (1971) Ltd, 1971–73 (Man. Dir, 1971–72); Director: Hambros Industrial Management Ltd, 1965–91; Hambros PLC, 1972–90 (Dep.

Chm., 1983–86); The Laird Gp, 1973– (Chm., 1975–87); DAF Trucks (GB), 1977–83; Zeus Management Ltd, 1985–; Psion PLC, 1987–; C. E. Heath Public Ltd Co., 1988–. Led Anglo-American Council on Productivity Team on Management Accounting to US, 1950. Council Member: British Electrical & Allied Manufacturers' Assoc., 1957–58; British Internal Combustion Engine Manufacturers' Assoc., 1957–58; Member: Grand Council, FBI, 1953–58; Council, Production Engineering Research Assoc., 1955–58; Council, Inst. of Cost and Works Accountants (now Inst. of Management Accountants), 1952–70 (Pres. 1956–57, Gold Medallist 1961); Performing Right Tribunal, 1968–74; Council, Inst. of Chartered Accountants of Scotland, 1968–72, 1979–82 (Vice-Pres. 1970–72, 1979–80, 1980–81, Pres., 1981–82); Inflation Accounting Steering Gp, 1976–79; Lay Member, Press Council, 1974–80; Freeman, City of London; Liveryman, Worshipful Co. of Spectaclemakers. DUniv. Stirling, 1979; Hon. DLitt Heriot-Watt, 1982. *Publications:* papers and addresses on professional and management subjects. *Recreations:* reading, music, golf, ski-ing. *Address:* 2 Albert Terrace Mews, NW1 7TA. *T:* 071–722 7110. *Clubs:* National Liberal, Royal Automobile; Royal and Ancient (St Andrews).

MORROW, Martin S.; Stipendiary Magistrate, Glasgow, since 1972; *b* 16 Nov. 1923; *s* of late Thomas Morrow and Mary Lavery; *m* 1952, Nancy May, BMus, LRAM; one *s* two *d*. *Educ:* St Aloysius' Coll., Glasgow; Glasgow Univ. Solicitor. Private practice, 1951–56; Asst Procurator Fiscal, 1956–72. *Recreations:* music, golf, reading. *Address:* 33 Leicester Avenue, Glasgow G12 0LU. *T:* 041–334 1324. *Club:* St Mungo (Glasgow).

MORSE, Sir Christopher Jeremy, KCMG 1975; Chairman, Lloyds Bank, since 1977 (Deputy Chairman, 1975–77); Director, ICI plc; Deputy Chairman, Business in the Community; Vice-President, British Bankers' Association, since 1991 (President, 1984–91); Warden, Winchester College, since 1987 (Fellow, 1966–82); Chancellor, Bristol University, since 1989; *b* 10 Dec. 1928; *s* of late Francis John Morse and Kinbarra (*née* Armfield-Marrow); *m* 1955, Belinda Marianne, *d* of Lt-Col R. B. Y. Mills; three *s* one *d* (and one *d* decd). *Educ:* Winchester; New Coll., Oxford (Hon. Fellow, 1979). 1st Class Lit. Hum. 1953. 2nd Lt KRRC, 1948–49. Fellow, All Souls Coll., Oxford, 1953–68, 1983–. Trained in banking at Glyn, Mills & Co., and made a director in 1964; Executive Dir, Bank of England, 1965–72; Lloyds Bank International: Chm., 1979–80; Dep. Chm., 1975–77 and 1980–85; Chm., Lloyds Merchant Bank Hldgs, 1985–88. Alternate Governor for UK of IMF, 1966–72; Chm. of Deputies of Cttee of Twenty, IMF, 1972–74; Chm., Cttee of London Clearing Bankers, 1980–82 (Dep. Chm., 1978–80); Mem., Council of Lloyd's, 1987–; President: London Forex Assoc., 1978–91; Institut Internat. d'Etudes Bancaires, 1982–83; British Overseas Bankers' Club, 1983–84; Internat. Monetary Conf., 1985–86; Banking Fedn of EC, 1988–90. Mem., NEDC, 1977–81. Chm., City Communications Centre, 1985–87; Director: Alexanders Discount Co. Ltd, 1975–84; Legal & General Assce Soc., 1964 and 1975–87. Hon. Mem., Lombard Assoc., 1989. Governor, Henley Management Coll., 1966–85. Chairman: Per Jacobsson Foundn, 1987–; Trustees, Beit Meml Fellowships for Med. Res., 1976–; Mem., British Selection Cttee, Harkness Fellowships, 1986–90. Freeman, City of London, 1978; Chm., City Arts Trust, 1976–79. FIDE Internat. Judge for chess compositions, 1975–; Pres., British Chess Problem Soc., 1977–79; Hon. Life Mem., British Chess Fedn, 1988. Pres., Classical Assoc., 1989–90. Hon. DLitt City, 1977; Hon. DSc Aston, 1984; Hon. LLD Bristol, 1989. *Recreations:* poetry, problems and puzzles, coarse gardening, golf. *Address:* 102a Drayton Gardens, SW10. *T:* 071–370 2265. *Club:* Athenæum.

MORSE, Sir Jeremy; *see* Morse, Sir C. J.

MORSON, Basil Clifford, CBE 1987; VRD 1963; MA, DM Oxon; FRCS; FRCPath; FRCP; Civilian Consultant in Pathology to the Royal Navy, 1976–86, now Emeritus; Consulting Pathologist and Research Consultant to St Mark's Hospital, since 1986 (Consultant Pathologist, 1956–86); Director, WHO International Reference Centre for Gastrointestinal Cancer, 1969–86; *b* 13 Nov. 1921; *s* of late A. Clifford Morson, OBE, FRCS; *m* 1st, 1950, Pamela Elizabeth Gilbert (marr. diss. 1982); one *s* two *d*; 2nd, 1983, Sylvia Dutton, MBE. *Educ:* Beaumont Coll.; Wadham Coll., Oxford; Middlesex Hosp. Medical Sch. House Surg., Middlesex Hosp., 1949; House Surg., Central Middlesex Hosp., 1950; Asst Pathologist, Bland-Sutton Institute of Pathology, Middlesex Hosp., 1950. Sub-Lt RNVR, 1943–46; Surgeon-Comdr RNR (London Div.), retd 1972. President: Sect. of Proctology, RSocMed, 1973–74; British Soc. of Gastroenterology, 1979–80 (Hon. Mem., 1987); British Div., Internat. Acad. of Pathology, 1978–; Treas., RCPath, 1983– (Vice-Pres., 1978–81). Vis. Prof. of Pathology, Univ. of Chicago, 1959; Sir Henry Wade Vis. Prof., RCSE, 1970; Vis. Prof of Pathology, Univ. of Texas System Cancer Center, 1980 (Joanne Vandenberg Hill Award); Lectures: Lettsomian, Med. Soc., 1970; Sir Arthur Hurst Meml, British Soc. of Gastroenterology, 1970; Richardson, Massachusetts Gen. Hosp., Boston, 1970; Skinner, RCR, 1983; Shelley Meml, Johns Hopkins Univ., 1983; Kettle, RCPath, 1987. FRCS 1972; FRCP 1979 (MRCP 1973); Hon. Fellow: Amer. Soc. of Colon and Rectal Surgeons, 1974; Amer. Coll. of Gastroenterology, 1978; French Nat. Soc. of Gastroenterology, 1982; RSM, 1989; RAeS, 1990. John Hunter Medal, RCS, 1987; Frederick Salmon Medal, Sect. of Coloproctology, RSM, 1991. *Publications:* Pathology of Alimentary Tract, in Systemic Pathology, ed W. St C. Symmers, 1966, 3rd edn 1987; (ed) Diseases of the Colon, Rectum and Anus, 1969; Textbook of Gastrointestinal Pathology, 1972, 3rd edn 1989; Histological Typing of Intestinal Tumours, 1976; The Pathogenesis of Colorectal Cancer, 1978; Pathology in Surgical Practice, 1985; Colour Atlas of Gastrointestinal Pathology, 1988; numerous articles in medical journals. *Recreations:* gardening, ornithology, travel. *Address:* 14 Crossways Park, West Chiltington, W Sussex RH20 2QZ. *T:* West Chiltington (0798) 813528.

MORT, Rt. Rev. John Ernest Llewelyn, CBE 1965; Assistant Bishop, Diocese of Leicester, since 1972; *b* 13 April 1915; *s* of late Trevor Ll. Mort, JP, and Ethel Mary Mort; *m* 1953, Barbara Gifford. *Educ:* Malvern Coll.; St Catharine's Coll., Cambridge (BA Hist. Tripos 1938; MA 1942); Westcott House, Cambridge. Asst Curate, Dudley, 1940–44; Worcester Diocesan Youth Organiser, 1944–48; Private Chaplain to Bishop of Worcester, 1943–52; Vicar of St John in Bedwardine, Worcester, 1948–52; Bishop of N Nigeria, 1952–69; Canon Residentiary and Treasurer of Leicester Cathedral, 1970–88. Hon. LLD Ahmadu Bello Univ., 1970. *Address:* 271 Forest Road, Old Woodhouse, Loughborough, Leics LE12 8TZ.

MORT, (Margaret) Marion; Co-ordinator, Decade of Evangelism (Church of England), since 1990; *b* 10 May 1937; *d* of Rev. Ivan H. Whittaker and Margaret Whittaker; *m* 1959, Colin James Mort; one *s* two *d*. *Educ:* St Mary's Sch., Wantage; Queen's Coll., Harley St; Edinburgh Univ. Nat. Sec., World Development Movement, 1970–72; Licensed Lay Reader, 1983–; Mem. Gen. Synod, 1985–90 (rep. in Partners in Mission consultation for Church in Kenya, 1988). World Develt Educn Adviser, Dio. Portsmouth, 1984–91. Dir, Ocean Sound (ILR), 1985–; Mem., Bd of Christian Aid, 1987–90. *Publications:* (jtly) Mission Audit, 1983; (jtly) Called to Order, 1988; church educnl papers; contribs to Church press. *Recreations:* good cars, good beer, good conversation. *Address:* Church House, Great Smith Street, Westminster SW1P 3NZ. *T:* 071–222 9011.

MORTIMER, Hon. Barry; *see* Mortimer, Hon. J. B.

MORTIMER, Clifford Hiley, DSc, DrPhil; FRS 1958; Distinguished Professor in Zoology, University of Wisconsin-Milwaukee, 1966–81, now Distinguished Professor Emeritus; *b* Whitchurch, Som, 27 Feb. 1911; *er s* of Walter Herbert and Bessie Russell; *m* 1936, Ingeborg Margarete Closs, Stuttgart, Germany; two *d*. *Educ:* Sibford and Sidcot Schs; Univ. of Manchester. BSc (Manchester) 1932, DSc (Manchester) 1946; Dr Phil (Berlin) 1935. Served on scientific staff of Freshwater Biological Assoc., 1935–41 and 1946–56. Seconded to Admiralty scientific service, 1941–46. Sec. and Dir, Scottish Marine Biological Assoc., 1956–66; Dir, Center for Great Lakes Studies, Univ. of Wisconsin-Milwaukee, 1966–79. Hon. DSc Wisconsin–Milwaukee, 1985; DèsSc *hc* Ecole Polytechnique Fédérale de Lausanne, 1987. *Publications:* scientific papers on lakes and the physical and chemical conditions which control life in them. *Recreations:* music, travel. *Address:* 2501 E Menlo Boulevard, Shorewood, Wisconsin 53211, USA.

MORTIMER, Gerald James, CBE 1979 (MBE (mil.) 1944); DL; FEng; Councillor, Surrey County Council, since 1973 (Chairman, Policy Committee, 1986–90); *b* 2 Sept. 1918; *s* of late Rev. Fernley Mortimer and Grace Mortimer (*née* Whiting); *m* 1st, 1942, Connie (*née* Dodd) (*d* 1989); two *s* two *d*; 2nd, 1990, Theresa Ella Walker. *Educ:* Caterham Sch.; Royal School of Mines, London Univ. (BSc (mining engrg), ARSM). Served War, Major, RE, UK and NW Europe, 1939–46. Mining official on Witwatersrand gold mines, S Africa, and in E Africa, 1946–55; Consolidated Gold Fields Ltd: Management staff, London, 1955–63; Exec. Dir, 1963–78; Dep. Chm., 1969–78; Gp Chief Exec., 1976–78; non. exec. Dir, 1978–80; Consultant, 1978–83; Dir, other Gp cos, 1957–79; in charge Goldsworthy iron ore project, W Australia, 1964–65; Exec. Chm., Amey Roadstone Corp. Ltd, 1967–75. President: Overseas Mining Assoc., 1972–73; Instn of Mining and Metallurgy, 1977–78; Inst. of Quarrying, 1980–81; Board Mem., 1978–83, Vice-Chm., 1981–82, Chm., 1982–83, CEI. Hon. Treas., Fellowship of Engrg, 1981–84. President: Old Caterhamians Assoc., 1970–71; RSM Assoc., 1976–77. Chm., E Surrey Cons. Assoc., 1980–82, Treasurer, 1982–83. DL Surrey, 1990. FRSA; Hon. FIMM; Hon. FIQ. *Recreations:* history, politics. *Address:* 40 Harestone Valley Road, Caterham, Surrey CR3 6HD. *T:* Caterham (0883) 44853.

MORTIMER, James Edward; General Secretary of the Labour Party, 1982–85; *b* 12 Jan. 1921; *m*; two *s* one *d*. *Educ:* Junior Techn. Sch., Portsmouth; Ruskin Coll., Oxford; London Sch. of Economics. Worked in Shipbuilding and Engrg Industries as Ship Fitter Apprentice, Machinist and Planning Engr; TUC Schol., Oxford, 1945–46; TUC Economic Dept, 1946–48; full-time Trade Union Official, Draughtsmen's and Allied Technicians' Assoc., 1948–68. Dir, London Co-operative Soc., 1968–71. Mem., NBPI, 1968–71; Mem., Bd, LTE, 1971–74. Chm., ACAS (formerly Conciliation and Arbitration Service), 1974–81. Member: Wilberforce Ct of Inquiry into the power dispute, 1970; Armed Forces Pay Review Body, 1971–74; EDC for Chemical Industry, 1973–74; Chm. EDC for Mechanical and Electrical Engineering Construction, 1974–82. Vis. Fellow, Admin. Staff Coll., Henley, 1976–82; Sen. Vis. Fellow, Bradford Univ., 1977–82; Vis. Prof., Imperial Coll. of Sci. and Technol., London Univ., 1981–83; Ward-Perkins Res. Fellow, Pembroke Coll., Oxford, 1981. Hon. DLitt Bradford, 1982. *Publications:* A History of Association of Engineering and Shipbuilding Draughtsmen, 1960; (with Clive Jenkins) British Trade Unions Today, 1965; (with Clive Jenkins) The Kind of Laws the Unions Ought to Want, 1968; Industrial Relations, 1968; Trade Unions and Technological Change, 1971; History of the Boilermakers' Society, vol. 1, 1973, vol. 2, 1982; (with Valerie Ellis) A Professional Union: the evolution of the Institution of Professional Civil Servants, 1980. *Address:* 5 Silverdale Drive, SE9 4DH. *T:* 081–851 7866.

MORTIMER, Hon. (John) Barry; Hon. Mr Justice Mortimer; a Judge of the Supreme Court of Hong Kong, since 1985; *b* 7 Aug. 1931; *s* of John William Mortimer and Maud (*née* Snarr) Mortimer; *m* 1958, Judith Mary (*née* Page); two *s* two *d*. *Educ:* St Peter's School, York (Headmasters' Exhibitioner 1945); Emmanuel College, Cambridge; BA 1955, MA 1959. Commissioned into 4 RTR, 1951; served in Egypt, 1951–52; 45/51 RTR (TA), 1952–57. Called to the Bar, Middle Temple, 1956 (Bencher 1980); Harmsworth Law Scholar 1957; Prosecuting Counsel on NE Circuit: to Post Office, 1965–69; to Inland Revenue, 1969–71; QC 1971; a Recorder, 1972–87. Chancellor, Dio. of Ripon, 1971–85. Chairman: Mental Health Review Tribunal, 1983–85; Overseas Trust Bank (Compensation) Tribunal, 1986–87; Member: Bar Council, 1970–75; Senate, 1979–85; Law Reform Commn, Hong Kong, 1990– (Chm., Sub-cttee on Privacy and Data Protection). *Recreations:* reading, shooting, tennis. *Address:* Supreme Court, Queensway, Hong Kong; The Grange, Staveley, Knaresborough, N Yorks HG5 9LD. *Club:* Hong Kong.

MORTIMER, John (Clifford), CBE 1986; QC 1966; barrister; playwright and author; *b* 21 April 1923; *s* of Clifford Mortimer and Kathleen May (*née* Smith); *m* 1st, 1949, Penelope Ruth Fletcher; one *s* one *d*; 2nd, Penelope (*née* Gollop); two *d*. *Educ:* Harrow; Brasenose Coll., Oxford. Called to the Bar, 1948; Master of the Bench, Inner Temple, 1975. Mem. Nat. Theatre Bd, 1968–88. Chairman: Council, RSL, 1989–; Royal Court Theatre, 1990–. Pres., Berks, Bucks and Oxon Naturalists' Trust, 1984–90. Hon. DLitt: Susquehanna Univ., 1985; St Andrews, 1987; Nottingham, 1989; Hon. LLD: Exeter, 1986; Brunel, 1990. Won the Italia Prize with short play, The Dock Brief, 1958; another short play What Shall We Tell Caroline, 1958. Full-length plays: The Wrong Side of the Park, 1960; Two Stars for Comfort, 1962; (trans.) A Flea in Her Ear, 1966; The Judge, 1967; (trans.) Cat Among the Pigeons, 1969; Come as You Are, 1970; A Voyage Round My Father, 1970 (filmed, 1982); (trans.) The Captain of Köpenick, 1971; I, Claudius (adapted from Robert Graves), 1972; Collaborators, 1973; Mr Luby's Fear of Heaven (radio), 1976; Heaven and Hell, 1976; The Bells of Hell, 1977; (trans.) The Lady from Maxim's, 1977; (trans.) A Little Hotel on the Side, 1984; opera (trans) Die Fledermaus, 1988. Film Scripts: John and Mary, 1970; Brideshead Revisited (TV), 1981; Edwin (TV), 1984. British Acad. Writers Award, 1979. *Publications: novels:* Charade, 1947; Rumming Park, 1948; Answer Yes or No, 1950; Like Men Betrayed, 1953, reissued 1987; Three Winters, 1956; Will Shakespeare: an entertainment, 1977; Rumpole of the Bailey, 1978 (televised; BAFTA Writer of the Year Award, 1980); The Trials of Rumpole, 1979; Rumpole's Return, 1980 (televised); Regina v Rumpole, 1981; Rumpole for the Defence, 1982; Rumpole and the Golden Thread, 1983 (televised); Paradise Postponed, 1985 (televised 1986); Rumpole's Last Case, 1987 (televised); Rumpole and the Age of Miracles, 1988 (televised); Summer's Lease, 1988 (televised 1989); Titmuss Regained, 1990; Rumpole à la Carte, 1990; *travel:* (in collab. with P. R. Mortimer) With Love and Lizards, 1957; *plays:* The Dock Brief and Other Plays, 1959; The Wrong Side of the Park, 1960; Lunch Hour and Other Plays, 1960; Two Stars for Comfort, 1962; (trans.) A Flea in Her Ear, 1965; A Voyage Round My Father, 1970; (trans.) The Captain of Köpenick, 1971; Five Plays, 1971; Collaborators, 1973; Edwin and Other Plays, 1984; (trans.) Die Fledermaus, 1989; *interviews:* In Character, 1983; Character Parts, 1986; *autobiography:* Clinging to the Wreckage (Book of the Year Award, Yorkshire Post), 1982; writes TV plays (incl. five Rumpole series); contribs to periodicals. *Recreations:* working, gardening, going to opera. *Address:* c/o A. D. Peters, 5th Floor, The Chambers, Chelsea Harbour, Lots Road, SW10 0XF. *Club:* Garrick.

MORTIMER, Katharine Mary Hope, (Mrs Robert Dean); Consultant/Financial Adviser, Know How Fund for Eastern Europe, since 1990; *b* 28 May 1946; *d* of Robert

Cecil Mortimer and Mary Hope (*née* Walker); *m* 1st, 1973, John Noel Nicholson (marr. diss. 1986); one *s*; 2nd, 1990, Robert Michael Dean. *Educ:* School of SS Mary and Anne, Abbots Bromley; Somerville Coll., Oxford. MA, BPhil Oxon. World Bank, 1969–72; Central Policy Review Staff, 1972–78; N. M. Rothschild Asset Management Ltd, 1978–84; Dir, N. M. Rothschild & Sons (International Corporate Finance, subseq. Internat. Asset Management), 1984–88; seconded as Dir of Policy, SIB, 1985–87; Chief Exec., Walker Books, 1988–89. Mem. Bd, Crown Agents, 1990–; Non-Executive Director: National Bus Company, 1979–91; Inst. of Development Studies, 1983–; Mast Develt Co., 1989–. Member: ESRC, 1983–86; Authorised Conveyancing Practitioners Bd, 1991–. Mem., Royal Commn for Exhibn of 1851, 1988–. Member, Governing Body: Centre for Economic Policy Res., 1986–; Imperial Coll., 1987–. Trustee, Inst. for Public Policy Res., 1989–. *Address:* Lower Corscombe, Okehampton, Devon EX20 1SD.

MORTIMER, Penelope (Ruth), FRSL; writer; *b* 19 Sept. 1918; *d* of Rev. A. F. G. and Amy Caroline Fletcher; *m* 1st, 1937, Charles Dimont (marr. diss. 1949); four *d*; 2nd, 1949, John Clifford Mortimer, QC (marr. diss. 1972); one *s* one *d*. *Educ:* Croydon High Sch.; New Sch., Streatham; Blencathra, Rhyl; Garden Sch., Lane End; St Elphin's Sch. for Daughters of Clergy; Central Educnl Bureau for Women; University Coll., London. *Screenplay:* Portrait of a Marriage, 1990. *Publications:* Johanna (as Penelope Dimont), 1947; A Villa in Summer, 1954; The Bright Prison, 1956; (with John Mortimer) With Love and Lizards, 1957; Daddy's Gone A-Hunting, 1958; Saturday Lunch with the Brownings, 1960; The Pumpkin Eater, 1962; My Friend Says It's Bulletproof, 1967; The Home, 1971; Long Distance, 1974; About Time (autobiog.), 1979 (Whitbread Prize); The Handyman, 1983; Queen Elizabeth: a life of the Queen Mother, 1986. *Address:* c/o Curtis Brown, 163–168 Regent Street, W1R 5TA. *T:* 071–872 0331.

MORTIMER, Air Vice-Marshal Roger, CBE 1972; Officer Commanding RAF Institute of Pathology and Tropical Medicine and Consultant Adviser in Pathology and Tropical Medicine, 1969–76; Dean of Air Force Medicine, 1975–76; *b* 2 Nov. 1914; *s* of Henry Roger Mortimer, tea planter, Dooars, India and Lily Rose (*née* Collier); *m* 1942, Agnes Emily Balfour (*d* 1985); two *d*. *Educ:* Uppingham; St Mary's Hosp. Med. School. MB, BS London, FRCPath, DCP, DTM&H. Joined RAF, 1942; Sqdn Med. Officer to Nos 23 and 85 Sqdns, 1942–44; Service Narrator and Editor to Official RAF Medical History of the War, 1944–47; specialised in Pathology and Tropical Medicine from 1947. Founder Mem. RCPath; Assoc. Editor and Council Mem., British Div. of Internat. Academy of Pathology, 1967–73; Editor, International Pathology, 1970–73; Mem. Council, Royal Soc. Trop. Med. and Hygiene, 1970–73. QHS 1973–76. *Publications:* papers on approved laboratory methods, practical disinfection, blood transfusion and infusion. *Recreations:* cars, anything mechanical, do-it-yourself, laboratory design. *Address:* 13 Welclose Street, St Albans, Herts AL3 4QD. *T:* St Albans (0727) 864247.

MORTIMORE, Simon Anthony; QC 1991; *b* 12 April 1950; *s* of Robert Anthony Mortimore and Katherine Elizabeth Mackenzie Mortimore (*née* Caine); *m* 1983, Fiona Elizabeth Jacobson; one *s* one *d*. *Educ:* Westminster School; Exeter Univ. (LLB). Called to the Bar, Inner Temple, 1972. *Publications:* contribs to Bullen and Leake and Jacobs Precedents of Pleading, 13th edn. *Recreations:* opera, general cultural interests, travel, golf. *Address:* 3/4 South Square, Gray's Inn, WC1R 5HP. *T:* 071–696 9900. *Clubs:* Hurlingham; Royal Mid Surrey Golf, Royal St George's Golf.

MORTLOCK, Herbert Norman; Civil Service, retired; *b* 1926. Ministry of Defence: Superintendent, Royal Armament Research & Development Estabt, 1964–71; Asst Director, Procurement Executive, 1971–73; Dep. Dir., Chemical Defence Estabt, 1973–78; Dep. Dir, 1978–79, Dir, 1979–84, Materials Quality Assurance Directorate; Dir, Quality Assurance (Technical Support), 1984.

MORTON, family name of **Baron Morton of Shuna**.

MORTON, 22nd Earl of, *cr* 1458 (*de facto* 21st Earl, 22nd but for the Attainder); **John Charles Sholto Douglas;** Lord Aberdour, 1458; Lord-Lieutenant of West Lothian, since 1985; *b* 19 March 1927; *s* of Hon. Charles William Sholto Douglas (*d* 1960) (2nd *s* of 19th Earl) and Florence (*d* 1985), *er d* of late Major Henry Thomas Timson; *S* cousin, 1976; *m* 1949, Sheila Mary, *d* of late Rev. Canon John Stanley Gibbs, MC, Didmarton House, Badminton, Glos; two *s* one *d*. DL West Lothian, 1982. *Recreation:* polo. *Heir: s* Lord Aberdour, *qv*. *Address:* Dalmahoy, Kirknewton, Midlothian. *Clubs:* Farmers'; Edinburgh Polo, Dalmahoy Country.

MORTON OF SHUNA, Baron *cr* 1985 (Life Peer), of Stockbridge in the District of the City of Edinburgh; **Hugh Drennan Baird Morton;** a Senator of the College of Justice in Scotland, since 1988; *b* 10 April 1930; *s* of late Rev. T. R. Morton, DD, and J. M. M. Morton (*née* Baird); *m* 1956, Muriel Miller; three *s*. *Educ:* Glasgow Academy; Glasgow Univ. (BL). Admitted Faculty of Advocates, 1965; QC 1974. *Address:* 25 Royal Circus, Edinburgh EH3 6TL. *T:* 031–225 5139.
See also G. M. Morton.

MORTON, Sir Alastair; *see* Morton, Sir R. A. N.

MORTON, Alastair; *see* Morton, S. A.

MORTON, Rev. Andrew Queen; Minister of Culross Abbey, 1959–87; *b* 4 June 1919; *s* of Alexander Morton and Janet Queen; *m* 1948, Jean, *e d* of George Singleton and late Jean Wands; one *s* two *d*. *Educ:* Glasgow Univ. MA 1942, BD 1947, BSc 1948. Minister of St Andrews, Fraserburgh, 1949–59. Dept of Computer Science, Univ. of Edinburgh, 1965–86. Hon. Res. Fellow, Glasgow Univ., 1990. FRSE 1973. *Publications:* The Structure of the Fourth Gospel, 1961; Authorship and Integrity in the New Testament, 1963; (with G. H. C. Macgregor) The Structure of Luke and Acts, 1965; Paul the Man and the Myth, 1965; (with S. Michaelson) The Computer in Literary Research, 1973; Literary Detection, 1979; (with S. Michaelson and N. Hamilton-Smith) Justice for Helander, 1979; (with James McLeman) The Genesis of John, 1980; (with S. Michaelson) The Cusom Plot, 1990; (with M. G. Farringdon) Fielding and the Federalist, 1990; contrib. ALLC Jl; TLS. *Recreations:* thinking, talking. *Address:* 4 Upper Adelaide Street, Helensburgh G84 7HT. *T:* Helensburgh (0436) 75152.

MORTON, Admiral Sir Anthony (Storrs), GBE 1982; KCB 1978; DL; King of Arms, Order of the British Empire, since 1983; Vice Admiral of the United Kingdom, since 1990; *b* 6 Nov. 1923; *s* of late Dr Harold Morton. *Educ:* Loretto School. Joined RN 1941; war service in Atlantic, Mediterranean and Far East (despatches, HMS Wrangler, 1945); Commander 1956; Comd HMS Appleton and 100th MSS 1957–58; HMS Undine 1960; HMS Rocket 1960–62; Captain 1964; Captain (F) 20th Frigate Squadron, 1964–66; Chief Staff Officer, Plans and Policy, to Commander Far East Fleet, 1966–68; Senior Naval Officer, Northern Ireland, 1968–70; Senior Naval Mem., RCDS, 1971–72; ACDS (Policy), 1973–75; Flag Officer, First Flotilla, 1975–77; Vice-Chief of Defence Staff, 1977–78; Vice-Chief of Naval Staff, 1978–80; UK Mil. Rep. to NATO, 1980–83. Rear Adm. of the UK, 1988–90. Chairman: Govs, Royal Star and Garter Home, 1986–91; Trustees, RN Museum, Portsmouth, 1985–; King George's Fund for Sailors, 1986–. DL Hants, 1989. *Recreations:* fishing, sailing, shooting, watching Association football. *Address:* c/o Barclays Bank, Winchester, Hants SO23 8RG. *Clubs:* Naval and Military, Royal Cruising; Royal Yacht Squadron; Irish Cruising.

MORTON, Rev. Arthur, CVO 1979; OBE 1961; Director, National Society for the Prevention of Cruelty to Children, 1954–79; *b* 29 June 1915; *s* of Arthur Morton and Kate Floyd Morton; *m* 1940, Medora Gertrude Harrison; two *d*. *Educ:* Imperial Service Coll., Windsor; Jesus Coll., Cambridge (MA); Wycliffe Hall, Oxford (GOE). Curate, St Catherine's, Neasden, NW2, 1938–41; Chaplain, Missions to Seamen, Manchester, 1941–51. Asst Dir, NSPCC, 1951–54. Member, Adv. Council in Child Care and of Central Trng Council, 1956–71; frequent broadcasts on work of NSPCC. Mem., Glaziers Co., 1976–. *Publication:* (with Anne Allen) This is Your Child: the story of the NSPCC, 1961. *Recreations:* golf, fishing, reading, gardening. *Address:* 25 Cottes Way, Hill Head, Fareham, Hants PO14 3NF. *T:* Stubbington (0329) 663511.

MORTON, Air Commodore Crichton Charles, CBE 1945; Command Electronics Officer, HQ Bomber Command, 1962–66, retired; *b* 26 July 1912; *s* of late Charles Crichton Morton, Ramsey, IOM; *m* 1956, Diana Yvonne, *d* of late Maj.-Gen. R. C. Priest, CB, RMS and *widow* of Group Captain N. D. Gilbart-Smith, RAF; no *c*. *Educ:* King William's Coll., IOM; RAF Coll., Cranwell. Various flying duties, 1932–36; RAF Officers Long Signals Course, Cranwell, 1936–37; signals duties, 1937–39; radar duties at HQ Fighter Comd, No 5 Signals Wing France, HQ 60 Signals Gp, Air HQ Iceland, HQ Air Comd SE Asia, 1939–45; Dir of Radar and Dep. Dir of Signals, Air Min., 1945–49; jssc Latimer, 1949–50; OC No 3 Radio Sch., RAF Compton Bassett, 1950–52; OC Communications Gp, Allied Air Forces Central Europe, 1952–55; Inspector of Radio Services, 1955–58; Dep. Chief Signals Office, HQ, SHAPE, 1958–60; Chm. of Brit. Jt Communications Electronics Board, Ministry of Defence, 1960–62. AMIEE 1955; AFRAeS 1965; MIERE 1965; CEng 1966. *Recreation:* researching Visigothic remains. *Address:* Apartamento 102, Torre Tramontana, Apartado 50, 17250 Playa de Aro, Gerona, Spain. *T:* (972) 817 871.

MORTON, Prof. Frank, CBE 1976 (OBE 1968); DSc 1952, PhD 1936 (Manchester); MSc Tech; FIChemE; Professor of Chemical Engineering, University of Manchester, 1956–73, now Professor Emeritus; a Pro-Vice-Chancellor, 1968–72; *b* Sheffield, 11 Aug. 1906; *s* of late Joseph Morton, Manchester; *m* 1936, Hilda May, *d* of John W. Seaston, Withington, Manchester; one *s*. *Educ:* Manchester Univ. Demonstrator in Chemical Technology, 1931–36; Research Chemist, Trinidad Leaseholds Ltd, 1936–40; Superintendent of Research and Development, Trinidad Leaseholds, Trinidad, 1940–45; Chief Chemist, Trinidad Leaseholds Ltd, UK, 1945–49; Prof. of Chemical Engineering, Univ. of Birmingham, 1949–56. Actg Principal, Manchester Coll. of Science and Technology, 1964–65; Dep. Principal, Univ. of Manchester Inst. of Science and Technology, 1966–71. Member: Council, Manchester Business Sch., 1964–72; Chemical and Allied Products Training Board, 1968–71; European Fedn of Chemical Engineering, 1968–72. Pres., IChemE, 1963–64 (Hon. FIChemE 1983). Society of Chemical Industry: Vice-Pres., 1967–; Jubilee Memorial Lectr, 1967; Medal, 1969. Hon. Fellow, UMIST, 1978. *Publications:* Report of Inquiry into the Safety of Natural Gas as a Fuel (Ministry of Technology), 1970; various papers on petroleum, organic chemistry, chemical engineering and allied subjects. *Recreation:* golf. *Address:* 47 Penrhyn Beach East, Llandudno, Gwynedd. *T:* Llandudno (0492) 548037. *Club:* Savage.

MORTON, George Martin; Senior Planner, Trafford Borough Council, since 1986; *b* 11 Feb. 1940; *s* of Rev. Thomas Ralph Morton, DD, and Janet Maclay MacGregor Morton (*née* Baird). *Educ:* Fettes Coll Edinburgh; Edinburgh Coll. of Art; Glasgow Univ. RIBA. Member: Manchester City Council, 1971–74; Greater Manchester Council, 1973–77. Sec., Tameside and Glossop CHC, 1984–86. MP (Lab) Manchester, Moss Side, July 1978–1983; an Opposition Whip, 1979–83. *Address:* 4 St Annes Road, Manchester M21 2TG. *T:* 061–881 8195.
See also Baron Morton of Shuna.

MORTON, Prof. Keith William; Professor of Numerical Analysis, and Professorial Fellow of Balliol College, Oxford University, since 1983; *b* 28 May 1930; *s* of Keith Harvey Morton and Muriel Violet (*née* Hubbard); *m* 1952, Patricia Mary Pearson; two *s* two *d*. *Educ:* Sudbury Grammar Sch.; Corpus Christi Coll., Oxford (BA 1952; MA 1954); New York Univ. (PhD 1964). Theoretical Physics Div., AERE, Harwell, 1952–59; Res. Scientist, Courant Inst. of Mathematical Sci., NY Univ., 1959–64; Head of Computing and Applied Maths, Culham Lab., UKAEA, 1964–72; Prof. of Applied Maths, Reading Univ., 1972–83. *Publications:* (with R. D. Richtmyer) Difference Methods for Initial-value Problems, 1967; (ed with M. J. Baines) Numerical Methods for Fluid Dynamics, Vol. I 1982, Vol. II 1986, Vol. III 1988; numerous articles on numerical analysis and applied maths in learned jls. *Recreations:* reading, tennis, walking, gardening, listening to music. *Address:* Roscarrock, 48 Jack Straw's Lane, Headington, Oxford OX3 0DW. *T:* Oxford (0865) 68823; Oxford University Computing Laboratory, 11 Keble Road, Oxford OX1 3QD. *T:* Oxford (0865) 273886.

MORTON, Kenneth Valentine Freeland, CIE 1947; OBE 1971; Secretary East Anglian Regional Hospital Board, 1947–72, retired; *b* 13 May 1907; *s* of Kenneth John Morton; *m* 1936, Mary Hadwin Hargreaves; four *s* one *d*. *Educ:* Edinburgh Academy; University Coll., Oxford. Joined ICS, 1930; Under-Sec. (Political) Punjab Govt, 1934–36; Deputy Commissioner, 1936–39; Colonisation Officer, 1939–43; Deputy Sec., Development Dept, 1943–46; Sec. Electricity and Industries Depts, 1946–47; retired, 1947. *Address:* Temple End House, 27 Temple End, Great Wilbraham, Cambridge CB1 5JF. *T:* Cambridge (0223) 880691. *Club:* East India, Devonshire, Sports and Public Schools.

MORTON, Sir (Robert) Alastair (Newton), Kt 1991; British Chairman of Eurotunnel, since 1987; Chief Executive and Deputy Chairman, Joint Eurotunnel Board, since 1990; *b* 11 Jan. 1938; *s* of late Harry Newton Morton and Elizabeth Martino; *m* 1964, Sara Bridget Stephens; one *s* one *d*. *Educ:* St John's Coll. and Witwatersrand Univ., Johannesburg (BA); Worcester Coll., Oxford (MA). Special grad. student, MIT, 1964. Anglo American Corp. of SA (mining finance), London and Central Africa, 1959–63; Internat. Finance Corp., Washington, 1964–67; Industrial Reorganisation Corp., 1967–70; Exec. Dir, 117 Group of investment trusts, 1970–72; Chm., Draymont Securities, 1972–76; Chm. or Dir, various engineering groups, 1968–76; Man. Dir, BNOC, 1976–80; Chief Exec., 1982–87, Chm., 1987, Guinness Peat Gp. Non-Exec. Member: Royal Ordnance Factories Bd, 1974–76; British Steel Corp., 1979–82; Dir, Massey Ferguson (later Varity Corp.), 1981–87. Currently non-executive Director: BNP UK Hldgs; Nova Corp. of Alberta; Nat. Power plc. Chm., Kent TEC. Mem., City and East London AHA, 1974–77. *Recreations:* sailing, walking, touring in 2CV. *Address:* Victoria Plaza, 111 Buckingham Palace Road, SW1W 0ST. *Club:* University (New York).

MORTON, His Honour (Stephen) Alastair, TD 1949; JP; a Circuit Judge (formerly Deputy Chairman, Greater London Quarter Sessions), 1971–87; *b* 28 July 1913; *o s* of late Philip Morton, Dorchester; *m* 1939, Lily Yarrow Eveline, *o d* of J. S. P. Griffith-Jones, Drews, Beaconsfield, Bucks; one *s* one *d*. *Educ:* private sch.; Trinity Hall, Cambridge. Commnd Dorset Heavy Bde, RA, TA, 1932; served War of 1939–45, Royal Artillery. Called to the Bar, Middle Temple, 1938; Western Circuit, 1938; Master of the Bench,

1964. Counsel to the Crown at County of London Sessions, 1954–59; Central Criminal Court: First Junior Treasury Counsel, 1959–64; Senior Treasury Counsel, 1964–71; Recorder of Devizes, 1957–71; Dep.-Chm. Quarter Sessions: Dorset, 1957–71; Norfolk, 1969–71. JP Dorset, 1957. *Recreation:* painting. *Address:* 1 Church Row, Moore Park Road, SW6 2JW. *T:* 071–736 8109; Cringles, Burnham Overy Staithe, near King's Lynn, Norfolk PE31 8JD. *T:* Fakenham (0328) 738339. *Clubs:* White's, Pratt's.

MORTON, Sir William (David), Kt 1990; CBE 1984; farmer; *b* 13 June 1926; *m* 1952, Catherine Mary Macbeth; three *s*. *Educ:* Northampton Town and County Grammar Sch. Farming in Northants and Bucks. County Chairman: Nat. Fedn of Young Farmers' Clubs, 1953–57; Northants NFU, 1970. Northamptonshire County Council: Member, 1964–; Dep. Leader, 1970–73; Chief Whip, 1973–81, Dep. Leader, 1981–84, Leader, 1984–, Cons. Gp; Chairman: Highways Cttee, 1969–73; Planning and Transportation Cttee, 1977–81. Conservative Party: Chairman: Daventry Constituency, 1975–79 (Dep. Chm., 1969–75); Northants Euro-Constituency, 1978–82; E Midlands Area, 1980–85 (Mem. Exec., 1975–; Treas., 1979–80); Nat. Agricl and Countryside Cttee, 1984–89; Mem., Exec. Cttee, Nat. Union, 1979–. High Sheriff, Northants, 1984–85. *Address:* Flore Fields House, Flore, Northants NN7 4JX. *T:* Weedon (0327) 40226.

MORTON BOYD, John; *see* Boyd, J. M.

MORTON JACK, David; His Honour Judge Morton Jack; a Circuit Judge, since 1986; *b* 5 Nov. 1935; *o s* of late Col W. A. Morton Jack, OBE, and late Mrs Morton Jack (*née* Happell); *m* 1972, Rosemary, *o d* of F. G. Rentoul; four *s*. *Educ:* Stowe (scholar); Trinity Coll., Oxford (Cholmeley Schol., MA). 2nd Lieut, RIF, 1955–57. Called to the Bar, Lincoln's Inn, 1962; a Recorder of the Crown Court, 1979–86. *Recreations:* country pursuits, sheep-keeping, reading, music, gardens. *Address:* 1 Harcourt Buildings, Temple, EC4Y 9DA.

MORTON-SANER, Robert, CVO 1966; CBE 1962 (OBE 1946; MBE 1941); HM Diplomatic Service, retired; *b* 30 December 1911; *o s* of late Major A. E. Saner; *m* 1943, Katharine Mary Gordon (*d* 1981); two *d*. *Educ:* Westminster Sch.; Christ Church, Oxford. ICS, 1935; served in United Provinces; Under Sec., Defence Department, Government of India, 1940; Deputy Secretary and Chief Administrative Officer, General Headquarters, New Delhi, 1943–45; served with Resettlement Directorate, 1945–47. Retired from Indian Civil Service and entered Foreign (subseq. Diplomatic) Service, 1947. Served in Madras, 1947–50; Foreign Office, 1950–52; Budapest, 1953–55; NATO Defence College, 1955; Counsellor and Consul-General, Djakarta, 1955–59; Counsellor, Buenos Aires, 1960–64; Consul-General, Antwerp, 1964–70. Acted as Chargé d'Affaires, 1953, 1954, 1956, 1958, 1959, 1960. Member, Skinners' Company. Commander, Order of Leopold II (Belgium). *Recreations:* gardening, old churches. *Address:* Hethe Cottage, Hethe, Oxon OX6 9EU. *Club:* Anglo-Belgian.

MOSAR, Nicolas; Member, Commission of the European Communities, 1985–88; *b* Luxembourg, 25 Nov. 1927; *m*; three *c*. *Educ:* Athénée Grand-Ducal; Faculté de Droit, Paris University. Called to Bar, 1955. Mem. Town Council, Luxembourg, 1959–70, 1975–85. Member of Luxembourg Parliament, 1964–74, 1976–85. Social Christian Party: Sec.-Gen., 1959–72; Chm., 1972–74; Chm., Party Parly Gp, 1979–85. *Publications:* political and legal papers.

MOSDELL, Lionel Patrick; Judge of the High Court of Kenya, 1966–72, Tanganyika, 1960–64; *b* 29 Aug. 1912; *s* of late William George Mosdell and late Sarah Ellen Mosdell (*née* Gardiner); *m* 1945, Muriel Jean Sillem; one *s* one *d*. *Educ:* Abingdon Sch.; St Edmund Hall, Oxford (MA). Solicitor, England, 1938. Served War of 1939–45, Gunner, Sussex Yeomanry RA, 1939–41; Commnd Rifle Bde, 1941; Libyan Arab Force; Force 133; No 1 Special Force; Egypt, Cyrenaica, Eritrea, Abyssinia, Italy (Capt.). Registrar of Lands and Deeds, N Rhodesia, 1946; Resident Magistrate, 1950; Senior Resident Magistrate, 1956; Barrister, Gray's Inn, 1952; Asst Solicitor, Law Soc., 1964–66. Part-time Chairman: Surrey and Sussex Rent Assessment Panel, 1972–82; Nat. Insce Local Tribunal, London S Region, 1974–84; Immigration Appeal Tribunal, 1975–84; Pensions Appeal Tribunals, 1976–86. *Recreation:* cycling. *Address:* 10 Orpen Road, Hove, East Sussex BN3 6NJ. *Clubs:* Special Forces, Commonwealth Trust.

MOSELEY, Sir George (Walker), KCB 1982 (CB 1978); Chairman, British Cement Association, since 1987; *b* 7 Feb. 1925; *o c* of late William Moseley, MBE, and Bella Moseley; *m* 1st, 1950, Anne Mercer (*d* 1989); one *s* one *d*; 2nd, 1990, Madge James. *Educ:* High Sch., Glasgow; St Bees Sch., Cumberland; Wadham Coll., Oxford (MA). Pilot Officer, RAF Levies, Iraq, 1943–48. Asst Principal, Min. of Town and Country Planning, 1950; Asst Private Sec. to Minister of Housing and Local Govt, 1951–52; Private Sec. to Parly Sec., 1952–54; Principal Private Sec. to Minister of Housing and Local Govt, 1963–65; Asst Sec. 1965; Under-Sec. 1970–76; Dep. Sec., DoE, 1976–78, CSD, 1978–80; Second Permanent Sec., DoE, 1980–81, Perm. Sec., 1981–85. Chm., Cement Makers' Fedn, 1987–88. Member: Adv. Council on Public Records, 1989–; Ancient Monuments Adv. Cttee, 1986–91; Historic Buildings and Monuments Commn for England, 1986–91. Trustee, Civic Trust, 1987– (Chm. Trustees, 1990–). *Recreations:* listening to music, gardening, watching sport. *Address:* Windy Ridge, Cornells Lane, Widdington, Saffron Walden, Essex CB11 3SP. *Club:* Royal Air Force.

MOSELEY, (Thomas) Hywel; QC 1985; **His Honour Judge Moseley;** a Circuit Judge, since 1989; *b* 27 Sept. 1936; *s* of Rev. Luther Moseley and late Megan Eiluned Moseley; *m* 1960, Monique Germaine Thérèse Drufin; three *d*. *Educ:* Caterham Sch.; Queens' Coll., Cambridge (MA, LLM). Called to the Bar, Gray's Inn, 1964; in private practice, Cardiff, 1965–89, and London, 1977–; a Recorder, 1981–89. Lectr in Law, 1960–65, Prof. of Law, 1970–82, UCW, Aberystwyth. *Publication:* (with B. Rudden) Outline of the Law of Mortgages, 4th edn 1967. *Recreation:* bee-keeping. *Address:* Nantceiro, Llanbadarn Fawr, Aberystwyth, Dyfed SY23 3HW. *T:* Aberystwyth (0970) 623532; 6 Belgrave Court, 25 Cowbridge Road East, Cardiff CF1 9BJ. *T:* Cardiff (0222) 237769.

MOSER, Sir Claus (Adolf), KCB 1973; CBE 1965; FBA 1969; Warden, Wadham College, Oxford, since 1984; Chancellor, University of Keele, since 1986; Director: N. M. Rothschild & Sons, 1978–90 (Vice-Chairman, 1978–84); The Economist Newspaper, since 1979; Chairman, Harold Holt Ltd, since 1990; *b* Berlin, 24 Nov. 1922; *s* of late Dr Ernest Moser and Lotte Moser; *m* 1949, Mary Oxlin; one *s* two *d*. *Educ:* Frensham Heights Sch.; LSE, Univ. of London. RAF, 1943–46. London Sch. of Economics: Asst Lectr in Statistics, 1946–49; Lectr, 1949–55; Reader in Social Statistics, 1955–61; Prof. of Social Statistics, 1961–70; Vis. Prof. of Social Statistics, 1970–75; Vis. Fellow, Nuffield Coll., Oxford, 1972–80. Dir, Central Statistical Office and Hd of Govt Statistical Service, 1967–78. Statistical Adviser, Cttee on Higher Educn, 1961–64. Chm., Economist Intelligence Unit, 1979–83; Director: Equity & Law Life Assurance Soc., 1980–87; International Medical Statistics Inc., 1982–88; Octopus Books Ltd, 1982–87; Property & Reversionary Investments plc, 1983–86. Chm., Royal Opera House, 1974–87; Member: Governing Body, Royal Academy of Music, 1967–79; BBC Music Adv. Cttee, 1971–83; Court of Governors, Royal Shakespeare Theatre, 1982–; British Amer. Arts Assoc.,

1982–; Pilgrim Trust, 1982–; Nat. Commission on Educn, 1991–. Trustee: BM, 1988–; LPO, 1988–; Glyndebourne Opera Arts Trust, 1989–. Pres., Royal Statistical Soc., 1978–80; Pres., BAAS, 1989–90. Hon. FRAM, 1970. Hon. Fellow, LSE, 1976; Hon. DSocSci Southampton, 1975; Hon. DSc: Leeds, 1977; City, 1977; Sussex, 1980; Wales, 1990; Liverpool, 1991; Hon. DSc(Econ) London, 1991; DUniv: Surrey, 1977; Keele, 1979; York, 1980; Hon. DTech Brunel, 1981; Dr *hc* Edinburgh, 1991. Comdr de l'Ordre National du Mérite (France), 1976; Commander's Cross, Order of Merit (FRG), 1985. *Publications:* Measurement of Levels of Living, 1957; Survey Methods in Social Investigation, 1958; (jtly) Social Conditions in England and Wales, 1958; (jtly) British Towns, 1961; papers in statistical jls. *Recreation:* music. *Address:* 3 Regent's Park Terrace, NW1 7EE. *T:* 071–485 1619; Wadham College, Oxford OX1 3PN. *Club:* Garrick.

MOSES, Alan George; QC 1990; a Recorder, since 1986; *b* 29 Nov. 1945; *s* of Eric George Rufus Moses, *qv*; two *s* one *d*. *Educ:* Bryanston Sch.; University Coll., Oxford (Quondam Exhibnr; BA). Called to the Bar, Middle Temple, 1968; Mem., Panel of Junior Counsel to the Crown, Common Law, 1981–90; Junior Counsel to Inland Revenue, Common Law, 1985–90.

MOSES, Eric George Rufus, CB 1973; Solicitor of Inland Revenue, 1970–79; *b* 6 April 1914; *s* of Michael and Emily Moses; *m* 1940, Pearl Lipton; one *s*. *Educ:* University Coll. Sch., London; Oriel Coll., Oxford. Called to Bar, Middle Temple, 1938, Hon. Bencher, 1979. Served Royal Artillery, 1940–46 (Major). Asst Solicitor, Inland Revenue, 1953–65, Principal Asst Solicitor, 1965–70. *Recreations:* walking, opera. *Address:* Broome Cottage, Castle Hill, Nether Stowey, Bridgwater, Somerset TA5 1NB.
See also A. G. Moses.

MOSES, Very Rev. Dr John Henry; Provost of Chelmsford; *b* 12 Jan. 1938; *s* of late Henry William Moses and of Ada Elizabeth Moses; *m* 1964, Susan Elizabeth; one *s* two *d*. *Educ:* Ealing Grammar School; Nottingham Univ. (Gladstone Meml Prize 1958, BA History 1959, PhD 1965); Trinity Hall and Dept of Education, Cambridge (Cert. in Education 1960); Lincoln Theological Coll. Deacon 1964, priest 1965; Asst Curate, St Andrew, Bedford, 1964–70; Rector of Coventry East Team Ministry, 1970–77; Examining Chaplain to Bishop of Coventry, 1972–77; Rural Dean of Coventry East, 1973–77; Archdeacon of Southend, 1977–82. Member, Gen. Synod, 1985–. Church Commissioner, 1988–. Chm. Council, Centre for Study of Theology, Univ. of Essex, 1987–. Vis. Fellow, Wolfson Coll., Cambridge, 1987. *Address:* The Provost's House, 3 Harlings Grove, Waterloo Lane, Chelmsford, Essex CM1 1YQ. *T:* Chelmsford (0245) 354318.

MOSES, Dr Kenneth, CBE 1988; FEng 1985; Member, British Coal Corporation, since 1986; *b* 29 Nov. 1931; *s* of Thomas and Mary Moses; *m* 1949, Mary Price; one *s* two *d*. *Educ:* Cowley Boys Grammar Sch., St Helens; Wigan Mining Coll. (Dip. in Mining; 1st Cl. Cert., Mines and Quarries Act); Nottingham Univ. (MPhil 1988; PhD 1990). Mineworker, 1954; Management Trainee, 1960; Undermanager, 1962; Dep. Manager, 1964; Colliery Manager, 1967; Mem. Directing Staff, NCB Staff Coll., 1971; National Coal Board: Chief Mining Engr, N Yorks, 1974; Dir of Planning, 1978; Dir, N Derbys, 1981. Mem., NRDC, 1990–. CBIM. Hon. FIMinE, 1990. Laurence Holland Medal, IMinE, 1961; Douglas Hay Medal, IMinE, 1982. *Publications:* contribs to learned journals. *Recreations:* gardening, walking, swimming, reading. *Address:* Oaktrees, 6 Heath Avenue, Mansfield NG18 3EU. *T:* Mansfield (0623) 653843; Flat 15, Listergate, 315–317 Upper Richmond Road, Putney, SW15 6ST. *T:* 081–785 3220.

MOSHINSKY, Elijah; Associate Producer, Royal Opera House, since 1979; *b* 8 Jan. 1946; *s* of Abraham and Eva Moshinsky; *m* 1970, Ruth Dyttman; two *s*. *Educ:* Melbourne Univ. (BA); St Antony's Coll., Oxford. Apptd to Royal Opera House, 1973: work includes original productions of: Peter Grimes, 1975; Lohengrin, 1978; The Rake's Progress, 1979; Macbeth, 1981; Samson et Dalila, 1981; Tannhäuser, 1984; Otello, 1987; Die Entführung aus dem Serail, 1987; for ENO: Le Grand Macabre, 1982; The Mastersingers of Nuremberg, 1984; The Bartered Bride, 1985, 1986; other opera productions include: Wozzeck, 1976; A Midsummer Night's Dream, 1978; Boris Godunov, 1980; Un Ballo in Maschera, Met. Opera, New York, 1980; Il Trovatore, Australian Opera, 1983; Samson, Met. Opera, NY; I Vespri Siciliani, Grand Théâtre, Geneva; Les Dialogues des Carmélites, Australian Opera; Die Meistersinger von Nürnberg, Holland Fest.; Benvenuto Cellini, 50th Maggio Musicale, Florence, 1987. Producer: Three Sisters, Albery, 1987; Light up the Sky, Globe, 1987; Ivanov, Strand, 1989; Much Ado About Nothing, Strand, 1989; Another Time, Wyndham's, 1989; Shadowlands, Queen's, 1989; productions at National Theatre: Troilus and Cressida, 1976; The Force of Habit, 1976; productions for the BBC: All's Well That Ends Well, 1980; A Midsummer Night's Dream, 1981; Cymbeline, 1982; Coriolanus, 1984; Love's Labour's Lost, 1985; Ghosts, 1986; The Rivals, 1987; The Green Man, 1990. Dir, Matador, Queen's, 1991. *Recreations:* painting, conversation. *Address:* 28 Kidbrooke Grove, SE3. *T:* 081–858 4179. *Club:* Garrick.

MOSIMANN, Anton; Owner, Mosimann's (formerly Belfry Club), since 1988; *b* 23 Feb. 1947; *s* of Otto and Olga Mosimann; *m* 1973, Kathrin Roth; two *s*. *Educ:* private school in Switzerland; youngest Chef to be awarded Chef de Cuisine Diplome; 3 degrees. Served apprenticeship in Hotel Baeren, Twann; worked in Canada, France, Italy, Japan, Sweden, Belgium, Switzerland, 1962–; cuisinier at: Villa Lorraine, Brussels; Les Près d'Eugénie, Eugénie-les-Bains; Les Frères Troisgros, Roanne; Paul Bocuse, Collonges au Mont d'Or; Moulin de Mougins; joined Dorchester Hotel, 1975, Maître Chef des Cuisines, 1976–88. Channel Four TV series, Cooking with Mosimann, 1989. World Pres., Les Toques Blanches Internationales, 1989–90; Hon. Mem., Chefs' Assoc., Canada, Japan, Switzerland, S Africa. Dr of Culinary Arts *hc* Johnson & Wales Univ., RI, 1990. Numerous Gold Medals in Internat. Cookery Competitions; Chef Award, Caterer and Hotelkeeper, 1985; Personnalité de l'année award, 1986; Glenfiddich Awards Trophy, 1986; Chevalier, Ordre des Coteaux de Champagne, 1990. Le Croix de Chevalier du Mérite Agricole (France), 1988. *Publications:* Cuisine à la Carte, 1981; A New Style of Cooking, 1983; Cuisine Naturelle, 1985; Anton Mosimann's Fish Cuisine, 1988; The Art of Anton Mosimann, 1989; Cooking with Mosimann, 1989. *Recreations:* jogging, travelling, collecting art. *Address:* 46 Abingdon Villas, W8 6XD. *T:* 071–937 4383. *Clubs:* Garrick, Reform.

MOSLEY, family name of **Baron Ravensdale.**

MOSLEY, Nicholas; *see* Ravensdale, 3rd Baron.

MOSS, Very Rev. Basil Stanley; Provost of Birmingham Cathedral, 1973–85; Rector, Cathedral parish of St Philip, 1973–85; *b* 7 Oct. 1918; *e s* of Canon Harry George Moss and Daisy Violet (*née* Jolly); *m* 1950, Rachel Margaret, *d* of Dr Cyril Bailey and Gemma (*née* Creighton); three *d*. *Educ:* Canon Slade Grammar Sch., Bolton; The Queen's Coll., Oxford. Asst Curate, Leigh Parish Church, 1943–45; Sub-Warden, Lincoln Theological Coll., 1946–51; Sen. Tutor, St Catharine's Cumberland Lodge, Windsor Gt Pk, 1951–53; Vicar of St Nathanael with St Katharine, Bristol, 1953–60; Dir, Ordination Training, Bristol Dioc., 1956–66; Residentiary Canon of Bristol Cath., 1960–66, Hon. Canon,

1966–72; Chief Secretary, Advisory Council for the Church's Ministry, 1966–72; Chaplain to Church House, Westminster, 1966–72; Examining Chaplain to Bishop of Bristol, 1956–72, to Bishop of Birmingham, 1985–. Chm., Birmingham Community Relations Council, 1973–81. *Publications*: Clergy Training Today, 1964; (ed) Crisis for Baptism, 1966; (contrib.) Living the Faith, 1980. *Recreations*: walking, music. *Address*: 25 Castle Grove, Old Swinford, Stourbridge DY8 2HH. *T*: Stourbridge (0384) 378799. *Club*: Stourbridge Rotary.

MOSS, Charles James, CBE 1977; Director, National Institute of Agricultural Engineering, 1964–77; *b* 18 Nov. 1917; *s* of James and Elizabeth Moss; *m* 1939, Joan Bernice Smith; two *d*. *Educ*: Queen Mary Coll., London Univ. (BSc). Rotol Ltd, Gloucester, 1939–43; RAE Farnborough, 1943–45; CIBA Ltd, Cambridge, 1945–51; ICI Ltd, Billingham, 1951–58; Central Engineering Estabt, NCB, Stanhope Bretby, 1958–61; Process Develt Dept, NCB, London, 1961–63; Vis. Prof., Dept of Agric. Engrg, Univ. of Newcastle upon Tyne, 1972–75; Head of Agr. Engineering Dept, Internat. Rice Res. Inst., Philippines, 1977–80; Liaison scientist and agr. engineer, Internat. Rice Res. Inst., Cairo, 1980–81. *Publications*: papers in learned jls, confs., etc. *Recreations*: gardening, walking. *Address*: 1 Laurel Court, Endcliffe Vale Road, Sheffield, South Yorks S10 3DU.

MOSS, David Christopher; Under Secretary, International Aviation, Department of Transport, since 1988; President, European Civil Aviation Conference, since 1990; *b* 17 April 1946; *s* of Charles Clifford Moss and Marjorie Sylvia Moss (*née* Hutchings); *m* 1971, Angela Mary Wood; one *s*. *Educ*: King's Sch., Chester; Magdalene Coll., Cambridge (BA). Asst Principal, MPBW, 1968; Principal, 1972, DoE, and subseq. Dept of Transport and HM Treasury; Asst Sec., 1980, Dept of Transport and DoE. *Recreations*: opera, ecclesiastical architecture, wine. *Address*: Department of Transport, 2 Marsham Street, SW1P 3EB. *T*: 071–276 5399; European Civil Aviation Conference, 3 bis, Villa Emile Bergerat, 92522 Neuilly-sur-Seine, France. *Club*: United Oxford & Cambridge University.

MOSS, David Francis; JP; Assistant Chief Executive, Dockyards, Ministry of Defence, Bath, 1981–82, retired; *b* 11 July 1927; *s* of Frank William and Dorothy May Moss; *m* 1950, Beryl Eloïse (*née* Horsley); one *s* one *d*. *Educ*: Manchester Grammar Sch.; Manchester Univ. (BSc Hons MechEng); RNC Greenwich (Naval Architecture Cert.). Devonport Dockyard, 1952; Director General Ships, Bath, 1956; HM Dockyards: Gibraltar, 1961; Devonport, 1964; Singapore, 1967; Rosyth, 1969; Chatham, 1973; Rosyth, 1975; Portsmouth, 1979. JP Bath 1983. *Recreations*: hill walking, handiwork; material and philosophical aspects of early Mediterranean sea power. *Address*: 16 Beaufort West, Grosvenor, Bath BA1 6QB.

MOSS, (Sir) David John E.; *see* Edwards-Moss.

MOSS, David Joseph, CMG 1989; HM Diplomatic Service; High Commissioner in New Zealand, Governor (non-resident) of the Pitcairn, Henderson, Ducie and Oeno Islands, and High Commissioner (non-resident) to Western Samoa, since 1990; *b* 6 Nov. 1938; *s* of Herbert Joseph and Irene Gertrude Moss; *m* 1961, Joan Lillian Moss; one *d* (one *s* decd). *Educ*: Hampton Grammar Sch. CS Commn, 1956; FO, 1957; RAF, 1957–59; FO, 1959–62; Third Sec., Bangkok, 1962–65; FO, 1966–69; First Sec., La Paz, 1969–70; FCO, 1970–73; First Sec. and Head of Chancery, The Hague, 1974–77; First Sec., FCO, 1978–79, Counsellor, 1979–83; Counsellor, Hd of Chancery and Dep. Perm. Rep., UK Mission, Geneva, 1983–87; Asst. Under-Sec. of State, FCO, 1987–90. *Recreations*: reading, listening to music. *Address*: c/o Foreign and Commonwealth Office, SW1.

MOSS, Edward Herbert St George; Under-Secretary, University Grants Committee, 1971–78; *b* 18 May 1918; *s* of late Sir George Moss, KBE, HM Consular Service in China, and late Lady (Gladys Lucy) Moss; *m* 1948, Shirley Evelyn Baskett; two *s* one *d*. *Educ*: Marlborough; Pembroke Coll., Cambridge. PhD Surrey, 1984. Army Service in UK and Middle East, 1940–45; entered HM Foreign (subseq. Diplomatic) Service, 1945; served in Japan, FO, Belgrade (Head of Chancery 1951–55), St Louis, Detroit, FO; transf. to Home Civil Service (MoD), 1960; Asst Sec. 1961; Dept of Educn and Science, 1969. *Publications*: (with Rev. Robert Llewelyn) Fire from a Flint: daily readings with William Law, 1986; Seeing Man Whole: a new model for psychology, 1989. *Recreations*: writing, gardening. *Address*: Prospect, 29 Guildown Avenue, Guildford, Surrey GU2 5HA. *T*: Guildford (0483) 66984.

MOSS, Elaine Dora; Children's Books Adviser to The Good Book Guide, 1980–86; *b* 8 March 1924; *d* of Percy Philip Levy and Maude Agnes Levy (*née* Simmons); *m* 1950, John Edward Moss, FRICS, FAI; two *d*. *Educ*: St Paul's Girls' Sch.; Bedford Coll. for Women (BA Hons); Univ. of London Inst. of Educn (DipEd); University College London Sch. of Librarianship (ALA). Teacher, Stoatley Rough Sch., Haslemere, 1945–47; Asst Librarian, Bedford Coll., 1947–50; freelance journalist and broadcaster (Woman's Hour, The Times, TES, TLS, The Spectator, Signal, etc.), 1956–; Editor and Selector, NBL's Children's Books of the Year, 1970–79; Librarian, Fleet Primary Sch., ILEA, 1976–82. Eleanor Farjeon Award, 1976. *Publications*: texts for several picture books, incl. Polar, 1976; catalogues for Children's Books of the Year, 1970–79; Picture Books for Young People 9–13, 1981, 2nd edn 1985; Part of the Pattern: a personal journey through the world of children's books 1960–1985, 1986. *Recreations*: walking, art galleries, reading, ballet. *Address*: 7 St Anne's Close, N6.

MOSS, Gabriel Stephen; QC 1989; *b* 8 Sept. 1949; *m* 1979, Judith; one *d*. *Educ*: University of Oxford (Eldon Schol. 1975; BA Jurisprudence, BCL, MA). Lectr, Univ. of Connecticut Law Sch., 1972–73. Called to the Bar, Lincoln's Inn, 1974; Hardwicke Schol., 1971, Cassel Schol., 1975. Jt DTI Inspector, Bestwood plc, 1989. *Publications*: (ed with David Marks) Rowlatt on Principal and Surety, 4th edn 1982; (with Gavin Lightman) The Law of Receivers of Companies, 1986; (with Martin Pascoe) Insolvency chapter, Ryde on Rating, 1990. *Recreations*: chess, gardening, foreign travel, tennis. *Address*: 3/4 South Square, Gray's Inn, WC1. *T*: 071–696 9900, *Fax*: 071–696 9911.

MOSS, James Richard Frederick, OBE 1955; FRINA; RCNC; Founder, and Chairman, Polynous, Cambridge, since 1978; Chief Executive, Balaena Structures (North Sea), 1974–77, retired; *b* 26 March 1916; *s* of late Lt-Cdr J. G. Moss, RN, and late Kathleen Moss (*née* Steinberg); *m* 1941, Celia Florence Lucas; three *d*. *Educ*: Marlborough College; Trinity Coll., Cambridge (1st Cl. Hons Mech. Sci. Tripos and Maths Pt I, MA); RCNC, 1941. Constructor Comdr to C-in-C, Far East Fleet, 1949–52; Chief Constructor, HM Dockyard, Singapore, 1955–58; Supt, Naval Construction Research Estab., Dunfermline, 1965–68; Dir, Naval Ship Production, 1968–74. *Recreations*: yachting, music. *Address*: 13 Beaufort Place, Thompsons Lane, Cambridge CB5 8AG. *T*: Cambridge (0223) 328583. *Clubs*: Royal Naval Sailing Association, Cruising Association.

MOSS, Jane Hope; *see* Bown, J. H.

MOSS, (John) Michael; Assistant Under-Secretary of State (Naval Personnel), Ministry of Defence, since 1989; *b* 21 April 1936; *s* of late Ernest and of Mary Moss. *Educ*: Accrington Grammar Sch.; King's Coll., Cambridge (Foundn Scholar; MA Math. Tripos, Pt I Cl. I, Pt II Wrangler, Pt III Hons with Dist.). National Service, RAF Educn Branch: Pilot Officer 1958; Flying Officer 1959; Flt Lieut 1960; RAF Technical Coll., Henlow,

1959–60. Asst Principal, Air Min., 1960–63; Private Sec. to Air Member for Supply and Orgn, 1962–63; Principal, Air Min., 1963–64, and MoD, 1964–70; Private Sec. to Parly Under-Sec. of State for Defence for the RAF, 1969–70; Asst Sec., MoD, 1971–72; Estab. Officer, Cabinet Office, 1972–75; Sec., Radcliffe Cttee of Privy Counsellors on Ministerial Memoirs, 1975; returned to MoD as Asst Sec., 1976–83; RCDS, 1983; Asst Under-Sec. of State (Air), MoD (PE), 1984–88; Fellow, Center for Internat. Affairs, Harvard Univ., 1988–89. Cantoris Bass, St Bartholomew-the-Great, Smithfield, 1968–. *Recreations*: travel, photography, choral singing. *Address*: c/o Royal Bank of Scotland, 119 Blackburn Road, Accrington, Lancs BB5 1JJ. *Clubs*: Royal Air Force, United Oxford & Cambridge University.

MOSS, John Ringer, CB 1972; adviser to companies in Associated British Foods Group, since 1980; *b* 15 Feb. 1920; 2nd *s* of late James Moss and Louisa Moss; *m* 1946, Edith Bland Wheeler; two *s* one *d*. *Educ*: Manchester Gram. Sch.; Brasenose Coll., Oxford (MA). War Service, mainly India and Burma, 1940–46; Capt., RE, attached Royal Bombay Sappers and Miners. Entered Civil Service (MAFF) as Asst Princ., 1947; Princ. Private Sec. to Minister of Agric., Fisheries and Food, 1959–61; Asst Sec., 1961; Under-Sec., Gen. Agricultural Policy Gp, 1967–70; Dep. Sec., 1970–80. Mem., Economic Develt Cttee for Agriculture, 1969–70. Specialist Adviser to House of Lords' Select Cttee on European Communities, 1982–90. Chm. Council, RVC, 1983–90. *Recreations*: music, travel. *Address*: 16 Upper Hollis, Great Missenden, Bucks HP16 9HP. *T*: Great Missenden (02406) 2676.

MOSS, Ven. Leonard Godfrey; Archdeacon of Hereford and Canon Residentiary of Hereford Cathedral, since 1991; *b* 11 July 1932; *s* of Clarence Walter Moss and Frances Lilian Vera Moss; *m* 1954, Everell Annette (*née* Reed); two *s* one *d*. *Educ*: Regent St Poly., London; King's Coll., London and Warminster (BD, AKC 1959). Quantity Surveyor's Asst, L. A. Francis and Sons, 1948–54; RE (National Service), 1954–56. Ordained: deacon, 1960; priest, 1961; Assistant curate: St Margaret, Putney, 1960–63; St Dunstan, Cheam, 1963–67; Vicar: Much Dewchurch with Llanwarne and Llandinabo, 1967–72; Marden with Amberley and Wisteston, 1972–84; Hereford Diocesan Ecumenical Officer, 1969–83; Prebendary of Hereford Cathedral, 1979–; Bishop of Hereford's Officer for Social Responsibility and Non-Residentiary Canon of Hereford Cathedral, 1984–91. Proctor in Convocation, 1970–. *Publications*: (contrib.) The People, the Land and the Church, 1987; articles and reviews in theol jls. *Recreations*: reading, listening to music, walking, folk-dancing. *Address*: The Archdeacon's House, The Close, Hereford HR1 2NG. *T*: Hereford (0432) 272873.

MOSS, Malcolm Douglas; MP (C) Cambridgeshire North East, since 1987; Chairman, Mandrake Group, plc, since 1986; *b* 6 March 1943; *s* of Norman Moss and Annie Moss (*née* Gay); *m* 1965, Vivien Lorraine (*née* Peake); two *d*. *Educ*: Audenshaw Grammar Sch.; St John's Coll., Cambridge (BA 1965, MA 1968). Teaching Cert 1966. Asst Master, 1966–68, Head of Dept, 1968–70, Blundell's Sch.; Insurance Consultant, 1970–72, Gen. Manager, 1972–74, Barwick Associates; Chairman: Mandrake Associates Ltd (formerly Mandrake (Insurance and Finance Brokers)), 1986– (Dir, 1974–); Fens Business Enterprise Trust, 1983–87 (Dir, 1983–). *Recreations*: tennis, ski-ing, amateur dramatics. *Address*: Boston House, South Brink, Wisbech, Cambs PE14 0RT; 88 St George's Square, SW1. *T*: 071–821 0269. *Club*: United Oxford & Cambridge University.

MOSS, Martin Grenville, CBE 1975; Director of National Trust Enterprises Ltd, 1985–89; *b* 17 July 1923; *s* of late Horace Grenville Moss and Gladys Ethel (*née* Wootton); *m* 1953, Jane Hope Bown, *qv*; two *s* one *d*. *Educ*: Lancing Coll. Served RAF, 1942–46 (Sqdn Ldr, pilot). Managing Director: Woollands Knightsbridge, 1953–66; Debenham & Freebody, 1964–66; Simpson (Piccadilly) Ltd, 1966–73, 1981–85; Chm. and Chief Exec. Officer, May Department Stores Internat., USA, 1974–80. Member: Export Council of Europe, 1960–64; Design Council, 1964–75 (Dep. Chm., 1971–75); Council, RCA, 1953–58; Royal Fine Art Commn, 1982–84; Council, RSA (Chm., 1983–85). Formerly Governor: Sevenoaks Sch.; Ravensbourne Coll. of Art and Design; W Surrey Coll. of Art and Design. Order of the Finnish Lion, 1970. *Recreations*: gardening, painting, classic cars. *Address*: Parsonage Farm, Bentworth, Alton, Hants GU34 5RB. *T*: Alton (0420) 62175. *Club*: Royal Air Force.

MOSS, Michael; *see* Moss, J. M.

MOSS, Norman J.; *see* Jordan-Moss.

MOSS, Ronald Trevor; Metropolitan Stipendiary Magistrate, since 1984; a Recorder, since 1990; Chairman, Inner London Juvenile Courts, since 1986; *b* 1 Oct. 1942; *s* of Maurice and Sarah Moss; *m* 1971, Cindy (*née* Fiddleman); one *s* one *d*. *Educ*: Hendon County Grammar School; Nottingham University (Upper Second BA; Hons Law). Admitted Solicitor, 1968; Partner, Moss Beachley, solicitors, 1973–84; Mem., Cttee of London Criminal Courts Solicitors' Assoc., 1982–84; Asst Recorder, 1986–90. *Recreations*: golf, Watford Football Club, lawn tennis. *Address*: c/o Horseferry Road Magistrates' Court, SW1. *Club*: Moor Park Golf.

MOSS, Stirling, OBE 1959; FIE; Racing Motorist, 1947–62, retired; Managing Director, Stirling Moss Ltd; Director: Designs Unlimited Ltd; SM Design & Interior Decorating Co.; Hankoe Stove Enamelling Ltd; Piccadilly Securities Ltd; *b* 17 Sept. 1929; *m* 1st, 1957, Kathleen Stuart (marr. diss. 1960), *y d* of F. Stuart Moison, Montreal, Canada; 2nd, 1964, Elaine (marr. diss. 1968), 2nd *d* of A. Barbarino, New York; one *d*; 3rd, 1980, Susan, *y d* of Stuart Paine, London; one *s*. *Educ*: Haileybury and Imperial Service Coll. Brit. Nat. Champion, 1950, 1951, 1952, 1954, 1955, 1956, 1957, 1958, 1959, 1961; Tourist Trophy, 1950, 1951, 1955, 1958, 1959, 1960, 1961; Coupe des Alpes, 1952, 1953, 1954; Alpine Gold Cup (three consecutive wins), 1954. Only Englishman to win Italian Mille Miglia, 1955. Competed in 494 races, rallies, sprints, land speed records and endurance runs, and won 222 of these. Successes include Targa Florio, 1955; Brit. Grand Prix, 1955, 1957; Ital. GP, 1956, 1957, 1959; NZ GP, 1956, 1959; Monaco GP, 1956, 1960, 1961; Leguna Seca GP, 1960, 1961; US GP, 1959, 1960; Aust. GP, 1956; Bari GP, 1956; Pescara GP, 1957; Swedish GP, 1957; Dutch GP, 1958; Argentine GP, 1958; Morocco GP, 1958; Buenos Aires GP, 1958; Melbourne GP, 1958; Villareal GP, 1958; Caen GP, 1958; Portuguese GP, 1959; S African GP, 1960; Cuban GP, 1960; Austrian GP, 1960; Cape GP, 1960; Watkins Glen GP, 1960; German GP, 1961; Modena GP, 1961. Twice voted Driver of the Year, 1954 and 1961. *Publications*: Stirling Moss's Book of Motor Sport, 1955; In the Track of Speed, 1957; Stirling Moss's Second Book of Motor Sport, 1958; Le Mans, 1959; My Favourite Car Stories, 1960; A Turn at the Wheel, 1961; All But My Life, 1963; Design and Behaviour of the Racing Car, 1964; How to Watch Motor Racing, 1975; Motor Racing and All That, 1980; My Cars, My Career, 1987; *relevant publication*: Stirling Moss, by Robert Raymond, 1953. *Recreations*: snow-ski-ing, water ski-ing, dancing, spear-fishing, model making, the theatre, and designing. *Address*: (business) Stirling Moss Ltd, 46 Shepherd Street, W1; (residence) 44 Shepherd Street, W1. *Clubs*: White Elephant; British Racing Drivers', British Automobile Racing, British Racing and Sports Car, Road Racing Drivers of America, 200 mph, Lord's Taverners, Royal Automobile; Internationale des Anciens Pilotes des Grand Prix; Chm. or Pres. of 36 motoring clubs.

MOSS, Trevor Simpson, PhD, ScD; FInstP; Editor, Journal of Infra Red Physics, since 1961; *b* 28 Jan. 1921; *s* of William Moss and Florence Elizabeth (*née* Simpson); *m* 1948, Audrey (*née* Nelson). *Educ:* Alleynes, Uttoxeter; Downing Coll., Cambridge. MA, PhD, ScD Cantab. Research on radar, Royal Aircraft Establishment, 1941–43; research on radar and semiconductors, Telecommunications Research Estabt, 1943–53; RAE, 1953–78; Dep. Dir, Royal Signals and Radar Estabt, 1978–81. Mem., Lloyd's, 1979–. Various hon. commissions in RAF, 1942–45. Max Born Medal, German and British Physical Societies, 1975; Dennis Gabor award, Internat. Soc. of Optical Engrs, 1988. Editor, Jl of Progress in Quantum Electronics, 1978–90. *Publications:* Photoconductivity, 1952; Optical Properties of Semiconductors, 1959; Semiconductor Optoelectronics, 1973; Handbook of Semiconductors, 4 vols, 1980–92; approx. 100 res. papers in internat. physics jls. *Address:* 2 Shelsley Meadow, Colwall, Malvern, Worcs WR13 6PX. *T:* Colwall (0684) 40079.

MÖSSBAUER, Rudolf L., PhD; Professor of Experimental Physics, Technische Universität München, since 1964; *b* Munich, 31 Jan. 1929; *m*; one *s* two *d*. *Educ:* High Sch. and Technische Hochschule, München (equiv. Bachelor's and Master's degrees). PhD (München) 1958. Thesis work, Max Planck Inst., Heidelberg, 1955–57; Research Fellow: Technische Hochschule, München, 1958–60, and at Caltech, 1960–61; Prof. of Physics, CIT, 1962–64; Prof. of Experimental Physics, München, 1964; Dir, Institut Max von Laue-Paul Langevin, and French-German-British High-Flux-Reactor at Grenoble, 1972–77. Member: Bavarian Acad. of Sci.; Amer. Acad. of Sci.; Amer. Acad. of Arts and Scis; Pontifical Acad.; Soviet Acad. of Sci.; Acad. Leopoldina, etc. Hon. degrees Oxford, Leuwen, Madrid, Grenoble, etc. Nobel Prize for Physics, 1961, and numerous other awards. Bavarian Order of Merit, 1962. *Publications:* on gamma resonance spectroscopy (Mössbauer effect) and on neutrino physics. *Recreations:* photography, music, mountaineering. *Address:* Technische Universität München, Physik-Department E 15, James-Franck-Strasse, 8046 Garching, Federal Republic of Germany.

MOSSELMANS, Carel Maurits, TD 1961; Chairman: N. M. Rothschild International Asset Management, since 1989; N. M. Rothschild Asset Management, since 1989; Director, Rothschilds Continuation Ltd, since 1990; *b* 9 March 1929; *s* of Adriaan Willem Mosselmans and Jonkvrouwe Nancy Henriette Mosselmans (*née* van der Wyck); *m* 1962, Hon. Prudence Fiona McCorquodale, *d* of 1st Baron McCorquodale of Newton, KCVO, PC; two *s*. *Educ:* Stowe; Trinity Coll., Cambridge (MA Modern Langs and Hist.). Queen's Bays 2nd Dragoon Guards, 1947–49; City of London Yeomanry (Rough Riders), TA, 1949; Inns of Court and City Yeomanry, 1961; Lt-Col comdg Regt, 1963. Joined Sedgwick Collins & Co., 1952 (Dir, 1963); Director: Sedgwick Forbes Hldgs, 1978; Sedgwick Forbes Bland Payne, 1979; Chm., Sedgwick Ltd, 1981–84; Dep. Chm., 1982, Chm., 1984–89, Sedgwick Group; Chairman: Sedgwick Lloyd's Underwriting Agents (formerly Sedgwick Forbes (Lloyd's Underwriting Agents)), 1974–89; The Sumitomo Marine & Fire Insurance Co. (Europe), 1981–90 (Dir, 1975–81); Dir, Coutts & Co., 1981–. *Recreations:* shooting, fishing, golf, tennis, music. *Address:* 15 Chelsea Square, SW3 6LF. *T:* 071–352 0621. *Clubs:* White's, Cavalry and Guards.

MOSTYN, 5th Baron, *cr* 1831; **Roger Edward Lloyd Lloyd-Mostyn,** Bt 1778; MC 1943; *b* 17 April 1920; *e s* of 4th Baron Mostyn; *S* father, 1965; *m* 1943, Yvonne Margaret Stuart (marr. diss., 1957), *y d* of A. Stuart Johnston, Henshall Hall, Congleton, Cheshire; one *s* one *d*; 2nd, 1957, Mrs Sheila Edmondson Shaw, DL, *o c* of Major Reginald Fairweather, Stockwell Manor, Silverton, Devon, and of Mrs Fairweather, Yew Tree Cottage, Fordcombe, Kent. *Educ:* Eton; Royal Military College, Sandhurst. 2nd Lt, 9th Queen's Royal Lancers, 1939. Served War 1939–45, France, North Africa, and Italy (wounded, despatches, MC). Temp. Major, 1946. *Heir: s* Hon. Llewellyn Roger Lloyd Lloyd-Mostyn [*b* 26 Sept. 1948; *m* 1974, Denise Suzanne, *d* of Roger Duvanel; one *s* one *d*. *Educ:* Eton. Called to the Bar, Middle Temple, 1973]. *Address:* Mostyn Hall, Mostyn, Clwyd, North Wales. *T:* Mostyn (0745) 222.

MOSTYN, Gen. Sir David; *see* Mostyn, Gen. Sir J. D. F.

MOSTYN, Gen. Sir (Joseph) David (Frederick), KCB 1984; CBE 1974 (MBE 1962); Adjutant General, 1986–88; Aide de Camp General to the Queen, 1987–89; *b* 28 Nov. 1928; *s* of late J. P. Mostyn, Arundel, and of Mrs J. D. S. Keenan, Farnham; *m* 1952, Diana Patricia Sheridan; four *s* two *d*. *Educ:* Downside; RMA Sandhurst; psc, rcds. Commnd Oxf. and Bucks LI, 1948; served BAOR, Greece, Cyprus, UK, 1948–58; Canadian Army Staff Coll., 1958; WO, 1959–61; Coy Comdr 1st Green Jackets, Malaya, Brunei, Borneo, 1962–63 (despatches); Instructor, Staff Coll., Camberley, 1964–67; MoD, 1967–69; CO 2 RGJ, BAOR and NI, 1969–71; Comdt Officers' Wing, Sch. of Infantry, 1972; Comdr 8 Inf. Bde, NI, 1972–74; Dep. Dir Army Training, 1974–75; RCDS 1976; BGS, HQ BAOR, 1977; Dir Personal Services (Army), 1978–80; GOC Berlin and Comdt British Sector, 1980–83; Military Sec., 1983–86. Col Commandant: The Light Div., 1983–86; Army Legal Corps, 1983–88. Special Comr, Duke of York's Royal Mil. Sch., Dover, 1989–. Chairman: Lyme Regis Hosp. Trust, 1990–; Council, Dorset Respite and Hosp. Trust, 1990–. Kt SMO Malta, 1974. *Publications:* articles in mil. and RUSI jls. *Recreations:* maintaining a home for the family; all field sports. *Address:* c/o Lloyds Bank Plc, 54 Broad Street, Lyme Regis, Dorset. *Club:* Army and Navy.

MOSTYN, Sir William Basil John, 15th Bt *cr* 1670, of Talacre, Flintshire; *b* 15 Oct. 1975; *s* of Sir Jeremy John Anthony Mostyn, 14th Bt and of Cristina, *o d* of Marchese Orengo, Turin; *S* father, 1988. *Heir: uncle* Trevor Alexander Richard Mostyn, *b* 23 May 1946. *Address:* The Coach House, Church Lane, Lower Heyford, Oxon.

MOTE, Harold Trevor, JP, DL; company director, company consultant and engineer, retired; *b* 28 Oct. 1919; *s* of late Harold Roland Mote; *m* 1944, Amplias Pamela, *d* of late Harold Johnson, Oswestry; three *s* one *d*. *Educ:* Upper Latymer Sch.; St Paul's Sch.; Regent Street Polytechnic; Army Staff Coll. RE, TA, 1935–39; Royal Signals, 1940–46 (Lt-Col); TA, 1948–54. Councillor, Harrow, 1953–67, Alderman 1967; 1st Mayor, London Bor. of Harrow, 1965–66; Opposition Leader, Harrow Council, 1971–73, Leader, 1973–77, resigned 1978. Greater London Council: Mem. for Harrow E, 1965–86; Member, Leader's Cttee, 1977–78, 1979–81 (formerly with special responsibility for Law and Order); Dep. Leader, Planning and Communications Policy Cttee, 1977–78, 1980–81; Chm., 1978–79; Chm., London Transport Cttee, 1979–81; Opposition Spokesman on Transport, 1981–82; Technical Services, 1985–86; Member: Staff Cttee, 1981–82; Planning Cttee, 1981–86; Shadow Leaders Cttee, 1981–82 and 1985–86; formerly: Chm., Scrutiny Cttee; Vice-Chm., Public Services Cttee; Member: Policy and Resources Cttee; West and North Area Planning Bds; Opposition Leader, Fire Bde Cttee; Chm., W Area Planning and Transportation Sub-Cttee; Member: Finance and Estabt Cttee; Public Services and Safety Cttee. Mem., Thames Water Authority, 1973–83 (Chm., Personnel Sub-Cttee, 1973–83; Nat. Rep. on Personnel Matters, 1973–83). JP Mddx 1965; DL Greater London 1967; Rep. DL Harrow 1969. *Address:* Mercury, 48A High Street, Pinner, Middlesex HA5 5PW. *T:* 081–866 8500.

MOTHERWELL, Bishop of, (RC), since 1983; **Rt. Rev. Joseph Devine;** *b* 7 Aug. 1937; *s* of Joseph Devine and Christina Murphy. *Educ:* Blairs Coll., Aberdeen; St Peter's Coll., Dumbarton; Scots Coll., Rome. Ordained priest in Glasgow, 1960; postgraduate work in Rome (PhD), 1960–64; Private Sec. to Archbishop of Glasgow, 1964–65; Assistant Priest in a Glasgow parish, 1965–67; Lecturer in Philosophy, St Peter's Coll., Dumbarton, 1967–74; a Chaplain to Catholic Students in Glasgow Univ., 1974–77; Titular Bishop of Voli and Auxiliary to Archbishop of Glasgow, 1977–83. Papal Bene Merenti Medal, 1962. *Recreations:* general reading, music, Association football. *Address:* 17 Viewpark Road, Motherwell ML1 3ER. *T:* Motherwell (0698) 63715.

MOTION, Andrew; editor, Faber & Faber, since 1989; *b* 26 Oct. 1952; *s* of Andrew Richard Motion and Catherine Gillian Motion; *m* 1st, 1973, Joanna Jane Powell (marr. diss. 1983); 2nd, 1985, Janet Elisabeth Dalley; two *s* one *d*. *Educ:* Radley Coll.; University Coll., Oxford (BA 1st Cl. Hons, MLitt). Lectr in English, Univ. of Hull, 1977–81; Editor of Poetry Review, 1981–83; Poetry Editor, 1983–89, Editl Dir, 1985–87, Chatto & Windus. FRSL 1982. *Publications: poetry:* The Pleasure Steamers, 1978, 3rd edn 1983; Independence, 1981; The Penguin Book of Contemporary British Poetry (anthology), 1982; Secret Narratives, 1983; Dangerous Play, 1984 (Rhys Meml Prize); Natural Causes, 1987 (Dylan Thomas Award); Love in a Life, 1991; *criticism:* The Poetry of Edward Thomas, 1981; Philip Larkin, 1982; *biography:* The Lamberts, 1986 (Somerset Maugham Award, 1987); *novels:* The Pale Companion, 1989; Famous for the Creatures, 1991. *Recreation:* cooking. *Address:* c/o Faber & Faber, 3 Queen Square, WC1N 3AU.

MOTT, Gregory George Sidney, CBE 1979; Managing Director, Vickers Shipbuilding and Engineering Ltd, 1979–84; *b* 11 Feb. 1925; *s* of Sidney Cyril George Mott and Elizabeth Rolinda Mott; *m* 1949, Jean Metcalfe. *Educ:* Univ. of Melbourne (BMechE Hons). Trainee Manager, Vickers Armstrong Ltd Naval Yard, 1948–49; Supervising Engr, A. E. Turner and John Coates, London, 1950–52; Sen. Draughtsman, Melbourne Harbour Trust Comrs, 1952–56; joined Vickers Armstrong Ltd, Barrow, trng on submarine construction, 1956; seconded to Naval Section Harwell, for shielding design DS/MP1 (specialised in computer technol.), 1957–59; returned to Barrow as Project Manager, Dreadnought, 1959–61; Technical Manager, Nuclear, 1961–64; Projects Controller, 1964–67; Local Dir, Vickers Ltd Shipbuilding Gp, 1966; responsible for Special Projects Div., incl. Oceanics Dept, 1968–72; Man. Dir, Vickers Oceanics Ltd, on formation of company, 1972–75; Dir, Vickers Ltd Shipbuilding Gp, and Gen. Manager, Barrow Shipbuilding Works (retained directorship, Vickers Oceanics Ltd, resigned later), 1975–77; Dir, Vickers Shipbuilding Gp Ltd, 1977; Gen. Manager and Dir, Barrow Engrg Works, Vickers Shipbuilding Gp Ltd, 1978.

MOTT, John Charles Spencer, FEng, FICE, FIStructE; CBIM; Chairman, William Sindall plc, since 1990 (Director, since 1989); *b* Beckenham, Kent, 18 Dec. 1926; *m* 1953, Patricia Mary (*née* Fowler); two *s*. *Educ:* Balgowan Central Sch., Beckenham, Kent; Brixton Sch. of Building; Battersea Polytechnic; Rutherford Coll. of Technology, Newcastle upon Tyne. Served war, Lieut, Royal Marines, 1943–46. Indentured as Engr with L. G. Mouchel & Partners, 1949–52; joined Kier Ltd, 1952; Agent on heavy civil engrg contracts, 1952–63; Chairman: French Kier Holdings plc, 1974–86 (Dir, on merger, 1973, Chief Exec., 1974–84); May Gurney Hldgs Ltd, 1986–89. Director: Kier Ltd, 1963; J. L. Kier & Co. Ltd (Holding Co.), 1968; RMC plc, 1986–. Mem. Council, Fellowship of Engrg, 1983–86; Mem. Council, 1973–75, 1986–87, and Vice Pres., 1986–87, ICE; Mem., Bragg Cttee on Falsework, 1972–74. *Address:* (home) 91 Long Road, Cambridge; (office) William Sindall plc, Babraham Road, Sawston, Cambs CB2 4LJ. *Club:* Danish.

MOTT, Sir John (Harmar), 3rd Bt, *cr* 1930; Regional Medical Officer, Department of Health and Social Security, 1969–84; *b* 21 July 1922; *s* of 2nd Bt and Mary Katherine (*d* 1972) *d* of late Rev. A. H. Stanton; *S* father, 1964; *m* 1950, Elizabeth (*née* Carson); one *s* two *d*. *Educ:* Radley Coll.; New Coll., Oxford. MA Oxford, 1948; BM, BCh, 1951. Served War of 1939–45: Pilot, Royal Air Force, 1943–46. Middlesex Hospital: House Physician, 1951; House Surgeon, 1952. Mem., RCGP. *Recreation:* photography. *Heir: s* David Hugh Mott [*b* 1 May 1952; *m* 1980, Amanda Jane, *d* of Lt-Comdr D. W. P. Fryer, RN; two *s*]. *Address:* Staniford, Brookside, Kingsley, Cheshire WA6 8BG. *T:* Kingsley (0928) 88123.

MOTT, Michael Duncan; His Honour Judge Mott; a Circuit Judge, since 1985; *b* 8 Dec. 1940; *s* of Francis J. Mott and Gwendolen Mott; *m* 1970, Phyllis Ann Gavin; two *s*. *Educ:* Rugby Sch.; Caius Coll., Cambridge (Exhibnr, MA). Called to Bar, Inner Temple, 1963; practised Midland and Oxford Circuit, 1964–69; Resident Magistrate, Kenya, 1969–71; resumed practice, Midland and Oxford Circuit, 1972; a Deputy Circuit Judge, 1976–80; a Recorder, 1980–85. *Recreations:* tennis, ski-ing, travel, music. *Address:* c/o Circuit Administrator, Midland and Oxford Circuit, 2 Newton Street, Birmingham B4 7LU. *Clubs:* Cambridge Union Society; Union and County (Worcester).

MOTT, Sir Nevill (Francis), Kt 1962; FRS 1936; MA Cantab; Cavendish Professor of Physics, Cambridge University, 1954–71; Senior Research Fellow, Imperial College, London, 1971–73, Fellow, 1978; *b* 30 Sept. 1905; *s* of C. F. Mott, late Dir of Educn, Liverpool, and Lilian Mary Reynolds; *m* 1930, Ruth Horder; two *d*. *Educ:* Clifton Coll.; St John's Coll., Cambridge. Lecturer at Manchester Univ., 1929–30; Fellow and Lecturer, Gonville and Caius Coll., Cambridge, 1930–33; Melville Wills Prof. of Theoretical Physics in the Univ. of Bristol, 1933–48; Henry Overton Wills Prof. and Dir of the Henry Herbert Wills Physical Laboratories, Univ. of Bristol, 1948–54. Master of Gonville and Caius Coll., Univ. of Cambridge, 1959–66. Corr. mem., Amer. Acad. of Arts and Sciences, 1954; Pres., International Union of Physics, 1951–57; Pres., Mod. Languages Assoc., 1955; Pres., Physical Soc., 1956–58; Mem. Governing Board of Nat. Inst. for Research in Nuclear Science, 1957–60; Mem. Central Advisory Council for Education for England, 1956–59; Mem. Academic Planning Cttee and Council of University Coll. of Sussex; Chm. Ministry of Education's Standing Cttee on Supply of Teachers, 1959–62; Chairman: Nuffield Foundation's Cttee on Physics Education, 1961–73; Physics Education Cttee (Royal Society and Inst. of Physics), 1965–71. Chairman, Taylor & Francis, Scientific Publishers, 1970–75, Pres., 1976–86. Foreign Associate, Nat. Acad. of Sciences of USA, 1957; Hon. Member: Akademie der Naturforscher Leopoldina, 1964; Société Française de Physique, 1970; Inst. of Metals, Japan, 1975; Sociedad Real Española de Fisica y Quimica, 1980; European Physical Soc., 1985; Hon. Fellow: St John's Coll., Cambridge, 1971; UMIST, 1975; Darwin Coll., Cambridge, 1977; For. Fellow, Indian Nat. Science Acad., 1982. Hon. DSc: Louvain, Grenoble, Paris, Poitiers, Bristol, Ottawa, Liverpool, Reading, Sheffield, London, Warwick, Lancaster, Heriot-Watt, Oxon, East Anglia, Bordeaux, St Andrews, Essex, William and Mary, Stuttgart, Sussex, Marburg, Bar Ilan, Lille, Rome, Lisbon; Hon. Doctorate of Technology, Linköping, Sweden. Hon. FInstP 1972. Hughes Medal of Royal Society, 1941; Royal Medal, 1953; Grande Médaille de la Société Française de Métallurgie, 1970; Copley Medal, 1972; Faraday Medal, IEE, 1973; (jtly) Nobel Prize for Physics, 1977. Chevalier, Ordre Nat. du Mérite, France, 1977. *Publications:* An Outline of Wave Mechanics, 1930; The Theory of Atomic Collisions (with H. S. W. Massey), 1933; The Theory of the Properties of Metals and Alloys (with H. Jones), 1936; Electronic Processes in Ionic Crystals (with R. W. Gurney), 1940; Wave Mechanics and its Applications (with I. N. Snedden), 1948; Elements of Wave Mechanics, 1952; Atomic Structure and the Strength of Metals, 1956; Electronic Processes in Non-Crystalline Materials (with E. A. Davis), 1971, 2nd edn 1979; Elementary Quantum Mechanics, 1972; Metal-Insulator Transitions, 1974, 2nd edn 1990; Conduction in Non-crystalline Materials, 1986; A Life in Science (autobiog.), 1986; (ed) Can Scientists Believe? some examples of the attitude of scientists to religion, 1991; various contribs to scientific periodicals about Atomic Physics, Metals, Semi-conductors, Superconductors and Photographic Emulsions and Glasses. *Recreation:* photography. *Address:* The Cavendish Laboratory, Madingley Road, Cambridge CB3 0HE; 63 Mount Pleasant, Aspley Guise, Milton Keynes MK17 8JX. *Club:* Athenæum.

MOTT, Philip Charles; QC 1991; a Recorder of the Crown Court, since 1987; *b* 20 April 1948; *s* of Charles Kynaston Mott and Elsie (*née* Smith); *m* 1977, Penelope Ann Caffery; two *d. Educ:* King's Coll., Taunton; Worcester Coll., Oxford (MA). Called to the Bar, Inner Temple, 1970; in practice on Western Circuit, 1970–. *Recreations:* the countryside, sailing. *Address:* Lamb Building, Temple, EC4Y 7AS. *T:* 071–353 6381. *Clubs:* Hampshire (Winchester); Exeter and County (Exeter); Bar Yacht.

MOTT-RADCLYFFE, Sir Charles (Edward), Kt 1957; DL; Captain Rifle Brigade, Reserve of Officers; *b* 1911; *o s* of Lt-Col C. E. Radclyffe, DSO, Rifle Brigade (killed in action 1915), Little Park, Wickham, Hants, and Theresa Caroline, *o d* of John Stanley Mott, JP, Barningham Hall, Norfolk; *m* 1940, Diana (*d* 1955), *d* of late Lt-Col W. Gibbs, CVO, 7th Hussars; three *d*; *m* 1956, Stella, *d* of late Lionel Harrisson, Caynham Cottage, Ludlow, Salop. *Educ:* Eton; Balliol Coll., Oxford. Hon. Attaché Diplomatic Service, Athens and Rome, 1936–38; Mem. Military Mission to Greece, 1940–41; served as Liaison Officer in Syria, 1941, and with Rifle Brigade in Middle East and Italy, 1943–44; MP (C) Windsor, 1942–70; Parliamentary Private Sec. to Sec. of State for India (Rt Hon. L. S. Amery), Dec. 1944–May 1945; Junior Lord of the Treasury, May-July 1945; Conservative Whip, Aug. 1945–Feb. 1946; Chm. Conservative Parly Foreign Affairs Cttee, 1951–59. Mem., Plowden Commn on Overseas Representational Services, 1963–64. A Governor of Gresham's Sch., Holt, 1957–87; Mem., Historic Buildings Council for England, 1962–70; President: Country Landowners Assoc. (Norfolk Branch), 1972–87; Norfolk CCC, 1972–74 (Chm., 1976–89); Royal Norfolk Show, 1979. High Sheriff, 1974, DL 1977, of Norfolk. Comdr, Order of Phoenix (Greece). *Publication:* Foreign Body in the Eye (a memoir of the Foreign Service), 1975. *Recreations:* cricket (Captain, Lords and Commons Cricket, 1952–70), shooting. *Address:* Barningham Hall, Matlaske, Norfolk. *T:* Matlaske 250; Flat 1, 38 Cadogan Square, SW1. *T:* 071–584 5834. *Clubs:* Turf, Buck's, Pratt's, MCC.

MOTTELSON, Prof. Ben R., PhD; Danish physicist; Professor, Nordic Institute for Theoretical Atomic Physics, Copenhagen, since 1957; *b* Chicago, Ill, USA, 9 July 1926; *s* of Goodman Mottelson and Georgia Mottelson (*née* Blum); *m* 1948, Nancy Jane Reno; three *c*; became a Danish citizen, 1971. *Educ:* High Sch., La Grange, Ill; Purdue Univ. (officers' trng, USN, V12 program; BSc 1947); Harvard Univ. (grad. studies, PhD 1950). Sheldon Trav. Fellowship from Harvard at Inst. of Theoretical Physics, Copenhagen (later, the Niels Bohr Inst.), 1950–51. His Fellowship from US Atomic Energy Commn permitted continuation of work in Copenhagen for two more years, after which he held research position in CERN (European Organization for Nuclear Research) theoretical study group, formed in Copenhagen. Visiting Prof., Univ. of Calif at Berkeley, Spring term, 1959. Nobel Prize for Physics (jtly), 1975; awarded for work on theory of Atomic Nucleus, with Dr Aage Bohr (3 papers publ. 1952–53). *Publications:* Nuclear Structure, vol. I, 1969; vol. II, 1975 (with A. Bohr); contrib. Rev. Mod. Phys (jt), etc. *Address:* Nordita, Copenhagen, Denmark.

MOTTERSHEAD, Frank William, CB 1957; Deputy Secretary, Department of Health and Social Security (formerly Ministry of Health), 1965–71; *b* 7 Sept. 1911; *o s* of late Thomas Hastings and Adeline Mottershead; unmarried. *Educ:* King Edward's Sch., Birmingham; St John's Coll., Cambridge. BA 1933, MA 1973. Entered Secretary's Dept of Admiralty, 1934; Principal Private Sec. to First Lord, 1944–46; idc 1949; Under Sec., 1950; Transferred to Ministry of Defence, 1956; Deputy Sec., 1958; Deputy Under-Sec. of State, 1964. *Address:* Old Warden, Grevel Lane, Chipping Campden, Glos GL55 6HS. *T:* Evesham (0386) 840548. *Club:* United Oxford & Cambridge University.

MOTTISTONE, 4th Baron, *cr* 1933, of Mottistone; **David Peter Seely,** CBE 1984; Lord Lieutenant for Isle of Wight, since 1986; *b* 16 Dec. 1920; 4th *s* of 1st Baron Mottistone; *S* half brother, 1966; *m* 1944, Anthea, *er d* of T. V. W. McMullan, Cultra, Co. Down, N Ireland; two *s* two *d* (and one *d* decd). *Educ:* RN Coll., Dartmouth. Convoy escorting, Atlantic and Mediterranean, 1941–44; qualified in Communications, 1944; Served in Pacific, 1945; in comd HMS Cossack, FE Flt, 1958–59; in comd HMS Ajax and 24th Escort Sqdn, FE Flt (offensive ops against Indonesian confrontation) (despatches), 1963–65; Naval Advr to UK High Comr, Ottawa, 1965–66; retired at own request as a Captain, 1967. Dir of Personnel and Training, Radio Rentals Gp, 1967–69; Director: Distributive Industry Trng Bd, 1969–75; Cake and Biscuit Alliance, 1975–81; Export Secretary: Biscuit, Cake, Chocolate and Confectionary Alliance, 1981–83. Chairman: Westminster Industrial Brief Ltd, 1981–86; Bureau of Applied Sciences, 1987–; Eyos Ltd, 1988–; CNL Group, 1990–. FIEE; FIPM; FBIM. DL Isle of Wight, 1981–86. KStJ 1989. *Recreation:* yachting. *Heir:* *s* Hon. Peter John Philip Seely [*b* 29 Oct. 1949; *m* 1st, 1972, Joyce Cairns (marr. diss. 1975); one *s*; 2nd, 1982, Linda, *d* of W. Swain, Bulphan Fen, Essex; one *s* three *d*]. *Address:* The Old Parsonage, Mottistone, Isle of Wight. *Clubs:* Commonwealth Trust; Royal Yacht Squadron, Royal Cruising, Island Sailing, Royal Navy Sailing Association.

MOTTRAM, Maj.-Gen. John Frederick, CB 1983; LVO 1976; OBE 1969; Chief Executive, General Council of the Bar, since 1987; *b* 9 June 1930; *s* of Frederick Mottram and Margaret Mottram (*née* Butcher); *m* 1956, Jennifer Thomas; one *s* one *d. Educ:* Enfield Central Sch.; Enfield Technical Coll. Joined RM, 1948; 42 Commando, Malaya, ME, 1951–54; Special Boat Squadron, 1955–56; HMS Loch Lomond, Persian Gulf, 1957–58; Adjutant, Commando Trng Centre, 1959–62; Student, Army Staff Coll., 1963; Staff of CGRM and RM Equerry to HRH The Duke of Edinburgh, 1964–65; Bde Major, 3 Commando Bde, Far East, 1966–68; Directing Staff, Army Staff Coll., 1969–71; CO, 40 Commando, NI and Plymouth, 1972–74 (mentioned in Despatches, 1973); Student, Naval War Coll., 1974; Jt Warfare Attaché, British Embassy, Washington DC, 1974–77; Col GS, DCGRM and RM ADC to HM The Queen, 1978–80; Maj.-Gen., 1980; Maj.-Gen. Training and Reserve Forces, RM, 1980–83, retd. Dir Gen., Fertiliser Manufacturers Assoc., 1983–86. *Recreation:* fishing. *Address:* c/o General Council of the Bar, 11 South Square, Gray's Inn, WC1R 5EL. *Club:* Army and Navy.

MOTTRAM, Richard Clive; Deputy Under Secretary of State (Policy), Ministry of Defence, since 1989; *b* 23 April 1946; *s* of John Mottram and Florence Yates; *m* 1971, Fiona Margaret Erskine; three *s* one *d. Educ:* King Edward VI Camphill Sch., Birmingham; Univ. of Keele (1st Cl. Hons Internat. Relns). Entered Home Civil Service by open competition, 1968, assigned to Ministry of Defence: Asst Private Sec. to Sec. of State for Defence, 1971–72; Principal, Naval Programme and Budget, 1973; Cabinet Office, 1975–77; Ministry of Defence: Private Sec. to Perm. Under Sec., 1979–81; Asst Sec., Manpower Control and Audit, Procurement Exec., 1981; Private Sec. to Sec. of State for Defence, 1982–86; Asst. Under Sec. of State, 1986–89. *Recreations:* cinema, tennis. *Address:* c/o Ministry of Defence, Whitehall, SW1A 2HB. *T:* 071–218 9000.

MOTYER, Rev. John Alexander; Minister of Christ Church, Westbourne, Bournemouth, 1981–89, retired; *b* 30 Aug. 1924; *s* of Robert Shankey and Elizabeth Maud Motyer; *m* 1948, Beryl Grace Mays; two *s* one *d. Educ:* High Sch., Dublin; Dublin Univ. (MA, BD); Wycliffe Hall, Oxford. Curate: St Philip, Penn Fields, Wolverhampton, 1947–50; Holy Trinity, Old Market, Bristol, 1950–54; Tutor, Clifton Theol Coll., Bristol, 1950–54, Vice-Principal, 1954–65; Vicar, St Luke's, Hampstead, 1965–70; Dep. Principal, Tyndale Hall, Bristol, 1970–71; Principal and Dean of College, Trinity Coll., Bristol, 1971–81. *Publications:* The Revelation of the Divine Name, 1959; After Death, 1965; The Richness of Christ (Epistle to the Philippians), 1966; The Tests of Faith (Epistle of James), 1970, 2nd edn 1975; (Old Testament Editor) New Bible Commentary Revised, 1970; The Day of the Lion (Amos), 1975; The Image of God: Law and Liberty in Biblical Ethics (Laing Lecture), 1976; The Message of Philippians, 1984; The Message of James, 1985; contributor: New Bible Dictionary; Expositor's Bible Commentary; Law and Life (monograph); New International Dictionary of New Testament Theology; Evangelical Dictionary of Theology. *Recreations:* reading, odd-jobbing. *Address:* 10 Littlefield, Bishopsteignton, Teignmouth, Devon TQ14 9SG. *T:* Teignmouth (0626) 770986.

MOULE, Rev. Prof. Charles Francis Digby, CBE 1985; FBA 1966; Lady Margaret's Professor of Divinity in the University of Cambridge, 1951–76; Fellow of Clare College, Cambridge, since 1944; Canon Theologian (non-residentiary) of Leicester, 1955–76; Honorary Member of Staff, Ridley Hall, Cambridge, 1976–80; *b* 3 Dec. 1908; *s* of late Rev. Henry William Moule and Laura Clements Pope; unmarried. *Educ:* Weymouth Coll., Dorset; Emmanuel Coll., Cambridge (scholar) (Hon. Fellow 1972); Ridley Hall, Cambridge. 1st Cl. Classical Tripos Part I, 1929; BA (1st Cl. Classical Tripos Part II), 1931; Evans Prize, 1931; Jeremie Septuagint Prize, 1932; Crosse Scholarship, 1933; MA 1934. Deacon, 1933, priest, 1934; Curate, St Mark's, Cambridge, and Tutor of Ridley Hall, 1933–34; Curate, St Andrew's, Rugby, 1934–36; Vice-Principal, Ridley Hall, 1936–44, and Curate of St Mary the Great, Cambridge, 1936–40. Dean of Clare Coll., Cambridge, 1944–51; Faculty Asst Lecturer in Divinity in the Univ. of Cambridge, 1944–47; Univ. Lecturer, 1947–51. Burkitt Medal for Biblical Studies, British Acad., 1970. Hon. DD: St Andrews, 1958; Cantab, 1988. *Publications:* An Idiom Book of New Testament Greek, 1953; The Meaning of Hope, 1953; The Sacrifice of Christ, 1956; Colossians and Philemon (Cambridge Greek Testament Commentary), 1957; Worship in the New Testament, 1961; The Birth of the New Testament, 1962, 3rd edn 1981; The Phenomenon of the New Testament, 1967; (co-editor) Christian History and Interpretation, 1968; The Origin of Christology, 1977 (Collins Theological Book Prize, 1977); The Holy Spirit, 1978; Essays in New Testament Interpretation, 1982; (co-editor) Jesus and the Politics of His Day, 1984; contrib., Encyclopædia Britannica, Interpreter's Dictionary of the Bible, Biblisch-Historisches Handwörterbuch. *Address:* 1 King's Houses, Pevensey, East Sussex.

MOULTON, Alexander Eric, CBE 1976; RDI; FEng; Managing Director, Moulton Developments Ltd, since 1956; *b* 9 April 1920; *s* of John Coney Moulton, DSc, The Hall, Bradford-on-Avon, and Beryl Latimer Moulton. *Educ:* Marlborough Coll.; King's Coll., Cambridge (MA). Bristol Aeroplane Co., 1939–44: Engine Research Dept; George Spencer, Moulton & Co. Ltd, 1945–56; became Techn. Dir; estab. Research Dept (originated work on rubber suspensions for vehicles, incl. own design Flexitor); formed Moulton Developments Ltd, 1956 to do develt work on own designs of rubber suspensions for BLMC incl. Hydrolastic and Hydragas (Queen's Award to Industry, 1967); formed Moulton Bicycles Ltd to produce own design Moulton Bicycle, 1962 (Design Centre Award, 1964); designer of Moulton Coach, 1968–70; Chm., Moulton report on engrg design educn, Design Council, 1975–76; launched Alex Moulton Bicycle, 1983. Dir, SW Regional Bd, National Westminster Bank, 1982–87. RDI 1968 (Master, 1982–83); FRSA 1968; FEng 1980. Hon. Dr, RCA, 1967; Hon. DSc Bath, 1971. SIAD Design Medal, 1976; (jointly): James Clayton Prize, Crompton-Lanchester Medal, and Thomas Hawksley Gold Medal, IMechE, 1979. *Publications:* numerous articles and papers on engineering and education. *Recreations:* cycling, canoeing, steam boating, shooting. *Address:* The Hall, Bradford-on-Avon, Wilts. *T:* Bradford-on-Avon (02216) 2991. *Club:* Brooks's.

MOULTON, Maj.-Gen. James Louis, CB 1956; DSO 1944; OBE 1950; retired; *b* 3 June 1906; *s* of Capt. J. D. Moulton, RN; *m* 1937, Barbara Aline (*née* Coode); one *s* one *d. Educ:* Sutton Valence Sch. Joined Royal Marines, 1924; Pilot, Fleet Air Arm, 1930; Staff Coll., Camberley, 1938; served War of 1939–45: GSO3 GHQ, BEF, 1940; GSO1, Force 121 (Madagascar), 1942; Commanding Officer, 48 Commando, NW Europe, 1944–45 (DSO); Comd 4th Commando Bde, NW Europe, 1945 (despatches); CO Commando Sch., 1947–49; Comd 3rd Commando Bde, Middle East, 1952–54; Maj.-Gen. Royal Marines, Portsmouth, 1954–57; Chief of Amphibious Warfare, 1957–61. Rep. Col Comdt RM, 1971–72. Mem. Council, RUSI, 1964–71 (Vice-Chm., 1965–67; Chm., 1967–69). Naval Editor, 1964–69, Editor, 1969–73, Brassey's Annual. *Publications:* Haste to the Battle, 1963; Defence in a Changing World, 1964; The Norwegian Campaign of 1940, 1966; British Maritime Strategy in the 1970s, 1969; The Royal Marines, 1972, 2nd rev. and enl. edn 1981; Battle for Antwerp, 1978. *Address:* Fairmile, Woodham Road, Woking, Surrey GU21 4DN. *T:* Woking (0483) 715174.

MOULTON, Air Vice-Marshal Leslie Howard, CB 1971; DFC 1941; with The Plessey Co., 1971–82, retired; *b* 3 Dec. 1915; *s* of late Peter Moulton, Nantwich, Cheshire; *m* Lesley, *d* of late P. C. Clarke, Ilford; two *s* two *d. Educ:* Nantwich and Acton School. Joined RAF, 1932; served War of 1939–45, Pilot; Operations with 14 Sqdn in Africa, 1940–42; CFS, 1942–44; specialised in Signals, 1945; Staff Coll., 1950; USAF, Strategic Air Comd, 1954–56; Dep. Dir Radio, Air Min., 1958–61; Comdt RAF Cosford, 1961–63; CSO Fighter Comd, 1963–65; Min. of Technology, 1965–68. Wing Comdr 1955; Gp Captain 1959; Air Cdre 1964; Air Vice-Marshal 1969; AOC No 90 (Signals) Group, RAF, 1969–71; retired 1971. FIEE, CEng, 1959. *Recreations:* gardening, golf, hill walking. *Address:* No 14 The Paddock, Willaston House, Willaston, Nantwich, Cheshire CW5 7EP. *T:* Nantwich (0270) 665308. *Club:* Royal Air Force.

MOUND, Laurence Alfred, DSc; FRES; Keeper of Entomology, Natural History Museum (formerly British Museum (Natural History)), since 1981; *b* 22 April 1934; *s* of John Henry Mound and Laura May Cape; *m* 1st, 1958, Agnes Jean Solari (marr. diss. 1985); one *s* two *d*; 2nd, 1987, Sheila Helen Halsey. *Educ:* Warwick Sch.; Sir John Cass Coll., London; Imperial Coll., London (DIC); DSc London; Imperial Coll. of Tropical Agriculture, Trinidad (DipTropAgric). Nigerian Federal Dept of Agricl Research, 1959–61; Empire Cotton Growing Corp., Republic of Sudan, 1961–64; Sen. Scientific Officer, BM (NH), 1964–69; Australian CSIRO Research Award, 1967–68; PSO, 1969–75, Dep. Keeper, Dept of Entomology, BM (NH), 1975–81. Sec., 1976–, Vice-Chm., 1988–, Council for Internat. Congresses of Entomology; Consultant Dir, Commonwealth Inst. of Entomology, 1981–. Hon. Prof., Sch. of Pure and Applied Biology, Univ. of Wales at Cardiff, 1990–. Editor, Jl of Royal Entomological Soc. of London, 1973–81 (Vice-Pres., RES, 1975–76). Numerous expedns studying thrips in tropical countries. *Publications:* over 90 technical books and papers on biology of thrips and whitefly, particularly in Bull. of BM (NH), incl. Whitefly of the World (with S. H. Halsey). *Recreations:* thrips with everything. *Address:* c/o Natural History Museum, Cromwell Road, SW7. *T:* 071–938 9474.

MOUND, Trevor Ernest John, CVO 1986; OBE 1977; HM Diplomatic Service, retired; writer and broadcaster; Chairman, Ephew II Consultants; *b* 27 July 1930; *e s* of late Harvey Mound and late Margaret Webb; *m* 1955, Patricia Kathleen de Burgh (marr. diss. 1972); two *s*. *Educ:* Royal Grammar Sch., Worcester; RMA Sandhurst; Univs of London and Hong Kong. Enlisted Coldstream Gds; 2nd Lt, Worcs Regt (Malayan Campaign), 1951–54; Parachute Regt (ME), 1954–56; Adjutant, Airborne Forces, 1956–58; GSO 3, 16 Parachute Bde (ME), 1958–60; MoD, 1965–67; retired 1967; joined HM Diplomatic Service, 1967; First Secretary and Head of Chancery: Luxembourg, 1969–71; Calcutta, 1971–73; FCO, 1973–76; Beirut, 1976–77; Counsellor (Commercial), Peking, 1978–81; Counsellor (Econ.), Oslo, 1981–83; Counsellor (Hong Kong negotiations), FCO, 1984; Consul General: Shanghai, 1985–87; Marseilles Principality of Monaco, 1987–90. *Recreation:* astericology. *Address:* 8 Beaufort East, Bath, BA1 6QD.

MOUNSEY, John Patrick David, MA, MD, FRCP; Provost, Welsh National School of Medicine, 1969–79, retired; *b* 1 Feb. 1914; *s* of late John Edward Mounsey and late Christine Frances Trail Robertson; *m* 1947, Vera Madeline Sara King (*d* 1990); one *s* one *d*. *Educ:* Eton Coll.; King's Coll., Cambridge; King's Coll. Hosp., London. Sherbrook Res. Fellow, Cardiac Dept, London Hosp., 1951; Royal Postgraduate Medical School: Lectr, 1960; Sen. Lectr and Sub-Dean, 1962; Cons. Cardiologist, Hammersmith Hosp., 1960; Dep. Dir, British Postgrad. Med. Fedn, 1967; Member: GMC, 1970–79; GDC, 1973–79; Council, St David's University Coll., Lampeter, 1975–83; South Glamorgan AHA (T); British Cardiac Soc.; Assoc. of Physicians; Soc. of Physicians in Wales. Corresp. Mem., Australasian Cardiac Soc.; late Asst Ed., British Heart Jl. Hon. LLD Wales, 1980. *Publications:* articles on cardiology mainly in British Heart Jl. *Recreations:* painting, gardening, music. *Address:* Esk House, Coombe Terrace, Wotton-under-Edge, Glos GL12 7NA. *T:* Dursley (0453) 842792. *Club:* Athenæum.

MOUNT, Air Cdre Christopher John, CBE 1956; DSO 1943; DFC 1940; DL; retired; *b* 14 Dec. 1913; *s* of Capt. F. Mount; *m* 1947, Audrey Mabel Clarke; two *s*. *Educ:* Eton; Trinity Coll., Oxford. Royal Auxiliary Air Force, 1935; Royal Air Force, 1938. Consultant, Wrights (formerly C. R. Thomas & Son), Solicitors, Maidenhead (partner, 1970–79). DL Berks, 1984. *Address:* Garden House, Bagshot Road, Sunninghill, Ascot, Berks SL5 9JL. *T:* Ascot (0990) 22225.

MOUNT, Ferdinand; *see* Mount, W. R. F.

MOUNT, Sir James (William Spencer), Kt 1979; CBE 1965; BEM 1946; VMH; *b* 8 Nov. 1908; *s* of Spencer William Mount and Kathleen Mount (*née* Ashenden) *m* 1931, Margaret Geikie (*d* 1973); one *s* three *d*; *m* 1975, Jane Mount. *Educ:* Tonbridge School. Chairman and Director, S. W. Mount & Sons Ltd, 1944–. Chairman: Horticultural Advisory Cttee, MAFF, 1963–69; National Fruit Trials Advisory Cttee, MAFF, 1973–78; Governing Body, E Malling Res. Station, 1960–80. VMH 1982. *Recreations:* fishing, gardening. *Address:* Woolton Farm, Bekesbourne, Canterbury, Kent. *T:* Canterbury (0227) 830202. *Club:* Farmers'.

MOUNT, Sir William (Malcolm), 2nd Bt, *cr* 1921; Lieutenant-Colonel Reconnaissance Corps; *b* 28 Dec. 1904; *s* of Sir William Mount, 1st Bt, CBE, and Hilda Lucy Adelaide (*d* 1950), OBE, *y d* of late Malcolm Low of Clatto, Fife; *S* father, 1930; *m* 1929, Elizabeth Nance, *o d* of Owen John Llewellyn, Badminton Vicarage, Glos; three *d*. *Educ:* Eton; New Coll., Oxford. Berkshire: DL 1946; High Sheriff, 1947–48; Vice-Lieutenant, 1960–76. *Recreation:* fishing. *Heir: nephew* William Robert Ferdinand Mount, *qv*. *Address:* Wasing Place, Aldermaston, Berks.

See also Sir W. S. Dugdale, Bt.

MOUNT, (William Robert) Ferdinand; journalist; Editor, Times Literary Supplement, since 1991; *b* 2 July 1939; *s* of late Robin and Lady Julia Mount; *heir pres.* to Sir William Mount, *qv*; *m* 1968, Julia Margaret, *d* of late Archibald Julian and Hon. Mrs Lucas; two *s* one *d* (and one *s* decd). *Educ:* Eton; Christ Church, Oxford. Has worked for Sunday Telegraph, Conservative Research Dept, Daily Sketch, National Review, Daily Mail, The Times; Political Columnist: The Spectator, 1977–82 and 1985–87; The Standard, 1980–82; Daily Telegraph, 1984–90; Head of Prime Minister's Policy Unit, 1982–83. *Publications:* Very Like a Whale, 1967; The Theatre of Politics, 1972; The Man Who Rode Ampersand, 1975; The Clique, 1978; The Subversive Family, 1982; The Selkirk Strip, 1987. *Address:* 17 Ripplevale Grove, N1. *T:* 071–607 5398.

MOUNT CHARLES, Earl of; Henry Vivian Pierpoint Conyngham; *b* 23 May 1951; *s* and *heir* of 7th Marquess Conyngham, *qv*; *m* 1st, 1971, Juliet Ann, *yr d* of Robert Kitson (marr. diss. 1985); one *s* one *d*; 2nd, 1985, Lady Iona Grimston, *yr d* of 6th Earl of Verulam; one *d*. *Educ:* Harrow; Harvard Univ. Irish Rep., 1976–78, Consultant, 1978–84, Sotheby's; Chairman: Slane Castle Ltd; Slane Castle Productions. Dir, Grapevine Arts Centre, Dublin. Trustee, Irish Youth Foundn. *Heir: s* Viscount Slane, *qv*. *Address:* Slane Castle, Co. Meath, Eire; Beau Parc House, Navan, Co. Meath, Eire. *Club:* Kildare Street and University (Dublin).

MOUNT EDGCUMBE, 8th Earl of, *cr* 1789; **Robert Charles Edgcumbe;** Baron Edgcumbe, 1742; Viscount Mount Edgcumbe and Valletort, 1781; Farm Manager, for Lands and Survey, New Zealand, 1975–84; *b* 1 June 1939; *s* of George Aubrey Valletort Edgcumbe (*d* 1977) and of Meta Blucher, *d* of late Robert Charles Lhoyer; *S* uncle, 1982; *m* 1960, Joan Ivy Wall (marr. diss. 1988); five *d*. *Educ:* Nelson College. Career from farm worker to farm manager, managing first farm, 1960; taking up family seat in Cornwall, 1984. *Recreations:* hunting game, restoring classic cars. *Heir: half-b* Piers Valletort Edgcumbe, *b* 23 Oct. 1946. *Address:* Empacombe House, Cremyll, Cornwall PL10 1H2.

MOUNTAIN, Sir Denis Mortimer, 3rd Bt *cr* 1922; Chairman and Managing Director: Eagle Star Insurance Co. Ltd, 1974–85; Eagle Star Holdings plc, 1979–85, Hon. President, since 1985; Chairman, Eagle Star Insurance Co. of America, 1978–85; *b* 2 June 1929; *er s* of Sir Brian Edward Stanley Mountain, 2nd Bt, and of Doris Elsie, *e d* of late E. C. E. Lamb; *S* father, 1977; *m* 1958, Hélène Fleur Mary Kirwan-Taylor; two *s* one *d*. *Educ:* Eton. Late Lieut, Royal Horse Guards. Chairman: Australian Eagle Insurance Co. Ltd, 1977–85; South African Eagle Insurance Co. Ltd, 1977–85, and other companies both in UK and overseas; Pres., Compagnie de Bruxelles Risques Divers SA d'Assurances (Belgium), 1977–85; Director: Rank Organisation PLC, 1968–; Grovewood Securities Ltd, 1969–85 (Dep. Chm.); Philip Hill Investment Trust plc, 1967–86; Bank of Nova Scotia (Toronto), 1978–; BAT Industries plc, 1984–85; Allied London Properties, 1986–, and other UK and overseas companies. *Recreations:* fishing, shooting. *Heir: s* Edward Brian Stanford Mountain [*b* 19 March 1961; *m* 1987, Charlotte Sarah Jesson, *d* of Judge Henry Pownall, *qv*; two *s*]. *Address:* The Manor, Morestead, Winchester, Hants SO2 1LZ. *T:* Twyford (0962) 777237; 12 Queens Elm Square, Old Church Street, Chelsea, SW3 6ED. *T:* 071–352 4331.

MOUNTBATTEN, family name of **Marquess of Milford Haven.**

MOUNTBATTEN OF BURMA, Countess (2nd in line) *cr* 1947; **Patricia Edwina Victoria Knatchbull,** CBE 1991; CD; JP; DL; Viscountess Mountbatten of Burma, 1946; Baroness Romsey, 1947; Vice Lord-Lieutenant of Kent, since 1984; *b* 14 Feb. 1924; *er d* of Admiral of the Fleet 1st Earl Mountbatten of Burma, KG, GCB, OM, GCSI, GCIE, GCVO, DSO, PC, FRS, and Countess Mountbatten of Burma, CI, GBE, DCVO, LLD (*d* 1960) (Hon. Edwina Cynthia Annette Ashley, *e d* of 1st and last Baron Mount Temple, PC); *S* father, 1979; *m* 1946, Baron Brabourne, *qv*; four *s* two *d* (and one *s* decd). *Educ:* Malta, England and New York City. Served War in WRNS, 1943–46. Colonel-in-Chief, Princess Patricia's Canadian Light Infantry. Vice-Pres., BRCS; Dep. Vice-Chm., NSPCC; Chm., Sir Ernest Cassel Educational Trust. President: SOS Children's Villages (UK); Friends of Cassel Hosp.; Friends of William Harvey Hosp.; Shaftesbury Homes and Arethusa; Kent Branches of NSPCC, Save the Children Fund and Marriage Guidance Council. Vice-President: FPA; Nat. Childbirth Trust; SSAFA; RLSS; Shaftesbury Soc.; Nat. Soc. for Cancer Relief; Kent Voluntary Service Council; The Aidis Trust; RCN; Royal Nat. Coll. for Blind. Hon. President: Soc. for Nautical Research; British Maritime Charitable Foundn; Patron: Commando Assoc.; HMS Cavalier Trust; Legion of Frontiersmen of the Commonwealth; Foudroyant Trust; HMS Kelly Reunion Assoc.; Nuclear Weapons Freeze; VADs (RN); Compassionate Friends; Nurses' Welfare Trust; Vice-Patron, Burma Star Assoc. Governor: Ashford School, Kent; Caldecott Community, Kent. JP 1971 and DL 1973, Kent. DStJ 1981. *Heir: s* Lord Romsey, *qv*. *Address:* Newhouse, Mersham, Ashford, Kent TN25 6NQ. *T:* Ashford (0233) 623466; 39 Montpelier Walk, SW7 1JH. *T:* 071–589 8829.

MOUNTEVANS, 3rd Baron *cr* 1945, of Chelsea; **Edward Patrick Broke Evans;** Assistant Marketing Manager, British Tourist Authority, since 1982; *b* 1 Feb. 1943; *s* of 2nd Baron Mountevans and of Deirdre Grace, *d* of John O'Connell, Cork; *S* father, 1974; *m* 1973, Johanna Keyzer, *d* of late Antonius Franciscus Keyzer, The Hague. *Educ:* Rugby; Trinity Coll., Oxford. Reserve Army Service, 1961–66; 74 MC Regt RCT, AER; Lt 1964. Joined management of Consolidated Gold Fields Ltd, 1966; British Tourist Authority, 1972: Manager, Sweden and Finland, 1973; Head of Promotion Services, 1976. *Heir: b* Hon. Jeffrey de Corban Richard Evans [*b* 13 May 1948; *m* 1972, Hon. Juliet, *d* of Baron Moran, *qv*; two *s*]. *Address:* c/o House of Lords, SW1A 0PW.

MOUNTFIELD, Peter; Under Secretary, HM Treasury, since 1980; *b* 2 April 1935; *s* of late Alexander Stuart Mountfield and Agnes Elizabeth (*née* Gurney); *m* 1958, Evelyn Margaret Smithies; three *s*. *Educ:* Merchant Taylors' Sch., Crosby; Trinity Coll., Cambridge (BA); Graduate Sch. of Public Admin, Harvard. RN, 1953–55. Asst Principal, HM Treasury, 1958; Principal, 1963; Asst Sec., 1970; Under Sec., Cabinet Office, 1977. *Recreations:* reading, walking, looking at buildings. *Address:* HM Treasury, Parliament Street, SW1P 3AG.

See also R. Mountfield.

MOUNTFIELD, Robin, CB 1988; Deputy Secretary, Department of Trade and Industry, since 1984; *b* 16 Oct. 1939; *s* of late Alexander Stuart Mountfield and Agnes Elizabeth (*née* Gurney); *m* 1963, Anne Newsham; three *c*. *Educ:* Merchant Taylors' Sch., Crosby; Magdalen Coll., Oxford (BA). Assistant Principal, Ministry of Power, 1961, Principal, 1965; Private Sec. to Minister for Industry, 1973–74; Asst Sec., Dept of Industry, 1974, seconded to Stock Exchange, 1977–78; Under Sec., DoI, later, DTI, 1980–84. *Address:* Department of Trade and Industry, 1–19 Victoria Street, SW1H 0ET. *T:* 071–215 4211.

See also P. Mountfield.

MOUNTFORD, Arnold Robert, CBE 1984; MA; Director, City Museum and Art Gallery, Stoke-on-Trent, 1962–87, retired; *b* 14 Dec. 1922; *s* of Ernest Gerald and Dorothy Gwendoline Mountford; *m* 1943, Joan (*née* Gray); one *s*. *Educ:* Hanley High School; Univ. of Keele (MA History). Royal Artillery, seconded to Special Liaison Unit and Special Communications Unit, 1942–47; demobilized 1947 (Captain). Joined staff of City Museum and Art Gallery, Stoke-on-Trent, specializing in archaeology and ceramics, 1949. Editor, Jl of Ceramic History, 1968–83. *Publications:* The Illustrated Guide to Staffordshire Saltglazed Stoneware, 1971; various ceramic journals. *Recreations:* touring inland waterways, gardening.

MOUNTFORT, Guy Reginald, OBE 1970; retired as Director, Ogilvy & Mather International Inc., New York (1964–66); and as Managing Director, Ogilvy and Mather Ltd, London (1964–66); *b* 4 Dec. 1905; *s* of late Arnold George Mountfort, artist, and late Alice Edith (*née* Hughes); *m* 1931, Joan Hartley (*née* Pink); two *d*. *Educ:* Grammar Sch. General Motors Corporation (France), 1928–38. War service, 1939–46, 12 Regt HAC and British Army Staff (Washington) Lt-Col; service in N Africa, Italy, Burma, Pacific, Germany. Procter & Gamble Inc., USA, 1946–47; Mather & Crowther Ltd, 1947, Dir, 1949; Vice-Chm., Dollar Exports Bd Advertising Cttee, 1948–49. Hon. Sec., Brit. Ornithologists' Union, 1952–62, Pres. 1970–75 (Union Medal, 1967); Leader of scientific expedns to Coto Doñana, 1952, 1955, 1956; Bulgaria, 1960; Hungary, 1961; Jordan, 1963, 1965; Pakistan, 1966, 1967. Vice Pres., World Wildlife Fund (Gold Medal, 1978); Scientific FZS (Stamford Raffles Award, 1969). Medal of Société d'Acclimatation, 1936. Commander, Order of the Golden Ark, Netherlands, 1980. *Publications:* A Field Guide to the Birds of Europe (co-author), 1954; The Hawfinch, 1957; Portrait of a Wilderness, 1958; Portrait of a River, 1962; Portrait of a Desert, 1965; The Vanishing Jungle, 1969; Tigers, 1973; So Small a World, 1974; Back from the Brink, 1977; Saving the Tiger, 1981; Wild India, 1985; Rare Birds of the World, 1988; Memories of Three Lives, 1991; contribs to ornithological and other scientific jls; television and radio broadcasts on ornithology and exploration. *Recreations:* ornithology, gardening, photography, travel. *Address:* 8 Park Manor, St Aldhelm's Road, Poole, Dorset BH13 6BS.

MOUNTGARRET, 17th Viscount (Ireland) *cr* 1550; Baron (UK) *cr* 1911; **Richard Henry Piers Butler;** *b* 8 Nov. 1936; *s* of 16th Viscount; *S* father, 1966; *heir-pres.* to earldoms of Marquess of Ormonde, *qv*; *m* 1st, 1960, Gillian Margaret (marr. diss. 1970), *o d* of Cyril Francis Stuart Buckley, London, SW3; two *s* one *d*; 2nd, 1970, Mrs Jennifer Susan Melville Fattorini (marr. diss. 1983), *yr d* of Captain D. M. Wills, Barley Wood, Wrington, near Bristol; 3rd 1983, Mrs Angela Ruth Waddington, *e d* of T. G. Porter, The Croft, Church Fenton, Tadcaster. *Educ:* Eton; RMA, Sandhurst. Commissioned, Irish Guards, 1957; retd rank Capt., 1964. Pres., Yorks CCC, 1984–90. *Recreations:* shooting, stalking, cricket, golf. *Heir: s* Hon Piers James Richard Butler, *b* 15 April 1961. *Address:* Stainley House, South Stainley, Harrogate, Yorks. *T:* Harrogate (0423) 770087; 15 Queensgate Place, SW7. *T:* 071–584 6998. *Clubs:* White's, Pratt's.

MOUNTSTUART, Lord; John Bryson Crichton-Stuart; *b* 21 Dec. 1989; *s* and *heir* of Earl of Dumfries, *qv*.

MOURANT, Arthur Ernest, DM, FRCP; FRS 1966; formerly Director, Serological Population Genetics Laboratory; Conseiller Scientifique Etranger, Institut d'Hématologie, Immunologie et Génétique Humaine, Toulouse, since 1974; *b* 11 April 1904; *er s* of Ernest Charles Mourant and Emily Gertrude (*née* Bray); *m* 1978, Mrs Jean E. C. Shimell. *Educ:* Victoria Coll., Jersey; Exeter Coll., Oxford; St Bartholomew's Hosp. Medical Coll. London. BA 1925, DPhil (Geol.) 1931, MA 1931, BM, BCh 1943, DM 1948, Oxford; FRCP 1960; FRCPath 1963. 1st cl. hons Chem., 1926; Sen. King Charles I Schol., Exeter Coll., Oxford, 1926; Burdett-Coutts Schol., Oxford Univ., 1926. Demonstrator in Geology, Univ. of Leeds, 1928–29; Geol Survey of Gt Brit., 1929–31; teaching posts, 1931–34; Dir, Jersey Pathological Lab., 1935–38; Med. Student, 1939–43; House med.

appts, 1943–44; Med. Off., Nat. Blood Transfusion Service, 1944–45; Med. Off., Galton Lab. Serum Unit, Cambridge, 1945–46; Dir, Blood Gp Reference Lab., Min. of Health and MRC, 1946–65 (Internat. Blood Gp Reference Lab., WHO, 1952–65); Hon. Adviser, Nuffield Blood Gp Centre, 1952–65; Hon. Sen. Lectr in Haematology, St Bartholomew's Hospital Medical Coll., 1965–77. Visiting Professor: Columbia Univ., 1953; Collège de France, 1978–79. Marett Meml Lectr, Exeter Coll., Oxford, 1978. Pres., Section H (Anthropology), Brit. Assoc., 1956; Vice-Pres., Mineralogical Soc., 1971–73; Mem. Hon., Société Jersiaise (Vice-Pres., 1977–80, 1984–87); Corresp. Mem., Académie des Sciences, Inscriptions et Belles-Lettres, Toulouse; Honorary Member: Internat. Soc. of Blood Transfusion; British Soc. for Haematology; Peruvian Pathological Soc.; Soc. for Study of Human Biol. (Vice-Pres., 1960–63); Human Biology Council, 1987. Past or present Mem. Ed. Bd of eight British, foreign and internat. scientific jls. His bronze bust by John Doubleday, 1990, Jersey Mus. Hon. Citizen, Toulouse, 1985. Oliver Meml Award, 1953; Huxley Memorial Medal, Royal Anthropological Institute, 1961; Landsteiner Meml Award, Amer. Assoc. of Blood Banks, 1973; Osler Meml Medal, Univ. of Oxford, 1980; R. H. Worth Prize, Geolog. Soc., 1982. *Publications:* The Distribution of the Human Blood Groups, 1954, (jtly) 2nd edn, 1976; (jtly) The ABO Blood Groups: Comprehensive Tables and Maps of World Distribution, 1958; (ed jtly) Man and Cattle, 1963; (jtly) Blood Groups and Diseases, 1978; (jtly) The Genetics of the Jews, 1978; Blood Relations, 1983; numerous papers in scientific jls on blood groups and other biol subjects, geology and archæology. *Recreations:* photography, geology, archæology, travel, reading in sciences other than own, alpine gardening. *Address:* The Dower House, Maison de Haut, Longueville, St Saviour, Jersey JE2 7SP, Channel Islands. *T:* Jersey (0534) 52280.

MOVERLEY, Rt. Rev. Gerald; *see* Hallam, Bishop of, (RC).

MOWAT, David McIvor; JP; consultant, journalist and broadcaster; Director, Contact Scotland Ltd, since 1991; *b* 12 March 1939; *s* of Ian M. Mowat and Mary I. S. Steel; *m* 1964, Elinor Anne Birtwistle; three *d. Educ:* Edinburgh Academy; University of Edinburgh (MA); BA Open Univ., 1984. Chief Executive: Edinburgh Chamber of Commerce and Manufactures, 1967–90; Chamber Developments Ltd, 1971; Edinburghs Capital Ltd, 1986; Who's Who in Business in Scotland Ltd, 1989–90. Dep. Chm., Edinburgh Tourist Gp, 1985–90. Pres., British Chambers of Commerce Execs, 1987–89. JP Edinburgh, 1969. FRSA. *Address:* 37 Orchard Road South, Edinburgh EH4 3JA. *T:* 031–332 6865.

MOWAT, John Stuart; QC (Scot.) 1988; Sheriff Principal of South Strathclyde, Dumfries and Galloway, since 1988; *b* 30 Jan. 1923; *s* of George Mowat and Annie Barlow; *m* 1956, Anne Cameron Renfrew; two *s* two *d. Educ:* Glasgow High Sch.; Belmont House; Merchiston Castle Sch.; Glasgow Univ. (MA, LLB). Served RAF Transport Comd, 1941–46; Flt-Lt 1944. Journalist, 1947–52; Advocate, 1952; Sheriff-Substitute, then Sheriff, of Fife and Kinross at Dunfermline, 1960–72; Sheriff of Fife and Kinross at Cupar and Kinross, 1972–74; Sheriff of Lanark and Glasgow, subseq. Glasgow and Strathkelvin, 1974–88. Chm., Sheriff Court Rules Council, 1989–. Contested (L) Caithness and Sutherland, 1955; Office-bearer, Scottish Liberal Party, 1954–58; Life Trustee: Carnegie Dunfermline Trust, 1967–73; Carnegie UK Trust, 1971–73. *Recreations:* golf, curling, watching football. *Address:* 31 Westbourne Gardens, Glasgow G12 9PF. *T:* 041–334 3743; Afton, Port Wemyss, Isle of Islay.

MOWBRAY (26th Baron *cr* 1283), **SEGRAVE** (27th Baron *cr* 1283), **AND STOURTON,** of Stourton, Co. Wilts (23rd Baron *cr* 1448); **Charles Edward Stourton,** CBE 1982; *b* 11 March 1923; *s* of William Marmaduke Stourton, 25th Baron Mowbray, 26th Baron Segrave and 22nd Baron Stourton, MC, and Sheila (*d* 1975), *er d* of Hon. Edward Gully, CB; *S* father, 1965; *m* 1952, Hon. Jane de Yarburgh Bateson, *o c* of 5th Baron Deramore, and of Nina Lady Deramore, OBE, *d* of Alastair Macpherson-Grant; two *s. Educ:* Ampleforth; Christ Church, Oxford. Joined Army, 1942; Commissioned Gren. Guards, 1943; served with 2nd Armd Bn Gren. Gds, as Lt, 1943–44 (wounded, France, 1944; loss of eye and invalided, 1945). Mem. of Lloyd's 1952; Mem. Securicor, 1961–64; Chm., Ghadeco (UK) Ltd, 1986–; Director: Securicor (Scotland) Ltd, 1964–70; General Development Co. Ltd (Ghana), 1980–; EIRC Ghana Ltd, 1982–; EIRC (Canada) Inc., 1983–; EIRC Hldgs Ltd (Jersey), 1986–. Mem., Nidderdale RDC, 1954–58. A Conservative Whip in House of Lords, 1967–70, 1974–78; a Lord in Waiting (Govt Whip), and spokesman for DoE, 1970–74; Dep. Chief Opposition Whip in House of Lords, 1978–79; a Lord in Waiting (Govt Whip), and spokesman for the arts, envt and transport, 1979–80. Chm., Govt Picture Buying Cttee, 1972–74; Mem., British Parly Delegn to Bicentennial Celebrations, Washington, 1976; Trustee: College of Arms Trust, 1975–; Church, Convent and Hosp., St John and St Elizabeth. Chancellor, Primrose League, 1974–80, 1981–83. Life Governor, Imperial Cancer Res. Fund, 1983–. Hon. Pres., Safety Glazing Assoc., 1975–78. Bicentennial Year Award of Baronial Order of Magna Charta, USA, 1976. Kt of Hon. and Devotion, SMO Malta, 1947; Kt Gr. Cross, Mil. Order of St Lazarus, 1970; Bailiff, Grand Cross of Justice, Constantinian Order of St George (Italy), 1985. *Recreations:* reading, shooting, gardening. *Heir: s* Hon. Edward William Stephen Stourton [*b* 17 April 1953; *m* 1980, Penelope, *e d* of Dr Peter Brunet; four *d*]. *Address:* Marcus, by Forfar, Angus DD8 3QH. *T:* Finavon (030785) 219; 23 Warwick Square, SW1V 2AB. *Clubs:* Turf, White's, Pratt's, Beefsteak, Pilgrims, Roxburghe.

See also F. P. Crowder, Hon. J. J. Stourton.

MOWBRAY, Sir John, Kt 1983; Chairman, Wellington Diocesan Board of Trustees (Anglican), since 1970; *b* 23 Sept. 1916; *s* of Harry Logan Campbell Mowbray and Therese Josephine Mowbray; *m* 1946, Audrey Burt Steel; two *s* one *d. Educ:* King's Coll., Auckland; Auckland University Coll. BCom, Dip. in Banking, Univ. of NZ; FCA NZ 1973. Served War, 2nd NZ Div. Field Artillery, ME, 1940–46 (Lieut). Joined staff of The National Bank of New Zealand, 1934; Gen. Man.'s Asst, 1957; Asst Gen. Man., 1961; Gen. Man. and Chief Exec., 1966–76. Chairman: Develt Finance Corp. of NZ, 1976–85; GEC New Zealand Ltd, 1976–86; Motor Hlldgs Ltd, 1980–84; DIC Ltd, 1982–86. Chairman: NZ Bankers' Assoc., 1966, 1972 and 1975; Higher Salaries Cttee in the State Services, 1972–78; Bd of Trustees, NZ Inst. of Econ. Res., 1978–; Asean NZ Business Council, 1984–88; NZ Technol. Advancement Trust, 1984–; Japan/NZ Business Council, 1974–78; NZ Cttee, Pacific Basin Econ. Council, 1972–74. Life Member: NZ Admin. Staff Coll. (formerly Chm.); Arthritis and Rheumatism Foundn of NZ. FNZIM 1974; Hon. Fellow, NZ Inst. of Bankers, 1975; FRSA 1970. A Lay Canon, Wellington Cathedral, 1985–. *Recreations:* golf, bridge, gardening. *Address:* 167 Karori Road, Karori, Wellington 5, New Zealand. *T:* 766–334. *Clubs:* Wellington, United Services Officers (Wellington); Northern (Auckland); Wellington Golf.

MOWBRAY, Sir John Robert, 6th Bt *cr* 1880; *b* 1 March 1932; *s* of Sir George Robert Mowbray, 5th Bt, KBE, and of Diana Margaret, *d* of Sir Robert Heywood Hughes, 12th Bt; *S* father, 1969; *m* 1957, Lavinia Mary, *d* of late Lt-Col Francis Edgar Hugonin, OBE, Stainton House, Stainton in Cleveland, Yorks; three *d. Educ:* Eton; New College, Oxford. *Address:* The Hill House, Duffs Hill, Glemsford, Suffolk CO10 7PP. *T:* Glemsford (0787) 281930.

MOWBRAY, William John, QC 1974; *b* 3 Sept. 1928; *s* of James Nathan Mowbray, sugar manufr and E. Ethel Mowbray; *m* 1960, Shirley Mary Neilan; one *s* three *d. Educ:* Upper Canada Coll.; Mill Hill Sch.; New Coll., Oxford. BA 1952. Called to Bar, Lincoln's Inn, 1953 (Bencher, 1983); called to Bahamian Bar, 1971. Chairman: Chancery Bar Assoc., 1985–; Westminster Assoc. for Mental Health, 1981–; Westminster Christian Council, 1986–87 (Vice-Chm., 1984–85). *Publications:* Lewin on Trusts, 16th edn, 1964; Estate Duty on Settled Property, 1969; articles in jls. *Recreations:* music, observing nature in Sussex garden. *Address:* 12 New Square, Lincoln's Inn, WC2A 3SW. *T:* 071–405 3808/9, 071–405 0988/9. *Club:* Travellers'.

MOWER, Brian Leonard; Head of News Department, Foreign and Commonwealth Office, since 1990; *b* 24 Aug. 1934; *s* of Samuel William and Nellie Elizabeth Rachel Mower; *m* 1960, Margaret Ann Wildman; one *s* one *d. Educ:* Hemel Hempstead Grammar Sch. Royal Air Force, 1954–56. Executive, Service Advertising Co., 1956–66; entered Civil Service, Sen. Information Officer, HM Treasury, 1966; Principal Information Officer, Central Statistical Office, 1969; Dep. Head of Information, HM Treasury, 1978; Head of Information, Dept of Employment, 1980; Dep. Press Sec. to Prime Minister, 1982; Dir of Information, Home Office, 1982. *Recreations:* bridge, walking. *Address:* 34 Wrensfield, Hemel Hempstead, Herts HP1 1RP. *T:* Hemel Hempstead (0442) 52277. *Club:* Reform.

MOWL, Colin John; Grade 3, and Head, Economic Analysis and Forecasting Group, HM Treasury, since 1990; *b* 19 Oct. 1947; *s* of Arthur Sidney and Ada Mowl; *m* 1980, Kathleen Patricia Gallagher; one *s* one *d. Educ:* Lawrence Sheriff Sch., Rugby; LSE (BSc Econs, MSc). Econ. Asst, MoT, 1970–72; Sen. Econ. Asst, Econ. Advr, HM Treasury, 1972–83; Res. Manager, Forex Research Ltd, 1983; Sen. Econ. Advr, HM Treasury, 1983–90. *Publications:* various Treasury working papers. *Recreations:* family, home, sport. *Address:* HM Treasury, Parliament Street, SW1P 3AG. *T:* 071–270 4459.

MOWLAM, Dr Marjorie; MP (Lab) Redcar, since 1987; *b* 18 Sept. 1949. *Educ:* Coundon Court Comprehensive Sch., Coventry; Durham Univ. (BA Social Anthrop. 1971); Iowa Univ. (MA; PhD 1978). Lecturer: Florida State Univ., 1977–78; Newcastle upon Tyne Univ., 1979–83; Administrator, Northern Coll., Barnsley, 1984–87. Opposition frontbench spokesman on NI, 1988–89, on city and corporate affairs, 1989–. Has held various Labour Party offices at constituency and dist levels. *Publications:* (ed jtly) Debate on Disarmament, 1982; (contrib.) Over Our Dead Bodies, ed D. Thompson, 1983. *Recreations:* travelling, swimming, jigsaws. *Address:* House of Commons, SW1A 0AA. *T:* 071–219 5066; Redcar (0642) 490404.

MOWLL, Christopher Martyn; Clerk to The Clothworkers' Company of the City of London and Secretary to The Clothworkers' Foundation, since 1978; *b* 14 Aug. 1932; *s* of late Christopher Kilvinton Mowll and Doris Ellen (*née* Hutchinson) *m* 1958, Margaret Frances (*née* Laird); four *s. Educ:* Epsom Coll.; Gonville and Caius Coll., Cambridge (MA). Admitted Solicitor, 1956. Member: Council, National Library for the Blind, 1964–79; Council, Metropolitan Society for the Blind, 1964– (Treas., 1965–79; Vice-Chm., 1971–79; Chm., 1979–); Exec. Council, RNIB, 1982–; Britain-Australia Bicentennial Cttee, 1984–88; Exec. Cttee, Assoc. of Charitable Foundns, 1989–. *Address:* Clothworkers' Hall, Dunster Court, Mincing Lane, EC3R 7AH. *T:* 071–623 7041.

MOXON, Prof. (Edward) Richard; Professor and Head of the Department of Paediatrics, University of Oxford, since 1984; *b* 16 July 1941; *s* of late Gerald Richard Moxon and of Margaret Forster Mohun; *m* 1973, Marianne Graham; two *s* one *d. Educ:* Shrewsbury Sch.; St John's Coll., Cambridge (BA 1963; MB, BChir 1966). MA Oxon 1984. FRCP 1984 (MRCP 1968). House Physician, Peace Meml Hosp., Watford, 1966; Sen. House Officer and Res. Pathologist, St Thomas' Hosp., 1967; Sen. House Officer in Paediatrics: Whittington Hosp., 1968; Hosp. for Sick Children, Gt Ormond St, 1969; Children's Hosp. Medical Center, Boston, Mass, USA: Asst Resident in Pediatrics, 1970; Res. Fellow in Infectious Diseases Div., 1971–74; Johns Hopkins Hosp., Baltimore, Md, USA: Asst Prof. in Paediatrics, 1974–80; Associate Prof. in Paediatrics, 1980–84; Chief, Eudowood Div. of Paediatric Infectious Diseases, 1982–84. *Publications:* contribs to: Barnett's Textbook of Paediatrics; Mandell's Principles and Practice of Infectious Diseases, 2nd edn, 1985; Sande's Bacterial Meningitis, 1985; Pathogenesis of Bacterial Infection, Bayer Symposium VIII, 1985; Lark's Protein-Carbohydrate Interactions in Biological Systems, 1986; McKhann's Diseases of the Nervous System, part II, 1986; Baron's Medical Microbiology, 2nd edn, 1986; Beecham Colloquia, Bacterial Meningitis, 1987; Cole's The Pathogenicity of Haemophilus, 1987; Kennedy's Infections of the Nervous System, 1987; Jann's Bacterial Capsules and Adhesins, 1988; articles in Jl of Infectious Diseases, Infection and Immunity, Jl of Clinical Investigation, Proc. National Acad. of Sciences, Cell, Lancet, Archives of Diseases in Childhood, Vaccine, Jl Bacteriology, Jl Gen. Microbiology, Microbial Pathogenesis, Jl Pediatrics, New England Jl of Medicine. *Recreations:* squash, tennis, music, literature. *Address:* 17 Moreton Road, Oxford OX2 7AX. *T:* Oxford (0865) 515344.

MOXON, Rev. Canon Michael Anthony; Canon, St George's Chapel, Windsor and Chaplain to Windsor Great Park, since 1990; Chaplain to the Queen, since 1986; *b* 23 Jan. 1942; *s* of Rev. Canon Charles Moxon and Phyllis Moxon; *m* 1969, Sarah-Jane Cresswell; twin *s* one *d. Educ:* Merchant Taylors' Sch., Northwood, Mddx; Durham Univ.; Salisbury Theol Coll. BD London. Deacon, 1970; Priest, 1971; Curate, Lowestoft gp of parishes, 1970–74; Minor Canon, St Paul's Cathedral, 1974–81; Sacrist of St Paul's, 1977–81; Warden of Coll. of Minor Canons, 1979–81; Vicar of Tewkesbury with Walton Cardiff, 1981–90. Member: Gen. Synod of C of E, 1985–90; Council for the Care of Churches, 1986–. *Recreations:* music, reading, cricket. *Address:* The Chaplain's Lodge, The Great Park, Windsor, Berks SL4 2HP. *T:* Egham (0784) 432434.

MOXON BROWNE, Robert William; QC 1990; a Recorder, since 1991; *b* 26 June 1946; *s* of Kendall Edward Moxon Browne and Sheila Heron Moxon Browne; *m* 1968, Kerstin Elizabet Warne; one *s* one *d. Educ:* Gordonstoun School; University College, Oxford (BA). Called to the Bar, Gray's Inn, 1969. *Recretations:* ski-ing, archery, walking, gardening, wine. *Address:* 2 Temple Gardens, EC4Y 9AY. *T:* 071–583 6041. *Club:* Hampstead Bowmen.

MOYA, (John) Hidalgo, CBE 1966; RIBA 1956; architect; *b* Los Gatos, Calif, 5 May 1920; *s* of Hidalgo Moya; *m* 1st, 1947, Janiffer Innes Mary Hall (marr. diss. 1985); one *s* two *d*; 2nd, 1988, Jean Conder (*née* MacArthur). *Educ:* Oundle Sch.; Royal West of England Coll. of Art; AA Sch. of Architecture; AA Dip., 1943. Partner, Powell and Moya, 1946, Powell Moya and Partners, 1976–. Major works include: Churchill Gardens Flats, Westminster, 1948–62; Houses at Chichester, 1950; Toys Hill, 1954; Mayfield Sch., Putney, 1955; Plumstead Manor Sch., Woolwich, 1970; Chichester Festival Theatre, 1962; Public Swimming Baths, Putney, 1967; British Nat. Pavilion, Expo 1970, Osaka; Dining Rooms, Bath Acad. of Art, 1970, Eton Coll., 1974; Psychiatric Hosp. extensions at Fairmile, 1957 and Borocourt, 1965; Brasenose Coll., 1961 and Corpus Christi Coll., 1969, Oxford extensions; Christ Church Coll., Oxford Picture Gall. and undergraduate rooms, 1967; St. John's Coll., 1967 and Queens' Coll., 1978, Cambridge, new buildings; Wolfson Coll., Oxford, 1974; General Hosps at Swindon, Slough, High Wycombe,

Wythenshawe, Woolwich and Maidstone; new headquarters for London & Manchester Assurance Co., near Exeter, 1978; extensions for Schools for Advanced Urban Studies and of Extra Mural Studies, Univ. of Bristol, 1980; Nat. West. Bank, Shaftesbury Ave, London, 1982, labs etc and Queen's Building, RHBNC, Egham, 1986; Queen Elizabeth II Conf. Centre, Westminster, 1986. Pimlico Housing Scheme, Winning Design in Open Competition, 1946; Skylon, Festival of Britain Winning Design, 1950 (Award, 1951); Mohlg Good Design in Housing Award, 1954; RIBA Bronze Medal, 1958, 1961 (Bucks, Berks, Oxon); Civic Trust Awards (Class I and II), 1961; Architectural Design Project Award, 1965; RIBA Architectural Award, (London and SE Regions), 1967; Royal Gold Medal for Architecture, RIBA, 1974. *Address:* Point Hill South, Rye, E Sussex; Powell, Moya and Partners, Architects, 21 Upper Cheyne Row, SW3 5JW. *T:* 071–351 3882.

MOYERS, Bill D., BJ, BD; journalist; Executive Editor, Public Affairs Television Inc., since 1987; *b* 5 June 1934; *s* of John Henry Moyers and Ruby Moyers (*née* Johnson); *m* 1954, Judith Suzanne Davidson; two *s* one *d*. *Educ:* High Sch., Marshall, Texas; Univ. of Texas; Univ. of Edinburgh; Southwestern Theological Seminary. BJ 1956; BD 1959. Personal Asst to Senator Lyndon B. Johnson, 1959–60; Executive Asst, 1960; US Peace Corps: Associate Dir, 1961–63; Dep. Dir, 1963. Special Asst to President Johnson, 1963–66; Press Sec., 1965–67; Publisher of Newsday, Long Island, 1967–70; Exec. Ed., Bill Moyers' Jl, Public Broadcasting Service, 1971–76, 1978–81; editor and chief reporter, CBS Reports, 1976–79; Sen. News Analyst, CBS Evening News, 1981–86. Contributing Editor, Newsweek Magazine. Eighteen Emmy Awards, incl. most outstanding broadcaster, 1974; Lowell Medal, 1975; ABA Gavel Award for distinguished service to American system of law, 1974; ABA Cert. of Merit, 1975; Awards for The Fire Next Door: Monte Carlo TV Festival Grand Prize, Jurors Prize and Nymph Award, 1977; Robert F. Kennedy Journalism Grand Prize, 1978, 1988; Christopher Award, 1978; Sidney Hillman Prize for Distinguished Service, 1978, 1981, 1987; Distinguished Urban Journalism Award, Nat. Urban Coalition, 1978; George Polk Award, 1981, 1987; Columbia—Du Pont Award, 1981, 1987, 1988; Peabody Award, 1977, 1981, annually 1986–89; Overseas Press Award, 1986. *Publications:* Listening to America, 1971; Report from Philadelphia, 1987; The Secret Government, 1988; Joseph Campbell and the Power of Myth, 1988; A World of Ideas, 1989, 1990. *Address:* 356 W 58th, New York, NY 10019, USA.

MOYES, Lt-Comdr Kenneth Jack, MBE (mil.) 1960; RN retd; Under-Secretary, Department of Health and Social Security, 1975–78; *b* 13 June 1918; *s* of Charles Wilfrid and Daisy Hilda Moyes; *m* 1943, Norma Ellen Outred Hillier; one *s* two *d*. *Educ:* Portsmouth Northern Grammar Sch. FCIS. Royal Navy, 1939–63. Principal, Dept of Health and Social Security, 1963; Asst Secretary, 1970. *Recreations:* gardening, tennis, squash, bridge. *Address:* Garden House, Darwin Road, Birchington, Kent CT7 9JL. *T:* Thanet (0843) 42015.

MOYLAN, His Honour (John) David (FitzGerald); a Circuit Judge (formerly Judge of the County Courts), 1967–88; *b* 8 Oct. 1915; *s* of late Sir John FitzGerald Moylan, CB, CBE, and late Lady Moylan (*née* FitzGerald); *m* 1946, Jean, *d* of late F. C. Marno-Edwards, Lavenham, Suffolk; one *s* two *d*. *Educ:* Charterhouse; Christ Church, Oxford. Served War of 1939–45, with Royal Marines. Inner Temple, 1946; practised on the Western Circuit. *Recreations:* travel and music. *Address:* Ufford Hall, Fressingfield, Diss, Norfolk IP21 5TA.

MOYLE, Rt. Hon. Roland (Dunstan); PC 1978; barrister-at-law; Deputy Chairman, Police Complaints Authority, 1985–91; *b* 12 March 1928; *s* of late Baron Moyle, CBE; *m* 1956, Shelagh Patricia Hogan; one *s* one *d*. *Educ:* Infants' and Jun. Elem. Schs, Bexleyheath, Kent; County Sch., Llanidloes, Mont.; UCW Aberystwyth (LLB); Trinity Hall, Cambridge (MA, LLM). Called to the Bar, Gray's Inn, 1954. Commnd in Royal Welch Fusiliers, 1949–51. Legal Dept, Wales Gas Bd, 1953–56; Industrial Relations Executive with Gas Industry, 1956–62, and Electricity Supply Industry, 1962–66. MP (Lab) Lewisham N, 1966–74, Lewisham E, 1974–83; PPS to Chief Secretary to the Treasury, 1966–69, to Home Secretary, 1969–70; opposition spokesman on higher educn and science, 1972–74; Parly Sec., MAFF, 1974; Min. of State, NI Dept, 1974–76; Min. of State for the Health Service, 1976–79; opposition spokesman on health, 1979–80; deputy foreign affairs spokesman, 1980–83; opposition spokesman on defence and disarmament, 1983. Mem., Select Cttee on Race Relations and Immigration, 1968–72; Vice-Chm., PLP Defence Group, 1968–72; Sec., 1971–74, Mem. Exec. Cttee, 1968–83, British Amer. Parly Gp. *Recreation:* pottering. *Address:* 19 Montpelier Row, Blackheath, SE3 0RL.

MOYNE, 2nd Baron, *cr* 1932, of Bury St Edmunds; **Bryan Walter Guinness**, MA; FRSL; poet and novelist; Vice-Chairman of Arthur Guinness, Son and Co., 1949–79, retired (Director, 1934–79); Trustee: Iveagh (Housing) Trust, Dublin; Guinness (Housing) Trust, London; Barrister-at-Law; *b* 27 Oct. 1905; *e s* of 1st Baron Moyne (3rd *s* of 1st Earl of Iveagh) and Lady Evelyn Erskine (*d* 1939), 3rd *d* of 14th Earl of Buchan; *S* father 1944; *m* 1st, 1929, Diana Freeman-Mitford (marr. diss. 1934); two *s*; 2nd, 1936, Elisabeth Nelson; three *s* five *d* (and one *s* decd). *Educ:* Eton; Christ Church, Oxford. Called to Bar, 1930. Capt., Royal Sussex Regiment, 1943. A Governor National Gallery of Ireland, 1955; Mem., Irish Acad. of Letters, 1968. Hon. FTCD 1979. Hon. LLD: TCD, 1958; NUI, 1961. *Publications:* (as Bryan Guinness): 23 Poems, 1931; Singing out of Tune, 1933; Landscape with Figures, 1934; Under the Eyelid, 1935; Johnny and Jemima, 1936; A Week by the Sea, 1936; Lady Crushwell's Companion, 1938; The Children in the Desert, 1947; Reflexions, 1947; The Animals' Breakfast, 1950; Story of a Nutcracker, 1953; Collected Poems, 1956; A Fugue of Cinderellas, 1956; Catriona and the Grasshopper, 1957; Priscilla and the Prawn, 1960; Leo and Rosabelle, 1961; The Giant's Eye, 1964; The Rose in the Tree, 1964; The Girl with the Flower, 1966; The Engagement, 1969; The Clock, 1973; Dairy Not Kept, 1975; Hellenic Flirtation, 1978; Potpourri from the Thirties, 1982; Personal Patchwork, 1986; *plays:* The Fragrant Concubine, 1938; A Riverside Charade, 1954. *Recreation:* travelling. *Heir:* *s* Hon. Jonathan Bryan Guinness, *qv*. *Address:* Biddesden House, Andover, Hants SP11 9DN. *T:* Andover (0264) 790237; Knockmaroon, Castleknock, Co. Dublin. *Clubs:* Athenæum, Carlton; Kildare Street and University (Dublin).

See also Hon. D. W. Guinness.

MOYNIHAN, family name of **Baron Moynihan.**

MOYNIHAN, 3rd Baron, *cr* 1929; **Antony Patrick Andrew Cairnes Berkeley Moynihan;** Bt 1922; *b* 2 Feb. 1936; *s* of 2nd Baron Moynihan, OBE, TD, and Ierne Helen Candy (*d* 1991); *S* father, 1965; *m* 1st, 1955, Ann Herbert (marr. diss., 1958); 2nd, 1958, Shirin Roshan Berry (marr. diss., 1967); one *d*; 3rd, 1968, Luthgarda Maria Fernandez (marr. diss. 1979); three *d*; 4th, Editha; one *s* decd; 5th, Jinna (*née* Sabiaga); one *s*. *Educ:* Stowe. Late 2nd Lt Coldstream Guards. *Recreation:* dog breeding. *Heir:* *s* Hon. Daniel Antony Patrick Berkeley Moynihan, *b* 12 Jan. 1991.

See also Hon. C. B. Moynihan.

MOYNIHAN, Hon. Colin Berkeley; MP (C) Lewisham East, since 1983; Parliamentary Under Secretary of State, Department of Energy, since 1990; *b* 13 Sept. 1955; *s* of 2nd Baron Moynihan, OBE, TD, and of June Elizabeth (who *m* 1965, N. B. Hayman), *d* of Arthur Stanley Hopkins. *Educ:* Monmouth Sch. (Music Scholar); University Coll., Oxford (BA PPE 1977, MA 1982). Pres., Oxford Union Soc., 1976. Personal Asst to Chm., Tate & Lyle Ltd, 1978–80; Manager, Tate & Lyle Agribusiness, resp. for marketing strategy and develt finance, 1980–82; Chief Exec., 1982–83, Chm., 1983–87, Ridgways Tea and Coffee Merchants; external consultant, Tate & Lyle PLC, 1983–87. Political Asst to the Foreign Sec., 1983; PPS to Minister of Health, 1985, to Paymaster General, 1985–87; Parly Under Sec. of State (Minister for Sport), DoE, 1987–90. Chm., All-Party Parly Gp on Afghanistan, 1986; Vice Chm., Cons. Food and Drinks Sub-Cttee, 1983–85; Sec. Cons. Foreign and Commonwealth Affairs Cttee, 1983–85. Member: Paddington Conservative Management Cttee, 1980–81; Bow Group, 1978– (Mem., Industry Cttee, 1978–79, 1985–87); Chm., Trade & Industry Standing Cttee, 1983–87. Hon. Sec., Friends of British Council. Patron, Land & City Families Trust. Gov., Feltonfleet Sch. Member: Sports Council, 1982–85; Major Spectator Sports Cttee, CCPR, 1979–82; CCPR Enquiry into Sponsorship of Sport, 1982–83; Steward, British Boxing Bd of Control, 1979–87; Trustee: Oxford Univ. Boat Club, 1980–84; Sports Aid Trust, 1983–87; Patron, Cambridge Univ. Women's Boat Club Assoc., 1989–; Governor, Sports Aid Foundn (London and SE), 1980–82. Oxford Double Blue, Rowing and Boxing, 1976 and 1977; World Gold Medal for Lightweight Rowing, Internat. Rowing Fedn, 1978; Olympic Silver Medal for Rowing, 1980; World Silver Medal for Rowing, 1981. Freeman, City of London, 1978; Liveryman, Worshipful Co. of Haberdashers, 1981. *Recreations:* collecting Nonesuch Books, music, sport. *Address:* House of Commons, SW1. *Clubs:* Brooks's, Commonwealth Trust (Mem. Council, 1980–82); Vincent's (Oxford).

MOYNIHAN, Senator Daniel Patrick; US Senator from New York State, since 1977; *b* Tulsa, Oklahoma, 16 March 1927; *s* of John Henry and Margaret Ann Phipps Moynihan; *m* 1955, Elizabeth Therese Brennan; two *s* one *d*. *Educ:* City Coll., NY; Tufts Univ.; Fletcher Sch. of Law and Diplomacy. MA, PhD. Gunnery Officer, US Navy, 1944–47. Dir of Public Relations, Internat. Rescue Commn, 1954; successively Asst to Sec., Asst Sec., Acting Sec., to Governor of NY State, 1955–58; Mem., NY Tenure Commn, 1959–60; Dir, NY State Govt Res. Project, Syracuse Univ., 1959–61; Special Asst to Sec. of Labor, 1961–62; Exec. Asst to Sec., 1962–63, Asst Sec. of Labor, 1963–65; Dir, Jt Center Urban Studies, MIT and Harvard Univ., 1966–69; Prof. of Govt, 1972–77 and Senior Mem., 1966–77, Harvard (Prof. of Education and Urban Politics, 1966–73). Asst to Pres. of USA for Urban Affairs, 1969–70; Counsellor to Pres. (with Cabinet rank), 1969–70; Consultant to Pres., 1971–73; US Ambassador to India, 1973–75; US Permanent Rep. to the UN and Mem. of Cabinet, 1975–76. Democratic Candidate for the Senate, NY, 1976. Mem., US delegn 26th Gen. Assembly, UN, 1971. Fellow, Amer. Acad. Arts and Scis; Member: Amer. Philosophical Soc.; AAAS (formerly Vice-Pres.); Nat. Acad. Public Admin; President's Sci. Adv. Cttee, 1971–73. Hon. Fellow, London Sch. of Economics, 1970. Holds numerous hon. degrees. Meritorius Service Award, US Dept of Labor, 1965; Internat. League for Human Rights Award, 1975; John LaFarge Award for Interracial Justice, 1980; Hubert Humphrey Award, Amer. Pol Sci. Assoc., 1983; Medallion, State Univ. of NY at Albany, 1984; Henry Medal, Smithsonian Instn, 1985; Seal Medallion, CIA, 1986; Meml Sloan-Kettering Cancer Center Medal, 1986; Britannica Award, 1986. *Publications:* (co-author) Beyond the Melting Pot, 1963; (ed) The Defenses of Freedom, 1966; (ed) On Understanding Poverty, 1969; Maximum Feasible Misunderstanding, 1969; (ed) Toward a National Urban Policy, 1970; (jt ed) On Equality of Educational Opportunity, 1972; The Politics of a Guaranteed Income, 1973; Coping: On the Practice of Government, 1974; (jt ed) Ethnicity: Theory and Experience, 1975; A Dangerous Place, 1979; Counting Our Blessings, 1980; Loyalties, 1984; Family and Nation, 1986; Came the Revolution, 1988. *Address:* United States Senate, Washington, DC 20510, USA. *Clubs:* Century, Harvard (NYC); Federal City (Washington).

MOYNIHAN, Martin John, CMG 1972; MC; HM Diplomatic Service, retired; *b* 17 Feb. 1916; *e s* of late William John Moynihan and Phebe Alexander; *m* 1946, Monica Hopwood; one *s* one *d*. *Educ:* Birkenhead Sch.; Magdalen Coll., Oxford (MA). India Office, 1939. War of 1939–45: Indian Army, 1940; QVO Corps of Guides; served with Punjab Frontier Force Regt, N-W Frontier and Burma (MC); Commonwealth Service: Delhi, Madras, Bombay and London, 1946–54; Deputy High Commissioner: Peshawar, 1954–56; Lahore, 1956–58; Kuala Lumpur, 1961–63; Port of Spain, 1964–66; HM Consul-General, Philadelphia, 1966–70; Ambassador to Liberia, 1970–73; High Comr in Lesotho, 1973–76. Administering Officer, Kennedy Meml Trust, 1977–79. Member: Council, Hakluyt Soc., 1976–81 and 1985–90; Charles Williams Soc., 1977; Pres., Lesotho Diocesan Assoc., 1976–83. Fellow: Internat. Scotist Congress, Padua, 1976; Internat. Arthurian Congress, Regensburg, 1979; inaugural session of Inklings-Gesellschaft, Aachen, 1983; Associate Mem. in S African Studies, Clare Hall, Cambridge, 1977–78. Hon. Knight Grand Band of Humane Order of African Redemption (Liberia), 1973. *Publications:* The Strangers, 1946; South of Fort Hertz, 1956; The Latin Letters of C. S. Lewis, 1987; Letters: C. S. Lewis and Don Giovanni Calabria, 1988. *Address:* 5 The Green, Wimbledon Common, SW19 5AZ. *T:* 081–946 7964. *Clubs:* Athenæum, Travellers'.

MOYNIHAN, Sir Noël (Henry), Kt 1979; MA, MB, BCh; FRCGP; Chairman, Save the Children Fund, 1977–82 (Member Council, 1972–86, Vice-Chairman, 1972–77); *b* 24 Dec. 1916; *o s* of Dr Edward B. Moynihan and Ellen (*née* Shea), Cork, Ireland; *m* 1941, Margaret Mary Lovelace, JP (*d* 1989), *d* of William John Lovelace, barrister-at-law, and Mary Lovelace, JP, Claygate, Surrey; two *s* two *d*. *Educ:* Ratcliffe; Downing Coll., Cambridge (BA English Tripos 1940, MA 1946; Pres., Downing Coll. Assoc., 1985–86; Associate Fellow, 1986–) (represented Cambridge in athletics (mile) and cross country, v Oxford, 1939, 1940); MB 1956, BChir 1955 London; MRCS, LRCP 1954, MRCGP 1965, FRCGP 1981. Cambridge Univ. Air Sqdn, 1938–39; served War, RAF, Sqdn Ldr, 1940–46 (despatches twice). Medically qual., St Thomas' Hosp., 1954; Newsholme Public Health Prize, 1954; Sutton Sams Prize (Obstet. and Gynaecol.), 1954. Upjohn Travelling Fellow, RCGP, 1967; Leverhulme Travelling Res. Fellow, 1974. Co-Founder, Med. Council on Alcoholism, 1963 (Mem. Council, 1963–79; Hon. Vice-Pres., 1972–); Mem. Bd, S London Faculty, RCGP, 1958–73; Chm., Public Relations and Fund Raising Cttee, African Med. and Res. Foundn, 1959–64; President: Harveian Soc. of London, 1967 (Mem. Council, 1963–68, 1978–79; Hon. Life Mem., 1988) Chelsea Clinical Soc., 1978 (Mem. Council, 1969–78; Hon. Life Mem., 1987); Hon. Sec., Council, 1981–82, Vice-Pres., 1982–85, Med. Soc. of London. Mem. Exec. Cttee, St Francis Leper Guild, 1964–85 (Vice-Pres., 1981). Mem. Bd, Royal Med. Benevolent Fund, 1973–77. Editor, St Thomas' Hosp. Gazette, 1952–54. Mem., Inner Temple, 1948; Yeoman, Worshipful Soc. of Apothecaries, 1956, Liveryman, 1959; Cttee of Liverymen, 1984–88; Freeman, City of London, 1959. CStJ 1971; Kt SMO Malta 1958 (Officer of Merit, 1964; Comdr of Merit, 1979); KSG 1966. *Publications:* The Light in the West, 1978; Rock Art of the Sahara, 1979; contribs to med. jls, 1953–89. *Recreations:* Save The Children Fund, rock art of the Sahara. *Address:* Herstmonceux Place, Church Road, Flowers Green, near Hailsham, East Sussex BN27 1RL. *T:* Herstmonceux (0323) 832017. *Clubs:* Brooks's, Carlton, MCC; Hawks (Cambridge), Achilles.

MOYOLA, Baron *cr* 1971 (Life Peer), of Castledawson; **James Dawson Chichester-Clark**, PC (Northern Ireland) 1966; DL; *b* 12 Feb. 1923; *s* of late Capt. J. L. C. Chichester-Clark, DSO and bar, DL, MP, and Mrs C. E. Brackenbury; *m* 1959, Moyra Maud Haughton (*née* Morris); two *d* one step *s*. *Educ:* Eton. Entered Army, 1942; 2nd Lieut

Irish Guards, Dec. 1942; wounded, Italy, 1944; ADC to Governor-General of Canada (Field-Marshal Earl Alexander of Tunis), 1947–49; attended Staff Coll., Camberley, 1956; retired as Major, 1960. MP (U), S Derry, NI Parlt, 1960–72; Asst Whip, March 1963; Chief Whip, 1963–67; Leader of the House, 1966–67; Min. of Agriculture, 1967–69; Prime Minister, 1969–71. DL Co. Derry, 1954. *Recreations:* shooting, fishing, ski-ing. *Address:* Moyola Park, Castledawson, Co. Derry, N Ireland.

See also Sir R. Chichester-Clark, P. Hobhouse.

MPUCHANE, Samuel Akuna; in business in Botswana, since 1991; *b* 15 Dec. 1943; *s* of Chiminya Thompson Mpuchane and Motshidiemang Phologolo; *m* Sisai Felicity Mokgokong; two *s* one *d.* *Educ:* Univ. of Botswana, Lesotho and Swaziland (BA Govt and Hist.); Southampton Univ. (MSc Internat. Affairs). External Affairs Officer, 1969–70; First Secretary: Botswana Mission to UN, 1970–71; Botswana Embassy, Washington, 1971–74; Under Sec., External Affairs, 1974–76; on study leave, 1976–77; Dep. Perm. Sec., Min. of Mineral Resources and Water Affairs, 1977–79; Admin. Sec., Office of Pres., 1979–80; Perm. Sec., Min. of Local Govt and Lands, 1980–81; High Comr for Botswana in UK, 1982–85; Perm. Sec. for External Affairs, 1986–90. Director, 1991–: Standard Chartered Bank (Botswana); Builders World; Building Materials Supplies; Royal Wholesalers; Parts World; Parts Distributors; Trade World; Blue Chip Investments; Continental Star Caterers. *Recreations:* playing and watching tennis, watching soccer.

MTAŴALI, Bernard Brenm; Malaŵi High Commissioner in London, 1987–90; *b* 18 Oct. 1935; *s* of Ernest Michael Mtaŵali and Rose Mtaŵali; *m* 1966, Ruth; four *s* one *d.* *Educ:* Allahabad Univ., India (BSc Agric., Dip. Agric.); Cambridge; courses with FAO in agric. planning. Agric. Extension Service, Malaŵi Govt, 1962–66; Agric. Admin. Project, Malaŵi Govt, 1966–72; Dep. Sec. and Sec., Ministry of Agric., 1972–78; Gen. Manager, Gen. Farming Co. Ltd, 1978–83; self employed in crop production and marketing, 1983–84; Admin. Sec., Tobacco Exporters Assoc. of Malaŵi, 1984–86; High Comr in Canada, 1986–87. *Recreations:* walking, jogging, swimming, reading. *Address:* c/o Malaŵi High Commission, 33 Grosvenor Street, W1X 0DE. *T:* 071–491 4172. *Clubs:* Royal Overseas League, Travellers'; Limbe Country (Malaŵi).

MTEKATEKA, Rt. Rev. Josiah; *b* 1903; *s* of Village Headman; *m* 1st, 1925, Maude Mwere Nambote (*d* 1940); one *s* four *d*; 2nd, 1944, Alice Monica Chitanda; six *s* two *d* (and five *c* decd). *Educ:* Likoma Island School; S Michael's Teachers' Training Coll., Likoma; St Andrew's Theological Coll., Likoma. Deacon, 1939; Priest, 1943. Asst Priest, Nkhotakota, Nyasaland Dio., 1943–45; Chiulu, Tanganyika, 1945–50; Priest, Mlangali, Tanganyika, Nyasaland Dio., 1950–52; Mlangali, SW Tanganyika Dio., 1952–60; rep. SW Tanganyika Dio. at UMCA Centenary Celebrations in England, 1957; Canon of SW Tanganyika Dio., 1959; Priest-in-charge, Manda, 1960–64, Njombe, 1964–65, SW Tanganyika Dio.; Archdeacon of Njombe, 1962–65; Suffragan Bishop, Nkhotakota, Dio. Malawi, 1965–71; Bishop of Lake Malaŵi, 1971–77. *Address:* Madimba 1, PO Box 5, Likoma Island, Malaŵi.

MUDD, (William) David; MP (C) Falmouth and Camborne, since 1970; *b* 2 June 1933; *o s* of Capt. W. N. Mudd and Mrs T. E. Mudd; *m*; one *s* one *d* (and one step *d*). *Educ:* Truro Cathedral Sch. Journalist, Broadcaster, TV Commentator; work on BBC and ITV (Westward Television). Editor of The Cornish Echo, 1952; Staff Reporter: Western Morning News, 1952–53 and 1959–62; Tavistock Gazette, 1963. Mem., Tavistock UDC, 1963–65. Secretary: Conservative West Country Cttee, 1973–76; Conservative Party Fisheries Sub-Cttee, 1974–75, 1981–82. PPS, Dept of Energy, 1979–81; Mem., Transport Select Cttee, 1982–. Patron, Court Interpreters' Assoc., Supreme Court of Hong Kong, 1979–. *Publications:* Cornishmen and True, 1971; Murder in the West Country, 1975; Facets of Crime, 1975; The Innovators, 1976; Down Along Camborne and Redruth, 1978; The Falmouth Packets, 1978; Cornish Sea Lights, 1978; Cornwall and Scilly Peculiar, 1979; About the City, 1979; Home Along Falmouth and Penryn, 1980; Around and About the Roseland, 1980; The Cruel Cornish Sea, 1981; The Cornish Edwardians, 1982; Cornwall in Uproar, 1983; Around and About ther Fal, 1989; Around and About the Smugglers' Ways, 1991. *Recreations:* jig-saw puzzles, boating, photography, ice skating, walking, cycling. *Address:* c/o House of Commons, SW1A 0AA.

MUELLER, Dame Anne Elisabeth, DCB 1988 (CB 1980); Second Permanent Secretary, HM Treasury, 1987–90; Chancellor, Leicester Polytechnic, since 1991; *b* 15 Oct. 1930; *d* of late Herbert Constantin Mueller and Phoebe Ann Beevers; *m* 1958, James Hugh Robertson (marr. diss. 1978). *Educ:* Wakefield Girls' High Sch.; Somerville Coll., Oxford (Hon. Fellow, 1984). Entered Min. of Labour and Nat. Service, 1953; served with Orgn for European Econ. Co-op., 1955–56; Treasury, 1962; Dept of Economic Affairs, 1964; Min. of Technology, 1969; DTI 1970; Under-Sec., DTI, later DoI, 1972–77; Dep. Sec., DoI, later DTI, 1977–84; Second Perm. Sec., Cabinet Office (MPO), 1984–87. Director: EIB, 1978–84; STC plc, 1990–91; CARE Britain, 1990–; Phonepoint Ltd, 1990–. Ind. Investigator, SIB, 1990–; Member: Bd, Business in the Community, 1984–88; Develt Commn, 1990–; Vice Pres., Industrial Participation Assoc., 1986–90. Member Council: Inst. of Manpower Studies, 1981–; Templeton Coll., Oxford, 1985–; Manchester Business Sch., 1985–; Queen Mary and Westfield Coll., 1990–; Trustee: Whitechapel Art Gall., 1985–; Duke of Edinburgh's Study Confs, 1986–. Gov., Leicester Polytechnic, 1988–. CBIM 1978; FRSA 1981; FIPM 1986. Hon. DLitt Warwick, 1985. *Address:* 46 Kensington Heights, Campden Hill Road, W8 7BD. *T:* 071–727 4780. *Club:* United Oxford & Cambridge University.

MUFF, family name of **Baron Calverley.**

MUGABE, Robert Gabriel; President of Zimbabwe, since 1988; President, Zimbabwe African National Union-Patriotic Front, since 1988; *b* Kutama, 1924; *m* Sarah Mugabe. *Educ:* Kutama and Empanden Mission School; Fort Hare Univ. (BA (Educ), BSc (Econ)); London Univ. (by correspondence: BSc(Econ); BEd; LLB; LLM; MSc(Econ)); Univ. of S Africa (by correspondence BAdm). Teacher, 1942–58: Kutama, Mapanzure, Shabani, Empandeni Mission, Hope Fountain Mission, Driefontein Mission, South Africa; Mbizi Govt Sch., Mambo Sch., Chalimbana Trng Coll., Zambia; St Mary's Teacher Trng Coll., Ghana. Publ. Sec. of Nat. Dem. Party, 1960–61; Publicity Sec. and acting Sec.-Gen., Zimbabwe African People's Union, 1961–62. Political detention, 1962, escaped to Tanzania, 1963; became Sec.-Gen. ZANU, Aug. 1963, but in detention in Rhodesia, 1964–74; resident in Mozambique, 1975–79. Prime Minister and Minister of Defence, 1980–87, Minister of Public Service, 1981–87, First Sec. of Politburo and Minister of Industry and Technology, 1984–87, Zimbabwe. Jt Leader (with Joshua Nkomo) of the Patriotic Front, Oct. 1976; Pres. (Co-Founder, 1963), ZANU, 1977–87. Attended Confs: Geneva Constitutional Conf. on Rhodesia, 1976; Malta Conf., 1978; London Conf., 1979. Hon. LLD Ahmadu Bello. *Address:* Office of the President, Harare, Zimbabwe.

MUGNOZZA, Carlo S.; *see* Scarascia-Mugnozza.

MUHEIM, Franz Emmanuel; Swiss Ambassador to the Court of St James's, since 1989; *b* 27 Sept. 1931; *s* of Hans Muheim and Hélène (*née* Ody); *m* 1962, Radmila Jovanovic. *Educ:* Univs of Fribourg (LèsL), Geneva and Paris (arts degree). Joined Swiss Federal Dept of Foreign Affairs, 1960; served successively in Belgrade, Rabat and London, 1961–70; Council of Europe, UN and Internat. Orgns Sect., Dept of Foreign Affairs, Berne, 1971–77; Dep. Head of Mission, Minister Plenipotentiary, Washington, 1978–81; Dep. Dir of Political Affairs and Head of Political Div. Europe and N America, with rank of Ambassador, Berne, 1982–83; Dir, Internat. Orgns, Dept of Foreign Affairs, 1984–89. Head of Swiss delegns to internat. confs, *inter alia* UNESCO, ESA, Red Cross, Non-Aligned Movement. Fellow, Center for Internat. Affairs, Harvard Univ., 1981–82. *Publication:* (ed jtly) Einblick in die Schweizerische Aussenpolitik: festschrift für Staatssekretär Raymond Probst, 1984. *Recreations:* walking, mountaineering, ski-ing, photography, music. *Address:* Swiss Embassy, 21 Bryanston Square, W1H 7FG. *T:* 071–723 0701.

MUIR, Alec Andrew, CBE 1968; QPM 1961; DL; Chief Constable of Durham Constabulary, 1967–70; *b* 21 Aug. 1909; *s* of Dr Robert Douglas Muir, MD, and Edith Muir, The Limes, New Cross, SE14; *m* 1948, Hon. Helen (who *m* 1st, 1935, Wm Farr; marr. diss., 1948), *er d* of Baron du Parcq (*d* 1949); one *s* one *d* (and one step *s* one step *d*). *Educ:* Christ's Hosp.; Wadham Coll., Oxford (MA). Receivers' Office, Metropolitan Police, 1933; Metropolitan Police Coll., 1934; Supt, 1948; Chief Constable, Durham Co. Constabulary, 1950. DL, Co. Durham, 1964. OStJ 1957. *Recreations:* cricket, bowls, squash, sailing. *Address:* 7 Newcombe Court, 300 Woodstock Road, Oxford OX2 7NR. *T:* Oxford (0865) 512518. *Clubs:* United Oxford & Cambridge University; County (Durham).

MUIR, Dr Alexander Laird, MD; FRCPE, FRCR; Postgraduate Dean of Medicine, University of Edinburgh, since 1990; Honorary Consultant Physician, Edinburgh Royal Infirmary, since 1974; Physician to the Queen in Scotland, since 1985; Honorary Physician to the Army in Scotland, since 1986; *b* 12 April 1937; *s* of Andrew Muir and Helena Bauld; *m* 1968, Berenice Barker Snelgrove, FRCR; one *s* one *d.* *Educ:* Morrisons Acad.; Fettes Coll.; Univ. of Edinburgh. MB ChB; MD 1970; FRCPE 1975 (MRCPE 1967); FRCR 1986. MO, British Antarctic Survey, 1963–65; MRC Fellow, McGill Univ., 1970–71; Consultant Physician, Manchester Royal Infirmary, 1973–74; Sen. Lectr in Medicine, 1974, Reader in Medicine, 1981–89, Univ. of Edinburgh. Canadian MRC Vis. Scientist, Univ. of British Columbia, 1982. Mem., Admin of Radioactive Substances Adv. Cttee, 1986–. Member Editorial Board: Thorax, 1981–86; British Heart Jl, 1986–. *Publications:* contribs on physiology and diseases of heart and lungs to medical books, symposia and jls. *Recreations:* gardening, reading, ski-ing, sailboarding. *Address:* 45 Cluny Drive, Edinburgh EH10 6DU. *T:* 031–447 2652. *Club:* Edinburgh University Staff (Edinburgh).

MUIR, Frank, CBE 1980; writer and broadcaster; *b* 5 Feb. 1920; *s* of Charles James Muir and Margaret Harding; *m* 1949, Polly McIrvine; one *s* one *d.* *Educ:* Chatham House, Ramsgate; Leyton County High Sch. Served RAF, 1940–46. Wrote radio comedy-series and compered TV progs, 1946. With Denis Norden, 1947–64; collaborated for 17 years writing comedy scripts, including: (for radio): Take it from Here, 1947–58; Bedtime with Braden, 1950–54; (for TV): And so to Bentley, 1956; Whack-O,! 1958–60; The Seven Faces of Jim, 1961, and other series with Jimmy Edwards; resident in TV and radio panel-games; collaborated in film scripts, television commercials, and revues (Prince of Wales, 1951; Adelphi, 1952); joint Advisors and Consultants to BBC Television Light Entertainment Dept, 1960–64; jointly received Screenwriters Guild Award for Best Contribution to Light Entertainment, 1961; together on panel-games My Word!, 1956–, and My Music, 1967–. Asst Head of BBC Light Entertainment Gp, 1964–67; Head of Entertainment, London Weekend Television, 1968–69, resigned 1969, and reverted to being self-unemployed; resumed TV series Call My Bluff, 1970; began radio series Frank Muir Goes Into . . ., 1971; The Frank Muir Version, 1976. Pres., Johnson Soc., Lichfield, 1975–76. Rector, Univ. of St Andrews, 1977–79. (With Simon Brett) Writers' Guild Award for Best Radio Feature Script, 1973; (with Denis Norden) Variety Club of GB Award for Best Radio Personality of 1977; Radio Personality of the Year, Radio Industries Club, 1977; Sony Gold Award, 1983. Hon. LLD St Andrews, 1978; Hon. DLitt Kent, 1982. *Publications:* (with Patrick Campbell) Call My Bluff, 1972; (with Denis Norden) You Can't Have Your Kayak and Heat It, 1973; (with Denis Norden) Upon My Word!, 1974; Christmas Customs and Traditions, 1975; The Frank Muir Book: an irreverant companion to social history, 1976; What-a-Mess, 1977; (with Denis Norden) Take My Word for It, 1978; (with Simon Brett) Frank Muir Goes Into . . ., 1978; What-a-Mess the Good, 1978; (with Denis Norden) The Glums, 1979; (with Simon Brett) The Second Frank Muir Goes Into . . ., 1979; Prince What-a-Mess, 1979; Super What-a-Mess, 1980; (with Simon Brett) The Third Frank Muir Goes Into . . ., 1980; (with Simon Brett) Frank Muir on Children, 1980; (with Denis Norden) Oh, My Word!, 1980; What-a-Mess and the Cat-Next-Door, 1981; (with Simon Brett) The Fourth Frank Muir Goes Into . . ., 1981; (with Polly Muir) The Big Dipper, 1981; A Book at Bathtime, 1982; What-a-Mess in Spring, What-a-Mess in Summer, What-a-Mess in Autumn, What-a-Mess in Winter, 1982; (with Simon Brett) The Book of Comedy Sketches, 1982; What-a-Mess at the Seaside, 1983; (with Denis Norden) The Complete and Utter "My Word!" Collection, 1983; What-a-Mess goes to School, 1984; What-a-Mess has Breakfast, 1986; What-a-Mess has Lunch, 1986; What-a-Mess has Tea, 1986; What-a-Mess has Supper, 1986; What-a-Mess goes on Television, 1989; (with Denis Norden) You Have "My Word", 1989; The Oxford Book of Humorous Prose: from William Caxton to P. G. Wodehouse, a conducted tour, 1990; What-a-Mess and the Hairy Monster, 1990. *Recreations:* book collecting, staring silently into space. *Address:* Anners, Thorpe, Egham, Surrey TW20 8UE. *T:* Chertsey (0932) 562759. *Club:* Garrick.

MUIR, (Isabella) Helen (Mary), CBE 1981; MA, DPhil, DSc; FRS 1977; Director, Kennedy Institute of Rheumatology, London, 1977–90 (Head of Division of Biochemistry, 1966–86); *b* 20 Aug. 1920; *d* of late G. B. F. Muir, ICS, and Gwladys Muir (*née* Stack). *Educ:* Downe House, Newbury; Somerville Coll., Oxford (Hon. Fellow, 1978). MA 1944, DPhil (Oxon) 1947, DSc (Oxon) 1973. Research Fellow, Dunn's Sch. of Pathology, Oxford, 1947–48; Scientific Staff, Nat. Inst. for Med. Research, 1948–54; Empire Rheumatism Council Fellow, St Mary's Hosp., London, 1954–58; Pearl Research Fellow, St Mary's Hosp., 1959–66; Vis. Prof., Queen Elizabeth Coll., Univ. of London, 1981–85. Hon. Prof., Charing Cross and Westminster Med. Sch., 1979–. Scientific Mem. Council, Med. Research Council (first woman to serve), Oct. 1973–Sept. 1977. Mem., Connective Tissue Res. Adv. Bd, 1971–85; Governor, Strangeways Res. Lab., 1980–; Trustee, Wellcome Trust, 1982–90. Heberden Orator, London, 1976; Bunim Lectr, US Arthritis Assoc., New Orleans, 1978. Member, Editorial Board: Biochemical Jl, 1964–69; Annals of the Rheumatic Diseases, 1971–77; Connective Tissue Res., 1971–85; Jl of Orthopaedic Res., 1983–. For. Mem., Royal Swedish Acad. of Scis, 1989; Honorary Member: Amer. Soc. of Biological Chemists, 1982; European Soc. of Arthrology, 1988. Hon. DSc: Edinburgh, 1982; Strathclyde, 1983; Brunel, 1990. Feldberg Foundn Award, 1977; Neil Hamilton Fairley Medal, RCP, 1981; Ciba Medal, Biochem. Soc., 1981; Steindler Award, Orthop. Soc., USA, 1982. *Publications:* many scientific papers, mainly on biochem. of connective tissues in reln to arthritis and inherited diseases in Biochem. Jl, Biochim. et Biophys. Acta, Nature, etc; contribs to several specialist books. *Recreations:* gardening, music, horses, natural history and science in general. *Address:* Department of Biochemistry, Charing Cross and Westminster Medical School, Fulham Palace Road, W6 8RF. *T:* 081–846 7053.

MUIR, Jean Elizabeth, (Mrs Harry Leuckert), CBE 1984; RDI; FCSD; Designer-Director and Co-Owner, Jean Muir Ltd, since 1967; *d* of Cyril Muir and Phyllis Coy; *m* 1955, Harry Leuckert. *Educ:* Dame Harper Sch., Bedford. Selling/sketching, Liberty & Co., 1950; Designer, Jaeger Ltd, 1956, then Jane & Jane; with Harry Leuckert as co-director, formed own company, 1966. Member: Art & Design Cttee, TEC, 1978–83; BTEC Bd for Design and Art, 1983–; Design Council, 1983–; Adv. Council, V&A Museum, 1979–83; Trustee, V&A Museum, 1984–. Awards: Dress of the Year, British Fashion Writers' Gp, 1964; Ambassador Award for Achievement, 1965; Harpers Bazaar Trophy, 1965; Maison Blanche Rex Internat. Fashion Award, New Orleans, 1967, 1968 and 1974 (also Hon. Citizen of New Orleans); Churchman's Award as Fashion Designer of the Year, 1970; Neiman Marcus Award, Dallas, Texas, 1973; British Fashion Industry Award for Services to the Industry, 1984; Hommage de la Mode, Féd. Française du Prêt-à-porter Feminin, 1985; Chartered Soc. of Designers' Medal, 1987; Textile Inst. Medal for Design, 1987; Australian Govt Bicentennial Award, 1988. Hon. DLit Newcastle, 1985; Hon. DLitt Ulster, 1987. RDI 1972; FRSA 1973; FCSD (FSIAD 1978); Hon. Dr RCA, 1981. *Address:* 59/61 Farringdon Road, EC1M 3HD. *T:* 071–831 0691.

MUIR, Sir John (Harling), 3rd Bt, *cr* 1892; TD; DL; Director, James Finlay & Co. Ltd, 1946–81 (Chairman, 1961–75); Member, Queen's Body Guard for Scotland (The Royal Company of Archers); *b* 7 Nov. 1910; *s* of James Finlay Muir (*d* 1948), Braco Castle, Perthshire, and of Charlotte Escudier, *d* of J. Harling Turner, CBE; *S* uncle 1951; *m* 1936, Elizabeth Mary, *e d* of late Frederick James Dundas, Dale Cottage, Cawthorne, near Barnsley; five *s* two *d*. *Educ:* Stowe. With James Finlay & Co. Ltd, in India, 1932–40. Served War of 1939–45: joined 3rd Carabiniers, Sept. 1940, Lieut; transferred 25th Dragoons, 1941, Capt.; Major, 1942; transferred RAC Depot, Poona, i/c Sqdn, 1942; transferred to Staff, HQ 109 L of C Area, Bangalore; held various Staff appointments terminating as AA and QMG with actg rank of Lt-Col; demobilised, 1946, with rank of Major. DL, Perthshire, 1966. *Recreations:* shooting, fishing, gardening. *Heir:* *s* Richard James Kay Muir [*b* 25 May 1939; *m* 1965, Susan Elizabeth (marr. diss.), *d* of G. A. Gardner, Leamington Spa; two *d*; *m* 1975, Lady Linda Mary Cole, *d* of 6th Earl of Enniskillen, MBE; two *d*]. *Address:* Bankhead, Blair Drummond, by Stirling, Perthshire FK9 4UX. *T:* Doune (0786) 841207. *Club:* Oriental.

See also Sir G. J. Aird, Bt.

MUIR, Prof. Kenneth, FBA 1970; King Alfred Professor of English Literature, University of Liverpool, 1951–74, now Professor Emeritus; *b* 5 May 1907; *s* of Dr R. D. Muir; *m* 1936, Mary Ewen; one *s* one *d*. *Educ:* Epsom Coll.; St Edmund Hall, Oxford (Hon. Fellow, 1987). Lectr in English, St John's Coll., York, 1930–37; Lectr in English Literature, Leeds Univ., 1937–51; Liverpool University: Public Orator, 1961–65; Dean of the Faculty of Arts, 1958–61. Visiting Professor: Univ. of Pittsburgh, 1962–63; Univ. of Connecticut, 1973; Univ. of Pennsylvania, 1977. Editor, Shakespeare Survey, 1965–80; Vice-Pres., Internat. Shakespeare Assoc., 1986– (Chm., 1974–85); Pres., English Assoc., 1987. Leeds City Councillor, 1945–47, 1950–51; Chm. of Leeds Fabian Soc., 1941–46; Pres., Leeds Labour Party, 1951; Birkenhead Borough Councillor, 1954–57. FRSL 1978. Docteur de l'Université: de Rouen, 1967; de Dijon, 1976. *Publications:* The Nettle and the Flower, 1933; Jonah in the Whale, 1935; (with Sean O'Loughlin) The Voyage to Illyria, 1937; English Poetry, 1938; Collected Poems of Sir Thomas Wyatt, 1949; Arden edn Macbeth, 1951; King Lear, 1952; Elizabethan Lyrics, 1953; (ed) Wilkins' Painful Adventures of Pericles, 1953; John Milton, 1955; The Pelican Book of English Prose I, 1956; Shakespeare's Sources, 1957; (ed with F. P. Wilson) The Life and Death of Jack Straw, 1957; (ed) John Keats, 1958; Shakespeare and the Tragic Pattern, 1959; trans. Five Plays of Jean Racine, 1960; Shakespeare as Collaborator, 1960; editor Unpublished Poems by Sir Thomas Wyatt, 1961; Last Periods, 1961; (ed) U. Ellis-Fermor's Shakespeare the Dramatist, 1961; (ed) Richard II, 1963; Life and Letters of Sir Thomas Wyatt, 1963; Shakespeare: Hamlet, 1963; (ed) Shakespeare: The Comedies, 1965; Introduction to Elizabethan Literature, 1967; (ed) Othello, 1968; (ed) The Winter's Tale, 1968; (ed with Patricia Thomson) Collected Poems of Sir Thomas Wyatt, 1969; The Comedy of Manners, 1970; (ed) The Rivals, 1970; (ed) Double Falsehood, 1970; (ed with S. Schoenbaum) A New Companion to Shakespeare Studies, 1971; Shakespeare's Tragic Sequence, 1972; Shakespeare the Professional, 1973; (ed) Essays and Studies, 1974; (ed) Three Plays of Thomas Middleton, 1975; The Singularity of Shakespeare, 1977; The Sources of Shakespeare's Plays, 1977; Shakespeare's Comic Sequence, 1979; Shakespeare's Sonnets, 1979; (trans.) Four Comedies of Calderón, 1980; (ed) U. Ellis-Fermor's Shakespeare's Drama, 1980; (ed with S. Wells) Aspects of the Problem Plays, 1982; (ed with M. Allen) Shakespeare's Plays in Quarto, 1982; (ed) Troilus and Cressida, 1982; (ed with S. Wells) Aspects of King Lear, 1982; (ed with J. Halio and D. Palmer) Shakespeare: man of the theater, 1983; Shakespeare's Didactic Art, 1984; (ed) King Lear: Critical Essays, 1984; (ed) Interpretations of Shakespeare, 1985; Shakespeare: contrasts and controversies, 1985; (trans. with A. L. Mackenzie) Three Comedies of Calderón, 1985; King Lear: a critical study, 1986; Antony and Cleopatra: a critical study, 1987; Negative Capability and the Art of the Dramatist, 1987; (trans. with A. L. Mackenzie) Calderón's La Cisma de Inglaterra, 1990. *Recreation:* theatre. *Address:* 6 Chetwynd Road, Oxton, Birkenhead, Merseyside L43 2JJ. *T:* 051–652 3301.

MUIR, Sir Laurence (Macdonald), Kt 1981; VRD 1954; company director; Deputy Chairman, Australian Science and Technology Advisory Committee, 1986–89; Founding Chairman, Canberra Development Board, 1979–86; *b* 3 March 1925; *s* of Andrew Muir and Agnes Campbell Macdonald; *m* 1948, Ruth Richardson; two *s* two *d*. *Educ:* Yallourn State Sch.; Scotch Coll., Melbourne; Univ. of Melbourne (LLB). Served RAN, 1942–46 (Lieut); Lt-Comdr, RANR, 1949–65. Admitted Barrister and Solicitor, Supreme Court of Victoria, 1950. Sharebroker, 1949–80; Mem., Stock Exchange of Melbourne, 1960–80; Partner, 1962–80, Sen. Partner, 1976–80, Potter Partners. Director: ANZ Banking Gp, 1980–; ACI Internat. Ltd (formerly ACI Ltd), 1980–88; Nat. Commercial Union Assce Co. of Aust. Ltd (formerly Commercial Union Assce Co. of Aust.), 1979–; Wormald Internat. Ltd, 1980–88; Herald and Weekly Times Ltd, 1982–87; ANZ Pensions Ltd, 1982–; Alcoa of Australia Ltd, 1982–; Hudson Conway Ltd (formerly Australian Asset Management Ltd), 1987–; Templeton Global Growth Fund, 1987–; Greening Australia; Chairman: Aust. Biomedical Corp. Ltd, 1983–87; Liquid Air Australia Ltd, 1982–; Elders Austral Chartering Pty Ltd, 1984–; University Paton Ltd, 1986–; Vic. Br., Greening Australia. Fellow: Securities Inst. of Australia, 1962; Australian Inst. of Dirs, 1967; FAIM 1965. Chm., John Curtin Sch. of Medical Res. Adv. Bd, 1982–88; Member: Parlt House Construction Authority (Chm., Artworks Adv. Cttee); Council, Gen. Motors, Aust.; L'Air Liquide World Adv. Cttee; Victoria Garden State Cttee; Vic. Appeals Cttee, Anti-Cancer Council; Consultant, Alfred Hosp. Bd, 1983–88. Patron: Baker Med. Res. Inst.; Microsurgery Foundn; Trustee and Board Member: Sir Robert Menzies Meml Trust; Earthwatch Australia; Founder and Trustee, Delta Soc. Aust.; Trustee, Aust. Scout Educn & Trng Foundn; Life Trustee, Cttee for Economic Develt of Aust. Pres., Australian Brain Foundn. Mem. Exec. Cttee, World Athletic Cup 1985; Council Mem., HRH Duke of Edinburgh's 6th Commonwealth Study Conf. (Chm., Aust. Finance Cttee). *Recreations:* gardening, fishing. *Address:* 1 Belle Avenue, Brighton, Vic 3186, Australia. *Clubs:* Melbourne, Melbourne Cricket, Lawn Tennis Association of Victoria (Melbourne).

MUIR, Richard John Sutherland; HM Diplomatic Service; Principal Finance Officer and Chief Inspector, Foreign and Commonwealth Office, since 1991; *b* 25 Aug. 1942; *s* of John Muir and Edna (*née* Hodges); *m* 1966, Caroline Simpson; one *s* one *d*. *Educ:* The Stationers' Co.'s Sch.; Univ. of Reading (BA Hons). Entered HM Diplomatic Service, 1964; FO, 1964–65; MECAS, Lebanon, 1965–67; Third, then Second Sec. (Commercial), Jedda, 1967–70; Second Sec., Tunis, 1970–72; FCO, 1972–75; First Sec., Washington, 1975–79; seconded to Dept of Energy, 1979–81; First Sec., Jedda, 1981–82; Counsellor, Jedda and Dir-Gen., British Liaison Office, Riyadh, 1983–85; FCO 1985–. *Address:* c/o Foreign and Commonwealth Office, SW1A 2AH.

MUIR, Tom; Under Secretary, External European Policy Division, Department of Trade and Industry, since 1989; *b* 15 Feb. 1936; *s* of late William and Maria Muir; *m* 1968, Brenda Dew; one *s* one *d*. *Educ:* King Edward VI Sch., Stafford; Leeds Univ. (BA Econs 1962). English Electric Co. Ltd, 1954–59; BoT, 1962–68; UK Perm. Delegn to OECD (on secondment to HM Diplomatic Service), 1968–71; DTI, 1972–75; UK Perm. Repn to EC, 1975–79 (on secondment); DoI, 1979–81; Dept of Trade, 1981–83; DTI, 1983–: Under Sec., Insce Div., 1982–87, Overseas Trade Div. 4, 1987–89. *Recreations:* walking, tennis, swimming, reading, looking at buildings and pictures. *Address:* c/o Department of Trade and Industry, 123 Victoria Street, SW1E 6RB.

MUIR BEDDALL, Hugh Richard; *see* Beddall.

MUIR MACKENZIE, Sir Alexander (Alwyne Henry Charles Brinton), 7th Bt *cr* 1805; *b* 8 Dec. 1955; *s* of Sir Robert Henry Muir Mackenzie, 6th Bt and Charmian Cecil de Vere (*d* 1962), *o d* of Col Cecil Charles Brinton; *S* father, 1970; *m* 1984, Susan Carolyn, *d* of John David Henzel Hayter; one *s* one *d*. *Educ:* Eton; Trinity Coll., Cambridge. *Heir:* *s* Archie Robert David Muir Mackenzie, *b* 17 Feb. 1989. *Address:* Buckshaw House, Holwell, near Sherborne, Dorset.

MUIR WOOD, Sir Alan (Marshall), Kt 1982; FRS 1980; FEng; FICE; Consultant, Sir William Halcrow & Partners (Partner, 1964–84, Senior Partner, 1979–84); *b* 8 Aug. 1921; *s* of Edward Stephen Wood and Dorothy (*née* Webb); *m* 1943, Winifred Leyton Lanagan; three *s*. *Educ:* Abbotsholme Sch.; Peterhouse, Cambridge Univ. (MA; Hon. Fellow 1982). FICE 1957; Fellow, Fellowship of Engrg, 1977 (a Vice-Pres., 1984–87). Engr Officer, RN, 1942–46. Asst Engr, British Rail, Southern Reg., 1946–50; Res. Asst, Docks and Inland Waterways Exec., 1950–52; Asst Engr, then Sen. Engr, Sir William Halcrow & Partners, 1952–64. Principally concerned with studies and works in fields of tunnelling, geotechnics, coastal engrg, energy, roads and railways; major projects include: (Proj. Engr) Clyde Tunnel and Potters Bar railway tunnels; (Partner) Cargo Tunnel at Heathrow Airport, and Cuilfail Tunnel, Lewes; studies and works for Channel Tunnel (intermittently from 1958); Dir, Orange-Fish Consultants, resp. for 80 km irrigation tunnel. Mem., SERC, 1981–84. Member: Adv. Council on Applied R & D, 1980–84; Governing Body, Inst. of Development Studies, 1981–87; Council, ITDG, 1981–84. Mem. Council, Royal Soc., 1983–84, a Vice-Pres., 1983–84; President: Internat. Tunnelling Assoc., 1975–77 (Hon. Life Pres., 1977); ICE, 1977–78. Fellow, Imperial Coll., 1981; Foreign Member, Royal Swedish Acad. of Engrg Sci., 1980; Hon. Fellow, Portsmouth Polytech., 1984. Hon. DSc: City, 1978; Southampton, 1986; Hon. LLD Dundee, 1985; Hon. DEng Bristol, 1991. Telford Medal, ICE, 1976; James Alfred Ewing Medal, ICE and Royal Soc., 1984. *Publications:* Coastal Hydraulics, 1969, (with C. A. Fleming) 2nd edn 1981; papers, mainly on tunnelling and coastal engrg, in Proc. ICE, and Geotechnique. *Address:* Franklands, Bere Court Road, Pangbourne, Berks RG8 8JY. *T:* Pangbourne (0734) 842833. *Club:* Athenæum.

MUIRHEAD, Sir David (Francis), KCMG 1976 (CMG 1964); CVO 1957; HM Diplomatic Service, retired; Special Representative of Secretary of State for Foreign and Commonwealth Affairs, since 1979; *b* 30 Dec. 1918; *s* of late David Muirhead, Kippen, Stirlingshire; *m* 1942, Hon. Elspeth Hope-Morley (*d* 1989), *d* of 2nd Baron Hollenden, and of Hon. Mary Gardner, *d* of 1st Baron Burghclere; two *s* one *d*. *Educ:* Cranbrook Sch. Commissioned Artists Rifles (Rifle Brigade), 1937; passed Officers Exam., RMC Sandhurst; apptd to Bedfs and Herts Regt, 1939; served War of 1939–45 in France, Belgium and SE Asia. Hon. Attaché, Brit. Embassy, Madrid, 1941. Passed Foreign Service Exam., 1946; appointed to Foreign Office, 1947; La Paz, 1948; Buenos Aires, 1949; Brussels, 1950; Foreign Office, 1953; Washington, 1955; Foreign Office, 1959; Under-Sec., Foreign Office, 1966–67; HM Ambassador: Peru, 1967–70; Portugal, 1970–74; Belgium, 1974–78. Mem. Council, St Dunstan's, 1981–89; Comr, Commonwealth War Graves Commn, 1981–86. Grand Cross, Military Order of Christ (Portugal); Grand Cross, Order of Distinguished Service (Peru). *Address:* 16 Pitt Street, W8. *T:* 071–937 2443. *Club:* Travellers'.

MUIRSHIEL, 1st Viscount, *cr* 1964, of Kilmacolm; **John Scott Maclay,** KT 1973; CH 1962; CMG 1944; PC 1952; DL; Lord-Lieutenant of Renfrewshire, 1967–80; shipowner; *b* 26 Oct. 1905; *s* of 1st Baron Maclay, PC; *m* 1930, Betty L'Estrange (*d* 1974), *d* of Major Delaval Astley, Wroxham, Norfolk. *Educ:* Winchester; Trinity Coll., Cambridge. MP (Nat. L and C) for Montrose Burghs, 1940–50, for Renfrewshire West, 1950–64. Capt., 57th Searchlight Regt RA, TA, seconded to Min. of War Transport, 1940; Mem., Brit. Merchant Shipping Mission, Washington, 1941, Head of Mission, 1944; Parliamentary Sec., Min. of Production, May-July 1945; Minister of Transport and Civil Aviation, Nov. 1951–May 1952; Minister of State for Colonial Affairs, Oct. 1956–Jan. 1957; Sec. of State for Scotland, Jan. 1957–July 1962. Pres., Assembly of WEU, 1955–56. Pres., National Liberal Council, 1957–67; Chm., Joint Exchequer Board for Northern Ireland, 1965–73. Former Director: Maclay & Macintyre; Nat. Provincial Bank; P&O Steamship Co.; Dir, Clydesdale Bank, 1970–82. Chm., Scottish Civic Trust, 1967–89; Trustee, Nat. Galls of Scotland, 1966–76. HDL Renfrewshire, 1981. Hon. LLD: Edinburgh, 1963; Strathclyde, 1966; Glasgow, 1970. *Heir:* none. *Address:* House of Lords, SW1A 0PW; Knapps Wood, Kilmacolm, Renfrewshire PA13 4NQ. *T:* Kilmacolm 2770. *Clubs:* Turf; Western (Glasgow).

MUKHERJEE, Pranab Kumar; Member, Rajya Sabha, since 1969 (Leader, 1980–88); Finance Minister, India, 1982–84; *b* 11 Dec. 1935; *s* of Kamda Kinkar Mukherjee, of an illustrious family which was involved actively in the Freedom Movement of India; *m* 1957, Suvra Mukherjee; two *s* one *d*. *Educ:* Vidyasagar Coll., Suri; Calcutta Univ. (MA (Hist. and Pol Sci.); LLB). Dep. Minister, Mins of Industrial Develt and of Shipping and Transport, 1973–74; Minister of State, Finance Min., 1974–77; Cabinet Minister i/c of Mins of Commerce, Steel and Mines, 1980–82; became youngest Minister to hold Finance Portfolio in Independent India, 1982. *Publications:* Crisis in Democracy; An Aspect of Constitutional Problems in Bengal, 1967; Mid-Term Poll, 1969. *Recreations:* music, gardening, reading. *Address:* 2 Jantar Mantar Road, New Delhi 110001, India. *T:* (home) 382875, 381328; (office) 372810.

MUKHERJEE, Tara Kumar, FLIA; Managing Director, Owl Financial Services Ltd, since 1988; President, Confederation of Indian Organisations (UK), since 1975; *b* 20 Dec. 1923; *s* of Sushil Chandra Mukherjee and Sova Moyee Mukherjee; *m* 1951, Betty Patricia Mukherjee; one *s* one *d*. *Educ:* Scottish Church Collegiate Sch., Calcutta, India; Calcutta Univ. (matriculated 1939). Shop Manager, Bata Shoe Co. Ltd, India, 1941–44; Buyer,

Brevitt Shoes, Leicester, 1951–56; Sundries Buyer, British Shoe Corp., 1956–66; Prodn Administrator, Priestley Footwear Ltd, Great Harwood, 1966–68; Head Stores Manager, Brit. Shoe Corp., 1968–70; Save & Prosper Group: Dist Manager, 1970–78; Br. Manager, 1978–84; Senior Sales Manager, 1984–85; Br. Manager, Guardian Royal Exchange PFM Ltd, 1985–88. Pres., India Film Soc., Leicester. Chairman: Charter 90 for Asians; Leicester Community Centre Project; Member: Brit. Europ. Movement, London; Exec. Council, Leics Europ. Movement; Dir, Coronary Prevention Gp, 1986–; Trustee, Haymarket Theatre, Leicester; Patron, London Community Cricket Assoc., 1987–. *Recreation:* cricket (1st Cl. cricketer; played for Bihar, Ranji Trophy, 1941; 2nd XI, Leics CCC, 1949). *Address:* Tallah, 1 Park Avenue, Hutton, Brentwood, Essex CM13 2QL. *T:* Brentwood (0277) 215438. *Club:* (Gen. Sec.) Indian National (Leicester).

MULCAHY, Geoffrey John; Chief Executive, since 1986, and Chairman, since 1990, Kingfisher (formerly Woolworth Holdings) plc (Group Managing Director, 1984–86); Chairman, F. W. Woolworth plc, since 1984; *b* 7 Feb. 1942; *s* of Maurice Frederick Mulcahy and Kathleen Love Mulcahy; *m* 1965, Valerie Elizabeth; one *s* one *d*. *Educ:* King's Sch., Worcester; Manchester Univ. (BSc); Harvard Univ. (MBA). Esso Petroleum, 1964–74; Norton Co., 1974–77; British Sugar, 1977–83; Woolworth Holdings, subseq. Kingfisher, 1983–. Director: British Telecom, 1988–; Bass, 1989–. *Recreations:* sailing, squash. *Club:* Lansdowne.

MULDOON, Rt. Hon. Sir Robert (David), GCMG 1984; CH 1977; PC 1976; MP Tamaki, since 1960; Shadow Minister of Foreign Affairs, since 1986; Prime Minister, and Minister of Finance, New Zealand, 1975–84; Leader of the National Party, 1974–84; *b* 25 Sept. 1921; *s* of James Henry and Mamie R. Muldoon; *m* 1951, Thea Dale Flyger; one *s* two *d*. *Educ:* Mt Albert Grammar School. FCANZ, CMANZ, FCIS, FCMA. Chartered Accountant. Pres., NZ Inst. of Cost Accountants, 1956. Parly Under-Sec. to Minister of Finance, 1963–66; Minister of Tourism, 1967; Minister of Finance, 1967–72; Dep. Prime Minister, Feb.–Nov. 1972; Dep. Leader, National Party and Dep. Leader of the Opposition, 1972–74; Leader of the Opposition, 1974–75 and 1984. Chm., Bd of Governors, IMF and World Bank, 1979–80; Chm., Ministerial Council, OECD, 1982. Chm., Global Econ. Action Inst., 1988–91. Pres., NZ Football Assoc., 1986–88. *Publications:* The Rise and Fall of a Young Turk, 1974; Muldoon, 1977; My Way, 1981; The New Zealand Economy: a personal view, 1985; No 38, 1986. *Recreation:* horticulture. *Address:* 7 Homewood Place, Birkenhead, Auckland 10, New Zealand.

MULDOWNEY, Dominic John; Music Director, National Theatre, since 1976; *b* 19 July 1952; *s* of William and Barbara Muldowney; *m* 1986, Diane Ellen Trevis; one *d*. *Educ:* Taunton's Grammar School, Southampton; York University. BA, BPhil. Composer in residence, Southern Arts Association, 1974–76; composer of chamber, choral, orchestral works, including work for theatre and TV; *music published:* Piano Concerto, 1983; The Duration of Exile, 1984; Saxophone Concerto, 1985; Sinfonietta, 1986; Ars Subtilior, 1987; Lonely Hearts, 1988; Violin Concerto, 1989. *Recreation:* France.

MULGRAVE, Earl of; Constantine Edmund Walter Phipps; *b* 24 Feb. 1954; *s* and *heir* of 4th Marquis of Normanby, *qv*; *m* 1990, Mrs Nicola St Aubyn, *d* of Milton Shulman, *qv* and Drusilla Beyfus, *qv*. *Educ:* Eton; Worcester Coll., Oxford. *Publications:* Careful with the Sharks, 1985; Among the Thin Ghosts, 1989. *Address:* Mulgrave Castle, Whitby, N Yorks YO21 3RJ. *Club:* Travellers'.

MULHOLLAND, family name of **Baron Dunleath.**

MULHOLLAND, Clare; Director of Programmes, Independent Television Commission, since 1991; *b* 17 June 1939; *d* of James Mulholland and Elizabeth (*née* Lochrin). *Educ:* Notre Dame High Sch., Glasgow; Univ. of Glasgow (MA Hons). Gen. trainee, then Press Officer, ICI, 1961–64; Press Officer: Granada Television, 1964–65; TWW, 1965–68; Press Officer, then Educn Officer, HTV, 1968–71; joined Independent Broadcasting Authority, later Independent Television Commission, 1971–: Reg. Exec., Bristol, 1971–77; Reg. Officer, Midlands, 1977–82; Chief Asst, Television, 1982–83; Dep. Dir of Television, 1983–91. Member: Arts Council of GB, 1986–; Scottish Film Prodn Fund, 1984–90. FRTS 1988. *Recreations:* travel, food. *Address:* c/o ITC, 70 Brompton Road, SW3 1EY. *T:* 071–584 7011.

MULHOLLAND, Major Sir Michael (Henry), 2nd Bt *cr* 1945; retired; *b* 15 Oct. 1915; *s* of Rt Hon. Sir Henry George Hill Mulholland, 1st Bt, and Sheelah (*d* 1982), *d* of Sir Douglas Brooke, 4th Bt; *S* father, 1971; *cousin* and *heir-pres.* to 4th Baron Dunleath, *qv*; *m* 1st, 1942, Rosemary Ker (marr. diss. 1948); 2nd, 1949, Elizabeth (*d* 1989), *d* of Laurence B. Hyde; one *s*. *Educ:* Eton; Pembroke College, Cambridge (BA). Regular Army Commission, 1937, Oxford and Bucks Light Infantry; retired, 1951, with rank of Major. *Heir:* *s* Brian Henry Mulholland [*b* 25 Sept. 1950; *m* 1976, Mary Joana, *y d* of Major R. J. F. Whistler; two *s* one *d*]. *Address:* Storbrooke, Massey Avenue, Belfast BT4 2JT. *T:* Belfast (0232) 63394. *Clubs:* Light Infantry (Shrewsbury); Green Jackets (Winchester).

MULKEARNS, Most Rev. Ronald Austin; see Ballarat, Bishop of, (RC).

MULKERN, John, CBE 1987; JP; FCIT; international airport and aviation consultant, since 1987; *b* 15 Jan. 1931; *s* of late Thomas Mulkern and Annie Tennant; *m* 1954, May Egerton (*née* Peters); one *s* three *d*. *Educ:* Stretford Grammar Sch. Dip. in Govt Admin. Harvard Business Sch. AMP, 1977. FCIT 1973 (Mem. Council, 1979–82). Ministries of Supply and Aviation, Civil Service, 1949–65: Exec. Officer, finally Principal, Audit, Purchasing, Finance, Personnel and Legislation branches; British Airports Authority, 1965–87: Dep. Gen. Man., Heathrow Airport, 1970–73; Dir, Gatwick Airport, 1973–77; Man. Dir and Mem. of Bd, 1977–87. Chairman: British Airports International Ltd, 1978–82; Manchester Handling Ltd, 1988–; Granik Ltd, 1990–; Board Mem., Airport Operators Council Internat., 1978–81; President: Western European Airports' Assoc., 1981–83; Internat. Civil Airports Assoc. (Europe), 1986–; Chm., Co-ordinating Council, Airports Assocs, 1982. CBIM 1981; FInstD 1982. JP Epsom, 1988. *Recreations:* family pursuits, opera, classical recorded music.

MULL, Very Rev. Gerald S.; see Stranraer-Mull.

MULLALY, Terence Frederick Stanley; art historian and critic; *b* 14 Nov. 1927; *s* of late Col B. R. Mullaly (4th *s* of Maj.-Gen. Sir Herbert Mullaly, KCMG, CB, CSI) and Eileen Dorothy (*née* Stanley); *m* 1949, Elizabeth Helen (*née* Burkitt). *Educ:* in India, England, Japan and Canada; Downing Coll., Cambridge (MA). FSA 1977; FRNS 1981. Archæological studies in Tripolitania, 1948, and Sicily, 1949; has specialised in study of Italian art, particularly Venetian and Veronese painting of 16th and 17th centuries; lecturer and broadcaster; Art Critic, Daily Telegraph, 1958–86. Pres. Brit. Section, Internat. Assoc. of Art Critics, 1967–73; Chm., British Art Medal Soc., 1986– (Vice Chm., 1982–86); Mem., Adv. Cttee: Cracow Art Festival, 1974; Palermo Art Festival, 1976; Mem. UK Delgn, Budapest Cultural Forum, 1985; Mem. Council: Attingham Summer Sch. Trust, 1984–90; Derby Porcelain Internat. Soc., 1985–; Artistic Adviser, Grand Tours, 1974–90; Director: Grand Tours, 1980–90; Specialtours, 1986. FRSA 1969; Commendatore, Order Al Merito, Italy, 1974 (Cavaliere Ufficiale, 1964); l'Ordre du Mérite Culturel, Poland, 1974; Order of Merit of Poland (Silver Medal), 1978;

Bulgarian 1300th Anniversary Medal, 1981; Sacro Militare Ordine Costantiniano di S Giorgio (Silver Medal), 1982; Premio Pietro Torta per il restauro di Venezia, 1983; Socio Straniero, Ateneo Veneto, 1986. *Publications:* Ruskin a Verona, 1966; catalogue of exhibition, Disegni veronesi del Cinquecento, 1971; contrib. to catalogue of exhibition Cinquant' anni di pittura veronese: 1580–1630, 1974; ed and contrib. to catalogue of exhibition, Modern Hungarian Medal, 1984; contrib. to Affreschi del Rinascimento a Verona: interventi di restauro, 1987; Caterina Cornaro, Queen of Cyprus, 1989; contribs on history of art, to Burlington Magazine, Master Drawings, Arte Illustrata, Antologia di Belle Arti, The Minneapolis Inst. of Arts Bulletin, Jl of British Art Medal Soc., Apollo, etc. *Recreations:* collecting and travel. *Address:* Waterside House, Pulborough, Sussex RH20 2BH. *T:* Pulborough (07982) 2104.

MULLAN, Charles Heron, CBE 1979; VRD 1950; DL; Resident Magistrate, 1960–82, retired; Lieutenant-Commander RNVR; retired, 1951; *b* 17 Feb. 1912; *s* of Frederick Heron Mullan, BA, DL, Solicitor, Newry, Co. Down, and Minnie Mullan, formerly of Stow Longa, Huntingdonshire; *m* 1940, Marcella Elizabeth Sharpe, *er d* of J. A. McCullagh, Ballycastle, Co. Antrim; one *s*. *Educ:* Castle Park, Dalkey, Co. Dublin; Rossall Sch., Fleetwood; Clare Coll., Cambridge. Hons Degree Law, Cambridge, 1934; MA 1939. Joined Ulster Div. RNVR, 1936; called up for active service with Royal Navy, Aug. 1939; served throughout the war, HMS Rodney 1939–40; destroyers and escort vessels, Channel, North Sea, North Atlantic, etc, 1940–44 (with Royal Norwegian Navy, 1941–43); King Haakon VII War Decoration 1944. MP (UU) Co. Down, 1946–50, Westminster Parlt; contested S Down, 1945, for NI Parlt. Mem. Ulster Unionist Council, 1946–60. Solicitor 1948; JP 1960; Chm., Belfast Juvenile Courts, 1964–79. Member: N Ireland Section of British Delegn to 3rd UN Congress on Prevention of Crime and Treatment of Offenders, Stockholm, 1965; initial N Ireland Legal Aid Adv. Cttee, 1967–75; Mem. Exec. Cttee, British Juvenile Courts Soc., 1973–79; Vice-Pres., NI Juvenile Courts Assoc., 1980–; NI Rep. to 9th Congress of Internat. Assoc. of Youth Magistrates, Oxford, 1974; Adviser, Internat. Assoc. of Youth Magistrates, 1974–82. Hon. Governor, South Down Hospitals Gp, 1965–73; Vice-Pres., Rossallian Club, 1974. DL Co. Down, 1974. *Recreations:* ornithology, walking, boating. *Address:* Casanbarra, Carrickmore Road, Ballycastle, Co. Antrim, Northern Ireland BT54 6QS. *T:* Ballycastle (02657) 62323.

MULLENS, Lt-Gen. Sir Anthony (Richard Guy), KCB 1989; OBE 1979 (MBE 1973); Deputy Chief of Defence Staff (Systems), Ministry of Defence, since 1989; *b* 10 May 1936; *s* of late Brig. Guy John de Wette Mullens, OBE, and of Gwendoline Joan Maclean; *m* 1964, Dawn Elizabeth Hermione Pease. *Educ:* Eton; RMA Sandhurst. Commnd 4th/7th Royal Dragoon Guards, 1956; regtl service, BAOR, 1956–58; ADC to Comdr 1st British Corps, 1958–60; Adjt 1962–65; sc 1967, psc; MA to VCGS, MoD, 1968–70; regtl service, 1970–72; Bde Major, 1972–73; Directing Staff, Staff Coll., 1973–76; CO 4/7 DG, BAOR, 1976–78; HQ BAOR, 1978–80; Comdr 7th Armd Bde, 1980–82; MoD (DMS(A)), 1982–85; Comdr 1st Armoured Div., 1985–87; ACDS (Operational Requirements), Land Systems, MoD, 1987–89. Niedersachsen Verdienstkreuz am Bande, 1982, Erste Klasse, 1987. *Recreations:* travel, riding, shooting, ski-ing. *Address:* c/o Lloyds Bank, 6 Pall Mall, SW1. *Clubs:* Cavalry and Guards, Hurlingham.

MÜLLER, Alex; see Müller, K. A.

MULLER, Franz Joseph; QC 1978; a Recorder of the Crown Court, since 1977; *b* England, 19 Nov. 1938; *yr s* of late Wilhelm Muller and Anne Maria (*née* Ravens); *m* 1985, Helena, *y d* of Mieczyslaw Bartosz; two *s*. *Educ:* Mount St Mary's Coll.; Univ. of Sheffield (LLB). Called to the Bar, Gray's Inn, 1961; called to NI Bar, 1982. Graduate Apprentice, United Steel Cos, 1960–61; Commercial Asst, Workington Iron and Steel Co. Ltd, 1961–63. Commenced practice at the Bar, 1964. Non-Executive Director: Richards of Sheffield (Holdings) PLC, 1969–77; Satinsteel Ltd, 1970–77; Joseph Rodgers and Son Ltd and Rodgers Wostenholm Ltd, 1975–77. Mem., Sen. Common Room, UC Durham, 1981. Gov., Mount St Mary's Coll., 1984–86. *Recreations:* the Georgians, fell walking, being in Greece, listening to music. *Address:* Slade Hooton Hall, Laughton en le Morthen, Yorks S31 7YQ; 11 King's Bench Walk, Temple, EC4Y 7EQ. *T:* 071–353 3337.

MÜLLER, (Karl) Alex, PhD; physicist at IBM Zurich Research Laboratory, since 1963; *b* 20 April 1927. *Educ:* Swiss Federal Institute of Technology, Zürich (PhD 1958). Battelle Inst., Geneva, 1958–63; Lectr, 1962, Titular Prof., 1970, Prof., 1987, Univ. of Zürich; joined IBM Res. Lab., Zürich, 1963; Manager, Physics Dept, 1973; IBM Fellow, 1982. Hon. degrees from eleven European and American univs. Prizes and awards include Nobel Prize for Physics (jtly), 1987. *Publications:* over 200 papers on ferroelectric and superconducting materials. *Address:* IBM Zurich Research Laboratory, Säumerstrasse 4, CH-8803 Rüschlikon, Switzerland.

MULLER, Dr Ralph Louis Junius, FIBiol; Director, International Institute of Parasitology, CAB International, since 1981; *b* 30 June 1933; *s* of Carl and Sarah Muller; *m* 1st, 1959, Gretta Shearer; one *s* one *d*; 2nd, 1979, Annie Badilla Delgado; one *s* one *d*. *Educ:* Summerhill Sch., Suffolk; London Univ. (BSc, PhD, DSc). Res. Fellow, KCL, 1958–59; ODM, 1959–61; Lectr, Univ. of Ibadan, 1961–66; Sen. Lectr, LSHTM, 1966–80. Pres., European Fedn of Parasitologists, 1988–. Editor: Advances in Parasitology; Jl of Helminthology. *Publications:* Worms and Disease, 1975, 2nd edn 1992; Onchocerciasis, 1987; Medical Parasitology, 1989. *Recreations:* beekeeping, writing instruments, sport, photography. *Address:* 22 Cranbrook Drive, St Albans, Herts AL4 0SS. *T:* St Albans (0727) 52605.

MULLER, Mrs Robert; see Whitelaw, Billie.

MULLETT, Aidan Anthony, (Tony), QPM 1982; Chief Constable, West Mercia Constabulary, since 1985; *b* 24 May 1933; *s* of Bartholomew Joseph and Mary Kate Mullett; *m* 1957, Monica Elizabeth Coney; one *s* one *d*. *Educ:* Moat Boys' Sch., Leicester. Served Royal Air Force, 1950–56; joined Leicester City Police, 1957; Leicestershire and Rutland Constabulary, 1966, Chief Superintendent, 1973; Asst Chief Constable, W Mercia Constabulary, 1975–82; Dep. Chief Constable, Dyfed Powys Police, 1982–85. Chairman: Birmingham Forensic Sci. Lab. User Bd, 1989–; Crime Cttee, ACPO (Hon. Sec., 1989); Mem., Home Office Policy Adv. Bd on Forensic Sci., 1989–91, on Forensic Pathology. *Recreations:* golf, swimming. *Address:* West Mercia Police Headquarters, Hindlip Hall, Worcester WR3 8SP. *T:* Worcester (0905) 723000.

MULLETT, Leslie Baden; consultant; Visiting Professor, University of Reading, since 1982; *b* 22 Aug. 1920; *s* of Joseph and Edith Mullett; *m* 1st, 1946, Katherine Lear (marr. diss. 1968); no *c*; 2nd, 1971, Gillian Pettit. *Educ:* Gram. Sch., Hales Owen, Worcs; Birmingham Univ. BSc (Hons Physics) 1941. Telecommunications Research Estab., 1941–46; AEA, 1946–60 (Head of Accelerator Div., 1958); Asst Dir, Rutherford High Energy Lab., SRC, 1960–68; on secondment to Res. Gp, Min. of Technology, 1966–68; CSO, Min. of Transport, 1968; CSO, Res. Requirements, DoE, 1970–74; Dep. Dir, Transport and Road Res. Lab., DoE/Dept of Transport, 1974–80. *Publications:* A Guide to Transport for Disabled People, 1982; papers in learned jls on particle accelerators and solar energy. *Recreation:* gardening. *Address:* 42 Grosvenor Avenue, Grosvenor Park, Bourne, Lincs PE10 9HU. *T:* Bourne (0778) 423054.

MULLETT, Tony; *see* Mullett, A. A.

MULLEY, family name of **Baron Mulley.**

MULLEY, Baron *cr* 1984 (Life Peer), of Manor Park in the City of Sheffield; **Frederick William Mulley;** PC 1964; barrister-at-law and economist; *b* 3 July 1918; *er s* of late William and M. A. Mulley, Leamington Spa; *m* 1948, Joan D., *d* of Alexander and Betty Phillips; two *d. Educ:* Bath Place Church of England Sch.; Warwick Sch. (Schol.); Christ Church, Oxford (Adult Scholar, 1945). 1st Class Hons Philosophy, Politics and Economics, 1947; Research Studentship, Nuffield Coll., Oxford, 1947; Fellowship (Economics), St Catharine's Coll., Cambridge, 1948–50. Called to Bar, Inner Temple, 1954. Son of general labourer; clerk, National Health Insurance Cttee, Warwicks; joined Labour Party and Nat. Union of Clerks, 1936. Served War of 1939–45, Worcs Regt; Lance-Sgt 1940 (prisoner of war in Germany, 1940–45, meanwhile obtaining BSc (Econ.) and becoming Chartered Sec.). Contested (Lab) Sutton Coldfield Division of Warwicks, 1945. MP (Lab) Sheffield, Park, 1950–83; PPS to Minister of Works, 1951; Deputy Defence Sec. and Minister for the Army, 1964–65; Minister of Aviation, Dec. 1965–Jan. 1967; Jt Minister of State, FCO (formerly FO), 1967–69; Minister for Disarmament, 1967–69; Minister of Transport, 1969–70; Minister for Transport, DoE, 1974–75; Sec. of State for Educn and Science, 1975–76; Sec. of State for Defence, 1976–79. Parly deleg. to Germany, 1951, to Kenya, 1957; deleg. to Council of Europe and WEU, 1958–61 and 1979–83; WEU Assembly: Vice-Pres., 1960 (also Vice-Pres., Econ. Cttee); Pres., 1980–83. Mem., Labour Party NEC, 1957–58, 1960–64, 1965–80; Chm., Labour Party, 1974–75. Dep. Chm., Sheffield Develt Corp., 1988–91. Director: Radio Hallam, Sheffield, 1980–90; Brassey's Defence Publications, 1983–. Chm., London Conf. for Overseas Students, 1984–87. *Publications:* The Politics of Western Defence, 1962; articles on economic, defence and socialist subjects. *Address:* House of Lords, SW1A 0PW.

MULLIGAN, Andrew Armstrong; President: Mulligan Communications Inc., since 1983; European Satellite Radio Ltd; EuroMedia Group, since 1989; *b* 4 Feb. 1936; *s* of Col Hugh Waddell Mulligan, CMG, MD, DSc and Rita Aimee Armstrong; *m* 1964, Pia Ursula Schioler; two *s* two *d. Educ:* Magdalene Coll., Cambridge (Geog. and Anthropol Tripos (Hons). Personal Asst to Man. Dir, De La Rue Co., London, 1958–60; special assignment to Australia and NZ for Irish Export Bd, 1961–62; Foreign Correspondent: Daily Telegraph and London Observer in Paris, 1962–68; Independent Television News at Ten, 1968; Producer and reporter, BBC's Panorama, 1969–73; Head of General Reports Div., EEC, Brussels, 1973–74; Dir of Press and Information, Delegn of Commn of European Communities to the US, 1975–83. Dir, American Ireland Fund (formerly Ireland Fund of the US), 1976–. Publisher, Europe magazine, 1975–82. *Publications:* Ouvert l'Après Midi, 1963; The All Blacks, 1964. *Recreations:* rugby, tennis, skiing, sailing, landscape painting. *Address:* 1855 Shepherd Street, Washington, DC 20011, USA. *Clubs:* Annabel's; Hawks (Cambridge); Kildare Street and University (Dublin); Anglo-American Press Association (Paris); National Press (Washington, DC).

MULLIGAN, Most Rev. Patrick; *b* 9 June 1912; *s* of James and Mary Martin. *Educ:* St Macartan's, Monaghan; Maynooth. Prof., St Macartan's, 1938; Bishop's Sec., 1943; Headmaster, Clones, 1948; Headmaster, St Michael's, Enniskillen, 1957; Parish Priest of Machaire Rois and Vicar General and Archdeacon, 1966; Bishop of Clogher, 1970–79. *Publications:* contribs to IER, JLAS, Seanchas Clochair. *Address:* Sacred Hearts' Home, Clones, Co. Monaghan, Ireland.

MULLIGAN, Prof. William, FRSE; Professor of Veterinary Physiology, 1963–86, and Vice-Principal, 1980–83, University of Glasgow, now Professor Emeritus; *b* 18 Nov. 1921; *s* of John Mulligan and Mary Mulligan (*née* Kelly); *m* 1948, Norah Mary Cooper one *s* two *d. Educ:* Banbridge Academy; Queen's Univ. of Belfast (BSc); PhD London. FIBiol 1988. Assistant, Dept of Chemistry, QUB, 1943–45; Demonstrator/Lectr, St Bartholomew's Med. Coll., London, 1945–51; Sen. Lectr, Veterinary Biochemistry, Univ. of Glasgow, 1951–63; McMaster Fellow, McMaster Animal Health Laboratory, Sydney, Aust., 1958–60; Dean of Faculty of Veterinary Medicine, Univ. of Glasgow, 1977–80. Dr. med. vet. *hc* Copenhagen, 1983. *Publications:* (jtly) Isotopic Tracers, 1954, 2nd edn 1959; numerous contribs to scientific jls on immunology and use of radiation and radioisotopes in animal science. *Recreations:* golf, tennis, gardening, pigeon racing, theatre. *Address:* 1 Daisy Green, Groton, near Boxford, Suffolk CO6 5EN. *T:* Boxford (0787) 210868.

MULLIN, Christopher John, (Chris); journalist and author; MP (Lab) Sunderland South, since 1987; *b* 12 Dec. 1947; *s* of Leslie and Teresa Mullin; *m* 1987, Nguyen Thi Ngoc, *d* of Nguyen Tang Minh, Kontum, Vietnam; one *d. Educ:* Univ. of Hull (LLB). Freelance journalist, travelled extensively in Indo-China and China; sub editor, BBC World Service, 1974–78; Editor, Tribune, 1982–84. Executive Member: Campaign for Labour Party Democracy, 1975–83; Labour Co-ordinating Cttee, 1978–82. Contested (Lab): Devon N, 1970; Kingston upon Thames, Feb. 1974. Editor: Arguments for Socialism, by Tony Benn, 1979; Arguments for Democracy, by Tony Benn, 1981. Chm., Britain-Vietnam Assoc., 1987–; Sec., Britain-Vietnam Br., IPU, 1988–. *Publications:* A Very British Coup (novel), 1982 (televised 1988); The Last Man Out of Saigon (novel), 1986; Error of Judgement—the truth about the Birmingham pub bombings, 1986, rev. edn 1990; The Year of the Fire Monkey (novel), 1991; pamphlets: How to Select or Reselect your MP, 1981; The Tibetans, 1981. *Address:* House of Commons, SW1A 0AA.

MULLIN, Prof. John William, DSc, PhD, FRSC, FEng, FIChemE; Ramsay Memorial Professor of Chemical Engineering, University College London, 1985–90, now Emeritus Professor; Hon. Research Fellow, University College London, since 1990; *b* Rock Ferry, Cheshire, 22 Aug. 1925; *er s* of late Frederick Mullin and Kathleen Nellie Mullin (*née* Oppy); *m* 1952, Averil Margaret Davies, Carmarthen; one *s* one *d. Educ:* Hawarden County Sch.; UCW Cardiff (Fellow, 1981); University Coll. London (Fellow, 1981). 8 yrs in organic fine chemicals industry; University College London: Lectr, 1956; Reader, 1961; Prof., 1969; Dean, Faculty of Engrg, 1975–77; Vice-Provost, 1980–86; Dean, Faculty of Engrg, London Univ., 1979–85. Vis. Prof., Univ. New Brunswick, 1967. Chm. Bd of Staff Examrs, Chem. Eng, Univ. London, 1965–70. Hon. Librarian, IChemE, 1965–77 (Mem. Council, 1973–76); Mem., Materials Sci. Working Gp, European Space Agency, 1977–81; Founder Mem., Brit. Assoc. for Crystal Growth. Member: Cttee of Management, Inst. of Child Health, 1970–83; Court of Governors, University Coll., Cardiff, 1982–; Council, Sch. of Pharmacy, Univ. of London, 1983– (Vice-Chm., 1988–). Chm., BS and ISO Cttees on industrial screens, sieves, particle sizing, etc. Moulton Medal, IChemE, 1970; Kurnakov Meml Medal, Inst. of Gen. and Inorganic Chem., USSR Acad. of Scis, 1991. Dr *hc* Inst Nat. Polytechnique de Toulouse, 1989. *Publications:* Crystallization, 1961, 2nd edn 1972; (ed) Industrial Crystallization, 1976; papers in Trans IChemE, Chem. Engrg Sci., Jl Crystal Growth, etc. *Address:* 4 Milton Road, Ickenham, Mddx UB10 8NQ. *T:* Uxbridge (0895) 634950. *Club:* Athenæum.

MULLINS, Rt. Rev. Daniel Joseph; *see* Menevia, Bishop of, (RC).

MULLINS, Edwin Brandt; author, journalist and film-maker; *b* 14 Sept. 1933; *s* of Claud and Gwendolen Mullins; *m* 1st, 1960, Gillian Brydone (*d* 1982); one *s* two *d*; 2nd, 1984, Anne Kelleher. *Educ:* Midhurst Grammar Sch.; Merton Coll., Oxford (BA Hons, MA). London Editor, Two Cities, 1957–58; Sub-editor and Art Correspondent, Illustrated London News, 1958–62; Art Critic: Sunday Telegraph, 1962–69; Telegraph Sunday Magazine, 1964–86; contributor, 1962–, to The Guardian, Financial Times, Sunday Times, Director, Apollo, Art and Artists, Studio, Radio Times, TV Times, Country Living. Regular broadcaster on radio and television; scriptwriter and presenter of numerous BBC and Channel 4 TV documentaries, incl. 100 Great Paintings, The Pilgrimage of Everyman, Gustave Courbet, Fake?, Prison, The Great Art Collection, A Love Affair with Nature, Masterworks, Paradise on Earth, Montparnasse Revisited. *Publications:* Souza, 1962; Alfred Wallis, 1967; Josef Herman, 1967; Braque, 1968; The Art of Elisabeth Frink, 1972; The Pilgrimage to Santiago, 1974; (ed) Great Paintings, 1981; (ed) The Arts of Britain, 1983; The Painted Witch, 1985; A Love Affair with Nature, 1985; *novels:* Angels on the Point of a Pin, 1979; Sirens, 1983; The Golden Bird, 1987; The Lands of the Sea, 1988. *Recreations:* everything except football. *Address:* 7 Lower Common South, SW15 1BP. *T:* 081–789 2553.

MULLINS, Leonard, CMG 1976; PhD, DSc; Director of Research, Malaysian Rubber Producers' Research Association, Brickendonbury, Hertford, 1962–83; *b* 21 May 1918; *s* of Robert and Eugenie Alice Mullins; *m* 1943, Freda Elaine Churchouse; two *d. Educ:* Eltham Coll.; University Coll., London; Inst. of Educn, London. BSc (Hons), PhD, DSc. CPhys; FInstP; FPRI. Experimental Officer, Min. of Supply, 1940–44; Scientific Officer, finally Head of Physics Gp, Research Assoc. of British Rubber Manufrs, 1944–49; Malaysian (previously British) Rubber Producers' Research Assoc., 1950–83; Foundn Lectr, Instn of Rubber Industry, 1968. Pres., Plastics and Rubber Inst., 1981–83 (Chm., 1976–77; Vice-Pres., 1977–81); Chm., Adv. Cttee, Nat. Coll. of Rubber Technology, 1976–87; Vice-Pres., Rubber and Plastics Research Assoc., 1983–. Member: Court, Cranfield Inst. of Technology; Adv. Bd, Inst. of Technol., Loughborough Univ.; Council, Rubber and Plastics Res. Assoc. Discovered Mullins Effect, relating to elastic behaviour of rubber. Moore Meml Lecture, Bradford Univ., 1982. Governor of local schools. Colwyn Medal, IRI, 1966; Médaille de la Ville de Paris, 1982; Outstanding Service Award, PRI, 1985; Charles Goodyear Medal Award, Rubber Div., American Chem. Soc., 1986; Carl Dietrich Harries Medal, Deutsche Kautschuk Ges., 1988; Eminent Citizen's Medal, Ho Chi Minh City, 1988. Comdr, Malaysian Order of Chivalry, JMN, 1975. *Publications:* numerous original scientific papers in field of rubber physics. *Address:* 32 Sherrardspark Road, Welwyn Garden City, Herts AL8 7JS. *T:* Welwyn Garden (0707) 323633. *Club:* Athenæum.

MULRONEY, Rt. Hon. (Martin) Brian, PC 1984; MP (Progressive Conservative) Charlevoix, since 1988 (Central Nova, 1983–84, Manicouagan, 1984–88); Prime Minister of Canada, since 1984; *b* 20 March 1939; *s* of Benedict Mulroney and Irene O'Shea; *m* 1973, Mila Pivnicki; three *s* one *d. Educ:* St Francis Xavier Univ. (BA); Université Laval (LLL). Partner, Ogilvy, Renault (Montreal law firm), 1965–76; Pres., Iron Ore Co. of Canada, 1976–83. Leader of the Opposition, 1983–84. Royal Comr, Cliche Commn investigating violence in Quebec construction industry, 1974. Hon. LLD: St Francis Xavier Univ., 1979; Meml Univ., 1980. *Publication:* Where I Stand, 1983. *Recreations:* tennis, swimming. *Address:* 24 Sussex Drive, Ottawa, Ont K1M 1M4, Canada. *Clubs:* Mount Royal (Montreal); Albany (Toronto); Garrison (Quebec).

MULVANEY, Prof. Derek John, CMG 1982; Professor of Prehistory, Australian National University, 1971–85, now Emeritus; *b* 26 Oct. 1925; *s* of Richard and Frances Mulvaney; *m* 1954, Jean Campbell; four *s* two *d. Educ:* Univ. of Melbourne (MA); Clare Coll., Univ. of Cambridge (BA, MA 1959, PhD 1970). FAHA 1970, FSA 1977, corr. FBA 1983. Navigator, RAAF, 1943–46 (Flying Officer); Lectr and Senior Lectr in History, Univ. of Melbourne, 1954–64; Senior Fellow, ANU, 1965–70; Vis. Prof., Cambridge, 1976–77; Chair of Australian Studies, Harvard, 1984–85; Mem. Council, Aust. Inst. of Aboriginal Studies, 1964–80 (Chm., 1982–84); Australian Heritage Commissioner, 1976–82; Mem., Cttee of Inquiry, Museums and National Collections, 1974–75; Sec., Australian Acad. of Humanities, 1989–. ANZAAS medal, 1988. *Publications:* Cricket Walkabout, 1967, 2nd edn 1987; The Prehistory of Australia, 1969, 2nd edn 1975; Australians to 1788, 1987; Encounters in Place, 1989; numerous excavation reports and historical articles. *Recreation:* gardening. *Address:* 128 Schlich Street, Yarralumla, ACT 2600, Australia. *T:* Canberra 2812352.

MUMFORD, Prof. Enid; Professor of Organizational Behaviour, Manchester Business School, 1979–88, now Emeritus; *d* of Arthur McFarland and Dorothy Evans; *m* 1947, Jim Mumford; one *s* one *d. Educ:* Wallasey High Sch.; Liverpool Univ. (BA, MA); Manchester Univ. (PhD). CIPM; FBCS. Personnel Officer, Rotol Ltd, 1946–47; Production Supervisor, J. D. Francis Ltd, 1947–48; Research Associate: Dept of Social Science, Liverpool Univ., 1948–56; Bureau of Public Health Economics, Univ. of Michigan, USA, 1956–57; Res. Lectr, Dept of Social Science, Liverpool Univ., 1957–65; Lectr, then Sen. Lectr and Reader, Manchester Business Sch., 1966–79. *Publications:* Chester Royal Infirmary 1856–1956, 1956; Living with a Computer, 1964; Computers Planning and Personnel Management, 1969; Systems Design for People, 1971; Job Satisfaction: a study of computer specialists, 1972; (with others) Coal and Conflict, 1963; (with O. Banks) The Computer and the Clerk, 1967; (with T. B. Ward) Computers: planning for people, 1968; (with E. Pettigrew) Implementing Strategic Decisions, 1975; (ed, with H. Sackman) Human Choice and Computers, 1975; (ed, with K. Legge) Designing Organizations for Efficiency and Satisfaction, 1978; (with D. Henshall) A Participative Approach to Computer Systems Design, 1978; (with M. Weir) Computer Systems in Work Design, 1979; (ed. with C. Cooper) The Quality of Working Life, 1979; (with others) The Impact of Systems Change in Organizations, 1980; Values, Technology and Work, 1980; Designing Secretaries, 1983; Designing Human Systems for New Technology, 1983; Using Computers for Business Success, 1986; (with W. B. MacDonald) XSEL's Progress, 1989; contribs to books and journals. *Address:* Manchester Business School, Booth Street West, Manchester M15 6PB. *T:* 061–273 8228.

MUMFORD, Rt. Rev. Peter; Bishop of Truro, 1981–89; *b* 14 Oct. 1922; *s* of late Peter Walter Mumford, miller, and of Kathleen Eva Mumford (*née* Walshe); *m* 1950, Lilian Jane, *d* of Captain George Henry Glover; two *s* one *d. Educ:* Sherborne School, Dorset; University Coll., Oxford; Cuddesdon Theological Coll. BA 1950, MA 1954 (Hons Theology). War Service, 1942–47, Captain, RA. Deacon, 1951; priest, 1952; Assistant Curate: St Mark, Salisbury, 1951–55; St Alban's Abbey, 1955–57; Vicar: Leagrave, Luton, 1957–63; St Andrew, Bedford, 1963–69; Rector of Crawley, Sussex, 1969–73; Canon and Prebendary of Ferring in Chichester Cathedral, 1972–73; Archdeacon of St Albans, 1973–74; Bishop Suffragan of Hertford, 1974–81. Vice Chm., Central Bd of Finance, 1984–89; Chm., Consultative Cttee, Foundation for Christian Communication, 1981–90. Pres., Royal Cornwall Agricl Assoc., 1985–86. *Address:* Greystones, Zeals, Wilts BA12 6LZ. *T:* Bourton (0747) 840392. *Club:* United Oxford & Cambridge University.

MUMFORD, William Frederick, CB 1989; government services consultant; Chairman's Panel, Civil Service Selection Board; Director, NHS Hospital Trust, South West

Bedfordshire; *b* 23 Jan. 1930; *s* of late Frederick Charles Mumford and Hester Leonora Mumford; *m* 1958, Elizabeth Marion, *d* of Nowell Hall; three *s* one *d*. *Educ:* St Albans Sch.; Lincoln Coll., Oxford (MA PPE). Nat. Service commission, Royal Artillery, 1949–50. Appointed to Home Civil Service, 1953; Asst Principal, 1953–58, Principal, 1958–60, Air Ministry; First Secretary, UK Delegn to NATO, Paris, 1960–65; Principal, 1965–67, Asst Sec., 1967–73, Defence Secretariat, MoD; Dep. Head of UK Delegn to MBFR Exploratory Talks, Vienna, 1973; Principal Private Sec. to Secretaries of State for Defence: Rt Hon. Lord Carrington, 1973–74, Rt Hon. Ian Gilmour, MP and Rt Hon. Roy Mason, MP, 1974–75; Under-Sec., Machinery of Govt Div., CSD, 1975–76; Asst Sec.-Gen. for Defence Planning and Policy, NATO, Brussels, 1976–80; Asst Under-Sec. of State (Material-Naval), MoD, 1980–84; Asst Under-Sec. of State (Estabts and Res.), MoD, 1984–90; Dep. Under-Sec. of State for Res. Estabs, MoD, 1989; retd. *Recreations:* antique book collecting, music. *Club:* Commonwealth Trust.

MUMMERY, Christopher John L.; *see* Lockhart-Mummery.

MUMMERY, Hon. Sir John Frank, Kt 1989; **Hon. Mr Justice Mummery;** a Judge of the High Court of Justice, Chancery Division, since 1989; *b* 5 Sept. 1938; *s* of Frank Stanley Mummery and Ruth Mummery (*née* Coleman) Coldred, Kent; *m* 1967, Elizabeth Anne Lamond Lackie, *d* of Dr D. G. L. Lackie and Ellen Lackie (*née* Easterbrook), Edinburgh; one *s* one *d*. *Educ:* Oakleigh House, Dover; Dover County Grammar Sch.; Pembroke Coll., Oxford, 1959–63 (MA, BCL; Winter Williams Prize in Law; Hon. Fellow, 1989). National Service, The Border Regt and RAEC, 1957–59. Called to Bar, Gray's Inn (Atkin Schol.), 1964, Bencher, 1985. Treasury Junior Counsel: in Charity Matters, 1977–81; Chancery, 1981–89; a Recorder, 1989. Member, Senate of Inns of Court and Bar, 1978–81. Member: Justice Cttee on Privacy and the Law, 1967–70; Art Registration Cttee, 1969–; Legal Adv. Commn, Gen. Synod of C of E, 1988–. *Publication:* (co-ed) Copinger and Skone James on Copyright, 13th edn 1991. *Recreation:* long walks with family, friends and alone. *Address:* c/o Royal Courts of Justice, Strand, WC2.

MUNBY, Dr John Latimer, OBE 1984; Director, British Council, Greece, since 1990; *b* 14 July 1937; *s* of late Lawrence St John Munby and Jennie Munby; *m* 1961, Lilian Cynthia Hogg; two *s*. *Educ:* King's Sch., Bruton; Lincoln Coll., Oxford (BA Jurisp., MA); Inst. of Educn, London Univ. (PGCE); Univ. of Essex (MA Applied Linguistics, PhD). Nat. service, 2nd Lieut, 1955–57. Educn Officer, Govt of Tanzania, 1961–68; joined British Council, 1969; seconded to Advanced Teachers' Coll., Zaria, then Ahmadu Bello Univ., Nigeria, 1969–72; Director: English Teaching Inf. Centre, 1974–76; English Lang. Consultancies Dept, 1976–78; Representative: Kuwait, 1978–81; Singapore, 1981–85; Dep. Controller, Home Div., 1985–87; Controller, Libraries, Books and Information Div., 1987–90. FRSA 1982. *Publications:* Read and Think, 1968; Communicative Syllabus Design, 1978; contrib. various jls. *Recreations:* music, sport, wine. *Address:* c/o The British Council, 10 Spring Gardens, SW1A 2BN. *T:* 071–930 8466.

MUNDAY, John, FSA; Keeper of Weapons and Antiquities, National Maritime Museum, Greenwich, 1976–84, now Keeper Emeritus; *b* 10 Aug. 1924; *s* of Rodney H. J. Munday and Ethel Emma Cutting; *m* 1953, Brenda Warden; two *s*. *Educ:* Portsmouth Northern Grammar Sch.; King's Coll., Newcastle; Durham Univ. (BA 1950; MA 1961). FSA 1972. Assistant, Portsmouth Public Libraries and Museums Dept, 1940–42. Served RN, 1942–46; Sub Lieut (Ex. Sp.), RNVR. National Maritime Museum, Greenwich: Asst Keeper, Librarian, 1951; Curator of Presentation, 1964; Dep. Keeper, 1969; Curator of Weapons and Antiquities, 1971. Hon. Vice Pres., Soc. for Nautical Res., 1985 (Hon. Sec., 1979–84); Member: Develt Cttee, SS Great Britain Project, 1980; HMS Victory Adv. Technical Cttee, 1985. *Publications:* For Those in Peril . . . lifesaving, then and now, 1963; Oar Maces of Admiralty, 1966; Dress of the British Sailor, rev. edn 1977; Heads & Tails—the Necessary Seating (with drawings), 1978; Naval Cannon, 1987. *Recreations:* painting, collecting, considering. *Address:* Fourteen The Beach, Walmer, Kent CT14 7HE. *T:* Deal (0304) 374493.

MUNFORD, William Arthur, MBE 1946; PhD; FLA; Librarian Emeritus, National Library for the Blind; *b* 27 April 1911; *s* of late Ernest Charles Munford and Florence Margaret Munford; *m* 1934, Hazel Despard Wilmer; two *s* one *d*. *Educ:* Hornsey County Sch.; LSE (BScEcon, PhD). Asst, Hornsey Public Libraries, 1927–31; Chief Asst, Ilford Public Libraries, 1931–34; Borough Librarian, Dover, 1934–45 (Food Exec. Officer, 1939–45); City Librarian, Cambridge, 1945–53; Dir-Gen., Nat. Library for the Blind, 1954–82. Hon. Sec., Library Assoc., 1952–55, Hon. Fellow 1977. Trustee, Ulverscroft Foundn. *Publications:* Books for Basic Stock, 1939; Penny Rate: aspects of British public library history, 1951; William Ewart, MP, 1960; Edward Edwards, 1963; (with W. G. Fry) Louis Stanley Jast, 1966; James Duff Brown, 1968; A History of the Library Association, 1877–1977, 1976; (with S. Godbolt) The Incomparable Mac (biog. of Sir J. Y. W. MacAlister), 1983; Who was Who in British Librarianship 1800–1985, 1987; contribs to Librarianship jls, 1933–. *Recreations:* reading, rough gardening, wood sawing, cycling, serendipity. *Address:* 11 Manor Court, Pinehurst, Grange Road, Cambridge CB3 9BE. *T:* Cambridge (0223) 62962. *Club:* National Liberal.

MUNIR, Ashley Edward; Under Secretary, Ministry of Agriculture, Fisheries and Food, since 1982; *b* 14 Feb. 1934; *s* of late Hon. Sir Mehmed Munir Bey, Kt, CBE, and late Lady (Vessime) Munir; *m* 1960, Sureyya S. V. Dormen; one *s*. *Educ:* Brentwood Sch.; St John's Coll., Cambridge (MA); King's Coll., London (MPhil). Called to the Bar, Gray's Inn, 1956. Practised as barrister, 1956–60; Crown Counsel, 1960–64; entered Govt Legal Service, 1964; Asst Solicitor, MAFF, 1975–82. *Publications:* Perinatal Rights, 1983; Fisheries after Factortame, 1991. *Recreations:* walking, playing the double-bass, listening to music. *Address:* Grassdale, 31 Kingwell Road, Hadley Wood, Herts EN4 0HZ. *T:* (office) 071–270 8369; L'Acapulco, Appt 506, Avenue du Casino, 34280 La Grande Motte, France. *Club:* United Oxford & Cambridge University.

MUNN, Sir James, Kt 1985; OBE 1976; MA; University Commissioner, since 1988; *b* 27 July 1920; *s* of Douglas H. Munn and Margaret G. Dunn; *m* 1946, Muriel Jean Millar Moles; one *d*. *Educ:* Stirling High Sch.; Glasgow Univ. (MA (Hons)). Entered Indian Civil Service, 1941; served in Bihar, 1942–47. Taught in various schools in Glasgow, 1949–57; Principal Teacher of Modern Languages, Falkirk High Sch., 1957–62, Depute Rector, 1962–66; Rector: Rutherglen Acad., 1966–70; Cathkin High Sch., Cambuslang, Glasgow, 1970–83. Chairman: Manpower Services Cttee for Scotland, 1984–88; MSC, subseq. Training Commn, 1987–88; Scottish Adv. Bd, Open Coll., 1989–91; Pres., Inst. of Trng and Develt, 1989–. Member: Consultative Cttee on Curriculum, 1968–80, Chm., 1980–87; University Grants Cttee, 1973–82; Chm., Cttee to review structure of curriculum at SIII and SIV, 1975–77. Mem. Court, Strathclyde Univ., 1983–91. Fellow: Paisley Coll. of Technology, 1988; SCOTVEC, 1989. Chevalier des Palmes Académiques, 1967. DUniv Stirling, 1978; Hon. LLD Strathclyde, 1988; Hon. DEd Napier Polytechnic, 1989. *Address:* 4 Kincath Avenue, High Burnside, Glasgow G73 4RP. *T:* 041–634 4654.

MUNNS, Victor George; Counsellor (Labour), Washington, 1983–86; *b* 17 June 1926; *s* of Frederick William Munns and Lilian Munns; *m* 1952, Pamela Ruth Wyatt; two *s*. *Educ:* Haberdashers' Aske's, Hatcham; University Coll., London (BA). Served HM Forces (Army Intell.), 1945–48. Min. of Labour Employment Service, 1951–61; ILO, Trinidad and Belize, 1962–63; Sec., Shipbldg Industry Trng Bd, 1964–66; Res. Staff, Royal Commn on Trade Unions, 1966; Principal, Dept of Employment (Indust. Trng and Indust. Relations), 1967–72; Dep. Chief Officer, Race Relations Bd, 1973–74; Sec., Health and Safety Commn, 1974–77; Asst Sec., Health and Safety Exec., 1977–82. *Club:* Royal Over-Seas League.

MUNRO, Sir Alan (Gordon), KCMG 1990 (CMG 1984); HM Diplomatic Service; Ambassador to Saudi Arabia, since 1989; *b* 17 Aug. 1935; *s* of late Sir Gordon Munro, KCMG, MC and Lilian Muriel Beit; *m* 1962, Rosemary Grania Bacon; twin *s* two *d*. *Educ:* Wellington Coll.; Clare Coll., Cambridge (MA). MIPM. Mil. Service, 4/7 Dragoon Guards, 1953–55; Middle East Centre for Arab Studies, 1958–60; British Embassy, Beirut, 1960–62; Kuwait, 1961; FO, 1963–65; Head of Chancery, Benghazi, 1965–66 and Tripoli, 1966–68; FO, 1968–73; Consul (Commercial), 1973–74, Consul-Gen., 1974–77, Rio de Janeiro; Head of E African Dept, FCO, 1977–78; Head of Middle East Dept, FCO, 1979; Head of Personnel Ops Dept, FCO, 1979–81; Regl Marketing Dir (ME), MoD, 1981–83; Ambassador to Algeria, 1984–87; Dep. Under-Sec. of State, ME/Africa, FCO, 1987–89. *Recreations:* historic buildings, gardening, music, history. *Address:* c/o Foreign and Commonwealth Office, SW1A 2AL. *Club:* Travellers'.

MUNRO of Lindertis, Sir Alasdair (Thomas Ian), 6th Bt *cr* 1825; Marketing Consultant; Chairman: Munro, Jennings & Doig, since 1983; Highland Development Group, since 1987; *b* 6 July 1927; *s* of Sir Thomas Torquil Alfonso Munro, 5th Bt and Beatrice Maude (*d* 1974), *d* of Robert Sanderson Whitaker; *S* father, 1985; *m* 1954, Marguerite Lillian, *d* of late Franklin R. Loy, Dayton, Ohio, USA; one *s* one *d*. *Educ:* Georgetown Univ., Washington, DC (BSS 1946); Univ. of Pennsylvania (MBA 1951); IMEDE, Lausanne. 2nd Lieut, USAF (previously US Army), 1946–53. Senior Vice-Pres., McCann-Erickson, New York, 1952–69; Pres., Jennings Real Estate, Waitsfield, Vermont, 1970–83. Founder, Dir (and Past Pres.), St Andrew's Soc. of Vermont, 1972–; Vice-Chm., Assoc. Bd of Directors, Howard Bank, Waitsfield, 1974–84; Founder, sometime Dir and Pres., Valley Area Assoc., Waitsfield, 1972–80. *Recreations:* gardening, travel, Scottish heritage matters. *Heir:* *s* Keith Gordon Munro, *b* 3 May 1959. *Address:* River Ridge, Box 940, Waitsfield, Vermont 05673, USA; Ruthven Mill, Meigle, Perthshire, Scotland.

MUNRO, Dame Alison, DBE 1985 (CBE 1964); Chairman, Chichester Health Authority, 1982–88; *d* of late John Donald, MD; *m* 1939, Alan Lamont Munro (killed on active service, 1941); one *s*. *Educ:* Queen's Coll., Harley Street; Wynberg Girls' High Sch., South Africa; St Paul's Girls' Sch.; St Hilda's Coll., Oxford (MA). Ministry of Aircraft Production, 1942–45; Principal, Ministry of Civil Aviation, 1945; Asst Sec., 1949; Under-Sec., Ministry of Transport and Civil Aviation, 1958; Under-Sec., Ministry of Aviation, 1960; High Mistress, St Paul's Girls' Sch. Hammersmith, 1964–74. Chm., Merton, Sutton and Wandsworth AHA(T), 1974–82. Chairman: Training Council for Teachers of the Mentally Handicapped, 1966–69; Cttee of Inquiry into Children's Footwear, 1972; Central Transport Consultative Cttee, 1980–85; Maternity Services Adv. Cttee, 1981–85; Code Monitoring Cttee on Infant Formulae, 1985–89; Member: Board, BEA, 1966–73; Board, British Library, 1973–79; British Tourist Authority, 1973–81. Governor, Charing Cross Group of Hospitals, 1967–74. *Recreations:* gardening, tennis, sailing, Scottish country dancing. *Address:* Harbour Way, Ellanore Lane, West Wittering, West Sussex PO20 8AN. *T:* Birdham (0243) 513274. *Club:* Commonwealth Trust.

MUNRO, Charles Rowcliffe; *b* 6 Nov. 1902; *s* of Charles John Munro, CA, Edinburgh, Hon. Sheriff Substitute, County of Selkirk, and of Edith Rowcliffe; *m* 1942, Moira Rennie Ainslie, *d* of Dr Alexander Cruickshank Ainslie; two *s*. *Educ:* Merchiston Castle Sch., Edinburgh. Hon. Treasurer W Edinburgh Unionist Assoc., 1945–61, Hon. Treas. Scottish Nat. Cttee English-Speaking Union of the Commonwealth 1952–64; Pres. Edinburgh Union of Boys' Clubs, 1957–66. *Recreation:* fishing. *Address:* 17 Succoth Place, Edinburgh EH12 6BJ. *T:* 031–337 2139.

MUNRO, Colin William Gordon R.; *see* Ross-Munro.

MUNRO, Graeme Neil, FSAScot; Director, Historic Scotland, since 1991; *b* 28 Aug. 1944; *s* of Daniel Munro and Nancy Kirkwood (*née* Smith); *m* 1972, Nicola Susan Wells; one *s* one *d*. *Educ:* Daniel Stewart's Coll., Edinburgh; Univ. of St Andrews (MA Hons 1967). FSAScot 1990. Joined Scottish Office as Asst Principal, 1968; Scottish Development Department: Housing, 1968; Planning, 1968–70; Private Sec. to Head of Dept, 1971; Principal, Roads, 1972–74; Scottish Home and Health Department: Hosp. Services, 1974–76; Criminal Justice, 1976–79; Asssistant Secrtetary: Dept of Agriculture and Fisheries for Scotland (Fisheries), 1979–83; NHS Funding, Scottish Home and Health Dept, 1983–87; Management and Orgn, Scottish Office Central Services, 1987–90; Dir, Historic Buildings and Monuments, Scotland, 1990–91. *Recreations:* gardening, walking, travel, reading. *Address:* 20 Brandon Street, Edinburgh EH3 5RA. *T:* 031–244 3068.

MUNRO, Ian Arthur Hoyle, MB, FRCP; Editor of The Lancet, 1976–88; *b* 5 Nov. 1923; *o s* of Gordon Alexander and Muriel Rebecca Munro; *m* 1948, Olive Isabel, MRCS, LRCP, *o d* of Ernest and Isabella Jackson; three *s* two *d*. *Educ:* Huddersfield Coll.; Paston Sch., North Walsham; Royal Liberty Sch., Romford; Guy's Hosp. (MB 1946). FRCP 1984 (MRCP 1980). Served with RAMC, 1947–50. Joined staff of The Lancet, 1951, Dep. Editor, 1965–76. Regents' Lectr, UCLA, 1982. *Recreations:* cricket, crosswords. *Address:* Oakwood, Bayley's Hill, Sevenoaks, Kent TN14 6HS. *T:* Sevenoaks (0732) 454993. *Clubs:* Athenæum; Yorkshire CC.

MUNRO of Foulis-Obsdale, Sir Ian Talbot, 15th Bt *cr* 1634; *b* 28 Dec. 1929; *s* of Robert Hector Munro (*d* 1965) (*n* of 12th and 13th Bts) and Ethel Amy Edith, *d* of Harry Hudson; *S* cousin, Sir Arthur Herman Munro, 14th Bt, 1972. *Heir:* *uncle* Malcolm Munro [*b* 24 Feb. 1901; *m* 1931, Constance, *d* of William Carter; one *d* (one *s* decd)].

MUNRO, John Bennet Lorimer, CB 1959; CMG 1953; *b* 20 May 1905; *s* of late Rev. J. L. Munro; *m* 1st, 1929, Gladys Maie Forbes Simmons (*d* 1965); three *s*; 2nd, 1965, Margaret Deacy Ozanne, *d* of John Deacy, Blackfort House, Foxford, County Mayo. *Educ:* Edinburgh Academy; Edinburgh University; Corpus Christi Coll., Oxford (MA). ICS: entered, 1928; Under-Sec. Public Dept, Fort St George, 1934; HM Treasury, 1939; Min. of Supply, 1943; idc, 1949; Div. of Atomic Energy Production, 1950; Chief Administrative Officer, UK High Commission for Germany, 1951; Under-Sec.: Min. of Supply, 1953; Bd of Trade, 1955–62; Export Credits Guarantee Dept, 1962–65; Consultant, Export Council for Europe, 1966–67. *Address:* 77 Shirley Drive, Hove, Sussex BN3 6UE. *T:* Brighton (0273) 556705.

MUNRO OF FOULIS, Captain Patrick, TD 1958; DL 1949; 30th Chief of Clan Munro; landowner and farmer; Vice-Lieutenant of Ross and Cromarty, 1968–77; *b* 30 Aug. 1912; *e s* of late Col C. H. O. Gascoigne, DSO, Seaforth Highlanders, and Eva Marion, *d* of Sir Hector Munro of Foulis, 11th Bt; assumed arms and designation of Munro of Foulis on death of his grandfather; *m* 1947, Eleanor Mary, *d* of Capt. Hon. William French, French Park, Co. Roscommon, Eire; three *s* one *d*. *Educ:* Imperial Service Coll., Windsor; RMC Sandhurst. 2nd Lt Seaforth Highlanders, 1933; Capt. 1939. Served War of 1939–45, France (POW). Mem. Ross and Cromarty T&AFA, 1938. Hon. Sheriff of Ross and Cromarty, 1973. *Address:* Foulis Castle, Evanton, Ross-shire. *T:* Evanton (0349) 212. *Club:* MCC.

MUNRO, Sir Robert (Lindsay), Kt 1977; CBE 1962; President of the Senate, Fiji, 1970–82; *b* NZ, 2 April 1907; *s* of Colin Robert Munro and Marie Caroline Munro; *m* 1937, Lucie Ragnhilde Mee; two *s* one *d*. *Educ:* Auckland Grammar Sch.; Auckland University Coll. (LLB). Barrister and Solicitor, 1929. Served War, 1940–46: 1st Lieut, FMF. Founder Chairman, Fiji: Town Planning Bd, 1946–53; Broadcasting Commn, 1953–61. Member: Educn Bd and Educn Adv. Council, 1943–70; Legislative Council, 1945–46; Nat. Health Adv. Cttee, 1976–80. President: Law Soc., 1960–62 and 1967–69; Family Planning Assoc. of Fiji, 1963–87. Internat. Planned Parenthood Federation: formerly Mem., Governing Body; Regional Vice-Pres., 1973–82. Govt Representative: Bangkok reg. pre-consultation World Population Conf., ECAFE, 1974; World Pop. Conf., Bucharest, 1974; E Asian and Pacific Copyright Seminar, Sydney, 1976. Order of St Olav, Norway, 1966. Rifle shooting Blue; Captain, NZ Hockey Team, 1932. *Recreations:* literature, garden, music. *Address:* Foulis, 6 Milne Road, Suva, Fiji. *T:* 314156. *Club:* Fiji (Suva).

MUNRO, Sir Sydney Douglas G.; *see* Gun-Munro, S. D.

MUNRO, William, QC (Scotland) 1959; *b* 19 April 1900; *s* of William Munro, JP, Kilmarnock, and Janet Thomson Munro; *m* 1950, Christine Frances, *d* of W. B. Robertson, MC, DL, Colton, Dunfermline; three *d*. *Educ:* Glasgow High Sch.; Glasgow Univ. (MA, LLB). Called to Scottish Bar, 1925; called to Bar of Straits Settlements, 1927; Johore, 1927. Practised in Singapore and Malaya, 1927–57; Partner, Allen & Gledhill, Singapore. 1933–57 (Prisoner of war, Feb. 1942–Aug. 1945). Resumed practice Scottish Bar, 1958. *Recreation:* reading. *Address:* 9 The Hawthorns, Muirfield Park, Gullane EH31 2DZ. *T:* Gullane (0620) 84 2398. *Clubs:* New (Edinburgh); Hon. Company of Edinburgh Golfers.

MUNROW, Roger Davis; Chief Master of the Supreme Court of Judicature (Chancery Division), since 1986 (Master, 1985–86); *b* 20 March 1929; *s* of late William Davis Munrow, CBE and Constance Caroline Munrow (*née* Moorcroft); *m* 1957, Marie Jane Beresford; three *d*. *Educ:* Bryanston School; Oriel College, Oxford. MA; Solicitor. Entered Treasury Solicitor's Dept as Legal Assistant, 1959; Senior Legal Assistant, 1965; Assistant Treasury Solicitor, 1973; Principal Asst Treasury Solicitor, 1981. *Recreations:* swimming, cycling. *Address:* 20 Monahan Avenue, Purley, Surrey CR8 3BA. *T:* 081–660 1872.

MUNSTER, 7th Earl of, *cr* 1831; **Anthony Charles FitzClarence;** Viscount FitzClarence, Baron Tewkesbury, 1831; stained glass conservator for Chapel Studio, Hertfordshire, 1983–90; *b* 21 March 1926; *s* of 6th Earl of Munster, and Monica Shiela Harrington (*d* 1958), *d* of Lt-Col Sir Henry Mulleneux Grayson, 1st Bt, KBE; *S* father, 1983; *m* 1st, 1949 (marr. diss. 1966); two *d*; 2nd, 1966 (marr. diss. 1979); one *d*; 3rd, 1979, Alexa Maxwell. *Educ:* St Edward's School, Oxford. Served RN, 1942–46, Mediterranean, Far East, Pacific. Graphic Designer: Daily Mirror Newspapers, 1957–66; IPC Newspapers Division (Sun), 1966–69; freelance 1971–79; stained glass conservator for Burrell collection, 1979–83. MSIA 1960–69. FRSA 1987. *Recreations:* field sports, carpentry. *Heir:* none. *Address:* House of Lords, SW1A 0PW.

MURCHIE, John Ivor; His Honour Judge Murchie; a Circuit Judge, since 1974; *b* 4 June 1928; *s* of Captain Peter Archibald Murchie, OBE, RD, RNR; *m* 1953, Jenifer Rosalie Luard; one *s* two *d*. *Educ:* Edinburgh Academy; Rossall Sch.; Exeter Coll., Oxford (MA). Called to the Bar, Middle Temple, 1953; Harmsworth Scholarship, 1956. Dep. Chm., Berkshire QS, 1969–71; a Recorder of the Crown Court, 1972–74; Dep. Sen. Judge, Sovereign Base Areas, Cyprus (non-res.), 1987–. Mem., Criminal Cttee, Judicial Studies Bd, 1988–. Chm. Council, Rossall Sch., 1979–. *Recreations:* versifying and diversifying.

MURDIN, Paul Geoffrey, OBE 1988; PhD; Acting Director, Royal Observatory, Edinburgh, since 1991; *b* 5 Jan. 1942; *s* of Robert Murdin and Ethel Murdin (*née* Chubb); *m* 1964, Lesley Carol Milburn; two *s* one *d*. *Educ:* Trinity School of John Whitgift; Wadham Coll., Oxford (BA Physics); Univ. of Rochester, NY (PhD Physics and Astronomy). Res. Associate, Univ. of Rochester, 1970–71; Sen. Res. Associate, Royal Greenwich Observatory, 1971–74; Sen. Res. Scientist, Anglo-Australian Observatory, NSW, 1975–78; Royal Greenwich Observatory: Prin. Sci. Officer, 1979–81; Hd of La Palma Operations, 1981–87; Hd of Astronomy Div., 1987–90. Mem. Bd of Trustees, Nat. Maritime Museum, 1990–. Mem., Royal Astronomical Soc., 1963–. *Publications:* The Astronomer's Telescope (with Patrick Moore), 1963; Radio Waves from Space, 1969; (with L. Murdin) The New Astronomy, 1974; (with D. Allen and D. Malin) Catalogue of the Universe, 1980; (with D. Malin) Colours of the Stars, 1985; End in Fire, 1989; over 150 pubns in astronom. and other sci. jls, principally Monthly Notices of RAS. *Recreations:* writing, music, natural history, history of art. *Address:* Royal Observatory, Blackford Hill, Edinburgh EH9 3HJ. *T:* 031–668 8260.

MURDOCH, Dame Elisabeth (Joy), AC 1989; DBE 1963 (CBE 1961); *b* 1909; *d* of Rupert Greene and Marie (*née* de Lancey Forth); *m* 1928, Sir Keith (Arthur) Murdoch (*d* 1952); one *s* three *d*. *Educ:* Clyde Sch., Woodend, Victoria. Pres., Royal Children's Hospital, Melbourne, Victoria, Australia, 1953–65. Trustee, National Gallery, Victoria, 1968–76. Hon. LLD Melbourne, 1982. *Recreation:* gardening. *Address:* Cruden Farm, Langwarrin, Victoria 3910, Australia. *Clubs:* Alexandra, Lyceum (Melbourne).
See also K. R. Murdoch.

MURDOCH, Dame Iris; *see* Murdoch, Dame J. I.

MURDOCH, Dame (Jean) Iris, (Dame Iris Bayley), DBE 1987 (CBE 1976); CLit 1987; novelist and philosopher; Fellow of St Anne's College, Oxford, since 1948, Hon. Fellow, 1963; *b* Dublin, 15 July 1919; *d* of Wills John Hughes Murdoch and Irene Alice Richardson; *m* 1956, John Oliver Bayley, *qv*. *Educ:* Froebel Educational Inst., London; Badminton Sch., Bristol; Somerville Coll., Oxford (Lit. Hum. 1st Class 1942), Hon. Fellow 1977. Asst Principal, Treasury, 1942–44; Administrative Officer with UNRRA, working in London, Belgium, Austria, 1944–46; Sarah Smithson studentship in philosophy, Newnham Coll., Cambridge, 1947–48; Lectr, RCA, 1963–67. Mem., Irish Academy, 1970; Hon. Member: Amer. Acad. of Arts and Letters, 1975; Amer. Acad. of Arts and Sciences, 1982. Hon. Fellow, Newnham Coll., Cambridge, 1986. Hon. DLitt Oxford, 1987. Shakespeare Prize, FVS Foundn, Hamburg, 1988. *Publications:* Sartre, Romantic Rationalist, 1953; Under the Net, 1954; The Flight from the Enchanter, 1955; The Sandcastle, 1957; The Bell, 1958; A Severed Head, 1961 (play, Criterion, 1963); An Unofficial Rose, 1962; The Unicorn, 1963; The Italian Girl, 1964 (play, Criterion, 1967); The Red and the Green, 1965; The Time of The Angels, 1966; The Nice and The Good, 1968; Bruno's Dream, 1969; A Fairly Honourable Defeat, 1970; The Sovereignty of Good, 1970; An Accidental Man, 1971; The Black Prince, 1973 (James Tait Black Meml Prize; play, Aldwych, 1989); The Sacred and Profane Love Machine, 1974 (Whitbread Prize); A Word Child, 1975; Henry and Cato, 1976; The Fire and the Sun, 1977; The Sea, the Sea, 1978 (Booker Prize, 1978); Nuns and Soldiers, 1980; The Philosopher's Pupil, 1983; The Good Apprentice, 1985; Acastos, 1986; The Book and the Brotherhood, 1987; The Message to the Planet, 1989; *plays:* The Servants and the Snow (Greenwich), 1970; The Three Arrows (Arts, Cambridge), 1972; Art and Eros (Nat. Theatre), 1980; *poems:* A Year of Birds, 1978; papers in Proc. Aristotelian Soc., etc. *Recreation:* learning languages.

MURDOCH, John Derek Walter; Assistant Director in charge of Collections, Victoria and Albert Museum, since 1989; *b* 1 April 1945; *s* of James Duncan and Elsie Elizabeth Murdoch; *m* 1st, 1967, Prue Smijth-Windham (marr. diss. 1986); one *s* two *d*; 2nd, 1990, Susan Lambert. *Educ:* Shrewsbury Sch.; Magdalen Coll., Oxford (BA); King's Coll., London (MPhil). Asst Keeper, Birmingham City Art Gall., 1969–73; Victoria & Albert Museum: Asst, then Dep. Keeper, Dept of Paintings, 1973–86; Keeper of Prints, Drawings, Photographs and Paintings, 1986–89. Vis. Fellow, British Art Center, Yale Univ., 1979. Trustee: William Morris Gall., Walthamstow, 1975–; Dove Cottage, Grasmere, 1982–. *Publications:* David Cox, 1970; Byron, 1974; English Watercolours, 1977; The English Miniature, 1981; Discovery of the Lake District, 1984; A Sort of National Property, 1985; Painters and the Derby China Works, 1986; contrib. to Rev. of English Studies, Jl of Warburg and Courtauld Insts, Burlington Magazine. *Address:* Brickhill, Burghclere, Newbury, Berks RG15 9HJ. *T:* Burghclere (063527) 295.

MURDOCH, (Keith) Rupert, AC 1984; publisher; Chairman, since 1991 and Group Chief Executive, since 1979, The News Corporation Ltd, Australia; Chief Executive and Managing Director, News International plc, UK, since 1969 (Chairman, 1969–87); Chairman and President, News America Publishing Inc.; Director, Times Newspapers Holdings Ltd, since 1981 (Chairman, 1982–90); *b* 11 March 1931; *s* of late Sir Keith Murdoch and of Dame Elisabeth (Joy) Murdoch, *qv*; *m* 1967, Anna Torv; two *s* two *d*. *Address:* 1211 6th Avenue, New York, USA; 1 Virginia Street, E1 9XY.

MURDOCH, Robert, (Robin Murdoch), TD 1946; MD; FRCSGlas, FRCOG; Consultant Obstetrician and Gynaecologist, Royal Maternity and Royal Samaritan Hospitals, Glasgow, 1946–76; *b* 31 July 1911; *s* of late James Bowman Young Murdoch and Christina Buntin Murdoch (*née* Wood); *m* 1941, Nora Beryl (*née* Woolley); two *s* (and one *s* decd). *Educ:* Hillhead High Sch., Glasgow; Glasgow Univ. MB ChB 1934, MD 1955; MRCOG 1940; FRCSGlas 1959; FRCOG 1961. Pres., Glasgow Univ. Union, 1933. Served War, 1939–45; Major RAMC. Examiner in Obstetrics and Gynaecology, Univs of Glasgow and Cambridge. Royal College of Gynaecologists: Examiner; Mem. Council, 1954–60, 1968–74; Jun. Vice-Pres., 1974–75; Sen. Vice-Pres., 1975–77. Pres., Scottish AAA, 1956; Mem., British Amateur Athletic Bd, 1956. *Publications:* contribs to medical jls. *Recreations:* angling, golf, gardening, athletics (rep. Scotland (British Empire Games, 1934), and GB (1931, 1933, 1934, 1935, 1938) in 220 yds). *Address:* Carrick Arden, Torwoodhill Road, Rhu, Helensburgh G84 8LE. *T:* Helensburgh (0436) 820481. *Clubs:* Oriental; Royal Scottish Automobile (Glasgow).

MURDOCH, Rupert; *see* Murdoch, K. R.

MURDOCH, William Ridley Morton, CBE 1963; DSC 1940 and Bar, 1942; VRD 1949; Sheriff of Grampian, Highland and Islands (formerly Ross and Cromarty), at Dingwall and Tain, 1971–78; *b* 17 May 1917; *s* of William Ridley Carr Murdoch and Margaret Pauline Mackinnon; *m* 1941, Sylvia Maud Pearson; one *s* one *d*. *Educ:* Kelvinside Academy, Glasgow; Glasgow Univ. (MA, LLB). War Service in Navy, 1939–45; Captain, RNR, 1959. Solicitor in private practice, 1947–71; Dir, Glasgow Chamber of Commerce, 1955–71; Dean, Royal Faculty of Procurators in Glasgow, 1968–71. DL, County of City of Glasgow, 1963–75. OStJ 1976. *Recreations:* sailing, gardening. *Address:* Aird House, Gairloch, Ross-shire IV21 2AB. *T:* Badachro (044583) 243.

MURE, Kenneth Nisbet; QC (Scot.) 1989; *b* 11 April 1947; *o s* of Robert and Katherine Mure. *Educ:* Glasgow High Sch.; Glasgow Univ. (MA, LLB). FTII 1971. Admitted to Scots Bar, 1975; called to English Bar, Gray's Inn, 1990. Lectr, Faculty of Law, Glasgow Univ., 1971–83. *Address:* Advocates' Library, Edinburgh EH1 1RF.

MURERWA, Dr Herbert Muchemwa; Minister for the Environment and Tourism, Zimbabwe, since 1990; *b* 31 May 1941; *m* 1969, Ruth Chipo; one *s* four *d*. *Educ:* Harvard University. EdD (Educational Planning). Economic Affairs Officer, UN Economic Commission for Africa, Addis Ababa, 1978–80; Permanent Sec., Min. of Manpower Planning, 1980–81; Permanent Sec., Min. of Labour and Social Services, 1982–84; High Comr in UK, 1984–90. *Address:* c/o Ministry of Environment and Tourism, Karigamombe Centre, Private Bag 7753, Causeway, Harare, Zimbabwe.

MURGATROYD, Prof. Walter, PhD; Professor of Thermal Power, Imperial College of Science and Technology, 1968–86, now Professor Emeritus; Rockefeller International Fellow, Princeton University, 1979; *b* 15 Aug. 1921; *s* of Harry G. Murgatroyd and Martha W. Strachan; *m* 1952, Denise Geneviève, *d* of late Robert Adolphe Schlumberger, Paris and Bénouville; one *s* one *d* (and one *s* decd). *Educ:* St Catharine's Coll., Cambridge. BA 1946, PhD 1952. Hawker Aircraft Ltd, 1942–44; Rolls Royce Ltd, 1944–46; Univ. of Cambridge (Liquid Metal and Reactor heat transfer research), 1947–54; UK Atomic Energy Authority, Harwell, 1954–56; Head of Dept of Nuclear Engineering, Queen Mary Coll., Univ. of London, 1956–67, and Dean of Engineering, 1966–67. Member: British-Greek Mixed Commn, 1963–78; British-Belgian Mixed Commn, 1964–78; British-Austrian Mixed Commn, 1965–78. Specialist Adviser to H of C Select Cttee on Energy, 1980–. *Publications:* contrib. to various scientific and technical journals. *Recreation:* music. *Address:* 7 Currie Hill Close, SW19 7DX. *T:* 081–946 0415.

MURLEY, John Tregarthen, CB 1988; DPhil; *b* 22 Aug. 1928; *s* of John Murley and Dorothea Birch; *m* 1954, Jean Patricia Harris; one *d*. *Educ:* University College, London (BA 1st Cl. Hons History); St Antony's Coll., Oxford (DPhil). Entered FO, 1955; Counsellor, Washington, 1976–80. *Publication:* The Origin and Outbreak of the Anglo-French War of 1793, 1959. *Recreations:* tennis, squash, piano.

MURLEY, Sir Reginald (Sydney), KBE 1979; TD 1946; FRCS; President, Royal College of Surgeons, 1977–80; *b* 2 Aug. 1916; *s* of Sydney Herbert Murley and Beatrice Maud Baylis; *m* 1947, Daphne, 2nd *d* of Ralph E. and Rowena Garrod; three *s* two *d* and one step *d*. *Educ:* Dulwich Coll.; Univ. of London; St Bartholomew's Hosp. (MB, BS Hons 1939, MS 1948). MRCS, LRCP 1939; FRCS 1946. Served War, RAMC, 1939–45: ME, E Africa, N Africa, Sicily, Italy and NW Europe; regtl and fld ambulance MO; Surgical Specialist, No 1 and 2 Maxillo-Facial Units and Fld Surg. Units; Major. St Bartholomew's Hospital: Jun. Scholarship, 1935; Sen. Schol., and Sir William Dunn Exhibn in Anat., Univ. of London, 1936; House Surg., 1939; Anat. Demonstrator, 1946; Surg. Chief Asst, 1946–49; Cattlin Res. Fellow and Mackenzie Mackinnon Res. Fellow, RCP and RCS, 1950–51; Surgeon: St Albans Hosp., 1947; Royal Northern Hosp., London, 1953; Hon. Consultant Surgeon, St Bartholomew's Hosp., 1979. Chm., Med. Council on Alcoholism, 1980. Royal Coll. of Surgeons: formerly Tutor and Reg. Adviser; Examiner, primary FRCS, 1966–72; Mem. Council, 1970–82; Hunterian Orator, 1981; Bradshaw Lectr, 1981; Mem. Ct of Patrons, 1981–; Chm., Trustees of Hunterian Mus., 1988– (Trustee, 1981–). Vis. Prof., Cleveland Clinic, USA, 1979, 1982 and 1986. Mitchiner Lectr, RAMC, 1981. FRSM, 1946–85; Fellow, Assoc. of Surgeons of GB and Ireland. Member: Hunterian Soc. (former Mem. Council; Pres., 1970–71; Orator, 1978); Med. Soc. of London (former Mem. Council; Pres., 1982); Harveian Soc. (former Mem.

Council; Pres., 1983); BMA (former Councillor); Exec. Cttee, Soc. Internat. de Chirurgie, 1979–83 (Vice-Pres., 1985–86); European and internat. cardiovascular socs.; Adv. Council, The Social Affairs Unit, 1981–; Adv. Council, Health and Welfare Unit (formerly Health Unit), Inst. of Economic Affairs, 1986–. Hon. Vice-Pres., Nat. Stroke Campaign, 1985; Hon. Member: Brit. Assoc. of Plastic Surgs, 1983; Brit. Assoc. of Clinical Anatomists, 1983; Reading Pathological Soc., 1985. Sundry eponymous lectures and orations; Hon. FRACS and Syme Orator, 1979; Hon. FCSSA 1979; Hon. FRCSI 1980; Hon. FDSRCS 1981; Hon. Fellow: Italian Soc. Surg., 1979; Polish Assoc. of Surgeons, 1983. President: Sir John Charnley Trust, 1983–; Alleyn Club, 1983; Fellowship for Freedom in Medicine 1972–86; Mem. Council, Freedom Assoc., 1982–; Patron: Med. Aid to Poland, 1984–; Jagiellonian Trust, 1984–; Sponsor, 1984, Trustee, 1986, Family & Youth Concern (The Responsible Soc.). Freeman, City of London, 1955; Hon. Freeman, Barbers' Co., 1986; Liveryman, Apothecaries' Co., 1955–. *Publications:* (contrib.) Financing Medical Care, 1962; Surgical Roots and Branches (autobiog.), 1990; contrib. surg. textbooks; articles in med. literature on breast, thyroid and vascular diseases; articles on med. politics and econs. *Recreations:* swimming, gardening, music, reading history and economics. *Address:* (home) Cobden Hill House, 63 Cobden Hill, Radlett, Herts WD7 7JN. *T:* Radlett (0923) 856532; (office) Consulting Suite, Wellington Hospital, Wellington Place, NW8 9LE. *T:* 071–586 5959. *Clubs:* Royal Automobile; Fountain (St Bart's Hospital).

MURPHY, Andrew John; Sheriff of Tayside Central and Fife at Falkirk, since 1991; *b* 16 Jan. 1946; *s* of Robert James Murphy and Robina Murphy (*née* Scott); *m* 1980, Susan Margaret Thomson; two *s* two *d*. *Educ:* Allan Glen's School, Glasgow; Edinburgh Univ. (MA, LLB). 2nd Lieut RA (V), 1971–73; Flt Lieut RAF, 1973–75. Admitted to Faculty of Advocates, Scottish Bar, 1970; called to Bar, Middle Temple, 1990; Crown Counsel, Hong Kong, 1976–79; Standing Junior Counsel to Registrar General for Scotland, 1982–85; Temporary Sheriff, 1983–85; Sheriff of Grampian, Highland and Islands at Banff and Peterhead, 1985–91. *Address:* c/o Sheriff's Chambers, Court House, Main Street, Camelon, Falkirk FK1 4AR. *Clubs:* Caledonian (Edinburgh); Royal Northern, University (Aberdeen).

MURPHY, Rear-Adm. Anthony Albert, CBE 1976; Special Project Executive, Ministry of Defence, 1977–82; retired, 1983; *b* 19 May 1924; *s* of Albert Edward Murphy and Jennie (*née* Giles); *m* 1954, Antonia Theresa (*née* Rayner); four *s*. *Educ:* Sir George Monoux Grammar Sch. National Provincial Bank, 1940–42; joined RN, 1942; commnd, 1944; Western Approaches, 1944–45; HMS Vanguard (Royal Tour of S Africa), 1945–49; HMS Bulwark (Suez); Comdr 1960; HMS Yarmouth/6th Frigate Sqdn, Kuwait, 1961–63; HMS Eagle, 1965–67; Captain 1967; Dir, Naval Guided Weapons, 1970–73; in comd HMS Collingwood, 1973–76; Rear-Adm. 1977; Vice-Pres., and Senior Naval Mem., Ordnance Board, 1977. *Recreations:* cricket, soccer (Chm. RNFA, 1973–76), country activities.

MURPHY, Mrs Brian Taunton; *see* Hufton, Prof. Olwen.

MURPHY, Christopher Philip Yorke; writer, lecturer and consultant; *b* 20 April 1947; *s* of Philip John and Dorothy Betty Murphy; *m* 1969, Sandra Gillian Ashton. *Educ:* Devonport High Sch.; The Queen's Coll., Oxford (MA). Formerly Associate Dir, D'Arcy MacManus & Masius. President, Oxford Univ. Conservative Assoc., 1967; held number of Conservative Party offices, 1968–72. Parish Councillor, Windlesham, Surrey, 1972–76. Contested (C): Bethnal Green and Bow, Feb. 1974, Oct. 1974. MP (C) Welwyn Hatfield, 1979–87. Vice-Chairman: Parly Urban and New Town Affairs Cttee, 1980–87; Parly Arts and Heritage Cttee, 1981–86; Mem., Select Cttee on Statutory Instruments, 1980–87 (rep of cttee on Commonwealth Delegated Legislation Cttee, 1980–87); UK Delegate to Council of Europe/WEU, 1983–87 (Hon. Associate, 1988). Vice-President: C of E Artistic Heritage Commn, 1984–87; C of E Youth & Drugs Commn, 1986–87. Member: Nat. Cttee for 900th Anniversary of Domesday Book, 1986; Chief Pleas of Sark (Parlt), 1989–90 (Vice-Pres., Internat. Cttee of Chief Pleas, 1989–90); Arts Council of Bailiwick of Guernsey, 1988–90; Council, Société Guernésiaise, 1988–90. Life Mem., CLA, 1987. Hon. Sec., Société Sercquiaise, 1988–90; Sec., Sodor & Man Diocesan Synod, 1991–. FRSA. Freeman, City of London, 1984. Hon. Citizen, Cork, 1985. *Recreations:* arts, heritage, travel, conservation, walking, horticulture. *Address:* Cooil Voorath, The Cronk, Ballaugh, Isle of Man. *Club:* Oxford Union Society.

MURPHY, Cornelius McCaffrey, (Neil Murphy), MBE 1982; Group Managing Director, The Builder Group Ltd, since 1990 (Director, since 1979); *b* 31 May 1936; 2nd *s* of Edward and Annie Murphy, Glasgow; *m* (marr. diss.); two *d*. *Educ:* Holyrood Sch.; Univ. of Glasgow (MA 1958). Joined The Builder Group, 1962, following spells of teaching and management trng; Editor, 1974–83, Editor-in-Chief, 1983–87, Building Magazine. Mem., Worshipful Co. of Tylers and Bricklayers. *Recreations:* reading, racing, golf. *Address:* 42 St John's Park, Blackheath, SE3 7JH. *T:* 081–853 2625. *Club:* Royal Automobile.

MURPHY, Dervla; *b* 28 Nov. 1931; *d* of Fergus Murphy and Kathleen Rochfort-Dowling; one *d*. *Educ:* Ursuline Convent, Waterford. American Irish Foundn Literary Award, 1975; Christopher Ewart-Biggs Meml Prize, 1978; Irish Amer. Cultural Inst. Literary Award, 1985. *Publications:* Full Tilt, 1965, 7th edn 1984; Tibetan Foothold, 1966, 3rd edn 1968; The Waiting Land, 1967, 3rd edn 1969; In Ethiopia with a Mule, 1968, 4th edn 1985; On a Shoe String to Coorg, 1976, 3rd edn 1985; Where the Indus is Young, 1977, 2nd edn 1984; A Place Apart, 1978, 5th edn 1984; Wheels Within Wheels, 1979, 5th edn 1984; Race to the Finish?, 1981; Eight Feet in the Andes, 1983, 2nd edn 1985; Muddling Through in Madagascar, 1985, 3rd edn 1987; Ireland, 1985; Tales from Two Cities, 1987; (ed) Embassy to Constantinople, the Travels of Lady Mary Wortley Montague, 1988; In Cameroon with Egbert, 1989. *Recreations:* reading, music, cycling, swimming, walking. *Address:* Lismore, Co. Waterford, Ireland.

MURPHY, Rev. Canon Gervase; *see* Murphy, Rev. Canon J. G. M. W.

MURPHY, Sheriff James Patrick; Sheriff of Glasgow and Strathkelvin, since 1989; *b* 24 Jan. 1932; *s* of Henry Francis Murphy and Alice (*née* Rooney); *m* 1956, Maureen Coyne; two *s* one *d*. *Educ:* Notre Dame Convent; St Aloysius' Coll., Glasgow; Univ. of Glasgow (BL 1953). Admitted Solicitor, 1953; assumed partner, R. Maguire Cook & Co., Glasgow, 1959; founded, with J. Ross Harper, firm of Ross Harper & Murphy, Glasgow, 1961; Sheriff of N Strathclyde, 1976–89. President: Glasgow Juridical Soc., 1962–63; Glasgow Bar Assoc., 1966–67; Sheriffs' Assoc., 1991–; Mem. Council, Law Soc. of Scotland, 1974–76. Governor, St Aloysius' Coll., Glasgow, 1978–86. *Recreations:* bird watching, canoeing, cycling, books, the history of writing, footering. *Address:* 1 Kelvin Crescent, Bearsden G61 1BT.

MURPHY, Most Rev. John A., DD; Archbishop Emeritus of Cardiff, (RC) (Archbishop, 1961–83); *b* Birkenhead, 21 Dec. 1905; *s* of John and Elizabeth Murphy. *Educ:* The English Coll., Lisbon. Ordained 1931; consecrated as Bishop of Appia and Coadjutor Bishop of Shrewsbury, 1948; Bishop of Shrewsbury, 1949–61. ChStJ 1974. *Address:* Ty Mair, St Joseph's Nursing Home, Malpas, Newport, Gwent NP9 6ZE.

MURPHY, Rev. Canon (John) Gervase (Maurice Walker), LVO 1987; MA; a Chaplain to the Queen, since 1987; Chaplain of the Chapel Royal of St Peter ad Vincula, Tower of London, since 1991; *b* 20 Aug. 1926; *s* of William Stafford and Yvonne Iris Murphy; *m* 1957, Joy Hilda Miriam Livermore; five *d*. *Educ:* Methodist Coll., Belfast; Trinity Coll., Dublin (BA 1952, MA 1955; Rugby football team, 1947–52 (Capt., 1951–52); cricket colours). Guardsman, Irish Guards, 1944–45; commissioned Royal Ulster Rifles, 1945–47. TCD, 1947–52 and Divinity Sch., TCD, 1949–52. Ordained, 1952; Curate, Shankill Parish, Lurgan, 1952–55. Royal Army Chaplains' Dept, 1955; served: Korea, 1955–57; Woolwich, 1957–59; Aden, 1959–62; Infantry Junior Leaders, Oswestry, 1962–64; Bagshot, 1964–65; Worthy Down, 1965; Commonwealth Bde Sen. Chaplain, 1965–67; Sen. Chaplain, Guards Depot, Pirbright, 1967–69; DACG, Rhine Area, 1969–72; Sen. Chaplain, RMA Sandhurst, 1972–74; Asst Chaplain General: BAOR, 1974–75; South East, 1975–77; Vicar of Ranworth and RD of Blofield, 1977–79; Chaplain for Holidaymakers on Norfolk Broads, 1977–79; Domestic Chaplain to the Queen, Rector of Sandringham and Leader of Sandringham Group of Parishes, 1979–87; RD of Heacham and Rising, 1985–87; Hon Canon of Norwich Cathedral, 1986, Emeritus, 1987–; Rector, Christ Church Cathedral, Falkland Is, 1987–91. Vice-Pres., British Assoc. for Physical Trng, 1988– (Hon. Fellow, 1988). Played: Internat. Rugby football for Ireland, 1952, 1954 and 1958; Rugby football for British Army 1957, and for Barbarians, 1958. *Recreations:* people; sport, walking, gardening, interior decorating, peat chopping! *Address:* HM Tower of London, EC3N 4AB. *Clubs:* British Sportsman's, London Irish RFC, Public School Wanderers RFC; Leprechauns Cricket (Ireland); Mid-Ulster Cricket.

MURPHY, Sir Leslie (Frederick), Kt 1978; Director, Petroleum Economics Ltd, since 1980 (Chairman, 1980–87); Chairman, National Enterprise Board, 1977–79 (Deputy Chairman, 1975–77); *b* 17 Nov. 1915; *s* of Frederick Charles and Lillian Annie Murphy; *m* 1940, Marjorie Iris Cowell (*d* 1991); one *s* one *d*. *Educ:* Southall Grammar Sch.; Birkbeck Coll., Univ. of London. Principal Private Sec. to Minister of Fuel and Power, 1947–49; Asst Sec., Min. of Fuel and Power, 1949–52; Chm., Mobil Supply Co. Ltd and Mobil Shipping Co. Ltd, 1955–59; Finance Dir, Iraq Petroleum Co. Ltd, 1959–64; Director: J. Henry Schroder Wagg & Co. Ltd, 1964–75 (Dep. Chm. 1972–73); Schroders plc, 1979–90 (Dep. Chm., 1973–75); Unigate Ltd, 1968–75; Simon Engrg Ltd, 1980–85; Folksam International Insurance (UK) Ltd, 1980–90. Mem., NEDC, 1977–79. Mem. Royal Commn on Distribution of Income and Wealth, 1974–76; Board Mem., Church Army, 1964–; Chm., Church Army Housing Ltd, 1973–82, Pres., 1982–84. Trustee, SDP, 1981–90. *Recreations:* music, golf. *Address:* Hedgerley, Barton Common Road, Barton-on-Sea, Hants.

MURPHY, Neil; *see* Murphy, C. McC.

MURPHY, Patrick James, CMG 1985; HM Diplomatic Service, retired; Adviser to Sultanate of Oman, 1987–90; *b* 11 March 1931; *e s* of late Dr James Murphy and Cicely Mary (*née* Crowley); *m* 1st, 1959, Barbara May Healey-Purse (marr. diss. 1969); two *s*; 2nd, 1974, Jutta Ulrike Oehlmann; one *s*. *Educ:* Cranbrook School; Gonville and Caius College, Cambridge (BA; Geography Tripos). Served RAF, 1950–52. Oxford and Cambridge Far Eastern Expedition, 1955–56; BBC Gen. Overseas Service, 1956; Joined FO, 1957; Frankfurt, 1958; Berlin, 1959; FO, 1962; Second Sec. (Commercial), Warsaw, 1962; First Sec., FO, 1965; First Sec. (Commercial) and Consul, Phnom Penh, 1966; Consul, Düsseldorf, 1969; Consul, Hamburg, 1971; FCO, 1974; First Sec., Vienna, 1977; Counsellor, FCO, 1981–87. *Recreations:* history, travel, wine, boating, skiing. *Address:* c/o Lloyds Bank, 1 Waterloo Place, Pall Mall, SW1Y 5NJ. *Club:* Royal Air Force.

MURPHY, Patrick Wallace; Under Secretary, Head of Pesticides, Veterinary Medicines, Emergencies and Biotechnology Group, Ministry of Agriculture, Fisheries and Food, since 1989; *b* 16 Aug. 1944; *s* of Lawrence Vincent Murphy and Agnes Dunn; *m* 1972, Denise Lillieth Fullarton-Fullarton; two *s*. *Educ:* St Chad's College, Wolverhampton; Trinity Hall, Cambridge (BA Hons). Joined MAFF, 1966; Asst Private Sec. to Minister of Agriculture, Fisheries and Food, 1970; First Sec. (Agriculture and Commercial), British Embassy, Washington, 1974–78; Controller of Plant Variety Rights, 1978–82; Head, Land Use and Tenure Div., 1982–86; Under Sec., 1986; Head, milk and Potatoes Gp, 1986–89. Non-Exec. Dir, IDV (UK), 1985–88. *Recreations:* cricket, tennis, gardening. *Address:* Moors Cottage, Moors Lane, Elstead, Surrey GU8 6DN. *T:* Elstead (0252) 703151.

MURPHY, Paul Peter; MP (Lab) Torfaen, since 1987; *b* 25 Nov. 1948; *s* of Ronald and Marjorie Murphy. *Educ:* St Francis RC Primary Sch., Abersychan; West Monmouth Sch., Pontypool; Oriel Coll., Oxford (MA). Management Trainee, CWS, 1970–71; Lectr in History and Govt, Ebbw Vale Coll. of Further Education, 1971–87. Mem., Torfaen Borough Council, 1973–87 (Chm., Finance Cttee, 1976–86); Sec., Torfaen Constituency Labour Party, 1974–87. Opposition front bench spokesman for Wales, 1988–. *Recreation:* music. *Address:* 42 Wiston Path, Fairwater, Cwmbran, Gwent NP44 4PY. *T:* Cwmbran (0633) 67145. *Clubs:* St Joseph's (St Dials); Fairwater Sports and Social.

MURPHY, Richard Holmes; Chairman, Industrial Tribunals, 1972–84; *b* 9 July 1915; *o s* of Harold Lawson Murphy, KC, and Elsie, 4th *d* of Rt Hon. Lord Justice Holmes; *m* 1967, Irene Sybil, *e d* of Reginald and Elizabeth Swift. *Educ:* Charterhouse; Emmanuel Coll., Cambridge (MA, LLB). Called to Bar, Inner Temple, 1939. Enlisted Inns of Court Regt, 1939; Commissioned 3rd County of London Yeomanry, 1940; served Middle East and Italy, 1941–45; Judge Advocate-Gen.'s Dept, WO, 1945–46; released, rank of Major. Resident Magistrate, Tanganyika, 1948; Chief Registrar, Gold Coast Supreme Ct and Registrar of W African Ct of Appeal, 1951; Sen. Magistrate, Gold Coast, 1955; Puisne Judge, Ghana, 1957–60; Judge of High Court, Tanganyika, 1960–64; Senior Lectr in Law, Polytechnic of Central London (formerly Holborn Coll.), 1965–72. *Address:* 3 Abingdon Court, Abingdon Villas, W8 6BS. *T:* 071–937 4540.

MURPHY, Thomas, CBE 1991; Managing Director, Civil Aviation Authority, since 1987; *b* 13 Nov. 1928; *s* of Thomas Murphy and Elizabeth Gray Murphy (*née* Leckie); *m* 1962, Sheila Jean Dorothy Young; one *s* three *d*. *Educ:* St Mirin's Acad., Paisley; Glasgow Univ. (MA Hons). Served Royal Artillery, 1951–53. Marks and Spencer, 1953–55; British Petroleum, 1955–86: appts in Territory of Papua New Guinea, Trinidad, Scotland, Algeria, USA, 1955–68; Asst Gen. Man., BP Tanker Co., 1968–76; Gen. Man., Gp Personnel, 1976–81; Advr, Organisation Planning, 1981–86; Non-Exec. Dir, CAA, 1986–87. Internat. Sen. Managers Programme, Harvard Business Sch., 1973. *Recreations:* walking, coarse golf, destructive gardening. *Address:* Woodruffe, Onslow Road, Sunningdale, Berks SL5 0HW. *T:* Ascot (0344) 23261. *Club:* Wentworth.

MURPHY, Thomas A(quinas); Chairman, General Motors Corporation, 1974–80; *b* Hornell, NY, 10 Dec. 1915; *s* of John Joseph Murphy and Alma (*née* O'Grady); *m* 1941, Catherine Rita Maguire; one *s* two *d*. *Educ:* Leo High Sch., Chicago; Univ. of Illinois. US Naval Reserve, 1943–46. Joined General Motors Corporation, 1938; Asst Treas., 1959; Comptroller, 1967; Treas., 1968–70; Vice-Pres. and Gp Exec., Car and Truck Div., 1970–72; Vice-Chm., 1972–74. *Address:* c/o General Motors Corporation, General Motors Building, Detroit, Mich 48202, USA.

MURPHY, Thomas James; sub-editor, The Times, since 1990; *b* 26 June 1956; *s* of James Murphy and Beatrice Murphy (*née* Strand); *m* 1976, Janet Sallis; four *s*. *Educ:* Salesian Sch., Chertsey; Sussex Univ. (BA History); Warwick Univ. (MBA). Kitchen porter and factory labourer, 1977; trainee journalist, Slough Observer, 1978; Sports editor, Buckinghamshire Advertiser, 1981; Editor: Staines Informer, 1983; East Grinstead Courier, 1984; Sub-editor, The Independent, 1986; Dep. Chief sub-editor, London Evening News, 1987; Editor, The Universe, 1988–90. *Recreation:* singing. *Address:* 17 Reynolds Road, Hove, Sussex BN3 5RT. *T:* Brighton (0273) 721858.

MURPHY-O'CONNOR, Rt. Rev. Cormac; *see* Arundel and Brighton, Bishop of, (RC).

MURRAY; *see* Beasley-Murray.

MURRAY; *see* Erskine-Murray.

MURRAY, family name of **Duke of Atholl,** of **Earl of Dunmore,** of **Earl of Mansfield and Mansfield** and of **Barons Murray of Epping Forest** and **Murray of Newhaven.**

MURRAY, Rt. Hon. Lord; Ronald King Murray, PC 1974; a Senator of the College of Justice in Scotland, since 1979; *b* 15 June 1922; *s* of James King Murray, MIEE, and Muriel (*née* Aitken), Glasgow; *m* 1950, Sheila Winifred Gamlin; one *s* one *d*. *Educ:* George Watson's Coll., Edinburgh; Univ. of Edinburgh; Jesus Coll., Oxford. MA (1st cl. hons Phil) Edinburgh, 1948; LLB Edinburgh, 1952. Served HM Forces, 1941–46; commnd in REME, 1942; India and SEAC, 1943–46. Asst in Moral Philosophy, Edinburgh Univ., 1949; called to Scottish Bar, 1953; QC (Scotland) 1967; Standing Jun. Counsel to BoT (Scotland), 1961–64; Advocate-Depute, 1964–67; Senior Advocate-Depute, 1967–70. MP (Lab) Leith, Edinburgh, 1970–79; Lord Advocate, 1974–79. Vice-Chm., Edinburgh Univ. Court, 1990– (Assessor, 1981)–. Mem., Scottish Records Adv. Council, 1987–. Hon. Pres., Leith Boys' Brigade, 1984–. *Publications:* articles in various jls. *Recreation:* boating. *Address:* 31 Boswall Road, Edinburgh EH5 3RP. *T:* 031-552 5602. *Clubs:* Royal Forth Yacht, Forth Corinthian Yacht.

MURRAY OF EPPING FOREST, Baron *cr* 1985 (Life Peer), of Telford in the County of Shropshire; **Lionel Murray,** OBE 1966; PC 1976; General Secretary of the Trades Union Congress, 1973–84; *b* 2 Aug. 1922; *m* 1945, Heather Woolf; two *s* two *d*. *Educ:* Wellington (Salop) Gram. Sch.; Univ. of London, 1940–41; NCLC; New Coll., Oxford, 1945–47 (Hon. Fellow, 1975). Economic Dept, TUC, 1947, Head of Dept, 1954–69; Asst Gen. Sec., TUC, 1969–73. Mem., NEDC, 1973–84; Vice-President: ICFTU, 1973; European Trade Union Confedn, 1974. Vice-Pres. and Vice-Chm., Nat. Children's Home; Vice-President: Hearing and Speech Trust; British Heart Foundn; Ironbridge Mus. Trust. Trustee: Carnegie UK Trust; NUMAST; Crisis at Christmas; Prison Service Trust. Governor: Ditchley Foundn; Nat. Youth Theatre. Fellow, QMW, 1988; Hon. Fellow, Sheffield City Polytechnic, 1979. Hon. DSc: Aston, 1977; Salford, 1978; Hon. LLD: St Andrews, 1979; Leeds, 1985. *Address:* 29 The Crescent, Loughton, Essex IG10 4PY. *T:* 081-508 4425.

MURRAY OF NEWHAVEN, Baron *cr* 1964 (Life Peer); **Keith Anderson Hope Murray,** KCB 1963; Kt 1955; Chancellor, Southampton University, 1964–74; Visitor, Loughborough University of Technology, 1968–78; *b* 28 July 1903; 2nd surv. *s* of late Rt Hon. Lord Murray, PC, CMG, LLD. *Educ:* Edinburgh Academy; Edinburgh Univ. (BSc); Ministry of Agriculture, 1925–26; Commonwealth Fund Fellowship, 1926–29, at Cornell Univ., New York (PhD); Oriel Coll. and Agricultural Economics Research Institute, 1929–32, University of Oxford (BLitt and MA); Research Officer, 1932–39; Fellow and Bursar, Lincoln Coll., 1937–53, and Rector, 1944–53; Chm., Univ. Grants Cttee, 1953–63. Oxford City Council, 1938–40; Min. of Food, 1939–40; RAFVR 1941–42; Dir of Food and Agriculture, Middle East Supply Centre, GHQ, MEF, 1942–45; Oxfordshire Education Cttee, 1946–49; JP, City of Oxford, 1950–53; Chm., Vice-Chancellor's Commission of Enquiry on Halls of Residence, 1947; Mem. of Commission of Enquiry into Disturbances in the Gold Coast, 1948; Development Commissioner, 1948–53; Chairman: Advisory Cttee on Colonial Colleges of Arts, Science and Technology, 1949–53, RAF Education Advisory Cttee, 1947–53; National Council of Social Service, 1947–53. Advisory Cttees on Agricultural Colls, 1954–60, Harkness Fellowship Cttee of Award, 1957–63, Cttee on Provincial Agricultural Economics Service, 1949–57, Cttee on Australian Univs, 1957; World Univ. Service, 1957–62; Dartmouth Review Cttee, 1958; Pres. Agric. Economics Soc., 1959–60; Pres. Agricultural History Soc., 1959–62; Chairman: Colonial Univ. Grants Cttee, 1964–66; London Conf. on Overseas Students, 1963–67; Academic Adv. Cttee for Stirling Univ., 1967–75. Vice-Pres., Wellington Coll., 1966–69; Governor, The Charterhouse, 1957–69. Mem. Bd, Wellcome Trustees, 1965–73; Dir, Leverhulme Trust Fund, 1964–72; Hon. Pres., Nat. 1.wUnion of Students, 1967–70. Chairman: Cttee of Enquiry into Governance of London Univ., 1970–72; Royal Commn for Exhibition of 1851, 1962–71. Director: Bristol Aeroplane Co., 1963–67; Metal Box Co., 1964–68. Hon. Fellow: Downing Coll., Cambridge; Oriel Coll., Oxford; Lincoln Coll., Oxford; Birkbeck Coll., London. Hon. LLD: Western Australia and of Bristol, 1963; Cambridge, Hull, Edinburgh, Southampton, Liverpool and Leicester, 1964; Calif., 1966; London and Strathclyde, 1973; Hon. DCL Oxford, 1964; Hon. DLitt Keele, 1966; Hon. DUniv. Stirling, 1968; Hon. DU Essex, 1971; Hon. FDSRCS, 1964; Hon. FUMIST, 1965. *Address:* 224 Ashley Gardens, SW1. *T:* 071–828 4113. *Club:* United Oxford & Cambridge University.

MURRAY, Bishop of The, since 1989; **Rt. Rev. Graham Howard Walden;** *b* 19 March 1931; *s* of Leonard Howard Walden and Mary Ellen Walden (*née* Cahalane); *m* 1964, Margaret Ann (*née* Brett); two *s* one *d*. *Educ:* Univ. of Queensland (BA 1952; MA 1954); Australian Coll. of Theol. (ThL 1954); Christ Church, Oxford (BLitt 1960; MLitt 1980). Ordained deacon 1954, priest 1955; Assistant Curate: West Hackney, 1954–56; St Saviour's, Poplar, 1957–58; permission to officiate, dio. of Oxford, 1955–59; Mem., Bush Brotherhood of the Good Shepherd, NSW, 1959–63; Vice Principal, Torres Strait Mission Theol Coll., 1963–65; Rector of Mudgee, NSW, 1965–70; Archdeacon of Barker, 1968–70; Archdeacon and Vicar-Gen. of Ballarat, 1970–89; Asst Bishop of Ballarat, 1981–89; Rector of Hamilton and Bishop in Hamilton, 1981–84. Nat. Chm., Anglican Men's Soc., 1983–; Anglican Chm., Jt Anglican RC Diocesan Commn, 1977–89; Member: Gen. Bd of Religious Educn, 1970–81; Anglican Lutheran Conversations constituted by Gen. Synod of Anglican Church of Australia, 1989–; Gen. Synod Commn on Doctrine, 1989–. *Publications:* contrib. to jls and church papers. *Address:* Bishop's Lodge, 23 Ellendale Avenue, Murray Bridge, SA 5253, Australia. *T:* 085 322240; PO Box 269, Murray Bridge, SA 5253, Australia. *T:* 085 322270.

MURRAY, Dame (Alice) Rosemary, DBE 1977; MA, DPhil; JP; DL; President, New Hall, Cambridge, 1964–81 (Tutor in Charge, 1954–64); Vice-Chancellor, Cambridge University, 1975–77; *b* 28 July 1913; *d* of late Adm. A. J. L. Murray and Ellen Maxwell Spooner. *Educ:* Downe House, Newbury; Lady Margaret Hall, Oxford (Hon. Fellow, 1968). MA (Oxon and Cantab); BSc, DPhil (Oxon). Lecturer in chemistry: Royal Holloway Coll., 1938–41; Sheffield Univ., 1941–42. Served War of 1939–45, Experimental Officer, Admiralty Signals Establishment, 1941; WRNS, 1942–46, Chief Officer. Lectr in Chemistry, Girton Coll., Cambridge, 1946–54, Fellow, 1949, Tutor, 1951, Hon. Fellow, 1976; Demonstrator in Chemistry, Univ. of Cambridge, 1947–52. Dir, Midland Bank Ltd, 1978–84; Independent Dir, The Observer, 1981–. Member: Lockwood Cttee on Higher Educn in NI, 1963–65; Wages Councils, 1968–; Council, GPDST, 1969–; Armed Forces Pay Review Body, 1971–81; Pres., Nat. Assoc. of Adult Educn, 1977–80, Vice-Pres., 1980–83. Governor and Chm., Keswick Coll. of Education, 1953–83; Mem. Delegacy, Goldsmiths' Coll., London Univ., 1986–89; Visitor, Homerton Coll., Cambridge, 1990–. Mem. Council, Toynbee Hall, 1983–89. Liveryman, Goldsmiths' Co., 1978–. JP City of Cambridge, 1953–83; DL Cambs, 1982. Hon. Fellow: LMH, Oxford, 1970; Girton Coll., Cambridge, 1975; New Hall, Cambridge, 1981; Robinson Coll., Cambridge, 1985. Hon. DSc: New Univ. of Ulster, 1972; Leeds, 1975; Pennsylvania, 1975; Wellesley Coll., 1976; Hon. DCL Oxon, 1976; Hon. DL Univ. Southern California, 1976; Hon. LLD: Sheffield, 1977; Cantab, 1988. *Recreations:* foreign travel, gardening, book binding and restoring. *Address:* 9 Grange Court, Cambridge CB3 9BD. *Club:* University Women's.

MURRAY, Andrew Robin; HM Diplomatic Service; Counsellor, Foreign and Commonwealth Office, since 1991; *b* 21 Sept. 1941; *s* of Robert Alexander Murray and Jean Agnes Murray (*née* Burnett); *m* 1965, Irene Dorothy Foy; one *s* one *d*. *Educ:* Trinity Coll., Glenalmond; Edinburgh Univ. (MA Hons 1965). Economist with Govt of Ontario, Canada, 1966; investment analyst, ICFC, 1969; joined HM Diplomatic Service, 1973; First Sec., Islamabad, 1975–78; Head of Chancery, Buenos Aires, 1979–81; FCO, 1982–84; Counsellor, UKMIS to UN, 1984–88; Caracas, 1988–91. *Recreation:* sporadic sport. *Address:* c/o Foreign and Commonwealth Office, SW1.

MURRAY, Sir Antony; *see* Murray, Sir J. A. J.

MURRAY, Athol Laverick, PhD; FRHistS; Keeper of the Records of Scotland, 1985–90; *b* Tynemouth, Northumberland, 8 Nov. 1930; *s* of late George Murray and Margery Laverick; *m* 1958, Irene Joyce Cairns; one *s* one *d*. *Educ:* Royal Grammar Sch., Lancaster; Jesus Coll., Cambridge (BA, MA); Univ. of Edinburgh (LLB, PhD). Research Assistant, Foreign Office, 1953; Assistant Keeper, Scottish Record Office, 1953–83; Deputy Keeper, 1983–84. Consultant Archivist, Jersey Archives Steering Gp, 1990–. Vice-Pres., Soc. of Antiquaries of Scotland, 1989–. FRHistS 1971. *Publications:* The Royal Grammar School, Lancaster, 1951; articles in Scottish Historical Review, etc. *Address:* 33 Inverleith Gardens, Edinburgh EH3 5PR. *T:* 031–552 4465. *Club:* Commonwealth Trust.

MURRAY, Brian; business consultant; *b* 7 Feb. 1933; *s* of Sidney Franklin Murray and Marjorie Manton Murray; *m* 1958, Pamela Anne Woodward (marr. diss. 1982); one *s* two *d*. *Educ:* Queen Mary College, London. BSc Chem. Central Research Labs, Bowater Corp., 1957–64; Dept. of Scientific and Industrial Research, 1964–66; Min. of Technology, 1967–70; Cabinet Office, 1971–74; DTI 1974–90; Under Sec., Minerals and Metals Div., 1983–87, Res. and Technol. Policy Div., 1987–90. Chm., Northumbria Cttee, The Prince's Trust, 1991–. *Recreations:* skiing, hill walking, travel. *Address:* 43 Lindisfarne Close, Newcastle upon Tyne NE2 2HT.

MURRAY, Charles Henry; Chairman, National Irish Bank (formerly Northern Bank (Ireland)) Ltd, 1986–89; *b* 1917; *s* of Charles and Teresa Murray; *m* 1942, Margaret Ryan; one *s* four *d*. *Educ:* Christian Brothers Sch., Synge Street, Dublin; London Univ. (BCom). Asst Secretary, Dept of Finance (Ireland), 1961, Secretary, 1969–76; Dir, 1969–76, Governor, 1976–81, Central Bank of Ireland. Dir, Northern Bank, 1982–88. Hon. LLD, NUI, 1977. *Recreations:* reading, theatre, golf. *Address:* 6 Washington Park, Dublin 14. *T:* 947781.

MURRAY, David Edward; Chairman, Murray International Holdings Ltd, since 1981; director of companies; *b* 14 Oct. 1951; *s* of late David Ian Murray and of Roma Murray; *m* 1972, Louise V. Densley; two *s*. *Educ:* Fettes Coll.; Broughton High Sch. Formed: Murray International Metals Ltd, 1976; Murray International Holdings Ltd, 1981. Young Scottish Businessman of the Year, 1984. Chairman: UK2000 (Scotland), 1987; Rangers FC, 1989–. Gov., Clifton Hall Sch., 1987. DUniv Heriot-Watt, 1986. *Recreations:* playing snooker, wine enthusiast. *Address:* Murray House, 4 Redheughs Rigg, South Gyle, Edinburgh EH12 9DQ. *T:* 031–317 7000.

MURRAY, Rt. Hon. Sir Donald (Bruce), Kt 1988; PC 1989; **Rt. Hon. Lord Justice Murray;** a Lord Justice of Appeal, Supreme Court of Northern Ireland, since 1989; a Judge of the Restrictive Practices Court, since 1987; *b* 24 Jan. 1923; *y s* of late Charles Benjamin Murray and late Agnes Mary Murray, Belfast; *m* 1953, Rhoda Margaret, *o c* of late Thomas and Anna Parke, Londonderry; two *s* one *d*. *Educ:* Belfast Royal Acad.; Queen's Univ. Belfast (LLB Hons); Trinity Coll. Dublin (BA). 1st Cl., Certif. of Honour, Gray's Inn Prize, English Bar Final Exam., 1944; Called to Bar, Gray's Inn, 1945, Hon Bencher, 1987. Asst Parly Draftsman to Govt of NI, 1945–51; Asst Lectr, Faculty of Law, QUB, 1951–53. Called to NI Bar, 1953, and to Inner Bar, NI, 1964; Bencher, Inn of Court, NI, 1971; Chm., Gen. Council of Bar of NI, 1972–75; Judge of the High Court of Justice, NI, 1975–89. Dep. Chm., Boundary Commn for NI, 1976–84. Chairman: Incorporated Council of Law Reporting for NI, 1974–87 (Mem., 1971); Bd, SLS Legal Publications (NI), 1988–. Member: UK Delegn to Commn Consultative des Barreaux des Pays des Communautés Européennes, 1972–75; Jt Standing Cttee of Bars of UK and Bar of Ireland, 1972–75; Deptl Cttee on Registration of Title to Land in N Ireland. Chm., Deptl Cttee on Reform of Company Law in NI; Inspector apptd to report on siting of new prison in NI. Mem., Legal Adv. Cttee of Standing Cttee of General Synod of Church of Ireland. Governor, Belfast Royal Academy. *Publications:* articles in various legal periodicals. *Recreations:* playing the piano, DXing. *Address:* Royal Courts of Justice, Chichester Street, Belfast, N Ireland.

MURRAY, Sir Donald (Frederick), KCVO 1983; CMG 1973; Channel Tunnel Complaints Commissioner, since 1987; *b* 14 June 1924; *s* of A. T. Murray and F. M. Murray (*née* Byfield); *m* 1949, Marjorie Culverwell; three *s* one *d*. *Educ:* Colfe's Grammar Sch.; King's Sch., Canterbury (King's and Entrance Schols); Worcester Coll., Oxford. Royal Marines, 1943–46 (41 (RM) Commando). Entered Foreign Office, 1948; Third Sec., Warsaw, 1948; FO 1951; Second Sec., Vienna, 1953; First Sec., Political Office, ME Forces, 1956; FO, 1957; First Sec. (Comm.), Stockholm, 1958; Head of Chancery, Saigon, 1962; FO 1964; Counsellor, 1965; Head of SE Asia Dept, 1966; Counsellor, Tehran, 1969–72; RCDS, 1973; Ambassador to Libya, 1974–76; Asst Under-Sec. of State, FCO, 1977–80; Ambassador to Sweden, 1980–84; retired HM Diplomatic Service, 1984. Assessor Chm., CS Selection Bd, 1984–86. Dir, Goodlass Wall and Co., 1985–. Kent County Chm., SSAFA, 1985–90; Trustee, World Resource Foundn, 1986–. Grand Cross, Order of North Star (Sweden), 1983. *Recreations:* gentle sports (Oxford v Cambridge cross-country, 1942; athletics, 1943; small-bore shooting, 1947), gardening, music. *Address:* Oxney House, Wittersham, Kent TN30 7ED.

MURRAY, George Sargent; Forestry Commissioner, 1981–84; *b* 2 Oct. 1924; *s* of James and Helen Murray; *m* 1951, Anita Garden Fraser; two *s*. *Educ:* Buckie High School. Inland Revenue, 1941–43; Royal Navy, 1943–46; Inland Revenue, 1946–49; Dept of Agriculture and Fisheries for Scotland, 1949–67; Scottish Development Dept, 1967–71; Scottish Economic Planning Dept, Scottish Office, 1971–76; Dept of Agriculture and

Fisheries for Scotland, 1976–81. *Recreation:* golf. *Address:* 30 Easter Currie Terrace, Currie, Midlothian EH14 5LE. *T:* 031–449 2538.

MURRAY, Gordon, PhD; Director, Scottish Courts Administration, since 1986; *b* 25 Aug. 1935; *s* of late James Murray, Aberdeen, and Annie Hardie (*née* Center); *m* 1964, Janet (*née* Yerrington); two *s* one *d*. *Educ:* Kirkcaldy High Sch.; Edinburgh Univ. (BSc (Hons), PhD). Research Fellow: Atomic Energy of Canada, 1960–62; UKAEA, Harwell, 1962–65; Lectr, Univ. of Manchester, 1965–69; Principal, Scottish Home and Health Dept, 1970–77; Assistant Secretary: Scottish Educn Dept, 1977–79; Central Services, Scottish Office, 1979–86. *Recreations:* reading, hill walking, gardening. *Address:* 26–27 Royal Terrace, Edinburgh EH7 5AH. *T:* 031–556 0755.

MURRAY, Sir James, KCMG 1978 (CMG 1966); HM Diplomatic Service, retired; Ambassador and Permanent UK Representative to UN and other International Organisations at Geneva, 1978–79; *b* 3 Aug. 1919; *er s* of late James Hamilton Murray, King's Cross, Isle of Arran, and Hester Macneill Buie; *m* 1982, Mrs Jill Charmian Chapuisat, *d* of Maj.-Gen. Frederick William Gordon-Hall, CB, CBE; two step *d*. *Educ:* Bellahouston Acad.; Glasgow Univ. Royal Regt of Artillery, 1939; served India and Burma, 1943–45; Staff Coll., Quetta, 1945; Bde Major (RA) 19 Ind. Div.; GSO II (RA) ALFSEA; GSO II War Office. HM Foreign (subseq. Diplomatic) Service, 1947; Foreign Office, 1947–49; First Sec. (Information), HM Embassy, Cairo, 1949–54; Foreign Office, 1954–56; attached National Defence Coll. of Can., 1956–57; First Sec., HM Embassy, Paris, 1957–61; HM Consul in Ruanda-Urundi, 1961–62; Special Ambassador for Independence celebrations in Ruanda, July 1962, and in Burundi, Sept. 1962; Ambassador to Rwanda and Burundi, 1962–63; Deputy Head of UK Delegation to European Communities, 1963–65; Counsellor, Djakarta, 1965–67; Head of Far Eastern Dept, FCO, 1967–70; Consul-Gen., San Francisco, 1970–73; Asst Under-Sec. of State, FCO, 1973–74; Dep. Perm. Representative to UN, 1974–78 (Ambassador, 1976). Special Envoy of 5 Western Govts for negotiations on Namibia, 1979–80. Withrow Prof. of Govt, Deep Springs Coll., Calif, 1990; Advr, Trade Policy Res. Centre, London, 1981–89; Hanson Industries, NY, 1983–. *Recreations:* horses, lawn tennis. *Address:* 220 Columbia Heights, Brooklyn Heights, New York, NY 11201, USA. *T:* (718) 852.3320. *Clubs:* Brooks's, Beefsteak, Pratt's; Brook (New York).

MURRAY, Prof. James Dickson, FRS 1985; FRSE 1979; Professor of Mathematical Biology, since 1986, Director, Centre for Mathematical Biology, since 1983, and Professorial Fellow, Corpus Christi College, since 1986, University of Oxford; *b* 2 Jan. 1931; *s* of Peter and Sarah Murray; *m* 1959, Sheila Todd Murray; one *s* one *d*. *Educ:* Dumfries Acad.; Univ. of St Andrews (BSc 1953; Carstairs Medal; Miller Prize; PhD 1956); Univ. of Oxford (MA 1961; DSc 1968). FIBiol 1988. Lectr, Applied Maths, Kings Coll., Durham Univ., 1955–56; Gordon MacKay Lectr and Res. Fellow, Tutor in Applied Maths, Leverett House, Harvard, 1956–59; Lectr, Applied Maths, UCL, 1959–61; Fellow and Tutor in Maths, Hertford College, Oxford, 1961–63; Res. Associate, Harvard, 1963–64; Prof. of Engineering Mechanics, Univ. of Michigan, 1964–67; Prof. of Maths, New York Univ., 1967–70; Fellow and Tutor in Maths, 1970–85, Sen. Res. Fellow, 1985–86, Corpus Christi Coll., Oxford; Reader in Maths, Univ. of Oxford, 1972–86. Vis. Fellow, St Catherine's Coll., Oxford, 1967; Guggenheim Fellow, Pasteur Inst., Paris, 1968; Vis. Professor: Nat. Tsing Hua Univ., 1975; Univ. of Florence, 1976; MIT, 1979; Winegard Prof., Univ. of Iowa, 1979; Univ. of Utah, 1979, 1985; Ida Beam Prof., Univ. of Guelph, 1980; Univ. of Heidelberg, 1980; CIT, 1983; Scott Hawkins Lectr, Southern Methodist Univ., Dallas, 1984; Stan Ulam Vis. Schol., Univ. of Calif. Berkeley's Los Alamos Nat. Lab., 1985; Philip Prof., Univ. of Washington, 1988–89; Landsdowne Lectr, Univ. of Victoria, 1990. Math. Comr, SERC, 1985–88; Pres., European Soc. for Theoretical and Mathematical Biol., 1991; Bd of Dirs, Soc. for Mathematical Biol., USA, 1986–89. Naylor Prize in Applied Math., London Math. Soc., 1989. Member Editorial Boards: Jl Theor. Biol.; Jl Math. Biol.; Jl Maths Applied in Medicine and Biol.; Bull. Math. Biol.; Lecture Notes in Biomaths; Biomaths Series; Applied Math. Letters; IMPACT of Computing in Sci. and Engrg; Biotheoretica; Jl Nonlinear Sci. *Publications:* Asymptotic Analysis, 1974, 2nd edn 1984; Nonlinear Differential Equation Models in Biology, 1977 (Russian trans. 1983); (ed with S. Brenner and L. Wolpert) Theories of Biological Pattern Formation, 1981; (ed with W. Jäger) Modelling of Patterns in Space and Time, 1984; Mathematical Biology, 1989; numerous articles in learned jls. *Address:* Centre for Mathematical Biology, Mathematical Institute, 24–29 St Giles', Oxford OX1 3LB. *T:* Oxford (0865) 273525.

MURRAY, James Patrick, CMG 1958; *b* 1906; *m* 1934, Margaret Ruth Buchanan; three *s*. *Educ:* St Edward's Sch., Oxford; Christ Church, Oxford. Cadet, Northern Rhodesia, 1929; District Officer, Northern Rhodesia, 1931; Provincial Commissioner, Northern Rhodesia, 1950; Senior Provincial Commissioner, Northern Rhodesia, 1955; Commissioner for Northern Rhodesia in London, 1961–64 (Country became Independent, as Zambia, 1964). *Address:* Trewen, Shaftesbury Road, Woking, Surrey. *T:* Woking (0483) 761988. *Club:* Commonwealth Trust.

MURRAY, Jennifer Susan, (Jenni); Presenter, Woman's Hour, BBC, Radio 4, since 1987; *b* 12 May 1950; *d* of Alvin Bailey and Win Bailey (*née* Jones); *m* 1971, Brian Murray (marr. diss. 1978); partner, David Forgham-Bailey; two *s*. *Educ:* Barnsley Girls' High Sch.; Hull Univ. (BA Hons French/Drama). BBC Radio Bristol, 1973–78; BBC TV South, 1978–82; BBC Newsnight, 1982–85; BBC Radio 4 Today, 1985–87. TV documentaries include: Everyman: Stand By Your Man, 1987, Breaking the Chain, 1988, As We Forgive Them, 1989; The Duchy of Cornwall, 1985, Women in Politics, 1989. *Recreations:* reading, theatre, riding, the children. *Address:* c/o Woman's Hour, BBC, Broadcasting House, Portland Place, W1A 1AA. *T:* 071–927 4314.

MURRAY, John; *see* Dervaird, Hon. Lord.

MURRAY, Sir (John) Antony (Jerningham), Kt 1987; CBE 1980; Hon. Adviser to Government of Barbados in United Kingdom, since 1961; *b* 21 Jan. 1921; *s* of Captain John Challenger Murray and Cecilia Annette Murray (*née* Jerningham); *m* 1943, Hon. Winifred Mary, *e d* of 2nd Baron Hardinge of Penshurst, PC, GCB, GCVO, MC; one *s*. *Educ:* Eton College; New College, Oxford (2 terms). Grenadier Guards, 1940–46 (Major); Dir, Christmas Island Phosphate Co. Ltd, 1947–51; Mem. Exec. Cttee, West India Cttee, 1957– (Chm., 1963–65; Vice-Pres., 1966–). *Recreation:* fishing. *Address:* Woodmancote Manor Cottage, Cirencester, Glos GL7 7ED. *T:* Cirencester (0285) 83226. *Clubs:* White's, Boodle's, Royal Automobile, MCC.

MURRAY, John (Arnaud Robin Grey), CBE 1975 (MBE 1945); FSA; FRSL; Senior Director of Publishing House of John Murray since 1968; *o s* of late Thomas Robinson Grey and Dorothy Evelyn Murray; *m* 1939, Diana Mary, 3rd *d* of late Col Bernard Ramsden James and Hon. Angela Kay-Shuttleworth; two *s* two *d*. *Educ:* Eton; Magdalen Coll., Oxford (BA Hist). Joined publishing firm of John Murray, 1930; Asst Editor, Cornhill Magazine, 1931; Asst Editor, Quarterly Review, 1933. Served with Royal Artillery and Army-Air Support, War Office, 1940–45. Relaunched Cornhill Magazine with Peter Quennell, 1945. Member: Council, Publishers' Assoc., to 1976; Council, RGS, to 1978; Pres., English Assoc., 1976. *Publications:* (editor, with Peter Quennell) Byron: A Self-Portrait, 1950; (editor, with Leslie A. Marchand) Complete Letters and Journals of Lord Byron, 12 vols, 1973–81. *Recreations:* Byron, archives, forestry, music. *Address:* (office) 50 Albemarle Street, W1X 4BD. *T:* 071–493 4361; (home) Cannon Lodge, 12 Cannon Place, NW3 1EJ. *T:* 071–435 6537. *Clubs:* Pratt's, Beefsteak, Brooks's; Roxburghe.

See also Viscount Mersey.

MURRAY, Katherine Maud Elisabeth, MA, BLitt, FSA; Principal, Bishop Otter College, Chichester, 1948–70; *b* 3 Dec. 1909; *d* of Harold J. R. Murray (former HMI of Schools) and Kate M. Crosthwaite. *Educ:* Colchester County High Sch.; Somerville Coll., Oxford. Tutor and Librarian, Ashburne Hall, Manchester, 1935–37; Mary Somerville Research Fellow, Somerville Coll., Oxford, 1937–38; Asst Tutor and Registrar, 1938–44, Domestic Bursar, 1942–44, and Junior Bursar, 1944–48, Girton Coll., Cambridge. Chairman of Council, Sussex Archæological Soc., 1964–77, Pres., 1977–80. Mem., Chichester District Council, 1973–87 (Chm. Planning Cttee, 1979–82, Vice-Chm., 1976–79). Hon. DLitt: Sussex, 1978; Coll. of Wooster, Ohio, 1979. *Publications:* The Constitutional History of the Cinque Ports, 1935; Register of Daniel Rough, Kent Record Soc., 1945; Caught in the Web of Words: James A. H. Murray and the Oxford English Dictionary, 1977; articles in Sussex Notes and Queries, Transactions of the Royal Historical Society, Archæologia Cantiana, English Historical Review. *Recreations:* walking, archæology, nature conservation. *Address:* Upper Cranmore, Heyshott, Midhurst, West Sussex. *T:* Midhurst (0730) 812325.

MURRAY, Prof. Kenneth, PhD; FRS 1979; FRSE; Professor of Molecular Biology, University of Edinburgh, since 1976; *b* 1930; *yr s* of Allen and Elizabeth Ann Murray; *m* 1958, Noreen Elizabeth Parker (*see* N. E. Murray). *Educ:* Birmingham. Dept of Molecular Biology, Univ. of Edinburgh: Sen. Lecturer, 1967–73; Reader, 1973–76; Prof., 1976–. Member: Biochemical Soc.; European Molecular Biology Organisation; British Biophysical Soc.; Academia Europaea. FRSE 1989. *Publications:* papers on nucleic acid biochem. and molecular genetics. *Address:* Institute of Cell and Molecular Biology, University of Edinburgh, Edinburgh EH9 3JR. *Clubs:* Athenæum; New (Edinburgh).

MURRAY, Kenneth Alexander George, CB 1977; MA, EdB; Special Adviser to the Home Office on Police Service, Prison Service, and Fire Service selection, 1977–80; Director, Civil Service Selection Board, and Civil Service Commissioner, 1964–77; *b* 16 June 1916; *s* of late George Dickie Murray and Isabella Murray; *m* 1942, Elizabeth Ward Simpson; one *d*. *Educ:* Skene Street and Central Schools, Aberdeen; Aberdeen Univ. (MA English (1st Cl. Hons), EdB Psychol. (1st Cl. Hons)). RAMC and War Office Selection Bd, 1940–45, Captain. Psychological Adviser, Govt of India, 1945–47; Lectr in Psychology, Univ. of Hull, 1948–50; Principal Psychologist and Chief Psychologist, CS Selection Bd, 1951–63. Adviser to Police Service in high-grade selection, 1963–, also to Fire and Prison Services, to Church of Scotland and C of E; Adviser (earlier) to Govts of Pakistan and Western Nigeria through their Public Service Commns. FBPs S 1984. *Recreations:* reading, walking, bridge, watching cricket and Rugby League. *Address:* 15 Melvinshaw, Leatherhead, Surrey KT22 8SX. *T:* Leatherhead (0372) 372995. *Clubs:* MCC, Commonwealth Trust.

MURRAY, Leo Joseph, CB 1986; QC (Aust.) 1980; legislation consultant, since 1989; Parliamentary Counsel, Queensland, Australia, 1975–89; *b* 7 April 1927; *s* of William Francis Murray and Theresa Agnes Murray (*née* Sheehy); *m* 1957, Janet Barbara Weir (marr. diss. 1987); two *d*. *Educ:* St Columban's Coll., Brisbane; Univ. of Queensland (BA, LLB). Admitted Barrister, Supreme Court, Queensland, 1951; Asst Crown Prosecutor, 1958; Asst Parly Counsel, 1963. *Publications:* contrib. to Australian Law Jl. *Recreations:* golf, ski-ing, music. *Address:* 99 Red Hill Road, Nudgee, Qld 4014, Australia. *T:* 07.267.5786. *Clubs:* Nudgee Golf (Brisbane); Southern Alps Ski (Sydney).

MURRAY, Nigel; Master of the Supreme Court, Queen's Bench Division, since 1991; *b* 22 Jan. 1944; *s* of Dr Ronald Ormiston Murray, *qv*; *m* 1970, Shirley Arbuthnot; one *s* one *d*. *Educ:* Stowe. Called to the Bar, Inner Temple, 1965; in practice, Western Circuit, 1987–91; Judge of High Court of Botswana, 1984–87. *Recreation:* golf. *Address:* Royal Courts of Justice, Strand, WC2A 2LL. *T:* 071–936 7472. *Clubs:* Garrick; Berkshire Golf, Rye Golf.

MURRAY of Blackbarony, Sir Nigel Andrew Digby, 15th Bt *cr* 1628; farmer; *b* 15 Aug. 1944; *s* of Sir Alan John Digby Murray of Blackbarony, 14th Bt, and of Mabel Elisabeth, *d* of late Arthur Bernard Schiele, Arias, Argentina; *S* father, 1978; *m* 1980, Diana Margaret, *yr d* of Robert C. Bray, Arias, Argentina; one *s* two *d*. *Educ:* St Paul's School, Argentina; Salesian Agricl Sch., Argentina; Royal Agricultural Coll., Cirencester. Farms dairy cattle, store cattle, crops and bees. Holds a private pilot's licence. *Heir: s* Alexander Nigel Robert Murray, *b* 1 July 1981. *Address:* Establecimiento Tinamú, cc 115, 2624 Arias, Provincia de Córdoba, Argentina. *T:* 0462–60031. *Clubs:* Venado Tuerto Polo and Athletic; Tigre Boat.

MURRAY, Prof. Noreen Elizabeth, PhD; FRS 1982; FRSE; Professor of Molecular Genetics, Institute of Cell and Molecular Biology (formerly Department of Molecular Biology), University of Edinburgh, since 1988; *b* 26 Feb. 1935; *d* of John and Lillian Grace Parker; *m* 1958, Kenneth Murray, *qv*. *Educ:* King's College London (BSc); Univ. of Birmingham (PhD). Research Associate: Stanford Univ., California, 1960–64; Univ. of Cambridge, 1964–67; Mem., MRC Molecular Genetics Unit, Edinburgh, 1968–74; Lectr, 1974, later Sen. Lectr, Reader, 1978–88, Dept. of Molecular Biology, Univ. of Edinburgh; scientist in European Molecular Biol. Lab., Heidelberg, 1980–82. Member: EMBO; Genetics Soc., USA; Pres., Genetical Soc., 1987–90. FRSE 1989. *Publications:* original research papers and reviews in field of genetics and molecular biology. *Recreation:* gardening. *Address:* Institute of Cell and Molecular Biology, University of Edinburgh, Mayfield Road, Edinburgh EH9 3JR. *T:* 031–650 5374.

MURRAY, Sir Patrick (Ian Keith), 12th Bt *cr* 1673; *b* 22 March 1965; *s* of Sir William Patrick Keith Murray, 11th Bt, and of Susan Elizabeth (who *m* 1976, J. C. Hudson, PhD), *d* of Stacey Jones; *S* father, 1977. *Educ:* Christ College, Brecon, Powys; LAMDA. *Heir: kinsman* Major Peter Keith-Murray, Canadian Forces [*b* July 1935; *m* 1960, Judith Anne, *d* of late Andrew Tinsley; one *s* one *d*]. *Address:* Sheephouse, Hay-on-Wye, Powys.

MURRAY, Peter, CMG 1959; HM Diplomatic Service, retired; *b* 18 July 1915; *m* 1960, E. M. Batchelor. *Educ:* Portsmouth Gram. Sch.; Merton Coll., Oxford. Burma Commission, 1937–49, Foreign Service, 1947; HM Ambassador to Cambodia, 1961–64; Ambassador to Ivory Coast, Upper Volta and Niger, 1970–72. *Address:* Brae Cottage, Lion Lane, Haslemere GU27 1JR.

MURRAY, Peter (John), PhD (London), FSA; Professor of the History of Art at Birkbeck College, University of London, 1967–80, now Emeritus; *b* 23 April 1920; *er s* of John Knowles Murray and Dorothy Catton; *m* 1947, Linda Bramley. *Educ:* King Edward VI Sch., Birmingham; Robert Gordon's Coll., Aberdeen; Gray's Sch. of Art, Aberdeen; Slade Sch. and Courtauld Inst., Univ. of London. Sen. Research Fellow, Warburg Inst., 1961. Trustee, British Architectural Library, 1979–83. Pres., Soc. of Architectural Historians of GB, 1969–72; Chm., Walpole Soc., 1978–81. Rhind Lecturer, Edinburgh, 1967; Vis.

Prof., Univ. of Victoria, BC, 1981. *Publications:* Watteau, 1948; Index of Attributions . . . before Vasari, 1959; Dictionary of Art and Artists (with Linda Murray), 1959 (6th edn 1989); History of English Architecture (with P. Kidson), 1962 (with P. Kidson and P. Thomson), 1965; The Art of the Renaissance (with L. Murray), 1963; The Architecture of the Italian Renaissance, 1963, 3rd edn 1986; Renaissance Architecture, 1971; The Dulwich Picture Gallery, a Catalogue, 1980; (ed) J. Burckhardt, The Architecture of the Italian Renaissance, 1985; contribs to New Cambridge Mod. Hist., Encycl. Britannica, etc.; translations; articles in Warburg and Courtauld Jl, Burlington Mag., Apollo, foreign jls. *Address:* The Old Rectory, Farnborough, Banbury OX17 1DZ.

MURRAY, Prof. Robin MacGregor, MD; Professor of Psychological Medicine, University of London, at King's College London and the Institute of Psychiatry, since 1989; *b* 31 Jan. 1944; *s* of James Alistair Campbell Murray and Helen Murray; *m* 1970, Shelagh Harris; one *s* one *d*. *Educ:* Royal High Sch., Edinburgh; Glasgow Univ. (MB, ChB 1968; MD 1974). MRCP 1971; MRCPsych 1976; MPhil London, 1976; DSc London, 1989. Registrar, Dept of Medicine, Univ. of Glasgow/Western Infirmary, 1971; Sen. House Officer, successively Registrar and Sen. Registrar, Maudsley Hosp., 1972–76; Vis. Fellow, National Inst. of Health, Washington, DC, 1977; Sen. Lectr, 1978–82, Dean, 1982–89, Inst. of Psych. *Publications:* (jtly) Essentials of Postgraduate Psychiatry, 1979; (jtly) Misuse of Psychotropic Drugs, 1981; Lectures on the History of Psychiatry, 1990; articles on schizophrenia, depression, alcoholism, genetics, analgesic abuse and psychiatric illness in doctors.

MURRAY, Roger; President, Cargill Europe Ltd, since 1982; Chairman, Cargill plc, since 1982; *b* 8 June 1936; *s* of Donald Murray and Nancy (*née* Irons); *m* 1960, Anthea Mary (*née* Turnbull); one *s* three *d*. *Educ:* Uppingham Sch.; Brasenose Coll., Oxford (MA). RNVR (Sub-Lieut), 1954–56. Joined Cargill Inc., Minneapolis, 1959; various positions in Hull and Geneva, 1960–70; Pres., Cargill Canada, 1973. Mem., Management Cttee, Cargill Inc., 1986–. Canadian and British citizen. *Recreations:* sailing, ski-ing. *Address:* 11 Pembridge Place, W2 4XB. *T:* 071–243 0026.

MURRAY, Rt. Hon. Ronald King; *see* Murray, Rt Hon. Lord.

MURRAY, Dr Ronald Ormiston, MBE (mil.) 1945; MD; FRCPE, DMR, FRCR; Consulting Radiologist: Royal National Orthopaedic Hospital, since 1977 (Consultant Radiologist, 1956–77); Lord Mayor Treloar's Orthopaedic Hospital, Alton, and Heatherwood Hospital, Ascot, since 1977 (Consultant Radiologist, 1951–77); *b* 14 Nov. 1912; *y s* of late John Murray and Elizabeth Ormiston Murray (*née* MacGibbon); *m* 1st, 1940, Catherine Joan Suzette Gauvain, FFCM (*d* 1980), *d* of late Sir Henry Gauvain, MD, FRCS, and Laura Louise Butler; one *s* two *d*; 2nd, 1981, Jane (*née* Tierney), *widow* of Dr J. G. Mathewson. *Educ:* Glasgow Acad.; Loretto Sch.; St John's Coll., Cambridge (MA); St Thomas's Hosp. Med. Sch. Casualty Officer and Ho. Surg., St Thomas' Hosp., 1938–39; RAMC (TA), 1939–45, MO 2nd Bn The London Scottish, Hon. Lt-Col. Associate Prof., Radiology, Amer. Univ. Hosp., Beirut, 1954–56. Sen. Lectr in Orthopaedic Radiology, Inst. of Orthopaedics, London Univ., 1963–77; Robert Jones Lectr, RCS, 1973; Baker Travelling Prof. in Radiology, Australasia, 1974; Caldwell Lectr, Amer. Roentgen Ray Soc., 1975, also Corresp. Mem. of the Soc., 1973–; Skinner Lectr, RCR, 1979; other eponymous lectures. Associate Editor, Brit. Jl of Radiology, 1959–71. Founder Vice-Pres., Internat. Skeletal Soc., 1973, Pres., 1977–78. Fellow: Brit. Orthopaedic Assoc.; RSocMed (Pres., Sect. of Radiol., 1978–79); Hon. Fellow: Amer. Coll. of Radiology, 1969; Royal Australasian Coll. of Radiol., 1979; Fac. Radiol., RCSI, 1981; Hon. Member: Mexican and Peruvian Rad. Socs, 1968; Rad. Soc. of N Amer., 1975; GETROA, France, 1976. *Publications:* chapters in: Modern Trends in Diagnostic Radiology, 1970; D. Sutton's Textbook of Radiology, 1969, 4th edn 1987; (jtly) Radiology of Skeletal Disorders: exercises in diagnosis, 1971, 3rd edn 1990; (jtly) Orthopaedic Diagnosis, 1984; papers in med. jls, mainly concerning radiological aspects of orthopaedics. *Recreations:* golf; formerly: Rugby football (Cambridge XV 1933–34, Scotland XV 1935), swimming (Cambridge Univ. Team 1933–34, British Univs Team, Turin, 1933). *Address:* Little Court, The Bury, Odiham, Hants RG25 1NB. *T:* Odiham (0256) 702982. *Clubs:* United Oxford & Cambridge University; Hawks (Cambridge), Berkshire Golf, Rye Golf.
See also N. Murray.

MURRAY, Dame Rosemary; *see* Murray, Dame A. R.

MURRAY, Sir Rowland William Patrick, 14th Bt *cr* 1630; retired hotel general manager; *b* 26 Oct. 1910; *s* of late Rowland William Murray, 2nd *s* of 12th Bt, and Gertrude Frances McCabe; *S* uncle 1958; *m* 1944, Josephine Margaret Murphy; four *s* two *d*. Served in US Army during War of 1939–45. Captain. *Heir: s* Rowland William Murray, [*b* 22 Sept. 1947; *m* 1970, Nancy Diane, *d* of George C. Newberry; two *s*].

MURRELL, Geoffrey David George, OBE 1987; HM Diplomatic Service; Minister-Counsellor, Moscow, since 1991; *b* 19 Dec. 1934; *s* of Stanley Hector Murrell and Kathleen Murrell (Martin); *m* 1962, Kathleen Ruth Berton; one *s* three *d*. *Educ:* Minchenden Grammar School, Southgate; Oxford Univ. BA French and Russian. FCO Research Dept, 1959–61; Moscow, 1961–64; FCO, 1964–68; Moscow, 1968–70; Head, Soviet Section, FCO Research Dept, 1970–75; First Sec., Belgrade, 1975–78; Regional Dir, Soviet and East European Region, Research Dept, 1978–83; Counsellor, Moscow, 1983–87; Counsellor, Res. Dept, FCO, 1987–91. *Recreations:* tennis, guitar. *Address:* c/o Foreign and Commonwealth Office, SW1A 2AH. *Club:* United Oxford & Cambridge University.

MURRELL, Prof. John Norman, PhD; FRS 1991; FRSC; Professor of Chemistry, University of Sussex, since 1965 (Pro-Vice-Chancellor (Science), 1985–88); *b* London, 1932. *Educ:* Univ. of London (BSc); Univ. of Cambridge (PhD). University of Sussex: Dean, Sch. of Molecular Scis, 1979–84; Acad. Dir of Univ. Computing, 1984–85. Chm., Science Bd Computing Cttee, SERC, 1981–84. *Publications:* Theory of Electronic Spectra of Organic Molecules, 1960; (jointly): Valence Theory, 1965; Semi-empirical Self-consistent-field-molecular Theory of Molecules, 1971; Chemical Bond, 1978; Properties of Liquids and Solutions, 1982; Molecular Potential Energy Surfaces, 1985; Introduction to the Theory of Atomic and Molecular Scattering, 1989. *Address:* School of Molecular Sciences, University of Sussex, Falmer, Brighton BN1 9QJ.

MURRIE, Sir William (Stuart), GCB 1964 (CB 1946); KBE 1952; Permanent Under-Secretary of State for Scotland, 1959–64, retired; *b* Dundee, 19 Dec. 1903; *s* of Thomas Murrie and Catherine Burgh; *m* 1932, Eleanore Boswell (*d* 1966). *Educ:* S America; Harris Acad., Dundee; Edinburgh Univ.; Balliol Coll., Oxford. Entered Scottish Office, 1927; transferred to Dept of Health for Scotland, 1935; Under-Sec., Offices of War Cabinet, 1944; Deputy Sec. (Civil), Cabinet Office, 1947; Deputy Under-Sec. of State, Home Office, 1948–52; Sec. to the Scottish Education Dept, 1952–57; Sec., Scottish Home Dept, 1957–59. Chm., Board of Trustees for Nat. Galls of Scotland, 1972–75; Member: Council on Tribunals, 1965–77; Adv. Cttee on Rhodesian Travel Restrictions, 1968–79 (Chm., 1979). General Council Assessor, Edinburgh Univ. Court, 1967–75. Hon. LLD, Dundee Univ., 1968. *Address:* 7 Cumin Place, Edinburgh EH9 2JX. *T:* 031–667 2612.

MURSELL, Sir Peter, Kt 1969; MBE 1941; Vice Lord-Lieutenant, West Sussex, 1974–90; *b* 20 Jan. 1913; *m* 1938, Cicely, *d* of late Mr and Mrs M. F. North; two *s* two *d*. *Educ:* Bedales Sch.; Downing Coll. Cambridge. Fruit growing, 1934. War Service: Air Transport Auxiliary, 1940–44, Sen. Comdr. West Sussex County Council: Mem., 1947–74; Chm., 1962–67 and 1969–74. Member: Cttee on Management in Local Govt, 1965–66; Royal Commn on Local Govt in England, 1966–69; Water Space Amenity Commn, 1973–76; Inland Waterways Amenity Adv. Council, 1974–77. DL West Sussex, 1962. *Recreations:* sailing, mountain walking, skiing, squash, canal cruising. *Address:* Taints Orchard, The Street, Washington, West Sussex RH20 4AS. *T:* Ashington (0903) 893062. *Club:* Farmers'.

MURTA, Prof. Kenneth Hall, FRIBA; Professor of Architecture, University of Sheffield, since 1974; *b* 24 Sept. 1929; *s* of John Henry Murta and Florence (*née* Hall); *m* 1955, Joan Wilson; two *s* two *d*. *Educ:* King's Coll., Univ. of Durham (BArch, DipArch). Architect in private practice and public service, 1954–59; Sen. Lectr, Nigerian Coll. of Arts, Science and Technology, then Ahmadu Bello Univ., 1959–62; University of Sheffield: Lectr, then Sen. Lectr, 1962–74; Dean, Faculty of Architectural Studies, 1974–77, 1984–88. Vice-Chm., Bd of Architectural Educn, ARCUK, 1990–91. *Publications:* contribs to Architectural Rev., Ecclesiologist, Churchbuilding, Trans RIBA, Architects' Jl, RIBA Jl. *Recreations:* cricket, soccer, churchwatching, travel, walking in cities on Sundays. *Address:* Underedge, Back Lane, Hathersage, Derbyshire S30 1AR. *T:* Hope Valley (0433) 50833. *Club:* Royal Over-Seas League.

MURTAGH, Miss Marion; Managing Director: Stats (MR) Ltd, 1985–87; CSB Data Processing Ltd, 1985–87; Chairman of both companies, 1970–85. *Educ:* Waverley Gram. Sch., Birmingham. Qualified as: Certified Accountant, 1947; Chartered Secretary, 1948. Proprietor, The Calculating Bureau, 1938–51, Joint Owner, 1951–61. Member: Anglo-Thai Soc.; West Midlands Bridge Club (Pres.). Pres., Dorridge Village Hall Assoc. *Recreation:* bridge. *Address:* 116 Chessetts Wood Road, Lapworth, Solihull, West Midlands B94 6EL. *T:* Lapworth (05643) 2089.

MURTON, family name of **Baron Murton of Lindisfarne.**

MURTON OF LINDISFARNE, Baron *cr* 1979 (Life Peer), of Hexham in the County of Northumberland; **(Henry) Oscar Murton,** PC 1976; OBE 1946; TD 1947 (Clasp 1951); JP; a Deputy Chairman of Committees, since 1981 and a Deputy Speaker, since 1983, House of Lords; *b* 8 May 1914; *o s* of late H. E. C. Murton, and of E. M. Murton (*née* Renton), Hexham, Northumberland; *m* 1st, 1939, Constance Frances (*d* 1977), *e d* of late F. O'L. Connell; one *s* (one *d* decd); 2nd, 1979, Pauline Teresa (Freeman, City of London, 1980; Chevalier, Nat. Order of Merit, France, 1976), *y d* of late Thomas Keenan. *Educ:* Uppingham Sch. Commissioned, TA, 1934; Staff Capt., 149 Inf. Bde, TA, 1937–39; Staff Coll., Camberley, 1939; tsc; active service, Royal Northumberland Fusiliers, 1939–46; Lt-Col, Gen. Staff, 1942–46. Managing Dir, Henry A. Murton Ltd, Departmental Stores, Newcastle-upon-Tyne and Sunderland, 1949–57. MP (C) Poole, 1964–79; Sec., Cons. Parly Cttee for Housing, Local Government and Land, 1964–67, Vice-Chm., 1967–70; Chm., Cons. Parly Cttee for Public Building and Works, 1970; PPS to Minister of Local Government and Development, 1970–71; an Asst Govt Whip, 1971–72; a Lord Comr, HM Treasury, 1972–73; Second Dep. Chm., 1973–74, First Dep. Chm., 1974–76, Dep. Speaker and Chm. of Ways and Means, House of Commons, 1976–79. Member: Exec. Cttee, Inter-Parliamentary Union British Group, 1970–71; Panel of Chairmen of Standing Cttees, 1970–71. Mem., Poole BC, 1961–63; Pres., Poole Cons. Assoc., 1983–; a former Vice-Pres., Assoc. of Municipal Corporations; Mem. Herrison (Dorchester) Hosp. Group Management Cttee, 1963–74. Governor, Canford Sch., 1972–76. Chancellor, Primrose League, 1983–88. Freeman, City of London, 1977; Freeman, Wax Chandlers' Co., 1978; Liveryman, 1979, Master, 1989, Clockmakers' Co. JP, Poole, 1963. *Recreations:* sailing, painting, military history. *Address:* 49 Carlisle Mansions, Carlisle Place, SW1P 1HY. *T:* 071–834 8226.

MUSCROFT, Harold Colin; barrister; *b* Leeds, 12 June 1924; *s* of Harold and Meta Catrina Muscroft; *m* 1958; three *d*. *Educ:* Dept of Navigation, Southampton Univ.; home; Exeter Coll., Oxford (MA). Volunteer, Royal Corps of Signals, 1942; commnd RA, 1943; served in India, Burma (wounded), Malay and Java; demobilised 1947 (Captain). Oxford, 1947–51. Called to Bar, Inner Temple, 1953; practised NE Circuit; a Recorder of the Crown Court, 1972–82. Called to Hong Kong Bar, 1982. Huddersfield Town Councillor, 1958–59. *Recreation:* writing. *Address:* 11 Chelmsford Road, Harrogate, North Yorks. *T:* Harrogate (0423) 503344; Les Oliviers, 28 Boulevard Eugene-Tripet, 06400 Cannes, France.

MUSEVENI, Lt-Gen. Yoweri Kaguta; President of the Republic of Uganda, since 1986; *b* 1945; *s* of Amos and Esteri Kaguta; *m* 1973, Janet Kataaha; one *s* three *d*. *Educ:* primary and secondary schs in Uganda; Univ. of Dar-es-Salaam, Tanzania (BA). Asst Sec. for Research in President's Office, 1970–71; Hd of Front for National Salvation and anti-Idi Amin armed gp, 1971–79; Minister of Defence, 1979–80, and Vice Chm. of ruling Military Commn; Chm., Uganda Patriotic Movement; Chm., High Comd of Nat. Resistance Army, 1981–. *Publications:* The Path of Liberation; Consolidating the Revolution; essays on Southern Africa; National Resistance Movement selected writings. *Recreations:* karate, football. *Address:* Office of the President, Parliamentary Buildings, PO Box 7168, Kampala, Uganda. *T:* 254881/241176/243926/243943.

MUSGRAVE, Sir Christopher (Patrick Charles), 15th Bt *cr* 1611; *b* 14 April 1949; *s* of Sir Charles Musgrave, 14th Bt and of Olive Louise Avril, *o d* of Patrick Cringle, Norfolk; *S* father, 1970; *m* 1978, Megan, *d* of Walter Inman, Hull; two *d*. *Recreations:* sailing, tennis, table-tennis, painting. *Heir: b* Julian Nigel Chardin Musgrave, *b* 8 Dec. 1951. *Address:* c/o Royal Bank of Scotland, Silver Street, Hull HU16 5PJ.

MUSGRAVE, Dennis Charles, FICE; Director, British Water Industries Group, 1981–85; *b* 10 Feb. 1921; *s* of Frederick Charles Musgrave and Jane Elizabeth (*née* Gulliver); *m* 1942, Marjorie Cynthia (*née* Chaston); one *s*. *Educ:* privately. MIStructE, FIWES. Engineering Assistant: Howard Humphreys and Sons, Consulting Engrs; Coode and Partners, Cons. Engrs, 1938–45; Asst Port Engr, Lagos, Nigeria, 1945–47; Engrg Asst, Borough of Willesden, 1947–49; Agent, Ruddock and Meighan, Civil Engrg Contractors, 1949–56; Associate Partner, Sandford, Fawcett and Partners, Cons. Engrs, in Canada, 1956–63, in Westminster, 1963–66. Engineering Inspector, Min. of Housing and Local Govt, 1966, Sen. Inspector, 1971; Asst Dir, DoE, 1974; Chief Water Engr, DoE, 1977–82. *Publications:* various technical papers. *Recreations:* music, literature. *Address:* Gaywoods, Ringshall Road, Little Gaddesden, near Berkhamstead, Herts HP4 1PE. *T:* Little Gaddesden (044284) 3501.

MUSGRAVE, Sir Richard James, 7th Bt, *cr* 1782; *b* 10 Feb. 1922; *s* of Sir Christopher Norman Musgrave, 6th Bt, OBE, and Kathleen (*d* 1967), 3rd *d* of late Robert Chapman, Co. Tyrone; *S* father 1956; *m* 1958, Maria, *d* of late Col M. Cambanis, and Mrs Cambanis, Athens, Greece; two *s* four *d*. *Educ:* Stowe. Capt., The Poona Horse (17th Queen Victoria's Own Cavalry), 1940–45. *Recreation:* shooting. *Heir: s* Christopher John Shane Musgrave, *b* 23 Oct. 1959. *Address:* Knightsbrook House, Trim, Co. Meath. *T:* 046 31372; Komito, Syros, Greece. *Club:* Kildare Street and University (Dublin).

MUSGRAVE, Rosanne Kimble, MA; Headmistress, Blackheath High School (GPDST), since 1989; *b* 31 Jan. 1952; *d* of Gp Captain John Musgrave, DSO, and Joanne Musgrave. *Educ:* Cheltenham Ladies' Coll.; St Anne's Coll., Oxford (MA); MA Reading Univ.; PGCE London Univ. Assistant teacher of English: Latymer Grammar Sch., 1976–79; Camden School for Girls (ILEA), 1979–82; Head of English: Channing Sch., Highgate, 1982–84; Haberdashers' Aske's School for Girls, Elstree, 1984–89. Corporate Mem., Cheltenham Ladies' Coll., 1989. *Recreations:* letterpress printing, DIY. *Address:* 14 Fortis Green, N2 9EL. *Club:* United Oxford & Cambridge University.

MUSGRAVE, Thea; composer; *b* 1928; *d* of James P. Musgrave and Joan Musgrave (*née* Hacking); *m* 1971, Peter, *s* of Irving Mark, NY. *Educ:* Moreton Hall, Oswestry; Edinburgh Univ.; Paris Conservatoire; privately with Nadia Boulanger. *Works include:* Cantata for a summer's day, 1954; The Abbot of Drimock (Chamber opera), 1955; Triptych for Tenor and orch., 1959; Colloquy for violin and piano, 1960; The Phoenix and the Turtle for chorus and orch., 1962; The Five Ages of Man for chorus and orch., 1963; The Decision (opera), 1964–65; Nocturnes and arias for orch., 1966; Chamber Concerto No. 2, in homage to Charles Ives, 1966; Chamber Concerto No 3 (Octet), 1966; Concerto for orchestra, 1967; Music for Horn and Piano, 1967; Clarinet Concerto, 1968; Beauty and the Beast (ballet), 1968; Night Music, 1969; Memento Vitae, a concerto in homage to Beethoven, 1970; Horn concerto, 1971; From One to Another, 1972; Viola Concerto, 1973; The Voice of Ariadne (opera), 1972–73; Rorate Coeli, for chorus, 1974; Space Play, 1974; Orfeo I and Orfeo II, 1975; Mary, Queen of Scots (opera), 1976–77; Christmas Carol (opera), 1979; An Occurrence at Owl Creek Bridge (radio opera), 1981; Peripeteia (orchestral), 1981; Harriet, the Woman called Moses (opera), 1984; Black Tambourine for women's chorus and piano, 1985; Pierrot, 1985; For the Time Being for chorus, 1986; The Golden Echo, 1987; Narcissus, 1988; The Seasons (orchestral), 1988; Rainbow (orchestral), 1990. Performances and broadcasts: UK, France, Germany, Switzerland, Scandinavia, USA, USSR, etc., Edinburgh, Cheltenham, Aldeburgh, Zagreb, Venice and Warsaw Festivals. Hon. MusDoc, CNAA. *Address:* c/o Novello & Co. Ltd, 8 Lower James Street, W1R 3PL.

MUSGRAVE, Prof. William Kenneth Rodgerson, PhD, DSc (Birmingham); Professor of Organic Chemistry, 1960–81, now Emeritus, and Head of Department of Chemistry, 1968–71, 1974–77, 1980–81, University of Durham; *b* 16 Sept. 1918; *s* of late Charles Musgrave and late Sarah Alice Musgrave; *m* 1944, Joyce Cadman; two *s*. *Educ:* Stanley Grammar Sch., Co. Durham; Univ. of Birmingham. British-Canadian Atomic Energy Project, 1944–45; Univ. of Durham: Lecturer in Chemistry, 1945–56; Senior Lecturer, 1956–60; Personal Readership in Organic Chem., 1960; Second Pro-Vice-Chancellor, 1970–73; Pro-Vice-Chancellor and Sub-Warden, 1973–78; Acting Vice-Chancellor, 1979. *Publications:* (joint) Advances in Fluorine Chemistry, Vol. I, edited by Stacey, Tatlow and Sharpe, 1960; Rodd's Chemistry of Carbon Compounds, vols Ia and IIIa, edited by Coffey; scientific papers in chemical journals. *Recreations:* gardening, rough shooting. *Address:* The Orchard, Potter's Bank, Durham City. *T:* Durham (091) 3843196.

MUSGROVE, Prof. Frank, DLitt; Sarah Fielden Professor of Education, University of Manchester, 1970–82, now Emeritus; Dean of the Faculty of Education, 1976–78; *b* 16 Dec. 1922; *e s* of late Thomas and Fanny Musgrove; *m* Dorothy Ellen (*née* Nicholls); one *d*. *Educ:* Henry Mellish Grammar Sch., Nottingham; Magdalen Coll., Oxford; Univ. of Nottingham. MA Oxon, PhD Nottingham, MEd Manchester. Served War, RAFVR, 1941–45; Navigator, Bomber Command (commnd), Ops 149 Sqdn (tour of bombing missions completed 1944). Educational appts in England and in the Colonial Educn Service, E Africa, 1947–57; Lectureships in Univs of Leicester and Leeds, 1957–65; Foundn Chair of Research in Educn, Univ. of Bradford, 1965–70. Visiting Professor: of Educn, Univ. of BC, 1965; of Sociology, Univ. of California (Davis), 1969; Guest lectr, Inst. of Sociology, Univ. of Utrecht, 1968; The Chancellor's Lectr, Univ. of Wellington, NZ, 1970; British Council Lectr, Univs of Grenoble, Aix-en-Provence, Nice, Paris, 1972; Raymond Priestley Lectr, Univ. of Birmingham, 1975. Hon. Prof., Univ. of Hull, 1985–88. Co-editor, Research in Education, 1971–76. FRAI 1952; FRSA 1971. DLitt Open, 1982. *Publications:* The Migratory Elite, 1963; Youth and the Social Order, 1964; The Family, Education and Society, 1966; Society and the Teacher's Role (with P. H. Taylor), 1969; Patterns of Power and Authority in English Education, 1971; Ecstasy and Holiness: counter culture and the open society, 1974; Margins of the Mind, 1977; School and the Social Order, 1979; Education and Anthropology, 1982; The North of England: from Roman to present times, 1990; research papers in: Africa; Sociological Review; Brit. Jl of Sociology; Brit. Jl of Educational Psychology; Economic History Review; Brit. Jl of Social and Clinical Psychology, etc. *Recreations:* fell walking, fly fishing. *Address:* Dibscar, The Cedar Grove, Beverley, E Yorks HU17 7EP. *T:* Hull (0482) 868799. *Club:* Driffield Anglers (Driffield).

MUSGROVE, Harold John; Chairman, Power Supplies and Lighting Group, Chloride plc, since 1991; *b* 19 Nov. 1930; *s* of Harold Musgrove; *m* 1959, Jacquelin Mary Hobbs; two *s* two *d*. *Educ:* King Edward Grammar Sch., Birmingham; Birmingham Tech. Coll. Nat. Cert. of Mech. Eng. Apprentice, Austin Motor Co., 1945; held various positions, incl. Chief Material Controller (Commission as Navigator, RAF, during this period); Senior Management, Truck and Bus Group, Leyland Motor Corp., 1963–78; Austin Morris: Dir of Manufacturing, 1978–79; Man. Dir, 1979–80; Chm. and Man. Dir, 1980–81; Chm., Light Medium Cars Group, 1981–82; Chm. and Chief Exec., Austin Rover Gp, 1982–86; Chm., Industrial Battery Sector, Chloride, 1988–91. Pres., Birmingham Chamber of Industry and Commerce, 1987–88. Director: Chloride plc, 1989–; Metalrax Gp, 1987–. Pres., Aston Villa FC, 1986–. FIMI 1985. Midlander of the Year Award, 1980; IProdE Internat. Award, 1981; Soc. of Engineers Churchill Medal, 1982. *Recreations:* golf, soccer. *Address:* The Lodge, Laverton, Broadway, Worcs WR12 7NA.

MUSGROVE, Prof. John, RIBA; Professor Emeritus, University of London; Haden-Pilkington Professor of Environmental Design and Engineering, 1978–85 and Head of the Bartlett School of Architecture and Planning, 1980–85, University College London; *b* 20 June 1920; *s* of James Musgrove and Betsy (*née* Jones); *m* 1941, Gladys Mary Webb; three *s*. *Educ:* Univ. of Durham (King's Coll.) (BArch, 1st Cl. Hons). Asst to late Baron Holford, RA, 1952–53; Research Architect, Nuffield Foundn, 1953–60; Sen. Lectr and Reader in Architecture, University Coll. London, 1960–70, Prof., 1970–78. Hon. Fellow, Inst. of Architects, Sri Lanka, 1972. *Publications:* (jtly) The Function and Design of Hospitals, 1955; (jtly) The Design of Research Laboratories, 1960; (ed) Sir Banister Fletcher's History of Architecture, 19th edn, 1987; numerous articles and papers in Architects' Jl, RIBA Jl, and reviews. *Recreations:* painting in oils, gardening. *Address:* Netherby, Green End Road, Boxmoor, Hemel Hempstead, Herts HP1 1QW.

MUSHIN, Prof. William W(oolf), CBE 1971; MA Oxon, 1946; MB, BS (Hons) London, 1933; FRCS 1966; FFARCS 1948; Professor and Director of Anaesthetics, Welsh National School of Medicine, University of Wales, 1947–75, now Emeritus; *b* London, Sept. 1910; *y s* of Moses Mushin and Jesse (*née* Kalmenson); *m* 1939, Betty Hannah Goldberg; one *s* three *d*. *Educ:* Davenant Sch.; London Hosp. Med. Sch. (Buxton Prize in Anatomy, Anderson Prize in Clinical Medicine). Various resident hosp. posts; formerly: Anaesthetist, Royal Dental Hosp.; first Asst, Nuffield Dept of Anaesthetists, Univ. of Oxford. Lectures: Clover, RCS, 1955; Kellogg, George Washington Univ., 1950; Guedel, Univ. of Calif, 1957; John Snow, 1964; Baxter Travenol, Internat. Anaesth. Research Soc., 1970; Macgregor, Univ. of Birmingham, 1972; Rovenstine, Amer. Soc. of Anesthesiol., 1973; Crawford Long, Emory Univ., USA, 1981. Visiting Professor or Consultant to univs, academic and other bodies in USA, Argentine, Uruguay, Brazil, Denmark, NZ, Australia, India, Germany, Ghana, Kenya, S Africa, and Holland. Examiner: Univ. of Oxford for MD and PhD; FFARCS, 1953–73; FFARCSI, 1962–67. Welsh Regional Hospital Board: Cons. Adviser in Anaesthetics, 1948–74; Mem., 1961–74. Member: Central Health Services Council, 1962–72; Safety of Drugs Cttee, Dept of Health and Social Security, 1964–76; Medicines Commn, 1976–83; Assoc. of Anaesthetists, 1936– (Mem. Council, 1946–59 and 1961–73; Vice-Pres., 1953–56); Anaesthetists Group Cttee, BMA, 1950–69; Bd of Governors, United Cardiff Hosps, 1956–65; Court, Univ. of Wales, 1957–58; Commonwealth Scholarships Commn, 1969–78. Welsh National School of Medicine: Mem. Senate, 1947–75; Mem. Council, 1957–58; Vice-Provost, 1958–60; Royal College of Surgeons: Mem. Bd, Faculty of Anaesthetists, 1954–71; Mem. Council, 1961–64; Dean, Faculty of Anaesthetists, 1961–64. Mem. Bd of Management and Consulting Editor, British Jl of Anaesthesia, 1947–75. Hon. Mem., various societies of anaesthetists. Hon. FFARACS 1959; Hon. FFA(SA) 1962; Hon. FFARCSI 1962; Hon. FRSM 1987. Hon. DSc Wales, 1982. John Snow Silver Medal, 1974; Henry Hill Hickman Medal, RSocMed, 1978. *Publications:* Anaesthesia for the Poor Risk, 1948; (with Sir R. Macintosh) Local Analgesia: Brachial Plexus, 1954, 4th edn 1967; Physics for the Anaesthetist, 1946, 4th edn 1987; Automatic Ventilation of Lungs, 1959, 3rd edn 1980; (ed) Thoracic Anaesthesia, 1963. Numerous papers on anaesthesia and allied subjects in British and foreign jls. *Address:* 30 Bettws-y-Coed Road, Cardiff CF2 6PL. *T:* Cardiff (0222) 751002.

MUSKER, Sir John, Kt 1952; banker; Chairman: Cater, Brightwen & Co. Ltd, Bankers, 1938–60; Cater, Ryder & Co., Ltd, Bankers, 1960–71 (Director, 1960–79); *b* 25 Jan. 1906; *o s* of late Capt. Harold Musker, JP, Snarehill Hall, Thetford, Norfolk; *m* 1st, 1932, Elizabeth (decd), *d* of Captain Loeffler, 51 Grosvenor Square, W1; two *d*; 2nd, 1955, Mrs Rosemary Pugh (*d* 1980), *d* of late Maj.-Gen. Merton Beckwith-Smith; 3rd 1982, Hon. Audrey Elizabeth Paget (*d* 1990), *d* of 1st Baron Queenborough, GBE. *Educ:* privately; St John's Coll., Cambridge (BA). Mem. LCC for City of London, 1944–49. Lt, RNVR, 1940. Hon. Treas., London Municipal Soc., 1936–46. *Address:* Shadwell Park, Thetford, Norfolk. *T:* Thetford (0842) 753257; 4 Cliveden Place, SW1. *Club:* White's.

MUSKERRY, 9th Baron *cr* 1781 (Ire.); **Robert Fitzmaurice Deane;** Bt 1710 (Ire.); *b* 26 March 1948; *s* of 8th Baron Muskerry and Betty Fairbridge, *e d* of George Wilfred Reckless Palmer; *S* father, 1988; *m* 1975, Rita Brink, Pietermaritzburg; one *s* two *d*. *Educ:* Sandford Park School, Dublin; Trinity Coll., Dublin (BA, BAI). *Heir:* *s* Hon. Jonathan Fitzmaurice Deane, *b* 7 June 1986. *Address:* 74 Bank Terrace, Manor Gardens, Durban, South Africa.

MUSKIE, Edmund Sixtus; Secretary of State, USA, 1980–81; lawyer and politician; *b* Rumford, Maine, 28 March 1914; *s* of Stephen Muskie and Josephine Czarnecki; *m* 1948, Jane Frances Gray; two *s* three *d*. *Educ:* Bates Coll., Maine (AB); Cornell Law Sch., Ithaca, New York (LLB). Served War, Lt USNR, 1942–45. Admitted to Bar: Massachusetts, 1939; Maine, 1940, and practised at Waterville, Maine, 1940 and 1945–55; Federal District Court, 1941. Mem., Maine House of Reps, 1947–51; Democratic Floor Leader, 1949–51; Dist. Dir for Maine, Office of Price Stabilisation, 1951–52; City Solicitor, Waterville, Maine, 1954–55; Governor of State of Maine, 1955–59; US Senator from Maine, 1959–80; Senate Assistant Majority Whip, 1966–80; Chm., Senate Budget Cttee, 1974–80. Cand. for Vice-Presidency of US, 1968. Mem., Senate Foreign Relations Cttee, 1970–74, 1979–80; Former Chm., and Mem. *ex officio*, Democratic Senatorial Campaign Cttee; Chairman, Senate Sub-Cttees on: Environmental Pollution, Senate Environment and Public Wks Cttee; Intergovtl Relations, Senate Governmental Affairs Cttee, 1959–78; Former Member: Special Cttee on Aging; Exec. Cttee, Nat. Governors' Conf.; Chm., Roosevelt Campobello Internat. Park Commn. Mem, Amer. Acad. of Arts and Sciences. Has numerous hon. doctorates. Phi Beta Kappa; Phi Alpha Delta. Presidential Medal of Freedom, 1981; Notre Dame Laetare Medal, 1981; Distinguished Service Award, Former Members of Congress Assoc., 1981. *Publication:* Journeys, 1972. *Address:* Chadbourne Parke, 1101 Vermont Avenue, NW, Washington, DC 20005, USA.

MUSSON, Maj.-Gen. Alfred Henry, CB 1958; CBE 1956; pac; late RA; President, Ordnance Board, 1957–58, retired (Vice-President, 1955–57); *b* 14 Aug. 1900; *s* of Dr A. W. Musson, Clitheroe, Lancs; *m* 1932, Joan Wright Taylor; three *s*. *Educ:* Tonbridge Sch.; RMA Woolwich. Served War of 1939–45. *Address:* Lyndon, 19 The Ridgeway, Tonbridge, Kent TN10 4NH. *T:* Tonbridge (0732) 364978.

MUSSON, Gen. Sir Geoffrey (Randolph Dixon), GCB 1970 (KCB 1965; CB 1959); CBE 1945; DSO 1944; BA; *b* 9 June 1910; *s* of late Robert Dixon Musson, Yockleton, Shrewsbury; *m* 1939, Hon. Elspeth L. Bailey, *d* of late Hon. Herbert Crawshay Bailey; one *s* (one *d* decd). *Educ:* Shrewsbury; Trinity Hall, Cambridge. 2nd Lt KSLI, 1930. Served War of 1939–45, North Africa and Italy; Comdr 2nd Bn DCLI, 1943–44; Comdr 36th Infantry Bde, 1944–46. Comdr Commonwealth Forces in Korea, 1954–55; Comdt Sch. of Infantry, 1956–58, Comdr 7th Armoured Div., BAOR, 1958; Maj.-Gen. 1958; Comdr, 5th Div., 1958–59. Chief of Staff, GHQ, Near East Land Forces, 1959–62; Vice-Adjutant-Gen., War Office, subseq. Min. of Defence, 1963–64; GOC-in-C, N Command, 1964–67; Adjutant-General, 1967–70, retired. Colonel: King's Shropshire Light Infantry, 1963–68; The Light Infantry, 1968–72. A Vice-Chm., Nat. Savings Cttee, 1970–78; Chairman: HM Forces Savings Cttee, 1970–78; Regular Forces Employment Assoc., 1978–80; Vice-Pres., Royal Patriotic Fund Corporation, 1974–83; Pres., Victory Services Club, 1970–80. *Address:* Barn Cottage, Hurstbourne Tarrant, Andover, Hants SP11 0BD. *T:* Hurstbourne (026476) Tarrant 354. *Club:* Army and Navy.

MUSSON, Rear Adm. John Geoffrey Robin; Senior Naval Directing Staff, Royal College of Defence Studies, since 1990; Chief Naval Supply and Secretariat Officer, since 1991; *b* 30 May 1939; *s* of Geoffrey William Musson and Winifred Elizabeth Musson (*née* Whyman); *m* 1965, Joanna Marjorie Ward; two *s* one *d*. *Educ:* Luton Grammar Sch.; BRNC, Dartmouth. Entered RN, 1957; served HM Ships: Bulwark, 1960–61; Decoy, 1961–62; Cavalier, 1966–67; Forth, 1967–69; Kent, 1975–76; NDC, 1979; MA, VCDS (Personnel and Logistics), 1980–81; Sec. to Chief of Fleet Support, 1982–83; CSO (Personnel and Admin), FONAC, 1984–86; Dir, Naval Officer Appts (Supply and WRNS), 1986–88; Captain, HMS Cochrane, 1988–90. *Recreations:* hill walking, mending things, history, natural history. *Address:* c/o Lloyds Bank, Cox's & King's, 7 Pall Mall, SW1Y 5NA.

MUSSON, John Nicholas Whitaker; Warden of Glenalmond College (formerly Trinity College, Glenalmond), 1972–87; *b* 2 Oct. 1927; *s* of late Dr J. P. T. Musson, OBE and

Gwendoline Musson (*née* Whitaker); *m* 1953, Ann Priest; one *s* three *d. Educ:* Clifton; Brasenose Coll., Oxford (MA). Served with Welsh Guards and Lancs Fusiliers, 1945–48 (commnd); BA Hons Mod. Hist., Oxford, 1951; HM Colonial Admin. Service, 1951–59; District and Provincial Administration, N Nigeria; Lectr, Inst. of Administration, N Nigeria; Staff Dept, British Petroleum, London, 1959–61; Asst Master and Housemaster, Canford Sch., 1961–72. Chm., Scottish Div. HMC, 1981–83; Scottish Dir, ISCO, 1987–. Gov. and Mem. Council, Clifton Coll., 1989–; Gov., George Watson's Coll., Edinburgh, 1989–. *Recreations:* hill walking, history, fine arts. *Address:* 47 Spylaw Road, Edinburgh EH10 5BP. *T:* 031–337 0089. *Club:* New (Edinburgh).

MUSSON, Samuel Dixon, CB 1963; MBE 1943; Chief Registrar of Friendly Societies and Industrial Assurance Commissioner, 1963–72; *b* 1 April 1908; *e s* of late R. Dixon Musson, Yockleton, Salop; *m* 1949, Joan I. S., 2nd *d* of late Col D. Davies-Evans, DSO, Penylan, Carmarthenshire. *Educ:* Shrewsbury Sch.; Trinity Hall, Cambridge. Called to Bar (Inner Temple), 1930; practised as Barrister, 1930–46; commnd, Pilot Officer, RAFVR, 1941; served Egypt, N Africa, Italy, 1942–45 (despatches). Ministry of Health: Senior Legal Asst, 1946; Asst Solicitor, 1952; Principal Asst Solicitor, 1957. Vice-Pres., Building Socs Assoc., 1972–87; Mem., Trustee Savings Bank Inspection Cttee, 1972–77. *Recreations:* golf, country pursuits. *Address:* The Beehive, 8 Fairview Road, Headley Down, Bordon, Hants GU35 8JP. *T:* Headley Down (0428) 713183. *Club:* Savile.

MUSTAFA, Nasr El-Din; Medal of Merit, First Class, 1972; Order of the Dedicated Son of Sudan, 1978; Order of the Two Niles, First Class, 1979; Ambassador of the Democratic Republic of Sudan to the Court of St James's, 1982–83; *b* 10 Oct. 1930; *m* 1962, Raga Yousif Sukkar; three *s* three *d. Educ:* University Coll. Khartoum. BSc(Eng), London; FICE. Sudan Railways (Civil Engrg), 1956–68; Messrs Goode & Partners, Consulting Engrs, UK, 1958–60; Sudanese Estate Bank, 1968–69; Sudanese People's Armed Forces, 1969–74; Chm., Sea Ports Corp., 1974–76; Minister of State for Planning, 1976–77; Minister of Nat. Planning, 1977–81 (and as such Governor for Sudan in IBRD, Arab Fund for Socio-Econ. Develt, IDB, ADB/F, and Nat. Authorising Officer, EDF); Dep. Pres., Ministerial Cttee for Economic Sector, 1979–81. Mem., Sudan Railway Bd of Dirs, 1973–76; Chm., Bd of Dirs, Khartoum Polytechnic, 1976–79. *Recreations:* reading, swimming. *Address:* c/o Ministry of Foreign Affairs, Khartoum, Sudan. *Club:* Royal Automobile.

MUSTILL, Rt. Hon. Sir Michael (John), Kt 1978; PC 1985; **Rt. Hon. Lord Justice Mustill;** a Lord Justice of Appeal, since 1985; *b* 10 May 1931; *o s* of Clement William and late Marion Mustill; *m* 1st, Beryl Reid Davies (marr. diss.); 2nd, Caroline Phillips; two *s* and one step *d. Educ:* Oundle Sch.; St John's Coll., Cambridge. Royal Artillery, 1949–51 (commissioned, 1950). Called to Bar, Gray's Inn, 1955, Bencher, 1976. QC 1968. Dep. Chm., Hants QS, 1971; a Recorder of the Crown Court, 1972–78; Judge of High Court, QBD, 1978–85. Presiding Judge, NE Circuit, 1981–84. Chairman: Civil Service Appeal Tribunal, 1971–78; Judicial Studies Board, 1985–89; Deptl Cttee on Law of Arbitration, 1985–90. *Publications:* The Law and Practice of Commercial Arbitration in England (with S. C. Boyd, QC), 1982, 2nd edn 1989; Anticipatory Breach of Contract, 1990; Joint Editor: Scrutton on Charterparties and Bills of Lading; Arnould on Marine Insurance; articles in legal periodicals. *Recreations:* visiting France, reading, music, active sports. *Address:* Royal Courts of Justice, Strand, WC2.

MUSTOE, Mrs Anne, MA; traveller, and educational consultant; *b* 24 May 1933; *d* of H.W. Revill; *m* 1960, Nelson Edwin Mustoe, QC (*d* 1976). *Educ:* Girton Coll., Cambridge (BA Classical Tripos 1955, MA 1958). DipIPM 1959. Guest, Keen & Nettlefolds Ltd, 1956–60; Head of Classics, Francis Holland School, NW1, 1965–69; independent travel agent, 1969–73; Dep. Headmistress, Cobham Hall, Kent, 1975–78; Headmistress, St Felix School, Southwold, 1978–87. Chm., ISIS, 1986–87; President, Girls' Schools Assoc., 1984–85; Mem., Board of Managers of Girls' Common Entrance Examinations, 1983–86. Governor: Hethersett Old Hall Sch., 1981–86; Cobham Hall, 1986–; James Allen's Girls' Sch., 1991–. JP Suffolk, 1981–85. *Publication:* A Bike Ride: 12,000 miles around the world, 1991. *Recreations:* music, cycling (world cycling tour, 1987–88). *Address:* c/o PCA Finance, 90 Gloucester Mews West, W2 6DY. *T:* 071–402 9082.

MUSTON, Rt. Rev. Gerald Bruce; *see* Australia, North-West, Bishop of.

MUTI, Riccardo; Music Director, Philadelphia Orchestra, 1980–autumn 1992, Conductor Laureate, from autumn 1992; Music Director, La Scala, Milan, since 1986; *b* 28 July 1941; *m* 1969, Cristina Mazzavillani; two *s* one *d. Educ:* Diploma in pianoforte, Conservatorio di Napoli; Diploma in conducting and composition, Milan. Principal Conductor, 1973–82, Music Dir, 1979–82, New Philharmonia, later Philharmonia Orchestra; Principal Conductor, Orchestra Maggio Musicale Fiorentino, 1969–81. Concert tours in USA: with Boston, Chicago, and Philadelphia orchestras; concerts at Salzburg, Edinburgh, Lucerne, Flanders and Vienna Festivals; concerts with Berlin Philharmonic, Vienna Philharmonic, Concertgebouw Amsterdam; opera in Florence, Salzburg, Vienna, Munich, Covent Garden, Milan. Hon. degrees from Bologna Univ. and univs in England and USA. Recording prizes from France, Germany, Italy, Japan and USA. Accademico: dell'Accademia di Santa Cecilia, Rome; dell'Accademia Luigi Cherubini, Florence. Grande Ufficiale, Repubblica Italiana; Verdienstkreuz, 1st class (Germany), 1976. *Address:* Teatro a la Scala, Via Filodrammtici 2, Milan 20121, Italy.

MWANZA, Dr Jacob Mumbi; Vice-Chancellor, University of Zambia, since 1976; *b* 2 Feb. 1937; *m* 1964, Elizabeth Maria; three *d. Educ:* Univ. of Munster, W Germany (MA Econ. 1968); Cornell Univ., USA (PhD 1973). Lectr, then Sen. Lectr, 1968–74, Head of Econs Dept, 1973–74, Univ. of Zambia. Man. Dir, Zambia Energy Corp., 1974–76; Dir, Zambia Nat. Commercial Bank, 1976–86. Mem., UN Cttee for Develt Planning, 1981–83; Vice-Chm., Senate, UN Inst. for Namibia, 1980–; Pres., Council for Develt of Economic and Social Research in Africa, 1982–. Mem. Council, Univ. of Dar es Salaam. *Publications:* Orienting Economics Teaching to Development Needs, in The Teaching of Economics in African Universities, 1973; The Operation of Public Enterprises in Zambia, 1978; contrib. Developing Economies. *Recreations:* fishing, tennis. *Address:* (home) Hawndsworth Park, Lumubashi Road 1–5, Lusaka, Zambia; (office) Box 32379, Lusaka, Zambia. *Clubs:* Flying, Economics (Lusaka).

MWINYI, Ndugu Ali Hassan; President, United Republic of Tanzania, since 1985; *b* 8 May 1925; *s* of late Hassan Mwinyi Chande and Asha Mwinyishehe; *m* 1960, Siti A. Mwinyi (*née* Abdulla); five *s* four *d. Educ:* Mangapwani Sch. and Dole Sch., Zanzibar; Teachers' Training Coll., Zanzibar; Durham Univ. Inst. of Education. Primary sch. teacher, head teacher, Tutor, Principal, Zanzibar, 1945–64; Acting Principal Sec., Min. of Educn, 1964–65; Dep. Gen. Manager, State Trading Corp., 1965–70; Minister of State, President's Office, Dar es Salaam, 1970–72; Minister for Health, 1972–75; Minister for Home Affairs, 1975–77; Ambassador to Egypt, 1977–81; Minister for Natural Resources and Tourism, 1982–83; Minister of State, Vice-President's Office, 1983; Vice-Pres., Union Govt, 1984. Chama cha Mapinduzi (Revolutionary Party): Member, 1977; Nat. Exec. Cttee, 1982; Central Cttee, 1984; Vice-Chm., 1984–90; Chm., 1990–; Mem., Afro-Shirazi Party, 1964. Chairman: Zanzibar Film Censorship Bd, 1964–65; E African Currency Bd, Zanzibar, 1964–67; Nat. Kiswahili Council, 1964–77; Tanzania Food and Nutrition Council, 1974–76. Mem.,Univ. Council of Dar es Salaam, 1964–65. *Address:* State House, Dar es Salaam, United Republic of Tanzania.

MYER, Sidney Baillieu, AC 1990; MA Cantab; Chairman: National Mutual Life Association of Australasia, since 1988 (Director, since 1978); Myer Emporium Ltd, since 1978 (Director, since 1955); Deputy Chairman, Coles Myer Ltd, since 1985; *b* 11 Jan. 1926; *s* of late Sidney Myer and late Dame (Margery) Merlyn Baillieu Myer, DBE; *m* 1955, Sarah J., *d* of late S. Hordern; two *s* one *d. Educ:* Geelong Grammar Sch.; Pembroke Coll., Cambridge (MA). Sub-Lieut, RANVR, 1944–46. Joined Myer Emporium, 1953; Vice-Pres., Myer Foundn, 1959–. Director: Elders IXL Ltd, 1972–82 and 1986–90; Cadbury Schweppes Aust. Ltd, 1976–82; Commonwealth Banking Corp., 1979–83; Network Ten Holdings Ltd and associated Cos, 1985–87. Part-time Mem. Executive, CSIRO, 1981–85. Pres., French Chamber of Commerce (Vic), 1962–64; Rep. Chm., Aust.-Japan Foundn, 1976–81; Member: Consultative Cttee on Relations with Japan, 1978–81; Aust.-China Council, 1979–81; Nat. Bicentennial Sci. Centre Adv. Cttee, 1986–89. Councillor: Aust. Conservation Foundn, 1964–73; Vic. Coll. of Arts, 1973–78; Chm., Art Foundn of Vic., 1986–88; Vice-Pres., Nat. Gall. Soc. of Vic., 1964–68; Trustee, Nat. Gall. of Vic., 1973–83 (Vice-Pres., 1977–83); Chm., Commonwealth Research Centres of Excellence Cttee, 1981–82. Chevalier de la Légion d'Honneur, 1976. *Address:* 250 Elizabeth Street, Melbourne, Victoria 3000, Australia. *Clubs:* Australian; Leander.

MYERS, Dr David Milton, CMG 1974; Vice-Chancellor, La Trobe University, Melbourne, 1965–76; *b* 5 June 1911; *s* of W. H. Myers, Sydney; *m* 1937, Beverley A. H., *d* of Dr T. D. Delprat; three *s. Educ:* Univs of Sydney and Oxford. BSc, BE, DScEng; FIE Aust., FIEE, FInstP. 1st Chief of Div. of Electrotechnology, CSIR, 1939–49; P. N. Russell Prof. of Elec. Engrg, Univ. of Sydney, 1949–59; Dean, Faculty of Applied Science, and Prof. of Elec. Engrg, Univ. of British Columbia, 1960–65. Mem. Adv. Council, CSIRO, 1949–55; Mem. Nat. Res. Council of Canada, 1965; Chairman: Cttee on Overseas Professional Qualifications, 1969–84; Inquiry into Unemployment Benefits, for Aust. Govt, 1977; Cttee of Inquiry into fluoridation of Victorian water supplies, 1979–80; Consultative Council on Victorian Mental Health Act, 1981. Pres., Aust. Inst. of Engineers, 1958. Kernot Meml Medal, 1974; P. N. Russell Meml Medal, 1977. *Publications:* various research papers in sci. jls. *Recreations:* golf, tennis, music. *Address:* 76 Glenard Drive, Heidelberg, Vic. 3084, Australia. *T:* 459 9629. *Club:* Melbourne (Melbourne).

MYERS, Brig. (Retired) Edmund Charles Wolf, CBE 1944; DSO 1943; BA Cantab; CEng, MICE; *b* 12 Oct. 1906; *er s* of late Dr C. S. Myers, CBE, FRS; *m* 1943, Louisa, *er d* of late Aldred Bickham Sweet-Escott; one *d. Educ:* Haileybury; Royal Military Academy, Woolwich; Caius Coll., Cambridge. Commissioned into Royal Engineers, 1926. Served Palestine, 1936 (despatches); War of 1939–45; Comdr, British Mil. Mission to Greek Resistance Forces, 1942–43; Middle East, including Balkans, until 1944 (African Star, Italy Star, DSO, CBE); North-West Europe, 1944–45 (France and Germany Star, Dutch Bronze Lion, Norwegian Liberty Medal); Far East, 1945; Korea, 1951–52 (despatches, American Legion of Merit). Chief Engineer, British Troops in Egypt, 1955–56; Dep. Dir, Personnel Administration in the War Office, 1956–59; retired 1959. Chief Civil Engineer Cleveland Bridge & Engineering Co. Ltd, 1959–64. Construction Manager, Power Gas Corp. Ltd, Davy-Ashmore Group, 1964–67. Regional Sec., British Field Sports Soc., 1968–71. *Publication:* Greek Entanglement, 1955. *Recreations:* horse training and riding, sailing, flying (1st Sec. RE Flying Club, 1934–35), fishing. *Address:* Wheatsheaf House, Broadwell, Moreton-in-Marsh, Glos GL56 0TY. *T:* Cotswold (0451) 30183. *Clubs:* Army and Navy, Special Forces.

MYERS, Geoffrey, CBE 1984; CEng; FCIT; Chairman, TRANSAID; Vice-Chairman, British Railways Board, 1985–87 (Member, 1980–87); *b* 12 July 1930; *s* of Ernest and Annie Myers; *m* 1959, Patricia Mary (*née* Hall); two *s. Educ:* Belle Vue Grammar Sch.; Bradford Technical Coll. (BScEng London). CEng, MICE 1963; FCIT 1973. RE, 1955–57. British Rail: civil engrg positions, 1957–64; Planning Officer, N Eastern Reg., 1964–66; Divl Movements Manager, Leeds Div., 1966–68; Dir of Studies, British Transport Staff Coll., 1968–70; Divl Man., Sheffield, 1970–76; Dep. Gen. Man., Eastern Reg., 1976–77, Gen. Man., 1977–78; Dir of Strategic Develt, 1978–80; Dep. Chief Exec. (Railways), 1983; Jt Managing Dir (Railways), 1984–85. Pres. Council, CIT, 1986–87. Mem., Carmen's Co., 1983. Hon. DEng Bradford, 1988. OStJ 1979. *Recreations:* golf, walking. *Address:* The Spinney, Lands Lane, Knaresborough, N Yorks. *T:* Harrogate (0423) 863719.

MYERS, Geoffrey Morris Price; Under-Secretary, Agricultural and Food Research Council, 1973–87; *b* 8 May 1927. *Educ:* Reigate Grammar Sch.; King's Coll., London. Civil Service, 1950; UKAEA, 1959–67; Nat. Econ. Develt Office, 1967–69; Agric. Research Council, 1970. *Address:* 4 Stanhope Road, Croydon CR0 5NS. *T:* 081-680 0827.

MYERS, Gordon Elliot, CMG 1979; Under-Secretary, Arable Crops, Pigs and Poultry Group, Ministry of Agriculture, Fisheries and Food, 1986–89, retired; *b* 4 July 1929; *s* of William Lionel Myers and Yvonne (*née* Arthur); *m* 1963, Wendy Jane Lambert; two *s* one *d Educ:* Kilburn Grammar Sch.; University Coll., Oxford (BA 1st Cl. Hons Modern History). Asst Principal, MAFF, 1951; Principal, 1958; Asst Sec., 1966; Head successively of Land Drainage Div., Sugar and Tropical Foods Div., and EEC Div., 1966–74; Under-Sec., MAFF, 1975; Minister (Agriculture), Office of UK Perm. Rep. to EEC, 1975–79; Under-Sec., Food Policy Gp, 1980–85, Cereals and Sugar Gp, 1985–86, MAFF. Mem., Cttee on Simplification of Common Agricl Policy, EEC. *Address:* Woodlands, Nugents Park, Hatch End, Pinner, Mddx. *Club:* United Oxford & Cambridge University.

MYERS, Harry Eric, QC 1967; QC Gibraltar 1977; *b* 10 Jan. 1914; *s* of Harry Moss Myers and Alice Muriel Serjeant; *m* 1951, Lorna Babette Kitson (*née* Blackburn); no *c. Educ:* Bedford Sch. HAC, City of London, 1931. Admitted Solicitor of Supreme Court, 1936; called to Bar, Middle Temple, 1945. Prosecuting Counsel to Bd of Inland Revenue on SE Circuit, 1965. *Address:* 202 Beatty House, Dolphin Square, SW1V 3PH; 10 King's Bench Walk, Temple, EC4Y 7EB.

MYERS, John David; Chairman of Industrial Tribunals, since 1982; *b* 30 Oct. 1937; *s* of Frank and Monica Myers; *m* 1974, Anne McGeough (*née* Purcell), *widow* of J. T. McGeough; one *s. Educ:* Marist College, Hull; Hull University. LLB Hons. Called to the Bar, Gray's Inn, 1968. Schoolmaster, 1958–64; University, 1964–67; pupillage with J. D. Walker (later Judge Walker); practice at Hull, 1969–82 (Junior, NE Circuit, 1975–76). *Recreations:* cooking, oenology. *Club:* Hull Golf.

MYERS, Sir Kenneth (Ben), Kt 1977; MBE 1944; FCA; Director, South British Insurance Co. Ltd, 1934–82 (Chairman, 1945–78); retired; *b* 5 March 1907; *s* of Hon. Sir Arthur Myers and Lady (Vera) Myers (*née* Levy); *m* 1933, Margaret Blair Pirie one *s* two *d. Educ:* Marlborough Coll.; Gonville and Caius Coll., Cambridge (BA 1928). FCA 1933. Returned to NZ, 1933; served War with 2nd NZEF, ME and Italy, 1940–45. *Recreation:* looking after my family. *Address:* 21 Upland Road, Auckland 5, New Zealand. *T:* Auckland 545499. *Clubs:* Boodle's; Northern (Auckland).

MYERS, Martin Trevor, FRICS; Chief Executive and Managing Director, Imry Holdings Ltd, since 1989; *b* 24 Sept. 1941; *s* of Bernard Myers and Sylvia Marjorie Myers (*née*

Pearman); *m* 1981, Nicole Josephine Yerna; one *s* one *d*. *Educ*: Arnold House, St John's Wood; Latymer Upper Sch.; Coll. of Estate Management, London Univ. (BSc). FRICS 1975. Jones Lang Wootton, 1965–83: Partner, 1969; Proprietory Partner, 1972; Chm. and Chief Exec., Arbuthnot Properties, 1983; merged with Imry Property Holdings, 1987, and with City Merchant Developers, 1988. *Recreations*: golf, tennis, riding, exercise. *Address*: 1 Durham Place, SW3 4ET. *T*: 071–351 1114; Kingsdown House, Upper Lambourn, Berks. *T*: Lambourn (0488) 72067. *Clubs*: Royal Automobile; Coombe Hill Golf (Kingston Hill).

MYERS, Sir Philip (Alan), Kt 1985; OBE 1977; QPM 1972; DL; one of Her Majesty's Inspectors of Constabulary, since 1982; *b* 7 Feb. 1931; *s* of John and Catherine Myers; *m* 1951, Hazel Gittings; two *s*. *Educ*: Grove Park, Wrexham. RAF, 1949–50. Shropshire Constabulary, 1950–67; West Mercia Police, 1967–68; Dep. Chief Constable, Gwynedd Constabulary, 1968–70; Chief Constable, North Wales Police, 1970–81. OStJ 1972. DL Clwyd, 1983.

MYERS, Sir Rupert (Horace), KBE 1981 (CBE 1976); FTS 1979; Professor Emeritus; Director: CSR Ltd, since 1982; Energy Resources of Australia Ltd, since 1982; *b* 21 Feb. 1921; *s* of Horace Alexander Myers and Dorothy (*née* Harris); *m* 1944, Io Edwina King; one *s* three *d*. *Educ*: Melbourne High Sch.; Univ. of Melbourne. BSc 1942; MSc 1943; PhD 1947; CEng, FIMMA, FRACI; FAIM; FAusIMM. Commonwealth Res. Fellow, Univ. of Melbourne, 1942–47; Principal Res. Officer, CSIRO, AERE Harwell, 1947–52; Univ. of New South Wales: Foundn Prof. of Metallurgy, 1952–81; Dean, Faculty of Applied Science, 1956–61; Pro-Vice-Chancellor, 1961–69; Vice-Chancellor and Principal, 1969–81. Chairman: NSW State Pollution Control Commn, 1971–89; Aust. Vice-Chancellors' Cttee, 1977–79; Cttee of Inquiry into Technol Change in Australia, 1979–80; Commonwealth Cttee of Review of Nat. Capital Devel Commn, 1982–83; Consultative Cttee for Nat. Conservation Strategy for Australia, 1983–85; Coastal Council of NSW, 1982–85; Cttee of Review of NZ Univs, 1987–88; Pres., Aust. Acad. of Technol Scis and Engrg, 1989– (Vice-Pres., 1985–88). Dir, IBM Australia Ltd, 1988–91. Member: Nat. Energy Adv. Cttee, 1980–82; Australian Manufacturing Council, 1980–82. Mem., Sydney Opera House Trust, 1976–83; Foundn Pres., Friends of Royal Botanic Gdns, Sydney, 1982–85. Hon. LLD Strathclyde, 1973; Hon. DSc Wollongong, 1976; Hon. DEng Newcastle, 1981; Hon. DLitt NSW, 1981. *Publications*: Technological Change in Australia, 1980; numerous on metallurgy and atomic energy (also patents). *Recreations*: tennis, bowls, music, working with silver. *Address*: 135 Neerim Road, Castlecove, NSW 2069, Australia. *T*: (02) 4176586, *Fax*: (02) 4178213. *Club*: Australian (Sydney).

MYERSON, Arthur Levey, QC 1974; **His Honour Judge Myerson**; a Circuit Judge, since 1978; *b* 25 July 1928; *o s* of Bernard and Eda Myerson; *m* 1960, Elaine Shirley Harris; two *s*. *Educ*: Blackpool Grammar Sch.; Queens' Coll., Cambridge. BA 1950, LLB 1951; BA (Open Univ.) 1985. Called to the Bar, 1952. A Recorder of the Crown Court, 1972–78. RAF, 1946–48. Pres., HM Council of Circuit Judges, 1991. *Recreations*: walking, reading, sailing. *Address*: Leeds Combined Court Centre, Oxford Row, Leeds LS1 3BE. *T*: Leeds (0532) 830040. *Clubs*: Commonwealth Trust; Moor Allerton Golf (Leeds).

MYLAND, Howard David, CB 1988; Deputy Comptroller and Auditor General, National Audit Office, 1984–89; *b* 23 June 1929; *s* of John Tarrant and Frances Grace Myland; *m* 1951, Barbara Pearl Mills; two *s* one *d*. *Educ*: Fairfields Schs; Queen Mary's Sch., Basingstoke. Served Intelligence Corps, 1948–50. Entered Exchequer and Audit Dept, 1948; Dep. Dir of Audit, 1972; Dir of Audit, 1977; Dep. Sec. of Dept, 1979; an Asst Auditor Gen., National Audit Office, 1984. Member: Basingstoke Round Table, 1962–70; Basingstoke Ex-Tablers, 1970–. *Publication*: Public Audit Law—Key Development Considerations, 1991. *Recreations*: travel, boating, contract bridge. *Clubs*: Sloane; Lanz (Bournemouth).

MYLES, David Fairlie, CBE 1988; tenant hill farmer; *b* 30 May 1925; *s* of Robert C. Myles and Mary Anne S. (*née* Fairlie); *m* 1951, Janet I. (*née* Gall); two *s* two *d*. *Educ*: Edzell Primary Sch.; Brechin High Sch. National Farmers Union of Scotland: Mem. Council, 1970–79; Convenor of Organisation and Publicity Cttee, 1976–79. MP (C) Banff, 1979–83; Sec., Cons. backbench Cttees on European Affairs and on Agriculture, Fisheries and Food (Jt Sec.); Mem., Select Cttees on Agriculture and on European Legislation. Contested (C) Orkney and Shetland, 1983. Councillor, Angus DC, 1984–. Chm., Dairy Produce Quota Tribunal for Scotland, 1984–; Member: Exec., Angus Tourist Bd, 1984–; North of Scotland Hydro-Electric Bd, 1985–88; Extra-Parly Panel (Scotland), 1986–; Potato Marketing Bd, 1988–. *Recreations*: curling, Scottish fiddle music. *Address*: Dalbog, Edzell, Brechin, Angus DD9 7UU; (home) The Gorse, Dunlappie Road, Edzell, Brechin, Angus DD9 7UB. *Clubs*: Farmers'; Brechin Rotary.

MYLLENT, Peter; *see* Hamylton Jones, K.

MYLNE, Nigel James; QC 1984; a Recorder, since 1985; *b* 11 June 1939; *s* of late Harold James Mylne and Dorothy Evelyn Mylne (later D. E. Hogg); *m* 1st, 1967, Julie Phillpotts (marr. diss. 1977); two *s* one *d*; 2nd, 1979, Judith Hamilton; one *s*. *Educ*: Eton College. National Service, 10th Royal Hussars, 1957–59. Called to the Bar, Middle Temple, 1963. *Recreation*: beekeeping. *Address*: 67 Thurleigh Road, SW12 8TZ. *T*: 081–673 2200. *Clubs*: White's, Pratt's, Garrick.

MYNORS, Sir Richard (Baskerville), 2nd Bt *cr* 1964, of Treago, Co. Hereford; Director of Music, Belmont Abbey School, Hereford, 1988–89; *b* 5 May 1947; *s* of Sir Humphrey Charles Baskerville Mynors, 1st Bt and Lydia Marian, *d* of Sir Ellis Minns, LittD, FSA, FBA; *S* father, 1989; *m* 1970, Fiona Bridget, *d* of late Rt. Rev. G. E. Reindorp; three *d*. *Educ*: Marlborough; Royal College of Music (ARCM, ARCO); Corpus Christi Coll., Cambridge (MA). Asst Director of Music, King's School, Macclesfield, 1970–73; Director of Music: Wolverhampton Grammar School, 1973–81; Merchant Taylors' School, Crosby, 1981–88. *Heir*: none. *Address*: Treago, St Weonards, Hereford HR2 8QB. *T*: St Weonards (09818) 208.

MYRES, Rear-Adm. John Antony Lovell; Hydrographer of the Navy, since 1990; *b* 11 April 1936; *yr s* of late Dr John Nowell Linton Myres, CBE and Joan Mary Lovell Myres (*née* Stevens); *m* 1965, Alison Anne, *d* of late Lieut David Lawrence Carr, RN and Mrs James Pertwee; three *s*. *Educ*: Winchester College. FRICS, MRIN. Entered RN 1954; specialised Hydrographic Surveying, 1959; CO HM Ships Woodlark, 1969–71, Fox, 1972–73, Hecla, 1974, 1978–79, 1981; Hydrographer, RAustN, 1982–85. FBIM. Younger Brother of Trinity House, 1990. Freeman, City of London, 1990; Liveryman, Chartered Surveyors' Co., 1990. *Publications*: articles in professional jls. *Recreations*: naval and medallic history, gardening. *Address*: Hydrographic Office, Ministry of Defence (Navy), Taunton, Somerset TA1 2DN.

MYRTLE, Brig. Andrew Dewe, CB 1988; CBE 1979 (MBE 1967); Chief Executive and Secretary, Tennis and Rackets Association, since 1989; *b* 17 Dec. 1932; *s* of Lt-Col John Young Elphinstone Myrtle, KOSB (killed in action in World War II) and Doreen May Lake; *m* 1973, Mary Rose Ford; two *d*. *Educ*: Horris Hill Prep. Sch.; Winchester Coll.; RMA, Sandhurst; Army Staff Coll. Co. Comdr, 1 KOSB, 1964–66; Bde Major, 24 Infantry Bde, 1966–68; Co. Comdr, 1 KOSB, 1968–69, CO, 1969–71; MA to Adjt Gen., 1971–74; Comdt, Jun. Div., Staff Coll., 1974–77; Comd 8 Infantry Bde, 1977–79; student, RCDS, 1979; DDMO, MoD, 1980–83; Asst Comdt, RMA, Sandhurst, 1983–85; Comdr Land Forces, Cyprus, 1986–88. ADC to the Queen, 1985–88. FBIM 1980. *Recreations*: golf, lawn tennis, (Real) tennis, rackets, fly-fishing. *Address*: Pen Guen, Stonor, Henley-on-Thames, Oxon RG9 6HB. *T*: Turville Heath (049163) 469. *Clubs*: Army and Navy, MCC; Huntercombe Golf.

N

NAAS, Lord; Charles Diarmuidh John Bourke; *b* 11 June 1953; *e s* and *heir* of 10th Earl of Mayo, *qv*; *m* 1st, 1975, Marie Antoinette Cronnelly (marr. diss. 1979); one *d*; 2nd, 1985, Marie Veronica Mannion; two *s*. *Educ:* St Aubyn's, Rottingdean; Portora Royal Sch., Enniskillen; QUB; Bolton Street Coll. of Technology, Dublin. *Heir: s* Hon. Richard Thomas Bourke, *b* 7 Dec. 1985. *Address:* Derryinver, Beach Road, Clifden, Co. Galway, Eire.

NABARRO, Prof. Frank Reginald Nunes, MBE 1946; FRS 1971; Professor of Physics, University of the Witwatersrand, 1953–84, now Hon. Professorial Research Fellow; *b* 7 March 1916; *s* of late Stanley Nunes Nabarro and Leah Nabarro; *m* 1948, Margaret Constance, *d* of late James Dalziel, ARAM; three *s* two *d*. *Educ:* Nottingham High Sch.; New Coll., Oxford (MA, BSc). DSc Birmingham. Sen. Exper. Officer, Min. of Supply, 1941–45; Royal Soc. Warren Research Fellow, Univ. of Bristol, 1945–49; Lectr in Metallurgy, Univ. of Birmingham, 1949–53; University of Witwatersrand: Prof. and Head of Dept of Physics, 1953–77, City of Johannesburg Prof. of Physics, 1970–77; Dean, Faculty of Science, 1968–70; Representative of Senate on Council, 1967–77; Deputy Vice-Chancellor, 1978–80. Vis. Prof., Nat. Research Council, Ottawa, 1956; Vice-Pres., S African Inst. of Physics, 1956–57; Republic Steel Vis. Prof., Dept of Metallurgy, Case Inst. of Techn., Cleveland, Ohio, 1964–65; Overseas Fellow of Churchill Coll., Cambridge, 1966–67; Gauss Prof., Akademie der Wissenschaften, Göttingen, 1970; Professeur-associé, Univ. Paris-Sud, 1971, Montpellier II, 1973; Vis. Prof. Dept of Material Science, Univ. of Calif., Berkeley, 1977; Vis. Fellow, Robinson Coll., Cambridge, 1981; Vis. Prof., Dept of Materials Engrg, Technion, Haifa, 1983. Hon. FRSSAf 1973 (Pres., 1989–). Hon. DSc: Witwatersrand, 1987; Natal, 1988; Cape Town, 1988. Beilby Memorial Award, 1950; South Africa Medal, 1972; De Beers Gold Medal, 1980; Claude Harris Leon Foundn Award of Merit, 1983; J. F. W. Herschel Medal, 1989. *Publications:* Theory of Crystal Dislocations, 1967, repr. 1987; scientific papers, mainly on solid state physics. *Recreation:* gardening. *Address:* 32 Cookham Road, Auckland Park, Johannesburg 2092, South Africa. *T:* (011) 726–7745.

NABARRO, Sir John (David Nunes), Kt 1983; MD; FRCP; Consultant Physician, The Middlesex Hospital, London, 1954–81, now Emeritus Consultant Physician; Hon. Research Associate, Departments of Medicine and Biochemistry, University College and Middlesex School of Medicine (formerly Middlesex Hospital Medical School), since 1981; Director, Cobbold Laboratories, Middlesex Hospital Medical School, 1970–81; Hon. Consultant Physician, Royal Prince Alfred Hospital, Sidney, since 1959; *b* 21 Dec. 1915; *s* of David Nunes Nabarro and Florence Nora Nabarro (*née* Webster); *m* 1948, Joan Margaret Cockrell; two *s* two *d*. *Educ:* Oundle Sch.; University Coll., London (Howard Cluff Meml Prize 1935; Fellow, UCL, 1963); University Coll. Hosp. Med. Sch. (Magrath Schol., Atkinson Morley Schol., Atchison Schol., 1938). MD London. Medical Specialist, OC Med. Div., RAMC, 1939–45: served in Iraq; 8th Army, Italy (Salerno Anzio); Middle East (despatches). UCH: House Phys., 1939; Med. Registrar, 1945–47; Res. Asst Phys., 1948–49; First Asst, Med. Unit, UCH Med. Sch., 1950–54; WHO Travelling Fellowship, 1952. Hon. Cons. Endocrinologist to Army, 1965–81. Examiner in Medicine, Univs of Cambridge, London and Sheffield. Chm., Jt Consultants Cttee, 1979–84. Mem., Assoc. of Physicians of GB and Ire., 1952; Pres., Sect. of Endocrinology, RSM, 1968–70; Chm., Med. and Sci. Sects, 1975–77, Chm. Council, 1986–90, Brit. Diabetic Assoc. RCP: Mem. Council, 1954–55; Oliver Sharpey Lectr, 1960; Joseph Senior White Fellow, 1960; Examiner for MRCP, 1964–81; Procensor, 1973; Censor, 1974; Croonian Lectr, 1976; Sen. Censor and First Vice-Pres., 1977. William McIlwrath Guest Prof., Royal Prince Alfred Hosp., Sidney, 1959; John Mathison Shaw Lectr, RCPE, 1963; Guest Visitor, St Vincent's Hosp., Sidney, 1963; Guest Lectr, Postgrad. Cttee, Christchurch Hosps, NZ, 1973; Banting Meml Lectr, Brit. Diabetic Assoc., 1978; Best Meml Lectr, Toronto Diabetes Assoc., 1984. Hon. FRSM 1988. *Publications:* Biochemical Investigations in Diagnosis and Treatment, 1954, 3rd edn, 1962; papers on endocrinology and diabetes in med. jls. *Recreation:* gardening. *Address:* 33 Woodside Avenue, N12 8AT. *T:* 081–445 7925.

NADER, Ralph; author, lecturer, lawyer; *b* Winsted, Conn, USA, 27 Feb. 1934; *s* of Nadra Nader and Rose (*née* Bouziane). *Educ:* Gilbert Sch., Winsted; Woodrow Wilson Sch. of Public and Internat. Affairs, Princeton Univ. (AB *magna cum laude*); Harvard Univ. Law Sch. (LLB). Admitted to: Bar of Conn, 1958; Bar of Mass, 1959; US Supreme Court Bar, 1963. Served US Army, 1959. Law practice in Hartford, Conn, 1959–; Lectr in History and Govt, Univ. of Hartford, 1961–63; Lectr, Princeton Univ., 1967–68. Member: Amer. Bar Assoc., 1959–; AAAS, 1964–; Phi Beta Kappa. Has pursued actively better consumer protection and improvement in the lot of the American Indian; lobbied in Washington for safer food, drugs, air, water and against nuclear reactors; played very important role in work for passing of: National Traffic and Motor Vehicle Safety Act, 1966; Wholesome Meat Act, 1967; Occupational Safety and Health Act, 1970; Safe Drinking Water Act, 1974; Freedom of Information Act, 1974. Niemen Fellows Award, 1965–66; named one of the Ten Outstanding Young Men of the Year by US Jun. Chamber of Commerce, 1967. *Publications:* Unsafe at Any Speed: the designed-in dangers of the American automobile, 1965, rev. edn 1972; (jtly) What to do with Your Bad Car, 1971; Working on the System: a manual for citizen's access to federal agencies, 1972; (jtly) Action for a Change, 1972; (jtly) Whistleblowing, 1972; (jtly) You and Your Pension, 1973; (ed) The Consumer and Corporate Accountability, 1973; (co-ed) Corporate Power in America, 1973; (jtly) Taming the Giant Corporation, 1976; (co-ed) Verdicts on Lawyers, 1976; (jtly) Menace of Atomic Energy, 1977; (co-ed) Who's Poisoning America?, 1981; (jtly) The Big Boys: power and position in American business, 1986; contrib. articles to many magazines; has weekly syndicated newspaper column. *Address:* PO Box 19367, Washington, DC 20036, USA.

NADESAN, Pararajasingam, CMG 1955; OBE 1954; Governor, Rotary International, District 321; Member, Legislative Council, Rotary International; Director: Cargills (Ceylon) Ltd; Associated Hotels Co. Ltd; Past Chairman: Low Country Products Association; Air Ceylon; *b* 20 Dec. 1917; *s* of Sir Sangarapillai Pararajasingam, *qv*; *m* 1st, 1941, Gauri Nair (decd); one *s* one *d*; 2nd, 1953, Kamala Nair; three *d*. *Educ:* Royal College, and Ceylon Univ. Coll.; Univ. of London (BA Hons). Tutor, Ceylon Univ. Coll., 1940; entered Ceylon Civil Service, 1941; held various appts in sphere of provincial administration, 1941–47; Asst Permanent Sec., Min. of Transport and Works, 1948–53; Dir of Civil Aviation in addition to duties as Asst Sec. Min. of Transport and Works, 1954–56; Sec. to the Prime Minister and Information Officer, Ceylon, 1954–56; Member: Ceylon Delegation to the Bandung Conf.; Commonwealth Prime Minister's Conf.; ICAO Gen. Assembly; ILO Cttee on Plantations. Past Mem., Nat. Planning Council. Pres. Emeritus and Life Mem., Ceylon Hotels Assoc.; FHCIMA. FCIT. President: Orchid Circle of Ceylon; Sri Lanka Horticultural Soc. Officer Order of Merit (Italy), 1954; Knight Comdr Order of the Crown, Thailand, 1955; Comdr Order of Orange Nassau, Netherlands, 1955; Defence Medal, 1947; Coronation Medal, 1953; Ceylon Armed Services Inauguration Medal, 1956. *Recreations:* golf, tennis, gardening, collecting antiques, stamps and coins. *Clubs:* Colombo, Orient, Rotary (Colombo); Gymkhana.

NAGDA, Kanti; Manager, Community Centre; *b* 1 May 1946; *s* of Vershi Bhoja Nagda and Zaviben Nagda; *m* 1972, Bhagwati Desai; two *s*. *Educ:* City High Sch., Kampala, Uganda; Coll. of Further Educn, Chippenham, Wilts; E African Univ., Uganda. Sec.-Gen., Confedn of Indian Organisations (UK), 1975–. Exec. Cttee Member: Harrow Community Relations Council, 1974–76; Gujarati Literary Acad. (GB), 1976–82. Mem., European Movement. President: Uganda Art Circle, 1968–71; Anglo Indian Circle, 1973–82 and 1985–; Indian Cricket Club, Harrow, 1976–80; Greenford (Willow Tree) Lions Club, 1988–89. Representative: Harrow Youth Council; Brent Youth Council; Harrow Arts Council. Hon. Editorial Consultant, International Asian Guide & Who's Who, 1975–; Asst Editor, Oswal News, 1977–84. *Publications:* Muratiyo Ke Nokar (Gujarati novel), Kenya 1967; stories and articles in newspapers and jls. *Recreations:* cricket, photography. *Address:* 170 Tolcarne Drive, Pinner, Middx HA5 2DR. *T:* 081–863 9089. *Club:* Indian National.

NAGY, János L.; *see* Lörincz-Nagy, J.

NAILATIKAU, Brig.-Gen. Ratu Epeli, LVO 1977; OBE 1979; MSD 1988; Ambassador of the Republic of Fiji to the Court of St James's, since 1988; concurrently Ambassador to the Holy See, Denmark, Federal Republic of Germany, Egypt and Israel; *b* 5 July 1941; *s* of Ratu Sir Edward Cakobau, KBE, MC, ED and Adi Lady Vasamaca Cakobau; *m* 1981, Adi Koila Nailatikau (*née* Mara), *d* of Ratu Sir Kamisese Mara, *qv*; one *s* one *d*. *Educ:* Levuka Public Sch.; Queen Victoria Sch., Fiji; Wadham Coll., Oxford. Enlisted in Royal Fiji Military Forces, 1962; commnd Fiji Infantry Regt, 1963; seconded to First Bn, Royal NZ Infantry Regt, Malaysia and Borneo, 1966; ADC to Governor of Fiji, 1968–69; Foreign Service Course, Oxford Univ., 1969–70; Second Secretary: Fiji High Commn, Canberra, 1970–72; Fiji Mission to UN, 1973–74; Australian Army Staff Coll., Queenscliffe, 1976 (psc); CO Fiji Bn, Fiji Infantry Regt serving with UNIFIL, 1978–79; Jt Services Staff Coll., Canberra, Australia, 1980 (jssc); Sen. Plans Officer, UNIFIL HQ, 1981; CS, 1981–82, Comdr, 1982–87, Royal Fiji Mil. Forces. Fiji Equerry: to the Prince of Wales during Fiji Independence visit, 1970; to the Queen during Jubilee visit, 1977. OStJ 1985. *Recreations:* golf, tennis. *Address:* Embassy of the Republic of Fiji, 34 Hyde Park Gate, SW7 5BN. *T:* 071–584 3661.

NAILOR, Prof. Peter; Provost of Gresham College, 1988; *b* 16 Dec. 1928; *o s* of Leslie Nailor and Lily Matilda (*née* Jones). *Educ:* Mercers' Sch.; Wadham Coll., Oxford (BA 1952, MA 1955). Home Civil Service, 1952; Asst Principal, Admiralty, 1952; First Lord's Representative on Admiralty Interview Bd, 1960–62; Polaris Executive, 1962–67; Asst Sec., MoD, 1967–69; Professor of Politics, Univ. of Lancaster, 1969–77; Prof. of Hist., 1977–88, Dean, 1982–84 and 1986–88, RNC, Greenwich. Visiting research appts and professorships in Canada, Australia and India; Member: Political Science Cttee, SSRC, 1975–81; FCO adv. panel on arms control and disarmament, 1975; MoD adv. panel on historical records, 1979; Chairman, British International Studies Assoc., 1983–86. Freeman and Liveryman, Mercers' Co., 1969. *Publications:* The Nassau Connection, 1988; articles in learned jls, pamphlets. *Address:* Gresham College, c/o Mercers' Hall, Ironmonger Lane, EC2V 8HE.

NAIPAUL, Sir Vidiadhar Surajprasad, (Sir Vidia), Kt 1990; author; *b* 17 Aug. 1932; *m* 1955, Patricia Ann Hale. *Educ:* Queen's Royal Coll., Trinidad; University Coll., Oxford (Hon. Fellow, 1983). Hon. Dr Letters Columbia Univ., NY, 1981; Hon. LittD Cambridge, 1983. *Publications:* The Middle Passage, 1962; An Area of Darkness, 1964; The Loss of El Dorado, 1969; The Overcrowded Barracoon, and other articles, 1972; India: a wounded civilization, 1977; The Return of Eva Perón, 1980; Among the Believers, 1981; Finding the Centre, 1984; A Turn in the South, 1989; India: a million mutinies now, 1990; *novels:* The Mystic Masseur, 1957 (John Llewelyn Rhys Memorial Prize, 1958); The Suffrage of Elvira, 1958; Miguel Street, 1959 (Somerset Maugham Award, 1961); A House for Mr Biswas, 1961; Mr Stone and the Knights Companion, 1963 (Hawthornden Prize, 1964); The Mimic Men, 1967 (W. H. Smith Award, 1968); A Flag on the Island, 1967; In a Free State, 1971 (Booker Prize, 1971); Guerrillas, 1975; A Bend in the River, 1979; The Enigma of Arrival, 1987. *Address:* c/o Aitken & Stone Ltd, 29 Fernshaw Road, SW10 0TG.

NAIR, Chengara Veetil Devan; President of Singapore, 1981–85; *b* Malacca, Malaysia, 5 Aug. 1923; *s* of Karunakaran Illath Vayalakkara and Devaki Chengara Veetil Nair; *m* 1953, Avadai Dhanam Lakshimi; three *s* one *d*. *Educ:* Victoria Sch., Singapore. Teacher, St Andrew's Sch., 1949–51; Gen. Sec., Singapore Teachers' Union, 1949–51; Convenor, and Mem. Central Exec. Cttee, People's Action Party, 1954–56; Political Sec., Min. of

Education, 1959–60; Chm., Singapore Adult Educn Bd, 1961–64; National Trades Union Congress: Sec. Gen., 1962–65, 1969–79; Dir, Res. Unit, 1969–81; Pres., 1979–81; Pres., Asian Regl Orgn, ICFTU, 1976–81. MP Malaysia, 1964–69, Singapore, 1979–81; first Sec. Gen., Democratic Action Party, Malaysia, 1964–69. Member: Nat. Wages Council, 1972–81; Housing and Develt Bd, 1975–81; Presidential Council for Minority Rights, 1979–81; Chm., Singapore Labour Foundn, 1977–81. Mem. Council, Nat. Univ. of Singapore, 1980–81; Chm., Hindu Adv. Bd, 1981. Life Member: Singapore Cancer Soc.; Ramakrishna Mission; Sri Aurobindo Soc. Hon. DLitt Nat. Univ. of Singapore, 1976. *Publications:* (ed) Who Lives if Malaysia Dies?, 1969; (ed) Singapore: Socialism that Works, 1976; (ed) Tomorrow: the peril and the promise, 1976; (ed) Asian Labour and the Dynamics of Change, 1977; (ed) Not by Wages Alone, 1982.

NAIRN, Air Vice-Marshal Kenneth Gordon, CB 1945; chartered accountant; *b* 9 Nov. 1898; *m* 1920, Mary Fleming Martin; two *s* one *d*. *Educ:* George Watson's Coll., Edinburgh; Univ. of Manitoba. Lived in Edinburgh till 1911; proceeded to Canada; service in Strathcona Horse and transferred to RFC 1916–19; Pilot, rank Lt; moved to Vancouver from Winnipeg, 1921; retired. Hon. Wing Commander of 111 Aux. Squadron RCAF 1933; Active Service, 1939–45; on Air Council as Air Mem. Accounts and Finance till Oct. 1944, then Special Adviser to Minister for Air on Finance. Hon. ADC for Province of BC to the Governor-General, Viscount Alexander, 1947. Norwegian Cross of Liberation, 1948. *Recreations:* golf, fishing, yachting. *Address:* 1611 Drummond Drive, Vancouver, BC V6T 1B7, Canada. *T:* 224–1500. *Clubs:* Royal Air Force; Vancouver, Royal Vancouver Yacht (Vancouver).

NAIRN, Margaret, RGN, SCM; Chief Area Nursing Officer, Greater Glasgow Health Board, 1974–84; *b* 20 July 1924; *d* of James R. Nairn and Anne G. Nairn. *Educ:* Aberdeen Academy. Nurse Training: general: Aberdeen Royal Infirmary, to 1945 (RGN); midwifery: Aberdeen Maternity Hosp., until 1948 (State Certified Midwife); Health Visitors: Aberdeen Coll. for Health Visitors, until 1952 (Health Visitors Cert.); administrative: Royal Coll. of Nursing, London, to 1959 (Nursing Admin. Cert.); 6 months study in USA as British Commonwealth and Empire Nurses Scholar, 1956. Ward Sister and Night Supt, Aberdeen Maternity Hosp., 1945–52; Director of Nursing Services in Aberdeen and Glasgow, 1952–74. *Publications:* articles in medical and nursing press: A Study of 283 Families with Rent Arrears; Liaison Services between Hospital and Community Nursing Services; Health Visitors in General Practice. *Recreations:* reading, gardening, swimming. *Address:* 12 Countesswells Terrace, Aberdeen AB1 8LQ.

NAIRN, Martin John L.; *see* Lambie-Nairn.

NAIRN, Sir Michael, 4th Bt *cr* 1904; *b* 1 July 1938; *s* of Sir Michael George Nairn, 3rd Bt, TD, and of Helen Louise, *yr d* of Major E. J. W. Bruce, Melbourne, Aust.; *S* father, 1984; *m* 1st, 1972, Diana (*d* 1982), *er d* of Leonard Bligh, NSW; two *s* one *d*; 2nd, 1986, Sally Jane, *d* of Major W. P. S. Hastings. *Educ:* Eton; INSEAD. *Heir: s* Michael Andrew Nairn, *b* 2 Nov. 1973. *Club:* Caledonian.

NAIRN, Sir Robert Arnold S.; *see* Spencer-Nairn.

NAIRNE, Lady (12th in line, of the Lordship *cr* 1681); **Katherine Evelyn Constance Bigham;** *b* 22 June 1912; *d* of 6th Marquess of Lansdowne and Elizabeth (she *m* 2nd, Lord Colum Crichton-Stuart, who *d* 1957; she *d* 1964); *S* to brother's Lordship of Nairne, 1944; *m* 1933, Hon. Edward Bigham (later 3rd Viscount Mersey, who *d* 1979); three *s*. *Heir: s* Viscount Mersey, *qv*. *Address:* Bignor Park, Pulborough, W Sussex. *T:* Sutton (Sussex) (07987) 214.

NAIRNE, Alexander Robert, (Sandy); Director of Visual Arts, Arts Council, since 1987; *b* 8 June 1953; *s* of Rt Hon. Sir Patrick Nairne, *qv*; partner since 1981, Sylvia Elizabeth (Lisa) Tickner; one *s* one *d*. *Educ:* Radley Coll.; University Coll., Oxford (BA Modern History and Economics 1974). Asst Dir, Museum of Modern Art, Oxford, 1974–76; Research Asst and Asst Keeper, Tate Gallery, 1976–79; Dir of Exhibitions, Inst. of Contemporary Arts, 1980–83; writer and associate producer, State of the Art, TV series, Channel 4, 1985–87. *Publication:* State of the Art, 1987. *Recreation:* punting. *Address:* 43 Lady Somerset Road, NW5 1TY. *T:* 071–485 7992. *Clubs:* Chelsea Arts; Leander (Henley).

NAIRNE, Rt. Hon. Sir Patrick (Dalmahoy), GCB 1981 (KCB 1975; CB 1971); MC 1943; PC 1982; Master, St Catherine's College, Oxford, 1981–88 (Hon. Fellow, 1988); Chancellor, Essex University, since 1983; *b* 15 Aug. 1921; *s* of late Lt-Col C. S. and Mrs E. D. Nairne; *m* 1948, Penelope Chauncy Bridges, *d* of Lt-Col R. F. and Mrs L. C. Bridges; three *s* three *d*. *Educ:* Radley Coll.; University Coll., Oxford (Exhibr; Hon. Fellow, 1981). Seaforth Highlanders, 1941–45 (Capt.). 1st cl. hons Mod. Hist. (Oxon), 1947. Entered Civil Service and joined Admty, Dec. 1947; Private Sec. to First Lord of Admty, 1958–60; Asst Sec., 1960; Private Sec. to Sec. of State for Defence, 1965–67; Assistant Under-Sec. of State (Logistics), MoD, 1967–70; Dep. Under-Sec. of State, MoD, 1970–73; Second Perm. Sec., Cabinet Office, 1973–75; Perm. Sec., DHSS, 1975–81. Mem., Falkland Isles Review Cttee, 1982; Govt Monitor, Hong Kong, 1984. Central Independent TV: Mem. Bd, 1990–; Dep. Chm., 1986–90, Chm., 1990–92, W Regl Bd. Chairman: Irene Wellington Educnl Trust, 1987–; Adv. Bd, Oxford Mus. of Modern Art, 1988–; Vice-Pres., Soc. for Italic Handwriting, 1987– (Chm., 1981–87); Trustee: Nat. Maritime Museum, 1981–91; Joseph Rowntree Foundn; Nat. AIDS Trust; Member: VSO Council; Council, Ditchley Foundn; President: Assoc. of CS Art Clubs, 1976–89; Radleian Soc., 1980–83; Seamen's Hosp. Soc. FRSA 1978. Hon. LLD: Leicester, 1980; St Andrews, 1984; DU Essex, 1983. *Recreations:* watercolour painting, calligraphy. *Address:* Yew Tree, Chilson, near Charlbury, Chipping Norton, Oxon OX7 3HU. *Club:* United Oxford & Cambridge University (Trustee, 1989–).

See also A. R. Nairne.

NAIRNE, Sandy; *see* Nairne, A. R.

NAIROBI, Archbishop of, (RC), since 1971; **HE Cardinal Maurice Otunga;** *b* Jan. 1923. Priest, 1950; Titular Bishop of Tacape, 1957; Bishop of Kisii, 1960; Titular Archbishop of Bomarzo, 1969; Cardinal 1973. *Address:* Archbishop's House, PO Box 14231, Nairobi, Kenya.

NAKAJIMA, Hiroshi, MD, PhD; Director-General of the World Health Organization, since 1988; *b* Japan, 16 May 1928; *m* Martha Ann (*née* De Witt); two *s*. *Educ:* Nat. Sen. High Sch., Urawa; Tokyo Med. Coll. (MD 1955; PhD 1960); Faculty of Medicine, Univ. of Paris. Research, Nat. Inst. of Health and Med. Res., Paris, 1958–67; Dir of Res. and Admin, Nippon Roche Res. Centre, Tokyo, 1967–73; Scientist, Evaluation and Control of Drugs, 1973–76, Chief, Drug Policies and Management, 1976–79, WHO HQ, Geneva; Regional Dir, Western Pacific Region, WHO, 1979–88. Vis. Prof. in Public Health, Tokyo Med. Coll., 1987. Kojima Prize, Japan, 1984. *Publications:* articles and reviews in Japanese, French and English pubns. *Address:* World Health Organization, 20 avenue Appia, CH-1211 Geneva 27, Switzerland. *T:* 791 21 11.

NAKASONE, Yasuhiro; Prime Minister of Japan, 1982–87; Chairman and President, International Institute for Global Peace, since 1988; *b* 27 May 1918; 2nd *s* of Matsugoroh Nakasone; *m* 1945, Tsutako Kobayashi; one *s* two *d*. *Educ:* Faculty of Law, Imperial Univ. (graduate). Joined Min. of Home Affairs, 1941; commd as Lt-Comdr, 1945. Elected to House of Representatives (first of 15 consecutive times), 1947; Minister of State, Dir-Gen. of Science and Technology Agency, 1959–60; Minister of Transport, 1967–68; Minister of State, Dir-Gen. of Defence Agency, 1970–71; Minister of Internat. Trade and Industry, 1972–74; Minister of State for Admin. Management Agency, 1980–82. Chm. Exec. Council, 1971–72, Sec. Gen., 1974–76, Liberal Democratic Party. Hon. DHL, Johns Hopkins, 1984. Médaille de la Chancellerie, Univs of Paris. *Publications:* The Ideals of Youth, 1947; Japan Speaks, 1954; The New Conservatism, 1978; Human Cities—a proposal for the 21st century, 1980. *Address:* 3-22-7, Kamikifazawa, Setagaya-ku, Tokyo, Japan.

NALDER, Hon. Sir Crawford David, Kt 1974; farmer; active in voluntary and charitable organisations; *b* Katanning, WA, 14 Feb. 1910; *s* of H. A. Nalder, Wagin; *m* 1st, 1934, Olive May (*d* 1973), *d* of S. Irvin; one *s* two *d*; 2nd, 1974, Brenda Wade. *Educ:* State Sch., Wagin; Wesley Coll., Perth, WA. Sheep, wheat and pig farmer, 1934–; Country rep. for Perth butchers. Entered parliament, 1947; MLA (CP) for Katanning, Parliament of Western Australia, 1950–73 (for Wagin, 1947–50); Dep. Leader, Country Party, 1956; Minister: for War Service Land Settlement, 1959–66; for Agriculture, 1959–71; for Electricity, 1962–71; Leader, Parly Country Party, 1962–73. Chm., Girls College Council. Knighted for services to the state and in local govt. *Recreations:* tennis, gardening. *Address:* 7 Morriett Street, Attadale, WA 6156, Australia.

NALL, Sir Michael (Joseph), 2nd Bt *cr* 1954; Vice Lord-Lieutenant of Nottinghamshire, 1989–91; *b* 6 Oct. 1921; *er s* of Colonel Sir Joseph Nall, 1st Bt; *S* father, 1958; *m* 1951, Angela Loveday Hanbury, *e d* of Air Chief Marshal Sir Alec Coryton, KCB, KBE, MVO, DFC; two *s*. *Educ:* Wellington College, Berks. Joined Royal Navy, 1939. Served War of 1939–45 (at sea); psc(mil.) 1949; Lt-Comdr, 1950–61, retired. General Manager, Guide Dogs for the Blind Association, 1961–64. Pres., Nottingham Chamber of Commerce and Industry, 1972–74. DL Notts, 1970; High Sheriff, Notts, 1971. Chm., Notts Scout Assoc., 1968–88 (Silver Acorn, 1979; Silver Wolf, 1989). *Recreations:* field sports, flying. *Heir: s* Edward William Joseph Nall, *b* 24 Oct. 1952. *Address:* Hoveringham Hall, Nottingham NG14 7JR. *T:* Nottingham (0602) 663634.

NALL-CAIN, family name of **Baron Brocket.**

NAMALIU, Rt. Hon. Rabbie Langanai, CMG 1979; PC 1989; MP; Prime Minister of Papua New Guinea, since 1988; *b* 3 April 1947; *s* of Darius Namaliu and Utul Ioan; *m* 1978, Margaret Nakikus; two *s*, and one step *d*. *Educ:* Univ. of Papua New Guinea (BA); Univ. of Victoria, BC (MA). Senior Tutor, later Lectr in History, Univ. of Papua New Guinea, 1973; Principal Private Sec. to Chief Minister (Hon. Michael Somare), 1974–75; Vis. Pacific Fellow, Centre for Pacific Studies, Univ. of California, Santa Cruz, 1975; Provincial Comr, East New Britain Province, 1976; Chm., Public Services Commn; Exec. Officer to Leader of the Opposition (Rt Hon. Michael Somare), 1980–81; MP for Kipoko (Pangu Pati), 1982–; Minister for Foreign Affairs and Trade, 1982–84, for Primary Industry, 1984–85. Hon. LLD Univ. of Victoria, BC, 1983. *Recreations:* swimming, walking, reading. *Address:* Office of the Prime Minister, PO Box 6605, Boroko, National Capital District, Papua New Guinea. *T:* 27 6715.

NANCE, His Honour Francis James, LLM; a Circuit Judge (formerly a Judge of County Courts and Commissioner, Liverpool and Manchester Crown Courts), 1966–90; *b* 5 Sept. 1915; *s* of late Herbert James Nance and Margaret Ann Nance, New Brighton; *m* 1st, 1943, Margaret Gertrude Roe (*d* 1978); two *s*; 2nd, 1988, Theodora McGinty (*née* Marchand). *Educ:* St Francis Xavier's College, Liverpool; University of Liverpool (LLM 1938). Called to the Bar, Gray's Inn, 1936. Served War of 1939–45, Royal Corps of Signals (Captain): Normandy invasion, NW Europe (despatches). Practised on Northern Circuit, 1936–66. Deputy Chairman, Lancashire QS, 1963–71; Pres., HM Council of Circuit Judges, 1984. *Recreation:* chess. *Address:* c/o Queen Elizabeth II Law Courts, Liverpool, Merseyside L2 1XA. *Club:* Athenæum (Liverpool).

NANDY, Dipak; Hon. Lecturer in Social Policy, University of Birmingham, since 1989; *b* 21 May 1936; *s* of B. C. Nandy and Leela Nandy; *m* 1st, 1964, Margaret Gracie (decd); 2nd, 1972, Hon. Luise Byers; two *d*. *Educ:* St Xavier's Coll., Calcutta; Univ. of Leeds BA 1st Cl. Hons English Literature, 1960; C. E. Vaughan Research Fellowship, 1960–62. Lectr, English Literature, Univ. of Leicester, 1962–66; Lectr and Fellow of Rutherford College, Univ. of Kent at Canterbury, 1966–68; founder-Director, The Runnymede Trust, 1968–73; Vis. Fellow, Adlai Stevenson Inst. of International Affairs, Chicago, 1970–73; Research Fellow, Social and Community Planning Research, 1973–75; Dep. Chief Exec., Equal Opportunities Commn, 1976–86; Chief Exec., Intermediate Technology Develt Gp, 1986–88. Member: Cttee of Inquiry into Future of Broadcasting, 1974–77; Council, Nat. Assoc. Citizens' Advice Bureaux, 1983–; BBC: Chm., Asian Programmes Adv. Cttee, 1983–88; Mem., General Adv. Council. Mem. Council, Northern Chamber Orch., 1980–84. Governor, BFI, 1984–87. Trustee, CSV, 1981–. Hon. Liaison, Employment and Labour Law Sect., Amer. Bar Assoc., 1980–. *Publications:* numerous essays in books, periodicals and newspapers on literature, political thought, race relations, urban problems, equality for women, broadcasting policy and development issues. *Recreations:* collecting records, opera, computing. *Club:* National Liberal.

NANKIVELL, Owen; JP; economic and business consultant; Executive Director, Hinksey Centre, since 1982; *b* 6 April 1927; *s* of John Hamilton Nankivell and Sarah Ann Mares; *m* 1956, Mary Burman Earnshaw; one *s* two *d*. *Educ:* Torquay Grammar Sch.; Univ. of Manchester. BA (Econ) 1951, MA (Econ) 1963. FRSS. Admty, 1951–52; Colonial Office, 1952–55; Central Statistical Office, 1955–65; DEA, 1965–69; HM Treasury, 1969–72; Asst Dir, Central Statistical Office, 1972–79; Gp Chief Economist, Lucas Industries, 1979–82. JP Worcester, 1984. *Publication:* All Good Gifts, 1978. *Recreations:* Christian, tennis, choral music, singing. *Address:* 18 Ash Hill Road, Torquay TQ1 3HZ. *T:* Torquay (0803) 297719.

NAPIER, family name of **Lord Napier and Ettrick** and **Baron Napier of Magdala.**

NAPIER, 14th Lord, *cr* 1627 (Scotland), **AND ETTRICK,** 5th Baron, *cr* 1872 (UK); **Francis Nigel Napier,** CVO 1985 (LVO 1980); DL; a Bt of Nova Scotia, 1666, 11th Bt of Thirlestane; Major, Scots Guards (Reserve of Officers); Private Secretary, Comptroller and Equerry to HRH the Princess Margaret, Countess of Snowdon, since 1973; *b* 5 Dec. 1930; *e s* of 13th Baron Napier and 4th Ettrick, TD, and Muir, *e d* of Sir Percy Newson, Bt; *S* father 1954; *m* 1958, Delia Mary, *yr d* of A. D. B. Pearson; two *s* two *d*. *Educ:* Eton; RMA, Sandhurst. Commissioned, 1950; served Malaya, 1950–51 (invalided); Adjt 1st Bn Scots Guards, 1955–57. Equerry to His late Royal Highness The Duke of Gloucester, 1958–60, retd, 1960. Deputy Ceremonial and Protocol Secretary, CRO, 1962–66; Purple Staff Officer at State Funeral of Sir Winston Churchill, 1966. A Cons. Whip, House of Lords, 1970–71. On behalf of HM The Queen, handed over Instruments of Independence to Tuvalu (formerly Ellice Is), 1978. Member: Royal Co. of Archers (Queen's Body

Guard for Scotland), 1953–; Cttee, Standing Council of the Baronetage, 1985–. Pres., St John Ambulance Assoc. and Brigade for County of London, 1975–83. DL Selkirkshire, 1974, Ettrick and Lauderdale, 1975–. Freeman, City of London; Liveryman, Worshipful Company of Grocers. CStJ 1988. *Heir: s* Master of Napier, *qv. Address:* Forest Lodge, The Great Park, Windsor SL4 2BU; Nottingham Cottage, Kensington Palace, W8 4PU; (seat) Thirlestane, Ettrick, Selkirkshire. *Clubs:* White's, Pratt's; Royal Caledonian Hunt (Edinburgh).

NAPIER OF MAGDALA, 6th Baron *cr* 1868; **Robert Alan Napier;** *b* 6 Sept. 1940; *s* of 5th Baron Napier of Magdala, OBE, and of Elizabeth Marian, *y d* of E. H. Hunt, FRCS; *S* father, 1987; *m* 1964, Frances Clare, *d* of late Alan Frank Skinner; one *s* one *d*. *Educ:* Winchester College; St John's Coll., Cambridge (BA 1st cl. Hons 1962; MA 1966). *Heir: s* Hon. James Robert Napier, *b* 29 Jan. 1966. *Address:* Fingerbread House, Rectory Lane, Woolpit, Suffolk IP30 9QP. *T:* Elmswell (0359) 40235. *Club:* Leander (Henley-on-Thames).

NAPIER, Master of; Hon. Francis David Charles Napier; *b* 3 Nov. 1962; *s* and *heir* of 14th Lord Napier (and 5th Baron Ettrick), *qv*. *Educ:* Stanbridge Earls School; South Thames Coll., Wandsworth, 1986–87 (City and Guilds Computer Diploma). With a Lloyd's agency, 1984–. *Recreations:* travelling, photography, squash, tennis. *Address:* Forest Lodge, The Great Park, Windsor. *Club:* Turf.

NAPIER, Barbara Langmuir, OBE 1975; Senior Tutor to Women Students in the University of Glasgow, 1964–74; Member, the Industrial Arbitration Board (formerly Industrial Court), 1963–76; *b* 21 Feb. 1914; *y c* of late James Langmuir Napier, Consultant Engineer, and late Siblie Agnes Mowat. *Educ:* Hillhead High Sch., Glasgow; Univ. of Glasgow (MA); Glasgow and West of Scotland Coll. of Domestic Science. Org. Sec. Redlands Hosp., Glasgow, 1937–41; Univ. of Glasgow: Warden, Queen Margaret Hall, 1941–44; Gen. Adv. to Women Students, 1942–64; Appts Officer (Women), 1942–65. Founder Mem. Assoc. of Principals, Wardens and Advisers to Univ. Women Students, 1942, Hon. Mem., 1977– (Pres. 1965–68); Local Rep. and later Mem. Coun., Women's Migration and Overseas Appts Soc., 1946–64; Winifred Cullis Lecture Fellowship (midwest USA) of Brit. Amer. Associates, 1950. Founder Dir, West of Scotland Sch. Co. Ltd, 1976–77. Member, Tribunal under National Insurance Acts, 1954–60; President, Standing Conference of Women's Organisations (Glasgow), 1955–57; Member: Scottish Committee, ITA, 1957–64; Executive Cttee, Nat. Advisory Centre on Careers for Women, (formerly Women's Employment Fedn), 1963–68, 1972–77; Indep. Member: Flax and Hemp Wages Council (GB), 1962–70 (Dep. Chm. 1964–70); Hat, Cap and Millinery Wages Council (GB), 1963–70; Laundry Wages Council (GB), 1968–70. Governor: Westbourne Sch., Glasgow, 1951–77 (Chm., 1969–77; Hon. Governor, 1981); Notre Dame Coll. of Educn, Glasgow, 1959–64. Admitted as Burgess and Guild Sister (*qua* Hammerman) of Glasgow, and Mem., Grand Antiquity Soc. of Glasgow, 1956. JP Glasgow 1955–75, Stirling 1975–80. *Publications:* (with S. Nisbet) Promise and Progress, 1970; contrib. The College Courant, etc. *Recreations:* reading, travel, gardening, painting, being with cats. *Address:* 67 Brisbane Street, Largs, Ayrshire KA30 8QP. *T:* Largs (0475) 675495. *Club:* College (Glasgow).

NAPIER, John; stage designer; *b* 1 March 1944; *s* of James Edward Thomas Napier and Lorrie Napier (*née* Godbold); *m* 1st, Andreane Neofitou; one *s* one *d*; 2nd, Donna King, one *s* one *d*. *Educ:* Hornsey Coll. of Art; Central Sch. of Arts and Crafts. Designed 1st production, A Penny for a Song, Pheonix, Leicester, 1967; London productions: Fortune and Men's Eyes, 1968; The Ruling Class, The Fun War, Muzeeka, George Frederick (ballet), La Turista, 1969; Cancer, Isabel's a Jezebel, 1970; Mister, The Foursome, The Lovers of Viorne, Lear, 1971; Jump, Sam Sam, Big Wolf, 1972; The Devils (ENO), Equus, The Party, 1973; Knuckle, 1974; Kings and Clowns, The Travelling Music Show, 1978; The Devils of Loudon, Lohengrin (Covent Garden); King John, Richard II, Cymbeline, Macbeth, Richard III, 1974; Hedda Gabler, 1975; Much Ado About Nothing, The Comedy of Errors, King Lear, Macbeth, 1976; A Midsummer Night's Dream, As You Like It, 1977; The Merry Wives of Windsor, Twelfth Night, Three Sisters, Once in a Lifetime, 1979; The Greeks, Nicholas Nickleby (SWET award, Tony Award), 1980; Cats (Tony award), 1981; Henry IV Parts I and II, Peter Pan, 1982; Idomeneo (Glyndebourne), 1983; Macbeth (Covent Garden), 1983; Starlight Express, 1984 (Tony Award, 1987); Les Misérables, 1985 (Tony Award, 1987); Time, 1986; Miss Saigon, 1989; Children of Eden, 1990; film designs incl. Hook, 1991; numerous designs for stage productions in Europe, Japan, Australia, USA and for TV. *Recreation:* photography. *Address:* c/o MLR, 200 Fulham Road, SW10.

NAPIER, Sir John Archibald Lennox, 14th Bt *cr* 1627 (NS), of Merchistoun; *b* 6 Dec. 1946; *s* of Sir William Archibald Napier, 13th Bt and of Kathleen Mabel, *d* of late Reginald Greaves; *S* father, 1990; *m* 1969, Erica, *d* of late Kurt Kingsfield; one *s* one *d*. *Educ:* St Stithians; Witwatersrand Univ., Johannesburg. MSc(Eng); PhD. *Heir: s* Hugh Robert Lennox Napier, *b* 1 Aug. 1977. *Address:* Merchistoun, PO Box 65177, Benmore 2010, Transvaal, South Africa.

NAPIER, Maj.-Gen. Lennox Alexander Hawkins, CB 1983; OBE 1970; MC 1957; DL; General Officer Commanding Wales, 1980–83, retired; Chairman, Central Transport Consultative Committee, since 1985; Inspector of Public Inquiries, since 1983; *b* 28 June 1928; *s* of Major Charles McNaughton Napier and D. C. Napier; *m* 1959, Jennifer Dawn Wilson; one *s* two *d*. *Educ:* Radley; RMA Sandhurst. Joined Army, 1946; commnd into South Wales Borderers, 1948; commanded 1st Bn S Wales Borderers and 1st Bn Royal Regt of Wales, 1967–70; Instructor, JSSC, 1970–72; served Min. of Defence, 1972–74; Brigade Commander, Berlin Infantry Bde, 1974–76; Prince of Wales's Division: Divisional Brigadier, 1976–80; Col Commandant, 1980–83; Col, The Royal Regt of Wales, 1983–89; Hon. Col, Cardiff Univ. OTC, 1985–. Gwent: DL 1983; High Sheriff 1988. *Recreations:* shooting, riding. *Address:* c/o Barclays Bank, Monmouth, Gwent. *Club:* Lansdowne.

NAPIER, Sir Oliver John, Kt 1985; Chairman, Standing Advisory Commission on Human Rights, 1988–June 1992; *b* 11 July 1935; *e s* of James J. and Sheila Napier; *m* 1961, Brigid (*née* Barnes); three *s* five *d* (and one *s* decd). *Educ:* Ballycruttle Public Elem. Sch., Downpatrick; St Malachy's Coll., Belfast; Queen's Univ., Belfast (LLB). Qual. Solicitor, NI, 1959; Lectr and Mem. Bd of Examrs, Incorp. Law Soc. of NI, 1965–71. Mem. Exec., Ulster Liberal Party, 1962–69; Founder Mem., New Ulster Movt, 1969; Founder Mem., Alliance Party, 1970, Leader 1973–84, Pres., 1989–March 1992. Mem. (Alliance), E Belfast, NI Assembly, 1973–75; Minister of Legal Affairs, NI Executive, Jan.-May 1974; Mem. (Alliance), N Ireland Constitutional Convention for E Belfast, 1975–76; Mem. (Alliance) Belfast E, NI Assembly, 1982–86. Contested (Alliance), E Belfast, 1979, 1983. Councillor for E Belfast, Belfast CC, 1977–89. *Recreations:* many and varied. *Address:* 83 Victoria Road, Holywood, Co. Down.

NAPIER, Robert Stewart; Group Managing Director, since 1987, Chief Executive, since 1991, Redland; *b* 21 July 1947; *s* of Andrew Napier and Lilian V. Napier (*née* Ritchie); *m* 1977, Patricia Stewart; one *d*. *Educ:* Sedbergh School; Sidney Sussex College, Cambridge (BA 1969; MA 1971); Harvard Business School (AMP 1987). RTZ Corp., 1969–73; Brandts, 1973–75; Fisons, 1975–81; Redland: Finance Dir, 1981–87; Managing Dir, 1987–. Trustee: World in Need; AIDS Care, Education and Training. *Recreations:* organ playing, hill walking. *Address:* Redland House, Reigate, Surrey RH2 0SJ. *T:* Reigate (0737) 242488.

NAPIER, Sir Robin (Surtees), 5th Bt *cr* 1867, of Merrion Square, Dublin; United Kingdom Representative for Rothschild Bank, AG (Zurich), since 1983; *b* 5 March 1932; *s* of Sir Joseph William Lennox Napier, 4th Bt, OBE and of Isabelle Muriel, *yr d* of late Major Siward Surtees; assumed forenames of Robin Surtees in lieu of Robert Aubone Siward; *S* father, 1986; *m* 1971, Jennifer Beryl, *d* of late H. Warwick Daw; one *s*. *Educ:* Eton College. 2nd Lt Coldstream Guards, 1951–52. Pearl Assurance Co., 1953–56; Charterhouse Japhet, 1956–83. *Recreations:* fishing, shooting, golf, gardening. *Heir: s* Charles Joseph Napier, *b* 15 April 1973. *Address:* Upper Chilland House, Martyr Worthy, Winchester, Hants SO21 1EB. *T:* Itchen Abbas (096278) 307. *Clubs:* City of London, Flyfishers', MCC, British Sportsman's; Union (Sydney, NSW).

NAPLEY, Sir David, Kt 1977; Solicitor; Senior Partner in Kingsley Napley; President of the Law Society, 1976–77 (Vice-President, 1975–76); *b* 25 July 1915; *s* of late Joseph and Raie Napley; *m* 1940, Leah Rose, *d* of Thomas Reginald Saturley; two *d*. *Educ:* Burlington College. Solicitor, 1937. Served with Queen's Royal (W Surrey) Regt, 1940; commnd 1942; Indian Army, 1942; Captain 1942; invalided 1945. Contested (C): Rowley Regis and Tipton, 1951; Gloucester, 1955. Pres., London (Criminal Courts) Solicitors Assoc., 1960–63; Chm. Exec. Council, British Academy of Forensic Sciences, 1960–74 (Pres. 1967; Director, 1974–); Mem. Council, Law Soc., 1962–86; Mem. Judicial Exchange with USA, 1963–64; Chm., Law Soc's Standing Cttee on Criminal Law, 1963–76; Mem. Editorial Bd, Criminal Law Review, 1967–; Chairman: Contentious Business, Law Soc., 1972–75; Legal Aid Cttee, 1969–72; Exam. Bd, Incorp. Soc. of Valuers and Auctioneers, 1981–84; Mem., Home Office Law Revision Cttee, 1971–. President: City of Westminster Law Soc., 1967–68; Law Services Assoc., 1987–90. Mem. Council and Trustee, Imperial Soc. of Kts Bachelor, 1981–, Chm., 1988–. Chairman: Mario & Franco Restaurants Ltd, 1968–77; Burton-Race Restaurants plc, 1986–; Dir, Covent Garden Fest. Ltd, 1989–. Trustee, W Ham Boys' Club, 1979–, Pres., 1981–; Pres., Burnham Ratepayers Assoc., 1987–. *Publications:* Law on the Remuneration of Auctioneers and Estate Agents, 1947; (ed) Bateman's Law of Auctions, 1954; The Law of Auctioneers and Estate Agents Commission, 1957; Crime and Criminal Procedure, 1963; Guide to Law and Practice under the Criminal Justice Act, 1967; The Technique of Persuasion, 1970, 3rd edn 1984; Not without Prejudice, 1982; The Camden Town Murder, 1987; Murder at the Villa Madeira, 1988; Rasputin in Hollywood, 1990; a section, Halsbury's Laws of England; contrib. legal and forensic scientific jls, press, legal discussions on radio and TV. *Recreations:* painting, reading, writing, music, eating. *Address:* 107–115 Long Acre, WC2E 9PT. *T:* 071–240 2411. *Club:* Garrick.

NAPOLITAN, Leonard, CB 1970; Director of Economics and Statistics, Ministry of Agriculture, Fisheries and Food, 1965–77; *b* 9 April 1919; *s* of Domenic and Rose G. Napolitan; *m* 1945, Dorothy Laycock; two *d*. *Educ:* Univ. of London (BSc Econ. 1944); LSE (MSc Econ. 1946). Asst Agric. Economist, Univ. of Bristol, 1947–48; joined Min. of Agric. and Fisheries as Agric. Economist, 1948. Pres., Agric. Econs Soc., 1974–75. FRSA 1984. *Address:* 4 Rectory Gardens, Burway Road, Church Stretton, Shropshire SY6 6DP.

NAPPER, John (Pelham); painter; *b* London, 17 Sept. 1916; *e s* of late John Mortimer Napper and late Dorothy Charlotte (*née* Hill); *m* 1st, 1935, Hedvig Sophie Armour; 2nd, 1945, Pauline Davidson. *Educ:* Frensham Heights, Surrey and privately; Dundee Sch. of Art; Royal Acad. Schs of Art. Served War of 1939–45: commnd RA, 1941; Ceylon, 1942, War Artist to Ceylon comd, 1943–44; seconded to RNVR, 1944, E Africa, 1944; demobilised, 1945. Taught life painting at St Martin's Sch. of Art, London, 1949–57. Lived in France, 1957–70. One-man exhibitions: Leicester Galleries, London, 1949, 1961, 1962; The Adams Gallery, London, 1957 and 1959; La Maison de la Pensée Française, Paris, 1960; Galerie Lahumière, Paris, 1963; Galleries Hervé and Lahumière, Paris, 1965; Larcada Gallery, New York, 1968, 1970, 1972, 1975, 1977; Browse and Darby Gall., 1978, 1980; Ludlow Fest., 1985; Thos Agnew and Sons, 1986; Albemarle Gall., 1988, 1990, 1991; retrospective exhibitions: Walker Art Gall., Liverpool, 1959; Oldham Art Gall., 1984. Paintings acquired by: BM; Contemp. Art Soc.; Courtauld Inst., Fitzwilliam Mus., Musée d'Art Moderne, Paris; Mus. of Art, Tel Aviv; Musée Municipale, Dieppe; Nat. Gall., Kenya; Columbus Gall. of Fine Arts, Ohio, and other public and pvte collections. Vis. Prof. of Fine Arts, Southern Illinois Univ., USA, 1968–69. Médaille d'argent, Salon des Artistes françaises, Paris, 1947; Awarded prize at International Exhibition of Fine Arts, Moscow, 1957; Awarded International Assoc. of Art Critics Prize, 1961. *Address:* c/o Albemarle Gallery, 18 Albemarle Street, W1X 3HA. *Club:* Beefsteak.

NARAIN, Sase, OR 1976; CMG 1969; SC (Guyana) 1985; JP (Guyana); solicitor; Speaker of the National Assembly, Guyana, since 1971; Chairman, National Bank of Industry and Commerce (Guyana), since 1986; *b* 27 Jan. 1925; *s* of Oudit and Sookdai Naraine; *m* 1952, Shamshun Narain (*née* Rayman); four *s*. *Educ:* Modern Educational Inst.; Gibson and Weldon Law Tutors. Solicitor, admitted in England and Guyana, 1957. Town Councillor, City of Georgetown, 1962–70; Member: History and Arts Council, 1969–; Republic Cttee of Guyana, 1969; Pres., Guyana Sanatan Dharma Maha Sabha, 1963–. Comr for Oaths to Affidavits, 1961; Notary Public, 1968. Dep. Chm., Public Service Commn, Guyana, 1966–71; Mem., Police Service Commn, 1961–71. Chm., Berger Paints (Guyana), 1966–78; Dir, Pegasus Hotels of Guyana, 1987–90. Member: Nat. Awards Cttee of Guyana, 1970–; Bd of Governors, President's Coll., Guyana, 1985–. JP 1962. *Recreations:* golf, cricket, swimming. *Address:* 217 South Street, Lacytown, Georgetown, Demerara, Guyana. *T:* 66611. *Clubs:* Georgetown, Georgetown Cricket, Everest Cricket (Guyana).

NARAIN, Sir Sathi, KBE 1980 (MBE 1971); Managing Director, Narain Construction Co. Ltd, since 1945; *b* 26 Sept. 1919; *s* of Suramma and Appalsamy Narain; *m* 1969, Hannah Shakuntla (*née* Pratap); three *s*. *Educ:* Suva, Fiji. Government apprentice carpenter, 1933–44; Man. Dir, Narain Construction Co. Ltd, 1945–, and of subsidiary companies (hotels, land development, road development, shipping), 1950–; Director: Burns Philps South Sea Co. Ltd; Queensland Insurance Co. Ltd. Suva City Councillor, 1956–59; Member of Parliament, 1963–67. Mem., CPA, 1970. Hon. Architect, Fiji Assoc. of Architects, 1983. *Recreations:* golf, bowling. *Address:* (business) Narain Construction Co. Ltd, Box 1288, Suva, Fiji. *T:* 381086; (residence) 20 Narain Place, Tamavua, Suva, Fiji. *T:* 381027. *Clubs:* Defence, Royal Yacht, Fiji (Suva, Fiji); Tattersall (Sydney, Aust.).

NARASIMHAN, Chakravarthi Vijayaraghava; Senior Fellow, UN Institute for Training and Research, since 1978; *b* 21 May 1915; *s* of Chakravarthi V. and Janaki Vijayaraghavachari; *m* 1938, Janaki, *d* of Dr M. T. Chari; two *d*. *Educ:* University of Madras (BA); Oxford (MA). Indian Civil Service, 1936; Dep. Sec., Development Dept, Government of Madras, 1945–48; Min. of Agriculture, Govt of India, 1950–53; Joint Sec., Economic Affairs Dept, Ministry of Finance, 1953–56; Executive Sec., UN Economic Commission for Asia and Far East, 1956–59; Under-Sec. for Special Political Affairs, UN,

1959–62; Chef de Cabinet of the Sec.-Gen., UN, 1961–73; Under-Sec., 1962–67, Under-Sec.-Gen. 1967–69, for Gen. Assembly Affairs, UN; Dep. Administrator, UN Develt Prog., 1969–72; Under-Sec.-Gen. for Inter-Agency Affairs and Co-ordination, UN, 1973–78; Organizing Exec. Sec., Cotton Develt Internat., UN Develt Programme, 1979–81. Hon. Doctor of Laws, Williams Coll. Williamstown, Mass, 1960; Hon. Dr of Humane Letters, Colgate Univ., 1966. *Publication:* The United Nations: an inside view, 1988. *Recreations:* Sanskrit literature, South Indian classical music, tennis. *Address:* 5527 Uppingham Street, Chevy Chase, Md 20815, USA. *T:* (301) 657–8571.

NARAYAN, R. K., (Rasipuram Krishnaswamy); author; *b* Madras, 10 Oct. 1906. *Educ:* Maharaja's College, Mysore, India. Padma Bushan award for distinguished services to literature. Hon. LittD Leeds, 1967. *Publications: novels:* Swami and Friends, 1935; The Bachelor of Arts, 1937; The Dark Room, 1939; The English Teacher, 1945; Mr Sampath, 1947; The Financial Expert, 1952; Waiting for the Mahatma, 1955; The Guide, 1958; The Man-Eater of Malgudi, 1961; Gods, Demons and Others, 1964; The Sweet Vendor, 1967; The Painter of Signs, 1977; A Tiger for Malgudi, 1983; (ed) The Ramayana, 1973; (ed) The Mahabharata, 1978; Talkative Man, 1986; The World of Nagaraj, 1990; *autobiography:* My Days, 1975; *short stories:* An Astrologer's Day; The Lawley Road; A Horse and Two Goats, 1970; Under the Banyan Tree and Other Stories, 1985, etc; *essays:* Next Sunday, 1955 (India); My Dateless Diary, 1960 (India). *Address:* c/o Anthony Sheil Associates, 43 Doughty Street, WC1N 2LF; Yadavagiri, Mysore 2, India.

NARAYAN, Rudy; barrister; *b* Guyana, 11 May 1938; *s* of Sase Narayan and Taijbertie (*née* Sawh); *m* 1988, Saeeda Begum Asif; two *d* by previous marriage. *Educ:* Lincoln's Inn. Came to UK, 1953; served HM Forces, BAOR and HQ MELF, 1958–65. Lincoln's Inn: Founder/1st Pres., Students Union, 1966; Chm. of Debates, and Captain of Cricket, 1967; called to the Bar, 1968. Vice-Chm., Lambeth Council for Community Relations 1974; Founder Chm., Lambeth Law Centre; Councillor, Lambeth, 1974–76. Founder, Black Rights (UK); Chm. and Dir, Civil Rights (UK); Legal Adviser: Caribbean Times, Asian Times, African Times (London). Formerly: Mem., Race Relations Bd; Legal Officer, W Indian Standing Conf.; Founder, Soc. of Black Lawyers (Pres., 1987–89). Contested (Ind) Vauxhall, June 1989. *Publications:* Black Community on Trial, 1976; Black England, 1977; Barrister for the Defence, 1985; Black Silk, 1985; When Judges Conspire, 1989. *Recreations:* cricket, debating, theatre, ballet, opera. *Address:* Justice House, 402 Brixton Road, SW9 7AW. *T:* 071–978 8545; 081–769 0444. *Club:* Wig and Pen.

NARJES, Karl-Heinz; Vice-President, Commission of the European Communities, 1985–88 (Member, 1981–88); *b* 30 Jan. 1924; *s* of Heinrich Narjes; *m* 1951, Eva-Maria Rahe; one *s* one *d*. *Educ:* Hamburg Univ. Entered Foreign Service, 1953; Chef du Cabinet, Pres. of EEC, 1963; Dir-Gen., Press and Inf. Directorate, EEC, 1968–69; Minister of Econs and of Transport, Schleswig-Holstein, 1969–73. Mem., Bundestag, 1972–88; Mem., For. Affairs Cttee, 1976–80; Pres., Econ. Affairs Cttee, 1972–76, 1980–88.

NARUEPUT, Owart S.; *see* Suthiwart-Narueput.

NASH, (Denis Frederic) Ellison, OBE 1982; AE; FRCS; Consulting Surgeon, St Bartholomew's Hospital; *b* 10 Feb. 1913; *m* 1938, Joan Mary Andrew; two *s* two *d*. *Educ:* Dulwich College; St Bartholomew's Medical College. MRCS, LRCP, 1935; FRCS 1938. Served war of 1939–45, RAFVR, Wing-Comdr (Air Efficiency Award, 1943). Hunterian Professor, 1949 and 1956. Arris and Gale Lecturer, 1950. Consultant Surgeon: St Bartholomew's Hosp., 1947–78; Chailey Heritage Hosp., 1952–78; Dean, St Bartholomew's Hospital Medical College, 1957–62; Special Trustee, St Bartholomew's Hosp., 1974–78; Regional Postgraduate Dean, and Asst Dir, British Postgraduate Medical Fedn, Univ. of London, 1948–74. Special interest in the education and care of the physically handicapped; Hon. Med. Adviser: Shaftesbury Soc.; John Groom's Assoc. for Disabled. Senior Member, British Assoc. of Urological Surgeons. Senior Fellow, British Orthopædic Assoc.; Fellow, Assoc. of Surgeons of GB. Hon. Fellow, Med. Artists Assoc. *Publications:* The Principles and Practice of Surgery for Nurses and Allied Professions, 1955, 7th revised edn, 1980; scientific papers in medical journals particularly concerned with surgery of childhood. *Recreations:* photography, fuchsias. *Address:* 28 Hawthorne Road, Bickley, Bromley, Kent BR1 2HH. *T:* 081–467 1142. *Club:* City of London Guild of Freemen.

NASH, John Edward; Member, Advisory Board, Bank S. G. Warburg Soditic AG; Chairman, S. G. Warburg Bank AG, 1980–87 (Director, 1977–87; Deputy Chairman, 1977–80); *b* 25 June 1925; *s* of Joseph and Madeleine Nash; *m* 1947, Ralda Everard Herring; two *s* two *d*. *Educ:* Univ. of Sydney (BEc); Balliol Coll., Oxford (BPhil). Teaching Fellow in Economics, Sydney Univ., 1947. Exec. Dir, Samuel Montagu & Co. Ltd, 1956; also Director, 1960–73: British Australian Investment Trust; Montagu Trust Ltd; Midland Montagu Industrial Finance Ltd; Capel Court Corp. (in Melb.); resigned all directorships on appt to Brussels, 1973; Dir of Monetary Affairs, EEC, 1973–77; Director: Reckitt & Colman plc, 1966–73 and 1977–86; S. G. Warburg & Co. Ltd, 1977–86. Dir, Oxford Univ. Business Summer Sch., 1965; Research Fellow, Nuffield Coll., Oxford (part-time), 1966–69. Hon. Treasurer, PEP, 1964–73. Mem. Bd of Trustees, WWF Internat., 1979– (Hon. Treas., 1985–). *Recreations:* golf, skiing, horse-racing, music. *Address:* Chalet Gstelli, 3781 Gsteig bei Gstaad, Switzerland. *T:* (030) 51162. *Clubs:* Turf, Buck's, MCC, University (Sydney).

NASH, Philip; Commissioner of Customs and Excise, 1986–90; *b* 14 March 1930; *s* of late John Hollett Nash and Edith Grace Nash (*née* Knee); *m* 1953, Barbara Elizabeth Bangs; one *s*. *Educ:* Watford Grammar School. National Service, RAF, 1949–50. HM Customs and Excise, 1950–90; on loan to Civil Service College, 1970–73; Asst Sec. and Head of Management Services, 1978–81; Asst Sec., Customs Directorate, 1981–86; Director, Customs, 1986–90. *Recreation:* collecting things. *Address:* 149 Merryhill Road, Bushey, Watford, Herts WD2 1DF. *T:* 081–950 1048.

NASH, Ronald Peter, LVO 1983; HM Diplomatic Service; Deputy Head of Mission and Consul General, Vienna, since 1987; *b* 18 Sept. 1946; *s* of John Henry Nash and Jean Carmichael Nash (*née* McIlwraith); *m* 1976, Annie Olsen; three *s*. *Educ:* Harefield Secondary Modern Sch.; Southall Tech. Sch.; Southall Grammar Tech. Sch.; Manchester Univ. FCO, 1970; Moscow, 1974–76; UK Delegn to MBFR, Vienna, 1976–79; FCO, 1979–83; New Delhi, 1983–86; FCO, 1986–87. *Address:* c/o Foreign and Commonwealth Office, SW1.

NASH, Thomas Arthur Manly, CMG 1959; OBE 1944; Dr (Science); retired; *b* 18 June 1905; *s* of late Col L. T. Nash, CMG, RAMC; *m* 1930, Marjorie Wenda Wayte; (one *s* decd). *Educ:* Wellington Coll.; Royal Coll. of Science. Entomologist, Dept Tsetse Research and Reclamation, Tanganyika Territory, 1927; Entomologist, Sleeping Sickness Service, Med. Dept, Nigeria, 1933. Doctorate of Science, 1933. In charge Anchau Rural Development Scheme, 1937–44; seconded as Chief Entomologist, W African Institute for Trypanosomiasis Research, 1948; Deputy Director, WAITR, 1953; Director, 1954–59; Dir, Tsetse Research Lab., Univ. of Bristol, Veterinary Field Station, Langford, 1962–71. *Publications:* Tsetse Flies in British West Africa, 1948; Africa's Bane, The Tsetse Fly, 1969; A Zoo without Bars, 1984; numerous scientific publications on tsetse and trypanosomiasis. *Recreation:* fishing. *Address:* Spring Head Farm, Upper Langford, near Bristol BS18 7DN. *T:* Churchill (0934) 852321.

NASH, Ven. Trevor Gifford; Executive Co-ordinator, Bishops' Advisers for Churches' Ministry of Healing in England, since 1990 (Adviser, since 1973); *b* 3 May 1930; *s* of Frederick Walter Gifford Nash and Elsie Violet Louise Nash; *m* 1957, Wanda Elizabeth (*née* Freeston); four *d*. *Educ:* Haileybury College, Hertford; Clare Coll., Cambridge (MA); Cuddesdon Coll., Oxford. Curate: Cheshunt, 1955–57; Kingston-upon-Thames, 1957–61; Priest-in-Charge, Stevenage, 1961–63; Vicar, Leagrave, Luton, 1963–67; Senior Chaplain, St George's Hosp. Gp, London, 1967–73; Rector, St Lawrence with St Swithun, Winchester, 1973–82; Priest-in-Charge, Holy Trinity, Winchester, 1977–82; RD of Winchester, 1978–82; Archdeacon of Basingstoke, 1982–90, Archdeacon Emeritus, 1990; Hon. Canon of Winchester, 1980–. RAChD (TA), 1956–61. *Recreations:* clay modelling, music, walking. *Address:* Corner Stone, 50B Hyde Street, Winchester, Hants SO23 7DY. *T:* Winchester (0962) 61759.

NASHA, Margaret Nnananyana, (Mrs Lawrence Nasha); High Commissioner for Botswana in the UK, since 1989; *b* 6 Aug. 1947; *d* of Sadinyana and Motlatshiping Ramontshonyana; *m* 1975, Lawrence Nasha; four *s*. *Educ:* Univ. of Botswana (BA 1976). Several posts as broadcaster, 1968–84; Dir of Information and Broadcasting, Botswana, 1985–89. *Recreations:* leisure walks, tennis. *Address:* Botswana High Commission, 6 Stratford Place, W1N 9AE. *T:* 071–499 0031; PO Box 917, Gabarone, Botswana.

NASMITH; *see* Dunbar-Nasmith.

NASMYTH, Dr Kim Ashley, FRS 1989; Senior Scientist, Institute of Molecular Pathology, Vienna, since 1987; *b* 18 Oct. 1952; *s* of James Nasmyth and Jenny Hughes; *m* 1982, Anna Dowson; two *d*. *Educ:* Eton Coll.; York Univ. (BA); Edinburgh Univ. (PhD). Jane Coffin Childs Postdoctoral Fellow, Dept of Genetics, Univ. of Washington, 1978–80; Robertson Fellow, Cold Spring Harbor Lab, NY, 1980–81; Staff Mem., MRC Lab. of Molecular Biol., Cambridge, 1982–87; Unofficial Fellow, King's Coll., Cambridge, 1984–87. Mem., European Molecular Biol. Orgn, 1985–. *Recreations:* climbing, ski-ing. *Address:* Linke Wien Zeile 4/2/5, A-1060 Vienna, Austria. *T:* (222) 56 94 98.

NASON, Justin Patrick Pearse, OBE 1980; HM Diplomatic Service; Ambassador to Guatemala, since 1991; *b* 29 March 1937; *s* of John Lawrence Nason and Catherine Agnes (*née* McFadden). *Educ:* Ampleforth; University Coll., Oxford. National Service, RAF, 1956–58. BICC, 1962–63; entered HM Foreign Service, 1963; FO, 1964–65; Prague, 1965–67; FCO, 1967–71; First Sec., Pretoria and Cape Town, 1971–74; Head of Chancery, Saigon, 1974–75; FCO, 1975–79; Head of Chancery, Kampala, 1979–81; Nat. Defence Coll. of Canada, 1981–82; Dep. High Comr, Colombo, 1982–85; Barclays Bank (on secondment), 1986–87; Minister Counsellor, Mexico City, 1988–90; temp. duty, Accra, 1990–91. *Recreation:* golf. *Address:* c/o Foreign and Commonwealth Office, SW1A 2AH. *Club:* United Oxford & Cambridge University.

NATAL, Bishop of, since 1982; **Rt. Rev. Michael Nuttall;** *b* 3 April 1934; *s* of Neville and Lucy Nuttall; *m* 1959, Dorris Marion Meyer; two *s* one *d*. *Educ:* Maritzburg Coll. (matric. 1951); Univ. of Natal (BA 1955); Rhodes Univ. (BA Hons in History 1956). MA (Cantab), MA, DipEd (Oxon), BD Hons (London). Teacher at Westville High Sch., Natal, 1958; Lectr in History, Rhodes Univ., 1959–62; Theological Student, St Paul's Coll., Grahamstown, 1963–64; ordained deacon, 1964, priest 1965; Assistant Priest, Cathedral of St Michael and St George, Grahamstown, 1965–68; Lectr in Ecclesiastical History, Rhodes Univ., 1969–74; Dean of Grahamstown, 1975; Bishop of Pretoria, 1975–81. *Publications:* chapters in: Better Than They Knew, Volume 2 (ed R. M. de Villiers), 1974; Authority in the Anglican Communion (ed Stephen W. Sykes), 1987; articles in Dictionary of S African Biography. *Recreations:* walking, bird watching. *Address:* Bishop's House, 52 Roberts Road, Pietermaritzburg, 3201, South Africa.

NATH, (Dhurma) Gian; High Commissioner of Mauritius to Australia, with concurrent accreditation to New Zealand, Brunei and Indonesia, since 1990; *b* Triolet, Mauritius, 29 May 1934; *s* of Anmole Facknath, OBE and Mrs B. Facknath; *m* 1961, Chitralekha, *d* of Dr and Mrs Chiranji Lal Sud; two *s* one *d*. *Educ:* Delhi Univ. (BA Hons English 1960, MA 1962); Postgrad. Inst. of Internat. Affairs, New Delhi. Educn Officer, John Kennedy Coll., Mauritius, 1963–66 (Head of Dept of English, 1965–66); entered Diplomatic Service, Mauritius, as trainee, 1966; apptd to Mauritius High Commn, London, 1968; Head of Chancery, 1969; Counsellor, Mauritius Mission to EEC, 1972–76; Dep. High Comr, London, 1976–82; Ambassador in Cairo, 1982–83; High Comr in UK, 1983–87; Ambassador to Pakistan and (non-resident), to China, 1988–90. Sec., OAU Gp, London, 1973–82. Mem., Television Bd, Mauritius Broadcasting Corp., 1965–66. Representative of Mauritius at various internat. meetings. Kt of Order of Pius IX (Vatican), 1987. *Recreations:* bridge, history of World War II, golf. *Address:* (office) 43 Hampton Circuit, Yarralumla, Canberra, ACT 2600, Australia. *T:* 2811203, 2824436; 5 Mugga Way, Forrest, ACT 2603, Australia.

NATHAN, family name of **Baron Nathan.**

NATHAN, 2nd Baron, *cr* 1940; **Roger Carol Michael Nathan;** *b* 5 Dec. 1922; *s* of 1st Baron Nathan, PC, TD, and Eleanor Joan Clara (*d* 1972), *d* of C. Stettauer; *S* father, 1963; *m* 1950, Philippa Gertrude, *d* of Major Joseph Bernard Solomon, MC, Pulborough, Sussex; one *s* two *d*. *Educ:* Stowe Sch.; New Coll., Oxford (MA). Served War of 1939–45: Capt., 17/21 Lancers (despatches, wounded twice). Admitted Solicitor (Hons), 1950; Senior Partner, Herbert Oppenheimer Nathan & Vandyk, 1978–86; Consultant, Denton Hall Burgin & Warrens, 1989–. Chm., Arbitration Panel, The Securities Assoc., 1988–. Associate Member: Bar Assoc. of City of New York; NY County Lawyers' Assoc.; FSA; FRSA; FRGS. Pres., Jewish Welfare Board, 1967–71; Chairman: Central British Fund for Jewish Relief and Rehabilitation, 1971–77 (Hon. Pres., 1977–); Exec. Cttee, Cancer Research Campaign (formerly British Empire Cancer Campaign), 1970–75 (Hon. Treasurer, 1979–87, Vice-Chm., 1987–); Working Party on Energy and the Envmt (reported 1974); Animal Procedures Cttee, 1990–; Wkg Party on Efficiency and Effectiveness in Voluntary Sector, 1989–90; Court of Discipline, Cambridge Univ., 1990–; Vice Chm., Cttee on Charity Law and Practice (reported 1976); Mem., Royal Commn on Envmtl Pollution, 1979–89. Mem., House of Lords Select Cttee on European Communities, 1983–88 and 1990– (Chm., *ad hoc* Sub-Cttee on European Co. Statute, 1989–90; Chm., Sub-Cttee F (Envmt), 1983–87 and 1990–); Chm., H of L Select Cttee on Murder and Life Imprisonment, 1988–89. Chm., RSA, 1975–77, Vice-Pres., 1977–. Chm., Inst. of Envmtl Assessment, 1990–; President: UK Envmtl Law Assoc., 1987–; Nat. Soc. for Clean Air, 1987–89; Soc. of Sussex Downsmen, 1987–. Chm., City Festival of Flowers, 1964; Master, Worshipful Company of Gardeners, 1963–64. Hon. LLD Sussex, 1988. *Heir:* *s* Hon. Rupert Harry Bernard Nathan, *b* 26 May 1957. *Address:* 5 Chancery Lane, WC2A 1LF. *T:* 071–242 1212; Collyers Farm, Lickfold, Petworth, West Sussex. *T:* Lodsworth (07985) 284. *Clubs:* Athenæum, Cavalry and Guards.

See also Hon. Lady Waley-Cohen.

NATHANS, Prof. Daniel; Professor of Molecular Biology and Genetics, The Johns Hopkins University School of Medicine, since 1980; Senior Investigator, Howard Hughes

Medical Institute, since 1982; *b* 30 Oct. 1928; *s* of Samuel Nathans and Sarah Nathans (*née* Levitan); *m* 1956, Joanne Gomberg; three *s*. *Educ:* Univ. of Delaware, Newark, Del (BS Chemistry); Washington Univ., St Louis, Mo (MD). Intern, 1954–55, and resident, 1957–59, in Medicine, Columbia-Presbyterian Medical Center, NYC; Clinical Associate, Nat. Cancer Inst., Bethesda, Md, 1955–57; Guest Investigator, Rockefeller Inst., NYC, 1959–62; Prof. of Microbiology, 1962 and Faculty Mem., Johns Hopkins Univ. Sch. of Medicine, Baltimore, Md, 1962–. Nobel Prize in Physiology or Medicine, 1978. *Address:* 2227 Crest Road, Baltimore, Md 21209, USA.

NATWAR-SINGH, Kanwar; Padma Bhushan, 1984; Union Minister of State for Foreign Affairs, India, 1986–89; *b* 16 May 1931; *s* of Govind Singh and Prayag Kaur; *m* 1967, Princess Heminder Kumari, *e d* of late Maharaja Yadvindra Singhji of Patiala; one *s* one *d*. *Educ:* St Stephen's Coll., Delhi Univ.; 1st cl. hons History Delhi. Joined Indian Foreign Service, 1953; 3rd Sec., Peking, 1956–58; Under Sec., Ministry of External Affairs, and Private Sec. to Sec. General, 1958–61; Adviser, Indian Delegn to UN, NY, 1961–66; Rapporteur, UN Cttee on Decolonisation, 1962–66; Rapporteur, UN Trusteeship Council, 1965; Alt. Deleg. of India to UN Session for 1962; Rep. of India on Exec. Bd of UNICEF, NY, 1962–66; Dep. Sec. to Prime Minister of India, 1966–67; Dir, Prime Minister's Secretariat, New Delhi, 1967–70; Jt Sec. to Prime Minister, 1970–71; Ambassador to Poland, 1971–73; Dep. High Comr in London, 1973–77; High Comr for India in Zambia and Botswana, 1977–80; Ambassador to Pakistan, 1980–82; Sec., Min. of External Affairs, India, 1982–84; Minister of State for Steel, 1984–85, for Fertilizers, 1985–86. Attended Commonwealth Heads of Govt Meetings: Jamaica, 1975; Lusaka, 1979; Member: Commonwealth Cyprus Cttee, 1977; Indian Delegn to Zimbabwe Indep. Celebrations, 1980; Sec.-Gen., 7th Non-Aligned Summit, New Delhi, 1983; Chief Co-ordinator, Commonwealth Heads of State and Govt Meeting, New Delhi, 1983; Pres., UN Conf. on Disarmament and Develt, 1987; Leader, Indian Delegn to 42nd Session of UN Gen. Assembly, 1987. Dir, Air India, 1982–84. Executive Trustee: UNITAR, 1981–; Jawaharlal Nehru Meml Fund, 1986. Pres., All India Tennis Fedn, 1988. Hon. Res. Fellow, UCL. E. M. Forster Literary Award, 1989. *Publications:* E. M. Forster: A Tribute, 1964; The Legacy of Nehru, 1965; Tales from Modern India, 1966; Stories from India, 1971; Maharaja Suraj Mal, 1707–1763, 1981; Curtain Raisers, 1984; writes and reviews for national and international papers. *Recreations:* tennis, reading, writing, walking, good conversations followed by prolonged periods of reflective uninterrupted silence. *Clubs:* Garrick, Royal Over-Seas League (Life Mem.); India International Centre (Life Mem.), Gymkhana (Life Mem; Pres., 1984) (Delhi).

NAUGHTIE, (Alexander) James; journalist and broadcaster; Presenter: The World at One, BBC Radio, since 1988; Opera News, BBC Radio 3, since 1990; *b* 9 Aug. 1951; *s* of Alexander and Isabella Naughtie; *m* 1986, Eleanor Updale; one *s* two *d*. *Educ:* Keith Grammar Sch.; Aberdeen Univ. (MA Hons); Syracuse Univ., New York (MA). The Press and Journal, 1975–77; The Scotsman, 1977–84; The Guardian, 1984–88, Chief Political Corresp., 1985–88. Columnist, Scotland on Sunday, 1990–. Laurence M. Stern Fellow, Washington Post, 1981; Mem. Bd, Anglo-Irish Encounter, 1984–87. Contributor to radio and TV current affairs programmes. Hon. LLD Aberdeen, 1990. Personality of the Year, Sony Radio Awards, 1991. *Publications:* (ed) Playing the Palace: a Westminster collection, 1984; contribs to newspapers, magazines, journals. *Recreations:* books, opera. *Address:* BBC, Broadcasting House, W1A 1AA.

NAUGHTON, Philip Anthony; QC 1988; *b* 18 May 1943; *s* of Francis and Madeleine Naughton; *m* 1968, Barbara, *d* of Prof. F. E. Bruce; two *s* one *d*. *Educ:* Wimbledon Coll.; Univ. of Nottingham (LLB). Called to the Bar, Gray's Inn, 1970. Marketing and public relations posts with BP Chemicals Ltd and Air Products Ltd, 1964–71; commenced practice as barrister, 1971. *Recreations:* walking with friends, sailing without them. *Address:* 3 Serjeants' Inn, EC4Y 1BQ. *T:* 071–353 5537.

NAVARRETE, Jorge Eduardo; Mexican Ambassador to China, since 1989; Member of South Commission; *b* 29 April 1940; *s* of Gabriel Navarrete and late Lucrecia López; *m* 1st, 1962, María Antonieta Linares (marr. diss. 1973); one *s*; 2nd, 1976, María de Navarrete (*d* 1985); 3rd, 1987, Angeles Salceda. *Educ:* Nat. Sch. of Economics, Nat. Autonomous Univ. of Mexico (equivalent BA Econ.); post-graduate studies in internat. economy. Center for Latin American Monetary Studies, Mexico, 1963–65; Nat. Foreign Trade Bank, Mexico, 1966–72; joined Mexican Foreign Service, 1972; Ambassador to: Venezuela, 1972–75; Austria, 1976–77; Yugoslavia, 1977–79; Dep. Perm Rep. to UN, NY, 1979; Under Sec. (Economics), Min. of Foreign Affairs, Mexico, 1979–85; Ambassador to UK and Republic of Ireland, 1986–89. Holds decorations from Argentina, Brazil, Ecuador, Federal Republic of Germany, Italy, Panama, Poland, Sweden, Venezuela. *Publications:* The International Transfer of Technology (with G. Bueno and M. S. Wionczeck), 1969; Mexico's Economic Policy, 2 vols, 1971, 1972; Cancun 1981: the international meeting on co-operation and development, 1982; The External Debt of Latin America: issues and policies, 1987; numerous essays on Mexican and Latin American economic issues, in Mexican and foreign jls. *Recreation:* chess. *Address:* Mexican Embassy, San Li Tun Dong, Wu Jie 5, Beijing, China.

NAYAR, Kuldip; syndicated columnist; President, Citizens for Democracy; *b* 14 Aug. 1924; *m* 1949, Bharti; two *s*. *Educ:* Northwestern Univ., USA (BA Hons, LLB, MSc in journalism). Press Officer to Home Minister, India, 1954–56, to Prime Minister, India, 1960–64; Editor and General Manager, United News of India, 1964–67; Delhi Editor, The Statesman, 1967–75; Editor, Indian Express News Service, 1975–81; syndicated columnist, 1981–; correspondent, The Times, London, 1968–89. High Comr in UK, 1990. Numerous journalism awards. *Publications:* Between the Lines, 1967; India: the critical years, 1968; The Supersession of Judges, 1971; Distant Neighbours, 1972; India After Nehru, 1974; The Judgement, 1977; In Jail, 1979; A report on Afghanistan, 1982; The Tragedy of Punjab, 1985. *Recreations:* music (Indian and Western); cricket, hockey. *Address:* D7/2 Vasant Vihar, New Delhi 57, India.

NAYLER, Georgina Ruth; Director, National Heritage Memorial Fund, since 1989; *b* 16 March 1959; *d* of Dennis Nayler and Yvonne (*née* Loader). *Educ:* Brentwood County High Sch. for Girls; Univ. of Warwick (BA). Joined Nat. Heritage Meml Fund, 1982; Asst Dir, 1987–88; Dep. Dir, 1988–89. Mem., Historic Bldgs Council for Scotland, 1990–. *Recreations:* gardening, interior decorating, collecting china and watercolours. *Address:* c/o National Heritage Memorial Fund, 10 St James's Street, SW1A 1EF. *T:* 071–930 0963.

NAYLOR, Bernard; University Librarian since 1977 and Co-ordinator of Information Services since 1988, Southampton University; *b* 7 May 1938; *s* of William Edward Naylor and Lilian Naylor (*née* Oakes); *m* 1967, Frances Gemma Trenaman; four *s* one *d*. *Educ:* Balliol Coll., Oxford (BA 1963; MA 1965); Sch. of Librarianship and Archive Administration, University Coll. London (Dip. Lib. 1966). ALA 1969. Asst, Foreign Accessions Dept, Bodleian Liby, 1964–66; Librarian and Bibliographer, Univ. of London Inst. of Latin American Studies, 1966–74; Sec., Library Resources Co-ordinating Cttee, Univ. of London, 1974–77. Member: British Liby Adv. Cttee on Lending Services, 1978–86 (Chm., 1981–85); Council, Standing Conf. of Nat. and Univ. Libraries, 1979–82, 1984–90 (Vice-Chm., 1984–86; Chm., 1986–88); British Council Libraries Adv. Cttee, 1982– (Chm., 1986–). Chm., Hants Area Tech. Res. Indust. Commercial Service Exec., 1981–. *Publications:* Accounts of Nineteenth Century South America, 1969; Directory of Libraries and Special Collections on Latin America and the West Indies, 1975; articles in liby jls. *Recreations:* playing the piano (in private), making wine, learning foreign languages. *Address:* 12 Blenheim Avenue, Highfield, Southampton SO2 1DU. *T:* Southampton (0703) 554697.

NAYLOR, (Charles) John; National Secretary, National Council of YMCAs, since 1982; *b* 17 Aug. 1943; *s* of late Arthur Edgar Naylor, MBE and Elizabeth Mary Naylor; *m* 1968, Margery Thomson; two *s*. *Educ:* Royal Grammar Sch., Newcastle upon Tyne; Haberdashers' Aske's Sch., Elstree; Clare Coll., Cambridge (MA History). Jun. and sen. exec. posts in industry, 1965–75; Dir, YMCA National Centre, Lakeside, Cumbria, 1975–80; Dep. National Sec., National Council of YMCAs, 1980–82. Vice-Chm., Nat. Council for Voluntary Youth Services, 1985–88; Mem., Nat. Adv. Council for Youth Service, 1985–88. Chair: Assoc. of Heads of Outdoor Educn Centres, 1979–80; MSC and DES Working Party on Residential Experience and Unemployment, 1980–81. *Publications:* contribs on outdoor educn to DES and MSC pubns; articles in national and internat. YMCA pubns. *Recreations:* running, the outdoors (partic. the mountains), theatre, church, a growing family, embryonic golf. *Address:* National Council of YMCAs, 640 Forest Road, E17 3DZ. *T:* 081–520 5599.

NAYLOR, Maj.-Gen. David Murray, MBE 1972; Director-General, Territorial Army and Organisation, Ministry of Defence, since 1989; *b* 5 March 1938; *s* of Thomas Humphrey Naylor and Dorothy Isobel Durning Naylor (*née* Holt); *m* 1965, Rosemary Gillian Hicks Beach; three *s*. *Educ:* Eton Coll. psc, rcds. Joined Scots Guards, 1956; commnd as National Service and later as Regular Officer; commanded: 2nd Bn Scots Guards, 1976–79; 22nd Armoured Bde, 1982–83; Dep. Mil. Sec. (A), 1985–87; GOC NE Dist and Comdr 2nd Inf. Div., 1987–89. *Recreations:* shooting, walking, tennis, travel. *Address:* c/o Barclays Bank, Heywoods, PO Box 99, 45 Victoria Street, Liverpool L69 1AN. *T:* 051–227 4641. *Club:* Cavalry and Guards.

NAYLOR, Prof. Ernest, PhD, DSc; FIBiol; Lloyd Roberts Professor of Marine Zoology (formerly Lloyd Roberts Professor of Zoology), since 1982, and Dean of Science, since 1989, University College of North Wales, Bangor; *b* 19 May 1931; *s* of Joseph and Evelyn Naylor; *m* 1956, Carol Gillian Bruce; two *d*. *Educ:* Univ. of Sheffield (BSc); Univ. of Liverpool (PhD, DSc). FIBiol 1972. Successively Asst Lectr, Lectr, Sen. Lectr and Reader in Zoology, University Coll. of Swansea, Wales, 1956–71; Prof. of Marine Biology, Univ. of Liverpool, 1971–82. Vis. Professor: Duke Univ., USA, 1969, 1970; Univ. of Otago, NZ, 1982. Mem. Council, NERC, 1976–82; Specialist Adviser to H of L Select Sub-Cttee on Marine Sci. and Technology, 1985; Indep. Mem., Co-ordinating Cttee on Marine Sci. and Technology, 1988–91; Pres., Soc. for Exptml Biology, 1989–91. *Publications:* British Marine Isopods, 1972; (co-ed with R. G. Hartnoll) Cyclic Phenomena in Marine Plants and Animals, 1979; over 100 papers in learned jls. *Recreation:* gardening. *Address:* School of Ocean Sciences, University College of North Wales, Bangor, Gwynedd LL57 2DG. *T:* Bangor (0248) 351151.

NAYLOR, John; *see* Naylor, C. J.

NAYLOR, Prof. Malcolm Neville, RD 1967; BSc, BDS, PhD; FDSRCS; Professor of Preventive Dentistry, University of London, since 1970; Head of Department of Periodontology and Preventive Dentistry, Guy's Hospital Dental School, since 1980; *b* 30 Jan. 1926; *er s* of late Roland B. Naylor, MBE and Mabel L. (*née* Neville), Walsall, Staffs; *m* 1956, Doreen Mary, *d* of late H. E. Jackson, CBE; one *s*. *Educ:* Queen Mary's Sch., Walsall; Univ. of Glasgow; Univ. of Birmingham (BSc 1951, BDS 1955; Nuffield Scholar, 1949–51); Univ. of London (PhD 1963). FDSRCS 1958. Hosp. appts, Birmingham and Dundee, 1955–59; Guy's Hosp. Dental School: Res. Fellow, 1959–62; Sen. Lectr in Preventive Dentistry, 1962–66; Reader in Preventive Dentistry, 1966–70; Hon. Consultant Dental Surgeon, Guy's Hosp., 1966–. William Waldorf Astor Fellow, USA, 1963. President: British Div., IADR, 1990– (Hon. Treas., 1975–90); Odontol Sect., RSocMed, 1984–85. Served RNVR and RNR, retiring as Surg. Captain (D), 1943–76; Hon. Dental Surgeon to the Queen, 1976; Hon. Col, Univ. of London OTC, 1979–; Sec., 1978–82, Chm., 1982–89, COMEC; Chairman: Mil. Educn Cttee, Univ. of London, 1979–; Sea Cadet Assoc., Sports Council, 1976–. Governor: Roehampton Inst. for Higher Educn, 1978–; Whitelands Coll., 1975–; Bacons Sch., Bermondsey, 1979–90 (Vice Chm., 1981–90); St Saviour's and St Olave's Sch., 1980–90 (Chm., 1988–). Lay Reader, C of E, 1974–. Mem., Southwark Diocesan Synod, 1983–. Freeman, City of London, 1983; Liveryman, Bakers' Co., 1983–. Colgate Prize, IADR, 1961; Tomes Medal, BDA, 1987. *Publications:* papers and articles in prof. and scientific jls. *Recreations:* sailing, music, family and home. *Address:* Carrick Lodge, Roehampton, SW15 5BN. *T:* 081–788 5045. *Clubs:* Royal Society of Medicine; Royal Naval Sailing Assoc.

NAYLOR, Maurice; *see* Naylor, W. M.

NAYLOR, Peter Brian, CBE 1987; Representative, British Council, Greece, 1983–86; *b* 10 July 1933; *s* of Eric Sydney Naylor and Phyllis Marian Jolly; *m* 1958, Barbara Pearson; two *s* one *d* (and one *s* decd). *Educ:* Grange High Sch., Bradford; Selwyn Coll., Cambridge (Open Exhibnr; BA 1957). Wool Top Salesman, Hirsch, Son & Rhodes, Bradford, 1957; British Council: Asst Rep., Bangkok, 1959; Courses Dept and E Europe Dept, London, 1962; Asst Rep., Warsaw, 1967; Reg. Rep., Dacca, E Pakistan, 1969; Actg Rep., Athens, 1971; Rep., Argentina, 1972, Brazil, 1975; Controller, European Div., 1978–83. *Recreations:* painting, music, books, games. *Address:* 3 Farmadine Court, Saffron Walden, Essex CB11 3HT. *T:* Saffron Walden (0799) 27708. *Club:* Saffron Walden Golf.

NAYLOR, (William) Maurice, CBE 1973; FHSM; JP; Director, National Association of Health Authorities, 1981–84; *b* 1920; *s* of late Thomas Naylor; *m* 1948, Maureen Ann, *d* of John Walsh; one *s* two *d*. *Educ:* St Joseph's Coll., Market Drayton; Manchester Univ. (BA Admin). FHSM 1956. Sec., Sheffield Regional Hosp. Bd, 1963–73; Regional Administrator, Trent RHA, 1973–81. Pres., Inst. of Health Services Management, 1975–76 (Chm., Educn Cttee, 1980–86); Hon. FHSM 1987. Hon. MBA Sheffield, 1982. *Address:* 8 Middlefield Croft, Dore, Sheffield S17 3AS. *T:* Sheffield (0742) 350778.

NAYLOR-LEYLAND, Sir Philip (Vyvian), 4th Bt *cr* 1895, of Hyde Park House; Director: Nantclwyd Farms Ltd; B. M. S. S. Ltd; Fitzwilliam Peterborough Properties; Milton Gate Development Co.; Milton (Peterborough) Estates Co.; *b* 9 Aug. 1953; *s* of Sir Vivyan Edward Naylor-Leyland, 3rd Bt and of Hon. Elizabeth Anne Fitzalan-Howard (who *m* 2nd, Sir Stephen Hastings, *qv*), *yr d* of 2nd Viscount FitzAlan of Derwent, OBE; *S* father, 1987; *m* 1980, Lady Isabella Lambton, *d* of Viscount Lambton, *qv*; two *s* one *d*. Vice-Chm., Peterborough Royal Foxhound Show Soc., 1988–; Pres., Nat. Coursing Club, 1988–. Jt Master, Fitzwilliam Hunt, 1987–. Heir: *s* Thomas Philip Naylor-Leyland, *b* 22 Jan. 1982. *Address:* Nantclwyd Hall, Ruthin, Clwyd LL15 2PR; The Ferry House, Milton Park, Peterborough PE6 7AB. *Club:* White's.

NAZARETH, Gerald Paul, CBE 1985 (OBE 1976); **Hon. Mr Justice Nazareth;** Judge of the High Court, Hong Kong, since 1985; *b* 27 Jan. 1932; *s* of Vincent Lionel Nazareth and Lily Isabel Monteiro; *m* 1959, Elba Maria Fonseca; three *d*. *Educ:* Nairobi; St Xavier's College, Bombay; LLB Bombay Univ. Called to the Bar, Lincoln's Inn, 1962. Public Prosecutor, and Senior Crown Counsel, Kenya, 1954–63; Solicitor General, British Solomon Islands, 1963–73; Attorney General and Legal Advisor, Western Pacific High Commn, 1973–76; Hong Kong: Law Draftsman, 1976–84; MLC, 1979–84; QC Hong Kong 1982; Mem., Law Reform Commn, 1982–84 (Chm., Sub-Cttee on Copyright Law, 1987–). Vice-Pres., Commonwealth Assoc. of Legislative Counsel, 1983–90. *Recreations:* music, reading, walking. *Address:* The Supreme Court, Hong Kong. *T:* Hong Kong 825–4432.

NAZIR-ALI, Rt. Rev. Dr Michael; General Secretary, Church Missionary Society, since 1989; *b* 19 Aug. 1949; *s* of James and Patience Nazir-Ali; *m* 1972, Valerie Cree; two *s*. *Educ:* St Paul's School and St Patrick's Coll., Karachi; Univ. of Karachi (BA 1970, Econs and Sociology); Fitzwilliam Coll. and Ridley Hall, Cambridge; St Edmund Hall, Oxford (BLitt 1974). MLitt Cantab 1976; MLitt Oxon 1981; PhD Aust. Coll. of Theol. (Univ. of NSW) with Centre for World Religions, Harvard, 1983. Assistant: Christ Church, Cambridge, 1970–72; St Ebbe's, Oxford, 1972–74; Burney Lectr in Islam, Cambridge, 1973–74; Tutorial Supervisor in Theology, Univ. of Cambridge, 1974–76; Assistant, Holy Sepulchre, Cambridge, 1974–76; Tutor, then Sen. Tutor, Karachi Theol Coll., 1976–81; Assoc. Priest, Holy Trinity Cathedral, Karachi, 1976–79; Priest-in-charge, St Andrew's, Akhtar Colony, Karachi, 1979–81; Provost of Lahore Cathedral, 1981–84; Bishop of Raiwind, Pakistan, 1984–86. Asst to Archbp of Canterbury, Co-ordinator of Studies and Editor for Lambeth Conf., 1986–89; Director-in-Residence, Oxford Centre for Mission Studies, 1986–89. Sec., Archbp's Commn on Communion and Women in the Episcopate (Eames Commn), 1988–. *Publications:* Islam: a Christian perspective, 1983; Frontiers in Muslim-Christian Encounter, 1987; Martyrs and Magistrates: toleration and trial in Islam, 1989; *edited:* Working Papers for the Lambeth Conference, 1988; The Truth shall Make you Free: Report of the Lambeth Conference, 1988; Trustworthy and True: Pastoral Letters from the Lambeth Conference, 1988; From Everywhere to Everywhere, 1990; articles and contribs to jls. *Recreations:* cricket, hockey, table tennis, reading detective fiction, humour and poetry, writing fiction and poetry. *Address:* 157 Waterloo Road, SE1 8UU. *T:* 071–928 8681.

NEAL, Prof. Bernard George, MA, PhD, ScD; FEng 1980; Emeritus Professor, since 1982 and Fellow, since 1986, Imperial College, London University (Professor of Applied Science, 1961–72, of Engineering Structures, 1972–81, of Civil Engineering, 1981–82, and Head of Civil Engineering Department, 1976–82); *b* 29 March 1922; *s* of late Horace Bernard Neal, Wembley, and Hilda Annie Webb; *m* 1948, Elizabeth Ann, *d* of late William George Toller, Woodbridge, and Bertha Catharine Toller; one *s* one *d*. *Educ:* Merchant Taylors'; Trinity College, Cambridge (Schol.). MA Cantab, 1947; PhD Cantab 1948; ScD Cantab 1965; FInstCE 1960; FIStructE 1966. Temp. Experimental Officer, Admiralty, 1942–45; Research Student, Univ. of Cambridge, 1945–48; Research Associate, Brown University, USA, 1948–49; Demonstrator, 1949–51, Lecturer, 1951–54, Univ. of Cambridge; Research Fellow, 1947–50, Staff Fellow, 1950–54, Trinity Hall, Cambridge; Prof. of Civil Engineering, University Coll. of Swansea, 1954–61. Pro-Rector, Imperial Coll., London, 1972–74. Dean of City and Guilds Coll., 1964–67; Visiting Prof., Brown Univ., USA, 1959–60. Telford Premium, 1951, Manby Premium, 1952, Instn Civil Engineers. *Publications:* The Plastic Methods of Structural Analysis, 1956; Structural Theorems and their Applications, 1964; technical papers on theory of structures, strength of materials. *Recreations:* lawn tennis, croquet. *Address:* 32 Napier Court, Ranelagh Gardens, SW6 3UU. *T:* 071–731 6188. *Clubs:* All England Lawn Tennis and Croquet (Mem. Cttee, 1982–), Hurlingham.

NEAL, Sir Eric (James), AC 1988; Kt 1982; Director, since 1972 and Chief Executive, since 1973, Boral Ltd (Managing Director, 1982–87); Chairman: Westpac Banking Corporation, since 1989 (Director, since 1985; Deputy Chairman, 1987–88); Atlas Copco Australia Pty Ltd, since 1989; Metal Manufacturers Ltd, since 1990 (Director, since 1987); *b* 3 June 1924; *s* of James and May Neal; *m* 1950, Thelma Joan, *d* of R. E. Bowden; two *s*. *Educ:* South Australian Sch. of Mines. CEng; FIGasE, FAIE, FAIM. Director: John Fairfax Ltd, 1987–88; BHP Co. Ltd, 1988–; Coca Cola Amatil Ltd, 1987–. Mem., Cttee apptd by Fed. Govt to advise on Higher Defence Orgn, 1982. Member: Amer. Bureau of Shipping, 1976–90; Aust. Gas Assoc. (former Mem. Bd); Inst. of Dirs; first Nat. Pres., Aust. Inst. of Co. Dirs, 1990. Chm. Exec. Cttee, Duke of Edinburgh's Sixth Commonwealth Study Conf. 1986; Nat. Chm., Duke of Edinburgh's Award Scheme in Australia. Chief Comr, City of Sydney, 1987–88. Hon. FIE (Aust). Hon. DEng Sydney, 1989. *Recreations:* naval history, travel, reading, shipping. *Address:* 286 Moore Park Road, Paddington, NSW 2021, Australia. *T:* 02 331 6404, *Fax:* 02 332 1804. *Clubs:* Melbourne (Melbourne); Union, Australian Jockey, Australasian Pioneers (Sydney).

NEAL, Frederick Albert, CMG 1990; FIL; UK Representative on Council of International Civil Aviation Organization, Montreal, since 1983; *b* 22 Dec. 1932; *s* of Frederick William George Neal and Frances Elizabeth (*née* Duke); *m* 1958, Gloria Maria Moirano. *Educ:* Royal Grammar Sch., High Wycombe; Birkbeck Coll., London (BA). FIL 1965. Min. of Supply, 1953; Asst Defence Supply Attaché, Bonn, 1958–64; Principal, Min. of Technology (subseq. DTI), 1967; Asst Sec., DTI, 1974; Counsellor (Economic and Commercial), Ottawa, 1975–80; Asst Sec., Dept of Trade, 1980–83. *Recreations:* golf, bridge, music. *Address:* International Civil Aviation Organization, Suite 928, 1000 Sherbrooke Street West, Montreal, Quebec H3A 3G4, Canada. *Clubs:* Naval and Military, Royal Over-Seas League; South Herts Golf, Royal Montreal Golf.

NEAL, Harry Morton, CBE 1991; FIC; Chairman, Harry Neal (City) Ltd; *b* 21 Nov. 1931; *s* of late Godfrey French Neal and Janet Bryce Morton; *m* 1954, Cecilia Elizabeth Crawford, *d* of late Col M. Crawford, DSO; one *s* three *d*. *Educ:* Uppingham Sch.; London Univ. (BSc(Eng)); City and Guilds Coll. (ACGI). Flying Officer, RAF, 1953. Chm., Connaught Hotel Ltd, 1980–; Dir, Savoy Hotel Ltd, 1982–; Chm., Harry Neal Ltd, 1985–90. Member of Lloyd's. Chm., City and Guilds of London Inst., 1979–; Member: Technician Educn Council, 1982–83; Business and Technician Educn Council, 1983–; Court of City Univ., 1982–; Bd of Governors, Willesden Tech. Coll., 1983–86; Bd of Govs, Francis Holland Sch., 1988–; Management Cttee, Courtauld Inst. of Art, 1983–. Pres., Greater London NW County Scout Council, 1983–. Liveryman, Carpenters' Co., 1955–. FCIOB, FRSA; FCGI 1983. Chevalier de Tastevin, 1981. *Recreations:* gardening, shooting. *Address:* Great Sarratt Hall, Sarratt, Rickmansworth, Herts WD3 4PD.

NEAL, Sir Leonard (Francis), Kt 1974; CBE 1971; FCIT; CIPM; Industrial Relations Consultant to number of industrial and commercial companies; *b* 27 Aug. 1913; *s* of Arthur Henry Neal and Mary Neal; *m* 1939, Mary Lilian Puttock; one *s* one *d*. *Educ:* London School of Economics; Trinity College, Cambridge (MA). Labour Manager, Esso, 1956; Employee Relations Manager, Fawley Refinery, 1961; Labour Relations Adviser, Esso Europe Inc. Mem., British Railways Board, 1967–71; Chm., Commn on Industrial Relations, 1971–74. Prof. (part-time) of Industrial Relations, UMIST, 1970–76; Chairman: MAT International Gp Ltd, 1974–85; Employment Conditions Abroad Ltd, 1977–84; Dir (non-exec.), Pilkington Bros, 1976–83; Dir (non-exec.), Rosgill Holdings Ltd, 1980–84. *Publication:* (with A. Robertson) The Managers Guide to Industrial Relations. *Recreations:* reading, gardening, motoring. *Address:* Towcester, Northants.

NEAL, Michael David; Headmaster, Cranborne Chase School, 1969–83; *b* 27 Jan. 1927; *s* of David Neal, FCA; *m* 1952, Barbara Lisette, *d* of late Harold Carter, MA; two *s* two *d*. *Educ:* Winchester; University Coll., Oxford (BA). Rifle Bde, 1945–48 (Captain); Asst Master, RNC Dartmouth, 1952–54; Eton Coll., 1954–69 (Housemaster, 1963–69). Mem., Eton UDC, 1960–63. *Address:* Wegnall's Mill, Presteigne, Powys LD8 2LD. *T:* Presteigne (0544) 267012.

NEALE, Sir Alan (Derrett), KCB 1972 (CB 1968); MBE 1945; Deputy Chairman, Association of Futures Brokers and Dealers Ltd, 1987–91, retired; *b* 24 Oct. 1918; *o s* of late W. A. Neale; *m* 1956, Joan, *o d* of late Harry Frost, Wisbech; one *s*. *Educ:* Highgate School; St John's College, Oxford. War Service, Intelligence Corps, 1940–45. Board of Trade, 1946–68; Second Sec., 1967; Dep. Sec., Treasury, 1968–71, Second Permanent Sec., 1971–72; Perm. Sec., MAFF, 1973–78. A Dep. Chm., Monopolies and Mergers Commn, 1982–86 (Mem., 1981–86). Commonwealth Fund Fellowship, USA, 1952–53; Fellow of Center for Internat. Affairs, Harvard Univ., 1960–61. *Publications:* The Anti-Trust Laws of the USA, 1960; The Flow of Resources from Rich to Poor, 1961; (jtly) International Business and National Jurisdiction, 1988. *Recreations:* music, bridge. *Address:* 95 Swains Lane, N6 6PJ. *T:* 081–340 5236. *Club:* Reform.

NEALE, Sir Gerrard Anthony, (Sir Gerry), Kt 1990; MP (C) North Cornwall, since 1979; *b* 25 June 1941; *s* of Charles Woodhouse Neale and Phyllis Muriel Neale; *m* 1965, Deirdre Elizabeth McCann; one *s* two *d*. *Educ:* Bedford Sch. Articled to solicitors, Bedford, 1961; admitted 1966; Partner, Heald Nickinson, Solicitors, London, 1988–. Dir, Telephone Rentals, 1979–89. Councillor, Borough of Milton Keynes, 1973–79, Mayor, 1976–77. Chm., Buckingham Constituency Cons. Assoc., 1974–76. Contested (C) N Cornwall, Oct. 1974; PPS to Minister for Consumer Affairs, 1981–82, to Minister of State for Trade, 1981–83, to Sec. of State for Transport, 1985–86, to Sec. of State for the Environment, 1986–87, to Sec. of State for Defence, 1987–89. *Recreations:* sailing, tennis. *Address:* House of Commons, SW1A 0AA.

NEALE, Rt. Rev. John Robert Geoffrey, AKC; Hon. Assistant Bishop, Dioceses of London and Southwark, since 1989; *b* 21 Sept. 1926; *s* of late Geoffrey Brockman Neale and Stella Beatrice (*née* Wild). *Educ:* Felsted Sch.; King's Coll., London Univ. Served War of 1939–45: Lieut RA; Army, 1944–48. Business, G. B. Neale & Co Ltd, EC2, 1948–51. King's Coll. London, 1951–55 (Jelf Prize, 1954). Deacon, 1955, priest, 1956; Curate, St Peter, St Helier, Dio. Southwark, 1955–58. Chaplain, Ardingly Coll., Sx, 1958–63; Recruitment Sec., CACTM (ACCM), 1963–67; Archbishops' Rep. for ordination candidates, 1967–68; Canon Missioner, Dio. Guildford, Hon. Canon of Guildford Cath. and Rector of Hascombe, Surrey, 1968–74; Suffragan Bishop (later Area Bishop) of Ramsbury, 1974–88; Hon. Canon of Salisbury Cathedral, 1974–88; Archdeacon of Wilts, 1974–80; Sec., Partnership for World Mission, 1989–91. FIC 1991. *Publication:* Ember Prayer (SPCK), 1965. *Recreation:* horticulture. *Address:* 26 Prospect, Corsham, Wilts SN13 9AF. *T:* Corsham (0249) 712557. *Club:* Commonwealth Trust.

NEALE, Keith Douglas; County Treasurer, Essex, since 1987; *b* 27 March 1947; *s* of Douglas Jeffrey and Dorothy Neale; *m* 1969, Mary Williamson; one *s* one *d*. East Midlands Electricity Board, 1964; Trainee Accountant, Blackwell RDC, 1965; County Treasurer's Dept, Lindsey CC, Lincs, 1968; Asst Dir of Finance, Humberside CC, 1974; Dep. County Treasurer, Essex, 1982. Jt Sec., Soc. of County Treasurers. Mem., CIPFA. *Address:* County Treasurer's Department, Essex County Council, County Hall, Chelmsford, Essex. *T:* Chelmsford (0245) 492211.

NEALE, Kenneth James, OBE 1959; FSA; consultant; author and lecturer; Assistant Under Secretary of State, Home Office, 1976–82; *b* 9 June 1922; *s* of late James Edward and Elsie Neale; *m* 1943, Dorothy Willett; three *s* one *d*. *Educ:* Hackney Downs (Grocers') Sch., London. Entered Civil Service as Clerical Officer, Tithe Redemption Commn, 1939. Lieut, RNVR, 1941–46. Exec. Officer, Min. of Nat. Insce, 1947–51; Asst Princ., 1951–55, Principal, 1955–64, Colonial Office; Sec. for Interior and Local Govt, Cyprus, 1957; Dep. Admin Sec., Cyprus, 1958–59; Central African Office, 1962–64; Asst Sec., Commonwealth Office, Diplomatic Service, 1964–67; Home Office: Asst Sec., 1967–70; Dir, Industries and Supply, 1970–75; Controller, Planning and Develt, 1976–80; Dir, Regimes and Services, 1980–82. Member: Prisons Bd, 1967–69, 1976–82; European Cttee on Crime Problems, 1976–84; Chairman: Council of Europe Select Cttee on Standard Minimum Rules for Treatment of Prisoners, 1978–80; Council of Europe Cttee for Co-operation in Prison Affairs, 1981–84; Consultant: Council of Europe, 1984–; Open Univ., 1990–. Chairman: Essex Archaeol and Historical Congress, 1984–87 (Pres., 1987–90); Friends of Historic Essex, 1986–; Member: Council, Essex Soc. for Archaeol. and Hist. (formerly Essex Archaeol Soc.), 1984–87; Library, Museum and Records Cttee, Essex CC, 1986–. Mem. Editl Bd, Essex Jl, 1989–. *Publications:* Discovering Essex in London, 1970; Victorian Horsham, 1975; Work in Penal Institutions, 1976; Essex in History, 1977; Her Majesty's Commissioners, 1978; (ed) Strategies for Education within Prison Regimes, 1986; (ed) An Essex Tribute, 1987; various articles and papers on local history, natural history, penology. *Recreations:* reading, local history, natural history. *Address:* Honeysuckle Cottage, Great Sampford, Saffron Walden, Essex. *T:* Great Sampford (079986) 304.

NEALE, Michael Cooper, CB 1987; CEng, FIMechE, FRAeS; Secretary, Royal Commission for Exhibition of 1851, since 1987; industrial consultant; non-executive director of companies; *b* 2 Dec. 1929; *s* of Frank and Edith Kathleen Neale; *m* 1956, Thelma Weare; one *s* two *d*. *Educ:* West Bridgford Grammar Sch., Nottingham; Queen Mary Coll., Univ. of London (BScEng, MScEng). Postgraduate research on fuel injection in diesel engines, 1951–53; Engr Officer, Royal Air Force, 1953–56; joined Civil Service, 1956; Aeroplane and Armament Experimental Estabt, Boscombe Down, 1956–58; joined Nat. Gas Turbine Estabt, Pyestock, 1958; Asst Director of Engine Develt, MoD Headquarters, 1971; Dep. Director (R&D), Nat. Gas Turbine Estabt, 1973–80; Dir Gen. Engines (PE), MoD, 1980–87. Silver medallist, RAeS, 1987. *Publications:* papers in Aeronautical Research Council reports and memoranda series and elsewhere in the technical press, mainly concerning engines. *Recreations:* old railways, cricket. *Address:* 108 Wargrave Road, Twyford, Reading, Berks RG10 9PJ. *T:* Twyford (0734) 341759. *Club:* Athenæum.

NEALON, Dr Catherina Theresa, (Rina), CBE 1979; JP; Chairman, Lothian Health Board, 1973–81; *d* of John and Margaret O'Reilly, Glasgow; *m* 1940, James Patrick Nealon (*d* 1989); one *s*. *Educ:* Convent of Mercy, Garnethill, Glasgow. Mem., Edinburgh Town Council for Pilton Ward, 1949–74; served as Magistrate, 1954–57; Licensing Court, 1954–57; Judge of Police, 1957–62; Chm., Health Cttee, 1972–73. Member: Educn Cttee, Civil Defence Commn, 1949–73; Royal Infirmary and Associated Hosp's Bd of Management, 1952–56; NHS Exec. Council for City of Edinburgh, 1953–74 (Vice-Chm., May 1966–74); Exec. Cttee of Scottish Assoc. of Exec. Councils, 1967–74 (Vice-Pres., 1971, Pres., 1972); SE Regional Hosp. Bd, Scotland, 1966–74 (Chm., 1969–74); Med. Educn Cttee, 1969–74 (Chm., 1972–74); Livingston New Town Jt Health Service Adv. Cttee, 1969–73; Scottish Health Service Planning Council, 1974–81; Common

Services Agency, Management Cttee, and Convenor, Estabt and Accommodation Sub-Cttee, Scottish Health Service, 1974–77; Univ. Liaison Cttee, 1974– (Chm., 1978–81); Edinburgh and SE District Cttee, Scottish Gas Consultative Council, 1967–74 (Chm., 1970–74; Mem. Council, 1969–74); Clean Air Council for Scotland, 1966–75; Nat. Soc. for Clean Air, Scottish Div., 1963– (Vice-Pres., 1970–72, Pres., 1972–74); A&C Whitley Council, 1973–81 (Vice-Chm., 1975–81); Nat. Negotiating Cttee; Ambulance Officers' Negotiating Cttee (Management Side Chm., 1979–81); Gen. Whitley Council (Mem., Gen. Purposes Cttee and Jt Negotiating Cttee, 1980–81); Nat. Appeals Panel; SE Dist Cttee, Gas Consumers' Council, 1981–87; Chm., Scottish Hosp. Supplies Steering Cttee, 1972–74. Former Member: Edin. and Lothian Probation Cttee; Animal Disease Res. Assoc.; Edin. Coll. of Art; Royal Blind Asylum and Sch.; Scottish Accident Prevention Council; Marriage Guidance Council; Nat. Assoc. for Maternal and Child Welfare; Nat. Council on recruitment of Nurses and Midwives; Scottish Assoc. for Mental Health; Assoc. of Sea and Airport Authorities; Edin. and Lothians Tourist Assoc.; Youth Employment Cttee; Extra-Mural Cttee, Edin. Univ., 1960–65; Mem. Bd of Governors: Napier Coll. of Science and Technology, 1964–73 (Vice-Chm., 1971–73); Telford Coll. for Further Education, 1969–72; Moray House Coll. of Educn; Wellington Farm Approved Sch.; Dr Guthrie's Girls' Sch. JP Edinburgh, 1957; Mem. Justices Cttee, 1975; Justice on District Court, 1975–83; Mem. Extra-Parliamentary Panel, 1976–86; Mem., Crossroads Cttee, 1987–. Attended 25th Anniv. Meeting, President's Cttee on Employment of Handicapped, Washington, 1972. Travelled to many countries with Internat. Hosp. Fedn study tours. Member, Church of Scotland. Dr *hc* Edinburgh, 1977. *Recreation:* dressmaking. *Address:* 34 Learmonth Crescent, Edinburgh EH4 1DE. *T:* 031–332 6191.

NEAME, Robert Harry Beale; Chairman, Shepherd Neame Brewers, since 1971; *b* 25 Feb. 1934; *s* of Jasper Beale Neame and Violet Evelyn Neame; *m* 1st, Sally Elizabeth Corben; one *s* two *d* (and one *s* decd); 2nd, 1974, Yvonne Mary Mackenzie; one *d. Educ:* Harrow (Head of School). Joined Shepherd Neame, 1956; Dir, 1957–. SE Regional Director: National Westminster Bank, 1982–; Royal Insurance Co., 1988–; Dir, Folkestone Racecourse, 1985– (Chm., 1988–). Chairman: SE England Tourist Bd, 1979–90; British Section: IULA, 1986–89; CEMR, 1986–89; Vice Chm., Consultative Council of Regl and Local Authorities, 1989. Mem. (C) for Faversham, Kent CC, 1965–89 (Leader, 1982–84). *Recreations:* cricket, squash, rackets (Army Rackets Champion, 1954), golf, shooting, ski-ing. *Address:* Dane Court Farmhouse, Kits Hill, Selling, Faversham, Kent ME13 9QP. *T:* Canterbury (0227) 752284. *Clubs:* Press; MCC, Free Foresters, I Zingari, Band of Brothers, Butterflies; Kandahar Ski; Escorts, Jesters; Royal St George's Golf (Sandwich).

NEAME, Ronald; film producer and director; *b* 23 Apr. 1911; *s* of Elwin Neame and Ivy Close; *m* 1933, Beryl Yolanda Heanly; one *s. Educ:* University College School; Hurstpierpoint College. Entered film industry, 1928; became Chief Cameraman, 1934. In charge of production on: In Which We Serve, This Happy Breed, Blithe Spirit, Brief Encounter, 1942–45; produced: Great Expectations, Oliver Twist, The Magic Box; directed: Take My Life, The Card, 1945–51; The Million Pound Note, 1953; The Man Who Never Was, 1954; Windom's Way, 1957; The Horse's Mouth, 1958; Tunes of Glory, 1960; I Could Go On Singing, 1962; The Chalk Garden, 1963; Mr Moses, 1964; Gambit, 1966; The Prime of Miss Jean Brodie, 1968; Scrooge, 1970; The Poseidon Adventure, 1972; Odessa File, 1973; Meteor, 1978; Hopscotch, 1979; First Monday in October, 1980; Foreign Body, 1985; The Magic Balloon, 1989. *Address:* 2317 Kimridge, Beverly Hills, Calif 90210, USA. *Club:* Savile.

NEARS, Colin Gray; television producer; Member of Council, and Chairman of Advisory Panel on Dance, Arts Council of Great Britain, 1982–90; *b* 19 March 1933; *s* of William Charles Nears and Winifred Mildred Nears (*née* Gray). *Educ:* Ipswich Sch.; King's Coll., Cambridge (MA). Admin. Asst, RIBA, 1956; BBC, 1958–87; Producer: Schools Television, 1960; Music and Arts, 1967. Author and director of programmes on literature, the visual arts, music and dance. Member: Ballet Bd, Royal Opera House, 1990–; Bd, Riverside Trust, 1991–. Editor, Review, 1971–72. FRSA. BAFTA award for Best Specialised Programme, 1973; Prix Italia music prize, 1982. *Recreations:* reading, gardening, painting, swimming. *Address:* 16 Ashchurch Terrace, W12 9SL. *T:* 081–749 3615.

NEARY, Martin Gerard James; conductor and organist; Organist and Master of the Choristers, Westminster Abbey, since 1988; *b* 28 March 1940; *s* of Leonard Walter Neary and Jeanne Marguerite (*née* Thébault); *m* 1967, Penelope Jane, *d* of Sir Brian Warren, *qv*, and Dame A. J. M. T. Barnes, *qv*; one *s* two *d. Educ:* HM Chapels Royal, St James's Palace; City of London Sch.; Gonville and Caius Coll., Cambridge (Organ Schol.; MA Theol. and Music). FRCO. Organist, St Mary's, Hornsey Rise, 1958; St Margaret's, Westminster: Asst Organist, 1963–65; Organist and Master of Music, 1965–71; Prof. of Organ, Trinity Coll., London, 1963–72; Organist and Master of Music, Winchester Cathedral, 1972–87. Organ Advr to dio. of Winchester, 1975–87. Conductor, Twickenham Musical Soc., 1966–72; Founder and Conductor, St Margaret's Westminster Singers, 1967–71; Conductor, Waynflete Singers, 1972–88; Dir, Southern Cathedrals Festival, 1972, 1975, 1978, 1981, 1984, 1987; Conductor, Aspen Music Festival, 1980; Dir, Westminster Baroque Ensemble, 1988–. President: Cathedral Organists' Assoc., 1985–88; RCO, 1988–90 (Mem. Council, 1982–; a Vice-Pres., 1990–); Organists' Benevolent League, 1988–. Many organ recitals and broadcasts in UK, incl. Royal Festival Hall; has conducted many premières of music by British composers incl. John Tavener's Ultimos Ritos, 1979, and Akathist, 1988, Jonathan Harvey's Hymn, 1979, and Passion and Resurrection, 1981; with Martin Neary Singers perf. madrigals and graces at 10 Downing Street, 1970–74. Toured US and Canada, 1963, 1968, 1971, 1973, 1975, 1977, 1979, 1982, 1984, 1986, 1988, appearances incl. Carnegie Hall, Lincoln Center, Kennedy Center, Roy Thomson Hall; BBC Promenade Concerts; sometime Conductor with: ECO; LSO; Bournemouth SO and Sinfonietta; Acad. of Ancient Music; Winchester Baroque Ensemble; many European tours; many recordings, incl. Lloyd Webber's Requiem (Golden Disc). Compositions include: What is man?; responses, carol arrangements, etc. Hon. FTCL, 1969; Hon. RAM, 1988. Hon. Citizen of Texas, 1971. Prizewinner, St Alban's Internat. Organ Festival, 1963; Conducting Scholarship, Berkshire Music Center, USA, 1963; Diploma, J. S. Bach Competn, Leipzig, 1968; UK/USA Bicentennial Fellow, 1979–80; Artist-in-residence, Univ. of California at Davis, 1984. *Publications:* edns of early organ music; contribs to organ jls. *Recreation:* watching cricket. *Address:* 2 Little Cloister, Westminster Abbey, SW1P 3PL. *T:* 071–222 6923. *Club:* Athenæum.

NEAVE, Sir Arundell Thomas Clifton, 6th Bt, *cr* 1795; JP; late Major Welsh Guards; *b* 31 May 1916; *e s* of Col Sir Thomas Lewis Hughes Neave, 5th Bt, and Dorina (*d* 1955) (author of 26 years on the Bosphorus, Remembering Kut, 1937, Romance of the Bosphorus, 1950), *d* of late George H. Clifton; *S* father, 1940; *m* 1946, Richenda, *o c* of Sir Robert J. Paul, 5th Bt; two *s* two *d. Educ:* Eton. Served in 1939–45 war, Welsh Guards (Major); Dunkirk, 1940, retired 1947. JP for Anglesey, 1950. *Heir: s* Paul Arundell Neave [*b* 13 December 1948; *m* 1976, Coralie Jane Louise, *e d* of Sir Robert Kinahan, *qv*; two *s*]. *Address:* Greatham Moor, Liss, Hants. *Clubs:* Carlton, Pratt's.

See also Sir Richard Williams-Bulkeley.

NEAVE, Julius Arthur Sheffield, CBE 1978 (MBE (mil.) 1945); JP; DL; General Manager, since 1966, Director since 1977, Mercantile & General Reinsurance Co. Ltd (Managing Director, 1980–82); Director, Prudential Corporation plc, since 1982; *b* 17 July 1919; *s* of Col Richard Neave and Helen Mary Elizabeth (*née* Miller); *m* 1951, Helen Margery, *d* of Col P. M. Acton-Adams, DSO, Clarence Reserve, Marlborough, NZ; three *d. Educ:* Sherborne School. Joined Mercantile & General Reinsurance Co. Ltd, 1938. Served War, 1939–46: called as Territorial, commnd 13th/18th Royal Hussars, Adjt 3 years, final rank Major (despatches 1945). Returned to Mercantile & General, 1946; Asst Gen. Manager, 1964. (First) Chairman, Reinsurance Offices Assoc., 1969–74, Hon. Pres., 1974–82; Chm., Reinsurance Panel, British Insce Assoc., 1971–82; representative, Gt Britain: Cttee, annual internat. meeting of reinsurers, Monte Carlo, 1969–82; Vice-Pres., Assoc. Internat. pour l'Etude de l'Assurance, Geneva, 1976–83, Pres., 1983. Dir and Governor, Internat. Insce Seminars, 1977–82 (Founder's Gold Medal, 1977); President: Insce Inst. of London, 1976–77, 1983–84; Chartered Insce Inst., 1983–84 (Mem. Council, 1975–); Mem. Court, Insurers' Co., 1979– (Master, 1984–85). Hon. Fellow, RSA, 1975. Essex: JP (Brentwood), 1975; DL, 1983; High Sheriff, 1987–88. OStJ 1988. *Publications:* Speaking of Reinsurance, 1980; Still Speaking of Reinsurance, 1983. *Recreations:* shooting, fishing, golf, needlework. *Address:* Mill Green Park, Ingatestone, Essex CM4 0JB. *T:* Ingatestone (0277) 353036. *Club:* Cavalry and Guards.

NEAVE AIREY, family name of **Baroness Airey of Abingdon.**

NEDD, Sir (Robert) Archibald, Kt 1985; Chief Justice of Grenada, 1979–86; *b* 7 Aug. 1916; *s* of late Robert and Ruth Nedd; *m* 1941, Annis (*née* McDowall); two *s* one *d. Educ:* King's Coll. London (LLB). Called to the Bar, Inner Temple, 1938. Registrar of High Court, and Addtl Magistrate, St Vincent, 1940–41, Dominica, 1941–43; Magistrate, St Lucia, 1943–44 (acted Crown Attorney); Crown Attorney, Dominica, 1944–49 (Officer administering Govt of Dominica, March 1945–Nov. 1946); Magistrate, full powers, Nigeria, 1949–53; private practice, Nigeria, 1953–70; Principal State Counsel, Rivers State, Nigeria, 1970–71 (exercising functions of legal draftsman); Legal draftsman, Rivers State, Nigeria, 1971–74 (occasionally perf. functions of Solicitor-Gen.); Puisne Judge of Supreme Court of Associated States of W Indies and Grenada, at Antigua, 1974–75, at Grenada, 1975–79. *Recreation:* reading. *Address:* Old Fort, St George's, Grenada, West Indies. *T:* 809–440–1225.

NEEDHAM, family name of **Earl of Kilmorey.**

NEEDHAM, Joseph, MA, PhD, ScD (Cantab); FRS 1941; FBA 1971; Emeritus Director, Needham Research Institute (East Asian History of Science Library), Cambridge (Director, 1976–90); Master of Gonville and Caius College, 1966–76; Hon. Counsellor, UNESCO; *b* 1900; *s* of late Joseph Needham, MD, of Harley Street and Clapham Park, and Alicia A. Needham; *m* 1924, Dorothy Mary, ScD, FRS (*d* 1987), *d* of John Moyle, Babbacombe, Devon; *m* 1989, Gwei-Djen Lu, *qv. Educ:* Oundle School. Fellow Gonville and Caius Coll., 1924–66, 1976– (Librarian, 1959–60, Pres., 1959–66); Univ. Demonstrator in Biochem., 1928–33; Sir William Dunn Reader in Biochemistry, 1933–66, now Emeritus; Vis. Prof. of Biochem. at Stanford Univ., California, USA, 1929; Hitchcock Prof., Univ. of California, 1950; Visiting Professor: Univ. of Lyon, 1951; Univ. of Kyoto, 1971; Collège de France, Paris, 1973; Univ. of British Columbia, Vancouver, 1975; Hon. Professor: Inst. of History of Science, Acad. Sinica, Peking, 1980–; Chinese Acad. of Soc. Sci., 1983–. Lectures: Terry and Carmalt, Yale Univ.; Goldwin-Smith, Cornell Univ.; Mead-Swing, Oberlin College, Ohio, USA, 1935; Oliver Sharpey, RCP, 1935–36; Herbert Spencer, Oxford, 1936–37; for Polskie Towarzystwo Biologicznej in the Universities of Warsaw, Lwów, Kraków and Wilno, 1937; Comte Memorial, London, 1940; Conway Memorial, London, 1947; Boyle, Oxford, 1948; Noguchi, Johns Hopkins Univ., 1950; Hobhouse, London Univ., 1950; Dickinson, Newcomen Soc., 1956; Colombo, Singapore, Peking and Jaipur Universities, 1958; Wilkins, Royal Society, 1958; Wilde, Manchester, 1959; Earl Grey, Newcastle upon Tyne, 1960–61; Henry Myers, Royal Anthropological Institute, 1964; Harveian, London, 1970; Rapkine, Paris, 1971; Bernal, London, 1971; Ballard Matthews, Bangor, 1971; Fremantle, Oxford, 1971; Irvine, St Andrews, 1973; Dressler, Leeds, 1973; Carr-Saunders, London, Gerald Walters, Bath, First John Caius, Padua, 1974; Bowra, Oxford, 1975; Danz, Seattle, 1977; Harris, Northwestern, 1978; First Wickramasinghe, Colombo, 1978; Ch'ien Mu and Huang Chan, Hong Kong, 1979; Creighton, London, 1979; Radhakrishnan, Oxford, 1980; Priestley, London, 1982; First E Asian Hist. of Sci. Foundn, Hongkong, 1983; First Julian Huxley Meml, 1987. Head of the British Scientific Mission in China and Scientific Counsellor, British Embassy, Chungking, and Adviser to the Chinese National Resources Commission, Chinese Army Medical Administration and Chinese Air Force Research Bureau, 1942–46; Director of the Dept of Natural Sciences, UNESCO, 1946–48. Mem., Internat. Commn for Investigation of Bacteriological Warfare in China and Korea, 1952; Chm. Ceylon Government University Policy Commission, 1958. Pres., Internat. Union of Hist. of Science, 1972–75. Foreign Member: Nat. Acad. of Science, USA; Amer. Acad. Arts and Sciences; Amer. Hist. Assoc.; National Academy of China (Academia Sinica); Royal Danish Acad.; Mem. Internat. Academies of Hist. of Science and of Med.; Hon. Member Yale Chapter of Sigma Xi. Hon. Fellow, UMIST. Hon. FRCP 1984. Hon. DSc, Brussels, Norwich, Chinese Univ. of Hong Kong; Hon. LLD Toronto and Salford; Hon. LittD Cambridge, Hongkong, Newcastle upon Tyne, Hull, Chicago Wilmington, NC and Peradeniya, Celon; DUniv Surrey; Hon. PhD Uppsala. Sir William Jones Medallist, Asiatic Society of Bengal, 1963; George Sarton Medallist, Soc. for History of Science, 1968; Leonardo da Vinci Medallist, Soc. for History of Technology, 1968; Dexter Award for History of Chemistry, 1979; Science Award (1st cl.), Nat. Sci. Commn of China, 1984; Fukuoka Municipality Medal for Asian Culture, 1990. Order of the Brilliant Star, 3rd cl. with sash (China); Friendship Ambassador, 1990 (title conferred by Chinese People's Cttee for friendship with other countries). *Publications:* Science, Religion and Reality (ed), 1925; Man a Machine, 1927; The Sceptical Biologist, 1929; Chemical Embryology (3 vols), 1931; The Great Amphibium, 1932; A History of Embryology, 1934; Order and Life, 1935; Christianity and the Social Revolution (ed), 1935; Adventures before Birth (tr.), 1936; Perspectives in Biochemistry (Hopkins Presentation Volume; ed), 1937; Background to Modern Science (ed), 1938; Biochemistry and Morphogenesis, 1942; The Teacher of Nations, addresses and essays in commemoration of John Amos Comenius (ed), 1942; Time, the Refreshing River, 1943; History is on Our Side, 1945; Chinese Science, 1946; Science Outpost, 1948; Hopkins and Biochemistry (ed), 1949; Science and Civilisation in China (7 vols, 25 parts; jtly), 1954–: vol. I, Introductory Orientations, 1954; vol. II, History of Scientific Thought, 1956; vol III, Mathematics and the Sciences of the Heavens and the Earth, 1959; vol. IV, Physics and Physical Technology, part 1, Physics, 1962, part 2, Mechanical Engineering, 1965, part 3, Civil Engineering and Nautics, 1971; vol. V, Chemistry and Chemical Technology, part 2, Spagyrical Discovery and Invention, 1974, part 3, History of Alchemy, 1976, part 4, Apparatus, Theory and Comparative Macrobiotics, 1980, part 5, Physiological Alchemy, 1983, part 6, Projectiles and Sieges, 1990, part 7, The Gunpowder Epic, 1988; vol. VI, part 1, Botany, 1985; The Development of Iron and Steel Technology in China, 1958; Heavenly Clockwork, 1960, rev. edn 1986; Within the Four Seas, 1970; The Grand Titration, 1970; Clerks and Craftsmen in China and the West (jtly), 1970; The Chemistry of Life (ed), 1970; Moulds of Understanding, 1976; Celestial Lancets, a history and rationale of Acupuncture and Moxa (jtly), 1980; The Hall of Heavenly Records: Korean astronomical instruments and clocks 1380–1780 (jtly), 1986; Trans-Pacific Echoes and Resonances, Listening Once Again (jtly), 1986. Chart to illustrate the History of Physiology and Biochemistry, 1926; original papers in scientific, philosophical and sinological journals. *Address:* 2A Sylvester Road, Cambridge CB3 9AF. *T:* Cambridge (0223) 352183; Needham Research Institute (East Asian History of Science Library), 8 Sylvester Road, Cambridge CB3 9AF. *T:* Cambridge (0223) 311545.

NEEDHAM, Noël Joseph Terence Montgomery; *see* Needham, Joseph.

NEEDHAM, Phillip; Director, Farm and Countryside Service, and Commercial Director, Agricultural Development and Advisory Service, Ministry of Agriculture, Fisheries and Food, since 1988; *b* 21 April 1940; *s* of Ephraim and Mabel Jessie Needham; *m* 1962, Patricia Ann (*née* Farr); two *s* two *d*. *Educ:* Dunstable Grammar Sch.; Univ. of Birmingham (BSc); Imperial Coll., London Univ. (MSc, DIC). National Agricultural Advisory Service, subseq. Agricultural Development and Advisory Service: Soil Scientist, 1961; Regional Soil Scientist, Reading, 1979; Hd of Soil Science, London, 1982; Sen. Agricl Scientist, 1985; Dep. Dir of R&D, 1987. *Publications:* contribs to books and jls on various aspects of crop nutrition and soil science. *Address:* Ministry of Agriculture, Fisheries and Food, Nobel House, 17 Smith Square, SW1P 3JR. *T:* 071–238 5776.

NEEDHAM, Richard Francis; (6th Earl of Kilmorey, but does not use the title); MP (C) Wiltshire North, since 1983 (Chippenham, 1979–83); Parliamentary Under-Secretary of State, Northern Ireland Office, since 1985; *b* 29 Jan. 1942; *e s* of 5th Earl of Kilmorey (*d* 1977), and of Helen (who *m* 2nd, 1978, Harold William Elliott, *qv*), *y d* of Sir Lionel Faudel-Phillips, 3rd Bt; *m* 1965, Sigrid Juliane Thiessen-Gairdner, *o d* of late Ernst Thiessen and of Mrs John Gairdner, Hamburg; two *s* one *d*. *Educ:* Eton College. Chm., R. G. M. Print Holdings Ltd, 1967–85. CC Somerset, 1967–74. Contested (C): Pontefract and Castleford, Feb. 1974; Gravesend, Oct. 1974; Personal Asst to Rt Hon. James Prior, MP, 1974–79. PPS: to Sec. of State for NI, 1983–84; to Sec. of State for the Environment, 1984–85. Cons. Vice-Chm., Employment Cttee, 1981–83; Mem., Public Accts Cttee, 1982–83. Founder Mem., Anglo-Japanese 2000 Gp, 1984–; Governor, British Inst. of Florence, 1983–85. *Publication:* Honourable Member, 1983. *Heir: s* Viscount Newry and Morne, *qv*. *Address:* House of Commons, SW1. *Club:* Pratt's.

NEEDHAM, Prof. Roger Michael, FRS 1985; Professor of Computer Systems, since 1981, Head of Computer Laboratory, since 1980, and Fellow of Wolfson College, since 1967, University of Cambridge; *b* 9 Feb. 1935; *s* of Leonard William Needham and Phyllis Mary Needham; *m* 1958, Karen Ida Boalth Spärck Jones. *Educ:* Cambridge Univ. (MA, PhD). FBCS. Cambridge University: Sen. Asst in Research, Computer Lab., 1963–64; Asst Dir of Research, 1964–73; Reader in Computer Systems, 1973–81. Mem., UGC, 1985–89. Member: Chesterton RDC, 1971–74; South Cambs DC, 1974–86. Hon. DSc Kent, 1983. *Publications:* (with M. V. Wilkes) The Cambridge CAP Computer and its operating system, 1979; (with A. J. Herbert) The Cambridge Distributed Computing System, 1982; contribs to publications on computer operating systems, communications, security and protection. *Recreations:* sailing, politics. *Address:* 7 Brook Lane, Coton, Cambridge CB3 7PY. *T:* Madingley (0954) 210366; (work) Cambridge (0223) 334607. *Clubs:* Naval; Royal Harwich Yacht.

NÉEL, Prof. Louis Eugène Félix, Grand Croix de la Légion d'Honneur; Croix de Guerre avec Palme; Président d'Honneur, Institut National Polytechnique de Grenoble; *b* Lyon, 22 Nov. 1904; *m* 1931, Hélène Hourticq; one *s* two *d*. *Educ:* Ecole Normale Supérieure. Agrégé de l'Université; Dr Sc. Prof., Univ. Strasbourg, 1937–45. Dir, Centre d'Etudes Nucléaires, Grenoble, 1956–71, and Delegate of High Comr for Atomic Energy at the centre, 1971–76; rep. France at Scientific Council, NATO, 1960–83; Prés., Conseil Sup. Sûreté Nucléaire, 1973–86. Mem., Acad. of Science, Paris, 1953; For. Member: Acad. of Science, USSR, 1959, Rumania, 1965, Poland, 1975; Royal Netherlands Acad., 1959; Deutsche Akademie der Naturforscher Leopoldina, 1964; Royal Society, 1966; Amer. Acad. of Arts and Sciences, 1966; Pres., Internat. Union of Pure and Applied Physics, 1963–66. Gold Medal, CNRS, 1965; Nobel Prize for Physics, 1970. Hon. Dr: Graz, 1948; Nottingham, 1951; Oxford, 1958; Louvain, 1965; Newcastle, 1965; Coïmbra, 1966; Sherbrooke, 1967; Madrid, 1978. *Publications:* numerous on magnetism. *Address:* 15 rue Marcel-Allégot, 92190 Meudon-Bellevue, France. *T:* 45 34 36 51.

NEGARA BRUNEI DARUSSALAM, HM Sultan of; Hassanal Bolkiah Mu'izzaddin Waddaulah, DKMB, DK, PSSUB, DPKG, DPKT, PSPNB, PSNB, PSLJ, SPMB, PANB; Hon. GCMG; DMN, DK (Kelantan), DK (Johor), DK (Negeri Sembilan), DK (Pahang); Ruler of Negara Brunei Darussalam (formerly Brunei), since 1967; Prime Minister, Finance and Home Affairs Minister, Negara Brunei Darussalam, since its independence, Jan. 1984; *b* 15 July 1946; *s* of Sultan Sir Muda Omar 'Ali Saifuddien Sa'adul Khairi Waddien, DKMB, DK, GCVO, KCMG, PSSUB, PHBS, PBLI (*d* 1986). *Educ:* Victoria Inst., Kuala Lumpur; RMA Sandhurst (Hon. Captain, Coldstream Guards, 1968; Hon. General 1984). Collar of the Supreme Order of the Chrysanthemum; Grand Order of Mugunghwa. *Address:* Istana Nurul Iman, Bandar Seri Begawan, Negara Brunei Darussalam.

NEGUS, Norma Florence, (Mrs D. J. Turner-Samuels); Her Honour Judge Negus; a Circuit Judge, since 1990; *b* 31 July 1932; *d* of late George David Shellabear and Kate (*née* Calvert); *m* 1st, 1956, Richard Negus (marr. diss. 1960); 2nd, 1976, David Jessel Turner-Samuels, *qv*. *Educ:* Malvern Girls' Coll., Malvern, Worcs. Fashion promotion and advertising in UK, Canada and USA, 1950–61; Merchandise Editor, Harper's Bazaar, 1962–63; Asst Promotion Manager, Vogue and House & Garden, 1963–65; Unit Manager, Trends Merchandising and Fashion Promotion Unit, 1965–67; Export Marketing Manager and Advertising Manager, Glenoit (UK) Ltd, 1967–68. Called to the Bar, Gray's Inn, 1970; Mem., Middle Temple, 1984. In practice on SE Circuit, 1971–84; a Metropolitan Stipendiary Magistrate, 1984–90; a Recorder, 1989–90. Mem., Central Criminal Court Bar Mess, 1978–84. *Recreations:* cooking, reading, writing, listening to music, travel, swimming. *Address:* c/o The Crown Court, Inner London Sessions House, Newington Causeway, SE1 6AZ.

NEGUS, Richard; consultant designer; Senior Partner, Negus & Negus, 1967–87; *b* 29 August 1927; *s* of Bertie and Kate Negus; *m* 1949, Pamela Wheatcroft-Hancock; two *s* one *d*. *Educ:* Battersea Grammar Sch.; Camberwell Sch. of Arts and Crafts. FSTD. Staff designer, Festival of Britain, 1948–51; Partner, Negus & Sharland, 1951–67; Lecturer, Central Sch. of Art, 1951–53. Consultant to: Cotton Board Design Centre, 1960–67; BNEC, 1969–75; British Airways, 1973–84, 1990–; Pakistan Airlines, 1975–79 and 1989–; Rank Organisation, 1979–86; City of Westminster, 1973–75; National Exhibition Centre, 1974–77; Lloyds Bank, 1972–75; Godfrey Davis, 1971–80; John Laing, 1970–73; Andry Montgomery, 1967–; Celltech, 1980–83; Vickers Ltd, 1980–83; SDP, 1981–88; Historic Buildings and Monuments Commn, 1984–; Nat. Maritime Mus., 1984–; Royal Armouries, 1984–; The Emirates (Airline), 1985–88; Tower of London, 1986–; Science Museum, 1987–; Northern Foods, 1986–; Waterford/Wedgwood, 1987; DoE Royal Parks, 1987–88; Nature Conservation Council, 1987–89; John Lewis Partnership, 1987–89; Nat. Theatre, 1989–91; Internat. Youth Hostels, 1989; Dubai Tourist Bd, 1990–; Blue Circle Properties, 1990–. Member: Design Council Poster Awards Cttee, 1970–72; PO Stamps Adv. Cttee, 1977–; CNAA, 1980–85; Design Council, 1981–86; Art and Design Cttee, Technician Educn Council, 1981–86. Advisor, Norwich Sch. of Art, 1969–71; External Assessor: Birmingham and Bradford Colls of Art, 1969–73; Medway Coll. of Design, 1989–; Governor: Camberwell Sch. of Art, 1964–78; Chelsea Sch. of Art, 1977–85; Mem. Court, RCA, 1979–82. PPCSD (Pres., SIAD, 1977–79, Vice Pres. 1966–68). *Publications:* Designing for Export Printing, 1972; Display of Text in Museums, 1989; contribs to: Design Mag., The Designer, Graphis, Gebrauchgraphick, Architectural Review, Rolls Royce Mag., Creative Review, Art and Artists. *Recreations:* the countryside, sailing. *Address:* Myddelton Cottage, 44 Canonbury Park South, N1 2JH. *T:* 071–226 2381; Little Gravenhurst, Bolney, Sussex. *T:* Bolney (0444) 881841.

NEHRU, Braj Kumar; Chairman: Indian Advisory Board, Grindlays Bank, since 1988; Hindustan Oil Exploration Co. Ltd, since 1987; Director, East India Hotels Ltd, since 1988; *b* Allahabad, 4 Sept. 1909; *s* of Brijlal and Rameshawri Nehru; *m* 1935, Magdalena Friedmann; three *s*. *Educ:* Allahabad Univ.; LSE (Fellow); Balliol Coll., Oxford. BSc; BSc(Econ.). Called to Bar, Inner Temple. Joined ICS, 1934; Asst Comr, 1934–39; Under-Sec., Dept of Education, Health and Lands, 1939; Mem., Indian Legislative Assembly, 1939; Officer on special duty, Reserve Bank of India, and Under-Sec., Finance Dept, 1940; Jt Sec., 1947; Exec. Dir, IBRD (World Bank), and Minister, Indian Embassy, Washington, 1949–54 and 1958–62; Sec., Dept of Econ. Affairs, 1957–58; Comr-Gen. for Econ. Affairs, Min. of Finance, 1958–61; Ambassador to USA, 1961–68; Governor: Assam and Nagaland, 1968–73; Meghalaya, Manipur and Tripura, 1972–73; High Comr in London, 1973–77; Governor: Jammu and Kashmir, 1981–84; Gujarat, 1984–86. Rep. of India: Reparations Conf., 1945; Commonwealth Finance Ministers Confs, UN Gen. Assembly, 1949–52, and 1960; FAO Confs, 1949–50; Sterling Balance Confs, 1947–49; Bandung Conf., 1955; deputed to enquire into Australian Fed. Finance, 1946; Mem., UN Adv. Cttee on Admin and Budgetry Questions, 1951–53; Advr to Sudan Govt, 1955; Mem., UN Investments Cttee, 1962– (Chm., 1977–). Pres., Dyal Singh Coll. Trust, 1990–; Trustee: Indira Gandhi Meml Trust, 1985–; Dyal Singh Library Trust, 1988–; Tribune Trust, 1988–; World War Meml Fund for Disaster Relief, 1989–. Hon. LLD Mo Valley Coll.; Hon. LittD Jacksonville; Hon. DLitt Punjab. *Publications:* Australian Federal Finance, 1947; Speaking of India, 1966; Thoughts on the Present Discontents, 1986. *Recreations:* bridge, reading, conversation. *Address:* Fair View, Kasauli-173204, India. *T:* 2189 (01793). *Club:* Gymkhana (Delhi).

NEIDPATH, Lord; Hon. James Donald Charteris, Lord Douglas of Neidpath, Lyne and Munard; *b* 22 June 1948; *s* and *heir* of 12th Earl of Wemyss and March, *qv*; *m* 1983, Catherine Ingrid (marr. diss. 1988), *d* of Hon. Jonathan Guinness, *qv*, and of Mrs Paul Channon; one *s* one *d*. *Educ:* Eton; University College, Oxford (BA 1969, MA 1974); St Antony's Coll., Oxford (DPhil 1975); Royal Agricultural Coll., Cirencester (Diploma, 1978); ARICS 1983. Page of Honour to HM Queen Elizabeth the Queen Mother, 1962–64. Mem., Royal Co. of Archers (Queen's Body Guard for Scotland), 1978–; Mem. Council, Nat. Trust for Scotland, 1987–. *Publication:* The Singapore Naval Base and the Defence of Britain's Eastern Empire 1919–42, 1981. *Heir: s* Hon. Francis Richard Percy Charteris, *b* 15 Sept. 1984. *Address:* Stanway, Cheltenham, Glos. *T:* Stanton (038673) 469. *Clubs:* Brooks's, Pratt's, Ognisko Polskie; Puffin's, New (Edinburgh).

NEIGHBOUR, Oliver Wray, FBA 1982; Music Librarian, Reference Division of the British Library, 1976–85; *b* 1 April 1923; *s* of Sydney William Neighbour, OBE, TD, and Gwenydd Joyce (*née* Prentis). *Educ:* Eastbourne Coll.; Birkbeck Coll., London (BA 1950). Entered Dept of Printed Books, BM, 1946; Asst Keeper in Music Room, 1951; Dep. Keeper, 1976. *Publications:* (with Alan Tyson) English Music Publishers' Plate Numbers, 1965; The Consort and Keyboard Music of William Byrd, 1978; (ed) Music and Bibliography: essays in honour of Alec Hyatt King, 1980; article on Schoenberg in New Grove Dictionary of Music and Musicians, 1980; editor of first publications of works by Schumann, Schoenberg and Byrd. *Recreations:* walking, ornithology. *Address:* 12 Treborough House, 1 Nottingham Place, W1M 3FP. *T:* 071–935 1772.

NEIL, Andrew Ferguson; Editor, The Sunday Times, since 1983; *b* Paisley, 21 May 1949; *s* of James and Mary Neil. *Educ:* Paisley Grammar Sch.; Univ. of Glasgow (MA Hons Politics and Economics, 1971). Conservative Res. Dept, 1971–72; joined The Economist, 1973; Reporter, Ulster, 1973–74; Lobby Correspondent, 1974–75; Labour Corresp., 1975–78; Amer. Corresp., Washington and New York, 1979–82; UK Editor, London, 1982–83. Presenter of and pundit on various current affairs television and radio programmes in Britain and America. Chm., Sky TV, 1988–90. *Publication:* The Cable Revolution, 1982. *Recreations:* dining out in London, Paris, New York and Aspen. *Address:* The Sunday Times, 1 Pennington Street, Wapping, E1. *Clubs:* Royal Automobile, Tramp.

NEIL, Matthew, CBE 1976; Secretary and Chief Executive, Glasgow Chamber of Commerce, 1954–83; *b* 19 Dec. 1917; *er s* of John Neil and Jean Wallace. *Educ:* John Neilson High Sch., Paisley; Glasgow Univ. (MA, LLB). Served War, 1939–46: Far East, ME, Mediterranean and Western Europe; RHA, RA and Air Observation Post; RAuxAF, 1950–57. Admitted solicitor, 1947. Mem., British Overseas Trade Adv. Council, 1975–82. LLD Glasgow, 1983. *Recreations:* skiing, golf, music. *Address:* 39 Arkleston Road, Paisley PA1 3TH. *T:* 041–889 4975. *Clubs:* East India, Devonshire, Sports and Public Schools; Lamlash Golf, Prestwick Golf.

NEIL, Ronald John Baille; Managing Director, Regional Broadcasting, BBC, since 1989; *b* 16 June 1942; *s* of John Clark Neil and Jean McMillan Taylor; *m* 1967, Isobel Anne Clark. *Educ:* High Sch. of Glasgow. Reporter, Daily Express, 1961; BBC, 1967–: Newsreader/Reporter, Reporting Scotland, 1967; Producer, Nationwide and 24 Hours, 1969; Output Editor, Nationwide, 1973; Dep. Editor, Newsnight, 1979; Editor: That's Life, 1981; Newsnight, 1981; Breakfast Time, 1983; Six O'Clock News, 1984; TV News, 1985; Dep. Dir, 1987–88, Dir, 1988–89, News and Current Affairs. *Recreations:* tennis, food, wine. *Address:* BBC, Broadcasting House, W1A 1AA. *T:* 071–580 4468. *Club:* Reform.

NEIL, Thomas, CMG 1962; TD 1951; Director, Thomson Foundation, 1963–79; *b* 23 December 1913; *s* of late W. R. Neil; *m* 1939, Phyllis Selina Gertrude Sargeant; one *d*. *Educ:* King's College, University of Durham (now University of Newcastle upon Tyne) (BSc, NDA). Lectr in Agriculture, Devon County Council, 1936–39; Chief Technical Officer, 1946. Colonial Service: District Officer, Kenya, 1947; Assistant Chief Secretary, 1957; Permanent Secretary, 1957; Permanent Secretary, Ministry of State, Kenya, 1959–63. Directed Africanisation of CS. Director, Kenya Famine Relief, 1961–63. Lay Mem., Immigration Appeal Tribunal, 1971–84. Served War of 1939–45 with Devonshire Regiment (TA), Lieutenant-Colonel, in UK, E Africa, Middle East. *Recreation:* country life. *Address:* Summerhill, Bourne End, Bucks SL8 5JL. *T:* Bourne End (06285) 20403.

NEILD, Prof. Robert Ralph; Professor of Economics, University of Cambridge, 1971–84, now Emeritus; Fellow and Steward of Trinity College, Cambridge; *b* 10 Sept. 1924; *o s* of Ralph and Josephine Neild, Letchmore Heath, Hertfordshire; *m* 1st, 1957,

Nora Clemens Sayre (marr. diss. 1961); 2nd, 1962, Elizabeth Walton Griffiths (marr. diss. 1986); one *s* four *d* (incl. twin *d*). *Educ:* Charterhouse; Trinity Coll., Cambridge. Royal Air Force, 1943–44; Operational Research, 1944–45. Secretariat of United Nations Economic Commission for Europe, Geneva, 1947–51; Economic Section, Cabinet Office and Treasury, 1951–56; Lecturer in Economics, and Fellow, Trinity College, Cambridge, 1956–58; National Institute of Economic and Social Research: at first as Editor of its Quarterly Economic Review; then as Deputy Director of the Institute, 1958–64; MIT Center for International Studies, India Project, New Delhi, 1962–63; Economic Adviser to HM Treasury, 1964–67; Dir, Stockholm Internat. Peace Research Inst., 1967–71. Vis. Fulbright Prof., Hampshire Coll. and Five Colls, Amherst, Mass, USA, 1985. Mem., Fulton Cttee on Reform of CS, 1966–68; Vice-Chm., Armstrong Cttee on Budgetary Reform in UK, Inst. for Fiscal Studies, 1979–80. Director: Nat. Mutual Life Assce Soc., 1959–64; Investing in Success Equities Ltd, 1961–64, 1972–87. *Publications:* Pricing and Employment in the Trade Cycle, 1964; (with T. S. Ward) The Measurement and Reform of Budgetary Policy, 1978; How to Make Up Your Mind about the Bomb, 1981; An Essay on Strategy, 1990; (ed with A. Boserup) The Foundations of Defensive Defence, 1990; various articles. *Address:* Trinity College, Cambridge CB2 1TQ.

NEILL, Alistair, FFA, FIA; General Manager, Scottish Widows' Fund & Life Assurance Society, since 1988; President, Faculty of Actuaries in Scotland, since 1990; *b* 18 Nov. 1932; *s* of Alexander Neill and Marion Wilson; *m* 1958, Mary Margaret Hunter; one *s* two *d*. *Educ:* George Watson's Coll., Edinburgh; Univ. of Edinburgh (John Welsh Math. Bursar; MA); Univ. of Wisconsin (Fulbright Grantee; MS). Instructor Lieut, RN, 1958–60. Actuarial management posts in Scottish Widows' Fund, 1961–. *Publication:* Life Contingencies, 1977, 5th edn 1989. *Recreations:* golf, squash, curling. *Address:* 24 Bonaly Crescent, Edinburgh EH13 0EW. *T:* 031–441 2038. *Club:* Caledonian.

NEILL, Rt. Hon. Sir Brian (Thomas), Kt 1978; PC 1985; **Rt. Hon. Lord Justice Neill;** a Lord Justice of Appeal, since 1985; *b* 2 Aug. 1923; *s* of late Sir Thomas Neill and Lady (Annie Strachan) Neill (*née* Bishop); *m* 1956, Sally Margaret, *d* of late Sydney Eric and Marguerite Backus; three *s*. *Educ:* Highgate Sch.; Corpus Christi Coll., Oxford (Hon. Fellow 1986). Rifle Brigade, 1942–46 (Capt.). MA Oxford. Called to the Bar, Inner Temple, 1949, Bencher, 1976. QC 1968; a Recorder of the Crown Court, 1972–78; a Judge of the High Court, Queen's Bench Div., 1978–84. A Judge of the Commercial and Admiralty Courts, 1980–84; a Judge of Employment Appeal Tribunal, 1981–84. Mem., Departmental Cttee to examine operation of Section 2 of Official Secrets Act, 1971; Chairman: Adv. Cttee on Rhodesia Travel Restrictions, 1973–78; IT and the Courts Cttee, 1985–; Supreme Court Procedure Cttee, 1986–90. Mem., Ct of Assts, 1972–, Master, 1980–81, Turners' Co. Governor, Highgate Sch., 1969–90. *Publication:* (with Colin Duncan) Defamation, 1978, 2nd edn (ed with R. Rampton), 1984. *Address:* c/o Royal Courts of Justice, Strand, WC2. *Clubs:* MCC, Hurlingham.

See also Sir F. P. Neill.

NEILL, Rev. Bruce Ferguson; QHC 1991; Principal Chaplain, Naval, Church of Scotland and Free Churches, since 1991; *b* 9 Jan. 1941; *s* of Thomas Ferguson Neill and Jane (*née* Bruce); *m* 1966, Ishbel Macdonald; two *s* one *d*. *Educ:* Lesmahagow Primary; Hamilton Academy; Glasgow Univ. and Trinity Coll., Glasgow (MA, BD). Probationer Asst, Drumchapel Old Parish Church, 1964–66; Minister, Dunfermline Townhill Parish Church, 1966–71; commnd as Chaplain, RN, 1971; Naval appts include: HMS Drake, 1972; RM, 1972; HMS Seahawk, 1974; HMS Cochrane, 1976; ships of 1st and 2nd Flotillas, 1979; HMS Dryad, 1981; Britannia RNC, 1983; HMS Cochrane, 1986; ships of Minor War Vessels Flotilla, 1989–91. *Recreations:* gardening, hill walking, off-shore sailing, woodwork, music, model making. *Address:* Room 725, Lacon House, Theobalds Road, WC1X 8RW. *T:* 071–430 6842.

NEILL, Prof. Derrick James, DFC 1943; Emeritus Professor of Prosthetic Dentistry, University of London; Sub-Dean of Dental Studies, Guy's Hospital Dental School, 1969–76; Consultant Dental Surgeon, Guy's Hospital, since 1960; *b* 14 March 1922; *s* of Jameson Leonard Neill, MBE, and Lynn Moyle; *m* 1st, 1952, Iris Jordan (*d* 1970); one *s* one *d*; 2nd, 1971, Catherine Mary Daughtry. *Educ:* East Sheen County Grammar Sch.; Guy's Hosp. Dental Sch., Univ. of London. LDSRCS 1952; FDSRCS 1955; MDS London, 1966. Served RAFVR, 1941–46, 150 Sqdn, Bomber Comd (Sqdn Ldr). Dept of Dental Prosthetics, Guy's Hosp. Dental School: Lectr, 1954; Sen. Lectr, 1959; Univ. Reader in Dental Prosthetics, 1967; Prof. of Prosthetic Dentistry, 1969. Council Member, Odontological Section, Royal Soc. of Medicine, 1966–73; Past Pres., British Soc. for Study of Prosthetic Dentistry. Mem. Council of Governors: Guy's Hosp. Med. Sch., 1980–82; United Med. Schs of Guy's and St Thomas's Hosps, 1982–87. Fellow, Internat. Coll. of Cranio-Mandibular Orthopedics, 1986. Mem. Editorial Bd, Internat. Jl of Prosthodontics. *Publications:* (jtly) Complete Dentures, 1968; Partial Denture Construction, 1976; Restoration of the Partially Dentate Mouth, 1984; numerous papers in dental jls. *Recreations:* golf, music. *Address:* Hurst, Clenches Farm Road, Kippington, Sevenoaks, Kent TN13 2LU. *T:* Sevenoaks (0732) 452374. *Club:* Royal Automobile.

NEILL, Sir (Francis) Patrick, Kt 1983; QC 1966; Warden of All Souls College, Oxford, since 1977; a Judge of the Courts of Appeal of Jersey and Guernsey, since 1977; *b* 8 Aug. 1926; *s* of late Sir Thomas Neill, JP, and Lady (Annie Strachan) Neill (*née* Bishop); *m* 1954, Caroline Susan, *d* of late Sir Piers Debenham, 2nd Bt, and Lady (Angela) Debenham; four *s* two *d*. *Educ:* Highgate Sch.; Magdalen College, Oxford (Hon. Fellow, 1988). Gibbs Law Scholar, 1949; Eldon Law Scholar, 1950. BA 1950; BCL 1951; MA 1972. Served Rifle Brigade, 1944–47 (Captain); GSO III (Training), British Troops Egypt, 1947. Fellow of All Souls, 1950–77, Sub-Warden 1972–74; Lectr in Air Law, LSE, 1955–58; Vice-Chancellor, Oxford Univ., 1985–89. Called to the Bar, Gray's Inn, 1951; Bencher, 1971; Vice-Treas., 1989; Treas., 1990; Member, Bar Council, 1967–71, Vice-Chm., 1973–74, Chm., 1974–75; Chm., Senate of the Inns of Court and the Bar, 1974–75; a Recorder of the Crown Court, 1975–78. Chm., Justice—All Souls Cttee for Rev. of Admin. Law, 1978–87. Chairman: Press Council, 1978–83; DTI Cttee of Inquiry into Regulatory Arrangements at Lloyd's, 1986–87; first Chm., Council for the Securities Industry, 1978–85; Vice-Chm., CVCP, 1987–89. Independent Nat. Dir, Times Newspaper Hldgs, 1988–. Hon. Prof. of Legal Ethics, Birmingham Univ., 1983–84. Hon. LLD Hull; Hon. DCL Oxon, 1987. *Publication:* Administrative Justice: some necessary reforms, 1988. *Recreations:* music and forestry. *Address:* All Souls College, Oxford OX1 4AL. *T:* Oxford (0865) 279379. *Clubs:* Athenæum, Garrick, Beefsteak.

See also Rt Hon. Sir Brian Neill.

NEILL, Hugh; *see* Neill, J. H.

NEILL, Major Rt. Hon. Sir Ivan, Kt 1973; PC (N Ireland) 1950; *b* Belfast 1 July 1906; *m* 1928, Margaret Helena Allen. *Educ:* Ravenscroft Nat. Sch., Belfast; Shaftesbury House Tutorial Coll., Belfast; Queen's Univ., Belfast (BSc Econ). FRGS. Served War of 1939–45: RE in UK and FE, 1939–46; Major. MP Ballynafeigh Div. of Belfast, Parlt of Northern Ireland, 1949–73; Government of Northern Ireland: Minister of Labour and National Insurance, 1950–62; Minister of Home Affairs, Aug.-Oct. 1952; Minister of Education, 1962–64; Minister of Finance, 1964–65; Leader of House of Commons, Oct. 1964; resigned from Govt, April 1965; Minister of Develt, Dec. 1968–March 1969; Speaker of House of Commons, 1969–73. Represented N Ireland at Internat. Labour Confs, 1950–61. Councillor and Alderman in Belfast Corp., 1946–50 (specialised in educn, housing and youth welfare). DL Belfast, 1966–86. *Address:* Greenlaw, Ballywilliam, Donaghadee, Co. Down, Northern Ireland BT21 0PQ.

NEILL, Very Rev. Ivan Delacherois, CB 1963; OBE 1958; Provost of Sheffield and Vicar of the Cathedral Church of St Peter and St Paul, 1966–74, now Emeritus; Chaplain to the Queen, 1962–66; *b* 10 July 1912; *s* of Rev. Robert Richard Neill and Bessie Montrose (*née* Purdon); *m* 1938, Enid Eyre Godson (*née* Bartholomew); one *s* one *d*. *Educ:* St Dunstan's College; Jesus College, Cambridge (MA); London College of Divinity. Curate: St Mary, West Kensington, 1936–38; Christ Church, Crouch End, 1938–39. CF 4th Cl., Chatham; served BEF and UK with 3rd Div., Orkneys, Sandhurst, 1941–43; Sen. Chaplain, N Aldershot, 1943; 43rd (Wessex) Div., 1943–45 (despatches); DACG, 1st British Corps, 1945–46; Sen. Chaplain, Guards Depot, Caterham, 1947–50; DACG, N Canal, Egypt, 1950–53; Catterick, 1953; Warden, Royal Army Chaplains Dept Trg Centre Depot, 1954–57; Sen. Chaplain, SHAPE 1957–58; Asst Chaplain-Gen., Middle East Land Forces, 1958–60; QHC 1960; Chaplain General to HM Forces, 1960–66. Chairman of Governors, Monkton Combe Sch., Bath, 1969–81; Pres. of Foundn, St Paul's and St Mary's C of E Coll. of Educn, Cheltenham, 1978–88. Knight Officer, Order of Orange Nassau (with Swords) 1946. *Address:* Greathed Manor, Lingfield, Surrey RH7 6PA. *T:* Lingfield (0342) 3992. *Club:* National.

NEILL, (James) Hugh, CBE 1969; TD 1950; JP; Lord-Lieutenant for South Yorkshire, since 1985; President, James Neill Holdings plc, since 1989 (Chairman, 1963–89); *b* 29 March 1921; *o s* of Col Sir Frederick Neill, CBE, DSO, TD, DL, JP, and Lady (Winifred Margaret) Neill (*née* Colver); *m* 1st, 1943, Jane Margaret Shuttleworth (*d* 1980); two *d*; 2nd, 1982, Anne O'Leary; one *s*. *Educ:* Rugby School. War service with RE and Royal Bombay Sappers and Miners, UK, Norway, India, Burma and Germany, 1939–46 (despatches, Burma, 1945). Mem., British Overseas Trade Bd, 1973–78; Pres., European Tool Cttee, 1972–76; Mem., Trent Regional Health Authority, 1974–80; Chm. Exec. Cttee, Sheffield Council for Voluntary Service, 1953–87; Mem. Council, CBI, 1965–83; Chm., E and W Ridings Regional Council, FBI, 1962–64; Pres., Nat. Fedn of Engrs Tool Manufrs, 1963–65; Pres., Fedn of British Hand Tool Manufrs, 1960–61. Pres., Sheffield Chamber of Commerce, 1984–85. FBIM. Hon. Col, 4th Bn Yorks Vol., 1988–. Hon. Fellow, Sheffield City Polytechnic, 1978; Hon. LLD Sheffield, 1982. Master Cutler of Hallamshire, 1958; High Sheriff of Hallamshire, 1971; DL South Yorkshire, 1974, JP 1985. KStJ 1986. *Recreations:* golf, horse trials, racing, shooting. *Address:* Barn Cottage, Lindrick Common, near Worksop S81 8BA. *T:* Dinnington (0909) 562806. *Clubs:* East India; Sheffield (Sheffield); Lindrick (Worksop); Royal and Ancient (St Andrews); Hon. Co. of Edinburgh Golfers (Muirfield).

NEILL, Rt. Rev. John Robert Winder; *see* Tuam, Killala and Achonry, Bishop of.

NEILL, Sir Patrick; *see* Neill, Sir F. P.

NEILSON, Ian (Godfrey), DFC 1944; TD 1951; *b* 4 Dec. 1918; *er s* of James Wilson Neilson, solicitor, Glasgow; *m* 1945, D. Alison St Clair Aytoun, Ashintully; one *s* one *d*. *Educ:* Glasgow Acad.; Glasgow Univ. (BL). Legal Trng, Glasgow, 1935–39; Territorial Army, 1938; War Service, 1939–45: Field Artillery; Air Observation Post, 1941; RA Staff, 1944; Lt-Col comdg War Crimes Investigation Unit, Germany, 1945–46; formed and commanded No 666 (Scottish) Sqdn, RAuxAF, 1948–53. Enrolled Solicitor, 1946. Royal Institution of Chartered Surveyors: Scottish Sec., Edinburgh, 1946–53; Asst Sec., London, 1953–61; Under-Sec., 1961–65; The Boys' Brigade: Brigade Sec., 1966–74; Officer, 5th Mid-Surrey Co., 1972–78; Nat. Hon. Vice-Pres., 1982–; Hon. Vice-Pres., W of England Dist, 1983–; Hon. Vice-Pres., Wilts Bn, 1985–. Clerk to Governors of the Cripplegate Foundn, Cripplegate Educnl Foundn, Trustees of St Giles and St Luke's Jt Parochial Charities, and Governors of the Cripplegate Schs Foundn, 1974–81. Hon. Treasurer, Thames Youth Venture Adv. Council (City Parochial Foundn), 1968–76. Vice-Chm., British Council of Churches Youth Dept, 1971–74; Trustee: St George's Chapel, London Airport, 1978– (Chm., 1983–); Douglas Haig Meml Homes, 1979–; Mem., Nat. Council for Voluntary Youth Services, 1966–74; Pres., London Br., Glasgow Academical Club, 1977–79; Chm. of Governors, Lucas-Tooth Leadership Training Fund for Boys, 1976–83; Governor, Kingsway-Princeton Coll. of Further Educn, 1977–83. Elder, United Reformed Church, St Andrew's, Cheam, 1972–83; Lay Mem., Provincial Ministerial Cttee, URC, 1974–83; Dir and Jt Sec., URC Trust, 1982–; Mem. Council: Christchurch, Marlborough, 1984–90; St Peter's and St Paul's Trust, Marlborough, 1985–. BIM: Hon. Sec., City of London Branch, 1976–79, Chm., 1979–81, Vice Pres., 1981–87; Chm., Inner London Branches Area Cttee, 1981–83; FBIM 1980. Sen. Instr, Royal Yachting Assoc., 1977–87; Vice-Pres., Air Observation Post Officers Assoc., 1978–; Chm., Epsom Choral Soc., 1977–81. Freeman, Guild of Air Pilots and Air Navigators, 1976–78, Liveryman, 1978–; Freeman, City of London, 1975; Chm., Queenhithe Ward Club, 1977–78. Hon. Editor, Tower and Town, Marlborough, 1984–. *Recreations:* golf, music, gardening, sailing. *Address:* The Paddock, Kingsbury Street, Marlborough, Wilts SN8 1HZ. *T:* Marlborough (0672) 515114. *Clubs:* Athenæum; Marlborough Golf; St Mawes Sailing.

NEILSON, Nigel Fraser, MC 1943; Chairman, Neilson Associates (formerly Neilson McCarthy), since 1962; Director, Phoenix Lloyd Associates, since 1986; *b* 12 Dec. 1919; *s* of Lt-Col W. Neilson, DSO, 4th Hussars and Maud Alice Francis Anson; *m* 1949, Pamela Catherine Georgina Sheppard; one *s* one *d*. *Educ:* Hereworth Sch.; Christ's Coll., New Zealand; RADA. Inns of Court Regt; commnd Staffs Yeomanry, 1939; seconded Cavalry Regt, Transjordanian Frontier Force; served Syrian Campaign; returned Staffs Yeo., Seventh Armoured Div., GSO 111 Ops; served desert and Italy; Staff Coll., 1944; served in Germany, Holland and France; C of S, Bergen area, Norway; served with SAS and French SAS. On demobilisation worked in theatre, cabaret, films, London, USA and NZ; joined J. Walter Thompson, 1951; became personal rep. to Aristotle Onassis, 1955, later consultant to his daughter, Christina; founded Neilson McCarthy Internat. Public Relations Consultants in UK, USA, Australia, NZ and SE Asia, 1962. Past Pres., NZ Soc., 1978–79. Chevalier de la Légion d'Honneur 1946, Croix de Guerre avec Palme 1946. *Recreations:* riding, shooting, music, theatre. *Address:* c/o Coutts & Co., 1 Old Park Lane, W1Y 4BS.

NEILSON, Richard Alvin, CMG 1987; LVO 1968; HM Diplomatic Service; Ambassador to Chile, since 1990; *b* 9 July 1937; *s* of Robert and Ethel Neilson; *m* 1961, Olive Tyler; one *s*. *Educ:* Burnley Grammar Sch.; Leeds Univ. (BA Hons 1958, MA 1960). Fulbright Fellow, Univ. of Wisconsin, 1959–60; Asst Lectr, Univ. of Edinburgh, 1960–61; joined FO, 1961; Third (later Second) Sec., Kinshasa, 1963–65; Treasury Centre for Admin. Studies, 1965; Second (later First) Sec. (Information), Santiago, 1966–69; First Sec., Canberra, 1969–73; FCO, 1973–77; Counsellor, seconded to NI Office as Head of Political Affairs Div., 1977–79; Dep. High Comr, Lusaka, 1979–80, Acting High Comr, Nov. 1979–June 1980; Dep. Governor and Political Advr, Gibraltar, 1981–84; Head of Southern European Dept, FCO, 1984–86; Ambassador to Colombia, 1987–90.

Publications: contribs to geomorphological literature. *Address:* c/o Foreign and Commonwealth Office, SW1A 2AH; Maynes Hill Farm, Hoggeston, Buckingham, Bucks. *T:* Winslow (029671) 2308. *Club:* Commonwealth Trust.

NELDER, John Ashworth, DSc; FRS 1981; Visiting Professor, Imperial College of Science, Technology and Medicine (formerly Imperial College of Science and Technology), since 1971; Head of Statistics Department, 1968–84, and of Division of Biomathematics, Jan.-Oct. 1984, Rothamsted Experimental Station; *b* 8 Oct. 1924; *s* of Reginald Charles and Edith May Ashworth Nelder; *m* 1955, Mary Hawkes; one *s* one *d. Educ:* Blundell's Sch., Tiverton; Cambridge Univ. (MA); DSc Birmingham. Head, Statistics Section, National Vegetable Research Station, 1950–68. Pres., Royal Statistical Soc., 1985–86. Hon. DSc Paul Sabatier, Toulouse, 1981. *Publications:* Computers in Biology, 1974; (with P. McCullagh) Generalized Linear Models, 1983; responsible for statistical programs (computer), Genstat and GLIM; numerous papers in statistical and biological jls. *Recreations:* piano-playing, music, natural history. *Address:* Cumberland Cottage, 33 Crown Street, Redbourn, St Albans, Herts AL3 7JX. *T:* Redbourn (0582) 792907.

NELIGAN, Desmond West Edmund, OBE 1961; National Insurance Commissioner, 1961–76, retired; *b* 20 June 1906; *s* of late Rt Rev. M. R. Neligan, DD (one time Bishop of Auckland, NZ), and Mary, *d* of Edmund Macrory, QC; *m* 1st, 1936, Penelope Ann, *d* of Henry Mason (marr. diss., 1946); two *s*; 2nd, 1947, Margaret Elizabeth, *d* of late Captain Snook, RN; one step *d. Educ:* Bradfield Coll.; Jesus Coll., Cambridge. BA Cantab, 1929; Barrister, Middle Temple, 1940. Practising Barrister until 1961. Appointed Umpire under National Service Acts, Nov. 1955. Dep. Comr for National Insurance, 1955–61. Served War of 1939–45, in 2 NZ Division, in Greece, Crete and Western Desert. *Publications:* (ed) 6th, 7th and 8th Editions Dumsday's Parish Councils Handbook; (with Sir A. Safford, QC) Town and Country Planning Act, 1944, and *ibid*, 1947; Social Security Case Law: digest of Commissioners' decisions, 1979; Lawful Lyrics and Cautionary Tales for Lawyers, 1984. *Recreations:* formerly: hockey, cricket, tennis and hunting. *Address:* The Cottage, 61 West Street, Storrington, Pulborough, West Sussex RH20 4DZ. *T:* Storrington (09066) 4514.

See also M. H. D. Neligan.

NELIGAN, Michael Hugh Desmond; His Honour Judge Neligan; a Circuit Judge, since 1990; *b* 2 Dec. 1936; *s* of Desmond West Edmund Neligan, *qv*; *m* 1965, Lynn (*née* Maidment); three *d. Educ:* Bradfield College; Jesus College, Cambridge. Commissioned Royal Sussex Regt, 1960–62; served East Africa with 23rd and 4th Bns, King's African Rifles. Called to the Bar, Middle Temple, 1965; Prosecuting Counsel to the Crown, 1972; Metropolitan Stipendiary Magistrate, 1987–90. *Recreations:* cabinet making, gardening, dog-walking. *Address:* The Law Courts, Barker Road, Maidstone, Kent ME16 8EQ.

NELLIST, David; MP (Lab) Coventry South East, since 1983; *b* 16 July 1952. Mem., MSF. Mem., W Midlands CC, 1982–86. *Address:* House of Commons, SW1A 0AA. *T:* 071–219 4214.

NELSON, family name of **Earl Nelson** and **Baron Nelson of Stafford.**

NELSON, 9th Earl *cr* 1805, of Trafalgar and of Merton; **Peter John Horatio Nelson;** Baron Nelson of the Nile and of Hilborough, Norfolk, 1801; Viscount Merton, 1805; *b* 9 Oct. 1941; *s* of Captain Hon. John Marie Joseph Horatio Nelson (*d* 1970) (*y s* of 5th Earl) and of Kathleen Mary, *d* of William Burr, Torquay; *S* uncle, 1981; *m* 1969, Maureen Diana, *d* of Edward Patrick Quinn, Kilkenny; one *s* one *d*. Chm., Retainacar Ltd, 1988–; Dir, British Navy Pusser's Rum, 1988–. President: Royal Naval Commando Assoc.; Nelson Soc.; Vice-Pres., Jubilee Sailing Trust; Mem. Council, Friends of Nat. Maritime Mus.; Hon. Life Member: Royal Naval Assoc.; Royal Naval Museum. *Heir: s* Viscount Merton, *qv. Address:* House of Lords, SW1A 0PW. *Club:* St James's.

NELSON OF STAFFORD, 2nd Baron, *cr* 1960; **Henry George Nelson,** Bt 1955; MA, FEng, FICE, Hon. FIMechE, Hon. FIEE, FRAeS; *b* Manchester, 2 Jan. 1917; *s* of 1st Baron Nelson of Stafford and late Florence Mabel, *o d* of late Henry Howe, JP; *S* father, 1962; *m* 1940, Pamela Roy Bird, *yr d* of late Ernest Roy Bird, formerly MP for Skipton, Yorks; two *s* two *d. Educ:* Oundle; King's Coll., Cambridge. Exhibnr 1935; Mechanical Sciences Tripos, 1937. Practical experience in England, France and Switzerland, 1937–39. Joined the English Electric Co. Ltd, 1939; Supt, Preston Works, 1939–40; Asst Works Man., Preston, 1940–41; Dep. Works Man., Preston, 1941–42; Man. Dir, D. Napier & Son Ltd, 1942–49; Exec. Dir, The Marconi Co. Ltd, 1946–58; Dep. Man. Dir, 1949–56, Man. Dir, 1956–62, Chm. and Chief Exec., 1962–68, The English Electric Co. Ltd; Chm., 1968–83, Dir, 1968–87, GEC. Dep. Chm., British Aircraft Corp., 1960–77; Chm., Royal Worcester Ltd, 1978–84; Director: Internat. Nickel Co. of Canada, 1966–74 and 1975–88; ICL, 1968–74; Nat. Bank of Australasia Ltd (London Bd of Advice), 1950–81; Bank of England, 1961–87; Enserch Corp., 1984–89; Humphreys & Glasgow International, 1991–. Outside Lectr, Univ. of Cambridge (Mech. Sciences Tripos course on Industrial Management), 1947–49. Chancellor of Aston Univ., 1966–79. Chm., Stafford Enterprise Agency, 1987–; Member: Govt. Adv. Council on Scientific Policy, 1955–58; Adv. Council on Middle East Trade, 1958–63 (Industrial Leader and Vice-Chm., 1959–63); Civil Service Commn (Part time Mem. Final Selection and Interview Bds), 1956–61; Engrg Adv. Council, 1958–61; Council, Inst. Electrical Engineers, 1959–76 (Vice-Pres. 1957–62 and 1965–70, Pres., 1970–71); Middle East Assoc. (Vice-Pres., 1962–); Gen. Bd of NPL, 1959–66; Council, SBAC, 1943–64 (Pres. 1961–62); Council, Foundn on Automation and Employment Ltd, 1963–68; Council, BEAMA, 1964–78 (Pres., 1966); Adv. Council, Min. of Technology, 1964–70; Engineering Industries Council, 1975–84; H of L Select Cttee on Sci. and Technology, 1984–91; Mem., 1954–87, Chm., 1971–74, British Nat. Cttee, World Power Conf.; Mem., Nat. Def. Industries Council, 1969–77 (Chm., 1971–77); President: Locomotive and Allied Manufacturers Assoc., 1964–66; British Electrical Power Convention, 1965–67; Orgalime (Organisme de Liaison des Industries Métalliques Européennes), 1968–70; Sino-British Trade Council, 1973–83. Liveryman: Worshipful Co. of Coachmakers and Coach Harness Makers of London, 1944; Worshipful Co. of Goldsmiths, 1961 (Prime Warden, 1983–84). Lord High Steward of Borough of Stafford, 1966–71. Hon. DSc: Aston, 1966; Keele, 1967; Cranfield, 1972; Hon. LLD Strathclyde, 1971; Fellow, Imp. Coll. of Science and Technology, 1969. Benjamin Franklin Medal, RSA, 1959. *Recreations:* shooting, fishing. *Heir: s* Hon. Henry Roy George Nelson [*b* 26 Oct. 1943; *m* 1968, Dorothy, *yr d* of Leslie Caley, Tibthorpe Manor, Driffield, Yorks; one *s* one *d*]. *Address:* 244 Cranmer Court, Whiteheads Grove, SW3 3HD. *T:* 071–581 2551. *Club:* Carlton.

NELSON, NZ, Bishop of, since 1990; **Rt. Rev. Derek Lionel Eaton,** QSM 1985; *b* 10 Sept. 1941; *s* of Henry Jackson Eaton and Ella Barbara (*née* McDouall); *m* 1964, Alice Janice Maslim; two *s* one *d. Educ:* Christchurch Boys' High Sch. (NZ); Univ. of Missouri (MA *cum laude*); Switzerland (Cert. Française); Univ. of Tunis (Cert. Arabic and Islamics); Missionary Training Coll., Australia (DipTheol): Trinity Theol Coll., Bristol. School teacher, 1964. Missionary with Worldwide Evangelisation Crusade, Tunisia, 1968–78; ordained deacon and priest, 1971; Curate, St Luke's, Bristol, 1971–72; Vicar of Tunis, 1972–78; Hon. Chaplain, British Embassy, Tunis, 1972–78; Provost, Cairo Cathedral, Egypt, 1978–83 (Emeritus, 1984); Hon. Chaplain, British Embassy, Egypt, 1978–83; with Church Missionary Society, 1980–84; Assoc. Vicar, Papanui, Bishopdale, NZ, 1984–85; Vicar, Sumner, Redcliffs, NZ, 1985–90. Hon. Canon, Cairo Cathedral, 1985. *Publications:* contrib. theol and missiological jls. *Recreations:* swimming, golf, reading, tennis. *Address:* Bishopdale, PO Box 100, Nelson, New Zealand. *T:* Nelson (0354) 88991.

NELSON, Anthony; *see* Nelson, R. A.

NELSON, Bertram James, OBE 1984; HM Diplomatic Service, retired; Consul-General, Antwerp, 1983–85; *b* 7 Dec. 1925; *s* of Herbert James Nelson and Adelaide Mabel Nelson (*née* Newton); *m* 1958, Constance Dangerfield; one *s* one *d. Educ:* North Kensington Central School. Grenadier Guards, 1944–47; Post Office and Cable and Wireless, 1947–54; Foreign Office, 1954; served Cairo, Budapest, Athens, Asunción, Zagreb, DSAO, 1966–69; Vice-Consul, Tokyo, 1969–71; Vice-Consul, Tehran, 1972–75; FCO, 1975–79; First Sec. and Consul, Brussels, 1979–83. *Recreation:* enjoying retirement. *Address:* 2 Hornbeam Close, Aldwick, Bognor Regis, West Sussex PO21 4AH.

NELSON, Air Cdre Eric Douglas Mackinlay, CB 1952; DL; retired, Sept. 1963; *b* 2 Jan. 1912; *e s* of late Rear-Adm. R. D. Nelson, CBE, and the late Ethel Nelson (*née* MacKinlay); *m* 1939, Margaret Yvonne Taylor (*d* 1988); one *s* one *d. Educ:* Dover Coll.; RAF Coll., Cranwell. Commissioned RAF, 1932; served War of 1939–45 (despatches); CO 103 (HB) Sqdn Elsham Wolds, 1943–44; Group Capt., 1944; ADC to the Queen, 1953–57; Air Commodore, 1956; Commandant, RAF, Halton, 1956–58; Commandant, Royal Air Force Staff College, Andover, 1958–60; AOA Transport Command, 1960–61; Air Officer Commanding and Commandant, Royal Air Force College, Cranwell, 1961–63. DL Lincs, 1966. *Recreations:* sailing, beagling. *Address:* (permanent) 23 The Link, Wellingore, Lincoln LN5 0BJ. *T:* Lincoln (0522) 810604. *Club:* Royal Air Force.

NELSON, Eric Victor, LVO 1975; HM Diplomatic Service, retired; *b* 11 Jan. 1927; *s* of Victor H. H. and E. Vera B. Nelson (*née* Collingwood); *m* 1960, Maria Teresa (Marité) Paul; two *d. Educ:* Western High School; George Washington University, Washington DC. Royal Air Force, 1945–48. Board of Trade, 1949; served FO, later FCO: Athens, Belgrade, Haiphong, Caracas; First Sec., Saigon, 1962; First Sec. and Consul, Bujumbura, 1964 (Chargé d'Affaires *ai*, 1966–67); FO 1968; First Sec. and Consul, Asunçion, 1971; First Sec., Mexico City, 1974; FCO, 1978; seconded to Brunei Govt Service as Special Adviser to HM Sultan of Brunei, for Establishment of Brunei Diplomatic Service, 1981–84; Consul-Gen., Bordeaux, 1984–87. Order of the Aztec Eagle, Mexico, 1975. *Recreations:* photography, giving illustrated talks, tourism, cartooning, sculpture. *Address:* 8 Purberry Grove, Ewell, Surrey KT17 1LU.

NELSON, Maj.-Gen. Sir (Eustace) John (Blois), KCVO 1966 (MVO 1953); CB 1965; DSO 1944; OBE 1948; MC 1943; *b* 15 June 1912; *s* of late Roland Hugh Nelson and late Hylda Letitia Blois; *m* 1936, the Lady Jane FitzRoy (granted rank and precedence of *d* of a duke, 1931), *er d* of (William Henry Alfred FitzRoy) Viscount Ipswich; two *d. Educ:* Eton; Trinity College, Cambridge. BA (Hons) History, MA 1983. Commissioned Grenadier Guards, Sept. 1933; served 1939–45 with 3rd and 5th Bns, Belgium, N Africa, Italy (wounded three times, despatches); comd 3rd Bn Grenadier Guards, 1944–45, Italy. Contested (C) Whitechapel, 1945. Comd 1st Guards Parachute Bn, 1946–48, Palestine; comd 1st Bn Gren. Gds, 1950–52, Tripoli, N Africa. Planning Staff Standing Group, Washington, DC, 1954–56, Imperial Defence College, 1958; comd 4th Guards Bde, 1959–61, Germany; GOC London District, and Maj.-Gen. comdg Household Brigade 1962–65; GOC Berlin (British Sector), 1966–68. Chm., Christian Youth Challenge Trust; Vice-Pres., Nat. Playing Fields Assoc. (Gen. Sec. 1969–72); Pres., Trident Trust, 1986–. Silver Star (USA), 1944. *Recreations:* the countryside, sailing. *Address:* Tigh Bhaan, Appin, Argyll PA38 4BL. *T:* Appin (063173) 252.

NELSON, Sir Jamie (Charles Vernon Hope), 4th Bt *cr* 1912, of Acton Park, Acton, Denbigh; *b* 23 Oct. 1949; *s* of Sir William Vernon Hope Nelson, OBE and Hon. Elizabeth Ann Bevil Cary, *er d* of 14th Viscount Falkland; *S* father, 1991; *m* 1983, Maralyn Hedge (*née* Pyatt); one *s. Heir: b* Dominic William Michael Nelson [*b* 13 March 1957; *m* 1981, Sarah, *e d* of late John Neil Hylton Jolliffe; three *s*]. *Address:* 39 Montacute Road, Tintinhull, Yeovil, Somerset BA22 8QD. *T:* Martock (0935) 822496.

NELSON, John Graeme; General Manager, British Rail Eastern Region, since 1987; *b* 19 June 1947; *s* of Charles and Jean Nelson; *m* 1971, Pauline Dickinson; two *s* one *d. Educ:* Aylesbury and Slough Grammar Schs; Univ. of Manchester (BA Econ Hons). Management trainee, BR Western Reg., 1968; Asst Station Man., Liverpool Street, 1971; Area Passenger Man., Shenfield, 1973; Passenger Sales Officer, Leeds, 1977; Passenger Man., Sheffield Div., 1979; Personal Asst, Chief Exec. BRB, 1981; Parcels Man., Southern Reg., 1982; Nat. Business Man., Red Star Parcels, 1984. *Recreations:* piano, football, badminton. *Address:* British Railways Eastern Region, Regional Headquarters, York YO1 1HT. *T:* York (0904) 653022, ext. 2200.

NELSON, Michael Edward; Chairman, Reuter Foundation, 1982–90; General Manager, 1976–89, and Deputy Managing Director, 1981–89, Reuters Ltd; *b* 30 April 1929; *s* of Thomas Alfred Nelson and Dorothy Pretoria Nelson; *m* 1960, Helga Johanna (*née* den Ouden); two *s* one *d. Educ:* Latymer Upper School; Magdalen College, Oxford (MA). Joined Reuters, London, as trainee financial journalist, 1952; assignments Asia, 1954–57; returned to London; Manager, Reuters Economic Services, 1962; Chairman, 1987–88: Reuters Asia; Reuters Europe; Reuters Overseas. Trustee: Visnews, 1990– (Chm., 1985–89); Internat. Inst. of Communications, 1989– (Chm., UK Chapter, 1989–); Chm. Adv. Council, World Link, 1990–. Trustee, St Bride's Church, 1989–. *Recreations:* walking, music, photography. *Address:* 44 Phillimore Gardens, W8 7QG. *T:* 071–937 1626; 17 route du Port, 74290 Veyrier du Lac, France. *T:* 50.60.19.70. *Club:* Garrick.

NELSON, Nicholas; Managing Director, Royal Mail Parcelforce (formerly Parcels, Post Office), since 1987; *b* 20 Jan. 1947; *s* of late Peter Nelson and of Margaret Nelson; *m* 1972, Charmian Alice (*née* Bell); one *s* two *d. Educ:* Pudsey Grammar Sch., Yorkshire; Reading Univ. (BA (Hons) History). BOAC: Management Trainee, 1969; Air Cargo Sales Rep., 1971; Cargo Sales Man., Japan/Dep. Marketing Man., Japan, 1973; British Airways: Cargo Manager: Eastern Scotland, 1978; Midlands, 1979; DHL International (UK) Ltd: Gen. Man., 1981; Man. Dir, 1982; Regional Dir (Europe), 1987. *Recreations:* cricket, golf, history. *Address:* Royal Mail Parcelforce, Solaris Court, Davy Avenue, Knowl Hill, Milton Keynes MK5 8PP.

NELSON, Air Marshal Sir Richard; *see* Nelson, Air Marshal Sir S. R. C.

NELSON, (Richard) Anthony; MP (C) Chichester, since Oct. 1974; *b* 11 June 1948; *o s* of late Gp Captain R. G. Nelson, BSc, CEng, FRAeS, MICE, and of Mrs J. M. Nelson; *m* 1974, Caroline Victoria Butler; one *s* one *d. Educ:* Harrow Sch.; Christ's Coll., Cambridge (MA (Hons) Economics and Law). State Scholarship to Harrow, 1961; Head of School, 1966; Rothschild Scholar, 1966. N. M. Rothschild & Sons Ltd, 1969–73. Mem., Bow Gp Council, 1973. Dir, Chichester Fest. Th., 1983–. Contested (C) E Leeds, Feb. 1974. PPS to Minister for Housing and Construction, 1979–83, to Minister of State for the Armed Forces, 1983–85. Member: Select Cttee on Science and Technology, 1975–79; Select

Cttee on Televising of Proceedings of the House, 1988–. FRSA 1979. *Recreations*: music, rugby. *Address*: The Old Vicarage, Easebourne, Midhurst, West Sussex.

NELSON, Dr (Richard) Stuart, FInstP; Managing Director, Industrial Business Group, since 1991; *b* 1 May 1937; *s* of Richard and Winifred Emily Nelson; *m* 1965, Veronica Mary Beck; one *s* two *d*. *Educ*: Univ. of Reading (BSc 1st Cl. Hons Physics, 1958; DSc 1969). FInstP 1968. Joined UKAEA, Harwell, 1958; Div. Head, Materials Develt Div., 1981; Dir, Nuclear Power Res., 1984; Dir, Northern Res. Labs, 1987–90 (including Risley, Springfield and Windscale Labs); Dep. Man. Dir, AEA Technology, 1990. Vis. Prof., Univ. of Sussex, 1970–. *Publications*: The Observation of Atomic Collisions in Crystalline Solids, 1968; Ion Implantation, 1973; 200 papers in scientific jls. *Recreations*: hockey (played for Berkshire), tennis. *Address*: Harwell Laboratory, Didcot, Oxfordshire OX11 0RA. *T*: Didcot (0235) 432814.

NELSON, Robert Franklyn; QC 1985; a Recorder, since 1986; *b* 19 Sept. 1942; *s* of Clarence William and Lucie Margaret Nelson; *m* 1968, Anne-Marie Sabina Hall; two *s*. *Educ*: Repton; St John's Coll., Cambridge (MA). Called to the Bar, Middle Temple, 1965 (Harmsworth Entrance Exhibn, 1963). *Recreations*: cricket, opera, golf. *Address*: 1 Paper Buildings, Temple, EC4Y 7EP. *T*: 071–583 7355.

NELSON, St Elmo Dudley, CMG 1964; Permanent Secretary, Military Governor's Office, Kano, 1968–76; Acting Secretary to Military Government, and Head of Kano State Civil Service, 1970, 1973 and 1975; *b* 18 March 1919; *s* of Dudley Nelson and late Dorothy Maida (*née* Browne), Highton, Victoria, Australia; *m* 1958, Lynette Margaret, *o d* of late Phillip Anthony Browne, Yarram and Frankston, Victoria, Australia. *Educ*: privately; Geelong School; Oxford University; Sorbonne. Served War of 1939–45 (despatches): 2/7 Australian Infantry Bn (Major); campaigns N Africa, Greece, Crete, New Guinea; Instructor Staff Coll., Cabalah, 1944. Joined HM Colonial Administrative Service. Nigeria: Cadet 1947; Administrative Officer (Class II), 1957; Resident, Plateau Province, 1961; Resident and Provincial Sec., Kabba Province, 1962; Provincial Sec., Kano Province, 1963–67, Sokoto, 1967–68. Chm., Cttee which divided assets of Northern Region between the six Northern States, 1967. Election supervisor, Rhodesian independence elecns, 1980. Gen. Tax Comr, S Wilts, 1980–. *Recreations*: fishing, polo, squash. *Address*: Buln Buln, 272/274 Roslyn Road, Highton, Geelong, Vic 3216, Australia. *Club*: MCC.

NELSON, Air Marshal Sir (Sidney) Richard (Carlyle), KCB 1963 (CB 1962); OBE 1949; Director-General, Royal Air Force Medical Services, 1962–67; Director of Research and Medical Services, Aspro-Nicholas Ltd, 1967–72; *b* Ponoka, Alberta, Canada, 14 Nov. 1907; *s* of M. O. Nelson, BA; *m* 1939, Christina Elizabeth Powell; two *s*. *Educ*: University of Alberta (MD). Commissioned in RAF, 1935; served: England 1935–36; Egypt and Western Desert, 1936–42; Fighter Command, 1943; UK Delegation (Canada), 1943–44; British Jt Services Mission (Washington), 1945–48; RAF Staff Coll., 1949; Air Ministry, 1949–52; Comd RAF Hosp., Nocton Hall, 1953–55; SMO British Forces, Arabian Peninsula, 1956–57; PMO Technical Training Comd, 1957–59; Bomber Comd, 1959–62, QHP 1961–67. *Recreations*: fishing, golf. *Address*: Caffyn's Copse, Shappen Hill Lane, Burley, Hants. *T*: Burley (04253) 3308. *Clubs*: Royal Air Force; Royal Lymington Yacht.

NELSON, Stuart; see Nelson, R. S.

NEMETZ, Hon. Nathaniel Theodore, CC 1989; Canada Medal 1967; Chief Justice of British Columbia and Administrator of the Province of British Columbia, 1979–88; *b* 8 Sept. 1913; *s* of Samuel and Rebecca (*née* Birch); *m* 1935, Bel Newman; one *s*. *Educ*: Univ. of British Columbia (BA 1st Cl. Hons History). Called to the Bar, BC, 1937; KC (Canada) 1950. Justice, Supreme Court of BC, 1963–68; Justice, Court of Appeal of BC, 1968–73; Chief Justice, Supreme Court of BC, 1973–78. Exec. Mem., Canadian Judicial Council, 1973–88 (Vice-Chm., 1985–88). Special counsel to: City of Vancouver, City of New Westminster and Municipality of Burnaby; Electrical Assoc.; BC Hosp. Assoc.; Public Utilities Commn of BC; Royal Commission on: Expropriation, 1961; Fishing, 1964; Election Regulations, 1965; Forest Industry, 1966. Chm., Educational Delegn to People's Republic of China, 1974; Advisor to Canadian Govt Delegn, ILO, Geneva, 1973. University of British Columbia: Mem. Senate and Bd of Govs, 1957–68 (Chm. Bd of Govs, 1965–68); Chancellor, 1972–75, now Chancellor Emeritus; Pres., Alumni Assoc., 1957; Hon. Mem., Faculty Assoc., 1972; Chancellor's Medal, 1988. Mem., Bd of Governors, Canadian Inst. for Advanced Legal Studies, Cambridge, England. Hon. Fellow, Hebrew Univ., Jerusalem, 1976. Hon. LLD: Notre Dame (Nelson), 1972; Simon Fraser, 1975; British Columbia, 1975; Victoria, 1976. Freeman, City of Vancouver, 1988. Hon. Consul, Singapore, 1989–. Silver Jubilee Medal, 1977; Medal of Yugoslav Flag with Ribbon, 1989. *Publications*: articles on: Swedish Labour Law and Practice, 1967; Judicial Administration and Judicial Independence, 1976; The Jury and the Citizen, 1985; The Concept of the Independence of the Judiciary, 1985. *Recreations*: reading, travelling. *Address*: 5688 Newton Wynd, Vancouver, BC V6T 1H5, Canada. *T*: (604) 224–5383. *Clubs*: Vancouver (Life Mem.), University (Life Mem.; Pres., 1961–62), Faculty of University of British Columbia (Hon. Life Mem.) (Vancouver).

NENDICK, David Alan Challoner, CBE 1990; Secretary for Monetary Affairs, Hong Kong Government, since 1985; *b* 31 July 1932; *s* of late Cyril Arthur and Kathleen Nendick; *m* 1964, Miriam Louise Gibbons; one *s* two *d*. *Educ*: Haileybury College. National Service, commissioned RA, 1950–52. Bank of England, 1953–89 (seconded Bank of Mauritius, 1970–72 and Hong Kong Govt, 1985–89); Hong Kong Govt, 1989–. *Recreations*: tennis, walking, watching cricket. *Address*: House L, 8 Mount Kellett Road, The Peak, Hong Kong. *T*: Hong Kong 8496013; 26 St Stephens Gardens, W2 5QX. *T*: 071–792 2940. *Clubs*: East India, Overseas Bankers; Hong Kong Country, Hong Kong Overseas Bankers.

NEPEAN, Lt-Col Sir Evan Yorke, 6th Bt, *cr* 1802; late Royal Signals; *b* 23 Nov. 1909; *s* of Sir Charles Evan Molyneux Yorke Nepean, 5th Bt, and Mary Winifred, *o d* of Rev. William John Swayne, formerly Vicar of Heytesbury, Wilts, and Custos of St John's Hospital, Heytesbury; *S* father 1953; *m* 1940, (Georgiana) Cicely, *o d* of late Major Noel Edward Grey Willoughby, Middlesex Regiment, of Chancel End House, Heytesbury, Wilts; three *d*. *Educ*: Winchester; Downing College, Cambridge. BA 1931, MA 1946. North West Frontier of India (Mohmand), 1935. Served War of 1939–45: GSO3, War Office, 1939–40; with Royal Signals (Lt-Col 1943), UK, and Middle East, Major 1946; on Staff Southern Command, 1947; GSO1 Royal Signals, Ministry of Defence, 1950–53; Lt-Col 1952; Cmdg 11 Air Formation Signal Regt, BAOR, 1955–56, retired. Civil Servant, 1957–59; CSO's branch at HQ Southern Command (Retired Officers' Staff appt), 1959–73. Mem., Salisbury Diocesan Guild of Ringers. CEng; MIEE. *Recreations*: bell-ringing, amateur radio. *Heir*: none. *Address*: Goldens, Teffont, Salisbury, Wilts. *T*: Teffont (0722) 716275.

NERINA, Nadia; (*née* Nadine Judd); Prima Ballerina; Ballerina with Royal Ballet, 1951–69; *b* Cape Town, Oct. 1927; *m* 1955, Charles Gordon. Joined Sadler's Wells Sch., 1946; after two months joined Sadler's Wells Theatre Ballet; transferred Sadler's Wells

Ballet, Royal Opera House (now Royal Ballet), as soloist, 1967. *Rôles*: Princess Aurora in The Sleeping Beauty; Ondine; Odette-Odile in Swan Lake; Swanhilda in Coppelia; Sylvia; Giselle; Cinderella; Firebird; Can Can Dancer in La Boutique Fantasque; Ballerina in Petrushka; Colombine in Carnaval; Mazurka, Little Waltz, Prelude, in Les Sylphides; Mam'zelle Angot; Ballet Imperial; Scènes de Ballet; Flower Festival of Genzano; Les Rendezvous; Polka in Façade; The Girl in Spectre de la Rose; Casse Noisette; Laurentia; Khadra; Vagabonds; The Bride in A Wedding Bouquet; *creations*: Circus Dancer in Mardi Gras; Fairy Spring in Cinderella; Queen of the Earth in Homage to the Queen; Faded Beauty in Noctambules; Variation on a Theme; Birthday Offering; Lise in La Fille Mal Gardée; Electra; The Girl in Home; Clorinda in Tancredi. Appeared with Royal Ballet: Europe; South Africa; USA; Canada; USSR; Bulgaria; Romania. Recital Tours with Alexis Rassine: South Africa, 1952–55; England, 1956–57; concert performances, Royal Albert Hall and Royal Festival Hall, 1958–60. *Guest appearances include*: Turkish Nat. Ballet, 1957; Bolshoi Ballet, Kirov Ballet, 1960; Munich Ballet, 1963; Nat. Finnish Ballet, Royal Danish Ballet, 1964; Stuttgart Ballet, 1965; Ballet Theatre, Opera House Chicago, 1967; Royal Command Variety Performances, 1963–66. Mounted, dir. and prod three Charity Gala performances, London Palladium, 1969, 1971, 1972. Many TV appearances, UK and USA. Hon. Consultant on Ballet, Ohio Univ., 1967–69. British Jury Member, 3rd Internat. Ballet Competition, Moscow, 1977. Fellow, 1959, Patron, 1964, Cecchetti Soc. Mem. Council, RSPCA, 1969–74. *Publications*: contrib.: La Fille Mal Gardée, 1960; Ballet and Modern Dance, 1974; *relevant publication*: Ballerina, ed Clement Crisp, 1975. *Address*: c/o Royal Opera House, Covent Garden, WC2.

NESS, Air Marshal Sir Charles, KCB 1980 (CB 1978); CBE 1967 (OBE 1959); Military Adviser, International Computers Ltd, since 1983; *s* of late Charles W. Ness and Jessica Ness; *m* 1951, Audrey, *d* of late Roy and Phyllis Parker; one *s*. *Educ*: George Heriot's Sch.; Edinburgh Univ. CBIM, MIPM. Joined RAF, 1943; flying and staff appts in Bomber Comd and with USAF, 1944–62; Commander, British Skybolt Trials Force, Florida, 1962–63; Station Commander, Royal Air Force, Steamer Point, Aden, 1965–67; Air Comdr, Gibraltar, 1971–73; Director of Organisation and Administrative Plans (RAF), MoD, 1974–75; Comdr, Southern Maritime Air Region, 1975–76; Dir Gen., Personnel Management (RAF), 1976–80; Air Mem. for Personnel, 1980–83. Chairman: Air League, 1987–90; Educn Cttee, RAF Benevolent Fund, 1987–. Chm., Bd of Govs, Duke of Kent Sch., 1987–. *Address*: Lloyds Bank plc, Cox's & Kings Branch, 7 Pall Mall, SW1Y 5NA. *Club*: Royal Air Force.

NETHERTHORPE, 3rd Baron *cr* 1959, of Anston, W Riding; **James Frederick Turner;** *b* 7 Jan. 1964; *s* of 2nd Baron Netherthorpe, and of Belinda, *d* of F. Hedley Nicholson; *S* father, 1982; *m* 1989, Elizabeth Curran Fahan, *d* of Edward Fahan, Connecticut. *Educ*: Heatherdown Prep. School; Harrow School. *Heir*: *b* Hon. Patrick Andrew Turner, *b* 4 June 1971. *Address*: Boothby Hall, Boothby Pagnell, Grantham, Lincs. *T*: Ingoldsby (047685) 374.

NEUBERGER, Albert, CBE 1964; PhD (London), MD (Würzburg); FRCP; FRS 1951; FRSC; Professor of Chemical Pathology, St Mary's Hospital, University of London, 1955–73, now Emeritus Professor; *b* 15 April 1908; *s* of late Max Neuberger and Bertha Neuberger; *m* 1943, Lilian Ida, *d* of late Edmund Dreyfus and Marguerite Dreyfus, London; four *s* (one *d* decd). *Educ*: Gymnasium, Würzburg; Univs of Würzburg and London. Beit Memorial Research Fellow, 1936–40; Research at the Biochemistry Department, Cambridge, 1939–42; Mem. of Scientific Staff, Medical Research Council, 1943; Adviser to GHQ, Delhi (Medical Directorate), 1945; Head of Biochemistry Dept, Nat. Inst. for Medical Research, 1950–55; Principal of the Wright Fleming Institute of Microbiology, 1958–62. Visiting Lectr on Medicine, 1960, on Biol Chemistry, 1964, Harvard Univ., and Physician-in-Chief (*pro tem.*), Peter Bent Brigham Hosp., Boston; Merck, Sharp and Dohme Vis. Prof., Sch. of Medicine, Univ. of Washington, 1965; Royal Soc./Israel Acad. Vis. Res. Prof., 1969; Julius Schultz Vis. Prof., Univ. of Miami Sch. of Medicine, 1988. Mem. of Editorial Bd, Biochemical Jl, 1947–55, Chm., 1952–55; Associate Man. Editor, Biochimica et Biophysica Acta, 1968–81. Member: MRC, 1962–66; Council of Scientific Policy, 1968–69; ARC, 1969–79; Indep. Cttee on Smoking and Health, 1973–82; Sci. Adv. Cttee, Rank Prize Funds, 1974–86; Chm., Jt ARC/MRC Cttee on Food and Nutrition Res., 1971–73; Chairman: Governing Body, Lister Inst., 1971–88 (Mem., 1968–); Advisory Board, Beit Memorial Fellowships, 1967–73; Biochemical Soc., 1967–69 (Hon. Mem., Biochemical Soc., 1973); Dep. Chm., Bd of Governors, Hebrew Univ., Jerusalem. Pres., Assoc. of Clinical Biochemists, 1972–73; Hon. Pres., British Nutrition Foundn, 1982–86. For. Hon. Mem., Amer. Acad. Arts and Sciences, 1972. FRCPath 1964; FRCP 1966. William Julius Mickle Fellowship of Univ. of London, 1946–47; Heberden Medal, 1959; Frederick Gowland Hopkins Medal, 1960; Kaplun Prize, 1973. Hon. LLD, Aberdeen, 1967; Hon. PhD, Jerusalem, 1968; Hon. DSc Hull, 1981. *Publications*: papers in Biochemical Jl, Proceedings of Royal Society and other learned journals. *Address*: 37 Eton Court, Eton Avenue, NW3 3HJ. *T*: 071–586 5470. *Club*: Athenæum.
See also D. E. Neuberger.

NEUBERGER, David Edmond; QC 1987; a Recorder, since 1990; *b* 10 Jan. 1948; *s* of Prof. Albert Neuberger, *qv*; *m* 1976, Angela, *d* of Brig. Peter Holdsworth; two *s* one *d*. *Educ*: Westminster; Christ Church, Oxford (MA). N. M. Rothschild & Sons, 1970–73; called to the Bar, Lincoln's Inn, 1974. *Address*: 11 King's Bench Walk, Temple, EC4. *T*: 071–353 2484.

NEUBERGER, Rabbi Julia Babette Sarah; Harkness Fellow, Harvard University, 1991–Feb. 1992; *b* 27 Feb. 1950; *d* of Walter and Alice Schwab; *m* 1973, Anthony John Neuberger; one *s* one *d*. *Educ*: South Hampstead High Sch.; Newnham Coll., Cambridge (BA, MA); Leo Baeck Coll., London (Rabbinic Dip.). Lectr and Associate Fellow, Leo Baeck Coll., 1979–; Associate, Newnham Coll., Cambridge, 1983–. Rabbi, South London Liberal Synagogue, 1977–89; Chm., Rabbinic Conf., Union of Liberal and Progressive Synagogues, 1983–85; Mem., Policy Planning Gp, Inst. of Jewish Affairs, 1986–. Member: Council, N London Hospice Gp, 1984–; Ethics Adv. Gp, RCN, 1986–; Council, St George's Hosp. Med. Sch., 1987–; Chairman: Patients' Assoc., 1988–91; RCN Commn on the Health Service, 1988. Member: Nat. Cttee, SDP, 1982–88; Policy Cttee, SDP, 1983–85; Convenor, SDP/Liberal Lawyers' Working Party on Legal Services, 1985–87; Mem., Editorial Bd, Political Qly, 1987–. Presenter, Choices, BBC TV, 1986 and 1987; Member: Interim (formerly Voluntary) Licensing Authority for IVF, 1987–91; Human Fertilization and Embryology Authority, 1990–; Exec., Anchor Housing Assoc. and Trust, 1985–87; Exec., NCVO, 1988–89; Exec., Unicef UK, 1989–91; Bd, Citizenship Foundn, 1989–; Council, St George's House, Windsor, 1989–; Council, Runnymede Trust, 1989–; Governor, British Inst. of Human Rights, 1989–. *Publications*: The Story of Judaism (for children), 1986, 2nd edn 1988; (ed) Days of Decision (4 in series), 1987; Caring for Dying Patients of Different Faiths, 1987; (ed with John A. White) A Necessary End, 1991; Whatever's Happening to Women?, 1991; contribs to various books on cultural, religious and ethical factors in nursing, reviews for variety of jls and newspapers. *Recreations*: riding, sailing, Irish life, opera, setting up the old girls' network, children. *Address*: 36 Orlando Road, SW4 0LF. *T*: 071–622 2995. *Club*: Groucho.

NEUBERT, Sir Michael (Jon), Kt 1990; MP (C) Romford, since Feb. 1974; *b* 3 Sept. 1933; *s* of Frederick Henry and Mathilda Marie Louise Neubert; *m* 1959, Sally Felicity Bilger; one *s*. *Educ:* Queen Elizabeth's Sch., Barnet; Bromley Grammar Sch.; Royal Coll. of Music; Downing Coll., Cambridge. MA (Cantab) Modern and Medieval Langs. Travel and industrial consultant. Councillor, Borough of Bromley, 1960–63; London Borough of Bromley: Councillor, 1964–68; Alderman, 1968–74; Leader of the Council, 1967–70; Mayor, 1972–73. Contested (C): N Hammersmith, 1966; Romford, 1970. PPS to: Minister for Social Security and for the Disabled, 1980; Ministers of State, NI Office, 1981; Minister of State for Employment, 1981–82; Sec. of State for Trade, 1982–83; Asst Govt Whip, 1983–86; a Lord Comr of HM Treasury, 1986–88; Vice-Chamberlain of HM Household, 1988; Parly Under-Sec. of State for the Armed Forces, 1988–89, for Defence Procurement, 1989–90, MoD. Chm., Bromley Conservative Assoc., 1968–69. *Publication:* Running Your Own Society, 1967. *Recreations:* music, literature, cinema, theatre, the countryside. *Address:* House of Commons, SW1A 0AA. *Club:* Romford Conservative and Constitutional.

NEUMANN, Prof. Bernhard Hermann, FACE 1970; FAA 1964; FRS 1959; Honorary Research Fellow, CSIRO Division of Mathematics and Statistics, since 1978; *b* Berlin-Charlottenburg, 15 Oct. 1909; *s* of late Richard Neumann and late Else (*née* Aronstein); *m* 1st, 1938, Hanna Neumann (*née* von Caemmerer) (*d* 1971), DPhil, DSc, FAA, formerly Prof. and Head of Dept of Pure Mathematics, Sch. of Gen. Studies, ANU; three *s* two *d*; 2nd, 1973, Dorothea Neumann (*née* Zeim), MA, PhD. *Educ:* Herderschule, Berlin; Univs of Freiburg, Berlin, Cambridge. Dr phil Berlin, 1932; PhD Cambridge 1935; DSc Manchester 1954. Asst Lectr, University Coll, Cardiff, 1937–40. Army Service, 1940–45. Lectr, University Coll., Hull, 1946–48; Lectr, Senior Lectr, Reader, Univ. of Manchester, 1948–61; Prof. and Hd of Dept of Maths, Inst. of Advanced Studies, ANU, Canberra, 1962–74, Emeritus Prof., 1975–; Sen. Res. Fellow, CSIRO Div. of Maths and Stats, 1975–77. Visiting Lecturer: Australian Univs, 1959; Univ. of Cambridge, 1970; Monash Univ., 1980; Visiting Professor: Tata Inst. of Fundamental Research, Bombay, 1959; New York Univ., 1961–62; Univ. of Wisconsin, 1966–67; Vanderbilt Univ., 1969–70; G. A. Miller Vis. Prof., Univ. of Illinois at Urbana-Champaign, 1975; Univ. of Manitoba, 1979; Vis. Fellow, Fitzwilliam Coll., Cambridge, 1970; SERC Visiting Fellow: Univ. of Glasgow, 1985; Univ. of Wales Coll. of Cardiff, 1991; Deutscher Akademischer Austauschs-Dienst Visitor, Univ. of Bielefeld, 1987. Wiskundig Genootschap te Amsterdam Prize, 1949; Adams Prize, Univ. of Cambridge, 1952–53. Mem., Aust. Subcommn, Internat. Commn Math. Instruct., 1967–75 (Chm.), and 1979–83; Mem.-at-large, Internat. Commn Math. Instruct., 1975–82, Mem. Exec. Cttee, 1979–82; Mem., Programme Adv. Cttee, Congress Math. Educn, Karlsruhe, 1976, Berkeley, Calif., 1980, Adelaide, Australia, 1984. Member Council: London Math. Society, 1954–61 (Vice-Pres., 1957–59); Aust. Math. Society, 1963–79 (Vice-Pres., 1963–64, 1966–68, 1971–73, Pres., 1964–66; Hon. Mem. 1981–); Aust. Acad. of Science, 1968–71 (a Vice-Pres., 1969–71). Mem. Aust. Nat. Cttee for Mathematics, 1963–75 (Chm., 1966–75); (Foundation) Pres., Aust. Assoc. Math. Teachers, 1966–68, Vice-Pres., 1968–69, Hon. Mem., 1975–; (Foundn) Pres., Canberra Math. Assoc., 1963–65, Vice-Pres., 1965–66, Hon. Mem., 1975–; Hon. Mem., NZ Math. Soc., 1975–; Member: Acad. Adv. Council, RAN Coll., 1978–87; Sci. and Industry Forum, 1989–. Chairman: Internat. Math. Olympiad Site Cttee, 1981–83; Aust. Math. Olympiad Cttee, 1980–86. Hon. DSc: Univ. of Newcastle, NSW, 1974; Monash Univ., 1982; Hon. DMath Univ. of Waterloo, 1986. Non-res. Fellow (Tutor), Bruce Hall, ANU, 1963–; Hon. Fellow: Dept of Maths, Inst. of Advanced Studies, ANU, 1975–; Inst. of Combinatorics and its Applications, 1990. Pres., Amateur Sinfonia of Canberra Inc., 1978–80, Vice-Pres., 1980–81, 1983–84, Hon. Mem., 1984–85; Vice-Pres., Friends of the Canberra Sch. of Music, 1983–. Hon. Editor, Proc. London Math. Soc., 1959–61; Assoc. Editor, Pacific Jl Math., 1964–; (Foundation) Editor, Bulletin of Aust. Math. Soc., 1969–79, Hon. Editor, 1979–; Member Editorial Board: Communications in Algebra, 1973–84; Houston Jl Math., 1974–; Mem., Adv. Bd, Zentralblatt Didaktik Math. 1970–84; Editorial Advr, SE Asian Math. Bull., 1987–; Founder Editor and Publisher, IMU Canberra Circular, 1972–; Mem. and Regional Chm., IMU Exchange Commn, 1975–78. *Publications:* Appendix to German and Hungarian translations of A. G. Kuroš: Teoriya Grupp, 1953, 1955: Topics in the Theory of Infinite Groups, Bombay, 1961; Special Topics in Algebra, Vol. I: Universal Algebra, Vol. II: Order Techniques, New York, 1962; Selected Works of B. H. Neumann and Hanna Neumann, 6 vols, 1988; papers, mainly on theory of groups, in various mathematical journals. *Recreations:* chess, cycling, music. *Address:* 20 Talbot Street, Forrest, ACT 2603, Australia. *T:* (06) Canberra 2733447.

NEUSTADT, Rt. Hon. Shirley Vivien Teresa Brittain; *see* Williams, Rt Hon. S. V. T. B.

NEVE, David Lewis; President, Immigration Appeal Tribunal, 1978–91; *b* 7 Oct. 1920; *s* of Eric Read Neve, QC, and Nellie Victorine Neve (*née* Uridge); *m* 1948, Betsy Davida Bannerman; one *s* (decd). *Educ:* Repton; Emmanuel Coll., Cambridge (BA). Served war, Royal Artillery, 1940–46. Called to Bar, Middle Temple, 1947; Resident Magistrate, Uganda, 1952–59; Sen. Resident Magistrate, Uganda, 1959–62; Acting Judge, Uganda, 1962. Immigration Appeals Adjudicator, 1970; Vice-Pres., Immigration Appeals Tribunal, 1976. *Recreations:* sailing, music, reading. *Address:* Deans, Lewes Road, Ditchling, Hassocks, East Sussex.

NEVILE, Henry Nicholas; Lord-Lieutenant of Lincolnshire, since 1975; High Steward, Lincoln Cathedral, since 1985; *b* 1920; *e s* of late Charles Joseph Nevile, Wellingore, Lincoln and Muriel (*née* O'Conor), *m* 1944, Jean Rosita Mary, MBE 1984, *d* of Cyril James Winceslas Torr and Maude (*née* Walpole); two *s* three *d*. *Educ:* Ampleforth; Trinity Coll., Cambridge. Served war, Scots Guards, in NW Europe, 1940–46 (despatches). Member: Upper Witham IDB, 1952–83 (Chm., 1964–76); Lincs River Bd and Authy, 1962–82; Kesteven CC, 1964–72. Liveryman, Farmers' Co., 1975–. JP 1950, DL 1962, High Sheriff, 1963, Lincolnshire. Hon. Col, Lincs ACF. KStJ. *Address:* Aubourn Hall, Lincoln LN5 9DZ. *T:* Bassingham (052285) 270. *Club:* Brooks's.

NEVILL, family name of **Marquess of Abergavenny.**

NEVILL, Prof. Bernard Richard, FCSD; designer; Professor of Textile Design, Royal College of Art, 1984–89 (Fellow, since 1984); Director, Bernard Nevill Ltd (own furnishing collections), since 1990; *b* 24 Sept. 1934; *s* of R. G. Nevill. *Educ:* privately; St Martin's Sch. of Art; Royal Coll. of Art. FSIA 1970. Designed exhibn, Opera and Ballet, for Cotton Bd, Manchester, 1950; lectured in art, fashion, history of costume, textile design and fashion drawing, Shoreditch Coll., 1954–56 (resp. for first dress show staged at GLC Chm's annual reception, County Hall); Lectr, St Martin's Sch. of Art and RCA, 1959–74 (liaised between Fashion and Textile Schs, devising projs and themes for finale to RCA annual diploma show); lectured in theatre design and book illustration, Central Sch. of Art and Design, 1957–60; freelance illustrator, Good Housekeeping, Woman's Jl, Vogue, Harper's Bazaar, incl. covers for Queen and Sketch, 1956–60; freelance journalist, Vogue, Sketch and textile and fashion periodicals, 1956–66; Art Critic, Vogue, 1965–66; Designer (later Design Dir), Liberty Prints, 1961: for next decade, produced collections which became fashion landmarks and re-estabd Liberty's as major source of fashion textiles worldwide; collections designed: Islamic, 1963 (anticipated Eastern revival in fashion); Jazz, 1964 (first re-appraisal of Art Deco); Tango, 1966; Renaissance, 1967; Chameleon, 1969 (co-ordinated prints); Designer and Design Dir, Ten Cate, Holland, 1969–71; Design Consultant in dress fabrics to Cantoni (founders of cotton industry in Italy), 1971–84: printed velvets and cottons have placed Cantoni in fore-front of internat. ready-to-wear; designed printed sheet collection for Cantoni Casa, 1977; textile consultant and designer of dress fabrics, Unitika Ltd, Japan, 1990–; redesign and supervision of restoration of interiors: Lennoxlove Castle, 1988–89; Eastnor Castle, 1989–. Designed: two collections for Internat. Wool Secretariat, 1975–77; English Country House Collection for Sekers Internat., 1981–82 (used this collection when redesigning Long Gall., Lutyen's British Embassy, Washington); Collections for Romanex de Boussac, France, 1982–87, including English Gardens, Botanic, Figurative Porcelain Prints and Printed Damasks; furnishing collection for restored Château de Bagnole, France. Designed costumes: films: Genevieve, 1953; Next To No Time, 1955; The Admirable Crichton, 1957; musical: Marigold, 1958; opera: Così fan tutte (Glyndebourne), 1962. Engaged in restoration of Fonthill Abbey and woodlands, 1976–. Mem., Adv. Panel, National Dip. of Design, 1964–66; Governor, Croydon Coll. of Art, 1966–67. FRSA 1966, resigned 1977. Book reviewer, TLS, 1987–. Illustrated articles on his work have appeared in the Press. *Recreations:* looking at large well-built walls and buildings; passionate conservationist and environmentalist, collector, bibliophil; tree-worship, chamber music. *Address:* West House, 35 Glebe Place, SW3; Fonthill Abbey, Fonthill Gifford, near Salisbury, Wilts.

NEVILL, Maj.-Gen. Cosmo Alexander Richard, CB 1958; CBE 1954; DSO 1944; War Office, 1958–60; Colonel, Royal Fusiliers, 1959–63, retired; *b* 14 July 1907; *s* of late Maj. Cosmo Charles Richard Nevill, DSO, OBE, Eccleston, Leamington Spa; *m* 1934, Grania, *d* of late Maj. G. V. Goodliffe, MC, Birdstown, co. Donegal; one *s* one *d*. *Educ:* Harrow; Royal Military College. Commissioned as Second Lieutenant, Royal Fusiliers, 1927; served War of 1939–45 (DSO, OBE): on staff, India; commanded 2nd battalion Devonshire Regiment, Normandy; Lieutenant-Colonel, 1944. A General Staff Officer, Military Staff Committee, United Nations, New York, 1946–48; Chief Instr, Sch. of Infantry, 1948–50; commanded 1st battalion Royal Fusiliers, 1950–51; a Brigade Commander, 1951–54; Commandant School of Infantry, 1954–56; Major-General 1957; GOC 2nd Infantry Division, 1956–58. CC West Suffolk, 1962–67. Lay Canon, St Edmundsbury Cathedral, 1979–85. *Address:* Holt, Edwardstone, Colchester, Essex CO6 5PJ. *T:* Boxford (0787) 210428. *Clubs:* Army and Navy; I Zingari.

NEVILLE, family name of **Baron Braybrooke.**

NEVILLE, Prof. Adam Matthew, TD 1963; FEng 1986; FRSE 1979; arbitrator and consultant on concrete and structural design and failures; Director, A & M Neville Engineering Ltd, since 1975; Principal and Vice-Chancellor, University of Dundee, 1978–87; *b* 5 Feb. 1923; *m* 1952, Mary Hallam Cousins; one *s* one *d*. BSc 1st cl. Hons, MSc, PhD, DSc (Eng) London; DSc Leeds; FICE, FIStructE, FCIArb. Served War; Major RE (TA), 1950–63. Lectr, Southampton Univ., 1950–51; Engr, Min. of Works, NZ, 1951–54; Lectr, Manchester Univ., 1955–60; Prof. of Civil Engrg, Nigerian Coll. of Technology, 1960–62; Dean of Engrg, Calgary Univ., 1963–67, also Dean of Graduate Studies, 1965–66; Vis. Prof., Swiss Federal Inst. of Technology, 1967–68; Prof. and Head of Dept of Civil Engineering, Univ. of Leeds, 1968–78. Chm., Cttee of Principals of Scottish Univs, 1984–86. Former Chm., Permanent Concrete Commn, RILEM (Internat. Union of Testing and Res. Labs for Materials and Structures); Dir, Petroleum Recovery Res. Inst.; Advr to Canadian Govt on management of concrete research. Member Council: Concrete Soc., 1968–77, (Pres., 1974–75); IStructE, 1976–79; Faculty of Building, 1976–80; Fellowship of Engrg, 1989–; Open University, 1979–87; Council of Europe Standing Conference on Univ. Problems, 1980–87 (Pres., 1984–86); Member: Bd, Architectural Educn, ARC, 1980–87; Exec. Cttee, IUPC, 1979–90 (Vice-Chm., 1983–85); British Library Adv. Council, 1989–; SERC Envmt Cttee, 1988–; Athlone-Vanier Fellowships Bd, 1990–. Mem. Editorial Boards of various technical jls. Fellow, Amer. Concrete Inst., 1973, Hon. Mem., 1986; Hon. Fellow: Inst. of Concrete Technologists, 1976; Singapore Concrete Inst., 1987; Hon. For. Mem., Académie Royale des Sciences d'Outre-Mer, Belgium, 1974. Hon. LLD St Andrews, 1987. IStructE Research Award, 1960; Reinforced Concrete Assoc. Medal, 1961; Senior Research Fellowship, Nat. Research Council of Canada, 1967. Stanton Walker Award (US) 1968; Medal of Univ. of Liège (Belgium), 1970; Arthur R. Anderson Award, Amer. Concrete Inst., 1972; President's Medal, Soc. of Engrs, 1985. OStJ 1983. *Publications:* Properties of Concrete, 1963, 3 edns, trans. into 10 languages; (with J. B. Kennedy) Basic Statistical Methods, 1964, 3 edns; Creep of Concrete: plain, reinforced and prestressed, 1970; (with A. Ghali) Structural Analysis: a unified classical and matrix approach, 1971, 3rd edn 1989, trans. into Chinese; Hardened Concrete: physical and mechanical aspects, 1971; High Alumina Cement Concrete, 1975; (with W. H. Dilger and J. J. Brooks) Creep of Plain and Structural Concrete, 1983; (with J. J. Brooks) Concrete Technology, 1987; numerous research papers on concrete and concrete structures. *Recreations:* ski-ing, travel (Travelers' Century Club Plaque, 1990). *Address:* 24 Gun Wharf, 130 Wapping High Street, E1 9NH. *T:* 071–265 1087. *Clubs:* Athenæum; New (Edinburgh).

NEVILLE, Prof. (Alexander) Munro, MD; FRCPath; Research Secretary and Administrator, Ludwig Institute for Cancer Research, since 1985; *b* 24 March 1935; *s* of Alexander Munro and Georgina Neville; *m* 1961, Anne Margaret Stroyan Black; one *s* one *d*. *Educ:* Hillhead High Sch.; Univ. of Glasgow (MB ChB 1959; PhD 1965; MD 1969); Harvard Med. Sch.; DSc London, 1985. MRCPath 1969, FRCPath 1981. Med. appts, Glasgow Royal and Victoria Infirmaries, 1960–65; Res. Fellow, Harvard Med. Sch., 1965–67; Sen. Lectr in Pathology, Univ. of Glasgow, 1967–70; Hon. Consultant Pathologist, Royal Marsden Hosp., 1970–85; Prof. of Experimental Pathology, Univ. of London, 1972–85; Dean, Inst. of Cancer Research, 1982–84; Dir, Ludwig Inst. for Cancer Research, London Branch, 1975–85. *Publications:* The Human Adrenal Cortex, 1982; numerous papers on oncology and pathology in primary jls. *Recreations:* golf, gardening. *Address:* (office) Hedges House, 153–155 Regent Street, W1R 7FD; 6 Woodlands Park, Tadworth, Surrey KT20 7TL. *T:* Tadworth (0737) 844113. *Clubs:* Athenæum; Banstead Downs.

NEVILLE, (Eric) Graham; His Honour Judge Neville; a Circuit Judge, since 1980; *b* 12 Nov. 1933; *s* of late Frederick Thomas Neville and Doris Winifred (*née* Toye); *m* 1966, Jacqueline Catherine, *d* of late Major Francis Whalley and Alexandrina Whalley (*née* MacLeod). *Educ:* Kelly Coll.; Sidney Sussex Coll., Cambridge. Served Royal Air Force, General Duties. Called to Bar, Middle Temple, 1958. A Recorder of the Crown Court, 1975–80. *Recreations:* sailing, fishing. *Address:* Trillow House, Nadderwater, Exeter EX4 2LD. *T:* Exeter (0392) 54403. *Clubs:* Royal Western Yacht (Plymouth); Royal Fowey Yacht.

NEVILLE, John, OBE 1965; actor, stage and film; Hon. Professor in Drama, Nottingham University, since 1967; Artistic Director, Festival Theatre, Stratford, Ontario, 1985–89; *b* Willesden, 2 May 1925; *s* of Reginald Daniel Neville and Mabel Lillian (*née* Fry); *m* 1949, Caroline Hooper; three *s* three *d*. *Educ:* Willesden and Chiswick County Schools; Royal Academy of Dramatic Art. Worked as a stores clerk before studying at RADA.

First appearance on stage, walking-on part in Richard II; subseq. parts at Open Air Theatre, in repertory at Lowestoft, and with Birmingham Repertory Co.; Bristol Old Vic Co., 1950–53; Old Vic Co., London, 1953–61; Nottingham Playhouse, 1961–63; Theatre Director, Nottingham Playhouse, 1963–68; Dir, Park Theatre Co., Fortune, 1969; Theatre Director: Citadel Theatre, Edmonton, Canada, 1973–78; Neptune Theatre, Halifax, NS, 1978–83. Parts with Old Vic include: Ferdinand in The Tempest, Macduff, Richard II, Orlando in As You Like It, Henry Percy in Henry IV, Part I, Mark Antony; during Old Vic tour of Europe, 1958, Hamlet, Sir Andrew Aguecheek. Played lead in Irma La Douce, Lyric, 1959–60; produced Henry V, Old Vic, 1960; The Lady From the Sea, Queen's, 1961; The School for Scandal, Haymarket, 1962; Alfie, Mermaid and Duchess, 1963. Acted in: The Chichester Festival Theatre, 1962; Beware of the Dog, St Martin's, 1967; Iago in Othello, Nottingham Playhouse, 1967; Mr and Mrs, Palace, 1968; The Apple Cart, Mermaid, 1970; The Beggar's Opera, The Doctor's Dilemma, Chichester, 1972; Sherlock Holmes, NY, 1975; Happy Days, Nat. Theatre, 1977; Grand Theatre, London, Ontario: acted in Dear Antoine and Arsenic and Old Lace, directed Hamlet, 1983; Stratford, Ontario: acted in Loves Labours' Lost, 1983, Merchant of Venice, 1984, Intimate Admiration, 1987, My Fair Lady, 1988; directed Mother Courage, and Othello, 1987, Three Sisters, 1989; acted in The School for Scandal, NT, 1990. Tour W Africa (Jt Dir and acting), 1963. *Films:* Oscar Wilde; Topaze; Billy Budd; A Study in Terror; Adventures of Baron of Munchausen. Has appeared on television, incl. The First Churchills, series for BBC 2. Hon. Dr Dramatic Arts Lethbridge Univ., 1979; Hon. DFA Nova Scotia Coll. of Art and Design, 1981. *Address:* 99 Norman Street, Stratford, Ont N5A 5R8, Canada. *Club:* Savage.

NEVILLE, (John) Oliver, MA, PhD; Principal, Royal Academy of Dramatic Art, since 1984; *b* 14 Aug. 1929; *s* of Frederick and Ethel Neville; *m* 1st, 1952, Shirley Hall; one *s* one *d*; 2nd, 1964, Pat Heywood. *Educ:* Price's Sch., Fareham; King's Coll., Cambridge (Le Bas Student; BA Eng. Lit., MA, PhD). After National Service, engaged in following with ultimate aim of becoming a theatre director: studied theatre design under Reginald Leefe, 1949–51; joined Old Vic Co., walking on in Tyrone Guthrie's Tamburlaine, with Donald Wolfit, 1951; studied singing with Clive Carey and Frank Titterton; seasons of rep. at York, Scarborough, Worthing, Bristol, Birmingham and Manchester, 1952–58; re-joined Old Vic Co., 1958 (roles included Warwick in Henry VI Trilogy and Claudius in Hamlet); toured America, Poland, Russia, India, Pakistan, Ceylon, with Old Vic and Bristol Old Vic, as stage dir, actor and dir; Associate Dir, Old Vic Co., 1960–62 (directed Macbeth and The Tempest); Director: Library Theatre, Manchester, 1963–66; Arts Theatre, Ipswich, 1966–69; Mature Student, Cambridge, 1969–76 (PhD on Ben Jonson's Masques and Poetry); Caroline Spurgeon Res. Fellow, Bedford Coll., London, 1977–79; Sen. Lectr in Drama, Univ. of Bristol, 1979–84. *Recreations:* mediaeval church architecture and stained-glass, gardening. *Address:* Royal Academy of Dramatic Art, 62–64 Gower Street, WC1E 6ED. *T:* 071–636 7076.

NEVILLE, Munro; *see* Neville, A. M.

NEVILLE, Air Vice-Marshal Patrick, CB 1988; OBE 1976; AFC 1960; Chief of Air Staff, Royal New Zealand Air Force, 1986–89, retired; *b* 23 Sept. 1932; *s* of Patrick Joseph Neville and Helena Neville; *m* 1954, Barbara Howell; one *s* one *d*. *Educ:* Purbrook Park County High Sch. (SchCert). Commnd 1951; Navigator: RAF, 1951–55; RNZAF, 1955; CO No 14 Sqdn RNZAF, 1966–69; Base Comdr, RNZAF Base Ohakea, NZ, 1969–70; Hon. ADC to Gov. Gen., 1972; Sen. ASO, Air HQ, ANZUK Force Singapore; later, Dep. Comdr NZ Force SE Asia in Singapore, 1973–75; RNZAF Air Staff, 1975–77; Base Comdr, RNZAF Base Auckland, 1978–79; AOC RNZAF Support Gp, 1980–82; Asst CDS for Operations and Plans, Defence HQ, Wellington, 1982–83; Hd of NZ Defence Liaison Staff, London, 1984–86. Gp Captain 1973, Air Cdre 1980, Air Vice-Marshal 1986. FNZIM; FRAeS. *Recreations:* golf, fishing. *Address:* 12 Mark Place, Lynmore, Rotorua, New Zealand. *T:* 459650. *Clubs:* Wellington (Wellington); Wellington Golf, Rotorua Golf.

NEVILLE, Sir Richard (Lionel John Baines), 3rd Bt *cr* 1927; *b* 15 July 1921; *s* of Sir Reginald James Neville Neville, 1st Bt (*d* 1950), and Violet Sophia Mary (*d* 1972), *widow* of Captain Richard Jocelyn Hunter, Rifle Bde and *d* of Lt-Col Cuthbert Johnson Baines, Gloucester Regt, The Lawn, Shirehampton, Glos; *S* half-brother, 1982; unmarried. *Educ:* Eton; Trinity Coll., Cambridge (BA 1941, MA 1948). Served War of 1939–45: joined Army, 1941; Captain, Oxford and Bucks Light Infantry; seconded Royal West African Frontier Force (1st Gold Coast Regt), Burma Campaign, 1944–45. Journalist and Director of English Broadcasts of Radio-Télévision Française (RTF), Indochina, 1953–55; Dir of Foreign Broadcasts, RTF (English, Spanish and Portuguese), French Equatorial Africa (Congo), 1956–57; Algeria, 1957–60. Master, Worshipful Co. of Bowyers, 1972–74. *Recreations:* history, genealogy, heraldry and supporting lost causes. *Heir:* none. *Address:* Sloley Hall, Norwich NR12 8HA. *T:* Swanton Abbott (069269) 236.

NEVILLE, Roger Albert Gartside, VRD 1965; FCA; Group Chief Executive, Sun Alliance Group, since 1987; *b* 23 Dec. 1931; *s* of Geoffrey Graham Gartside Neville and Veronica Lily Neville; *m* 1957, Brenda Mary Parke Hamilton; one *s* three *d*. Royal Navy, 1950–52; joined Sun Alliance Insurance, 1962; General Manager, 1977; Dep. Chief General Manager, 1984. *Recreations:* sailing, fly fishing, cabinet making. *Address:* Sun Alliance Insurance Group, 1 Bartholomew Lane, EC2N 2AB. *T:* 071–588 2345. *Clubs:* Royal Automobile, Royal Ocean Racing.

NEVILLE, Royce Robert; Agent-General for Tasmania, in London, 1971–78; Governing Director, Neville Constructions Pty Ltd, Burnie; *b* 5 Oct. 1914; *s* of R. P. Neville, Launceston, Tasmania; *m* 1941, Joan, *d* of G. A. Scott; two *s* two *d*. *Educ:* Launceston Technical Coll. Served War, Sqdn Ldr (OC Flying, Chief Flying Instr, Gen Reconnaissance Sqdn), RAAF, 1941–45. OC Air Trg Corps, Burnie, 1947. Past President: Air Force Assoc., 1947; Tas. Apex, 1948; Tas. Master Builders' Assoc., 1965–67; Master Builders' Fedn of Aust., 1965–66; Comr of Oaths for Tasmania, 1971; Mem., Australia Soc., London; Life Mem., Tasmanian Master Builders' Assoc. FInstD, FRAIB, AFAIM, Fellow, Inst. of Dirs, Aust., 1971; MIEx 1973; FFB 1976; FIArb 1977. Freeman, City of London, 1975; Freeman, Guild of Air Pilots and Air Navigators, 1976. JP 1974. *Recreations:* boating, fishing, painting. *Address:* 57 Illabunda Drive, Malua Bay, NSW 2536, Australia. *Clubs:* Wig and Pen; Naval, Military and Air Force (Hobart).

NEVILLE-JONES, (Lilian) Pauline, CMG 1987; HM Diplomatic Service; Deputy Under Secretary, Cabinet Office (on secondment), since 1991; *b* 2 Nov. 1939; *d* of Roland Neville-Jones and Cecilia Emily Millicent Rath. *Educ:* Leeds Girls' High Sch.; Lady Margaret Hall, Oxford (BA Hons Mod. History). Harkness Fellow of Commonwealth Fund, USA, 1961–63; joined FO, 1963; Third Sec., Salisbury, Rhodesia, 1964–65; Third, later Second Sec., Singapore, 1965–68; FCO, 1968–71; First Sec., Washington, 1971–75; FCO, 1975–77; Mem. Cabinet, later Chef de Cabinet to Christopher Tugendhat, European Comr for Budget, Financial Control, Financial Instns and Taxation, 1977–82; Vis. Fellow, RIIA, and Inst. français des relations internationales, 1982–83; Head of Planning Staff, FCO, 1983–87; Minister (Econ.), 1987–88, Minister, 1988–91, Bonn. FRSA 1986. *Recreations:* antiques, cooking, gardening. *Address:* Cabinet Office, 70 Whitehall, SW1A 2AS.

NEVILLE-ROLFE, Marianne Teresa, (Mrs D. W. J. Blake); Chief Executive and Principal, Civil Service College, and Under Secretary, Cabinet Office (Office of the Minister for the Civil Service), since 1990; *b* 9 Oct 1944; *d* of Edmund Neville-Rolfe and Margaret (*née* Evans); *m* 1972, David William John Blake. *Educ:* St Mary's Convent, Shaftesbury; Lady Margaret Hall, Oxford (BA). CBI, 1965–73 (Head, Brussels Office, 1971–72); Principal, DTI, 1973, Asst Sec., 1982, Under Sec., Internal European Policy Div., 1987. *Recreations:* travel, opera. *Address:* Sunningdale Park, Ascot, Berks SL5 0QE. *T:* Ascot (0344) 23444.

NEVIN, His Honour (Thomas) Richard, TD 1949 (and Bar); JP; LLB; retired 1984, as senior Circuit Judge on NE Circuit; a Judge of County Courts, later a Circuit Judge, 1967–84; a Deputy High Court Judge, 1974–84; Hon. Life Member, Council of HM Circuit Judges; *b* 9 Dec. 1916; *e s* of late Thomas Nevin, JP, and Phyllis (*née* Strickland), Ebchester Hall and Mirfield; *m* 1955, Brenda Micaela (marr. diss. 1979), *e d* of Dr B. C. Andrade-Thompson, MC, Scarborough; one *s* (and one *s* decd). *Educ:* Bilton Grange; Shrewsbury School; Leeds University. LLB 1939. 2nd Lt, W Yorks Regt (Leeds Rifles) TA, 1935. Served London Bombardment, India and Burma, 1939–46; Indian Artillery, Lt-Col 1944 (despatches), SEAC; DJAG, XII Army, 1945. Major, TARO, 1951. WR Special Constab., 1938–66. Articled Clerk to Sir A. M. Ramsden, CB, Solicitor, 1935. Called to Bar, Inner Temple, 1948; practised 19 years on NE Circuit (Junior, 1951); Law Lectr, Leeds Coll. of Commerce, 1949–51; Asst Recorder of Leeds, 1961–64; Recorder of Doncaster, 1964–67; Dep. Chm., Quarter Sessions: W Riding, 1965–71; E Riding, 1968–71, Yorkshire; Chm., Northern Agricultural Land Tribunal, 1963–67 (Dep. Chm. 1961–63); a special Divorce Comr, 1967–72; Mem., County Court Rule Cttee, 1974–80; Chm., Lord Chancellor's Adv. Cttee on JP's, Hull, 1968–74; apptd by Minister of Transport to conduct enquiries under Merchant Shipping Acts, 1986–89. Founder Chm., Leeds Family Mediation Service, 1979–84. Director, Bowishott Estates Ltd; Member: Leeds Gp Hospital Management Cttee, 1965–67; Thoresby Soc.; Yorks Archæological Soc.; President, Yorks Numismatic Soc., 1968; Life Mem., Guild of Freemen of London; Vice-Pres. Leeds Univ. Law Graduates; Mem., Leeds Univ. Adv. Cttee on Law. FRNS; FRSA; FCIArb. Freeman of City of London. JP West Yorks 1965–. *Publications:* Hon. Editor, Yorkshire Numismatic Soc.; and various articles. *Recreations:* coinage, our past, retirement, and rest. *Address:* The Court House, 1 Oxford Row, Leeds; 11 King's Bench Walk, Temple, EC4.

NEW, Maj.-Gen. Sir Laurence (Anthony Wallis), Kt 1990; CB 1986; CBE 1980; Lieutenant Governor of the Isle of Man, and President of the Tynwald Court, 1985–90; General Secretary, Officers' Pensions Society Ltd, since 1990; International President, Association of Christian Military Fellowships, since 1991; *b* 25 Feb. 1932; *s* of Lt-Col S. W. New, MBE and Mrs C. M. New; *m* 1956, Anna Doreen Verity; two *s* two *d*. *Educ:* King William's College, Isle of Man; RMA Sandhurst, 1950–52; commissioned, RTR, 1952; service in Hong Kong, Germany, Malaya, Borneo; CO 4 RTR, 1971–73; Bde Major, 20th Armd Bde, 1969–70; Sec., Defence Policy Staff, 1970–71; Defence and Military Attaché, Tel Aviv, 1974–77; Col GS, MoD, 1977–79; Brig. GS, MoD, 1981–82; ACGS (Op. Reqs), 1983–84; ACDS (Land Systems), MoD, 1984–85; graduate Staff Coll., JSSC, RCDS. Col Comdt, RTR, 1986–; Vice Pres., TA&VRA, 1985–90. Licenced Reader, C of E; Church Warden, St Peter upon Cornhill, 1986–; Pres., Soldiers' and Airmen's Scripture Readers Assoc., 1985–; Vice Pres., Officers' Christian Union, 1988–. County Pres., St John Ambulance Brigade and Assoc., 1985–90; Patron, I of M Red Cross, 1985–90; President: Manx Music Fest., 1985–90; Mananan Internat. Fest. of Music and the Arts, 1986–90; Sunninghill Comrades Club, 1991–; Chairman: Bishop Barrow's Trustees, 1985–90; Royal Jubilee and Prince's Trust (I of M), 1986–90; Pres., White House School, Wokingham, 1985–. Freeman, City of London, 1985; Liveryman, Glass Sellers' Co., 1985. FBIM 1979; CBIM 1986. KStJ 1986. *Recreations:* music, water colour painting, walking. *Club:* Army and Navy.

NEW WESTMINSTER, Archbishop of, since 1981; **Most Rev. Douglas Walter Hambidge,** DD; Metropolitan of the Ecclesiastical Province of British Columbia, since 1981; *b* London, England, 6 March 1927; *s* of Douglas Hambidge and Florence (*née* Driscoll); *m* 1956, Denise Colvill Lown; two *s* one *d*. *Educ:* London Univ.; London Coll. of Divinity. BD, ALCD; DD, Anglican Theol. Coll. of BC, 1970. Asst Curate, St Mark's, Dalston, 1953–56; Rector: All Saints, Cassiar, BC, 1956–58; St James, Smithers, BC, 1958–64; Vicar, St Martin, Fort St John, BC, 1964–69; Canon, St Andrew's Cathedral, Caledonia, 1965–69; Bishop of Caledonia, 1969–80; Bishop of New Westminster, 1980. Mem., ACC, 1990– (Mem., Standing Cttee). Pres., Missions to Seamen, 1980–; Mem. Bd of Governors, Vancouver Sch. of Theology, 1980–85. *Address:* #302–814 Richards Street, Vancouver, BC V6B 3A7, Canada. *T:* (604) 684–6306. *Clubs:* Vancouver, Arbutus (Vancouver).

NEW ZEALAND, Primate and Archbishop of, since 1986; **Most Rev. Brian Newton Davis;** Bishop of Wellington, since 1986; *b* 28 Oct. 1934; *s* of Leonard Lancelot and Ethel May Davis; *m* 1961, Marie Lynette Waters: four *d*. *Educ:* Stratford Primary and Technical High School; Ardmore Teachers' Training Coll., Auckland; Victoria Univ. of Wellington (MA 1st class Hons Geog.); Christchurch Theol Coll. (LTh). Teacher, Stratford Primary School, 1954; Laboratory Asst, Victoria Univ., 1958. Deacon 1960, priest 1961; Assistant Curate: St Mark's, Wellington, 1960–62; Parish of Karori West and Makara, 1962–64; Vicar: Karon West and Makara, 1964–67; Dannevirke, 1967–73; Cathedral Parish of St John the Evangelist and Dean of Waiapu, 1973; Vicar General of Waiapu, 1979–80; Bishop of Waikato, 1980–86. *Publication:* (contrib.) An Encyclopaedia of New Zealand, 1966. *Recreations:* tennis, wood carving and turning, water colour painting. *Address:* Bishopscourt, PO Box 12–046, Wellington, New Zealand.

NEWALL, family name of **Baron Newall.**

NEWALL, 2nd Baron, *cr* 1946; **Francis Storer Eaton Newall;** DL; company director and Chairman of several companies; Chairman, British Greyhound Racing Board, since 1985; *b* 23 June 1930; *o s* of 1st Baron (Marshal of the RAF Lord) Newall, GCB, OM, GCMG, CBE, AM; *S* father, 1963; *m* 1956, Pamela Elizabeth, *e d* of E. H. L. Rowcliffe, Pinkney Park, Malmesbury, Wilts; two *s* one *d*. *Educ:* Eton College; RMA Sandhurst. Commissioned into 11th Hussars (Prince Albert's Own), 1950; served in: Germany, 1950–53; Malaya, 1953–55; on staff of GHQ FarELF, Singapore, 1955–56; Adjt Royal Gloucestershire Hussars, 1956–58; retired 1961. Introduced Farriers Registration Acts and Betting Gaming and Lotteries Amendment Acts (Greyhound Racing) in House of Lords. Cons. Whip and front bench spokesman, 1976–79; Founder Mem., House of Lords all party Defence Study Group; official visits to NATO, SHAPE, Norway, Morocco, Bonn, Cyprus, BAOR, Qatar, Oman, Bahrain and Romania; Deleg. to Council of Europe and WEU, 1983. Mem., Select Cttee on Laboratory Animals Protection Bill. Hon. Pres., Corp. of Insurance and Financial Advisors (formerly Corp. of Mortgage Brokers). Mem., Merchant Taylors' Co (Master, 1985–86). DL Greater London, 1988. *Recreations:* shooting, travel, meeting people. *Heir:* *s* Hon. Richard Hugh Eaton Newall, *b* 19 Feb.

1961. *Address:* 18 Lennox Gardens, SW1X 0DG; Wotton Underwood, near Aylesbury, Bucks. *Club:* Cavalry and Guards.

NEWALL, Paul Henry, TD 1967; DL; Director, Shearson Lehman International Ltd, since 1985; *b* 17 Sept. 1934; *s* of late Leopold Newall and Frances Evelyn Newall (*née* Bean); *m* 1969, Penelope Moyra, *o d* of Sir Julian Ridsdale, *qv*; two *s*. *Educ:* Harrow; Magdalene Coll., Cambridge (MA Econs). Nat. Service, commnd Royal Fusiliers, 1953–55; TA 1955–70, Major. Partner, Loeb Rhoades & Co. (mem., NY Stock Exchange), 1971; Overseas Director: Shearson Loeb Rhoades Inc., 1978; Shearson Lehman American Express (UK) Hldgs, 1981; Exec. Dir, Lehman Brothers Securities, 1990–. Mem., Adv. Cttee, Energy Internat. NV, 1978–. City of London: Mem., Court of Common Council, 1980–81; Alderman, Ward of Walbrook, 1981–; Sheriff, 1989–90; Chm., City of London TAVRA, 1986–89; Vice-Chm., TA&VRA for Gtr London, 1989–; Master, Bakers' Co., 1990–91; Mem. Court, Guild of Freemen, 1988–; Liveryman, Gold and Silver Wyre Drawers' Co., 1980–. Vice-Pres., City of London Sector, British Red Cross, 1986–; Governor: MENCAP City Foundn, 1982–; City of London Boys' Sch., 1985–86; City of London Freemen's Sch., 1987–88; Patron, Samaritans Nat. Appeal, 1989–. One of HM Lieutenants of City of London, 1975; DL Gtr London, 1977; JP City of London, 1981; Hon. Vis. Magistrate, HM Tower of London. OStJ 1989. Churchwarden, St Stephen's, Walbrook. *Recreations:* fencing, fly fishing, shooting, water-skiing, tennis, trees. *Address:* (office) One Broadgate, EC2M 7HA. *T:* 071–260 2667. *Clubs:* City Livery, United Wards, Walbrook Ward (Pres.), MCC.

NEWARK, Archdeacon of; *see* Hawtin, Ven. D. C.

NEWBERRY, Raymond Scudamore, OBE 1989; Director, British Council in Brazil, since 1990; *b* 8 Feb. 1935; *s* of James Henry Newberry and late Doris Ada Newberry; *m* 1967, Angelina Nanca; one *s* one *d*. *Educ:* Bristol Grammar Sch.; Selwyn Coll., Cambridge (BA); Univ. of Leeds (DipESL); Univ. of Bristol (DipEd). National Service, 1953–55. Lectr, Coll. of Arts, Baghdad Univ., 1959–62; joined British Council, 1962; Lectr, Teheran, 1963–64; Educn Officer, Calcutta, 1964–66; Head of English Dept, Advanced Teacher Trng Coll., Winneba, Ghana, 1966–70; Advr on English Lang., Min. of Educn, Singapore, 1970–74; Rep., Colombia, 1975–80; Director: North and Latin American Dept, 1980–82; America and Pacific Dept, 1982–84; Rep., Australia, 1984–89. *Publication:* (with A. Maley) Between You and Me, 1974. *Recreations:* bookbinding, golf. *Address:* c/o The British Council, 10 Spring Gardens, SW1A 2BN. *T:* 071–930 8466.

NEWBERY, Prof. David Michael Garrood, FBA 1991; Professor of Economics and Director of Department of Applied Economics, Cambridge, since 1988; Fellow, Churchill College, Cambridge, since 1966; *b* 1 June 1943; *s* of Alan James Garrood Newbery and Betty Amelia Newbery; *m* 1975, Dr Terri Eve Apter; two *d*. *Educ:* Portsmouth Grammar Sch.; Trinity Coll., Cambridge (BA, MA, PhD). Economist, Treasury, Tanzania, 1965–66; Cambridge University: Asst Lectr, 1966–71; Lectr, 1971–86; Reader, 1986–88. Associate Prof., Stanford Univ., 1976–77; Div. Chief, World Bank, Washington, 1981–83; Vis. Prof., Princeton, 1985; Vis. Scholar, IMF, 1987; Ford Vis. Prof., Univ. of California, Berkeley, 1987–88. Mem. Council, REconS, 1984–; Fellow: Centre for Economic Policy Res., 1984–; Econometric Soc., 1989 (Frisch Medal, 1990). Bd Mem, Review of Economic Studies, 1968–79; Associate Editor: Economic Jl, 1977–; European Economic Review, 1988–. *Publications:* Project Appraisal in Practice, 1976; (with J. E. Stiglitz) The Theory of Commodity Price Stabilization, 1981; (with N. H. Stern) The Theory of Taxation for Developing Countries, 1987; articles in learned jls. *Address:* 9 Huntingdon Road, Cambridge. *T:* Cambridge (0223) 60216.

NEWBIGGING, David Kennedy, OBE 1982; Chairman: Rentokil PLC, since 1987 (Director, since 1986); NM UK Ltd, since 1990; Ivory & Sime plc, since 1992 (Director, since 1987; Deputy Chairman, 1990–91); *b* 19 Jan. 1934; *s* of late David Locke Newbigging, CBE, MC, and Lucy Margaret; *m* 1968, Carolyn Susan (*née* Band); one *s* two *d*. *Educ:* in Canada; Oundle Sch., Northants. Joined Jardine, Matheson & Co. Ltd, Hong Kong, 1954; Dir, 1967; Man. Dir, 1970; Chm. and Sen. Man. Dir, 1975–83; Chairman: Hongkong & Kowloon Wharf & Godown Co. Ltd, 1970–80; Jardine Matheson & Co. Ltd, 1975–83; Jardine Fleming Holdings Ltd, 1975–83; Hongkong Land Co. Ltd, 1975–83; Hongkong Electric Holdings Ltd, 1982–83 (Dir, 1975–83); Redfearn PLC, 1988; Dep. Chm., Provincial Gp plc, 1985–91 (Dir, 1984–); Director: Hongkong & Shanghai Banking Corp., 1975–83; Hong Kong Telephone Co., 1975–83; Safmarine and Rennies Holdings (formerly Rennies Consolidated Holdings), 1975–85; PACCAR (UK) Ltd, 1986–; Internat. Financial Markets Trading Ltd, 1986–; United Meridian Corp., USA, 1987–; Faupel Trading Gp, 1989–; Provincial Insurance, 1984–86; Provincial Life Insurance Co., 1984–86; CIN Management, 1985–87. Dir, British Coal Corp. (formerly NCB), 1984–87. Mem., Internat. Council, Morgan Guaranty Trust Co. of NY, 1977–85. Vice Chm. Council, and Chm. Gen. Cttee, Missions to Seamen, 1986–. Chm. of Trustees, Wilts Community Foundn, 1991–. Member: Hong Kong Exec. Council, 1980–84; Hong Kong Legislative Council, 1978–82. Chairman: Hong Kong Tourist Assoc., 1977–82; Hong Kong Gen. Chamber of Commerce, 1980–82; Steward, Royal Hong Kong Jockey Club, 1975–84. JP (unofficial) Hong Kong, 1971. *Recreations:* most outdoor sports; Chinese art. *Address:* 26 Little Chester Street, SW1X 7AP. *T:* 071–823 2545. *Clubs:* Boodle's, Turf, Hurlingham; Hongkong (Hong Kong).

NEWBIGIN, Rt. Rev. (James Edward) Lesslie, CBE 1974; DD; Minister, United Reformed Church, Winson Green, since 1980; *b* 8 Dec. 1909; *s* of Edward Richmond Newbigin, Shipowner, Newcastle, and Annie Ellen Newbigin (*née* Affleck); *m* 1936, Helen Stewart, *d* of Rev. Robert Henderson; one *s* three *d*. *Educ:* Leighton Park Sch.; Queens' Coll., Cambridge; Westminster Coll., Cambridge. Intercollegiate Secretary, Student Christian Movement, Glasgow, 1931–33. Ordained by Presbytery of Edinburgh and appointed to Madras Mission of Church of Scotland, 1936; served as missionary in Chingleput and Kancheepuram, 1936–46; Bishop in Madura and Ramnad, Church of South India, 1947. Chairman, Advisory Cttee on Main Theme for Second Assembly, World Council of Churches, 1954; Vice-Chairman, Commission on Faith and Order, 1956; Chairman, International Missionary Council, 1958. Resigned from See of Madura, 1959. General Secretary, International Missionary Council, 1959; Associate General Secretary, World Council of Churches, 1961–65; Bishop in Madras, 1965–74; Lectr in Theology, Selly Oak Colls, Birmingham, 1974–79. Moderator, Gen. Assembly of URC, 1978. Hon. DD: Chicago Theological Seminary, 1954; St Andrews Univ., 1958; Hamburg, 1960; Basel, 1965; Hull, 1975; Newcastle, 1981. *Publications:* Christian Freedom in the Modern World, 1937; The Reunion of the Church, 1948; South India Diary, 1951; The Household of God, 1953; Sin and Salvation, 1956; A Faith for This One World?, 1962; Honest Religion for Secular Man, 1966; The Finality of Christ, 1969; The Good Shepherd, 1977; The Open Secret, 1978; The Light has come, 1982; The Other Side of 1984, 1983; Unfinished Agenda, 1985; Foolishness to the Greeks, 1986; The Gospel in a Pluralist Society, 1989. *Recreations:* music, walking. *Address:* 15 Fox Hill, Birmingham B29 4AG.

NEWBOLD, Sir Charles Demorée, KBE 1970; Kt 1966; CMG 1957; QC (Jamaica) 1947; President, Court of Appeal for East Africa, 1966–70; *b* 11 June 1909; *s* of late Charles Etches and Laura May Newbold; *m* 1936, Ruth, *d* of Arthur L. Vaughan; two *d*. *Educ:* The Lodge Sch., Barbados; Keble Coll., Oxford (BA). Called to Bar, Gray's Inn, 1931. Private practice at the Bar, Trinidad, 1931–35; joined Colonial Legal Service, 1936, as Principal Officer, Supreme Court Registry, Trinidad; Magistrate, Trinidad, 1937; Legal Draftsman, Jamaica, 1941; Solicitor-General Jamaica, 1943; Member of Commission of Enquiry into Land Taxation, Jamaica, 1942–43; represented Jamaica at Quarantine Conf. in Trinidad, 1943; at US Bases Conf. in Trinidad, 1944; at Washington, USA, for labour contracts, 1945; Actg Attorney-Gen., 1946; Legal Secretary, East Africa High Commn, 1948–61. Mem. of East Africa Central Legislative Assembly, 1948–61 (Chm. of Committee of Supply, 1948–61); Commissioner for Revision of High Commn Laws, 1951; Vice-Chm. Governing Council of Royal Technical Coll., 1954–59; Justice of Appeal, Court of Appeal for Eastern Africa, 1961–65; Vice-Pres., 1965–66. Star of Africa (Liberia). *Publications:* Joint Editor of Trinidad Law Reports, 1928–33; Editor of East African Tax Cases Reports, 1948–61. *Recreations:* cricket, tennis, croquet, reading. *Address:* 7 St Mary's Garden, Chichester, W Sussex PO19 1NY.

NEWBOROUGH, 7th Baron, *cr* 1776; **Robert Charles Michael Vaughan Wynn,** Bt 1742; DSC 1942; *b* 24 April 1917; *er s* of 6th Baron Newborough, OBE, JP, DL, and Ruby Irene (*d* 1960), 3rd *d* of Edmund Wigley Severne, of Thenford, Northamptonshire and Wallop, Shropshire; *S* father, 1965; *m* 1st, 1945, Rosamund Lavington Barbour (marr. diss. 1971); one *s* two *d*; 2nd, 1971, Jennifer, *y d* of late Captain C. C. A. Allen, RN, and Lady Morgan. *Educ:* Oundle. Served as 2nd Lt, SR, 1935–39, with 9th Lancers, 5th Inniskilling Dragoon Guards, then as Lt with 16th/5th Lancers after 6 months attachment with Royal Dragoon Guards; invalided out of Army, 1940. Took command of vessel attached to Fleet Air Arm, 1940, as civilian, and took part in Dunkirk evacuation; then joined RNVR as Sub Lieut; later had command of MTB 74 and took part in St Nazaire raid, 1942 (wounded, despatches, DSC, POW, escaped from Colditz 1944). High Sheriff of Merionethshire, 1963. *Recreation:* yachting. *Heir:* *s* Hon. Robert Vaughan Wynn [*b* 11 Aug. 1949; *m* 1st, 1981, Sheila Christine (marr. diss. 1988), *d* of William A. Massey; one *d*; 2nd, 1988, Mrs Susan Elizabeth Hall, *d* of late Andrew Francis Lloyd]. *Address:* Rhug, Corwen, Clwyd, North Wales. *T:* Corwen (0490) 2510. *Clubs:* Goat, Naval and Military.

NEWBURGH, 12th Earl of, *cr* 1660 (Scot.); **Don Filippo Giambattista Francesco Aldo Maria Rospigliosi;** Viscount Kynnaird, Baron Levingston, 1660; 11th Prince Rospigliosi (Holy Roman Empire), 11th Duke of Zagarolo, 14th Prince of Castiglione, Marquis of Giuliana, Count of Chiusa, Baron of La Miraglia and Valcorrente, Lord of Aidone, Burgio, Contessa and Trappeto, and Conscript Roman Noble, Patrician of Venice, Genoa and Pistoia; *b* 4 July 1942; *s* of 11th Earl of Newburgh and of Donna Giulia, *d* of Don Guido Carlo dei Duchi, Visconti di Mondrone, Count of Lonate Pozzolo; *S* father, 1986; *m* 1972, Baronessa Donna Luisa, *d* of Count Annibale Caccia Dominioni; one *d*. *Heir:* *d* Princess Donna Benedetta Francesca Maria Rospigliosi, *b* 4 June 1974. *Address:* Piazza Sant'Ambrogio 16, 20123 Milan, Italy.

NEWBY, (George) Eric, MC 1945; FRSL 1972; FRGS 1975; writer; *b* 6 Dec. 1919; *o s* of George Arthur Newby and Hilda Pomroy, London; *m* 1946, Wanda, *d* of Viktor Skof and Gisella Urdih, Trieste; one *s* one *d*. *Educ:* St Paul's School. With Dorland Advertising, London, 1936–38; apprentice and ord. seaman, 4-masted Finnish barque, Moshulu, 1938–39; served War of 1939–45, The Black Watch and Special Boat Section, POW 1942–45; Women's Fashion Business, 1946–56 (with Worth Paquin, 1955–56); explored in Nuristan and made unsuccessful attempt to climb Mir Samir, Afghan Hindu Kush, 1956; with Secker & Warburg, 1956–59; with John Lewis Partnership (Central Buyer, Model Dresses), 1959–63; descended Ganges with wife, 1963. Travel Editor, The Observer, and Gen. Editor, Time Off Books, 1964–73. Mem., Assoc. of Cape Horners. *Publications:* The Last Grain Race, 1956; A Short Walk in the Hindu Kush, 1958; Something Wholesale, 1962; Slowly Down the Ganges, 1966; Time Off in Southern Italy, 1966; Grain Race: Pictures of Life Before the Mast in a Windjammer, 1968; (jointly) The Wonders of Britain, 1968; (jointly) The Wonders of Ireland, 1969; Love and War in the Apennines, 1971; (jointly) The World of Evelyn Waugh, 1973; Ganga (with photographs by Raghubir Singh), 1973; World Atlas of Exploration, 1975; Great Ascents, 1977; The Big Red Train Ride, 1978; A Traveller's Life, 1982; On the Shores of the Mediterranean, 1984; A Book of Travellers' Tales, 1985; Round Ireland in Low Gear, 1987; What the Traveller Saw, 1989. *Recreations:* walking, running, cycling, gardening. *Address:* West Bucknowle House, Bucknowle, Wareham, Dorset BH20 5PQ. *T:* Corfe Castle (0929) 480374. *Club:* Garrick.

NEWBY, Prof. Howard Joseph; Chairman, Economic and Social Research Council, since 1988; *b* 10 Dec. 1947; *s* of Alfred Joseph Newby and Constance Annie (*née* Potts); *m* 1970, Janet Elizabeth (*née* Craddock); two *s*. *Educ:* John Port Grammar Sch., Etwall, Derbyshire; Atlantic Coll., St Donat's, Glamorgan; Univ. of Essex (BA, PhD). University of Essex: Lectr in Sociology, 1972–75; Sen. Lectr, 1975–79; Reader, 1979–83; Prof. of Sociology, 1983–88; Dir, ESRC Data Archive, 1983–88. Prof. of Sociology and Rural Sociology, Univ. of Wisconsin-Madison, 1980–83; visiting appointments: Univ. of NSW, 1976; Sydney, 1976; Newcastle upon Tyne, 1983–84. Mem., UFC, 1991–. *Publications:* (jtly) Community Studies, 1971; The Deferential Worker, 1977; (jtly) Property, Paternalism and Power, 1978; Green and Pleasant Land?, 1979, 2nd edn 1985; (jtly) The Problem of Sociology, 1983; (jtly) Approximación Teoretica a la Sociologia Rural, 1983; Country Life, 1987; The Countryside in Question, 1988; (jtly) Social Class in Modern Britain, 1988; *edited jointly:* The Sociology of Community, 1974; Doing Sociological Research, 1977; International Perspectives in Rural Sociology, 1978; The Rural Sociology of the Advanced Societies, 1980; Political Action and Social Identity, 1985; Restructuring Capital, 1985; over 50 papers in learned jls. *Recreations:* family life, gardening, Derby County and railway enthusiasms. *Address:* The Old Mill, Mill Lane, Corston, Malmesbury, Wilts SN16 0HH. *T:* Swindon (0793) 513838. *Club:* Athenæum.

NEWBY, Percy Howard, CBE 1972; novelist; *b* 25 June 1918; *o s* of Percy Newby and Isabel Clutsam Newby (*née* Bryant); *m* 1945, Joan Thompson; two *d*. *Educ:* Hanley Castle Grammar Sch., Worcester; St Paul's Coll., Cheltenham. Served War of 1939–45, RAMC, 1939–42; BEF, France, 1939–40; MEF, 1941–42; seconded as Lecturer in English Literature, Fouad 1st University, Cairo, 1942–46. Joined BBC, 1949; Controller: Third Programme, 1958–69; Radio Three, 1969–71; Dir of Programmes, Radio, 1971–75; Man. Dir, BBC Radio, 1975–78. Chm., English Stage Co., 1978–84. Atlantic Award, 1946; Somerset Maugham Prize, 1948; Yorkshire Post Fiction Award, 1968; Booker Prize, 1969 (first recipient). *Publications:* A Journey to the Interior, 1945; Agents and Witnesses, 1947; The Spirit of Jem, 1947; Mariner Dances, 1948; The Snow Pasture, 1949; The Loot Runners, 1949; Maria Edgeworth, 1950; The Young May Moon, 1950; The Novel, 1945–50, 1951; A Season in England, 1951; A Step to Silence, 1952; The Retreat, 1953; The Picnic at Sakkara, 1955; Revolution and Roses, 1957; Ten Miles from Anywhere, 1958; A Guest and his Going, 1959; The Barbary Light, 1962; One of the Founders, 1965; Something to Answer For, 1968; A Lot to Ask, 1973; Kith, 1977; (with F. Maroon) The Egypt Story, 1979; Warrior Pharaohs, 1980; Feelings Have Changed, 1981; Saladin in his Time, 1984; Leaning in the Wind, 1986; Coming in with the Tide, 1991. *Address:* Garsington House, Garsington, Oxford OX9 9AB. *T:* Garsington (086736) 420.

NEWBY, Richard Mark, OBE 1990; Executive, Rosehaugh plc, since 1988; *b* 14 Feb. 1953; *s* of Frank and Kathleen Newby; *m* 1978, Ailsa Ballantyne Thomson; two *s*. *Educ:* Rothwell Grammar Sch.; St Catherine's Coll., Oxford (MA). HM Customs and Excise: Administration trainee, 1974; Private Sec. to Permanent Sec., 1977–79; Principal, Planning Unit, 1979–81; Sec. to SDP Parly Cttee, 1981; joined SDP HQ Staff, 1981; Nat. Sec., SDP, 1983–88. *Recreations:* cricket, music. *Address:* 4 Rockwells Gardens, Dulwich Wood Park, SE19 1HW. *T:* 081–670 6152. *Club:* MCC.

NEWCASTLE, Bishop of, since 1981; **Rt. Rev. Andrew Alexander Kenny Graham;** *b* 7 Aug. 1929; *o s* of late Andrew Harrison and Magdalene Graham; unmarried. *Educ:* Tonbridge Sch.; St John's Coll., Oxford (Hon. Fellow, 1986); Ely Theological College. Curate of Hove Parish Church, 1955–58; Chaplain and Lectr in Theology, Worcester Coll., Oxford, 1958–70; Fellow and Tutor, 1960–70, Hon. Fellow, 1981; Warden of Lincoln Theological Coll., 1970–77; Canon and Prebendary of Lincoln Cathedral, 1970–77. Examining Chaplain to: Bishop of Carlisle, 1967–77; Bishop of Bradford, 1972–77; Bishop of Lincoln, 1973–77; Bishop Suffragan of Bedford, 1977–81. Chairman: ACCM, 1984–87; Doctrine Commn, 1987–. *Recreation:* hill walking. *Address:* Bishop's House, 29 Moor Road South, Newcastle upon Tyne NE3 1PA. *T:* 091–285 2220. *Club:* United Oxford & Cambridge University.

NEWCASTLE, NSW, Bishop of, since 1978; **Rt. Rev. Alfred Charles Holland;** *b* 23 Feb. 1927; *s* of Alfred Charles Holland and Maud Allison; *m* 1954, Joyce Marion Embling; three *s* one *d*. *Educ:* Raine's Sch., London; Univ. of Durham (BA 1950, DipTh 1952). RNVR, 1945–47; Univ. of Durham, 1948–52; Assistant Priest, West Hackney, London, 1952–54; Rector of Scarborough, WA, 1955–70; Asst Bishop, Dio. Perth, WA, 1970–77. Life Member: Stirling Rugby Football Club, 1969; Durham Univ. Society, 1984. *Publications:* Luke Through Lent, 1980; (ed) The Diocese Together, 1987. *Recreations:* reading, painting. *Address:* Bishopscourt, Newcastle, NSW 2300, Australia. *T:* (office) 263733, (home) 262767. *Clubs:* Australian (Sydney); Newcastle (NSW).

NEWCASTLE, Provost of; *see* Coulton, Very Rev. N. G.

NEWDEGATE; *see* FitzRoy Newdegate, family name of Viscount Daventry.

NEWELL, Christopher William Paul; Director of Headquarters Casework, Crown Prosecution Service, since 1989; *b* 30 Nov. 1950; *s* of Nicolas Gambier Newell and Edith Alice Newell (*née* Edgill). *Educ:* Wellington College; Southampton Univ. (LLB Hons). Called to the Bar, Middle Temple, 1973; Department of Director of Public Prosecutions: Legal Asst, 1975–78; Sen. Legal Asst, 1978–79; Law Officers' Dept, 1979–83; Sen. Legal Asst, DPP, 1983–86; Asst DPP, 1986; Branch Crown Prosecutor, Crown Prosecution Service, 1986–87; Asst Legal Sec., Law Officers' Dept, 1987–89. *Recreations:* sport, travel. *Address:* Crown Prosecution Service, 4/12 Queen Anne's Gate, SW1H 9AZ. *T:* 071–417 7158. *Club:* Royal Automobile.

NEWELL, Rt. Rev. Phillip Keith; *see* Tasmania, Bishop of.

NEWENS, (Arthur) Stanley; Member (Lab) London Central, European Parliament, since 1984; *b* 4 Feb. 1930; *s* of Arthur Ernest and Celia Jenny Newens, Bethnal Green; *m* 1st, 1954, Ann (*d* 1962), *d* of J. B. Sherratt, Stoke-on-Trent; two *d*; 2nd, 1966, Sandra Christina, *d* of J. A. Frith, Chingford; one *s* two *d*. *Educ:* Buckhurst Hill County High Sch.; University Coll., London (BA Hons History); Westminster Training Coll. (Post-Graduate Certificate of Education). Coal face worker in N Staffs mines, 1952–55. Secondary Sch. Teacher, 1956–65, 1970–74. MP (Lab) Epping, 1964–70 (NUT sponsored); MP (Lab and Co-op) Harlow, Feb. 1974–1983. Contested (Lab) Harlow, 1983 and 1987. Chairman: Eastern Area Gp of Lab. MPs, 1974–83; Tribune Gp of MPs, 1982–83 (Vice-Chm., 1981–82); PLP Foreign Affairs Gp, 1982–83 (Vice-Chm., 1976–77); Dep. Leader, British Lab. Gp of MEPs, 1988–89 (Chm., 1985–87); Vice-Chairman: E Reg. Council, Lab. Party; Labour Action for Peace. Active Member: Labour Party, holding numerous offices, 1949–; NUM, 1952–55; NUT, 1956–. Chm., Liberation (Movement for Colonial Freedom), 1967–. Dir, London Co-operative Soc., 1971–77 (Pres., 1977–81); Mem., Central Exec., Co-op. Union, 1974–80. Sec., Harlow Council for Voluntary Service, 1983–84. *Publications:* The Case Against NATO (pamphlet), 1972; Nicolae Ceausescu, 1972; Third World: change or chaos, 1977; A History of North Weald Bassett and its People, 1985; A Short History of the London Co-op Society Political Committee, 1988; pamphlets and articles. *Recreations:* local historical research, family, reading. *Address:* The Leys, 18 Park Hill, Harlow, Essex. *T:* Harlow (0279) 420108.

NEWEY, John Henry Richard, QC 1970; **His Honour Judge Newey;** London Official Referee, since 1980; Commissary General of the City and Diocese of Canterbury, since 1971; *b* 20 Oct. 1923; *s* of late Lt-Col T. H. Newey, ED and of Mrs I. K. M. Newey (*née* Webb); *m* 1953, Mollie Patricia (*née* Chalk), JP; three *s* two *d*. *Educ:* Dudley Grammar Sch.; Ellesmere Coll.; Queens' Coll., Cambridge (MA, LLM (1st class); Foundn Scholar). Served Central India Horse, Indian Army, 1942–47 in India, Middle East, Italy and Greece, Captain (US Bronze Star, 1944). Called to Bar, Middle Temple, 1948, Bencher 1977. Prosecuting Counsel to Post Office, South Eastern Circuit, 1963–64; Standing Counsel to Post Office at Common Law, 1964–70; Personal Injuries Junior to Treasury, 1968–70; Dep. Chm., Kent County QS, 1970–71; a Recorder of the Crown Court, 1972–80. Legal Assessor, GMC and GDC, 1973–80; an Advr to the Home Sec. under Prevention of Terrorism Act, 1978–80; Parly Boundary Comr for England, 1980–88. Chm., Cheshire Structure Plan Exam., 1977; Inspector: Calder Valley Motorway Inquiry, 1978; Gatwick Air Port Inquiry, 1980. Legal Mem., Rhodesian Travel Facilities Cttee, 1978–80. Lectr, (part-time), Coll. of Estate Mgt, Univ. of London, 1951–59. FCIArb 1989 (ACIArb 1988). Contested (C and L) Cannock Div. of Staffs, 1955. Alternate Chm., Burnham and other Teachers' Remuneration Cttees, 1969–80. Chairman: Sevenoaks Preservation Soc., 1962–65; Sevenoaks Div. Conservative Assoc., 1965–68. *Publications:* Official Referees Courts—practice and procedure, 1988; (jtly) Construction Disputes, 1989. *Recreations:* history, excursions. *Address:* St David's, 68 The Drive, Sevenoaks, Kent TN13 3AF. *T:* Sevenoaks (0732) 454597.

NEWEY, Sidney Brian; Assistant to Chief Executive, Railways, British Rail, since 1990; *b* 8 Jan. 1937; *s* of Sidney Frank Newey and Edith Mary Newey; *m* 1967, Margaret Mary Stevens; one *s*. *Educ:* Burton upon Trent Grammar Sch.; Worcester Coll., Oxford (MA Mod. History). MCIT. British Rail: Traffic apprentice, Western Region, 1960; Stationmaster, Southall, Mddx, 1964; Freight Marketing Manager, Western Region, 1971; Divl Manager, Birmingham, 1978; Dep. General Manager, London Midland Region, 1980; Gen. Manager, Western Region, 1985–87; Director, Provincial, 1987–90. *Recreations:* fell walking, history, reading, carpentry. *Address:* Chestnut Cottage, The Green South, Warborough, Oxon OX10 7DN. *T:* Warborough (086732) 8322.

NEWFOUNDLAND, CENTRAL, Bishop of, since 1990; **Rt. Rev. Edward Frank Marsh;** *b* 25 Oct. 1935; *m* 1962, Emma Marsh; one *s* two *d*. *Educ:* Dalhousie Univ., NS (BCom 1956); Univ. of Newfoundland (BA 1960); Queen's Coll., Newfoundland (LTh 1961; BD 1969). Deacon 1959, priest 1960; Curate, Corner Brook, 1959–63; Incumbent, Harbour Breton, 1963–69; Curate, Wickford, 1969–71; Incumbent, Indian Bay, 1971–73; Curate, St John the Baptist Cathedral, St John's, 1973–77; Rector of Cartwright, dio. East Newfoundland, 1977–81; Rector, Holy Trinity, Grand Falls, 1981–90. *Address:* 34 Fraser Road, Gander, Newfoundland A1V 2E8, Canada.

NEWFOUNDLAND, EASTERN, AND LABRADOR, Bishop of, since 1980; **Rt. Rev. Martin Mate;** *b* 12 Nov. 1929; *s* of John Mate and Hilda Mate (*née* Toope); *m* 1962, Florence Hooper, Registered Nurse; two *s* three *d*. *Educ:* Meml Univ. of Newfoundland and Queen's Coll., St John's, Newfoundland (LTh); Bishop's Univ., Lennoxville, PQ. BA (1st Cl. Hons), MA. Deacon 1952, priest 1953; Curate, Cathedral of St John the Baptist, St John's, Newfoundland, 1952–53; Deacon-in-charge and Rector, Parish of Pushthrough, 1953–58; Incumbent, Mission of St Anthony, 1958–64; Rural Dean, St Barbe, 1958–64; Rector of Cookshire, Quebec, 1964–67; Rector of Catalina, Newfoundland, 1967–72; RD of Bonavista Bay, 1970–72; Rector of Pouch Cove/Torbay, 1972–76; Treasurer, Diocesan Synod of E Newfoundland and Labrador, 1976–80. *Publication:* Pentateuchal Criticism, 1967. *Recreations:* carpentry, hunting, fishing, camping. *Address:* 19 King's Bridge Road, St John's, Newfoundland A1C 3K4, Canada.

NEWFOUNDLAND, WESTERN, Archbishop of, since 1990; **Rt. Rev. S(idney) Stewart Payne;** Metropolitan of the Ecclesiastical Province of Canada; *b* 6 June 1932; *s* of Albert and Hilda Payne; *m* 1962, Selma Carlson Penney, St Anthony, Newfoundland; two *s* two *d*. *Educ:* Elementary and High School, Fogo, Newfoundland; Memorial Univ. of Newfoundland (BA); Queen's Coll., Newfoundland (LTh); BD(General Synod). Incumbent of Mission of Happy Valley, 1957–65; Rector, Parish of Bay Roberts, 1965–70; Rector, Parish of St Anthony, 1970–78; Bishop of Western Newfoundland, 1978–. DD *hc* Univ. of King's Coll., Halifax, NS, 1981. *Address:* 13 Cobb Lane, Corner Brook, Newfoundland A2H 2V3, Canada. *T:* 709–639–9987.

NEWHOUSE, Ven. Robert John Darrell; Archdeacon of Totnes and Canon Residentiary of Exeter Cathedral, 1966–76, now Archdeacon Emeritus and Canon Emeritus; Treasurer of Exeter Cathedral, 1970–76; *b* 11 May 1911; *s* of Rev. R. L. C. Newhouse; *m* 1938, Winifred (*née* Elton); two *s*. *Educ:* St Edward's Sch.; Worcester Coll., Oxford; Cuddesdon College. Ordained, 1936. Curate of: St John's, Peterborough, 1936–40; St Giles, Cambridge, 1940–46; Chaplain, RNVR, 1941–46; Rector of Ashwater, Devon, 1946–56; Rural Dean of Holsworthy, 1954–56; Vicar of Littleham-cum-Exmouth, 1956–66; Rural Dean of Aylesbeare, 1965–66. *Address:* Pound Cottage, Northlew, Okehampton, Devon EX20 3NR. *T:* Beaworthy (0409) 221532.

NEWING, John Frederick; QPM 1988; Chief Constable, Derbyshire Constabulary, since 1990; *b* 1 March 1940; *s* of Frederick George Newing and Emily Beatrice Newing (*née* Bettles); *m* 1963, Margaret May Kilborn; two *s* one *d*. *Educ:* Kettering Grammar Sch.; Leeds Univ. (BA Hons Social and Public Administration). Joined Metropolitan Police, 1963; Police Staff Coll., 1967–68; Bramshill Scholarship, Leeds Univ., 1969–72; Community Relations Bd, 1974; Staff Officer to Commissioner, 1977; Chief Supt i/c Marylebone Div., 1980; Senior Command Course, Police Staff Coll., 1981; Comdr, Community Relations, 1982, Public Order Branch, 1984; Dep. Asst Comr i/c W London Area, 1985–87; seconded to Home Office Science and Technology Gp, 1987–90. *Publications:* articles in Policing and other professional jls. *Recreations:* reading, walking the dog, voluntary youth work, such sports as age allows. *Address:* Derbyshire Constabulary HQ, Butterley Hall, Ripley, Derbyshire DE5 3RS. *T:* Ripley (0773) 570100.

NEWING, Rt. Rev. Dom Kenneth Albert, OSB; *b* 29 Aug. 1923; *s* of Albert James Pittock Newing and Nellie Louise Maude Newing; unmarried. *Educ:* Dover Grammar School; Selwyn College, Cambridge (MA); Theological College, Mirfield, Yorks. Assistant Curate, Plymstock, 1955–63; Rector of Plympton S Maurice, Plymouth, 1963–82; Archdeacon of Plymouth, 1978–82; Bishop Suffragan of Plymouth, 1982–88; joined Order of St Benedict, 1988; solemn (life) profession, 1989. *Address:* Elmore Abbey, Church Lane, Speen, Newbury, Berks RG13 1SA.

NEWINGTON, Michael John, CMG 1982; HM Diplomatic Service; Ambassador to Brazil, since 1987; *b* 10 July 1932; *er s* of J. T. Newington, Spalding, Lincs; *m* 1956, Nina Gordon-Jones; one *s* one *d*. *Educ:* Stamford Sch.; St John's Coll., Oxford. MA. RAF, 1951–52, Pilot Officer. Joined Foreign Office, 1955; Economic Survey Section, Hong Kong, 1957–58; resigned 1958. ICI, 1959–60. Rejoined FO, 1960; Second, later First Sec. (Economic), Bonn, 1961–65; First Sec., Lagos, 1965–68; Asst Head of Science and Technology Dept, FCO, 1968–72; Counsellor (Scientific), Bonn, 1972–75; Counsellor and Consul-Gen., Tel Aviv, 1975–78; Head of Republic of Ireland Dept, FCO, 1978–81; Consul-Gen., Düsseldorf, 1981–85; Ambassador to Venezuela and concurrently (non-resident) to Dominican Republic, 1985–87. *Recreations:* ski-ing, golf, gardening. *Address:* c/o Foreign and Commonwealth Office, SW1.

NEWIS, Kenneth, CB 1967; CVO 1970 (MVO 1958); *b* 9 Nov. 1916; *o s* of late H. T. and G. Newis, Manchester; *m* 1943, Kathleen, *o d* of late John Barrow, Davenport, Cheshire; two *d*. *Educ:* Manchester Grammar Sch.; St John's Coll., Cambridge (Scholar). BA 1938, MA 1942. Entered HM Office of Works, 1938; Private Sec. to Minister of Works (Rt Hon. C. W. Key), 1948–49; Asst Sec., 1949; Under-Sec., 1959; Dir of Management Services, MPBW, 1969–70; Under-Sec., Scottish Develt Dept, 1970–73, Sec., 1973–76. Chairman: Queen's Hall (Edinburgh) Ltd; MHA Housing Assoc. Vice-Chm., Cockburn Assoc., 1986–; Member: Historic Buildings Council for Scotland, 1978–88; Cockburn Conservation Trust; Bd, Methodist Homes for the Aged; Bd, RSAMD, 1977–88; Scottish Churches' Council, 1984–87 (Chm., Friends of Scottish Churches' Council, 1984–87). Conservator of Wimbledon and Putney Commons, 1963–70. Governor: Farrington's School, 1964–70; Richmond College, 1964–70. *Recreation:* music. *Address:* 11 Abbotsford Park, Edinburgh EH10 5DZ. *Club:* New (Edinburgh).

NEWLAND, Prof. David Edward, MA; ScD; FEng 1982; FIMechE, FIEE; Professor of Engineering (1875), University of Cambridge, since 1976; Fellow, Selwyn College, Cambridge, since 1976; consulting engineer (part-time), since 1963; *b* 8 May 1936; *s* of late Robert W. Newland and of Marion A. Newland (*née* Dearman); *m* 1959, Patricia Frances Mayne; two *s*. *Educ:* Alleyne's Sch., Stevenage; Selwyn Coll., Cambridge (Lyttleton Scholar, 1956; Mech. Sciences Tripos: Rex Moir Prize, 1956, Ricardo Prize, 1957; MA 1961; ScD 1990); Massachusetts Inst. of Technol. (ScD thesis on nonlinear vibrations, 1963). English Electric Co., 1957–61; Instr and Asst Prof. of Mech. Engrg, MIT, 1961–64; Lectr and Sen. Lectr, Imperial Coll. of Science and Technol., 1964–67; Prof. of Mech. Engrg, Sheffield Univ., 1967–76. Visitor, Transport and Road Res. Lab., 1990–. Past or present mem., cttees of IMechE, DTI, BSI, SERC, Design Council, Engrg Council and Fellowship of Engineering, including: Mem., Editorial Panel, 1968–82 and Consultant Editor, 1983–87, Jl Mech. Engrg Sci., Proc. IMechE, Part C; Member: SRC Transport Cttee, 1969–72; Mech. Engrg and Machine Tools Requirements Bd, 1977, 1978; Engrg Awards Panel, Design Council, 1977–79; Council, Fellowship of Engrg, 1985–88; Chairman: BSI Tech. Cttee on bellows expansion jts, 1976–85; Working Party on Engineers and Risk Issues, Engrg Council, 1990–. Technical witness, Flixborough Inquiry, 1974–75, and other legal cases; Mem., Royal Commn on Environmental Pollution, 1984–89. Governor, St Paul's Schs, 1978–; Churchwarden, Ickleton, 1979–87. *Publications:* An Introduction to Random Vibrations and Spectral Analysis, 1975, 2nd edn

1984; Mechanical Vibration Analysis and Computation, 1989; technical papers, mostly in British and Amer. engrg jls. *Recreations:* walking, sport, engineering memorabilia. *Address:* c/o University Engineering Department, Trumpington Street, Cambridge CB2 1PZ. *T:* Cambridge (0223) 332670. *Club:* Athenæum.

NEWLEY, Edward Frank, CBE 1960; consultant; *b* 9 June 1913; *s* of Frederick Percy Newley; *m* 1946, Sybil Madge Alvis; two *s* one *d*. *Educ:* King's Coll., London. 1st class hons BSc; MSc. GPO Engrg Dept, Radio Research Br, 1937–44; GPO Factories Dept, 1944–49; Royal Naval Scientific Service, 1949–55; joined UKAEA, 1955; Dep. Dir, AWRE, 1959; Dir, Atomic Weapons Establishment, Aldermaston, 1965–76. Mem., Nat. Savings Cttee, 1976–78. *Publications:* sundry scientific and technical papers. *Address:* Rosapenna, Leigh Woods, Bristol BS8 3PX.

NEWLEY, (George) Anthony; actor since 1946; author, composer; *b* 24 Sept. 1931; *m* 1956, Ann Lynn; *m* 1963, Joan Collins; one *s* one *d*; *m* Dareth Rich; one *s* one *d*. *Educ:* Mandeville Street Sch., Clapton, E5. Appeared on West End stage in: Cranks, 1955; Stop the World, I Want to Get Off (co-author and co-composer, with Leslie Bricusse), 1961–62; subseq. starred in New York production, 1962–63, new production, Lyric, 1989 (also co-dir); The Good Old Bad Old Days (co-author and co-composer with Leslie Bricusse), 1972; The Roar of the Greasepaint-the Smell of the Crowd (co-author and composer, with Leslie Bricusse, star and director), New York, 1965; Chaplin, Los Angeles, 1983. Has acted in over 40 films in last 17 years. *Films include:* Adventures of Dusty Bates; Oliver Twist; Up To His Neck; Cockleshell Heroes; High Flight; Idle on Parade; Jazz Boat; The Small World of Sammy Lee; Dr Doolittle; Sweet November; (wrote, produced and acted) Can Heironymus Merkin ever forget Mercy Humppe and find True Happiness?; (directed) Summertree, 1970; (score) Willy Wonka and the Chocolate Factory (Academy Award nomination, 1972); Quilp, 1974; It Seemed Like a Good Idea at the Time, 1974. *TV appearances include:* Anthony Newley Shows; The Strange World of Gurney Slade, 1960–61; Johnny Darling Show, 1962; Lucy in London, 1966; appears on TV and stars in leading night clubs and theatres in US. He is also a successful recording star. *Recreations:* photography, painting, fishing. *Address:* c/o Raymond Katz Enterprises, Suite 1115, 9255 Sunset Boulevard, Los Angeles, Calif 90069, USA.

NEWMAN, Dr Barry Hilton; consultant; Director, Propellants, Explosives and Rocket Motor Establishment, and Head of Rocket Motor Executive, Ministry of Defence, 1980–84, retired; *b* 16 Sept. 1926; *s* of Charles Ernest Newman and Kathleen (*née* Hilton); *m* 1950, Dorothy Ashworth Truesdale; one *s* one *d*. *Educ:* Bishop Vesey's Grammar Sch., Sutton Coldfield; Univ. of Birmingham (BSc (Hons) 1947, PhD 1950). Joined Scientific Civil Service, 1950; Explosives R&D Estabt, 1950–63; Defence Research Staff, Washington, 1963–66; Supt Explosives Br., Royal Armament R&D Estabt, 1966–71; Asst Dir, Directorate General Weapons (Army), 1971–72; Dir, Research Armaments, 1972–74; RCDS 1975; Head of Terminal Effects Dept, RARDE, 1976–77; Dep. Dir, RARDE, 1977–80. FRSA. *Publications:* official reports. *Recreations:* cricket, bridge, reading, music. *Address:* c/o Barclays Bank, 80 High Street, Sevenoaks, Kent. *Club:* MCC.

NEWMAN, Cyril Wilfred Francis; QC 1982; **His Honour Judge Newman;** a Circuit Judge, since 1986; *b* 2 July 1937; *s* of late Wilfred James Newman and Cecilia Beatrice Lily Newman; *m* 1966, Winifred de Kok; two *s* one *d*. *Educ:* Sacred Heart Coll., Droitwich; Lewes County Grammar Sch. for Boys; Merton Coll., Oxford (BA 1959, MA 1964). President: OU Law Soc., 1959; OU Middle Temple Soc., 1959. Blackstone Entrance Scholar, Blackstone Pupillage Prize, and Harmsworth Major Scholar, Middle Temple, 1958–60; called to the Bar, Middle Temple, 1960; a Recorder, 1982–86. Asst Comr, Boundary Commn for England, 1976; Mem., Criminal Injuries Compensation Bd, 1985–86. Hon. Treasurer, Bar Yacht Club, 1973–88 (Rear-Cdre, 1985–86). *Recreations:* sailing, ski-ing, game keeping, shooting, swimming, opera, church music. *Address:* c/o Court Administrator, Law Courts, Maidstone, Kent ME16 8EW. *Club:* Bar Yacht.

See also G. M. Newman.

NEWMAN, Edward; Member (Lab) Greater Manchester Central, European Parliament, since 1984; *b* 14 May 1953. Formerly in light engineering, cable making; postal worker, Manchester. *Address:* European Parliament, Centre européen, Plateau du Kirchberg, Luxembourg.

NEWMAN, Sir Francis (Hugh Cecil), 4th Bt *cr* 1912, of Cecil Lodge, Newmarket; *b* 12 June 1963; *s* of Sir Gerard Robert Henry Sigismund Newman, 3rd Bt and of Caroline Philippa, *d* of late Brig. Alfred Geoffrey Neville, CBE, MC; *S* father, 1987; *m* 1990, Katharine, *d* of Timothy Edwards. *Educ:* Eton; Univ. of Pennsylvania (BA Econs). *Recreation:* rowing. *Heir: b* Geoffrey John Newman, *b* 12 Dec. 1966. *Address:* Burloes, Royston, Herts SG8 9NE. *Club:* Eton Vikings.

NEWMAN, Frederick Edward Fry, CBE 1986; MC 1945; Chairman: Dan-Air Services, 1953–90; Davies & Newman Holdings, 1971–89; *b* 14 July 1916; *s* of Frank Newman and Katharine Newman; *m* 1947, Margaret Helen (*née* Blackstone); two *s* one *d*. *Educ:* The Leys School, Cambridge. Joined Davies & Newman, 1937; served HAC and 9th Field Regt, RA, 1939–46; formed Dan-Air Services, 1953. *Recreation:* golf. *Address:* Cranstone, Hook Heath Road, Woking, Surrey. *T:* Woking (04862) 72605.

NEWMAN, Sir Geoffrey (Robert), 6th Bt, *cr* 1836; *b* 2 June 1947; *s* of Sir Ralph Alured Newman, 5th Bt, and of Hon. Ann Rosemary Hope, *d* of late Hon. Claude Hope-Morley; *S* father, 1968; *m* 1980, Mary, *y d* of Colonel Sir Martin St John Valentine Gibbs, *qv*; one *s* three *d*. *Educ:* Heatherdown, Ascot; Kelly Coll., Tavistock. 1st Bn, Grenadier Guards, 1967–70. FRGS. *Recreations:* sub-aqua, sailing, all sports. *Heir: s* Robert Melvil Newman, *b* 4 Oct. 1985. *Address:* Blackpool House, Dartmouth, Devon.

NEWMAN, George Michael; QC 1981; a Recorder, since 1985; *b* 4 July 1941; *s* of late Wilfred James Newman and Cecilia Beatrice Lily Newman; *m* 1966, Hilary Alice Gibbs (*née* Chandler); two *s* one *d*. *Educ:* Lewes County Grammar Sch.; St Catharine's Coll., Cambridge (BA Law). Called to the Bar, Middle Temple, 1965, Bencher, 1989. *Recreations:* tennis, skiing, the countryside. *Address:* 1 Crown Office Row, Temple, EC4Y 7HH. *T:* 071–583 9292.

See also C. W. F. Newman.

NEWMAN, Graham Reginald, FICS; Chairman, Tatham Bromage & Co. Ltd and group of companies, since 1953; *b* 26 July 1924; *m* 1952, Joycelyn Helen Sandison, MB, ChB, DPH. *Educ:* Canford Sch.; Hertford Coll., Oxford. War service, Royal Signals, India and Far East, 1941–46, retd Captain. Elected to Baltic Exchange, 1947; Dir, 1967; Chm., 1977–79; Chm., Baltic Exchange Clerks' Pension Fund, 1966–68. Pres., Baltic Charitable Soc., 1982–84. Mem. Cttee of Management, RNLI and sub-cttees, 1977–. Prime Warden, Shipwrights' Co., 1988–89. *Recreation:* sailing. *Address:* Irwin House, 2nd Floor, 118 Southwark Street, SE1 0SW.

NEWMAN, Sir Jack, Kt 1977; CBE 1963; FCIT 1955; JP; Founder, 1938, President, 1981, Newman Group Ltd (formerly TNL), Nelson, New Zealand; *b* 3 July, 1902; *s* of Thomas Newman and Christina Thomson; *m* 1926, Myrtle O. A. Thomas; four *d*. *Educ:* Nelson Coll. for Boys, NZ. Joined Newman Bros Ltd (family business), 1922; Manager, 1927; Managing Director, 1935. Past President and Life Member: NZ Cricket Council; NZ Travel Assoc.; NZ Passenger Transport Fedn; former Dir, Pacific Area Travel Assoc. Represented: NZ, at cricket, 1931–33; Nelson, Canterbury and Wellington, at cricket; Nelson, at Rugby football, golf, and lawn bowls. JP Nelson, 1950. *Recreation:* lawn bowls. *Address:* 364 Trafalgar Square, Nelson, New Zealand. *Clubs:* MCC; Wellesley (Wellington); Nelson (Nelson).

NEWMAN, Karl Max, CB 1979; Second Counsel to the Chairman of Committees and Legal Adviser to the European Communities Committee, House of Lords, 1982–87; *b* 26 March 1919; *s* of Karl Neumann, DrJur, and Licie Neumann; *m* 1952, Annette, *d* of late Ronald Cross Sheen; one *s* one *d*. *Educ:* Ottershaw Coll., Surrey; Christ Church, Oxford (MA). Bacon Scholar of Gray's Inn, 1939. Served War in Army, 1940–42. Called to Bar, Gray's Inn, 1946, Bencher 1987; joined Lord Chancellor's Office, 1949; Asst Solicitor, 1962; Under-Sec., 1972–82; part-time Legal Adviser to European Unit of Cabinet Office, 1972–82; Head of Delegn negotiating UK accession to EEC Convention on Jurisdiction and Judgments, 1972–78. Member: UK delegns to Internat. Diplomatic Confs on Nuclear Liability, 1962–63; expert Cttees of Council of Europe, 1961–68; 10th and 11th Session of Hague Conf. on Private Internat. Law, 1964–68. Mem., EEC expert cttees, 1972–82. *Publications:* Das Englisch-Amerikanische Beweisrecht, 1949 (Heidelberg); contribs to legal publications on EEC law, internat. jurisdiction and recognition of judgments. *Recreations:* philately, looking at paintings. *Address:* 17 Marryat Road, Wimbledon, SW19 5BB. *T:* 081–946 3430. *Club:* United Oxford & Cambridge University.

NEWMAN, Sir Kenneth (Leslie), GBE 1987; Kt 1978; QPM 1982; Commissioner of the Metropolitan Police, 1982–87; non-executive director of various companies; *b* 15 Aug. 1926; *s* of John William Newman and Florence Newman; *m* 1949, Eileen Lilian. *Educ:* London Univ. (LLB Hons). Served War, RAF, 1942–46. Palestine Police, 1946–48; Metropolitan Police, 1948–73; Comdr, New Scotland Yard, 1972; Royal Ulster Constab., 1973–79; Sen. Dep. Chief Constable, 1973; Chief Constable, 1976–79; Comdt, Police Staff Coll., and HM Inspector of Constabulary, 1980–82. Vis. Prof. of Law, Bristol University, 1987–88. Chairman: Disciplinary Cttee, Security Systems Inspectorate, British Security Industry Assoc., 1987–; Assoc. for Prevention of Theft in Shops, 1987–91; Vice Pres., Defence Manufacturers Assoc., 1987–. Trustee: Police Foundn, 1982–; Community Action Trust (Crime Stoppers), 1987–. CBIM (FBIM 1977). Freeman of the City of London, 1983. KStJ 1987 (CStJ 1984). Communicator of the Year, BAIE, 1984. Order of: Bahrain, Class 2, 1984; the Aztec Eagle, Cl. 2, Mexico, 1985. King Abdul Aziz, Cl. 1, Saudi Arabia, 1987; Grand Officer: Order of Orange-Nassau, Netherlands, 1982; Grand Order of the Lion, Malaŵi, 1985; Order of Ouissam Alouite, Morocco, 1987; Commander: National Order of Legion of Honour, France, 1984; Order of Military Merit, Spain, 1986; Kt Comdr, Order of Merit, West Germany, 1986; Medal of Merit, Cl. 1, Qatar, 1985. *Recreations:* swimming, walking, reading.

NEWMAN, Dr Lotte Therese, (Mrs N. E. Aronsohn), OBE 1991; FRCGP; general practitioner since 1958; Member, General Medical Council, since 1984; *b* 22 Jan. 1929; *d* of Dr George Newman and Dr Tilly Newman; *m* 1959, Norman Edward Aronsohn; three *s* one *d*. *Educ:* North London Collegiate Sch.; Univ. of Birmingham; King's College London and Westminster Hosp. Med. Schs. BSc 1951, MB BS 1957; LRCP, MRCS 1957; FRCGP 1977; FRSM 1977. Casualty Officer, Westminster Hosp.; Paediatric House Officer, Westminster Children's Hosp.; gen. medicine, St Stephen's Hosp. Director: Private Patients Plan, 1983–; Private Patients Plan (Lifetime) plc, 1991–. Hon. Sec., 1981–86, Pres. elect, 1986–87, Pres., 1987–88, Medical Women's Fedn; Pres., Internat. Soc. of Gen. Practice, 1988–; Member: Council, RCGP, 1980– (Vice-Chm., 1987–89; former Provost, NE London Faculty; formerly examr, RCGP); Council, BMA, 1985–89; Member: Med. Ethics Cttee; General Med. Services Cttee, 1983–86 and 1988–; Private Practice and Prof. Fees Cttee, 1985–; Forensic Medicine Sub-Cttee, 1989–; Chm., Camden and Islington Local Med. Cttee, 1986– (Vice-Chm., 1983–86); Chm., Regional Co-ordinating Cttee of Area Local Med. Cttees, 1985–87; Lectr, Royal Army Med. Coll., 1976– (first woman to give Sir David Bruce Lecture in Gen. Practice, 1989); temp. Adviser, WHO; formerly UK rep., OECD and Mem., Expert Cttees studying Primary Health Care in Germany, Switzerland, Sweden. Member: Hunterian Soc.; Hampstead Medical Soc.; Assurance Med. Soc., 1987–. Freeman, City of London; Liveryman, Apothecaries' Soc. of London. Sir David Bruce Medal, RAMC, 1990; Purkinje Medal for Services to Medicine, Czech Soc. of Gen. Practice, 1985. *Publications:* papers on: women doctors; multidisciplinary training and courses of Primary Health Care Team; breast feeding; ENT conditions and management of mental health handicap in gen. practice. *Recreations:* listening, music, boating. *Address:* 1 Cholmley Gardens, Mill Lane, NW6 1AE. *T:* 071–794 6256. *Clubs:* Royal Automobile, City Livery, Little Ship.

NEWMAN, Malcolm, CIPFA; City Treasurer, since 1987, and Deputy Chief Executive, since 1990, Sheffield City Council; *b* 2 April 1946; *s* of John George and Elizabeth Newman; *m* 1980, Marilyn Wilson; one *s* one *d*. *Educ:* Jarrow Grammar Sch. Clerk, Hebburn UDC, 1962–66; Newcastle upon Tyne City Council: various positions, 1966–71; Sen. Audit Asst, 1971–72; Sen. Management Accountant, 1972–73; Chief Accountant, 1973–77; Asst City Treas. (Accounting), 1977–79; Man. (Cons.) and Gen. Man., Wilson Johnson, 1979–80; Asst Finance Officer (Audit and Tech.), Sefton MDC, 1980–82; Hd of Financial Services 1982–85, Bor. Treas. 1985–87, London Borough of Southwark. Director: Hallamshire Investments plc, 1988–; Sheffield Heat and Power, 1988–. Governor, Sheffield Polytechnic, 1989–. *Recreations:* old house, young family, squash, jogging, reading. *Address:* 113 Knowle Lane, Sheffield S11 9SN.

NEWMAN, Nanette, (Mrs Bryan Forbes); actress and writer; *b* 29 May 1939; *d* of Sidney and Ruby Newman; *m* 1958, Bryan Forbes, *qv*; two *d*. *Educ:* Sternhold Coll., London; Italia Conti Stage Sch.; RADA. Appeared as a child in various films for Children's Film Foundn; other film appearances include: The L-Shaped Room, 1962; The Wrong Arm of the Law, 1962; Seance on a Wet Afternoon, 1963; The Wrong Box, 1965; The Whisperers, 1966; Deadfall, 1967; The Madwoman of Chaillot, 1968; The Raging Moon, 1971 (Variety Club Best Film Actress Award); The Stepford Wives, 1974; International Velvet, 1978 (Evening News Best Film Actress Award); *television:* Call My Bluff, What's My Line, The Fun Food Factory (own series), London Scene, Stay with me till Morning (Yorkshire), Jessie (title role, BBC), Let There Be Love (Thames series), A Breath of Fresh Air (TSW), Late Expectations (BBC); The Endless Game (Channel 4). *Publications:* God Bless Love, 1972 (repr. 16 times); Lots of Love, 1973 (repr. 7 times); Vote for Love, 1976 (repr. 4 times); All Our Love, 1978; Fun Food Factory, 1976 (repr. twice); Fun Food Feasts, 1978; The Root Children, 1978; The Pig Who Never Was, 1979; Amy Rainbow, 1980; The Facts of Love, 1980; That Dog, 1980; Reflections, 1981; The Dog Lovers Coffee Table Book, 1982; The Cat Lovers Coffee Table Book, 1983; My Granny was a Frightful Bore, 1983; A Cat and Mouse Love Story, 1984; Nanette Newman's Christmas Cook Book, 1984; Pigalev, 1985; The Best of Love, 1985; The Summer Cookbook, 1986; Archie, 1986; Small Beginnings, 1987; Bad Baby, 1988; Entertaining with Nanette Newman and her Daughters Sarah and Emma, 1988; Sharing, 1989; Charlie the Noisy Caterpillar, 1989; ABC, 1990; 123, 1991; Cooking for Friends, 1991. *Recreation:*

needlepoint. *Address:* c/o The Bookshop, Virginia Water, Surrey. *T:* Wentworth (0344) 842463.

NEWMAN, Paul; American actor and director; *b* 26 Jan. 1925; *s* of Arthur Newman and Theresa (*née* Fetzer); *m* 1st, 1949, Jacqueline Witte; two *d* (one *s* decd); 2nd, 1958, Joanne Woodward; three *d*. *Educ:* Kenyon Coll. (BA); Yale Drama Sch. Mil. Service, USNR, 1943–46. Chairman: Newman's Own; Salad King. *Stage appearances include:* Picnic, 1953–54; Sweet Bird of Youth, 1959; *films include:* Somebody Up There Likes Me, 1956; Cat on a Hot Tin Roof, 1958; The Hustler, 1961; Sweet Bird of Youth, 1962; Hud, 1963; Torn Curtain, 1966; Cool Hand Luke, 1967; Butch Cassidy and the Sundance Kid, 1969; The Sting, 1973; Drowning Pool, 1975; Quintet, 1979; Fort Apache, the Bronx (also dir), 1980; Absence of Malice, 1981; The Verdict, 1982; Harry and Son (also wrote and directed), 1984; The Color of Money, 1986 (Academy Award, 1987); Blaze, 1990; Shadow Makers, 1990; Mr and Mrs Bridge, 1991; *films directed include:* Rachel, Rachel, 1968; When Time Ran Out, 1980; The Glass Menagerie, 1987. Hon. Academy Award for career achievement, 1986. *Address:* c/o Rogers & Cowan Inc., 1000 Santa Monica Boulevard No 400, Los Angeles, Calif 90067–7007, USA.

NEWMAN, Philip Harker, CBE 1976; DSO 1940; MC; FRCS; FCS(SA); formerly Consulting Orthopædic Surgeon, Middlesex Hospital, Royal National Orthopædic Hospital, King Edward VII's Hospital for Officers, W1, retired; *b* 22 June 1911; *s* of John Harker Newman, Mannofield, Ingatestone, Essex; *m* 1943, Elizabeth Anne (*d* 1991), *er d* of Rev. G. H. Basset, Turners, Belchamp St Paul, Suffolk; two *s* one *d*. *Educ:* Cranleigh; Middlesex Hospital Medical School (Senior Broderip Scholar and 2nd Year Exhibitioner), MRCS, LRCP, 1934; FRCS, 1938; Hunterian Prof., RCS, 1954; late Lt-Col RAMC; Served War of 1939–45 (DSO, MC); FRSM (formerly Pres., Section of Orthopaedics); Fellow Brit. Orthopædic Assoc. (Pres., 1975–76); Chm., British Editorial Soc. of Bone and Joint Surgery, 1973–75; Chm., Medical Br., St John, 1976–82; Member British Medical Association. Corresp. Member: Amer. Orthopaedic Assoc.; S African Orthopaedic Assoc. *Publications:* The Prisoner of War Mentality, 1944; Early Treatment of Wounds of the Knee Joint, 1945; The Etiology of Spondylolisthesis, 1962; The Spine, the Wood and the Trees, 1968; Spinal Fusion, Operative Surgery, 1969; Safer than a Known Way, 1983; Orthopaedic Surgery, in British Encyclopædia of Medical Practice, 1956; (contrib.) Total Hip Replacement, 1971; (contrib.) The Scientific Basis of Medicine, Annual Review, 1973. *Recreations:* sailing, golf. *Address:* 72A Saxmundham Road, Aldeburgh, Suffolk. *T:* Aldeburgh (072885) 3373.

NEWMAN, Vice Adm. Roy Thomas, CB 1991; Chief of Staff to Commander-in-Chief Fleet, since 1990; *b* 8 Sept. 1936; *s* of Mr and Mrs T. U. Newman; *m* 1960, Heather (*née* Macleod); four *s*. *Educ:* Queen Elizabeth's Grammar Sch., Barnet, Herts. Joined RN, 1954; specialised in anti-submarine warfare, 1963; joined Submarine Service, 1966; Comdr 1971, Captain 1979; commanded: HMS Onyx, 1970–71; HMS Naiad, 1978–79; First Submarine Sqn and HMS Dolphin, 1981–83; Seventh Frigate Sqn and HMS Cleopatra, 1984–85; Dir of Naval Warfare, 1986–88; Flag Officer Sea Trng, 1988–89. Freeman, City of London, 1989. *Recreations:* cricket, golf, music, reading. *Clubs:* Army and Navy, Institute of Directors.

NEWMAN, Sydney Cecil, OC 1981; film and television producer and executive; President, Sydney Newman Enterprises; *b* Toronto, 1 April 1917; *m* 1944, Margaret Elizabeth (*d* 1981), *d* of Rev. Duncan McRae, DD; three *d*. *Educ:* Ogden Public School and Central Technical School, Toronto. Painter, stage, industrial and interior designer; still and cinema photographer, 1935–41. National Film Board of Canada: joined under John Grierson as splicer-boy, 1941. Editor and Dir of Armed Forces training films and war information shorts, 1942; Exec. Producer in charge of all films for cinemas, including short films, newsreels, films for children and travel, 1947–52 (assigned to NBC in New York by Canadian govt, to report on American television techniques, 1949–50); TV Dir of Features and Outside Broadcasts, Canadian Broadcasting Corp., 1953; Superviser of Drama and Producer of General Motors Theatre, On Camera, Ford Theatre, Graphic, 1954; Superviser of Drama and Producer, Armchair Theatre, ABC Television, England, 1958–62 (devised, The Avengers, 1961); Head of Drama Group, TV, BBC, 1963–67 (devised Dr Who, 1963, and Adam Adamant Lives!, 1966); Producer, Associated British Productions Ltd, Elstree, 1968–69; Special Advr to Chm. and Dir, Broadcast Programmes Branch, Canadian Radio and Television Commn, 1970; Canadian Govt Film Comr and Chm., Nat. Film Bd of Canada, 1970–75; Special Advr on Film to Sec. of State for Canada, 1975–77; Chief Creative Consultant, Canadian Film Develt Corp., 1978–84 (Dir, Montreal, 1970–75). Dir, Canadian Broadcasting Corp., 1972–75. Producer: Canada Carries On. 1945; over 300 documentaries, including: Suffer Little Children (UN), It's Fun to Sing (Venice Award), Ski Skill, After Prison What? (Canada Award); Stephen D, BBC TV, 1963; The Rise and Fall of the City of Mahagonny, BBC TV, 1965; The Tea Party, BBC TV, 1965; Britten's The Little Sweep, Channel 4, 1989; produced first plays by Arthur Hailey, inc. Flight into Danger, Course for Collision; commissioned and prod. first on-air plays of Alun Owen, Harold Pinter, Angus Wilson, Robert Muller, Peter Luke, and plays by Clive Exton, David Perry and Hugh Leonard. Trustee, Nat. Arts Center, Ottawa, 1970–75; Gov., Canadian Conf. of the Arts; Member New Western Film and TV Foundn; BAFTA; FRTS 1990; FRSA 1970; Fellow Soc. of Film and Television Arts, 1958. Ohio State Award for Religious Drama, 1956; Liberty Award, Best Drama Series, 1957; Desmond Davis Award, 1967, Soc. of Film and Television Arts; President's Award, 1969, and Zeta Award, 1970, Writers Guild of GB; Canadian Picture Pioneers Special Award, 1973; Special Recognition Award, SMPTE, 1975. Kt of Mark Twain, USA. *Address:* 3 Nesbitt Drive, Toronto, Ont M4W 2G2, Canada.

NEWMARCH, Michael George, (Mick); Chief Executive, Prudential Corporation Plc, since 1990; *b* 19 May 1938; *s* of George Langdon Newmarch and Phyllis Georgina Newmarch; *m* 1959, Audrey Clarke; one *s* two *d*. *Educ:* Univ. of London (BSc (Econs) external). Joined Prudential, 1955, Econ. Intelligence Dept; Exec. Dir, Prudential Corp., 1985–; Chief Executive: Prudential Financial Servs, 1987–89; Prudential Portfolio Managers, 1982–89; Chm., Prudential Holborn, 1986–89. *Recreations:* salmon and trout fishing, flytying, bridge, theatre, concerts. *Club:* Flyfishers'.

NEWNHAM, Captain Ian Frederick Montague, CBE 1955; RN Retired; *b* 20 Feb. 1911; *s* of late John Montague Newnham, OBE, DL, JP, and Hilda Newnham; *m* 1947, Marjorie Warden; no *c*. *Educ:* RN College, Dartmouth. Served War of 1939–45 (despatches). Captain, 1952; retd 1961. Lent to Indian Navy as Chief of Material, 1952–55; Chief of Staff to Admiral, British Joint Service Mission, and Naval Attaché, Washington, 1959–61. Gen. Manager, Precision Engineering Div., Short Brothers and Harland, Belfast, 1961–68. *Recreation:* fishing. *Address:* The Lodge, Mill Lane, Stedham, Midhurst, West Sussex GU29 0PS. *T:* Midhurst (0730) 813663.

NEWNS, Sir (Alfred) Foley (Francis Polden), KCMG 1963 (CMG 1957); CVO 1961; MA Cantab; *b* 30 Jan. 1909; *s* of late Rev. Alfred Newns, AKC; *m* 1st, 1936, Jean (*d* 1984), *d* of late A. H. Bateman, MB, BS; one *s* one *d*; 2nd, 1988, Beryl Wattles, BEd Cantab, MSc London (Head of Dyslexia Centre, King's Coll. Sch., Cambridge). *Educ:* Christ's Hospital; St Catharine's College, Cambridge. Colonial Administrative Service, Nigeria, 1932; served E Reg. and Colony; Enugu Secretariat, 1947; Lagos Secretariat, 1949; attached Cabinet Office, London, 1951; Resident, 1951; Secretary to Council of Ministers, 1951; Secretary to Governor-General and the Council of Ministers, Federation of Nigeria, 1955–59; Dep. Governor, Sierra Leone, 1960–61; Acting Gov. during 1960; Adviser to the Government of Sierra Leone after Independence, 1961–63; Sec. to Cabinet, Govt of the Bahamas, 1963–71. President: St Catharine's Coll. Soc., 1986–87 (Sec., 1976–85); Foxton Gardens Assoc., 1989–91 (Chm., 1973–89); Member: Cambridgeshire Wild Life Fundraising Cttee (formerly Trust Appeal), 1986–90; Cttee, UK Br., Nigerian Field Soc., 1983–90 (Life Mem., 1934); Life Member: Britain–Nigeria Assoc.; Sierra Leone Soc., and other societies. Hon. Treasurer, Cambridge Specific Learning Disabilities Gp, 1986–; Hon. Auditor, Cambridge Decorative and Fine Arts Soc., 1984–. FRSA 1969. *Publications:* various papers on Cabinet procedure and government machinery, circulated in Commonwealth. *Address:* 47 Barrow Road, Cambridge CB2 2AR. *T:* Cambridge (0223) 356903.

See also J. Ounsted.

NEWPORT, Viscount; Alexander Michael Orlando Bridgeman; *b* 6 Sept. 1980; *s* and *heir* of 7th Earl of Bradford, *qv*.

NEWRY AND MORNE, Viscount; Robert Francis John Needham; Sales Manager, Lewmar Marine Ltd; *b* 30 May 1966; *s* and *heir* to Earl of Kilmorey (*see* R. F. Needham); *m* 1991, Laura Mary, *o d* of Michael Tregaskis. *Educ:* Sherborne Prep. School; Eton College; Lady Margaret Hall, Oxford (BA). *Recreations:* squash, theatre, travelling.

NEWSAM, Sir Peter (Anthony), Kt 1987; Director, London Institute of Education, since 1989; *b* 2 Nov. 1928; *s* of late W. O. Newsam and of Mrs D. E. Newsam; *m* 1st, 1953, Elizabeth Joy Greg (marr. diss. 1987); four *s* one *d*; 2nd, 1988, Sue Addinell; one *d*. *Educ:* Clifton Coll.; Queen's Coll., Oxford (MA, DipEd). Asst Principal, BoT, 1952–55; teacher, 1956–63; Asst Educn Officer, N Riding of Yorks, 1963–66; Asst Dir of Educn, Cumberland, 1966–70; Dep. Educn Officer: W Riding of Yorks, 1970–72; ILEA, 1972–76; Educn Officer, ILEA, 1977–82; Chm., CRE, 1982–87; Sec., ACC, 1987–89. *Address:* 14 Endsleigh Street, WC1.

NEWSOM, George Harold, QC 1956; Chancellor: Diocese of St Albans, since 1958; Diocese of London, since 1971; Diocese of Bath and Wells, since 1971; *b* 29 Dec. 1909; *e s* of late Rev. G. E. Newsom, Master of Selwyn Coll., Cambridge; *m* 1939, Margaret Amy, *d* of L. A. Allen, OBE; two *s* one *d*. *Educ:* Marlborough; Merton College, Oxford. 2nd Class Lit Hum, 1931; 1st Class Jurisprudence, 1932; Harmsworth Senior Scholar; Merton College, 1932; Cholmeley Student, 1933, called to Bar, 1934, Lincoln's Inn; Bencher, 1962; Treasurer, 1980; practised at Chancery Bar, 1934–79. Min. of Economic Warfare, 1939–40; Trading with the Enemy Dept, Treasury and Bd of Trade, 1940–45; Junior Counsel to Charity Comrs, 1947–56; Conveyancing Counsel to PO, 1947–56; Dep. Chm., Wilts QS, 1964–71; a Recorder of the Crown Court, 1972–74. Member Gen. Council of the Bar, 1952–56. Vis. Prof. in Law, Auckland Univ., NZ, 1971. *Publications:* Restrictive Covenants affecting freehold land, 1st edn (with late C. H. S. Preston), 1940, 7th edn 1982; Limitation of Actions, 1st edn (with late C. H. S. Preston), 1939, 2nd edn 1943, 3rd edn (with L. Abel-Smith), 1953; The Discharge and Modification of Restrictive Covenants, 1957; (with J. G. Sherratt) Water Pollution, 1972; The Faculty Jurisdiction of the Church of England, 1988. *Recreations:* wine, walking. *Address:* The Old Vicarage, Bishop's Cannings, Devizes, Wilts SN10 2LA. *T:* Devizes (0380) 860660. *Club:* Athenæum.

NEWSOM-DAVIS, Prof. John Michael, MD; FRCP; FRS 1991; Professor of Clinical Neurology, University of Oxford, since 1987; *b* 18 Oct. 1932; *s* of John Kenneth and Dorothy Eileen Newsom-Davis; *m* 1963, Rosemary Elisabeth (*née* Schmid); one *s* two *d*. *Educ:* Sherborne Sch.; Pembroke Coll., Cambridge (BA 1957 Nat. Scis); Middlesex Hosp. Med. Sch. (MB BChir 1960, MD 1966); FRCP 1973. RAF, 1951–53 (Pilot). Lectr, Univ. Dept of Clinical Neurology, Nat. Hosp. for Nervous Diseases, 1967–69; Neurological Research Fellow, Cornell Med. Center, New York Hosp., 1969–70; Consultant Neurologist, Royal Free Hosp. and Nat. Hosp. for Nervous Diseases, 1970–80; MRC Clinical Res. Prof. of Neurology, Royal Free Hosp. Med. Sch. and Inst. of Neurology, 1980–87; Hon. Consultant, Nat. Hosp. for Nervous Diseases, 1987–. Mem., MRC, 1983–87 (Mem., Neurosciences Grants Cttee, 1978–80; Neurosciences Bd Mem., 1980–83, Chm., 1983–85); Pres., Biomedical Section, BAAS, 1982–83; Hon. Sec., Assoc. of British Neurologists, 1981–84; Vice-Pres., Internat. Soc. for Neuroimmunology, 1987–. Hon. Mem., Aust. Assoc. of Neurologists; Corr. Mem., Amer. Acad. of Neurology. Mem., Governing Body, BPMF, 1987–. Mem. Editorial Bds of Brain, Jl of Neurological Sci., Jl of Neuroimmunology. *Publications:* (with E. J. M. Campbell and E. Agostoni) Respiratory Muscles: mechanics and neural control, 1970; numerous papers in Neurol. and Immunol. jls. *Recreations:* music and France. *Address:* Department of Neurology, University of Oxford, Radcliffe Infirmary, Oxford OX2 6HE.

NEWSOME, David Hay, MA; LittD Cantab 1976; FRSL 1981; Master of Wellington College, 1980–89; *b* 15 June 1929; *s* of Captain C. T. Newsome, OBE; *m* 1955, Joan Florence, *d* of Lt-Col L. H. Trist, DSO, MC; four *d*. *Educ:* Rossall Sch., Fleetwood; Emmanuel Coll., Cambridge (Scholar). First Cl. in Hist. Tripos Parts I and II, 1952, 1953. Asst Master, Wellington Coll., 1954–59 (Head of History Dept, 1956–59); Fellow of Emmanuel Coll., Cambridge, 1959–70; Asst Lectr in Ecclesiastical History, Univ. of Cambridge, 1961–66; Univ. Lectr, 1966–70; Sen. Tutor, Emmanuel Coll., Cambridge, 1965–70; Headmaster of Christ's Hospital, 1970–79. Lectures: Gore Memorial, Westminster Abbey, 1965; Bishop Westcott Memorial, Cambridge, 1968; Birkbeck, Univ. of Cambridge, 1972. Council of: Ardingly Coll., 1965–69; Eastbourne Coll., 1966–70; Epsom Coll., 1966–70. FRHistS, 1970. *Publications:* A History of Wellington College, 1859–1959, 1959; Godliness and Good Learning, Four Studies in a Victorian Ideal, 1961; The Parting of Friends, a study of the Wilberforces and Henry Manning, 1966; Bishop Westcott and the Platonic Tradition, 1969; Two Classes of Men: Platonism and English Romantic Thought, 1974; On the Edge of Paradise: A. C. Benson the Diarist, 1980 (Whitbread Book of the Year Award); (ed) Edwardian Excursions, 1981; articles in Jl of Theological Studies, Jl of Ecclesiastical History, Theology, History Today, Historical Jl. *Recreations:* music, fell-walking. *Address:* The Retreat, Thornthwaite, Keswick, Cumbria CA12 5SA. *T:* Braithwaite (059682) 372. *Club:* East India.

NEWSOME, William Antony; Director-General, Association of British Chambers of Commerce, 1974–84; *b* 8 Nov. 1919; *s* of William F. Newsome and Elizabeth (*née* Thompson); *m* 1951, Estella Ann (*née* Cope); one *s*. *Educ:* King Henry VIII Sch., Coventry; Bedford Modern Sch. Student Engineer, W. H. Allen, Sons & Co. Ltd, Bedford, 1937–40. Served War, Royal Engineers: N Africa, Sicily, Italy campaigns, 1940–47. Engrg Dept, Crown Agents for Oversea Governments and Administrations, 1949–61; Principal: Home Office, 1961–64; Min. of Technology, 1964–70; Dept of Trade and Industry, 1970–71; Asst Sec., Dept of Trade, 1971–74. Member: SITPRO, 1972–84; Production Statistics Adv. Cttee, 1975–84; Home Office Standing Cttee on Crime Prevention, 1978–84. *Recreations:* photography, swimming, golf. *Address:* Bourdon Lacey, Old Woking Road, Woking, Surrey GU22 8HR. *T:* Woking (0483) 762237.

NEWSON-SMITH, Sir John (Kenneth), 2nd Bt *cr* 1944; DL; Member of HM Commission of Lieutenancy for City of London, since 1947; *b* 9 Jan. 1911; *s* of Sir Frank Newson-Smith, 1st Bt and Dorothy (*d* 1955), *d* of late Sir Henry Tozer; *S* father, 1971; *m* 1st, 1945, Vera Margaret Allt (marr. diss. 1971); one *s* two *d*; 2nd, 1972, Anne (*d* 1987), *d* of late Harold Burns; 3rd, 1988, Sarah Ramsay, *d* of late Robert Bicknell. *Educ:* Dover Coll.; Jesus Coll., Cambridge (MA). Joined Newson-Smith & Co, 1933, Partner 1938. Served War, Royal Navy, 1939–40; RNVR 1940. Rejoined Newson-Smith & Co, 1946 (which subseq. became Fielding Newson-Smith & Co.). Master of Turners Co., 1969–70; Liveryman: Merchant Taylors' Co.; Spectaclemakers' Co. Court of Common Council, 1945–78; Deputy, Ward of Bassishaw, 1961–76. DL City of London, 1947. *Recreations:* travelling, gardening. *Heir: s* Peter Frank Graham Newson-Smith [*b* 8 May 1947; *m* 1974, Mrs Mary-Ann Owens, *o d* of Cyril C. Collins; one *s* one *d*]. *Address:* East End, 67 East Street, Warminster BA12 9BZ. *Club:* City Livery.

NEWTON, 4th Baron, *cr* 1892; **Peter Richard Legh;** *b* 6 April 1915; *er s* of 3rd Baron Newton, TD, DL, JP, and Hon. Helen Meysey-Thompson (*d* 1958); *S* father 1960; *m* 1948, Priscilla, *yr d* of late Capt. John Egerton-Warburton and *widow* of William Matthew Palmer, Visc. Wolmer; two *s*. *Educ:* Eton; Christ Church, Oxford (MA). 2nd Lt, Grenadier Guards (SR), 1937; Captain, 1941; Major, 1945. JP 1951; CC Hampshire, 1949–52 and 1954–55. Chairman East Hampshire Young Conservatives, 1949–50. MP (C) Petersfield Division of Hants, Oct. 1951–June 1960; PPS to Fin. Sec. to Treasury, 1952–53; Asst Govt Whip, 1953–55; a Lord Comr of Treasury, 1955–57; Vice-Chamberlain of the Household, 1957–59; Treasurer of the Household, 1959–60; Capt. Yeomen of the Guard and Govt Asst Chief Whip, 1960–62; (Joint) Parly Sec., Min. of Health, 1962–64; Min. of State for Education and Science, April-Oct. 1964. *Recreations:* photography, clock repairing, making gadgets. *Heir: s* Hon. Richard Thomas Legh [*b* 11 Jan. 1950; *m* 1978, Rosemary Whitfoot Clarke, *yr d* of Herbert Clarke, Eastbourne; one *s* one *d*]. *Address:* Vernon Hill House, Bishop's Waltham, Hampshire. *T:* Bishop's Waltham (04893) 2301. *Clubs:* Carlton, St Stephen's Constitutional, Pratt's; Hampshire (Winchester).

See also Earl of Selborne.

NEWTON, Rt. Hon. Antony Harold, (Rt. Hon. Tony Newton), OBE 1972; PC 1988; MP (C) Braintree since Feb. 1974; Secretary of State for Social Security, since 1989; economist; *b* Aug. 1937; *m* 1st, 1962, Janet Huxley (marr. diss. 1986); two *d*; 2nd, 1986, Mrs Patricia Gilthorpe. *Educ:* Friends' Sch., Saffron Walden; Trinity Coll., Oxford. Hons PPE. President: OU Conservative Assoc., 1958; Oxford Union, 1959. Formerly Sec. and Research Sec., Bow Group. Head of Conservative Research Dept's Economic Section, 1965–70; Asst Dir, Conservative Research Dept, 1970–74. Chm. Coningsby Club, 1965–66. Contested (C) Sheffield, Brightside, 1970. An Asst Govt Whip, 1979–81; a Lord Comr of HM Treasury, 1981–82; Parly Under-Sec. of State for Social Security, 1982–84, and Minister for the Disabled, 1983–84, Minister of State (Minister for Social Security and the Disabled), 1984–86, Minister of State (Minister for Health) and Chm., NHS Management Bd, 1986–88, DHSS; Chancellor of Duchy of Lancaster and Minister of Trade and Industry, 1988–89. Vice-Chm., Fedn of Univ. Conservative and Unionist Assocs, 1959. Gov., Felsted Sch. Interested in taxation and social services. *Address:* House of Commons, SW1A 0AA.

NEWTON, Air Vice-Marshal Barry Hamilton, CB 1988; OBE 1975; Gentleman Usher to The Queen, since 1989; *b* 1 April 1932; *s* of late Bernard Hamilton Newton, FCA and Dorothy Mary Newton; *m* 1959, Constance Lavinia, *d* of late Col J. J. Aitken, CMG, DSO, OBE; one *s* one *d*. *Educ:* Highgate; RAF College Cranwell. Commissioned 1953; 109 Sqn, 1954; 76 Sqn, Australia and Christmas Island, 1956; Flying Instr, RAF Coll. and No 6 Flying Trng Sch., 1959–63; HQ Flying Trng Comd, 1964; Staff Coll., Bracknell, 1966; Personal Staff Officer to Comdr, Second Allied Tactical Air Force, 1967; OC Ops Wing, RAF Cottesmore, 1969; Air Warfare Course, 1971; Defence Policy Staff, 1972; Cabinet Office, 1975; Asst Dir, Defence Policy, 1978; Cabinet Office, 1979; Air Cdre Flying Trng, HQ RAF Support Comd, 1982; Sen. Directing Staff (Air), RCDS, 1984; Comdt, JSDC, 1986–88; Special Project Officer, RCDS, 1988—89. Mem. Council, TA&VRA, 1989–. *Recreations:* shooting, walking, philately. *Address:* c/o National Westminster Bank, Blue Boar Row, Salisbury, Wilts. *Club:* Royal Air Force.

NEWTON, (Charles) Wilfrid, CBE 1988; Chairman and Chief Executive, London Regional Transport, and Chairman, London Underground Ltd, since 1989; *b* 11 Dec. 1928; *s* of late Gore Mansfield Newton and Catherine Knox Newton; *m* 1954, Felicity Mary Lynn Thomas; two *s* two *d*. *Educ:* Orange Grove Prep. Sch.; Highlands North High Sch.; Univ. of Witwatersrand, Johannesburg. Chartered Accountant (South Africa). Chartered Accountant, Saml Thomson & Young, 1947–55; Territory Accounting and Finance Manager, Mobil Oil Corp., S Africa, 1955–62; Controller, Mobil Sekiyu KK, Tokyo, 1962–63; Financial Manager/Dep. Gen. Manager, Mobil Oil, E Africa, Nairobi, 1963–65; Finance Dir, Mobil Sekiyu KK, Tokyo,, 1965–68; Turner & Newall: Finance Dir, 1968; Man. Dir of Finance and Planning, 1974, of Plastics, Chemicals and Mining, 1976; Gp Man. Dir, 1979; Gp Man. Dir and Chief Exec., 1982; Chairman: Mass Transit Railway Corp., Hong Kong, 1983–89; Hong Kong Futures Exchange Ltd, 1987–89; Non-exec. Director: Hongkong & Shanghai Banking Corp., 1986–; Sketchley PLC, 1990–; MetroPower Ltd, 1990–; HSBC Hldgs plc, 1990–. FRSA 1990. JP Hong Kong, 1986–89. *Recreations:* sailing, reading. *Address:* Newtons Gate, 12 Ramley Road, Pennington, Lymington, Hants SO41 8GQ. *T:* Lymington (0590) 679750; 7A Balmoral House, Windsor Way, Brook Green, W14 0UF. *T:* 071–602 4996. *Clubs:* Carlton; Wanderers (Johannesburg); Hong Kong, Aberdeen Boat, Royal Hong Kong Yacht (Hong Kong); Royal Lymington Yacht.

NEWTON, Clive Trevor, CB 1991; Under Secretary, Head of Consumer Affairs Division, Department of Trade and Industry, 1986–91; *b* 26 Aug. 1931; *s* of late Frederick Norman and of Phyllis Laura Newton; *m* 1961, Elizabeth Waugh Plowman; one *s* one *d*. *Educ:* Hove Grammar School for Boys. LLB London; called to Bar, Middle Temple, 1969; certified accountant. Examiner, Insolvency Service, Board of Trade, 1952, Sen. Examiner, 1963, Asst Official Receiver, 1967; Principal, Marine Div., BoT, 1969; Sen. Principal, Marine Div., Dept of Trade, 1973; Asst Director of Consumer Credit, Office of Fair Trading, 1974; Asst Sec., Regional Development Grants Div., Dept of Industry, 1978; Dir of Consumer Affairs, OFT, 1980. *Recreations:* golf, watching cricket and football. *Address:* 115 Hangleton Way, Hove, E Sussex BN3 8AF. *Clubs:* Royal Automobile; Surrey County Cricket, East Brighton Golf.

NEWTON, Derek Henry; Chairman, C. E. Heath plc, 1984–87; *b* 14 March 1933; *s* of Sidney Wellington Newton and Sylvia May Newton (*née* Peacock); *m* 1957, Judith Ann, *d* of Roland Hart, Kingston, Surrey; two *d*. *Educ:* Emanuel School. FCII. Commissioned Royal Artillery, 1952–54 (Lieut). Clerical, Medical & General Life Assurance Society, 1954–58; C. E. Heath Urquhart (Life & Pensions), 1958–83, Chm., 1971–84; Dir. C. E. Heath, 1975, Dep. Chm., 1983–84; Director: Glaxo Insurance (Bermuda), 1980–; Glaxo Trustees, 1980–; Clarges Pharmaceutical Trustees, 1985. Governor, BUPA Med. R&D, 1981–. *Recreations:* cricket, golf. *Address:* Pantiles, Meadway, Oxshott, Surrey KT22 0LZ. *T:* Oxshott (0372) 842273. *Clubs:* Surrey County Cricket (Chm. 1979–), MCC.

NEWTON, Douglas Anthony, CB 1976; Senior Registrar, Principal Registry, Family Division of High Court, 1972–75, retired; *b* 21 Dec. 1915; *s* of John and Janet May Newton; *m* 1946, Barbara Sutherland; one *s* one *d*. *Educ:* Westminster Sch. Joined Civil Service, 1934. Served War, British and Indian Armies, 1940–46. Apptd Registrar, 1959; Sen. Registrar, 1972. *Recreations:* beer, boats, building.

NEWTON, Sir Gordon; *see* Newton, Sir L. G.

NEWTON, Sir (Harry) Michael (Rex), 3rd Bt, *cr* 1900; Director Thos Parsons & Sons Ltd; *b* 7 Feb. 1923; 2nd and *e* surv. *s* of Sir Harry K. Newton, 2nd Bt, OBE, DL, and Myrtle Irene (*d* 1977), *e d* of W. W. Grantham, Balneath Manor, Lewes; *S* father, 1951; *m* 1958, Pauline Jane, *o d* of late R. J. F. Howgill, CBE; one *s*; three adopted *d*. *Educ:* Eastbourne College. Served War of 1939–45, with KRRC, in 8th Army and Middle East, 1941–46 (wounded). Master, Girdlers' Company, 1975–76; Freeman of City of London. *Recreations:* shooting, sailing (winner of 1953 Fastnet Race), ski-ing, fencing. *Heir: s* George Peter Howgill Newton [*b* 26 March 1962; *m* 1988, Jane, twin *d* of John Rymer; one *d*]. *Address:* Cliff House, Old Lyme Road, Charmouth, Dorset DT6 6BW. *T:* Charmouth (0297) 60704. *Club:* Royal Ocean Racing.

NEWTON, Rev. Dr John Anthony; Chairman of the Liverpool District of the Methodist Church, since 1986; a President, Churches Together in England, since 1990; *b* 28 Sept. 1930; *s* of late Charles Victor Newton and of Kathleen Marchant; *m* 1963, Rachel, *d* of late Rev. Maurice H. Giddings and of Hilda Giddings, Louth, Lincs; four *s*. *Educ:* Grammar School, Boston, Lincs; University Coll., Hull; London Univ.; Wesley House, Cambridge. BA, PhD (Lond), MA (Cantab). Jun. Research Fellow, Inst. of Historical Research, London Univ., 1953–55; Housemaster and actg Chaplain, Kent Coll., Canterbury, 1955–56; trained for Methodist Ministry, Wesley House, 1956–58; Asst Tutor, Richmond Coll., Surrey, 1958–61, having been ordained, 1960; Circuit Minister at Louth, Lincs, 1961–64, and Stockton-on-Tees, 1964–65; Tutor at Didsbury Coll. (from 1967, Wesley Coll.), Bristol, 1965–72; taught Church History, St Paul's United Theolog. Coll., Limuru, Kenya, and Univ. of Nairobi, 1972–73; Principal of Wesley Coll., Bristol, 1973–78; Superintendent Minister, London Mission (W London) Circuit, 1978–86. President of the Methodist Conference, 1981–82; Jt Pres., Merseyside and Region Churches' Ecumenical Assembly, 1987–; Moderator, Free Church Fed. Council, 1989–90. Hon. Canon, Lincoln Cathedral, 1988. Chm. of Governors, Westminster Coll., Oxford, 1979–88; Trustee, Wesley House, Cambridge, 1979–88. Governor, Rydal School, Colwyn Bay, 1986–. Hon. DLitt Hull, 1982. *Publications:* Methodism and the Puritans, 1964; Susanna Wesley and the Puritan Tradition in Methodism, 1968; The Palestine Problem, 1972; Search for a Saint: Edward King, 1977; The Fruit of the Spirit in the Lives of Great Christians, 1979; A Man for All Churches: Marcus Ward, 1984; The Wesleys for Today, 1989. *Recreations:* music, gardening, walking, book-collecting. *Address:* 49 Queen's Drive, Mossley Hill, Liverpool L18 2DT. *T:* 051–722 1219. *Clubs:* Penn; Athenæum (Liverpool).

NEWTON, John David; a Recorder of the Crown Court, since 1983; *b* 4 April 1921; *s* of late Giffard and Mary Newton; *m* 1942, Mary Bevan; one *s* one *d*. *Educ:* Berkhamsted School; University College London. LLB 1947. Served war of 1939–45 in Royal Artillery and Indian Army (Major); called to the Bar, Middle Temple, 1948; Lectr in Law, University College, Hull, 1948–51; Lectr then Senior Lectr in Law, Liverpool University, 1951–82. Dir, Liverpool Philharmonic Hall Trust, 1986–88. *Publications:* (ed) Halsbury's Laws of England, 4th edn, 1982, Vol. 39, Rent Charges and Annuities; (ed jtly) Encyclopaedia of Forms and Precedents, 5th edn, 1988, Vol. 33, Rent Charges and Annuities. *Recreations:* fishing, golf. *Address:* 10 Rose Mount, Oxton, Birkenhead, Merseyside L43 5SW. *T:* 051–652 4675. *Clubs:* Athenæum (Liverpool); Royal Liverpool Golf.

NEWTON, Prof. John Michael, DSc; Professor of Pharmaceutics, School of Pharmacy, University of London, since 1984; *b* 26 Dec. 1935; *s* of Richard and Dora Newton; *m* 1959, Janet Hinninghan (marr. diss. 1986); one *s* two *d*. *Educ:* Leigh Grammar Sch., Lancs; Sch. of Pharmacy, Univ. of London (BPharm; DSc 1990); Univ. of Nottingham (PhD). FPS. Apprentice pharmacist, Royal Albert Edward Infirmary, Wigan, 1953–55; Demonstrator, Univ. of Nottingham, 1958–62; Sen. Lectr, Sunderland Polytechnic, 1962–64; Lectr, Univ. of Manchester, 1964–67; Sen. Scientist, Lilly Research Centre Ltd, 1968–71; Lectr, Univ. of Nottingham, 1972–78; Prof. of Pharmaceutics, Univ. of London, at Chelsea College, 1978–83. *Publications:* numerous articles in sci. jls associated with pharmaceutical technology. *Recreations:* fell walking, long distance running (Belgrave Harriers), gardening.

NEWTON, Sir Kenneth (Garnar), 3rd Bt *cr* 1924; OBE 1970 (MBE 1944); TD; Chairman, Garnar Booth plc, 1972–87 (Managing Director, 1961–83); *b* 4 June 1918; *s* of Sir Edgar Henry Newton, 2nd Bt, and Gladys Maud (*d* 1966), *d* of late Sir James Garnar; *S* father, 1971; *m* 1944, Margaret Isabel (*d* 1979), *d* of Rev. Dr George Blair, Dundee; two *s*. *Educ:* Wellington College, Berks. Served War of 1939–45 (MBE); Lt-Col, RASC (TA). General Commissioner for Income Tax, 1961–. Chm. Governors, Colfe's Sch., 1982–. Pres., Internat. Council of Tanners, 1972–78; Past President, British Leather Federation (1968–69); Liveryman and Member of Court of Assistants, Leathersellers' Company (Master, 1977–78) and Feltmakers' Company (Master, 1983–84). *Heir: s* John Garnar Newton [*b* 10 July 1945; *m* 1972, Jacynth A. K. Miller; three *s* (incl. twins)]. *Address:* Wildways, High Broom Lane, Crowborough, Sussex TN6 3SP. *T:* Crowborough (0892) 661089.

NEWTON, Sir (Leslie) Gordon, Kt 1966; Editor of The Financial Times, 1950–72, Director 1967–72; *b* 1907; *s* of John and Edith Newton; *m* 1935, Peggy Ellen Warren; (one *s* decd). *Educ:* Blundell's School; Sidney Sussex College, Cambridge. Chm., LBC, 1974–77; Director: Trust Houses Forte Ltd, 1973–80; Mills & Allen (Internat.) Ltd, 1974–81. Hannen Swaffer Award for Journalist of the Year, 1966; Granada Television special award, 1970. *Address:* 51 Thames House, Phyllis Court Drive, Henley-on-Thames, Oxon RG9 2NA.

NEWTON, Margaret; Schools Officer, Diocese of Oxford, 1984–88, retired; *b* 20 Dec. 1927; 2nd *d* of F. L. Newton, KStJ, MB, ChB, and Mrs A. C. Newton, MBE, BA. *Educ:* Sherborne School for Girls; St Andrews Univ.; Oxford University. MA Hons St Andrews, 1950; Educn Dip. Oxon 1951. Asst Mistress, King Edward VI Grammar School, Handsworth, Birmingham, 1951–54; Classics Mistress, Queen Margaret's Sch., York, 1954–60 (House Mistress, 1957); House Mistress, Malvern Girls' College, 1960–64 (Head of Classics Dept, 1962); Headmistress, Westonbirt Sch., 1965–80; Gen. Sec., Friends of the Elderly, 1981–83. *Address:* The Comedy, Sherborne Street, Lechlade, Glos GL7 3AN.

NEWTON, Sir Michael; *see* Newton, Sir H. M. R.

NEWTON, Peter Marcus; HM Diplomatic Service; Deputy High Commissioner, Ottawa, since 1989; *b* 16 Sept. 1942; *s* of Leslie Marcus Newton and Edith Mary Newton; *m* 1972, Sonia Maria Freire de Castilho; two *s* one *d*. *Educ:* Hamilton Academy; Glasgow Univ. (MA Hons); McGill Univ. (postgrad. studies). Third Sec., CRO, later CO, 1965; Kinshasa, 1967; Lima, 1968; First Sec., FCO, 1972; First Sec. (Econ.), Tokyo, 1975; First

Sec. and Head of Chancery, Caracas, 1979; FCO, 1981; Counsellor, FCO, 1985–87; Consul-Gen., Montreal, 1987–89. *Address:* c/o Foreign and Commonwealth Office, SW1. *Club:* Mount Royal (Montreal).

NEWTON, Richard James; Chairman, National and Provincial Building Society, since 1988; *b* 17 Nov. 1927; *s* of Alfred Richard Newton and Rosamond Newton (*née* Tunstill); *m* 1961, Elizabeth Seraphine Meuwissen (*d* 1986); four *s*. *Educ:* Clifton; St John's College, Cambridge (MA). Managerial positions at: Courtaulds, 1951–58; Midland Silicones, 1959–62; Chemstrand, 1963–66; Keith Shipton & Co., 1967–69; Director: Bury & Masco (Holdings), 1970–77; Sketchley, 1978–87 (Chm., 1983–87); National & Provincial Building Soc., 1985–. Fellow and Bursar, Trinity Hall, Cambridge, 1977–89. Gov., Clifton Coll., 1990–. *Recreations:* music, fell-walking, playing the piano. *Address:* The White House, Beeston, Norfolk PE32 2NF. *T:* Fakenham (0328) 701215.

NEWTON, Wilfrid; *see* Newton, C. W.

NEWTON-CLARE, Herbert Mitchell, (Bill), CBE 1976; MC 1943; Executive Chairman, Albemarle Group; *b* 5 May 1922; *s* of Herbert John and Eileen Margaret Newton-Clare; *m*; three *d*. *Educ:* Cheltenham Coll. TA, Middlesex Regt, 1938; served War of 1939–45: mobilised, 1939; commnd, Wiltshire Regt, 1941; wounded, Normandy, 1944; demobilised, 1945 (Major). Joined Bowyers (Wiltshire) Ltd. as trainee, 1945; Factory Manager, 1955, Gen. Manager, 1957, Man. Dir, 1960, Chm., 1966; following take-over by Unigate of Scot Bowyers (formerly Bowyers (Wiltshire) Ltd), became Director of Unigate, 1973, Vice-Chm., 1974–76; Dir, FMC Ltd, and ancillary cos, 1976–77. Chm., Meat Manufrs Assoc., 1970–82; Member: Exec. and Council, Food Manufrs Fedn, 1970–82; Food and Drink Industries Fedn, 1970–82; Exec. Centre de Liaison des Industries Transformatrice de Viandes de la Commune Européenne, 1970–82. *Recreations:* golf, tennis, swimming, fishing. *Address:* 4A Walham Grove, SW6 1QP. *T:* 071–381 0131. *Club:* Sunningdale Golf.

NEWTON DUNN, William Francis; Member (C) Lincolnshire, European Parliament, since 1979, and representative for Gibraltar, since 1984; *b* 3 Oct. 1941; *s* of Lt-Col Owen Newton Dunn, OBE, and Barbara (*née* Brooke); *m* 1970, Anna Terez Arki; one *s* one *d*. *Educ:* Marlborough Coll. (scholar); Gonville and Caius Coll., Cambridge (MA); INSEAD Business Sch., Fontainebleau (MBA). With Fisons Ltd (Fertilizer Division), 1974–79. European Parliament: Cons. Spokesman: on Transport, 1984–87; on Rules of Procedure, 1987–89; on Political Affairs, 1989–;91; Chm., 1979 Cttee (Cons. backbench MEPs), 1983–88; Mem. Bureau, Cons. MEP Gp, 1988–; Dep. Leader, EDG, 1991–. Contested (C): general elections: Carmarthen, Feb. 1974; Cardiff West, Oct. 1974. *Publications:* Greater in Europe, 1986; pamphlet on the EEC's democratic deficit. *Recreation:* spending time with his children. *Address:* 10 Church Lane, Navenby, Lincoln LN5 0EG. *T:* Lincoln (0522) 810812.

NGAIZA, Christopher Pastor; Chairman and Managing Director, PES Consultants Ltd, Tanzania, since 1986; *b* 29 March 1930; parents decd; *m* 1952, Thereza; three *s* two *d* (and one *s* decd). *Educ:* Makerere University Coll.; Loughborough Co-operative College. Local Courts Magistrate, 1952–53; Secretary/Manager, Bahaya Co-operative Consumer Stores, 1955–57; Loughborough Co-operative Coll., 1957–59; Auctioneer and Representative of Bukoba Native Co-operative Union, Mombasa, 1959–61; Foreign Service, 1961–; Counsellor, Mission to UN, 1961–62; Counsellor, Tanganyika High Commn, London, 1962–63; High Commissioner for United Republic of Tanganyika and Zanzibar in London, 1964–65; Tanzanian Ambassador: to Netherlands, 1965–67, to Arab Republic of Egypt, 1972–77; Mem., E African Common Market Tribunal, 1968–69; Tanzania's first High Comr to Zambia, 1969–72; Special Personal Assistant to Pres. of Tanzania, 1977–83; Comr for Kagera River Basin Orgn, 1978–83. *Recreations:* music, tennis. *Address:* PES Consultants Ltd, PO Box 4647, Dar-es-Salaam, Tanzania.

NGATA, Sir Henare Kohere, KBE 1982 (OBE); chartered accountant, retired; *b* Waiomatatini, 19 Dec. 1917; *s* of Sir Apirana Ngata and Arihia, *d* of Tuta Tamati; *m* 1940, Rora Lorna, *d* of Maihi Rangipo Mete Kingi; one *s*. *Educ:* Waiomatatini Sch.; Te Aute Coll., Victoria Univ. of Wellington, BA; BCom; FCA (NZ Soc. of Accountants). Served 28th Maori Bn, 1939–45: POW, Greece; Germany, 1941–45. Chm., Mangatu 1, 3 & 4 Blocks Incorp., 1959–87; Director: Fieldair Ltd, 1960–79; Gisborne Sheepfarmers Mercantile Co. Ltd; Gisborne Sheepfarmers Freezing Co. Ltd. Member: Gisborne Reg. Commn, NZ Historic Places Trust, 1962–70; NZ Maori Council, 1962–85; C of E Provincial Commn on Maori Schs, 1964–; Gisborne/East Coast Regional Develt Council, 1973–78; Finance Cttee, Bishopric of Aotearoa. Nat. Pres., 28th Maori Bn Assoc., 1964–66. Vice-Pres., NZ Nat. Party, 1967–69. Hon. LLD, Victoria Univ. of Wellington, 1979. *Address:* Grant Road, Gisborne, New Zealand.

NG'ETHE NJOROGE; businessman; High Commissioner for Kenya in London, 1970–78; *m* 1972, Dr Njeri Ng'ethe Njoroge; one *s*. *Educ:* Kenya and Uganda (Cambridge Sch. Cert., 1949); United States: Central State Coll., Wilberforce, Ohio (BSc (Gen. Sci.) 1955); Univ. of Dayton, Dayton, Ohio (Sociology, 1955–56); Boston Univ. (MSc (Pol. Sci. and Journalism) 1962). Began as journalist, Patriot Ledger, Quincy, Mass; subseq., Kenya Govt: Asst Sec. (Admin), in Min. of Lands and Settlement, and Min. of Works, 1963–64; Min. of Foreign Affairs, 1964; Head of Africa Div., 1964–67; Counsellor, Kenya Embassy, Bonn, 1968–70. Delegate: Commonwealth Conf., 1965, 1966, 1971; Organization of African Unity Confs, 1964–67; UN Gen. Assembly, 1964, 1965, 1966. *Recreations:* music (collector of jazz and classical records), photography (colour slides), reading; interest in current public and international issues. *Address:* PO Box 30384, Nairobi, Kenya.

NGONDA, Putteho Muketoi; Zambian Ambassador to USA, Peru, Brazil and Venezuela, since 1977; *b* 16 Aug. 1936; *m* 1965, Lungowe Mulala; three *s*. *Educ:* Mongu and Munali Secondary Schs, Zambia; UC of Rhodesia and Nyasaland, Salisbury. BScEcon (Hons). District Officer, 1963–64; 2nd Sec., Zambia Perm. Mission to UN, 1964–65; 1st Sec., Zambian Embassy, Washington, 1967–68; Asst Sec. (Political), Min. of Foreign Affairs, 1968–70; Under-Sec., Min. of Foreign Affairs, 1970–72; Ambassador to Ethiopia, 1972–74; High Comr to UK, 1974–75; Perm. Sec., Ministry of Foreign Affairs, 1975–77. *Recreation:* mainly tennis. *Address:* Embassy of the Republic of Zambia, 2419 Massachusetts Avenue, NW, Washington, DC 20008, USA.

NIALL, Sir Horace Lionel Richard, Kt 1974; CBE 1957 (MBE 1943); Civil Servant (retd); *b* 14 Oct. 1904; *s* of late Alfred George Niall and Jane Phyllis Niall; *m* 1965, Una Lesley Niall (*née* de Salis); one *d*. *Educ:* Mudgee High Sch., NSW; Sydney Univ., NSW. Served War of 1939–45: with AIF, four yrs in New Guinea, rank Major. No NGX 373, all campaigns in New Guinea. NSW Public Service (Water Conservation Commn), 1923–27. Public Service of Papua, New Guinea, 1927–64: joined as a Cadet and retd as Dist Comr; rep. PNG at South Pacific Commn, 1954, and UN Trusteeship Council, 1957; Mem. for Morobe in first House of Assembly and Speaker First House, 1964. *Recreations:* golf, surfing. *Address:* 9 Commodore, 50 Palm Beach Road, Palm Beach, NSW 2108, Australia. *T:* 919 5462. *Clubs:* Palm Beach Golf, RSL Palm Beach (NSW).

NIARCHOS, Stavros Spyros; Grand Cross of Order of the Phœnix (Greece), 1957; Commander of Order of George I of Greece, 1954; Commander of Order of St George and St Constantine (Greece), 1964; Head of Niarchos Group of Shipping Companies which controls over 5.75 million tons of shipping (operational and building); *b* 3 July 1909; *s* of late Spyros Niarchos and of Eugenie Niarchos; *m* 1st, 1939, Melpomene Capparis (marr. diss., 1947); no *c*; 2nd, 1947, Eugenie Livanos (*d* 1970); three *s* one *d*; 3rd, 1965, Charlotte Ford (marr. diss., 1967); one *d*; 4th, 1971, Mrs Athina Livanos (*d* 1974). *Educ:* Univ. of Athens (Dr of Laws). On leaving Univ. joined family grain and shipping business; started independent shipping concern, 1939. Joined Royal Hellenic Navy Volunteer Reserve, 1941; served on destroyer engaged in North Atlantic convoy work (despatches). Demobilised, 1945, with rank of Lieut-Comdr. Returned to Shipping business. Pioneered super-tankers. *Recreations:* yachting, ski-ing. *Address:* c/o Niarchos (London) Ltd, 41/43 Park Street, W1A 2JR. *T:* 071–629 8400. *Clubs:* Athenian, Royal Yacht Club of Greece (both in Athens).

NIBLETT, Prof. William Roy, CBE 1970; BA, MLitt; Professor of Higher Education, University of London, 1967–73, now Professor Emeritus; *b* 25 July 1906; *m* 1938, Sheila Margaret, OBE 1975, *d* of A. C. Taylor, Peterborough; one *s* one *d*. *Educ:* Cotham Sch., Bristol; University of Bristol (1st cl. hons English; DipEd cl. I; John Stewart Schol.); St Edmund Hall, Oxford. Lectr in Educn, King's Coll., Newcastle, 1934–45 (Registrar, Durham Univ., 1940–44); Prof. of Educn, University Coll., Hull, 1945–47; Prof. of Education, and Dir, Inst. of Education, Univ. of Leeds, 1947–59; Dean, Univ. of London Inst. of Education, 1960–68. Hibbert Lectr, 1965; Fulbright Schol. (Harvard) and Kellogg International Fellow, 1954; sometime Visiting Professor, Universities of California, Melbourne, Otago and Univs of Japan. Mem., UGC, 1949–59; Chairman: UGC Sub-Cttee on Halls of Residence, 1956 (Report 1957); Educn Dept, BCC, 1965–71; Higher Educn Policy Gp, 1969–72; President: European Assoc. for Res. in Higher Educn, 1972; Higher Educn Foundn, 1984– (Chm. Trustees, 1980–81). Vice-President: World Univ. Service (UK), 1963–90; Soc. for Res. in Higher Educn, 1978–; Gloucestershire Historic Churches Preservation Trust, 1981–. Member: Nat. Advisory Coun. on Trng and Supply of Teachers, 1950–61; Adv. Council on Army Educn, 1961–70; Council, Royal Holloway College, 1963–76; Council, Cheltenham Ladies' College, 1967–79; Trustee, Westhill Coll., Birmingham, 1979–. Chm., Editorial Bd, Studies in Higher Education, 1975–82. *Publications:* Education and the Modern Mind, 1954; Christian Education in a Secular Society, 1960; (ed) Moral Education in a Changing Society, 1963; (ed) Higher Education: Demand and Response, 1969; (ed with R. F. Butts) World Year Book of Education, 1972–73; Universities Between Two Worlds, 1974; (with D. Humphreys and J. Fairhurst) The University Connection, 1975; (ed) The Sciences, The Humanities and the Technological Threat, 1975; (contrib.) International Encyclopedia of Higher Education, 1977; (contrib.) The Study of Education, 1980; (contrib.) Validation in Higher Education, 1983. *Address:* 7 Blenheim Road, Bristol BS6 7JL. *T:* Bristol (0272) 735891.

NIBLOCK, Henry, (Pat), OBE 1972; HM Diplomatic Service, retired; HM Consul-General, Strasbourg, 1968–72; *b* 25 Nov. 1911; *s* of Joseph and Isabella Niblock, Belfast; *m* 1940, Barbara Mary Davies, *d* of late Captain R. W. Davies, Air Ministry; two *s*. Vice-Consul: Bremen, 1947–50; Bordeaux, 1951; Second Sec. (Commercial), Copenhagen, 1951–53; Consul, Frankfurt-on-Main, 1954–57; First Sec. and Consul, Monrovia, 1957–58; Consul, Houston, 1959–62; Chargé d'Affaires, Port-au-Prince, 1962–63; First Sec. and Consul, Brussels, 1964; Consul (Commercial), Cape Town, 1964–67. *Recreations:* walking, photography. *Address:* 10 Clifton House, 2 Park Avenue, Eastbourne, East Sussex BN22 9QN. *T:* Eastbourne (0323) 505695. *Club:* Civil Service.

NICCOL, Kathleen Agnes; *see* Leo, Dame Sister M.

NICE, Geoffrey; QC 1990; a Recorder, since 1987; *b* 21 Oct. 1945; *s* of William Charles Nice and Mahala Anne Nice (*née* Tarryer); *m* 1974, Philippa Mary Gross; three *d*. *Educ:* St Dunstan's College, Catford; Keble College, Oxford. Called to the Bar, Inner Temple, 1971; Contested (SDP/Liberal Alliance) Dover, 1983, 1987. *Address:* Manor Farm, Adisham, Canterbury, Kent CT3 3JJ; Farrar's Building, Temple, EC4Y 7BD. *T:* 071–583 9241.

NICHOL, Duncan Kirkbride, CBE 1989; Chief Executive, National Health Service Management Executive, since 1989 (Member, since 1985); *b* 30 May 1941; *s* of James and Mabel Nichol; *m* 1972, Elizabeth Wilkinson; one *s* one *d*. *Educ:* Bradford Grammar Sch.; St Andrews Univ. (MA Hons). AHSM (AHA 1967); FFPHM 1991. Asst Gp Sec. and Hosp. Sec. to Manchester Royal Infirmary, 1969–73; Dep. Gp Sec. and Actg Gp Sec., Univ. Hosp. Management Cttee of S Manchester, 1973–74; Dist Administrator, Manchester S Dist, 1974–77; Area Administrator, Salford AHA(T), 1977–81; Regional Administrator, 1981–84, Regional Gen. Manager, 1984–89, Mersey RHA. Hon. Lectr, Dept of Social Admin, Manchester Univ., 1977–. Member: Central Health Services Council, 1980–81; NHS Training Authy, 1983–85; Nat. Council, Inst. of Health Services Management, 1976– (Pres., 1984–85); Educn Cttee, King Edward's Hosp. Fund for London, 1981– (Chm., 1987–). *Publications:* contributed: Health Care in the United Kingdom, 1982; Management for Clinicians, 1982; Working with People, 1983; Managers as Strategists, 1987. *Recreations:* walking, golf, squash. *Address:* Department of Health, Richmond House, 79 Whitehall, SW1; 1 Pipers Close, Heswall, Wirral, Merseyside L60 9LJ. *T:* 051–342 2699. *Club:* Athenæum.

NICHOL, Prof. Lawrence Walter, DSc; FRACI; FAA; Vice-Chancellor, Australian National University, since 1988; *b* 7 April 1935; *s* of Lawrence Gordon Nichol and Mavis Lillian Nichol (*née* Burgess); *m* 1963, Rosemary Esther (*née* White); three *s*. *Educ:* Univ. of Adelaide (BSc 1956, Hons 1957; PhD 1962; DSc 1974). Postdoctoral Fellow, Clark Univ., Mass, 1961–62; Res. Fellow, ANU, 1963–65; Sen. Lectr, then Reader, Univ. of Melbourne, 1966–70; Prof. of Phys. Biochem., ANU, 1971–85; Vice-Chancellor, Univ. of New England, 1985–88. FRACI 1971; FAA 1981; Fellow, Royal Soc. of NSW, 1986. David Syme Res. Prize, 1966; Lemberg Medal, Aust. Biochem. Soc., 1977. *Publications:* Migration of Interacting Systems, 1972; Protein-Protein Interactions, 1981; over 100 papers in internat. sci. jls. *Recreations:* philately, cinema, art, Spanish language. *Address:* 21 Balmain Crescent, Acton, ACT 2601, Australia. *T:* (062) 498 749. *Club:* North Sydney (New South Wales).

NICHOL, Mrs Muriel Edith; JP; *e d* of late R. C. Wallhead, MP Merthyr Tydfil, 1922–34; *m* James Nichol, MA; one *s*. Counsellor, Welwyn Garden City UDC, 1937–45 (Chm. 1943–44); formerly Dep. Chm., Welwyn Magistrates' Court. MP (Lab) North Bradford, 1945–50; Mem. Parly Delegation to India, Jan.-Feb. 1946; Mem. "Curtis" Cttee (Home Office) on Care of Children, 1945–46. JP Herts, 1944. *Recreations:* local government, social welfare, education.

NICHOLAS, (Angela) Jane (Udale), OBE 1990; Dance Director, Arts Council of Great Britain, 1979–89, retired; *b* 14 June 1929; *d* of late Bernard Alexander Royle Shore, CBE; *m* 1964, William Alan Nicholas. *Educ:* Norland Place Sch.; Rambert Sch. of Ballet; Arts Educnl Trust; Sadler's Wells Ballet Sch. Founder Mem., Sadler's Wells Theatre Ballet, 1946–50; Mem., Sadler's Wells Ballet at Royal Opera House, 1950–52; freelance dancer, singer, actress, 1952–60; British Council Drama Officer, 1961–70; Arts Council of Great

Britain: Dance Officer, 1970–75; Asst Dance Dir, 1975–79. FRSA 1990. *Recreations:* pruning, weeding, collecting cracked porcelain. *Address:* 21 Stamford Brook Road, W6 0XJ. *T:* 081–741 3035.

NICHOLAS, Barry; *see* Nicholas, J. K. B. M.

NICHOLAS, Sir David, Kt 1989; CBE 1982; Chief Executive, 1979–91, Chairman, 1989–91, Independent Television News; *b* 25 Jan. 1930; *m* 1952, Juliet Davies; one *s* one *d. Educ:* Neath Grammar School; University Coll. of Wales, Aberystwyth. BA (Hons) English. National Service, 1951–53. Journalist with Yorkshire Post, Daily Telegraph, Observer; joined ITN, 1960; Deputy Editor, 1963–77; Editor, 1977–89. Produced ITN General Election Results, Apollo coverage, and ITN special programmes. FRTS 1980. Fellow, UC Aberystwyth, 1990. Hon. LLD Wales, 1990. Producers' Guild Award 1967, on return of Sir Francis Chichester; Cyril Bennett Award, RTS, 1985; Judges' Award, RTS, 1991. *Recreations:* walking, sailing, riding.

NICHOLAS, Sir Harry; *see* Nicholas, Sir Herbert Richard.

NICHOLAS, Prof. Herbert George, FBA 1969; Rhodes Professor of American History and Institutions, Oxford University, 1969–78; Fellow of New College, Oxford, 1951–78, Emeritus 1978–80, Honorary Fellow since 1980; Director, New College Development Fund, since 1989; *b* 8 June 1911; *s* of late Rev. W. D. Nicholas. *Educ:* Mill Hill Sch.; New Coll., Oxford. Commonwealth Fund Fellow in Modern History, Yale, 1935–37; MA Oxon, 1938; Exeter College, Oxford: Lectr, 1938, Fellow, 1946–51; Amer. Div., Min. of Information, and HM Embassy, Washington, 1941–46; Faculty Fellow, Nuffield Coll., Oxford, 1948–57; Nuffield Reader in the Comparative Study of Institutions at Oxford Univ., 1956–69. Chm., British Assoc. for American Studies, 1960–62; Vice-Pres., British Academy, 1975–76. Vis. Prof., Brookings Instn, Washington, 1960; Albert Shaw Lectr in Diplomatic History, Johns Hopkins, 1961; Vis. Fellow, Inst. of Advanced Studies, Princeton, 1964; Vis. Faculty Fellow, Inst. of Politics, Harvard, 1968. Hon. DCL Pittsburgh, 1968. *Publications:* The American Union, 1948; The British General Election of 1950, 1951; To the Hustings, 1956; The United Nations as a Political Institution, 1959, 5th edn 1975; (ed) Tocqueville's De la Démocratie en Amérique, 1961; Britain and the United States, 1963; The American Past and The American Present, 1971; The United States and Britain, 1975; The Nature of American Politics, 1980, 2nd edn 1986; (ed) Washington Despatches, 1941–45, 1981; La Naturaleza de la Política Norteamericana, 1985; articles. *Recreations:* gardening, listening to music. *Address:* 3 William Orchard Close, Old Headington, Oxford OX3 9DR. *T:* Oxford (0865) 63135. *Club:* Athenæum.

NICHOLAS, Sir Herbert Richard, (Sir Harry Nicholas), Kt 1970; OBE 1949; General Secretary of the Labour Party, 1968–72; *b* 13 March 1905; *s* of Richard Henry and Rosina Nicholas; *m* 1932, Rosina Grace Brown. *Educ:* Elementary sch., Avonmouth, Bristol; Evening Classes; Correspondence Courses. Clerk, Port of Bristol Authority, 1919–36. Transport and Gen. Workers Union: District Officer, Gloucester, 1936–38; Regional Officer, Bristol, 1938–40; National Officer, London: Commercial Road Transport Group, 1940–42; Chemical Section, 1942–44; Metal and Engineering Group, 1944–56; Asst Gen. Sec., 1956–68 (Acting Gen. Sec., Oct. 1964–July 66). Mem., TUC General Council, 1964–67. Mem., Labour Party Nat. Exec. Cttee, 1956–64, 1967–; Treasurer, Labour Party, 1960–64. *Publications:* occasional articles in press on Industrial Relations subjects. *Recreations:* Rugby football, fishing, reading, gardening. *Address:* 33 Madeira Road, Streatham, SW16. *T:* 081–769 7989.

NICHOLAS, Jane; *see* Nicholas, A. J. U.

NICHOLAS, (John Keiran) Barry (Moylan), FBA 1990; Principal of Brasenose College, Oxford, 1978–89 (Fellow, 1947–78; Hon. Fellow, 1989); *b* 6 July 1919; *s* of Archibald John Nicholas and Rose (*née* Moylan); *m* 1948, Hildegart, *d* of Prof. Hans Cloos, Bonn; one *s* one *d. Educ:* Downside; Brasenose Coll., Oxford (Scholar). 1st cl. Class. Mods, 1939 and Jurisprudence, 1946. Royal Signals, 1939–45: Middle East, 1941–45; Major, 1943. Called to Bar, Inner Temple, 1950, Hon. Bencher, 1984. Tutor, 1947–71 and Vice-Principal, 1960–63, Brasenose Coll.; All Souls Reader in Roman Law, Oxford Univ., 1949–71; Prof. of Comparative Law, Oxford, 1971–78; Mem., Hebdomadal Council, 1975–83. Vis. Prof.: Tulane Univ., 1960; Univ. of Rome Inst. of Comparative Law, 1964; Fordham Univ., 1968; Georgetown Univ., 1990; Bacon-Kilkenny Dist. Vis. Prof., Fordham Univ., 1985. UK Deleg. to UN Conf. on Internat. Sales Law, 1980. Mem., Louisiana State Law Inst., 1960. Dr *hc* Paris V, 1987. *Publications:* Introduction to Roman Law, 1962; (trans. Spanish, 1987); Jolowicz's Historical Introduction to Roman Law, 3rd edn, 1972; French Law of Contract, 1982. *Address:* 18A Charlbury Road, Oxford OX2 6UU. *T:* Oxford (0865) 58512.

NICHOLAS, Sir John (William), KCVO 1981; CMG 1979; HM Diplomatic Service, retired; *b* 13 Dec. 1924; *m* 1947, Rita (*née* Jones); two *s. Educ:* Birmingham Univ. Served 7th Rajput Regt, Indian Army, 1944–47; joined Home Civil Service, 1949; War Office, 1949–57; transf. to CRO 1957; First Sec., Brit. High Commn, Kuala Lumpur, 1957–61; Economic Div., CRO, 1961–63; Dep. High Comr in Malawi, 1964–66; Diplomatic Service Inspector, 1967–69; Dep. High Comr and Counsellor (Commercial), Ceylon, 1970–71; Dir, Establishments and Finance Div., Commonwealth Secretariat, 1971–73; Hd of Pacific Dependent Territories Dept, FCO, 1973–74; Dep. High Comr, Calcutta, 1974–76; Consul Gen., Melbourne, 1976–79; High Comr to Sri Lanka and (non-resident) to Republic of the Maldives, 1979–84. *Club:* Royal Over-Seas League.

NICHOLAS, William Ford, OBE 1954; Director, London Chamber of Commerce and Industry, 1974–84; *b* 17 March 1923; *s* of William and Emma Nicholas; *m* 1954, Isobel Sybil Kennedy; two *s. Educ:* Stockport Grammar School. Called to Bar, Middle Temple, 1965. Joined S Rhodesia Civil Service, 1947; Private Sec. to Prime Minister, S Rhodesia, 1950; Private Sec. to Prime Minister, Fedn of Rhodesia and Nyasaland, 1953; Counsellor, High Comr's Office, London, 1960; retd 1963. Dir, UK Cttee, Fedn of Commonwealth Chambers of Commerce, 1964; Dep. Dir, London Chamber of Commerce, 1966. *Address:* 2 Lime Close, Frant, Tunbridge Wells, Kent. *T:* Frant (089275) 428; Les Collines de Capitou, Bâtiment A, Appt 06, 06210 Mandelieu, France.

NICHOLL, Anthony John David; His Honour Judge Nicholl; a Circuit Judge, since 1988; *b* 3 May 1935; *s* of late Brig. and Mrs D. W. D. Nicholl; *m* 1961, Hermione Mary (*née* Landon); one *s* two *d. Educ:* Eton; Pembroke Coll., Oxford. Called to Bar, Lincoln's Inn, 1958. Practising in London, 1958–61, in Birmingham, 1961–88; Head of Chambers, 1976–87; Chm., Fountain Court Chambers (Birmingham) Ltd, 1984–88. A Recorder, 1978–88. *Recreations:* history, gardening and other rural pursuits. *Address:* c/o Birmingham Crown Court, Newton Street, Birmingham B4 6NE.

NICHOLLS; *see* Harmar-Nicholls.

NICHOLLS, Brian; Director: John Brown Engineering Ltd, since 1979; John Brown Engineering Gas Turbines Ltd, since 1979; Rugby Power Co. Ltd, since 1990; *b* 1928; *s* of Ralph and Kathleen Nicholls; *m* 1961, Mary Elizabeth Harley; one *s* two *d. Educ:* Haberdashers' Aske's Sch., Hampstead; London Univ. (BSc Econ); Harvard Business Sch. George Wimpey & Co., 1951–55; Constructors John Brown Ltd, 1955–75; Director: CJB Projects Ltd, 1972–75; CJB Pipelines Ltd, 1974–75; Industrial Adviser, Dept of Trade, 1975–78; Dep. Chm., CJB Mohandessi Iran Ltd, 1974–75; Vice Pres., John Brown Power Ltd, 1987–90. Member: Council, British Rly Industry Export Gp, 1976–78; Overseas Projects Bd, 1976–78; BOTB, 1978. Member: Council, British Chemical Engineering Contractors Assoc., 1973–75; Trade and Industry Cttee, British Algerian Soc., 1974–75; Scottish Council (Develt and Industry), 1983–. *Recreations:* writing, walking, music. *Address:* Croy, Shandon, by Helensburgh, Dunbartonshire. *T:* Rhu (0436) 820388. *Club:* Royal Northern and Clyde Yacht (Rhu).

NICHOLLS, Christine Stephanie, DPhil; Editor, Dictionary of National Biography, since 1989 (Joint Editor, 1977–89); *b* 23 Jan. 1943; *d* of Christopher James Metcalfe, Mombasa, Kenya, and Olive Metcalfe (*née* Kennedy); *m* 1966, Anthony James Nicholls, *s* of Ernest Alfred Nicholls, Carshalton; one *s* two *d. Educ:* Kenya High School; Lady Margaret Hall, Oxford (BA); St Antony's Coll., Oxford (MA, DPhil). Henry Charles Chapman res. fellow, Inst. of Commonwealth Studies, London Univ., 1968–69; freelance writer for BBC, 1970–74; res. asst, 1975–76. *Publications:* The Swahili Coast, 1971; (with Philip Awdry) Cataract, 1985; Power: a political history of the 20th Century, 1990. *Recreation:* reading novels. *Address:* 27 Davenant Road, Oxford OX2 8BU. *T:* Oxford (0865) 511320; DNB, Clarendon Building, Bodleian Library, Oxford OX1 3BG. *T:* Oxford (0865) 277232.

NICHOLLS, Clive Victor, QC 1982; a Recorder, since 1984; *b* 29 Aug. 1932; twin *s* of late Alfred Charles Victor Nicholls and of Lilian Mary (*née* May); *m* 1960, Alison Virginia, *d* of late Arthur and Dorothy Oliver; three *s* three *d. Educ:* Brighton Coll.; Trinity Coll., Dublin (MA, LLB); Sidney Sussex Coll., Cambridge (BA *ad eund*; LLM). Called to the Bar, Gray's Inn, 1957; Bencher, 1990. Chm. of Trustees, Bob Champion Cancer Trust, 1982–. *Recreations:* sailing, fishing. *Address:* Queen Elizabeth Building, Temple, EC4Y 9BS. *T:* 071–583 9744. *Clubs:* Garrick; Royal Western Yacht (Plymouth).
See also C. A. A. Nicholls.

NICHOLLS, Colin Alfred Arthur, QC 1981; a Recorder, since 1984; *b* 29 Aug. 1932; twin *s* of late Alfred Charles Victor Nicholls and of Lilian Mary (*née* May); *m* 1976, Clarissa Allison Spenlove, *d* of late Clive and of Theo Dixon; two *s. Educ:* Brighton Coll.; Trinity Coll., Dublin. MA, LLB. Called to the Bar, Gray's Inn, 1957 (Albion Richardson Schol.), Bencher, 1989. Auditor, 1956, and Hon. Mem., 1958–, TCD Historical Soc. *Recreations:* painting (exhib. RHA), sailing. *Address:* 3 Raymond Buildings, Gray's Inn, WC1R 5BH. *T:* 071–831 3833. *Club:* Garrick.
See also C. V. Nicholls.

NICHOLLS, David Alan, CB 1989; CMG 1984; Associate Fellow, Royal Institute for International Affairs, since 1990; Senior Political-Military Associate, Institute for Foreign Policy Analysis, Cambridge, Mass, USA, since 1991; *s* of Thomas Edward and Beatrice Winifred Nicholls; *m* 1955, Margaret (*née* Lewis); two *d. Educ:* Cheshunt Grammar School; St John's Coll., Cambridge (Schol., Wright's Prizeman 1952, 1953; BA Hons 1954; MA 1989). Served RAF (Flying Officer), 1950–51. Admiralty, 1954–64; Asst Principal, 1954; Private Sec. to Parliamentary Sec., 1958–59; Principal, 1959; MoD, 1964–75; Private Sec. to Minister of Defence for Admin, 1968–69; Asst Sec., 1969; Cabinet Office, 1975–77; Asst Under-Sec. of State, MoD, 1977–80; Asst Sec., Gen. for Defence Planning and Policy, NATO, 1980–84; Dep. Under Sec. of State (Policy), MoD, 1984–89. Vis. Fellow (Fellow Commoner), Magdalene Coll., Cambridge, 1989–90. Chm., Soc. for Italic Handwriting, 1987–. *Recreations:* sketching, printmaking. *Address:* c/o Midland Bank, Church Stretton, Shropshire. *Club:* National Liberal.

NICHOLLS, Rt. Hon. Sir Donald (James), Kt 1983; PC 1986; **Rt. Hon. Lord Justice Nicholls;** a Lord Justice of Appeal, since 1986; *b* 25 Jan. 1933; *yr s* of William Greenhow Nicholls and late Eleanor Jane; *m* 1960, Jennifer Mary, *yr d* of late W. E. C. Thomas, MB, BCh, MRCOG, JP; two *s* one *d. Educ:* Birkenhead Sch.; Liverpool Univ.; Trinity Hall, Cambridge (Foundn Schol.; Hon. Fellow, 1986). LLB 1st cl. hons Liverpool, BA 1st cl. hons with dist., Pt II Law Tripos Cantab, LLB 1st cl. hons with dist. Cantab. Certif. of Honour, Bar Final, 1958; called to Bar, Middle Temple, 1958, Bencher, 1981; in practice, Chancery Bar, 1958–83; QC 1974; Judge of High Court of Justice, Chancery Div., 1983–86. Mem., Senate of Inns of Court and the Bar, 1974–76. Pres., Birkenhead Sch., 1986–. Hon. LLD Liverpool, 1987. *Recreations:* gardening, history, music. *Address:* Royal Courts of Justice, Strand, WC2A 2LL. *Club:* Athenæum.

NICHOLLS, Rear-Adm. (Francis) Brian (Price) B.; *see* Brayne-Nicholls.

NICHOLLS, Rt. Rev. John; *see* Lancaster, Bishop Suffragan of.

NICHOLLS, Prof. John Graham, FRS 1988; Professor of Pharmacology, Biocenter, University of Basel, since 1983; *b* 19 Dec. 1929; *s* of late Dr Nicolai and ofCharlotte Nicholls; *m* (marr. diss.); two *s. Educ:* Berkhamsted Sch.; Charing Cross Hosp.; King's Coll. and University Coll., London. BSc (1st cl. Hons); PhD; MB, BS. Research and teaching in Neurobiology at: Oxford, 1962; Harvard, 1962–65; Yale, 1965–68; Harvard, 1968–73; Stanford, 1973–83. *Publications:* From Neuron to Brain (with S. Kuffler), 1976, 2nd edn 1984; The Search for Connections, 1987. *Recreations:* Latin American history, music. *Address:* Biocenter, Klingelbergstrasse 70, CH-4055 Basel, Switzerland . *T:* 41–61–2672230. *Club:* Athenæum.

NICHOLLS, Air Marshal Sir John (Moreton), KCB 1978; CBE 1970; DFC 1953; AFC 1965; Director in Charge, British Aircraft Co. (British Aerospace), Saudi Arabia, 1980–82; *b* 5 July 1926; *s* of Alfred Nicholls and Elsie (*née* French); *m* 1st, Enid Jean Marjorie Rose (*d* 1975); two *d*; 2nd, Shelagh Joyce Hall (*née* Strong). *Educ:* Liverpool Collegiate; St Edmund Hall, Oxford. RAF Coll., 1945–46; No 28 Sqdn and No 257 Sqdn; 335th Ftr Sqdn USAF, Korea, 1952; Fighter Leader Sch.; 435th and 83rd Ftr Sqdns USAF, 1956–58; attached British Aircraft Co., Lightning Project, 1959–61; psa 1961; Comd, Air Fighting Develt Sqdn; jssc 1964; MoD; comd RAF Leuchars, 1967–70; idc 1970; SASO 11 Gp, 1971; Principal Staff Officer to CDS, 1971–73; SASO, Strike Comd, 1973–75; ACAS (Op. Requirements), 1976–77; Air Mem. for Supply and Orgn, 1977–79; Vice-Chief of the Air Staff, 1979–80. CBIM. DFC (USA) and Air Medal (USA), 1953. *Address:* Dove Barn, Old Coast Road, Ormesby St Margaret, Norfolk NR29 3QH. *Club:* Royal Air Force.

NICHOLLS, Nigel Hamilton, CBE 1982; Assistant Under Secretary of State (Systems), Ministry of Defence, since 1989; *b* 19 Feb. 1938; *s* of late Bernard Cecil Hamilton Nicholls and Enid Kathleen Nicholls (*née* Gwynne); *m* 1967, Isobel Judith, *d* of Rev. Canon Maurice Dean; two *s. Educ:* King's School, Canterbury; St John's College, Oxford (Exhibr). BA 1962; MA 1966. Asst Principal, Admiralty, 1962, MoD, 1964; Asst Private Sec. to Minister of Defence for RN, 1965–66; Principal, 1966; Directing Staff, RCDS, 1971–73; Asst Private Sec. to Sec. of State for Defence, 1973–74; Asst Sec., 1974; Defence Counsellor, UK Delegation to MBFR Talks, Vienna, 1977–80; Asst Under-Sec. of State, MoD, 1984; Under Sec., Cabinet Office, 1986–89. *Recreations:* choral singing, genealogy. *Address:* Ministry of Defence, Main Building, Whitehall, SW1A 2HB. *Club:* United Oxford & Cambridge University.

NICHOLLS, Patrick Charles Martyn; MP (C) Teignbridge, since 1983; *b* 14 Nov. 1948; *s* of late Douglas Charles Martyn Nicholls and Margaret Josephine Nicholls; *m* 1976, Bridget Elizabeth Fergus Owens; one *s* two *d*. *Educ:* Redrice College, Andover. Qualified solicitor, 1974. Partner, Dunn & Baker, 1976, Partner, Dunn & Baker in association with Roger M. L. Williams & Co., 1979–. Mem., E Devon District Council, 1980–84. PPS to Ministers of State: Home Office, 1984–86; MAFF, 1986–87; Parliamentary Under-Secretary of State: Dept of Employment, 1987–90; DoE, 1990. Vice Chm., Social Security Select Cttee, 1990–. Vice Chm., Soc. of Cons. Lawyers, 1986–87. Steward, British Boxing Bd of Control, 1985–87. *Recreations:* theatre, opera, historical research, ski-ing. *Address:* c/o House of Commons, SW1A 0AA. *T:* 071–219 4077. *Club:* Carlton.

NICHOLLS, Philip, CB 1976; *b* 30 Aug. 1914; *yr s* of late W. H. Nicholls, Radlett; *m* 1955, Sue, *yr d* of late W. E. Shipton; two *s*. *Educ:* Malvern; Pembroke Coll., Cambridge. Asst Master, Malvern, 1936; Sen. Classical Master, 1939; resigned, 1947. Served in Army, 1940–46: 8th Bn, The Worcestershire Regt; HQ, East Africa Command; Allied Commn for Austria. Foreign Office (German Section), 1947; HM Treasury, 1949; a Forestry Commissioner (Finance and Administration), 1970–75, retired. Mem. Council, Malvern Coll., 1960–90 (Vice-Chm., 1963–88). *Address:* Barnards Green House, Barnards Green, Malvern, Worcs. *T:* Malvern (0684) 574446.

NICHOLLS, Robert Michael; Regional General Manager, Oxford Regional Health Authority, since 1988; *b* 28 July 1939; *s* of late Herbert Edgar Nicholls and of Bennetta L'Estrange (*née* Burges); *m* 1961, Dr Deirín Deirdre (*née* O'Sullivan); four *s*. *Educ:* Hampton Sch.; University Coll. of Wales (BA 1961); Univ. of Manchester (DSA 1962). AHA 1963. Asst Sec., Torbay Hosp., 1964; House Governor, St Stephen's Hosp., Chelsea, 1966; Asst Clerk to the Governors, St Thomas' Hosp., 1968; Dep. Gp Sec., Southampton Univ. Hosp. Management Cttee, 1972; Dist Administrator, Southampton and SW Hampshire Health Dist, 1974; Area Administrator, Newcastle upon Tyne AHA(T), 1977; Regl Administrator, SW RHA, 1981; Dist Gen. Man., Southmead DHA, 1985. Mem., Health Educn Council, 1984–87. National Council, Inst. of Health Service Management (formerly IHA): Mem., 1976–86; Pres., 1983–84. Mem., Education Cttee, King Edward's Hosp. Fund for London, 1975–81. *Publications:* (contrib.) Resources in Medicine, 1970; (contrib.) Working with People, 1983; contrib. Hosp. and Health Services Rev., Health and Soc. Services Jl and The Health Services. *Recreations:* bird-watching, jazz, opera, sport. *Address:* Charlton on Otmoor, Oxon.

NICHOLLS, Rt. Rev. Vernon Sampson; Hon. Assistant Bishop of Coventry, since 1983; *b* 3 Sept. 1917; *s* of Ernest C. Nicholls, Truro, Cornwall; *m* 1943, Phyllis, *d* of Edwin Potter, Stratford-on-Avon; one *s* one *d*. *Educ:* Truro Sch.; Univ. of Durham and Clifton Theological Coll., Bristol. Curate: St Oswald Bedminster Down, Bristol, 1941–42; Liskeard, Cornwall, 1942–43. CF, 1944–46 (Hon. CF 1946). Vicar of Meopham, 1946–56; Rural Dean of Cobham, 1953–56; Mem., Strood RDC, 1948–56; Vicar and Rural Dean of Walsall, and Chaplain to Walsall Gen. Hosp., 1956–67; Preb. of Curborough, Lichfield Cath., 1964–67; Archdeacon of Birmingham, 1967–74; Diocesan Planning Officer and Co-ordinating Officer for Christian Stewardship, 1967–74; Bishop of Sodor and Man, 1974–83; Dean of St German's Cathedral, Peel, 1974–83. MLC, Tynwald, IoM, 1974–83; Member: IoM Bd of Educn, 1974–83; Bd of Social Security, 1974–81; IoM Health Services Bd, 1981–83; Founder Chm., IoM Council on Alcoholism, 1979. Mem., S Warwicks Drug Adv. Cttee, 1984–. JP, IoM, 1974–83 Provincial Grand Master, Warwicks Province of Freemasons, 1985. *Recreations:* meeting people, gardening, motoring. *Address:* 4 Winston Close, Hathaway Park, Shottery, Stratford-upon-Avon, Warwickshire CV37 9ER. *T:* Stratford-upon-Avon (0789) 294478.

NICHOLS, Clement Roy, CMG 1970; OBE 1956; Chairman, Alpha Spinning Mills Pty Ltd; *b* 4 Jan. 1909; *s* of C. J. Nichols, Melbourne; *m* 1933, Margareta, *d* of A. C. Pearse, Melbourne; one *s* one *d*. *Educ:* Scotch Coll., Melbourne. CText; ATI Lifetime in wool worsted manufacturing. Past Pres., Wool Textile Mfrs of Australia; Vice-Pres., Internat. Wool Textile Organisation, 1970–75; President: Victorian Chamber of Mfrs, 1970–72, 1977–78; Associated Chambers of Mfrs of Australia, 1971–74. Mem., World Scouts' Cttee, 1959–65, 1967–73; Chm., Asia Pacific Region, 1962–64; Chief Comr, Scout Assoc., 1963–66; Chief Comr, Victorian Br., 1952–58; Nat. Chm., 1973–79; Vice-Pres., Scout Assoc. of Australia, 1979–88. *Address:* 82 Studley Park Road, Kew, Victoria 3101, Australia. *Clubs:* Australian (Melbourne); Rotary (Heidelberg).

NICHOLS, Dinah Alison; Deputy Secretary, Property, Construction and Central Support Services, Department of the Environment, since 1991; *b* 28 Sept. 1943; *d* of late Sydney Hirst Nichols and of Freda Nichols. *Educ:* Wyggeston Girls' Grammar Sch., Leicester; Bedford Coll., Univ. of London (Reid Arts Schol.; BA Hons History, 1965). Ministry of Transport: Asst Principal, 1965–69; Asst Private Sec. to Minister, 1969–70; Principal, 1970–74; Cabinet Office, 1974–77; Asst Sec., DoE, 1978–83; Principal Private Sec. to Sec. of State for Transport, 1983–85; Under Sec., DoE, 1985–91. Dir, John Laing ETE, 1987–90. Winston Churchill Meml Fellow, 1969. *Recreations:* mountaineering and walking, choral singing (Goldsmiths' Choral Union), music, theatre. *Address:* Department of the Environment, 2 Marsham Street, SW1P 3EB. *T:* 071–276 3623. *Clubs:* Swiss Alpine; Hampstead Cricket.

NICHOLS, Sir Edward (Henry), Kt 1972; TD; Town Clerk of City of London, 1954–74; *b* 27 Sept. 1911; *o s* of Henry James and Agnes Annie Nichols, Notts; *m* 1941, Gwendoline Hetty, *d* of late Robert Elgar, Leeds; one *s*. *Educ:* Queen Elizabeth's Gram. Sch., Mansfield; Selwyn Coll., Cambridge (BA, LLB). Articled Town Clerk, Mansfield, 1933; Asst Solicitor, Derby, 1936–40. Served War of 1939–45, Hon. Lt-Col RA. Dep. Town Clerk, Derby, 1940–48, Leicester, 1948–49; Town Clerk and Clerk of the Peace, Derby, 1949–53. Hon. DLitt City Univ., 1974. Chevalier, Order of N Star of Sweden; holds other foreign orders. *Address:* 4 Victoria Place, Esher Park Avenue, Esher, Surrey KT10 9PX. *T:* Esher (0372) 65102. *Club:* City Livery.

NICHOLS, Jeremy Gareth Lane, MA; Headmaster, Stowe School, since 1989; *b* 20 May 1943; *yr s* of late Derek Aplin Douglas Lane Nichols and of Ruth Anne Nichols (formerly Baiss); *m* 1972, Patricia Anne, *d* of Cdre Alan Swanton, DSO, DFC and bar, RN; one *s* three *d*. *Educ:* Lancing Coll., Sussex; Fitzwilliam Coll., Cambridge (BA English Lit. 1966; MA); Perugia Univ. Assistant Master: Livorno Naval Acad., 1965; Rugby Sch., 1966–67; Eton Coll., 1967–89, House Master, 1981–89; Gilman Sch., Baltimore, USA, 1979–80. *Recreations:* outdoor pursuits, sport, music, old cars. *Address:* Kinloss, Stowe, Buckingham MK18 5EH. *Clubs:* Hawks (Cambridge); Free Foresters, Corinthian Casuals.

NICHOLS, John; *see* Nichols, K. J. H.

NICHOLS, John Winfrith de Lisle, BSc (Eng); CEng; FIEE; retired; Director: National Maritime Institute, 1976–79; Computer Aided Design Centre, Cambridge, 1977–79; *b* 7 June 1919; *er s* of late John F. Nichols, MC, PhD, FRHistS, FSA, Godalming; *m* 1942, Catherine Lilian (*d* 1984), *er d* of Capt. A. V. Grantham, RNR, Essex; two *s* two *d*. *Educ:* Sir Walter St John's Sch., Battersea; London Univ. Royal Navy, 1940–46; GPO, Dollis Hill, 1946–47; RN Scientific Service, 1947–55; Chief Research Officer, Corp. of Trinity House, 1955–59; UKAEA, 1959–65; Min. of Technology, later DTI and Dept of Industry, 1965–; Under-Sec., and Chm., Requirement Bd for Computers, Systems and Electronics, 1972–74; Under Sec., Research Contractors Div., DoI, 1974–76. *Recreations:* gardening, sailing, caravanning. *Address:* Leybourne End, Wormley, Godalming, Surrey GU8 5TP. *T:* Wormley (042879) 3252.

NICHOLS, (Kenneth) John (Heastey); Metropolitan Stipendiary Magistrate, since 1972; *b* 6 Sept. 1923; *s* of Sidney Kenneth Nichols, MC and Dorothy Jennie Heastey Richardson; *m* 1st, 1946, Audrey Heather Powell; one *d*; 2nd, 1966, Pamela Marjorie Long, *qv*. *Educ:* Westminster School. Served War of 1939–45: 60th Rifles, 1941–43; Parachute Regt, NW Europe, SE Asia Comd, 1943–46 (Captain). Admitted Solicitor, 1949; Partner, Speechly, Mumford & Soames (Craig), 1949–69. Mem., Inner London Probation Service Cttee, 1975–91. Mem. Council of Law Soc., 1959–68. Pres., Newheels, 1980–86; Vice-Pres., David Isaacs Fund, 1982–86. *Recreations:* cricket, music, walking. *Address:* Marlborough Street Magistrates' Court, Great Marlborough Street, W1. *Club:* MCC.

NICHOLS, Pamela Marjorie, (Mrs John Nichols); *see* Long, P. M.

NICHOLS, Peter Richard, FRSL 1983; playwright since 1959; *b* 31 July 1927; *s* of late Richard George Nichols and Violet Annie Poole; *m* 1960, Thelma Reed; one *s* two *d* (and one *d* decd). *Educ:* Bristol Grammar Sch.; Bristol Old Vic Sch.; Trent Park Trng College. Actor, mostly in repertory, 1950–55; worked as teacher in primary and secondary schs, 1958–60. Mem., Arts Council Drama Panel, 1973–75. Playwright in residence, Guthrie Theatre, Minneapolis, 1976. *TV plays:* Walk on the Grass, 1959; Promenade, 1960; Ben Spray, 1961; The Reception, 1961; The Big Boys, 1961; Continuity Man, 1963; Ben Again, 1963; The Heart of the Country, 1963; The Hooded Terror, 1963; The Brick Umbrella, 1964; When the Wind Blows, 1964 (later adapted for radio); Daddy Kiss It Better, 1968; The Gorge, 1968; Hearts and Flowers, 1971; The Common, 1973; Greeks Bearing Gifts (Inspector Morse series), 1981; *films:* Catch Us If You Can, 1965; Georgy Girl, 1967; Joe Egg, 1971; The National Health, 1973; Privates on Parade, 1983; *stage plays:* A Day in The Death of Joe Egg, 1967 (Evening Standard Award, Best Play; Tony Award, Best Revival, 1985); The National Health, 1969 (Evening Standard Award, Best Play); Forget-me-not Lane, 1971; Chez Nous, 1973; The Freeway, 1974 (radio broadcast, 1991); Privates on Parade, 1977 (Evening Standard Best Comedy, Soc. of West End Theatres Best Comedy and Ivor Novello Best Musical Awards); Born in the Gardens, 1979 (televised 1986); Passion Play, 1980 (Standard Best Play award, 1981); A Piece of My Mind, 1986; *musical:* Poppy, 1982 (SWET Best Musical Award). *Publications:* Feeling You're Behind (autobiog.), 1984; some TV plays in anthologies; all above stage plays published separately and in 2 vols, Nichols: Plays One and Two, 1991. *Recreations:* listening to jazz, looking at cities. *Address:* c/o Rochelle Stevens & Co., 2 Terretts Place, Upper Street, N1 1QZ.

NICHOLS, Rt. Rev. Mgr Vincent Gerard; General Secretary, Roman Catholic Bishops' Conference of England and Wales, since 1984; *b* 8 Nov. 1945; *s* of Henry Joseph Nichols and Mary Nichols (*née* Russell). *Educ:* St Mary's College, Crosby; Gregorian Univ., Rome (STL PhL); Manchester Univ. (MA Theol); Loyola Univ., Chicago (MEd). Chaplain, St John Rigby VI Form College, Wigan, 1972–77; Priest, inner city of Liverpool, 1978–81; Director, Upholland Northern Inst., with responsibility for in service training of clergy and for adult Christian educn, 1981–84. Advr to Cardinal Hume and Archbishop Worlock, Internat. Synods of Bishops, 1980, 1983, 1985, 1987. *Publications:* articles in The Clergy Review. *Address:* Bishops' Conference Secretariat, 39 Eccleston Square, SW1V 1PD. *T:* 071–630 8220.

NICHOLS, William Henry, CB 1974; *b* 25 March 1913; *s* of William and Clara Nichols. *Educ:* Owens School. Entered Inland Revenue, 1930; Exchequer and Audit Dept, 1935, Secretary, 1973–75, retired. *Address:* 17 Park House, Winchmore Hill Road, N21 1QL. *T:* 081–886 4321; 11 Old Street, Haughley, Stowmarket, Suffolk IP14 3NT.

NICHOLS, William Reginald, CBE 1975; TD; MA; Clerk of the Worshipful Company of Salters, 1946–75, Master, 1978–79; *b* 23 July 1912; *s* of late Reginald H. Nichols, JP, FSA, Barrister-at-Law; *m* 1946, Imogen, *d* of late Rev. Percy Dearmer, DD, Canon of Westminster, and late Nancy (who *m* 1946, Sir John Sykes, KCB; he died, 1952); one *s* one *d*. *Educ:* Harrow; Gonville and Caius Coll., Cambridge (Sayer Classical Scholar). MA 1938. Called to the Bar, Gray's Inn, 1937. Served War of 1939–45 with Hertfordshire Regt (despatches) and on staff 21st Army Group. Former Jt Hon. Sec., CGLI; Governor of Christ's Hospital; former Governor of Grey Coat Hospital Foundation. *Address:* The Farriers Cottage, St Nicholas-at-Wade, Birchington, Kent CT7 0NR.

NICHOLSON, Air Commodore Angus Archibald Norman, CBE 1961; AE 1945; Deputy Secretary-General, International Shipping Secretariat, 1971–80; *b* 8 March 1919; *s* of Major Norman Nicholson and Alice Frances Nicholson (*née* Salvidge), Hoylake, Cheshire; *m* 1943, Joan Mary, *d* of Ernest Beaumont, MRCVS, DVSM; one *s* one *d*. *Educ:* Eton; King's Coll., Cambridge. Cambridge Univ. Air Sqn, 1938–39; commissioned, 1939. Served War 1939–45: flying duties in Bomber Command and Middle East. Air Cdre, 1966; Dir of Defence Plans (Air), Min. of Defence, 1966–67; Defence Adviser to British High Comr in Canada and Head of British Defence Liaison Staff, 1968–70; retired from RAF, 1970. MBIM 1967, FBIM 1980. *Recreations:* sailing, golf, music. *Address:* 8 Courtenay Place, Lymington, Hants. *Clubs:* Army and Navy; Leander (Henley); Royal Lymington Yacht.

NICHOLSON, Anthony Thomas Cuthbertson; a Recorder of the Crown Court, 1980–84; *b* 17 May 1929; *s* of Thomas and Emma Cuthbertson Nicholson, Stratford, E; *m* 1955, Sheila Rose, *er d* of Albert and Rose Pigram, Laindon, Essex; two *s* one *d*. *Educ:* St Bonaventure's Grammar Sch., Forest Gate, E7. Journalist, 1944–62. Served Army, 1947–49, RAF, 1950–53. Called to the Bar, Gray's Inn, 1962. *Publications:* (play) Van Call, 1954; Esprit de Law, 1973. *Recreation:* wildfowling. *Address:* The Old Vicarage, Southminster, Essex CM0 7ES; 3 Hare Court, Temple, EC4.

NICHOLSON, Brian Thomas Graves; Head of Public Affairs, Lloyd's of London, since 1990; *b* 27 June 1930; *s* of late Ivor Nicholson, CBE, and of Mrs Alan McGaw; *m* Henrietta, *d* of late Nevill Vintcent, OBE, DFC, and of Mrs Ralph Dennis; two *s* (and one *s* decd). *Educ:* Charterhouse. Reporter, Newcastle Evening Chronicle, 1949–53; Montreal Star, Toronto Telegram, and Victoria Times, 1953–54; Manchester Evening Chronicle, 1954–56; Sunday Graphic, 1956–57; Advertisement Manager, Sunday Times, 1957–65; Director: Sunday Times, 1963–65; Beaverbrook Newspapers, 1967–77; Man. Dir, Evening Standard, 1972–77; Jt Man. Dir, Observer, 1977–84; Director: CompAir, 1977–85; Center for Communication (USA), 1981–; Lloyd's of London Press, 1982–; London Broadcasting Co., 1983–90; Royal Opera House Covent Garden, 1984–89; Royal Ballet, 1984–; News (UK), 1985–87; CCA Galleries, 1986–89; Logie Bradshaw Media, 1986–; Messenger Newspapers Gp, 1986–89; Aurora Productions, 1987–; Messenger Television Ltd, 1989–; Whitespace Software Ltd, 1990–; Chairman: Audit Bureau of Circulation, 1975–77; Marlar Internat. Ltd, 1985–90; Carthusian Trust, 1987–; Advertising Standards Bd of Finance, 1989–; SE Arts Assoc., 1989–; Publicitas Hldg

(UK) Ltd, 1989–. Vice President: CAM Foundn, 1975–; Royal Gen. Theatrical Fund Assoc., 1986–; Member: Council of Commonwealth Press Union, 1975–; Adv. Cttee on Advertising, COI, 1977–; Adv. Bd, New Perspective Fund (USA), 1984–; Trustee, Glyndebourne Opera Co., 1977–; Gov., British Liver Foundn, 1989–. Mem., Editorial Adv. Bd, Focus in Education Ltd, 1986–. Churchwarden, St Bride's Church, Fleet Street, 1978–. *Recreations:* travelling, listening, playing games. *Address:* One Lime Street, EC3M 7HA. *Clubs:* Beefsteak, Brooks's, Pratt's, MCC; Royal Western Yacht; Piltdown Golf; Wentworth Golf.

NICHOLSON, Sir Bryan Hubert, Kt 1987; Chairman and Chief Executive, Post Office, since 1987; *b* 6 June 1932; *s* of late Reginald Hubert and Clara Nicholson; *m* 1956, Mary Elizabeth, *er d* of A. C. Harrison of Oxford; one *s* one *d* (and one *s* decd). *Educ:* Palmers School, Grays, Essex; Oriel College, Oxford (MA PPE; Hon. Fellow, 1989). 2nd Lieut, RASC, 1950–52; Unilever Management Trainee, 1955–58; Dist. Manager, Van den Berghs, 1958–59; Sales Manager, Three Hands/Jeyes Group, 1960–64; Sperry Rand: Sales Dir, UK, Remington Div., 1964–66; Gen. Manager, Australia, Remington Div., 1966–69; Managing Dir, UK and France, Remington Div., 1969–72; Dir, Ops, Rank Xerox (UK), 1972–76; Dir, Overseas Subsidiaries, Rank Xerox, 1976; Exec. Main Bd Dir, Rank Xerox, 1976–84; Chm., Rank Xerox (UK) and Chm., Rank Xerox GmbH, 1979–84; Non-executive Director: Rank Xerox, 1984–87; Baker Perkins Holdings, 1982–84; Evode, 1981–84; Internat. Post Corp. SA, 1988–; GKN, 1991–. Chairman: MSC, 1984–87; CNAA, 1988–91; NICG, 1988–90; CBI Task Force on Vocational Educn and Training, 1988–89; CBI Educn and Training Affairs Cttee, 1990–; NCVQ, 1990–; Member: NEDC, 1985–; Council, Inst. of Manpower Studies, 1985–; Adv. Cttee on Women's Employment, Dept of Employment, 1985–87; Race Relations Adv. Gp, Dept of Employment, 1985–87; Governing Council, Business in the Community, 1985–; Council, Prince's Youth Business Trust, 1986–; Council, CBI, 1987–; President's Cttee, CBI, 1990–; Council, Industrial Soc., 1988– (Chm., 1990–); Editl Bd, European Business Jl, 1988–. President: Involvement and Participation Assoc., 1990–; ACFHE, 1992–; Vice President: Re-Solv (Soc. for Prevention of Solvent Abuse), 1985–; Nat. Children's Home, 1989–. Pres., Oriel Soc., 1988–; Patron, Rathbone Soc., 1987–; Trustee, Babson Coll., Mass, USA, 1990–. Hon. Fellow, Manchester Polytechnic, 1990. UK Hon. Rep., W Berlin, 1983–84. CBIM 1985; FRSA 1985. FCGI (CGIA 1988). *Recreations:* tennis, bridge, political history. *Address:* c/o Post Office, 33 Grosvenor Place, SW1X 1PX. *Club:* United Oxford & Cambridge University.

NICHOLSON, (Charles) Gordon (Brown); QC (Scot.) 1982; Sheriff Principal of Lothian and Borders and Sheriff of Chancery, since 1990; *b* 11 Sept. 1935; *s* of late William Addison Nicholson, former Director, Scottish Tourist Board, and Jean Brown; *m* 1963, Hazel Mary Nixon; two *s*. *Educ:* George Watson's Coll., Edinburgh; Edinburgh Univ. (Hon. Fellow, Faculty of Law, 1988). MA Hons (English Lit.) 1956, LLB 1958. 2nd Lieut Queen's Own Cameron Highlanders, 1958–60. Admitted Faculty of Advocates, Edinburgh, 1961; in practice at Bar; Standing Junior Counsel, Registrar of Restrictive Trading Agreements, 1968; Advocate-Depute, 1968–70; Sheriff of: South Strathclyde, Dumfries and Galloway, 1970–76; Lothian and Borders, 1976–82; Mem., Scottish Law Commn, 1982–90. Vice-Pres., Sheriffs' Assoc., 1979–82 (Sec., 1975–79). Member: Scottish Council on Crime, 1972–75; Dunpark Cttee on Reparation by Offenders, 1974–77; May Cttee of Inquiry into UK Prison Service, 1978–79; Kincraig Review of Parole in Scotland, 1988–89; Hon. President: Scottish Assoc. of Victim Support Schemes, 1989– (Chm., 1987–89); Scottish Assoc. for Study of Delinquency, 1988– (Chm., 1974–79; Hon. Vice-Pres., 1982–88); Chm., Edinburgh CAB, 1979–82. Comr, Northern Lighthouse Bd, 1990–. *Publications:* The Law and Practice of Sentencing in Scotland, 1981; contrib. to legal periodicals. *Recreation:* music. *Address:* 1A Abbotsford Park, Edinburgh EH10 5DX. *T:* 031–447 4300. *Club:* New (Edinburgh).

NICHOLSON, Hon. Sir David (Eric), Kt 1972; Speaker of the Legislative Assembly of Queensland, 1960–72 (record term); MLA (CP) for Murrumba, 1950–72; *b* 26 May 1904; *s* of J. A. Nicholson; *m* 1934, Cecile F., *d* of M. E. Smith; two *s* two *d*. *Recreations:* bowls, swimming, gardening. *Address:* Villa 37, Peninsular Gardens, 56 Miller Street, Kippa Ring, Qld 4021, Australia. *Clubs:* Redcliffe Trotting (Life Mem.), Redcliffe Agricl, Horticultural and Industrial Soc. (Life Mem.); Caboolture, Returned Servicemen's (Life Mem.), Caboolture Bowls (Caboolture).

NICHOLSON, David John; MP (C) Taunton, since 1987; *b* 17 Aug. 1944; *s* of John Francis Nicholson and Lucy Warburton Nicholson (*née* Battrum); *m* 1981, Frances Mary, *d* of late Brig. T. E. H. Helby, MC; one *s* one *d*. *Educ:* Queen Elizabeth's Grammar School, Blackburn; Christ Church, Oxford (MA Hons Mod. Hist.). Dept of Employment, 1966; Research Fellow, Inst. of Historical Res., 1970; Cons. Res. Dept, 1972 (Head, Political Section, 1974–82); Assoc. of British Chambers of Commerce, 1982–87 (Dep. Dir-Gen., 1986–87). PPS to Minister for Overseas Develt, 1990–. Sec., Cons. Backbench Social Services Cttee, 1988–90. *Publication:* (ed with John Barnes) The Diaries of L. S. Amery: vol. I, 1896–1929, 1980; vol. II, The Empire at Bay, 1929–45, 1988. *Recreations:* travel, gardening, music, the country. *Address:* Allshire, near Brushford, Somerset EX16 9JG. *Clubs:* Reform; Taunton Conservative; Wellington Conservative.

NICHOLSON, (Edward) Max, CB 1948; CVO 1971; a Principal, Land Use Consultants (Chairman, 1966–89); *b* 1904; *m* 1st, 1932, Eleanor Mary Crawford (marr. diss., 1964); two *s*; 2nd, Marie Antoinette Mauerhofer; one *s*. *Educ:* Sedbergh; Hertford Coll., Oxford. Head of Allocation of Tonnage Division, Ministry of War Transport, 1942–45; Secretary of Office of The Lord President of the Council, 1945–52. Member Advisory Council on Scientific Policy, 1948–64; Dir-Gen., Nature Conservancy, 1952–66; Convener, Conservation Section, Internat. Biological Programme, 1963–74; Secretary, Duke of Edinburgh's Study Conference on the Countryside in 1970, 1963; Albright Lecturer, Univ. of California, 1964; a Dir and Managing Editor, Environmental Data Services Ltd, 1978–80. President: RSPB, 1980–85; Simon Population Trust, 1985–; Trust for Urban Ecology (formerly Ecological Parks Trust), 1987–88 (Chm., 1977–87); Vice-President: RSA, 1978–82; Wildfowl and Wetlands Trust; WWF, UK; Trustee, Earthwatch Europe, 1985–; Member: Council, Internat. Inst. of Environment and Develt, 1972–88; Internat. Council, WWF, 1983–86. Chairman: Environmental Cttee, London Celebrations for the Queen's Silver Jubilee, 1976–77; London Looks Forward Conf., 1977; UK Standing Cttee for World Conservation Strategy Prog., 1981–83; Common Ground Internat., 1981–. Hon. Member: IUCN; British Ecol Soc.; WWF; RTPI. Scientific FZS; Corr. Fellow, American Ornithologists' Union. Hon. Fellow RIBA; Hon. LLD Aberdeen, 1964; Hon. Dr, RCA, 1970; Hon. DL Birmingham, 1983. John C. Phillips Medallist International Union for Conservation of Nature and Natural Resources, 1963; Europa Preis für Landespflege, 1972. Comdr, Order of Golden Ark, Netherlands, 1973. *Publications:* Birds in England, 1926; How Birds Live, 1927; Birds and Men, 1951; Britain's Nature Reserves, 1958; The System, 1967; The Environmental Revolution, 1970 (Premio Europeo Cortina-Ulisse, 1971); The Big Change, 1973; The New Environmental Age, 1987; (ed jtly) The Birds of the Western Palearctic, Vol. I, 1977, Vol. II, 1980, Vol. III, 1983, Vol. IV, 1985, Vol. V, 1988, Vol. VI, 1991, and other books, scientific papers and articles. *Address:* 13 Upper Cheyne Row, SW3 5JW. *Club:* Athenæum.

NICHOLSON, (Edward) Rupert, FCA; Partner, Peat Marwick Mitchell & Co. (UK), 1949–77; *b* 17 Sept. 1909; *s* of late Alfred Edward Nicholson and late Elise (*née* Dobson); *m* 1935, Mary Elley (*d* 1983); one *s* one *d*. *Educ:* Whitgift Sch., Croydon. Articled to father, 1928–33; joined Peat Marwick Mitchell & Co., 1933. Apptd by BoT, jointly, Inspector of Majestic Insurance Co. Ltd and two others, 1961; apptd Liquidator, Davies Investments Ltd, 1967; apptd Receiver, Rolls-Royce Ltd, 1971; Receiver, Northern Developments (Holdings), 1975. Chm., Techn. Adv. Cttee, Inst. Chartered Accountants, 1969–70; Liquidator, Court Line Ltd, 1974; Mem., Post Office Review Cttee, 1976. Dep. Chm., Croydon Business Venture, 1990– (Chm., 1983–90). Governor, Whitgift Foundn, 1976– (Chm., 1978–91). Master, Horners' Co., 1984–85. *Publications:* articles in learned jls. *Address:* Grey Wings, The Warren, Ashtead, Surrey KT21 2SL. *T:* Ashtead (0372) 272655. *Club:* Caledonian.

NICHOLSON, Emma Harriet; MP (C) Devon West and Torridge, since 1987; *b* 16 Oct. 1941; *d* of Sir Godfrey Nicholson, 1st Bt and late Lady Katharine Constance Lindsay, 5th *d* of 27th Earl of Crawford; *m* 1987, Sir Michael Harris Caine, *qv*. *Educ:* St Mary's School, Wantage; Royal Academy of Music. LRAM, ARCM. Computer Programmer, Programming Instructor, Systems Analyst, ICL, 1963–66; Computer consultant, John Tyzack & Partners, 1967–69; Gen. Management Consultant and Computer Consultant, McLintock Mann and Whinney Murray, 1969–74; joined Save the Children Fund, 1974, Dir of Fund Raising, 1977–85, Pres., Hatherleigh Dist Br. Vice-Chm., Conservative Party, 1983–87. Member: Council, Howard League; Council, PITCOM; Centre for Policy Studies; RIIA; Adv. Bd, Women of Tomorrow Awards; RAM Appeal Cttee. Dir, Cities in School. Fellow Elect, Industry and Parliament Trust. Vice Pres., Small Farmers' Assoc. Deputy Chairman: Duke of Edinburgh's Award 30th Anniv. Tribute Project, 1986-88; Duke of Edinburgh's Internat. Project '87, 1987–88; Chm., Friends of Duke of Edinburgh's Award. President: Plymouth and W Devon Cassette, Talking Newspaper; W Regl Assoc. for the Deaf; Patron: Hospice Care Trust, N Devon; CRUSAID; Devon Care Trust; Trustee: Suzy Lamplugh Trust; Ross McWhirter Foundn; Chm. Adv. Cttee, Carnegie UK Trust Venues Improvement Programmes. *Recreations:* music, walking. *Address:* c/o House of Commons, SW1A 0AA. *T:* 071–219 3000. *Club:* Reform.

NICHOLSON, Rev. Prof. Ernest Wilson, DD; FBA 1987; Provost of Oriel College, Oxford, since 1990; *b* 26 Sept. 1938; *s* of Ernest Tedford Nicholson and Veronica Muriel Nicholson; *m* 1962, Hazel (*née* Jackson); one *s* three *d*. *Educ:* Portadown Coll.; Trinity Coll., Dublin (Scholar, BA 1960, MA 1964); Glasgow Univ. (PhD 1964). MA (by incorporation) 1967, BD 1971, DD 1978, Cambridge; DD Oxford (by incorporation) 1979. Lectr in Hebrew and Semitic Languages, TCD, 1962–67; Univ. Lectr in Divinity, Cambridge Univ., 1967–79; Fellow: University Coll. (now Wolfson Coll.), Cambridge, 1967–69; Pembroke Coll., Cambridge, 1969–79; Chaplain, Pembroke Coll., Cambridge, 1969–73, Dean, 1973–79; Oriel Prof. of the Interpretation of Holy Scripture, and Fellow of Oriel Coll., Oxford Univ., 1979–90. At various times vis. prof. at univs and seminars in Europe, USA, Canada and Australia. Pres., SOTS, 1988. Comdr, Order of Merit (Italian Republic). *Publications:* Deuteronomy and Tradition, 1967; Preaching to the Exiles, 1971; Exodus and Sinai in History and Tradition, 1973; (with J. Baker) The Commentary of Rabbi David Kimḥi on Psalms 120–150, 1973; Commentary on Jeremiah 1–25, 1973; Commentary on Jeremiah 26–52, 1975; God and His People: covenant and theology in the Old Testament, 1986; articles in biblical and Semitic jls. *Recreations:* music, the English countryside. *Address:* Oriel College, Oxford OX1 4EW. *Club:* United Oxford & Cambridge University.

NICHOLSON, Gordon; *see* Nicholson, C. G. B.

NICHOLSON, Dr Howard, FRCP; Physician, University College Hospital, since 1948; Physician, Brompton Hospital, 1952–77, retired; Fellow of University College, London, since 1959; *b* 1 Feb. 1912; *s* of Frederick and Sara Nicholson; *m* 1941, Winifrid Madeline Piercy. *Educ:* University Coll., London, and University Coll. Hospital. MB, BS, London, 1935; MD London 1938; MRCP 1938, FRCP 1949. House appointments and Registrarship, UCH, 1935–38; House Physician at Brompton Hosp., 1938. Served War, 1940–45, RAMC; Physician to Chest Surgical Team and Officer i/c Medical Div. (Lt-Col). Registrar, Brompton Hosp., and Chief Asst, Inst. of Diseases of Chest, 1945–48. Goulstonian Lecturer, RCP, 1950. *Publications:* sections on Diseases of Chest in The Practice of Medicine (ed J. S. Richardson), 1961, and in Progress in Clinical Medicine, 1961; articles in Thorax, Lancet, etc. *Recreations:* reading, going to the opera. *Address:* Chelwood, Laughton, Lewes, E Sussex BN8 6BE.

NICHOLSON, Jack; American film actor, director and producer; *b* 22 April 1937; *s* of John and Ethel May Nicholson; *m* 1961, Sandra Knight (marr. diss. 1966); one *d*. *Films include:* Cry-Baby Killer, 1958; Studs Lonigan, 1960; The Shooting (also produced); Easy Rider, 1969; Five Easy Pieces, 1970; The Last Detail, 1973; Chinatown, 1974; One Flew Over the Cuckoo's Nest, 1975 (Acad. Award for Best Actor, 1976); The Passenger, 1975; The Shining, 1980; The Postman Always Rings Twice, 1981; Reds, 1981; Terms of Endearment (Acad. Award for Best Supporting Actor), 1984; Prizzi's Honor, 1985; Heartburn, 1986; The Witches of Eastwick, 1986; Ironweed, 1987; Batman, 1988. *Address:* c/o Bresler Kelly & Associates, 15760 Ventura Boulevard, Suite 1730, Encino, Calif 91436, USA.

NICHOLSON, James Frederick; farmer; Member (OU) Northern Ireland, European Parliament, since 1989; *b* 29 Jan. 1945; *s* of Thomas and Matilda Nicholson; *m* 1968, Elizabeth Gibson; six *s*. *Educ:* Aghavilly Primary Sch. Member: Armagh Dist Council, 1975–; Southern Health and Social Services Bd, 1977–. Mem. (OU) Newry and Armagh, NI Assembly, 1982–86. Contested (OUP) Newry and Armagh, 1987. MP (OU) Newry and Armagh, 1983–85.

NICHOLSON, Hon. Sir (James) Michael (Anthony), Kt 1988; **Hon. Mr Justice Nicholson;** a Judge of the High Court of Justice in Northern Ireland, since 1986; *b* 4 Feb. 1933; *s* of late Cyril Nicholson, QC, DL and late Eleanor Nicholson (*née* Caffrey); *m* 1973, Augusta Mary Ada, *d* of late Thomas F. Doyle and of Mrs Elizabeth Doyle, Co. Cork; one *s* two *d*. *Educ:* Downside; Trinity College, Cambridge (MA). Called to the Bar of N Ireland, 1956; to English Bar, Gray's Inn, 1962; to Bar of Ireland, 1975; QC (NI), 1971; Bencher, Inn of Court of NI, 1978; Chm., Exec. Council of Inn of Court of NI and of Bar Council, 1983–85; Senior Crown Counsel: Co. Fermanagh, 1971–73; Co. Tyrone, 1973–77; Co. Londonderry, 1977–86. Chm., Mental Health Review Tribunal (NI), 1973–76; Mem., Standing Adv. Commn for Human Rights (NI), 1976–78. High Sheriff, Co. Londonderry, 1972. President: Irish Cricket Union, 1978; NW ICU, 1986–. *Recreations:* cricket, chess. *Address:* Royal Courts of Justice, Chichester Street, Belfast, Northern Ireland. *Club:* MCC.

NICHOLSON, Sir John (Norris), 2nd Bt, *cr* 1912; KBE 1971; CIE 1946; JP; Lord-Lieutenant, 1980–86, and Keeper of the Rolls, 1974–86, of the Isle of Wight; *b* 19 Feb. 1911; *o c* of late Captain George Crosfield Norris Nicholson, RFC, and Hon. Evelyn Izme Murray, *y d* of 10th Baron and 1st Viscount Elibank (she *m* 2nd 1st Baron Mottistone, PC); *S* grandfather, 1918; *m* 1938, Vittoria Vivien (*d* 1991), *y d* of late Percy Trewhella, Villa Sant' Andrea, Taormina; two *s* two *d*. *Educ:* Winchester Coll., Trinity Coll.,

Cambridge. Captain 4th Cheshires (TA), 1939–41. BEF Flanders 1940 (despatches). Min. of War Transport, India and SE Asia, 1942–46. Chairman: Ocean Steam Ship Co. Ltd, 1957–71; Liverpool Port Employers Assoc., 1957–61; Martins Bank Ltd, 1962–64 (Dep. Chm., 1959–62); Management Cttee, HMS Conway, 1958–65; British Liner Cttee, 1963–67; Cttee, European Nat. Shipowners' Assoc., 1965–69; IoW Develt Bd, 1986–88; Mem., Shipping Advisory Panel, 1962–64; Pres., Chamber of Shipping of the UK, 1970–71; Mem., Economic and Social Cttee, EEC, 1973–74. Director: Barclays Bank Ltd, 1969–81; Royal Insurance Co. Ltd, 1955–81. Pres., E Wessex TA&VRA, 1982–84. Governor, IoW Technical Coll., 1974–89. Vice Lord-Lieutenant, IoW, 1974–79. Silver Jubilee Medal, 1977. *Heir:* *s* Charles Christian Nicholson [*b* 15 Dec. 1941; *m* 1975, Martie, *widow* of Niall Anstruther-Gough-Calthorpe and *d* of Stuart Don]. *Address:* Mottistone Manor, Isle of Wight. *T:* Isle of Wight (0983) 740322. *Clubs:* Army and Navy; Royal Yacht Squadron (Commodore, 1980–86).

NICHOLSON, Lewis Frederick, CB 1963; *b* 1 May 1918; *s* of Harold and May Nicholson; *m* 1947, Diana Rosalind Fear; one *s* two *d*. *Educ:* Taunton Sch.; King's Coll., Cambridge. Research Laboratories of GEC, 1939; Royal Aircraft Establishment, 1939–59; Head of Aerodynamics Dept, RAE, 1953–59; Imperial Defence Coll., 1956; Director-General of Scientific Research (Air), Ministry of Aviation, 1959–63; Dep. Director (Air) Royal Aircraft Establishment, 1963–66; Chief Scientist, RAF, 1966–69; Vice Controller Aircraft, MoD (PE), 1969–78, retired. *Publications:* (Joint) Compressible Airflow-Tables; Compressible Airflow-Graphs; papers on aerodynamic subjects. *Address:* 15 Silver Birches Way, Elstead, Godalming, Surrey GU8 6JA. *T:* Elstead (0252) 702362

NICHOLSON, Max; *see* Nicholson, E. M.

NICHOLSON, Hon. Sir Michael; *see* Nicholson, Hon. Sir J. M. A.

NICHOLSON, Michael Constantine; a Recorder of the Crown Court, since 1980; *b* 3 Feb. 1932; *m* 1960, Kathleen Mary Strong; two *d*. *Educ:* Wycliffe Coll., Stonehouse; University Coll. of Wales, Aberystwyth (LLB). Called to the Bar, Gray's Inn, 1957; Crown Counsel, Nyasaland, 1960–63; Wales and Chester circuit, 1963–. *Recreations:* opera, cinema, theatre. *Address:* (chambers) 33 Park Place, Cardiff CF1 3BA. *T:* Cardiff (0222) 233313. *Club:* Cardiff Golf.

NICHOLSON, Paul Douglas, DL; Chairman and Managing Director, Vaux Group, since 1976; *b* 7 March 1938; *s* of late Douglas Nicholson, TD and Pauline Nicholson; *m* 1970, Sarah, *y d* of Sir Edmund Bacon, Bt, KG, KBE, TD; one *d*. *Educ:* Harrow; Clare College, Cambridge (MA). FCA. Lieut, Coldstream Guards, 1956–58; joined Vaux Breweries, 1965. Chm., Northern Investors Co., 1984–89; Director: Tyne Tees Television, 1981–; Northern Development Co. Ltd, 1986–; Northern Electric, 1990–. Chm., Urban Develt Corp. for Tyne and Wear, 1987–; Chm., N Region, CBI, 1977–79; Chm., N Regional Bd, British Technology Group, 1979–84. High Sheriff, Co. Durham, 1980–81; DL Co. Durham, 1980. *Recreations:* deerstalking, driving horses (Pres., Coaching Club, 1990–), flying. *Address:* Quarry Hill, Brancepeth, Durham DH7 8DW. *T:* Durham (091) 3780275. *Clubs:* Boodle's; Northern Counties (Newcastle upon Tyne).

NICHOLSON, Ralph Lambton Robb; Secretary, United Kingdom Atomic Energy Authority, 1984–86; *b* 26 Sept. 1924; *s* of Ralph Adam Nicholson and Kathleen Mary Nicholson (*née* Robb); *m* 1951, Mary Kennard; one *s* two *d*. *Educ:* Sherborne School; Cambridge Univ.; Imperial College, London (BSc; ACGI). FIChemE. Royal Engineers, 1943–47. Chemical engineer, Distillers Co., 1950–51; Wellcome Foundation, 1951–54; Fisons, 1954–58; planning and commercial manager, UKAEA, 1958–67; Dir, Min. of Technology Programmes Analysis Unit, 1967–71; Principal Programmes and Finance Officer, UKAEA, 1971–84. *Publications:* contribs to energy and management jls. *Recreations:* gardening, music, canals. *Address:* The Garth, Midgham, Reading, Berks RG7 5UJ. *T:* Woolhampton (0734) 712211.

NICHOLSON, Robert; publisher, designer, artist, writer; *b* Sydney, Australia, 8 April 1920; *m* 1951 (marr. diss. 1976); one *s* one *d*; *m* 1989. Educ: Troy Town Elementary Sch., Rochester; Rochester Tech. Sch.; Medway Sch. of Art. Served 1939–45, RAMC (mainly pathology in Middle East). Responsible with brother for major design projects during post-war design boom, 1945–55, including Festival of Britain Exhibition in Edinburgh, 1951 and Design Centre, London, 1956. Writer and publisher of guide books including: Nicholson's London Guide; Street Finder; Guide to Great Britain, guides to the Thames, the canals, etc. Benjamin Franklin medal, 1960. Exhibns of landscape painting in London, 1976, Madrid, 1982, and annually in Kent and Sussex. Lives in Kent.

NICHOLSON, Sir Robin (Buchanan), Kt 1985; PhD; FRS 1978; FEng 1980; Director, Pilkington plc (formerly Pilkington Brothers plc), since 1986; *b* 12 Aug. 1934; *s* of late Carroll and of Nancy Nicholson; *m* 1958, Elizabeth Mary (*d* 1988), *d* of late Sir Sydney Caffyn; one *s* two *d*. *Educ:* Oundle Sch.; St Catharine's Coll., Cambridge. BA 1956, PhD 1959, MA 1960. FIM; MInstP; CBIM. University of Cambridge: Demonstrator in Metallurgy, 1960; Lectr in Metallurgy, 1964; Fellow of Christ's Coll., 1962–66, Hon. Fellow 1984; Prof. of Metallurgy, Univ. of Manchester, 1966. Inco Europe Ltd: Dir of Research Lab., 1972; Dir, 1975; Man. Dir, 1976–81; Co-Chm., Biogen NV, 1979–81. Chief Scientific Advr to Cabinet Office, 1983–85 (Central Policy Review Staff, 1981–83). Director: Rolls-Royce plc, 1986–; BP plc, 1987–. Chairman: CEST, 1987–; ACOST, 1990–. Mem., SERC (formerly SRC), 1978–81. Mem. Council: Royal Soc., 1983–85; Fellowship of Engrg, 1986–89; Foreign Associate, Nat. Acad. of Engrg, USA, 1983. Hon. FIChemE; Hon. Fellow UMIST, 1988. Hon. DSc: Cranfield, 1983; Aston, 1983; Manchester, 1985; Hon. DMet Sheffield, 1984; Hon. DEng Birmingham, 1986; DUniv. Open, 1987. Rosenhain Medallist, Inst. of Metals, 1971; Platinum Medal, Metals Soc., 1982. *Publications:* Precipitation Hardening (with A. Kelly), 1962; (jtly) Electron Microscopy of Thin Crystals, 1965; (ed and contrib. with A. Kelly) Strengthening Methods in Crystals, 1971; numerous papers to learned jls. *Recreations:* family life, gardening, music. *Address:* Whittington House, 8 Fisherwick Road, Whittington, near Lichfield, Staffs WS14 9LH. *T:* Whittington (0543) 432081. *Club:* MCC.

NICHOLSON, Rupert; *see* Nicholson, E. R.

NICKELL, Prof. Stephen John; Professor of Economics, Director of the Institute of Economics and Statistics and Fellow of Nuffield College, University of Oxford, since 1984; *b* 25 April 1944; *s* of John Edward Hilary Nickell and Phyllis Nickell; *m* 1976, Susan Elizabeth (*née* Pegden); one *s* one *d*. *Educ:* Merchant Taylors' Sch.; Pembroke Coll., Cambridge (BA); LSE (MSc). Maths teacher, Hendon County Sch., 1965–68; London School of Economics: Lectr, 1970–77; Reader, 1977–79; Prof. of Economics, 1979–84. Member: Academic Panel, HM Treasury, 1981–89; Council, REconS, 1984–; ESRC, 1990–. Fellow, Econometric Soc., 1980. *Publications:* The Investment Decisions of Firms, 1978; (with R. Layard and R. Dombusch) The Performance of the British Economy, 1988; (with R. Jackman and R. Layard) Unemployment, 1991; articles in learned jls. *Recreations:* reading, riding, cooking. *Address:* Church Wing, Old Rectory, Somerton, Oxon OX5 4NB.

NICKERSON, Albert Lindsay; retired as Chairman and Chief Executive Officer, Mobil Oil Corporation; *b* 17 Jan. 1911; *s* of Albert Lindsay Nickerson and Christine (*née* Atkinson); *m* 1936, Elizabeth Perkins; one *s* three *d*. *Educ:* Noble and Greenough Sch., Mass; Harvard. Joined Socony-Vacuum Oil Co. Inc. as Service Stn Attendant, 1933; Dist. Man., 1940; Div. Manager, 1941; Asst General Manager, Eastern Marketing Div., 1944; Director, 1946; name of company changed to Socony Mobil Oil Co. Inc., 1955; President, 1955–61; Chairman Exec. Cttee and Chief Exec. Officer, 1958–69; Chm. Bd, 1961–69; name of company changed to Mobil Oil Corporation, 1966. Chairman, Vacuum Oil Co. Ltd, London (later Mobil Oil Co. Ltd), 1946. Director, Placement Bureau War Manpower Commission, Washington, 1943. Chm., Federal Reserve Bank of NY, and Federal Reserve Agent, 1969–71; Mem., The Business Council (Chm. 1967–69). Director: American Management Assoc., NY, 1948–51, 1953–56, 1958–61; Federal Reserve Board of NY, 1964–67; Metrop. Life Insurance Co., 1965–81; Mobil Oil Corp., 1946–75; Raytheon Co., 1970–90; State Street Investment Corp.; State Street Growth Fund Inc.; Harvard Management Co., 1974–84; Transportation Assoc. of America, 1969; State Street Exchange Fund; Trustee: International House, NY City, 1952–62; Cttee for Economic Development, NY, 1961–65; Brigham and Women's Hosp., Boston, 1969–89; Rockefeller Univ., 1964–84; (Emeritus) Boston Symphony Orch.; American Museum of Natural History, 1958–62, 1964–69; Mem. Emeritus, Corp. of Woods Hole Oceanographic Instn, Mass; former Director and Treas., American Petroleum Institute; former Member: Council on Foreign Relations; National Petroleum Council; Harvard Corp., 1965; Fellow, Harvard Univ., 1965–75; Overseer Harvard Univ., 1959–65. Hon. LLD: Hofstra Univ., 1964; Harvard Univ., 1976. Comdr, Order of Vasa (Sweden), 1963; Grand Cross of the Republic (Italy), 1968. *Recreations:* golfing, fishing, sailing, camping. *Address:* 3 Lexington Road, Lincoln Center, Mass 01773, USA. *T:* (617) 259–9664. *Clubs:* Thames Rowing; Harvard Varsity, Cambridge Boat (Cambridge, Mass); Country (Brookline, Mass); Harvard (NY City); Harvard (Boston); 25 Year Club of Petroleum Industry.

NICKLAUS, Jack William; golfer; *b* 21 Jan. 1940; *s* of Louis Charles Nicklaus and Helen (*née* Schoener); *m* 1960, Barbara Jean Bash; four *s* one *d*. *Educ:* Upper Arlington High Sch.; Ohio State Univ. Won US Amateur golf championship, 1959, 1961; became professional golfer, 1961; designs golf courses in USA, Europe, and Far East; Chm., Golden Bear Internat. Inc. Captained US team which won 25th Ryder Cup, 1983. *Major wins include:* US Open, 1962, 1967, 1972, 1980; US Masters, 1963, 1965, 1966, 1972, 1975, 1986; US Professional Golfers' Assoc., 1963, 1971, 1973, 1974, 1975, 1980; British Open, 1966, 1970, 1978, and many other championships in USA, Europe, Australia and Far East. Hon. Dr Athletic Arts Ohio State, 1972; Hon. LLD St Andrews, 1984. *Publications:* My 55 Ways to Lower Your Golf Score, 1962; Take a Tip from Me, 1964; The Greatest Game of All, 1969; Golf My Way, 1974; The Best Way to Better Your Golf, vols 1–3, 1974; Jack Nicklaus' Playing Lessons, 1976; Total Golf Techniques, 1977; On and Off the Fairway, 1979; The Full Swing, 1982; My Most Memorable Shots in the Majors, 1988. *Address:* (office) 11780 US Highway #1, North Palm Beach, Florida 33408, USA.

NICKOLS, Herbert Arthur; Headmaster, Westonbirt School, Tetbury, Gloucestershire, 1981–86; *b* 17 Jan. 1926; *s* of Herbert and Henrietta Elizabeth Nickols; *m* 1953, Joyce Peake; two *s* one *d*. *Educ:* Imperial Coll., Univ. of London (BSc). ACGI. Res. Demonstrator, Imperial Coll., 1947–49; Housemaster, Sen. Science Master and later Dep. Headmaster, St Edmund's Sch., Canterbury, Kent, 1949–81. *Recreations:* music, travel, cricket. *Address:* 146 New Dover Road, Canterbury, Kent CT1 3EJ. *T:* Canterbury (0227) 452605.

NICKSON, Sir David (Wigley), KBE 1987 (CBE 1981); DL; CBIM; FRSE; Chairman: Clydesdale Bank plc, since 1991 (Director, 1981–89; Deputy Chairman, 1990–91); Top Salaries Review Body, since 1989; Scottish Enterprise, since 1990 (Scottish Development Agency, 1989–90); *b* 27 Nov. 1929; *s* of late Geoffrey Wigley Nickson and of Janet Mary Nickson; *m* 1952, Helen Louise Cockcraft; three *d*. *Educ:* Eton; RMA, Sandhurst. Commnd Coldstream Guards, 1949–54. Joined Wm Collins, 1954; Dir, 1961–85; Jt Man. Dir, 1967; Vice Chm., 1976–83; Gp Man. Dir, 1979–82; Chm., Pan Books, 1982. Director: Scottish United Investors plc, 1970–83; General Accident Fire and Life Assurance Corp. plc, 1971–; Scottish & Newcastle Breweries plc, 1981– (Dep. Chm., 1982–83; Chm., 1983–89); Radio Clyde PLC, 1982–85; Edinburgh Investment Trust plc, 1983–91; Hambro's plc, 1989–. Chm., CBI in Scotland, 1979–81; Pres., CBI, 1986–88 (Dep. Pres., 1985–86). Member: Scottish Indust. Develt Adv. Bd, 1975–80; Scottish Econ. Council, 1980–; NEDC, 1985–88; Scottish Cttee, Design Council, 1978–81; Nat. Trng Task Force, 1989–91. Chairman: Countryside Commn for Scotland, 1983–85; Atlantic Salmon Trust, 1989– (Mem., Council of Management, 1982–); Vice Chm., Assoc. of Scottish Dist Salmon Fishery Bds, 1989–; Trustee, Game Conservancy, 1988–91. Mem., Queen's Body Guard for Scotland, Royal Co. of Archers. DL Stirling and Falkirk, 1982. CBIM 1980; FRSE 1987. DUniv Stirling, 1986; Hon. DBA Napier Polytechnic, 1990. *Recreations:* fishing, shooting, bird watching, the countryside. *Clubs:* Boodle's, Flyfishers', MCC; Western (Glasgow).

NICKSON, Francis; Chief Executive and Town Clerk, London Borough of Camden, 1977–90; *b* 9 Sept. 1929; *s* of Francis and Kathleen Nickson; *m* 1957, Helena (*née* Towers). *Educ:* Preston Catholic College; Liverpool Univ. (LLB). LMRTPI. Admitted Solicitor (Hons), 1953; Asst Solicitor, Newcastle-under-Lyme, 1953–56; Senior Asst Solicitor, Wood Green, 1956–60; Assistant Town Clerk, Enfield, 1960–71; Deputy Town Clerk, Camden, 1971–77. Hon. Clerk, Housing and Works Cttee, London Boroughs Assoc., 1979–84; Hon. Sec., London Boroughs Children's Regional Planning Cttee, 1977–90. FRSA. *Recreations:* listening to music, country walking. *Address:* 14 Waggon Road, Hadley Wood, Barnet, Herts EN4 0HL. *T:* 081–449 9390.

NICOL, family name of **Baroness Nicol.**

NICOL, Baroness *cr* 1982 (Life Peer), of Newnham in the County of Cambridgeshire; **Olive Mary Wendy Nicol;** FRGS; JP; Opposition Environment Team spokesman on green issues, since 1990; *b* 21 March 1923; *d* of James and Harriet Rowe-Hunter; *m* 1947, Alexander Douglas Ian Nicol (CBE 1985); two *s* one *d*. Civil Service, 1943–48. Opposition Whip, 1983–87, Opposition Dept. Chief Whip, 1987–89, H of L. Trustee, Cambridge United Charities, 1967–86; Director, Cambridge and District Co-operative Soc., 1975–81, Pres. 1981–85; Member: Supplementary Benefits Tribunal, 1976–78; Cambridge City Council, 1972–82; Assoc. of District Councils, Cambridge Branch, 1974–76 and 1980–82; various school Governing Bodies, 1974–80; Council, Granta Housing Soc., 1975–; Careers Service Consultative Group, 1978–81. JP Cambridge City, 1972–. *Recreations:* reading, walking. *Address:* c/o House of Lords, SW1A 0PW.

NICOL, Andrew William, BSc; FICE, FIMechE, FIEE; Chairman, since 1987, and Chief Executive, South Western Electricity plc; *b* 29 April 1933; *s* of Arthur Edward Nicol and Ethel Isabel Gladstone Nicol (*née* Fairley); *m* 1960; Jane Gillian Margaret Mann; one *s*. *Educ:* King's College School, Wimbledon; Durham Univ. (BSc). W. S. Atkins & Partners, 1960–67; Electricity Council, 1967–69; London Electricity Board, 1969–81; Dep. Chm., SE Electricity Board, 1981–87. JP Surrey 1976. *Recreation:* Honourable Artillery

Company. *Address:* South Western Electricity plc, 800 Park Avenue, Aztec West, Almondsbury, Bristol BS12 4SE. *Club:* Caledonian.

NICOL, Angus Sebastian Torquil Eyers; barrister; a Recorder of the Crown Court, since 1982; *b* 11 April 1933; *s of* Henry James Nicol and Phyllis Mary Eyers; *m* 1968, Eleanor Denise Brodrick; two *d. Educ:* RNC, Dartmouth. Served RN, 1947–56. Called to the Bar, Middle Temple, 1963. A Chairman: Disciplinary Cttee, Potato Marketing Bd, 1988–; VAT Tribunal, 1988–. Founder Vice-Chm. and Mem. Council, Monday Club, 1961–68. Lectr in Gaelic, Central London Adult Educn Inst., 1983–; Sen. Steward, Argyllshire Gathering, 1983; Dir, 1981–, and Jt Sec., 1984–, Highland Soc. of London; Conductor, London Gaelic Choir, 1985–; Comr of Clan MacNicol for all Territories of GB south of River Tweed, 1988–. FSA (Scot.). *Publications:* Gaelic poems and short stories in Gairm, etc. *Recreations:* music, Gaelic language and literature, shooting, fishing, sailing, gastronomy. *Address:* 5 Paper Buildings, Temple, EC4Y 7HB. *T:* 071–353 8494. *Clubs:* Flyfishers'; Royal Highland Yacht.

NICOL, Davidson Sylvester Hector Willoughby, CMG 1964; MA, MD, PhD (Cantab); FRCPath; Under-Secretary-General of the United Nations and Executive Director, United Nations Institute for Training and Research (UNITAR), 1972–82; Senior Fellow, UNITAR, 1983; Hon. Consultant Pathologist, Sierra Leone Government; Associate Lecturer, Centre of International Studies, University of Cambridge, since 1985; *b* 14 Sept. 1924, of African parentage; *m*; three *s* two *d. Educ:* Schools in Nigeria and Sierra Leone; Cambridge and London Univs. Science Master, Prince of Wales Sch., Sierra Leone, 1941–43. Cambridge: Foundation Schol., Prizeman, 1943–47; Fellow and Supervisor in Nat. Sciences and Med., 1957–59, Christ's Coll. (Hon. Fellow, 1972); BA 1946; 1st Cl. Hons (Nat. Sciences), 1947; Beit Meml Fellow for Medical Research, 1954; Benn Levy Univ. Studentship, Cambridge, 1956; Univ. Schol., House Physician (Medical Unit and Clinical Pathology), Receiving Room Officer, and Research Asst (Physiology), London Hosp., 1947–52; Univ. Lectr, Medical School, Ibadan, Nigeria, 1952–54; Visiting Lecturer: Univs of Toronto, California (Berkeley), Mayo Clinic, 1958; Aggrey-Fraser-Guggisberg Meml Lectr, Univ. of Ghana, 1963; Danforth Fellowship Lectr in African Affairs, Assoc. of Amer. Colls, USA, 1968–71. Sen. Pathologist, Sierra Leone, 1958–60; Principal, Fourah Bay Coll., Sierra Leone, 1960–68, and first Vice-Chancellor, Univ. of Sierra Leone, 1966–68; Perm. Rep. and Ambassador for Sierra Leone to UN, 1969–71 (Security Council, 1970–71), Pres. Sept. 1970; Chm., Cttee of 24 (Decolonisation); Mem., Economic and Social Council, 1969–70); High Comr for Sierra Leone in London, and Ambassador to Norway, Sweden and Denmark, 1971–72. Margaret Wrong Prize and Medal for Literature in Africa, 1952; Chm., Sierra Leone Nat. Library Bd, 1959–65; Member: Governing Body, Kumasi Univ., Ghana; Public Service Commn, Sierra Leone, 1960–68; W African Council for Medical Research, 1959–62; Exec. Council, Assoc. of Univs of British Commonwealth, 1960 and 1966; Commn for proposed Univ. of Ghana, 1960; Chm., Univ. of E Africa Visiting Cttee, 1962; Chm., UN Mission to Angola, July 1976. Director: Central Bank of Sierra Leone; Consolidated African Selection Trust Ltd (London); Davesme Corp. President: W African Science Assoc., 1964–66; Sierra Leone Red Cross Soc., 1962–66; World Fedn of UNAs, 1983–87 (Hon. Pres., 1987–); Vice-Pres., Royal African Soc., 1986; Chm., W African Exams Council, 1964–69. Consultant, Ford Foundn, NY. Member, Internat. Board: African-Amer. Inst., NY; Fund for Peace, NY. Conference Delegate to: WHO Assembly, 1960; UNESCO Higher Educn Conf., Tananarive, 1963; Commonwealth Prime Ministers' Conf., London, 1965 and 1969, Singapore 1971. Guest Scholar: Woodrow Wilson Internat. Center, Washington, 1983; Hoover Instn, Stanford Univ., 1984; Distinguished Vis. Prof. in Internat. Studies, Calif State Univ., 1987–88; Vis. Fellow, Johns Hopkins Sch. of Advanced Internat. Studies, Washington, 1983; Vis. Prof., Univ. of S Carolina, 1990, 1991. Hon. Fellow, Ghana Acad. of Scis. Hon. LLD: Leeds; Barat, Ill; Univ. of West Indies (St Augustine), 1981; Tuskegee, Ala, 1981; Hon. DSc: Newcastle upon Tyne; Kalamazoo, Mich; Laurentian, Ont; Sierra Leone; Hon. DLitt Davis and Elkins Coll., W Va. Independence Medal, Sierra Leone, 1961; World Peace Gold Medal, Indian Fedn of UN Assocs, New Delhi, 1986. Grand Commander: Order of Rokel, Sierra Leone, 1974; Star of Africa, Liberia, 1974. *Publications:* Africa, A Subjective View, 1964; contribs to: Malnutrition in African Mothers and Children, 1954; HRH the Duke of Edinburgh's Study Conference, Vol. 2, 1958; The Mechanism of Action of Insulin, 1960; The Structure of Human Insulin, 1960; Africanus Horton and Black Nationalism (1867), 1969; New and Modern Rôles for Commonwealth and Empire, 1976; The United Nations and Decision Making: the role of women, 1978; Nigeria and the Future of Africa, 1980; (ed) Paths to Peace, 1981; (ed) Essays on the UN Security Council and its Presidency, 1981; (ed) Regionalism and the New International Economic Order, 1981; The United Nations Security Council: towards greater effectiveness, 1981; Creative Women, 1982; also to Jl Trop. Med., Biochem. Jl, Nature, Jl of Royal African Soc., Times, Guardian, New Statesman, Encounter, West Africa, etc. *Recreation:* creative writing (under *nom-de-plume* Abioseh Nicol). *Address:* Christ's College, Cambridge CB2 3BU. *Clubs:* United Oxford & Cambridge University, Commonwealth Trust; Senior Dinner (Freetown).

NICOL, Prof. Donald MacGillivray, FBA 1981; FKC 1980; Director, Gennadius Library, Athens, since 1989; Koraës Professor of Modern Greek and Byzantine History, Language and Literature, University of London, King's College, 1970–88, now Emeritus; Vice Principal, King's College, 1980–81 (Assistant Principal, 1977–80); *b* 4 Feb. 1923; *s* of late Rev. George Manson Nicol and Mary Patterson (*née* MacGillivray); *m* 1950, Joan Mary Campbell, *d* of Sir Walter Campbell, KCIE; three *s. Educ:* King Edward VII Sch., Sheffield; St Paul's Sch., London; Pembroke Coll., Cambridge (MA, PhD). Friends' Ambulance Unit, 1942–46; Scholar at British Sch. of Archæology, Athens, 1949–50; Lectr in Classics, University Coll., Dublin, 1952–64; Vis. Fellow, Dumbarton Oaks, Washington, DC, 1964–65; Vis. Prof. of Byzantine History, Indiana Univ., 1965–66; Sen. Lectr and Reader in Byzantine History, Univ. of Edinburgh, 1966–70. Birkbeck Lectr, Cambridge, 1976–77. Pres., Ecclesiastical Hist. Soc., 1975–76. MRIA 1960; FRHistS 1971. Hon. Citizen of Arta, Greece, 1990. Editor, Byzantine and Modern Greek Studies, 1973–83. *Publications:* The Despotate of Epiros, 1957; Meteora, the Rock Monasteries of Thessaly, 1963, rev. edn, 1975; The Byzantine Family of Kantakouzenos (Cantacuzenus) ca 1100–1460: a genealogical and prosopographical study, 1968; The Last Centuries of Byzantium, 1261–1453, 1972; Byzantium: Its Ecclesiastical History and Relations with the Western World, 1972; Church and Society in the Last Centuries of Byzantium, 1979; The End of the Byzantine Empire, 1979; The Despotate of Epiros 1267–1479: a contribution to the history of Greece in the middle ages, 1984; Studies in Late Byzantine History and Prosopography, 1986; Byzantium and Venice: a study in diplomatic and cultural relations, 1988; Joannes Gennadios—The Man: a biographical sketch, 1990; A Biographical Dictionary of the Byzantine Empire, 1991; articles in Byzantine, classical and historical jls. *Recreation:* bookbinding. *Address:* Gennadius Library, American School of Classical Studies, Athens 106 76, Greece; 16 Courtyards, Little Shelford, Cambridge CB2 5ER. *T:* Cambridge (0223) 843406. *Club:* Athenæum.

NICOL, Dr Joseph Arthur Colin, FRS 1967; Professor of Zoology, University of Texas Institute of Marine Science, 1967–80, now Professor Emeritus; *b* 5 Dec. 1915; *s* of George Nicol and Noele Petrie; *m* 1941, Helen Wilhelmina Cameron; one *d. Educ:* Universities

of McGill, Western Ontario and Oxford. BSc (hons Zool.) 1938, McGill; MA 1940, Western Ontario; DPhil 1947, DSc 1961, Oxford. Canadian Army, RCCS, 1941–45. Asst Professor in Zoology, University of British Columbia, 1947–49; Experimental Zoologist, Marine Biological Assoc., UK, 1949 (research on marine animals, comparative physiology, luminescence, vision, at Plymouth Laboratory, 1949–66). Guggenheim Fellow, Scripps Inst. Oceanography, 1953–54. Vis. Prof., Univ. of Texas, 1966–67. *Publications:* Biology of Marine Animals, 1960; Eyes of Fishes, 1989; papers on comparative physiology and anatomy in Jl Marine Biol. Assoc. UK, Proc. Royal Soc, Jl Exp. Biol., Biol. Review, etc. *Recreation:* English literature. *Address:* Ribby, Lerryn, Lostwithiel, Cornwall PL22 0PG. *T:* Bodmin (0208) 872319.

NICOLI, Eric Luciano; Group Chief Executive, United Biscuits (Holdings) Plc, since 1991; *b* 5 Aug. 1950; *s* of Virgilio and Ida Nicoli; *m* 1977, Rosalind West; one *s* one *d. Educ:* Diss Grammar Sch.; King's College London (BSc Hons 1st class Physics). Rowntree Mackintosh: Market Research Asst, 1972; Brand Manager, Marketing, 1973; Product Group Manager, 1977; United Biscuits: Sen. Marketing Controller, 1980; Marketing Dir, Biscuits Div., 1981; UK Group Business Planning Dir, 1984; Managing Dir, Frozen Food Div., 1985, Biscuit and Confectionery Div., 1986; Chief Exec., Eur. Ops and Group Chief Exec. designate, 1989–91. *Recreations:* sport, food, music. *Address:* United Biscuits (Holdings) plc, Park Place, Church Road, West Drayton, Middlesex UB7 7PR; 24 Amersham Road, High Wycombe, Bucks HP13 6QU.

NICOLL, Douglas Robertson, CB 1980; retired; *b* 12 May 1920; *s* of James George Nicoll and Mabel Nicoll (*née* Styles); *m* 1949, Winifred Campion (*d* 1987); two *s. Educ:* Merchant Taylors' School; St John's College, Oxford (MA 1946). FCO (GCHQ), 1946–80; Joint Services' Staff College, 1953; Under Secretary, 1977–80. *Address:* c/o National Westminster Bank, 31 The Promenade, Cheltenham, Glos GL50 1LH. *Club:* Travellers'.

NICOLL, Prof. Ronald Ewart, MSc, FRTPI, FRICS; Professor of Urban and Regional Planning, University of Strathclyde, 1966–80; Partner, 1980–85, Consultant, since 1985, PIEDA; *b* 8 May 1921; *s* of William Ewart Nicoll and Edith May Choat; *m* 1943, Isabel Christina McNab; one *s* one *d. Educ:* Southend Municipal Coll.; Hammersmith Sch. of Architecture and Building; Royal College of Science and Technology, Glasgow. Served War, Royal Navy, 1939–46. Planning Asst, 1949–53: Southend CB; Derbyshire CC; Northamptonshire CC. Dep. Dir of Planning, Glasgow City, 1953–64; Chief Planning Officer, Scottish Development Dept, 1964–66. Consultant to UN and WHO. Member: Scottish Social Advisory Council, 1970; Scottish Council on Crime, 1971; Scottish Council (Develt and Industry), 1971; Glasgow Chamber of Commerce, 1971; Royal Commn on Environmental Pollution, 1973–79. RICS Gold Medal, 1975. FRSA. *Publications:* Oceanspan, 1970; Energy and the Environment, 1975; contribs to: The Future of Development Plans, 1965 (HMSO); How Do You Want to Live?, 1972 (HMSO); A Future for Scotland, 1973. *Recreations:* travel, photography, hill walking. *Address:* 78 Victoria Park Drive North, Glasgow G14 9PJ. *T:* 041–959 7854. *Clubs:* Commonwealth Trust; Western (Glasgow).

NICOLL, William, CMG 1974; Fulbright Fellow, George Mason University, Virginia, USA, 1991–May 1992; *b* 28 June 1927; *s* of Ralph Nicoll and Christina Mowbray Nicoll (*née* Melville); *m* 1954, Helen Morison Martin; two *d. Educ:* Morgan Acad., Dundee; St Andrews Univ. Entered BoT, 1949; British Trade Comr, India, 1955–59; Private Sec. to Pres. of BoT, 1964–67; Commercial Inspector, FCO, 1967–69; DTI, 1969–72; Office of UK Perm. Rep. to European Communities, 1972–75; Under Sec., Dept of Prices and Consumer Protection, 1975–77; Dep. UK Rep. to EEC, 1977–82; a Dir Gen., Council of Eur. Communities, 1982–91. Assoc. Res. Fellow, Univ. of St Andrews, 1991–. Hon. LLD Dundee, 1983. *Publications:* (contrib.) Government and Industry (ed W. Rodgers), 1986; (ed and contrib.) Competition Policy Enquiry, 1988; (with T. C. Salmon) Understanding the European Communities, 1990; contribs to various jls on European subjects. *Address:* Flat 15, Lees Court, Sheldwich, Kent ME13 0NQ.

NICOLLE, Anthony William; Commissioner of Banking, Hong Kong, 1987–91; *b* 13 April 1935; *s* of late Roland Nicolle and Dorothy May Pearce; *m* 1960, Josephine Anne (*née* Read); one *s* one *d. Educ:* Tiffin Sch.; King's Coll., London (LLB). Served RA, 1956–58. Joined Bank of England, 1958; seconded to NEDO, 1968–70; Econ. Intelligence Dept, 1970–77; seconded to Royal Commn on Distribn of Income and Wealth, 1974–75; banking supervision, 1977–80; Banking Dept, 1980–83; banking supervision, 1983–87. *Recreations:* walking (a little), gardening (occasionally). *Club:* Overseas Bankers' (Hong Kong).

NICOLSON, family name of **Baron Carnock.**

NICOLSON, Sir David (Lancaster), Kt 1975; FEng 1977; *b* 20 Sept. 1922; *s* of Charles Tupper Nicolson, consulting engineer, and Margaret Lancaster Nicolson; *m* 1945, Joan Eileen (*d* 1991), *d* of Major W. H. Griffiths, RA; one *s* two *d. Educ:* Haileybury; Imperial Coll., London Univ. (BSc; Hon. Fellow 1971). FCGI, FIMechE, FIProdE; FBIM; FRSA. Constructor Lt, Royal Corps Naval Constructors, 1942–45; served N Atlantic and Normandy, 1944 (despatches). Production Manager, Bucyrus-Erie Co., Milwaukee, 1950–52; Manager, later Dir, Production-Engineering Ltd, 1953–62; Chairman: P-E Consulting Gp, 1963–68; British Airways Board, 1971–75; BTR plc, 1969–84 (Dep. Chm., 1965–69, Dir, 1984–); Rothmans International plc, 1975–84; Bulk Transport Ltd, 1984–89; German Securities Investment Trust, 1985–89; Lazard Leisure Fund, 1985–91; VSEL (Vickers Shipbuilding and Engineering), 1986–87; British Rail Engineering, 1987–89; Union Group, 1988–; DRG Ltd, 1989–; TACE PLC, 1991–; Director: Delta Metal Co., 1967–79; Bank of Montreal, 1970–85; Richard Costain, 1970–78; MEPC, 1976–80; Todd Shipyards Corp., 1976–91; CIBA-Geigy (UK), 1978–90; GKN Plc, 1984–89; London & Scottish Marine Oil, 1983–; Northern Telecom Ltd, 1987–; Britannia Arrow Holdings plc, later Invesco MIM PLC, 1987–; STC PLC, 1987–91; Dawnay Day & Co., 1988–; Brel Group Ltd, 1989–; Southern Water plc, 1989–; Churchill Leisure Internat., 1989–90; Strategic Hldgs SA, 1991–. European Adviser, NY Stock Exchange, 1985–. Mem. (C) London Central, European Parlt, 1979–84. Mem. Council: CBI, 1972– (Chm., Environment Cttee, 1976–79); Inst. of Directors, 1971–76; Brit. Inst. of Management, 1964–69; Inst. of Production Engrs, 1966–68; City and Guilds of London Inst., 1968–76; Mem., SRC Engineering Bd, 1969–71; Chm. Management Consultants Assoc., 1964; Mem. Brit. Shipbuilding Mission to India, 1957; Chairman: Cttee for Hosiery and Knitwear, NEDC, 1966–68; BNEC Cttee for Canada, 1967–71. Pres., ABCC, 1983–86. Chm., Amer. European Community Assoc., 1981–; Chm., European Movement, 1985–. Mem. Council, Templeton Coll. (formerly Oxford Centre for Management Studies), 1982–; Governor: Imperial Coll., London Univ., 1966–77; Cranleigh Sch., 1979–; Pro-Chancellor, Surrey Univ., 1987–. *Publications:* contribs to technical jls; lectures and broadcasts on management subjects in UK, USA, Australia, etc. *Recreation:* sailing. *Address:* 3 Kingston House North, Prince's Gate, SW7 1LN. *T:* 071–225 3870; Howicks, Dunsfold, Surrey. *Clubs:* Brooks's; Royal Thames Yacht.

NICOLSON, Malise Allen, MC 1945; Chairman: Bangor-on-Dee Races Ltd, since 1984 (Director, since 1972); *b* 31 Oct. 1921; *e s* of late Sir Kenneth Nicolson, MC; *m* 1946,

Vivien Bridget, *y d* of late Arthur Hilton Ridley, CBE; one *s* two *d*. *Educ:* Eton. Served War, Probyn's Horse, 1940–45 (MC; Burma); served 1st Royal Dragoons, 1946–47. Gladstone, Lyall Ltd, Calcutta, 1948–55; joined Booker McConnell, 1956; Dir, 1968–83; Chairman: Booker Line, 1968–83 (Dir, 1957–83); Coe Metcalf Shipping, 1977–83; McConnell Salmon Ltd, 1980–90 (Dir, 1973–90); Govt 'A' Dir, Mersey Docks and Harbour Co., 1974–80. Chairman: Liverpool Steam Ship Owners, 1971–72; Employers Assoc., Port of Liverpool, 1972–74; Vice-Chm., British Shipping Fedn, 1968–71; Pres., Gen. Council of British Shipping, 1982–83; Mem., Nat. Dock Labour Bd, 1986–90. Dir, The Race Course Assoc. Ltd, 1984–90. *Recreation:* country sports. *Address:* Frog Hall, Tilston, Malpas, Cheshire SY14 7HB. *T:* Tilston (0829) 250320. *Club:* Cavalry and Guards.

NICOLSON, Nigel, MBE 1945; FSA; FRSL; author; Director of Weidenfeld and Nicolson Ltd since 1948; *b* 19 Jan. 1917; 2nd *s* of late Hon. Sir Harold Nicolson, KCVO, CMG and Hon. V. Sackville-West, CH; *heir-pres.* to 4th Baron Carnock, *qv*; *m* 1953, Philippa Janet (marr. diss. 1970; she *d* 1987), *d* of Sir Gervais Tennyson d'Eyncourt, 2nd Bt; one *s* two *d*. *Educ:* Eton Coll.; Balliol Coll., Oxford. Capt. Grenadier Guards. Served War of 1939–45 in Tunisian and Italian Campaigns (MBE). Contested (C) NW Leicester, 1950, and Falmouth and Camborne, 1951; MP (C) Bournemouth East and Christchurch, Feb. 1952–Sept. 1959. Chm. Exec. Cttee, UNA, 1961–66. *Publications:* The Grenadier Guards, 1939–45, 1949 (official history); People and Parliament, 1958; Lord of the Isles, 1960; Great Houses of Britain, 1965, revd edn 1978; (editor) Harold Nicolson: Diaries and Letters, 3 vols, 1966–68; Great Houses, 1968; Alex (FM Alexander of Tunis), 1973; Portrait of a Marriage, 1973; (ed) Letters of Virginia Woolf, 1975–80 (6 vols); The Himalayas, 1975; Mary Curzon, 1977 (Whitbread Award); Napoleon: 1812, 1985; (with Adam Nicolson) Two Roads to Dodge City, 1986; Kent, 1988; The World of Jane Austen, 1991; Vita and Harold: Selected Letters, 1991. *Recreation:* archæology. *Address:* Sissinghurst Castle, Cranbrook, Kent TN17 2AB. *T:* Cranbrook (0580) 714239. *Club:* Beefsteak.

NICOLSON, Roy Macdonald; Managing Director, Scottish Amicable Life Assurance Society, since 1990; *b* 12 June 1944; *s* of Alan Neil Nicolson and Mary Nicholson; *m* 1972, Jennifer Margaret Miller; one *s* one *d*. *Educ:* Paisley Grammar School. FFA, FPMI. Joined Scottish Amicable, 1960; Asst London Secretary, 1971; Asst Actuary, 1973; Pensions Manager (Operations), 1976; Asst Gen. Manager (Pensions), 1982; Gen. Manager (Systems), 1985; Dep. Chief Gen. Manager, 1990. *Recreations:* golf, bridge. *Address:* Scottish Amicable, 150 St Vincent Street, Glasgow G2 5NQ; Ardgarten, Doune Road, Dunblane, Perthshire FK15 9HR. *T:* Dunblane (0786) 823849. *Clubs:* Dunblane New Golf; Dun Whinny (Gleneagles).

NIEDUSZYŃSKI, Anthony John; Head of Business Task Forces Division 2, Department of Trade and Industry, since 1990; *b* 7 Jan. 1939; *er s* of Tadeusz Adolf Antoni Nieduszyński, LLD and Madaleine Gladys Lilian (*née* Huggler); *m* 1980, Frances, *yr d* of Wing Comdr Max Oxford, OBE; one *d*. *Educ:* St Paul's School (Foundation Scholar); Merton College, Oxford (Postmaster; 1st cl. Hon. Mods 1959; 1st cl. Lit Hum 1961; MA). Board of Trade, 1964; Private Sec. to Pres. of BoT, 1967–68; Principal Private Sec. to Minister for Trade and Consumer Affairs, 1972–74 and to Sec. of State for Trade, 1974; Asst Sec., Dept of Prices and Consumer Protection, 1974, Dept of Industry, 1977, Home Office, 1982; Under Sec., DTI, 1985–; Head: of Radiocommunications Div., 1985; of Air Div., 1988. *Recreations:* gardening, fell walking, skating, linguistics, opera. *Address:* c/o Department of Trade and Industry, 151 Buckingham Palace Road, SW1W 9SS.

NIELD, Sir Basil Edward, Kt 1957; CBE 1956 (MBE 1943); DL; Judge of High Court of Justice, Queen's Bench Division, 1960–78; *b* 7 May 1903; *yr s* of late Charles Edwin Nield, JP, and Mrs F. E. L. Nield, MBE, Upton-by-Chester. *Educ:* Harrow Sch.; Magdalen Coll., Oxford (MA). Officers Emergency Reserve, 1938; served War of 1939–45: commnd Captain, 1940; GHQ MEF (Major), HQs E Africa Force, Palestine; Pres., Palestine Military Courts in Jerusalem; 9th Army, Beirut; HQs Eritrea and 8th Army; 1943: HQ Persia and Iraq; Asst Dep. Judge Advocate-Gen., ME (Lt-Col; despatches; MBE (mil.)); 21 Army Gp; HQ Lines of Communication, BLA, Normandy; HQ 2nd Army, Low Countries, Rhine; RARO until 1948. Called to Bar, Inner Temple, 1925, Master of the Bench, 1952, Reader, 1976, Treasurer, 1977; Northern Circuit, Chambers in Liverpool; KC 1945; Recorder of Salford, 1948–56; Recorder and first permanent Judge of Crown Court at Manchester, 1956–60; the only Judge to have presided at all sixty-one Assize towns in England and Wales before abolition of Assize system, 1972. Mem., Gen. Council of Bar, 1951. MP (C) City of Chester, 1940–56; sponsored as Private Member's Bill the Adoption of Children Act, 1949; Hon. Parly Chm., Dock and Harbour Authorities Assoc., 1944–50; Mem. Exec., 1922 Cttee; Mem., Special Cttee under Reorganisation Areas Measure for Province of York, 1944. Member: Magistrates' Rules Cttee, 1952–56; Legal Bd, Church Assembly, 1952–56; Home Secretary's Adv. Cttee on Treatment of Offenders, 1957. Chancellor, Diocese of Liverpool, 1948–56. Vice-President: Nat. Chamber of Trade, 1948–56; Graduate Teachers Assoc., 1950–56; Corp. of Secretaries, 1950; Assoc. of Managers of Approved Schools, 1956; Cheshire Soc. in London; Spastics Soc., Manchester. Chm., Chester Conservative Assoc., 1930–40. Member: Court, Liverpool Univ., 1948–56; Adv. Council, E-SU, 1951; Oxford Soc.; Imperial Soc. of Knights Bachelor; Life Mem., Royal Soc. of St George. Governor, Harrow Sch., 1961–71. FAMS. DL County Palatine of Chester, 1962–. Freeman, City of London, 1963. *Publication:* Farewell to the Assizes, 1972. *Address:* Osborne House, Isle of Wight PO32 6JY. *T:* Isle of Wight (0983) 200056. *Clubs:* Carlton; City, Grosvenor (Chester).

NIELD, Sir William (Alan), GCMG 1972; KCB 1968 (CB 1966); Deputy Chairman, Rolls Royce (1971) Ltd, 1973–76; *b* 21 Sept. 1913; *s* of William Herbert Nield, Stockport, Cheshire, and Ada Nield; *m* 1937, Gwyneth Marion Davies; two *s* two *d*. *Educ:* Stockport Gram. Sch.; St Edmund Hall, Oxford (Hon. Fellow, 1990). Research and Policy Dept of Labour Party, 1937–39; K-H News Letter Service, 1939. Served Royal Air Force and Royal Canadian Air Force, 1939–46 (despatches, 1944); demobilised as Wing Comdr, 1946. Min. of Food, 1946–47; HM Treasury, 1947–49; Min. of Food and Min. of Agric., Fisheries and Food, 1949–64 (Under-Sec., 1959–64); Dept of Economic Affairs: Under-Sec., 1964–65; Dep. Under-Sec. of State, 1965–66; a Dep. Sec., Cabinet Office, 1966–68; Permanent Under-Sec. of State, DEA, 1968–69; Permanent Secretary: Cabinet Office, 1969–72; NI Office, 1972–73. Pres., St Edmund Hall Assoc., 1981–83. *Address:* South Nevay, Stubbs Wood, Chesham Bois, Bucks. *T:* Amersham (0494) 433869. *Club:* Farmers'.

NIELSEN, Aksel Christopher W.; *see* Wiin-Nielsen.

NIELSEN, Hon. Erik H., DFC; PC 1984; QC 1962; President, Canadian Transport Commission, since 1987; MP (Progressive Conservative Party) for Yukon, 1957–87; Deputy Prime Minister of Canada, 1984–86; Minister of Defence, 1985–86; *b* 24 Feb. 1924; *m* 1st, Pamela Hall (*d* 1969); three *c*; 2nd, 1983, Shelley Coxford. *Educ:* Dalhousie Univ. (LLB). Royal Canadian Air Force, 1942–51; flew Lancaster bombers, War of 1939–45. Called to the Bar of Nova Scotia, 1951; legal practice in Whitehorse, Yukon, 1952–. Minister of Public Works, 1979; Dep. House Leader, 1980–81; Opposition appts, 1981–83. Member: Canadian Bar Assoc; Yukon Law Soc.; Hon. Member: Internat. Union of Mine, Mill and Smelter Workers; Whitehorse Chamber of Commerce. Vice-Pres., Dawson City Museum and Hist. Soc. *Publications:* Water Boy, 1987; The House is Not a Home, 1989. *Address:* 103/107 Main Street, Whitehorse, Yukon Y1A 2A5, Canada.

NIEMEYER, Oscar; architect; *b* Rio de Janeiro, 15 Dec. 1907; *s* of Oscar Niemeyer Soares; *m* Anita Niemeyer; one *d*. *Educ:* Escola Nacional de Beles Artes, Univ. of Brazil. Joined office of Lúcio Costa, 1935; worked on Min. of Education and Health Building, Rio de Janeiro, Brazilian Pavilion, NY World Fair, etc., 1936–41. Major projects include: Pamphulha, Belo Horizonte, 1941–43; also Quintandinha, Petrópolis; Exhibition Hall, São Paulo, 1953; Brasilia (Dir of Architecture), 1957–. Brazilian Rep., UN Bd of Design Consultants, 1947. Lenin Peace Prize, 1963; Prix Internat. de l'Architecture Aujourd'hui, 1966. *Address:* 3940 avenida Atlântica, Rio de Janeiro, Brazil.

NIGERIA, Metropolitan Archbishop and Primate of, since 1988; **Most Rev. Joseph Abiodun Adetiloye;** Bishop of Lagos, since 1985. *Educ:* Melville Hall, Ibadan; King's Coll., London (BD); Wycliffe Hall, Oxford. Ordained, dio. of Lagos, 1954; Lect, 1962, Vice Principal, 1963–66, Immanuel Coll., Ibadan; Provost, Ibadan Cathedral, 1966–70; Bishop of Ekiti, 1970–85. Mem., Eames Commn. *Address:* PO Box 13 (Bishopscourt, 29 Marina), Lagos, Nigeria. *Fax:* (1) 631 264.

NIGHTINGALE, Benedict; *see* Nightingale, W. B. H.

NIGHTINGALE, Sir Charles (Manners Gamaliel), 17th Bt *cr* 1628; Senior Executive Officer, Department of Health, since 1989; *b* 21 Feb. 1947; *s* of Sir Charles Athelstan Nightingale, 16th Bt, and of Evelyn Nadine Frances, *d* of late Charles Arthur Diggens; *S* father, 1977. *Educ:* St Paul's School. BA Hons Open Univ., 1990. Entered DHSS as Executive Officer, 1969; Higher Executive Officer, 1977. *Heir: cousin* Edward Lacy George Nightingale, *b* 11 May 1938. *Address:* 14 Frensham Court, 27 Highbury New Park, N5 2ES.

NIGHTINGALE, Edward Humphrey, CMG 1955; Farmer in Kenya since 1954; *b* 19 Aug. 1904; *s* of Rev. Edward Charles Nightingale and Ada Mary Nightingale; *m* 1944, Evelyn Mary Ray; three *s* one *d*. *Educ:* Rugby Sch.; Emmanuel Coll., Cambridge. Joined Sudan Political Service, 1926; Dep. Civil Sec., Sudan Government, 1951–52; Gov., Equatoria Province, Sudan, 1952–54. Order of the Nile, 4th Class, 1940. *Recreations:* carpentry, ornithology, photography. *Address:* Nunjoro Farm, PO Box 100, Naivasha, Kenya. *T:* Kerati, Naivasha 2Y1. *Clubs:* Muthaiga Country (Nairobi); Naivasha Sports.

NIGHTINGALE, Sir John (Cyprian), Kt 1975; CBE 1970; BEM 1941; QPM 1965; DL; Chief Constable, Essex, 1962–69 and 1974–78, retired (Essex and Southend-on-Sea Joint Constabulary, 1969–74); *b* 16 Sept. 1913; *s* of Herbert Paul Nightingale, Sydenham, London; *m* 1947, Patricia Mary, *d* of Norman Maclaren, Glasgow University. *Educ:* Cardinal Vaughan Sch., Kensington; University Coll., London. Joined Metropolitan Police, 1935; Asst Chief Constable, Essex, 1958. Chm., Police Council, 1976–78; Mem., Parole Bd, 1978–82. Served with RNVR, 1943–45. DL Essex 1975. *Publications:* various police pubns. *Address:* Great Whitman's Farm, Purleigh, Essex.

NIGHTINGALE of Cromarty, Michael David, OBE 1960; BSc; BLitt; FSA; Baron of Cromarty; Esquire Bedell, University of London, since 1953; Director, The Chillington Corporation plc, since 1986 (Chairman, 1986–89); *b* 6 Dec. 1927; *s* of late Victor Russell John Nightingale, Wormshill, Kent; *m* 1956, Hilary Marion Olwen, *d* of late John Eric Jones, Swansea; two *s* three *d*. *Educ:* Winchester; Wye Coll.; Magdalen Coll., Oxford. Organised Exhibition from Kent Village Churches, Canterbury, 1951; Asst to Investment Manager, Anglo-Iranian Oil Co., 1951–53; Investment Adviser, Univ. of London, 1954–66; Dir, Charterhouse Japhet Ltd, 1965–70. Secretary: Museums Assoc. (and Editor of Museums Jl), 1954–60; Museum Cttee, Carnegie UK Trust, 1954–60; Member: Advisory Council on Export of Works of Art, 1954–60; British Cttee of International Council of Museums, 1956–60; Canterbury Diocesan Advisory Cttee, 1964–79; Exec. Cttee, SE Arts Assoc., 1974–77; Area Archaeol. Adv. Cttee for SE England, 1975–79; Investment Cttee, Univs Superannuation Scheme, 1977–84; Mem. Bd, Commonwealth Develt Corp., 1985–. Mem., Gen. Synod of C of E, 1979–85 (Panel of Chairmen, 1984–85). Member: Kent CC, 1973–77; Maidstone Borough Council, 1973– (Chm., Planning Cttee, 1973–77; Leader, 1976–77; Mayor, 1984–85). Vice-Pres., North Downs Soc.; Chm., Churches Cttee, Kent Archaeological Soc. Dep. Steward, Royal Manor of Wye, 1954–; Warden, Rochester Bridge, 1989–92; a Lord of the Level of Romney Marsh. *Publications:* articles on agrarian and museum subjects. *Address:* Wormshill Court, Sittingbourne, Kent ME9 0TS. *T:* Wormshill (062784) 235; Perceval House, 21 Dartmouth Row, Greenwich, SE10. *T:* 081–692 6033; Cromarty House, Ross and Cromarty IV11 8XS. *T:* Cromarty (03817) 265. *Club:* Athenæum.

NIGHTINGALE, Roger Daniel; economist and strategist; *b* 5 June 1945; *s* of Douglas Daniel John Nightingale and Edna Kathleen Vincent; *m* 1971, Pauline Mary Cross; two *d*. *Educ:* Welwyn Garden City Grammar Sch.; Keele Univ. (BA double hons Maths and Econs); University Coll. London (MSc Stats). Economist, Hoare & Co., 1968; Datastream, 1972, Dir, 1975; Hoare Govett, 1976, Dir, 1980; Head of Economics and Strategy Dept, Smith New Court, 1988–. *Publications:* articles in financial magazines and newspapers. *Recreations:* snooker, collecting dictionaries, European history. *Address:* 182 Ashley Gardens, SW1P 1PD. *T:* 071–828 0259. *Club:* Reform.

NIGHTINGALE, (William) Benedict (Herbert); theatre critic, The Times, since 1990; *b* 14 May 1939; *s* of late Ronald Nightingale and of Hon. Evelyn Nightingale, *d* of 1st Baron Burghclere; *m* 1964, Anne Bryan Redmon; two *s* one *d*. *Educ:* Charterhouse Sch.; Magdalene College, Cambridge (BA Hons); Univ. of Pennsylvania. General writer and northern drama critic, The Guardian, 1963–66; Literary Editor, New Society, 1966–68; theatre critic, New Statesman, 1968–86; Sunday theatre critic, New York Times, 1983–84; Prof. of English, Theatre and Drama, Univ. of Michigan, 1986–89. *Publications:* Charities, 1973; Fifty Modern British Plays, 1981; Fifth Row Center, 1985. *Address:* 40 Broomhouse Road, SW6 3QX. *Club:* Hurlingham.

NIKLASSON, Frau Bertil; *see* Nilsson, Birgit.

NIKLAUS, Prof. Robert, BA, PhD London; LèsL Lille; DrUniv Rennes *hc* 1963; Hon. DLitt Exon 1981; Officier de l'Ordre National du Mérite, 1972; Professor of French, 1952–75, now Emeritus, also Head of Department of French and Spanish, 1958–64, French and Italian, 1964–75, University of Exeter (formerly University College of the South West); *b* 18 July 1910; *s* of late Jean Rodolphe and Elizabeth Niklaus; *m* 1st, 1935, Thelma (*née* Jones) (*d* 1970); two *s* one *d*; 2nd, 1973, Kathleen (*née* Folta). *Educ:* Lycée Français de Londres; University Coll., London; Univ. of Lille. Sen. Tutor, Toynbee Hall, London, 1931–32; Asst and Asst Lecturer at University Coll., 1932–38; Asst Lecturer, Lecturer, Univ. of Manchester, 1938–52. Dean of the Faculty of Arts, Exeter, 1959–62; Dep. Vice-Chancellor, 1965–67. Visiting Professor: Univ. of Calif., Berkeley, 1963–64; Case Western Reserve Univ., Ohio, 1971; Univ. of British Columbia, 1975–76; Hd of Dept of Langs, Univ. of Nigeria, Nsukka, 1977–78. Pres., Assoc. of Univ. Teachers,

1954–55, Mem. Executive Cttee, 1948–62; Pres. Internat. Assoc. of Univ. Profs and Lecturers, 1960–64 (Vice-Pres., 1958–60, 1964–66); Member: Cttee of Modern Humanities Research Association, 1956–71; Cttee, Soc. for French Studies, 1965–72 (Vice-Pres., 1967–68 and 1970–71, Pres. 1968–70); Pres., British Soc. for XVIIIth Century Studies, 1970–72; Treasurer, Internat. Soc. for Eighteenth-century Studies, 1969–79; Post-graduate Awards Cttee of Min. of Education, 1956–61; Management Cttee, British Inst., Paris, 1965–67. Gen. Editor, Textes Français Classiques et Modernes, Hodder & Stoughton. *Publications:* Jean Moréas, Poète Lyrique, 1936; The Nineteenth Century (Post-Romantic) and After (in The Year's Work in Modern Language Studies, VII-XIII), 1937–52; Diderot and Drama, 1942; Beaumarchais, Le Barbier de Séville, 1968; A Literary History of France, the Eighteenth Century, 1970; Beaumarchais, Le Mariage de Figaro, 1983; critical editions of: J.-J. Rousseau, Les Rêveries du Promeneur Solitaire, 1942; Denis Diderot, Pensées Philosophiques, 1950; Denis Diderot, Lettre sur les Aveugles, 1951; Marivaux, Arlequin poli par l'Amour, 1959 (in collab. with Thelma Niklaus); Sedaine, La Gageure imprévue, 1970; (contrib.) Diderot: Œuvres Complètes, vol. II, 1975, vol. IV, 1979; articles in Encyclopaediæ and learned journals; textbooks for schools and universities. *Recreations:* aviculture, the theatre, the cinema. *Address:* 17 Elm Grove Road, Topsham, Exeter, Devon EX3 0EQ. *T:* Topsham (0392) 873627.

NIKOLAYEVA-TERESHKOVA, Valentina Vladimirovna; Hero of the Soviet Union; Order of Lenin; Gold Star Medal; Order of October Revolution; Joliot-Curie Peace Medal; Soviet cosmonaut; *b* Maslennikovo, 6 March 1937; *d* of late Vladimir and of Elena Fyodorovna Tereshkova; *m* 1963, Andrian Nikolayev; one *d.* Formerly textile worker, Krasny Perekop mill, Yaroslavl; served on cttees; Sec. of local branch, Young Communist league, 1960; Member: CPSU, 1962–; Central Cttee, CPSU, 1971; Deputy, 1966, Mem. of Presidium, 1970, Supreme Soviet of Russia; Pres., Soviet Women's Cttee, 1968. Joined Yaroslavl Air Sports Club, 1959, and started parachute jumping; joined Cosmonaut Training Unit, 1962; became first woman in the world to enter space when she made 48 orbital flights of the earth in spaceship Vostok VI, 16–19 June 1963. Nile Collar (Egypt), 1971; holds honours and citations from other countries. *Address:* Soviet Women's Committee, 6 Nemirovich-Danchenko Street, 103009 Moscow, USSR.

NILSSON, Birgit, (Fru Bertil Niklasson); Swedish operatic soprano; *b* Karup, Kristianstadslaen, 1922. *Educ:* Stockholm Royal Academy of Music. Debut as singer, 1946; with Stockholm Opera, 1947–51. Has sung at Glyndebourne, 1951; Bayreuth, 1953, 1954, 1957–70; Munich, 1954–58; Hollywood Bowl, Buenos Aires, Florence, 1956; La Scala, Milan, 1958–; Covent Garden, 1957, 1960, 1962, 1963, 1973 and 1977; Edinburgh, 1959; Metropolitan, New York, 1959–; Moscow, 1964; also in most leading opera houses and festivals of the world. Particularly well-known for her Wagnerian rôles. Austrian Kammersängerin, 1968; Bavarian Kammersängerin, 1970. Hon. RAM, 1970. Hon. Dr: Andover Univ., Mass, 1970; Manhattan Sch. of Music, NY, 1982; East Lansing Univ. of Fine Arts, Mich, 1982. Swedish Royal Acad. of Music's Medal for Promotion of Art of Music, 1968; Swedish Golden Medal (cl. 18 *illis quorum*) (only lady to be so honoured). Comdr of the Vasa Order (1st cl.), Sweden, 1974.

NIMMO, Derek Robert; actor, author and producer; *b* 19 Sept. 1932; *s* of Harry Nimmo and Marjorie Sudbury (*née* Hardy); *m* 1955, Patricia Sybil Ann Brown; two *s* one *d.* *Educ:* Quarry School, Liverpool. *Stage:* First appearance, Hippodrome, Bolton, as Ensign Blades in Quality Street, 1952; repertory and variety; Waltz of the Toreadors, Criterion, 1957; Duel of Angels, Apollo, 1958; How Say You?, Aldwych, 1959; The Amorous Prawn, Saville, 1959; The Irregular Verb to Love, Criterion, 1961; See How They Run, Vaudeville, 1964; Charlie Girl, Adelphi, 1965–71 and overseas, 1971–72; Babes in the Wood, Palladium, 1972; Why Not Stay for Breakfast?, Apollo, 1973, and overseas tours; Same Time Next Year, Prince of Wales, 1978; Shut Your Eyes and Think of England, Australia, 1979; See How They Run, Shaftesbury, 1984; A Friend Indeed, Shaftesbury, 1984; produced and appeared in numerous plays and countries for Intercontinental Entertainment, 1976–; *television: series include:* All Gas and Gaiters; Oh Brother; Oh Father; Sorry I'm Single; The Bed Sit Girl; My Honorable Mrs; The World of Wooster; Blandings Castle; Life Begins at Forty; Third Time Lucky; Hell's Bells; *interview series:* If it's Saturday it must be Nimmo; Just a Nimmo; numerous other appearances; *radio:* Just A Minute, 1968–; *films include:* Casino Royale; The Amorous Prawn; The Bargee; Joey Boy; A Talent for Loving; The Liquidator; Tamahine; One of our Dinosaurs is Missing. RTS Silver Medal, 1970; Variety Club Show Business Personality of the Year, 1971. *Publications:* Derek Nimmo's Drinking Companion, 1979; Shaken and Stirred, 1984; (ed) Oh, Come On All Ye Faithful!, 1986; Not in Front of the Servants, 1987; Up Mount Everest Without a Paddle, 1988; As the Actress said to the Bishop, 1989; Wonderful Window Boxes, 1990; Table Talk, 1990. *Recreations:* sailing, collecting English 17th and 18th century walnut furniture and Derby porcelain. *Address:* c/o Barry Burnett Ltd, Suite 42, 2 Golden Square, W1. *Clubs:* Garrick; Beefsteak; Lord's Taverners; Athenæum (Liverpool).

NIMMO, Hon. Sir John (Angus), Kt 1972; CBE 1970; Justice of the Federal Court of Australia, 1977–80; Justice of Australian Industrial Court, 1969–80; *b* 15 Jan. 1909; *s* of John James Nimmo and Grace Nimmo (*née* Mann); *m* 1st, 1935, Teanie Rose Galloway (*d* 1984); two *s*; 2nd, 1985, Maude Pearce. *Educ:* Univ. of Melbourne. Admitted to practise at Victorian Bar, 1933. QC 1957. Mem., Commonwealth Taxation Bd of Review No 2, 1947–54; Actg Supreme Court Justice, Victoria, 1963; Dep. Pres., Commonwealth Conciliation and Arbitration Commn, 1964–69; Chm., Health Insce Cttee of Enquiry, 1968–69. Dep. Pres., Trade Practices Tribunal, 1966–73, also a Justice of Supreme Courts of ACT and NT, 1966–74; on secondment as Chief Justice of Fiji, 1972–74. Royal Comr into future of Norfolk Is, 1975–76; Chm., Commonwealth Legal Aid Commn, 1978–79; Mem., Cttee on Overseas Professional Qualifications, 1978–82. OStJ 1945. *Recreations:* reading, bowls, walking. *Address:* 3/22 Albert Street, Mornington, Vict 3931, Australia. *T:* (059) 754530.

NIMMO SMITH, William Austin, QC (Scot.) 1982; *b* 6 Nov. 1942; *s* of Dr Robert Herman Nimmo Smith and Mrs Ann Nimmo Smith; *m* 1968, Jennifer Main; one *s* one *d.* *Educ:* Eton Coll. (King's Scholar, 1956); Balliol Coll., Oxford (BA 1965); Edinburgh Univ. (LLB 1967). Admitted to Faculty of Advocates, 1969; Standing Junior Counsel to Dept of Employment, 1977–82; Advocate-Depute, 1983–86. Chairman: Medical Appeal Tribunals, 1986–; Vaccine Damage Tribunals, 1986–; Mem. (part-time), Scottish Law Commn, 1988–. *Recreations:* hill-walking, music. *Address:* 29 Ann Street, Edinburgh EH4 1PL. *Club:* New (Edinburgh).

NIND, Philip Frederick, OBE 1979; TD 1946; Director, Foundation for Management Education, 1968–83; Secretary, Council of Industry for Management Education, 1969–83; *b* 2 Jan. 1918; *s* of W. W. Nind, CIE; *m* 1944, Fay Allardice Crofton (*née* Errington) (*d* 1991); two *d.* *Educ:* Blundell's Sch.; Balliol Coll., Oxford (MA). War service, 1939–46, incl. Special Ops in Greece and Albania (despatches), 1943–44, Mil. Govt Berlin, 1945–46 (Major). Shell Gp of Cos in Venezuela, Cyprus, Lebanon, Jordan and London, 1939–68. Educn and Trng Cttee, CBI (formerly FBI), 1961–68; OECD Working Gp on Management Educn, 1966–69; Nat. Adv. Council on Educn for Industry and Commerce, 1967–70; UGC Management Studies Cttee, 1968–83; NEDO Management Educn Trng and Develt Cttee, 1968–83; Chm., NEDO Management Teacher Panel, 1969–72; Member: Council for Techn. Educn and Trng for Overseas Countries, 1970–75; CNAA Management Studies Bd, 1971–83; Vice-Pres., European Foundn for Management Develt, 1978–83. Member: Oxford Univ. Appts Cttee, 1967–83; Grand Council, Royal Academy of Dancing, 1988– (Mem. Exec. Cttee, 1970–88); Governor: Univ. of Keele, 1961–; Bedford Coll., London Univ., 1967–85. Hon. Fellow, London Business School, 1988. FRSA. Chevalier, Order of Cedars of Lebanon, 1959; Grand Cross, Orders of St Mark and Holy Sepulchre, 1959. *Publications:* (jtly) Management Education and Training Needs of Industry, 1963; Fourth Stockton Lecture, 1973; A Firm Foundation, 1985; Never a Dull Moment, 1991; articles in various jls. *Club:* Special Forces.

NINEHAM, Rev. Prof. Dennis Eric, DD (Oxon); BD (Cantab); Hon. DD (Birmingham); Hon. DD (BDS Yale); Professor of Theology and Head of Theology Department, Bristol University, 1980–86, now Emeritus; Honorary Canon of Bristol Cathedral, 1980–86, now Emeritus; *b* 27 Sept. 1921; *o c* of Stanley Martin and Bessie Edith Nineham, Shirley, Southampton; *m* 1946, Ruth Corfield, *d* of Rev. A. P. Miller; two *s* two *d.* *Educ:* King Edward VI Sch., Southampton; Queen's Coll., Oxford (Hon. Fellow, 1991). Asst Chaplain of Queen's Coll., 1944; Chaplain, 1945; Fellow and Praelector, 1946; Tutor, 1949; Prof. of Biblical and Historical Theology, Univ. of London (King's Coll.), 1954–58; Prof. of Divinity, Univ. of London, 1958–64; Regius Prof. of Divinity, Cambridge Univ., and Fellow, Emmanuel Coll., 1964–69; Warden of Keble Coll., Oxford, 1969–79, Hon. Fellow, 1980. FKC 1963. Examining Chaplain: to Archbishop of York and to Bishop of Ripon; to Bishop of Sheffield, 1947–54; to Bishop of Norwich, 1964–73; to Bishop of Bristol, 1981–. Select Preacher to Univ. of Oxford, 1954–56, 1971, and to Univ. of Cambridge, 1959; Proctor in Convocation of Canterbury: for London Univ., 1955–64; for Cambridge Univ., 1965–69. Mem. General Synod of Church of England for Oxford Univ., 1970–76; Mem., C of E Doctrine Commn, 1968–76. Roian Fleck Resident-in-Religion, Bryn Mawr Coll., Pa, 1974. Governor of Haileybury, 1966–. *Publications:* The Study of Divinity, 1960; A New Way of Looking at the Gospels, 1962; Commentary on St Mark's Gospel, 1963; The Use and Abuse of the Bible, 1976; Explorations in Theology, no 1, 1977; (Editor) Studies in the Gospels: Essays in Honour of R. H. Lightfoot, 1955; The Church's Use of the Bible, 1963; The New English Bible Reviewed, 1965; contrib. to: Studies in Ephesians (editor F. L. Cross), 1956; On the Authority of the Bible, 1960; Religious Education, 1944–1984, 1966; Theologians of Our Time, 1966; Christian History and Interpretation, 1967; Christ for us To-day, 1968; Christian Believing, 1976; The Myth of God Incarnate, 1977; Imagination and the Future, 1980; God's Truth, 1988; A Dictionary of Biblical Interpretation, 1990. *Recreation:* reading. *Address:* 4 Wootten Drive, Iffley Turn, Oxford OX4 4DS. *T:* Oxford (0865) 715941.

See also Very Rev. J. H. Drury.

NINIS, Ven. Richard Betts; Archdeacon of Lichfield (formerly Stafford) and Treasurer of Lichfield Cathedral, since 1974; *b* 25 Oct. 1931; *s* of late George Woodward Ninis and Mary Gertrude Ninis; *m* 1967, Penelope Jane Harwood; two *s* one *d.* *Educ:* Lincoln Coll., Oxford (MA); Bishop's Hostel, Lincoln (GOE). Curate, All Saints, Poplar, 1955–62; Vicar of: St Martins, Hereford, 1962–71; Bullinghope and Dewsall with Callow, 1966–71. Diocesan Missioner for Hereford, 1971–74. Chm., USPG, 1988–91. *Recreations:* gardening, viticulture, travel. *Address:* 24 The Close, Lichfield, Staffs. *T:* Lichfield (0543) 258813.

NIRENBERG, Dr Marshall Warren; Research Biochemist; Chief, Laboratory of Biochemical Genetics, National Heart, Lung and Blood Institute, National Institutes of Health, Bethesda, Md, since 1966; *b* New York, 10 April 1927; *m* 1961, Perola Zaltzman; no *c.* *Educ:* Univs of Florida (BS, MS) and Michigan (PhD). Univ. of Florida: Teaching Asst, Zoology Dept, 1945–50; Res. Associate, Nutrition Lab., 1950–52; Univ. of Michigan: Teaching and Res. Fellow, Biol Chemistry Dept, 1952–57; Nat. Insts of Health, Bethesda: Postdoctoral Fellow of Amer. Cancer Soc., Nat. Inst. Arthritis and Metabolic Diseases, 1957–59, and of Public Health Service, Section of Metabolic Enzymes, 1959–60; Research Biochemist, Section of Metabolic Enzymes, 1960–62 and Section of Biochem. Genetics, 1962–66. Member: Amer. Soc. Biol Chemists; Amer. Chem. Soc.; Amer. Acad. Arts and Sciences; Biophys. Soc.; Nat. Acad. Sciences; Washington Acad. Sciences; Sigma Xi; Soc. for Study of Development and Growth; (Hon.) Harvey Soc.; Leopoldina Deutsche Akademie der Naturforscher; Neurosciences Research Program, MIT; NY Acad. Sciences; Pontifical Acad. Science, 1974. Robbins Lectr, Pomona Coll., 1967; Remsden Mem. Lectr, Johns Hopkins Univ., 1967. Numerous awards and prizes, including Nobel Prize in Medicine or Physiology (jtly), 1968. Hon. Dr Science: Michigan, Yale, and Chicago, 1965; Windsor, 1966; Harvard Med. Sch., 1968; Hon. PhD, Weitzmann Inst. of Science, Israel, 1978. *Publications:* numerous contribs to learned jls and chapters in symposia. *Address:* Laboratory of Biochemical Genetics, National Heart, Lung and Blood Institute, Bethesda, Md 20014, USA; 7001 Orkney Parkway, Bethesda, Maryland, USA.

NISBET, Prof. Hugh Barr; Professor of Modern Languages, University of Cambridge, since 1982; Professorial Fellow, Sidney Sussex College, since 1982; *b* 24 Aug. 1940; *s* of Thomas Nisbet and Lucy Mary Hainsworth; *m* 1962, Monika Luise Ingeborg Uecker; two *s.* *Educ:* Dollar Acad.; Univ. of Edinburgh. MA, PhD 1965. University of Bristol: Asst Lectr in German, 1965–67; Lectr, 1967–72; Reader, 1972–73; Prof. of German Lang. and Lit., Univ. of St Andrews, 1974–81. Mem., Gen. Teaching Council for Scotland, 1978–81. Pres., British Soc. for Eighteenth Century Studies, 1986–88. Governor, Dollar Acad., 1978–81. Jt Editor, Cambridge Studies in German, 1983–; Germanic Editor, 1973–80, Gen. Editor, 1981–84, Modern Language Rev. *Publications:* Herder and the Philosophy and History of Science, 1970; (ed with Hans Reiss) Goethe's Die Wahlverwandtschaften, 1971; Goethe and the Scientific Tradition, 1972; (ed) German Aesthetic and Literary Criticism: Winckelmann to Goethe, 1985; (ed with Peter Brooks and Claude Rawson) Cambridge History of Literary Criticism, 9 vols, 1989–; *translations:* Kant, Political Writings, 1970, 2nd edn 1991; Hegel, Lectures on the Philosophy of World History, 1975, 2nd edn 1980; Hegel, Elements of the Philosophy of Right, 1991; articles and reviews on German literature and thought. *Recreations:* music, art history, cycling. *Address:* Sidney Sussex College, Cambridge CB2 3HU. *T:* Cambridge (0223) 338877.

NISBET, Prof. John Donald, OBE 1981; MA, BEd, PhD; FEIS; Professor of Education, Aberdeen University, 1963–88; *b* 17 Oct. 1922; *s* of James Love Nisbet and Isabella Donald; *m* 1952, Brenda Sugden; one *s* one *d.* *Educ:* Dunfermline High Sch.; Edinburgh Univ. (MA, BEd); PhD (Aberdeen); Teacher's Certif. (London). FEIS 1975; Royal Air Force, 1943–46. Teacher, Fife, 1946–48; Lectr, Aberdeen Univ., 1949–63. Editor: British Jl of Educnl Psychology, 1967–74; Studies in Higher Education, 1979–84; Chairman: Educnl Research Bd, SSRC, 1972–75; Cttee on Primary Educn, 1974–80; Scottish Council for Research in Educn, 1975–78; President: British Educnl Research Assoc., 1975; Scottish Inst. of Adult and Continuing Educn, 1991. *Publications:* Family Environment, 1953; Age of Transfer to Secondary Education, 1966; Transition to Secondary Education, 1969; Scottish Education Looks Ahead, 1969; Educational Research Methods, 1970; Educational Research in Action, 1972; Impact of Research, 1980;

Towards Community Education, 1980; (ed) World Yearbook of Education, 1985; Learning Strategies, 1986; papers in jls on educnl psychology and curriculum develt. *Recreations:* golf, orienteering. *Address:* 7 Lawson Avenue, Banchory AB3 3TW. *T:* Banchory (03302) 3145.
See also S. D. Nisbet.

NISBET, Prof. Robin George Murdoch, FBA 1967; Corpus Christi Professor of Latin, Oxford, 1970–Sept. 1992; Fellow of Corpus Christi College, Oxford, 1952–Sept. 1992; *b* 21 May 1925; *s* of R. G. Nisbet, Univ. Lecturer, and A. T. Husband; *m* 1969, Anne, *d* of Dr J. A. Wood. *Educ:* Glasgow Academy; Glasgow Univ.; Balliol Coll., Oxford (Snell Exhibitioner; Hon. Fellow, 1989). Tutor in Classics, Corpus Christi College, Oxford, 1952–70. *Publications:* Commentary on Cicero, *in Pisonem*, 1961; (with M. Hubbard) on Horace, *Odes I*, 1970; *Odes II*, 1978; articles and reviews on Latin subjects. *Recreation:* 20th century history. *Address:* 80 Abingdon Road, Cumnor, Oxford OX2 9QW. *T:* Oxford (0865) 862482.

NISBET, Prof. Stanley Donald; Professor of Education, University of Glasgow, 1951–78; *b* 26 July 1912; *s* of Dr J. L. and Isabella Nisbet; *m* 1942, Helen Alison Smith; one *s* one *d*. *Educ:* Dunfermline High Sch., Edinburgh Univ. MA (1st Cl. Hons Classics), 1934; Diploma in Education, 1935; BEd (with distinction in Education and Psychology), 1940. Taught in Moray House Demonstration Sch., Edinburgh, 1935–39. Served War in RAF, 1940–46; research officer at Air Ministry, 1944–46. Lecturer in Education, Univ. of Manchester, Feb.-Sept. 1946; Prof. of Education, Queen's Univ. of Belfast, 1946–51. FRSE 1955; FEIS 1976. *Publications:* Purpose in the Curriculum, 1957; (with B. L. Napier) Promise and Progress, 1970; articles in psychological and educational journals. *Recreations:* walking, sailing. *Address:* 6 Victoria Park Corner, Glasgow G14 9NZ.
See also J. D. Nisbet.

NISBET-SMITH, Dugal; Director, Newspaper Society, since 1983; *b* 6 March 1935; *s* of David and Margaret Homeward Nisbet-Smith; *m* 1959, Dr Ann Patricia Taylor; one *s* two *d*. *Educ:* Southland Boys' High Sch., Invercargill, NZ. Journalist on Southland Daily News, NZ, 1952–56; Features writer and reporter, Beaverbrook Newspapers, London, 1956–60; variously Asst Editor, Gen. Manager and Man. Dir, Barbados Advocate Co., Barbados, WI, Gen. Manager, Sierra Leone Daily Mail Ltd, W Africa, Dep. Gen. Manager, Trinidad Mirror Co., 1960–66; Sen. Industrial Relations Manager, Mirror Gp Newspapers, London, 1966–68; Develt Manager, 1969–71, Production Dir, 1971–73, Man. Dir, 1974–78, Scottish Daily Record and Sunday Mail Ltd, Glasgow; joined Bd, Mirror Gp Newspapers, 1976; Dir/General Manager, 1978–80, Man. Dir, 1980–81, Times Newspapers Ltd; Publishing Advr to HH the Aga Khan, Aiglemont, France, 1981–83. *Recreations:* travel, sculpture, painting. *Address:* 19 Highgate Close, Hampstead Lane, N6. *T:* 081–340 9457. *Club:* Royal Automobile.

NISSAN, Prof. Alfred Heskel, PhD, DSc (Chem. Eng, Birmingham), FIChemE, FAIChE, FACS; Member Sigma XI; Consultant to WESTVACO (formerly West Virginia Pulp and Paper), New York (Vice-President, 1967–79, and Corporate Director of Research, 1962–79); Professor, College of Environmental Science and Forestry, Syracuse, New York, since 1979; *b* 14 Feb. 1914; *s* of Heskel and Farha Nissan, Baghdad, Iraq; *m* 1940, Zena Gladys Phyllis, *o d* of late Phillip and Lillian Frances Pursehouse-Ahmed, Birmingham; one *d*. *Educ:* The American Sch. for Boys, Baghdad, Iraq; Univ. of Birmingham. Instn of Petroleum Scholarship, 1936; first cl. Hons BSc 1937; Sir John Cadman Medal, 1937; Instn of Petroleum Medal and Prize and Burgess Prize, 1937; Research Fellow, 1937, Lectr, 1940, Univ. of Birmingham; Head of Central Research Laboratories, Bowater Paper Corporation Ltd, 1947; Technical Director in charge of Research, Bowaters Development and Research Ltd, 1950; Research Prof. of Wool Textile Engineering, the Univ. of Leeds, 1953; Prof. of Chemical Engineering, Rensselaer Polytechnic Inst., Troy, NY, USA, 1957. Hon. Vis. Prof., Uppsala Univ., 1974; ERCO Res. Fellow, Univ. of Toronto, 1987. Schwarz Memorial Lectr, Amer. Soc. of Mech. Engrs, 1967; Dow Dist. Lectr, Univ. of British Columbia, 1989. Member: Adv. Council for Advancement of Industrial R&D, State of NY, 1965–; Board of Directors: Technical Assoc. of Pulp & Paper Industry, 1968–71 (R&D Div. Award, 1976); Industrial Res. Inst., 1973–77. Bd of Trustees, Amer. Inst. of Chemists Foundn, 1989–91. Alexander Mitscheslich Medal, Zellcheming, W Germany, 1980; Gold Medal, Technical Assoc. of Pulp and Paper Industry, 1982. *Publications:* (ed) Textile Engineering Processes, 1959; (ed) Future Technical Needs and Trends in the Paper Industry, 1973; Lectures on Fiber Science in Paper, 1977; papers on physical chemistry and chemical engineering problems of petroleum, paper and textile technology in scientific jls. *Address:* 6A Dickel Road, Scarsdale, NY 10583, USA.

NISSEN, David Edgar Joseph; Legal Adviser to Department of Energy (Principal Assistant Treasury Solicitor), since 1990; *b* 27 Nov. 1942; *s* of Tunnock Edgar Nissen and Elsie Nissen (*née* Thorne); *m* 1969, Pauline Jennifer (*née* Meaden); two *d*. *Educ:* King's School, Chester; University College London (LLB). Solicitor, admitted 1969. Asst Solicitor, W Midlands Gas Board, 1969–70; Prosecuting Solicitor, Sussex Police Authority, 1970–73; HM Customs and Excise, 1973–90; Asst Solicitor, 1983–87; Principal Asst Solicitor, 1987–90. *Recreations:* photography, music, gardening. *Address:* Department of Energy, 1 Palace Street, SW1E 5HE.

NISSEN, George Maitland, CBE 1987; Chairman, Investment Management Regulatory Organisation, since 1989; Consultant, Morgan Grenfell Group, since 1987 (Director, 1984–87); *b* 29 March 1930; *s* of Col Peter Norman Nissen, DSO, and Lauretta Maitland; *m* 1956, Jane Edmunds, *d* of late S. Curtis Bird, New York; two *s* two *d*. *Educ:* Eton; Trinity Coll., Cambridge (MA). National Service, KRRC, 1949–50, 2/Lieut. Sen. Partner, Pember & Boyle, Stockbrokers, 1982–86; Chm., New Frontiers Develt Trust (formerly CDFC Trust) plc, 1987–; Director: Union Discount Co., 1988–; Trades Union Unit Trust Managers Ltd. Mem., Stock Exchange, 1956– (Dep. Chm., 1978–81; Mem. Council, 1973–); Chm., Gilt-Edged Market Makers Assoc., 1986–; Dir, The Securities Assoc., 1986–89; Mem., Inflation Accounting Steering Gp, 1976–80. Governor: Reed's Sch., Cobham; St Paul's Girls' Prep. Sch., Hammersmith; Godolphin and Latymer School, Hammersmith. *Recreations:* railways, music. *Address:* Swan House, Chiswick Mall, W4 2PS. *T:* 081–994 8203.

NISSEN, Karl Iversen, MD, FRCS; retired Surgeon, Royal National Orthopædic Hospital, W1, 1946–71; Orthopædic Surgeon: Harrow Hospital 1946–71; Peace Memorial Hospital, Watford, 1948–71; *b* 4 April 1906; *s* of Christian and Caroline Nissen; *m* 1935, Margaret Mary Honor Schofield (*d* 1981); one *s* one *d*. *Educ:* Otago Boys' High Sch., Dunedin, NZ; Univ. of Otago, NZ. BSc (NZ) 1927; MB, ChB (NZ) 1932; MD (NZ) 1934; FRCS 1936. Served as Orthopædic Specialist, RNVR, 1943–45. Corresp. mem. Belgian, French, Swiss, German, Scandinavian, Norwegian, Finnish, Danish Socs of Orthopædics. Writes articles and gives talks on primary osteoarthrosis of the hip, Morton's metatarsalgia, and the carpal tunnel syndrome. *Recreation:* French. *Address:* Prospect House, The Avenue, Sherborne, Dorset DT9 3AJ. *T:* Sherborne (0935) 813539. *Club:* Naval.

NIVEN, Alastair Neil Robertson, PhD; Literature Director, Arts Council of Great Britain, since 1987; *b* 25 Feb. 1944; *s* of Harold Robertson Niven and Elizabeth Isobel Robertson Niven (*née* Mair); *m* 1970, Helen Margaret Trow; one *s* one *d*. *Educ:* Dulwich Coll.; Gonville and Caius Coll., Cambridge (MA); Univ. of Ghana (Commonwealth Schol.; MA); Univ. of Leeds (PhD). Lecturer in English: Univ. of Ghana, 1968–69; Univ. of Leeds, 1969–70; Lectr in English Studies, Univ. of Stirling, 1970–78; Dir Gen., Africa Centre, London, 1978–84; Chapman Fellow 1984–85, Hon. Fellow 1985, Inst. of Commonwealth Studies; Special Asst to Sec. Gen., ACU, 1985–87. Vis. Prof., Univ. of Aarhus, 1975–76; Vis. Fellow, Aust. Studies Centre, Univ. of London, 1985; Hon. Lectr, SOAS, 1979–85; Hon. Fellow, Univ. of Warwick, 1988. Editor, Jl of Commonwealth Literature, 1979–. Chairman: Public Schools Debating Assoc., 1961–62; Literature Panel, GLAA, 1981–84; Welfare Policy Cttee, 1983–87, Exec. Cttee, 1987–91, UK Council for Overseas Student Affairs; Member: Public Affairs Cttee, Royal Commonwealth Soc., 1979–; Laurence Olivier Awards Theatre Panel, 1989–91; British Library Adv. Cttee for the Centre for the Book, 1990–. *Publications:* The Commonwealth Writer Overseas (ed), 1976; D. H. Lawrence: the novels, 1978; The Yoke of Pity: the fiction of Mulk Raj Anand, 1978; D. H. Lawrence: the writer and his work, 1980; (with Sir Hugh W. Springer) The Commonwealth of Universities, 1987; (ed) Under Another Sky: the Commonwealth Poetry Prize anthology, 1987; articles in Afr. Affairs, Ariel, Brit. Book News, Jl of Commonwealth Lit., Jl of Indian Writing in English, Jl of RSA, Lit. Half-Yearly, TES, THES, World Lit. Written in English, etc; study guides on Elechi Amadi, Wm Golding, R. K. Narayan, Raja Rao. *Recreations:* theatre, travel. *Address:* Eden House, 28 Weathercock Lane, Woburn Sands, Bucks MK17 8NT. *T:* Milton Keynes (0908) 582310. *Club:* Commonwealth Trust.

NIVEN, Sir (Cecil) Rex, Kt 1960; CMG 1953; MC 1918; *b* 20 Nov. 1898; *o s* of late Rev. Dr G. C. and Jeanne Niven, Torquay, Devon; *m* 1st, 1925, Dorothy Marshall (*d* 1977), *e d* of late D. M. Mason, formerly MP (Coventry and E Edinburgh); one *d* (and one *d* decd); 2nd, 1980, Mrs Pamela Beerbohm, *d* of late G. C. Leach, ICS, Sibton Park, Lyminge, Kent, and Mrs Leach, and *widow* of Dr O. H. B. Beerbohm. *Educ:* Blundell's Sch., Tiverton; Balliol Coll. Oxford (MA Hons). Served RFA 1917–19, France and Italy. Colonial Service Nigeria, 1921–54; served Secretariats, and Provinces; PRO, Nigeria, 1943–45; Senior Resident, 1947; twice admin. Northern Govt; Mem. N House of Assembly, 1947–59 (Pres. 1952–58; Speaker, 1958–59); Mem., N Executive Council, 1951–54; Comr for Special Duties in N Nigeria, 1959–62; Dep. Sec., Southwark Dio. Bd of Finance, 1962–68. Life Mem., BRCS; Member: Council, RSA, 1963–69; Council, N Euboea Foundation; Council, Imp. Soc. of Knights Bachelor, 1969–; Gen. Synod of C of E, 1975–80; St Charles's (formerly Paddington) Group Hosp. Management Cttee, 1963–72. Chm., NE Kent Oxford Soc., 1986–89, Pres., 1989–; Patron, Deal Soc., 1985–. FRGS. *Publications:* A Short History of Nigeria, 1937, 12th edn 1971; Nigeria's Story, 1939; Nigeria: the Outline of a Colony, 1946; How Nigeria is Governed, 1950; West Africa, 1958; Short History of the Yoruba Peoples, 1958; You and Your Government, 1958; Nine Great Africans, 1964; Nigeria (in Benn's Nations of the Modern World), 1967; The War of Nigerian Unity, 1970; (collab.) My Life, by late Sardauna of Sokoto, 1962; A Nigerian Kaleidoscope, 1982. *Recreations:* walking, architecture, philately. *Address:* 12 Archery Square, Walmer, Kent CT14 7HP. *T:* Deal (0304) 361863. *Club:* Royal Over-Seas League.

NIVEN, Ian; *see* Niven, J. R.

NIVEN, John Robertson, (Ian Niven); Under-Secretary, Department of the Environment, formerly Ministry of Housing and Local Government, 1974–79; *b* 11 May 1919; *s* of Robert Niven and Amelia Mary Hill; *m* 1946, Jane Bicknell; three *s*. *Educ:* Glasgow Academy; Jesus Coll., Oxford. Entered Min. of Town and Country Planning, 1946; Sec., Royal Commn on Local Govt in Greater London, 1957–60. *Address:* White Gates, Parham, Woodbridge, Suffolk.

NIVEN, Margaret Graeme, ROI 1936; Landscape and Portrait Painter; *b* Marlow, 1906; *yr d* of William Niven, FSA, ARE, JP, Marlow Place, Marlow, Bucks, and Eliza Mary Niven. *Educ:* Prior's Field, Godalming. Studied at Winchester Sch. of Art, Heatherley Sch. of Fine Art, and under Bernard Adams, RP, ROI; Mem. of National Soc. Painters, Sculptors, and Engravers, 1932. Exhibitor at Royal Academy and Royal Soc. of Portrait Painters. Works purchased by Bradford Art Gallery, The Ministry of Works, Homerton Coll., Cambridge, and Bedford Coll., London. Served with WRNS, 1940–45. *Address:* Broomhill, Sandhills, Wormley, near Godalming, Surrey GU8 5UF.

NIVEN, Sir Rex; *see* Niven, Sir C. R.

NIVISON, family name of **Baron Glendyne.**

NIX, Prof. John Sydney; Emeritus Professor, University of London, since 1989 (Professor of Farm Business Management, 1982–89, and Head, Farm Business Unit, 1974–89, Wye College); *b* 27 July 1927; *s* of John William Nix and Eleanor Elizabeth (*née* Stears); *m* 1950, Mavis Marian (*née* Cooper); one *s* two *d*. *Educ:* Brockley County Sch.; University Coll. of the South-West. BSc Econ (London), MA Cantab. Instr Lieut, RN, 1948–51. Farm Economics Branch, Sch. of Agriculture, Univ. of Cambridge, 1951–61; Wye College: Farm Management Liaison Officer and Lectr, 1961–70; Sen. Tutor, 1970–72; Sen. Lectr, 1972–75; Reader, 1975–82; apptd to personal chair, the first in Farm Business Management in UK, 1982. Founder Mem., Farm Management Assoc., 1965; formerly Member: Study Groups etc. for Natural Resources (Tech.) Cttee; Agric. Adv. Council; ARC Tech. Cttee; ADAS Exptl and Develt Cttee; Meat and Livestock Commn; Countryside Commn. Programme Advr, Southern Television, 1966–81; Specialist Advr, Select Cttee on Agric., 1990–91. British Inst. of Management: Chm., Jl Cttee of Centre of Management of Agric., 1971–; Chm., Bd of Farm Management, 1979–81; Nat. Award for outstanding and continuing contrib. to advancement of management in agric. industry, 1982 (1st recipient). Pres., Agricl Economics Soc., 1990–91. CBIM 1983. FRSA 1984; FRAgS 1985. *Publications:* Farm Management Pocketbook, 1966, 22nd edn 1991; (with C. S. Barnard) Farm Planning and Control, 1973, 2nd edn 1979, Spanish edn 1984; (with W. Butterworth) Farm Mechanisation for Profit, 1983; (with G. P. Hill and N. T. Williams) Land and Estate Management, 1987, 2nd edn 1989; articles in Jl of Agricl Econs, Jl of RASE, Farm Management, etc. *Recreations:* theatre, cinema, travel, rugby, cricket. *Address:* Wye College, Wye, Ashford, Kent TN25 5AH. *T:* Wye (0233) 812401. *Club:* Farmers'.

NIXON, Sir Edwin (Ronald), Kt 1984; CBE 1974; DL; Deputy Chairman, National Westminster Bank PLC, since 1987 (Director, since 1975); Chairman, Amersham International plc, since 1988 (Director, since 1987); *b* 21 June 1925; *s* of William Archdale Nixon and Ethel (*née* Corrigan); *m* 1952, Joan Lilian (*née* Hill); one *s* one *d*. *Educ:* Alderman Newton's Sch., Leicester; Selwyn Coll., Cambridge (MA; Hon. Fellow 1983). Man. Accountant, Dexion Ltd, 1950–55; IBM United Kingdom Ltd, 1955–90; Chm., IBM UK Hldgs Ltd, 1986–90 (Man. Dir, 1965–78; Chm. and Chief Exec., 1979–86); Director: Royal Insurance PLC, 1980–; International Westminster Bank PLC, 1987–; UK-Japan 2000 Gp Ltd, 1987–; Partnership Sourcing, 1990–; Alternate Dir, BCH Property Ltd, 1988–. Member Council: Foundn for Automation and Employment,

1967–77; Electronic Engineering Assoc., 1965–76; CBI, 1971– (Chm. Standing Cttee on Marketing and Consumer Affairs, 1971–78; Mem., Cttee on Industrial Policy, 1978–85; President's Cttee, 1986–88); Foundn for Management Educn, 1973–84. Member: British Cttee of Awards for Harkness Fellowships, 1976–82; Adv. Council, Business Graduates Assoc., 1976–87; Board of Governors, United World Coll. of Atlantic, 1977–; Bd of Trustees, Internat. Inst. for Management Develt, 1990–; Member Council: Manchester Business Sch., 1974–86 (Chm., 1979–86); Business in the Community, 1981–; Westfield Coll., London, 1969–82 (Vice Chm., 1980–82; Hon. Fellow 1983); William Temple Coll., Manchester, 1972–80; Oxford Centre for Management Studies, 1973–83; Open Univ., 1986–. Member: The Civil Service Coll., 1979–; Adv. Council, New Oxford English Dictionary, 1985–; Council for Industry and Higher Educn, 1986–. Trustee, Inst. of Econ. Affairs, 1986–. Member: Chichester Cathedral Develt Trust, 1986–; The Prince's Youth Business Trust, 1987–; Lloyd's of London Tercentary Foundn. Pres., Nat. Assoc. for Gifted Children, 1980–91; Vice-Pres., Opportunities for the Disabled, 1980–; Chm., Jt Bd for Pre-Vocational Educn, 1983–87; Mem., Study Commn on the Family, 1979–83. Chm. of Bd of Trustees and a Dir, Royal Opera House, Covent Garden, 1984–87 (Trustee, 1980–87); Chm., Bd of Trustees, Monteverdi Choir and Orch., 1988– (Trustee, 1980–); Vice-Pres., Portsmouth Internat. String Quartet Competition, 1979–. Patron, Assoc. Internationale des Etudiantes en Sciences Economiques et Commerciales, 1980–. DL Hampshire, 1987. Hon. Fellow: Inst. of Marketing, 1982 (Hon. Vice-Pres., 1980–); Portsmouth Polytechnic, 1986; Leeds Polytechnic, 1991. Hon. DSc Aston, 1985; DUniv Stirling, 1985; Hon. DTech Brunel, 1986; Hon. LLD Manchester, 1987. *Recreations:* music, tennis, golf, sailing. *Address:* National Westminster Bank, 41 Lothbury, EC2P 2BP. *T:* 071–726 1000; Starkes Heath, Rogate, Petersfield, Hants. *T:* Rogate (0730) 821504. *Club:* Athenæum.

NIXON, Rev. Sir Kenneth Michael John Basil, SJ; 4th Bt *cr* 1906; Teaching Member of the Jesuit Community at St George's College, Harare, since 1954; *b* 22 Feb. 1919; *s* of Sir Christopher William Nixon, 2nd Bt, DSO, and Louise (*d* 1949), *d* of Robert Clery, JP, The Glebe, Athlacca, Limerick; *S* brother, 1978. *Educ:* Beaumont College; Heythrop College, Oxon. Catholic priest and member of the Society of Jesus; ordained, 1952. *Recreation:* cricket. Heir: *b* Major Cecil Dominic Henry Joseph Nixon, MC [*b* 5 Feb. 1920; *m* 1953, Brenda, *d* of late Samuel Lycett Lewis and *widow* of Major M. F. McWhor; three *s* one *d*]. *Address:* St George's College, PB 7727, Causeway, Zimbabwe. *T:* Harare 724650.

NIXON, Patrick Michael, CMG 1989; OBE 1984; HM Diplomatic Service; Counsellor, Foreign and Commonwealth Office, since 1990; *b* 1 Aug. 1944; *s* of John Moylett Gerard Nixon and late Hilary Mary (*née* Paterson); *m* 1968, Elizabeth Rose Carlton; four *s*. *Educ:* Downside; Magdalene Coll., Cambridge (Exhibnr; MA Classical Tripos Pt I and Historical Tripos Pt II). Joined HM Diplomatic Service, 1965; MECAS, Lebanon, 1966; Third Sec., Cairo, 1968; Second Sec. (Commercial), Lima, 1970; First Sec., FCO, 1973; Hd of Chancery, Tripoli, Libya, 1977; Dir, British Inf. Services, New York, 1980; Asst, later Hd, Near East and N Africa Dept, FCO, 1983; Ambassador and Consul-Gen. at Doha, Qatar, 1987–90. *Address:* c/o Foreign and Commonwealth Office, SW1.

NIXON, Richard M.; President of the United States of America, 1969–74, resigned 10 Aug. 1974; *b* 9 Jan. 1913; *s* of Francis A. and Hannah Milhous Nixon; *m* 1940, Patricia Ryan; two *d*. *Educ:* Whittier Coll., Whittier, California (AB); Duke University Law Sch., Durham, North Carolina (LLB). Lawyer, Whittier, California, 1937–42; Office of Price Administration, 1942; Active duty, US Navy, 1942–46. Member 80th, 81st Congresses, 1947–50; US Senator from California, 1950–53. Vice-President of the USA, 1953–61; Republican candidate for the Presidency of the USA, 1960. Lawyer, Los Angeles, 1961–63, NY, 1963–68. Republican Candidate for Governor of California, 1962. Member: Board of Trustees, Whittier Coll., 1939–68; Society of Friends; Order of Coif. *Publications:* Six Crises, 1962; Memoirs, 1978; The Real War, 1980; Leaders, 1982; Real Peace: a strategy for the West, 1983; No More Vietnams, 1986; 1999: Victory Without War, 1988; In the Arena: a memoir of victory, defeat and renewal, 1990. *Address:* 577 Chestnut Ridge Road, Woodcliff Lake, NJ 07675, USA.

NOAD, Sir Kenneth (Beeson), Kt 1970; Consulting Physician, 1931–84; Patron, Australian Postgraduate Federation in Medicine; *b* 25 March 1900; *s* of James Beeson and Mary Jane Noad; *m* 1935, Eileen Mary Ryan; no *c. Educ:* Maitland, NSW; Sydney University. MB, ChM 1924, MD 1953, Sydney; MRCP 1929; FRCP 1948; Foundn FRACP 1938 (PRACP 1962–64). Hon FACP 1964; Hon. FRCPE 1968. Served War of 1939–45, Palestine, Egypt, Greece, Crete, New Guinea; Lt-Col Comdr Medical Div. of an Australian General Hospital. Hon. DLitt and Hon. AM Singapore. *Publications:* papers in Brain, Med. Jl of Australia. *Recreations:* walking, music. *Address:* 22 Billyard Avenue, Elizabeth Bay, NSW 2011, Australia. *Clubs:* Australian (Sydney); Royal Sydney Golf.

NOAKES, Rt. Rev. George; Archbishop of Wales, 1987–91; Bishop of St Davids, 1982–91; *b* 13 Sept. 1924; *s* of David John and Elizabeth Mary Noakes; *m* 1957, Jane Margaretta Davies. *Educ:* Tregaron Secondary School; University Coll. of Wales, Aberystwyth (BA); Wycliffe Hall, Oxford. Curate of Lampeter, 1950–56; Vicar: Eglwyswrw, 1956–59; Tregaron, 1959–67; Dewi Sant, Cardiff, 1967–76; Rector of Aberystwyth, 1976–79; Canon of St Davids Cathedral, 1977–79; Archdeacon of Cardigan, 1979–82; Vicar of Llanychaearn, 1980–82. Hon. DD Wales, 1989. *Recreations:* cricket, angling. *Address:* Hafodlon, Rhydargaeau, Carmarthen, Dyfed. *T:* Carmarthen (0267) 253302.

NOAKES, John Edward, FRCGP; Partner, group medical practice in Harrow, since 1961; Vice-Chairman of Council, Royal College of Medical Practitioners, since 1990; *b* 27 April 1935; *s* of Edward and Mary Noakes; *m* 1960, Margaret Ann Jenner; two *s* one *d. Educ:* Wanstead County High Sch.; Charing Cross Hospital Medical Sch. (MB BS); DObstRCOG. House Surgeon, Mount Vernon Hosp., 1960; House Physician, Charing Cross Hosp., 1960; House Obstetric Officer, Bromley Hosp., 1961. Trainer, Gen. Practice Vocational Trng Scheme, Northwick Park Hosp., 1974–82. Member: Brent Harrow Local Med. Cttee, 1972–; Harrow HA, 1982–90. Mem. Council, RCGP, 1989– (Chm., NW London Faculty, 1989–91). Mem., 71 Club, Northwick Park Hosp. *Recreations:* music (mainly opera), horticulture (Alpine plants). *Address:* Dykeside Cottage, 113 Rowlands Avenue, Pinner, Middx HA5 4AW. *T:* 081–428 4289.

NOAKES, Michael, PPROI, RP; portrait and landscape painter; *b* 28 Oct. 1933; *s* of late Basil and Mary Noakes; *m* 1960, Vivien Noakes (*née* Langley), writer; two *s* one *d. Educ:* Downside; Royal Academy Schs, London. Nat. Dipl. in Design, 1954; Certificate of Royal Academy Schools, 1960. Commnd: National Service, 1954–56. Has broadcast and appeared on TV on art subjects in UK and USA; Art Correspondent, BBC TV programme Town and Around, 1964–68; subject of BBC films: (with Eric Morley) Portrait, 1977, 1978; (with JAK) Changing Places, 1989. Member Council: ROI, 1964–78 (Vice-Pres. 1968–72; Pres., 1972–78; Hon. Mem. Council, 1978–); RP, 1969–71, 1972–74, 1978–80; NS, 1962–76 (Hon. Mem., 1976–); Chm., Contemp. Portrait Soc., 1971; a Dir, Fedn of British Artists, 1981–83 (a Governor, 1972–83). *Exhibited:* Royal Acad.; Royal Inst. Oil Painters; Royal Soc. Portrait Painters; Contemp. Portrait Soc.; Nat. Society; Young

Contemporaries, Grosvenor Galleries, Upper Grosvenor Galls, Woodstock Galls, Royal Glasgow Inst. of Fine Arts, Nat. Portrait Gall.; Roy. Soc. of British Artists; Grafton Gall.; New Grafton Galls; Art Exhibitions Bureau, touring widely in Britain, USA and Canada. Judge, Miss World Contest, 1976. Platinum disc, 1977 (record sleeve design Portrait of Sinatra). *Portraits include:* The Queen (unveiled Silver Jubilee year, for Manchester; Queen's Lancs Regt); Queen Elizabeth The Queen Mother (as Chancellor, Univ. of London; as Patron, RADAR); Prince of Wales (for 2nd KEO Gurkhas); Princess Anne (for Saddlers' Co.; Royal Signals); Duke and Duchess of York; Duchess of Kent; Lord Aberconway; Lord Aldington; Lord Amory; Princess Ashraf; Lord Benson; Lord Barnetson; Lord Boothby; Lord Bowden; Lord Boyd; FM Lord Carver; Lord Charteris; Lord Chuter-Ede; Lord Denning; Paul Dirac; Lord Elwyn-Jones; Archbishop Lord Fisher; Lord Fulton; Sir Alec Guinness; Gen. Sir John Hackett; Gilbert Harding; Robert Hardy; Sir Alan Hodgkin; Cardinal Hume; Amb. John J. Louis, USA; Lord Selwyn-Lloyd; Cliff Michelmore; Eric Morley; Robert Morley; Malcolm Muggeridge; Sir Gerald Nabarro; Sir David Napley; Ambassador Charles Price, USA; J. B. Priestley; Valerie Profumo; Lord Pym; Sir Ralph Richardson; Dom John Roberts, Abbot of Downside; Edmund de Rothschild; Lord Runcie; Dame Margaret Rutherford; Very Rev. M. Sullivan; Margaret Thatcher (as Prime Minister); Lord Todd; Dennis Wheatley; Sir Mortimer Wheeler; Lord Wolfenden; Sir Donald Wolfit; *major group portraits:* Royal Family, with Lord and Lady Mayoress, for Guildhall; Members and Officers, Metropolitan Water Board (47 figures); Lords of Appeal in Ordinary (for Middle Temple); Queen Elizabeth the Queen Mother opening Overlord Embroidery to public view, with Princess Alice, Lord Mountbatten, Duke of Norfolk, etc.; Company of Woolmen showing Princess Royal. *Represented in collections:* The Queen, for Royal Collection Windsor; The Prince of Wales; British Mus.; Nat. Portrait Gall. (incl. Hugill Fund Purchase, RA, 1972); numerous Oxford and Cambridge colleges; County Hall, Westminster; various livery companies and Inns of Court; House of Commons; Univs of London, Nottingham, East Anglia; City Univ.; Frank Sinatra. *Publications:* A Professional Approach to Oil Painting, 1968; contributions to various art journals. *Recreation:* idling. *Address:* 146 Hamilton Terrace, St John's Wood, NW8 9UX. *T:* 071–328 6754. *Club:* Garrick.

NOAKES, Philip Reuben, OBE 1962; HM Diplomatic Service, retired; *b* 12 Aug. 1915; *y s* of late Charles William and Elizabeth Farey Noakes; *m* 1940, Moragh Jean Dickson; two *s. Educ:* Wyggeston Grammar Sch.; Wycliffe Coll.; Queens' Coll., Cambridge (Open Schol.). Mod. Langs Tripos Part I, Hist. Tripos Part II; BA 1937; MA 1945; Pres., Cambridge Union Soc., 1937. Served War, 1940–46; Capt.-Adjt 2nd Fife and Forfar Yeomanry, RAC (despatches). Public Relations Officer, Royal Over-Seas League, 1947–48; Sen. Information Officer, Colonial Office, 1948; Prin. Information Officer, CO, 1953; Information Adviser to Governor of Malta, 1960–61; Chief Information Officer, CO, 1963–66; Commonwealth Office, 1967; Counsellor (Information), Ottawa, 1967–72; Consul-Gen., Seattle, 1973–75. *Recreations:* bird-watching, fishing, shooting. *Address:* Little St Mary's, St Mary's Lane, Uplyme, Lyme Regis, Dorset DT7 3XH. *T:* Axminster (0297) 33371. *Club:* Royal Over-Seas League.

NOAKES, Sheila Valerie, (Mrs C. B. Noakes); see Masters, S. V.

NOAKES, His Honour Sidney Henry; a Circuit Judge (formerly County Court Judge), 1968–77; *b* 6 Jan. 1905; *s* of Thomas Frederick Noakes (Civil Servant) and Ada Noakes. *Educ:* Merchant Taylors' Sch.; St John's Coll., Oxford (MA). Called to Bar, Lincoln's Inn, 1928; SE Circuit; Bencher, 1963. War Service, Lt-Col., Intelligence Corps, England and NW Europe. Deputy Chairman: Surrey QS, 1963; Herts QS, 1964; Recorder of Margate, 1965–68. *Publication:* Fire Insurance, 1947. *Recreations:* regretfully now only walking and gardening. *Address:* 14 Meadway Crescent, Hove, E Sussex BN3 7NL. *T:* Brighton (0273) 736143.

NOBAY, Prof. (Avelino) Robert, PhD; Brunner Professor of Economic Science, University of Liverpool, since 1980; *b* 11 July 1942; *s* of Theodore Anastasio Nobay and Anna Gracia D'Silva; *m* 1965, Susan Clare Saunders; two *s. Educ:* Univ. of Leicester (BA); Univ. of Chicago; PhD Southampton. Jun. Economist, Electricity Council, London, 1964–66; Res. Officer, NIESR, 1966–70; Sen. Lectr, Univ. of Southampton, 1970–80. Vis. Associate Prof., Univ. of Chicago, 1977–79. *Publications:* (with H. G. Johnson) The Current Inflation; (with H. G. Johnson) Issues in Monetary Economics. *Recreations:* sailing, golf, music. *Address:* Springfield, 28 Knowsley Road, Cressington Park, Liverpool L19 0PG. *T:* 051–427 2093.

NOBBS, David Gordon; writer; *b* 13 March 1935; *s* of Gordon and Gwen Nobbs; *m* 1968, Mary Blatchford; two step *s* one step *d. Educ:* Marlborough; St John's Coll., Cambridge (BA English). Wrote scripts for: That Was the Week That Was, BBC TV, 1963; The Frost Report, The Two Ronnies, The Fall and Rise of Reginald Perrin, 1976–78; BBC TV: The Hello Goodbye Man, Dogfood Dan and The Carmarthen Cowboy; Yorkshire TV: Sez Les, Cupid's Darts, A Bit of a Do, 1982–90; Rich Tea and Sympathy, 1991; Granada: Our Young Mr Wignall, The Glamour Girls; Fairly Secret Army, Channel 4. *Publications:* The Itinerant Lodger, 1965; Ostrich Country, 1968; A Piece of the Sky is Missing, 1969; The Fall and Rise of Reginald Perrin, 1975; The Return of Reginald Perrin, 1977; The Better World of Reginald Perrin, 1978; Second From Last in the Sack Race, 1983; A Bit of a Do, 1986; Pratt of the Argus, 1988; Fair Do's, 1990. *Recreations:* cricket, football, bird-watching, travel, food, drink, bridge, theatre, weeding. *Address:* c/o Jonathan Clowes, Iron Bridge House, Bridge Approach, NW1 8BD. *Club:* Hereford United Football.

NOBES, (Charles) Patrick; Deputy Headmaster, Northaw School, West Tytherley, since 1990; *b* 17 March 1933; *o c* of Alderman Alfred Robert Nobes, OBE, JP, and Marguerite Violet Vivian (*née* Fathers), Gosport, Hants; *m* 1958, Patricia Jean (*née* Brand); three *s. Educ:* Price's Sch., Fareham, Hants; University Coll., Oxford. MA. With The Times, reporting and editorial, 1956–57; Head of English Dept, King Edward VI Grammar Sch., Bury St Edmunds, 1959–64; Head of English and General Studies and Sixth Form Master, Ashlyns Comprehensive Sch., Berkhamsted, 1964–69; Headmaster: The Ward Freman Sch., Buntingford, Herts, 1969–74; Bedales Sch., 1974–81; Weymouth Grammar Sch., 1981–85, later The Budmouth Sch., 1985–86; St Francis' Coll., Letchworth, 1986–87. Chairman: HMC Co-ed Schs Gp, 1976–80; Soc. of Headmasters of Independent Schs, 1978–80; Mem., SHA Council, 1985–86. General Editor and adapter, Bulls-Eye Books (series for adults and young adults with reading difficulties), 1972–. *Recreations:* writing, cricket and hockey, King Arthur, Hampshire, music, First World War. *Address:* 8 Glen Court, Glenmore Road, Salisbury, Wilts SP1 3HG. *T:* Salisbury (0722) 327363.

NOBES, Peter John, QPM 1986; Chief Constable, West Yorkshire Police, since 1989; *b* 1 Oct. 1935; *s* of Cornelius James Nobes and Ivy Kathleen (*née* Eke); *m* 1955, Ruth Winifred Barnett; two *d. Educ:* Fakenham Modern Secondary Sch.; University Coll. London (Bramshill Scholarship; LLB 1968). Nat. Service, Royal Corps of Signals. W Suffolk (later Suffolk) Constabulary, 1956; Constable to Inspector, Newmarket, Brandon, Ipswich; Police Staff Coll., Bramshill, 1963–64 (Cert. with Dist.); University, 1965–68; Essex and Southend-on-Sea Jt Constabulary (later Essex Police), 1969; Chief Inspector to Chief Supt, Harlow, Basildon, Chelmsford; courses at Police Staff Coll., 1970, 1976; Asst

Chief Constable, W Yorks Metropolitan Police, 1977 (management services, criminal investigation, complaints and discipline); Dep. Chief Constable, 1983; Chief Constable, N Yorks Police, 1985. *Publication:* A Policeman's Lot, 1973. *Recreations:* music, gardening, taking exercise. *Address:* West Yorkshire Police Headquarters, Laburnum Road, Wakefield WF1 3QP. *T:* Wakefield (0924) 375222.

NOBLE, Adrian Keith; Artistic Director, Royal Shakespeare Company, since 1991; *b* 19 July 1950; *s* of late William John Noble and of Violet Ena (*née* Wells). *Educ:* Chichester High Sch. for Boys; Bristol Univ. (BA); Drama Centre, London. Associate Dir, Bristol Old Vic, 1976–79; Resident Dir, RSC, 1980–82; Guest Dir, Royal Exchange Theatre, Manchester, 1980–81; Associate Dir, RSC, 1982–90. *Stage productions include:* Ubu Rex, A Man's A Man, 1977; A View from the Bridge, Titus Andronicus, The Changeling, 1978; Love for Love, Timon of Athens, Recruiting Officer (Edinburgh Fest.), 1979; Duchess of Malfi, 1980; Dr Faustus, The Forest, A Doll's House, 1981; King Lear, Antony and Cleopatra, 1982; A New Way to Pay Old Debts, Comedy of Errors, Measure for Measure, 1983; Henry V, The Winter's Tale, The Desert Air, 1984; As You Like It, 1985; Mephisto, The Art of Success, Macbeth, 1986; Kiss Me Kate, 1987; The Plantagenets, 1989; The Master Builder, 1989; The Three Sisters, 1990; Henry IV, parts 1 and 2, 1991; *opera:* Don Giovanni, Kent Opera, 1983; The Fairy Queen, Aix-en-Provence Fest., 1989. *Address:* Barbican Theatre, EC2.

NOBLE, Barrie Paul; HM Diplomatic Service; Counsellor, Paris, since 1989; *b* 17 Oct. 1938; *s* of late Major F. A. Noble and Mrs Henrietta Noble; *m* 1965, Alexandra Helene Giddings; one *s*. *Educ:* Hele's, Exeter; New Coll., Oxford (BA Jurisprudence); Univ. of Dakar. RAF, 1957–59. Joined HM Diplomatic Service, 1962; Third, later Second Sec., (Leopoldville) Kinshasa, 1965–67; Second Sec. (Commercial), Kaduna, 1967–69; FCO, 1969–72; First Sec., 1972–75 and Head of Chancery, 1975, Warsaw; FCO, 1976–80; Counsellor, UK Mission to UN, Geneva, 1980–84; Counsellor, FCO, 1984–89. *Publication:* Droit Coutumier, Annales Africaines, 1965. *Recreations:* grass cutting, bridge, skiing. *Address:* c/o Foreign and Commonwealth Office, SW1. *Clubs:* Royal Air Force, Ski Club of Great Britain; Rolls-Royce Enthusiasts'.

NOBLE, David, WS, JP; Sheriff of North Strathclyde at Oban, Campbeltown and Fort William, since 1983; *b* 11 Feb. 1923; *s* of late Donald Noble, Solicitor, Inverness, and Helen Kirk Lynn Melville or Noble; *m* 1947, Marjorie Scott Smith or Noble; two *s* one *d*. *Educ:* Inverness Royal Academy; Edinburgh Univ. (MA, LLB *summa cum laude*). Royal Air Force Bomber Command, 1942–46. Partner in Miller Thomson & Robertson, WS, Edinburgh, 1953–82. JP Midlothian, 1970. *Address:* Woodhouselee, North Connel, Argyll PA37 1QZ. *T:* Connel (063171) 678.

NOBLE, David, CBE 1989; Under Secretary and Head of Administrative Division, Medical Research Council, 1981–89, retired; *b* 12 June 1929; *s* of late William Ernest Noble and of Maggie (*née* Watt); *m* 1969, Margaret Patricia Segal. *Educ:* Buckhurst Hill County High Sch., Essex; University Coll., Oxford (BA Hons English, 1952). Admin. Assistant, UCH, 1952–58; Mem., Operational Res. Unit, Nuffield Provincial Hosps Trust, 1958–61; Project Sec., Northwick Park Hosp. and Clinical Res. Centre, NW Thames RHA and MRC, 1961–68; Medical Research Council: Principal, 1968–72; Asst Sec., 1972–81. Member: Nat. Biological Standards Bd, 1983–90; PHLS Bd, 1990–. *Publications:* contribs to literature on operation and design of hosps and res. labs. *Recreations:* music, reading, travel. *Address:* 173 Bittacy Hill, NW7 1RT. *T:* 081–346 8005.

NOBLE, Sir David (Brunel), 6th Bt *cr* 1902, of Ardmore and Ardadan Noble, Cardross, Co. Dunbarton; sales consultant, Allied Maples Group Ltd, since 1989; *b* 25 Dec. 1961; *s* of Sir Marc Brunel Noble, 5th Bt, CBE and of Jennifer Lorna, *d* of late John Mein-Austin; *S* father, 1991; *m* 1987, Virginia Ann, *yr d* of late Roderick Wetherall; two *s*. *Educ:* Eton Coll.; Cambridge Tutors, Croydon. Sales Exec., Gabriel Communications Ltd, 1986–88. *Recreations:* golf, photography, gardening. *Heir:* *s* Roderick Lancaster Brunel Noble, *b* 12 Dec. 1988. *Address:* 1 New Walk, Wrotham, Sevenoaks, Kent TN15 7DA. *T:* Sevenoaks (0732) 884796. *Club:* HAC.

NOBLE, Prof. Denis, FRS 1979; Burdon Sanderson Professor of Cardiovascular Physiology, Oxford University, since 1984; Tutorial Fellow, 1963–84, Professorial Fellow, since 1984, Balliol College, Oxford; *b* 16 Nov. 1936; *s* of George and Ethel Noble; *m* 1965, Susan Jennifer Barfield, BSc, BA, DPhil; one *s* one *d*. *Educ:* Emanuel Sch., London; University Coll. London (BSc, MA, PhD; Fellow 1985) Asst Lectr, UCL, 1961–63; Tutor in Physiology, Balliol Coll., and Univ. Lectr, Oxford Univ., 1963–84; Praefectus of Holywell Manor (Balliol Graduate Centre), 1971–89; Vice-Master, Balliol Coll., 1983–85. Visiting Professor: Alberta, 1969–70; Univs of BC, Calgary, Edmonton, and SUNY at Stonyhook, 1990; Univ. of Auckland, 1990. Lectures: Darwin, British Assoc., 1966; Nahum, Yale, 1977; Bottazzi, Pisa, 1985; Ueda, Tokyo, 1985; Lloyd Roberts, London Med. Soc., 1987; Allerdale Wyld, Northern Industrial and Technical Soc., 1988; Bowden, UMIST, 1988. Chm., Jt Dental Cttee (MRC, SERC, Depts of Health), 1985–90. Hon. Sec., 1974–80, Foreign Sec., 1986–, Physiol Soc.; Founder Mem., Save British Science; Pres., Med. Section, BAAS, 1991–92. Hon. MRCP 1988; Mem., Academia Europaea, 1989; Correspondent Etranger (Fellow), Royal Acad. of Medicine, Belgium, 1985. Editor, Progress in Biophysics, 1967–. Scientific Medal, Zoolog. Soc., 1970; Gold Medal, British Heart Foundn, 1985. *Publications:* Initiation of the Heartbeat, 1975, 2nd edn, 1979; Electric Current Flow in Excitable Cells, 1975; Electrophysiology of Single Cardiac Cells, 1987; Goals, No Goals and Own Goals, 1989; Sodium-Calcium Exchange, 1989; papers mostly in Jl of Physiology; contribs on sci. res. and funding to New Scientist, nat. press, radio and TV. *Recreations:* Indian and French cooking, Occitan language and music, classical guitar. *Address:* 49 Old Road, Oxford OX3 7JZ. *T:* Oxford (0865) 62237.

NOBLE, Sir Fraser; *see* Noble, Sir T. A. F.

NOBLE, Sir Iain (Andrew), 3rd Bt *cr* 1923, of Ardkinglas and Eilean Iarmain; OBE 1988; Proprietor of Fearann Eilean Iarmain, Isle of Skye, since 1972; Chairman, Noble and Co. Ltd, Edinburgh, since 1980; Director: Adam and Co. plc, Edinburgh, since 1983; New Scotland Insurance Group PLC, since 1986, and other companies; *b* 8 Sept. 1935; *s* of Sir Andrew Napier Noble, 2nd Bt, KCMG and of Sigrid, 2nd *d* of Johan Michelet, Norwegian Diplomatic Service; *S* father, 1987; *m* 1990, Lucilla Charlotte James, *d* of late Col H. A. C. Mackenzie, OBE, MC, TD, DL, JP, Dalmore. *Educ:* China, Argentina and England (Eton); University Coll., Oxford (MA 1959). Matthews Wrightson, 1959–64; Scottish Council (Develt and Industry), Edinburgh, 1964–69; Jt Founder and Jt Man. Dir, Noble Grossart Ltd, merchant bankers, Edinburgh, 1969–72; Jt Founder and Chm., Seaforth Maritime Ltd, Aberdeen, 1972–78; Chm., Lennox Oil Co. plc, Edinburgh, 1980–85; Dep. Chm., Traverse Theatre, Edinburgh, 1966–68; Mem., Edinburgh Univ. Court, 1970–73; Trustee: College of Sabhal Mor Ostaig, Isle of Skye, 1974–84; Nat. Museums of Scotland, 1987–91. Scotsman of the Year Award, 1981. *Publication:* Sources of Finance, 1968. *Recreations:* Comhradh, beul-aithris is ceol le deagh chompanaich. *Heir:* *b* Timothy Peter Noble [*b* 21 Dec. 1943; *m* 1976, Elizabeth Mary, *d* of late Alexander Wallace Aitken; two *s* one *d*]. *Address:* (home) An Lamraig, Eilean Iarmain, An t-Eilean Sgitheanach IV43 3QR; (office) 5 Darnaway Street, Edinburgh EH3 6DW. *T:* (offices) Isle Ornsay (04713) 266 and 031–225 9677. *Club:* New (Edinburgh).

NOBLE, Kenneth Albert, CBE 1975; Member, Price Commission, 1973–77 (Deputy Chairman, 1973–76); Director, 1954–73, Vice-Chairman, 1966–73, Co-operative Wholesale Society Ltd; Director of associated organisations and subsidiaries. Member: CoID, 1957–65; Post Office Users Nat. Council, 1965–73; Monopolies Commn, 1969–73; London VAT Tribunals Panel, 1977–82. Served War, 1940–46 (despatches); Major RASC. *Publication:* (jtly) Financial Management Handbook, 1977, 2nd edn 1980.

NOBLE, Sir (Thomas Alexander) Fraser, Kt 1971; MBE 1947; Principal and Vice-Chancellor, University of Aberdeen, 1976–81, now Principal Emeritus; *b* 29 April 1918; *s* of late Simon Noble, Grantown-on-Spey and Jeanie Graham, Largs, Ayrshire; *m* 1945, Barbara A. M. Sinclair, Nairn; one *s* one *d*. *Educ:* Nairn Acad; Univ. of Aberdeen. After military service with Black Watch (RHR), entered Indian Civil Service, 1940. Served in NW Frontier Province, 1941–47, successively as Asst Comr, Hazara; Asst Polit. Agent, N Waziristan; Controller of Rationing, Peshawar; Under-Sec., Food Dept and Develt Dept; Sec., Home Dept; Joint Dep. Comr, Peshawar; Civil Aide to Referendum Comr. Lectr in Political Economy, Univ. of Aberdeen, 1948–57; Sec. and Treas., Carnegie Trust for Univs of Scotland, 1957–62; Vice-Chancellor, Leicester Univ., 1962–76. Mem. and Vice-Chm., Bd of Management, Aberdeen Mental Hosp. Group, 1953–57. Sec., Scottish Economic Soc., 1954–58; Vice-Pres., 1962–. Chm., Scottish Standing Conf. of Voluntary Youth Organisations, 1958–62; Vice-Chm., Standing Consultative Council on Youth Service in Scotland, 1959–62. Mem., Departmental Cttee on Probation Service, 1959–62; Chairman: Probation Advisory and Training Board, 1962–65; Television Research Cttee, 1963–69; Advisory Council on Probation and After-Care, 1965–70; Univs Council for Adult Education, 1965–69; Min. of Defence Cttee for Univ. Assistance to Adult Educn in HM Forces, 1965–70; Advisory Board, Overseas Students' Special Fund, 1967–71, Fees Awards Scheme, 1968–75; Cttee of Vice-Chancellors and Principals of Univs of UK, 1970–72; British Council Cttee on Exchanges between UK and USSR, 1973–78; Scottish Council for Community Educn, 1979–80. Member: Academic Advisory Cttee, Univs of St Andrews and Dundee, 1964–66; E Midlands Economic Planning Council, 1965–68; Council, Assoc. Commonwealth Univs, 1970–79; Exec. Cttee, Inter-Univ. Council for Higher Educn Overseas, 1972–79; Exec. Cttee, British Council, 1973–79; British Council Cttee for Commonwealth Univ. Interchange, 1973–79; US-UK Educnl Commn, 1973–76. Hon. LLD: Aberdeen, 1968; Leicester, 1976; Glasgow, 1981; Washington Coll., Maryland, 1981. *Publications:* articles in economic journals and on education. *Recreation:* golf. *Address:* Hedgerley, Victoria Street, Nairn IV12 4HH. *Clubs:* Royal Northern and University (Aberdeen); Royal Aberdeen Golf, Nairn Golf.

NODDER, Timothy Edward, CB 1982; Deputy Secretary, Department of Health and Social Security, 1978–84; *b* 18 June 1930; *s* of Edward Nodder. *Educ:* St Paul's Sch.; Christ's Coll., Cambridge. Under-Sec., DHSS, 1972. *Recreation:* natural history. *Address:* 10 Frognal Lane, NW3 7DU.

NOEL, family name of **Earl of Gainsborough.**

NOEL, Rear-Adm. Gambier John Byng, CB 1969; retired; *b* 16 July 1914; *s* of late G. B. E. Noel; *m* 1936, Miss Joan Stevens; four *d*. *Educ:* Royal Naval Coll., Dartmouth. Joined Royal Navy, 1928; served in War of 1939–45, HMS Aurora and HMS Norfolk (despatches twice); Captain 1959; Imperial Defence Coll., 1962; Staff of Commander Far East Fleet, 1964–67; Rear-Admiral 1967; Chief Staff Officer (Technical) to C-in-C, Western Fleet, 1967–69. *Recreation:* gardening. *Address:* Woodpeckers, Church Lane, Haslemere, Surrey. *T:* Haslemere (0428) 3824. *Club:* Anglo-Belgian.

NOEL, Geoffrey Lindsay James; Metropolitan Stipendiary Magistrate, since 1975; *b* 19 April 1923; *s* of Major James Noel and Maud Noel; *m* 1st, 1947; two *d*; 2nd, 1966, Eileen Pickering (*née* Cooper); two step *s*. *Educ:* Crewkerne Sch., Somerset. Enlisted Royal Regt of Artillery, 1941; commnd, 1942; attached 9th Para Bn, 6 Airborne Div., 1944, Captain; POW Oflag 79; Major 1957; retd 1960. Called to Bar, Middle Temple, 1962; practised London and SE circuit. Chm., Juvenile Courts, 1977–79; Dep. Circuit Judge, 1980–82. *Recreation:* gardening. *Address:* c/o 1 Garden Court, Temple, EC4.

NOEL, Hon. Gerard Eyre Wriothesley; author, publisher and journalist; Editor, Catholic Herald, 1971–76 and 1982–84, Editorial Director, since 1984; *b* 20 Nov. 1926; *s* of 4th Earl of Gainsborough, OBE, TD, and Alice (*née* Eyre); *m* 1958, Adele Julie Patricia, *d* of Major V. N. B. Were; two *s* one *d*. *Educ:* Georgetown, USA; Exeter Coll., Oxford (MA, Modern History). Called to Bar, Inner Temple, 1952. Director: Herder Book Co., 1959–66; Search Press Ltd, 1972–. Literary Editor, Catholic Times, 1958–61; Catholic Herald: Asst Editor, 1968; Editorial Dir, 1976–81. Mem. Exec. Cttee, 1974–, Hon. Treasurer, 1979–81, Council of Christians and Jews. Contested (L) Argyll, 1959. Liveryman, Co. of Stationers and Newspapermakers. Freeman, City of London. *Publications:* Paul VI, 1963; Harold Wilson, 1964; Goldwater, 1964; The New Britain, 1966; The Path from Rome, 1968; Princess Alice: Queen Victoria's Forgotten Daughter, 1974; contrib. The Prime Ministers, 1974; The Great Lock-Out of 1926, 1976; The Anatomy of the Roman Catholic Church, 1980; Ena: Spain's English Queen, 1984; Cardinal Basil Hume, 1984; *translations:* The Way to Unity after the Council, 1967; The Holy See and the War in Europe (Official Documents), 1968; articles in: Church Times, Catholic Times, Jewish Chronicle, Baptist Times, Catholic Herald, Literary Review, European, International Mind. *Recreations:* walking, travel, exploring London. *Address:* 105 Cadogan Gardens, SW3 2RF. *T:* 071–730 8734; Westington Mill, Chipping Campden, Glos. *T:* Evesham (0386) 840240. *Clubs:* Beefsteak, Garrick.

NOEL-BAKER, Hon. Francis Edward; Director: North Euboean Enterprises Ltd, since 1973; Fini Fisheries, Cyprus, since 1976; *b* 7 Jan. 1920; *o s* of late Baron Noel-Baker, PC, and late Irene, *o d* of Frank Noel, British landowner, of Achmetaga, Greece; *m* 1957, Barbara Christina, *yr d* of late Joseph Sonander, Sweden; four *s* (one *d* decd). *Educ:* Westminster Sch.; King's Coll., Cambridge (Exhibitioner; 1st cl. hons History). Founder and Chm., CU Lab. Club, 1939; left Cambridge to join Army, summer 1940, as Trooper, Royal Tank Regt; Commissioned in Intelligence Corps and served in UK, Force 133, Middle East (despatches); returned to fight Brentford and Chiswick Div.; MP (Lab) Brentford and Chiswick Div. of Mddx, 1945–50; Editor, United Nations World/World Horizon, 1945–47, Go! magazine, 1947–48; PPS Admiralty, 1949–50; BBC European Service, 1950–54; MP (Lab) Swindon, 1955–68, resigned from Labour Party, 1969; Sec., 1955–64, Chm., 1964–68, UN Parly Cttee; Vice-Chm., Lab. Cttee for Europe, 1976–78; Member: SDP 1981–83; Conservative Party, 1984–; NUJ, 1946–81. Chm., Advertising Inquiry Council, 1951–68. Chairman: North Euboean Foundation Ltd, 1965–; Candili Craft Centre, Philip Noel-Baker Centre, Euboea, 1983–; Founder Pres., European Council for Villages and Small Towns, 1984–; Pres., Internat. Campaign for Environmental Health, 1985–; Hon. Pres., Union of Forest Owners of Greece, 1968–. Member: Parochial Church Council, St Martin in the Fields, 1960–68; Freedom from Hunger Campaign UK Cttee Exec. Cttee, 1961; Ecology Party, 1978–; Soil Assoc., 1979–. Governor, Campion Sch., Athens, 1973–78. Archives Fellow Commoner, Churchill Coll., Cambridge, 1989. Wine Constable, Guyenne, 1988–. *Publications:* Greece, the Whole Story, 1946; Spanish

Summary, 1948; The Spy Web, 1954; Land and People of Greece, 1957; Nansen, 1958; Looking at Greece, 1967; My Cyprus File, 1985; Book Eight: a taste of hardship, 1987; Three Saints and Poseidon, 1988. *Recreation:* gardening. *Address:* Achmetaga Estate, GR 340–04 Procopi, Greece. *T* and *Fax:* 30 227 41204; 5 Cresswell Gardens, SW5 0BJ. *T:* 071–373 6345; (office) 27 Bryanston Square, W1H 7LS. *T:* 071–723 9405; Penrith (0768) 66608, *Fax:* Penrith (0768) 68291. *Clubs:* Travellers', Special Forces; Athens.

NOEL-BUXTON, family name of **Baron Noel-Buxton.**

NOEL-BUXTON, 3rd Baron *cr* 1930; **Martin Connal Noel-Buxton;** *b* 8 Dec. 1940; *s* of 2nd Baron Noel-Buxton and Helen Nancy (*d* 1949), *yr d* of late Col K. H. M. Connal, CB, OBE, TD; *S* father, 1980; *m* 1st, 1964, Miranda Mary (marr. diss. 1968), *er d* of H. A. Chisenhale-Marsh; 2nd, 1972, Sarah Margaret Surridge (marr. diss. 1982), *o d* of N. C. W. Barrett, TD; one *s* one *d*; 3rd, 1986, Abigail Marie, *yr d* of E. P. R. Clent; one *d*. *Educ:* Bryanston School; Balliol College, Oxford (MA). Admitted a Solicitor, 1966. *Heir: s* Hon. Charles Connal Noel-Buxton, *b* 17 April 1975.

NOEL-PATON, family name of **Baron Ferrier.**

NOEL-PATON, Hon. (Frederick) Ranald; Group Managing Director, John Menzies, since 1986; *b* 7 Nov. 1938; *s* of Baron Ferrier, *qv*; *m* 1973, Patricia Anne Stirling; four *d*. *Educ:* Rugby School; McGill Univ. (BA). Various posts, British United Airways, 1965–70; various sen. exec. posts, British Caledonian Airways, 1970–86; Director: John Menzies plc, 1986–; Pacific Assets Trust, 1986–; General Accident plc, 1987–; Macallan-Glenlivet, 1990–; Royal Bank of Scotland Gp, 1991–. *Recreations:* fishing, walking, gardening, bird watching, the arts. *Address:* John Menzies, 108 Princes Street, Edinburgh EH2 3AA. *T:* 031–225 8555. *Clubs:* New (Edinburgh); Skek-O Country, Hong Kong (Hong Kong).

NOEST, Peter John, FRICS; Director, Lambert Smith Hampton, since 1988; *b* 12 June 1948; *s* of Major A. J. F. Noest and Mrs M. Noest-Gerbrands; *m* 1972, Lisabeth Penelope Moody; one *s* one *d*. *Educ:* St George's Coll., Weybridge; Royal Agricl Coll., Cirencester. FRICS 1978 (ARICS 1973). Joined Knight Frank & Rutley, 1971; Partner i/c Dutch office, Amsterdam, 1972; London Partner, 1977; full equity Partner, 1981; Consultant, 1983, full equity Partner, 1984, Hampton & Sons; Dir, Hampton & Sons Holdings, 1987 (subseq. merged with Lambert Smith to form Lambert Smith Hampton). *Publication:* (contrib.) Office Development, 1985. *Recreations:* hunting, shooting, farming, travel. *Address:* Little Park, Wootton Bassett, Wilts SN4 7QW. *T:* Swindon (0793) 852348. *Clubs:* Turf, Oriental.

NOGUEIRA, Albano Pires Fernandes; Ambassador of Portugal; *b* 8 Nov. 1911; *m* 1937, Alda Maria Marques Xavier da Cunha. *Educ:* Univ. of Coimbra. 3rd Sec., Washington, 1944; 2nd Sec., Pretoria, 1945; 1st Sec., Pretoria, 1948; Head of Mission, Tokyo, 1950; Counsellor, London, 1953; Consul-Gen., Bombay, 1955; Consul-Gen., NY, 1955; Dep. Perm. Rep. UN, NY, 1955; Asst Dir-Gen., Econ. Affairs, Lisbon, 1959; Dir Gen., Econ. Affairs, Lisbon, 1961; Ambassador to: European Communities, Brussels, 1964; NATO, 1970; Court of St James's, 1974–76; Sec.-Gen., Ministry for Foreign Affairs, 1977. Vis. Prof., Univ. of Minho, Braga, 1979, 1980. Mem., Internat. Assoc. of Literary Critics, 1981–. Grand Cross: Merito Civil (Spain), 1961; Order of Infante Dom Henrique (Portugal), 1964; Isabel la Católica (Spain), 1977; Merit (Germany), 1977; St Olav (Norway), 1978; Christ (Portugal), 1981; the Flag with golden palm (Yugoslavia), 1978; Grand Officer: Cruzeiro do Sul (Brazil), 1959; White Elephant (Thailand), 1960. *Publications:* Imagens em Espelho Côncavo (essays); Portugal na Arte Japonesa (essay); Uma Agulha no Céu (novel); contribs to: NATO and the Mediterranean, 1985; NATO's Anxious Birth—the Prophetic Vision of the 1940s, 1985; contrib. leading Portuguese papers and reviews. *Recreations:* reading, writing. *Address:* Avenida Gaspar Corte-Real 18, Apt 4D, 2750 Cascais, Portugal. *T:* 4868264; 5 Rua Alberto de Oliveira, 5–3-E, 3000 Coimbra, Portugal. *T:* 715035. *Clubs:* Grémio Literário, Automóvel de Portugal (Lisbon).

NOLAN, Brig. Eileen Joan, CB 1976; Director, Women's Royal Army Corps, 1973–77; *b* 19 June 1920; *d* of late James John and Ethel Mary Nolan. *Educ:* King's Norton Grammar Sch. for Girls. Joined ATS, Nov. 1942; commissioned, 1945. Lt-Col, 1967; Col, 1970; Brig., 1973. Hon. ADC to the Queen, 1973–77; Chm., NATO Senior Women Officers' Cttee, 1975–77; Dep. Controller Comdt, WRAC, 1977–84. *Address:* c/o Barclays Bank, High Street, Crowthorne, Berkshire.

NOLAN, Rt. Hon. Sir Michael (Patrick), Kt 1982; PC 1991; **Rt. Hon. Lord Justice Nolan;** a Lord Justice of Appeal, since 1991; *b* 10 Sept. 1928; *yr s* of James Thomas Nolan and Jane (*née* Walsh); *m* 1953, Margaret, *yr d* of Alfred Noyes, CBE, and Mary (*née* Mayne); one *s* four *d*. *Educ:* Ampleforth; Wadham Coll., Oxford. Served RA, 1947–49; TA, 1949–55. Called to Bar, Middle Temple, 1953 (Bencher, 1975); QC 1968; called to Bar, NI, 1974; QC (NI) 1974; a Recorder of the Crown Court, 1975–82; Judge, High Court of Justice, QBD, 1982–91; Presiding Judge, Western Circuit, 1985–88. Member: Bar Council, 1973–74; Senate of Inns of Court and Bar, 1974–81 (Treasurer, 1977–79). Mem., Sandilands Cttee on Inflation Accounting, 1973–75. Mem. Governing Body, Convent of the Sacred Heart, Woldingham, 1973–83; Governor, Combe Bank Sch., 1974–83. *Recreation:* fishing. *Address:* c/o Royal Courts of Justice, WC2A 2LL. *Club:* MCC.

NOLAN, Sir Sidney (Robert), OM 1983; AC 1988; Kt 1981; CBE 1963; RA 1991 (ARA 1987); artist; *b* Melbourne, 22 April 1917; *s* of late Sidney Henry Nolan; *m* 1939, Elizabeth Patterson (marr. diss. 1942); *m* 1948, Cynthia Hansen (*d* 1974); *m* 1977, Mary Elizabeth à Beckett Perceval. *Educ:* State and technical schools, Melbourne; National Art Gallery Sch., Victoria. Italian Government Scholar, 1956; Commonwealth Fund Fellow, to USA, 1958; Fellow: ANU, 1965 (Hon. LLD, 1968); York Univ., 1971; Bavarian Academy, 1971. Hon. DLit London, 1971. Exhibited: Paris, 1948, 1961; New Delhi, 1953; Pittsburgh International, 1953, 1954, 1955, 1964, 1967, 1970; Venice Biennale, 1954; Rome, 1954; Pacific Loan Exhibition, 1956; Brussels International Exhibition, 1958; Documenta II, Kassel, 1959; Retrospective, Art Gallery of New South Wales, Sydney, 1967; Retrospective, Darmstadt, 1971; Ashmolean Museum, Oxford, 1971; Retrospective, Royal Dublin Soc., 1973; Perth Festival, 1982; Retrospective, Vic. Nat. Gall., 1987. Exhibits Tate Gallery, Marlborough New London Gallery, Marlborough Gallery, New York. Ballet Designs for Icare, Sydney, 1941; Orphée (Cocteau), Sydney, 1948; The Guide, Oxford, 1961; Rite of Spring, Covent Garden, 1962, 1987; The Display, Adelaide Festival, 1964; opera designs for: Samson et Delilah, Covent Garden, 1981; Il Trovatore, Sydney Op. House, 1983; Die Entführung aus dem Serail, Covent Garden, 1987; mural for Victorian Cultural Centre Concert Hall, 1982. Works in Tate Gallery, Museum of Modern Art, New York, Australian national galleries, Contemporary Art Society and Arts Council of Great Britain, etc. Film, Nolan at 60, BBC and ABC, 1977. Hon. DLitt: Sydney, 1977; Perth, 1988. *Publication:* Paradise Garden (poems, drawings and paintings), 1972; *Illustrated:* Near the Ocean, by Robert Lowell, 1966; The Voyage, by Baudelaire, trans. Lowell, 1968; Children's Crusade, by Benjamin Britten, 1973; *Relevant publications:* Kenneth Clark, Colin MacInnes, Bryan Robertson: Nolan, 1961; Robert Melville: Ned Kelly, 1964; Elwyn Lynn: Sydney Nolan: Myth and Imagery, 1967; Melville and Lynn: The Darkening Ecliptic: Ern Malley Poems, Sidney Nolan Paintings, 1974; Cynthia Nolan: Open Negative, 1967; Sight of China, 1969; Paradise, and yet, 1971. *Address:* c/o Marlborough Fine Art Ltd, 6 Albemarle Street, W1. *Clubs:* Athenæum, Garrick.

NONWEILER, Prof. Terence Reginald Forbes, BSc; PhD; CEng; FRAeS; FIMA; Professor of Mathematics, Victoria University of Wellington, 1975–91, now Emeritus; *b* 8 Feb. 1925; *s* of Ernest James Nonweiler and Lilian Violet Amalie Nonweiler (*née* Holfert); *m* 1949, Patricia Hilda Frances (*née* Neame); four *s* two *d*. *Educ:* Bethany Sch., Goudhurst, Kent; University of Manchester, BSc 1944, PhD 1960. Scientific Officer, Royal Aircraft Establishment, Farnborough, Hants, 1944–50; Scientific Officer, Scientific Advisor's Dept, Air Ministry, 1950–51; Senior Lecturer in Aerodynamics, College of Aeronautics, Cranfield, Beds, 1951–57; Senior Lecturer in Aeronautical Engineering, The Queen's Univ. of Belfast, 1957–61; Mechan Prof. of Aeronautics and Fluid Mechanics, Glasgow Univ., 1961–75. Consultant: to Admiralty, 1951; to Ministry of Aviation, 1959; to Ministry of Agriculture, 1966; to Wellington City Corp., 1977. Vis. Prof., Cranfield Inst. of Technology, 1991. Member, International Academy of Astronautics. *Publications:* Jets and Rockets, 1959; Computational Mathematics, 1984; numerous technical papers on aeronautics, space flight, and submarine motion. *Recreations:* acting and stage production. *Address:* 15 Tui Road, Raumati Beach 6150, New Zealand.

NOOR, Rusli; Indonesian Order of Satya Lencana Karya Satya, 1974; Secretary General, Association of South East Asian Nations, since 1989; *b* 1 May 1927; *s* of Pangeran Mohamad Noor and Gusti Aminah; *m* 1952, Aji Ratna Kemala Afloes; two *s* five *d*. *Educ:* Columbia Univ., NY (MA; Cert. Russian Inst.). Indonesian Ministry of Foreign Affairs: served London, Moscow, The Hague, Jakarta, 1951–74; Ambassador to Denmark and Norway, 1974–78; Dir Gen. for Foreign Economic, Social and Cultural Relations, 1978–83; Ambassador to Belgium, Luxembourg and EC, 1983–86; Dir Gen for Foreign Economic Relations, 1986–88; Consultant to Minister for Foreign Affairs, 1988–89. Foreign Orders from Belgium, France, Netherlands and Venezuela. *Recreations:* reading, fishing. *Address:* Jln Imam Bonjol 49, Jakarta, Indonesia. *T:* 334805.

NORBURN, Prof. David, PhD; Director, The Management School, Imperial College of Science, Technology and Medicine, and Professor of Management, University of London, since 1987; Director: Newchurch & Co., since 1985; *b* 18 Feb. 1941; *s* of late Richard Greville and Constance Elizabeth Norburn; *m* 1st, 1962, Veronica Ellis (marr. diss. 1975); one *s* one *d*; 2nd, 1975, Prof. Susan Joyce Birley, *qv*. *Educ:* Bolton Sch.; LSE (BSc); City Univ. (PhD). Salesman, Burroughs Corp., 1962–66; Management Consultant, Price Waterhouse, 1966–67; Sen. Lectr, Regent Street Polytechnic, 1967–70; Sen. Res. Fellow, City Univ., 1970–72; Lectr, Sen. Lectr, Dir, MBA programme, London Business Sch., 1972–82; Inaugural Chairholder, Franklin D. Schurz Prof. in Strategic Management, Univ. of Notre Dame, Indiana, 1982–85; Prof. of Strategic Management, Cranfield Inst. of Technology, 1985–87. Freeman, Clockmakers' Co. CBIM, FRSA. *Publications:* British Business Policy (with D. Channon and J. Stopford), 1975; articles in professional jls. *Recreations:* antiquarian horology, competitive tennis, carpentry. *Address:* The Management School, Imperial College of Science, Technology and Medicine, 53 Prince's Gate, SW7 2PG. *T:* 071–589 5111. *Club:* Athenæum.

NORBURN, Susan Joyce, (Mrs David Norburn); *see* Birley, S. J.

NORBURY, 6th Earl of, *cr* 1827; **Noel Terence Graham-Toler;** Baron Norwood, 1797; Baron Norbury, 1800; Viscount Glandine, 1827; *b* 1 Jan. 1939; *s* of 5th Earl and Margaret Greenhalgh (*d* 1984); *S* father 1955; *m* 1965, Anne Mathew; one *s* one *d*. *Heir: s* Viscount Glandine, *qv*. *Address:* Stock Exchange, EC2.

NORBURY, Brian Martin; Head of Schools Branch 2, Department of Education and Science, since 1988; *b* 2 March 1938; *s* of Robert Sidney Norbury and Doris Lilian (*née* Broughton). *Educ:* Churcher's Coll., Petersfield; King's Coll., London (BA; AKC 1959). National Service, RAEC, 1959–61. Asst Principal, WO, 1961; Private Sec. to Under Sec. of State for War, 1962; Asst Private Sec. to Dep. Sec. of State for Defence, 1964; Principal, MoD, 1965, Cabinet Office, 1969; Private Sec. to Sec. of the Cabinet, 1970–73; Asst Sec., MoD, 1973; Private Sec. to Sec. of State for Def., 1979–81; Under Sec., MoD, 1981, DES, 1984–. *Address:* 63 Aberdeen Road, N5. *Club:* Reform.

NORCROSS, Lawrence John Charles, OBE 1986; Headmaster, Highbury Grove School, 1975–87; *b* 14 April 1927; *s* of Frederick Marshall Norcross and Florence Kate (*née* Hedges); *m* 1958, Margaret Wallace; three *s* one *d*. *Educ:* Ruskin Coll., Oxford; Univ. of Leeds (BA Hons English). Training Ship, Arethusa, 1941–42; RN, 1942–49 (E Indies Fleet, 1944–45); clerical asst, 1949–52; Asst Teacher: Singlegate Sch., 1957–61; Abbey Wood Sch., 1961–63; Housemaster, Battersea County Sch., 1963–74; Dep. Headmaster, Highbury Grove Sch., 1974–75. Member: NAS/UWT, 1970–86; Secondary Heads' Assoc., 1975–87; HMC, 1985–87; Trustee and Mem. Exec. Cttee, Nat. Council for Educnl Standards, 1976–89; Trustee: Educnl Res. Trust, 1986–; Ind. Primary and Secondary Educn Trust, 1987–; Grant Maintained Schools Trust, 1988–; Member: Educn Study Gp, Centre for Policy Studies, 1980–; Univ. Entrance and Schs Examinations Council, Univ. of London, 1980–84; Steering Cttee, Campaign for a Gen. Teaching Council. Mem., Adv. Council, Educn Unit, IEA, 1986–90. Founder and Hon. Sec., John Ireland Soc., 1960–; former Chm., Contemp. Concerts Co-ordination. Occasional broadcasts and television appearances. *Publications:* (with F. Naylor) The ILEA: a case for reform, 1981; (with F. Naylor and J. McIntosh) The ILEA after the Abolition of the GLC, 1983; (contrib.) The Wayward Curriculum, 1986; GCSE: the Egalitarian Fallacy, 1990; occasional articles. *Recreations:* talking to friends, playing bridge badly, watching cricket, listening to music. *Address:* 3 St Nicholas Mansions, 6–8 Trinity Crescent, SW17 7AF. *T:* 081–767 4299; Crockwell Cottage, Crockwell Street, Long Compton, Warwicks CV36 5JN. *T:* Long Compton (060884) 662. *Club:* Surrey County Cricket.

NORDEN, Denis, CBE 1980; scriptwriter and broadcaster; *b* 6 Feb. 1922; *s* of George Norden and Jenny Lubell; *m* 1943, Avril Rosen; one *s* one *d*. *Educ:* Craven Park Sch., London; City of London Sch. Theatre Manager, 1939–42; served RAF, 1942–45; staff-writer in Variety Agency, 1945–47. With Frank Muir, 1947–64: collaborated for 17 years writing comedy scripts, including: (for radio): Take It From Here, 1947–58; Bedtime with Braden, 1950–54; (for TV): And So To Bentley, 1956; Whack-O!, 1958–60; The Seven Faces of Jim, 1961, and other series with Jimmy Edwards; resident in TV and radio panel-games; collaborated in film scripts, television commercials, and revues; joint Advisors and Consultants to BBC Television Light Entertainment Dept, 1960–64; jointly received Screenwriters Guild Award for Best Contribution to Light Entertainment, 1961; together on panel-games My Word!, 1956–, and My Music, 1967–. Since 1964, solo writer for television and films; Chm., Looks Familiar (Thames TV), 1973–87; It'll Be Alright on the Night (LWT), 1977–90; It'll Be Alright on the Day, 1983; In On The Act, 1988; Pick of the Pilots, 1990. Film Credits include: The Bliss of Mrs Blossom; Buona Sera, Mrs Campbell; The Best House in London; Every Home Should Have One; Twelve Plus One; The Statue; The Water Babies. Variety Club of GB Award for Best Radio Personality (with Frank Muir), 1978; Male TV Personality of the Year, 1980. *Publications:* (with Frank Muir): You Can't Have Your Kayak and Heat It,

1973; Upon My Word!, 1974; Take My Word for It, 1978; The Glums, 1979; Oh, My Word!, 1980; The Complete and Utter My Word Stories, 1983; Coming to You Live! behind-the-screen memories of 50s and 60s Television, 1986; You Have My Word, 1989. *Recreations:* reading, loitering. *Address:* 53 Frith Street, W1V 5TE. *Club:* Saturday Morning Odeon.

NORELL, Dr Jacob Solomon, (Jack), FRCGP; principal in general practice, 1956–90; *b* 3 March 1927; *s* of Henry (formerly Habib) Norell and Malka Norell; *m* 1948, Brenda Honeywell (marr. diss. 1973); three *s*. *Educ:* South Devon Technical Coll.; Guy's Hosp. Med. Sch. (MB, BS 1953). MRCS, LRCP 1953; LMSSA 1952; MRCGP 1972, FRCGP 1982. Principal in general practice, 1956–. Dean of Studies, RCGP, 1974–81; Exec. Officer, Jt Cttee on Postgrad. Educn for Gen. Practice, 1976–81. Mem. Council, RCGP, 1984–90; Pres., Section of Gen. Practice, RSM, 1989–90. Pres., Balint Soc., 1984–87, Internat. Balint Fedn, 1989–. Fellow, Hunterian Soc., 1987. William Pickles Lectr, RCGP, 1984. Editor, The Practitioner, 1982–83. *Publications:* (co-ed) Six Minutes for the Patient, 1973; Entering General Practice, 1981; papers and chapters on general practice topics: the Balint philosophy, consultation, practice orgn, postgrad. educn, women doctors, measuring quality of med. care, professional self-regulation, doctor-patient relationship. *Recreations:* rural walks, driving open-topped cars, spotting unclad emperors. *Address:* 50 Nottingham Terrace, York Gate, Regent's Park, NW1 4QD. *T:* 071–486 2979.

NORFOLK, 17th Duke of, *cr* 1483; **Miles Francis Stapleton Fitzalan-Howard,** KG 1983; GCVO 1986; CB 1966; CBE 1960; MC 1944; DL; Earl of Arundel, 1139; Baron Beaumont, 1309; Baron Maltravers, 1330, Earl of Surrey, 1483; Baron FitzAlan, Clun, and Oswaldestre, 1627; Earl of Norfolk, 1644; Baron Howard of Glossop, 1869; Earl Marshal and Hereditary Marshal and Chief Butler of England; Premier Duke and Earl; *b* 21 July 1915; *s* of 3rd Baron Howard of Glossop, MBE, and Baroness Beaumont (11th in line), OBE; *S* to barony of mother, 1971, and of father, 1972, and to dukedom of cousin, 1975; *m* 1949, Anne Mary Teresa, *e d* of late Wing Commander Gerald Joseph Constable Maxwell, MC, DFC, AFC; two *s* three *d*. *Educ:* Ampleforth Coll.; Christ Church, Oxford (MA; Hon. Student, 1983). 2nd Lieut, Grenadier Guards, 1937. Served War of 1939–45, France, North Africa, Sicily, Italy (despatches, MC), NW Europe. Appointed Head of British Military Mission to Russian Forces in Germany, 1957; Commanded 70 Bde KAR, 1961–63; GOC, 1 Div., 1963–65 (Maj.-Gen.); Dir, Management and Support Intelligence, MoD, 1965–66; Director, Service Intelligence, MoD, 1966–67; retd 1967. Chm., Arundel Castle Trustees, Ltd, 1976–. Pres., Building Socs Assoc., 1982–86. Prime Warden, Fishmongers' Co., 1985–86. Hon. Fellow, St Edmund's House, Cambridge, 1983; Hon. Bencher, Inner Temple, 1984. DL West Sussex, 1977. Knight of the Sovereign Order of Malta. *Heir: s* Earl of Arundel and Surrey, *qv*. *Address:* Arundel Castle, Sussex BN18 9AB. *T:* Arundel (0903) 882173; Carlton Towers, Goole, North Humberside DN14 9LZ. *T:* Goole (0405) 860 243; Bacres House, Hambleden, Henley-on-Thames, Oxfordshire RG9 6RY. *T:* Henley-on-Thames (0491) 571350. *Club:* Pratt's.

See also Lord Michael Fitzalan-Howard, D. P. Frost.

NORFOLK, Lavinia Duchess of; Lavinia Mary Fitzalan-Howard, LG 1990; CBE 1971; Lord-Lieutenant of West Sussex, 1975–90; *b* 22 March 1916; *d* of 3rd Baron Belper and of Eva, Countess of Rosebery, DBE; *m* 1937, 16th Duke of Norfolk, KG, PC, GCVO, GBE, TD (*d* 1975); four *d*. *Educ:* Abbotshill, Hemel Hempstead, Herts. President: Nat. Canine Defence League, 1969–; Pony Riding for the Disabled Trust, Chigwell, 1964–; BHS, 1980–82. Vice-President: ASBAH, 1970–; Spastic Soc., 1969–; NSPCC, 1967–. Patron, Riding for the Disabled, 1986– (Pres., 1970–86). Chairman, King Edward VII Hosp., Midhurst, 1975–. Steward, Goodwood, 1976–78. BRCS Certificate of Honour and Badge, Class 1, 1969. Silver Jubilee Medal, 1977. *Address:* Arundel Park, Sussex. *T:* Arundel (0903) 882041.

See also Earl of Ancram, Lady Herries of Terregles.

NORFOLK, Archdeacon of; *see* Dawson, Ven. Peter.

NORFOLK, Ven. Edward Matheson; Archdeacon of St Albans, 1982–87, Emeritus since 1987; *b* 29 Sept. 1921; *s* of Edward and Chrissie Mary Wilson Norfolk; *m* 1947, Mary Louisa Oates; one *s* one *d* (and one *s* decd). *Educ:* Latymer Upper School; Leeds Univ. (BA); College of the Resurrection, Mirfield. Deacon, 1946; priest, 1947; Assistant Curate: Greenford, 1946–47; King Charles the Martyr, South Mymms, 1947–50; Bushey, 1950–53; Vicar: Waltham Cross, 1953–59; Welwyn Garden City, 1959–69; Rector, Great Berkhamsted, 1969–81; Vicar, King's Langley, 1981–82. Hon. Canon of St Albans, 1972–82. *Recreations:* walking, bird-watching. *Address:* 5 Fairlawn Court, Sidmouth, Devon EX10 1UR.

NORFOLK, Leslie William, CBE 1973 (OBE 1944); TD 1946; CEng; engineering consultant; *b* 8 April 1911; *e s* of late Robert and Edith Norfolk, Nottingham; *m* 1944, A. I. E. W. (Nancy) Watson (then WRNS), *d* of late Sir Hugh Watson, IFS (retd); two *s* one *d*. *Educ:* Southwell Minster Grammar Sch., Notts; University Coll., Nottingham (BSc). MICE; MIMechE; MIEE. Assistant and later Partner, E. G. Phillips, Son & Norfolk, consulting engineers, Nottingham, 1932–39. 2nd Lieut 1931, 5 Foresters TA, transferred and served with RE, France, Gibraltar, Home Forces, 1939–45, Lt-Col. Engineer, Dyestuffs Div., ICI Ltd, 1945–53; Resident Engineer, ICI of Canada, Kingston, Ont., 1953–55; Asst Chief Engr, Metals Div., ICI Ltd, 1955–57; Engineering Manager, Severnside Works, ICI Ltd, 1957–59; Engineering Director, Industrias Quimicas Argentinas Duperial SAIC, Buenos Aires, 1959–65; Director, Heavy Organic Chemicals Div., ICI Ltd, 1965–68; retired from ICI, 1968; Chief Exec., Royal Dockyards, MoD, 1969–72. *Recreations:* home workshop, industrial archaeology. *Address:* Beechwoods, Beechwood Road, Combe Down, Bath, Avon BA2 5JS. *T:* Combe Down (0225) 832104. *Club:* Bath & County (Bath).

NORGARD, John Davey, AO 1982; Chairman, Australian Broadcasting Commission, 1976–81; retired as Executive General Manager, Operations, BHP Co. Ltd, and as Chairman, Associated Tin Smelters, 1970; *b* 3 Feb. 1914; *s* of John Henry and Ida Elizabeth Norgard; *m* 1943, Irena Mary Doffkont; one *s* three *d*. *Educ:* Adelaide Univ. (BE); SA Sch. of Mines (FSASM). Part-time Chm., Metric Conversion Bd, Australia, 1970–81; Chairman: Commonwealth Employment Service Review, 1976–77; Pipeline Authority, 1976–81; Mem., Nat. Energy Adv. Cttee, 1977–80. Dep. Chancellor, La Trobe Univ., 1972–75. Chm., Grad. Careers Council of Australia, 1979–86. *Recreation:* golf. *Address:* 29 Montalto Avenue, Toorak, Victoria 3142, Australia. *T:* (03) 2414937. *Clubs:* Australian, Royal Melbourne Golf, Sciences (Melbourne).

NORLAND, Otto Realf; London representative, Deutsche Schiffsbank (formerly Deutsche Schiffahrtsbank) AG, since 1984; Chairman, Otto Norland Ltd, since 1984; *b* 24 Feb. 1930; *s* of Realph I. O. Norland and Aasta S. Sæther; *m* 1955, Gerd Ellen Andenæs; one *s* two *d*. *Educ:* Norwegian University College of Economics and Business Administration, Bergen. FCIB. Hambros Bank Ltd, 1953–84, Dir, 1964–84. Director: Alcoa of Great Britain Ltd, 1968–84 (Chm., 1978–84); Banque Paribas Norge A/S, Oslo, 1986–88; Oivind Lorentzen Shipping UK Ltd, 1988–. Dir, Aluminium Fedn Ltd, 1979–84 (Pres., 1982). *Recreations:* tennis, skiing, books (polar explorations). *Address:* Grocers' Hall, Princes Street, EC2R 8AQ. *T:* 071–726 8726. *Clubs:* Den Norske; Norske Selskab (Oslo).

NORMAN, (Alexander) Vesey (Bethune); Inspector of the Wallace Collection's Armouries, since 1977; *b* 10 Feb. 1930; *s* of Lt-Col A. M. B. Norman and Sheila M. Maxwell; *m* 1st, 1954, Catherine Margaret Barne (marr. diss. 1987); one *s*; 2nd, 1988, Elizabeth Anne Buddle. *Educ:* Alford Sch.; Trinity Coll., Glenalmond; London Univ. (BA Gen.). FSA; FSAScot. Asst Curator, Scottish United Services Museum, Edinburgh Castle, 1957; Hon. Curator of Arms and Armour, Abbotsford, 1957–63; Asst to Dir, Wallace Collection, 1963; Master of the Armouries, The Royal Armouries, HM Tower of London, 1977–88, retd; Pres., Church Monuments Soc., 1986–91; Vice-President: NADFAS, 1984–89; Arms and Armour Soc., 1983–. Liveryman, Gunmakers' Co., 1981–. *Publications:* Arms & Armour, 1964 (also foreign edns); (with Don Pottinger) Warrior to Soldier, 449–1660, 1966 (USA edn as A History of War and Weapons, 449–1660, reprinted as English Weapons and Warfare, 449–1660, 1979); Small Swords and Military Swords, 1967; The Medieval Soldier, 1971 (also USA); Arms and Armour in the Royal Scottish Museum, 1972; A Catalogue of Ceramics, Wallace Collection, Pt I, 1976; (with C. M. Barne) The Rapier and Small-Sword, 1460–1820, 1980; Catalogue of European Arms and Armour, supplement, Wallace Collection, 1986; articles in learned jls. *Recreation:* study of arms and armour. *Address:* The Wallace Collection, Manchester Square, W1.

NORMAN, Rear-Adm. Anthony Mansfeldt, CB 1989; Bursar and Fellow, St Catharine's College, Cambridge, since 1989; *b* 16 Dec. 1934; *s* of Cecil and Jean Norman; *m* 1961, Judith Pye; one *s* one *d*. *Educ:* Royal Naval Coll., Dartmouth. Graduate ndc. Various sea/shore appts, 1952–73; Staff of Dir Underwater Weapons, 1973–74; student ndc, 1974–75; CO HM Ships Argonaut and Mohawk, 1975–76; Fleet Anti-Submarine Warfare Officer, 1976–78; CO (Captain), HMS Broadsword, 1978–80; Asst Dir Naval Plans, MoD, 1980–83; Captain: 2nd Frigate Sqdn, HMS Broadsword, 1983–85; Sch. of Maritime Ops, HMS Dryad, 1985–86; Dir Gen., Naval Personal Services, MoD (Navy), 1986–89. *Recreations:* tennis, squash, hill walking, travel. *Address:* c/o National Westminster Bank, 208 Piccadilly, W1A 2DG. *Clubs:* Army and Navy, Anchorites.

NORMAN, Archibald Percy, MBE 1945; FRCP; MD; Hon. Medical Adviser, Tadworth Court Children's Hospital, since 1984 (Member of the Board of Trustees, since 1988); Physician, Hospital for Sick Children, 1950–77, now Hon. Physician; Paediatrician, Queen Charlotte's Maternity Hospital, 1951–77, now Hon. Paediatrician; *b* 19 July 1912; *s* of Dr George Percy Norman and Mary Margaret MacCallum; *m* 1950, Aleida Elisabeth M. M. R. Bisschop; five *s*. *Educ:* Charterhouse; Emmanuel Coll., Cambridge. Served War of 1939–45, in Army, 1940–45. Chairman: Med. and Res. Cttee, Cystic Fibrosis Res. Trust, 1976–84; E Surrey Cttee, Mencap Homes Foundn, 1987–; Tadworth Court Hosp. Trust, 1991–; Mem., Attendance Allowance Appeals Bd, 1978–84. *Publications:* (ed) Congenital Abnormalities, 1962, 2nd edn 1971; (ed) Moncreiff's Nursing and Diseases of Sick Children, 1966; (ed) Cystic Fibrosis, 1983; contributions to medical journals. *Address:* White Lodge, Heather Close, Kingswood, Surrey KT20 6NY. *T:* Mogador (0737) 832626.

NORMAN, Sir Arthur (Gordon), KBE 1969 (CBE 1966); DFC 1943; and Bar 1944; Chairman, The De La Rue Company, 1964–87; *b* N Petherton, Som, 18 Feb. 1917; *m* 1944, Margaret Doreen Harrington (*d* 1982); three *s* two *d*. *Educ:* Blundell's Sch. Joined Thomas De La Rue & Co., 1934. RAF 1939–45 (DFC and Bar); Wing-Comdr, 1943. Rejoined Thomas De La Rue & Co., 1946; Director, 1951; Managing Director, 1953–77. Vice-Chm., Sun Life Assurance Society, 1984–87 (Dir, 1966–87); Director: SKF (UK) Ltd, 1970–87; Kleinwort, Benson, Lonsdale plc, subseq. Kleinwort Benson Gp, 1985–88. Pres., CBI, 1968–70. Bd mem., Internat. Inst. for Environment and Develt, 1982–; Chairman: WWF UK, 1977–84, 1987–90. UK CEED, 1984–; Mem., Nature Conservancy Council, 1980–86. Trustee, King Mahendra Trust for Nature Conservation (Nepal). *Recreations:* tennis, golf, country life. *Address:* Fir Tree Cottage, Hammoon, Sturminster Newton, Dorset DT10 2DB. *Club:* East India.

NORMAN, Barry (Leslie); author, journalist and broadcaster; *b* 21 Aug. 1933; *s* of Leslie and Elizabeth Norman; *m* 1957, Diana, *o d* of late A. H. and C. A. Narracott; two *d*. *Educ:* Highgate Sch. Entertainments Editor, Daily Mail, 1969–71, then made redundant; Writer and Presenter of Film, 1973–81, and Film 1983–88, BBC1; Presenter of: Today, Radio 4, 1974–76; Going Places, Radio 4, 1977–81; Breakaway, Radio 4, 1979–80; Omnibus, BBC1, 1982; The Chip Shop, Radio 4, 1984; How Far Can You Go?, Radio 4, 1990; Writer and Presenter of: The Hollywood Greats, BBC1, 1977–79, 1984, 1985; The British Greats, 1980; Tallking Pictures (series), BBC1, 1988. Weekly columnist, The Guardian, 1971–80. Richard Dimbleby Award, BAFTA, 1981. *Publications:* The Matter of Mandrake, 1967; The Hounds of Sparta, 1968; Tales of the Redundance Kid, 1975; End Product, 1975; A Series of Defeats, 1977; To Nick a Good Body, 1978; The Hollywood Greats, 1979; The Movie Greats, 1981; Have a Nice Day, 1981; Sticky Wicket, 1984; The Film Greats, 1985; Talking Pictures, 1988. *Recreation:* playing village cricket. *Address:* c/o Curtis Brown Ltd, 162–168 Regent Street, W1.

NORMAN, Desmond; *see* Norman, N. D.

NORMAN, Rev. Dr Edward Robert; Dean of Chapel, Christ Church College, Canterbury, since 1988; *b* 22 Nov. 1938; *o s* of Ernest Edward Norman and Yvonne Louise Norman. *Educ:* Chatham House Sch.; Monoux Sch.; Selwyn Coll., Cambridge (MA, PhD, DD). FRHistS. Lincoln Theological Coll., 1965. Deacon, 1965; Priest, 1971. Asst Master, Beaconsfield Sec. Mod. Sch., Walthamstow, 1957–58; Fellow of Selwyn Coll., Cambridge, 1962–64; Fellow of Jesus Coll., Cambridge, 1964–71; Lectr in History, Univ. of Cambridge, 1965–88; Dean of Peterhouse, Cambridge, 1971–88. Wilkinson Prof. of Church History, Wycliffe Coll., Univ. of Toronto, 1981–82; Associated Schol., Ethics and Public Policy Center, Washington, 1986–. NATO Res. Fellow, 1966–68. Asst Chaplain, Addenbrooke's Hosp., Cambridge, 1971–78. Reith Lectr, 1978; Prideaux Lectr, 1980; Suntory-Toyota Lectr, LSE, 1984. Six Preacher in Canterbury Cathedral, 1984–90. *Publications:* The Catholic Church and Ireland, 1965; The Conscience of the State in North America, 1968; Anti-Catholicism in Victorian England, 1968; The Early Development of Irish Society, 1969; A History of Modern Ireland, 1971; Church and Society in Modern England, 1976; Christianity and the World Order, 1979; Christianity in the Southern Hemisphere, 1981; The English Catholic Church in the Nineteenth Century, 1983; Roman Catholicism in England, 1985; The Victorian Christian Socialists, 1987; The House of God: church architecture, style and history, 1990. *Recreation:* watching television. *Address:* Christ Church College, Canterbury, Kent CT1 1QU. *Club:* Athenæum.

NORMAN, Vice-Adm. Sir Geoffrey; *see* Norman, Vice-Adm. Sir H. G.

NORMAN, Geoffrey; JP; Deputy Secretary of Commissions (Training), Lord Chancellor's Department, since 1990; *b* 25 March 1935; *s* of late William Frederick Trafalgar Norman and of Vera May Norman (*née* Goodfellow); *m* 1958, Dorothy Frances King (*d* 1978); two *s* two *d*. *Educ:* Harrow County Sch.; Brasenose Coll., Oxford (MA). Admitted

Solicitor, 1959. Deputy Clerk to the Justices, Uxbridge, 1961–66; Clerk to the Justices, N Hertfordshire and Stevenage, 1966–77; Sec., Magistrates' Assoc., 1977–86; Asst Sec. of Commns (Trng), Lord Chancellor's Dept, 1986–90. Member: Duty Solicitor Scheme-making Cttee, 1984–86; Magisterial Cttee, Judicial Studies Bd, 1986–; Magistrates' Courts Rules Cttee, 1989–. JP Inner London, 1982. Freeman, City of London, 1981; Liveryman, Curriers' Co., 1983. *Publication:* The Magistrate as Chairman (with Lady Ralphs), 1987. *Address:* Easter Cottage, Gosmore, Hitchin, Herts SG4 7QH. *T:* Hitchin (0462) 450783.

NORMAN, George Alfred B.; *see* Bathurst Norman.

NORMAN, Vice-Admiral Sir (Horace) Geoffrey, KCVO 1963; CB 1949; CBE 1943; *b* 25 May 1896; *m* 1924, Noreen Frances, *o d* of late Brig.-General S. Geoghegan; one *s* one *d*. *Educ:* Trent Coll.; RN Coll., Keyham. HMS Queen Elizabeth and destroyers, 1914–18; Long Gunnery Course, 1921; passed RN Staff Coll., 1929; Commander, 1932; Captain, 1938; idc 1939; Rear-Admiral, 1947; Chief of Staff to C-in-C, Mediterranean Station, 1948–50; Admiralty, 1950; Vice-Admiral (retired), 1951. Sec., Nat. Playing Fields Assoc., 1953–63. *Recreations:* fishing and outdoor sports. *Address:* Chantry Cottage, Wickham, Hants PO17 6JA. *T:* Wickham (0329) 832248.

NORMAN, Jessye; soprano, concert and opera singer; *b* Augusta, Ga, USA, 15 Sept. 1945; *d* of late Silas Norman Sr and Janie King Norman. *Educ:* Howard Univ., Washington, DC (BM *cum laude*). Peabody Conservatory, 1967; Univ. of Michigan, 1967–68 (MMus). Operatic début, Deutsche Oper, Berlin, 1969; La Scala, Milan, 1972; Royal Opera House, Covent Garden, 1972; NY Metropolitan Opera, 1983; American début, Hollywood Bowl, 1972; Lincoln Centre, NYC, 1973. Tours include North and South America, Europe, Middle East, Australia, Israel, Japan. Many international festivals, including Aix-en-Provence, Aldeburgh, Berlin, Edinburgh, Flanders, Helsinki, Lucerne, Salzburg, Tanglewood, Spoleto, Hollywood, Ravinia. Hon. Fellow: Newnham Coll., Cambridge, 1989; Jesus Coll., Cambridge, 1989. Hon. DMus: Howard Univ., 1982; Univ. of the South, Sewanee, 1984; Boston Conservatory, 1984; Univ. of Michigan and Brandeis Univ., Mass, 1987; Harvard Univ., 1988; Cambridge, 1989; Hon DHL Amer. Univ. of Paris, 1989. Hon. RAM 1987. Musician of the Year, Musical America, 1982; prizes include: Grand Prix du Disque (Acad. du Disque Français), 1973, 1976, 1977, 1982, 1984; Grand Prix du Disque (Acad. Charles Cros), 1983; Deutscher Schallplattenpreis, 1975, 1981; Cigale d'Or, Aix-en-Provence Fest., 1977; IRCAM record award, 1982; Grammy, 1984, 1988. Commandeur de l'Ordre des Arts et des Lettres, France, 1984. *Address:* c/o Shaw Concerts Incorporated, 1900 Broadway, New York, NY 10023, USA.

NORMAN, Prof. Kenneth Roy, FBA 1985; Professor of Indian Studies, University of Cambridge, since 1990; *b* 21 July 1925; *s* of Clement and Peggy Norman; *m* 1953, Pamela Raymont; one *s* one *d*. *Educ:* Taunton School; Downing College, Cambridge (MA 1954). Fellow and Tutor, Downing College, Cambridge, 1952–64; Lectr in Indian Studies (Prakrit), 1955–78, Reader, 1978–90, Univ. of Cambridge. Foreign Mem., Royal Danish Acad. of Sciences and Letters, 1983. *Publications:* Elders' Verses I (Theragāthā), 1969; Elders' Verses II (Therīgāthā), 1971; (trans.) Jain Cosmology, 1981; Pāli Literature, 1983; The Group of Discourses (Sutta-nipāta), 1984; (ed) Pāli Tipiṭakaṁ Concordance, Vol. II 4–9, 1963–73; (ed) Critical Pāli Dictionary Vol. II 11–17, 1981–90. *Recreations:* reading, walking. *Address:* Faculty of Oriental Studies, Sidgwick Avenue, Cambridge CB3 9DA. *T:* Cambridge (0223) 335133.

NORMAN, Air Cdre Sir Mark (Annesley), 3rd Bt, *cr* 1915; DL; farmer; *b* 8 Feb. 1927; *s* of Sir Nigel Norman, 2nd Bt, CBE, and Patricia Moyra (*d* 1986) (who *m* 2nd, 1944, Sir Robert Perkins), *e d* of late Colonel J. H. A. Annesley, CMG, DSO; *S* father, 1943; *m* Joanna Camilla, *d* of late Lt-Col I. J. Kilgour; two *s* one *d*. *Educ:* Winchester Coll.; RMC. Coldstream Guards, 1945–47; Flying Officer, 601 (County of London) Sqdn, RAuxAF, 1953–56. Hon. Air Cdre, No 4624 (County of Oxford) Movements Sqdn, RAuxAF; Air Cdre RAuxAF, 1984. Chm., Anglo-US Cttee, RAF Upper Heyford, 1984–. Director: Gotaas-Larsen Shipping Corp., 1979–88; Supermarine Motor Yacht Co., 1989–90. Chm., IU Europe Ltd, 1973–87. Mem., Council, St Luke's, Oxford, 1985– (Chm., 1986–88). Patron and Churchwarden, St Peter's, Wilcote, 1972–. High Sheriff, 1983–84, DL 1985, Oxon. *Recreations:* gardening, workshop, the building of minor follies, offshore cruising. *Heir:* *s* Nigel James Norman, late Major 13/18th Royal Hussars (Queen Mary's Own), *b* 5 Feb. 1956. *Address:* Wilcote Manor, Charlbury, Oxon OX7 3EB. *T:* Ramsden (0993868) 357. *Clubs:* White's, Pratt's, Royal Air Force, MCC; St Moritz Tobogganing; Royal Southern Yacht.

See also N. D. Norman, W. R. Norman.

NORMAN, Mark Richard, CBE 1977 (OBE 1945); Managing Director of Lazard Brothers & Co. Ltd, 1960–75; Chairman, Gallaher Ltd, 1963–75; Director of other public companies, 1947–75; Deputy Chairman, National Trust, 1977–80 (Chairman, Finance Committee, 1969–80); *b* 3 April 1910; *s* of late Ronald C. Norman; *m* 1933, Helen, *d* of late Thomas Pinckney Bryan, Richmond, Virginia; two *s* three *d*. *Educ:* Eton; Magdalen Coll., Oxford. With Gallaher Ltd, 1930–32; Lazard Brothers & Co. Ltd, 1932–39. Served War of 1939–45: Hertfordshire Yeomanry; wounded Greece, 1941; an Asst Military Secretary, War Cabinet Offices, 1942–45 (Lieut-Colonel). Partner Edward de Stein & Co., 1946–60. *Address:* Garden House, Moor Place, Much Hadham, Herts SG10 6AA. *T:* Much Hadham (027984) 2703. *Club:* Brooks's.

NORMAN, (Nigel) Desmond, CBE 1970; CEng; FRAeS; Chairman and Managing Director, AeroNorTec Ltd, 1988; *b* 13 Aug. 1929; 2nd *s* of Sir Nigel Norman, 2nd Bt (*d* 1943), CBE, and Patricia Moyra (*d* 1987) (who *m* 2nd, 1944, Sir Robert Perkins); *m* 1st, Anne Fogg-Elliott; two *s*; 2nd, 1965, Mrs. Boel Elizabeth Holmsen; two *s* two *d*. *Educ:* Eton; De Havilland Aeronautical Technical Sch. (1946–49). RAF GD Pilot, thereafter 601 Sqdn, RAuxAF Fighter Sqdn, until disbandment, 1948–57. Export Asst at SBAC, 1951–53; Founder of Britten-Norman Ltd with F. R. J. Britten, 1954, Jt Man. Dir, 1954–71; Dep. Chm. and Man. Dir, NDN Aircraft, IoW, subseq. Norman Aeroplane Co., 1979. *Recreations:* aviation, sailing, shooting. *Address:* Wistaria House, 105 High Street, Bembridge, Isle of Wight PO35 5SF. *Clubs:* Royal Air Force, Royal Yacht Squadron.

See also Sir Mark Norman, Bt, W. R. Norman.

NORMAN, Sir Richard (Oswald Chandler), KBE 1987; DSc; FRS 1977; CChem, FRSC; Rector, Exeter College, University of Oxford, since 1987; Chief Scientific Adviser, Department of Energy, since 1988; *b* 27 April 1932; *s* of Oswald George Norman and Violet Maud Chandler; *m* 1982, Jennifer Margaret Tope. *Educ:* St Paul's Sch.; Balliol Coll., Oxford (MA, DSc; Hon. Fellow, 1989). CChem; FRIC 1963. Jun. Res. Fellow, Merton Coll., Oxford, 1956–58, Fellow and Tutor, 1958–65; Univ. Lectr in Chemistry, Oxford, 1958–65; Prof. of Chemistry, Univ. of York, 1965–87; seconded as Chief Scientific Advr, MoD, 1983–88. Mem., SERC, 1983–88. President: RIC, 1978–80; RSC, 1984–86; Dir, Salters' Inst. of Indust. Chemistry, 1975–. Tilden Lectr, Chemical Soc., 1976. Hon. Fellow, Merton Coll., Oxford, 1988. Meldola Medal, RIC, 1961; Corday-Morgan Medal, Chemical Soc., 1967. Encomienda, Orden del Mérito Civil (Spain), 1990. *Publications:* Principles of Organic Synthesis, 1968; (with D. J. Waddington) Modern Organic Chemistry, 1972; papers in Jl Chem. Soc. *Recreations:* cricket, music, gardening. *Address:* The Rector's Lodgings, Exeter College, Oxford OX1 3DP. *T:* Oxford (0865) 279644. *Club:* United Oxford & Cambridge University.

NORMAN, Sir Robert (Henry), Kt 1989; OBE 1957; Chairman, Cairns Campus Co-ordinating Committee, James Cook University of North Queensland, since 1987; *b* 30 Jan. 1914; *s* of Robert Moreton Norman and Dora Muriel Hoole; *m* 1942, Betty Merle Kimmins; one *s* three *d*. *Educ:* Christian Brothers' Coll. Joined RAAF, 1941; commnd, 1942; 459 Sqdn, 1943; discharged, 1945. Founded Bush Pilot Airways, 1952, retd 1984. Cairns Centenary Co-ordinator, 1976. Past Pres., Rotary Club of Cairns, Marlin Coast; Dist Gov., D9550, Rotary Internat., 1991–92. *Publication:* Bush Pilot, 1976. *Recreations:* motoring, reading. *Address:* 12 Gloucester Street, Whitfield, Qld 4870, Australia; PO Box 133, Edge Hill, Qld 4871, Australia.

NORMAN, Sir Robert (Wentworth), Kt 1970; JP; *b* 10 April 1912; *s* of William Henry Norman and Minnie Esther Brown; *m* 1942, Grace Hebden, *d* of Sidney Percy Hebden; one *s* one *d*. *Educ:* Sydney Grammar Sch. Served Army 1940–46: Captain, AIF. Joined Bank of New South Wales, 1928; Manager, Head Office, 1961; Dep. Gen. Manager, 1962; Chief Gen. Manager, 1964–77; Dir, 1977–84. Councillor: Science Foundn for Physics within Univ. of Sydney; Inst. of Public Affairs; Senator and Life Mem., Junior Chamber Internat. FAIM. JP NSW, 1956. 3rd Order of the Rising Sun (Japan), 1983. *Recreations:* bowls, reading. *Address:* 26/16 Rosemont Avenue, Woollahra, NSW 2025, Australia. *T:* 3631900. *Clubs:* Union, Royal Sydney Golf, Australian Jockey (Sydney).

NORMAN, Vesey; *see* Norman, A. V. B.

NORMAN, Willoughby Rollo; Hon. President, The Boots Co. Ltd, since 1972 (Chairman, 1961–72); Deputy Chairman, English China Clays Ltd; 2nd *s* of Major Rt Hon. Sir Henry Norman, 1st Bt; *m* 1st, 1934, Hon. Barbara Jacqueline Boot, *er d* of 2nd and last Baron Trent, KBE; one *s* two *d*; 2nd, 1973, Caroline Haskard, *d* of William Greville and Lady Diana Worthington. *Educ:* Eton; Magdalen Coll., Oxford. Served War of 1939–45, Major, Grenadier Guards. Director: National Westminster Bank (Chm. Eastern Region), 1963–79; Sheepbridge Engineering Ltd, 1979; Guardian Royal Exchange Assurance, 1961–79. Vice-Chairman Boots Pure Drug Co. Ltd, 1954–61. High Sheriff of Leicestershire, 1960. *Recreations:* shooting, farming, gardening. *Address:* The Grange, South Harting, Petersfield, Hants GU31 5NR; 28 Ranelagh House, Elystan Place, SW3. *T:* 071–584 9410. *Clubs:* White's, Pratt's.

See also Sir Mark Norman, Bt, N. D. Norman.

NORMANBY, 4th Marquis of, *cr* 1838; **Oswald Constantine John Phipps,** KG 1985; CBE 1974 (MBE (mil.) 1943); Baron Mulgrave (Ireland), 1767; Baron Mulgrave (Great Britain), 1794; Earl of Mulgrave and Viscount Normanby, 1812; Lord-Lieutenant of North Yorkshire, 1974–87 (of North Riding of Yorkshire, 1965–74); *b* 29 July 1912; *o s* of Rev. the 3rd Marquess and Gertrude Stansfeld, OBE, DGStJ (*d* 1948), *d* of Johnston J. Foster of Moor Park, Ludlow; *S* father, 1932; *m* 1951, Hon. Grania Maeve Rosaura Guinness, *d* of 1st Baron Moyne; two *s* five *d*. *Educ:* Eton; Christ Church, Oxford. Served War of 1939–45, The Green Howards (wounded, prisoner, repatriated). PPS to Sec. of State for Dominion Affairs, 1944–45, to Lord President of the Council, 1945; a Lord-in-Waiting to the King, 1945. High Steward of York Minster, 1980–88. Mem., Council of St John for N Yorks (formerly NR of Yorks), 1948–87 (Chm., 1948–77; Pres., 1977–87); Chairman: KCH, 1948–74; Nat. Art-Collections Fund, 1981–86; Pres., Nat. Library for the Blind, 1977–88; Vice-President: St Dunstans, 1980– (Mem. Council, 1944–80); RNLI, 1984– (Mem. Cttee of Management, 1972–84). N Riding CC, 1937–46. Hon. Col Comdt, The Green Howards, 1970–82; Dep. Hon. Col, 2nd Bn Yorks Volunteers, 1971–72; President: TA&VRA for N of England, 1971–74 (Vice-Pres., 1968–71); TA&VRA N Yorks and Humberside, 1980–83. KStJ. Fellow, KCH Med. Sch., 1982. Hon. DCL: Durham Univ, 1963; York Univ., 1985. *Heir:* *s* Earl of Mulgrave, *qv*. *Address:* Lythe Hall, near Whitby, N Yorks YO21 3RL; Argyll House, 211 King's Road, SW3. *T:* 071–352 5154. *Club:* Yorkshire (York).

NORMANTON, 6th Earl of, *cr* 1806; **Shaun James Christian Welbore Ellis Agar;** Baron Mendip, 1794; Baron Somerton, 1795; Viscount Somerton, 1800; Baron Somerton (UK), 1873; Royal Horse Guards, 1965; Blues and Royals, 1969; left Army, 1972, Captain; *b* 21 Aug. 1945; *er s* of 5th Earl of Normanton; *S* father, 1967; *m* 1970, Victoria Susan, *o d* of J. H. C. Beard, Turmer House, Somerley, Ringwood, Hants; one *s* two *d*. *Educ:* Eton. *Recreations:* shooting, skiing, motor boating. *Heir:* *s* Viscount Somerton, *qv*. *Address:* Somerley, Ringwood, Hants BH24 3PL. *T:* Ringwood (0425) 473253. *Clubs:* White's; Royal Yacht Squadron.

NORMANTON, Sir Tom, Kt 1987; TD; BA (Com); past chairman of a group of companies; *b* 12 March 1917; *m* 1942, Annabel Bettine (*née* Yates); two *s* one *d*. *Educ:* Manchester Grammar Sch.; Manchester Univ. (BA (Com); Chm., Cons. Assoc., 1937–38; Vice-Pres. Students' Union, 1938). Joined family group of textile cos, 1938. Served War of 1939–45: Army (commnd TA 1937) Europe and N Africa; GS appts, GHQ BEF, HQ First and Eighth Armies; HQ 21 Army Gp (wounded, Calais, 1940; despatches, 1944); demob., rank Major, 1946. Chm., Rochdale YC, 1948; Mem. Rochdale CB Council, 1950–53; contested (C) Rochdale, 1959 and 1964. MP (C) Cheadle, 1970–87. Hon. Sec., Cons. Backbencher Industry Cttee, 1972–74; Mem., Expenditure Cttee, 1972–73; opposition front bench spokesman on energy, 1975–79. Contested (C) Cheshire E, European parly elecn, 1989. MEP (C) 1973–89 (elected for Cheshire E, 1979); Member: Cttee on Energy and Research, 1973–79 (Vice-Chm., 1976–79 and (as elected Member), 1979–89); Cttee on Economic and Monetary Affairs, 1973–79; Budgets Cttee, 1986–89; Pol Affairs Cttee, 1986–89; Jt Africa, Caribbean, Pacific States Standing Conf., 1975–79; spokesman on Competition Policy, 1975; Deleg. to US Congress, 1975–78; Mem., delegn to Turkey, 1987–89; Mem. European Cons. Gp, resp. Indust. Policy; special interests energy and defence; Chm., European All-Party Gp Friends with Israel, 1979–89; Vice-Pres., Pan European Union eV, 1980– (Hon. Treas., 1989–). Mem. Supervisory Bd, European Inst. for Security. Manager, Lancashire Fusiliers Compassionate Fund, 1964–; Trustee, Cotton Industry War Memorial Fund, 1965; apptd Employer panel, NBPI, 1966–68; Member: Council, British Employers Confedn, 1959–64; Council, CBI, 1964–86 (Mem. Europe Cttee, 1964–86, and 1989–, and Econ. Policy Cttee, 1964–70); Stockport Chamber of Commerce, 1970–87; Central Training Council, 1968–74; Exec., UK Automation Council, 1966–73 (Vice-Chm., 1970–73); Cotton and Allied Textiles Ind. Trng Bd, 1966–70; Exec. Council, British Textile Confederation, 1972–76; Mem. Cttee, 1955–, Vice-Chm., 1969–71, Manchester Br. of Inst. of Dirs; Chm., European Textile Industries Cttee; President: British Textile Employers Assoc., 1970–71; Internat. Fedn of Cotton & Allied Textiles Industries, 1970– (Vice-Pres., 1972–76, Pres., 1976–78). Director: Industrial Training Services Ltd, 1972–; N Reg. Bd, Commercial Union Assurance Ltd, 1974–86; Manchester Chamber of Commerce, 1970–89. Consultant, Midland Bank Gp, EEC, Brussels, 1979–91. Mem. Cttee, Anglo-Austrian Soc.; Patron, Assoc. for Free Russia. Pres., New Forest Br., Normandy Veterans Assoc., 1990–; Chm., British Sect., Confedn of European Ex-servicemen, 1986–90. Speaks French and German. AMBIM. *Recreations:* sailing, walking, gardening. *Address:* Nelson House, Nelson Place,

Lymington, Hants SO41 9RT. *T:* Lymington (0590) 675095. *Clubs:* Beefsteak; St James's (Manchester); Royal Yacht Squadron.

NORMINGTON, David John; Head of Strategy and Employment Policy Division, Department of Employment, since 1990; *b* 18 Oct. 1951; *s* of Ronald Normington and Kathleen Normington (*née* Towler); *m* 1985, Winifred Anne Charlotte Harris. *Educ:* Bradford Grammar Sch.; Corpus Christi College, Oxford (BA Hons Mod. Hist.) Department of Employment: joined 1973; Private Sec. to Perm. Sec., 1976–77; Principal Private Sec. to Sec. of State for Employment, 1984–85; Employment Service Regional Dir for London and SE Region, 1987–89. *Recreations:* gardening, ballet, theatre, cricket. *Address:* Department of Employment, Caxton House, Tothill Street, SW1H 9NF. *T:* 071–273 5766.

NORREYS, Lord; Henry Mark Willoughby Bertie; *b* 6 June 1958; *s* and *heir* of the Earl of Lindsey (14th) and Abingdon (9th), *qv*; *m* 1989, Lucinca, *d* of Christopher Moorsom. *Educ:* Eton; Univ. of Edinburgh. *Address:* Gilmilnscroft, Sorn, Mauchline, Ayrshire KA5 6ND. *Club:* Puffin's (Edinburgh).

NORRIE, family name of **Baron Norrie.**

NORRIE, 2nd Baron, *cr* 1957; **George Willoughby Moke Norrie;** Director: Conservation Practice Ltd, since 1989; Hilliers (Fairfield) Ltd, since 1989; *b* 27 April 1936; *s* of 1st Baron Norrie, GCMG, GCVO, CB, DSO, MC, and Jocelyn Helen (*d* 1938), *d* of late R. H. Gosling; *S* father, 1977; *m* 1964, Celia Marguerite, JP, *d* of John Pelham Mann, MC; one *s* two *d.* *Educ:* Eton College; RMA Sandhurst. Commissioned 11th Hussars (PAO), 1956; ADC to C-in-C Middle East Comd, 1960–61; GSO 3 (Int.) 4th Guards Brigade, 1967–69; retired, 1970. Director: Fairfield Nurseries (Hermitage) Ltd, 1976–89; International Garden Centre (British Gp) Ltd, 1984–86. Mem., H of L EC Cttee, Sub Cttee F (Environment), 1988–. President: British Trust for Conservation Volunteers, 1987–; Royal British Legion (Newbury Branch), 1972–. Mem., Tree Council, 1991. *Recreations:* skiing, tennis. *Heir:* *s* Hon. Mark Willoughby John Norrie, *b* 31 March 1972. *Address:* Eastgate House, Hamstead Marshall, Newbury, Berks RG15 0JD. *T:* Kintbury (0488) 57026. *Clubs:* Cavalry and Guards, MCC.

NORRIE, Marian Farrow, (Mrs W. G. Walker); Her Honour Judge Norrie; a Circuit Judge, since 1986; *b* 25 April 1940; *d* of Arthur and Edith Jackson; *m* 1st, 1964; two *d*; 2nd, 1983, William Guy Walker; one step *s* two step *d.* *Educ:* Manchester High Sch. for Girls; Nottingham Univ. (LLB). Admitted Solicitor of Supreme Court, 1965; a Recorder, 1979–86. Consultant, Norrie, Bowler & Wrigley, Solicitors, Sheffield, 1983–86 (Sen. Partner, 1968–83). Member: Parole Bd, 1983–85; Appts Commn, Press Council, 1985–. *Address:* Croydon Crown Court, Barclay Road, Croydon CR9 3NE.

NORRINGTON, Humphrey Thomas; Deputy Group Managing Director, Barclays Bank, since 1991; *b* 8 May 1936; *s* of Sir Arthur Norrington and Edith Joyce, *d* of William Moberly Carver; *m* 1963, Frances Guenn Bateson; two *s* two *d.* *Educ:* Dragon School, Oxford; Winchester; Worcester College, Oxford (MA). Barclays Bank: joined, 1960; general management, 1978–87; Dir, 1985–; Exec Dir, Overseas Ops, 1987–91. Chm., Exec. Cttee, British Bankers' Assoc., 1990–91. Chairman: Springhead Trust, 1983–88; Southwark Cathedral Develt Trust, 1986–; Dir, City Arts Trust, 1988–; Mem., Archbishops' Commn on Rural Areas, 1988–90. *Recreations:* music, countryside. *Address:* Hill House, Frithsden Copse, Berkhamsted, Herts HP4 2RQ. *T:* Berkhamsted (0442) 871855. *Club:* United Oxford & Cambridge University.

See also R. A. C. Norrington.

NORRINGTON, Roger Arthur Carver, CBE 1990 (OBE 1980); Musical Director, London Classical Players, since 1978; Music Director, Orchestra of St Luke's, New York, since 1990; Musical Director, Schütz Choir of London, since 1962; Co-Director: Early Opera Project, since 1984; Historic Arts, since 1986; *b* 16 March 1934; *s* of late Sir Arthur Norrington and Edith Joyce, *d* of William Moberly Carver; *m* 1st, 1964, Susan Elizabeth McLean May (marr. diss. 1982); one *s* one *d*; 2nd, 1986, Karalyn Mary Lawrence. *Educ:* Dragon Sch., Oxford; Westminster; Clare Coll., Cambridge (BA; Hon. Fellow, 1990); Royal Coll. of Music. Freelance singer, 1962–72. Principal Conductor: Kent Opera, 1966–84; Bournemouth Sinfonietta, 1985–89. Guest conducts many British, European and American orchestras, appears at Covent Garden, Coliseum, Proms and festivals; broadcasts regularly at home and abroad. Debuts: British, 1962; BBC Radio, 1964; TV 1967; Germany, Austria, Denmark, Finland, 1966; Portugal, 1970; Italy, 1971; France and Belgium, 1972; USA, 1974; Holland, 1975; Switzerland, 1976. Many gramophone recordings. Hon. RAM 1988. Cavaliere, Order al Merito della Repubblica Italiana, 1981. *Publications:* occasional articles in various musical journals. *Recreations:* gardening, reading, walking.

See also H. T. Norrington.

NORRIS, Air Chief Marshal Sir Christopher Neil F.; *see* Foxley-Norris.

NORRIS, Rt. Rev. Mgr David Joseph; Protonotary Apostolic to the Pope; Vicar General of Westminster Diocese, since 1972; General Secretary to RC Bishops' Conference of England and Wales, 1967–83; *b* 17 Aug. 1922; *s* of David William and Anne Norris. *Educ:* Salesian Coll., Battersea; St Edmund's Coll., Ware; Christ's Coll., Cambridge (MA). Priest, 1947; teaching at St Edmund's Coll., Ware, 1948–53; Cambridge, 1953–56; Private Secretary to Cardinal Godfrey, 1956–64; National Chaplain to Catholic Overseas Students, 1964–65; Private Secretary to Cardinal Heenan, 1965–72. *Recreations:* reading, music, sport. *Address:* Cathedral Clergy House, 42 Francis Street, SW1P 1QW. *T:* 071–834 7452.

NORRIS, Sir Eric (George), KCMG 1969 (CMG 1963); HM Diplomatic Service, retired; Director: Inchcape & Co., 1977–88 (Deputy Chairman, 1981–86); London Sumatra Plantations Ltd, 1978–88; Gray Mackenzie Ltd, 1978–88; *b* 14 March 1918; *s* of late H. F. Norris, Bengeo, Hertford; *m* 1941, Pamela Crane; three *d.* *Educ:* Hertford Grammar Sch.; St Catharine's Coll., Cambridge. Served Royal Corps of Signals, 1940–46 (Major). Entered Dominions Office, 1946. Served in British Embassy, Dublin, 1948–50; UK High Commission in Pakistan, 1952–55; UK High Commission in Delhi, 1956–57; Dep. High Commissioner for the UK, Bombay, 1957–60; IDC 1961; British Dep. High Comr, Calcutta, 1962–65; Commonwealth Office, 1966–68; High Comr, Kenya, 1968–72; Dep. Under Sec. of State, FCO, 1972–73; High Comr, Malaysia, 1974–77. Chm., Royal Commonwealth Soc., 1980–84. PMN (Malaysia), 1974. *Address:* Homestead, Great Amwell, Herts SG12 9SN. *T:* Ware (0920) 870739. *Clubs:* East India, Commonwealth Trust.

NORRIS, Gilbert Frank; Chief Road Engineer, Scottish Development Department, 1969–76; *b* 29 May 1916; *s* of Ernest Frank Norris and Ada Norris; *m* 1941, Joan Margaret Catherine Thompson; one *s.* *Educ:* Bemrose Sch., Derby; UC Nottingham. FICE. Served with Notts, Bucks and Lindsey County Councils, 1934–39; Royal Engineers, 1939–46; Min. of Transport: Highways Engr in Nottingham, Edinburgh and Leeds, 1946–63; Asst Chief Engr, 1963–67; Dep. Chief Engr, 1967; Dir, NE Road Construction Unit, 1967–69. *Recreations:* motoring, photography. *Address:* Woodhead Lee, Lamlash, Isle of Arran KA27 8JU. *T:* Lamlash (07706) 323.

NORRIS, Col Graham Alexander, OBE (mil.) 1945; JP; Vice Lord-Lieutenant of County of Greater Manchester, 1975–87; *b* 14 April 1913; *er s* of late John O. H. Norris and Beatrice H. Norris (*née* Vlies), Manchester; *m* 1st, 1938, Frances Cicely, *d* of late Walter Gorton, Minchinhampton, Glos; one *d*; 2nd, 1955, Muriel, *d* of late John Corris, Manchester. *Educ:* William Hulme's Grammar Sch.; Coll. of Technology, Manchester; Regent St Polytechnic, London; Merchant Venturers Techn. Coll., Bristol. CEng, FIMechE. Trng as automobile engr, Rolls Royce Ltd, Bristol Motor Co. Ltd; Joseph Cockshoot & Co. Ltd: Works Man., 1937, Works Dir 1946, Jt. Man. Dir 1964, Chm. and Man. Dir, 1968; Dir, Lex Garages Ltd, 1968–70; Dir, Red Garages (N Wales) Ltd, 1973–88. War service, RAOC and REME, UK, ME and Italy, 1940–46 (Lt-Col); Comdr REME 22 (W) Corps Tps (TA), 1947–51; Hon. Col, 1957–61. Mem., NEDC for Motor Vehicle Distrib. and Repair, 1966–74; Pres., Motor Agents Assoc., 1967–68; Vice-Pres., Inst. of Motor Industry, 1973–76; Mem., Industrial Tribunal Panel, 1976–82. Pres., Manchester and Dist Fedn of Boys' Clubs, 1968–74; Vice-Pres., NABC, 1972–; Chm. Council, UMIST, 1971–83; Member Court: Univ. of Manchester; UMIST. Master, Worshipful Co. of Coachmakers and Coach Harness Makers, 1961–62; Freeman, City of London, 1938. JP, Lancashire 1963; DL Co. Palatine of Lancaster, 1962. *Recreations:* walking, social service activities. *Address:* 5 Brook Court, Brook Road, Windermere, Cumbria LA23 2BP.

NORRIS, Herbert Walter; Regional Director, South East Region, National Westminster Bank Ltd, 1969–73; Deputy Chief General Manager, 1962–65, Director, 1965–68, Westminster Bank Ltd; *b* 9 Dec. 1904; *s* of Walter Norris, Farnworth, Widnes, Lancs; *m* 1935, Laura Phyllis Tardif (*d* 1986), *d* of A. Tardif, St Martin's, Guernsey; no *c.* *Educ:* Liverpool Collegiate School. Joined Westminster Bank, Liverpool Office, 1921; Joint General Manager, Westminster Bank Ltd, 1949. FCIB; Mem. Council, Inst. of Bankers, 1952–65, Dep. Chairman, 1959–61. Master of Coopers' Company, 1973–74. *Recreations:* reading, music. *Address:* c/o Ashurst Park Nursing Home, Fordcombe, Tunbridge Wells, Kent TN3 0RD.

NORRIS, John Hallam Mercer, CBE 1987; DL; Crown Estate Commissioner, since 1991; Board member, National Rivers Authority, since 1989; *b* 30 May 1929; *s* of late William Hallam Norris and Dorothy Edna Norris (*née* Mercer); *m* 1954, Maureen Joy Banyard; two *d.* *Educ:* Brentwood School. Partner, W. H. Norris & Sons. Chm., Essex River Authy, 1971–74; Member: Anglian Water Authy, 1974–85; Nat. Rivers Authy Adv. Cttee, 1988; Chairman: Essex Land Drainage Cttee, 1974–89; Crouch Harbour Authy, 1981–88. Pres., CLA, 1985–87 (Mem., Exec. Cttee, 1973–; Chm., 1983–85). ARAgS 1990. DL Essex, 1989. *Recreations:* fishing, sailing. *Address:* Mountnessing Hall, Brentwood, Essex CM13 1UN. *T:* Brentwood (0277) 352152. *Clubs:* Boodle's, Farmers'; Royal Burnham Yacht.

NORRIS, John Robert, CBE 1991; PhD, DSc; Director, Group Research, Cadbury Schweppes Ltd, 1979–90; *b* 4 March 1932; *s* of Albert Norris and Winifred May Perry; *m* 1956, Barbara Jean Pinder; two *s* one *d* (and one *s* decd). *Educ:* Depts of Bacteriology and Agriculture, Univ. of Leeds (BSc 1st Cl. Hons 1954, PhD 1957, DSc 1987). Lectr in Bacteriology, Univ. of Glasgow, 1957–63; Microbiologist, Shell Research Ltd, 1963–73 (Dir, Borden Microbiol Lab., 1970–73); Dir, Meat Res. Inst., ARC, 1973–79. Editor, Methods in Microbiology, 1969–. *Publications:* papers in microbiol jls. *Recreations:* walking, wood carving, Yoga. *Address:* 41 Bulmershe Road, Reading RG1 5RH. *T:* Reading (0734) 660672. *Club:* Farmers'.

NORRIS, Steven John; MP (C) Epping Forest, since Dec. 1988; *b* 24 May 1945; *s* of John Francis Birkett Norris and Eileen Winifred (*née* Walsh); *m* 1969, Peta Veronica (*née* Cecil-Gibson); two *s.* *Educ:* Liverpool Institute; Worcester College, Oxford. MA. Private company posts, 1967–82. Mem., Berks CC, 1977–85; Dep. Leader, Cons. Group, 1983–85. Mem., Berks AHA, 1979–82; Vice-Chm., W Berks District HA, 1982–85. Chm., Steve Norris Ltd, 1982–. Contested (C) Oxford E, 1987. MP (C) Oxford E, 1983–87. PPS to Hon. William Waldegrave, MP, Minister of State, DoE, 1985–87, to Rt Hon. Nicholas Ridley, Sec. of State for Trade and Industry, 1990, to Rt Hon. Kenneth Baker, Home Sec., 1991–. Mem., Select Cttee on Social Services, 1984–85. Chairman: Grant Maintained Schools Trust, 1988–89; Crime Concern Trust, 1988–; Alcohol and Drug Addiction Prevention and Treatment, 1990–. Freeman, City of London; Liveryman, Coach and Harness Makers' Co. *Recreations:* reading, not walking. *Address:* House of Commons, SW1A 0AA. *Clubs:* Brooks's, Carlton, United and Cecil.

NORRIS, Sydney George; Assistant Under Secretary of State, Principal Finance Officer, Home Office, since 1990; *b* 22 Aug. 1937; *s* of late George Samuel Norris, FCA and of Agnes Rosa Norris; *m* 1965, Brigid Molyneux FitzGibbon; two *s* one *d.* *Educ:* Liverpool Inst. High Sch. for Boys; University Coll., Oxford (MA); Trinity Hall and Inst. of Criminology, Cambridge (Dip. in Criminology); Univ. of California, Berkeley (MCrim). Intelligence Corps, 1956–58; Home Office, 1963–; Private Sec. to Parly Under Sec. of State, 1966; Harkness Fellow, 1968–70; Sec., Adv. Council on Penal System, 1970–73; Principal Private Sec. to Home Sec., 1973–74; Asst Sec., 1974; seconded to HM Treasury, 1979–81; Asst Under Sec. of State, 1982; seconded to NI Office as Principal Estabt and Finance Officer, 1982–85; Dir of Operational Policy, Prison Dept, 1985–88; Police Dept, 1988–90. *Recreations:* running, fell walking, gardening, piano. *Address:* Home Office, SW1H 9AT. *Club:* Thames Hare and Hounds.

NORTH, family name of **Earl of Guilford.**

NORTH, Lord; Piers Edward Brownlow North; *b* 9 March 1971; *s* and *heir* of Earl of Guilford, *qv.* *Address:* Waldershare Park, Dover, Kent CT15 5BA. *T:* Dover (0304) 820244.

NORTH, John Joseph; Senior Visiting Fellow, Department of Land Economy, University of Cambridge, since 1985; *b* 7 Nov. 1926; *s* of Frederick James North and Annie Elizabeth North (*née* Matthews); *m* 1958, Sheila Barbara Mercer; two *s.* *Educ:* Rendcomb College; Univ. of Reading (BSc, DipAgric); Univ. of California (MS). FIBiol 1972. Agricultural Adviser, Nat. Agricultural Advisory Service, 1951; Kellogg Fellowship, USA, 1954–55; Regional Agricultural Officer, Cambridge, 1972; Senior Agricultural Officer, 1976; Chief Agricl Officer, ADAS, MAFF, 1979. *Recreations:* golf, gardening. *Address:* 28 Hauxton Road, Little Shelford, Cambridge. *T:* Cambridge (0223) 843369.

NORTH, Sir Jonathan; *see* North, Sir W. J. F.

NORTH, Dr Peter Machin, CBE 1989; DCL; FBA 1990; Principal of Jesus College, Oxford, since 1984; Pro-Vice-Chancellor, University of Oxford, since 1988; *b* Nottingham, 30 Aug. 1936; *o s* of late Geoffrey Machin North and Freda Brunt (*née* Smith); *m* 1960, Stephanie Mary, *e d* of T. L. Chadwick; two *s* one *d.* *Educ:* Oakham Sch.; Keble Coll., Oxford (BA 1959, BCL 1960, MA 1963, DCL 1976). National Service, Royal Leics Regt, 2nd Lieut, 1955–56. Teaching Associate, Northwestern Univ. Sch. of Law, Chicago, 1960–61; Lecturer: University Coll. of Wales, Aberystwyth, 1961–63;

Univ. of Nottingham, 1963–65; Tutor in Law, 1965–76, Fellow, 1965–84, Hon. Fellow: Keble Coll., Oxford, 1984; UCNW, Bangor, 1988. Mem., Hebdomadal Council, 1985–. A Law Comr, 1976–84. Vis. Professor: Univ. of Auckland, 1969; Univ. of BC, 1975–76; Dir of Studies, Hague Acad. of Internat. Law, 1970 (general course in private internat. law, 1990); Lectures: Hague Acad. of Internat. Law, 1980; Horace Read Meml, Dalhousie Univ., 1980; Colston, Bristol Univ., 1984; Frances Moran Meml, TCD, 1984; Philip James, Leeds Univ., 1985; James Smart, 1988; MacDermott, QUB, 1991. Chairman: Road Traffic Law Review, 1985–88; Conciliation Project Adv. Cttee, 1985–88; Management Cttee, Oxford CAB, 1985–88; Appeal Cttee, Assoc. of Certified Accountants, 1990– (Mem., 1987–); Member: Lord Chancellor's Adv. Cttee on Legal Educn, 1973–75; Social Scis and the Law Cttee, ESRC (formerly SSRC), 1982–85; Govt and Law Cttee, ESRC, 1985–87; Council, British Inst. of Internat. and Comparative Law, 1986– (Chm., Private Internat. Law Section, Adv. Bd, 1986–); Council, Univ. of Reading, 1986–. Associate Mem., Inst. of Internat. Law, 1985. Hon. Bencher, Inner Temple, 1987. Mem., Editorial Cttee, British Yearbook of Internat. Law, 1983–; General Editor, Oxford Jl of Legal Studies, 1987–. *Publications:* (ed jtly) Chitty on Contracts, 23rd edn 1968 - 26th edn 1989; Occupiers' Liability, 1971; The Modern Law of Animals, 1972; Private International Law of Matrimonial Causes, 1977; Cheshire and North's Private International Law, 11th edn 1987; Contract Conflicts, 1982; (with J. H. C. Morris) Cases and Materials on Private International Law, 1984; articles and notes in legal jls. *Recreations:* children, gardening, cricket (both playing and sleeping through). *Address:* Jesus College, Oxford. *T:* Oxford (0865) 279701. *Club:* United Oxford & Cambridge University.

NORTH, Robert, (Robert North Dodson); dancer and choreographer; Ballet Director, Gothenburg Ballet, since 1991; *b* 1 June 1945; *s* of Charles Dodson and Elizabeth Thompson; *m* 1978, Janet Smith. *Educ:* Pierrepont Sch. (A levels in Maths, Physics and Art); Central Sch. of Art; Royal Ballet Sch. Dancer and choreographer, London Contemporary Dance Co., 1966–81; seasons with Martha Graham Dance Co., 1967 and 1968; Teacher of Modern Dance, Royal Ballet Sch., 1979–81; Artistic Dir, Ballet Rambert, 1981–86; Ballet Dir, Teatro Regio, Turin, 1990–91. Has choreographed about 50 ballets, including: Troy Game; Death and the Maiden; The Annunciation; Running Figures; Pribaoutki; Colour Moves; Entre dos Aguas; choreography for other cos, including: Royal Ballet; Dance Theatre of Harlem; Royal Danish Ballet; San Francisco Ballet; Oakland Ballet; Helsinki Ballet; Batsheva; Janet Smith and Dancers; also choreography for films, television, theatre and musicals (incl. For My Daughter).

NORTH, Sir Thomas (Lindsay), Kt 1982; FAIM, FRMIA; Chairman, G. J. Coles & Coy Limited, Melbourne, Australia, 1979–83, Hon. Chairman, 1983–84; *b* 11 Dec. 1919; *s* of John North and Jane (*née* Irwin); *m* 1944, Kathleen Jefferis; two *d*. *Educ:* Rutherglen, Vic. FAIM 1972. Joined G. J. Coles & Co. Ltd, 1938; Gen. Man., 1966; Dep. Man. Dir, 1969; Man. Dir, 1975–79; Dir, various G. J. Coles subsid. cos. Dep. Chm., KMart (Australia) Ltd, 1975–; Chairman: Island Cooler Pty Ltd, 1985–; Smurfit Australia Pty Ltd. 1986–. *Recreations:* horse racing, swimming. *Address:* 31 Power Street, Toorak, Vic 3142, Australia. *T:* 03.8223161. *Clubs:* Athenæum, Royal Automobile Club of Victoria (Melbourne); Australian, Australian Armoured Corps (Sydney); Victorian Amateur Turf (Dep. Chm.), Victorian Racing Club, Moonee Valley Race; Melbourne Cricket, Sydney Cricket.

NORTH, Sir (William) Jonathan (Frederick), 2nd Bt, *cr* 1920; *b* 6 Feb. 1931; *s* of Muriel Norton (*d* 1989) (2nd *d* of 1st Bt) and Hon. John Montagu William North (*d* 1987) (who *m* 2nd, 1939, Marion Dyer Chase, Boston, Mass; she *d* 1986); *g s* of Sir William Hicking, 1st Bt; *S* grandfather, 1947 (under special remainder); *m* 1956, Sara Virginia, *d* of Air Chief Marshal Sir Donald Hardman, GBE, KCB, DFC; one *s* two *d*. *Educ:* Marlborough Coll. *Heir:* *s* Jeremy William Francis North [*b* 5 May 1960; *m* 1986, Lucy, *d* of G. A. van der Meulen, Holland; two *s*]. *Address:* Frogmore, Weston-under-Penyard, Herefordshire HR9 5TQ.

NORTH-EASTERN CARIBBEAN AND ARUBA (formerly **ANTIGUA**), **Bishop of;** *see* West Indies, Archbishop of.

NORTHAMPTON, 7th Marquess of, *cr* 1812; **Spencer Douglas David Compton;** DL; Earl of Northampton, 1618; Earl Compton, Baron Wilmington, 1812; *b* 2 April 1946; *s* of 6th Marquess of Northampton, DSO, and of Virginia, *d* of Lt-Col David Heaton, DSO; *S* father, 1978; *m* 1st, 1967, Henriette Luisa Maria (marr. diss. 1973), *o d* of late Baron Bentinck; one *s* one *d*; 2nd, 1974, Annette Marie (marr. diss. 1977), *er d* of C. A. R. Smallwood; 3rd, 1977, Hon. Mrs Rosemary Dawson-Damer (marr. diss. 1983); one *d*; 4th, 1985, Hon. Mrs Michael Pearson (marr. diss. 1988); one *d*; 5th, 1990, Pamela Martina Raphaela Kyprios. *Educ:* Eton. DL Northants 1979. *Heir:* *s* Earl Compton, *qv*. *Address:* Compton Wynyates, Tysoe, Warwicks CV35 0UD. *T:* Tysoe (029588) 629. *Club:* Turf.

NORTHAMPTON, Bishop of, (RC), since 1990; **Rt. Rev. (Patrick) Leo McCartie;** *b* 5 Sept. 1925; *s* of Patrick Leo and Hannah McCartie. *Educ:* Cotton College; Oscott College. Priest, 1949; on staff of Cotton College, 1950–55; parish work, 1955–63; Director of Religious Education, 1963–68; Administrator of St Chad's Cathedral, Birmingham, 1968–77; Aux. Bp of Birmingham, and Titular Bp of Elmham, 1977–90. Pres., Catholic Commn for Racial Justice, 1978–83; Chm., Cttee for Community Relations, Dept for Christian Responsibility and Citizenship, Bishops' Conf. on Eng. and Wales, 1983–. *Recreations:* music, walking. *Address:* Bishop's House, Marriott Street, Northampton NN2 6AW.

NORTHAMPTON, Archdeacon of; *see* Chapman, Ven. M. R.

NORTHARD, John Henry, CBE 1987 (OBE 1979); FEng 1983; FIMinE; Deputy Chairman, British Coal Corporation, since 1988, and Board Member, National Coal Board, since 1986; *b* 23 Dec. 1926; *s* of William Henry Northard and Nellie Northard; *m* 1952, Marian Josephine Lay; two *s* two *d*. *Educ:* St Bede's Grammar School, Bradford; Barnsley Mining and Technical College (Certificated Colliery Manager, first class). CEng. Colliery Manager, Yorks, 1955–57, Leics, 1957–63; Group Manager, Leics Collieries, 1963–65; Dep. Chief Mining Engineer, NCB, Staffs Area, 1965–70; Area Dep. Dir (Mining), NCB, N Derbyshire Area, 1970–73; Area Dir, NCB, N Derbyshire Area, 1973–81, Western Area, 1981–85; Operations Dir, British Coal, 1985–88. Pres., IMinE, 1982. CBIM. SBStJ 1981. *Publications:* contribs to mining engineering instns and tech. jls. *Address:* Rydal, 196 Ashgate Road, Chesterfield, Derbyshire. *T:* Chesterfield (0246) 232260.

NORTHBOURNE, 5th Baron *cr* 1884; **Christopher George Walter James;** Bt 1791; FRICS; Chairman: Betteshanger Farms Ltd, since 1975; Kent Salads Ltd, since 1987; *b* 18 Feb. 1926; *s* of 4th Baron Northbourne and Katherine Louise (*d* 1980), *d* of late George A. Nickerson, Boston, Mass; *S* father, 1982; *m* 1959, Aliki Louise Hélène Marie Sygne, *e d* of Henri Claudel, Chatou-sur-Seine, and *g d* of late Paul Claudel; three *s* one *d*. *Educ:* Eton; Magdalen Coll., Oxford (MA). Director: Anglo Indonesian Corp., 1971–; Chillington Corp. PLC, 1986–; Center Parcs Ltd, 1987–; Center Parcs PLC, 1988–; Regl Dir, Lloyds Bank plc, 1986–. *Heir:* *s* Hon. Charles Walter Henri James [*b* 14 June 1960; *m* 1987, Catherine Lucy, *d* of Ralph Burrows; one *s*]. *Address:* 11 Eaton Place, SW1. *T:* 071–235 6790; Coldharbour, Northbourne, Deal, Kent. *T:* Sandwich (0304) 611277. *Clubs:* Brooks's, Farmers'.

NORTHBROOK, 6th Baron *cr* 1866; **Francis Thomas Baring;** Bt 1793; Senior Investment Manager, Taylor Young Investment Management Ltd, since 1990; *b* 21 Feb. 1954; *s* of 5th Baron Northbrook and of Rowena Margaret, 2nd *d* of Brig.-Gen. Sir William Manning, GCMG, KBE, CB; *S* father, 1990; *m* 1987, Amelia Sarah Elizabeth, *er d* of Dr Reginald Taylor; two *d*. *Educ:* Winchester Coll.; Bristol Univ. (BA Hons 1976). Trainee accountant, Dixon Wilson & Co., 1976–80; Baring Brothers and Co. Ltd, 1981–89. *Heir:* (to baronetcy) *kinsman* Peter Baring [*b* 12 Sept. 1939; *m* 1973, Rose, *d* of George Nigel Adams; one *s*]. *Address:* House of Lords, SW1A 0PW. *Club:* City University.

NORTHCOTE, family name of **Earl of Iddesleigh.**

NORTHCOTE, Prof. Donald Henry, FRS 1968; Master of Sidney Sussex College, Cambridge, 1976–July 1992; Professor of Plant Biochemistry, University of Cambridge, 1972–89 (Reader, 1965–72), Emeritus Professor, 1989; *b* 27 Dec. 1921; *m* Eva Marjorie Mayo; two *d*. *Educ:* Sir George Monoux Grammar Sch., London; London Univ.; Cambridge Univ. Fellow, St John's College, Cambridge, 1960–76. Hon. Fellow, Downing Coll., Cambridge, 1976. Mem. Governing Council, John Innes Inst., 1980–. *Publication:* Differentiation in Higher Plants, 1974, 2nd edn 1980. *Recreations:* sitting and chatting; strolling about. *Address:* Sidney Sussex College, Cambridge. *T:* (until July 1992) Cambridge (0223) 355860, (from Aug. 1992) 338847. *Club:* United Oxford & Cambridge University.

NORTHCOTE, His Honour Peter Colston; a Circuit Judge 1973–89; *b* 23 Oct. 1920; *s* of late William George Northcote and late Edith Mary Northcote; *m* 1947, Patricia Bickley; two *s*. *Educ:* Ellesmere Coll.; Bristol Univ. Called to Bar, Inner Temple, 1948. Chm., Nat. Insce Tribunal; Chm., W Midland Rent Tribunal; Dep. Chm., Agric. Land Tribunal. Commnd KSLI, 1940; served 7th Rajput Regt, Far East (Major). *Recreations:* music, travel, ski-ing. *Address:* Wroxeter Grange, Wroxeter, Shrewsbury, Salop. *T:* Cross Houses (0743) 761279. *Club:* Army and Navy.

NORTHCOTT, Prof. Douglas Geoffrey, MA, PhD, Cambridge; FRS 1961; Town Trust Professor of Mathematics, University of Sheffield, 1952–82, now Emeritus; *b* London, 1916; *m* 1949, Rose Hilda Austin, Twickenham, Middlesex; two *d*. *Educ:* Christ's Hospital; St John's Coll., Cambridge; Princeton Univ., USA. *Publications:* Ideal Theory, 1953; An Introduction to Homological Algebra, 1960; Lessons on Rings, Modules and Multiplicities, 1968; A First Course of Homological Algebra, 1973; Finite Free Resolutions, 1976; Affine Sets and Affine Groups, 1980; Multilinear Algebra, 1984. *Address:* 25 Parkhead Road, Sheffield S11 9RA.

NORTHERN ARGENTINA, Bishop of, since 1990; **Rt. Rev. Maurice Walter Sinclair;** *b* 20 Jan. 1937; *s* of Maurice and Dorothea Sinclair; *m* 1962, Gillian (*née* Spooner); four *s*. *Educ:* Chigwell Sch.; Nottingham Univ. (BSc 1959); Leicester Univ. (PGCE 1960); Tyndale Hall, Bristol. Asst Master, Brays Grove County Secondary Sch., Harlow, Essex, 1960–62. Ordained, 1964; Asst Curate, St John's Church, Boscombe, 1964–67; Missionary, South American Missionary Soc., serving in Argentina, 1967–78; Personnel Sec., 1979–83, Asst Gen. Sec., 1983–84, South American Missionary Soc.; Principal, Crowther Hall, Selly Oak Colls, 1984–90. Ibo chief, Nigeria, 1987. *Publications:* Green Finger of God, 1980; Ripening Harvest Gathering Storm, 1988. *Recreations:* gardening, hill walking, veteran football. *Address:* Iglesia Anglicana, Casilla 187, CP 4400 Salta, Argentina. *T:* 087 310167.

NORTHERN TERRITORY (AUSTRALIA), Bishop of the, since 1983; **Rt. Rev. Clyde Maurice Wood,** BA, ThL; *b* 7 Jan. 1936; *s* of Maurice O. Wood and Helen M. Wood; *m* 1957, Margaret Joan Burls; two *s* one *d*. *Educ:* Perry Hall, Melbourne (ThL 1964); Monash Univ. (BA 1974). Deacon 1965, priest 1965; Curate: St John's, Bentleigh, 1965–66; St Paul's, Ringwood, 1966–67; in Dept of Evangelism and Extension, 1967–70; Curate-in-Charge: St Philip's, Mount Waverley, 1967–70; Armadale/Hawksburn, 1970–73; Rector and Canon Res., Christ Church Cathedral, Darwin, 1974, Dean 1978–83. On leave, Rector St Timothy's Episcopal Church, Indianapolis, USA, 1981. OStJ 1980; ChStJ 1985. *Recreations:* golf, sailing. *Address:* PO Box 39352, Winnellie, NT 0821, Australia. *T:* (office) (089) 852044; 5 Rankin Street, Nightcliff, NT 0810, Australia. *T:* (089) 85 3099.

NORTHESK, 13th Earl of, *cr* 1647; **Robert Andrew Carnegie;** Lord Rosehill and Inglismaldie, 1639; Landowner, Farmer; *b* 24 June 1926; *yr s* of 12th Earl of Northesk and Dorothy Mary (*d* 1967), *er d* of late Col Sir William Robert Campion, KCMG, DSO; *S* father, 1975; *m* 1st, 1949, Jean Margaret (*d* 1989), *yr d* of Captain (John) Duncan George MacRae, Ballimore, Otter Ferry, Argyll; one *s* two *d* (and one *s* decd); 2nd, 1989, Brownie (*née* Grimason), *widow* of Carl Heimann. *Educ:* Pangbourne RNR Coll.; Tabor Naval Acad., USA. Served with Royal Navy, 1942–45. Member: Council, Fédération Internationale des Assocs d'éléveurs de la race bovine Charolaise; Council, Game Research Assoc., 1955–57; Council, British Charolais Cattle Soc., 1972–74. Chm. Bd, Chandler, Hargreaves (IOM) Ltd, 1980–; Director: NEL Britannia International Assurance Ltd, 1984–89; Royal Skandia Life Assurance Ltd, 1989–; Member: Bd of Dirs, IOM Bank, 1980–; IOM Br., CPA; Bd of Governors, Buchan Sch., IOM, 1980–86. President: Save the Children Fund, Douglas, IoM, 1977–; Friends of the Physically Disabled, IOM, 1985–. Trustee, Pain Relief Foundn, 1985–. Midhurst RDC, 1968–75 (Chm., 1972–74). *Publication:* Diary of an Island Glen, 1988. *Heir:* *s* Lord Rosehill, *qv*. *Address:* Springwaters, Ballamodha, Isle of Man.

See also Baron Fisher.

NORTHFIELD, Baron *cr* 1975 (Life Peer), of Telford, Shropshire; **(William) Donald Chapman;** Chairman: Telford Development Corporation, 1975–87; Consortium Developments Ltd, since 1986; *b* 25 Nov. 1923; *s* of Wm H. and Norah F. E. Chapman, Barnsley. *Educ:* Barnsley Grammar Sch.; Emmanuel Coll., Cambridge, MA (1st Cl. Hons) Economics, also degree in Agriculture; Senior Scholar of Emmanuel Coll. Research in Agric. Economics, Cambridge, 1943–46. Cambridge City Councillor, 1945–47; Sec., Trades Council and Labour Party, 1945–57; MP (Lab) Birmingham (Northfield), 1951–70. Research Sec. of the Fabian Soc., 1948–49, Gen. Sec., 1949–53. Gwilym Gibbon Fellow, Nuffield Coll., Oxford, 1971–73; Vis. Fellow, Centre for Contemporary European Studies, Sussex Univ., 1973–79. Special Adviser to EEC Commn, 1978–84; Chairman: Develt Commn, 1974–80; Inquiry into recent trends in acquisition and occupancy of agric. land, 1977–79. *Publications:* The European Parliament: the years ahead, 1973; The Road to European Union, 1975; articles and Fabian pamphlets. *Recreation:* travel. *Address:* House of Lords, SW1.

NORTHLAND, Viscount; title of heir to Earldom of Ranfurly.

NORTHOLT, Archdeacon of; *see* Shirras, Ven. E. S.

NORTHROP, Filmer S(tuart) C(uckow), PhD, LittD, LLD; Sterling Professor of Philosophy and Law Emeritus, the Law School and the School of Graduate Studies, Yale University, USA, since 1962; *b* 27 Nov. 1893; *s* of Marshall Ellsworth Northrop and Ruth Cuckow; *m* 1st, 1919, Christine Johnston; two *s*; 2nd, 1969, Marjorie Carey. *Educ:* Beloit Coll. (BA 1915, LittD 1946); Yale (MA 1919); Harvard (MA 1922, PhD 1924); Imperial Coll. of Science and Technology, London; Trinity Coll., Cambridge. Instr. at Yale, 1923–26; Asst Prof., Yale, 1926–29; Associate Prof., Yale, 1929–32, Prof., 1932–47; Master of Silliman Coll., 1940–47; Sterling Prof. of Philosophy and Law, Yale, 1947–62; Visiting Prof., summer session, Univ. of Iowa, 1926; Univ. of Michigan, 1932; Univ. of Virginia, 1931–32; Visiting Prof. and Mem. of East-West Conf. on Philosophy at Univ. of Hawaii, 1939; Prof. Extraordinario, La Universidad Nacional Autonoma de Mexico, 1949; Fellow: American Acad. of Arts and Sciences, 1951; American Acad. of Political and Social Science, 1957; Pres., American Philosophical Assoc. (Eastern Div.), 1952. Hon. Founder: Macy Foundn Conferences, 1944–53; Amer. Soc. of Cybernetics, 1964; Mem., SEATO Round Table, Bangkok, 1958. Hon. LLD: Univ. of Hawaii, 1949, Rollins Coll., 1955; Hon. LittD: Beloit Coll., 1946; Pratt Inst., 1961. Order of the Aztec Eagle (Mexican), 1946. *Publications:* Science and First Principles, 1931; The Meeting of East and West, 1946; The Logic of the Sciences and the Humanities, 1947; The Taming of the Nations, A Study of the Cultural Bases of International Policy, 1952 (Wilkie Memorial Building Award, 1953); European Union and United States Foreign Policy, 1954; The Complexity of Legal and Ethical Experience, 1959; Philosophical Anthropology and Practical Politics, 1960; Man, Nature and God, 1962; Co-Editor, Cross-cultural Understanding: Epistemology in Anthropology, 1964; Chapter 5 in Contemporary American Philosophy, second series, 1970; (with J. Sinões da Fonseca) Interpersonal Relations in Neuropsychological and Legal Science, 1975; ed, Ideological Differences and World Order, 1949; Prolegomena to a Philosophia Naturales, 1985. *Recreations:* travel, baseball. *Address:* 8 Hampton Road, Exeter, NH 03833, USA. *Clubs:* Century (New York); Beaumont, Berzilius, Elizabethan, Graduates, Mory's (New Haven); American Academy of Arts and Sciences (Philosophy Section) (Boston).

NORTHUMBERLAND, 11th Duke of, *cr* 1766; **Henry Alan Walter Richard Percy;** Bt 1660; Baron Percy 1722; Earl of Northumberland, Baron Warkworth 1749; Earl Percy 1766; Earl of Beverly 1790; Lord Lovaine, Baron of Alnwick 1784; *b* 1 July 1953; *s* of 10th Duke of Northumberland, KG, GCVO, TD, PC, FRS and of Lady Elizabeth Diana Montagu-Douglas-Scott, *er d* of 8th Duke of Buccleuch and Queensberry, KT, GCVO, PC; *S* father, 1988. *Educ:* Eton; Christ Church, Oxford. President: Alnwick & Dist Cttee for the Disabled; Alnwick Working Men's Club & Inst.; Northumbria Club; Northumbrian Anglers' Fedn; Natural History Soc. of Northumbria; Northumberland Assoc. of Boys Clubs; Northumberland County Victims' Support Scheme; N of England CRC; Craster Br., RNLI; Surrey Farming & Wildlife Adv. Gp; Royal Northumberland Yacht Club; Tyne Mariners' Benevolent Instn; Vice President: Ancient Monuments Soc.; Internat. Sheep Dog Soc.; Patron: Assoc. of Northumberland Local History Socs; Berwick-upon-Tweed Preservation Trust; Internat. Centre for Child Studies; NE Br., Mental Health Foundn; Northumberland Buildings Preservation Trust; Hounslow and Feltham Victim Support Scheme; Hounslow and Twickenham Br., Arthritis Care; Northern Counties Sch. for the Deaf; Royal Northumberland Fusiliers Aid Soc. and Regimental Assoc.; Theatre W4; Tyneside Cinema. MFH 1989; FRSA 1989. *Recreations:* tennis, shooting, movies. *Heir: b* Lord Ralph George Algernon Percy [*b* 16 Nov. 1956; *m* 1979, Jane, *d* of John W. M. M. Richard; two *s* two *d*]. *Address:* Alnwick Castle, Northumberland; Syon House, Brentford, Mddx.

NORTHUMBERLAND, Archdeacon of; *see* Thomas, Ven. W. J.

NORTHWAY, Eileen Mary, CBE 1990; RRC 1982 (ARRC 1969); Principal Nursing Officer and Matron-in-Chief, Queen Alexandra's Royal Naval Nursing Service, 1986–90; *b* 22 July 1931; *d* of Ernest and Margaret Northway. *Educ:* St Michael's Convent, Newton Abbot. SRN 1952, SCM 1954; joined QARNNS 1956. QHNS, 1986–90. OStJ 1985. *Recreations:* gardening, reading.

NORTON; *see* Hill-Norton.

NORTON, family name of **Barons Grantley** and **Rathcreedan.**

NORTON, 7th Baron, *cr* 1878; **John Arden Adderley,** OBE 1964; *b* 24 Nov. 1915; *s* of 6th Baron Norton; *S* father, 1961; *m* 1946, Betty Margaret, *o d* of late James McKee Hannah; two *s*. *Educ:* Radley; Magdalen Coll., Oxford (BA). Oxford University Greenland Expedition, 1938; Assistant Master, Oundle School, 1938–39. Served War, 1940–45 (despatches); RE (N Africa, Europe). Major, 1944. Asst Secretary, Country Landowners Assoc., 1947–59. *Recreations:* mountaineering, shooting, heraldry and genealogy. *Heir: s* Hon. James Nigel Arden Adderley [*b* 2 June 1947; *m* 1971, Jacqueline Julie Willett, *e d* of Guy W. Willett, Woking, Surrey; one *s* one *d*]. *Address:* Fillongley Hall, Coventry, West Midlands. *T:* Fillongley (0676) 40303.

NORTON, Donald; Regional Administrator, Oxford Regional Health Authority, 1973–80, retired; *b* 2 May 1920; *s* of Thomas Henry Norton and Dora May Norton (*née* Prentice); *m* 1945, Miriam Joyce, *d* of Herbert and Florence Mann; two *s* one *d*. *Educ:* Nether Edge Grammar Sch., Sheffield; Univs of Sheffield and London. LLB, DPA; FHA. Senior Administrator Sheffield Regional Hosp. Bd, 1948–51; Sec. Supt, Jessop Hosp. for Women and Charles Clifford Dental Hosp., Sheffield, 1951–57; Dep. Sec., Archway Gp of Hosps, London, 1957–60; Gp Sec., Dudley Road Gp of Hosps, Birmingham 1960–70; Sec., Oxford Regional Hosp. Bd, 1970–73. *Recreations:* marriage, golf, gardening. *Address:* The Squirrels, 14 Pullens Field, Headington, Oxford OX3 0BU. *T:* Oxford (0865) 67291. *Clubs:* Victory; Clarendon (Oxford); Frilford Heath.

NORTON, Captain Gerard Ross, VC 1944; MM; 1/4th Hampshire Regiment; *b* S Africa, 7 Sept. 1915; *m* 1942, Lilia Morris, East London, S Africa; one *d*. *Educ:* Selborne Coll., East London, S Africa. Bank clerk. *Recreations:* Rugger-provincial, tennis, cricket. *Address:* Annandale Farm, Box 112, Banket, Zimbabwe.

NORTON, Hugh Edward; Managing Director, British Petroleum Co. plc, since 1989; *b* 23 June 1936; *s* of Lt-Gen. Edward F. Norton, CB, DSO, MC and of I. Joyce Norton; *m* 1965, Janet M. Johnson; one *s*. *Educ:* Winchester Coll.; Trinity Coll., Oxford (BA Hons Lit.Hum.). British Petroleum Co., 1959–: Regl Co-ordinator, ME, 1977–78; Man. Dir, BP Singapore, 1978–81; Director: Planning, 1981–84; Admin, 1984–86; Chief Exec., BP Exploration Co., 1986–89. *Recreations:* painting, ornithology, tennis, travel. *Address:* c/o British Petroleum Co., Britannic House, 1 Finsbury Circus, EC2M 7BA. *T:* 071–496 4000.

NORTON, John Lindsey; Chairman, BDO Binder, since 1988; *b* 21 May 1935; *s* of Frederick Raymond Norton and Doris Ann Norton; *m* 1959, Judith Ann Bird; three *d*. *Educ:* Winchester College; Cambridge Univ. (MA). Blackburn Robson Coates & Co., 1959–63; BDO Binder Hamlyn, 1963–. *Recreations:* walking, gardening. *Address:* BDO Binder, 20 Old Bailey, EC4M 7BH; 8 Conway House, 5/6 Ormonde Gate, SW3 4EU. *T:* 071–352 1878.

NORTON, Mary; children's writer; *b* 10 Dec. 1903; *d* of Reginald Spencer Pearson and Minnie Savile Hughes; *m* 1st, 1926, Robert Charles Norton; two *s* two *d*; 2nd, 1970, Lionel Bonsey (*d* 1989). *Educ:* St Margaret's Convent, East Grinstead. Old Vic Co. under Lilian Baylis, 1925–26; domiciled family home in Portugal, 1926–39; war job and acting for BBC, 1940; war job, British Purchasing Commn, New York, 1941; returned to London, 1942, caring for own children and acting for H. M. Tennant. *Publications:* Bonfires and Broomsticks, 1947; The Borrowers, 1952 (Library Assoc. Carnegie Medal, 1952; Hans Christian Anderson Honours Award); The Borrowers Afield, 1955; The Borrowers Afloat, 1959; The Borrowers Aloft, 1961; Poor Stainless, 1971; Are All the Giants Dead?, 1975; The Borrowers Avenged, 1982. *Recreations:* (formerly) swimming and training for show-jumping. *Address:* 102 West Street, Hartland, N Devon EX39 6BQ. *Clubs:* Lansdowne, Sloane.

NORTON-GRIFFITHS, Sir John, 3rd Bt *cr* 1922; FCA; President and Chief Executive Officer, Main Street Data Services Inc.; *b* 4 Oct. 1938; *s* of Sir Peter Norton-Griffiths, 2nd Bt, and Kathryn (*d* 1980), *e d* of late George F. Schrafft; *S* father, 1983; *m* 1964, Marilyn Margaret, *er d* of Norman Grimley. *Educ:* Eton. FCA 1966. Lately Sub Lieutenant RN. *Heir: b* Michael Norton-Griffiths [*b* 11 Jan. 1941; *m* 1965, Ann, *o d* of late Group Captain Blair Alexander Fraser; one *s*]. *Address:* 17 Royal Drive, Bricktown, NJ 08723, USA.

NORWICH, 2nd Viscount, *cr* 1952, of Aldwick; **John Julius Cooper,** FRSL, FRGS; writer and broadcaster; *b* 15 Sept. 1929; *s* of 1st Viscount Norwich, PC, GCMG, DSO, and Lady Diana Cooper (*d* 1986), *d* of 8th Duke of Rutland; *S* father, 1954; *m* 1st, 1952, Anne (Frances May) (marr. diss. 1985), *e d* of late Hon. Sir Bede Clifford, GCMG, CB, MVO; one *s* one *d*; 2nd, 1989, Mollie Philipps, *e d* of Baron Sherfield, *qv*. *Educ:* Upper Canada Coll., Toronto, Canada; Eton; University of Strasbourg; New Coll., Oxford. Served 1947–49 as Writer, Royal Navy. Entered Foreign Office, 1952; Third Secretary, British Embassy, Belgrade, 1955–57; Second Secretary, British Embassy, Beirut, 1957–60; worked in Foreign Office (First Secretary from 1961) and in British Delegation to Disarmament Conference, Geneva, from 1960 until resignation from Foreign Service 1964. Chairman: Venice in Peril Fund; British Theatre Museum, 1966–71; Member: Exec. Cttee, National Trust, 1969– (Properties Cttee, 1970–87); Franco-British Council, 1972–79; Bd, English Nat. Opera, 1977–81. Has made some thirty documentary films for television, mostly on history and architecture. Editor, New Shell Guides to Britain, 1987–. Commendatore, Ordine al Merito della Repubblica Italiana. *Publications:* (as John Julius Norwich): Mount Athos (with Reresby Sitwell), 1966; The Normans in the South (as The Other Conquest, US), 1967; Sahara, 1968; The Kingdom in The Sun, 1970; A History of Venice, vol. I, The Rise to Empire, 1977, vol. II, The Greatness and the Fall, 1981; Christmas Crackers, 1970–79, 1980; Fifty Years of Glyndebourne, 1985; A Taste for Travel (anthology), 1985; General Editor: Great Architecture of the World, 1975; The Architecture of Southern England, 1985; Byzantium, the Early Centuries, 1988; (ed) Britain's Heritage, 1982; (ed) The Italian World: history, art and the genius of a people, 1983; More Christmas Crackers 1980–89, 1990; Venice: a traveller's companion, 1990; (ed) The Oxford Illustrated Encyclopaedia of the Arts, 1990; Byzantium: the apogee, 1991. *Recreations:* sight-seeing, walking at night through Venice. *Heir: s* Hon. Jason Charles Duff Bede Cooper, *b* 27 Oct. 1959. *Address:* 24 Blomfield Road, W9 1AD. *T:* 071–286 5050. *Clubs:* Beefsteak, Garrick.

NORWICH, Bishop of, since 1985; **Rt. Rev. Peter John Nott;** *b* 30 Dec. 1933; *s* of Cecil Frederick Wilder Nott and Rosina Mabel Bailey; *m* 1961, Elizabeth May Maingot; one *s* three *d*. *Educ:* Bristol Grammar School; Dulwich Coll.; RMA Sandhurst; Fitzwilliam House, Cambridge; Westcott House, Cambridge (MA). Curate of Harpenden, 1961–64; Chaplain of Fitzwilliam Coll., Cambridge, 1964–69; Fellow of Fitzwilliam Coll., 1967–69; Chaplain of New Hall, Cambridge, 1966–69; Rector of Beaconsfield, 1969–77; Bishop Suffragan of Taunton, 1977–85. Archbishop's Adviser to HMC, 1980–85; President: SW Region, Mencap, 1978–84; Somerset Rural Music Sch., 1981–85. Vice-Chm., Archbishops' Commn for Rural Areas, 1988–90. *Address:* Bishop's House, Norwich NR3 1SB. *T:* Norwich (0603) 629001.

NORWICH, Dean of; *see* Burbridge, Very Rev. J. P.

NORWICH, Archdeacon of; *see* Handley, Ven. A. M.

NORWOOD, Suzanne Freda, (Mrs John Lexden Stewart); Her Honour Judge Norwood; a Circuit Judge, since 1973; *b* 24 March 1926; *d* of late Frederic Francis Norwood and of Marianne Freda Norwood (*née* Thomas); *m* 1954, John Lexden Stewart (*d* 1972); one *s*. *Educ:* Lowther Coll., Bodelwyddan; St Andrews Univ. MA English, MA Hons History. Called to Bar, Gray's Inn, 1951; practised at Bar, SE Circuit. Member: Parole Bd, 1976–78; Mental Health Review Tribunal, 1983–. Member: Greenwich and Bexley AHA, 1979–82; Greenwich DHA, 1982–85; Bexley DHA, 1985–90. *Recreations:* walking, housekeeping, opera. *Address:* Crown Court, Middlesex Guildhall, Broad Sanctuary, SW1.

NORWOOD, Sir Walter (Neville), Kt 1971; *b* 14 July 1907; *s* of late Sir Charles Norwood; *m* 1935, Rana Muriel, *d* of David Redpath; two *s* one *d*. *Educ:* Wellington and Wanganui. Trustee: Nuffield Trust for Crippled Children; Laura Fergusson Trust for Disabled Persons; C. J. B. Norwood Crippled Children's Trust; Norwood Cricket Trust. Past President: Wellington Rotary Club; Wellington Racing Club. *Recreations:* racing, farming, sailing. *Address:* Hillcrest, 24 Mataroa Avenue, Wellington, New Zealand. *Clubs:* Wellesley, Wellington (Wellington, NZ).

NOSS, John Bramble; HM Diplomatic Service; Deputy Head of Mission and Commercial Counsellor, Helsinki, 1988–91; *b* 20 Dec. 1935; *s* of John Noss and Vera Ethel (*née* Mattingly); *m* 1957, Shirley May Andrews; two *s* one *d*. *Educ:* Portsmouth Grammar School. Foreign Office, 1954; RAF, 1955–57; served FO, Beirut, Copenhagen, FCO; Russian language training, 1965; Moscow, 1965–68; Santiago, 1968–70; FCO, 1970–73; First Sec. (Economic), Pretoria, 1974–77; First Sec. (Commercial), Moscow, 1977–78; FCO, 1978–81; Consul (Inward Investment), New York, 1981–85; High Comr, Solomon Is, 1986–88. *Recreations:* photography, reading, golf. *Address:* c/o Foreign and Commonwealth Office, SW1A 2AH.

NOSSAL, Sir Gustav (Joseph Victor), AC 1989; Kt 1977; CBE 1970; FRS 1982; FAA; Director, The Walter and Eliza Hall Institute of Medical Research, Melbourne, since 1965; Professor of Medical Biology, University of Melbourne, since 1965; *b* Austria, 4 June 1931; *m* 1955, Lyn B. Dunnicliff; two *s* two *d*. *Educ:* Sydney Univ. (1st Cl. Hons BScMed (Bacteriology), 1952; 1st Cl. Hons MB, BS 1954 (Mills Prize)); Melbourne Univ. (PhD 1960). FAA 1967; FRACP 1967; Hon. FRCPA 1971; FRACMA 1971; FRCP 1980; FTS 1981; Hon. FRSE 1983. Jun., then Sen. Resident Officer, Royal Prince Alfred Hosp., Sydney, 1955–56; Res. Fellow, Walter and Eliza Hall Inst. of Med. Res., 1957–59; Asst Prof., Dept of Genetics, Stanford Univ. Sch. of Medicine, Calif, 1959–61; Dep. Dir (Immunology), Walter and Eliza Hall Inst. of Med. Res., 1961–65. Vis. scientist and vis. professor to several univs and res. insts; has given many lectures to learned societies, assocs and univs. Dir, CRA Ltd, 1977–. World Health Organisation: Member: Expert Adv. Panel on Immunology, 1967; Adv. Cttee Med. Res., 1973–80; Special

Consultant, Tropical Disease Res. Prog., 1976. Chm., West Pac Adv. Co. Med. Res., 1976–80; Member: Aust. Science and Technol. Council, 1975–83; Adv. Bd, John Curtin Sch. of Med. Res., 1981–; Centre for Recombinant DNA Res., Res. Sch. of Biol Sciences, ANU, 1981– (Founder Mem.); Baker Med. Res. Inst., 1982–; Scientific Adv. Cttee, Centenary Res. Inst. of Cancer Medicine and Cell Biol., Sydney, 1983–; Aust. Industrial Res. Develt Incentives Bd, 1983–. Mem., Aust. Soc. of Immunology; Hon. Mem., Amer. (1975), French (1979), Indian (1976), Soc. of Immunology; Foreign Hon. Mem., Amer. Acad. of Arts and Scis, 1974. For. Associate, US Nat. Acad. of Scis, 1979; Fellow, New York Acad. of Scis, 1977; For. Fellow, Indian Nat. Sci. Acad., 1980. Hon. MD Johannes Gutenberg Univ., Mainz, 1981. Emil von Behring Prize, Philipps Univ., Marburg, Germany, 1971; Rabbi Shai Shacknai Memorial Prize, Univ. of Jerusalem, 1973; Ciba Foundn Gold Medal, 1978; Burnet Medal, Aust. Acad. of Sci., 1979. Mem. Editorial Bd of several med. jls. *Publications:* Antibodies & Immunity, 1968 (rev. edn 1977); Antigens Lymphoid Cells & The Immune Response, 1971; Medical Science & Human Goals, 1975; Nature's Defences (Boyer Lectures), 1978; Reshaping Life: key issues in genetic engineering, 1984. *Recreations:* golf, literature. *Address:* 46 Fellows Street, Kew, Vic 3101, Australia. *T:* 861 8256. *Clubs:* Melbourne (Melbourne); Rosebud Country.

NOSSITER, Bernard Daniel; journalist; *b* 10 April 1926; *s* of Murry and Rose (Weingarten) Nossiter; *m* 1950, Jacqueline Robinson; four *s*. *Educ:* Dartmouth Coll., Hanover, NH (BA); Harvard Univ., Cambridge, Mass. (MA Econ). Washington Post: Nat. Econs Corresp., 1955–62; European Econs Corresp., 1964–67; S Asia Corresp., 1967–68; Nat. Bureau Reporter, 1968–71; London Corresp., 1971–79; UN Bureau Chief, NY Times, 1979–83. Nieman Fellow, Harvard, 1962–63. *Publications:* The Mythmakers, 1964; Soft State, 1970; Britain: a future that works, 1978; The Global Struggle for More, 1987; Fat Years and Lean: the economy since Roosevelt, 1990; contribs to Amer. Econ. Rev., Harvard Business Rev., Annals Amer. Acad. Pol. Sci. *Address:* 300 East 75 Street, New York, NY 10021, USA. *T:* 879 1491. *Club:* Reform.

NOSWORTHY, Harold George, CMG 1965; FCCA; FCA; *b* 15 March 1908; *m* 1941, Marjorie Anjelique; two *d*. *Educ:* Kingston Technical High Sch.; private tuition. Entered Jamaica Civil Service, 1929; 2nd class Clerk, 1938; Examiner of Accounts, 1943; Asst Commissioner, Income Tax, 1947; Asst Trade Administrator, 1950; Trade Administrator and Chairman Trade Control Board, 1953; Principal Asst Secretary, Ministry of Finance, 1955; Auditor-General, 1957–66; Dir, Internal Audit Service, UN, 1966–68. Mem., Parly Integrity Commn, 1973 (Chm., 1988–91). Queen's Coronation Medal, 1953; Jamaica Independence Medal, 1962. *Recreations:* reading, billiards, bridge, swimming. *Address:* 18 Hyperion Avenue, PO Box 127, Kingston 6, Jamaica. *T:* 9279889. *Club:* Kingston Cricket (Jamaica).

NOTT, Charles Robert Harley, CMG 1959; OBE 1952; retired, New Zealand; *b* 24 Oct. 1904; *e s* of late John Harley Nott, JP, Leominster, Herefordshire and late Mrs Nott, formerly of Bodenham Hall, Herefordshire; *m* 1935, Marion (*née* Macfarlane), Auckland, NZ; one *s* one *d*. *Educ:* Marlborough; Christ's Coll., Cambridge (MA). Colonial Administrative Service: Fiji, 1926; Administrative Officer (Grade II), 1938, (Grade I), 1945. Member of the Legislative Council, Fiji, 1950; HBM's Agent and Consul, Tonga, 1954–57; Sec. for Fijian Affairs, 1957–59; MLC, MEC, retired, 1960. *Recreation:* trout fishing. *Address:* PO Box 8106, Havelock North, New Zealand.

NOTT, Rt. Hon. Sir John (William Frederic), KCB 1983; PC 1979; Chairman and Chief Executive, Lazard Brothers & Co. Ltd, 1985–90 (Director, 1983–90); *b* 1 Feb. 1932; *s* of Richard Nott, Bideford, Devon, and late Phyllis (*née* Francis); *m* 1959, Miloska Sekol, Maribor, Yugoslavia; two *s* one *d*. *Educ:* King's Mead, Seaford; Bradfield Coll.; Trinity Coll., Cambridge. Lieut, 2nd Gurkha Rifles (regular officer), Malayan emergency, 1952–56; Trinity Coll., Cambridge, 1957–59 (BA Hons Law and Econs); Pres., Cambridge Union, 1959; called to the Bar, Inner Temple, 1959; Gen. Manager, S. G. Warburg & Co. Ltd, Merchant Bankers, 1960–66. MP (C) Cornwall, St Ives, 1966–83; Minister of State, HM Treasury, 1972–74; Cons. front bench spokesman on: Treasury and Economic Affairs, 1975–76; Trade, 1976–79; Sec. of State for Trade, 1979–81; Sec. of State for Defence, 1981–83. Dep. Chm., Royal Insurance PLC, 1986–89 (Dir, 1985–). *Address:* 21 Moorfields, EC2. *T:* 071–588 2721.

NOTT, Kathleen Cecilia, FRSL; author, broadcaster, lecturer and journalist; *d* of Philip and Ellen Nott; *m* Christopher Bailey (marr. diss.). *Educ:* Mary Datchelor Sch., London; Somerville Coll., Oxford (BA Hons, PPE); King's Coll., London. FRSL 1977. President: Progressive League, 1959–61; English PEN, 1974–75. Editor, PEN International (formerly Internat. PEN Bulletin of Selected Books), 1960–. *Publications: poetry:* Landscapes and Departures, 1947; Poems from the North, 1956; Creatures and Emblems, 1960; Elegies and Other Poems, 1980; *novels:* Mile End, 1938; The Dry Deluge, 1947; Private Fires, 1960; An Elderly Retired Man, 1963; *criticism and philosophy:* The Emperor's Clothes, 1954; A Soul in the Quad, 1969; Philosophy and Human Nature, 1970; The Good Want Power, 1977; *general:* A Clean Well-lighted Place, 1961 (Sweden); contribs to collections of essays, and to periodicals. *Recreations:* playing the piano, gardening. *Address:* 17 Roman Crescent, Old Town, Swindon, Wilts SN1 4HH. *Clubs:* University Women's, PEN, Society of Authors.

NOTT, Rt. Rev. Peter John; *see* Norwich, Bishop of.

NOTTAGE, Raymond Frederick Tritton, CMG 1964; Deputy Chairman, Association of Lloyd's Members, since 1985; Chairman, Bobath Centre for Children with Cerebral Palsy, since 1987; Treasurer, Arkwright Arts Trust, Hampstead, since 1975; *b* 1 Aug. 1916; *s* of Frederick and Frances Nottage; *m* 1941, Joyce Evelyn, *d* of Sidney and Edith Philpot; three *d*. *Educ:* Hackney Downs Secondary Sch. Civil servant, Post Office Headquarters, 1936–49; Editor of Civil Service Opinion, and Member Exec. Cttee, Soc. of Civil Servants, 1944–49; Dir-Gen., RIPA, 1949–78. Mem. Hornsey Borough Council, 1945–47. Mem. Cttee on Training in Public Admin. for Overseas Countries, 1961–63; Vice-Pres. Internat. Inst. of Admin. Sciences, 1962–68; Mem. Governing Body, Inst. of Development Studies, Univ. of Sussex, 1966–76; travelled abroad as Consultant and Lectr. *Publications:* Sources of Local Revenue (with S. H. H. Hildersley), 1968; Financing Public Sector Pensions, 1975; (with Gerald Rhodes) Pensions: a plan for the future, 1986; articles in Public Administration and similar jls. *Recreations:* music, swimming. *Address:* 36e Arkwright Road, NW3. *T:* 071–794 7129.

NOTTINGHAM, Bishop of, (RC), since 1974; **Rt. Rev. James Joseph McGuinness;** *b* 2 Oct. 1925; *s* of Michael and Margaret McGuinness. *Educ:* St Columb's College, Derry; St Patrick's College, Carlow; Oscott College, Birmingham. Ordained, 1950; Curate of St Mary's, Derby, 1950–53; Secretary to Bishop Ellis, 1953–56; Parish Priest, Corpus Christi Parish, Clifton, Nottingham, 1956–72; Vicar General of Nottingham Diocese, 1969; Coadjutor Bishop of Nottingham and Titular Bishop of St Germans, 1972–74. *Recreations:* gardening, golf. *Address:* Bishop's House, 27 Cavendish Road East, The Park, Nottingham NG7 1BB.

NOTTINGHAM, Archdeacon of; *see* Walker, Ven. T. O.

NOULTON, John David; Director, Transmanche Link, since 1989; *b* 5 Jan. 1939; *s* of John Noulton and Kathleen (*née* Sheehan); *m* 1961, Anne Elizabeth Byrne; three *s* one *d*. *Educ:* Clapham Coll. MCIT. Asst Principal, Dept of Transport, 1970–72; Principal, DoE, 1972–78; Pvte Sec. to Minister of State, DoE, 1976–78; Asst Sec., Depts of the Environment and of Transport, 1978–85; Under Sec., Dept of Transport, 1985–89. British Co-Chm., Channel Tunnel Intergovtl Commn, 1987–89. *Recreations:* boating, swimming, walking, reading. *Address:* 12 Ladderstile Ride, Coombe, Surrey KT2 7LP. *T:* 081–541 0734.

NOURSE, Rt. Hon. Sir Martin (Charles), PC 1985; Kt 1980; **Rt. Hon. Lord Justice Nourse;** a Lord Justice of Appeal, since 1985; *b* 3 April 1932; *yr s* of late Henry Edward Nourse, MD, MRCP, of Cambridge, and Ethel Millicent, *d* of Rt Hon. Sir Charles Henry Sargant, Lord Justice of Appeal; *m* 1972, Lavinia, *yr d* of late Comdr D. W. Malim; one *s* one *d*. *Educ:* Winchester; Corpus Christi Coll., Cambridge (Hon. Fellow, 1988). National Service as 2nd Lieut, Rifle Bde, 1951–52; Lieut, London Rifle Bde Rangers (TA), 1952–55. Called to Bar, Lincoln's Inn, 1956; Bencher, 1978; Mem., General Council of the Bar, 1964–68; a Junior Counsel to BoT in Chancery matters, 1967–70; QC 1970; Attorney Gen., Duchy of Lancaster, 1976–80; a Judge of the Courts of Appeal of Jersey and Guernsey, 1977–80; Judge of the High Court of Justice, Chancery Div., 1980–85. *Address:* Royal Courts of Justice, Strand, WC2.

See also Sir Edmund Sargant.

NOVA SCOTIA, Bishop of, since 1984; **Rt. Rev. Arthur Gordon Peters;** *b* 21 Dec. 1935; *s* of William Peters and Charlotte Peters (*née* Symes); *m* 1962, Elizabeth Baert; one *s* two *d*. *Educ:* High School, North Sydney, NS; Univ. of King's College, Halifax, NS (BA 1960, BST 1963, BD 1973). Student, Parish of Waverley, 1961–63; deacon 1962, priest 1963, Nova Scotia; Morris Scholar, 1963, at Canterbury (Eng.), Geneva, Jerusalem, Norton (dio. Durham, Eng.); Rector: Weymouth, NS, 1964–68; Annapolis-Granville, NS, 1968–73; Christ Church, Sydney, NS, 1973–82; Bishop Coadjutor of Nova Scotia, 1982–84. Hon. DD Univ. of King's College, 1982. *Recreations:* swimming, ski-ing, reading, skating, photography. *Address:* 5732 College Street, Halifax, NS B3H 1X3, Canada. *T:* 902–420–0717.

NOVA SCOTIA, Assistant Bishop of; *see* Allan, Rt Rev. H. J. P.

NOVE, Prof. Alexander, FRSE 1982; FBA 1978; Professor of Economics, University of Glasgow, 1963–82, now Emeritus; Hon. Senior Research Fellow, Glasgow University, since 1982; *b* Leningrad, 24 Nov. 1915; *s* of Jacob Novakovsky; *m* 1951, Irene MacPherson; three *s*. *Educ:* King Alfred Sch., London; London Sch. of Economics (Hon. Fellow, 1982). BSc (Econ) 1936. Army, 1939–46. Civil Service (mainly BoT), 1947–58; Reader in Russian Social and Economic Studies, Univ. of London, 1958–63. Hon. Dr.agr Giessen, 1977. *Publications:* The Soviet Economy, 1961; (with J. A. Newth) The Soviet Middle East, 1965; Was Stalin Really Necessary?, 1965; Economic History of the USSR, 1969; (ed, with D. M. Nuti) Socialist Economics, 1972; Efficiency Criteria for Nationalised Industries, 1973; Stalinism and After, 1976; The Soviet Economic System, 1977, 3rd edn 1986; Political Economy and Soviet Socialism, 1979; The Economics of Feasible Socialism, 1983; Socialism, Economics and Development, 1986. *Recreations:* walking in Scottish hills, travel, music, theatre, exotic dishes. *Address:* 55 Hamilton Drive, Glasgow G12 8DP. *T:* 041–339 1053. *Club:* Commonwealth Trust.

NOWAR, Maj.-Gen. Ma'an Abu, Jordanian Star 1st Class; Minister of Tourism and Antiquities, and of Culture and Youth, Hashemite Kingdom of Jordan, 1981–84; *b* 26 July 1928; *m* Vivian Ann Richards; two *s* seven *d*; *m* 1976, Susan Ann Coombs, Bath, Som; one *d*. *Educ:* London Univ. (Dip. World Affairs, 1963). Joined Jordanian Armed Forces, 1943; comd Regt, 1956; comd Bde, 1957; Counsellor, Jordan Embassy, London, 1963; Dir of Civil Defence, 1964; Dir of Public Security, 1967; Asst Chief of Staff, Jordan Armed Forces, 1969; Minister of Culture and Information, 1972–73; Ambassador of Jordan to the Court of St James's, 1973–76; Mayor of Amman, 1976–80; Minister of Public Works, 1980–81. *Publications:* The Battle of Karameh, 1968; For Jerusalem, 1969; 40 Armoured Brigade, 1970; The State in War and Peace, 1971; History of the Jordan Army, 1972; The Olympic Games Old and Modern, 1983. *Recreation:* swimming. *Address:* c/o Ministry of Tourism and Antiquities, Amman, Jordan.

NOWELL-SMITH, Prof. Patrick Horace, AM (Harvard); MA (Oxon); Professor of Philosophy, York University, Toronto, 1969–85, now Emeritus; *b* 17 Aug. 1914; *s* of Nowell Charles Smith; *m* 1st, 1946, Perilla Thyme (marr. diss. 1968), *d* of Sir Richard Vynne Southwell; three *s* one *d*; 2nd, 1968, Felicity Margret (marr. diss. 1986), *d* of Dr Richard Leonard Ward; two *d*. *Educ:* Winchester Coll.; New College, Oxford. Commonwealth Fellow, Harvard Univ., 1937–39. Served War of 1939–45, in Army, 1939–45. Fellow and Lecturer, Trinity Coll., Oxford, 1946–57, Estates Bursar, 1951–57; Professor of Philosophy: University of Leicester, 1957–64; University of Kent, 1964–69. *Publications:* Ethics, 1954; articles in Mind, Proc. Aristotelian Soc., Theoria, etc. *Address:* 5 Thackley End, 119 Banbury Road, Oxford OX2 6LB.

See also S. H. Nowell-Smith, Sir S. S. T. Young.

NOWELL-SMITH, Simon Harcourt, FSA; *b* 5 Jan. 1909; *s* of late Nowell Charles Smith, sometime Headmaster of Sherborne; *m* 1st, 1938, Marion Sinclair (*d* 1977), *d* of late W. S. Crichton, Liverpool; two *s* one *d*; 2nd, 1986, Judith Adams, *d* of Frederick B. Adams, *qv*. *Educ:* Sherborne; New Coll., Oxford (MA). Editorial Staff of The Times, 1932–44; Assistant Editor, Times Literary Supplement, 1937–39; attached to Intelligence Division, Naval Staff, 1940–45; Secretary and Librarian, The London Library, 1950–56; Secretary, Hospital Library Services Survey, 1958–59; President, Bibliographical Society, 1962–64; Lyell Reader in Bibliography, Oxford Univ., 1965–66. Pres., Oxford Bibliographical Soc., 1972–76. Trustee, Dove Cottage Trust, 1974–82. OStJ. *Publications:* Mark Rutherford, a bibliography, 1930; The Legend of the Master (Henry James), 1947; The House of Cassell, 1958; (ed) Edwardian England, 1964; Letters to Macmillan, 1967; International Copyright Law and the Publisher, 1968; Postscript to Autobiography of William Plomer, 1975. *Address:* 2 Emden House, Barton Lane, Old Headington, Oxford OX3 9JU.

See also Prof. P. H. Nowell-Smith.

NOYES, Ralph Norton; writer; *b* 9 June 1923; *s* of late Sidney Ralph Noyes and Nova (*née* Pearce); *m* 1948, Margaret Isaacs; two *s* one *d*. *Educ:* Haberdashers' Aske's Hampstead Sch.; London School of Economics (BScEcon). War service, RAF (aircrew), 1940–46. Air Ministry, 1949–63: Private Sec. to VCAS, 1950–52, and to CAS, 1953; Air Force Dept, 1964–69; idc 1966; Defence Secretariat, 1969–77: Asst Under-Sec. of State (Logistics), 1975–77; UK Rep., NATO Maintenance and Supply Org., 1975–77. Hon. Secretary: SPR, 1990–; Centre for Crop Circle Studies, 1990–. Member: Folklore Soc., 1987–; British UFO Res. Assoc., 1983–. *Publications:* A Secret Property, 1985; (ed) The Crop Circle Enigma, 1990; several short stories, articles, papers and broadcasts on speculative themes, in Punch, Country Life, Argosy, Fiction Magazine, etc, BBC2, Jl of Soc. for Psych. Res., several times reprinted in anthologies. *Recreations:* travel, research into anomalous topics. *Address:* 9 Oakley Street, SW3 5NN. *T:* 071–351 6659.

NSEKELA, Amon James, OURT 1985; Chairman and Managing Director, National Bank of Commerce, 1967–74 and since 1981; Chairman, Tanzania Investment Bank, since 1982; *b* 4 Jan. 1930; *s* of Ngonile Reuben Nsekela and Anyambilile Nsekela (*née* Kalinga); *m* 1957, Christina Matilda Nsekela (*née* Kyusa); two *s*. *Educ:* Rungwe Dist Sch.; Malangali Secondary Sch.; Tabora Govt Sen. Sec. Sch.; Makerere UC (DipEd); Univ. of Pacific (Scholar, MA). Schoolteacher, Rungwe Middle Sch. and Alliance Secondary Sch., 1954–57; entered Civil Service as DO, Moshi, 1960; Perm. Sec., Min. of External Affairs and Defence, 1963; Perm. Sec. to Min. of Commerce, 1964; Prin. Sec. to Treasury (also ex-officio Paymaster Gen.), 1966–67. MP 1973–75, and Mem. E African Legis. Assembly, 1967–70. High Comr, UK, 1974–81, and Ambassador Extraordinary and Plenipotentiary to Ireland, 1980–81. Chm. or Dir of many cos and corporations, 1967–, incl.: Chm., Nat. Insurance Corp. of Tanzania, 1967–72; Director: Nat. Develt Corp. (past Chm. when Tanganyika Develt Corp.); Bd of Internal Trade; E African Airways Corp.; Tanzania Zambia Railway Authority, 1982–; Bd, African Medical Res. Fund, 1986–. Mem./Sec., Presidential Commn on Estabt of Democratic One-Party State in Tanzania; Mem., Internat. Council of Trustees, Internat. Defence and Aid Fund for Southern Africa, 1985–. Chairman: Council, Inst. of Finance Management, 1971–; Inst. of Develt Management, 1982–; Public Service Salaries Review Commn, 1985–86. Pres., Tanzania Soc. for Internat. Develt; Past Pres., Economic Assoc. of Tanzania; Chm., Britain–Tanzania Soc., 1982–. Mem., TANU, 1955–. Mem., NEC, Chama Cha Mapinduzi, 1987–. Chm. Council, Univ. of Dar es Salaam; Vice-Chm., Council, Sokoine Univ. of Agriculture, 1982–. *Publications:* Minara ya Historia ya Tanganyika: Tanganyika hadi Tanzania, 1965, new edns 1966 and 1971; Demokrasi Tanzania, 1973; (with A. L. Nhonoli) The Development of Health Services in Mainland Tanzania: Tumetoka Mbali, 1976; Socialism and Social Accountability in a Developing Nation, 1978; (ed) Southern Africa: toward economic liberation, 1981; Towards Rational Alternatives, 1984; A Time to Act, 1984; contribs to Jl of Administration Overseas (ODM), African Review, Development Dialogue. *Recreations:* swimming, darts, reading, writing. *Address:* 9 Lupa Way, Box 722, Mbeya, Tanzania.

NTIWANE, Nkomeni Douglas; Minister for Commerce, Industry and Tourism, Swaziland, since 1987; *b* 16 Feb. 1933; *s* of Isaiah Myotha and Jane Dlamini; *m* 1st, 1960, Sophia Pulane Kali (*d* 1981); three *s*; 2nd, 1983, Phindile T. Mamba. *Educ:* DOT Coll., Middelburg, Transvaal, SA; Columbia Univ. (1967–68; Carnegie Fellow in Dipl.). Certificate Teacher: Mbekelweni Sch., 1962–63; Mhlume Central Sch., 1964–66; Lozitha Central Sch., Jan.-Sept. 1967. High Commissioner for Swaziland in London, 1968–71; Ambassador: Federal Republic of Germany, March 1969; Republic of France, April 1969. Permanent Secretary: Dept of Foreign Affairs, Swaziland, 1971–72; Ministry of Health, 1972–77; Ministry of Commerce, Industry, Mines and Tourism, 1977–80; retired from Civil Service, 1980; Group Personnel, Training and Localisation Manager, Swaki Gp of Cos, 1980–87. Swaziland Independence Medal, 1968; Meritorious Service Medal, Royal Swaziland Umbutfo Defence Force, 1978. *Publications:* Asive Ngwane (Siswati poetry), 1978; (jtly) Takitsi, 1986. *Address:* Emangweni, PO Box 41, Malkerns, Swaziland.

NUGEE, Edward George, TD 1964; QC 1977; *b* 9 Aug. 1928; *o s* of late Brig. George Travers Nugee, CBE, DSO, MC, RA, and of Violet Mary (*née* Richards, now Brooks); *m* 1955, Rachel Elizabeth Makower (*see* R. E. Nugee); four *s*. *Educ:* Brambletye; Radley Coll. (Open Scholar); Worcester Coll., Oxford (Open Exhibnr; Law Mods, Distinction, 1950; 1st Cl. Hons Jurisprudence, 1952; Eldon Law Scholar, 1953; MA 1956). National Service, RA, 1947–49 (Office of COS, GHQ, FARELF); service with 100 Army Photographic Interpretation Unit, TA, 1950–64 (retd Captain, Intell. Corps, 1964). Read as pupil with Lord Templeman and Lord Brightman; called to the Bar, Inner Temple, 1955, Bencher 1976; *ad eundem* Lincoln's Inn, 1968. Jun. Counsel to Land Commn (Chancery and Conveyancing), 1967–71; Counsel for litigation under Commons Registration Act, 1965, 1968–77; Conveyancing Counsel to Treasury, WO, MAFF, Forestry Commn, MoD (Admiralty), and DoE, 1972–77; Conveyancing Counsel of Court, 1976–77. Poor Man's Lawyer, Lewisham CAB, 1954–72. Member: CAB Adv. Cttee, Family Welfare Assoc., 1969–72; Management Cttee, Greater London Citizens Advice Bureaux Service Ltd, 1972–74; Man. Cttee, Forest Hill Advice Centre, 1972–76; Bar Council, 1962–66 (Mem., External Relations Cttee, 1966–71); Council of Legal Educn, 1967–90 (Vice-Chm. 1976–82, and Chm. of Bd of Studies, 1976–82); Adv. Cttee on Legal Educn, 1971–90; Common Professional Exam. Bd, 1976–89 (Chm., 1981–87); Lord Chancellor's Law Reform Cttee, 1973–; various working parties and consultative groups of Law Commn, 1966–; Inst. of Conveyancers, 1971– (Pres., 1986–87); Chm., Cttee of Inquiry into Management Problems of Privately Owned Blocks of Flats, 1984–85. Church Comr, 1990–. Chm. Governors, Brambletye Sch., 1972–77; Mem. Council, Radley Coll., 1975–. *Publications:* (jtly) Nathan on the Charities Act 1960, 1962; (ed jtly) Halsbury's Laws of England, titles Landlord and Tenant (3rd edn 1958), Real Property (3rd edn 1960, 4th edn 1982); contribs to legal jls. *Recreations:* travel, cooking, the family. *Address:* Wilberforce Chambers, 3 New Square, Lincoln's Inn, WC2A 3RS. *T:* 071–405 5296; 10 Heath Hurst Road, Hampstead, NW3 2RX. *T:* 071–435 9204.

NUGEE, Rachel Elizabeth, JP, MA; *b* 15 Aug. 1926; *d* of John Moritz Makower and Adelaide Gertrude Leonaura Makower (*née* Franklin); *m* 1955, Edward George Nugee, *qv*; four *s*. *Educ:* Roedean Sch., Brighton; Lady Margaret Hall, Oxford; MA (EngLang and Lit); Reading Univ. (Dip. Soc. Studies). Joined Mothers' Union, 1956; Diocesan Pres., London Dio., 1974–76; Central Pres., 1977–82; MU rep. on Women's Nat. Commn, 1983–88. Chm., Edmonton Area Social Responsibility Policy Cttee, 1987–90; Member: Royal Free Hosp. (Hampstead Gen. Hosp.) House Cttee and Patients' Services Cttee, 1961–72; London Diocesan Bd for Social Responsibility, 1984–85, 1987–90; Law of Marriage Gp, General Synod, 1985–88; Lord Chancellor's Adv. Cttee on Conscientious Objectors, 1986–. Trustee, Marriage Res. Fund, 1984–. JP Inner London (Thames), 1971, Dep. Chm. of Bench, 1985–. *Publications:* several religious articles and booklets. *Recreations:* active support of Church and family life; reading, especially history; visiting friends. *Address:* 10 Heath Hurst Road, Hampstead, NW3 2RX. *T:* 071–435 9204.

NUGENT, family name of **Earl of Westmeath** and **Baron Nugent of Guildford.**

NUGENT OF GUILDFORD, Baron, *cr* 1966 (Life Peer), of Dunsfold; **George Richard Hodges Nugent;** Bt 1960; PC 1962; *b* 6 June 1907; *s* of late Colonel George H. Nugent, RA; *m* 1937, Ruth, *d* of late Hugh G. Stafford, Tilford, Surrey. *Educ:* Imperial Service Coll., Windsor; RMA, Woolwich. Commissioned RA, 1926–29. MP (C) Guildford Division of Surrey, 1950–66. Parliamentary Secretary: Ministry of Agriculture, Fisheries and Food, 1951–57; Min. of Transport, 1957–Oct. 1959. A Dep. Speaker, House of Lords. JP Surrey; CC and sometime Alderman, Surrey, 1944–51. Member: Exec. Council, NFU, 1945–51; Agricl Improvement Council, 1947–51; Vice-Chairman: Nat. Fedn of Young Farmers, 1948–51; Wye Agricl Coll., 1946–51; Harper Adams Agric. Coll., 1947–51; Chairman: Thames Conservancy Board, 1960–74; Nat. Water Council, 1973–78; House of Commons Select Cttee for Nationalised Industries, 1961–64; Agricultural Market Development Cttee, 1962–68; Animal Virus Research Institute, 1964–77; Standing Conf. on London and SE Regional Planning, 1962–81; Defence Lands Cttee, 1971–73; President, Assoc. of River Authorities, 1965–74; Chm. Management Bd, Mount Alvernia Hosp., Guildford, 1987–; Mem., Guildford Diocesan Synod, 1970–. Pres., RoSPA, 1980–82. FRSA 1962. Hon. FIWEM (Hon. FIPHE; Hon. FIWES). DUniv Surrey, 1968. Hon. Freeman, Borough of Guildford, 1985. *Address:* Blacknest Cottage, Dunsfold, Godalming, Surrey GU8 4PE. *Club:* Royal Automobile (Vice-Pres., 1974).

NUGENT, Sir John (Edwin Lavallin), 7th Bt *cr* 1795; Chairman, Lambourn Holdings Ltd, since 1980; *b* 16 March 1933; *s* of Sir Hugh Charles Nugent, 6th Bt, and of Margaret Mary Lavallin, *er d* of late Rev. Herbert Lavallin Puxley; *S* father, 1983; *m* 1959, Penelope Anne, *d* of late Brig. Richard Nigel Hanbury, CBE, TD; one *s* one *d*. *Educ:* Eton. Short service commn, Irish Guards, Lieut, 1953–56. PA to William Geoffrey Rootes (later 2nd Baron Rootes), Chm. of Rootes Gp, 1957–59; joined board of Lambourn group of cos, 1959. High Sheriff of Berks, 1981–82; JP Berks, 1962. *Recreations:* garden and fishing. *Heir:* *s* Nicholas Myles John Nugent, *b* 17 Feb. 1967. *Address:* Ballinlough Castle, Clonmellon, Navan, Co. Meath, Ireland. *T:* Trim (046) 33135. *Club:* Kildare Street and University (Dublin).

NUGENT, Sir Peter Walter James, 5th Bt, *cr* 1831; *b* 26 Jan. 1920; *s* of Sir Walter Richard Nugent, 4th Bt and of Aileen Gladys, *y d* of late Middleton Moore O'Malley, JP, Ross, Westport, Co. Mayo; *S* father, 1955; *m* 1947, Anne Judith, *o d* of Major Robert Smyth, Gaybrook, Mullingar, Co. Westmeath; two *s* two *d*. *Educ:* Downside. Served War of 1939–45; 2nd Lieut, Hampshire Regt, 1941; Major, 1945. *Heir:* *s* Walter Richard Middleton Nugent, *b* 15 Nov. 1947. *Address:* Bay Bush, Straffan, Co. Kildare, Eire.

NUGENT, Sir Robin (George Colborne), 5th Bt *cr* 1806; *b* 11 July 1925; *s* of Sir Guy Nugent, 4th Bt and of Maisie, Lady Nugent, *d* of J. A. Bigsby; *S* father, 1970; *m* 1st, 1947, Ursula Mary (marr. diss. 1967), *d* of late Lt-Gen. Sir Herbert Fothergill Cooke, KCB, KBE, CSI, DSO; two *s* one *d*; 2nd, 1967, Victoria Anna Irmgard, *d* of late Dr Peter Cartellieri. *Educ:* Eton; RWA School of Architecture. Lt Grenadier Guards, 1943–48; served Italy, 1944–45. ARIBA 1959. *Recreation:* fishing. *Heir:* *s* Christopher George Ridley Nugent, *b* 5 Oct. 1949. *Address:* Bannerdown House, Batheaston, Bath, Avon.

NUNAN, Manus; lecturer; *b* 26 March 1926; *s* of Manus Timothy Nunan, Dist Justice, and Nan (*née* FitzGerald); *m* 1987, Valerie (*née* Robinson); one *s* one *d* by previous marriages. *Educ:* St Mary's Coll., Dublin; Trinity Coll., Dublin (BA, LLB). Called to the Irish Bar, King's Inns, 1950; called to the English Bar, Gray's Inn, 1956. Asst d'Anglais, Lycée Masséna, Nice, 1949–50; practised at Irish Bar, 1950–53; Crown Counsel, Nigeria, 1953–62; Solicitor-Gen., Northern Nigeria, 1962–64; Minister of Govt, Northern Nigeria, 1962; QC (Nigeria) 1962; practised at English Bar, 1965–85; a Recorder, 1978–84; since 1985 has lectured throughout Australia and North America on the life and trials of Oscar Wilde, Dr Samuel Johnson and his circle, Talleyrand; Evelyn Wrench Lectr, E-SU of USA, 1988; Vis. Lectr, Broward Community Coll., Fla, 1989; Lecturer: Amer. Irish Historical Soc., NY, 1990; Nat. Portrait Gall., 1991. *Address:* La Calmeraie, Route de L'Aude, 09110 Ax-les-Thermes, France. *T:* 61 64 24 93. *Club:* Kildare Street and University (Dublin).

NUNBURNHOLME, 4th Baron *cr* 1906; **Ben Charles Wilson;** Major, Royal Horse Guards, retired; *b* 16 July 1928; *s* of 3rd Baron Nunburnholme, and Lady Mary Thynne, *y d* of 5th Marquess of Bath, KG, PC, CB; *S* father, 1974; *m* 1958, Ines Dolores Jeanne, *d* of Gerard Walravens, Brussels; four *d* (including twin *d*). *Educ:* Eton. *Heir:* *b* Hon. Charles Thomas Wilson [*b* 27 May 1935; *m* 1969, Linda Kay, *d* of Cyril James Stephens; one *s* one *d*]. *Address:* c/o House of Lords, SW1.

NUNN, John Francis, PhD; MD; FRCS; FFARCS; Head of Division of Anaesthesia, Medical Research Council Clinical Research Centre, since 1968; *b* 7 Nov. 1925; *s* of late Francis Nunn, Colwyn Bay; *m* 1949, Sheila, *d* of late E. C. Doubleday; one *s* two *d*. *Educ:* Wrekin Coll.; Birmingham Univ. MO, Birmingham Univ. Spitzbergen Expedition, 1948; Colonial Med. Service, Malaya, 1949–53; University Research Fellow, Birmingham, 1955–56; Leverhulme Research Fellow, RCS, 1957–64; Part-time Lectr, Postgrad. Med. Sch., Univ. of London, 1959–64; Consultant Anæsth., Hammersmith Hosp., 1959–64; Prof. of Anaesthesia, Univ. of Leeds, 1964–68. Member: Council, RCS, 1977–82 (Mem. Board, Faculty of Anaesthetists, Vice-Dean, 1977–79, Dean, 1979–82); Council, Assoc. of Anaesthetists, 1973–76 (Vice Pres., 1988–90); Pres., Sect. Anaesthesia, RSM, 1984–85. Hunterian Professor, RCS, 1960; Visiting Professor to various American Universities, 1960–; British Council Lecturer: Switzerland, 1962; USSR, 1963; Czechoslovakia, 1969; China, 1974. Joseph Clover Lectr, RCS, 1968. Mem., Egypt Exploration Soc. Hon. FFARACS; Hon. FFARCSI. (1st) Sir Ivan Magill Gold Medal, Assoc. of Anaesthetists of GB and Ireland, 1988. *Publications:* Applied Respiratory Physiology, 1969, 3rd edn 1987; Jt Editor, General Anaesthesia, 3rd edn 1971, 5th edn 1989; several chapters in medical text-books, and publications in Journal Appl. Physiol., Lancet, Nature, British Journal Anæsth., etc. *Recreations:* archaeology, geology, model engineering, ski-ing. *Address:* MRC Clinical Research Centre, Northwick Park, Harrow, Middx; 3 Russell Road, Moor Park, Northwood, Mddx. *T:* Northwood (09274) 26363.

NUNN, Rear-Adm. John Richard Danford, CB 1980; Bursar and Official Fellow, Exeter College, Oxford, 1981–88, retired; *b* 12 April 1925; *s* of Surg. Captain Gerald Nunn and Edith Florence (*née* Brown); *m* 1951, Katharine Mary (*née* Paris); three *d*. *Educ:* Epsom Coll. CEng, FIMechE; MPhil Cantab, 1981; MA Oxon, 1982. Entered RN, 1943; RN Engrg Coll., Keyham, 1943–47; HMS Devonshire, Second Cruiser Sqdn, 1945; HMS Vengeance, 1947; Advanced Engineering Course, RNC Greenwich, 1949–51. HMS Amethyst, Korea, 1952–53; HMS Tiger, 1957–59; Commander, 1960; HMS Glamorgan, 1967–68; Captain, 1969; Sea Dart and Seaslug Chief Engineer, 1970–72; Cabinet Office, 1973–74; Staff of SACLANT, 1975–77; Rear-Adm., 1978; Port Adm., Rosyth, 1977–80. Fellow Commoner, Downing Coll., Cambridge, 1980–. Editor, The Naval Review, 1980–83. *Recreations:* sailing, tennis, gliding, travel. *Address:* Warner's Cottage, Corhampton, Hants SO3 1LL; 2 Sadler Walk, St Ebbes, Oxford OX1 3TX. *Clubs:* Naval; Royal Naval Sailing Association (Portsmouth).

NUNN, Trevor Robert, CBE 1978; Associate Director, Director Emeritus and Advisory Director, Royal Shakespeare Company, since 1987 (Artistic Director, 1968–78; Joint Artistic Director, 1978–87; Chief Executive, 1968–86); *b* 14 Jan. 1940; *s* of Robert Alexander Nunn and Dorothy May (*née* Piper); *m* 1st, 1969, Janet Suzman, *qv* (marr. diss. 1986); one *s*; 2nd, 1986, Sharon Lee Hill (marr. diss. 1991); two *d*. *Educ:* Northgate Grammar Sch., Ipswich; Downing Coll., Cambridge (BA). Producer, Belgrade Theatre, Coventry; subseq. Associate Dir, Royal Shakespeare Company. Hon. MA: Newcastle upon Tyne, 1982; Warwick. *Address:* Homevale Ltd, Gloucester Mansions, Cambridge Circus, WC2H 8HD.

NUNNELEY, John Hewlett, FCIT; Chairman, AMF Microflight Ltd, since 1987; *b* Sydney, NSW, 26 Nov. 1922; *o s* of late Wilfrid Alexander Nunneley and Audrey Mary (*née* Tebbitt); *m* 1945, Lucia, *e d* of Enrico Ceruti, Milan, Italy; one *s* one *d*. *Educ:* Lawrence Sheriff Sch., Rugby. Served War of 1939–45: Somerset LI, seconded KAR; Abyssinia, Brit. Somaliland, 1942; Burma campaign, 1944 (wounded, despatches); Captain and Adjt. Various management posts in aircraft, shipping, printing and publishing industries, 1946–55. Exec., Beaverbrook Newspapers, 1955–62; joined BTC, 1962: Chief Publicity

Officer, 1962–63; Chief Development Officer (Passenger) BR Bd, 1963–64; Chief Passenger Manager, 1964–69; Pres. and Chm., BR-Internat. Inc., New York, USA, 1966–69; Man. Dir, British Transport Advertising Ltd, 1969–87. Principal Advertising Consultant, Hong Kong Govt, 1981–83. Member: Passenger Co-ordination Cttee for London, 1964–69; Outdoor Advertising Council, 1969–88. Pres., European Fedn of Outdoor Advertising (FEPE), 1984–87. Introduced BR Corporate Identity, 1964 and Inter-City concept, 1965. FRSA. City of Paris Medal, 1986. *Publications:* numerous articles on aviation, transport and advertising subjects. *Recreations:* gliding (FAI Gold C and Two Diamonds), powered flight. *Address:* 6 Ashfield Close, Petersham, Surrey TW10 7AF.

NUREYEV, Rudolf Hametovich; ballet dancer and choreographer; Directeur Artistique de la Danse, Théâtre National de l'Opéra, Paris, 1983–89; *b* Razdolnaia, 1938, of a farming family. Joined Kirov Ballet School at age 17; appeared with the Company in 1959; when on tour, in Paris, sought political asylum, June 1961. Joined Le Grand Ballet du Marquis de Cuevas Company and has made frequent appearances abroad; London debut at Royal Academy of Dancing Gala Matinée, organised by Dame Margot Fonteyn, Dec. 1961; debut at Covent Garden in Giselle with Margot Fonteyn, Feb. 1962; Choreographic productions include: La Bayadère, Raymonda, Swan Lake, Tancredi, Sleeping Beauty, Nutcracker, Don Quixote, Romeo and Juliet, Manfred, The Tempest, Washington Square, Cinderella; guest artist in England and America in wide variety of rôles. Has danced in many countries of the world. Gold Star, Paris, 1963. *Films:* Romeo and Juliet, 1965; Swan Lake, 1966; I am a Dancer, 1972; Don Quixote, 1972; Valentino, 1977; Exposed, 1983. Légion d'Honneur (France), 1988. *Publication:* Nureyev, 1962. *Recreations:* listening to and playing music. *Address:* c/o S. A. Gorlinsky Ltd, 34 Dover Street, W1X 4NJ.

NURJADIN, Air Chief Marshal Roesmin; Minister of Communications, Indonesia, 1983–88, retired (of Transport, Communications and Tourism, 1978–83); *b* 31 May 1930; *m* 1962, Surjati Subali; two *s* one *d*. *Educ:* Indonesian Air Force Academy; Techn. Coll., Univ. Gadjahmada. Student Army, 1945–50. Comdr 3rd Fighter Sqdn, 1953; RAF CFS, England, 1954; Law Sch., 1956; Instructor, Jet Sqdn, 1957–59; Junior Staff Sch., 1959; Defence Services Staff Coll., Wellington, India, 1960–61; Dir Operation AF HQ, 1961–62; Dep. Comdr Operational Comd, Chief of Staff Air Defence Comd, 1962–64; Air Attaché: Bangkok, 1964–65; Moscow, 1965–66; Minister/C-in-C/Chief of Staff, Indonesian Air Force, 1966–70; Ambassador to the UK, 1970–74, to the USA, 1974–78. *Recreations:* golf, swimming. *Address:* c/o Ministry of Communications, Jl Merdeka Barat 8, Jakarta, Indonesia. *Clubs:* Highgate Golf; Djakarta Golf.

NURSAW, James, CB 1983; QC 1988; HM Procurator General and Treasury Solicitor, since 1988; *b* 18 Oct. 1932; *s* of William George Nursaw, *qv*; *m* 1959, Eira, *yr d* of late E. W. Caryl-Thomas, MD, BSc, Barrister-at-law; two *d*. *Educ:* Bancroft's School; Christ's Coll., Cambridge (Schol.; MA, LLB). Called to Bar, Middle Temple, 1955 (Blackstone Entrance Schol. and Prize, Harmsworth Schol.), Bencher 1989. Senior Research Officer, Cambridge Univ. Dept of Criminal Science, 1958. Joined Legal Adviser's Branch, Home Office, 1959; Principal Asst Legal Advr, HO and NI Office, 1977–80; Legal Secretary, Law Officers' Dept, 1980–83; Legal Adviser, Home Office and NI Office, 1983–88. Liveryman, Loriners' Co. *Address:* Queen Anne's Chambers, 28 Broadway, SW1H 9JS. *Clubs:* United Oxford & Cambridge University, MCC.

NURSAW, William George; investment consultant since 1961; financial writer and company director; *b* 5 Sept. 1903; *s* of George Edward Nursaw and Amy Elizabeth (*née* Davis); *m* 1931, Lilian May (*née* Howell); one *s* two *d*. *Educ:* Rushmore Road LCC Primary Sch.; Holloway Grammar Sch. (Schol.). Insurance, 1920–61: Trustee Man., Atlas Assce Co.; subseq. Dir Throgmorton Management (Man. Dir, 1962–71) and Hogg Robinson Gardner Mountain Pensions Management (Chm., 1963–71); Hon. Financial Adviser, RAF Escapers Soc., 1964–83, and National Birthday Trust, 1946–90 (and Hon. Treas.); Co-founder and Hon. Financial Advr, 1945–, Jt Pres., 1987–, Covenanters Educational Trust and Perry Foundn; Freeman, City of London; Past Warden, Loriners' Co.; Deacon, Chingford Congregational Church, 1944–62; Youth Leader, 1942–67; Sec. and Treas., 1934–58, Chm., 1959–79, Chingford and Waltham Forest Playing Fields Assoc. (completed 51 yrs as an hon. officer for the dist); Exec., Essex County Playing Fields Assoc., then Greater London Playing Fields, 1948–85. Civil Defence (Post Warden), 1938–65. FSS; ACII; FCIS (Mem. Council, 1962–70, Chm., London, 1968–69); FCIArb (Mem. Council, 1968–74); AMSIA. Mem., Royal Soc. of St George. *Publications:* Investment in Trust: problems and policies, 1961; Art and Practice of Investment, 1962, 4th edn 1974; Purposeful Investment, 1965; Principles of Pension Fund Investment, 1966, 2nd edn 1976; Investment for All, 1972; articles for national press on investment and insurance, incl. over 200 articles for The Guardian, Observer, etc. *Recreations:* rose-growing, cricket (Pres. and Captain, Chingford Park CC), writing, portrait painting, playing-fields movement, 1934–85 (Duke of Edinburgh award). *Address:* 603 Mountjoy House, Barbican, EC2Y 8BP. *T:* 071–628 7638; 6 Carlton Road East, Westgate, Kent. *T:* Thanet (0843) 32105. *Clubs:* City Livery, Aldersgate Ward, MCC, Pen International.

See also James Nursaw.

NURSE, Prof. Paul Maxime, FRS 1989; Fellow of Linacre College, since 1987, and Napier Research Professor of Microbiology, since 1991, University of Oxford; *b* 25 Jan. 1949; *s* of Maxime Nurse and Cissie Nurse (*née* White); *m* 1971, Anne Teresa (*née* Talbott); two *d*. *Educ:* Harrow County Grammar Sch.; Univ. of Birmingham (BSc): Univ. of East Anglia (PhD). Research Fellow, Univ. of Edinburgh, 1973–79; SERC Advanced Fellow and MRC Sen. Fellow, Univ. of Sussex, 1979–84; Hd of Cell Cycle Control Laboratory, Imp. Cancer Res. Fund, London, 1984–87; Iveagh Prof. of Microbiology, Univ. of Oxford, 1987–91. SAC Mem. EMBL. Guest Prof., Univ. of Copenhagen, 1980; Fleming Lectr, 1984, Marjory Stephenson Lectr, 1990, Soc. of Gen. Microbiology; Florey Lectr, Royal Soc., 1990. Pres., Genetical Soc., 1990–. Ciba Medal, Biochemical Soc., 1991; Feldberg Foundn Prize, 1991. *Publications:* numerous, in sci. jls, concerned with cell and molecular biology. *Recreations:* gliding, astronomy, talking. *Address:* Department of Biochemistry, University of Oxford, South Parks Road, Oxford OX1 3QU. *T:* Oxford (0865) 275296.

NURSTEN, Prof. Harry Erwin, PhD, DSc; CChem, FRSC; FIFST; FSLTC; Professor of Food Science, Reading University, since 1976; *s* of Sergius Nursten and Helene Nursten; *m* 1950, Jean Patricia Frobisher. *Educ:* Ilkley Grammar Sch.; Leeds Univ. (BSc 1st Cl. Hons Colour Chemistry, 1947; PhD 1949; DSc 1973). FRIC 1957; FIFST 1972; FSLTC 1986. Bradford Dyers Assoc. Res. Fellow, Dept of Colour Chem. and Dyeing, Leeds Univ., 1949–52; Lectr in Textile Chem. and Dyeing, Nottingham and Dist Tech. Coll., 1952–54; Lectr 1955–65, Sen. Lectr 1965–70, and Reader 1970–76, Procter Dept of Food and Leather Science, Leeds Univ.; Head of Dept of Food Sci., 1976–86, Head of Dept of Food Science and Technology, 1986–89, Head of Sub-Dept of Food Sci., 1989–91, Reading Univ. Res. Associate, Dept of Nutrition, Food Science and Technol., MIT, 1961–62; Vis. Prof., Dept of Food Science and Technol., Univ. of Calif, Davis, 1966. Chief Examiner, Mastership in Food Control, 1982–90. Pres., Soc. of Leather Technologists and Chemists, 1974–76. Bill Littlejohn Memorial Medallion Lectr, Brit. Soc. of Flavourists, 1974. *Publications:* (ed jtly) Progress in Flavour Research, 1979; papers in Jl Sci. Food Agric., and Jl Chromatog. *Address:* Department of Food Science and Technology, University of Reading, Whiteknights, PO Box 226, Reading, Berks RG6 2AP. *T:* Reading (0734) 318715.

NUTMAN, Dr Phillip Sadler, FRS 1968; Head of Department of Soil Microbiology, Rothamsted Experimental Station, Harpenden, 1957–79; *b* 10 Oct. 1914; *s* of John William Nutman and Elizabeth Hester Nutman (*née* Hughes); *m* 1940, Mary Meta Stanbury; two *s* one *d*. *Educ:* Teignmouth Grammar Sch.; Imperial Coll., London Univ. Research Asst, Rothamsted Experimental Station, 1940; Senior Research Fellow, Canberra, Australia, 1953–56; Rothamsted, 1956–79; Hannaford Res. Fellow, Waite Inst., Adelaide, 1980. Huxley Medal, 1959. *Publications:* research papers in plant physiological, genetical and microbiological journals. *Recreations:* music, woodworking. *Address:* Great Hackworthy Cottage, Tedburn St Mary, Exeter EX6 6DW. *T:* Tedburn St Mary (0647) 61364.

NUTTALL, Christopher Peter; Assistant Under Secretary of State and Director of Research and Statistics, Home Office, since 1989; *b* 20 April 1939; *s* of Barbara Goodwin and David Nuttall; *m* 1966, Caryn Thomas; two *s*. *Educ:* Queen Elizabeth Grammar Sch., Wakefield; Univ. of Keele (BA); Univ. of California at Berkeley (MA). Home Office Res. Unit, 1963–75 (Principal Res. Officer, 1971–75); Dir of Res., 1975–80, Dir Gen., Res. and Stats, 1980–82, Min. of Solicitor Gen., Ottawa; Asst Dep. Solicitor Gen. of Canada, 1982–89. UN Human Rights Fellow, 1967–68. *Publications:* Parole in England and Wales, 1977; articles on parole, deterrence, crime prevention and imprisonment. *Recreations:* The United States, television, taking baths, books. *Address:* Home Office, 50 Queen Anne's Gate, SW1H 9AT. *T:* 071–273 2616.

NUTTALL, Rev. Derek, MBE 1990; Minister, United Reformed Church, Windsor, since 1990; *b* 23 Sept. 1937; *s* of Charles William Nuttall and Doris Nuttall; *m* 1965, Margaret Hathaway Brown; two *s* one *d*. *Educ:* Ironville Sch.; Somercotes Sch.; Overdale Coll., Selly Oak (Diploma). Semi-skilled worker in industry, 1953–60; office clerk, 1960–61; college, 1961–65; ministry in Falkirk, 1965–67; ordained, 1967; ministry and community work in Aberfan, 1967–74: Gen. Sec., Community Assoc.; mem., church and community cttees; Nat. Organiser, 1974–78, Dir, 1978–90, Cruse—the Nat. Orgn for the widowed and their children, subseq. Cruse—Bereavement Care. Member: Exec., Internat. Fedn of Widow/Widower Orgns, 1980–90; Internat. Workgroup on Death and Dying, 1980–90; Internat. Liaison Gp on Disasters, 1986–90; Sec., Wkg Party on Social and Psychological Aspects of Disasters, 1989–91. *Publications:* The Early Days of Grieving, 1986; articles and papers on bereavement and on needs of widows, widowers and bereaved children. *Recreations:* music, reading, golf, keeping up with the family's activities. *Address:* The Manse, 10 Clifton Rise, Windsor, Berks SL4 5TD. *T:* Windsor (0753) 854558. *Club:* Royal Society of Medicine.

NUTTALL, Dr Geoffrey Fillingham, FBA 1991; Ecclesiastical historian, retired; Visiting Professor, King's College, London, 1977–80; *b* Colwyn Bay, Wales, 8 Nov. 1911; *s* of Harold Nuttall and Muriel Fillingham (*née* Hodgson); *m* 1944, Mary (*née* Preston) (*d* 1982), *widow* of George Philip Powley. *Educ:* Bootham Sch., York; Balliol Coll., Oxford (MA 1936); Mansfield Coll., Oxford (BD 1938, DD 1945). Ordained Congregational Minister, 1938; Warminster, Wilts, 1938–43; Fellow, Woodbrooke, Selly Oak Colls, Birmingham, 1943–45; Lectr in Church Hist., New Coll. (Sch. of Divinity), London Univ., 1945–77; Chm., Bd of Studies in Theol., Univ. of London, 1957–59; Dean, Faculty of Theol., 1960–64; FKC 1977. University Preacher: Leeds, 1950; Cambridge, 1958; London, 1968; Oxford, 1972, 1980. Lectures: Friends of Dr Williams's Library, 1951; Drew, New Coll., London, 1956; Hibbert, 1962; W. M. Llewelyn, Memorial Coll., Swansea, 1966; Charles Gore, Westminster Abbey, 1968; Owen Evans, Aberystwyth, 1968; F. D. Maurice, King's Coll., London, 1970; R. T. Jenkins, Bangor, 1976; Ethel M. Wood, London, 1978; Dr Williams Meml, Swansea, 1978. External Examiner: Belfast, Birmingham, Cambridge, Canterbury, Durham, Edinburgh, Leeds, McMaster, Manchester, Nottingham, Oxford, Salford, St Andrews, Wales. President: Friends' Hist. Soc., 1953; Congregational Hist. Soc., 1965–72; London Soc. for Study of Religion, 1966; Eccles. History Soc., 1972; United Reformed Church History Soc., 1972–77. Trustee, Dr Daniel Williams's Charity. A Vice-Pres., Hon. Soc. of Cymmrodorion, 1978–. Mem., Adv. Editorial Bd, Jl of Eccles. History, 1950–86. For. Hon. Mem., Kerkhistorisch Gezelschap, 1981–. Hon. DD Wales, 1969. *Publications:* (ed) Letters of John Pinney 1679–1699, 1939; The Holy Spirit in Puritan Faith and Experience, 1946 (2nd edn 1947); The Holy Spirit and Ourselves, 1947 (2nd edn 1966); Studies in Christian Enthusiasm illustrated from Early Quakerism, 1948; (ed) Philip Doddridge 1702–1751: his contribution to English religion, 1951; Richard Baxter and Philip Doddridge: a study in a tradition, 1951; The Reality of Heaven, 1951; James Nayler: a fresh approach, 1954; (contrib.) Studies in Christian Social Commitment, 1954; Visible Saints: the Congregational Way 1640–1660, 1957; The Welsh Saints 1640–1660: Walter Cradock, Vavasor Powell, Morgan Llwyd, 1957; Christian Pacifism in History, 1958 (2nd edn 1971); (ed with Owen Chadwick) From Uniformity to Unity 1662–1962, 1962; Better Than Life: the lovingkindness of God, 1962; (contrib.) Man's Faith and Freedom: the theological influence of Jacobus Arminius, 1962; (contrib.) The Beginnings of Nonconformity, 1964; (contrib.) Choose your Weapons, 1964; Richard Baxter (Leaders of Religion), 1965; Howel Harris 1714–1773: the last enthusiast, 1965; The Puritan Spirit: essays and addresses, 1967; Congregationalists and Creeds, 1967; (contrib.) A Declaration of Faith (Congregational Church in England and Wales), 1967; The Significance of Trevecca College 1768–91, 1969; The Faith of Dante Alighieri, 1969; Christianity and Violence, 1972; (contrib.) Violence and Oppression: a Quaker Response, 1973; New College, London and its Library, 1977; The Moment of Recognition: Luke as story-teller, 1978; contrib. Studies in Church History: Vol. VII, 1971; Vol. X, 1973; (contrib.) Pietismus und Réveil, 1978; (ed) Calendar of the Correspondence of Philip Doddridge, DD 1702–1751, 1979; (contrib.) Philip Doddridge, Nonconformity and Northampton, 1981; Handlist of the Correspondence of Mercy Doddridge 1751–1790, 1984; (with J. van den Berg) Philip Doddridge (1702–1751) and the Netherlands, 1987; (ed with N. H. Keeble) Calendar of the Correspondence of Richard Baxter, 1991; contrib. to Festschriften for: Gordon Rupp, 1975; Martin Schmidt, 1975; C. W. Dugmore, 1979; A. G. Dickens, 1980; R. Buick Knox, 1985; R. Tudur Jones, 1986; J. van den Berg, 1987; contrib. Dict. of Nat. Biog., Encyc. Brit., Dict. d'Histoire et de Géog. Ecclés., Evang. Kirchenlexikon; articles and revs in Jl Eccles. History and Jl Theol Studies; *Festschrift:* Reformation, Conformity and Dissent: essays in honour of Geoffrey Nuttall, 1977. *Recreations:* walking, genealogy, motoring (as passenger), languages. *Address:* 35 Queen Mother Court, 151 Selly Wood Road, Birmingham B30 1TH. *T:* 021–472 2320. *Club:* Penn.

NUTTALL, Rt. Rev. Michael; *see* Natal, Bishop of.

NUTTALL, Sir Nicholas Keith Lillington, 3rd Bt, *cr* 1922; *b* 21 Sept. 1933; *s* of Lieut-Colonel Sir E. Keith Nuttall, 2nd Bt, RE (who died on active service, Aug. 1941), and Gytha Primrose Harrison (*d* 1967), *e d* of Sidney H. Burgess, of Heathfield, Bowdon, Cheshire; *S* father, 1941; *m* 1st, 1960, Rosemary Caroline (marr. diss. 1971), *e d* of Christopher York, *qv*; one *s* one *d*; 2nd, 1971, Julia Jill Beresford (marr. diss. 1975), *d* of Thomas Williamson; 3rd, 1975, Miranda, *d* of Richard St John Quarry and Diana

Elizabeth (who *m* subseq. 2nd Baron Mancroft, KBE, TD); three *d*; 4th, 1983, Eugenie Marie Alicia, *e d* of William Thomas McWeeney; one *s*. *Educ:* Eton; Royal Military Academy, Sandhurst. Commissioned Royal Horse Guards, 1953; Captain, 1959; Major 1966; retd 1968. *Heir: s* Harry Nuttall, *b* 2 Jan. 1963. *Address:* PO Box N7776, Nassau, Bahamas. *T:* (809) 32 67938. *Club:* White's.

NUTTALL, Simon James; Director, Relations with China, Japan and the other countries of the Far East, Directorate General for External Relations, Commission of the European Communities, since 1988; *b* 6 Oct. 1940; *s* of John C. Nuttall and Amy L. Nuttall. *Educ:* Glossop Grammar Sch.; St John's Coll., Oxford (BA). HM Diplomatic Service, 1963–71; Office of Clerk of the Assembly, Council of Europe, 1971–73; EEC, 1973–. *Publications:* articles on European political co-operation in Yearbook of European Law. *Recreation:* strolling in the mountains. *Address:* Commission of the European Communities, 200 Rue de la Loi, 1049 Brussels, Belgium. *Club:* United Oxford & Cambridge University.

NUTTER, Most Rev. Harold Lee, DD; Archbishop of Fredericton and Metropolitan of the Ecclesiastical Province of Canada, 1980–89, retired (Bishop of Fredericton, 1971); *b* 29 Dec. 1923; *s* of William L. Nutter and Lillian A. Joyce; *m* 1946, Edith M. Carew; one *s* one *d*. *Educ:* Mount Allison Univ. (BA 1944); Dalhousie Univ. (MA 1947); Univ. of King's College (MSLitt 1947). Rector: Simonds and Upham, 1947–51; Woodstock, 1951–57; St Mark, Saint John, NB, 1957–60; Dean of Fredericton, 1960–71. Co-Chairman, NB Task Force on Social Development, 1970–71; Mem., Adv. Cttee to Sec. of State for Canada on Multi-culturalism, 1973. Member: Bd of Governors, St Thomas Univ., 1979–; Bd of Regents, Mount Allison Univ., 1978–84; Vice-Chm., Bd of Governors, Univ. of King's Coll., 1971–89. Pres., Atlantic Ecumenical Council, 1972–74, 1984–86. Vice-Chm., NB Police Commn, 1988–; Co-Chm., Dialogue New Brunswick, 1989–90. Hon. DD: Univ. of King's College, 1960; Montreal Diocesan Coll., 1982; Wycliffe Coll., 1983; Trinity Coll., Toronto, 1985; Hon. LLD, Mount Allison Univ., 1972. *Publication:* (jointly) New Brunswick Task Force Report on Social Development, 1971. *Address:* Comp. 25, Site 7, RR4, Fredericton, NB E3B 4X5, Canada.

NUTTGENS, Patrick John, CBE 1983; Director, Leeds Polytechnic, 1969–86; *b* 2 March 1930; 2nd *s* of late Joseph Edward Nuttgens, stained glass artist, and of Kathleen Mary Nuttgens (*née* Clarke); *m* 1954, Bridget Ann Badenoch; five *s* three *d*. *Educ:* Ratcliffe Coll., Leicester; Univ. of Edinburgh; Edinburgh Coll. of Art. MA, PhD, DA(Edin), ARIBA. Lectr, Dept of Architecture, Univ. of Edinburgh, 1956–61; Dir, Inst. of Advanced Architectural Studies, Univ. of York, 1962–68; Prof. of Architecture, Univ. of York, 1968–69; Hoffman Wood Prof. of Architecture, Univ. of Leeds, 1968–70. Member: Royal Commn on Ancient and Historical Monuments of Scotland, 1967–76; Ancient Monuments Bd, 1975–78; Royal Fine Art Commn, 1983–90. Chairman: BBC North Region Adv. Council, 1970–75; BBC Continuing Educn Adv. Council, 1977–82; CNAA Cttee for Art and Design, 1981–84. Hon. Prof., York Univ., 1986–. Hon. Fellow, Leeds Polytechnic. DUniv: York, 1986; Open, 1986; Hon. DLitt: Sheffield, 1987; Heriot-Watt, 1990. *Publications:* Reginald Fairlie, a Scottish Architect, 1959; York, City Building Series, 1971; The Landscape of Ideas, 1972; (contrib.) Spirit of the Age, 1975; York: the continuing city, 1976; Leeds, Old and New, 1976; Leeds, 1979; Yorkshire section, Shell Book of English Villages, 1980; Pocket Guide to Architecture, 1980; (Gen. Editor) World's Great Architecture, 1980; (contrib.) Study Service, 1982; The Story of Architecture, 1983; What should we teach and How should we teach it?, 1988; Understanding Modern Architecture, 1988; The Home Front, 1989; regular contributor to jls on architecture, planning, education and environmental studies. *Recreations:* drawing, painting, broadcasting. *Address:* Roselea Cottage, Terrington, York YO6 4PP. *Club:* Yorkshire (York).

NUTTING, Rt. Hon. Sir (Harold) Anthony, 3rd Bt *cr* 1902; PC 1954; *b* 11 Jan. 1920; 3rd and *y s* of Sir Harold Stansmore Nutting, 2nd Bt, and Enid Hester Nina (*d* 1961), *d* of F. B. Homan-Mulock; *S* father, 1972; *m* 1st, 1941, Gillian Leonora (marr. diss., 1959), *d* of Edward J. Strutt, Hatfield Peverel, Essex; two *s* one *d*; 2nd, 1961, Anne Gunning (*d* 1990), *d* of Arnold Parker, Cuckfield, Sussex. *Educ:* Eton; Trinity College, Cambridge. Leics. Yeo., 1939; invalided, 1940. In HM Foreign Service on special duties, 1940–45; MP (C) Melton Division of Leics, 1945–56, resigned. Chairman: Young Conservative and Unionist Movement, 1946; National Union of Conservative and Unionist Associations, 1950; Conservative National Executive Cttee, 1951. Parliamentary Under-Secretary of State for Foreign Affairs, 1951–54; Minister of State for Foreign Affairs, 1954–56, resigned. Leader, UK Delegn to UN General Assembly and to UN Disarmament Commn, 1954–56. *Publications:* I Saw for Myself, 1958; Disarmament, 1959; Europe Will Not Wait, 1960; Lawrence of Arabia, 1961; The Arabs, 1964; Gordon, Martyr and Misfit, 1966; No End of a Lesson, 1967; Scramble for Africa: the Great Trek to The Boer War, 1970; Nasser, 1972. *Recreation:* fishing. *Heir: s* John Grenfell Nutting, *qv*. *Club:* Boodle's.

NUTTING, Prof. Jack, MA, ScD, PhD; FEng, FIM; Professor of Metallurgy, Houldsworth School of Applied Science, University of Leeds, 1960–89, now Emeritus; consultant metallurgist; *b* 8 June 1924; *o s* of Edgar and Ethel Nutting, Mirfield, Yorks; *m* 1950, Thelma Kippax, *y d* of Tom and Florence Kippax, Morecambe, Lancs; one *s* two *d*. *Educ:* Mirfield Grammar School, Yorks; Univ. of Leeds. BSc Leeds, 1945; PhD Leeds, 1948; MA Cantab, 1952; ScD Cantab, 1967. Research at Cavendish Laboratory, Cambridge, 1948–49; University Demonstrator, 1949–54, University Lecturer, 1954–60, Department of Metallurgy, Cambridge University. President: Metals Soc., 1977–78; Instn of Metallurgists, 1980–81; Historical Metallurgy Soc., 1984–86. Awarded Beilby medal and prize, 1961; Hadfield medal and prize, 1964. Hon. DSc: Acad. of Mining and Metallurgy, Cracow, 1969; Moratuwa Univ., Sri Lanka, 1981. Institute of Metals Platinum Medal, 1988; Wilkinson Medal, 1989. *Publications:* numerous papers in Jls of Iron and Steel Inst., Inst. of Metals and Metals Soc. *Recreations:* foreign travel, mountain walking. *Address:* St Mary's, 57 Weetwood Lane, Headingley, Leeds LS16 5NP. *T* and *Fax:* Leeds (0532) 751400.

NUTTING, John Grenfell; Senior Treasury Counsel, since 1988; a Recorder of the Crown Court, since 1986; *b* 28 August 1942; *s* and *heir* of Rt Hon. Sir Anthony Nutting, *qv*; *m* 1974, Diane, Countess Beatty, *widow* of 2nd Earl Beatty, DSC; one *s* one *d*, and one step-*s* one step-*d*. *Educ:* Eton Coll.; McGill Univ. (BA 1964). Called to the Bar, Middle Temple, 1968, Hon. Bencher 1991; Jun. Treasury Counsel, 1981; First Jun. Treasury Counsel, 1987–88. Mem., Bar Council, 1976–80, 1986–87; Chm., Young Bar, 1978–79. *Recreations:* fishing, stalking, stamp collecting. *Address:* 3 Raymond Buildings, Grays Inn, WC1R 3BH. *T:* 071–831 3833. *Club:* White's.

NYAKYI, Anthony Balthazar; Permanent Tanzanian Representative to the United Nations, since 1989; *b* 8 June 1936; *m* 1969, Margaret Nyakyi; two *s* two *d*. *Educ:* Makerere Coll., Univ. of E Africa (BA Gen.). Admin. Office, Prime Minister's Office and Min. of Educn, 1962–63; Head of Political Div., Foreign Service Office, 1963–68; Ambassador: to the Netherlands, 1968–70; to Fed. Republic of Germany, 1970–72; Principal Sec., Foreign Affairs, 1972–78; Principal Sec., Defence, 1978–80; High Comr to Zimbabwe, 1980–81, in London, 1981–89. *Address:* Tanzanian Mission to UN, 205 E 42nd Street, 13th Floor, New York, NY 10017, USA.

NYE, Prof. John Frederick, FRS 1976; Melville Wills Professor of Physics, University of Bristol, 1985–88 (Professor of Physics, 1969–88), now Professor Emeritus; *b* 26 Feb. 1923; *s* of Haydn Percival Nye and Jessie Mary, *d* of Anderson Hague, painter; *m* 1953, Georgiana Wiebenson; one *s* two *d*. *Educ:* Stowe; King's Coll., Cambridge (Maj. Schol.; MA, PhD 1948). Research, Cavendish Laboratory, Cambridge, 1944–49; Univ. Demonstrator in Mineralogy and Petrology, Cambridge, 1949–51; Bell Telephone Laboratories, NJ, USA, 1952–53; Lectr, 1953, Reader, 1965, Univ. of Bristol; Visiting Professor: in Glaciology, California Inst. of Technol., 1959; of Applied Sciences, Yale Univ., 1964; of Geophysics, Univ. of Washington, 1973. President: Internat. Glaciological Soc., 1966–69; Internat. Commn of Snow and Ice, 1971–75. For. Mem., Royal Swedish Acad. of Scis, 1977. Kirk Bryan Award, Geol. Soc. of Amer., 1961; Seligman Crystal, Internat. Glaciol Soc., 1969; Antarctic Service Medal, USA, 1974; NPL Metrology Award, 1986; Charles Chree Medal, Inst. of Physics, 1989. *Publications:* Physical Properties of Crystals, 1957, rev. edn 1985; papers on physics of crystals, glaciology, and applications of catastrophe theory in scientific jls. *Address:* 45 Canynge Road, Bristol BS8 3LH. *T:* Bristol (0272) 733769.

See also P. H. Nye.

NYE, Ven. Nathaniel Kemp; retired; *b* 4 Nov. 1914; *s* of Charles Frederick and Evelyn Nye; *m* 1941, Rosa Jackson; two *s* one *d*. *Educ:* Merchant Taylors' Sch.; King's College London (AKC 1935); Cuddesdon College, Oxford. Ordained 1937 to St Peter's, St Helier Estate, Morden, Surrey; Chaplain RAF, 1940–46 (POW 1941–43; escaped from Italy at liberation); Rector, Holy Trinity, Clapham, 1946–54; Vicar, St Peter's, St Helier Estate, 1954–60; Vicar, All Saints, Maidstone (Parish Church), Canon, and Rural Dean, 1960–66; Tait Missioner, Canterbury Diocese, 1966–72; Archdeacon of Maidstone, 1972–79. Hon. Canon of Canterbury, 1960; Canon Emeritus, 1979; Archdeacon Emeritus, dio. Canterbury, 1982. *Recreations:* woodcraft, sailing, travel; family life! *Address:* Lees Cottage, Boughton Lees, Ashford, Kent TN25 4HX. *T:* Ashford (0233) 626175.

NYE, Peter Hague, FRS 1987; Reader in Soil Science, University of Oxford, 1961–88; Fellow of St Cross College, Oxford, 1966–88 (Senior Fellow, 1982–83), now Emeritus Fellow; *b* 16 Sept. 1921; *s* of Haydn Percival Nye and Jessie Mary (*née* Hague); *m* 1953, Phyllis Mary Quenault; one *s* two *d*. *Educ:* Charterhouse; Balliol Coll., Oxford (MA, BSc (Domus Exhibnr)); Christ's Coll., Cambridge. Agricl Chemist, Gold Coast, 1947–50; Lectr in Soil Science, University Coll. of Ibadan, Nigeria, 1950–52; Sen. Lectr in Soil Science, Univ. of Ghana, 1952–60; Res. Officer, Internat. Atomic Energy Agency, Vienna, 1960–61. Vis. Professor, Cornell Univ., 1974, 1981, Messenger Lectures, 1989; Commonwealth Vis. Prof., Univ. of Western Aust., 1979; Vis. Prof., Royal Vet. and Agricl Univ., Copenhagen, 1990. Pres., British Soc. Soil Science, 1968–69; Mem. Council, Internat. Soc. Soil Science, 1968–74. Governor, Nat. Vegetable Res. Station, 1972–87. *Publications:* The Soil under Shifting Cultivation, 1961; Solute Movement in the Soil-Root System, 1977; articles, mainly in Jl of Soil Science, Plant and Soil, Jl of Agricl Science. *Recreations:* computing; formerly cricket, tennis, squash. *Address:* Hewel Barn, Common Road, Beckley, Oxon OX3 9UR. *T:* Stanton St John (086735) 607.

See also J. F. Nye.

NYE, Robert; writer; *b* 15 March 1939; *s* of Oswald William Nye and Frances Dorothy Weller; *m* 1st, 1959, Judith Pratt (marr. diss. 1967); three *s*; 2nd, 1968, Aileen Campbell; one *d*. *Educ:* Southend High School, Essex. Freelance writer, 1961–. FRSL 1977. *Publications: poetry:* Juvenilia 1, 1961; Juvenilia 2, 1963 (Eric Gregory Award, 1963); Darker Ends, 1969; Divisions on a Ground, 1976; A Collection of Poems 1955–1988, 1989; *fiction:* Doubtfire, 1967; Tales I Told My Mother, 1969; Falstaff, 1976 (The Guardian Fiction Prize, 1976; Hawthornden Prize, 1977); Merlin, 1978; Faust, 1980; The Voyage of the Destiny, 1982; The Facts of Life and Other Fictions, 1983; The Memoirs of Lord Byron, 1989; The Life and Death of My Lord Gilles de Rais, 1990; *plays:* (with Bill Watson) Sawney Bean, 1970; The Seven Deadly Sins: A Mask, 1974; Penthesilea, Fugue and Sisters, 1976; *children's fiction:* Taliesin, 1966; March Has Horse's Ears, 1966; Wishing Gold, 1970; Poor Pumpkin, 1971; Out of the World and Back Again, 1977; Once Upon Three Times, 1978; The Bird of the Golden Land, 1980; Harry Pay the Pirate, 1981; Three Tales, 1983; *translation:* Beowulf, 1968; *editions:* A Choice of Sir Walter Ralegh's Verse, 1972; William Barnes: Selected Poems, 1973; A Choice of Swinburne's Verse, 1973; The English Sermon 1750–1850, 1976; The Faber Book of Sonnets, 1976; PEN New Poetry 1, 1986; contribs to British and American periodicals. *Recreation:* gambling. *Address:* 2 Westbury Crescent, Wilton, Cork, Ireland.

NYERERE, Julius Kambarage; President, United Republic of Tanzania (formerly Tanganyika and Zanzibar), 1964–85; President, Tanganyika African National Union, 1954–77; *b* 1922; *m* 1953, Maria Magige; five *s* two *d*. *Educ:* Tabora Secondary School; Makerere University College; Edinburgh University (MA). Began as Teacher; became President African Association, Dar es Salaam, 1953; formed Tanganyika African National Union, left teaching and campaigned for Nationalist Movement, 1954; addressed Trusteeship Council, 1955, and Cttee of UN Gen. Assembly, 1956. MLC Tanganyika, July-Dec. 1957, resigned in protest; elected Mem. for E Prov. in first elections, 1958, for Dar es Salaam, 1960; Chief Minister, 1960; Prime Minister of Tanganyika, 1961–62; President, Tanganyika Republic, 1962–64. Chm., Chama cha Mapinduzi (The Revolutionary Party) (born of merger between mainland's TANU and Zanzibar Afro-Shiraz Party), 1977–90. Chm., OAU, 1984. First Chancellor, Univ. of East Africa, 1963–70; Chancellor: Univ. of Dar es Salaam, 1970–85; Sokoine Univ. of Agriculture, 1984–. Chm., South Commn, 1987–. Holds hon. degrees. *Publications:* Freedom and Unity-Uhuru Na Umoja, 1966; Freedom and Socialism-Uhuru na Ujamaa, 1969; Essays on Socialism, 1969; Freedom and Development, 1973; Swahili trans of Julius Caesar and The Merchant of Venice, 1969. *Address:* PO Box 71000, Dar es Salaam, United Republic of Tanzania.

NYMAN, Michael; composer; *b* 23 March 1944; *s* of Mark and Jeanette Nyman; *m* 1970; two *d*. *Educ:* Royal Academy of Music; King's College London (BMus); Conservatorul Ciprian Porumbescu, Bucharest. FRAM 1991. Music critic, Spectator, New Statesman, The Listener, 1968–78; formed Michael Nyman Band, 1977. *Film scores include:* The Draughtsman's Contract, 1982; Drowning by Numbers, 1988; The Cook, The Thief, His Wife and Her Lover, 1989; Monsieur Hire, 1989; The Hairdresser's Husband, 1990; Prospero's Books, 1990; *other compositions:* A Broken Set of Rules, Royal Ballet, 1983; The Man Who Mistook his Wife for a Hat (opera), 1986; String Quartets, 1985, 1988, 1990; Six Celan Songs, 1990–91; La Princesse de Milan (opera ballet), 1991; Where the Bee Dances, for saxophone and orch., 1991. *Publication:* Experimental Music: Cage and beyond, 1974. *Recreation:* QPR. *Club:* Groucho.

O

OAKELEY, Sir John (Digby Atholl), 8th Bt *cr* 1790, of Shrewsbury; Manager, Dehler Yachts UK, since 1988; *b* 27 Nov. 1932; *s* of Sir Atholl Oakeley, 7th Bt and of Mabel, (Patricia), *d* of Lionel H. Birtchnell; *S* father, 1987; *m* 1958, Maureen Frances, *d* of John and Ellen Cox; one *s* one *d*. *Educ:* private tutor. Own charter business, 1958–61; Contracts Manager, Proctor Masts, 1961–72; Managing Director: Freedom Yachts Internat. Ltd, 1981–88; Miller & Whitworth, 1972–81. *Publications:* Winning, 1968; Sailing Manual, 1980; Downwind Sailing, 1981. *Recreation:* yachting (holder of national, international, European and world titles; twice represented Great Britain in Olympic Games). *Heir: s* Robert John Atholl Oakeley [*b* 13 Aug. 1963; *m* 1989, Catherine Amanda, *d* of late William Knowles]. *Address:* 10 Bursledon Heights, Long Lane, Bursledon, Hants SO3 8DB. *Club:* Warsash Sailing (Warsash, Hants).
See also M. Oakeley.

OAKELEY, Mary, MA Oxon; Headmistress, St Felix School, Southwold, 1958–78; *b* 2 April 1913; *d* of Maj. Edward Francis Oakeley, S Lancs Regt, and Everilde Anne (*née* Beaumont); *sister* of Sir Atholl Oakeley, 7th Bt. *Educ:* St John's Bexhill-on-Sea; St Hilda's Coll., Oxford. MA Hons History. Asst Mistress: St James's, West Malvern, 1935–38; St George's, Ascot, 1938–39; Headmistress, Craighead Diocesan Sch., Timaru, NZ, 1940–55; Head of American Section, La Châtelainie, St Blaise, Switzerland, 1956–58. *Recreations:* gardening, embroidery. *Address:* 8 Newland Close, Eynsham, Oxon OX8 1LE. *T:* Oxford (0865) 880759. *Club:* Royal Over-Seas League.
See also Sir J. D. A. Oakeley, Bt.

OAKES, Sir Christopher, 3rd Bt, *cr* 1939; *b* 10 July 1949; *s* of Sir Sydney Oakes, 2nd Bt, and Greta (*d* 1977), *yr d* of Gunnar Victor Hartmann, Copenhagen, Denmark; *S* father, 1966; *m* 1978, Julie Dawn, *d* of Donovan Franklin Cowan, Regina, Canada; one *s* one *d*. *Educ:* Bredon, Tewkesbury; Georgia Mil. Acad., USA. *Heir: s* Victor Oakes, *b* 6 March 1983.

OAKES, Rt. Hon. Gordon James; PC 1979; MP (Lab) Halton, since 1983 (Widnes, Sept. 1971–1983); *b* 22 June 1931; *o s* of late James Oakes and Florence (*née* Hewitt), Widnes, Lancs; *m* 1952, Esther O'Neill, *e d* of late Councillor Joseph O'Neill; three *s*. *Educ:* Wade Deacon Gram. Sch., Widnes; Univ. of Liverpool. BA (Hon.) English, 1952; Admitted Solicitor, 1956. Entered Widnes Borough Council, 1952 (Mayor, 1964–65). Chm. Widnes Constituency Labour Party, 1953–58; contested (Lab): Bebington, 1959; Moss Side (Manchester) by-election, 1961; MP (Lab) Bolton West, 1964–70; PPS, Home Office, 1966–67, DES, 1967–70; Front Bench Opposition spokesman on local govt and the environment, 1970–74; Parly Under-Secretary of State: DoE, 1974–76; Dept of Energy, 1976; Minister of State, DES, 1976–79; Front Bench Opposition spokesman on Environment, 1979–83. British Deleg., NATO Parliamentarians, 1967–70; Member: Select Cttee on Race Relations, 1969–70; Executive, NW Region of Labour Party, 1971–73; Exec. Cttee, CPA, 1979–; Chairman: All-Party Energy Efficiency Gp, 1980–; All-Party Chem. Industry Gp, 1990– (Vice-Chm., 1982–90); Jt Chm., All-Party Gp for the Licensing Trade, 1986–. Vice-President: Rural District Councils Assoc., 1972–74; County Councils Assoc., 1982–; Environmental Officers' Assoc. (formerly Inst. of Public Health Inspectors), 1973–; Building Societies Assoc., 1984–; Jt Chm., Nat. Waste Management Adv. Council, 1974–76. Hon. Alderman, Borough of Halton. *Publications:* The Management of Higher Education in the Maintained Sector, 1978; various articles. *Recreations:* conversation, motoring with the family, caravanning, maps. *Address:* Upton Bridle Path, Widnes, Cheshire.

OAKES, Joseph Stewart; barrister-at-law; *b* 7 Jan. 1919; *s* of Laban Oakes and Mary Jane Oakes; *m* 1950, Irene May Peasnall. *Educ:* Royal Masonic Sch., Bushey; Stretford Grammar Sch.; Manchester Univ., 1937–40 (BA Hons). Royal Signals, 1940–48, Captain. Called to Bar, Inner Temple, 1948; practised on Northern Circuit, 1948–; a Recorder, 1975–82. Presiding Legal Mem., Mental Health Review Tribunal, 1971–91. *Recreations:* horticulture, photography, music. *Address:* 38 Langley Road, Sale, Greater Manchester M33 5AY. *T:* 061–962 2068; 28 St John Street, Manchester M3 4DJ. *T:* 061–834 8418.

OAKHAM, Archdeacon of; *see* Fernyhough, Ven. B.

OAKLEY, Brian Wynne, CBE 1981; Director, Logica (Cambridge) Ltd; *b* 10 Oct. 1927; *s* of Bernard and Edna Oakley; *m* 1953, Marian Elizabeth (*née* Woolley); one *s* three *d*. *Educ:* Exeter Coll., Oxford. MA. FInstP, FBCS. Telecommunication Res. Establishment, 1950; Head, Industrial Applications Unit, RRE, 1966–69; Head, Computer Systems Branch, Min. of Technology, 1969–72; Head, Res. Requirements Div., DTI, 1972–78; Sec., SRC, later SERC, 1978–83; Dep. Sec., DTI, and Dir, Alvey Programme, 1983–87. Pres., BCS, 1988. DUniv York, 1988. *Publication:* (with Kenneth Owen) Alvey, 1990. *Recreations:* theatre, sailing. *Address:* 120 Reigate Road, Ewell, Epsom, Surrey KT17 3BX. *T:* 081–393 4096.

OAKLEY, Christopher John; Editor-in-Chief, since 1989, Managing Director, since 1990, Birmingham Post & Mail; *b* 11 Nov. 1941; *s* of late Ronald Oakley and of Joyce Oakley; *m* 1st, 1962, Linda Margaret Viney (marr. diss. 1986); one *s* two *d*; 2nd, 1990, Moira Jean Martingale. *Educ:* Skinners' School, Tunbridge Wells. Kent and Sussex Courier, 1959; Bromley and Kentish Times, 1963; Kent and Sussex Courier, 1963; Evening Argus, Brighton, 1966; Evening Echo, Basildon, 1969; Evening Post, Leeds, 1970; Dep. Editor, Yorkshire Post, 1976; Editor, Lancashire Evening Post, 1981; Dir, Lancashire Evening Post, 1981–83; Editor, Liverpool Echo, 1983–89; Dir, Liverpool Daily Post and Echo Ltd, 1984–89.

OAKLEY, John Davidson, CBE 1981; DFC 1944; Chairman: Grosvenor Development Capital, 1981–91; Grosvenor Technology Ltd, 1986–91; Gardners Transformers Ltd, 1986–91 (Deputy Chairman, 1984–86; Director, since 1982); Third Grosvenor Ltd, 1987–91; *b* 15 June 1921; *s* of Richard Oakley and Nancy Davidson; *m* 1943, Georgina Mary Hare; two *s*. *Educ:* Green Lane Sch. Joined Briggs Motor Bodies Ltd, 1937. Served War in RAF, 1941–46: commissioned 1942; Flt Lt 1943; actg Sqdn Leader 1944; apptd to Air Min. Directorate Staff, 1945. Engrg Buyer, Briggs Motor Bodies Ltd, 1946–53; Dep. Purchase Manager, Body Div., Ford Motor Co. Ltd, 1953–56; Production Dir/General Manager, Standard Triumph (Liverpool) Ltd, until 1962; Managing Director: Copeland & Jenkins Ltd, 1963–71; R. Woolf & Co. Ltd, 1964–67; Gp Man. Dir, L. Sterne & Co., 1967–69; Chairman: General Electric & Mechanical Systems Ltd, 1970–73; Berwick Timpo Ltd, 1970–82; Edgar Allen Balfour Ltd, 1974–79; Australian British Trade Assoc., 1977–81 (Vice-Pres., British Council, 1981–); BOTB Adv. Gp Australia and NZ, 1977–81; Mem., British Overseas Trade Adv. Council, 1977–83. Director: Blairs Ltd, 1976–82; Eagle & Globe Steel Ltd, NSW, 1978–79; Ionian Securities Ltd, 1978–88; Nexos Office Systems Ltd, 1981–82; Isis Gp PLC (formerly Industrial Services plc), 1982–; Beau Brummel Ltd, 1972–85; Robert Jenkins (Hldgs) Ltd, 1976– (Dep. Chm., 1978–83, Chm., 1983–90). Oxford Univ. Business Summer School: Dir for 1978; Mem., Steering Cttee, 1981–, Chm., 1984–87. Cons. Mem., Essex CC, 1982–85. Member: Glovers' Co.; Cutlers' Co. in Hallamshire; Inst. of British Carriage & Automobile Manufacturers. CBIM; FIPS. FRSA. *Recreations:* golf, tennis, walking, bridge. *Address:* 25 Manor Links, Bishop's Stortford, Herts CM23 5RA. *T:* Bishop's Stortford (0279) 507552. *Clubs:* Reform, Royal Air Force; Bishop's Stortford Golf (Bishop's Stortford, Herts).

OAKLEY, Robin Francis Leigh; Political Editor, The Times, since 1986; *b* 20 Aug. 1941; *s* of Joseph Henry Oakley, civil engineer and Alice Barbara Oakley; *m* 1966, Carolyn Susan Germaine Rumball; one *s* one *d*. *Educ:* Wellington College; Brasenose College, Oxford (MA). Liverpool Daily Post, 1964–70; Sunday Express, 1970–79; Assistant Editor: Now! magazine, 1979–81, Daily Mail, 1981–86. Contribs to radio and TV; columnist, People and Politics, BBC World Service, 1986–; presenter: The Week in Westminster, BBC Radio, 1987–; Power of Patronage series, BBC, 1991. *Publications:* (with Peter Rose) The Political Year 1970; (with Peter Rose) The Political Year 1971; contribs to educnl series. *Recreations:* theatre, horse racing, sports, bird watching. *Address:* Quarry House, Lynwood Road, Epsom, Surrey. *Club:* Royal Automobile.

OAKLEY, Wilfrid George, MD, FRCP; Hon. Consulting Physician, King's College Hospital, since 1971; Vice President, British Diabetic Association, since 1971; *b* 23 Aug. 1905; *s* of late Rev. Canon G. D. Oakley and Mrs Oakley; *m* 1931, Hermione Violet Wingate-Saul; one *s*. *Educ:* Durham School; Gonville and Caius College, Cambridge; St Bartholomew's Hospital. Tancred studentship in Physic, Gonville and Caius Coll., 1923; Bentley Prize and Baly Research Schol., St Bart's Hosp., 1933. Formerly Physician i/c Diabetic Dept, King's College Hosp., 1957–70. Examr, Cambridge and Glasgow Univs. MD (Hon. Mention) Cantab 1934; FRCP 1942. Pres., Med. Soc., London, 1962; Mem. Assoc. of Physicians of Great Britain; Vice-Pres., British Diabetic Assoc., 1971. *Publications:* (jtly) Clinical Diabetes and its Biochemical Basis, 1968; Diabetes and its Management, 1973, 3rd edn 1978; scientific articles and chapters on diabetes in various text-books. *Address:* 111 Clifton Hill, St John's Wood, NW8 0JS. *T:* 071–624 3033.

OAKSEY, 2nd Baron *cr* 1947 (properly **TREVETHIN,** 4th Baron *cr* 1921, **AND OAKSEY); John Geoffrey Tristram Lawrence,** OBE 1985; JP; Racing Correspondent to Daily Telegraph since 1957; Columnist, Racing Post, since 1988; racing commentator for ITV, since 1970; Director, HTV, 1980–91; *b* 21 March 1929; *o s* of 1st Baron Oaksey and 3rd Baron Trevethin and Marjorie (*d* 1984), *d* of late Commander Charles N. Robinson, RN; *S* father, 1971; *m* 1st, 1959, Victoria Mary (marr. diss. 1987), *d* of late Major John Dennistoun, MBE; one *s* one *d*; 2nd, 1988, Rachel Frances Crocker, *d* of late Alan Hunter. *Educ:* Horris Hill; Eton; New College, Oxford (BA); Yale Law School. Racing Correspondent: Horse and Hound, 1959–88; Sunday Telegraph, 1960–88. JP Malmesbury, 1978. *Publications:* History of Steeplechasing (jointly), 1967; The Story of Mill Reef, 1974. *Recreations:* skiing, riding. *Heir: s* Hon. Patrick John Tristram Lawrence [*b* 29 June 1960; *m* 1987, Lucinda, *e d* of Demetri Marchessini and Mrs Nicholas Peto; one *d*]. *Address:* Hill Farm, Oaksey, Malmesbury, Wilts SN16 9HS. *T:* Crudwell (06667) 303, *Fax:* Crudwell (06667) 7962. *Club:* Brooks's.
See also Sir H. S. L. Dundas.

OAKSHOTT, Hon. Sir Anthony (Hendrie), 2nd Bt *cr* 1959; *b* 10 Oct. 1929; *s* of Baron Oakshott, MBE (Life Peer), and Joan (*d* 1986), *d* of Marsden Withington; *S* to baronetcy of father, 1975; *m* 1965, Mrs Valerie de Pret-Roose (marr. diss. 1981; she *d* 1988), *d* of Jack Vlasto. *Educ:* Rugby. *Heir: b* Hon. Michael Arthur John Oakshott [*b* 12 April 1932; *m* 1st, 1957, Christina Rose Methuen (*d* 1985), *d* of late Thomas Banks; three *s*; 2nd, 1988, Mrs (Helen) Clare Jones, *d* of late Edward Ravell]. *Address:* Beckley House, Bledington, Oxfordshire OX7 6UX. *T:* Kingham (0608) 658527. *Club:* White's.

OATES, Prof. (Edward Ernest) David (Michael), FSA; FBA 1974; Professor of Western Asiatic Archaeology, University of London, 1969–82; *b* 25 Feb. 1927; *s* of Thomas Oates and Dora B. Strike; *m* 1956, Joan Louise Lines; one *s* two *d*. *Educ:* Callington County Sch.; Oundle Sch.; Trinity Coll., Cambridge (BA, MA). Fellow of Trinity Coll., Cambridge, 1951–65; Director, British School of Archaeology in Iraq, 1965–69 (Chm., 1988–). Director, British Archaeological Expedition to Tell Brak, Syria, 1976–. FSA 1954. *Publications:* Studies in the Ancient History of N Iraq, 1968; (with J. Oates) The Rise of Civilisation, 1976; contribs to The Dark Ages, ed D. Talbot Rice, 1965; Papers of the British School at Rome, Iraq, etc. *Recreations:* history, carpentry. *Address:* 86 High Street, Barton, Cambridge CB3 7BG. *T:* Cambridge (0223) 262273.
See also Sir Thomas Oates.

OATES, Rev. Canon John; Rector of St Bride's Church, Fleet Street, since 1984; *b* 14 May 1930; *s* of John and Ethel Oates; *m* 1962, Sylvia Mary, *d* of Herbert Charles and Ada

Harris; three *s* one *d*. *Educ:* Queen Elizabeth School, Wakefield; SSM, Kelham. Curate, Eton College Mission, Hackney Wick, 1957–60; Development Officer, C of E Youth Council and mem. staff, Bd of Education, 1960–64; Development Sec., C of E Council for Commonwealth Settlement, 1964–65, Gen. Sec. 1965–70; Sec., C of E Cttee on Migration and Internat. Affairs, Bd for Social Responsibility, 1968–71; Vicar of Richmond, Surrey, 1970–84; RD, Richmond and Barnes, 1979–84. Commissary: of Archbishop of Perth and Bishop of NW Australia, 1968–; to Archbishop of Jerusalem, 1969–75; to Bishop of Bunbury, 1969–. Hon. Canon, Bunbury, 1969–. Chaplain: Inst. of Journalists, 1984–; Inst. of Public Relations, 1984–; Publicity Club of London, 1984–; London Press Club, 1984–. Chaplain: Co. of Marketors, 1984–; Co. of Stationers and Newspapermakers, 1989–. Freeman, City of London, 1985. *Recreations:* broadcasting, walking, exploring, squash. *Address:* St Bride's Rectory, Fleet Street, EC4Y 8AU. *T:* 071–353 1301. *Clubs:* Athenæum, Wig and Pen.

OATES, (John) Keith; Managing Director, Marks and Spencer plc, since 1991; a Governor of the BBC, since 1988; *b* 3 July 1942; *s* of late John Alfred Oates and Katherine Mary (*née* Hole); *m* 1968, Helen Mary (*née* Blake); one *s* three *d*. *Educ:* King's Sch., Chester; Arnold Sch., Blackpool; London School of Economics (BScEcon); Univ. of Manchester Inst. of Sci. and Technology (DipTech Industrial Admin); Bristol Univ. (MSc Management Accounting). FCT 1982. Work Study trainee, Reed Paper Gp, 1965–66; Budgets and Planning Man., IBM (UK) Ltd, 1966–73; Gp Financial Controller, Rolls Royce (1971) Ltd, 1973–74; Controller, Black and Decker Europe, 1974–78; Vice Pres., Finance, Thyssen Bornemisza NV, 1978–84; Finance Dir, Marks and Spencer plc, 1984–91: Founder Chm., Marks and Spencer Financial Services. Non Exec. Dir, John Laing plc, 1987–89. Mem. Council, CBI, 1988–; Chm., Europ. Council of Financial Execs, 1984; Mem., 100 Gp Chartered Accountants, 1985–. *Recreations:* tennis, ski-ing, spectator sports (esp. Association Football, cricket). *Address:* Michael House, Baker Street, W1A 1DN. *T:* 071–268 6427. *Club:* Tennis Club de Monaco.

OATES, Laurence Campbell; Under Secretary and Head of Legislation Group, Lord Chancellor's Department, since 1988; *b* 14 May 1946; *s* of Stanley Oates and late Norah Christine Oates (*née* Meek); *m* 1968, Brenda Lilian Hardwick; one *s* one *d*. *Educ:* Beckenham and Penge Grammar School; Bristol Univ. (LLB 1967). Called to the Bar, Middle Temple, 1968; Dept. of Employment, 1976–80; Law Officers' Dept, 1980–83; Asst Treasury Solicitor, Dept of Transport, 1983–88. *Recreations:* music, golf. *Address:* Lord Chancellor's Department, House of Lords, SW1A 0PW.

OATES, Sir Thomas, Kt 1972; CMG 1962; OBE 1958 (MBE 1946); Governor and Commander-in-Chief of St Helena, 1971–76; *b* 5 November 1917; *er s* of late Thomas Oates, Wadebridge, Cornwall; unmarried. *Educ:* Callington Grammar School, Cornwall; Trinity College, Cambridge (MA). Mathematical Tripos (Wrangler). Admiralty Scientific Staff, 1940–46; HMS Vernon, Minesweeping Section, 1940–42; British Admiralty Delegn, Washington, DC, 1942–46; Temp. Lieut, RNVR. Colonial Administrative Service, Nigeria, 1948–55; seconded to HM Treasury, 1953–55; Adviser to UK Delegn to UN Gen. Assembly, 1954. Financial Sec. to Govt of: British Honduras, 1955–59, Aden, 1959–63; Dep. High Comr, Aden, 1963–67; Permanent Sec., Gibraltar, 1968–69; Dep. Governor, Gibraltar, 1969–71. *Recreations:* photography, walking. *Address:* Tristan, Trevone, Padstow, Cornwall PL28 8QX. *Clubs:* East India, Devonshire, Sports and Public Schools, Commonwealth Trust.
See also E. E. D. M. Oates.

OATLEY, Brian; County Education Officer, Kent, 1984–88; *b* 1 June 1935; *s* of Arnold and Vivian Oatley. *Educ:* Bolton School; King's College, Cambridge. BA, PGCE. Teacher, North Manchester Grammar School, 1959–64; Assistant, Senior Assistant and Deputy County Education Officer, Kent County Council, 1964–84. Member: RHS; Kent Trust for Nature Conservation; Weald Singers, Maidstone. *Recreations:* music, travel, gardening. *Address:* 45 Beresford Road, Aylesford, Maidstone, Kent ME20 7EP.

OATLEY, Sir Charles (William), Kt 1974; OBE 1956; MA; FRS 1969, FEng, FIEE, FIEEE; Professor of Electrical Engineering, University of Cambridge, 1960–71, now Emeritus; Fellow of Trinity College, Cambridge, since 1945; *b* 14 Feb. 1904; *s* of William Oatley and Ada Mary Dorrington; *m* 1930, (Dorothy) Enid West; two *s*. *Educ:* Bedford Modern Sch.; St John's Coll., Cambridge. Demonstrator, later lecturer, Dept of Physics, KCL, 1927–39. Min. of Supply, Radar Research and Development Establishment, 1939–45. Actg Superintendent in charge of scientific work, 1944–45. Lecturer, later Reader, Dept of Engineering, Cambridge Univ., 1945–60. Director, English Electric Valve Company, 1966–85. Member: Council, Inst. of Electrical Engineers, 1954–56, 1961–64 (Chm. of Radio Section, 1954–55); Council, Royal Society, 1970–72. FEng 1976. Hon. Fellow, Royal Microscopical Soc., 1970; FKC 1976; Foreign Associate, Nat. Acad. of Engineering, USA, 1979. Hon. DSc: Heriot-Watt, 1974; Bath 1977; Hon. ScD Cambridge, 1990. Achievement Award, Worshipful Co. of Scientific Instrument Makers, 1966; Duddell Medal, Inst. of Physics and Physical Soc., 1969; Royal Medal, Royal Soc., 1969; Faraday Medal, IEE, 1970; Mullard Award, Royal Soc., 1973; James Alfred Ewing Medal, ICE, 1981; Distinguished Scientist Award, Electron Microscopy Soc. of America, 1984; Howard N. Potts Medal, Franklin Inst., 1989. *Publications:* Wireless Receivers, 1932; The Scanning Electron Microscope, 1972; Electric and Magnetic Fields, 1976; papers in scientific and technical journals. *Recreation:* gardening. *Address:* 16 Porson Road, Cambridge. *T:* Cambridge (0223) 356194. *Club:* Athenæum.
See also M. C. Oatley.

OATLEY, Michael Charles, CMG 1991; OBE 1975; HM Diplomatic Service, retired; Director of Operations, Kroll Associates UK Ltd, since 1991; *b* 18 Oct. 1935; *s* of Sir Charles Oatley, *qv* and Lady Oatley (*née* Enid West); *m* 1st, 1965, Pippa Howden (marr. diss. 1990); two *s* one *d*; 2nd, 1990, Mary Jane Laurens; one *s*. *Educ:* The Leys Sch.; Trinity Coll., Cambridge. Joined HM Foreign, later Diplomatic, Service, 1959, retired 1991. *Address:* Manor Farmhouse, Caundle Marsh, Sherborne, Dorset DT9 5LX.

OBAN (St John's Cathedral), Provost of; *see* Maclean of Dochgarroch, Very Rev. A. M.

OBASANJO, Gen. Olusegun; Nigerian Head of State, Head of the Federal Military Government and Commander-in-Chief of the Armed Forces, Nigeria, 1976–79; Member, Advisory Council of State, since 1979; farmer; *b* Abeokuta, Ogun State, Nigeria, 5 March 1937; *m*; two *s* three *d*. *Educ:* Abeokuta Baptist High Sch.; Mons Officers' Cadet Sch., England. Entered Nigerian Army, 1958; commission, 1959; served in Zaire (then, the Congo), 1960. Comdr, Engrg Corps, 1963; Comdr of 2nd (Rear) Div. at Ibadan; GOC 3rd Inf. Div., 1969; Comdr, 3rd Marine Commando Div.; took surrender of forces of Biafra, in Nigerian Civil War, 1969–70; Comdr Engrg Corps, 1970–75. Political post as Federal Comr for Works and Housing, Jan.-July 1975. Chief of Staff, Supreme HQ, July 1975–Feb. 1976. Mem., Internat. Indep. Commn on Disarmament and Security. Part-time Associate, Univ. of Ibadan. *Publication:* My Command (autobiog.), 1980. *Recreations:* squash, table tennis, billiards, snooker. *Address:* PO Box 2286, Abeokuta, Nigeria.

OBASI, Godwin Olu Patrick; Secretary-General, World Meteorological Organization, since 1984; *b* 24 Dec. 1933; *s* of Albert B. Patrick Obasi and Rhoda A. Akande; *m* 1967, Winifred O. Akande; one *s* five *d*. *Educ:* McGill Univ., Canada (BSc Hons Maths and Physics); Massachusetts Inst. of Technology (MSc, DSc Meteorology). Mem., Inst. of Statisticians. University of Nairobi: WMO/UNDP Expert and Sen. Lectr, 1967–74; Acting Head of Dept of Meteorology, 1972–73; Dean, Faculty of Science, Prof. of Meteorology and Chm., Dept of Meteorology, 1974–76; Adviser in Meteorology to Nigerian Govt and Head of Nigerian Inst. for Met. Res. and Training, 1976–78; Dir, Educn and Training Dept, WMO, 1978–83. Carl Rossby Award, MIT, 1963; Gold plaque merit award medal, Czechoslovakian Acad. of Sciences, 1986. *Publications:* numerous contribs to learned jls. *Recreations:* tennis, gardening. *Address:* Chemin en Vuaracaux, 1297 Founex, Vaud, Switzerland. *T:* (022) 76 28 25.

OBEEGADOO, (Louis) Claude; High Commissioner for Mauritius in UK, 1982–83; *b* 12 June 1928; *m* 1955, Primerose Moutousamy; two *s*. *Educ:* London University. BSc 1955. Teacher, 1948–73, Manager, 1952–82, Trinity College Group, Mauritius. *Publication:* The Pupil and the Total Environment, 1977. *Recreations:* community service, reading, yoga. *Address:* Royal Road, Moka, Mauritius. *Club:* Rotary (Port Louis, Mauritius).

O'BEIRNE, Cornelius Banahan, CBE 1964; QC; consultant on international and comparative law; *b* 9 September 1915; *e s* of late Captain C. B. O'Beirne, OBE; *m* 1949, Ivanka (*d* 1991), *d* of Miloc Tupanjanin, Belgrade; one *s* one *d*. *Educ:* Stonyhurst Coll. Solicitor (Eng.), 1940. Served War, 1940–46; Maj. RA, Eur., Mid. E; Polit. Adviser's Office, Brit. Emb., Athens, 1945–46. Colonial Office, 1947–48. Called to Bar, Lincoln's Inn, 1952. Crown Counsel: Nigeria, 1949–53; High Commn Territories, SA, 1953–59; Solicitor-Gen., 1959; Attorney-General, High Commission Territories, South Africa, 1961–64; Counsellor (Legal), British Embassy, SA, 1964–65; Senior Legal Asst, Lord Chancellor's Office, 1966–71 (seconded as Attorney-Gen., Gibraltar, 1966–70); Council on Tribunals, 1971–78; Asst Dir, British Inst. of Internat. and Comparative Law, 1978–82, Dir of its Commonwealth Legal Adv. Service, 1982–86. QC: Basutoland, Bechuanaland and Swaziland, 1962; Gibraltar, 1967. Member: RIIA; Justice; Plowden Soc.; Commonwealth Parly Assoc. *Publications:* Laws of Gibraltar, rev. edn 1968; Survey of Extradition and Fugitive Offenders Legislation in the Commonwealth, 1982, 3rd edn 1989; contribs to jls. *Recreations:* reading, photography. *Address:* Nanhoran Cottage, 23 Claremont Lane, Esher, Surrey KT10 9DP. *T:* Esher (0372) 462268.

O'BEIRNE RANELAGH, John, (John Ranelagh), PhD; Associate, Hydra Associates, since 1989; *b* 3 Nov. 1947; *o s* of James O'Beirne Ranelagh and Elaine Lambert O'Beirne Ranelagh; *m* 1974, Elizabeth Grenville, *y d* of Sir William Hawthorne, *qv*. *Educ:* St Christopher's Sch.; Cambridgeshire Coll. of Arts and Technology; Christ Church, Oxford (MA); Eliot Coll., Univ. of Kent (PhD). Chase Manhattan Bank, 1970; Campaign Dir, Outset Housing Assoc., 1971; Univ. of Kent Studentship, 1972–74; BBC TV, 1974; Conservative Res. Dept, 1975–79; Associate Producer, Ireland: a television history, BBC TV, 1979–81; Commissioning Editor, Channel Four TV Co., 1981–88 (Sec. to the Bd, 1981–83); Dep. Chief Exec. and Dir of Programmes, TV2 Denmark, 1988; Exec. Producer. and writer, The Agency, BBC TV/NRK/Primetime, 1989–. Dir, Broadcasting Research Unit, 1988–90 (Mem., Exec. Cttee, 1984–87). Mem., Political Cttee, UNA, 1978–90. Governor, Daneford Sch., 1977–81. *Publications:* Science, Education and Industry, 1978; (with Richard Luce) Human Rights and Foreign Policy, 1978; Ireland: an illustrated history, 1981; A Short History of Ireland, 1983; The Agency: the rise and decline of the CIA, 1986 (Nat. Intelligence Book Award, and New York Times Notable Book of the Year, 1987); (contrib.) Freedom of Information, ed by Julia Neuberger, 1987; (contrib.) The Revolution in Ireland 1879–1923, ed D. G. Boyce, 1988; Den Anden Kanal, 1989; Thatcher's People, 1991. *Recreations:* old Bentley motor cars, quarter horses. *Address:* The Garner Cottages, Mill Way, Grantchester, Cambridge CB3 9NB. *Club:* Travellers'.

OBOLENSKY, Sir Dimitri, Kt 1984; MA, PhD, DLitt; FBA 1974; FSA; FRHistS; Emeritus Professor, University of Oxford, since 1985 (Professor of Russian and Balkan History, 1961–85, and Student of Christ Church, 1950–85); *b* Petrograd, 1 April 1918; *s* of late Prince Dimitri Obolensky and late Countess Mary Shuvalov; *m* 1947, Elisabeth Lopukhin (marr. diss. 1989). *Educ:* Lycée Pasteur, Paris; Trinity College, Cambridge. Cambridge: 1st Class Modern and Medieval Langs Tripos Parts I and II; Amy Mary Preston Read and Allen Schol.; Fellow of Trinity Coll., 1942–48; Faculty Asst Lecturer, 1944; Lecturer, Trinity Coll., 1945; Univ. Lecturer in Slavonic Studies, 1946; Reader in Russian and Balkan Medieval History in Univ. of Oxford, 1949–61. Vis. Schol., Dumbarton Oaks Center for Byzantine Studies, Harvard Univ., 1952, 1964, 1977, Vis. Fellow, 1981–82; Vis. Prof. of Russian History, Yale Univ., 1957; Vis. Prof. of European Hist., Univ. of California, Berkeley, 1973; Davis Prof. in Slavic Studies, Wellesley Coll., Mass, 1982; Vis. Mellon Prof., Inst. for Advanced Study, Princeton, 1985–86; Birkbeck Lecturer in Ecclesiastical History, Trinity Coll., Cambridge, 1961; Raleigh Lectr, British Acad., 1981. Vice-Pres., British Acad., 1983–85. Gen. Sec. Thirteenth Internat. Congress of Byzantine Studies, Oxford, 1966; British Co-Chairman: Anglo-Bulgarian Conf. of Historians, 1973; Anglo-Romanian Conf. of Historians, 1975. Corresp. Mem., Acad. of Athens; Foreign Member: Serbian Acad. of Scis and Arts, 1988; Amer. Philosophical Soc., 1990. Hon. Dr Univ: Paris, Sorbonne, 1980; Sofia, 1989; Hon. DLitt Birmingham, 1988. *Publications:* The Bogomils, A Study in Balkan Neo-Manichaeism, 1948; (ed) The Penguin Book of Russian Verse, 1962; (jointly) The Christian Centuries, vol. 2: The Middle Ages, 1969; Byzantium and the Slavs, 1971; The Byzantine Commonwealth, 1971; (ed jtly) Companion to Russian Studies, 3 vols, 1976–80; The Byzantine Inheritance of Eastern Europe, 1982; Six Byzantine Portraits, 1988. *Address:* 29 Belsyre Court, Woodstock Road, Oxford OX2 6HU. *T:* Oxford (0865) 56496. *Club:* Athenæum.

OBOTE, Dr (Apollo) Milton; President of Uganda and Minister of Foreign Affairs, 1980–85; former Leader, Uganda People's Congress Party; *b* 1924; *m*; three *s*. Migrated to Kenya and worked as labourer, clerk and salesman, 1950–55; Founder Mem., Kenya Africa Union. Mem., Uganda Nat. Congress, 1952–60; Mem., Uganda Legislative Council, 1957–71; Founder and Mem., Uganda People's Congress, 1960–71; Leader of the Opposition, 1961–62; Prime Minister, 1962–66; Minister of Defence and Foreign Affairs, 1963–65; President of Uganda, 1966–71 (deposed by military coup); in exile in Tanzania, 1971–80; returned to Uganda, 1980.

O'BRIEN, family name of **Barons Inchiquin** and **O'Brien of Lothbury.**

O'BRIEN OF LOTHBURY, Baron *cr* 1973 (Life Peer), of the City of London; **Leslie Kenneth O'Brien,** PC 1970; GBE 1967; President, British Bankers' Association, 1973–80; *b* 8 Feb. 1908; *e s* of late Charles John Grimes O'Brien; *m* 1st, 1932, Isabelle Gertrude Pickett (*d* 1987); one *s*; 2nd, 1989, Marjorie Violet Taylor. *Educ:* Wandsworth School. Entered Bank of England, 1927; Deputy Chief Cashier, 1951; Chief Cashier, 1955; Executive Director, 1962–64; Deputy Governor, 1964–66; Governor, 1966–73; Director: Commonwealth Develt Finance Co. Ltd, 1962–64; The Prudential Assurance Co. Ltd, 1973–80; The Prudential Corp. Ltd, 1979–83; The Rank Organisation, 1974–78;

Bank for International Settlements, 1966–73, 1974–83 (Vice-Chm., 1979–83); Saudi Internat. Bank, 1975–84; Vice-Chm., Banque Belge, 1981–88; Mem., Adv. Bd, Unilever Ltd, 1973–78; Consultant to J. P. Morgan & Co., 1973–79; Chm., Internat. Council of Morgan Guaranty Trust Co., NY, 1974–78; Mem. Internat. Adv. Council, Morgan Grenfell & Co. Ltd, 1974–87. Chm., Cttee of Inquiry into export of animals for slaughter, 1973. Member: Finance and Appeal Cttee, RCS, 1973–85; Council, RCM, 1973–90; Bd of National Theatre, 1973–78; Council, Marie Curie Meml Foundn, 1963–78; Investment Adv. Cttee, Mercers' Co., 1973–; City of London Savings Cttee, 1966–78. A Trustee of Glyndebourne Arts Trust, 1974–78; Hon. Treasurer and Mem. Exec. Cttee, Royal Opera House Develt Appeal, 1977–87. Pres., United Banks' Lawn Tennis Assoc., 1958–81; Vice-Pres., Squash Rackets Assoc., 1972–78. One of HM Lieutenants for City of London, 1966–73; Freeman, City of London in Co. of Mercers; Hon. Liveryman, Leathersellers Co. Hon. DSc City Univ., 1969; Hon. LLD Univ. of Wales, 1973. FRCM 1979. Hon. FCIB. Cavaliere di Gran Croce al Merito della Repubblica Italiana, 1975; Grand Officier, Ordre de la Couronne (Belgium), 1976. *Address:* 3 Peter Avenue, Oxted, Surrey RH8 9LG. *T:* Oxted (0883) 712535. *Clubs:* Athenæum, Boodle's, Garrick, Grillions, MCC, All England Lawn Tennis.

O'BRIEN, Brian Murrough Fergus; Special Commissioner of Income Tax since 1981; *b* 18 July 1931; *s* of Charles Murrough O'Brien, MB, BCh and late Elizabeth Joyce O'Brien (*née* Peacocke). *Educ:* Bedford Sch.; University Coll., Oxford (BA 1954, MA 1959). Nat. Service, Royal Inniskilling Fusiliers, 1950–51. Called to the Bar, Lincoln's Inn, 1955; Office of Solicitor of Inland Revenue, 1956–70; Asst Solicitor, Law Commn, 1970–80; Secretary, Law Commn, 1980–81. Mem., Senate of Inns of Court and Bar Council, 1977–80; Hon. Gen. Sec., 1962–67 and Chm., 1974–76, CS Legal Soc.; Chm., Assoc. of First Div. Civil Servants, 1979–81. Lay Chm., Westminster (St Margaret's) Deanery Synod, 1978–82. Chm., Trustees, St Mary's, Bourne St, 1968–. *Recreations:* music, travel, light-hearted bridge. *Address:* 20 Manchester Street, W1M 5PG. *T:* 071–935 4285. *Clubs:* Reform; Kildare Street and University (Dublin).

O'BRIEN, Charles Michael, MA; FIA, FPMI; General Manager (formerly Manager), and Actuary, 1955–84, Council Member, since 1984, Royal National Pension Fund for Nurses; *b* 17 Jan. 1919; *s* of late Richard Alfred O'Brien, CBE, MD, and Nora McKay; *m* 1950, Joy, *d* of late Rupert Henry Prebble and Phyllis Mary Langdon; two *s*. *Educ:* Westminster Sch.; Christ Church, Oxford (MA). Commissioned, Royal Artillery, 1940 (despatches, 1945). Asst Actuary, Equitable Life Assce Soc., 1950; Royal National Pension Fund for Nurses: Asst Manager, 1953; Manager and Actuary, 1955. Dir, M & G Assurance Gp plc, 1984–. Institute of Actuaries: Fellow, 1949; Hon. Sec., 1961–62; Vice-Pres., 1965–68; Pres., 1976–78. Mem., Governing Body, Westminster Sch., 1970–. *Address:* The Boundary, Goodley Stock, Crockham Hill, Edenbridge, Kent TN8 6TA. *T:* Edenbridge (0732) 866349.

O'BRIEN, Conor Cruise; Contributing Editor, The Atlantic, Boston; Editor-in-Chief, The Observer, 1979–81; Pro-Chancellor, University of Dublin, since 1973; *b* 3 November 1917; *s* of Francis Cruise O'Brien and Katherine Sheehy; *m* 1st, 1939, Christine Foster (marr. diss. 1962); one *s* two *d*; 2nd, 1962, Máire Mac Entee; one adopted *s* one adopted *d*. *Educ:* Sandford Park School, Dublin; Trinity College, Dublin (BA, PhD). Entered Department of External Affairs of Ireland, 1944; Counsellor, Paris, 1955–56; Head of UN section and Member of Irish Delegation to UN, 1956–60; Asst Sec., Dept of External Affairs, 1960; Rep. of Sec.-Gen. of UN in Katanga, May-Dec. 1961; resigned from UN and Irish service, Dec. 1961. Vice-Chancellor, Univ. of Ghana, 1962–65; Albert Schweitzer Prof. of Humanities, New York Univ., 1965–69. TD (Lab) Dublin North-East, 1969–77; Minister for Posts and Telegraphs, 1973–77. Mem. Senate, Republic of Ireland, 1977–79. Vis. Fellow, Nuffield Coll., Oxford, 1973–75; Fellow, St Catherine's Coll., Oxford, 1978–81; Vis. Prof. and Montgomery Fellow, Dartmouth Coll., USA, 1984–85. Member: Royal Irish Acad.; Royal Soc. of Literature. Hon. DLitt: Bradford, 1971; Ghana, 1974; Edinburgh, 1976; Nice, 1978; Coleraine, 1981; QUB, 1984. Valiant for Truth Media Award, 1979. *Publications:* Maria Cross (under pseud. Donat O'Donnell), 1952 (reprinted under own name, 1963); Parnell and his Party, 1957; (ed) The Shaping of Modern Ireland, 1959; To Katanga and Back, 1962; Conflicting Concepts of the UN, 1964; Writers and Politics, 1965; The United Nations: Sacred Drama, 1967 (with drawings by Felix Topolski); Murderous Angels, 1968; (ed) Power and Consciousness, 1969; Conor Cruise O'Brien Introduces Ireland, 1969; (ed) Edmund Burke, Reflections on the Revolution in France, 1969; Camus, 1969; A Concise History of Ireland, 1972; (with Máire Cruise O'Brien) The Suspecting Glance, 1972; States of Ireland, 1972; Herod, 1978; Neighbours: the Ewart-Biggs memorial lectures 1978–79, 1980; The Siege: the saga of Israel and Zionism, 1986; Passion and Cunning, 1988; God Land: reflections on religion and nationalism, 1988. *Recreation:* travelling. *Address:* Whitewater, Howth Summit, Dublin, Ireland. *T:* Dublin 322474. *Club:* Athenæum.

O'BRIEN, Prof. Denis Patrick, FBA 1988; Professor of Economics, University of Durham, since 1972; *b* Knebworth, Herts, 24 May 1939; *s* of Patrick Kevin O'Brien and Dorothy Elizabeth Crisp; *m* 1961, Eileen Patricia O'Brien (*d* 1985); one *s* two *d*. *Educ:* Douai Sch.; University Coll. London (BSc (Econ) 1960); PhD Queen's Univ., Belfast, 1969. In industry, 1960–62; Queen's University, Belfast: Assst Lectr, 1963–65; Lectr, 1965–70; Reader, 1970–72. *Publications:* (with D. Swann) Information Agreements, 1969; J. R. McCulloch, 1970; Correspondence of Lord Overstone, 3 vols, 1971; (jtly) Competition in British Industry, 1974; (ed) J. R. McCulloch: Treatise on Taxation, 1975; The Classical Economists, 1975; Competition Policy, Profitability and Growth, 1979; (with J. Presley) Pioneers of Modern Economics in Britain, 1981; (with A. C. Darnell) Authorship Puzzles in the History of Economics, 1982; (with J. Creedy) Economic Analysis in Historical Perspective, 1984; Lionel Robbins, 1988. *Recreation:* the violin. *Address:* Department of Economics, University of Durham, 23–26 Old Elvet, Durham DH1 3HY. *T:* Durham (091) 3742274.

O'BRIEN, Dermod Patrick; QC 1983; a Recorder of the Crown Court, since 1978; *b* 23 Nov. 1939; *s* of Lieut D. D. O'Brien, RN, and Mrs O'Brien (*née* O'Connor); *m* 1974, Zoë Susan Norris; two *s*. *Educ:* Ampleforth Coll., York; St Catherine's Coll., Oxford. BA (Jurisprudence); MA. Called to Bar, Inner Temple, 1962; joined Western Circuit, 1963. *Recreations:* fishing, shooting, skiing. *Address:* Little Daux Farm, Billingshurst, West Sussex RH14 9DB. *T:* Billingshurst (0403) 784800; (chambers) 2 Temple Gardens, Temple, EC4Y 9AY. *T:* 071–583 6041.

O'BRIEN, Edna; writer; *b* Ireland; marr. diss.; two *s*. *Educ:* Irish convents; Pharmaceutical Coll. of Ireland. Yorkshire Post Novel Award, 1971. *Publications:* The Country Girls, 1960 (screenplay for film, 1983); The Lonely Girl, 1962; Girls in Their Married Bliss, 1963; August is a Wicked Month, 1964; Casualties of Peace, 1966; The Love Object, 1968; A Pagan Place, 1970; (play) A Pagan Place, 1971; Night, 1972; (short stories) A Scandalous Woman, 1974; Mother Ireland, 1976; Johnnie I hardly knew you, 1977; Mrs Reinhardt and other stories, 1978; Virginia (play), 1979; The Dazzle, 1981; Returning, 1982; A Christmas Treat, 1982; A Fanatic Heart (selected stories), 1985; Tales for the Telling, 1986; Flesh and Blood (play), 1987; Madame Bovary (play), 1987; The High Road, 1988; Lantern Slides (short stories), 1990. *Recreations:* reading, writing, remembering. *Address:* c/o Duncan Heath Associates, 162–170 Wardour Street, W1V 3AT.

O'BRIEN, Sir Frederick (William Fitzgerald), Kt 1984; QC (Scotland) 1960; Sheriff Principal of Lothian and Borders, 1978–89; Sheriff of Chancery in Scotland, 1978–89; Hon. Sheriff at Edinburgh and Paisley, since 1990; *b* 19 July 1917; *s* of Dr Charles Henry Fitzgerald O'Brien and Helen Jane; *m* 1950, Audrey Muriel Owen; two *s* one *d*. *Educ:* Royal High Sch.; Univ. of Edinburgh; MA 1938; LLB 1940. Admitted Faculty of Advocates, 1947. Comr, Mental Welfare Commission of Scotland, 1962–65; Home Advocate Depute, 1964–65; Sheriff-Principal of Caithness, Sutherland, Orkney and Shetland, 1965–75; Interim Sheriff-Principal of Aberdeen, Kincardine and Banff, 1969–71; Sheriff Principal of N Strathclyde, 1975–78; Interim Sheriff Principal of S Strathclyde, 1981. Hon. Mem., Sheriffs' Assoc., 1990–. Member: Scottish Medical Practices Cttee, 1973–76; Scottish Records Adv. Council, 1974–83; Convener of Sheriffs Principal, 1972–89; Chm., Sheriff Court Rules Council, 1975–81. Chm., Northern Lighthouse Bd, 1983–84 and 1986–87. Convener, Gen. Council Business Cttee, Edinburgh Univ., 1980–84. Hon. Pres., Royal High Sch. Former Pupils Club, 1982 (Pres. 1975–76); Chm., Edinburgh Sir Walter Scott Club, 1989–. *Recreations:* golf, music. *Address:* 22 Arboretum Road, Edinburgh EH3 5PN. *T:* 031–552 1923. *Clubs:* New (Edinburgh); Bruntsfield Golf, Scottish Arts.

O'BRIEN, Rt. Rev. James Joseph; Auxiliary Bishop of Westminster (Bishop in Hertfordshire) (RC), and Titular Bishop of Manaccenser, since 1977; *b* 5 Aug. 1930; *s* of John and Mary Elizabeth O'Brien. *Educ:* St Ignatius College, Stamford Hill; St Edmund's Coll., Ware. Priest, 1954; Assistant, St Lawrence's, Feltham, 1954–62; Catholic Missionary Society, 1962–68; Director of Catholic Enquiry Centre, 1967–68; Rector of Allen Hall, 1968–77. Bishops' Conference of England and Wales: Chm., Dept for Internat. Affairs, 1984–88; Chm., Cttee for Ministerial Formation, 1988–. Prelate of Honour, 1969. *Address:* The Gate House, All Saints Pastoral Centre, London Colney, St Albans, Herts AL2 1AG. *T:* Bowmansgreen (0727) 24664.

O'BRIEN, Prof. John W., PhD; Rector Emeritus, Concordia University (incorporating Loyola College and Sir George Williams University, Montreal), since 1984 (Rector and Vice-Chancellor, 1969–84); Professor of Economics, since 1965; *b* 4 Aug. 1931; *s* of Wilfred Edmond O'Brien and Audrey Swain; *m* 1956, Joyce Helen Bennett; two *d*. *Educ:* McGill Univ., Montreal, Que. BA 1953, MA 1955, PhD 1962. Sir George Williams Univ.: Lectr in Economics, 1954; Asst Prof. of Economics, 1957; Associate Prof. of Economics and Asst Dean, 1961; Dean, Faculty of Arts, 1963; Vice-Principal (Academic), 1968–69. Hon. DCL Bishop's Univ., 1976; Hon. LLD McGill Univ., 1976. *Publication:* Canadian Money and Banking, 1964 (2nd edn, with G. Lermer, 1969). *Address:* Concordia University, 1455 de Maisonneuve Boulevard West, Montreal, Que H3G 1M8, Canada. *T:* (514) 848–2424.

O'BRIEN, Most Rev. Keith Michael Patrick; *see* St Andrews and Edinburgh, Archbishop of, (RC).

O'BRIEN, Rt. Rev. Kevin; *see* O'Brien, Rt Rev. T. K.

O'BRIEN, (Michael) Vincent; racehorse trainer; *b* 9 April 1917; *s* of Daniel P. O'Brien and Kathleen (*née* Toomey); *m* 1951, Jacqueline (*née* Wittenoom), Perth, Australia; two *s* three *d*. *Educ:* Mungret Coll., Ireland. Started training in Co. Cork, 1944; moved to Co. Tipperary, 1951. Won all major English and Irish hurdle and steeple-chases, incl. 3 consecutive Grand Nationals, Gold Cups and Champion Hurdles. From 1959 has concentrated on flat racing and has trained winners of 44 Classics, incl. 6 Epsom Derbys, 6 Irish Derbys and 1 French Derby; also 3 Prix de l'Arc de Triomphe and Washington International; trainer of Nijinsky, first triple crown winner since 1935. Hon. LLD NUI, 1983. *Recreations:* fishing, golf. *Address:* Ballydoyle House, Cashel, Co. Tipperary, Ireland. *T:* 062–61222, *Telex:* 70714, *Fax:* 062–61677.

O'BRIEN, Oswald; Director, Workplace Advisory Service, Alcohol Concern (national charity), since 1986 (Director, Education Division, 1984–86); freelance lecturer, since 1983; *b* 6 April 1928; *s* of Thomas and Elizabeth O'Brien; *m* 1950, Freda Rosina Pascoe; one *s*. *Educ:* St Mary's Grammar Sch., Darlington; Fircroft Coll., Birmingham; Durham Univ. BA Hons Politics and Economics. Royal Navy, 1945–48; various posts in industry, 1948–59; College and University, 1959–63; Tutor, WEA, 1963–64; Staff Tutor, Durham Univ., 1964–78; Senior Industrial Relations Officer, Commn on Indust. Relations, 1970–72 (secondment); Dir of Studies and Vice-Principal, Co-operative Coll., 1978–83. Dept of Employment and ACAS Arbitrator in Shipbuilding, 1968–78; Indust. Relations Adviser to various statutary bodies, 1965–78; Chm., Soc. of Indust. Tutors, 1978–82. Mem., Durham CC, 1990–. MP (Lab) Darlington, March-June 1983; contested (Lab) Darlington, 1987. FBIM. *Publications:* (jtly) Going Comprehensive, 1970; (jtly) Drink and Drugs at Work, 1988; various papers, reports and case studies. *Recreations:* reading, talking, opera. *Address:* 6 Hillclose Avenue, Darlington, Co. Durham DL3 8BH. *T:* Darlington (0325) 315540.

O'BRIEN, Prof. Patrick Karl, DPhil; FBA 1991; Professor of Economic History, University of London, and Director of the Institute of Historical Research, since 1990; *b* 12 Aug. 1932; *s* of William O'Brien and Elizabeth Stockhausen; *m* 1959, Cassy Cobham; one *s* two *d*. *Educ:* London Sch. of Economics (Lilian Knowles Schol.; BSc 1958); Nuffield Coll., Oxford (DPhil). London University: Res. Fellow, 1960–63; Lectr, 1963–70; Reader in Econs and Econ. Hist., 1967–70; Oxford University: Univ. Lectr in Econ. Hist., 1970–84; Reader, 1984–90; Faculty Fellow, 1970–84, Professorial Fellow, 1984–90, Emeritus Fellow, 1991, St Antony's Coll. *Publications:* The Revolution in Egypt's Economic System, 1966; The New Economic History of the Railways, 1977; (with C. Keyder) Economic Growth in Britain and France 1780–1914, 1978; (ed jtly) Productivity in the Economies of Europe in the 19th and 20th Centuries, 1983; (ed) Railways and the Economic Development of Western Europe 1830–1914, 1983; (ed) International Productivity Comparisons 1750–1939, 1986; The Economic Effects of the Civil War, 1988; contribs to many learned jls. *Recreations:* theatre, Western art, tennis, squash, foreign travel. *Address:* 66 St Bernards Road, Oxford OX2 6EJ. *T:* Oxford (0865) 512004.

O'BRIEN, Patrick William; His Honour Judge O'Brien; a Circuit Judge, since 1991; *b* 20 June 1945; *s* of William C. O'Brien and Ethel M. O'Brien; *m* 1970; one *s* two *d*. *Educ:* St Joseph's Academy, Blackheath; Queens' College, Cambridge (MA, LLM). Called to the Bar, Lincoln's Inn, 1968; practised SE Circuit; a Recorder, 1987. *Recreations:* cricket, choral singing, musical theatre. *Address:* Chelmsford Crown Court, New Street, Chelmsford, Essex. *T:* Chelmsford (0245) 358222. *Club:* MCC.

O'BRIEN, Raymond Francis; DL; Chief Executive, Financial Intermediaries, Managers and Brokers Regulatory Association, 1987–90; *b* 13 Feb. 1936; *s* of Ignatius and Anne O'Brien; *m* 1959, Mary Agnes, (Wendy), *d* of late James and of Agnes Alcock; two *s* two *d*. *Educ:* St Mary's Coll., Great Crosby, Liverpool; St Edmund Hall, Oxford (BA Hons 1959; MA 1962). IPFA. Accountant, Cheshire CC, 1959–65; Head of Data Processing, Staffs CC, 1965–67; Asst County Treas., Notts CC, 1967–70; Dep. Clerk, Notts CC, 1970–73; Clerk of CC and Chief Executive, Notts, 1973–77; Chief Exec., Merseyside

MCC, 1978–86; Chief Exec. and Bd Mem., Severn-Trent Water Authy, 1986–87. Mem., Merseyside Area Bd, MSC, 1980–86; Director: Merseyside Economic Development Co. Ltd, 1981–86; Merseyside Cablevision Ltd, 1982–86; Anfield Foundation, 1983–. DL Merseyside, 1980. *Recreations*: sports critic, gardening, music, reading. *Address*: 20 Oldway Drive, Solihull, West Midlands B91 3HP. *T*: 021–704 4925.

O'BRIEN, Sir Richard, Kt 1980; DSO 1944, MC 1942 (Bar 1944); Chairman, Manpower Services Commission, 1976–82; *b* 15 Feb. 1920; *s* of late Dr Charles O'Brien and of Marjorie Maude O'Brien; *m* 1951, Elizabeth M. D. Craig; two *s* three *d*. *Educ*: Oundle Sch.; Clare Coll., Cambridge (MA). Served, 1940–45, with Sherwood Foresters and Leicesters, N Africa, ME, Italy and Greece; Personal Asst to Field Marshal Montgomery, 1945–46. Develt Officer, Nat. Assoc. of Boys' Clubs, 1946–48; Richard Sutcliffe Ltd, Wakefield (latterly Prodn Dir), 1948–58; Dir and Gen. Man., Head Wrightson Mineral Engrg Ltd, 1958–61; Dir, Industrial Relns, British Motor Corp., 1961–66; Industrial Adviser (Manpower), DEA, 1966–68; Delta Metal Co. Ltd (subseq. Dir of Manpower, and Dir 1972–76), 1968–76. Chairman: CBI Employment Policy Cttee, 1971–76; Crown Appointments Commn, 1979; Concordia (Youth Service Volunteers), 1981–87; Engineering Industry Trng Bd, 1982–85; Archbishop's Commn on Urban Priority Areas, 1983–85; Industrial Participation Assoc., 1983–86; Policy Studies Inst., 1984–90; Employment Inst. and Charter for Jobs, 1985–87; Community Educn Develt Centre, 1989–; Deputy Chairman: AMARC, 1988–; Church Urban Fund, 1988–. Member: NEDC, 1977–82; Engrg Council, 1985–88; President: British Inst. of Industrial Therapy, 1982–87; Inst. of Trng and Develt, 1983–84; Nat. Assoc. of Colls of Further and Higher Educn, 1983–85; Campaign for Work, 1988–. Member Council: Industrial Soc., 1962–86; Univ. of Birmingham, 1969–88; Hymns Ancient & Modern, 1984–. Mem. Ct of Governors, ASC, 1977–83. Hon. DSc Aston, 1979; Hon. LLD: Bath, 1981; Liverpool, 1981; Birmingham, 1982; Hon. DLitt: Warwick, 1983; CNAA (Coll. of St Mark and St John), 1988; DCL Lambeth, 1987; Hon. Fellow Sheffield City Polytech., 1980. JP Wakefield, 1955–61. *Publications*: contrib: Conflict at Work (BBC pubn), 1971; Montgomery at Close Quarters, 1985; Seekers and Finders, 1985; articles in various jls. *Recreations*: reading, theatre, cinema, tennis. *Address*: 53 Abingdon Villas, W8 6XA. *T*: 071–937 8944.

O'BRIEN, (Robert) Stephen, CBE 1987; Chief Executive, Business in the Community, since 1983; *b* 14 Aug. 1936; *s* of Robert Henry and Clare Winifred O'Brien; *m* 1st, 1958, Zoë T. O'Brien (marr. diss. 1989); two *s* two *d*; 2nd, 1989, Meriel Barclay. *Educ*: Sherborne Sch., Dorset. Joined Charles Fulton & Co. Ltd, 1956; Dir, 1964; Chm., 1970–82. Chairman: Foreign Exchange and Currency Deposit Brokers Assoc., 1968–72; Project Fullemploy, 1973–; Home Sec.'s Adv. Bd on Community Radio, 1985–86; Dir, Kirkland-Whittaker Co. Ltd, 1981–82. Ordained Deacon, 1971; Hon. Curate, St Lawrence Jewry, 1973–82; Chm., Christian Action, 1976–88. Pres., Esher Assoc. for Prevention of Addiction, 1979–90. Chm., UK 2000, 1988– (Mem. Bd, 1986–); Member: Administrative Council, Royal Jubilee Trusts, 1984–89; Management Cttee, Action Resource Centre, 1986–; Council, RSA, 1987–; Trustee, Prince's Youth Business Trust, 1987–. *Recreations*: causes, gentle gardening, tennis. *Address*: 13 Tredegar Square, E3. *T*: 081–980 1435.

O'BRIEN, Terence John, CMG 1971; MC 1945; HM Diplomatic Service, retired; *b* 13 Oct. 1921; *s* of Joseph O'Brien; *m* 1950, Phyllis Mitchell (*d* 1952); *m* 1953, Rita Emily Drake Reynolds; one *s* two *d*. *Educ*: Gresham's Sch., Holt; Merton Coll., Oxford. Ayrshire Yeo., 1942–45. Dominions Office, 1947; CRO, 1947–49; British High Comr's Office, Ceylon, 1950–52; Princ., Treasury, 1953–56; 1st Sec. (Financial), Canberra, 1956–58; Planning Officer, CRO, 1958–60; 1st Sec., Kuala Lumpur, 1960–62; Sec. to Inter-Governmental Cttee, Jesselton, 1962–63; Head of Chancery, New Delhi, 1963–66; Imp. Def. Coll., 1967; Counsellor, FCO (formerly FO), 1968–70; Ambassador: Nepal, 1970–74; Burma, 1974–78; Indonesia, 1978–81. *Address*: Beaufort House, Woodcutts, Dorset SP5 5RP. *T*: Handley (Dorset) (0725) 52234.

O'BRIEN, Rt. Rev. (Thomas) Kevin; Auxiliary Bishop of Middlesbrough, (RC), and Titular Bishop of Ard Carna, since 1981; *b* Cork City, Republic of Ireland, 18 Feb. 1923; *s* of Jack and Mary O'Brien. *Educ*: Christian Brothers Coll., Cork. Ordained, All Hallows College, Dublin, 1948; Curate at Batley, Yorks, 1948–51, and St Anne's Cathedral, Leeds, 1951–56; Catholic Missionary Society, 1956–71, Superior 1960–71; Vicar General, Diocese of Leeds, 1971–81; Parish Priest: St Patrick's, Huddersfield, 1971–79; St Francis, Bradford, 1979–81. Chm., Home Mission Cttee of Bishops' Conference, 1983–. *Address*: St Charles Rectory, Jarratt Street, Hull HU1 3HB.

O'BRIEN, Timothy Brian; designer; *b* 8 March 1929; *s* of Brian Palliser Tiegue O'Brien and Elinor Laura (*née* Mackenzie). *Educ*: Wellington Coll.; Corpus Christi, Cambridge (MA); Yale Univ. Design Dept, BBC TV, 1954; Designer, Associated Rediffusion, 1955–56; Head of Design, ABC Television, 1956–66 (The Flying Dutchman, 1958); partnership in stage design with Tazeena Firth estabd 1961; output incl.: The Bartered Bride, The Girl of the Golden West, 1962; West End prodns of new plays, 1963–64; London scene of Shakespeare Exhibn, 1964; Tango, Days in the Trees, Staircase, RSC, and Trafalgar at Madame Tussaud's, 1966; All's Well that Ends Well, As You Like It, Romeo and Juliet, RSC, 1967; The Merry Wives of Windsor, Troilus and Cressida (also Nat. Theatre, 1976), The Latent Heterosexual, RSC, 1968; Pericles (also Comédie Française, 1974), Women Beware Women, Bartholomew Fair, RSC, 1969; 1970: Measure for Measure, RSC; Madame Tussaud's in Amsterdam; The Knot Garden, Royal Opera; 1971: Enemies, Man of Mode, RSC; 1972: La Cenerentola, Oslo; Lower Depths, The Island of the Mighty, RSC; As You Like It, OCSC; 1973: Richard II, Love's Labour's Lost, RSC; 1974: Next of Kin, NT; Summerfolk, RSC; The Bassarids, ENO; 1975: John Gabriel Borkman, NT; Peter Grimes, Royal Opera (later in Göteborg, Paris); The Marrying of Ann Leete, RSC; 1976: Wozzeck, Adelaide Fest.; The Zykovs, RSC; The Force of Habit, NT; 1977: Tales from the Vienna Woods, Bedroom Farce, NT; Falstaff, Berlin Opera; 1978: The Cunning Little Vixen, Göteborg; Evita, London (later in Australia, Austria, USA); A Midsummer Night's Dream, Sydney Opera House; 1979: The Rake's Progress, Royal Opera; 1981: Lulu, Royal Opera; 1982: La Ronde, RSC; Le Grand Macabre, ENO; 1983: Turandot, Vienna State Opera; 1984: The Mastersingers of Nuremberg, ENO; Tannhäuser, Royal Opera; 1985: Samson, Royal Opera; Sicilian Vespers, Grande Théâtre, Geneva; Old Times, Haymarket; Lucia di Lammermoor, Köln Opera; 1986: The Threepenny Opera, NT; Die Meistersinger von Nürnberg, Netherlands Opera; The American Clock, NT; 1987: Otello (revived 1990), and Die Entführung aus dem Serail, Royal Opera; 1988: Three Sisters, RSC; 1989: Cymbeline, RSC; Exclusive, Strand; 1990: King, Piccadilly; Love's Labours Lost, RSC; 1991: Twelfth Night, Playhouse; War and Peace, Kirov, Leningrad. Chm., Soc. of British Theatre Designers, 1984–. (Jtly) Gold Medal for Set Design, Prague Quadriennale, 1975. *Recreation*: sailing. *Address*: 33 Lansdowne Gardens, SW8 2EQ. *T*: 071–622 5384.

O'BRIEN, Sir Timothy John, 7th Bt *cr* 1849; *b* 6 July 1958; *s* of John David O'Brien (*d* 1980) and of Sheila Winifred, *o d* of Sir Charles Arland Maitland Freake, 4th Bt; *S* grandfather, 1982. *Heir*: *b* James Patrick O'Brien, *b* 22 Dec. 1964.

O'BRIEN, Turlough Aubrey, CBE 1959; Public Relations Consultant, 1972–82; *b* 30 Sept. 1907; *er s* of late Lieut-Colonel A. J. O'Brien, CIE, CBE; *m* 1945, Phyllis Mary (*d* 1986), twin *d* of late E. G. Tew; two *s* one *d*. *Educ*: Charterhouse; Christ Church, Oxford. Assistant to Director of Public Relations, Board of Trade, 1946–49; Public Relations Officer: Home Office, 1949–53; Post Office, 1953–64; Chief Public Relations Officer, 1964–66; Director, Public Relations, 1966–68; Public Relations Manager, Bank of London and South America, 1968–72. President, Institute of Public Relations, 1965. *Recreation*: fishing. *Address*: Claremount, 11 Kiln Gardens, Hartley Wintney, Basingstoke, Hants RG27 8RG. *Club*: United Oxford & Cambridge University.

O'BRIEN, Vincent; *see* O'Brien, M. V.

O'BRIEN, William, (Bill), JP; MP (Lab) Normanton, since 1983; *b* 25 Jan. 1929; *m* Jean; three *d*. *Educ*: state schools; Leeds Univ. Coalminer, 1945–83. Wakefield DC: Mem., 1973–83; former Dep. Leader and Chm., Finance and Gen. Purposes Cttee. Mem., NUM, 1945–; Local Branch Official, 1956–83. Opposition front bench spokesman on the Environment, 1987–. Member: Public Accounts Cttee, 1983–88; Energy Select Cttee, 1986–88. JP Wakefield, 1979. *Recreations*: reading, organising. *Address*: House of Commons, SW1A 0AA. *T*: 071–219 3000; 29 Limestrees, Ferrybridge Road, Pontefract WF8 2QB.

O'BRIEN, Adm. Sir William (Donough), KCB 1969 (CB 1966); DSC 1942; Commander-in-Chief, Western Fleet, Feb. 1970–Sept. 71, retd Nov. 1971; Vice-Admiral of the United Kingdom and Lieutenant of the Admiralty, 1984–86; *b* 13 Nov. 1916; *s* of late Major W. D. O'Brien, Connaught Rangers and I. R. Caroe (*née* Parnis); *m* 1943, Rita Micallef, Sliema, Malta; one *s* two *d*. *Educ*: Royal Naval Coll., Dartmouth. Served War of 1939–45: HM Ships Garland, Wolsey, Witherington, Offa, 1939–42; Cottesmore i/c, 1943–44; Arakan Coast, 1945. HMS Venus i/c, 1948–49; Commander 1949; HMS Ceylon, 1952; Admiralty, 1953–55; Captain, 1955; Captain (D) 8th DS in HMS Cheviot, 1958–59; HMS Hermes i/c, 1961–64; Rear-Admiral 1964; Naval Secretary, 1964–66; Flag Officer, Aircraft Carriers, 1966–67; Comdr, Far East Fleet, 1967–69; Admiral 1969. Rear-Admiral of the UK, 1979–84. Chairman: Kennet and Avon Canal Trust, 1974–; King George's Fund for Sailors, 1974–86. Pres., Assoc. of RN Officers, 1973–88. *Address*: The Black Barn, Steeple Ashton, Trowbridge, Wilts BA14 6EU. *T*: Devizes (0380) 870496. *Club*: Army and Navy.

O'BRIEN QUINN, Hon. James Aiden; *see* Quinn, Hon. J. A. O'B.

O'CATHAIN, Baroness *cr* 1991 (Life Peer), of The Barbican in the City of London; **Detta O'Cathain,** OBE 1983; Managing Director, Barbican Centre, since 1990; *b* 3 Feb. 1938; *d* of late Caoimhghin O'Cathain and Margaret O'Cathain; *m* 1968, William Bishop. *Educ*: Laurel Hill, Limerick; University College, Dublin (BA). Aer Lingus, Dublin, 1961–66; Group Economist, Tarmac, 1966–69; Economic Advr, Rootes Motors, 1969–72; Sen. Economist, Carrington Vyella, 1972–73; Economic Advr, British Leyland, 1973–74; Dir, Market Planning, Leyland Cars, 1974–76; Corporate Planning Exec., Unigate, 1976–81; Milk Marketing Board: Head of Strategic Planning, 1981–83; Dir and Gen. Manager, 1984; Man. Dir Milk Marketing, 1985–88. Advr on Agricl Marketing to Minister of Agriculture, 1979–83. Director: Midland Bank, 1984–; Channel 4, 1985–86; Tesco, 1985–; Sears, 1987–. FCIM 1987; FRSA 1986. *Recreations*: music, tennis, reading. *Address*: Eglantine, Tower House Gardens, Arundel, W Sussex BN18 9RU. *T*: Arundel (0903) 883775.

OCHOA, Dr Severo; Hon. Director, Centro de Biología Molecular, Universidad Autónoma, Madrid, since 1985; *b* Luarca, Spain, 24 Sept. 1905; *s* of Severo Ochoa and Carmen (*née* Albornoz); *m* 1931, Carmen G. Coblan. *Educ*: Malaga Coll.; University of Madrid. AB, Malaga, 1921; MD, Madrid, 1929. Lecturer in Physiology, University of Madrid Medical School, 1931–35; Head of Physiology Div., Institute for Medical Research, 1935–36; Guest Research Asst, Kaiser Wilhelm Inst., Heidelberg, 1936–37; Marine Biological Lab., Plymouth, July-Dec. 1937; Demonstrator and Nuffield Research Assistant in Biochemistry, University of Oxford Medical School, 1938–41; Instructor and Research Assoc. in Pharmacology, Washington Univ. School of Medicine, St Louis, 1941–42; New York University School of Medicine: Research Assoc. in Medicine, 1942–45; Asst Professor of Biochemistry, 1945–46; Professor of Pharmacology, and Chairman of Dept of Pharmacology, 1946–54; Prof. of Biochemistry, and Chm. of Dept of Biochemistry, 1954–74; Distinguished Mem., Roche Inst. of Molecular Biology, New Jersey, 1974–85. Carlos Jimenez Diaz lectr, Madrid Univ., 1969. Pres., Internat. Union of Biochemistry, 1961–67. Member: US National Academy of Sciences; American Academy of Arts and Sciences; American Philosophical Society; Deutsche Akademie der Naturforscher (Leopoldina), etc. Nobel Prize (joint) in Physiology or Medicine, 1959. Hon. degrees from universities and colleges in Argentina, Brazil, Chile, England, Italy, Peru, Philippines, Scotland, Spain and USA. Foreign Member: Royal Society, 1965; USSR Academy of Science, 1966; Polish Acad. of Science; Acad. of Science, DDR, 1977; Acad. of Med. Scis, Argentina, 1977; Chilean Acad. of Scis, 1977; Indian Nat. Sci. Acad., 1977. Hon. Mem., Royal Acad. Med., Sevilla, 1971. Gold Medal, Madrid Univ., 1969; Quevedo Gold Medal, Madrid, 1969; Albert Gallatin Medal, NY Univ., 1970. Order of Rising Sun, 2nd class, 1967. *Publications*: papers on biochemistry and molecular biology. *Recreations*: colour photography and swimming. *Address*: Miguel Angel 1 Bis, 28010 Madrid, Spain. *T*: 410–0709; Universidad Autónoma, Campus de Cantoblanco, 28049 Madrid, Spain. *T*: 734–9300.

O'CONNELL, Desmond Henry, Jr; Group Managing Director, BOC Group, 1986–90; *b* 22 Feb. 1936; *s* of Desmond H. and Rosemary O'Connell; *m* 1964, Roberta M. Jaeger; two *s* one *d*. *Educ*: University of Notre Dame, Indiana; Harvard Business School. BS Elec. Eng., MBA. McKinsey & Co., Chicago, 1962–69; Walsh, Killian & Co., 1969–70; Baxter Travenol Labs, Deerfield, 1970–80; Airco, Montvale, NJ, 1980–86. Non-exec. Dir, Lucas Industries, 1988–. *Recreations*: golf, ski-ing. *Clubs*: East India; Leander; Indian Hill Country (Winnetka, Ill); Ridgewood Country (Ridgewood, NJ); Harvard (New York); Bay Head Yacht (Bay Head, NJ).

O'CONNELL, John Eugene Anthony, MS (London), FRCS; Consulting Neurological Surgeon, St Bartholomew's Hospital; *b* 16 Sept. 1906; *s* of Thomas Henry and Catherine Mary O'Connell (*née* O'Sullivan); *m* Marjorie Hutchinson Cook, MBE (*d* 1986). *Educ*: Clongowes Wood and Wimbledon Colleges; St Bartholomew's Hospital. Held posts of House Surgeon, Senior Demonstrator of Anatomy, and Surgical Chief Assistant, St Bartholomew's Hospital, 1931–39; Studied at Universities of Michigan and Chicago on Rockefeller Foundation Travelling Fellowship, 1935–36; Surgeon in charge of an EMS Neurosurgical Unit, 1941–46; Surgeon i/c Dept of Neurol Surgery, St Bartholomew's Hosp., 1946–71; Hunterian Professor, Royal College of Surgeons, 1943 and 1950. Emeritus Mem., Soc. of Brit. Neurol Surgeons (ex-Pres.); FRSM (ex-Vice-Pres.); Hon. Member: Neurosurgical Soc. Australasia; Deutsche Gesellschaft für Neurochirurgie; Corresp. Mem., Amer. Assoc. Neurol Surgeons. *Publications*: papers in neurological, surgical and other journals and books. *Recreations*: fly-fishing, bird watching. *Address*: Fishing Cottage, Itchen Abbas, Winchester, Hants. *T*: Itchen Abbas (096278) 227.

O'CONNELL, Sir Maurice (James Donagh MacCarthy), 7th Bt *cr* 1869, of Lakeview, Killarney and Ballybeggan, Tralee; *b* 10 June 1958; *s* of Sir Morgan Donal Conail

O'Connell, 6th Bt and of Elizabeth, *o d* of late Major John MacCarthy O'Leary; *S* father, 1989. *Heir: b* John Morgan Ross MacCarthy O'Connell, *b* 17 April 1960. *Address:* 41 Lowndes Street, SW1; Lakeview House, Killarney, Co. Kerry.

O'CONNOR, Surgeon Rear-Adm. Anthony, LVO 1967; Director, Red Cross Blood Transfusion Service, Western Australia, 1981–84 (Deputy Director, 1975–81); *b* 8 Nov. 1917; *s* of Armel John O'Connor and Lucy Violet O'Connor (*née* Bullock-Webster); *m* 1946, Catherine Jane (*née* Hayes); three *d. Educ:* Kings Coll., Strand, London; Westminster Hosp. Med. Sch. MRCS, LRCP, MB, BS, FFARCS, MFCM. Qualified Medical Practitioner, 1941; joined Royal Navy (RNVR), 1942; Permanent Commn, 1945; Dep. Medical Director General (Naval), 1969; MO i/c, Inst. of Naval Med. and Dean of Naval Med., 1972–75. QHP 1970–75. *Recreations:* gardening, photography. *Address:* c/o Lloyds Bank, Ludlow, Shropshire.

O'CONNOR, Rev. Canon (Brian) Michael (McDougal); Vicar of Rainham, Kent, since 1979; *b* 20 June 1942; *s* of Brian McDougal O'Connor and Beryl O'Connor; *m* 1968, Alison Margaret Tibbutt; two *s. Educ:* Lancing Coll.; St Catharine's Coll., Cambridge (BA, MA); Cuddesdon Coll., Oxford. Admitted Solicitor, 1964; Asst Curate, St Andrew, Headington, 1969–72; Sec., Oxford Dio. Pastoral Cttee, 1972–79; Rural Dean of Gillingham, 1981–88. Hon. Canon of Rochester Cathedral, 1988–. Member: General Synod, 1975–90 (Mem., Standing Cttee, 1985–90); Crown Appointments Commn, 1987–90; ACC, 1988–. Deleg., WCC Assembly, Canberra, 1991. *Address:* The Vicarage, 80 Broadview Avenue, Rainham, Gillingham, Kent ME8 9DE. *T:* Medway (0634) 31538. *Club:* National Liberal.

O'CONNOR, Rt. Rev. Cormac Murphy; *see* Murphy-O'Connor.

O'CONNOR, Professor Daniel John; Professor of Philosophy, University of Exeter, 1957–79, now Emeritus; *b* 2 April 1914; *m* 1948, Kathleen Kemsley; no *c. Educ:* Birkbeck Coll., University of London. Entered Civil Service, 1933; Commonwealth Fund Fellow in Philosophy, University of Chicago, 1946–47; Professor of Philosophy, University of Natal, SA, 1949–51; Professor of Philosophy, University of the Witwatersrand, Johannesburg, 1951–52; Lecturer in Philosophy, Univ. Coll. of North Staffordshire, 1952–54; Professor of Philosophy, University of Liverpool, 1954–57. Visiting Professor, University of Pennsylvania, 1961–62. *Publications:* John Locke, 1952; Introduction to Symbolic Logic (with A. H. Basson), 1953; Introduction to the Philosophy of Education, 1957; A Critical History of Western Philosophy (ed), 1964; Aquinas and Natural Law, 1968; Free Will, 1971; (ed jtly) New Essays in the Philosophy of Education, 1973; The Correspondence Theory of Truth, 1975; various papers in philosophical journals. *Address:* c/o Department of Philosophy, University of Exeter, Queen's Building, The Queen's Drive, Exeter EX4 4QH.

O'CONNOR, Francis Brian, PhD; Chief Officer, Joint Nature Conservation Committee, since 1991; *b* 27 Dec. 1932; *s* of Francis Arthur and Marjorie O'Connor; *m* 1957, Dilys Mary Mathew-Jones; one *s* one *d. Educ:* Quarry Bank High Sch., Liverpool; University Coll. of N Wales, Bangor (BSc, PhD). Univ. of Wales Res. Fellow, 1956–58; Lecturer in Zoology: TCD, 1958–60; UCL, 1960–67; Prof. of Soil Biology, Univ. of Aarhus, Denmark, 1968–69; Dir of Studies in Conservation, UCL, 1969–75; Nature Conservancy Council: Dep. Dir Gen., 1975–84; Dir (England), 1984–90; Dir of Policy, Planning and Services, 1990–91. *Publications:* numerous scientific. *Recreations:* boating, motoring, restoration of old houses. *Address:* Manor Farm Cottage, 52 Main Street, Ailsworth, Peterborough PE5 7AF. *T:* Peterborough (0733) 380248. *Club:* Savile.

O'CONNOR, Gillian Rose; Editor, Investors Chronicle, since 1982; *b* 11 Aug. 1941; *d* of Thomas McDougall O'Connor and Kathleen Joan O'Connor (*née* Parnell). *Educ:* Sutton High School for Girls; St Hilda's College, Oxford. *Address:* Investors Chronicle, Greystoke Place, Fetter Lane, EC4A 1ND. *T:* 071–405 6969.

O'CONNOR, Rt. Rev. Kevin, JCL; Titular Bishop of Glastonbury and an Auxiliary Bishop of Liverpool, (RC), since 1979; *b* 20 May 1929. *Educ:* St Francis Xavier, Liverpool; Junior and Senior Seminaries, Upholland; Gregorian Univ., Rome. Priest, 1954; Member, Archdiocesan Marriage Tribunal; Parish Priest, St Anne's and Chancellor of Archdiocese of Liverpool, 1977. *Address:* 12 Richmond Close, Eccleston, St Helens WA10 5JE.

O'CONNOR, Rev. Canon Michael; *see* O'Connor, Rev. Canon B. M. McD.

O'CONNOR, Air Vice-Marshal Patrick Joseph, CB 1976; OBE 1943; MD; FRCPE, FRCPsych; Civil Consultant in Neuropsychiatry, Royal Air Force, since 1978; Consultant in Neurology and Psychiatry to Civil Aviation Authority and to British Airways, since 1978; *b* 21 Aug. 1914; *s* of Charles O'Connor, Straffan, Co. Kildare, Eire, farmer; *m* 1946, Elsie, *o d* of David Craven, Leeds, Yorks; one *s* two *d* (and one *d* decd). *Educ:* Roscrea Coll.; University of Dublin. MB, BCh 1938. Joined RAF, 1940; Air Cdre 1966; Air Vice-Marshal 1971; Consultant Adviser in Neurology and Psychiatry to RAF, 1964–78; Senior Consultant to RAF at Central Medical Establishment, 1975–78, Hon. Consultant, 1978–; retired from RAF, 1978. MD 1950; MRCPE 1950; DPM 1953; FRCPE 1960; MRCP 1960; FRCPsych 1970. QHP 1967–78. Member: Med. Council to Migraine Trust; Med. Council on Alcoholism; The EEG Soc.; Assoc. of British Neurologists; Internat. Acad. of Aviation and Space Med., 1977; Internat. League against Epilepsy; Flying Personnel Res. Cttee. Fellow, Aerospace Med. Assoc; FRSM. *Publications:* contrib.: Journal Neurology, Psychiatry and Neurosurgery; British Journal Psychiatry; BMJ. *Recreations:* gardening, shooting. *Address:* 10 Harley Street, W1N 1AA. *T:* 071–636 6504; St Benedicts, Bacombe Lane, Wendover, Bucks. *T:* Aylesbury (0296) 623329. *Club:* Royal Air Force.

O'CONNOR, Rt. Hon. Sir Patrick McCarthy, Kt 1966; PC 1980; a Lord Justice of Appeal, 1980–89; *b* 28 Dec. 1914; *s* of late William Patrick O'Connor; *m* 1938, Mary Garland (*d* 1984), *d* of William Martin Griffin, KC, of Vancouver, BC; two *s* two *d. Educ:* Downside; Merton Coll., Oxford (Hon. Fellow 1987). Called to the Bar, Inner Temple, 1940; Master of the Bench, 1966. Junior Counsel to the Post Office, 1954–60; QC 1960; Recorder: of King's Lynn, 1959–61; of Southend, 1961–66; a Judge of the High Ct of Justice, QBD, 1966–80; Dep. Chairman, IoW QS, 1957–71. Vice-Chm., Parole Bd, 1974–75. A Governor of Guy's Hospital, 1956–60. *Recreation:* golf. *Address:* 210 Rivermead Court, Ranelagh Gardens, SW6 3SG. *T:* 071–731 3563. *Club:* Huntercombe.

O'CONNOR, Rory, CBE 1991; Judge of the High Court of Hong Kong, 1977–90; *b* Co. Down, 26 Nov. 1925; *s* of late James O'Connor and Mary (*née* Savage); *m* 1963, Elizabeth, *d* of late Frederick Dew; one *s* two *d. Educ:* Blackrock Coll., Dublin; Univ. Coll., Dublin (BCom). Called to Irish Bar, King's Inns, 1949. Resident Magistrate, Kenya, 1956–62; Hong Kong: Magistrate, 1962–70; District Judge, 1970–77. *Address:* 12 Windermere Crescent, Bangor, Co Down, N Ireland.

O'CONNOR, Sandra Day; Associate Justice of the Supreme Court of the United States, since 1981; *b* 26 March 1930; *d* of Harry and Ada Mae Day; *m* 1952, John Jay O'Connor III; three *s. Educ:* Stanford Univ. (BA 1950; LLB 1952). Legal appts in Calif and Frankfurt, 1952–57; in private practice, 1959–65; Asst Attorney-Gen., Arizona, 1965–69; Judge: Maricopa County Superior Ct, 1974–79; Arizona Ct of Appeals, 1979–81. Mem. Senate, Arizona, 1969–74 (majority leader, 1973–74). Director: Nat. Bank of Arizona, Phoenix, 1971–74; Blue Cross/Blue Shield, Arizona, 1975–79. Chm., Maricopa County Juvenile Detention Home, 1966–68; Pres., Heard Museum, Phoenix, 1979–81; Mem. Nat. Bd, Smithsonian Assocs, 1981–82. Trustee, Stanford Univ., 1976–80. Hon. Bencher, Gray's Inn, 1982. *Address:* Supreme Court Building, 1 First Street NE, Washington, DC 20543, USA.

O'CONNOR HOWE, Mrs Josephine Mary; HM Diplomatic Service, retired; *b* 25 March 1924; *d* of late Gerald Frank Claridge and late Dulcie Agnes Claridge (*née* Waldegrave); *m* 1947, John O'Connor Howe (decd); one *d. Educ:* Wychwood Sch., Oxford; Triangle Coll. (course in journalism). Inter-Allied Information Cttee, later, United Nations Information Office, 1942–45; Foreign Office: The Hague, 1945–46; Internat. News Service and freelance, 1946–50; FO, 1952; Counsellor, FCO, 1974–1979. Reader's Digest, 1979–83; Dir, Council for Arms Control, 1983–84; Exec. Editor, Inst. for the Study of Conflict, 1985–89; Freelance Editor specialising in internat. affairs, arms control, etc., 1985–. *Publication:* (ed) Armed Peace—the search for world security, 1984. *Recreations:* theatre, gardening, grandchildren. *Address:* Dering Cottage, Little Chart, Ashford, Kent TN27 0PT. *T:* Pluckley (023384) 328. *Club:* Commonwealth Trust.

ODDIE, Christopher Ripley; His Honour Judge Oddie; a Circuit Judge, since 1974; Judge, Mayor's and City of London Court, since 1989; *b* Derby, 24 Feb. 1929; *o s* of Dr and Mrs J. R. Oddie, Uttoxeter, Staffs; *m* 1957, Margaret Anne, *d* of Mr and Mrs J. W. Timmis; one *s* three *d. Educ:* Giggleswick Sch.; Oriel Coll., Oxford (MA). Called to Bar, Middle Temple, 1954, Oxford Circuit. Contested (L) Ludlow, Gen. Election, 1970. A Recorder of the Crown Court, 1972–74. Chm., County Court Rule Cttee, 1985–87 (Mem., 1981–87). Member: Judicial Studies Bd, 1989–91; Cttee, Council of Her Majesty's Circuit Judges, 1989–91. Mem. Council, St Mary's Hosp. Med. Sch., 1980–88. *Recreations:* reading, gossip, opera, walking. *Address:* 89 The Vineyard, Richmond, Surrey. *T:* 081–940 4135; Lower Riddings, Woodside, Clun, Shropshire. *Club:* Reform.

ODDIE, Prof. Guy Barrie, BArch, DipTP; architect and designer; Robert Adam Professor of Architecture, 1968–82, now Emeritus, and Head of Department of Architecture, 1968–80, University of Edinburgh; *b* 1 Jan. 1922; *o s* of Edward Oddie and Eleanor Pinkney; *m* 1952, Mabel Mary Smith (*d* 1990); two step *d. Educ:* Hookergate Grammar Sch.; Univ. of Newcastle upon Tyne. Demonstrator, Univ. of Newcastle upon Tyne, 1944; Research Architect, Building Res. Stn, 1947–50; Sen. Lectr, Birmingham Sch. of Architecture, 1950–52; Develt Gp, Min. of Educn, 1952–58; Staff architect, UGC, 1958–63; Consultant to OECD, 1963–66; Dir, Laboratories Investigation Unit, DES, 1966–68. Sen. Advr to OECD Prog. on Educnl Bldg, 1972–84. Participant in and advocate for 1950's architectural movement led by school-designers and aimed at producing quality buildings on time and in the numbers needed to satisfy social needs. *Publications:* School Building Resources and their Effective Use, 1966; Development and Economy in Educational Building, 1968; Industrialised Building for Schools, 1975; contrib. Architects Jl, Architectural Rev., RIBA Jl. *Recreations:* dry-fly fishing, gardening. *Address:* The Causeway, Edinburgh EH15 3QA.

ODDY, Christine Margaret; Member (Lab) Midlands Central, European Parliament, since 1989; *b* 20 Sept. 1955; *d* of Eric Lawson Oddy and Audrey Mary Oddy. *Educ:* Stoke Park Sch., Coventry; University Coll. London (LLB Hons); Licence Spéciale en droit européen, Inst. d'Etudes européennes, Brussels; Birkbeck Coll., London (MSc (Econ)). Stagiaire (grad. trainee) in EC, 1979–80; Articled Clerk, Clifford Turner, 1980–82; admitted Solicitor, 1982; Lectr in Law, City of London Poly., 1984–89. Member: Legal Affairs Cttee; Social Affairs Cttee; Women's Rights Cttee; Central America Delegn. *Recreations:* travel, wine, theatre, cinema. *Address:* 3 Copthall House, Station Square, Coventry CV1 2FZ. *T:* Coventry (0203) 552328.

ODDY, Revel, FSA; Keeper, Department of Art and Archaeology, Royal Scottish Museum, Edinburgh, 1974–83; *b* 11 April 1922; *s* of Sidney Oddy and Muriel Barnfather; *m* 1949, Ariadne Margaret, *d* of late Sir Andrew Gourlay Clow, KCSI, CIE; two *s* two *d. Educ:* Worksop Coll.; Pembroke Coll., Cambridge (MA). FSA 1982. Served War, Loyal Regt and King's African Rifles, 1941–46. Mod. langs master, Dr Challoner's Grammar Sch., Amersham, 1949; Res. Asst, V&A Mus., London, 1950–55; Asst Keeper, Royal Scottish Mus., Edinburgh, 1955–74. *Recreations:* mild gardening, reading. *Address:* 44 Findhorn Place, Edinburgh EH9 2NT. *T:* 031–667 5815. *Clubs:* Civil Service; University of Edinburgh Staff (Edinburgh).

ODDY, William Andrew, FSA; Keeper of Conservation, British Museum, since 1985; *b* 6 Jan. 1942; *s* of late William T. Oddy and of Hilda F. Oddy (*née* Dalby); *m* 1965, Patricia Anne Whitaker; one *s* one *d. Educ:* Bradford Grammar Sch.; New Coll., Oxford (BA 1964; BSc 1965; MA 1969). FSA 1973; FIIC 1974. Joined British Museum Research Lab., 1966, research into conservation and ancient technology; Head of Conservation, 1981. Member: Scientific Cttee, Internat. Congress on Deterioration and Preservation of Stone, 1976–; Dept of Transport Adv. Cttee on Historic Wrecks, 1981–; Exec. Cttee, Textile Conservation Centre, 1985–; Cons. Cttee, Council for Care of Churches, 1985–; Cons. Cttee, Cons. Unit, Mus. and Gall. Commn, 1987–. Freeman, Goldsmiths' Co., 1986. *Publications:* editor: Problems in the Conservation of Waterlogged Wood, 1975; Aspects of Early Metallurgy, 1980; Scientific Studies in Numismatics, 1980; Metallurgy in Numismatics 2, 1988; joint editor: Conservation in Museums and Galleries, 1975; Metallurgy in Numismatics I, 1980; Aspects of Tibetan Metallurgy, 1981; A Survey of Numismatic Research 1978–1984, 1986; (jtly) Romanesque Metalwork: copper alloys and their decoration, 1986; papers in learned jls. *Recreation:* travel. *Address:* c/o The British Museum, WC1B 3DG.

O'DEA, Sir Patrick Jerad, KCVO 1974; retired public servant, New Zealand; Extra Gentleman Usher to the Queen, since 1981; *b* 18 April 1918; 2nd *s* of late Patrick O'Dea; *m* 1945, Jean Mary, *d* of Hugh Mulholland; one *s* three *d. Educ:* St Paul's Coll. and Univ. of Otago, Dunedin, NZ; Victoria Univ., Wellington, NZ. Joined NZ Public Service, 1936; served in Agriculture Dept, 1936–47. Served War in Royal New Zealand Artillery of 2 NZEF, 1941–45. With Industries and Commerce Dept, 1947–49; subseq. served with Dept of Internal Affairs in various posts interrupted by 2 years' full-time study at Victoria Univ. of Wellington (DPA). Group Exec. Officer, Local Govt, 1959–64; Dep. Sec., 1964–67; Sec. for Internal Affairs, NZ, 1967–78; formerly Sec. for: Local Govt; Civil Defence; Sec. of Recreation and Sport; Clerk of the Writs; NZ Sec. to the Queen, 1969–78, reapptd 1981, for visit of Queen and Duke of Edinburgh to NZ. Pres., Keep NZ Beautiful Inc.; Chairman: Dorothy Daniels Foundn; Duke of Edinburgh's Award NZ Foundn; Mem., Vicentian Foundn. *Publications:* several papers on local govt in New Zealand. *Recreations:* gardening, golf, bowls. *Address:* 1 Tensing Place, Khandallah, Wellington, New Zealand. *T:* Wellington 792–424. *Clubs:* Shandon Golf (Petone, NZ); Khandallah Bowling (Khandallah, NZ); Wellesley (Wellington).

ODELL, John William, (Jack), OBE 1969; Chairman, Lledo (London) Ltd, since 1982. Joint Vice-Chairman, Lesney Products & Co. Ltd, Diecasting Engineers, London E9,

1981–82 (Joint Managing Director, 1947–73; Deputy Chairman, 1973–81). *Address:* Lledo (London) Ltd, Woodhall Road, South Street, Ponders End, Enfield, Middx.

O'DELL, Mrs June Patricia, OBE 1990; Deputy Chairman, Equal Opportunities Commission, 1986–90; *b* 9 June 1929; *d* of Leonard Vickery, RN and Myra Vickery; *m* 1951 (marr. diss. 1963); one *s* two *d.* *Educ:* Edgehill Girls College; Plymouth Technical College. Estate Agent. Dir, Eachdale Developments Ltd. Nat. Pres., Fedn of Business and Professional Women, 1983–85; Chm., Employment Cttee, Internat. Fedn of Business Professional Women, 1983–87; Member: Women's Nat. Commn, 1983–85; Industry Matters Women's Wkg Gp, 1985–; European Adv. Cttee for Equal Treatment between Women and Men, 1986–90; Authorised Conveyancing Practitioners Bd, 1991–. FRSA 1986; FNAEA 1986. *Recreations:* music, particularly opera and choral; writing, literature, the countryside, equestrian events. *Address:* Vale Farm, Kimblewick, Aylesbury, Bucks HP17 8SX. *Club:* University Women's.

ODELL, Prof. Peter Randon; Professor Emeritus, Erasmus University, Rotterdam (Director, Centre for International Energy Studies, 1981–90); *b* 1 July 1930; *s* of late Frank James Odell and late Grace Edna Odell; *m* 1957, Jean Mary McKintosh; two *s* two *d.* *Educ:* County Grammar Sch., Coalville; Univ. of Birmingham (BA, PhD); Fletcher Sch. of Law and Diplomacy, Cambridge, Mass (AM). FInstPet. RAF 1954–57. Economist, Shell International Petroleum Co., 1958–61; Lectr, LSE, 1961–65; Sen. Lectr, LSE, 1965–68; Prof. of Economic Geography, Erasmus Univ., 1968–81. Visiting Professor: LSE, 1983–; College of Europe, Bruges, 1983–90; Scholar in Residence, Rockefeller Centre, Bellagio, 1984; Killam Vis. Scholar, Univ. of Calgary, 1989. Stamp Meml Lectr, London Univ., 1975. Canadian Council Fellow, 1978. Adviser, Dept of Energy, 1977–78. Contested (Lib Dem) Suffolk, European Elecn, 1989. European Editor, Energy Jl, 1988–90. FRSA 1983. *Publications:* An Economic Geography of Oil, 1963; Natural Gas in Western Europe, 1969; Oil and World Power, 1970, 8th edn 1986; (with D. A. Preston) Economies and Societies in Latin America, 1973, 2nd edn 1978; Energy: Needs and Resources, 1974, 2nd edn 1977; (with K. E. Rosing) The North Sea Oil Province, 1975; The West European Energy Economy: the case for self-sufficiency, 1976; (with K. E. Rosing) The Optimal Development of the North Sea Oilfields, 1976; (with L. Vallenilla) The Pressures of Oil: a strategy for economic revival, 1978; British Oil Policy: a Radical Alternative, 1980; (with K. E. Rosing) The Future of Oil, 1980–2080, 1980, 2nd edn 1983; (ed with J. Rees) The International Oil Industry: an interdisciplinary perspective 1986; Global and Regional Energy Supplies: recent fictions and fallacies revisited, 1991. *Address:* De Lairesselaan 191, 3062 PH Rotterdam, The Netherlands. *T:* Rotterdam 4525341.

ODELL, Sir Stanley (John), Kt 1986; farmer and landowner; *b* 20 Nov. 1929; *s* of George Frederick Odell and Florence May Odell; *m* 1952, Eileen Grace Stuart; four *d.* *Educ:* Bedford Modern School. Chairman: Mid Beds Young Conservatives, 1953–59; Mid Beds Cons. Assoc., 1964–69 (Pres., 1991); Beds Cons. European Constituency Council, 1979; E of England Provincial Council, Cons. Party, 1983–86 (Pres., 1991–); Nat. Union of Cons. and Unionist Assocs, 1989–90 (Vice Chm., 1986–89). *Recreations:* politics, shooting. *Address:* Woodhall Farm, Campton, Shefford, Beds SG17 5PB. *T:* Hitchin (0462) 813230. *Club:* Farmers'.

ODGERS, Graeme David William; Chief Executive, Alfred McAlpine plc, since 1990; *b* 10 March 1934; *s* of late William Arthur Odgers and Elizabeth Minty (*née* Rennie); *m* 1957, Diana Patricia Berge; one *s* two *d* (and one *d* decd). *Educ:* St John's Coll., Johannesburg; Gonville and Caius Coll., Cambridge (Mech. Scis Tripos); Harvard Business Sch. (MBA, Baker Scholar). Investment Officer, Internat. Finance Corp., Washington DC, 1959–62; Management Consultant, Urwick Orr and Partners Ltd, 1962–64; Investment Executive, Hambros Bank Ltd, 1964–65; Director: Keith Shipton and Co. Ltd, 1965–72; C. T. Bowring (Insurance) Holdings Ltd, 1972–74; Chm., Odgers and Co. Ltd (Management Consultants), 1970–74; Dir, Industrial Develt Unit, DoI, 1974–77; Assoc. Dir (Finance), General Electric Co., 1977–78; Gp Finance Dir, 1979–86, Gp Man. Dir, 1983–86, Tarmac; British Telecommunications: pt-time Mem. Bd, 1983–86; Govt Dir, 1984–86; Dep. Chm. and Chief Finance Officer, 1986–87; Gp Man. Dir, 1987–90. Non-executive Director: Dalgety, 1987–; Nat. & Provincial Bldg Soc., 1990–. Mem., Listed Cos' Adv. Cttee, Stock Exchange, 1987–. *Recreation:* golf. *Address:* Brome House, West Malling, Kent ME19 6NE. *Clubs:* City of London, Reform; Wildernesse (Sevenoaks).

ODGERS, Paul Randell, CB 1970; MBE 1945; TD 1949; Deputy Secretary, Department of Education and Science, 1971–75; *b* 30 July 1915; *e s* of late Dr P. N. B. Odgers and Mrs M. A. Odgers (*née* Higgins); *m* 1944, Diana, *d* of late R. E. F. Fawkes, CBE; one *s* one *d.* *Educ:* Rugby; New Coll., Oxford. Entered CS, Board of Education, 1937. Army Service, 1939–45 (despatches three times). Asst Secretary: Min. of Educn, 1948; Cabinet Office, 1956; Under-Secretary: Min. of Educn, 1958; Office of First Secretary of State, 1967; Office of Lord President of the Council, 1968; Office of Sec. of State for Social Services, 1968; Cabinet Office, 1970. Vice-Pres., Soc. for Promotion of Roman Studies; Mem. Council, GPDST, 1976–89. *Address:* Stone Walls, Aston Road, Haddenham, Bucks HP17 8AF. *T:* Haddenham (0844) 291830. *Club:* United Oxford & Cambridge University.

See also C. D. Compston.

ODLING, Thomas George, CB 1974; *b* 18 Sept. 1911; *yr s* of late Major W. A. Odling, Paxford, Glos and late Mary Bennett Odling (*née* Case); *m* 1st, Camilla Haldane Paterson (marr. diss.); two *s*; 2nd, Hilary Katharine, *d* of late W. J. Palgrave-Ker, Lilliput, Dorset. *Educ:* Temple Grove; Rugby Sch.; New Coll., Oxford (MA). House of Commons: Asst Clerk, 1935; Clerk of Private Bills, Examr of Petitions for Private Bills and Taxing Officer, 1961–73; Clerk of Select Cttee on Parly Comr for Admin, 1969–73; Clerk of Committees, 1974–76, retired 1976. Temp. attached to Consultative Assembly of Council of Europe during 1949 and later sessions. *Recreations:* music, gardening. *Address:* Paxford, Campden, Glos. *Clubs:* Athenæum, MCC.

See also Maj.-Gen. W. Odling.

ODLING, Maj.-Gen. William, CB 1963; OBE 1951; MC; DL; President, English-Speaking Union (Eastern Counties); Chairman: Roman River (Colchester) Conservation Zone; Friends of Essex Churches; Vice-Chairman of School, and Chairman of Hall, Fingringhoe; Treasurer/Secretary, Fingringhoe Ancient Charities; *b* 8 June 1909; *s* of late Major and Mrs W. A. Odling, Paxford, Campden, Glos; *m* 1939, Margaret Marshall (*née* Gardner); one *s* two *d.* *Educ:* Temple Grove; Wellington Coll.; RMA, Woolwich. Subaltern RHA and RA, chiefly in India until 1938; Captain, 1938; Major, 1946; Lieut-Colonel, 1951; Colonel, 1953; Brigadier 1957; Maj.-General, 1961; Adjutant, TA, 1939; CRA, Madagascar Force, 1942 (MC); GSO 1, RA, COSSAC, Planning Staff for Operation Overlord, 1943; NW Europe Campaign (despatches), 1944; GSO 1, War Office, 1945; GSO 1, Training, GHQMELF, 1948; AQMG, MELF, 1950; AAG Colonel, War Office, 1953; CRA E Anglian Div., 1957; Brig. AQ, HQ E Comd, 1959; Maj.-Gen. i/c Admin, GHQ FELF, 1961–62; COS GHQ FELF 1962–64. DL Essex, 1975. *Recreations:* sailing (Cdre, Atalanta (Yacht) Owners Assoc.), print collecting, gardening, brick building, economising. *Address:* Gun House, Fingringhoe, Colchester CO5 7AL. *T:* Peldon (020635) 320. *Club:* Army and Navy.

See also T. G. Odling.

ODLING-SMEE, John Charles; Senior Adviser, International Monetary Fund, since 1990; *b* 13 April 1943; *s* of late Rev. Charles William Odling-Smee and of Katharine Hamilton Odling-Smee (*née* Aitchison). *Educ:* Durham School; St John's College, Cambridge. BA Cantab 1964, MA Oxon 1966. Junior Research Officer, Dept of Applied Economics, Cambridge, 1964–65; Asst Research Officer, Inst. of Economics and Statistics, Oxford, 1965–66; Fellow in Economics, Oriel College, Oxford, 1966–70; Research Officer, Inst. of Economics and Statistics, Oxford, 1968–71 and 1972–73; Economic Research Officer, Govt of Ghana, 1971–72; Senior Research Officer, Centre for Urban Economics, LSE, 1973–75; Economic Adviser, Central Policy Review Staff, Cabinet Office, 1975–77; Senior Economic Adviser, HM Treasury, 1977–80; Senior Economist, IMF, 1981–82; Under-Sec., HM Treasury, 1982–89; Dep. Chief Economic Advr, HM Treasury, 1989–90. *Publications:* (with A. Grey and N. P. Hepworth) Housing Rents, Costs and Subsidies, 1978, 2nd edn 1981; (with R. C. O. Matthews and C. H. Feinstein) British Economic Growth 1856–1973, 1982; articles in books and learned jls. *Address:* 2210 R Street NW, Washington, DC 20008, USA. *T:* (202) 234–7059.

O'DONNELL, Augustine Thomas; Press Secretary to the Prime Minister, since 1990; *b* 1 Oct. 1952; *s* of Helen O'Donnell (*née* McClean) and James O'Donnell; *m* 1979, Melanie Joan Elizabeth Timmis; one *d.* *Educ:* Univ. of Warwick (BA Hons); Nuffield Coll., Oxford (MPhil). Lectr, Dept of Political Economy, Univ. of Glasgow, 1974–79; Economist, HM Treasury, 1979–85; First Sec. (Econ.), British Embassy, Washington, 1985–88; Sen. Economic Adviser, 1988–89, Press Sec., 1989–90, HM Treasury. *Publications:* articles in economic jls. *Recreations:* football, cricket, tennis. *Address:* 10 Downing Street, SW1A 2AA. *Club:* Old Salesians FC.

O'DONNELL, Prof. Barry, FRCS, FRCSI; Professor of Paediatric Surgery, Royal College of Surgeons in Ireland; Consultant Paediatric Surgeon, Our Lady's Hospital for Sick Children, Dublin, since 1957; Director, West Deutsche Landesbank, since 1990; *b* 6 Sept. 1926; *e s* of Michael J. O'Donnell and Kathleen O'Donnell (*née* Barry); *m* 1959, Mary Leydon, BA, BComm, BL, *d* of John Leydon, LLD, KCSG; three *s* one *d.* *Educ:* Christian Brothers College, Cork; Castleknock College, Dublin; University College, Cork (MB Hons 1949). MCh NUI, 1954. FRCS 1953, FRCSI 1953. Ainsworth Travelling Scholar, Boston (Lahey Clinic and Boston Floating Hosp., 1955–56); Sen. Registrar, Hosp. for Sick Children, London, 1956–57. Vis. Prof. of Surgery, Boston Children's Hosp. and Harvard Med. Sch., 1985; Hunterian Prof., RCS, 1986. Jt Pres., British, Canadian and Irish Med. Assocs, 1976–77; President: British Assoc. of Paediatric Surgeons, 1980–82; Surgical Sect., Royal Acad. of Medicine of Ireland, 1990–92; Chm., Jl Cttee, BMA, 1982–88. Hon. Fellow, Amer. Acad. of Pediatrics, 1974. People of the Year Award, New Ireland Insce Co., 1984; Denis Browne Gold Medal, British Assoc. of Paediatric Surgeons, 1989. *Publications:* Essentials of Paediatric Surgery, 1961, 4th edn 1989; Abdominal Pain in Children, 1985. *Recreations:* sailing, golf. *Address:* Children's Research Centre, Our Lady's Hospital for Sick Children, Crumlin, Dublin 12, Ireland. *T:* Dublin 558111; 58 Ailesbury Road, Ballsbridge, Dublin 4, Ireland. *T:* Dublin 694000. *Clubs:* Royal Ocean Racing; Royal Irish Yacht; Portmarnock Golf.

O'DONNELL, James Anthony, FRCO; Master of Music, Westminster Cathedral, since 1988 (Assistant Master of Music, 1982–88); *b* 15 Aug. 1961; *s* of Dr James Joseph Gerard O'Donnell and Dr Gillian Anne O'Donnell (*née* Moody). *Educ:* Westcliff High Sch,, Essex; Jesus Coll., Cambridge (Organ Scholar and Open Scholar in Music; BA 1982, MA). FRCO 1983. Member Council: Guild of Church Musicians, 1988–; RCO, 1989–. Royal Coll. of Organists Performer of the Year, 1987. *Recreations:* opera, food, wine. *Address:* Westminster Cathedral Clergy House, 42 Francis Street, SW1P 1QW. *T:* 071–834 4008/7452.

O'DONNELL, Dr Michael; author and broadcaster; *b* 20 Oct. 1928; *o s* of late James Michael O'Donnell and Nora (*née* O'Sullivan); *m* 1953, Catherine Dorrington Ward; one *s* two *d.* *Educ:* Stonyhurst; Trinity Hall, Cambridge (Lane Harrington Schol.); St Thomas's Hosp. Med. Sch., London (MB, BChir). FRCGP 1990. Editor, Cambridge Writing, 1948; Scriptwriter, BBC Radio, 1949–52. General Medical Practitioner, 1954–64. Editor, World Medicine, 1966–82. Member: General Medical Council, 1971–; Longman Editorial Adv. Bd, 1978–82. Inaugural lecture, Green Coll., Oxford, 1981. John Rowan Wilson Award, 1982; John Snow Medal, 1984. Scientific Adviser: O Lucky Man (film), 1972; Inside Medicine (BBC TV), 1974; Don't Ask Me (Yorkshire TV), 1977; Don't Just Sit There (Yorkshire TV), 1979–80; Where There's Life (Yorkshire TV), 1981–83. *Television plays:* Suggestion of Sabotage, 1963; Dangerous Reunion, 1964; Resolution, 1964; *television documentaries:* You'll Never Believe It, 1962; Cross Your Heart and Hope to Live, 1975; The Presidential Race, 1976; From Europe to the Coast, 1976; Chasing the Dragon, 1979; Second Opinion, 1980; Judgement on Las Vegas, 1981; Is Your Brain Really Necessary, 1982; Plague of Hearts, 1983; Medical Express, 1984; Can You Avoid Cancer?, 1984; O'Donnell Investigates . . . booze, 1985; O'Donnell Investigates . . . food, 1985; O'Donnell Investigates . . . the food business, 1986; O'Donnell Investigates . . . age, 1988; Health, Wealth and Happiness, 1989; What is this thing called health, 1990; *radio:* contributor to Stop the Week (BBC), 1976–; Chm., My Word (BBC), 1983–; Presenter, Relative Values (BBC), 1987–. Medical Journalists Assoc. Award, 1971, 1982 and 1990; British Science Writers' Award, 1979. *Publications:* Cambridge Anthology, 1952; The Europe We Want, 1971; My Medical School, 1978; The Devil's Prison, 1982; Doctor! Doctor! an insider's guide to the games doctors play, 1986; The Long Walk Home, 1988; Dr Michael O'Donnell's Executive Health Guide, 1988; contrib. Punch, New Scientist, The Listener, The Times, The Guardian, Daily Telegraph, Daily Mail. *Recreations:* golf, walking, listening to music, loitering (with and without intent). *Address:* Handon Cottage, Markwick Lane, Loxhill, Godalming, Surrey GU8 4BD. *T:* Hascombe (048632) 295. *Club:* Garrick.

O'DONNELL, Rt. Hon. Turlough; PC 1979; Lord Justice of Appeal, Supreme Court of Northern Ireland, 1979–89; *b* 5 Aug. 1924; *e s* of Charles and Eileen O'Donnell; *m* 1954, Eileen McKinley; two *s* two *d.* *Educ:* Abbey Grammar Sch., Newry; Queen's Univ., Belfast (LLB). Called to Bar of Northern Ireland, 1947; called to Inner Bar, 1964; Puisne Judge, NI, 1971–79. Chairman: NI Bar Council, 1970–71, Council of Legal Educn, NI, 1980–. *Recreations:* golf, folk music. *Address:* c/o Royal Courts of Justice (Ulster), Belfast BT1 3JF.

O'DONOGHUE, Michael; His Honour Judge O'Donoghue; a Circuit Judge, since 1982; *b* 10 June 1929; *s* of late Dr James O'Donoghue, MB, ChB and Vera O'Donoghue. *Educ:* Rhyl County School; Univ. of Liverpool. LLB (Hons) 1950. Called to the Bar, Gray's Inn, 1951; National Service as Flying Officer, RAF, 1951–53; practised at the Chancery Bar, 1954–82; Lectr in Law (part time), Univ. of Liverpool, 1966–82. *Recreations:* music, sailing, photography. *Address:* c/o Chancery Listing Clerk, High Court of Justice, Crown Square, Manchester. *Clubs:* Athenæum (Liverpool); Royal Welsh Yacht (Caernarfon) (Commodore, 1980–82).

O'DONOGHUE, Philip Nicholas, CBiol, FIBiol; General Secretary, Institute of Biology, 1982–89; *b* 9 Oct. 1929; *s* of Terence Frederick O'Donoghue and Ellen Mary (*née* Haynes); *m* 1955, Veronica Florence Campbell; two *d*. *Educ:* East Barnet Grammar Sch.; Univ. of Nottingham (BSc; MSc 1959). FIBiol 1975. Experimental Officer, ARC's Field Stn, Compton, 1952–55 and Inst. of Animal Physiology, Babraham, 1955–61; Scientific Officer, National Inst. for Res. in Dairying, Shinfield, 1962–66; Lectr in Exptl Vet. Science and later Sen. Lectr in Lab. Animal Science, Royal Postgrad. Med. Sch., Univ. of London, 1966–82. Hume Meml Lect., UFAW, 1990. Vice-Pres., Inst. of Animal Technicians, 1969–; Hon. Sec., Inst. of Biology, 1972–76; Member: TEC, 1973–79 (Chm., Life Sciences Cttee, 1973–80); Council, Section of Comparative Medicine, RSM, 1983– (Pres., 1985–86); President: Lab. Animal Sci. Assoc., 1989–90; Fedn of European Lab. Animal Sci. Assocs, 1990–. Editor, Laboratory Animals, 1967–82. *Publications:* editor of books and author of articles chiefly on the law relating to and the effective use and proper care of laboratory animals. *Recreations:* music, local history, talking, limited gardening. *Address:* 21 Holyrood Road, New Barnet, Herts EN5 1DQ. *T:* 081–449 3692. *Clubs:* Athenæum, Royal Society of Medicine.

O'DONOVAN, Rev. Canon Oliver Michael Timothy, DPhil; Regius Professor of Moral and Pastoral Theology, University of Oxford, since 1982; Canon of Christ Church, Oxford, since 1982; *b* 28 June 1945; *s* of Michael and Joan M. O'Donovan; *m* 1978, Joan Elizabeth Lockwood; two *s*. *Educ:* University Coll. Sch., Hampstead; Balliol Coll., Oxford (MA, DPhil); Wycliffe Hall, Oxford; Princeton Univ. Ordained deacon 1972, priest 1973, dio. of Oxford. Tutor, Wycliffe Hall, Oxford, 1972–77; Prof. of Systematic Theology, Wycliffe Coll., Toronto, 1977–82. Member: C of E Bd for Social Responsibility, 1976–77, 1982–85; Anglican-Roman Catholic Internat. Commn, 1985–; Anglican-Orthodox Jt Doctrinal Discussions, 1982–84. *Publications:* The Problem of Self-Love in Saint Augustine, 1980; Begotten or Made?, 1984; Resurrection and Moral Order, 1986; On the Thirty Nine Articles, 1986; Peace and Certainty, 1989; contrib. Jl of Theol Studies, Jl of Religious Ethics and Studies in Christian Ethics. *Address:* Christ Church, Oxford OX1 1DP.

O'DRISCOLL, Rt. Rev. P. R.; *see* Huron, Bishop of.

OEHLERS, Maj.-Gen. Gordon Richard, CB 1987; Director of Security and Investigation, British Telecom, since 1987; *b* 19 April 1933; *s* of late Dr Roderic Clarke Oehlers and Hazel Ethne Oehlers (*née* Van Geyzel); *m* 1956, Doreen, (Rosie), Gallant; one *s* one *d*. *Educ:* St Andrews School, Singapore. CEng, FIEE, MIERE. Commissioned Royal Corps of Signals, 1958; UK and Middle East, 1958–64; Adjutant, 4th Div. Signals Regt, 1964–66; Instructor, School of Signals, 1966–68; OC 7th Armd Bde HQ and Signals Sqdn, 1968–70; GSO2 (Weapons), 1970–72; CO 7th Signal Regt, 1973–76; Commander Corps Royal Signals, 1st (British) Corps, 1977–79; Dir, Op. Requirements 4 (Army), 1979–84; ACDS (Comd Control, Communications and Inf. Systems), 1984–87. Col Comdt, RCS, 1987–; Hon. Col 31st (Greater London) Signal Regt (Volunteers), 1988–. Chm., Royal Signals Instn, 1990–. Pres., British Wireless Dinner Club, 1986–87. *Recreations:* interested in all games esp. badminton (Captain Warwicks County Badminton Team, 1954–56), lawn tennis (Chm., Army Lawn Tennis Assoc., 1980–86). *Address:* c/o National Westminster Bank, 4 High Street, Petersfield, Hants GU32 3JF.

OESTREICHER, Rev. Canon Paul; Director of the International Ministry of Coventry Cathedral, since 1986; Canon Residentiary of Coventry Cathedral, since 1986; Member of the Society of Friends (Quakers), since 1982; journalist; *b* Germany, 29 Sept. 1931; *s* of Paul Oestreicher and Emma (*née* Schnaus); *m* 1958, Lore Feind; two *s* two *d*. *Educ:* King's High Sch., Dunedin; Otago and Victoria Univs, NZ; Bonn Univ. (Humboldt Res. Fellow); Lincoln Theol College. BA Mod. Langs Otago 1953; MA Hons Polit. Sci. Victoria 1955. Ordained 1959. Fled to NZ with refugee parents, 1939; returned to Europe, 1955. Fraternal worker with German Lutheran Church at Rüsselsheim, trng in problems of industrial soc. (Opel, Gen. Motors), 1958–59; Curate, Dalston, E London, 1959–61; Producer, Relig. Dept, BBC Radio, 1961–64; Assoc. Sec., Dept of Internat. Affairs, Brit. Council of Churches with special resp. for East-West Relations, 1964–69; Vicar, Church of the Ascension, Blackheath, 1968–81; Asst Gen. Sec. and Sec. for Internat. Affairs, BCC, 1981–86; Dir of (Lay) Trng, Dio. Southwark, 1969–72; Hon. Chaplain to Bp of Southwark, 1975–81; Public Preacher in Dio. Southwark, 1981–86; Hon. Canon of Southwark Cathedral, 1978–83, Canon Emeritus 1983–86. Mem. Gen. Synod of C of E, 1970–86. Member: Brit. Council of Churches working parties on Southern Africa and Eastern Europe; Anglican Pacifist Fellowship (sometime exec. mem.), 1960–; Exec. Mem., Christian Concern for Southern Africa, 1978–81; Chm., of Trustees, Christian Inst. (of Southern Africa) Fund, 1984–; Chm., British Section, Amnesty International, 1974–79. Mem. Council, Keston Coll. (Centre for the Study of Religion and Communism), 1976–82. Vice-Chm., Campaign for Nuclear Disarmament, 1980–81, Vice-Pres. 1983–; Mem. Alternative Defence Commn, 1981–87; Vice-Chm., Ecumenical Commn for Church and Society in W Europe (Brussels), 1982–86. Shelley Lectr, Radio NZ, 1987. Editor, Critic (Otago Univ. newspaper), 1952–53; subseq. free-lance journalist and broadcaster. *Publications:* (ed English edn) Helmut Gollwitzer, The Demands of Freedom, 1965; (trans.) H. J. Schultz, Conversion to the World, 1967; (ed, with J. Klugmann) What Kind of Revolution: A Christian-Communist Dialogue, 1968; (ed) The Christian Marxist Dialogue, 1969; (jtly) The Church and the Bomb, 1983; The Double Cross, 1986. *Address:* Coventry Cathedral Office, 7 Priory Row, Coventry, W Midlands CV1 5ES. *T:* Coventry (0203) 227597; 20 Styvechale Avenue, Coventry CV5 6DX. *T:* Coventry (0203) 673704.

O'FERRALL, Very Rev. Basil Arthur, CB 1979; MA; Dean of Jersey, and Rector of St Helier, Jersey, since 1985; Hon. Canon of Winchester, since 1986; *b* 25 Aug. 1924; *s* of Basil James and Mabel Violet O'Ferrall, Dublin; *m* 1952, Joyce Forbes (*née* Taylor); one *s* two *d*. *Educ:* St Patrick's Cathedral Gram. Sch., Dublin; Trinity Coll., Dublin (BA 1948, MA 1966). Curate Assistant, St Patrick's, Coleraine, 1948; Chaplain RN, 1951; served: HMS Victory, 1951; Ganges, 1952; Gambia, 1952–54; Curlew, 1955; Daedalus, 1956; Amphibious Warfare Sqdn, 1956–58; HMS Adamant, 1958–60; 40 Commando, RM, 1960–62; RN Hosp., Bighi, 1962; HMS Victorious, 1963–64; Condor, 1964–66; Maidstone, 1966–68; St Vincent, 1968; Commando Training Centre, RM, 1969–71; HM Naval Base, Portsmouth, 1971–74; CTC, RM, 1975; Chaplain of the Fleet and Archdeacon of the Royal Navy, 1975–80; Vicar of Ranworth wih Panxworth and Woodbastwick (Norwich) and Bishop's Chaplain for the Broads, 1980–85; Chaplain to the Queen, 1980–85. Hon. Canon of Gibraltar, 1977–80. QHC 1975–80. Mem., Gen. Synod of C of E, 1990–. *Recreations:* sailing, ornithology. *Address:* The Deanery, Jersey, Channel Islands JE2 4TE. *T:* Jersey (0534) 20001.

OFFALY, Earl of; Thomas FitzGerald; *b* 12 Jan. 1974; *s* of Marquess of Kildare, *qv*.

OFFORD, Albert Cyril, DSc London; PhD Cantab; FRS 1952; FRSE; Emeritus Professor of Mathematics, University of London; Professor, 1966–73, Hon. Fellow, 1978, London School of Economics and Political Science; *b* 9 June 1906; *s* of Albert Edwin and Hester Louise Offord; *m* 1945, Marguerite Yvonne Pickard; one *d*. *Educ:* Hackney Downs School, London; University Coll. London (Fellow, 1969); St John's Coll., Cambridge. Fellow of St John's Coll., Cambridge, 1937–40; Lectr, UC N Wales, Bangor, 1940–41; Lectr, King's Coll., Newcastle upon Tyne, 1941–45; Professor: King's College, Newcastle upon Tyne, 1945–48; Birkbeck Coll., Univ. of London, 1948–66. *Publications:* papers in various mathematical journals. *Recreation:* early, especially Renaissance, music. *Address:* West Cottage, 24A Norham Gardens, Oxford OX2 6QD. *T:* Oxford (0865) 513703.

O'FLAHERTY, Prof. Coleman Anthony; Deputy Vice-Chancellor, University of Tasmania, Australia, since 1991; *b* 8 Feb. 1933; *s* of Michael and Agnes O'Flaherty; *m* 1957, Nuala Rose Silke. *Educ:* Nat. Univ. of Ireland (BE); Iowa State Univ. (MS, PhD). FICE; FIE(Aust); FIHT; FRSA; FAIM; FCIT. Engineer: Galway Co. Council, Ireland, 1954–55; Canadian Pacific Railway Co., Montreal, 1955–56; M. W. Kellogg Co., USA, 1956–57; Asst Prof., Iowa State Univ., 1957–62; Leeds University: Lectr, 1962–66; Prof. of Transport Engineering, Inst. for Transport Studies and Dept of Civil Engineering, 1966–74; First Asst Comr (Engineering), Nat. Capital Develt Commn, Canberra, 1974–78; Dir and Principal, Tasmanian Coll. of Advanced Educn, subseq. Tasmanian State Inst. of Technology, 1978–90. Vis. Prof., Univ. of Melbourne, 1973. *Publications:* Highways, 1967, 2nd edn 1974, vol. I of 3rd edn (Traffic Planning and Engineering), 1986, vol. II of 3rd edn (Highway Engineering), 1988; (jtly) Passenger Conveyors, 1972; (jtly) Introduction to Hovercraft and Hoverports, 1975; contribs to professional jls. *Recreation:* walking. *Address:* University of Tasmania at Launceston, PO Box 1214, Launceston, Tasmania 7250, Australia. *T:* (003) 260531. *Club:* Launceston.

O'FLYNN, Hon. Francis Duncan; QC 1968; *b* 1918; *s* of Hon. Francis E. O'Flynn, MLC; *m* 1942, Sylvia Elizabeth Hefford; one *s* three *d*. *Educ:* Christchurch Boys' High School; Victoria University of Wellington (BA, LLM). Flight Lieut, RNZAF, 1942–46; Flying Instructor, NZ and 6 Flying Boat Sqdn, Pacific. Barrister and Solicitor, 1948; in practice on own account, 1954–. MP (Lab): Kapiti, 1972–75; Island Bay, 1978–87. Minister of State and of Defence, NZ, 1984–87. Member: Otaki Borough Council, 1968–71; Wellington City Council, 1977–83. Mem. Council, Wellington District Law Soc., 1970–74. *Recreations:* golf, bowls. *Address:* 105 Grant Road, Thorndon, New Zealand. *T:* (04) 720344.

of MAR, family name of **Countess of Mar.**

OGDEN, Sir (Edward) Michael, Kt 1989; QC 1968; Barrister since 1950; a Recorder (formerly Recorder of Hastings), since 1971; *b* 9 Apr. 1926; *er s* of late Edward Cannon Ogden and Daisy (*née* Paris); *m* 1951, Joan Kathleen, *er d* of late Pius Charles Brodrick and Kathleen (*née* Moran); two *s* two *d*. *Educ:* Downside Sch.; Jesus Coll., Cambridge (MA). Served in RAC (Royal Glos Hussars and 16th/5th Lancers), 1944–47 (Capt.); Inns of Court Regt (TA) 1950–56. Jesus Coll., Cambridge, 1948–49; called to Bar, Lincoln's Inn, 1950; Bencher, 1977. Mem. Bar Council, 1960–64, 1966–70, 1971–78 (responsible for fee negotiations, 1968–72, Treas., 1972–74, Chm., Internat. Relns Cttee, 1974–75); Mem. Senate of the Inns of Court, 1966–70, 1972–78. Leader, SE Circuit, 1975–78. Member: Council of Union Internationale des Avocats, 1962–83; Council of Legal Educn, 1969–74; Council, Internat. Bar Assoc., 1983–87. Chairman: Criminal Injuries Compensation Bd, 1975–89 (Mem., 1968–89); Inter-Professional Wkg Party publishing Actuarial Tables for Personal Injury and Fatal Accident Cases, 1982–84; Mem., Lord Chancellor's Adv. on Legal Education, 1972–74. Dir, Internat. Assoc. of Crime Victim Compensation Bds, 1978–89 (Co-Chm. 1983–87). Assessor for Home Sec. of compensation for persons wrongly convicted, 1978–89, and for Minister of Defence, 1986–89. *Address:* 2 Crown Office Row, Temple, EC4Y 7HJ. *T:* 071–353 9337. *Club:* Cavalry and Guards.

OGDEN, Eric; *b* 23 Aug. 1923; *s* of Robert and Jane Lillian Ogden, Rhodes, Co. Lancaster; *m*; one *s*; *m* Marjorie (*née* Smith); two *s* two step *d*. *Educ:* Queen Elizabeth's Grammar School, Middleton, Lancs; Leigh Tech. Coll.; Wigan Mining and Tech. Coll. Merchant Service, 1942–46. Textiles, 1946–52; NCB, 1952–64. Mem., Nat. Union of Mineworkers. Councillor, Borough of Middleton, 1958–65. NUM sponsored candidate, West Derby, Liverpool, 1962. MP (Lab 1964–81, SDP 1981–83) Liverpool, Derby W, 1964–83; contested (SDP) Liverpool, Derby W, 1983. Dir, Ogden's, Fotografica & Fulcrum Ltd. Mem., PO Stamps Adv. Cttee. Chairman: Falkland Islands Assoc., 1983–87; UK Falkland Islands Cttee, 1983–88 (Mem., 1982–); Vice-Pres., Tristan da Cunha Assoc. FRGS 1987. *Recreations:* Central European affairs, photography, motoring, heraldry, surviving. *Club:* Europe House.

OGDEN, Sir Michael; *see* Ogden, Sir E. M.

OGILVIE, Sir Alec (Drummond), Kt 1965; Chairman, Powell Duffryn Ltd, 1969–78 (Deputy Chairman, 1967–69); *b* 17 May 1913; *s* of late Sir George Drummond Ogilvie, KCIE, CSI; *m* 1945, Lesley Constance, *d* of E. B. Woollan; two *s*. *Educ:* Cheltenham College. Served War of 1939–45; 2/2nd Gurkha Rifles (Indian Army), 1940–45; Captain 1941; PoW, Singapore, 1942–45. Joined Andrew Yule & Co. Ltd, Calcutta, 1935, Man. Dir, 1956, and Chm., 1962–65. Director: Westinghouse Brake & Signal Co. Ltd, 1966–79; Lindustries Ltd, 1973–79; J. Lyons & Co. Ltd, 1977–78. Pres., Bengal Chamber of Commerce and Industry, 1964–65; Pres., Associated Chambers of Commerce and Industry of India, 1964–65. Member: Council, King Edward VII Hosp. for Officers, 1967– (Vice-Pres., 1979–); Council, Cheltenham Coll., 1973–85 (Dep. Pres., 1983–85). *Recreations:* golf, walking. *Address:* Townlands, High Street, Lindfield, West Sussex RH16 2HT. *T:* Lindfield (04447) 3953. *Clubs:* Oriental, MCC; Bengal (Calcutta).

OGILVIE, Dr Bridget Margaret, FIBiol; Director, Wellcome Trust, since 1991; *b* 24 March 1938; *er d* of late John Mylne Ogilvie and of Margaret Beryl (*née* McRae). *Educ:* New England Girls' Sch., Armidale, NSW; Univ. of New England, Armidale (BRurSc 1960). PhD 1964, ScD 1981, Cambridge. FIBiol 1985. Parasitology Div., Nat. Inst. for Med. Res., London, 1963–81; Ian McMaster Fellow, CSIRO Div. of Animal Health, Australia, 1971–72; with Wellcome Trust, 1979–: Co-ordinator, Tropical Med. Prog., 1979–81; Dep. Sec. and Asst Dir, 1981–84; Dep. Dir, Science, 1984–89; Dir, Science Progs, 1989–91. Vis. Prof., Dept of Biology, Imperial Coll., London, 1985–. Hon. Mem., British Soc. for Parasitology, 1990. *Publications:* contrib. scientific papers to parasitological and immunological jls. *Recreations:* the company of friends, looking at landscapes, music, gardening. *Address:* The Wellcome Trust, PO Box 39, NW9 4LW. *T:* 071–486 4902. *Club:* Queen's (Sydney).

OGILVIE-GRANT, family name of **Earl of Seafield.**

OGILVIE-LAING of Kinkell, Gerald, NDD; ARBS 1987; sculptor; *b* 11 Feb. 1936; *s* of Gerald Francis Laing and Enid Moody (*née* Foster); adopted name of Ogilvie-Laing, 1968; *m* 1st, 1962, Jenifer Anne Redway; one *d*; 2nd, 1969, Galina Vassilovna Golikova; two *s*; 3rd, 1988, Adaline Havemeyer Frelinghuysen; one *s*. *Educ:* Berkhamsted Sch.; RMA, Sandhurst; St Martin's Sch. of Art, London (NDD) 1964). Served Royal Northumberland Fusiliers, 1955–60, resigned; lived in NYC, 1964–69; Pop painting, 1962–65, abstract sculpture, 1965–69; Artist in Residence, Aspen Inst., 1966; restored Kinkell Castle, Scotland, 1969–70 (Civic Trust Award, 1971); established Tapestry Workshop, 1970–74; changed to figurative sculpture, 1973. Vis. Prof. of Painting and Sculpture, Univ. of New Mexico, 1976–77; Prof. of Sculpture, Columbia Univ., 1986–87. Installed: Callanish sculpture, Strathclyde Univ., 1971; Frieze of Wise and Foolish Virgins,

Edinburgh, 1979; Fountain of Sabrina, Bristol, 1980; Conan Doyle Meml, and Axis Mundi, Edinburgh, 1991; exhibits frequently; work in many public and private collections worldwide; divides time between Scotland and New York. Member Art Cttee, Scottish Arts Council, 1978–80; Royal Fine Art Commn for Scotland, 1987–. Chm., Black Isle Civic Trust. *Publication:* Kinkell—the Reconstruction of a Scottish castle, 1974, 2nd edn 1984. *Address:* Kinkell Castle, Ross and Cromarty IV7 8AT. *T:* Dingwall (0349) 61485; 139 East 66th Street, New York, NY 10021, USA. *T:* 212–628–5593. *Club:* Chelsea Arts.

OGILVIE THOMPSON, Julian; Chairman, Anglo American Corporation of SA Ltd, since 1990 (Deputy Chairman, 1983–90); Chairman, De Beers Consolidated Mines Ltd, since 1985 (Deputy Chairman, 1982–85); *b* 27 Jan. 1934; *s* of Hon. N. Ogilvie Thompson, formerly Chief Justice of S Africa, and Eve Ogilvie Thompson; *m* 1956, Hon. Tessa Mary Brand, *yr surv. d* of 4th Viscount Hampden, CMG and Leila, Viscountess Hampden; two *s* two *d. Educ:* Diocesan Coll., Rondebosch; Univ. of Cape Town; Worcester Coll., Oxford. MA. Diocesan Coll. Rhodes Scholar, 1953. Joined Anglo American Corp. of SA Ltd, 1956; Dir, 1970; Exec. Dir, 1971–82; Chairman: Anglo American Gold Investment Co. Ltd, 1976–90; Minorco SA (formerly Minerals and Resources Corp. Ltd), 1982–; Vice Chm., First Nat. Bank Ltd, 1977–. *Recreations:* shooting, fishing, golf. *Address:* Froome, Froome Street, Athol Extension 3, Sandton, Transvaal, S Africa. *T:* 884–3925. *Clubs:* White's; Rand (Johannesburg); Kimberley (Cape Province); The Brook (NY).
See also Baroness Dacre.

OGILVY, family name of **Earl of Airlie.**

OGILVY, Lord; David John Ogilvy; Managing Director, Richard L. Feigen UK Ltd, Art Dealers; *b* 9 March 1958; *s* and *heir* of 13th Earl of Airlie, *qv*; *m* 1981, Hon. Geraldine Harmsworth (marr. diss. 1991), *d* of Viscount Rothermere, *qv*; one *d*; *m* 1991, Tarka Kings. *Educ:* Eton and Oxford (MA). *Address:* Airlie Castle, Kirriemuir, Angus.

OGILVY, Hon. Sir Angus (James Bruce), KCVO 1989; *b* 14 Sept. 1928; *s* of 12th (*de facto* 9th) Earl of Airlie, KT, GCVO, MC; *m* 1963, HRH Princess Alexandra of Kent; one *s* one *d. Educ:* Eton Coll.; Trinity Coll., Oxford (MA). Scots Guards 1946–48; Mem., HM Body Guard for Scotland (The Royal Company of Archers). President: Imperial Cancer Res. Fund, 1964–; Youth Clubs UK (formerly NAYC), 1969–89 (Chm. 1964–69); Carr-Gomm Soc., 1983–; Vice-Pres., Friends of the Elderly & Gentlefolk's Help, 1969– (Treasurer, 1952–63; Chm. 1963–69); Patron: Arthritis Care (formerly British Rheumatism and Arthritis Soc.), 1978– (Chm. 1963–69; Pres., 1969–78); Scottish Wildlife Trust, 1974 (Pres., 1969–74); Vice-Patron, Nat. Children's Homes, 1986–. Chm., Council, The Prince's Youth Business Trust, 1986–; Member Governing Council: Business in the Community, 1984–; Society for Promoting Christian Knowledge, 1984–. Trustee: Leeds Castle Foundn, 1975–; GB-Sasakawa Foundn, 1985–. Director of various public cos. *Recreations:* architecture, reading, music. *Address:* Thatched House Lodge, Richmond, Surrey. *T:* 081–546 8833. *Club:* White's.
See also under Royal Family.

OGILVY, Sir David (John Wilfrid), 13th Bt, *cr* 1626; DL; farmer and landowner; *b* 3 February 1914; *e s* of Gilbert Francis Molyneux Ogilvy (*d* 1953) (4th *s* of 10th Bt) and Marjory Katharine, *d* of late M. B. Clive, Whitfield, Herefordshire; *S* uncle, Sir Herbert Kinnaird Ogilvy, 12th Bt, 1956; *m* 1966, Penelope Mary Ursula, *d* of Arthur Lafone Frank Hills, White Court, Kent; one *s. Educ:* Eton; Trinity College, Oxford. Served in the RNVR in War of 1939–45. JP 1957, DL 1971, East Lothian. *Heir: s* Francis Gilbert Arthur Ogilvy, *b* 22 April 1969. *Address:* Winton Cottage, Pencaitland, East Lothian EH34 5AT. *T:* Pencaitland (0875) 340222.

OGILVY, David Mackenzie, CBE 1967; Founder, Ogilvy and Mather, 1948, Chairman to 1973; Chairman, WPP Group, since 1989; *b* 23 June 1911; *s* of Francis John Longley Ogilvy and Dorothy Fairfield; *m* 1973, Herta Lans; one *s. Educ:* Fettes College, Edinburgh; Christ Church, Oxford (Scholar). British Security Coordination, 1942–45. Dir, NY Philharmonic, 1957–67. Chm., Utd Negro Coll. Fund, 1968. Mem. of Honor, WWF. Dr of letters (*hc*), Adelphi Univ., USA, 1977. Officier, l'Ordre des Arts et des Lettres (France), 1990. *Publications:* Confessions of an Advertising Man, 1963; Blood, Brains and Beer (autobiog.), 1978; Ogilvy On Advertising, 1983. *Recreation:* gardening. *Address:* Château de Touffou, 86300 Bonnes, France.

OGILVY-WEDDERBURN, Sir Andrew John Alexander, 13th and 7th Bt *cr* 1704 and 1803; *b* 4 Aug. 1952; *s* of Sir (John) Peter Ogilvy-Wedderburn, 12th and 6th Bt, and of Elizabeth Katharine, *e d* of late John A. Cox, Drumkilbo; *S* father, 1977; *m* 1984, Gillian Meade, *yr d* of Richard Adderley, Pickering, N Yorks; three *s* (incl. twins) one *d. Educ:* Gordonstoun. *Heir: s* Peter Robert Alexander Ogilvy-Wedderburn, *b* 20 April 1987. *Address:* Silvie, Alyth, Perthshire PH11 8NA.

OGLE-SKAN, Peter Henry, CVO 1972; TD 1948; Director, Scottish Services, Department of the Environment, 1970–75; *b* 4 July 1915; 2nd *s* of Dr H. W. Ogle-Skan, Hendon; *m* 1941, Pamela Moira Heslop; one *s* one *d. Educ:* Merchant Taylors' Sch., London. Clerk with Arbuthnot-Latham & Co. Ltd, London, 1933–39. Commnd into Royal Engineers (TA), 1936; War Service, 1939–46; England, 1939–42; India, 1942–45. Min. of Works: Temp. Principal, 1946; Principal, 1948; Asst Sec., 1955; Under-Sec., Scottish HQ, MPBW, 1966–70. *Recreations:* golf, walking, photography. *Address:* 44 Ravelston Garden, Edinburgh EH4 3LF. *T:* 031–337 6834.

OGLESBY, Peter Rogerson, CB 1982; *b* 15 July 1922; *s* of late Leonard William Oglesby and late Jessie Oglesby (*née* Rogerson); *m* 1947, Doreen Hilda Hudson; three *d. Educ:* Woodhouse Grove Sch., Apperley Bridge. Clerical Officer, Admlty, 1939–47; Exec. Officer, Min. of Nat. Ins., 1947–56; Higher Exec. Officer, MPNI, 1956–62, Principal 1962–64; Principal Private Secretary: to Chancellor of Duchy of Lancaster, 1964–66; to Minister without Portfolio, 1966; to First Sec. of State, 1966–68; to Lord President, 1968; Asst Sec., Cabinet Office, 1968–70, Asst Sec., DHSS, 1970–73; Sec., Occupational Pensions Bd, 1973–74; Under Sec., 1974–79; Dep. Sec., 1979–82, DHSS. *Address:* 41 Draycot Road, Wanstead, E11 2NX. *T:* 081–989 5526.

OGMORE, 2nd Baron *cr* 1950, of Bridgend; **Gwilym Rees Rees-Williams;** *b* 5 May 1931; *er s* of 1st Baron Ogmore, PC, TD, and of Constance, *er d* of W. R. Wills; *S* father, 1976; *m* 1967, Gillian Mavis, *d* of M. K. Slack; two *d. Educ:* Mill Hill School. *Heir: b* Hon. Morgan Rees-Williams [*b* 19 Dec. 1937; *m* 1964, Patricia (marr. diss. 1970), *o d* of C. Paris Jones; *m* 1972, Roberta (marr. diss. 1976), *d* of Captain Alec Cunningham-Reid, DFC; *m* 1990, Beata, *o d* of Z. Solski]. *Address:* 4 Foster Road, Chiswick, W4 4NY.

OGNALL, Sir Harry Henry, Kt 1986; **Hon. Mr Justice Ognall;** a Judge of the High Court of Justice, Queen's Bench Division, since 1986; *b* 9 Jan. 1934; *s* of Leo and Cecilia Ognall; *m* 1977, Elizabeth Young; two step *s* and two *s* one *d* of former marriage. *Educ:* Leeds Grammar Sch.; Lincoln Coll., Oxford (MA (Hons)); Univ. of Virginia, USA (LLM). Called to Bar (Gray's Inn), 1958; Bencher, 1983. Joined NE Circuit; a Recorder, 1972–86; QC 1973. Member: Criminal Injuries Compensation Bd, 1976; Planning Cttee, Senate of Inns of Court and Bar, 1980–83; Professional Conduct Cttee, 1985; Judicial Studies Bd (Chm., Criminal Cttee), 1986–89; Parole Bd, 1989– (Vice-Chm., 1990–). Arbitrator, Motor Insurers' Bureau Agreement, 1979–85. *Recreations:* golf, music, travel. *Address:* Royal Courts of Justice, Strand, WC2A 2LL. *Clubs:* Garrick; Ilkley Golf, Ilkley Bowling.

O'GRADY, Prof. Francis William, CBE 1984; TD 1970; MD; FRCP, FRCPath, FFPM; Hon. Consultant Microbiologist: Public Health Laboratory Service, since 1974; to the Army, since 1982; *b* 7 Nov. 1925; *s* of Francis Joseph O'Grady and Lilian Maud Hitchcock; *m* 1951, Madeleine Marie-Thérèse Becquart; three *d. Educ:* Middlesex Hosp. Med. Sch., London (BSc 1st Cl. Hons; MB, BS Hons; MSc; MD). FRCP 1976; FRCPath 1972; FFPM 1989. House Physician, Mddx and North Mddx Hosps, 1951; Asst Pathologist, Bland-Sutton Inst. of Pathol., Mddx Hosp., 1952–53, 1956–58 and 1961–62; Pathologist, RAMC, 1954–55, AER, 1956–72; Asst Prof. of Environmental Medicine, Johns Hopkins Univ., Baltimore, 1959–60; Reader, 1962–66, and Prof. of Bacteriology, 1967–74, Univ. of London; Bacteriologist, St Bartholomew's Hosp., 1962–74; Foundation Prof. of Microbiology, Univ. of Nottingham, 1974–88; Chief Scientist, DHSS, subseq. DoH, 1986–90. Mem., MRC, 1980–84, 1986–; Chm., MRC Physiol Systems and Disorders Bd, 1980–82 (Mem., 1977–80; Mem., Grants Cttee, 1975–76); Chm., MRC Cttee on Hosp. Infection, 1977–80 (Mem., 1967–77). Member: Antibiotics Panel, Cttee on Med. Aspects of Food Policy, 1968–72; Sub-Cttee on Toxicity, Clin. Trials and Therapeutic Efficacy, 1971–75, and Sub-Cttee on Biol Substances, 1971–81, Cttee on Safety of Medicines; Jt Sub-Cttee on Antimicrobial Substances, Cttee on Safety of Medicines and Vet. Products Cttee, 1973–80; Cttee on Rev. of Medicines, 1975–81; Public Health Lab. Service Bd, 1980–86; Nat. Biological Standards Bd, 1983–87. William N. Creasy Vis. Prof. of Clin. Pharmacology, Duke Univ., NC, 1979. Erasmus Wilson Demonstrator, RCS, 1967; Foundn Lectr, Univ. of Hong Kong, 1974; Sydney Watson Smith Lectr, RCPE, 1975; Jacobson Vis. Lectr, Univ. of Newcastle upon Tyne, 1979; Berk Lectr, British Assoc. of Urol Surgeons, 1980; Garrod Lectr, British Soc. for Antimicrobial Chemotherapy, 1983; Jenner Lectr, St George's Hosp. Med. Sch., 1988. Pres. Council, British Jl of Exper. Pathol., 1980– (Mem., 1968–80); Mem. Editorial Boards: Jl of Med. Microbiol., 1970–75; Pathologie Biologie, 1973–78; British Jl of Clin. Pharmacol., 1974–84; Drugs, 1976–88; Gut, 1977–83; Jl of Infection, 1978–; Revs of Infectious Diseases, 1979–88. *Publications:* Airborne Infection: transmission and control, 1968; Antibiotic and Chemotherapy, 1968, 6th edn 1991; (ed) Urinary Tract Infection, 1968; (ed) Microbial Perturbation of Host Defences, 1981; papers on clin. and exper. infection and on antimicrobial chemotherapy. *Recreation:* watching the vines grow. *Address:* Department of Physiology and Pharmacology, Medical School, Queen's Medical Centre, Nottingham NG7 2UH; des Bouysses, 46700 Puy-l'Evêque, Lot, France.

OGSTON, Alexander George, MA, DSc; FRS 1955; President of Trinity College, Oxford, 1970–78, Hon. Fellow 1978; Fellow, 1937, and Bedford Lecturer, 1950, Balliol College; *b* 30 January 1911; *s* of late Walter Henry Ogston and late Josephine Elizabeth Ogston (*née* Carter); *m* 1934, Elizabeth Wicksteed; one *s* three *d. Educ:* Eton College (King's Scholar); Balliol College, Oxford. DPhil 1936, MA 1937, DSc 1970. Demonstrator, Balliol College, 1933; Freedom Research Fellow, London Hospital, 1935; Departmental Demonstrator (Biochemistry), 1938; University Demonstrator, 1944, Oxford; Reader in Biochemistry, University of Oxford, 1955–59; Prof. of Physical Biochemistry, John Curtin School of Medical Research, ANU, 1959–70, Prof. Emeritus, 1970. Vis. Fellow, Inst. for Cancer Research, Philadelphia, Nov. 1978–Jan. 1979 and March–June 1981; Silver Jubilee Vis. Fellow, University House, ANU, March–Aug. 1979. Chairman, Editorial Bd, Biochemical Journal, 1955–59 (Member of Board, 1951–55). Chm., Central Council, Selly Oak Colleges, Birmingham, 1980–84 (Vice-Chm., 1976–80). Fellow, Australian Acad. of Science, 1962; Hon. Fellow: Balliol Coll., Oxford, 1969; Univ. of York, 1980; Selly Oak Colls, 1984; Hon. Mem. American Soc. of Biological Chemists, 1965; Hon. DMed Uppsala, 1977. Davy Medal, Royal Soc., 1986. *Publications:* scientific papers on physical chemistry and biochemistry. *Address:* 6 Dewsbury Terrace, York YO1 1HA.

OGSTON, Prof. Derek, MD, PhD, DSc; FRCP; FRSE 1982; Professor of Medicine, since 1983 and Vice Principal, since 1987, University of Aberdeen; *b* 31 May 1932; *s* of Frederick John Ogston and Ellen Mary Ogston; *m* 1963, Cecilia Marie Clark; one *s* two *d. Educ:* King's Coll. Sch., Wimbledon; Univ. of Aberdeen (MA, MD, PhD, DSc). FRCP Edin 1973; FRCP 1977; FIBiol 1987. Univ. of Aberdeen: Res. Fellow, 1959–62; Lectr in Medicine, 1962–69; Sen. Lectr in Med., 1969–75; Reader in Med., 1975–76; Regius Prof. of Physiology, 1977–83. Dean, Faculty of Medicine, 1984–87. MRC Trav. Fellow, 1967–68. Member: GMC, 1984–; Grampian Health Bd, 1991–. Mem. Governing Body, Rowett Res. Inst., 1977–. *Publications:* Physiology of Hemostasis, 1983; Antifibrinolytic Drugs, 1984; Venous Thrombosis, 1987; scientific papers on haemostasis. *Recreation:* home maintenance. *Address:* 64 Rubislaw Den South, Aberdeen AB2 6AX. *T:* Aberdeen (0224) 316587.

O'HAGAN, 4th Baron, *cr* 1870; **Charles Towneley Strachey;** Member (C) Devon, European Parliament, since 1979; *b* 6 Sept. 1945; *s* of Hon. Thomas Anthony Edward Towneley Strachey (*d* 1955; having assumed by deed poll, 1938, the additional Christian name of Towneley, and his mother's maiden name of Strachey, in lieu of his patronymic) and of Lady Mary (who *m* 1981, St John Gore, *qv*), *d* of 3rd Earl of Selborne, PC, CH; *S* grandfather, 1961; *m* 1st, 1967, Princess Tamara Imeretinsky (marr. diss. 1984); one *d*; 2nd, 1985, Mrs Mary Claire Parsons (*née* Roose-Francis); one *d. Educ:* Eton; (Exhibitioner) New College, Oxford. Page to HM the Queen, 1959–62. Independent Member, European Parliament, 1973–75; Junior Opposition Whip, House of Lords, 1977–79. *Recreations:* life in Devon, Rashleigh, walking. *Heir: brother* Hon. Richard Towneley Strachey [*b* 29 Dec. 1950; *m* 1983, Sally Anne, *yr d* of Frederick Cecil Cross]. *Address:* 12 Lyndhurst Road, Exeter, Devon EX2 4PA. *T:* Exeter (0392) 410532; Rashleigh Barton, Wembworthy, Chulmleigh, N Devon EX18 7RW. *Clubs:* Beefsteak, Pratt's.

O'HAGAN, Desmond, CMG 1957; *b* 4 Mar. 1909; *s* of Captain Claud O'Hagan, Nyeri, Kenya and Eva O'Hagan (*née* Napier Magill); *m* 1942, Pamela, *d* of Major A. H. Symes-Thompson, DSO, Kiambu, Kenya; one *s* two *d. Educ:* Wellington Coll.; Clare Coll., Cambridge. Entered Colonial Administrative Service, Kenya, 1931. Called to Bar, Inner Temple, 1935. Private Secretary to British Resident, Zanzibar, 1937; served with E African Forces in N Province, Kenya, 1940–42; Native Courts Adviser, 1948–51; Provincial Commissioner, Coast Province, Kenya, 1952–59; Chairman, Transport Licensing Authority, Tanganyika, 1959–63. *Recreations:* bridge, golf. *Address:* Kianjibbi, Kiambu, Kenya. *Clubs:* East India, Devonshire, Sports and Public Schools; Muthaiga, Nairobi (life mem.).

O'HALLORAN, Sir Charles (Ernest), Kt 1982; Chairman, Irvine Development Corporation, 1983–85; *b* 26 May 1924; *s* of Charles and Lily O'Halloran; *m* 1943, Annie Rowan; one *s* two *d. Educ:* Conway St Central Sch., Birkenhead. Telegraphist, RN, 1942–46. Elected Ayr Town Council, 1953; Provost of Ayr, 1964–67; Mem., Strathclyde Regional Council, 1974–82 (Convener, 1978–82). Freeman of Ayr Burgh, 1975. Parly Cand. (Lab) Ayr Burghs, 1966. Dir, Radio Clyde, 1980–85; Mem., BRB(Scot.), 1981–85.

Recreations: politics, golf, soccer spectating. *Address:* 40 Savoy Park, Ayr. *T:* Ayr (0292) 266234. *Clubs:* Royal Scottish Automobile (Glasgow); Labour, Ex-Servicemen's (Ayr).

O'HALLORAN, Michael Joseph; Building and Construction Works Manager; *b* 20 Aug. 1933; British; *m* 1956, Stella Beatrice McDonald; three *d. Educ:* Clohanes National School, Eire; self-educated. Railway worker, 1948–63; building works manager, 1963–69; returned to building industry, 1983. MP (Lab 1969–81, SDP 1981–82, Ind. Lab 1983) Islington N, Oct. 1969–1983; contested (Ind. Lab) Islington N, 1983. *Recreations:* boxing, football. *Address:* 149 Cheam Road, Sutton, Surrey SM1 2BP. *Club:* Challoner.

O'HARA, Bill; National Governor of the BBC for Northern Ireland, 1973–78; *b* 26 Feb. 1929; *s* of William P. O'Hara and Susanna Agnes O'Hara (*née* Gill); *m* 1953, Anne Marie Finn; two *s* two *d. Address:* Ashvale, 14 Raglan Road, Bangor, Co. Down, N Ireland. *T:* Bangor (0247) 60869. *Clubs:* Royal Ulster Yacht, Royal Belfast Golf, Sunnyland Beagles.

O'HARA, Air Vice-Marshal Derek Ive, CB 1981; *b* 14 Feb. 1928; *s* of late William Edward O'Hara and Daisy Bathurst O'Hara (*née* Ive); *m* 1953, Angela Elizabeth (*née* Marchand); two *s* one *d. Educ:* Ardingly Coll., Sussex; RAF Coll., Cranwell. Commnd RAF Coll., 1950; RAF Horsham St Faith and Tuddenham, 1950–54; Egypt, 1954–56; HQ Bomber Comd, 1956–59; Instructor, RAF Coll., 1959–61; RAF Staff Coll., Andover, 1961; Jt Planning HQ ME, Aden, 1962–64; OC Supply, RAF Finningley, 1964; Manchester Univ., 1965; OC Supply, 14 MU RAF Carlisle, 1966–68; Directing Staff, RAF Staff Coll., Andover, 1968–70; Comd of RAF Stafford, 1970–72; Dep. Dir, Supply Management, MoD Harrogate, 1972; RCDS, 1973; Air Commodore Supply and Movements, HQ Strike Comd, 1974–75; Dir, Engrg and Supply Policy, 1975–79; Dir Gen. of Supply, RAF, 1979–82. *Recreations:* sailing, fishing, gardening. *Club:* Royal Air Force.

O'HARA, Edward; MP (Lab) Knowsley South, since Sept. 1990; *b* 1 Oct. 1937; *s* of Robert Edward O'Hara and Clara O'Hara (*née* Davies); *m* 1962, Lillian Hopkins; two *s* one *d. Educ:* Magdalen Coll., Oxford (MA 1962); PGCE 1966, DipED (Adv.) 1970, London. Assistant Teacher: Perse Sch., Cambridge, 1962–65; Birkenhead Sch., 1966–70; Lectr and Principal Lectr, C. F. Mott Coll. of Educn, 1970–74; Principal Lectr and Sen. Tutor, Dean of Postgrad. Studies, City of Liverpool Coll. of Higher Educn, 1974–83; Head of Curriculum Studies, Sch. of Educn and Community Studies, Liverpool Polytechnic, 1983–90. Knowsley Borough Council: Mem., 1975–91; Mem., all Standing Cttees; Chm., Libraries and Arts, Finance, Youth, Educn and Econ. Develt and Planning Cttees. Mem., Educn and Planning, and Econ. Develt Cttees, AMA; Parly Advr, Fire and Emergency Services Cttee, AMA; Member: Bd of Management, NFER; European Assoc. of Teachers; Socialist Educn Assoc.; Hon. Mem. and Parly Advr, Assoc. of Chief Educn Social Workers; Member: Labour Movement in Europe; Communauté de Travail des Régions Européennes de Tradition Industrielle; Perm. Cttee of Assembly of European Regions. Member: Fabian Soc.; Bd of Management, Royal Liverpool Philharmonic Soc. *Recreations:* music, reading, theatre, travel, Greek language and culture. *Address:* 69 St Mary's Road, Huyton, Merseyside L36 5SR. *T:* 051–489 8021. *Clubs:* Halewood Labour, Huyton Labour, Lyme Grove Labour (Knowsley).

O'HARA, Prof. Michael John, PhD; FRS 1981; FRSE 1969; Professor of Geology, University College of Wales, Aberystwyth, since 1978; *b* 22 Feb. 1933; *s* of Michael Patrick O'Hara, OBE, and Winifred Dorothy O'Hara; *m* 1st, 1962, Janet Tibbits; one *s* two *d*; 2nd, 1977, Susan Howells; two *s* one *d. Educ:* Dulwich Coll. Prep. Sch.; Cranleigh; Peterhouse, Cambridge (MA, PhD). Asst, Lectr, Reader and Prof. (1971), Edinburgh Univ., 1958–78; Principal Investigator, NASA Lunar Science Prog., 1968–75; Prof. of Geology, Sultan Qaboos Univ., Oman, 1988–90. Sherman-Fairchild Vis. Scholar, Calif Inst. of Technology, 1984–85; Vis. Prof., Harvard Univ., 1986. Member: Council, NERC, 1986–88; UGC, 1987–89. Associate Mem., Geol Soc. of France. Murchison Medal, Geol Soc., 1983; Bowen Medal, Amer. Geophys. Union, 1984. *Publications:* numerous in learned jls. *Recreation:* mountaineering. *Address:* Institute of Earth Sciences, University College of Wales, Aberystwyth, Dyfed SY23 3DB. *T:* Aberystwyth (0970) 623111.

O'HIGGINS, Prof. Paul; Professor of Law, King's College London, since 1987; *b* 5 Oct. 1927; *s* of Richard Leo O'Higgins, MC, MRCVS and Elizabeth O'Higgins, MA (*née* Deane); *m* 1952, Rachel Elizabeth Bush; one *s* three *d. Educ:* St Ignatius' Coll., Galway; St Columba's Coll., Rathfarnham; Trinity Coll., Dublin (MA, LLB, LLD); MA, PhD, LLD Cantab. MRIA 1986. Called to the Bar, King's Inns, 1957, and Lincoln's Inn, 1959. University of Cambridge: Fellow, Christ's College, 1959–; Dir of Studies in Law, Peterhouse, 1960–74; Steward, Christ's Coll., 1964–68; Tutor for Advanced Students, Christ's, 1970–79; University Lectr, 1965–79; Reader in Labour Law, 1979–84; Regius Prof. of Laws, TCD, 1984–87. Co-founder, Cambridge Law Surgery, 1969. Lectr in Labour Law, Inns of Court Sch. of Law, 1976–84; Vis. Prof., Univ. of Kent at Canterbury, 1973–74; Mem. Bureau, European Inst. of Social Security, 1970–; Mem., Staff Side Panel, Civil Service Arbitration Tribunal, 1972–84; Vice-Pres., Inst. of Shops, Health and Safety Acts Admin, 1973–; Chm., Irish Soc. for Labour Law, 1985–87. Patron, Cambridge Univ. Graduate Union, 1973–84; Trustee, Cambridge Union Soc., 1973–84; Vice-Pres., Haldane Soc., 1976–; Gov., British Inst. of Human Rights, 1988–; Vice-Pres., Inst. of Employment Rights, 1989–. Hon. Mem., Grotian Soc., 1968. Gilbert Murray Prize (jt), 1968; Joseph L. Andrews Bibliographical Award, Amer. Assoc. of Law Libraries, 1987. Grand Consul honorifique du consulat de la Vinée de Bergerac, 1983. *Publications:* Bibliography of Periodical Literature relating to Irish Law, 1966, 2nd supp. 1983; (with B. A. Hepple) Public Employee Trade Unionism in the UK: the legal framework, 1971; (with B. A. Hepple) Employment Law, 1971, 4th edn 1981; Censorship in Britain, 1972; Workers' Rights, 1976, 2nd edn 1986; Cases and Materials on Civil Liberties, 1980; Bibliography of Irish Trials, 1986; (with A. D. Dubbins and J. Gennard) Fairness at Work: even-handed industrial relations, 1986; (with M. Partington) Bibliography of Social Security Law, 1986; (ed jtly) The Common Law Tradition: Essays in Irish Legal History, 1990; British and Irish Labour Law, 1979–88: a bibliography, 1991; (ed jtly) Lessons from Northern Ireland, 1991. *Recreations:* wine, talking and travelling, particularly in France and Italy. *Address:* Christ's College, Cambridge CB2 3BU. *T:* Cambridge (0223) 67641. *Club:* Royal Dublin Society (Dublin).

O'HIGGINS, Hon. Thomas Francis, SC (Ireland) 1954; a Judge of the European Court of Justice, since 1985; *b* 23 July 1916; *e s* of Dr Thomas F. O'Higgins and Agnes McCarthy; *m* 1948, Thérese Keane; five *s* two *d. Educ:* St Mary's Coll., Rathmines, Clongowes Wood Coll.; University Coll., Dublin (BA); King's Inns, Dublin (BL). Called to Irish Bar, 1938; Bencher of King's Inns, 1967; Judge of High Court, 1973; Chief Justice of Ireland, 1974–85. Elected to Dail Eireann, 1948; Minister for Health, 1954; contested Presidency, 1966 and 1973. *Recreations:* fishing, golf. *Address:* European Court of Justice, L-2925 Luxembourg; Glenville Cottage, 75 Monkstown Road, Monkstown, Co. Dublin. *T:* 809119. *Clubs:* Stephen's Green, Miltown Golf.

OHLSON, Sir Brian (Eric Christopher), 3rd Bt *cr* 1920; money broker, retired; *b* 27 July 1936; *s* of Sir Eric James Ohlson, 2nd Bt, and of Marjorie Joan, *d* of late C. H. Roosmale-Cocq; *S* father, 1983. *Educ:* Harrow School; RMA Sandhurst. Commissioned into Coldstream Guards, 1956–61. Started money broking, 1961; *Recreations:* sport of kings, cricket, squash, bridge. *Heir: b* Peter Michael Ohlson [*b* 18 May 1939; *m* 1968, Sarah, *o d* of Maj.-Gen. Thomas Brodie, *qv*]. *Address:* 1 Courtfield Gardens, SW5. *Clubs:* MCC, Naval and Military, Hurlingham, Cavalry and Guards.

OISTRAKH, Igor Davidovich; Soviet Violinist; *b* Odessa, 27 April 1931; *s* of late David Oistrakh. *Educ:* Music Sch. and State Conservatoire, Moscow. Many foreign tours (USSR, Europe, the Americas, Japan); many gramophone recordings. 1st prize, Violin Competition, Budapest, 1949; 1st prize, Wieniawski Competition, Poznan, 1952; People's Artist of RSFSR.

OKA, Prof. Takeshi, PhD; FRS 1984; FRSC 1977; Professor of Astronomy and Astrophysics, since 1981, and Robert A. Millikan Distinguished Service Professor of Chemistry, since 1989, University of Chicago; *b* 10 June 1932; *s* of Shumpei and Chiyoko Oka; *m* 1960, Keiko Nukui; two *s* two *d. Educ:* University of Tokyo. BSc, PhD. Fellow, Japanese Soc. for Promotion of Science, 1960–63; National Research Council of Canada: Postdoctorate Fellow, 1963–65; Asst Research Physicist, 1965–68; Associate Research Physicist, 1968–71; Senior Research Physicist, 1971–75; Herzberg Inst. of Astrophysics, 1975–81. Centenary Lectr, Royal Soc., 1982; Chancellor's Distinguished Lectr, Univ. of California, 1985–86. Fellow, Amer. Acad. of Arts and Scis, 1987. Steacie Prize, Steacie Fund, NRSC, 1972; Earle K. Plyler Prize, Amer. Physical Soc., 1982. *Recreation:* running. *Address:* 1463 East Park Place, Chicago, Illinois 60637, USA. *T:* (312)-752-5963.

O'KEEFE, John Harold; TV consultant; *b* 25 Dec. 1938; *s* of Terence Harold O'Keefe and Christian Frances (*née* Foot); *m* 1959, Valerie Anne Atkins; two *s* two *d. Educ:* Acton County Grammar School. Dir, Newspaper Publishers Assoc., 1974; Hd of Industrial Relations, 1974–81, Production Dir, Central London, 1981, Thames TV, 1982; Man. Dir, Limehouse Studios, 1982–86. *Address:* The White House, Dymock, Glos GL18 2AQ.

O'KEEFFE, (Peter) Laurence, CMG 1983; CVO 1974; HM Diplomatic Service, retired; *b* 9 July 1931; *s* of Richard O'Keeffe and Alice (*née* Chase); *m* 1954, Suzanne Marie Jousse; three *d. Educ:* St Francis Xavier's Coll., Liverpool; University Coll., Oxford (schol.). HM Customs and Excise, 1953–62; 2nd, later 1st Sec. (Economic), Bangkok, 1962–65; FO, 1965–68; 1st Sec. and Head of Chancery, Athens, 1968–72; Commercial Counsellor, Jakarta, 1972–75; Head of Hong Kong and Indian Ocean Dept, FCO, 1975–76; Dir-Gen., British Information Services, and Dep. Consul General (Information), New York, 1976–78; Counsellor, Nicosia, 1978–81; Research Associate, Inst. for the Study of Diplomacy, Georgetown Univ., Washington, DC, 1981–82; Ambassador to Senegal, 1982–85, and concurrently (non-resident) to Guinea, Guinea-Bissau, Mali, Mauritania and Cape Verde, 1982–85; Diplomatic Service Chm., CSSB, 1985–86; Head, British Delegn to CSCE Rev. Conf., Vienna, 1986–88; Ambassador to Czechoslovakia, 1988–91. *Publications:* (as Laurence Halley): Simultaneous Equations (novel), 1975; Ancient Affections, 1985; Abiding City (novel), 1986. *Recreations:* photography, music. *Address:* Wylye Cottage, Great Wishford, Salisbury, Wilts SP2 0PD.

O'KELLY, Surgeon Rear-Adm. Francis Joseph, OBE 1965; Royal Navy, retired 1980; Occupational Health Consultant, Medical and Health Department, Government of Hong Kong, 1980–86; *b* 24 Dec. 1921; *s* of Francis John O'Kelly and Elizabeth Mary O'Kelly (*née* Rogan); *m* 1954, Winifred Mary Teresa Henry; one *s* three *d. Educ:* St Patrick's Coll., Cavan; University Coll., Dublin. MB, BCh 1945; FFCM, FFOM (RCPI), MFOM (RCPE); Hon. FACOM; DPH, DIH. Hosp. appts in Dublin, 1946–48; joined RN 1948; served with RM Commandos, Middle and Far East, 1948–52; HM Ships Unicorn, St Bride's Bay and Centaur, RNB Chatham and RN Air Station, Brawdy, 1952–63; Naval MOH appts, Far East Fleet, Scotland and NI Comd, Portsmouth and Chatham Comd, 1963–72; Dep. Dir, Health and Research, 1972–74; MO i/c RN Hosp. Gibraltar, 1974–77; Surgeon Rear-Adm. (Ships and Establishments), 1977–78; Surg. Rear-Adm. (Naval Hosps), 1978–80; QHP 1977–80. Adviser in Preventive and Industrial Medicine to Med. Dir Gen. (Naval), 1972–77, in Community Medicine, 1977–80. *Publications:* articles in med jls. *Recreations:* reading and travel. *Address:* Breffni, 38 Seamead, Stubbington, Fareham, Hants PO14 2NG.

O'KENNEDY, Michael E.; TD (Fianna Fáil) Tipperary North, 1969–80 and since 1982; Minister for Agriculture and Food, since 1987; *b* Nenagh, Co. Tipperary, 21 Feb. 1936; *s* of Éamonn and Helena O'Kennedy; *m* 1965, Breda, *d* of late Andrew Heavey and of Mary Heavey; one *s* two *d. Educ:* St Flannan's College, Ennis, Co. Clare; Univ. Coll., Dublin. MA 1957. Called to Irish Bar, 1961; Senior Counsel 1973. Elected to Seanad Éireann, 1965; Mem., Oireachtas Select Constitutional Cttee, 1966. Parly Sec. to Minister for Educn, 1970–72; Minister without Portfolio, Dec. 1972–Jan. 1973; Minister for Transport and Power, Jan.-March 1973; Opposition spokesman on Foreign Affairs, 1973–77; Minister for Foreign Affairs, 1977–79; Pres., Council of Ministers of the European Communities, July-Dec. 1979; Minister for Finance, 1979–81; opposition spokesman on finance, 1983–87; Pres., Council of Agriculture Ministers, EC, Jan.–June 1990. Mem., Commn of the European Communities, 1981–82. Member: All-Party Cttee on Irish Relns, 1973–77; Dáil and Seanad Jt Cttee on Secondary Legislation of the European Communities, 1973–77; Chm., Inter-Party Cttee on Implications of Irish Unity, 1972–73. *Address:* Gortlandroe, Nenagh, Co. Tipperary, Ireland.

OKEOVER, Sir Peter Ralph Leopold W.; *see* Walker-Okeover.

OKOGIE, Most Rev. Anthony Olubunmi; *see* Lagos, Archbishop of, (RC).

OKOTH, Most Rev. Yona; *see* Uganda, Archbishop of.

OLAGBEGI II, The Olowo of Owo, (Sir Olateru), Kt 1960; Oba Alaiyeluwa, Olagbegi II, Olowo of Owo, since 1941; Minister of State, Western Region (now Western Provinces) of Nigeria, 1952; President of the House of Chiefs, Western Region (now Western Provinces), 1965; *b* 1910; *s* of Oba Alaiyeluwa, Olagbegi I, Olowo of Owo; married; many *s* and *d* (some decd). *Educ:* Owo Government School. A Teacher in 1934; Treasury Clerk in Owo Native Administration, 1935–41. Queen's Medal, 1957. *Recreations:* lawn tennis, squash racquets. *Address:* PO Box 1, Afin Oba Olowo, Owo, Western Provinces of Nigeria. *T:* Owo 1.

OLANG', Most Rev. Festo Habakkuk; *b* 11 Nov. 1914; *m* 1937, Eseri D. Olang'; four *s* eight *d. Educ:* Alliance High School. Teacher, 1936–43; ordained 1945; consecrated Assistant Bishop of Mombasa in Namirembe Cathedral, by Archbishop of Canterbury, 1955; Bishop of Maseno, 1961; Bishop of Nairobi, 1970; Archbishop of Kenya, 1970–79. Hon. DD Univ. of the South Sewanee, USA. *Address:* PO Box 1, Maseno, Kenya.

OLAYAN, Suliman Saleh, Hon. KBE 1987; Founder and Chairman, The Olayan Group, since 1947; *b* 5 Nov. 1918; *s* of Saleh Olayan and Haya Al Ghanim; *m* 1974, Mary Perdikis; one *s* three *d. Educ:* Bahrain. Founding Chairman: Arab Commercial Enterprises, 1950–84; Nat. Gas Co., 1951–54; Saudi British Bank, 1978–; Saudi Spanish Bank, 1979–84; Director: Al Khobar Power Co., 1950–54; Riyadh Bank, 1963–78; Saudi Arabian Airlines, 1965–81; Mobil Corp., 1980–83; CS First Boston, 1989–. Member: Internat. Council of Morgan Guaranty Trust Co., 1979–90; Internat. Adv. Bd, Amer.

Internat. Gp, 1982–; Adv. Bd, Energy Internat. NV, 1983–. Chairman: Riyadh Chamber of Commerce and Industry, 1981–89; Council of Saudi Chambers of Commerce and Industry, 1984–87. Member: Internat. Industrial Conf., 1961–; Gp of Thirty, 1984–87; Bd, Inst. for Internat. Econs, 1987–. Mem., Rockefeller Univ. Council, 1974–87 (Alumnus Mem., 1987–). Founding Vice Chm., Handicapped Children's Assoc., Riyadh, 1983–89. Medal of Honour, Madrid Chamber of Commerce and Industry, 1985. Grand Cross, Order of Merit (Spain), 1984; Comdr First Class, Royal Order of Polar Star (Sweden), 1988. *Publications:* contribs on energy to Washington Qly. *Recreations:* swimming, reading, walking. *Address:* PO Box 8772, Riyadh, Saudi Arabia. *Clubs:* Royal Automobile; Equestrian (Riyadh); Knickerbocker (New York); Pacific Union (San Francisco).

OLDENBOURG-IDALIE, Zoë; Chevalier, Légion d'Honneur, 1980; Commandeur du Mérite des Arts et des Lettres, 1978; writer (as Zoë Oldenbourg); *b* 31 March 1916; *d* of Sergius Oldenbourg, writer and historicist, and of Ada (*née* Starynkevitch); *m* 1948, Heinric Idalie; one *s* one *d*. *Educ:* Lycée Molière and Sorbonne, Paris. Prix Fémina, 1953. *Publications:* Argile et cendres, 1946 (The World is Not Enough, 1949); La Pierre angulaire, 1953 (The Cornerstone, 1954); Réveillés de la Vie, 1956 (The Awakened, trans. E. Hyams, 1957); Les Irréductibles, 1958 (The Chains of Love, 1959); Bûcher de Montségur, 1959 (Massacre at Montségur, 1962); Les Brûlés, 1961 (Destiny of Fire, trans. P. Green, 1961); Les Cités charnelles, 1961 (Cities of the Flesh, 1963); Les Croisades: un essai historique, 1963 (The Crusades, trans. Anne Carter, 1966); Catherine de Russie, 1965 (Catherine the Great, 1965); Saint Bernard, 1969; La Joie des pauvres, 1970 (The Heirs of the Kingdom, trans. Anne Carter, 1972); L'Epopée des cathédrales, 1973; Que vous a donc fait Israël?, 1974; Visages d'un autoportrait (autobiog.), 1977; La Joie-Souffrance, 1980; Le Procès du Rêve, 1982; Que nous est Hécube?, 1984; Les Amours égarées, 1987; Déguisements, 1989. *Recreation:* painting. *Address:* c/o Victor Gollancz Ltd, 14 Henrietta Street, WC2; 4 rue de Montmorency, 92100 Boulogne, France.

OLDENBURG, Richard Erik; Director, Museum of Modern Art, New York, since 1972; *b* 21 Sept. 1933; *s* of Gösta Oldenburg and Sigrid Elisabeth (*née* Lindforss); *m* 1960, Harriet Lisa Turnure. *Educ:* Harvard Coll. (AB 1954). Manager, Design Dept, Doubleday & Co., NYC, 1958–61; Man. Editor, Trade Div., Macmillan Co., NYC, 1961–69; Dir, Publications, Museum of Modern Art, NYC, 1969–72. *Address:* Museum of Modern Art, 11 W 53rd Street, New York, NY 10019, USA.

OLDFIELD, Bruce, OBE 1990; designer; *b* 14 July 1950; parents unknown; brought up by Dr Barnado's, Ripon, Yorks. *Educ:* Ripon Grammar School; Sheffield City Polytechnic (Hon. Fellow 1987); Ravensbourne College of Art; St Martin's College of Art. Established fashion house, 1975; produced designer collections of high fashion clothes for UK and overseas; began exporting clothes worldwide, 1975; began making couture clothes for individual clients, 1981; opened first Bruce Oldfield retail shop, selling ready to wear and couture to international clientèle, 1984. Exhibitor: British Design Exhibn, Vienna, 1986; Australian Bicentennial Fashion Show, Sydney Opera House, 1988. Lectures: Fashion Inst., NY, 1977; Los Angeles County Museum, 1983; Internat. Design Conf., Aspen, Colorado, 1986 (Speaker and show). Hon. Fellow RCA, 1990. Designed for films: Jackpot, 1974; The Sentinel, 1976. *Publication:* (with Georgina Howell) Bruce Oldfield's Season, 1987. *Recreations:* music, reading, driving, working. *Address:* 27 Beauchamp Place, SW3. *T:* 071–584 1363.

OLDFIELD, John Richard Anthony; *b* July 1899; *s* of late Major H. E. Oldfield; *m* 1953, Jonnet Elizabeth, *d* of late Maj. H. M. Richards, DL, JP. *Educ:* Eton; Trinity College, Cambridge; Served in: Coldstream Guards, 1918–20; RN, 1939–45. MP (Lab) South-East Essex, 1929–31; Parliamentary Private Secretary to Sec. of State for Air, 1929–30. Mem. LCC, 1931–58 (Vice-Chairman, 1953); CC (C) Kent, 1965–81. *Address:* Doddington Place, near Sittingbourne, Kent ME9 0BB.

OLDFIELD, Michael Gordon, (Mike); musician and composer; *b* 15 May 1953; *s* of Dr Raymond Henry Oldfield and Maureen Bernadine Liston; one *d* by Anita Hegerland; two *s* one *d* by Sally A. Cooper. *Educ:* St Edward's, Reading; Presentation Coll., Reading. Records include: Tubular Bells, 1973 (over 10 million copies sold to date); Hergest Ridge; Ommadawn; Incantations; Platinum; QE2, 1980; Five Miles Out, 1982; Crises, 1983; Discovery, 1984; The Killing Fields (film sound track), 1984; Islands, 1987; The Wind Chimes (video album), 1988. Extensive world wide concert tours, 1979–. Mem., Assoc. of Professional Composers. Freeman, City of London, 1982. Hon. Pict. *Recreations:* helicopter pilot, squash, ski-ing, cricket. *Address:* c/o Ross, Bennet-Smith, 46/47 Upper Berkeley Street, W1. *Club:* Jacobs Larder (Ealing).

OLDHAM, Rev. Canon Arthur Charles Godolphin; *b* 5 Apr. 1905; *s* of late Sidney Godolphin and Lilian Emma Oldham; *m* 1934, Ursula Finch Wigham Richardson (*d* 1984), *d* of late George and Isabel Richardson, Newcastle upon Tyne; one *s* two *d*. *Educ:* King's College School; King's College, London. Business, music and journalism to 1930. Ordained, to Witley, Surrey, 1933; Vicar of Brockham Green, 1936; Rector of Merrow, 1943; Rural Dean of Guildford, 1949; Vicar of Godalming, 1950; Rural Dean of Godalming, 1957; Director of Ordination Training, and Bishop's Examining Chaplain, 1958; Hon. Canon of Guildford, 1959; Canon Residentiary of Guildford Cathedral, 1961–71, retired. *Recreations:* music, sketching. *Address:* Dora Cottage, Beech Hill, Hambledon, Surrey GU8 4HL. *T:* Wormley (0428) 682087.

OLDHAM, Prof. (Charles Herbert) Geoffrey, CBE 1990; Director, Science Policy Research Unit, University of Sussex, since 1980; *b* 17 Feb. 1929; *s* of Herbert Cecil Oldham and Evelyn Selina Oldham (*née* Brooke); *m* 1951, Brenda Mildred Raven; two *s* one *d* (and one *s* decd). *Educ:* Bingley Grammar Sch.; Reading Univ. (BSc Hons); Toronto Univ. (MA, PhD). Research geophysicist, Chevron Research Corp., 1954–57; Sen. Geophysicist, Standard Oil Co. of California, 1957–60; Fellow, Inst. of Current World Affairs, studying Chinese lang. and sci., 1960–66; Scientific Directorate, OECD, 1965–66; Dep. Dir, Science Policy Res. Unit, 1966–80; Associate Dir, Internat. Develt Res. Centre, Ottawa, 1970–80. Vis. Prof., Stanford Univ., 1979; Vis. Researcher, Aust. Sci. and Tech. Adv. Council, 1988. Chm., UN Adv. Ctte on Sci. and Tech. for Develt, 1991–. *Publications:* articles in jls on science, technology and Chinese development. *Recreations:* travel, esp. long distance train journeys, golf. *Address:* The Clock House, Barcombe Place, Barcombe, near Lewes, E Sussex BN8 5DL. *T:* Barcombe (0273) 400975.

O'LEARY, Michael; barrister; TD (FG) for Dublin South West, since 1982 (TD (Lab), Dublin North Central, 1965–82); *b* 8 May 1936; *s* of John O'Leary and Margaret McCarthy; unmarried. *Educ:* Presentation Coll., Cork; University Coll., Cork; Columbia Univ., NY. Called to the Bar, King's Inns, Dublin, 1979. Educn Officer, Irish TUC, 1962–65. Minister for Labour, 1973–77; Dep. Leader, Labour Party, 1977–81, Leader, 1981–82 (resigned); Tánaiste (Dep. Prime Minister) and Minister for Industry and Energy, 1981–82; joined Fine Gael, 1982. President, ILO, 1976. Mem. for Ireland, European Parlt, 1979–81. *Address:* Leinster House, Kildare Street, Dublin 2, Ireland. *T:* Dublin 789911.

O'LEARY, Peter Leslie; Under-Secretary, Inland Revenue, 1978–84; *b* 12 June 1929; *s* of Archibald and Edna O'Leary; *m* 1960, Margaret Elizabeth Debney; four *d*. *Educ:* Portsmouth Southern Grammar Sch.; University Coll., London (BA). Joined Inland Revenue as Inspector, 1952; Sen. Principal Inspector, 1974. *Recreations:* horology, gardening, wine-making. *Address:* 17 Sleaford Road, Heckington, Sleaford, Lincs NG34 9QP. *T:* Sleaford (0529) 61213.

O'LEARY, Terence Daniel, CMG 1982; MA; HM Diplomatic Service, retired 1988; Chairman, Petworth Preservation, since 1989; *b* 18 Aug. 1928; 2nd *s* of late Daniel O'Leary; *m* 1960, Janet Douglas Berney, *d* of Dr H. B. Berney, Masterton, NZ; twin *s* one *d*. *Educ:* Dulwich; St John's Coll., Cambridge. BA 1950. Army, commnd Queen's Royal Regt, 1946–48. Commerce, 1951–53; Asst Principal, CRO, 1953; 2nd Sec., British High Commn, Wellington, 1956–58; Principal, PSO's Dept, CRO, 1958; 1st Sec., New Delhi, 1960–63; 1st Sec., Dar es Salaam, 1963–64; CRO, 1964–65; 1st Sec. and Defence Sec., Canberra, 1965–68; Actg Head, S Asia Dept, FCO, 1969; Asst Sec., Cabinet Office, 1970–72; Counsellor, Pretoria/Cape Town, 1972–74; Dep. High Comr, Wellington, 1974–78; Senior Civil Mem., Directing Staff, Nat. Defence Coll., 1978–81; High Comr in Sierra Leone, 1981–84; High Comr in New Zealand and concurrently to Western Samoa, and Governor of Pitcairn, 1984–87. *Recreations:* cutting grass, tennis, Pacific history. *Address:* The Old Rectory, Petworth, W Sussex. *T:* Petworth (0798) 43335. *Clubs:* Travellers'; Wellington (New Zealand).

OLINS, Wallace, (Wally), MA Oxon; FCSD; Chairman, Wolff Olins Ltd; *b* 19 Dec. 1930; *s* of Alfred Olins and Rachel (*née* Muscovitch); *m* 1st, 1957, Maria Renate Olga Laura Steinert (marr. diss. 1989); two *s* one *d*; 2nd, 1990, Dornie Watts; one *d*. *Educ:* Highgate Sch.; St Peter's Coll., Oxford (Hons History, MA). National Service, Army, in Germany, 1950–51. S. H. Benson Ltd, London, 1954–57; Benson, India, 1957–62; Caps Design Group, London, 1962–65; Wolff Olins, London, 1965–. Vis. Lectr, Design Management, London Business Sch., 1984–; Vis. Prof., Management Sch., Imperial Coll., 1987–. Vice-Pres., SIAD, 1982–85. Chm., Design Dimension Educnl Trust, 1987–. Trustee, Design Mus., 1988–. Mem., Council, RSA, 1989–. *Publications:* The Corporate Personality, 1978; The Wolff Olins Guide to Corporate Identity, 1983; The Wolff Olins Guide to Design Management, 1985; Corporate Identity, 1989; numerous articles in Design and Management publications. *Recreations:* looking at buildings, shopping for books, theatre, old cars. *Address:* Wolff Olins, 22 Dukes Road, WC1H 9AB. *T:* 071–387 0891. *Club:* Groucho.

OLIPHANT, Air Vice-Marshal David Nigel Kington B.; *see* Blair-Oliphant.

OLIPHANT, Sir Mark, (Marcus Laurence Elwin), AC 1977; KBE 1959; FRS 1937; FAA 1954; FTS 1976; Governor of South Australia, 1971–76; *b* Adelaide, 8 Oct. 1901; *e s* of H. G. Oliphant; *m* 1925, Rosa Wilbraham (*d* 1987), Adelaide, S Australia; one *s* one *d*. *Educ:* Unley and Adelaide High Schools; University of Adelaide; Trinity Coll., Cambridge (1851 Exhibitioner, Overseas 1927, Senior 1929; PhD 1929). Messel Research Fellow of Royal Society, 1931; Fellow and Lecturer St John's Coll., 1934. Hon. Fellow, 1952; Assistant Director of Research, Cavendish Laboratory, Cambridge, 1935, Poynting Professor of Physics, University of Birmingham, 1937–50; Dir, Research Sch. of Physical Sciences, ANU, Canberra, 1950–63; Prof. of Physics of Ionised Gases, Inst. of Advanced Studies, ANU, 1964–67, now Professor Emeritus. Pres., Aust. Acad. of Sciences, 1954–57. Hon. DSc (Toronto, Belfast, Melbourne, Birmingham, New South Wales, ANU, Adelaide, Flinders); Hon. LLD (St Andrews). KStJ 1972. *Publications:* Rutherford: recollections of the Cambridge days, 1972; various papers on electricity in gases, surface properties and nuclear physics. *Address:* 28 Carstensz Street, Griffith, ACT 2603, Australia. *Club:* Adelaide (Adelaide).

OLIVE, Prof. David Ian, FRS 1987; Professor of Theoretical Physics, Imperial College of Science, Technology and Medicine, since 1984; *b* 16 April 1937; *s* of Ernest Edward Olive and Lilian Emma Olive (*née* Chambers); *m* 1963, Jenifer Mary Tutton; two *d*. *Educ:* Royal High Sch., Edinburgh; Univ. of Edinburgh (MA); Univ. of Cambridge (BA, PhD). Fellow of Churchill Coll., 1963–70; Lectr, Univ. of Cambridge, 1965–71; Staff Mem., CERN, 1971–77; Imperial College: Lectr, 1977; Reader, 1980. Visiting Professor: Univ. of Virginia, 1982–83; Univ. of Geneva, 1986. *Publications:* (jtly) The Analytic S-Matrix, 1966; many articles on theoretical physics in learned jls. *Recreations:* listening to music, golf. *Address:* Blackett Laboratory, Imperial College of Science, Technology and Medicine, SW7 2BZ. *T:* 071–589 5111, ext. 6974.

OLIVER, family name of **Baron Oliver of Aylmerton.**

OLIVER OF AYLMERTON, Baron *cr* 1986 (Life Peer), of Aylmerton in the County of Norfolk; **Peter Raymond Oliver;** Kt 1974; PC 1980; a Lord of Appeal in Ordinary, since 1986; *b* 7 March 1921; *s* of David Thomas Oliver, Fellow of Trinity Hall, Cambridge, and Alice Maud Oliver; *m* 1st, 1945, Mary Chichester Rideal (*d* 1985), *d* of Sir Eric Keightley Rideal, MBE, FRS; one *s* one *d*; 2nd, 1987, Wendy Anne, *widow* of I. Lewis Lloyd Jones. *Educ:* The Leys, Cambridge; Trinity Hall, Cambridge (Hon. Fellow, 1980). Military Service, 1941–45, 12th Bn RTR (despatches). Called to Bar, Lincoln's Inn, 1948, Bencher 1973; QC 1965; Judge of the High Ct of Justice, Chancery Div., 1974–80; a Lord Justice of Appeal, 1980–86. Mem., Restrictive Practices Court, 1976–80; Chm., Review Body on Chancery Div. of High Court, 1979–81. Hon. LLD: City of London Poly., 1989; UEA, 1991. *Recreations:* gardening, music. *Address:* House of Lords, SW1A 0PW.

See also Hon. D. K. R. Oliver.

OLIVER, Benjamin Rhys; Stipendiary Magistrate for Mid-Glamorgan, since 1983; a Recorder of the Crown Court, since 1972; *b* 8 June 1928; *m* 1955; one *s* one *d*. *Educ:* Llandovery and Aberystwyth. Called to the Bar, Inner Temple, 1954. *Recreation:* golf.

OLIVER, Hon. David Keightley Rideal; QC 1986; *b* 4 June 1949; *o s* of Baron Oliver of Aylmerton, *qv*; *m* 1st, 1972, Marisa Mirasierras (marr. diss. 1987); two *s*; 2nd, 1988, Judith Britannia Caroline Powell; one *s*. *Educ:* Westminster School; Trinity Hall, Cambridge; Institut d'Etudes Européennes, Brussels. Called to the Bar, Lincoln's Inn, 1972; Junior Counsel to Dir-Gen. of Fair Trading, 1980–86. *Recreations:* gardening, bird watching, shooting. *Address:* 13 Old Square, Lincoln's Inn, WC2A 3UA. *T:* 071–404 4800.

OLIVER, Dennis Stanley, CBE 1981; PhD, FEng, FIM, FInstP; Director, Pilkington Brothers plc, 1977–86; *b* 19 Sept. 1926; *s* of late James Thomas Oliver and Lilian Mabel Oliver (*née* Bunn); *m* 1st, 1952, Enid Jessie Newcombe (marr. diss. 1984); 2nd, 1988, Elizabeth Emery. *Educ:* Deacon's School, Peterborough; Birmingham Univ. BSc, PhD. Research Fellowship, Univ. of Bristol, 1949–52; Senior Scientific Officer, UKAEA, Culcheth, 1952–55; Head of Metallurgy Div., UKAEA, Dounreay, 1955–63; Chief R & D Officer, Richard Thomas & Baldwin Ltd, 1963–68; Group R & D Dir, Pilkington Brothers plc, 1968–77. Member: Board, British Technology Gp (Member: NEB, 1981–; NRDC, 1981–; Court and Council, Cranfield Inst. of Technology, 1976–88. Vis. Prof., Cranfield Inst. of Technology, 1984–88. Director: Anglo-American Venture Fund Ltd, 1980–84; Monotype Corp., 1985–90. Chm., Industrial Experience Projects Ltd, 1981–86; Pres., European Industrial Res. Management Assoc., 1977–81. Patron, Science and Technology Educn on Merseyside, 1982– (Pres., 1978–81); Governor: Liverpool Inst. of Higher Educn, 1979–85; Christ's and Notre Dame Coll., Liverpool, 1979–87; Royal Nat.

Coll. for the Blind, 1981–85; Dir, L'Ecole Supérieure du Verre, Belgium, 1971–86; Governor, Community of St Helens Trust Ltd, 1978–86; Founder Trustee, Anfield Foundn, 1983–88. Freeman of City of London; Liveryman: Spectaclemakers Co. (Court of Assts, 1985–88); Co. of Engrs, 1984. FBIM. KSG 1980. *Publications:* The Use of Glass in Engineering, 1975; Glass for Construction Purposes, 1977; various publications on technical subjects and technology transfer. *Recreations:* music, poetry, travel. *Address:* Castell Bach, Bodfari, Denbigh, Clwyd LL16 4HT. *T:* Bodfari (075475) 354.

OLIVER, Sir (Frederick) Ernest, Kt 1962; CBE 1955; TD 1942; DL; Chairman, George Oliver (Footwear) Ltd, 1950–73; *b* 31 Oct. 1900; *s* of late Colonel Sir Frederick Oliver and late Lady Oliver, CBE; *m* 1928, Mary Margaret (*d* 1978), *d* of late H. Simpson; two *d* (one *s* decd). *Educ:* Rugby School. Member Leicester City Council, 1933–73, Lord Mayor, 1950. Officer, Territorial Army, 1922–48. Served UK and Burma, 1939–45. President: Multiple Shoe Retailers' Assoc., 1964–65; Leicester YMCA, 1955–76; Leicester Conservative Assoc., 1952–66. Leicester: DL 1950; Hon. Freeman, 1971. *Address:* c/o 20 New Walk, Leicester LE1 6TX. *Club:* Leicestershire (Leicester).

OLIVER, Dr John Andrew, CB 1968; *b* 25 Oct. 1913; *s* of Robert John Oliver, Limavady, Co. Londonderry and Martha Sherrard, Magilligan, Co. Londonderry; *m* 1943, Stella Ritson; five *s. Educ:* Royal Belfast Academical Institution; Queen's Univ., Belfast; Bonn Univ.; Königsberg Univ.; Zimmern School of International Studies, Geneva; Imperial Defence Coll., London. BA 1936; DrPhil, 1951; IDC, 1954. Ministry of Development, NI: Second Sec., 1964–71; Permanent Sec., 1971–74; Permanent Sec., Housing, Local Govt and Planning, NI, 1974–75; Chief Adviser, NI Constitutional Convention, 1975–76. Hon. Sec., Assoc. of Governing Bodies of Voluntary Grammar Schs in NI, 1964–77; Chm., Bd of Governors, Royal Belfast Academical Instn, 1970–77. UK Election Supervisor, Que Que, Rhodesia, 1980. Chm. Management Review, Royal Victoria Hosp. Gp, Belfast, 1981–82. Chm., S Lakeland Council for Voluntary Action, 1980; Vice-Chm., Voluntary Action Cumbria, 1980–. Proposer and interim Governor, new Dallam Schs, Cumbria, 1983–84. Retired deliberately from all cttees and exec. positions on reaching 70, to make way for younger people. Hon. MRTPI, 1964; Hon. Member, Assoc. for Housing and Town Planning, W Germany, 1966. Rhodesia Medal, 1980; Zimbabwe Independence Medal, 1980. *Publications:* Ulster Today and Tomorrow, 1978; Working at Stormont, 1978; many articles in learned jls on Ulster Admin and on family history. *Recreations:* swimming, maps, languages, family history. *Address:* Laundry Cottage, Hale, Milnthorpe, Cumbria LA7 7BL. *T:* Milnthorpe (05395) 62698. *Club:* Royal Over-Seas League.

OLIVER, Rt. Rev. John Keith; *see* Hereford, Bishop of.

OLIVER, John Laurence; Journalist; *b* 14 Sept. 1910; *s* of late Harold and Teresa Oliver; *m* 1946, Renée Mary Webb; two *s. Educ:* Haberdashers' Aske's Hampstead School. Publicity Manager, The Book Society, 1934; Art Editor, The Bystander, 1935–39. War of 1939–45: served in the Field Security Corps; commissioned 1941, The Suffolk Regt (transferred The Cambridgeshire Regt). Joined staff of The Sphere, 1946; Art Editor, 1947; Assistant Editor, 1956; Editor, 1960–64; Editor, The Tatler, 1961–65. *Publications:* Saint John's Wood Church (with Rev. Peter Bradshaw), 1955; Malcolm Morley at the Everyman, 1977; occasional short stories and articles. *Recreations:* reading, theatre going, watching cricket. *Address:* 10 Wellington Place, NW8 9JA. *T:* 071–286 5891. *Clubs:* Garrick, MCC.

OLIVER, Group Captain John Oliver William, CB 1950; DSO 1940; DFC 1940; RAF retired; *b* 1911; *e s* of William and Cicely Oliver; *m* 1935 (marr. diss., 1951); one *s* two *d; m* 1962, Anne Fraser Porteous; one *s* two *d* (of whom *s* and *yr d* are twins). *Educ:* Christ's Hospital; Cranwell. Commissioned from Cranwell, General Duties Pilot Branch permanent commn, 1931; served 43 (F) Squadron and 55 (B) Squadron, Iraq; qualified CFS. Served War of 1939–45 (despatches thrice); commanded 85 (F) Squadron, 1940; Fighter Command and Tactical Air Force; Wing Commander, 1940; Group Captain, 1942. Assistant Commandant, RAF Coll., Cranwell, 1948–50; ACOS Ops, Allied Forces Northern Europe, 1958–60; retired, 1961. Personnel Officer, ENV (Engineering) Ltd, 1961; Staff Institute Personnel Management, 1962; Personnel Manager, Humber Ltd, 1963; Manager, Training and Administrative Service, Rootes, Coventry, 1965; Senior Training Officer, Engineering Industry Training Board, 1968; Personnel and Trng Manager, Thorn Gp, 1970–76, retired. *Recreations:* painting, sailing.

OLIVER, Prof. Michael Francis, CBE 1985; MD; FRCP, FRCPEd, FFCM; FRSE; Director, Wynn Institute for Metabolic Research, since 1989; Hon. Professor, National Heart and Lung Institute, since 1989; Professor Emeritus, University of Edinburgh, since 1990; *b* 3 July 1925; *s* of late Captain Wilfrid Francis Lenn Oliver, MC (DLI), and Cecilia Beatrice Oliver (*née* Daniel); *m* 1st; two *s* one *d* (and one *s* decd); 2nd, Helen Louise Daniel. *Educ:* Marlborough Coll.; Univ. of Edinburgh. MB, ChB 1947, MD (Gold Medal) 1957. Edinburgh University: Consultant Physician, Royal Infirmary and Sen. Lectr in Medicine, 1961; Reader in Medicine, 1973; Personal Prof. of Cardiology, 1977; Duke of Edinburgh Prof. of Cardiology, 1979–89. Mem., Cardiovascular Panel, Govt Cttee on Medical Aspects of Food Policy, 1971–74, 1982–84; UK Rep. Mem., Adv. Panel for Cardiovascular Disease, WHO, 1972–; Chm., BBC-Medical Adv. Gp in Scotland, 1975–81; Mem. Scientific Bd, Internat. Soc. of Cardiology, 1968–78 (Chm., Council on Atherosclerosis and Ischaemic Heart Disease, 1968–75); Chairman: Brit. Atherosclerosis Gp, 1970–75; Science Cttee, Fondation Cardiologique Princess Lilian, Belgium, 1976–85; MoT Panel on driving and cardiovascular disease, 1985–90; Jt Cttee on Higher Medical Training, 1987–90. Convener, Cardiology Cttee, Scottish Royal Colls, 1978–81; Council Mem., Brit. Heart Foundn, 1976–85. Pres., British Cardiac Soc., 1981–85; Pres., RCPEd, 1986–88. FRSE 1987. Hon. FRCPI 1988; Hon. FRACP 1988. Hon. Fellow, Amer. Coll. of Cardiology, 1973. Hon. MD: Karolinska Inst., Stockholm, 1980; Univ. Bologna, 1985. Purkinje Medal, 1981; Polish Cardiac Soc. Medal, 1984. *Publications:* Acute Myocardial Infarction, 1966; Intensive Coronary Care, 1970, 2nd edn 1974; Effect of Acute Ischaemia on Myocardial Function, 1972; Modern Trends in Cardiology, 1975; High-Density Lipoproteins and Atherosclerosis, 1978; Coronary Heart Disease in Young Women, 1978; Strategy for Screening of Coronary Heart Disease, 1986; contribs to sci. and med. jls on causes of coronary heart disease, biochemistry of fats, myocardial metabolism, mechanisms of sudden death, clinical trials of drugs, and population studies of vascular diseases. *Recreations:* talking, travelling, Northern Italy. *Address:* Barley Mill House, Pencaitland, East Lothian EH34 5EP. *T:* Pencaitland (0875) 340433; 28 Chalcot Road, NW1. *T:* 071–722 4460. *Clubs:* Athenæum; New (Edinburgh).

OLIVER, Peter Richard, CMG 1965; HM Diplomatic Service, retired; Ambassador to Uruguay, 1972–77; *b* 3 June 1917; *yr s* of William Henry Oliver and Muriel Daisy Elisabeth Oliver (*née* Widdicombe); *m* 1940, Freda Evelyn Gwyther; two *s* two *d. Educ:* Felsted Sch.; Hanover; Berlin; Trinity Hall, Cambridge. Indian Civil Service, 1939–47; served in Punjab and Bahawalpur State. Transferred to HM Foreign (subsequently Diplomatic) Service, 1947; served in Karachi, 1947–49; Foreign Office, 1949–52; The Hague, 1952–56; Havana, 1956–59; Foreign Office, 1959–61; Djakarta, 1961–64; Bonn, 1965–69; Dep. High Comr, Lahore, 1969–72. *Recreations:* gardening, Bumbloclasm.

Address: Bridge Cottage, Little Petherick, Wadebridge, Cornwall PL27 7QT. *T:* Rumford (0841) 540358. *Clubs:* Commonwealth Trust; Hawks (Cambridge); Union (Cambridge).

OLIVER, Prof. Emeritus Richard Alexander Cavaye; Professor of Education and Director of the Department of Education in the University of Manchester, 1938–70; Dean of Faculty of Education, 1938–48, 1962–65; Dean of Faculty of Music, 1952–62, 1966–70; *b* 9 Jan. 1904; *s* of Charles Oliver and Elizabeth Smith; *m* 1929, Annabella Margaret White, MA Edin, MA Oxon; one *s* one *d. Educ:* George Heriot's Sch.; University of Edinburgh; Stanford Univ., California, USA. Held Commonwealth Fund Fellowship at Stanford Univ., 1927–29; research educational psychologist in Kenya, 1929–32; Asst Master Abbotsholme Sch. and in Edinburgh, 1933–34; University Extension Lecturer, 1933–34; Asst Director of Education, Wilts Education Cttee, 1934–36; Dep. Secretary, Devon Education Cttee, 1936–38. Director, University of Manchester School of Education, 1947–51; Pro Vice-Chancellor, 1953–57 and 1960–61; Presenter of Hon. Graduands, 1959–64, 1966. Member National Advisory Council on Training and Supply of Teachers, 1949–59; Member, Northern Universities Joint Matriculation Board, 1942–70 (Chm., 1952–55); Member Secondary School Examinations Council, 1958–64. FBPsS. Hon. Research Fellow, Princeton Univ., 1961. Hon. LLD Manchester, 1981. *Publications:* (with others) The Educational Guidance of the School Child, 1936; Research in Education, 1946; The Content of Sixth Form General Studies, 1974; Joint Matriculation Board Occasional Publications; contrib. to East Africa Medical Journal, Africa, British Journal of Psychology, Yearbook of Education, Universities Quarterly, Research in Education, etc. *Recreations:* gardening, painting. *Address:* Waingap, Crook, Kendal, Cumbria LA8 9HT. *T:* Kendal (0539) 821277.
See also H. A. Hetherington.

OLIVER, Prof. Roland Anthony, MA, PhD (Cantab); Professor of the History of Africa, London University, 1963–86; *b* Srinagar, Kashmir, 30 March 1923; *s* of late Major D. G. Oliver and Lorimer Janet (*née* Donaldson); *m* 1st, 1947, Caroline Florence (*d* 1983), *d* of late Judge John Linehan, KC; one *d*; 2nd, 1990, Suzanne Doyle, *widow* of Brig. Richard Miers. *Educ:* Stowe; King's Coll., Cambridge. Attached to Foreign Office, 1942–45; R. J. Smith Research Studentship, King's Coll., Cambridge, 1946–48; Lecturer, School of Oriental and African Studies, 1948–58; Reader in African History, University of London, 1958–63; Francqui Prof., University of Brussels, 1961; Visiting Professor: Northwestern Univ., Illinois, 1962; Harvard Univ., 1967; travelled in Africa, 1949–50 and 1957–58; org. international Conferences on African History and Archæology, 1953–61; Haile Selassie Prize Trust Award, 1966; Distinguished Africanist Award, American African Studies Assoc., 1989. President: African Studies Assoc., 1967–68; British Inst. in Eastern Africa, 1981–. Member: Perm. Bureau, Internat. Congress of Africanists, 1973–78; Council, Royal African Society; Chm., Minority Rights Group. Corresp. Member, Académie Royale des Sciences d'Outremer, Brussels. Editor (with J. D. Fage) Jl of African History, 1960–73. *Publications:* The Missionary Factor in East Africa, 1952; Sir Harry Johnston and the Scramble for Africa, 1957; (ed) The Dawn of African History, 1961; (with J. D. Fage) A Short History of Africa, 1962; (ed with Gervase Mathew) A History of East Africa, 1963; (with A. E. Atmore) Africa since 1800, 1967; (ed) The Middle Age of African History, 1967; (with B. M. Fagan) Africa in the Iron Age, 1975; (with A. E. Atmore) The African Middle Ages, 1400–1800, 1981; The African Experience, 1991; Gen. Editor (with J. D. Fage), Cambridge History of Africa, 8 vols, 1975–86. *Address:* Frilsham Woodhouse, Newbury, Berks RG16 9XB. *T:* Hermitage (0635) 201407.

OLIVER, Dr Ronald Martin, CB 1989; RD 1973; Deputy Chief Medical Officer (Deputy Secretary), Department of Health and Social Security, 1985–89, retired; *b* 28 May 1929; *s* of late Cuthbert Hanson Oliver and Cecilia Oliver; *m* 1957, Susanna Treves Blackwell; three *s* one *d. Educ:* King's Coll. Sch., Wimbledon; King's Coll., London; St George's Hosp. Med. Sch. (MB, BS 1952). MRCS, LRCP 1952; DCH 1954; DPH 1960; DIH 1961; MD London 1965; MFOM 1978; MRCP 1987; MFCM 1987. Served RNR: Surg. Lieut, 1953–55; Surg. Lt-Comdr, retd 1974. St George's Hosp., London: House Surgeon and Physician, 1952–53; Resident Clin. Pathologist, 1955–56; trainee asst, gen. practice, 1956–57; Asst County MO, Surrey CC, 1957–59; MO, London Transport Exec., 1959–62; MO, later SMO, Treasury Med. Service (later CS Med. Adv. Service), 1962–74; seconded Diplomatic Service as Physician, British Embassy, Moscow, 1964–66; SMO, 1974–79, SPMO, 1979–85, DHSS; Chief Med. Advr, ODA, 1983–85. *Publications:* papers in med. jls on epidemiology of heart disease, public health, toxicology, and health service admin. *Recreations:* golf, sailing, gardening, bad bridge. *Address:* Greenhill House, Beech Avenue, Effingham, Surrey KT24 5PH. *T:* Bookham (0372) 452887. *Club:* Effingham Golf.

OLIVER, Stephen John Lindsay, QC 1980; barrister-at-law; a Recorder, since 1989; *b* 14 Nov. 1938; *s* of Philip Daniel Oliver and Audrey Mary Oliver; *m* 1967, Anne Dawn Harrison Taylor; one *s* two *d. Educ:* Rugby Sch.; Oriel Coll., Oxford (MA Jurisprudence). National Service, RN, 1957–59: served submarines; Temp. Sub-Lieut. Called to the Bar, Middle Temple, 1963; Bencher, 1987. Asst Boundary Comr, Parly Boundary Commn, 1977. Chm. Blackheath Concert Halls Charity, 1986–. *Recreations:* music, sailing. *Address:* 4 Pump Court, Temple, EC4Y 7AN. *T:* 071–583 9770.

OLIVIER, Henry, CMG 1954; DScEng, PhD London, DEng; FICE, FASCE, Beit Fellow; FRSA; specialist consulting engineer in water resources engineering, Henry Olivier & Associates, since 1974; *b* 25 Jan. 1914; *s* of J. Olivier, Umtali, S Rhodesia; *m* 1st, 1940, Lorna Renée Collier; one *d* (one *s* decd); 2nd, 1979, Johanna Cecilia van der Merwe. *Educ:* Umtali High Sch.; Cape Town Univ. (BSc 1936; MSc 1947); University College, London (PhD 1953); DEng Witwatersrand, 1967. Beit Engineering Schol., 1932–38; Beit Fellow for two Rhodesias, 1939. Engineering post-grad. training with F. E. Kanthack & Partners, Consulting Engineers, Johannesburg, 1937; Sir Alex. Gibb & Partners, Cons. Engineers, London: training 1938, Asst Engineer, 1939. Experience covers design and construction of steam-electric power-stations, hydro-electric, floating harbour, irrigation, and water resources development schemes in UK, Africa, Middle East, and USA; Chief Engineer in charge civil engineering contracts, Owen Falls Hydro-Electric Scheme, Uganda, 1950–54; Partner in firm of Sir Alexander Gibb and Partners (Africa), 1954–55; Resident Director and Chief Engineer (Rhodesia), in firm of Gibb, Coyne & Sogei (Kariba), 1955–60; Consultant (mainly in connection with Indus Basin Project in Pakistan) to Sir Alexander Gibb and Partners, London, 1960–69 (Sen. Consultant, 1967); Partner, Gibb Hawkins and Partners, Johannesburg, 1963–69, associated with design and construction of Hendrik Verwoerd and P. K. le Roux dams on Orange River, RSA; Chm. LTA Ltd and LTA Engineering Ltd, 1969–73; major projects: Cahora Bassa Hydro-electric Scheme in Mozambique as mem. of Internat. Consortium Zamco; Orange-Fish Tunnel in South Africa; Sen. Partner, Henry Olivier and Associates, 1974–86, acting for Dept of Water Affairs, RSA, on concept plans for water and power projects in Lesotho, Transkei, Swaziland and Botswana; major concept plans accepted and implemented Lesotho Highlands Water Scheme. Mem., Exec. Cttee, SA Nat. Cttee on Large Dams, 1972–81; Pres., SA Inst. of Civil Engineers, 1979. Hon. DSc: Cape, 1968; Rhodesia, 1977. *Publications:* Irrigation and Climate, 1960; Irrigation and Water Resources Engineering, 1972; Damit, 1975; Great Dams in Southern Africa, 1977; Papers to Institution Civil

Engineering Journal; Int. Commn on Irrigation and Drainage; Water for Peace Conference, Washington, DC. *Recreation:* bowls. *Address:* PO Box 523, Jeffreys Bay, Cape, 6330, South Africa. *Club:* Country (Johannesburg).

OLIVIER, Lady, (Joan); *see* Plowright, Joan.

OLLARD, Richard Laurence, FRSL, FSA; author and editor; *b* 9 Nov. 1923; *s* of Rev. Dr S. L. Ollard and Mary Ollard (*née* Ward); *m* 1954, Mary, *d* of Sir Walter Buchanan Riddell, 12th Bt; two *s* one *d*. *Educ:* Eton College; New College, Oxford. MA. Lectr in History and English, Royal Naval College, Greenwich, 1948–59; Senior Editor, Collins, 1960–83. *Publications:* The Escape of Charles II, 1966; Man of War: Sir Robert Holmes and the Restoration Navy, 1969; Pepys: a biography, 1974, new edn 1984; This War Without an Enemy, 1976; The Image of the King: Charles I and II, 1979; An English Education: a perspective of Eton, 1982; (ed jtly) For Veronica Wedgwood These Studies in Seventeenth-Century History, 1986; Clarendon and his Friends, 1987; (ed) Clarendon's Four Portraits, 1989; Fisher and Cunningham: a study in the personalities of the Churchill era, 1991. *Address:* Norchard Farmhouse, Morcombelake, Bridport, Dorset DT6 6EP. *T:* Chideock (0297) 263; c/o Curtis Brown Ltd, 162–168 Regent Street, W1. *Club:* Brooks's.

OLLERENSHAW, Dame Kathleen (Mary), DBE 1971; DL; MA, DPhil; FIMA, FCP; Freeman of the City of Manchester, 1984; Chairman, Council for St John Ambulance in Greater Manchester, 1974–89; Member, Manchester City Council, 1956–80, Leader of Conservative Opposition, 1977–79; Alderman, 1970–74, Hon. Alderman since 1980; Lord Mayor, 1975–76, Deputy Lord Mayor, 1976–77; *b* 1 Oct. 1912; *d* of late Charles Timpson, JP, and late Mary Elizabeth Timpson (*née* Stops); *m* 1939, Robert Ollerenshaw (*d* 1986); one *s* (one *d* decd). *Educ:* Ladybarn House Sch., Manchester; St Leonards Sch., St Andrews; (open schol. in maths) Somerville Coll., Oxford (Hon. Fellow, 1978). BA (Hons) 1934, MA 1943, DPhil 1945; Foundation Fellow, Institute of Mathematics and its Applications (FIMA), 1964 (Mem. Council, 1973–75, Vice-Pres., 1976–77, Pres., 1978–79; Hon. Fellow 1986). Research Assistant, Shirley Institute, Didsbury, 1937–40. Chairman: Educn Cttee, Assoc. of Municipal Corporations, 1968–71; Assoc. of Governing Bodies of Girls' Public Schs, 1963–69; Manchester Educn Cttee, 1967–70 (Co-opted Mem., 1954–56); Manchester Coll. of Commerce, 1964–69; Court, Royal Northern Coll. of Music, Manchester, 1968–86 (Companion, 1978); Council, Science and Technology Insts, 1980–81; Member: Central Adv. Council on Educn in England, 1960–63; CNAA, 1964–74; SSRC, 1971–75; Tech. Educn Council, 1973–75; (Vice-Pres.,) British Assoc. for Commercial and Industrial Educn (Mem. Delegn to USSR, 1963); Exec., Assoc. of Educn Cttees, 1967–71; Nat. Adv. Council on Educn for Industry and Commerce, 1963–70; Gen. Adv. Council of BBC, 1966–72; Schools Council, 1968–71; Management Panel, Burnham Cttee, 1968–71; Nat. Foundn of Educnl Res., 1968–71; Layfield Cttee of Inquiry into Local Govt Finance, 1974–76; Court, Univ. of Salford, 1967– (Mem. Council, 1967–89; a Pro-Chancellor, 1983–89); Court, Univ. of Manchester, 1964–; Manchester Polytechnic, 1968–86 (Chm., 1969–72; Dep.-Chm., 1972–75; Hon. Fellow, 1979); Court, UMIST, 1971–87 (Vice-Pres., 1976–86; Hon. Fellow, 1987); Council, Lancaster Univ., 1975– (a Dep. Pro-Chancellor, 1978–); Council, CGLI, 1972–84 (Hon. Fellow, 1978; Vice-Pres., 1979–84); Sen. Res. Fellow (part-time), 1972–75, Hon. Res. Fellow, 1975–77, Lancaster Univ.; Rep. Governor, Royal Coll. of Advanced Technol., Salford, 1959–67; Governor: St Leonards Sch., St Andrews, 1950–72 (Pres., 1980–); Manchester High Sch. for Girls, 1959–69; Ladies Coll., Cheltenham, 1966–68; Chethams Hosp. Sch., Manchester, 1967–77; Further Educn Staff Coll., Blagdon, 1960–74; Mem., Manchester Statistical Soc., 1950– (Mem. Council, 1977–; Vice-Pres., 1977, Pres., 1981–83); Hon. Member: Manchester Technology Assoc., 1976– (Pres., 1982); Manchester Literary and Philosophical Soc., 1981–; Hon. Col, Manchester and Salford Univs OTC, 1977–81; Mem., Mil. Educn Cttee, 1979–. Dir, Greater Manchester Independent Radio, Ltd, 1972–83. Winifred Cullis Lecture Fellow to USA, 1965; Fourth Cockroft Lecture, UMIST and Manchester Tech. Assoc., 1977. DStJ 1983 (CStJ 1978) (Mem., Chapter Gen., 1974–). Hon. LLD CNAA, 1975; Hon. DSc Salford, 1975; Hon LLD Manchester, 1976. DL Greater Manchester, 1987. Mancunian of the Year, Jnr Chamber of Commerce, 1977. *Publications:* Education of Girls, 1958; Education for Girls, 1961; The Girls' Schools, 1967; Returning to Teaching, 1974; The Lord Mayor's Party, 1976; First Citizen, 1977; papers in mathematical journals, 1945–54 and 1977–, incl. Proc. RI 1981 (on form and pattern), Phil. Trans Royal Soc. 1982 (on magic squares), and Proc. Royal Soc. 1986 (on pandiagonal magic squares); articles on education and local govt in national and educational press. *Address:* 2 Pine Road, Didsbury, Manchester M20 0UY. *T:* 061–445 2948. *Club:* English-Speaking Union.

OLLIS, Prof. William David, BSc, PhD; FRS 1972; CChem; FRSC; Professor of Organic Chemistry, University of Sheffield, 1963–90 (Head of Department of Chemistry, 1966–69, 1973–75); *b* 22 Dec. 1924; *s* of Albert George and Beatrice Charlotte Ollis; *m* 1951, Sonia Dorothy Mary Weekes (marr. diss. 1974); two *d*. *Educ:* Cotham Grammar Sch., Bristol; University of Bristol. Assistant Lecturer in Organic Chemistry, University of Bristol, 1946–49, Lecturer, 1949–62, Reader, 1962–63. Research Fellow, Harvard, 1952–53; Visiting Professor: UCLA, 1962; University of Texas, 1966; Universidade Federal Rural do Rio de Janeiro, Brasil, 1967–70 (Hon. Prof., 1969); Wesleyan Univ., Conn, 1970–71; Univ. of Sri Lanka, 1974; Univ. of Kuwait, 1986. Lectures: Robert Gnehm, 1965; Chemical Soc. Tilden, 1969; Peboc, 1982; Irvine, 1984; Syntex, 1985, Pedler, RSC, 1988. Consultant, MoD, 1952–76; Scientific Advr, Home Office, 1954–76; Member: Individual Merit Promotion Panel Scientific CS, 1971–; Adv. Council for Misuse of Drugs, 1981–; Scientific Adv. Gp, 1985–, Policy Adv. Gp, 1986–, Forensic Sci. Service. Founder-Chm., Phytochem. Soc., 1966–67; Chm., Publication Cttee, Chem. Soc., 1972–74; Pres., Organic Chem. Div., RSC, 1983–85. Organic Synthesis Medal, RSC, 1982. FRSA. *Publications:* Recent Developments in the Chemistry of Natural Phenolic Compounds, 1961; Structure Determination in Organic Chemistry, 1973; (ed with Sir Derek Barton) Comprehensive Organic Chemistry, vols 1–6, 1979; (contrib.) Advances in Medicinal Phytochemistry, 1986; scientific papers mainly in Jl of Chemical Soc., Perkin Transl, Tetrahedron. *Address:* c/o Department of Chemistry, University of Sheffield, Sheffield S3 7HF. *Club:* Athenæum.

O'LOGHLEN, Sir Colman (Michael), 6th Bt, *cr* 1838; *b* 6 April 1916; *s* of Henry Ross O'Loghlen (*d* 1944; 6th *s* of 3rd Bt) and of Doris Irene, *d* of late Major Percival Horne, RA; *S* uncle 1951; *m* 1939, Margaret, *d* of Francis O'Halloran, Melbourne, Victoria; six *s* two *d*. *Educ:* Xavier Coll., Melbourne; Melbourne Univ. (LLB). Formerly Captain AIF. Sometime Magistrate and Judge of Supreme Court, PNG. *Heir:* *s* Michael O'Loghlen, *b* 21 May 1945.

OLSSON, Curt Gunnar; Chairman, Skandinaviska Enskilda Banken, since 1984; *b* 20 Aug. 1927; *s* of N. E. and Anna Olsson; *m* 1954, Asta Engblom; two *d*. *Educ:* Stockholm Sch. of Econs (BSc Econs 1950). Managing Director, Stockholm Group: Skandinaviska Banken, 1970–72; Skandinaviska Enskilda Banken, 1972–76; Man. Dir and Chief Exec., Head Office, 1976–82, and first Dep. Chm., 1982–84, Skandinaviska Enskilda Banken. Director: Atlas Copco AB, 1976–; Fastighets AB Hufvudstaden, 1983–. Chm., Stockholm Chamber of Commerce, 1986–; Swedish Bankers' Association: Dir, 1978–; Chm., 1978–80, 1989–91; Vice-Chm., 1987–89. Hon. Consul Gen. for Finland, 1989. Kt Order of Vasa, Sweden, 1976; King Carl XVI Gustaf's Gold Medal, Sweden, 1982; Comdr, Royal Norwegian Order of Merit, 1985; Comdr, Order of the Lion, Finland, 1986. *Address:* Skandinaviska Enskilda Banken, S-106 40 Stockholm, Sweden. *T:* 22 19 00.

OLUFOSOYE, Most Rev. Timothy, OON 1964; *b* 31 March 1918; *s* of Chief D. K. Olufosoye and Felecia O. Olufosoye; *m* 1947; one *s* three *d*. *Educ:* St Andrew's Coll., Oyo, Nigeria; Vancouver School of Theology, Univ. of BC (STh). Headmaster, 1942–44; deacon 1946, priest 1947; appointments in Ondo, Lagos, and overseas in St Helens, Lancs, Sheffield Cathedral, Yorks, and Christ Church Cathedral, Vancouver, BC; Canon, 1955; Provost, St Stephen's Cathedral, Ondo, 1959; Vicar-Gen., 1963; Bishop of Gambia and Rio Pongas, 1965–70; Bishop of Ibadan, 1971–88; Archbishop of Nigeria, 1979–88. Member: World Council of Churches; Gen. and Exec. Cttee, All Africa Conf. of Churches. Hon. DD, St Paul's Univ., Tokyo, 1958. Knight Comdr, Humane order of African Redemption, Republic of Liberia. *Publications:* Egbobi fun Ibanuje, 1967; Glossary of Ecclesiastical Terms, 1988; My Memoirs; editor of the Beacon, Ibadan Ecclesia Anglicana, The Rubric. *Recreation:* poultry farming. *Address:* 12 Awosika Avenue, Bodija Estate, PO Box 1666, Ibadan, Oyo State, Nigeria. *Club:* Ibadan Dining.

OLVER, Sir Stephen (John Linley), KBE 1975 (MBE 1947); CMG 1965; HM Diplomatic Service, retired; *b* 16 June 1916; *s* of late Rev. S. E. L. Olver and Mrs Madeleine Olver (*née* Stratton); *m* 1953, Maria Morena, Gubbio, Italy; one *s*. *Educ:* Stowe. Indian Police, 1935–44; Indian Political Service, Delhi, Quetta, Sikkim and Bahrain, 1944–47; Pakistan Foreign Service, Aug.-Oct. 1947; Foreign Service, Karachi, 1947–50; Foreign Office, 1950–53; Berlin, 1953–56; Bangkok, 1956–58; Foreign Office, 1958–61; Washington, 1961–64; Foreign Office, 1964–66; The Hague, 1967–69; High Comr, Freetown, 1969–72; High Comr, Nicosia, 1973–75. *Recreations:* golf, photography, painting. *Address:* 6 Saffrons Court, Compton Place Road, Eastbourne, Sussex BN21 1DX.

OLYOTT, Ven. Leonard Eric; Archdeacon of Taunton and Prebendary of Milverton, since 1977; *b* 11 Jan. 1926; *s* of Thomas Olyott and Maude Ann Olyott (*née* Purser); *m* 1951, Yvonne Winifred Kate Keele; two *s* one *d*. *Educ:* Colchester Royal Grammar School; London Univ. (BA 1950); Westcott House, Cambridge. Served RNVR, 1944–47; commissioned, 1945. Asst Curate, St George, Camberwell, 1952–55; Priest-in-Charge, St Michael and All Angels, Birchwood, Hatfield, Herts, 1955–60; Vicar of Chipperfield, Herts, 1960–68; Vicar of Crewkerne, 1968–71; Rector of Crewkerne with Wayford, 1971–77; Rural Dean of Crewkerne, 1972–77; Prebendary of Timberscombe, 1976. Hospital Chaplains Adviser to Bishop of Bath and Wells, 1983–. *Recreations:* sailing, gardening, music. *Address:* 4 Westerkirk Gate, Staplegrove, Taunton, Somerset TA2 6BQ. *T:* Taunton (0823) 323838, *Fax:* Taunton (0823) 325420.

O'MALLEY, Stephen Keppel; His Honour Judge O'Malley; a Circuit Judge, since 1989; *b* 21 July 1940; *s* of late D. K. C. O'Malley and Mrs R. O'Malley; *m* 1963, Frances Mary, *e d* of late James Stewart Ryan; four *s* two *d*. *Educ:* Ampleforth Coll.; Wadham Coll., Oxford (MA). Called to Bar, Inner Temple, 1962; Mem. Bar Council, 1968–72; Co-Founder, Bar European Gp, 1977; a Recorder, Western Circuit, 1978–89. Wine Treasurer, Western Circuit, 1986–89. *Publications:* Legal London, a Pictorial History, 1971; European Civil Practice, 1989. *Address:* 24 Montague Road, Richmond, Surrey TW10 6QW. *T:* 081–940 2727.

OMAN, Julia Trevelyan, (Lady Strong), CBE 1986; RDI 1977; designer; Director, Oman Productions Ltd; *b* 11 July 1930; *d* of late Charles Chichele Oman and Joan Trevelyan; *m* 1971, Sir Roy Colin Strong, *qv*. *Educ:* Royal College of Art, London. Royal Scholar, 1953 and Silver Medal, 1955, RCA. Designer: BBC Television, 1955–67; Mefistofele, WNO, 1957; Alice in Wonderland, BBC TV Film, 1966; Brief Lives, London and New York, 1967; Country Dance, London and Edinburgh, 1967; Art Director (England), The Charge of the Light Brigade, 1967; Art Director, Laughter in the Dark, 1968; Designer: 40 Years On, 1968; (Production designer) Julius Caesar, 1969; The Merchant of Venice, National Theatre, 1970; Eugene Onegin, Covent Garden, 1971; The Straw Dogs (film), 1971; Othello, Stratford, 1971; Samuel Pepys Exhibn, Nat. Portrait Gall., 1971; Getting On, Queen's, 1971; Othello, RSC, Aldwych, 1972; Un Ballo in Maschera, Hamburgische Staatsoper, 1973; La Bohème, Covent Garden, 1974; The Importance of Being Earnest, Burgtheater, Vienna, 1976; Die Fledermaus, Covent Garden, 1977; Mme Tussaud's hist. tableaux, 1979; Danish TV, 1979; Hay Fever and The Wild Duck, Lyric, Hammersmith, 1980; The Shoemakers' Holiday, Nat. Theatre, 1981; The Bear's Quest for Ragged Staff, Warwick, 1981; Die Csardasfürstin, Kassel, 1982; Separate Tables, 1982; Otello, Stockholm, 1983; Arabella, Glyndebourne, 1984, 1985, 1989; The Consul, Connecticut Grand Opera, USA, 1985; Mr and Mrs Nobody, Garrick, 1986; A Man for All Seasons, Chichester and Savoy, 1987. The Best of Friends, Apollo, 1988; *ballet:* Enigma Variations, 1968; A Month in the Country, 1976; Sospiri, 1980; Swan Lake, 1981; The Nutcracker, 1984. Mem., DES Vis. Cttee for RCA, 1981–85. DesRCA (1st class), 1955; FCSD. Hon. DLitt Bristol, 1987. Designer of the Year Award for Alice in Wonderland, 1967; Award for Cable Excellence, for Best Art Direction, NCTA, 1983. *Publications:* Street Children (photographs by Julia Trevelyan Oman; text by B. S. Johnson), 1964; (with Roy Strong) Elizabeth R, 1971; (with Roy Strong) Mary Queen of Scots, 1972; introd. The Merchant of Venice, Folio Soc. edn, 1975; (with Roy Strong) The English Year, 1982; contrib. Architectural Review (photographs), Vogue (text and photographs). *Address:* c/o Oman Productions ltd, The Laskett, Much Birch, Hereford HR2 8HZ.

OMAND, David Bruce; Assistant Under Secretary of State (Management Strategy), Ministry of Defence, since 1988; *b* 15 April 1947; *s* of late J. Bruce Omand, JP, and of Esther Omand; *m* 1971, Elizabeth, *er d* of late Geoffrey Wales, RE, ARCA; one *s* one *d*. *Educ:* Glasgow Acad.; Corpus Christi Coll., Cambridge (BAEcon). Asst Principal, MoD, 1970; Private Sec. to Chief Exec. (PE), 1973; Asst Private Sec. to Sec. of State, 1973–75, 1979–80; Principal, 1975; Asst Sec., 1981; Private Sec. to Sec. of State, 1981–82; on loan to FCO as Defence Counsellor, UK Delegn to NATO, Brussels, 1985–88. *Recreations:* opera, hill-walking. *Address:* Ministry of Defence, Whitehall, SW1. *Club:* Reform.

OMOLODUN, John Olatunji, (Chief), The Ottun-Balogun of Awe (Oyo State, Nigeria); Director, Department of Asian and Pacific Affairs, Ministry of External Affairs, Lagos, 1981–82; *b* 24 June 1935; *s* of of late Chief Omolodun and Mrs Emmanuel Owolabi Omolodun; *S* father, 1965; *m* 1959, Risikatu Fowoshere; two *s* three *d*. *Educ:* King's Coll., Lagos; Univ. of London (LLB); Council of Legal Educn. Called to the Bar, Lincoln's Inn, 1959. Barrister and Solicitor, Supreme Court of Nigeria, 1960–65; Chm., Tax Appeal Bd, W Reg. Nigeria, 1963–65; Director: Nat. Bank of Nigeria, 1964–65; Wrought Iron Co. of Nigeria, 1964–65; Councillor, Oyo Div. Council, 1964–65; Agent-General for Western Reg. of Nigeria, UK, 1965–66; Actg High Commissioner of Nigeria: Pakistan, 1966–67; Sierra Leone, 1967–70; Chargé d'Affaires, Ivory Coast, 1971–73; Dep. Dir of African Affairs Dept, Min. of Ext. Affairs, Lagos, 1973–75; Actg High Comr, UK, 1976–77; High Comr, India, with concurrent accreditation to Sri Lanka, Burma, Thailand and Bangladesh, 1977. Order of Grand Star of Africa, Liberia, 1971. Sec.-Gen., UN Assoc. of Nigeria, 1960–63; Vice-Pres., World Fedn of UN Assocs, 1963–64. *Publications:* Economic Prospects in Sub-Saharan Africa, 1978; Nigeria, Africa and the World, 1981; pamphlet on overseas students in UK, and paper on International Court of Justice.

Recreations: cricket, golf, cycling, table tennis. *Heir: s* Folarin Owolabi Omolodun, *b* 13 March 1968. *Address:* PO Box 3159, General Post Office, Marina, Lagos, Nigeria. *Clubs:* Royal Over-Seas League (Hon. Mem); Yoruba Tennis, Island (Lagos).

O'MORCHOE, David Nial Creagh, CB 1979; MBE 1967; (The O'Morchoe); Chief of O'Morchoe of Oulartleigh and Monamolin; sheep farmer; *b* 17 May 1928; *s* of Nial Creagh O'Morchoe and Jessie Elizabeth, *d* of late Charles Jasper Joly, FRS, FRIS, MRIA, Astronomer Royal of Ireland; *S* father as Chief of the Name (O'Morchoe), 1970; *m* 1954, Margaret Jane, 3rd *d* of George Francis Brewitt, Cork; two *s* one *d. Educ:* St Columba's Coll., Dublin (Fellow 1983; Chm. of Fellows, 1989); RMA Sandhurst. Commissioned Royal Irish Fusiliers, 1948; served in Egypt, Jordan, Gibraltar, Germany, Kenya, Cyprus, Oman; psc 1958, jssc 1966; CO 1st Bn RIrF, later 3rd Bn Royal Irish Rangers, 1967–68; Directing Staff, Staff Coll., Camberley, 1969–71; RCDS 1972; Brigade Comdr, 1973–75; Brig. GS, BAOR, 1975–76; Maj.-Gen. 1977; Comdr, Sultan of Oman's Land Forces, 1977–79, retired. Dep. Col, 1971–76, Col 1977–79, The Royal Irish Rangers. Mem. Council: Concern, Dublin, 1984– (Sec., 1989–); Irish Grassland and Animal Prodn Assoc., 1985–89. *Recreations:* sailing and an interest in most sports. *Heir: s* Dermot Arthur O'Morchoe, *b* 11 Aug. 1956. *Address:* c/o Ulster Bank, Patrick Street, Cork. *Clubs:* Friendly Brothers (Dublin); Irish Cruising.

O'NEIL, Most Rev. Alexander Henry, MA, DD; *m* 1931, Marguerite (*née* Roe); one *s. Educ:* Univ. of W Ontario; BA 1928, BD 1936, MA 1943; Huron Coll., London, Ont; LTh 1929. Deacon, 1929; Priest, 1930; Principal, Huron Coll., London, Ont, 1941–52; Gen. Sec., British and Foreign Bible Soc. in Canada, 1952–57; Bishop of Fredericton, 1957–63; Archbishop of Fredericton and Metropolitan of the Province of Canada, 1963–71. Hon. DD: Univ. of W Ontario, 1945; Wycliffe Coll., Toronto, 1954; King's Coll., Halifax, 1958; Hon. LLD: W Ontario, 1962; St Thomas Univ., Fredericton, 1970; Hon. DCL Bishop's Univ., Lennoxville, 1964. *Address:* Apt 807 Grosvenor Gates, 1 Grosvenor Street, London, Ont N6A 1Y2, Canada.

O'NEIL, Hon. Sir Desmond (Henry), Kt 1980; Chairman: Western Australia Lotteries Commission, 1981–84; Western Australia Greyhound Racing Association, 1981–84; *b* 27 Sept. 1920; *s* of late Henry McLelland O'Neil and Lilian Francis O'Neil; *m* 1944, Nancy Jean Culver; two *d. Educ:* Aquinas Coll., Perth; Claremont Teachers Coll., WA. Served War, Australian Army, 1939–46: Captain, Aust. Corps of Signals. Educn Dept, WA, 1939–58; Mem., Legislative Assembly, WA, 1959–80; Govt Whip, 1962–65; Minister for Housing and Labour, 1965–71; Dep. Leader of Opposition, 1972–73; Minister for: Works and Housing, 1974–75; Works, Housing and the North-West, 1975–77; Dep. Premier, Chief Sec., Minister for Police and Traffic, Minister for Regional Admin and the NW, Western Australia, 1977–80. Col Comdt, Royal Aust. Corps of Signals 5 Mil. Dist, 1980–82. *Recreations:* power boating, fishing. *Address:* 42 Godwin Avenue, South Como, WA 6152, Australia. *T:* 450–4682. *Club:* South of Perth Yacht.

O'NEIL, Roger; Director and Vice President, Mobil Europe PLC, since 1990; *b* 22 Feb. 1938; *s* of James William O'Neil and Claire Kathryn (*née* Williams); *m* 1976, Joan Mathewson; one *s* one *d. Educ:* Univ. of Notre Dame (BS Chemical Engrg, 1959); Cornell Univ. (MBA 1961). Joined Mobil Corp., New York, 1961; Various staff and exec. positions in Japan, Hong Kong, Australia, Paris, Cyprus, London and New York, 1963–73; Chm., Mobil cos in SE Asia, Singapore, 1973–78; Dir/Vice Pres., Mobil Europe Inc., London, 1978–81; Manager, Corporate Econs and Planning, Mobil Corp., New York, 1981–82; Gp Vice Pres., Container Corp. of America, Chicago, 1982–84; Pres., Mobil Oil Italiana SpA, Rome, 1984–87; Chm. and Chief Exec., Mobil Oil Co., London, 1987–90. Vice-President: President's Council, Asia Soc., NY, 1982–; Inst. of Petroleum, 1989–; Adv. Bd, Johnson Business Sch., Cornell Univ., 1990–. *Recreations:* archæology, ski-ing, tennis. *Address:* 3 Ormonde Gate, SW3 4EU. *Clubs:* Royal Automobile, Hurlingham.

O'NEILL, family name of **Barons O'Neill** and **Rathcavan.**

O'NEILL, 4th Baron *cr* 1868; **Raymond Arthur Clanaboy O'Neill,** TD 1970; DL; *b* 1 Sept. 1933; *s* of 3rd Baron and Anne Geraldine (she *m* 2nd, 1945, 2nd Viscount Rothermere, and 3rd, 1952, late Ian Fleming, and *d* 1981), *e d* of Hon. Guy Charteris; *S* father, 1944; *m* 1963, Georgina Mary, *er d* of Lord George Montagu Douglas Scott; three *s. Educ:* Eton; Royal Agricultural Coll. 2nd Lieut, 11th Hussars, Prince Albert's Own; Major, North Irish Horse, AVR; Lt-Col, RARO, Hon. Col D, 1986–; Hon. Col, NI Horse Sqn, RYR and 69 Signal Sqn, NI Horse, Chm., Ulster Countryside Cttee, 1971–75. Vice-Chm., Ulster Folk and Transport Mus., 1987–90 (Trustee, 1969–90); Member: NI Tourist Bd, 1973–80 (Chm., 1975–80); NI Nat. Trust Cttee, 1980–91 (Chm., 1981–91); Museums and Galleries Commn, 1987–; President: NI Assoc. of Youth Clubs, 1965–; Royal Ulster Agricl Soc., 1984–86 (Chm. Finance Cttee, 1974–83). DL Co. Antrim. *Recreations:* vintage motoring, railways, gardening. *Heir: s* Hon. Shane Sebastian Clanaboy O'Neill, *b* 25 July 1965. *Address:* Shanes Castle, Antrim, N Ireland BT41 4NE. *T:* Antrim (08494) 63264. *Clubs:* Turf; Ulster Reform (Belfast).

See also Sir J. A. L. Morgan.

O'NEILL, Alan Albert; Clerk to the Drapers' Company, 1973–80, Member, Court of Assistants, since 1981; *b* 11 Jan. 1916; *o s* of late Albert George O'Neill; *m* 1939, Betty Dolbey (*d* 1986); one *s. Educ:* Sir George Monoux Grammar Sch., Walthamstow. Joined staff Drapers' Co., 1933, Dep. Clerk 1967. Clerk to Governors, Bancroft's School, 1951–73, Governor, 1980–; Governor, Queen Mary Coll., 1973–80. Served War of 1939–45, Royal Navy: Telegraphist, RNV(W)R, 1939; DEMS Gunnery Officer, SS Aquitania and SS Nieuw Amsterdam; Lt-Comdr, RNVR, 1943; DEMS Staff Officer, Aberdeen and NE Coast Scotland, 1945. *Recreation:* gardening. *Address:* Wickenden, 36 Main Road, Sundridge, Sevenoaks, Kent TN14 6EP. *T:* Westerham (0959) 63530.

O'NEILL, Hon. Hugh (Detmar Torrens); Founder Director, Lamont Holdings; Chairman: Northern Ireland Airports, since 1986; Northern Ireland Tourist Board, since 1988; *b* 14 June 1939; *o s* and *heir* of Baron Rathcavan, *qv*; *m* 1983, Sylvie Marie-Thérèse Wichard; one *s. Educ:* Eton. Captain, Irish Guards. Financial journalism, Observer, Irish Times, FT; Dep. Chm., IPEC Europe, 1978–82; Chm., FRX Internat., 1988–; Director: St Quentin, 1980–; The Spectator; 1982–84; Old Bushmills Distillery Co., 1988–; Savoy Management, 1989–. *Recreations:* food, travel. *Address:* Cleggan Lodge, Ballymena, Co. Antrim BT43 7JW; 14 Thurloe Place, SW7 2RZ. *Clubs:* Beefsteak, Garrick.

O'NEILL, Martin (John); MP (Lab) Clackmannan, since 1983 (Stirlingshire, East and Clackmannan, 1979–83); *b* 6 Jan. 1945; *s* of John and Minnie O'Neill; *m* 1973, Elaine Marjorie Samuel; two *s. Educ:* Trinity Academy, Edinburgh; Heriot Watt Univ. (BA Econ.); Moray House Coll. of Education, Edinburgh. Insurance Clerk, Scottish Widows Fund, 1963–67; Asst Examiner, Estate Duty Office of Scotland, 1971–73; Teacher of Modern Studies, Boroughmuir High School, Edinburgh, 1974–77; Social Science Tutor, Craigmount High School, Edinburgh, 1977–79; Open Univ., 1976–79. Opposition spokesman on Scottish affairs, 1980–84, on defence matters, 1984–88; Chief opposition spokesman on defence, 1988–. Mem., Select Cttee, Scottish Affairs, 1979–80. Member: GMB; MATSA; EIS. *Recreations:* watching football, reading, listening to jazz, the cinema. *Address:* House of Commons, SW1. *T:* 071–219 4548; 19 Mar Street, Alloa, Clackmannanshire FK10 1HR. *T:* Alloa (0259) 721536.

O'NEILL, Prof. Patrick Geoffrey, BA, PhD; Professor of Japanese, School of Oriental and African Studies, University of London, 1968–86, now Emeritus; *b* 9 Aug. 1924; *m* 1951, Diana Howard; one *d. Educ:* Rutlish Sch., Merton; Sch. of Oriental and African Studies, Univ. of London. Lectr in Japanese, Sch. of Oriental and African Studies, Univ. of London, 1949. First Sakura Award, Nihon Zenkoku Gakushikai, 1976. Order of the Rising Sun (Japan), 1987. *Publications:* A Guide to Nō, 1954; Early Nō Drama, 1958; (with S. Yanada) Introduction to Written Japanese, 1963; A Programmed Course on Respect Language in Modern Japanese, 1966; Japanese Kana Workbook 1967; A Programmed Introduction to Literary-style Japanese, 1968; Japanese Names, 1972; Essential Kanji, 1973; (ed) Tradition and Modern Japan, 1982; (with H. Inagaki) A Dictionary of Japanese Buddhist Terms, 1984; A Reader of Handwritten Japanese, 1984; (trans.) Japan on Stage, by T. Kawatake, 1990. *Address:* School of Oriental and African Studies, London University, WC1E 7HP.

O'NEILL, Robert James, CMG 1978; HM Diplomatic Service; Ambassador to Belgium, since 1989; *b* 17 June 1932; *m* 1958, Helen Juniper; one *s* two *d. Educ:* King Edward VI Sch., Chelmsford; Trinity Coll., Cambridge (Schol.). 1st cl. English Tripos Pts I and II. Entered HM Foreign (now Diplomatic) Service, 1955; FO, 1955–57; British Embassy, Ankara, 1957–60; Dakar, 1961–63; FO, 1963–68, Private Sec. to Chancellor of Duchy of Lancaster, 1966, and to Minister of State for Foreign Affairs, 1967–68; British Embassy, Bonn, 1968–72; Counsellor Diplomatic Service, 1972; seconded to Cabinet Office as Asst Sec., 1972–75; FCO, 1975–78; Dep. Governor, Gibraltar, 1978–81; Under Sec., Cabinet Office, 1981–84; Asst Under-Sec. of State, FCO, 1984–86; Ambassador to Austria, and concurrently Head of UK Delegn, MBFR, Vienna, 1986–89. *Recreations:* diplomatic history, hill-walking. *Address:* c/o Foreign and Commonwealth Office, SW1A 2AH. *T:* Brussels 217.9000. *Club:* Travellers'.

O'NEILL, Prof. Robert John, AO 1988; FASSA; FIE (Aust); FRHistS; Chichele Professor of the History of War, University of Oxford, since 1987; Fellow, All Souls College, Oxford, since 1987; Director of Graduate Studies, Modern History Faculty, Oxford, since 1990; *b* 5 Nov. 1936; *s* of Joseph Henry and Janet Gibbon O'Neill; *m* 1965, Sally Margaret Burnard; two *d. Educ:* Scotch Coll., Melbourne; Royal Military Coll. of Australia; Univ. of Melbourne (BE); Brasenose Coll., Oxford (MA, DPhil 1965; Hon. Fellow, 1990). FASSA 1978; FIE(Aust) 1981; FRHistS 1990. Served Australian Army, 1955–68; Rhodes Scholar, Vic, 1961; Fifth Bn Royal Australian Regt, Vietnam, 1966–67 (mentioned in despatches); Major 1967; resigned 1968. Sen. Lectr in History, Royal Military Coll. of Australia, 1968–69; Australian National University: Sen. Fellow in Internat. Relations, 1969–77, Professorial Fellow, 1977–82; Head, Strategic and Defence Studies Centre, 1971–82; Dir, IISS, 1982–87. Official Australian Historian for the Korean War, 1969–82. Member: Council, IISS, 1977–82; Exec. Cttee, British Internat. Studies Assoc., 1983–88; Commonwealth Sec.-Gen.'s Adv Gp on Small State Security, 1984–85. Chairman: Management Cttee, Sir Robert Menzies Centre for Australian Studies, Univ. of London, 1990–; Bd, Centre for Defence Studies, KCL, 1990–. Governor: Ditchley Foundn, 1989–; Internat. Peace Acad., 1990–; Trustee: Imperial War Museum, 1990–; Commonwealth War Graves Commn, 1991–. Chm., Round Table Moot, 1986–. *Publications:* The German Army and the Nazi Party 1933–1939, 1966; Vietnam Task, 1968; General Giap: politician and strategist, 1969; (ed) The Strategic Nuclear Balance, 1975; (ed) The Defence of Australia: fundamental new aspects, 1977; (ed) Insecurity: the spread of weapons in the Indian and Pacific Oceans, 1978; (ed jtly) Australian Dictionary of Biography, Vols 7–12, 1891–1939, 1979–91; (ed with David Horner) New Directions in Strategic Thinking, 1981; Australia in the Korean War 1950–1953, Vol. 1, Strategy and Diplomacy, 1981, Vol. II, Combat Operations, 1985; (ed with David Horner) Australian Defence Policy for the 1980s, 1982; (ed) Security in East Asia, 1984; (ed) The Conduct of East-West Relations in the 1980s, 1985; (ed) New Technology and Western Security Policy, 1985; (ed) Doctrine, the Alliance and Arms Control, 1986; (ed) East Asia, the West and International Security, 1987; (ed) Security in the Mediterranean, 1989; (ed with R. J. Vincent) The West and the Third World, 1990; articles in many learned jls. *Recreations:* local history, walking. *Address:* All Souls College, Oxford OX1 4AL. *Club:* Garrick.

O'NEILL, Thomas P(hilip), Jr; Speaker, House of Representatives, USA, 1976–86; *b* Cambridge, Mass, 9 Dec. 1912; *s* of Thomas P. O'Neill and Rose Anne (*née* Tolan); *m* 1941, Mildred Anne Miller; three *s* two *d. Educ:* St John's High Sch.; Boston Coll., Mass. Grad. 1936. In business, insurance, in Cambridge, Mass. Mem., State Legislature, Mass, 1936–52: Minority Leader, 1947 and 1948; Speaker of the House, 1948–52. Member, Camb. Sch. Cttee, 1946, 1949. Member of Congresses: 83rd-87th, 11th Dist, Mass; 88th-99th, 8th Dist, Mass. Democrat: Majority Whip, 1971–73, Majority Leader, 1973–77. *Address:* 1310 19th Street NW, Washington, DC 20036–1602, USA.

ONGLEY, Sir Joseph (Augustine), Kt 1987; Judge of the High Court of New Zealand, 1975–86; *b* 1918; *s* of Arthur Montague Ongley, OBE and Nora Crina Ongley; *m* 1943, Joan Muriel Archer; four *s* one *d. Educ:* St Patrick's Coll., Silverstream; Victoria Univ. of Wellington (LLB). Admitted Barrister and Solicitor of Supreme, now High, Court of NZ, 1939; Crown Solicitor, Palmerston North, 1960–75; retired, 1986, now serving in temp. capacity. Former Pres., NZ Cricket Council. *Recreations:* formerly cricket (represented NZ), golf. *Address:* 48 Atotara Crescent, Lower Hutt, New Zealand. *T:* Wellington 664–501. *Clubs:* Wellington; Manawatu (Palmerston North).

O'NIONS, Prof. Robert Keith, PhD; FRS 1983; Royal Society Research Professor, Cambridge University, since 1979; Official Fellow, Clare Hall, Cambridge, since 1980; *b* 26 Sept. 1944; *s* of William Henry O'Nions and Eva O'Nions; *m* 1967, Rita Margaret Bill; three *d. Educ:* Univ. of Nottingham (BSc 1966); Univ. of Alberta (PhD 1969). Post-doctoral Fellow, Oslo Univ., 1970; Demonstr in Petrology, Oxford Univ., 1971–72, Lectr in Geochem., 1972–75; Associate Prof., then Prof., Columbia Univ., NY, 1975–79. Mem., Norwegian Acad. of Sciences, 1980. Macelwane Award, Amer. Geophys. Union, 1979; Bigsby Medal, Geol. Soc. London, 1983. *Publications:* contrib. to jls related to earth and planetary sciences. *Address:* Department of Earth Sciences, Cambridge University, Cambridge CB2 3EQ. *T:* Cambridge (0223) 333400.

ONSLOW, family name of **Earl of Onslow.**

ONSLOW, 7th Earl of, *cr* 1801; **Michael William Coplestone Dillon Onslow,** Bt 1660; Baron Onslow, 1716; Baron Cranley, 1776; Viscount Cranley, 1801; *b* 28 Feb. 1938; *s* of 6th Earl of Onslow, KBE, MC, TD, and of Hon. Pamela Louisa Eleanor Dillon, *o d* of 19th Viscount Dillon, CMG, DSO; *S* father, 1971; *m* 1964, Robin Lindsay, *o d* of Major Robert Lee Bullard III, US Army, and of Lady Aberconway; one *s* two *d. Educ:* Eton; Sorbonne. Life Guards, 1956–60, served Arabian Peninsula. Farmer; director, various cos. Governor, Royal Grammar Sch., Guildford; formerly Governor, University Coll. at Buckingham. Mem., Univ. of Surrey Res. Park Exec. High Steward of Guildford. *Heir: s* Viscount Cranley, *qv. Address:* Temple Court, Clandon Park, Guildford, Surrey. *Clubs:* White's, Beefsteak.

See also A. A. Waugh.

ONSLOW, Rt. Hon. Cranley (Gordon Douglas), PC 1988; MP (C) Woking since 1964; *b* 8 June 1926; *s* of late F. R. D. Onslow and Mrs M. Onslow, Effingham House, Bexhill; *m* 1955, Lady June Hay, *yr d* of 13th Earl of Kinnoull; one *s* three *d*. *Educ:* Harrow; Oriel Coll., Oxford; Geneva Univ. Served in RAC, Lieut 7th QO Hussars, 1944–48, and 3rd/4th Co. of London Yeo. (Sharpshooters) (TA) as Captain, 1948–52. Joined HM Foreign Service, 1951; Third Sec. Br. Embassy, Rangoon, 1953–55; Consul at Maymyo, N Burma, 1955–56; resigned, 1960. Served on Dartford RDC, 1960–62, and Kent CC, 1961–64. Parly Under-Sec. of State, Aerospace and Shipping, DTI, 1972–74; an Opposition spokesman on health and social security, 1974–75, on defence, 1975–76; Minister of State, FCO, 1982–83. Chairman: Select Cttee on Defence, 1981–82; Cons. Aviation Cttee, 1970–72, 1979–82. Mem. Exec., 1922 Cttee, 1968–72, 1981–82, 1983–, Chm., 1984–. Mem., UK delegn to Council of Europe and WEU, 1977–81. Director: Argyll Group PLC, 1983–; Redifon Ltd (formerly Rediffusion), 1985– (Chm., 1988–). Chm., Nautical Museums Trust, 1983–. Council Member: Nat. Rifle Assoc.; Salmon & Trout Assoc.; Anglers' Co-operative Assoc.; British Field Sports Soc. Mem. Council, St John's Sch., Leatherhead. MRAeS. Liveryman, Fishmongers' Co., 1991–. *Publication:* Asian Economic Development (ed), 1965. *Recreations:* fishing, shooting, watching cricket. *Address:* Highbuilding, Fernhurst, W Sussex. *Club:* English-Speaking Union.

ONSLOW, Sir John (Roger Wilmot), 8th Bt, *cr* 1797; Captain, Royal Yacht of Saudi Arabia; *b* 21 July 1932; *o s* of Sir Richard Wilmot Onslow, 7th Bt, TD, and Constance (*d* 1960), *o d* of Albert Parker; *S* father, 1963; *m* 1955, Catherine Zoia (marr. diss. 1973), *d* of Henry Atherton Greenway, The Manor, Compton Abdale, near Cheltenham, Gloucestershire; one *s* one *d*; *m* 1976, Susan Fay, *d* of E. M. Hughes, Frankston, Vic, Australia. *Educ:* Cheltenham College. *Heir: s* Richard Paul Atherton Onslow, *b* 16 Sept. 1958. *Address:* c/o Barclays Bank, Fowey, Cornwall.

ONTARIO, Metropolitan of; *see* Niagara, Archbishop of.

ONTARIO, Bishop of, since 1981; **Rt. Rev. Allan Alexander Read;** *b* 19 Sept. 1923; *s* of Alex P. Read and Lillice M. Matthews; *m* 1949, Mary Beverly Roberts; two *s* two *d*. *Educ:* Trinity Coll., Univ. of Toronto (BA, LTh). Incumbent, Mono East and Mono West, 1947–54; Rector, Trinity Church, Barrie, 1954–71; Canon of St James Cathedral, Toronto, 1957; Archdeacon of Simcoe, 1961–72; Bishop Suffragan of Toronto, 1972–81. Hon. DD: Trinity Coll., Toronto, 1972; Wycliffe Coll., Toronto, 1972; Hon. STD Thornloe Coll., Sudbury, 1982. Citizen of the Year, Barrie, 1969; Honorary Reeve, Black Creek, Toronto, 1980. *Publication:* Shepherds in Green Pastures, 1952. *Recreation:* organ music. *Address:* 90 Johnston Street, Kingston, Ont. K7L 1X7, Canada.

OPENSHAW, (Charles) Peter (Lawford); QC 1991; *b* 21 Dec. 1947; *s* of late Judge William Harrison Openshaw and Elisabeth Joyce Emily Openshaw; *m* 1979, Caroline Jane Swift; one *s* one *d*. *Educ:* Harrow; St Catharine's College, Cambridge (MA). Called to the Bar, Inner Temple, 1970; practising on Northern Circuit, Junior 1973; Assistant Recorder, 1985; Recorder, 1988. *Recreations:* fishing, gardening, village life. *Address:* 2 Old Bank Street, Manchester. *T:* 061–832 3791. *Club:* United Oxford & Cambridge University.

OPIE, Alan John; Principal Baritone with English National Opera, since 1973; *b* 22 March 1945; *s* of Jack and Doris Winifred Opie; *m* 1970, Kathleen Ann Smales; one *s* one *d*. *Educ:* Truro Sch.; Guildhall Sch. of Music (AGSM); London Opera Centre. Principal rôles include: Papageno in The Magic Flute, Sadler's Wells Opera, 1969; Tony in the Globolinks, Santa Fé Opera, 1970; Officer in the Barber of Seville, Covent Garden, 1971; Don Giovanni, Kent Opera, and Demetrius, English Opera Gp, 1972; *English National Opera:* Figaro; Papageno; Gugliemo; Beckmesser; Valentin; Lescaut in Manon; Eisenstein and Falke in Die Fledermaus; Danilo; Silvio; Junius in Rape of Lucretia; Cecil in Gloriana; Faninal in Der Rosenkavalier; Germont in La Traviata; Marcello and Schaunard in La Bohème; Kovalyov in The Nose; Strephon in Iolanthe; Grosvenor in Patience; Tomsky in Queen of Spades; Paolo in Simon Boccanegra; Harlequin in Ariadne auf Naxos; Dr Faust by Busoni; Sharpless in Madame Butterfly; *Royal Opera, Covent Garden:* Hector in King Priam, 1985; Ping in Turandot, 1986; Mangus in The Knot Garden, 1988; Falke in Die Fledermaus, 1989; Paolo in Simon Boccanegra; *Glyndebourne Festival Opera:* Sid in Albert Herring, 1985, 1990; rôles in Death in Venice, 1989; Figaro in Le Nozze di Figaro, 1991; *Scottish Opera:* Baron in La Vie Parisienne, 1985; Storch in Intermezzo, 1986; Forester in Cunning Little Vixen, 1991; has also appeared at Bayreuth Fest., Berlin (Unter den Linden, Berlin Staatsoper, 1990) and in Amsterdam (rôles include Beckmesser), and at Buxton Fest. and in Brussels, Chicago, Vienna and Paris. *Address:* Quanda, Old Court, Ashtead, Surrey KT21 2TS. *T:* Ashtead (0372) 274038.

OPIE, Geoffrey James; freelance lecturer on 19th and 20th century art and design; *b* 10 July 1939; *s* of Basil Irwin Opie and Florence Mabel Opie (*née* May); *m* 1st, 1964, Pamela Green; one *s* one *d*; 2nd, 1980, Jennifer Hawkins; one *s*. *Educ:* Humphry Davy Grammar School, Penzance; Falmouth Sch. of Art (NDD); Goldsmiths' Coll., London (ATC). Asst Designer, Leacock & Co., 1961; Curator, Nat. Mus. of Antiquities of Scotland, 1963; Designer, Leacock & Co., 1967; Curator, Victoria and Albert Mus., 1969, Educn Dept, 1978–89, Head of Educn Services, 1983–89. *Publications:* The Wireless Cabinet 1930–1956, 1979; contribs to various jls. *Recreations:* painting, literature, music, motorcycling. *Address:* 130 Kingston Road, Teddington, Middx TW11 9JA.

OPIE, Iona Margaret Balfour; folklorist; *b* 13 Oct. 1923; *d* of late Sir Robert Archibald, CMG, DSO, MD, and of Olive Cant; *m* 1943, Peter Mason Opie (*d* 1982); two *s* one *d*. *Educ:* Sandecotes Sch., Parkstone. Served 1941–43, WAAF meteorological section. Hon. Mem., Folklore Soc., 1974. Coote-Lake Medal (jtly with husband), 1960. Hon. MA: Oxon, 1962; OU, 1987; Hon. DLitt Southampton. *Publications:* (all with Peter Opie): I Saw Esau, 1947; The Oxford Dictionary of Nursery Rhymes, 1951; The Oxford Nursery Rhyme Book, 1955; Christmas Party Games, 1957; The Lore and Language of Schoolchildren, 1959; Puffin Book of Nursery Rhymes, 1963 (European Prize City of Caorle); Children's Games in Street and Playground, 1969 (Chicago Folklore Prize); The Oxford Book of Children's Verse, 1973; Three Centuries of Nursery Rhymes and Poetry for Children (exhibition catalogue), 1973, enl. edn 1977; The Classic Fairy Tales, 1974; A Nursery Companion, 1980; The Oxford Book of Narrative Verse, 1983; The Singing Game, 1985 (Katharine Briggs Folklore Award; Rose Mary Crawshay Prize; Children's Literature Assoc. Book Award); Tail Feathers from Mother Goose, 1988; (ed jtly) The Treasures of Childhood, 1989; A Dictionary of Superstitions, 1989; Babies: an unsentimental anthology (from notes assembled with Peter Opie), 1990. *Recreation:* opsimathy. *Address:* Westerfield House, West Liss, Hants GU33 6JQ. *T:* Liss (0730) 893309.

OPIE, Roger Gilbert, CBE 1976; Fellow and Lecturer in Economics, New College, Oxford, since 1961; *b* Adelaide, SA, 23 Feb. 1927; *o s* of late Frank Gilbert Opie and late Fanny Irene Grace Opie (*née* Tregoning); *m* 1955, Norma Mary, *o d* of late Norman and late Mary Canter; two *s* one *d*. *Educ:* Prince Alfred Coll. and Adelaide Univ., SA; Christ Church and Nuffield Coll., Oxford. BA 1st Cl. Hons 1948, MA Adelaide 1950; SA Rhodes Schol., 1951; Boulter Exhibnr, 1952; George Webb Medley Jun. Schol., 1952, Sen. Schol., 1953; PPE 1st Cl. 1953; Nuffield Coll. Studentship, 1954; BPhil 1954. Tutor and Lectr, Adelaide Univ., 1949–51; Asst Lectr and Lectr, LSE, 1954–61; Econ. Adviser, Econ. Section, HM Treasury, 1958–60; Asst Dir, HM Treasury Centre for Administrative Studies, 1964; Asst Dir, Planning Div., Dept of Economic Affairs, 1964–66; Advr, W. Pakistan Planning Commn, 1966; Economic Adviser to Chm., NBPI, 1967–70; Special Univ. Lectr in Econs, Oxford, 1970–75; Tutor and Sen. Tutor, Oxford Univ. Business Summer Sch., 1974–79. Visiting Professor: Brunel Univ., 1975–77; Univ. of Strathclyde, 1984–87. Member: Monopolies and Mergers Commn, 1968–81; Price Commn, 1977–80. Mem., ILO Mission to Ethiopia, 1982. City Councillor, Oxford, 1972–74; Oxford Dist Councillor, 1973–76. Economic Correspondent, New Statesman, 1967–71, 1974–76; Editor: The Bankers' Magazine, 1960–64; International Currency Review, 1970–71. Governor, Bryanston Sch. FRSA 1980. *Publications:* co-author of a number of works in applied economics. *Recreations:* sailing, photography, hiding in Cornwall. *Address:* New College, Oxford OX1 3BN. *T:* Oxford (0865) 279555.

OPPÉ, Prof. Thomas Ernest, CBE 1984; FRCP; Professor of Paediatrics, University of London at St Mary's Hospital Medical School, 1969–90, now Emeritus Professor; *b* 7 Feb. 1925; *s* of late Ernest Frederick Oppé and Ethel Nellie (*née* Rackstraw); *m* 1948, Margaret Mary Butcher; three *s* one *d*. *Educ:* University Coll. Sch., Hampstead; Guy's Hosp. Med. Sch. (MB BS, hons dist. in Medicine, 1947). DCH 1950; FRCP 1966. Sir Alfred Fripp Meml Fellow, Guy's Hosp., 1952; Milton Res. Fellow, Harvard Univ., 1954; Lectr in Child Health, Univ. of Bristol, 1956–60; Consultant Paediatrician, United Bristol Hosps, 1960; Asst Dir, 1960–64, Dir, 1964–69, Paediatric Unit, St Mary's Hosp. Med. Sch.; Consultant Paediatrician, St Mary's Hosp., 1960–90. Consultant Adviser in Paediatrics, DHSS, 1971–86; Member, DHSS Committees: Safety of Medicines, 1974–79; Med. Aspects of Food Policy, 1966–88 (Chm., Panel on Child Nutrition); Child Health Services, 1973–76. Royal College of Physicians: Chm., Cttee on Paediatrics, 1970–74; Pro-Censor and Censor, 1975–77; Sen. Censor and Sen. Vice-Pres., 1983–84; University of London: Mem., Bd of Studies in Medicine, 1964–90 (Chm., 1978–80); elected Mem. of Senate, 1981–89; Dean, Faculty of Medicine, 1984–86; Mem. of Court, 1984–89. Member: BMA (Dep. Chm., Bd of Sci. and Educn, 1974–82); British Paediatric Assoc. (Hon. Sec., 1960–63); European Soc. for Paediatric Res., 1969–; GMC, 1984–88; sometime Mem., Governing Bodies, St Mary's Hosp., Inst. of Med. Ethics, Paddington Coll.; Examiner in Paediatrics, Univs of Glasgow, Leicester, Liverpool, London, Sheffield, Wales, Colombo, Singapore. *Publications:* Modern Textbook of Paediatrics for Nurses, 1961; Neurological Examination of Children (with R. Paine), 1966; chapters in books and papers on paediatrics and child health. *Address:* 2 Parkholme Cottages, Fife Road, Sheen Common, SW14 7ER. *T:* 081–392 1626.

OPPENHEIM, Tan Sri Sir Alexander, Kt 1961; OBE 1955; FRSE; MA, DSc (Oxon); PhD (Chicago); retired; Visiting Professor, University of Benin, Nigeria, 1973–77; Vice-Chancellor, University of Malaya, 1957–65 (Acting Vice-Chancellor, 1955); *b* 4 Feb. 1903; *o s* of late Rev. H. J. and Mrs F. Oppenheim; *m* 1930, Beatrice Templer (marr. diss. 1977), *y d* of Dr Otis B. Nesbit, Indiana, USA; one *d*; and two *s*. *Educ:* Manchester Grammar Sch.; Balliol Coll., Oxford (Scholar). Sen. Mathematical Schol., Oxf., 1926; Commonwealth Fund Fell., Chicago, 1927–30; Lectr, Edinburgh, 1930–31; Prof. of Mathematics, 1931–42, 1945–49; Dep. Principal, 1947, 1949, Raffles Coll., Singapore; Prof. of Mathematics, 1949–57; Dean, Faculty of Arts, 1949, 1951, 1953. Hon. degrees: DSc (Hong Kong) 1961; LLD: (Singapore) 1962; (Leeds) 1966; DLitt (Malaya) 1965. L/Bdr, SRA(V), POW (Singapore, Siam), 1942–45; Dean POW University, 1942; Pres. Malayan Mathematical Soc., 1951–55, 1957. Pres. Singapore Chess Club, 1956–60; Pres., Amer. Univs. Club, 1956. Chm. Bd of Management, Tropical Fish Culture Research Institute (Malacca), 1962; Member: Unesco-International Assoc. of Universities Study of Higher Education in Development of Countries of SE Asia, 1962; Academic Adv. Cttee, Univ. of Cape Coast, 1972. Visiting Professor: Univ. of Reading, in Dept of Mathematics, 1965–68; Univ. of Ghana, 1968–73. Alumni Medal, Univ. of Chicago Alumni Assoc., 1977. Panglima Mangku Negara (Fedn of Malaya), 1962; FWA, 1963. *Publications:* papers on mathematics in various periodicals. *Recreations:* chess, bridge. *Address:* Matson House, Remenham, Henley-on-Thames RG9 3HB. *T:* Henley-on-Thames (0491) 572049. *Clubs:* Royal Over-Seas League; Selangor (Kuala Lumpur).

OPPENHEIM, Sir Duncan (Morris), Kt 1960; Adviser to British-American Tobacco Co. Ltd, 1972–74 (Chairman 1953–66, President, 1966–72); Chairman, Tobacco Securities Trust Co. Ltd, 1969–74; Deputy Chairman, Commonwealth Development Finance Co., 1968–74; *b* 6 Aug. 1904; *s* of Watkin Oppenheim, BA, TD, and Helen, 3rd *d* of Duncan McKechnie; *m* 1st, 1932, Joyce Mary (*d* 1933), *d* of Stanley Mitcheson; no *c*; 2nd, 1936, Susan May (*d* 1964), *e d* of Brig.-Gen. E. B. Macnaghten, CMG, DSO; one *s* one *d*. *Educ:* Repton Sch. Admitted Solicitor of the Supreme Court, 1929; Messrs Linklaters & Paines, London, Assistant Solicitor, 1929–34; joined British-American Tobacco Ltd group as a Solicitor, 1934; Director: British-American Tobacco Co. Ltd, 1943; Lloyds Bank Ltd, 1956–75; Equity and Law Life Assurance Society, 1966–80. Chairman: Council, Royal College of Art, 1956–72; Council of Industrial Design, 1960–72 (Mem. 1959); British Nat. Cttee of Internat. Chamber of Commerce, 1963–74; Overseas Investment Cttee CBI, 1964–74; RIIA (Chatham House), 1966–71; Member: Adv. Council, V&A Mus., 1967–79 (Chm. V&A Associates, 1976–81); Crafts Council (formerly Crafts Adv. Cttee), 1972–83 (acting Chm., 1977; Dep. Chm., 1978); Governing Body of Repton School, 1959–79; Chm. Court of Governors, Admin. Staff Coll., 1963–71. Hon. Dr and Senior Fellow, Royal College of Art; Hon. FCSD (Hon. FSIAD 1972). Bicentenary Medal, RSA, 1969. *Recreations:* painting, sailing. *Address:* 43 Edwardes Square, Kensington, W8 6HH. *T:* 071–603 7431. *Clubs:* Athenæum; Royal Yacht Squadron.

OPPENHEIM, Hon. Phillip Anthony Charles Lawrence; MP (C) Amber Valley, since 1983; *b* 20 March 1956; *s* of late Henry Oppenheim and of Baroness Oppenheim-Barnes, *qv*. *Educ:* Harrow; Oriel College, Oxford. BA Hons. Company director, author. PPS to Sec. of State for Health, 1988–90, to Sec. of State for Educn and Sci., 1990–. Vice Pres., Videotex Industry Assoc., 1985–. Co-editor, What to Buy for Business, 1980–85. *Publications:* A Handbook of New Office Technology, 1982; Telecommunications: a user's handbook, 1983; A Word Processing Handbook, 1984; The New Masters: can the West match Japan?, 1991. *Recreations:* Rugby, tennis, travel, ski-ing, tropical plants. *Address:* House of Commons, SW1A 0AA.

OPPENHEIM-BARNES, Baroness *cr* 1989 (Life Peer), of Gloucester in the county of Gloucestershire; **Sally Oppenheim-Barnes;** PC 1979; non-executive Director and Member of the Main Board, Boots Co. plc, since 1982; *b* 26 July 1930; *d* of Mark and Jeanette Viner; *m* 1st, 1949, Henry M. Oppenheim (*d* 1980); one *s* two *d*; 2nd, 1984, John Barnes. *Educ:* Sheffield High Sch.; Lowther Coll., N Wales. Formerly: Exec. Dir, Industrial & Investment Services Ltd; Social Worker, School Care Dept, ILEA. Trustee, Clergy Rest House Trust. MP (C) Gloucester, 1970–87. Vice Chm., 1971–73, Chm., 1973–74, Cons. Party Parly Prices and Consumer Protection Cttee; Opposition Spokesman on Prices and Consumer Protection, 1974–79; Mem. Shadow Cabinet, 1975–79; Min. of State (Consumer Affairs), Dept of Trade, 1979–82. Chairman: Nat. Consumer Council, 1987–89; Council of Management, Nat. Waterways Museums Trust, 1988–89. Non-exec. Dir, Fleming High Income Trust, 1989–. Nat. Vice-Pres., NUTG, 1973–79 and 1989–90; Pres., Glos Dist Br., BRCS, 1973–. *Recreations:* tennis, bridge. *Address:* Quietways, The Highlands, Painswick, Glos.

See also Hon. P. A. C. L. Oppenheim.

OPPENHEIMER, Harry Frederick; Chairman: Anglo-American Corporation of SA Ltd, 1957–82 (Director, 1934–82); De Beers Consolidated Mines, Ltd, 1957–84 (Director, 1934–85); *b* Kimberley, S Africa, 28 Oct. 1908; *s* of late Sir Ernest Oppenheimer, DCL, LLD; *m* 1943, Bridget, *d* of late Foster McCall; one *s* one *d*. *Educ:* Charterhouse; Christ Church, Oxford (MA; Hon. Student). MP (SA) Kimberley City, 1948–58. Served 4th SA Armoured Car Regt 1940–45. Chancellor, Univ. of Cape Town; Hon. DEcon, Univ. of Natal; Hon. DLaws, Univs of Leeds, Rhodes and Witwatersrand. Instn MM Gold Medal, 1965. *Recreations:* horse breeding and racing. *Address:* Brenthurst, Parktown, Johannesburg, South Africa. *Clubs:* Brooks's; Rand, Inanda (Johannesburg); Kimberley (SA); Harare (Zimbabwe).

OPPENHEIMER, (Lætitia) Helen, (Lady Oppenheimer); writer on moral and philosophical theology; *b* 30 Dec. 1926; *d* of Sir Hugh Lucas-Tooth (later Munro-Lucas-Tooth), 1st Bt; *m* 1947, Sir Michael Oppenheimer, Bt, *qv*; three *d*. *Educ:* Cheltenham Ladies' Coll.; Lady Margaret Hall, Oxford (Schol.; BPhil, MA). Lectr in Ethics, Cuddesdon Theological Coll., 1964–69. Served on: Archbp of Canterbury's Gp on the law of divorce (report, Putting Asunder, 1966); C of E Marriage Commn (report, Marriage, Divorce and the Church, 1971); Wkg Party, ACCM (report, Teaching Christian Ethics, 1974); C of E Wkg Party on Educn in Personal Relationships (Chm.), 1978–82; Inter-Anglican Theol and Doctrinal Commn (report, For the Sake of the Kingdom, 1986); General Synod Wkg Party on the law of marriage (report, An Honourable Estate, 1988). Pres., Soc. for the Study of Christian Ethics, 1989–91. John Coffin Meml Lectr, London Univ., 1977; First Mary Sumner Lectr, Mothers' Union, 1978; preached University Sermon, Oxford, 1979, Cambridge, 1983. *Publications:* Law and Love, 1962; The Character of Christian Morality, 1965, 2nd edn 1974; Incarnation and Immanence, 1973; The Marriage Bond, 1976; The Hope of Happiness: a sketch for a Christian humanism, 1983; Looking Before and After: The Archbishop of Canterbury's Lent Book for 1988; Marriage, 1990; contributor: New Dictionary of Christian Theology, 1983; New Dictionary of Christian Ethics, 1986; articles in Theology, Religious Studies, etc, and in various collections of essays. *Address:* L'Aiguillon, Grouville, Jersey, CI JE3 9AP. *Club:* Victoria (Jersey).

OPPENHEIMER, Sir Michael (Bernard Grenville), 3rd Bt, *cr* 1921; *b* 27 May 1924; *s* of Sir Michael Oppenheimer, 2nd Bt, and Caroline Magdalen (who *m* 2nd, 1935, late Sir Ernest Oppenheimer), *d* of Sir Robert G. Harvey, 2nd Bt; *S* father, 1933; *m* 1947, Laetitia Helen Lucas-Tooth (*see* L. H. Oppenheimer); three *d*. *Educ:* Charterhouse; Christ Church, Oxford (BLitt, MA). Served with South African Artillery, 1942–45. Lecturer in Politics: Lincoln Coll., Oxford, 1955–68; Magdalen Coll., Oxford, 1966–68. *Heir:* none. *Address:* L'Aiguillon, Grouville, Jersey, CI JE3 9AP. *Clubs:* Victoria (Jersey); Kimberley (Kimberley).

OPPENHEIMER, Peter Morris; Student of Christ Church, Oxford, and University Lecturer in Economics, since 1967; on secondment as Chief Economist, Shell International Petroleum Co., 1985–Dec. 1986; *b* 16 April 1938; *s* of Friedrich Rudolf and Charlotte Oppenheimer; *m* 1964, Catherine, *er d* of late Dr Eliot Slater, CBE, FRCP, and Dr Lydia Pasternak; two *s* one *d*. *Educ:* Haberdashers' Aske's Sch.; The Queen's Coll., Oxford (BA 1961). National Service, RN, 1956–58. Bank for International Settlements, Basle, 1961–64; Research Fellow, Nuffield Coll., Oxford, 1964–67; Vis. Prof., London Graduate Sch. of Business Studies, 1976–77; Temp. Econ. Attaché, British Embassy, Moscow, 1991. Director: Panfida plc (formerly Investing in Success Equities Ltd), 1975–; Target Hldgs, 1982–84; J. Rothschild Investment Management, 1982–86; Jewish Chronicle Ltd, 1986–; Delbanco, Meyer and Co. Ltd, 1986–; Dixons Group plc, 1987–. Delegate, OUP, 1987–. Mem., Royal Commn on Legal Services, 1976–79. Mem. Council, Trade Policy Research Centre, 1976–89, and co-Editor, The World Economy, 1977–89; Member: Econ. Adv. Bd, RIIA, 1989–; Editl Bd, International Affairs, 1989–; Exec. Cttee, Inst. of Jewish Affairs, 1991–. Governor: St Edward's Sch., Oxford, 1979–; St Clare's Hall, Oxford, 1985–; Haberdashers' Monmouth Schs, 1987–. Freeman, Haberdashers' Co., 1987. Presenter: (BBC radio): File on 4, 1977–80; Third Opinion, 1983; Poles Apart, 1984; (BBC TV) Outlook, 1982–85; (Granada TV) Under Fire, 1988; (participant) Round Britain Quiz, Radio 4, 1979–. *Publications:* (ed) Issues in International Economics, 1980; contribs to symposia, conference procs, prof. jls, bank reviews, etc. *Recreations:* music, opera, amateur dramatics, swimming, ski-ing. *Address:* 6 Linton Road, Oxford OX2 6UG. *T:* Oxford (0865) 58226.

OPPENHEIMER, Sir Philip (Jack), Kt 1970; Chairman, The Diamond Trading Co. (Pty) Ltd, since 1975; President, CSO Valuations AG, since 1989; *b* 29 Oct. 1911; *s* of Otto and Beatrice Oppenheimer; *m* 1935, Pamela Fenn Stirling; one *s* one *d*. *Educ:* Harrow; Jesus Coll., Cambridge. Director: De Beers Consolidated Mines Ltd; Anglo American Corp. of SA Ltd. Bronze Cross of Holland, 1943; Commandeur, Ordre de Léopold, 1977. *Recreations:* golf, horse-racing and breeding. *Address:* (office) 17 Charterhouse Street, EC1N 6RA. *Clubs:* Jockey, Portland, White's.

OPPERMAN, Hon. Sir Hubert (Ferdinand), Kt 1968; OBE 1952; Australian High Commissioner in Malta, 1967–72; *b* 29 May 1904; Australian; *m* 1928, Mavys Paterson Craig; one *s* (one *d* decd). *Educ:* Armadale, Vic.; Bailieston, Vic. Served RAAF 1940–45; commissioned 1942. Commonwealth Public Service: PMG's Dept, 1918–20; Navigation Dept, Trade and Customs, 1920–22. Cyclist: Australian Road Champion, 1924, 1926, 1927, 1929; Winner French Bol d'Or, 1928, and Paris-Brest-Paris, 1931; holder, numerous world's track and road unpaced and motor paced cycling records. Director, Allied Bruce Small Pty Ltd, 1936–60. MHR for Corio, Vic., 1949–67; Mem. Australian Delegn to CPA Conf., Nairobi, 1954; Chief Govt Whip, 1955–60; Minister for Shipping and Transport, 1960–63; Minister for Immigration, 1963–66. Convenor, Commonwealth Jubilee Sporting Sub-Cttee, 1951; Nat. Patron, Aust. Sportsmen's Assoc., 1980–; Chm. Selection Cttee, Aust. Hall of Sporting Fame, 1985–; Hon. Master of Sport, Confedn of Aust. Sport, 1984. Selected as one of 200 People Who Made Australia Great, Heritage 200, 1988. GCSJ 1980 (KSJ 1973); Bailiff Prior, Victoria, 1980–83; Bailiff, Aust. Grand Council, 1983–. Hon. Rotarian, St Kilda Rotary, 1984. Coronation Medal, 1953; Medals of City of Paris, 1971, Brest, 1971, Verona, 1972; Médaille Mérite, French Cycling Fedn, 1978. *Publication:* Pedals, Politics and People (autobiog.), 1977. *Recreations:* cycling, swimming. *Address:* Unit 52, Salford Park, 100 Harold Street, Wantirna, Vic. 3152, Australia. *T:* 801–4010. *Clubs:* USI, Air Force (Victoria); Naval and Military (Melbourne).

ORAM, family name of **Baron Oram.**

ORAM, Baron *cr* 1975 (Life Peer), of Brighton, E Sussex; **Albert Edward Oram;** *b* 13 Aug. 1913; *s* of Henry and Ada Edith Oram; *m* Frances Joan, *d* of Charles and Dorothy Barber, Lewes; two *s*. *Educ:* Burgess Hill Element. Sch.; Brighton Grammar Sch.; University of London (London School of Economics and Institute of Education). Formerly a teacher. Served War 1942–45; Royal Artillery, Normandy and Belgium. Research Officer, Co-operative Party, 1946–55. MP (Lab and Co-op) East Ham South, 1955–Feb. 1974; Parly Secretary, ODM, 1964–69; a Lord in Waiting (Govt Whip), 1976–78. Chm., Co-op. Develt Agency, 1978–81. Co-ordinator, Develt Programmes, Internat. Co-operative Alliance, 1971–73; Develt Administrator, Intermediate Technol. Develt Gp. Mem., Commonwealth Develt Corp., 1975–76. *Publication:* (with Nora Stettner) Changes in China, 1987. *Recreations:* country walking, cricket, chess. *Address:* 19 Ridgeside Avenue, Patcham, Brighton BN1 8WD. *T:* Brighton (0273) 505333.

ORAM, Rt. Rev. Kenneth Cyril; Assistant Bishop, Diocese of Lichfield, since 1987; *b* 3 March 1919; *s* of Alfred Charles Oram and Sophie Oram; *m* 1943, Kathleen Mary Malcolm; three *s* one *d*. *Educ:* Selhurst Grammar Sch., Croydon; King's Coll., London; Lincoln Theol Coll. BA Hons English, 1st Cl. AKC. Asst Curate: St Dunstan's, Cranbrook, 1942–45; St Mildred's, Croydon, 1945–46; Upington with Prieska, S Africa, 1946–48; Rector of Prieska and Dir of Prieska Mission District, 1949–51; Rector of Mafeking, 1952–59; Dir of Educn, dio. Kimberley and Kuruman, 1953–62; Archdeacon of Bechuanaland, 1953–59; Dean and Archdeacon: of Kimberley, 1960–64; of Grahamstown, 1964–74; Bishop of Grahamstown, 1974–87. *Address:* 10 Sandringham Road, Baswich, Stafford ST17 0AA. *T:* Stafford (0785) 53974.

ORAM, Samuel, MD (London); FRCP; Consultant Cardiologist and Emeritus Lecturer; former Senior Physician, and Director, Cardiac Department, King's College Hospital; Censor, Royal College of Physicians; Medical Adviser, Rio Tinto Zinc Corporation Ltd; *b* 11 July 1913; *s* of Samuel Henry Nathan Oram, London; *m* 1940, Ivy, *d* of Raffaele Amato; two *d*. *Educ:* King's College, London; King's College Hospital, London. Senior Scholar, KCH, London; Sambrooke Medical Registrar, KCH. Served War of 1939–45, as Lt-Col, RAMC. Examiner in Medicine for RCP and Univs of Cambridge and London; Examiner: in Pharmacology and Materia Medica, The Conjoint Bd; in Medicine, The Worshipful Soc. of Apothecaries. Member: Assoc. of Physicians; Br. Cardiac Society; American Heart Assoc.; Corresp. Member Australasian Cardiac Soc. Gold Medal, RCP. *Publications:* Clinical Heart Disease (textbook), 1971, 2nd edn 1981; various cardiological and medical articles in Quart. Jl Med., British Heart Jl, BMJ, Brit. Encyclopaedia of Medical Practice, The Practitioner, etc. *Recreation:* golf (execrable). *Address:* 73 Harley Street, W1. *T:* 071–935 9942.

ORANMORE and BROWNE, 4th Baron (Ireland), *cr* 1836; Baron Mereworth of Mereworth Castle (UK), *cr* 1926; **Dominick Geoffrey Edward Browne;** *b* 21 Oct. 1901; *e s* of 3rd Baron and Lady Olwen Verena Ponsonby (*d* 1927), *e d* of 8th Earl of Bessborough; *S* father, 1927; *m* 1st, 1925, Mildred Helen (who obtained a divorce, 1936; she *d* 1980), *e d* of Hon. Thomas Egerton; two *s* one *d* (and two *d* decd); 2nd, 1936, Oonagh (marr. diss., 1950), *d* of late Hon. Ernest Guinness; one *s* (and two *s* decd); 3rd, 1951, Sally Gray, 5b Mount Street, London, W. *Educ:* Eton; Christ Church, Oxford. *Heir: s* Hon. Dominick Geoffrey Thomas Browne [*b* 1 July 1929; *m* 1957, Sara Margaret (marr. diss. 1974), *d* of late Dr Herbert Wright, 59 Merrion Square, Dublin, and late Mrs C. A. West, Cross-in-Hand, Sussex]. *Address:* 52 Eaton Place, SW1X 8AL.

ORCHARD, Edward Eric, CBE 1966 (OBE 1959); *b* 12 Nov. 1920. *Educ:* King's Sch., Grantham; Jesus Coll., Oxford (MA). War Service, 1941–46; FO and HM Embassy, Moscow, 1948–51; Lectr in Russian, Oxford, 1951–52; HM Embassy Moscow and FCO, 1953–76 (Dir of Research, 1970–76). Mem., Waverley Borough Council, 1978–87; Mayor, Haslemere, 1987. *Publications:* articles and reviews. *Recreations:* swimming, gardening, local government and welfare. *Address:* Sturt Meadow House, Haslemere, Surrey GU27 3RT. *T:* Haslemere (0428) 643034.

ORCHARD, Peter Francis, CBE 1982; Chairman, The De La Rue Co. plc, since 1987 (Director, since 1963; Chief Executive, 1977–87); *b* 25 March 1927; *s* of Edward Henslowe Orchard and Agnes Marjory Willett; *m* 1955, Helen Sheridan; two *s* two *d*. *Educ:* Downside Sch., Bath; Magdalene Coll., Cambridge (MA). CBIM. Service, KRRC, 1944–48. Joined Thomas De La Rue & Co. Ltd, 1950; Managing Director: Thomas De La Rue (Brazil), 1959–61; Thomas De La Rue International, 1962–70. Dir, Delta plc, 1981–. Mem., Court of Assistants, Drapers' Co., 1974–, Master 1982. Hon. Col 71st (Yeomanry) Signal Regt, TA, 1984–88. *Recreations:* gardening, swimming, building, cricket. *Address:* Willow Cottage, Little Hallingbury, Bishop's Stortford, Herts CM22 7PX. *T:* Bishop's Stortford (0279) 654101. *Clubs:* Travellers', MCC.

ORCHARD, Stephen Michael; Chief Executive, Legal Aid Board, since 1989; *b* 5 Aug. 1944; *s* of Stephen Henry Orchard and Ellen Frances Orchard; one *s* one *d*. *Educ:* Swanage Grammar School. Lord Chancellor's Dept, 1961–89. *Recreations:* walking, food and wine. *Address:* Legal Aid Board, 5th and 6th Floors, 29/37 Red Lion Street, WC1R 4PP. *T:* 071–831 4209.

ORCHARD-LISLE, Brig. Paul David, CBE 1988; TD 1961; DL; Senior Partner, Healey & Baker, since 1988; *b* 3 Aug. 1938; *s* of Mervyn and Phyllis Orchard-Lisle. *Educ:* Marlborough College; Trinity Hall, Cambridge (MA). FRICS. Nat. Service, RA, 1956–58. Joined Healey & Baker, 1961. RA (TA), 1958–88; ADC (TA), 1985–87; Brig. (TA), UKLF, 1985; Chm., TAVRA Greater London, 1988–91. Pres., RICS, 1986–87. Hon. Fellow, Coll. of Estate Management, 1985–. Mem. Council, Marlborough Coll., 1991–; Governor: West Buckland Sch., 1986–; Harrow Sch., 1988–. DL Gtr London, 1987. *Recreations:* golf, squash. *Address:* Bedford House, Bidwell, Houghton Regis, Beds LU5 6JP. *T:* Dunstable (0582) 867317. *Club:* Athenæum.

ORD, Andrew James B.; *see* Blackett-Ord.

ORDE, Alan C. C.; *see* Campbell Orde.

ORDE, Denis Alan; His Honour Judge Orde; a Circuit Judge, since 1979; *b* 28 Aug. 1932; *s* of John Orde, CBE, Littlehoughton Hall, Northumberland, and late Charlotte Lilian Orde, County Alderman; *m* 1961, Jennifer Jane, *d* of late Dr John Longworth, Masham, Yorks; two *d*. *Educ:* Oxford Univ. (MA). Served Army, 1950–52, 2nd Lieut 1951; TA, 1952–64 (RA). Pres., Oxford Univ. Conserv. Assoc., 1954; Mem. Cttee, Oxford Union, 1954–55; Vice-Chm., Fedn of Univ. Conserv. Assocs., 1955. Called to Bar, Inner Temple, 1956; Pupil Studentship, 1956; Profumo Prize, 1959. North-Eastern Circuit, 1958. Asst Recorder: Kingston upon Hull, 1970; Sheffield, 1970–71; a Recorder of the Crown Court, 1972–79. Contested (C): Consett, Gen. Elec. 1959, Newcastle upon Tyne West, Gen. Elec. 1966, Sunderland South, Gen. Elec. 1970. *Recreations:* listening to music; cricket, golf, painting. *Address:* Chollerton Grange, Chollerton, near Hexham, Northumberland NE46 4TF; 11 King's Bench Walk, Temple, EC4. *Clubs:* Carlton, Coningsby, United and Cecil; Northern Counties (Newcastle).

ORDE, Sir John (Alexander) Campbell-, 6th Bt *cr* 1790, of Morpeth; *b* 11 May 1943; *s* of Sir Simon Arthur Campbell-Orde, 5th Bt, TD, and of Eleanor, *e d* of Col Humphrey Watts, OBE, TD, Haslington Hall, Cheshire; *S* father, 1969; *m* 1973, Lacy Ralls, *d* of Grady Gallant, Nashville, USA; one *s* three *d*. *Educ:* Gordonstoun. *Heir: s* John Simon Arthur Campbell-Orde, *b* 15 Aug. 1981. *Address:* Bee's Wing Farm, Route 2, Box 380, Kingston Road, Fairview, Tenn 37062, USA. *Clubs:* Caledonian, Lansdowne.

ORDE-POWLETT, family name of **Baron Bolton.**

O'REGAN, Hon. Sir (John) Barry; Kt 1984; Judge of the Court of Appeal, Cook Islands, since 1986; *b* 2 Dec. 1915; *s* of John O'Regan; *m* Catherine, *d* of John O'Donnell; four *s* one *d*. *Educ:* Sacred Heart College, Auckland; Victoria University, Wellington (LLB). Army service, 1941–45 (Captain). Partner, Bell O'Regan & Co., 1945–73; Judge of High Court, NZ, 1973–84; Judge of Ct of Appeal, Fiji, 1983–87. Chairman: Prisons Parole Bd, 1977–83; War Pensions Appeal Bd, 1984–90. Member: Council, Wellington Law Soc., 1959–69 (Pres., 1968); Council, NZ Law Soc., 1967–69; Council of Legal Education, 1969–73; Legal Aid Board, 1970–73. Consul-Gen. for Ireland, 1965–73. *Address:* Apt A/4 Lincoln Courts, 1 Washington Avenue, Wellington 2, New Zealand.

O'REILLY, Dr Anthony John Francis, (Dr Tony O'Reilly); Chairman, since 1987, President and Chief Executive Officer, since 1979, H. J. Heinz Co. Inc.; *b* Dublin, 7 May 1936; *o c* of J. P. O'Reilly, former Inspector-General of Customs; *m* 1962, Susan, *d* of Keith Cameron, Australia; three *s* three *d* (of whom two *s* one *d* are triplets). *Educ:* Belvedere Coll., Dublin; University Coll., Dublin (BCL 1958); Bradford Univ. (PhD 1980). Admitted Solicitor, 1958. Industrial Consultant, Weston Evans UK, 1958–60; PA to Chm., Suttons Ltd, Cork, 1960–62; Chief Exec. Officer, Irish Dairy Bd, 1962–66; Man. Dir, Irish Sugar Bd, 1966–69; Man. Dir, Erin Foods Ltd, 1966–69; Jt Man. Dir, Heinz-Erin, 1967–70; Man. Dir, H. J. Heinz Co. Ltd, UK, 1969–71; Sen. Vice-Pres., N America and Pacific, H. J. Heinz Co., 1971–72; Exec. Vice-Pres. and Chief Op. Off., 1972–73, Pres. and Chief Operating Officer, 1973–79, H. J. Heinz Co. Lectr in Business Management, UC Cork, 1960–62. Director: Robt McCowen & Sons Ltd, 1961–62; Agricl Credit Corp. Ltd, 1965–66; Nitrigin Eireann Teoranta, 1965–66; Allied Irish Investment Bank Ltd, 1968–71; Thyssen-Bornemisza Co., 1970–72; Independent Newspapers (Vice Chm., 1973–80; Chm., 1980–); Nat. Mine Service Co., 1973–76; Mobil, 1979–; Bankers Trust Co., 1980–; Allegheny Internat. Inc., 1982–; GEC, 1990–; Chairman: Fitzwilliam Securities Ltd, 1971–77; Fitzwilton Ltd, 1978– (Dep. Chm., 1972–78); Atlantic Resources PLC, 1981–. Member: Incorp. Law Soc.; Council, Irish Management Inst.; Hon. LLD: Wheeling Coll., 1974; Rollins Coll., 1978; Trinity Coll., 1978; Allegheny Coll., 1983. *Publications:* Prospect, 1962; Developing Creative Management, 1970; The Conservative Consumer, 1971; Food for Thought, 1972. *Recreations:* Rugby (played for Ireland 29 times), tennis. *Address:* 835 Fox Chapel Road, Pittsburgh, Pa 15238, USA; Castlemartin, Kilcullen, Co. Kildare, Ireland. *Clubs:* Reform, Annabels, Les Ambassadeurs; Stephen's Green (Dublin); Union League (New York); Duquesne, Allegheny, Fox Chapel, Pittsburgh Golf (Pittsburgh); Carlton (Chicago); Rolling Rock (Ligonier); Lyford Cay (Bahamas).

O'REILLY, Most Rev. Colm; *see* Ardagh and Clonmacnoise, Bishop of, (RC).

O'REILLY, Francis Joseph; Chancellor, University of Dublin, Trinity College, since 1985 (Pro-Chancellor, 1983–85); Chairman, Ulster Bank Ltd, 1982–89 (Deputy Chairman, 1974–82; Director, 1961–90); Director, National Westminster Bank, 1982–89; *b* 15 Nov. 1922; *s* of Lt-Col Charles J. O'Reilly, DSO, MC, MB, KSG and Dorothy Mary Martin; *m* 1950, Teresa Mary, *e d* of Captain John Williams, MC; three *s* seven *d*. *Educ:* St Gerard's Sch., Bray; Ampleforth Coll., York; Trinity Coll., Dublin (BA, BAI). Served HM Forces, RE, 1943–46. John Power & Son, 1946–66 (Dir, 1952–66, Chm., 1955–66); Chm., Player & Wills (Ire.) Ltd, 1964–81; Chm., 1966–83, Dir, 1983–88, Irish Distillers Gp. President: Marketing Inst. of Ireland, 1983–85; Inst. of Bankers in Ireland, 1985–86. President: Equestrian Fedn of Ireland, 1963–79; Royal Dublin Soc., 1986–89 (Mem. Cttees, 1959–80; Chm. of Soc., 1980–86); Chm., Collège des Irlandais, Paris, 1987–. Hon. Life Delegate, Fédn Equestre Internationale, 1979–. MRIA 1987–. LLD *hc*: Univ. of Dublin, 1978; NUI, 1986. *Recreations:* fox-hunting, racing, gardening. *Address:* Rathmore, Naas, Co. Kildare, Ireland. *T:* Naas 62136. *Clubs:* Kildare Street and University (Dublin); Irish Turf (The Curragh, Co. Kildare).

O'REILLY, William John, CB 1981; OBE 1971; FASA; Commissioner of Taxation, Australian Taxation Office, 1976–84, retired; *b* 15 June 1919; *s* of William O'Reilly and Ruby (*née* McCrudden). *Educ:* Nudgee Coll., Brisbane, Qld; Univ. of Queensland (Associate in Accountancy). FASA 1983. Served RAAF, 1942–44. Joined Australian Public Service, 1946; Australian Taxation Office: Brisbane, 1946–55; Melbourne, 1955–61; Canberra, 1961–84; Asst Comr of Taxation, 1963; First Asst Comr of Taxation, 1964; Second Comr of Taxation (Statutory Office), 1967. *Recreations:* reading, walking. *Address:* c/o Mrs L. C. Bennedick, 1240 Waterworks Road, The Gap, Qld 4061, Australia. *T:* 300–1607. *Clubs:* Commonwealth, Canberra (Canberra).

OREJA AGUIRRE, Marcelino; Grand Cross: Order of Charles III, 1980; Order of Isabella the Catholic, 1982; Member (Partido Popular) European Parliament, since 1989; Chairman, Institutional Affairs Committee; *b* 13 Feb. 1935; *m* 1967, Silvia Arburua; two *s*. *Educ:* Univ. of Madrid (LLD). Prof. of Internat. Affairs, Diplomatic Sch., Madrid, 1962–70; Dir of Internat. Service, Bank of Spain, 1970–74; Minister of Foreign Affairs, 1976–80; Governor-Gen., Basque Country, 1980–82; Sec. Gen., Council of Europe, 1984–89. Grand Officier de la Légion d'Honneur (France), 1976; Grand Cross: Order of Christ (Portugal), 1978; Order of the Crown (Belgium); (1st Cl.), Order of Service (Austria); (1st Cl.), Order of Merit (Federal Republic of Germany); Order of Orange-Nassau (Netherlands); (1st Cl.) Order of Polar Star (Sweden); Order of Dannebrog (Denmark); Order of Merit (Italy); Order of the Oak Crown (Luxembourg); Order of Merit (Liechtenstein). *Address:* 81 Nunez de Balboa, E-28006 Madrid, Spain. *T:* Madrid 5759101; 97–113 rue Belliard, 1040 Brussels, Belgium.

ORESCANIN, Bogdan; Ambassador of Yugoslavia to the Court of St James's, 1973–76; *b* 27 Oct. 1916; *m* 1947, Sonja Dapcevic; no *c*. *Educ:* Faculty of Law, Zagreb; Higher Mil. Academy. Organised uprising in Croatia; i/c various mil. and polit. duties in Nat. Liberation Struggle, War of 1939–45; Asst, then DCGS and Asst Defence Sec. of State, Yugoslav People's Army (Col General); formerly Mem. Fed. Parlt, Mem. Council of Fedn, Chm. Parly Cttee for Nat. Defence, Mem. For. Affairs Cttee of Fed. Parlt and Mem. Exec. Bd, Yugoslav Gp of IPU; Mil. Attaché in Gt Britain, 1952–54; Yugoslav Ambassador, People's Republics of China, Korea and Vietnam, 1970–73. Holds various Yugoslav and foreign decorations. *Publications:* articles on military-political theory; (study) Military Aspects of the Struggle for World's Peace, National Independence and Socialism. *Address:* Federal Secretariat for Foreign Affairs, Kneza Milosa 24, 11000 Belgrade, Yugoslavia.

ORGAN, (Harold) Bryan; painter; *b* Leicester, 31 Aug. 1935; *o c* of late Harold Victor Organ and Helen Dorothy Organ; *m* (marr. diss. 1981); *m* 1982, Sandra Mary Mills. *Educ:* Wyggeston Sch., Leicester; Coll. of Art, Loughborough; Royal Academy Schs, London. Lectr in Drawing and Painting, Loughborough Coll. of Art, 1959–65. One-man exhibns: Leicester Museum and Art Gallery, 1959; Redfern Gallery, 1967, 1969, 1971, 1973, 1975, 1978, 1980; Leicester 1973, 1976; New York, 1976, 1977; Turin, 1981. Represented: Kunsthalle, Darmstadt, 1968; Mostra Mercatao d'Arte Contemporanea, Florence, 1969; 3rd Internat. Exhibn of Drawing, Germany, 1970; Sao Paolo Museum of Art, Brazil; Baukunst Gallery, Cologne, 1977. Works in public and private collections in England, USA, Germany, France, Canada, Italy. Portraits include: Malcolm Muggeridge, 1966; Sir Michael Tippett, 1966; David Hicks, 1968; Mary Quant, 1969; Nadia Nerina, 1969; Princess Margaret, 1970; Dr Roy Strong, 1971; Elton John, 1973; Lester Piggott, 1973; Lord Ashby, 1975; Sir Rex Richards, 1977; Harold Macmillan, 1980; Prince of Wales, 1981; Lady Diana Spencer, 1981; Lord Denning, 1982; Jim Callaghan, 1982; Duke of Edinburgh, 1983. Hon. MA Loughborough, 1974; Hon. DLitt Leicester, 1985. *Address:* c/o Redfern Gallery, 20 Cork Street, W1. *T:* 071–734 1732.

ORGEL, Leslie Eleazer, DPhil Oxon, MA; FRS 1962; Senior Fellow, Salk Institute, La Jolla, California, USA, and Adjunct Professor, University of California, San Diego, Calif, since 1964; *b* 12 Jan. 1927; *s* of Simon Orgel; *m* 1950, Hassia Alice Levinson; two *s* one *d*. *Educ:* Dame Alice Owen's Sch., London. Reader, University Chemical Laboratory, Cambridge, 1963–64, and Fellow of Peterhouse, 1957–64. Fellow, Amer. Acad. of Arts and Sciences, 1985; Mem., Nat. Acad. of Scis, USA, 1990. *Publications:* An Introduction to Transition-Metal Chemistry, Ligand-Field Theory, 1960; The Origins of Life: molecules and natural selection, 1973; (with Stanley L. Miller) The Origins of Life on the Earth, 1974. *Address:* Salk Institute, PO Box 85800, San Diego, Calif 92138, USA.

O'RIORDAN, Rear-Adm. John Patrick Bruce, CBE 1982; Chief Executive, St Andrew's Hospital, Northampton, since 1990; *b* 15 Jan. 1936; *yr s* of Surgeon Captain Timothy Joseph O'Riordan, RN and Bertha Carson O'Riordan (*née* Young); *m* 1959, Jane, *e d* of John Alexander Mitchell; one *s* two *d*. *Educ:* Kelly College. Nat. Service and transfer to RN, 1954–59; served in submarines, Mediterranean, Home and Far East; HM Ships Porpoise (i/c) and Courageous, NDC, HMS Dreadnought (i/c), MoD, 1960–76; Captain (SM), Submarine Sea Training, 1976–78; RCDS, 1979; HMS Glasgow (i/c), 1980–81; ACOS (Policy), Saclant, USA, 1982–84; Dir, Naval Warfare, MoD, 1984–86; Mil. Dep. Comdt, NATO Defence Coll., Rome, 1986–89. Consultant, Spencer Stuart and Associates, 1989. FBIM. *Recreations:* sailing, Rugby football, travel, painting. *Address:* The Manor House, Islip, Kettering, Northants NN14 3JL. *T:* Thrapston (08012) 2325; Fulham Park Studios, 903A Fulham Road, SW6 5HU. *Clubs:* Army and Navy, Royal Navy of 1765 and 1785; Royal Yacht Squadron, Royal Naval Sailing Association.
See also Sir J. A. N. Graham.

O'RIORDAN, Prof. Timothy; Professor of Environmental Sciences, University of East Anglia, since 1980; *s* of Kevin Denis O'Riordan and Norah Joyce O'Riordan (*née* Lucas); *m* 1967, Ann Morison Philip; two *d*. *Educ:* Univ. of Edinburgh (MA 1963); Cornell Univ. (MS 1965); Univ. of Cambridge (PhD 1967). Asst Lectr and Associate Prof., Dept of Geography, Simon Fraser Univ., Canada, 1967–74; Reader, Sch. of Environmental Scis, UEA, 1974–80. Gill Meml Award, RGS, 1982. FRSA. *Publications:* Environmentalism 1976, 2nd edn 1981; (jtly) Sizewell B: an anatomy of the inquiry, 1988; (jtly) Countryside Conflicts, 1986. *Recreation:* classical double bass playing. *Address:* Wheatlands, Hethersett Lane, Colney, Norwich NR4 7TJ. *T:* Norwich (0603) 810534.

ORKNEY, 8th Earl of, *cr* 1696; **Cecil O'Bryen Fitz-Maurice;** Viscount of Kirkwall and Baron of Dechmont, 1696; *b* 3 July 1919; *s* of Douglas Frederick Harold FitzMaurice (*d* 1937; *g g s* of 5th Earl) and Dorothy Janette (who *m* 2nd, 1939, Commander E. T. Wiggins, DSC, RN), *d* of late Capt. Robert Dickie, RN; *S* kinsman 1951; *m* 1953, Rose Katharine Durk, *yr d* of late J. W. D. Silley, Brixham. Joined RASC, 1939; served in North Africa, Italy, France and Germany, 1939–46, and in Korea, 1950–51. *Heir: kinsman* Oliver Peter St John [*b* 27 Feb. 1938; *m* 1st, 1963, Mary Juliet (marr. diss. 1985), *d* of late W. G. Scott-Brown, CVO, MD, FRCS, FRCSE; one *s* three *d* (and one *d* decd); 2nd, 1985, Mrs Mary Barbara Huck, *d* of Dr David B. Albertson; one step *s* three step *d*]. *Address:* Ferndown, Dorset.

ORLEBAR, Sir Michael Keith Orlebar S.; *see* Simpson-Orlebar.

ORMAN, Stanley, PhD; Chief Executive Officer, General Technology Systems Inc., Maryland, since 1990; *b* 6 Feb. 1935; *s* of Jacob and Ettie Orman; *m* 1960, Helen (*née* Hourman); one *s* two *d*. *Educ:* Hackney Downs Grammar School; King's College London. BSc (1st Cl. Hons) 1957; PhD (Organic Chem.) 1960. MICorrST; FRIC 1969. Research Fellowship, Brandeis Univ., 1960–61; AWRE Aldermaston, research in corrosion and mechano-chemical corrosion, 1961–74, project work, 1974–78; Director Missiles, 1978–81, Chief Weapon System Engineer Polaris, 1981–82, MoD; Minister-Counsellor, Hd of Defence Equip. Staff, British Embassy, Washington, 1982–84; Dep. Dir, AWRE, MoD, 1984–86; Dir Gen., SDI Participation Office, MoD, 1986–90. Founder Chm., Reading Ratepayers' Assoc., 1974; Pres., Reading Hebrew Congregation, 1970–74. *Publications:* Faith in G.O.D.S.: stability in the nuclear age, 1991; numerous papers on free radical chemistry, materials science and mechano-chemical corrosion, in learned jls. *Recreations:* sporting—originally athletics, now tennis and badminton; designing bow ties, woodwork. *Address:* 17825 Stoneridge Drive, Gaithersburg, Md 20878, USA. *T:* 301 670 0685.

ORME, Jeremy David, FCA; Group Director, Compliance and Enforcement, Securities and Investments Board, since 1987; *b* 27 Dec. 1943; 2nd *s* of John Samuel Orme, CB, OBE, and of Jean Esther (*née* Harris); *m* 1967, Susan Diane Knights (marr. diss. 1978); two *s*. *Educ:* Winchester Coll.; Christ Church, Oxford (MA). Robson Rhodes, chartered accountants, 1966–87, Man. Partner, 1982–87; Asst Sec. (on secondment), Dept of Transport, 1979–81. Member: National Bus Co., 1984–86 (Dep. Chm. 1985–86); Audit Commn for Local Authorities in England and Wales, 1989–. *Address:* c/o Royal Bank of Scotland, Holts, Farnborough, Hants GU14 7NR.

ORME, Rt. Hon. Stanley, PC 1974; MP (Lab) Salford East, since 1983 (Salford West, 1964–83); *b* 5 April 1923; *s* of Sherwood Orme, Sale, Cheshire; *m* 1951, Irene Mary, *d* of Vernon Fletcher Harris, Worsley, Lancashire. *Educ:* elementary and technical schools; National Council of Labour Colleges and Workers' Educational Association classes. Warrant Officer, Air-Bomber Navigator, Royal Air Force Bomber Command, 1942–47. Joined the Labour party, 1944; contested (Lab) Stockport South, 1959. Minister of State: NI Office, 1974–76; DHSS, 1976; Minister of State for Social Security, 1976–77, Minister for Social Security, and Mem. Cabinet, 1977–79; Opposition Spokesman on Health and Social Services, June 1979–Dec. 1980, on Industry, 1980–83, on Energy, 1983–87; Chm., PLP, 1987–. Member of Sale Borough Council, 1958–65; Member: AEU; District Committee, Manchester; shop steward. Hon. DSc Salford, 1985. *Address:* House of Commons, SW1; 8 Northwood Grove, Sale, Cheshire. *Clubs:* ASE (Altrincham); Ashfield Labour (Salford).

ORMEROD, Alec William; Metropolitan Stipendiary Magistrate, since 1988; Chairman, Family Court, since 1991; *b* 19 July 1932; *s* of William and Susan Ormerod; *m* 1976, Patricia Mary Large. *Educ:* Nelson Grammar Sch.; Christ's Coll., Cambridge (MA, LLM). Solicitor. Local Govt Service, 1958–64; Sen. Partner, Boyle and Ormerod, Solicitors, Aylesbury, 1964–88. Councillor, Aylesbury Borough Council, 1966–72. Freeman, City of London, 1973. *Recreations:* travel, fine art. *Address:* c/o Inner London Magistrates Courts, Bush House, WC2B 4PJ. *T:* 071–836 9331. *Club:* Naval and Military.

ORMESSON, Comte Jean d'; Chevalier des Palmes académiques 1962; Commandeur des Arts et Lettres 1973; Officier de la Légion d'honneur 1988; Officier de l'Ordre national du Mérite, 1978; Membre Académie française 1973; Secretary-General, International

Council for Philosophy and Humanistic Studies (UNESCO), since 1971 (Deputy, 1950–71); writer and journalist; *b* 16 June 1925; 2nd *s* of Marquis d'Ormesson, French diplomat and Ambassador; *m* 1962, Françoise Béghin; one *d*. *Educ:* Ecole Normale Supérieure. MA (History), Agrégé de philosophie. Mem. French delegns to various internat. confs, 1945–48; Mem. staff of various Govt Ministers, 1958–66; Mem. Council ORTF, 1960–62; Mem. Control Cttee of Cinema, 1962–69; Mem. TV Programmes Cttee, ORTF, 1973–74. Mem., Brazilian Acad. of Letters, 1979. Diogenes: Dep. Editor, 1952–72; Mem. Managing Cttee, 1972–80; Editor, 1980–82; Editor-in-Chief, 1982–; Le Figaro: Dir, 1974–77; Editor-in-Chief, 1975–77. *Publications:* L'Amour est un plaisir, 1956; Du côté de chez Jean, 1959; Un amour pour rien, 1960; Au revoir et merci, 1966; Les Illusions de la mer, 1968; La Gloire de l'Empire, 1971 (Grand Prix du Roman de l'Académie française), Amer. edn (The Glory of the Empire), 1975, Eng. edn 1976; Au Plaisir de Dieu, 1974, Amer. edn (At God's Pleasure), 1977, Eng. edn 1978; Le Vagabond qui passe sous une ombrelle trouée, 1978; Dieu, sa vie, son œuvre, 1981; Mon dernier rêve sera pour vous, 1982; Jean qui grogne et Jean qui rit, 1984; Le Vent du soir, 1985; Tous les hommes en sont fous, 1986; Le Bonheur à San Miniato, 1987; Garçon de quoi écrire, 1989; Histoire du Juif errant, 1991; articles and essays, columns in Le Figaro, Le Monde, Le Point, La Revue des Deux Mondes, La Nouvelle Revue Française. *Recreation:* ski-navigation. *Address:* CIPSH-UNESCO, 1 rue Miollis, 75732 Paris Cedex 15, France. *T:* 45.68.26.85; (home) 10 avenue du Parc Saint-James, 92200 Neuilly-sur-Seine, France.

ORMOND, Sir John (Davies Wilder), Kt 1964; BEM 1940; JP; Chairman: Shipping Corporation of New Zealand Ltd, since 1973; Container Terminals Ltd, since 1975; Exports and Shipping Council, since 1964; *b* 8 Sept. 1905; *s* of J. D. Ormond and Gladys Wilder; *m* 1939, Judith Wall; four *s* one *d*. *Educ:* Christ's Coll., Christchurch, New Zealand. Chairman, Waipukurau Farmers Union, 1929; President, Waipukurau Jockey Club, 1950; Member, New Zealand Meat Producers Board, 1934–72, Chm., 1951–72. Active Service Overseas (Middle East), 1940. JP, NZ, 1945. DSc (*hc*), 1972. *Recreations:* tennis, polo, Rugby Union football. *Address:* Wallingford, Waipukurau, New Zealand. *T:* Waipukurau 542M. *Club:* Hawke's Bay (New Zealand).

ORMOND, Richard Louis; Director, National Maritime Museum, since 1986 (Head of Picture Department, 1983–86); *b* 16 Jan. 1939; *s* of late Conrad Eric Ormond and Dorothea (*née* Gibbons); *m* 1963, Leonée Jasper; two *s*. *Educ:* Oxford University. MA. Assistant Keeper, 1965–75, Dep. Director, 1975–83, Nat. Portrait Gallery. *Publications:* J. S. Sargent, 1970; Catalogue of Early Victorian Portraits in the National Portrait Gallery, 1973; Lord Leighton, 1975; Sir Edwin Landseer, 1982; The Great Age of Sail, 1986; F. X. Winterhalter and the Courts of Europe, 1987. *Recreations:* cycling, opera, theatre. *Address:* 8 Holly Terrace, N6 6LX. *T:* 081–340 4684. *Club:* Garrick.

ORMONDE, 7th Marquess of, *cr* 1825; **James Hubert Theobald Charles Butler,** MBE 1921; Earl of Ormonde, 1328; Viscount Thurles, 1525; Earl of Ossory, 1527; Baron Ormonde (UK), 1821; 31st Hereditary Chief Butler of Ireland; retired; *b* 19 April 1899; *s* of Lord Theobald Butler (4th *s* of 2nd Marquess) and Annabella Brydon (*d* 1943), *o d* of Rev. Cosmo Reid Gordon, DD; *S* cousin, 1971; *m* 1st, 1935, Nan Gilpin (*d* 1973); two *d*; 2nd, 1976, Elizabeth Liles (*d* 1980). *Educ:* Haileybury College; RMC Sandhurst. Commissioned Dec. 1917, King's Royal Rifle Corps; resigned commission, May 1926 (Lieut). Various business connections in USA. *Heir:* (to earldoms of Ormonde and Ossory) Viscount Mountgarret, *qv*. *Address:* King-Bruwaert House, 6101 South County Line Road, Burr Ridge, Ill 60521, USA. *Club:* Naval and Military.

ORMROD, Rt. Hon. Sir Roger (Fray Greenwood), PC 1974; Kt 1961; a Lord Justice of Appeal, 1974–82; *b* 20 Oct. 1911; *s* of late Oliver Fray Ormrod and Edith Muriel (*née* Pim); *m* 1938, Anne, *d* of Charles Lush; no *c*. *Educ:* Shrewsbury Sch.; The Queen's Coll., Oxford. BA Oxon (Jurisprudence) 1935. Called to Bar, Inner Temple, 1936; QC 1958; Judge of High Court of Justice, Family Division (formerly Probate, Divorce and Admiralty Division), 1961–74. Hon. Fellow, Queen's Coll., Oxford, 1966. BM, BCh Oxon, 1941; FRCP 1969. House Physician, Radcliffe Infirmary, Oxford, 1941–42. Served in RAMC, 1942–45, with rank of Major. DADMS 8 Corps. Lecturer in Forensic Medicine, Oxford Medical Sch., 1950–59. Hon. Prof. of Legal Ethics, Univ. of Birmingham, 1973–74. Chairman: Lord Chancellor's Cttee on Legal Education, 1968; Notting Hill Housing Trust, 1968–88. Pres., British Acad. of Forensic Science, 1970–71; Chm., Cttee of Management, Institute of Psychiatry, 1973–84. Visitor, Royal Postgrad. Med. Sch., 1975–90; Chm., British Postgrad. Med. Fedn, 1980–86. Hon. Fellow: RPMS, 1990; Manchester Polytechnic, 1972; Hon. FRCPsych 1975; Hon. FRCPath 1983. Hon. LLD Leicester, 1978. *Publications:* ed, (with E. H. Pearce) Dunstan's Law of Hire-Purchase, 1938; (with Harris Walker) National Health Service Act 1946, 1949; (with Jacqueline Burgoyne and Martin Richards) Divorce Matters, 1987. *Address:* 4 Aubrey Road, W8 7JJ. *T:* 071–727 7876. *Club:* Garrick.

ORMSBY GORE, family name of **Baron Harlech.**

O'ROURKE, Andrew; Ambassador of Ireland to Denmark, since 1991; *b* 7 May 1931; *s* of Joseph O'Rourke and Elizabeth (*née* O'Farrell); *m* 1962, Hanne Stephensen; one *s* two *d*. *Educ:* Trinity Coll., Dublin (BA, BComm). Joined diplomatic service, 1957; Third Sec., Berne, 1960; First Sec., London, 1964; First Sec., later Counsellor, Dept of Foreign Affairs, Dublin, 1969–73; Counsellor, later Dep. Perm. Rep., Perm. Rep. of Ireland to EEC, 1973–78; Sec.-Gen., Dept of For. Affairs, 1978–81; Perm. Rep. to EEC, 1981–86; Ambassador to: France, OECD and UNESCO, 1986–87; UK, 1987–91. Grand Cross: Order of Civil Merit, Spain, 1985; OM, Luxembourg, 1986. *Recreations:* walking, golf. *Address:* Embassy of Ireland, Østbanegade 21 1 T.H., DK-2100 Copenhagen, Denmark. *Clubs:* Garrick, Royal Automobile; Kildare Street and University (Dublin).

ORR, Sir David (Alexander), Kt 1977; MC and bar 1945; LLB; Chairman, British Council, 1985–Feb. 1992; Deputy Chairman, Inchcape PLC, since 1986 (Chairman, 1983–86); Director: Shell Transport & Trading Co., since 1982; Rio Tinto-Zinc Corporation PLC, since 1981; *b* 10 May 1922; *s* of late Canon Adrian William Fielder Orr and Grace (*née* Robinson); *m* 1949, Phoebe Rosaleen Davis; three *d*. *Educ:* High Sch., Dublin; Trinity Coll., Dublin (Hon. LLD 1978). Served Royal Engineers attached QVO Madras Sappers and Miners, 1941–46. With various Unilever companies, 1948–82; Hindustan Lever, 1955–60; Mem. Overseas Cttee, Unilever, 1960–63; Lever Bros Co., New York, 1963, Pres. 1965–67; Dir, 1967–82, Vice-Chm. 1970–74, Chm., 1974–82, Unilever Ltd; Vice-Chm., Unilever NV, 1974–82; Mem. Court, Bank of Ireland, 1982–85. Chm., Armed Forces Pay Review Body, 1982–84; Member: Cttee to Review Functioning of Financial Instns, 1977–80; Top Salaries Review Body, 1982–85; Adv. Cttee on Business Appointments of Crown Servants, 1984–. Chairman: Leverhulme Trust, 1982–; Shakespeare Globe Theatre Trust, 1982–; Jt Chm., Anglo-Irish Encounter, 1983–87. Dir, Five Arrows Chile Fund, 1990–; Pres., Children's Medical Charity, 1991–. Pres., Liverpool Sch. of Tropical Medicine, 1981–89; Governor, LSE, 1980–. FRSA. Hon. LLD: TCD, 1978; Liverpool, 1989; DUniv Surrey, 1981. Comdr, Order of Oranje Nassau, 1979. *Recreations:* golf, Rugby, travel. *Address:* 81 Lyall Mews West, SW1; Home Farm House, Shackleford, near Godalming, Surrey. *Clubs:* Athenæum; Sunningdale Golf.

ORR, Iain Campbell; HM Diplomatic Service; Deputy High Commissioner, Wellington, since 1991; *b* 6 Dec. 1942; *s* of David Campbell Orr and late Hilda Dora Moore; *m* 1978, Susan Elizabeth Gunter; one *s* one *d*. *Educ:* Kirkcaldy High Sch.; St Andrews Univ. (MA); Linacre Coll., Oxford (BPhil). Asst Lectr, Dept of Politics, Glasgow Univ., 1967–68; entered HM Diplomatic Service, 1968; language student, Hong Kong, 1969–71; Second, later First Sec., Peking, 1971–74; FCO, 1974–78; Asst Political Adviser, Hong Kong, 1978–81; Dublin, 1981–84; FCO, 1984–87; Consul-Gen., Shanghai, 1987–90. *Recreations:* natural history, islands, anthologies, reading poetry. *Address:* c/o Foreign and Commonwealth Office, SW1.

ORR, James Bernard Vivian, CVO 1968 (MVO 1962); Secretary, Medical Commission on Accident Prevention, 1970–82; *b* 19 Nov. 1917; *s* of Dr Vivian Bernard Orr and Gladys Constance Orr (*née* Power); unmarried. *Educ:* Harrow; Gordonstoun; RMC, Sandhurst. British South Africa Police, Southern Rhodesia, 1939–46. Attached occupied Enemy Territory Administration in Ethiopia and Eritrea Police Forces, 1941–49; Kenya Police, 1954–57. Private Secretary to HRH The Duke of Edinburgh, 1957–70, an Extra Equerry, 1970–. *Recreations:* horse racing, watching cricket. *Address:* 10 Mulberry Trees, Shepperton, Mddx TW17 8JN. *T:* Walton-on-Thames (0932) 245274.

ORR, Dr James Henry; Consultant in forensic psychiatry, since 1982; *b* 2 Feb. 1927; *s* of Hubert Orr and Ethel Maggs; *m* 1950, Valerie Elizabeth Yates; two *s* one *d*. *Educ:* Bristol Grammar Sch.; Bristol Univ. (MB, ChB 1955). DPM; FRCPsych. Enlisted, 1944; commnd RE, 1947; demobilised, 1949. Hosp. appts, 1955–56; gen. practice, 1956–58; Medical Officer, HM Prison: Leeds, 1958; Winchester, 1962; Lincoln, 1966; SMO, Leeds, 1967; Asst Dir, Prison Med. Services, 1973; Dir, Prison Med. Services, and Mem., Prisons Bd, 1976–82; Mem., Parole Bd, 1983–86. *Recreation:* gardening.

ORR, Jean Fergus Henderson; Director, Office of Manpower Economics, 1973–80; *b* 3 April 1920; *yr d* of late Peter Orr, OBE and Janet Muir Orr (*née* Henderson). *Educ:* privately; University Coll., London (BA; Fellow, 1982). Min. of Aircraft Prodn, temp. Asst Principal, 1942; Min. of Supply: Asst Principal, 1946; Principal, 1949; HM Treasury, 1954: Principal, Official Side Sec. to Civil Service Nat. Whitley Council negotiations on Report of Royal Commn on Civil Service, 1953–55; Asst Sec. 1961; on loan to Office of Manpower Econs as Sec. to Top Salaries Review Body, 1971. *Publication:* (contrib.) Edward Boyle: his life by his friends, ed Ann Gold, 1991. *Recreations:* music, travel, natural history. *Address:* 21 Bathwick Hill, Bath, Avon BA2 6EW. *T:* Bath (0225) 463664. *Club:* United Oxford & Cambridge University.

ORR, Sir John Henry, Kt 1979; OBE 1972; QPM 1977; Chief Constable, Lothian and Borders Police, 1975–83; *b* 13 June 1918; *m* 1942, Isobel Margaret Campbell; one *s* one *d*. *Educ:* George Heriot's Sch., Edinburgh. Edinburgh City Police, 1937; served in RAF 1943–45 (Flying Officer; Defence and War Medals); Chief Constable: of Dundee, 1960; of Lothians and Peebles, 1968. Hon. Sec., Assoc. of Chief Police Officers (Scotland), 1974–83. FBIM 1978. Coronation Medal, 1953; Police Long Service and Good Conduct Medal, 1959; Jubilee Medal, 1977; OStJ, 1975. Comdr, Polar Star, class III, Sweden, 1975; Legion of Honour, France, 1976. *Recreations:* Rugby (capped for Scotland; Past Pres., Scottish Rugby Union); golf. *Address:* 12 Lanark Road West, Currie, Midlothian EH14 5ET.

ORR, Prof. Robin, (Robert Kemsley Orr), CBE 1972; MA, MusD (Cantab); FRCM; Hon. RAM; Hon. FRSAM; Hon. DMus, Hon. LLD; Composer; Professor of Music, Cambridge University, 1965–76, now Professor Emeritus; Fellow of St John's College, Cambridge, 1965–76, Hon. Fellow 1987; *b* Brechin, Scotland, 2 June 1909; *s* of Robert Workman Orr and Florence Mary Kemsley; *m* 1st, 1937, Margaret (marr. diss. 1979), *er d* of A. C. Mace; one *s* two *d*; 2nd, 1979, Doris Winny-Meyer, *d* of Leo Meyer-Bechtler, Zürich. *Educ:* Loretto Sch.; Royal Coll. of Music; Pembroke Coll., Cambridge (Organ Scholar; Hon. Fellow, 1988); Accademia Musicale Chigiana, Siena. Studied privately with Casella and Nadia Boulanger. Dir of Music, Sidcot Sch., Somerset, 1933–36; Asst Lecturer in Music, Univ. of Leeds, 1936–38. Served War of 1939–45, RAFVR, Photographic Intelligence (Flight Lieut). Organist and Dir of Studies in Music, St John's Coll., 1938–51, and Fellow, 1948–56, Univ. Lecturer in Music, 1947–56, Cambridge; Prof. of Theory and Composition, RCM, 1950–56; Gardiner Prof. of Music, Univ. of Glasgow, 1956–65. Mem., Carl Rosa Trust, 1953–; Chm., Scottish Opera, 1962–76; Director: Arts Theatre, Cambridge, 1970–75; Welsh Nat. Opera, 1977–83. Compositions include: Sonatina for violin and piano, 1941; Three Chinese Songs, 1943; Sonata for viola and piano, 1947; Winter's Tale (Incidental Music), BBC, 1947; Overture, The Prospect of Whitby, 1948; Oedipus at Colonus (Cambridge Univ. Greek Play), 1950; Four Romantic Songs (for Peter Pears), 1950; Festival Te Deum, 1950; Three Pastorals for soprano, flute, viola and piano, 1951; Deirdre of the Sorrows (Incidental Music), BBC, 1951; Italian Overture, 1952; Te Deum and Jubilate in C, 1953; Motet, I was glad, 1955; Spring Cantata, 1955; Sonata for violin and clavier, 1956; Rhapsody for string orchestra; Antigone (Bradfield College Greek Play), 1961; Symphony in one movement, 1963; Full Circle (opera), 1967; From the Book of Philip Sparrow, 1969; Journeys and Places (mezzo-sop. and strings), 1971; Symphony No 2, 1971; Hermiston (opera), 1975; Symphony No 3, 1978; Versus from Ogden Nash for medium voice and strings, 1978; Songs of Zion (choir), 1978; On the Razzle (opera), 1986; Sinfonietta Helvetica, 1990; ed, The Kelvin Series of Scots Songs. Hon. DMus Glasgow, 1972; Hon. LLD Dundee, 1976. *Recreations:* gardening, mountain walks. *Address:* 16 Cranmer Road, Cambridge CB3 9BL. *T:* Cambridge (0223) 352858.

ORR-EWING, family name of **Baron Orr-Ewing.**

ORR-EWING, Baron *cr* 1971 (Life Peer), of Little Berkhamsted; **(Charles) Ian Orr-Ewing,** OBE 1945; 1st Bt *cr* 1963; Consultant and Director various companies; Chairman, Metrication Board, 1972–77; *b* 10 Feb. 1912; *s* of Archibald Ian Orr Ewing and Gertrude (*née* Runge); *m* 1939, Joan McMinnies; four *s*. *Educ:* Harrow; Trinity Coll., Oxford. MA (Physics). Graduate apprentice, EMI, Hayes, 1934–37; BBC Television Service, 1938–39, 1946–49. Served RAFVR, 1939–46, N Africa, Italy, France and Germany, Wing Comdr, 1941; Chief Radar Officer, Air Staff, SHAEF, 1945 (despatches twice); BBC Television Outside Broadcasts Manager, 1946–48. MP (C) North Hendon, 1950–70; Joint Secretary, Parliamentary Scientific Cttee, 1950; Vice-Pres., Parliamentary and Scientific Cttee, 1965–68; Vice-Chm., 1922 Cttee, 1966–70 (Secretary, 1956); Vice-Chairman, Defence Cttee, 1966–70. PPS to Sir Walter Monckton, Minister of Labour and National Service, Nov. 1951–1955; Parliamentary Under-Secretary of State, for Air, Air Ministry, 1957–59; Parliamentary and Financial Secretary to Admiralty, 1959; Civil Lord of the Admiralty, 1959–63. Dep. Chm., Assoc. of Cons. Peers, 1980–86. Mem., Royal Commn on Standards of Conduct in Public Life, 1975–76. Pres. and Chm. of Council, Electronic Engineering Assoc., 1969–70. Pres., Nat. Ski Fedn of GB, 1972–76. FIEE. *Publication:* (ed) A Celebration of Lords and Commons Cricket 1850–1988, 1989. *Recreations:* tennis, light-hearted cricket and ski-ing. *Heir* (to baronetcy only): *s* (Alistair) Simon Orr-Ewing [*b* 10 June 1940; *m* 1968, Victoria, *er d* of late Keith Cameron, Fifield House, Milton-under-Wychwood, Oxon; two *s* one *d*]. *Address:* House of Lords, SW1. *Clubs:* Boodle's, MCC; All England Lawn Tennis; Vincent's (Oxford).

ORR EWING, Major Edward Stuart; landowner and farmer, since 1969; Lord-Lieutenant of Wigtown, since 1989; *b* 28 Sept. 1931; *s* of late Captain David Orr Ewing, DSO, DL and of Mary Helen Stuart Orr Ewing (*née* Noaks); *m* 1st, 1958, Fiona Anne Bowman (*née* Farquhar) (marr. diss. 1981); one *s* two *d*; 2nd, 1981, Diana Mary Waters. *Educ:* Sherborne; Royal Military Coll. of Science. Regular soldier, The Black Watch, 1950–69. DL Wigtown, 1970. *Recreations:* country sports, ski-ing, painting. *Address:* Dunskey, Portpatrick, Wigtownshire. *T:* Portpatrick (077681) 211. *Club:* New (Edinburgh).

ORR-EWING, Hamish; *b* 17 Aug. 1924; *o s* of Hugh Eric Douglas Orr-Ewing and Esme Victoria (*née* Stewart), Strathgarry, Killiecrankie, Perthshire; *m* 1st, 1947, Morar Margaret Kennedy; one *s* (one *d* decd); 2nd, 1954, Ann Mary Teresa Terry. *Educ:* Heatherdown, Ascot; Eton. Served War, Captain Black Watch. Salesman, EMI, 1950; Ford Motor Co., 1954; Ford Light Car Planning Manager, 1959–63; Leyland Motor Corp. Ltd, 1963–65; joined Rank Xerox, 1965; apptd to Bd as Dir of Product Planning, 1968; Dir of Personnel, 1970; Man. Dir, Rank Xerox (UK) Ltd, 1971; Reg. Dir for Rank Xerox Ops in UK, France, Holland, Sweden and Belgium, 1977; Chairman: Rank Xerox Ltd, 1980–86; Jaguar plc, 1984–85; White Horse Hldgs, 1987–91; Dir, Tricentrol PLC, 1975–86. Chairman: Work and Society, 1982–85; European Govt Business Relations Council, 1980–84; Member: MSC, 1983–85; Engrg Council, 1984–87; Envmt Awards Panel, RSA, 1987–; President: Inst. of Manpower Studies, 1986–89; Inst. of Training and Develt, 1987–89. CBI: Member: Bd, Educn Foundn (UBI), 1982–87; Council, 1985–87; Chm., Educn and Trng Cttee, 1985–87. Trustee: Shaw Trust, 1985–; Roman Res. Trust, 1985–. Governor: Interphil, 1985–; New Coll., Swindon, 1984– (Chm. of Govs, 1986–); Bradon Forest Sch., 1989–. CBIM 1981. *Recreations:* anything mechanical, country life, the Roman Empire. *Address:* Fox Mill, Purton, near Swindon, Wilts SN5 9EF. *T:* Swindon (0793) 770496.

ORR EWING, Major Sir Ronald Archibald, 5th Bt, *cr* 1886; Major (retired) Scots Guards; *b* 14 May 1912; *e s* of Sir Norman Orr Ewing, 4th Bt, CB, DSO, and Lady Orr Ewing (*née* Robarts), Tile House, Buckingham; *S* father, 1960; *m* 1938, Marion Hester, *yr d* of late Colonel Sir Donald Walter Cameron of Lochiel, KT, CMG, and of Lady Hermione Cameron of Lochiel, *d* of 5th Duke of Montrose, KT; two *s* two *d*. *Educ:* Eton; RMC, Sandhurst. Scots Guards, 1932–53, Major. Served War of 1939–45, Middle East (POW 1942). JP Perthshire, 1956; DL Perthshire, 1963. Grand Master Mason of Scotland, 1965–69. *Recreation:* forestry. *Heir: s* Archibald Donald Orr Ewing [*b* 20 Dec. 1938; *m* 1st, 1965, Venetia Elizabeth (marr. diss. 1972), *y d* of Major and Mrs Richard Turner, Co. Dublin; 2nd, 1972, Nicola Jean-Anne, *d* of Reginald Baron Black, Fovant, near Salisbury; one *s*]. *Address:* Cardross, Port of Menteith, Kippen, Stirling FK8 3JY. *T:* Port of Menteith (08775) 220. *Club:* New (Edinburgh).

ORREGO-VICUÑA, Prof. Francisco; Professor of International Law, School of Law and Institute of International Studies, University of Chile, since 1969; President, Chilean Council on Foreign Relations; *b* 12 April 1942; *s* of Fernando Orrego Vicuña and Raquel Vicuña Viel; *m* 1965, Soledad Bauzá; one *s* two *d*. *Educ:* Univ. of Chile (Degree in Law); LSE (PhD). Admitted to legal practice, 1965. Sen. Legal Advisor, OAS, 1965–69 and 1972–74; Dir, Inst. of Internat. Studies, Univ. of Chile, 1974–83; Ambassador of Chile to UK, 1983–85. Advisor on legal matters to Min. of Foreign Affairs, 1974–83. *Publications:* Derecho de la Integraciòn Latinoamericana, 1969; Los Fondos Marinos, 1976; Antarctic Resources Policy, 1983; The Exclusive Economic Zone, 1984; Antarctic Mineral Exploration, 1988; The Exclusive Economic Zone in International Law, 1989; contrib. Amer. Jl of Internat. Law and Annuaire Français de Droit Internat. *Recreations:* golf, ski-ing. *Address:* Institute of International Studies, University of Chile, PO Box 14187, Suc. 21, Santiago 9, Chile. *T:* 2740–730. *Club:* Athenæum.

ORRELL, James Francis Freestone; His Honour Judge Orrell; a Circuit Judge, since 1989; *b* 19 March 1944; *s* of Francis Orrell and late Marion Margaret Orrell; *m* 1970, Margaret Catherine Hawcroft; two *s*. *Educ:* Ratcliffe; Univ. of York (BA History). Called to the Bar, Gray's Inn, 1968; Recorder, Midland and Oxford Circuit, 1988. *Address:* c/o Leicester Crown Court, 90 Wellington Street, Leicester.

ORSON, Rasin Ward, CBE 1985; CompIEE; consultant; Member, The Electricity Council, 1976–89; *b* 16 April 1927; *s* of Rasin Nelson Orson and Blanche Hyre; *m* 1st, 1950, Marie Goodenough; two *s*; 2nd, 1979, Lesley Jean Vallance. *Educ:* Stratford Grammar Sch.; London School of Economics (BScEcon 1948). Asst Statistician, Min. of Civil Aviation, 1948, Statistician, 1953; Electricity Council: Head of Economics and Forecasting Branch, 1963; Dep. Commercial Adviser, 1968; Commercial Adviser, 1972. Dir, Chloride Silent Power, 1974–89. *Recreations:* music, photography. *Address:* The Old Garden, Dunorlan Park, Tunbridge Wells, Kent TN2 3QA. *T:* Tunbridge Wells (0892) 24027.

ORTIZ DE ROZAS, Carlos; Argentine Ambassador to France, 1984–88; *b* 26 April 1926; *m* 1952, María del Carmen Sarobe. *Educ:* School of Diplomacy, Min. of Foreign Affairs, Buenos Aires (grad. 1949). Lawyer, Faculty of Law, Univ. of Buenos Aires, 1950. Entered Argentine Foreign Service, 1948; served Bulgaria, Greece, UAR and UK (Minister); Ambassador to Austria, 1967–70; Permanent Rep. to UN, 1970–77; Pres. UN Security Council, 1971–72; Chairman: First (Polit. and Security) Cttee of 29th Gen. Assembly, 1974; Preparatory Cttee of Special Session on Disarmament, 1977–78; Cttee on Disarmament, Geneva, 1979; Mem. Adv. Bd on Disarmament Studies, New York, 1978–81; Ambassador to UK, 1980–82; Head, Argentine Special Mission to the Holy See, 1982–83. Universidad del Salvador, Buenos Aires: Prof. of History and Constitutional Law, 1958, Prof. of Political Science, 1958–, Faculty of Law; Prof. of Internat. Relations, School of Political Sciences, 1962–, and at School of Diplomacy, 1962–. Holds many foreign decorations incl. Grand Cross, Order of Pius IX, 1985, and Commandeur, Légion d'Honneur, 1985. *Address:* c/o Ministry of Foreign Affairs, Reconquista 1088, 1003 Buenos Aires, Argentina. *Clubs:* Jockey, Círculo de Armas (Buenos Aires); Cercle de l'Union Interalliée (Paris); Doubles (New York).

ORTOLI, François-Xavier; Hon. Chairman, Total Compagnie Française des Pétroles, since 1990 (Président Directeur Général, 1984–90); *b* 16 Feb. 1925. *Educ:* Hanoi Faculty of Law; Ecole Nationale d'Administration. Inspector of Finances, 1948–51; Tech. Adv., Office of Minister of Econ. Affairs and Information, 1951–53; Asst Dir to Sec. of State for Econ. Affairs and Sec.-Gen., Franco-Italian Cttee of EEC, 1955; Head, Commercial Politics Service of Sec. of State for Econ. Affairs, 1957; Dir-Gen., Internal Market Div., EEC, 1958; Sec.-Gen., Inter-Ministerial Cttee for Questions of European Econ. Co-operation, Paris, 1961–; Dir of Cabinet to Prime Minister, 1962–66; Comr-Gen. of the Plan, 1966–67; Minister: of Works, 1967–68; of Educn, 1968; of Finance, 1968–69; of Industrial and Scientific Develt, 1969–72; Pres., EEC, 1973–76, a Vice-Pres., with responsibility for econ. and financial affairs, 1977–84. Hon. Fellow, Worcester Coll., Oxford, 1991. Hon. DCL Oxon, 1975; Hon Dr Sch. of Political Scis, Athens, 1975. Commandeur de la Légion d'Honneur; Médaille Militaire; Croix de Guerre, 1945; Médaille de la Résistance. *Address:* 18 rue de Bourgogne, 75007 Paris, France.

OSBORN, Frederic Adrian, (Derek Osborn), CB 1991; Director General (Deputy Secretary), Environmental Protection, Department of the Environment, since 1990; *b* 14 Jan. 1941; *s* of late Rev. George R. Osborn and E. M. Osborn, MBE; *m* 1971, Caroline Niebuhr Tod; one *d* one *s*. *Educ:* Leys School, Cambridge; Balliol College, Oxford. BA Maths 1963, BPhil 1965. Asst Principal, Min. of Housing and Local Govt, 1965; Private Sec. to Minister of State and Perm. Sec., 1967; Royal Commn on Standards of Conduct in Public Life, 1974; Dept of Transport, 1975–77; Department of the Environment, 1977–: Under Sec., Finance, 1982–86, Housing Gp, 1986–87; Dep. Sec., Local Govt and Finance, 1987–89. *Recreations:* music, reading, chess.

OSBORN, Sir John (Holbrook), Kt 1983; semi-retired scientist, soldier, industrialist and politician; *b* 14 Dec. 1922; *s* of Samuel Eric Osborn and Aileen Decima, *d* of Colonel Sir Arthur Holbrook, KBE, MP; *m* 1st, 1952, Molly Suzanne (*née* Marten) (marr. diss.); two *d*; 2nd, 1976, Joan Mary MacDermot (*née* Wilkinson) (*d* 1989); 3rd, 1989, Patricia Hine (*née* Read). *Educ:* Rugby; Trinity Hall, Cambridge. MA Cantab; Part 2 Tripos in Metallurgy; Diploma in Foundry Technology, National Foundry Coll., 1949. Served in Royal Corps of Signals, 1943–47 (West Africa, 1944–46; Captain); served in RA (TA) Sheffield, 1948–55, Major. Joined 1947, and Technical Dir, 1951–79, Samuel Osborn & Co. Ltd, and associated companies. Chairman, Hillsborough Divisional Young Conservative and Liberal Association, 1949–53. MP (C) Hallam Div. of Sheffield, 1959–87 (NL and U, 1959–64); PPS to the Secretary of State for Commonwealth Relations and for the Colonies, 1963–64. Chairman: Cons. Parly Transport Cttee, 1970–74; Parly Gp for Energy Studies, 1985–87 (Vice-Chm., Cons. Parly Energy Gp, 1979–81); Anglo-Swiss Parly Gp, 1981–87; (or Vice-Chm.) Anglo-Soviet Parly Gp, 1968–87; Vice Chm., Parly and Scientific Cttee, 1963–66, 1982 (Officer, 1959–87; Life Mem., 1987); Jt Sec., 1922 Cttee, 1968–87; Member: Science and Technol. Select Cttee, 1970–73; Educn, Science and Arts Select Cttee, 1979–83; Chm., All Party Channel Tunnel Gp, 1985–87. Mem., UK Delegn to Council of Europe and WEU, 1973–75, 1980–87; Council of Europe: Vice Chm., Science and Technol. Cttee, 1981–87; Chm., Eur. Scientific Contact Gp, 1982–87; Hon. Associate, 1987. Chm., Econ. Affairs and Develt Sub-Cttee (North/South: Europe's role), 1985–87. Mem., European Parlt, 1975–79; Mem. Exec., British Br., IPU, 1968–75, 1979–83; Mem. Cttee, European Atlantic Gp, 1990–. Mem., Interim (formerly Voluntary) Licensing Authy, MRC/RCOG, 1987–. Chairman: Friends of Progress, 1989–; Business and Develt Cttee, UK Chapter, Soc. for Internat. Develt, 1990–. Mem., RIIA, 1985–. Freeman Co. of Cutlers in Hallamshire, 1987 (Asst Searcher, 1951–65; Searcher, 1965–70 and 1973–87). Fellow, Institute of British Foundrymen, 1948–72 (Member Council, Sheffield Branch, 1954–64); FIM 1986 (MISI 1947); Fellow, Institute of Directors; Member Council: Sheffield Chamber of Commerce, 1956–89 (Hon. Life Mem., 1989); Assocs British Chambers of Commerce, 1960–62 (Hon. Secretary, 1962–64); British Iron and Steel Res. Association, 1965–68; CBI and Yorks and WR Br., CBI, 1968–79; Industrial Soc., 1963–79 (Life Mem.). Pres., Sheffield Inst. of Advanced Motorists, 1960–; Chm., H of C Motor Club, 1979–84. Mem., Court and Council Sheffield Univ., 1951–79. Chm., Zackery Merton Trust, 1988–. Travelled widely in business and politics. *Recreations:* golf, tennis, photography, gardening, ski-ing, gymnasium, swimming. *Address:* Flat 13, 102 Rochester Row, SW1P 1JP. *T:* 071–828 0464. *Clubs:* Carlton; Sheffield.

OSBORN, Sir Richard (Henry Danvers), 9th Bt *cr* 1662, of Chicksands Priory, Co. Bedford; fine art consultant; *b* 12 Aug. 1958; surv. *s* of Sir Danvers Lionel Rouse Osborn, 8th Bt, and Constance Violette, JP, OStJ (*d* 1988), *d* of late Major Leonard Frank Rooke, KOSB and RFC; *S* father, 1983. *Educ:* Eton. Christie's, 1978–83. *Recreations:* cricket, tennis, squash, horse racing, real tennis. *Heir: kinsman* William Danvers Osborn [*b* 4 June 1909; *m* 1939, Jean Burns, *d* of R. B. Hutchinson, Vancouver; one *d*]. *Address:* The Dower House, Moor Park, Farnham, Surrey GU10 1QX; 25 Queens Gardens, W2. *Clubs:* MCC, Turf, Queen's.

OSBORNE, Hon. Lord; Kenneth Hilton Osborne; a Senator of the College of Justice in Scotland, since 1990; *b* 9 July 1937; *s* of Kenneth Osborne and Evelyn Alice (*née* Hilton); *m* 1964, Clare Ann Louise Lewis; one *s* one *d*. *Educ:* Larchfield Sch., Helensburgh; Merchiston Castle Sch., Edinburgh; Edinburgh Univ. (MA, LLB). Admitted to Faculty of Advocates in Scotland, 1962; QC (Scotland) 1976. Standing Junior Counsel to Min. of Defence (Navy) in Scotland, 1974–76; Advocate-Depute, 1982–84. Chairman: Disciplinary Cttee, Potato Marketing Bd, 1975–90; (part-time), VAT Tribunals, 1985–90; Medical Appeal Tribunals, 1987–90; Mem., Lands Tribunal for Scotland, 1985–87. Chm., Local Govt Boundary Commn for Scotland, 1990–. *Recreations:* ski-ing, fishing, gardening, music, cooking. *Address:* 42 India Street, Edinburgh EH3 6HB. *T:* 031–225 3094; Primrose Cottage, Bridgend of Lintrathen, by Kirriemuir, Angus. *T:* Lintrathen (05756) 316. *Club:* New (Edinburgh).

OSBORNE, Anthony David; Principal Assistant Treasury Solicitor; Under Secretary (Legal), Head of Property Division, Treasury Solicitor's Department, Taunton, since 1990; *b* 21 March 1935; *s* of Frederick Charles Osborne and Eva Mary Osborne (*née* Tutt); *m* 1958, Ethelwyn Grieve; two *s* one *d*. *Educ:* Brighton College. Articled: Aldrich and Crowther, Brighton; Ashurst, Morris, Crisp & Co., London; admitted Solicitor, 1958; private practice, London, 1958–65; joined Treasury Solicitor's Dept, 1965; Asst Treasury Solicitor, 1975; Solicitor to Health and Safety Commn and Health and Safety Exec., 1985–90. *Recreations:* music, theatre, travel, photography. *Address:* Bartletts, Milverton, Somerset TA4 1JX. *T:* Taunton (0823) 400887.

OSBORNE, Charles (Thomas); author; Theatre Critic, The Daily Telegraph, since 1987; *b* 24 Nov. 1927; *s* of Vincent Lloyd Osborne and Elsa Louise Osborne; *m* 1970, Marie Korbelářová (marr. diss. 1975). *Educ:* Brisbane State High Sch. Studied piano and voice, Brisbane and Melbourne; acted in and directed plays, 1944–53; wrote poetry and criticism, published in Aust. and NZ magazines; co-owner, Ballad Bookshop, Brisbane, 1947–51; actor, London, provincial rep. and on tour, also TV and films, 1953–57; Asst Editor, London Magazine, 1958–66; Asst Lit. Dir, Arts Council of GB, 1966–71, Lit. Dir, 1971–86. Broadcaster, musical and literary progs, BBC, 1957–; Dir, Poetry International, 1967–74; Sec., Poetry Book Soc., 1971–84; opera critic, Jewish Chronicle, 1985–. Mem. Editorial Board: Opera, 1970–; Annual Register, 1971–87. *Publications:* (ed) Australian Stories of Today, 1961; (ed) Opera 66, 1966; (with Brigid Brophy and Michael Levey) Fifty Works of English Literature We Could Do Without, 1967; Kafka, 1967; Swansong (poems), 1968; The Complete Operas of Verdi, 1969 (Italian trans. 1975, French trans. 1989); Ned Kelly, 1970; (ed) Australia, New Zealand and the South Pacific, 1970; (ed) Letters of Giuseppe Verdi, 1971; (ed) The Bram Stoker Bedside Companion, 1973; (ed) Stories and Essays by Richard Wagner, 1973; The Concert Song Companion, 1974; Masterpieces of Nolan, 1976; Masterpieces of Drysdale, 1976; Masterpieces of Dobell, 1976; Wagner and his World, 1977 (USA 1977; trans. Spanish 1985); Verdi, 1977 (trans. Spanish 1985); (ed) Dictionary of Composers, 1977; The Complete Operas of Mozart, 1978 (trans. Ital. 1982); (ed) Masterworks of Opera: Rigoletto, 1979; The Opera House Album, 1979 (trans. Dutch 1981); W. H. Auden: the Life of a Poet, 1980; (ed with Kenneth Thomson) Klemperer Stories, 1980 (trans. German 1981); The Complete Operas of Puccini, 1981; The Life and Crimes of Agatha Christie, 1982; The World Theatre of

Wagner, 1982; How to Enjoy Opera, 1983 (trans. Spanish 1985); The Dictionary of Opera, 1983 (trans. Finnish 1984; trans. Portuguese 1987); Letter to W. H. Auden and Other Poems, 1984; Schubert and his Vienna, 1985 (trans. German 1986); Giving It Away (memoirs), 1986; (ed) The Oxford Book of Best-Loved Verse, 1986; Verdi: a life in the theatre, 1987; The Complete Operas of Richard Strauss, 1988; Max Oldaker: last of the matinée idols, 1988; The Complete Operas of Wagner, 1990; poems in: The Oxford Book of Australian Verse, 1956; Australian Poetry, 1951–52, etc; The Queensland Centenary Anthology, 1959; Australian Writing Today, 1968; various jls; contrib.: TLS, Observer, Sunday Times, Times, Guardian, New Statesman, Spectator, London Mag., Encounter, Opera, Chambers Encyc. Yearbook, and Enciclopedia dello spettacolo; also cassettes. *Recreations:* travelling, planning future projects. *Address:* 125 St George's Road, SE1 6HY. *T:* 071–928 1534.

OSBORNE, Maj.-Gen. the Rev. Coles Alexander, CIE 1945; Indian Army, retired; *b* 29 July 1896; *s* of late W. E. Osborne, formerly of Dover, Kent; *m* 1930, Joyce, *o d* of late R. H. Meares of Forbes and Sydney, NSW, Australia; two *d. Educ:* Dover County Sch. European War, 1914–18: served with HAC, Royal West Kent Regt, and RFC (wounded); transferred to 15th Sikhs, 1918; served in Afghan War 1919 and in NW Frontier Operations 1920–22 and 1939; Palestine 1938; Middle East 1940. Tactics Instructor at Royal Military Coll., Duntroon, Australia, 1928–30; Bt Major 1933; General Staff (Operations), War Office, 1934–38; Bt Lieut-Col 1936; Comd 1 Bombay Grenadiers, 1940; Deputy Director Military Training, India, 1940; Colonel, 1940; Commandant, Staff Coll., Quetta, 1941–42; Brigadier, 1941; Director Military Operations, GHQ, India and Burma, 1942–43; Temp. Maj.-Gen. 1942; Comd Kohat District, 1943–45; retired 1946. Student at Moore Theological Coll., Sydney, 1947; ordained, 1947; Hon. Asst Minister St Andrew's Cathedral, Sydney, Australia, 1947–53; Hon. Asst Minister, St Mark's Church, Darling Point, 1953–66; Personal Chaplain to Anglican Archbishop of Sydney, 1959–66. Director, Television Corp., 1956–75. Fellow of St Paul's Coll., Sydney Univ., 1953–69. Chairman, Freedom from Hunger Campaign, NSW, 1970–72. *Address:* 11 Charles Street, Warner's Bay, NSW 2282, Australia. *Club:* Australian (Sydney).

OSBORNE, Denis Gordon, CMG 1990; Royal Institute of Public Administration (International Services), since 1990; *b* 17 Sept. 1932; *s* of A. Gordon Osborne and Frances A. Osborne (*née* Watts); *m* 1970, Christine Susannah, *d* of P. Rae Shepherd and C. Elaine Shepherd; two *d. Educ:* Dr Challoner's Grammar Sch., Amersham; University Coll., Durham (BSc 1st Cl. Hons Physics, PhD). FInstP 1966. Lectr in Physics, Univ. of Durham, 1957; Lectr, Fourah Bay Coll., Sierra Leone, 1957–58; Lectr, 1958–63, Sen. Lectr, 1963–64, Univ. of Ghana; Reader in Physics, 1964–66, Prof., 1966–71, Dean of Science, 1968–70, Univ. of Dar es Salaam; Res. Fellow, UCL, 1971–72; Cons. for World Bank missions to Malaysia and Ethiopia, 1971, 1972; Overseas Development Administration: Principal, 1972; Multilateral Aid Dept, 1972–75; Mediterranean and Near East Dept, 1975–77; Sci. and Technology Dept, 1977–80; Asst Sec., 1980; Hd of Dept in Natural Resources Div., 1980–84; Hd of E and W Africa Dept, 1984–87; HM Diplomatic Service, High Comr in Malaŵi, 1987–90. *Publications:* Way Out: some parables of science and faith, 1977; research papers on geophysics, particularly the equatorial ionosphere; gen. papers on science, technology, educn and develt. *Recreations:* reading, writing, attempts at windsurfing. *Address:* Royal Institute of Public Administration, Regent's College, Inner Circle, Regent's Park, NW1 4NS. *Club:* Athenæum.

OSBORNE, Helena; *see* Moore, G. M.

OSBORNE, John (James); dramatist and actor; Director of Woodfall Films; *b* 12 Dec. 1929; *s* of Thomas Godfrey Osborne and Nellie Beatrice Grove; *m* 1st, 1951, Pamela Elizabeth Lane (marr. diss. 1957); 2nd, 1957, Mary Ure (marr. diss. 1963, she *d* 1975); 3rd, 1963, Penelope Gilliatt, *qv* (marr. diss. 1968); 4th, 1968, Jill Bennett (marr. diss. 1977; she *d* 1990); 5th, 1978, Helen Dawson. *Educ:* Belmont Coll., Devon. First stage appearance at Lyceum, Sheffield, in No Room at the Inn, 1948; toured and in seasons at: Ilfracombe, Bridgwater, Camberwell, Kidderminster, Derby, etc; English Stage Company season at Royal Court: appeared in Death of Satan, Cards of Identity, Good Woman of Setzuan, The Making of Moo, A Cuckoo in the Nest; directed Meals on Wheels, 1965; appeared in: The Parachute (BBC TV), 1967; First Night of Pygmalion (TV), 1969; First Love (film, as Maidanov), 1970; Get Carter (film), 1971; Lady Charlotte (TV), 1977; Tomorrow Never Comes (film), 1978. First play produced, 1949, at Theatre Royal, Huddersfield; other plays include, Personal Enemy, Opera House, Harrogate, 1955. *Plays filmed:* Look Back in Anger, 1958; The Entertainer, 1959, 1975; Inadmissible Evidence, 1965; Luther, 1971. *Film:* Tom Jones, 1964 (Oscar for best screenplay). Hon. Dr RCA, 1970. *Publications:* Look Back in Anger (play), 1957 (produced 1956); The Entertainer (play), 1957 (also produced); Epitaph for George Dillon (with A. Creighton), 1958 (produced 1957); The World of Paul Slickey (comedy of manners with music), 1959 (produced 1959); Luther (play), 1960 (produced 1961, New York, 1964); A Subject of Scandal and Concern (TV play), 1960; Plays for England, 1963; Inadmissible Evidence (play), 1964 (produced 1965); A Patriot for Me (play), 1964 (produced 1965, 1983); A Bond Honoured, 1966 (produced 1966); The Hotel in Amsterdam, 1967 (produced 1968); Time Present, 1967 (produced 1968); Hedda Gabler (adaptation), 1970 (produced 1972); The Right Prospectus and Very Like a Whale (TV plays), 1971; West of Suez, 1971 (produced 1971); The Gift of Friendship (TV play), 1971; A Sense of Detachment, 1972 (produced 1972); A Place Calling Itself Rome, 1972; The Picture of Dorian Gray (play), 1973; The Gift of Friendship (TV play), 1974; Jill and Jack (TV play), 1974; The End of Me Old Cigar (play), 1975; Watch it come down (play), 1975; You're Not Watching Me, Mummy and Try a Little Tenderness (TV plays), 1978; A Better Class of Person (autobiog.), 1981 (televised, 1985); God Rot Tunbridge Wells! (TV play), 1985; The Father (adapted and trans.), 1989. Contrib. to various newspapers, journals. *Address:* c/o Peters, Fraser and Dunlop, 5th Floor, The Chambers, Chelsea Harbour, Lots Road, SW10 0XF. *Club:* Garrick.

OSBORNE, Kenneth Hilton; *see* Osborne, Rt Hon. Lord.

OSBORNE, Prof. Michael John, FAHA 1985; Vice-Chancellor, La Trobe University, Australia, since 1990; *s* of Samuel Osborne and Olive May Osborne (*née* Shove); *m* 1978, Dawn Brindle. *Educ:* Eastbourne Grammar Sch.; Christ Church, Oxford (MA); Catholic Univ. of Leuven (DPhil and Lett.). Lectr, Dept of Classics, Bristol, 1966–67; Lectr, then Sen. Lectr, Dept of Classics and Archaeology, Univ. of Lancaster, 1967–82; University of Melbourne: Prof. and Chm., Dept of Classical and NE Studies, 1983–90, now Prof. Emeritus; Dep./Associate Dean, Faculty of Arts, 1985–89; Pro-Vice-Chancellor and Vice-Pres., Academic Bd, 1989. Mem., Inst. for Advanced Study, Princeton, 1978–79; Visiting Professor: Maximilians Univ., Munich, 1973; Leuven, 1975, 1988; Vis. Fellow, other univs, 1972–85. Laureate, Royal Acad. of Sci., Letters and Fine Arts, Belgium, 1980. *Publications:* Naturalization in Athens, 4 vols, 1981–83; numerous articles in learned jls on Greek history, Greek epigraphy and Greek archaeology. *Recreations:* tennis, travel, Australian Rules football. *Address:* Office of the Vice-Chancellor, La Trobe University, Bundoora, Vic 3083, Australia. *T:* 61–3–479.2000. *Club:* Essendon Football.

OSBORNE, Sir Peter (George), 17th Bt, *cr* 1629; Chairman and Managing Director, Osborne & Little plc (design company), since 1967; *b* 29 June 1943; *s* of Lt-Col Sir George Osborne, 16th Bt, MC, and Mary (Grace) (*d* 1987), *d* of C. Horn; *S* father, 1960; *m* 1968, Felicity, *d* of Grantley Loxton-Peacock; four *s. Educ:* Wellington Coll., Berks; Christ Church Coll., Oxford. *Heir: s* George Gideon Oliver Osborne, *b* 23 May 1971. *Address:* 36 Porchester Terrace, W2. *T:* 071–402 3903. *Club:* White's.

OSBORNE, Trevor; Chairman and Managing Director, Speyhawk plc, since 1981 (Chairman, Speyhawk Ltd, 1973–81); *b* 7 July 1943; *s* of Alfred Osborne and Annie Edmondson; *m* 1969, Pamela Ann Stephenson; one *s* one *d. Educ:* Sunbury Grammar School. FRICS. South Area Estate Manager, Middx County Council, 1960–65; Partner, A. P. C., 1966–67; Principal, Private Property Interests, 1967–73; Chm., St George plc; non-exec. Dir, Redland plc. Member: Royal Opera House Develt Bd; Assoc. of City Property Owners; Vice-Pres., British Property Fedn. BPF Vis. Fellow, Land Management Course, Reading Univ., 1987–90. Trustee, Wokingham Cons. Assoc.; Pres., Windsor Arts Centre. Leader, Wokingham DC, 1980–82. Freeman, City of London; Liveryman, Chartered Surveyors' Co. FRSA. *Recreations:* travel, theatre, opera, tennis. *Address:* Speyhawk plc, Osprey House, Lower Square, Old Isleworth, Middlesex TW7 6BN; Pinewood House, Nine Mile Ride, Wokingham, Berks RH11 3EA. *T:* Crowthorne (0344) 774320. *Clubs:* Carlton, Arts.

O'SHEA, David Michael; Solicitor to the Metropolitan Police, 1982–87, retired; *b* 27 Jan. 1927; *s* of late Francis Edward O'Shea and Helen O'Shea; *m* 1953, Sheila Winifred; two *s. Educ:* St Ignatius Coll., London; King's Coll., London Univ. (LLB). Served RN, 1946–48. Articled H. C. L. Hanne & Co., London, 1949–52; admitted solicitor, 1952; in practice with H. C. L. Hanne & Co., 1952–56; joined Solicitor's Dept, Metropolitan Police Office, 1956; Dep. Solicitor, 1976–82. *Recreation:* travel. *Address:* c/o New Scotland Yard, SW1.

OSIFELO, Sir Frederick (Aubarua), Kt 1977; MBE 1972; Speaker of Legislative Assembly, Solomon Islands, 1974–78; Chairman: Public Service Commission, since 1975; Police and Prison Service Commission, since 1977; Member, Judicial and Legal Service Commission, since 1977; *b* 15 Oct. 1928; *s* of late Paul Iromea and Joy Ngangale Iromea; *m* 1949, Margaret Tanai; three *s* three *d. Educ:* Torquay Technical Coll., England (Dip. Public Admin). Office cleaner, 1945; clerk, 1950; 1st Cl. Magistrate, 1967; Admin. Officer, Cl. B, 1967; Admin. Officer, Cl. A, 1972; District Comr, Eastern Solomons, 1972; Sen. Sec., 1973; Comr of Lands, 1974. Chairman: Cttee of Prerogative of Mercy, 1979; ad hoc cttee on Solomon Islands Honours and Awards, 1979. Pres., Amateur Sports Assoc., 1975–. Lay Canon, 1977. *Address:* PO Box 548, Honiara, Solomon Islands. *T:* (office) 21529, (home) 22018.

OSMAN, Sir (Abdool) Raman (Mahomed), GCMG 1973; CBE 1963; Governor-General of Mauritius, 1972–77; *b* 29 Aug. 1902, of Mauritian parents; unmarried. *Educ:* Royal College, Mauritius; Inns of Court, London. District Magistrate, Mauritius, 1930–38; Additional Substitute Procureur and Advocate General, 1938–50; Actg Procureur and Advocate-General, 1950–51; Actg Chief Justice, Apr.-Nov. 1958; Puisne Judge, Supreme Court of Mauritius, 1950–59, Sen. Puisne Judge, 1959–60, retired. Hon. DCL Mauritius, 1975. *Address:* Le Goulet Terrace, Tombeau Bay, Mauritius. *Club:* Port Louis Gymkhana.

OSMAN, Louis, BA (Arch.); FRIBA; artist, architect, goldsmith, medallist; *b* 30 January 1914; *s* of Charles Osman, Exeter; *m* 1940, Dilys Roberts, *d* of Richard Roberts, Rotherfield, Sussex; one *d. Educ:* Hele's School, Exeter; London University (Fellow, UCL, 1984–). Open exhibn at Bartlett School of Architecture, University Coll. London, 1931, and at Slade School; Donaldson Medallist of RIBA, 1935. With British Museum and British School of Archæology Expeditions to Syria, 1936, 1937; designed private and public buildings, 1937–39. Served War of 1939–45, Major in Intelligence Corps: Combined Ops HQ and Special Air Service as specialist in Air Photography, Beach Reconnaissance Cttee, prior to invasion of Europe. Resumed practice in London, 1945, designed buildings, furniture, tapestries, glass, etc; work in Westminster Abbey, Lincoln, Ely and Exeter Cathedrals; Staunton Harold for National Trust; Bridge, Cavendish Square, with Jacob Epstein; Newnham Coll., Cambridge; factory buildings for Cambridge Instrument Co., aluminium Big Top for Billy Smart's Circus, two villages on Dartmoor, etc; consultant architect to British Aluminium Co.; executed commissions as goldsmith and jeweller, 1956–; commissioned by De Beers for 1st Internat. Jewellery Exhibn, 1961; designed and made Prince of Wales' crown for investiture, 1969; British Bicentennial Gift to America housing Magna Carta, 1976; Verulam Medal for Metals Soc., 1975; EAHY Medal, 1975; Olympic Medal, 1976; works in art galleries, museums and private collections in GB, Europe, Canada, USA, S Africa, Australia, Japan, etc; one-man retrospective exhibn, Goldsmiths' Hall, 1971. Mem. Exec. Cttee: The Georgian Group, 1952–56; City Music Soc., 1960–70. *Publications:* reviews and contributions to learned jls. *Recreation:* music. *Address:* Harpton Court, near New Radnor, Presteigne, Powys LD8 2RE. *T:* New Radnor (054421) 380.

OSMAN, Dr Mohammad Kheir; Member of Foundation Committee, 1981–86, and Professor and Dean of Students since 1985, Sultan Qaboos University, Muscat, Sultanate of Oman; *b* Gedarif, Sudan, 1928; *s* of Osman Khalifa Taha and Khadija Al Shareef; *m* 1953, Sara Ahmed. *Educ:* Khartoum Univ. (BA); London Univ. (PGCE; AcDip; MA); Univ. of California, LA (PhD). Director: Educational Research and Planning, 1970–71; Sudan/ILO Productivity Centre, Khartoum, 1972; Minister of Education, 1972–75; Mem., Sudan Nat. Assembly, 1972–75; Ambassador to UK, 1975–76; Manager, UNDP/UNESCO Educnl Project, Oman, 1977–84; Adviser to Min. of Educn, Oman, 1984–85. Professional interests include Western educnl experience and indigenous Afro/Arab conditions, and the problems of change through institutional educnl systems. Constitution Decoration, 1973; Two-Niles Decoration for Public Service, 1979; Sultan Qaboos Decoration, 1986. *Address:* Sultan Qaboos University, PO Box 32491, Al-Khod, Sultanate of Oman. *Club:* Athenæum.

OSMAN, Sir Raman; *see* Osman, Sir A. R. M.

OSMOND, Prof. Charles Barry, PhD; FRS 1984; FAA; Arts and Sciences Professor, Department of Botany, Duke University, Durham, USA, since 1988; *b* 20 Sept. 1939; *s* of Edmund Charles Osmond and Joyce Daphne (*née* Krauss); *m* 1st, 1962, Suzanne Alice Ward; two *s* one *d* (and one *s* decd); 2nd, 1983, Ulla Maria Cornelia Gauhl (*née* Büchen). *Educ:* Morisset Central Sch.; Wyong High Sch.; Univ. of New England, Armidale (University Medal in Botany, 1961; BSc 1961, MSc 1963); Univ. of Adelaide (PhD 1965). FAA 1978. Post-doctoral Res. Associate, Botanical Sciences Dept, Univ. of Calif, LA, 1965; Royal Commn for Exhibn of 1851 and CSIRO Fellow, Botany Sch., Cambridge Univ., 1966; successively Res. Fellow, Fellow and Sen. Fellow, Dept of Environmental Biol., ANU, Canberra, 1967–78, Prof. of Biology, 1978–87; Exec. Dir, Biol Sciences Center, Desert Res. Inst., Reno, 1982–86. Fulbright Sen. Scholar, Univ. of Calif, Santa Cruz, 1973–74; Carnegie Instn Fellow (Plant Biol.), Stanford, 1973–74; Richard Mereton Guest Prof., Technical Univ., Munich, 1974; Overseas Fellow, Churchill Coll., Cambridge, 1980. Goldacre Award, Aust. Soc. of Plant Physiologists, 1972; Edgeworth David Medal, Royal Soc. of NSW, 1974. *Publications:* (ed jtly) Photosynthesis and Photorespiration, 1971; (ed jtly) Photorespiration in Marine Plants, 1976; (jtly) Physiological Processes in Plant Ecology, 1980; (ed jtly) Encyclopedia of Plant Physiology, Vols 12 A-D,

Physiological Plant Ecology, 1981–83; (ed jtly) Photoinhibition, 1987; (ed jtly) New Vistas in Measurement of Photosynthesis, 1989; (ed jtly) Plant Biology of the Basin and Range, 1990; articles on plant metabolic biology and its ecological implications in learned jls. *Recreations:* biological research, social cricket, music of romantic composers, confections of Continental Europe. *Address:* Department of Botany, Duke University, Durham, NC 27706, USA. *T:* (919) 684 2377.

OSMOND, Sir Douglas, Kt 1971; CBE 1968 (OBE 1958); QPM 1962; DL; Chief Constable, Shropshire, 1946–62, Hampshire, 1962–77; *b* 27 June 1914. *Educ:* University Coll., London. Metropolitan Police Coll., Metropolitan Police, RN, Control Commn for Germany (Public Safety Branch); Dep. Asst Inspector Gen., 1944–46. Pres., Assoc. of Chief Police Officers of England and Wales, 1967–69; Chm., Police Council for UK, 1972, 1974; Provincial Police Representative, Interpol, 1968–70; Member: Inter-Deptl Cttee on Death Certification and Coroners, 1964–71; Bd of Governors, Police Coll., 1968–72 (Adv. Cttee, 1959–77); Royal Commn on Criminal Procedure, 1978–81. DL Hants, 1981. OStJ 1971. *Address:* Woodbine Cottage, Ovington, Alresford, Hants SO24 0RF. *T:* Winchester (0962) 733729.

OSMOND, Mervyn Victor, OBE 1978; Secretary, Council for the Protection of Rural England, 1966–77 (Assistant Secretary, 1946; Deputy Secretary 1963); *b* 2 July 1912; *s* of Albion Victor Osmond and Florence Isabel (*née* Edwards), Bristol; *m* 1940, Aimée Margaret Moir; one *d*. *Educ:* Clifton Coll. (Schol.); Exeter Coll., Oxford (Schol.). 1st cl. Hon. Class. Mods; 2nd cl. Lit. Hum.; 2nd cl. Jurisprudence; Poland Prizeman (Criminal Law), 1937; called to Bar (Inner Temple), 1938; MA 1939. Practising Barrister, Western Circuit, 1938–40. Joined Gloucestershire Regt, TA, 1931; served war of 1939–45; Royal Fusiliers; DAAG (Major) 352 L of C Sub-Area and 303 L of C Area (Calcutta). *Recreations:* reading, enjoying rural England. *Address:* 39 Stonehill Road, East Sheen, SW14 8RR. *T:* 081–876 7138.

OSMOND, Michael William Massy, CB 1977; Solicitor to the Department of Health and Social Security, and to the Office of Population Censuses and Surveys, and the General Register Office, 1974–78; *b* 1918; *s* of late Brig. W. R. F. Osmond, CBE, and Mrs C. R. E. Osmond; *m* 1943, Jill Ramsden (*d* 1989); one *s* one *d*. *Educ:* Winchester; Christ Church, Oxford. 2nd Lieut Coldstream Guards, 1939–40. Called to Bar, Inner Temple, 1941; Asst Principal, Min. of Production, 1941–43; Housemaster, HM Borstal Instn, Usk, 1943–45; Legal Asst, Min. of Nat. Insce, 1946; Sen. Legal Asst, 1948; Asst Solicitor, Min. of Pensions and Nat. Insce, 1958; Principal Asst Solicitor, DHSS, 1969. *Recreations:* music, fishing. *Address:* Waylands, Long Newnton, near Tetbury, Glos GL8 8RN. *T:* Tetbury (0666) 503308. *Club:* United Oxford & Cambridge University.

OSMOND, Sir (Stanley) Paul, Kt 1980; CB 1966; *b* 13 May 1917; *o s* of late Stanley C. and Susan Osmond; *m* 1942, Olivia Sybil, JP, *yr d* of late Ernest E. Wells, JP, Kegworth, Leicestershire; two *s*. *Educ:* Bristol Grammar School; Jesus College, Oxford. Served War of 1939–45, in Army (Gloucestershire Regiment and staff), 1940–46. Home Civil Service, 1939–75: Ministry of Education, 1946–48; Private Secretary to Prime Minister, 1948–51; Admiralty, 1951, Asst Secretary, 1954; Under-Secretary, 1959; HM Treasury, 1962, Third Secretary, 1965; Deputy Secretary: Civil Service Dept, 1968–70; Office of the Lord Chancellor, 1970–72; DHSS, 1972–75. Sec. to the Church Commissioners, 1975–80. Member: Lord Chancellor's Cttee on Public Records, 1978–80; Adv. Council on Public Records, 1983–88. Royal Institution: a Manager, 1966–69, 1970–73; Hon. Treas., 1981–86; Vice-Pres., 1981–86, 1989–; Mem. Council, 1989– (Chm., 1989–). Chm., Nat. Marriage Guidance Council, 1982–88. Mem., Clergy Orphan Corp., 1980–; Hon. Treasurer, Central London YMCA, 1982–85; Governor, Bristol Grammar Sch., 1972– (Vice-Chm., 1984–); Chm., Lingfield Hosp. Sch., 1981–87. CBIM 1978. *Recreations:* theatre, travel, gardening. *Address:* 20 Beckenham Grove, Bromley, Kent BR2 0JU. *T:* 081–460 2026. *Club:* Athenæum.

OSMOTHERLY, Edward Benjamin Crofton; Deputy Secretary, Public Transport and Research, Department of Transport, since 1989; *b* 1 Aug. 1942; *s* of Crofton and Elsie Osmotherly; *m* 1970, Valerie (*née* Mustill); one *d* one *s*. *Educ:* East Ham Grammar School; Fitzwilliam College, Cambridge (MA). Asst Principal, Ministry of Housing and Local Govt, 1963–68 (Private Sec. to Parly Sec., 1966–67, to Minister of State, 1967–68); Principal, 1968–76; Harkness Fellow, 1972–73 (Guest Scholar, Brookings Instn, Washington DC; Exec. Fellow, Univ. of California at Berkeley); Asst Sec., DoE, 1976–79; seconded to British Railways Bd, 1979; Head of Machinery of Govt Div., CSD, 1980–81; Under Sec. (Railways), Dept of Transport, 1982–85; Under Sec., Dir of Personnel, Management and Training, Depts of the Environment and of Transport, 1985–89. *Recreation:* reading. *Address:* Department of Transport, 2 Marsham Street, SW1P 3EB. *Club:* United Oxford & Cambridge University.

OSOLA, (Victor) John, (Väinö Juhani), CBE 1980; FEng, FIMechE; Chairman, John Osola & Associates Ltd, since 1983; Director, Cranfield Precision Engineering Ltd, since 1990; *b* 24 Jan. 1926; *s* of Väinö Kaarlo Osola and Violet Agenoria (*née* Jones); *m* 1948, Brenda Lilian Davison; two *s* one *d*. *Educ:* Hymers Coll., Hull; Sunderland Technical Coll., Univ. of Durham (BSc). FEng 1979; FIMechE 1966; Fellow ASME; MInstE. Technical Commn, RE, 1945–48. Gas Turbine Res. Engr, C. A. Parsons & Co. Ltd, 1951–52; Sen. Proj. Design Engr, Procter & Gamble Ltd, 1952–57; Chief Engr, Lankro Chemicals Ltd, 1957–65; Technical Director: Fibreglass Ltd, 1965–72; Triplex Safety Glass Co. Ltd, 1972–79; Chm., Fibreglass Pilkington Ltd, Bombay, 1967–72; Director: Triplex Ireland Ltd, 1976–79; Triclover Safety Glass Co. Ltd, 1976–79; (non-exec.) Kongsberg Systems Technology Ltd, 1983–85; Mem., Pilkington Brothers European Safety Glass Bd, 1977–79; Group Chief Exec., Redman Heenan Internat. plc, 1979–82, non-exec. Dir, 1982–84. Pres., IMechE, 1982–83; Ind. Mem., Mech. Engrg and Machine Tool Requirements Bd, Dept of Industry, 1974–77, Chm. 1977–79; Chm., NEDO Adv. Manufacturing Systems Cttee, 1983–86; Member: Parly and Scientific Cttee, 1983–; (Founder), Parly Gp for Engrg Develt, 1985–; Court of Cranfield Inst. of Technol., 1979–85; Policy Bd, Cranfield Product Engrg Centre, 1980–. Sec., Fellowship of Engrg, 1983–89. Foreign Mem., Finnish Nat. Acad. of Technology, 1989. Associate, St George's House, Windsor, 1980–; Governor, Malvern Coll., 1981–87. Freeman, City of London, 1984; Liveryman, Worshipful Co. of Engineers, 1984–. FRSA 1976. Hon. Fellow, Humberside Coll. of Higher Educn, 1986. MacRobert Award, 1978. *Publications:* papers in specialised engrg jls. *Recreations:* offshore sailing (BoT yachtmaster), music, theatre. *Address:* Whiddon End, Yarhampton Cross, near Stourport-on-Severn, Worcs DY13 0UY. *T:* Great Witley (0299) 896293. *Clubs:* Army and Navy; Royal Dee Yacht (Cheshire); Royal Irish Yacht (Dublin); North West Venturers Yacht (Beaumaris).

OSTLERE, Dr Gordon; *see* Gordon, Richard.

OSTROWSKI, Joan Lorraine; *see* Walley, J. L.

O'SULLEVAN, Peter John, CBE 1991 (OBE 1977); Racing Correspondent: Daily Express, 1950–86; Today, 1986–87; BBC Television Commentator; *b* 3 March 1918; *o s* of late Col John Joseph O'Sullevan, DSO, formerly Resident Magistrate, Killarney, and Vera, *o d* of Sir John Henry, DL, JP; *m* 1951, Patricia, *o d* of Frank Duckworth, Winnipeg, Manitoba, Canada. *Educ:* Hawtreys; Charterhouse; Collège Alpin, Switzerland. Specialised in ill-health in early life and not accepted for fighting forces in 1939–45 war, during which attached to Chelsea Rescue Services. Subsequently worked for John Lane, the Bodley Head, on editorial work and MSS reading. Joined Press Assoc. as Racing Correspondent, 1945, until appointed Daily Express, 1950, in similar capacity. Race-broadcasting 1946– (incl. Australia, S Africa, Italy, France, USA); in 1953 became first regular BBC TV and horse-racing commentator to operate without a race-reader; commentated: first television Grand National, 1960; world's first televised electronic horse race from Atlas computer at Univ. of London, transmitted by BBC TV Grandstand, 1967; first horse race transmitted live via satellite, from NY, to invited audience in London, 1980. Director: Internat. Racing Bureau, 1979–; Racing Post Ltd, 1985–. Mem., Jockey Club, 1986–. Derby Award for Racing Journalist of the Year, 1971 (with late Clive Graham), 1986; Racehorse Owner of the Year Award, Horserace Writers' Assoc., 1974; Timeform Racing Personality, 1974; Clive Graham Meml Award for services to racing, Press Club, 1978, 1985; Evening News Sports Commentator of the Year, 1978; William Hill Golden Spurs for services to racing, 1985. *Publication:* Calling the Horses: a racing autobiography, 1989. *Recreations:* racehorse owning, in minor way (happiest broadcasting experience commentating success of own horses, Be Friendly, 1966–67, and Attivo, 1974); travel, reading, art, food and wine. *Address:* 37 Cranmer Court, SW3 3HW. *T:* 071–584 2781.

O'SULLIVAN, (Carrol Austin) John (Naish), CB 1973; LLB (London); Public Trustee, 1971–75; *b* 24 Jan. 1915; *s* of late Dr Carrol Naish O'Sullivan and late Stephanie O'Sullivan (*née* Manning); *m* 1939, Lillian Mary, *y d* of Walter Frank Yate Molineux, Ulverston; one *s* one *d*. *Educ:* Mayfield College. Admitted Solicitor, 1936. Served War of 1939–45, Gordon Highlanders and HQ Special Force SEAC (Captain). Joined Public Trustee Office, 1945; Chief Administrative Officer, 1963–66; Asst Public Trustee, 1966–71. Pres., Holborn Law Soc., 1965–66. Chm. of Governors of St Thomas More High Sch. for Boys, Westcliff-on-Sea, 1964–66. *Publications:* articles in legal jls; short stories. *Recreations:* golf (playing), cricket (watching), wrestling (with crossword puzzles). *Address:* 13 Orchid Place, South Woodham Ferrers, Essex CM3 5LQ. *T:* Chelmsford (0245) 321530.

O'SULLIVAN, Rt. Rev. Mgr. James, CBE 1973 (MBE 1963); Officiating Chaplain (RC), RAMC Depot and Training Centre, since 1973; *b* 2 Aug. 1917; *s* of Richard O'Sullivan and Ellen (*née* Ahern). *Educ:* St Finnbarr's Coll., Cork; All Hallows Coll., Dublin. Ordained, 1941; joined Royal Army Chaplain's Dept, 1942; 49 Infantry Div., Normandy, 1944; Senior RC Chaplain, Malaya, 1952–54 (despatches 1953); Chaplain Irish Guards, 1954–56; Senior RC Chaplain, Berlin, 1956–59; Staff Chaplain (RC), War Office, 1959–64; Senior RC Chaplain, BAOR, 1965–69; Principal RC Chaplain (Army), 1969–73. *Recreation:* golf. *Address:* Osgil, Vicarage Lane, Ropley, Alresford, Hants SO24 0DU.

O'SULLIVAN, John; *see* O'Sullivan, C. A. J. N.

O'SULLIVAN, Sally Angela, (Mrs Charles Wilson); Editor in Chief, Good Housekeeping, since 1991; *b* 26 July 1949; *d* of Lorraine and Joan Connell; *m* 1st, 1973, Thaddeus O'Sullivan (marr. diss.); 2nd, 1980, Charles Martin Wilson, *qv*; one *s* one *d*. *Educ:* Ancaster House Sch.; Trinity Coll., Dublin (BA). Dep. Editor, Woman's World, 1977–78; Women's Editor: Daily Record, 1980; Sunday Standard, 1981; Editor, Options, 1982–88; Launch Editor, Country Homes & Interiors, 1986; Editor: She, 1989; Harpers & Queen, 1989–91. Magazine Editor of the Year, 1986. *Recreations:* family, horses. *Address:* National Magazine House, 72 Broadwick Street, W1V 1FA. *T:* 071–439 5000.
See also M. B. Connell.

OSWALD, Adm. Sir (John) Julian (Robertson), GCB 1989 (KCB 1987); First Sea Lord and Chief of Naval Staff, and First and Principal Naval Aide-de-Camp to the Queen, since 1989; *b* 11 Aug. 1933; *s* of George Hamilton Oswald and Margaret Elliot Oswald (*née* Robertson), Newmore, Invergordon; *m* 1958, Veronica Therese Dorette Thompson; two *s* three *d*. *Educ:* Beaudesert Park, Minchinhampton; Britannia RNC, Dartmouth. Junior Officer, 1951; served in HM Ships Devonshire, Vanguard, Verulam, Newfoundland, Jewel, Victorious, Naiad; specialised in Gunnery, 1960; Commanded HMS Yarnton, 1962–63, HMS Bacchante, 1971–72; MoD, 1972–75; RCDS, 1976; Commanded HMS Newcastle, 1977–79; RN Presentation Team, 1979–80; Captain, Britannia RNC, 1980–82; ACDS (Progs), 1982–84; ACDS (Policy and Nuclear), 1985; Flag Officer, Third Flotilla, and Comdr, Anti-Submarine Warfare, Striking Fleet, 1985–87; C-in-C, Fleet, Allied C-in-C, Channel, and C-in-C, E Atlantic, 1987–89. Member: RUSI (Mem. Council, 1983–86 and 1990–); European Atlantic Gp., Catholic Union; Mensa. Book reviewer for various publications. *Publications:* articles on strategy and defence policy. *Recreations:* tennis, gliding, walking, stamp collecting, family. *Address:* c/o Naval Secretary, Old Admiralty Building, Whitehall, SW1.

OSWALD, Maj.-Gen. Marshall St John, CB 1965; CBE 1961; DSO 1945; MC 1943; retired as Director of Management and Support Intelligence, Ministry of Defence, 1966; *b* 13 Sept. 1911; *s* of William Whitehead Oswald and Katharine Ray Oswald; *m* 1st, 1938, Mary Georgina Baker (*d* 1970); one *s* two *d*; 2nd, 1974, Mrs Barbara Rickards. *Educ:* Rugby Sch.; RMA, Woolwich. Commissioned RA, 1931; served in RHA and Field Artillery, UK and India, 1931–39. Served War of 1939–45 (despatches, MC, DSO): Battery Comdr 4 RHA and Staff Officer in Egypt and Western Desert, 1939–42; GSO1, Tactical HQ, 8th Army, 1942–43; 2nd in Comd Field Regt, Italy, 1943–44; CO South Notts Hussars, Western Europe, 1944–45; Col on staff of HQ 21 Army Group, 1945. Mil. Govt Comdr (Col) of Cologne Area, 1946–47; Staff Officer, War Office (Lt-Col) 1948–49; Instructor (Col) Staff Coll., Camberley 1950–52; CO 19 Field Regt, Germany/Korea, 1953–55; GHQ, MELF (Col), 1955–56 (despatches 1957); IDC 1958; CCRA and Chief of Staff (Brig.) 1st Corps in Germany, 1959–62; DMI, War Office, 1962–64, Min. of Defence (Army), 1964–65. *Recreations:* fishing, shooting, ski-ing. *Address:* Eastfield House, Longparish, near Andover, Hants SP11 6NN. *T:* Longparish (026472) 228. *Club:* Army and Navy.

OSWALD, Dr Neville Christopher, TD 1946; MD Cantab 1946; FRCP 1947; retired 1975; formerly: Consultant Physician: St Bartholomew's Hospital; Brompton Hospital; King Edward VII's Hospital for Officers, London; King Edward VII's Hospital, Midhurst; *b* 1 Aug. 1910; *s* of late Col Christopher Percy Oswald, CMG; *m* 1st, 1941, Patricia Rosemary Joyce Cooke (*d* 1947); one *s* one *d*; 2nd, 1948, Marjorie Mary Sinclair; one *d*. *Educ:* Clifton Coll.; Queens' Coll., Cambridge. Research Fellow, USA, 1938–39. Royal Army Medical Corps, 1939–45. Hon. Physician to the Queen, 1956–58; Hon. Consultant in Diseases of the Chest to the Army, 1972–75. Hon. Col, 17th (London) General Hospital RAMC (TA), 1963–70, 217 (Eastern) General Hospital RAMC (V), 1967–70. President: British Tuberculosis Assoc., 1965–67; Thoracic Soc., 1974. DL Greater London, 1973–78. RCP: Mitchell Lectr; Tudor Edwards Lectr. *Publications:* Recent Trends in Chronic Bronchitis, 1958; Diseases of the Respiratory System, 1962; many articles upon respiratory diseases. *Recreations:* travel, golf. *Address:* The Old Rectory, Thurlestone, South Devon TQ7 3NJ. *T:* Kingsbridge (0548) 560555.

OSWALD, Richard Anthony; Deputy Health Service Commissioner, since 1989; b 12 Jan. 1941; s of Denis Geoffrey Oswald and late Dorothy Lettice Oswald (née Shaw); m 1963, Janet Iris Penticost; three s one d (and one d decd). Educ: The Leys School, Cambridge. AHSM. NHS admin. posts, 1961–77; Dist Administrator, Leeds West, 1977–84; Gen. Manager, Leeds Western HA, 1985–89. Recreations: music, acting, bird-watching, DIY. Address: South View Farm, Draughton, Skipton, N Yorks BD23 6EB. T: Bolton Abbey (075671) 256.

OSWALD, William Richard Michael, CVO 1988 (LVO 1979); Manager, Royal Studs, since 1970; b 21 April 1934; s of Lt-Col William Alexander Hugh Oswald, ERD and Rose-Marie (née Leahy); m 1958, Lady Angela Mary Rose Cecil, d of 6th Marquess of Exeter, KCMG; one s one d. Educ: Eton; King's College, Cambridge (MA). 2nd Lieut The King's Own Royal Regt, 1953; Captain, Royal Fusiliers (TA), 1957. Manager, Lordship and Egerton Studs, 1962–70. Mem. Council, Thoroughbred Breeders' Assoc., 1965–; Chm., Bloodstock Industry Cttee, Animal Health Trust, 1989–. Recreations: shooting, painting. Address: Flitcham Hall, King's Lynn, Norfolk PE6 3BY. T: Hillington (0485) 600319. Club: White's.

O'TOOLE, (Seamus) Peter; actor; b 1932; s of Patrick Joseph O'Toole; m Sian Phillips, qv (marr. diss.); two d. Educ: Royal Academy of Dramatic Art. With Bristol Old Vic Company, 1955–58; first appearance on London stage as Peter Shirley in Major Barbara, Old Vic, 1956. Associate Dir, Old Vic Co., 1980. Plays include: Oh, My Papa!, Garrick, 1957; The Long and the Short and the Tall, Royal Court and New, 1959; season with Shakespeare Memorial Theatre Company, Stratford-on-Avon, 1960; Baal, Phœnix, 1963; Hamlet, National Theatre, 1963; Ride a Cock Horse, Piccadilly, 1965; Juno and the Paycock, Man and Superman, Pictures in the Hallway, Gaiety, Dublin, 1966; Waiting for Godot, Happy Days (dir.), Abbey, Dublin, 1969; Uncle Vanya, Plunder, The Apple Cart, Judgement, Bristol Old Vic, 1973; Uncle Vanya, Present Laughter, Chicago, 1978; Macbeth, Old Vic, 1980; Man and Superman, Haymarket, 1982; Pygmalion, Shaftesbury, 1984, Yvonne Arnaud, Guildford, and NY, 1987; The Apple Cart, Haymarket, 1986; Jeffrey Bernard is Unwell, Apollo, 1989, Shaftesbury, 1991. Films include: Kidnapped, 1959; The Day They Robbed the Bank of England, 1959; The Savage Innocents, 1960; Lawrence of Arabia, 1962; Becket, 1963; Lord Jim, 1964; What's New, Pussycat?, 1965; How to Steal a Million, 1966; The Bible . . . in the Beginning, 1966; The Night of the Generals, 1967; Great Catherine, 1968; The Lion in Winter, 1968; Goodbye Mr Chips, 1969; Brotherly Love, 1970; Murphy's War, 1971; Under Milk Wood, 1971; The Ruling Class, 1972; Man of La Mancha, 1972; Rosebud, 1975; Man Friday, 1975; Foxtrot, 1975; The Stunt Man, 1977; Coup d'Etat, 1977; Zulu Dawn, 1978; Power Play, 1978; The Antagonists, 1981; My Favorite Year, 1981; Supergirl, 1983; Club Paradise, 1986; The Last Emperor, 1987; High Spirits, 1988; Creator, 1990; King Ralph, 1991; Wings of Fame, 1991; television: Rogue Male, 1976; Strumpet City, 1979; Masada, 1981; Svengali, 1982; Pygmalion, 1983; Kim, 1983; Banshee, 1986; The Dark Angel, 1989. Club: Garrick.

OTTAWA, Archbishop of, (RC), since 1967; **Most Rev. Joseph Aurèle Plourde;** b 12 Jan. 1915; s of Antoine Plourde and Suzanne Albert. Educ: Bathurst Coll.; Bourget Coll., Rigaud; Major Seminary of Halifax; Inst. Catholique, Paris; Gregorian Univ., Rome. Auxiliary Bishop of Alexandria, Ont., 1964. Hon. DEducn, Moncton Univ., 1969. Address: Archbishop's Residence, 1247 Kilborn Place, Ottawa, Ont K1H 6K9, Canada. T: 738–5025.

OTTAWA, Bishop of, since 1981; **Rt. Rev. Edwin Keith Lackey.** Educ: Bishop's Univ., Lennoxville (BA 1953). Deacon 1953, priest 1954, Ottawa; Curate of Cornwall, 1953–55; Incumbent of Russell, 1955–60, Vankleek Hill, 1960–63; Rector of St Michael and All Angels, Ottawa, 1963–72; Director of Programme, dio. Ottawa, 1972–78; Hon. Canon, 1972–78; Archdeacon of the Diocese, 1978–81. Hon. DCL Bishop's Univ., 1988. Address: Bishop's Office, 71 Bronson Avenue, Ottawa, Ontario K1R 6G6, Canada.

OTTAWAY, Richard Geoffrey James; Legal Adviser, Coastal States Petroleum (UK) Ltd, since 1988; b 24 May 1945; s of late Professor Christopher Ottaway, PhD, FRCVS and of Grace Ottaway; m 1982, Nicola E. Kisch. Educ: Backwell Secondary Modern School, Somerset; Bristol University. LLB (Hons). Entered RN as an Artificer apprentice, 1961; commissioned and entered RNC, Dartmouth, 1966; served with Western Fleet, HM Ships Beechampton, Nubian and Eagle, 1967–70; Bristol Univ., 1971–74; articled to Norton Rose Botterell & Roche, 1974; admitted Solicitor, 1977; specialist in international, maritime and commercial law; Partner, William A. Crump & Son, 1981–87. Contested (C) Nottingham N, 1987; Prospective Parly Candidate (C) Croydon South, 1991–; MP (C) Nottingham N, 1983–87. PPS to Ministers of State, FCO, 1985–87. Publications: (jtly) Road to Reform, 1987; papers on combating internat. maritime fraud, on financial matters and on the environment. Recreations: jazz, ski-ing, yacht racing. Clubs: Carlton; Royal Corinthian Yacht.

OTTER, Air Vice-Marshal Victor Charles, CBE 1967 (OBE 1945); Air Officer Engineering, Air Support Command Royal Air Force, 1966–69, retired; b 9 February 1914; s of Robert and Ada Annie Otter; m 1943, Iris Louise Dykes; no c. Educ: Weymouth Gram. School. RAF Aircraft Apprentice, 1929–32; flying duties, 1935–37; commissioned Engr. Br., 1940; SO (Techn) Controller Research and Development (MAP), 1942–47; Asst Air Attaché, Budapest, 1947–48; Officer Comdg Central Servicing Develt Establt, 1953–55; Chief Engrg Officer, Bomber Comd, 1956–59; OC No 32 Maintenance Unit, 1959–61; STSO Flying Trng Comd, 1961–63; Project Dir, P1154/P1127, 1963–66. CEng, FRAeS, psc. Address: Harpenden, 21 Keats Avenue, Littleover, Derby DE3 7EE. T: Derby (0332) 512048. Club: Royal Air Force.

OTTEWILL, Prof. Ronald Harry, OBE 1989; PhD; FRS 1982; FRSC; Leverhulme Professor of Physical Chemistry, since 1982, and Head, School of Chemistry, since 1990, University of Bristol; b 8 Feb. 1927; m Ingrid Geraldine Roe; one s one d. Educ: Southall Grammar Sch.; Queen Mary Coll., London (BSc 1948; PhD 1951); Fitzwilliam Coll., Cambridge (MA 1955; PhD 1956). Sen. Asst in Res., 1955–58, Asst Dir of Res., 1958–63, Dept of Colloid Sci., Cambridge Univ.; Bristol University: Lectr, 1964–66; Reader, 1966–70; Prof. of Colloid Science, 1970–82; Head of Dept of Physical Chem., 1973; Dean, Faculty of Science, 1988–90. Chm., SERC Neutron Beam Res. Cttee, 1982–85. Pres., Faraday Soc., 1989– (Hon. Treas. 1985–89; Vice Pres., 1986–89). Lectures: A. E. Alexander, RACI, 1982; Liversidge, RSC, 1985–86; Canadian High Polymer Forum, 1987; Langmuir, ACS, 1988; Rideal, RSC/SCI, 1990. Medal for Surface and Colloid Chemistry, RSC, 1972; Wolfgang Ostwald Medal, Kolloid Gesellschaft, W Germany, 1979; Bude Medal, Collège de France, Paris, 1981. Publications: contribs to learned jls. Address: School of Chemistry, The University, Bristol BS8 1TS.

OTTON, Sir Geoffrey (John), KCB 1981 (CB 1978); Second Permanent Secretary, Department of Health and Social Security, 1979–86, retired; b 10 June 1927; s of late John Alfred Otton and Constance Alma Otton; m 1952, Hazel Lomas (née White); one s one d. Educ: Christ's Hosp.; St John's Coll., Cambridge (MA). Home Office, 1950–71 (seconded to Cabinet Office, 1959–61; Principal Private Sec. to Home Sec., 1963–65); Dept of Health and Social Security, 1971–86 (Chief Advr to Supplementary Benefits Commn,

1976–79). Chairman: Bromley CVS, 1987–; Management Cttee, St Piers (Special Sch.), Lingfield, 1987–. Recreation: music. Address: 72 Cumberland Road, Bromley, Kent BR2 0PW. T: 081–460 9610.

OTTON, Hon. Sir Philip (Howard), Kt 1983; **Hon. Mr Justice Otton;** a Judge of the High Court of Justice, Queen's Bench Division, since 1983; Judge in Charge of Official Solicitors Courts, since 1991; b 28 May 1933; o s of late Henry Albert Otton, Kenilworth and of Leah Otton; m 1965, Helen Margaret, d of late P. W. Bates, Stourbridge; two s one d. Educ: Bablake School, Coventry; Birmingham Univ. LLB 1954. 2nd Lieut, 3rd Dragoon Guards, 1955–57. Called to the Bar, Gray's Inn, 1955, Bencher 1983; QC 1975. Dep. Chm., Beds QS, 1970–72; Junior Counsel to the Treasury (Personal Injuries), 1970–75; a Recorder of the Crown Court, 1972–83; Presiding Judge, Midland and Oxford Circuit, 1986–88. Chairman: Royal Brompton and National Heart and Lung Hospitals SHA, 1991–; Nat. Heart and Lung Inst., 1991–. Governor, Nat. Heart and Chest Hosps, 1979–85. Hon. Mem., Amer. Bar Assoc. Recreations: theatre, opera, music. Address: Royal Courts of Justice, Strand, WC2A 2LL. Clubs: Garrick, Pilgrims, Roehampton.

OTUNGA, HE Cardinal Maurice; see Nairobi, Archbishop of, (RC).

OULTON, Sir (Antony) Derek (Maxwell), GCB 1989 (KCB 1984; CB 1979); QC 1985; MA, PhD; Permanent Secretary, Lord Chancellor's Office, and Clerk of the Crown in Chancery, 1982–89; barrister-at-law; Fellow, Magdalene College, Cambridge, since 1990; b 14 Oct. 1927; y s of late Charles Cameron Courtenay Oulton and Elizabeth, d of T. H. Maxwell, KC; m 1955, Margaret Geraldine (d 1989), d of late Lt-Col G. S. Oxley, MC, 60th Rifles; one s three d. Educ: St Edward's Sch., Oxford; King's Coll., Cambridge (scholar; BA (1st Cl.), MA; PhD 1974). Called to Bar, Gray's Inn, 1952, Bencher, 1982; in private practice, Kenya, 1952–60; Private Sec. to Lord Chancellor, 1961–65; Sec., Royal Commn on Assizes and Quarter Sessions, 1966–69; Asst Solicitor, 1969–75. Dep. Sec., 1976–82, and Dep. Clerk of the Crown in Chancery, 1977–82, Lord Chancellor's Office. Vis. Prof. in Law, Bristol Univ., 1990–91. Chm., Mental Health Foundn Cttee on the Mentally Disordered Offender, 1989–. Trustee, Nat. Gallery, 1989–. Pres., Electricity Arbitration Assoc., 1990–. Publication: (jtly) Legal Aid and Advice, 1971. Address: Magdalene College, Cambridge CB3 0AG. T: Cambridge (0223) 332100.

OULTON, Air Vice-Marshal Wilfrid Ewart, CB 1958; CBE 1953; DSO 1943; DFC 1943; FEng; FRIN; FIEE; Chairman, Medsales Executive Ltd, since 1982; b 27 July 1911; s of Llewellin Oulton, Monks Coppenhall, Cheshire; m 1935, Sarah, d of Rev. E. Davies, Pitsea, Essex; three s. Educ: University Coll., Cardiff; Cranwell. Commissioned, 1931; Director, Joint Anti-Submarine School, 1946–48; Joint Services Staff College, 1948–50; Air Attaché, Buenos Aires, Montevideo, Asuncion, 1950–53; idc 1954; Director of Operations, Air Ministry, 1954–56; commanded Joint Task Force "Grapple" for first British megaton weapon tests in the Pacific, 1956–58; Senior Air Staff Officer, RAF Coastal Command, HQ, 1958–60; retd. Publication: Christmas Island Cracker, 1987. Recreations: music, squash, golf, travel. Address: Farthings, Hollywood Lane, Lymington, Hants. T: Lymington (0590) 673498. Clubs: Royal Air Force; Royal Lymington Yacht.

OUNSTED, John, MA Cantab; HM Inspector of Schools, 1971–81, retired; b London, 24 May 1919; e s of late Rev. Laurence J. Ounsted, Dorchester Abbey, Oxon (ordained 1965); formerly with Sun Life Assurance); m 1940, Irene, 3rd d of late Rev. Alfred Newns; one s four d. Educ: Winchester (Scholar); Trinity College, Cambridge (Major Scholar). Math. Tripos Part I, 1st Class; Science Tripos Part II, 1st Class; Senior Scholarship, Trinity College. Assistant Master, King Edward's School, Birmingham, 1940–48; Headmaster, Leighton Park School, 1948–70. First layman ever to be Select Preacher, Oxford Univ., 1964. Page Scholarship to visit USA, 1965. Liveryman, Worshipful Company of Mercers. Vice-Pres., Botanical Soc. of British Isles, 1989–. Publications: verses from various languages in the 2 vols of Translation, 1945 and 1947; contributions to Watsonia, The Proceedings of the Botanical Society of the British Isles, and various other educational and botanical periodicals. Recreations: botany, camping, being overtaken when motoring. Address: Apple Tree Cottage, Woodgreen Common, Fordingbridge, Hants SP6 2BD. T: Downton (0725) 22271.

See also Sir A. Foley Newns.

OUTERIÑO, Felix C.; see Candela Outeriño.

OUTRAM, Sir Alan James, 5th Bt, cr 1858; MA; Master, Harrow School (Housemaster, 1979–91); b 15 May 1937; s of late James Ian Outram and late Evelyn Mary Littlehales; S great-uncle, 1945; m 1976, Victoria Jean, d of late George Dickson Paton, Bexhill-on-Sea; one s one d. Educ: Spyway, Langton Matravers, Swanage; Marlborough College, Wilts; St Edmund Hall, Oxford. Lt-Col TAVR. Recreations: golf, tennis, bridge. Heir: s Douglas Benjamin James Outram, b 15 March 1979. Address: Harrow School, Harrow-on-the-Hill, Middlesex HA1 3HW.

OVENDEN, John Frederick; County Councillor, Kent, since 1985; b 17 Aug. 1942; s of late Richard Ovenden and Margaret Louise Ovenden (née Lucas); m 1963, Maureen (née White); one d. Educ: Salmestone County Primary Sch., Margate; Chatham House Grammar Sch., Ramsgate. Asst Exec. Engr, Post Office, 1961–74. MP (Lab) Gravesend, Feb. 1974–1979. Contested (Lab) Gravesham, 1983. Manager, Post Office, subseq. British Telecom, 1979–90. Recreations: football (as a spectator), cricket (Kent), theatre, gardening, books. Club: Gillingham Labour (Gillingham).

OVENS, Maj.-Gen. Patrick John, OBE 1968; MC 1951; Commandant, Joint Warfare Establishment, 1976–79; retired; b 4 Nov. 1922; s of late Edward Alec Ovens and late Mary Linsell Ovens, Cirencester; m 1952, Margaret Mary White; one s two d. Educ: King's Sch., Bruton. Commnd into Royal Marines, 1941; HMS Illustrious, 1942–43; 46 Commando, 1945; HQ 3rd Commando Bde, 1946–48; 41 Indep. Commando, Korea, 1950–52; HQ Portsmouth Gp, 1952–55; psa 1955–56; Staff of CGRM, 1959–61; Amphibious Warfare Sqdn, 1961–62; 41 Commando, 1963–65, CO 1965–67; C-in-C Fleet Staff, 1968–69; Comdr 3 Commando Bde, 1970–72; RCDS 1973; COS to Comdt Gen., RM, MoD, 1974–76. Recreations: sailing, music, gardening.

OVERALL, Sir John (Wallace), Kt 1968; CBE 1962; MC and Bar; architect, town planner and company director; b 15 July 1913; s of late W. Overall, Sydney; m 1943, Margaret J. (d 1988), d of C. W. Goodman; four s. Educ: Sydney Techn. College. AIF, 1940–45: CO, 1 Aust. Para. Bn (Lt-Col). Chief Architect, S Australian Housing Trust, 1946–48; private practice, Architect and Town Planner, 1949–52; Dir of Architecture, Commonwealth Dept of Works, 1952–57; Comr, Nat. Capital Develt Commn, 1958–72; Chm., Nat. Capital Planning Cttee, 1958–72; Comr, Cities Commn (Chm., Adv. Cttee), 1972–73; Principal, John Overall and Partners, 1973–81; Director: Lend Lease Corp. Ltd, 1973–83; General Property Trust, 1975–83; Alliance Holdings Ltd, 1975–83 (Chm., 1980–83); CSR Ltd, 1973–85. Mem., Parliament House Construction Authority (Commonwealth Govt of Australia), 1979–85; Chm. Assessors, Parlt House Design Competition, 1979–80. Chm. of Olympic Fine Arts Architecture and Sculpture Exhibn, Melb., 1956. Life Fellow, RAIA and API; Hon. Fellow, AIA, 1984; Pres., Austr. Inst. of Urban Studies, 1970–71. Past Pres., Canberra Legacy Club. Sydney Luker Meml Medal,

1970; Sir James Barrett Medal, 1970; Gold Medal, RAIA, 1982. *Publications:* Observations on Redevelopment Western Side of Sydney Cove, 1967; sundry papers to professional jls. *Recreations:* golf, tennis. *Address:* Unit 1, Kingston Tower, 9 Jardine Street, Kingston, ACT 2604, Australia. *Clubs:* Commonwealth (Canberra); Royal Sydney Golf.

OVERBURY, (Henry) Colin (Barry), OBE (mil.) 1974; Director, Directorate-General for Competition, Commission of the European Communities, since 1986; *b* 13 Jan. 1931; *s* of Stanley and Daisy Overbury; *m* 1st, 1954, Dawn Rhodes Dade (marr. diss. 1981); three *s*; 2nd, 1989, Louise Jane Rosewarne. *Educ:* Dragon Sch., Oxford; Eastbourne Coll.; Law Society's Coll. of Law. Admitted Solicitor of the Supreme Court, 1955. HM Army Legal Services, 1955–74: progressively, Captain, Major, Lt-Col; Retired List, Lt-Col, 1974. European Commission: Prin. Administrator, 1974–82; Adviser, 1982–84; Hd of Div., 1984–86. Sen. Fellow of the Salzburg Seminar, 1984. *Publications:* articles in Common Market Law Rev., 1977, Fordham Univ. Law Inst. Jl, 1984, 1989. *Recreations:* travel, boating, good living. *Address:* Broke Hall, Nacton, Suffolk IP10 0ET; 200 rue de la Loi, 1049 Brussels. *T:* Brussels 235–5891. *Clubs:* Lansdowne; Cercle Royal Gaulois (Brussels).

OVEREND, Prof. (William) George; Professor of Chemistry in the University of London, 1957–87, now Professor Emeritus; Master, Birkbeck College, 1979–87 (Vice-Master, 1974–79; Hon. Fellow, 1988); *b* 16 Nov. 1921; *e s* of late Harold George Overend, Shrewsbury, Shropshire; *m* 1949, Gina Olava, *y d* of late Horace Bertie Cadman, Birmingham; two *s* one *d. Educ:* Priory School, Shrewsbury; Univ. of Birmingham. BSc (Hons) 1943, PhD 1946, DSc 1954, Birmingham; CChem; FRSC (FRIC 1955). Asst Lecturer, Univ. Coll., Nottingham, 1946–47; Research Chemist with Dunlop Rubber Co. Ltd and subsequently British Rubber Producers' Assoc., 1947–49; Hon. Research Fellow, 1947–49, Lecturer in Chemistry, 1949–55, Univ. of Birmingham; Vis. Associate Prof., Pennsylvania State Univ., 1951–52; Reader in Organic Chemistry, Univ. of London, 1955–57; Hd of Dept of Chem., Birkbeck Coll., London, 1957–79. Univ. of London: Mem., Academic Council, 1963–67, 1976–79 and 1984–87; Mem., Collegiate Council, 1979–87; Mem., University Entrance and Schools Examination Council, 1966–67 and 1985–87; Mem., F and GP Cttee, 1976–87; Mem., External Cttee, 1984–87; Chm., Bd of Studies in Chemistry, 1974–76; Mem., Senate, 1976–87; Mem., Jt Cttee of Court and Senate for collective planning, 1976–79; Dean, Faculty of Science, 1978–79; Chm., Acad. Adv. Bd in Sci., 1978–79; Mem., Extra-Mural Council, 1979–87, Chm., 1983–84; Chm., Cttee for Extra-Mural Studies, 1984–87. Mem. Council, Inst. of Educn, 1979–82; Leverhulme Emeritus Fellow, 1987–89. Member Council: National Inst. of Adult Continuing Educn, 1983–88; London and E Anglian Gp for GCSE, 1986–87; Mem. Chem. Bd, 1981–84, Mem. Adv. Bd on Credit Accumulation and Transfer, 1986–87, CNAA. Rep. of South Bank Poly, Assoc. of Colls of Further and Higher Educn, 1981–. Royal Institute of Chemistry: Examiner, 1958–62; Assessor, 1959–72; Mem., Institutions and Examinations Cttee, 1969–75 (Chm., 1976–85); Mem. Council, 1977–80; Mem. Qual. and Admissions Cttee, 1977–80; Mem. Qual. and Exam. Bd, RSC, 1980–85; Chemical Society (subseq. Royal Society of Chemistry): Mem. Council, 1967–70, 1972–77; Mem. Publications Bd, 1967–78; Hon. Sec. and Hon. Treasurer, Perkin Div., 1972–75; Vice-Pres., 1975–77; Mem., Interdivisional Council, 1972–75; Mem., Educn and Trng Bd, 1972–78; Soc. of Chemical Industry: Mem., Council, 1955–65; Mem., Finance Committee, 1956–65; Mem., Publications Cttee, 1955–65 (Hon. Sec. for publications and Chairman of Publications Committee, 1958–65); Member: Brit. Nat. Cttee for Chemistry, 1961–66, 1973–78; Brit. Nat. Cttee for Biochemistry, 1975–81; Chemical Council, 1960–63 and 1964–69 (Vice-Chm. 1964–69); European Cttee for Carbohydrate Chemists, 1970–85 (Chm.); Hon. Sec., Internat. Cttee for Carbohydrate Chemistry, 1972–75 (Pres., 1978–80); Mem., Jt IUPAC-IUB Commn on Carbohydrate Nomenclature, 1971–. Jubilee Memorial Lecturer, Society of Chemical Industry, 1959–60; Lampitt Medallist, Society of Chemical Industry, 1965; Member: Pharmacopœia Commission, 1963–81; Home Office Poisons Board, 1973–. Governor: Polytechnic of the South Bank, 1970– (Chm., 1980–89; Hon. Fellow 1989); Thomas Huxley Coll., 1971–77; Mem., Council of Governors, Queen Elizabeth Coll., Univ. of London, 1983–85. Mem., Cttee of Management, Inst. of Archaeology, 1980–86. FBIM 1988. Hon. FCollP 1986. DUniv Open, 1988. *Publications:* The Use of Tracer Elements in Biology, 1951; papers in Nature, and Jl of Chemical Soc. *Recreation:* gardening. *Address:* Birkbeck College, Gordon House, Gordon Street, WC1. *T:* 071–380 7479; The Retreat, Nightingales Lane, Chalfont St Giles, Bucks HP8 4SR. *Clubs:* Athenæum, Royal Automobile.

OVERTON, Sir Hugh (Thomas Arnold), KCMG 1983 (CMG 1975); HM Diplomatic Service, retired; Member of Council, Barnardo's, since 1985 (Executive Finance Committee, since 1988); *b* 2 April 1923; *e s* of late Sir Arnold Overton, KCB, KCMG, MC; *m* 1948, Claire-Marie Binet; one *s* two *d. Educ:* Dragon Sch., Oxford; Winchester; Clare Coll., Cambridge. Royal Signals, 1942–45. HM Diplomatic Service, 1947–83; served: Budapest; UK Delegn to UN, New York; Cairo; Beirut; Disarmament Delegn, Geneva; Warsaw; Bonn; Canadian Nat. Defence Coll.; Head of N America Dept, FCO, 1971–74; Consul-Gen., Düsseldorf, 1974–75; Minister (Econ.), Bonn, 1975–80; Consul-Gen., New York, and Dir-Gen., British Trade Develt in USA, 1980–83. Trustee: Bell Educnl Trust, 1986–; Taverner Concerts Trust, 1987–. Mem., RIIA. *Recreations:* reading, handwork, sailing, fishing. *Club:* Royal Automobile.

OWEN, (Alfred) David; Chairman and Group Chairman, Rubery Owen Holdings Ltd, since 1975; *b* 26 Sept. 1936; *m* 1966, Ethne (*née* Sowman); two *s* one *d. Educ:* Brocksford Hall; Oundle; Emmanuel Coll., Cambridge Univ. (MA). Joined Rubery Owen Gp, 1960; Gen. Man., Rubery Owen Motor Div., 1962–67; Dep. Man. Dir, Rubery Owen & Co. Ltd, 1967; Acting Chm. and Man. Dir, Rubery Owen Holdings Ltd, 1969; Dir, Brooke Tool Engineering (Holdings) plc, 1968–; Chm., Severn Valley Railways (Holdings) plc, 1989–. Dir, W Midlands Bd, Central Indep. Television, 1986–. Trustee, Community Projects Foundn, 1978–; Member: Council, Univ. of Aston, 1981–; Bd, British Library, 1982–90; Bd, Nat. Exhibn Centre, 1982–. Pres., Comité de Liaison Eur. de la Distrib. Ind. de Pièces de rechange et équipements pour Autos, 1988–90. Hon. DSc Aston, 1988. *Recreations:* walking, photography, music, industrial archaeology, local history, collecting books. *Address:* Mill Dam House, Mill Lane, Aldridge, Walsall, West Midlands WS9 0NB. *T:* 021–353 1221. *Clubs:* National, Royal Automobile.

OWEN, Alun, MC 1945; retired; Under-Secretary, Land Use Planning Group, Welsh Office, 1975–79; *b* 14 March 1919; *m* 1946, Rhona Evelyn Griffiths; one *s* four *d. Educ:* West Monmouth Grammar Sch.; Bridgend Grammar Sch.; LSE (BScEcon). Mil. Service, 1939–46: Ches. Regt, 1940–46 (Captain) (despatches, Normandy, 1944); Civil Service, Min. of Labour NW Region, 1946–48; Min. of Fuel and Power, 1948–50; Customs and Excise, 1950–59; Welsh Office, Min. of Housing and Local Govt, 1959–62; Welsh Bd of Health, 1962–69; Welsh Office, 1969–79. *Address:* 12 Knowbury Avenue, Penarth, South Glam CF6 2RX.

OWEN, Alun (Davies); writer since 1957; *b* 24 Nov. 1925; *s* of Sidney Owen and Ruth (*née* Davies); *m* 1942, (Theodora) Mary O'Keeffe; two *s. Educ:* Cardigan County School, Wales; Oulton High School, Liverpool. Worked as Stage Manager, Director and Actor,

in theatre, TV and films, 1942–59. Awards: Screenwriters and Producers Script of the Year, 1960; Screenwriters Guild, 1961; Daily Mirror, 1961; Golden Star, 1967. *Acted in: stage:* Birmingham Rep., 1943–44; Humoresque, 1948; Snow White and the Seven Dwarfs, 1951; Old Vic season, 1953; Tamburlaine the Great, As You Like It, King Lear, Twelfth Night, The Merchant of Venice, Macbeth, The Wandering Jew, The Taming of the Shrew, 1957; Royal Court Season, 1957; Man with a Guitar, The Waiting of Lester Abbs, The Samson Riddle, 1972; The Ladies, 1977; *films:* Every Day Except Christmas, 1957; I'm All Right Jack, 1959; The Servant, 1963; *television:* Glas y Dorlan, BBC Wales. *Author of productions: stage:* The Rough and Ready Lot, 1959 (Radio 1958), publ. 1960; Progress to the Park, 1959 (Radio 1958), publ. 1962; The Rose Affair, 1966 (TV 1961), publ. 1962; A Little Winter Love, 1963, publ. 1964; Maggie May, 1964; The Game, 1965; The Goose, 1967; Shelter, 1971 (TV 1967), publ. 1968; There'll Be Some Changes Made, 1969; Norma, 1969 (extended version, Nat. Theatre, 1983); We Who Are About To (later title Mixed Doubles), 1969, publ. 1970; The Male of the Species, 1974 (TV 1969), publ. 1972; Lucia, 1982; *screen:* The Criminal, 1960; A Hard Day's Night, 1964 (Oscar nomination); Caribbean Idyll, 1970; *radio:* Two Sons, 1957; It Looks Like Rain, 1959; Earwig (series), 1984; *television:* No Trams to Lime Street, 1959, After the Funeral, 1960, Lena, Oh My Lena, 1960, publ. as Three TV Plays, 1961; The Ruffians, 1960; The Ways of Love, 1961; Dare to be a Daniel, 1962, publ. in Eight Plays, Book 1, 1965; The Hard Knock, You Can't Wind 'em All, 1962; The Strain, Let's Imagine Series, The Stag, A Local Boy, 1963; The Other Fella, The Making of Jericho, 1966; The Wake, 1967, publ. in A Collection of Modern Short Plays, 1972; George's Room, 1967, publ. 1968; The Winner, The Loser, The Fantasist, Stella, Thief, 1967; Charlie, Gareth, Tennyson, Ah There You Are, Alexander, Minding the Shop, Time for the Funny Walk, 1968; Doreen, 1969, publ. in The Best Short Plays, 1971; The Ladies, Joan, Spare Time, Park People, You'll Be the Death of Me, Male of the Species, 1969; Hilda, And a Willow Tree, Just the Job, Female of the Species, Joy, 1970; Ruth, Funny, Pal, Giants and Ogres, The Piano Player, 1971; The Web, 1972; Ronnie Barker Show (3 scripts), Buttons, Flight, 1973; Lucky, Norma, 1974; Left, 1975; Forget Me Not (6 plays), 1976; The Look, 1978; Passing Through, publ. 1979; The Runner, 1980; Sealink, 1980; Lancaster Gate End, 1982; Cafe Society, 1982; Kish-Kisch, 1982; Colleagues, 1982; Soft Impeachment, 1983; Tiger (musical drama), 1984; (adap.) Lovers of the Lake, 1984 (Banff award, 1985); Widowers, 1985; Unexplained Laughter, 1989; (adap.) Come home Charlie, and face them, 1990. *Recreations:* languages and history. *Address:* c/o Julian Friedmann, Blake Friedmann Literary Agency, 37–41 Gower Street, WC1E 6HH. *Club:* Chelsea Arts.

OWEN, Aron, PhD; **His Honour Judge Owen;** a Circuit Judge, since 1980; *b* 16 Feb. 1919; *m* 1946, Rose (*née* Fishman), JP; one *s* two *d. Educ:* Tredegar County Grammar Sch.; Univ. of Wales (BA Hons, PhD). Called to the Bar, Inner Temple, 1948. Freeman, City of London, 1963. *Recreations:* travel, gardening. *Address:* 44 Brampton Grove, Hendon, NW4 4AQ. *T:* 081–202 8151.

OWEN, Bernard Laurence; a Chairman of Industrial Tribunals, since 1982; *b* 8 Aug. 1925; *s* of Albert Victor Paschal Owen and Dorothy May Owen; *m* 1950, Elsie Yarnold; one *s* two *d. Educ:* King Edward's School, Birmingham; solicitor. Commissioned Royal Warwickshire Regt, 1945, service in Sudan, Eritrea, Egypt; staff appts in GHQs Middle East and Palestine, 1946–47; retired 1947 (Major); qualified as solicitor, 1950; a Senior Partner, C. Upfill Jagger Son & Tilley, 1952–82. *Recreations:* gardening, photography, bird watching.

OWEN, David; *see* Owen, A. D.

OWEN, Rt. Hon. David Anthony Llewellyn, PC 1976; MP Plymouth, Devonport, since 1974 (Plymouth, Sutton, 1966–74) (Lab, 1966–81, SDP, 1981–90, Social Democrat, since 1990); *b* Plympton, South Devon, 2 July 1938; *s* of Dr John William Morris Owen and Mary Llewellyn; *m* 1968, Deborah Schabert; two *s* one *d. Educ:* Bradfield College; Sidney Sussex College, Cambridge (Hon. Fellow, 1977); St Thomas' Hospital. BA 1959; MB, BChir 1962; MA 1963. St Thomas' Hospital: house appts, 1962–64; Neurological and Psychiatric Registrar, 1964–66; Research Fellow, Medical Unit, 1966–68. Contested (Lab) Torrington, 1964. PPS to Minister of Defence, Administration, 1967; Parly Under-Sec. of State for Defence, for RN, 1968–70; Opposition Defence Spokesman, 1970–72, resigned over EEC, 1972; Parly Under-Sec. of State, DHSS, 1974; Minister of State: DHSS, 1974–76; FCO, 1976–77; Sec. of State for Foreign and Commonwealth Affairs, 1977–79; Opposition spokesman on energy, 1979–80. Sponsored 1973 Children's Bill; ministerially responsible for 1975 Children's Act. Co-founder, SDP, 1981; Chm., Parly Cttee, SDP, 1981–82; Dep. Leader, SDP, 1982–83; Leader, SDP, 1983–87, resigned over issue of merger with Liberal Party, re-elected 1988. Chm., Decision Technology Internat., 1970–72. Member: Independent Commn on Disarmament and Security Issues, 1980–89; Ind. Commn on Internat. Humanitarian Issues, 1983–88. Chm., Humanitas, 1990–. Governor of Charing Cross Hospital, 1966–68; Patron, Disablement Income Group, 1968–. Chairman of SW Regional Sports Council, 1967–71. *Publications:* (ed) A Unified Health Service, 1968; The Politics of Defence, 1972; In Sickness and in Health, 1976; Human Rights, 1978; Face the Future, 1981; A Future That Will Work, 1984; A United Kingdom, 1986; Personally Speaking to Kenneth Harris, 1987; Our NHS, 1988; contrib. to Social Services for All, 1968; articles in Lancet, Neurology, Clinical Science, and Economic Affairs. *Recreation:* sailing. *Address:* 78 Narrow Street, Limehouse, E14. *T:* 071–987 5441; House of Commons, SW1. *T:* 071–219 5531.

OWEN, David Harold Owen; Registrar of the Privy Council, since 1983; *b* 24 May 1933; *er* twin *s* of late Lloyd Owen Owen and Margaret Glyn Owen, Machynlleth, Powys; *m* 1961, Ailsa Ransome Wallis; three *d. Educ:* Harrow Sch.; Gonville and Caius Coll., Cambridge. Called to the Bar, Gray's Inn, 1958. Served Royal Welch Fusiliers, 1951–53 (2nd Lieut). Campbell's Soups Ltd, King's Lynn, 1958–68; Lord Chancellor's Dept, 1969–80 (Private Sec. to Lord Chancellor, 1971–75); Chief Clerk, Judicial Cttee of Privy Council, 1980–83. *Recreations:* music, travel. *Address:* Judicial Committee of the Privy Council, Downing Street, SW1. *T:* 071–270 0487. *Club:* Reform.

OWEN, Maj.-Gen. David Lanyon Ll.; *see* Lloyd Owen.

OWEN, Rt. Rev. Edwin, MA; *b* 3 Nov. 1910; *s* of late William Rowland Owen; *m* 1940, Margaret Mary Williams, BA; one *s* one *d. Educ:* Royal School, Armagh; Trinity College, Dublin (MA). Deacon 1934, priest 1935, Dublin; Curate of Glenageary, 1934–36; Christ Church, Leeson Park, Dublin, 1936–38; Minor Canon of St Patrick's Cathedral, Dublin, 1935–36; Chancellor's Vicar, 1936–38; Succentor, 1938–42; Incumbent of Birr with Eglish, 1942–57; Canon, Killaloe Cathedral, 1954–57; Rector of Killaloe and Dean of Killaloe Cathedral, 1957–72; Diocesan Secretary of Killaloe and Kilfenora, 1957–72; Bishop of Killaloe, Kilfenora, Clonfert and Kilmacduagh, 1972–76, when diocese amalgamated with Limerick, Ardfert and Aghadoe, and Emly; Bishop of Limerick and Killaloe, 1976–81. *Recreation:* classical music. *Address:* 5 Frankfort Avenue, Rathgar, Dublin 6.

OWEN, Dr Gareth, CBE 1988; DSc; MRIA; FIBiol; Principal, University College of Wales, Aberystwyth, 1979–March 1989; Vice-Chancellor, University of Wales, 1985–87; *b* 4 Oct. 1922; *s* of J. R. and B. M. Owen; *m* 1953, Beti Jones; one *s* two *d. Educ:*

Pontypridd Boys' Grammar Sch.; University Coll., Cardiff (BSc 1950; Fellow, 1982). DSc Glasgow, 1959. FIBiol 1964. Served War, RAF Pilot, 1942–47. Lectr in Zoology, Univ. of Glasgow, 1950–64; Prof. of Zool., 1964–79, and Pro-Vice-Chancellor, 1974–79, Queen's Univ. of Belfast. Welsh Supernumerary, Jesus Coll., Oxford, 1981–82 and 1986–87. Mem., Nature Conservancy Council, 1984–91 (Chm., Adv. Cttee for Wales, 1985–91). Pres., Welsh Centre of Internat. Affairs, 1989–. MRIA 1976. Hon. Fellow, UCW, Cardiff, 1982; Hon. Mem. of the Gorsedd, 1983. Hon. DSc QUB, 1982; Hon. LLD Wales, 1989. *Publications:* contrib. Trans Royal Soc., Proc. Malacol. Soc. London, Jl Mar. Biol. Soc., and Qly Jl Micro. Sci. *Recreation:* photography. *Address:* 6A St Margaret's Place, Whitchurch, Cardiff CF4 7AD. *T:* Cardiff (0222) 692199. *Club:* Commonwealth Trust.

OWEN, Sir Geoffrey (David), Kt 1989; Director, Business Policy Programme, Centre for Economic Performance, London School of Economics and Political Science, since 1991; *b* 16 April 1934; *s* of L. G. Owen; *m* 1961, Dorothy Jane; two *s* one *d.* *Educ:* Rugby Sch.; Balliol Coll., Oxford (MA). Joined Financial Times, 1958, feature writer, industrial correspondent; US Correspondent, 1961; Industrial Editor, 1967; Executive, Industrial Reorganisation Corp., 1967–69; Dir of Admin, Overseas Div., 1969, Dir of Personnel and Admin, 1972, British Leyland Internat.; Dep. Editor, 1974–80, Editor, 1981–90, Financial Times. *Publication:* Industry in the USA, 1966. *Address:* London School of Economics and Political Science, Houghton Street, WC2A 2AE.

OWEN, Gerald Victor; QC 1969; a Recorder of the Crown Court, since 1979; *b* London, 29 Nov. 1922; *m* 1946, Phyllis (*née* Ladsky); one *s* one *d.* *Educ:* Kilburn Grammar Sch.; St Catharine's Coll., Cambridge. Exhibr, St Catharine's Coll., Cambridge, 1940; Drapers' Company Science Schol., Queen Mary Coll., London, 1940. 1st cl. Maths Tripos I, 1941; Senior Optimes Tripos II, 1942; BA 1943, MA 1946, Cantab; Royal Statistical Soc. Certif., 1947; LLB London (Hons) 1949. Research Ballistics, Min. of Supply, 1942–45; Statistical Officer, LCC, 1945–49. Called to Bar, Gray's Inn, 1949; *ad eundem* Inner Temple, 1969. A Dep. Circuit Judge, 1971. Chairman: Dairy Produce Quota Tribunal, 1984–85; Medical Appeals Tribunal, 1984–. Member, Cttees of Justice on: Legal Aid in Criminal Cases; Complaints against Lawyers, 1970; False Witness, the problem of perjury, 1973. *Address:* 3 Paper Buildings, Temple, EC4. *T:* 071–583 1183. *Club:* Maccabaeans.

OWEN, Gordon Michael William, CBE 1991; Group Managing Director, Cable and Wireless PLC, 1990–91 (Director, 1986–91; Joint Managing Director, 1987–88; Deputy Chief Executive, 1988–90); Chairman, Mercury Communications Ltd, since 1990 (Managing Director, 1984–90); *b* 9 Dec. 1937; *s* of Christopher Knowles Owen and late Mrs Margaret Joyce Milward (*née* Spencer); *m* 1963, Jennifer Pearl, (Jane), Bradford; one *s* one *d.* *Educ:* Cranbrook Sch. Cable & Wireless, 1954–91. *Recreations:* bee keeping, stamp collecting, sailing, bad golf. *Address:* Braye House, Egypt Lane, Farnham Common, Bucks SL2 3LF.

OWEN, Maj.-Gen. Harry, CB 1972; Chairman, Medical Appeal Tribunal, 1972–84; *b* 17 July 1911; *m* 1952, Maureen (*née* Summers); one *s* one *d.* *Educ:* University Coll., Bangor. BA Hons Philosophy, 1934. Solicitor of Supreme Court, 1939. Commissioned in Queen's Own Cameron Highlanders, 1940–43; joined Mil. Dept of Office of Judge Advocate General, 1943; served in: W Africa, 1945–46; Middle East, 1947–50; Austria, 1952–53; Dep. Dir of Army Legal Services: Far East, 1960–62; HQ, BAOR, 1962–67; Brig. Legal Staff, 1968–69; Maj.-Gen. 1969; Dir, Army Legal Services, 1969–71, retd. *Recreations:* philosophy, history of art, walking, gardening. *Address:* 1 The Beeches, Slab Lane, West Wellow, near Romsey, Hants SO51 6RN. *T:* Romsey (0794) 23562.

OWEN, Sir Hugh (Bernard Pilkington), 5th Bt *cr* 1813; *b* 28 March 1915; *s* of Sir John Arthur Owen, 4th Bt and Lucy Fletcher (*d* 1985), *e d* of F. W. Pilkington; *S* father, 1973. *Educ:* Chillon Coll., Switzerland. *Heir:* *b* John William Owen [*b* 7 June 1917; *m* 1963, Gwenllian Mary, *er d* of late E. B. Phillips]. *Address:* 63 Dudsbury Road, Ferndown, Dorset BH22 8RD.

OWEN, Sir Hugo Dudley C.; *see* Cunliffe-Owen.

OWEN, Idris Wyn; a director of a company in the construction industry; *b* 1912; *m.* *Educ:* Stockport Sch. and Coll. of Technology; Manchester Sch. of Commerce. Contested (C): Manchester Exchange, 1951; Stalybridge and Hyde, 1955; Stockport North 1966; MP (C) Stockport North, 1970–Feb. 1974; contested (C) Stockport North, Oct. 1974. Member, Stockport Borough Council, 1946; Mayor, 1962–63. Vice-Pres., Nat. Fedn of Building Trades Employers, 1965. FCIOB.

OWEN, Ivor Henry, CEng, FIMechE; Director General, Design Council, since 1988; *b* 14 Nov. 1930; *s* of Thomas and Anne Owen; *m* 1954, Jane Frances Graves; two *s* one *d.* *Educ:* Liverpool College of Technology; Manchester College of Science and Technology. Engineering apprentice, later design engineer, Craven Bros (Manchester), Stockport, 1947–57; Manufacturing Develt Engr, Steam Turbine Div., English Electric, Rugby, 1957–62; Manager, Netherton Works, English Electric, Bootle, 1962–66 (hydro electric plant, steam turbine components, condensers, nuclear equipment); Manager, English Electric Computers, Winsford, 1966–69; Manager, Winsford Kidsgrove Works, ICL, 1969–70; Man. Dir, RHP Bearings, 1970–81; Thorn EMI: Chief Exec., Gen. Engineering Div., 1981–83; Chm., Appliance and Lighting Group, 1984–87; Dir, 1984–87. Chm., Ball Roller Bearing Manufrs Assoc., 1978–80; Vice-Pres., Fedn European Bearing Manufrs Assoc., 1978–80. CBIM; FRSA. *Recreations:* theatre, reading, running, gardening. *Address:* Design Council, 28 Haymarket, SW1Y 4SU. *T:* 071–839 8000. *Club:* Carlton.

OWEN, Hon. Sir John (Arthur Dalziel), Kt 1986; **Hon. and Rt. Worshipful Mr Justice John Owen;** a Judge of the High Court of Justice, Queen's Bench Division, since 1986; Dean of the Arches Court of Canterbury and Auditor of the Chancery Court of York, since 1980; *b* 22 Nov. 1925; *s* of late R. J. Owen and Mrs O. B. Owen; *m* 1952, Valerie, *d* of W. Ethell; one *s* one *d.* *Educ:* Solihull Sch.; Brasenose Coll., Oxford. MA, BCL 1949. Commnd 2nd King Edward VII's Own Goorkha Rifles, 1944. Called to Bar, Gray's Inn, 1951, Bencher, 1980. Dep. Chm., Warwickshire QS, 1967–71; QC 1970; a Recorder, 1972–84; Dep. Leader, Midland and Oxford Circuit, 1980–84; a Circuit Judge, 1984–86; a Presiding Judge, Midland and Oxford Circuit, 1988–. Mem. Senate of the Inns of Court and the Bar, 1977–80. Chm., West Midlands Area Mental Health Review Tribunal, 1972–80. Mem., General Synod of Church of England, Dio. Coventry, 1970–80; Chancellor, Dio. Derby, 1973–80, Dio. Coventry, 1973–80, Dio. Southwell, 1979–80. *Address:* Royal Courts of Justice, Strand, WC2A 2LL. *Club:* Garrick.

See also Baroness Seccombe.

OWEN, John Aubrey; Under Secretary, Directorate of Personnel Management, Department of the Environment, since 1991; *b* 1 Aug. 1945; *s* of late Prebendary Douglas Aubrey Owen and Patricia Joan Owen; *m* 1971, Julia Margaret Jones; one *s* one *d.* *Educ:* City of London Sch., St Catharine's Coll., Cambridge (MA). Joined Min. of Transport, 1969; Asst Private Sec. to Minister for Transport Industries, 1972; DoE, 1973–75; Dept of Transport, 1975–78; seconded to Cambridgeshire CC, 1978–80; DoE, 1980–; Regional Dir, Northern Regional Office, Depts of the Environment and Transport, 1987–91. *Recreations:* gardening, opera, reading. *Address:* 33 Valley Road, Welwyn Garden City, Herts AL8 7DH. *T:* Welwyn Garden (0707) 321768.

OWEN, Prof. John Benjamin Brynmor, DSc (Oxon), MSc (Wales); CEng; John William Hughes Professor of Civil Engineering, University of Liverpool, 1950–77, now Emeritus Professor; *b* 2 Sept. 1910; *s* of David Owen, (Degwyl), and Mary Alice Owen; *m* 1938, Beatrice Pearn (*née* Clark); two *d.* *Educ:* Universities of Oxford and Wales. Drapers Company Scholar, Page Prize and Medal, University College, Cardiff, 1928–31 (Fellow, 1981); Meyricke Scholar, Jesus Coll., Oxford, 1931–32; British Cotton Industry Research Association, 1933–35; Messrs A. V. Roe, Manchester, 1935–36; Royal Aircraft Establishment, Farnborough, 1936–48; Naval Construction Research Establishment, 1948–50. *Publications:* Light Structures, 1965; many contributions to learned journals on design of structures, on helicopters and on investigation of aircraft accidents. *Address:* The University of Liverpool, PO Box 147, Liverpool L69 3BX. *T:* 051–709 6022.

OWEN, John Gethin M.; *see* Morgan-Owen.

OWEN, John Halliwell, OBE 1975; HM Diplomatic Service, retired; *b* 16 June 1935; *e s* of late Arthur Llewellyn Owen, OBE and Doris Spencer (*née* Halliwell); *m* 1st, 1963 (marr. diss. 1971); one *s* one *d*; 2nd, 1972, Dianne Elizabeth (*née* Lowry); one *d.* *Educ:* Sedbergh School; The Queen's Coll., Oxford (Hastings Scholar). MA. 2nd Lieut, RA, 1954–56; HMOCS, Tanganyika Govt Service, 1960; Dist Officer, Provincial Administration, 1960–61; Dist Comr, 1962; Dist Magistrate and Regional Local Courts Officer, 1963–65; HM Foreign Service, 1966; Second Sec., Dar-es-Salaam, 1968–70; FCO, 1970–73; First Sec., Dacca, 1973–75; FCO 1976; First Sec., Accra, 1976–80; FCO, 1980–82; Counsellor, Pretoria, 1982–86; Counsellor, FCO, 1986–90. *Recreations:* music, travel, wildlife, gardening. *Address:* c/o Foreign and Commonwealth Office, SW1A 2AH. *Club:* Dar-es-Salaam Yacht.

OWEN, Maj.-Gen. John Ivor Headon, OBE 1963; Director, Opus Resource Management Ltd; Editor, Current Military and Political Literature, since 1983; *b* 22 Oct. 1922; *s* of Major William H. Owen; *m* 1948, Margaret Jean Hayes; three *d.* *Educ:* St Edmund's Sch., Canterbury. FBIM; psm, jssc, idc. Joined Royal Marines (as Marine), 1942; temp. 2nd Lieut RM, 1942; 44 Commando RM, Far East, 1942–46; demobilised 1946 (Captain RM); Constable, Metropolitan Police, 1946–47; rejoined Royal Marines as Lieut, 1947; regimental service, 1948–55; Staff Coll., Camberley, 1956; Bde Major, HQ 3 Cdo Bde, 1959–62; Naval Plans, Admty/MoD, 1962–64; 42 Cdo RM, 1964–66; Instructor, Jt Services Staff Coll., 1966–67; CO 45 Cdo RM, 1967–68 (despatches); Col GS, Staff of CGRM, 1969–70; Royal Coll. of Defence Studies, 1971–72; Maj.-Gen, Commando Forces RM, Plymouth, 1972–73. Lt-Col 1966; Col 1970; Maj.-Gen. 1972; Col Comdt, RM, 1983–84, Rep. Col Comdt, 1985–86. UK Partnership Sec. to KMG Thomson McLintock, Chartered Accountants, 1974–87 (the British Mem. of KMG Klynveld Main Goerdeler, 1979–87). Chm. Exec. Cttee, Bowles Outdoor Centre, 1984–; Treas., Clergy Orphan Corp., 1980–; Mem., Ct of Assistants, Sons of the Clergy, 1981–; Chairman of Governors: St Edmund's Sch., Canterbury, 1980–; St Margaret's Sch., Bushey, 1980–. *Publications:* Brassey's Infantry Weapons of the World, 1975; contrib. Seaford House Papers, 1971; articles in Contemporary Review and the press. *Recreations:* woodworking, gardening. *Address:* c/o Midland Bank, 89 Queen Victoria Street, EC4V 4AQ. *Club:* Army and Navy.

OWEN, Prof. John Joseph Thomas, FRS 1988; Sands Cox Professor and Head of Department of Anatomy, University of Birmingham, since 1978; *b* 7 Jan. 1934; *s* of Thomas and Alice Owen; *m* 1961, Barbara Schofield Forster; two *s.* *Educ:* Univ. of Liverpool (BSc, MD); MA Oxon 1963. Lecturer: Univ. of Liverpool, 1960–63; Univ. of Oxford, 1963–72; Fellow, St Cross Coll., Oxford, 1968–72; Sen. Scientist, Imperial Cancer Res. Fund's Tumour Immunology Unit, UCL, 1972–74; Prof. of Anatomy, Univ. of Newcastle upon Tyne 1974–78. Mem., Physiol Systems and Disorders Bd, 1978–83, Chm., Grants Cttee, B, 1980–83, MRC; Member: Wellcome Trust's Biochemistry and Cell Biology Panel, 1987–; Council, Nat. Kidney Res. Fund, 1987–. *Publications:* numerous contribs to sci. literature. *Recreations:* sport, travel. *Address:* 20 Farquhar Road, Edgbaston, Birmingham B15 3RB.

OWEN, John Simpson, OBE 1956; conservationist; *b* 1912; *s* of late Archdeacon Walter Edwin Owen and late Lucy Olive (*née* Walton); *m* 1946, May Patricia, *d* of late Francis Gilbert Burns and late May (*née* Malone); three *d.* *Educ:* Christ's Hospital; Brasenose Coll., Oxford. Sudan Political Service, 1936–55; Director of National Parks, Tanzania, 1960–70, Asst to Director, 1971; Consultant on National Parks in Eastern and Central Africa, 1972–74; Woodrow Wilson Internat. Centre for Scholars, Washington, DC, 1973; Council of the Fauna Preservation Soc., 1975–80. Founder Mem., Royal Tunbridge Wells Dept of Civic Virtue, 1985. Hon. DSc (Oxon) 1971; World Wildlife Fund Gold Medal, 1971; Special Freedom of Information Award, 1987. *Publications:* papers and articles on National Parks and African Zoology. *Recreations:* implacably opposing the Channel Tunnel, walking, reading. *Address:* 5 Calverley Park Crescent, Tunbridge Wells TN1 2NB. *T:* Tunbridge Wells (0892) 29485.

OWEN, Prof. John V.; *see* Vallance-Owen.

OWEN, John Wyn; Director, National Health Service Wales, Welsh Office, since 1985; Chairman, Welsh Health Common Services Authority, since 1985; *b* 15 May 1942; *s* of late Idwal Wyn Owen and of Myfi Owen (*née* Hughes); *m* 1967, Elizabeth Ann (*née* MacFarlane); one *s* one *d.* *Educ:* Friars School, Bangor; St John's Coll., Cambridge (BA 1964, MA 1968); Hosp. Admin. Staff Coll. (DipHA 1967). Trainee, King Edward VII's Hosp. Fund for London, 1964–66; Dep. Hosp. Sec., West Wales Gen. Hosp., Carmarthen, 1966–67; Hosp. Sec., Glantawe HMC, Swansea, 1967–70; Staff Training Officer, Welsh Hosp. Bd, Cardiff, 1968–70; Divl Administrator, Univ. of Wales, Cardiff, HMC, 1970–72; St Thomas' Hospital: Asst Clerk, and King's Fund Fellow, 1972–74; Dist Administrator, St Thomas' Health Dist, Teaching, 1974–79; Trustee, Refresh, 1976–78; Hon. Tutor, Med. Sch., 1974–79; Praeceptor, Sch. of Health Administration, Univ. of Minnesota, 1974–79. Vis. Fellow, Univ. of NSW, 1979; Exec. Dir, United Medical Enterprises, London, 1979–85; Trustee, Florence Nightingale Museum Trust, 1983–90; Chm., Health Bldg Educn Gp, British Consultants' Bureau, 1983–85. FRGS 1968. Hon. FFPHM. *Publications:* contribs to professional jls. *Recreations:* organ playing, opera, travel. *Address:* Newton Farm, Newton, Cowbridge CF7 7RZ. *T:* Cowbridge (0446) 775113. *Club:* Athenæum.

OWEN, Joslyn Grey, CBE 1979; Chief Education Officer, Devon, 1972–89; Visiting Professor, Polytechnic of the South-West, since 1989; *b* 23 Aug. 1928; *s* of W. R. Owen, (Bodwyn), and Nell Evans Owen; *m* 1961, Mary Patricia Brooks; three *s.* *Educ:* Cardiff High Sch.; Worcester Coll., Oxford (MA). Asst Master, Chigwell Sch., and King's Sch., Canterbury, 1952–58; Asst Educn Officer, Croydon, 1959–62, and Somerset, 1962–66; Jt Sec., Schs Council, 1966–68; Dep. Chief Educn Officer, Devon, 1968–72; Dep. Chief Exec., Devon CC, 1975–89. Adviser, ACC and Council of Local Educn Authorities, 1977–89. Pres., BAAS Educn Section, 1978–79; Chairman: Further Educn Unit, 1982–87; IBA Educnl Adv. Council, 1982–86; County Educn Officers' Soc., 1980–81; Member:

Assessment of Perf. Unit Consultative Cttee, 1974–80; NFER Management Cttee, 1973–86; Council of Educnl Technol., 1972–82; Gulbenkian Working Party, Arts in the Curriculum, 1978–81; Macfarlane Working Party, 16–19 Educn, 1979–80; Educnl Research Board of SSRC, 1976–82; Nat. Adv. Bd for Local Auth. Higher Educn, 1982–88; Nat. Joint Council, Further Education, 1980–84; Cttee for Academic Policy, CNAA, 1981–84; Exec., Soc. of Educn Officers, 1987–89; Council of Management, United World Coll. of the Atlantic, 1988–; Bd of Dirs, Exeter and Devon Centre for the Arts, 1989–. Mem. Council, Univ. of Exeter, 1976–. Governor: The Open Sch., 1989–; Dartington Coll. of Arts, 1990–. FRSA 1977; Hon. FCP 1979; Hon. Fellow Plymouth Polytechnic, 1981. OStJ 1985. *Publications:* The Management of Curriculum Development, 1973; many chapters in edited works, papers and contribs to jls. *Address:* 4 The Quadrant, Exeter EX2 4LE. *Club:* Reform.

OWEN, Patricia, (Mrs Peter Owen); *see* Hodge, P.

OWEN, Peter Francis, CB 1990; Deputy Secretary, Cabinet Office, since 1990; *b* 4 Sept. 1940; *s* of Arthur Owen and Violet (*née* Morris); *m* 1963, Ann Preece; one *s* one *d*. *Educ:* The Liverpool Inst.; Liverpool Univ. (BA French). Joined MPBW, 1964; Cabinet Office, 1971–72; Private Sec. to successive Ministers of Housing and Construction, 1972–74; Asst Sec., Housing Policy Review, 1975–77, Local Govt Finance, 1977–80; Under Sec. and Regional Dir of Northern and Yorks eight Humberside Regs, Depts of the Environment and of Transport, 1980–82; Under Secretary: Rural Affairs, DoE, 1983; Local Govt Finance Policy, DoE, 1984–86; Dep. Sec., Housing and Construction, DoE, 1986–90. *Recreations:* reading, gardening, French language and literature. *Address:* Cabinet Office, 70 Whitehall, SW1A 2AS.

OWEN, Philip Loscombe Wintringham, TD 1950; QC 1963; *b* 10 Jan. 1920; *er s* of late Rt Hon. Sir Wintringham Stable, MC, and Lucie Haden (*née* Freeman); assumed surname of Owen in lieu of Stable by deed poll, 1942; *m* 1949, Elizabeth Jane, *d* of late Lewis Trelawny Widdicombe, Effingham, Surrey; three *s* two *d*. *Educ:* Winchester; Christ Church, Oxford (MA). Served War of 1939–45, Royal Welch Fusiliers: W Africa, India, Ceylon, Burma, 1939–47; Major TARO. Received into Roman Catholic Church, 1943. Called to Bar, Middle Temple, 1949; Bencher, 1969; Mem., Gen. Council of the Bar of England and Wales, 1971–77; a Deputy Chairman of Quarter Sessions: Montgomeryshire, 1959–71; Cheshire, 1961–71; Recorder of Merthyr Tydfil, 1971; a Recorder of the Crown Court, 1972–82; Leader, Wales and Chester Circuit, 1975–77. Chm., Adv. Bd constituted under Misuse of Drugs Act, 1974–. Legal Assessor to: Gen. Med. Council, 1970–; Gen. Dental Council, 1970–; RICS, 1970–. Contested (C) Montgomeryshire, 1945. JP Montgomeryshire, 1959; JP Cheshire, 1961. Vice-Pres., Montgomeryshire Cons. and Unionist Assoc.; Pres., Montgomeryshire Soc., 1974–75. Dir, Swansea City AFC Ltd, 1976–87. *Recreations:* shooting, fishing, forestry, music, Association football. *Address:* 15–19 Devereux Court, WC2R 3JJ. *T:* 071–583 0777; Plas Llwyn Owen, Llanbrynmair, Powys SY19 7BE. *T:* Llanbrynmair (06503) 542. *Clubs:* Carlton, Pratt's; Cardiff and County; Welshpool and District Conservative; Bristol Channel Yacht (Mumbles).

See also R. O. C. Stable.

OWEN, Rear-Adm. Richard Arthur James, CB 1963; *b* 26 Aug. 1910; *s* of late Captain Leonard E. Owen, OBE, JP; *m* 1941, Jean Sophia (*née* Bluett); one *s* two *d*. *Educ:* Sevenoaks Sch. Joined RN, 1927; Commander (S) 1945; Captain, 1954; Rear-Admiral, 1961; Director-General, Personal Services, Admiralty, 1962–64; retired. *Address:* High Bank, Martin, near Fordingbridge, Hants SP6 3LA. *T:* Martin Cross (072589) 295.

OWEN, Richard Wilfred, FCA; National Director, Personnel, Touche Ross & Co., Chartered Accountants, since 1987 (Chairman, 1988–90); *b* 26 Oct. 1932; *s* of Wilfred Owen and Ivy (*née* Gamble); *m* 1966, Sheila Marie Kerrigan; four adopted and fostered *s*, two adopted and fostered *d*. *Educ:* Gunnersbury Catholic Grammar Sch. Lloyds Bank, 1949–51; RAF Russian translator, 1951–53; accountancy articles, 1953–58; Thomson McLintock, 1958–62; Crompton Parkinson, 1962–64; Touche Ross & Co., Chartered Accountants and Management Consultants, 1964–: admitted to Partnership, 1969; seconded to CSD, 1971; Partner-in-Charge, Management Consultancy, 1974–87. Chm., Management Consultancies Assoc., 1987. Trustee, Civic Trust, 1990–. *Address:* Touche Ross & Co., Hill House, 1 Little New Street, EC4A 3TR. *T:* 071–936 3000.

OWEN, Robert John Richard; Chairman, Securities and Futures Commission, Hong Kong, since 1989; *b* 11 Feb. 1940; *s* of Richard Owen and Margaret Owen (*née* Fletcher); *m* 1962, Beatrice; two *s* one *d*. *Educ:* Repton School; Oxford University. Foreign Office, 1961–68, incl. HM Embassy, Washington, 1965–68; HM Treasury, 1968–70; Morgan Grenfell & Co., 1970–79 (Dir, 1974); Lloyds Bank International, 1979–85 (Dir); Chm. and Chief Exec., Lloyds Merchant Bank, 1985–88; Comr for Securities, Hong Kong, 1988–89. *Recreations:* oriental paintings, mountain walking. *Address:* c/o Securities and Futures Commission, Two Exchange Square, 38F, Hong Kong.

OWEN, Robert Michael; QC 1988; *b* 19 Sept. 1944; *s* of Gwynne Llewellyn Owen and Phoebe Constance Owen; *m* 1969, Sara Josephine Rumbold; two *s*. *Educ:* Durham Sch.; Exeter Univ. (LLB). Called to Bar, Inner Temple, 1968; Judicial Mem., Transport Tribunal, 1985; a Recorder, 1987. *Address:* 1 Crown Office Row, Temple, EC4Y 7HH. *T:* 071–353 1801.

OWEN, Robert Penrhyn; Director and Secretary, The Water Companies' Association, 1974–83, retired; *b* 17 Dec. 1918; *s* of late Captain Richard Owen; *m* 1949, Suzanne, *d* of late L. H. West; one *s* one *d*. *Educ:* Friar's School. War service in Royal Welch Fusiliers, 1939–46, in Madagascar, India, The Arakan and North and Central Burma. Admitted Solicitor, 1947. Asst Solicitor: Berks CC, 1948–50; Leics CC, 1950–54; Chief Asst Solicitor, Lancs CC, 1954–60; 2nd Dep. Clerk and 2nd Dep. Clerk of the Peace, Lancs CC, 1960–63; Gen. Manager, Telford Develt Corp. (New Town), 1963–69; Sec., Chief Exec. Officer and Solicitor, Thames Conservancy, 1969–74. *Recreations:* all sport, gardening, reading. *Address:* Pilgrims Wood, Three Gables Lane, Streatley, Reading RG8 9LJ. *T:* Goring (0491) 874294. *Clubs:* MCC; Phyllis Court (Henley-on-Thames).

OWEN, Rowland Hubert, CMG 1948; Deputy Controller, HM Stationery Office, 1959–64, retired; *b* 3 June 1903; *s* of William R. and Jessie M. Owen, Armagh, NI; *m* 1st, 1930, Kathleen Margaret Evaline Scott (*d* 1965); no *c*; 2nd, 1966, Shelagh Myrle Nicholson. *Educ:* Royal Sch., Armagh; Trinity Coll., Dublin (BA, LLB). Entered Dept of Overseas Trade, 1926; Private Secretary to Comptroller-General, 1930; Secretary Gorell Cttee on Art and Industry, 1931; idc, 1934; Commercial Secretary, Residency, Cairo, 1935; Ministry of Economic Warfare, 1939; Rep. of Ministry in Middle East, 1942; Director of Combined (Anglo-American) Economic Warfare Agencies, AFHQ, Mediterranean, 1943; transferred to Board of Trade and appointed Senior UK Trade Commissioner in India, Burma and Ceylon, 1944; Economic Adviser to UK High Commissioner in India, 1946; Adviser to UK Delegation at International Trade Conf., Geneva, 1947. Comptroller-General, Export Credits Guarantee Dept, 1953–58; Member Managing Cttee, Union d'Assureurs des Crédits Internationaux, 1954–58. Staff, NPFA, 1964–68. Chm., Haslemere Br., British Heart Foundn Appeal. Vice-President, Tilford Bach Society, 1962–69; Organist: St Mary's, Bramshott, 1964–70; St John the Evangelist, Farncombe, 1970–75; St Luke's, Grayshott, 1975–87; Holy Trinity, Bramley, 1987–; Pres., Surrey Organists' Assoc., 1976, Secretary, 1977–83. US Medal of Freedom. *Publications:* Economic Surveys of India, 1949 and 1952; Insurance Aspects of Children's Playground Management, 1966; Children's Recreation: Statutes and Constitutions, 1967; miscellaneous church music miniatures. *Recreations:* music, theatre, gardening. *Address:* Oak Tree Cottage, Holdfast Lane, Haslemere, Surrey GU27 2EU.

OWEN, Samuel Griffith, CBE 1977; MD, FRCP; Second Secretary, Medical Research Council, 1968–82, retired; *b* 3 Sept. 1925; *e s* of late Rev. Evan Lewis Owen and of Marjorie Lawton; *m* 1954, Ruth, *e d* of late Merle W. Tate, Philadelphia, Pa, USA; two *s* two *d*. *Educ:* Dame Allen's Sch.; Durham Univ. MB, BS Dunelm 1948; MRCP 1951; MD Dunelm 1954; FRCP 1965; clinical and research appts at Royal Victoria Infirmary, Newcastle upon Tyne, 1948–49 and 1950–53; RAMC, SMO, HM Troopships, 1949–50; Med. Registrar, Nat. Heart Hosp., 1953–54; Instr in Pharmacology, Univ. of Pennsylvania Sch. of Med., 1954–56; Reader in Med., Univ. of Newcastle upon Tyne, 1964–68 (First Asst, 1956, Lectr, 1960, Sen. Lectr, 1961); Hon. Cons. Physician, Royal Victoria Infirmary, Newcastle upon Tyne, 1960–68; Clin. Sub-Dean of Med. Sch., Univ. of Newcastle upon Tyne, 1966–68 (Academic Sub-Dean, 1964–66); Examr in Med., Univ. of Liverpool, 1966–68; Examr in Membership, RCP, 1967–68 and Mem., Research Cttee, RCP, 1968–76; Member: Brit. Cardiac Soc., 1962–82; Assoc. of Physicians of GB, 1965–; European Molec. Biol. Conf., 1971–82; European Molec. Biol. Lab., 1974–82; Exec. Council, European Science Foundn, 1974–78; Comité de la Recherche Médicale et de la Santé Publique, EEC, 1977–82; Scientific Coordinating Cttee, Arthritis and Rheumatism Council, 1978–82; NW Thames RHA, 1978–82. Consultant to WHO, SE Asia, 1966 and 1967–68; Commonwealth Fund Fellow, Univ. of Illinois, 1966; Fellow, Hunterian Soc., 1978. Chm., Feldberg Foundn, 1974–78; Governor, Queen Charlotte's Hosp. for Women, 1979–82. Liveryman, Soc. of Apothecaries, 1976–. *Publications:* Essentials of Cardiology, 1961 (2nd edn 1968); Electrocardiography, 1966 (2nd edn 1973); contribs to med. jls on heart disease, cerebral circulation, thyroid disease, med. research, etc. *Recreations:* chess, gastronomy, music, theatre. *Address:* 60 Bath Road, Chiswick, W4 1LH. *T:* 081–995 3228. *Club:* Royal Society of Medicine.

OWEN, Thomas Arfon; Director, Welsh Arts Council, since 1984; *b* 7 June 1933; *s* of late Hywel Peris Owen and Jennie Owen; *m* 1955, Joy (*née* Phillips); three *s* one *d*. *Educ:* Ystalyfera Grammar School; Magdalen College, Oxford. MA Oxon, MA Wales. Deputy Registrar, 1959, Registrar 1967, UCW Aberystwyth; Chm., Mid-Wales Hosp. Management Cttee, 1972–74; Member: East Dyfed Health Authy, 1982–84; S Glam Health Authy, 1984–87 (Vice-Chm., 1986–87); Consumers' Cttee for GB, 1975–; Vice-Chm., Coleg Harlech, 1984–; Member Council: UWIST, 1987–88; Univ. of Wales Coll. of Cardiff, 1988–; UCW, Aberystwyth, 1991–; Nat. Library of Wales, 1987–. Vice-Pres., Llangollen Internat. Eisteddfod, 1984–; Mem., Gorsedd of Bards, Royal National Eisteddfod, 1984–. FRSA 1991. High Sheriff, Dyfed, 1976–77. *Publications:* articles in educ. jls. *Recreations:* the arts, crossword puzzles. *Address:* Welsh Arts Council, Museum Place, Cardiff CF1 3NX. *T:* Cardiff (0222) 394711. *Club:* Cardiff and County (Cardiff).

OWEN, Trevor Bryan, CBE 1987; Chairman, Bethlem Royal and Maudsley Special Health Authority, since 1988; *b* 3 April 1928; *s* of Leonard Owen, CIE and Dilys (*née* Davies Bryan); *m* 1955, (Jennifer) Gaie (*née* Houston); one *s* one *d*. *Educ:* Rugby Sch.; Trinity Coll., Oxford (Scholar; MA). Sch. Student, British Sch. of Archaeology, Athens, 1953–54; ICI, 1955–78: wide range of jobs culminating in, successively: Chm., J. P. MacDougall Ltd; Dir, Paints, Agricl and Plastics Divs; Co. Personnel Manager; Man. Dir, Remploy Ltd, 1978–88. Member: Higher Educn Review Gp, Govt of NI, 1979–81; CNAA, 1973–79; Continuing Educn Adv. Council, BBC, 1977–85; Council, CBI, 1982–88; Council, Industrial Soc., 1967–88; Council, Inst. of Manpower Studies, 1975–88 (Chm., 1977–78); Chairman: Bd of Governors, Nat. Inst. for Social Work, 1985–91 (Mem., 1982–; Mem., Working Party on Role and Tasks of Social Workers, 1981–82); Cttee of Management, Inst. of Psychiatry, 1990–. Chm., Phab, 1988–91. *Publications:* Business School Programmes—the requirements of British manufacturing industry (with D. Casey and N. Huskisson), 1971; Making Organisations Work, 1978; The Manager and Industrial Relations, 1979; articles in jls. *Address:* 8 Rochester Terrace, NW1 9JN.

OWEN, Prof. Walter Shepherd, PhD, DEng; Professor Emeritus of Materials Science, Massachusetts Institute of Technology; *b* 13 March 1920; *s* of Walter Lloyd and Dorothea Elizabeth Owen; *m*; one *d*. *Educ:* Alsop High Sch.; University of Liverpool. Metallurgist, D. Napier and Sons and English Electric Co., 1940–46; Asst Lecturer and Lecturer in Metallurgy, Univ. of Liverpool, 1946–54; Commonwealth Fund Fellow, Metallurgy Dept, Mass Inst. of Technol., 1951–52; on research staff, 1954–57, and Henry Bell Wortley Professor of Metallurgy, 1957–66, Univ. of Liverpool; Thomas R. Briggs Prof. of Engineering and Dir of Materials Science and Engineering, Cornell Univ., 1966–70; Dean of Technological Inst., Northwestern Univ., 1970–71; Vice Pres. for Science and Research, Northwestern Univ., 1971–73; Head of Dept, 1973–82, and Prof. of Physical Metallurgy, 1973–85, Mass Inst. of Technol. Mem., Nat. Acad. of Engineering, USA, 1977. *Publications:* papers in British and American journals on aspects of physical metallurgy. *Recreation:* sailing. *Address:* 1 Marine Terrace, Porthmadog, Gwynedd LL49 9BL. *Club:* St Botolph (Boston).

OWEN-JONES, John Eryl, CBE 1969; JP; DL; Clerk of Caernarvonshire County Council, 1956–74, and Clerk of Lieutenancy; *b* 19 Jan. 1912; *s* of late John Owen-Jones, Hon. FTSC, Rhydwenfa, Old Colwyn; *m* 1944, Mabel Clara, *d* of Grant McIlvride, Ajmer, Rajputana; one *s* one *d*. *Educ:* Portmadoc Grammar Sch.; University Coll. of Wales, Aberystwyth; Gonville and Caius Coll., Cambridge. LLB Wales 1933; MA Cantab 1939. Admitted Solicitor, 1938; Asst Solicitor, Chester Corp., 1939. Sqdn Ldr, RAFVR, 1945; Legal Staff Officer, Judge Advocate General's Dept, Mediterranean. Dep. Clerk, Caernarvonshire CC, 1946; Clerk of the Peace, Caernarvonshire, 1956–71; formerly: Sec., N Wales Combined Probation and After-Care Cttee; Dep. Clerk, Snowdonia Jt Adv. Cttee; Clerk, Gwynedd Police Authority, 1956–67. Member: Central Council, Magistrates' Cts Cttees, 1980–82; Bd, Civic Trust for Wales, 1982–; Bd, Gwynedd Archaeological Trust Ltd, 1982–. Hon. Sec., Caernarvonshire Historical Soc. Mem., Gorsedd of Royal National Eisteddfod of Wales. FRSA 1987. DL Caernarvonshire, 1971; JP 1974, DL 1974, Gwynedd. *Recreations:* music, gardening, photography. *Address:* Rhiw Dafnau, Caernarfon, Gwynedd LL55 1LF. *T:* Caernarfon (0286) 673370. *Club:* National Liberal.

OWEN-JONES, Lindsay Harwood; Chairman and Chief Executive Officer, L'Oréal, since 1988; *b* 17 March 1946; *s* of Hugh A. Owen-Jones and Esmee Owen-Jones (*née* Lindsay); *m* 1984, Violaine de Dalmas; one *d*. *Educ:* Oxford Univ. (BA); European Inst. of Business Admin. Product Manager, L'Oréal, 1969; Head, Public Products Div., Belgium, 1971–74; Manager, SCAD (L'Oréal subsid.), Paris, 1974–76; Marketing Manager, Public Products Div., Paris, 1976–78; Gen. Manager, SAIPO (L'Oréal subsid.), Italy, 1978–81; Pres., COSMAIR (L'Oréal agent), USA, 1981–83; Vice-Pres., L'Oréal Man. Cttee and Mem. Bd of Dirs, 1984; Pres. and Chief Operating Officer, 1984–88. Dir, Banque Nationale de Paris, 1989–. *Recreation:* private helicopter pilot. *Address:* L'Oréal, 41 rue Martre, 92117 Clichy, France. *T:* 47.56.70.00.

OWENS, Bernard Charles; Member, Monopolies and Mergers Commission, since 1981; Chairman and Managing Director, Bernard Owens & Partners Ltd, since 1962; *b* 20 March 1928; *s* of Charles A. Owens and late Sheila (*née* O'Higgins); *m* 1954, Barbara Madeline Murphy; two *s* four *d*. *Educ:* Solihull Sch.; London Sch. of Econs and Pol Science. Commnd 2nd Lieut, RASC, 1947; transf. RARO, 1949 (Lieut). Managing Director: Stanley Bros, 1962–67; Coronet Industrial Securities, 1965–67; Chairman: Unochrome Industries, 1964–79; Silverthorne Group, 1972–79; Director: Hobbs Savill & Bradford, 1957–62; Trinidad Sugar Estates, 1965–67; Cornish Brewery, 1987–; Land & Leisure—Tir a Hamdden Ltd, 1990–; Local Dir, Alexander Stenhouse UK (formerly Reed Stenhouse UK), 1980–87. Mem. of Lloyd's, 1978–. Chm., Metal Finishing Assoc., 1982–85 (Vice-Chm., 1981–82; Dep. Chm., 1985–88); Pres., British Jewellery and Giftware Fedn, 1991– (Vice-Pres., 1990–91; Dir, 1987–); Member: Cttee, Nat. Clayware Fedn, 1962–67; Council, Zoological Society, 1987–90. Mem., Solihull Council, 1953–63 (Chm., Finance Cttee, 1957–63); contested (C) Birmingham, Small Heath, 1959 and March 1961. Freeman, City of London, 1981; Liveryman, Worshipful Co. of Gardeners, 1982; Mem., HAC, 1984–. Governor, RNLI, 1984–. FRSA 1972; FRGS 1980; FZS 1980; FLS 1989. Mem., SMO Malta, 1979. *Recreations:* fine food and wine. *Address:* The Vatch House, Stroud, Glos GL6 7JY. *T:* Stroud (045376) 3402. *Clubs:* Carlton, Wig and Pen, City Livery, City Livery Yacht (Hon. Sec.), MCC; Stroud Rugby Football.

OWENS, Frank Arthur Robert, CBE 1971; Editor, Birmingham Evening Mail, 1956–74; Director, Birmingham Post & Mail Ltd, 1964–75; *b* 31 Dec. 1912; *s* of Arthur Oakes Owens; *m* 1st, 1936, Ruby Lilian Long; two *s*; 2nd, Olwen Evans, BSc; one *s* one *d*. *Educ:* Hereford Cathedral School. Served with RAF, 1940–46 (despatches). Member: Defence, Press and Broadcasting Cttee, 1964–75; Deptl Cttee on Official Secrets Act 1911, 1970–71; West Midlands Econ. Planning Council, 1975–77; Press Council, 1976–79. Pres., Guild of British Newspaper Editors, 1974–75. Hon. Mem., Mark Twain Soc. Hon. Mem., Barnt Green Fishing and Sailing Club. *Address:* 31 The Dreel, Edgbaston, Birmingham B15 3NS.

OWENS, John Ridland; Director General, Building Employers Confederation, since 1990; *b* 21 May 1932; *s* of Dr Ridland Owens and late Elsie Owens; *m* 1st, 1958, Susan Lilian (*née* Pilcher); two *s* one *d*; 2nd, 1985, Cynthia Rose (*née* Forbes); one *s*. *Educ:* Merchant Taylors' Sch.; St John's Coll., Oxford (MA). National Service, RA (Lieut), 1951–52. ICI, 1955–67; Managing Dir, Cape Asbestos Fibres, 1967–73; Dir Gen., Dairy Trade Fedn, 1973–83; Dep. Chm., Assilec, Paris, 1973–83; Exec. Dir, Nat. Dairy Council, 1975–83; Dep. Dir Gen., CBI, 1983–90; Dir, UK Skills Ltd, 1990–. Vice-Chm., EEC Adv. Cttee on Milk and Milk Products; Member: Food and Drink Industry Council, 1973–83; RSA Industry Cttee for Industry Year, 1986; Council, Assoc. of Business Sponsorship of the Arts, 1985–; RA Adv. Bd, 1987; Exec. Cttee, PRONED, 1983–90; Council, CBI, 1990–. Member: Council, CGLI, 1988–; Court, City Univ., 1988–. FRSA. Mem. Court, Merchant Taylors' Co., 1982–. *Publications:* articles for The Times Review of Industry. *Recreations:* painting, music, walking. *Address:* 40 Blenheim Terrace, NW8 0EG. *T:* 071–372 6993.

OWER, Dr David Cheyne, TD 1975; Senior Principal Medical Officer, Department of Health and Social Security, 1976–87; *b* 29 July 1931; *s* of Ernest Ower and Helen Edith Cheyne (*née* Irvine); *m* 1954, June Harris; two *s* two *d*. *Educ:* King's Coll. Sch., Wimbledon; King's Coll., London; King's Coll. Hosp. Med. Sch. (MB, BS 1954). DObstRCOG 1959; FFCM 1983 (MFCM 1976). Jun. hosp. appts, King's Coll. Hosp. and Kingston Hosp., 1955; RAF Med. Br., 1956–58; gen. practice, 1959–64; DHSS (formerly Min. of Health) Med. Staff, 1965–87. T&AVR, and RAMC(V), 1962–; Lt-Col RAMC(V); CO 221 (Surrey) Field Amb., 1973–75. *Recreations:* music, bridge, thinking about playing golf. *Address:* Merlewood, 94 Coombe Lane West, Kingston-upon-Thames, Surrey. *T:* 081–942 8552.

OWERS, Anne Elizabeth; General Secretary, Joint Council for the Welfare of Immigrants, since 1986; *b* 23 June 1947; *d* of William Spark and Anne Smailes Spark (*née* Knox); *m* 1968, Rev. Ian Humphrey Owers; two *s* one *d*. *Educ:* Washington Grammar Sch., Co. Durham; Univ. of Cambridge (BA Hons). Research and teaching in Zambia, 1968–71; Mem., Southwark Race Relations Commn, 1976–90; work at JCWI, 1981–. Bd Mem., Centre for Research into Ethnic Relations, Warwick Univ., 1990–. *Publications:* chapters and papers on immigration and nationality matters. *Recreations:* theatre, music, books. *Address:* Joint Council for the Welfare of Immigrants, 115 Old Street, EC1V 9JR. *T:* 071–251 8708.

OWO, The Olowo of; *see* Olagbegi II.

OXBURGH, Prof. Ernest Ronald, PhD; FRS 1978; Professor of Mineralogy and Petrology, University of Cambridge, since 1978; Professorial Fellow, Queens' College, Cambridge, since 1989; Chief Scientific Adviser, Ministry of Defence, since 1988; *b* 2 Nov. 1934; *m* Ursula Mary Brown; one *s* two *d*. *Educ:* Liverpool Inst.; Univ. of Oxford (BA 1957, MA 1960); Univ. of Princeton (PhD 1960). Departmental Demonstrator, 1960–61, Lectr in Geology, 1962–78, Univ. of Oxford; Fellow of St Edmund Hall, Oxford, 1964–78, Emeritus Fellow, 1978, Hon. Fellow, 1986; University of Cambridge: Fellow of Trinity Hall, 1978–82, Hon. Fellow, 1983; Hd of Dept of Earth Scis, 1980–88; Pres., Queens' Coll., 1982–89. Vis. Professor: CIT, 1967–68; Stanford and Cornell Univs, 1973–74; Sherman Fairchild Distinguished Vis. Scholar, CIT, 1985–86. Pres., Eur. Union of Geosciences, 1985–87. FGS; Fellow: Geol. Soc. of America; Amer. Geophys. Union. Hon. Mem., Geologists' Assoc.; Foreign Corresp., Geologische Bundesanstalt, Austria and of Geological Soc. of Vienna. Hon. Fellow, Univ. Coll., Oxford, 1983. DSc (*hc*): Univ. of Paris, 1986; Leicester, 1990; Loughborough, 1991. Bigsby Medal, Geol Soc., 1979. *Publications:* contribs to Nature, Jl Geophys Res., Phil Trans Royal Soc., Annual Reviews, Science, Bull. Geol Soc. America, Jl Fluid Mechanics, Jl Geol Soc. London. *Recreations:* mountaineering, orienteering, reading, theatre. *Address:* Department of Earth Sciences, Downing Street, Cambridge CB2 3EQ. *T:* Cambridge (0223) 333400.

OXBURY, Harold Frederick, CMG 1961; Deputy Director-General, British Council, 1962–66 (Assistant Director-General, 1959); *b* 11 Nov. 1903; *s* of Fredric Thomas Oxbury; *m* 1st, 1928, Violet Bennets (*d* 1954); one *s* one *d*; 2nd, 1954, Helen Shipley (*d* 1975), *d* of Amos Perry, FLS, VMH. *Educ:* Norwich Sch.; Trinity Coll., Cambridge (Senior Scholar). Entered Indian Civil Service, 1928; Chief Collector of Customs, Burma, 1940; in charge of civilian evacuation from N Burma, 1942; Government of Burma Representative, Burma Office, 1942–44; Dep. Controller Finance (Colonel), Military Administration, Burma, 1945; Finance Secretary, Government of Burma, 1946; British Council: Director, Colonies Dept, 1947; Controller Finance, 1956. *Publications:* (ed) Concise Dictionary of National Biography 1901–1970, 1982; Great Britons: twentieth century lives, 1985; contribs to biographical works. *Recreations:* gardening, writing, painting. *Address:* 122B Woodstock Road, Oxford OX2 7NF.

OXFORD, Bishop of, since 1987; **Rt. Rev. Richard Douglas Harries;** *b* 2 June 1936; *s* of Brig. W. D. J. Harries, CBE and late Mrs G. M. B. Harries; *m* 1963, Josephine Bottomley, MA, MB, BChir, DCH; one *s* and *d*. *Educ:* Wellington Coll,; RMA, Sandhurst; Selwyn Coll., Cambridge (MA 1965); Cuddesdon Coll., Oxford. Lieut, Royal Corps of Signals, 1955–58. Curate, Hampstead Parish Church, 1963–69; Chaplain, Westfield Coll., 1966–69; Lectr, Wells Theol Coll., 1969–72; Warden of Wells, Salisbury and Wells Theol Coll., 1971–72; Vicar, All Saints, Fulham, 1972–81; Dean, King's Coll., London, 1981–87. GOE examnr in Christian Ethics, 1972–76; Dir, Post Ordination Trng for Kensington Jurisdiction, 1973–79. Vice-Chairman: Council of Christian Action, 1979–87; Council for Arms Control, 1982–87; Mem., Home Office Adv. Cttee for reform of law on sexual offences, 1981–85; Chairman: Southwark Ordination Course, 1982–87; Shalom; ELTSA (End Loans to Southern Africa), 1982–87. Pres., Johnson Soc., 1988–89. Consultant to Archbishops of Canterbury and York on Interfaith Relns, with special resp. for Jewish Christian relns, 1986–. Radio and TV work. Lectures: Hockerill, 1982; Drawbridge, 1982. FKC 1983. *Publications:* Prayers of Hope, 1975; Turning to Prayer, 1978; Prayers of Grief and Glory, 1979; Being a Christian, 1981; Should Christians Support Guerillas?, 1982; The Authority of Divine Love, 1983; Praying Round the Clock, 1983; Prayer and the Pursuit of Happiness, 1985; Morning has Broken, 1985; Christianity and War in a Nuclear Age, 1986; C. S. Lewis: the man and his God, 1987; Christ is Risen, 1988; *edited:* (jtly) Seasons of the Spirit, 1984; The One Genius; Through the Year with Austin Farrer, 1987; *edited and contributed:* What Hope in an Armed World?, 1982; Reinhold Niebuhr and the Issues of Our Time, 1986; *contributed to:* Stewards of the Mysteries of God, 1979; Unholy Warfare, 1983; The Cross and the Bomb, 1983; Dropping the Bomb, 1985; Julian, Woman of our Time, 1985; If Christ be not raised, 1986; The Reality of God, 1986; articles in Theology, The Times, The Observer and various other periodicals. *Recreations:* theatre, literature, sport. *Address:* Diocesan Church House, North Hinksey, Oxford OX2 0NB. *T:* Oxford (0865) 244566.

OXFORD, Archdeacon of; *see* Weston, Ven. F. V.

OXFORD AND ASQUITH, 2nd Earl of, *cr* 1925; **Julian Edward George Asquith,** KCMG 1964 (CMG 1961); Viscount Asquith, *cr* 1925; Governor and Commander-in-Chief, Seychelles, 1962–67; Commissioner, British Indian Ocean Territory, 1965–67; *b* 22 April 1916; *o s* of late Raymond Asquith and Katharine Frances (*d* 1976), *d* of late Sir John Horner, KCVO; *S* grandfather, 1928; *m* 1947, Anne Mary Celestine, CStJ, *d* of late Sir Michael Palairet, KCMG; two *s* three *d*. *Educ:* Ampleforth; Balliol Coll., Oxford (Scholar), 1st Class Lit. Hum., 1938. Lieut, RE, 1941; Assistant District Commissioner, Palestine, 1942–48; Dep. Chief Secretary, British Administration, Tripolitania, 1949; Director of the Interior, Government of Tripolitania, 1951; Adviser to Prime Minister of Libya, 1952; Administrative Secretary, Zanzibar, 1955; Administrator of St Lucia, WI, 1958. KStJ. *Heir:* *s* Viscount Asquith, *qv*. *Address:* The Manor House, Mells, Frome, Somerset. *T:* Mells (0373) 812324. *Club:* Naval and Military.

See also Baron Hylton.

OXFORD, Sir Kenneth (Gordon), Kt 1988; CBE 1981; QPM 1976; DL; Chief Constable, Merseyside Police, 1976–89; Regional Director, Lloyds Bank plc, 1989–91; *b* Lambeth, 25 June 1924; *s* of late Ernest George Oxford and Gladys Violet (*née* Seaman); *m* 1954, Muriel (*née* Panton). *Educ:* Caldecot Sch., Lambeth. RAF, VR Bomber Comd, SEAC, 1942–47. Metropolitan Police, 1947–69, with final rank Det. Ch. Supt, following Intermed. Comd Course, 1966, Sen. Staff Course, 1968, The Police Coll., Bramshill; Asst Chief Constable (Crime), Northumberland Constabulary, 1969; Northumbria Police, 1974; Dep. Chief Constable, Merseyside Police, 1974–75. Member: Forensic Science Soc., 1970; Medico-Legal Soc., 1975; Chairman: Crime Cttee, Assoc. of Chief Police Officers of Eng., Wales and NI, 1977–83; Jt Standing Cttee on Police Use of Firearms, 1979–89; Anti-Terrorist Cttee, 1982–89; Rep., ICPO (Interpol), 1983–86; President: NW Police Benevolent Fund, 1978–89; Assoc. of Chief Police Officers of England, Wales and NI, 1982–83. Pres., Merseyside Br., BIM, 1983– (Chm., 1978–81; Vice-Chm., 1975–78); CBIM 1980. Merseyside County Dir, St John Ambulance Assoc., 1976–84 (County Vice Pres., 1985). Chm., Merseyside Community Trust, 1988–. Hon. Col, 156 (Liverpool and Greater Manchester) Transport Regt, RCT (Volunteers), 1989–. Freeman, City of London, 1983. FRSA 1983. OStJ 1977. DL Merseyside, 1988. *Publications:* contrib. articles and papers to prof. papers on crime and kindred matters. *Recreations:* shooting, cricket, music, books, roses. *Address:* c/o Chief Constable's Office, PO Box 59, Liverpool L69 1JD. *Clubs:* Commonwealth Trust, Special Forces; Surrey CC, Lancashire CC, Rainford CC, Liverpool St Helens Rugby Union Football.

OXFUIRD, 13th Viscount of, *cr* 1651; **George Hubbard Makgill;** Bt 1627; Lord Macgill of Cousland, 1651; *b* 7 Jan. 1934; *s* of Richard James Robert Haldane Makgill, RNZAF (*d* 1948) (*yr s* of 11th Bt) and Elizabeth Lyman (*d* 1981), *d* of Gorham Hubbard, Boston, USA; *S* uncle, 1986; *m* 1st, 1967, Alison Campbell (marr. diss. 1977), *er d* of late Neils Max Jensen, Randers, Denmark; three *s* (inc. twin *s*); 2nd, 1980, Venetia Cunitia Mary, *o d* of Major Charles Anthony Steward, Crondall, Farnham, Surrey; one *s*. *Educ:* St Peter's School, Cambridge, NZ; Wanganui Collegiate School. Commissioned RAF, 1955–58. A Deputy Speaker, House of Lords, 1990–. *Recreations:* fishing, gardening, shooting. *Heir:* *s* Master of Oxfuird, *qv*. *Address:* Hill House, St Mary Bourne, Andover, Hants. *Club:* Caledonian.

OXFUIRD, Master of; Hon. Ian Arthur Alexander Makgill; *b* 14 Oct. 1969; *s* and *heir* of 13th Viscount of Oxfuird, *qv*.

OXLADE, Zena Elsie, CBE 1984; SRN, RNT; Regional Nursing Officer, East Anglian Regional Health Authority, 1981–87, retired; *b* 26 April 1929; *d* of James and Beatrice May Oxlade. *Educ:* Latymer Grammar Sch., N9. SRN 1950; RNT (London Univ.). Ward Sister, 1952; Theatre Sister 1953; Night Sister, 1954; Sister Tutor, 1956; Principal Tutor, 1963; Principal Nursing Officer, 1969; Chief Nursing Officer, 1973; District Nursing Officer, 1974; Area Nursing Officer, Suffolk AHA, 1978–81. Chm., GNC, 1977–83 (Mem., 1975–83); Mem., UK Council for Nurses, Midwives and Health Visitors, 1983–. *Publication:* Ear, Nose and Throat Nursing, 1972. *Recreations:* motoring, reading, handicrafts. *Address:* 5 Morgan Court, Claydon, Suffolk IP6 0AN. *T:* Ipswich (0473) 831895.

OXLEE, Colin Hamilton; Technical Director, Military Division, Defence Research Agency, since 1991; *b* 14 July 1935; *s* of Leonard William and Margaret Hamilton Oxlee; *m* 1960, Robyn Rosemary Gardner; one *s* one *d*. *Educ:* St Lawrence College, Ramsgate; Univ. of Nottingham (BSc Hons 1959; MScMet 1961). MIM 1960; CEng 1977. Technical apprentice, Appleby-Frodingham Steel Co., 1954–56; Materials Res. Scientist, RARDE, 1961–71; PSO to Chief Scientist (Army), 1971–74; Supt Materials Res., 1974–77, Supt Ammunition, 1977–81, RARDE; Dep. Dir, Scientific and Technical Intell., 1981–84, Dir, Heavy Weapons Projects, 1984–89, MoD; Dep. Dir (Armaments), RARDE, 1989–91. *Publications:* Low Alloy Steels, 1968; procs of Iron and Steel Institute Council of Scientific and Industrial Research, India, 1966, and Iron and Steel Institute of Japan, 1970; official reports. *Recreations:* hockey, tennis, jazz, guitar. *Address:* Defence Research Agency, Military Division, Royal Armament Research and Development Establishment, Fort Halstead, Sevenoaks, Kent TN14 7BP.

OXLEY, Humphrey Leslie Malcolm, CMG 1966; OBE 1956; HM Diplomatic Service, retired; *b* 9 Oct. 1909; *s* of W. H. F. Oxley, MRCS, LRCP, FRCOG, and Lily Malcolm; *m* 1945, Frances Olga, *d* of George Bowden, San Jose, Costa Rica; twin *s*. *Educ:* Epsom

Coll. Admitted Solicitor, 1933; Junior Legal Assistant, India Office, 1933; Commissioner for Oaths, 1934; Assistant Solicitor, 1944; Commonwealth Relations Office, 1947; Assistant Legal Adviser, 1961; Legal Counsellor, Commonwealth Office, 1965–67; HM Diplomatic Service, 1967; Dep. Legal Adviser, FCO, 1967–69. Legal Consultant to HM Comr, Magistrate, various legal appts, Anguilla, 1971–72. *Recreations:* sailing, gardening. *Address:* Sandpipers, Crooked Lane, Birdham, Chichester, West Sussex PO20 7ET. *Club:* Civil Service.

OXLEY, James Keith R.; *see* Rice-Oxley.

OXLEY, Julian Christopher; Director-General, Guide Dogs for the Blind Association, since 1989; Chairman, International Federation of Guide Dog Schools, since 1990; *b* 23 Nov. 1938; *s* of Horace Oxley and Lilian Oxley (*née* Harris); *m* 1979, Carol (*née* Heath); one *d*; one *s* two *d* from previous marr. *Educ:* Clifton Coll., Bristol; Oriel Coll., Oxford (Organ Scholar, MA). FCA. Dir and Sec., Williams & James plc, 1970–84; Dir and Sec., Guide Dogs for the Blind Assoc., 1984–89. Mem. Council, Gloucester Civic Trust, 1972–75. Chm. of Govs, Selwyn Sch., Gloucester, 1980–84. *Recreations:* music, old furniture, railways. *Address:* Alexandra House, Park Street, Windsor, Berks SL4 1JR. *T:* Windsor (0753) 855711. *Clubs:* Kennel; Constitutional (Windsor).

OXMANTOWN, Lord; Laurence Patrick Parsons; *b* 31 March 1969; *s* and *heir of* Earl of Rosse, *qv*.

OZAWA, Seiji; Japanese conductor; Music Director, Boston Symphony Orchestra, since 1973; *b* Shenyang, China, 1 Sept. 1935; *m* 1st, Kyoko Edo; 2nd, Vera Ilyan; one *s* one *d*. *Educ:* Toho School of Music, Tokyo; studied with Hideo Saito, Eugène Bigot, Herbert von Karajan, Leonard Bernstein. Won Besançon Internat. Comp., 1959, Koussevitsky Meml Scholarship, 1960. Asst Conductor, NY Philharmonic Orch., 1961–62 and 1964–65; music dir, Ravinia Fest., Chicago, 1964–68; conductor, Toronto Symph. Orch., 1965–69; music dir, San Francisco Symph. Orch., 1970–76, music advisor, 1976–77; Artistic Advr, Tanglewood Fest., 1970–73. Tours with Boston Symphony Orchestra: Europe, 1976 and 1982; Japan, 1978; China (musical and cultural exchange), 1979; European music festivals, 1979 and 1984; 14 USA cities (orchestra's hundredth birthday), 1982; Japan, 1982 and 1986. Guest conductor with major orchestras in Canada, Europe, Far East and USA. Opera highlights: La Scala, Milan; Covent Garden, London; Paris Opera (incl. world première of Messiaen's Saint François d'Assise); many recordings (awards). Evening at Symphony, PBS television series with Boston Symphony Orch. (Emmy award). Hon. DMus: Univ. of Mass; New England Conservatory of Music; Wheaton Coll., Norton, Mass. *Address:* c/o Ronald A. Wilford, Columbia Artists Management Inc. Conductors Division, 165 West 57th Street, New York, USA; c/o Harold Holt Ltd, 31 Sinclair Road, W14.

P

PACK, Prof. Donald Cecil, CBE 1978 (OBE 1969); MA, DSc, FIMA, FEIS, FRSE; Professor of Mathematics, University of Strathclyde, Glasgow, 1953–82, Hon. Professor, 1982–86, Professor Emeritus, 1986 (Vice-Principal, 1968–72); *b* 14 April 1920; *s* of late John Cecil and late Minnie Pack, Higham Ferrers; *m* 1947, Constance Mary Gillam; two *s* one *d*. *Educ:* Wellingborough School; New Coll., Oxford. Lecturer in Mathematics, University College, Dundee, University of St Andrews, 1947–52; Visiting Research Associate, University of Maryland, 1951–52; Lecturer in Mathematics, University of Manchester, 1952–53. Guest Professor: Technische Universität, Berlin, 1967; Bologna Univ. and Politecnico Milano, 1980; Technische Hochschule Darmstadt, 1981; other vis. appts at Warsaw Univ., 1977, Kaiserslautern, 1980, 1984. Member: Dunbartonshire Educn Cttee, 1960–66; Gen. Teaching Council for Scotland, 1966–73; Chairman: Scottish Certificate of Educn Examn Bd, 1969–77; Cttee of Inquiry into Truancy and Indiscipline in Schools in Scotland, 1974–77; Member: various Govt Scientific Cttees, 1952–84; British Nat. Cttee for Theoretical and Applied Mechanics, 1973–78; Council, Gesellschaft für Angewandte Mathematik und Mechanik, 1977–83; Council, RSE, 1960–63; Scottish Arts Council, 1980–85; Hon. Mem., European Consortium for Mathematics in Industry, 1988. Founder Chm., NYO of Scotland, 1978–88 (Hon. Pres., 1988–); Mem., European Music Year UK Cttee (Chm., Scottish Sub-Cttee), 1982–86; First Hon. Treasurer, IMA, 1964–72; Governor, Hamilton Coll. of Education, 1977–81; Pres., Milngavie Music Club, 1983–. *Publications:* papers on fluid dynamics. *Recreations:* music, gardening, golf. *Address:* 18 Buchanan Drive, Bearsden, Glasgow G61 2EW. *T:* 041–942 5764.

PACKARD, Lt-Gen. Sir (Charles) Douglas, KBE 1957 (CBE 1945; OBE 1942); CB 1949; DSO 1943; retired as GOC-in-C Northern Ireland Command, 1958–61; *b* 17 May 1903; *s* of late Capt. C. T. Packard, MC, Copdock, near Ipswich; *m* 1st, 1937, Marion Lochhead (*d* 1981); one *s* two *d*; 2nd, 1982, Mrs Patricia Miles Sharp. *Educ:* Winchester; Royal Military Academy, Woolwich. 2nd Lieut, RA, 1923; served War of 1939–45, in Middle East and Italy (despatches, OBE, DSO, CBE); Dep.-Chief of Staff, 15th Army Group, 1944–45; Temp. Maj.-Gen. and Chief of Staff, Allied Commission for Austria (British Element), 1945–46; Director of Military Intelligence, WO, 1948–49; Commander British Military Mission in Greece, 1949–51; Chief of Staff, GHQ, MELF, 1951–53; Vice-Quarter-Master-General War Office, 1953–56; Military Adviser to the West African Governments, 1956–58. Lt-Gen. 1957. Col Comdt, RA, 1957–62. Officer Legion of Merit (USA). *Address:* Park Side, Lower Road, Ufford, Woodbridge, Suffolk IP13 6DL. *T:* Eyke (0394) 460418.

PACKARD, Vance (Oakley); Author; *b* 22 May 1914; *s* of Philip and Mabel Packard; *m* 1938, Mamie Virginia Mathews; two *s* one *d*. *Educ:* Pennsylvania State Univ.; Columbia Univ. Reporter, The Boston Record, 1938; Feature Editor, The Associated Press, 1939–42; Editor and Staff Writer, The American Magazine, 1942–56; Staff writer, Colliers, 1956; Distinguished Alumni Award, Pennsylvania State University, 1961; Outstanding Alumni Award, Columbia University Graduate School of Journalism, 1963. LittD Monmouth Coll., 1974. *Publications:* (books on social criticism): The Hidden Persuaders, 1957; The Status Seekers, 1959; The Waste Makers, 1960; The Pyramid Climbers, 1962; The Naked Society, 1964; The Sexual Wilderness, 1968; A Nation of Strangers, 1972; The People Shapers, 1977; Our Endangered Children, 1983; The Ultra Rich, 1989; numerous articles for The Atlantic Monthly. *Recreations:* reading, boating. *Address:* 87 Mill Road, New Canaan, Conn 06840, USA. *T:* WO 6–1707.

PACKER, Ven. John Richard; Archdeacon of West Cumberland, since 1991; *b* 10 Oct. 1946; *s* of John and Muriel Packer; *m* 1971, Barbara Jack; two *s* one *d*. *Educ:* Manchester Grammar Sch.; Keble Coll., Oxford (MA); Ripon Hall, Oxford; York Univ. (DSA). Ordained deacon, 1970, priest, 1971; Curate, St Peter, St Helier, 1970–73; Director of Pastoral Studies: Ripon Hall, 1973–75; Ripon Hall, Cuddesdon, 1975–77; Chaplain, St Nicolas, Abingdon, 1973–77; Vicar, Wath Upon Dearne with Adwick Upon Dearne, 1977–86; Rural Dean of Wath, 1983–86; Rector, Sheffield Manor, 1986–91; Rural Dean of Attercliffe, 1990–91. Mem., Gen. Synod of C of E, 1985–91. *Recreations:* history, cricket, walking. *Address:* 50 Stainburn Road, Workington, Cumbria CA14 1SN. *T:* Workington (0900) 66190.

PACKER, Prof. Kenneth John, PhD; FRS 1991; CChem, FRSC; Chief Research Associate, Analytical Research Division, BP Research, since 1990; *b* 18 May 1938; *s* of late Harry James Packer and Alice Ethel Packer (*née* Purse); *m* 1962, Christine Frances Hart; one *s* one *d*. *Educ:* Harvey Grammar Sch., Folkestone; Imperial Coll., London (BSc Hons Chemistry, 1st cl., 1959); Cambridge Univ. (PhD 1962). CChem 1985, FRSC 1985. Post-doctoral Res. Fellow, Central Res. Dept, E. I. duPont de Nemours, Wilmington, USA, 1962–63; University of East Anglia: SERC Res. Fellow, 1963–64; Lectr in Chemistry, 1964–71; Sen. Lectr, 1971–78; Reader, 1978–82; Prof., 1982–84; Sen. Res. Associate, Spectroscopy, 1984–87, Prin. Res. Associate, 1987–90, BP Research. Visiting Professor in Chemistry: UEA; Southampton Univ.; KCL; Imperial Coll., London. Science and Engineering Research Council: Member: Physical Chem. Cttee, 1976–81; Chem. Cttee, 1979–82; Sci. Bd, 1988–91; Chm., Central Services Panel, 1980–82; Cttee Mem. and Sec., British Radiofrequency Spectroscopy Gp; Mem. Council, Faraday Div., RSC, 1988–91. Gov., Hampton Sch., Hanworth, 1990–. Ed., Molecular Physics, 1982–88. *Publications:* contrib. approx. 120 papers on topics involving devel t and application of NMR spectroscopy to internat. jls. *Recreations:* fly-fishing, ski-ing, gardening, music. *Address:* Periwinkle Cottage, Perry Hill, Worplesdon, Guildford, Surrey GU3 3RG. *T:* Guildford (0483) 233320; BP Research, Chertsey Road, Sunbury-on-Thames, Middx TW16 7LN. *T:* Sunbury-on-Thames (0932) 762420.

PACKER, Kerry Francis Bullmore, AC 1983; Chairman, Consolidated Press Holdings Ltd, since 1974; publisher of magazines and journals, for specialist, technical, fashion and trends; *b* 17 Dec. 1937; *s* of late Sir Douglas Frank Hewson Packer, KBE, and Lady (Gretel Joyce) Packer (*née* Bullmore); *m* 1963, Roslyn Redman Weedon; one *s* one *d*. *Educ:* Cranbrook Sch., Sydney, NSW; Geelong C of E Grammar Sch., Vic. Largest shareholder in Nine Network Australia Ltd and in Australian National Industries; producer of free standing coupon inserts for week-end newspapers in USA and of intermediate petrochemical products. *Recreations:* golf, tennis, cricket, polo. *Address:* 54 Park Street, Sydney, NSW 2000, Australia. *T:* (02) 282 8000. *Clubs:* Athenæum (Melbourne); Royal Sydney Golf, Australian Golf, Elanora Country, Tattersall's (NSW).

PACKER, Richard John; Deputy Secretary (Agricultural Commodities, Trade and Food Production), Ministry of Agriculture, Fisheries and Food, since 1989; *b* 18 Aug. 1944; *s* of George Charles Packer and Dorothy May Packer (*née* Reynolds); *m* 1st, Alison Mary Sellwood; two *s* one *d*; 2nd, Lucy Jeanne Blackett-Ord (*née* Neville-Rolfe); three *s*. *Educ:* City of London School; Manchester Univ. (BSc 1965, MSc 1966). MAFF, 1967; 1st Sec., Office of Perm Rep. to EEC, 1973–76; Principal Private Sec. to Minister, 1976–78; Asst Sec., 1979; Under Sec., MAFF, 1985–89. *Recreation:* living intensely. *Address:* Ministry of Agriculture, Fisheries and Food, Whitehall Place, SW1A 2HH. *T:* 071–270 8109.

PACKER, William John; painter and critic; art critic, Financial Times, since 1974; *b* 19 Aug. 1940; *o s* of late (Harold George Edward) Rex Packer and Evelyn Mary Packer (*née* Wornham); *m* 1965, Clare, *er d* of late Thomas Winn and Cecily Philip; three *d*. *Educ:* Windsor Grammar Sch.; Wimbledon Sch. of Art (NDD 1963); Brighton Coll. of Art (ATC 1964). First exhibited, RA, 1963; teaching full-time, 1964–67, part-time in art schs, 1967–77; external assessor, 1980–87. Member: Fine Art Board, CNAA, 1976–83; Adv. Cttee, Govt Art Collection, 1977–84; Crafts Council, 1980–87. Exhibn selector, incl. first British Art Show, 1979–80. London corrresp., Art & Artists, 1969–74. Inaugural Henry Moore lectr, Florence, 1986. Hon. Fellow, RCA, 1988. *Publications:* The Art of Vogue Covers, 1980; Fashion Drawing in Vogue, 1983; Henry Moore: a pictorial biography, 1985; Carl Erickson, and René Bouët-Willaumez, 1989. *Recreations:* hockey, cricket, riding, walking. *Address:* 39 Elms Road, Clapham, SW4 9EP. *T:* 071–622 1108. *Clubs:* Brooks's, Chelsea Arts, Academy.

PACKSHAW, Robin David; Consultant, Business in the Community, 1990; *b* 20 March 1933; *s* of late Savil Packshaw and Fay Mary Packshaw; *m* 1980, Susan Granville Louise Osborne; three *s* one *d* by previous marriage. *Educ:* Diocesan Coll., Cape Town; Bradfield Coll., Berks. Served RM, 1951–53; commnd and served in Special Boat Service, 1952; RMFVR, 1953–58. Iraq Petroleum Co. Ltd, 1953–63; Long Till and Colvin Ltd, 1963–69; founded Packshaw & Associates Ltd, Sterling Money Brokers, 1969; apptd Main Bd Dir, Charles Fulton, when Packshaw & Associates merged with Charles Fulton Sterling and became Fulton Packshaw Ltd, 1973; additl responsibility for Charles Fulton Middle East Develt, 1973–79; Chm., Charles Fulton (UK) Ltd, Internat. For. Exch. and Currency Deposit Brokers, 1982; as Chm., developed Charles Fulton (UK) Ltd into International City Holdings Gp (full Stock Exchange listing, 1985), 1982–85; Chm., Internat. City Holdings, Money and Securities Brokers, 1985–89. Chm., Radionics Assoc., 1991 (Mem. Finance Cttee, 1979–91). Chm., Stours Br., N Dorset Conservation Assoc., 1989–. Church Warden, All Saints, Stour Row, Dorset, 1984–. Freeman, City of London, 1983; Life Mem., Guild of Freemen of City of London. *Recreations:* farm in Dorset, travel, people, the Church of England. *Address:* Baskerville Farm, Stour Row, Shaftesbury, Dorset. *T:* East Stour (074785) 483; 25 Lennox Gardens, SW1. *T:* 071–584 3969. *Club:* Royal Automobile.

PADFIELD, Nicholas David; QC 1991; *b* 5 Aug. 1947; *s* of David Padfield and Sushila, *d* of Sir Samuel Runganadhan; *m* 1st, 1978, Nayana Parekh (*d* 1983); one *d*; 2nd, 1986, Mary Barran, JP, *d* of Sir Edward Playfair, *qv*; two *s*. *Educ:* Charterhouse; University Coll., Oxford (Open Scholar, MA); Trinity Hall, Cambridge (LLB Internat. Law). Called to the Bar, Inner Temple, 1972; Mem. Panel, Treasury Counsel (Common Law), 1985–90; Assistant Recorder, 1990–. *Address:* 1 Hare Court, Temple, EC4Y 7BE. *T:* 071–353 3171. *Clubs:* MCC; Vincent's (Oxford).

PADMORE, Elaine Marguirite; Artistic Director: Wexford Festival Opera, since 1982; Classical Productions, since 1990; Artistic Consultant, London International Opera Festival, since 1991; *b* Haworth, Yorks, 3 Feb. 1947; *d* of Alfred and Florence Padmore. *Educ:* Newland High Sch., Hull; Arnold Sch., Blackpool; Birmingham Univ. (MA; BMus); Guildhall Sch. of Music; LTCL. Liberal Studies Lectr, Croydon and Kingston Colls of Art, 1968–70; Books Editor, OUP Music Dept, 1970–71; Producer, BBC Music Div., 1971–76; Announcer, Radio 3, 1982–90. Major BBC Radio 3 series include: Parade, Music of Tchaikovsky's Russia, England's Pleasant Land, Journal de mes Mélodies; Presenter of numerous programmes, incl. Festival Comment, Edinburgh Fest., 1973–81; Chief Producer, Opera, BBC Radio, 1976–83: series incl. complete operas of Richard Strauss and first performances of works by Delius and Havergal Brian; active as professional singer (soprano), particularly of opera; Lectr in Opera, RAM, 1979–. Artistic Dir, Dublin Grand Opera Soc., 1989–90. Hon. ARAM. Hungarian Radio Pro Musica Award for prog. Summertime on Bredon, 1973; Prix Musical de Radio Brno for prog. The English Renaissance, 1974; Sunday Independent Award for services to music in Ireland, 1985. *Publications:* Wagner (Great Composers' Series), 1970; Music in the Modern Age: chapter on Germany, 1973; contributor to: New Grove Dict. of Music, Proc. of Royal Musical Assoc., Music and Letters, The Listener. *Recreations:* gardening, travel, art exhibitions. *Address:* 11 Lancaster Avenue, Hadley Wood, Barnet, Herts EN4 0EP. *T:* 081–449 5369.

PADMORE, Sir Thomas, GCB 1965 (KCB 1953; CB 1947); MA; FCIT; *b* 23 April 1909; *e s* of Thomas William Padmore, Sheffield; *m* 1st, 1934, Alice (*d* 1963), *d* of Robert Alcock, Ormskirk; two *d* (one *s* decd); 2nd, 1964, Rosalind Culhane, *qv*. *Educ:* Central Sch., Sheffield; Queens' Coll., Cambridge (Foundation Scholar; Hon. Fellow, 1961).

Secretaries' Office, Board of Inland Revenue, 1931–34; transferred to Treasury, 1934; Principal Private Secretary to Chancellor of Exchequer, 1943–45; Second Secretary, 1952–62; Permanent Sec., Min. of Transport, 1962–68. Dir, Laird Gp Ltd, 1970–79; Dep. Chm., Metropolitan Cammell Ltd, 1969–80. Chairman: Rehearsal Orchestra, 1961–71; Handel Opera Soc., 1963–86. Hon. Treas., Inst. of Cancer Res., 1973–81. *Address:* 39 Cholmeley Crescent, Highgate, N6 5EX. *T:* 081–340 6587. *Club:* Reform.

PADMORE, Lady (Thomas); *see* Culhane, Rosalind.

PADOVAN, John Mario Faskally; Chairman, Merchant Banking Division, Barclays de Zoete Wedd Group, since 1986; Deputy Chairman, Barclays de Zoete Wedd, since 1989; *b* 7 May 1938; *s* of Umberto Mario Padovan and Mary Nina Liddon Padovan; *m* 1964, Sally Kay (*née* Anderson); three *s*. *Educ:* St George's College, Weybridge; King's College London (LLB); Keble College, Oxford (BCL). FCA. County Bank, 1970–84: Dir, 1971; Dep. Chief Exec., 1974; Chief Exec., 1976; Chm., 1984; Dep. Chm., Hambros Bank and Dir, Hambros, 1984–86. Director: Tesco, 1982–; M. S. Instruments, 1985–; Mabey Hldgs, 1989–. *Recreations:* golf, squash, walking. *Address:* 61 Cleaver Square, SE11 4EA. *T:* 071–735 2611. *Clubs:* United Oxford & Cambridge University; Royal St George's Golf, West Surrey Golf.

PAFFARD, Rear-Admiral (retired) Ronald Wilson, CB 1960; CBE 1943; *b* Ludlow, 14 Feb. 1904; 4th *s* of Murray Paffard and Fanny (*née* Wilson); *m* 1933, Nancy Brenda Malim; one *s* one *d*. *Educ:* Maidstone Grammar Sch. Paymaster Cadetship in RN, 1922; Paymaster Commander, 1940; Captain (S), 1951; Rear-Admiral, 1957. Secretary to Adm. of the Fleet Lord Tovey in all his Flag appointments, including those throughout the War of 1939–45; Supply Officer of HMS Vengeance, 1946–48; Portsmouth Division, Reserve Fleet, 1948–50; HMS Eagle, 1950–51; Asst Director-General, Supply and Secretarial Branch, 1952–54; Commanding Officer, HMS Ceres, 1954–56; Chief Staff Officer (Administration) on staff of Commander-in-Chief, Portsmouth, 1957–60, retired. *Recreations:* painting, golf. *Address:* 2 Little Green Orchard, Alverstoke, Hants PO12 2EY.

PAFFORD, John Henry Pyle, MA, DLit (London); FSA; FLA; Goldsmiths' Librarian of the University of London, 1945–67; *b* 6 March 1900; *s* of John Pafford and Bessie (*née* Pyle); *m* 1941, Elizabeth Ford, *d* of R. Charles Ford and Margaret Harvey; one *d* (and one *d* decd). *Educ:* Trowbridge High Sch.; University Coll., London (Fellow, 1956). Library Asst, University College, London, 1923–25; Librarian, and Tutor, Selly Oak Colleges, 1925–31 (Hon. Fellow 1985); Sub-Librarian, National Central Library, 1931–45; Lecturer at University of London School of Librarianship, 1937–61. Editor, Year's Work in Librarianship, 1935–38 (jointly), and 1939–46; Library Adviser, Inter-Univ. Council for Higher Education Overseas, 1960–68. *Publications:* Bale's King Johan, 1931, and The Sodder'd Citizen, 1936 (Malone Society); Library Co-operation in Europe, 1935; Accounts of Parliamentary Garrisons of Great Chalfield and Malmesbury, 1645–46, 1940; Books and Army Education, 1946; W. P. Ker, A Bibliography, 1950; The Winter's Tale (Arden Shakespeare), 1963; Watts's Divine Songs for Children, 1971; L. Bryskett's Literary Works, 1972; (with E. R. Pafford) Employer and Employed, 1974. *Address:* Hillside, Allington Park, Bridport, Dorset DT6 5DD. *T:* Bridport (0308) 22829.

PAGE, family name of **Baron Whaddon.**

PAGE, Sir Alexander Warren, (Sir Alex Page), Kt 1977; MBE 1943; Chairman, PFC International Portfolio Fund Ltd, since 1985; *b* 1 July 1914; *s* of Sydney E. Page and Phyllis (*née* Spencer); *m* 1st, 1940, Anne Lewis Hickman (marr. diss.); two *s* one *d*; 2nd, 1981, Mrs Andrea Mary Wharton. *Educ:* Tonbridge; Clare Coll., Cambridge (MA). Served REME, with Guards Armoured Div., 1940–45, Lt-Col REME. Joined The Metal Box Co. Ltd, 1936; joined board as Sales Dir, 1957; Man. Dir 1966; Dep. Chm. 1969; Chief Exec., 1970–77; Chm., 1970–79. Director: J. Lyons & Co. Ltd, Feb.-Oct. 1978; C. Shippam Ltd, 1979–85; Chairman: Electrolux, 1978–82; G. T. Pension Services Ltd, 1981–85; Paine & Co. Ltd, 1981–87. Mem., IBA (formerly ITA), 1970–76; Mem., Food Science and Technology Bd, 1973–. Pres., BFMIRA, 1980. FIMechE; CBIM. Governor, Colfe's Grammar Sch., Lewisham, 1977–. *Recreations:* golf, tennis. *Address:* 2 Montagu Square, W1. *T:* 071–935 9894; Merton Place, Dunsfold, Godalming, Surrey. *T:* Dunsfold (048649) 211.

PAGE, Annette, (Mrs Ronald Hynd); Ballerina of the Royal Ballet until retirement, 1967; Ballet Mistress, Ballet of the Bayerischestaatsoper, Munich, 1984–86; *b* 18 Dec. 1932; *d* of James Lees and Margaret Page; *m* 1957, Ronald Hynd, *qv*; one *d*. *Educ:* Royal Ballet School. Audition and award of scholarship to Roy. Ballet Sch., 1944. Entry into touring company of Royal Ballet (then Sadler's Wells Theatre Ballet), 1950; promotion to major Royal Ballet Co. (Sadler's Wells Ballet), 1955. Mem., Arts Council of GB, 1976–79. *Roles included:* The Firebird, Princess Aurora in Sleeping Beauty, Odette-Odile in Swan Lake, Giselle, Lise in La Fille Mal Gardée, Juliet in Romeo and Juliet, Cinderella. *Recreations:* music, books, gardening, choral singing.

PAGE, Anthony (Frederick Montague); stage, film and television director; *b* India, 21 Sept. 1935; *s* of Brig. F. G. C. Page, DSO, OBE, and P. V. M. Page. *Educ:* Oakley Hall, Cirencester; Winchester Coll. (Schol.); Magdalen Coll., Oxford (Schol., BA); Neighborhood Playhouse Sch. of the Theater, NY. Asst, Royal Court Theatre, 1958: co-directed Live Like Pigs, directed The Room; Artistic Dir, Dundee Repertory Theatre, 1962; The Caretaker, Oxford and Salisbury; Women Beware Women, and Nil Carborundum, Royal Shakespeare Co., 1963; BBC Directors' Course, then several episodes of Z-Cars, Horror of Darkness and 1st TV prodn Stephen D; Jt Artistic Dir, Royal Court, 1964–65; directed Inadmissible Evidence (later Broadway and film), A Patriot for Me, 1st revival of Waiting for Godot, Cuckoo in the Nest; Diary of a Madman, Duchess, 1966; Artistic Dir, two seasons at Royal Court: Uncle Vanya, 1970; Alpha Beta (also film); Hedda Gabler; Krapp's Last Tape; Not I; Cromwell; other plays transf. from Royal Court to West End: Time Present; Hotel in Amsterdam; revival, Look Back in Anger; West of Suez; directed Hamlet, Nottingham, 1970; Rules of the Game, National Theatre; King Lear, Amer. Shakespeare Fest., 1975; Cowardice, Ambassadors, 1983; Heartbreak House, Broadway, 1984 (televised); Mrs Warren's Profession, Nat. Theatre, 1985; *television:* The Parachute; Emlyn; Hotel in Amsterdam; Speaking of Murder; You're Free; The Changeling; Headmaster; Sheppey; in USA: Missiles of October (nominated for Emmy award); Pueblo (nominated for Emmy award); FDR, the Last Year; Bill (starring Mickey Rooney (Golden Globe Award); Johnny Belinda; Bill on His Own; The Nightmare Years; Patricia Neal Story; Murder by Reason of Insanity; Second Serve; Pack of Lies; Chernobyl: The Final Warning, 1990; Absolute Hell, 1991; *films:* Inadmissible Evidence; I Never Promised You a Rose Garden; Absolution; The Lady Vanishes; Forbidden. Directors' and Producers' Award for TV Dir of Year, 1966. *Recreations:* movies, reading, riding, travelling. *Address:* 6 Arundel Gardens, W11.

PAGE, Sir (Arthur) John, Kt 1984; *b* 16 Sept. 1919; *s* of Sir Arthur Page, QC (late Chief Justice of Burma), and Lady Page, KiH; *m* 1950, Anne, *d* of Charles Micklem, DSO, JP, DL, Longcross House, Surrey; four *s*. *Educ:* Harrow, Magdalene College, Cambridge. Joined RA as Gunner, 1939, commissioned, 1940; served War of 1939–45, Western Desert (wounded), France, Germany; demobilised as Major, comdg 258 Battery Norfolk Yeomanry, 1945; various positions in industry and commerce, 1946–. Chm. Bethnal Green and E London Housing Assoc., 1957–70; contested (C) Eton and Slough, Gen. Election, 1959. MP (C) Harrow W, March 1960–1987. PPS to Parly Under-Sec. of State, Home Office, 1961–63; Conservative Parly Labour Affairs Cttee: Sec., 1960–61, 1964–67, Vice-Chm., 1964–69, Chm., 1970–74; Sec., Conservative Broadcasting Cttee, 1974–76. Pres., Cons. Trade Unionists Nat. Adv. Council, 1967–69; Member: Parly Select Cttee on Race Relations and Immigration, 1970–71; British Delegn to Council of Europe and WEU, 1972–87 (Chm. Budget Cttee, 1973–74, Social and Health Cttee, 1975–78). Mem. Exec., IPU, British Gp, 1970 (Treasurer, 1974–77; Vice-Chm., 1977–79; Chm., 1979–82); Acting Internat. Pres., IPU, 1984 (Dep. Internat. Pres., 1982–84). Vice-Pres., British Insurance Brokers Assoc., 1980–; President: Water Companies Assoc., 1986–89 (Dep. Pres., 1984–86); Independent Schools Assoc., 1971–78; Chm., Council for Indep. Educn, 1974–80. *Recreations:* painting and politics. *Address:* Hitcham Lodge, Taplow, Maidenhead, Berks SL6 0HG. *T:* Burnham (0628) 605056. *Clubs:* Brooks's, MCC.

PAGE, Bertram Samuel; University Librarian and Keeper of the Brotherton Collection, University of Leeds, 1947–69, Emeritus Librarian, since 1969; *b* 1 Sept. 1904; *s* of Samuel and Catherine Page; *m* 1933, Olga Ethel, *d* of E. W. Mason. *Educ:* King Charles I School Kidderminster; University of Birmingham. BA 1924, MA 1926. Asst Librarian (later Sub-Librarian), Univ. of Birmingham, 1931–36; Librarian, King's College, Newcastle upon Tyne, 1936–47. Pres. Library Assoc., 1960 (Hon. Fellow, 1961); Chairman: Standing Conf. of Nat. and Univ. Libraries, 1961–63; Exec. Cttee, Nat. Central Library, 1962–72 (Trustee, 1963–75); Librarianship Bd, Council for Nat. Academic Awards, 1966–71. Mem. Court of Univ. of Birmingham, 1954–69. Hon. DUniv. York, 1968. *Publications:* contrib. to Stephen MacKenna's trans. of Plotinus, vol. 5, 1930 (revised whole trans. for 2nd, 3rd, 4th edns, 1958, 1962, 1969); A Manual of University and College Library Practice (jt ed.), 1940; articles and reviews in classical and library jls. *Address:* 24 St Anne's Road, Headington, Oxford. *T:* Oxford (0865) 65981.

PAGE, Bruce; journalist; Managing Director, Paul Rose Pagesystems Ltd, since 1986; *b* 1 Dec. 1936; *s* of Roger and Beatrice Page; *m* 1969, Anne Louise Darnborough; one *s* one *d*. *Educ:* Melbourne High Sch.; Melbourne Univ. The Herald, Melbourne, 1956–60; Evening Standard, 1960–62; Daily Herald, 1962–64; Sunday Times, 1964–76; Daily Express, 1977; Editor, The New Statesman, 1978–82. *Publications:* (jtly) Philby, 1968, 3rd edn 1977; (jtly) An American Melodrama, 1969; (jtly) Do You Sincerely Want to be Rich?, 1971; (jtly) Destination Disaster, 1976; contrib. Ulster, 1972; The Yom Kippur War, 1974; The British Press, 1978. *Recreations:* sailing, reading. *Address:* 35 Duncan Terrace, N1 8AL. *T:* 071–359 1000.

PAGE, Maj.-Gen. Charles Edward, CB 1974; MBE 1944; DL; *b* 23 Aug. 1920; *s* of late Sir (Charles) Max Page, KBE, CB, DSO, FRCS and Lady (Helen) Page; *m* 1948, Elizabeth Marion, *d* of late Sir William Smith Crawford, KBE; two *s* one *d*. *Educ:* Marlborough Coll.; Trinity Coll., Cambridge. BSc (Eng) London 1949; CEng, FIEE 1968. Commissioned 2nd Lieut Royal Signals from TA, 1941; regimental appts Guards Armd Divisional Signals, 1941–45; CO 19 Indian Div. Signals, 1945–46; psc 1951; GSO2 Staff Coll., 1955–58; GSO1 Combat Develt Directorate, WO, 1960–63; CO 1st Div. Signal Regt, 1963–65; CCR Signals 1 (BR) Corps, 1966–68; Sec., NATO Mil. Cttee, Brussels, 1968–70; DCD(A) MoD, 1971–74; retired 1974. Col Comdt, Royal Corps of Signals, 1974–80. Hon. Col, Women's Transport Service (FANY), 1976. DL W Sussex, 1986. *Recreations:* shooting, golf, fishing. *Address:* Church Farm House, Old Bosham, Chichester, W Sussex PO18 8HL. *T:* Chichester (0243) 573191. *Clubs:* Army and Navy; Royal and Ancient (St Andrews).

PAGE, Cyril Leslie, OBE 1965; Controller, Personnel, Television, BBC Television Service, 1971–76, retired; *b* 20 Oct. 1916; *s* of Cyril Herbert Page and Rosamund Clara Page; *m* 1939, Barbara Mary Rowland; one *s* one *d*. *Educ:* Sherborne Sch. Royal Air Force, 1936–46 (Wing Comdr). British Broadcasting Corporation, 1946–: Asst, Appts Dept, 1947; Asst Admin. Officer, Overseas Services, 1949; Asst Head of TV Admin., 1951; Estabt Officer, TV, 1958; Head of TV Estabt Dept, 1961; Asst Controller, TV Admin., 1964. Chm., Osborne Management Ltd, 1984–. Mem. Council, Royal Postgrad. Med. Sch., 1975–Sept. 1989. *Recreations:* reading, gardening. *Address:* 95 Fountain Gardens, Windsor, Berks SL4 3SU.

PAGE, Rt. Rev. Dennis Fountain; *b* 1 Dec. 1919; *s* of Prebendary Martin Fountain Page and Lilla Fountain Page; *m* 1946, Margaret Bettine Clayton; two *s* one *d*. *Educ:* Shrewsbury Sch.; Gonville and Caius Coll., Cambridge (MA); Lincoln Theological Coll. Curate, Rugby Parish Church, 1943; Priest-in-Charge, St George's Church, Hillmorton, Rugby, 1945; Rector of Hockwold, Vicar of Wilton and Rector of Weeting, Norfolk, 1949; Archdeacon of Huntingdon and Vicar of Yaxley, 1965–75; Hon. Canon of Ely Cathedral, 1968; Bishop Suffragan of Lancaster, 1975–85. *Publication:* Reflections on the Reading for Holy Communion in the Alternative Service Book 1980, 1983. *Recreations:* music, astronomy, gardening. *Address:* Larkrise, Hartest Hill, Hartest, Bury St Edmunds, Suffolk IP29 4ES.

PAGE, Brig. (Edwin) Kenneth, CBE 1951 (OBE 1946); DSO 1945; MC 1918; *b* 23 Jan. 1898; *s* of G. E. Page, Baldock, Herts; *m* 1921, Kate Mildred (*d* 1975), *d* of G. H. Arthur, Yorkshire, Barbados, BWI; two *s*; *m* 1987, Joan, *d* of W. H. Goodall and *widow* of Bryan Rose. *Educ:* Haileybury College; RMA, Woolwich. 2nd Lt, RFA, 1916; BEF, France, 1916–18. Adjt TA, 1924–27; Staff College, Camberley, 1928–29; Staff Captain, India, 1931–35; GSO2, War Office, 1936–39; Lt-Col, 1939; served War of 1939–45: BEF, France, 1940; Col, 1945; Brig., 1946; Dep. Director, WO, 1946–48; Commander, Caribbean Area, 1948–51; employed War Office, 1951; retired pay, 1952. CC 1961–74, CA 1968–74, Dorset. *Address:* Durrant End, Durrant, Sturminster Newton, Dorset DT10 1DQ. *T:* Sturminster Newton (0258) 73146. *Club:* Army and Navy.

See also Prof. J. K. Page.

PAGE, Ewan Stafford, PhD, MA, BSc; Vice-Chancellor, University of Reading, since 1979; *b* 17 Aug. 1928; *s* of late Joseph William Page and Lucy Quayle (*née* Stafford); *m* 1955, Sheila Margaret Smith; three *s* one *d*. *Educ:* Wyggeston Grammar Sch., Leicester; Christ's Coll., Cambridge (MA, PhD, Raleigh Prize 1952); Univ. of London (BSc). Instr, RAF Techn. Coll., 1949–51; Lectr in Statistics, Durham Colls, 1954–57; Director: Durham Univ. Computing Lab., 1957–63; Newcastle Univ. Computing Lab., 1963–78; Visiting Prof., Univ. of N Carolina, Chapel Hill, USA, 1962–63; University of Newcastle upon Tyne: Prof. of Computing and Data Processing, 1965–78; Pro-Vice Chancellor, 1972–78 (Actg Vice-Chancellor, 1976–77). Mem. Bd, Aycliffe and Peterlee Develt Corp., 1969–78. Chairman: Food Adv. Cttee, 1988–; Univs' Authorities Panel, 1988–. Pres., British Computer Soc., 1984–85 (Dep. Pres., 1983–84); Mem., Gen. Optical Council, 1984– (Vice-Chm., 1989–); Hon. Treasurer, Royal Statistical Soc., 1983–89. CBIM 1986; Hon. Fellow, Amer. Statistical Assoc., 1974; Hon. FBCS, 1976; Hon. Fellow, Newcastle upon Tyne Polytechnic, 1979. Chevalier, Académiques l'Ordre des Palmes (France), 1991. *Publications:* (jtly) Information Representation and Manipulation in a Computer, 1973, 2nd edn 1978; (jtly) Introduction to Computational Combinatorics, 1978; papers in statistical and computing jls. *Recreations:* golf, music, reading, vegetable gardening, country wine and beer making. *Address:* University of Reading, Whiteknights, Reading, Berks RG6 2AH. *T:* Reading (0734) 875123.

PAGE, Sir Frederick (William), Kt 1979; CBE 1961; FRS 1978; FEng, Hon. FRAeS; Member of the Board, British Aerospace PLC, 1977–83; Chairman and Chief Executive, Aircraft Group of British Aerospace PLC, 1977–82; retired 1983; *b* 20 Feb. 1917; *s* of Richard Page and Ellen Potter; *m* 1940, Kathleen Edith de Courcy; three *s* one *d. Educ:* Rutlish Sch., Merton; St Catharine's Coll., Cambridge (MA). Hawker Aircraft Co., 1938; English Electric, 1945; Chief Engr, 1950, and Dir and Chief Exec. (Aircraft), English Electric Aviation, 1959; Managing Dir, Mil. Aircraft Div. of BAC, 1965–72, Chm., 1967; apptd Managing Dir (Aircraft), BAC, and Chm., Commercial Aircraft Div., 1972. Jt Chm. of SEPECAT, the Anglo-French co. formed for management of Jaguar programme, 1966–73; apptd to Bd of Panavia Aircraft GmbH, 1969, Chm. 1977; apptd Chm. BAC Ltd (a co. of Brit. Aerospace), 1977. Mem. Council, Soc. of Brit. Aerospace Cos Ltd; apptd to Bd of BAC (Operating) Ltd, 1963; Dir, BAC (USA) Inc., 1975–77. FRAeS, 1951–80, Hon. FRAeS, 1980 (Gold Medal, 1974); Fellow, Fellowship of Engrg, 1977. Hon. Fellow, UMIST, 1970. Hon. DSc Cranfield, 1979. British Gold Medal for Aeronautics, 1962. *Recreation:* gardening. *Address:* Renvyle, 60 Waverley Lane, Farnham, Surrey GU9 8BN. *T:* Farnham (0252) 714999. *Club:* United Oxford & Cambridge University.

PAGE, Howard William Barrett; QC 1987; *b* 11 Feb. 1943; *s* of Leslie Herbert Barrett Page and Phyllis Elizabeth Page; *m* 1969, Helen Joanna Shotter; two *s* one *d. Educ:* Radley Coll.; Trinity Hall, Cambridge (BA, LLB). Called to the Bar, Lincoln's Inn, 1967 (Mansfield Schol.). *Recreations:* music, walking. *Address:* 1 Hare Court, Temple, EC4Y 7BE.

PAGE, Jennifer Anne; Chief Executive, English Heritage (Historic Buildings and Monuments Commission), since 1989; *b* 12 Nov. 1944; *d* of Edward and Olive Page. *Educ:* Barr's Hill Grammar School, Coventry; Royal Holloway College, Univ. of London (BA Hons). Entered Civil Service, 1968; Principal, DoE, 1974; Asst Sec., Dept of Transport, 1980; seconded BNOC, 1981; LDDC, 1983. Senior Vice-Pres., Pallas Invest SA, 1984–89. *Address:* English Heritage, Fortress House, 23 Savile Row, W1X 1AB.

PAGE, Sir John; *see* Page, Sir (Arthur) John and Page, Sir John (Joseph Joffre).

PAGE, John Brangwyn; Chairman, Agricultural Mortgage Corporation, 1982–85; Director: Standard Chartered Bank, 1982–89; Nationwide Anglia (formerly Nationwide Building Society), since 1982; *b* 23 Aug. 1923; *s* of late Sidney John Page, CB, MC; *m* 1948, Gloria Vail; one *s* one *d. Educ:* Highgate Sch. (Foundation Schol.); King's Coll., Cambridge (BA). RAF, 1942–46; Cambridge, 1946–48; Bank of England, 1948; seconded to IMF, 1953; Chief Cashier, 1970–80; Exec. Dir, 1980–82. FCIB; CBIM; FRSA. *Recreations:* gardening, music, travel.

PAGE, Maj.-Gen. John Humphrey, CB 1977; OBE 1967; MC 1952; Director of the London Law Trust, 1979–88; *b* 5 March 1923; *s* of late Captain W. J. Page, JP, Devizes and late Alice Mary Page (*née* Richards); *m* 1956, Angela Mary Bunting; three *s* one *d. Educ:* Stonyhurst. Commnd into RE, 1942; served in NW Europe, India, Korea, Middle East and UK, 1942–60; Instr, Staff Coll., Camberley, 1960–62; comd 32 Armd Engr Regt, 1964–67; idc 1968; CCRE 1st Br. Corps, 1969–70; Asst Comdt, RMA Sandhurst, 1971–74; Dir of Personal Services (Army), MoD, 1974–78, retd. Col Comdt, RE, 1980–85. Dir, RBM (Holdings), 1980–86. Mem. Council, Officers' Pension Soc.; Vice-Chm., SSAFA, 1983–87. Chm. Trustees, Home-Start Consultancy, 1982–90; Mem., Management Cttee, Stacpole Trust, 1981–. Chm., Bd of Governors, St Mary's Sch., Shaftesbury, 1985–; Mem., Bd of Governors, Stonyhurst Coll., 1980–90. *Address:* c/o Lloyds Bank, Somerton, Somerset.

PAGE, Sir John (Joseph Joffre), Kt 1979; OBE 1959; Chairman, Christie Hospital NHS Trust, since 1991; *b* 7 Jan. 1915; 2nd *s* of late William Joseph and Frances Page; *m* 1939, Cynthia Maynard, *d* of late L. M. Swan, CBE; two *s. Educ:* Emanuel School. RAF, 1933–38 and 1939–46 (despatches, 1943); Group Captain. Iraq Petroleum Group of Cos, 1938–39 and 1946–70; served in Palestine, Jordan, Lebanon, Syria, Iraq, Qatar, Bahrain and Abu Dhabi; Head Office, London, 1958–61; Gen. Man., 1955–58; Chief Representative, 1961–70. Chm., 1972–77 and 1980–84, Chief Exec., 1975–77, Mersey Docks and Harbour Co.; Dep. Chm., British Ports Assoc., 1974–77; Chm., Nat. Ports Council, 1977–80. Chairman: Chester DHA, 1981–82; North Western RHA, 1982–88. *Recreations:* photography, fishing, music. *Address:* The Cottage, Hockenhull Lane, Tarvin, Chester CH3 8LB. *Clubs:* Oriental, Royal Air Force, MCC.

PAGE, Prof. John Kenneth; energy and environmental consultant; Initiating Director, Cambridge Interdisciplinary Environmental Centre, since 1991; Professor of Building Science, University of Sheffield, 1960–84, now Emeritus; *b* 3 Nov. 1924; *s* of Brig. E. K. Page, *qv; m* 1954, Anita Bell Lovell; two *s* two *d. Educ:* Haileybury College; Pembroke College, Cambridge. Served War of 1939–45, Royal Artillery, 1943–47. Asst Industrial Officer, Council of Industrial Design, 1950–51; taught Westminster School, 1952–53; Sen. Scientific Officer, Tropical Liaison Section, Building Research Station, 1953–56; Chief Research Officer, Nuffield Div. for Architectural Studies, 1956–57; Lecturer, Dept. of Building Science, Univ. of Liverpool, 1957–60. Former Chairman: Environmental Gp, and Mem., Econ. Planning Council, Yorks and Humberside Region, 1965–78; UK Section, Internat. Solar Energy Soc. Consultant author working with UN internat. agencies on energy use in Third World and on environmental health in tropical bldgs. Farrington Daniels Internat. Award, for distinguished contribs to solar energy studies, 1989. *Publications:* 200 papers on Energy policy, Environmental Design and Planning, Building Climatology and Solar Energy. *Address:* 15 Brincliffe Gardens, Sheffield S11 9BG. *T:* Sheffield (0742) 551570.

PAGE, Kenneth; *see* Page, Edwin Kenneth.

PAGE, Prof. Raymond Ian, LittD; Director, Leverhulme Trust Research Group on Manuscript Evidence, Parker Library, since 1989; Elrington and Bosworth Professor of Anglo-Saxon, University of Cambridge, 1984–91; Fellow, Corpus Christi College, Cambridge, since 1962; *b* 25 Sept. 1924; *s* of Reginald Howard Page and Emily Louise Page; *m* 1953, Elin Benedicte Hustad, *d* of Tormod Kristoffer Hustad and Anne Margarethe Hustad, Oslo; two *d* (one *s* decd). *Educ:* King Edward VII Sch., Sheffield; Rotherham Technical Coll.; Univ. of Sheffield. LittD Cambridge 1974. Assistant Lecturer and Lecturer, Univ. of Nottingham, 1951–61; successively Lectr, Reader and Professor, Dept of Anglo-Saxon, Norse and Celtic, Cambridge, 1961–91; Librarian, Corpus Christi Coll., Cambridge, 1965–91; Sandars Reader in Bibliography, 1989–90. *Address:* Ashton House, Newnham Road, Cambridge.

PAGE, Richard Lewis; MP (C) Hertfordshire South West, since Dec. 1979; Director of family company, since 1964; *b* 22 Feb. 1941; *s* of Victor Charles and Kathleen Page; *m* 1964, Madeleine Ann Brown; one *s* one *d. Educ:* Hurstpierpoint Coll.; Luton Technical Coll. Apprenticeship, Vauxhall Motors, 1959–64; HNC Mech. Engineering. Young Conservatives, 1964–66; Councillor, Banstead UDC, 1968–71; contested (C)

Workington, Feb. and Oct. 1974; MP (C) Workington, Nov. 1976–1979; PPS: to Sec. of State for Trade, 1981–82; to Leader of the House, 1982–87. Mem., Public Accounts Cttee, 1987–; Vice-Chm., Cons. Trade and Industry Cttee, 1988–89. Hon. Treasurer, Leukaemia Res. Fund, 1987–. *Recreation:* most sport. *Address:* House of Commons, SW1A 0AA.

PAGE, Simon Richard; District Judge (formerly Registrar), Guildford, Epsom and Reigate County Courts, and High Court of Justice, since 1980; a Recorder of the Crown Court, since 1980; *b* 7 March 1934; *s* of Eric Rowland Page and Vera (*née* Fenton); *m* 1st, 1963, (marr. diss. 1977); three *s* one *d*; 2nd, 1984. *Educ:* Lancing; LSE (LLB External, 1956). Admitted solicitor (hons), 1957. National Service, Second Lieut RA, 1957–59. Private practice as solicitor, 1959–75; Pres., West Surrey Law Soc., 1972–73; Registrar, Croydon County Court, 1975–80; Pres., Assoc. of County Court and District Registrars, 1983–84. *Recreations:* squash racquets, cricket, bridge. *Address:* c/o The Law Courts, Mary Road, Guildford.

PAGE WOOD, Sir Anthony John, 8th Bt, *cr* 1837; *b* 6 Feb. 1951; *s* of Sir David (John Hatherley) Page Wood, 7th Bt and Evelyn Hazel Rosemary, *d* of late Captain George Ernest Bellville; *S* father 1955. *Heir: uncle,* Matthew Page Wood [*b* 13 Aug. 1924; *m* 1947; two *d*].

PAGEL, Prof. Bernard Ephraim Julius; Professor of Astrophysics, NORDITA (Nordic Institute for Theoretical Physics), Copenhagen, since 1990; Visiting Professor of Astronomy, University of Sussex, since 1970; *b* 4 Jan. 1930; *s* of Walter T. U. Pagel and Magdalene M. E. Pagel; *m* 1958, Annabel Ruth Tuby; two *s* one *d. Educ:* Merchant Taylors' Sch., Northwood; Sidney Sussex Coll., Cambridge (MA, PhD). Res. Fellow, Sidney Sussex Coll., 1953–56; Radcliffe Student, Pretoria, 1955; PSO, Royal Greenwich Observ., 1955–61; Astrophysicist, Sacramento Peak Observ., New Mexico, 1960; SPSO, 1961–71, DCSO, 1971–89, Royal Greenwich Observ.; Vis. Reader in Astronomy, Univ. of Sussex, 1966–70. Kelvin Lectr, BAAS, 1962; Vice-Pres. and For. Corresp., RAS, 1974–75. Gold Medal, RAS, 1990. *Publications:* Théorie des Atmosphères Stellaires, 1971; articles in Nature, Encycl. Britannica, Monthly Notices of RAS, New Scientist, and procs of astronomical confs. *Recreations:* music, ski-ing, bicycling. *Address:* Groombridge, Lewes Road, Ringmer, East Sussex BN8 5ER. *T:* Ringmer (0273) 812729.

PAGET, family name of **Marquess of Anglesey.**

PAGET DE BEAUDESERT, Lord; Benedict Dashiel Paget; *b* 11 April 1986; *s* and *heir* of Earl of Uxbridge, *qv.*

PAGET, David Christopher John; Fourth Senior Prosecuting Counsel to the Crown at the Central Criminal Court, since 1991; a Recorder, since 1986; *b* 3 Feb. 1942; *s* of Henry Paget and Dorothy Paget (*née* Colenutt), Johannesburg, S Africa; *m* 1968, Dallas Wendy (*née* Hill); two *d. Educ:* St John's Coll., Johannesburg. Called to Bar, Inner Temple, 1967; Jun. Prosecuting Counsel to the Crown, 1982, Sen. Prosecuting Counsel to the Crown, 1989, Central Criminal Court. *Recreations:* walking, bird watching, listening to music. *Address:* Queen Elizabeth Building, Temple, EC4Y 9BS. *T:* 071–583 5766.

PAGET, Sir John (Starr), 3rd Bt *cr* 1886; CEng, FIMechE; Director, Somerset Fruit Machinery Ltd, since 1986; Proprietor, Sir John Paget Woodworker; Senior Partner, Haygrass Cider Orchards; *b* 24 Nov. 1914; *s* of Sir Richard Paget, 2nd Bt and Lady Muriel Paget, CBE; *S* father 1955; *m* 1944, Nancy Mary Parish, JP, *d* of late Lieutenant-Colonel Francis Parish, DSO, MC; two *s* five *d. Educ:* Oundle; Chateau D'Oex; Trinity College, Cambridge (MA). Joined English Electric Co. Ltd, 1936; Asst Works Supt, English Electric, Preston, 1941; Joined D. Napier & Son Ltd, 1943; Assistant Manager, D. Napier & Son Ltd, Liverpool, 1945; Manager, D. Napier & Son Ltd, London Group, 1946; Works Director, Napier Aero Engines, 1961–62 (Dir and Gen. Man. D. Napier & Son Ltd, 1959–61). Director: Thermal Syndicate Ltd, Wallsend, 1939–84 (Chm., 1973–80; Chm. Emeritus, 1980–84); Glacier Metal Group, 1963–65; Hilger & Watts, 1965–68; Rank Precision Industries Ltd, 1968–70. Hon. DTech Brunel, 1976. Silver Medal, Instn of Production Engineers, 1950. *Recreations:* music, cooking. *Heir: s* Richard Herbert Paget [*b* 17 February 1957; *m* 1985, Richenda, *d* of Rev. J. T. C. B. Collins; three *d*]. *Address:* Haygrass House, Taunton, Somerset TA3 7BS. *T:* Taunton (0823) 331779. *Club:* Athenæum.

PAGET, Lt-Col Sir Julian (Tolver), 4th Bt *cr* 1871; CVO 1984; Gentleman Usher to the Queen, since 1971; author; *b* 11 July 1921; *s* of General Sir Bernard Paget, GCB, DSO, MC (*d* 1961) (*g s* of 1st Bt), and Winifred (*d* 1986), *d* of Sir John Paget, 2nd Bt; *S* uncle, Sir James Francis Paget, 3rd Bt, 1972; *m* 1954, Diana Frances, *d* of late F. S. H. Farmer; one *s* one *d. Educ:* Radley College; Christ Church, Oxford (MA). Joined Coldstream Guards, 1940; served North West Europe, 1944–45; retired as Lt-Col, 1968. *Publications:* Counter-Insurgency Campaigning, 1967; Last Post: Aden, 1964–67, 1969; The Story of the Guards, 1976; The Pageantry of Britain, 1979; Yeoman of the Guard, 1984; Discovering London's Ceremonial and Traditions, 1989; Wellington's Peninsular War: the battles and battlefields, 1990. *Recreations:* fishing, shooting, travel, writing. *Heir: s* Henry James Paget, *b* 2 Feb. 1959. *Address:* 4 Trevor Street, SW7. *T:* 071–584 3524. *Clubs:* Cavalry and Guards, Pratt's, Flyfishers'.

PAGET-WILKES, Ven. Michael Jocelyn James; Archdeacon of Warwick, since 1990; *b* 11 Dec. 1941; *s* of Arthur Hamilton Paget-Wilkes and Eleanor Bridget Paget-Wilkes; *m* 1969, Ruth Gillian Macnamara; one *s* two *d. Educ:* Harper Adams Agricultural Coll. (NDA); London Coll. of Divinity (ALCD). Agricultural Extension Officer, Tanzania, 1964–66; attended London Coll. of Divinity, 1966–69; Curate, All Saints', Wandsworth, 1969–74; Vicar: St James', Hatcham, New Cross, 1974–82; St Matthew's, Rugby, 1982–90. *Publications:* The Church and Rural Development, 1968; Poverty, Revolution and the Church, 1981. *Recreations:* squash, tennis, music, ski-ing, gardening. *Address:* 10 Northumberland Road, Leamington Spa, Warwicks CV32 6HA.

PAGNAMENTA, Peter John; Executive Producer, BBC Television Documentary Department, 1981–85, and since 1987; *b* 12 April 1941; *s* of Charles Francis Pagnamenta and Daphne Pagnamenta; *m* 1966, Sybil Healy; one *s* one *d. Educ:* Shrewsbury; Trinity Hall, Cambridge (MA). Joined BBC, 1965; Prodn Asst, Tonight and 24 Hours, 1965–67; Asst Editor, 24 Hours, 1967; New York office, 1968–71 (Producer, US Election coverage and Apollo flights); Editor: 24 Hours, 1971; Midweek, 1972–75; Panorama, 1975–77; Dir of News and Current Affairs, Thames Television, 1977–80; Exec. Producer, All Our Working Lives (eleven part series), BBC2, 1984; Editor, Real Lives (documentary strand), BBC 1, 1984–85; Head of Current Affairs Gp, BBC TV, 1985–87; Exec. Producer, Nippon (eight part series), BBC 2, 1990. *Publication:* (with Richard Overy) All Our Working Lives, 1984. *Recreations:* walking, fishing. *Address:* BBC, Kensington House, Richmond Way, W14 0AX. *T:* 081–743 1272.

PAIBA, Denis Anthony; His Honour Judge Paiba; a Circuit Judge, since 1982; *b* 10 Dec. 1926; *e s* of late Geoffrey Paiba and Geraldine Paiba; *m* 1955, Lesley Patricia Dresden; two *s. Educ:* University Coll. Sch. (Junior); Magdalen Coll. Sch., Oxford; Jesus Coll., Cambridge. 44 Royal Marine Commando, 1945–47. Financial Times, 1957–58. Called to the Bar, Gray's Inn, 1958; a Recorder of the Crown Court, 1980–82. *Recreations:* theatre, music, gardening, archery, watching rugby and cricket, wining and dining. *Address:* Roehampton, SW15; 3 Temple Gardens, Temple, EC4Y 5BG. *T:* 071–353 3102.

PAICE, James Edward Thornton, MP (C) Cambridgeshire South East, since 1987; *b* 24 April 1949 *s* of Edward and Winifred Paice; *m* 1973, Ava Barbara Patterson; two *s. Educ:* Framlingham College, Suffolk; Writtle Agricultural College. Farm Manager, 1970–73; Farmer 1973–79; with United Framlingham Farmers Ltd (non-exec. Dir, 1989–), then with Framlingham Management and Training Services Ltd: Training Officer, 1979–82; Training Manager, 1982–85; Gen. Manager/Exec. Dir, 1985–87; Non-Exec. Dir, 1987–89. PPS to Minister of State, 1989–91, to Minister, 1991–, MAFF. Mem., Select Cttee on Employment, 1987–89. *Recreations:* shooting, windsurfing. *Address:* House of Commons, SW1A 0AA.

PAICE, Karlo Bruce; Assistant Under-Secretary of State, Home Office, 1955–66; *b* 18 August 1906; *s* of H. B. Paice, Horsham, Sussex; *m* 1st, 1935, Islay (*d* 1965), *d* of late Paymaster Comdr Duncan Cook; four *s*; 2nd, 1966, Mrs Gwen Morris (*née* Kenyon) (*d* 1991). *Educ:* Collyer's School, Horsham; Jesus Coll., Cambridge (MA). Second Clerk, Metropolitan Police Courts, 1928; Assistant Principal, Home Office, 1929; Asst Sec. to the Poisons Bd, 1933–35; Private Sec. to successive Parliamentary Under-Secretaries of State for Home Affairs, 1935–39. Principal, 1936; Assistant Secretary, 1941, serving in London Civil Defence Region, Fire Service Department, and Aliens Department. Secretary to the Prison Commission and a Prison Commissioner, 1949–55. *Recreations:* history, music. *Address:* Flat 5, Windsor Lodge, Third Avenue, Hove, East Sussex. *T:* Brighton (0273) 733194. *Clubs:* Athenæum; Hove.

PAIGE, Prof. Edward George Sydney, PhD; FRS 1983; Professor of Electrical Engineering, University of Oxford, since 1977; *b* 18 July 1930; *s* of Sydney and Maude Paige; *m* 1953, Helen Gill; two *s* two *d. Educ:* Reading University (BSc, PhD). FInstP; FIEE. Junior Research Fellow to DCSO, Royal Radar Establishment, Malvern, 1955–77. *Address:* Department of Engineering Science, University of Oxford, Parks Road, Oxford OX1 3PJ. *T:* Oxford (0865) 273113.

PAIGE, Rear-Adm. Richard Collings, CB 1967; *b* 4 October 1911; *s* of Herbert Collings Paige and Harriet Pering Paige; *m* 1937, Sheila Brambles Ward, *d* of late Dr Ernest Ward, Paignton; two *s. Educ:* Blundell's School, Tiverton; RNE College, Keyham. Joined Navy, 1929. Served in HMS Neptune, Curaçao, Maori, King George V, Superb, Eagle (despatches twice); Captain, 1957; Commanding Officer, RNE College, 1960–62; Commodore Supt, HM Naval Base, Singapore, 1963–65; Admiral Supt HM Dockyard, Portsmouth, 1966–68. Rear-Adm. 1965.

PAIGE, Victor Grellier, CBE 1978; Chairman, National Health Service Management Board, and Second Permanent Secretary, Department of Health and Social Security, 1985–86; *b* 5 June 1925; *s* of Victor Paige and Alice (*née* Grellier); *m* 1948, Kathleen Winifred, 3rd *d* of Arthur and Daisy Harris; one *s* one *d. Educ:* East Ham Grammar Sch.; Univ. of Nottingham. CIPM, FCIT, CBIM, FAIM. Roosevelt Mem. Schol. 1954. Dep. Personnel Manager, Boots Pure Drug Co. Ltd, 1957–67; Controller of Personnel Services, CWS Ltd, 1967–70; Dir of Manpower and Organisation, 1970–74, Exec. Vice-Chm. (Admin), 1974–77, Nat. Freight Corp.; Dep. Chm., Nat. Freight Corp., later Nat. Freight Co., 1977–82; Dir, 1977–88 (non.-exec., 1985–88), and Dep. Chm., 1982–85, Nat. Freight Consortium; Chm., Iveco (UK), 1984–85. Chm., PLA, 1980–85; Member: Manpower Services Commn, 1974–80; Thames Water Authy, 1983–85. Member: Notts Educn Cttee, 1957–63; Secondary Schs Examn Council, 1960–63; UK Adv. Council for Educn in Management, 1962–65; Careers Adv. Bd, Univ. of Nottingham, 1975–81; Chairman: Regional Adv. Council for Further Educn, E Mids, 1967; Exec. Council, British Assoc. for Commercial and Industrial Educn, 1974 (Vice-Pres. 1980) Pres., Inst. of Admin. Management, 1984–90; Vice-Pres., Chartered Inst. of Transport, 1984–85 (Mem. Council, 1976–79); Mem. Council, CBI, 1983–85 (Chm., Educn and Trng Cttee, 1983–85). Mem. Court, of Henley, The Management College, 1985–. Governor, British Liver Foundn, 1990–. Vice-Pres., London Fedn of Boys' Clubs. Freeman, Co. of Watermen and Lightermen of the River Thames; Freeman, City of London, 1981. Commander, Order of Orange Nassau, The Netherlands, 1982. *Publications:* contrib. techn. press on management. *Recreations:* reading, sport generally, athletics in particular (Pres. Notts Athletic Club, 1962–67). *Address:* Queen's Wood, Frithsden, Berkhamsted, Herts. *T:* Berkhamsted (0442) 865030. *Clubs:* Royal Automobile, MCC.

PAIN, Barry Newton, CBE 1979; QPM 1976; Commandant, Police Staff College, Bramshill, and HM Inspector of Constabulary, 1982–87, retired; *b* 25 Feb. 1931; *s* of Godfrey William Pain and Annie Newton; *m* 1952, Marguerite Agnes King; one *s* one *d. Educ:* Waverley Grammar Sch., Birmingham. Clerk to Prosecuting Solicitor, Birmingham, 1947–51; 2nd Lieut (Actg Captain) RASC, Kenya, 1949–51. Birmingham City Police, 1951–68; Staff Officer to HM Inspector of Constabulary, Birmingham, 1966–68; Asst Chief Constable, Staffordshire and Stoke-on-Trent Constabulary, 1968–74; Chief Constable of Kent, 1974–82; JSSC 1970. Adviser to Turkish Govt on Reorganization of Police, 1972. Pres., Assoc. of Chief Police Officers, 1981–82. *Recreations:* golf, shooting, boating.

PAIN, Lt-Gen. Sir (Horace) Rollo (Squarey), KCB 1975 (CB 1974); MC 1945; late 4th/7th Royal Dragoon Guards; Head of British Defence Staff, Washington, 1975–78, retired; *b* 11 May 1921; *s* of late Horace Davy Pain, Levenside, Haverthwaite, Ulverston, and late Audrey Pain (*née* Hampson); *m* 1950, Denys Sophia (*née* Chaine-Nickson); one *s* two *d.* Commissioned into Reconnaissance Corps during War of 1939–45: served NW Europe (MC). After War, served for two years in E Africa and Brit. Somaliland before joining 4th/7th Royal Dragoon Gds in Palestine, 1947; attended Staff Coll., Camberley, 1951; subseq. served in Mil. Ops Directorate, in War Office; served with his Regt in BAOR, 1955–56; Mem. Directing Staff, Staff Coll., Camberley, 1957; GSO1, Brit. Army Staff, Washington, DC, 1960; commanded his Regt in BAOR, 1962; commanded one of the three divs, Staff Coll., Camberley, 1964; commanded 5 Inf. Bde in Borneo, 1965; IDC, 1968; ADC to the Queen, 1969; BGS, HQ, BAOR, 1969–70; GOC 2nd Div., 1970–72; Dir of Army Training, MoD, 1972–75; Col Comdt, Mil. Provost Staff Corps, 1974–83; Col. 4th/7th Royal Dragoon Guards, 1979–83. *Address:* Eddlethorpe Hall, Malton, North Yorkshire YO17 9QS. *T:* Burythorpe (065385) 218. *Club:* Cavalry and Guards.

PAIN, Hon. Sir Peter (Richard), Kt 1975; a Judge of the High Court of Justice, Queen's Bench Division, 1975–88; *b* 6 Sept. 1913; *s* of Arthur Richard Pain and Elizabeth Irene Pain (*née* Benn); *m* 1941, Barbara Florence Maude Riggs; two *s. Educ:* Westminster; Christ Church, Oxford. Called to the Bar, Lincoln's Inn, 1936, Bencher 1972. QC 1965. Chairman: Race Relations Board Conciliation Cttee for Greater London, 1968–71; South Metropolitan Conciliation Cttee, 1971–73; Mem., Parole Bd, 1978–80. Pres., Holiday Fellowship, 1977–83. *Publications:* Manual of Fire Service Law, 1951; The Law Relating to the Motor Trade (with K. C. Johnson-Davies), 1955. *Recreations:* forestry, cricket,

mountain walking. *Address:* Loen, St Catherine's Road, Frimley, Surrey. *T:* Deepcut (0252) 835639.

PAIN, Sir Rollo; *see* Pain, Sir H. R. S.

PAINE, George, CB 1974; DFC 1944; *b* 14 Apr. 1918; 3rd *s* of late Jack Paine and Helen Margaret (*née* Hadow), East Sutton; *m* 1969, Hilary (*née* Garrod), widow of Dr A. C. Frazer. *Educ:* Bradfield Coll.; Peterhouse, Cambridge. External Ballistics Dept, Ordnance Bd, 1941; RAF, 1942–46; Min. of Agriculture, 1948; Inland Revenue, 1949; Central Statistical Office, 1954; Board of Trade, 1957; Dir of Statistics and Intelligence, Bd of Inland Revenue, 1957–72; Dir, OPCS and Registrar Gen. for Eng. and Wales, 1972–78. Hon. Treasurer, Royal Statistical Soc., 1974–78. *Recreations:* fruit growing, beekeeping. *Address:* Springfield House, Broad Town, near Swindon, Wilts SN4 7RU. *T:* Swindon (0793) 731377.

PAINE, Peter Stanley, CBE 1981; DFC 1944; Chairman, Oracle Teletext Ltd, since 1984; *b* 19 June 1921; *s* of Arthur Bertram Paine and Dorothy Helen Paine; *m* 1942, Sheila Mary, *d* of Frederick Wigglesworth, MA; two *s* two *d. Educ:* King's Sch., Canterbury. Served 1940–46, 2 Gp RAF (Flt-Lt). Worked in Punch Publishing Office, 1945–47; Sales Promotion Man., Newnes Pearson, 1948–52, Odhams Press, then Sales Dir and Dir of Tyne Tees Television, 1958–67; Sales Dir and Dir of Yorkshire Television, 1967–74; Managing Director: Tyne Tees Television, 1974–83; Tyne Tees Television Holdings, 1981–84. Director: Trident Television, 1970–81; Independent Television News Ltd, 1982–83; Independent Television Publications Ltd, 1977–83; Broadcasters Audience Res. Bd, 1980–86; Member: Council, Independent Television Companies Assoc., 1974–83 (4 yrs Chm. Marketing Cttee); Cable Authority, 1984–90. *Recreations:* golf, fishing, theatre, music, reading. *Address:* Briarfield, Ashwood Road, Woking, Surrey GU22 7JW. *T:* Woking (0483) 773183. *Club:* Worplesdon Golf.

PAINE, Roger Edward; Chief Executive, Cardiff City Council, since 1988; *b* 20 Oct. 1943; *s* of Ethel May Jones and Edward Paine. *Educ:* Stockport Sch.; Univ. of Wales (BA Hons); Univ. of Manchester (part time; Dip TP); Univ. of Birmingham (MSocSci). Town Planner: Lancs CC, 1964– 66; Stockport CB, 1966–68; Lancs CC, 1968–70; Salford City, 1970; Stockport Borough: Corporate Planner, 1971–73; Head of Corporate Planning, 1973–75; Co-ordinator of Central Units, 1975–77; Dep. Chief Exec., Camden, 1977–80; Chief Exec., Wrekin Council, 1980–88. Hon. Fellow, Inst. of Local Govt Studies, Birmingham. *Recreations:* music, travel, sport. *Address:* Cardiff City Council, City Hall, Cardiff CF1 3ND.

PAINE, Dr Thomas Otten; Chairman, Thomas Paine Associates, Los Angeles, since 1982; *b* 9 Nov. 1921; *s* of George Thomas Paine, Cdre, USN retd and Ada Louise Otten; *m* 1946, Barbara Helen Taunton Pearse; two *s* two *d. Educ:* Maury High, Norfolk, Va; Brown Univ.; Stanford Univ. Served War of 1939–45 (US Navy Commendation Ribbon 1944; Submarine Combat Award with two stars, 1943–45). Research Associate: Stanford Univ., 1947–49; General Electric Res. Lab., Schenectady, 1949–50; Manager, TEMPO, GE Center for Advanced Studies, Santa Barbara, 1963–67; Dep. Administrator, US Nat. Aeronautics and Space Admin., Washington, 1968, Administrator 1968–70; Group Executive, GE, Power Generation Group, 1970–73, Sen. Vice-Pres., GE, 1974–76; Pres. and Chief Operating Officer, Northrop Corp., 1976–82. Member, Board of Directors: Eastern Air Lines, 1981–86; Quotron Systems, Inc., 1982–; RCA, 1982–86; NBC, 1982–86; Director: Arthur D. Little Inc., 1982–85; NIKE Inc., 1982–; Orbital Sciences Corp., 1987–. Chairman: Pacific Forum, 1980–86; US National Commn on Space, 1985–86. MInstMet; Member: Newcomen Soc.; Nat. Acad. of Engineering; Acad. of Sciences, NY; Sigma Xi; Trustee: Occidental Coll.; Brown Univ.; Asian Inst. Tech. Hon. Dr of Science: Brown, 1969; Clarkson Coll. of Tech., 1969; Nebraska Wesleyan, 1970; New Brunswick, 1970; Oklahoma City, 1970; Hon. Dr Engrg: Worcester Polytechnic Inst., 1970; Cheng Kung Univ., 1978. Harvey Mudd Coll. Outstanding Contribution to Industrial Science Award, AAS, 1956; NASA DSM, 1970; Washington Award, Western Soc. of Engrs, 1972; John Fritz Medal, United Engrg Soc., 1976; Faraday Medal, IEE, 1976; NASA Distinguished Public Service Award, 1987; Konstantin Tsiolkovsky Award, USSR, 1987; John F. Kennedy Astronautics Award, Amer. Astronautical Soc., 1987; Assoc. of Space Explorers Award, 1988. Grand Ufficiale della Ordine Al Merito della Repubblica Italiana, 1972. *Publications:* various technical papers and patents. *Recreations:* sailing, beachcombing, skin diving, photography, book collecting, oil painting. *Address:* (office) Thomas Paine Associates, Suite 178, 2401 Colorado Avenue, Santa Monica, Calif 90404, USA; (home) 1275 Las Alturas, Santa Barbara, Calif 93103, USA. *Clubs:* Sky, Lotos, Explorers (New York); Army and Navy, Space, Cosmos (Washington); California, Regency (Los Angeles).

PAINTAL, Prof. Autar Singh, Padma Vibhushan 1986; MD, PhD, DSc; FRS 1981; FRSE; Director-General, Indian Council for Medical Research, New Delhi, since 1986; *b* 24 Sept. 1925; *s* of Dr Man Singh and Rajwans Kaur; *m* 1st; one *s* two *d*; 2nd, 1988, Ashima Anand. *Educ:* SSBS Khalsa High Sch., Lahore; Forman Christian Coll., Lahore; Lucknow Univ. (MB, BS, MD); Edinburgh Univ. (PhD, DSc). Lectr in Physiol., King George's Med. Coll., Lucknow Univ., 1949; Rockefeller Fellow, 1950; Lectr in Physiol., Edinburgh Univ., 1951; Control Officer, Technical Develt Estabt Labs, Min. of Defence, Kanpur, 1952–54; Prof. of Physiology, All-India Inst. of Med. Sciences, New Delhi, 1958–64; Prof. of Physiology and Dir, Vallabhbhai Patel Chest Inst., Delhi Univ., 1964–90 (Asst Dir, 1954–56); Dean, Faculty of Med. Sciences, Delhi Univ., 1966–77. Associate Prof., Albert Einstein Coll. of Medicine, New York, 1956; Vis. Associate Prof. of Physiol., Univ. of Utah, 1957; Commonwealth Vis. Prof., St Bartholomew's Hosp. Med. Sch., London, 1966. FRSE 1966; Fellow: Indian Acad. of Med. Sciences, 1966; Indian National Science Acad., 1971 (Vice Pres., 1981–83; Pres., 1987–88); President: Nat. Coll. of Chest Physicians, 1981–86; Indian Sci. Congress, 1984–85; Member: Physiol Soc., UK, 1953; Ergonomics Res. Soc., UK, 1954; Foreign Mem., USSR Acad. of Scis, 1988; Hon. Mem., Amer. Physiol. Soc., 1990. B. C. Roy Orator, New Delhi, 1973; Sharpey-Schafer Lectr, Univ. of Edin., 1981; Dr Zakir Husain Meml Lectr, Jawaharlal Nehru Univ., 1984. Hon. FRCP, 1987. Hon. DSc: Benares Hindu Univ., 1982; Delhi Univ., 1984; Aligarh Muslim Univ., 1986; N Bengal Univ., 1990. Basanti Devi Amir Chand Prize, 1967; Silver Jubilee Res. Award, 1978; Barclay Medal, Asiatic Soc., 1982; R. D. Birla Award, 1982; Nehru Sci. Award, 1983; Maharishi Dayanand Centenary Gold Medal, 1983; Acharya J. C. Bose Medal, 1985. *Publications:* (ed) Morphology and Mechanisms of Chemoreceptors, 1976; (ed) Respiratory Adaptations, Capillary Exchange and Reflex Mechanisms, 1977; papers in Jl of Physiol. and in other physiol jls. *Recreations:* swimming, rowing, bird watching. *Address:* DST Centre for Visceral Mechanisms, Vallabhbhai Patel Chest Institute, Delhi University, PO Box 2101, Delhi 110007, India. *T:* Delhi 2523856 and 231749. *Club:* Roshanara (Delhi).

PAINTER, George Duncan, OBE 1974; Biographer and Incunabulist; Assistant Keeper in charge of fifteenth-century printed books, British Museum, 1954–74; *b* Birmingham, 5 June 1914; *s* of George Charles Painter and Minnie Rosendale (*née* Taylor); *m* 1942, Isabel Joan, *d* of Samuel Morley Britton, Bristol; two *d. Educ:* King Edward's Sch., Birmingham; Trinity Coll., Cambridge (Schol.). Bell Exhibr; John Stewart of Rannoch

Schol.; Porson Schol.; Waddington Schol.; 1st cl. hons Class. Tripos pts I and II; Craven Student; 2nd Chancellor's Class. Medallist, 1936; MA Cantab 1945. Asst Lectr in Latin, Univ. of Liverpool, 1937; joined staff of Dept of Printed Books, BM, 1938. FRSL 1965. Hon. DLitt Edinburgh, 1979. *Publications:* André Gide, A Critical Biography, 1951, rev. edn 1968; The Road to Sinodun, Poems, 1951; André Gide, Marshlands and Prometheus Misbound (trans.), 1953; Marcel Proust, Letters to his Mother (trans.), 1956; Marcel Proust, A Biography, vol. 1, 1959, vol. 2, 1965 (Duff Cooper Memorial Prize), rev. and enl. edn in 1 vol., 1989; The Vinland Map and the Tartar Relation (with R. A. Skelton and T. E. Marston), 1965; André Maurois, The Chelsea Way (trans.), 1966; William Caxton, a Quincentenary Biography, 1976; Chateaubriand, A Biography, vol. 1, The Longed-for Tempests, 1977 (James Tait Black Meml Prize); Studies in Fifteenth-Century Printing, 1984; articles on fifteenth-century printing in The Library, Book Collector, Gutenberg-Jahrbuch. *Recreations:* family life, walking, gardening, music. *Address:* 10 Mansfield Road, Hove, East Sussex BN3 5NN. *T:* Brighton (0273) 416008.

PAINTER, Terence James, CB 1990; a Deputy Chairman and Director General, Board of Inland Revenue, since 1986; *b* 28 Nov. 1935; *s* of late Edward Lawrence Painter and Ethel Violet (*née* Butler); *m* 1959, Margaret Janet Blackburn; two *s* two *d*. *Educ:* City of Norwich Sch.; Downing Coll., Cambridge (BA (History)). Nat. Service Commn, Royal Norfolk Regt, 1958–59. Entered Inland Revenue as Asst Principal, 1959; Principal, 1962; seconded to Civil Service Selection Bd, 1967–68; Asst Sec., 1969; seconded to HM Treasury, 1973–75; Under-Sec., 1975–86. *Recreations:* music, books, walking.

PAISLEY, Bishop of (RC), since 1988; **Rt. Rev. John Aloysius Mone;** Auxiliary Bishop of Glasgow, 1984–88; *b* 22 June 1929; *s* of Arthur Mone and Elizabeth Mone (*née* Dunn). *Educ:* Holyrood Secondary School, Glasgow; Séminaire Saint Sulpice, Paris; Institut Catholique, Paris (Faculty of Social Studies). Ordained Priest, Glasgow, 1952. Scottish National Chaplain, Girl Guides, 1971–; Chm., Scottish Catholic Internat. Aid Fund, 1974–75, Pres./Treas., 1985–; Chm., Scottish Catholic Marriage Advisory Council, 1982–84; Pres., Scottish Justice and Peace Commn, 1987–. *Recreations:* watching soccer (attending if possible), playing golf (when time!), playing the piano. *Address:* Bishop's House, Porterfield Road, Kilmacolm, Renfrewshire PA13 4PD. *T:* Kilmacolm (050587) 2494.

PAISLEY, Rev. Ian Richard Kyle; MP (Democratic Unionist) North Antrim, since 1974 (ProtU 1970–74) (resigned seat Dec. 1985 in protest against Anglo-Irish Agreement; re-elected Jan. 1986); Member (DemU) Northern Ireland, European Parliament, since 1979; Minister, Martyrs Memorial Free Presbyterian Church, Belfast, since 1946; *b* 6 April 1926; 2nd *s* of late Rev. J. Kyle Paisley and Mrs Isabella Paisley; *m* 1956, Eileen Emily Cassells; two *s* three *d* (incl. twin *s*). *Educ:* Ballymena Model Sch.; Ballymena Techn. High Sch.; S Wales Bible Coll.; Reformed Presbyterian Theol. Coll., Belfast. Ordained, 1946. Moderator, Free Presbyterian Church of Ulster, 1951; Pres., Whitefield Coll. of the Bible, 1979–. Commenced publishing The Protestant Telegraph, 1966. Contested (Prot U) Bannside, NI Parlt, 1969; MP (Prot U), Bannside, Co. Antrim, NI Parlt, 1970–72; Leader of Opposition, 1972; Chm., Public Accounts Cttee, 1972. Co-Founder, Democratic Unionist Party, NI, 1972. Mem. (Democratic Unionist), N Antrim, NI Assembly, 1973–75; Mem. (UUUC), N Antrim, NI Constitutional Convention, 1975–76; Mem. (DemU) N Antrim, NI Assembly, 1982–86. Hon. DD Bob Jones Univ., SC. FRGS. Mem., Internat. Cultural Soc., Korea, 1977. *Publications:* History of the 1859 Revival, 1959; Christian Foundations, 1960; Ravenhill Pulpit, Vol. 1, 1966, Vol. 2, 1967; Exposition of the Epistle to the Romans, 1968; Billy Graham and the Church of Rome, 1970; The Massacre of St Bartholomew, 1972; America's Debt to Ulster, 1976; (jtly) Ulster—the facts, 1981; No Pope Here, 1982; Dr Kidd, 1982; Those Flaming Tennents, 1983; Mr Protestant, 1985; Be Sure, 1986; Paisley's Pocket Preacher, 1987, vol. II, 1988, vol. III, 1989; Jonathan Edwards: the theologian of revival, 1987; Union with Rome, 1989. *Address:* House of Commons, SW1; The Parsonage, 17 Cyprus Avenue, Belfast BT5 5NT.

PAISLEY, Robert, OBE 1977; Board Member, Liverpool Football Club, since 1983 (Manager, 1974–83, Team Consultant, 1985–87); *b* 23 Jan. 1919; *s* of Samuel and Emily Paisley; *m* 1946, Jessie Chandler; two *s* one *d*. *Educ:* Eppleton Sen. Mixed Sch., Tyne and Wear. Apprentice bricklayer, 1934; also Hetton Juniors Amateur FC, 1934–37; Bishop Auckland Amateur FC, 1937–39; signed as professional for Liverpool FC, 1939; Army Service, RA, 1939–46; Liverpool FC: 2nd Team Trainer, 1954–59; 1st Team Trainer, 1959–70; Asst Manager, 1970–74. Successes as manager: UEFA Cup, 1976; League Championship, 1976, 1977, 1979, 1980, 1982, 1983; European Cup, 1977, 1978, 1981; League Cup (later known as Milk Cup, then Littlewoods Cup), 1981, 1982, 1983. Manager of the Year Award, 1976, 1977, 1979, 1980, 1982, 1983; Special Merit Award, PFA Award, 1983. Hon. Fellow, Liverpool Polytechnic, 1988. Hon. MSc Liverpool, 1983. Freeman, City of Liverpool, 1983. *Publications:* Bob Paisley's Liverpool Scrap Book, 1979; Bob Paisley: an autobiography, 1983; Bob Paisley's Assessment of the 1986–1987 Liverpool Team, 1987; Fifty Golden Reds, 1990. *Recreations:* all types of sport.

PAKENHAM, family name of **Earl of Longford.**

PAKENHAM, Elizabeth; *see* Longford, Countess of.

PAKENHAM, Henry Desmond Verner, CBE 1964; HM Diplomatic Service, retired; *b* 5 Nov. 1911; *s* of Hamilton Richard Pakenham and Emilie Willis Stringer; *m* 1st, 1946, Crystal Elizabeth Brooksbank (marr. diss., 1960); one *s* one *d* (and one *s* decd); 2nd, 1963, Venetia Maude; one *s* one *d*. *Educ:* Monkton Combe; St John Baptist College, Oxford. Taught modern languages at Sevenoaks School, 1933–40. Served in HM Forces, 1940–45. Entered Foreign Service, 1946; served in Madrid, Djakarta, Havana, Singapore, Tel Aviv, Buenos Aires and Sydney; retired 1971. Chm., Suffolk Preservation Soc., 1979–82. Asst Editor, Satow's Guide to Diplomatic Practice, 5th edn, 1979. *Address:* Rose Farm, Brettenham, Suffolk.

PAKENHAM, Hon. Michael Aidan; HM Diplomatic Service; Ambassador to Luxembourg, since 1991; *b* 3 Nov. 1943; *s* of 7th Earl of Longford, *qv* and Countess of Longford, *qv*; *m* 1980, Meta (Mimi) Landreth Doak, *d* of William Conway Doak of Maryland, USA; two *d* two step *d*. *Educ:* Ampleforth College; Trinity College, Cambridge (MA Classics); Rice University, Texas. Washington Post, 1965; Foreign Office, 1965; Nairobi, 1966; Warsaw, 1967; FCO, 1970; Asst Private Sec., later Private Sec. to Chancellor of Duchy of Lancaster (European Community Affairs), on secondment to Cabinet Office, 1971–74; Geneva (CSCE), 1974; New Delhi, 1974; Washington, 1978; Head of Arms Control and Disarmament Dept, FCO, 1983–87; Counsellor (External Relations), UK Perm. Rep. to EC, Brussels, 1987–91. *Recreations:* tennis, golf, bridge, reading history, museums. *Address:* c/o Foreign and Commonwealth Office, SW1A 2AH. *Clubs:* MCC; Delhi Golf.

PAKENHAM, Thomas (Frank Dermot); writer; *b* 14 Aug. 1933; *e s* of 7th Earl of Longford, *qv* and of Countess of Longford, *qv*; (does not use courtesy title); *m* 1964, Valerie, *d* of Major R. G. McNair Scott; two *s* two *d*. *Educ:* Dragon School, Oxford; Belvedere Coll., Dublin; Ampleforth Coll., York; Magdalen Coll., Oxford (BA Greats 1955). Travelled, Near East and Ethiopia, 1955–56 (discovered unrecorded medieval Ethiopian church at Bethlehem, Begemdir, 1956). Free-lance writing, 1956–58. Editorial staff: Times Educational Supplement, 1958–60; Sunday Telegraph, 1961; The Observer, 1961–64. Founder Mem. 1958, and Member Cttee 1958–64, Victorian Soc.; Founder Mem., and Mem. Cttee 1968–72, Historic Irish Tourist Houses and Gardens Assoc. (HITHA); Treas., British-Irish Assoc., 1972–; Sec. (co-founder), Christopher Ewart-Biggs Memorial Trust, 1976–; Founder and Chm., Irish Tree Soc. Chm., Ladbroke Assoc., 1988–. Sen. Associate Mem., St Antony's Coll., Oxford, 1979–81. *Publications:* The Mountains of Rasselas: an Ethiopian adventure, 1959; The Year of Liberty: the story of the Great Irish Rebellion of 1798, 1969; The Boer War, 1979 (Cheltenham Prize, 1980); (selected and introd with Valerie Pakenham) Dublin: a travellers' companion, 1988; The Scramble for Africa, 1991. *Recreation:* water. *Address:* 111 Elgin Crescent, W11. *T:* 071–727 7624; Tullynally, Castlepollard, Westmeath, Ireland. *T:* Mullingar (044) 61159. *Clubs:* Beefsteak, Brooks's; Stephen's Green (Dublin).

PAKENHAM-WALSH, John, CB 1986; Standing Counsel to General Synod of the Church of England, since 1988; *b* 7 Aug. 1928; *s* of late Rev. W. P. Pakenham-Walsh, formerly ICS, and Guendolen (*née* Elliott); *m* 1951, Deryn, *er d* of late Group Captain R. E. G. Fulljames, MC, and Mrs Muriel Fulljames; one *s* four *d*. *Educ:* Bradfield Coll.; University Coll., Oxford (MA). Called to the Bar, Lincoln's Inn, 1951. Crown Counsel, Hong Kong, 1953–57; Parly Counsel, Fedn of Nigeria, 1958–61; joined Legal Adviser's Br., Home Office, 1961; Under Sec. (Legal), Home Office, 1980–87. *Address:* Crinken House, Pathfields Close, Haslemere, Surrey GU27 2BL. *T:* Haslemere (0428) 642033; Flat 06, Howard House, Dolphin Square, SW1V 3PE. *T:* 071–798 8702. *Clubs:* Athenæum; Liphook Golf (Hants).

PAKINGTON, family name of **Baron Hampton.**

PALADE, Prof. George Emil; scientist, USA; Professor, Division of Cellular and Molecular Medicine and Dean for Scientific Affairs, School of Medicine, University of California at San Diego, since 1990; *b* Iassy, Romania, 19 Nov. 1912; *s* of Emil Palade and Constanta Cantemir; *m* 1st, 1941, Irina Malaxa (decd); one *s* one *d*; 2nd, 1970, Dr Marilyn Farquhar. *Educ:* Liceul Al. Hasdeu, Buzau, Romania; Med. Sch., Univ. of Bucharest (MD). Arrived in US, 1946; naturalized US citizen, 1952. Instructor, Asst Prof., then Lectr in Anatomy, Sch. of Med., Univ. of Bucharest, 1940–45; Visiting Investigator, Rockefeller Inst. for Med. Research, 1946–48; continuing as an Assistant (later the Inst. became Rockefeller Univ., NYC); promoted to Associate, 1951, and Associate Mem., 1953; Prof. of Cell Biology, Rockefeller Univ. and full Member of Rockefeller Inst., 1956; Prof. of Cell Biology, Yale Univ. Med. Sch., 1973. Fellow, Amer. Acad. of Arts and Sciences; Member: Nat. Acad. of Sciences; Pontifical Acad. of Sciences; Leopoldina Acad.; Romanian Acad.; For. Mem., Royal Soc., 1984. Awards include: Albert Lasker Basic Research, 1966; Gairdner Award, 1967; Hurwitz Prize, 1970; Nobel Prize for Medicine, 1974; Nat. Medal of Science, USA, 1986. *Publications:* Editor: Annual Review of Cell Biology; Jl of Cell Biology (co-founder); Jl of Membrane Biology; numerous contribs med. and sci. jls. *Address:* School of Medicine, University of California, San Diego, La Jolla, Calif 92093–0602, USA. *T:* (619) 534 7708, *Fax:* (619) 534 6573.

PALETHORPE-TODD, Richard Andrew; *see* Todd, Richard.

PALETTE, John, OBE 1986; Director of Personnel, British Rail, 1982–86; *b* 19 May 1928; *s* of Arthur and Beatrice Palette; *m* 1950, Pamela Mabel Palmer; three *s*. *Educ:* Alexandra Sch., Hampstead. MCIT. Gen. Railway Admin, 1942–69; Divl Manager, Bristol, 1969–72; Asst Gen. Manager, Western Region, 1972–74; Divl Manager, Manchester, 1974–76; Gen. Manager, Scottish Region, 1976–77, Southern Region, 1977–82, British Railways. Chm., British Transport Ship Management (Scotland) Ltd, 1976. *Recreations:* walking, reading, gardening, watching sport. *Address:* 90 Wargrave Road, Twyford, Reading, Berks. *T:* Twyford (Berks) (0734) 340965.

PALIN, Michael Edward; writer and actor; *b* 5 May 1943; *s* of late Edward and Mary Palin; *m* 1966, Helen M. Gibbins; two *s* one *d*. *Educ:* Birkdale Sch., Sheffield; Shrewsbury; Brasenose Coll., Oxford (BA 2nd Cl. Hons Mod. Hist.). Pres., Transport 2000. Actor and writer: Monty Python's Flying Circus, BBC TV, 1969–74; Ripping Yarns, BBC TV, 1976–80; actor: Three Men in a Boat, BBC, 1975; GBH, Channel 4, 1991; writer: East of Ipswich, BBC TV, 1987; Number 27, BBC1, 1988. *Films:* actor and jt author: And Now for Something Completely different, 1970; Monty Python and the Holy Grail, 1974; Monty Python's Life of Brian, 1978; Time Bandits, 1980; Monty Python's "The Meaning of Life," 1982; American Friends, 1991; actor, writer and co-producer: The Missionary, 1982; actor: Jabberwocky, 1976; A Private Function, 1984; Brazil, 1985; A Fish Called Wanda, 1988 (Best Supporting Film Actor, BAFTA Award, 1988). Contributor, Great Railway Journeys of the World, BBC TV, 1980; retraced Phileas Fogg's journey for Around the World in Eighty Days, BBC TV, 1989. *Publications:* Monty Python's Big Red Book, 1970; Monty Python's Brand New Bok, 1973; Dr Fegg's Encyclopaedia of *All* World Knowledge, 1984; Limericks, 1985; Around the World in Eighty Days, 1989; *for children:* Small Harry and the Toothache Pills, 1981; The Mirrorstone, 1986; The Cyril Stories, 1986. *Recreations:* reading, running, railways—preferably all three in a foreign country. *Address:* 68A Delancey Street, NW1 7RY.

PALIN, Air Chief Marshal Sir Roger Hewlett, KCB 1989; OBE 1978; Air Member for Personnel, since 1991; Air Aide-de-Camp to the Queen, since 1991. *Educ:* Canford Sch.; St John's Coll., Cambridge (BA 1967; MA 1979); psc. Flight Lieut, 1964; Sqn Leader, 1970; Wing Comdr, 1975; Group Captain, 1980; ADC to the Queen, 1981–82; a Dir, Dept of ACDS (Progs), MoD, 1983–84; Air Cdre, 1984; Dir of Defence Progs, 1984–86; Air Vice-Marshal, 1986; ACDS (Progs), 1986–87; AOC No 11 Gp, 1987–89; Air Marshal, 1989; C-in-C, RAF Germany and Comdr Second Allied Tactical Air Force, 1989–91; Air Chief Marshal, 1991. *Recreations:* sport, travel.

PALING, Helen Elizabeth, (Mrs W. J. S. Kershaw); Her Honour Judge Paling; a Circuit Judge, since 1985; *b* 25 April 1933; *o d* of A. Dale Paling and Mabel Eleanor Thomas; *m* 1961, William John Stanley Kershaw, PhD; one *s* three *d*. *Educ:* Prince Henry's Grammar Sch., Otley; London Sch. of Economics. LLB London 1954. Called to Bar, Lincoln's Inn, 1955; a Recorder, 1972–85. *Address:* Quayside Law Courts, Newcastle upon Tyne. *T:* 091–201 2000.

PALING, William Thomas; *b* 28 Oct. 1892; *s* of George Thomas Paling, Sutton-in-Ashfield, Notts; *m* 1919, Gladys Nellie, MBE (decd), *d* of William Frith, James Street, Nuncar Gate, Nottinghamshire; one *s* one *d*. MP (Lab) Dewsbury, 1945–59, retired.

PALLEY, Dr Claire Dorothea Taylor; Principal of St Anne's College, Oxford, 1984–91; *b* 17 Feb. 1931; *d* of Arthur Aubrey Swait, Durban; *m* 1952, Ahrn Palley (marr. diss. 1985); five *s*. *Educ:* Durban Girls' Coll.; Univs of Cape Town and London. BA 1950, LLB 1952, Cape Town; PhD London 1965; MA Oxon 1984. Called to Bar, Middle Temple; Advocate, S Africa and Rhodesia. Lecturer: UC Rhodesia and Nyasaland, 1960–65; QUB, 1966–67; Reader, QUB, 1967–70, Prof. of Public Law, 1970–73, and Dean of Faculty of Law, 1971–73; Prof. of Law, 1973–84, and Master of Darwin Coll., 1974–82, Univ. of Kent. Hamlyn Lectr, Reading, 1990. Chm., SE Area Cttee, Nat. Assoc.

of Citizens' Advice Bureaux, 1974–79; Member: Council, Minority Rights Group, 1975–; UK Nat. Commn for UNESCO, 1984–86; UN Sub-Commn on Prevention of Discrimination and Protection of Minorities, 1988–; (Lay), Disciplinary Appeals Tribunal, Securities Assoc., 1988–; Lord Chancellor's Adv. Cttee on Legal Educn and Conduct, 1991–. Constitutional Adviser to: African Nat. Council at Const. Talks on Rhodesia, 1976; Govt of Republic of Cyprus, 1980–. Hon. LLD QUB, 1991. *Publications:* The Constitutional History and Law of Southern Rhodesia, 1966; The United Kingdom and Human Rights, 1991; contrib. learned jls. *Address:* 9/10 Regent Square, WC1.

PALLISER, Rt. Hon. Sir (Arthur) Michael, GCMG 1977 (KCMG 1973; CMG 1966); PC 1983; HM Diplomatic Service, retired; Chairman, Samuel Montagu & Co. Ltd, since 1986 (Director, since 1983; Vice Chairman, 1984; Chairman, 1984–85); Deputy Chairman, Midland Montagu (Holdings), since 1987; *b* 9 April 1922; *s* of late Admiral Sir Arthur Palliser, KCB, DSC, and of Lady Palliser (*née* Margaret Eva King-Salter); *m* 1948, Marie Marguerite, *d* of late Paul-Henri Spaak; three *s*. *Educ:* Wellington Coll.; Merton Coll., Oxford (Hon. Fellow 1987). Served with Coldstream Guards, 1942–47; Capt. 1944. Entered HM Diplomatic Service, 1947; SE Asia Dept, Foreign Office, 1947–49; Athens, 1949–51; Second Sec., 1950; Foreign Office: German Finance Dept, 1951–52; Central Dept, 1952–54; Private Sec. to Perm. Under-Sec., 1954–56; First Sec., 1955; Paris, 1956–60; Head of Chancery, Dakar, 1960–62 (Chargé d'Affaires in 1960, 1961 and 1962); Counsellor, and seconded to Imperial Defence College, 1963; Head of Planning Staff, Foreign Office, 1964; a Private Sec. to PM, 1966; Minister, Paris, 1969; Ambassador and Head of UK Deleg. to European Communities, Brussels, 1971; Ambassador and UK Permanent Representative to European Communities, 1973–75; Permanent Under-Sec. of State, FCO and Head of Diplomatic Service, 1975–82. Dep. Chm., Midland Bank, 1987–91. Director, since 1983: BAT Industries plc; Booker plc; Eagle Star Hldgs; Shell Transport & Trading Co. plc; Director: United Biscuits (Hldgs), 1983–89; Arbor Acres Farm Inc., 1985–91; UK–Japan 2000 Gp, 1987–. Dep. Chm., British Invisible Exports Council, 1987–. Member: Council, IISS, 1982–91 (Chm., 1983–90); Trilateral Commn, 1982–; Security Commn, 1983–; Council, British N American Cttee and Res. Assoc., 1987– (British Chm., 1990). Mem., Royal Nat. Theatre Bd, 1988–. Pres., Internat. Social Service of GB, 1982–; Chm., City and E London Confedn of Medicine and Dentistry, 1989–. Governor, Wellington Coll., 1982–. FRSA 1983. Fellow, QMW, 1990. Chevalier, Order of Orange Nassau, 1944; Chevalier, Légion d'Honneur, 1957. *Address:* Samuel Montagu & Co. Ltd, 10 Lower Thames Street, EC3R 6AC. *Club:* Buck's.

PALLOT, Arthur Keith, CB 1981; CMG 1966; Secretary and Director-General, Commonwealth War Graves Commission, 1975–82 (Director of Finance and Establishments, 1956–75); *b* 25 Sept. 1918; *s* of Harold Pallot, La Tourelle, Jersey; *m* 1945, Marjorie, *d* of J. T. Smith, Rugby; two *d*. *Educ:* Newton College. Royal Navy, 1936; retired as Lt-Comdr, 1947. Commonwealth War Graves Commission, 1947. Awarded the Queen's Commendation for brave conduct, 1958. *Recreations:* walking, squash, cricket, golf. *Address:* Northways, Stubbles Lane, Cookham Dean, Berks SL6 9PX. *T:* Marlow (0628) 486529.

PALMAR, Sir Derek (James), Kt 1986; FCA; President Bass PLC, 1987–89 (Chairman, 1976–87; Chairman and Chief Executive, 1976–84; Director, 1970–76); Chairman: Yorkshire Television, since 1981; Boythorpe, since 1986; Vice President, Brewers' Society, since 1982 (Chairman, 1980–82); *b* 25 July 1919; *o s* of late Lt-Col Frederick James Palmar and Hylda (*née* Smith); *m* 1946, Edith Brewster (*d* 1990); one *s* one *d*. *Educ:* Dover College. FCA 1957 (ACA 1947). Served RA and Staff, 1941–46; psc; Lt-Col 1945. Peat, Marwick, Mitchell & Co., 1937–57; Director: Hill Samuel Group, 1957–70; Grindlays Bank, 1970–85. Adviser, Dept of Economic Affairs, 1965–67; Mem., British Railways Bd, 1969–72; Chm., BR Southern Regional Adv. Bd, 1972–79. Director: Drayton Consolidated Trust, 1982–; Consolidated Venture Trust, 1984–; CM Group Holdings, 1985–; United Newspapers, 1986–. Dir, Centre for Policy Studies, 1983–88; Chm., NEDC for Food and Drink Packaging Equipment, 1986–87. Chairman: Zool Soc. of London Develt Trust, 1986–89; Leeds Univ. Foundn, 1986–89; Member: Accounting Standards Cttee, 1982–84; Alcohol Educn and Res. Council, 1982–87. Dir, Business in the Community, 1984–; Mem., Adv. Council, Prince's Youth Business Trust, 1984–. Mem., Ct, Brewers' Co., 1982–89. Trustee, Civic Trust, 1979–89. Freeman, City of London. *Recreations:* shooting, gardening. *Address:* Quarry House, Kirkbymoorside, N Yorks YO6 6JF. *Club:* Boodle's.

PALMER, family name of **Earl of Selborne, Baron Palmer** and **Baroness Lucas of Crudwell.**

PALMER, 4th Baron, *cr* 1933, of Reading; **Adrian Bailie Nottage Palmer;** *b* 8 Oct. 1951; *s* of Col the Hon. Sir Gordon Palmer, KCVO, OBE, TD, MA, FRCM and of the Hon. Lady Palmer, DL; *S* uncle, 1990; *m* 1977, Cornelia Dorothy Katherine, *d* of R. N. Wadham, DFC, Exning, Newmarket; two *s* one *d*. *Educ:* Eton; Edinburgh Univ. Member: Exec. Council, HHA for Scotland, 1980–; Exec. Council, HHA, 1981–. Scottish Rep. to European Landowning Orgn, 1986–. Sec., The Royal Caledonian Hunt, 1989–. *Recreations:* gardening, shooting, hunting. *Heir:* *s* Hon. Hugo Bailie Rohan Palmer, *b* 5 Dec. 1980. *Address:* Manderston, Duns, Berwickshire TD11 3PP. *T:* Duns (0361) 83450. *Clubs:* MCC; New (Edinburgh).

PALMER, Andrew Eustace, CMG 1987; CVO 1981; HM Diplomatic Service; Ambassador to the Holy See, since 1991; *b* 30 Sept. 1937; *s* of late Lt-Col Rodney Howell Palmer, MC, and of Mrs Frances Pauline Ainsworth (*née* Gordon-Duff); *m* 1962, Davina, *d* of Sir Roderick Barclay, *qv*; two *s* one *d*. *Educ:* Winchester Coll.; Pembroke Coll., Cambridge (MA). Second Lieut. Rifle Bde, 1956–58. Joined HM Foreign (later Diplomatic) Service, 1961; American Dept, FO, 1962–63; Third, later Second, Secretary (Commercial), La Paz, 1963–65; Second Sec., Ottawa, 1965–67; Treasury Centre for Administrative Studies, 1967–68; Central Dept, FO, later Southern European Dept, FCO, 1968–72; First Sec. (Information), Paris, 1972–76; Asst Head of Defence Dept, FCO, 1976–77; RCDS 1978; Counsellor, Head of Chancery and Consul-Gen., Oslo, 1979–82; Hd, Falkland Is Dept, FCO, 1982–85; Fellow, Harvard Center for Internat. Affairs, 1985–86; Ambassador to Cuba, 1986–88; seconded as Pvte Sec. to the Duke and Duchess of Kent, 1988–90. *Recreations:* fishing, tennis, following most other sports, photography. *Address:* c/o Foreign and Commonwealth Office, SW1A 2AH. *Clubs:* Brooks's, MCC.

PALMER, Anthony Thomas Richard, (Tony); film and television director; author; *b* 29 Aug. 1941; brought up by godparents, late Bert Spencer (railway engineer) and Elsie Spencer. *Educ:* Lowestoft Grammar Sch. *Films include:* All My Loving, 1968; Farewell Cream, 1968; A Time There Was, 1979 (Italia Prize); At the Haunted End of the Day, 1980 (Italia Prize); Once at a Border, 1981 (Special Jury Prize, San Francisco); Wagner, 1982 (Best Drama, NY Film and TV Fest.); God Rot Tunbridge Wells, 1985 (Best Drama, NY); Maria, 1986 (Gold Medal, NY); Testimony, 1987 (Fellini Prize); The Children, 1989 (Best Director, NY); Menuhin, 1990 (Grand Award, NY); dir operas, Berlin, Karlsruhe, Munich, Hamburg, Zürich. *Publications:* Born Under a Bad Sign, 1970; Trials of Oz, 1971; Electric Revolution, 1972; Biography of Liberace, 1976; All You Need is Love, 1976; Charles II, 1979; A Life on the Road (biog. of Julian Bream), 1982; Menuhin: a family portrait, 1991. *Recreation:* walking. *Address:* Nanjizal, St Levan, Cornwall. *T:* c/o 071–727 3541. *Club:* Garrick.

PALMER, Anthony Wheeler, QC 1979; a Recorder of the Crown Court, since 1980; *b* 30 Dec. 1936; *s* of late Philip Palmer and of Doris Palmer; *m* Jacqueline, *d* of Reginald Fortnum, Taunton; one *s* two *d*. *Educ:* Wrekin Coll., Salop. Called to the Bar, Gray's Inn, 1962. *Address:* 17 Warwick Avenue, Coventry CV5 6DJ. *T:* Coventry (0203) 75340.

PALMER, Arnold Daniel; professional golfer since 1954; golf course designer; *b* 10 Sept. 1929; *s* of Milfred J. and Doris Palmer; *m* 1954, Winifred Walzer; two *d*. *Educ:* Wake Forest Univ. Winner of numerous tournament titles, including: British Open Championship, 1961, 1962; US Open Championship, 1960; Masters Championship, 1958, 1960, 1962, 1964; Spanish Open Championship, 1975; Professional Golfers' Assoc. Championship, 1975; Canadian PGA, 1980; USA Seniors' Championship, 1981. Hon. Dr of Laws: Wake Forest; Nat. Coll. of Educn; Hon. Dr Hum: Thiel Coll.; Florida Southern College. Hon. Member: Royal and Ancient Golf Club, 1979; Troon Golf Club, 1982; Royal Birkdale Golf Club, 1983. *Publications:* (all jointly) Arnold Palmer Golf Book, 1961; Portrait of a Professional Golfer, 1964; My Game and Yours, 1965; Situation Golf, 1970; Go for Broke, 1973; Arnold Palmer's Best 54 Golf Holes, 1977; Arnold Palmer's Complete Book of Putting, 1986; Play Great Golf, 1987. *Recreations:* aviation (speed record for flying round world in twin-engine jet, 1976), bridge, hunting, fishing. *Address:* PO Box 52, Youngstown, Pa 15696, USA. *T:* (412) 537–7751. *Clubs:* (Owner and Pres.) Latrobe Country; (Pres. and Part-Owner) Bay Hill and Isleworth (Orlando, Fla); (Tournament Professional) Laurel Valley Golf; numerous other country, city, golf.

PALMER, Arthur Montague Frank, CEng, FIEE, FInstE; *b* 4 Aug. 1912; *s* of late Frank Palmer, Northam, Devon; *m* 1939, Dr Marion Ethel Frances Woollaston, medical consultant; two *d*. *Educ:* Ashford Gram. Sch.; Brunel Technical College (now Brunel Univ.). Is a Chartered Engineer and a Chartered Fuel Technologist. Studied electrical supply engineering, 1932–35, in London; Member technical staff of London Power Co., 1936–45; former Staff Mem., Electrical Power Engineers Assoc. Member Brentford and Chiswick Town Council, 1937–45. MP (Lab) for Wimbledon, 1945–50; MP (Lab and Co-op): Cleveland Div. of Yorks, Oct. 1952–Sept. 1959; Bristol Central, 1964–74; Bristol NE, 1974–83; Frontbench Opposition Spokesman on fuel and power, 1957–59; Chairman: Parly and Scientific Cttee, 1965–68; House of Commons Select Cttee on Science and Technology, 1966–70, 1974–79; Co-operative party Parly Gp, 1970–73; Vice-Chm., Select Cttee on Energy, 1979–83. Defence Medal, 1946; Coronation Medal, 1953. *Publications:* The Future of Electricity Supply, 1943; Modern Norway, 1950; Law and the Power Engineer, 1959; Nuclear Power: the reason why, 1984; Energy Policy in the Community, 1985; articles on political, industrial, and economic subjects. *Recreations:* walking, motoring, gardening, reading novels, history and politics. *Address:* Manton Thatch, Manton, Marlborough, Wilts SN8 4HR. *T:* Marlborough (0672) 513313. *Club:* Athenæum.

PALMER, Bernard Harold Michael, OBE 1989; MA; Editor of the Church Times, 1968–89; *b* 8 Sept. 1929; *e s* of late Christopher Harold Palmer; *m* 1954, Jane Margaret, *d* of late E. L. Skinner; one *s* one *d*. *Educ:* St Edmund's School, Hindhead; Eton (King's Scholar); King's College, Cambridge. BA 1952; MA 1956. Member of editorial staff, Church Times, 1952–89; Managing Director, 1957–89; Editor-in-Chief, 1960–68; Chm., 1962–89. DLitt Lambeth, 1988. *Publication:* Gadfly for God: a History of the Church Times, 1991. *Recreations:* cycling, penmanship. *Address:* Three Corners, 15 East Hill, Charminster, Dorchester, Dorset DT2 9QL. *T:* Dorchester (0305) 260948. *Club:* Commonwealth Trust.

PALMER, Brian Desmond; formerly Under Secretary, Northern Ireland Office; *b* 1 May 1939; *m* 1964, Hilary Eileen Latimer; one *s* one *d*. *Educ:* Royal Belfast Academical Instn; Queen's Univ. of Belfast (LLB 1962). Joined Northern Ireland Civil Service, 1957: Estate Duty Office, 1957–62; Min. of Home Affairs, 1962–65; Dept of the Environment, 1965–77; Head of Central Secretariat, 1977–81. *Recreation:* golf.

PALMER, Sir (Charles) Mark, 5th Bt, *cr* 1886; *b* 21 Nov. 1941; *s* of Sir Anthony Frederick Mark Palmer, 4th Bt, and of Henriette (*see* Lady Abel Smith); *S* father 1941; *m* 1976, Hon. Catherine Elizabeth Tennant, *y d* of 2nd Baron Glenconner; one *s* one *d*. *Heir:* *s* Arthur Morris Palmer, *b* 9 March 1981. *Address:* Mill Hill Farm, Sherborne, Northleach, Glos. *T:* Windrush (04514) 395.

PALMER, Gen. Sir (Charles) Patrick (Ralph), KBE 1987 (CBE 1982; OBE 1974); CBIM; Commander-in-Chief, Allied Forces Northern Europe, since 1989; *b* 29 April 1933; *s* of late Charles Dudley Palmer and Catherine Anne (*née* Hughes-Buller); *m* 1st, 1960, Sonia Hardy Wigglesworth (*d* 1965); one *s*; 2nd, 1966, Joanna Grace Baines; two *d*. *Educ:* Marlborough Coll.; RMA, Sandhurst. psc 1963. Commnd Argyll and Sutherland Highlanders, 1953; served British Guiana, Berlin, Suez Operation and Cyprus; Instructor, RMA Sandhurst, 1961–62; BM 153(H) Inf. Bde, 1964–65; 1 Argyll and Sutherland Highlanders, Borneo, Singapore and Aden, 1965–68; MA to Dep. CDS (Intell.), MoD, 1968–70; Instructor, Staff Coll., 1970–72; reformed and commanded 1st Bn Argyll and Sutherland Highlanders, 1972–74; Chief of Staff to Comd British Forces Hong Kong, 1974–76; RCDS, 1977; Comd 7th Armoured Bde, 1977–78; Dep. Comd 1 Armoured Div., 1978–80; Comd British Mil. Adv. and Training Team, Zimbabwe, 1980–82; GOC NE Dist, 1982 and Comd 2nd Inf. Div., 1983; Comdt, Staff Coll., Camberley, 1984–86; Military Sec., 1986–89. Col of the Argyll and Sutherland Highlanders, 1982–; Captain of Tarbert Castle, 1982–. *Recreations:* travel, outdoor interests. *Address:* c/o Royal Bank of Scotland, Comrie, Perthshire PH6 2DW. *Club:* Army and Navy.

PALMER, Charles Stuart William, OBE 1973; Vice-President, British Olympic Association, since 1988 (Vice-Chairman, 1977–83; Chairman, 1983–88); President, British Judo Association, since 1977 (Chairman, 1962–85); *b* London, 15 April 1930; *s* of Charles Edward Palmer and Emma Byrne. *Educ:* Drayton Manor County Sch. Represented GB in internat. judo comps, 1949–59; studied judo in Japan, 1951–55; obtained 1st Dan 1948, 4th Dan 1955, 8th Dan 1980; Mem. 1957, Capt. 1958, 1959, European Judo Champs winning team. Pres., Internat. Judo Fedn, 1965–79 (Hon. Life Pres., 1979–); Vice-Pres., British Schs Judo Assoc., 1967–; Chm., British Univs Judo Assoc., 1968–75. Sec.-Gen., Gen. Assoc of Internat. Sports Fedns, 1975–84; Member: IOC Tripartite Commn, 1974–81; Sports Council, 1983–; Exec. Council, Assoc. of European Nat. Olympic Cttees, 1985–89 (Pres., Scientific and Medical Commn, 1988–89); Exec. Cttee, CCPR, 1975– (Chm., Games and Sports Div., 1980–; Chm., cttee studying amateurism and eligibility in sport (Palmer Report published, 1988)); Programme Commn, IOC, 1989–. Governor, Sports Aid Foundn, 1979–. Mem., Lloyd's, 1988–. Mem. Council, Royal Albert Hall, 1987–. Manning Award, Sports Writers' Assoc., 1976. Olympic Order (silver), 1980; Gold Medal, European Judo Union, 1982. Key of City of Taipei, 1974, Key of City of Seoul, 1981; Diploma and Bronze Medal, City of Bordeaux, 1970; Distinguished Service Gold Medal (China), 1974; Merito Deportivo Gold Medal (Spain), 1976. *Publications:* technical papers and articles on judo and sports politics. *Recreations:* judo, ski-ing, sport generally, flying light aircraft, orchestral music, opera, languages.

Address: 4 Hollywood Road, SW10 9HY. *T:* 071–352 6238. *Clubs:* Budokwai, Kandahar, Ski of Great Britain.

PALMER, Charles William; Sheriff of North Strathclyde at Dunoon and Dumbarton, since 1986; *b* 17 Dec. 1945; *s* of Charles J. S. Palmer and Patricia Palmer; *m* 1969, Rosemary Ann Holt; one *s* two *d. Educ:* Inverness Royal Academy; Edinburgh University (LLB 1971). Prior to University, short stints in banking and Police Force; Partner, Allan McDougall & Co., SSC, 1975; temporary Sheriff, 1984. *Recreations:* hill walking, ski-ing, amateur opera, choral singing, photography. *Address:* 6 Great Stuart Street, Edinburgh EH3 6AW. *T:* 031–225 4962.

PALMER, David Erroll Prior; Chief Executive, The Financial Times, since 1990; *b* 20 Feb. 1941; *s* of Sir Otho Prior-Palmer, DSO, and Sheila Peers (*née* Weller-Poley), OBE; *m* 1974, Elizabeth Helen Young; two *s* one *d. Educ:* Eton; Christ Church, Oxford (MA PPE). Joined Financial Times, 1964: New York Correspondent, 1967; Management Editor, 1970; News Editor, 1972; Foreign Editor, 1979; Dep. Editor, 1981; Gen. Manager and Dir, 1983; Dep. Chief Exec., 1989. First British finisher, seventh over-all, Observer Singlehanded Transatlantic Race, 1976. *Publication:* The Atlantic Challenge, 1977. *Recreations:* sailing, travelling. *Address:* c/o Financial Times, No 1 Southwark Bridge, SE1 9HL. *Clubs:* Itchenor Sailing (near Chichester); Slocum Society.

PALMER, David Vereker; Chairman, 1982–88, and Chief Executive, 1978–88, Willis Faber plc; *b* 9 Dec. 1926; *s* of late Brig. Julian W. Palmer and Lena Elizabeth (*née* Vereker); *m* 1950, Mildred Elaine O'Neal; three *d. Educ:* Stowe. ACII 1950. Commnd The Life Guards, 1944; served as regular officer in Europe and ME, 1944–49; joined Edward Lumley & Sons, 1949; Manager, New York office, 1953–59; joined Willis, Faber & Dumas Ltd, 1959; Dir, 1961; Partner, 1965; Dep. Chm., 1972. Mem. Lloyd's, 1953. Chm., British Insurance & Investment Brokers Assoc., 1987–90 (Dep. Chm., 1984–87); Pres., Insurance Inst. of London, 1985–86. Commissioner, Royal Hosp. Chelsea, 1982–88. Master, Worshipful Co. of Insurers, 1982. *Recreations:* farming, shooting. *Address:* Burrow Farm, Hambleden, near Henley-on-Thames, Oxon RG9 6LT. *T:* Henley (0491) 571256. *Clubs:* City of London, Cavalry and Guards.

PALMER, Rev. Derek George; Chaplain to the Queen, since 1990; Team Rector of Dronfield with Holmesfield, since 1987; *b* 24 Jan. 1928; *s* of late George Palmer, MBE and Edna Palmer; *m* 1952, June Cecilie Goddard; two *s* two *d. Educ:* Clifton Coll.; Selwyn Coll., Cambridge (MA); Wells Theological Coll. Deacon 1952, priest 1953; Priest in Charge, Good Shepherd, Bristol, 1954–58; first Vicar of Hartcliffe, 1958–68; Vicar of Christ Church, Swindon, 1968–77; Archdeacon of Rochester and Canon Residentiary of Rochester Cathedral, 1977–83; Home Secretary, Bd for Mission and Unity, 1983–87. Mem., General Synod, 1971–81. Hon. Canon of Rochester Cathedral, 1983–87. Chm., Christian Enquiry Agency, 1988–. *Publications:* All Things New, 1963; Quest, 1971; Strangers No Longer, 1990. *Recreation:* canals. *Address:* The Rectory, Church Street, Dronfield, Sheffield S18 6QB.

PALMER, Edward Hurry, CB 1972; retired Civil Servant; *b* 23 Sept. 1912; *s* of late Harold G. Palmer and late Ada S. Palmer; *m* 1940, Phyllis Eagle; no *c. Educ:* Haileybury. Dep. Chief Surveyor of Lands, Admty, 1942; Chief Surveyor of Lands, Admty, 1950; Chief Surveyor of Defence Lands, MoD, 1964; Comptroller of Defence Lands and Claims, MoD, 1968–72; Property Services Agency, DoE: Dir, Defence Lands Services, 1972–73; Dir, Estate Surveying Services, 1973–74. *Recreations:* gardening, walking. *Address:* 4 Barrowdene Close, Pinner, Middlesex HA5 3DD. *T:* 081–866 5961.

PALMER, Felicity Joan; mezzo-soprano; *b* 6 April 1944. *Educ:* Erith Grammar Sch.; Guildhall Sch. of Music and Drama. AGSM (Teacher/Performer), FGSM. Kathleen Ferrier Meml Prize, 1970; major appearances at concerts in Britain, America, Belgium, France, Germany, Italy, Russia and Spain, firstly as soprano and then as mezzo-soprano; début as soprano, Dido in Dido and Aeneas, Kent Opera, 1972; début in USA, Marriage of Figaro, Houston, 1973; soprano roles included: Pamina in The Magic Flute, ENO, 1975; Cleopatra in Julius Caesar, Herrenhausen Hanover, and Frankfurt Opera, 1978; title role, Alcina, Bern Opera, 1978; Elektra in Idomeneo, Zurich Opera, 1980; the Countess in The Marriage of Figaro, ENO; Elvira in Don Giovanni, Scottish Opera and ENO; Marguerite in Damnation of Faust, ENO; mezzo-soprano roles include: ENO: Tristan und Isolde, 1981; Rienzi, 1983; Mazeppa, 1984; Herodias in Salome, and The Witch in Hansel and Gretel, 1987; Orfeo, Opera North, 1984; King Priam, Royal Opera, 1985; Albert Herring, Glyndebourne, 1985; Tamburlaine, Opera North, 1985; Katya Kabanova, Chicago Lyric Opera, 1986; début at La Scala, Milan, as Marguerita in world première of Riccardo III by Flavio Testi, 1987; Last Night of the Proms, 1987; début, Netherlands Opera, as Kabanicha in Katya Kabanova, 1988, same role, Glyndebourne, 1988; Mistress Quickly in Falstaff, 1988 and 1990; Marcellina in The Marriage of Figaro, 1989, Glyndebourne; world première of Tippett's New Year, Houston, USA, 1989; The Marriage of Figaro and The Gambler (Prokofiev), Chicago, 1991; recitals in Amsterdam, Paris, Vienna, 1976–77, Tokyo, 1991; concert tours with BBC SO, Europe, 1973, 1977 and 1984, Australasia, Far East and Eastern Europe, 1977–; ABC tour of Australia, 1978. Recordings include: Poèmes pour Mi, with Pierre Boulez; Holst Choral Symphony, with Sir Adrian Boult; title role in Gluck's Armide; Elektra in Idomeneo, with Nikolaus Harnoncourt; The Music Makers; Sea Pictures; Britten's Phaedra; recitals, with John Constable, of songs by Poulenc, Ravel and Fauré, and of Victorian ballads. *Address:* 27 Fielding Road, W4 1HP.

PALMER, Rev. Preb. Francis Harvey; Prebendary of Sawley in Lichfield Cathedral, 1986–89; Prebendary Emeritus since 1989; *b* 13 Jan. 1930; *s* of Harry Hereward North Palmer and Ada Wilhelmina Annie Utting; *m* 1955, Mary Susan Lockhart; three *d. Educ:* Nottingham High Sch.; Jesus Coll., Cambridge (Exhibr); Wycliffe Hall, Oxford. MA. Deacon, 1955; Priest, 1956. Asst Curate: Knotty Ash, Liverpool, 1955–57; St Mary, Southgate, Crawley, 1958–60; Chaplain, Fitzwilliam House, Cambridge, 1960–64; Vicar of Holy Trinity, Cambridge and Chaplain to Cambridge Pastorate, 1964–71; Principal, Ridley Hall, Cambridge, 1971–72; Rector of Worplesdon, Surrey, 1972–80; Diocesan Ecumenical Officer, Guildford, 1974–80; Diocesan Missioner, Lichfield, 1980–89. *Publication:* (contrib.) New Bible Dictionary, 1959. *Recreation:* stamp collecting. *Address:* The Old Vicarage, Claverley, Wolverhampton WV5 7DT.

PALMER, Prof. Frank Robert, FBA 1975; Professor and Head of Department of Linguistic Science, University of Reading, 1965–87; *b* 9 April 1922; *s* of George Samuel Palmer and Gertrude Lilian (*née* Newman); *m* 1948, Jean Elisabeth Moore; three *s* two *d. Educ:* Bristol Grammar Sch.; New Coll., Oxford (Ella Stephens Schol., State Schol.) 1942–43 and 1945–48; Merton Coll., Oxford (Harmsworth Sen. Schol.) 1948–49. MA Oxon 1948; Craven Fellow, 1948. Served war, E Africa, 1943–45. Lectr in Linguistics, Sch. of Oriental and African Studies, Univ. of London, 1950–60 (study leave in Ethiopia, 1952–53); Prof. of Linguistics, University Coll. of N Wales, Bangor, 1960–65; Dean of Faculty of Letters and Social Sciences, Univ. of Reading, 1969–72. Linguistic Soc. of America Prof., Buffalo, 1971; Distinguished Visiting Professor: Foreign Languages Inst., Beijung, 1981; Univ. of Delaware, 1983. Professional visits to Canada, USA, Mexico, Venezuela, Peru, Chile, Argentine, Uruguay, Brazil, India, Japan, China, Indonesia, Morocco, Tunisia, Uganda, Kuwait and most countries of Europe. *Publications:* The Morphology of the Tigre Noun, 1962; A Linguistic Study of the English Verb, 1965; (ed) Selected Papers of J. R. Firth, 1968; (ed) Prosodic Analysis, 1970; Grammar, 1971, 2nd edn 1984; The English Verb, 1974, 2nd edn 1987; Semantics, 1976, 2nd edn 1981; Modality and the English Modals, 1979, 2nd edn 1990; Mood and Modality, 1986; articles and reviews on Ethiopian langs, English and linguistic theory, in learned jls. *Recreations:* gardening, crosswords. *Address:* Whitethorns, Roundabout Lane, Winnersh, Wokingham, Berks RG11 5AD. *T:* Wokingham (0734) 786214.

PALMER, Sir Geoffrey (Christopher John), 12th Bt, *cr* 1660; *b* 30 June 1936; *er s* of Lieutenant-Colonel Sir Geoffrey Frederick Neill Palmer, 11th Bt, and Cicely Katherine (who *m* 1952, Robert W. B. Newton; she *d* 1989), *o d* of late Arthur Radmall, Clifton, nr Watford; *S* father 1951; *m* 1957, Clarissa Mary, *er d* of Stephen Villiers-Smith, Knockholt, Kent; four *d. Educ:* Eton. *Recreations:* squash, racquets, cricket, shooting. *Heir: b* Jeremy Charles Palmer [*b* 16 May 1939; *m* 1968, Antonia, *d* of late Ashley Dutton; two *s*]. *Address:* Carlton Curlieu Hall, Leicestershire. *T:* Great Glen (053759) 2656. *Clubs:* Boodle's; MCC, I Zingari, Free Foresters, Eton Ramblers, Butterflies, Gentlemen of Leicestershire, Lincolnshire Gentlemen's Cricket, Derbyshire Friars, Oakham Cricket, XL, Frogs, Pedagogues, Market Harborough CC, Stoneygate, Old Etonian Golfing Society, Old Etonian Racquets and Tennis, Langtons CC, Northants Amateurs' CC, Knockturnes CC.

PALMER, Rt. Hon. Sir Geoffrey (Winston Russell), AC 1991; KCMG 1991; PC 1985; Professor of Law: University of Iowa, USA, 1969–73, and since 1991; Victoria University of Wellington, New Zealand, 1974–79, and since 1991; PC 1985; *b* 21 April 1942; *s* of Leonard Russell and Jessie Patricia Palmer; *m* 1963, Margaret Eleanor Hinchcliff; one *s* one *d. Educ:* Nelson Coll.; Victoria Univ. of Wellington (BA; LLB); Univ. of Chicago (JD). Barrister and Solicitor, High Court of New Zealand. Vis. Professor of Law, Univ. of Virginia, 1972–73. MP (Lab) Christchurch Central, NZ, 1979–90; Dep. Prime Minister, 1984–89; Attorney-Gen., 1984–89; Minister of Justice, 1984–89; Minister for the Environment, 1987–90; Prime Minister, 1989–90. *Publications:* Unbridled Power?—an interpretation of New Zealand's constitution and government, 1979, 2nd edn 1987; Compensation for Incapacity—a study of law and social change in Australia and New Zealand, 1979; Environmental Politics—a greenprint for New Zealand, 1990. *Recreations:* cricket, golf, playing the trumpet. *Address:* 72 Elizabeth Street, Wellington, New Zealand. *T:* 8015185.

PALMER, Horace Anthony; Chief Executive, Taylor Woodrow Group, since 1990; *b* 20 Feb. 1937; *s* of Horace Charles and Violet Victoria Palmer; *m* 1961, Beryl Eileen; two *d. Educ:* Pinner County Grammar School; Hammersmith Sch. of Building. FRICS; FCIOB. Trainee Quantity Surveyor, 1954; Taylor Woodrow: Contracts Manager, 1970; Subsidiary Dir, 1974; Subsidiary Man. Dir, 1987; Man. Dir, 1989. *Recreations:* sports, reading biography, carpentry. *Address:* San Julia, Stratton Road, Beaconsfield, Bucks. *T:* Beaconsfield (0494) 678202.

PALMER, John, CB 1986; Managing Director, Channel Tunnel, British Rail, since 1990; *b* 13 Nov. 1928; 2nd *s* of late William Nathaniel Palmer and Grace Dorothy May Palmer (*née* Procter); *m* 1958, Lyliane Marthe Jeanjean, *o d* of René Jeanjean and Jeanne Jeanjean (*née* Larrouy); two *d. Educ:* Heath Grammar Sch., Halifax; The Queen's Coll., Oxford (Lit. Hum.) (MA). Entered Min. of Housing and Local Govt, 1952; Cabinet Office, 1963–65; Asst Sec., 1965; Under Secretary: DoE, 1971; Dept of Transport, 1976–82; Dep. Sec., Dept of Transport, 1982–89. Liveryman, Carmens' Co., 1987–. *Club:* United Oxford & Cambridge University.

PALMER, Sir John (Chance), Kt 1979; solicitor; Consultant, Bevan Ashford, Tiverton, Exeter, Taunton, Bristol, Swindon and London; Vice Lord-Lieutenant of Devon, since 1991; *b* 21 March 1920; *s* of Ernest Clephan Palmer and Claudine Pattie Sapey; *m* 1945, Mary Winifred Ellyatt; four *s. Educ:* St Paul's Sch.; St Edmund Hall, Oxford (MA). Served War, RNVR, Atlantic and Mediterranean, 1939–46. Admitted a Solicitor, 1948; Elected Council of Law Society, 1963, President, 1978–79; Member: Criminal Injuries Compensation Board, 1981–; SW Region Mental Health Tribunal, 1983–. Governor, Coll. of Law, 1965–83; Pres., Devon and Exeter Law Society, 1972; Pres., S Western Law Societies, 1973; Chm., Governors of Blundells Sch., 1980–91; Chairman, Trustees: London Sailing Project, 1982–; Internat. Technol Univ., 1988–; Mem. Council, Exeter Univ., 1983–. Hon. Member: Amer. Bar Assoc., 1978; Canadian Bar Assoc., 1979; Florida Defence Lawyers Assoc., 1981. Hon. Sec., Soc. for Protection of Animals in N Africa, 1989–. Hon. Citizen, Texas, 1980. FRGS 1989. DL Devon, 1984. Hon. LLD Exeter, 1980. *Recreations:* gardening, sailing. *Address:* Hensleigh, Tiverton, Devon EX16 5NJ. *T:* Tiverton (0884) 252959. *Clubs:* Athenæum, Royal Over-Seas League, Naval; Western (Glasgow); Royal Yacht Squadron.

PALMER, Sir John (Edward Somerset), 8th Bt, *cr* 1791; retired; Director, Atkins Land and Water Management, 1979–88; *b* 27 Oct. 1926; *e s* of Sir John A. Palmer, 7th Bt; *S* father, 1963; *m* 1956, Dione Catherine Skinner; one *s* one *d. Educ:* Canford School; Cambridge Univ. (MA); Durham Univ. (MSc). Colonial Service, Northern Nigeria, 1952–61. R. A. Lister & Co. Ltd, Dursley, Glos, 1962–63; Min. Overseas Develt, 1964–68. *Recreations:* fishing, sailing. *Heir: s* Robert John Hudson Palmer, *b* 20 Dec. 1960. *Address:* Gayton House, Gayton, Northampton NN7 3EZ. *T:* Northampton (0604) 858336.

PALMER, Maj.-Gen. Sir (Joseph) Michael, KCVO 1985; Chairman: Copley Marshall & Co. Ltd, since 1980; The Chadwick Group, since 1991; *b* 17 Oct. 1928; *s* of late Lt-Col William Robert Palmer, DSO, and late Joan Audrey Palmer (*née* Smith); *m* 1953, Jillean Monica Sherston; two *s* one *d. Educ:* Wellington College. Commissioned 14th/20th King's Hussars, 1948; Adjutant 14th/20th King's Hussars, 1953–55; Adjutant Duke of Lancaster's Own Yeomanry, 1956–59; psc 1960; jssc 1965; CO 14th/20th King's Hussars, 1969–72; Comdr RAC 1st (BR) Corps, 1974–76; Asst Chief of Staff, Allied Forces Central Europe, 1976–78; Director, Royal Armoured Corps, 1978–81; Defence Services Sec., 1982–85. Col, 14th/20th King's Hussars, 1981–; Hon. Col, Duke of Lancaster's Own Yeomanry, 1988–. Director: Alexanders, Laing & Cruickshank Service Co., 1986–89; Credit Lyonnais Construction Co., 1988–90. Chm. of Governors, Sandroyd Sch., 1984–. Liveryman, Salters' Co., 1965 (Master, 1989–90). FBIM. *Recreations:* riding, shooting, music, reading. *Club:* Cavalry and Guards.

PALMER, Leslie Robert, CBE 1964; Director-General, Defence Accounts, Ministry of Defence, 1969–72; *b* 21 Aug. 1910; *s* of Robert Palmer; *m* 1937, Mary Crick; two *s* one *d. Educ:* Battersea Grammar School; London University. Entered Admiralty Service, 1929; Assistant Dir of Victualling, 1941; Dep. Dir of Victualling, 1954; Dir of Victualling, Admiralty, 1959–61; Principal Dir of Accounts, Admiralty, 1961–64; Principal Dir of Accounts (Navy) MoD, 1964–68. Hon. Treasurer and Chm., Finance and Admin Dept, United Reformed Church, 1973–79; Hon. Treasurer, BCC, 1980–82. *Recreation:* music. *Address:* 3 Trossachs Drive, Bath BA2 6RP. *T:* Bath (0225) 461981.

PALMER, Sir Mark; *see* Palmer, Sir C. M.

PALMER, Maj.-Gen. Sir Michael; *see* Palmer, Maj.-Gen. Sir J. M.

PALMER, Michael Julian Barham, CMG 1990; writer, lecturer and art consultant; *b* 2 Feb. 1933; *s* of Cecil Barham Palmer and Phyllis Palmer; *m* 1983, Dr Karin Reichel. *Educ:* Corpus Christi College, Oxford (MA). Research Officer, Political and Economic Planning, 1957–61; Sec., Political Cttee, Council of Europe, 1961–66; Councillor for Defence and Armaments, WEU, 1966–68; Dir of Cttees, N Atlantic Assembly, 1968–72; Dir-Gen. of Research European Parlt, 1972–90. Jean Monnet Prof., European Univ. Inst., Florence, 1989. Austrian Order of Merit, 1990; Order of Oak Leaf Crown (Luxembourg), 1990. *Publications:* European Organisations, 1959; European Unity, 1968; Prospects for a European Security Conference, 1971; The European Parliament, 1981; articles in The World Today, Foreign Policy, The Times, Christie's International. *Recreations:* music, art, cooking, climbing. *Address:* 8 rue des Franciscaines, L-1539 Luxembourg Grand Duchy; Glebe House, Easton-on-the-Hill, Stamford, Lincs.

PALMER, Monroe Edward, OBE 1982; FCA; Partner, Wilson Green Gibbs (formerly Palmer Marshall), Chartered Accountants, London; *b* 30 Nov. 1938; *s* of William and Sybil Polikoff; *m* 1962, Susette Sandra (*née* Cardash); two *s* one *d. Educ:* Orange Hill Grammar Sch. FCA 1963. Chm., Hendon CAB, 1981–83; Vice-Chm., Barnet CAB, 1986–88; Treasurer: Disablement Assoc., London Borough of Barnet, 1971–88; Liberal Parly Party, 1977–83; Jt Treasurer, Liberal Party, 1977–83; Chm., Lib Dem Friends of Israel, 1987–. Councillor (L, then Lib Dem) London Borough of Barnet, 1986–. Contested (L) Hendon South, 1979, 1983, 1987. Prospective Parly Cand. (Lib Dem) Hastings and Rye, 1991–. *Recreations:* politics, fishing. *Address:* 31 The Vale, NW11 8SE. *T:* 081–455 5140. *Club:* National Liberal.

PALMER, Most Rev. Norman Kitchener, CMG 1981; MBE 1975; *b* 2 Oct 1928; *s* of Philip Sydney and Annie Palmer; *m* 1960, Elizabeth Lucy Gorringe; three *s* one *d. Educ:* Kokeqolo, Pawa, Solomon Is; Te Aute, NZ; Ardmore, NZ (Teachers' Cert,); St John's Theological Coll., NZ (LTh; ordained deacon, 1964). Appts in Solomon Islands: Deacon/Teacher, Pawa Secondary (Anglican), 1966; priest, Pawa, 1966; Priest/Headmaster: Alanguala Primary, 1967–69; St Nicholas Primary, 1970–72; Dean, St Barnabas Cathedral, 1973–75; Bishop of Central Melanesia, 1975–87; Archbishop of Melanesia, 1975–87. Member, Public Service Advisory Bd, 1971–75. *Address:* Varei Village, Bauro District, General Post Office, Kira Kira, Makira Province, Solomon Islands.

PALMER, Lt.-Gen. Sir Patrick; *see* Palmer, Lt.-Gen. Sir C. P. R.

PALMER, Maj.-Gen. (Retd) Philip Francis, CB 1957; OBE 1945; Major-General late Royal Army Medical Corps; *b* 8 Aug. 1903. MB, BCh, BAO, Dublin, 1926; DPH 1936. Served North West Frontier of India, 1930–31 (medal and clasp). Adjutant Territorial Army, 1932–36. War of 1939–45 (OBE). Director of Medical Services, Middle East Land Forces, Dec. 1955; QHS, 1956–60, retired. Col Comdt, RAMC, 1963–67. *Address:* c/o Royal Bank of Scotland, Whitehall, SW1.

PALMER, Robert Henry Stephen; His Honour Judge Palmer; a Circuit Judge, since 1978; *b* 13 Nov. 1927; *s* of Henry Alleyn Palmer and Maud (*née* Obbard); *m* 1955, Geraldine Elizabeth Anne Evens; one *s* two *d. Educ:* Charterhouse; University Coll., Oxford. Called to the Bar, 1950. Dep. Chm., Berks QS, 1970. A Recorder of the Crown Court, 1972–78. Resident Judge, Harrow Crown Court; Pres., Mental Health Rev. Tribunal, 1983–. *Publications:* Harris's Criminal Law, 1960; Guide to Divorce, 1965. *Recreation:* self-sufficiency.

PALMER, Sidney John, CB 1972; OBE 1953; Deputy Director General, Ships, and Head of Royal Corps of Naval Constructors, 1968–73; *b* 28 Nov. 1913; *m* 1941, Mavis Beatrice Blennerhassett Hallett; four *s. Educ:* RNC Greenwich. WhSch 1937. Admty Experiment Works, Haslar, 1938; Portsmouth Dockyard, 1942; Chief Constructor, Sydney, 1945; Constructor Comdr, Hong Kong, 1946; Chief Constructor Aircraft Carriers, 1948; Prof. of Naval Architecture, RNC Greenwich, 1952; Asst Dir Dreadnought Project, 1959; Dep. Dir Polaris Programme, 1963; Dir Naval Ship Production, 1966; Dep. Dir General Ships, 1968. Mem. Council, RINA, 1960; Liveryman, Shipwrights' Co., 1968; Hon. Research Fellow, UCL, 1968. Mem., Cttee of Management, RNLI, 1974–78. *Address:* 89 Bloomfield Avenue, Bath, Avon BA2 3AE. *T:* Bath (0225) 312592.

PALMER, Thomas Joseph, (Joe), CBE 1990; Director, National Power plc, since 1991; *b* 11 Sept. 1931; *m* 1955, Hilary Westrup; two *s* two *d. Educ:* King's School, Bruton; Trinity College, Cambridge. MA. Asst Gen. Man. (Planning), Legal and General Assurance Soc., 1969–72, Dir and Gen. Man. (Admin.), 1972–78; Dir and Gen. Man. (Internat.), Legal & General Group plc, 1978–83, Dir and Group Chief Exec., 1984–91. Dir, SIB, 1991–. Chairman: London Business Sch. Assoc., 1974–78; Assoc. of British Insurers, 1989–91; Pres., Insurance Inst. of London, 1982–83. Gov., King's Sch., Bruton, 1989–. Hon. Fellow, London Business Sch., 1990. *Recreations:* tennis, gardening, long-distance walking, cross country ski-ing. *Address:* 5 High Pewley, Guildford GU1 3SH. *T:* Guildford (0483) 504448.

PALMER, Maj.-Gen. Tony Brian, CB 1984; CEng, FIMechE; consultant; conducted a study on maintenance philosophy and organisation in the Army, 1986; retired 1986; *b* 5 Nov. 1930; *s* of Sidney Bernard Palmer and Ann (*née* Watkins); *m* 1953, Hazel Doris Robinson; two *s. Educ:* Wolverton Technical College; Luton College of Technology; General Motors Inst. of Technology, USA. General Motors UK, 1948–51 and 1953–54; commissioned REME 1954; RMCS, 1960–62; Tank Gunnery Trials, Infantry Workshop, staff duties MoD, JSSC, Ops and Plans MoD, 1962–70; Head, DG FVE Secretariat, 1970–72; Comdr REME, 3 Div., 1972–74; Head, Tech. Intell. (Army), 1974–76; Dir, Elect. and Mech. Engineering (Organisation and Training), 1977–79; Comdt, REME Training Centre, 1979–83; Dir-Gen. of Elect. and Mech. Engrg, MoD (Army), 1983–85. Col Comdt, REME, 1986–91. Vice-Pres., S Region, British Sports Assoc. for Disabled, 1980–; Chm., Dorset Cttee for Employment of Disabled People, 1989–. MBIM. *Recreations:* history, gardening, bird watching. *Address:* c/o Barclays Bank, PO Box 756, Hamilton Road, Slough, Bucks. *Club:* Army and Navy.

PALMER, William John, CBE 1973; Judge of Her Majesty's Chief Court for the Persian Gulf, 1967–72; Member, Court of Appeal for Anguilla, 1973–81; *b* 25 April 1909; *o s* of late William Palmer and late Mary Louisa Palmer (*née* Dibb), Suffolk House, Cheltenham; *m* 1st, 1935, Zenaida Nicolaevna (*d* 1944), *d* of late Nicolai Maropoulo, Yalta, Russia; 2nd, 1949, Vanda Ianthe Millicent, *d* of late William Matthew Cowton, Kelvin Grove, Queensland; one *s* two *d. Educ:* Pate's Grammar School, Cheltenham; Christ's College, Cambridge (Lady Margaret Scholar). Barrister, Gray's Inn. Joined Indian Civil Service, 1932; Deputy Commissioner, Jalpaiguri, 1943, Chief Presidency Magistrate, Calcutta, 1945; retired from ICS, 1949. Joined Colonial Legal Service as Magistrate, Nigeria, 1950; Chief Registrar, High Court, Eastern Region, 1956; Judge, 1958; Acting Chief Justice of Eastern Nigeria, Oct.-Dec. 1963 and Aug.-Nov. 1965. Judge of HM's Court for Bahrain and Assistant Judge of the Chief Court for the Persian Gulf, 1965–67. A part-time Chm. of Industrial Tribunals, 1975–78. *Recreations:* travel, history. *Address:* Guys Farm, Icomb, Glos GL54 1JD. *T:* Cotswold (0451) 30219. *Clubs:* East India, Commonwealth Trust.

PALMES, Peter Manfred Jerome; Principal Assistant Director, Public Prosecutions Department, 1979–81; *b* 28 Feb. 1920; *s* of late Manfred Palmes and Gwendoline Robb; *m* 1st, 1945, Sylvia Theodor (decd); 2nd, 1969, Brenda Laban; one step *d. Educ:* Charterhouse; Worcester Coll., Oxford. Served War of 1939–45: Oxford and Bucks LI and 1/8th Gurkha Rifles, 1940–45. Called to Bar, Inner Temple, 1948. Public Prosecutions Dept: Legal Assistant, 1948; Sen. Legal Asst, 1958; Asst Solicitor, 1969; Asst Director, 1977. Jubilee Medal, 1977. *Address:* Chapel Lodge, Cross Colwood Lane, Bolney, West Sussex RH17 5RY.

PALUMBO, family name of **Baron Palumbo.**

PALUMBO, Baron *cr* 1991 (Life Peer), of Walbrook in the City of London; **Peter Garth Palumbo,** MA; Chairman, Arts Council of Great Britain, since 1989; *b* 20 July 1935; *s* of late Rudolph and of Elsie Palumbo; *m* 1st, 1959, Denia (*d* 1986), *d* of late Major Lionel Wigram; one *s* two *d*; 2nd, 1986, Hayat, *er d* of late Kamel Morowa; two *d. Educ:* Eton College; Worcester College, Oxford. MA Hons Law. Governor, London School of Economics and Political Science, 1976–; Chairman: Tate Gallery Foundn, 1986–87; Painshill Park Trust Appeal, 1986–; Trustee: Mies van der Rohe Archive, 1977–; Tate Gallery, 1978–85; Whitechapel Art Gallery Foundation, 1981–87; Trustee and Hon. Treas., Writers and Scholars Educnl Trust, 1984–. Hon. FRIBA. *Recreations:* music, travel, gardening, reading. *Address:* Bagnor Manor, Bagnor, Newbury, Berks RG16 8AG. *T:* Newbury (0635) 40930. *Clubs:* White's, Turf, City Livery.

PANAYIDES, Tasos Christou, Hon. GCVO 1990; Permanent Secretary of the Ministry of Foreign Affairs of Cyprus, since 1990; Ambassador to Iceland, since 1979; High Comr in UK and Ambassador to Sweden, Norway and Denmark, 1979–90; *b* 9 April 1934; *s* of Christos Panayides and Efrosini Panayides; *m* 1969, Pandora Constantinides; two *s* one *d. Educ:* Paphos Gymnasium; Teachers' Training Coll.; Univ. of London (Diploma in Education); Univ. of Indiana, USA (MA Political Science, Diploma in Public Administration). Teacher, 1954–59; First sec. to Pres., 1960–68; Director President's Office, 1969; Ambassador of Cyprus to Federal Republic of Germany, Switzerland, Austria, and Atomic Energy organisation, Vienna, 1969–78. Doyen of the Diplomatic Corps in London and Sen. High Comr, 1988–90. Chairman: Commonwealth Foundn Grants Cttee, 1985–88; Commonwealth Fund Tech. Co-operation Bd of Reps, 1986–89. Hon. Fellow, Ealing Coll. of Higher Educn, 1983. Freeman, City of London, 1984. 1st Cl., Grand Order and Grand Cross with Star and Sash, Federal Republic of Germany, 1978; Grand Cross in Gold with Star and Sash, Austria, 1979; Golden Cross of the Archdiocese of Thyateira and Great Britain, 1981; Grand Cross in Gold of Patriarchate of Antioch, 1984. *Publications:* articles in newspapers and magazines. *Recreations:* swimming, reading books. *Address:* Ministry of Foreign Affairs of the Republic of Cyprus, Nicosia, Cyprus.

PANDEY, Ishwari Raj, Hon. GCVO 1986; Prasiddha Prabala Gorakha-Dakshina Bahu, 1982; Vikhyata Trishakti-Patta, 1974; Additional Foreign Secretary to HM's Government, Kingdom of Nepal, since 1988; *b* 15 Aug. 1934; *s* of Rajguru Sri Hem Raj Panditgue and Nayab Bada Guruma Khaga Kumari Pandit; *m* 1953, Gita Rajya Laxmi Devi Rana; three *s* two *d. Educ:* Bombay Univ. (MA); Univ. of Pittsburgh (MPIA). Planning Officer, Min. of Planning and Develt, 1959; Under Sec., Min. of Finance (Foreign Aid Co-ordination), 1961; Dir, Dept of Industries, 1964; Head of Section for Econ. Relations, Min. of Foreign Affairs, 1966; First Secretary: Royal Nepalese Embassy, London, 1968; Perm. Mission of Kingdom of Nepal to UN, New York, 1972; Head of Section for Neighbouring Countries, Min. of For. Affairs, 1974; Chargé d'Affaires (Counsellor), Royal Nepalese Embassy, Tehran, 1975; Jt Sec., Div for Europe and the Americas, Min. of For. Affairs, 1979; Minister, Royal Nepalese Embassy, New Delhi, 1980; Ambassador to the UK, 1983–88 (concurrently Ambassador to Denmark, Finland, Norway, Iceland and Sweden). Coronation Medal, Bhutan, 1975. *Publications:* The Economic Impact of the Tourist Industry (with special reference to Puerto Rico and Nepal), 1961 (Univ. of Pittsburgh); contrib. to many jls. *Recreations:* reading, travelling. *Address:* Bharatee Bhawan, Dhokatole, Kathmandu, Nepal. *T:* 211297. *Club:* Hurlingham.

PANDOLFI, Filippo Maria; a Vice-President of the Commission of the European Communities, since 1989; *b* 1 Nov. 1927; *m* 1963, Carola Marziani; three *s* one *d. Educ:* Catholic Univ. of Milan (BA in philosophy). Member, Italian Parliament (Christian Democrats), 1968–88; Under Secretary of State, Min. of Finance, 1974–76; Minister of Finance, 1976–78; Minister of the Treasury, 1978–80; Chm. of Interim Cttee of IMF, 1979–80; Minister of Industry, 1980–82; Minister of Agriculture, 1983–88. *Recreations:* music, classical Greek, rock climbing. *Address:* EEC, 200 rue de la Loi, 1049 Brussels, Belgium. *T:* Brussels 235.24.65.

PANK, Maj.-Gen. (John) David (Graham), CB 1989; Chief Executive, Newbury Racecourse plc, since 1990; *b* 2 May 1935; *s* of late Edward Graham Pank and Margaret Sheelah Osborne Pank; *m* 1963, Julia Letitia Matheson; two *s* one *d. Educ:* Uppingham Sch. Commnd KSLI, 1958; served in Germany, Borneo, Singapore and Malaya; commanded: 3rd Bn The Light Infantry, 1974–76; 33rd Armoured Bde, 1979–81; Dir Gen. of Personal Services, Army, 1985–88; Dir of Infantry, 1988–90. Col, The LI, 1987–90. President: Army Cricket Assoc., 1987–89; Combined Services Cricket Assoc., 1988. *Recreations:* racing, fishing, cricket. *Address:* c/o Royal Bank of Scotland, Holt's Branch, Whitehall, SW1A 2EB. *Clubs:* Army and Navy, Victory Services; Mounted Infantry; Free Foresters, I Zingari, Mount Cricket.

PANKHURST, Air Vice-Marshal (Retd) Leonard Thomas, CB 1955; CBE 1944; *b* 26 August 1902; *s* of late Thomas William Pankhurst, Teddington, Middlesex; *m* 1939, Ruth, *d* of late Alexander Phillips, Cromer, Norfolk; one *s* two *d. Educ:* Hampton Grammar School. Joined Royal Air Force, 1925; Group Captain, 1942; Air Commodore, 1947; Actg Air Vice-Marshal, 1954. Served War of 1939–45 (despatches, CBE); Directorate of War Organisation, Air Ministry, 1938–41; Coastal Command, 1941–42; Mediterranean Air Forces, 1942–45. Air Officer Commanding 44 Group Transport Command, 1945–46; Asst Comdt RAF Staff Coll., 1946; idc, 1947; Dir Staff Trg, Air Ministry, 1948–50; Air Officer Commanding RAF E Africa, 1950–52; Dir of Postings, Air Ministry, 1953–54; Director-General of Personnel (I), Air Ministry, 1954–57. *Address:* Earl's Eye House, 8 Sandy Lane, Chester CH3 5UL. *T:* Chester (0244) 320993.

PANNETT, Juliet Kathleen, FRSA; painter; *b* Hove; 2nd *d* of Charles Somers and May (*née* Brice); *m* 1938, Major M. R. D. Pannett (*d* 1980), late the Devonshire Regt; one *s* one *d. Educ:* Harvington Sch., Ealing; Wistons Sch., Brighton; Brighton College of Art. Special Artist to Illustrated London News, 1957–64. *Exhibitions:* Royal Festival Hall, 1957, 1958; Qantas Gallery, 1959; New York, 1960; Cleveland, Ohio, 1960; Cooling Gallery, London, 1961; Coventry Cathedral Festival, 1962; Gloucester Three Choirs Festival, 1962; Brighton Corporation Gallery, Rottingdean, 1967; Arun Art Centre, 1967, 1969, 1972; Fine Art Gall., London, 1969; Mignon Gall., Bath, 1970; Brotherton Gall., London, 1980; Pacific and Fringe Clubs, Hong Kong, 1986; Wigmore Hall, 1989, 1991; RNCM, 1989. Exhibitor: Royal Academy; Royal Society of Portrait Painters; Royal Inst. of Painters in Watercolours, etc. Official Artist on Qantas Inaugural Jet Flight, London to Sydney, 1959, London to Hong Kong, 1964; Air Canada Inaugural Flight, London to Vancouver, 1968. Freeman: City of London, 1960; Painter Stainers' Company, 1960. *Work in Permanent Collections:* 22 portraits in National Portrait Gall.; Bodleian

Library; Maudsley Hospital; Army Phys. Training Sch., Aldershot; Gurkha Mus., Aldershot; Painter Stainers' Hall, London; Edinburgh Univ.; D Day painting for Devon and Dorset Regt, 1963; Commemorative Stained Glass Window (St Alban), Garrison Church, Munster, 1967; painting of Duke of Kent presenting new colours to Devon and Dorset Regt, 1982; Portraits, many for official bodies, include: HM The Queen, 1989; HRH Princess Alexandra, 1984; HRH Prince Andrew, HRH Prince Edward, for HM The Queen, 1974; HRH Princess Marina, Duchess of Kent, 1968; Lord Alport; Lord Annan; Lord Baden-Powell; Lady Baden-Powell; Group Captain Sir Douglas Bader; Maj.-Gen. T. A. Boam; Sir Denys Buckley; Lord Butler; Lord Caldecote; Lord David Cecil; Group Captain Leonard Cheshire; Lord Dacre; Lord Delfont; Lord Denning; Gen. Sir Martin Farndale; Lord Goodman; Lord Hailsham; Lady Heseltine; Ivon Hitchens; Bishop Huddleston; Sir John Kendrew; C. S. Lewis; Dr Quett Masire, President of Botswana; Lord Montagu; Lady Montagu; Patrick Moore; Sir Nevill Mott; Lord Mountbatten of Burma; Sir David Napley; Dr David Newsome; Lavinia Duchess of Norfolk; Lord Sackville; Lord Salmon; Lord Shawcross; Gilbert Spencer; Lord Spencer; Rt Hon. Margaret Thatcher; Col Digby Thompson; Lord Tonypandy; Sir Barnes Wallis. Has broadcast on art subjects on TV in UK and USA. *Publications*: cover portraits for books by Sir Thomas Beecham, Charles Causley, Henry Cecil, Canon Collins, Mary Drewery, Louis Golding, Gerald Pawle and Cyril Scott; drawings reproduced in The Times, Daily Telegraph, Birmingham Mail, Radio Times, The Lancet, Leisure Painter, The Artist, Law Guardian, Guardian Gazette, etc. *Recreation*: painting surgical operations, musicians and old barns. *Address*: Pound House, Angmering Village, Sussex BN16 4AL. *T*: Rustington (0903) 784446.

PANT, Apasaheb Balasaheb; Padma Shri 1954; retired 1975; *b* 11 Sept. 1912; *s* of Pratinidhis of Aundh; *m* 1942, Nalini Pant, MB, BS, FRCS; one *s* two *d*. *Educ*: Univ. of Bombay (BA); Univ. of Oxford (MA). Barrister-at-Law, Lincoln's Inn. Educn Minister, Aundh State; Prime Minister, 1944–48 (when State was merged into Bombay State). Member, AICC, 1948; an alternate Deleg., of India, at UN, 1951 and 1952; Comr for Govt of India in Brit. E Africa, 1948–54; apptd Consul-Gen. for Belgian Congo and Ruanda-Urundi, Nov. 1950, and Comr for Central Africa and Nyasaland, Dec. 1950; Officer on Special Duty, Min. of Ext. Affairs, 1954–55; Polit. Officer in Sikkim and Bhutan with control over Indian Missions in Tibet, 1955–61; Ambassador of India: to Indonesia, Oct. 1961–June 1964; to Norway, 1964–66; to UAR, 1966–69; High Comr in London, 1969–72; Ambassador to Italy, 1972–75. Dr of Laws *hc* Univ. of Syracuse, NY, 1988. *Publications*: Tensions and Tolerance, 1965; Aggression and Violence: Gandhian experiments to fight them, 1968; Yoga, 1968 (Arabic, Italian, German, Danish, Norwegian and Marathi edns); Surya Namaskar, 1969, 2nd edn 1987 (Marathi, Italian, German, Danish, Norwegian, Swahili edns, 3rd edn, as A Yogic Exercise, 1988); Mahatma Gandhi; A Moment in Time, 1973; Mandala, An Awakening, 1976; Progress, Power, Peace and India, 1978; Survival of the Individual, 1981; Un-Diplomatic Incidents, 1985; Story of the Pants: an extended family and fellow pilgrims, 1985; Energy: Intelligence: Love, 1986; An Unusual Raja and the Mahatma, 1987; A Tale of Two Houses, 1990. *Recreations*: photography, yoga, tennis, ski-ing, gliding. *Address*: Natesh, 211 Road No 2, Sindh Society, Aundh, Poona 411 007, India. *T*: 345115.

PANTER-DOWNES, Mollie Patricia, (Mrs Clare Robinson); London Correspondent, The New Yorker, 1939–87; *b* 25 Aug. 1906; *o c* of late Major Edward Panter-Downes, Royal Irish Regt and Kathleen Cowley; *m* 1927, Clare, 3rd *s* of late Aubrey Robinson; two *d*. *Educ*: mostly private. Wrote novel, The Shoreless Sea, at age of 16 (published John Murray, 1924); wrote in various English and American publications. *Publications*: Letter from England, 1940; Watling Green (children's book), 1943; One Fine Day, 1947; Ooty Preserved, 1967; At the Pines, 1971; London War Notes, 1972; contributed to The New Yorker Book of War Pieces, 1947. *Address*: Roppelegh's, near Haslemere, Surrey.

See also J. M. F. Baer.

PANTIN, Most Rev. Anthony; *see* Port of Spain, Archbishop of.

PANTON, Air Cdre Alastair Dyson, CB 1969; OBE 1950; DFC 1939; Provost Marshal and Director of RAF Security, 1968–71; retired; *Educ*: Bedford School; RAF Coll., Cranwell. Pilot Officer, No 53 Sqdn RAF, 1937; POW 1940–45; OC, Nos 58 and 540 Sqdns, 1946–47; Air Staff, Hong Kong, 1948–50; Wing Comdr Flying, RAF Coningsby, 1951–53; Staff Coll., 1953–54; Air Ministry, 1954–57; Station Comdr, RAF Cranwell, 1957–60, RAF Bircham Newton, 1961–62, RAF Tern Hill, 1963–64; HQ Far East Air Force, 1965–67. *Recreations*: gardening, poetry, carpentry. *Address*: Old Post Horns, Belle Hill, Giggleswick, Settle, N Yorks BD24 0BA.

PANTON, Dr Francis Harry, MBE 1948; Consultant, Cabinet Office, since 1985; Director, Royal Armament Research and Development Establishment, Ministry of Defence, 1980–83; *b* 25 May 1923; 3rd *s* of George Emerson Panton and Annie Panton; *m* 1952, Audrey Mary Lane (*d* 1989); two *s*. *Educ*: City Sch., Lincoln; University College and Univ. of Nottingham. PhD Nottingham 1952. Served War of 1939–45: commissioned, Bomb Disposal, Royal Eng., 1943–47. Pres., Univ. of Nottingham Union, 1950–51; Vice-Pres., Nat. Union of Students, 1952–54; Technical Officer, ICI, Billingham, 1952–53; Permanent Under-Secretary's Dept, FO, 1953–55; Office of Political Adviser, Berlin, 1955–57; Dep. Head, Technical Research Unit, MoD, 1957–58; Attaché, British Embassy, Washington, DC, 1958–59; Technical Adviser, UK Delegn to Conf. on Discontinuance of Nuclear Tests, Geneva, 1959–61; Permanent Under-Secretary's Dept, FO, 1961–63; Counsellor (Defence), British Embassy, Washington, DC, 1963–66; Head of Defence Science 6, MoD, 1966–68; Asst Chief Scientific Adviser (Nuclear), MoD, 1969–76; Dir Gen., Estabs, Resources and Programmes (B), MoD, April-Sept. 1976; Dir, Propellants, Explosives and Rocket Motor Estabt, and Head, Rocket Motor Exec., MoD, 1976–80. FRSC (FRIC 1961); FRSA 1973; FRAeS 1982. *Recreations*: bridge, reading local history. *Address*: Cantis House, 1 St Peter's Lane, Canterbury, Kent. *T*: Canterbury 452902. *Club*: Reform.

PANTRIDGE, Prof. (James) Frank, CBE 1978; MC 1942; MD, FRCP, FACC; *b* 3 Oct. 1916. *Educ*: Queen's Univ., Belfast (MD). FRCP 1957; FACC 1967. Research Fellow, Univ. of Mich, 1948–49; Dir, Regional Medical Cardiology Centre, NI, 1977–82; Hon. Prof. of Cardiol., QUB. Canadian Heart Foundn Orator; St Cyres Orator, National Heart Hosp., London. Chm., British Cardiac Soc., 1978. Developer of the Portable Defibrillator, and initiator (with J. S. Geddes) of pre-hospital coronary care. Hon. FRCPI. DUniv Open, 1981; Hon. DSc NUU, 1981. *Publications*: The Acute Coronary Attack, 1975; An Unquiet Life (autobiog), 1989, 3rd edn 1991. *Recreation*: fishing. *Address*: Hillsborough, Co. Down, N Ireland BT26 6EH. *T*: Hillsborough (0846) 682911.

PANUFNIK, Sir Andrzej, Kt 1991; composer and conductor; *b* 24 Sept. 1914; 2nd *s* of Tomasz Panufnik and Mathilda Thonnes Panufnik; *m* 1963, Camilla Ruth Jessel, FRPS, *yr d* of late Commander R. F. Jessel, DSO, OBE, DSC, RN; one *s* one *d*. *Educ*: Warsaw State Conservatoire; Vienna State Acad. for Music (under Professor Felix von Weingartner). Diploma with distinction, Warsaw Conservatoire, 1936. Conductor of the Cracow Philharmonic, 1945–46; Director and Conductor of the Warsaw Philharmonic Orchestra,

1946–47. Conducting leading European orchestras such as L'Orchestre National, Paris, Berliner Philharmonisches Orchester, L'Orchestre de la Suisse Romande, Geneva, and all principal British orchestras, 1947–. Polish decorations: Standard of Labor 1st class (1949), twice State Laureate (1951, 1952). Left Poland and settled in England, 1954; naturalized British subject, 1961. Vice-Chairman of International Music Council of UNESCO, Paris, 1950–53; Musical Director and Conductor, City of Birmingham Symphony Orchestra, 1957–59. Hon. Member of International Mark Twain Society (USA), 1954; Knight of Mark Twain, 1966; Hon. RAM 1984. DPhil *hc* Polish Univ. in Exile, London, 1985. The Sibelius Centenary Medal, 1965; Prix de composition musical Prince Pierre de Monaco, 1983. *Ballets*: Elegy, NY, 1967; Cain and Abel, Berlin, 1968; Miss Julie, Stuttgart, 1970; Homage to Chopin (SW Royal Ballet), 1980; Adieu (Royal Ballet), 1980; Polonia (SW Royal Ballet), 1980; Dances of the Golden Hall (Martha Graham), NY, 1982; Sinfonia Mistica (NY City Ballet), 1987. *Compositions*: Piano Trio, 1934; Five Polish Peasant Songs, 1940; Tragic Overture, 1942; Twelve Miniature Studies for piano, 1947; Nocturne for orchestra, 1947; Lullaby for 29 stringed instruments and 2 harps, 1947; Sinfonia Rustica, 1948; Hommage à Chopin-Five vocalises for soprano and piano, 1949; Old Polish Suite for strings, 1950; Concerto in modo antico, 1951; Heroic Overture, 1952; Rhapsody for orchestra, 1956; Sinfonia Elegiaca, 1957; Polonia-Suite for Orchestra, 1959; Piano Concerto, 1961; Autumn Music, 1962; Landscape, 1962; Two Lyric Pieces, 1963; Sinfonia Sacra, 1963 (first prize, Prix de Composition Musicale Prince Rainier III de Monaco, 1963); Song to the Virgin Mary, 1964; Katyn Epitaph, 1966; Jagiellonian Triptych, 1966; Reflections for piano, 1967; The Universal Prayer, 1969; Thames Pageant, 1969; Violin Concerto, 1971; Triangles, 1972; Winter Solstice, 1972; Sinfonia Concertante, 1973; Sinfonia di Sfere, 1974; String Quartet No 1, 1976, No 2, 1980, No 3, 1990; Dreamscape, 1976; Sinfonia Mistica, 1977; Metasinfonia, 1978; Concerto Festivo, 1979; Concertino, 1980; Sinfonia Votiva, 1981; A Procession for Peace, 1982; Arbor Cosmica, 1984; Pentasonata, 1985; Bassoon Concerto, 1985; Symphony No 9, 1986; String Sextet, 1987; Symphony No 10, 1988; Harmony, 1989; String Quartet No 3, 1990. *Publication*: Composing Myself (autobiog.), 1987. *Address*: Riverside House, Twickenham, Middlesex TW1 3DJ. *T*: 081–892 1470. *Club*: Garrick.

See also O. R. Jessel, T. F. H. Jessel.

PAO, Sir Yue-Kong, Kt 1978; CBE 1976; JP; LLD; Chairman of Supervisory Board, World-Wide Shipping Group, since 1974; Group Deputy Chairman, Standard Chartered Bank, 1986–88; *b* Chekiang, China, 10 Nov. 1918; *s* of late Sui-Loong Pao and Chung Sau-Gin Pao; *m* 1940, Sue-Ing Haung; four *d*. *Educ*: Shanghai, China. Banking career in China until went to Hong Kong, 1949; engaged in import and export trade; shipowner, 1955–. Dep. Chm., Hongkong & Shanghai Banking Corp., 1980–84; Adviser, Indust. Bank of Japan. Member: Adv. Council, Nippon Kaiji Kyokai of Japan; (Life), Court of Univ. of Hong Kong; Rockefeller Univ. Council, New York; Hon. Mem., INTERTANKO. Hon. Vice-Pres., Maritime Trust. Overseas Hon. Trustee, Westminster Abbey Trust. Trustee, Hong Kong Arts Centre. Hon. LLD: Univ. of Hong Kong, 1975; Chinese Univ. of Hong Kong, 1977. JP Hong Kong, 1971. Commander: National Order of Cruzeiro do Sul, Brazil, 1977; Order of the Crown, Belgium, 1982; Vasquo Nunez de Balboa, Panama, 1982. *Recreations*: swimming, golf. *Address*: World-Wide Shipping Agency Ltd, Wheelock House, 6/F, 20 Pedder Street, Hong Kong. *T*: 5–8423888. *Clubs*: Royal Automobile; Woking Golf (Surrey); Royal and Ancient Golf (St Andrews, Fife); Sunningdale Golf (Berks).

PAOLOZZI, Sir Eduardo (Luigi), Kt 1989; CBE 1968; RA 1979 (ARA 1972); sculptor; HM Sculptor in Ordinary for Scotland, since 1986; Visiting Professor, Royal College of Art, since 1989 (Tutor in Ceramics, 1968–89); *b* 7 March 1924; *s* of Rudolpho Antonio Paolozzi and Carmella (*née* Rossi), both Italian; *m*; three *d*. *Educ*: Edinburgh School of Art; Slade Sch. Worked in Paris, 1947–50; Instructor, Central School of Arts and Crafts, London, 1950–55; Lecturer, St Martin's School of Art, 1955–56; Prof. of Ceramics at Fachhochschule, Cologne, 1977–81; Prof. of Sculpture, Akad. der Bildenden Künste, Munich, 1981–91. Trustee, Nat. Portrait Gall., 1988–. Fellow, UCL, 1986. Hon. Dr RCA, 1979; Hon. RSA; Hon. DLitt: Glasgow, 1980; Heriot-Watt, 1987; London, 1987. British Critics Prize, 1953; David E. Bright Foundn Award, 1960; Watson F. Blaire Prize, 1961; Purchase Prize, Internat. Sculpture Exhibn at Solomon R. Guggenheim Mus., 1967; First Prize for Sculpture, Carnegie Internat. Exhibn, 1967; Sculpture Prize, European Patent Office, Munich, 1978; First Prize, Rhinegarten Cologne comp., 1981; Grand Prix d'Honneur, Print Biennale at Ljubljana, Yugoslavia, 1983. *One-man exhibitions*: first in London, Mayor Gallery, 1947; first in New York, Betty Parsons Gallery, 1960, also 1962; Tate Gallery, 1971; V&A Mus., 1973, 1977 (print retrospective); Nationalgal., W Berlin, 1975; Fruit Market Gall., Edinburgh, 1976; Marlborough Fine Art Gallery, 1976; Anthony d'Offay Gall., 1977; Kassel, Germany, 1978; Glasgow League of Artists, 1979; Edinburgh Univ., 1979; Cologne, Germany, 1979; Museum for Künste und Gewerbe, Hamburg, 1982; Aedes Gall., Berlin, 1983; Invited artist, 6th Internat. Drawing Biennale, Cleveland (UK), 1983; Wissenschaftskolleg zu Berlin, 1983; Architectural Assoc., London; Royal Scottish Acad., Stadische Galerie im Lenbachhaus, Munich; New Metropole Arts Centre, Folkestone, 1984; Mus. Ludwig, Cologne; De Beyerd Mus., Breda, Holland; Contemporary Art Centre, Lyon, France; Ivan Dougherty Gall., Sydney, Aust., 1985; Cork, Ireland, 1985; Mus. of Mankind, 1986; RA, 1986; Serpentine Gall., 1987; Nat. Portrait Gall., 1988; Talbot Rice Art Gall., Edinburgh, 1989; Scottish Gall., 1990. *Group exhibitions include*: Whitechapel Gall., 1981; Ashmolean Mus., 1982; Museo Municipal of Madrid, 1983; Mus. of Contemp. Art, LA, 1984; designed: glass mosaics for Tottenham Ct Road Underground Station, London; film sets for Percy Adlon's Herschel and the Music of the Stars, 1984–85. Work in permanent collections: Tate Gallery; Contemporary Art Society; Museum of Modern Art, New York; Kowloon Park, Hong Kong, etc. Work exhibited in: British Pavilion, Venice Biennale, 1952; Documenta 2, Kassel, 1959; New Images of Man, New York, 1959; British Pavilion, 30th Venice Biennale; International Exhibition of Sculpture, Boymans Museum, Rotterdam; Open Air Sculpture, Battersea Park, London; Critics Choice, Tooths Gallery, London; City Art Gallery, Manchester, Oct. 1960; British Sculpture in the Sixties, Tate Gallery, March 1965; Chelsea School of Art, 1965; Hanover Gallery, 1967; Tate Gall., 1971. Corresponding Mem., Bayerische Akad. der Schöner Künste, 1990. Hon. Mem., AA, 1980; Hon. RIAS, 1991. Eduardo Paolozzi Art Sch. inaugurated at Ipswich Sch., 1987. Goethe Medal, 1991. *Relevant publications*: Eduardo Paolozzi, by Winfried Konnertz, 1984. *Recreation*: music. *Address*: 107 Dovehouse Street, SW3 6JZ. *Club*: Athenæum.

PAPADOPOULOS, Achilles Symeon, CMG 1980; LVO 1972; MBE 1954; HM Diplomatic Service, retired; High Commissioner in the Bahamas, 1981–83; *b* 16 Aug. 1923; *s* of late Symeon Papadopoulos and Polyxene Papadopoulos; *m* 1954, Joyce Martin (*née* Stark); one *s* two *d*. *Educ*: The English School, Nicosia, Cyprus. British Mil. Admin, Eritrea, 1943; HMOCS: Cyprus, 1953; Dar es Salaam, 1959; Malta, 1961; HM Diplomatic Service: Malta, 1965; Nairobi, 1965; FCO, 1968; Colombo, 1971; Washington, 1974; Havana, 1974; Ambassador to El Salvador, 1977–79; to Mozambique, 1979–80; attached UK Mission to UN, Sept.-Dec. 1980. *Recreations*: golf, bridge. *Address*: 14 Mill Close, Great Bookham, Leatherhead, Surrey KT23 3JX.

PAPANDREOU, Dr Andreas George; Leader of the Opposition, 1977–81 and since 1989; *b* 5 Feb. 1919; *s* of late George Papandreou and Sophia (*née* Mineiko); *m* 2nd, 1951,

Margaret Chant (marr. diss. 1989); three *s* one *d*; *m* 3rd, 1989, Mrs Dimitra Liani. *Educ:* Athens Univ. Law Sch.; Harvard, USA. Associate Professor: Univ. of Minnesota, 1947–50; Northwestern Univ., 1950–51; Professor: Univ. of Minnesota, 1951–55; Univ. of California, 1955–63; Dir, Centre of Econ. Res., Athens, 1961–64; Minister to Prime Minister, Greece, Feb.–Nov. 1964; Minister of Economic Co-ordination, 1965; Deputy for Ahaia, 1965–67; in prison, April–Dec. 1967; Founder and Chm., Pan-Hellenic Liberation Movement, 1968–74; Prof., Univ. of Stockholm, 1968–69; Prof. of Economics, York Univ., Canada, 1969–74; Founder and Pres., Panhellenic Socialist Movement, 1974–; Minister of Defence, 1981–86; Prime Minister, 1981–89. *Publications:* Economics as a Science, 1958; A Strategy for Greek Economic Development, 1962; Fundamentals of Model Construction in Microeconomics, 1962; The Greek Front, 1970; Man's Freedom, 1970; Democracy at Gunpoint, 1971; Paternalistic Capitalism, 1972; Project Selection for National Plans, 1974; Socialist Transformation, 1977. *Address:* Office of the Leader of the Opposition, Parliament Building, Athens, Greece.

PAPANDREOU, Vasso; Member, Commission of the European Communities, since 1989; *d* of Andreas and Anastasia. *Educ:* Athens Univ. (BSc 1969); London Univ. (MSc 1971); Reading Univ. (PhD 1980). Economics Tutor, Exeter Univ., 1971–73; Res. Asst, Oxford Univ., 1973–74; Lectr, High Business and Econs Sch., Athens, 1981–85; MP, Greece, 1985–89. Panhellenic Socialist Movement: Mem., Central Cttee, 1981–85; Mem., Exec. Bureau of Central Cttee, 1984–88. Dir, Hellenic Orgn for Small and Medium Size Firms, 1981–85. Mem., Bd of Dirs, Commercial Bank of Greece, 1982–85. *Publications:* Multinational Companies and Less Developed Countries: the case of Greece, 1981; numerous papers and articles. *Address:* Commission of the European Communities, 200 rue de la Loi, 1049 Brussels, Belgium.

PAPE, (Jonathan) Hector (Carruthers), OBE 1980; FCIT; Advocate; Chief General Manager, National Dock Labour Board, 1975–82 (General Manager and Secretary, 1970–75); *b* 8 March 1918; *er s* of Jonathan Pape, MA and Florence Muriel Myrtle; *m* 1st, 1944, Mary Sullins (*née* Jeffries) (*d* 1985); one *s*; 2nd, 1987, Yvonne (*née* Bartlett). *Educ:* Merchant Taylors' Sch., Crosby. Mercantile Marine, 1934–46; Master Mariner (FG), 1944 (Liverpool Qualif.). Manager, Master Stevedoring Co., Liverpool, 1947–51; National Dock Labour Board: Dep. Port Manager, London, 1952–57; Asst Gen. Manager, Bd HQ, 1957–69; Dep. Gen. Manager and Secretary, Bd HQ, 1969. Mem., Honourable Co. of Master Mariners, 1965. Freeman, City of London. *Address:* 42 Homedane House, Denmark Place, Hastings, East Sussex TN34 1PQ.

PAPOULIAS, George Dimitrios; Commander, Order of Phoenix; Order of George I; Greek Ambassador to the Court of St James's and non-resident Ambassador to Iceland, since 1990; *b* 19 May 1927; *s* of Dimitrios G. Papoulias and Caterina Kontopoulou; *m* 1974, Emily Pilavachi; one *d*. *Educ:* Athens Univ. (Law degree; Econ. and Comm. Scis degree). Military service, 2nd Lieut, 1950–51. Entered Greek Diplomatic Service, 1955; served Athens, New Delhi, Bonn; Dep. Perm. Deleg. to UN and to Internat Orgns, Geneva, 1964–69; Counsellor, 1967; Dir, Political Affairs, Min. of N Greece, 1969–70; Minister, Paris and Perm. Rep. to Unesco, 1971–74; Mem., Bd of Dirs, Resettlement Fund, Council of Europe, 1971–74; Ambassador to UN, NY, 1975–79, to Turkey, 1979–83, to USA, 1983–89; Alternate Minister and Minister for Foreign Affairs, 1989, 1990. Holds foreign orders and decorations. *Recreations:* archaeology, history. *Address:* 51 Upper Brook Street, W1Y 1PG. *T:* 071–629 0793; Rigillis 16, Athens 106 74, Greece. *T:* 031–72298888. *Clubs:* Brooks's; Athenian (Greece).

PAPUA NEW GUINEA, Archbishop of, since 1990; **Most Rev. Bevan Meredith;** Primate of the Province of Papua New Guinea, since 1990; Bishop of New Guinea Islands, since 1977; *b* Alstonville, NSW, 14 Aug. 1927; 3rd *c* of Stanley Meredith and Edith Meredith (*née* Witchard). *Educ:* Univ. of Queensland; St Francis Theol Coll., Brisbane. Teacher, Slade Sch., Warwick, Qld and Housemaster, Highfields House, 1948–53; Staff, Martyrs' Meml Sch., PNG, 1954–58; deacon 1961, priest 1962, St Thomas, Toowong; Priest-in-charge, Managalas, PNG, 1963–67; Asst Bp of New Guinea, 1969–77. *Recreations:* music, photography, philately. *Address:* Bishop's Street, Rabaul, Papua New Guinea; PO Box 159, Rabaul, Papua New Guinea. *T:* (675) 922237.

PAQUET, Dr Jean-Guy, OC 1984; FRSC; Executive Vice-President, The Laurentian Mutual Insurance; *b* Montmagny, Qué, 5 Jan. 1938; *s* of Laurent W. Paquet and Louisianne Coulombe. *Educ:* Université Laval (BSc Engrg Physics, 1959; DSc Elec. Engrg, 1963); Ecole Nat. Sup. de l'Aéronautique, Paris (MSc Aeronautics, 1960). FRSC 1978; FAAAS 1981. Université Laval: Asst Prof. of Elec. Engrg, 1962; Associate Prof., 1967; Head, Elec. Engrg Dept, 1967–69; Vice-Dean (Research), Faculty of Science, 1969–72; Prof. of Elec. Engrg, 1971; Vice-Rector (Academic), 1972–77; Rector, 1977–87. Fellowships: French Govt, 1959; NATO, 1962; Nat. Science Foundn, 1964; Québec Govt, 1965. Def. Res. Bd of Canada Grant, 1965–76. National Research Council of Canada: Fellowship, 1961; Grant, 1964–77; Mem., Associate Cttee on Automatic Control, 1964–70; Special Asst to Vice-Pres. (Scientific), 1971–72. Pres., Conf. of Rectors and Principals of Univs of Prov. of Québec, 1979–81. Member: Council, Univs of Prov. of Qué, 1973–77; Bd, Assoc. of Scientific, Engrg and Technol Community of Canada, 1970–77 (Pres., 1975–76); Bd, French Canadian Assoc. for Advancement of Science, 1969–71; Canadian Assoc. of Univ. Res. Administrators; Special Task Force on Res. and Develt, Science Council of Canada, 1976; Order of Engrs, Qué; Amer. Soc. for Engrg Educn; Amer. Management Assoc., 1980–; Soc. for Res. Administrators. Member Board: Hockey Canada, 1980–; Interamerican Univs Assoc., 1980–; Assoc. des universités partiellement ou entièrement de langue française, 1981– (Vice-Pres., 1983–); Assoc. of Commonwealth Univs, 1981–; Social Sciences and Humanities Res. Council of Canada, 1982–; Inst. of Canadian Bankers, 1980–; Founding Mem., Corporate Higher Educn Forum. Pres., Selection Cttee, Outstanding Achievement Awards, Canada, 1984 (Mem., 1983). DSc *hc* McGill Univ., 1982; DLaw *hc*, York Univ., 1983. *Publications:* (with P. A. Roy) Rapport d'études bibliographiques: l'automation dans la production et la distribution de l'énergie électrique, 1968; (with J. F. Le Maître) Méthodes pratiques d'étude des oscillations non-linéaires: application aux systèmes par plus-ou-moins, 1970; more than fifty pubns in scientific jls, on control systems engrg; articles on research, develt and scientific policy. *Recreations:* jogging, travels, golf. *Address:* The Laurentian Mutual Insurance, 500 Grande-Allee East, Québec G1R 2J7, Canada. *Clubs:* Cercle de la Garnison de Québec, Club de Golf Cap-Rouge (Québec).

PARAGUAY, Bishop of, since 1988; **Rt. Rev. John Alexander Ellison;** *b* 24 Dec. 1940; *s* of Alexander and Catherine Ellison; *m* 1964, Judith Mary Cox; one *s* two *d*. *Educ:* London College of Divinity (ALCD); Borough Road College (Teacher's Cert.). Secondary school teacher, 1961–64. Deacon 1967, priest 1968; Curate, St Paul, Woking, 1967–71; missionary, church planter, evangelist; Bible school/Bible institute lecturer, 1971–79; Asst to Archdeacon, St Saviour, Belgrano, Dio. Argentina, 1979–82; Rector, Aldridge, Dio. Lichfield, 1983–88. *Recreations:* walking, gardening, family, dining out, club. *Address:* Diocesan Office, Casilla de Correo 1124, Asunción, Paraguay. *Club:* Garden (Asunción).

PARARAJASINGAM, Sir Sangarapillai, Kt 1955; Senator, Ceylon, 1954–59; Chairman, Board of Directors, Colonial Motors Ltd, 1961–74; former Member, Board of Trustees, Ceylon Social Service League; *b* 25 June 1896; *s* of late W. Sangarapillai, social worker and philanthropist; *m* 1916, Padmavati, *d* of Sir Ponnambalam Arunachalam; one *s* one *d*. *Educ:* St Thomas' Coll., Mt Lavinia. Past President, Board of Directors, Manipay Hindu Coll., Manager, 1929–61; Past President Ceylon Poultry Club; Member National Savings Cttee; Past Chairman, Board Governors, Ceylon Inst. of Scientific and Industrial Research. Formerly Chairman: Board of Directors, Agricultural and Industrial Credit Corporation of Ceylon; Education Cttee, Ceylon Social Service League; Low Country Products Assoc., 1943–44 and 1944–45; Ceylon Coconut Board; Coconut Commn; Past Member: Textile Tribunal; Land Advisory Cttee; Ceylon Tea Propaganda Board; Coconut Research Scheme; Radio Advisory Board; Excise Advisory Cttee; Central Board of Agriculture; Income Tax Board of Review; Rice Advisory Board; Services Standing Wages Board; Board for Approval of Credit Agencies; Commn on Broadcasting; Past President Vivekananda Society; Rotary Club of Colombo; Governor, Rotary Internat. District 320, 1951–52; formerly Trustee and Hon. Treasurer, Ceylon Society of Arts; formerly Manager, all Schools managed by Ceylon Social Service League. JP Ceylon 1923. Travelled widely in the UK, Europe, USA, India, Far East. Coronation Medals, 1937 and 1953. *Recreations:* gardening, agriculture and farming. *Address:* No 50, Pathmalaya, Flower Road, Colombo 7, Sri Lanka. *T:* 23159.

See also P. Nadesan.

PARAYRE, Jean-Paul Christophe; Chevalier de la Légion d'Honneur; Officier, l'Ordre National du Mérite, 1978; French building and civil engineering executive; Member, Supervisory Board, Peugeot SA, since 1984; Chairman, Dumez SA, since 1988; *b* Lorient, 5 July 1937; *s* of Louis Parayre and Jehanne Malarde; *m* 1962, Marie-Françoise Chaufour; two *s* two *d*. *Educ:* Lycées in Casablanca and Versailles; Ecole Polytechnique, Paris; Ecole Nationale des Ponts et Chaussées. Engr, Dept of Highways, 1963–67; Technical Adviser: Min. of Social Affairs, 1967; Min. of Economy and Finance, 1968; Dir of Mech. Industries, Min. of Industry and Res., 1970–74; Chief Adviser to Pres. and Gen. Man., Banque Vernes et Commerciale de Paris, 1974; Manager of Planning, Automobile Div. of Peugeot, 1975; Manager, Automobile Div., Peugeot-Citroën, 1976; Chm., Peugeot SA, 1977–84; Mem., Supervisory Bd, 1977–84, Dir-Gen., 1984–88, Dumez SA. Mem., Board of Directors: Crédit National, 1978–; Valeo, 1986–91; Alcatel Alsthom (formerly Compagnie Générale d'Electricité), 1986–; GTM, 1986–; LVMH, 1987–89; Jean Lefebvre, 1988–; Vallourec, 1989–; Inchcape plc, 1991–. *Recreations:* tennis, golf. *Address:* (office) Lyonnaise des Eaux-Dumez, 32 Avenue Pablo Picasso, 92022 Nanterre, France; 3 Rond-Point Saint-James, 92200 Neuilly-sur-Seine, France. *Clubs:* Polo de Paris, Golf de Morfontaine.

PARBO, Sir Arvi (Hillar), Kt 1978; Non-Executive Chairman, Western Mining Corporation Ltd, since 1990 (Chairman and Managing Director, 1974–86; Executive Chairman, 1986–90); Chairman, The Broken Hill Pty Co. Ltd, since 1989 (Director, since 1987); *b* 10 Feb. 1926; *s* of Aado and Hilda Parbo; *m* 1953, Saima Soots; two *s* one *d*. *Educ:* Clausthal Mining Acad., Germany; Univ. of Adelaide (BE Hons). Western Mining Corporation: Underground Surveyor, 1956; Underground Manager, Nevoria Mine, 1958–60; Techn. Asst to Man. Dir, 1960–64; Dep. Gen. Supt, WA, 1964–68; Gen. Manager, 1968–71 (Dir, 1970–); Dep. Man. Dir, 1971; Man. Dir, 1971. Director: Aluminium Co. of America, 1980–; Hoechst Australian Investments Pty Ltd, 1981–; Chase AMP Bank Ltd, 1985–; Chairman: Munich Reinsurance Company of Australia Ltd, 1984 (Dir, 1983–); Zurich Insurance Australian Group, 1985–; Alcoa of Australia Ltd, 1978–. Member: Chase Internat. Adv. Bd; Degussa AG Supervisory Bd. Hon. DSc: Deakin, 1989; Curtin, 1989; Hon. DEng Monash, 1989; DUniv Flinders, 1991. Comdr, Order of Merit, Germany, 1979; Grand Cordon, Order of the Sacred Treasure, Japan, 1990; Australian Achiever, 1990. *Recreations:* reading, carpentry. *Address:* Western Mining Corporation Ltd, 360 Collins Street, Melbourne, Vic 3000, Australia; GPO Box 860K, Melbourne, Vic 3001. *T:* 602 0316. *Clubs:* Melbourne, Australian (both Melbourne); Weld (Perth); Commonwealth (Canberra); Hannans (Kalgoorlie); Duquesne (Pittsburgh, USA).

PARDOE, Alan Douglas William; QC 1988; a Recorder of the Crown Court, since 1990; *b* 16 Aug. 1943; *s* of William Pardoe and Grace Pardoe, DSc, FRSC; *m* 1st, 1972, Mary Ensor (marr. diss. 1976); 2nd, 1991, Catherine Williams (*née* Steuart); one step *s* one step *d*. *Educ:* Oldbury Grammar Sch.; St Catharine's Coll., Cambridge (MA, LLB). Called to the Bar, Lincoln's Inn, 1971 (Hardwicke Schol.). Asst Lectr and Lectr in Law, Univ. of Exeter, 1965–70; Vis. Lectr in Law, Univ. of Auckland, NZ, 1970; Lectr in Law, Univ. of Sussex, 1970–74; began practice at the Bar, 1973. *Publications:* A Practical Guide to the Industrial Relations Act 1971; articles in legal periodicals. *Recreations:* mountain-walking, cooking. *Address:* 50 Northumberland Place, W2; Devereux Chambers, Devereux Court, Temple, WC2R 3JJ. *T:* 071–353 7534. *Club:* Travellers'.

PARDOE, Dr Geoffrey Keith Charles, OBE 1988; PhD; FEng, FRAeS; FBIS; Chairman: General Technology Systems Ltd, since 1973 (Managing Director, 1973–88); General Technology Systems (Scandinavia) A/S, since 1985; President: General Technology Systems SA, Belgium, since 1979; General Technology Systems Inc. (USA), since 1986; Deputy Chairman, Surrey Satellite Technology Ltd, since 1987 (Managing Director, 1985–87); *b* 2 Nov. 1928; *s* of James Charles Pardoe and Ada Violet Pardoe; *m* 1953, Dorothy Patricia Gutteridge; one *s* one *d*. *Educ:* Wanstead County High Sch., London; London Univ. (BScEng Hons); Loughborough Coll. (DLC Hons Aeronautics; PhD (Astronautics) Loughborough Univ., 1984). FRAeS 1968; FEng 1988. Sen. Aerodynamicist, Armstrong Whitworth Ltd, 1949–51; Chief Aerodynamicist, Guided Weapons, De Havilland Props Ltd, 1951–56, Proj. Manager, Blue Streak, 1956–60; Hawker Siddeley Dynamics Ltd: Chief Engr, Weapons and Space Research, 1960–63; Chief Proj. Engr, Space Div., 1963–69; Sales Exec., 1969–73; Exec. Dir, British Space Develt Co. Ltd, 1960–74. Chm., Procogen Computer Systems Ltd, 1981–86; Director: Philip A. Lapp Ltd, Canada, 1973–; Gen. Technology Systems (Netherlands) BV, Den Haag, 1982–; Eurosat SA, Switzerland, 1971–83; Eurotech Develts Ltd, 1981–83. Vice Pres., Eurospace (Paris), 1961–73; Pres., RAeS, 1984–85 (Vice-Pres., 1981–83). Dep. Chm., 1981–86, Chm., 1986–, Watt Cttee on Energy. FRSA; FInstD. *Publications:* The Challenge of Space, 1964; Integration of Payload and Stages of Space Carrier Vehicles, 1964; Project Apollo: The way to the Moon, 1969, 2nd edn 1970; The Future for Space Technology, 1984; over 50 main pubns in learned society pubns and jls; about 100 articles; about 2000 TV and radio interviews 1959–. *Recreations:* skiing, flying, badminton, photography, wind-surfing. *Address:* 23 Stewart Road, Harpenden, Herts AL5 4QE. *T:* Harpenden (0582) 460719. *Clubs:* Royal Air Force, Institute of Directors, Ski of GB.

PARDOE, John George Magrath, CBE 1975; FRAeS; Director-General, Airworthiness, Civil Aviation Authority, 1972–79. *Educ:* Coll. of Aeronautical Engineering. Entered design work in Aircraft Industry, 1935; joined Accidents Inspection Br. of Air Ministry, 1942; joined Staff, Air Registration Bd, 1945; Chief Technical Officer, 1969. Médaille de l'aéronautique, 1980.

PARDOE, John Wentworth; Chairman, Sight and Sound Education Ltd; Senior Research Fellow of Policy Studies Institute; *b* 27 July 1934; *s* of Cuthbert B. Pardoe and Marjorie E. W. (*née* Taylor); *m* 1958, Joyce R. Peerman; two *s* one *d*. *Educ:* Sherborne; Corpus Christi Coll., Cambridge (MA). Television Audience Measurement Ltd, 1958–60;

Osborne Peacock Co. Ltd, 1960–61; Liberal News, 1961–66. MP (L) Cornwall N, 1966–79; Treasurer of the Liberal Party, 1968–69. Presenter, Look Here, LWT, 1979–81. Consultant to Nat. Assoc. of Schoolmasters, 1967–73. Director: William Schlackman Ltd, 1968–71; Gerald Metals, 1972–83; Mem. London Metal Exchange, 1973–83. Mem., Youth Trng Bd, 1985–. *Recreations:* cricket, walking, singing. *Address:* 18 New End Square, NW3.

PARE, Rev. Philip Norris; *b* 13 May 1910; *s* of Frederick William and Florence May Pare; *m* 1943, Nancy Eileen, *d* of late Canon C. Patteson; two *s* two *d*. *Educ:* Nottingham High Sch.; King's Coll., Cambridge; Cuddesdon Theological Coll. Curate, All Saints, W Dulwich, 1934–37; Chaplain and Vice-Principal, Bishops Coll., Cheshunt, 1937–39; Curate, St Mary the Less, Cambridge, 1939–40. Chaplain RNVR, 1940–46. Vicar of Cheshunt, Herts, 1946–57; Rural Dean of Ware, 1949–56; Examining Chaplain to Bishop of St Albans, 1952–56; Missioner Canon Stipendiary, Diocese of Wakefield, 1957–62; Diocesan Adviser for Christian Stewardship, 1959–68; Provost, and Vicar of Cathedral Church of All Saints, Wakefield, 1962–71; Vicar of Cholsey, dio. Oxford, 1973–82. A Church Commissioner, 1968–71; Member Board of Ecclesiastical Insurance Office, 1966–83; Provost of Woodard Schools (Northern Div.), 1977–82; Trustee, Ely Stained Glass Museum, 1980–87. *Publications:* Eric Milner-White, A Memoir (with Donald Harris), 1965; Re-Thinking Our Worship, 1967; God Made the Devil?: a ministry of healing, 1985; articles in Theology, The Reader, etc. *Recreations:* modern stained glass and architecture; railways, motor cars; church music. *Address:* 73 Oakland Drive, Ledbury, Herefordshire HR8 2EX. *T:* Ledbury (0531) 3619.

PAREKH, Prof. Bhikhu Chhotalal; Professor of Political Theory, University of Hull, since 1982; *b* 4 Jan. 1935; *s* of Chhotalal Parekh and Gajaraben Parekh; *m* 1959, Pramila (*née* Dalal); three *s*. *Educ:* Univ. of Bombay (BA 1954, MA 1956); Univ. of London (PhD 1966). Tutor, LSE, 1962–63; Asst Lectr, Univ. of Glasgow, 1963–64; Univ. of Hull: Lectr, Sen. Lectr and Reader, 1964–82. Vice-Chancellor, Univ. of Baroda, 1981–84. Visiting Professor: Univ. of BC, 1968–69; Concordia Univ., 1974–75; McGill Univ., 1976–77. Mem. Council, PSI, 1985–90; Chm., British Assoc. of S Asia Scholars, 1989–91. Dep. Chm., CRE, 1985–90. Trustee: Runnymede Trust, 1985–; Inst. for Public Policy Res., 1988–; Gandhi Foundn, 1988–. FRSA 1988. *Publications:* Politics and Experience, 1968; Dissent and Disorder, 1971; The Morality of Politics, 1972; Knowledge and Belief in Politics, 1973; Bentham's Political Thought, 1973; Colour, Culture and Consciousness, 1974; Jeremy Bentham: ten critical essays, 1974; The Concept of Socialism, 1975; Hannah Arendt and the Search for a New Political Philosophy, 1981; Karl Marx's Theory of Ideology, 1982; Contemporary Political Thinkers, 1982; Political Discourse, 1986; Gandhi's Political Philosophy, 1988; Colonialism, Tradition and Reform, 1989; articles in learned jls incl. Political Studies, British Jl of Political Science, Social Research, Jl of History of Ideas, Internat. Review of Sociology and Cross Currents. *Recreations:* reading, music. *Address:* 211 Victoria Avenue, Hull HU5 3EF.

PARES, Peter; *b* 6 Sept. 1908; 2nd *s* of late Sir Bernard Pares, KBE, DCL, and late Margaret Pares (*née* Dixon); unmarried. *Educ:* Lancing Coll.; Jesus Coll., Cambridge (Scholar). Entered Consular Service, 1930; served in Philadelphia, 1930; Havana, 1932; Consul, Liberec and Bratislava, Czechslovakia, 1936–39; Budapest, 1939; Cluj, Rumania, 1940; New York, 1941; Washington, as First Secretary, 1944; Control Commission for Germany, 1946; Foreign Office, 1949; Casablanca, 1952; Strasbourg, 1956; Deputy Consul-General, Frankfurt, 1957; Consul-General, Asmara, Eritrea, 1957–59; Head of Education and Cultural Relations Dept, CRO, 1960–63. *Address:* 3 Ashburnham Gardens, Eastbourne, East Sussex BN21 2NA.

PARFIT, Derek Antony, FBA 1986; Senior Research Fellow, All Souls College, Oxford, since 1984; *b* 11 Dec. 1942; *s* of Norman and Jessie Parfit. *Educ:* Eton; Balliol College, Oxford. BA Modern History, 1964. Fellow of All Souls, 1967–. *Publication:* Reasons and Persons, 1984. *Recreation:* architectural photography. *Address:* All Souls College, Oxford. *T:* Oxford (0865) 279282.

PARGETER, Edith; *b* 28 Sept. 1913; 3rd *c* of Edmund Valentine Pargeter and Edith Hordley; unmarried. *Educ:* Dawley C of E Elementary Sch.; County High School for Girls, Coalbrookdale. Worked as a chemist's assistant, and at twenty succeeded in finding a publisher for first-and unsuccessful-book. WRNS Aug. 1940, teleprinter operator (BEM 1944); dispersed from the Service, Aug. 1945. FIIAL 1962. Gold Medal and Ribbon, Czechoslovak Society for International Relations, 1968. *Publications:* Hortensius, Friend of Nero, Iron Bound, 1936; The City Lies Foursquare, 1939; Ordinary People, 1941; She Goes to War, 1942; The Eighth Champion of Christendom, 1945; Reluctant Odyssey, 1946; Warfare Accomplished, 1947; By Firelight, 1948; The Fair Young Phoenix, 1948; The Coast of Bohemia, 1949; Lost Children, 1950; Fallen Into the Pit, 1951; Holiday with Violence, 1952; This Rough Magic, 1953; Most Loving Mere Folly, 1953; The Soldier at the Door, 1954; A Means of Grace, 1956; Tales of the Little Quarter (trans. from the Czech of Jan Neruda), 1957; Don Juan (trans. from the Czech of Josef Toman), 1958; Assize of the Dying, 1958; The Heaven Tree, 1960; The Green Branch 1962; The Scarlet Seed, 1963; The Terezín Requiem (trans. from the Czech of Josef Bor), 1963; The Lily Hand and other stories, 1965; Close Watch on the Trains (trans from the Czech of Bohumil Hrabal), 1968; Report on my Husband (trans. from the Czech of Josefa Slánská), 1969; A Bloody Field by Shrewsbury, 1972; Sunrise in the West, 1974; The Dragon at Noonday, 1975; The Hounds of Sunset, 1976; Afterglow and Nightfall, 1977; The Marriage of Meggotta, 1979; *as Ellis Peters:* many crime and mystery novels including: Monk's-hood, 1980 (Silver Dagger, Crime Writers Assoc.); Saint Peter's Fair, 1981; The Leper of Saint Giles, 1981; The Virgin in the Ice, 1982; The Sanctuary Sparrow, 1982; The Devil's Novice, 1983; Dead Man's Ransom, 1984; The Pilgrim of Hate, 1984; An Excellent Mystery, 1985; The Raven in the Foregate, 1986; The Rose Rent, 1986; The Hermit of Eyton Forest, 1987; The Confession of Brother Haluin, 1988; The Heretic's Apprentice, 1989; The Potter's Field, 1989; The Summer of the Danes, 1991. *Recreations:* collecting gramophone records, particularly of voice; reading anything and everything; theatre. *Address:* Troya, 3 Lee Dingle, Madeley, Telford, Salop TF7 5TW. *T:* Telford (0952) 585178.

PARGETER, Rt. Rev. Philip; Auxiliary Bishop of Birmingham, (RC), and Titular Bishop of Valentiniana, since 1989; *b* 13 June 1933; *s* of Philip William Henry Pargeter and Ellen Pargeter. *Educ:* St Bede's Coll., Manchester; Oscott Coll., Sutton Coldfield. Priest, 1959; on staff of Cotton College, 1959–85; Administrator, St Chad's Cathedral, Birmingham, 1985–90; Canon, 1986. *Recreations:* reading, listening to music, walking. *Address:* Grove House, 90 College Road, Sutton Coldfield B73 5AH. *T:* 021–354 4363.

PARIS, Archbishop of; *see* Lustiger, His Eminence Cardinal J.-M.

PARISH, Sir David (Elmer) W.; *see* Woodbine Parish.

PARK, family name of **Baroness Park of Monmouth.**

PARK OF MONMOUTH, Baroness *cr* 1990 (Life Peer), of Broadway in the County of Hereford and Worcester; **Daphne Margaret Sybil Désirée Park,** CMG 1971; OBE 1960; HM Diplomatic Service, retired; Principal of Somerville College, Oxford, 1980–89; Chairman, Royal Commission on the Historical Monuments of England, since 1989; *b* England, 1 Sept. 1921; British parents; unmarried. *Educ:* Rosa Bassett Sch.; Somerville Coll., Oxford (Hon. Fellow, 1990). WTS (FANY), 1943–47 (Allied Commn for Austria, 1946–48). FO, 1948; UK Delegn to NATO, 1952; 2nd Sec., Moscow, 1954; FO, 1956; Consul and 1st Sec., Leopoldville, 1959; FO, 1961; Lusaka, 1964; FO, 1967; Consul-Gen., Hanoi, 1969–70; Hon. Res. Fellow, Univ. of Kent, 1971–72, on sabbatical leave from FCO; Chargé d'Affaires *ai*, Ulan Bator, Apr.–June 1972; FCO, 1973–79. Chm., Legal Aid Adv. Cttee to the Lord Chancellor, 1985–90. Member: British Library Bd, 1983–89; Sheffield Develt Corp. Bd, 1989–; RIIA; Royal Asiatic Soc.; Mem. Council, VSO, 1981–84; Dir, Zoo Develt Trust, 1989–90. Governor, BBC, 1982–87. Pro-Vice-Chancellor, Univ. of Oxford, 1985–89. Trustee: Royal Armouries Develt Trust; Jardine Educnl Trust. MRSA. Hon. LLD Bristol, 1988. *Recreations:* good talk, politics, and difficult places. *Address:* House of Lords, SW1A 0PW. *Clubs:* United Oxford & Cambridge University, Naval and Military, Commonwealth Trust, Special Forces.

PARK, Andrew Edward Wilson, QC 1978; a Recorder, since 1989; *b* 27 Jan. 1939; *m* 1962, Ann Margaret Woodhead; two *s* one *d* (and one *s* decd). *Educ:* Leeds Grammar Sch.; University Coll., Oxford. Winter Williams Law Schol., 1959; BA (Jurisp.) 1960, MA 1964. Various academic posts in UK and abroad, 1960–68. Called to the Bar, Lincoln's Inn, 1964, Bencher, 1986; practice at Revenue Bar, 1965–; Chairman: Taxation and Retirement Benefits Cttee of the Bar Council, 1978–82; Revenue Bar Assoc., 1987–; Treasurer, Senate of the Inns of Court and Bar, 1982–85. *Publications:* The Sources of Nigerian Law, 1963; various articles, notes and reviews in legal periodicals, mainly concerning taxation. *Recreations:* squash, tennis. *Address:* Blandford Cottage, Weston Green Road, Thames Ditton, Surrey KT7 0HX. *T:* 081–398 5349; Gray's Inn Chambers, Gray's Inn, WC1R 5JA. *T:* 071–242 2642.

PARK, George Maclean; *b* 27 Sept. 1914; *s* of James McKenzie Park and Mary Gorman Park; *m* 1941, Joyce, *d* of Robert Holt Stead and Gertrude Stead; one *d*. *Educ:* Onslow Drive Sch., Glasgow; Coventry Techn. College. Sen. AEU Shop Steward, Chrysler UK Ltd, Ryton, 1968–73. Coventry City Councillor, 1961–74; Coventry District Councillor, 1973–74; Leader of Council Labour Gp, 1967–74; W Mids Metropolitan CC, 1973–77; Chm. Coventry and District Disablement Adv. Cttee, 1960–74; Leader, Coventry City and District Councils, 1972–74; Chm. Policy Adv. Cttee, 1972–74. MP (Lab) Coventry North East, Feb. 1974–1987. PPS to Dr J. Gilbert, Minister for Transport, 1975–76; PPS to E. Varley, Sec. of State for Industry, 1976–79. Chm., W Midland Regional Council of the Labour Party, 1983–84. Chairman: Coventry Mental Health Assoc. (MIND), 1987–88; Coventry CHC, 1990– (Mem., 1987–; Vice-Chm., 1989–90). Chm. Belgrade Theatre Trust, 1972–74. JP Coventry, 1961–84. AEU Award of Merit, 1967. *Recreations:* reading, walking. *Address:* 170 Binley Road, Coventry CV3 1HG. *T:* Coventry (0203) 458589.

PARK, Hon. Sir Hugh (Eames), Kt 1965; Judge of the High Court of Justice, Queen's Bench Division, 1973–85 (Family Division, 1965–73); retired; *b* 24 April 1910; *er s* of late William Robert and Helen Beatrice Park; *m* 1938, Beryl Josephine, *d* of late Joseph and Margery Coombe; three *d*. *Educ:* Blundell's; Sidney Sussex Coll., Cambridge (Hon. Fellow, 1968). Called to the Bar, Middle Temple, 1936; QC 1960; Bencher, 1965. Member Western Circuit. Served War, 1940–45; Sqdn Leader, 1945. Recorder of Penzance, 1959–60; of Exeter, 1960–64; of Southampton, 1964–65. Member, Court of Exeter Univ., 1961; Member, Board of Governors, Blundell's Sch., 1961–81. Commn of Assize, North East Circuit, 1963; Judge of the Courts of Appeal, Channel Islands, 1964–65; Chairman, County of Devon Quarter Sessions, 1964–71; Deputy Chairman, Cornwall County Quarter Sessions, 1959–71; Presiding Judge, Western Circuit, 1970–75. Hon. LLD Exeter, 1984. *Recreation:* fishing. *Address:* 34 Ordnance Hill, St John's Wood, NW8 6PU. *T:* 071–586 0417; 1 Church Street, Gorran Haven, Cornwall PL26 6JH. *T:* Mevagissey (0726) 842333.
See also C. O. Hum.

PARK, Ian Grahame; Managing Director, Northcliffe Newspapers Group Ltd, since 1982; Director, Associated Newspaper Holdings plc, since 1983; *b* 15 May 1935; *s* of William Park and Christina (*née* Scott); *m* 1965, Anne Turner; one *s*. *Educ:* Lancaster Royal Grammar Sch.; Queens' Coll., Cambridge. 1st Bn Manchester Regt, Berlin (Nat. Service Commn), 1954–56. Trainee Journalist, Press and Journal, Aberdeen, 1959; Asst Lit. Editor, Sunday Times, 1960–63; various management posts, Thomson Newspapers, 1963–65; Liverpool Daily Post and Echo, 1965–, Man. Dir and Editor in Chief, 1972–82. Mem. Council, Newspaper Soc., 1967– (Pres., 1980–81); Dir, Press Assoc., 1973–83 (Chm., 1978–79 and 1979–80); Dir, Reuters, 1978–82, 1988–. Mem. Newspaper Panel, Monopolies and Mergers Commn, 1986–. Dir, Radio City (Sound of Merseyside Ltd), 1973–82; Dir, Liverpool Playhouse, 1973–80; Trustee, Blue Coat Soc. of Arts, Liverpool, 1973–82. FRSA. *Recreations:* eighteenth-century English pottery, twentieth-century English pictures. *Address:* 31 John Street, WC1N 2QB. *Club:* Reform.

PARK, (Ian) Michael (Scott), CBE 1982; Consultant, Paull & Williamsons, Advocates, Aberdeen, since 1991 (Partner, 1964–91); *b* 7 April 1938; *m* 1964, Elizabeth Mary Lamberton Struthers; two *s*. *Educ:* Aberdeen Grammar Sch.; Aberdeen Univ. (MA, LLB). Admitted Mem. Soc. of Advocates, Aberdeen, 1962. Law Society of Scotland: Mem. Council, 1974–85; Vice-Pres., 1979–80; Pres., 1980–81. Chm., Aberdeen Citizens Advice Bureau, 1976–88; Mem., Criminal Injuries Compensation Bd, 1983–. Frequent broadcaster on legal topics. *Recreations:* golf, gardening. *Address:* Beechwood, 46 Rubislaw Den South, Aberdeen AB2 6AX. *T:* Aberdeen (0224) 313799. *Club:* New (Edinburgh).

PARK, Dame Kiri; *see* Te Kanawa, Dame K.

PARK, Dame Merle (Florence), (Dame Merle Bloch), DBE 1986 (CBE 1974); Principal, Royal Ballet; Director, Royal Ballet School, since 1983; *b* Salisbury, S Rhodesia, 8 Oct. 1937; *d* of P. J. Park, Eastlea, Salisbury, S Rhodesia, C Africa; *m* 1st, 1965, James Monahan, CBE (marr. diss. 1970; he *d* 1985); one *s*; 2nd, 1971, Sidney Bloch. *Educ:* Elmhurst Ballet Sch. Founder, Ballet Sch., St Peter's Sq., W6, 1977–83. Joined Sadler's Wells Ballet, 1955; first rôle, a Mouse (Sleeping Beauty prologue); first solo, Milkmaid (Façzce); principal soloist, 1959. First danced: Blue Bird (Act III, Sleeping Beauty), 1956; Swanhilda (Coppelia), Mamzelle Angot (Mamzelle Angot), 1958; Lise (Fille Mal Gardée), 1960; Cinderella, 1962; Juliet (Romeo and Juliet), 1965; Giselle, Celestial (Shadow Play), 1967; Clara (Nutcracker), Aurora (Sleeping Beauty), 1968; Odette (Swan Lake), 1971; A Walk to Paradise Garden, 1972; Firebird, Odette/Odile (Swan Lake), Dances at a Gathering, 1973; Manon, Emilia (The Moor's Pavane), Aureole, Terpsichore (Apollo), Elite Syncopations, 1974; Lulu, 1976; Kate (The Taming of the Shrew), La Bayadère, Tuesday's Child (Jazz Calendar), Triad, Symphonic Variations, Waltzes of Spring (in Royal Opera Fledermaus), Le Papillon, 1977; Countess Larisch (Mayerling), 1978; La Fin du Jour, 1979; Mary Vetsera (Mayerling), Natalia (A Month in the Country), Adieu, 1980; Chloë (Daphnis and Chloë), Isadora, 1981; Raymonda, 1983. Queen Elizabeth Award, Royal Acad. of Dancing, 1982. *Recreations:* gardening, reading. *Address:* c/o Royal Ballet School, 144 Talgarth Road, W14.

PARK, Michael; *see* Park, I. M. S.

PARK, Trevor; Lecturer in Industrial Relations, 1972–86 and Senior Fellow, 1983–86, Department of Adult Education and Extramural Studies, University of Leeds; *b* 12 Dec. 1927; *s* of late Stephen Clifford Park and Annie Park (*née* Jackson); *m* 1953, Barbara Black; no *c*. *Educ:* Bury Grammar Sch.; Manchester Univ. (MA). History Master, Bacup and Rawtenstall Grammar Sch., 1949–56; WEA, Tutor and Organiser (NW District), 1956–60; Lecturer, Extramural Dept, Univ. of Sheffield (politics and internat. relations), 1960–64; WEA Tutor and Organiser, Manchester, 1970–72. Parliamentary Labour Candidate: Altrincham and Sale, General Election, 1955; Darwen, General Election, 1959; MP (Lab) South East Derbyshire, 1964–70. Mem. (Lab) Leeds CC, 1979–86 (Chairman: Mun. Services Cttee, 1980–83; Planning and Develt Cttee, 1983–86). Member: TGWU; Select Cttees on Nationalised Industries, 1966–68, and on Education and Science, 1968–70; Yorkshire and Humberside Economic Planning Council, 1977–79. Chm. ATAE, 1972–75. *Recreation:* walking.

PARKE, Prof. Dennis Vernon William, PhD, DSc; CChem, FRSC, FIBiol, FRCPath; (first) Professor and Head of Department of Biochemistry, University of Surrey, 1967–87; University Professor of Biochemistry, 1986–90; Emeritus Professor, since 1990; *b* London, 15 Nov. 1922; *e s* of William Parke and Florence Parke; *m* 1943, Doreen Joan Dunn; two *s* one *d*. *Educ:* West Ham Municipal Secondary Sch. (Gurney Scholar); Chelsea and University Colls, Univ. of London 1940–48; St Mary's Hosp. Med. Sch., London (PhD DSc). War Service, RA RAMC, 1942–47. Head, Dept of Microbiol Chem., Glaxo Labs Ltd, 1948–49; St Mary's Hosp. Med. Sch., Univ. of London: Res. Asst to Prof. R. T. Williams, FRS, 1949–52; Lectr in Biochem., 1952–58, Sen. Lectr, 1958–62; Reader in Biochem., 1962–67; Dean, Faculty of Biol and Chem. Sciences, Univ. of Surrey, 1971–75. Visiting Professor: Univ. of Calif, Davis, 1978; Edmonton, Canada, 1984. Sometime Examnr, Univs of Dublin (Trinity), Edinburgh, Glasgow, Liverpool, London, Newcastle upon Tyne, Reading, Strathclyde, Wales, Auckland, Ibadan, Nairobi, Singapore, Sydney and Wellington. Sigma Xi Lectr, Univ. of Calif (Davis), 1978. Member: Cttee on Safety of Drugs, 1968–70; Cttee on Safety of Medicines, 1970–83; Cttee on Med. Aspects of Chemicals in Food and Environment, DHSS, 1972–86; Food Additives and Contaminants Cttee, MAFF, 1972–80; WHO Expert Panel on Food Additives, 1975–88; WHO Sci. Gp on Toxicity Evaluation of Chemicals, 1975; WHO Cons. in Indust. Toxicol., 1974, 1979, 1981, 1983; Sci. Dir, NATO Workshop on Ecotoxicology, July-Aug. 1977; Consultant to Environmental Protection Agency, Washington, 1985. Dir, Food and Veterinary Labs Ltd, 1988–. Mem., Internat. Acad. of Environmental Safety. Scheele Lectr and Medal, Uppsala, 1989. Hon. MRCP 1985; Hon. Mem., Polish Soc. of Toxicology, 1984; Hon. Fellow, Polish Soc. of Occupational Medicine, 1984. Editor, Xenobiotica, 1970–. *Publications:* The Biochemistry of Foreign Compounds, 1968; (ed) Enzyme Induction, 1975; Drug Metabolism from Microbe to Man, 1977; Mucus in Health and Disease, 1977; Immunotoxicology, 1983; The Future of Predictive Safety Evaluation, 1987; chapters in books and res. papers in biochem., pharm. and med. jls. *Recreations:* landscape gardening, music. *Address:* Trevelen, Poyle Road, Guildford, Surrey. *T:* Guildford (0483) 573667. *Club:* Athenæum.

PARKER, family name of **Earls of Macclesfield** and **Morley.**

PARKER, Viscount; Richard Timothy George Mansfield Parker; *b* 31 May 1943; *s* and *heir* of 8th Earl of Macclesfield, *qv*; *m* 1967, Tatiana Cleone, *d* of Major Craig Wheaton-Smith; three *d* (including twins); *m* 1986, Mrs Sandra Hope Mead. *Educ:* Stowe; Worcester Coll., Oxford. *Address:* Portobello Farm, Shirburn, Watlington, Oxon.

PARKER, A(gnes) Miller, RE; Artist and Wood-engraver; *b* Irvine, Ayrshire, 25 March 1895; *d* of William McCall and Agnes Mitchell Parker; *m* 1918, William McCance, Artist (marr. diss. 1963, and she legally assumed maiden name); no *c*. *Educ:* Glasgow School of Art (Diploma, Haldane Scholar). Instructress, Glasgow School of Art, 1918–20; Art Mistress, Maltmans Green School, Gerrards Cross, 1920–28; Art Mistress, Clapham High School and Training Coll., 1928–30; Walter Brewster Prize, 1st International Exhibition of Engraving and Lithography, Chicago, 1929; Wood-engraver to Gregynog Press, Newtown, Montgomeryshire, 1930–33. *Publications:* Chief Illustrated Editions; Esopes Fables by Caxton, 1931; Daisy Matthews and three other tales by Rhys Davies, 1932; XXI Welsh Gypsy Folk-Tales, collected by John Sampson, 1933; The House with the Apricot by H. E. Bates, 1933; Forest Giant-translated from the French by J. H. Ross (Colonel T. E. Lawrence), 1935; Through the Woods by H. E. Bates, 1936; Down the River by H. E. Bates, 1937; Gray's Elegy written in a Country Church-yard (Limited Editions Club of NY), 1938; Richard II-Shakespeare (Limited Editions Club of NY), 1940; A Shropshire Lad by A. E. Housman, 1940; The Return of the Native by Thomas Hardy (Limited Editions Club of NY), 1942; Essays in Russet by Herbert Furst, 1944; Spring of the Year by Richard Jefferies, 1946; The Life of the Fields, 1947, Field and Hedgerow, 1948, The Open Air, 1948, The Old House at Coate, 1948, by Richard Jefferies; Animals Under the Rainbow by Aloysius Roche, 1952; The Faerie Queene by Edmund Spenser, vols I and II, 1953; Lucifer by J. C. Powys, 1956; Tess of the D'Urbervilles, 1956, and Far From the Madding Crowd, 1958, by Thomas Hardy (New York); The Tragedies of Shakespeare (New York), 1959; The Mayor of Casterbridge by Thomas Hardy (Limited Editions Club of NY), 1964; Poems of Shakespeare (Limited Editions Club of NY), 1967; Jude the Obscure by Thomas Hardy (Limited Editions Club of NY), 1969. *Recreations:* fishing and cats.

PARKER, Alan William; film director and writer; *b* 14 Feb. 1944; *s* of William and Elsie Parker; *m* 1966, Annie Inglis; three *s* one *d*. *Educ:* Owen's Sch., Islington. Advertising Copywriter, 1965–67; Television Commercials Director, 1968–78. Wrote screenplay, Melody, 1969; wrote and directed: No Hard Feelings, 1972; Our Cissy, 1973; Footsteps, 1973; Bugsy Malone, 1975; A Turnip Head's Guide to the British Cinema, 1985; Angel Heart, 1987; Come See the Paradise, 1990; directed: The Evacuees, 1974; Midnight Express, 1977; Fame, 1979; Shoot the Moon, 1981; The Wall, 1982; Birdy, 1984; Mississippi Burning, 1989; The Commitments, 1991. Vice-Chm., Directors Guild of Great Britain, 1982–; Mem., British Screen Adv. Council, 1985–. BAFTA Michael Balcon Award for Outstanding Contribution to British Film, 1985. *Publications: novels:* Bugsy Malone, 1976; Puddles in the Lane, 1977; *cartoon:* Hares in the Gate, 1983.

PARKER, Cameron Holdsworth; Managing Director, Lithgows Ltd, since 1984; *b* 14 April 1932; *s* of George Cameron Parker and Mary Stevenson Parker; *m* 1st, 1957, Elizabeth Margaret Thomson (*d* 1985); three *s*; 2nd, 1986, Marlyne Honeyman, Mem. Stock Exchange. *Educ:* Morrison's Acad., Crieff; Glasgow Univ. (BSc Hons). John G. Kincaid & Co. Ltd, Greenock: Asst Manager, 1958; Asst Gen. Man., 1961; Dir, 1963; Man. Dir, 1967; Chm., 1976; Chm. and Chief Exec., Scott Lithgow Ltd, Port Glasgow, 1980–83. Bd Mem., British Shipbuilders, 1977–80, 1981–83. Chairman, 1984–: Campbeltown Shipyard Ltd; J. Fleming Engrg Ltd; Glasgow Iron & Steel Co. Ltd; Landcatch Ltd; Lithgow Electronics Ltd; Malakoff & Wm Moore Ltd; McKinlay & Blair Ltd; Prosper Engrg Ltd; Dir, Lithgows Pty Ltd. Mem. Scottish Council, CBI, 1986–. Mem., Argyll and Clyde Health Bd, 1991–. Freeman, City of London, 1981; Liveryman, Worshipful Co. of Shipwrights, 1981–. *Recreation:* golf. *Address:* Heath House, Rowantreehill Road, Kilmacolm, Renfrewshire PA13 4PE. *T:* Kilmacolm (050587) 3197. *Club:* Caledonian.

PARKER, Christopher William Oxley, MA; JP; DL; *b* 28 May 1920; *s* of late Lieut-Col John Oxley Parker, TD, and Mary Monica (*née* Hills); *m* 1947, Jocelyn Frances Adeline, *d* of late Colonel C. G. Arkwright, Southern Rhodesia; one *s* two *d*. *Educ:* Eton; Trinity Coll., Oxford. Served War of 1939–45, 147th Field Regt (Essex Yeomanry) RA, 1939–42. Director: Strutt and Parker (Farms) Ltd; Lord Rayleighs Farm Inc.; Local Dir, Chelmsford Bd, Barclays Bank, 1951–83. Mem., Nat. Trust Properties Cttee, 1974–89; Mem. Exec. Cttee, CLA, 1959–73; Pres., Essex CLA, 1987–. JP Essex, 1952; High Sheriff of Essex, 1961; DL Essex 1972. *Recreations:* shooting, golf; estate management. *Address:* Faulkbourne Hall, Witham, Essex CM8 1SP. *T:* Witham (0376) 513385. *Club:* Boodle's.

PARKER, Clifford Frederick, MA, LLB Cantab; JP; Bracton Professor of Law at the University of Exeter, 1957–85 (Deputy Vice-Chancellor, 1963–65, Public Orator, 1977–81); *b* 6 March 1920; *yr s* of late Frederick James Parker and Bertha Isabella (*née* Kemp), Cardiff; *m* 1945, Christine Alice (*née* Knowles); two *d*. *Educ:* Cardiff High Sch.; Gonville and Caius Coll., Cambridge. Royal Air Force, 1940–43. Solicitor of Supreme Court, 1947. Lecturer in Common Law, University of Birmingham, 1951–57; Senior Tutor and Asst Director of Legal Studies, Faculty of Law, University of Birmingham, 1956–57. Pres., Soc. of Public Teachers of Law, 1974–75. Chm., Exeter Area, Supplementary Benefit Appeal Tribunal, 1978–. JP Devon, 1969. *Publications:* contrib. to legal periodicals. *Recreation:* touring. *Address:* Lynwood, Exton, Exeter EX3 0PR. *T:* Exeter (0392) 874051.

PARKER, (Diana) Jean, CBE 1989; Chairman, North Lincolnshire Health Authority, 1987–90; *b* 7 June 1932; *d* of Lewis William Reeve Morley and Amy (*née* Southwood); *m* 1959, Dudley Frost Parker (*d* 1971); one *s* one *d*. *Educ:* Kesteven and Grantham Girls' Sch.; Birmingham Univ. (BCom). CBIM 1986. Director: Vacu-Lug Traction Tyres Ltd, 1957–; Central Independent Television Plc, 1982–; British Steel (Industry) Ltd, 1986–90. Mem. Bd, E Midlands Electricity, 1983–90; Mem., E Midlands Adv. Bd, National Westminster Bank, 1985–; Chm., Lincs Jt Develt Cttee, 1983–; Chm., CBI Smaller Firms Council, 1986–88. Non-exec. Dir, Lincs Ambulance and Health Service Trust, 1991–. *Address:* 93 Manthorpe Road, Grantham, Lincs NG31 8DE. *T:* Grantham (0476) 62424. *Club:* University Women's.

PARKER, Sir Douglas D.; *see* Dodds-Parker.

PARKER, Rear-Adm. Douglas Granger, CB 1971; DSO 1945; DSC 1945; AFC 1952; Assistant Chief of Naval Staff (Operations and Air), 1969–71, retired; *b* 21 Nov. 1919; *s* of R. K. Parker; *m* 1953, Margaret Susan, *d* of late Col W. Cooper; one *s* one *d*. *Educ:* W Hartlepool Technical Coll. Joined Royal Navy, 1940; Command Fleet Air Arm Fighter Squadrons, 1948–51; Commanded: HMS Cavendish, 1961–62; RN Air Station, Lossiemouth, 1965–67; HMS Hermes, 1967–69. Captain 1959; Rear-Adm. 1969. *Address:* High Meadow, Walhampton, Lymington, Hants. *T:* Lymington (0590) 73259. *Club:* Royal Lymington Yacht.

PARKER, Sir Eric (Wilson), Kt 1991; FCA; Chief Executive, since 1983, and Deputy Chairman, since 1988, Trafalgar House PLC; *b* 8 June 1933; *s* of Wilson Parker and Edith Gladys (*née* Wellings); *m* 1955, Marlene Teresa (*née* Neale); two *s* two *d*. *Educ:* The Priory Grammar Sch. for Boys, Shrewsbury. FCA 1967 (ACA 1956); CBIM 1983. Articled Clerk with Wheeler, Whittingham & Kent, Shrewsbury, 1950–55; National Service, Pay Corps, 1956–58; Taylor Woodrow Gp, 1958–64; Trafalgar House Gp, 1965–: Finance/Admin Dir, 1969; Dep. Man. Dir, 1973; Gp Man. Dir, 1977; Dir, Associated Container Transportation (Aust.), 1983–. Non-Executive Director: European Assets Trust NV, 1972–85; Sealink UK Ltd, 1979–81; British Rail Investments Ltd, 1980–84; Evening Standard Co. Ltd, 1982–85; Touche Remnant Hldgs Ltd, 1985–89; MB-Caradon plc (formerly Metal Box plc, then MB Group), 1985–; The Royal Automobile Club (formerly The Automobile Pty Ltd), 1986–; Hardy Oil & Gas plc, 1989–. FRSA 1983. *Recreations:* sports (including golf and horseracing), wines. *Address:* Trafalgar House, 1 Berkeley Street, W1A 1BY; Crimbourne House, Wisborough Green, Billingshurst, W Sussex. *Clubs:* Royal Automobile, MCC; Tyrrell's Wood Golf (Leatherhead).

PARKER, Frederick John, (Jack), FICE, FIStructE, FIHT; Chief Highway Engineer (Under Secretary), Department of Transport, 1988–91; *b* 6 Sept. 1927; *s* of Charles Fred Parker and Eleanor Emily (*née* Wright); *m* 1955, Ann Shirley Newnham; three *d*. *Educ:* Shene Grammar School; Univ. of Liverpool (BEng 1948; MEng 1951). Engineer with Scott, Wilson, Kirkpatrick & Partners in London, Hong Kong and elsewhere, 1952–65; Sen. Engineer, then Partner, with Husband & Co., 1965–78; Director, W. S. Atkins & Partners, 1978–88. Institution of Highways and Transportation: Chm., Greater London Br., 1975–77; Vice-Pres., 1985; Pres., 1988. Mem., Transportation Group Bd, ICE, 1983–86; Vice-Chm., Brit. Nat. Cttee of Permanent Internat. Assoc of Road Congresses, 1988. *Publications:* professional papers in engineering jls. *Recreations:* athletics (Olympics 1952 and 1956, European silver medallist 1954); local affairs, music. *Address:* 43 York Avenue, East Sheen, SW14 7LQ. *T:* 081–876 1059. *Club:* South London Harriers.

PARKER, Geoffrey; *see* Parker, N. G.

PARKER, Prof. Geoffrey Alan, FRS 1989; Professor in the Department of Environmental and Evolutionary Biology, University of Liverpool, since 1989; *b* 24 May 1944; *s* of late Dr Alan Parker and of G. Ethel Parker (*née* Hill); *m* 1967, Susan Mary Wallis; one *s* one *d*. *Educ:* Stockton Heath Primary Sch.; Lymm Grammar Sch.; Univ. of Bristol (BSc (1st Cl. Hons Zoology); PhD); Univ. of Cambridge (MA). Asst Lectr 1968, Lectr 1969, Sen. Lectr 1976, Reader 1980, Univ. of Liverpool. Fellow of King's Coll., Cambridge, 1978–79; Nuffield Sci. Res. Fellow, 1982–83; SERC Sen. Res. Fellow, 1990–. *Publications:* many scientific papers in learned jls. *Recreations:* playing jazz in local bands (clarinet), mainly Dixieland; breeding, showing and judging exhibition bantams (Hon. Sec./Treasurer, Partridge Wyandotte Club, 1987–; Mem. Council, Poultry Club, 1986–90). *Address:* Saunton, The Runnel, Neston, South Wirral, Cheshire L64 3TG. *T:* 051–336 4202.

PARKER, Geoffrey John, CBE 1985; Chairman and Chief Executive, Maritime Transport Services Ltd, since 1989; *b* 20 March 1937; *s* of Stanley John Parker and Alice Ellen Parker; *m* 1957, Hazel Mary Miall; two *s* two *d*. *Educ:* County Grammar Sch., Hendon. Commercial Dir, Townsend Car Ferries Ltd, 1972–74; Man. Dir, Atlantic Steam Navigation Co., 1974–87; Man. Dir, 1976–87, Chm., 1983–87, Felixstowe Dock & Rly Co.; Chairman: Larne Harbour Bd, 1983–87; European Ferries PLC, 1986–87; Chief Exec., Highland Participants, 1987–89. Mem., Nat. Bus Co., 1980–87. FCIT 1982. *Recreation:* golf. *Address:* 101 Valley Road, Ipswich, Suffolk IP1 4NF. *T:* Ipswich (0473) 216003. *Club:* Ipswich Golf (Purdis Heath, Ipswich).

PARKER, Herbert John Harvey; *see* Parker, John.

PARKER, Hugh; Chairman, Corporate Renewal Associates Ltd, since 1989; Director, VSEL (Vickers Shipbuilding & Engineering) PLC, since 1986; *b* 12 June 1919; *s* of Ross Parker and Ruth Baker Parker; *m* 1957, Elsa del Carmen Mijares Osorio; one *s* one *d*. *Educ:* Tabor Academy; Trinity Hall, Cambridge; Massachusetts Inst. of Technology. North Carolina Shipbuilding Co., 1941–43; General Electric Co., 1945–46; Ludlow

Manufacturing Co., 1947–50; McKinsey & Co. Inc., 1951–84 (Sen. Dir, 1974–84). Pres., American Chamber of Commerce (UK), 1976–79. Pres., MIT Alumni Club of GB, 1962–84. Governor, Ditchley Foundn. *Publications:* Letters to a New Chairman, 1979; numerous articles on management. *Recreations:* reading, sculling, cooking. *Address:* 9 Cheyne Walk, SW3 5QZ. *Clubs:* The Pilgrims, United Oxford & Cambridge University; Leander; Racquet and Tennis (New York); Eastern Yacht (Mass).

PARKER, Jack; *see* Parker, F. J.

PARKER, James Geoffrey; High Master, Manchester Grammar School, since 1985; *b* 27 March 1933; *s* of late Ian Sutherland Parker and Kathleen Lilian Parker; *m* 1956, Ruth Major; two *d*. *Educ:* Alderman Newton's Sch., Leicester; Christ's Coll., Cambridge (Exhibnr); Wadham Coll., Oxford. National Service, RA, 1954–56. Asst Master, Bedford Modern Sch., 1957–66; Head of History Dept, Tonbridge Sch., 1966–75; Headmaster, Queen Elizabeth Grammar Sch., Wakefield, 1975–85. Chm., HMC, 1991. *Recreation:* sailing. *Address:* 143 Old Hall Lane, Manchester M14 6HL. *T:* 061–224 3929.

PARKER, James Mavin, (Jim Parker); composer and conductor; *b* Hartlepool, 18 Dec. 1934; *s* of James Robertson Parker and Margaret Mavin; *m* 1969, Pauline George; two *d*; one *d* by a previous marriage. *Educ:* various grammar schools; Guildhall Sch. of Music (AGSM 1959; Silver Medal; Hon. GSM 1986). LRAM 1959. Professional oboeist, 1959; joined the Barrow Poets, 1963. Wrote musical settings of Sir John Betjeman's poems, Banana Blush, 1973 (recorded these and subsequent settings with Sir John as speaker); wrote music for Chichester Theatre, 1974–77; music for television and films, 1977–, includes: Credo; Another Six English Towns; Good Behaviour; Wynne and Penkovsky; Mapp and Lucia; Time After Time; Betjeman's Britain; Late Flowering Love; The Miser; España Viva; The Blot (silent film made in 1921); Wish Me Luck; House of Cards; Parnell and the Englishwoman. *Compositions* include: with William Bealby-Wright: Moonshine Rock, 1972; Mister Skillicorn Dances, 1974; with Cicely Herbert: Mayhew's London, 1978; La Comédie Humaine, 1986; (with John Betjeman) Poems (ballet), 1981; In The Gold Room (words by Oscar Wilde), 1983; (with Jeremy Lloyd) The Woodland Gospels, 1984, re-written as Heaven's Up, 1990; Lullingstone (for concert band), 1985; (with John Edmunds) Pelican Five, 1986; Mississippi Five (woodwind quintet), 1991. Recordings with Barrow Poets, Keith Michell, Peter Sellers, Harry Secombe, Twiggy, etc. *Publications:* (with Wally K. Daly) Follow the Star, 1975; (with Jeremy Lloyd) Captain Beaky, 1977; with Tom Stanier: The Shepherd King, 1979; The Burning Bush, 1980; All Aboard, 1983; Blast Off, 1986; A Londoner in New York (suite for brass), 1986; (with Tom Stanier and Chris Ellis) BabylonTimes, 1988; English Towns (for flute and piano), 1988. *Recreations:* tennis, literature, 20th Century art. *Address:* 19 Laurel Road, Barnes, SW13 0EE. *T:* 081–876 8571.

PARKER, James Roland Walter, CMG 1978; OBE 1968; HM Diplomatic Service, retired; Governor and Commander-in-Chief, Falkland Islands and Dependencies, and High Commissioner, British Antarctic Territory, 1976–80; *b* 20 Dec. 1919; *s* of late Alexander Roland Parker, ISM; *m* 1941, Deirdre Mary Ward. Served War of 1939–45: 1st London Scottish, 1940–41. Ministry of Labour, 1938–57; Labour Attaché, Tel Aviv, 1957–60; Labour Adviser: Accra, 1960–62; Lagos, 1962–64; seconded to Foreign Office, 1965–66; Dep. High Comr, Enugu, 1966–67; Commonwealth Office (later FCO), 1968–70; Head of Chancery, Suva, Fiji, 1970–71; High Comr in The Gambia, 1972–75; Consul-Gen., Durban, 1976. *Address:* Crockers Hill, Yarlington, Somerset BA9 8DJ; 1 St Edmund's Court, NW8 7QL.

PARKER, Jean; *see* Parker, D. J.

PARKER, John; *see* Parker, T. J.

PARKER, Sir John; *see* Parker, Sir W. J.

PARKER, Comdr (John) Michael (Avison), CVO 1957 (MVO 1953); RN (retired); *b* 23 June 1920; *s* of late Capt. C. A. Parker, CBE, Royal Australian Navy, Melbourne; *m* 1st, 1943, Eileen Margaret Anne (*née* Allan) (marr. diss. 1958); one *s* one *d*; 2nd, 1962, Carol (marr. diss.; she *d* 1977); one *d* (one *s* decd); 3rd, 1976, Mrs Jean Lavinia Grice Ramsay. *Educ:* Xavier College, Melbourne, Australia. Royal Navy, 1938–47. Equerry-in-Waiting to Princess Elizabeth and the Duke of Edinburgh, 1947–52; Private Sec. to Duke of Edinburgh, 1947–57. Dir., Brain Behavioural Res. Cttee, La Trobe Univ., 1984–. Chm., Australian Dredging and Gen. Services Co., 1987–. Member: Aust.-Britain Soc. (Vice-Pres.); Navy League; RSL; Australian Ballet Trust; Chm. of Trustees, Melbourne Maritime Trust; Trustee: World Wildlife Australia; The World Ship Trust (UK). Chm., Plain English Speaking Award, Aust. *Recreations:* painting, tennis, golf, sailing. *Address:* Santosa, 33 Albany Road, Toorak, Vic 3142, Australia; Lapwing, Robe, SA 5276, Australia. *Clubs:* Melbourne; Sandringham Yacht (Melbourne); Robe Golf (SA).

PARKER, Jonathan Frederic; QC 1979; Attorney General of the Duchy of Lancaster, since 1989; a Recorder, since 1989; *b* 8 Dec. 1937; *s* of late Sir (Walter) Edmund Parker, CBE and late Elizabeth Mary Butterfield; *m* 1967, Maria-Belen Burns; three *s* one *d*. *Educ:* Winchester College; Magdalene College, Cambridge (MA). Called to Bar, Inner Temple, 1962, Bencher, 1985; practising member of the Bar, 1962–. *Recreations:* painting, gardening. *Address:* 11 Old Square, Lincoln's Inn, WC2A 3TS. *T:* 071–430 0341. *Club:* Garrick.

PARKER, Sir Karl (Theodore), Kt 1960; CBE 1954; MA, PhD; FBA 1950; Hon. DLitt Oxon, 1972; Hon. Antiquary to the Royal Academy, 1963; Hon. Fellow, Oriel College, Oxford; Trustee, National Gallery, 1962–69; Keeper of the Ashmolean Museum, Oxford, 1945–62 (retired); Keeper of the Department of Fine Art, Ashmolean Museum, and of the Hope Collection of Engraved Portraits, 1934–62; *b* 1895; *s* of late R. W. Parker, FRCS, and Marie Luling; *m* Audrey (*d* 1976), *d* of late Henry Ashworth James, of Hurstmonceux Place; two *d*. *Educ:* Bedford; Paris; Zürich. Studied art at most continental centres and at the British Museum; edited Old Master Drawings, a Quarterly Magazine for Students and Collectors, since its inception, 1926; late Asst Keeper, Dept of Prints and Drawings, British Museum. *Publications:* North Italian Drawings of the Quattrocento; Drawings of the Early German Schools; Alsatian Drawings of the XV and XVI Centuries; Drawings of Antoine Watteau; Catalogue of Drawings in the Ashmolean Museum, Vol. I, 1938, Vol. II, 1956; Catalogue of Holbein's Drawings at Windsor Castle, 1945; The Drawings of Antonio Canaletto at Windsor Castle, 1948; Antoine Watteau: Catalogue Complet de son œuvre Dessiné, Vol. I (with J. Mathey), 1957, Vol. II, 1958; and articles, mostly on Old Master drawings, in various English and continental periodicals. *Address:* 4 Saffrons Court, Compton Place Road, Eastbourne.

PARKER, Keith John; Editor, Express and Star, Wolverhampton, since 1977; *b* 30 Dec. 1940; *s* of Sydney John Parker and Phyllis Mary Parker; *m* 1962, Marilyn Ann Edwards; one *s*. Various editorial appointments; Editor, Shropshire Star, 1972–77. Pres., Guild of British Newspaper Editors, 1987–88 (Vice-Pres., 1986–87); Mem., Assoc. of British Editors. FRSA. *Recreations:* reading, travel. *Address:* 94 Wrottesley Road, Tettenhall, Wolverhampton, West Midlands WV6 8SJ. *T:* Wolverhampton (0902) 758595.

PARKER, Kenneth Alfred Lamport, CB 1959; Receiver for the Metropolitan Police District, 1967–74; *b* 1 April 1912; *e s* of A. E. A. and Ada Mary Parker; *m* 1938, Freda Silcock (OBE 1975); one *s* one *d*. *Educ:* Tottenham Grammar Sch.; St John's College, Cambridge (Scholar; MA 1937). Home Office, 1934; London Civil Defence Region, 1938–45; (Assistant Secretary, 1942, Deputy Chief Administrative Officer, 1943); Assistant Under-Secretary of State, Home Office, 1955–67 (Head of Police Dept, 1961–66). Imperial Defence College, 1947. Mem., Chairman's Panel, CS Selection Bd, 1974–82. *Publications:* articles on police matters. *Recreations:* garden, cellar, library. *Address:* 18 Lichfield Road, Kew, Surrey TW9 3JR. *T:* 081–940 4595. *Club:* United Oxford & Cambridge University.

PARKER, Margaret Annette McCrie Johnston, (Margaret Johnston); actress; *d* of James and Emily Dalrymple Johnston; *m* 1946, Albert E. W. Parker (*d* 1974). *Educ:* North Sydney and Neutral Bay High School; Sydney University, Australia. Student, RADA; studied with Dr Stefan Hock; in repertory and acted as understudies. *Plays:* Murder without Crime, 1943; Fifth Column, 1944; Last of Summer, 1944; Time of Your Life, 1946; Shouting Dies, 1946; Barretts of Wimpole Street, 1947; Always Afternoon, 1949; Summer and Smoke, 1950; Second Threshold, 1951; The Dark is Light Enough, 1954; Sugar in the Morning, 1959; The Ring of Truth, 1959; Masterpiece, 1961. Stratford Memorial Theatre, 1956 season: Othello, The Merchant of Venice, Measure for Measure; Chichester Festival Theatre, 1966 Season: Lady Macbeth. *Films:* Rake's Progress, 1945; Man About the House, 1946; Portrait of Clare, 1949; Magic Box, 1951; Knave of Hearts, 1953; Touch and Go, 1955; Nose on her Face; Life at the Top, 1965; Psychopath; Sebastian. Television plays. *Address:* c/o Al Parker Ltd, 55 Park Lane, W1.

PARKER, Comdr Michael; *see* Parker, Comdr (J.) M. (A.).

PARKER, Michael Clynes, QC 1973; **His Honour Judge Parker;** a Circuit Judge, since 1978; *b* 2 Nov. 1924; *s* of Herbert Parker and Elsie Vera Parker (sometime Pres., NUT); *m* 1950, Molly Leila Franklin; one *s* two *d*. *Educ:* City of London Sch.; Pembroke Coll., Cambridge (BA, LLB). Sec., Cambridge Union, 1943. Flt-Sgt/Air Gunner, RAF, 1943–47. Called to Bar, Gray's Inn, 1949; practised in London and SE Circuit. A Recorder of the Crown Court, 1972–78. Contested (Lab) S Kensington, 1951. *Recreations:* theatre, watching cricket. *Address:* 17 Courtnell Street, W2. *Club:* United Oxford & Cambridge University.

See also B. Tizard.

PARKER, Major Michael John, CVO 1991; MBE 1968; Producer: Royal Tournament, since 1974; Edinburgh Tattoo, since 1991; *b* 21 Sept. 1941; *s* of Capt. S. J. Wilkins and V. S. M. Wilkins (*née* Parker); name changed by Deed Poll, 1959. *Educ:* Dulwich Coll. Prep. Sch.; Hereford Cathedral Sch.; RMA Sandhurst. Captain, Queen's Own Hussars, 1961–71 (produced Berlin Tattoo, 1965, 1967 and 1971); Major, TA, Special List, attached QOH, 1973–. Producer of international events, 1972–: Berlin Tattoo, 1972–88; Aldershot Army Display, 1974–83; Queen's Bonfire, Windsor and others, Queen's Silver Jubilee, 1977; Wembley Musical Pageant, 1979, 1981, 1985; Great Children's Party for Internat. Year of the Child, 1979; Carols for the Queen, 1979; Royal Fireworks (Prince of Wales's wedding), 1981; Heart of the Nation, son et lumière, Horse Guards, 1983, 1985; America's Cup, Newport, 1983; Great St John Party (180,000 children), Hyde Park, 1985; King Hussein of Jordan's 50th Celebration, 1985; Finale, Christmas Horse Show, Olympia, 1986–; Jordanian Royal Wedding, 1987; Coronation Anniversary Celebration, Jordan, 1988; Joy to the World, Royal Albert Hall, 1988–; Royal Equestrian Day, Oman, 1990; Fortress Fantasia, Gibraltar, 1990; Queen Mother's 90th Birthday Celebration, Horse Guards, 1990; Opening Ceremony, World Equestrian Games, 1990; Economic Summit Spectacular, Buckingham Palace, 1991. Vice-Pres., Morriston Orpheus Choir. KStJ 1985 (OStJ 1982). Grand Officer, Order of el Istiqlal (Jordan), 1987. *Publication:* The Awful Troop Leaders Gunnery Crib, 1969. *Recreations:* painting, antiques, giving parties. *Club:* Cavalry and Guards.

PARKER, Michael Joseph Bennett; Managing Director since 1970, and Chairman since 1980, Favor Parker Ltd; *b* 22 June 1931; *s* of Henry Gordon Parker and Alice Rose Parker; *m* 1960, Tania Henrietta Tiarks; two *s* one *d*. *Educ:* Eton; Magdalene Coll., Cambridge (BA Agric., MA). Chm., Sovereign Chicken Gp, 1977–. Chm., Land Settlement Assoc., 1982–85; Mem., UKAEA, 1985–88. *Recreations:* country sports, windsurfing, lying in the sun. *Address:* Gooderstone Manor, King's Lynn, Norfolk. *T:* Gooderstone (036621) 255.

PARKER, Michael St J.; *see* St John Parker.

PARKER, Prof. (Noel) Geoffrey, PhD, LittD; FBA 1984; Charles E. Nowell Distinguished Professor of History, University of Illinois at Urbana-Champaign, since 1986 (Department Chair, 1989–91); *b* 25 Dec. 1943; *s* of late Derek Geoffrey Parker and Kathleen Betsy Symon; *m* 1st, 1965, Angela Maureen Chapman (marr. diss. 1980); one *s* one *d*; 2nd, 1986, Jane Helen Ohlmeyer; one *s*. *Educ:* Nottingham High Sch.; Christ's Coll., Cambridge (BA 1965; MA; PhD 1968; LittD 1981). Fellow of Christ's Coll., Cambridge, 1968–72; Lectr in Mod. Hist., 1972–78, Reader in Mod. Hist., 1978–82, and Prof. of Early Mod. Hist., 1982–86, St Andrews Univ. British Acad. Exchange Fellow, Newberry Library, Chicago, 1981; Visiting Professor: Vrije Universiteit, Brussels, 1975 (Dr phil and letters *hc*, 1990); Univ. of BC, Vancouver, Canada, 1979–80; Keio Univ., Tokyo, 1984. Lees Knowles Lectr in Mil. Hist., Univ. of Cambridge, 1984. Television scripts and broadcasts. Corres. Fellow, Spanish Royal Acad. of History, 1988–. Encomienda, Order of Isabel the Catholic (Spain), 1988. *Publications:* The Army of Flanders and the Spanish Road 1567–1659, 1972, 3rd edn 1990; The Dutch Revolt, 1977, 3rd edn 1985; Philip II, 1978, 2nd edn 1988; Europe in Crisis 1598–1648, 1979; Spain and the Netherlands 1559–1659, 1979, 2nd edn 1990; The Thirty Years' War, 1984; (ed) The World: an illustrated history, 1986; The Military Revolution: military innovation and the rise of the West 1500–1800, 1988, 2nd edn 1990 (Dexter Prize, 1987–90); (with Colin Martin) The Spanish Armada, 1988; edited numerous other works; articles and reviews. *Recreations:* travel, archaeology. *Address:* Department of History, University of Illinois, 309 Gregory Hall, 810 South Wright Street, Urbana, Ill 61801, USA. *T:* (217) 333–4193.

PARKER, Sir Peter; *see* Parker, Sir W. P. B.

PARKER, Sir Peter, Kt 1978; LVO 1957; Chairman: Rockware Group plc, 1971–76, and since 1983 (Director, since 1976); Mitsubishi Electric (UK), since 1984; Whitehead Mann Group Plc, since 1984; Evered Bardon plc (formerly Evered), since 1989; *b* 30 Aug. 1924; *s* of late Tom and Dorothy S. Parker; *m* 1951, Gillian Rowe-Dutton, *d* of late Sir Ernest Rowe-Dutton, KCMG, CB, and of Lady Rowe-Dutton; three *s* one *d*. *Educ:* Bedford Sch.; London Univ.; Lincoln Coll., Oxford (Hon. Fellow, 1980). Major, Intelligence Corps, 1943–47. Commonwealth Fund Fellowship to Cornell and Harvard, 1950–51. Contested (Lab) Bedford, 1951. Phillips Electrical, 1951–53; Head of Overseas Dept, Industrial Soc. 1953–54; Sec., Duke of Edinburgh's Study Conf. on Human Problems of Industry, 1954–56 (Vice-Chm., UK Trustees, Commonwealth Study Confs, 1986–); joined Booker McConnell Ltd, 1956; Chairman: Bookers Engineering &

Industrial Holdings Ltd, 1966–70; Associated British Maltsters Ltd, 1971–73; Curtis Brown Ltd, 1971–76; Victoria Deep Water Terminal Ltd, 1971–76; Dawnay Day Group, 1971–76; BRB, 1976–83; Target Gp, 1984–87; Oakland Develt Capital Fund, 1985–; Parkdale Hldgs PLC, 1988–89; Group 4 Total Security Ltd, 1988–89; Horace, Holman Gp Ltd, 1988–; Whitehead Rice Ltd, 1988–90; Fidelity Japan OTC and Regional Markets Fund; Apricot Computers, 1990–; Arcadian Internat., 1990–; Vice-Chm., H. Clarkson & Co. (Hldgs), 1984– (Dir, 1976–; Chm., 1975–76); Director: Booker Bros McConnell & Co. Ltd, 1960–70; Renold Group Ltd; Group 4 Securitas, 1984–; Art Advisers Ltd, 1989–. Chm.-designate, Nat. Ports Authority, 1970; Chm., Clothing EDC, 1971–78; Member: BSC, 1967–70; British Tourist Authy Bd, 1969–75; British Airways Bd, 1971–81; Royal Nat. Theatre Bd, 1986–91; Political and Econ. Plannning Exec. (Vice-Chm., 1969–70; Hon. Treasurer, 1973–78); Council, BIM (Chm., 1984–86); Foundn on Automation & Human Develt, 1971–; Engineering Industries Council, 1975–76; NEDC, 1980–83; Honeywell Adv. Council, 1984–. Dir, UK-Japan 2000 Gp, 1986–; Chm., Organising Cttee, Japan Fest. 1991. Founder Mem., Council of Foundn for Management Educn; Chairman: Westfield College, 1969–76 (Hon. Fellow, 1979); Ct of Governors, LSE, 1988–; Dep. Chm., Ct of London Univ., 1970–; Chm., Adv. Council, Business Graduates Assoc. Vis. Fellow, Nuffield Coll., Oxford, 1980 (Hon. Fellow, 1980). Mem. Council, Oxford Mus. of Modern Art, 1984–; Trustee: Conran Foundn Boilerhouse Proj., 1980–; British Architecture Library Trust, 1984; Dir, Design Mus., 1989–; Vice-Chm., Friends of the Earth Trust Ltd, 1988–; Pres., Industry Council for Packaging and Envmt, 1990–. Dimbleby Lecture, BBC TV, 1984. Hon. Fellow: SIAD; SOAS, 1991; London Business Sch., 1991. Hon. LLD: London, 1981; Manchester Polytechnic, 1981; Bath, 1983. Communicator of the Year Award, British Assoc. of Indust. Editors, 1981; Bicentenary Medal, RSA, 1990. CStJ 1983. *Publication:* For Starters (autobiog.), 1989. *Recreations:* Rugby (played for Bedford and E Mids); swimming, browsing. *Address:* Rockware Group plc, 5 Chandos Street, W1M 9DG. *T:* 071–637 0369.

PARKER, Rev. Reginald Boden; *b* Wallasey, Cheshire, 4 June 1901; *s* of Joseph William and Ada Parker. *Educ:* Wallasey Grammar School; St Catherine's College, Oxford University; Ripon Hall, Oxford. BSc (London), 1923; MA (Oxon), 1938. Assistant Master, Ashton Gram. Sch., Lancs, 1925–30; Asst Master, Newton Gram. Sch., Lancs, 1930–32; Curate, Childwall, Liverpool, 1935–37; Curate, St Margaret's, Westminster, 1937–39; Asst Master and Chaplain, Oundle School, 1940–48; Headmaster, Igbobi College, Lagos, 1948–58; Bishop's Chaplain in Liverpool University, 1958–61; Residentiary Canon, Liverpool Cathedral, 1958–61; Precentor, Liverpool Cathedral, 1959–61; Asst Master, Wellington Coll., 1961–64; Rector of Bentham, dio. of Bradford, 1964–72. Hon. Lecturer in Hellenistic Greek, Liverpool University, 1959; Select Preacher, Oxford University, 1960. Member of Headmasters' Conference, 1950. *Publications:* (with J. P. Hodges): The Master and the Disciple, 1938 (SPCK); The King and the Kingdom, 1939 (SPCK); The Holy Spirit and The Kingdom, 1941 (SPCK). *Address:* 3 Yew Tree Cottages, Sheepscombe, Stroud, Glos GL6 7RB. *T:* Painswick (0452) 812650.

PARKER, Sir Richard (William) Hyde, 12th Bt, *cr* 1681; *b* 5 April 1937; *o s* of Sir William Stephen Hyde Parker, 11th Bt, and Ulla Ditlef, *o d* of C. Ditlef Nielsen, Dr of Philosophy, Copenhagen; *S* father 1951; *m* 1972, Jean, *d* of late Sir Lindores Leslie, 9th Bt; one *s* three *d* (incl. twin *d*). *Educ:* Millfield; Royal Agricultural College. *Heir: s* William John Hyde Parker, *b* 10 June 1983. *Address:* Melford Hall, Long Melford, Suffolk CO10 9AA.

PARKER, Robert Stewart; Deputy Parliamentary Counsel, since 1987; *b* 13 Jan. 1949; *o s* of Robert Arnold Parker and Edna Parker (*née* Baines). *Educ:* Brentwood School; Trinity College, Oxford (Scholar; First in Mods; MA 1974). Called to the Bar, Middle Temple, 1975 (Harmsworth Exhibnr; Astbury Senior Law Scholarship); Lincoln's Inn *ad eundem*, 1977. Classics Master, Brentwood School, 1971–74; in practice at the Bar, 1975–80; Office of Parly Counsel, 1980; Law Commn, 1985–87. Freeman, City of London, 1984; Liveryman, Wheelwrights' Co., 1984. MBIM. *Publication:* Cases and Materials on General Principles of English Law (with C. R. Newton), 1980. *Recreations:* the Livery, cricket, bridge, books, music. *Address:* Office of the Parliamentary Counsel, 36 Whitehall, SW1A 2AY. *Clubs:* Athenæum, City Livery.

PARKER, Rt. Hon. Sir Roger (Jocelyn), Kt 1977; PC 1983; **Rt. Hon. Lord Justice Parker;** a Lord Justice of Appeal, since 1983; *b* 25 Feb. 1923; *s* of Captain Hon. T. T. Parker, DSC, RN (Retired) and Marie Louise Leonie (*née* Kleinwort); *m* 1948, Ann Elizabeth Frederika (*née* White); one *s* three *d*. *Educ:* Eton; King's Coll., Cambridge. Served Rifle Bde, 1941–46. Called to Bar, Lincoln's Inn, 1948, Bencher, 1969; QC 1961. Dep. Chm., Herts QS, 1969–71; Judge of the Courts of Appeal, Jersey and Guernsey, 1974–83; a Judge of the High Court, QBD, 1977–83. Member, Bar Council, 1968–69, Vice-Chm., 1970–72, Chm., 1972–73. Vice-Pres., Senate of Four Inns of Court, 1972–73. Treas., Lincoln's Inn, 1990–91. Conducted Windscale Nuclear Fuel Reprocessing Inquiry, 1977. Chm., Court of Inquiry into Flixborough Explosion, 1974. *Clubs:* Lansdowne; Leander.

PARKER, Ronald William, CBE 1959; JP; *b* 21 Aug. 1909; *s* of late Ernest Edward Parker, MBE, Accountant of Court, and Margaret Parker (*née* Henderson); *m* 1937, Phyllis Mary (*née* Sherren); two *s*. *Educ:* Royal High School, Edinburgh. Chartered Accountant, 1933. Secretary, later Dir, Weston Group of Companies, 1935; Asst Dir of Finance, Ministry of Fuel and Power, 1942; Partner, J. Aikman, Smith & Wells, CA, 1946. National Coal Board: Finance Dir, Scottish Division, 1947; Dep. Chm., North Western Division, 1954; Chm., Scottish Division, 1955–67; Regional Chm., Scottish Region, 1967–68; Chm., Scottish Gas Region (formerly Scottish Gas Bd), 1968–74. JP City and County of Edinburgh, 1972. *Recreations:* golf, gardening, fishing. *Address:* Claremont, 3 South Lauder Road, Edinburgh EH9 2LL. *T:* 031–667 7666. *Club:* New (Edinburgh).

PARKER, (Thomas) John, FEng; Chairman and Chief Executive, Harland and Wolff, since 1983; *b* 8 April 1942; *s* of Robert Parker and Margaret Elizabeth Parker (*née* Bell); *m* 1967, Emma Elizabeth (*née* Blair); one *s* one *d*. *Educ:* Belfast Coll. of Technology. FEng 1983; FRINA; FIMarE. Harland & Wolff, Belfast: Student Apprentice Naval Architect, 1958–63; Ship Design Staff, 1963–69 (Nat. Physical Lab. (Ship Hydrodynamics), on secondment, 1964); Numerical Applications Manager, 1969–71; Prodn Drawing Office Manager, 1971–72; Gen. Manager, Sales and Projects, 1972–74; Man. Dir, Austin-Pickersgill Ltd, Sunderland, 1974–78; British Shipbuilders: Dir of Marketing, 1977–78; Bd Mem. for Shipbuilding, 1978–83; Dep. Chief Exec., 1980–83. Mem., British Coal Corp., 1986–. Member: Council, RINA, 1978–80, 1982–; Bd of Governors, Sunderland Polytechnic, 1976–81; Internat. Cttee, Bureau Veritas, Paris, 1979–83; Gen. Cttee, Lloyd's Register of Shipping, 1983–; Industrial Develt Bd of NI, 1983–87. Hon. DSc (Eng) Queen's Univ. Belfast, 1985; Hon. ScD Trinity Coll. Dublin, 1986. *Publications:* papers to Trans IES, RINA. *Recreations:* reading, motoring in the countryside, ships, sailing, music. *Address:* Harland and Wolff Holdings Plc, Queen's Island, Belfast BT3 9DU. *T:* Belfast (0232) 457032.

PARKER, Vice-Adm. Sir (Wilfred) John, KBE 1969 (OBE 1953); CB 1965; DSC 1943; *b* 12 Oct. 1915; *s* of Henry Edmond Parker and Ida Mary (*née* Cole); *m* 1943, Marjorie Stuart Jones, Halifax, NS, Canada; two *d*. *Educ:* RN College, Dartmouth. Joined Royal Navy, 1929; War Service in N Atlantic, N Russia, Mediterranean, Pacific, Korea (OBE); sunk in HMS Edinburgh and HMS Trinidad; mined in HMS Sheffield; torpedoed in HMS Newfoundland; DSC (Capture of Sicily); twice mentioned in despatches (HMS Edinburgh on N Russian convoys, and destruction of an Italian convoy, HMS Aurora 1942); Imperial Defence College, 1957; Commodore West Indies, 1958–60; Captain RNC Dartmouth, 1961–63; an Asst Chief of Defence Staff, Min. of Defence, 1963–66; Flag Officer, Medway, and Adm. Supt HM Dockyard, Chatham, 1966–69, retd 1969. Pres., RN Communication Chief Petty Officers Assoc., 1969–. *Recreation:* 7 grandchildren (3 Mayo, 3 Panton, 1 Polak). *Address:* Flint Cottage, East Harting, Petersfield, Hants GU31 5LT. *Club:* Royal Navy.

PARKER, Sir (William) Peter (Brian), 5th Bt *cr* 1844, of Shenstone Lodge, Staffordshire; Partner, Stephenson, Nuttall & Co., chartered accountants, Newark; *b* 30 Nov. 1950; *s* of Sir (William) Alan Parker, 4th Bt and of Sheelagh Mary, *o d* of late Dr Sinclair Stevenson; *S* father, 1990; *m* 1976, Patricia Ann, *d* of R. Filtness and Mrs D. Filtness; one *s* ond *d*. *Educ:* Eton. FCA 1974. *Heir: s* John Malcolm Parker, *b* 14 May 1980. *Address:* Apricot Hall, Sutton-cum-Beckingham, Lincoln LN5 0RE.

PARKER-JERVIS, Roger, DL; Deputy Chairman, CGA plc, 1982–90; *b* 11 Sept. 1931; *s* of George Parker-Jervis and late Ruth, *d* of C. E. Farmer; *m* 1958, Diana, *d* of R. St V. Parker-Jervis; two *s* one *d*. *Educ:* Eton; Magdalene College, Cambridge. Served Rifle Brigade, 1950–51, Queen Victoria Rifles, 1951–54; ADC to Governor of Tasmania, 1954–56. Bucks County Council: Mem., 1967; Chm., Planning and Transp. Cttee, 1974; Chm., Policy and Resources Cttee, 1977; Vice-Chm. Council, 1979; Chm. Council, 1981–85. Mem., Milton Keynes Develt Corp., 1976–; Pres., Timber Growers of England and Wales, 1981–83; Vice-Chm., Forestry Cttee of GB, 1981–83. High Sheriff of Bucks, 1973–74, DL Bucks, 1982. *Recreations:* painting, shooting. *Address:* The Gardener's Cottage, Great Hampden, Great Missenden, Bucks HP16 9RJ. *T:* High Wycombe (0494) 488531. *Clubs:* Farmers', Naval and Military, Greenjackets.

PARKES, Sir Basil (Arthur), Kt 1971; OBE 1966; *b* 20 Feb. 1907; *s* of late Sir Fred Parkes, Boston, Lincs, and Blackpool, Lancs, and late Gertrude Mary Parkes (*née* Bailey); *m* 1933, May Lewis McNeill (*d* 1988); two *s* one *d*. *Educ:* Boston Grammar Sch., Lincs. Joined family trawler owning Co., 1924 (Dir, 1928; Man. Dir, 1946). Pres., North British Maritime Gp Ltd (formerly United Towing Ltd), 1960–. Hon. Brother, Hull Trinity House. Mem., Worshipful Co. of Fishmongers; Mem., Worshipful Co. of Poulters; Officier de l'ordre du Mérite National Français, 1973; Ordre de la Couronne, Belgium, 1979. *Recreations:* golf, shooting. *Address:* Loghan-y-Yuiy, The Garey, Lezayre, near Ramsey, Isle of Man. *T:* Ramsey (0624) 815449. *Clubs:* City Livery, St Stephen's Constitutional, Royal Over-Seas League.

PARKES, Sir Edward (Walter), Kt 1983; DL; FEng; Vice-Chancellor, University of Leeds, 1983–91; Chairman, Committee of Vice-Chancellors and Principals of the Universities of the United Kingdom, 1989–91 (Vice-Chairman, 1985–89); *b* 19 May 1926; *o s* of Walter Frederick Parkes; *m* 1950, Margaret Parr (*see* Margaret Parkes); one *s* one *d*. *Educ:* King Edward's, Birmingham; St John's College, Cambridge; Scholar; 1st cl. hons Mech. Sci. Tripos, 1945; MA, PhD, ScD; FIMechE. At RAE and in the aircraft industry, 1945–48; research student and subsequently Univ. Lecturer, Cambridge, 1948–59; Fellow and Tutor of Gonville and Caius College; Vis. Prof., Stanford Univ., 1959–60; Head of the Department of Engineering, Univ. of Leicester, 1960–65; Prof. of Mechanics, Cambridge, and Professorial Fellow, Gonville and Caius Coll., 1965–74 (Mem. Gen. Bd, Dep. head of Dept of Engineering); Vice-Chancellor, City Univ., 1974–78; Chm., UGC, 1978–83. Member: Brynmor Jones Cttee, 1964–65; Adv. Bd for Res. Councils, 1974–83; University and Polytechnic Grants Cttee for Hong Kong, 1974–; Chm., Clinical Academic Staff Salaries Cttee, 1985–90. Chm., Adv. Panel on Limestone Workings in the W Midlands, 1983–. DL W Yorks, 1990. Hon. DTech Loughborough, 1984; Hon. DSc: Leicester, 1984; City, 1988; Hon. LLD Wales, 1984. *Publications:* Braced Frameworks, 1965, 2nd edn 1974; papers on elasticity, dynamic plasticity or thermal effects on structures in Proc. and Phil. Trans. Royal Society and other jls. *Club:* Athenæum.

PARKES, John Alan; Chief Executive, Humberside County Council, and Clerk to Humberside Lieutenancy, since 1988; *b* 18 Jan. 1939; *s* of Arthur and Alice Parkes: *m* 1963, Margaret Jill (*née* Clayton); two *d*. *Educ:* Nottingham High Sch.; Oriel Coll., Oxford (MA). IPFA 1965. Various posts from graduate traineeship, Council Finance, Derbyshire, 1961–68; Asst County Treasurer, Glos, 1968–71; Dep., then County Treasurer, Lindsey, 1971–74; Dir of Finance, Humberside, 1974–88. Member: Phildrew Ventures Adv. Cttee, 1986–; Financial Reporting Council, 1990–. Advr, ACC, 1976–; Sec., 1980–86, Pres., 1987–88, Soc. of County Treasurers; Dir, Humberside TEC, 1990–. Freeman, City of London, 1988. *Publications:* articles on local govt finance in prof. jls. *Recreations:* walking, cars, railways. *Address:* County Hall, Beverley, North Humberside HU17 9BA. *T:* Hull (0482) 884830. *Clubs:* Royal Over-Seas League; Rotary (Beverley).

PARKES, John Hubert, CB 1984; Permanent Secretary, Department of Education, Northern Ireland, 1979–90; *b* 1 Oct. 1930; 2nd *s* of Frank Hubert Parkes and Mary Edith (*née* Barnes), Birmingham; *m* 1956, Elsie Griffiths Henderson; two *s*. *Educ:* George Dixon Sch., Birmingham; Magdalen Coll., Oxford (MA). Joined NI Civil Service, 1953; Asst Sec. 1966; RCDS 1972; Dep. Sec., 1973. Hon. DLitt Ulster, 1991. *Address:* c/o Department of Education, Rathgael House, Balloo Road, Bangor, Co. Down, Northern Ireland BT19 2PR. *Club:* United Oxford & Cambridge University.

PARKES, Margaret, (Lady Parkes), CBE 1990; JP; Chairman, National Council for Educational Technology, since 1991; a Governor of the BBC, 1984–89; *b* 26 Sept. 1925; *d* of John and Dorothy Parr; *m* 1950, Sir Edward Walter Parkes, *qv*; one *s* one *d*. *Educ:* Perse School for Girls, Cambridge; Leicester Univ. (MEd). Homerton Coll., Cambridge, 1965–74. Pres., Leeds Marriage and Personal Counselling Service, 1987–91; Chairman: London Diocesan Bd of Educn, 1976–80; Colleges Adv. Cttee, Gen. Synod Bd of Educn, 1982–86; Radio London Adv. Council, 1979–83; Ripon Diocesan Bd of Educn, 1988–91; Leeds Parish Church Commn, 1988. Member: Press Council, 1978–84; Secondary Exams Council, 1983–88; Voluntary Sector Consultative Council, 1984–88; Chm., Design and Technology Wkg Gp for Nat. Curriculum, 1988–89. Chm. of Governors, Whitelands Coll., London, 1981–87. JP Inner London 1977.

PARKES, Norman James, CBE 1976 (OBE 1960); Clerk of the Australian House of Representatives, 1971–76, retired; *b* 29 July 1912; *s* of Ernest William Parkes; *m* 1937, Maida Cleave, *d* of James Nicholas Silk; two *s*. *Educ:* Victorian State Schools. AASA. Parliamentary officer, 1934: with Reporting Staff, 1934–37; with House of Representatives, 1937–76. *Recreation:* bowls. *Address:* 1/3 Nuyts Street, Red Hill, Canberra, ACT 2603, Australia. *T:* Canberra 06–2957320. *Clubs:* Canberra Bowling, National Press (Canberra).

PARKHOUSE, James, MD, FFARCS; Hon. Director, Medical Careers Research Group, Oxford, since 1989 (Director, 1984–89); *b* 30 March 1927; *s* of Charles Frederick

Parkhouse and Mary Alice Sumner; *m* 1952, Hilda Florence Rimmer; three *s* two *d*. *Educ:* Merchant Taylors' Sch., Great Crosby; Liverpool Univ. (MD 1955). MB ChB, 1950; MA Oxon 1960; MSc Manchester 1974. DA; FFARCS 1952. Anaesthetist, RAF Med. Br., 1953–55. Sen. Resident Anaesth., Mayo Clinic, 1957–58; First Asst, Nuffield Dept of Anaesths, Oxford, and Hon. Cons. Anaesth., United Oxford Hosps, 1958–66; Prof. and Head of Dept of Anaesths, Univ. of Manitoba, and Chief Anaesth., Winnipeg Gen. Hosp., 1967–68; Postgrad. Dean, Faculty of Med., Sheffield Univ., and Hon. Cons. Anaesth., United Sheffield Hosps, 1969–70; Prof. of Anaesths, Manchester Univ., and Hon. Cons. Anaesth., Manchester and Salford AHAs (Teaching), 1970–80; Prof. of Postgraduate Med. Educn, Univ. of Newcastle upon Tyne, and Postgrad. Dean and Dir, Northern Postgrad. Inst. for Medicine and Dentistry, 1980–84. Consultant, postgrad. med. trng, WHO, 1969–89; Specialist Adviser, H of C Social Services Cttee, 1980–81, 1984. Member: Sheffield Reg. Hosp. Bd, 1969–70; Bd, Faculty of Anaesthetists, 1971–82; Neurosciences Bd, MRC, 1977–80; GMC, 1979–89; Nat. Trng Council, NHS, 1981–84; North Tyneside HA, 1982–84. *Publications:* A New Look at Anaesthetics, 1965; Medical Manpower in Britain, 1979; Doctors' Careers, 1990; contrib. to The Lancet, BMJ and specialist jls. *Recreations:* music, golf. *Address:* 145 Cumnor Hill, Oxford OX2 9JA. *Club:* Royal Birkdale Golf.

PARKHOUSE, Peter; Under Secretary, Ministry of Agriculture, Fisheries and Food, 1973 and 1979–84, retired; *b* 22 July 1927; *s* of late William Richard Parkhouse, MBE, and late Alice Vera Parkhouse (*née* Clarke); *m* 1950, Mary Alison Holland (*d* 1987); one *s* one *d*. *Educ:* Blundell's Sch.; Peterhouse, Cambridge (organist, 1944–45); Cologne Univ. BA 1947, MA 1950. Instr Lieut, RN, 1947–50; Asst Master, Uppingham Sch., 1951–52; Asst Principal, Min. of Food, 1952; transf. to MAFF, 1955; served in private office of successive Ministers and Parly Secs, 1954–58; Principal 1958; Principal Private Sec. to Minister, 1966–67; Asst Sec. 1967; Under-Sec. 1973; Dir in Directorate-Gen. for Agriculture, Commn of European Communities, 1973–79; Under Sec., 1979–84. Mem., EDC for Agriculture, 1982–84. *Recreations:* music (sub-organist of Tetbury Parish Church), fishing. *Address:* Stafford House, The Chipping, Tetbury, Glos GL8 8ET. *T:* Tetbury (0666) 502540. *Club:* United Oxford & Cambridge University.

PARKHURST, Raymond Thurston, BSc(Agr), MSc, PhD; Director of South Central Poultry Research Laboratory, State University, Mississippi, 1960–68, retired; *b* Everett, Massachusetts, USA, 24 April 1898; *o s* of Fred Lincoln and Celeste Elizabeth Parkhurst; *m* 1922; one *s* one *d*; *m* 1985, Christine Jennings. *Educ:* Fitchburg (Massachusetts) High School; Universities of Massachusetts, Idaho and Edinburgh. Extension Poultryman, Iowa State College, 1919–21; Professor of Poultry Husbandry, Experiment Station Poultry Husbandman, and Head, Dept of Poultry Husbandry, University of Idaho, 1921–27; Director, Brit. Nat. Institute of Poultry Husbandry, 1927–32; Head, Department Agricultural Research, National Oil Products Co., 1932–38; Head, Dept of Poultry Husbandry, University of Massachusetts, Amherst, 1938–44; Director, Nutrition and Research, Flory Milling Co., Bangor, Pa, 1944–49; Director of Nutrition and Research, Lindsey-Robinson and Company, Roanoke, Va, USA, 1949–60; Member: Amer. Poultry Science Assoc.; Amer. Assoc. of Retired Persons; Nat. Assoc. of Retired Persons, etc.; First President of British Poultry Education Association. *Publications:* Vitamin E in relation to Poultry; The Comparative Value of various Protein Feeds for Laying Hens; Factors Affecting Egg Size; Mixed Protein Foods for Layers; Ricketts and Perosis in Growing Chickens; Rexing the Rabbit; Corn Distillers By-Products in Poultry Rations; Calcium and Manganese in Poultry Nutrition; Crabmeal and Fishmeal in Poultry Nutrition; Commercial Broiler Raising; Gumboro Disease, etc. *Recreations:* roses, bridge, stamps, coins. *Address:* 119 Kirk Side, Starkville, Miss 39759, USA. *Club:* Kiwanis International.

PARKIN, John Mackintosh; Administrator, Royal Courts of Justice, 1982–85, retired; *b* 18 June 1920; *s* of Thomas and Emily Cecilia Parkin; *m* Biancamaria Giuganino, Rome; two *d*. *Educ:* Nottingham High Sch.; Emmanuel Coll., Cambridge (Sen. Schol.; MA). Royal Artillery, 1939–46 (Captain). Asst Principal, WO, 1949; Registrar, RMCS, 1957–60; Principal Private Sec. to Sec. of State for War, 1960–62; Asst Sec. 1962; Sen. Fellow, Harvard Univ., 1966–67; Comd Sec., BAOR, 1967–70; Asst Under-Sec. of State, MoD, 1974–80. Mem., Royal Patriotic Fund Corpn, 1977–80. *Recreation:* history of architecture and art. *Address:* 18 Dulwich Mead, 48–50 Halfmoon Lane, SE24 9HS.

PARKIN, Sara Lamb; Speaker of the Green Party, UK, since 1990; *b* 9 April 1946; *d* of Dr George Lamb McEwan and Mairie Munro Rankin; *m* 1969, Dr Donald Maxwell Parkin; two *s*. *Educ:* Barrs Hill School, Coventry; Edinburgh Royal Infirmary (RGN). Ward Sister, Royal Infirmary, Edinburgh, and Res. Asst, Nursing Res. Unit, Univ. of Edinburgh, 1973–74; Council Mem., 1974–76; Family Planning Nurse, Brook Clinic, Edinburgh and Leeds AHA, 1976–80. Internat. Liaison Sec., Green Party, UK, 1983–90; Co-Sec., European Green Co-ordination, 1985–90. *Publication:* Green Parties: an international guide, 1989. *Recreations:* reading, films, theatre, opera, walking, camping, squash, gardening. *Address:* 18 Boulevard Pinel, 69003 Lyon, France. *T:* (33) 72.33.65.97.

PARKINS, Graham Charles; QC 1990; a Recorder, since 1989; *b* 11 Nov. 1942; *s* of John Charles Parkins and Nellie Elizabeth Parkins; *m* 1st, 1964, Carole Ann Rowe (marr. diss.); two *s* one *d*; 2nd, 1977, Susan Ann Poole; two *d*. *Educ:* Harwich County High Sch.; Mid-Essex Coll. of Law; LLB Hons London. Called to the Bar, Inner Temple, 1972; an Asst Recorder, 1986–89. *Recreations:* golf, sailing, relaxing. *Address:* 24 King Coel Road, Lexden, Colchester CO3 5AQ. *Club:* North Countryman's (Colchester).

PARKINSON, Rt. Hon. Cecil (Edward), PC 1981; MP (C) Hertsmere, since 1983 (Enfield West, Nov. 1970–1974; Hertfordshire South, 1974–83); Secretary of State for Transport, 1989–90; *b* 1 Sept. 1931; *s* of Sidney Parkinson, Carnforth, Lancs; *m* 1957, Ann Mary, *d* of F. A. Jarvis, Harpenden, Herts; three *d*. *Educ:* Royal Lancaster Grammar Sch., Lancaster; Emmanuel Coll., Cambridge. BA 1955, MA 1961. Joined Metal Box Company as a Management Trainee; joined West, Wake, Price, Chartered Accountants, 1956; qualified 1959; Partner, 1961–71; founded Parkinson Hart Securities Ltd, 1967; Director of several cos, 1965–79, 1984–87. Constituency Chm., Hemel Hempstead Conservative Assoc.; Chm., Herts 100 Club, 1968–69; contested (C) Northampton, 1970. PPS to Minister for Aerospace and Shipping, DTI, 1972–74; an Asst Govt Whip, 1974; an Opposition Whip, 1974–76; Opposition Spokesman on trade, 1976–79; Minister for Trade, Dept of Trade, 1979–81; Paymaster General, 1981–83; Chancellor, Duchy of Lancaster, 1982–83; Sec. of State for Trade and Industry, June-Oct. 1983, for Energy, 1987–89. Chm. of Cons. Party, 1981–83. Sec., Cons. Parly Finance Cttee, 1971–72; Chm., Anglo-Swiss Parly Gp, 1979–82; Pres., Anglo-Polish Cons. Soc., 1986–. *Recreations:* reading, golf, skiing; ran for combined Oxford and Cambridge team against Amer. Univs, 1954 and 1955; ran for Cambridge against Oxford, 1954 and 1955. *Address:* House of Commons, SW1A 0AA. *Clubs:* Beefsteak, Carlton, Garrick, Pratt's; Hawks (Cambridge).

PARKINSON, Cyril Northcote, MA, PhD, FRHistS; author, historian and journalist; Professor Emeritus and Hon. President, Troy State University, Alabama, since 1970; *b* 30 July 1909; *yr s* of late W. Edward Parkinson, ARCA and late Rose Emily Mary Curnow; *m* 1st, 1943, Ethelwyn Edith Graves (marr. diss.); one *s* one *d*; 2nd, 1952, Elizabeth Ann Fry (*d* 1983); two *s* one *d*; 3rd, 1985, Iris (Ingrid) Hilda Waters. *Educ:* St Peter's School, York; Emmanuel College, Cambridge; King's College, London. Fellow of Emmanuel Coll., Cambridge, 1935; Sen. History Master, Blundell's Sch., Tiverton, 1938; Master, RNC, Dartmouth, 1939. Commissioned as Captain, Queen's Roy. Regt, 1940; Instructor in 166 OCTU; attached RAF, 1942–43; Major, 1943; trans. as GSO2 to War Office (General Staff), 1944; demobilised, 1945; Lectr in History, Univ. of Liverpool, 1946; Raffles Professor of History, University of Malaya, Singapore, 1950–58. Visiting Professor: Univ. of Harvard, 1958; Univs of Illinois and California, 1959–60. Mem. French Académie de Marine and US Naval Inst.; Mem. Archives Commission of Govt of India. Hon. LLD Maryland, 1974; Hon. DLitt Troy State, 1976. *Plays:* Helier Bonamy, Guernsey, 1967; The Royalist, Guernsey, 1969. *Publications:* many books including: Edward Pellew Viscount Exmouth, 1934; Trade in the Eastern Seas, 1937; (ed.) The Trade Winds, 1948; The Rise of the Port of Liverpool, 1952; War in the Eastern Seas, 1954; Britain in the Far East, 1955; Parkinson's Law, the Pursuit of Progress, 1958; The Evolution of Political Thought, 1958; British Intervention in Malaya, 1867–1877, 1960; The Law and the Profits, 1960; In-laws and Outlaws, 1962; East and West, 1963; Ponies Plot, 1965; A Law unto Themselves, 1966; Left Luggage, 1967; Mrs Parkinson's Law, 1968; The Law of Delay, 1970; The Life and Times of Horatio Hornblower, 1970; Big Business, 1974; Gunpowder, Treason and Plot, 1977; Britannia Rules, 1977; The Rise of Big Business, 1977; (with Nigel Rowe) Communicate, 1977; Jeeves: a Gentleman's Personal Gentleman, 1979; (with H. Le Compte) The Law of Longer Life, 1980; *novels:* Devil to Pay, 1973; The Fireship, 1975; Touch and Go, 1977; Dead Reckoning, 1978; So Near So Far, 1981; The Guernseyman, 1982; The Fur-Lined Mousetrap, 1983; Man Hunt, 1990; contribs to Encyclopædia Britannica, Economist, Guardian, New York Times, Fortune, Saturday Evening Post, Punch and Foreign Policy. *Recreations:* painting, travel, sailing, music. *Address:* Delancey, 36 Harkness Drive, Canterbury, Kent CT2 7RW. *Club:* Army and Navy.

PARKINSON, Dr David Hardress; science writer and consultant; formerly Director General, Establishments Resources and Programmes, A, Ministry of Defence (1973–77); *b* Liverpool, 9 March 1918; *s* of E. R. H. Parkinson; *m* 1st, 1944, Muriel Gwendoline Patricia (*d* 1971), *d* of Captain P. W. Newenham; two *s*; 2nd, 1974, Daphne Margaret Scott-Gall (marr. diss. 1978). *Educ:* Gravesend County Grammar Sch.; Wadham Coll., Oxford (MA, DPhil). CPhys, FInstP. Royal Artillery, 1939–45 (Major); Oxford Univ., 1937–39 and 1945–49; Civil Service: TRE, Malvern, 1949; Supt Low Temp. and Magnetics Div., RRE, Malvern, 1956–63; Head Physics Gp, RRE, 1963–68; Head Physics and Electronics Dept, RRE and Dep. Dir, 1968–72. Hon. Prof. Physics, Birmingham Univ., 1966–73. Chm. Midland Br., Inst. Physics, 1968–70; Vice-Pres. (Exhibns), Inst. Physics, 1973–78; Chm. Adv. Cttee on Physics and Society, European Physical Soc., 1982–88. *Publications:* (with B. Mulhall) Generation High Magnetic Fields, 1967; many scientific papers and articles. *Recreations:* antiques, silversmithing. *Address:* South Bank, 47 Abbey Road, Great Malvern, Worcs WR14 3HH. *T:* Malvern (0684) 575423. *Club:* Commonwealth Trust.

PARKINSON, Desmond Frederick, CMG 1975; HM Diplomatic Service, retired; *b* 26 Oct. 1920; *m* 1977, Patricia Jean Campbell Taylor; two *s* two *d* of former *m*. HM Forces, 1939–49; served FO, 1949–51; Rangoon, 1951–53; Jakarta, 1954–55; FO, 1955–57; Rabat, 1957–60; Lagos, 1960–61; FO, 1961–63; Singapore, 1963–65; Delhi, 1965–67; FCO, 1967–78. *Address:* Woodrow, Silchester, near Reading. *T:* Reading (0734) 700257. *Club:* Huntercombe Golf.

PARKINSON, Desmond John, OBE 1950; Under-Secretary, Agricultural Research Council, 1971–73; *b* 8 March 1913; *s* of late Frederick A. Parkinson, Rio de Janeiro; *m* 1st, 1940, Leonor Hughes (marr. diss. 1954); 2nd, 1955, Lorna Mary Britton (*née* Wood); no *c*. *Educ:* Hereford Cathedral Sch.; St John's Coll., Cambridge; Brasenose Coll., Oxford. BA Cantab 1935; Colonial Admin. Service, 1936–60 (Gold Coast, Colonial Office, British Guiana, Nigeria); UK MAFF, 1960–63; ARC, 1963–73. *Recreation:* gardening. *Address:* Glebe House, North Cadbury, Yeovil, Somerset BA22 7DW. *T:* North Cadbury (0963) 40181. *Club:* United Oxford & Cambridge University.

PARKINSON, Ewart West, BSc, DPA, CEng, FICE, PPRTPI, FIMunE; OStJ; development adviser; Director of Environment and County Engineer, County of South Glamorgan, 1973–85; *b* 9 July 1926; *s* of Thomas Edward Parkinson and Esther Lilian West; *m* 1948, Patricia Joan Wood; two *s* one *d*. *Educ:* Wyggeston Sch., Leicester; Coll. of Technology, Leicester (BSc, DPA). Miller Prize (bridge design), Instn CE, 1953. After working with Leicester, Wakefield, Bristol and Dover Councils, he became Dep. Borough Engr, Chelmsford, 1957–60; Dep. City Surveyor Plymouth, 1960–64; City Planning Officer, Cardiff, 1964–73, specialising in Central Area Redevelt. Mem. Council, RTPI, 1971–83 (Vice-Pres., 1973–75, Pres., 1975–76, Chm. Internat. Affairs Bd, 1975–80); Member: Sports Council for Wales, 1966–78 (Chm., Facilities Cttee); Internat. Soc. of City and Regional Planners, 1972; Govt Deleg. to UN Conf. on Human Settlements, 1976; Watt Cttee for Energy, 1977–83 (Chm., Working Gp on Energy and Envt, 1980–83); UK mem., Internat. Wkg Party on Urban Land Policy, Internat. Fedn for Housing and Planning, 1979–85; Chairman: Internat. Wkg Party on Energy and the Environment, Internat. Fedn for Housing and Planning, 1982–85 (Life Mem. 1986); Wkg Party on Land Policy, Royal Town Planning Inst., 1983–85; led Study Tours to Soviet Union, 1977, India and Bangladesh, 1979, China, 1980, Kenya, Zimbabwe and Tanzania, 1981; lecture visits to People's Republic of China at invitation of Ministry of Construction, 1982, 1986, 1989, 1990, 1991. Director: Moving Being Theatre Co., 1986–90; W. S. Atkins (Wales), 1988–. Chairman: STAR Community Trust Ltd, 1979–; Intervol, 1985–89; Wales Sports Centre for the Disabled Trust, 1986–; Vice-Pres., Wales Council for the Disabled, 1982–. Managing Trustee, Norwegian Church Rebuilding Trust. Diamond Jubilee Silver Medal, Nat. Housing and Town Planning Council, 1978. OStJ 1980 (S Glamorgan Council, 1975–). *Publications:* The Land Question, 1974; And Who is my Neighbour?, 1976; articles in prof. jls on land policy, energy and the environment, and public participation. *Recreations:* working, travelling, being with family, talking with friends. *Address:* 42 South Rise, Llanishen, Cardiff CF4 5RH. *T:* Cardiff (0222) 756 394.

PARKINSON, Graham Edward; Metropolitan Stipendiary Magistrate, since 1982; a Recorder, since 1989; *b* 13 Oct. 1937; *s* of Norman Edward Parkinson and Phyllis (*née* Jaquiss); *m* 1963, Dinah Mary Pyper; one *s* one *d*. *Educ:* Loughborough Grammar Sch. Admitted Solicitor of the Supreme Court, 1961. Articled to J. Tempest Bouskell, Leicester, 1955–60; Asst Solicitor: Slaughter & May, 1961–63; Amery Parkes & Co., 1963–67; Partner, Darlington and Parkinson, Ealing, 1967–82. Pres., Central and S Mddx Law Soc., 1978–79; Vice Chm. Exec. Cttee, Soc. of Conservative Lawyers, 1978–82; Mem. Cttee, London Criminal Courts Solicitors Assoc., 1978–80. *Recreations:* going to the opera, reading, piano playing, listening to music. *Address:* Thames Magistrates' Court, 58 Bow Road, E3 4DJ.

PARKINSON, Dr James Christopher, MBE 1963; TD 1962; Deputy Director, Brighton Polytechnic, 1970–83, retired; *b* 15 Aug. 1920; *s* of late Charles Myers Parkinson, Pharmacist, Blackburn, Lancs; *m* 1950, Gwyneth Margot, *d* of late Rev. John Raymond Harrison, Macclesfield, Ches; three *s*. *Educ:* Queen Elizabeth's Gram. Sch.,

Blackburn; Univ. Coll., Nottingham. BPharm, PhD (London), FRPharmS. Served in Mediterranean area, Parachute Regt, 1943–46; Parachute Regt TA: 16 AB Div. and 44 Parachute Bde, 1949–63 (Major). Lectr, Sch. of Pharmacy, Univ. of London, 1948–54; Head of Sch. of Pharmacy, Brighton Coll. of Technology, 1954–64; Dep. Sec., Pharmaceutical Soc. of Gt Britain, 1964–67; Principal, Brighton Coll. of Technology, 1967–70. Mem. various pharmaceutical cttees of British Pharmacopœia, British Pharmaceutical Codex and British Veterinary Codex, 1956–64; Examr, Pharmaceutical Soc. of Gt Britain, 1954–64; Mem. Bds of Studies in Pharmacy and Librarianship, CNAA, 1965–75. Mem., Mid-Downs DHA, 1984–87. Member, Gen. Synod of Church of England, 1970–85. *Publications:* research papers on applied microbiology in Jl Appl. Bact. and Jl Pharm. (London) and on pharmaceutical education in Pharm. Jl. *Recreation:* do-it-yourself. *Address:* 92 Wickham Hill, Hurstpierpoint, West Sussex BN6 9NR. *T:* Hurstpierpoint (0273) 833369.

PARKINSON, Michael; interviewer, television presenter, writer; *b* 28 March 1935; *m* Mary Heneghan; three *s*. *Educ:* Barnsley Grammar School. Journalist on local paper; The Guardian; Daily Express; columnist on Sunday Times; radio work; has written for Punch, The Listener, New Statesman; Columnist: Daily Mirror, 1986–90; Daily Telegraph, 1991–; Editor, Catalyst, 1988–; Producer and interviewer: Granada's Scene; Granada in the North; World in Action; What the Papers Say; reporter on 24 Hours (BBC); Exec. producer and presenter, London Weekend Television, 1968; Presenter: Cinema, 1969–70; Tea Break, Where in the World, The Movie Quiz, 1971; host of own chat show, Parkinson, 1971–82; TV-am, 1983–84; Parkinson in Australia, 1979–84; Give Us a Clue, 1984–; All Star Secrets, 1984–86; The Skag Kids, 1985; Parkinson One-to-One, 1987–88; Desert Island Discs, BBC Radio 4, 1986–88. Founder-Director, Pavilion Books, 1980–. *Publications:* Football Daft, 1968; Cricket Mad, 1969; (with Clyde Jeavons) Pictorial History of Westerns, 1972; Sporting Fever, 1974; (with Willis Hall) Football Classified, 1974; George Best: an intimate biography, 1975; (with Willis Hall) A-Z of Soccer, 1975; Bats in the Pavilion, 1977; The Woofits, 1980; Parkinson's Lore, 1981; The Best of Parkinson, 1982. *Address:* c/o Michael Parkinson Enterprises Ltd, IMG, 23 Eyot Gardens, W6 9TR.

PARKINSON, Sir Nicholas (Fancourt), Kt 1980; consultant; *b* 5 Dec. 1925; *s* of late Rev. C. T. Parkinson, MA Oxon, and Dorothy Fancourt (*née* Mitchell); *m* 1952, Roslyn Sheena Campbell; two *d*. *Educ:* King's Sch., Parramatta, NSW; Univ. of Sydney (BA). Entered Aust. Foreign Service, 1951; Third Sec., Cairo, 1953–56; First Sec., Hong Kong, 1958–61; Counsellor, Moscow, Wellington, Kuala Lumpur, 1963–67; Chm., Jt Intell. Cttee, Dept of Defence, Canberra, 1967–70; High Comr, Singapore, 1970–74; Dep. Sec., Dept of For. Affairs, Canberra, 1974–76; Ambassador to the US, 1976–77 and 1979–82; Sec., Dept of For. Affairs, Canberra, 1977–79. Dir, Sears World Trade (Australia), 1983–86. Mem., ABC Adv. Council, 1991–. *Recreation:* bridge. *Address:* 62 Collings Street, Pearce, ACT 2607, Australia. *T:* Canberra 861004; Shiloh, Mount Tomah, NSW 2758, Australia. *Club:* Commonwealth (Canberra).

PARKINSON, Ronald Dennis; Assistant Curator of Paintings, Victoria and Albert Museum, since 1978; *b* 27 April 1945; *s* of Albert Edward Parkinson and Jennie Caroline Clara Meager. *Educ:* St Dunstan's Coll.; Clare Coll., Cambridge (MA). Res. Assistant: Paul Mellon Foundn for British Art, 1971–72; V&A Mus., 1972–74; Asst Keeper, Tate Gall., 1974–78. *Publications:* (ed jtly) Richard Redgrave, 1988; Catalogue of British Oil Paintings 1820–1860 in the Victoria and Albert Museum, 1990; articles in Apollo, Burlington Mag., Cambridge Res., Connoisseur, Country Life, Times Higher Educn Sup. *Recreations:* reading, shopping. *Address:* Victoria and Albert Museum, South Kensington, SW7 2RL. *T:* 071–938 8474. *Club:* Algonquin.

PARKINSON, Thomas Harry, CBE 1972; DL; Town Clerk, 1960–72, Clerk of the Peace, 1970–72, Birmingham; *b* Bilston, 25 June 1907; *y s* of G. R. J. Parkinson; *m* 1936, Joan Catherine, *d* of C. J. Douglas-Osborn; two *s* one *d*. *Educ:* Bromsgrove; Birmingham University. LLB Hons 1929. Admitted Solicitor, 1930. RAF, 1939–45. Asst Solicitor, Birmingham Corp., 1936–49; Dep. Town Clerk, Birmingham, 1949–60. Pres., Birmingham Law Soc., 1969–70. Sec., W Midlands Passenger Transport Authority, 1969–72; Member: Water Services Staff Adv. Commn, 1973–78; W Midlands Rent Assessment Panel, 1972–78; Sec., Nat Exhibn Centre Ltd, 1972–78; Hon. Member: Birmingham Assoc. of Mech. Engrs; Inst. of Housing. DL Warwickshire, 1970. Hon. DSc Aston, 1972. *Recreations:* walking, sailing, gardening. *Address:* Roseland Nursery, Upper Castle Road, St Mawes, Truro, Cornwall TR2 5AE. *T:* St Mawes (0326) 270592.

PARKYN, Brian (Stewart); General Manager, Training Services, British Caledonian Airways Ltd, 1981–88; *b* 28 April 1923; *o s* of Leslie and Gwen Parkyn, Whetstone, N20; *m* 1951, Janet Anne, *o d* of Charles and Jessie Stormer, Eastbourne; one *s* one *d*. *Educ:* King Edward VI Sch., Chelmsford; technical colleges. Principal, Glacier Inst. of Management (Associated Engineering Ltd), 1976–80. Director: Scott Bader Co. Ltd, 1953–83; Hunting Industrial Plastics Ltd, 1979–83; Halmatic Ltd, 1983–88. British Plastics Federation: Chm., Reinforced Plastics Gp, 1961–63; Mem. Council, 1959–75. Vice Pres., Rubber and Plastics Inst., 1972–75. Has travelled widely and lectured in N and S America, Africa, Australasia, India, Japan, USSR and China, etc.; Plastics Lectr, Worshipful Co. of Horners, 1967. Contested (Lab) Bedford, 1964; MP (Lab) Bedford, 1966–70; Mem., Select Cttee on Science and Technology, 1967–70; Chm., Sub-Cttee on Carbon Fibres, 1969; contested (Lab) Bedford, Oct. 1974. Member: Council, Cranfield Inst. of Technology, 1971–; Council, RSA, 1976–82 (Hon. Treas., 1977–82). FPRI. *Publications:* Democracy, Accountability and Participation in Industry, 1979; various papers and books on polyester resins and reinforced plastics. *Recreations:* writing, industrial democracy. *Address:* 9 Clarendon Square, Leamington Spa, Warwicks CV32 5QJ. *T:* Leamington (0926) 330066.

PARMOOR, 4th Baron *cr* 1914; **Milo Cripps;** *b* 18 June 1929; *s* of 3rd Baron Parmoor, DSO, TD, DL, and Violet Mary Geraldine, *d* of Sir William Nelson, 1st Bt; *S* father, 1977. *Educ:* Ampleforth; Corpus Christi College, Oxford. *Heir: cousin* (Matthew) Anthony Leonard Cripps, *qv*. *Address:* Dairy, Sutton Veny, Wilts.

PARNABY, Dr John, CBE 1987; FEng 1986; FIProdE, FIMechE; MIEE; Group Director, Technology, Lucas Industries, since 1983; Chairman, Lucas Metier; Managing Director, Lucas Engineering and Systems Ltd; *b* 10 July 1937; *s* of John Banks Parnaby and Mary Elizabeth Parnaby; *m* 1959, Lilian Armstrong; three *s* one *d*. *Educ:* Durham Univ. (BSc Mech. Engrg, 1961); Glasgow Univ. (PhD Control Engrg, 1966). FIProdE 1978; FIMechE 1978; MIEE 1966. Technical Apprentice, 1954–58, Ironworks Develt Engr, 1961–62, United Steel Co.; Res. Asst, Univ. of Durham, 1962–63; Lectr in Mech. Engrg, Univ. of Glasgow, 1963–66; Sen. Projects Engr, Albright & Wilson Ltd, 1966–67; Works Man., Solway Chemicals Ltd, 1967–70; Univ. of Bradford: Sen. Lectr, 1970–73; Prof. of Manufg Systems Design, 1973–80 (Chm., Sch. of Manufacturing Systems Engrg, 1975–80); Technical and Marketing Dir, subseq. Jt Man. Dir, Rieter Scragg Ltd, 1980–82; Gen. Man., Dunlop Ltd, 1982–83. Vis. Hon. Prof. of Manufacturing Systems Engrg, Univ. of Birmingham, 1984–. Pres., IProdE, 1989. *Publications:* Minicomputers and Microcomputers in Engineering and Manufacture, 1986; over 40 papers in engrg and management jls on manufg systems, control engrg, process engrg and machinery design. *Recreations:* hockey, sailing. *Address:* Crest Edge, Beechnut Lane, Solihull, W Midlands B91 2NN. *T:* 021–705 4348.

PARNELL, family name of **Baron Congleton.**

PARNIS, Alexander Edward Libor, CBE 1973; *b* 25 Aug. 1911; *s* of Alexander T. J. Parnis and Hetty Parnis (*née* Dams). *Educ:* Malvern Coll.; London Univ. BSc(Econ); MA (Cantab). Entered HM Consular Service, 1933: Acting British Vice-Consul, Paris, 1933–34; transferred to HM Treasury, 1937; Finance Officer, Friends' Ambulance Unit, 1941–45; returned to HM Treasury, 1945. Sec., Gowers Cttee on Houses of Outstanding Historic or Architectural Interest, 1950; Sec., Waverley Cttee on Export of Works of Art, etc., 1952; Treasurer, Univ. of Cambridge, 1953–62; Fellow, King's Coll., Cambridge, 1959–62; Asst Sec., Univ. Grants Cttee, 1962–72. Sec., Church's Main Cttee, 1973–81. *Recreations:* music, travel, cycling, walking. *Address:* 4 Jordan Close, Kenilworth, Warwicks CV8 2AE. *T:* Kenilworth (0926) 58354. *Clubs:* Reform; Casino Maltese (Malta).

PARR, (Thomas) Donald, CBE 1986; Chairman, William Baird PLC, since 1981; *b* 3 Sept. 1930; *s* of Thomas and Elizabeth Parr; *m* 1954, Gwendoline Mary Chaplin; three *s* one *d*. *Educ:* Burnage Grammar Sch. Own business, 1953–64; Chm., Thomas Marshall Investments Ltd, 1964–76; Director: William Baird PLC, 1976–; Dunhill Holdings PLC, 1986–; Hepworth PLC, 1989–; Kwik Save Group, 1991–. Chm., British Clothing Industry Assoc., 1987–; Member: NW Industrial Develt Bd, 1975–87; Ct of Governors, UMIST, 1984–. *Recreation:* sailing. *Address:* Homestead, Homestead Road, Disley, Stockport, Cheshire SK12 2JP. *T:* Disley (0663) 765211. *Clubs:* Boodle's; Royal Ocean Racing (Admiral); Royal Yacht Squadron (Cowes).

PARRAMATTA, Bishop of; *see* Watson, Rt Rev. P. R.

PARRETT, John; Managing Director and Clerk of the Course, Aintree Racecourse, since 1989; *b* 18 Sept. 1947; *s* of Peter John and Gladys Mary Parrett; *m* 1968, Deborah Phyllis Gibb; one *s* one *d*. *Educ:* Clarks Coll., Southampton. Fellow, Chartered Inst. of Certified Accountants, 1972; Associate, CIMA, 1970. Various management positions and directorships held in engrg and marine industries from 1968 until entered racing, 1983. *Recreations:* fox hunting, racing, reading, gardening. *Address:* Barrs Farm, Soberton, Southampton SO3 1PN. *T:* Droxford (0489) 878548; Winterbourne Cottage, Aintree Racecourse, Aintree, Liverpool L9 5AS.

PARRINDER, Prof. (Edward) Geoffrey (Simons); Professor of Comparative Study of Religions, University of London, at King's College, 1970–77, Professor Emeritus, 1977; *b* 30 April 1910; *s* of William Patrick and Florence Mary Parrinder; *m* 1936, Esther Mary Burt; two *s* one *d*. *Educ:* private sch.; Richmond Coll., London Univ.; Faculté libre de théologie protestante, Montpellier. MA, PhD, DD London. Minister of Methodist Church, Dahomey and Ivory Coast, 1933; ordained 1936; Principal, Séminaire Protestant, Dahomey, 1936–40, 1945–46; Methodist Church: Redruth, 1940; Dahomey, 1943; Guernsey, 1946; Lectr in Religious Studies, 1949, Sen. Lectr, 1950–58, UC Ibadan; Reader in Comparative Study of Religions, Univ. of London, 1958–70; Dean, Faculty of Theology, KCL, 1972–74. Mem. Editorial Bd of Religious Studies and Jl of Religion in Africa. Hon. Sec., Internat. Assoc. for History of Religions, British Br., 1960–72, Pres., 1972–77; President: London Soc. for Study of Religion, 1980–82; London Soc. of Jews and Christians, 1981–90. Lectures: Charles Strong (Australian Church), 1964; Wilde, in Natural and Comparative Religion, Oxford Univ., 1966–69; Teape, Delhi, Madras, 1973. Vis. Prof., Internat. Christian Univ., Tokyo, 1977–78; Vis. Lectr, Surrey Univ., 1978–83. FKC 1972; Hon. DLitt Lancaster, 1975. *Publications:* West African Religion, 1949; Bible and Polygamy, 1950; West African Psychology, 1951; Religion in an African City, 1953; African Traditional Religion, 1954; Story of Ketu, 1956; Introduction to Asian Religions, 1957; Witchcraft, 1958; (ed) African Ideas of God, 1961; Worship in the World's Religions, 1961; Comparative Religion, 1962; Upanishads, Gītā and Bible, 1962; What World Religions Teach, 1963; The Christian Debate, 1964; The World's Living Religions, 1965; A Book of World Religions, 1965; Jesus in the Qur'ān, 1965; African Mythology, 1967; Religion in Africa, 1969, repr. as Africa's Three Religions, 1976; Avatar and Incarnation, 1970; Dictionary of Non-Christian Religions, 1971; (ed) Man and his Gods, 1971, repr. as Illustrated History of the World's Religions, 1983; The Indestructible Soul, 1973; Themes for Living, 1973; The Bhagavad Gita, a Verse Translation, 1974; Something after Death?, 1974; The Wisdom of the Forest, 1975; Mysticism in the World's Religions, 1976; The Wisdom of the Early Buddhists, 1977; Sex in the World's Religions, 1980; Storia Universale delle Religioni, 1984; Encountering World Religions, 1987; A Dictionary of Religious and Spiritual Quotations, 1989; The Sayings of the Buddha, 1991; articles and reviews in Times Lit. and Educnl Supplements, and jls of theology, African and Asian religions and Annual Register, 1958–. *Recreations:* travel, gardening, literature. *Address:* 31 Charterhouse Road, Orpington, Kent BR6 9EJ. *T:* Orpington (0689) 823887.

See also D. M. Boston.

PARRIS, Matthew Francis; author, journalist and broadcaster; *b* 7 Aug. 1949; *s* of Leslie Francis Parris and Theresa Eunice Parris (*née* Littler). *Educ:* Waterford School, Swaziland; Clare Coll., Cambridge (BA Hons); Yale Univ., USA (Paul Mellon Fellowship). Foreign Office, 1974–76; Conservative Research Dept, 1976–79; MP (C) West Derbyshire, 1979–86; Presenter, Weekend World, LWT, 1986–88. *Publications:* Inca-Kola, 1990; A Traveller's Tale of Peru, 1990. *Recreation:* distance running. *Address:* 6 Masters Lodge, Johnson Street, E1 0BE.

PARROTT, Andrew Haden; conductor and musicologist; *b* 1947. *Educ:* Merton Coll., Oxford (schol.; BA 1969). Formerly: Dir of Music, Merton Coll., Oxford; musical assistant to Sir Michael Tippett; member of Electric Phoenix (vocal gp specialising in modern music). Founded Taverner Choir, 1973, then Taverner Consort and Taverner Players, for performance of music ranging from medieval to late 18th century; Associate Conductor, London Mozart Players, 1989–. Début: BBC Prom. concerts, 1977; EBU, 1979; La Scala, 1985; Salzburg, 1987; Guest Conductor: ECO; Scottish Chamber Orch.; London Sinfonietta; BBC Philharmonic; Kent Opera; orchs in Czechoslovakia, Holland, USA, etc, and at festivals throughout Europe. 30 recordings. *Address:* c/o Norman McCann International Artists Ltd, The Coach House, 56 Lawrie Park Gardens, SE26 6XJ.

PARROY, Michael Picton; QC 1991; *b* 22 Oct. 1946; *s* of Gerard May and Elizabeth Mary Parroy; *m* 1978, Susan Patricia Blades. *Educ:* Malvern College; Brasenose College, Oxford. Called to the Bar, Middle Temple, 1969; a Recorder, 1990. *Publication:* Road Traffic, in Halsbury's Laws of England, 4th edn. vol. 40, 1983. *Recreations:* gardening, food and wine, dog walking. *Address:* First Floor, 3 Paper Buildings, Temple, EC4Y 7EU.

PARRY; *see* Jones Parry and Jones-Parry.

PARRY, family name of **Baron Parry.**

PARRY, Baron *cr* 1975 (Life Peer), of Neyland, Dyfed; **Gordon Samuel David Parry;** Chairman: Milford Docks Company, since 1984; Taylor Plan Services, since 1987; *b* 30 Nov. 1925; *s* of Thomas Lewis Parry and Anne Parry (*née* Evans); *m* 1948, Glenys Parry (*née* Incledon); one *d. Educ:* Neyland Board Sch.; Pembroke County Intermediate Sch.; Trinity Coll., Carmarthen; Univ. of Liverpool (Dipl. Advanced Educn). Teacher: Coronation Sch., Pembroke Dock, 1945–46; Llanstadwell Voluntary Primary Sch., Neyland, 1946–47; Barn St Voluntary Sch., Haverfordwest, 1947; County Primary Sch., Neyland, 1947–52; Librarian, Housemaster, County Sec. Sch., Haverfordwest, 1952–62 and 1963–68; Inst. of Educn, Univ. of Liverpool, 1962–63; Warden, Pembs Teachers' Centre, 1969–78. Former member: Welsh Develt Authority; Gen. Adv. Council, IBA; Welsh Arts Council; Schs Council Cttee for Wales; Member: Fac. of Educn, Univ. Coll. of Wales Aberystwyth; Council, Open Univ. (Chm., Adv. Cttee on Studies in Educn, 1978–83); British Tourist Authority, 1978–84; President: Pembs Br., Multiple Sclerosis Soc.; Pembs Spastics Soc.; Spastics Soc., Wales; Commonwealth Games Appeal Cttee for Wales, 1979; Keep Wales Tidy Cttee, 1979– (Chm., 1979–86); BICSc, 1981–; Chairman: Wales Tourist Bd, 1978–84; British Cleaning Council, 1983–; Keep Britain Tidy, 1986–; Tidy Britain (formerly Keep Britain Tidy Gp), 1986–; Keep Britain Beautiful Campaign, 1986–; British Travel Educn Trust; Vice President: Nat. Chamber of Trade, 1980; Internat. Year of Disabled People in Wales, 1979; Nat. Soc. for Mentally Handicapped Children, S Wales Region; Soc. of Handicapped Drivers in Wales; Welsh Nat. Council of YMCAs; Dir, Guidehouse. Contested (Lab) Monmouth 1959, Pembroke 1970, and Feb. and Oct. 1974. Writer, broadcaster, and TV panel Chm. FRSA; Fellow: Tourism Soc., 1979; HCIMA, 1980; BICSc, 1981; James Cook Univ., N Qld, Aust, 1989; Hon. Fellow, Trinity Coll., Carmarthen, 1990. Hon. Fellow, Inst. of Wastes Management. *Recreations:* travel; watching Welsh Rugby XV win the Grand Slam; reading. *Address:* Willowmead, 52 Port Lion, Llangwm, Haverfordwest, Pembrokeshire, Dyfed SA62 4JT. *T:* Neyland (0646) 600667.

PARRY, Alan; President, Johnson & Higgins Ltd, since 1989 (Chairman, 1987–89); *b* 30 Oct. 1927; *s* of George Henry James Edgar Parry and Jessica Cooke; *m* 1954, Shirley Yeoman; one *s* one *d. Educ:* Reedham School. Leonard Hammond Ltd, 1941; Sedgwick Collins Ltd, 1948, Dir, 1960; Dir, Man. Dir, Dep. Chm. and Chm., Sedgwick companies and subsidiaries, to 1981; Chm., Carter Brito e Cunha, 1982–87. Mem., Lloyd's Insurance Brokers' Assoc., 1961–64, 1970–73, 1975–78 (Chm., 1977); Mem. Council, BIBA, and LIBA and BIBA rep. on Cttee on Invisible Exports, 1977; Mem., Cttee of Lloyd's, 1979–82, 1985–88 (Dep. Chm., 1987–88). *Recreations:* farming, flyfishing, drama. *Address:* Upper Gatton Park, Reigate, Surrey RH2 0TZ. *T:* Merstham (07374) 5388. *Club:* Naval and Military.

PARRY, Anthony Joseph, QFSM 1990; County Fire Officer, 1985–90, and Chief Executive, County Fire Service, 1986–90, Greater Manchester; *b* 20 May 1935; *s* of Henry Joseph Parry and Mary Elizabeth McShane; *m* 1959, Elizabeth Therese Collins; three *s* one *d. Educ:* St Francis Xavier's Coll., Liverpool. MIFireE. Liverpool Fire Bde, 1958; Fire Service Technical Coll., 1967; Gloucestershire Fire Service, 1969; Avon Fire Service, 1974; Lancashire County Fire Service, 1975. Long Service and Good Conduct Medal, 1978. *Address:* 18 Oakenclough Drive, Bolton BL1 5QY.

PARRY, Prof. Eldryd Hugh Owen, OBE 1982; MD, FRCP; Visiting Professor, London School of Hygiene and Tropical Medicine, since 1985; *b* 28 Nov. 1930; *s* of Dr Owen Parry and Dr Constance Parry (*née* Griffiths); *m* 1960, Helen Madeline, *d* of Humphry and Madeline House; one *s* three *d. Educ:* Shrewsbury; Emmanuel Coll., Cambridge; Welsh Nat. Sch. of Medicine (BChir 1955; MA; MD). FWACP. Junior posts, Cardiff Royal Infirmary, Nat. Heart Hosp., Hammersmith Hosp., 1956–65; seconded to UCH, Ibadan, 1960–63; Tutor in Medicine, Univ. of London, 1964; Associate Prof., Haile Selassie I Univ., Addis Ababa, 1966–69; Prof. of Medicine, Ahmadu Bello Univ., 1969–77; Foundn Dean, Faculty of Health Sciences, Univ. of Ilorin, Nigeria, 1977–80; Dean and Prof. of Medicine, Sch. of Med. Scis, Kumasi, 1980–85; Dir, Wellcome Tropical Inst., 1985–90. Albert Cook Meml Lectr, Kampala, 1974; Mem., Med. and Dental Council, Ghana, 1980–85; Chairman: Tropical Health and Educn Trust, 1989–; Council, All Nations Christian Coll., 1986–. Frederick Murgatroyd Prize, RCP, 1973. *Publications:* Principles of Medicine in Africa, 1976; papers on medicine in the tropics in med. jls. *Recreations:* tennis, Wales, old Welsh furniture. *Address:* 21 Edenhurst Avenue, SW6 3PD. *Club:* Hurlingham.

See also J. P. H. House.

PARRY, Emyr Owen; solicitor; a Recorder of the Crown Court, since 1979; *b* 26 May 1933; *s* of Ebenezer Owen Parry and Ellen Parry; *m* 1959, Enid Griffiths; one *s* one *d. Educ:* Caernarfon Grammar Sch.; University Coll. of Wales, Aberystwyth (LLB Hons Wales, 1954). Admitted solicitor, 1957. Estabd own practice in Llangefni, Anglesey, 1958; formed partnership (Emyr Parry & Davies) with Mrs Elinor C. Davies, 1964; Dep. Circuit Judge, 1975. Chairman: Social Security (formerly National Insurance) Appeals Tribunal, Holyhead Area, 1969–; Medical Appeal Tribunal, 1986–; Solicitor Mem., Lord Chancellor's County Court Rule Cttee, 1975–80. *Recreations:* cricket, music, theatre. *Clubs:* Llangefni Cricket (Chm., Life Mem.); Anglesey County Cricket (Vice Pres.).

PARRY, Sir Ernest J.; *see* Jones-Parry.

PARRY, Sir Hugh (Nigel), Kt 1963; CBE 1954; *b* 26 Aug. 1911; *s* of Charles Frank Parry and Lilian Maud Parry (*née* Powell); *m* 1945, Ann Maureen Forshaw; two *d. Educ:* Cheltenham Coll.; Balliol Coll., Oxford. Entered Colonial Administrative Service, 1939. Chief Secretary, Central African Council, Salisbury, S Rhodesia, 1951–53; Secretary, Office of Prime Minister and External Affairs, Federal Government of Rhodesia and Nyasaland, 1953–63; Ministry of Overseas Development, 1965; Acting Head, Middle East Develt Div., 1969–71, retd 1971. *Recreations:* sailing, motoring. *Address:* c/o Grindlays Bank, 13 St James's Square, SW1.

PARRY, John Alderson, CBE 1985; BBC National Governor for Wales, since 1986; *b* 3 Jan. 1934; *s* of Albert Parry and Mary Parry (*née* Alderson); *m* 1959, Joan Rathbone; one *s* one *d. Educ:* Leighton Park, Reading; Christ's College, Cambridge (MA, Vet MB). MRCVS; FRAgS 1986. Veterinary practice, Brecon, 1958–. Mem., Agricl Adv. Council, 1969–73; Chairman: Hill Farming Res. Orgn, 1981–87 (Mem., 1971–); Welsh Agricl Adv. Cttee, BBC, 1978–85; Welsh Office Hydatid Control Steering Cttee, 1981–; Member: Sec. of State for Wales' Agricl Adv. Cttee, 1978–; AFRC, 1982– (Chm., Animals Res. Cttee, 1983–87); Develt Bd for Rural Wales, 1985–88; Council, Royal Welsh Agricl Soc., 1986–; Dir, Animal Disease Res. Assoc., 1987–. President: BVA, 1976–77; RCVS, 1986–87. Chm., Governing Body, Inst. of Grassland and Animal Prodn, AFRC, 1987–; Gov., McCauley Land Use Res. Inst., 1987–. *Recreations:* field sports. *Address:* Watergate Mill, Brecon, Powys LD3 9AN. *T:* Brecon (0874) 2113. *Clubs:* United Oxford & Cambridge University, Farmers'; Hawks (Cambridge); Cardiff & County (Cardiff).

PARRY, Mrs Margaret Joan; Headmistress of Heathfield School, Ascot, 1973–82; *b* 27 Nov. 1919; *d* of W. J. Tamplin, Llantrisant, Glamorgan; *m* 1946, Raymond Howard Parry; two *s* one *d. Educ:* Howell's Sch., Llandaff, Cardiff; Univ. of Wales. Hons English Cl I. Married to a schoolmaster at Eton; taught and coached interesting people from time to time; Examiner for: Civil Service, LCC, Schools Examination Boards. Patron, Univ. of Buckingham, 1983. *Recreations:* books, music, tapestry. *Address:* Carreg Gwaun, 23a Murray Court, Ascot, Berks SL5 9BP. *T:* Ascot (0990) 26299.

PARRY, Robert; MP (Lab) Liverpool, Riverside, since 1983 (Liverpool Exchange, 1970–74; Liverpool, Scotland Exchange, 1974–83); *b* 8 Jan. 1933; *s* of Robert and Sarah Parry (*née* Joyce); *m* 1956, Marie (*née* Hesdon) (*d* 1987). *Educ:* Bishop Goss RC School, Liverpool. Became a building trade worker. Full-time organizer for National Union of Public Employees, 1960–67; now sponsored Member, Transport and General Workers' Union. Member of Co-operative Party. Member, Liverpool City Council, 1963–74. Chm., Merseyside Gp of Labour MPs, 1976–87. Mem., UK Delegn to Council of Europe Assembly and WEU, 1984–. Pres., Assoc. for Democracy in Hong Kong, 1980–; Co-President: Internat. Cttee for Human Rights in S Korea, 1984–; Internat. Cttee for Peaceful and Indep. Reunification of Korea, 1984–. Patron: UNA Hong Kong, 1977–; Rotunda Boxing Club, 1975–; KIND (Kids in Need and Distress); President: Liverpool and Dist Sunday Football League (largest in Europe), 1973–; Liverpool Transport Boxing and Sporting Club, 1982–. Special interests: human rights, peace and disarmament, civil liberties, foreign affairs, particularly Central and SE Asia, overseas aid and the third world. *Address:* House of Commons, SW1A 0AA.

PARRY, Victor Thomas Henry, MA Oxon; FLA; Director of Central Library Services and Goldsmiths' Librarian, University of London, 1983–88; *b* 20 Nov. 1927; *s* of Thomas and Daisy Parry; *m* 1959, Mavis K. Russull; two *s* one *d. Educ:* St Julian's High Sch., Newport; St Edmund Hall, Oxford (MA); University College, London (DipLib). FLA 1959. Manchester Public Libraries, 1950–56; Colonial Office and CRO Library, 1956–60; Librarian, Nature Conservancy, 1960–63; British Museum (Natural History), 1963–74; Chief Librarian and Archivist, Royal Botanic Gdns, Kew, 1974–78; Librarian, SOAS, Univ. of London, 1978–83. Chm., Circle of State Librarians, 1966–68; Mem., Adv. Cttee, British Library Dept of Humanities and Social Scis (formerly Reference Div.), 1983–90; Council Member: Sir Anthony Panizzi Foundn, 1983–89; London Soc., 1984–88. FRSA. *Publications:* contrib. prof. books and jls. *Recreations:* ball games, books, bridge, railways. *Address:* 69 Redway Drive, Twickenham TW2 7NN. *T:* 081–894 0742. *Club:* Commonwealth Trust.

PARRY, Prof. William, PhD; FRS 1984; Professor of Mathematics, University of Warwick, since 1970; *b* 3 July 1934; *s* of late Richard Parry and Violet Irene Parry; *m* 1958, Benita (*née* Teper); one *d. Educ:* University Coll. London (BSc 1956); Univ. of Liverpool (MSc 1957); Imperial Coll. of Science and Technol., London (PhD 1960). Lectr, Univ. of Birmingham, 1960–65; Sen. Lectr, Univ. of Sussex, 1965–68; Reader, Univ. of Warwick, 1968–70. Member: Labour Party; NCCL. *Publications:* Entropy and Generators in Ergodic Theory, 1969; Topics in Ergodic Theory, 1981; (with S. Tuncel) Classification Problems in Ergodic Theory, 1982; articles in Trans Amer. Math. Soc., Amer. Jl of Maths, and Annals of Maths. *Recreations:* theatre, concerts, walking. *Address:* Manor House, High Street, Marton CV23 9RR. *T:* Marton (0926) 632501.

PARRY BROWN, Arthur Ivor; *see* Brown, A. I. P.

PARRY-EVANS, Air Chief Marshal Sir David, GCB 1991 (KCB 1985); CBE 1978; Ministry of Defence (Central Staffs), since 1991; *b* 19 July 1935; *s* of late Group Captain John Parry-Evans, MRCS, LRCP, DLO, and of Dorothy Parry-Evans; *m* 1960, Ann, 2nd *d* of late Charles Reynolds and of Gertrude Reynolds; two *s. Educ:* Berkhamsted School. Joined RAF, 1956; served FEAF, Coastal Command, United States Navy, RN Staff Coll., 1958–70; Headquarters Strike Command, 1970–74; OC 214 Sqn, 1974–75; OC RAF Marham, 1975–77; MoD, 1977–81 (Director of Defence Policy, 1979–81); Comdt, RAF Staff Coll., 1981–82; AOC Nos 1 and 38 Groups, RAF Strike Comd, 1982–85; C-in-C RAF Germany, and Comdr, Second ATAF, 1985–87; Dep. Chief of Defence Staff (Progs and Personnel), 1987–89; Air Mem. for Personnel, 1989–91. *Recreation:* Rugby (Chairman, RAFRU, 1978–83). *Address:* c/o National Westminster Bank, 26 Spring Street, W2. *Club:* Royal Air Force.

PARRY EVANS, Mary Alethea, (Lady Hallinan); a Recorder of the Crown Court, since 1978; *b* 31 Oct. 1929; *o c* of Dr Evan Parry Evans, MD, JP, and Dr Lilian Evans; *m* 1955, Sir Adrian Lincoln Hallinan, *qv*; two *s* two *d. Educ:* Malvern Girls' Coll.; Somerville Coll., Oxford (BCL, MA). Called to Bar, Inner Temple, 1953; Wales and Chester Circuit. Member: Cardiff City Council, 1961–70; S Glamorgan CC, 1972–81; S Glamorgan Health Authority, 1977–81. Lady Mayoress of Cardiff, 1969–70. *Address:* (chambers) 33 Park Place, Cardiff. *T:* Cardiff (0222) 33313.

PARRY JONES, Terence Graham; *see* Jones, Terry.

PARSLOE, Prof. Phyllida; Professor of Social Work, since 1978, and Warden of Wills Hall, since 1991, Bristol University; *b* 25 Dec. 1930; *d* of late Charles Guy Parsloe and of Mary Zirphie (*née* Munro). *Educ:* Bristol Univ. (BA, PhD); London Univ. (Cert. in Mental Health). Probation Officer, Devon CC, 1954–59; Psychiatric Social Worker, St George's Hospital, 1959–65; Lectr, London Sch. of Economics, 1965–70; Associate Prof., Sch. of Law, Indiana Univ., 1970–73; Prof. of Social Work, Univ. of Aberdeen, 1973–78; Pro-Vice Chancellor, Bristol Univ., 1988–91. Member: Central Council for Educn and Training in Social Work, 1986–; Commonwealth Scholarships Commn. *Publications:* The Work of the Probation and After Care Officer, 1967; Juvenile Justice in Britain and America, 1978; (with Prof. O. Stevenson) Social Service Teams: the practitioner's view, 1978; Social Service Area Teams, 1981; report to the Sec. of State for Scotland on Social Work in Prisons, 1987; (with S. Macara *et al*) Data Protection in Health and Social Services, 1988; Aiming for Partnership, 1990; contribs to: British Jl of Social Work, Community Care, Social Work Today, British Jl Criminology. *Recreations:* hill walking, crafts, gardening. *Address:* 15 Elliston Road, Bristol BS6 6QG.

PARSONS, family name of **Earl of Rosse.**

PARSONS, Adrian; *see* Parsons, C. A. H.

PARSONS, Alan; *see* Parsons, T. A.

PARSONS, Alfred Roy, AO 1986; High Commissioner for Australia in the UK, 1984–87, retired; *b* 24 May 1925; *s* of W. G. R. Parsons and R. E. Parsons; *m* 1958, Gillian Tryce Pigot; two *s* one *d. Educ:* Hobart High School; Univ. of Tasmania (postgraduate research; BCom); Canberra University College. Dept of Foreign Affairs, 1947; Djakarta, 1950–53, Rangoon, 1956–58, Berlin, 1961–62; Aust. Mission to UN, NY, 1962–64; Counsellor, Djakarta, 1964–66; High Comr, Singapore, 1967–70; First Asst Sec., Canberra, 1970–73; High Comr, Kuala Lumpur, 1973–76; Dep. Sec., periodically Acting Sec., Dept of Foreign Affairs, 1978–83. Chm., Commonwealth Observer Gp on Namibia, 1989. Member: Australia Japan Foundn, 1978–83; Australia China Council. Pres., ACT Br., Lord's Taverners Australia. *Recreations:* golf, reading. *Address:* 11 Hotham Crescent, Deakin, Canberra, ACT 2600, Australia. *Clubs:* Commonwealth; Royal Canberra Golf, Canberra Wine and Food.

PARSONS, Sir Anthony (Derrick), GCMG 1982 (KCMG 1975; CMG 1969); LVO 1965; MC 1945; HM Diplomatic Service, retired; Research Fellow, University of Exeter, since 1984 (Lecturer, 1984–87); *b* 9 Sept. 1922; *s* of late Col H. A. J. Parsons, MC; *m* 1948, Sheila Emily Baird; two *s* two *d*. *Educ:* King's Sch., Canterbury; Balliol Coll., Oxford (Hon. Fellow 1984). HM Forces, 1940–54; Asst Mil. Attaché, Baghdad, 1952–54; Foreign Office, 1954–55; HM Embassy: Ankara, 1955–59; Amman, 1959–60; Cairo, 1960–61; FO, 1961–64; HM Embassy, Khartoum, 1964–65; Political Agent, Bahrain, 1965–69; Counsellor, UK Mission to UN, NY, 1969–71; Under-Sec., FCO, 1971–74; Ambassador to Iran, 1974–79; FCO, 1979; UK Perm. Rep. to UN, 1979–82; Special Advr to PM on foreign affairs, 1982–83. Bd Mem., British Council, 1982–86. Order of the Two Niles (Sudan), 1965. *Publications:* The Pride and the Fall, 1984; They Say the Lion, 1986. *Recreations:* gardening, golf, tennis. *Address:* Highgrove, Ashburton, South Devon. *Clubs:* MCC, Royal Over-Seas League.

PARSONS, (Charles) Adrian (Haythorne); consultant on charity matters, Wilde Sapte, solicitors, since 1989; *b* 15 June 1929; *s* of Dr R. A. Parsons and Mrs W. S. Parsons (*née* Haythorne); *m* 1951, Hilary Sharpe; one *d*. *Educ:* Bembridge Sch.; Wadham Coll., Oxford. Called to Bar, Gray's Inn, 1964. Coutts & Co., Bankers, 1952–64; joined Charity Commn, 1964; Dep. Comr, 1972; Comr, 1974–89; Head of Legal Staff, 1981; Unit Trust Ombudsman, 1989. *Address:* c/o Wilde Sapte, Queensbridge House, 60 Upper Thames Street, EC4V 3BD. *Club:* United Oxford & Cambridge University.
See also Sir R. E. C. F. Parsons.

PARSONS, Geoffrey Penwill, AO 1990; OBE 1977; concert accompanist; *b* 15 June 1929; *s* of Francis Hedley Parsons and Edith Vera Buckland. *Educ:* Canterbury High Sch., Sydney; State Conservatorium of Music (with Winifred Burston), Sydney. Winner ABC Concerto Competition, 1947; first tour of Australia, 1948; arrived England, 1950; made 25th tour of Australia, 1983; has accompanied many of world's greatest singers and instrumentalists, incl. Elisabeth Schwarzkopf, Victoria de los Angeles, Janet Baker, Jessye Norman, Hans Hotter, Olaf Bär, in 40 countries of world on all six continents. Master Classes: South Bank Summer Festival, 1977 and 1978; Sweden, 1984, 1985, 1987, 1989; Austria, 1985; USA, 1987, 1988; Denmark, 1990; Geoffrey Parsons and Friends, internat. song recital series, Barbican Concert Hall opening season 1982, 1983. FRCM 1987. Hon. RAM, 1975; Hon. GSM, 1983. *Address:* 176 Iverson Road, NW6 2HL. *T:* 071–624 0957.

PARSONS, John Christopher; Deputy Keeper of the Privy Purse and Deputy Treasurer to the Queen, since 1988; *b* 21 May 1946; *s* of Arthur Christopher Parsons and Veronica Parsons; *m* 1982, Hon. Anne Manningham-Buller, *d* of 1st Viscount Dilhorne, PC; two *s* one *d*. *Educ:* Harrow; Trinity College, Cambridge. BA (Mech. Scis) 1968. FCA, MIMC. Dowty Group Ltd, 1968–72; Peat, Marwick, Mitchell & Co., 1972–85; Asst Treas. to the Queen, 1985–87. *Address:* The Old Stables, Kensington Palace, W8 4PU. *Club:* Brooks's.

PARSONS, Mrs J. D.; *see* Beer, Patricia.

PARSONS, Prof. John David, DSc; FEng 1988; FIEE; David Jardine Professor of Electrical Engineering, since 1982, Pro-Vice-Chancellor, since 1990, University of Liverpool; *b* 8 July 1935; *s* of Oswald Parsons and Doris Anita (*née* Roberts); *m* 1969, Mary Winifred Stella Tate. *Educ:* University College of Wales, Cardiff (BSc); King's College London (MSc (Eng), DSc (Eng)). FIEE 1986. GEC Applied Electronics Labs, 1959–62; Regent Street Poly., 1962–66; City of Birmingham Poly., 1966–68; Lectr, Sen. Lectr and Reader in Electronic Engrg, Univ. of Birmingham, 1969–82; University of Liverpool: Head, Dept of Electrical Engrg and Electronics, 1983–86; Dean, Faculty of Engrg, 1986–89. Vis. Prof., Univ. of Auckland, 1982; Vis. Res. Engr, NTT, Japan, 1987. UN Expert in India, 1977; Hon. SPSO, RSRE, Malvern, 1978–82. Member Council: IERE, 1985–88; IEE, 1988–89. *Publications:* Electronic and Switching Circuits, 1975; Mobile Radio Communications, 1989; The Mobile Radio Propagation Channel, 1991; many papers on radio communication systems and radio propagation in learned jls. *Recreations:* golf, bridge, ski-ing. *Address:* Department of Electrical Engineering and Electronics, University of Liverpool, PO Box 147, Liverpool L69 3BX. *T:* 051–794 4503.

PARSONS, Sir (John) Michael, Kt 1970; Deputy Chairman and Chief Executive, 1979–81, Senior Managing Director, 1976–81, Director, 1971–81, Inchcape & Co. Ltd; *b* 29 Oct. 1915; *s* of late Rt Rev. Richard Godfrey Parsons, DD, Bishop of Hereford; *m* 1st, 1946, Hilda Mary Frewen (marr. diss. 1964); one *s* two *d*; 2nd, 1964, Caroline Inagh Margaret Frewen. *Educ:* Rossall Sch.; University Coll., Oxford. Barry & Co., Calcutta, 1937. Served in Royal Garhwal Rifles (Indian Army), 1939–45: Bde Major, 1942; POW, Singapore, 1942. Macneill & Barry Ltd, Calcutta, 1946–70; Chm. & Managing Dir, 1964–70; Chm., Macdonald Hamilton & Co. Pty Ltd, 1970–72; Chairman and Director: Assam Investments, 1976–81; Paxall Investments Ltd, 1982–84; Dep. Chm. and Dir, Inchcape Insurance Hldgs Ltd, 1979–83; Dir, Commonwealth Develt Finance Co. Ltd, 1973–86. Vice-Chm., Indian Jute Mills Assoc., 1960–61; President: Bengal Chamber of Commerce, 1968–69; Associated Chambers of Commerce of India, 1969; Chm., UK Cttee, Fedn of Commonwealth Chambers of Commerce, 1974; Mem., Advisory Council on Trade, Bd of Trade, India, 1968–69. Chm. Council, Royal Commonwealth Soc., 1976–80, Vice Pres., 1980–; Pres., India, Pakistan and Bangladesh Assoc., 1973–78, Vice Pres., 1978. Dep. Chm., Internat. Bd, United World Colls, 1981–86. *Recreation:* golf. *Address:* Tall Trees, Warren Hill Lane, Aldeburgh, Suffolk IP15 5QB. *T:* Aldeburgh (0728) 2917. *Clubs:* Oriental; Bengal, Tollygunge (Calcutta); Union (Sydney).

PARSONS, Kenneth Charles, CMG 1970; OBE 1962; HM Diplomatic Service, retired; Counsellor, Foreign and Commonwealth Office, 1972–80; *b* 9 Jan. 1921; *m* 1st, 1949, Monica (*née* Howell) (decd); two *d*; 2nd, 1977, Mary Woolhouse. *Educ:* Haverfordwest Grammar Sch.; Exeter Coll., Oxford. Served War of 1939–45: with Oxfordshire and Buckinghamshire LI, 1941–46. 1st Class Hons, Mod. Langs (at Oxford), 1948. Joined Diplomatic Service, 1949; served FO, Moscow, Tokyo, Rangoon and Athens, 1951–72; FCO, 1972–77; Counsellor, with British Forces, Hong Kong, 1977–79. *Recreations:* rowing, swimming, walking. *Address:* 46 Lackford Road, Chipstead, Surrey CR5 3TA. *T:* Downland (0737) 555051. *Club:* Carlton.

PARSONS, Sir Michael; *see* Parsons, Sir J. M.

PARSONS, Air Comdt Dame Pauline, (formerly **Air Comdt Dame Pauline Giles**), DBE 1967; RRC; Matron-in-Chief, Princess Mary's Royal Air Force Nursing Service, 1966–70, retired; *b* 17 Sept. 1912; *m* 1987, Daniel G. Parsons, OBE. *Educ:* Sheffield. Joioned PMRAFNS, Nov. 1937; later appointments included Principal Matron for Royal Air Force Command in Britain and Western Europe; became Matron-in-Chief, PMRAFNS, Sept. 1966. *Address:* Coma Colat, La Massana, Andorra.

PARSONS, Prof. Peter John, FBA 1977; Regius Professor of Greek, University of Oxford, since 1989; Student of Christ Church, Oxford, since 1964; *b* 24 Sept. 1936; *s* of Robert John Parsons and Ethel Ada (*née* Frary). *Educ:* Raynes Park County Grammar Sch.; Christ Church, Oxford (MA 1961). Oxford University: Craven Scholar, 1955; 1st Cl. Hons Mods and de Paravicini Scholar, 1956; Chancellor's Prize for Latin Verse and Gaisford Prize for Greek Verse, 1st Cl. Lit. Hum., Derby Scholar, Dixon and Sen. Scholar of Christ Church, 1958; Passmore Edwards Scholar, 1959; Lectr in Documentary Papyrology, 1960–65; Lectr in Papyrology, 1965–89. J. H. Gray Lectr, Univ. of Cambridge, 1982; Heller Lectr, Univ. of Calif, Berkeley, 1988. Hon. PhD Bern, 1985. *Publications:* (jtly) The Oxyrhynchus Papyri XXXI, 1966, XXXIII and XXXIV, 1968; The Oxyrhynchus Papyri XLII, 1973; (with H. Lloyd-Jones) Supplementum Hellenisticum, 1983; articles in learned jls. *Recreations:* music, cinema, cooking and eating. *Address:* Christ Church, Oxford OX1 1DP. *T:* Oxford (0865) 296223.

PARSONS, Sir Richard (Edmund Clement Fownes), KCMG 1982 (CMG 1977); HM Diplomatic Service, retired; Ambassador to Sweden, 1984–87; *b* 14 March 1928; *s* of Dr R. A. Parsons; *m* 1960, Jenifer Jane Mathews (*d* 1981); three *s*. *Educ:* Bembridge Sch.; Brasenose Coll., Oxford. Served in Army, 1949–51; joined HM Foreign (subseq. Diplomatic) Service, 1951; FO, 1951–53; 3rd Sec., Washington, 1953–56; 2nd Sec., Vientiane, 1956–58; FO, 1958–60; 1st Sec., Buenos Aires, 1960–63; FO, 1963–65; 1st Sec., Ankara, 1965–67; FO, 1967–69; Counsellor, Lagos, 1969–72; Head of Personnel Ops Dept, FCO, 1972–76; Ambassador to: Hungary, 1976–79; Spain, 1980–84. *Publications:* The Moon Pool, 1988; *as John Haythorne:* None of Us Cared for Kate, 1968; The Strelsau Dimension, 1981; Mandrake in Granada, 1984; Mandrake in the Monastery, 1985. *Recreations:* reading, writing, music, travel. *Address:* 152 De Beauvoir Road, N1. *Club:* Garrick.
See also C. A. H. Parsons.

PARSONS, Roger, PhD, DSc; FRS 1980; FRSC; Professor of Chemistry, University of Southampton, 1985–Sept. 1992; *b* 31 Oct. 1926; *s* of Robert Harry Ashby Parsons and Ethel Fenton; *m* 1953, Ruby Millicent Turner; three *s* one *d*. *Educ:* King Alfred Sch., Hampstead; Strathcona High Sch., Edmonton, Alta; Imperial Coll. of Science and Technol., (BSc, PhD). DSc Bristol 1962; ARCS 1946; FRIC 1962. Asst Lectr, Imp. Coll. of Science and Technol., 1948–50; Deedes Fellow, Dundee Univ., 1950–54; Lectr, then Reader in Electrochem., Bristol Univ., 1954–79; Dir, Lab. d'Electrochimie Interfaciale, Centre Nat. de la Recherche Scientifique, Meudon, France, 1977–84. Unesco Specialist, Buenos Aires, 1961; Vis. Prof., Calif Inst. of Technol., 1966–67. Royal Society of Chemistry: Pres., Faraday Div., 1991– (Vice-Pres., 1984–91); Liversidge Lectr, 1989–90. Hon. Fellow, Polish Chem. Soc., 1981. Palladium Medal, US Electrochem. Soc., 1979; Bruno Breyer Medal, Electrochem. Div., RACI, 1980; Prix Paul Pascal de l'Acad. des Scis, 1983; Galvani Medal, Electrochem. Div., Italian Chem. Soc., 1986. Editor, Jl of Electroanal. Chem., 1962–. *Publications:* Electrochemical Data, 1956; (with J. Lyklema) Electrical Properties of Interfaces, 1983; (ed jtly) Standard Potentials in Aqueous Solution, 1985; (ed with R. Kalvoda) Electrochemistry in Research and Development, 1985; *circa* 200 papers in scientific jls. *Recreations:* listening to music, going to the opera. *Address:* Department of Chemistry, The University, Southampton SO9 5NH.

PARSONS, (Thomas) Alan, CB 1984; LLB; Chief Adjudication Officer, Department of Health and Social Security, 1984–86; *b* 25 Nov. 1924; *s* of late Arthur and Laura Parsons; *m* 1st, 1947, Valerie Vambeck; one *s*; 2nd, 1957, Muriel Lewis; two *s*. *Educ:* Clifton Coll.; Bristol Univ. (LLB). Called to the Bar, Middle Temple, 1950. Served, Royal Marines, 1943–46. Legal Asst, Min. of Nat. Insurance, 1950; Sen. Legal Asst, Min. of Pensions and Nat. Insurance, 1955; Asst Solicitor, 1968, Principal Asst Solicitor, 1977, DHSS. *Recreations:* walking, listening to music. *Address:* 11 Northiam Street, Pennethorne Place, E9. *T:* 081–986 0930. *Club:* University Women's (Dining Mem.).

PARSONS-SMITH, (Basil) Gerald, OBE (mil.) 1945; MA, MD, FRCP; Hon. Consulting Neurologist, Charing Cross Hospital; Hon. Consulting Physician, St Mary's Hospital Group; Teacher in Medicine, London University; *b* 19 Nov. 1911; *s* of late Dr Basil Parsons-Smith, FRCP, and Marguerite, *d* of Sir David Burnett, 1st Bt; *m* 1939, Aurea Mary, *d* of late William Stewart Johnston, Sunningdale; two *s* one *d*. *Educ:* Harrow; Trinity Coll., Cambridge. St George's Hospital: Entrance Exhib., 1933; Brackenbury Prize in Medicine, 1936; House Surgeon, House Physician, Med. Registrar. Physician: Western Ophthalmic Hospital (St Mary's), 1938–60; Electro Encephalograph Dept, Middlesex Hospital Medical Sch., 1950–55; Dept of Neurology, West London and Charing Cross Hosps, 1950–77; Graylingwell Hosp., Chichester, 1950; West End Hosp. for Neurology, 1951–72; Neurologist, Florence Nightingale Hosp., 1955. MRCP 1939. Served War of 1939–45, as Blood Transfusion Officer, Chelsea EMS, then as medical specialist i/c medical divisions in RAF Hospitals in ME; Sqdn Leader RAFVR (despatches, OBE). MD (Cantab) 1949, Prox. Acc. Raymond Horton-Smith Prize; FRCP 1955. Examiner, RCP. FRSocMed. Member: Med. Appeals Trib., 1966–83; Vaccine Damage Tribunal, 1979–83; Association of British Neurologists; Ophthalmic Society of UK. Liveryman, Society of Apothecaries. Appeared in Hospital 1922, BBC TV, 1972. *Publications:* EEG of Brain Tumours, 1949; Sir Gordon Holmes, in, Historical Aspects of the Neurosciences, 1982; 58 contribs to medical, neurological and ophthalmic jls mostly on the immediate treatment of acute stroke of the brain (1979) and eye (1952). *Recreation:* managing wife's equitation centre. *Address:* Roughets House, Bletchingley, Surrey RH1 4QX. *T:* Caterham (0883) 343929. *Clubs:* Royal Society of Medicine; Pitt (Cambridge).

PARTINGTON, Prof. Thomas Martin; Professor of Law, since 1987 and Dean, Faculty of Law, since 1988, Bristol University; *b* 5 March 1944; *s* of Thomas Paulett Partington and Alice Emily Mary Partington; *m* 1st, 1970, Marcia Carol Leavey (marr. diss.); one *s*; 2nd, 1978, Daphne Isobel Scharenguivel; one *s* one *d*. *Educ:* King's Sch., Canterbury; Peterhouse, Cambridge (BA 1965; LLB 1966). Called to the Bar, Middle Temple, 1984. Asst Lectr, Bristol Univ., 1966–69; Lectr, Warwick Univ., 1969–73, LSE, 1973–80; Prof. of Law, Brunel Univ., 1980–87 (Dean, Faculty of Soc. Scis, 1985–87). Visiting Professor: Osgoode Hall Law Sch., Canada, 1976; Univ. of NSW, 1983. Chm., Cttee of Heads of Univ. Law Schools, 1990–. Vice-Chm., Legal Action Gp, 1982–83; Member: Lord Chancellor's Adv. Cttee on Legal Aid, 1988–; Tribunals Cttee, Judicial Studies Bd, 1988–; Law Society's Trng Cttee, 1989–; Law Society's Academic Consultative Cttee, 1989–; External Adviser, Educn and Trng Cttee, Inst. of Housing, 1985–89; Part time Chm., Soc. Security Appeals Tribunal, 1990– (Adviser on trng to Pres. 1984–). Gen. Editor, Anglo-American Law Review, 1984–. *Publications:* Landlord and Tenant, 1975; Claim in Time, 1978; (with A. Arden) Housing Law, 1983; (with P. O'Higgins) Bibliography of Social Security Law, 1986; Secretary of State's Powers of Adjudication in Social Security Law, 1990; (with J. Hill) Housing Law: cases, materials and commentary, 1991; articles on public law, housing law, social security law, Legal Aid and Legal Services. *Recreations:* playing the violin, reading fiction, gardening, cooking. *Address:* Little Court, Grib Lane, Blagdon, Avon BS18 6SA. *T:* Blagdon (0761) 62916.

PARTON, Prof. John Edwin; Professor of Electrical Engineering, University of Nottingham, 1954–78, now Emeritus; *b* Kingswinford, Staffordshire, 26 Dec. 1912; *s* of Edwin and Elizabeth Parton; *m* 1940, Gertrude Brown; one *s* one *d*. *Educ:* Huntington Church of England Sch.; Cannock Chase Mining Coll.; University of Birmingham. BSc (1st Class Hons), 1936, PhD, 1938, Birmingham; DSc Glasgow, 1971. Training: Littleton Collieries, 1934; Electrical Construction Co., 1935; Asst Engineer, PO Engineering Dept, Dollis Hill Research Station, 1938–39; Part-time Lecturer: Cannock Chase Mining Coll., 1931–38; Northampton Polytechnic, 1938–39. Served RNVR Electrical Branch, Sub-Lt,

1939, to Lt-Comdr, 1943–45. Sen. Sci. Officer, British Iron and Steel Research Assoc., 1946; Lecturer, 1946–54, Senior Lecturer, 1954, University of Glasgow. Sen. Vis. Scientist, Nat. Sci. Foundn at Univ. of Tennessee, 1965–66; Vis. Prof., Univ. of W Indies, Trinidad, 1979, 1980. Chairman, East Midland Centre Institution of Electrical Engineers, 1961–62. FIEE 1966; Life MIEEE 1990; FIMechE 1967. *Publications:* Applied Electromagnetics (jtly), 1975; papers in Proc. IEE, Trans. IEEE, Trans. IES, Instrument Practice, International Journal of Electrical Engineering Education, etc. *Recreations:* golf, gardening, bowls, bridge. *Address:* 93 Parkside, Wollaton, Nottingham NG8 2NQ. *T:* Nottingham (0602) 286693.

PARTRIDGE, Rt. Rev. Arthur; *see* Partridge, Rt Rev. W. A.

PARTRIDGE, Bernard B.; *see* Brook-Partridge.

PARTRIDGE, Derek William, CMG 1987; HM Diplomatic Service, retired; *b* 15 May 1931; *o s* of late Ernest and Ethel Elizabeth Partridge (*née* Buckingham), Wembley. *Educ:* Preston Manor County Grammar Sch., Wembley. Entered Foreign Service (later Diplomatic Service), 1949. Royal Air Force, 1949–51. Served: Foreign Office, 1951–54; Oslo, 1954–56; Jedda, 1956; Khartoum, 1957–60; Sofia, 1960–62; Bangkok, 1962; Manila, 1962–65; Djakarta, 1965–67; FCO, 1967–70; Diplomatic Service Inspectorate, 1970–72; British Consul-General, Brisbane, 1972–74; First Sec. (Economic and Commercial), Colombo, 1974–77; FCO, 1977–86: Counsellor and Head of Migration and Visa Dept, 1981–83; Counsellor and Head of Nationality and Treaty Dept, 1983–86; High Comr, Sierra Leone, 1986–91. *Address:* 54 Chester Court, Albany Street, NW1 4BU.

PARTRIDGE, Ian Harold; concert singer (tenor); *b* 12 June 1938; *s* of Harold Partridge and Ena Stinson; *m* 1959, Ann Glover; two *s. Educ:* New Coll., Oxford (chorister); Clifton Coll. (music scholar); Royal Coll. of Music; Guildhall Sch. of Music (LGSM, singing and teaching). Began as piano accompanist, although sang tenor in Westminster Cath. Choir, 1958–62; full-time concert singer, 1963–; performs in England and all over the world, both in recitals (with sister Jennifer) and in concerts; has worked with many leading conductors, incl. Stokowski, Boult, Giulini, Boulez and Colin Davis. Opera debut at Covent Garden as Iopas in Berlioz, Les Troyens, 1969. Title role, Britten's St Nicolas, Thames Television (Prix Italia, 1977). Over 100 records, *including:* Schubert, Die Schöne Müllerin, Die Winterreise; Schumann, Dichterliebe; Beethoven, An die ferne Geliebte; Vaughan-Williams, On Wenlock Edge; Warlock, The Curlew; Fauré and Duparc Songs; Britten, Serenade and Winter Words. Innumerable radio broadcasts, many TV appearances. Governor, Clifton Coll., 1981–. *Recreations:* bridge, horse racing, theatre, cricket. *Address:* 127 Pepys Road, SW20 8NP.

PARTRIDGE, John Albert, CBE 1981; RA; FRIBA; architect in private practice; a Senior and Founder Partner, Howell, Killick, Partridge & Amis (HKPA), since 1959; *b* 26 Aug. 1924; *s* of George and Gladys Partridge; *m* 1953, Doris (*née* Foreman); one *s* one *d. Educ:* Shooter's Hill Grammar Sch., Woolwich; Polytechnic School of Architecture, Regent Street. FRIBA 1966 (ARIBA 1951); RA 1988 (ARA 1980). London County Council Housing Architects Dept, 1951–59; Design Tutor, Architectural Assoc., 1958–61. The work of HKPA includes universities, colleges, public buildings, housing and leisure buildings; principal commissions include: Wolfson, Rayne and Gatehouse building, St Anne's Coll., Oxford; New Hall and Common Room building, St Antony's Coll., Oxford; Wells Hall, Reading Univ.; Middlesex Polytechnic College of Art, Cat Hill; Medway Magistrates' Court; The Albany, Deptford; Hall of Justice, Trinidad and Tobago; Warrington Court House; Basildon Magistrates' Courthouse; Berlin Mineral Spa; Haywards Heath Magistrates' Courthouse; Japanese University Coll., Univ. of Kent, Canterbury. RIBA: Vice-Pres., 1977–79; Hon. Librarian, 1977–81; Chm. Res. Steering Gp, 1977–84. Vice-Pres., Concrete Soc., 1979–81. External Examiner in Architecture: Bath Univ., 1975–78; Thames Polytechnic, 1978–86; Cambridge Univ., 1979–81; Manchester Univ., 1982–; South Bank Polytechnic, 1982–86; Brighton Polytechnic, 1987–. Governor, Building Centre Trust, 1982–; Chm., Assoc. of Consultant Architects, 1983–85. Mem., NEDO Construction Res. Strategy Cttee, 1983–86; Architect Mem., FCO Adv. Bd on the Diplomatic Estate, 1985–. *Publications:* articles in technical press. *Recreations:* looking at buildings, travel, sketching and taking photographs. *Address:* Cudham Court, Cudham, near Sevenoaks, Kent TN14 7QF. *T:* Biggin Hill (0959) 71294. *Club:* Arts.

PARTRIDGE, Dr Linda; Reader in Zoology, Edinburgh University, since 1987; *b* 18 March 1950; *d* of George and Ida Partridge; *m* 1983, Dr V. K. French (marr. diss.). *Educ:* Convent of the Sacred Heart, Tunbridge Wells; St Anne's Coll., Oxford (MA); Wolfson Coll., Oxford (DPhil 1974). Post-doctoral Fellow, York Univ., 1974–76; Lectr, Edinburgh Univ., 1976–87. Pres., Internat. Soc. in Behavioural Ecology, 1990–92. *Publications:* on evolutionary biology in scientific jls. *Recreations:* wind-surfing, hill walking, gardening. *Address:* 135 Mayfield Road, Edinburgh EH9 3AN. *T:* 031–667 1696.

PARTRIDGE, Sir Michael (John Anthony), KCB 1990 (CB 1983); Permanent Secretary, Department of Social Security, since 1988; *b* 29 Sept. 1935; *s* of late Dr John Henry Partridge, DSc, PhD, and of Ethel Green; *m* 1968, Joan Elizabeth Hughes; two *s* one *d. Educ:* Merchant Taylors'; St John's Coll., Oxford. BA (1st Cl. Hons Mods and Lit Hum) 1960, MA 1963. Entered Home Civil Service (Min. of Pensions and Nat. Insce), 1960; Private Sec. to Permanent Sec., 1962–64; Principal, 1964–71 (MPNI, Min. of Social Security and DHSS); DHSS: Asst Sec., 1971–76; Under Sec., 1976–81; Dep. Sec., 1981–83; Dep. Under-Sec. of State, Home Office, 1983–87; Second Permanent Sec., DHSS, 1987–88. Senior Treasurer, Methodist Ch. Finance Div., 1980–. Liveryman, Merchant Taylors' Co., 1987–. *Recreations:* Do-it-Yourself, Greece, reading, skiing. *Address:* Department of Social Security, Richmond House, 79 Whitehall, SW1A 2NS. *Club:* United Oxford & Cambridge University.

PARTRIDGE, Prof. (Stanley) Miles, FRS 1970; Professor of Biochemistry, University of Bristol, since 1976; *b* Whangarei, NZ, 2 Aug. 1913; *s* of Ernest Joseph Partridge and Eve Partridge (later Eve McCarthy) (*d* 1977); *m* 1940, Ruth Dowling; four *d. Educ:* Harrow County Sch.; Battersea Coll. of Technology. PhD Chemistry 1937; MA 1946, ScD 1964, Cantab. Beit Memorial Fellow, Lister Inst. of Preventive Medicine, 1940; Techn. Adviser, Govt of India, 1944; returned to Low Temperature Stn, Cambridge, 1946; Principal Scientific Officer 1952; Dep. Chief Scientific Officer, ARC, 1964; Head of Dept of Biochem. and Physiol., ARC Meat Research Inst., 1968–78. Member: Biochemical Soc. Cttee, 1957–61; Nuffield Foundn Rheumatism Cttee, 1965–77. Fourth Tanner Lectr and Award, Inst. of Food Technologists, Chicago, 1964. Hon. DSc Reading, 1984. Laurea ad Honorem in Medicine and Surgery, Univ. of Padua, 1986. *Publications:* scientific papers, mainly in Biochemical Jl. *Recreation:* gardening. *Address:* Millstream House, St Andrew's Road, Cheddar, Somerset BS27 3NG. *T:* Cheddar (0934) 742130.

PARTRIDGE, Rt. Rev. (William) Arthur; Assistant Bishop of Hereford, 1963–75; Prebendary Emeritus, Hereford Cathedral, since 1977; *b* 12 Feb. 1912; *s* of Alfred and Sarah Partridge; *m* 1945, Annie Eliza Joan Strangwood (*d* 1984); one *s. Educ:* Alcester Grammar Sch.; Birmingham Univ.; Scholæ Cancellarii, Lincoln. Curate of Lye, Worcs, 1935; SPG Studentship at Birmingham Univ. Education Dept, 1938–39; Educational Missionary, Dio. Madras, 1939–43; Chaplain, RAFVR, 1943–46; Lecturer Meston Training Coll., Madras, 1947–51; Metropolitan's Commissary and Vicar-General in Nandyal, 1951; Asst Bishop of Calcutta (Bishop in Nandyal), 1953–63; Vicar of Ludford, 1963–69. *Publication:* The Way in India, 1962. *Recreation:* the organ. *Address:* Flat 3, Capel Court, The Burgage, Prestbury, Cheltenham, Glos GL52 3EL. *T:* Cheltenham (0242) 576505.

PASCO, Richard Edward, CBE 1977; actor; Hon. Associate Artist, Royal Shakespeare Company; *b* 18 July 1926; *s* of Cecil George Pasco and Phyllis Irene Pasco; *m* 1st, Greta (*née* Watson) (marr. diss.); one *s*; 2nd, 1967, Barbara (*née* Leigh-Hunt). *Educ:* Colet Court; King's Coll. Sch., Wimbledon; Central Sch. of Speech and Drama (Gold Medallist). Served HM Forces, 1944–48. 1st stage appearance, She Stoops to Conquer, 1943; 1st London appearance, Zero Hour, Lyric, 1944; 1st New York appearance, The Entertainer, 1958. London appearances include: leading roles, English Stage Co., Royal Court, 1957; The Entertainer, Palace, 1957; The Lady from the Sea, Queen's, 1961; Teresa of Avila, Vaudeville, 1961; Look Homeward, Angel, Phoenix, 1962; The New Men, Strand, 1962; The Private Ear and the Public Eye, Globe, 1963; Bristol Old Vic: Henry V (title role), Berowne in Love's Labour's Lost, 1964; Peer Gynt (title role), Angelo in Measure for Measure, Hamlet (title role), 1966 (and world tour); Ivanov, Phoenix, 1965; The Italian Girl, Wyndham's, 1968. Joined RSC, 1969; leading roles include: Becket, Murder in the Cathedral, Aldwych, 1972; (alternated with Ian Richardson) Richard and Bolingbroke in Richard II, Stratford-on-Avon, 1973, and Stratford and Aldwych, 1974; tour of Amer. univs; Jack Tanner in Man and Superman, Malvern Festival, tour and Savoy, 1977; Timon in Timon of Athens, Clarence in Richard III, Arkady Schatslivtses in The Forest, Stratford, 1980–81; La Ronde, Aldwych, 1982; National Theatre: The Father in Six Characters in Search of an Author, Pavel in Fathers and Sons, 1987; Rt Rev. Charlie Allen in Racing Demon, 1990. Many foreign tours; accompanied HSH Princess Grace of Monaco at Edinburgh, Stratford and Aldeburgh Festivals and on tour of USA, 1977–78. Frequent appearances at Aldeburgh, Brighton, Windsor and Harrogate festivals, Stratford-upon-Avon Poetry Festival etc. Recent films: A Watcher in the Woods; Wagner. Countless TV and radio appearances; recent television series: Sorrell & Son; Drummonds; Hannay, etc. Many recordings of poems, plays, recitals, etc. *Recreations:* music, gardening, reading. *Address:* c/o Michael Whitehall Ltd, 125 Gloucester Road, SW7 4TE. *Club:* Garrick.

PASCO, Rowanne; Religious Editor, TV-am, since 1987; *b* 7 Oct. 1938; *d* of John and Ann Pasco. *Educ:* Dominican Convent, Chingford; Ursuline Convent, Ilford; Open Univ. (BA). Reporter, 1956–57, Editor, 1957–58, Chingford Express; Publicity Officer, NFU, 1958–59; Account Exec., Leslie Frewin PR, 1959–60; Travel Rep., Horizon Holidays, 1960–64; Publicity Asst, Paramount Pictures Corp., Hollywood, 1964–66; Publicity Officer, Religious Progs, Radio and TV, BBC, 1966–71; Reporter, BBC Radio London, 1971–72; TV Editor, Ariel, BBC Staff Newspaper, 1972–74; Radio 4 Reporter, 1974–76; Researcher, Religious Progs, BBC TV, 1976–77; Producer and Presenter, Religious Progs, BBC Radio, 1977–78; Dep. Editor, 1979–81, Editor, 1981–87, The Universe. *Publication:* (ed with Fr John Redford) Faith Alive, 1988. *Recreations:* gardening, Italy, creative cooking. *Address:* Breakfast Television Centre, Hawley Crescent, NW1 8EF.

PASCOE, Alan Peter, MBE 1975; Managing Director, Alan Pascoe Associates Ltd, since 1983 (Director, 1976–83); Chairman, Pascoe Nally International Ltd, since 1987; Board Member, WCRS Group plc, since 1986; *b* 11 Oct. 1947; *s* of Ernest George Frank Pascoe and Joan Rosina Pascoe; *m* 1970, Della Patricia (*née* James); one *s* one *d. Educ:* Portsmouth Southern Grammar Sch.; Borough Road Coll. (Cert. in Educn); London Univ. (Hons degree in Educn). Master, Dulwich Coll., 1971–74; Lectr in Physical Educn, Borough Road Coll., Isleworth, 1974–80. Member: Sports Council, 1974–80; Minister for Sport's Working Party on Centres of Sporting Excellence; BBC Adv. Council, 1975–79. European Indoor Champion, 50m Hurdles, 1969; Europ. Games Silver Medallist, 110m Hurdles, 1971; Silver Medal, Olympic Games, Munich, 4 × 400m Relay, 1972; Europa Gold Cup Medallist, 400m Hurdles, 1973; Commonwealth Games Gold Medal, 400m Hurdles, and Silver Medal, 4 × 400m Relay, 1974; Europ. Champion and Gold Medallist in both 400m Hurdles and 4 × 400m Relay, 1974; Europa Cup Gold Medallist, 400m Hurdles, 1975; Olympic Finalist (injured), Montreal, 1976; Europe's Rep., World Cup Event, 1977. *Publication:* An Autobiography, 1979. *Recreations:* theatre, sport. *Address:* c/o Alan Pascoe Associates Ltd, 141–143 Drury Lane, WC2B 5TB. *T:* 071–379 5220.

PASCOE, Dr Michael William; Head of Science, Camberwell College of Arts (formerly Camberwell School of Arts and Crafts), 1981–90; *b* 16 June 1930; *s* of Canon W. J. T. Pascoe and Mrs D. Pascoe; *m* 1st, 1956, Janet Clark (marr. diss. 1977); three *d*; 2nd, 1977, Brenda Hale Reed; one *d. Educ:* St John's, Leatherhead; Selwyn Coll., Cambridge (BA, PhD). MInstP. Res. Student (Tribology), Cambridge, 1951–55; Physicist: Mount Vernon Hosp., Northwood, 1956–57; British Nylon Spinners Ltd, 1957–60; Chemist/Physicist, ICI Paints Div., 1960–67; Lectr (Polymer Science), Brunel Univ., 1967–77; Principal Scientific Officer, 1976–79, Keeper of Conservation and Technical Services, 1979–81, British Museum. Tutor and Counsellor, Open Univ., 1971–76. Occasional Lectr: Winchester Coll., 1989–90; Univ. of Stirling, 1991–; Camberwell Coll. of Arts. Consultant to: Royal Acad. of Arts (Great Japan exhibn), 1982–; Mary Rose Trust, 1978–83; Council for the Care of Churches, 1980–; Public Record Office (Domesday exhibn), 1986; Science Museum, 1988. FRSA. *Publications:* contrib. to books on polymer tribol. and technol.; articles in scientific, engrg and conservation jls on tribol., materials technol. and on conservation methods. *Recreations:* painting and drawing *inter alia. Address:* 15 Parkfield Road, Ickenham, Uxbridge UB10 8LN. *T:* Uxbridge (0895) 674723.

PASCOE, Nigel Spencer Knight; QC 1988; a Recorder of the Crown Court, since 1979; *b* 18 Aug. 1940; *er s* of late Ernest Sydney Pascoe and of Cynthia Pascoe; *m* 1964, Elizabeth Anne Walter; two *s* four *d. Educ:* Epsom Coll. Called to the Bar, Inner Temple, 1966. County Councillor for Lyndhurst, Hants, 1979–84. Founder and Editor, All England Qly Law Cassettes, 1976–85. *Publications:* The Trial of Penn and Mead, 1985; articles in legal jls. *Recreations:* theatre, devising and presenting with Elizabeth Pascoe legal anthologies, after-dinner speaking, cricket, writing. *Address:* 3 Pump Court, Temple, EC4 7AJ. *T:* 071–353 0711. *Club:* Garrick.

PASCOE, Gen. Sir Robert (Alan), KCB 1985; MBE 1968; Adjutant General, 1988–90; Aide de Camp General to the Queen, 1989–91, retired; Director, Executive Action Ltd, since 1991; *b* 21 Feb. 1932; *er s* of late C. and Edith Mary Pascoe; *m* 1955, Pauline (*née* Myers); one *s* three *d. Educ:* Tavistock Grammar Sch.; RMA, Sandhurst. rcds, psc. Commissioned Oxford and Bucks LI, 1952; served with 1 Oxf. Bucks, 1 DLI and 4 Oxf. Bucks (TA), 1953–57; Middle East Centre for Arab Studies, Lebanon, 1958–59; 1st Cl. Interpretership (Arabic); GSO2 Land Forces Persian Gulf, 1960–62; sc Camberley, 1963; Co. Comd 2RGJ, UK and Malaysia, 1964–66 (despatches (Borneo) 1966); GSO2 HQ 2 Div. BAOR, 1967–68; Co. Comd 1RGJ, UK and UNFICYP, 1968–69; Second in Comd 2RGJ, BAOR, 1969; MA to QMG, 1970–71; Comd 1RGJ, 1971–74, BAOR and NI (despatches (NI) 1974); Col General Staff HQ UKLF, 1974–76; Comd 5 Field Force

BAOR, 1976–79; rcds 1979; Asst Chief of Gen. Staff (Operational Requirements), MoD, 1980–83; Chief of Staff, HQ, UKLF, 1983–85; GOC Northern Ireland, 1985–88. Rep. Col Comdt, RGJ, 1988–90; Colonel Commandant: 1st Bn Royal Green Jackets, 1986–91; Army Legal Corps, 1988–90. Co. Comdt, Oxfordshire ACF, 1991–. Chm. of Governors, Royal Sch., Bath, 1988– (Governor, 1981–). President: Army LTA, 1986–91; Army Boxing Assoc., 1989–90. Vice-Chm., Reg. Forces Employment Agency, 1991–. Mem., Royal Patriotic Fund Corp., 1991–. Hon. Liveryman, Fruiterers' Co., 1992–. *Recreations:* gardening, golf, fishing, tennis, windsurfing, ski-ing. *Clubs:* Army and Navy; Queen's.

PASHLEY, Prof. Donald William, FRS 1968; Professor of Materials, Imperial College of Science, Technology and Medicine, since 1979; *b* 21 Apr. 1927; *s* of late Harold William Pashley and Louise Pashley (*née* Clarke); *m* 1954, Glenys Margaret Ball; one *s* one *d*. *Educ:* Henry Thornton Sch., London; Imperial Coll., London (BSc). 1st cl. hons Physics, 1947; PhD 1950. Research Fellow, Imp. Coll., 1950–55; TI Res. Labs, Hinxton Hall: Res. Scientist, 1956–61; Gp Leader and Div. Head, 1962–67; Asst Dir, 1967–68; Dir, 1968–79 (also Dir of Research, TI Ltd, 1976–79); Imperial College: Hd, Dept of Materials, 1979–90; Dean, Royal Sch. of Mines, 1986–89; Mem. Governing Body, 1986–89. Mem. Council, Royal Soc., 1981–83. Rosenhain Medal, Inst. of Metals, 1968. *Publications:* (jtly) Electron Microscopy of Thin Crystals, 1965; numerous papers on electron microscopy and diffraction, thin films and epitaxy in Phil. Mag., Proc. Roy. Soc., etc. *Address:* 11 The Gables, Oxshott, Leatherhead, Surrey KT22 0SD. *T:* Oxshott (0372) 844518; Department of Materials, Imperial College, SW7 2AZ.

PASLEY, Sir (John) Malcolm (Sabine), 5th Bt *cr* 1794; FBA 1991; Emeritus Fellow, Magdalen College, Oxford; *b* 5 April 1926; *s* of Sir Rodney Marshall Sabine Pasley, 4th Bt, and Aldyth Werge Hamber (*d* 1983); *S* father, 1982; *m* 1965, Virginia Killigrew Wait; two *s*. *Educ:* Sherborne Sch.; Trinity Coll., Oxford (MA). War service, Royal Navy, 1944–46. Laming Travelling Fellow, Queen's Coll., Oxford, 1949–50; Lectr in German, Brasenose and Magdalen Colls, 1950–58; Fellow and Tutor, 1958–86, Vice-Pres., 1979–80, Magdalen Coll. Mem., Deutsche Akademie für Sprache und Dichtung, 1983–. Hon. DPhil Giessen, 1986. Austrian Ehrenkreuz für Wissenschaft und Kunst, 1st cl., 1987. *Publications:* (co-author) Kafka-Symposion, 1965; (ed) Germany: A Companion to German Studies, 1972, 2nd edn 1982; (trans.) Kafka Shorter Works, vol. 1, 1973; (ed) Nietzsche: Imagery and Thought, 1978; (ed) Franz Kafka, Das Schloss, 1982; (ed) Max Brod, Franz Kafka, Reiseaufzeichnungen, 1987; Briefwechsel, 1989; (ed) Franz Kafka, Der Process, 1990. *Heir:* *s* Robert Killigrew Sabine Pasley, *b* 23 Oct. 1965. *Address:* 25 Lathbury Road, Oxford OX2 7AT.

PASMORE, (Edwin John) Victor, CH 1981; CBE 1959; RA 1984; Artist; *b* Chelsham, Surrey, 3 Dec. 1908; *s* of late E. S. Pasmore, MD; *m* 1940, Wendy Blood; one *s* one *d*. *Educ:* Harrow; attended evening classes, LCC Central School of Arts & Crafts. Local government service, LCC County Hall, 1927–37; joined the London Artists' Assoc., 1932–34, and the London Group, 1932–52. Associated with the formation of the Euston Road School, 1937–39, and the first post-war exhibitions of abstract art, 1948–53; joined the Penwith Society, St Ives, 1951–53. Visiting teacher, LCC Camberwell School of Art, 1945–49; Central School of Arts and Crafts, 1949–53. Master of Painting, Durham University, 1954–61; consultant urban and architectural designer, South West Area, Peterlee New Town, 1955–77. Trustee, Tate Gall., 1963–66. Hon. degrees from Newcastle-upon-Tyne, 1967; Surrey, 1969; RCA; Warwick, 1985. *Retrospective exhibitions:* Venice Biennale, 1960; Musée des Arts Décoratifs, Paris, 1961; Stedelijk Museum, Amsterdam, 1961; Palais des Beaux Arts, Brussels, 1961; Louisiana Museum, Copenhagen, 1962; Kestner-Gesellschaft, Hanover, 1962; Kunsthalle, Berne, 1963; Tate Gallery, 1965; São Paolo Biennale, 1965; Cartwright Hall, Bradford, 1980; Royal Acad., London, 1980; Musée des Beaux Arts, Calais, 1985; Yale Center for British Art, USA, 1988; Phillips Mus., Washington, 1988; Center for Internat. Contemp. Art, NY, 1990; Serpentine Gall., 1991. Marlborough Galleries, London, Rome, NY, Zurich, Toronto and Tokyo. *Retrospective graphic exhibitions:* Marlborough Gallery, Tate Gallery, Galleria 2RC, Rome, Milan, Lubjlana, Messina, Oslo, Osaka. Stage backcloth designs for Young Apollo, Royal Ballet, Covent Gdn, 1984. Works represented in: Tate Gallery and other public collections in Gt Britain, Canada, Australia, Holland, Italy, Austria, Switzerland, France and the USA. Carnegie Prize for painting, Pittsburgh International, 1964. Grand Prix d'Honneur, International Graphics Biennale, Lubjlana, 1977; Charles Wollaston Award, Royal Acad., 1983. *Publication:* Monograph and Catalogue Raisonnée, 1980. *Address:* Dar Gamri, Gudja, Malta; 12 St Germans Place, Blackheath, SE3. *Club:* Arts.

PASQUILL, Frank, DSc; FRS 1977; retired from Meteorological Office, 1974; *b* 8 Sept. 1914; *s* of late Joseph Pasquill and Elizabeth Pasquill (*née* Rudd), both of Atherton, Lancs; *m* 1937, Margaret Alice Turnbull, West Rainton, Co. Durham; two *d*. *Educ:* Henry Smith Sch., Hartlepool; Durham Univ. BSc (1st Cl. Hons Physics) 1935, MSc, 1949, DSc 1950. Meteorological Office, 1937–74, with posts at Chem. Defence Res. Estabt, Porton, 1937–46 (incl. overseas service in Australia); Sch. of Agric., Cambridge Univ., 1946–49; Atomic Energy Res. Estabt, Harwell, 1949–54; Chem. Defence Res. Estabt, Porton, 1954–61; Meteorological Office HQ Bracknell, 1961–74 (finally Dep. Chief Scientific Officer, and Head of Boundary Layer Research Br.). Visiting Prof., Pennsylvania State Univ., Autumn, 1974, N Carolina State Univ., Spring, 1975; Visiting Scientist, Penn. State Univ., 1975, Winter, 1976, Winter, 1977, Savannah River Lab., S Carolina, Winter, 1976. Royal Meteorological Society: Editor, 1961–64; Pres., 1970–72; Hon. Mem., 1978; Chm., Aero Res. Council's Gust Res. Cttee, 1963–68; Chm., CEGB's Adv. Panel on Environmental Res., 1962–80. Symons Medal, RMetS, 1983. *Publications:* Atmospheric Diffusion, 1962, 3rd edn (with F. B. Smith) 1983; papers on atmospheric turbulence and diffusion in various jls. *Address:* Woodwell, 37 Arbor Lane, Winnersh, Wokingham, Berks RG11 5JE.

PASTERFIELD, Rt. Rev. Philip John; an Assistant Bishop, Diocese of Exeter, since 1984; *b* 1920; *s* of Bertie James Pasterfield and Lilian Bishop Pasterfield (*née* Flinn); *m* 1948, Eleanor Maureen, *d* of William John Symons; three *s* one *d*. *Educ:* Denstone Coll., Staffs; Trinity Hall, Cambridge (MA); Cuddesdon Coll., Oxford. Army Service, 1940–46; commnd in Somerset Light Infantry. Deacon 1951, Priest 1952. Curate of Streatham, 1951–54; Vicar of West Lavington, Sussex, and Chaplain, King Edward VII Hosp., Midhurst, 1954–60; Rector of Woolbeding, 1955–60; Vicar of Oxton, Birkenhead, 1960–68; Rural Dean of Birkenhead, 1966–68; Canon Residentiary and Sub Dean of St Albans, 1968–74; Rural Dean of St Albans, 1972–74; Bishop Suffragan of Crediton, 1974–84. *Recreations:* ornithology, music. *Address:* 2 Brixton Court, Brixton, Plymouth PL8 2AH.

PASTINEN, Ilkka, KCMG (Hon.) 1976; Finnish Ambassador to the Court of St James's, 1983–91; *b* 17 March 1928; *s* of Martti and Ilmi Pastinen; *m* 1950, Eeva Marja Viitanen; two *d*. Entered Diplomatic Service, 1952; served Stockholm, 1955; Perm. Mission to UN, 1957–60; Peking, 1962–64; London, 1966–69; Ambassador and Dep. Representative of Finland to UN, 1969–71; Special Representative of Sec. Gen. of UN to Cttee of Disarmament, 1971–75; Ambassador and Perm. Representative of Finland at UN, NY, 1977–83. Kt Comdr of Order of White Rose of Finland, 1984. *Address:* Maneesikatu 1–3B, Helsinki, Finland. *Clubs:* Athenæum, Travellers'; Swinley Forest Golf.

PASTON-BEDINGFELD, Sir Edmund George Felix, 9th Bt, *cr* 1661; Major late Welsh Guards; Managing Director, Handley Walker (Europe) Ltd, 1969–80; *b* 2 June 1915; *s* of 8th Bt and Sybil (*d* 1985), *e d* of late H. Lyne Stephens of Grove House, Roehampton; *S* father, 1941; *m* 1st, 1942, Joan Lynette (*née* Rees) (*d* 1965); one *s* one *d*; 2nd, 1957, Agnes Kathleen (*d* 1974), *d* of late Miklos Gluck, Budapest; 3rd, 1975, Mrs Peggy Hannaford-Hill (*d* 1991), Fort Victoria, Rhodesia. *Educ:* Oratory School; New College, Oxford. Under-Sec., Head of Agricultural Div., RICS, 1966–69. Liveryman, Bowyers' Co., 1988–. *Heir:* *s* Henry Edgar Paston-Bedingfeld, *qv*. *Address:* 153 Southgate Street, Bury St Edmunds, Suffolk. *T:* Bury St Edmunds (0284) 754764. *Club:* Naval and Military.

PASTON-BEDINGFELD, Henry Edgar; Rouge Croix Pursuivant of Arms, since 1983; *b* 7 Dec. 1943; *s* and *heir* of Sir Edmund Paston-Bedingfeld, Bt, *qv*; *m* 1968, Mary Kathleen, *d* of Brig. R.D. Ambrose, CIE, OBE, MC; two *s* two *d*. *Educ:* Ampleforth College, York. Chartered Surveyor. Founder Chairman, Norfolk Heraldry Soc., 1975–80, Vice-Pres. 1980–; Member Council: Heraldry Soc., 1976–85; Norfolk Record Soc., 1990–; Sec., Standing Council of the Baronetage, 1984–88; Vice-Pres., Cambridge Univ. Heraldic and Genealogical Soc., 1988–. Freeman of the City of London; Liveryman: Scriveners' Co; Bowyers' Co. Kt of Sovereign Mil. Order of Malta. *Publication:* Oxburgh Hall, The First 500 Years, 1982. *Address:* The College of Arms, Queen Victoria Street, EC4V 4BT. *T:* 071–236 6420; Oxburgh Hall, King's Lynn, Norfolk PE33 9PS. *T:* Gooderstone (036621) 269. *Club:* Norfolk (Norwich).

PASTON BROWN, Dame Beryl, DBE 1967; *b* 7 March 1909; *d* of Paston Charles Brown and Florence May (*née* Henson). *Educ:* Streatham Hill High School; Newnham Coll., Cambridge (MA); London Day Training College. Lecturer: Portsmouth Training Coll., 1933–37; Goldsmiths' Coll., Univ. of London, 1937–44 and 1946–51. Temp. Asst Lecturer, Newnham Coll., 1944–46. Principal of City of Leicester Training Coll., 1952–61; Principal, Homerton College, Cambridge, 1961–71. Chairman, Assoc. of Teachers in Colleges and Depts of Educn, 1965–66. *Address:* 21 Keere Street, Lewes, East Sussex BN7 1TY. *T:* Lewes (0273) 473608.

PATCHETT, Terry; MP (Lab) Barnsley East, since 1983; *b* 11 July 1940; *s* of Wilfred and Kathleen Patchett; *m* 1961, Glenys Veal; one *s* two *d*. *Educ:* State schools; Sheffield University (Economics and Politics). Miner; NUM Houghton Main Branch Delegate, 1966–83; Mem., Yorkshire Miners' Exec., 1976–83; former Member: Appeals Tribunals; Community Health Council. Mem., Wombwell UDC, 1969–73. Mem., H of C Expenditure Cttee (Social Services Sub-Cttee), 1985–87. *Recreations:* walking, gardening, golf. *Address:* 71 Upperwood Road, Darfield, near Barnsley, S Yorks. *T:* Barnsley (0226) 757684. *Clubs:* Darfield Working Men's, Mitchell and Darfield Miners' Welfare.

PATE, Prof. John Stewart, FRS 1985; FAA 1980; FLS; Professor of Botany, University of Western Australia, since 1974; *b* 15 Jan. 1932; *s* of Henry Stewart Pate and Muriel Margaret Pate; *m* 1959, Elizabeth Lyons Sloan, BSc; three *s*. *Educ:* Campbell College; Queen's Univ., Belfast (BSc, MSc, PhD, DSc). FLS 1990. Lectr, Sydney Univ., 1956–60; Lectr, Reader, Personal Chair in Plant Physiology, Queen's Univ. Belfast, 1960–73. Vis. Fellow, Univ. of Cape Town, 1973. *Publications:* (ed with J. F. Sutcliffe) Physiology of the Garden Pea, 1977; (ed with A. J. McComb) Biology of Australian Plants, 1981; (with K. W. Dixon) Tuberous, Cormous and Bulbous Plants, 1983; (ed with J. S. Beard) Kwongan: plant life of the sandplain, 1984; reviews on carbon:nitrogen metabolism. *Recreations:* music, nature study, hobby farming. *Address:* 83 Circe Circle, Dalkeith, WA 6009, Australia. *T:* 3866070 (Perth, WA).

PATEL, Indraprasad Gordhanbhai, Hon. KBE 1990; PhD; Director, London School of Economics and Political Science, 1984–90 (Hon. Fellow, 1990); *b* 11 Nov. 1924; *s* of F. Patel Gordhanbhai Tulsibhai and M. Patel Kashiben Jivabhai; *m* 1958, Alaknanda Dasgupta; one *d*. *Educ:* Bombay Univ. (BA Hons); King's Coll., Cambridge (BA, PhD; Hon. Fellow, 1986). Prof. of Economics and Principal, Baroda Coll., Maharaja Sayajirao Univ. of Baroda, 1949; Economist, later Asst Chief, IMF, 1950–54; Dep. Economic Adviser, Min. of Finance, India, 1954–58; Alternate Exec. Dir for India, IMF, 1958–61; Chief Economic Adviser, Min. of Finance and Planning Commn, 1962–64, 1965–67; Special Sec. and Sec., Dept of Economic Affairs, 1967–72; Dep. Administrator, UN Develt Programme, 1972–77; Governor, Reserve Bank of India, 1977–82; Dir, Indian Inst. of Management, Ahmedabad, 1982–84. Vis. Prof., Delhi Univ., 1964. Chm., Aga Khan Rural Support Project, India, 1990–. Hon. DLitt Sardar Patel Univ.; Hon. DCL, Univ. of Mauritius, 1990. Padma Vibhushan, 1991. *Publications:* Essays in Economic Policy and Economic Growth, 1986; articles in IMF staff papers etc. on inflation, monetary policy, internat. trade. *Recreations:* music, reading, watching cricket. *Address:* 12 Amee Co-operative Housing Society, Diwalipuya, Old Padra Road, Vadodara 390015, India.

PATEL, Praful Raojibhai Chaturbhai; Company Director; Investment Adviser in UK, since 1962; Hon. Secretary, All-Party Parliamentary Committee on UK Citizenship, since 1968; *b* Jinja, Uganda, 7 March 1939; *s* of Raojibhai Chaturbhai Patel, Sojitra, Gujarat, India, and Maniben Jivabhai Lalaji Patel, Dharmaj, Gujarat; unmarried. *Educ:* Government Sec. Sch., Jinja, Uganda; London Inst. of World Affairs, attached to University Coll., London (Extra Mural Dept). Sec., Uganda Students Union, 1956–58; Deleg. to Internat. Youth Assembly, New Delhi, 1958; awarded two travel bursaries for visits to E, Central and S Africa, and Middle East, to study and lecture on politics and economics; arrived in Britain as student, then commenced commercial activities, 1962; increasingly involved in industrial, cultural and educational projects affecting immigrants in Britain. Spokesman for Asians in UK following restriction of immigration resulting from Commonwealth Immigrants Act 1968; Council Mem., UK Immigrants Advisory Service, 1970–; Mem., Uganda Resettlement Bd, 1972–74; Hon. Sec., Uganda Evacuees Resettlement Advisory Trust, 1974–; Pres., Nava Kala India Socio-Cultural Centre, London, 1962–75; Chm. Bd of Trustees, Swaminarayan Hindu Mission, UK, 1970–76; Jt Convener, Asian Action Cttee, 1976; Convener, Manava Trust, 1979–. Contested (Lab) Brent North, 1987. *Publications:* articles in newspapers and journals regarding immigration and race relations. *Recreations:* cricket; campaigning and lobbying; current affairs; and inter-faith co-operation. *Address:* 60 Bedford Court Mansions, Bedford Avenue, Bedford Square, WC1B 3AD. *T:* 071–580 0897. *Club:* Commonwealth Trust.

PATEMAN, Jack Edward, CBE 1970; FEng; Chairman, Kent County Engineering Society, since 1989; *b* 29 Nov. 1921; *s* of William Edward Pateman and Lucy Varley (*née* Jetten); *m* 1949, Cicely Hope Turner; one *s* one *d*. *Educ:* Gt Yarmouth Grammar Sch. Served War of 1939–45, RAF, 1940–46. Research Engineer: Belling & Lee, 1946–48; Elliott Bros (London) Ltd, 1948–51; formed Aviation Div. of EBL at Borehamwood, 1951–62; Dep. Chm. and Jt Man. Dir, Elliott Flight Automation Ltd, 1962–71; Man. Dir, 1971–86, Dep. Chm., 1986–87, GEC Avionics; Director: Canadian Marconi Co., 1971–87; GEC Computers Ltd, 1971–89 (Chm., 1978–82); Elliott Brothers (London) Ltd, 1979–89; Marconi Electronic Devices, 1980–87; GEC Avionics Projects Ltd, 1980–89; GEC Information Systems, 1982–86; GEC Avionics Projects (UK) Ltd, 1984–89; General Electric Co. Plc, 1986–88. GEC-Marconi Ltd, 1987–89. British Gold

Medal, RAeS, 1981. *Recreation:* sailing. *Address:* Spindles, Ivy Hatch, Sevenoaks, Kent TN15 0PG. *T:* Plaxtol (0732) 810364.

PATEMAN, Prof. John Arthur Joseph, FRS 1978; FRSE 1974; Emeritus Professor of Genetics, Australian National University; *b* 18 May 1926; *s* of John and Isobel May Pateman; *m* 1952, Mary Phelps; one *s* two *d. Educ:* Clacton County High Sch., Essex; University Coll., Leicester. BSc, PhD(Lond); MA(Cantab). Lectr, Univ. of Sheffield, 1954–58; Sen. Lectr, Univ. of Melbourne, Australia, 1958–60; Lectr, Univ. of Cambridge, 1960–67; Prof., Flinders Univ., S Australia, 1967–70; Prof. of Genetics, Univ. of Glasgow, 1970–79; Prof. of Genetics, ANU, 1979–88 (Exec. Dir, Centre for Recombinant DNA Res., 1982–88). Fellow, Churchill Coll., Cambridge, 1961–67. *Publications:* scientific papers in genetical, biochemical and microbiological jls. *Recreations:* reading, music, walking. *Address:* 7 South Park Court, East Avenue, Oxford OX4 1YZ. *T:* Oxford (0865) 726728.

PATERSON, Alexander Craig, (Alastair), CBE 1987; FEng 1983; Senior Partner, Bullen and Partners, Consulting Engineers, 1969–88, retired (Partner 1960–69); *b* 15 Jan. 1924; *s* of Duncan McKellar Paterson and Lavinia (*née* Craig); *m* 1947, Betty Hannah Burley; two *s* two *d. Educ:* Glasgow High Sch.; Royal Coll. of Science and Technol. (ARCST); Glasgow Univ. (BSc). FICE 1963; FIMechE 1964; FIStructE 1970; FCIArb 1968. Commd REME, 1944; served India and Burma, attached Indian Army, 1944–47. Engineer: with Merz and McLellan, 1947–58; with Taylor Woodrow, 1958–60. Mem., Overseas Projects Bd, 1984–87. Institution of Structural Engineers: Mem. Council, 1976–89; Vice Pres., 1981–84; Pres., 1984–85; Institution of Civil Engineers: Mem. Council, 1978–81 and 1982–; Vice-Pres., 1985–88; Pres., 1988–89. Pres., British Section, Société des Ingénieurs et Scientifiques de France, 1980; Chm., British Consultants Bureau, 1978–80; Member: Council, British Bd of Agrément, 1982–; Engrg Council, 1987–90. Mem. Court, Cranfield Inst. of Technol., 1970–80. Hon. DSc Strathclyde, 1989. *Publications:* professional and technical papers in engrg jls. *Recreations:* sailing, gardening. *Address:* Willows, The Byeway, West Wittering, Chichester, West Sussex PO20 8LJ. *T:* Birdham (0243) 514199. *Club:* Caledonian.

PATERSON, Dame Betty (Fraser Ross), DBE 1981 (CBE 1973); DL; Chairman: NW Thames Regional Health Authority, 1973–84; National Staff Advisory Committee for England and Wales (Nurses and Midwives), 1975–84; *b* 14 March 1916; *d* of Robert Ross Russell and Elsie Marian Russell (*née* Fraser); *m* 1940, Ian Douglas Paterson; one *s* one *d. Educ:* Harrogate Coll.; Western Infirmary, Glasgow. Mem. Chartered Soc. of Physiotherapy (MCSP). County Comr, Herts Girl Guides, 1950–57. Member: Herts CC, 1952–74 (Alderman 1959–74; Chm., 1969–73); NE Metropolitan Regional Hosp. Bd, 1960–74; Governing Body, Royal Hosp. of St Bartholomew, 1960–74; Commn for the New Towns, England and Wales, 1961–75 (Dep. Chm., 1971–75); Governing Body, Bishop's Stortford Coll., 1967–81; Central Health Services Council, 1969–74; Gen. Council, King Edward's Hosp. Fund for London, 1975–84 (Management Cttee, 1975–80); Pres., Herts Assoc. of Local Councils, 1980–90; Vice-Pres., Herts Magistrates' Assoc., 1987–. JP Herts, 1950–86 (Chm. Bishop's Stortford Bench, 1978–86); DL Herts, 1980. *Recreations:* music, cooking, foreign travel. *Address:* 52 Free Trade Wharf, The Highway, E1 9ES. *T:* 071–791 0367.

PATERSON, Prof Sir Dennis (Craig), Kt 1976; MB, BS 1953, MD 1983; FRCS, FRACS; Director and Chief Orthopaedic Surgeon, Adelaide Children's Hospital, since 1970; Consultant Orthopaedic Surgeon, Queen Victoria Hospital, since 1968; Clinical Associate Professor, University of Adelaide, since 1990; *b* 14 Oct. 1930; *s* of Gilbert Charles Paterson and Thelma Drysdale Paterson; *m* 1955, Mary, *d* of Frederick Mansell Hardy; one *s* three *d. Educ:* Collegiate Sch. of St Peter; Univ. of Adelaide (MB, BS 1953; MD 1983). FRCS 1958, FRACS 1961. Res. Med. Officer: Royal Adelaide Hosp., 1954; Adelaide Children's Hosp., 1955; Registrar, Robert Jones & Agnes Hunt Orthop. Hosp., Oswestry, Shropshire, 1958–60; Royal Adelaide Hospital: Sen. Registrar, 1960–62; Cons. Orthop. Surg., 1964–86; Cons. Orthop. Surg., Repatriation Gen. Hosp., Adelaide, 1962–70; Adelaide Children's Hospital: Asst Hon. Orthop. Surg., 1964–66; Sen. Hon. Orthop. Surg., 1966–70; Mem. Bd of Management, 1976–84; Chm., Med. Adv. Cttee, 1976–84; Chm., Med. Staff Cttee, 1976–84. Amer./British/Canadian Trav. Prof., 1966. Royal Australasian Coll. of Surgeons: Mem., Bd of Orthop. Surg., 1974–82, 1984–85 (Chm., 1977–82); Mem., Court of Examnrs, 1974–84; Mem., SA Cttee, 1974–78; Fellow: British Orthopaedic Assoc.; RSocMed; Member: Aust. Orthopaedic Assoc. (Censor-in-Chief, 1976–80; Dir, Continuing Educn, 1982–85); AMA; Internat. Scoliosis Res. Soc.; SICOT (Aust. Nat. Delegate, 1975–84, First Vice-Pres., 1984–87; Pres., 1987–90); Paediatric Orthopaedic Soc.; W Pacific Orthopaedic Soc.; Hon. Mem., American Acad. of Orthopaedic Surgeons, 1981. Pres., Crippled Children's Assoc. of South Australia Inc., 1970–84 (Mem. Council, 1966–70). Life Mem., S Aust. Cricket Assoc. Queen's Jubilee Medal, 1977. *Publications:* over 80 articles in Jl of Bone and Joint Surg., Clin. Orthopaedics and Related Res., Aust. and NZ Jl of Surg., Med. Jl of Aust., Western Pacific Jl of Orthop. Surg. *Recreations:* tennis, golf, gardening, vigneron. *Address:* 31 Myall Avenue, Kensington Gardens, SA 5068, Australia. *T:* 08 3323364. *Clubs:* Adelaide, Royal Adelaide Golf, Kooyonga Golf (Adelaide).

PATERSON, Francis, (Frank), FCIT; General Manager, Eastern Region, British Rail, York, 1978–85; Member, British Railways (Eastern) Board, 1978–85; Chairman, North Yorkshire Family Practitioner Committee, 1987–91; *b* 5 April 1930; *s* of Francis William Paterson and Cecilia Eliza Reid Brownie; *m* 1950, Grace Robertson; two *s* two *d. Educ:* Robert Gordon's Coll., Aberdeen. Joined LNER as Junior Clerk, 1946; clerical and supervisory positions in NE Scotland; management training, Scotland, 1956–59; various man-management, operating and marketing posts, Scotland, Lincs and Yorks, 1960–66; Operating Supt, Glasgow North, 1967–68; Sales Manager, Edinburgh, 1968; Asst Divl Manager, S Wales, 1968–70; Dir, United Welsh Transport, 1968–70; Harbour Comr, Newport Harbour, 1968–70; Divl Manager, Central Div., Southern Region, 1970–75; Director: Southdown Motor Services Ltd, 1970–73; Brighton, Hove & District Omnibus Co., 1970–73; Dep. Gen. Man., Southern Region, 1975–77; Chief Freight Manager, British Railways Bd, 1977–78. Vice-Chm., Nat. Railway Mus. Cttee, 1984– (Mem., 1978–); Member: CBI Southern Regional Council, 1975–77; CBI Transport Policy Cttee, 1977–78; BBC NE Adv. Council, 1987–91; Chm., BBC Local Radio Adv. Council, Radio York, 1987–91. Pres., St Andrews Soc. of York, 1989–90. Trustee, Friends of Nat. Railway Museum, 1988–. Mem. Court, Univ. of York, 1981–. OStJ 1980. FCIT 1978 (Mem. Council, CIT, 1979–84). *Publications:* papers to transport societies. *Recreations:* transport, travel, hill walking, country pursuits, Scottish culture, enjoying grandchildren. *Address:* Alligin, 97 Main Street, Askham Bryan, York YO2 3QS. *T:* York (0904) 708478.

PATERSON, Frank David; His Honour Judge Paterson; a Circuit Judge (formerly County Court Judge), since 1968; *b* 10 July 1918; *yr s* of late David Paterson and Dora Paterson, Liverpool; *m* 1953, Barbara Mary, 2nd *d* of late Oswald Ward Gillow and Alice Gillow, Formby; one *s* two *d. Educ:* Calderstones Preparatory Sch. and Quarry Bank High Sch., Liverpool; Univ. of Liverpool (LLB). Called to Bar, Gray's Inn, 1941; Warden, Unity Boys' Club, Liverpool, 1941; Asst Warden, Florence Inst. for Boys, Liverpool, 1943. Practised on Northern Circuit. Chairman: Min. of Pensions and Nat. Insce Tribunal, Liverpool, 1957; Mental Health Review Tribunal for SW Lancashire and Cheshire, 1963. Asst Dep. Coroner, City of Liverpool, 1960. Pres., Merseyside Magistrates' Assoc., 1978–. *Address:* Vailima, 2 West Lane, Formby, Liverpool L37 7BA. *T:* Formby (07048) 74345. *Club:* Athenæum (Liverpool).

PATERSON, Sir George (Mutlow), Kt 1959; OBE 1946; QC (Sierra Leone) 1950; Chairman, Industrial Tribunals, 1965–79; *b* 3 Dec. 1906; *e s* of late Dr G. W. Paterson; *m* 1935, Audrey Anita, *d* of late Major C. C. B. Morris, CBE, MC; one *s* two *d. Educ:* Grenada Boys' School; St John's College, Cambridge. Appointed to Nigerian Administrative Service, 1929. Called to the Bar, Inner Temple, 1933. Magistrate, Nigeria, 1936; Crown Counsel, Tanganyika, 1938. War of 1939–45: served with the King's African Rifles, 1939 (wounded 1940); Occupied Enemy Territories Admin., 1941; Lieutenant-Colonel 1945. Solicitor-General, Tanganyika, 1946; Attorney-General, Sierra Leone, 1949, Ghana, 1954–57; Chief Justice of Northern Rhodesia, 1957–61, retired 1961; appointed to hold an inquiry into proposed amendments to the Potato Marketing Scheme, 1962; appointed legal chairman (part-time), Pensions Appeal Tribunals, 1962; appointed chairman Industrial Tribunals, South Western Region, 1965. *Recreations:* shooting, gardening, genealogy. *Address:* St George's, Westbury, Sherborne, Dorset DT9 3RA. *T:* Sherborne (0935) 814003. *Club:* Bath and County (Bath).

See also T. P. P. Clifford.

PATERSON, Sqdn-Ldr Ian Veitch, CBE 1969; DL; JP; Deputy Chairman, Local Government Boundary Commission for Scotland, 1974–80; *b* 17 Aug. 1911; *s* of Andrew Wilson Paterson; *m* 1940, Anne Weir, *d* of Thomas Brown; two *s* one *d. Educ:* Lanark Grammar School; Glasgow University. Served RAF, 1940–45. Entered local govt service, Lanark, 1928; Principal Legal Asst, Aberdeen CC; Lanarkshire: Dep. County Clerk, 1949; County Clerk, 1956, resigned 1974. Chm., Working Party which produced The New Scottish Local Authorities Organisation and Management structures, 1973. DL Lanarkshire (Strathclyde), 1963; JP Hamilton (formerly Lanarkshire).

PATERSON, (James Edmund) Neil, MA; author; *b* 31 Dec. 1915; *s* of late James Donaldson Paterson, MA, BL; *m* 1939, Rosabelle, MA, 3rd *d* of late David MacKenzie, MC, MA; two *s* one *d. Educ:* Banff Academy; Edinburgh Univ. Served in minesweepers, War of 1939–45, Lieut RNVR, 1940–46. Dir, Grampian Television, 1960–86; Films of Scotland: (Mem., 1954–76; Dir, 1976–78); Consultant, 1978–80. Member: Scottish Arts Council, 1967–76 (Vice-Chm., 1974–76; Chm., Literature Cttee, 1968–76); Arts Council of Great Britain, 1974–76; Governor: Nat. Film Sch., 1970–80; Pitlochry Festival Theatre, 1966–76; British Film Institute, 1958–60; Atlantic Award in Literature, 1946; Award of American Academy of Motion Picture Arts and Sciences, 1960. *Publications:* The China Run, 1948; Behold Thy Daughter, 1950; And Delilah, 1951; Man on the Tight Rope, 1953; The Kidnappers, 1957; film stories and screen plays. *Recreations:* golf, fishing. *Address:* St Ronans, Crieff, Perthshire PH7 4AF. *T:* Grieff (0764) 2615.

PATERSON, James Rupert; HM Diplomatic Service; Consul-General, Geneva, 1989–Aug. 1992; *b* 7 Aug. 1932; *s* of late Major Robert Paterson, MC, Seaforth Highlanders and Mrs Josephine Paterson; *m* 1956, Kay Dineen; two *s* two *d. Educ:* Nautical Coll., Pangbourne; RMA, Sandhurst. Commnd RA, 1953 (Tombs Meml Prize); Staff Coll., Camberley, 1963; retd from Army with rank of Major, 1970; joined FCO, 1970; First Sec., Pakistan, 1972; Dep. High Comr, Trinidad and Tobago, 1975; Ambassador to the Mongolian People's Republic, 1982; Consul-General, Istanbul, 1985. *Recreations:* ballet, golf. *Address:* c/o Foreign and Commonwealth Office, King Charles Street, SW1A 2AH; c/o Barclays Bank, Carshalton Beeches, Surrey SM5 3LA.

PATERSON, James Veitch; Sheriff of the Lothian and Borders (formerly Roxburgh, Berwick and Selkirk) at Jedburgh, Selkirk and Duns, since 1963; *b* 16 April 1928; *s* of late John Robert Paterson, ophthalmic surgeon, and of Jeanie Gouinlock; *m* 1956, Ailie, *o d* of Lt-Comdr Sir (George) Ian Clark Hutchison, *qv*; one *s* one *d. Educ:* Peebles High School; Edinburgh Academy; Lincoln College, Oxford; Edinburgh University. Admitted to Faculty of Advocates, 1953. *Recreations:* fishing, shooting, gardening. *Address:* Sunnyside, Melrose, Roxburghshire TD6 9BE. *T:* Melrose (089682) 2502. *Club:* New (Edinburgh).

PATERSON, John Mower Alexander, OBE 1985; JP; Vice Lord-Lieutenant of Buckinghamshire, since 1984; *b* 9 Nov. 1920; *s* of Leslie Martin Paterson and Olive Harriette Mower; *m* 1944, Daisy Miriam Ballanger Marshall; one *s* two *d. Educ:* Oundle; Queens' Coll., Cambridge (MA Hons). Served War, RE, 1941–46. Cincinnati Milling Machines, Birmingham, 1946–48; Dir, 1945–87, Chm., 1960–85, Bifurcated Engineering, later BETEC PLC, Aylesbury; Dir and Works Man., Bifurcated & Tubular Rivet Co. Ltd, Aylesbury, 1948–60; Chm., Rickmansworth Water Co., 1988–90 (Dir, 1984–90; Dep. Chm., 1986–88); Dir, Three Valleys Water Service plc, 1991–. Member: Southern Regional Council, CBI, 1971–85 (Chm., 1974–76); Grand Council, CBI, 1971–84. Gen. Comr of Taxes, Aylesbury Div., 1959–. Mem., Lloyd's, 1960–. Pres., Aylesbury Divl Cons. and Unionist Assoc., 1984–85; Chairman: Bucks Council for Voluntary Youth Services, 1978–; Council, Order of St John in Buckinghamshire, 1981– (Mem., 1980–); Member: Management Cttee, Waddesdon Manor (NT), 1980–; Governing Body, Aylesbury Coll. of Further Educn, 1961–88 (Chm., 1977–87); Governing Body, Aylesbury GS, 1974– (Chm., 1984–). JP 1962, High Sheriff 1978, DL 1982, Bucks. KStJ 1991. *Recreations:* sailing, veteran cars, gardening. *Address:* Park Hill, Potter Row, Great Missenden, Bucks HP16 9LT. *T:* Great Missenden (02406) 2995. *Clubs:* Royal Ocean Racing; Royal Yacht Squadron (Cowes); Royal Lymington Yacht (Cdre, 1973–76).

PATERSON, Very Rev. John Munn Kirk; Minister Emeritus of St Paul's Parish Church, Milngavie (Minister, 1970–87); Moderator of the General Assembly of the Church of Scotland, 1984–85; *b* 8 Oct. 1922; *s* of George Kirk Paterson and Sarah Ferguson Paterson (*née* Wilson); *m* 1946, Geraldine Lilian Parker; two *s* one *d. Educ:* Hillhead High School, Glasgow; Edinburgh Univ. MA, BD. RAF, 1942–46 (Defence and Victory medals, Italy Star, 1945). Insurance Official, 1940–58 (ACII 1951); Assistant Minister, 1958–64; Ordained Minister of Church of Scotland, 1964–. Hon. DD Aberdeen, 1986. *Recreations:* fishing, hill walking. *Club:* Royal Over-Seas League (Edinburgh).

PATERSON, Very Rev. John Thomas Farquhar; Dean of Christ Church, Dublin, since 1989; *b* Portadown, Co. Armagh, 21 Dec. 1938; *s* of Henry Paterson and Margreta Elizabeth Paterson (*née* Bell); unmarried. *Educ:* Portadown College; Trinity College, Dublin (BA, MA, BD). Curate-Assistant: Drumglass (Dungannon), 1963; St Bartholomew, Dublin, 1966; Priest-in-charge, St Mark, Dublin and Asst Chaplain, TCD, 1968; Vicar, St Bartholomew with Christ Church, Leeson Park, Dublin, 1972; Dean and Rector of Kildare, 1978. *Publications:* articles in Irish theological jls (Search, The Furrow, Doctrine and Life). *Recreations:* travel, reading, music. *Address:* The Chapter House, Christ Church Cathedral, Christchurch Place, Dublin 8. *T:* Dublin 778099. *Clubs:* Kildare Street and University, Friendly Brothers of St Patrick (Dublin).

PATERSON, Sir John (Valentine) J.; *see* Jardine Paterson.

PATERSON, Neil; *see* Paterson, James Edmund N.

PATERSON, Robert Lancelot, OBE 1980; MC 1945; ERD 1957; part-time Adjudicator, Home Office Immigration Appeals, 1970–83; Director, Merseyside Chamber of Commerce and Industry, 1967–81; *b* 16 May 1918; *e s* of Lancelot Wilson and Sarah Annie Paterson; *m* 1940, Charlotte Orpha, *d* of James and Elizabeth Nicholas; three *s*. *Educ:* Monmouth Sch.; University Coll. of Wales, Aberystwyth (BA); London School of Economics. Commissioned into Border Regt, SR, Dec. 1937; served War of 1939–45, 4th Bn, Border Regt, France, ME, Syria, Tobruk, Burma and India (Chindits, 1943–44); Asst Chief Instr 164 (Inf.), OCTU, 1946. Entered Colonial Admin. Service, Tanganyika, 1947; Dist Officer, 1947–60; Principal Asst Sec., Min. of Home Affairs, 1960–62; prematurely retired on attainment of Independence by Tanganyika. Dep. Sec., Liverpool Chamber of Commerce, 1963–67; Member, Nat. Council, Assoc. of Brit. Chambers of Commerce, 1969–81; Pres., Brit. Chambers of Commerce Executives, 1977–79; Governor, Liverpool Coll. of Commerce, 1967–71; Mem., Liverpool Univ. Appts Bd, 1968–72; *Recreations:* archaeology, gardening. *Address:* 4 Belle Vue Road, Henley-on-Thames, Oxon RG9 1JG.

PATERSON, William Alexander; *see* Alexander, Bill.

PATERSON-BROWN, Dr June, CBE 1991; DL; Chief Commissioner, Girl Guides Association, and Commonwealth Chief Commissioner, 1985–90; *b* 8 Feb. 1932; *d* of Thomas Clarke Garden and Jean Martha (*née* Mallace); *m* 1957, Dr Peter N. Paterson-Brown; three *s* one *d*. *Educ:* Esdaile Sch.; Edinburgh Univ. (MB, ChB). MO in Community Health, 1960–85. Scottish Chief Comr, Girl Guides Assoc., 1977–82. Non-Exec. Dir, Border Television, 1980–; Chm., Borders Children's Panel Adv. Cttee, 1982–85; Vice Chm. and Trustee, Prince's Trust, 1982–; Trustee, MacRobert's Trust, 1987–; Chm., Scottish Standing Conf. Voluntary Youth Organisations, 1982–85. DL Roxburgh, Ettrick and Lauderdale, 1990. *Recreations:* ski-ing, golfing, fishing, tennis, music, reading. *Address:* Norwood, Hawick, Roxburghshire TD9 7HP. *T:* Hawick (0450) 72352. *Clubs:* Lansdowne, New Cavendish.

PATEY, Very Rev. Edward Henry; Dean of Liverpool, 1964–82, now Dean Emeritus; *b* 12 Aug. 1915; *s* of Walter Patey, MD, and Dorothy Patey; *m* 1942, Margaret Ruth Olivia Abbott, OBE; one *s* three *d*. *Educ:* Marlborough College; Hertford College, Oxford; Westcott House, Cambridge. Assistant Curate, St Mary-at-the-Walls, Colchester, 1939; MA (Oxon) 1941; Assistant Curate Bishopwearmouth Parish Church, Sunderland, 1942; Youth Chaplain to the Bishop of Durham, 1946; Vicar of Oldland, with Longwell Green, Bristol, 1950; Secretary, Youth Department, The British Council of Churches, 1952; Assistant Gen. Secretary, The British Council of Churches, 1955; Canon Residentiary of Coventry Cathedral, 1958. Hon. LLD Liverpool, 1980. *Publications:* Religion in the Club, 1956; Boys and Girls Growing Up, 1957; Worship in the Club, 1961; A Doctor's Life of Jesus, 1962; Young People Now, 1964; Enquire Within, 1966; Look out for the Church, 1969; Burning Questions, 1971; Don't Just Sit There, 1974; Christian Lifestyle, 1975; All in Good Faith, 1978; Open the Doors, 1978; Open the Book, 1981; I Give You This Ring, 1982; My Liverpool Life, 1983; Becoming An Anglican, 1985; Preaching on Special Occasions, 1985; Questions For Today, 1986; For the Common Good, 1989; Faith in a Risk-Taking God, 1991. *Recreations:* reading, listening to music, walking. *Address:* 139 High Street, Malmesbury, Wilts SN16 9AL.

PATHAK, Raghunandan Swarup; Judge of the International Court of Justice, The Hague, since 1989; *b* 25 Nov. 1924; *s* of Gopal Swarup Pathak and Prakashwati; *m* 1955, Asha Paranjpe; three *s*. *Educ:* St Joseph's Coll., Allahabad; Ewing Christian Coll., Allahabad; Allahabad Univ. (BSc 1945; LLB 1947; MA (Pol. Sci.) 1948; Sastri Medal in Internat. Law, 1947). Enrolled Advocate: Allahabad High Court, 1948; Supreme Court of India, 1957; Additional Judge, 1962, Judge, 1963, Allahabad High Court; Chief Justice, Himachal Pradesh High Court, 1972; Judge, Supreme Court of India, 1978; Chief Justice of India, 1986–89. Chm., All India Univ. Professors' Internat. Law Res. Gp, 1969–89; Visitor, Nat. Law Sch. of India, Bangalore, 1986–89; Pro-Chancellor, Univ. of Delhi, 1986–89; Distinguished Vis. Prof., Inst. of Advanced Studies in the Humanities, Edinburgh Univ. President: Indian Law Inst., 1986–89; Indian Council of Legal Aid and Advice; Indian Soc. of Internat. Law, 1989–; International Law Association, London: Mem., 1952–; Pres., India Regl Br., 1986–89; Mem., Cttee on Space Law, and Cttee on Enforcement of Human Rights; Vice-Pres., Indian Acad. of Environmental Law and Research. Chm., World Congress on Law and Medicine, New Delhi, 1985; Member: Indo-Soviet Internat. Law Confs; Indo-W German Internat. Law Colloquia; UN Univ. project on Internat. Law, Common Patrimony and Intergenerational Equity; UN Univ. project on Internat. Law and Global Change, 1989. Lectures worldwide on law and on human rights. Hon. Bencher, Gray's Inn, 1988. Hon. LLD: Agra; Panjab; Hon. DLitt Kashi Vidyapeeth, Varanasi. *Publications:* papers on internat. law, law of the sea, etc, in learned jls. *Recreations:* golf, photography. *Address:* 5 Janpath, New Delhi 110011, India. *T:* 301 9224. *Clubs:* Delhi Gymkhana, India International Centre, Delhi Golf (New Delhi).

PATIENCE, Andrew; QC 1990; a Recorder of the Crown Court, since 1986; *b* 28 April 1941; *s* of late William Edmund John Patience and of Louise Mary Patience; *m* 1975, Jean Adèle Williams; one *s* one *d*. *Educ:* Whitgift School, Croydon; St John's College, Oxford (MA). Called to the Bar, Gray's Inn, 1966. *Recreations:* mimicry, complaining, sleeping. *Address:* 5 Paper Buildings, Temple, EC4Y 7HB. *T:* 071–353 5638. *Club:* United Oxford & Cambridge University.

PATMORE, Prof. (John) Allan; Professor of Geography, University of Hull, 1973–91, Professor Emeritus, since 1991; Vice-Chairman, Sports Council, since 1988 (Member, since 1978); *b* 14 Nov. 1931; *s* of John Edwin Patmore and Marjorie Patmore; *m* 1956, Barbara Janet Fraser; one *s* two *d*. *Educ:* Harrogate Grammar Sch.; Pembroke Coll., Oxford (MA, BLitt). Served RAF, Educn Br., 1952–54. Dept. of Geography, Univ. of Liverpool: Tutor, 1954–55; Asst Lectr, 1955–58; Lectr, 1958–69; Sen. Lectr, 1969–73; Dean of Social Science, 1979–81, Pro-Vice-Chancellor, 1982–85, Univ. of Hull. Visiting Professor: Univ. of Southern Illinois, 1962–63; Univ. of Canterbury, NZ, 1978. Pres. 1979–80, Trustee 1979–88, Hon. Mem., 1991, Geographical Assoc.; Pres., Sect. E, BAAS, 1987–88. Member: N York Moors National Park Cttee, 1977–; Nat. Parks Review Panel, 1990–91. *Publications:* Land and Leisure, 1970; People, Place and Pleasure, 1975; Recreation and Resources, 1983. *Recreations:* pursuing railway history, enjoying the countryside. *Address:* 4 Aston Hall Drive, North Ferriby, North Humberside HU14 3EB. *T:* Hull (0482) 632269.

PATNICK, (Cyril) Irvine, OBE 1980; MP (C) Sheffield, Hallam, since 1987; a Lord Commissioner of HM Treasury (Government Whip), since 1990; *b* 6 Oct. 1929; *m* 1960, Lynda Margaret (*née* Rosenfield); one *s* one *d*. *Educ:* Sheffield Poly. FCIOB. Dir, Eversure Textiles Ltd, Sheffield, 1980–. Member: Sheffield City Council, 1967–70; Sheffield MDC, 1971–88; S Yorks CC, until abolition in 1986 (Opposition Leader, 1973–86); Dep. Chm., S Yorks Residuary Bd, 1985–87. Contested (C) Sheffield, Hillsborough, 1970, 1979. An Asst Govt Whip, 1989–90. Vice-Chm., Cons. Party Back-bench Envmt Cttee, 1988–89. Mem., Cons. Party NEC, 1982–89; Chm., Cons. Party Nat. Local Govt Adv. Cttee, 1989–. Chm., Yorks and Humberside Council for Sport and Recreation, 1979–85; Member: Sheffield Community Health Council, 1974–75; Yorks and Humberside Tourist Bd, 1977–79; Governor, Sports Aid Foundn, Yorks and Humberside, 1980–. *Address:* House of Commons, SW1A 0AA.

PATON; *see* Noel-Paton.

PATON, Alasdair Chalmers, CEng, FICE, Chief Engineer, Scottish Office Environment Department, since 1991; *b* Paisley, 28 Nov. 1944; *o s* of David Paton and Margaret Elizabeth Paton (*née* Chalmers); *m* 1969, Zona Gertrude Gill; one *s* one *d*. *Educ:* John Neilson Instn, Paisley; Univ. of Glasgow (BSc). MIWEM. Assistant Engineer: Clyde Port Authy, 1967–71; Dept of Agric. and Fisheries for Scotland, 1971–72; Sen. Engineer, Scottish Develt Dept, 1972–77; Engineer, Public Works Dept, Hong Kong Govt, 1977–80; Scottish Development Department: Sen. Engineer, 1980–84; Principal Engineer, 1984–87; Dep. Chief Engineer, 1987–91. *Recreations:* Rotary, sailing, golf. *Address:* Scottish Office Environment Department, 27 Perth Street, Edinburgh EH3 5RB. *T:* 031–244 3035.

PATON, Sir Angus; *see* Paton, Sir T. A. L.

PATON, Ann; QC (Scot.) 1990; *d* of James McCargow and Ann Dunlop or McCargow; *m* 1974, Dr James Y. Paton; no *c*. *Educ:* Laurel Bank Sch.; Univ. of Glasgow (MA 1972; LLB 1974). Admitted to the Scottish Bar, 1977. Standing Junior Counsel: to the Queen's and Lord Treasurer's Remembrancer (excluding *Ultimus Haeres*), 1979; in Scotland to Office of Fair Trading, 1981. *Publications:* Map of Sheriffdoms and Sheriff Court Districts in Scotland, 1977, 2nd edn 1980; (Jt Asst Editor) Gloag and Henderson, Law of Scotland, 8th edn 1980, 9th edn 1987; (with R. G. McEwan) A Casebook on Damages in Scotland, 1983, 2nd edn as Damages in Scotland (sole author), 1989; contrib. Session Cases, and Scots Law Times. *Recreations:* sailing, tennis. *Address:* 23 Drummond Place, Edinburgh EH3 6PN. *Club:* Grange Tennis.

PATON, Rev. Canon David Macdonald; Chaplain to the Queen, 1972–83; Rector of St Mary de Crypt and St John the Baptist, Gloucester, 1970–81; Vicar of Christ Church, Gloucester, 1979–81; Hon. Canon of Canterbury Cathedral, 1966–80 (now Canon Emeritus); *b* 9 Sept. 1913; *e s* of late Rev. William Paton, DD and Grace Mackenzie Paton (*née* Macdonald); *m* 1946, Alison Georgina Stewart; three *s*. *Educ:* Repton; Brasenose Coll., Oxford. BA 1936, MA 1939. SCM Sec., Birmingham, 1936–39; Deacon 1939, Priest 1941; Missionary in China, 1940–44 and 1947–50; Chaplain and Librarian, Westcott House, Cambridge, 1945–46; Vicar of Yardley Wood, Birmingham, 1952–56; Editor, SCM Press, 1956–59; Sec., Council for Ecumenical Co-operation of Church Assembly, 1959–63; Sec., Missionary and Ecumenical Council of Church Assembly, 1964–69; Chairman: Churches' China Study Project, 1972–79; Gloucester Civic Trust, 1972–77. Hon. Fellow, Selly Oak Colls, 1981. *Publications:* Christian Missions and the Judgment of God, 1953; (with John T. Martin) Paragraphs for Sundays and Holy Days, 1957; (ed) Essays in Anglican Self-Criticism, 1958; (ed) The Ministry of the Spirit, 1960; Anglicans and Unity, 1962; (ed) Reform of the Ministry, 1968; (ed) Breaking Barriers (Report of WCC 5th Assembly, Nairobi, 1975), 1976; (ed with C.H. Long) The Compulsion of the Spirit, 1983; (ed) The 1483 Gloucester Charter in History, 1983; R.O.: The Life and Times of Bishop Ronald Hall of Hong Kong, 1985.

See also Rt. Rev. H. W. Montefiore, Ven. M. J. M. Paton, Prof. Sir W. D. M. Paton.

PATON, Douglas Shaw F.; *see* Forrester-Paton.

PATON, Maj.-Gen. Douglas Stuart, CBE 1983 (MBE 1961); FFPHM; Commander Medical HQ BAOR, 1983–85; retired 1986; *b* 3 March 1926; *s* of Stuart Paton and Helen Kathleen Paton (*née* Hooke); *m* 1957, Jennifer Joan Land; two *d*. *Educ:* Sherborne; Bristol University. MB ChB 1951; FFPHM 1989 (FFCM 1982, MFCM 1973). Commissioned RAMC, 1952; served Middle East (Canal Zone), Malaya, Hong Kong and UK, 1952–61; 16 Para Bde, 1961–66; jssc 1966; CO BMH Terendak, Malaysia, 1967–70; MoD, 1970–73; CO Cambridge Mil. Hosp., Aldershot, 1973–76; rcds 1977; DDMS HQ 1 (BR) Corps, 1978–81; Dep. Dir-Gen., Army Med. Services, MoD, 1981–83. QHP 1981–86. Hon. Col 221 (Surrey) Field Amb. RAMC(V), TA, 1988–. Chm., RAMC Assoc., 1988–. Mem. Bd of Governors, Moorfields Eye Hosp., 1988–91. CStJ 1986. *Publications:* contribs to Jl RAMC. *Recreations:* golf, skiing, travel, opera, gardening. *Address:* Brampton, Springfield Road, Camberley, Surrey GU15 1AB.

PATON, Ven. Michael John Macdonald; Archdeacon of Sheffield, 1978–87, Archdeacon Emeritus since 1988; *b* 25 Nov. 1922; *s* of late Rev. William Paton, DD, and Grace Mackenzie Paton (*née* Macdonald); *m* 1952, Isobel Margaret Hogarth; one *s* four *d*. *Educ:* Repton School; Magdalen Coll., Oxford (MA). Indian Army, 1942–46; HM Foreign Service, 1948–52; Lincoln Theological Coll., 1952–54; Deacon 1954, priest 1955; Curate, All Saints', Gosforth, Newcastle upon Tyne, 1954–57; Vicar, St Chad's, Sheffield, 1957–67; Chaplain, United Sheffield Hosps, 1967–70; Vicar, St Mark's, Broomhill, Sheffield, 1970–78. *Publications:* contrib. to: Essays in Anglican Self-criticism, 1958; Religion and Medicine, 1976. *Recreations:* hill walking, music, birdwatching. *Address:* 947 Abbeydale Road, Sheffield S7 2QD. *T:* Sheffield (0742) 366148.

See also Rt. Rev. H. W. Montefiore, Rev. Canon D. M. Paton, Prof. Sir W. D. M. Paton.

PATON, Sir (Thomas) Angus (Lyall), Kt 1973; CMG 1960; FRS 1969; FEng; Consulting Civil Engineer, since 1984; *b* 10 May 1905; *s* of Thomas Lyall Paton and Janet (*née* Gibb); *m* 1932, Eleanor Joan Delmé-Murray (*d* 1964); two *s* two *d*. *Educ:* Cheltenham Coll.; University College, London. Fellow of University College. Joined Sir Alexander Gibb & Partners as pupil, 1925; after experience in UK, Canada, Burma and Turkey on harbour works, hydro-electric projects and industrial development schemes, was taken into partnership, 1938; Senior Partner, 1955–77; Senior Consultant, 1977–84. Responsible for design and supervision of construction of many large industrial factories and for major hydro-electric and irrigation projects, including Owen Falls and Kariba Schemes, and for overall supervision of Indus Basin Project in W. Pakistan; also for economic surveys in Middle East and Africa on behalf of Dominion and Foreign Governments. Member UK Trade Mission to: Arab States, 1953; Egypt, Sudan and Ethiopia, 1955. Mem. NERC, 1969–72. Pres. ICE, 1970–71; Chm., Council of Engineering Instns, 1973; Past Chairman Assoc. of Consulting Engineers. FICE (Hon. FICE, 1975); FIStructE, Fellow Amer. Soc. of Civil Engineers, Past Pres., British Section, Soc. of Civil Engineers (France); a Vice-Pres., Royal Soc., 1977–78; For. Associate, Nat. Acad. of Engineering, USA, 1979. Founder Fellow, Fellowship of Engineering, 1976; FRSA. Fellow, Imperial Coll., London, 1978. Hon. DSc: London, 1977; Bristol, 1981. *Publications:* Power from Water, 1960; technical articles on engineering subjects. *Address:* L'Epervier, Route Orange, St Brelade, Jersey JE3 8GQ. *T:* 45619.

PATON, Prof. Sir William (Drummond Macdonald), Kt 1979; CBE 1968; MA, DM; FRS 1956; FRCP 1969; JP; Professor of Pharmacology in the University of Oxford, and Fellow of Balliol College, 1959–84, now Emeritus Professor and Emeritus Fellow; Honorary Director, Wellcome Institute for History of Medicine, 1983–87; *b* 5 May 1917; 3rd *s* of late Rev. William Paton, DD, and Grace Mackenzie Paton; *m* 1942, Phoebe Margaret, *d* of Thomas Rooke and Elizabeth Frances (*née* Pearce); no *c*. *Educ:* Winchester House Sch., Brackley; Repton Sch.; New Coll., Oxford (Scholar; Hon. Fellow, 1980); University College Hospital Medical Sch. BA (Oxon) Natural Sciences, Physiology, 1st class hons, 1938; Scholarships: Theodore Williams (Physiology), 1938; Christopher Welch, 1939; Jesse Theresa Rowden, 1939; Demonstrator in Physiology, Oxford, 1938–39; Goldsmid Exhibition, UCH Medical Sch., 1939; Ed. UCH Magazine, 1941; Fellowes Gold Medal in Clinical Med., 1941; BM, BCh Oxon, 1942; House physician, UCH Med. Unit, 1942. Pathologist King Edward VII Sanatorium, 1943–44; Member scientific staff, National Institute for Medical Research, 1944–52; MA 1948. Reader in Pharmacology, University College and UCH Med. Sch., 1952–54; DM 1953; Professor of Pharmacology, RCS, 1954–59. Delegate, Clarendon Press, 1967–72; Rhodes Trustee, 1968–87 (Chm., 1978–82). Chm., Cttee for Suppression of Doping, 1970–71; Member: Pharmacological Soc. (Chm. Edtl Bd, 1969–74, Hon. Mem., 1981); Physiological Soc. (Hon. Sec. 1951–57; Hon. Mem., 1985); British Toxicological Soc., 1980– (Chm., 1982–83, Hon. Mem., 1987); MRC, 1963–67; Council, Royal Society, 1967–69; British Nat. Cttee for History of Science, 1972–87 (Chm., 1980–85); Council, Inst. Study of Drug Dependence, 1969–75; Central Adv. Council for Science and Technology, 1970; DHSS Independent Cttee on Smoking, 1978–83; Adv. Cttee on Animal Experiments, 1980–85; Advr, HO Breath-alcohol Survey, 1984–85. Pres., Inst. of Animal Technicians, 1969–75, Vice-Pres., 1976–; Chm., Research Defence Soc., 1972–78 (Paget Lectr, 1978, Boyd Medal, 1987). Wellcome Trustee, 1978–87. Consultant, RN (Diving), 1978–82. Hon. Member: Soc. Franc. d'Allergie; Australian Acad. Forensic Sci.; Corresp. Mem., German Pharmacological Soc.; Hon. Lectr, St Mary's Hosp. Med. Sch., 1950; Visiting Lecturer: Swedish Univs, 1953; Brussels, 1956. Robert Campbell Oration, 1957; Lectures: Clover, 1958; Bertram Louis Abrahams, RCP, 1962; Ivison Macadam, RCSE, 1973; Osler, RCP, 1978; Cass, Dundee, 1981; Scheuler, Tulane, 1981; Hope Winch, Sunderland, 1982. Editor with R. V. Jones, Notes and Records of Royal Soc., 1971–89. FRSA 1973; Hon. FFARCS 1975; Hon. FRSM 1982. JP St Albans, 1956. Hon. DSc: London, 1985; Edinburgh, 1987; DUniv Surrey, 1986. Bengue Meml Prize, 1952; Cameron Prize, 1956; Gairdner Foundn Award, 1959; Gold Medal, Soc. of Apothecaries, 1976; Baly Medal, RCP, 1983; Osler Meml Medal, Univ. of Oxford, 1986. *Publications:* Pharmacological Principles and Practice (with J. P. Payne), 1968; Man and Mouse: animals in medical research, 1984; papers on diving, caisson disease, histamine, synaptic transmission, drug action and drug dependence in physiological and pharmacological journals. *Recreations:* music, old books. *Address:* 13 Staverton Road, Oxford OX2 6XH.

See also Rt. Rev. H. W. Montefiore, Rev. Canon D. M. Paton, Ven. M. J. M. Paton, Dr J. F. Stokes.

PATON WALSH, Jill; self-employed author, since 1966; *b* 29 April 1937; *d* of John Llewelyn Bliss and Patricia Paula DuBern; *m* 1961, Antony Paton Walsh (separated); one *s* two *d.* *Educ:* St Michael's Convent, Finchley; St Anne's Coll., Oxford (BA English; MA; DipEd). Schoolteacher, Enfield Girls' Grammar Sch., 1959–62. Arts Council Creative Writing Fellowship, Brighton Poly., 1976–77, 1977–78; Gertrude Clark Whitall Meml Lectr, Library of Congress, 1978; vis. faculty mem., Center for Children's Lit., Simmons Coll., Boston, Mass, 1978–86. A Judge, Whitbread Lit. Award, 1984; Chm., Cambridge Book Assoc., 1987–89; former Mem., Management Cttee, Soc. of Authors; Member: Cttee, Children's Writers' and Illustrators' Gp; Adjunct British Bd, Children's Literature New England. *Publications: fiction:* Farewell, Great King, 1972; Lapsing, 1986; A School for Lovers, 1989; *for children:* The Island Sunrise: pre-historic Britain, 1975; *fiction:* Hengest's Tale, 1966; The Dolphin Crossing, 1967; (with Kevin Crossley-Holland) Wordhoard, 1969; Fireweed (Book World Fest. Award), 1970; Goldengrove, 1972; Toolmaker, 1973; The Dawnstone, 1973; The Emperor's Winding Sheet (jtly, Whitbread Prize), 1974; The Butty Boy, 1975 (US edn as The Huffler); Unleaving (Boston Globe/Horn Book Award), 1976; Crossing to Salamis, The Walls of Athens, and Persian Gold, 1977–78 (US combined edn as Children of the Fox, 1978); A Chance Child, 1978; The Green Book, 1981 (re-issued as Shine, 1988); Babylon, 1982; Lost & Found, 1984; A Parcel of Patterns (Universe Prize), 1984; Gaffer Samson's Luck, 1985 (Smarties Prize Grand Prix, 1984); Five Tides, 1986; Torch, 1987; Birdy and the Ghosties, 1989. *Recreations:* photography, gardening, reading. *Address:* 72 Water Lane, Histon, Cambridge CB4 4LR. *T:* Cambridge (0223) 233034.

PATRICK, Graham McIntosh, CMG 1968; CVO 1981; DSC 1943; Under Secretary, Department of the Environment, 1971–81, retired; *b* 17 Oct. 1921; *m* 1945, Barbara Worboys; two *s.* *Educ:* Dundee High Sch.; St Andrews Univ. RNVR (Air Branch), 1940–46. Entered Ministry of Works, 1946; Regional Director: Middle East Region, 1965–67; South West Region, DoE, 1971–75; Chm., South West Economic Planning Bd, 1971–75; Dir, Scottish Services, PSA, 1975–81. *Address:* 3 Blueberry Downs, Coastguard Road, Budleigh Salterton, Devon EX9 6NU. *Club:* New (Edinburgh).

PATRICK, (James) McIntosh, ROI 1949; ARE; RSA 1957 (ARSA 1949); Painter and Etcher; *b* 1907; *s* of Andrew G. Patrick and Helen Anderson; *m* 1933, Janet (*d* 1983), *d* of W. Arnot Watterston; one *s* one *d.* *Educ:* Morgan Academy, Dundee; Glasgow School of Art. Awarded Guthrie Award RSA, 1935; painting Winter in Angus purchased under the terms of the Chantrey Bequest, 1935; paintings purchased for Scottish Nat. Gall. of Modern Art; National Gallery, Millbank; National Gallery of South Africa, Cape Town; National Gallery of South Australia; Scottish Contemp. Art Assoc.; and Municipal collections Manchester, Aberdeen, Hull, Dundee, Liverpool, Glasgow, Greenock, Perth, Southport, Newport (Mon.), Arbroath, also for Lady Leverhulme Art Gallery, etc.; etchings in British Museum and other print collections. Served War of 1939–46, North Africa and Italy; Captain (General List). Fellow, Duncan of Jordanstone Coll. of Art, Dundee, 1987. Hon. LLD Dundee, 1973. *Recreations:* gardening, music. *Address:* c/o Fine Art Society, 148 New Bond Street, W1; The Shrubbery, Magdalen Yard Road, Dundee. *T:* Dundee (0382) 68561. *Club:* Scottish Arts (Edinburgh).

PATRICK, John Bowman; Sheriff of North Strathclyde (formerly Renfrew and Argyll) at Greenock, 1968–83; *b* 29 Feb. 1916; *s* of late John Bowman Patrick, Boot and Shoe maker, Greenock, and late Barbara Patrick (*née* James); *m* 1945, Sheina Struthers McCrea; one *d.* *Educ:* Greenock Academy; Edinburgh Univ.; Glasgow Univ. MA Edinburgh, 1937. Served War in Royal Navy, Dec. 1940–Dec. 1945; conscripted as Ordinary Seaman, finally Lieut RNVR. LLB Glasgow 1946. Admitted as a Solicitor in Scotland, June 1947; admitted to Faculty of Advocates, July 1956. Sheriff of Inverness, Moray, Nairn, Ross and Cromarty at Fort William and Portree (Skye), 1961–68. *Address:* 77 Union Street, Greenock, Renfrewshire PA16 8BG. *T:* Greenock (0475) 20712.

PATRICK, Margaret Kathleen, OBE 1976; District/Superintendent Physiotherapist, Central Birmingham Health Authority (Teaching) (formerly United Birmingham Hospitals Hospital Management Committee), 1951–88, retired; *b* 5 June 1923; *d* of late Roy and Rose Patrick. *Educ:* Godolphin and Latymer Sch., London; Guy's Hosp. Sch. of Physiotherapy. BA, Open Univ., 1980. MCSP (Hon. FCSP). Chm. Physio. Adv. Cttee, and Mem. Health Care Planning for Elderly, Birmingham AHA (T). Member: Exec., Whitley Council PTA, 1960–75 (Chm., PTA Cttee C, 1960–75); Tunbridge Cttee on Rehab. Services, 1971–72; Hosp. Adv. Service on Geriatrics, 1972; DHSS Working Party on Stat. Data in Physio., 1969–76; Council, Chartered Soc. of Physio., 1953–75 (Exec. Mem., 1960–75; Vice Chm., 1971–75); Birmingham AHA (Teaching), 1979–82; Vice-Chm., Bromsgrove and Redditch HA, 1982–90. Assoc. of Supt Chartered Physiotherapists: Chm., 1964–75; Pres., 1971–72. *Publications:* Ultrasound Therapy: a textbook for physiotherapists, 1965; (contrib.) Physiotherapy in some Surgical Conditions, ed Joan Cash, 1977, 2nd edn 1979; contrib. Physiotherapy, and articles on ultrasound therapy, geriatric care, and paediatrics. *Recreation:* gardening.

PATTEN, Brian; poet; *b* 7 Feb. 1946. Regents Lectr, Univ. of Calif (San Diego), 1985. *Publications: poetry:* Penguin Modern Poets, 1967; Little Johnny's Confession, 1967; Notes to the Hurrying Man, 1969; The Irrelevant Song, 1971; The Unreliable Nightingale, 1973; Vanishing Trick, 1976; The Shabby Angel, 1978; Grave Gossip, 1979; Love Poems, 1981; Clare's Countryside: a book on John Clare, 1982; New Volume, 1983; Storm Damage, 1988; Grinning Jack (Selected Poems), 1990; *novel:* Mr Moon's Last Case, 1975 (Mystery Writers of Amer. Special Award, 1976); *for younger readers:* The Elephant and the Flower, 1969; Jumping Mouse; 1971; Emma's Doll, 1976; The Sly Cormorant and the Fish: adaptations of The Aesop Fables, 1977; (ed) Gangsters, Ghosts and Dragonflies, 1981; Gargling with Jelly, 1985; Jimmy Tag-along, 1988; Thawing Frozen Frogs, 1990; (ed) The Puffin Book of Twentieth Century Children's Verse, 1991; *plays:* The Pig And The Junkle, 1975; (with Roger McGough) The Mouth Trap, 1982; Blind Love, 1983; Gargling with Jelly, 1989; *records:* Brian Patten Reading His Own Poetry, 1969; British Poets Of Our Time, 1974; Vanishing Trick, 1976; The Sly Cormorant, 1977. *Address:* c/o Unwin Hyman Ltd, Publishers, 15–17 Broadwick Street, W1V 1FP. *Club:* Chelsea Arts.

PATTEN, Rt. Hon. Christopher (Francis), PC 1989; MP (C) Bath, since 1979; Chancellor of the Duchy of Lancaster, since 1990; Chairman of the Conservative Party, since 1990; *b* 12 May 1944; *s* of late Francis Joseph Patten and Joan McCarthy; *m* 1971, Mary Lavender St Leger Thornton; three *d.* *Educ:* St Benedict's School, Ealing; Balliol College, Oxford. Conservative Research Dept, 1966–70; Cabinet Office, 1970–72; Home Office, 1972; Personal Asst to Chairman of Conservative Party, 1972–74; Director, Conservative Research Dept, 1974–79. PPS to Chancellor of Duchy of Lancaster and Leader of House of Commons, 1979–81, to Secretary of State for Social Services, 1981; Parly Under-Sec. of State, NI Office, 1983–1985; Minister of State, DES, 1985–86; Minister of State (Minister for Overseas Develt), FCO, 1986–89; Sec. of State for the Envmt, 1989–90. Vice Chm., Cons. Parly Finance Cttee, 1981–83; Mem., Select Cttees on Defence and Procedure, 1982–83. *Publication:* The Tory Case, 1983. *Recreations:* reading, tennis, travelling in France and Spain. *Address:* c/o House of Commons, SW1. *Club:* Beefsteak.

PATTEN, Rt. Hon. John (Haggitt Charles); PC 1990; MP (C) Oxford West and Abingdon, since 1983 (City of Oxford, 1979–83); Minister of State, Home Office, since 1987; Fellow of Hertford College, Oxford, since 1972; *b* 17 July 1945; *s* of Jack Patten and late Maria Olga (*née* Sikora); *m* 1978, Louise Alexandra Virginia, 2nd *d* of late John Rowe, Norfolk, and of Claire Rowe, Oxfordshire; one *d.* *Educ:* Wimbledon Coll.; Sidney Sussex Coll., Cambridge (PhD 1972). University Lectr, Univ. of Oxford, 1969–79. Oxford City Councillor, 1973–76. PPS to Mr Leon Brittan and Mr Tim Raison, Ministers of State at the Home Office, 1980–81; Parliamentary Under-Secretary of State: NI Office, 1981–83; DHSS, 1983–85; Minister of State for Housing, Urban Affairs and Construction, DoE, 1985–87. Editor, Journal of Historical Geography, 1975–80. Mem. Council, Univ. of Reading. *Publications:* The Conservative Opportunity (with Lord Blake), 1976; English Towns, 1500–1700, 1978; Pre-Industrial England, 1979; (ed) The Expanding City, 1983; (with Paul Coones) The Penguin Guide to the Landscape of England and Wales, 1986. *Recreation:* talking with my wife. *Address:* House of Commons, SW1; Hertford College, Oxford. *Clubs:* Beefsteak; Clarendon (Oxford).

PATTEN, Nicholas John; QC 1988; *b* 7 Aug. 1950; *s* of Peter Grenville Patten and Dorothy Patten (*née* Davenport); *m* 1984, Veronica Mary Schoeneich; two *s* one *d.* *Educ:* Tulse Hill Sch.; Christ Church, Oxford (Open Schol.; MA; BCL (1st Cl. Hons Jurisprudence)). Called to the Bar, Lincoln's Inn, 1974. *Recreations:* gardening, ski-ing, motor cars. *Address:* 9 Old Square, Lincoln's Inn, WC2A 3SR. *T:* 071–405 4682.

PATTEN, Prof. Tom, CBE 1981; PhD; FEng 1986; FIMechE; FRSE; consultant; Director, Pict Petroleum plc, since 1981; Professor and Head of Department of Mechanical Engineering, Heriot-Watt University, 1967–82, now Emeritus; *b* 1 Jan. 1926; *s* of late William Patten and Isabella (*née* Hall); *m* 1950, Jacqueline McLachlan (*née* Wright); one *s* two *d.* *Educ:* Leith Acad.; Edinburgh Univ. (BSc, PhD). CEng, FIMechE 1965; FRSE 1967. Captain REME, 1946–48: served Palestine and Greece. Barry Ostlere & Shepherd Ltd, Kirkcaldy, 1949; Asst Lectr, Lectr and Sen. Lectr, Dept of Engrg, Univ. of Edinburgh, 1950–67; Dir, Inst. of Offshore Engineering, Heriot-Watt Univ., 1972–79; Vice-Principal, Heriot-Watt Univ., 1978–80, Acting Principal, 1980–81. Vis. Res. Fellow, McGill Univ., Canada, 1958. Researches in heat transfer, 1950–83; British and foreign patents for heat exchange and fluid separation devices. Man. Dir, Compact Heat Exchange Ltd, 1970–87; Chm., Sealand Industries plc, 1987–; Director: Melville Street Investments plc, 1983–; New Darien Oil Trust plc, 1985–88; Seaboard Lloyd Ltd, 1986–87; Brown Brothers & Co. Ltd, 1986–88; Marine Technology Directorate Ltd, 1988–; Chm., Environment and Resource Technology Ltd, 1982–91. Member: Council, IMechE, 1971–73, 1975–88 and 1989– (Pres., 1991–); Oil Develt Council for Scotland, 1973–78; SRC Marine Technol. Task Force, 1975–76; Design Council (Scottish Cttee), 1979–82; Offshore Technol. Bd, Dept of Energy, 1985–88; Co-ordinating Cttee on Marine Sci. and Technol., 1987–91; Supervisory Bd, NEL, 1989–91; Pres., Engrg Cttee on Oceanic Resources, 1987–90. Council, RSE, 1969–79 (Vice-Pres. RSE, 1976–79); Pres., Soc. for Underwater Technol., 1985–87. Hon. DEng Heriot-Watt, 1987. *Publications:* technical and scientific papers in field of heat transfer in Proc. IMechE, and Internat. Heat Transfer Conf. Proc.; also papers on offshore engineering. *Recreations:* squash, music. *Address:* 146/4 Whitehouse Loan, Edinburgh EH9 2AN. *T:* 031–447 0769. *Clubs:* Caledonian; New (Edinburgh).

PATTENDEN, Prof. Gerald, FRS 1991; Sir Jesse Boot Professor of Organic Chemistry, Nottingham University, since 1988; *b* 4 March 1940; *s* of Albert James and Violet Eugene Pattenden; *m* 1969, Christine Frances Doherty; three *d.* *Educ:* Brunel Univ.; Queen Mary College London. BSc, PhD, DSc; CChem, FRSC. Lectr, UC, Cardiff, 1966–72; Nottingham University: Lectr, 1972–75; Reader, 1975–80; Prof., 1980–88. *Publications:* numerous contribs in organic chem.; editor of several books and jls. *Recreations:* sport, entertainment, gardening. *Address:* Chemistry Department, The University, Nottingham NG7 2RD. *T:* Nottingham (0602) 484848.

PATTERSON, Arthur, CMG 1951; Assistant Secretary, Department of Health and Social Security, 1968–71; *b* 24 June 1906; 2nd *s* of late Alexander Patterson; *m* 1942, Mary Ann Stocks, *er d* of late J. L. Stocks; two *s* one *d.* *Educ:* Methodist Coll., Belfast; Queen's Univ., Belfast; St John's Coll., Cambridge. Entered Ministry of Labour, 1929; Assistant Secretary, 1941; transferred to Ministry of National Insurance, 1945; lent to Cyprus, 1953; Malta, 1956; Jamaica, 1963; Kuwait, 1971. *Address:* 8 Searles Meadow, Dry Drayton, Cambs CB3 8BU. *T:* Crafts Hill (0954) 89911.

PATTERSON, Maj.-Gen. Arthur Gordon, CB 1969; DSO 1964; OBE 1961; MC 1945; Director of Army Training, 1969–72; retired; *b* 24 July 1917; *s* of late Arthur

Abbey Patterson, Indian Civil Service; *m* 1949, Jean Mary Grant; two *s* one *d*. *Educ:* Tonbridge Sch.; RMC Sandhurst. Commnd, 1938; India and Burma, 1939–45; Staff Coll., Camberley, 1949; jssc 1955; CO 2nd 6th Queen Elizabeth's Own Gurkha Rifles, 1959–61; Comdr 99 Gurkha Inf. Brigade, 1962–64; idc 1965; GOC 17 Div. and Maj.-Gen., Bde of Gurkhas, 1965–69. Col, 6th Queen's Own Gurkha Rifles, 1969–73. *Address:* Burnt House, Benenden, Cranbrook, Kent. *Club:* Naval and Military.

PATTERSON, Ben; *see* Patterson, G.B.

PATTERSON, Rt. Rev. Cecil John, CMG 1958; CBE 1954; DD (Lambeth), 1963; DD (University of Nigeria, Nsukka), 1963; Commander of the Federal Republic (CFR) (Nigeria), 1965; *b* 9 Jan. 1908. *Educ:* St Paul's School; St Catharine's Coll., Cambridge; Bishop's Coll., Cheshunt. London Curacy, 1931–34; Missionary in S Nigeria, 1934–41; Asst Bishop on the Niger, 1942–45; Bishop on the Niger, 1945–69; Archbishop of West Africa, 1961–69; Representative for the Archbishops of Canterbury and York for Community Relations, 1970–72; Hon. Asst Bishop, Diocese of London, 1970–76. Hon. Fellow, St Catharine's Coll., Cambridge, 1963. *Address:* 6 High Park Road, Kew, Surrey TW9 4BH. *T:* 081–876 1697.

PATTERSON, (Constance) Marie, (Mrs Barrie Devney), CBE 1978 (OBE 1973); National Officer, Transport and General Workers' Union, 1976–84 (National Woman Officer, 1963–76); Member of General Council of TUC 1963–84 (Chairman, 1974–75 and 1977); *b* 1 April 1934; *d* of Dr Richard Swanton Abraham; *m* 1st, 1960, Thomas Michael Valentine Patterson (marr. diss. 1976); 2nd, 1984, Barrie Devney. *Educ:* Pendleton High Sch.; Bedford Coll., Univ. of London (BA). Member: Exec., Confedn of Shipbuilding and Engrg Unions, 1966–84 (Pres., 1977–78); Hotel and Catering Trng Bd, 1966–87; Equal Opportunities Commn, 1975–84; Central Arbitration Commn, 1976–; Legal Aid Adv. Cttee, 1988–90. Dir of Remploy, 1966–87. Lay Mem., Press Council, 1964–70. Hon. DSc Salford, 1975. *Recreations:* cooking, sight-seeing.

PATTERSON, Eric, MBE 1970; HM Diplomatic Service, retired; Consul-General, 1982–88 and Counsellor (Commercial), 1986–88, Auckland; *b* 2 May 1930; *s* of Richard and Elizabeth Patterson; *m* 1953, Doris (*née* Mason); two *s*. *Educ:* Hookergate Grammar Sch., Co. Durham. Served Royal Signals, 1948–50. Local govt service, 1947–50; Lord Chancellor's Dept, 1950–52; BoT, 1952–62; Asst Trade Comr, Halifax, NS, 1962–67; Second Sec. (Commercial), Khartoum, 1967–70; First Sec. (Commercial), The Hague, 1970–74; FCO, 1974–76; First Sec. (Commercial), Warsaw, 1976–80; FCO, 1980–82. *Recreations:* golf, sailing, photography, fly-fishing. *Address:* 3 Prebble Place, Auckland 5, New Zealand. *Clubs:* Royal Over-Seas League, Northern, Auckland, Auckland Golf, Royal New Zealand Yacht Squadron (Auckland).

PATTERSON, George Benjamin, (Ben); Member (C) Kent West, European Parliament, since 1979; *b* 21 April 1939; *s* of late Eric James Patterson and of Ethel Patterson; *m* 1970, Felicity Barbara Anne Raybould; one *s* one *d*. *Educ:* Westminster Sch.; Trinity Coll., Cambridge (MA); London Sch. of Economics. Lecturer, Swinton Conservative Coll., 1961–65; Editor (at Conservative Political Centre), CPC Monthly Report, 1965–74; Dep. Head, London Office of European Parlt, 1974–79. *Publications:* The Character of Conservatism, 1973; Direct Elections to the European Parliament, 1974; Europe and Employment, 1984; Vredeling and All That, 1984; VAT: the zero rate issue, 1988; A Guide to EMU, 1990. *Recreations:* squash, reading science fiction. *Address:* Elm Hill House, High Street, Hawkhurst, Kent TN18 4XU. *T:* Hawkhurst (0580) 753260. *Club:* Institute of Directors.

PATTERSON, Harry; novelist; *b* 27 July 1929; *s* of Henry Patterson and Rita Higgins Bell; *m* 1st, 1958, Amy Margaret Hewitt (marr. diss. 1984); one *s* three *d*; 2nd, 1985, Denise Lesley Anne Palmer. *Educ:* Roundhay Sch., Leeds; Beckett Park Coll. for Teachers; London Sch. of Economics as external student (BSc(Hons) Sociology). FRSA. NCO, The Blues, 1947–50. 1950–58: tried everything from being a clerk to a circus tent-hand; 1958–72: variously a schoolmaster, Lectr in Liberal Studies, Leeds Polytechnic, Sen. Lectr in Education, James Graham Coll. and Tutor in Sch. Practice, Leeds Univ.; since age of 41, engaged in full-time writing career. Dual citizenship, British/Irish. *Publications include:* (as Jack Higgins): Prayer for the Dying, 1973 (filmed 1985); The Eagle has Landed, 1975 (filmed 1976); Storm Warning, 1976; Day of Judgement, 1978; Solo, 1980; Luciano's Luck, 1981; Touch the Devil, 1982; Exocet, 1983; Confessional, 1985 (filmed 1985); Night of the Fox, 1986 (filmed 1989); A Season in Hell, 1989; Cold Harbour, 1990; The Eagle Has Flown, 1990; (as Harry Patterson) The Valhalla Exchange, 1978; To Catch a King, 1979 (filmed 1983); Dillinger, 1983; Walking Wounded (stage play), 1987; and many others (including The Violent Enemy, filmed 1969, and The Wrath of God, filmed 1972) under pseudonyms (Martin Fallon, Hugh Marlowe, Henry Patterson); some books trans. into 42 languages. *Recreations:* tennis, old movies. *Address:* c/o Ed Victor Ltd, 162 Wardour Street, W1V 3AT.

PATTERSON, Hugh Foggan, MA; Secretary, King's College London, 1977–83; *b* 8 Nov. 1924; *s* of late Sir John Robert Patterson, KBE, CMG, and late Esther Margaret Patterson; *m* 1956, Joan Philippa Abdy Collins; one *s* two *d*. *Educ:* Royal Grammar Sch., Newcastle upon Tyne; King's Coll., Cambridge (MA). Served War, Royal Artillery, 1943–47. HMOCS, Nigeria, 1950–61; Universities of: Birmingham, 1962–63; Warwick, 1964–69; London, 1969–83 (Clerk of the Senate, 1976–77). *Recreations:* music, golf, tennis. *Address:* 11 Sandwell Mansions, West End Lane, NW6 1XL.

PATTERSON, John Allan, CB 1989; Director of Savings and Head of Department for National Savings, 1986–91; *b* 10 Oct. 1931; *s* of William Gilchrist Patterson and May (*née* Eggie); *m* 1956, Anne Marie Lasson; one *s* two *d*. *Educ:* Epsom Coll.; Clare Coll., Cambridge (Major Scholar in Classics, Stewart of Rannoch Scholar; BA 1954). HM Diplomatic Service, 1954–65: served in Bangkok, 1957–61 and in Rome, 1961–64 (Private Sec. to the Ambassador); HM Treasury, 1965–81 (on loan to Cabinet Office, 1974–78); Dep. Dir of Savings, Dept for Nat. Savings, 1981–86. FRSA 1989. *Recreations:* gardening, walking, languages, church.

PATTERSON, Marie; *see* Patterson, C. M.

PATTERSON, Dr Mark Lister; *b* 2 March 1934; *s* of Alfred Patterson and Frederica Georgina Mary Lister Nicholson; *m* 1958, Jane Teresa Scott Stokes; one *s* two *d*. *Educ:* privately; St Bartholomew's Hosp. Med. Coll., Univ. of London (MB 1959). MRCP. Jun. hosp. appts at St Bartholomew's Hosp., Royal Postgrad. Med. Sch., and MRC Exptl Haematol. Unit; Consultant Haematologist to Nat. Heart and Chest Hosps, 1967–84. Mem., GLC, 1970–73 and 1977–81; Parly Candidate (C) Ealing N, 1974. *Recreations:* medicine, politics. *Address:* Wolverton Manor, Shorwell, Newport, Isle of Wight. *T:* Isle of Wight (0983) 740609. *Club:* Carlton.

PATTERSON, Paul Leslie; composer; Professor of Composition, since 1970, Head of Composition and Twentieth Century Music, since 1985, Royal Academy of Music; formed: Manson Ensemble, 1968; The Patterson Quintet, 1982; *b* 15 June 1947; *s* of Leslie and Lilian Patterson; *m* 1981, Hazel Wilson; one *s* one *d*. *Educ:* Royal Academy of Music. FRAM 1980. Freelance composer, 1968–; Arts Council Composer in Association, English Sinfonia, 1969–70; Director, Contemporary Music, Warwick Univ., 1974–80; Composer in Residence: SE Arts Assoc., 1980–82; Bedford School, 1984–85; Southwark Fest., 1989–91; James Allen School, Dulwich, 1990–91; Guest Prof., Yale Univ., 1989–90. Member: Exec. Cttee, Composers Guild, 1972–75; Council, SPNM, 1975–81, 1985–; Adv. Council, BBC Radio London, 1986–; Adv. Cttee, Arts Council's Recordings Panel, 1986–; Artistic Director of RAM Festivals: Lutosławski, 1984; Penderecki, 1986; Messiaen, 1987; Henze, 1988; Berio, 1989; Carter, 1990. Featured Composer at: Three Choirs Fest., Patterson at South Bank Fest., 1988; Cheltenham Fest., 1988, 1990; Peterborough Fest., 1989; Exeter Fest, 1991 (Artistic Dir, 1991–). Performances world wide by leading orchestras and soloists and ensembles; also film and TV music. Numerous recordings. FRSA 1989. OM, Polish Ministry of Culture, 1987. *Publications:* Rebecca, 1968; Trumpet Concerto, 1969; Time Piece, 1972; Kyrie, 1972; Requiem, 1973; Comedy for Five Winds, 1973; Requiem, 1974; Fluorescences, 1974; Clarinet Concerto, 1976; Cracowian Counterpoints, 1977; Voices of Sleep, 1979; Concerto for Orchestra, 1981; Canterbury Psalms, 1981; Sinfonia, 1982; Mass of the Sea, 1983; Deception Pass, 1983; Duologue, 1984; Mean Time, 1984; Europhony, 1985; Missa Brevis, 1985; Stabat Mater, 1986; String Quartet, 1986; Magnificat and Nunc Dimittis, 1986; Propositions, 1987; Trombone Quartet, 1987; Suite for Cello, 1987; Sorriest Cow, 1987; Tides of Mananan, 1988; Te Deum, 1988; Tunnel of Time, 1989; White Shadows, 1989; Symphony, 1990; The End, 1990. *Recreations:* sailing, croquet, swimming. *Address:* 31 Cromwell Avenue, Highgate, N6 5HN. *T:* 081–348 3711, *Fax:* 081–340 6489.

PATTERSON, Very Rev. William James, CBE 1991; Dean of Ely, 1984–90; Vicar of Abbotsley, Everton and Waresley, since 1990; *b* 25 Sept. 1930; *s* of William Moscrop and Alice Patterson; *m* 1955, Elisabeth Roederer; one *s* two *d*. *Educ:* Haileybury; Balliol College, Oxon. MA. Asst Curate of St John Baptist, Newcastle upon Tyne, 1955–58; Priest-in-Charge, Rio Claro with Mayaro, Dio. Trinidad, 1958–65; Rector of Esher, 1965–72; RD of Emly, 1968–72; Rector of Little Downham, 1972–80; Priest-in-Charge of Coveney, 1978–80; Archdeacon of Wisbech, 1979–84; Vicar of Wisbech St Mary, 1980–84. *Recreation:* cycling. *Address:* The Vicarage, Everton, Sandy, Beds SG19 3JZ. *T:* Sandy (0767) 621827.

PATTIE, Rt. Hon. Sir Geoffrey (Edwin), Kt 1987; PC 1987; MP (C) Chertsey and Walton since Feb. 1974; Vice-Chairman, Conservative Party, since 1990; Joint Chairman, GEC-Marconi, since 1991 (Chairman, 1990); *b* 17 Jan. 1936; *s* of late Alfred Edwin Pattie, LDS, and Ada Clive (*née* Carr); *m* 1960, Tuëma Caroline (*née* Eyre-Maunsell); one *s* (one *d* decd). *Educ:* Durham Sch.; St Catharine's Coll., Cambridge (MA). BA Cantab 1959. Called to Bar, Gray's Inn, 1964. Served: Queen Victoria's Rifles (TA), 1959–61; (on amalgamation) Queen's Royal Rifles (TA), now 4th Royal Green Jackets, 1961–65; Captain, 1964. Mem. GLC, Lambeth, 1967–70; Chm. ILEA Finance Cttee, 1968–70. Chm. of Governors, London Coll. of Printing, 1968–69. Contested (C) Barking, 1966 and 1970. Sec., Cons. Parly Aviation Cttee, 1974–75, 1975–76, Vice Chm., 1976–77, 1977–78; Jt Sec., Cons. Parly Defence Cttee, 1975–76, 1976–77, 1977–78, Vice Chm., 1978–79; Mem., Cttee of Public Accounts, 1976–79; Vice-Chm., All Party Cttee on Mental Health, 1977–79. Parly Under Sec. of State for Defence for the RAF, 1979–81, for Defence Procurement, 1981–83; Minister of State: for Defence Procurement, 1983–84; DTI (Minister for IT), 1984–87. Mem. General Synod of Church of England, 1970–75. *Publications:* Towards a New Defence Policy, 1976; (with James Bellini) A New World Role for the Medium Power: the British Opportunity, 1977. *Recreations:* travel, opera, cricket. *Address:* c/o House of Commons, SW1A 0AA. *Clubs:* Reform, Royal Green Jackets, MCC.

PATTINSON, Hon. Sir Baden, KBE 1962; LLB; Member, legal firm Pattinson, McLaughlin & Reid Smith; *b* 22 Dec. 1899; *m* 1926, Florence, *d* of T. A. Doman. Mayor of Maitland, 1928–30, and 1933; Mayor of Glenelg, 1944–47; MHA, South Australia: for Yorke Peninsula, 1930–38; for Glenelg, 1947–65; Minister of Education, SA, 1953–65. *Recreations:* horse riding, reading. *Address:* 12 Maturin Road, Glenelg, Adelaide, SA 5045, Australia.

PATTINSON, Sir Derek; *see* Pattinson, Sir W. D.

PATTINSON, John Mellor, CBE 1943; MA; *b* 1899; *s* of late J. P. Pattinson, JP, Mobberley, Cheshire; *m* 1927, Wilhelmina (*d* 1983), *d* of late W. J. Newth, Cheltenham; two *s*. *Educ:* Rugby Sch.; RMA; Cambridge Univ. RFA with BEF, 1918–19. Anglo-Iranian Oil Co., South Iran, 1922–45, General Manager, 1937–45. Director until 1969: British Petroleum Co. of Canada Ltd; Triad Oil Co. Ltd; BP Germany AG; Dep. Chm. 1960–65, and Man. Dir 1952–65, British Petroleum Co. Ltd; Dir, Chartered Bank, 1965–73. *Recreations:* gardening, travel. *Address:* Oakhurst, Oakcroft Road, West Byfleet, Surrey. *Club:* East India, Devonshire, Sports and Public Schools.

PATTINSON, Peter L. F.; *see* Foden-Pattinson, P. L.

PATTINSON, Rev. Sir (William) Derek, Kt 1990; Secretary-General, General Synod of Church of England, 1972–90; *b* 31 March 1930; *s* of late Thomas William and Elizabeth Pattinson. *Educ:* Whitehaven Grammar Sch.; Queen's Coll., Oxford (Stanhope Historical Essay Prize, 1951). BA 1952; MA 1956. Entered Home Civil Service, 1952; Inland Revenue Dept, 1952–62 and 1965–68; HM Treasury, 1962–65 and 1968–70; Assoc. Sec.-Gen., General Synod, 1970–72. Chm., William Temple Assoc., 1966–70; Member: Archbishops' Commn on Church and State, 1966–70; British Council of Churches, 1972–90; London Diocesan Synod, 1972–91. Ordained deacon, 1991; Asst Curate, St Gabriel's Pimlico, 1991–. Vice-Chm., Grosvenor Chapel Cttee, 1973–81; Vice-Pres., SPCK; Chm. of Governors, Liddon House, 1972–; Chm., English Friends of Anglican Centre in Rome, 1985; Governor: Sir John Cass Foundn; Greycoat Foundn. Freeman, City of London, 1973; Master, Parish Clerks' Co., 1986–87; Mem., Woolmens' Co. Mem., Alcuin Club. Churchwarden, St Michael's Cornhill, 1988–91. *Address:* 4 Strutton Court, Great Peter Street, SW1P 2HH. *T:* 071–222 6307. *Clubs:* Savile, Nikaean.

PATTISON, Prof. Bruce; Professor of Education, University of London Institute of Education, 1948–76, now Emeritus; *b* 13 Nov. 1908; *s* of Matthew and Catherine Pattison; *m* 1937, Dorothy Graham (*d* 1979). *Educ:* Gateshead Grammar Sch.; King's Coll., Newcastle upon Tyne; Fitzwilliam House, Cambridge. Henry Mellish Sch., Nottingham, 1933–35; Hymers Coll., Hull, 1935–36; Lecturer in English, University College, London, 1936–48 (Reader, 1948). Board of Trade, 1941–43; Ministry of Supply, 1943–45. *Publications:* Music and Poetry of the English Renaissance, 1948, 2nd edn 1970; Special Relations, 1984. *Address:* 62 The Vale, Coulsdon, Surrey CR5 2AW. *T:* 081–660 2991. *Clubs:* Athenæum, National Liberal.

PATTISON, David Arnold, PhD; Partner, Cobham Resource Consultants, since 1990; *b* 9 Feb. 1941; *s* of David Pattison and Christina Russell Bone; *m* 1967, Anne Ross Wilson; two *s* one *d*. *Educ:* Glasgow Univ. (BSc 1st Cl. Hons, PhD). Planning Assistant, Dunbarton County Council, 1966–67; Lecturer, Strathclyde Univ., 1967–70; Head of Tourism Division, Highlands and Islands Development Board, 1970–81; Chief Exec., Scottish Tourist Board, 1981–85; Dir of Leisure and Tourism Consulting, Arthur Young Group, 1985–90. Chm., Hotel Industry Liaison Cttee, Napier Polytechnic, 1990–; Hon. Vice

Pres., Scottish Youth Hostels Assoc., 1990–. *Publications:* Tourism Development Plans for: Argyll, Bute, Ayrshire, Burgh of Ayr, Ulster. *Recreations:* reading, watching soccer and Rugby, golf, gardening. *Address:* 7 Cramond Glebe Gardens, Cramond, Edinburgh EH4 6NZ.

PATTISON, Rev. Dr George Linsley; Dean of Chapel, King's College, Cambridge, since 1991; *b* 25 May 1950; *s* of George William Pattison and Jean Pattison; *m* 1971, Hilary Christine Cochrane; one *s* two *d. Educ:* Perse Sch., Cambridge; Edinburgh Univ. (MA, BD); Durham Univ. (PhD). Curate, St James' Church, Benwell, Newcastle upon Tyne, 1977–80; Priest-in-charge, St Philip and St James' Church, Kimblesworth, Co. Durham, 1980–83; Res. Student, Durham Univ., 1980–83; Rector, Badwell Ash, Great Ashfield, Hunston and Stowlangtoft with Langham, Suffolk, 1983–91. Has broadcast on BBC Radio 4 on subjects of art and religion. *Publications:* Art, Modernity and Faith, 1991; Kierkegaard: the aesthetic and the religious, 1991; articles on theology, philosophy of religion and the arts in specialist and non-specialist jls. *Recreations:* family life, running, music, films, theatre. *Address:* King's College, Cambridge CB2 1ST. *T:* Cambridge (0223) 350411.

PATTISON, Michael Ambrose; Secretary General, Royal Institution of Chartered Surveyors, since 1985; Director, Surveyors Holdings Ltd, since 1985; *b* 14 July 1946; *s* of Osmond John Pattison and Eileen Susanna Pattison (*née* Cullen); *m* 1975, Beverley Jean, *d* of Genevieve and Hugh Webber, Florida, USA; one *d. Educ:* Sedbergh School; University of Sussex (BA Hons 1968). Min. of Overseas Develt, 1968; Asst Private Sec. to Minister, 1970; seconded to HM Diplomatic Service as First Sec., Perm. Mission to UN, New York, 1974; ODA, 1977; Private Sec. to successive Prime Ministers, 1979–82; ODA, 1982, Establishment Officer, 1983–85. Mem. Council, British Consultants Bureau, 1985–. Dir, Battersea Arts Centre Trust, 1988–. Mem., Cambridge Univ. Careers Service Syndicate, 1989–; Governor, Thames Polytechnic, 1989– (Vice-Chm., 1991–). Vis. Fellow, City Univ., 1990–. FRSA 1990. *Recreations:* countryside, cricket, real tennis. *Address:* Royal Institution of Chartered Surveyors, 12 Great George Street, SW1P 3AD. *T:* 071–222 7000. *Club:* Warwickshire CC.

PATTON, Joseph Alexander, CBE 1982; FRAgS; farmer; *b* 17 Jan. 1936; *s* of Marshall Lyons and Bessie Robinson Patton; *m* 1967, Mary Morton Kirkpatrick; one *s* two *d.* Member: Milk Marketing Board, NI, 1982–; Council, Food From Britain, 1983–; Broadcasting Council of NI, 1982–84. President: Young Farmers' Clubs of Ulster, 1969–71; Ulster Farmers' Union, 1980–81. FRAgS 1984. *Address:* Roseyards, 107 Kirk Road, Ballymoney, Co. Antrim, Northern Ireland BT53 8HN. *T:* Dervock (02657) 41263.

PATTON, Thomas William Saunderson, OBE 1985; Member, Belfast City Council, since 1973; Lord Mayor of Belfast, 1982–83; *b* 27 July 1914; *s* of Florence and Robert Patton; *m* 1940, Alice Glover; three *s* three *d* (and one *d* decd). *Educ:* Templemore Avenue School, Belfast. Harland and Wolff Ltd, 1932–61; Ulster Folk and Transport Museum, 1962–82. *Recreations:* gardening, football. *Address:* 89 Park Avenue, Belfast BT4 1JJ. *T:* Belfast (0232) 658645.

PATTULLO, (David) Bruce, CBE 1989; Group Chief Executive, since 1988, and Governor, since 1991, Bank of Scotland; *b* 2 Jan. 1938; *s* of late Colin Arthur Pattullo and of Elizabeth Mary Bruce; *m* 1962, Fiona Jane Nicholson; three *s* one *d. Educ:* Rugby Sch.; Hertford Coll., Oxford (BA). FIB (Scot.). Commnd Royal Scots and seconded to Queen's Own Nigeria Regt. Gen. Man., Bank of Scotland Finance Co. Ltd, 1973–77; Dir, 1977–, Chief Exec., 1977–78, British Linen Bank Ltd; Bank of Scotland: Dep. Treas., 1978; Treas. and Gen. Manager (Chief Exec.), 1979–88; Dir, 1980–; Dep. Governor, 1988–91. Director: Melville Street Investments, 1973–90; Bank of Wales, 1986–; Standard Life Assurance Co., 1985–. Chm., Cttee, Scottish Clearing Bankers, 1981–83, 1987–89; Pres., Inst. of Bankers in Scotland, 1990–92 (a Vice-Pres., 1977–90). First Prizeman (Bilsland Prize), Inst. of Bankers in Scotland, 1964. FRSE 1990. *Recreation:* tennis. *Address:* 6 Cammo Road, Edinburgh EH4 8EB. *T:* 031–339 6012. *Clubs:* Caledonian; New (Edinburgh).

PAUK, György, Hon. RAM 1990; international concert violinist; Professor at Guildhall School of Music and Drama; Professor, Royal Academy of Music, since 1987; *b* 26 Oct. 1936; *s* of Imre and Magda Pauk; *m* 1959, Susanne Mautner; one *s* one *d. Educ:* Franz Liszt Acad. of Music, Budapest. Toured E Europe while still a student; won three internat. violin competitions, Genoa 1956, Munich 1957, Paris 1959; soon after leaving Hungary, settled in London, 1961, and became a British citizen. London début, 1961; seasonal appearances there and in the provinces, with orchestra, in recital and chamber music; also plays at Bath, Cheltenham and Edinburgh Fests and London Promenade Concerts; performs in major European music venues; US début, under Sir George Solti, with Chicago Symph. Orch., 1970, followed by further visits to USA and Canada to appear with major orchs; holds master classes, in Colo; plays regularly in Hungary following return in 1973; overseas tours to Australia, NZ, S America, S Africa, Middle and Far East; many performances for BBC, incl. Berg and Bartók concertos, with Boulez. As conductor/soloist, has worked with the English, Scottish and Franz Liszt chamber orchs and London Mozart Players; guest dir, Acad. of St Martin-in-the-Fields. Has made many recordings including: Bartok Sonatas (among top records in US, 1982); Tippett Concerto (Best Gramophone Record Award, 1983); Berg Concerto (Caecilia Prize, Belgium, 1983); complete sonatas for violin and harpsichord by Handel; all violin concertos and orch. works by Mozart. With Peter Frankl and Ralph Kirshbaum, formed chamber music trio, 1973; performances at major fests; public concerts in Gt Britain have incl. complete Brahms and Beethoven Cycles; the trio has also made many broadcasts for the BBC. First performances: Penderecki's Violin Concerto, Japan, 1979, UK, 1980; Tippett's Triple Concerto, London, 1980; Lutosawski's Chain 2, with composer conducting, Britain, The Netherlands and Hungary, 1986–87; Sir Peter Maxwell Davies' Violin Concerto, Switzerland, 1988. Hon. GSM, 1980. *Address:* c/o Artist Management International Ltd, 12/13 Richmond Buildings, W1V 5AF. *T:* 071–439 7515.

PAUL, Alan Roderick; HM Diplomatic Service; Head of Hong Kong Department, Foreign and Commonwealth Office, since 1989; *b* 13 May 1950; *s* of late Roderick Ernest Paul and of Hilda May Paul (*née* Choules); *m* 1979, Rosana Yuen-Ling Tam; one *s* one *d. Educ:* Wallington High Sch. for Boys; Christ Church, Oxford (Scholar; MA Modern Langs, 1st class Hons). FCO, 1972–73; language training, Univs of Cambridge and Hong Kong, 1973–75; FCO, 1975–77; Peking, 1977–80; FCO, 1980–84; Head of Chancery, The Hague, 1984–87; Asst Head, Hong Kong Dept, FCO, 1987–89. *Recreations:* gardening, genealogy, philately, music. *Address:* c/o Foreign and Commonwealth Office, King Charles Street, SW1A 2AH.

PAUL, Dr David Manuel; HM Coroner: City of London, since 1966; Northern District of London, since 1968; *b* 8 June 1927; *s* of Kenneth and Rachael Paul; *m* 1948, Gladys Audrey Garton, MCSP; two *d. Educ:* Selhurst Grammar Sch. for Boys, Croydon; St Bartholomew's Hosp. Med. Coll.; The London Hosp. Med. Coll. MRCS, LRCP 1953; DRCOG 1962; DA 1962; DMJ (Clin.) 1965. Served Manchester Regt, 1946–49 (Lieut). House Surgeon, Beckenham Hosp., 1954; Obstetric House Surgeon, Luton and Dunstable Hosp., 1955; gen. practice, Drs Duncan & Partners, Croydon, 1955–67; Clin. Asst Anaesthetist, Croydon Gp of Hosps, 1956–68; GP Obstetrician, Purley Hosp., 1958–68; Divl Surgeon, Z Div., Met. Police, 1956–68. Hon. Lectr, Court Practice and Clin. Forensic Medicine, Guy's Hosp. Med. Sch., 1966–; Hon. Consultant, Clin. Forensic Medicine, Surrey Constab., 1967–; Hon. Sen. Lectr, Clin. Forensic Medicine, Charing Cross and Westminster Hosp. Med. Sch., 1990–. Chm., Med. Section, 1973–76, Chm., Exec. Council, 1979–83, and 1989–, and Pres., 1987–88, British Acad. of Forensic Sciences. *Publications:* contrib. medico-legal jls and text books on forensic medicine. *Recreations:* travel, equitation, fishing, photography. *Address:* Cobhambury Farm, Edenbridge, Kent TN8 5NG. *T:* Edenbridge (0732) 863280; The Coroner's Court, Milton Court, Moor Lane, EC2Y 9BL. *T:* 071–606 3030; The Coroner's Court, Myddelton Road, Hornsey, N8 7PY. *T:* 081–348 4411; Shirley Oaks Hospital, Poppy Lane, Shirley Oaks Village, Croydon CR9 8AB. *T:* 081–655 2255.

PAUL, Geoffrey David, OBE 1991; United States Affairs Editor, Jewish Chronicle, since 1991; *b* 26 March 1929; *s* of Reuben Goldstein and Anne Goldstein; *m* 1st, 1952, Joy Stirling (marr. diss. 1972); one *d*; 2nd, 1974, Rachel Mann; one *s. Educ:* Liverpool, Kendal, Dublin. Weekly newspaper and news agency reporter, 1947–57; asst editor, Jewish Observer and Middle East Review, 1957–62; Jewish Chronicle, 1962–: successively sub-editor, foreign editor, Israel corresp., deputy editor; Editor, 1977–90. *Publication:* Living in Jerusalem, 1981. *Address:* 130 Dwight Place, Englewood, New Jersey, USA. *T:* (201) 894 1343.

PAUL, George William; Chief Executive, Harrisons & Crosfield, since 1987; *b* 25 Feb. 1940; *s* of William Stuart Hamilton Paul and Diana Violet Anne Martin; *m* 1963, Mary Annette Mitchell (*d* 1989); two *s* one *d. Educ:* Harrow; Wye Coll., Univ. of London (BSc Agric Hons). Pauls & Whites Foods: Marketing Dir, 1968; Managing Dir, 1972; Pauls & Whites: Dir, 1972; Group Managing Dir, 1982; Chm., Pauls, 1985; Harrisons & Crosfield: Dir, 1985; Jt Chief Exec., 1986. High Sheriff, Suffolk, 1990. *Recreations:* farming, hunting, shooting, fishing, sailing. *Address:* Bluegates, Wherstead, Ipswich, Suffolk IP9 2AU. *T:* Copdock (047386) 274. *Clubs:* Boodle's, Farmers'.

PAUL, Air Cdre Gerard John Christopher, CB 1956; DFC 1944; MA; FRAeS; FRMetS; *b* 31 Oct. 1907; *s* of E. W. Paul, FRCS; *m* 1st, 1937, Rosemary (*d* 1975), *d* of Rear-Admiral H. G. E. Lane, CB; two *s* one *d*; 2nd, 1987, Mollie Denise Samuels, *d* of Joseph Samuels, MM. *Educ:* Cheltenham Coll.; St John's Coll., Cambridge. Entered Royal Air Force, 1929; Fleet Air Arm, 1931–36; served War of 1939–45 in England and N.W. Europe; Commandant, Central Flying School, 1954–56; retired, 1958. Secretary-General of the Air League, 1958–71. Life Vice-Pres., RAF Gliding and Soaring Assoc.; Pres., Popular Flying Assoc., 1969–78. Croix de Guerre avec Palme (Belgium), 1944; Military Cross (Czechoslovakia), 1945. *Recreations:* dogs, garden. *Address:* Wearne House, Old Alresford, Hants SO24 9DH. *Club:* Royal Air Force.

PAUL, Hugh Glencairn B.; *see* Balfour-Paul.

PAUL, Very Rev. John Douglas; Dean of Moray, Ross and Caithness, since 1991; Rector of Holy Trinity, Elgin, with St Margaret's, Lossiemouth, since 1980; *b* 13 Sept. 1928; *s* of George Anson Moncrieff Paul and Vivian (*née* Ward); *m* 1969, Mary Susan Melody Woodhouse. *Educ:* Winchester Coll.; Edinburgh Univ. (MA); Ely Theol Coll. Asst Curate, Portsmouth, 1954–56; Missionary Priest, Mozambique, 1956–70; Archdeacon, Mozambique, 1965–70; Rector: Castle Douglas, 1970–75; Portobello, 1975–80; Hon. Canon and Synod Clerk, Dio. of Moray, Ross and Caithness, 1989–91. *Publication:* Mozambique: Memoirs of a Revolution, 1975. *Recreation:* travel. *Address:* The Rectory, 8 Gordon Street, Elgin IV30 1JQ. *T:* Elgin (0343) 547505.

PAUL, Sir John (Warburton), GCMG 1965 (KCMG 1962); OBE 1959; MC 1940; Lieutenant Governor, Isle of Man, 1974–80; *b* 29 March 1916; 2nd *s* of Walter George Paul and Phoebe (*née* Bull), Weymouth; *m* 1946, Kathleen Audrey, CStJ 1962, *d* of Dr A. D. Weeden, Weymouth; three *d. Educ:* Weymouth Coll., Dorset; Selwyn Coll., Cambridge (MA; Hon. Fellow, 1982). Secretary, Maddermarket Theatre, Norwich, 1936. Commissioned Royal Tank Regt (Suppl. Res.), 1937; regular commission, RTR, 1938; BEF 1940 (despatches, prisoner-of-war); ADC and Private Secretary to Governor of Sierra Leone, 1945 (seconded). Called to the Bar, Inner Temple, 1947. Colonial Administrative Service, Sierra Leone, 1947; District Commissioner, 1952; Permanent Secretary, 1956; Provincial Commissioner, 1959; Secretary to the Cabinet, 1960; Governor and C-in-C, The Gambia, 1962–65; Governor-General of The Gambia, 1965–66; Governor and C-in-C: British Honduras, 1966–72; The Bahamas, 1972–73; Governor-General, The Bahamas, July–Oct. 1973. Dir, Overseas Relns, St John Ambulance, 1981–89. Member Board, West African Airways Corporation, 1954–56. Chm., St Christopher Motorists' Security Assoc., and associated cos, 1980–. A Patron, Pain Relief Foundn, 1980–. Mem., Bd of Governors, Pangbourne Coll., 1981–86. KStJ 1962 (Member: Chapter-Gen., 1981–; St John Council, Hants, 1990–). *Recreation:* painting. *Address:* Sherrens Mead, Sherfield-on-Loddon, Hampshire RG27 0ED. *Clubs:* Athenæum, MCC; Hawks (Cambridge).

PAUL, Noël Strange, CBE 1978; Director, Press Council, 1976–79 (Assistant Secretary, 1964, Secretary, 1968–76), retired; *b* 1914; *y s* of late S. Evan Paul, SSC, and Susan, *d* of Dr Henry Habgood; *m* 1950, Mary, *yr d* of Philip J. Bone, FRSA, MRST, Luton. *Educ:* Kingston Grammar School. Journalist, Press Assoc., 1932; served War of 1939–45, Iran and Italy, Major seconded RAF (despatches). Home Counties Newspapers, 1949; Liverpool Daily Post, 1958. Mem., Steering Cttee on the Mass Media, Council of Europe, 1976–82; Governor, English-Speaking Union, 1980–82. *Publications:* Self-regulation of the Press, 1982; Principles for the Press, 1985. *Recreations:* sailing, photography. *Address:* The Lodge, St Catherine's, Strachur, Argyllshire PA25 8AZ. *T:* Inveraray (0499) 2208.

PAUL, Robert Cameron, FEng 1990; Managing Director, Albright & Wilson, since 1986; *b* 7 July 1935; *s* of late Dr F. W. Paul, MB ChB and Maureen K. Paul (*née* Cameron); *m* 1965, Diana Kathleen Bruce; two *d. Educ:* Rugby Sch.; Corpus Christi Coll., Cambridge (BA, MA). Nat. Service, 2nd Lieut RE, BAOR, 1953–55. Chemical Engineer, ICI, Runcorn, 1959; Dir, ICI Fibres, 1976; Dep. Chm., Mond Div., ICI, 1979; Dep. Chm. and Man. Dir, Albright & Wilson, 1986. Non-Exec. Dir, Mersey Docks and Harbour Co., 1985–88. Pres., IChemE, 1990–91. Hon DEng Birmingham, 1990. *Recreations:* music (piano), golf. *Address:* Albright & Wilson, 1 Knightsbridge Green, SW1X 7QD. *T:* 071–589 6393. *Clubs:* Oriental; Royal Wimbledon Golf.

PAUL, Roderick Sayers; Chief Executive, Severn Trent Water, since 1988; *b* 22 April 1935; *s* of Dr Robert Andrew Patrick Paul and Dr Margaret Louisa Paul; *m* 1965, Ann Broadway; one *s* one *d. Educ:* Wellington College; St Edmund Hall, Oxford (MA Jurisp.). Glynwed plc, 1962; British Oxygen, 1969; British Oxygen, S Africa, 1977; Mitchell Cotts, 1984–88, Chief Exec., 1986–88. *Recreations:* model making, boating, golf. *Address:* Severn Trent Water, 2297 Coventry Road, Birmingham B26 3PU. *T:* 021–722 4102.

PAUL, Air Marshal Sir Ronald Ian S.; *see* Stuart-Paul.

PAUL, Swraj; Padma Bhushan; Chairman: Caparo Group Ltd, since 1978; Caparo Industries Plc, since 1981; Caparo Inc., USA, since 1988; Armstrong Equipment Ltd, since 1989; CREMSA, Spain, since 1989; ENSA, Spain, since 1989; *b* 18 Feb. 1931; *s* of Payare and Mongwati Paul; *m* 1956, Aruna Vij; three *s* one *d* (and one *d* decd). *Educ:* Punjab Univ. (BSc); Mass Inst. of Technol. (BSc, MSc (Mech. Engrg)). Began work as Partner in family-owned Apeejay Surrendra Gp, India, 1953; came to UK in 1966 and estabd first business, Natural Gas Tubes Ltd; Caparo Group Ltd formed in 1978 as holding co. for UK businesses involved in engrg, hotel and property develt, investment, tea and shipping; Caparo Industries Plc (engrg, metals) formed in 1981. Chairman: Barton Tubes, Canada, 1983–; United Merchant Bar, 1985–; Bull Moose Tube Co., USA, 1988–; Bock Industries Inc., USA, 1990–. Founder Chm., Indo-British Assoc., 1975–. FRSA. Padma Bhushan (equivalent to British Peerage), 1983. Hon. PhD Amer. Coll. of Switzerland, Leysin, 1986. Corporate Leadership Award, MIT, 1987. *Publication:* Indira Gandhi, 1984, 2nd edn 1985. *Address:* Caparo House, 103 Baker Street, W1M 1FD. *T:* 071–486 1417. *Clubs:* MCC, Royal Automobile; Royal Calcutta Turf, Royal Calcutta Golf (Calcutta); Cricket of India (Bombay).

PAUL, Prof. Wolfgang, Grosses Verdienstkreuz mit Stern, 1981; Emeritus Professor of Physics, University of Bonn, since 1981; *b* 10 Aug. 1913; *m* 1940, Liselotte Hirsche; two *s* two *d*; *m* 1979, Dr Doris Walch. *Educ:* Tech. Hochschule, München (DrIng); Tech. Hochschule, Berlin. Asst, Univ. of Göttingen, 1942–44, Dozent, 1944–52; Prof. of Exptl Physics, Univ. of Bonn, 1952–81; Director: Kern Forschungs Anlage, Tülich, 1960–62; Nuclear Physics Div., CERN, Geneva, 1964–67; DESY, Hamburg, 1970–73. Hon. Degrees: Uppsala, 1978; Aachen, 1981; Poznan, 1990. (Jtly) Nobel Prize for Physics, 1990. *Publications:* numerous in physics jls. *Address:* Stationsweg 13, 53 Bonn, Germany.

PAULET, family name of **Marquess of Winchester.**

PAULIN, Prof. Roger Cole, DrPhil, LittD; Schröder Professor of German, University of Cambridge, since 1989; Fellow, Trinity College, Cambridge since 1989; *b* 18 Dec. 1937; *s* of Thomas Gerald Paulin and Paulina (*née* Duff); *m* 1966, Traute Fielitz; one *s* one *d*. *Educ:* Otago Boys' High Sch., Dunedin, NZ; Univ. of Otago (MA); Heidelberg Univ. (DrPhil); MA, LittD (Cantab). Asst Lectr, Univ. of Birmingham, 1963–64; Lectr, Univ. of Bristol, 1965–73; Fellow and Coll. Lectr in German, Trinity Coll., Cambridge, 1974–87; Univ. Lectr, Univ. of Cambridge, 1975–87; Henry Simon Prof. of German, Univ. of Manchester, 1987–89. Mem., Editl Bd, Literatur-Lexikon, 1988–. *Publications:* Ludwig Tieck: a literary biography, 1985, 2nd edn 1986 (trans. German, 1988); The Brief Compass, 1985; Ludwig Tieck, 1987; Theodor Storm, 1991. *Recreation:* gardening. *Address:* 45 Fulbrooke Road, Cambridge CB3 9EE. *T:* Cambridge (0223) 322564.

PAULING, Linus (Carl); Research Professor, Linus Pauling Institute of Science and Medicine, since 1974; *b* 28 Feb. 1901; *s* of Herman William Pauling and Lucy Isabelle Darling; *m* 1923, Ava Helen Miller (*d* 1981); three *s* one *d*. *Educ:* Oregon State Coll.; California Institute of Technology. BS Oregon State Coll., 1922; PhD California Inst. of Technology, 1925; Hon. DSc: Oregon State Coll., 1933; Univ. of Chicago, 1941; Princeton Univ., 1946; Yale, 1947; Cambridge, 1947; London, 1947; Oxford, 1948; Brooklyn Polytechnic Inst., 1955; Humboldt Univ. (Berlin), 1959; Melbourne, 1964; York (Toronto), 1966; LLD Reed Coll., 1959; LHD Tampa, 1949; Dr *hc*: Paris, 1948; Toulouse, 1949; Liège, 1955; Montpellier, 1958; Warsaw, 1969; Lyon, 1970; UJD, NB, 1950; DFA, Chouinard Art Inst., 1958. Asst in Chemistry and in Mechanics and Materials, Oregon State Coll., 1919–22; Graduate Asst, California Inst. Technology, 1922–23; Teaching Fellow, 1923–25; Research Associate, 1925–26; Nat. Res. Fellow in Chemistry, 1925–26; Fellow of John Simon Guggenheim Meml Foundn, 1926–27 (Univs of Munich, Zürich, Copenhagen); Asst Prof., California Inst. of Technology, 1927–29; Associate Prof., 1929–31; Prof. of Chemistry, 1931–63; Dir of Gates and Crellin Labs of Chemistry, and Chm., Div. of Chemistry and Chemical Engrg, 1936–58; Prof. of Chemistry, Stanford Univ., 1969–74. George Fisher Baker Lectr in Chemistry, Cornell Univ., Sept. 1937–Feb. 1938; George Eastman Prof., Oxford Univ., Jan.-June 1948, etc. Amer. Chem. Soc. Award in Pure Chemistry, 1931; William H. Nichols Medal, 1941; J. Willard Gibbs Medal, 1946; Theodore William Richards Medal, 1947; Davy Medal of Royal Society, 1947; Presidential Medal for Merit, 1948; Gilbert Newton Lewis Medal, 1951; Thomas Addis Medal, 1955; Amedeo Avogadro Medal, 1956; Pierre Fermat Medal, Paul Sabatier Medal, 1957; International Grotius Medal, 1957; Nobel Prize for Chemistry, 1954; Nobel Peace Prize for 1962, 1963; Linus Pauling Medal, 1966; Internat. Lenin Peace Prize, 1971; 1st Martin Luther King Jr Medical Award, 1972; Nat. Medal of Science, 1975; Lomonosov Gold Medal, Soviet Acad. of Scis, 1978; Vannevar Bush Medal, Nat. Sci. Bd, 1989. Member: Nat. Acad. of Sciences; Amer. Phil. Soc.; Amer. Acad. of Arts and Sciences, etc.; Hon. Fellow: Chemical Society (London), Royal Institution, etc.; For. Member: Royal Society, Akademia Nauk, USSR, etc.; Associé étranger, Acad. des Sciences, 1966. War of 1939–45, Official Investigator for projects of National Defense Research Cttee on Medical Research, and Office of Scientific Research and Development. Grand Officer, Order of Merit, Italian Republic. *Publications:* The Structure of Line Spectra (with S. Goudsmit), 1930; Introduction to Quantum Mechanics (with E. B. Wilson, Jun), 1935; The Nature of the Chemical Bond, 1939 (3rd ed., 1960); General Chemistry, 1947 (2nd ed., 1953); College Chemistry, 1950 (3rd ed., 1964); No More War!, 1958 (revised edn, 1962); The Architecture of Molecules (with Roger Hayward), 1964; The Chemical Bond, 1967; Vitamin C and the Common Cold, 1971; (with Peter Pauling) Chemistry, 1975; Vitamin C, the Common Cold and the Flu, 1976; (with Ewan Cameron) Cancer and Vitamin C, 1979; How to Live Longer and Feel Better, 1986; also numerous scientific articles in the fields of chemistry, physics, and biology including the structure of crystals, quantum mechanics, nature of the chemical bond, structure of gas molecules, structure of antibodies and nature of serological reactions, etc. *Address:* Linus Pauling Institute of Science and Medicine, 440 Page Mill Road, Palo Alto, California 94306, USA.

PAULUSZ, Jan Gilbert; a Recorder of the Crown Court, since 1980; *b* 18 Nov. 1929; *s* of Jan Hendrik Olivier Paulusz and Edith (*née* Gilbert); *m* 1973, Luigia Maria Attanasio. *Educ:* The Leys Sch., Cambridge. Called to the Bar, Lincoln's Inn, 1957; South Eastern Circuit, 1959–. *Recreations:* mountain walking, photography. *Address:* 50 Royston Gardens, Redbridge, Ilford, Essex IG1 3SY.

PAUNCEFORT, Bernard Edward, OBE 1983; HM Diplomatic Service, retired 1986; Administrator, Tristan da Cunha, South Atlantic, since 1989; *b* 8 April 1926; *o s* of Frederick George Pauncefort and Eleanor May (*née* Jux); *m* 1956, Patricia Anne, *yr d* of Charles Ernest Leah and Alice (*née* Kendal-Banks). *Educ:* Wandsworth School. RAFVR 1942–44; Royal Fusiliers, 1944–48. Metropolitan Police Civil Staff, 1948–53; HM Colonial Service, 1953; Malaya, 1953–56; Tanganyika, 1956–63; CRO, 1963–67; First Sec., Zambia, 1967–68; Consul, Cape Town, 1969–72; Lord Pearce's staff, Rhodesia, 1971–72; Head of Chancery, Madagascar, 1972–73; FCO, 1973–76; Head of Chancery, Burma, 1976–78; Dir, British Inf. Services, S Africa, 1978–80; Lord Soames' staff, Rhodesia-Zimbabwe, 1979–80; Administrator, Ascension Island, 1980–82; FCO, 1982–83; Counsellor and Chief Sec., Falkland Is, 1983–85; Counsellor, FCO, 1985–86; Under-Sec., Govt of the Turks & Caicos Is. W Indies, 1986–88. Zimbabwe Medal, 1980. *Recreations:* dogs, showing and breeding; birds, waterways. *Address:* The Residency, Tristan da Cunha, South Atlantic.

PAUNCEFORT-DUNCOMBE, Sir Philip; *see* Duncombe.

PAVAROTTI, Luciano; Italian tenor; *b* 12 Oct. 1935; *s* of Fernando Pavarotti and Adele (*née* Venturi); *m* 1961, Adua Veroni; three *d*. *Educ:* Istituto Magistrale. Teacher, 1955–57. Professional début, Teatro Municipale, Reggio Emilia, 1961; sang throughout Europe, 1961–64; US début and Australian tour 1965; rôles include Rodolfo in La Bohème, Cavaradossi in Tosca, Duke of Mantua in Rigoletto, Radames in Aïda, Ernani, Alfredo in La Traviata, Manrico in Il Trovatore, Rodolfo in Luisa Miller, Arturo in I Puritani, Elvino in La Sonnambula, Nemorino in L'Elisir d'Amore, Idomeneo, Enzo in La Gioconda, Riccardo (Gustavo) in Un Ballo in Maschera, etc. Chevalier des Grieux in Manon. Grammy Award for best classical vocal soloist, 1978, 1979, 1981, 1988, 1990. *Publications:* (jtly) Pavarotti: my own story, 1981; Grandissimo Pavarotti, 1986. *Address:* c/o Herbert Breslin, 119 West 57th Street, New York, NY 10019, USA.

PAVEY, Martin Christopher; Headmaster, Latymer Upper School, Hammersmith, 1988–91; *b* 2 Dec. 1940; *s* of Archibald Lindsay Pavey and Margaret Alice Pavey (*née* Salsbury); *m* 1969, Louise Margaret (*née* Bird); two *s*. *Educ:* Magdalen College Sch., Oxford; University Coll., London (Hons English); Nottingham Univ. (MA English); Univ. of Cambridge (Dip. Educn). Wigglesworth & Co., London and E. Africa (Shipping and Finance), 1956–62; Assistant Master: King's Sch., Ely, 1962–64; Lancing Coll., 1968–71; Fairham Comprehensive School, Nottingham: Head of English, 1971–75; Dep. Headmaster, 1975–76; Headmaster, 1976–81; Headmaster, Cranbrook School, 1981–88. *Recreations:* art architecture, cinema. *Address:* 5 The Vineyards, Bath, Avon.

PAWLEY, Robert John; Deputy Chief Executive (Technical), Valuation Office Agency (formerly Deputy Chief Valuer, Inland Revenue Valuation Office), since 1989; *b* 10 Sept. 1939; *s* of Frederick Clifford and Marjorie Pawley; *m* 1965, Simone Elizabeth Tayar; two *s*. *Educ:* Plymouth Coll.; Exeter Univ. (BA). FRICS. Private practice, Plymouth, 1962–71; joined Valuation Office, 1972; Dist Valuer, Waltham Forest, 1977, Haringey, 1978–81; Suptg Valuer, Chief Valuer's Office, London, 1981–84, Cambridge, 1984–87; Asst Chief Valuer, 1987–88. *Recreations:* 18th century English naval history and exploration, period model boats, antiques. *Address:* Chief Valuer's Office, New Court, Carey Street, WC2A 2JE. *T:* 071–324 1151.

PAWSEY, James Francis; MP (C) Rugby and Kenilworth, since 1983 (Rugby, 1979–83); *b* 21 Aug. 1933; *s* of William Pawsey and Mary Mumford; *m* 1956, Cynthia Margaret Francis; six *s* (including twins twice). *Educ:* Coventry Tech. School; Coventry Tech. Coll. Director: Autobar Group Ltd, 1983–; St Martins Hosps Ltd, 1989–. Parliamentary Private Secretary: DES, 1982–83; DHSS, 1983–84; to Minister of State for NI, 1984–86. Member: Parly Scientific Cttee, 1982–; Select Cttee of Parly Comr for Admin, 1983–; Select Cttee on Standing Orders, 1987–; Exec., 1922 Cttee, 1989–; Chm., Cons Parly Educn Cttee, 1985–; Vice-Chm., IPU, 1990– (Mem. Exec., 1984–); Secretary: British Solidarity with Poland Campaign, 1982–; British Portuguese Parly Gp, 1984–; Cons. Back Bench Social Services and Educn Cttees, 1982–83; Treas., British/Bangladesh Parly Gp, 1984–. Member: Rugby RDC, 1965–73; Rugby Borough Council, 1973–75; Warwickshire CC, 1974–79; former Chm. and Pres., Warwickshire Assoc. of Parish Councils. MInstD. KLJ. *Publication:* The Tringo Phenomenon, 1983. *Address:* Rugby and Kenilworth Conservative Association, Albert Buildings, Albert Street, Rugby. *T:* Rugby (0788) 569556. *Club:* Carlton.

PAXMAN, Jeremy Dickson; journalist, author and broadcaster; *b* 11 May 1950; *s* of Arthur Keith Paxman and Joan McKay Dickson. *Educ:* Malvern College; St Catharine's College, Cambridge (Exhibnr). Reporter: N Ireland, 1974–77; BBC TV Tonight, 1977–79; Panorama, 1979–85; The Bear Next Door; presenter: Breakfast Time, 1986–89; Newsnight, 1989–. Mem. Council, RUSI, 1990–. Award for Internat. Current Affairs, RTS, 1985. *Publications:* (jtly) A Higher Form of Killing: the secret story of gas and germ warfare, 1982; Through the Volcanoes: a Central American journey, 1985; Friends in High Places: who runs Britain?, 1990. *Recreations:* fishing, ski-ing, snoozing. *Address:* c/o BBC TV, W12. *Club:* Groucho.

PAXTON, John; author, also writing as Jack Cherrill; Editor, The Statesman's Year-Book, 1969–90; *b* 23 Aug. 1923; *m* 1950, Joan Thorne; one *s* one *d*. Head of Economics department, Millfield, 1952–63. Joined The Statesman's Year-Book, 1963, Dep. Ed., 1968; Consultant Editor, The New Illustrated Everyman's Encyclopaedia, 1981–84. *Publications:* (with A. E. Walsh) Trade in the Common Market Countries, 1965; (with A. E. Walsh) The Structure and Development of the Common Market, 1968; (with A. E. Walsh) Trade and Industrial Resources of the Common Market and Efta Countries, 1970; (with John Wroughton) Smuggling, 1971; (with A. E. Walsh) Into Europe, 1972; (ed) Everyman's Dictionary of Abbreviations, 1974, 2nd edn 1986, as Penguin Dictionary of Abbreviations, 1989; World Legislatures, 1974; (with C. Cook) European Political Facts 1789–1990, 3 vols, 1975–91; The Statesman's Year-Book World Gazetteer, 1975, 4th edn, 1991; (with A. E. Walsh) Competition Policy: European and International Trends and Practices, 1975; The Developing Common Market, 1976; A Dictionary of the European Economic Community, 1977, 2nd edn, A Dictionary of the European Communities, 1982 (commended, McColvin Medal Cttee); (with C. Cook) Commonwealth Political Facts, 1979; (with S. Fairfield) Calendar of Creative Man, 1980; Companion to Russian History, 1984; Companion to the French Revolution, 1988; The Statesman's Year-Book Historical Companion, 1988; (with G. Payton) Penguin Dictionary of Proper Names, 1991; contrib. to Keesing's Contemporary Archives, TLS. *Address:* Moss Cottage, Hardway, Bruton, Somerset BA10 0LN. *T:* Bruton (0749) 813423. *Clubs:* Royal Over-Seas League, PEN.

PAXTON, Peter James, FCIS; FCCA; FCIB; Finance Director and Secretary, Don Ridgway Associates Ltd, since 1988 (Chief Executive, 1986–88); Founder, Peter Paxton Marketing, 1986, now Peter Paxton Associates; *b* 27 April 1923; *m* 1st, 1947, Betty Jane Madden (marr. diss. 1980); one *s* one *d*; 2nd, 1985, Sylvia June Stock. *Educ:* Lawrence Sherriff Sch., Rugby. Served RAF, 1941–46. Accountant, Rugby Co-operative Society Ltd, 1949–55; Chief Accountant, 1955, Chief Exec. Officer, 1972–86, Cambridge and District Co-operative Society Ltd; Chairman: CWS, 1980–86; Co-operative Bank, 1980–86; First Co-op. Finance, 1980–86; Co-op. City Investments, 1983–86; Dep. Chm., Co-op. Insce Soc., 1983–86. *Address:* Harvest Home, 37 Green End, Fen Ditton, Cambridge CB5 8SX.

PAYE, Jean-Claude; Chevalier de la Légion d'Honneur; Officier de l'Ordre National du Mérite; Chevalier de l'Ordre National du Mérite agricole; Croix de la Valeur militaire; Secretary-General, OECD, since 1984; *b* 26 Aug. 1934; *s* of late Lucien Paye and of Suzanne Paye (*née* Guignard); *m* 1963, Laurence Hélène Marianne Jeanneney; two *s* two *d*. *Educ:* Lycée Bugeaud, Algiers; Lycée Carnot, Tunis; Faculté de droit, Tunis; Institut d'Etudes Politiques, Paris; Ecole Nationale d'Administration. Government service, 1961–64; Technical Adviser to: Sec. of State for Scientific Research, 1965; Minister of Social Affairs, 1966; Chief Adviser to Vice-Pres., EEC, 1967–73; Adviser, Embassy, Bonn,

1973; Asst Principal Private Sec. to Minister of Foreign Affairs, 1974–76; Diplomatic Advr to Prime Minister, 1976–79; Head of Economic and Financial Affairs, Ministry of Foreign Affairs, 1979–84; Pres., Exec. Cttee in special Session, OECD, 1979–84. *Address:* OECD, 2 rue André-Pascal, 75775 Paris cedex 16, France.

PAYKEL, Prof. Eugene Stern, FRCP; FRCPE; FRCPsych; Professor of Psychiatry and Head of Department, University of Cambridge, since 1985; Professorial Fellow, Gonville and Caius College, Cambridge, since 1985; *b* 9 Sept. 1934; *s* of late Joshua Paykel and Eva Stern Paykel; *m* 1969, Margaret, *d* of late John Melrose and Joan Melrose; two *s*. *Educ:* Auckland Grammar Sch.; Univ. of Otago (MB ChB, MD; Stuart Prize, Joseph Pullar Schol., 1956); DPM London. Maudsley Hosp., 1962–65; Asst Prof. of Psychiatry and Co-Dir/Dir, Depression Res. Unit, Yale Univ., 1966–71; Consultant and Sen. Lectr, 1971–75, Reader, 1975–77, Prof. of Psychiatry, 1977–85, St George's Hosp. Med. Sch., Univ. of London. Chm., Social and Community Psych. Section, RCPsych, 1984–88 (Mem. Council, Exec. and Finance Cttee); Chief Scientist's Adviser and Mem., Mental Illness Res. Liaison Gp, DHSS, 1984–88; previously examiner Univs of Edinburgh, Nottingham, Manchester, London, and RCPsych. Pres., British Assoc. for Psychopharmacology, 1982–84 (Hon. Sec., 1979–82); Mem., Neurosciences Bd, MRC, 1981–85. Trustee, Mental Health Foundn, 1988–. Foundations Fund Prize for Res. in Psychiatry, 1978; BMA Film Competition Bronze Award, 1981; Anna Monika Stiftung 2nd Prize, 1985. Jt Editor in Chief, Jl of Affective Disorders, 1979–; Member, Editorial Board: Social Psychiatry; Psychopharmacology; Jl of Psychosomatic Research. *Publications:* The Depressed Woman, 1974; Psychopharmacology of Affective Disorders, 1979; Monoamine Oxidase Inhibitors: the state of the art, 1981; Handbook of Affective Disorders, 1982; Community Psychiatric Nursing for Neurotic Patients, 1983; papers on depression, psychopharmacology, social psychiatry, life events, evaluation of treatment. *Recreations:* opera, music, theatre. *Address:* Department of Psychiatry, University of Cambridge, Addenbrooke's Hospital, Hills Road, Cambridge CB2 2QQ. *T:* Cambridge (0223) 336961. *Club:* Athenæum.

PAYNE, Alan Jeffrey, CMG 1988; HM Diplomatic Service, retired; Secretary General, International Primary Aluminium Institute, since 1989; *b* 11 May 1933; *s* of Sydney Ellis Payne and Lydia Payne; *m* 1959, Letitia Freeman; three *s*. *Educ:* Enfield Grammar Sch.; Queens' Coll., Cambridge (Exhibnr). FIL 1962. RN, 1955–57. EMI, London, later Paris, 1957–62; Secretariat, NATO, Paris, 1962–64; joined Diplomatic Service, 1965; Commonwealth Relations Office (later FCO), 1965–67; British High Commn, Kuala Lumpur, 1967–70; FCO, 1970–72; British Embassy, Budapest, 1972–75; Counsellor, Mexico City, 1975–79; FCO, 1979–82; Consul-General, Lyons, 1982–87; High Comr, Jamaica, and Ambassador (non-resident) to Haiti, 1987–89. *Recreations:* music, theatre. *Clubs:* United Oxford & Cambridge University, Commonwealth Trust; Liphook Golf.

PAYNE, Arthur Stanley, OBE 1977; HM Diplomatic Service, retired; Director, Southern Africa Association, since 1988; *b* 17 Nov. 1930; *s* of late Arthur and Lilian Gertrude Payne; *m* 1964, Heather Elizabeth Cavaghan; one *d*. *Educ:* Chatham Tech. Sch.; Gillingham Grammar Sch.; Nat. Defence Coll. HM Forces, 1949–50. Joined BoT, 1949; Raw Materials Dept, Washington, 1951–52; Min. of Materials, London, 1953–55; British Trade Commns, New Delhi, Bombay, Port of Spain, and Georgetown (First Sec.), 1956–67; joined HM Diplomatic Service, 1965; First Sec. (Inf.), Auckland, 1967–70; FCO, 1971–74; Dacca, 1974–76; Bonn, 1976–78; FCO, 1978–79; Dep. High Comr and Head of Chancery, Gabarone, 1980–83; Counsellor and Hd of Commercial Dept, Manila, 1983–87. *Recreations:* bridge, golf, music. *Address:* Hoders Gate, Woodhurst Park, Oxted, Surrey, RH8 9HA. *Club:* Commonwealth Trust.

PAYNE, Dr Christopher Charles; Chief Executive, Horticulture Research International, since 1990; *b* 15 May 1946; *s* of Rupert George Payne and Evelyn Violet (*née* Abbott); *m* 1969, Margaret Susan Street; one *s* one *d*. *Educ:* Wadham Coll., Oxford (MA, DPhil). CBiol, MIBiol; FIHort. Post-Doctoral Fellow, Univ. of Otago, NZ, 1972; SSO, NERC, Oxford, 1973–77; PSO, 1977–83, Head, Entomology Dept, 1983–86, Glasshouse Crops Res. Inst., Littlehampton; Head, Crop Protection Div., Inst. of Horticultural Res., E Malling, 1987–90. Editor in Chief, Biocontrol Science and Technology, 1991–. *Publications:* (with R. Hull and F. Brown) Virology: directory and dictionary of animal, bacterial and plant viruses, 1989; numerous contribs to books and learned jls. *Recreations:* gardening, walking. *Address:* The Coach House, Chestnut Square, Wellesbourne, Warwick CV35 9QS. *T:* Stratford-upon-Avon (0789) 842562.

PAYNE, Christopher Frederick, CBE 1987; QPM 1975; DL; Chief Constable of Cleveland Constabulary, 1976–90; *b* 15 Feb. 1930; *o s* of late Gerald Frederick Payne, OBE, BEM, QPM, and Amy Florence Elizabeth Payne (*née* Parker); *m* 1952, Barbara Janet Saxby; one *s* three *d*. *Educ:* Christ's Coll., Finchley; Hendon Technical Coll. CBIM 1987. Joined Metropolitan Police, 1950; Sen. Comd. course, 1965; Home Office R&D Br., 1968–70; Comdr 'X' Div., 1971–74; Comdr Airport Div., 1974–76. Dep. Chm., Metrop. Police Friendly Soc., 1971–76; Police Advr to ACCs' Social Services Cttee, 1979–90; Chm., Public Order Sub-Cttee, ACPO, 1981–88; Pres., Chief Constables' Club, 1989–90. Adviser to: Chemical Hazards Unit, Qld Govt, 1989–90; UN Disaster Relief Org. External Services, 1990–; Emergency Planning Advr, BRCS, Cleveland, 1990–. County Dir, St John Ambulance, Cleveland, 1978–85; Comdr, SJAB, Cleveland, 1985–89; Chm., St John Council, Cleveland, 1986–89. Chm., Cleveland Mental Health Support Gp, 1981–86; Vice-Pres., Cleveland Youth Assoc., 1983–; Vice Chm., Royal Jubilee and Prince's Trusts Cttee for Durham and Cleveland, 1984–90. Freeman, City of London, 1988. DL Cleveland 1983. CStJ 1985 (OStJ 1980). *Publications:* various articles on contingency planning and management. *Recreations:* painting, philately, gardening. *Address:* c/o The Chief Constable's Office, PO Box 70, Ladgate Lane, Middlesbrough, Cleveland TS8 9EH. *Clubs:* Commonwealth Trust; Cleveland.

PAYNE, Maj.-Gen. George Lefevre, CB 1966; CBE 1963; Director of Ordnance Services, Ministry of Defence, 1964–68; retired, 1968; *b* 23 June 1911; *s* of Dr E. L. Payne, MRCS, LRCP, Brunswick House, Kew, Surrey; *m* 1st, 1938, Betty Maud (*d* 1982), *d* of Surgeon Captain H. A. Kellond-Knight, RN, Eastbourne, Sussex; two *s* (and one *s* decd); 2nd, 1990, Antoinette Georgina, *d* of Roger Cookson, and *widow* of D. Mitchell. *Educ:* The King's Sch., Canterbury; Roy. Mil. Coll., Sandhurst. Royal Leicestershire Regiment: England, Northern Ireland, 1931–33; India, 1933–37; Royal Army Ordnance Corps: England, 1938–39; France, 1939–40; England, 1941–. Deputy Director Ordnance Services: HQ, BAOR, 1952–54; War Office, 1955–57; Commandant, Central Ordnance Depot, Chilwell, 1957–59; Deputy Director Ordnance Services, War Office, 1959–63; Commander, Stores Organization, RAOC, 1963–64; Col Comdt, RAOC, 1968–72. *Recreations:* fishing, cricket. *Address:* 10 Highlands Heath, Bristol Gardens, SW15 3TG. *T:* 081-785 3196. *Clubs:* Army and Navy, Commonwealth Trust.

PAYNE, Henry Salusbury Legh D.; *see* Dalzell Payne.

PAYNE, Ian; barrister; *b* 15 July 1926; *s* of late Douglas Harold Payne and of Gertrude (*née* Buchanan); *m* 1st, 1951, Babette (marr. diss. 1975), *d* of late Comte Clarence de Chalus; four *s* two *d*; 2nd, 1977, Colette Eugénie, *d* of late Marinus Jacobus van der Eb, Rotterdam. *Educ:* Wellington Coll. Commnd 60th Rifles, 1944–48. Called to the Bar, Lincoln's Inn, 1953, Hong Kong, 1981; Dep. Recorder of Derby, 1969–72; a Recorder, 1972–81. *Address:* 2 Crown Office Row, Temple, EC4; 1601 Hang Chong Building, 5 Queen's Road C, Hong Kong. *T:* 5221 778. *Clubs:* Garrick; Hong Kong; Refreshers Cricket.

PAYNE, Rev. James Richmond, MBE 1982; ThL; JP; General Secretary, Bible Society in Australia, 1968–88; Chairman, United Bible Societies World Executive Committee, 1976–88; *b* 1 June 1921; *s* of late R. A. Payne, Sydney, New South Wales; *m* 1943, Joan, *d* of late C. S. Elliott; three *s*. *Educ:* Drummoyne High School; Metropolitan Business College, Moore Theological College, Sydney. Served War of 1939–45: AIF, 1941–44. Catechist, St Michael's, Surry Hills, NSW, 1944–47; Curate, St Andrew's, Lismore, NSW, 1947–50; Rector, St Mark's, Nimbin, NSW, 1950–52; Chaplain, RAAF, Malta and Amberley, Qld, 1952–57; Rector, St Stephen's, Coorparoo, Qld, 1957–62; Dean of Perth, Western Australia, 1962–68. Hon. Commissary in Australia for Anglican Bp of Central Tanganyika, E Africa, 1988–. JP, ACT, 1969. *Publications:* Around the World in Seventy Days, 1965; And Now for the Good News, 1982. *Recreations:* sport, walking, reading, family. *Address:* 10/42 Jinka Street, Hawker, ACT 2614, Australia. *T:* (06) 2546722. *Clubs:* Weld (Perth); Commonwealth (Canberra).

PAYNE, Jane Marian, (Mrs A. E. Payne); *see* Manning, J. M.

PAYNE, Keith, VC 1969; *b* 30 Aug. 1933; *s* of Henry Thomas Payne and Remilda Payne (*née* Hussey); *m* 1954, Florence Catherine Payne (*née* Plaw); five *s*. *Educ:* State School, Ingham, North Queensland. Soldier, Department of Army, Aug. 1951–75; 1 RAR, Korea, 1952–53; 3 RAR, Malaya, 1963–65; Aust. Army Trng Team, Vietnam, 1969 (Warrant Officer); WO Instructor: RMC, Duntroon, ACT, 1970–72; 42 Bn, Royal Qld Regt, Mackay, 1973–75; Captain, Oman Army, 1975–76. Member: VC and GC Assoc.; Returned Services League; Korea and South East Asia Forces Assoc. Freeman City of Brisbane and of Shire of Hinchinbrook. Vietnamese Cross of Gallantry, with bronze star, 1969; US Meritorious Unit Citation; Vietnamese Unit Citation Cross of Gallantry with Palm. *Recreations:* football, fishing, hunting. *Address:* 11 Canberra Street, North Mackay, Qld 4740, Australia. *T:* (079) 578497.

PAYNE, Leonard Sidney, CBE 1983; Director, J. Sainsbury Ltd, 1974–86; Adviser on Distribution and Retailing, Coopers & Lybrand, since 1986; *b* 16 Dec. 1925; *s* of Leonard Sydney Payne and Lillian May Leggatt; *m* 1944, Marjorie Vincent; two *s*. *Educ:* Woodhouse Grammar School. FCCA, CBIM, FCIT, MBCS. Asst Accountant, Peek Frean & Co. Ltd, 1949–52; Chief Accountant, Administrator of various factory units, head office appts, Philips Electrical Industries, 1952–62; Dep. Gp Comptroller, Morgan Crucible Co. Ltd, 1962–64; British Road Services Ltd: Finance Dir, 1964–67; Asst Man. Dir, 1967–69; Man. Dir, 1969–71; Dir of Techn. Services and Develt, Nat. Freight Corp., 1971–74, Vice-Chm. Executive 1974. President: Freight Transport Assoc., 1980–82; Chartered Inst. of Transport, 1983–84. Chm., CBI Transport Policy Cttee, 1980–86. *Recreations:* gardening, swimming, squash, chess. *Address:* Flat 4N, Maple Lodge, Lythe Hill Park, Haslemere, Surrey GU27 3TE. *T:* Haslemere (0428) 56841.

PAYNE, Sir Norman (John), Kt 1985; CBE 1976 (OBE 1956; MBE (mil.) 1944); FEng; Chairman, BAA plc (formerly British Airports Authority), 1977–91 (Chief Executive, 1972–77); *b* 9 Oct. 1921; *s* of late F. Payne, Folkestone; *m* 1946, Pamela Vivien Wallis (separated); four *s* one *d*. *Educ:* John Lyon Sch., Harrow; City and Guilds Coll., London. BSc Eng Hons; FCGI, FICE, MIHE, FCIT, FEng, MSocCE (France); Mem. Architectural Assoc. Royal Engrs (Captain), 1939–45 (despatches twice); Imperial Coll. of Science and Technology London (Civil), 1946–49; Sir Frederick Snow & Partners, 1949, Partner 1955; British Airports Authority: Dir of Engrg, 1965; Dir of Planning, 1969, and Mem. Bd 1971. Pres., West European Airports Assoc., 1975–77; Chairman: Airports Assoc. Co-ordinating Council, 1976; Aerodrome Owners' Assoc., 1983–84. Chm., British Sect., Centre for European Public Enterprise, 1979–82. Chm., NICG, 1982–83; Comr, Manpower Services Commn, 1983–85. Pres., CIT, 1984–85. CBIM (FBIM 1975); RAeS 1987. FIC 1989; FRSA 1990. Hon. FIStructE, 1988; Hon. FRIBA 1991. Hon. DTech Loughborough, 1985. *Publications:* various papers on airports and air transport. *Recreations:* travel, gardening. *Address:* L'Abri, La route des Merriennes, St Martin, Guernsey, CI. *Clubs:* Reform, RAC.

PAYNE, Peter Charles John, PhD; MSc(AgrEng); agricultural consultant, arbitrator and farmer, since 1975; *b* 8 Feb. 1928; *s* of late C. J. Payne, China Clay Merchant, and Mrs F. M. Payne; *m* 1961, Margaret Grover; two *s* one *d*. *Educ:* Plymouth Coll.; Teignmouth Grammar School; Reading University. BSc Reading 1948; Min. of Agriculture Scholar, Durham Univ., MSc(AgrEng) 1950; Scientific Officer, Nat. Institute of Agricultural Engineering, 1950–55; PhD Reading 1954; Lecturer in Farm Mechanisation, Wye College, London Univ., 1955–60; Lecturer in Agricultural Engineering, Durham Univ., 1960–61; Principal, Nat. Coll. of Agricultural Engineering, Silsoe, 1962–75; Visiting Professor: Univ. of Reading, 1969–75; Cranfield Inst. of Technology, 1975–80. Chm., Agricl Panel, Intermed. Technol. Develt Gp, 1979–86; Mem., British Inst. of Agricl Consultants, 1978. Vice-Pres., Section III, Commn Internationale du Génie Rural, 1969. FIAgrE 1968; FRAgSs 1971; CEng 1980; ACIArb 1986. *Publications:* various papers in agricultural and engineering journals. *Recreation:* sailing. *Address:* Garlidna Farm, Porkellis, Helston TR13 0JX. *T:* Falmouth (0326) 40301. *Club:* Farmers'.

PAYNE, Rt. Rev. (Sidney) Stewart; *see* Newfoundland, Western, Archbishop of.

PAYNE, (Trevor) Ian; *see* Payne, I.

PAYNE-BUTLER, George William; County Treasurer, Surrey County Council, 1973–79 (Assistant, 1962; Deputy, 1970); *b* 7 Oct. 1919; *s* of late George and Letitia Rachel Payne; *m* 1947, Joyce Louise Cockburn; one *s* two *d*. *Educ:* Woking Sch. for Boys. Joined Surrey CC, 1937. Served War, RAF, 1940–45. Chartered Municipal Treasurer, 1950 (CIPFA). *Recreations:* gardening, handicraft work in wood, reading. *Address:* Janston, Hillier Road, Guildford, Surrey GU1 2JQ. *T:* Guildford (0483) 65337.

PAYNE-GALLWEY, Sir Philip (Frankland), 6th Bt, *cr* 1812; Director, British Bloodstock Agency plc, since 1968; *b* 15 March 1935; *s* of late Lt-Col Lowry Philip Payne-Gallwey, OBE, MC and of Janet, *d* of late Albert Philip Payne-Gallwey; *S* cousin, 1964. *Educ:* Eton; Royal Military Academy, Sandhurst. Lieut, 11th Hussars, 1957. *Recreations:* hunting, shooting, golf. *Heir:* none. *Address:* The Little House, Boxford, Newbury, Berks. *T:* Boxford (048838) 315; British Bloodstock Agency plc, 1 Chapel View, High Street, Lambourn, Newbury, Berks RG16 7XL. *T:* Lambourn (0488) 73111. *Club:* Cavalry and Guards.

PAYNTER, Prof. John Frederick, OBE 1985; Professor of Music Education and Head of Department of Music, University of York; *b* 17 July 1931; *s* of late Frederick Albert Paynter and late Rose Alice Paynter; *m* 1956, Elizabeth Hill; one *d*. *Educ:* Emanuel Sch., London; Trinity Coll. of Music, London (GTCL 1952). DPhil York, 1971. Teaching appts, primary and secondary schs, 1954–62; Lectr in Music, City of Liverpool C. F. Mott Coll. of Educn, 1962–65; Principal Lectr (Head of Dept of Music), Bishop Otter Coll., Chichester, 1965–69; Lectr, Dept of Music, Univ. of York, 1969, Sen. Lectr, 1974–82.

Composer and writer on music-educn. Dir, Schs Council Proj., Music in the Secondary School Curriculum, 1973–82. Gen. Editor, series, Resources of Music; Jt Editor, British Jl of Music Educn. FRSA 1987. Hon. GSM 1985. *Publications:* (with Peter Aston) Sound and Silence, 1970; Hear and Now, 1972; (with Elizabeth Paynter) The Dance and the Drum, 1974; All Kinds of Music, vols 1–3, 1976, vol. 4, 1979; Sound Tracks, 1978; Music in the Secondary School Curriculum: trends and developments in class music teaching, 1982; Sound and Structure, 1991; articles and revs in Music in Educn, Music Teacher, Times Educnl Sup., Music Now (Aust. Contemp. Music Qtly), Music Educn Rev., Canadian Music Educator, Muziek en Onderwijs, beQuadro, Kreativ Musik Undervining, Muzikale vorming, Proposte di musica creativa nella scuola, Investigating Music (Australian Broadcasting Commn); scripts and commentaries for schs broadcasts and TV; *musical compositions:* choral and instrumental works including: Landscapes, 1972; The Windhover, 1972; May Magnificat, 1973; God's Grandeur, 1975; Sacraments of Summer, 1975; Galaxies for Orchestra, 1977; The Voyage of Brendan, 1978; The Visionary Hermit, 1979; The Inviolable Voice, 1980; String Quartet no 1, 1981; Cantata for the Waking of Lazarus, 1981; The Laughing Stone, 1982; Contrasts for Orchestra, 1982; Variations for Orchestra and Audience, 1983; Conclaves, 1984; Piano Sonata, 1987; Time After Time, 1991; String Quartet no 2, 1991. *Address:* Westfield House, Newton upon Derwent, York YO4 5DA.

PAYNTER, Air Cdre Noel Stephen, CB 1946; DL; retired; *b* 26 Dec. 1898; *s* of late Canon F. S. Paynter, sometime Rector of Springfield, Essex; *m* 1925, Barbara Grace Haagensen; one *s* one *d. Educ:* Haileybury; RMC, Sandhurst. Flying Brevet, 1917; France and Russia, 1918–19 (St Anne 3rd Class); North-West Frontier, 1919–21; North-West Frontier, 1925–30; Malta, 1934; Directorate of Intelligence, Air Ministry, 1936–39; Chief Intelligence Officer, Middle East, 1939–42 (despatches); Chief Intelligence Officer, Bomber Command, 1942–45 (CB); Directorate of Intelligence, Air Ministry, 1946. Chm. Buckinghamshire Playing Fields Assoc., 1958–65; Chm. Bucks Army Cadet Force (TA), 1962–65. High Sheriff, Bucks, 1965. DL Buckinghamshire, 1963. *Address:* Lawn House, Edgcott, near Aylesbury, Bucks. *T:* Grendon Underwood (029677) 238.

PAYTON, Stanley Walden, CMG 1965; Chief of Overseas Department, Bank of England, 1975–80, retired; *b* 29 May 1921; *s* of late Archibald Walden Payton and late Ethel May Payton (*née* Kirtland); *m* 1941, Joan (*née* Starmer); one *s* one *d. Educ:* Monoux School. Fleet Air Arm, 1940–46; Entered Bank of England, 1946; UK Alternate on Managing Board of European Payments Union, Paris, 1957–59; First Governor of Bank of Jamaica, 1960–64.

PAZ, Octavio; Mexican author; poet; Director, Revista Vuelta; *b* Mexico City, 31 March 1914; *s* of Octavio Paz and Josefina Lozano; *m* Marie José Tramini; one *d. Educ:* National Univ. of Mexico. Founded and directed Mexican literary reviews: Barandal, 1931; Taller, 1938; El Hijo Pródigo, 1943. Guggenheim Fellowship, USA, 1944. Sec., Mexican Embassy, Paris, 1946; New Delhi, 1952; Chargé d'Affaires *ad interim*, Japan, 1952; posted to Secretariat for External Affairs México, 1953–58; Extraordinary and Plenipotentiary Minister to Mexican Embassy, Paris, 1959–62; Ambassador to India, 1962–68; in Oct. 1968 resigned in protest at bloody students' repression in Tlatelolco. Simon Bolivar Prof. of Latin-American Studies, Cambridge, 1970; Vis. Prof. of Spanish American Lit., Univ. of Texas, Austin, and Pittsburgh Univ., 1968–70; Charles Eliot Norton Prof. of Poetry, Harvard Univ., 1971–72. Editor, Plural, Mexico City, 1971–75. Prizes include: Internat. Poetry Grand Prix, 1963; Nat. Prize for Literature, Mexico, 1977; Jerusalem Prize, 1977; Critics' Prize, Spain, 1977; Golden Eagle, Nice, 1978; Ollin Yoliztli, Mexico, 1980; Cervantes, Spain, 1982; Neustadt Internat. Prize for Literature, US, 1982; T. S. Eliot Prize, Ingersoll Foundn, USA, 1987; Nobel Prize for Literature, 1990. *Publications: poetry:* Luna Silvestre, 1933; Bajo tu Clara Sombra y otras poemas sobre Espanã, 1937; Raiz del Hombre, 1937; Entre la Piedra y la Flor, 1941; A la Orilla del Mundo, 1942; Libertad bajo Palabra, 1949; Aguila o Sol?, 1951; Semillas para un Himno, 1956; Piedra de Sol, 1957 (trans. as Sun Stone, 1960); La Estación Violenta, 1958; Libertad bajo Palabra (poetical works 1935–57), 1960; Salamandra (poetical works 1958–61), 1962; Viento Entero, 1965; Blanco, 1967; Discos Visuales, 1968; Ladera Este, 1969; La Centena, 1969; Topoemas, 1971; Renga, 1971; New Poetry of Mexico (Anthol.), 1972; Pasado en Claro, 1975; Vuelta, 1976; Poemas 1935–1975, 1979; Arbol adentro, 1987; *in English:* Early Poems (1935–57), 1963; Eagle or Sun?, 1970; Configurations, 1971; A Draft of Shadows and Other Poems, 1979; Airborn/Hijos del Aire, 1981; Selected Poems, 1984; Collected Poems (1957–87), 1987; *prose:* El Laberinto de la soledad, 1950 (trans. as Labyrinth of Solitude, 1961); El Arco y la Lira, 1956 (trans. as The Bow and The Lyre, 1975); Las Peras del Olmo, 1957; Cuadrivio, 1965; Los Signos en Rotación, 1965; Piertas al campo, 1966; Corriente Alterna, 1967 (trans. as Alternating Current, 1972); Claude Lévi-Strauss o el Nuevo Festín de Esopo, 1967 (trans. as On Lévi-Strauss, 1970); Marcel Duchamp o El Castillo de la Pureza, 1968 (trans. as Marcel Duchamp or the Castle of Purity, 1970); Conjunciones y Disyunciones (essay), 1969 (trans. as Conjunctions and Disjunctions, 1974); Postdata, 1970 (trans. as The Other Mexico, 1972); El Mono Gramático, 1971 (trans. as The Monkey Grammarian, 1989); Las Cosas en su Sitio, 1971; Traducción: Literatura y Literalidad, 1971; El Signo y el Garabato, 1973; Los Hijos del Limo, 1974 (trans. as Children of the Mire, 1974); Marcel Duchamp: Apariencia Desnuda, 1978 (trans. as Marcel Duchamp: Appearance Stripped Bare, 1981); Xavier Villaurrutia en Persona y en Obra, 1978; El Ogro Filantrópico, 1979; In mediaciones, 1979; Sombras de Obra, 1983; Tiempo Nublado, 1983 (trans. as One Earth, Four or Five Worlds); Hombres en su siglo, 1984; Pasión Critica, 1985; On poets and others (essays on literature), 1986; Convergences, 1987; Sor Juana: her life and world, 1988; *translations:* Versiones y Diversiones, 1974. *Address:* c/o Revista Vuelta, Avenida Contreras 516, Tercer Piso, San Jerónimo 10200 DF, México City, México.

PEACH, Captain Charles Lindsay K.; *see* Keighly-Peach.

PEACH, Denis Alan, CB 1985; Chief Charity Commissioner, 1982–88; *b* 10 Jan. 1928; *s* of late Richard Peach and Alice Ellen Peach; *m* 1957, Audrey Hazel Chamberlain. *Educ:* Selhurst Grammar Sch., Croydon. Home Office, 1946–82: Asst Principal, 1951; Private Sec. to Perm. Under Sec of State, 1956; Principal, 1957; Sec. to Anglo-Egyptian Resettlement Bd, 1957–58; Prison Commn, 1958–62; Asst Sec., 1967; Asst Under Sec. of State, 1974–82 (Prin. Finance Officer, 1974–80). *Recreations:* painting, gardening. *Address:* 10 Morkyns Walk, Alleyn Park, SE21 8BG. *T:* 081–670 5574. *Club:* Reform.

PEACH, Sir Leonard (Harry), Kt 1989; Director of Personnel and Corporate Affairs, IBM, since 1989; *b* 17 Dec. 1932; *s* of late Harry and Beatrice Peach; *m* 1958, Doreen Lilian (*née* Barker); two *s. Educ:* Queen Mary's Grammar Sch., Walsall; Pembroke Coll., Oxford (MA); LSE (Dip. Personnel Management). Research Asst to Randolph S. Churchill, 1956; personnel management posts, 1956–62; IBM UK Ltd: personnel management posts, 1962–71; Dir of Personnel, 1971–72; Gp Dir, Personnel, IBM Europe, Africa, Middle East (based Paris), 1972–75; Dir, Personnel and Corporate Affairs, 1975–85; seconded to DHSS, 1985–89: Dir, Personnel, NHS Management Bd, 1985; Chief Exec., NHS Management Bd, 1986–89 (in rank of 2nd Perm. Sec.); Chairman: NHS Training Authy, 1986–91; Skillbase Ltd, 1990–; Standards Develt Cttee, Management Charter Initiative, 1989–. Chm., PSI, 1991–. Director: IBM UK Rentals, 1971–76; IBM UK Holdings, 1976–85, and 1989–; IBM UK Pensions Trust, 1989–; IBM UK Trust, 1989–; non-exec. Dir, Nationwide Anglia Bldg Soc, 1990–. Pres., IPM, and Chm., IPM Services Ltd, 1983–85 (President's Gold Medal, 1988); Mem., Data Protection Tribunal, 1985–. Vice-Chm. Ct of Governors, Polytechnic of Central London, 1987–. CBIM; CIPM; FRSA. Hon. Fellow, Thames Polytechnic, 1990. Hon. DSc Aston, 1991. *Publications:* articles on personnel management and social responsibility. *Recreations:* opera, theatre, cricket, gardening. *Address:* Crossacres, Meadow Road, Wentworth, Virginia Water, Surrey GU25 4NH. *T:* Wentworth (09904) 2258.

PEACOCK, Prof. Sir Alan (Turner), Kt 1987; DSC 1945; MA; FBA 1979; FRSE; Hon. Research Professor in Public Finance, Heriot-Watt University, since 1987; Chairman, Scottish Arts Council, since 1986; *b* 26 June 1922; *s* of late Professor A. D. Peacock, FRSE and of Clara Mary (*née* Turner); *m* 1944, Margaret Martha Astell Burt; two *s* one *d. Educ:* Dundee High School; University of St Andrews (1939–42, 1945–47). Royal Navy, 1942–45 (Lieut RNVR). Lecturer in Economics: Univ. of St Andrews, 1947–48; London Sch. of Economics, 1948–51 (Hon. Fellow, 1980); Reader in Public Finance, Univ. of London, 1951–56; Prof. of Economic Science, Univ. of Edinburgh, 1957–62; Prof. of Economics, Univ. of York, 1962–78; Prof. of Economics, and Principal-designate, University Coll. at Buckingham, 1978–80, Principal, 1980–83; Vice-Chancellor, Univ. of Buckingham, 1983–84, Professor Emeritus, 1985–; Exec. Dir, David Hume Inst., Edinburgh, 1985–90. Seconded from Univ. of York as Chief Economic Adviser, Depts of Industry and Trade, 1973–76. Visiting Prof. of Economics, Johns Hopkins Univ., 1958. Member: Commission of Enquiry into land and population problems of Fiji, 1959; Adv. Council, Inst. Economic Affairs, 1959–87 (Trustee, 1987–); Departmental Committee on Electricity in Scotland, 1961; Council, REconS, 1961–78; Cttee of Enquiry on impact of rates, 1964; Commn on the Constitution, 1970–73; SSRC, 1972–73; Cttee of Inquiry on Retirement Provision, 1984; Chm., Rowntree Inquiry into Corporate Takeovers, 1990–91. Pres., Internat. Inst. of Public Finance, 1966–69. Mem., Arts Council, 1986–; Chairman: Arts Council Enquiry on Orchestral Resources, 1969–70; Cttee on Financing the BBC, 1985–86. Non-exec. Director: Economist Intelligence Unit Ltd, 1977–84; Caledonian Bank plc. FRSE 1989. DUniv: Stirling, 1974; Brunel, 1989; Hon. DEcon Zürich, 1984; Hon. DSc: Buckingham, 1986; Edinburgh, 1990; Hon. LLD: St Andrews, 1990; Dundee, 1990; Dr *hc* Catania, 1991. *Publications:* Economics of National Insurance, 1952; (ed) Income Redistribution and Social Policy 1954; National Income and Social Accounting (with H. C. Edey), 1954, 3rd imp. 1967; The National Income of Tanganyika (1952–54) (with D. G. M. Dosser), 1958; The Growth of Public Expenditure in the UK, 1890–1955 (with J. Wiseman), 1961; Economic Theory of Fiscal Policy (with G. K. Shaw), 1971, 2nd edn, 1976; The Composer in the Market Place (with R. Weir), 1975; Welfare Economics: a liberal re-interpretation (with C. K. Rowley), 1975; Economic Analysis of Government, 1979; (ed and contrib.) Structural Economic Policies in West Germany and the UK, 1980; (ed jtly) Political Economy of Taxation, 1981; (ed and contrib.) The Regulation Game, 1984; (ed jtly) Public Expenditure and Government Growth, 1985; Waltz Contrasts (for piano solo), 1988; Public Choice Analysis in Historical Perspective, 1990; (with G. Bunnock) Corporate Takeovers and the Public Interest, 1991; articles on applied economics in Economic Jl, Economica and other journals. *Recreations:* trying to write music, wine spotting. *Address:* 8 Gilmour Road, Edinburgh EH16 5NF. *T:* 031–667 0544. *Clubs:* Reform, Naval.

PEACOCK, Hon. Andrew Sharp; MP (L) Kooyong, Australia, since 1966; Shadow Attorney General and Shadow Minister for Justice, since 1990; *b* 13 Feb. 1939; *s* of late A. S. Peacock and Iris Peacock. *Educ:* Scotch Coll., Melbourne, Vic; Melbourne Univ. (LLB). Former Partner, Rigby & Fielding, Solicitors; Chm., Peacock and Smith Pty Ltd, 1962–69. CMF Reserve (Captain), 1966. Pres., Victorian Liberal Party, 1965–66; Minister for Army and Minister assisting Prime Minister, 1969–71; Minister for Army and Minister asstg Treasurer, 1971–72; Minister for External Territories, Feb.-Dec. 1972; Mem., Opposition Exec., 1973–75; Oppos. Shadow Minister for For. Affairs, 1973–75, 1985–87; Minister for: Foreign Affairs, 1975–80; Industrial Relns, 1980–81; Industry and Commerce, 1982–83; Leader of the Parly Liberal Party, and of the Opposition, 1983–85; Dep. Leader, Liberal Party and Dep. Leader, Opposition, 1987–89; Leader, Parly Liberal Party, and of the Opposition, 1989–90. Chm., Internat. Democrat Union, 1989–. *Recreations:* horse racing, sailboarding, Australian Rules football. *Address:* 400 Flinders Street, Melbourne, Vic 3000, Australia. *T:* 6292521. *Clubs:* Melbourne, Melbourne Cricket (Melbourne).

PEACOCK, Elizabeth Joan, JP; MP (C) Batley and Spen, since 1983; *b* 4 Sept. 1937; *d* of late John and Dorothy Gates; *m* 1963, Brian D. Peacock; two *s. Educ:* St Monica's Convent, Skipton. Asst to Exec. Dir, York Community Council, 1979–83; Administrator, four charitable trusts, York, 1979–83. County Councillor, N Yorks, 1981–84. Mem., Select Cttee on Employment, 1983–87. Chairman: All Party Trans Pennine Gp, 1988; All Party Wool Textile Gp, 1989. Hon. Sec., Yorks Cons. MPs, 1983–88; Vice Chm., Cons. Back-bench Party Organisation Cttee, 1985–87; Mem. Exec. Cttee, 1922 Cttee, 1987–; Mem. Exec., CPA, 1987–. Mem., BBC Gen. Adv. Council, 1987–. Vice Pres., Yorks Area Young Conservatives, 1984–87; Pres., Yorks Area Cons. Trade Unionists, 1991– (Vice Pres., 1987–91). Hon. Pres., Nat. Assoc. of Approved Driving Instructors, 1984–88. FRSA 1990. JP Macclesfield, 1975–79, Bulmer East 1983. *Recreations:* reading, motoring. *Address:* House of Commons, SW1A 0AA. *T:* 071–219 4092; (constituency office) 27A Northgate, Cleckheaton, West Yorks BD19 3HH. *T:* Cleckheaton (0274) 872968.

PEACOCK, (Ian) Michael; Chairman: Unique Broadcasting Co. Ltd, since 1989; Publishing Projecte plc, since 1990; *b* 14 Sept. 1929; *e s* of Norman Henry and Sara Barbara Peacock; *m* 1956, Daphne Lee; two *s* one *d. Educ:* Kimball Union Academy, USA; Welwyn Garden City Grammar School; London School of Economics (BSc Econ.). BBC Television: Producer, 1952–56; Producer Panorama, 1956–58; Asst Head of Television Outside Broadcasts, 1958–59; Editor, Panorama, 1959–61; Editor, BBC Television News, 1961–63; Chief of Programmes, BBC-2, 1963–65; Controller, BBC-1, BBC Television Service, 1965–67; Managing Dir, London Weekend Television Ltd, 1967–69; Chm., Monitor Enterprises Ltd, 1970–89; Man. Dir, Warner Bros TV Ltd, 1972–74; Exec. Vice-Pres., Warner Bros Television Inc., 1974–76. Dir, Video Arts Ltd, 1972–89; Pres., Video Arts Inc., 1976–78; Man. Dir, Dumbarton Films Ltd (formerly Video Arts Television), 1978–87; Chm., Video Answers, 1989–90. Dep. Chm., Piccadilly Radio, 1988–89. IPPA: First Chm., 1981–82; Mem. Council, 1983–. Member: Council, Counsel and Care for the Elderly, 1986–; Ct of Governors, LSE, 1982–. *Recreations:* sailing, theatre, cinema, concerts, gardening. *Address:* 21 Woodlands Road, Barnes, SW13 0JZ. *T:* 081–876 2025. *Clubs:* Savile, Royal Ocean Racing, Royal Thames Yacht; Royal Southern Yacht; Royal Lymington Yacht.

PEACOCK, Prof. Joseph Henry, MD, FRCS; Professor of Surgical Science, University of Bristol, 1969–84, now Emeritus; *b* 22 Oct. 1918; *s* of Harry James Peacock and Florence Peacock; *m* 1950, Gillian Frances Pinckney; one *s* one *d. Educ:* Bristol Grammar Sch.; Univ. of Birmingham (MB, ChB 1941, ChM 1957, MD 1963). MRCS, LRCP 1941, FRCS 1949. House appts, 1942; served RAMC, 1942–47: surgical and orthopaedic specialist, England and Far East; Hon. Major; Demonstr in Anat., Univ. of Birmingham, 1947; Surg. Registrar, 1948–51, and Sen. Surg. Registrar, 1952–53, United Bristol Hosp.; Rockefeller Fellow, Ann Arbor, 1951; Lectr in Surgery, 1953, and Reader in Surg., 1965, Univ. of Bristol; Consultant Surgeon: United Bristol Hosp., 1955; SW Reg. Hosp. Bd, 1960. Member: GMC, 1975–85 (Chm., Sub-cttee F, 1980–85); SW RHA, 1975–84 (Chm., Res. Cttee, 1981–84); Vascular Surgical Soc. of GB (also Pres.); Founder Member: Surgical Res. Soc.; European Soc. of Surg. Res.; Fellow, Assoc. of Surgeons of GB. Royal Coll. of Surgeons of England: Jacksonian Prize, 1954 and 1967; Hunterian Prof., 1956; Arris and Gale Lectr, 1960; Examr, LDS, 1958–63, and primary FRCS, 1965–71; Mem., Ct of Examrs, 1976–82 (Chm., 1982). Examr in Surg., Univs of Bristol, Birmingham, London, Wales, Ghana, Sudan and Liverpool. *Publications:* Raynaud's Disease: British surgical practice, 1960; scientific pubns on vascular surgery and liver transplantation. *Recreations:* short wave radio, gardening. *Address:* The Old Manor, Ubley, near Bristol BS18 6PJ. *T:* Blagdon (0761) 62733. *Club:* Army and Navy.

PEACOCK, Michael; *see* Peacock, I. M.

PEACOCK, Ronald, MA, LittD (Leeds), MA (Manchester), DrPhil (Marburg); Professor of German, Bedford College, University of London, 1962–75, now Emeritus Professor; Fellow of Bedford College, 1980; *b* 22 Nov. 1907; *s* of Arthur Lorenzo and Elizabeth Peacock; *m* 1933, Ilse Gertrud Eva, *d* of Geheimer Oberregierungsrat Paul Freiwald; no *c. Educ:* Leeds Modern Sch.; Universities of Leeds, Berlin, Innsbruck, Marburg. Assistant Lecturer in German, University of Leeds, 1931–38; Lecturer, 1938–39; Professor, 1939–45; Henry Simon Professor of German Language and Literature, University of Manchester, 1945–62; Dean of the Faculty of Arts, 1954–56; Pro-Vice-Chancellor, 1958–62; Visiting Professor of German Literature, Cornell Univ. (USA), 1949; Visiting Professor of German Literature and Comparative Literature, University of Heidelberg, 1960–61; Professor of Modern German Literature, University of Freiburg, 1965, 1967–68. Pres., MHRA, 1983. Hon. LittD Manchester, 1977. *Publications:* The Great War in German Lyrical Poetry, 1934; Das Leitmotiv bei Thomas Mann, 1934; Hölderlin, 1938; The Poet in the Theatre, 1946 (reprinted with additional essays, 1960), 1986; The Art of Drama, 1957; Goethe's Major Plays, 1959; Criticism and Personal Taste, 1972; various articles on literature contributed to reviews and periodicals. *Recreations:* music, theatre, travel. *Address:* Greenshade, Woodhill Avenue, Gerrards Cross, Bucks SL9 8DR. *T:* Gerrards Cross (0753) 884886.

PEACOCK, Dr William James, BSc, PhD; FRS 1982; FAA; Chief, Division of Plant Industry, Commonwealth Scientific and Industrial Research Organization, since 1978; *b* 14 Dec. 1937; *m* 1961, Margaret Woodward; one *s* two *d. Educ:* Katoomba High Sch.; Univ. of Sydney (BSc, PhD). FAA 1976. CSIRO Postdoctoral Fellow, 1963 and Vis. Associate Prof. of Biology, 1964–65, Univ. of Oregon; Res. Consultant, Oak Ridge National Lab., USA, 1965; res. staff, Div. of Plant Industry, CSIRO, 1965–. Adjunct Prof. of Biology, Univ. of Calif, San Diego, 1969; Vis. Professor: of Biochem., Stanford Univ., 1970; of Molecular Biol., Univ. of Calif, LA, 1977. For. Associate, US Nat. Acad. of Scis, 1990; FTS 1988; FAIAS 1989. Edgeworth David Medal, Royal Soc. of NSW, 1967; Lemberg Medal, Aust. Biochem. Soc., 1978; BHP Bicentennial Prize for Pursuit of Excellence in Science and Technol., 1988; CSIRO Medal for Leadership of Div. of Plant Industry, 1989; Burnet Medal, Aust. Acad. of Sci., 1989. *Publications:* editor of 5 books on genetics and molecular biology; approx. 160 papers. *Recreations:* squash, sailing, bush-walking. *Address:* 16 Brassey Street, Deakin, ACT 2600, Australia. *T:* (home) (06) 2814485, (office) (06) 2465250.

PEACOCKE, Rev. Dr Arthur Robert, DSc, ScD, DD; SOSc; Warden, Society of Ordained Scientists, since 1987; Hon. Chaplain, Christ Church Cathedral, Oxford, since 1988; Catechist, Exeter College, Oxford, since 1989; *b* 29 Nov. 1924; *s* of Arthur Charles Peacocke and Rose Elizabeth (*née* Lilly); *m* 1948, Rosemary Winifred Mann; one *s* one *d. Educ:* Watford Grammar Sch.; Exeter Coll., Oxford (Scholar; BA Chem., BSc 1946; MA, DPhil 1948). DSc Oxon, 1962; ScD Cantab (incorp.), 1973; DD Oxon, 1982. DipTh 1960, BD 1971, Birmingham. Asst Lectr, Lectr and Sen. Lectr in Biophys. Chemistry, Univ. of Birmingham, 1948–59; Lectr in Biochem., Oxford Univ., and Fellow and Tutor in Chem., subseq. in Biochem., St Peter's Coll., 1959–73; Lectr in Chem., Mansfield Coll., Oxford, 1964–73; Dean and Fellow, Clare Coll., Cambridge, 1973–84; Dir, Ian Ramsey Centre, St Cross Coll., Oxford, and Fellow, St Cross Coll., 1985–88. Rockefeller Fellow, Univ. of Calif at Berkeley, and Univ. of Wis, 1951–52; Vis. Fellow, Weizmann Inst., Israel, 1956; Prof. of Judeo-Christian Studies, Tulane Univ., 1984; J. K. Russell Fellow in Religion and Science, Center for Theology and Natural Sci., Berkeley, 1986; Lectures: Bishop Williams Meml, Rikkyo (St Paul's) Univ., Japan, 1981; Shann, Univ. of Hong Kong, 1982; Mendenhall, DePauw Univ., Indiana, 1983; McNair, Univ. of N Carolina, 1984; Nina Booth Bricker Meml, Tulane Univ., 1986, 1989; Norton, Southern Baptist Seminary, Louisville, 1986; Sprigg, Virginia Theol Seminary, 1987; Rolf Buchdahl, N Carolina State Univ., 1987; Drawbridge, KCL, 1987; Alister Hardy Meml, 1989. Lay Reader, Oxford Dio., 1960–71; ordained, 1971; Mem., Archbps' Commn on Christian Doctrine, 1969–76 (Mem. sub-gp on Man and Nature, 1972–74); Chm., Science and Religion Forum, 1972–78, Vice-Pres., 1981–; Vice-Pres., Inst. of Religion in an Age of Science, USA, 1984–87 (Academic Fellow, 1987). Select Preacher, Oxford Univ., 1973, 1985; Hulsean Preacher, Cambridge Univ., 1976; Bampton Lectr, Oxford Univ., 1978; Judge, Templeton Foundn Prize, 1979–82. Meetings Sec., Sec. and Chm., Brit. Biophys. Soc., 1965–69. Hon. DSc DePauw Univ., Indiana, 1983; Hon. DHumLit Georgetown Univ., Washington, 1991. Mem. Editorial Bd, Biochem. Jl, and Biopolymers, 1966–71, Zygon, 1973–. Editor, Monographs in Physical Biochemistry (OUP), 1967–82. Lecomte du Noüy Prize, 1973. *Publications:* Molecular Basis of Heredity (with J. B. Drysdale), 1965 (repr. 1967); Science and the Christian Experiment, 1971; (with M. P. Tombs) Osmotic Pressure of Biological Macromolecules, 1974; (with J. Dominian) From Cosmos to Love, 1977; Creation and the World of Science, 1979; (ed) The Sciences and Theology in the Twentieth Century, 1982; The Physical Chemistry of Biological Organization, 1983; Intimations of Reality, 1984; (ed) Reductionism in Academic Disciplines, 1985; God and the New Biology, 1986; (ed with G. Gillett) Persons and Personality, 1987; (ed with S. Andersen) Evolution and Creation: a European perspective, 1987; Theology for a Scientific Age, 1990; articles and papers in scientific and theol jls, and symposia vols. *Recreations:* piano, music, walking, churches. *Address:* 55 St John Street, Oxford OX1 2LQ.

See also C. A. B. Peacocke.

PEACOCKE, Prof. Christopher Arthur Bruce, FBA 1990; Waynflete Professor of Metaphysical Philosophy, University of Oxford and Fellow of Magdalen College, Oxford, since 1989; *b* 22 May 1950; *s* of Rev. Dr Arthur Robert Peacocke, *qv*; *m* 1980, Teresa Anne Rosen; one *s* one *d. Educ:* Magdalen College Sch., Oxford; Exeter Coll., Oxford (MA, BPhil, DPhil). Kennedy Schol., Harvard Univ., 1971; Sen. Schol., Merton Coll., Oxford, 1972; Jun. Res. Fellow, Queen's Coll., Oxford, 1973; Prize Fellow, All Souls Coll., Oxford, 1975; Fellow and Tutor, New Coll., Oxford, and CUF Lectr in Philosophy, 1979–85; Susan Stebbing Prof. of Philosophy, KCL, 1985–88. Visiting Professor: Berkeley, 1975; Ann Arbor, 1978; UCLA, 1981; Maryland, 1987; Vis. Fellow, ANU, 1981; Fellow, Center for Advanced Study in the Behavioral Sciences, Stanford, 1983; Vis. Res. Associate, Center for Study of Language and Information, Stanford, 1984. Pres., Mind Assoc., 1986. *Publications:* Holistic Explanation: action, space, interpretation, 1979; Sense and Content, 1983; Thoughts: an essay on content, 1986; A Study of Concepts, 1992; papers on philosophy of mind and language, and philosophical logic, in Jl of Philosophy, Philosophical Rev., etc. *Recreations:* music, visual arts. *Address:* Magdalen College, Oxford OX1 4AU. *T:* Oxford (0865) 276000.

PEACOCKE, Rt. Rev. Cuthbert Irvine, TD; MA; *b* 26 April 1903; *er s* of late Rt Rev. Joseph Irvine Peacocke, DD; *m* 1931, Helen Louise Gaussen (*d* 1988); one *s* one *d. Educ:* St Columba's Coll., Dublin; Trinity Coll., Dublin; Curate, Seapatrick Parish, 1926–30; Head of Southern Mission, 1930–33; Rector, Derriaghy, 1933–35; Rector, St Mark's, Dundela, 1935–56; CF, 1939–45; Archdeacon of Down, 1950–56; Dean of St Anne's Cathedral, Belfast, 1956–69; Bishop of Derry and Raphoe, 1970–75. *Publication:* The Young Parson, 1936. *Recreations:* games, garden and reading. *Address:* 32 Lisburn Road, Hillsborough, Co. Down BT26 6HW.

PEAKE, family name of **Viscount Ingleby.**

PEAKE, David Alphy Edward Raymond; Chairman, Kleinwort Benson Group plc, since 1989; *b* 27 Sept. 1934; *s* of Sir Harald Peake, AE and Mrs Resy Peake, OBE; *m* 1962, Susanna Kleinwort; one *s* one *d. Educ:* Ampleforth Coll.; Christ Church, Oxford (MA History, 1958). 2nd Lieut Royal Scots Greys, 1953–55. Banque Lambert, Brussels, 1958–59; J. Henry Schroder Wagg & Co. Ltd, 1959–63; Kleinwort Benson Ltd, 1963–: Dir, 1971–; Vice-Chm., 1985–87; Chm., 1988–89; Hargreaves Group, 1964–86: Dir, 1964–86; Vice-Chm., 1967–74; Chm., 1974–86; Director: Kleinwort Benson Lonsdale, now Kleinwort Benson Gp, 1986–; Banque Nationale de Paris, 1974–; M & G Gp, 1979–87. Pt-time Mem. of Bd, British Liby, 1990–. Chm., City and Inner London N TEC, 1990–. *Recreations:* reading, country sports. *Address:* 15 Ilchester Place, W14 8AA. *T:* 071–602 2375. *Clubs:* Brooks's, Pratt's, Cavalry and Guards.

PEAKE, Air Cdre (retired) Dame Felicity (Hyde), (Lady Peake), DBE 1949 (MBE 1941); AE; *b* 1 May 1913; *d* of late Colonel Humphrey Watts, OBE, TD, and Mrs Simon Orde; *m* 1st, 1935, John Charles Mackenzie Hanbury (killed on active service, 1939); no *c*; 2nd, 1952, Sir Harald Peake, AE (*d* 1978); one *s. Educ:* St Winifreds, Eastbourne; Les Grands Huguenots, Vaucresson, Seine et Oise, France. Joined ATS Company of the RAF, April 1939; commissioned in the WAAF, Aug. 1939; served at home and in the Middle East; Director, Women's Auxiliary Air Force, 1946–49; Director Women's Royal Air Force, from its inception, 1949, until her retirement, 1950; Hon. ADC to King George VI, 1949–50. Member Advisory Cttee, Recruitment for the Forces, 1958. Trustee: Imperial War Museum, 1963–85 (Chm., 1986–88, Pres., 1988–, Friends of Imperial War Museum); St Clement Danes church, 1989–. Governor, London House, 1958–76, 1978–; Mem. Council, RAF Benevolent Fund (a Vice-Pres., 1978–); Mem. Council, Union Jack Club, 1950–78.

PEAKE, John Fordyce; Associate Director (Scientific Development), Natural History Museum, since 1989; *b* 4 June 1933; *s* of late William Joseph Peake and of Helena (*née* Fordyce); *m* 1963, Pamela Joyce Hollis; two *d. Educ:* City of Norwich Grammar Sch.; University Coll. London (BSc). National Trust, 1955–56; Norwich Technical Coll., 1956–58; Nature Conservancy Studentship, 1958–59; British Museum (Natural History): Research Fellow, 1959–61; Sen. Scientific Officer, 1961–69; PSO, 1969–71; Dep. Keeper, 1971–85; Keeper of Zoology, 1985–89. Hon. Research Associate, Bernice P. Bishop Mus., Honolulu, 1972–. Royal Society: Member: Aldabra Research Cttee, 1972–77; Southern Zones Cttee, 1982–; Unitas Malacologica: Treas. 1962–63, Mem. Council, 1963–75; Vice Pres., Malacological Soc. of London, 1976–78; Council Mem., Zoological Soc. of London, 1985–. *Publications:* (editor and contributor with Dr V. Fretter) Pulmonates, 3 vols, 1975–79; papers on taxonomy, biogeography and ecology of terrestrial molluscs in sci. jls. *Recreation:* gardening. *Address:* Spring Cottage, Trycewell Lane, Ightham, Sevenoaks, Kent TN15 9HN. *T:* Borough Green (0732) 882423.

PEAKE, John Morris, CBE 1986; Chairman, Baker Perkins PLC, 1984–87; *b* 26 Aug. 1924; *s* of late Albert Edward Peake and Ruby Peake (*née* Morris); *m* 1953, Elizabeth Rought; one *s* one *d. Educ:* Repton School; Clare College, Cambridge (Mech. Scis Tripos; MA 1949); Royal Naval College, Greenwich (Dip. Naval Arch.). FIMechE; FIMA; CBIM. Royal Corps of Naval Constructors, 1944–50; Personnel Administration Ltd, 1950–51; Baker Perkins (BP): joined 1951; Dir, parent co., 1956; Jt Man. Dir, BP Ltd, 1963–66; Man. Dir, BP Pty, 1969–74, in Australia; Pres., BP Inc., 1975–77, in USA; Dep. Man. Dir, BP Holdings, 1978–79, Man. Dir, 1980–85. Member: Chemicals and Minerals Requirements Bd, 1978–81; Council, CBI, 1980–89 (Chairman: Overseas Schols Bd, 1981–87; Educn and Trng Cttee, 1986–88); Council, BTEC, 1986–89 (Chm., Bd for Engineering, 1985–91); MSC, subseq. Trng Commn, 1986–88; RSA Exams Bd, 1987– (Chm., 1989–); RSA Council, 1989–; Adv. Council, British Library, 1989–; Vice Chm., Gtr Peterborough TEC, 1990–. Chm., Nene Park Trust, 1988–. Hockey Silver Medal, London Olympics, 1948. FRSA. Hon. DTech CNAA, 1986. *Recreations:* sport, travel. *Address:* Old Castle Farmhouse, Stibbington, Peterborough PE8 6LP. *T:* Stamford (0780) 782683. *Clubs:* East India, MCC.

PEAKER, Prof. Malcolm, PhD; FZS, FLS, FIBiol, FRSE; Director, Hannah Research Institute, Ayr, since 1981; Hannah Professor, University of Glasgow, since 1981; *b* 21 Aug. 1943; *s* of Ronald Smith Peaker and Marian (*née* Tomasin); *m* 1965, Stephanie Jane Large; three *s. Educ:* Henry Mellish Grammar Sch., Nottingham; Univ. of Sheffield (BSc Zoology); Univ. of Hong Kong (SRC NATO Scholar; PhD). FZS 1969; FIBiol 1979; FRSE 1983; FLS 1989. Inst. of Animal Physiology, ARC, 1968–78; Head, Dept of Physiol., Hannah Res. Inst., 1978–81. Mem. Editorial Board: Jl of Dairy Science, 1975–78; Internat. Zoo Yearbook, 1978–82; Jl of Endocrinology, 1981–; Editor: British Jl of Herpetology, 1977–81; Internat. Circle of Dairy Research Leaders, 1982–. *Publications:* Salt Glands in Birds and Reptiles, 1975; (ed) Avian Physiology, 1975; (ed) Comparative Aspects of Lactation, 1977; (ed jtly) Physiological Strategies in Lactation, 1984; papers in physiol, endocrinol, zool, biochem., vet. and agricl science jls. *Recreations:* vertebrate zoology, natural history, golf, grumbling about bureaucrats. *Address:* 13 Upper Crofts, Alloway, Ayr KA7 4QX. *T:* Alloway (0292) 43999. *Club:* Farmers'.

PEARCE, family name of **Baron Pearce.**

PEARCE, Andrew; European Community Affairs Adviser, Littlewoods plc, Liverpool, since 1989; *b* 1 Dec. 1937; *s* of late Henry Pearce, Liverpool cotton broker, and Evelyn Pearce; *m* 1966, Myra Whelan; three *s* one *d. Educ:* Rydal School, Colwyn Bay; University of Durham. BA. Formerly in construction industry; in Customs Dept, EEC, Brussels, 1974–79. Contested (C) Islington North, 1969 and 1970; Mem. (C) Cheshire W, Eur. Parlt, 1979–89; contested (C) Cheshire W, European Parly elecn, 1989. Founder and Vice-Pres., British Cons. Assoc. in Belgium; Vice-Pres., Consultative Assembly of Lomé Convention, 1980–89. Governor: Archway Comprehensive School, 1967–70; Woodchurch High Sch., Birkenhead, 1985–. *Address:* Devon House, 13 Lingdale Road, West Kirby, Wirral L48 5DG.

PEARCE, (Ann) Philippa, (Mrs M. J. G. Christie); freelance writer of children's fiction, since 1967; *d* of Ernest Alexander Pearce and Gertrude Alice (*née* Ramsden); *m* 1963, Martin James Graham Christie (decd); one *d. Educ:* Perse Girls' Sch., Cambridge; Girton Coll., Cambridge (MA Hons English Pt I, History Pt II). Temp. civil servant, 1942–45; Producer/Scriptwriter, Sch. Broadcasting, BBC Radio, 1945–58; Editor, Educn Dept, Clarendon Press, 1958–60; Children's Editor, André Deutsch Ltd, 1960–67. Also lectures. *Publications:* Minnow on the Say, 1955 (3rd edn 1974); Tom's Midnight Garden, 1958 (3rd edn 1976); Carnegie Medal, 1959); Mrs Cockle's Cat, 1961 (2nd edn 1974); A Dog So Small, 1962 (2nd edn 1964); (with Sir Harold Scott) From Inside Scotland Yard, 1963; The Strange Sunflower, 1966; (with Sir Brian Fairfax-Lucy) The Children of the House, 1968 (2nd edn 1970) (reissued as The Children of Charlecote, 1989); The Elm Street Lot, 1969 (enlarged edn, 1979); The Squirrel Wife, 1971; What the Neighbours Did and other stories, 1972 (2nd edn 1974); (ed) Stories from Hans Christian Andersen, 1972; Beauty and the Beast (re-telling), 1972; The Shadow Cage and other stories of the supernatural, 1977; The Battle of Bubble and Squeak, 1978 (Whitbread Award, 1978); Wings of Courage (trans. and adapted from George Sand's story), 1982; The Way to Sattin Shore, 1983; Lion at School and other stories, 1985; Who's Afraid? and other strange stories, 1986; The Toothball, 1987; Emily's Own Elephant, 1987; Freddy, 1988; Old Belle's Summer Holiday, 1989; reviews in TLS and Guardian. *Address:* c/o Viking-Kestrel Books, 27 Wright's Lane, W8 5TZ. *T:* 071–938 2200.

PEARCE, Sir Austin (William), Kt 1980; CBE 1974; PhD; Chairman, Oxford Instruments Group, 1987–91; *b* 1 Sept. 1921; *s* of William Thomas and Florence Annie Pearce; *m* 1st, 1947, Maglona Winifred Twinn (*d* 1975); three *d*; 2nd, 1979, Dr F. Patricia Grice (*née* Forsythe). *Educ:* Devonport High Sch. for Boys; Univ. of Birmingham. BSc (Hons) 1943, PhD 1945; Cadman Medallist. Joined Agwi Petroleum Corp., 1945 (later Esso Petroleum Co., Ltd): Asst Refinery Manager, 1954–56; Gen. Manager Refining, 1956–62; Dir, 1963; Man. Dir, 1968–71; Chm., 1972–80; Chm., British Aerospace, 1980–87; Director: Esso Europe Inc., 1972–80; Esso Africa Inc., 1972–80; Pres., Esso Holding Co. UK Inc., 1971–80; Chairman: Esso Pension Trust Ltd, 1972–80; Irish Refining Co. Ltd, 1965–71; Director: Williams & Glyn's Bank, 1974–85 (a Dep. Chm., 1980–83; Chm., 1983–85); Royal Bank of Scotland Gp (formerly Nat. & Commercial Banking Gp), 1978–, a Vice-Chm., 1985–; Pearl Assurance PLC, 1985–; Jaguar PLC, 1986–; Smiths Ind. PLC, 1987–. Part-time Mem., NRDC, 1973–76; Member: Adv. Council for Energy Conservation, 1974–79; Energy Commn, 1977–79; British Aerospace, 1977–87 (Mem., Organising Cttee, 1976); Standing Commn on Energy and the Environment, 1978–81; Takeover Panel, 1987–. Chm., UK Petroleum Industry Adv. Cttee, 1977–80; Pres., UK Petroleum Industry Assoc. Ltd, 1979–80; CBI: Chm., Industrial Policy Cttee, 1982–85; Chm., Industrial Steering Policy Gp, 1985–86. President: Inst. of Petroleum, 1968–70; The Pipeline Industries Guild, 1973–75; Oil Industries Club, 1975–77; Pres., SBAC, 1982–83. Mem., Bd of Governors, English-Speaking Union, 1974–80; Chm., Bd of Trustees, Science Museum, 1986–. Treas., RSA, 1988–. Mem. Council, Surrey Univ., 1981– (Pro-Chancellor, 1986–). Hon. DSc: Southampton, 1978; Exeter, 1985; Salford, 1987; Cranfield, 1987; Hon. DEng Birmingham, 1986. *Recreations:* golf, woodwork. *Address:* 25 Caroline Terrace, Belgravia, SW1W 8JT. *Club:* Royal Wimbledon Golf.

PEARCE, Brian; *see* Pearce, J. B.

PEARCE, Sir (Daniel Norton) Idris, Kt 1990; CBE 1982; TD 1972; DL; Partner, Richard Ellis, Chartered Surveyors and International Property Consultants, since 1961 (Managing Partner, 1981–87); Chairman, English Estates, since 1989;*b* 28 Nov. 1933; *s* of late Lemuel George Douglas Pearce and Evelyn Mary Pearce; *m* 1963, Ursula Helene Langley; two *d. Educ:* West Buckland Sch.; College of Estate Management. FRICS. Commnd RE, 1958; comd 135 Field Survey Sqdn, RE(TA), 1970–73. Joined Richard Ellis 1959. Dir, The Phoenix Initiative, 1991–. Royal Instn of Chartered Surveyors: Member: Gen. Council, 1980–; Management Bd, 1984–; Chm., Parly and Public Affairs Cttee, 1984–89; Vice Pres., 1986–90; Pres., 1990–91. Chm., Internat. Assets Valuation Standards Cttee, 1981–86. Member: Adv. Panel for Instnl Finance in New Towns, 1974–80; Sec. of State for Health and Social Security Inquiry into Surplus Land in the NHS, 1982; PSA Adv. Bd, 1981–86; FCO Adv. Panel on Diplomatic Estate, 1985–; Financial Reporting Review Panel, 1991–; Property Advr, NHS Management Bd, 1985–90. Mem., UFC, 1991–. Vice Chm., Greater London TA&VRA, 1991– (Mem. 1970–; Chm., Works and Bldgs Sub-Cttee, 1983–90). Chm. Develt Bd, Nat. Art-Collections Fund, 1988–. Mem. Court, City Univ., 1987–. Chm. Governors, Stanway Sch., Dorking, 1982–85. Contested (C) Neath, 1959. DL Greater London, 1986. Hon. Fellow, Coll. of Estate Management, 1987; Centenary Fellow, Thames Poly., 1991. Hon. Col, 135 Indep. Topographic Sqn, RE(V), TA, 1989–. FRSA 1989. Hon. DSc: City, 1990; Oxford Poly., 1991. *Publications:* various articles on valuation and property matters. *Recreations:* reading, opera, ballet, travel. *Clubs:* Brooks's, Carlton, City of London.

PEARCE, Sir Eric (Herbert), Kt 1979; OBE 1970; Consultant to General Television Corporation, Channel Nine, Melbourne, Australia, since 1990 (Director of Community Affairs, 1979–90); *b* 5 March 1905; *s* of Herbert Clement Pearce and Louise Mary Pearce; *m* 1956, Betty Constance Ham (decd). *Educ:* Raynes Sch., Hants. Served War, FO RAAF, 1942–44. Studio Manager/Chief Announcer, Radio Stn 3DB, Melbourne, 1944–50; Gen. Man., Radio Stns 5KA-AO-RM, SA, 1950–55; Dir of Progs, major broadcasting network, Australia, 1955–56; Chief Announcer/Sen. Newsreader, General TV, Channel Nine, 1957–79. *Recreations:* walking, swimming, golf. *Address:* c/o General Television Corporation, Channel Nine, 22 Bendigo Street, Richmond, Vic 3121, Australia. *Clubs:* Athenæum, Toorak Services (Melbourne).

PEARCE, Most Rev. George; former Archbishop of Suva; *b* 9 Jan. 1921; *s* of George H. Pearce and Marie Louise Duval. *Educ:* Marist Coll. and Seminary, Framingham Center, Mass, USA. Entered Seminary, 1940; Priest, 1947; taught in secondary sch. in New England, USA, 1948–49; assigned as missionary to Samoa, 1949; consecrated Vicar Apostolic of Samoa, 1956; first Bishop of Apia, 1966; Archbishop of Suva, 1967–76, retired 1976. *Address:* Cathedral Rectory, 30 Fenner Street, Providence, RI 02903, USA. *T:* (401) 331–2434.

PEARCE, Howard Spencer; Director for Wales, Property Services Agency, Department of Environment, 1977–85; *b* 23 Sept. 1924; *m* 1951, Enid Norma Richards; one *s. Educ:* Barry County Sch.; College of Estate Management. ARICS. Armed Services, Major RE, 1943–47. Ministry of Works: Cardiff, 1953–61; Salisbury Plain, 1961–64; Ministry of Public Building and Works: Hong Kong, 1964–67; Abingdon, 1967–70; Area Officer, Abingdon, 1970–72; Regional Works Officer, SW Region, Bristol, PSA, Dept of Environment, 1972–77. *Recreations:* music, playing golf and watching Rugby football. *Address:* 2 Longhouse Close, Lisvane, Cardiff CF4 5XR. *T:* Cardiff (0222) *Club:* Cardiff Golf.

PEARCE, Sir Idris; *see* Pearce, Sir D. N. I.

PEARCE, (John) Brian; Director, The Inter Faith Network for the United Kingdom, since 1987; *b* 25 Sept. 1935; *s* of late George Frederic Pearce and Constance Josephine Pearce; *m* 1960, Michelle Etcheverry; four *s. Educ:* Queen Elizabeth Grammar Sch., Wakefield; Brasenose Coll., Oxford (BA). Asst Principal: Min. of Power, 1959; Colonial Office, 1960; Private Sec. to Parly Under-Sec. of State, 1963; Principal: Colonial Office, 1964; Dept of Economic Affairs, 1967; Principal Private Sec. to Sec. of State for Economic Affairs, 1968–69; Asst Sec., Civil Service Dept, 1969, Under-Sec., 1976; Under-Sec., HM Treasury, 1981–86, retd. *Recreations:* comparative theology, music, architecture. *Address:* 124 Court Lane, SE21 7EA.

PEARCE, John Dalziel Wyndham, MA, MD, FRCP, FRCPEd, FRCPsych, DPM, FBPsS; Consulting Psychiatrist: St Mary's Hospital; Queen Elizabeth Hospital for Children; *b* 21 Feb. 1904; *s* of John Alfred Wyndham Pearce and Mary Logan Dalziel; *m* 1929, Grace Fowler (marr. diss.), 1964), no *c*; *m* 1964, Ellinor Elizabeth Nancy Draper. *Educ:* George Watson's Coll.; Edinburgh Univ. Formerly: Physician-in-charge, Depts of Psychiatry, St Mary's Hosp. and Queen Elizabeth Hosp. for Children; Cons. Psychiatrist, Royal Masonic Hosp.; Hon. physician, Tavistock Clinic and West End Hospital for Nervous Diseases; Medical co-director Portman Clinic, Institute for Study and Treatment of Delinquency (ISTD); medico-psychologist, LCC remand homes; Mem. Academic Boards, Inst. of Child Health, and St Mary's Hosp. Med. Sch. (Univ. of London); Examiner in Medicine: RCP; Univ. of London; Royal Coll. of Psychiatrists; Chm., Adv. Cttee on delinquent and maladjusted children, Internat. Union for Child Welfare; Mem., Army Psychiatry Adv. Cttee; Lt-Col, RAMC; adviser in psychiatry, Allied Force HQ, CMF (despatches). Member: Council, National Assoc. for Mental Health; Home Sec's Adv. Council on Treatment of Offenders. *Publications:* Juvenile Delinquency, 1952; technical papers in scientific journals. *Recreations:* golf, painting. *Address:* 2/28 Barnton Avenue West, Edinburgh EH4 6EB. *T:* 031–317 7116. *Clubs:* Caledonian; New (Edinburgh).

PEARCE, John Trevor Archdall, CMG 1964; *b* 7 May 1916; *s* of late Rev. W. T. L. A. Pearce, Seven Hills, NSW, Australia, and late N. B. Pearce, Prahran, Victoria, Australia; *m* 1st, 1948, Isabel Bundey Rankine(*d* 1983), Hindmarsh Island, S Australia; no *c*; 2nd, 1984, Judith Burland Kingsley-Strack, Sydney, NSW. *Educ:* The King's Sch., Parramatta, Australia; Keble Coll., Oxford. MA. District Officer, Tanganyika, 1939. War Service: Kenya, Abyssinia, Ceylon, India, Burma, 1940–46, Major RE. Tanganyika: District Commissioner, 1950; Provincial Commissioner, 1959; Permanent Secretary (Admin), Office of the Vice-President, 1961; Chairman, Public Service Commn, Basutoland, 1963, Swaziland, 1965; Registrar, Papua and New Guinea Univ. of Technology, 1969–73. *Recreations:* golf, piano music, solitude, travel in remote places. *Address:* Clippings, 14 Golf Street, Buderim, Qld 4556, Australia.

PEARCE, Maj.-Gen. Leslie Arthur, CB 1973; CBE 1971 (OBE 1964; MBE 1956); Chief of General Staff, NZ Army, 1971–73, retd; *b* 22 Jan. 1918; British parents; *m* 1944, Fay Mattocks, Auckland, NZ; two *s* one *d. Educ:* in New Zealand. Joined Army, 1937; served War: Greece, Western Desert, Italy, 1939–45. Staff Coll., Camberley, 1948. Directing Staff, Australia Staff Coll., 1958–59; Commandant, Army Schools, NZ, 1960; Comdg Officer, 1 NZ Regt, in NZ and Malaysia, 1961–64; Dep. QMG, NZ Army, 1964–65; Dir of Staff Duties, NZ Army, 1966; IDC, 1967; QMG, 1968–69; Dep. Chief of Defence Staff, 1970. Chm., Vocational Training Council, 1975–81. Company director. Dep. Chm., NZ Council for Educnl Res., 1983–85 (Mem., 1977–85). *Recreations:* golf, fishing, gardening; Provincial and Services Rugby representative, in youth. *Address:* 1064A Beach Road, Torbay, Auckland, New Zealand.

PEARCE, Rev. Neville John Lewis; Assistant Curate, St Swithin, Walcot, Bath, since 1991; Chief Executive, Avon County Council, 1982–89; *b* 27 Feb. 1933; *s* of John and Ethel Pearce; *m* 1958, Eileen Frances Potter; two *d. Educ:* Queen Elizabeth's Hosp., Bristol; Silcoates Sch., Wakefield; Univ. of Leeds (LLB Hons 1953, LLM 1954). Asst Solicitor: Wakefield CBC, 1957–59; Darlington CBC, 1959–61; Chief Asst Solicitor, Grimsby CBC, 1961–63, Dep. Town Clerk, 1963–65; Dep. Town Clerk, Blackpool CBC, 1965–66; Town Clerk, Bath CBC, 1967–73; Dir of Admin and County Solicitor, Avon CC, 1973–82. Ordained (C of E), 1991. *Recreations:* home, family, Anglican church affairs. *Address:* Penshurst, Weston Lane, Bath BA1 4AB. *T:* Bath (0225) 26925.

PEARCE, Philippa; *see* Pearce, A. P.

PEARCE, Prof. Robert Penrose, FRMetS; FRSE; Professor of Meteorology and Head of Department of Meteorology, University of Reading, 1970–90, now Emeritus Professor; *b* 21 Nov. 1924; *s* of Arthur Penrose Pearce and Ada Pearce; *m* 1951, Patricia Frances Maureen Curling; one *s* two *d. Educ:* Bishop Wordsworth Sch., Salisbury; Imperial Coll., London (BSc, ARCS, DIC, PhD). Asst, Meteorological Office, 1941–43. Served RAF, 1943–47 (commnd 1945). Lectr, then Sen. Lectr in Mathematics, Univ. of St Andrews, 1952–66; Reader in Phys. Climatology, Imperial Coll., 1966–70. Pres., Royal Meteorological Soc., 1972–74; Chm., World Meteorol Org. Working Gp in Trop. Meteorology, 1978–90. *Publications:* Observer's Book of Weather, 1980; (co-ed) Monsoon Dynamics, 1981; sci. papers in meteorol jls. *Recreations:* walking, gardening, bridge, music. *Address:* Schiehallion, 27 Copped Hall Way, Camberley, Surrey GU15 1PB. *T:* Camberley (0276) 63103.

PEARD, Rear-Admiral Sir Kenyon (Harry Terrell), KBE 1958 (CBE 1951); retired; *b* 1902; *s* of Henry T. Peard; *m* 1935, Mercy Leila Bone; one *s* one *d. Educ:* RN Colleges, Osborne and Dartmouth. Went to sea, 1919; Torpedo Specialist, 1929; transferred to Electrical Branch, 1946, Director, Naval Electrical Dept, Admiralty, 1955–58; retired 1958. *Address:* Finstead, Shorefield Crescent, Milford-on-Sea, Hants SO41 0PD.

PEARL, Valerie Louise, DPhil; President, New Hall, Cambridge, since 1981; *b* 31 Dec. 1926; *d* of Cyril R. Bence, *qv*, and late Florence Bence; *m* 1949, Morris Leonard Pearl; one *d. Educ:* King Edward VI High Sch., Birmingham; St Anne's Coll., Oxford (Exhibnr). BA Hons Mod. History; MA, DPhil (Oxon). Allen Research Studentship, St Hugh's Coll., Oxford, 1951; Eileen Power Studentship, 1952; Sen. Research Studentship, Westfield Coll., London, 1962; Leverhulme Research Award, 1962; Graham Res. Fellow and Lectr in History, Somerville Coll., Oxford, 1965; Reader in History of London, 1968–76, Prof. of History of London, 1976–81, University College London. Convenor of confs to found The London Journal, Chm. of Editorial Bd, Editor-in-Chief, 1973–77; McBride Vis. Prof., Cities Program, Bryn Mawr Coll., Pennsylvania, 1974; Woodward Lectr, Yale Univ., New Haven, 1974; Lectr, Indian Council for Soc. Sci., Calcutta, Research on Indian Cities, New Delhi, 1977; John Stow Commem. Lectr, City of London, 1979; James Ford Special Lectr, Oxford, 1980; Sir Lionel Denny Lectr, Barber Surgeons' Co., 1981. Literary Dir, Royal Historical Soc., 1975–77; Pres., London and Mddx Archaeol. Soc., 1980–82; Governor, Museum of London, 1978–; Member: Royal Commn on Historical MSS, 1983–; Syndic: Cambridge Univ. Library, 1982–; Cambridge Univ. Press, 1984–. FSA 1976. *Publications:* London and the Outbreak of the Puritan Revolution, 1625–43, 1961; (ed jtly) History and Imagination: essays for Hugh Trevor-Roper, 1981; (ed) J. Stow, The Survey of London, 1987; contribs to: Nuove Questione (ed L. Bulferetti), 1965; Studies in London History (ed W. Kellaway, A. Hollaender), 1969; The Interregnum (ed G. Aylmer), 1972; Puritans and Revolutionaries (ed K. Thomas, D. Pennington), 1978; also to learned jls and other works, including Trans Royal Hist. Soc., Eng. Historical Review, History of English Speaking Peoples, Past and Present, Archives, Economic Hist. Review,

History, Jl of Eccles. History, Times Literary Supplement, The London Journal, London Review of Books, Albion, Listener, BBC. *Recreations:* walking and swimming. *Address:* New Hall, Cambridge CB3 0DF. *T:* Cambridge (0223) 351721.

PEARLMAN, Valerie Anne; Her Honour Judge Pearlman; a Circuit Judge, since 1985; *b* 6 Aug. 1936; *d* of Sidney and Marjorie Pearlman; *m* 1972; one *s* one *d. Educ:* Wycombe Abbey Sch. Called to the Bar, Lincoln's Inn, 1958; a Recorder, 1982–85. Mem., Parole Bd, 1989–. Mem. Council, Marlborough Coll., 1989–. Patron, Suzy Lamplugh Trust. *Recreations:* gardening, painting, reading. *Address:* Crown Court at Southwark, English Grounds, SE1 2HU. *Club:* English-Speaking Union.

PEARMAN, Sir James (Eugene), Kt 1973; CBE 1960; Senior Partner, Conyers, Dill & Pearman; *b* 24 Nov. 1904; *o s* of Eugene Charles Pearman and Kate Trott; *m* 1st, 1929, Prudence Tucker Appleby (*d* 1976); two *s*; 2nd, 1977, Mrs Antoinette Trott, *d* of Dr and Mrs James Aiguier, Philadelphia, Pa. *Educ:* Saltus Grammar Sch., Bermuda; Bromsgrove Sch., Worcs; Merton Coll., Oxford; Middle Temple. Law partnership with N. B. Dill, 1927–29; law partnership with Sir Reginald Conyers and N. B. Dill, 1929 and still continuing as firm of Conyers, Dill & Pearman. Member Colonial Parlt, Bermuda, 1943–72; MEC, 1955–63 and 1968–72; MLC, 1972–. Hon. Consul for Bolivia. *Recreations:* deep-sea fishing, bridge. *Address:* Tideway, 19 Lone Palm Drive, Pembroke HM05, Bermuda. *T:* 21125. *Clubs:* Carlton; Anglers' (New York); Rod and Reel (Miami); Royal Bermuda Yacht.

PEARS, David Francis, FBA 1970; Student of Christ Church, Oxford, 1960–88, now Emeritus; Professor of Philosophy, Oxford University, 1985–88; *b* 8 Aug. 1921; *s* of late Robert and Gladys Pears; *m* 1963, Anne Drew; one *s* one *d. Educ:* Westminster Sch.; Balliol Coll., Oxford. Research Lecturer, Christ Church, 1948–50; Univ. Lectr, Oxford, 1950–72, Reader, 1972–85; Fellow and Tutor, Corpus Christi Coll., 1950–60. Visiting Professor: Harvard, 1959; Univ. of Calif, Berkeley, 1964; Rockefeller Univ., 1967; Los Angeles, 1979; Hill Prof., Univ. of Minnesota, 1970; Humanities Council Res. Fellow, Princeton, 1966. Mem., l'Inst. Internat. de Philosophie, 1978– (Prés., 1988–90). *Publications:* (trans. with B. McGuinness), Wittgenstein, Tractatus Logico-Philosophicus, 1961, repr. 1975; Bertrand Russell and the British Tradition in Philosophy, 1967, 2nd edn 1972; Ludwig Wittgenstein, 1971; What is Knowledge?, 1971; (ed) Russell's Logical Atomism, 1973; Some Questions in the Philosophy of Mind, 1975; Motivated Irrationality, 1984; The False Prison: a study of the development of Wittgenstein's philosophy, vol. I, 1987, vol. II, 1988; Hume's System, 1990. *Address:* 7 Sandford Road, Littlemore, Oxford. *T:* Oxford (0865) 778768.

PEARSALL, Phyllis Isobel, MBE 1986; FRGS; painter, water colourist, etcher, writer; Founder and Director, since 1936, and Chairman and Managing Director, since 1958, Geographers' A to Z Map Co. Ltd; Founder and Director, since 1966, and Chairman, since 1987, Geographers' Map Trust; *b* 25 Sept. 1906; *d* of Alexander Gross and Isobel (*née* Crowley); *m* 1926, Richard Montague Stack Pearsall (marr. diss. 1938). *Educ:* Roedean; Collège de Jeunes Filles, Fécamp; Sorbonne. One-man shows: continuously 1926–88, when opened by Minister for the Arts; Sally Hunter Fine Art Gall., 1989; Little Gall., Arundel, 1990; exhibn, New Ashgate Gall., Farnham, 1990. Work in V&A Mus. and Mus. of London. 50th Anniversary Exhibn of A to Z develt at RGS (opened by Speaker of the H of C), 1986. Hd of Sect., MOI, 1942–45. FRGS 1936. *Publications:* Castilian Ochre, 1934; Fleet Street, Tite Street, Queer Street, 1983; Only the Unexpected Happens, 1985; Women 1939–40, 1985; Women at War, 1990; From Bedsitter to Household Name: the personal story of A to Z Maps, 1990; short stories in Cornhill Mag., New Yorker. *Recreations:* cooking, opera, theatre. *Address:* Geographers' A to Z Map Co. Ltd, Vestry Road, Sevenoaks, Kent TN14 5EP. *T:* Sevenoaks (0732) 451152. *Clubs:* Arts, University Women's.

PEARSE, Prof. Anthony Guy Everson, MA, MD (Cantab); FRCP, FRCPath; DCP (London); Professor of Histochemistry, University of London, Royal Postgraduate Medical School, 1965–81, now Emeritus; *b* 9 Aug. 1916; *o s* of Captain R. G. Pearse, DSO, MC, Modbury, Devon, and Constance Evelyn Steels, Pocklington, Yorks; *m* 1947, Elizabeth Himmelhoch, MB, BS (Sydney), DCP (London); one *s* three *d. Educ:* Sherborne Sch.; Trinity Coll., Cambridge. Kitchener Scholar. Posts, St Bart's Hospital, 1940–41; Surg.-Lt, RNVR, 1941–45 (21st and 24th Destroyer Flotillas). Registrar, Edgware General Hospital, 1946; Asst Lecturer in Pathol., PG Med. School, London, 1947–51, Lecturer, 1951–57; Cons. Pathol., Hammersmith Hospital, 1951; Fulbright Fellow and Visiting Prof. of Path., University of Alabama, 1953–54; Guest Instructor in Histochemistry: University of Kansas, 1957, 1958; Vanderbilt Univ., 1967; Reader in Histochemistry, University of London, 1957–65; Middleton Goldsmith Lectr, NY Path. Soc., 1976; Feulgen Lectr, Deutsch Ges. Histochem., 1983, Hon. Mem., 1986. Member: Path. Society (GB), 1949 (Hon. Mem., 1990); Biochem. Society (GB), 1957; European Gastro Club, 1969; Hon. Member or Member various foreign societies incl. Deutsche Akademie der Naturforscher Leopoldina, 1973 and Amer. Assoc. Endocrine Surgeons, 1981; Corresp. Mem., Deutsche Gesellschaft für Endokrinologie, 1978; Hon. Fellow, Royal Microscop. Society, 1964 (Vice-Pres., 1970–72; Pres., 1972–74). Hon. Mem., Mark Twain Soc., 1977. Hon. MD: Basel, 1960; Krakow, 1978. Raymond Horton-Smith Prize, Univ. of Cambridge, 1950; John Hunter Medal and Triennial Prize, RCS, 1976–78; Ernest Jung Foundn Prize and Medal for Medicine, 1979; Fred W. Stewart Medal and Prize, Sloan-Kettering Cancer Center, NY, 1979; Jan Swammerdam Medal, Soc. for Advancement of Nat. Scis, Amsterdam, 1988; Schleiden Medal, Deutsche Akademie der Naturforscher Leopoldina, 1989. Member Editorial Board: Histochemie, 1958–73; Histochemical Jl, 1968–; Histochemistry, 1974–; Progress in Histochem. Cytochem., 1973–; Acta Histochem., 1980–; Basic and Applied Histochem., 1979–; Jl Histochem. Cytochem., 1959–68; Enzymol. biol. clin., 1961–67; Brain Research, 1968–76; Cardiovascular Research, 1968–75; Virchow's Archiv 'B', 1968–; Jl of Royal Microscopical Soc., 1967–69; Jl Microscopy, 1969–81; Jl of Neuro-visceral Relations, 1969–73; Jl of Molecular and Cellular Cardiology, 1970–79; Scand. Jl Gastroenterol., 1971–81; Jl Neural Transmission, 1973–76; Jl of Pathology, 1973–83; Mikroscopie, 1977–88; Editor, Medical Biology, 1974–84. *Publications:* Histochemistry Theoretical and Applied, 1953, 2nd edn, 1960; 3rd edn, vol. I, 1968, vol. II, 1972; 4th edn vol. I, 1980, vol. II, 1984, vol. III, 1991; numerous papers on theoretical and applied histochemistry, esp. endocrinology (The Neuroendocrine System). *Recreations:* horticulture (plant hybridization, Liliaceae, Asclepiadaceae); ship modelling, foreign touring. *Address:* Gorwyn House, Cheriton Bishop, Exeter EX6 6JL. *T:* Cheriton Bishop (0647) 24231. *Club:* Naval.

PEARSE, Barbara Mary Frances, (Mrs M. S. Bretscher), PhD; FRS 1988; Staff Scientist, Medical Research Council Laboratory of Molecular Biology, Cambridge, since 1981; *b* 24 March 1948; *d* of Reginald William Blake Pearse and Enid Alice (*née* Mitchell); *m* 1978, Mark Steven Bretscher, *qv*; one *s* one *d. Educ:* The Lady Eleanor Holles Sch., Hampton, Mddx; University Coll. London (BSc Biochemistry, PhD). MRC Res. Fellowship, 1972–74; Beit Meml Fellowship, 1974–77; SRC Advanced Fellowship, 1977–82; CRC Internat. Fellowship Vis. Prof., Stanford Med. Centre, USA, 1984–85. Mem., EMBO, 1982–. EMBO Medal, 1987. *Publications:* contribs to sci. jls. *Recreations:* wild flowers, planting trees, fresh landscapes. *Address:* Ram Cottage, 63 Commercial End, Swaffham Bulbeck, Cambridge CB5 0ND. *T:* Cambridge (0223) 811276.

PEARSE, Brian Gerald, FCIB; Chief Executive, Midland Bank, since 1991; *b* 23 Aug. 1933; *s* of Francis and Eileen Pearse; *m* 1959, Patricia M. Callaghan; one *s* two *d. Educ:* St Edward's Coll., Liverpool. Martin's Bank Ltd, 1950; Barclays Bank, 1969–91: Local Dir, Birmingham, 1972; Gen. Man., 1977; Chief Exec. Officer, N America, 1983; Finance Dir, 1987–91. *Recreations:* Rugby football, opera. *Club:* Royal Automobile.

PEARSE, Rear-Adm. John Roger Southey G.; *see* Gerard-Pearse.

PEARSON, family name of **Viscount Cowdray** and **Baron Pearson of Rannoch.**

PEARSON OF RANNOCH, Baron *cr* 1990 (Life Peer), of Bridge of Gaur in the district of Perth and Kinross; **Malcolm Everard MacLaren Pearson;** Chairman, PWS Holdings plc, since 1988; *b* 20 July 1942; *s* of Col John MacLaren Pearson; *m* 1st, 1965, Francesca Frua De Angeli (marr. diss. 1970); one *d*; 2nd, 1977, Hon. Mary, *d* of Baron Charteris of Amisfield, *qv*; two *d. Educ:* Eton. Founded Pearson Webb Springbett (PWS) group of reinsurance brokers, 1964; Dir, Highland Venison Ltd, 1984–89. Chm., Rannoch Protection Group, 1979–; founded Rannoch Trust, 1984 (Exec. Trustee). Mem., CNAA, 1983– (Hon. Treas., 1986–). *Recreations:* stalking, fishing, golf. *Address:* Rannoch Barracks, Rannoch Station, Perthshire PH17 2QE. *Clubs:* White's; Swinley Forest Golf.

PEARSON, Brig. Alastair Stevenson, CB 1958; DSO; OBE 1953; MC; TD; farmer; Lord Lieutenant of Dunbartonshire, 1979–90; Keeper of Dumbarton Castle, since 1981; *b* 1 June 1915; *m* 1944, Mrs Joan Morgan Weld-Smith; three *d. Educ:* Kelvinside Acad.; Sedbergh. Co. Director, 1936–39; served War of 1939–45 (MC, DSO, and three Bars); embodied 6th Bn Highland LI, TA, 1939; transferred to Parachute Regt, 1941; Lt-Col 1942; CO 1st and 8th Para Bns, 1942–45, CO 15th (Scottish) Bn The Parachute Regt (TA), 1947–53; Dep. Comd 46 Parachute Bde (TA), 1953–59. Comd Scotland Army Cadet Force, Brigadier, 1967–81. ADC to the Queen, 1956–61. Hon. Col, 15th (Scottish) Bn The Parachute Regt (TA), 1963–77 and 1983–90. DL Glasgow, 1951, Dunbartonshire, 1975. KStJ 1980. *Address:* Tullochan, Gartocharn, by Alexandria, Dunbartonshire. *T:* Gartocharn (038983) 205.

PEARSON, Rev. Brian William; Archbishop's Officer for Mission and Evangelism and Tait Missioner for Canterbury Diocese, since 1991; *b* 18 Aug. 1949; *s* of Victor William Charles Pearson and Florence Irene (*née* Webster); *m* 1974, Althea Mary Stride; two *s. Educ:* Roan Sch. for Boys, Blackheath; Brighton Polytechnic (BSc Hons); City Univ. (MSc); Ordination Training (Southwark Ordination Course). CEng; MBCS; FHSM. Systems Engineer: IBM UK, 1967–71; Rohm and Haas UK, 1971–72; Lectr, Thames Polytechnic, 1972–81; College Head of Dept, Northbrook Coll., W Sussex, 1981–88; Bishop's Research Officer and Communications Officer, Bath and Wells, 1988–91. *Publication:* Yes Manager: Management in the local church, 1986. *Recreations:* cricket, theatre, cinema, music, learning about life through the experiences of two young sons, travel, enjoying the humour God has placed in His world. *Address:* c/o The Old Palace, Canterbury, Kent CT1 2EE.

PEARSON, David Compton Froome; Deputy Chairman, Robert Fleming Holdings Ltd, 1986–90 (Director, 1974–90); *b* 28 July 1931; *s* of late Compton Edwin Pearson, OBE and of Marjorie (*née* Froome); *m* 1966, Venetia Jane Lynn; two *d. Educ:* Haileybury; Downing Coll., Cambridge (MA). Linklaters & Paines, Solicitors, 1957–69 (Partner, 1961–69); Dir, Robert Fleming & Co. Ltd, 1969–90; Chairman: The Fleming Property Unit Trust, 1971–90; Gill & Duffus Group Plc, 1982–85 (Dir, 1973–85); Robert Fleming Securities, 1985–90; Dep. Chm., Austin Reed Group Plc, 1977– (Dir, 1971–); Director: Blue Circle Industries Plc, 1972–87; Lane Fox and Partners Ltd, 1987–. Mem., Finance Act 1960 Tribunal, 1978–84. *Recreations:* gardening, walking. *Address:* The Manor, Berwick St John, Shaftesbury, Dorset SP7 0EX. *T:* Donhead (0747) 828363. *Club:* Brooks's.

PEARSON, Sir Denning; *see* Pearson, Sir J. D.

PEARSON, Derek Leslie, CB 1978; Deputy Secretary, Overseas Development Administration (formerly Ministry of Overseas Development), 1977–81; *b* 19 Dec. 1921; *s* of late George Frederick Pearson and Edith Maud Pearson (*née* Dent); *m* 1956, Diana Mary, *d* of late Sir Ralph Freeman; no *c. Educ:* William Ellis Sch.; London Sch. of Economics. BSc (Econ). Served War of 1939–45; Lieut (A) (O) RNVR. Colonial Office, 1947; seconded to Kenya, 1954–56; Principal Private Sec. to Sec. of State for Colonies, 1959–61; Dept of Technical Cooperation, 1961; Asst Sec., 1962; ODM, 1964; Under Secretary: CSD, 1970–72; Min. of Overseas Develt, 1972–75; Dep. Sec., Cabinet Office, 1975–77. *Address:* Langata, Little London Road, Horam, Heathfield, East Sussex TN21 0BG. *T:* Horam Road (04353) 2276. *Clubs:* Naval, Civil Service.

PEARSON, (Edward) John (David); Director, Fisheries Directorate-General, Commission of the European Communities, since 1981; *b* 1 March 1938; *s* of Sydney Pearson and Hilda Beaumont; *m* 1963, Hilary Stuttard; three *s* two *d. Educ:* Huddersfield Coll.; Emmanuel Coll., Cambridge (MA). Admin. Trainee, London Transport Exec., 1959; Asst Principal, MoT, 1960, Principal 1965; Sen. Principal, DoE, 1971; Head of Div., Transport Directorate-Gen., Commn of Eur. Communities, 1973. *Recreation:* orienteering (Pres., Belgian Orienteering Assoc., 1982–87; Chm., Develt and Promotion Cttee, 1986–88, Mem. Council, 1988–, Internat. Orienteering Fedn). *Address:* Rue du Repos 56, 1180 Brussels, Belgium. *T:* 375.11.82.

PEARSON, Sir (Francis) Nicholas (Fraser), 2nd Bt *cr* 1964, of Gressingham, Co. Palatine of Lancaster; Managing Director, Saison Holdings BV, since 1990; *b* 28 Aug. 1943; *s* of Sir Francis Fenwick Pearson, 1st Bt, MBE and of Katharine Mary, *d* of Rev. D. Denholm Fraser; *S* father, 1991; *m* 1978, Henrietta Elizabeth, *d* of Comdr Henry Pasley-Tyler. *Educ:* Radley Coll. Commnd The Rifle Brigade, 1961; active service, Cyprus, Zambia, Borneo, 1961–67; ADC to: Army Comdr, Far East, 1967; C-in-C, Far East, 1968. Dir, Hill & Delamain Ltd, 1970–75; Dep. Chm., Claughton Manor Brickworks, 1978; Chm., Turner Gp Ltd. 1979; Director: Intercontinental Hotel Group Ltd, 1989–; Virgin Atlantic Airlines, 1989–. Prospective Parly Cand. (C), Oldham West, 1976–79. *Recreations:* walking, poetry, fishing. *Heir:* none. *Address:* 9 Upper Addison Gardens, Holland Park, W14 8AL. *Clubs:* Carlton; Vanderbilt Racquet.

PEARSON, Dr Graham Scott, CB 1990; CChem, FRSC; Director General, Chemical and Biological Defence Establishment, Porton Down (formerly Director, Chemical Defence Establishment), since 1984; *b* 20 July 1935; *s* of Ernest Reginald Pearson and Alice (*née* Maclachlan); *m* 1960, Susan Elizabeth Meriton Benn; two *s. Educ:* Woodhouse Grove Sch., Bradford; St Salvator's Coll., Univ. of St Andrews (BSc 1st Cl. Hons Chemistry, 1957; PhD 1960). Postdoctoral Fellow, Univ. of Rochester, NY, USA, 1960–62; joined Scientific Civil Service, 1962; Rocket Propulsion Estab., 1962–69; Def. Res. and Develt Staff, Washington, DC, 1969–72; PSO to Dir Gen. Res. Weapons, 1972–73; Asst Dir, Naval Ordnance Services/Scientific, 1973–76; Technical Adviser/Explosives, Materials and Safety (Polaris), 1976–79; Principal Supt, Propellants

Explosives and Rocket Motor Estab., Westcott, 1979–80; Dep. Dir 1, 1980–82 and Dep. Dir 2, 1982–83, RARDE, Fort Halstead; Dir Gen., ROF (Res. and Develt), 1983–84. FRSA 1989. *Publications*: contrib. to: Advances in Photochemistry, vol. 3, 1964; Advances in Inorganic and Radio Chemistry, vol. 8, 1966; Oxidation and Combustion Reviews, vol. 3, 1968 and vol. 4, 1969; articles on combustion in scientific jls; official reports. *Recreations*: long distance walking, reading, gardening. *Address*: Chemical and Biological Defence Establishment, Porton Down, Salisbury, Wilts SP4 0JQ. *T*: Idmiston (0980) 610211.

PEARSON, Air Commodore Herbert Macdonald, CBE 1944; RAF retired; *b* Buenos Aires, Argentina, 17 Nov. 1908; *s* of John Charles Pearson; *m* 1st, 1939, Jane Leslie (*d* 1978); one *s* two *d*; 2nd, 1982, Elizabeth Griffiths, JP, *widow* of E. P. Griffiths, MRCS, LRCP. *Educ*: Cheltenham Coll.; Cranwell. Left Cranwell, 1928; Malta, 1929–31; Central Flying Sch., 1932; Instructor, Cranwell, 1933–34; attached to Peruvian Government, 1935–36; Asst Air Attaché in Spain, 1936–38; comd No. 54 Sqdn, 1938–39. War of 1939–45, in Fighter Command; then France, Belgium and Germany (despatches 1942, 1943, 1946); Air Attaché, Lima, Peru, 1946; Deputy Director Air Foreign Liaison, Air Ministry, 1949; Commanding Royal Air Force, Kai Tak, Hong Kong, 1951–53; Assistant Chief of Staff Intelligence, Headquarters of Allied Air Forces, Central Europe, 1953–55. Air Commodore, 1953; retired, 1955. *Publication*: Pilot-Diplomat and Garage Rat, 1989. *Address*: Mapleridge Barn, Horton, Chipping Sodbury, Bristol BS17 6QH. *Club*: Naval and Military.

PEARSON, Sir (James) Denning, Kt 1963; JP; FEng 1976; Chairman and Chief Executive, Rolls-Royce Ltd, 1969–70; Chairman, Gamma Associates, 1972–80; *b* 8 Aug. 1908; *s* of James Pearson and Elizabeth Henderson; *m* 1932, Eluned Henry; two *d*. *Educ*: Canton Secondary Sch., Cardiff; Cardiff Technical Coll. Senior Wh. Scholarship; BSc Eng. Joined Rolls-Royce Ltd, 1932; Technical Production Engineer, Glasgow Factory, 1941; Chief Quality and Service Engineer (resident in Canada for one year), 1941–45; Gen. Man. Sales and Service, 1946–49; Director, 1949; Director and Gen. Man., Aero Engine Division, 1950; Managing Director (Aero Engine Div.), 1954–65; Chief Exec. and Dep. Chm., 1957–68. President, SBAC, 1963; Mem., NEDC, 1964–67. FRAeS, 1957–64, Hon. FRAeS, 1964; Hon. FIMechE; DrIngEh Brunswick Univ., 1962–86. Member: Council, Manchester Business Sch.; Governing Body, London Graduate Sch. of Business Studies, 1968–70; Governing Body, Admin. Staff Coll., Henley, 1968–73; Council, Voluntary Service Overseas. Fellow, Imperial Coll. of Science and Technology, 1968–; Hon. Fellow, Manchester Univ. Inst. of Science and Technology, 1969; Hon. DSc: Nottingham, 1966; Wales, 1968; Cranfield Inst. of Technology, 1970; Hon. DTech: Loughborough, 1968; CNAA, 1969. Gold Medal, Royal Aero Club, 1969; Benjamin Franklin Medal, RSA, 1970. FRSA 1970. *Recreations*: reading, golf, tennis, sailing. *Address*: Green Acres, Holbrook, Derbyshire DE5 0TF. *T*: Derby (0332) 881137.

PEARSON, Prof. James Douglas; Emeritus Professor of Bibliography, with reference to Asia and Africa, School of Oriental and African Studies, University of London (Professor, 1972–79); *b* 17 Dec. 1911; *m* 1st, Rose Betty Burden (marr. diss.); one *s*; 2nd, Hilda M. Wilkinson; three *s*. *Educ*: Cambridge Univ. (MA). Asst Under-librarian, Cambridge Univ. Library, 1939–50; Librarian, Sch. of Oriental and African Studies, Univ. of London, 1950–72. Hon. FLA, 1976. *Publications*: Index Islamicus, 1958–82; Oriental and Asian Bibliography, 1966; Oriental Manuscripts in Europe and North America, 1971; (ed jtly) Arab Islamic Bibliography, 1977; (ed) South Asia Bibliography, 1978; Creswell's Bibliography of the Architecture, Arts and Crafts of Islam, Supplement II, 1984; A Guide to Manuscripts and Documents in the British Isles relating to South and SE Asia, Vol. I, 1989, Vol. II, 1990. *Recreations*: natural history, travel. *Address*: 79 Highsett, Hills Road, Cambridge CB2 1NZ.

PEARSON, John; *see* Pearson, E. J. D.

PEARSON, Captain John William, CBE 1981; Regional Administrator, Mersey Regional Health Authority, 1977–81; *b* 19 Sept. 1920; *s* of Walter and Margaret Jane Pearson; *m* 1945, Audrey Ethel Whitehead; two *s*. *Educ*: Holloway Sch. FCIS, FHA, FCCA, IPFA. Served War, RA (Field), 1939–46. Hospital Service, LCC, 1947–48; NW Metropolitan Regional Hosp. Bd, 1948–49; Northern Gp, HMC, Finance Officer, 1949–62; Treasurer: St Thomas' Bd of Governors, 1962–73; Mersey Regional Health Authority, 1973–77. Pres., Assoc. of Health Service Treasurers, 1970–71. *Recreations*: tennis, golf, gardening, snooker. *Address*: 20 Weare Gifford, Shoeburyness, Essex SS3 8AB. *T*: Southend (0702) 585039.

PEARSON, Keith Philip, MA; Headmaster, George Heriot's School, Edinburgh, since 1983; *b* 5 Aug. 1941; *s* of Fred G. and Phyllis Pearson; *m* 1965, Dorothy (*née* Atkinson); two *d*. *Educ*: Madrid Univ. (Dip. de Estudios Hispanicos); Univ. of Cambridge (MA; Cert. of Educn). Teacher, Rossall Sch., 1964–72 (Head of Mod. Langs, 1968–72); George Watson's College: Head of Mod. Langs, 1972–79; Dep. Principal, 1979–83. *Recreations*: sport, mountains, music, DIY. *Address*: 11 Pentland Avenue, Edinburgh EH13 0HZ. *T*: 031–441 2630.

PEARSON, Sir Nicholas; *see* Pearson, Sir F. N. F.

PEARSON, Norman Charles, OBE 1944; TD 1944; Member, Air Transport Licensing Board, 1971–72; Lay Member, Restrictive Practices Court, 1968–86; *b* 12 Aug. 1909; *s* of late Max Pearson and Kate Pearson; *m* 1951, Olive May, *d* of late Kenneth Harper and Ruth Harper, Granston Manor, Co. Leix; one *s* one *d*. *Educ*: Harrow Sch. (Scholar); Gonville and Caius Coll., Cambridge (Sayer Scholar). Commnd Royal Signals (TA), 1932; Middx Yeomanry; served War of 1939–45, N Africa (despatches, OBE), Italy, Greece; Lt-Col, comd 6th Armd Div. Signals, 1942; 10 Corps Signals, 1944; Mil. Comd Athens Signals; 4th Div. Signals, 1945; subseq. re-formed 56 Div. Signals Regt (TA). Boots Pure Drug Co. Ltd, 1931–37; Borax (Holdings) Ltd, 1937–69, Director, 1951–69; Director: UK Provident Instn, 1965–80; Cincinnati Milacron Ltd, 1968–83 (Dep. Chm., 1972–83). *Recreation*: gardening. *Address*: Brook House, Norton, Malmesbury, Wilts SN16 0JP. *Club*: Carlton.

PEARSON, Maj.-Gen. Ronald Matthew, CB 1985; MBE 1959; Director Army Dental Service, 1982–85, retired; *b* 25 Feb. 1925; *s* of Dr John Pearson and Sheila Pearson (*née* Brown); *m* 1956, Florence Eileen Jack; two *d*. *Educ*: Clifton Hall Sch., Ratho, Midlothian; Glasgow Acad.; Glasgow Univ./Glasgow Dental Hosp. LDS RFPS(Glas) 1948; FBIM 1979. Civilian Dental Practice, 1948–49. Commnd RADC, 1949; served: RWAFF, 1950–53; UK, 1953–57; BAOR, 1957–60; UK, 1961–67; CO No 1 Dental Gp, BAOR, 1967–70; CO Army Dental Centres, Cyprus, 1970–73; CO No 8 Dental Gp, UK, 1973–75; CO No 4 Dental Gp, UK, 1975–76; Dep. Dir Dental Service, UKLF, 1976–78; Dep. Dir Dental Service, BAOR, 1978–82. QHDS, 1978–85. CStJ 1983. *Recreations*: trout fishing, photography, gardening, caravanning. *Address*: c/o Royal Bank of Scotland, Holts Branch, Victoria Road, Farnborough, Hants.

PEARSON, Gen. Sir Thomas (Cecil Hook), KCB 1967 (CB 1964); CBE 1959 (OBE 1953); DSO 1940, and Bar, 1943; DL; retired 1974; *b* 1 July 1914; *s* of late Vice-Admiral J. L. Pearson, CMG; *m* 1947, Aud, *d* of late Alf Skjelkvale, Oslo; two *s*. *Educ*: Charterhouse;

Sandhurst. 2nd Lieutenant Rifle Bde, 1934. Served War of 1939–45, M East and Europe; CO 2nd Bn The Rifle Bde, 1942; Dep. Comdr 2nd Independent Parachute Bde Gp 1944; Dep. Comdr 1st Air-landing Bde 1945; GSO1 1st Airborne Div. 1945; CO 1st Bn The Parachute Regt 1946; CO 7th Bn The Parachute Regt 1947; GSO1 (Land Air Warfare), WO, 1948; JSSC, GSO1, HQ Malaya, 1950; GSO1 (Plans), FARELF, 1951; Directing Staff, JSSC, 1953; Comdr 45 Parachute Bde TA 1955; Nat. Defence Coll., Canada, 1956; Comdr 16 Indep. Parachute Bde 1957; Chief of Staff to Dir of Ops Cyprus, 1960; Head of Brit. Mil. Mission to Soviet Zone of Germany, 1960; Major-General Commanding 1st Division, BAOR, 1961–63; Chief of Staff, Northern Army Group, 1963–67; Comdr, FARELF, 1967–68; Military Sec., MoD, 1968–72; C-in-C, Allied Forces, Northern Europe, 1972–74; psc 1942; jssc 1950; ndc Canada 1957. ADC Gen. to the Queen, 1974. Col Comdt, the Royal Green Jackets, 1973–77. Fisheries Mem., Welsh Water Auth., 1980–83. DL Hereford and Worcester, 1983. Haakon VII Liberty Cross, 1948; Medal of Honour, Norwegian Defence Assoc., 1973. *Recreations*: field sports, yachting. *Clubs*: Naval and Military; Kongelig Norsk Seilforenning.

PEART, Brian; Under-Secretary, Ministry of Agriculture, Fisheries and Food, 1976–85; *b* 17 Aug. 1925; *s* of late Joseph Garfield Peart and Frances Hannah Peart (*née* English); *m* 1952, Dorothy (*née* Thompson); one *s* one *d*. *Educ*: Wolsingham Grammar Sch.; Durham Univ. (BA). Served War, RAF, 1943–47. Agricultural Economist, Edinburgh Sch. of Agric., 1950–57; Sen. Agricultural Economist, 1957–64; Regional Farm Management Adviser, MAFF, West Midlands Region, 1964–67; Chief Farm Management Adviser, MAFF, 1967–71; Regional Manager, MAFF, Yorks/Lancs Region, 1971–74; Head of Intelligence and Trng Div., 1974–76; Chief Administrator, ADAS, 1976–80; Under Sec., Lands Gp, MAFF, 1980–85. *Recreations*: golf, genealogy, bridge, The Times crossword. *Address*: 18 Derwent Close, Claygate, Surrey KT10 0RF. *Club*: Farmers'.

PEART, Prof. Sir (William) Stanley, Kt 1985; MD; FRS 1969; Professor of Medicine, University of London, at St Mary's Hospital Medical School, 1956–87, now Emeritus; *b* 31 March 1922; *s* of J. G. and M. Peart; *m* 1947, Peggy Parkes; one *s* one *d*. *Educ*: King's College School, Wimbledon; Medical School, St Mary's Hospital. MB, BS (Hons), 1945; FRCP, 1959; MD (London), 1949. Lecturer in Medicine, St Mary's Hospital, 1950–56. Master, Hunterian Inst., RCS, 1988–. Trustee, Wellcome Trust, 1975–; Beit Trustee, 1986–. Goulstonian Lectr, 1959, Croonian Lectr, 1979, RCP. Hon. For. Mem., Académie Royale de Médicine de Belgique, 1984. Hon. FIC, 1988. Stouffer Prize, Amer. Heart Assoc., 1968. *Publications*: chapters in: Cecil-Loeb, Textbook of Medicine; Renal Disease; Biochemical Disorders in Human Disease; articles in Biochemical Journal, Journal of Physiology, Lancet. *Recreations*: ski-ing, reading, tennis. *Address*: 17 Highgate Close, N6 4SD.

PEASE, family name of **Barons Daryngton, Gainford,** and **Wardington.**

PEASE, Sir (Alfred) Vincent, 4th Bt *cr* 1882; *b* 2 April 1926; *s* of Sir Alfred (Edward) Pease, 2nd Bt (*d* 1939), and of his 3rd wife, Emily Elizabeth (Dowager Lady Pease, JP) (*d* 1979); *S* half-brother, 1963; unmarried. *Educ*: Bootham School, York. *Heir*: *b* Joseph Gurney Pease [*b* 16 Nov. 1927; *m* 1953, Shelagh Munro, *d* of C. G. Bulman; one *s* one *d*]. *Address*: 149 Aldenham Road, Guisborough, Cleveland TS14 8LB. *T*: Guisborough (0287) 636453.

PEASE, Dr Rendel Sebastian, FRS 1977; Programme Director for Fusion, UKAEA, 1981–87; *b* 1922; *s* of Michael Stewart Pease and Helen Bowen (*née* Wedgwood); *m* 1952, Susan Spickernell; two *s* three *d*. *Educ*: Bedales Sch.; Trinity Coll., Cambridge (MA, ScD). Scientific Officer, Min. of Aircraft Prodn at ORS Unit, HQ, RAF Bomber Comd, 1942–46; research at AERE, Harwell, 1947–61; Div. Head, Culham Lab. for Plasma Physics and Nuclear Fusion, UKAEA, 1961–67; Vis. Scientist, Princeton Univ., 1964–65; Asst Dir, UKAEA Research Gp, 1967; Dir, Culham Lab., UKAEA, 1968–81. Gordon Godfrey Vis. Prof. of Theoretical Physics. Univ. NSW, 1984, 1988 and 1991. Chairman: Adam Hilger Ltd, 1976–77; Plasma Physics Commn, Internat. Union of Pure and Applied Physics, 1975–78; Internat. Fusion Res. Council, Internat. Atomic Energy Agency, 1976–83; British Pugwash Gp, 1988–. Member: Council, Royal Soc., 1985–87 (a Vice-Pres., 1986–87); Fabian Soc.; Inst. of Physics (Vice-Pres., 1973–77; Pres., 1978–80); Amer. Inst. of Physics; IEE. DUniv Surrey, 1973; Hon. DSc: Aston, 1981; City Univ., 1987. *Publications*: articles in physics jls. *Recreation*: music. *Address*: The Poplars, West Ilsley, Newbury, Berks RG16 0AW.

PEASE, Sir Richard Thorn, 3rd Bt *cr* 1920; DL; Chairman, Yorkshire Bank, 1986–90 (Director, since 1977; Deputy Chairman, 1981–86); *b* 20 May 1922; *s* of Sir Richard Arthur Pease, 2nd Bt, and Jeannette Thorn (*d* 1957), *d* of late Gustav Edward Kissel, New York; *S* father, 1969; *m* 1956, Anne, *d* of late Lt-Col Reginald Francis Heyworth; one *s* two *d*. *Educ*: Eton. Served with 60th Rifles, Middle East, Italy and Greece, 1941–46 (Captain). Director: Owners of the Middlesbrough Estate Ltd, 1954–86; Barclays Bank, 1965–89; Bank of Scotland, 1977–85; Grainger Trust PLC, 1986–; Vice-Chairman: Barclays Bank Ltd, 1970–82; Barclays Bank UK Management, 1971–82; Chm., Foreign and Colonial High Income Trust, 1990–. DL Northumberland, 1990. *Heir*: *s* Richard Peter Pease, *b* 4 Sept. 1958. *Address*: Hindley House, Stocksfield-on-Tyne, Northumberland NE43 7SA.

PEASE, Robert John Claude; HM Diplomatic Service, retired; Counsellor (Administration) and Consul-General, British Embassy, Moscow, 1977–80; *b* 24 April 1922; *s* of Frederick Robert Hellier Pease and Eileen Violet Pease (*née* Beer); *m* 1945, Claire Margaretta Whall; one *s* two *d*. *Educ*: Cattedown Road Sch., Plymouth; Sutton High Sch., Plymouth. Served War of 1939–45; Telegraphist, RN, 1942; commnd Sub Lt RNVR, 1944. Clerk, Lord Chancellor's Dept, Plymouth County Court, 1939, Truro County Court, 1946; Foreign Office, 1948; Moscow, 1952; HM Consul, Sarajevo, 1954; 2nd Sec., Bangkok, 1958; HM Consul, Gdynia, 1959, Düsseldorf, 1961; 1st Sec., Pretoria, 1964, Bombay, 1966; FCO, 1969; Dep. High Commissioner, Mauritius, 1973. *Recreations*: golf, opera. *Address*: 5 Springfield Road, Camberley, Surrey.

PEASE, Rosamund Dorothy Benson; Under Secretary, Department of Health, since 1989; *b* 20 March 1935; *d* of Helen Bowen (*née* Wedgwood) and Michael Stewart Pease; one *s*. *Educ*: Chester Sch., Nova Scotia; Perse Sch., Cambridge; Mount Sch., York; Newnham Coll., Cambridge (BA Classical Tripos). Asst Principal, Min. of Health, 1958; Principal, 1965; Asst Sec., Pay Board, 1973; Office of Manpower Economics, 1974; Cabinet Office, 1975–76; DHSS, 1976; Office of Population Censuses and Surveys, 1983; Under Sec., DHSS, 1985. *Recreations*: gardening, family. *Address*: Department of Health, Eileen House, 80–94 Newington Causeway, SE1 6EF.

See also R. S. Pease.

PEASE, Sir Vincent; *see* Pease, Sir A. V.

PEAT, Sir Gerrard (Charles), KCVO 1988; FCA; Partner, Peat Marwick McLintock (formerly Peat Marwick Mitchell) & Co., Chartered Accountants, 1956–87; Auditor to the Queen's Privy Purse, 1980–88 (Assistant Auditor, 1969–80); *b* 14 June 1920; *s* of Charles Urie Peat, MC, FCA, and Ruth (*née* Pulley); *m* 1949, Margaret Josephine Collingwood; one *s*. *Educ*: Sedbergh Sch. FCA 1961. Served War, RAF and ATA (pilot),

1940–45 (Service Medals); Pilot, 600 City of London Auxiliary Sqdn, 1948–51. Underwriting Mem. of Lloyd's, 1973–; Member: Cttee, Assoc. of Lloyd's Members, 1983–89; Council of Lloyd's, 1989–. Member: Corp. of City of London, 1973–78; Worshipful Co. of Turners, 1970–. Hon. Treasurer, Assoc. of Conservative Clubs, 1971–78. Jubilee Medal, 1977. *Recreations:* travel, shooting, fishing, golf, flying. *Address:* (office) Britannia House, Glenthorne Road, W6 0LF. *T:* 081–748 9898; Flat 10, 35 Pont Street, SW1X 0BB. *T:* 071–245 9736; Home Farm, Upper Basildon, Pangbourne, Berks RG8 8ND. *T:* Upper Basildon (0491) 671241. *Club:* Boodle's.

PEAT, Ven. Lawrence Joseph; Archdeacon of Westmorland and Furness, since 1989; *b* 29 Aug. 1928; *s* of Joseph Edward and Lilian Edith Peat; *m* 1953, Sheila Shipway; three *s* three *d*. *Educ:* Lincoln Theological College. Curate of Bramley, Leeds, 1958–61; Rector of All Saints', Heaton Norris, Stockport, 1961–65; Vicar of Bramley, Leeds, 1965–73; Team Rector of Southend-on-Sea, 1973–79; Vicar of Skelsmergh, Selside and Longsleddale, Cumbria, 1979–86; RD of Kendal, 1984–88; Team Vicar of Kirkby Lonsdale, 1986–88. Canon of Carlisle Cathedral, 1988–. *Recreations:* walking, music. *Address:* Woodcroft, Levens, Kendal LA8 8NQ. *T:* Sedgwick (0595) 61281.

PEAT, Michael Charles Gerrard, FCA; Director of Finance and Property Services, HM Household, since 1990; *b* 16 Nov. 1949; *m* 1976, Deborah Sage (*née* Wood); two *s* one *d* (and one *s* decd). *Educ:* Eton; Trinity Coll., Oxford (MA); INSEAD, Fontainebleau (MBA). FCA 1975. KPMG Peat Marwick McLintock, 1972–, Partner, 1985–; Auditor to the Privy Purse, 1987–90; Administrative Advr to Royal Household, 1987–90. *Recreations:* sport, history, literature. *Address:* 1 Puddle Dock, EC4V 3PD. *T:* 071–236 8000.

PEAT, (William Wood) Watson, CBE 1972; FRAgS; JP; farmer; broadcaster; Scottish Governor of the BBC, 1984–89; Chairman, Broadcasting Council for Scotland, 1984–89; *b* 14 Dec. 1922; *o s* of William Peat and Margaret Hillhouse; *m* 1955, Jean Frew Paton McHarrie; two *s* one *d*. *Educ:* Denny Public School. Served with Royal Signals, Europe and India, 1941–46; Lieut 1944. Member: Nat. Council, Scottish Assoc. of Young Farmers' Clubs, 1949– (Chm., 1953–54; Vice-Pres., 1975; Pres., 1979); Stirling CC, 1959–74 (Vice-Convenor, 1967–70); Council, NFU Scotland, 1959–78 (Pres., 1966–67); Scottish River Purification Adv. Cttee, 1960–79; Bd of Management, Royal Scottish Nat. Hosp., 1962–72; Council, Hannah Research Inst., 1963–82; Council, Scottish Agricultural Organisation Soc. Ltd, 1963– (Pres., 1974–77); Bd of Management, British Farm Produce Council, 1964–87 (Vice-Chm., 1980–87); Agric. Marketing Develt Exec. Cttee, 1966–67; Central Council for Agric. and Horticultural Co-operation, 1967–; Food from Britain Co-operative Development Board, 1983–89; Bd of Management, Oatridge Agric. Coll., 1967–75; Gen. Comr of Income Tax, 1962; Governor, West of Scotland Agric. Coll., 1964–90 (Vice Chm., 1975, Chm., 1983–88); Chm. Council, Scottish Agricl Colls, 1984–90; Dir, Agri-Finance (Scotland) Ltd, 1968–79; Chm., BBC Scottish Agric. Adv. Cttee, 1971–75; Chm., Scottish Adv. Cttee, Assoc. of Agriculture, 1974–79, Vice Pres., 1979–; Director: Fedn of Agricultural Co-operatives (UK) Ltd, 1974–77; FMC PLC, 1974–83; Mem., British Agricl Council, 1974–84. FRAgS 1987. JP Stirlingshire, 1963. *Recreations:* amateur radio, flying. *Address:* Carbro, 61 Stirling Road, Larbert, Stirlingshire FK5 4SG. *T:* Larbert (0324) 562420. *Clubs:* Farmers'.

PECK, His Honour David (Edward); a Circuit Judge (formerly Judge of County Courts), 1969–85; *b* 6 April 1917; *m* 1st, 1950, Rosina Seton Glover Marshall (marr. diss.); one *s* three *d*; 2nd, 1973, Frances Deborah Redford (*née* Mackenzie) (marr. diss.); one *s*; 3rd, 1983, Elizabeth Charlotte Beale (*née* Boost). *Educ:* Charterhouse School; Balliol College, Oxford. Served Army (Cheshire Regiment), 1939–46. Called to Bar, Middle Temple, 1949. Mem., County Court Rule Cttee, 1978–84 (Chm., 1981–84); Jt Editor, County Court Practice, 1982–90. *Address:* 8 New Square, Lincoln's Inn, WC2.

PECK, Sir Edward (Heywood), GCMG 1974 (KCMG 1966; CMG 1957); HM Diplomatic Service, retired; *b* 5 Oct. 1915; *s* of Lt-Col Edward Surman Peck, IMS, and Doris Louise Heywood; *m* 1948, Alison Mary MacInnes; one *s* two *d*. *Educ:* Clifton College; The Queen's College, Oxford. 1st Cl. Hons (Mod. Langs), 1937; Laming Travelling Fellow, 1937–38. Entered Consular Service, 1938; served in Barcelona, 1938–39; Foreign Office, 1939–40; Sofia, 1940; Ankara, 1940–44; Adana, 1944; Iskenderun, 1945; Salonica, 1945–47; with UK Deleg. to UN Special Commn on the Balkans, 1947; Foreign Office, 1947–50; seconded to UK High Commissioner's Office, Delhi, 1950–52; Counsellor, Foreign Office, 1952–55; Dep. Comdt, Brit. Sector, Berlin, 1955–58; on staff of UK Commissioner-General for S-E Asia, 1959–60; Assistant Under-Secretary of State, Foreign Office, 1961–66; British High Commissioner in Kenya, 1966–68; Dep. Under-Secretary of State, FCO, 1968–70; British Perm. Rep. to N Atlantic Council, 1970–75. Dir, Outward Bound (Loch Eil), 1976–90; Mem. Council, Nat. Trust for Scotland, 1982–87. Hon. Vis. Fellow in Defence Studies, Aberdeen Univ., 1976–85. *Publications:* North-East Scotland (Bartholomew's Guides Series), 1981; Avonside Explored, 1983. *Recreations:* mountaineering, travel, reading history and writing guide books. *Address:* Easter Torrans, Tomintoul, Banffshire AB37 9HJ. *Club:* Alpine.

PECK, Gregory; film actor, US, since 1943; *b* 5 April 1916; *s* of Gregory P. Peck and Bernice Ayres; *m* 1st, 1942, Greta Konen Rice (marr. diss. 1954); two *s* (and one *s* decd); 2nd, 1955, Veronique Passani; one *s* one *d*. *Educ:* Calif Public Schools; Univ. of Calif (BA). Broadway stage, 1941–43. *Films:* Days of Glory, 1943; Keys of the Kingdom, Valley of Decision, 1944; Spellbound, 1945; Duel in the Sun, The Yearling, 1946; The Macomber Affair, Gentlemen's Agreement, 1947; The Paradine Case, 1948; Yellow Sky, The Great Sinner, Twelve O'Clock High, 1949; The Gun Fighter, 1950; Only the Valiant, Captain Horatio Hornblower, David and Bathsheba, 1951; The World in his Arms, 1952; The Snows of Kilimanjaro, 1952; Roman Holiday, 1953; The Million Pound Note, 1953; Night People, 1954; The Purple Plain, 1954; The Man in the Grey Flannel Suit, 1956; Moby Dick, 1956; Designing Woman, 1957; The Bravados, 1958; The Big Country (co-producer), 1958; Pork Chop Hill, 1959; On the Beach, 1959; Guns of Navarone, 1960; Cape Fear, 1961; To Kill a Mocking Bird, 1962 (Academy Award for best performance); Captain Newman, MD, 1963; Behold a Pale Horse, 1964; Mirage, 1965; Arabesque, 1965; Mackenna's Gold, 1967; The Chairman, 1968; The Stalking Moon, 1968; Marooned, 1970; I Walk the Line, 1971; Shoot Out, 1971; The Trial of the Catonsville Nine, 1972; Billy Two-Hats, 1974; The Boys From Brazil, 1978; The Sea Wolves, 1980; Amazing Grace and Chuck, 1987; Old Gringo, 1989; *television:* The Blue and the Gray, 1982; The Scarlet and the Black, 1983; *produced:* The Dove, 1974; The Omen, 1976; MacArthur, 1977. Nat. Chm., Amer. Cancer Soc., 1966. Mem., Nat. Council on Arts, 1965–67, 1968–; Pres., Acad. Motion Pictures Arts and Sciences, 1967–70; Chm., Board of Trustees, Amer. Film Inst., 1967–69. Medal of Freedom Award, 1969; Jean Hersholt Humanitarian Award, Acad. of Motion Picture Arts and Sciences, 1968. *Recreations:* riding, swimming, bicycling, gardening. *Club:* Players (New York).

PECK, Sir John (Howard), KCMG 1971 (CMG 1956); HM Diplomatic Service, retired; *b* Kuala Lumpur, 16 Feb. 1913; *o s* of late Howard and Dorothea Peck; *m* 1st, 1939, Mariska Caroline (*d* 1979), *e d* of Josef Somló; two *s*; 2nd, 1987, Catherine, *y d* of Edward McLaren. *Educ:* Wellington College; CCC, Oxford. Assistant Private Secretary to First Lord of Admiralty, 1937–39; to Minister for Coordination of Defence, 1939–40; to the Prime Minister, 1940–46; transferred to Foreign Service, 1946; served in United Nations Dept, 1946–47; in The Hague, 1947–50; Counsellor and Head of Information Research Dept, 1951–54; Counsellor (Defence Liaison) and Head of Political Division, British Middle East Office, 1954–56; Director-General of British Information Services, New York, 1956–59; UK Permanent Representative to the Council of Europe, and Consul-General, Strasbourg, 1959–62; Ambassador to Senegal, 1962–66, and Mauritania, 1962–65; Asst Under-Sec. of State, FO, then FCO, 1966–70; Ambassador to the Republic of Ireland, 1970–73. *Publications:* Dublin from Downing Street (memoirs), 1978; various essays and light verse. *Recreations:* photography, gardening. *Address:* Stratford, Saval Park Road, Dalkey, Co. Dublin. *T:* Dublin 2852000. *Club:* Stephen's Green (Dublin).

PECK, Maj.-Gen. Richard Leslie, CB 1991; FRGS; CEng, FICE; Engineer-in-Chief (Army), 1988–91; *b* 27 May 1937; *s* of Frank Archibald Peck and Molly Peck (*née* Eyels); *m* 1962, Elizabeth Ann, *d* of Major Denis James Bradley and Barbara Edith Amy Bradley (*née* Metcalfe); two *s* one *d*. *Educ:* Wellingborough Sch.; Royal Mil. Acad., Sandhurst; Royal Mil. Coll. of Science, Shrivenham. BScEng. Commnd RE, 1957; served Cyprus, Libya, Germany, UK; psc 1969; Bde Major 5 Inf. Bde, 1969–71; Sqn Comd BAOR, 1972–73; Directing Staff, Staff Coll., 1973–77; CO 21 Engr Regt, 1977–79; Asst Mil. Sec., 1979–81; Comd 19 Inf. Bde, 1981–83; RCDS 1984; Dir Army Service Conditions, MoD, 1985; Dir Personnel, Staff of CDS, 1985–87. Col Comdt, RE, 1991–; Col, Queen's Gurkha Engineers, 1991–. *Recreations:* Association football, cricket, golf, shooting, skiing, Rugby football. *Address:* c/o National Westminster Bank, Rushden, Northamptonshire. *Clubs:* Army and Navy, MCC; I Zingari, Free Foresters, Cryptics; Royal Mid-Surrey Golf.

PECK, Stanley Edwards, CBE 1974; BEM 1954; QPM 1964; DL; HM Inspector of Constabulary, 1964–78; *b* 1916; *er s* of late Harold Edwards Peck, Edgbaston and Shanghai; *m* 1939, Yvonne Sydney Edwards, *er d* of late John Edwards Jessop, LDS; two *s* two *d*. *Educ:* Solihull School; Birmingham University. Served with RAF, 1941–45 (Flt-Lt). Joined Metropolitan Police, 1935; Chief Inspector and Supt, New Scotland Yard, 1950–54; Asst Chief Constable, Staffs, 1954–61; Chief Constable, Staffs, 1961–64. DL Staffs, 1962. Pres., Royal Life Saving Soc., UK, 1969–74 (Chm., East Midlands Region, RLSS, 1968–80). OStJ. *Recreations:* golf and dog walking. *Address:* Lodge Gardens, Walnut Grove, Radcliffe-on-Trent, Nottinghamshire NG12 2AD. *Club:* Royal Air Force.

PECKFORD, Hon. (Alfred) Brian; PC (Can.) 1982; Premier of the Province of Newfoundland and Labrador, 1979–89; *b* Whitbourne, Newfoundland, 27 Aug. 1942; *s* of Ewart Peckford and Allison (*née* Young), St John's; *m* 1969, Marina, *d* of Raymond Dicks and Hope (*née* Adams), Halls Bay; two *d*; *m* Carol Ellsworth; one *s*. *Educ:* Lewisporte High Sch.; Memorial Univ. of Newfoundland (BAEd). Schoolmaster, 1962–63 and 1966–72. MHA (Progressive C) Green Bay, 1972–89; Special Asst to Premier, 1973; Minister: of Dept of Municipal Affairs and Housing, 1974; of Mines and Energy, 1976, also of Rural Development, 1978. Leader of Progressive Cons. Party, Newfoundland and Labrador, 1979–89. Pres., Peckford Inc., 1989–. Hon. LLD Meml Univ. of Newfoundland, 1986. *Recreations:* reading, sport, swimming, ski-ing. *Address:* Peckford Incorporated, Box 102, 570 Newfoundland Drive, St John's, Newfoundland A1A 5B1, Canada.

PECKHAM, Arthur John; UK Permanent Representative, Food and Agriculture Organisation, Rome, 1977–80; *b* 22 Sept. 1920; *s* of Richard William Peckham and Agnes Mercy (*née* Parker); *m* 1949, Margaret Enid Quirk; two *s* one *d*. *Educ:* The Judd Sch., Tonbridge. RAF (Pilot), 1942–46, 59 Sqdn Coastal Command. Cadet, Min. of Labour and Nat. Service, 1948; Colonial Office: Asst Principal, 1950; Private Sec. to Perm. Under-Sec., 1952; Principal, 1954; Counsellor (Technical Assistance), Lagos, 1964; Asst Sec., Min. of Overseas Develt, 1966; Minister, FAO, Rome, 1977. *Recreations:* gardening, hill walking. *Address:* 7 Yardley Park Road, Tonbridge, Kent TN9 1NE. *T:* Tonbridge (0732) 353735.

PECKHAM, Prof. Michael John, FRCP, FRCPGlas, FRCR; Director, Research and Development, Department of Health, since 1991; *b* 2 Aug. 1935; *s* of William Stuart Peckham and Gladys Mary Peckham; *m* 1958, Catherine Stevenson King; three *s*. *Educ:* St Catharine's Coll., Cambridge (MA); University College Hosp. Med. Sch., London (MD). MRC Clin. Res. Schol., Inst. Gustav Roussy, Paris, 1965–67; Institute of Cancer Research, London: Lectr, 1967–71; Sen. Lectr, 1971–74; Prof. of Radiotherapy, 1974–86; Dean, 1984–86; Dir, BPMF, 1986–90. Consultant: Royal Marsden Hosp., 1971–86; to Royal Navy, 1974–. Mem., MRC Cell Biology and Disorders Bd, 1977–81. Member, Special Health Authority: Gt Ormond St Hosp., 1988–90; Brompton Nat. Heart and London Chest Hosps, 1986–90; Hammersmith and Queen Charlotte's Hosps, 1989–90. President: European Radiotherapy Gp, 1978; European Soc. of Therapeutic Radiology and Oncology, 1983–85; British Oncological Assoc., 1986–88; Fedn of European Cancer Socs, 1989–91 (Pres.-elect, 1987–89). Vice-Chm., Council, Imperial Cancer Research Fund, 1988–91. Founder: Bob Champion Cancer Trust, 1983; British Oncological Assoc., 1985. Editor-in-Chief, European Jl of Cancer, 1989–. Dr *hc* Besançon, 1991. *Publications:* Management of Testicular Tumours, 1981; (jtly) The Biological Basis of Radiotherapy, 1983; (jtly) Primary Management of Early Breast Cancer, 1985; articles on cancer research and cancer treatment. *Recreation:* painting (one-man exhibitions: 1964, 1967, 1970, 1976, 1982, 1983, 1989). *Address:* Richmond House, Whitehall, SW1. *Club:* Reform.

PECKOVER, Dr Richard Stuart; Site Director, Winfrith Technology Centre, UKAEA, since 1990; *b* 5 May 1942; *s* of Rev. Cecil Raymond Peckover and Grace Lucy (*née* Curtis). *Educ:* King Edward VII Sch., King's Lynn; Wadham Coll., Oxford (MA); Corpus Christi Coll., Cambridge (PhD). FInstP, FIMA, FRMetS, FRAS, FSaRS. United Kingdom Atomic Energy Authority: Res. Scientist, Culham Lab., 1969–81; Res. Associate, MIT, 1973–74; Safety and Reliability Directorate, 1982, Br. Head, 1983–87; Asst Dir, AEE Winfrith, 1987, Dep. Dir, 1989. Mem., Amer. Nucl. Soc. *Recreations:* walking, talking, listening to music. *Address:* 6 The Square, Puddletown, Dorset DT2 8SL; Winfrith Technology Centre, AEA Technology, Dorchester, Dorset DT2 8DH. *T:* Dorchester (0305) 251888. *Club:* United Oxford & Cambridge University.

PEDDER, Vice-Adm. Sir Arthur (Reid), KBE 1959; CB 1956; retired as Commander, Allied Naval Forces, Northern Europe (1957–59); *b* 6 July 1904; *s* of late Sir John Pedder, KBE, CB; *m* 1934, Dulcie, *d* of O. L. Bickford; two *s*. *Educ:* Osborne and Dartmouth. Served in various ships, 1921–; qualified as Naval Observer, 1930; promoted Commander and appointed Admiralty, 1937–40; Executive Officer, HMS Mauritius, 1940–42; Admiralty Asst, Dir of Plans (Air), 1942–45; Capt. 1944; comd HM Ships Khedive and Phoebe, 1945–47; idc 1948; Admiralty (Dep. Dir of Plans), 1949–50; Fourth Naval Member of Australian Commonwealth Naval Board, 1950–52; Rear-Adm. 1953; Asst Chief of Naval Staff (Warfare), Admiralty, 1953–54; Flag Officer, Aircraft Carriers, December 1954–May 1956; Vice-Adm. 1956. *Recreation:* everything outdoors. *Address:* Langhurst Barn Cottage, Hascombe, Godalming, Surrey GU8 4JP. *T:* Hascombe (048632) 294. *Club:* Athenæum.

PEDDER, Air Marshal Sir Ian (Maurice), KCB 1982; OBE 1963; DFC 1949; Chairman, Dan-Air Services, 1989–90 (Deputy Chairman, 1986–89); Director, Davies & Newman Ltd, since 1989; *b* 2 May 1926; *s* of Maurice and Elsie Pedder; *m* 1949, Jean Mary (*née* Kellett); one *s* two *d*. *Educ:* Royal Grammar Sch., High Wycombe; Queen's Coll., Oxford. Service in Nos 28, 60, 81, 213 Sqdns, CFS, and with Burma Air Force, 1946–59; Staff Coll., Andover, and MoD, 1959–62; Far East, 1962–64; Staff appts, 1965–70; RCDS, 1971; Comdg RAF Chivenor, 1972–74; Nat. Air Traffic Services, 1974–84, Dep. Controller, 1977–81, Controller, 1981–84. *Publications:* contribs to Service jls, UK and US. *Recreations:* study of Victorian times, photography, riding (a bicycle). *Address:* The Chestnuts, Cheddar, Somerset. *Club:* Royal Air Force.

PEDDIE, Robert Allan; Chairman, South Eastern Electricity Board, 1977–83; general management consultant since 1983; *b* 27 Oct. 1921; *s* of Robert Allan Peddie and Elizabeth Elsie (*née* Sharp); *m* 1946, Ilene Ivy Sillcock (*d* 1990); one *d*. *Educ:* Nottingham Univ. (BSc Eng). Electricity Dept, Hull Corp., 1946; joined nationalised electricity supply industry, 1948, and held various appts; Supt, Bradwell Nuclear Power Stn, 1958; Asst Reg. Dir, NW Region, 1962; Dep. Reg. Dir, Mids Region, 1967; Dir-Gen., SE Region, 1970; Mem. CEGB, 1972–77; part-time Mem., UKAEA, 1972–77. *Recreations:* swimming, golf, walking. *Address:* Torness, 5 The Mount Drive, Reigate, Surrey RH2 0EZ. *T:* Reigate (0737) 244996.

PEDERSEN, (Knud) George, PhD; FCCT; FRSA; President, The University of Western Ontario, since 1985; *b* 13 June 1931; *s* of Hjalmar Nielsen Pedersen and Anna Marie (*nee* Jensen); *m* 1st, 1953, Joan Elaine Vanderwarker (*d* 1988); one *s* one *d*; 2nd, 1988, Penny Ann Jones. *Educ:* Vancouver Normal Sch. (Dip. in Teaching 1952); Univ. of BC (BA History and Geography, 1959); Univ. of Washington (MA 1964); Univ. of Chicago (PhD 1969). FCCT 1977; FRSA 1983. Schools in North Vancouver: Teacher, Highlands Elem. Sch., 1952–56; Vice-Principal, North Star Elem. Sch., 1956–59; Principal, Carisbrooke Elem. Sch., 1959–61; Vice-Principal, Handsworth Sec. Sch., 1961–63; Principal, Balmoral Sec. Sch., 1963–65; Univ. of Chicago: Teaching Intern, 1966; Staff Associate, Midwest Admin Center, 1965–66, Res. Associate (Asst Prof.), 1966–68; Asst Prof., Ontario Inst. for Studies in Educn and Univ. of Toronto, 1968–70; Asst Prof. and Associate Dir, Midwest Admin Center, Div. of Social Sciences, Univ. of Chicago, 1970–72; Faculty of Educn, Univ. of Victoria: Associate Prof., 1972–75; Dean, 1972–75; Vice-Pres. (Academic), and Prof., Univ. of Victoria, 1975–79; Pres. and Prof., Simon Fraser Univ., 1979–83; Pres. and Prof., Univ. of British Columbia, 1983–85. Universities Council of British Columbia: Mem., Prog. Co-ordinating Cttee, 1975–78; Mem., Business Affairs Cttee, 1975–78; Mem., Long-range Planning Cttee, 1979—85. Chm., Adv. Cttee on Educnl Planning, Min. of Educn (Prov. of BC), 1977–78; Member: Jt Bd of Teacher Educn, Prov. of BC, 1972–75; Planning Cttee, Canadian Teachers' Fedn, 1974; Planning Cttee, 1973–74, and Bd of Dirs, 1974–75 and 1979–80, BC Council for Leadership in Educn; Interior Univ. Progs Bd, Min. of Educn, 1977–78. Member, Board of Directors: Assoc. of Univs and Colls of Canada, 1979–84 (Mem., Adv. Cttee, Office of Internat. Develt, 1979–83); Inter-American Orgn for Higher Educn, 1979–85; Public Employers' Council of BC, 1979–84; Vancouver Bd of Trade, 1983–85; Pulp and Paper Res. Inst. of Canada, 1983–85; President: N Vancouver Teachers' Assoc., 1962–63; N Vancouver Principals' and Vice-Principals' Assoc., 1963–64; Sec.-Treasurer, Canadian Assoc. of Deans and Directors of Educn, 1972–73 and 1973–74. Member: Amer. Educnl Res. Assoc., 1965–; National Soc. for Study of Educn, 1965–; Canadian Assoc. of Sch. Administrators, 1968–; Canadian Educn Assoc., 1968–; Canadian Educnl Researchers' Assoc., 1968–; Canadian Soc. for Study of Educn, 1968–; Internat. Council on Educn for Teaching, 1968–; Canadian Bureau for Internat. Educn, 1970–; Canadian Foundn for Econ. Educn, 1970–; Canadian Soc. for Study of Higher Educn, 1975–; Inst. of Public Admin. of Canada, 1976–; Internat. Assoc. of Univ. Presidents, 1979–; Assoc. of Commonwealth Univs, 1979–; Comparative and Internat. Educn Soc., 1980–; Assoc. for Advancement of Scandinavian Studies in Canada, 1981–; Bd of Dirs, Corporate and Higher Educn Forum, 1988–. Member: BoT, Vancouver, 1983–85; Nat. Council, Canadian Human Rights Foundn, 1984–. Mem., Bd of Dirs, MacMillan Bloedel Ltd, 1984–86. Member, Board of Governors: Arts, Sciences and Technol. Centre, 1980–85; Leon and Thea Koerner Foundn, 1981–85; Mem., Bd of Trustees, Discovery Foundn, 1980–85. *Publications:* The Itinerant Schoolmaster: a socio-economic analysis of teacher turnover, 1973; chapters in books on educn; articles in Administrator's Notebook (Univ. of Chicago), Selected Articles for Elem. Sch. Prinicipals, Res. in Educn, Educn and Urban Soc., Educn Canada, Teacher Educn, Resources in Educn, Elem. Sch. Jl, Jl of Educnl Admin, and Canadian Jl of Univ. Continuing Educn; book reviews; proc. of confs and symposia; governmental and institutional studies and reports. *Address:* President's Office, Room 113, Stevenson-Lawson Building, The University of Western Ontario, London, Ontario N6A 5B8, Canada. *T:* (519) 661–3106; (home) Gibbons Lodge, 1836 Richmond Street, London, Ontario N6A 4B6, Canada. *T:* (519) 433–5062. *Clubs:* London Hunt and Country, London, University (London, Ont.); University (Toronto).

PEDLEY, Alan Sydney, DFC 1946; Lord Mayor of Leeds, 1975–1976; District Insurance Manager, 1974–82, retired; *b* 16 Aug. 1917; *s* of Herbert Leonard Pedley and Edith Mary (*née* Skipsey); *m* 1st, 1949, Evelyn Anderson (*née* Scott) (*d* 1977); 2nd, 1981, Shirley Elizabeth, *widow* of Reg Howard. *Educ:* Leeds Modern Sch. Entered Insurance, 1934; retd (Commercial Union), 1971; joined Barclays Insurance Services Co. Ltd, 1971. Member: Leeds City Council, 1951–81; W Yorkshire Metropolitan CC, 1973–81; Dep. Lord Mayor, 1971–72. FCII 1949. *Recreations:* cricket, Association football, Rugby League, music, theatre, the Arts, after dinner speaking. *Address:* Whitelea, 8 Bentcliffe Close, Leeds LS17 6QT. *T:* Leeds (0532) 685424. *Club:* Leeds Taverners.

PEDLEY, Rev. (Geoffrey) Stephen; Chaplain to the Queen, since 1984; Rector of Whickham, since 1988; *b* 13 Sept. 1940; *s* of Geoffrey Heber Knight and Muriel Pedley; *m* 1970, Mary Frances Macdonald; two *s* one *d*. *Educ:* Marlborough College; Queens' College, Cambridge (MA); Cuddesdon Theological College. Curate: Liverpool Parish Church, 1966; Holy Trinity, Coventry, 1969; Rector of Kitwe, Zambia, 1971–77; Vicar of St Peter's, Stockton, 1977–88. *Recreations:* architecture, English literature, travel. *Address:* The Rectory, Church Chare, Whickham, Newcastle upon Tyne NE16 4SH. *T:* 091–488 7397.

PEDLEY, Stephen; *see* Pedley, G. S.

PEEBLES, Prof. Phillip James Edwin, FRS 1982; Professor of Physics, since 1965, and Albert Einstein Professor of Science, since 1984, Princeton University; *b* Winnipeg, 25 April 1935; *s* of Andrew Charles Peebles and Ada Marian (*née* Green); *m* 1958, Jean Alison Peebles; three *d*. *Educ:* Univ. of Manitoba (BSc 1958); Princeton Univ. (Ma 1959; PhD 1962). Member: Amer. Phys. Soc.; Amer. Astron. Soc.; AAAS; Amer. Acad. of Arts and Scis; Internat. Astron. Union. Hon. DSc: Univ. of Toronto, 1986; Univ. of Chicago, 1986. *Publications:* Physical Cosmology, 1971; The Large Scale Structure of the Universe, 1979; (ed jtly) Objects of High Redshift, 1980. *Address:* 24 Markham Road, Princeton, NJ 08540, USA; Joseph Henry Laboratories, Physics Department, Princeton University, Princeton, NJ 08544, USA.

PEECH, Alan James; *b* 24 August 1905; *s* of late Albert Orlando Peech; *m* 1948, Betty Leese; no *c*. *Educ:* Wellington College; Magdalen College, Oxford (BA). Former Governor, Wellington College, retd 1975. Independent Chm., Cement Makers' Fedn, 1970–76; former Dep. Chm., Steetley Co. Ltd, retd 1976; Pres., British Iron and Steel Fedn, Jan.-June 1967; Jt Man. Dir, United Steel Cos Ltd, 1962–67, Chm., 1962–71; a Dep. Chm., BSC, 1967–70; Man. Dir, Midland Gp BSC, 1967–70. Hon. LLD Sheffield, 1966. *Recreations:* fishing and shooting. *Address:* High House, Blyth, Worksop, Notts S81 8HG. *T:* Blyth (090976) 255. *Club:* MCC.

PEECH, Neil Malcolm; President for life, Steetley PLC, since 1976 (Managing Director, 1935–68, Chairman, 1935–76); *b* 27 Jan. 1908; *s* of Albert Orlando Peech; *m* 1932, Margaret Josephine, *d* of late R. C. Smallwood, CBE, Worplesdon, Surrey; one *s* one *d*. *Educ:* Wellington College; Magdalen College, Oxford. Developed the production of magnesia from seawater and dolomite, 1939. Consul for Sweden, 1974–76 (Vice Consul, 1949–74). Underwriting member of Lloyd's, 1950–69; Director, Sheepbridge Engineering Ltd, 1949–79, and Albright & Wilson Ltd, 1958–79. Chairman, Ministry of Power Solid Smokeless Fuel Committee, 1959. High Sheriff of Yorkshire, 1959. Chevalier, Order of Vasa, Sweden, 1963. *Recreations:* fishing and shooting. *Address:* Park House, Firbeck, Worksop, Notts S81 8JW. *T:* Worksop (0909) 730338. *Club:* MCC.

PEEK, Sir Francis (Henry Grenville), 4th Bt, *cr* 1874; *b* 16 Sept. 1915; *o s* of 3rd Bt and Edwine Warner (*d* 1959), *d* of late W. H. Thornburgh, St Louis, USA; *S* father, 1927; *m* 1st, 1942, Ann (marr. diss., 1949), *d* of late Captain Gordon Duff and *widow* of Sir Charles Mappin, Bt (she *m* 1951, Sir William Rootes, later 1st Baron Rootes); 2nd, Marilyn (marr. diss., 1967; she *m* 1967, Peter Quennell), *d* of Dr Norman Kerr, London and Bahamas; one *s* decd; 3rd, Mrs Caroline Kirkwood, *d* of late Sir Robert Kirkwood, KCMG, OJ. *Educ:* Eton; Trinity College, Cambridge. ADC to Governor of Bahamas, 1938–39; served Irish Guards, 1939–46. *Heir: cousin* William Grenville Peek [*b* 15 Dec. 1919; *m* 1950, Lucy Jane, *d* of late Major Edward Dorrien-Smith, DSO; one *s* three *d*]. *Address:* Le Schuylkill, Boulevard de Suisse, Monte Carlo; Apartado Postal 5–203, Cuernavaca, Morelos 62051, Mexico. *Club:* White's.

PEEK, Vice-Adm. Sir Richard (Innes), KBE 1972 (OBE 1944); CB 1971; DSC 1945; pastoralist; *b* 30 July 1914; 2nd *s* of late James Norman and Kate Ethel Peek; *m* 1943, Margaret Seinor (*née* Kendall) (*d* 1946); one *s*; *m* 1952, Mary Catherine Tilley (*née* Stops); two *d*. *Educ:* Royal Australian Naval College. Joined RAN, 1928; served War of 1939–45 in HMS Revenge, HMAS Cerberus, Hobart, Australia, Navy Office; Korean War Service in HMAS Tobruk, 1951; Flag Officer Comdg HMA Fleet, 1967–68; Chief of Naval Staff, Australia, 1970–73. Legion of Merit (US), 1951. *Recreations:* gardening, golf. *Address:* Rothlyn, RMB, Monaro Highway, via Cooma, NSW 2630, Australia. *Clubs:* Royal Automobile (Sydney); Royal Commonwealth Society (Canberra).

PEEL, family name of **Earl Peel.**

PEEL, 3rd Earl *cr* 1929; **William James Robert Peel;** Bt 1800; Viscount Peel, 1895; Viscount Clanfield, 1929; *b* 3 Oct. 1947; *s* of 2nd Earl Peel and Kathleen (*d* 1972), *d* of Michael McGrath; *S* father, 1969; *m* 1st, 1973, Veronica Naomi Livingston (marr. diss. 1987), *d* of Alastair Timpson; one *s* one *d*; 2nd, 1989, Hon. Mrs Charlotte Hambro, *yr d* of Baron Soames, PC, GCMG, GCVO, CH, CBE and of Lady Soames, *qv*. *Educ:* Ampleforth; University of Tours; Cirencester Agric. Coll. Mem., Nature Conservancy Council for England, 1991–. *Heir: s* Viscount Clanfield, *qv*. *Address:* Gunnerside Lodge, Richmond, North Yorks. *Club:* Turf.

PEEL, David Alexander Robert; Under Secretary, Director of Administration Resources, Department of the Environment, since 1990; *b* 12 Nov. 1940; *s* of late Maj. Robert Edmund Peel and of Sheila Mary (*née* Slattery); *m* 1971, Patricia Muriel Essery; two *s*. *Educ:* St Edmund's Coll., Ware; University Coll., Oxford. Building labourer, New Scotland Yard develt, 1963; joined MoT, 1964; Private Sec. to Minister of State, 1967; Principal, 1968; DoE, 1970; First Sec., UK Perm. Repn to EC, Brussels, 1972; Private Sec. to Minister for Transport, 1975; Asst Sec., Depts of Transport and the Environment, 1976–90: Nat. Roads Prog. and Highway Policy, 1982; Okehampton Bypass (Confirmation of Orders) Act, 1985; Interdeptl Review on Using Private Enterprise in Govt, 1986; Office Services, 1987–90. *Recreations:* allotment gardening, music, baroque architecture. *Address:* Department of the Environment, 2 Marsham Street, SW1P 3EB. *T:* 071–276 3544.

PEEL, Prof. Edwin Arthur, DLit; Professor of Education, University of Birmingham, 1950–78, and Chairman of School of Education, 1965–70; *b* 11 March 1911; *s* of late Arthur Peel and Mary Ann Miller; *m* 1939, Nora Kathleen Yeadon (*d* 1988); two *s* two *d*. *Educ:* Prince Henry's Grammar School, Otley, Yorks; Leeds University; London University. Teaching in various London Schools, 1933–38; LCC School of Building, 1938–41; MA London, 1938; Ministry of Supply, 1941–45; PhD London 1945; Part-time Lecturer London Univ. Institute of Education, 1945; Lecturer in Education, King's College, Newcastle, 1946; Reader in Psychology, Durham University, 1946–48; Professor of Educational Psychology, University of Durham, 1948–50. President British Psychological Society 1961–62. DLit, London, 1961. *Publications:* The Psychological Basis of Education, 1956; The Pupil's Thinking, 1960; The Nature of Adolescent Judgment, 1971; various in leading British and foreign journals of psychology; Editor and contrib., Educational Review. *Recreation:* painting. *Address:* 47 Innage Road, Birmingham B31 2DY. *T:* 021–475 2820.

See also J. D. Y. Peel.

PEEL, Jack Armitage, CBE 1972; DL; industrial relations consultant; *b* 8 Jan. 1921; *s* of Martha and George Henry Peel; *m* 1950, Dorothy Mabel Dobson; one *s* one *d*. *Educ:* elem. and modern sch.; Ruskin Coll., Oxford (Schol., Social Sci.), 1948–49. Railwayman, 1936–47. National Union of Dyers, Bleachers and Textile Workers: full-time Officer, 1950; Asst Gen.-Sec., 1957–66, Gen. Sec., 1966–73; Mem. Gen. Council of TUC, 1966–72; Dir, Industrial Relations, in the Social Affairs Directorate, EEC, 1973–79, Chief Adviser, 1979–81. Part-time Director: British Wool Marketing Board, 1968–73; NCB, 1969–73. Served on several courts of inquiry, incl. Rochdale Cttee of Inquiry into Merchant Navy; Special Adviser to Sec. of State for Transport on long term industrial relns strategy, May 1983 - Jan. 1984. Senior Vis. Fellow in Industrial Relns, Bradford Univ., 1984–. Hon. MA Bradford, 1979. DL West Yorks, 1971; JP Bradford, 1960–72. *Publications:* The Real Power Game, 1979; What Makes Man Work?, 1989; Europe—the wider perspective, 1990. *Recreations:* cricket, painting, guitar music, swimming. *Address:* Timberleigh, 39 Old Newbridge Hill, Bath, Avon BA1 3LU. *T:* Bath (0225) 423959.

PEEL, Sir John; *see* Peel, Sir W. J.

PEEL, John; *see* Ravenscroft, J. R. P.

PEEL, Prof. John David Yeadon, FBA 1991; Professor of Anthropology and Sociology, with reference to Africa, School of Oriental and African Studies, University of London, since 1989; *b* 13 Nov. 1941; *e s* of Prof. Edwin Arthur Peel, *qv*; *m* 1969, Jennifer Christine

Ferial, *d* of K. N. Pare, Leicester; three *s*. *Educ:* King Edward's Sch., Birmingham; Balliol Coll., Oxford (Scholar; BA 1963, MA 1966); LSE (PhD 1966); DLit London 1985. Asst Lectr, then Lectr in Sociology, Nottingham Univ., 1965–70; Lectr in Sociology, LSE, 1970–73; Charles Booth Prof. of Sociology, 1975–89, Dean, Faculty of Social and Envmtl Studies, 1985–88, Univ. of Liverpool. Vis. Reader in Sociology and Anthropology, Univ of Ife, Nigeria, 1973–75; Vis. Prof. in Anthropology and Sociology, Univ. of Chicago, 1982–83. Associate, Inst. of Develt Studies, 1973–; Mem. Council, African Studies Assoc. of UK, 1978–81. Editor, Africa, and Officer, Internat African Inst., 1979–86; Gen. Editor, Internat. African Library, 1986–; Advising Editor, African Studies Series, 1986–. Amaury Talbot Prize for African Anthropology, 1983; Herskovits Award, African Studies Assoc., USA, 1984. *Publications:* Aladura: a religious movement among the Yoruba, 1968; Herbert Spencer: the evolution of a sociologist, 1971; (ed) Herbert Spencer on Social Evolution, 1972; Ijeshas and Nigerians, 1983; articles in anthropological, sociological and Africanist jls. *Recreations:* gardening, old churches. *Address:* 23 Mount Road, Upton, Wirral, Merseyside L49 6JA. *T:* 051–678 6783.

PEEL, Sir John (Harold), KCVO 1960; MA, BM, BCh; FRCP 1971; FRCS 1933; FRCOG 1944; Surgeon-Gynæcologist to the Queen, 1961–73; Consulting Obstetric and Gynæcological Surgeon, King's College Hospital, since 1969; Emeritus Consulting Gynæcologist, Princess Beatrice Hospital, since 1965; *b* 10 December 1904; *s* of Rev. J. E. Peel; *m* 1st, 1936, Muriel Elaine Pellow; one *d*; *m* 2nd, 1947, Freda Margaret Mellish; *Educ:* Manchester Grammar Sch.; Queen's Coll., Oxford. MA, BM, BCh Oxon 1932. King's College Hospital Med. Sch., qualified 1930; MRCS, LRCP. Obstetric and Gynæcological Surgeon: King's Coll. Hosp., 1936–69; Princess Beatrice Hosp., 1937–65; Queen Victoria Hosp., East Grinstead, 1941–69; Surgeon EMS, 1939–45. Director of Clinical Studies, King's College Hospital Medical School, 1948–67. Mem., Economic and Social Cttee, EEC, 1973–78. Litchfield Lecturer, Oxford University, 1961 and 1969; Sir Kadar Nath Das Lecturer, Bengal O and G Soc., 1962; Sir A. Mudaliar Lecturer, Madras Univ., 1962; Vis. Prof., Cape Town Univ., 1963; Travelling Prof., S African Council, RCOG, 1968. Past Examiner, Universities of Oxford, Cambridge, London, Liverpool, Bristol, Glasgow, Newcastle, Nat. Univ. of Ireland, Birmingham, Dundee, Sheffield, Conjoint Board, RCOG and CMB. Nuffield visitor to Colonies, 1950 and 1953. President, RCOG, 1966–69 (Hon. Treasurer, 1959–66, Councillor, 1955–); President: Internat. Fedn of Obstetrics and Gynæcology, 1970–73; Chelsea Clinical Society, 1960; BMA 1970 (Chm., Bd of Science and Educn, 1972–76); Family Planning Assoc., 1971–74; Chm., DHSS Cttees of Enquiry: Domiciliary Midwifery and Bed Needs, 1971; The Use of Fetus and Fetal Material for Research, 1972. FKC 1980; Hon. Fellow: American Association of Obstetricians and Gynæcologists, 1962 (Joseph Price Oration, 1961); Edinburgh Obstetrical Soc., 1971; RSM, 1973; Hon. Member: Canadian Assoc. of O and G, 1955; Italian Assoc O and G, 1960; Hon. Treas., GMC, 1972–75; Hon. FRCS (Canada), 1967; Hon. FCOG (SA), 1968; Hon. MMSA 1970; Hon. FACS 1970; Hon. FACOG 1971; Hon. Fellow, American Gynæcological Soc., 1974. Hon. DSc Birmingham, 1972; Hon. DM Southampton, 1974; Hon. DCh Newcastle, 1980. *Publications:* Textbook of Gynæcology, 1943; Lives of the Fellows of Royal College of Obstetricians and Gynaecologists 1929–69, 1976; Biography of William Blain-Bell, 1986; numerous contributions to Medical Journals. *Recreations:* fishing, gardening. *Address:* Flat 2, The Old House, 3 Rougemont Close, Salisbury, Wilts SP1 1LY. *Club:* Naval and Military.

PEEL, Jonathan Sidney, MC 1957; Vice Lord-Lieutenant of Norfolk, since 1981; Director, Norwich Union Insurance Group, since 1973; *b* 21 June 1937; *s* of Major D. A. Peel (killed in action 1944) and Hon. Mrs David Peel (*née* Vanneck); *m* 1965, Jean Fulton Barnett, *d* of Air Chief Marshal Sir Denis Barnett, *qv*; one *s* four *d*. *Educ:* Norwich Sch.; Eton; St John's Coll., Cambridge (BA Land Economy; MA 1970). Commnd, Rifle Bde, Royal Green Jackets, 1956; served Malaya, 1956–57; UN forces, Congo (Zaire), 1960–61; Cyprus, 1962–63; resigned, 1966. Chm., Pleasureworld plc, 1986–89. Vice Pres., Norfolk Naturalists Trust, 1984–; National Trust: Mem. Exec. Cttee, 1982–; Mem. Council, 1984–; Chm., Cttee for East Anglia, 1981–90; Chm., Properties Cttee, 1990–. Chairman: Norfolk Police Authority, 1983–89; The Broads Authority, 1985–; Norwich Sch., 1985–; How Hill Trust, 1987–. Mem., Norfolk CC, 1973– (Chm., Planning and Transportation Cttee, 1990–). JP North Walsham, 1973–86. High Sheriff, Norfolk, 1984. *Publication:* (with M. J. Sayer) Towards a Rural Policy for Norfolk, 1973. *Recreations:* forestry, music. *Address:* Barton Hall, Barton Turf, Norwich NR12 8AU. *T:* Smallburgh (069260) 250, and 298. *Clubs:* Boodle's; Norfolk (Norwich).

PEEL, Sir (William) John, Kt 1973; *b* 16 June 1912; *s* of late Sir William Peel, KCMG, KBE, and Violet Mary Drake, *er d* of W. D. Laing; *m* 1936, Rosemary Mia Minka, *er d* of Robert Readhead; one *s* three *d*. *Educ:* Wellington College; Queens' College, Cambridge. Colonial Administrative Service, 1933–51; on active service, 1941–45; British Resident, Brunei, 1946–48; Res. Comr, Gilbert and Ellice Is Colony, 1949–51. Personal Asst to Man. Dirs of Rugby Portland Cement Co. Ltd, 1952–54. Contested (C) Meriden Division of Warwickshire, 1955; MP (C) Leicester SE, 1957–Feb. 1974; Parliamentary Private Secretary to: Economic Secretary to the Treasury, 1958–59; Minister of State, Board of Trade, 1959–60; Asst Govt Whip (unpaid), 1960–61; a Lord Comr of the Treasury, Nov. 1961–Oct. 1964. Parly Delegate to: Assemblies of Council of Europe, 1961–74; WEU 1961–74 (Vice-Pres., 1967, Pres. 1972, Chm., Defence and Armaments Cttee, 1970–72, WEU); N Atlantic Assembly, 1959–74 (Leader, 1970–74; Pres., N Atlantic Assembly, Nov. 1972); Mem., British Delegn to European Parlt, Strasbourg, 1973–74; Hon. Dir, Cons. Party Internat. Office, 1975–76. Member Council: Victoria League for Commonwealth Friendship, 1974–83 (Dep. Chm., 1976–81; Chm., 1982–83; Dep. Pres. and Mem., Chairman's Adv. Cttee, 1983–); British Atlantic Cttee; Mem. Central Council, Royal Over-Seas League, 1980–86; Chairman: Hospitality and Branches Cttee of Victoria League, 1974–78, Hospitality Cttee, 1978–81; Overseas Students Adv. Cttee, 1980–81; Jt Standing Cttee of Victoria League and Royal Commonwealth Soc., 1975–83; Westminster for Europe Branch, European Movement, 1974–77. Mem. Ct of Assistants, Framework Knitters' Co. (Master, 1983). Dato Seri Laila Jasa Brunei 1969; Dato Setia Negara Brunei 1971. *Recreations:* varied. *Address:* 51 Cambridge Street, SW1V 4PR. *T:* 071–834 8762. *Clubs:* Carlton, Hurlingham; Hawks (Cambridge).

PEELER, Joseph; Regional Director for the South-East Region, Departments of the Environment and Transport, and Chairman of Regional Board, 1979–86, retired; *b* 22 April 1930; *s* of late Edward Francis Peeler and Marjorie Cynthia Peeler; *m* 1958, Diana Helen (*née* Wynne); three *s* one *d*. *Educ:* King Edward VI Grammar Sch., Stratford-on-Avon; Wimbledon Coll.; Jesus Coll., Oxford (Scholar, 1948; BA 1st Cl. Hons Modern History, 1951; MA 1955). RAF, 1951–53. Entered Civil Service (Min. of Transport and Civil Aviation), 1953; Private Sec. to Parly Sec., 1956–58; Principal, 1958; seconded to Home Office, 1964–66; Asst Sec., 1966; Under Sec., 1978. Chm., Burford and Dist Soc., 1990–. *Recreations:* history, crosswords, bridge, walking. *Address:* Cocklands, Fulbrook, Burford, Oxon OX8 4BE. *T:* Burford (0993) 82612.

PEERS, Most Rev. Michael Geoffrey; Primate of the Anglican Church of Canada, since 1986; *b* 31 July 1934; *s* of Geoffrey Hugh Peers and Dorothy Enid Mantle; *m* 1963, Dorothy Elizabeth Bradley; two *s* one *d*. *Educ:* University of British Columbia (BA Hons); Universität Heidelberg (Zert. Dolm.-Interpreter's Certificate); Trinity Coll., Toronto (LTh). Deacon 1959, priest 1960; Curate: St Thomas', Ottawa, 1959–61; Trinity, Ottawa, 1961–65; University Chaplain, Diocese of Ottawa, 1961–66; Rector: St Bede's, Winnipeg, 1966–72; St Martin's, Winnipeg, with St Paul's Middlechurch, 1972–74; Archdeacon of Winnipeg, 1969–74; Rector, St Paul's Cathedral, Regina, 1974–77; Dean of Qu'Appelle, 1974–77; Bishop of Qu'Appelle, 1977–82; Archbishop of Qu'Appelle and Metropolitan of Rupert's Land, 1982–86. Hon. DD: Trinity Coll., Toronto, 1978; St John's Coll., Winnipeg, 1981; Wycliffe Coll., Toronto, 1987; Univ. of Kent, 1988; Montreal Dio. Coll., 1989; Coll. of Emmanuel and St Chad, Saskatoon, 1990. *Address:* 600 Jarvis Street, Toronto, Ontario M4Y 2J6, Canada. *T:* 416–924–9192.

PEET, Ronald Hugh, CBE 1974; Chairman: Stockley Plc, 1984–87; PWS Holdings plc, 1987–88; *b* 12 July 1925; *s* of Henry Leonard and Stella Peet; *m* 1st, 1949, Winifred Joy Adamson (*d* 1979); two *s* two *d*; 2nd, 1981, Lynette Judy Burgess Kinsella. *Educ:* Doncaster Grammar Sch.; Queen's Coll., Oxford (MA). Served in HM Forces, Captain RA, 1944–47. Legal and General Assurance Society Limited: joined 1952; emigrated to Australia, 1955; Sec., Australian Branch, 1955–59; Asst Life Manager, 1959–65; Manager and Actuary for Australia, 1965–69; returned to UK as General Manager (Ops), 1969; Dir, 1969–84; Chief Exec., 1972–84; Chm., 1980–84; Dir and Chief Exec., Legal & General Gp Plc, 1980–84. Chm., Aviation & General Insurance Co. Ltd, 1978–80; Director: AMEC Plc, 1984–; Howard Gp plc, 1985–86. Director: City Arts Trust Ltd, 1976–90 (Chm., 1980–87); Royal Philharmonic Orchestra Ltd, 1977–88; English National Opera, 1978–84, 1985–. Chm., British Insurance Assoc., 1978–79. FIA. *Recreations:* music, opera. *Address:* 9 Marlowe Court, Petyward, SW3 3PD. *Clubs:* Hurlingham, City of London.

PEGG, Michael Anstice, PhD; University Librarian and Director, John Rylands University Library, University of Manchester, 1981–90; *b* 3 Sept. 1931; *s* of Benjamin and Rose Pegg; *m* 1st, 1955, Jean Williams; three *s*; 2nd, 1986, Margaret Rae. *Educ:* Burton-on-Trent Grammar Sch.; Univ. of Southampton. BA (London); PhD (Southampton); MA (Manchester) 1985. Captain, Royal Army Education Corps, Educn Officer, SHAPE, Paris, 1958–61; Asst Keeper, Nat. Library of Scotland, Edinburgh, 1961–67; Sec. and Estabt Officer, Nat. Library of Scotland, Edinburgh, 1967–76; Librarian, Univ. of Birmingham, 1976–80. Vis Fellow, Beinecke Library, Yale Univ., 1989. Member: British Library Bd, 1981–84; Standing Conference of Nat. and Univ. Libraries' Council, 1981–83. *Publications:* Les Divers Rapports d'Eustorg de Beaulieu (édn critique), 1964 (Geneva); Catalogue of German Reformation Pamphlets in Libraries of Great Britain and Ireland, 1973 (Baden Baden); Catalogue of Sixteenth-century German Pamphlets in Collections in France and England, 1977 (Baden Baden); Catalogue of Reformation Pamphlets in Swiss Libraries, 1983; Catalogue of Sixteenth-century German and Dutch books in the Royal Library Copenhagen, 1989; occasional papers to learned jls. *Recreations:* travel, reading, railway modelling. *Address:* c/o John Rylands University Library, University of Manchester, Oxford Road, Manchester M13 9PP.

PEGGIE, Robert Galloway Emslie, CBE 1986; Commissioner for Local Administration (Ombudsman) in Scotland, since 1986; *b* 5 Jan. 1929; *s* of John and Euphemia Peggie; *m* 1955, Christine Jeanette Simpson; one *s* one *d*. *Educ:* Lasswade High Sch. Certified accountant; Accountancy apprenticeship, 1946–52; Accountant in industry, 1952–57; Public Service, Edinburgh City, 1957–74; Chief Exec., Lothian Regl Council, 1974–86. Mem., Gen. Convocation and Court, Heriot-Watt Univ., 1988–. (Convener, Finance Cttee, 1989–). Governor, Edinburgh Coll. of Art, 1989–. *Recreation:* golf. *Address:* 54 Liberton Drive, Edinburgh EH16 6NW. *T:* 031–664 1631.

PEGLER, Alfred Ernest, OBE 1978; DL; Councillor: Crawley Borough Council, since 1956; West Sussex County Council, since 1959; *b* 18 Jan. 1924; *s* of Frank Walter James Pegler and Violet Maud Pegler; *m* 1944, E. E. McDonald; one *s* one *d*. *Educ:* Cork Street Sch., Peckham; Oliver Goldsmith Sch., Peckham. Engrg apprentice, 1938–42; served War, RAF Air Crew, 1942–46; toolmaker, 1946–62; Civil Service Engrg Inspector, 1963–81. Chm., Crawley Council, 1959 and 1966; Chm. Housing Cttee, 1971–77. Leader, Labour Gp, W Sussex CC, 1977–. Mem., Crawley Cttee, New Towns Commn, 1962– (Chm., 1974–). Mayor, Crawley Borough Council, 1982–83, 1983–84. Mem., Sussex Police Authority, 1973–77. Parly Candidate (Labour): Horsham, 1959 and 1964; Gloucester, Feb. 1974. DL West Sussex, 1982. *Recreations:* gardening, politics. *Address:* 7 Priors Walk, Three Bridges, Crawley, West Sussex RH10 1NX. *T:* Crawley (0293) 27330.

PEGLER, James Basil Holmes, TD; BA; FIA, FSS, FIS, FIMA; Professor of Actuarial Science, City University, 1976–79, Visiting Professor, 1979–86; *b* 6 Aug. 1912; *s* of late Harold Holmes Pegler and late Dorothy Cecil (*née* Francis); *m* 1937, Enid Margaret Dell; one *s* three *d*. *Educ:* Charterhouse; Open Univ. Joined Clerical, Medical and Gen. Life Assce Soc., 1931; Gen. Man. and Actuary, 1950–69; Man. Dir, 1970–75; non-exec. Dir, 1975–83. War service, Queen's Royal Regt and RA, 1939–45 (Major). Inst. of Actuaries: Fellow, 1939; Hon. Sec., 1955–57; Pres., 1968–70. Chm., Life Offices' Assoc., 1959–61; Chm., Life Gp of Comité Européen des Assurances, 1964–70. *Publications:* contribs to Jl Inst. Actuaries. *Recreations:* mathematics, languages, lawn tennis, tap dancing. *Address:* Dormers, 28 Deepdene Wood, Dorking, Surrey RH5 4BQ. *T:* Dorking (0306) 885955. *Club:* Army and Navy.

PEIERLS, Sir Rudolf (Ernst), Kt 1968; CBE 1946; FRS 1945; MA Cantab; DSc Manchester, DPhil Leipzig; Wykeham Professor of Physics, Oxford University, and Fellow, New College, Oxford, 1963–74, now Emeritus Fellow (Hon. Fellow 1980); Professor of Physics (part-time), University of Washington, Seattle, 1974–77; *b* Berlin, 5 June 1907; *s* of H. Peierls; *m* 1931, Eugenia, *d* of late N. Kannegiesser (*d* 1986); one *s* three *d*. *Educ:* Humboldt School, Oberschöneweide, Berlin; Universities of Berlin, Munich, Leipzig. Assistant, Federal Institute of Technology, Zürich, 1929–32; Rockefeller Fellow, 1932–33; Honorary Research Fellow, Manchester University, 1933–35; Assistant-in-Research, Royal Society Mond Laboratory, 1935–37; Professor of Mathematical Physics (formerly Applied Mathematics), University of Birmingham, 1937–63; worked on Atomic Energy Project in Birmingham, 1940–43, in USA, 1943–46. Royal Society: Royal Medal, 1959; Copley Medal, 1986; Lorentz Medal of Royal Netherlands Academy of Sciences, 1962; Max Planck Medal, Assoc. of German Physical Societies, 1963; Guthrie Medal, IPPS, 1968; first British recipient of Enrico Fermi Award, US Dept of Energy, 1980. Hon. FInstP 1973 (Paul Dirac Medal, 1991). Hon. DSc: Liverpool, 1960; Birmingham, 1967; Edinburgh, 1969; Sussex, 1978; Chicago, 1981; Coimbra, 1988. Foreign Hon. Mem., American Academy of Arts and Sciences, 1962; Hon. Associate, College of Advanced Technology, Birmingham, 1963; Foreign Associate: Nat. Acad. of Sciences, USA, 1970; French Acad. of Sciences, 1984; Hon. Mem., French Phys. Soc., 1979; Foreign Member: Royal Danish Acad., 1980; USSR Acad. of Sciences, 1988; Mem., Leopoldina Acad., E Germany, 1981; Corresponding Member: Yugoslav Acad. of Arts and Sciences, 1983; Lisbon Academy of Sciences, 1988. *Publications:* Quantum Theory of Solids, 1955; The Laws of Nature, 1955; Surprises in Theoretical Physics, 1979; Bird of Passage, 1985; papers on Quantum Theory. *Address:* 2B Northmoor Road, Oxford OX2 6UP; Nuclear Physics Laboratory, Keble Road, Oxford. *Club:* Athenæum.

PEIRCE, Rev. Canon (John) Martin; Canon Residentiary of Christ Church, Oxford, since 1987, and Oxford Diocesan Director of Ordinands, since 1985; *b* 9 July 1936; *s* of Martin Westley and Winifred Mary Peirce; *m* 1968, Rosemary Susan Milne; two *s*. *Educ:* Brentwood Sch.; Jesus Coll., Cambridge; Westcott House, Cambridge. MA Cantab. Served Royal Air Force, 1954–56. Teacher, St Stephen's Coll., Hong Kong, 1960–64; Curate, St John Baptist, Croydon, 1966–70; Team Vicar, St Columba, Fareham, 1970–76; Team Rector, Langley, Slough, 1976–85. *Recreations:* walking, gardening. *Address:* 70 Yarnells Hill, Oxford OX2 9BG. *T:* Oxford (0865) 721330.

PEIRSE, Sir Henry G. de la P. B.; *see* Beresford-Peirse.

PEIRSE, Air Vice-Marshal Sir Richard (Charles Fairfax), KCVO 1988; CB 1984; Gentleman Usher of the Scarlet Rod, Order of the Bath, since 1990; *b* 16 March 1931; *s* of late Air Chief Marshal Sir Richard Peirse, KCB, DSO, AFC and late Lady Peirse; *m* 1st, 1955, Karalie Grace Cox (marr. diss. 1963); two *d*; 2nd, 1963, Deirdre Mary O'Donovan (*d* 1976); (one *s* decd); 3rd, 1977, Anna Jill Margaret Long (*née* Latey). *Educ:* Bradfield Coll.; RAF Coll., Cranwell. Commnd 1952; 2nd TAF No 266 Sqdn and HQ 2 Gp, 1952; Flying Instructor, Cranwell, 1956; Air Staff No 23 Gp, 1960; Staff Coll., 1962; Flt Comdr No 39 Sqdn and OC Ops Wg, Luqa, Malta, 1963; Air Sec.'s Dept, 1965; jssc 1968; OC No 51 Sqdn, 1968; Dep. Captain, The Queen's Flight, 1969; RCDS 1972; OC RAF Waddington, 1973; Dep. Dir, Op Requirements, 1976; Dir of Personnel (Air), 1977; Dir of Op Requirements, 1980; AOC and Comdt, RAF Coll. Cranwell, 1982; Defence Services Sec., 1985–88, retd. *Recreations:* theatre, archaeology. *Address:* The Old Mill House, Adderbury, near Banbury, Oxon OX17 3LW. *T:* Banbury (0295) 810196. *Club:* Royal Air Force.

PEIRSON, Margaret Ellen; Under Secretary, Department of Social Security (on secondment), since 1990; *b* 28 Nov. 1942; *e d* of late David Edward Herbert Peirson, CBE and of Norah Ellen Peirson (*née* Corney). *Educ:* North London Collegiate Sch.; Somerville Coll., Oxford (MA Maths); Yale Univ. Joined HM Treasury, 1965; secondment to Bank of England, 1982–84; Under Sec., 1986. *Recreations:* choral singing, theatre. *Address:* Dept of Social Security, The Adelphi, 1–11 John Adam Street, WC2N 6HT.

PELHAM, family name of **Earls of Chichester** and **Yarborough.**

PELHAM, Hugh Reginald Brentnall, PhD; FRS 1988; Member, Scientific Staff, Medical Research Council Laboratory of Molecular Biology, Cambridge, since 1981; *b* 26 Aug. 1954; *s* of late Reginald A. and of Pauline M. Pelham; *m* 1976, Alison Mary Slowe (marr. diss. 1989). *Educ:* Marlborough Coll., Wiltshire; Christ's Coll., Cambridge (MA, PhD). Research Fellow, Christ's Coll., 1978–84; Dept of Embryology, Carnegie Instn of Washington Baltimore, Md, 1979–81; Visitor, Univ. of Zürich, 1987–88. Colworth Medal, Biochemical Soc., 1988; EMBO medal, 1989; Louis Jeantet Prize for Medicine, 1991. *Publications:* papers in sci. jls on molecular and cell biology. *Address:* MRC Laboratory of Molecular Biology, Hills Road, Cambridge CB2 2QH. *T:* Cambridge (0223) 248011.

PELHAM BURN, Angus Maitland; JP; farmer; Vice-Lord-Lieutenant for Kincardineshire, since 1978; Director, Bank of Scotland, since 1977 (Director, since 1973, Chairman, since 1977, Aberdeen Local Board); Chairman and Director, Pelett Administration Ltd, since 1973; Director: Scottish Provident Institution, since 1975; Aberdeen Trust plc (formerly Aberdeen Fund Managers, then Abtrust Holdings, subseq. Aberdeen Trust Holdings), since 1985; Status Timber Systems, since 1986; Deputy Chairman, Accounts Commission, since 1987 (Member, since 1980); *b* 13 Dec. 1931; *s* of late Brig. Gen. H. Pelham Burn, CMG, DSO, and late Mrs K. E. S. Pelham Burn; *m* 1959, Anne R. Pelham Burn (*née* Forbes-Leith); four *d*. *Educ:* Harrow; N of Scotland Coll. of Agriculture. Hudson's Bay Co., 1951–58. Director: Aberdeen and Northern Marts Ltd, 1970–86 (Chm., 1974–86); Jessfield Ltd, 1970–88; Aberdeen Meat Marketing Co. Ltd, 1973–86 (Chm., 1974–86); Prime Space Design (Scotland) Ltd, 1981–87; Skeendale Ltd, 1987–88; Abtrust Scotland Investment Co., 1989–; Chairman and Director: MacRobert Farms (Douneside) Ltd, 1970–87; Taw Meat Co., 1984–86. Chm., Aberdeen Airport Consultative Cttee, 1986–. Mem. Council, Winston Churchill Meml Trust, 1984–; Dir., Aberdeen Assoc. for Prevention of Cruelty to Animals, 1975– (Chm., 1984–89). Pres., Aberdeen Br., Inst. of Marketing, 1987–90. Member: Kincardine CC, 1967–75 (Vice Convener, 1973–75); Grampian Regional Council, 1974–. Member, Queen's Body Guard for Scotland (Royal Co. of Archers), 1968–. Hon. FInstM. JP Kincardine and Deeside, 1984; DL Kincardineshire 1978. OStJ 1978. *Recreations:* fishing, vegetable gardening, photography, stalking. *Address:* Knappach, Banchory, Kincardineshire AB31 3JS. *T:* Crathes (033044) 555. *Clubs:* New (Edinburgh); Royal Northern (Aberdeen).

PELIZA, Major Robert John, OBE 1989; ED 1955; company director, since 1962; Speaker, House of Assembly, Gibraltar, since 1989; *b* 16 Nov. 1920; *s* of late Robert Peliza; *m* 1950, Irma Risso; three *s* four *d*. *Educ:* Christian Brothers' Coll., Gibraltar. Served in Gibraltar Defence Force (now Gibraltar Regt), 1939–61. Founder Mem., Integration with Britain Party (first leader), 1967; Chief Minister, 1969–72, apptd following Gen. Elections, 1969; Leader of the Opposition, 1972–73. *Recreations:* walking, painting, reading, jogging, cycling, rowing. *Address:* 203 Water Gardens, Gibraltar.

PELLEREAU, Maj.-Gen. Peter John Mitchell, MA, CEng, FIMechE, FBIM; Secretary, Association of Consulting Engineers, 1977–87; *b* Quetta, British India, 24 April 1921; *s* of late Col J. C. E. Pellereau, OBE and Mrs A. N. V. Pellereau (*née* Betham), Penshurst; *m* 1949, Rosemary, *e d* of late S. R. Garnar; two *s*. *Educ:* Wellington Coll.; Trinity Coll., Cambridge. BA 1942, MA 1957. Commnd into Royal Engrs, 1942; War Service in NW Europe, 1944–45; OC 26 Armd Engr Sqdn, RE, 1946; ptsc, psc, 1950–51; Sec., Defence Research Policy Cttee, 1960; Asst Mil. Sec., WO, 1961; CO 131 Parachute Engr Regt RE TA, 1963; Mil. Dir of Studies, RMCS, 1965; Asst Dir RE Equipment Develt, 1967; Sen. Mil. Officer, Royal Armament R&D Estabt, 1970; Vice-Pres., 1973–75, Pres., 1975–76, Ordnance Board; retired 1976. Hon. Col, RE (Vol.) (Explosive Ordnance Disposal), 1980–86. Liveryman: Worshipful Co. of Plumbers, 1977; Worshipful Co. of Engineers, 1984. Mem., Smeatonian Soc. of Civil Engineers, 1981–. Vice-Pres., Surrey Hockey Umpires' Assoc., 1979–85; Pres., Oxted Hockey Club, 1975–84. Mem., Wolfe Soc. Cttee, 1978–. *Recreation:* lawn tennis. *Address:* Woodmans Folly, Crockham Hill, Edenbridge, Kent. *T:* Edenbridge (0732) 866309.

PELLEW, family name of **Viscount Exmouth.**

PELLEW, Mark Edward, LVO 1980; HM Diplomatic Service; *b* 28 Aug. 1942; *s* of Comdr Anthony Pownoll Pellew, RN retd, and Margaret Julia Critchley (*née* Cookson); *m* 1965, Jill Hosford Thistlethwaite, *d* of Prof. Frank Thistlethwaite, *qv*; two *s*. *Educ:* Winchester; Trinity Coll., Oxford (BA). Entered HM Diplomatic Service, 1965; FO, 1965–67; Third Sec., Singapore, 1967–69; Second Sec., Saigon, 1969–70; FCO, 1970–76; First Sec., Rome, 1976–80; Asst Head of Personnel Ops Dept, FCO, 1981–83; Counsellor: Washington, 1983–89; on secondment to Hambros Bank, 1989–91. *Recreations:* singing, playing the horn. *Address:* c/o Foreign and Commonwealth Office, King Charles Street, SW1A 2AH. *Club:* Hurlingham.

PELLING, Anthony Adair; Director, London Region, Department of the Environment, since 1987; *b* 3 May 1934; *s* of Brian and Alice Pelling; *m* 1st, 1958, Margaret Lightfoot (*d* 1986); one *s* one *d*; 2nd, 1989, Virginia Glen-Calvert. *Educ:* Purley Grammar Sch.; London Sch. of Economics. BSc (Econ); MIPM. National Coal Board, 1957–67: O & M Officer, W Midlands; Head of Manpower Planning, Industrial Relations Dept; entered MPBW as Principal, 1967; Asst Sec., 1970, Under Sec., 1981, DoE; seconded as Dep. Dir, Business in the Community, 1981–83; Under Secretary: Highways, Contracts, Admin and Maintenance, Dept of Transport, 1983–85; Construction Industry and Sports & Recreation Directorates, DoE, 1985–87. Mem., Croydon FHSA. Dir, Croydon Business Venture. Chm., Adv. Cttee, Acad. of London Orch. *Recreations:* music, theatre. *Clubs:* Reform; Surrey County Cricket.

PELLING, Henry Mathison; Fellow of St John's College, Cambridge, 1966–80 and since 1980; *b* 27 Aug. 1920; *s* of late D. L. Pelling, Prenton, Cheshire, and late Mrs M. M. Pelling; unmarried. *Educ:* Birkenhead School; St John's Coll., Cambridge. Class. Tripos Part I, 1941; History Tripos Part II, 1947 (MA 1945; PhD 1950; LittD 1975). Army service, 1941–45; Commnd RE, 1942; served NW Europe campaign, 1944–45. Fellow, Queen's Coll., Oxford, 1949–65; Tutor, 1950–65; Dean, 1963–64; Supernumerary Fellow, 1980; Asst Dir of Research (History), Cambridge, 1966–76; Reader in Recent British History, Cambridge, 1976–80. Smith-Mundt Schol., University of Wisconsin, USA, 1953–54; Fellow, Woodrow Wilson Center, Washington, DC, 1983. Hon. DHL New Sch. for Social Res., New York, 1983. *Publications:* Origins of the Labour Party, 1954; Challenge of Socialism, 1954; America and the British Left, 1956; British Communist Party, 1958; (with Frank Bealey) Labour and Politics, 1958; American Labor, 1960; Modern Britain, 1885–1955, 1960; Short History of the Labour Party, 1961, 9th edn 1991; History of British Trade Unionism, 1963, 4th edn 1987; Social Geography of British Elections, 1967; Popular Politics and Society in Late Victorian Britain, 1968, 2nd edn 1979; Britain and the Second World War, 1970; Winston Churchill, 1974, 2nd edn 1989; The Labour Governments 1945–51, 1984; Britain and the Marshall Plan, 1988; articles and reviews in learned journals. *Recreations:* theatre, films. *Address:* St John's College, Cambridge CB2 1TP. *T:* Cambridge (0223) 338600. *Clubs:* National Liberal, Commonwealth Trust.

PELLY, Derek Roland, (Derk); Deputy Chairman, Barclays Bank PLC, 1986–88 (Vice Chairman, 1984–85); *b* 12 June 1929; *s* of late Arthur Roland Pelly and late Elsie Pelly; *m* 1953, Susan Roberts; one *s* two *d*. *Educ:* Marlborough; Trinity Coll., Cambridge. Served RA, 1947–49 (2nd Lieut). Entered Barclays Bank, 1952; Local Director: Chelmsford, 1959; Luton, 1969; Vice Chm., 1977–85, Chm., 1986–87, Barclays Internat. Ltd. Dir, The Private Bank & Trust Co., 1989–. Member: Milton Keynes Develt Corp., 1976–85; Council, ODI, 1984–89. Mem. Cttee, Family Assce Soc., 1988–. Dir, Chelmsford Dio. Bd of Finance, 1989–. Governor, London House for Overseas Graduates, 1985–. *Recreation:* painting. *Address:* The Bowling Green, 8 The Downs, Great Dunmow, Essex CM6 1DT. *T:* Great Dunmow (0371) 872662.

PELLY, Major Sir John (Alwyne), 6th Bt *cr* 1840; JP, DL; landowner and farmer; *b* 11 Sept. 1918; *s* of Sir (Harold) Alwyne Pelly, 5th Bt, MC, and Caroline (*d* 1976), *d* of late Richard Heywood Heywood-Jones; *S* father, 1981; *m* 1st, 1945, (Ava) Barbara (Ann) (marr. diss. 1950), *o d* of Brig. Keith Frederick William Dunn, CBE; 2nd, 1950, Elsie May, (Hazel) (*d* 1987), *d* of late L. Thomas Dechow, Rhodesia; one *d* (and two *d* decd); 3rd, 1990, 1st wife Barbara (Mrs Cazenove). *Educ:* Canford; RMC Sandhurst; Royal Agricultural Coll. Commissioned Coldstream Guards, 1938; served War of 1939–45; Malaya, 1948–50; retired (Major), 1950. Rhodesia, 1950–61; Royal Agric. Coll., 1962–63 (Certificate of Merit). Mem., Lands Tribunal, 1981–90. JP 1966, High Sheriff 1970–71, DL 1972, Hants. *Recreations:* ski-ing, shooting. *Heir: nephew* Richard John Pelly [*b* 10 April 1951; *m* 1983, Clare Gemma, *d* of late H. W. Dove; three *s*]. *Address:* The Manor House, Preshaw Park, Upham, Hants SO3 1HP. *T:* Bramdean (0962) 771757. *Club:* Royal Over-Seas League.

PEMBERTON; *see* Leigh-Pemberton.

PEMBERTON, Col Alan Brooke, CVO 1988; MBE 1960; *b* 11 Sept. 1923; *s* of Eric Harry Pemberton (Canadian by birth) and Phyllis Edith Pemberton (*née* Brooke-Alder); *m* 1952, Pamela Kirkland Smith, of Winnipeg, Canada; two *s*. *Educ:* Uppingham School; Trinity College, Cambridge. Commissioned Coldstream Guards, 1942; war service in Italy and NW Europe; ADC to Earl Alexander of Tunis, Governor-General of Canada, 1951–52; ADC to Gen. Sir Gerald Templer, High Comr to Malaya, 1952–53; Commanded 1st Bn Coldstream Guards, 1963–66; Regtl Lt-Col, 1966–67; retired 1967 (Hon. Col). Queen's Body Guard, Yeomen of the Guard: Exon, 1967; Ensign; Clerk of the Cheque; Lieutenant, 1985–. Chm. and Man. Dir, Diversified Corporate Services Ltd, 1970–85. Special Constable, A Div., Metropolitan Police, 1975–76. *Recreations:* gardening, reading, travel. *Address:* Eastfields, Stoke-by-Nayland, Colchester, Essex CO6 4TB. *Clubs:* Boodle's, Pratt's.

PEMBERTON, Rev. Desmond Valdo; Assistant National Superintendent, Wesleyan Church, since 1990; a President, Churches Together in England, since 1990; *b* 23 March 1927; *s* of Charles and Lilla Pemberton; *m* 1951, Inez Pauline Fieulleteau; six *s* four *d*. *Educ:* Dept of Education and Ministry, Wesleyan Church HQ, USA. Clergyman, ordained 1969. Voluntary work for Church, 1958–66; Pastoral work, 1966–72; Dist Superintendent, Wesleyan Holiness Church, 1972–Aug. 1990 when Church adopted Nat. status. Distinguished Service Award, Wesleyan Church, 1983. *Publication:* contrib. Faith in The City of Birmingham, 1990. *Recreations:* walking, reading. *Address:* c/o Churches Together in England, Inter-Church House, 35–41 Lower Marsh, SE1 7RL. *T:* 021–444 3883.

PEMBERTON, Sir Francis (Wingate William), Kt 1976; CBE 1970; DL; FRICS; company director; *b* 1 Oct. 1916; *s* of late Dr William Warburton Wingate (assumed Arms of Pemberton, by Royal Licence, 1921) and Viola Patience Campbell Pemberton; *m* 1941, Diana Patricia, *e d* of late Reginald Salisbury Woods, MD, and Irene Woods, CBE, TD; two *s*. *Educ:* Eton; Trinity Coll., Cambridge (MA). Senior Consultant, Bidwells, Chartered Surveyors, 1980–89. Director: Agricultural Mortgage Corp. Ltd, 1969–; Barclays Bank UK Ltd, 1977–81. Hon. Dir, Royal Show, 1963–68; Royal Agricultural Society of England: Mem. Council, 1951– (Pres., 1974–75, Dep. Pres., 1975–76); Chm. Exec. Bd, 1969–71; Trustee, 1969–; Gold Medal for distinguished services to agric., 1989. Trustee, Robinson Coll., Cambridge, 1973–85. Member: Water Resources Board, 1964–74; Winston Churchill Meml Trust, 1965–80; Economic Planning Council for East Anglia, 1965–74; National Water Council, 1974–81; Water Authorities Superannuation Pension Fund (Dep. Chm, Fund Management and Policy Cttee), 1983–89. High Sheriff, Cambridgeshire and Isle of Ely, 1965–66; DL Cambs, 1979. *Address:* Trumpington Hall, Cambridge CB2 2LH. *T:* Cambridge (0223) 841941. *Club:* Farmers'.

PEMBERTON, Prof. John, MD London; FRCP, FFCM; DPH Leeds; Professor of Social and Preventive Medicine, The Queen's University, Belfast, 1958–76; *b* 18 Nov. 1912; British; *m* 1937, Winifred Ethel Gray; three *s*. *Educ:* Christ's Hospital; University College and UCH, London. House Physician and House Surgeon, University College Hospital, 1936–37; Rowett Research Institute under the late Lord Boyd Orr, 1937–39; Rockefeller Travelling Fellow in Medicine, Harvard, Mass., USA, 1954–55; Director of MRC Group for research on Respiratory Disease and Air Pollution, and Reader in Social Medicine, University of Sheffield, 1955–58. Mem., Health Educn Council, DHSS, 1973–76. Milroy Lectr, RCP, 1976. *Publications:* (with W. Hobson) The Health of the Elderly at Home, 1954; (ed) Recent Studies in Epidemiology, 1958; (ed) Epidemiology: Reports on Research and Teaching, 1963; Will Pickles of Wensleydale, 1970; articles in Lancet, BMJ, etc. *Recreations:* reading, TV, walking, visual arts. *Address:* Iona, Cannon Fields, Hathersage, Sheffield S30 1AG.

PEMBROKE, 17th Earl of, *cr* 1551, **AND MONTGOMERY,** 14th Earl of, *cr* 1605; **Henry George Charles Alexander Herbert;** Baron Herbert of Caerdiff, 1551; Baron Herbert of Shurland, 1605; Baron Herbert of Lea (UK), 1861; Hereditary Grand Visitor of Jesus College, Oxford; *b* 19 May 1939; *s* of 16th Earl of Pembroke and Montgomery, CVO, and of Mary Countess of Pembroke, *qv*; *S* father, 1969; *m* 1st, 1966, Claire Rose (marr. diss. 1981), *o d* of Douglas Pelly, Swaynes Hall, Widdington, Essex; one *s* three *d*; 2nd, 1988, Miranda Juliet, *d* of Comdr John Oram, Bulbridge House, Wilton; one *d*. *Educ:* Eton Coll.; Oxford Univ. Royal Horse Guards, 1958–60 (National Service); Oxford University, 1960–63. *Recreations:* photography, gardening, horse racing. *Heir: s* Lord Herbert, *qv*. *Address:* Wilton House, Salisbury, Wilts. *T:* Salisbury (0772) 743211.

PEMBROKE, Mary Countess of; Mary Dorothea Herbert, CVO 1947; DL; Extra Lady-in-Waiting to Princess Marina, Duchess of Kent, 1950–68 (Lady-in-Waiting, 1934–50); *o d* of 1st Marquess of Linlithgow; *m* 1936, Lord Herbert (later 16th Earl of Pembroke and Montgomery, who *d* 1969); one *s* one *d*. DL Wilts, 1980. *Address:* The Old Rectory, Wilton, near Salisbury, Wilts SP2 0HT. *T:* Salisbury (0772) 743157.

PEÑA, Paco; musician; flamenco guitar player, since 1954; Professor of Flamenco, Rotterdam Conservatory, since 1985; *b* 1 June 1942; *s* of Antonio Peña and Rosario Perez; *m* 1982, Karin Vaessen; two *d*. *Educ:* Córdoba, Spain. London début, 1963; founded Paco Peña Flamenco Co., 1970; founded Centro Flamenco Paco Peña, Córdoba, 1981; Ramón Montoya Prize, 1983. *Address:* c/o Karin Vaessen, 4 Boscastle Road, NW5 1EG. *Fax:* 071–485 2320.

PENDER, 3rd Baron, *cr* 1937; **John Willoughby Denison-Pender;** Joint Chairman, Bremar Trust Ltd, 1977–83; Chairman, J. J. L. D. Frost plc, 1983–84; *b* 6 May 1933; *s* of 2nd Baron and of Camilla Lethbridge (*d* 1988), *o d* of late Willoughby Arthur Pemberton; *S* father, 1965; *m* 1962, Julia, *yr d* of Richard Nevill Cannon; one *s* two *d*. *Educ:* Eton. Formerly Lieut, 10th Royal Hussars and Captain, City of London Yeomanry (TA). Dir, Globe Investment Trust Ltd, 1969–70. Steward: Folkestone Racecourse, 1985–; Lingfield Park, 1989–. *Heir: s* Hon. Henry John Richard Denison-Pender, *b* 19 March 1968. *Address:* North Court, Tilmanstone, Kent. *T:* Sandwich (0304) 611726. *Clubs:* White's, Pratt's.

PENDERECKI, Krzysztof; Rector, State Academy of Music, Kraków, since 1972; Professor of Composition, School of Music, Yale University, New Haven, Conn, 1973–78; *b* Debica, Poland, 23 Nov. 1933; *s* of Tadeusz Penderecki and Zofia Penderecki; *m* 1965, Elzbieta Solecka; one *s* one *d*. *Educ:* State Acad. of Music, Kraków, Poland (Graduate 1958). Compositions include: Threnody to the Victims of Hiroshima, 1959–61 (52 strings); Passion According to St Luke, 1965–66 (oratorio); Utrenja, 1969–71 (oratorio); Devils of Loudun, 1969 (opera); Cello Concerto No 1, 1971–72; First Symphony, 1972; Magnificat, 1974 (oratorio); Awakening of Jacob, 1974 (orchestra); Paradise Lost, 1976–78 (rappresentazione for Chicago Lyric Opera; Milton libretto, Christopher Fry); Violin Concerto, 1977; Te Deum, 1979–80; (Christmas) Symphony No 2, 1980; Lacrimosa, 1980; Agnus Dei (for chorus a cappella), 1981; Cello Concerto No 2, 1982; Viola Concerto, 1983; Polish Requiem, 1983–84; Die schwarze Maske, 1986 (opera); Veni creator and Song of Cherubin (for chorus a cappella), 1987. Hon. Dr: Univ. of Rochester, NY; St Olaf Coll., Northfield, Minn; Katholieke Univ., Leuven; Univ. of Bordeaux; Georgetown Univ., Washington; Univ. of Belgrade; Universidad Autónoma, Madrid. Member: RAM (Hon.); Akad. der Künste, Berlin (Extraordinary); Akad. der Künste der DDR, Berlin (Corresp.); Kungl. Musikaliska Akad., Stockholm; Accad. Nazionale di Santa Cecilia, Rome (Hon.); Acad. Nacional de Bellas Artes, Buenos Aires (Corresp.). Grosser Kunstpreis des Landes Nordrhein-Westfalen, 1966; Prix Italia, 1967/68; Gottfried von Herder Preis der Stiftung FvS zu Hamburg, 1977; Prix Arthur Honegger, 1977; Sibelius Prize, Wihouri Foundn, 1983; Premio Lorenzo Magnifico, 1985; Wolf Prize, 1987. *Publications:* all works published. *Recreation:* collecting old furniture, clocks and paintings. *Address:* Cisowa 22, 30229 Kraków, Poland. *T:* 225760; 324 Livingston Street, New Haven, Conn 06511, USA. *T:* 203–789 0354.

PENDERED, Richard Geoffrey; Chairman, Bunge & Co., 1987–90; *b* 26 Sept. 1921; *s* of Richard Dudley Pendered and Adèle Pendered (*née* Hall); *m* 1953, Jennifer Preston Mead; two *s* two *d*. *Educ:* Winchester College (Scholar); Magdalene College (Scholar). GCCS Bletchley, 1940–52 (renamed GCHQ); Bunge & Co., 1952–90, Dir, 1957, Man. Dir, 1963–86. *Recreations:* fishing, shooting, golf. *Address:* 41 Sandy Lodge Lane, Northwood, Middx HA6 2HX. *Club:* Moor Park Golf.

PENDLEBURY, Edward; Assistant Under Secretary of State (Sales Administration), Ministry of Defence, 1983–85, retired; *b* 5 March 1925; *s* of Thomas Cecil Pendlebury and Alice (*née* Sumner); *m* 1957, Joan Elizabeth Bell; one *s*. *Educ:* King George V Sch., Southport; Magdalen Coll., Oxford (MA). Served War, RNVR, 1943–46. Asst Principal, Min. of Food, 1949–53; Principal: MAFF, 1953–56; MoD (British Defence Staff, Washington), 1956–60; MAFF, 1960–66; Asst Secretary: DEA, 1966–70; MoD, 1970–80; Exec. Dir (Civilian Management), MoD, 1980–83. *Recreations:* gramophone, gardening, gazing. *Address:* Bosworth House, Draycott, near Moreton-in-Marsh, Glos GL56 9LF. *T:* Blockley (0386) 701059.

PENDOWER, John Edward Hicks, FRCS; Dean, Charing Cross and Westminster Medical School, since 1989; *b* 6 Aug. 1927; *s* of Thomas Curtis Hicks Pendower and Muriel May Pendower (*née* Newbury); *m* 1st, 1960, Kate Tuohy (*d* 1987); one *s* two *d*; 2nd, 1989, Mrs Paulette Gleave. *Educ:* Dulwich College; King's College London; Charing Cross Hosp. Med. Sch. (MB BS (Hons Med.) 1950). FRCS 1955. Called to the Bar, Inner Temple, 1972. Served RAMC. Charing Cross Hosp. and St Mark's Hosp., 1950–62; Harvey Cushing Fellow, Harvard Med. Sch., 1959–60; Consultant Surgeon: Mayday Hosp., Croydon, 1964–89; Charing Cross Hosp., 1965–87 (Vice Dean, 1979–84; Sub Dean, Charing Cross and Westminster Med. Sch., 1984–87); former examr in surgery, London Univ. Mem., Hammersmith and Fulham, subseq. Riverside, HA, 1983–90. Special Trustee, Charing Cross Hosp.; Trustee, Malcolm Sargent Cancer Fund for Children. *Recreations:* formerly squash rackets, now walking; collecting campaign medals. *Address:* Rosemary, Promenade de Verdun, Purley, Surrey CR8 3LN. *T:* 081–660 8949.

PENDRED, Piers Loughnan; Director (formerly Controller) of Finance, British Council, since 1987; *b* 24 Aug. 1943; *s* of Loughnan Wildig Pendred and Dulcie Treen Hall; *m* 1973, Carol Ann Haslam; one *s* one *d*. *Educ:* Ardingly College; Trinity Hall, Cambridge (MA Fine Arts and Architecture). VSO teacher, S India, 1965–67; British Council: Television Officer, Sudan, 1967–69, Ethiopia, 1969–71; TV Training Officer, London, 1972–76; Head of Production, 1976–81; Dir, Design, Production and Publishing, 1981–84; Dir, Press and Inf., 1984–87. Sen. Exec. Programme, London Business Sch., 1987.

PENDRY, Prof. John Brian, PhD; FRS 1984; Professor of Theoretical Solid State Physics, Department of Physics, Imperial College of Science, Technology and Medicine, University of London, since 1981; *b* 4 July 1943; *s* of Frank Johnson Pendry and Kathleen (*née* Shaw); *m* 1977, Patricia Gard. *Educ:* Downing Coll., Cambridge (MA; PhD 1969). Res. Fellow in Physics, Downing Coll., Cambridge, 1969–72; Mem. of Technical Staff, Bell Labs, USA, 1972–73; Sen. Asst in Res., Cavendish Lab., Cambridge Univ., and Fellow in Physics and Praelector, Downing Coll., 1973–75; SPSO and Head of Theory Gp, Daresbury Lab., 1975–81. *Publications:* Low Energy Electron Diffraction, 1974; Surface Crystallographic Information Service, 1987; scientific papers. *Recreations:* music, gardening. *Address:* The Blackett Laboratory, Imperial College of Science, Technology and Medicine, SW7 2BZ. *T:* 071–589 5111, ext. 6901.

PENDRY, Thomas; MP (Lab) Stalybridge and Hyde since 1970; *b* 10 June 1934; *m* 1966, Moira Anne Smith; one *s* one *d*. *Educ:* St Augustine's, Ramsgate; Oxford Univ. RAF, 1955–57. Full time official, Nat. Union of Public Employees, 1960–70; Mem., Paddington Borough Council, 1962–65; Chm., Derby Labour Party, 1966. An Opposition Whip, 1971–74; a Lord Comr of the Treasury and Govt Whip, 1974, resigned 1977; Parly Under-Sec. of State, NI Office, 1978–79; Opposition Spokesman on NI, 1979–81, on overseas development, 1981–82, on regional affairs and devolution, 1982–84. Member: Select Cttee on Envmt, 1987–; Select Cttee on Members' Interests, 1987–. Chairman: All Party Football Cttee, 1980–; PLP Sports Cttee, 1984–. Member: Speaker's Conf., 1973; UK delegn to WEU and Council of Europe, 1973–75; Industrial Law Soc. Mem., Nat. Adv. Cttee, Duke of Edinburgh's Award Scheme; Steward, British Boxing Bd of Control, 1987–. Pres., Stalybridge Public Band. *Recreations:* sport; football, cricket, boxing (sometime Middleweight Champion, Hong Kong; boxed for Oxford Univ.). *Address:* 2 Cannon Street, Hollingworth, Hyde, Cheshire SK14 8LR. *Club:* Lord's Taverners.

PENFOLD, Maj.-Gen. Robert Bernard, CB 1969; LVO 1957; *b* 19 Dec. 1916; *s* of late Bernard Hugh Penfold, Selsey, and late Ethel Ives Arnold; *m* 1940, Ursula, *d* of late Lt-Col E. H. Gray; two *d*. *Educ:* Wellington; RMC, Sandhurst. 2nd Lieut, Royal Leics Regt, 1936; commnd into 11th Sikh Regt, Indian Army, 1937; served in NWFP and during War of 1939–45 in Middle East, Central Mediterranean Forces; Instructor, Staff Coll., Quetta, 1946–47; transf. to British Army, RA, 1947; RN Staff Coll., 1953; Secretary, British Joint Services Mission, Washington, 1957–59; comdg 6 King's African Rifles, Tanganyika, 1959–61; Comdr 127 Inf. Bde (TA), 1962–64; Security Ops Adviser to High Commissioner, Aden, 1964–65; Imperial Defence Coll., 1966; Chief of Defence Staff, Kenya, 1966–69; GOC South East District, 1969–72. Gen. Manager and Chief Exec., Royal Hong Kong Jockey Club, 1972–80. Chm., Horseracing Adv. Council, 1980–86. *Recreations:* shooting, golf, gardening. *Address:* Park House, Amport, Andover, Hants SP11 8BW. *Club:* Army and Navy.

PENGELLY, Richard Anthony; Under Secretary, Welsh Office, 1977–85; *b* 18 Aug. 1925; *s* of Richard Francis Pengelly and Ivy Mildred Pengelly; *m* 1st, 1952, Phyllis Mary Rippon; one *s*; 2nd, 1972, Margaret Ruth Crossley; two *s* one *d*. *Educ:* Plymouth Coll.; School of Oriental and African Studies; London Sch. of Economics and Political Science (BScEcon). Served War: Monmouthshire Regt and Intell. Corps, 1943–47. Joined Min. of Supply as Asst Principal, 1950, Principal, 1954; NATO Defence Coll., 1960–61; Asst Sec., Min. of Aviation, 1964; RCDS 1971; Min. of Defence, 1972. *Recreations:* skiing, golf. *Address:* Byways, Wern Goch Road, Cyncoed, Cardiff, S Wales CF2 6SD. *T:* Cardiff (0222) 764418.

PENINGTON, Prof. David Geoffrey, AC 1988; Vice-Chancellor, University of Melbourne, since 1988; *b* 4 Feb. 1930; *s* of Geoffrey Alfred Penington and Marjorie Doris (*née* Fricke); *m* 1st, 1956, Audrey Mary Grummitt (marr. diss.); two *s* two *d*; 2nd, 1984, Sonay Hussein. *Educ:* Magdalen Coll., Oxford (BA 1953; BM BCh 1955; MA 1957; DM 1969). MRCP 1957; MRACP 1968; FRCPA 1971; FRCP 1972; FRACP 1972. Consultant physician, London Hosp., 1963–67; Melbourne University: 1st Assistant in Medicine, 1968–70; Prof. and Chm. of Dept of Medicine, 1970–87; Dean, Faculty of Medicine, 1978–85. Vis. Res. Fellow, Wolfson Coll., Oxford, 1975–76; Sims Commonwealth Travelling Prof., RCS, 1981. Chief Advr, Health Policy & Progs, Health Dept, Victoria, 1986–87; Chairman: Cttee of Inquiry into Rights of Private Practice in Public Hosps, 1984; AIDS Task Force, 1984–87; Nat. Blood Transfusion Cttee of Australian Red Cross Soc., 1976–87. Member of Board: Walter and Eliza Hall Inst. for Med. Res.; Ludwig Inst., Royal Melbourne Hosp. *Publications:* (ed) De Gruchy's Clinical Haematology in Medical Practice, 5th edn, 1989; res. pubns on clin. and exptl haematology. *Recreations:* music, painting, fishing. *Address:* Vice-Chancellor's Office, University of Melbourne, Parkville, Vic 3052, Australia. *T:* (03) 344 6134. *Club:* Melbourne (Melbourne).

PENLEY, William Henry, CB 1967; CBE 1961; PhD; FEng; engineering consultant, since 1985; *b* 22 March 1917; *s* of late William Edward Penley and late Clara (*née* Dodgson), Wallasey, Cheshire; *m* 1st, 1943, Raymonde Evelyn (*d* 1975), *d* of late Frederick Richard Gough, Swanage, Dorset; two *s* one *d*; 2nd, 1977, Marion Claytor, *d* of late Joseph Enoch Airey, Swanage, Dorset. *Educ:* Wallasey Grammar Sch.; Liverpool Univ.; BEng, 1937; PhD, 1940. FIEE (MIEE 1964); FRAeS 1967; FRSA 1975; FEng 1978. Head of Guided Weapons Department, Royal Radar Establishment, 1953–61; Director, Royal Radar Establishment, 1961–62; Director-General of Electronics Research and Development, Ministry of Aviation, 1962–64; Deputy Controller of Electronics, Ministry of Aviation, then Ministry of Technology, 1964–67; Dir, Royal Armament R&D Establishment, 1967–70; Chief Scientist (Army), 1970–75, Dep. Controller, Establishments and Res. B, 1971–75, MoD; Controller, R&D Establishments, and Research, MoD, and Professional Head of Science Gp of the Civil Service, 1976–77; Chm., Appleton Lab. Establishment Cttee, 1977–79; Dep. Dir, Under Water Weapons, Marconi Space and Defence Systems Ltd, Stanmore, 1979–82; Engrg Dir, Marconi Underwater Systems Ltd, 1982–85. Sec., Swanage Choral and Operatic Soc., 1986–. Silver Jubilee Medal, 1977. *Address:* 28 Walrond Road, Swanage, Dorset BH19 1PD. *T:* Swanage (0929) 425042. *Club:* Commonwealth Trust.

PENLINGTON, Ross Grange, OBE (mil.) 1980; AE 1972 (Clasp 1979); **Hon. Mr Justice Penlington;** a Judge of the Court of Appeal of Hong Kong, since 1988; *b* 3 March 1931; *s* of Cedric Grange Penlington and Elsie May Penlington; *m* 1956, Valerie Ann Wacher; two *d*. *Educ:* Christ Coll., NZ; Univ. of Canterbury, NZ. LLB 1954. Barrister and Solicitor, Christchurch, NZ, 1954–59; Legal Officer, Magistrate and Attorney Gen., Western Samoa, 1959–64; Hong Kong: Crown Counsel, 1965–75; Dir of Public Prosecutions, 1976–77; District Court Judge, 1977–80; High Court Judge, 1980–88. Commnd Hong Kong RAuxAF, 1964; Pilot's Brevet, 1965; CO (Wing Comdr), 1975–83; Hon. Air Cdre, 1983–. *Recreations:* flying, golf, tennis, fishing, racing.

Address: 76F Peak Road, Hong Kong. *T:* 5–8498484. *Clubs:* Royal Air Force; Hong Kong, Shek-O, Royal Hong Kong Jockey (Hong Kong).

PENMAN, Ian Dalgleish, CB 1987; temporary Chief Executive, Scottish Homes, since 1991; *b* 1 Aug. 1931; *s* of late John B. Penman and of Dorothy Dalgleish; *m* 1963, Elisabeth Stewart Strachan; three *s*. *Educ:* Glasgow Univ. (MA Classics); Balliol Coll., Oxford (MA Lit. Hum.; Snell Exhibnr and Ferguson Scholar). National Service, RAF, 1955–57 (Educn Br.). Asst Principal, HM Treasury, 1957–58; Scottish Office, 1958–91; Private Sec. to Parly Under-Sec. of State, 1960–62; Principal, Scottish Develt Dept, 1962–69; Asst Sec., Estab. Div., 1970–72; Asst Sec., Scottish Home and Health Dept, 1972–78; Under-Sec., Scottish Develt Dept, 1978–84; Dep. Sec., Central Services, Scottish Office, 1984–91. *Recreations:* walking, music, swimming. *Address:* 4 Wardie Avenue, Edinburgh EH5 2AB. *T:* 031–552 2180. *Club:* New (Edinburgh).

PENMAN, John, FRCP; Consulting Neurologist to The Royal Marsden Hospital; *b* 10 Feb. 1913; *er s* of late William Penman, FIA; *m* 1st, 1938, Joan, *d* of late Claude Johnson (marr. diss. 1975); one *s* two *d*; 2nd, 1975, Elisabeth Quin. *Educ:* Tonbridge Sch.; University College, Oxford (Senior Classical Scholar); Queen Mary Coll., E1; The London Hospital. MB, BS (London) 1944; MRCP 1948, FRCP 1969. Neurologist to The Royal Marsden Hospital, 1954–77. Member of Association of British Neurologists. *Publications:* The Epodes of Horace: a new English version, 1980; A Late Harvest: poems, 1987; contributions to medical journals, mainly on tic douloureux and brain tumours; section on trigeminal injection, in Operative Surgery, 1957; chapters in Handbook of Clinical Neurology, 1968. *Recreations:* poetry; etymology; Japanese flower arrangement. *Address:* Forest View, Upper Chute, Andover, Hants. *Club:* Royal Automobile.

PENN, Lt-Col Sir Eric, GCVO 1981 (KCVO 1972; CVO 1965); OBE 1960; MC 1944; Extra Equerry to The Queen since 1963; *b* 9 Feb. 1916; *o s* of Capt. Eric F. Penn (killed in action 1915), Grenadier Guards, and late Gladys Ebden; *m* 1947, Prudence Stewart-Wilson, *d* of late Aubyn Wilson and late Muriel Stewart-Stevens, Balnakeilly, Pitlochry, Perthshire; two *s* one *d*. *Educ:* Eton; Magdalene Coll., Cambridge. Grenadier Guards, 1938–60: France and Belgium, 1939–40; Italy and Austria, 1943–45; Germany, 1945–46; Libya and Egypt, 1950–52; Germany, 1953–55. Assistant Comptroller, Lord Chamberlain's Office, 1960–64, Comptroller, 1964–81. *Address:* 6 Rosscourt Mansions, 4 Palace Street, SW1E 5HZ. *T:* 071–828 6262. *Clubs:* White's, Pratt's.

PENN, Richard; Chief Executive, City of Bradford Metropolitan Council, since 1989; *b* 4 Oct. 1945; *s* of George Stanley; *m* 1968, Jillian Mary Elias; three *s* one *d*. *Educ:* Canton High Sch., Cardiff; University Coll., Cardiff (BSc Econs Jt Hons); University Coll., Swansea (DipEd). MBPS. Lectr, University Coll., Cardiff, 1968–70; Glamorgan, then W Glamorgan, CC, 1970–76; Asst Chief Exec., Cleveland CC, 1976–78; Dep. Chief Exec., W Midlands CC, 1978–81; Chief Exec., Knowsley Metropolitan Council, 1981–89. FBIM. *Recreations:* family, Liverpool Football Club, theatre, good food. *Address:* City Hall, Bradford, West Yorks BD1 1HY. *T:* Bradford (0274) 752002. *Club:* Royal Over-Seas League.

PENNANT; *see* Douglas-Pennant.

PENNANT, His Honour David Edward Thornton; a Circuit Judge (formerly County Court Judge), 1961–84; *b* 2 Aug. 1912; *s* of David Falconer Pennant, DL, JP, Barrister-at-law, late of Nantlys, St Asaph, N. Wales, and late Lilla Agnes Pennant; *m* 1938, Alice Catherine Stainer; three *s* one *d*. *Educ:* Charterhouse; Trinity Coll., Cambridge. Called to Bar, Inner Temple, 1935. Served, 1939–45, with Royal Signals (TA); OC, Signals Officers' Training Sch., Mhow, India, 1944–45. Chancellor, Dio. Monmouth, 1949–77. Governing, and Representative Bodies, Church in Wales, 1946–83. Chm., Radnorshire QS, 1962–64; Deputy Chairman: Brecknockshire QS, 1956–64; Flintshire QS, 1962–71; Dorset QS, 1971. Joint Chairman, Medical Appeals Tribunal for Wales, 1957–61; Mem., County Court Rule Cttee, 1970–78. *Recreation:* gardening. *Address:* 12 Ettrick Road, Branksome Park, Poole, Dorset BH13 6LG. *T:* Bournemouth (0202) 765614.

PENNANT-REA, Rupert Lascelles; Editor, The Economist, since 1986; *b* 23 Jan. 1948; *s* of Peter Athelwold Pennant-Rea and Pauline Elizabeth Pennant-Rea; *m* 1st, 1970, Elizabeth Louise Greer (marr. diss. 1975); 2nd, 1979, Jane Trevelyan Hamilton (marr. diss. 1986); one *s* one *d*; 3rd, 1986, Helen Jay; one *s* and two step *d*. *Educ:* Peterhouse, Zimbabwe; Trinity Coll., Dublin (BA); Manchester Univ. (MA). Confedn of Irish Industry, 1970–71; Gen. and Municipal Workers Union, 1972–73; Bank of England, 1973–77; The Economist, 1977–. *Publications:* Gold Foil, 1979; (jtly) Who Runs the Economy?, 1980; (jtly) The Pocket Economist, 1983; (jtly) The Economist Economics, 1986. *Recreations:* music, tennis, fishing, family. *Address:* (office) 25 St James's Street, SW1A 1HG. *T:* 071–839 9118. *Clubs:* MCC, Reform.

PENNELL, Rev. Canon (James Henry) Leslie, TD and Bar, 1949; Rector of Foxearth and Pentlow (Diocese of Chelmsford), 1965–72, and of Borley and Lyston (Diocese of Chelmsford), 1969–72; Hon. Canon, Inverness Cathedral, since 1965 (Provost, 1949–65); *b* 9 Feb. 1906; *s* of late J. H. L. Pennell and late Elizabeth Esmé Gordon Steel; *m* 1939, Ursula Mary, *d* of Rev. A. E. Gledhill; twin *s* and *d*. *Educ:* Edinburgh Academy; Edinburgh University (BL); Edinburgh Theological College. Precentor, Inverness Cathedral, 1929–32; Rector, St Mary's, Dunblane, and Offic. Chaplain to Queen Victoria School, 1932–49; Officiating Chaplain, Cameron Barracks, 1949–64. TA, 1934; BEF, 1940; SCF, 1943; DACG, 34th Ind. Corps, 1945; SCF Corps Troops, Scottish Comd, 1946–50. *Recreations:* reading and travel. *Address:* The Croft, Hundon, Sudbury, Suffolk CO10 8EW. *T:* Hundon (044086) 221.

PENNEY, family name of **Baron Penney.**

PENNEY, Most Rev. Alphonsus Liguori; *see* St John's (Newfoundland), Archbishop of, (RC).

PENNEY, Jennifer Beverly; Senior Principal, Royal Ballet, retired 1988; *b* 5 April 1946; *d* of Beverley Guy Penney and Gwen Penney. *Educ:* in Canada (grades 1–12). Entered Royal Ballet Sch., 1962; joined Royal Ballet, 1963; became soloist during 1967, principal dancer during 1970, and senior principal dancer during 1974. Evening Standard Award, 1980. *Recreation:* painting (water-colours). *Address:* Mountain Park Drive, RR #1 Ganges, Salt Spring Island, British Columbia V0S 1E0, Canada.

PENNEY, Reginald John; Assistant Under-Secretary of State, Ministry of Defence, 1964–73, retired; *b* 22 May 1919; *s* of Herbert Penney and Charlotte Penney (*née* Affleck); *m* 1941, Eileen Gardiner; one *s* two *d*. *Educ:* Westminster School. War Service, Royal West Kent Regt, 1939–46. Civil Servant, Air Ministry, until 1964, including service with Far East Air Force, Singapore, 1960–63. Chm., Sherborne Soc., CPRE, 1976. *Recreation:* golf. *Address:* Rumbow Cottage, Acreman Street, Sherborne, Dorset DT9 3NX.

PENNICOTT, Maj.-Gen. Brian Thomas; Defence Services Secretary, since 1991; *b* 15 Feb. 1938; *s* of Thomas Edward Pennicott and Vera Ethel (*née* Gale); *m* 1962, Patricia Anne Chilcott; two *s* three *d*. *Educ:* Portsmouth Northern Grammar Sch.; RMA, Sandhurst. Commnd, RA, 1957; RMCS, Shrivenham, 1969–70; Staff Coll., Camberley, 1971; GSO2 (W), Project Management Team 155mm Systems, 1972–73; NDC, Latimer, 1976–77; CO 29 Commando Regt, RA, 1977–80; SO1 Mil. Sec.'s Br. 6, MoD, 1980–82; Comdr Artillery, Falkland Is, 1982; Asst Mil. Attaché, Washington, 1982–83; Comdr Artillery, 1 Armd Div., 1983–86; NDC, Canada, 1986–87; Dep. Mil. Sec. (A), 1987–89; Dir, RA, 1989–91. *Recreations:* tennis, golf, bridge. *Address:* c/o Lloyds Bank, Cox's & King's Branch, PO Box 1190, 7 Pall Mall, SW1Y 5NA. *Club:* Army and Navy.

PENNING-ROWSELL, Edmund Lionel; wine writer; Wine Correspondent: Country Life, 1954–87; Financial Times, since 1964; *b* 16 March 1913; *s* of Edmund Penning-Rowsell and Marguerite Marie-Louise Penning-Rowsell (*née* Egan); *m* 1937, Margaret Wintringham; one *s* two *d*. *Educ:* Marlborough College. Journalist, Morning Post, 1930–35; Book Publisher, Frederick Muller Ltd, 1935–50; Sales Manager, B. T. Batsford, 1952–57; Dir, book publisher, Edward Hulton & Co./Studio-Vista, 1957–63; Manager, World Book Fair, Earl's Court, 1964. Mem. Cttee of Management, Internat. Exhibition Co-op. Wine Soc., 1959–87 (Chm., 1964–87); Chm., Internat. Co-operative Wine Soc., 1964–87; Founder Mem., William Morris Soc., 1954 (Vice-Pres.). Chevalier de l'Ordre du Mérite Agricole (France), 1971; Chevalier de l'Ordre du Mérite National (France), 1981. *Publications:* Red, White and Rosé, 1967; The Wines of Bordeaux, 1969, 6th edn 1989. *Recreation:* drinking wine, particularly claret. *Address:* Yew Trees House, Wootton, Woodstock, Oxford OX7 1EG. *T:* Woodstock (0993) 811281. *Club:* Travellers'.

PENNINGTON, Michael Vivian Fyfe; freelance actor and writer; *b* 7 June 1943; *s* of late Vivian Maynard Cecil Pennington and Euphemia Willock (*née* Fyfe); *m* Katharine Ann Letitia Barker (marr. diss.); one *s*. *Educ:* Marlborough Coll.; Trinity Coll., Cambridge (BA English). RSC, 1964–65; BBC, ITV, Woodfall Films Ltd, West End Theatre, Royal Court Theatre, etc, 1966–74; RSC, 1974–81: roles included Berowne, Angelo and Hamlet; Crime and Punishment, Lyric Hammersmith, 1983; National Theatre: Strider, 1984; Venice Preserv'd, 1984; Anton Chekhov, 1984; The Real Thing, Strand, 1985; Jt Artistic Dir (also acting, Prince Hal and Henry V), English Shakespeare Co., 1986–87, Dir, 1987–89 (also title rôle in Richard II); Playing with Trains, RSC, 1989; Vershinin, The Three Sisters, Gate, Dublin, 1990; Leontes, Winter's Tale, Coriolanus (title rôle), English Shakespeare Co., UK and world tour, 1990–91. *Publications:* Rossya—A Journey Through Siberia, 1977; The English Shakespeare Company, 1990. *Recreations:* music, literature. *Address:* c/o James Sharkey Associates Ltd, 15 Golden Square, W1R 3AG.

PENNINGTON, Prof. Robert Roland; Professor of Commercial Law, Birmingham University, since 1968; *b* 22 April 1927; *s* of R. A. Pennington; *m* 1965, Patricia Irene; one *d*. *Educ:* Birmingham Univ. (LLB, LLD). Solicitor. Reader, Law Soc.'s Sch. of Law, 1951–62; Mem. Bd of Management, Coll. of Law, 1962; Sen. Lectr in Commercial Law, 1962–68 and Dean, Faculty of Law, Birmingham Univ., 1979–82. Govt Adviser on Company Legislation, Trinidad, 1967 and Seychelles, 1970; UN Adviser on Commercial Law, 1970–; Special Legal Adviser to EEC, 1972–79. Editor, European Commercial Law Library, 1974–. *Publications:* Company Law, 1959, 5th edn 1985; Companies in the Common Market, 1962, 3rd edn as Companies in the European Communities, 1982; The Investor and the Law, 1967; Stannary Law: A History of the Mining Law of Cornwall and Devon, 1973; Commercial Banking Law, 1978; Gesellschaftsrecht des Vereinigten Königreichs, 1981 (in Jura Europae: Gesellschaftsrecht); The Companies Acts 1980 and 1981: a practitioners' manual, 1983; Stock Exchange Listing: the new regulations, 1985; Directors' Personal Liability, 1987; Company Liquidations: the substantive law: the procedure (2 vols), 1987; The Law of the Investment Markets, 1990. *Recreations:* travel, walking, history, archaeology. *Address:* Gryphon House, Langley Road, Claverdon, Warwicks CV35 8QA.

PENNISON, Clifford Francis, CBE 1977; *b* 28 June 1913; *s* of Henry and Alice Pennison; *m* 1940, Joan Margaret Hopkins; three *d*. *Educ:* Taunton Sch.; Bristol Univ. (BA, 1st Cl. Hons, Hist.). Barrister-at-Law, Inner Temple, 1951. Appointed senior management trainee, Unilever Ltd, 1938. Field Security Officer, Army, 1940–46 (Captain). Principal, Home Civil Service, 1946; Assistant Secretary, and Director of Organisation and Methods, Ministry of Food, 1949; Ministry of Agriculture: Director of Statistics Div., 1953; Director of Public Relations Div., 1958; Director of External Relations Div., 1961; FAO: Permanent UK representative, 1963–66; Director, Economic Analysis Div., 1966–67; Asst Dir-Gen., Admin and Finance, 1967–74; Consultant, EEC/FAO relations, 1974–76; retired 1976. Diplôme, Lettres Modernes, and Diplôme, Langue allemande, Univ. of Nice, 1977–81; Final examination (French), Inst. of Linguists, 1984. *Recreations:* travel, reading, foreign languages. *Address:* 9 Arden Drive, Wylde Green, Sutton Coldfield B73 5ND. *T:* 021–384 2289.

PENNOCK, family name of **Baron Pennock.**

PENNOCK, Baron *cr* 1982 (Life Peer), of Norton in the County of Cleveland; **Raymond William Pennock;** Kt 1978; Senior Adviser, Morgan Grenfell Group plc, since 1990 (Director, 1984–90); *b* 16 June 1920; *s* of Frederick Henry Pennock and Harriet Ann Pennock (*née* Mathison); *m* 1943, Lorna Pearse; one *s* two *d*. *Educ:* Coatham Sch.; Merton Coll., Oxford (Hon. Fellow, 1979). MA; 2nd cl. hons History, Dipl. Educn. Royal Artillery (Captain), 1941–46 (despatches 1945). Joined ICI Ltd, 1947; Personnel Management and Commercial Duties, 1947–61; Commercial Dir, Billingham Div., 1961–64; Dep. Chm., Billingham Div., 1964–68; Chm., Agric. (formerly Billingham) Div. 1968–72; Director, ICI Ltd, 1972, Dep. Chm., 1975–80; Chm., BICC plc, 1980–84. Dep. Chm., Plessey Co., 1985–89 (Dir, 1979–89); Director: Standard Chartered plc, 1982–91 (Dep. Chm., 1989–91); Willis Corroon (formerly Willis Faber) plc, 1985–90; Eurotunnel plc, 1986–91. President: CIA, 1978–79; CBI, 1980–82 (Chm., Economic Situation Cttee, 1977–80); UNICE, 1984–86. Mem., NEDC, 1979–82. Mem. Nat. Council, Oxford Soc. *Recreations:* tennis, music, ballet. *Address:* 23 Great Winchester Street, EC2P 2AX. *Clubs:* Boodle's; Vincent's (Oxford); Queen's, Royal Tennis Court, All England Lawn Tennis & Croquet.

PENNY, family name of **Viscount Marchwood.**

PENNY, (Francis) David, CBE 1982; FRSE; FEng 1980; consulting engineer; *b* 20 May 1918; *s* of late David Penny and Esther Colley; *m* 1949, Betty E. Smith, *d* of late Oswald C. Smith. *Educ:* Bromsgrove County High School; University Coll., London (BSc), Fellow 1973. Engineering Apprenticeship, Cadbury Bros Ltd, 1934–39; Armament Design Establishment, Ministry of Supply, 1939–53; Chief Development Engineer, Fuel Research Station, 1954–58; Dep. Dir, Nat. Engineering Laboratory, 1959–66, Dir, 1967–69; Man. Dir, Yarrow Public Ltd Co., 1979–83. Chairman: Control Systems Ltd, 1979–83; Automatic Revenue Controls Ltd, 1979–83. FIMarE; FIMechE; Member Council, IMechE, 1964–85 (a Vice-Pres., 1977–81, Pres., 1981–82); Mem. Bd, BSI, 1982–. *Publications:* various technical papers. *Recreations:* gardening, walking. *Address:* The Park, Dundrennan, Kirkcudbright. *T:* Dundrennan (05575) 244.

PENNY, Joseph Noel Bailey, QC 1971; *b* 25 Dec. 1916; *s* of Joseph A. Penny, JP and Isabella Downie, JP; *m* 1st, 1947, Celia (*d* 1969), *d* of Mr and Mrs R. H. Roberts; three *s* one *d*; 2nd, 1972, Sara Margaret, *d* of Sir Arnold France, *qv*; one *d*. *Educ:* Worksop

College; Christ Church, Oxford; MA (Oxon). Major, Royal Signals, 1939–46 (despatches). Called to Bar, Gray's Inn, 1948. A Social Security (formerly Nat. Ins.) Comr, 1977–89. *Recreations:* wine and song, travel and amateur dramatics. *Address:* Fair Orchard, Camden Road, Lingfield, Surrey RH7 6AF. *T:* Lingfield (0342) 832191.
See also N. B. Penny.

PENNY, Nicholas Beaver, MA, PhD; Clore Curator of Renaissance Painting, National Gallery, since 1990; *b* 21 Dec. 1949; *s* of Joseph Noel Bailey Penny, *qv*; *m* 1971, Anne Philomel Udy (marr. diss.); two *d*. *Educ:* Shrewsbury Sch.; St Catharine's Coll., Cambridge (BA, MA); Courtauld Inst., Univ. of London (MA, PhD). Leverhulme Fellow in the History of Western Art, Clare Hall, Cambridge, 1973–75; Lectr, History of Art Dept, Univ. of Manchester, 1975–82; Sen. Res. Fellow, History of Western Art, King's Coll., Cambridge, 1982–84; Keeper of Western Art, Ashmolean Mus., Oxford, and Professorial Fellow, Balliol Coll., Oxford, 1984–89. Slade Prof. of Fine Art, Univ. of Oxford, 1980–81. *Publications:* Church Monuments in Romantic England, 1977; Piranesi, 1978; (with Francis Haskell) Taste and the Antique, 1981; Mourning, 1981; (ed jtly) The Arrogant Connoisseur, 1982; (with Roger Jones) Raphael, 1983; (ed) Reynolds, 1986; Alfred and Winifred Turner, 1988; (with Robert Flynn Johnson) Lucian Freud, Works on Paper, 1988; Ruskin's Drawings, 1988; (jtly) From Giotto to Dürer, 1991; reviews for London Review of Books; articles in Apollo, Burlington Magazine, Connoisseur, Jl of Warburg and Courtauld Insts, Past and Present, and elsewhere. *Address:* The National Gallery, Trafalgar Square, WC2.

PENNYCUICK, Prof. Colin James, FRS 1990; Maytag Professor of Ornithology, University of Miami, since 1983; *b* 11 June 1933; *s* of Brig. James Alexander Charles Pennycuick, DSO and Marjorie Pennycuick; one *s*. *Educ:* Wellington College; Merton College, Oxford (MA); Peterhouse, Cambridge (PhD). Lectr in Zoology, 1964–83, Reader, 1975–83, Bristol Univ.; seconded as Lectr in Zoology, Univ. of Nairobi, 1968–71, as Dep. Dir, Serengeti Res. Inst., 1971–73. *Publications:* Animal Flight, 1972; Bird Flight Performance, 1989. *Recreations:* gliding. *Address:* Department of Biology, University of Miami, PO Box 249118, Coral Gables, Fla 33124, USA.

PENRHYN, 6th Baron *cr* 1866; **Malcolm Frank Douglas-Pennant,** DSO 1945; MBE 1943; *b* 11 July 1908; 2nd *s* of 5th Baron Penrhyn and Alice Nellie (*d* 1965), *o d* of Sir William Charles Cooper, 3rd Bt; *S* father 1967; *m* 1954, Elisabeth Rosemary, *d* of late Brig. Sir Percy Laurie, KCVO, CBE, DSO, JP; two *d*. *Educ:* Eton; RMC, Sandhurst. Colonel (retd), KRRC. *Heir:* *b* Hon. Nigel Douglas-Pennant [*b* 22 Dec. 1909; *m* 1st, 1935, Margaret Dorothy (*d* 1938), *d* of T. G. Kirkham; one *s*; 2nd, 1940, Eleanor Stewart (*d* 1987), *d* of late Very Rev. H. N. Craig; one *s* one *d*]. *Address:* Littleton Manor, Winchester, Hants SO22 6QU. *T:* Winchester (0962) 880205. *Clubs:* Naval and Military, Flyfishers'.
See also Sir T. R. Troubridge, Bt.

PENRICE, Geoffrey, CB 1978; consultant, since 1981, including International Monetary Fund Adviser, Ministry of Finance, Thailand, 1984–86; *b* Wakefield, 28 Feb. 1923; *s* of Harry and Jessie Penrice; *m* 1947, Janet Gillies Allardice; three *s*. *Educ:* Thornes House Grammar Sch.; London Sch. of Economics. Control Commn for Germany, 1947; Asst Lectr in Statistics, LSE, 1952; Statistician, Inland Revenue, 1956; Statistician and Chief Statistician, Central Statistical Office, 1964; Chief Statistician, Min. of Housing and Local Govt, 1968; Under-Sec., BoT, Min. of Technology, DTI, 1968–73; Principal Dir of Stats, DoE, later DoE and Dept of Transport, 1973–78; Dir of Stats, and Dep. Sec., DoE, 1978–81. Statistical Adviser to Cttee on Working of Monetary System, 1957–59; OECD Consultant, Turkey, 1981–83. *Publications:* articles on wages, earnings, financial statistics and housing statistics. *Address:* 10 Dartmouth Park Avenue, NW5. *T:* 071–267 2175. *Club:* Reform.

PENRITH, Bishop Suffragan of, since 1979; **Rt. Rev. George Lanyon Hacker;** *b* 27 Dec. 1928; *s* of Edward Sidney Hacker and Carla Lanyon; *m* 1969, June Margaret Erica Smart; one *s* one *d*. *Educ:* Kelly College, Tavistock; Exeter College, Oxford (BA 1952, MA 1956); Cuddesdon College, Oxford. Deacon 1954, priest 1955, Bristol; Curate of St Mary Redcliffe, Bristol, 1954–59; Chaplain, King's College London at St Boniface Coll., Warminster, 1959–64; Perpetual Curate, Church of the Good Shepherd, Bishopwearmouth, 1964–71; Rector of Tilehurst, Reading, 1971–79. Pres., Rural Theol. Assoc., 1989–; Chm., Age Concern Cumbria, 1987–91; Episcopal Advr, Anglican Young People's Assoc., 1987–. *Recreations:* photography, boating. *Address:* Great Salkeld Rectory, Penrith, Cumbria CA11 9NA. *T:* Lazonby (076883) 273.

PENROSE, Hon. Lord; George William Penrose; a Senator of the College of Justice in Scotland, since 1990; *b* 2 June 1938; *s* of late George W. Penrose and Janet L. Penrose; *m* 1964, Wendy Margaret Cooper; one *s* two *d*. *Educ:* Glasgow Univ. (MA, LLB). CA. Advocate, 1964; QC 1978; Advocate Depute, 1986; Home Advocate Depute, 1988. Procurator to Gen. Assembly of Ch. of Scotland, 1984–90. Pres., Scottish procs of Aircraft and Shipbuilding Industries Arbitration Tribunal, 1977–83; Mem., panel of Chairmen, Financial Services Tribunal, 1988–90. *Recreation:* walking. *Address:* 5 Cobden Road, Edinburgh EH9 2BJ. *T:* 031–667 1819.

PENROSE, Prof. Edith Tilton; economic consultant; Hon. Visiting Fellow in Management Economics, University of Bradford, 1989–June 1992; Professor, 1977–84, Associate Dean for Research and Development, 1982–84, Professor Emeritus, since 1984, Institut Européen d'Administration des Affaires, Fontainebleau; Professor of Economics (with reference to Asia), School of Oriental and African Studies, University of London, 1964–78, Professor Emeritus, since 1978; *b* 29 Nov. 1914; *d* of George Albert Tilton and Hazel Sparling Tilton; *m* 1st, 1934, David Burton Denhardt (*d* 1938); 2nd, 1944, Ernest F. Penrose (*d* 1984); three *s*. *Educ:* Univ. of California, Berkeley (AB); Johns Hopkins Univ. (MA, PhD). Research Assoc., ILO, Geneva and Montreal, 1939–41; Special Asst, US Ambassador, London, 1941–46; US Delegn to UN, NY, 1946–47; research at Johns Hopkins Univ., 1948–50; Lectr and Res. Assoc., Johns Hopkins Univ., 1950–60; Vis. Fellow, Australian Nat. Univ., 1955–56; Assoc. Prof. of Econs, Univ. Baghdad, 1957–59; Reader in Econs, Univ. of London (LSE and SOAS), 1960–64; Head, Dept of Econs, SOAS, 1964–79. Associate Fellow, Oxford Centre of Management Studies, later Templeton College, Oxford, 1982–85; Visiting Professor: Univ. Dar Es Salaam, 1971–72; Univ. of Toronto, 1977. Member: Sainsbury Cttee of Enquiry into Relationship of Pharmaceutical Industry with Nat. Health Service, 1965–67; SSRC, 1974–76 (Econ. Cttee, 1970–76, Chm., 1974–76); Medicines Commn, 1975–78; Dir, Commonwealth Develt Corp., 1975–78; Mem. Council, Royal Economic Soc., 1975–; Governor, NIESR, 1974–. Dr *hc*: Uppsala, 1984; Helsinki Sch. of Econs, 1991. Award for distinguished contribs to lit. of energy econs, Internat. Assoc. of Energy Economists, 1986. *Publications:* Food Control in Great Britain, 1940; Economics of the International Patent System, 1951; The Theory of the Growth of the Firm, 1959; The Large International Firm in Developing Countries: The International Petroleum Industry, 1968; The Growth of Firms, Middle East Oil and Other Essays, 1971; (with E. F. Penrose) Iraq: international relations and national development, 1978; articles and contributions to books. *Recreations:* travel, theatre, gardening. *Address:* The Barn, 30A Station Road, Waterbeach, Cambridge CB5 9HT. *T:* Cambridge (0223) 861618. *Club:* Commonwealth Trust.

PENROSE, George William; *see* Penrose, Hon. Lord.

PENROSE, Maj.-Gen. (retd) John Hubert, OBE 1956; MC 1944; *b* 24 Oct. 1916; *e s* of late Brig. John Penrose, MC and late Mrs M. C. Penrose (*née* Hendrick-Aylmer); *m* 1941, Pamela Elizabeth, *d* of late H. P. Lloyd, Neath, Glam.; four *d*. *Educ:* Winchester Coll.; RMA Woolwich, 2nd Lieut, RA, 1936; war service in European Theatre, BEF, 1939–40, and BLA, 1944; subseq. service in India, Germany, Malaya and UK; idc 1964; Defence Adviser to British High Comr, New Delhi, 1968–71; retired 1972. *Publication:* (with Brigitte Mitchell) Letters from Bath, 1766–1767, by the Rev. John Penrose, 1983. *Address:* West Hoe House, Bishop's Waltham, Southampton SO3 1DT. *T:* Bishop's Waltham (0489) 892363.

PENROSE, Prof. Oliver, FRS 1987; FRSE; Professor of Mathematics, Heriot-Watt University, since 1986; *b* 6 June 1929; *s* of Lionel S. Penrose, FRS, and Margaret Penrose (*née* Leathes); *m* 1953, Joan Lomas Dilley; two *s* one *d* (and one *s* decd); *Educ:* Central Collegiate Inst., London, Ont; University Coll. London (BSc); Cambridge Univ. (PhD). FRSE 1989. Mathematical Physicist, English Electric Co., Luton, 1952–55; Res. Asst, Yale Univ., 1955–56; Lectr, then Reader, in Mathematics, Imperial Coll., London 1956–69; Prof. of Mathematics, Open Univ., 1969–86. *Publications:* Foundations of Statistical Mechanics, 1970; about 50 papers in physics jls; a few book reviews. *Recreations:* making music, chess. *Address:* 29 Frederick Street, Edinburgh EH2 2ND. *T:* 031–225 5879.
See also R. Penrose.

PENROSE, Prof. Roger, FRS 1972; Rouse Ball Professor of Mathematics, University of Oxford, since 1973; *b* Colchester, Essex, 8 Aug. 1931; *s* of Lionel Sharples Penrose, FRS; *m* 1959, Joan Isabel Wedge (marr. diss. 1981); three *s*; *m* 1988, Vanessa Dee Thomas. *Educ:* University Coll. Sch.; University Coll., Univ. of London (BSc spec. 1st cl. Mathematics), Fellow 1975; St John's Coll., Cambridge (PhD; Hon. Fellow, 1987). NRDC (temp. post, Feb.-Aug. 1956); Asst Lectr (Pure Mathematics), Bedford Coll., London, 1956–57; Research Fellow, St John's Coll., Cambridge, 1957–60; NATO Research Fellow, Princeton Univ. and Syracuse Univ., 1959–61; Research Associate King's Coll., London, 1961–63; Visiting Associate Prof., Univ. of Texas, Austin, Texas, 1963–64; Reader, 1964–66, Prof. of Applied Mathematics, 1966–73, Birkbeck Coll., London. Visiting Prof., Yeshiva, Princeton, Cornell, 1966–67 and 1969; Lovett Prof., Rice Univ., Houston, 1983–87; Distinguished Prof. of Physics and Maths, Syracuse Univ., NY, 1987–. Member: London Mathematical Soc.; Cambridge Philosophical Soc.; Inst. for Mathematics and its Applications; International Soc. for General Relativity and Gravitation. Adams Prize (Cambridge Univ.), 1966–67; Dannie Heineman Prize (Amer. Phys. Soc. and Amer. Inst. Physics), 1971; Eddington Medal (with S. W. Hawking), RAS, 1975; Royal Medal, Royal Soc., 1985; Wolf Foundn Prize for Physics (with S. W. Hawking), 1988; Dirac Medal and Prize, Inst. of Physics, 1989; Einstein Medal, 1990. *Publications:* Techniques of Differential Topology in Relativity, 1973; (with W. Rindler) Spinors and Space-time, Vol. 1, 1984, Vol. 2, 1986; The Emperor's New Mind, 1989 (Science Book Prize, 1990); many articles in scientific jls. *Recreations:* 3 dimensional puzzles, doodling at the piano. *Address:* Mathematical Institute, 24–29 St Giles, Oxford OX1 3LB. *T:* Oxford (0865) 273546.

PENRY-DAVEY, David Herbert; QC 1988; barrister; a Recorder, since 1986; *b* 16 May 1942; *s* of Watson and Lorna Penry-Davey; *m* 1970, Judy Walter; two *s* one *d*. *Educ:* Hastings Grammar Sch.; King's Coll., London (LLB Hons). British Univs debating tour of Canada, 1964. Called to the Bar, Inner Temple, 1965. *Recreations:* music, golf, cycling. *Address:* 15 Carson Road, SE21 8HT. *T:* 081–670 4929.

PENTECOST, David Henry; Executive Director, European Foundantion for Quality Management, since 1990; *b* 17 March 1938; *s* of Walter Henry Pentecost and Emily Louisa Pentecost; *m* 1st, 1959, Maureen Monica Taylor (marr. diss. 1979); one *s* one *d*; 2nd, 1980, Ann Carol Ansell (*née* Hills); one *s* one *d*. *Educ:* Battersea Grammar Sch.; Wandsworth Sch.; King's Coll., London (LLB, AKC); FInstPS. Called to Bar, Gray's Inn, 1962. Post Office: Asst Principal, 1962; Asst Private Sec. to Postmaster General, 1969; Dep. Telephone Man., 1972; Dir, Major Systems Procurement, British Telecom, 1982, subseq. British Telecom Plc, 1984; Chief Procurement Officer, 1986–88, Gp Dir of Quality, 1988–90, British Telecom Plc. *Recreations:* walking, period house restoration. *Address:* Mount Pleasant Farmhouse, Lamberhurst, Kent TN3 8LX. *T:* Lamberhurst (0892) 890953.

PENZER, Dr Geoffrey Ronald, CChem, FRSC; Partner, Penzer Allen, since 1992; *b* 15 Nov. 1943; *s* of Ronald and Dora Penzer; *m* 1966, Sylvia Elaine (*née* Smith); one *s* one *d*. *Educ:* Merchant Taylors' Sch.; St John's Coll., Oxford (MA; DPhil 1969). CChem, FRSC 1979. Jun. Res. Fellow, Merton Coll., Oxford, 1967–69; Res. Chemist, Univ. of Calif, 1969–70; Lectr in Biol Chem., Univ. of York, 1970–75; British Council: Science Officer, Cairo, 1975–80; Science Officer, Mexico, 1980–84; Dir, Technical Co-operation Training Dept, 1984–87; Dir, Management Div., and Manager, HQ Location Project, 1987–91. *Publications:* contrib. scientific books and jls. *Recreations:* music, landscapes, walking. *Address:* Laston House, Heslington, York YO1 5DT; c/o Penzer Allen, 75 Westow Hill, SE19 1TX.

PENZIAS, Dr Arno Allan; Vice-President, Research, AT&T Bell Laboratories, since 1981; *b* 26 April 1933; *s* of Karl and Justine Penzias; *m* 1954, Anne Barras Penzias; one *s* two *d*. *Educ:* City Coll. of New York (BS Physics, 1954); Columbia Univ. (MA Physics, 1958; PhD Physics, 1962). Bell Laboratories: Mem., Technical Staff, 1961–72; Head, Radio Physics Res., 1972–76; Dir, Radio Res. Lab., 1976–79; Exec. Dir, Research, Communications Sciences, 1979–81. Lectr, Princeton Univ., 1967–72, Vis. Prof., Astrophysical Scis Dept, 1972–85; Res. Associate, Harvard Univ., 1968–80; Adjunct Prof., State Univ. of NY, Stony Brook, 1974–84. Lectures: Kompfner, Stanford Univ., 1979; Gamow, Colorado Univ., 1980; Jansky, NRAO, 1983; Michelson Meml, Dept US Navy, 1985; Tanner, Southern Utah State Coll., 1987; Klopsteg, Northwestern Univ., 1987; NSF Distinguished, 1987; Regent's, Univ. of Calif., Berkeley, 1989. Member: Sch. of Engrg and Applied Science (Bd Overseers), Univ. Pennsylvania, 1983–86; Union Councils for Soviet Jews Adv. Bd, 1983–; NSF Industrial Panel on Science and Technology, 1982–; CIT Vis. Cttee, 1977–79; NSF Astronomy Adv. Panel, 1978–79; MNAS, 1975–; Wissenschaftliche Fachbeirat, Max-Planck Inst., Bonn, 1978–85 (Chm., 1981–83); Bd of Dirs, IMNET, 1986–. Vice-Chm., Cttee of Concerned Scientists, 1976– (Mem., 1975–). Mem., National Acad. of Engrg, 1990. Trustee, Trenton State Coll., 1977–79. Dir, Grad. Faculties Alumni, Columbia Univ., 1987–. Hon. degrees: Paris Observatory, 1976; Wilkes Coll., City Coll. of NY, Yeshiva Univ., and Rutgers Univ., 1979; Bar Ilan Univ., 1983; Monmouth Coll., 1984; Technion-Israel Inst. of Technology, Pittsburgh Univ., Ball State Univ., Kean Coll., 1986; Ohio State Univ., Iona Coll., 1988; Drew Univ., 1989; Lafayette Coll., 1990. Henry Draper Medal, National Acad. of Sciences, 1977; Herschel Medal, RAS, 1977; (jtly) Nobel Prize for Physics, 1978; Townsend Harris Medal, City Coll. NY, 1979; Newman Award, City Coll. NY, 1983; Joseph Handleman Prize in the Scis, 1983; Grad. Faculties Alumni Award, 1984; Big Brothers Inc. of NY, City Achievement in Science Award, 1985; Priestly Award, Dickinson Coll., 1989; Pake Prize, APS, 1990. Mem. Editorial Bd, Annual Revs of Astronomy and Astrophysics,

1974–78; Associate Editor, Astrophysical Jl Letters, 1978–82. *Publications:* Ideas and Information: managing in a high-tech world, 1989; 100 published articles, principally in Astrophysical Jl. *Address:* AT&T Bell Laboratories, 600 Mountain Avenue, Murray Hill, NJ 07974, USA. *T:* (201) 582–3361.

PEPLOE, Denis (Frederic Neil), RSA 1966 (ARSA 1956); former Teacher of drawing and painting at Edinburgh College of Art; *b* 25 March 1914; *s* of late Samuel John Peploe, RSA, and late Margaret Peploe (*née* Mackay); *m* 1957, Elizabeth Marion (*née* Barr); one *s* one *d*. *Educ:* Edinburgh Academy. Studied at Edinburgh College of Art and Académie André Lhote, 1931–37. Served War of 1939–45: Royal Artillery and Intelligence Corps. Lectr, Edinburgh College of Art, 1954–79, retd, Governor 1982–85. *Recreations:* hill-walking, mycology. *Address:* 18 Mayfield Gardens, Edinburgh EH9 2BZ. *T:* 031–667 6164.

PEPPARD, Nadine Sheila, CBE 1970; race relations consultant; *b* 16 Jan. 1922; *d* of late Joseph Anthony Peppard and May Peppard (*née* Barber). *Educ:* Macclesfield High Sch.; Manchester Univ. (BA, Teacher's Dip.). French teacher, Maldon Grammar Sch., 1943–46; Spanish Editor, George G. Harrap & Co. Ltd, 1946–55; Trg Dept, Marks and Spencer, 1955–57; Dep. Gen.-Sec., London Council of Social Service, 1957–64; Nat. Advisory Officer for Commonwealth Immigrants, 1964–65; Gen. Sec., Nat. Cttee for Commonwealth Immigrants, 1965–68; Chief Officer, Community Relations Commn, 1968–72; Adviser on Race Relations, Home Office, 1972–83, retd. *Publications:* (trans.) Primitive India, 1954; (trans.) Toledo, 1955; various professional articles. *Recreations:* cookery, writing. *Address:* 20 Park House, Park Place, Cheltenham, Glos. *T:* Cheltenham (0242) 242583.

PEPPER, Prof. Gordon Terry, CBE 1990; Director, Centre for Financial Markets, since 1988, and Professor, since 1991, City University Business School (Hon. Visiting Professor, 1987–90); Chairman, Payton Pepper & Sons Ltd, since 1987; *b* 2 June 1934; *s* of Harold Terry Pepper and Jean Margaret Gordon Pepper (*née* Furness); *m* 1958, Gillian Clare Huelin; three *s* one *d*. *Educ:* Repton; Trinity College, Cambridge (MA); FIA, Fellow, Soc. of Investment Analysts. Equity & Law Life Assurance Soc., 1957–60; W. Greenwell & Co.: Partner, 1962; Joint Senior Partner, 1980–86; Chairman, Greenwell Montagu & Co., 1986–87; Dir and Sen. Advr, Midland Montagu, 1985–90. Member: Cttee on Industry and Finance, NEDC, 1988–90; ESRC, 1989–. *Publications:* Money, Credit and Inflation, 1990; papers to Jl of Inst. of Actuaries. *Recreations:* sailing, tennis, family. *Address:* Staddleden, Sissinghurst, Cranbrook, Kent TN17 2AN. *T:* Cranbrook (0580) 712852. *Clubs:* Reform, Royal Ocean Racing.

PEPPER, Kenneth Bruce, CB 1965; Commissioner of HM Customs and Excise, 1957–73; *b* 11 March 1913; *s* of late E. E. Pepper; *m* 1945, Irene Evelyn Watts; two *s*. *Educ:* County High Sch., Ilford; London Sch. of Economics. Joined HM Customs and Excise, 1932; Asst Sec., 1949; Commissioner, 1957. Lieutenant, Intelligence Corps, 1944. *Address:* Fairfield, Cae Mair, Beaumaris, Gwynedd LL58 8YN.

PEPPER, Prof. Michael, FRS 1983; Professor of Physics, University of Cambridge, since 1987; Professorial Fellow of Trinity College, Cambridge, since 1987 (Senior Research Fellow, 1982–87); Managing Director, Toshiba Cambridge Research Centre Ltd, since 1990; *b* 10 Aug. 1942; *s* of Morris and Ruby Pepper; *m* 1973, Jeannette Denise Josse, MB, BS, MRCPsych; two *d*. *Educ:* St Marylebone Grammar Sch.; Reading Univ. (BSc Physics, 1963; PhD Physics, 1967); ScD Cantab 1989. FInstP. Res. Physicist, Mullard Ltd, 1967–69; res. in solid state physics, The Plessey Co., Allen Clark Res. Centre, 1969–73; Cavendish Lab., 1973–87 (in association with The Plessey Co., 1973–82); Warren Res. Fellow of Royal Soc., Cavendish Lab., 1978–86; Principal Res. Fellow, GEC plc, Hirst Res. Centre, 1982–87. Vis. Prof., Bar-Ilan Univ., Israel, 1984; Inaugural Mott Lectr, Inst. of Physics, 1985; Royal Soc. Review Lectr, 1987; Rankin Lectr, Liverpool Univ., 1987; G. I. Taylor Lectr, Cambridge Philosophical Soc., 1988. Past and present mem. of various cttees and panels of Inst. of Physics, Royal Soc. (Associate Editor, 1983–89), Rutherford Meml Cttee, 1987–, and SERC (Cttees on Solid State Devices, Semiconductors, 1984–89). Guthrie Prize and Medal, Inst. of Physics, 1985; Hewlett-Packard Prize, European Physical Soc., 1985; Hughes Medal, Royal Soc., 1987. *Publications:* papers on semiconductors and solid state physics in jls. *Recreations:* whisky tasting, reading, travel, homework with two *d*. *Address:* Cavendish Laboratory, Madingley Road, Cambridge CB3 0HE. *T:* Cambridge (0223) 337330; Toshiba Cambridge Research Centre, 260 Cambridge Science Park, Milton Road, Cambridge CB4 4WE. *T:* Cambridge (0223) 424666.

PEPPIATT, Hugh Stephen Kenneth; Chairman, Moorfields Eye Hospital, since 1991; *b* 18 Aug. 1930; *s* of late Sir Leslie Peppiatt, MC and Lady (Cicely) Peppiatt; *m* 1960, Claire, *e d* of late Ian Douglas Davidson, CBE and Claire Davidson; three *s* two *d*. *Educ:* Winchester College; Trinity College, Oxford; Univ. of Wisconsin. Partner, Freshfields, Solicitors, 1960–90: Resident Partner, New York, 1977–81; Sen. Partner, 1982–90. Dir, Greig Fester, 1990–; Chm., Butten Trustees, PA Consulting Gp, 1986–. Trustee, Help the Aged, 1991–. *Recreations:* hillwalking, fly fishing, birdwatching. *Address:* 28 Bathgate Road, Wimbledon, SW19 5PN. *T:* 081–947 2709. *Clubs:* City of London; Royal Wimbledon Golf; Racquet and Tennis, Larchmont Yacht (New York).

PEPPITT, John Raymond, QC 1976; **His Honour Judge Peppitt;** a Circuit Judge, since 1991; *b* 22 Sept. 1931; *s* of late Reginald Peppitt and Phyllis Claire Peppitt; *m* 1960, Judith Penelope James; three *s*. *Educ:* St Paul's Sch.; Jesus Coll., Cambridge (BA Classical Tripos). Called to the Bar, Gray's Inn, 1958, Bencher, 1982; a Recorder, 1976–91. *Recreation:* collecting water-colours.

PEPYS, family name of **Earl of Cottenham.**

PEPYS, Lady (Mary) Rachel, DCVO 1968 (CVO 1954); Lady-in-Waiting to Princess Marina, Duchess of Kent, 1943–68; *b* 27 June 1905; *e d* of 15th Duke of Norfolk, KG, GCVO, PC (*d* 1917); *m* 1st, 1939, as Lady Rachel Fitzalan Howard, Lieutenant-Colonel Colin Keppel Davidson, CIE, OBE, RA (killed in action, 1943), *s* of Col Leslie Davidson, CB, RHA, and Lady Theodora, *d* of 7th Earl of Albemarle; one *s* one *d*; 2nd, 1961, Brigadier Anthony Hilton Pepys, DSO (*d* 1967). *Address:* Highfield House, Crossbush, Arundel, W Sussex. *T:* Arundel (0903) 883158.

PERAHIA, Murray, FRCM; pianist; co-artistic director, Aldeburgh Festival, 1981–89; *b* New York, 19 April 1947; *s* of David and Flora Perahia; *m* 1980, Naomi Shohet (Ninette); one *s*. *Educ:* High Sch. of Performing Arts; Mannes College (MS); studied piano with Jeanette Haien, M. Horszowski, Arthur Balsam. Won Kosciusko Chopin Prize, 1965; début Carnegie Recital Hall, 1966; won Leeds Internat. Piano Festival, 1972; Avery Fisher Award, 1975; regular tours of Europe, Asia, USA; numerous recordings include complete Mozart Piano Concertos (records as conductor and pianist) and complete Beethoven Piano Concertos. *Address:* c/o Harold Holt, 31 Sinclair Road, W14.

PERCEVAL, family name of **Earl of Egmont.**

PERCEVAL, Viscount; Thomas Frederick Gerald Perceval; *b* 17 Aug. 1934; *e s* of 11th Earl of Egmont, *qv*.

PERCEVAL, Michael; HM Diplomatic Service; Consul-General, São Paulo, since 1990; *b* 27 April 1936; *o s* of late Hugh Perceval and Guida Brind; *m* 1968, Alessandra Grandis; one *s* one *d*. *Educ:* Downside Sch.; Christ Church, Oxford (Schol.; 2nd Cl. Hons English Lit.). Served Royal Air Force, Nicosia, 1956–60; film production asst, Athens, 1960; freelance correspondent, Madrid, 1961–69. Joined FCO, 1970; First Sec. (Press), UK Rep. to EC, Brussels, 1972–74; First Sec. and subseq. Head of Chancery, British High Commission, Nicosia, 1974–78; Asst Head of Mexico and Caribbean Dept, FCO, 1978–79; Counsellor, Havana, 1980–82; Counsellor (Political and Economic) and Consul-Gen., Brasilia, 1982–85; Counsellor (Commercial), Rome, 1985–89. *Publication:* The Spaniards, 1969, 2nd edn 1972. *Recreations:* music, walking, the Mediterranean. *Address:* c/o Foreign and Commonwealth Office, King Charles Street, Whitehall, SW1. *Club:* Commonwealth Trust.

PERCEVAL, Robert Westby, TD 1968; Clerk Assistant, House of Lords, 1964–74; retired; *b* 28 Aug. 1914; *m* 1948, Hon. J. I. L. Littleton, *er d* of 5th Baron Hatherton; two *s* two *d*. *Educ:* Ampleforth; Balliol College, Oxford. Joined Parliament Office, House of Lords, 1938. Royal Artillery, 1939–44; General Staff, War Office, 1944–45. *Address:* Pillaton Old Hall, Penkridge, Staffs ST19 5RZ. *Clubs:* Beefsteak, Turf.

PERCHARD, Colin William, OBE 1984; British Council Director and Cultural Counsellor, Turkey, since 1990; *b* 19 Oct. 1940; *m* 1970, Elisabeth Penelope Glynis, *d* of Sir Glyn Jones, *qv*; three *s*. *Educ:* Victoria Coll., Jersey; Liverpool Univ. (BA Hons History); Internat. Inst. for Educnl Planning, UNESCO, Paris (DipEd Planning and Admin). British Council: Asst Rep., Blantyre, Malawi, 1964–68; Regional Officer, Africa S of the Sahara, 1968–71: Asst Rep., Calcutta, 1971–72; Officer i/c Dhaka, 1972; Rep., Seoul, 1973–76; Dir, Technical Co-operation Trng Dept, 1976–79; Internat. Inst. for Educnl Planning, Paris, 1979–80; Rep., Harare, 1980–86; Controller, Africa Div., 1986–90. *Recreations:* theatre, music, cooking. *Address:* The British Council, 10 Spring Gardens, SW1A 2BN. *T:* 071–930 8466.

PERCIVAL, Allen Dain, CBE 1975; Chairman, Stainer & Bell Publishers, since 1978; *b* 23 April 1925; *s* of Charles and Gertrude Percival, Bradford; *m* 1st, 1952, Rachel Hay (*d* 1987); 2nd, 1990, Margaret Pickett. *Educ:* Bradford Grammar Sch.; Magdalene Coll., Cambridge. MusB Cantab 1948. Served War of 1939–45, RNVR. Music Officer of British Council in France, 1948–50; Music Master, Haileybury and Imp. Service Coll., 1950–51; Dir of Music, Homerton Coll., Cambridge, 1951–62; Conductor, CUMS, 1954–58; Dir of Music Studies, GSM, 1962–65, Principal, GSMD, 1965–78; Gresham Prof. of Music, City Univ., 1980–85; Dir, Hong Kong Academy for Performing Arts, 1987–89. Also professional continuo playing, broadcasting and conducting. FRCM; FGSM; FLCM 1986; Hon. RAM 1966; Hon. FTCL 1967; Fellow: Hong Kong Conservatory of Music, 1980; Curwen Inst., 1981. Hon. DMus City, 1978. *Publications:* The Orchestra, 1956; The Teach Yourself History of Music, 1961; Music at the Court of Elizabeth I, 1975; Galliard Book of Carols, 1980; English Love Songs, 1980; contribs to musical and educnl jls. *Recreations:* travel, gardening. *Address:* Water Gate, Water Lane, Charlton Horethorne, near Sherborne, Dorset DT9 4NX. *T:* Corton Denham (096322) 219.

PERCIVAL, Sir Anthony (Edward), Kt 1966; CB 1954; Chairman, Gordon & Gotch Holdings Ltd, 1971–81; *b* 23 Sept. 1910; *m* 1935, Doris Cuff (*d* 1988); one *d*. *Educ:* Manchester Gram. Sch.; Cambridge. Entered Board of Trade, 1933; Assistant Secretary, 1942; Commercial Counsellor, Washington, on Secondment, 1946–49; Under-Secretary, Board of Trade, 1949–58; Sec., Export Credits Guarantee Dept, 1962–71. Formerly: Director: Simon Engineering; Trade Indemnity Co., 1973–81; Bank of Adelaide; Switzerland (General) Insurance Co. President: Berne Union of Export Credit Insurance Organisations, 1966–68; Export Credit Gp, OECD, Paris, 1967–70. *Address:* 120 Rue Boecklin, Strasbourg 67000, France.

PERCIVAL, Rt. Hon. Sir Ian, Kt 1979; PC 1983; QC 1963; *b* 11 May 1921; *s* of Eldon and Chrystine Percival; *m* 1942, Madeline Buckingham Cooke; one *s* one *d*. *Educ:* Latymer Upper School; St Catharine's College, Cambridge (MA). Served HM Forces, 1940–46: 2nd Bn the Buffs, N Africa and Burma; Major. Called to the Bar, Inner Temple, 1948, Bencher, 1970, Reader, 1989, Treas., 1990. Recorder of Deal, later of the Crown Court, 1971–. MP (C) Southport, 1959–87. Solicitor-General, 1979–83; Conservative Parly Legal Committee: Sec., 1964–68; Vice-Chm., 1968–70; Chm., 1970–74 and 1983–87. Mem., Sidley & Austin, US and Internat. Attorneys at Law, 1984–. Fellow, Inst. of Taxation (Chm., Parly Cttee, 1965–71); Mem., Royal Economic Soc.; FCIArb 1983. Pres., Masonic Trust for Girls and Boys. Freeman, City of London, 1987; Liveryman, Co. of Arbitrators, 1987–. *Recreations:* golf, parachuting, windsurfing, tennis. *Address:* 2 Harcourt Buildings, Temple, EC4Y 7HB. *T:* 071–583 2939; (chambers) 5 Paper Buildings, Temple, EC4. *T:* 071–583 9275; Oxenden, Stone-in-Oxney, near Tenterden, Kent. *Clubs:* Carlton, Beefsteak, City Livery; Rye Golf; Royal Birkdale Golf.

PERCIVAL, Prof. Ian Colin, PhD; FRS 1985; Professor of Applied Mathematics, Queen Mary and Westfield (formerly Queen Mary) College, University of London, since 1974; *b* 27 July 1931; *m* 1955, Jill Cuff (*née* Herbert); two *s* one *d*. *Educ:* Ealing County Grammar Sch.; UCL (BSc, PhD; Fellow, 1986). FRAS. Lectr in Physics, UCL, 1957–61; Reader in Applied Maths, QMC, 1961–67; Prof. of Theoret. Physics, Univ. of Stirling, 1967–74. Naylor Prize, London Mathematical Soc., 1985. *Publications:* (with Derek Richards) Introduction to Dynamics, 1983; (with Owen Greene and Irene Ridge) Nuclear Winter, 1985; papers in learned jls on scattering theory, atomic and molecular theory, statistical mechanics, classical dynamics and theory of chaos. *Address:* Queen Mary and Westfield College, Mile End Road, E1 4NS. *T:* 081–980 4811.

PERCIVAL, Prof. John, FSA; Professor and Head of School of History and Archaeology, University of Wales College of Cardiff, since 1988; *b* 11 July 1937; *s* of Walter William Percival and Eva Percival (*née* Bowers); *m* 1st, 1962, Carole Ann Labrum (*d* 1977); two *d*; 2nd, 1988, Jacqueline Anne Gibson (*née* Donovan). *Educ:* Colchester Royal Grammar Sch.; Hertford Coll., Oxford (Lucy Schol.; 1st Cl. Lit. Hum.; MA; DPhil). FSA 1977. Harmsworth Sen. Schol., Merton Coll., Oxford, 1961; University College, Cardiff: Asst Lectr in Ancient History, 1962; Lectr, 1964; Sen. Lectr, 1972; Reader, 1979; Dean of Faculty of Arts, 1977–79; Dep. Principal, Univ. of Wales Coll. of Cardiff, 1987–90. Vice-Pres., 1989–, Chm. Council, 1990–, Classical Assoc. (Jt Sec., 1979–89). *Publications:* The Reign of Charlemagne (with H. R. Loyn), 1975; The Roman Villa, 1976, 2nd edn 1988; articles in historical and archaeol jls. *Recreation:* music. *Address:* 26 Church Road, Whitchurch, Cardiff CF4 2EA. *T:* Cardiff (0222) 617869.

PERCIVAL, Robert Clarendon, FRCS, FRCOG; Consulting Obstetric Surgeon, The London Hospital; *b* 16 Sept. 1908; British; *m* 1st, 1944, Beryl Mary Ind (*d* 1967); one *d*; 2nd, 1972, Beatrice Myfanwy Evans, FFARCS. *Educ:* Barker College, NSW; Sydney University; The London Hospital (qualified 1933). Resident appointments: Poplar Hospital; Hosp. for Sick Children, Gt Ormond St; The London Hosp.; Southend Gen. Hosp. Obstetric and Gynæcological 1st Asst, The London Hosp., 1937–41; Surgeon-Lt-Comdr, RNVR, 1941–45 (Surgical Specialist); Obstetric Surgeon, The London Hospital, 1947–73, Director, Obstetric Unit, 1968–73. Chm., Obst. Adv. Cttee, NE Region Met.

Hosp. Bd, 1967–73; President: Section of Obst. and Gyn., RSocMed, 1973–74; The London Hosp. Clubs' Union, 1965 (Treasurer, 1955–73); United Hosps RFC, 1969–72; London Hosp. Cricket Club, 1946–72. *Publications:* (jtly) Ten Teachers' Midwifery, 1958, new edition as Ten Teachers' Obstetrics, 1972; (jtly) Ten Teachers' Diseases of Women, 1965, new edition as Ten Teachers' Gynæcology, 1971; (jtly) British Obstetric Practice, 1963; (ed) Holland and Brews Obstetrics, 1969, 14th edn 1979; contribs to Lancet, British Jl of Obst. and Gynæcol. *Recreations:* fishing, golf. *Address:* Coker Wood Cottage, Pendomer, near Yeovil, Somerset BA22 9PD. *T:* Corscombe (093589) 328. *Clubs:* Gynaeological Travellers' of GB and Ireland; Royal Navy Ski.

PERCIVAL, Sir (Walter) Ian; *see* Percival, Sir Ian.

PERCIVAL-PRESCOTT, Westby William, FIIC; practising conservator and painter; *b* 22 Jan. 1923; *s* of William Percival-Prescott and Edith Percival; *m* 1948, Silvia Haswell Miller; one *s. Educ:* Edinburgh Coll. of Art (DA Hons). FIIC 1957. Andrew Grant Scholar, National Gall., 1945; restoration of Rubens Whitehall ceiling, 1947–51; Restorer i/c House of Lords frescos, 1953; worked in National Gall. Conservation Dept, 1954–56; directed restoration of Painted Hall, Greenwich, 1957–60; National Maritime Museum: estabd Picture Conservation Dept, 1961; Keeper and Head of Picture Dept, 1977–83; organised first internat. conf. on Comparative Lining Techniques, 1973 (Ottawa, 1974); produced and designed historical exhibitions: Idea and Illusion, 1960; Four Steps to Longitude, 1963; The Siege of Malta, 1970; Captain Cook and Mr Hodges, 1979; The Art of the Van de Veldes, 1982. Vis. Sen. Lectr, Dept of Fine Art, Univ. of Leeds, 1980. Internat. Council of Museums: Co-ordinator, Conservation Cttee, 1975–84; Mem., Directory Bd, Conservation Cttee, 1981–84. *Publications:* The Coronation Chair, 1957; The Lining Cycle, 1974, Swedish edn 1975; Handbook of Lining Terms, 1974; Thornhill at Greenwich, 1978; Micro X-Ray Techniques, 1978; Techniques of Suction Lining, 1981; The Art of the Van de Veldes, 1982; technical papers. *Recreations:* listening to music, travel. *Address:* 34 Compayne Gardens, NW6 3DP. *T:* 071–624 4577.

PERCY, family name of **Duke of Northumberland.**

PERCY, Algernon Eustace Hugh H.; *see* Heber-Percy.

PERCY, John Pitkeathly, (Ian), CA; London Senior Partner, Grant Thornton, since 1988; *b* 16 Jan. 1942; *s* of John Percy and Helen Glass Percy (*née* Pitkeathly); *m* 1965, Sheila Isobel Horn; two *d. Educ:* Edinburgh Acad. Qualified as a Chartered Accountant with Graham Smart & Annan, Edinburgh, 1968; Grant Thornton: Partner, Edinburgh, 1970–78; London, 1978–: Managing Partner, 1981–88. Hon. Prof. of Accounting and Auditing, Aberdeen Univ., 1988–. Pres., Inst. of Chartered Accountants of Scotland, 1990–91 (Sen. Vice-Pres., 1989–91). Freeman, City of London, 1983; Liveryman, Painter Stainers' Co., 1983. FRSA 1989. *Recreations:* golf, fishing. *Address:* Grant Thornton, Grant Thornton House, Melton Street, Euston Square, NW1 2EP. *T:* 071–383 5100; 30 Midmar Drive, Edinburgh EH10 6BU. *T:* 031–447 3645. *Clubs:* Royal Automobile, Institute of Directors, Caledonian; New (Edinburgh); Denham Golf; Royal & Ancient (St Andrews), Hon. Company of Edinburgh Golfers.

PERCY, Rodney Algernon; His Honour Judge Percy; a Circuit Judge, since 1979; *b* 15 May 1924; 3rd *s* of late Hugh James Percy, Solicitor, Alnwick; *m* 1948, Mary Allen, *d* of late J. E. Benbow, Aberystwyth; one *s* three *d. Educ:* Uppingham; Brasenose Coll., Oxford (MA). Lieut, Royal Corps of Signals, 1942–46, served in Burma, India, Malaya, Java. Called to Bar: Middle Temple, 1950; Lincoln's Inn, 1987 (*ad eund*). Dep. Coroner, N Northumberland, 1957; Asst Recorder, Sheffield QS, 1964; Dep. Chm., Co. Durham QS, 1966–71; a Recorder of the Crown Court, 1972–79. Pres., Tyneside Marriage Guidance Council, 1983–87; Founder Mem., Family Conciliation Service for Northumberland and Tyneside, 1982– (Pres., 1988–). *Publications:* (ed) Charlesworth on Negligence, 4th edn 1962, 5th edn 1971, 6th edn 1977, 7th edn (Charlesworth & Percy on Negligence) 1983, 8th edn 1990; (contrib.) Atkin's Court Forms, 2nd edn, Vol. 20, 1982, rev. edn 1987 (title Health and Safety at Work), and Vol. 29, 1983, rev. edn 1991 (title Negligence). *Recreations:* golf, gardening, hill walking, King Charles Cavalier spaniels, beach-combing. *Address:* Brookside, Lesbury, Alnwick, Northumberland NE66 3AT. *T:* Alnwick (0665) 830326.

PERDUE, Rt. Rev. Richard Gordon; *b* 13 Feb. 1910; *s* of Richard Perdue; *m* 1943, Evelyn Ruth Curry, BA; two *d. Educ:* Trinity Coll., Dublin. BA 1931; MA and BD 1938. Deacon 1933, priest 1934, Dublin. Curate of Drumcondra with N Strand, 1933–36; Rathmines, 1936–40; Incumbent of Castledermot with Kinneagh, 1940–43; Roscrea, Diocese of Killaloe, 1943–54; Archdeacon of Killaloe and Kilfenora, 1951–54; Examining Chaplain to Bishop of Killaloe, 1951–54; Bishop of Killaloe, Kilfenora, Clonfert and Kilmacduagh, 1953–57; Bishop of Cork, Cloyne and Ross, 1957–78. *Address:* 23 Le Cren Street, Timaru, New Zealand.

PEREGRINE, Gwilym Rhys, DL; Member: Independent Broadcasting Authority, 1982–89 (Chairman, Welsh Advisory Committee, 1982–89); Welsh Fourth Channel Authority, 1982–89; *b* 30 Oct. 1924; *s* of Rev. and Mrs T. J. Peregrine; *m* 1958, Gwyneth Rosemary Williams; one *s* one *d. Educ:* Caterham Sch., Surrey; Gwendraeth Valley Grammar Sch. Admitted Solicitor, 1949. Carmarthenshire County Council: Asst Solicitor, 1949–56; Dep. Clerk, 1956–72 (also Dep. Clerk of the Peace); Clerk and Chief Exec., 1972–74; Chief Exec., Dyfed CC, 1974–81. DL Dyfed, 1974. *Recreations:* golf, cricket, Rugby, music, reading. *Address:* Dôl-y-Coed, 37 Bronwydd Road, Carmarthen, Dyfed SA31 2AL. *Clubs:* Carmarthen Golf; Glamorgan Cricket, Bronwydd Cricket.

PEREIRA, Arthur Leonard, FRCS; Consulting Ear, Nose and Throat Surgeon to St George's Hospital, London; *b* 10 March 1906; British; *m* 1973, Mrs Jane Wilson (*née* Lapworth). *Educ:* Merchant Taylors' School. MRCS, LRCP 1929; MB, BS London 1931; FRCS 1936. Otologist to: the Metropolitan Hospital, E8, 1941–47; St George's Hospital, 1946–71. *Address:* Dormers, The Drive, Old Bosham, Sussex.

PEREIRA, Sir Charles; *see* Pereira, Sir H. C.

PEREIRA, Helio Gelli, DrMed; FRS 1973; FIBiol 1975; Consultant, Department of Virology, Fundação Oswaldo Cruz, Rio de Janeiro, 1979–88; *b* 23 Sept. 1918; *s* of Raul Pereira and Maria G. Pereira; *m* 1946, Marguerite McDonald Scott, MD (*d* 1987); one *s* one *d* (and one *d* decd). *Educ:* Faculdade Fluminense de Medicina, also Instituto Oswaldo Cruz, Rio de Janeiro, Brazil. British Council Scholarship, Dept of Bacteriology, Manchester Univ. and Div. of Bacteriology and Virus Research, Nat. Inst. for Med. Research, London, 1945–47; Rickettsia Laboratory, Instituto Oswaldo Cruz, 1948–51; Asst to Prof. of Microbiology, Faculdade Fluminense de Medicina, 1943–45 and 1948–51. Nat. Inst. for Med. Research, Mill Hill, London: Mem. Scientific Staff, 1951–73; Head of Div. of Virology, 1964–73; Dir, World Influenza Centre, 1961–70; Hd of Dept of Epidemiology and of World Reference Centre for Foot-and-Mouth Disease, Animal Virus Res. Inst., 1973–79. Carlos Findlay Prize, Unesco, 1987. *Publication:* (with C. H. Andrewes) Viruses of Vertebrates (3rd edn), 1972, 4th edn (with C. H. Andrewes and P. Wildy) 1978. *Recreations:* swimming, music. *Address:* 3 Ducks Walk, Twickenham, Mddx TW1 2DD. *T:* 081–892 4511.

PEREIRA, Sir (Herbert) Charles, Kt 1977; DSc; FRS 1969; Consultant, tropical agriculture research; *b* 12 May 1913; *s* of H. J. Pereira and Maud Edith (*née* Machin), both of London; *m* 1941, Irene Beatrice, *d* of David Sloan, Belfast; three *s* one *d. Educ:* Prince Albert Coll., Saskatchewan; St Albans Sch.; London Univ. Attached Rothamsted Expl Stn for PhD (London) 1941. Royal Engineers, 1941–46 (despatches). Colonial Agric. Service, Coffee Research Stn, Kenya, 1946–52; Colonial Research Service, established Physics Div. at East African Agriculture and Forestry Research Org., Kenya, 1952–61; DSc London 1961; Dir, ARC of Rhodesia and Nyasaland, 1961–63; Dir, ARC of Central Africa (Rhodesia, Zambia and Malawi), 1963–67; Dir, East Malling Research Station, 1969–72; Chief Scientist (Dep. Sec.), MAFF, 1972–77. Member: Natural Environment Res. Council, 1971–77; ARC, 1973–77; ABRC, 1973–77; Chm., Sci. Panel, Commonwealth Develt Corp., 1978–91; Pres., Tropical Agricl Assoc., 1990–. Mem. Bd of Trustees, Royal Botanic Gdns, Kew, 1983–86. FInstBiol; FRASE 1977; CompICE, 1971; Hon. DSc Cranfield, 1977. Haile Selassie Prize for Research in Africa, 1966. *Publications:* (jtly) Hydrological Effects of Land Use Changes in East Africa, 1962; Land Use and Water Resources, 1973; Policy and Practice in the Management of Tropical Watersheds, 1989; papers in research jls; Founding Editor, Rhodesian Jl Agric. Research. *Recreations:* swimming, sailing. *Address:* Peartrees, Nestor Court, Teston, Maidstone, Kent ME18 5AD. *T:* Maidstone (0622) 813333. *Clubs:* Athenæum; Harare (Zimbabwe).

PEREIRA, Margaret, CBE 1985; BSc; FIBiol; Controller, Home Office Forensic Science Service, 1982–88; *b* 22 April 1928. *Educ:* La Sainte Union Convent, Bexley Heath; Dartford County Grammar School for Girls; Chelsea Coll. of Science and Technol. BSc 1953. Joined Metropolitan Police Forensic Science Lab., New Scotland Yard, 1947; Dep. Dir, Home Office Forensic Science Central Res. Estab., 1976; Director, Home Office Forensic Science Laboratory: Aldermaston, 1977; Chepstow, 1979. *Address:* 24 Kingswood Close, Englefield Green, Egham, Surrey TW20 0NQ.

PEREIRA GRAY, Denis John; *see* Gray.

PEREIRA-MENDOZA, Vivian, MScTech, CEng, FIEE; Director, Polytechnic of the South Bank, 1970–80; *b* 8 April 1917; *o s* of Rev. Joseph Pereira-Mendoza, Manchester; *m* 1942, Marjorie, *y d* of Edward Lichtenstein; two *d. Educ:* Manchester Central High Sch.; Univ. of Manchester. Asst Lectr, Univ. of Manchester, 1939. Served War, 1940–45, in Royal Corps of Signals; Major, and GSO II (War Office). Sen. Lectr, Woolwich Polytechnic, 1948; Head of Dept: of Electrical Engrg, NW Kent Coll. of Technology, 1954; of Electrical Engrg and Physics, Borough Polytechnic, 1957; Vice-Principal, Borough Polytechnic, 1964; Principal, Borough Polytechnic, 1966–70. Mem. Council, Chelsea Coll., Univ. of London, 1972–85. Pres., Bd of Elders, Spanish and Portuguese Jews' Congregation, 1988–89 (Vice-Pres., 1986–88). *Address:* Flat 20, Whitegates, Wilmslow Road, Cheadle, Cheshire SK8 1HG. *T:* 061–491 2900.

PERES, Shimon; Vice Premier, 1986–90, Minister of Finance, 1988–90, Israel; Member of Knesset, since 1959; *b* 1923; *s* of Yitzhak and Sarah Persky; *m* 1945, Sonia Gelman; two *s* one *d. Educ:* New York Univ.; Harvard Univ. Head of Naval Services, 1948–49; Head of Israel Defense Min. delegn to US, 1949–52; Dep. Dir-Gen., Defense Min., 1953–59; Dep. Defense Minister, 1959–65; Sec. Gen., Rafi Party, 1965–67; Minister: of Immigrant Absorption, 1969–70; of Transport and Communications, 1970–74; of Information, 1974; of Defense, 1974–77; Acting Prime Minister, 1977; Prime Minister, 1984–86; Minister of Foreign Affairs, 1986–88. Chm, Israel Labour Party, 1977–; Vice-Pres., Socialist Internat., 1978–. *Publications:* The Next Phase, 1965; David's Sling, 1970; Tomorrow is Now, 1978; From These Men, 1980. *Recreation:* reading. *Address:* The Knesset, Jerusalem, Israel. *T:* 02–554111, 03–210261/2/4.

PERETZ, David Lindsay Corbett; UK Executive Director, International Monetary Fund and World Bank, and Economic Minister, Washington, since 1990; *b* 29 May 1943; *s* of Michael and April Peretz; *m* 1966, Jane Wildman; one *s* one *d. Educ:* The Leys Sch., Cambridge; Exeter Coll., Oxford (MA). Asst Principal, Min. of Technol., 1965–69; Head of Public Policy and Institutional Studies, IBRO, 1969–76; HM Treasury: Principal, 1976–80; Asst Sec., External Finance, 1980–84; Principal Pvte Sec. to Chancellor of Exchequer, 1984–85; Under-Secretary: Home Finance, 1985–86; Monetary Gp, Public Finance, 1986–90. *Recreations:* walking, sailing, listening to music. *Address:* c/o British Embassy, 3100 Massachusetts Avenue, NW, Washington, DC 20008, USA.

PÉREZ DE CUÉLLAR, Javier; Secretary-General, United Nations, 1982–91; *b* 19 Jan. 1920; *m* Marcela (*née* Temple); one *s* one *d. Educ:* Law Faculty, Catholic Univ., Lima, Perú. Joined Peruvian Foreign Ministry, 1940; Diplomatic Service, 1944; Sec., Peruvian Embassies in France, UK, Bolivia and Brazil and Counsellor, Embassy, Brazil, 1944–60; Mem., Peruvian Delegn to First Session of Gen. Assembly, UN, 1946; Dir, Legal, Personnel, Admin, Protocol and Political Affairs Depts, Min. of Foreign Affairs, Perú, 1961–63; Peruvian Ambassador to Switzerland, 1964–66; Perm. Under-Sec. and Sec.-Gen. of Foreign Office, 1966–69; Ambassador of Perú to USSR and to Poland, 1969–71; Perm. Rep. of Perú to UN, 1971–75 (Rep. to UN Security Council, 1973–74); Special Rep. of UN Sec.-Gen. in Cyprus, 1975–77; Ambassador of Perú to Venezuela, 1978–79; UN Under-Sec.-Gen. for Special Political Affairs, 1979–81. Prof. of Diplomatic Law, Academia Diplomática del Perú, 1962–63; Prof. of Internat. Relations, Academia de Guerra Aérea del Perú, 1963–64. LLD *hc:* Univ. of Nice, France, 1983; Carleton Univ., Ottawa, 1985; Osnabruck Univ., 1986; Coimbra Univ., 1986; other hon. degrees include: Jagiellonian Univ., Poland, 1984; Charles Univ. Czechoslovakia, 1984; Sofia Univ., Bulgaria, 1984; Universidad Nacional Mayor de San Marcos, Perú, 1984; Vrije Universiteit Brussel, Belgium, 1984; Sorbonne Univ., Paris, 1985; Mongolian State Univ., 1987; Cambridge Univ., 1989. Various internat. awards including: Prince of Asturias Prize, 1987; Olof Palme Prize, 1989; Jawaharlal Nehru, Award, 1989. *Publication:* Manual de Derecho Diplomático, 1964. *Address:* c/o United Nations, New York, NY 10017, USA. *T:* (212) 754–5012. *Clubs:* Nacional, Ecuestre Huachipa, Villa, Jockey (Lima, Perú).

PÉREZ ESQUIVEL, Adolfo; sculptor; Hon. President: Servicio Paz y Justicia en América Latina, since 1986; Servicio Paz y Justicia Argentina, since 1973; President, International League for the Rights and Liberation of Peoples, since 1987; *b* 26 Nov. 1931; *m* 1956, Amanda Guerreño; three *s. Educ:* Nat. Sch. of Fine Arts, Buenos Aires. Prof. of Art, Manuel Belgrano Nat. Sch. of Fine Arts, Buenos Aires, 1956–76; Prof., Faculty of Architecture and Urban Studies, Univ. Nacional de la Plata, 1969–73; Gen. Co-ordinator, Servicio Paz y Justicia en América Latina, 1974–86. Work in permanent collections: Buenos Aires Mus. of Modern Art; Mus. of Fine Arts, Córdoba; Fine Arts Mus., Rosario. Joined group dedicated to principles of militant non-violence, and engaged in projects to promote self-sufficiency in urban areas, 1971; founded Paz y Justicia magazine, 1973. Co-founder, Ecumenical Movement for Human Rights, Argentina; Pres., Permanent Assembly for Human Rights. Premio la Nación de Escultura; Pope John XXIII prize, Pax Christi Orgn, 1977; Nobel Peace Prize, 1980. *Address:* Servicio Paz y Justicia, Calle México 479, Buenos Aires, Argentina.

PERHAM, Prof. Richard Nelson, ScD, FRS 1984; Professor of Structural Biochemistry, since 1989, Head of Department of Biochemistry, since 1985, Cambridge University;

Fellow, St John's College, Cambridge, since 1964; *b* 27 April 1937; *s* of Cyril Richard William Perham and Helen Harrow Perham (*née* Thornton); *m* 1969, Nancy Jane, *d* of Temple Haviland Lane, Halifax, Nova Scotia; one *s* one *d*. *Educ:* Latymer Upper School; St John's College, Cambridge; BA 1961, MA 1965, PhD 1965, ScD 1976; Scholar; Slater Studentship, 1961–64; Henry Humphreys Prize, 1963. Nat. Service RN, 1956–58. Cambridge University: MRC Scholar, Lab. of Molecular Biol., 1961–64; Univ. Demonstrator in Biochem., 1964–69, Lectr, 1969–77; Reader in Biochemistry of Macromolecular Structures, 1977–89; Res. Fellow, St John's Coll., 1964–67, Tutor, 1967–77, Pres., 1983–87. Helen Hay Whitney Fellow, Dept of Molecular Biophysics, Yale Univ., 1966–67; EMBO Fellow, Max-Planck-Institut für Medizinische Forschung, Heidelberg, 1971; Drapers' Vis. Prof., Univ. of New South Wales, 1972; Biochem. Soc. Visitor, Aust. and NZ, 1979; Fogarty Internat. Scholar, NIH, USA, 1990–. Member: EMBO, 1983; SRC Enzyme Chem. and Tech. Cttee, 1973–75; Enzyme Panel, Biol. Scis Cttee, 1975–76; SERC Science Bd, 1985–90; Biochem. Soc. Cttee, 1980–84; British Nat. Cttee for Biochem., 1982–87; Dir's Adv. Gp, AFRC Inst. of Animal Physiology, 1983–86; Exec. Council, CIBA Foundn, 1989–; Chm., Biol Scis Cttee, SERC, 1987–90 (Mem., 1983–85); Pres., Section D (Biological Scis), BAAS, 1987–88. Syndic, CUP, 1988–. Lectures: Aust. Biochem. Soc., 1979; Alberta Heritage Foundn for Med. Res., 1982; Philip E. Wilcox Meml, Univ. of Washington, Seattle, 1983; Rosenheim, KCL, 1989; Kaplan Meml, Univ. of California, San Diego, 1990. FRSA 1988. *Publications:* (ed) Instrumentation in Amino Acid Sequence Analysis, 1975; papers in sci. jls. *Recreations:* gardening, rowing (Lady Margaret BC), theatre, nosing around in antique shops. *Address:* Department of Biochemistry, Tennis Court Road, Cambridge CB2 1QW. *T:* Cambridge (0223) 333663; St John's College, Cambridge CB2 1TP. *T:* Cambridge (0223) 338600; 107 Barton Road, Cambridge CB3 9LL. *T:* Cambridge (0223) 63752. *Club:* Hawks (Cambridge).

PERINAT, Marqués de, Luis Guillermo; Member, European Parliament, since 1986 (a Vice-President, since 1987); *b* 27 Oct. 1923; *s* of Luis Perinat and Ana Maria, Marquesa de Campo Real; *m* 1955, Blanca Escriva de Romani, Marquesa de Alginet; two *s* one *d*. *Educ:* Univs of Salamanca and Valladolid. Barrister-at-law. Sec., Spanish Embassy, Cairo, 1949–51; Dep. Consul-Gen., New York, 1954–56; Counsellor, Spanish Embassy, Paris, 1962–65; Permanent Sec., Spanish-American Jt Defence Cttee, 1965–70; Dir-Gen., N American and Far Eastern Affairs, Min. of Foreign Affairs, Madrid, 1973–76; Spanish Ambassador: to the Court of St James's, 1976–81; to the Soviet Union, 1981–83. Senator, 1983–87. Grand Cross: Order of Civil Merit (Spain); Merito Militar (Spain); Kt Comdr: Order of Isabel La Católica (Spain); Order of Merito Aeronautico (Spain); also holds foreign decorations. *Heir: s* Guillermo Perinat y Escriva de Romani, Count of Casal. *Address:* Calle del Prado 26, Madrid, Spain. *Clubs:* White's, Travellers'; Puerto de Hierro, Nuevo (Madrid).

PERKINS, Alice Elizabeth; Director of Personnel, Department of Social Security, since 1990; *b* 24 May 1949; *d* of Derrick Leslie John Perkins and Elsa Rose Perkins, CBE (*née* Rink); *m* 1978, John Whitaker Straw, *qv*; one *s* one *d*. *Educ:* North London Collegiate Sch. for Girls; St Anne's Coll., Oxford (BA Hons Modern Hist. 1971). Admin. Trainee, DHSS, 1971; Private Sec. to Minister of State for Social Security, 1974–75; Asst to Chm. of Supplementary Benefits Commn, 1975–77; Principal, 1976–84; Manager, Bromley Local Office, 1982–84; Asst Sec., DHSS, then DSS, 1984–90. Parent Governor, Henry Fawcett Jun. and Infant Schs, 1988–. *Recreations:* gardening, cooking, riding, looking at paintings. *Address:* Department of Social Security, Richmond House, 79 Whitehall, SW1A 2NS. *T:* 071–210 5831.

PERKINS, Bernard James; Chairman, Harlow Development Corporation, 1972–79; *b* 25 Jan. 1928; *y s* of George and Rebecca Perkins; *m* 1956, Patricia (*née* Payne); three *d*. *Educ:* Strand School. Member: Lambeth Council, 1962–71 (Leader, 1968–71); Community Relations Commn, 1970–72; SE Econ. Planning Council, 1971–79; Alderman, GLC, 1971–73; Chm., GLC Housing Cttee, 1972–73. *Recreation:* social service. *Address:* 38 Cedar Close, Dulwich, SE21 8HX. *T:* 081–761 8695.

PERKINS, Surg. Vice-Adm. Sir Derek Duncombe S.; *see* Steele-Perkins.

PERKINS, Prof. Donald Hill, CBE 1991; FRS 1966; Professor of Elementary Particle Physics, and Fellow of St Catherine's College, Oxford University, since 1965; *b* 15 Oct. 1925; *s* of George W. and Gertrude Perkins; *m* 1955, Dorothy Mary (*née* Maloney); two *d*. *Educ:* Malet Lambert High School, Hull. BSc London 1945; PhD London 1948; 1851 Senior Scholar, 1948–51. G. A. Wills Research Associate in Physics, Univ. of Bristol, 1951–55; Lawrence Radiation Lab., Univ. of California, 1955–56; Lectr in Physics, 1956–60, Reader in Physics, 1960–65, Univ. of Bristol. Mem., SERC, 1985–89. Hon. DSc Sheffield, 1982. Guthrie Medal, Inst. of Physics, 1979. *Publications:* The Study of Elementary Particles by the Photographic Method (with C. F. Powell and P. H. Fowler), 1959; Introduction to High Energy Physics, 1972, 3rd edn 1986; about 50 papers and review articles in Nature, Physical Review, Philosophical Magazine, Physics Letters, Proc. Royal Soc., Nuovo Cimento, etc. *Recreations:* squash, tennis. *Address:* c/o Department of Nuclear Physics, Keble Road, Oxford OX1 3RH.

PERKINS, Francis Layton, CBE 1977; DSC 1940; Chairman: British Insurance Brokers' Association, 1976–80; Insurance Brokers' Registration Council, 1977–84; Solicitor since 1937; *b* 7 Feb. 1912; *s* of Montague Thornton and Madge Perkins; *m* 1st, 1941, Josephine Brice Miller (marr. diss. 1971); one *s* two *d*; 2nd, 1971, Jill Patricia Greenish. *Educ:* Charterhouse. Served War of 1939–45, Comdr RNVR, in command of minesweepers. Partner in Clifford Turner & Co., 1946, Consultant, Clifford Chance, 1983; Dir, Hogg Robinson & Capel-Cure Ltd, 1962; Chairman: Hogg Robinson and Gardner Mountain Ltd, 1967–74; Hogg Robinson Group Ltd (formerly Staplegreen Insurance Holdings Ltd), 1971–77; Dir, Transport Holding Co., 1971–73. Master of Skinners' Company, 1966; Dep. Pres., 1971, Pres., 1972–77, Corp. of Insurance Brokers; Chairman: UK Insurance Brokers European Cttee, 1973–80; Common Mkt Cttee, Bureau International des Producteurs d'Assurances et de Réassurances, 1977–79; Dep. Chm., Cttee of Management, Inst. of Laryngology and Otology, 1976–78 (Mem., 1974–78); Mem. Council: Industrial Soc., 1976– (Treasurer, 1976–85); Common Law Inst. of Intellectual Property, 1983–. Governor and Chm. of Cttee, Tonbridge Sch.; Governor: Sutton's Hospital in Charterhouse, 1974–; Royal National Throat, Nose and Ear Hospital, 1974–80; Chairman: Fund Raising Cttee, St Bartholomew's Hosp., 1980; City of London and Thames Estuary Panel, Duke of Edinburgh's 1974 Commonwealth Conf.; Trustee, Barts Res. Develt Trust. *Recreations:* tennis, golf, fishing. *Address:* Flat 4, 34 Sloane Court West, SW3 4TB. *T:* 071–730 9775. *Clubs:* Boodle's, MCC, All England Lawn Tennis; Royal St George's Golf; Hon. Co. of Edinburgh Golfers.

PERKINS, Air Vice-Marshal Irwyn Morse, MBE 1957; Royal Air Force, retired; Medical Officer, Royal Military College of Science, 1981–85; *b* 15 Dec. 1920; *s* of William Lewis Perkins and Gwenllian Perkins, Ystalyfera, Swansea; *m* 1948, Royce Villiers Thompson, *d* of William Stanley Thompson and Zöe Thompson, The Mountain, Tangier; one *s* one *d*. *Educ:* Pontardawe, Swansea; St Mary's Hospital, Paddington, W2. MRCS, LRCP 1945; MFCM 1973. Commnd RAF, 1946; SMO: RAF Gibraltar, 1946–49; several flying stations in UK; DGMS Dept, MoD, 1955–57; RAF Laarbruch, Germany, 1958–61; RAF Khormaksar, Aden, 1964–66; DPMO, Bomber and Strike Commands, 1966–69; CO RAF Hospital, Ely, Cambs, 1969–72; PMO RAF Germany, 1972–75; CO PMRAF Hospital, Halton, 1975–77; PMO, Support Comd, 1977–80. Hon. Surgeon to HM the Queen, 1975–80. *Recreations:* study of archival medical records, woodworking, DIY. *Address:* 5 Redlands Close, Highworth, Swindon, Wilts SN6 7SN. *T:* Swindon (0793) 765097. *Club:* Royal Air Force.

PERKINS, James Alfred, MA, PhD; Chairman and Chief Executive Officer, International Council for Educational Development, 1970, now Chairman Emeritus; *b* 11 Oct. 1911; *s* of H. Norman Perkins and Emily (*née* Taylor); *m* 1st, 1938, Jean Bredin (*d* 1970); two *s* three *d*; 2nd, 1971, Ruth B. Aall; one step *s* three step *d*. *Educ:* Swarthmore Coll., Pa (AB); Princeton Univ., NJ (MA, PhD). Instructor Polit. Sci., Princeton Univ., 1937–39; Asst Prof. and Asst Dir, Sch. of Public and Internat. Affairs, Princeton, 1939–41; Dir, Pulp and Paper Div., Office of Price Admin., 1941–43; Asst to Administrator, For. Econ. Admin., 1943–45; Vice-Pres. Swarthmore Coll., 1945–50; Exec. Associate, Carnegie Corp. of NY, 1950–51; Dep. Chm. (on leave) Res. and Develt Bd, Dept of Defense, 1951–52; Vice-Pres., Carnegie Corp. of NY, 1951–63; Pres., Cornell Univ., 1963–69. Carnegie Foundn for the Advancement of Teaching: Sec. 1954–55; Vice-Pres., 1955–63. Chm., Pres. Johnson's Gen. Adv. Cttee on Foreign Assistance Prog., 1965–68; Trustee: Rand Corp., 1961–71; United Negro Coll. Fund (Chm. of Bd), 1965–69; Educl Testing Service, 1964–68; Dir Emeritus, Council on Foreign Relations; Mem. Gen. Adv. Cttee of US Arms Control and Disarmament Agency, 1963–66; Chm. NY Regents Adv. Cttee on Educational Leadership, 1963–67. Member: Bd of Directors, Chase Manhattan Bank, 1967–75; Stevenson Memorial Fund, 1966–69; Trustee, Aspen Inst., 1973–; Director: Overseas Develt Council, 1969–; Center for Inter-Amer. Relations, 1969–76; Inst. of Internat. Educn, 1981–87; Vice Chm., Acad. for Educnl Develt. Chm., President Carter's Commn on Foreign Language and Internat. Studies, 1978–79. Mem. Society of Friends, Swarthmore, Pa. Hon. LLD and Hon. LHD various colls and univs. *Publications:* The University in Transition, 1966; Higher Education: from Autonomy to Systems, 1972; The University as an Organization, 1973; contrib. to: Public Admin. Review, Amer. Polit. Sci. Review, Educational Record, etc. *Address:* (home) 94 North Road, Princeton, NJ 08540, USA; (office) 20 Nassau Street, Princeton, NJ 08540, USA. *Clubs:* University (NYC); Nassau (Princeton).

PERKINS, Maj.-Gen. Kenneth, CB 1977; MBE 1955; DFC 1953; Commander, Sultan's Armed Forces, Oman, 1975–77 (successfully concluded Dhofar War); *b* 15 Aug. 1926; *s* of George Samuel Perkins and Arabella Sarah Perkins (*née* Wise); *m* 1st, 1949, Anne Theresa Barry (marr. diss. 1984); three *d*; 2nd, 1985, Hon. Celia Sandys, *d* of Rt Hon. Lord Duncan-Sandys, CH, PC and Diana, *d* of Rt Hon. Sir Winston Churchill, KG, OM, CH, FRS; one *s* one *d*. *Educ:* Lewes County Sch. for Boys; New Coll., Oxford. Enlisted 1944; commnd RA 1946; various appts in Middle and Far East, BAOR and UK until 1965, incl. Korean War, Malayan Emergency, and Staff Coll. Quetta 1958; Instructor, Staff Coll. Camberley, 1965–66; CO 1st Regt Royal Horse Artillery, 1967–69; GSO 1 Singapore, 1970; Comdr 24 Bde, 1971–72; RCDS 1973; Central Staff, MoD, 1974; Maj.-Gen., 1975; Asst Chief of Defence Staff (Ops), 1977–80; Dir, Military Assistance Office, MoD, 1980–82. Col Comdt, RA, 1980–85. Mil. Advr, The Sun newspaper. Selangor Distinguished Conduct Medal (Malaya), 1955; Hashemite Order of Independence, first class, 1975; Order of Oman, 1977. *Publications:* Weapons and Warfare, 1987; A Fortunate Soldier, 1988; Khalida, 1991; articles in professional jls. *Recreations:* writing, painting (exhibited RA), cycling, family pursuits. *Address:* Carscombe, Stoodleigh, Devon EX16 9PR. *T:* Stoodleigh (03985) 404. *Club:* Army and Navy.

PERKS, His Honour (John) Clifford, MC 1944; TD; a Circuit Judge (formerly County Court Judge), 1970–85, retired; *b* 20 March 1915; *s* of John Hyde Haslewood Perks and Frances Mary Perks; *m* 1940, Ruth Dyke Perks (*née* Appleby); two *s* (one *s* two *d* decd). *Educ:* Blundell's; Balliol Coll., Oxford. Called to Bar, Inner Temple, 1938; joined Western Circuit; Chancellor, diocese of Bristol, 1950–71; Dep. Chm., Devon QS, 1965–71. *Recreation:* castles. *Address:* 32 Melbury Close, Chislehurst, Kent BR7 5ET.

PERLMAN, Itzhak; violinist; *b* Tel Aviv, 31 Aug. 1945; *s* of Chaim and Shoshana Perlman; *m* 1967, Toby Lynn Friedlander; two *s* three *d*. Studied at Tel Aviv Acad. of Music with Ryvka Goldgart, and at Juilliard Sch., NY, under Dorothy Delay and Ivan Galamian. First solo recital at age of 10 in Israel; New York début, 1958. Leventritt Meml Award, NY, 1964. Has toured extensively in USA and played with all major American symphony orchestras; recital tours of Canada, South America, Europe, Israel, Far East and Australia; recorded many standard works for violin. Has received numerous Grammy Awards. Hon. degrees: Harvard; Yale; Brandeis. *Recreation:* cooking. *Address:* c/o IMG Artists, 22 East 71st Street, New York, NY 10021, USA.

PEROWNE, Rear-Adm. Benjamin Cubitt, CB 1978; Member, Defence Advisory Group, ML Holdings, since 1988; Chairman, Faversham Oyster Fishery Co., since 1991; *b* 18 Feb. 1921; *s* of late Bernard Cubitt Perowne and of Gertrude Dorothy Perowne; *m* 1946, Phyllis Marjorie, *d* of late Cdre R. D. Peel, RNR, Southampton; two *s* one *d*. *Educ:* Culford Sch. Joined RN, 1939; Sec. to Adm. Sir Deric Holland-Martin, GCB, DSO, DSC, 1955–64; Acting Captain, 1957–64, Captain 1966; Staff, Chief of Personnel and Logistics, 1967–70; (Cdre, 1969–70); comd, HMS Cochrane, 1971–73; Dir of Defence Policy, 1973–75 (Cdre); Dir, Management and Support Intelligence, 1976–78, also Chief Naval Supply and Secretariat Officer, 1977–78. Gen. Sec., then Dir, RUKBA, 1978–88. *Recreations:* shooting, gardening. *Address:* c/o Barclays Bank, Haslemere, Surrey. *Club:* Army and Navy.

PEROWNE, Dame Freya; *see* Stark, Dame Freya.

PERRETT, Desmond Seymour; QC 1980; a Recorder of the Crown Court, since 1978; *b* 22 April 1937; *s* of His Honour John Perrett, *qv*; *m* 1961, Pauline Merriel, *yr d* of late Paul Robert Buchan May, ICS, and of Esme May; one *s* one *d*. *Educ:* Westminster Sch. National Service, RN, 1955–57: midshipman RNVR, 1955; Suez, 1956, and Cyprus, 1957. Called to the Bar, Gray's Inn, 1962, Bencher, 1989; Oxford Circuit, 1963–72; Midland and Oxford Circuit, 1972–; Mem., Senate of the Inns of Court and of the Bar, 1983–87. Chm. Disciplinary Appeals Cttee, Cricket Council, 1986–. Mem. Governing Body, Horris Hill Sch., 1986–. *Recreations:* cricket, fishing, shooting. *Address:* 2 Crown Office Row, Temple, EC4Y 7HJ. *T:* 071–353 9337. *Club:* MCC.

PERRETT, His Honour John, JP; a Circuit Judge (formerly a Judge of County Courts), 1969–81; *b* 22 Oct. 1906; *er s* of late Joseph and Alice Perrett, Birmingham; *m* 1933, Elizabeth Mary, *y d* of late William Seymour, Nenagh, Co. Tipperary; two *s* two *d*. *Educ:* St Anne's RC and Stratford Road Schools, Birmingham; King's Coll., Strand, WC2. Entered office of Philip Baker & Co., Solicitors, Birmingham, 1922; joined late Alfred W. Fryzer, Solicitor, Arundel St, WC2, 1925; joined Herbert Baron & Co., Solicitors, Queen Victoria St, EC4, 1934. Served War of 1939–45: RAPC, 1939–45; RASC, 1945. Called to Bar, Gray's Inn, 1946; practised in London and on Midland Circuit; Dep. Chm., Warwicks QS, 1970–71; JP Warwicks, 1970. *Address:* 5B Vicar's Close, Lichfield, Staffs WS13 7LE. *T:* Lichfield (0543) 252320.

See also D. S. Perrett, G. H. Rooke.

PERRIN, Charles John; Deputy Chairman, Hambros Bank Ltd, since 1986; *b* 1 May 1940; *s* of late Sir Michael Perrin, CBE, and of Nancy May, *d* of late Rt Rev. C. E. Curzon; *m* 1966, Gillian Margaret, *d* of late Rev. M. Hughes-Thomas; two *d*. *Educ:* Winchester; New Coll., Oxford (Schol.; MA). British Council Travelling Scholarship, 1962–63; called to the Bar, Inner Temple, 1965. Joined Hambros Bank, 1963, Dir, 1973–; Chm., Hambro Pacific, Hong Kong, 1983–; Dir, Hambros PLC, 1985–. Non-exec. Dir, Harland and Wolff, 1984–89. Hon. Treas., UK Assoc. for International Year of the Child, 1979; Vice-Chm., UK Cttee for UNICEF, 1972–91. Mem. Council/Management Cttee, Zoological Soc. of London, 1981–88; Governor: Queen Anne's Sch., Caversham, 1981–; London Hosp. Med. Coll., 1991–. *Publication:* Darwinism Today (Endeavour Prize Essay, 1958). *Recreation:* sailing. *Address:* 4 Holford Road, Hampstead, NW3 1AD. *T:* 071–435 8103. *Club:* Athenæum.

PERRIN, John Henry; *b* 14 Jan. 1916; *s* of Walter William Perrin, Faringdon and Sonning, Berks, and Amelia (*née* Honey), Oxford; *m* 1940, Doris Winifred Barrington-Brider; two *s*. *Educ:* Minchenden Sch.; London Univ. HM Customs and Excise; Royal Navy, 1939–46; Min. of Agriculture, 1948–76: Principal Private Sec. to Minister (Lord Amory), 1955–57; Regional Controller, Eastern Region, 1957–68; Under Sec., 1968–76. Dir-Gen., British Agricl Export Council, 1976–77. Inspector, Public Inquiries, Depts of the Environment and Transport, 1978–84. *Clubs:* Naval, Civil Service, Royal Yachting; RNVR Yacht; Cambridge University Cricket.

PERRIN, Air Vice-Marshal Norman Arthur; Director, Telecommunication Engineering and Manufacturing Association, since 1987; *b* 30 Sept. 1930; *s* of late Albert Arthur and Mona Victoria (*née* Stacey); *m* 1956, Marie (*née* Bannon), *d* of late Peter and Lucy Bannon; one *s*. *Educ:* Liverpool Collegiate School; Hertford College, Oxford; RAF Technical College. BA; CEng, FRAeS. Nat. Service commn, Airfield Construction Branch, RAF, Suez Canal Zone, 1951–53; perm. commn, Tech. Branch, 1953; Advanced GW course, 1956–57; Air Ministry, 1958–61; HQ 11 Group, 1961–62; Staff Coll., 1963; FEAF, 1964–65; OC Eng Wing, RAF Seletar, 1966–67; JSSC 1967; Op. Requirements, SAGW, 1967–70; Chief Instructor, Systems Engineering, RAF Coll., 1970–72; Group Captain Plans, HQ Maintenance Comd, 1972–75; C. Mech. Eng., HQ Strike Comd, 1975–78; RCDS 1979; Dir Air GW MoD (PE), 1980–83; Vice-Pres. (Air), Ordnance Board, 1983: Pres., Ordnance Board, 1984–86. *Recreations:* bridge, crosswords, Liverpool FC watching. *Address:* c/o Barclays Bank, 84 High Street, Princes Risborough, Aylesbury, Bucks HP17 0BD. *Club:* Royal Air Force.

PERRING, Franklyn Hugh, OBE 1988; writer; broadcaster; environmental consultant; *b* 1 Aug. 1927; *s* of Frank Arthur and Avelyn Millicent Perring; *m* 1st, 1951, Yvonne Frances Maud Matthews (marr. diss. 1972); one *s*; 2nd, 1972, Margaret Dorothy Barrow; one *d*. *Educ:* Earls Colne Grammar Sch.; Queens' Coll., Cambridge (MA, PhD). FLS; FIBiol 1979. Botanical Society of British Isles Distribution Maps Scheme: Hd, 1954–59; Dir, 1959–64; Hd, Biological Records Centre, Monks Wood Experimental Station, 1964–79; Botanical Sec., Linnean Soc. of London, 1973–78; Gen. Sec., RSNC, 1979–87. Hon. DSc Leicester, 1989. *Publications:* (jtly) Atlas of the British Flora, 1962; (jtly) A Flora of Cambridgeshire, 1964; Critical Supplement to the Atlas of the British Flora, 1968; (ed) The Flora of a Changing Britain, 1970; (ed jtly) The British Oak, 1974; (jtly) English Names of Wild Flowers, 1974, 2nd edn 1986; (jtly) British Red Data Book of Vascular Plants, 1977, 2nd edn 1983; (ed jtly) Ecological Effects of Pesticides, 1977; RSNC Guide to British Wild Flowers, 1984; (jtly) Ecological Flora of the Shropshire Region, 1985; (ed jtly) Changing Attitudes to Nature Conservation, 1988; (jtly) The Macmillan Guide to British Wildflowers, 1989; (ed jtly) The Nature of Northamptonshire, 1989; (ed jtly) Tomorrow is Too Late, 1990; Britain's Conservation Heritage, 1991; sci. papers in Jl of Ecology, Watsonia, etc. *Recreations:* opera-going, poetry reading, plant-hunting in the Mediterranean. *Address:* 24 Glapthorn Road, Oundle, Peterborough PE8 4JQ. *T:* Oundle (0832) 273388.

PERRING, John Raymond, TD 1965; Chairman: Perrings Finance Ltd, since 1987; Avenue Trading Ltd, since 1987; *b* 7 July 1931; *e s* and *heir* of Sir Ralph Perring, Bt, *qv*; *m* 1961, Ella Christine, *e d* of late Tony and Ann Pelham; two *s* two *d*. *Educ:* Stowe School. Nat. Service, then TA, RA, 1949–60; Royal Fusiliers (City of London), 1960–65. Joined family business, Perring Furnishings, 1951, Dir 1957, Jt Man. Dir 1964, Vice-Chm., 1972, Chm., 1981–88. Nat. Pres., Nat. Assoc. of Retail Furnishers, 1971–73; Mem. Council, Retail Consortium, 1972–91 (Chm., non-food policy cttee, 1987–91); Mem. EDC (Distributive Trades), 1974–78. City of London: Sheriff, 1991–Sept. 1992; One of HM Lieutenants, 1963–; Assistant, Merchant Taylors' Co., 1980, Master, 1988; Master, Furniture Makers' Co., 1978. Trustee, Ranyard Meml Charitable Trust, 1983– (Chm., 1990–). FRSA. *Recreations:* outdoor pursuits. *Address:* 21 Somerset Road, Wimbledon, SW19 5JZ. *T:* 081–946 8971. *Clubs:* City Livery, Royal Automobile; Royal Wimbledon Golf; Bembridge Sailing.

PERRING, Sir Ralph (Edgar), 1st Bt *cr* 1963; Kt 1960; Chairman, Perring Furnishings Ltd, 1948–81; *b* 23 March 1905; *yr s* of late Colonel Sir John Perring, DL, JP; *m* 1928, Ethel Mary, OStJ (*d* 1991), *o d* of late Henry T. Johnson, Putney; two *s* (and one *s* decd). *Educ:* University College Sch., London. Lieut, RA (TA) 1938–40, invalided. Member Court of Common Council (Ward of Cripplegate), 1948–51; Alderman of City of London (Langbourn Ward), 1951–75, one of HM Lieutenants of the City of London, and Sheriff, 1958–59. Lord Mayor of London, 1962–63. Chairman, Spitalfields Market Cttee, 1951–52; JP County of London, 1943–; Member: LCC for Cities of London and Westminster, 1952–55; County of London Licensing Planning Cttee; New Guildford Cathedral Council; Consumer Advisory Council, BSI, 1955–59; Bd of Governors, E-SU, 1976–81. Governor: St Bartholomew's Hospital, 1964–69; Imperial College of Science and Technology, 1964–67; Christ's Hospital; Vice-Chairman, BNEC Cttee for Exports to Canada, 1964–67, Chairman, 1968–70; Dir, Confederation Life Insurance Co. of Canada, 1969–81. Vice-President, Royal Bridewell Hospital (King Edward's Sch., Witley, 1964–75); Trustee, Morden Coll., Blackheath, 1970–, Chm. 1979–. Master Worshipful Co. of Tin Plate Workers, 1944–45; Master, Worshipful Co. of Painters-Stainers, 1977–78; Sen. Past Master and Founder Mem., Worshipful Co. of Furniture Makers; Mem. Court, Farmers' Co.; President Langbourn Ward Club, 1951–75. FRSA 1975. KStJ. Grand Cross of Merit (Republic of Germany), 1959; Order of Homayoun (Iran), 1959; Grand Officer, Order of Leopold (Belgium), 1963; Knight Commander, Royal Order of George I (Greece), 1963; Commander de la Valeur Camerounaise, 1963. *Heir: s* John Raymond Perring, *qv*. *Address:* 15 Burghley House, Somerset Road, Wimbledon, SW19 5JB. *T:* 081–946 3433. *Clubs:* St Stephen's Constitutional, Royal Automobile, City Livery (President, 1951–52).

PERRINS, Dr Christopher Miles, LVO 1987; Director, Edward Grey Institute of Field Ornithology, since 1974, and Fellow of Wolfson College, University of Oxford; *b* 11 May 1935; *s* of Leslie Howard Perrins and Violet Amy (*née* Moore); *m* 1963, Mary Ceresole Carslake; two *s*. *Educ:* Charterhouse; QMC (BSc Hons Zool.); Oxford Univ. (DPhil). Edward Grey Institute of Field Ornithology, University of Oxford: Research Officer, 1963–66; Sen. Res. Officer, 1966–84; Reader, 1984–. Mem., General Bd of Faculties, Oxford Univ., 1983–91. Hon. Corresp. Mem. 1976–83, Hon. Fellow 1983–, Amer. Ornithologists Union. Godman-Salvin Medal, British Ornithologists Union, 1988. *Publications:* (ed with B. Stonehouse) Evolutionary Ecology, 1977; British Tits, 1979; (with T. R. Birkhead) Avian Ecology, 1983; (ed with A. L. A. Middleton) The Encyclopaedia of Birds, 1985; (with M. E. Birkhead) The Mute Swan, 1986; New Generation Guide: Birds, 1987. *Recreations:* photography, walking. *Address:* Edward Gray Institute of Field Ornithology, Department of Zoology, University of Oxford, South Parks Road, Oxford OX1 3PS. *T:* Oxford (0865) 271169.

PERRIS, Sir David (Arthur), Kt 1977; MBE 1970; JP; Secretary, Trades Union Congress West Midlands Regional Council, since 1974; *b* 25 May 1929; *s* of Arthur Perris; *m* 1955, Constance Parkes, BPharm, FRPharmS, MCPP; one *s* one *d*. *Educ:* Sparkhill Commercial Sch., Birmingham. Film distribution industry, 1944–61; Reed Paper Group, 1961–65; Vice-Chm., ATV Midlands Ltd, 1980–81; Dir, Central Independent Television plc, 1982–83 (Vice Chm., W Midlands Bd). Sec., Birmingham Trades Council, 1966–83; a Chm., Greater Birmingham Supplementary Benefits Appeal Tribunal, 1982–89. Chairman: Birmingham Regional Hosp. Bd, 1970–74; West Midlands RHA, 1974–82; NHS National Trng Council, 1975–82; Mem. Bd of Governors, United Birmingham Hosps, 1965–74; Mem., Birmingham Children's Hosp. House Cttee, 1958–71 (Chm. 1967–71); Chm., Birmingham Hosp. Saturday Fund, 1985– (Vice-Chm., 1975–85). Chm., Central Telethon Trust, 1987–. Member: W Mids Econ. Planning Council, 1968–70; Midlands Postal Bd, 1974–81. Life Governor, Univ. of Birmingham, 1972; Elective Gov. Birmingham & Midland Inst., 1989–. President: Public Service Announcements Assoc., subseq. Community Media Assoc., 1983–; Magistrates' Assoc., Birmingham Br., 1986– (Chm., 1975–86). Life Fellow, British Fluoridation Soc., 1987. Hon. LLD Birmingham, 1981. JP Birmingham, 1961. *Recreations:* cinema, reading. *Address:* Broadway, 21 Highfield Road, Moseley, Birmingham B13 9HL. *T:* 021–449 3652.

PERRIS, John Douglas; HM Diplomatic Service, retired; *b* 28 March 1928; *s* of Frank William Perris and Alice Perris; *m* 1954, Kathleen Mary Lewington; one *s* two *d*. *Educ:* St Paul's, Knightsbridge; Westminster City Sch. Entered FO, 1945; Bahrain, 1951; Bucharest, 1953; Hamburg, 1955; FO, 1957; Tehran, 1960; Second Sec. (Admin), Caracas, 1963; Second Sec. (Econ.), Berlin, 1966; First Sec. (Admin), Baghdad, 1969; FCO (Inspectorate), 1972; First Sec./Head of Chancery/Consul, Tegucigalpa, 1974; First Sec. (Consular and Immigration), New Delhi, 1976; FCO, 1979; Counsellor (Admin), Bonn, 1982–86. *Recreations:* sport (non-active), reading (thrillers), bridge, DIY. *Address:* 128 Wakehurst Road, SW11 6BS. *T:* 071–228 0521.

PERROW, (Joseph) Howard; Chairman, Co-operative Union Ltd, 1975–83; Chief Executive Officer and Secretary, Greater Lancastria Co-operative Society Ltd, 1976–83; *b* 18 Nov. 1923; *s* of Joseph and Mary Elizabeth Perrow; *m* 1947, Lorraine Strick; two *s*. *Educ:* St Just, Penzance, Cornwall; Co-operative Coll., Stanford Hall, Leics (CSD). Joined Penzance Co-operative Soc., 1940. Served RAF, 1943–47. Various managerial positions in Co-operative Movement: in W Cornwall, with CRS N Devon, Carmarthen Soc., Silverdale (Staffs) and Burslem Socs; Mem., Co-operative Union Central Exec., 1966–83, Vice-Chm., 1973–75; Vice-Chm., NW Sectional Bd, 1970–75; Director: CWS, 1970–83; Nat. Co-operative Chemists, 1973–83; Greater Manchester Independent Radio, 1973–83; Mem., Central Cttee, Internat. Co-operative Alliance, 1975–83; Mem. Council (rep. Co-operative Union), Retail Consortium, 1976–83. President, Co-operative Congress, 1979. *Recreations:* football, cricket. *Address:* Blue Seas, Cliff Road, Mousehole, Penzance, Cornwall TR19 6QT. *T:* Penzance (0736) 731330. *Club:* Bolitho's (St Just).

PERRY, family name of **Baroness Perry of Southwark** and **Baron Perry of Walton.**

PERRY OF SOUTHWARK, Baroness *cr* 1991 (Life Peer), of Charlbury in the County of Oxfordshire; **Pauline Perry;** Director, South Bank Polytechnic, since 1987; *b* 15 Oct. 1931; *d* of John George Embleton Welch and Elizabeth Welch; *m* 1952, George Walter Perry; three *s* one *d*. *Educ:* Girton Coll., Cambridge (MA). Teacher in English Secondary Sch., Canadian and American High Schs, 1953–54 and 1959–61; High School Evaluator, New England, USA, 1959–61; Research Fellow, Univ. of Manitoba, 1956–57; Lecturer in Philosophy: Univ. of Manitoba, 1957–59; Univ. of Massachusetts at Salem, 1960–62; Lectr in Education (part-time), Univ. of Exeter, 1962–66; Tutor for In-Service Trng, Berks, 1966–70; Part-time Lectr in Educn, Dept of Educational Studies, Oxford Univ., 1966–70; HM Inspector of Schools, 1970–86; Staff Inspector, 1975; Chief Inspector, 1981. Chairman: Teacher Educn Study Gp, SRHE, 1988–; Management Cttee of Trng Unit, Cttee of Dirs of Polytechnics, 1990–; Member: Cttee on Internat. Co-operation in Higher Educn, British Council, 1987–; British Council Task Force on Women in Develt, 1990–91. Member: ESRC, 1988–; Governing Body, Institute of Develt Studies, 1987–; Examination Bd, RSA, 1987–; Council, Foundn for Educn Business Partnerships, 1990–. Rector's Warden, Southwark Cath., 1990–. Hon. FCollP, 1987; Hon. FRSA, 1988. Hon. Fellow, Sunderland Polytechnic, 1990. Hon LLD Bath, 1991. Mem., Editl Adv. Bd, Higher Education, 1990–. *Publications:* Case Studies in Teaching, 1969; Case Studies in Adolescence, 1970; Your Guide to the Opposite Sex, 1970; (contrib.) Advances in Teacher Education, 1989; (contrib.) Women in Education Management, 1990; (contrib.) Public Accountability and Quality Control in Higher Education, 1990; (contrib.) The Future of Higher Education, 1991; articles in various educnl jls; freelance journalism for radio and TV (incl. appearances on Question Time, BBC). *Recreations:* music, walking, cooking. *Address:* 98 Bramfield Road, SW11 6PY. *Club:* National Liberal.

PERRY OF WALTON, Baron *cr* 1979 (Life Peer), of Walton, Bucks; **Walter Laing Macdonald Perry,** Kt 1974; OBE 1957; FRS 1985; FRSE 1960; Vice-Chancellor, The Open University, 1969–80, Fellow, since 1981; *b* 16 June 1921; *s* of Fletcher S. Perry and Flora M. Macdonald; *m* 1st, 1946, Anne Elizabeth Grant (marr. diss. 1971); three *s*; 2nd, 1971, Catherine Hilda Crawley; two *s* one *d*. *Educ:* Ayr Acad.; Dundee High Sch. MB, ChB 1943, MD 1948, DSc 1958 (University of St Andrews); MRCP (Edinburgh), 1963; FRCPE 1967; FRCP 1978; Fellow, UCL, 1981–. Medical Officer, Colonial Medical Service (Nigeria), 1944–46; Medical Officer, RAF, 1946–47; Member of Staff, Medical Research Council, 1947–52; Director, Department of Biological Standards, National Institute for Medical Research, 1952–58. Prof. of Pharmacology, University of Edinburgh, 1958–68, Vice-Principal, 1967–68. Member, British Pharmacopœia Commission, 1952–68; Secretary, British Pharmacological Society, 1957–61. Chairman: Community Radio Milton Keynes, 1979–82; Living Tapes Ltd, 1980–; The Envmtl Partnership, 1990–. Chairman: Research Defence Soc., 1979–82; Delegacy of Goldsmiths' Coll., 1981–84; Standing Cttee on Continuing Educn, UGC and Nat. Adv. Body for Public Sector Higher Educn, 1985–89. Dep. Leader, SDP peers in House of Lords, 1981–83, 1988–89. Hon. DSc Bradford, 1974; Hon. LLD Dundee, 1975; Hon. DHL: Maryland, 1978; State Univ. of NY, 1982; Hon. Dr Athabasca, 1979; DUniv: Stirling, 1980; Open, 1981; Hon. DLitt: Deakin Univ., Australia, 1981; Andhra Pradesh Open Univ., 1987. *Publications:* Open University, 1976; papers in Journal of Physiology, British Journal of Pharmacology and Chemo-therapy, etc. *Recreations:* making music and playing games. *Address:* The Open University, 60 Melville Street, Edinburgh EH3 7HF. *Clubs:* Savage; Scottish Arts (Edinburgh).

PERRY, Alan Joseph; Director of Public Sector Services, Ernst & Young; *b* 17 Jan. 1930; *s* of late Joseph and Elsie Perry; *m* 1961, Vivien Anne Ball; two *s. Educ:* John Bright Grammar Sch., Llandudno; Dartford Grammar Sch. Served RE, 1948–50. HM Treasury, 1951–68 and 1970–78; CSD, 1968–70; Principal 1968, Asst Sec. 1976; Counsellor (Economic), Washington, 1978–80; Asst Sec., HM Treasury, 1980–86; Advr on Govt Affairs, Ernst & Whinney, 1986–88. Chm., Review of BBC External Services, 1984. *Address:* c/o Ernst & Young, Becket House, Lambeth Palace Road, SE1 7EU.
   See also P. G. Perry.

PERRY, Charles Bruce; Professor of Medicine, University of Bristol, 1935–69, Emeritus since 1969; *b* 1903; *s* of Charles E. and Sarah Duthie Perry; *m* 1929, Mildred Bernice Harvey; three *d. Educ:* Bristol Grammar Sch.; University of Bristol, MB, ChB 1926, MD 1928; FRCP, 1936. Physician, Bristol Royal Hospital for Sick Children and Women, 1928; Physician, Winford Orthopædic Hospital, 1930; Buckston Browne Prize, Harveian Society of London, 1929; Markham Skeritt Memorial Prize, 1931; Asst Physician, Bristol General Hospital, 1933. Lectures: Long Fox Memorial, 1943; Bradshaw, RCP, 1944; Lumleian, RCP, 1969; Carey Coombs, Univ. of Bristol, 1969; Cyril Fernando Meml, Ceylon, 1971. Pro-Vice-Chancellor, University of Bristol, 1958–61 (Hon. Fellow, 1986); President Assoc. of Physicians of Great Britain and Ireland, 1961–62; Chairman, British Cardiac Society, 1961–62; Censor, RCP, 1962–64; Medical Mem., Pensions Appeals Tribunals, 1969–79; Trustee, Jenner Appeal, 1982–. *Publications:* Bacterial Endocarditis, 1936; The Bristol Royal Infirmary 1904–1974, 1981; The Voluntary Medical Institutions of Bristol, 1984; The Bristol Medical School, 1984; Edward Jenner, 1986; various papers in the Medical Press dealing with research in Diseases of the Heart. *Address:* Beechfield, 54 Grove Road, Coombe Dingle, Bristol BS9 2RR. *T:* Bristol (0272) 682713.

PERRY, Sir David (Howard), KCB 1986; Chief of Defence Equipment Collaboration, Ministry of Defence, 1985–87, retired; *b* 13 April 1931; *s* of Howard Dace Perry and Annie Evelyn Perry; *m* 1961, Rosemary Grigg; one *s* two *d. Educ:* Berkhamsted Sch.; Pembroke Coll., Cambridge (MA). CEng, FRAeS. Joined Aero Dept, RAE, 1954; Aero Flt Div., 1954–66; Aero Projs Div., 1966–71; Head of Dynamics Div., 1971–73; RCDS, 1974; Head of Systems Assessment Dept, RAE, 1975–77; Ministry of Defence (Procurement Executive): Dir-Gen. Future Projects, 1978–80; Dir-Gen. Aircraft 1, 1980–81; Dep. Controller of Aircraft, 1981–82, Controller of Aircraft 1982; Chief of Defence Procurement, 1983–85. *Recreations:* gardening, painting. *Address:* 23 Rectory Road, Farnborough, Hants GU14 7BU.

PERRY, Sir David Norman; *see* Perry, Sir Norman.

PERRY, Ernest George; *b* 25 April 1908; British; *m* 1950, Edna Joyce Perks-Mankelow; one *s. Educ:* LCC secondary school. Textiles, 1923–33; Insurance, 1933–64. Member Battersea Borough Council, 1934–65 (Mayor of Battersea, 1955–56); Alderman, London Borough of Wandsworth, 1964–72. MP (Lab) Battersea S, 1964–74, Wandsworth, Battersea S, 1974–79; Asst Govt Whip, 1968–69; Lord Commissioner, HM Treasury, 1969–70; an Opposition Whip, 1970–74; an Asst Govt Whip, 1974–75. Served with Royal Artillery, 1939–46: Indian Army and Indian Artillery (Troop Sgt); Far East, 1942–45. *Recreations:* local government, sport, reading. *Address:* 6 Brinkley Road, Worcester Park, Surrey KT4 8JF. *T:* 081–337 4679.

PERRY, Frances Mary, (Mrs Roy Hay), MBE 1962; VMH 1971; horticulturist; *b* 19 Feb. 1907; *d* of Richard and Isabella Everett; *m* 1st, 1930, Gerald Amos Perry (*d* 1964); one *s* (and one *s* decd); 2nd, 1977, Robert Edwin Hay, MBE, VMH (*d* 1989). *Educ:* Enfield County Sch.; Swanley Horticultural Coll. (later Wye Coll.). Diploma in Horticulture. Organiser for Agricl and Horticultural Educn, Mddx CC, 1943; Principal, Norwood Hall Inst. and Coll. of Horticulture, 1953–67. Veitch Meml Medal in Gold, RHS, 1964; Sara Francis Chapman Medal, Garden Club of America, 1973. *Publications:* Water Gardening, 1938; The Herbaceous Border, 1949; The Garden Pool, 1954; The Woman Gardener, 1955; (as Charles Hewitt) Flower Arrangement, 1955; Guide to Border Plants, 1957; Making Things Grow, 1960; Shrubs and Trees for the Smaller Garden, 1961; Penguin Water Gardens, 1962; Colour in the Garden, 1964; Book of Flowering Bulbs, Corms and Tubers, 1966; Flowers of the World, 1972; Gardening in Colour, 1972; Plants & Flowers, 1974; Good Gardeners Guide, 1976; Beautiful Leaved Plants, 1979; Water Garden, 1981; (with Roy Hay) Tropical and Subtropical Plants, 1982; Scent in the Garden, 1989. *Recreations:* flower stamps, photography. *Address:* Lussacombe, Lustleigh, Devon TQ13 9SQ.

PERRY, Frederick John; professional tennis coach, TV and BBC Radio commentator, since 1946; *b* Stockport, 18 May 1909; *s* of Samuel Frederick Perry, sometime MP for Kettering, and Hannah Perry; *m. Educ:* elementary school. Started to play tennis at age of 14; World Table Tennis Champion, 1929; first played at Wimbledon Lawn Tennis championships, 1929; Wimbledon Champion, 1934, 1935, 1936; also won Mixed Doubles, with Dorothy Round, Wimbledon, 1935, 1936; Australian Champion, 1934; French Champion, 1935; American Champion, 1933, 1934, 1936; first player to win all four major titles; Mem., British Davis Cup team, 1931–36; winner: Australian Doubles, 1934, and French Doubles, 1935, with Pat Hughes; French Mixed Doubles, with Betty Nuthall; American Mixed Doubles, with Sarah Palfrey, 1932; became professional, 1936. Co-Founder, with Theodore Wegner, Fred Perry Sportswear, 1950. *Publications:* My Story, 1934; Perry on Tennis, 1934; Perry Wins, 1935; Fred Perry: an autobiography, 1984. *Address:* c/o All England Lawn Tennis Club, Church Road, Wimbledon, SW19 5AE.

PERRY, George Henry; *b* 24 Aug. 1920; *s* of Arthur and Elizabeth Perry; *m* 1944, Ida Garner; two *d. Educ:* elementary sch. and technical college. Engineering Apprentice, 1934–41. Naval Artificer, 1941–46 (Atlantic and Italy Stars; 1939–45 Star). Railway Fitter, 1946–66. Derby Town Councillor, 1955–66. Chairman: Derby Water Cttee, 1957–61; S Derbys Water Board, 1961–66; Derby Labour Party, 1961–62; Secretary, Derby Trades Council, 1961–66. Contested (Lab) Harborough, 1964; MP (Lab) Nottingham South, 1966–70. *Recreation:* walking. *Address:* 123 Hawthorn Street, Derby. *T:* Derby (0332) 44687.

PERRY, John; *see* Perry, R. J.

PERRY, Rt. Rev. John Freeman; *see* Southampton, Bishop Suffragan of.

PERRY, Rev. John Neville; *b* 29 March 1920; *s* of Robert and Enid Perry; *m* 1946, Rita Dyson Rooke; four *s* four *d. Educ:* The Crypt Gram. Sch., Gloucester; Univ. of Leeds (BA 1941), College of the Resurrection, Mirfield. Asst Curate, All Saints', Poplar, 1943–50; Vicar, St Peter De Beauvoir Town, Hackney, 1950–63; Vicar, St Dunstan with St Catherine, Feltham, Mddx, 1963–75; Rural Dean of Hounslow, 1967–75; Archdeacon of Middlesex, 1975–82; Rector of Orlestone with Ruckinge and Warehorne, Kent, 1982–86. Mem. Latey Cttee on the Age of Majority, 1966–67. *Recreations:* D-I-Y handyman. *Address:* 73 Elizabeth Crescent, East Grinstead, West Sussex RH19 3JG.

PERRY, John William; Chairman and Managing Director, Unisys, since 1987; *b* 23 Sept. 1938; *s* of John and Cecilia Perry; *m* 1961, Gillian Margaret; two *d. Educ:* Wallington

Grammar Sch.; Brasenose Coll., Oxford (MA). Burroughs: Dir of Marketing, UK, 1967–71, Europe Africa Div., 1977–78; Group Dir, Internat. Marketing, 1978–80; Vice-President: Strategic Planning, 1981; Financial Systems Gp., 1983; Central USA, 1985–86; Man. Dir, Burroughs UK, 1986. Director: Sperry; Burroughs Machines; BMX Information Systems; BMX Holdings; Unisys Holdings; Convergent Technologies (UK). Trustee, Information Age Project, 1989. Mem., Bd of Governors, Polytechnic of East London, 1989. *Recreations:* gardening, golf, reading, music. *Address:* The Great Barn, Sandpit Lane, Bledlow, Bucks HP17 9AA. *T:* Princes Risborough (08444) 7037.

PERRY, Ven. Michael Charles, MA; Archdeacon of Durham and Canon Residentiary of Durham Cathedral since 1970; *b* 5 June 1933; *o s* of late Charlie Perry; *m* 1963, Margaret, *o d* of late John Middleton Adshead; two *s* one *d. Educ:* Ashby-de-la-Zouch Boys' Grammar Sch.; Trinity Coll., Cambridge (Sen. Schol.); Westcott House, Cambridge. Asst Curate of Berkswich, Stafford, 1958–60; Chaplain, Ripon Hall, Oxford, 1961–63; Chief Asst for Home Publishing, SPCK, 1963–70; Examining Chaplain to Bishop of Lichfield, 1965–74. Sec., Archbishops' Commn on Christian Doctrine, 1967–70. Diocesan Chm., 1970–81, Mem. Council, 1975–81, USPG; Mem., 1981–88, Vice-Chm., 1982–88, Hosp. Chaplaincies Council, Gen. Synod; Mem. Council for the Deaf, Gen. Synod, 1986–90. Mem., Durham HA, 1982–88. Trustee, 1970–, Chm., 1982–, Lord Crewe's Charity; Chm., Churches' Fellowship for Psychical and Spiritual Studies, 1986–. Lectures: Selwyn, NZ, 1976; Marshall Meml, Melbourne, 1976; Beard Meml, London, 1977; Maurice Elliott Meml, London, 1986; Shepherd Meml, Worcester, 1988. Editor, Church Quarterly, 1968–71; Editor, Christian Parapsychologist, 1977–. *Publications:* The Easter Enigma, 1959; The Pattern of Matins and Evensong, 1961; (co-author) The Churchman's Companion, 1963; Meet the Prayer Book, 1963; (contrib.) The Miracles and the Resurrection, 1964; (ed) Crisis for Confirmation, 1967; (co-author) Declaring The Faith: The Printed Word, 1969; Sharing in One Bread, 1973; The Resurrection of Man, 1975; The Paradox of Worship, 1977; A Handbook of Parish Worship, 1977, 2nd edn 1989; (contrib.) Yes to Women Priests, 1978; (co-author) A Handbook of Parish Finance, 1981; Psychic Studies: a Christian's view, 1984; Miracles Then and Now, 1986; (ed) Deliverance, 1987. *Address:* 7 The College, Durham DH1 3EQ. *T:* Durham (091) 3861891.

PERRY, Sir Norman, Kt 1977; MBE; retired. Knighthood awarded for services to the community and the Maori people, New Zealand. *Address:* Waiotahi, Opotiki, New Zealand.

PERRY, Norman Henry, PhD; Chief Executive and Policy Co-ordinator, Wolverhampton Metropolitan Borough Council, since 1990; *b* 5 March 1944; *s* of late Charles and Josephine Perry; *m* 1970, Barbara Ann Marsden; two *s. Educ:* Quintin Sch., NW8; University Coll. London (BA 1965; PhD 1969). Lectr in Geography, UCL, 1965–69; Sen. Res. Officer, GLC, 1969–73; Sen. Res. Fellow, SSRC Survey Unit, 1973–75; joined DoE, 1975; Principal, London and Birmingham, 1975–80; Asst Sec., W Midlands Regl Office, 1980–86; Head of Inner Cities Unit (G4), Dept of Employment, then DTI, 1986–88; Under Sec., and Dir W Midlands, DTI, 1988–90. *Publications:* (contrib.) European Glossary of Legal and Administrative Terminology, 1974, 1979, 1988; contribs to books and learned jls in fields of geography, planning, organisational sociology and urban policy. *Address:* Civic Centre, St Peter's Square, Wolverhampton WV1 1SH. *T:* Wolverhampton (0902) 314000. *Clubs:* Civil Service; Arden (Solihull).

PERRY, Mrs Pauline; Director, South Bank Polytechnic, since 1987; *b* 15 Oct. 1931; *d* of John George Embleton Welch and Elizabeth Welch; *m* 1952, George Walter Perry; three *s* one *d. Educ:* Girton Coll., Cambridge (MA). Teacher in English Secondary Sch., Canadian and American High Schs, 1953–54 and 1959–61; High School Evaluator, New England, USA, 1959–61; Research Fellow, Univ. of Manitoba, 1956–57; Lecturer in Philosophy: Univ. of Manitoba, 1957–59; Univ. of Massachusetts at Salem, 1960–62; Lectr in Education (part-time), Univ. of Exeter, 1962–66; Tutor for In-Service Trng, Berks, 1966–70; Part-time Lectr in Educn, Dept of Educational Studies, Oxford Univ., 1966–70; HM Inspector of Schools, 1970–86; Staff Inspector, 1975; Chief Inspector, 1981. Chairman: Teacher Educn Study Gp, SRHE, 1988–; Management Cttee of Trng Unit, Cttee of Dirs of Polytechnics, 1990–; Member: Cttee on Internat. Co-operation in Higher Educn, British Council, 1987–; British Council Task Force on Women in Develt, 1990–91. Member: ESRC, 1988–; Governing Body, Institute of Develt Studies, 1987–; Examination Bd, RSA, 1987–; Council, Foundn for Educn Business Partnerships, 1990–. Rector's Warden, Southwark Cath., 1990–. Hon. FCollP, 1987; Hon. FRSA, 1988. Hon. Fellow, Sunderland Polytechnic, 1990. Hon LLD Bath, 1991. Mem., Editl Adv. Bd, Higher Education, 1990–. *Publications:* Case Studies in Teaching, 1969; Case Studies in Adolescence, 1970; Your Guide to the Opposite Sex, 1970; (contrib.) Advances in Teacher Education, 1989; (contrib.) Women in Education Management, 1990; (contrib.) Public Accountability and Quality Control in Higher Education, 1990; (contrib.) The Future of Higher Education, 1991; articles in various educnl jls; freelance journalism for radio and TV (incl. appearances on Question Time, BBC). *Recreations:* music, walking, cooking. *Address:* 98 Bramfield Road, SW11 6PY. *Club:* National Liberal.

PERRY, Peter George, CB 1983; Under Secretary, Department of Health and Social Security, 1975–84; *b* 15 Dec. 1923; *s* of late Joseph and Elsie Perry; *m* 1957, Marjorie Margaret Stevens; no *c. Educ:* Dartford Grammar Sch.; London Univ. (LLB). Normandy with Northants Yeomanry, 1944. Joined Min. of Health, 1947; Private Sec. to Minister of State, 1968–70; Asst Sec., 1971. Chm., Investigation Cttee, 1988–91, Chm., Policy Adv. Cttee, 1991–, Solicitors' Complaints Bureau; Member: Industrial Tribunals, 1984–; Parole Bd, 1988–91. JP City of London, 1974–87; Freeman, City of London, 1975. *Recreations:* sailing, squash, opera. *Address:* 50 Great Brownings, College Road, Dulwich, SE21. *T:* 081–670 3387. *Club:* Little Ship (Commodore, 1984–87; Vice-Pres., 1988–).
   See also A. J. Perry.

PERRY, Prof. Roger, FRSC; Professor of Environmental Control and Waste Management (formerly of Public Health and Water Technology), Imperial College of Science, Technology and Medicine, since 1981; Director, Centre for Toxic Waste Management, since 1990; *b* 21 June 1940; *s* of Charles William and Gladys Perry; *m* (separated); one *s* one *d. Educ:* King Edward's Grammar Sch., Birmingham; Univ. of Birmingham (BSc, PhD). FRSH, FIWEM. Held number of industrial appts in chem. industry until 1964; Depts of Chemistry and Chem. Engineering, Univ. of Birmingham, 1964–70; Mem., academic staff, Imperial Coll., 1970–. Cons. to number of major chemical and engrg based industries and govt depts, UK and overseas, also to UNEP and WHO, resulting in involvement in major environmental projects in some 30 countries. Mem., Univ. of London Senate and Academic Council, 1984–. *Publications:* Handbook of Air Pollution Analysis (ed jtly with R. Young), 1977, 2nd edn (ed jtly with R. M. Harrison), 1986; approx. 200 papers in various scientific jls. *Recreations:* travel, gardening, cooking, building. *Address:* Imperial College of Science, Technology and Medicine, Centre for Toxic Waste Management, South Kensington, SW7 2BU. *T:* 071–589 5111. *Club:* Athenæum.

PERRY, (Rudolph) John; QC 1989; an Assistant Recorder, since 1988; *b* 20 Feb. 1936; *s* of Rudolph Perry and Beatrice (*née* Tingling, now Robertson); *m* (marr. diss.); one *d.*

Educ: Ruseas High Sch., Lucea, Jamaica; Southgate Technical Coll.; London Sch. of Economics (LLB (Hons), LLM); Univ. of Warwick (MA (Industrial Relations)). Lectr (part-time), LSE, 1970–78; Lectr, 1971, Sen. Lectr, 1974–78, City of London Poly. Called to the Bar, Middle Temple, 1975; in practice, 1976–. *Recreations:* watching cricket, travel, cinema. *Address:* 11 South Square, Gray's Inn, WC1R 5EU. *T:* 071–831 2311.

PERRY, Prof. Samuel Victor, BSc (Liverpool), PhD, ScD (Cantab); FRS 1974; Professor of Biochemistry, 1959–85, now Emeritus, and Head of Department of Biochemistry, 1968–85, University of Birmingham; *b* 16 July 1918; *s* of late Samuel and Margaret Perry; *m* 1948, Maureen Tregent Shaw; one *s* two *d. Educ:* King George V Sch., Southport; Liverpool Univ.; Trinity Coll., Cambridge. Served in War of 1939–45, home and N. Africa; Royal Artillery, 1940–46, Captain; POW 1942–45. Research Fellow, Trinity Coll., Cambridge, 1947–51; Commonwealth Fund Fellow, University of Rochester, USA, 1948–49; University Lecturer, Dept of Biochemistry, Cambridge, 1950–59. Member: Standing Cttee for Research on Animals, ARC, 1965–72; Biol Scis and Enzyme Cttees, SRC, 1968–71; Medical Res. Cttee, Muscular Dystrophy Gp of GB, 1970–; Systems Bd, MRC, 1974–77; Research Funds Cttee, British Heart Foundn, 1974–82; British Nat. Cttee for Biochemistry, 1978–87 (Chm., 1982–87); Council, Royal Soc., 1986–88; Chairman: Cttee of Biochemical Soc., 1980–83; Adv. Bd, Meat Res. Inst., 1980–85. Croonian Lectr, Royal Soc., 1984. FAAAS 1987. Hon. Mem., Amer. Soc. of Biol Chemists, 1978; Corresponding Mem., Société Royale des Sciences, Liège, 1978; Mem., Accad. Virgiliana, Mantova, 1979; Foreign Mem., Accademia Nazionale dei Lincei, 1989. CIBA Medal, Biochemical Soc., 1977. *Publications:* scientific papers in Biochemical Journal, Nature, Biochemica Biophysica Acta, etc. *Recreations:* gardening, building stone walls, Rugby football (Cambridge, 1946, 1947, England, 1947, 1948). *Address:* 64 Meadow Hill Road, King's Norton, Birmingham B38 8DA. *T:* 021–458 1511.

PERRY, William Arthur; Assistant Secretary, Air Secretariat Division 3, Ministry of Defence, Procurement Executive, since 1988; *b* 5 Aug. 1937; *s* of Arthur Perry and Elizabeth Grace (*née* Geller); *m* 1962, Anne Rosemary Dight; two *d. Educ:* St Dunstan's Coll. Min. of Aviation, 1960–61; Second Sec. (Defence Supply), Bonn, 1964–66; Min. of Technology, then MoD, 1966–74; First Sec., UK Delegn to NATO, 1974–77; Head, Defence Secretariat 8, MoD, 1978–80; Counsellor (Defence Supply), Bonn, 1980–84; Regl Marketing Dir, Defence Exports Orgn, 1984–88. *Recreations:* opera, gardening, philately, genealogy. *Address:* c/o Ministry of Defence, St Giles Court, 1–13 St Giles High Street, WC2H 8LD.

PERRYMAN, (Francis) Douglas; Director, Homes Assured Corporation, since 1988; *b* 23 April 1930; *s* of Frank Smyth Perryman and Caroline Mary Anderson; *m* 1955, Margaret Mary Lamb; two *d. Educ:* West Hartlepool Grammar School; Durham Univ. BCom (Hons); FCA. Articled Clerk, 1951–55; Nat. Service, commnd RAPC, 1955–57; National Coal Board: Area Chief Accountant, Fife and Scottish South Areas, 1963–72; Finance Dir, Opencast Exec., 1972; Dir Gen. of Finance, 1978–81; Board Mem. for Finance, PO, 1981; Bd Mem., then Corporate Dir, for Finance, 1981–86, Corporate Commercial Dir, 1986–88, BT. Mem. Council, CBI, 1987–88. FRSA. *Recreations:* golf, Rugby football, music, Francophile. *Address:* Long Mynd, 69 Copperkins Lane, Amersham, Bucks. *T:* Amersham (0494) 721611.

PERSSON, Rt. Rev. William Michael Dermot; *see* Doncaster, Bishop Suffragan of.

PERTH, 17th Earl of, *cr* 1605; **John David Drummond,** PC 1957; Baron Drummond of Cargill, 1488; Baron Maderty, 1609; Baron Drummond, 1686; Lord Drummond of Gilston, 1685; Lord Drummond of Rickertoun and Castlemaine, 1686; Viscount Strathallan, 1686; Hereditary Thane of Lennox, and Hereditary Steward of Menteith and Strathearn; Representative Peer for Scotland, 1952–63; First Crown Estate Commissioner, 1962–77; Chairman, Ditchley Foundation, 1963–66; *b* 13 May 1907; *o s* of 16th Earl of Perth, PC, GCMG, CB, and Hon. Angela Constable-Maxwell (*d* 1965), *y d* of 11th Baron Herries; *S* father 1951; *m* 1934, Nancy Seymour, *d* of Reginald Fincke, New York City; two *s. Educ:* Downside; Cambridge Univ. Lieut, Intelligence Corps, 1940; seconded to War Cabinet Offices, 1942–43, Ministry of Production, 1944–45; Minister of State for Colonial Affairs, 1957–62 (resigned). Chm., Reviewing Cttee on Export of Works of Art, 1972–76. Member: Court of St Andrews Univ., 1967–86; Adv. Council, V&A Museum, 1971–72; Trustee, Nat. Library of Scotland, 1968–. Hon. FRIBA 1978; Hon. FRIAS 1988. Hon. LLD St Andrews, 1986. *Heir: s* Viscount Strathallan, *qv. Address:* 14 Hyde Park Gardens Mews, W2 2NU. *T:* 071–262 4667; Stobhall, by Perth PH2 6DR.

PERTH (Australia), Archbishop of, and Metropolitan of Western Australia, since 1981; **Most Rev. Peter Frederick Carnley;** *b* 17 Oct. 1937; *s* of Frederick Carnley and Gweyenneth Lilian Carnley (*née* Read); *m* 1966, Carol Ann Dunstan; one *s* one *d. Educ:* St John's Coll., Morpeth, NSW (ThL 1st Cl., ACT, 1962); Univ. of Melbourne (BA, 1st Cl. Hons, 1966); Univ. of Cambridge (PhD 1969). Deacon 1962, priest 1964, Bath; Licence to Officiate, dio. Melbourne, 1963–65; Asst Curate of Parkes, 1966; Licence to Officiate, dio. Ely, 1966–69; Chaplain, Mitchell Coll. of Advanced Education, Bath, 1970–72; Research Fellow, St John's Coll., Cambridge, 1971–72; Warden, St John's College, St Lucia, Queensland, 1972–81; Residentiary Canon, St John's Cathedral, Brisbane, 1975–81; Examining Chaplain to Archbishop of Brisbane, 1975–81. DD *hc*, Gen. Theological Seminary, NY, 1984. ChStJ 1982. *Publications:* The Poverty of Historical Scepticism, in Christ, Faith and History (ed S. W. Sykes and J. P. Clayton), 1972; The Structure of Resurrection Belief, 1987. *Recreations:* gardening, swimming. *Address:* 52 Mount Street, West Perth, WA 6005, Australia. *T:* 322 1777. *Clubs:* Weld, Western Australian (Perth); Royal Perth Yacht; St John's (Brisbane).

PERTH (Australia), Archbishop of, (RC); *no new appointment at time of going to press.*

PERTH (Australia), Assistant Bishops of; *see* Kyme, Rt Rev. B. R.; Wright, Rt Rev. B.

PERTH, (St Ninian's Cathedral), Provost of; *see* Franz, Very Rev. K. G.

PERU AND BOLIVIA, Bishop of, since 1988; **Rt. Rev. Alan Leslie Winstanley;** *b* 7 May 1949; *s* of John Leslie Winstanley and Eva Winstanley; *m* 1972, Vivien Mary Parkinson; two *s* one *d. Educ:* St John's College, Nottingham (BTh, ALCD). Deacon 1972, priest 1973, Blackburn; Curate: St Andrew's, Livesey, Blackburn, 1972–75; St Mary's, Great Sankey, dio. Liverpool, with responsibility for St Paul's, Penketh, 1975–77; Vicar of Penketh, 1978–81. SAMS Missionary in Peru: Lima, 1981–85; Arequipa, 1986–87. *Recreations:* caravanning, steam locomotives. *Address:* Iglesia Cristiana Episcopal, Apdo 18–1032, Lima 18, Peru. *T:* Lima 45–38–78, *Fax:* Lima 45–30–44.

PERUTZ, Max Ferdinand, OM 1988; CH 1975; CBE 1963; PhD; FRS 1954; Member, scientific staff, Medical Research Council Laboratory of Molecular Biology, 1979– (Chairman, 1962–79); *b* 19 May 1914; *s* of Hugo and Adèle Perutz; *m* 1942, Gisela Peiser; one *s* one *d. Educ:* Theresianum, Vienna; Univ. of Vienna; Univ. of Cambridge (PhD 1940). Hon. Fellow: Peterhouse, Cambridge, 1962; Darwin Coll., Cambridge, 1984. Dir, MRC Unit for Molecular Biology, 1947–62; Chm., European Molecular Biology Orgn, 1963–69. Reader, Davy Faraday Res. Lab., 1954–68, and Fullerian Prof. of Physiology, 1973–79, Royal Instn. Hon. FRSE, 1976; Hon. Member American Academy of Arts and Sciences, 1963; Corresp. Member, Austrian Acad. of Sciences, 1963; Mem., Akademie Leopoldina, Halle, 1964; Foreign Member: American Philosophical Society, 1968; Royal Netherlands Acad., 1972; French Acad. of Sciences, 1976; Bavarian Acad. of Sciences, 1983; National Acad. of Sciences, Rome, 1983; Accademia dei Lincei, Rome, 1984; Acad. of Science of DDR, 1985; For. Associate, Nat. Acad. of Sciences, USA, 1970; Mem., Pontifical Acad. of Sciences, Rome, 1981. Hon. degrees: in philosophy: Vienna, 1965; Salzburg, 1972; in science: Edinburgh, 1965; East Anglia, 1967; Cambridge, 1981; York, 1990; in medicine, Rome, 1988. Nobel Prize for Chemistry (jointly), 1962; Ehrenzeichen für Wissenschaft und Kunst (Austria), 1966; Royal Medal, 1971, Copley Medal, 1979, Royal Soc. Actonian Prize, Royal Instn, 1984. Pour le Mérite, FRG, 1988. *Publications:* Proteins and Nucleic Acids, Structure and Function, 1962; (jtly) Atlas of Haemoglobin and Myoglobin, 1981; Is Science Necessary?, 1988; Mechanisms of Co-operativity and Allosteric Control in Proteins, 1990. *Address:* 42 Sedley Taylor Road, Cambridge; Laboratory of Molecular Biology, Hills Road, Cambridge.

PERY, family name of **Earl of Limerick.**

PESARAN, Prof. (Mohammad) Hashem, PhD; Professor of Economics, Cambridge University, and Fellow of Trinity College, Cambridge, since 1988; Professor of Economics, and Director, Program in Applied Econometrics, University of California, Los Angeles, since 1989; *b* 30 March 1946; *s* of Jamal and Effat Pesaran; *m* 1969, Marion Fay Swainston; two *s* two *d. Educ:* Salford Univ. (BSc 1968); Cambridge Univ. (PhD 1972). Jun. Res. Officer, Dept of Applied Econs, Cambridge Univ., and Lektor, Trinity Coll., Cambridge, 1971–73; Asst to Vice-Governor, 1973–74, and Head of Econ. Res. Dept, 1974–76, Central Bank of Iran; Under-Sec., Min. of Educn, Iran, 1977–78; Teaching Fellow, and Dir of Studies in Econs, Trinity Coll., Cambridge, 1979–88; Lectr in Econs, 1979–85, and Reader in Econs, 1985–88, Cambridge Univ. Visiting Lecturer: Harvard Univ., 1982; Dutch Network for Quantitative Econs, Groningen, 1985; Vis. Fellow, ANU, 1984 and 1988; Visiting Professor: Univ. of Rome, 1986; Univ. of Calif, LA, 1987–88. Fellow, Econometric Soc., 1990. Founding Ed., Jl of Applied Econometrics, 1985–. *Publications:* World Economic Prospects and the Iranian Economy—a short term view, 1974 (also Persian); (with L. J. Slater) Dynamic Regression: theory and algorithms, 1980 (trans. Russian, 1984); (ed with T. Lawson) Keynes' Economics: methodological issues, 1985; The Limits to Rational Expectations, 1987; (with B. Pesaran) Data–FIT: an interactive software econometric package, 1987 (paperback edn, as Microfit, 1989); (ed with T. Barker) Disaggregation in Economic Modelling, 1990; scientific papers in econ. and econometric jls. *Recreations:* basketball (half-blue, Cambridge University), squash, swimming. *Address:* Trinity College, Cambridge CB2 1TQ; 39 Leys Avenue, Cambridge CB4 2AN. *T:* Cambridge (0223) 322937.

PESCOD, Prof. Mainwaring Bainbridge, OBE 1977; CEng, FICE, FIWEM; Tyne and Wear Professor of Environmental Control Engineering, since 1976, and Head of Department of Civil Engineering, since 1983, University of Newcastle upon Tyne; *b* 6 Jan. 1933; *s* of Bainbridge and Elizabeth Pescod; *m* 1957, Mary Lorenza (*née* Coyle); two *s. Educ:* Stanley Grammar Sch., Co. Durham; King's Coll., Univ. of Durham (BSc); MIT (SM). CEng 1973, FICE 1980; FIWEM 1987 (FIPHE 1971; FIWES 1983; MIWPC 1967); MRSH 1964; MInstWM 1985. Lectr in Engrg, Fourah Bay Coll, Freetown, Sierra Leone, 1957–61; Asst Engr, Babtie, Shaw & Morton, CCE, Glasgow, 1961–64; Asst and Associate Prof. of Environmental Engrg, 1964–72, Prof. and Head of Div. of Environmental Engrg, 1972–76, Asian Inst. of Technol., Bangkok, Thailand. Mem., Northumbrian Water Authority, 1986–89; Director: Northumbrian Water Group, 1989–; Motherwell Bridge Envirotec, 1991–; Chm. and Man. Dir, Envmtl Technology Cosultants, 1988–. *Publications:* (ed with D. A. Okun) Water Supply and Wastewater Disposal in Developing Countries, 1971; (ed. with A. Arar) Treatment and Use of Sewage Effluent for Irrigation, 1988; (ed) Urban Solid Waste Management, 1991; pubns on water supply, wastewater treatment, environmental pollution control and management in learned jls and conf. proc. *Recreations:* squash, reading, advisory assignments in developing countries. *Address:* Tall Trees, High Horse Close Wood, Rowlands Gill, Tyne and Wear NE39 1AN. *T:* Rowlands Gill (0207) 542104. *Clubs:* British, Royal Bangkok Sports (Bangkok, Thailand).

PEŠEK, Libor; Music Director, Royal Liverpool Philharmonic Society and Orchestra, since 1987; *b* 22 June 1933. *Educ:* Academy of Musical Arts, Prague (studied conducting, piano, 'cello, trombone). Worked at Pilsen and Prague Opera Houses; Founder Director, Prague Chamber Harmony, 1958–64; Chief Conductor, Slovak Philharmonic, 1980–81; Conductor in residence, Czech Philharmonic, 1982– (tours and fests, Europe, Russia, Far East); guest conductor, USA and other orchestras; numerous recordings incl. much Czech repertoire. Hon. DMus Liverpool Polytechnic, 1989. *Recreations:* physics, eastern philosophical literature, Kafka, Dostoyevsky. *Address:* c/o IMG Artists (Europe), Media House, 3 Burlington Lane, W4 2TH.

PESKETT, Stanley Victor, MA; Principal, Royal Belfast Academical Institution, 1959–78; *b* 9 May 1918; *o s* of Sydney Timber and Mary Havard Peskett; *m* 1948, Prudence Eileen, OBE 1974, *o d* of C. R. A. Goatly, Calcutta; two *s* one *d* (and one *d* decd). *Educ:* Whitgift Sch.; St Edmund Hall, Oxford. Served War, 1939–46 (despatches) in Royal Marines, Norway, Shetland, Normandy, India and Java; Lt-Col, 1944; two Admiralty awards for inventions. Senior English Master, 1946–59, Housemaster 1954–59, The Leys School. Mem. Cttee, Headmasters' Conf., 1976; Mem. Council, Headmasters' Assoc., and Pres., Ulster Headmasters' Assoc., 1973–75; Chm., Northern Ireland Cttee, Voluntary Service Overseas, 1969–78; Founder Pres., Irish Schools Swimming Assoc., 1968–69 (Chm., Ulster Branch, 1968–78); Chm., NI Branch, School Library Assoc., 1964–73; Governor, Belfast Sch. of Music, 1974–77; Mem. Adv. Council, UDR, 1975–78. *Publications:* The Metfield Clock, 1980; (contrib.) People, Poverty and Protest in Hoxne Hundred 1780–1880, 1982; articles in educational jls. *Address:* Huntsman and Hounds Cottage, Metfield, Harleston, Norfolk IP20 0LB. *T:* Fressingfield (037986) 425.

PESKIN, Richard Martin; Chairman, since 1986, and Managing Director, since 1985, Great Portland Estates PLC; *b* 21 May 1944; *s* of Leslie and Hazel Peskin; *m* 1979, Penelope Howard Triebner; one *s* two *d. Educ:* Charterhouse; Queens' Coll., Cambridge (MA, LLM). Great Portland Estates, 1967–: Dir, 1968; Asst Man. Dir, 1972. FRSA. CBIM. *Recreations:* racing, golf. *Address:* 41 Circus Road, NW8 9JH. *T:* 071–289 0492. *Clubs:* Royal Automobile; Wentworth Golf.

PESTELL; *see* Wells-Pestell.

PESTELL, Catherine Eva, CMG 1984; HM Diplomatic Service, retired; Principal, Somerville College, Oxford, since 1989; *b* 24 Sept. 1933; *d* of Edmund Ernest Pestell and Isabella Cummine Sangster. *Educ:* Leeds Girls' High Sch.; St Hilda's Coll., Oxford (MA). FO, 1956; Third Sec., The Hague, 1958; Second Sec., Bangkok, 1961; FO, 1964; First Sec., UK Delegn to OECD, Paris, 1969; FCO, 1971; St Antony's Coll., Oxford, 1974; Counsellor, East Berlin, 1975–78; Cabinet Office, 1978–80; Diplomatic Service Inspector, 1980–82; Minister (Economic), Bonn, 1983–87; Asst Under-Sec. (Public Depts), FCO, 1987–89. *Address:* Somerville College, Oxford OX2 6HD. *Clubs:* Reform, United

Oxford & Cambridge University.
See also J. E. Pestell.

PESTELL, John Edmund; Partnership Secretary, Linklaters & Paines, since 1990; *b* 8 Dec. 1930; *s* of late Edmund Pestell and Isabella (*née* Sangster); *m* 1958, Muriel Ada (*née* Whitby); three *s*. *Educ:* Roundhay Sch.; New Coll., Oxford (MA). National Service, 1949–50. Jt Intell. Bureau, 1953–57; Asst Principal, WO, 1957–60; Private Sec. to Parly Under Sec. of State for War, 1958–60; Principal, WO and MoD, 1960–70; Admin. Staff Coll., Henley, 1963; Private Sec. to Minister of Defence (Equipment), 1969–70; Asst Sec., MoD, 1970–72; Press Sec. (Co-ordination), Prime Minister's Office, 1972–74; Asst Sec., CSD, 1974–76, Under Sec., 1976–81; Under Sec., HM Treasury, 1981–84; Asst Under-Sec. of State, MoD, 1984–88; Resident Chm., CSSB, 1988–90. Mem., CS Pay Res. Unit Bd, 1978–80. Governor, Cranleigh Sch., 1975–. *Address:* New House, Bridge Road, Cranleigh, Surrey GU6 7HH. *T:* Cranleigh (0483) 273489. *Club:* Athenæum.
See also C. E. Pestell.

PESTELL, Sir John Richard, KCVO 1969; an Adjudicator, Immigration Appeals, Harmondsworth, 1970–87; *b* 21 Nov. 1916; *s* of late Lt-Comdr Frank Lionel Pestell, RN, and Winifred Alice Pestell; *m* 1951, Betty Pestell (*née* Parish); three *d*. *Educ:* Portsmouth Northern Secondary Sch. Joined British South Africa Police, Southern Rhodesia, 1939; retired, 1965, with rank of Asst Commissioner. Served, 1944–47, Gen. List, MELF, in Cyrenaica Defence Force. Secretary/Controller to Governor of S Rhodesia, Rt Hon. Sir H. V. Gibbs, 1965–69. *Recreation:* walking. *Address:* Batch Cottage, North Road, Charlton Horethorne, near Sherborne, Som DT9 4NS.

PESTON, family name of **Baron Peston.**

PESTON, Baron *cr* 1987 (Life Peer), of Mile End in Greater London; **Maurice Harry Peston;** Professor of Economics at Queen Mary College, University of London, 1965–88, now Emeritus; *b* 19 March 1931; *s* of Abraham and Yetta Peston; *m* 1958, Helen Conroy; two *s* one *d*. *Educ:* Belle Vue School, Bradford; Hackney Downs School; London School of Economics (BSc Econ); Princeton Univ., NJ, USA. Scientific Officer, then Sen. Scientific Officer, Army Operational Research Group, 1954–57; Asst Lecturer, Lectr, Reader in Economics, LSE, 1957–65. Economic Adviser: HM Treasury, 1962–64; Min. of Defence, 1964–66; H of C Select Cttee on Nationalised Industries, 1966–70, 1972–73; Special Adviser to Sec. of State for Education, 1974–75, to Sec. of State for Prices 1976–79. Chairman: Pools Panel, 1991–; NFER, 1991–; Member: CNAA (and Chm. of Economics Bd), 1967–73; SSRC (Chm. of Economics Bd), 1976–79; Council of Royal Pharmaceutical Soc. of GB, 1986–. *Publications:* Elementary Matrices for Economics, 1969; Public Goods and the Public Sector, 1972; Theory of Macroeconomic Policy, 1974, 2nd edn 1982; Whatever Happened to Macroeconomics?, 1980; The British Economy, 1982, 2nd edn 1984; ed and contrib. to many other books; articles in economic jls. *Address:* House of Lords, SW1A 0PW. *T:* 071–219 3000.

PETCH, Barry Irvine, FCA; General Manager, IBM Financing International Ltd, since 1989; *b* 12 Oct. 1933; *s* of Charles Reginald Petch and Anne (*née* Fryer); *m* 1966, Anne Elisabeth (*née* Johannessen); two *s* one *d*. *Educ:* Doncaster Grammar Sch. FCA 1967. IBM United Kingdom Ltd, 1959–80; Controller, IBM Europe, 1981–83; Vice-Pres., Finance, IBM Europe, 1983–89. Part-time Mem., Price Commn, 1973–77. *Recreations:* tennis, golf, sailing. *Address:* IBM, West Cross House, 2 West Cross Way, Brentford, Middx TW8 9DY. *Club:* Reform.

PETCH, Prof. Norman James, FRS 1974; FEng; Professor of Metallurgy, University of Strathclyde, 1973–82, now Emeritus Professor; *b* 13 Feb. 1917; 3rd *s* of George and Jane Petch, Bearsden, Dunbartonshire; *m* 1st, 1942, Marion Blight (marr. diss. 1947); 2nd, 1949, Eileen Allen (*d* 1975); two *d*; 3rd, 1976, Marjorie Jackson. *Educ:* Queen Mary Coll., London; Sheffield Univ. Research at Cavendish Lab., Cambridge, 1939–42; Royal Aircraft Establishment, 1942–46; Cavendish Laboratory, 1946–48; British Iron and Steel Research Assoc., Sheffield, 1948–49; Reader in Metallurgy, Leeds Univ., 1949–56; First Professor of Metallurgy, Leeds Univ., 1956–59; Cochrane Prof. of Metallurgy, 1959–73, a Pro-Vice-Chancellor, 1968–71, Univ. of Newcastle upon Tyne. Former Member: Basic Properties of Metals Cttee, Interservice Metallurgical Res. Council; Ship Steels Cttee, Admiralty; Physics Cttee, Aeronautical Res. Council; Carbon Steel Cttee, BSC; Plasticity Div. Cttee, Nat. Engrg Lab.; former UK Editor: Acta Metallurgica; Internat. Jl of Fracture. Royal Society: Mem. Council, 1979–81; Chm., Scientific Relief Cttee, 1983–88. Rosenhain Medal, Inst. of Metals; Gold Medal, Amer. Soc. of Metals. *Address:* Findon Cottage, Culbokie, Conon Bridge, Ross-shire IV7 8JJ. *T:* Culbokie (034987) 259.

PETERBOROUGH, Bishop of, since 1984; **Rt. Rev. William John Westwood;** *b* 28 Dec. 1925; *s* of Ernest and Charlotte Westwood; *m* 1954, Shirley Ann, *yr d* of Dr Norman Jennings; one *s* one *d*. *Educ:* Grove Park Grammar Sch., Wrexham; Emmanuel Coll. (Exhibnr 1944; Hon. Fellow 1989) and Westcott House, Cambridge. MA. Soldier, 1944–47. Curate of Hull, 1952–57; Rector of Lowestoft, 1957–65; Vicar of S Peter Mancroft, Norwich, 1965–75; Hon. Canon, Norwich Cathedral, 1969–75; Rural Dean of Norwich, 1966–70, City Dean, 1970–73; Area Bishop of Edmonton, 1975–84. Member: General Synod, 1970–75 and 1977–; Archbishop's Commission on Church and State, 1966–70; Press Council, 1975–81; Church Commissioner, 1973–78 and 1985–; Chm., C of E Cttee for Communications, 1979–86; Member: IBA Panel of Religious Advisers, 1983–87; Video Consultative Council, 1985–89; Broadcasting Standards Council, 1988–. Pres., Nat. Deaf-Blind League, 1991–. Chm. Governors, Coll. of All Saints, Tottenham, 1976–78. Pres., Church Housing Assoc., 1985–; Chairman: Lowestoft Church and Town Charities, 1957–65; Norwich Housing Soc., 1969–74; Cotman Housing Assoc., Norwich, 1972–75. Freeman, City of London, 1977. Hon. LLD Leicester, 1991. *Recreations:* the countryside, simple demographic studies, art galleries, wine bars. *Address:* The Palace, Peterborough, Cambs PE1 1YA.

PETERBOROUGH, Dean of; *see* Wise, Very Rev. R. G.

PETERKEN, Laurence Edwin, CBE 1990; General Manager, Greater Glasgow Health Board, since 1986; *b* 2 Oct. 1931; *s* of Edwin James Peterken and Constance Fanny (*née* Giffin); *m* 1st, 1955, Hanne Birgithe Von Der Recke (decd); one *s* one *d*; 2nd, 1970, Margaret Raynal Blair; one *s* one *d*. *Educ:* Harrow Sch. (Scholar); Peterhouse, Cambridge (Scholar); MA. Pilot Officer, RAF Regt, Adjt No 20 LAA Sqdn, 1950–52. Service Div. Manager, Hotpoint Ltd, 1961–63, Commercial Dir, 1963–66; Man. Dir, British Domestic Appliances Ltd, 1966–68; Dir, British Printing Corporation Ltd, 1969–73; Debenhams Ltd: Man. Dir, Fashion Multiple Div., 1974–76; Management Auditor, 1976–77; Controller, Operational Services, GLC, 1977–85. Chairman: Working Party on Disposal of Clinical Waste in London, 1982–83; GLC Chief Officers' Guild, 1983–85. Acting Dir, Royal Festival Hall, 1983–85, to implement open foyer policy. Churchwarden, Haslemere Parish Church, 1985–86. *Recreations:* music, golf. *Address:* 25 Kingsborough Gardens, Glasgow G12 9NH. *Club:* Athenæum.

PETERKIEWICZ, Prof. Jerzy; novelist and poet; Professor of Polish Language and Literature, University of London, 1972–79; *b* 29 Sept. 1916; *s* of late Jan Pietrkiewicz and Antonina (*née* Politowska). *Educ:* Dlugosz Sch., Wloclawek; Univ. of Warsaw; Univ. of St Andrews (MA 1944); King's Coll., London (PhD 1947). Freelance writer until 1950; Reader (previously Lectr) in Polish Language and Literature, Sch. of Slavonic and East European Studies, Univ. of London, 1952–72, Head of Dept of E European Lang. and Lit., 1972–77. *Publications:* Prowincja, 1936; Wiersze i poematy, 1938; Pogrzeb Europy, 1946; The Knotted Cord, 1953; Loot and Loyalty, 1955; Polish Prose and Verse, 1956; Antologia liryki angielskiej, 1958; Future to Let, 1958; Isolation, 1959; (with Burns Singer) Five Centuries of Polish Poetry, 1960 (enlarged edn 1970); The Quick and the Dead, 1961; That Angel Burning at my Left Side, 1963; Poematy londynskie, 1965; Inner Circle, 1966; Green Flows the Bile, 1969; The Other Side of Silence (The Poet at the Limits of Language), 1970; The Third Adam, 1975; (ed and trans.) Easter Vigil and other Poems, by Karol Wojtyla (Pope John Paul II), 1979; Kula magiczna (Poems 1934–52), 1980; (ed and trans.) Collected Poems, by Karol Wojtyla (Pope John Paul II), 1982; Poezje wybrane (Selected Poems), 1986; Literatura polska w perspektywie europejskiej (Polish Literature in its European context; essays trans. from English), 1986; essays, poems and articles in various periodicals; radio plays, BBC Radio 3. *Recreation:* travels, outward and inward. *Address:* 7 Lyndhurst Terrace, NW3 5QA.

PETERKIN, Sir Neville (Allan Mercer), Kt 1981; Chief Justice, West Indies Associated States, 1980–84; *b* 27 Oct. 1915; *s* of Joseph Allan Peterkin and Evelyn Peterkin; *m* 1942, Beryl Thompson; two *s* one *d*. *Educ:* Wellington Sch., Somerset, England. Called to Bar, Middle Temple, 1939. Registrar, St Lucia, 1943; Magistrate, Trinidad and Tobago, 1944; Resident Magistrate, Jamaica, 1954; High Court Judge: Trinidad, 1957; Associated States, 1967; Justice of Appeal, Associated States, 1975. *Recreations:* golf, bridge. *Address:* Reduit, St Lucia, West Indies. *T:* 28113.

PETERS, Rt. Rev. Arthur Gordon; *see* Nova Scotia, Bishop of.

PETERS, Prof. David Keith, FRCP; Regius Professor of Physic, University of Cambridge, and Fellow, Christ's College, Cambridge, since 1987; *b* 26 July 1938; *s* of Herbert Lionel and Olive Peters; *m* 1st, 1961, Jean Mair Garfield (marr. diss. 1978); one *s* one *d*; 2nd, 1979, Pamela Wilson Ewan; two *s* one *d*. *Educ:* Welsh National Sch. of Medicine. MB, BCh, 1961; MRCP 1964; FRCP 1975. Junior posts in United Cardiff Hosps, 1961–65; Med. Research Council, Clinical Res. Fellowship, 1965–68; Lectr in Med., Welsh Nat. Sch. of Med., 1968–69; Royal Postgraduate Medical School: Lectr, 1969; Sen. Lectr, 1974; Reader in Med., 1975; Prof. of Medicine and Dir, Dept of Medicine, 1977–87; Consultant Physician, Hammersmith Hosp., 1969–87. Member: MRC, 1984–88 (Chm., MRC Physiological Systems Bd, 1986–88); ACOST, 1987–. Hon. MD Wales, 1987. *Publications:* in various jls on immunology of renal and vascular disease. *Recreations:* tennis, chess. *Address:* 7 Chaucer Road, Cambridge CB2 2EB. *T:* Cambridge (0223) 356117. *Club:* Garrick.

PETERS, Ellis; *see* Pargeter, E.

PETERS, Prof. George Henry; Research Professor in Agricultural Economics and Head of Agricultural Economics Unit, Queen Elizabeth House, University of Oxford, since 1986; Fellow, since 1980, Vicegerent, since 1991, Wolfson College, Oxford; *b* 2 Sept. 1934; *s* of William and Mary Peters; *m* 1959, Judith Mary Griffiths; two *d*. *Educ:* Mold Grammar Sch., Clwyd; University Coll. of Wales, Aberystwyth (BSc, MSc); King's Coll., Cambridge. National Service, Educn Br., RAF, 1957–59. Inst. for Res. in Agricl Econs, Univ. of Oxford, 1959–67; University of Liverpool: Lectr in Econs, 1967–69; Sen. Lectr, 1969–70; Brunner Prof. of Economic Science, 1970–79; Hd of Dept of Econs and Commerce, 1976–79; Dir, Inst. of Agricl Econs, Univ. of Oxford, 1980–86. Pres., Agricl Econs Soc., 1991–. Ed., Procs of Internat. Assoc. of Agricl Economists, 1991–. *Publications:* Cost Benefit Analysis and Public Expenditure (IEA Eaton Paper 8), 1966, 3rd edn 1973; Private and Public Finance, 1971, 2nd edn 1975; ESRC/RSS Reviews of UK Statistical Sources, vol. 23, Agriculture, 1988; articles in Jl of Agricl Econs, Oxford Agrarian Studies, etc. *Recreations:* all sport, increasingly as a spectator. *Address:* Gable End Cottage, 33 The Moors, Kidlington, Oxford OX5 2AH. *T:* Kidlington (08675) 2232.

PETERS, Kenneth Jamieson, CBE 1979; JP; DL; FSAScot; Member: Scottish Region Board, British Rail, since 1982; Peterhead Bay Authority Board, since 1983 (Vice-Chairman, since 1989); *b* 17 Jan. 1923; *s* of William Jamieson Peters and Edna Rosa Peters (*née* Hayman); *m* 1951, Arunda Merle Jane Jones. *Educ:* Aberdeen Grammar Sch.; Aberdeen Univ. Served War of 1939–45: last rank Captain/Adjutant, 2nd Bn King's Own Scottish Borderers. Editorial staff, Daily Record and Evening News Ltd, 1947–51; Asst Editor: Evening Express, Aberdeen, 1951–52; Manchester Evening Chronicle, 1952–53; Editor: Evening Express, Aberdeen, 1953–56; The Press and Journal, Aberdeen, 1956–60; Dir, 1960–90, Man. Dir, 1960–80, Chm., 1980–81, Aberdeen Journals Ltd. Director: Highland Printers Ltd (Inverness), 1968–83; Aberdeen Assoc. of Social Service, 1973–78; Thomson Regional Newspapers, 1974–80; Thomson Scottish Petroleum Ltd, 1981–86; Thomson N Sea, 1981–88; Thomson Forestry Hldgs, 1982–88; Mem., Girobank, Scotland Bd, 1984–90. Pres., Scottish Daily Newspaper Soc., 1964–66 and 1974–76; Mem., Press Council, 1974–77; Pres., Publicity Club of Aberdeen, 1972–81; Member: Scottish Adv. Cttee of British Council, 1967–84; Cttee, Films of Scotland, 1970–82; Chm., NE Cttee, 1982–88, Mem. Exec., 1982–88, Fellow, 1988, Scottish Council (Develt and Industry). FSAScot 1980; FBIM 1980; ACIT 1985; FRSA 1989. JP City of Aberdeen, 1961; DL Aberdeen, 1978. *Publications:* The Northern Lights, 1978; (ed) Great North Memories, vol. 1, 1978, vol. 2, 1981; Burgess of Guild, 1982. *Recreations:* cricket, Rugby football, walking. *Address:* 47 Abergeldie Road, Aberdeen AB1 6ED. *T:* Aberdeen (0224) 587647. *Clubs:* MCC; Royal Northern and University (Aberdeen).

PETERS, Martin Trevor, CB 1991; CEng, FRAeS; aerospace consultant, since 1991; *b* 23 Dec. 1936; *s* of Reginald Thomas Peters and Catherine Mary Peters (*née* Ings); *m* 1958, Vera Joan Horton; one *s*. *Educ:* Aylesbury Grammar Sch.; Watford Tech. Coll.; High Wycombe Coll. of Further Educn. MIMechE. Airtech, 1953–55; RAF, 1955–57; Airtech, 1957–59; RPE Westcott, 1959–64; NGTE Pyestock, 1964–71; MoD, 1971–77; Supt of Engineering, A&AEE Boscombe Down, 1977–79; NAMMA, Munich, 1979–81; Dir, Aircraft Post Design Services, MoD (PE), 1981–83; RCDS, 1984; Dir-Gen. Aircraft, 1984–87; Dep. Controller Aircraft, 1987–89; Dir, RAE, 1989–91. *Recreations:* ski-ing, walking, music, 18th century ship modelling. *Address:* Eynesbury, Wych Hill Way, Woking, Surrey GU22 0AE.

PETERS, Mary Elizabeth, CBE 1990 (MBE 1973); self employed; Managing Director, Mary Peters Sports Ltd, since 1977; *b* 6 July 1939; *d* of Arthur Henry Peters and Hilda Mary Peters. *Educ:* Portadown Coll., Co. Armagh; Belfast Coll. of Domestic Science (DipDomSc). Represented Great Britain: Olympic Games: 4th place, Pentathlon, 1964; 1st, Pentathlon (world record), 1972; Commonwealth Games: 2nd, Shot, 1966; 1st, Shot, 1st Pentathlon, 1970; 1st, Pentathlon, 1974. Member: Sports Council, 1974–80, 1987–; Northern Ireland Sports Council, 1974– (Vice-Chm., 1977–81); Ulster Games Foundn, 1984–; NI BBC Broadcasting Council, 1981–84. Dir, Churchill Foundn Fellowship Scholarship, Calif, 1972. Asst Sec., Multiple Sclerosis Soc., 1974–78; Pres., Old-Age Pensioners' Coal and Grocery Fund. Hon. Senior Athletic Coach, 1975–; BAAB Pentathlon Coach, 1976; Team Manager: GB women's athletic team, European Cup, 1979; GB women's athletic team, Moscow, 1980 and Los Angeles, 1984. Pres., NIWAAA,

1985–87; Vice-President: Assoc. of Youth Clubs; NI Assoc. of Youth Clubs; Riding for the Disabled; Driving for the Disabled; Trustee, Ulster Sports Trust, 1972; Patron: NIAAA, 1981–; Friends of Royal Victoria Hosp., Belfast, 1988–. Awards: BBC Sports personality, 1972; Athletic Writers', 1972; Sports Writers', 1972; Elizabeth Arden Visible Difference, 1976; Athletics, Dublin (Texaco), 1970 and 1972; British Airways Tourist Endeavour, 1981; Living Action, 1985; Evian Health, 1985. Hon. DSc, New Univ. of Ulster, 1974. *Publication:* Mary P., an autobiography, 1974. *Address:* Willowtree Cottage, River Road, Dunmurry, Belfast, N Ireland.

PETERS, Prof. Raymond Harry; Professor of Polymer and Fibre Science, University of Manchester, 1955–84, now Emeritus; *b* 19 Feb. 1918. *Educ:* County High Sch., Ilford; King's Coll., London Univ.; Manchester Univ. BSc (London) 1939, PhD (London), 1942, in Chemistry; BSc (Manchester), 1949, BSc (London), 1949, in Mathematics; DSc (London), 1968. Scientist at ICI Ltd, 1941–46 and 1949–55. Visiting Professor: UMIST, 1984–86; Univ. of Strathclyde, 1984–. President, Society of Dyers and Colourists, 1967–68. *Publications:* Textile Chemistry: Vol. I, The Chemistry of Fibres, 1963; Vol. II, Impurities of Fibres: Purification of Fibres, 1967; Vol. III, Physical Chemistry of Dyeing, 1975; contributions to Journals of Chemical Society, Society of Dyers and Colourists, Textile Institute, British Journal of Applied Physics, etc. *Recreation:* gardening. *Address:* 1 Vale Road, Wilmslow, Cheshire SK9 5QA.

PETERS, Prof. Richard Stanley, BA (Oxon), BA (London), PhD (London); Professor of the Philosophy of Education, University of London Institute of Education, 1962–82, now Emeritus Professor; Dean, Faculty of Education, London University, 1971–74; *b* 31 Oct. 1919; *s* of late Charles Robert and Mabel Georgina Peters; *m* 1943, Margaret Lee Duncan; one *s* two *d*. *Educ:* Clifton Coll., Bristol; Queen's Coll., Oxford; Birkbeck Coll., University of London. War service with Friends' Ambulance Unit and Friends' Relief Service in E. London, 1940–44. Classics Master, Sidcot School, Somerset, 1944–46; Birkbeck Coll., University of London: Studentship and part-time Lecturer in Philos. and Psychol., 1946–49; full-time Lecturer in Philos. and Psychol., 1949–58; Reader in Philosophy, 1958–62. Visiting Prof. of Education: Grad. School of Education, Harvard Univ., 1961; Univ. of Auckland, 1975; Visiting Fellow, Australian National Univ., 1969. Part-time lectureships, Bedford Coll., LSE; Tutor for University of London Tutorial Classes Cttee and Extension Cttee. Member, American National Academy of Education, 1966. *Publications:* (revised) Brett's History of Psychology, 1953; Hobbes, 1956; The Concept of Motivation, 1958; (with S. I. Benn) Social Principles and the Democratic State, 1959; Authority, Responsibility and Education, 1960; Ethics and Education, 1966; (ed) The Concept of Education, 1967; (ed) Perspectives on Plowden, 1969; (with P. H. Hirst) The Logic of Education, 1970; (ed with M. Cranston) Hobbes and Rousseau, 1971; (ed with R. F. Dearden and P. H. Hirst) Education and the Development of Reason, 1972; Reason and Compassion (Lindsay Meml Lectures), 1973; (ed) The Philosophy of Education, 1973; Psychology and Ethical Development, 1974; (ed) Nature and Conduct, 1975; (ed) The Role of the Head, 1976; Education and the Education of Teachers, 1977; (ed) John Dewey Reconsidered, 1977; Essays on Educators, 1981; Moral Development and Moral Education, 1981. *Address:* 16 Shepherd's Hill, N6.

PETERS, Air Vice-Marshal Robert Geoffrey; Commandant, Royal Air Force Staff College, since 1990; *b* 22 Aug. 1940; *s* of Geoffrey Ridgeway Peters and Henriette Catharine Peters; *m* 1966, Mary Elizabeth (*née* Fletcher); three *s* one *d*. *Educ:* St Paul's Sch., London; RAF Coll., Cranwell (Gen. Duties/Pilot). Beverley C Mk1 Pilot Nos 34 and 37 Sqdns, Singapore and UK, 1961–66; Flt Comdr, No 46 Sqdn (Andovers), RAF Abingdon, 1967–68; MoD Central Staffs (Asst MA to Chief Adviser Personnel and Logistics), 1968–69; OC Flying Trng Sqdn, Air Electronics and Air Engr Trng Sch., RAF Topcliffe, 1970–72; RAF Staff Coll., Bracknell, 1973; Air Sec.'s Dept, MoD, 1974–76; OC 10 Sqdn (VC10), RAF Brize Norton, 1977–78; Directorate of Forward Policy (RAF), MoD, 1979–81; PSO to Dep. SACEUR(UK), SHAPE, Belgium, 1981–83; OC RAF St Mawgan, 1984–85; RCDS 1986; Comdr, RAF Staff and Air Attaché, Washington, 1987–90. President: RAF Fencing Union, 1986–; Combined Services Fencing Assoc., 1988–. Freeman, City of London; Liveryman, Co. of Coachmakers and Coach Harness Makers. QCVSA 1973. *Recreations:* squash, golf, sailing. *Address:* RAF Staff College, Bracknell, Berks RG12 3DD. *T:* Bracknell (0344) 54593. *Club:* Royal Air Force.

PETERS, Theophilus, CMG 1967; HM Diplomatic Service, retired; freelance lecturer on Chinese Art and History; *b* 7 Aug. 1921; *er s* of late Mark Peters and Dorothy Knapman; *m* 1953, Lucy Bailey Summers, *d* of late Lionel Morgan Summers, Winter Park, Fla; two *s* three *d*. *Educ:* Exeter Sch., Exeter; St John's Coll., Cambridge (MA). Served War of 1939–45: 2nd Lieut, Intelligence Corps, 1942; Captain, 8 Corps HQ, 1944; Normandy, 1944; Holland, 1944–45 (despatches); Germany; Major. Entered HM Foreign (subseq. Diplomatic) Service; Vice-Consul/2nd Secretary, Peking, 1948; FO, 1951–52; Tripoli and Benghazi (Libya), 1953; FO, 1956; Dep. Secretary-General, Cento, 1960; Head of Chancery, Manila, 1962; Counsellor (Commercial), Peking, 1965; Dir, Diplomatic Service Language Centre, 1968–71, and Head of Training Dept, FCO, 1969–71; Counsellor and Consul-Gen., Buenos Aires, 1971–73; Consul-Gen., Antwerp, 1973–78. Dir, Theophilus Knapman & Co., 1979–87. *Address:* Henlo Pen House, Church Road, Ketton, Stamford, Lincs PE9 3RD.

PETERS, Prof. Wallace, MD, DSc; FRCP; Professor of Medical Protozoology, London School of Hygiene and Tropical Medicine, University of London, 1979–89, now Emeritus; Joint Director, Malaria Reference Laboratory, Public Health Laboratory Service, 1979–89; *b* 1 April 1924; *s* of Henry and Fanny Peters; *m* 1954, Ruth (*née* Scheidegger). *Educ:* Haberdashers' Aske's Sch.; St Bartholomew's Hosp., London. MB BS, 1947; MRCS, DTM&H. Served in RAMC, 1947–49; practised tropical medicine in West and East Africa, 1950–52; Staff Mem., WHO, Liberia and Nepal, 1952–55; Asst Dir (Malariology), Health Dept, Territory of Papua and New Guinea, 1956–61; Research Associate, CIBA, Basle, Switzerland, 1961–66; Walter Myers Prof. of Parasitology, Univ. of Liverpool, 1966–79. Dean, Liverpool Sch. of Tropical Medicine, 1975–78. Vice-Pres. and Pres., Brit. Soc. Parasit., 1972–76; President: Brit. Sect., Soc. Protozool., 1972–75; Royal Soc. of Trop. Medicine and Hygiene, 1987–89 (Vice-Pres., 1982–83, 1985–87). Chm., WHO Steering Cttee on Chemotherapy of Malaria, 1975–83; Member: Expert Adv. Panel, WHO, 1967–; WHO Steering Cttees on Leishmaniasis, 1979; Editorial Bd, Ann. Trop. Med. Parasit., 1966–79; Trop. Med. Research Bd, MRC, 1973–77; Scientific Council, Inst. of Cellular and Molecular Path., 1981–84; Parasitol. Bd, Institut Pasteur, 1979–87; Sec., European Fedn Parasit., 1979–84 (Vice-Pres., 1975–79). Hon. Consultant on malariology to the Army, 1986–89. Rudolf Leuckart Medal, German Soc. of Parasitol., 1980; King Faisal Internat. Prize in Medicine, 1983. *Publications:* A Provisional Checklist of Butterflies of the Ethiopian Region, 1952; Chemotherapy and Drug Resistance in Malaria, 1970, 2nd edn 1987; (with H. M. Gilles) A Colour Atlas of Tropical Medicine and Parasitology, 1976, 3rd edn 1989; (ed with R. Killick-Kendrick) Rodent Malaria, 1978; (ed with W. H. G. Richards) Antimalarial Drugs, 2 vols, 1984; (ed with R. Killick-Kendrick) The Leishmaniases in Biology and Medicine, 1987; numerous papers in jls, on trop. med. and parasitology. *Recreation:* photography. *Address:* London School of Hygiene and Tropical Medicine, Keppel Street, WC1E 7HT. *T:* 071–636 8636.

PETERS, William, CMG 1981; LVO 1961; MBE 1959; HM Diplomatic Service, retired; Chairman, Executive Committee, Lepra, since 1984; *b* 28 Sept. 1923; *o s* of John William Peters and Louise (*née* Woodhouse), Morpeth, Northumberland; *m* 1944, Catherine B. Bailey; no *c*. *Educ:* King Edward VI Grammar Sch., Morpeth; Balliol Coll., Oxford. MA Lit. Hum. 1948. War Service, Queen's Royal Rifles, KOSB, and 9th Gurkha Rifles, 1942–46. Joined HMOCS as Asst District Comr, Gold Coast, 1950; served in Cape Coast, Bawku and Tamale; Dep. Sec., Regional Comr, Northern Region, 1958–59; joined CRO as Asst Prin., 1959; Prin., 1959; 1st Sec., Dacca, 1960–63; 1st Sec., Cyprus, 1963–67; Head of Zambia and Malawi Dept, CRO, 1967–68; Head of Central African Dept, FCO, 1968–69; Dir, Internat. Affairs Div., Commonwealth Secretariat, 1969–71; Counsellor and Head of Chancery, Canberra, 1971–73; Dep. High Comr, Bombay, 1974–77; Ambassador to Uruguay, 1977–80; High Comr in Malaŵi, 1980–83. Member: Royal African Soc., 1980–85 (Hon. Treas., 1983–85); RSAA, 1987– (Mem., Editl Bd, 1990–); Council: S Atlantic Council, 1985–; USPG, 1988– (Chm., 1991–); Chm., Tibet Soc. of UK, 1985–; President: Downs Br., Royal British Legion, 1986–; Rotary Club of Deal, 1989–90. Governor, Walmer Sch., 1989–. FBIM 1984. *Publications:* Diplomatic Service: Formation and Operation, 1971; contribs to Jls of Asian Affairs and of African Administration; Illustrated Weekly of India; Noticias (Uruguay); Army Qly and Defence Jl; Christian Aid; Asian Affairs; Network. *Recreations:* music, carpentry. *Address:* 12 Crown Court, Middle Street, Deal, Kent CT14 7AG. *T:* Dover (0304) 362822. *Clubs:* United Oxford & Cambridge University, Commonwealth Trust.

PETERSEN, Sir Jeffrey (Charles), KCMG 1978 (CMG 1968); HM Diplomatic Service, retired; *b* 20 July 1920; *s* of Charles Petersen and Ruby Petersen (*née* Waple); *m* 1962, Karin Kristina Hayward; two *s* four *d*. *Educ:* Westcliff High Sch.; London School of Economics. Served RN (Lieut, RNVR), 1939–46. Joined Foreign Office, 1948; 2nd Secretary, Madrid, 1949–50; 2nd Secretary, Ankara, 1951–52; 1st Secretary, Brussels, 1953–56; NATO Defence College, 1956–57; FO, 1957–62; 1st Secretary, Djakarta, 1962–64; Counsellor, Athens, 1964–68; Minister (Commercial), Rio de Janeiro, 1968–71; Ambassador to: Republic of Korea, 1971–74; Romania, 1975–77; Sweden, 1977–80. Chairman: GVA Internat. Ltd; North Sea Assets PLC, 1989–; Ake Larson Ltd, 1990–; other directorships. Chm., British Materials Handling Bd; President: Anglo Swedish Soc.; Anglo-Korean Soc.; Vice Pres., Swedish Chamber of Commerce for UK. Knight Grand Cross, Order of Polar Star (Sweden), 1984; Order of Diplomatic Merit (Republic of Korea), 1985. *Recreations:* painting, making things, totting. *Address:* 32 Longmoore Street, SW1V 1JF. *T:* 071–834 8262; Crofts Wood, Petham, Kent CT4 5RX. *T:* Petham (022770) 537. *Clubs:* Travellers'; Kent and Canterbury.

PETERSEN, Hon. Sir Johannes B.; *see* Bjelke-Petersen.

PETERSHAM, Viscount; Charles Henry Leicester Stanhope; *b* 20 July 1945; *s* and *heir* of 11th Earl of Harrington, *qv*; *m* 1966, Virginia Alleyne Freeman Jackson, Mallow (marr. diss. 1983); one *s* one *d*; *m* 1984, Anita Countess of Suffolk and Berkshire. *Educ:* Eton. *Heir:* *s* Hon. William Henry Leicester Stanhope, *b* 14 Oct. 1967. *Address:* Baynton House, Coulston, Westbury, Wilts BA13 4NY. *T:* Bratton (0380) 830273. *Club:* House of Lords Yacht.

PETERSON, Cathryn Mary; *see* Pope, C. M.

PETERSON, Colin Vyvyan, CVO 1982; Lay Assistant to Bishop of Winchester, since 1985; *b* 24 Oct. 1932; *s* of late Sir Maurice Drummond Peterson, GCMG; *m* 1966, Pamela Rosemary Barry; two *s* two *d*. *Educ:* Winchester Coll.; Magdalen Coll., Oxford. Joined HM Treasury, 1959; Sec. for Appointments to PM and Ecclesiastical Sec. to the Lord Chancellor, 1974–82; Under Sec., Cabinet Office (MPO), 1982–85. *Recreation:* fishing. *Address:* Balldown Farmhouse, Sparsholt, Hants SO21 2LZ. *T:* Sparsholt (096272) 368.

PETERSON, Hon. David Robert; Premier of Ontario, 1985–90; *b* 28 Dec. 1943; *s* of Clarence Marwin Peterson and Laura Marie (*née* Scott); *m* 1974, Shelley Christine Matthews; two *s* one *d*. *Educ:* Univ. of Western Ontario (BA Phil./PolSci); Univ. of Toronto (LLB). Called to Bar, Ontario, 1969. Former Pres., C. M. Peterson Co. Ltd. MLA for London Centre, Ontario, 1975–90. Leader, Liberal Party of Ontario, until 1990; Leader of the Opposition, 1982–85. *Address:* c/o Parliament Buildings, Queen's Park, Toronto, Ontario M7A 1A1, Canada. *Club:* London (Ontario) Hunt.

PETERSON, Rt. Rev. Leslie Ernest; *see* Algoma, Bishop of.

PETERSON, Oscar Emmanuel, CC (Canada) 1984 (OC 1972); concert jazz pianist; *b* 15 Aug. 1925; *s* of Daniel Peterson and Kathleen Peterson; *m* 1st, 1947, Lillian Alice Ann; two *s* three *d*; 2nd, 1966, Sandra Cythia, *d* of H. A. King; 3rd, Charlotte; one *s*. *Educ:* (academic) Montreal High Sch.; (music) private tutors. 1st prize, amateur show, 1940; Carnegie Hall debut, 1950; 1950–: numerous jazz awards; TV shows; composer and arranger; yearly concert tours in N America, Europe, GB and Japan; has performed also in S America, Mexico, WI, Australia, NZ and Russia. *Television series:* (Canada): Oscar Peterson Presents, 1974; Oscar Peterson and Friends, 1980; (BBC) Oscar Peterson's Piano Party, 1974. Faculty Member: Sch. of Jazz, Lenox, Mass.; Banff Centre, Toronto; Mem., Bd of Govs, Credit Valley Hosp., Mississauga, Ont., 1984–. Oscar Peterson scholarship established, Berklee Coll. of Mus., 1982. Grammy award, 1974, 1975, 1977. Hon. LLD: Carleton Univ., 1973; Queen's Univ., Kingston, 1976; Concordia, 1979; MacMaster, 1981; Victoria, 1981; York, 1982; Toronto, 1985; Hon. DMus; Sackville, 1980; Laval, 1985; Hon. DFA Northwestern, Ill, 1983. Civic Award of Merit, Toronto, 1972, second mention, 1983; Diplôme d'Honneur, Canadian Conf. of the Arts, 1974. *Publications:* Oscar Peterson New Piano Solos, 1965; Jazz Exercises and Pieces, 1965. *Recreations:* audio, photography, ham radio, sports. *Address:* Regal Recordings Ltd, 2421 Hammond Road, Mississauga, Ont L5K 1T3, Canada. *T:* 416/855 2370.

PETHERBRIDGE, Edward; actor and director; *b* 3 Aug. 1936; *s* of William and Hannah Petherbridge; *m* 1st, 1957, Louise Harris (marr. diss. 1980); one *s*; 2nd, 1981, Emily Richard, actress; one *d*. *Educ:* Grange Grammar Sch., Bradford; Northern Theatre Sch. Early experience in repertory and on tour; London début, Dumain in Love's Labours Lost and Demetrius in A Midsummer Night's Dream, Regent's Park Open Air Theatre, 1962; All in Good Time, Mermaid, and Phoenix, 1963; with Nat. Theatre Co. at Old Vic, 1964–70, chief appearances in: Trelawny of the Wells, Rosencrantz and Guildenstern are Dead, A Flea in her Ear, Love for Love, Volpone, The Advertisement, The Way of the World, The White Devil; Alceste in The Misanthrope, Nottingham, Lulu, Royal Court, and Apollo, 1970; John Bull's Other Island, Mermaid, Swansong, opening of Crucible, Sheffield, 1971; Founder Mem., Actors' Co., 1972; chief appearances at Edinburgh Fests, NY, and on tour, 1972–75: 'Tis Pity she's a Whore, Rooling the Roost, The Way of the World, Tartuffe, King Lear; also devised, dir. and appeared in Knots (from R. D. Laing's book), The Beanstalk, a wordless pantomime, and dir. The Bacchae; RSC tour of Australia and NZ, 1976; dir. Uncle Vanya, Cambridge Theatre Co., 1977; Chasuble in The Importance of Being Earnest, and dir., devised and appeared in Do You Love Me (from R. D. Laing's book), Actors' Co. tour and Round House, 1977; Crucifer of Blood, Haymarket, 1979; Royal Shakespeare Company: tour, 1978, Twelfth Night; Three

Sisters, 1979; Suicide, Newman Noggs in Nicholas Nickleby (Best Supporting Actor, London Drama Critics' Award, 1981), No Limits to Love, 1980; Nicholas Nickleby, Broadway, 1981; Twelfth Night, British Council tour (Philippines, Singapore, Malaysia, China and Japan), followed by season at Warehouse, London, 1982; Peter Pan, Barbican, 1983; Strange Interlude, Duke of York's, 1984, Broadway, 1985 (Olivier Award, 1984); Love's Labours Lost, Stratford, 1984; Busman's Honeymoon, Lyric, Hammersmith, 1988; The Eight O'Clock Muse, one-man show, Riverside Studios, 1989; The Power and the Glory, Chichester, 1990; Cyrano de Bergerac (title rôle), Greenwich, 1990; Point Valaine, and Valentine's Day, Chichester, 1991; National Theatre: The Rivals, 1983; Co-Dir, McKellen Petherbridge Co. at NT, 1984–86, acting in Duchess of Malfi, The Cherry Orchard, The Real Inspector Hound, and The Critic, 1985, company appeared at Internat. Theatre Fests, Paris and Chicago, 1986; Alceste in The Misanthrope, co-prodn with Bristol Old Vic, 1989. Numerous television appearances include: Vershinin in Three Sisters (from RSC prod.); Lytton Strachey in No Need to Lie; Newman Noggs in Nicholas Nickleby (from RSC prod.); Gower in Pericles; Lord Peter Wimsey; Marsden in Strange Interlude; Uncle in Journey's End; No Strings. Member: Theatre Performers Working Group, Arts Council, 1978–; Specialist Allocations Bd, Arts Council, 1980–. Hon. DLitt Bradford, 1989. *Recreations:* listening to music, photography, theatre history. *Address:* c/o Jonathan Altaras Associates, 2 Goodwins Court, WC2N 4LL. *T:* 071–497 8878.

PETHICK, Brig. Geoffrey Loveston, CBE 1960; DSO 1944; *b* 25 Nov. 1907; *s* of late Captain E. E. Pethick, RN and May (*née* Brook); *m* 1st, 1939, Nancy Veronica Ferrand (*d* 1980); one *d*; 2nd, 1981, Mrs Paula Usborne. *Educ:* Newton College. Commissioned, Royal Artillery, 1927; RHA 1934; served War of 1939–45: Staff Coll., Camberley, 1940; CO, Field Regt, 1942; Far East, 1945; Jt Services Staff Coll., 1946; Dep. Dir, WO, 1948; idc, 1950; Comdr 3 Army Group, RA, 1951; Comdr RA 3 Div. 1953; Army Council Staff, 1957; retired, 1960. Dir, British Paper Makers' Association, 1960–74. *Address:* Little Croft, Fireball Hill, Sunningdale, Berks. *T:* Ascot (0344) 22018.

PETIT, Sir Dinshaw Manockjee, 4th Bt *cr* 1890; *b* 13 Aug. 1934; *s* of Sir Dinshaw Manockjee Petit, 3rd Bt and Sylla (*d* 1963), *d* of R. D. Tata; *S* father, 1983; *m* 1st, 1964, Nirmala Nanavatty (marr. diss. 1985); two *s*; 2nd, 1986, Elizabeth Maria Tinkelenberg. President: N. M. Petit Charities, 1983–; Sir D. M. Petit Charities, 1983–; F. D. Petit Sanatorium, 1983–; Persian Zoroastrian Amelioration Fund, 1983–; Petit Girls' Orphanage, 1983–; D. M. Petit Gymnasium, 1983–; J. N. Petit Institute, 1983–; Native Gen. Dispensary, 1983–; Trustee, Soc. for Prevention of Cruelty to Animals; Mem., Managing Cttee, B. D. Petit Parsi Gen. Hospital. Pres., Ripon Club, Bombay. *Heir: s* Jehangir Petit, *b* 21 Jan. 1965. *Address:* Petit Hall, 66 Nepean Sea Road, Bombay 400 006, India.

PETIT, Roland; Chevalier de la Légion d'honneur; Chevalier des Arts et des Lettres; French choreographer and dancer; Artistic Director and Choreographer, Ballet National de Marseille; *b* Villemomble, 13 Jan. 1924; *m* 1954, Renée (Zizi) Jeanmaire; one *d*. *Educ:* Ecole de Ballet de l'Opéra de Paris, studying under Ricaux and Lifar. Premier danseur, l'Opéra de Paris, 1940–44; founded Les Vendredis de la Danse, 1944, Les Ballets des Champs-Elysées, 1945, Les Ballets de Paris de Roland Petit, 1948; Artistic Dir and Choreographer, Ballets de Marseille. Choreographic works include: Les Forains, Le Jeune Homme et la Mort, Les Demoiselles de la nuit, Carmen, Deuil en 24 heures, Le Loup, L'éloge de la Folie, Les Chants de Maldoror, Notre Dame de Paris, Paradise Lost, Les Intermittences du coeur, La Symphonie fantastique, La Dame de Pique, Die Fledermaus, L'Arlésienne, Le Chat Botté, Coppelia, The Blue Angel, etc; choreographer and dancer: La Belle au Bois Dormant; Cyrano de Bergerac. Appeared in films Hans Christian Andersen; Un, Deux, Trois, Quatre (arr. ballets, for film, and danced in 3); 4 ballets, Black Tights. *Address:* Ballet National de Marseille, 1 place Auguste-François Carli, 13001 Marseille, France.

PETO, Sir Henry (George Morton), 4th Bt *cr* 1855; *b* 29 April 1920; *s* of Comdr Sir Henry Francis Morton Peto, 3rd Bt, RN, and Edith (*d* 1945), *d* of late George Berners Ruck Keene; *S* father, 1978; *m* 1947, Frances Jacqueline, JP, *d* of late Ralph Haldane Evers; two *s*. *Educ:* Sherborne; Corpus Christi College, Cambridge. Served War with Royal Artillery, 1939–46. Manufacturing industry, 1946–80. *Heir: s* Francis Michael Morton Peto [*b* 11 Jan. 1949; *m* 1974, Felicity Margaret, *d* of late Lt-Col John Alan Burns; two *s*]. *Address:* Stream House, Selborne, Alton, Hants. *T:* Selborne (042050) 246.

PETO, Sir Michael (Henry Basil), 4th Bt *cr* 1927; *b* 6 April 1938; *s* of Brig. Sir Christopher Henry Maxwell Peto, 3rd Bt, DSO, and of Barbara, *yr d* of Edwyn Thomas Close; *S* father, 1980; *m* 1st, 1963, Sarah Susan (marr. diss. 1970), *y d* of Major Sir Dennis Stucley, 5th Bt; one *s* two *d*; 2nd, 1971, Lucinda Mary, *yr d* of Major Sir Charles Douglas Blackett, 9th Bt; two *s*. *Educ:* Eton; Christ Church, Oxford (MA). Called to the Bar, Inner Temple, 1960. Mem., Stock Exchange, 1965–; Dir, Barnett Consulting Gp, 1985–. *Heir: s* Henry Christopher Morton Bampfylde Peto, *b* 8 April 1967. *Address:* Lower Church Cottage, Cliddesden, near Basingstoke, Hants. *Club:* Pratt's.

PETO, Richard, FRS 1989; Reader in Cancer Studies, University of Oxford, since 1975; *b* 14 May 1943; *s* of Leonard Huntley Peto and Carrie Clarinda Peto; *m* 1970, Sallie Messum (marr. diss.); two *s*, and two *s* by Gale Mead. *Educ:* Trinity Coll., Cambridge (MA Natural Sci.); Imperial Coll., London (MSc Statistics). Research Officer: MRC, 1967–69; Univ. of Oxford, 1969–72; Lectr, Dept of Regius Prof. of Medicine, Univ. of Oxford, 1972–75. *Publications:* Natural History of Chronic Bronchitis and Emphysema, 1976; Quantification of Occupational Cancer, 1981; The Causes of Cancer, 1983; Diet, Lifestyle and Mortality in China, 1990. *Recreations:* science, children. *Address:* Radcliffe Infirmary, Oxford OX2 6HE. *T:* Oxford (0865) 52830/58379.

PETRE, family name of **Baron Petre.**

PETRE, 18th Baron *cr* 1603; **John Patrick Lionel Petre;** *b* 4 Aug. 1942; *s* of 17th Baron Petre and of Marguerite Eileen, *d* of late Ion Wentworth Hamilton; *S* father, 1989; *m* 1965, Marcia Gwendolyn, *d* of Alfred Plumpton; two *s* one *d*. *Educ:* Eton; Trinity College, Oxford (MA). *Heir: s* Hon. Dominic William Petre, *b* 9 Aug. 1966. *Address:* Writtle Park, Highwood, Chelmsford, Essex CM1 3QF.

PETRE, Francis Herbert Loraine; His Honour Judge Petre; a Circuit Judge, since 1972; Chairman, Police Complaints Authority, since 1989; *b* 9 March 1927; *s* of late Maj.-Gen. R. L. Petre, CB, DSO, MC and Mrs Katherine Sophia Petre; *m* 1958, Mary Jane, *d* of late Everard C. X. White and Sydney Mary Carleton White (*née* Holmes), three *s* one *d*. *Educ:* Downside; Clare Coll., Cambridge. Called to Bar, Lincoln's Inn, 1952; Dep. Chm., E Suffolk QS, 1970; Dep. Chm., Agricultural Lands Tribunal (Eastern Area), 1972; a Recorder, 1972; Regular Judge, Central Criminal Court, 1982. *Address:* 10 Great George Street, SW1P 3AE.

PETRIE, Joan Caroline, (Lady Bathurst); HM Diplomatic Service, retired 1972; *b* 2 Nov. 1920; *d* of late James Alexander Petrie, Barrister-at-law, and Adrienne Johanna (*née* van den Bergh); *m* 1968, Sir Maurice Edward Bathurst, *qv*; one step *s*. *Educ:* Wycombe Abbey Sch.; Newnham Coll., Cambridge (Mary Ewart Schol.). 1st cl. Med. and Mod. Langs Tripos, 1942, MA 1964. Entered HM Foreign Service, 1947: FO, 1947–48; 2nd Sec., The Hague, 1948–50; FO, 1950–54; 1st Sec., 1953; Bonn, 1954–58; FO (later FCO), 1958–71; Counsellor 1969; Head of European Communities Information Unit, FCO, 1969–71. Mem., UK Delegn to Colombo Plan Consultative Cttee, Jogjakarta, 1959. Adviser, British Group, Inter-Parly Union, 1962–68. Officer, Order of Leopold (Belgium), 1966. *Recreations:* music, genealogy, gardening. *Address:* Airlie, The Highlands, East Horsley, Surrey KT24 5BG. *T:* East Horsley (04865) 3269. *Club:* United Oxford & Cambridge University.

PETRIE, Sir Peter (Charles), 5th Bt *cr* 1918, of Carrowcarden; CMG 1980; European Adviser to Governor of Bank of England, since 1989; HM Diplomatic Service, retired; *b* 7 March 1932; *s* of Sir Charles Petrie, 3rd Bt, CBE, FRHistS and Jessie Cecilia (*d* 1987), *d* of Frederick James George Mason; *S* half-brother, 1988; *m* 1958, Countess Lydwine Maria Fortunata v. Oberndorff, *d* of Count v. Oberndorff, The Hague and Paris; two *s* one *d*. *Educ:* Westminster; Christ Church, Oxford. BA Lit. Hum., MA. 2nd Lieut Grenadier Guards, 1954–56. Entered HM Foreign Service, 1956; served in UK Delegn to NATO, Paris 1958–61; UK High Commn, New Delhi (seconded CRO), 1961–64; Chargé d'Affaires, Katmandu, 1963; Cabinet Office, 1965–67; UK Mission to UN, NY, 1969–73; Counsellor (Head of Chancery), Bonn, 1973–76; Head of European Integration Dept (Internal), FCO, 1976–79; Minister, Paris, 1979–85; Ambassador to Belgium, 1985–89. *Recreations:* country pursuits. *Heir: s* Charles James Petrie [*b* 16 Sept. 1959; *m* 1981, France de Hauteclocque; two *s* (one *d* decd)]. *Address:* 16A Cambridge Street, SW1V 4QH; 40 rue Lauriston, 75116 Paris, France; Le Hameau du Jardin, Lestre, 50310 Montebourg, France. *Clubs:* Brooks's; Jockey (Paris).

PETT, Maj.-Gen. Raymond Austin, MBE 1976; Deputy Chief of Staff Support and Senior British Officer, Headquarters Allied Forces Northern Europe, since 1991; *b* 23 Sept. 1941; *s* of late Richard John Austin Pett and Jessie Lyle Pett (*née* Adamson); *m* 1965, (Joan) Marie McGrath Price, *d* of FO Bernard Christopher McGrath, RAF (killed in action 1943) and of Mrs Robert Henry Benbow Price; one *s* one *d*. *Educ:* Christ's Coll.; RMA Sandhurst; rcds, psc. Commnd Lancashire Regt (POW Vols), 1961; regtl service in GB, BAOR, Swaziland and Cyprus; seconded 2nd Bn 6th QEO Gurkha Rifles, Malaysia and Hong Kong, 1967–69; Instr, RMA Sandhurst, 1969–72; Staff Coll., 1972–73; DAA&QMG, HQ 48 Gurkha Inf. Bde, 1974–75; 1st Bn, Queen's Lancashire Regt, 1976–78; GSO2 ASD 3, MoD, 1978–80; CO, 1st Bn King's Own Royal Border Regt, 1980–82; Staff Coll. (HQ and Directing Staff), 1983–84; Col ASD 2, MoD, 1984; Col Army Plans, MoD, 1985; Comd Gurkha Field Force, 1985–86, and Comd 48 Gurkha Inf. Bde, 1986–87, Hong Kong; RCDS 1988; Dir, Army Staff Duties, MoD, 1989–91. Col, 6th QEO Gurkha Rifles, 1988–. *Recreations:* stage impressario, the arts, military history, house restoration, ski-ing. *Clubs:* Army and Navy, Ronnie Scott's.

PETTIFER, Julian; freelance writer and broadcaster; *b* 21 July 1935; *s* of Stephen Henry Pettifer and Diana Mary (*née* Burton); unmarried. *Educ:* Marlborough; St John's Coll., Cambridge. Television reporter, writer and presenter: Southern TV, 1958–62; Tonight, BBC, 1962–64; 24 Hours, BBC, 1964–69; Panorama, BBC, 1969–75; Presenter, Cuba—25 years of revolution (series), ITV, 1984; Host, Busman's Holiday, ITV, 1985–86. Numerous television documentaries, including: Vietnam, War without End, 1970; The World About Us, 1976; The Spirit of '76, 1976; Diamonds in the Sky, 1979; Nature Watch, 1981–82, 1985–86, 1988, 1990; Automania, 1984; The Living Isles, 1986; Missionaries, 1990; See for Yourself, 1991; Assignment, 1991. Pres., Berks, Bucks and Oxfordshire Naturalists Trust. Reporter of the Year Award, Guild of Television Directors and Producers, 1968; Cherry Kearton Award for Contribution to Wildlife Films, RGS, 1990. *Publications:* (jtly) Diamonds in the Sky: a social history of air travel, 1979; (jtly) Nature Watch, 1981; (jtly) Automania, 1984; (jtly) Missionaries, 1990. *Recreations:* travel, sport, cinema. *Address:* c/o Curtis Brown, 163–168 Regent Street, W1R 5TA. *T:* 071–437 9700. *Club:* Queen's.

PETTIGREW, Prof. John Douglas, FRS 1987; FAA 1987; Professor of Physiology, since 1983, Director, Vision, Touch and Hearing Research Centre, since 1988, University of Queensland; *b* 2 Oct. 1943; *s* of John James Pettigrew and Enid Dellmere Holt; *m* 1968, Rona Butler; one *s* two *d*. *Educ:* Katoomba High Sch.; Univ. of Sydney (BSc Med., MSc, MB BS). Jun. Resident MO, Royal Prince Alfred Hosp., 1969; Miller Fellow 1970–72, Res. Associate 1973, Univ. of California, Berkeley; Asst Prof. of Biology 1974, Associate Prof. of Biology 1978, CIT; Actg Dir, National Vision Res. Inst. of Aust., 1981. *Publications:* Visual Neuroscience, 1986; numerous pubns in Nature, Science, Jl of Physiol., Jl of Comp. Neurol., Exp. Brain Res., etc. *Recreations:* bird watching, mountaineering. *Address:* 423 Savages Road, Brookfield, Qld 4069, Australia. *T:* (07) 374 1561.

PETTIGREW, Sir Russell (Hilton), Kt 1983; FInstD; FCIT; Director, Union Shipping Group Company, since 1981; Chairman, Chep Handling Systems NZ Ltd, since 1980; *b* 10 Sept. 1920; *s* of Albert and Bertha Pettigrew; *m* 1965, Glennis Olive Nicol; one *s* one *d*. *Educ:* Hangatiki Sch., King Country. Served War, Naval Service, 1941–45 (Service Medals). Hawkes Bay Motor Co., 1935–40; Pettigrews Transport, 1946–63; formed Allied Freightways (now Freightways Holdings Ltd), 1964. Chairman: NZ Maritime Holdings Ltd, 1981–89; AGC NZ, 1984–88; Dep. Chm., NZ Forest Products, 1980–88 (Dir, 1975–90). FCIT 1972; Fellow, NZ Inst. of Dirs, 1972; Life Mem., NZ Road Transport Assoc., 1981. Knighthood for services to the Transport Industry. *Publication:* article in The Modern Freight Forwarder and the Road Carrier, 1971. *Recreations:* farming, deer farming, stud breeding (Herefords), Rugby, surfing, jogging, horse racing. *Address:* PO Box 16, Bay View, Napier, New Zealand. *T:* Napier 4151, 266–426. *Clubs:* Auckland, Hawkes Bay (New Zealand).

PETTIT, Sir Daniel (Eric Arthur), Kt 1974; Chairman, PosTel Investment Management (formerly Post Office Staff Superannuation Fund), 1979–83; *b* Liverpool, 19 Feb. 1915; *s* of Thomas Edgar Pettit and Pauline Elizabeth Pettit (*née* Kerr); *m* 1940, Winifred, *d* of William and Sarah Bibby; two *s*. *Educ:* Quarry Bank High Sch., Liverpool; Fitzwilliam Coll., Cambridge (MA; Hon. Fellow, 1985). School Master, 1938–40 and 1946–47; War Service, Africa, India, Burma, 1940–46 (Major, RA); Unilever: Management, 1948–57; Associated Company Dir and Chm., 1958–70. Chm., Nat. Freight Corp., 1971–78 (part-time Mem. Bd, 1968–70); Member: Freight Integration Council, 1971–78; National Ports Council, 1971–80; Bd, Foundn of Management Educn, 1973–84; Waste Management Adv. Council, 1971–78; Chm., EDC for Distributive Trades, 1974–78. Chairman: Incpen, 1979–90; RDC Properties, 1987–; Director: Lloyds Bank Ltd, 1977–78 (Chm., Birmingham & W Midlands Bd, 1978–85); Lloyds Bank (UK) Ltd, 1979–85; Black Horse Life Assurance Co. Ltd, 1983–85; Lloyds Bank Unit Trust Managers Ltd, 1981–85; Bransford Farmers Ltd. Mem. Council, British Road Fedn Ltd. Hon. Col, 162 Regt RCT (V). Freeman, City of London, 1971; Liveryman, Worshipful Co. of Carmen, 1971. CBIM; FCIT (Pres. 1971–72); FRSA; FIM; MIPM. *Publications:* various papers on transport and management matters. *Recreations:* cricket, Association football (Olympic Games, 1936; Corinthian FC, 1935–); fly-fishing. *Address:* Bransford Court Farm, Worcester WR6 5JL. *Clubs:* Farmers', MCC; Hawks (Cambridge).

PETTITT, Gordon Charles, OBE 1991; Managing Dir, Regional Railways, British Rail, since 1991; *b* 12 April 1934; *s* of Charles and Annie Pettitt; *m* 1956, Ursula Margareta

Agnes Hokamp; three *d. Educ:* St Columba's Coll., St Albans; Pitman's Coll., London. MCIT. British Rail, 1950–: Freight Sales Manager, Eastern Reg., 1976; Chief Passenger Manager, Western Reg., 1978; Divl Manager, Liverpool Street, Eastern Reg., 1979; Dep. Gen. Manager, 1983, Gen. Manager, 1985, Southern Reg.; Dir, Provincial, 1990–91. Dir, Middlesex Polytechnic, 1989. *Recreations:* walking, foreign travel. *Address:* PO Box 100, Euston House, 24 Eversholt Street, NW1 1DZ.

PETTY, Very Rev. John Fitzmaurice; Provost of Coventry Cathedral, since 1988; *b* 1935; *m* 1963, Susan Shakerley; three *s* one *d. Educ:* RMA Sandhurst; Trinity Hall, Cambridge (BA 1959, MA 1965); Cuddesdon College. Commnd RE, 1955; seconded Gurkha Engineers, 1959–62; resigned commission as Captain, 1964. Deacon 1966, priest 1967; Curate: St Cuthbert, Sheffield, 1966–69; St Helier, Southwark Dio., 1969–75; Vicar of St John's, Hurst, Ashton-under-Lyne, 1975–87; Area Dean of Ashton-under-Lyne, 1983–87; Hon. Canon of Manchester Cathedral, 1986. *Recreations:* squash, ski-ing. *Address:* c/o Coventry Cathedral, 7 Priory Row, Coventry CV1 5ES. *T:* Coventry (0203) 227597.

PETTY, William Henry, CBE 1981; County Education Officer, Kent, 1973–84; *b* 7 Sept. 1921; *s* of Henry and Eveline Ann Petty, Bradford; *m* 1948, Margaret Elaine, *o d* of Edward and Lorna Bastow, Baildon, Yorks; one *s* two *d. Educ:* Bradford Grammar Sch.; Peterhouse, Cambridge; London Univ. MA 1950, BSc 1953. Served RA, India and Burma, 1941–45. Admin, teaching and lectrg in London, Doncaster and N R Yorks, 1946–57; Sen. Asst Educn Officer, W R Yorks CC 1957–64; Dep. County Educn Officer, Kent CC, 1964–73. Member: Council and Court, Univ. of Kent at Canterbury, 1974–84; Local Govt Trng Bd, Careers Service Trng Cttee, 1975–84; Careers Service Adv. Council, 1976–84; Trng and Further Educn Cons. Gp, 1977–83; Vital Skills Task Gp, 1977–78; Manpower Services Commn, SE Counties Area Bd, 1978–83; Bd of Dirs, Industrial Trng Service, 1978–; Exec. Mem. and Sec. for SE Reg., Soc. of Educn Officers, 1978–82; Pres., Soc. of Educn Officers, 1980–81; Chm., Assoc. of Educn Officers, 1979–80 (Vice-Chm., 1978–79); Member: JNC for Chief Officers, Officers' side, 1974–84 (Chm., 1981–84); C of E Bd of Educn, Schs Cttee, 1981–86; County Educn Officers' Soc., 1974–84 (Chm., 1982–83); Youth Trng Task Gp, 1982; National Youth Trng Bd, 1983–84; Kent Area Manpower Bd, 1983–84; Canterbury Diocesan Bd of Educn, 1984– (Vice-Chm., 1989–); Consultant, Further Educn Unit, 1984–90. Dir, Sennocke Services Ltd, 1989–. Governor: Christ Church Coll., Canterbury, 1974– (Vice-Chm., 1988–); Sevenoaks Sch., 1974–. Hon. DLitt Kent, 1983. Prizewinner: Cheltenham Fest. of Lit., 1968; Camden Fest. of Music and Arts, 1969. Greenwood Prize, 1978; Lake Aske Meml Award, 1980. *Publications:* No Bold Comfort, 1957; Conquest, 1967; (jtly) Educational Administration, 1980; Executive Summaries, 1984–90; contrib. educnl and lit. jls and anthologies. *Recreations:* literature, travel. *Address:* Willow Bank, Moat Road, Headcorn, Kent TN27 9NT. *T:* Headcorn (0622) 890087. *Club:* United Oxford & Cambridge University.

PETTY-FITZMAURICE; *see* Mercer Nairne Petty-Fitzmaurice, family name of Marquess of Lansdowne.

PEYREFITTE, (Pierre-) Roger; French author; *b* 17 Aug. 1907; *o s* of Jean Peyrefitte, landowner, and Eugénie Jamme; unmarried. *Educ:* Collège St Benoit, Ardouane, Hérault (Lazarist); Collège du Caousou, Toulouse, Hte. Garonne (Jesuit); Lycée de Foix, Ariège; Université de Toulouse; Ecole libre des Sciences Politiques, Paris. Bachelier de l'enseignement secondaire; Diplôme d'études supérieures de langue et de littérature française; Diplômé de l'Ecole libre des Sciences Politiques (major de la section diplomatique). Concours diplomatique, 1931; attached to Ministry of Foreign Affairs, 1931–33; Secretary, French Embassy, Athens, 1933–38; attached to Ministry of Foreign Affairs, 1938–40 and 1943–45. *Publications:* Du Vésuve à l'Etna, 1952; Chevaliers de Malte, 1957; La Nature du Prince, 1963; Les Juifs, 1965; Notre Amour, 1967; Manouche, 1972; Un Musée de l'Amour, 1972; La Muse garçonnière, 1973; Catalogue de la collection de monnaies grecques et romaines de l'auteur, 1974; Tableaux de chasse, ou la vie extraordinaire de Fernand Legros, 1976; Propos secrets, 1977; La Jeunesse d'Alexandre, 1977; L'Enfant de coeur, 1978; Les Conquêtes d'Alexandre, 1980; Propos secrets 2, 1980; Alexandre le Grand, 1981; Henry de Montherlant-Roger Peyrefitte: Correspondence, 1983; Voltaire, Sa Jeunesse et son Temps, 1985; L'Innominato, nouveaux propos secrets, 1989; *novels:* Les Amitiés particulières, 1944 (Prix Théophraste Renaudot, 1945); Mademoiselle de Murville, 1947; L'Oracle, 1948; Les Amours singulières, 1949; La Mort d'une mère, 1950; Les Ambassades, 1951; La Fin des Ambassades, 1953; Les Clés de Saint Pierre, 1955; Jeunes proies, 1956; L'Exilé de Capri, 1959; Les Fils de la lumière, 1962; Les Américains, 1968; Des Français, 1970; La Coloquinte, 1971; Roy, 1979; L'Illustre écrivain, 1982; La Soutane rouge, 1983; L'Innominato, nouveaux propos secrets, 1989; *plays:* Le Prince des neiges, 1947; Le Spectateur nocturne, 1960; Les Ambassades (adaptation of A. P. Antoine), 1961. *Recreations:* travel, walks, collecting antiques. *Address:* 9 Avenue du Maréchal Maunoury, 75016 Paris, France.

PEYTON, family name of **Baron Peyton of Yeovil.**

PEYTON OF YEOVIL, Baron *cr* 1983 (Life Peer), of Yeovil in the County of Somerset; **John Wynne William Peyton;** PC 1970; Chairman, British Alcan Aluminium, 1987–91; *b* 13 Feb. 1919; *s* of late Ivor Eliot Peyton and Dorothy Helen Peyton; *m* 1947, Diana Clinch (marr. diss., 1966); one *s* one *d* (and one *s* decd); *m* 1966, Mrs Mary Cobbold. *Educ:* Eton; Trinity College, Oxford. Commissioned 15/19 Hussars, 1939; Prisoner of War, Germany, 1940–45. Called to the Bar, Inner Temple, 1945. MP (C) Yeovil, 1951–83; Parly Secretary, Ministry of Power, 1962–64; Minister of Transport, June-Oct. 1970; Minister for Transport Industries, DoE, 1970–74. Chm., Texas Instruments Ltd, 1974–90. Treas., Zoological Society of London, 1984–91. *Address:* The Old Malt House, Hinton St George, Somerset TA17 8SE. *T:* Crewkerne (0460) 73618; 6 Temple West Mews, West Square, SE11 4TJ. *T:* 071–582 3611. *Club:* Boodle's.

PEYTON, Kathleen Wendy; writer (as K. M. Peyton); *b* 2 Aug. 1929; *d* of William Joseph Herald and Ivy Kathleen Herald; *m* 1950, Michael Peyton; two *d. Educ:* Wimbledon High Sch.; Manchester Sch. of Art (ATD). Taught art at Northampton High Sch., 1953–55; started writing seriously after birth of first child, although had already had 4 books published. *Publications: as Kathleen Herald:* Sabre, the Horse from the Sea, 1947, USA 1963; The Mandrake, 1949; Crab the Roan, 1953; *as K. M. Peyton:* North to Adventure, 1959, USA 1965; Stormcock Meets Trouble, 1961; The Hard Way Home, 1962; Windfall, 1963, USA (as Sea Fever), 1963; Brownsea Silver, 1964; The Maplin Bird, 1964, USA 1965 (New York Herald Tribune Award, 1965); The Plan for Birdsmarsh, 1965, USA 1966; Thunder in the Sky, 1966, USA 1967; Flambards Trilogy (Guardian Award, 1970): Flambards, 1967, USA 1968; The Edge of the Cloud, 1969, USA 1969 (Carnegie Medal, 1969); Flambards in Summer, 1969, USA 1970; Fly-by-Night, 1968, USA 1969; Pennington's Seventeenth Summer, 1970, USA (as Pennington's Last Term), 1971; The Beethoven Medal, 1971, USA 1972; The Pattern of Roses, 1972, USA 1973; Pennington's Heir, 1973, USA 1974; The Team, 1975; The Right-Hand Man, 1977; Prove Yourself a Hero, 1977, USA 1978; A Midsummer Night's Death, 1978, USA 1979; Marion's Angels, 1979, USA 1979; Flambards Divided, 1981; Dear Fred, 1981, USA 1981; Going Home, 1983, USA 1983; Who, Sir? Me, Sir?, 1983; The Last Ditch, 1984, USA (as Free Rein), 1983; Froggett's Revenge, 1985; The Sound of Distant Cheering, 1986; Downhill All the Way, 1988; Darkling, 1989, USA 1990; Skylark, 1989; No Roses Round the Door, 1990. *Recreations:* riding, walking, gardening, sailing. *Address:* Rookery Cottage, North Fambridge, Chelmsford, Essex CM3 6LP.

PFLIMLIN, Pierre; *b* 5 Feb. 1907; *s* of Jules Pflimlin and Léonie Schwartz; *m* 1939, Marie-Odile Heinrich; one *s* two *d. Educ:* Mulhouse; University of Strasbourg. Dr of Laws, 1932. Mem. for Bas-Rhin Dept, French Parliament (Nat. Assembly), 1945–67; Under Sec. of State, Ministries for Public Health and for Economics, 1946; Minister: of Agriculture, 1947–49 and 1950–51; of Trade and External Economic Relations, 1951–52; of State in charge of relations with Council of Europe, 1952; for Overseas Territories, 1952–53; of Finance and Economics, 1955–56 and 1957–58; Prime Minister, May-June 1958; Minister of State in de Gaulle Govt, 1958–59; Minister of State for Co-operation with Overseas Countries, 1962. Mem., Consultative Assembly of Council of Europe (President, 1963–66) and of European Parliament, 1959–67; European Parliament: Mem., 1979–89; Vice-Pres., 1979–84; Pres., 1984–87. Mayor, City of Strasbourg, 1959–83. *Publications:* Industry in Mulhouse, 1932; The Economic Structure of the Third Reich, 1938; Alsace: destiny and will, 1963; The Europe of the Communities, 1966. *Address:* 24 avenue de la Paix, 67000 Strasbourg, France. *T:* 88/35–63–68.

PHAROAH, Prof. Peter Oswald Derrick, MD, FFCM; Professor of Public Health (formerly of Community Health), University of Liverpool, since 1979; *b* 19 May 1934; *s* of Oswald Higgins Pharoah and Phyllis Christine Gahan; *m* 1960, Margaret Rose McMinn; three *s* one *d. Educ:* Lawrence Memorial Royal Military School, Lovedale, India; Palmers School, Grays, Essex; St Mary's Hospital Medical School. MD, MSc. Graduated, 1958; Med. House Officer and Med. Registrar appointments at various London Hosps, 1958–63; MO and Research MO, Dept of Public Health, Papua New Guinea, 1963–74; Sen. Lectr in Community Health, London School of Hygiene and Tropical Medicine, 1974–79. *Publication:* Endemic Cretinism, 1971. *Recreations:* squash, walking, philately. *Address:* 11 Fawley Road, Liverpool L18 9TE. *T:* 051–724 4896.

PHELAN, Andrew James; His Honour Judge Phelan; a Circuit Judge, since 1974; *b* 25 July 1923; *e s* of Cornelius Phelan, Kilganey House, Clonmel, Eire; *m* 1950, Joan Robertson McLagan; one *s* two *d. Educ:* Clongoweswood, Co. Kildare; National Univ. of Ireland (MA); Trinity Coll., Cambridge. Called to: Irish Bar, King's Inn, 1945; English Bar, Gray's Inn, 1949. Jun. Fellow, Univ. of Bristol, 1948–50; in practice at English Bar, 1950–74. *Publication:* The Law for Small Boats, 2nd edn, 1970. *Recreations:* sailing, mountain walking. *Address:* 17 Hartington Road, Chiswick, W4 3TL. *T:* 081–994 6109. *Clubs:* Royal Cruising, Bar Yacht.

PHELPS, Anthony John, CB 1976; Deputy Chairman, Board of Customs and Excise, 1973–82; *b* 14 Oct. 1922; *s* of John Francis and Dorothy Phelps, Oxford; *m* 1st, 1949, Sheila Nan Rait (*d* 1967), *d* of late Colin Benton Rait, Edinburgh; one *s* two *d*; 2nd, 1971, Janet M. T., *d* of late Charles R. Dawson, Edinburgh. *Educ:* City of Oxford High Sch.; University Coll., Oxford. HM Treasury, 1946; Jun. Private Sec. to Chancellor of the Exchequer, 1949–50; Principal, 1950; Treasury Rep. in Far East, 1953–55; Private Sec. to the Prime Minister, 1958–61; Asst Sec., 1961; Under-Sec., 1968. Freeman, City of Oxford, 1971. *Recreations:* music, watching sport. *Address:* 1 Woodsyre, Sydenham Hill, SE26 6SS. *T:* 081–670 0735. *Clubs:* City Livery, MCC.

PHELPS, Charles Frederick, DPhil, DSc; Consultant to Rector on International Affairs, Imperial College of Science, Technology and Medicine, since 1990; *b* 18 Jan. 1934; *s* of Seth Phelps and Rigmor Kaae; *m* 1960, Joanna Lingeman; one *s* one *d. Educ:* Bromsgrove Sch.; Oxford Univ. (MA, DPhil; DSc 1990). Lecturer, Univ. of Bristol: in Chemical Physiology, 1960–63; in Biochemistry, 1963–70; Reader in Biochemistry, Univ. of Bristol, 1970–74; Prof. of Biochemistry, Univ. of Lancaster, 1974–80; Principal, Chelsea Coll., London, 1981–84; Pro-Rector (Internat. Affairs), Imperial Coll., 1984–89. Visiting Fellow, Univ. of Rome, 1968–69. Consultant, World Bank Educational Mission to China, 1980 and to Korea, 1982. Mem. Senate, 1980–84, Mem., F and GP Cttee, 1983–88, Chm., Univ. Trng Cttee, 1984–, London Univ. Member: Cttee, Biochemical Soc., 1980–84; Cttee, British Biophysical Soc., 1974–84 (Chm., 1983–84); Research Cttee of Arthritis and Rheumatism Council, 1974–78. Trustee, America European Community Assoc. Trust, 1986–. Mem. Governing Body, Royal Postgraduate Med. Fedn, 1986–; Mem. Council, Queen Elizabeth Coll., 1983–85; Governor: Furzedown Sch., 1980–85; King Edward Sch., Witley, 1984–; Mill Hill Sch., 1985–; Royal Grammar Sch., Guildford, 1989–. FKC 1985. Editorial Board: Biochim. Biophys. Acta, 1976–80, 1983–84; Internat. Research Communications Systems Jl of Med. Scis, 1980–. *Publications:* numerous papers in medical and science jls. *Recreations:* enjoying things Italian, 17th Century science, landscape gardening. *Address:* Brockhurst, The Green, Chiddingfold, near Guildford, Surrey GU8 4TU. *T:* Wormley (0428) 683092. *Club:* Athenæum.

PHELPS, Howard Thomas Henry Middleton; Executive Vice-Chairman Brewery Court Ltd, since 1990; *b* 20 Oct. 1926; *s* of Ernest Henry Phelps, Gloucester, and Harriet (*née* Middleton); *m* 1949, Audrey (*née* Ellis); one *d. Educ:* Crypt Grammar Sch., Gloucester; Hatfield Coll.; Durham Univ. BA Hons Politics and Econs 1951. National Coal Board, Lancs, Durham and London, 1951–72, finally Dep. Dir-Gen. of Industrial Relations; Personnel Dir, BOAC, 1972; British Airways: Gp Personnel Dir, 1972; Bd Mem., 1973–83; Dir of Operations, 1979–86. Chairman: Sutcliffe Catering Gp, 1986–88; Sterling Guards Ltd, 1986–89; Earls Court and Olympia Ltd, 1986–89; Niccol Centre Ltd, 1989–90. Non-Exec. Chm., QA Training Ltd, Cirencester, 1989–; Dir, P&OSN Co., 1986–89; Non-Exec. Dir, Alden Press Ltd, Oxford, 1990–. FRAeS; FIPM; FCIT; CBIM. Chm., Alice Ruston Housing Assoc., 1973–84; President: Durham Univ. Soc., 1988– (Chm., 1975–88); Pres., Hatfield Assoc., 1983–. Mem. Council, Durham Univ., 1985–88; Dep. Chm., Governing Body, Middlesex Polytechnic, 1987–89 (Vis. Prof., 1987–); Chm., Cirencester Tertiary Coll., 1990–; Governor: Rendcomb Coll., Cirencester; Cotswold Sch. *Recreations:* gardening, musical appreciation. *Address:* Tall Trees, Chedworth, near Cheltenham, Glos GL54 4AB. *T:* Fossebridge (0285) 720324. *Club:* Royal Over-Seas League.

PHELPS, Maj.-Gen. Leonard Thomas Herbert, CB 1973; OBE 1963; CBIM; *b* 9 Sept. 1917; *s* of Abijah Phelps; *m* 1945, Jean Irene, *d* of R. Price Dixon; one *s* one *d.* CBIM 1980 (FBIM 1973). Served War, Hong Kong, 1940–41; India/Burma, 1941–47. Student, Staff Coll., Quetta, 1946; DAQMG, HQ Land Forces Hong Kong, 1951–53; Second in Command, 4th Trng Bn, RAOC, 1955–57; War Office: DAAG, 1957–59; ADOS, 1961–63; AA & QMG Singapore Mil. Forces, 1963; Chief of Staff and Dep Comdr, 4th Malaysian Inf. Bde, 1964; ADOS, WO, 1965–67; Chief Inspector, Land Service Ammunition, 1967–70; Comdr, Base Organisation, RAOC, 1970; Dir, Ordnance Services, MoD (Army), 1971–73; retired 1973; Col Comdt, RAOC, 1976–78. Man. Dir, The Warrior Gp, 1975–78; Director: Leon Davis & Co., 1975–82; Debenhams Business Systems Ltd, 1982–84. Parchment Award for life saving, Royal Humane Soc., 1936. *Publication:* A History of the Royal Army Ordnance Corps 1945–1982, 1991.

PHELPS, Maurice Arthur; Human Resource Consultant, since 1989: Maurice Phelps Associates; Emslie Phelps Associates; *b* 17 May 1935; *s* of H. T. Phelps; *m* 1960, Elizabeth

Anne Hurley; two *s* one *d*. *Educ:* Wandsworth School; Corpus Christi College, Oxford Univ. BA Hons Modern History. Shell Chemical Co. Ltd, 1959–68; Group Personnel Planning Adviser, Pilkington Bros Ltd, 1968–70; Group Personnel Dir, Unicorn Industries Ltd, 1970–72; Dir of Labour and Staff Relations, W Midland Passenger Transport Exec., 1973–77; Dir of Personnel, Heavy Vehicle Div., Leyland Vehicles Ltd, 1977–80; Bd Mem. for Personnel and Industrial Relations, 1980–87, non-exec. Bd Mem., 1987–, British Shipbuilders; Dir of Personnel and Employee Relations, Sealink UK Ltd, 1987–89. *Address:* Abbotsfield, Goring Heath, S Oxon RG8 7SA.

PHELPS, Richard Wintour, CBE 1986; General Manager, Central Lancashire New Town Development Corporation, 1971–86; consultant in management of urban development and housing, since 1986; *b* 26 July 1925; *s* of Rev. H. Phelps; *m* 1955, Pamela Marie Lawson; two *d*. *Educ:* Kingswood Sch.; Merton Coll., Oxford (MA). 14th Punjab Regt, IA, 1944–46. Colonial Admin. Service, Northern Region and Fed. Govt. of Nigeria, 1948–57 and 1959–61; Prin., HM Treasury, 1957–59 and 1961–65; Sen. Administrator, Hants CC, 1965–67; Gen. Manager, Skelmersdale New Town Develt Corp., 1967–71. Advr (part-time) on housing to Govt of Vanuatu, 1986–89; Consultant on housing policy to Falkland Is Govt, 1988–89; Chm., Examn in Public Replacement Structure Plan, Derbys CC, 1989, Notts CC and Northants CC, 1990. Contested (SDP) Barrow and Furness, 1987. Winston Churchill Trust Travelling Fellowship, 1971. *Recreations:* reading, travel, music. *Address:* Fell Foot House, Newby Bridge, Ulverston, Cumbria LA12 8NL. *T:* Newby Bridge (05395) 31274. *Club:* Commonwealth Trust.

PHELPS BROWN, Sir Ernest Henry; *see* Brown, Sir E. H. P.

PHILBIN, Most Rev. William J., DD; *b* 26 Jan. 1907; *s* of late James Philbin and Brigid (*née* O Hora). *Educ:* St Nathy's Coll., Ballaghaderreen; St Patrick's, Maynooth. Priest, 1931; DD Maynooth, 1933. Curate, Eastbourne, 1933; Secondary teacher, Ballaghaderreen, 1934; Prof. of Dogmatic Theology, Maynooth, 1936; Bishop of Clonfert, 1953; Bishop of Down and Connor, 1962–82. *Publications:* Does Conscience Decide?, 1969; To You Simonides, 1973; The Bright Invisible, 1984; pamphlets on socio-moral questions; Mise Padraig, 3 edns; contributor to The Irish Theological Quarterly, Studies, The Irish Ecclesiastical Record. *Address:* 81 Highfield Road, Rathgar, Dublin 6, Ireland.

PHILIP, Alexander Morrison; QC (Scot) 1984; *b* 3 Aug. 1942; *s* of late Alexander Philip, OBE and of Isobel Thomson Morrison; *m* 1971, Shona Mary Macrae; three *s*. *Educ:* High School of Glasgow; St Andrews University (MA 1963); Glasgow University (LLB 1965). Solicitor, 1967–72; Advocate 1973; Standing Junior Counsel to Scottish Education Dept, 1982; Advocate-Depute, 1982–85. *Recreations:* golf, skiing, piping. *Address:* 15 Russell Place, Edinburgh. *T:* 031–552 8164. *Club:* Scottish Arts (Edinburgh).

PHILIP, John Robert, DSc; FRS 1974; FAA 1967; Fellow, Commonwealth Scientific and Industrial Research Organization, Australia, since 1991; *b* 18 Jan. 1927; *e s* of late Percival Norman Philip and Ruth (*née* Osborne), formerly of Ballarat and Maldon, Vic., Australia; *m* 1949, Frances Julia, *o d* of late E. Hilton Long; two *s* one *d*. *Educ:* Scotch Coll., Melbourne; Univ. of Melbourne (Queen's Coll.). BCE 1946, DSc 1960. Research Asst, Melb. Univ., 1947; Engr, Qld Irrig. Commn, 1948–51; Research Staff, CSIRO, 1951–; Sen. Prin. Res. Scientist, 1961–63; Chief Res. Scientist and Asst Chief, Div. of Plant Industry, 1963–71; Chief, Dir. of Envmtl Mechanics, subseq. Centre for Envmtl Mechanics, 1971–80 and 1983–91; Associate Mem., CSIRO Exec., 1978; Dir, Inst. of Physical Scis, 1980–83. Visiting Scientist, Cambridge Univ., 1954–55; Res. Fellow, Calif. Inst. Techn., 1957–58; Vis. Prof., Univ. of Illinois, 1958 and 1961; Nuffield Foundn Fellow, Cambridge Univ., 1961–62; Res. Fellow, Harvard Univ., 1966–67; Vis. Prof., Univ. of Florida, 1969; Vinton-Hayes Fellow, Harvard Univ., 1972; Vis. Res. Fellow, Cornell Univ., 1979. Mem. Council, Australian Acad. of Sci., 1972–78 (Biol. Sec., 1974–78); ANZAAS: Pres. Section 1 (Physics), 1970; Pres. Sect. 8 (Maths), 1971. FRMetS; Fellow, Amer. Geophys. Union, 1981. Hon. DEng Melbourne, 1983. Horton Award, 1957, Horton Medal, 1982, Amer. Geophys. Union; David Rivett Medal, 1966; Thomas Ranken Lyle Medal, 1981; Eminent Researcher Award, Aust. Water Res. Adv. Council, 1990. *Publications:* papers in scientific jls on soil and porous medium physics, fluid mechanics, hydrology, micrometeorology, mathematical and physical aspects of physiology and ecology. *Recreations:* reading, writing, architecture. *Address:* CSIRO Centre for Environmental Mechanics, GPO Box 821, Canberra, ACT 2601, Australia. *T:* (06) 246–5645; 42 Vasey Crescent, Campbell, ACT 2601. *T:* (06) 247–8958.

PHILIPPE, André J., Hon. GCVO 1972; Luxembourg Ambassador to the United States of America, 1987–91; *b* Luxembourg City, 28 June 1926. Dr-en-Droit. Barrister-at-Law, Luxembourg, 1951–52. Joined Luxembourg Diplomatic Service, 1952; Dep. to Dir of Polit. Affairs, Min. of Foreign Affairs, 1952–54; Dep. Perm. Rep. to NATO, 1954–61 and to OECD, 1959–61; Dir of Protocol and Legal Adviser, Min. of For. Affairs, 1961–68; Ambassador and Perm. Rep. to UN and Consul-Gen., New York, 1968–72 (Vice-Pres., 24th Session of Gen. Assembly of UN, 1969); Ambassador to UK, Perm. Rep. to Council of WEU, and concurrently Ambassador to Ireland and Iceland, 1972–78; Ambassador to France, 1978–84; Ambassador to UN, NY, 1984–87. Commander: Order of Adolphe Nassau (Luxembourg); Légion d'Honneur (France); Grand Officer: Order of Merit (Luxembourg), 1983; Order of Oaken Crown (Luxembourg), 1988.

PHILIPPS, family name of **Viscount St Davids** and **Baron Milford.**

PHILIPPS, Hon. Hanning; *see* Philipps, Hon. R. H.

PHILIPPS, Lady Marion (Violet), FRAgS; JP; farmer, since 1946; *b* 1 Feb. 1908; *d* of 12th Earl of Stair, KT, DSO; *m* 1930, Hon. Hanning Philipps, *qv*; one *s* one *d*. *Educ:* privately. FRAgS 1973. War Service: original Mem., WVS HQ Staff, i/c Canteen and Catering Information Services, 1938–41; Min. of Agriculture, 1942–45. Mem., Narberth Rural Dist Council, 1970–73. Chm., Picton Land & Investment Pty Ltd, WA. Trustee, Picton Castle Trust (Graham Sutherland Gallery), 1976–. Founder Mem., British Polled Hereford Soc., 1950– (also first Pres.); Member: Welsh Council, Historic Houses Assoc., 1975; Gardens Cttee, National Council of Historic Houses Assoc., 1975. Pres., Royal Welsh Agricultural Soc., 1978–. JP Dyfed (formerly Pembrokeshire), 1965. CStJ; Order of Mercy, 1926. *Recreation:* gardening. *Address:* Picton Castle, The Rhos, Haverfordwest, Dyfed SA62 4AS. *T:* Rhos (0437) 751201.

PHILIPPS, Hon. (Richard) Hanning, MBE 1945; JP; Hon. Major Welsh Guards; Lord-Lieutenant of Dyfed, 1974–79 (HM Lieutenant of Pembrokeshire, 1958–74); *b* 14 Feb. 1904; 2nd *s* of 1st Baron and *b* of 2nd Baron Milford, *qv*; *m* 1930, Lady Marion Violet Dalrymple (*see* Lady Marion Philipps); one *s* one *d*. *Educ:* Eton. Contested (Nat) Brecon and Radnor, 1939. Served War of 1939–45, NW Europe, 1944–45 (MBE). Vice-Lieutenant of Pembrokeshire, 1957. Hon. Colonel Pembroke Yeomanry, 1959. Chairman: Dun & Bradstreet Ltd, 1946–69; Milford Haven Conservancy Bd, 1963–75; Northern Securities Trust Ltd, 1950–80; Hon. Pres. (former Chm.) Schweppes Ltd; Dir, Picton Land and Investment Pty Ltd, W Australia; Trustee, Picton Castle Trust, Graham and Kathleen Sutherland Foundn. Pres., Order of St John, Pembrokeshire, 1958–. CStJ. *Recreations:* painting, forestry, gardening. *Address:* Picton Castle, Haverfordwest, Pembrokeshire, Dyfed SA62 4AS. *T:* Rhos (0437) 751201. *Club:* Boodle's.

PHILIPS, Prof. Sir Cyril (Henry), Kt 1974; Professor of Oriental History, University of London, 1946–80; Director, School of Oriental and African Studies, London, 1957–76; Vice-Chancellor, University of London, 1972–76 (Deputy Vice-Chancellor, 1969–70); *b* Worcester, 27 Dec. 1912; *s* of William Henry Philips; *m* 1st, 1939, Dorcas (*d* 1974), *d* of John Rose, Wallasey; one *d* (one *s* decd); 2nd, 1975, Joan Rosemary, *d* of William George Marshall. *Educ:* Rock Ferry High School; Univs of Liverpool (MA) and London (PhD). Bishop Chavasse Prizeman; Gladstone Memorial Fellow. Frewen Lord Prizeman (Royal Empire Soc.), 1935; Alexander Prizeman (Royal Hist. Soc.), 1938; Sir Percy Sykes Meml Medal (RSAA), 1976; Asst Lectr, Sch. of Oriental Studies, 1936. Served in Suffolk Infantry, Army Education Corps, 1940–43; Col Commandant, Army School of Education, 1943. Chief Instructor, Dept of Training, HM Treasury, 1943–46. Colonial Office Mission on Community Development, Africa, 1947. Lectures: Montague Burton, Univ. of Leeds, 1966; Creighton, Univ. of London, 1972; James Smart, on Police, 1979; Home Office Bicentenary, 1982; Police, Univ. of Bristol, 1982; Dawtry Meml, Univ. of Leeds, 1983. Chairman: UGC Cttee on Oriental, African and Slavonic Studies, 1965–70; UGC Cttee on Latin American Studies, 1966–70; India Cttee of Inter-University Council and British Council, 1972–; Royal Commn on Criminal Procedure, 1978–80; Police Complaints Bd, 1980–85; Council on Tribunals, 1986–89; Inst. of Archaeology, 1979–85, Inst. of Latin American Studies, 1978–87 (Univ. of London); Member: Social Development Cttee, Colonial Office, 1947–55; Colonial Office Research Council, 1955–57; University Grants Cttee, 1960–69; Commonwealth Education Commn, 1961–70; Postgraduate Awards Cttee (Min. of Education), 1962–64; Modern Languages Cttee (Min. of Education), 1964–67; Inter-Univ. Council, 1967–77; Court, London Univ., 1970–76; Governor: Chinese Univ. of Hong Kong, 1965–; Mill Hill Sch., 1980–91 (Chm., 1982); Governor and Trustee, Richmond Coll., 1979–84. Pres., Royal Asiatic Soc., 1979–82, 1985–88. Hon. DLitt: Warwick, 1967; Bristol, 1983; Sri Lanka, 1986; Hon. LLD Hong Kong, 1971. India Tagore Medal, 1968; Bombay Freedom Medal, 1977. *Publications:* The East India Company, 1940 (2nd edn 1961); India, 1949; Handbook of Oriental History, 1951 (2nd edn 1962); Correspondence of David Scott, 1951; Historians of India, Pakistan and Ceylon, 1961; The Evolution of India and Pakistan, 1962; Politics and Society in India, 1963; Fort William-India House Correspondence, 1964; History of the School of Oriental and African Studies, 1917–67, 1967; The Partition of India, 1970; The Correspondence of Lord William Bentinck, Governor General of India 1828–35, 1977. *Address:* School of Oriental and African Studies, Malet Street, WC1E 7HP. *T:* 071–637 2388. *Club:* Athenæum.

PHILIPS, Justin Robin Drew; Metropolitan Stipendiary Magistrate, since 1989; *b* 18 July 1948; *s* of late Albert Lewis Philips, Solicitor and of Henrietta Philips (*née* Woolfson). *Educ:* John Lyon School, Harrow; College of Law, London. Called to the Bar, Gray's Inn, 1969; practised criminal bar, 1970–89. Hon. Sec., Hendon Reform Synagogue, 1990– (Mem. Council, 1979–90). *Recreations:* music, reading, travel. *Address:* c/o Camberwell Green Magistrates' Court, 15 D'Eynsford Road, SE5 7UP. *T:* 071–703 0909.

PHILIPSON, Garry, DFC 1944; Managing Director (formerly General Manager), Aycliffe and Peterlee Development Corporation, 1974–85; *b* 27 Nov. 1921; *s* of George and Marian Philipson; *m* 1949, June Mary Miller Somerville; one *d*. *Educ:* Stockton Grammar Sch.; Durham Univ. (BA(Hons)). Jubilee Prize, 1947. Served War, RAFVR (2 Gp Bomber Comd), 1940–46. Colonial Service and Overseas Civil Service, 1949–60. Various Dist and Secretariat posts, incl. Clerk, Exec. Council and Cabinet Sec., Sierra Leone; Principal, Scottish Develt Dept, 1961–66; Under Sec., RICS, 1966–67; Dir, Smith and Ritchie Ltd, 1967–70; Sec., New Towns Assoc., 1970–74; Vice-Chm. (NE), North Housing Assoc., 1985–. Trustee, Dales-Care, 1988–. *Publications:* Aycliffe and Peterlee New Towns 1946–88, 1988; Press articles and contribs to various jls. *Recreations:* country pursuits, history. *Address:* Tunstall Grange, Tunstall, Richmond, North Yorks DL10 7RF. *T:* Richmond (0748) 833327. *Club:* Royal Air Force.

PHILIPSON, John Trevor Graham; QC 1989; *b* 3 March 1948; *s* of William Arnold Philipson and Rosalind Philipson; *m* 1974, Victoria Caroline Haskard (marr. diss. 1983). *Educ:* Newcastle Royal Grammar Sch.; Wadham Coll., Oxford (BA Jurisprudence 1970; BCL 1st cl. 1971). Called to the Bar, Middle Temple, 1972, Sen. Harmsworth Schol. *Recreations:* walking, gardening, travel. *Address:* Fountain Court, Temple, EC4Y 9DH. *T:* 071–583 3335; 239 Knightsbridge, SW7 1DJ. *Club:* Royal Automobile.

PHILIPSON, Sir Robert James, (Sir Robin Philipson), Kt 1976; RA 1980 (ARA 1973); PRSA 1973 (RSA 1962; ARSA 1952); RSW 1954; Head of the School of Drawing and Painting, The College of Art, Edinburgh, 1960–82; President, Royal Scottish Academy, 1973–83 (Secretary, 1969–73); *b* 17 Dec. 1916; *s* of James Philipson; *m* 1949, Brenda Mark; *m* 1962, Thora Clyne (marr. diss. 1975); *m* 1976, Diana Mary Pollock; one *s*, and one adopted *s* one adopted *d*. *Educ:* Whitehaven Secondary School; Dumfries Academy; Edinburgh College of Art, 1936–40. Served War of 1939–45: King's Own Scottish Borderers, 1942–46, in India and Burma; attached to RIASC. Member of teaching staff, Edinburgh College of Art, 1947. Exhibits with Browse & Darby Ltd, London, Scottish Gallery and Fine Art Soc., Edinburgh. Mem., Royal Fine Art Commn for Scotland, 1965–80. Hon. RA 1973; Hon. Mem., RHA 1979; Hon. Mem., RCA 1980. Commandeur de l'Ordre National du Mérite de la République Française, 1976. FRSA 1965; FRSE 1977. DUniv: Stirling, 1976; Heriot-Watt, 1985; Hon. LLD Aberdeen 1977. *Address:* 23 Crawfurd Road, Edinburgh EH16 5PQ. *T:* 031–667 2373. *Club:* Scottish Arts (Edinburgh).

PHILIPSON-STOW, Sir Christopher, 5th Bt *cr* 1907; DFC 1944; retired; *b* 13 Sept. 1920; *s* of Henry Matthew Philipson-Stow (*d* 1953) (3rd *s* of 1st Bt) and Elizabeth Willes (*d* 1979), *d* of Sir Thomas Willes Chitty, 1st Bt; *S* cousin, 1982; *m* 1952, Elizabeth Nairn, *d* of late James Dixon Trees and *widow* of Major F. G. McLaren, 48th Highlanders of Canada; two *s*. *Educ:* Winchester. *Heir:* *er s* Robert Matthew Philipson-Stow, *b* 29 Aug. 1953. *Address:* RR2, Port Carling, Ontario P0B 1J0, Canada. *T:* 705–765–3000.

PHILLIMORE, family name of **Baron Phillimore.**

PHILLIMORE, 4th Baron *cr* 1918, of Shiplake, Oxfordshire; **Claud Stephen Phillimore;** Bt 1881; architect; *b* 15 Jan. 1911; *s* of 2nd Baron Phillimore and Dorothy Barbara, *d* of Lt-Col A. B. Haig, CMG, CVO; *S* nephew, 1990; *m* 1944, Anne Elizabeth, *e d* of late Maj. Arthur Algernon Dorrien-Smith, DSO; one *s* one *d*. *Educ:* Winchester Coll.; Trinity Coll., Cambridge. RIBA. Major, City of London Yeomanry, 1939–45. 1939–45 Star; Defence Medal; Africa Star, 8th Army. *Recreation:* travel. *Heir:* *s* Francis Stephen Phillimore [*b* 25 Nov. 1944; *m* 1971, Nathalie Pequin; two *s* one *d*]. *Address:* 39 Ashley Gardens, SW1P 1QE. *Club:* Brooks's.

PHILLIMORE, John Gore, CMG 1946; a Managing Director of Baring Brothers & Co. Ltd, 1949–72; *b* 16 April 1908; 2nd *s* of late Adm. Sir Richard and Lady Phillimore, Shedfield, Hants; *m* 1951, Jill, *d* of late Captain Mason Scott, Royal Navy retd, Buckland Manor, Broadway, Worcs, and of Hon. Mrs Scott; two *s* two *d*. *Educ:* Winchester

College; Christ Church, Oxford. Partner of Roberts, Meynell & Co., Buenos Aires, 1936–48; Representative of HM Treasury and Bank of England in South America, 1940–45. Prime Warden, Fishmongers' Co., 1974–75. High Sheriff of Kent, 1975, DL Kent, 1979–84. Condor de los Andes (Bolivia), 1940; Commander, Orden de Mayo (Argentina), 1961. *Address:* Brooklyn House, Kingsclere, near Newbury, Berks RG15 8QY. *T:* Newbury (0635) 298321. *Club:* White's.

PHILLIPS, family name of Baroness Phillips.

PHILLIPS, Baroness *cr* 1964 (Life Peer); **Norah Phillips,** JP; Director, Association for the Prevention of Theft in Shops; President (and former General Secretary), National Association of Women's Clubs; President: Institute of Shops, Health and Safety Acts Administration; Association for Research into Restricted Growth; Keep Fit Association; International Professional Security Association; Pre-Retirement Association; Vice-President: National Chamber of Trade; Fair Play for Children; *d* of William and Catherine Lusher; *m* 1930, Morgan Phillips (*d* 1963); one *s* one *d* (*see* G. P. Dunwoody). *Educ:* Marist Convent; Hampton Training College. A Baroness in Waiting (Govt Whip), 1965–70. Lord-Lieutenant of Greater London, 1978–85. *Address:* House of Lords, SW1A 0PW. *T:* (office) 081–741 4815.

PHILLIPS, Adrian Alexander Christian; freelance environmental consultant; teaching and research, City and Regional Planning Department, University of Wales College of Cardiff, since 1992; *b* 11 Jan. 1940; *s* of Eric Lawrance Phillips, *qv*; *m* 1963, Cassandra Frances Elaïs Hubback, MA Oxon, *d* of D. F. Hubback, CB; two *s*. *Educ:* The Hall, Hampstead; Westminster Sch.; Christ Church, Oxford (1st Cl. Hons MA Geography). MRTPI; FRSA; FRGS. Planning Services, Min. of Housing and Local Govt, 1962–68; Sen. Research Officer and Asst Director, Countryside Commission, 1968–74; Special Asst, Executive Director, United Nations Environment Programme (UNEP), Nairobi, Kenya, 1974–75; Head, Programme Coordination Unit, UNEP, Nairobi, 1975–78; Director of Programmes, IUCN, Switzerland, 1978–81; Dir, then Dir Gen., Countryside Commn, 1981–91. Dep. Chm., Commn on Nat. Parks and Protected Areas, IUCN, 1988–. *Publications:* articles on countryside planning and conservation in professional jls. *Recreations:* walking, skiing, stroking the cat. *Address:* 2 The Old Rectory, Dumbleton, near Evesham, Worcs WR11 6TG. *T:* Evesham (0386) 881973. *Club:* Royal Over-Seas League.

PHILLIPS, Alan; *see* Phillips, D. A.

PHILLIPS, Andrew Bassett; Director, Humanities and Social Sciences, British Library, since 1990; *b* 26 Sept. 1945; *s* of William Phillips and Doreen (*née* Harris); *m* 1976, Valerie Cuthbert; two *s* one *d*. *Educ:* Newport High Sch.; Reading Univ. (BA). ALA. British Nat. Bibliography Ltd, 1969–70; Research Officer, Nat. Libraries ADP Study, 1970–71; Admin. Officer, Nat. Council for Educnl Technol., 1971–73; British Library: various posts in Bibliographic Servs and Ref. (subseq. Humanities and Social Scis) Divs, 1973–86; Dir, Public Services and Planning and Admin, 1987–90. Part-time Lectr, West London Coll, 1972–75. *Publications:* various reviews, articles. *Address:* 23 Meynell Road, E9. *T:* 081–985 7413.

PHILLIPS, Anne, (Mrs David Phillips); *see* Dickinson, V. A.

PHILLIPS, Rev. Canon Anthony Charles Julian; Headmaster, King's School, Canterbury, since 1986; Canon Theologian, Diocese of Truro, since 1986; Hon. Canon, Canterbury Cathedral, since 1987; *b* 2 June 1936; *s* of Arthur Reginald Phillips and Esmée Mary Phillips; *m* 1970, Victoria Ann Stainton; two *s* one *d*. *Educ:* Kelly Coll., Tavistock (schol.); King's Coll., London (BD, 1st cl.; AKC, 1st cl.); Archibald Robertson Prize, 1962; Jun. McCaul Hebrew Prize, 1963; Gonville and Caius Coll., Cambridge (PhD 1967); College of the Resurrection, Mirfield. Curate, Good Shepherd, Cambridge, 1966–69; Dean, Chaplain and Fellow, Trinity Hall, Cambridge, 1969–74; Chaplain and Fellow, 1975–86, Domestic Bursar, 1982–84, St John's Coll., Oxford; Lecturer in Theology: Jesus Coll., Oxford, 1975–86; Hertford Coll., Oxford, 1984–86; S. A. Cook Bye Fellow, Gonville and Caius Coll., 1984. Hon. Chaplain to Bishop of Norwich, 1970–71; Examining Chaplain to: Bp of Oxford, 1979–86; Bp of Manchester, 1980–86; Bp of Wakefield, 1984–86. Archbps of Canterbury and York Interfaith Cons. for Judaism, 1984–86. *Publications:* Ancient Israel's Criminal Law, 1970; Deuteronomy (Cambridge Bible Commentary), 1973; God BC, 1977; (ed) Israel's Prophetic Tradition, 1982; Lower Than the Angels, 1983; Preaching from the Psalter, 1987; contrib. to: Words and Meanings (ed P. R. Ackroyd and B. Lindars), 1968; Witness to the Spirit (ed W. Harrington), 1979; The Ministry of the Word (ed G. Cuming), 1979; Heaven and Earth (ed A. Linzey and P. Wexler), 1986; Tradition and Unity (ed Dan Cohn-Sherbok), 1991; articles in theol jls, The Times, Expository Times, etc. *Recreations:* gardening, beachcombing. *Address:* The King's School, Canterbury, Kent CT1 2ES. *T:* Canterbury (0227) 475501. *Club:* Athenæum.

PHILLIPS, Prof. Calbert Inglis, FRCS, FRCSE; Professor of Ophthalmology, University of Edinburgh and Ophthalmic Surgeon, Royal Infirmary, Edinburgh, 1972–90, now Professor Emeritus; *b* 20 March 1925; *o s* of Rev. David Horner Phillips and Margaret Calbert Phillips; *m* 1962, Christina Anne Fulton, MB, FRCSE; one *s*. *Educ:* Glasgow High Sch.; Robert Gordon's Coll., Aberdeen; Aberdeen Univ. MB, ChB Aberdeen 1946; DPH Edinburgh 1950; FRCS 1955; MD Aberdeen 1957; PhD Bristol 1961; MSc Manchester 1969; FRCSE 1973. Lieut and Captain, RAMC, 1947–49. House Surgeon: Aberdeen Royal Infirmary, 1946–47 (House Phys., 1951); Aberdeen Maternity Hosp., 1949; Glasgow Eye Infirmary, 1950–51; Asst, Anatomy Dept, Glasgow Univ., 1951–52; Resident Registrar, Moorfields Eye Hosp., 1953–54; Sen. Registrar, St Thomas' Hosp. and Moorfields Eye Hosp., and Res. Asst, Inst. of Ophthalmology, 1954–58; Consultant Surg., Bristol Eye Hosp., 1958–63; Alexander Piggott Wernher Trav. Fellow, Dept of Ophthal., Harvard Univ., 1960–61; Consultant Ophthalmic Surg., St George's Hosp., 1963–65; Prof. of Ophthal., Manchester Univ., and Hon. Consultant Ophthalmic Surg. to United Manchester Hosps, 1965–72. Hon. FBOA 1975. *Publications:* (ed jtly) Clinical Practice and Economics, 1977; Basic Clinical Ophthalmology, 1984; papers in Brit. and Amer. Jls of Ophthal., Nature, Brain, BMJ, etc, mainly on intra-ocular pressure and glaucoma, retinal detachments, ocular surgery and hereditary diseases. *Address:* 5 Braid Mount Crest, Edinburgh EH10 6JN.

PHILLIPS, Prof. Charles Garrett, DM; FRCP; FRS 1963; Dr Lee's Professor of Anatomy, University of Oxford, 1975–83, now Emeritus; Fellow of Hertford College, Oxford, 1975–83, now Emeritus; *b* 13 October 1916; *s* of Dr George Ramsey Phillips and Flora (*née* Green); *m* 1942, Cynthia Mary, *d* of L. R. Broster, OBE, FRCS; two *d*. *Educ:* Bradfield; Magdalen College, Oxford; St Bartholomew's Hospital. Captain, RAMC, 1943–46. Reader in Neurophysiology, 1962–66, Prof., 1966–75, Oxford Univ.; Fellow, Trinity Coll., 1946–75, Emeritus Fellow, 1975. Mem., MRC, 1980–84. Hon. Sec., Physiological Society, 1960–66; President: Sect. of Neurology, RSocMed, 1978–79; Assoc. of British Neurologists, 1980–81. Mem., Norwegian Acad. of Sci. and Letters, 1984; Hon. Member: Canadian Neurol Soc.; Belgian Soc. of Electromyography and Clin. Neurophysiology. Editor, Brain, 1975–81. Hon. DSc Monash, 1971. Lectures: Ferrier, 1968; Hughlings Jackson (and Medal), 1973; Victor Horsley Meml, 1981; Sherrington, Univ. of Liverpool, 1982. Feldberg Prize, 1970. *Publications:* Papers on neurophysiology in Jl of Physiology, etc. *Address:* 10 Hawkeswell Gardens, Oxford OX2 7EX. *Club:* United Oxford & Cambridge University.

PHILLIPS, Prof. David; Professor of Physical Chemistry, Imperial College of Science, Technology and Medicine, since 1989; *b* 3 Dec. 1939; *s* of Stanley and Daphne Ivy Phillips; *m* 1970, Caroline Lucy Scoble; one *d*. *Educ:* South Shields Grammar-Technical Sch.; Univ. of Birmingham (BSc, PhD). Post doctoral Fellow, Univ. of Texas, 1964–66; Vis. Scientist, Inst. of Chemical Physics, Acad. of Scis of USSR, Moscow, 1966–67; Lectr 1967–73, Sen. Lectr 1973–76, Reader 1976–80, in Phys. Chem., Univ. of Southampton; Royal Institution of Great Britain: Wolfson Prof. of Natural Philosophy, 1980–89; Actg Dir, Jan.–Oct. 1986; Dep. Dir, 1986–89. Vice-Pres. and Gen. Officer, BAAS, 1988–89. Mem., Faraday Council, RSC, 1990–. *Publications:* Time-Correlated Single-Photon Counting (jtly), 1984; Polymer Photophysics, 1985; over 300 res. papers and revs in sci. lit. on photochem., photophys. and lasers. *Recreations:* music, travel. *Address:* 195 Barnett Wood Lane, Ashtead, Surrey KT21 2LP. *T:* Ashtead (0372) 74385. *Club:* Athenæum.

PHILLIPS, (David) Alan; His Honour Judge Phillips; a Circuit Judge, since 1983; Chancellor, diocese of Bangor, since 1988; *b* 21 July 1926; *s* of Stephen Thomas Phillips, MC and Elizabeth Mary Phillips; *m* 1960, Jean Louise (*née* Godsell); two *s*. *Educ:* Llanelli Grammar Sch.; University Coll., Oxford (MA). Left school, 1944. Served War, Army, 1944; commnd, 1946, RWF; Captain (GS), 1947; demobilised, 1948. Oxford, 1948–51. Lectr, 1952–59. Called to Bar, Gray's Inn, 1960. Stipendiary Magistrate for Mid-Glamorgan, 1975–83; a Recorder of the Crown Court, 1974–83. *Recreations:* music, chess, swimming. *Address:* The Crown Court, The Castle, Chester.

PHILLIPS, Prof. Sir David (Chilton), KBE 1989; Kt 1979; FRS 1967; BSc, PhD (Wales); FInstP; Professor of Molecular Biophysics and Fellow of Corpus Christi College, Oxford, 1966–90, now Hon. Fellow; Chairman, Advisory Board for the Research Councils, since 1983 (part-time, 1983–90); *b* 7 March 1924; *o s* of late Charles Harry Phillips and Edith Harriet Phillips (*née* Finney), Ellesmere, Shropshire; *m* 1960, Diana Kathleen (*née* Hutchinson); one *d*. *Educ:* Ellesmere C of E Schools; Oswestry Boys' High Sch.; UC, Cardiff. Radar Officer, RNVR, 1944–47. UC, Cardiff, 1942–44 and 1947–51. Post-doctoral Fellow, National Research Council of Canada, 1951–53; Research Officer, National Research Laboratories, Ottawa, 1953–55; Research Worker, Davy Faraday Research Lab., Royal Institution, London, 1955–66; Mem., MRC, 1974–78; Royal Soc. Assessor, MRC, 1978–83; Member: ACARD, 1983–87; Technology Requirements Bd, 1985–88; ACOST, 1987–. UK Co-ordinator, Internat. Science Hall, Brussels Exhibition, 1958; Member, European Molecular Biology Organization (EMBO), 1964, Mem. Council, 1972–78; Royal Society: Vice-Pres., 1972–73, 1976–83; Biological Sec., 1976–83; Fullerian (Vis.) Prof. of Physiology, Royal Institution, 1979–85, Christmas lectures, 1980. Foreign Hon. Member: Amer. Academy of Arts and Sciences, 1968; Royal Swedish Acad. of Scis, 1989; Hon. Mem., Amer. Society of Biological Chemists, 1969 (Lecturer, 1965); For. Associate, Amer. Nat. Acad. of Science, 1985; Mem., Academia Europaea, 1989. Lectures: Almroth Wright Meml, 1966; Plenary, Internat. Biochem. Congress, Tokyo, 1967, Hamburg, 1976, Internat. Crystallography Congress, Kyoto, 1972; Hassel, Oslo, 1968; Dunham, Harvard Med. Sch., 1989; Romanes, Edinburgh, 1990; Rutherford, Royal Soc. UK–Canada, 1990; Irvine, St Andrews, 1991; Krebs Lecture and Medal, FEBS, 1971; Feldberg Prize, 1968; CIBA Medal, Biochem. Soc., 1971; Royal Medal, Royal Society, 1975; (jtly) Prix Charles Léopold Mayer, French Académie des Sciences, 1979; (jtly) Wolf Prize for Chemistry, Wolf Foundn, Israel, 1987. Hon. FRSE 1991; Hon. FRCP 1991. Hon. DSc: Leicester, 1974; Univ. of Wales, 1975; Chicago, 1978; Exeter, 1982; Warwick, 1982; Essex, 1983; Birmingham, 1987; Glasgow, 1990. Member, Ed. Board, Journal of Molecular Biology, 1966–76. *Publications:* papers in Acta Cryst. and other journals. *Address:* Advisory Board for the Research Councils, Elizabeth House, York Road, SE1 7PH. *T:* 071–934 9851; 35 Addisland Court, Holland Villas Road, W14 8DA. *T:* 071–602 0738. *Club:* Athenæum.

PHILLIPS, Prof. Dewi Zephaniah; Professor of Philosophy, since 1971, Vice-Principal, since 1989, University College, Swansea; *b* 24 Nov. 1934; *s* of David Oakley Phillips and Alice Frances Phillips; *m* 1959, Margaret Monica Hanford; three *s*. *Educ:* Swansea Grammar Sch.; UC Swansea (MA); St Catherine's Society, Oxford (BLitt). Asst Lectr, Queen's Coll., Dundee, Univ. of St Andrews, 1961–62; Lectr: at Queen's Coll., Dundee, 1962–63; UC Bangor, 1963–65; UC Swansea, 1965–67; Sen. Lectr, UC Swansea, 1967–71. Visiting Professor: Yale Univ., 1985; Claremont Graduate Sch., 1986. Hintz Meml Lectr, Univ. of Arizona, Tucson, 1975; Vis. Prof. and McMartin Lectr, Univ. of Carleton, 1976; Agnes Cuming Visitor, Univ. Coll. Dublin, 1982; Lectures: William James, Lousiana State Univ., 1982; Marett, Oxford, 1983; Riddell Meml, Newcastle, 1986; Aquinas, Oxford, 1987; Cardinal Mercier, Leuven, 1988. Editor, Philosophical Investigations, 1982–. *Publications:* The Concept of Prayer, 1965; (ed) Religion and Understanding, 1967; (ed) Saith Ysgrif Ar Grefydd, 1967; (with H. O. Mounce) Moral Practices, 1970; Death and Immortality, 1970; Faith and Philosophical Enquiry, 1970; (with Ilham Dilman) Sense and Delusion, 1971; Athronyddu Am Grefydd, 1974; Religion Without Explanation, 1976; Through A Darkening Glass: Philosophy, Literature and Cultural Change, 1981; Dramau Gwenlyn Parry, 1981; Belief, Change and Forms of Life, 1986; R. S. Thomas: poet of the hidden God, 1986; Faith after Foundationalism, 1988; From Fantasy to Faith, 1990; Interventions in Ethics, 1991; General Editor: Studies in Ethics and the Philosophy of Religion, 1968–74; Values and Philosophical Enquiry, 1976–86; Swansea Studies in Philosophy, 1989; papers in philosophical jls. *Recreations:* lawn tennis and supporting Swansea City AFC. *Address:* 45 Queen's Road, Sketty, Swansea. *T:* Swansea (0792) 203935.

PHILLIPS, Diane Susan; Under Secretary and Principal Finance Officer, Property Holdings, Department of the Environment, since 1990; *b* 29 Aug. 1942; *d* of Michael Keogh and Jessie (*née* Tite); *m* 1967, John Phillips; two *d*. *Educ:* Univ. of Wales. NEDO, 1967–72; Civil Service, 1972–: Principal, DoE, 1972–77, Cabinet Office, 1977–78; Asst Sec., Dept of Transport, 1978–80, DoE 1981–88; Grade 4, Local Govt Finance, 1988–90. *Address:* Department of the Environment, 2 Marsham Street, SW1P 3EB.

PHILLIPS, Edward Thomas John, CBE 1985; Controller, English Language and Literature Division, British Council, 1985–89; *b* 5 Feb. 1930; *s* of late Edward Emery Kent Phillips and of Margaret Elsie Phillips; *m* 1952, Sheila May (*née* Abbott); two *s* two *d*. *Educ:* Exmouth Grammar Sch., University Coll. London; Inst. of Education, London; School of Oriental and African Studies London (BA Hons; postgraduate Cert. of Educn; Dip. in linguistics). RAF, 1948–49. HMOCS, Educn Officer, Nigeria, 1953–62; British Council: Head, Cultural and Educn Unit, Overseas Students' Dept, 1962–65; English Lang. Officer, Enugu, Nigeria, 1966–67; Sen. Lectr, Coll. of Educn, Lagos Univ., Nigeria, 1967–70; English Lang. Teaching Advr, Min. of Educn, Cyprus, 1970–72; Chief Inspector, English Teaching Div., London, 1972–75; Rep., Bangladesh, Dacca, 1975–77; Dir, Personnel Dept and Dep. Controller Personnel Staff Recruitment Div., 1977–80; Rep, Malaysia, 1980–85. Consultant, BESO. Member: British-Malaysia Soc.; Anti-Slavery Soc.; Britain-Nigeria Assoc. *Publications:* (ed jtly) Organised English, Books I and II, 1973;

contribs to English Language Teaching Jl. *Recreations:* music, theatre, tennis, golf, swimming. *Address:* 1 Bredune, off Church Road, Kenley, Surrey CR8 4DU. *T:* 081–660 1929.

PHILLIPS, Edwin William, MBE 1946; Chairman: Friends Provident Life Office, 1968–88; United Kingdom Provident Institution, 1986–88; Director, Lazard Bros & Co. Ltd, 1960–83; *b* 29 Jan. 1918; *s* of C. E. Phillips, Chiswick; *m* 1951, P. M. Matusch; two *s*. *Educ:* Latymer Upper Sch. Joined Edward de Stein & Co., Merchant Bankers, 1934. Army, 1939–46; Major, Sherwood Rangers Yeomanry. Rejoined Edward de Stein & Co., 1946, Partner, 1954; merged into Lazard Bros & Co. Ltd, 1960. Director: British Rail Property Bd, 1970; Phoenix Assurance, 1975–85; Woolwich Equitable Building Soc., 1977 (Vice-Chm., 1984–86; Sen. Vice-Chm., 1986–88); Chm., Higgs and Hill, 1975–82. *Recreation:* cricket. *Address:* Down House, Downsway, Merrow, Surrey. *T:* Guildford (0483) 301196. *Club:* MCC.

PHILLIPS, Eric Lawrance, CMG 1963; retired; *b* 23 July 1909; *s* of L. Stanley Phillips and Maudie Phillips (*née* Elkan), London, NW1; *m* 1938, Phyllis Bray, Artist; two *s* one step *d*. *Educ:* Haileybury Coll.; Balliol Coll., Oxford (Scholar, BA). With Erlangers Ltd, 1932–39. Served War of 1939–45, Captain, RA. Principal, Bd of Trade, 1945, Monopolies Commn, 1949; Asst Secretary, Monopolies Commn, 1951, Bd of Trade, 1952; Under-Sec., Bd of Trade, 1964–69; Sec., Monopolies Commn, 1969–74; consultant to Monopolies and Mergers Commn, 1974–75. Hon. Chm., Abbeyfield West London Soc., 1980–86. *Recreations:* looking at pictures, places and buildings. *Address:* 46 Platts Lane, NW3 7NT. *T:* 071–435 7873. *Club:* Royal Automobile.

See also A. A. C. Phillips.

PHILLIPS, Sir Fred (Albert), Kt 1967; CVO 1966; QC; Senior Legal Adviser, Cable and Wireless (West Indies); *b* 14 May 1918; *s* of Wilbert A. Phillips, Brighton, St Vincent. *Educ:* London Univ. (LLB); Toronto Univ.; McGill Univ. (MCL); Hague Acad. of International Law. Called to the Bar, Middle Temple. Legal Clerk to Attorney-General of St Vincent, 1942–45; Principal Officer, Secretariat, 1945–47; Windward Island: Chief Clerk, Governor's Office, 1948–49; District Officer/Magistrate of District III, 1949–53; Magistrate, Grenada, and Comr of Carriacou, 1953–56; Asst Administrator and MEC, Grenada, 1957–58 (Officer Administrating the Govt, April 1958); Senior Asst Sec., Secretariat, Fedn of W Indies (dealing with constitutional development), 1958–60; Permanent Sec. (Sec. to Cabinet), 1960–62 (when Fedn dissolved); actg Administrator of Montserrat, 1961–62; Sen. Lectr, Univ. of W Indies and Sen. Resident Tutor, Dept of Extra-mural Studies, Barbados, 1962–63; Registrar, Coll. of Arts and Science, Univ. of W Indies, 1963–64; Sen. Res. Fellow, Faculty of Law and Centre for Developing Area Studies, McGill Univ., 1964–65; Guggenheim Fellow, 1965; Administrator of St Kitts, 1966–67; Governor, St Kitts/Nevis/Anguilla, 1967–69. Has attended numerous conferences as a Legal or Constitutional Adviser. KStJ 1968. *Publications:* Freedom in the Caribbean: a study in constitutional change, 1977; The Evolving Legal Profession in the Commonwealth, 1978; West Indian Constitutions: post-Independence reforms, 1985; papers in various jls. *Recreations:* reading, bridge. *Address:* Chambers, Kingstown, St Vincent, West Indies; PO Box 206, Bridgetown, Barbados.

PHILLIPS, (Gerald) Hayden, CB 1989; Deputy Secretary, HM Treasury, since 1988; *b* 9 Feb. 1943; *s* of Gerald Phillips and Dorothy Phillips; *m* 1st, 1967, Dr Ann Watkins (marr. diss.); one *s* one *d*; 2nd, 1980, Hon. Laura Grenfell; one *s* two *d*. *Educ:* Cambridgeshire High Sch.; Clare Coll., Cambridge (MA); Yale Univ., USA (MA). Home Office: Asst Principal, 1967; Economic Adviser, 1970–72; Principal, 1972–74; Asst Sec., and Principal Private Sec. to Sec. of State for Home Dept, 1974–76; Dep. Chef de Cabinet to Pres., Commn of European Communities, 1977–79; Asst Sec., Home Office, 1979–81, Asst Under-Sec. of State, 1981–86; Dep. Sec., Cabinet Office (MPO, subseq. Office of the Minister for the Civil Service), 1986–88. *Address:* c/o HM Treasury, Parliament Street, SW1P 3AG. *Club:* Brooks's.

PHILLIPS, Hayden; *see* Phillips, G. H.

PHILLIPS, Sir Henry (Ellis Isidore), Kt 1964; CMG 1960; MBE 1946; Vice-Chairman, SIFIDA Investment Co. (SA); Chairman, Assured Property Trust plc; director of other companies; *b* 30 Aug. 1914; *s* of late Harry J. Phillips, MBE; *m* 1st, 1941, Vivien Hyamson (marr. diss., 1965); two *s* one *d*; 2nd, 1966, Philippa Cohen. *Educ:* Haberdashers' Sch., Hampstead; University College London (BA 1936; MA 1939; Fellow 1991). FRHistS. Inst. of Historical Research, 1936–39. Commissioned in Beds and Herts Regt, 1939; served War of 1939–45, with 5th Bn, becoming Adjutant; POW, Singapore, 1942. Joined Colonial Administrative Service and appointed to Nyasaland, 1946 (until retirement in 1965); Development Secretary, 1952; seconded to Federal Treasury of Rhodesia and Nyasaland, 1953–57, Dep. Sec., 1956; Financial Sec., Nyasaland Govt, 1957–64, and Minister of Finance, 1961–64. Man. Dir, Standard Bank Finance and Development Corp., 1966–72. Dir, Nat. Bank of Malaŵi, 1983–88; Chm., Ashley Industrial Trust plc, 1986–88. Member: Civil Aviation Authority, 1975–80; Finance Cttee, UCL, 1985–. Dep. Chm., Stonham Housing Assoc., 1984–; Hon. Treasurer: Stonham Meml Trust, 1977–; SOS Sahel Internat. (UK), 1987–. Mem., Royal Commonwealth Soc. *Address:* 34 Ross Court, Putney Hill, SW15. *T:* 081–789 1404. *Club:* MCC.

PHILLIPS, Sir Horace, KCMG 1973 (CMG 1963); HM Diplomatic Service, retired; Lecturer in Diplomacy, Bilkent Univ., Ankara, since 1988; *b* 31 May 1917; *s* of Samuel Phillips; *m* 1944, Idina Doreen Morgan; one *s* one *d*. *Educ:* Hillhead High Sch., Glasgow. Joined Board of Inland Revenue, 1935. Served War of 1939–45, Dorsetshire and 1st Punjab Regts, 1940–47. Transf. to FO, Oct. 1947; Acting Vice-Consul, Shiraz, Nov. 1947; Vice-Consul, Bushire, 1948 (Acting Consul, 1948); 1st Secretary and Consul, 1949; Kabul, Oct. 1949; Foreign Office, 1951; 1st Secretary, and Consul, Jedda, 1953; Counsellor, 1956; seconded to Colonial Office, Dec. 1956, as Protectorate Secretary, Aden, until Aug. 1960; Counsellor, British Embassy, Tehran, Oct. 1960; Deputy Political Resident in the Persian Gulf, at Bahrain, 1964–66; Ambassador to Indonesia, 1966–68; High Comr in Tanzania, 1968–72; Ambassador to Turkey, 1973–77. Resident Rep., Taylor Woodrow Internat. Ltd: Iran, 1978–79, Hong Kong, 1979–84, Bahrain, 1984–85, China (at Peking), 1985–87, retd. Hon. LLD Glasgow, 1977. Order of the Taj (Iran), 1961. *Recreations:* languages, long-distance car driving. *Address:* 34a Sheridan Road, Merton Park, SW19 3HP. *T:* 081–542 3836. *Clubs:* Travellers'; Hong Kong (Hong Kong).

PHILLIPS, Ian, FCA; Director of Finance, British Broadcasting Corporation, since 1988; Chairman, BBC Enterprises Ltd, since 1991; *b* 16 July 1938; *s* of Wilfrid and Dorothy Phillips; *m* 1961, Fay Rosemary Stoner; two *s*. *Educ:* Whitgift Sch., South Croydon. Articled clerk, Hatfield Dixon Roberts Wright & Co., Accountants, 1955–61; Senior Asst, Robert J. Ward & Co., Accountants, 1961–65; Management Services Dept, John Lewis' Partnership, 1965–69; London Transport Executive: Director of Corporate Planning, 1969–75; Chief Business Planning Officer, 1975–78; Group Planning Director, 1978–80; Mem. Board, LTE, later LRT, 1980–84; Dir, Finance and Planning, BRB, 1985–88. *Recreations:* playing golf, watching any sport, the country, spending time with my family. *Address:* 113 Lower Camden, Chislehurst, Kent. *T:* 081–467 0529; Bakers Cottage, Church Road, Quenington, near Cirencester, Glos.

PHILLIPS, Jeremy Patrick Manfred, QC 1980; *b* 27 Feb. 1941; *s* of late Manfred Henry Phillips, CA, and late Irene Margaret (*née* Symondson); *m* 1968, Virginia Gwendoline (*née* Dwyer) (marr. diss. 1974); one *s* (and one *s* decd); *m* 1976, Judith Gaskell (*née* Hetherington); two *s* two *d*. *Educ:* St Edmund's Sch., Hindhead, Surrey; Charterhouse. Apprentice Accountant, Thomson McLintock & Co., 1957–61. Called to Bar, Gray's Inn, 1964; in practice, 1964–. Owner of Kentwell Hall, Long Melford, Suffolk, 1971–; organizer of Kentwell's Annual Historical Re-Creations of Tudor Domestic Life. Dir, CARE Britain. *Publications:* contrib. Cooper's Students' Manual of Auditing, Cooper's Manual of Auditing and various pamphlets, papers, guides, etc, on Kentwell Hall and Tudor period. *Recreations:* Kentwell Hall, historic buildings, Tudor history and Tudor domestic life. *Address:* Kentwell Hall, Long Melford, Suffolk.

PHILLIPS, John, RIBA; architect in private practice, since 1955; *b* 25 Nov. 1926; *s* of John Tudor Phillips and Bessie Maud Phillips; *m* 1955, Eileen Margaret Fryer. *Educ:* Christ's Coll., Finchley; Northern Polytechnic, Holloway. ARIBA 1954. Studied under Romilly B. Craze, Architect, 1948–52. Surveyor to the Fabric: Truro Cathedral, 1961 (Consultant Architect, 1979–); Westminster Cathedral, 1976–; RIBA 1979–; Consultant Architect to Brisbane Cathedral, 1988–. Pres., Ecclesiastical Architects' and Surveyors' Assoc., 1982. *Recreations:* looking at churches, choral singing. *Address:* (home) 8 Friary Way, North Finchley, N12 9PH. *T:* 081–445 3414; (office) 208/209 Upper Street, N1 1RL. *T:* 071–359 2299.

PHILLIPS, John Fleetwood Stewart, CMG 1965; HM Diplomatic Service, retired; *b* 16 Dec. 1917; *e s* of late Major Herbert Stewart Phillips, 27th Light Cavalry, and Violet Gordon, *d* of late Sir Alexander Pinhey, KCSI; *m* 1948, Mary Gordon Shaw, MB, BS; two *s* two *d*. *Educ:* Brighton; Worcester Coll., Oxford (Open Exhibition in Classics, MA). Represented Univ. and County intermittently at Rugby football, 1938–39. Served with 1st Bn, Argyll and Sutherland Highlanders in N Africa and Crete (wounded and captured, 1941). Appointed to Sudan Political Service, 1945; served in Kordofan and Blue Nile Provinces. HM Diplomatic Service, 1955, served in Foreign Office; Oriental Secretary in Libya, 1957; Consul-General at Muscat, 1960–63; Counsellor, British Embassy, Amman, 1963–66; Imperial Defence Coll., 1967; Dep. High Comr, Cyprus, 1968; Ambassador to Southern Yemen, 1969–70, to Jordan, 1970–72, to Sudan, 1973–77. *Recreations:* gardening and feuding. *Address:* Southwood, Gordon Road, Horsham, Sussex RH12 2EF. *T:* Horsham (0403) 52894. *Club:* Travellers'.

PHILLIPS, John Francis, CBE 1977 (OBE 1957); QC 1981; arbitrator; Chairman: London Court of International Arbitration, 1984–87; Private Patients Plan (formerly Provident Association for Medical Care), 1977–84, now President (Vice-Chairman, 1972–77; Director, since 1958); *b* 1911; *e s* of late F. W. Phillips and late Margaret (*née* Gillan); *m* 1937, Olive M. Royer; one *s* two *d*. *Educ:* Cardinal Vaughan Sch.; London Univ.; Trinity Hall, Cambridge. LLB (Hons) London; LLB (1st Cl. Hons), LLM Cantab. Barrister-at-law, Gray's Inn, 1944. Civil Servant (Lord Chancellor's Dept, Royal Courts of Justice), 1933–44; Parly Sec. and Asst Gen. Sec., Nat. Farmers' Union of England and Wales, 1945–57; Institute of Chartered Secretaries and Administrators: Sec. and Chief Exec., 1957–76; Mem. Council, 1976–81; Pres., 1977. Member: Council, Chartered Inst. of Arbitrators, 1969–83 (Vice-Pres., 1974–76; Pres., 1976–77); Gen. Cttee, Bar Assoc. for Commerce, Finance and Industry, 1967– (Vice-Chm., 1976–78 and 1980–81; Chm., 1978–80; Vice-Pres., 1982–88); Senate of the Inns of Court and the Bar; Bar Council; Cttees of Senate and Council, 1978–83; Council for Accreditation of Correspondence Colls, 1969–80 (Hon. Treas., 1969–74; Chm., 1975–80); British Egg Marketing Bd, 1969–71; Departmental Cttee of Enquiry into Fowl Pest, 1971; Vice-Chm. and Mem., Business Educn Council, 1974–80; Chairman: Jt Cttee for Awards in Business Studies and Public Admin., 1968–75 (Mem. Jt Cttee for Awards, 1960–75); Associated Examining Bd, GCE, 1976– (Mem., 1958–; Vice-Chm., 1973–76); Houghton Poultry Res. Station, 1976–82 (Governor, 1973–82); Dep. Chm., Eggs Authority, 1971–80. Governor: Christ's Hospital, 1957–; Crossways Trust, 1959–71 (Financial Advisor, 1966–71); Nuffield Nursing Homes Trust, 1975–81 (Vice-Pres., 1981–84); Mem. Council and Exec. Cttee, Animal Health Trust, 1976–; Deleg. to Internat. Labour Conf., 1950–56. FCIS 1958; FCIArb (FIArb 1966); CBIM (Council of Inst., 1969–74). Master, Co. of Chartered Secretaries and Administrators, 1978 and 1986–87; Founder Master, Worshipful Co. of Arbitrators, 1980–82; Master, Co. of Scriveners, 1982–83. OStJ. DCL City Univ., 1985. *Publications:* The Agriculture Act, 1947, 1948; Heywood and Massey's Lunacy Practice, 1939; Arbitration: Law, Practice and Precedents, 1988; many articles on aspects of law relating to land, agriculture and arbitration. *Recreation:* travel. *Address:* 17 Ossulton Way, Hampstead Garden Suburb, N2 0DT. *T:* 081–455 8460; (office) Private Patients Plan, Tavistock House, Tavistock Square, WC1H 9LJ; (chambers) 1 Verulam Buildings, Gray's Inn, WC1. *Clubs:* Athenæum, United Oxford & Cambridge University, City Livery.

PHILLIPS, John Randall; Leader, Cardiff City Council, since 1990 and Leader, Labour Group; *b* 22 April 1940; *s* of James Phillips and Charlotte Phillips (*née* Phelps); *m* 1967, Margaret Ray Davies; one *s* one *d*. *Educ:* Cardiff High Sch.; University Coll., Cardiff (BA Econ. 1961). Dip. Soc. Studies 1967. Dist Social Services Officer, Cynon Valley, Mid Glam CC. Mem., Cardiff Bay Develt Corp., 1990–. *Recreations:* politics, listening to music, wine making. *Address:* 15 Kyle Crescent, Whitchurch, Cardiff. *T:* Cardiff (0222) 624878.

PHILLIPS, Marisa, DLitt; President, Mental Health Review Tribunal, since 1990; *b* 14 April 1932; *d* of Dr and Mrs J. Fargion; *m* 1956, Philip Harold Phillips; one *s* one *d*. *Educ:* Henrietta Barnet Sch., London; Univ. of Redlands, California (Fulbright Schol.; BA Hons); Rome Univ. (DLitt). Called to Bar, Lincoln's Inn, 1963. On return from Redlands Univ., worked for US Inf. Service, Rome, 1954–56; spent one year in Berlin, as husband then in Army; period of work with Penguin Books; read for the Bar, joining DPP as Legal Asst, 1964; Legal Adviser, Police Complaints Bd, 1977; returned to DPP, 1979; Asst Dir, DPP, 1981; Principal Asst DPP, 1985; Asst Hd of Legal Services, 1986–87, Dir of Legal Casework, 1987–90, Crown Prosecution Service. Sen. Legal Advr, Banking Ombudsman, 1990–. Mem., Mental Health Commn, 1991–. *Recreations:* music, theatre, foreign travel.

PHILLIPS, Captain Mark Anthony Peter, CVO 1974; ADC(P); Managing Director, Gleneagles Mark Phillips Equestrian Centre, since 1988; *b* 22 Sept. 1948; *s* of P. W. G. Phillips, MC, and late Anne Patricia (*née* Tiarks); *m* 1973, HRH The Princess Anne; one *s* one *d*. *Educ:* Marlborough Coll.; RMA Sandhurst. Joined 1st The Queen's Dragoon Guards, July 1969; Regimental duty, 1969–74; Company Instructor, RMA Sandhurst, 1974–77; Army Trng Directorate, MoD, 1977–78, retired. Personal ADC to HM the Queen, 1974–. Student, RAC Cirencester, 1978. Chm., British Olympic Equestrian Fund, 1989–. In Three Day Equestrian Event, GB winning teams: Team Championships: World, 1970; European, 1971; Olympic Gold Medallists (Team), Olympic Games, Munich, 1972; Olympic Silver Medallists (Team), Olympic Games, Seoul, 1988; Mem., Equestrian Team (Reserve), Olympic Games, Mexico, 1968 and Montreal, 1976. Winner, Badminton Three Day Event, 1971, 1972, 1974, 1981. Chm., Glos Youth Assoc.; Patron: BAFPA; Everyman Theatre, Cheltenham. Liveryman: Farriers' Co.; Farmers' Co; Carmen's Co.; Loriners' Co.; Freeman: Loriners Co.; City of London; Yeoman, Saddlers' Co. *Recreations:* riding, Rugby football, athletics. *Address:* Aston Farm, Minchinhampton,

Stroud, Glos. *Club:* (Hon. Mem.) Buck's.
See also under Royal Family.

PHILLIPS, Max; Assistant Under Secretary of State, Ministry of Defence, 1977–84; *b* 31 March 1924; *m* 1953, Patricia Moore; two *s* two *d.* *Educ:* Colston's Sch., Bristol; Christ's Hospital; Magdalene Coll., Cambridge (Schol.; 1st cl. Hist. Tripos, pts I and II; MA). Served War, RA, 1943–46. Appointed to Home Civil Service, 1949; Colonial Office, 1949–59; Sec., Nigeria Fiscal Commn, 1957–58; UKAEA, 1959–73; Procurement Exec., MoD, 1973–74; HM Treasury, 1974–77; retired 1984, re-employed as Asst Sec., MoD, 1984–87. Governor and Almoner, Christ's Hospital. *Recreations:* modern myths, exploring the imagination and the countryside. *Address:* 2 Wilderness Farmhouse, Onslow Village, Guildford, Surrey GU2 5QP. *T:* Guildford (0483) 61308.

PHILLIPS, Mervyn John, AM 1987; FAIB; Deputy Governor and Deputy Chairman, Reserve Bank of Australia, since 1987; *b* 1 April 1930; *m* 1956, Moya, *d* of A. C. Bleazard; one *s* one *d.* *Educ:* De La Salle Coll., Ashfield; Univ. of Sydney (BEc). Commonwealth Bank of Australia, 1946–60; Reserve Bank of Australia, 1960–: Manager for PNG, 1962–64; Asst Manager, PNG Div., 1965–70, Manager, 1972–73; Asst Sec., 1970–72; Chief Manager, Internat. Dept, 1976–79, Securities Markets Dept, 1980–82, Financial Markets Group, 1983–85; Adviser, 1982; Chief Admin. Officer, 1985–87. Dir, CBOA Credit Union, 1964–73 (Chm., 1967–72); Chm., Note Printing Australia, 1990–; Member: PNG Currency Conversion Commn, 1965–66; NSW Credit Union Adv. Cttee, 1968–72; Govt Cttees on PNG Banking, 1971–73; Off-shore Banking in Australia, 1984. Mem., Senate, Australian Catholic Univ., 1991–. *Address:* Reserve Bank of Australia, 65 Martin Place, GPO Box 3947, Sydney, NSW 2001, Australia. *T:* Sydney 234 9333.

PHILLIPS, Prof. Neville Crompton, CMG 1973; Vice-Chancellor and Rector, University of Canterbury, Christchurch, New Zealand 1966–77; retired; *b* 7 March 1916; 2nd *s* of Samuel and Clara Phillips, Christchurch, NZ; *m* 1940, Pauline Beatrice, 3rd *d* of Selby and Dorothy Palmer, Te Aratipi, Havelock North, NZ; one *s* two *d.* *Educ:* Dannevirke High Sch.; Palmerston North Boys' High Sch.; Canterbury University College; Merton Coll., Oxford. BA (NZ) 1936; MA 1938; Hon. LittD (Cantuar) 1977; NZ University Post-Grad. Schol. in Arts, Arnold Atkinson Prizeman, 1938; Journalist, Sun and Press, Christchurch, 1932–38; read PPE at Oxford, 1938–39; RA (Gunner, subseq. Major), 1939–46; service in Tunisia and Italy (despatches). Lecturer in History and Political Science, Canterbury University College, 1946–47; Senior Lecturer, 1948; Prof. of History and Political Science, 1949–62; Prof. of History, 1962–66; Emeritus Prof., 1966; presented with Festschrift, 1984. Chairman: Canterbury Centennial Provincial Historical Cttee, 1948–66; Management Cttee, Canterbury Archaeological Trust, Kent, 1980–83; 1st Pres., Canterbury Historical Assoc., 1953; Editorial Adviser, NZ War Histories, 1957–67; US Dept of State Leader Grantee, 1966; Member: Council, Canterbury Manufacturers' Assoc., 1967–77; Christchurch Teachers' Coll. Council, 1968–76; NZ Vice-Chancellors' Cttee, 1966–77 (Chm., 1973–74); Council, Assoc. of Commonwealth Univs, 1973–74; NZ Council Educational Research, 1973–77. *Publications:* Italy, vol. 1 (The Sangro to Cassino), 1957 (New Zealand War Histories); Yorkshire and English National Politics, 1783–84, 1961; The Role of the University in Professional Education, 1970; (ed) A History of the University of Canterbury, 1873–1973, 1973; articles, mainly on eighteenth-century English politics, in English and NZ jls. *Recreations:* walking, watching cricket, things Italian. *Address:* Tyle House, Hackington Road, Tyler Hill, Canterbury, Kent CT2 9NF. *T:* Canterbury (0227) 471708.

PHILLIPS, Hon. Sir Nicholas (Addison), Kt 1987; **Hon. Mr Justice Phillips;** a Judge of the High Court of Justice, Queen's Bench Division, since 1987; *b* 21 Jan. 1938; *m* 1972, Christylle Marie-Thérèse Rouffiac (*née* Doreau); two *d*, and one step *s* one step *d.* *Educ:* Bryanston Sch.; King's Coll., Cambridge (MA). Nat. Service with RN; commnd RNVR, 1956–58. Called to Bar, Middle Temple (Harmsworth Scholar), 1962, Bencher, 1984. In practice at Bar, 1962–87; Jun. Counsel to Minister of Defence and to Treasury in Admiralty matters, 1973–78; QC 1978; a Recorder, 1982–87. Chm., Law Adv. Cttee, British Council, 1991–. Mem., Panel of Wreck Comrs, 1979. Governor, Bryanston Sch., 1975– (Chm. of Governors, 1981–). *Recreations:* sea and mountains. *Address:* Royal Courts of Justice, Strand, WC2A 2LL. *Club:* Brooks's.

PHILLIPS, Prof. Owen Martin, FRS 1968; Decker Professor of Science and Engineering, Johns Hopkins University, since 1975; *b* 30 Dec. 1930; *s* of Richard Keith Phillips and Madeline Lofts; *m* 1953, Merle Winifred Simons; two *s* two *d.* *Educ:* University of Sydney; Trinity Coll., Cambridge Univ. ICI Fellow, Cambridge, 1955–57; Fellow, St John's Coll., Cambridge, 1957–60; Asst Prof., 1957–60, Assoc. Prof., 1960–63, Johns Hopkins Univ.; Asst Director of Research, Cambridge, 1961–64; Prof. of Geophysical Mechanics, Johns Hopkins Univ., 1963–68, of Geophysics, 1968–75. Assoc. Editor Jl of Fluid Mechanics, 1964–; Mem. Council, Nat. Center of Atmospheric Research, Boulder, Colorado, 1964–68; Member: US Nat. Cttee Global Atmospheric Research Project, 1968; Res. Co-ord. Panel, Gas Research Inst., 1981–85; Principal Staff, Applied Phys. Lab., 1982–. Mem.-at-large, Amer. Meteorol. Soc. Publications Commn, 1971–75; Pres., Maryland Acad. of Scis, 1979–85. Sec., Bd of Trustees, Chesapeake Res. Consortium, 1973–74 (Trustee, 1972–75). Adams Prize, Univ. of Cambridge, 1965; Sverdrup Gold Medal, Amer. Metereol. Soc., 1975. *Publications:* The Dynamics of the Upper Ocean, 1966, 3rd edn 1976, Russian edn 1968; The Heart of the Earth, 1968, Italian edns 1970, 1975; The Last Chance Energy Book, 1979; (ed) Wave Dynamics and Radio Probing of the Ocean Surface, 1985; Flow and Reactions in Permeable Rocks, 1990; various scientific papers in Jl Fluid Mechanics, Proc. Cambridge Philos. Soc., Jl Marine Research, Proc. Royal Society, Deep Sea Research, Journal Geophys. Research. *Address:* 23 Merrymount Road, Baltimore, Maryland 21210, USA. *T:* 433–7195. *Clubs:* Johns Hopkins (Baltimore), Hamilton Street (Baltimore); Quissett Yacht (Mass).

PHILLIPS, Sir Peter (John), Kt 1990; OBE 1983; Chairman, A. B. Electronic Products Group, since 1987; *b* 18 June 1930; *s* of Walter Alfred Phillips and Victoria Mary Phillips; *m* 1956, Jean Gwendoline Williams; one *s* one *d.* *Educ:* Radley College; Pembroke College, Oxford (MA). Joined Aberthaw and Bristol Channel Portland Cement Co., 1956, Jt Man. Dir, 1964–83; Western Area Dir, Blue Circle Industries, 1983–84; Dep. Chm., A. B. Electronic Products Group, 1985. Chm., Principality Building Soc., 1991– (Dep. Chm., 1988–91). *Recreations:* walking, fishing, reading. *Address:* Great House, Llanblethian, near Cowbridge, South Glam CF7 7JG. *T:* Cowbridge (0446) 775163. *Club:* Cardiff and County.

PHILLIPS, Surgeon Rear-Adm. Rex Philip, CB 1972; OBE 1963; Medical Officer-in-Charge, Royal Naval Hospital, Plymouth, 1969–72, retired; *b* 17 May 1913; 2nd *s* of William John Phillips, late Consultant Anaesthetist at Royal Victoria Infirmary, Newcastle upon Tyne, and Nora Graham Phillips; *m* 1939, Gill Foley; two *s.* *Educ:* Epsom Coll.; Coll. of Med., Newcastle upon Tyne, Univ. of Durham (now Univ. of Newcastle upon Tyne). Qual. MB, BS 1937; Ho. Surg., Ingham Infirmary, S Shields, 1938. Joined RN, 1939; served War of 1939–45: HMS Rochester, 1939–41; Royal Marines, 1941–43; HMS Simba, 1943–45. HMS Excellent, 1945–47; qual. Dip. in Ophthalmology (London), 1948; HMS Implacable, Fleet MO, 1949–51; Specialist in Ophthalmology: HMS Ganges, 1951–53; Central Air Med. Bd, 1953–55; RN Hosp., Malta (Senior), 1955–57; Admty Adv. in Ophth. to Med. Dir-Gen., 1957–65; Surg. Captain 1963; SMO, RN Hosp., Malta, 1965–68; Staff MO to Flag Officer Submarines, 1968–69. QHS 1969–72. CStJ 1970. *Recreations:* golf, bridge. *Address:* Langstone House, 25 Langstone High Street, Havant, Hants PO9 1RY. *T:* Havant (0705) 484668.

PHILLIPS, Richard Charles Jonathan; QC 1990; *b* 8 Aug. 1947; *yr s* of Air Commodore M. N. Phillips, MD, ChB, DMRD and Dorothy E. Phillips; *m* 1978, Alison Jane Francis (OBE 1991). *Educ:* King's School, Ely; Sidney Sussex College, Cambridge (Exhibnr). Called to the Bar, Inner Temple, 1970. *Recreations:* travel, natural history, photography, walking. *Address:* 2 Harcourt Buildings, Temple, EC4Y 9DB. *T:* 071–353 8415.

PHILLIPS, Robin; actor and director; *b* 28 Feb. 1942; *s* of James William Phillips and Ellen Anne (*née* Barfoot). *Educ:* Midhurst Grammar School, Sussex. Trained as director, actor and designer, Bristol Old Vic Co.; first appearance, Bristol, as Mr Puff in The Critic, 1959; Associate Dir, Bristol Old Vic, 1960–61; played at Lyric, Hammersmith, 1961, Chichester Fest., 1962, and with Oxford Playhouse Co., 1964. Asst Dir, Timon of Athens and Hamlet, Royal Shakespeare Co., Stratford upon Avon, 1965; Dir or Associate Dir, Hampstead, Exeter, (Thorndike) Leatherhead, 1966–69; Artistic Dir, Stratford Festival, Canada, 1974–80; *London prodns include:* Tiny Alice, RSC, Aldwych, 1970; Abelard and Heloise, Wyndhams and Broadway; The Two Gentlemen of Verona, Stratford and Aldwych, 1970; Miss Julie, for RSC (also directed film); Virginia, Haymarket, 1981; *Chichester:* Caesar and Cleopatra and Dear Antoine, 1971; played Dubedat in The Doctor's Dilemma and directed The Lady's Not for Burning and The Beggar's Opera, 1972; The Jeweller's Shop, 1982; Antony and Cleopatra, 1985; *Greenwich:* formed Company Theatre and apptd Artistic Dir, 1973: plays directed include: The Three Sisters, Rosmerholm, Zorba; *Stratford Festival prodns incl.:* 1975: The Two Gentlemen of Verona and The Comedy of Errors (both also Nat. tour), Measure for Measure, Trumpets and Drums and The Importance of Being Earnest; 1976–78: Hamlet, The Tempest, Antony and Cleopatra, A Midsummer Night's Dream, The Way of the World, Richard III, The Guardsman, As You Like It, Macbeth, The Winter's Tale, Uncle Vanya, The Devils, Private Lives, Hay Fever, Judgement; 1979: Love's Labours Lost, The Importance of Being Earnest, King Lear; 1980: Virginia, Long Day's Journey into Night; Farther West, Theatre Calgary, 1982; King Lear, Stratford, 1988. Directorate, NY, 1978. *Films:* as actor: Decline and Fall, David Copperfield (title part), Tales from the Crypt. *TV:* Wilfred Desert in The Forsyte Saga, Constantin in The Seagull. *Address:* PO Box 51, Stratford, Ontario N5A 6S8, Canada.

PHILLIPS, Sir Robin Francis, 3rd Bt, *cr* 1912; Owner and Principal, Ravenscourt Theatre School, London; *b* 29 July 1940; *s* of Sir Lionel Francis Phillips, 2nd Bt, and Camilla Mary, *er d* of late Hugh Parker, 22 Chapel Street, Belgrave Square, SW1; *S* father, 1944. *Educ:* Aiglon Coll., Switzerland. Chief Air Traffic Control Officer, Biggin Hill, 1970–78; Hazel Malaone Management, 1978–81; Devonair Radio, 1981–83; Radio Luxembourg, 1984; Hd of Casting, Corona Stage School, 1985–89. *Heir:* none. *Address:* 12 Manson Mews, Queens Gate, SW7.

PHILLIPS, (Ronald) William; management consultant, since 1991; *b* 21 April 1949; *s* of Ronald Phillips and Phoebe Nora Haynes; *m* 1979, Dorothy Parsons. *Educ:* Steyning Grammar Sch.; University College of Wales, Aberystwyth (BScEcon). Joined CS, 1971; served in Dept of Transport, PSA, DoE, Develt Commn (Private Sec. to Lord Northfield); Asst County Sec., Kent CC, 1979–80; UK Expert to EC Council of Ministers Wkg Party on Environmental Impact Assessment, 1980–83; Greater London Reg. Office, DoE (Local Govt Reorganisation), 1983–86; Head of Policy Unit, 1986–87, Man. Dir, 1987–91, Westminster CC. FRSA 1990; FBIM 1990. *Recreation:* travel. *Address:* Livesey Cottage, Livesey Street, Teston, Kent ME18 5AY.

PHILLIPS, Siân; actress; *d* of D. Phillips and Sally Phillips; *m* 1st, 1960, Peter O'Toole, *qv* (marr. diss. 1979); two *d*; 2nd, 1979, Robin Sachs. *Educ:* Pontardawe Grammar Sch.; Univ. of Wales (Cardiff Coll.) (BA Hons English; Fellow, 1982); RADA (Maggie Albanesi Scholarship, 1956; Bancroft Gold Medal, 1958). BBC Radio Wales, mid 1940s-, and BBC TV Wales, early 1950s-; Newsreader and Announcer, and Mem. Rep. Co., BBC, 1953–55; toured for Welsh Arts Council with National Theatre Co., 1953–55; Arts Council Bursary to study drama outside Wales, 1955. Mem., Arts Council Drama Cttee, 1970–75. Governor, St David's Trust, 1970–73. London productions: Hedda Gabler, 1959; Ondine, and the Duchess of Malfi, 1960–61 (1st RSC season at Aldwych); The Lizard on the Rock, 1961; Gentle Jack, Maxibules, and The Night of the Iguana, 1964; Ride a Cock Horse, 1965; Man and Superman, and Man of Destiny, 1966; The Burglar, 1967; Epitaph for George Dillon, 1972; A Nightingale in Bloomsbury Square, 1973; The Gay Lord Quex, 1975; Spinechiller, 1978; You Never Can Tell, Lyric, Hammersmith, 1979; Pal Joey, Half Moon, 1980 and Albery, 1981; Dear Liar, Mermaid, 1982; Major Barbara, NT, 1982; Peg, Phoenix, 1984; Gigi, Lyric, Shaftesbury Ave., 1985; Thursday's Ladies, Apollo, 1987; Brel, Donmar, 1987; The Glass Menagerie, Cambridge Theatre Co. nat. tour, 1989; Paris Match, Garrick, 1989; Vanilla, Lyric, 1990; The Manchurian Candidate, Lyric, Hammersmith, and nat. tour, 1991. *TV drama series* include: Shoulder to Shoulder, 1974; How Green was my Valley, 1975; I, Claudius, 1976; Boudicca, and Off to Philadelphia in the Morning, 1977; The Oresteia of Aeschylus, 1978; Crime and Punishment, 1979; Sean O'Casey (RTE), 1980; Winston Churchill, The Wilderness Years, 1981; Language and Landscape (6 bilingual films, Welsh and English), 1985; The Snow Spider, 1988; Shadow of the Noose, 1989; Emlyn's Moon, 1990; Perfect Scoundrels, 1990; Hands Across the Sea, 1991; The Astonished Heart, 1991; Ways and Means, 1991; *TV films* include: A Painful Case (RTE), 1985; While Reason Sleeps; Return to Endor, 1986 (USA); Siân (biographical), 1987. *Films* include: Becket, 1963; Goodbye Mr Chips, and Laughter in the Dark, 1968; Murphy's War, 1970; Under Milk Wood, 1971; The Clash of the Titans, 1979; Dune, 1984; Ewocks Again, and The Doctor and the Devils, 1985; Valmont, 1989. Has made recordings, incl. Peg, Gigi, I remember Mama, Pal Joey and A Little Night Music. Hon. Fellow, Polytechnic of Wales, 1988. Fellow, Welsh Nat. Coll. of Music and Drama, 1991. Hon. DLitt Wales, 1984. Critics Circle Award, New York Critics Award, and Famous 7 Critics Award, for Goodbye Mr Chips, 1969; BAFTA Award for How Green was my Valley and I, Claudius, 1978; Royal Television Soc. Award for I, Claudius (Best Performer), 1978. Mem., Gorsedd of Bards, 1960 (for services to drama in Wales). *Publications:* Siân Phillips' Needlepoint, 1987; gen. journalism (Vogue, Cosmopolitan, Daily Mail, 3 years for Radio Times, Country Living, Options). *Recreations:* gardening, needlepoint, drawing. *Address:* c/o Saraband Ltd, 265 Liverpool Road, Barnsbury, N1 1HS.

PHILLIPS, Tom, RA 1989 (ARA 1984); RE 1987; painter, writer and composer; *b* 25 May 1937; *s* of David John Phillips and Margaret Agnes (*née* Arnold); *m* 1961, Jill Purdy (marr. diss. 1988); one *s* one *d.* *Educ:* St Catherine's College, Oxford (MA); Camberwell School of Art. NDD. One man shows: AIA Galleries, 1965; Angela Flowers Gall., 1970–71; Marlborough Fine Art, 1973–75; Dante Works, Waddington Galleries, 1983; retrospective exhibitions: Gemeente Museum, The Hague, 1975; Kunsthalle, Basel, 1975; Serpentine, 1975; 50 years of Tom Phillips, Angela Flowers Gall., 1987; Mappin Art Gall., Sheffield, 1987; Nat. Gall., Jamaica, 1987; Bass Mus., Miami, 1988; Nat. Gall.,

Australia, 1988; City Art Inst., Sydney, 1988; Nat. Portrait Gall., 1989; N Carolina Mus., 1990; work in collections: British Museum, Tate Gall., V&A, Nat. Portrait Gall., Imperial War Mus., Mus. Fine Arts, Budapest, MOMA NY, Philadelphia Museum, Bibliothèque Nationale, Paris, Gemeente Museum, Boymans Museum, Rotterdam, Nat. Museum, Stockholm, Nat. Gall. of Australia; designed tapestries for St Catherine's, Oxford; music: first perf. opera Irma, 1973; York, 1974; ICA, 1983; recordings incl. Irma, 1980 (new version, 1988); Intervalles/Music of Tom Phillips 1982; television: collaborating on Dante series, 1984–; film scripts: Tom Phillips (Grierson Award, BFI, 1976; Golden Palm Award, Chicago, 1976); The Artist's Eye (TV film), 1988; Twenty Sites (TV film), 1989. Chm., RA Library, 1987; Vice-Chm., British Copyright Council, 1984–88. Hon. Pres., S London Artists, 1987–. Francis Williams Prize, V&A 1983; First Prize, Hunting Gp of Cos, 1988. *Publications:* Trailer, 1971; A Humument, 1980, rev. edn 1987; illustr. trans. Dante's Inferno, 1982; Works/Texts to 1974, 1975; Heart of a Humument, 1985; The Class of Forty-Seven, 1990. *Recreation:* collecting African sculpture. *Address:* 57 Talfourd Road, SE15 5NN. *T:* 071–701 3978. *Clubs:* Chelsea Arts, Groucho; Surrey County Cricket.

PHILLIPS, William; *see* Phillips, R. W.

PHILLIPS GRIFFITHS, Allen; *see* Griffiths.

PHILLIS, Robert Weston; Chief Executive, Independent Television News, since 1991; *b* 3 Dec. 1945; *s* of Francis William Phillis and Gertrude Grace Phillis; *m* 1966, Jean (*née* Derham); three *s*. *Educ:* John Ruskin Grammar Sch.; Nottingham Univ. (BA Industrial Econs 1968). Apprentice, printing industry, 1961–65; Thomson Regional Newspapers Ltd, 1968–69; British Printing Corp. Ltd, 1969–71; Lectr in Industrial Relations, Edinburgh Univ. and Scottish Business Sch., 1971–75; Vis. Fellow, Univ. of Nairobi, 1974; Personnel Dir, later Man. Dir, Sun Printers Ltd, 1976–79; Managing Director: Independent Television Publications Ltd, 1979–82 (Dir, 1979–87); Central Independent Television plc, 1981–87 (non-exec. Mem. Bd, 1987–91); Gp Man. Dir, Carlton Communications, 1987–91. Chairman: ITV Network Programming Cttee, 1984–86; ITV Film Purchase Gp, 1985–87; Zenith Productions Ltd, 1984–91. Director: ITN Ltd, 1982–87; Periodical Publishers Assoc., 1979–82; Ind. Television Cos Assoc., 1982–87; Internat. Council, Nat. Acad. of Television Arts and Scis, 1985–. FRSA 1984; FRTS 1988 (Chm., 1989–). *Recreations:* family, sport, news. *Address:* Independent Television News Ltd, 200 Gray's Inn Road, WC1X 8XZ. *T:* 071–833 3000.

PHILLPOTTS, (Mary) Adelaide Eden, (Mrs Nicholas Ross); writer; *b* Ealing, Middlesex, 23 April 1896; *d* of late Eden Phillpotts; *m* 1951, Nicholas Ross. *Publications: novels:* The Friend, 1923; Lodgers in London, 1926; Tomek, the Sculptor, 1927; A Marriage, 1928; The Atoning Years, 1929; Yellow Sands, 1930; The Youth of Jacob Ackner, 1931; The Founder of Shandon, 1932; The Growing World, 1934; Onward Journey, 1936; Broken Allegiance, 1937; What's Happened to Rankin?, 1938; The Gallant Heart, 1939; The Round of Life, 1940; Laugh with Me, 1941; Our Little Town, 1942; From Jane to John, 1943; The Adventurers, 1944; The Lodestar, 1946; The Fosterling, 1949; Stubborn Earth, 1951; Village Love, 1988; The Beacon of Memory, 1990; *plays:* Arachne, 1920; Savitri the Faithful, 1923; Camillus and the Schoolmaster, 1923; Akhnaton, 1926; (with Eden Phillpotts) Yellow Sands, 1926; Laugh With Me, 1938; *poetry:* Illyrion, and other Poems, 1916; A Song of Man, 1959; *travel:* Panorama of the World, 1969; *miscellaneous:* Man, a Fable, 1922; (selected with Nicholas Ross) Letters to Nicholas Ross from J. C. Powys (ed A. Uphill), 1971; A Wild Flower Wreath, 1975; Reverie: An Autobiography, 1981. *Address:* Trelana Home, Poughill, near Bude, Cornwall EX23 9EL.

PHILO, Gordon Charles George, CMG 1970; MC 1944; HM Diplomatic Service, retired; *b* 8 Jan. 1920; *s* of Charles Gilbert Philo and Nellie Philo (*née* Pinnock); *m* 1952, Mavis (Vicky) Ella (*d* 1986), *d* of John Ford Galsworthy and Sybel Victoria Galsworthy (*née* Strachan). *Educ:* Haberdashers' Aske's Hampstead Sch.; Wadham Coll., Oxford. Methuen Scholar in Modern History, Wadham Coll., 1938. Served War, HM Forces, 1940–46: Royal West African Frontier Force, 1942–43; Airborne Forces, Normandy and Europe, 1944–45; India 1945–46. Alexander Korda Scholar, The Sorbonne, 1948–49; Lectr in Modern History, Wadham Coll., 1949–50; Foundn Mem., St Antony's Coll., Oxford, 1950–51. Foreign Office, 1951; Russian course, Christ's Coll., Cambridge, 1952–53; Istanbul, Third Sec., 1954–57; Ankara, Second Sec., 1957–58; FO, 1958–63; Kuala Lumpur, First Sec., 1963–67; FO, 1968; Consul-Gen., Hanoi, 1968–69; FCO, 1969–78. Extended Interview Assessor, Home Office Unit, CSSB, 1978–90. Chm. Council, Kipling Soc., 1986–88. Kesatria Mangku Negara (Hon.), Order of Malaysia, 1968. *Publications:* (jtly with wife, as Charles Forsyte): Diplomatic Death, 1960; Diving Death, 1962; Double Death, 1965; Murder with Minarets, 1968; The Decoding of Edwin Drood, 1980; articles in various jls. *Recreations:* travel, writing. *Address:* 10 Abercorn Close, NW8 9XS. *Club:* Athenæum.

PHILPOT, Oliver Lawrence Spurling, MC 1944; DFC 1941; Managing Director, Remploy Ltd, 1974–78; *b* Vancouver, BC, Canada, 6 March 1913; *s* of Lawrence Benjamin Philpot, London, and Catherine Barbara (*née* Spurling), Bedford; *m* 1st, 1938 (marr. diss. 1951); one *s* two *d*; 2nd, 1954, Rosl Widhalm, BA Hons History, PhD (Lond.), Vienna; one *s* one *d*. *Educ:* Queen Mary Sch., N Vancouver; Aymestrey Court, Worcester; Radley Coll.; Worcester Coll., Oxford (BA Hons PPE; MA). RAFVR: Pilot, 42 Torpedo/Bomber Sqdn, RAF Coastal Comd, 1940; shot down off Norway, 1941; 5 prison camps, Germany and Poland; escaped to Sweden and Scotland, as 3rd man in Wooden Horse, from Stalag Luft III at Sagan, Silesia, 1943; Sen. Scientific Officer, Air Min., 1944 (wrote 33 RAF Stations Manpower Survey, 1944). Management Trainee, Unilever Ltd, 1934; Asst (commercial) Sec., Unilever Home Margarine Exec., 1936; Exec., Maypole Dairy Ltd, 1946; Chm., Trufood Ltd, 1948; Office Manager, Unilever House, EC4, 1950; Gen. Manager (admin.), T. Walls & Sons Ltd, 1951; Coast-to-Coast Lecture Tour in N America on own book, Stolen Journey, with Peat Agency, Canadian Clubs and USAAF, 1952; Dir, Arthur Woollacott & Rappings Ltd, 1953; Chm. and Man. Dir, Spirella Co. of Great Britain Ltd, 1956; Man. Dir, Venesta (later Aluminium) Foils Ltd, 1959; Exec., Union International Ltd, 1962 (also Dep. Chm. and Chief Exec., Fropax Eskimo Frood Ltd, 1965–67), i/c Lonsdale & Thompson Ltd, John Layton Ltd, Merseyside Food Products Ltd, Union Distribution Co. Ltd, Weddel Pharmaceuticals Ltd, John Gardner (Printers) Ltd, and Union Internat. Res. Centre. Chairman: Royal Air Forces Escaping Soc., and RAFES Charitable Fund, 2 terms, 1963–69. Overseas Administrator, Help the Aged, 1979–82; Manager, St Bride Foundn Inst., 1982–89; Mem., Nat. Adv. Council on Employment of Disabled People, 1978; Chm., London NW Area Cttee for Employment of Disabled People, 1981–86. Mem., Gen. Adv. Council, IBA, 1982–85. Supports European Community; fights local environmental battles. *Publication:* Stolen Journey, 1950 (5th edn 1951, repr. 1970; Swedish, Norwegian and Amer. edns, 1951–52; paperback 1954, repr. 4 times, 1962–66). *Recreations:* political activity incl. canvassing, sculling Boat Race course and return (No 452 in Head of the River Race for Scullers, 1986), talking, idling, listening to sermons, reading Financial Times and obituaries in Lancet. *Address:* 30 Abingdon Villas, Kensington, W8 6BX. *T:* 071–937 6013. *Clubs:* London Rowing, Ends of the Earth, Society of Authors, United Oxford & Cambridge University, Institute of Directors, Goldfish, Guild of St Bride, RAF Escaping Society, RAF ex-POW Association, Aircrew Association; Worcester College Society (London and Oxford).

PHILPS, Dr Frank Richard, MBE 1946; retired; Consultant in Exfoliative Cytology, University College Hospital, WC1, 1960–73; Director, Joint Royal Free and University College Hospitals, Department of Cytology, 1972–73; *b* 9 March 1914; *s* of Francis John Philps and Matilda Ann Philps (*née* Healey); *m* 1941, Emma L. F. M. Schmidt; two *s* one *d*. *Educ:* Christ's Hospital, Horsham, Sussex. MRCS, LRCP, 1939; MB, BS, 1939; DPH 1947; MD London, 1952; FRCPath, 1966; Fellow, International Academy of Cytology, 1967. RAF Medical Service, 1940–46. Junior Hospital Appointments, UCH, 1950–54; Consultant Pathologist, Eastbourne, 1954–64; Research Asst, UCH, 1955–60. Hon. Cons. in Cytology, Royal Free Hosp., 1972–73. Producer, with wife, Wild Life Series of Educational Nature Films and films on pottery making, for Educational Foundation for Visual Aids; made BBC films, The Magic of a Dartmoor Stream, 1977, The Magic of a Dartmoor Wood, 1979. Exhibitor in the annual exhibition of the Royal Inst. of Painters in Watercolours, 1980–84. BBC Nature Film Prize, 1963; Council for Nature Film Prize, 1966. *Publications:* A Short Manual of Respiratory Cytology, 1964; Watching Wild Life, 1968, 3rd edn 1984; papers on Cytology to several medical journals, 1954–67. *Recreations:* living in the country; watching wild animals and filming them, painting. *Address:* Woodlands, Sydenham Wood, Lewdown, Okehampton EX20 4PP. *T:* Chillaton (082286) 347.

PHIPPS, family name of **Marquess of Normanby.**

PHIPPS, Colin Barry, PhD; Chairman: Clyde Petroleum plc, since 1983 (Deputy Chairman and Chief Executive, 1979–83); Phipps & Co. Ltd, since 1983; Greenwich Resources plc, since 1989; *b* 23 July 1934; *s* of Edgar Reeves Phipps and Winifred Elsie Phipps (*née* Carroll); *m* 1956, Marion May Phipps (*née* Lawrey); two *s* two *d*. *Educ:* Townfield Elem. Sch., Hayes, Mddx; Acton County; Swansea Grammar; University Coll. London; Birmingham Univ. BSc, 1st cl. Hons Geol. London 1955; PhD, Geol. Birm. 1957. Royal Dutch/Shell Geologist: Holland, Venezuela, USA, 1957–64; Consultant Petroleum Geologist, 1964–79. Chm., Brindex (Assoc. of British Independent Oil Exploration Cos), 1983–86. MP (Lab) Dudley W, Feb. 1974–1979. Mem., Council of Europe/WEU, 1976–79. Contested: (Lab) Walthamstow E, 1969; (SDP/L Alliance) Worcester, 1983; (SDP/L Alliance) Stafford, 1987. Founder mem., SDP; Mem. SDP Nat. Cttee, 1984–89; Chm., W Midland Regional council, SDP, 1986–89. FGS 1956, FInstPet 1972; Mem. Instn of Geologists, 1978. Chairman: Twentieth Century British Art Fair, 1988–; Falkland Islands Foundn, 1990– (Trustee, 1983–); English String Orch., 1990– (Dir, 1985–). *Publications:* (co-ed) Energy and the Environment: democratic decision-making, 1978; What Future for the Falklands?, 1977 (Fabian tract 450); contrib.: Qly Jl Geol Sci., Geol. Mag., Geol. Jl, etc. *Recreations:* various and changing with age. *Address:* Mathon Court, Mathon, Malvern WR13 5NZ. *T:* Malvern (0684) 892267; 38 Cheyne Walk, SW3. *T:* 071–352 5381. *Clubs:* Reform, Chelsea Arts.

PHIPPS, Air Vice-Marshal Leslie William, CB 1983; AFC 1959; *b* 17 April 1930; *s* of late Frank Walter Phipps and Beatrice Kate (*née* Bearman). *Educ:* SS Philip and James Sch., Oxford. Commnd RAF, 1950; served, 1951–69: Fighter Sqdns; Stn Comdr, RAF Aqaba, Jordan; OC No 19 (F) Sqdn; Central Fighter Estab.; RN Staff Coll.; HQ 1 (British) Corps; Stn Comdr, RAF Labuan, Borneo; OC No 29 (F) Sqdn; Jt Services Staff Coll.; Dir, RAF Staff Coll., 1970–72; Comdr, Sultan of Oman's Air Force, 1973–74; RCDS, 1975; Comdr, UK Team to Kingdom of Saudi Arabia, 1976–78; Dir of Air Def. and Overseas Ops, 1978–79; Air Sec., (RAF), 1980–82; Sen. Directing Staff, RCDS, 1983; retired. BAe (Mil. Aircraft Div.), 1984–91. *Recreations:* sailing, squash, music. *Address:* 33 Knole Wood, Devenish Road, Sunningdale, Berks SL5 9QR. *Clubs:* Royal Air Force; Royal Air Force Yacht (Hamble).

PHIPPS, Rt. Rev. Simon Wilton, MC 1945; Assistant Bishop, Dioceses of Chichester and Southwark, since 1986; *b* 6 July 1921; *s* of late Captain William Duncan Phipps, CVO, RN, and late Pamela May Ross; *m* 1973, Mary, *widow* of Rev. Dr James Welch and *d* of late Sir Charles Eric Palmer. *Educ:* Eton; Trinity Coll., Cambridge; Westcott House, Cambridge. Joined Coldstream Guards, 1940; commnd, 1941; Capt., 1944; ADC to GOC-in-C Northern Comd India, Nov. 1945; Mil. Asst to Adjt Gen. to the Forces, War Office, 1946; Major, 1946. BA (History) Cantab, 1948; MA 1953; Pres., Cambridge Univ. Footlights Club, 1949. Ordained 1950. Asst Curate, Huddersfield Parish Church, 1950; Chaplain, Trinity Coll., Cambridge, 1953; Industrial Chaplain, Coventry Dio., 1958; Hon. Canon, Coventry Cath., 1965; Bishop Suffragan of Horsham, 1968–74; Bishop of Lincoln, 1974–86. Chm. Council, William Temple Foundation, 1985–89; Pres., Assoc. of Pastoral Care and Counselling, 1985–; Mem., Home Sec's Cttee of Inquiry into Liquor Licensing Laws, 1971–72; formerly Mem. Council, Industrial Soc. *Publication:* God on Monday, 1966. *Recreations:* gardening, painting, cooking. *Address:* Sarsens, Shipley, W Sussex RH13 8PX. *T:* Coolham (0403) 741354. *Club:* Army and Navy.

PHIZACKERLEY, Ven. Gerald Robert; Archdeacon of Chesterfield, since 1978; *b* 3 Oct. 1929; *s* of John Dawson and Lilian Mabel Ruthven Phizackerley; *m* 1959, Annette Catherine, *d* of Cecil Frank and Inez Florence Margaret Baker; one *s* one *d*. *Educ:* Queen Elizabeth Grammar School, Penrith; University Coll., Oxford (MA); Wells Theological Coll. Curate of St Barnabas Church, Carlisle, 1954–57; Chaplain of Abingdon School, 1957–64; Rector of Gaywood, Norfolk, 1964–78; Rural Dean of Lynn, 1968–78; Hon. Canon of Norwich Cathedral, 1975, of Derby Cathedral, 1978; Priest-in-charge, Ashford-in-the-Water with Sheldon, 1978–90. Fellow, Woodard Corporation, 1981. JP Norfolk, 1972. *Recreations:* books, theatre, Border collies. *Address:* The Old Parsonage, Taddington, Buxton, Derbys SK17 9TW. *T:* Taddington (0298) 85607.

PHYSICK, John Frederick, CBE 1984; DrRCA; FSA; Deputy Director, Victoria and Albert Museum, 1983; *b* 31 Dec. 1923; *s* of Nino William Physick and Gladys (*née* Elliott); *m* 1954, Eileen Mary Walsh; two *s* one *d*. *Educ:* Battersea Grammar Sch. Royal Navy, 1942–46 (Petty Officer Airman). Joined Victoria and Albert Museum, as Museum Asst, Dept of Engraving, Illustration and Design, 1948; Research Asst, 1949; Sen. Research Asst, 1965; Asst Keeper, Dept of Public Relations and Educn, 1967; Keeper, Dept of Museum Services, 1975–83; Sec. to Adv. Council, 1973–83; Asst to Dir, 1974–83. Leverhulme Trust Emeritus Fellow, 1984–86. Pres., Church Monument Soc., 1984–86; Member: Rochester Dio. Adv. Cttee for the Care of Churches, 1965– (Vice-Chm., 1987–); RIBA Drawings Cttee, 1975; Cathedrals Adv. Cttee, 1977–81; Council for Care of Churches Monuments Sub-Cttee, 1978– (Chm., 1984–); Council for Care of Churches Conservation Cttee, 1984–; Council, British Archaeol Assoc., 1985–88; Westminster Abbey Architectural Adv. Panel, 1985–; Rochester Cathedral Fabric Cttee, 1987–; Council, Soc. of Antiquaries, 1991–. Trustee, London Scottish Regt, 1977–87. FRSA. *Publications:* Catalogue of the Engravings of Eric Gill, 1963; (ed) Handbook to the Departments Prints and Drawings and Paintings, 1964; The Duke of Wellington in caricature, 1965; Designs for English Sculpture 1680–1860, 1969; The Wellington Monument, 1970; (jtly) Victorian Church Art, 1971; Five Monuments from Eastwell, 1973; (with M. D. Darby) Marble Halls, 1973; Photography and the South Kensington

Museum, 1975; (with Sir Roy Strong) V&A Souvenir Guide, 1977; The Victoria and Albert Museum—the history of its building, 1982; (ed) V&A Album II, 1983; (ed) Sculpture in Britain 1530–1830, 2nd edn 1988; (contrib.) Change and Decay, the Future of our Churches, 1977; (contrib.) Westminster Abbey, 1986; (contrib.) The Royal College of Art, 1987; (introd.) Westminster Abbey: the monuments, 1989. *Recreations:* photography, looking at church monuments. *Address:* 49 New Road, Meopham, Kent DA13 0LS. *T:* Meopham (0474) 812301; 14 Park Street, Deal, Kent CT14 6AG. *T:* Deal (0304) 381621.

PIACHAUD, Prof. David François James; Professor of Social Administration, London School of Economics, since 1987; *b* 2 Oct. 1945; *s* of Rev. Preb. François A. Piachaud and Mary R. Piachaud; *m* 1988, Louise K. Carpenter; one *d*. *Educ:* Westminster Sch.; Christ Church, Oxford (MA); Univ. of Michigan (MPA). Economic Asst, DHSS, 1968–70; Lectr, 1970–83, Reader, 1983–87, LSE. Policy Advr, Prime Minister's Policy Unit, 1974–79. *Publications:* The Causes of Poverty (jtly), 1978; The Cost of a Child, 1979; (jtly) Child Support in the European Community, 1980; The Distribution and Redistribution of Incomes, 1982; (jtly) The Fields and Methods of Social Planning, 1984; (jtly) The Goals of Social Policy, 1989; contribs to learned jls. *Recreations:* carpentry, travelling hopefully. *Address:* London School of Economics, Houghton Street, WC2A 2AE. *T:* 071–405 7686.

PICACHY, His Eminence Lawrence Trevor, Cardinal, SJ; former Archibishop of Calcutta; *b* 7 Aug. 1916; Indian. *Educ:* St Joseph's College, Darjeeling and various Indian Seminaries. 1952–60: Headmaster of St Xavier's School, Principal of St Xavier's College, Rector of St Xavier's, Calcutta. Parish Priest of Basanti, large village of West Bengal, 1960–62; (first) Bishop of Jamshedpur, 1962–69, Apostolic Administrator of Jamshedpur, 1969–70; Archibishop of Calcutta, 1969. Cardinal, 1976. Pres., Catholic Bishops' Conf. of India, 1976–81 (Vice-Pres., 1972–75). *Address:* c/o Archbishop's House, 32 Park Street, Calcutta 700016, India.

PICCARD, Dr Jacques; scientist; President, Foundation for the Study and Preservation of Seas and Lakes; *b* Belgium, 1922; Swiss Citizen; *s* of late Prof. Auguste Piccard (explorer of the stratosphere, in lighter-than-air craft, and of the ocean depths, in vehicles of his own design); *m* 1953, Marie Claude (*née* Maillard); two *s* one *d*. *Educ:* Brussels; Switzerland. Grad., Univ. of Geneva, 1946; Dip. from Grad. Inst. of Internat. Studies. Asst Prof., Univ. of Geneva, 1946–48. With his father, he participated in design and operation of the first deep diving vessels, which they named the bathyscaph (deep ship); this vessel, like its successor, operated independently of a mother ship; they first constructed the FNRS-2 (later turned over to the French Navy) then the Trieste (ultimately purchased by US Navy); Dr J. Piccard piloted the Trieste on 65 successive dives (the last, 23 Jan. 1960, was the record-breaking descent to 35,800 feet in the Marianas Trench, off Guam in the Pacific Ocean). He built in 1963, the mesoscaph Auguste Piccard, the first civilian submarine, which made, in 1964–65, over 1,100 dives carrying 33,000 people into the depths of Lake Geneva; built (with Grumman) 2nd mesoscaph, Ben Franklin, and in 1969 made 1.500 miles/30 days drift dive in Gulf Stream. Founded: Fondation pour l'Etude et la Protection de la Mer et des Lacs, 1966 (built research submersible, F. A.-FOREL, 1978); Institut International d'Ecologie, 1972. Hon. doctorate in Science, Amer. Internat. Coll., Springfield, Mass, 1962; Hon. DSc, Hofstra Univ., 1970. Holds Distinguished Public Service Award, etc. *Publications:* The Sun beneath the Sea, 1971; technical papers and a popularized account (trans. many langs) of the Trieste, Seven Miles Down (with Robert S. Dietz). *Address:* (home) 19 avenue de l'Avenir, 1009 Pully-Lausanne, Switzerland. *T:* (021) 28 80 83; (office) Fondation pour l'Etude et la Protection de la Mer et des Lacs, 1096 Cully, Switzerland. *T:* (021) 799 2565.

PICK, Charles Samuel; Managing Director, Heinemann Group of Publishers, 1979–85; Founder, Charles Pick Consultancy, 1985; Consultant to Wilbur Smith; *b* 22 March 1917; *s* of Samuel and Ethel Pick; *m* 1938, Hilda Beryl Hobbs; one *s* one *d*. *Educ:* Masonic School, Bushey. Started in publishing with Victor Gollancz, 1933; founder member, Michael Joseph Ltd, 1935. Served War, 1939–46; commnd RA, AA Command; apptd Staff Captain; served ALFSEA, India, Ceylon and Singapore. Jt Man. Director, Michael Joseph Ltd, 1959; resigned, 1962; joined William Heinemann Ltd as Man. Director, 1962; Director, Heinemann Group of Publishers, 1962; Director, Pan Books, 1968–85; Chairman: Secker & Warburg, 1973–80; William Heinemann, 1973–80; William Heinemann, Australia and South Africa, 1973–80; William Heinemann International, 1979–85; Heinemann Educational Books International, 1979–85; Heinemann Inc., 1980–85; Heinemann Distribution Ltd, 1980–85; Chm. and Pres., Heinemann Holdings Inc., 1980–85. Mem. Council, Publishers' Assoc., 1980–83. *Recreations:* walking, reading, theatre. *Address:* Littlecot, 28 Compton Road, Lindfield, Sussex RH16 2JZ *T:* Lindfield (0444) 482218; 3 Bryanston Place, W1H 7FN. *T:* 071–402 8043. *Clubs:* Savile, MCC.

PICKARD, Sir Cyril (Stanley), KCMG 1966 (CMG 1964); HM Diplomatic Service, retired; British High Commissioner in Nigeria, 1971–74; *b* 18 Sept. 1917; *s* of G. W. Pickard and Edith Pickard (*née* Humphrey), Sydenham; *m* 1st, 1941, Helen Elizabeth Strawson (*d* 1982); three *s* one *d* (and one *s* decd); 2nd, 1983, Mary Rosser (*née* Cozens-Hardy). *Educ:* Alleyn's Sch., Dulwich; New Coll. Oxford. 1st Class Hons Modern History, 1939. Asst Principal, Home Office, 1939. War of 1939–45: Royal Artillery, 1940–41, Captain; appointment in Office of Minister of State, Cairo, 1941–44 Principal, 1943; with UNRRA in Middle East and Germany, 1944–45; transf. to Commonwealth Relations Office, 1948; Office of UK High Comr in India, New Delhi, 1950; Local Asst Sec., Office of UK High Comr, Canberra, 1952–55; Commonwealth Relations Office, Head of South Asian Dept, 1955–58; Deputy High Commissioner for the UK in New Zealand, 1958–61; Asst Under Sec. of State, CRO, 1962–66 (Acting High Commissioner in Cyprus, 1964); British High Comr, Pakistan, 1966–71. Vice President: Commonwealth Trust; Parkinson's Disease Soc.; Pakistan Soc.; Tibet Soc. *Recreation:* gardening. *Address:* 3 Orwell Road, Norwich NR2 2ND.

PICKARD, Prof. Huia Masters, FDSRCS; Professor of Conservative Dentistry, University of London, 1963–74, now Emeritus; *b* 25 March 1909; *o s* of late Ernest Pickard and Sophie Elizabeth Robins; *m* 1945, Daphne Evelyn, *d* of Hugh F. Marriott; two *d*. *Educ:* Latymer Sch.; Royal Dental Hosp. of London Sch. of Dental Surgery; Charing Cross Hosp. MRCS, LRCP, FDSRCS. Private dental practice, pre-1940; EMS, East Grinstead, 1939. Served War, in RAMC, 8th Army (despatches), 1940–45. Dental practice and teaching, 1945; Dir, Dept of Conservative Dentistry, Royal Dental Hosp., and Consultant, 1955; Reader, London Univ., 1957–63; Dir of Dept of Restorative Dentistry, Royal Dental Hosp., 1965–74. Mem. Bd of Governors, St George's Hosp., 1969; First Pres., British Soc. for Restorative Dentistry, 1969; Pres., Odontological Section of Royal Soc. Med., 1971; Examr for Univs of London, Newcastle, Glasgow, Birmingham, Wales; also RCS. Governor, Latymer Sch., Edmonton, 1968–84 (Chm., 1980–83). Tomes Medal, BDA, 1983. *Publications:* Manual of Operative Dentistry, 1961, 6th edn 1990; contribs: Dental Record, Brit. Dental Jl, Internat. Dental Jl. *Address:* 14 Kingsdown, 115A Ridgway, Wimbledon, SW19 4RL. *T:* 081–879 1790.

PICKARD, (John) Michael, FCA; Chief Executive, Sears plc, since 1988 (Deputy Chief Executive, 1986–88); *b* 29 July 1932; *s* of John Stanley Pickard and Winifred Joan Pickard; *m* 1959, Penelope Jane (*née* Catterall); three *s* one *d*. *Educ:* Oundle School. Finance Dir, British Printing Corp., 1965–68; Man. Dir, Trusthouses Ltd/Trusthouse Forte Ltd, 1968–71; Founder Chm., Happy Eater Ltd, 1972–86; Chairman: Grattan plc, 1978–84; Courage Ltd and Imperial Brewing & Leisure Ltd, 1981–85. Director: Brown Shipley Hlgs, 1986–; Electra Investment Trust, 1989–; Nationwide Anglia Building Soc., 1991–. Chm. Council, Roedean Sch., 1980–91. Mem., Bd, BTA, 1968–71. Mem., Court of Assistants, Co. of Grocers. *Recreations:* cricket, squash, tennis, golf. *Address:* c/o Sears plc, 40 Duke Street W1A 2HP. *Clubs:* Pilgrims, MCC; Walton Heath Golf; Headley Cricket.

PICKAVANCE, Thomas Gerald, CBE 1965; MA, PhD; FRS 1976; Fellow, St Cross College, Oxford, 1967–84, now Emeritus; *b* 19 October 1915; *s* of William and Ethel Pickavance, Lancashire; *m* 1943, Alice Isobel (*née* Boulton); two *s* one *d*. *Educ:* Cowley School, St Helens; Univ. of Liverpool. BSc (Hons Phys) 1937; PhD 1940. Research Physicist, Tube Alloys Project, 1941–46; Lecturer in Physics, University of Liverpool, 1943–46; Atomic Energy Research Establishment, Harwell: Head of Cyclotron Group, 1946–54; Head of Accelerator Group, 1954–57; Deputy Head of General Physics Division, 1955–57; Dir, Rutherford High Energy Lab., SRC, 1957–69; Dir of Nuclear Physics, SRC, 1969–72. Chm., European Cttee for Future Accelerators, 1970–71. Hon. DSc, City Univ., 1969. *Publications:* papers and articles in learned journals on nuclear physics and particle accelerators. *Recreations:* motoring, travel, photography. *Address:* 3 Kingston Close, Abingdon, Oxon OX14 1ES. *T:* Abingdon (0235) 523934.

PICKEN, Dr Laurence Ernest Rowland, FBA 1973; Fellow of Jesus College, Cambridge, 1944–76, now Emeritus (Hon. Fellow, 1989); *b* 1909. *Educ:* Oldknow Road and Waverley Road, Birmingham; Trinity Coll., Cambridge. BA 1931; PhD 1935; ScD 1952. Asst Dir of Research (Zoology), Cambridge Univ., 1946–66; Asst Dir of Research (Oriental Music), Cambridge Univ., 1966–76. FIBiol. Hon. Fellow, SOAS, 1991. DUP *hc* 1988. Editor: Musica Asiatica, 1977–84; Music from the Tang Court, 1981–. *Publications:* The Organization of Cells and Other Organisms, 1960; Folk Musical Instruments of Turkey, 1975; contribs to many learned jls. *Address:* Jesus College, Cambridge CB5 8BL.

PICKERING, Sir Edward (Davies), Kt 1977; Executive Vice-Chairman, Times Newspapers Ltd, since 1982; Chairman, The Times Supplements Ltd, since 1989; *b* 4 May 1912; 3rd *s* of George and Louie Pickering; *m* 1st, 1936, Margaret Soutter (marr. diss., 1947); one *d*; 2nd, 1955, Rosemary Whitton; two *s* one *d*. *Educ:* Middlesbrough High Sch. Chief Sub-Editor Daily Mail, 1939. Served Royal Artillery 1940–44; Staff of Supreme Headquarters Allied Expeditionary Force, 1944–45. Managing Editor: Daily Mail, 1947–49; Daily Express, 1951–57; Editor, Daily Express, 1957–62; Dir, Beaverbrook Newspapers, 1956–64; Editorial Dir, The Daily Mirror Newspapers Ltd, 1964–68, Chm., 1968–70; Director: Scottish Daily Record and Sunday Mail Ltd, 1966–69; IPC, 1966–75; Times Newspapers Holdings Ltd, 1981–; William Collins Sons & Co. Ltd, 1981–89; Harper Collins Publishers Ltd, 1989–; Chairman: International Publishing Corporation Newspaper Div., 1968–70; IPC Magazines, 1970–74; Mirror Group Newspapers, 1975–77. Member: Press Council, 1964–69, 1970–82 (Vice-Chm., 1976–82); Press Complaints Commn, 1991–. Treasurer, Fédération Internationale de la Presse Periodique, 1971–75; Chm. Council, Commonwealth Press Union, 1977–86. Hon. Freeman, Stationers' and Newspaper Makers' Co., 1985. Master, Guild of St Bride, 1981–. Astor Award for distinguished service to Commonwealth Press, CPU, 1986. Hon. DLitt City, 1986. *Club:* Garrick.

PICKERING, Errol Neil, PhD; Director General, International Hospital Federation, since 1987; *b* 5 May 1938; *s* of Russell Gordon and Sylvia Mary Pickering. *Educ:* York Univ., Canada (BA Hons); Univ. of Toronto (DipHA); Univ. of New South Wales (PhD). Asst Administrator, St Michael's Hosp., Toronto, 1971–73; Executive Director: Aust. Council on Hosp. Standards, 1973–80; Aust. Hosp. Assoc., 1980–87. Pres., UNICEF Australia, 1984–86. *Publications:* many articles on hosp. and health policy issues. *Recreations:* classical music, tennis, bridge. *Address:* 4 Abbot's Place, NW6 4NP. *T:* 071–372 7181. *Club:* Royal Society of Medicine.

PICKERING, Ven. Fred; Archdeacon of Hampstead, 1974–84; Archdeacon Emeritus since 1984; *b* 18 Nov. 1919; *s* of Arthur and Elizabeth Pickering; *m* 1948, Mabel Constance Threlfall; one *s* one *d*. *Educ:* Preston Grammar Sch.; St Peter's Coll., Oxford; St Aidan's Theol Coll., Birkenhead. BA 1941 (PPE), MA 1945. Curate: St Andrew's, Leyland, 1943–46; St Mary's, Islington, 1946–48; Organising Sec. for Church Pastoral Aid Soc. in NE England, 1948–51; Vicar: All Saints, Burton-on-Trent, 1951–56; St John's, Carlisle, 1956–63; St Cuthbert's, Wood Green, 1963–74; Rural Dean of East Haringey, 1968–73; Exam. Chaplain to Bp of Edmonton, 1973–84. *Address:* 23 Broadgate Way, Warmington, near Peterborough, Cambs PE8 6UN. *T:* Oundle (0832) 280548.

PICKERING, Herbert Kitchener; Chief of Protocol, Government of Alberta, 1983–85; *b* 9 Feb. 1915; *s* of Herbert Pickering, Hull, and Ethel Bowman, Carlisle; *m* 1963, Florence Marion Carr; two *s* two *d*. *Educ:* Montreal; Bishop's Univ. (Business Admin); Cornell Univ. (Hotel Admin); Michigan State Univ. (Hotel and Business Admin). Canadian National Railways: Gen. Passenger Traffic Dept, Montreal, 1930; various cities in Canada and US; served War of 1939–45, RCAF; returned to CNR; assisted in creation and management of Maple Leaf Tour Dept, 1953–59; created Sales Dept for Canadian National Hotels in Western Canada and then for System, 1960–67; Man., Bessborough Hotel, Saskatoon, 1968; Gen. Man., Jasper Park Lodge, until 1973; Agent-Gen. for Alberta in London, 1973–80; opened Govt Office, Hong Kong, and served as Agent General, 1980–82; Senior Dir, International Operations, Edmonton, 1982–83. Charter Mem., Lion's International; Life Mem., Royal Canadian Legion, 1974 (Mem., 1946); Liveryman, Plaisterers' Co., 1980–; Freeman, City of London, 1978. Hon. Mem., Wheelwrights' Co., 1979. *Recreations:* golf, ski-ing, swimming, philately. *Address:* 3074 McMillan Road, Abbotsford, BC V2S 6A8, Canada. *Clubs:* East India and Sports, MCC; Kelowna Canadian, International Skal (Vancouver, BC).

PICKERING, Prof. John Frederick; Deputy President, Portsmouth Polytechnic, since 1991 (Vice-President (Business and Finance), 1988–90; acting President, 1990–91); *b* 26 Dec. 1939; *er s* of William Frederick and Jean Mary Pickering; *m* 1967, Jane Rosamund Day; two *d*. *Educ:* Slough Grammar Sch.; University Coll. London (BSc Econ; PhD; DSc Econ); MSc Manchester. In indust. market res., 1961–62; Lectr, Univ. of Durham, 1964–66, Univ. of Sussex, 1966–73; Sen. Directing Staff, Admin. Staff Coll., Henley, 1974–75. UMIST: Prof. of Industrial Economics, 1975–88; Vice-Principal, 1983–85; Dep. Principal, 1984–85; Dean, 1985–87. Mem., UGC Business and Management Studies sub-cttee, 1985–88. Dir, Staniland Hall Ltd, 1988–; Dir and Chm., Portsmouth Polytechnic Enterprise Ltd, 1989–. Mem., Gen. Synod of Church of England, 1980–90; Church Comr for England, 1983–90; Mem., Archbishop's Commn on Urban Priority Areas, 1983–85; Pres., BCMS-Crosslink (formerly BCMS), 1986–. Member: Council of Management, Consumers' Assoc., 1969–73, 1980–83; Retail Prices Index Adv. Cttee, 1974–; Monopolies and Mergers Commn, 1990–. *Publications:* Resale Price Maintenance in Practice, 1966; (jtly) The Small Firm in the Hotel and Catering Industry, 1971; Industrial Structure and Market Conduct, 1974; The Acquisition of Consumer Durables, 1977; (jtly) The

Economic Management of the Firm, 1984; papers and articles in learned jls in economics and management. *Recreations:* family life, music, cricket. *Address:* c/o Portsmouth Polytechnic, Ravelin House, Museum Road, Portsmouth PO1 2QQ. *T:* Portsmouth (0705) 843203. *Club:* Commonwealth Trust.

PICKERING, His Honour John Robertson; a Circuit Judge, 1972–84; *b* 8 Jan. 1925; *s* of late J. W. H. Pickering and Sarah Lilian Pickering (*née* Dixon); *m* 1951, Hilde (*widow* of E. M. Wright); one *s* two step *s*. *Educ:* Winchester; Magdalene Coll., Cambridge. Degree in Classics (wartime) and Law, MA. Served War, Lieut RNVR, Russia, Europe and Far East, 1942–47. Called to Bar, Inner Temple, 1949. Subseq. with Nat. Coal Bd and Dyson Bell & Co (Parliamentary Agents). Mem. Parliamentary Bar. Dep. Chm. of Pneumoconiosis, Byssinosis and Miscellaneous Diseases Benefit Bd, and Workmen's Compensation (Supplementation) Bd, 1970; apptd Dep. Chm. NE London Quarter Sessions, 1971.

PICKERING, Richard Edward Ingram; His Honour Judge Richard Pickering; a Circuit Judge, since 1981; *b* 16 Aug. 1929; *s* of late Richard and Dorothy Pickering; *m* 1962, Jean Margaret Eley; two *s*. *Educ:* Birkenhead Sch.; Magdalene Coll., Cambridge (MA). Called to the Bar, Lincoln's Inn, 1953; has practised on Northern Circuit, 1955–81; a Recorder of the Crown Court, 1977–81. Admitted as advocate in Manx Courts (Summerland Fire Inquiry), 1973–74. Councillor, Hoylake UDC, 1961–64; Legal Chm., Min. of Pensions and Nat. Insurance Tribunal, Liverpool, 1967–77; pt-time Chm., Liverpool Industrial Tribunal, 1977–79; Nominated Judicial Mem., Merseyside Mental Health Rev. Tribunal, 1984 (Legal Mem., 1967–79; Regional Chm., 1979–81); Northern Circuit Rep., Cttee, Council of Circuit Judges, 1984–89. *Recreations:* walking, gardening, study of military history. *Address:* c/o The Crown Court, Liverpool. *Clubs:* United Oxford & Cambridge University; Athenæum (Liverpool); Union (Cambridge).

PICKERING, Thomas Reeve; Ambassador and United States Permanent Representative to the United Nations, since 1989; *b* Orange, NJ, 5 Nov. 1931; *s* of Hamilton R. Pickering and Sarah C. (*née* Chasteney); *m* 1955, Alice J. Stover; one *s* one *d*. *Educ:* Bowdoin Coll. (AB); Fletcher Sch. of Law and Diplomacy (MA); Univ. of Melbourne (MA). Served to Lt-Comdr, USNR, 1956–59. Joined US For. Service, 1959; For. Affairs Officer, Arms Control and Disarmament Agency, 1961; Political Advr, US Delegn to 18 Nation Disarmament Conf., Geneva, 1962–64; Consul, Zanzibar, 1965–67; Counselor, Dep. Chief of Mission, Amer. Embassy, Dar-es-Salaam, 1967–69; Dep. Dir Bureau, Politico-Mil. Affairs, State Dept, 1969–73; Special Asst to Sec. of State and Exec. Sec., Dept of State, 1973–74; Amb. to Jordan, 1974–78; Asst Sec. for Bureau of Oceans, Internat. Environmental and Sci. Affairs, Washington, 1978–81; Ambassador: to Nigeria, 1981–83; to El Salvador, 1983–85; to Israel, 1986–88. Mem. Council, For. Relns, IISS, 1973–. Phi Beta Kappa. Hon. LLD: Bowdoin Coll., 1984; Atlantic Union Coll., 1990; Tufts Univ., 1990. *Address:* US Permanent Representative to the United Nations, United States Mission to the United Nations, 799 United Nations Plaza, New York, NY 10017, USA. *T:* (212) 415–4000. *Club:* Cosmos (Washington).

PICKETT, Thomas, CBE 1972; retired,1986; Senior Regional Chairman, North West Area, Industrial Tribunals (England and Wales), 1975–85 (Chairman for Manchester, 1972); *b* 22 November 1912; *s* of John Joseph Pickett and Caroline Pickett (*née* Brunt); *m* 1940, Winifred Irene Buckley, *yr d* of late Benjamin Buckley; no *c*. *Educ:* Glossop Grammar School; London University (LLB). Barrister-at-Law, Lincoln's Inn; called to Bar, 1948. Served in Army, 1939–50, retiring with permanent rank of Major. Dep. Asst Dir of Army Legal Services, 1948; Dist Magistrate, Gold Coast, 1950; Resident Magistrate, Northern Rhodesia 1955; Sen. Res. Magistrate, 1956; Acting Puisne Judge, 1960; Puisne Judge, High Courts of Northern Rhodesia, 1961–64, Zambia, 1964–69; Justice of Appeal, 1969–71, Acting Chief Justice, 1970, Judge President, Court of Appeal, 1971, Zambia. Chairman: Tribunal on Detainees, 1967; Electoral Commn (Supervisory); Delimitation Commn for Zambia, 1968; Referendum Commn, 1969; Local Govt Commn, 1970. *Recreations:* walking, swimming. *Address:* Bryn Awelon, Aber Place, Craigside, Llandudno, Gwynedd LL30 3AR. *T:* Llandudno (0492) 44244. *Clubs:* Royal Over-Seas League; Victoria, County (Llandudno).

PICKFORD, David Michael, FRICS; Chairman: Lilliput Property Unit Trust, since 1984; Exeter Park Estates, since 1986; Compco Holdings PLC, since 1987; Gulliver Developments Property Unit Trust, since 1987; *b* 25 Aug. 1926; *s* of Aston Charles Corpe Pickford and Gladys Ethel Pickford; *m* 1956, Elizabeth Gwendoline Hooson; one *s* two *d*. *Educ:* Emanuel Sch., London; Coll. of Estate Management. FRICS 1953. Hillier Parker May & Rowden, 1943–46; LCC, 1946–48; London Investment & Mortgage Co., 1948–57; Haslemere Estates plc, 1957–86: Man. Dir, 1968–83; Chm., 1983–86; Dir, City & Metropolitan Building Soc., 1986–90. President: London Dist, The Boys' Bde, 1967–; Christians in Property, 1978–; Chairman: Mission to London, 1982–; Drug and Alcohol Foundn, 1987– (Vice-Pres., 1990–); Prison Fellowship England & Wales, 1989–; Dir, Youth with a Mission, 1986–; Trustee, CARE Trust, 1987–. *Recreations:* sheep farming, youth work, gardening. *Address:* 33 Grosvenor Square, Mayfair, W1X 9LL. *T:* 071–493 1156; Elm Tree Farm, Mersham, near Ashford, Kent TN25 7HS. *T:* Aldington (023372) 0200, *Fax:* Aldington (023372) 0522.

PICKFORD, Prof. (Lillian) Mary, DSc; FRS 1966; Professor, Department of Physiology, University of Edinburgh, 1966–72 (Reader in Physiology, 1952–66); retired 1972, now Emeritus Professor; *b* 14 Aug. 1902; *d* of Herbert Arthur Pickford and Lillian Alice Minnie Wintle. *Educ:* Wycombe Abbey Sch.; Bedford and University Colls, Univ. of London. BSc (1st cl., Gen.) 1924; BSc (2nd cl., Physiology Special) 1925; MSc (Physiology) 1926; MRCS, LRCP 1933; DSc London 1951. FRSE 1954; FRCPE 1977. House Physician and Casualty Officer, Stafford Gen. Infirmary, 1935; Jun. Beit Memorial Research Fellow, 1936–39; Lectr, Dept of Physiology, Univ. of Edinburgh, 1939; Personal Chair, Dept of Physiology, Univ. of Edinburgh, 1966. Special Prof. of Endocrinology, Nottingham Univ., 1973–83. Fellow, University Coll., London, 1968–. Hon. DSc Heriot-Watt, 1991. *Publications:* The Central Role of Hormones, 1969; papers in Jl Physiology, British Jl Pharmacology, Jl Endocrinology. *Recreations:* walking, travel, painting. *Address:* 12 Ormidale Terrace, Edinburgh EH12 6EQ.

PICKFORD, Prof. Mary; *see* Pickford, Prof. L. M.

PICKLES, His Honour James; a Circuit Judge, 1976–91; *b* 18 March 1925. Practised at Bradford, 1949–76; a Recorder of the Crown Court, 1972–76. *Publication:* Straight from the Bench, 1987. *Address:* Hazelwood, Halifax HX3 0BA.

PICKTHORN, Sir Charles (William Richards), 2nd Bt *cr* 1959; *b* 3 March 1927; *s* of Rt Hon. Sir Kenneth William Murray Pickthorn, 1st Bt, and Nancy Catherine Lewis (*d* 1982), *d* of late Lewis Matthew Richards; *S* father, 1975; *m* 1951, Helen Antonia, *o d* of late Sir James Mann, KCVO; one *s* two *d*. *Educ:* King's Coll. Sch., Cambridge; Eton; Corpus Christi Coll., Cambridge (Major Schol., BA). Served RNVR, 1945–48. Called to the Bar, Middle Temple, 1952. Dir, J. Henry Schroder Wagg & Co. Ltd, 1971–79. Occasional journalism. Contested (C) Hemsworth Div., W Riding of Yorks, 1966. Treas., Salisbury Gp, 1978–. Chm., R. S. Surtees Soc., 1980–. *Recreations:* smoking tobacco, sailing, reading. *Heir:* *s* James Francis Mann Pickthorn, *b* 18 Feb. 1955. *Address:* Manor House, Nunney, near Frome, Somerset. *T:* Nunney (037384) 574; 3 Hobury Street, SW10. *T:* 071–352 2795.

PICKUP, David Cunliffe; Director General, Sports Council, since 1988; *b* 17 Sept. 1936; *s* of Robert and Florence Pickup; *m* 1960, Patricia Moira Aileen (*née* Neill); three *s*. *Educ:* Bacup and Rawtenstall Grammar Sch. Min. of Education, 1955–63; MPBW, 1964–71 (incl. periods as Pvte Sec. to four Ministers); Department of the Environment: Prin. Pvte Sec. to Minister for Housing and Construction, 1971–72; Asst Sec., 1972; Housing, 1972–75; Personnel, 1975–77; Under Sec., 1977; Regl Dir, Northern Reg., 1977–80; Housing, 1980–84; Local Govt, 1984–85; Dep. Sec., Assoc. of Dist Councils, 1986–88. *Recreations:* reading, music, sport, walking. *Address:* 15 Sandford Road, Bromley, Kent BR2 9AL. *T:* 081–466 5433.

PICKUP, David Francis William; Principal Assistant Treasury Solicitor, and Legal Adviser to the Ministry of Defence, since 1991; *b* 28 May 1953; *s* of Joseph and Muriel Pickup; *m* 1975, Anne Elizabeth Round. *Educ:* Poole Grammar Sch.; Polytechnic of Central London (Univ. of London External LLB Hons). Called to the Bar, Lincoln's Inn, 1976. Joined Treasury Solicitor's Dept as Legal Asst, 1978, Sen. Legal Asst, 1981; Grade 5 1987; Estabt Finance and Security Officer, 1988–90; Grade 3, Chancery Litigation Div., 1990. *Recreations:* playing and watching cricket, ski-ing, listening to music, food and wine, travel. *Address:* Queen Anne's Chambers, 28 Broadway, SW1H 9JS. *T:* 071–218 0723. *Club:* Pyrford Cricket.

PICKUP, Ronald Alfred; actor; *b* 7 June 1940; *s* of Eric and Daisy Pickup; *m* 1964, Lans Traverse, USA; one *s* one *d*. *Educ:* King's Sch., Chester; Leeds Univ. (BA); Royal Academy of Dramatic Art. Repertory, Leicester, 1964; Royal Court, 1964 and 1965–66; National Theatre, 1965, 1966–73, 1977: appearances include: Rosalind, in all-male As You Like It, 1967; Richard II, 1972; Edmund, in Long Day's Journey into Night, 1971; Cassius, in Julius Caesar, 1977; Philip Madras, in The Madras House, 1977; Norman, in Norman Conquests, Globe, 1974; Play, Royal Court, 1976; Hobson's Choice, Lyric, Hammersmith, 1981; Astrov, in Uncle Vanya, Haymarket, 1982; Allmers in Little Eyolf, Lyric, Hammersmith, 1985; Gayev, in The Cherry Orchard, Aldwych, 1989; *films:* Three Sisters, 1969; Day of the Jackal, 1972; Joseph Andrews, 1976; 39 Steps, Zulu Dawn, 1978; Nijinsky, 1979; Never Say Never Again, John Paul II, 1983; Eleni, Camille (remake), 1984; The Mission, 1985; The Fourth Protocol, 1986; *television:* series and serials: Dragon's Opponent, 1973; Jennie, Fight Against Slavery, 1974; Tropic, 1979; Life of Giuseppe Verdi, 1982; Wagner, 1982; Life of Einstein, 1983; Moving, 1984; The Fortunes of War, 1987; Behaving Badly, 1988; other: The Philanthropist, Ghost Trio, The Discretion of Dominic Ayres, 1977; Memories, Henry VIII, 1978; England's Green and Pleasant Land, Christ Hero, 1979; The Letter, Ivanhoe, 1981; Orwell on Jura, 1983; The Rivals, 1986; The Attic, Chekov in Yalta, 1988; A Murder of Quality, 1990; Absolute Hell, 1991; The War that Never Ends, 1991. *Recreations:* listening to music, walking, reading.

PICTET, François-Charles; Ambassador of Switzerland to the Netherlands, since 1989; *b* Geneva, 21 July 1929; *e s* of Charles Pictet, Geneva, and Elisabeth (*née* Decazes), France; *m* 1st, 1954, Elisabeth Choisy (*d* 1980), Geneva; three *s*; 2nd, 1983, Countess Marie-Thérèse Althann, Austria. *Educ:* College Calvin, Geneva; Univ. of Geneva (Faculty of Law). Called to the Swiss Bar, 1954. Joined Swiss Federal Dept of Foreign Affairs, 1956; Attaché, Vienna, 1957; Sec., Moscow, 1958–60; 1st Sec., Ankara, 1961–66; Dep. Dir, Internat. Orgns, Dept of For. Affairs, Berne, 1966–75; Minister Plenipotentiary, 1975; Ambassador to Canada and (non-resident) to the Bahamas, 1975–79; Ambassador, Perm. Rep. to Internat. Orgns in Geneva, 1980–84; Ambassador to UK, 1984–89. *Address:* Swiss Embassy, Lange Voorhout 42, The Hague, 2514 EE, Netherlands. *T:* (70) 64 28 31.

PICTON, Jacob Glyndwr, (Glyn Picton), CBE 1972; Senior Lecturer in Industrial Economics, University of Birmingham, 1947–79; *b* Aberdare, 28 Feb. 1912; *s* of David Picton; *m* 1939, Rhiannon Mary James (Merch Megan), LRAM, ARCM (*d* 1978); one *s* one *d*. *Educ:* Aberdare Boys' County Sch.; Birmingham Univ. (MCom). Chance Bros Ltd, 1933–47, Asst Sec. 1945–47. Pres., W Midland Rent Assessment Panel, 1965–72 (Chm. Cttee 1973–81); Governor, United Birmingham Hosps, 1953–74; Chm., Children's Hosp., 1956–66; Teaching Hosps Rep. Professional and Techn. Whitley Council, 1955–61; Mem., Birmingham Regional Hosp. Bd, 1958–74 (Vice-Chm. 1971–74); Mem., NHS Nat. Staff Cttee, 1964–73 (Vice-Chm. 1968–73); Chm., Birmingham Hosp. Region Staff Cttee, 1964–74; Vice-Chm., W Mids RHA, 1973–79 (Mem., 1979–82); Vice-Chm., NHS Nat. Staff Cttee (Admin. and Clerical), 1973–82; NHS Nat. Assessor (Admin), 1973. Chm., Birmingham Industrial Therapy Assoc. Ltd, 1965–79 and W Bromwich Industrial Therapy Assoc. Ltd, 1969–79; Indep. Mem., Estate Agents Council, 1967–69; Chm. of Wages Councils, 1953–82; Dep. Chm., Commn of Inquiry concerning Sugar Confectionery and Food Preserving Wages Council, 1961; Chm., Commn of Inquiry concerning Licensed Residential Estabts and Restaurants Wages Council, 1963–64; sole Comr of Inquiry into S Wales Coalfield Dispute, 1965; Dep. Chm., Commn of Inquiry concerning Industrial and Staff Canteens Wages Council, 1975; Independent Arbitrator, Lock Industry, 1976–81. Has donated working papers: on Picton family to Nat. Liby of Wales; on academic and public service to Univ. of Birmingham. *Publications:* various articles and official reports. *Recreations:* music, gardening, Pembrokeshire history. *Address:* 54 Chesterwood Road, Kings Heath, Birmingham B13 0QE. *T:* 021–444 3959.

PIDDINGTON, Philip Michael, CBE 1988; HM Diplomatic Service, retired; Counsellor, Foreign and Commonwealth Office, 1987–90; *b* 27 March 1931; *s* of Percy Howard Piddington and Florence Emma (*née* Pearson); *m* 1955, Sylvia Mary Price; one *s* one *d*. *Educ:* Waverley Grammar Sch., Birmingham. Served HM Forces, 1949–51. Entered Min. of Works, 1947; FO, 1952; Jedda, 1956; Tokyo, 1962–66; First Sec., Lagos, 1969–71; Consul: NY, 1971–73; Istanbul, 1973–77; First Sec., FCO, 1978–83; Counsellor and Consul-Gen., Brussels, 1983–87. *Recreations:* riding, walking, photography. *Address:* The Pump House, St Mary's Road, East Claydon, Bucks MK18 2NA. *T:* Aylesbury (0296) 712302.

PIDGEON, Sir John (Allan Stewart), Kt 1989; Chairman, since 1980, and Managing Director, since 1960, F. A. Pidgeon & Son and associated companies; *b* 15 July 1926; *s* of Frederick Allan Pidgeon and Margaret Ellen Pidgeon, MBE; *m* 1952, Sylvia Dawn; one *s* four *d*. *Educ:* Church of England Grammar Sch., Brisbane. Fellow, Aust. Inst. of Building. Joined F. A. Pidgeon & Son Pty, 1946. Director: Suncorp Building Soc., 1976–; Folkestone Ltd, 1985–. Chm., Builders' Registration Bd of Qld, 1985–. Pres., Qld Master Builders' Assoc., 1970–72 (Trustee, 1978–). Chm., Salvation Army Adv. Bd., 1988–. *Recreations:* ski-ing, tennis, swimming. *Address:* 43 Beesley Street, West End, Brisbane, Qld 4101, Australia. *T:* 844 8001. *Clubs:* Brisbane, Tattersalls (Brisbane).

PIËCH, Ferdinand; Chairman, Board of Management, Audi AG, since 1988; *b* Vienna, 17 April 1937; *s* of Dr jur Anton Piëch and Louise (*née* Porsche). *Educ:* in Switzerland; Tech. Univ. of Zurich. Mem., Management Bd i/c R and D, Audi NSU Auto Union AG/Audi AG, 1975–88. Dr *hc* Vienna Technical Univ., 1984. *Address:* c/o Audi Aktiengesellschaft, Postfach 100 220, W-8070 Ingolstadt, Germany. *T:* 0841–89–3300.

PIEŃKOWSKI, Jan Michal; author and illustrator, since 1958; Founder Director, Gallery Five Ltd, 1961; *b* 8 Aug. 1936; *s* of late Jerzy Dominik Pieńkowski and of Wanda Maria Pieńkowska. *Educ:* Cardinal Vaughan Sch., London; King's Coll., Cambridge (MA Classics and English). Art Dir, J. Walter Thompson, William Collins, and Time and Tide, London, 1958–61. Work includes graphics and murals, posters and greeting cards, children's TV, and book illustration. *Stage designs:* Meg and Mog Show, 1981–88; Beauty and the Beast, Royal Opera House, 1986; Théâtre de Complicité, 1988. Kate Greenaway Medal, Library Assoc., 1972 and 1979. *Publications:* illustrator: The Kingdom under the Sea, 1971; Meg and Mog series, 1973–90; Tale of a One Way Street, 1978; Ghosts and Bogles, 1985; Past Eight O'Clock, 1986; A Foot in the Grave, 1989, etc; illustrator/author: Nursery series, 1973–91; Haunted House, 1979; Robot, 1981; Dinner Time, 1981; Christmas, 1984; Little Monsters, 1986; Small Talk, 1988; Easter, 1989; Fancy That, 1990; Christmas Kingdom, 1991; Phone Book, 1991. *Recreations:* movies, ski-ing, gardening, painting. *Address:* Oakgates, 45 Lonsdale Road, Barnes, SW13 9JR. *Clubs:* Chelsea Arts, Polish Hearth.

PIERCE, Francis William, MA (Belfast and Dublin); Hughes Professor of Spanish, University of Sheffield, 1953–80, now Emeritus Professor; Dean of the Faculty of Arts, 1964–67; *b* 21 Sept. 1915; *s* of late Robert Pierce, JP and Catherine Ismay Pierce; *m* 1944, Mary Charlotte Una, *o d* of late Rev. J. C. Black, Asyut, Upper Egypt; three *s*. *Educ:* Royal Belfast Academical Institution; Queen's University, Belfast. BA, 1st Cl. Hons, Spanish studies, QUB, 1938; Postgrad. Schol., Columbia Univ., New York, 1938–39; MA, QUB, 1939; Asst Lectr in Spanish, Univ. of Liverpool, 1939–40. Dep. to Prof. of Spanish, TCD, 1940–45; MA *jure officii*, Univ. of Dublin, 1943; Hughes Lectr in Spanish, Univ. of Sheffield, 1946. Visiting Professor: Brown Univ., Providence, RI, 1968; Case Western Reserve Univ., Cleveland, O, 1968. President: Anglo-Catalan Soc., 1955–57; Assoc. of Hispanists of GB and Ireland, 1971–73. Commander, Orden de Isabel la Católica (Spain), 1986. *Publications:* The Heroic Poem of the Spanish Golden Age: Selections, chosen with Introduction and Notes, 1947; Hispanic Studies: Review and Revision, 1954; (ed) Hispanic Studies in Honour of I. González Llubera, 1959; La poesía épica del siglo de oro, 1961 (Madrid), 2nd edn 1968; The Historie of Aravcana, transcribed with introd. and notes, 1964; (ed with C. A. Jones) Actas del Primer Congreso Internacional de Hispanistas, 1964; (ed) Two Cervantes Short Novels, 1970, 2nd edn 1976; (ed) La Cristiada by Diego de Hojeda, 1971; (ed) Luís de Camões: Os Lusíadas, 1973, 2nd edn 1981; Amadís de Gaula, 1976; Alonso de Ercilla y Zúñiga, 1984; (ed) Repertorio de Hispanistas de Gran Bretaña e Irlanda, 1984; Asociación Internacional de Hispanistas: fundación e historia, 1986; articles and reviews in Hispanic Review, Mod. Language Review, Bulletin of Hispanic Studies, Bulletin Hispanique, Ocidente, Estudis Romànics, Quaderni Ibero-Americani. *Address:* 357 Fulwood Road, Sheffield S10 3BQ. *T:* Sheffield (0742) 664239.

PIERCE, Hugh Humphrey; *b* 13 Oct. 1931; *s* of Dr Gwilym Pierce, Abercynon, Glam; *m* 1958, Rachel Margaret Procter; two *s*. *Educ:* Clifton; King's Coll., Univ. of London. LLB Hons 1954; Pres. Faculty of Laws Soc.; Pres. Union. Called to Bar, Lincoln's Inn, 1955. Diploma Personnel Management, 1962; MIPM 1963. Army Service, 2nd Lieut Intell. Corps (Cyprus), 1955–57; Kodak Ltd, legal and personnel work, 1957–63; joined BBC, 1963, personnel and industrial relations; Admin. Officer, Local Radio, 1967–68; Local Radio Develt Manager, 1968–69; General Manager, Local Radio, 1970–74; Asst Controller, Staff Admin, 1974–78; Asst Controller, Employment Policy and Appts, 1978–80. Chm., First Framework Ltd, 1988–; Member: Indep. Cttee for Supervision of Telephone Information Standards, 1987–; Indep. Manpower Commn, Coll. of Occupational Therapists, 1988–89; Exec. Cttee, Howard League, 1979–90; Treas., Prisoners' Advice and Law Service, 1986–89; Member: Justice; Amnesty; Trustee: Community Develt Trust; Nat. Council for the Welfare of Prisoners Abroad. *Recreations:* chamber music, narrow boats. *Address:* 11 Wood Lane, Highgate, N6 5UE. *T:* 081–444 6001; Pant y Bryn, Llanwnog, Caersws, Powys. *T:* Newtown (0686) 688229.

PIERCE, Rt. Rev. Reginald James, Hon. DD (Winnipeg), 1947; retired; *b* 1909; *s* of James Reginald Pierce and Clara (*née* Whitehand) Plymouth; *m* 1932, Ivy Bell, *d* of Edward and Lucy Jackson, Saskatoon, Canada; one *d*. *Educ:* University of Saskatchewan (BA 1931); Emmanuel Coll., Saskatoon (LTh 1932); Univ. of London (BD 1942). Deacon, 1932; priest, 1934; Curate of Colinton, 1932–33; Priest-in-charge, 1933–34; Rector and Rural Dean of Grande Prairie, 1934–38; Rector of South Saanich, 1938–41; Rector of St Barnabas, Calgary, 1941–43; Canon of St John's Cathedral, Winnipeg, and Warden of St John's Coll., 1943–50; Priest-in-charge of St Barnabas, Winnipeg, 1946–50; Bishop of Athabasca, 1950–74; Acting Rector: All Saints, Victoria, BC, 1975–76; St David's, Victoria, BC, 1976–78. Examining Chaplain: to Bishop of Athabasca, 1935–38; to Archbishop of Rupertsland, 1943–50. *Address:* 1735 Green Oaks Terrace, Victoria, BC V8S 2A9, Canada.

PIERCY, family name of **Baron Piercy.**

PIERCY, 3rd Baron *cr* 1945, of Burford; **James William Piercy;** *b* 19 Jan. 1946; *s* of 2nd Baron Piercy and Oonagh Lavinia (*d* 1990), *d* of late Major Edward John Lake Baylay, DSO; *S* father, 1981. *Educ:* Shrewsbury; Edinburgh Univ. (BSc 1968). AMIEE; ACCA. *Heir:* *b* Hon. Mark Edward Pelham Piercy [*b* 30 June 1953; *m* 1979, Vivien Angela, *d* of His Honour Judge Evelyn Faithfull Monier-Williams, *qv*; one *s* three *d*]. *Address:* 13 Arnold Mansions, Queen's Club Gardens, W14 9RD.

PIERCY, Hon. Joanna Elizabeth; *see* Turner, Hon. J. E.

PIERCY, Hon. Penelope Katherine, CBE 1968; Under-Secretary, Ministry of Technology, 1965–68; *b* 15 Apr. 1916; *d* of 1st Baron Piercy, CBE. *Educ:* St Paul's Girls' School; Somerville College, Oxford. War of 1939–45, various appointments, Military Intelligence. Foreign Office, 1945–47; Economist, Colonial Development Corp., 1948–54; Department of Scientific and Industrial Research, 1955–65 (Sen. Prin. Scientific Officer, 1960). *Address:* Charlton Cottage, Tarrant Rushton, Blandford Forum, Dorset DT11 8SD.

PIERRE, Abbé; (Henri Antoine Grouès); Officier de la Légion d'Honneur, 1980; French priest; Founder of the Companions of Emmaüs; *b* Lyon, 5 Aug. 1912; 5th *c* of Antoine Grouès, Soyeux. *Educ:* Collège des Jésuites, Lyon. Entered Capuchin Monastery, 1930; studied at Capuchin seminary, Crest, Drôme, and Faculté de Théologie, Lyon. Secular priest, St Joseph Basilica, Grenoble. Served war of 1939–45 (Officier de la Légion d'Honneur, Croix de Guerre, Médaille de la Résistance); Alsatian and Alpine fronts; Vicar of the Cathedral, Grenoble; assumed name of Abbé Pierre and joined resistance movement, 1942; Chaplain of French Navy at Casablanca, 1944; of whole Free French Navy, 1945. Elected (Indep.) to 1st Constituent Assembly of 4th French Republic, 1945; elected as candidate of Mouvement Républicain Populaire to 2nd Constituent Assembly; re-elected 1946; contested (Indep.), 1951. Président de l'Exécutif du Mouvement Universel pour une Confédération Mondiale, 1947–51. Founded the Companions of Emmaüs, a movement to provide a roof for the "sanslogis" of Paris, 1949. *Publications:* 23 Mois de Vie Clandestine; L'Abbé Pierre vous Parle; Vers l'Homme; Feuilles Eparses; Emmaüs ou Venger l'homme. *Address:* 2 avenue de la Liberté, 94220 Charenton-le-Pont, Val de Marne, France. *T:* 368.62.44.

PIERS, Sir Charles Robert Fitzmaurice, 10th Bt, *cr* 1660; Lt-Comdr RCNVR; *b* 30 Aug. 1903; *s* of Sir Charles Piers, 9th Bt, and Hester Constance (Stella) (*d* 1936), *e d* of late S. R. Brewis of Ibstone House, Ibstone; *S* father, 1945; *m* 1936, Ann Blanche Scott (*d* 1975), *o d* of late Capt. Thomas Ferguson (The Royal Highlanders); one *s* (one *d* decd). *Educ:* RN Colleges, Osborne and Dartmouth. Served European War, 1939–45. *Heir:* *s* James Desmond Piers, [*b* 24 July 1947; *m* 1975, Sandra Mae Dixon; one *s* one *d*]. *Address:* PO Box 748, Duncan, British Columbia V9L 3Y1, Canada.

PIERS, Rear-Adm. Desmond William, DSC 1943; CM 1982; CD; RCN, retd; Agent General of Nova Scotia in the United Kingdom and Europe, 1977–79; *b* 12 June 1913; *s* of William Harrington Piers and Florence Maud Piers (*née* O'Donnell), MD; *m* 1941, Janet, *d* of Dr and Mrs Murray Macneill, Halifax, NS; one step *d*. *Educ:* Halifax County Acad.; RMC of Canada; RN Staff Coll.; Nat. Defence Coll. of Canada. Joined RCN as cadet, 1932; CO, HMC Destroyer Restigouche, and Sen. Officer, Fourth Canadian Escort Gp on N Atlantic convoy routes, 1941–43 (DSC); CO, HMC Destroyer Algonquin with Brit. Home Fleet, Scapa Flow, and participated in invasion of Normandy and convoys to N Russia, 1944–45, Comdr 1945; Exec. Officer, HMC Aircraft Carrier Magnificent (Comdr), 1947–48; Dir, Naval Plans and Ops, Naval Headquarters, Ottawa (Captain), 1949–50; Asst COS (Personnel and Admin.) to SACLANT, 1952–53; CO, HMC Cruiser Quebec, 1955–56; Sen. Canadian Offr Afloat (Atlantic), 1956–57; Comdt, RMC Canada, and Hon. ADC to the Governor General (Cdre), 1957–60; Asst Chief of Naval Staff (Plans), Naval HQ, 1960–62; Chm., Can. Def. Liaison Staff, Washington DC, and Can. Rep. on NATO Mil. Cttee (Rear-Adm.), 1962–66; retd 1967. Hon. Life Mem., Nat. Trust for Scotland, 1984. Hon. DScMil, RMC of Canada, 1978. Freeman of City of London, 1978; KCLJ 1989. *Recreations:* golf, tennis, figure skating, photography. *Address:* The Quarter Deck, Chester, Nova Scotia B0J 1J0, Canada. *T:* 902–275–4462. *Clubs:* Halifax (Halifax); Halifax Golf and Country, Chester Golf, Chester Tennis, Chester Curling (Nova Scotia).

PIGGOTT, Donald James; Director-General, British Red Cross Society, 1980–85; *b* 1 Sept. 1920; *s* of James Piggott and Edith Piggott (*née* Tempest); *m* 1974, Kathryn Courtenay-Evans (*née* Eckford). *Educ:* Bradford Grammar School; Christ's College, Cambridge (MA); London School of Economics. Served Army in NW Europe and India, 1941–46. PA to Finance and Supply Director, London Transport, 1947–50; Shell-Mex and BP Ltd, 1951–58; Manager Development Div., Marketing Dept, British Petroleum Co. Ltd, 1958–73; BRCS: Dir, Internat. Affairs, 1973; Head of Internat. Div., 1975; Asst Dir-Gen. International, 1980. Member: Central Appeals Adv. Cttee, BBC and IBA, 1980–83; Jt Cttee, St John and Red Cross, 1980–; Open Sect., RSocMed, 1982–; Dep. Pres., Suffolk Br., BRCS, 1987–. Liveryman, Co. of Carmen, 1988–. OStJ 1983. *Recreations:* music, theatre. *Address:* Beech Tree House, The Green, Tostock, Bury St Edmunds, Suffolk IP30 9NY. *T:* Beyton (0359) 70589. *Club:* City Livery.

PIGGOTT, Maj.-Gen. Francis James Claude, CB 1963; CBE 1961; DSO 1945; *b* Tokyo, Japan, 11 Oct. 1910; *s* of late Maj.-Gen. F. S. G. Piggott, CB, DSO; *m* 1940, Muriel Joan, *d* of late Wilfred E. Cottam, Rotherham, Yorks; one *s* one *d*. *Educ:* Cheltenham; RMC Sandhurst. 2nd Lieut The Queen's Royal Regt, 1931; Language Officer, Japan, 1935–37; Captain, 1939; served 1939–45 in France (despatches), New Zealand, India and Burma (DSO); in Japan, UK and Egypt (OBE and Bt Lt-Col), 1946–52; attended 1st Course, Joint Services Staff Coll., 1947; Lt-Col comdg 1st Bn The Queen's Royal Regt, 1952, BAOR and Malaya; Colonel, War Office, 1954; Comd 161 Infantry Bde (TA), 1956; Dep. Director of Military Intelligence, War Office (Brigadier), 1958; Major-General, 1961; Assistant Chief of Staff (Intelligence), SHAPE, 1961–64; retired, 1964; served in Civil Service (Security), 1965–75. Col, The Queen's Royal Surrey Regt, 1964–66; Dep. Col (Surrey) The Queen's Regt, 1967–69. *Recreations:* cricket and foreign travel. *Address:* Pondside, Quay Lane, Kirby-le-Soken, Essex CO13 0DP. *T:* Frinton-on-Sea (0255) 679303. *Clubs:* Army and Navy, Free Foresters.

PIGGOTT, Lester Keith; jockey, 1948–85, and since 1990; trainer, 1985–87; *b* 5 Nov. 1935; *s* of Keith Piggott and Iris Rickaby; *m* 1960, Susan Armstrong; two *d*. Selection of races won: the Derby (9 times): 1954 (on Never Say Die); 1957 (on Crepello); 1960 (on St Paddy); 1968 (on Sir Ivor); 1970 (on Nijinsky); 1972 (on Roberto); 1976 (on Empery); 1977 (on The Minstrel); 1983 (on Teenoso); St Leger (8 times); The Oaks (6 times); 2,000 guineas (4 times); 1,000 guineas (twice). In many seasons 1955–85 he rode well over 100 winners a year, in this country alone; rode 4,000th winner in Britain, 14 Aug. 1982; Champion Jockey 11 times, 1960, 1964–71, 1981, 1982; rode frequently in France; won Prix de l'Arc de Triomphe on Rheingold, 1973, on Alleged, 1977 and 1978; won Washington, DC, International on Sir Ivor, 1968 (first time since 1922 an English Derby winner raced in USA), on Karabas, 1969, on Argument, 1980. *Relevant publication:* Lester, the Official Biography, by Dick Francis, 1986. *Recreations:* swimming, water skiing, golf. *Address:* Florizel, Newmarket, Suffolk. *T:* Newmarket (0638) 662584.

PIGGOTT, Prof. Stuart, CBE 1972; FBA 1953; Abercromby Professor of Prehistoric Archæology, University of Edinburgh, 1946–77; *b* 28 May 1910; *s* of G. H. O. Piggott. *Educ:* Churchers Coll., Petersfield; St John's Coll., Oxford (Hon. Fellow, 1979). On staff on Royal Commn on Ancient Monuments (Wales), 1929–34; Asst Dir of Avebury excavations, 1934–38; from 1939 in ranks and later as Intelligence Officer in Army in charge of military air photograph interpretation, South-East Asia. Conducted archæological excavations in southern England and carried out research on European prehistory up to 1942; in India, 1942–45; studied Oriental prehistory. FRSE; FSA (Gold Medal, 1983); Fellow, UCL, 1985. Mem. German Archæolog. Inst., 1953; Hon. Mem. Royal Irish Acad., 1956; Foreign Hon. Member: American Academy of Arts and Sciences, 1960; Archæolog. Inst. of America, 1990. Trustee, British Museum, 1968–74. Travelled in Europe and Asia. Hon. DLittHum, Columbia, 1954; Hon. DLitt Edinburgh, 1984. *Publications:* Some Ancient Cities of India, 1946; Fire Among the Ruins, 1948; British Prehistory, 1949; William Stukeley: an XVIII Century Antiquary, 1950; Prehistoric India, 1950; A Picture Book of Ancient British Art (with G. E. Daniel), 1951; Neolithic Cultures of British Isles, 1954; Scotland before History, 1958; Approach to Archæology, 1959; (ed) The Dawn of Civilization, 1961; The West Kennet Long Barrow, 1962; Ancient Europe, 1965; Prehistoric Societies (with J. G. D. Clark), 1965; The Druids, 1968; Introduction to Camden's Britannia of 1695, 1971; (ed jtly) France Before the Romans, 1974; Ruins in a Landscape, 1977; Antiquity Depicted, 1978; (ed and contrib.) Agrarian History of England and Wales Ii, 1981; The Earliest Wheeled Transport, 1983; Ancient Britons and the Antiquarian Imagination, 1989; numerous technical papers in archæological jls. *Recreation:* reading. *Address:* The Cottage, West Challow, Wantage, Oxon. *Club:* United Oxford & Cambridge University.

PIGNATELLI, Frank; Director of Education, Strathclyde Region, since 1988; *b* 22 Dec. 1946; *s* of Frank and Elizabeth Pignatelli; *m* 1969, Rosetta Anne McFadyen; one *s* one *d*. *Educ:* Univ. of Glasgow (MA; DipEd, MEd); Jordanhill Coll. of Educn (Secondary Teachers Cert.). Teacher, St Mungo's Acad., Glasgow, 1970; Hd of Dept, St Gregory's Secondary Sch., Glasgow, 1974; Asst Headteacher, St Margaret Mary's Secondary Sch, Glasgow, 1977; Strathclyde Region: Educn Officer, Renfrew Div., 1978; Asst Dir of Educn, 1983; Depute Dir of Educn, 1985. Hon. Lectr in Educn, 1988–90, Vis Prof.,

1990–, Univ. of Glasgow. Chm., RIPA (West of Scotland). FBIM 1989 (Pres., Renfrewshire). *Publications:* Basic Knowledge 'O' French, 1974; Higher French Past Papers, 1975; contributor, World Year Book in Education, TES. *Recreations:* swimming, genealogy, do-it-yourself, reading. *Address:* 10 Whittingehame Drive, Glasgow G12 0XX. *T:* 041–334 3458.

PIGOT, Sir George (Hugh), 8th Bt *cr* 1764, of Patshull, Staffs; engaged in aquaculture; *b* 28 Nov. 1946; *s* of Maj.-Gen. Sir Robert Pigot, 7th Bt, CB, OBE, DL, and Honor (*d* 1966), *d* of Captain Wilfred St Martin Gibbon; *S* father, 1986; *m* 1st, 1967, Judith Sandeman-Allen (marr. diss. 1973); one *d*; 2nd, 1980, Lucinda Jane, *d* of D. C. Spandler; two *s*. *Educ:* Stowe. Hon. Treas., British Trout Assoc., 1990–. *Recreations:* classic cars, golf. *Heir:* *s* George Douglas Hugh Pigot, *b* 17 Sept. 1982. *Address:* Mill House, Mill Lane, Padworth, near Reading RG7 4JX.

PIGOT, His Honour Thomas Herbert, QC 1967; a Circuit Judge, 1972–90; Common Serjeant in the City of London, 1984–90; Senior Judge (non-resident), Sovereign Base Area, Cyprus, 1984–90 (Deputy Senior Judge, 1971–84); *b* 19 May 1921; *e s* of late Thomas Pigot and of Martha Ann Pigot; *m* 1950, Zena Marguerite, *yr d* of late Tom and Dorothy Gladys Wall; three *d*. *Educ:* Manchester Gram. Sch. (Schol.); Brasenose Coll., Oxford (Somerset Schol.). BA (1st cl. hons Jurisprudence) 1941; MA 1946; BCL 1947. Commissioned Welch Regt, 1942; served N Africa with Royal Lincs Regt; wounded and taken prisoner, 1943; released, 1945. Called to Bar, Inner Temple, 1947, Bencher, 1985; practised in Liverpool on Northern Circuit until 1967. Mem., Bar Council, 1970. One of HM Comrs of Lieutenancy, City of London, 1984–90. Hon. Liveryman, Cutlers' Co. *Recreation:* golf. *Clubs:* MCC; Vincent's (Oxford); Huntercombe Golf; Harlequin FC.

PIGOTT, Sir (Berkeley) Henry (Sebastian), 5th Bt *cr* 1808; farmer; *b* 24 June 1925; *s* of Sir Berkeley Pigott, 4th Bt, and Christabel (*d* 1974), *d* of late Rev. F. H. Bowden-Smith; *S* father, 1982; *m* 1954, (Olive) Jean, *d* of John William Balls; two *s* one *d*. *Educ:* Ampleforth College. Served War with Royal Marines, 1944–45. *Recreation:* sailing (blue water). *Heir:* *er s* David John Berkeley Pigott [*b* 16 Aug. 1955; *m* 1st, 1981 (marr. diss.); 2nd, 1986, Julie Wiffen]. *Address:* Brook Farm, Shobley, Ringwood, Hants. *T:* Ringwood (0425) 3268.

PIGOTT, Dr Christopher Donald; Director, University Botanic Garden, Cambridge, since 1984; *b* 7 April 1928; *s* of John Richards Pigott and Helen Constance Pigott (*née* Lee); *m* 1st, 1954, Margaret Elsie Beatson (*d* 1981); one *d*; 2nd, 1986, Sheila Lloyd (*née* Megaw). *Educ:* Mill Hill School; University of Cambridge. MA, PhD. Asst Lectr, and Lectr, Univ. of Sheffield, 1951–60; Univ. Lectr, Cambridge, 1960–64; Fellow of Emmanuel Coll., Cambridge, 1962–64; Prof. of Biology, Univ. of Lancaster, 1964–84; Professorial Fellow, Emmanuel Coll., Cambridge, 1984–; Member: Nature Conservancy, 1971–73; Nature Conservancy Council, 1979–82; Council, Nat. Trust, 1980–; Home Grown Timber Adv. Cttee, Forestry Commn, 1987–; Foreign Mem., Acad. d'Agriculture de France (Silviculture), 1982–. *Publications:* contribs to sci. jls (ecology and physiology of plants). *Recreations:* walking, travelling in Europe. *Address:* Emmanuel College, Cambridge CB2 3AP.

PIGOTT-BROWN, Sir William Brian, 3rd Bt, *cr* 1902; *b* 20 Jan. 1941; *s* of Sir John Pigott-Brown, 2nd Bt (killed in action, 1942) and Helen (who *m* 1948, Capt. Charles Raymond Radclyffe), *o d* of Major Gilbert Egerton Cotton, Priestland, Tarporley, Cheshire; *S* father, 1942. *Heir:* none. *Address:* 47 Eaton Mews North, SW1X 8LL.

PIHL, Brig. Hon. Dame Mary Mackenzie, DBE 1970 (MBE 1958); Director, Women's Royal Army Corps, 1967–Aug. 1970, retired; *b* 3 Feb. 1916; *d* of Sir John Anderson, later 1st Viscount Waverley, PC, GCB, OM, GCSI, GCIE, FRS, and Christina Mackenzie Anderson; *m* 1973, Frithjof Pihl (*d* 1988). *Educ:* Sutton High Sch.; Villa Brillantmont, Lausanne. Joined Auxiliary Territorial Service, 1941; transferred to Women's Royal Army Corps, 1949. Hon. ADC to the Queen, 1967–70. *Clubs:* English-Speaking Union, Naval.

PIKE, Baroness *cr* 1974 (Life Peer), of Melton, Leics; **Irene Mervyn Parnicott Pike,** DBE 1981; Chairman, Broadcasting Complaints Commission, 1981–85; *b* 16 Sept. 1918; *d* of I. S. Pike, Company Director, Okehampton, Devonshire. *Educ:* Hunmanby Hall; Reading University. BA Hons Economics and Psychology, 1941. Served WAAF, 1941–46. Mem., WRCC, 1955–57. Contested (C): Pontefract, 1951; Leek, Staffordshire, 1955. MP (C) Melton, Leics, Dec. 1956–Feb. 1974; Assistant Postmaster-General, 1959–63; Joint Parliamentary Under-Secretary of State, Home Office, 1963–64. Director: Watts, Blake, Bearne & Co. Ltd; Dunderdale Investments. Chairman: IBA Gen. Adv. Council, 1974–79; WRVS, 1974–81. *Recreations:* gardening, walking. *Address:* Hownam, near Kelso, Roxburgh TD5 8AL.

PIKE, Prof. Edward Roy, PhD; FRS 1981; Clerk Maxwell Professor of Theoretical Physics, University of London at King's College, since 1986; with Royal Signals and Radar Establishment Physics Group, since 1960; *b* 4 Dec. 1929; *s* of Anthony Pike and Rosalind Irene Pike (*née* Davies); *m* 1955, Pamela Sawtell; one *s* two *d*. *Educ:* Southfield Grammar Sch., Oxford; University Coll., Cardiff (BSc, PhD; Fellow, 1981). CPhys, FInstP, FIMA. Served Royal Corps of Signals, 1948–50. Fulbright Schol., Physics Dept, MIT, 1958–60; Royal Signals and Radar Estabt Physics Group, 1960: theoretical and experimental research condensed matter physics and optics; Individual Merit: SPSO 1967; DCSO 1973; CSO, 1984–. Vis. Prof. of Maths, Imperial Coll., London, 1985–86. Chm., Oval (114) Ltd, 1984–85; non-exec. Dir, Richard Clay plc, 1985–86. Govt assessor, SRC Physics Cttee, 1973–76. Mem. Council: Inst. of Physics, 1976–85; European Physical Soc., 1981–83; Vice-Pres. for Publications and Chm., Adam Hilger Ltd, 1981–85; Director: NATO Advanced Study Insts, 1973, 1976; NATO Advanced Res. Workshops, 1987–88 and 1991. Hon. Editor: Journal of Physics A, 1973–78; Optica Acta, 1978–83; Quantum Optics, 1989–. Nat. Science Foundn Vis. Lectr, USA, 1959; Lectures: Univ. of Rome, 1976; Univ. of Bordeaux, 1977; Simon Fraser Univ., 1978; Univ. of Genoa, 1980. Royal Society Charles Parsons medal and lecture, 1975; MacRobert award (jtly) and lecture, 1977; Worshipful Co. of Scientific Instrument Makers Annual Achievement award (jtly), 1978; Committee on Awards to Inventors award, 1980; Confrérie St-Etienne, 1980–. *Publications:* (jtly) Introduction to High Temperature Superconductivity Theory, 1990; (ed) High Power Gas Lasers, 1975; edited jointly: Photon Correlation and Light Beating Spectroscopy, 1974; Photon Correlation Spectroscopy and Velocimetry, 1977; Frontiers in Quantum Optics, 1986; Fractals, Noise and Chaos, 1987; Quantum Measurement and Chaos, 1987; Squeezed and Non-classical Light, 1988; Photons and Quantum Fluctuations, 1988; Inverse Problems, 1991; numerous papers in scientific jls. *Recreations:* music, languages, woodwork. *Address:* 3a Golborne Mews, North Kensington, W10.

PIKE, Air Cdre James Maitland Nicholson, CB 1963; DSO 1942; DFC 1941; RAF, retired; with Ministry of Defence, 1969–78; *b* 8 Feb. 1916; *s* of late Frank Pike, Glendarary, Achill Island, Co. Mayo, Eire, and Daphne (*née* Kenyon Stow), Worcester; *m* 1st, 1942, Mary Bettina Dell; one *d*; 2nd, 1955, Amber Pauline Bettesworth Hellard; one *s* one step *d*; 3rd, 1972, Dorothy May Dawson (*née* Holland); one step *d*. *Educ:* Stowe; RAF Coll., Cranwell. Commnd 1937; War Service: Aden, Middle East, UK (Coastal Command), Malta and Azores. Directing staff, RAF Staff Coll., 1945–47; Group Capt. 1955; Comd RAF Station, St Mawgan and RAF Station, Kinloss, 1955–57; SASO, RAF Malta, 1958–60; Air Cdre 1961; AOC, RAF Gibraltar, 1961–62; Imperial Defence College, 1963; Air Cdre Intelligence (B), Ministry of Defence, 1964; Dir of Security, RAF, 1965–69. *Recreations:* shooting, fishing, gundog training. *Address:* The Hyde, 31 Brookside, Watlington, Oxford OX9 5AQ.

PIKE, Sir Michael (Edmund), KCVO 1989; CMG 1984; HM Diplomatic Service, retired; Political Affairs Adviser, Sun International Exploration and Production Co., since 1991; *b* 4 Oct. 1931; *s* of Henry Pike and Eleanor Pike; *m* 1962, Catherine (*née* Lim); one *s* two *d*. *Educ:* Wimbledon Coll.; London Sch. of Econs and Polit. Science; Brasenose Coll., Oxford (MA 1956). Service in HM Armed Forces, 1950–52. Editor, Cherwell, Oxford Univ., 1954; part-time News Reporter, Sunday Express, 1954–55; Feature Writer and Film Critic, Surrey Comet, 1955–56; joined HM Foreign (now Diplomatic) Service, 1956; Third Secretary: FO, 1956–57; Seoul, 1957–59; Second Secretary: Office of Comr Gen. for Singapore and SE Asia, 1960–62; Seoul, 1962–64; FO, 1964–68; First Sec., Warsaw, 1968–70; FCO, 1970–73; First Sec., Washington, 1973–75; Counsellor: Washington, 1975–78; Tel Aviv, 1978–82; RCDS, 1982; Ambassador to Vietnam, 1982–85; Minister and Dep. UK Perm. Rep. to NATO, Brussels, 1985–87; High Comr, Singapore, 1987–90. Pres., Union of Catholic Students of GB, 1955–56. *Recreations:* reading, running, contemplating London. *Address:* c/o Sun International Exploration and Production, Sun Oil House, 80 Hammersmith Road, W14 8YS.

PIKE, Peter Leslie; MP (Lab) Burnley, since 1983; *b* 26 June 1937; *s* of Leslie Henry Pike and Gladys (*née* Cunliffe); *m* 1962, Sheila Lillian Bull; two *d*. *Educ:* Hinchley Wood County Secondary Sch. (Commercial Dept); Kingston Technical Coll. Pt 1 Exam., Inst. of Bankers. National Service, RM, 1956–58. Midland Bank, 1954–62; Twinings Tea, 1962–63; Organiser/Agent, Labour Party, 1963–73; Mullard (Simonstone) Ltd, 1973–83. Mem., GMBATU (Shop Steward, 1976–83). Member: Merton and Morden UDC, 1962–63; Burnley Bor. Council, 1976–84 (Leader, Labour Gp, 1980–83; Gp Sec., 1976–80). Opposition frontbench spokesperson on Rural Affairs, 1990–; Chm., Parly Labour Party Environment Cttee, 1987–90; Mem., Environment Select Cttee, 1985–90. Member: Nat. Trust, 1974–; CND; Anti-Apartheid. *Recreation:* Burnley Football Club supporter. *Address:* 73 Ormerod Road, Burnley, Lancs BB11 2RU. *T:* Burnley (0282) 34719. *Clubs:* Byerden House Socialist; Philips Sports and Social.

PIKE, Sir Philip Ernest Housden, Kt 1969; Chief Justice of Swaziland, 1970–72, retired; *b* 6 March 1914; *s* of Rev. Ernest Benjamin Pike and Dora Case Pike (*née* Lillie); *m* 2nd, 1959, Millicent Locke Staples; one *s* one *d* of 1st marriage. *Educ:* De Carteret School, and Munro Coll., Jamaica; Middle Temple, London. Barrister at Law, 1938. Crown Counsel, Jamaica, 1947–49; Legal Draftsman, Kenya, 1949–52; Solicitor General, Uganda, 1952–58; QC (Uganda) 1953; Attorney General, Sarawak, 1958–65; QC (Sarawak) 1958; Chief Justice, High Court in Borneo, 1965–68; Judge, High Court of Malawi, 1969–70, Actg Chief Justice, 1970. Coronation Medal, 1953. PNBS-Sarawak, 1965; Malaysia Commemorative Medal, 1967; PMN Malaysia 1968. *Recreations:* golf, gardening. *Address:* 3 Earlewood Court, 180/184 Ron Penhaligon Way, Robina Waters, Qld 4226, Australia.

PIKE, Rt. Rev. St John Surridge; DD *jure dig* 1958; Assistant Bishop, Diocese of Guildford, 1963–83; *b* 27 Dec. 1909; *s* of late Rev. Canon William Pike, Thurles, Co. Tipperary; *m* 1958, Clare, *d* of late William Henry Jones; one *s* one *d* (and one *s* decd). *Educ:* The Abbey, Tipperary; Bishop Foy School, Waterford; Trinity Coll., Dublin (MA). Deacon, 1932; Priest, 1934; Curate of Taney, 1932–37; Head of Southern Church Mission, Ballymacarrett, Belfast, 1937–47; SPG Missionary, Diocese of Gambia, 1947–52; Rector of St George's, Belfast, 1952–58; Commissary for Gambia in N Ireland, 1954–58; Bishop of Gambia and the Rio Pongas, 1958–63; Vicar of St Mary the Virgin, Ewshot, 1963–71; Vicar of Holy Trinity, Botleys and Lyne, and Christ Church, Longcross, 1971–83. Hon. Canon, Guildford, 1963–83. *Address:* Wisteria Cottage, Old Rectory Lane, Twyford, near Winchester, Hampshire SO21 1NS. *T:* Twyford (0962) 712253.

PIKE, Lt-Gen. Sir William (Gregory Huddleston), KCB 1961 (CB 1956); CBE 1952; DSO 1943; Chief Commander, St John Ambulance, 1969–75; b 24 June 1905; *s* of late Captain Sydney Royston Pike, RA, and Sarah Elizabeth Pike (*née* Huddleston); *m* 1939, Josephine Margaret, *er d* of late Maj.-Gen. R. H. D. Tompson, CB, CMG, DSO, and Mrs B. D. Tompson; one *s* two *d*. *Educ:* Bedford School; Marlborough Coll.; RMA Woolwich. Lieutenant RA, 20th and 24th Field Brigades, RA and "A" Field Brigade, Indian Artillery, 1925–36; Staff College, Camberley, 1937–38; Command and Staff Appointments in UK, France and Belgium, North Africa, USA and Far East, 1939–50; CRA, 1st Commonwealth Div., Korea, 1951–52; idc 1953; Director of Staff Duties, War Office, 1954–57; Chief of Staff, Far East Land Forces, Oct. 1957–60; Vice-Chief of the Imperial General Staff, 1960–63; Col Comdt RA, 1962–70. Lieutenant of HM Tower of London, 1963–66; Commissioner-in-Chief, St John Ambulance Brigade, 1967–73. Jt Hon. Pres., Anglo-Korean Society, 1963–69. Hon. Col 277 (Argyll and Sutherland Highlanders) Regt RA (TA), 1960–67; Hon. Col Lowland Regt RA (T), 1967–70. Member Honourable Artillery Company; Chm., Lord Mayor Treloar Trust, 1976–82; Corps of Commissionaires, 1964–81 (Mem. Administrative Bd). Officer, US Legion of Merit, 1953. GCStJ 1976. *Recreations:* field sports and gardening. *Address:* Ganwells, Bentley, Hants.

PILBROW, Richard Hugh; Chairman, Theatre Projects Consultants, since 1957; *b* 28 April 1933; *s* of Arthur Gordon Pilbrow and Marjorie Pilbrow; *m* 1st, 1958, Viki Brinton; one *s* one *d*; 2nd, 1974, Molly Friedel; one *d*. *Educ:* Cranbrook Sch.; Central Sch. of Speech and Drama. Stage Manager, Teahouse of the August Moon, 1954; founded Theatre Projects, 1957. Lighting Designer for over 200 prodns in London, New York, Paris and Moscow, incl.: Brand, 1959; Blitz, 1962; Zorba, 1968; Annie, 1978; Oklahoma!, 1980; The Little Foxes, Windy City, 1982; Singin' In the Rain, 1983; for Nat. Theatre Co., 1963–70, incl. Hamlet, 1963; Rosencrantz and Guildenstern are Dead, 1966; Heartbreak House, 1975; Love for Love, 1985; Heliotrope Bouquet, 1991. Theatrical Producer in London of prodns incl.: A Funny Thing Happened on the Way to the Forum, 1963, 1986; Cabaret, 1968; Company, 1972; A Little Night Music, 1975; West Side Story, 1984; The Mysteries, Lyceum, 1985; I'm Not Rappaport, 1986. Film Prod., Swallows and Amazons, 1973; TV Productions: All You Need is Love—the story of popular music, 1975; Swallows and Amazons for Ever, 1984; Dir, Mister, 1971. Theatre Projects Consultants have been consultants on many theatres incl. Toronto Opera House, Nat. Theatre of GB, Barbican Theatre, Royal Opera House, and theatres and arts centres in Canada, Iran, Hong Kong, Saudi Arabia, Mexico, Iceland, Nigeria, Norway, USA, etc. Vice President: Assoc. of British Theatre Technicians: Nat. Youth Theatre; Co-founder, Soc. of Brit. Theatre Designers, 1975; Mem., Assoc. of Lighting Designers (Chm., 1982–85); Member: Drama Panel, Arts Council of GB, 1968–70; Soc. of West End Theatre; Council, London Acad. of Music and Drama. FRSA. *Publication:* Stage Lighting, 1970, 3rd edn 1991. *Recreations:* The Hebrides, cooking, dogs. *Address:* Theatre Projects

Consultants Ltd, 3 Apollo Studios, Charlton Kings Road, NW5 2SW. *T:* 071–482 4224. *Club:* Garrick.

PILCHER, Sir (Charlie) Dennis, Kt 1974; CBE 1968; FRICS; Chairman, Commission for the New Towns, 1971–78; Consultant, late Senior Partner (Partner 1930), Graves, Son & Pilcher (Chartered Surveyors); Director, Save and Prosper Group Ltd, 1970–80; *b* 2 July 1906; *s* of Charlie Edwin Pilcher, Fareham, Hants; *m* 1929, Mary Allison Aumonier (*d* 1991), *d* of William Aumonier, London; two *d. Educ:* Clayesmore Sch. Served War: Major, RA (despatches, Normandy), 1940–45. Hemel Hempstead Development Corp., 1949–56; Bracknell Development Corp., 1956–71 (Chm. 1968–71); Dir, Sun Life Assurance Soc. Ltd, 1968–77. Pres., RICS, 1963–64; Mem., Milner Holland Cttee on London Housing, 1963–64; Vice-Pres., London Rent Assessment Panel, 1966–70; Adviser to Business Rents Directorate of DoE, 1973–77. Mem. Council, Glyndebourne Fest. Opera, 1969–. *Recreations:* opera, golf, fishing. *Address:* Brambles, Batts Lane, Mare Hill, Pulborough, West Sussex. *T:* Pulborough (07982) 2126. *Club:* West Sussex Golf.
See also Earl of Strafford.

PILCHER, Robin Sturtevant, MS, FRCS, FRCP; Emeritus Professor of Surgery, University of London; Professor of Surgery and Director of the Surgical Unit, University College Hospital, London, 1938–67; *b* 22 June 1902; *s* of Thorold and Helena Pilcher; *m* 1929, Mabel Pearks; one *s* one *d. Educ:* St Paul's Sch.; University Coll., London. Fellow University Coll., London. *Publications:* various surgical papers. *Address:* Swanbourne, 21 Church End, Haddenham, Bucks HP17 8AE. *T:* Haddenham (0844) 291048.

PILDITCH, James George Christopher, CBE 1983; Founder, AIDCOM International plc (Chairman, 1980–83); *b* 7 Aug. 1929; *s* of Frederick Henry Pilditch and Marie-Thérèse (*née* Priest); *m* 1st, 1952, Molly (marr. diss.); one *d*; 2nd, 1970, Anne Elisabeth W :son Johnson. *Educ:* Slough Grammar Sch.; Reading Univ. (Fine Arts); INSEAD. Nat. Service, commnd RA, 1950; Royal Canadian Artillery Reserve, 1953–56. Journalism in Canada including Maclean-Hunter Publishing Co., 1952–56; work in design offices, Orr Associates (Toronto), THM Partners (London), Jim Nash Assocs (New York), 1956–59; started Package Design Associates (later Allied International Designers), in London, 1959. Chairman: Design Bd, Business and Technician Educn Council, 1983–86; Furniture EDC, NEDO, 1985–88; Design Working Party, NEDO, 1985–86; Financial Times/London Business Sch. Design Management Award, 1987–; Member: Council, Marketing Gp of GB, 1979–84; Adv. panel, Design Management Unit, London Business School, 1982–; Design Council, 1984–89; Design Management Gp, CSD (formerly (SIAD), 1984–86; Council, RSA, 1984–89; Council, Heritage of London Trust, 1985–; Chm.'s design panel, BAA, 1987–; Council, and Treasurer, RCA, 1990–; Final Judge, Prince of Wales' Award for Innovation, 1990–; Trustee, Parnham Trust, 1988. FRSA; Hon FCSD (Hon. FSIAD 1985 (ASIAD 1968)); First Hon. Fellow, Design Management Inst., USA, 1985. Medal of Conf. for Higher Educn in Art and Design, for distinguished services to higher educn, 1988. *Publications:* The Silent Salesman, 1961, 2nd edn 1973; (with Douglas Scott) The Business of Product Design, 1965; Communication By Design, 1970; Talk About Design, 1976; Hold Fast the Heritage, 1982; Winning Ways, 1987, 2nd edn 1989; I'll be over in the morning, 1990. *Recreations:* real tennis, watching West Indies cricket, travel, writing, sketching. *Address:* 62 Cadogan Square, SW1X 0EA. *T:* 071–584 9279; Brookhampton House, North Cadbury, Som. *T:* North Cadbury (0963) 40225. *Clubs:* Army and Navy, Travellers', MCC; Falkland Palace Royal Tennis; Barbados Cricket Assoc.

PILDITCH, Sir Richard (Edward), 4th Bt, *cr* 1929; *b* 8 Sept. 1926; *s* of Sir Philip Harold Pilditch, 2nd Bt, and Frances Isabella, *d* of J. G. Weeks, JP, Bedlington, Northumberland; *S* brother (Sir Philip John Frederick Pilditch, 3rd Bt) 1954; *m* 1950, Pauline Elizabeth Smith; one *s* one *d. Educ:* Charterhouse. Served War of 1939–45, with Royal Navy, in India and Ceylon, 1944–45. *Recreations:* shooting, fishing. *Heir: s* John Richard Pilditch, *b* 24 Sept. 1955. *Address:* 4 Fishermans Bank, Mudeford, Christchurch, Dorset.

PILE, Colonel Sir Frederick (Devereux), 3rd Bt *cr* 1900; MC 1945; *b* 10 Dec. 1915; *s* of Gen. Sir Frederick Alfred Pile, 2nd Bt, GCB, DSO, MC; *S* father, 1976; *m* 1st, 1940, Pamela (*d* 1983), *d* of late Philip Henstock; two *d*; 2nd, 1984, Mrs Josephine Culverwell. *Educ:* Weymouth; RMC, Sandhurst. Joined Royal Tank Regt, 1935; served War of 1939–45, Egypt and NW Europe; commanded Leeds Rifles, 1955–56; Colonel GS, BJSM, Washington, DC, 1957–60; Commander, RAC Driving and Maintenance School, 1960–62. Secretary, Royal Soldiers' Daughters' School, 1965–71. *Recreations:* fishing, cricket, travelling. *Heir: nephew* Anthony John Devereux Pile [*b* 7 June 1947; *m* 1977, Jennifer Clare Youngman; two *s* one *d*]. *Club:* MCC.

PILE, Sir William (Dennis), GCB 1978 (KCB 1971; CB 1968); MBE 1944; Chairman, Board of Inland Revenue, 1976–79; *b* 1 Dec. 1919; *s* of James Edward Pile and Jean Elizabeth Pile; *m* 1948, Joan Marguerite Crafter; one *s* two *d. Educ:* Royal Masonic School; St Catharine's College, Cambridge. Served Border Regt, 1940–45. Ministry of Education, 1947–50, 1951–66; Cabinet Office, 1950; Asst Under-Sec. of State: Dept of Education and Science, 1962; Ministry of Health, 1966; Dep. Under-Sec. of State, Home Office, 1967–70; Director-General, Prison Service, 1969–70; Permanent Under-Sec. of State, DES, 1970–76. Director: Nationwide Building Soc., 1980–88; Distillers' Co. Ltd, 1980–85. *Address:* The Manor House, Riverhead, near Sevenoaks, Kent. *T:* Sevenoaks (0732) 54498. *Clubs:* United Oxford & Cambridge University; Hawks (Cambridge).

PILGER, John Richard; journalist, author and film-maker; *b* 9 Oct. 1939; *s* of Claude Pilger and Elsie (*née* Marheine); *m* Scarth Flett; one *s*; one *d* by Yvonne Roberts. *Educ:* Sydney High Sch. Cadet journalist, Sydney Daily Telegraph, Australia, qualified, 1961; freelance journalist, Italy, 1962; Reuter, London, 1962; feature writer, chief foreign correspondent, Daily Mirror, London, 1962–86 (reporter, Vietnam War, 1966–75, Cambodia, 1979–91, etc). Campaigns incl. Thalidomide 'X list' victims, and Australian Aboriginal land rights. Films include: The Quiet Mutiny, 1970; A Faraway Country (Czechoslovakia), 1977; Year Zero: the silent death of Cambodia, 1979; The Last Dream, 1988. Awards include: Descriptive Writer of the Year, 1966; Reporter of the Year, 1967; Journalist of the Year, 1967, 1979; Internat. Reporter of the Year, 1970; News Reporter of the Year, 1974; Campaigning Journalist of the Year, 1977; UN Media Peace Prize and Gold Medal, 1979–80; George Foster Peabody Award, USA, 1990; Reporters Sans Frontiers Award, France, 1990; Richard Dimbleby Award, 1991. *Publications:* The Last Day, 1975; Aftermath: the struggle of Cambodia and Vietnam, 1981; The Outsiders, 1984; Heroes, 1986; A Secret Country, 1989. *Recreations:* swimming, sunning, mulling. *Address:* 57 Hambalt Road, SW4 9EQ. *T:* 081–673 2848.

PILGRIM, Cecil Stanley, CCH 1986; High Commissioner for Guyana in London, since 1986, and concurrently Ambassador (non-resident) to France, the Netherlands and Yugoslavia; *b* 1 Feb. 1932; *s* of Errol Pilgrim and Edith Pilgrim; *m* 1979, Cita I. Pilgrim; one *d. Educ:* Queen's Coll., Guyana; Univ. of Guyana (BSc; post graduate course in Internat. Relations). Diplomatic Cadet, Guyana, 1967; Second Sec., Jamaica, 1969; First Sec., China, 1974; Counsellor, USSR, 1978; Ambassador, Cuba, 1979. *Recreations:* reading, music, badminton, walking, cricket, enjoys sports of all types. *Address:* Guyana High Commission, 3 Palace Court, Bayswater, W2 4LP. *T:* 071–229 3777.

PILKINGTON, Sir Alastair; *see* Pilkington, Sir L. A. B.

PILKINGTON, Sir Antony (Richard), Kt 1990; DL; Chairman, Pilkington plc (formerly Pilkington Brothers plc), since 1980; *b* 20 June 1935; *s* of Arthur Cope Pilkington and Otilia Dolores Pilkington; *m* 1960, Alice Kirsty, *er d* of Sir Thomas Dundas, 7th Bt, MBE and of Lady Dundas; three *s* one *d. Educ:* Ampleforth Coll.; Trinity Coll., Cambridge (MA History). Coldstream Guards, 1953–55. Joined Pilkington Brothers, 1959; Dir, 1973–; Dep. Chm., 1979–80. Director: BSN Gervais Danone (France), 1975–80 (Mem., Internat. Consultative Cttee, 1982–); GKN, 1982–91; National Westminster Bank, 1984–; Libbey-Owens-Ford Co. (USA), 1984–89; ICI, 1991–; Deputy Chairman: Pilkington Deutschland GmbH, 1989–90; Flachglas AG, 1980–90; Dahlbusch AG, 1980–90. Chm., Community of St Helens Trust, 1978–. Mem. Council, Liverpool Univ., 1977–79. Hon. LLD Liverpool, 1987. DL Merseyside, 1988. *Recreations:* interesting motor cars, ski-ing, sailing, reading P. G. Wodehouse. *Address:* Pilkington plc, Prescot Road, St Helens, Lancs WA10 3TT. *T:* St Helens (0744) 28882. *Clubs:* Pratt's, MCC.

PILKINGTON, Godfrey; *see* Pilkington, R. G.

PILKINGTON, Lawrence Herbert Austin, CBE 1964; JP; Director, Pilkington Brothers Ltd, 1943–81; *b* 13 Oct. 1911; 2nd *s* of Richard Austin and Hon. Hope Pilkington; *m* 1936, Norah Holden, Whitby, Ont., Canada; two *d. Educ:* Bromsgrove School; Magdalene College, Cambridge. Volunteer with Grenfell Mission, 1933–34. Joined Pilkington Brothers Limited, 1935. Chairman: Glass Delegacy, 1949–54; Glass Industry Research Assoc., 1954–58; British Coal Utilisation Research Assoc., 1963–68; Soc. of Acoustic Technology, 1963–; Member: Building Research Board, 1958–62; Wilson Cttee on Noise, 1960–63; Adv. Council on R&D for Fuel and Power, 1973–75. President, Soc. of Glass Technology, 1960–64. JP Lancs, 1942. Hon. LLD Sheffield, 1956; Hon. DSc Salford, 1970. *Publications:* mainly on glass in various technical jls. *Recreations:* sailing, climbing, amateur radio, shooting. *Address:* Coppice End, Colborne Road, St Peter Port, Guernsey, CI. *Club:* Royal Dee Yacht.

PILKINGTON, Sir Lionel Alexander Bethune, (Sir Alastair), Kt 1970; FRS 1969; President, Pilkington plc (formerly Pilkington Brothers), St Helens, since 1985; Director, British Petroleum, since 1976; *b* 7 Jan. 1920; *yr s* of late Col L. G. Pilkington and Mrs L. G. Pilkington, Newbury, Berks; *m* 1945, Patricia Nicholls (*née* Elliott) (*d* 1977); one *s* one *d*; *m* 1978, Kathleen, *widow* of Eldridge Haynes. *Educ:* Sherborne School; Trinity Coll., Cambridge (Hon. Fellow). War service, 1939–46. Joined Pilkington Brothers Ltd, Glass Manufacturers, St Helens, 1947; Production Manager and Asst Works Manager, Doncaster, 1949–51; Head Office, 1952; Sub-Director, 1953; Director, 1955–85; Dep. Chm., 1971–73; Chm., 1973–80. Dir, Bank of England, 1974–84. Member: Central Adv. Council for Science and Technology, 1970–; SRC, 1972–; British Railways Bd, 1973–76; Court of Governors, Administrative Staff Coll., 1973–; Chairman: Council for Business in the Community, 1982–85; CNAA, 1984–87; Pres., BAAS, 1983–; Vice-Pres., Foundn of Science and Technology, 1986–. Pro-Chancellor, Lancaster Univ., 1980–90. Hon. FUMIST, 1969; Hon. Fellow: Imperial Coll., 1974; LSE, 1980; Sheffield Poly., 1987; Lancashire Poly., 1987. FBIM 1971. Hon. DTech: Loughborough, 1968; CNAA, 1976; Hon. DEng Liverpool, 1971; Hon. LLD Bristol, 1979; Hon. DSc (Eng) London, 1979. Toledo Glass and Ceramic Award, 1963; Mullard Medal, Royal Soc., 1968; John Scott Medal, 1969; Wilhelm Exner Medal, 1970; Phoenix Award, 1981. *Recreations:* gardening, sailing, music. *Address:* 74 Eaton Place, SW1; Goldrill Cottage, Patterdale, near Penrith, Cumbria. *T:* Glenridding (08532) 263. *Club:* Athenæum.

PILKINGTON, Air Vice-Marshal Michael John, CB 1991; CBE 1982; Air Officer Commanding Training and Units, Royal Air Force Support Command, since 1989; *b* 9 Oct. 1937; *s* of David and Mary Pilkington; *m* 1960, Janet Rayner; one *d. Educ:* Bromley Grammar Sch. psc rcds. Commnd Royal Air Force, 1956; Bomber Sqdns, No 35, No 83, No 27, 1959–70; RAF sc 1971; HQ Near East Air Force, 1972–73; CO No 230 Vulcan OCU, 1974–75; Defence Policy Staff, 1977–78; CO RAF Waddington, 1979–81; RCDS 1982; Branch Chief Policy, SHAPE, 1982–85; DG of Trng, RAF, 1986–89. *Recreations:* golf, tennis, gardening, theatre, wine. *Address:* c/o Lloyds Bank, Royston, Herts. *Club:* Royal Air Force.

PILKINGTON, Rev. Canon Peter; High Master of St Paul's School, since 1986; Hon. Canon of Canterbury Cathedral, 1975–90, now Canon Emeritus; *b* 5 Sept. 1933; *s* of Frank and Doris Pilkington; *m* 1966, Helen, *d* of Charles and Maria Wilson; two *d. Educ:* Dame Allans Sch., Newcastle upon Tyne; Jesus Coll., Cambridge. BA 1955, MA 1958. Schoolmaster, St Joseph's Coll., Chidya, Tanganyika, 1955–57; ordained 1959; Curate in Bakewell, Derbs, 1959–62; Schoolmaster, Eton College, 1962–75, Master in College, 1965–75; Headmaster, King's Sch., Canterbury, 1975–86. *Address:* The High Master's House, St Paul's School, Lonsdale Road, Barnes, SW13 9JT. *T:* 081–748 9162. *Clubs:* Beefsteak, Garrick.

PILKINGTON, (Richard) Godfrey; Partner and Director, Piccadilly Gallery, since 1953; *b* 8 Nov. 1918; *e s* of Col Guy R. Pilkington, DSO and Margery (*née* Frost); *m* 1950, Evelyn Edith (Eve) Vincent; two *s* two *d. Educ:* Clifton; Trinity Coll., Cambridge (MA). Lieut, RA, N Africa and Central Mediterranean, 1940–46. Joined Frost & Reed, art dealers, 1947; edited Pictures and Prints, 1951–60; founded Piccadilly Gallery, 1953. Master, Fine Art Trade Guild, 1964–66; Chm., Soc. of London Art Dealers, 1974–77. *Publications:* numerous exhibn catalogues and magazine articles. *Recreations:* walking, boating, tennis, golf. *Address:* 45 Barons Court Road, W14 9DZ. *Clubs:* Athenæum, Garrick, Hurlingham.

PILKINGTON, Dr Roger Windle; author; *b* 17 Jan. 1915; 3rd *s* of Richard Austin Pilkington and Hon. Hope (*née* Cozens-Hardy); *m* 1937, Theodora Miriam Jaboor; one *d* (and one *s* decd); *m* 1973, Fru Ingrid Geijer, Stockholm. *Educ:* Rugby; Freiburg, Germany; Magdalene Coll., Cambridge (MA, PhD). Research, genetics, 1937; Chm., London Missionary Soc., 1962; Chm. of Trustees, Homerton Coll., Cambridge, 1962; Chm. of Govs, Hall Sch., 1962; jt author, Sex and Morality Report, Brit. Council of Churches, 1966; Vice-Pres., River Thames Soc., 1967; Master, Glass Sellers' Co., 1967. *Publications:* Males and Females, 1948; Stringer's Folly, Biology, Man and God, Sons and Daughters, 1951; How Your Life Began, 1953; Revelation Through Science, 1954; Jan's Treasure, In the Beginning, 1955; Thames Waters, The Facts of Life, 1956; Small Boat Through Belgium, The Chesterfield Gold, The Great South Sea, The Ways of the Sea, 1957; The Missing Panel, 1958; Small Boat Through Holland, Robert Boyle: Father of Chemistry, How Boats Go Uphill, 1959; Small Boat to the Skagerrak, World Without End, The Dahlia's Cargo, Don John's Ducats, 1960; Small Boat to Sweden, Small Boat to Alsace, The Ways of the Air, Who's Who and Why, 1961; Small Boat to Bavaria, Nepomuk of the River, Boats Overland, How Boats are Navigated, 1962; The River, (with Noel Streatfeild) Confirmation and After, Facts of Life for Parents, Small Boat to Germany, The Eisenbart Mystery, 1963; Heavens Alive, Small Boat Through France, 1964; Small Boat in Southern France, Glass, 1965; Small Boat on the Thames, The Boy from Stink Alley, 1966; Small Boat on the Meuse, Small Boat to Luxembourg, 1967; Small Boat on the Moselle, 1968; Small Boat to Elsinore, 1968; Small Boat in Northern Germany, 1969;

Small Boat on the Lower Rhine, 1970; Small Boat on the Upper Rhine, 1971; Waterways in Europe, 1972; The Ormering Tide, 1974; The Face in the River, 1976; Geijer in England, 1983; Small Boat Down the Years, 1987; Small Boat in the Midi, 1989; I Sailed on the Mayflower, 1990; One Foot in France, 1991; contribs to Guardian, Daily Telegraph, Times, Family Doctor, Yachting World, etc. *Recreations:* inland waterways, walking. *Address:* Les Cactus, Montouliers, 34310 Capestang, France. *T:* (33) 67.89.49.98.

PILKINGTON, Sir Thomas Henry Milborne-Swinnerton-, 14th Bt, *cr* 1635; Chairman, Thos & James Harrison Ltd, since 1980 (Director, since 1963); Chairman, Charente Steamship Co. Ltd, since 1977; Deputy Chairman, Cluff Resources plc, since 1988; *b* 10 Mar. 1934; *s* of Sir Arthur W. Milborne-Swinnerton-Pilkington, 13th Bt and Elizabeth Mary (she *m* 1950, A. Burke), *d* of late Major J. F. Harrison, King's Walden Bury, Hitchin; *S* father 1952; *m* 1961, Susan, *e d* of N. S. R. Adamson, Durban, South Africa; one *s* two *d*. *Educ:* Eton College. *Recreations:* golf, racing. *Heir: s* Richard Arthur Milborne-Swinnerton-Pilkington, *b* 4 Sept. 1964. *Address:* King's Walden Bury, Hitchin, Herts SG4 8JU. *Club:* White's.

PILL, Hon. Sir Malcolm (Thomas), Kt 1988; **Hon. Mr Justice Pill;** a Judge of the High Court of Justice, Queen's Bench Division, since 1988; Presiding Judge, Wales and Chester Circuit, since 1989; *b* 11 March 1938; *s* of late Reginald Thomas Pill, MBE and Anne Pill (*née* Wright); *m* 1966, Roisin Pill (*née* Riordan); two *s* one *d*. *Educ:* Whitchurch Grammar Sch.; Trinity Coll., Cambridge. MA, LLM, Dip. Hague Acad. of Internat. Law. Served RA, 1956–58; Glamorgan Yeomanry (TA), 1958–67. Called to Bar, Gray's Inn, 1962, Bencher, 1987; Wales and Chester Circuit, 1963 (Treas., 1985–87); a Recorder, 1976–87; QC 1978. 3rd Sec., Foreign Office, 1963–64. Chm., UNA (Welsh Centre) Trust, 1969–77, 1980–87; Chm., Welsh Centre for Internat. Affairs, 1973–76. Chm., UK Cttee, Freedom from Hunger Campaign, 1978–87. *Address:* Royal Courts of Justice, Strand, WC2. *Clubs:* Commonwealth Trust; Cardiff and County (Cardiff).

PILLAI, Sir (Narayana) Raghavan, KCIE 1946 (CIE 1939); CBE 1937; Padma Vibhushan, 1960; *b* 24 July 1898; *s* of M. C. Narayana Pillai, Trivandrum, S India; *m* 1928, Edith Minnie Arthurs (*d* 1976); two *s*. *Educ:* Madras Univ.; Trinity Hall, Cambridge (schol.). BA (Madras) 1st Cl. English, 1918; Natural Sciences Tripos Pt 1 (Cambridge), 1st Cl., 1921; Law Tripos Pt 2, 1st Cl., 1922; ICS 1921; various appointments under the Government of Central Provinces and the Government of India. Secretary General, Ministry of External Affairs, New Delhi, 1952–60. Hon. DLitt Kerala University, 1953. Hon. Fellow, Trinity Hall, Cambridge, 1970. *Recreation:* walking. *Address:* 26 Hans Place, SW1X 0JY. *Clubs:* Oriental; Gymkhana (New Delhi).

PILLAR, Rt. Rev. Kenneth Harold; Bishop Suffragan of Hertford, 1982–89; *b* 10 Oct. 1924; *s* of Harold and Mary Pillar; *m* 1955, Margaret Elizabeth Davies; one *s* three *d*. *Educ:* Devonport High School; Queens' Coll., Cambridge (MA); Ridley Hall, Cambridge. Asst Curate, Childwall, Liverpool, 1950–53; Chaplain, Lee Abbey, Lynton, N Devon, 1953–57; Vicar: St Paul's, Beckenham, 1957–62; St Mary Bredin, Canterbury, 1962–65; Warden of Lee Abbey, Lynton, N Devon, 1965–70; Vicar of Waltham Abbey, Essex, 1970–82; RD of Epping Forest, 1976–82. *Recreation:* walking. *Address:* 75 Dobcroft Road, Millhouses, Sheffield S7 2LS. *T:* Sheffield (0742) 367902.

PILLAR, Adm. Sir William (Thomas), GBE 1983; KCB 1980; CEng, FIMechE; FIMarE; Lieutenant-Governor and Commander-in-Chief, Jersey, 1985–90; *b* 24 Feb. 1924; *s* of William Pillar and Lily Pillar; *m* 1946, Ursula, *d* of Arthur B. Ransley, MC; three *s* one *d*. *Educ:* Blundells Sch., Tiverton; RNEC. FIMechE 1969, FIMarE 1972. Entered RN, 1942; HMS Illustrious, 1946–48; staff RNEC, 1948–51; HMS Alert, 1951–53; HM Dockyard, Gibraltar, 1954–57; HMS Corunna, 1957–59; BEO, HMS Lochinvar, 1959–61; staff of C-in-C, SASA, Cape Town, 1961–64; HMS Tiger, 1964–65; staff of Dir of Naval Officer Appts (Eng), 1965–67; Sowc 1967; Naval Ship Prodn Overseer, Scotland and NI, 1967–69, IDC 1970; Asst Dir, DG Ships, 1971–73; Captain RNEC, 1973–75; Port Adm., Rosyth, 1976–77; Asst Chief of Fleet Support, 1977–79; Chief of Fleet Support (Mem., Admiralty Bd of Defence Council), 1979–81; Comdt, RCDS, 1982–83. Cdre, RNSA, 1980–83 (Life Vice Cdre, 1990). Mem. Council, RUSI, 1984–87 (Vice Chm., 1986–87). President: RN Modern Pentathlon Assoc., 1978–83; Square Rigger Club (Support of Trng Ship Royalist), 1988–; Forces Help Soc. and Lord Roberts Workshops, 1991–. KStJ 1985. *Recreations:* sailing, rough gardening and fixing things. *Address:* Selwood, Zeals Row, Zeals, Warminster, Wilts BA12 6PE. *Clubs:* Army and Navy; Royal Yacht Squadron, Royal Naval Sailing Association (Portsmouth).

PILLING, Joseph Grant; Director-General, HM Prison Service, Home Office, since 1991; *b* 8 July 1945; *s* of Fred and Eva Pilling; *m* 1968, Ann Cheetham; two *s*. *Educ:* Rochdale Grammar Sch.; King's Coll., London; Harvard. Asst Principal, 1966, Pvte Sec. to Minister of State, 1970, Home Office; Asst. Pvte Sec. to Home Sec., 1970–71; NI Office, 1972; Harkness Fellow, Harvard Univ. and Univ. of Calif at Berkeley, 1972–74; Home Office, 1974–78; Pvte Sec. to Sec. of State for NI, 1978–79; Home Office, 1979–84; Under Sec., DHSS, 1984–87; Dir of Personnel and Finance, HM Prison Service, Home Office, 1987–90; Dep. Under Sec. of State, NI Office, 1990–91. *Address:* HM Prison Service, Cleland House, Page Street, SW1P 4LN. *Club:* Athenæum.

PIMENTA, His Eminence Simon Ignatius Cardinal; *see* Bombay, Archbishop of, (RC).

PIMLOTT, Prof. Benjamin John; Professor of Politics and Contemporary History, Birkbeck College, University of London, since 1987; *b* 4 July 1945; *s* of late John Alfred Ralph Pimlott, CB, and Ellen Dench Howes Pimlott; *m* 1977, Jean Ann Seaton; three *s*. *Educ:* Rokeby Sch., Wimbledon; Marlborough Coll., Wilts; Worcester Coll., Oxford (Open Schol.; MA, BPhil); PhD Newcastle. Lectr, Newcastle Univ., 1970–79; Res. Associate, LSE, 1979–81; Lectr 1981–86, Reader 1986–87, Birkbeck Coll., London Univ. British Acad. Thank Offering to Britain Fellow, 1972–73; Nuffield Foundn Res. Fellow, 1977–78. Contested (Lab): Arundel, Feb. 1974; Cleveland and Whitby, Oct. 1974, and 1979. Mem. Exec., Fabian Soc., 1987–. Political columnist: Today, 1986–87; The Times, 1987–88; New Statesman (political editor), 1987–88; Sunday Times, 1988–89. Editor, Samizdat, 1988–90. *Publications:* Labour and the Left in the 1930s, 1977, 2nd edn 1986; (ed with Chris Cook) Trade Unions in British Politics, 1982; (ed) Fabian Essays in Socialist Thought, 1984; Hugh Dalton, 1985, 2nd edn 1986 (Whitbread Biography Prize, 1985); (ed) The Second World War Diary of Hugh Dalton 1940–45, 1986; (ed) The Political Diary of Hugh Dalton 1918–40, 1945–60, 1987; (ed with Jean Seaton) The Media in British Politics, 1987; (ed with A. Wright and T. Flower) The Alternative, 1990; (ed with S. MacGregor) Tackling the Inner Cities, 1990; articles in learned jls and articles and reviews in Guardian, Observer, Sunday Times, TLS, New Statesman and Society, etc. *Address:* 9 Milner Place, Islington, N1. *T:* 071–609 1793.

PINA-CABRAL, Rt. Rev. Daniel (Pereira dos Santos) de; an Auxiliary Bishop, Diocese of Gibraltar in Europe, since 1976; Archdeacon of Gibraltar, since 1986; *b* 27 Jan. 1924; *m* 1951, Ana Avelina Pina-Cabral; two *s* two *d*. *Educ:* University of Lisbon (Licentiate in Law). Archdeacon of the North in the Lusitanian Church, 1965; Suffragan Bishop of Lebombo (Mozambique), Church of the Province of Southern Africa, 1967; Diocesan Bishop of Lebombo, 1968; Canon of Gibraltar, 1976–. *Address:* Rua Fernão Lopes Castanheda 51, 4100 Porto, Portugal. *T:* Porto 677772.

PINAY, Antoine; Médiateur, French Republic, 1973–74; leather manufacturer; *b* Department of the Rhône, 30 Dec. 1891. *Educ:* Marist Fathers' Sch., St-Chamond. Joined a tannery business there; became Mayor, 1929–77; later became gen. councillor, Dept of the Loire (Pres. 1949–79). Was returned to Chamber of Deputies, 1936, Ind. Radical party; Senator, 1938; elected to 2nd Constituent Assembly, 1946; then to 1st Nat. Assembly; re-elected to Nat. Assembly as an associate of Ind. Republican group; Sec. of State for Economic Affairs, Sept. 1948–Oct. 1949; in several successive ministries, July 1950–Feb. 1952, he was Minister of Public Works, Transportation, and Tourism; Prime Minister of France, March-Dec. 1952; Minister of Foreign Affairs, 1955–56; Minister of Finance and Economic Affairs, 1958–60. Served European War, 1914–18, in artillery as non-commnd officer (Croix de Guerre, Médaille Militaire). *Address:* 17 avenue de Tourville, 75007 Paris, France.

PINCHAM, Roger James, CBE 1982; Chairman: Venture Consultants Ltd, since 1980; UK Radio Developments Ltd, since 1990; Associate Director, Gerrard Vivian Gray, since 1988; Director: Market Access International (formerly David Boddy PR), since 1985; CFI Ltd, since 1987; *b* 19 Oct. 1935; *y s* of Sam and Bessie Pincham; *m* 1965, Gisela von Ulardt (*d* 1974); one *s* two *d*. *Educ:* Kingston Grammar School. National Service, RAF, 1954–56. With Phillips & Drew, 1956–88, Partner, 1967–76, consultant, 1976–88. Contested (L) Leominster, 1970, Feb. and Oct. 1974, 1979, 1983. Liberal Party: Nat. Exec., 1974–75 and 1978–87; Assembly Cttee, 1974–87; Standing Cttee, 1975–83; Chm. of Liberal Party, 1979–82; Jt Negotiating Cttee with SDP, and signatory to A Fresh Start for Britain, 1981. Founder Chm., Gladstone Club, 1973–; First Chairman: Indep. Educnl Assoc., 1974–; St James and St Vedast Schools, 1974–; Treasurer, Roma Housing Soc., 1977–80; Pres., Kington Eisteddfod, 1978. Freeman, City of London. Liveryman: Barbers' Co. (Middle Warden, 1991–92); Founders' Co.; Freeman, Co. of Watermen and Lightermen. *Publications:* (jtly) New Deal for Rural Britain, 1977; (ed) New Deal for British Farmers, 1978. *Recreations:* gardening, cricket, theatre. *Address:* 7 The Postern, Wood Street, Barbican, EC2Y 8BJ. *T:* 071–638 8154. *Clubs:* Reform, National Liberal, City of London, City Livery, Royal Automobile; Surrey County Cricket, Woolhope Naturalists' Field, Grange Cricket.

PINCHER, (Henry) Chapman; freelance journalist, novelist and business consultant; Assistant Editor, Daily Express, and Chief Defence Correspondent, Beaverbrook Newspapers, 1972–79; *b* Ambala, India, 29 March 1914; *s* of Major Richard Chapman Pincher, E Surrey Regt, and Helen (*née* Foster), Pontefract; *m* 1965, Constance, (Billee), Wolstenholme; one *s* one *d* (by previous *m*). *Educ:* Darlington Gram. Sch.; King's Coll., London (FKC 1979); Inst. Educn; Mil. Coll. of Science. Carter Medallist, London, 1934; BSc (hons Botany, Zoology), 1935. Staff Liverpool Inst., 1936–40. Joined Royal Armoured Corps, 1940; Techn SO, Rocket Div., Min. of Supply, 1943–46; Defence, Science and Medical Editor, Daily Express, 1946–73. Hon. DLitt Newcastle upon Tyne, 1979. Granada Award, Journalist of the Year, 1964; Reporter of the Decade, 1966. *Publications:* Breeding of Farm Animals, 1946; A Study of Fishes, 1947; Into the Atomic Age, 1947; Spotlight on Animals, 1950; Evolution, 1950; (with Bernard Wicksteed) It's Fun Finding Out, 1950; Sleep, and how to get more of it, 1954; Sex in Our Time, 1973; Inside Story, 1978; (jtly) Their Trade is Treachery, 1981; Too Secret Too Long, 1984; The Secret Offensive, 1985; Traitors—the Labyrinths of Treason, 1987; A Web of Deception, 1987; The Truth about Dirty Tricks, 1991; One Dog and Her Man, 1991; *novels:* Not with a Bang, 1965; The Giantkiller, 1967; The Penthouse Conspirators, 1970; The Skeleton at the Villa Wolkonsky, 1975; The Eye of the Tornado, 1976; The Four Horses, 1978; Dirty Tricks, 1980; The Private World of St John Terrapin, 1982; Contamination, 1989; original researches in genetics, numerous articles in scientific and agricultural jls. *Recreations:* fishing, shooting, natural history, country life; ferreting in Whitehall and bolting politicians. *Address:* The Church House, 16 Church Street, Kintbury, near Hungerford, Berks RG15 0TR. *T:* Kintbury (0488) 58855.

PINCHIN, Malcolm Cyril; County Education Officer, Surrey, since 1982; *b* 4 May 1933; *s* of Cyril Pinchin and Catherine Pinchin; *m* 1957, Diana Elizabeth Dawson; three *s*. *Educ:* Cheltenham Grammar Sch.; Univ. of Bristol (BSc). Education Officer, HMOCS, Malawi, 1958–67; Asst Educn Officer, Northampton, 1967–70; Asst Dir of Educn, 1970–74, Asst Dep. Dir of Educn, 1974–76, Leicestershire; Dep. Chief Educn Officer, Devon, 1976–82. Trustee, Duke of Edinburgh Award, 1989–. FRSA 1986. *Recreations:* gardening, fly fishing, bee keeping, opera. *Address:* Firbank, 41 Knoll Road, Dorking, Surrey RH4 3ES. *T:* Dorking (0306) 882768.

PINCOTT, Leslie Rundell, CBE 1978; non-executive company director; Managing Director, Esso Petroleum Co. Ltd, 1970–78; *b* 27 March 1923; *s* of Hubert George Pincott and Gertrude Elizabeth Rundell; *m* 1944, Mary Mae Tuffin; two *s* one *d*. *Educ:* Mercers' Sch., Holborn. Served War, Royal Navy, 1942–46. Broads Paterson & Co. (Chartered Accountants), 1946–50; joined Esso Petroleum Co. Ltd, 1950; Comptroller, 1958–61; Asst Gen. Manager (Marketing), 1961–65; Dir and Gen. Manager, Cleveland Petroleum Co. Ltd, 1966–68; Standard Oil Co. (NJ): Exec. Asst to Pres., and later, to Chm., 1968–70; Vice-Chm., Remploy Ltd, 1979–87 (Dir, 1975–87); Chairman: Canada Permanent Trust Co. (UK) Ltd, 1978–80; Stone-Platt Industries PLC, 1980–82; Edman Communications Gp PLC, 1982–87; Investment Cttee, London Development Capital Fund (Guinness Mahon), 1985–; BR Southern Bd, 1986–89 (Dir, 1977–89). Director: George Wimpey PLC, 1978–85; Highlands Fabricators Ltd, 1984–. A Dep. Chm., 1978–79, Chm., 1979–80, Price Commn; Chairman: Hundred Gp of Chartered Accountants, 1978–79; Oxford Univ. Business Summer Sch., 1975–78; Printing Industries EDC, NEDO, 1982–88. Pres., District Heating Assoc., 1977–79. Vice-Pres., English Schs Athletics Assoc., 1977–; Mem. Council, ISCO, 1982–. Mem., The Pilgrims, 1971–. FCA, MCIM; CBIM. *Recreation:* tennis. *Address:* 6 Lambourne Avenue, Wimbledon, SW19 7DW. *Clubs:* Arts, Hurlingham (Chm., 1988–).

PINDER, Andrew; *see* Pinder, J. A.

PINDER, Ven. Charles; Archdeacon of Lambeth, 1986–88, now Archdeacon Emeritus; *b* 5 May 1921; *s* of Ernest and Gertrude Pinder; *m* 1943, Ethel, *d* of Albert and Emma Milke; four *d*. *Educ:* King's College London (AKC). Ordained, 1950; Curate, St Saviour, Raynes Park, 1950–53; Vicar: All Saints, Hatcham Park, 1953–60; St Laurence, Catford, 1960–73; Sub-Dean of Lewisham, 1968–73; Borough Dean of Lambeth, 1973–86. Hon. Chaplain to Bishop of Southwark, 1963–80; Hon. Canon of Southwark, 1973–86. Member of Parole Board, 1976–80; Chm., Brixton Prison Bd of Visitors, 1983–86. *Recreations:* most outdoor sports and selective indoor games; listening to music. *Address:* 22 Somerstown, Chichester, West Sussex PO19 4AG. *T:* Chichester (0243) 779708.

PINDER, (John) Andrew; Director of Systems, since 1990, and Director, Group Management Services, since 1991, Prudential Corporation (formerly Prudential Assurance Co.); *b* 5 May 1947; *s* of Norah Joan Pinder and William Gordon Pinder; *m* 1st, 1970, Patricia Munyard (marr. diss. 1980); one *d*; 2nd, 1981, Susan Ellen Tyrrell; one *d* and one step *s*. *Educ:* De La Salle Coll., Sheffield; Coleshill Grammar Sch., Warwicks; Univ. of

Liverpool (BA Hons Social Studies). Inspector of Taxes, 1972–76; Board of Inland Revenue: Policy Div., 1976–79; Management Div., 1979–90, Under Sec., Dir of IT, 1989. *Recreations:* music, walking, gardening. *Address:* 61 Andrewes House, Barbican, EC2Y 8AY. *Club:* Institute of Directors.

PINDLING, Rt. Hon. Sir Lynden Oscar, KCMG 1983; PC 1976; Prime Minister and Minister of Economic Affairs of the Commonwealth of The Bahamas, since 1969; *b* 22 March 1930; *s* of Arnold Franklin and Viola Pindling; *m* 1956, Marguerite McKenzie; two *s* two *d. Educ:* Western Senior Sch., Nassau Govt High Sch.; London Univ. (LLB 1952; LLD 1970; DHL 1978). Called to the Bar, Middle Temple, 1953. Practised as Lawyer, 1952–67. Parly Leader of Progressive Liberal Party, 1956; elected to Bahamas House of Assembly, 1956, re-elected 1962, 1967, 1968, 1972 and 1977. Worked for human rights and self-determination in the Bahamas; Mem., several delegns to Colonial Office, 1956–66; took part in Constitutional Conf., May 1963; Leader of Opposition, 1964; Mem., Delegns to UN Special Cttee of Twenty-four, 1965, 1966; Premier of the Bahamas and Minister of Tourism and Development, 1967; led Bahamian Delegn to Constitutional Conf., London, 1968; to Independence Conf., 1972 (first Prime Minister after Independence). Chm., Commonwealth Parly Assoc., 1968. *Recreations:* swimming, boating, travel. *Address:* Office of the Prime Minister, Rawson Square, Nassau, Bahamas.

PINEAU, Christian Paul Francis, Grand Officier, Légion d'Honneur; Compagnon de la Libération; Croix de Guerre (French), Médaille de la Résistance (Rosette); French Statesman and Writer; *b* Chaumont (Haute-Marne), 14 Oct. 1904; *m* 1962, Mlle Blanche Bloys; one *d* (and five *s* one *d* of previous marriages). Minister of Food and Supplies, June-Nov. 1945; General Rapporteur to Budget Commission 1945–46; Chm. Nat. Assembly Finance Commn, 1946–47; Minister of Public Works, Transport, and Tourism (Schuman Cabinet), 1947–48, also (Marie Cabinet) July-Aug. 1948, also (Queuille Cabinet), Sept. 1948, also (Bidault Cabinet), Oct. 1949; Minister of Finance and Economic Affairs (Schuman Cabinet), Aug. 1946; Chm. Nat. Defence Credits Control Commn, 1951–55; Designated Premier, Feb. 1955; Minister for Foreign Affairs, Feb. 1956–June 1957. Holds GCMG (Hon.) Great Britain, and numerous other foreign decorations. *Publications: books for children:* Contes de je ne sais quand; Plume et le saumon; L'Ourse aux pattons verts; Cornerousse le Mystérieux; Histoires de la forêt de Bercé; La Planète aux enfants perdus; La Marelle et le ballon; La Bête à bêtises; *other publications;* The SNCF and French Transport; Mon cher député; La simple verite, 1940–45; L'escalier des ombres; Khrouchtchev; 1956: Suez, 1976; economic and financial articles; contrib. to various papers. *Address:* 55 rue Vaneau, 75007 Paris, France.

PININFARINA, Sergio; Cavaliere del Lavoro, 1976; engineer; Member, European Parliament (Liberal and Democratic Group), 1979–88; President, Pininfarina SpA; *b* 8 Sept. 1926; *s* of Battista Pininfarina and Rosa Copasso; *m* 1951, Giorgia Gianolio; two *s* one *d. Educ:* Polytechnic of Turin; graduated in Mech. Eng., 1950. President: Federpiemonte, 1983–88; OICA, 1987–89; Confindustria, 1988–; Board Member: Ferrari; Banca Passadore; Banca Popolare di Novara; Toro Assicurazioni; CMB Packaging. Foreign Mem., Royal Swedish Acad. of Engrg Scis, 1988. Légion d'Honneur, 1979. Hon. RDI 1983. *Recreation:* golf. *Address:* PO Box 295, 10100 Turin, Italy. *T:* 11–70911. *Clubs:* Società Whist Accademia Filarmonica, Rotary Torino; Circolo Golf Torino, Associazione Sportiva I Roveri.

PINKER, Sir George (Douglas), KCVO 1990 (CVO 1983); FRCS, FRCSEd, FRCOG; Surgeon-Gynaecologist to the Queen, 1973–90; Consulting Gynaecological Surgeon and Obstetrician, St Mary's Hospital, Paddington and Samaritan Hospital, since 1958; Consulting Gynaecological Surgeon, Middlesex and Soho Hospitals, since 1969; Consultant Gynæcologist, King Edward VII Hospital for Officers, since 1974; *b* 6 Dec. 1924; *s* of late Ronald Douglas Pinker and of Queenie Elizabeth Pinker (*née* Dix); *m* Dorothy Emma (*née* Russell); three *s* one *d* (incl. twin *s* and *d*). *Educ:* Reading Sch.; St Mary's Hosp., London Univ. MB BS London 1947; DObst 1949; MRCOG 1954; FRCS(Ed) 1957; FRCOG 1964; FRCS 1989. Late Cons. Gyn. Surg., Bolingbroke Hosp., and Res. Off., Nuffield Dept of Obst., Radcliffe Infirmary, Oxford; late Cons. Gyn. Surg., Queen Charlotte's Hosp. Arthur Wilson Orator, 1972 and 1989, Turnbull Scholar, and Hon. Consultant Obstetrician and Gynaecologist, 1972, Royal Women's Hosp., Melbourne. Examiner in Obst. and Gynae.: Univs of Cambridge, Dundee, London, and FRCS Edinburgh; formerly also in RCOG, and Univs of Birmingham, Glasgow and Dublin. Sims Black Travelling Prof., RCOG, 1979; Vis. Prof., SA Regional Council, RCOG, 1980. Pres., RCOG, 1987–90 (Hon. Treas., 1970–77; Vice-Pres., 1980–83). Pres., British Fertility Soc., 1987; Mem. Council, Winston Churchill Trust, 1979–; Mem., Blair Bell Res. Soc.; FRSocMed (Pres. elect, 1991); Hon. Mem., British Paediatric Assoc., 1988. Hon. FRCSI 1987; Hon. FRACOG 1989; Hon. FACOG 1990; Hon. Fellow, S African Soc. of Obstetricians and Gynaecologists, 1990; Hon. FCMSA 1991. Chm., Editorial Bd, Modern Medicine (Obs. and Gynae.), 1989–91 (Mem., 1980–91). *Publications:* (all jtly) Ten Teachers Diseases of Women, 1964; Ten Teachers Obstetrics, 1966; A Short Textbook of Obstetrics and Gynaecology, 1967. *Recreations:* music, gardening, sailing, ski-ing, fell walking. *Address:* 96 Harley Street, W1N 1AF. *T:* 071–935 2292; Sycamore House, Willersey, Broadway, Worcs. *Club:* Garrick.

PINKER, Prof. Robert Arthur; Professor of Social Work Studies, London School of Economics and Political Science, since 1978; *b* 27 May 1931; *s* of Dora Elizabeth and Joseph Pinker; *m* 1955, Jennifer Farrington Boulton; two *d. Educ:* Holloway County Sch.; LSE (Cert. in Social Sci. and Admin. 1959; BSc Sociology 1962; MSc Econ 1965). University of London: Head of Sociology Dept, Goldsmiths' Coll., 1964–72; Lewisham Prof. of Social Admin, Goldsmiths' Coll. and Bedford Coll., 1972–74; Prof. of Social Studies, Chelsea Coll., 1974–78; Pro-Director, LSE, 1985–88; Pro-Vice-Chancellor for Social Scis, London Univ., 1989–90. Chm., British Library Project on Family and Social Research, 1983–86; Member: Council, Advertising Standards Authority, 1988–; Press Complaints Commn, 1991–; Council, Direct Mail Services Standards Bd, 1990–; Bd of Management, LSHTM, 1990–; Chm. Governors, Centre for Policy on Ageing, 1988–; Governor: BPMF, 1990–; Inst. of Educn, 1990–. Trustee, Highgate Cemetery Charity, 1991–. Chairman, Editorial Board, Jl of Social Policy, 1981–86. *Publications:* English Hospital Statistics 1861–1938, 1964; Social Theory and Social Policy, 1971; The Idea of Welfare, 1979; Social Work in an Enterprise Society, 1990. *Recreations:* reading, writing, travel, unskilled gardening. *Address:* 76 Coleraine Road, Blackheath, SE3 7PE. *Tel:* 081–858 5320.

PINKERTON, Prof. John Henry McKnight, CBE 1983; Professor of Midwifery and Gynæcology, Queen's University, Belfast, 1963–85, now Emeritus; Gynæcologist: Royal Victoria and City Hospitals, Belfast, 1963–85; Ulster Hospital for Women and Children, 1963–85; Surgeon, Royal Maternity Hospital, Belfast, 1963–85; *b* 5 June 1920; *s* of late William R. and Eva Pinkerton; *m* 1947, Florence McKinstry, MB, BCh, BAO; four *s. Educ:* Royal Belfast Academical Institution; Queen's Univ., Belfast. Hyndman Univ. Entrance Scholar, 1939; MB, BCh, BAO Hons; Magrath Scholar in Obstetrics and Gynæcology, 1943. Active service in HM Ships as Surg.-Lt, RNVR, 1945–47. MD 1948; MRCOG 1949; FRCOG 1960; FZS 1960; FRCPI 1977. Sen. Lectr in Obstetrics and Gynæcology, University Coll. of the West Indies, and Consultant Obstetrician and Gynæcologist to University Coll. Hosp. of the West Indies, 1953–59; Rockefeller Research Fellow at Harvard Medical Sch., 1956–57; Prof. of Obstetrics and Gynæcology, Univ. of London, at Queen Charlotte's and Chelsea Hosps and the Inst. of Obstetrics and Gynæcology, 1959–63; Obstetric Surgeon to Queen Charlotte's Hosp.; Surgeon to Chelsea Hosp. for Women. Vice-Pres., RCOG, 1977–80; Chm., Inst. of Obstetrics and Gynæcol., RCPI, 1984–87. Hon. DSc NUI, 1986. *Publications:* various papers on obstetrical and gynæcological subjects. *Address:* 41c Sans Souci Park, Belfast BT9 5BZ. *T:* Belfast (0232) 682956.

See also W. R. Pinkerton.

PINKERTON, William Ross, CBE 1977; JP; HM Nominee for Northern Ireland on General Medical Council, 1979–83, retired; a director of companies; *b* 10 April 1913; *s* of William Ross Pinkerton and Eva Pinkerton; *m* 1943, Anna Isobel Lyness; two *d.* Managing Director, H. Stevenson & Co. Ltd, Londonderry, 1941–76. Mem., Baking Wages Council (NI), 1957–74. Mem. later Chm, Londonderry/Gransha Psychiatric HMC, 1951–69; Vice-Chm., then Chm., North West HMC, 1969–72; Chm., Western Health and Social Services Board, 1972–79; Member: Central Services Agency (NI), 1972–79; NI Health and Social Services Council, 1975–79; Lay Mem., Health and Personal Social Services Tribunal, NI, 1978–. Member, New Ulster Univ. Court, 1973–85, Council, 1979–85. Hon. Life Governor: Altnagelvin, Gransha, Waterside, St Columb's, Roe Valley, Strabane, Foyle and Stradreagh Hosps. JP Co. Londonderry, 1965–84, Div. of Ards, 1984–. *Recreations:* yachting, fishing. *Address:* 2 Ard-Na-Ree, The Brae, Groomsport, Co. Down, N Ireland BT19 2JL. *T:* Bangor (0247) 464525. *Club:* Royal Highland Yacht (Oban).

See also J. H. McK. Pinkerton.

PINNER, Hayim, OBE 1989; consultant, administrator, linguist, educator, lecturer, journalist, broadcaster; Director, Sternberg Charitable Trust; *b* London, 25 May 1925; *s* of late Simon Pinner and Annie Pinner (*née* Wagner); *m* 1956, Rita Reuben, Cape Town (marr. diss. 1980); one *s* one *d. Educ:* Davenant Foundation School; London University; Yeshivah Etz Hayim; Bet Berl College, Israel. Served RAOC, 1944–48; Editor, Jewish Vanguard, 1950–74; Exec. Dir, B'nai B'rith, 1957–77; Sec. Gen., Board of Deputies of British Jews, 1977–91. Hon. Vice-Pres., Zionist Fedn of GB and Ireland, 1975– (Hon. Treasurer, 1971–75); Vice-Pres., Labour Zionist Movement; Member: Jewish Agency and World Zionist Orgn; Exec., Council of Christians and Jews; Adv. Council, World Congress of Faiths; Trades Adv. Council; Hillel Foundn; Jt Israel Appeal; Lab. Party Middle East Cttee; 'B' List of Parly Candidates; UNA; Founder Mem. Exec., Inter-Faith. Freeman, City of London. Contribs to Radio 4, Radio London, London Broadcasting, BBC TV. *Publications:* contribs to UK and foreign periodicals, Isra-Kit. *Recreations:* travelling, swimming, reading, talking. *Address:* 95 Millway, NW7 3QT.

PINNER, Ruth Margaret, (Mrs M. J. Pinner); *see* Kempson, R. M.

PINNINGTON, Geoffrey Charles; Editor, Sunday People, 1972–82; *b* 21 March 1919; *s* of Charles and Beatrice Pinnington; *m* 1941, Beryl, *d* of Edward and Lilian Clark; two *d. Educ:* Harrow County Sch.; Rock Ferry High Sch., Birkenhead; King's Coll., Univ. of London. Served War as Air Navigator, RAF Bomber and Middle East Commands, 1940–45 (Sqdn Ldr, 1943). On staff of (successively): Middlesex Independent; Kensington Post (Editor); Daily Herald: Dep. News Editor, 1955; Northern Editor, 1957; Dep. Editor, 1958; Daily Mirror: Night Editor, 1961, Assistant Editor, 1964, Dep. Editor, 1968; Dir, Mirror Group Newspapers, 1976–82. Mem., Press Council, 1982–86 (Jt Vice-Chm., 1983–86). *Recreations:* his family, travel, reading, music, theatre and the arts, amateur cine-photography. *Address:* 23 Lauderdale Drive, Richmond, Surrey TW10 7BS.

PINNINGTON, Roger Adrian, TD 1967; Chairman:Petrocon Group plc, since 1989; Aqualisa Products, since 1990; *b* 27 Aug. 1932; *s* of William Austin Pinnington and Elsie Amy Pinnington; *m* 1974, Marjorie Ann Pearson; one *s* three *d. Educ:* Rydal Sch., Colwyn Bay; Lincoln Coll., Oxford (MA). Marketing Dir, Jonas Woodhead & Sons, 1963–74; 1975–82: Vice Pres., TRW Europe Inc.; Man. Dir, CAM Gears Ltd; Pres., TRW Italia SpA; Dir Gen., Gemmer France; Pres., Torfinasa; Dep. Chm. and Ch. Exec., UBM Group, 1982–85; Dir, Norcros, 1985–86; Dir and Chief Exec., Royal Ordnance PLC, 1986–87; Dir and Gp Chief Exec., RHP, subseq. Pilgrim House Gp, 1987–89. Chm., Blackwood Hodge, 1988–90. *Recreations:* gardening, arguing with Sally, collecting sad irons. *Address:* 46 Willoughby Road, Hampstead, NW3 1RU. *T:* 071–431 3999. *Club:* Vincent's (Oxford).

PINNINGTON-HUGHES, John; *see* Hughes.

PINNOCK, Comdr Harry James, RN retd; Director, Cement Makers' Federation, 1979–87; *b* 6 April 1927; *s* of Frederick Walter Pinnock and Kate Ada (*née* Shepherd); *m* 1962, Fru Inger Connie Åhgren (*d* 1978); one *d. Educ:* Sutton Valence Sch. Joined RN, 1945; Midshipman, HMS Nelson, 1945–47; Sub-Lieut/Lieut, HMS Belfast, Far East, 1948–50; RN Rhine Flotilla, 1951–52; Staff of First Sea Lord, 1952–55; Lt-Comdr, Mediterranean Minesweepers, 1955–57; HMS Ceylon, E of Suez, 1957–59; Staff of C-in-C Plymouth, 1960–61; HQ Allied Naval Forces, Northern Europe, Oslo, 1961–63; Comdr, MoD, 1964–67, retd. Cement Makers' Fedn, 1970–87. *Recreations:* ski-ing, gardening, travel. *Address:* Windy Ridge, Bells Lane, Tenterden, Kent TN30 6EX. *T:* Tenterden (05806) 3025. *Club:* Army and Navy.

PINNOCK, Trevor, ARCM; harpsichordist; conductor; Director, The English Concert, since 1973; Artistic Director and Principal Conductor, National Arts Centre Orchestra, Ottawa, since 1991; *b* Canterbury, 16 Dec. 1946; *m* 1988, Pauline Nobes. *Educ:* Canterbury Cathedral Choir Sch.; Simon Langton Grammar Sch., Canterbury; Royal Coll. of Music, London (Foundn Scholar; Harpsichord and Organ Prizes). ARCM Hons (organ) 1965. London début with Galliard Harpsichord Trio (Jt Founder with Stephen Preston, flute and Anthony Pleeth, 'cello), 1966; solo début, Purcell Room, London, 1968. Formed The English Concert for purpose of performing music of baroque period on instruments in original condition or good modern copies, 1972, making its London début in English Bach Festival, Purcell Room, 1973. NY début at Metropolitan Opera, conducting Handel Giulio Cesare, 1988. Recordings of complete keyboard works of Rameau; Bach Toccatas, Partitas, Goldberg Variations, Concerti, Handel Messiah and Suites, Purcell Dido and Aeneas, orchestral and choral works of Bach, Handel, Vivaldi, etc. *Address:* c/o Ms Jan Burnett, 8 St George's Terrace, NW1 8XJ. *T:* 071–911 0901, *Fax:* 071–911 0903.

PINSENT, Sir Christopher (Roy), 3rd Bt *cr* 1938; Lecturer and Tutor, Camberwell School of Art, 1962–86, retired; *b* 2 Aug. 1922; *s* of Sir Roy Pinsent, 2nd Bt, and Mary Tirzah Pinsent (*d* 1951), *d* of Dr Edward Geoffrey Walls, Spilsby, Lincs; *S* father, 1978; *m* 1951, Susan Mary, *d* of John Norton Scorer, Fotheringhay; one *s* two *d. Educ:* Winchester College. *Heir: s* Thomas Benjamin Roy Pinsent, *b* 21 July 1967. *Address:* The Chestnuts, Castle Hill, Guildford, Surrey GU1 3SX.

PINSENT, Roger Philip; HM Diplomatic Service, retired; *b* 30 Dec. 1916; *s* of late Sidney Hume Pinsent; *m* 1941, Suzanne Smalley; one *s* two *d. Educ:* Downside Sch.; Lausanne, London and Grenoble Univs. London Univ. French Scholar, 1938; BA Hons

London, 1940. HM Forces, 1940–46; HM Diplomatic Service, May 1946; 1st Sec., HM Legation, Havana, 1948–50; HM Consul, Tangier, 1950–52; 1st Sec., HM Embassy, Madrid, 1952–53; FO, 1953–56; 1st Sec., Head of Chancery, HM Embassy, Lima (Chargé d'Affaires, 1958, 1959), 1956–59; Dep. Head of UK Delegation to the European Communities, Luxembourg, 1959–63; HM Ambassador to Nicaragua, 1963–67; Counsellor (Commercial), Ankara, 1967–70; Consul-Gen., São Paulo, 1970–73. Mem., Inst. of Linguists, 1976–79. *Recreations:* music, photography, book-binding, golf. *Address:* Cranfield Cottage, Maugersbury, Stow-on-the-Wold, Glos GL54 1HR. *T:* Cotswold (0451) 30992. *Clubs:* Canning; Broadway Golf; Stow on the Wold RFC.

PINSON, Barry, QC 1973; *b* 18 Dec. 1925; *s* of Thomas Alfred Pinson and Alice Cicily Pinson; *m* 1950, Miriam Mary; one *s* one *d*; *m* 1977, Anne Kathleen Golby. *Educ:* King Edward's Sch., Birmingham; Univ. of Birmingham. LLB Hons 1945. Fellow Inst. Taxation. Mil. Service, 1944–47. Called to Bar, Gray's Inn, 1949, Bencher 1981. Trustee, RAF Museums, 1980–; Chm., Addington Soc., 1987–90. *Publications:* Revenue Law, 17 edns. *Recreations:* music, photography. *Address:* 11 New Square, Lincoln's Inn, WC2A 3QB. *T:* 071–242 3981. *Club:* Arts.

PINTER, Lady Antonia; *see* Fraser, Antonia.

PINTER, Harold, CBE 1966; actor, playwright and director; Associate Director, National Theatre, 1973–83; *b* 10 Oct. 1930; *s* of J. Pinter; *m* 1st, 1956, Vivien Merchant (marr. diss. 1980; she *d* 1982); one *s*; 2nd, 1980, Lady Antonia Fraser, *qv. Educ:* Hackney Downs Grammar Sch. Actor (mainly repertory), 1949–57. Directed: The Collection (co-dir with Peter Hall), Aldwych, 1962; The Birthday Party, Aldwych, 1964; The Lover, The Dwarfs, Arts, 1966; Exiles, Mermaid, 1970; Butley, Criterion, 1971; Butley (film), 1973; Next of Kin, Nat. Theatre, 1974; Otherwise Engaged, Queen's, 1975, NY 1977; Blithe Spirit, Nat. Theatre, 1977; The Rear Column, Globe, 1978; Close of Play, Nat. Theatre, 1979; The Hothouse, Hampstead, 1980; Quartermaine's Terms, Queen's, 1981; Incident at Tulse Hill, Hampstead, 1981; The Trojan War Will Not Take Place, Nat. Theatre, 1983; The Common Pursuit, Lyric Hammersmith, 1984; Sweet Bird of Youth, Haymarket, 1985; Circe and Bravo, Wyndham's, 1986. Shakespeare Prize, Hamburg, 1970; Austrian State Prize for European Literature, 1973; Pirandello Prize, 1980; Donatello Prize, 1982; Elmer Holmes Bobst Award, 1984. Hon. DLitt: Reading, 1970; Birmingham, 1971; Glasgow, 1974; East Anglia, 1974; Stirling, 1979; Brown, 1982; Hull, 1986. *Plays:* The Room (stage 1957, television 1965 and 1987); The Birthday Party (stage 1958, television 1960 and 1987, film 1968); The Dumb Waiter, 1957 (stage 1960, television 1964 and 1987); The Hothouse, 1958 (stage 1980, television 1981); A Slight Ache (radio 1958, stage 1961, television 1966); A Night Out (radio and television, 1961); The Caretaker, 1960 (stage 1960, film 1963, television 1966 and 1982); Night School (television 1960 and 1982, radio 1966); The Dwarfs (radio 1960, stage 1963); The Collection (television 1961, stage 1962); The Lover (television, stage 1963) (Italia Prize for TV); Tea Party (television 1964); The Homecoming, 1964; Landscape (radio 1968, stage 1969); Silence (stage 1969); Old Times (stage 1971); Monologue (television 1972); No Man's Land (stage 1975, television 1978); Betrayal (stage 1978 (SWET Award, 1979), filmed 1983); Family Voices (radio 1981 (Giles Cooper Award, 1982), stage 1982); Victoria Station, 1982; A Kind of Alaska, 1982; One for the Road, 1984 (television 1985); Mountain Language, 1988 (television 1988); Party Time, 1991; The New World Order (stage 1991). *Screenplays:* The Caretaker, The Servant, 1962; The Pumpkin Eater, 1963; The Quiller Memorandum, 1966; Accident, 1967; The Birthday Party, The Homecoming, 1968; The Go-Between, 1969; Langrishe, Go Down, 1970 (adapted for television, 1978); A la Recherche du Temps Perdu, 1972; The Last Tycoon, 1974; The French Lieutenant's Woman, 1981; Betrayal, 1981; Turtle Diary, 1985; The Handmaid's Tale, 1987; The Heat of the Day, 1988; Reunion, 1989; The Comfort of Strangers, 1990. *Publications:* The Caretaker, 1960; The Birthday Party, and other plays, 1960; A Slight Ache, 1961; The Collection, 1963; The Lover, 1963; The Homecoming, 1965; Tea Party, and, The Basement, 1967; (co-ed) PEN Anthology of New Poems, 1967; Mac, 1968; Landscape, and, Silence, 1969; Five Screenplays, 1971; Old Times, 1971; Poems, 1971; No Man's Land, 1975; The Proust Screenplay: A la Recherche du Temps Perdu, 1978; Betrayal, 1978; Poems and Prose 1949–1977, 1978; I Know the Place, 1979; Family Voices, 1981; Other Places, 1982; French Lieutenant's Woman and other screenplays, 1982; One For The Road, 1984; Collected Poems and Prose, 1986; (co-ed) 100 Poems by 100 Poets, 1986; Mountain Language, 1988; The Heat of the Day, 1989; The Dwarfs (novel), 1990. *Recreation:* cricket. *Address:* c/o Judy Daish Associates Ltd, 83 Eastbourne Mews, W2 6LQ.

PIPER, Bright Harold, (Peter Piper), CBE 1979; FCIB; Director, 1970–84, Chief Executive, 1973–78, Lloyds Bank Group; *b* 22 Sept. 1918; 2nd *s* of Robert Harold Piper; *m* 1st, 1945, Marjorie Joyce, 2nd *d* of Captain George Arthur; one *s* one *d*; 2nd, 1979, Leonie Mary Lane, *d* of Major C. V. Lane. *Educ:* Maidstone Grammar School. Served with RN, 1939–46. Entered Lloyds Bank, 1935: Asst Gen. Man., 1963; Jt Gen. Man., 1965; Asst Chief Gen. Man., 1968; Dep. Chief Gen. Man., 1970; Chief Gen. Man., 1973. Director: Lewis' Bank, 1969–75; Lloyds and Scottish, 1970–75; Chm., Lloyds First Western (US), 1973–78. Freeman, City of London; Liveryman, Spectacle Makers' Company. *Recreation:* sailing. *Address:* Greenways, Hawkshill Close, Esher, Surrey KT10 8JY. *Clubs:* Overseas Bankers, Australia.

PIPER, John Egerton Christmas, CH 1972; painter and writer; Member of the Oxford Diocesan Advisory Committee, since 1950; *b* 13 Dec. 1903; *s* of late C. A. Piper, Solicitor; *m* 1935, Mary Myfanwy Evans; one *s* two *d* (and one *s* decd). *Educ:* Epsom Coll.; Royal College of Art. Paintings, drawings, exhibited in London since 1925; pictures bought by Tate Gallery, Contemporary Art Society, Victoria and Albert Museum, etc.; series of watercolours of Windsor Castle commissioned by the Queen, 1941–42; windows for nave of Eton College Chapel commissioned 1958; windows and interior design, Nuffield College Chapel, Oxford, completed, 1961; window, Coventry Cathedral, completed, 1962; windows for King George VI Memorial Chapel, Windsor, 1969; windows for Robinson Coll., Cambridge, 1981. Designed Tapestry for High Altar, Chichester Cathedral, 1966, and for Civic Hall, Newcastle upon Tyne. Designer for opera and ballet. Mem., Royal Fine Art Commn, 1959–78; a Trustee: Tate Gallery, 1946–53, 1954–61, 1968–74; National Gallery, 1967–74, 1975–78; Arts Council art panel, 1952–57. Hon. Fellow, Robinson Coll., Cambridge, 1980. Hon. ARIBA, 1957, Hon. FRIBA 1971; Hon. ARCA 1959; Hon. DLitt: Leicester, 1960; Oxford, 1966; Sussex, 1974; Reading, 1977; Wales (Cardiff), 1981. *Publications:* Wind in the Trees (poems), 1921; 'Shell Guide' to Oxfordshire, 1938; Brighton Aquatints, 1939; British Romantic Painters, 1942; Buildings and Prospects, 1949; (ed with John Betjeman) Buckinghamshire Architectural Guide, 1948; Berkshire Architectural Guide, 1949; (illus.) The Castles on the Ground by J. M. Richards, 1973; (jtly) Lincolnshire Churches, 1976; (illus.) John Betjeman's Church Poems, 1981; (with Richard Ingrams) Piper's Places: John Piper in England and Wales, 1983; *relevant publications:* John Piper: Paintings, Drawings and Theatre Designs, 1932–54 (arr. S. John Woods), 1955; John Piper, by Anthony West, 1979. *Address:* Fawley Bottom Farmhouse, near Henley-on-Thames, Oxon. *Club:* Athenæum.

PIPER, Peter; *see* Piper, Bright Harold.

PIPKIN, (Charles Harry) Broughton, CBE 1973; Chairman: BICC Ltd, 1977–80; Electrak International Ltd, 1982–84 (Director, 1982–85); *b* 29 Nov. 1913; *er s* of late Charles Pipkin and Charlotte Phyllis (*née* Viney), Lewisham; *m* 1941, Viola, *yr d* of Albert and Florence Byatt, Market Harborough; one *s* one *d. Educ:* Christ's Coll., Blackheath; Faraday House. CEng, FIEE; FBIM. Various appts with BICC, 1936–73, Dep. Chm. and Chief Exec., 1973–77. War service, 1940–46: Major REME, 14th Army (despatches). President: British Non-ferrous Metals Fedn, 1965–66; Electric Cable Makers' Fedn, 1967–68; BEAMA, 1975–76. *Recreations:* travel, reading, racing. *Address:* Pegler's Barn, Bledington, Oxon OX7 6XQ. *T:* Kingham (0608) 658304. *Club:* City Livery.

PIPPARD, Prof. Sir (Alfred) Brian, Kt 1975; FRS 1956; Cavendish Professor of Physics, University of Cambridge, 1971–82, now Emeritus; *b* 7 Sept. 1920; *s* of late Prof. A. J. S. Pippard; *m* 1955, Charlotte Frances Dyer; three *d. Educ:* Clifton Coll.; Clare Coll., Cambridge (Hon. Fellow 1973). BA (Cantab) 1941, MA 1945. PhD 1949; ScD 1966. Scientific Officer, Radar Research and Development Establishment, Great Malvern, 1941–45; Stokes Student, Pembroke Coll., Cambridge, 1945–46; Demonstrator in Physics, University of Cambridge, 1946; Lecturer in Physics, 1950; Reader in Physics, 1959–60; John Humphrey Plummer Prof. of Physics, 1960–71; Pres., Clare Hall, Cambridge, 1966–73. Visiting Prof., Institute for the Study of Metals, University of Chicago, 1955–56. Fellow of Clare Coll., Cambridge, 1947–66. Cherwell-Simon Memorial Lectr, Oxford, 1968–69; Eddington Meml Lectr, Cambridge, 1988. Pres., Inst. of Physics, 1974–76. Hughes Medal of the Royal Soc., 1959; Holweck Medal, 1961; Dannie-Heineman Prize, 1969; Guthrie Prize, 1970. *Publications:* Elements of Classical Thermodynamics, 1957; Dynamics of Conduction Electrons, 1962; Forces and Particles, 1972; The Physics of Vibration, vol. 1, 1978, vol. 2, 1983; Response and Stability, 1985; Magnetoresistance, 1989; papers in Proc. Royal Soc., etc. *Recreation:* music. *Address:* 30 Porson Road, Cambridge CB2 2EU. *T:* Cambridge (0223) 358713.

PIRATIN, Philip; *b* 15 May 1907; *m* 1929, Celia Fund; one *s* two *d. Educ:* Davenant Foundation Sch., London, E1. Was a Member of Stepney Borough Council, 1937–49; MP (Com) Mile End Division of Stepney, 1945–50.

PIRELLI, Leopoldo; Knight, Order of Labour Merit, 1977; engineer; Chairman, Pirelli SpA, since 1965; *b* 27 Aug. 1925; *s* of Alberto Pirelli and Ludovica Zambeletti; *m* 1947, Giulia Ferlito; two *c. Educ:* Milan University (Politecnico); graduated in Mech. Eng. 1950. Mem., Bd of Dirs, 1954, Vice-Chm., 1956, Pirelli SpA; Partner, Pirelli Inc., 1957–; Mem., Bd of Dirs, 1956, Vice-Chm., 1979–, Soc. Internat. Pirelli. Member, Board of Directors: Generale Industrie Metallurgiche, 1949–; Mediobanca, 1958–; Riunione Adriatica Sicurtà, 1959–; Banca Commerciale Italiana, 1982–; Società Metallurgica Italiana, 1983–; Compagnia Finanziaria De Bendetti, 1987–. Mem., Exec. Council, Confedn of Italian Industries, 1957– (Dep. Chm., 1974–80; Mem. Bd, 1974–82). *Address:* Piazza Cadorna 5, 20123 Milan, Italy. *T:* (02) 8535 1. *Clubs:* Dadi, Rotary, Unione (Milan); Yacht Club Italiano.

PIRIE, Group Captain Sir Gordon (Hamish Martin), Kt 1984; CVO 1987; CBE 1946; JP; DL; Deputy High Bailiff of Westminster, 1978–87; Member, Westminster City Council, 1949–82 (Mayor, 1959–60; Leader of Council, 1961–69; Alderman, 1963–78; Lord Mayor, 1974–75); Director, Parker Gallery; *b* 10 Feb. 1918; *s* of Harold Victor Campbell Pirie and Irene Gordon Hogarth; *m* 1st, 1953, Margaret Joan Bomford (*d* 1972); no *c*; 2nd, 1982, Joanna, *widow* of John C. Hugill. *Educ:* Eton (scholar); RAF Coll., Cranwell. Permanent Commission, RAF, 1938. Served War of 1939–45: Dir of Ops, RNZAF, Atlantic and Pacific (despatches, CBE); retired as Group Captain, 1946. Comr No 1 (POW) Dist SJAB, 1960–69; Comdr St John Ambulance, London, 1969–75; Chm., St John Council for London, 1975–85. Vice-Pres., Services Sound and Vision Corp., (Chm., 1979–90). A Governor of Westminster Sch., 1962–; Mem., Bd of Green Cloth Verge of Palaces, 1962–87; Vice-Pres., Engineering Industries Assoc., 1966–69; Mem., Council of Royal Albert Hall, 1965– (a Vice-Pres., 1985–); a Trustee, RAF Museum, 1965–; Vice-Chm., London Boroughs Assoc., 1968–71; Pres., Conf. of Local and Regional Authorities of Europe, 1978–80 (Vice-Pres., 1974–75, 1977–78, 1980–82); a Vice-Pres., British Sect., IULA/CEM, 1980–88; Mem. Solicitors' Disciplinary Tribunal, 1975–. Contested (LNat&U) Dundee West, 1955. DL, JP Co. of London, 1962; Mem., Inner London Adv. Cttee on appointment of Magistrates, 1969–87; Chm., S Westminster PSD, 1974–77. Liveryman, Worshipful Company of Girdlers. FRSA. KStJ 1969. Pro Merito Medal, Council of Europe, 1982. Comdr, Legion of Honour, 1960; Comdr, Cross of Merit, SMO Malta, 1971; JSM Malaysia, 1974. *Recreations:* motoring, bird-watching. *Address:* Cottage Row, Tarrant Gunville, Blandford, Dorset DT11 8JJ. *T:* Tarrant Hinton (025889) 212. *Clubs:* Carlton, Royal Air Force.

PIRIE, Henry Ward; crossword compiler, journalist and broadcaster; Sheriff (formerly Sheriff-Substitute) of Lanarkshire at Glasgow, 1955–74; *b* 13 Feb. 1922; *o surv. s* of late William Pirie, Merchant, Leith; *m* 1948, Jean Marion, *y d* of late Frank Jardine, sometime President of RCS of Edinburgh; four *s. Educ:* Watson's Coll., Edinburgh; Edinburgh Univ. MA 1944; LLB 1947. Served with Royal Scots; commnd Indian Army, 1944; Lieut, Bombay Grenadiers, 1944–46. Called to Scottish Bar, 1947. Sheriff-Substitute of Lanarkshire at Airdrie, 1954–55. OStJ 1967. *Recreations:* curling, golf, bridge. *Address:* 16 Poplar Drive, Lenzie, Kirkintilloch, Dunbartonshire. *T:* 041–776 2494.

PIRIE, Iain Gordon; Sheriff of Glasgow and Strathkelvin, since 1982; *b* 15 Jan. 1933; *s* of Charles Fox Pirie and Mary Ann Gordon; *m* 1960, Sheila Brown Forbes, MB, ChB; two *s* one *d. Educ:* Harris Acad., Dundee; St Andrews Univ. (MA, LLB). Legal Asst, Stirling, Eunson & Belford, Solicitors, Dunfermline, 1958–60; Depute Procurator Fiscal, Paisley, 1960–67; Sen. Depute Procurator Fiscal, Glasgow, 1967–71; Procurator Fiscal: Dumfries, 1971–76; Ayr, 1976–79; Sheriff of S Strathclyde, Dumfries and Galloway, 1979–82. *Recreations:* golf, tennis, reading, gardening, playing the violin.

PIRIE, Madsen (Duncan), PhD; President, Adam Smith Institute, since 1978; *b* 24 Aug. 1940; *s* of Douglas Gordon Pirie and Eva (*née* Madsen). *Educ:* Univ. of Edinburgh (MA Hons 1974); Univ. of St Andrews (PhD). With Republican Study Cttee, Capitol Hill, 1974; Distinguished Vis. Prof. of Philosophy, Hillsdale Coll., Michigan, 1975–78. *Publications:* Trial and Error and the Idea of Progress, 1978; The Book of the Fallacy, 1985; Privatization, 1988; Micropolitics, 1988. *Recreations:* calligraphy, Tae Kwon Do, Mensa. *Address:* PO Box 316, London SW1P 3DJ.

PIRIE, Norman Wingate, FRS 1949; *b* 1 July 1907; *yr s* of late Sir George Pirie, painter, Torrance, Stirlingshire; *m* 1931, Antoinette Patey; one *s. Educ:* Emmanuel Coll., Cambridge. Demonstrator in Biochemical Laboratory, Cambridge, 1932–40; Virus Physiologist, 1940–46, Head of Biochemistry Dept, 1947–73, Rothamsted Experimental Station, Harpenden. Vis. Prof., Indian Statistical Inst., Calcutta, 1971–. Copley Medal, 1971; Rank Prize for Nutrition, 1976. *Publications:* Food Resources: conventional and novel, 1969, 2nd edn 1976; Leaf Protein and other aspects of fodder fractionation, 1978, 2nd edn, Leaf Protein and its by-products in human and animal nutrition, 1987; ed several works on world food supplies; scientific papers on various aspects of Biochemistry but especially on separation and properties of macromolecules; articles on viruses, the origins of life, biochemical engineering, and the need for greatly extended research on food production and contraception. *Address:* Rothamsted Experimental Station, Harpenden, Herts AL5 2JQ. *T:* Harpenden (0582) 763133.

PIRIE, Psyche; Consultant Design and Decoration Editor, Woman's Journal (IPC Magazines), 1979–84, retired; *b* 6 Feb. 1918; *d* of late George Quarmby; *m* 1940, James Mansergh Pirie; one *d. Educ:* Kensington High Sch.; Chelsea Sch. of Art. Air Ministry, 1940–44. Teaching, Ealing Sch. of Art and Willesden Sch. of Art, 1944–46; Indep. Interior Designer, 1946–56; Furnishing Editor, Homes and Gardens, 1956–68, Editor, 1968–78. *Recreations:* conversation, cinema, theatre, junk shops; or doing absolutely nothing. *Address:* 2 Chiswick Square, W4 2QG. *T:* 081–995 7184.

PIRNIE, Rear Adm. Ian Hugh, FIEE; Chief, Strategic Systems Executive, Ministry of Defence, since 1988; *b* 17 June 1935; *s* of late Hugh and Linda Pirnie; *m* 1958, Sally Patricia (*née* Duckworth); three *d. Educ:* Christ's Hosp., Horsham; Pembroke Coll., Cambridge (MA). FIEE 1986. Qualified in submarines, 1964; post-graduate educn, RMCS, Shrivenham, 1964–65; sea service in aircraft carriers, destroyers and submarines; commanded RNEC, Manadon, 1986–88. Comdr 1972, Captain 1979, Rear Adm. 1988. *Recreations:* fell walking, bird watching, opera, classical music, topiary. *Club:* Army and Navy.

PIRRIE, David Blair, FCIB; Director of UK Retail Banking, Lloyds Bank Plc, since 1989; *b* 15 Dec. 1938; *s* of John and Sylvia Pirrie; *m* 1966, Angela Sellos; three *s* one *d. Educ:* Strathallen Sch., Perthshire; Harvard Univ. (Management Develt). FCIB 1950. Lloyds Bank: Gen. Man., Brazil, 1975–81; Dir, Lloyds Bank International, 1981–83; Gen. Man., Gp HQ, 1983–85; Sen. Dir, Internat. Banking, 1985–87; Sen. Gen. Man., UK Retail Banking, 1987–89. *Recreations:* golf, theatre, music. *Address:* 12 Calonne Road, Wimbledon, SW19 5HJ. *T:* 081–946 9562; Lloyds Bank Plc, PO Box 112, Canons House, Canons Way, Bristol BS99 7LB.

PIRZADA, Syed Sharifuddin, SPk 1964; Attorney-General of Pakistan, 1965–66, 1968–71 and since 1977; Secretary-General, Organization of the Islamic Conference, 1984–88; *b* 12 June 1923; *s* of Syed Vilayat Ali Pirzada; *m* 1960; two *s* two *d. Educ:* University of Bombay. LLB 1945; barrister-at-law. Secretary, Provincial Muslim League, 1946; Managing Editor, Morning Herald, 1946; Prof., Sind Muslim Law Coll., 1947–55; Advocate: Bombay High Court, 1946; Sind Chief Court, 1947; West Pakistan High Court, 1955; Supreme Court of Pakistan, 1961; Senior Advocate Supreme Court of Pakistan; Foreign Minister of Pakistan, 1966–68; Minister for Law and Parly Affairs, 1979–85. Advr to Chief Martial Law Administrator and Federal Minister, 1978. Represented Pakistan: before International Tribunal on Rann of Kutch, 1965; before Internat. Ct of Justice regarding Namibia, SW Africa, 1971; Pakistan Chief Counsel before ICAO Montreal in complaint concerning overflights over Indian territory; Leader of Pakistan delegations to Commonwealth Conf. and General Assembly of UN, 1966; Mem., UN Sub-Commn on Prevention of Discrimination and Protection of Minorities, 1972– (Chm., 1968). Hon. Advisor, Constitutional Commn, 1961; Chm., Pakistan Company Law Commn, 1962; Mem., Internat. River Cttee, 1961–68; President: Pakistan Br., Internat. Law Assoc., 1964–67; Karachi Bar Assoc., 1964; Pakistan Bar Council, 1966; Inst. of Internat. Affairs. Led Pakistan Delegn to Law of the Sea Conferences, NY, 1978 and 1979, and Geneva, 1980. Member: Pakistan Nat. Gp, Panel of the Permanent Ct of Arbitration; Panel of Arbitrators and Umpires, Council of Internat. Civil Aviation Organisation; Panel of Arbitrators, Internat. Centre for Settlement of Investment Disputes, Washington; Internat. Law Commn, 1981–. Chm., Cttee of Experts constituted by Organisation of Islamic Conf. for drafting statute of the Islamic Internat. Ct of Justice, 1980. *Publications:* Pakistan at a Glance, 1941; Jinnah on Pakistan, 1943; Leaders Correspondence with Jinnah, 1944, 3rd edn 1978; Evolution of Pakistan, 1962 (also published in Urdu and Arabic); Fundamental Rights and Constitutional Remedies in Pakistan, 1966; The Pakistan Resolution and the Historic Lahore Session, 1970; Foundations of Pakistan, vol. I, 1969, vol. II, 1970; Some Aspects of Quaid-i-Azam's Life, 1978; Collected Works of Quaid-i-Azam Mohammad Ali Jinnah, vol. I, 1985, vol. II, 1986. *Recreation:* bridge. *Address:* First Floor, Press Centre Building, Shahrah-E-Kamal Attaturk Road, Karachi, Pakistan. *Clubs:* Sind (Karachi); Karachi Boat, Karachi Gymkhana.

PISANI, Edgard (Edouard Marie Victor); Chevalier de la Légion d'honneur; *b* Tunis, 9 Oct. 1918; *s* of François and Zoë Pisani; *m* Isola Chazereau (decd); three *s* one *d; m* 1984, Carmen Berndt; one *s. Educ:* Lycée Carnot, Tunis; Lycée Louis-le-Grand, Paris. LèsL. War of 1939–45 (Croix de Guerre; Médaille de la Résistance). Chef du Cabinet, later Dir, Office of Prefect of Police, Paris, 1944; Dir, Office of Minister of Interior, 1946; Prefect: of Haute-Loire, 1946; of Haute-Marne, 1947; Senator (democratic left) from Haute-Marne, 1954; Minister of Agriculture, 1961; (first) Minister of Equipment, 1966; Deputy, Maine et Loire, 1967–68; Minister of Equipment and Housing, 1967; Conseiller Général, Maine et Loire, 1964–73; Mayor of Montreuil Bellay, 1965–75; Senator (socialist) from Haute-Marne, 1974–81; Mem., European Parlt, 1978–79 (Pres., Econ. and Monetary Affairs Cttee); Mem. for France, EEC, 1981–84; High Comr and Special Envoy to New Caledonia, 1984–85; Minister for New Caledonia, 1985–86. Mem., Commn on Develt Issues (Brandt Commn), 1978–80. Mem., Club of Rome, 1975. Pres., Inst. du Monde Arabe, 1988. Dir, L'Evénement Européen, 1988. *Publications:* La région: pourquoi faire?, 1969; Le général indivis, 1974; Utopie foncière, 1977; Socialiste de raison, 1978; Défi du monde, campagne d'Europe, 1979; (contrib.) Pour la science, 1980; La main et l'outil, 1984; Pour l'Afrique, 1988. *Address:* (home) 225 rue du Faubourg St Honoré, 75008 Paris, France.

PITBLADO, Sir David (Bruce), KCB 1967 (CB 1955); CVO 1953; Comptroller and Auditor-General, 1971–76; *b* 18 Aug. 1912; *o s* of Robert Bruce and Mary Jane Pitblado; *m* 1941, Edith (*d* 1978), *yr d* of Captain J. T. and Mrs Rees Evans, Cardigan; one *s* one *d. Educ:* Strand Sch.; Emmanuel Coll., Cambridge (Hon. Fellow 1972); Middle Temple. Entered Dominions Office, 1935; Asst Private Secretary to Secretary of State, 1937–39; served in War Cabinet Office, 1942; transferred to Treasury, 1942; deleg. to UN Conf., San Francisco, 1945; Under-Secretary, Treasury, 1949; Principal Private Secretary to the Prime Minister (Mr Clement Attlee, Mr Winston Churchill, and Sir Anthony Eden), 1951–56; Vice Chm., Managing Bd, European Payments Union, 1958; Third Secretary, Treasury, 1960; Economic Minister and Head of Treasury Delegation, Washington, and Executive Dir for the UK, IMF and World Bank, 1961–63; Permanent Sec., Min. of Power, 1966–69, Permanent Sec. (Industry), Min. of Technology, 1969–70; Civil Service Dept, 1970–71. Advr on non-exec. directorships, Inst. of Dirs, 1977–81. Chm., Davies's Educnl Trust, 1979–89. Member: Data Protection Cttee, 1976–78; Victoria County Histories Cttee, 1974–; Finance Cttee, RPMS, 1980–; Council, SSAFA, 1976–90 (Hon. Treasurer). Jt Editor, The Shetland Report, 1978. Companion Inst. of Fuel. *Address:* 23 Cadogan Street, SW3 2PP; Pengoitan, Borth, Dyfed. *Club:* Athenæum.

PITCHER, Desmond Henry, CEng, FIEE, FBCS; Group Chief Executive, and Board Member, The Littlewoods Organisation, since 1983; Chairman: Mersey Barrage Co., since 1986; Merseyside Development Corporation, since 1991; *b* 23 March 1935; *s* of George Charles and Alice Marion Pitcher; *m* (marr. diss.); two *s* twin *d; m* 1991, Norma Barbara Niven. *Educ:* Liverpool Coll. of Technology. MIEEE (USA). A. V. Roe & Co.,

Develt Engr, 1955; Automatic Telephone and Elec. Co. (now Plessey), Systems Engr, 1958; Univac Remington Rand (now Sperry Rand Ltd), Systems Engr, 1961; Sperry Univac: Dir, Systems, 1966; Managing Dir, 1971; Vice-Pres., 1974; Dir, Sperry Rand, 1971–78, Dep. Chm., 1974–78; Man. Dir, Leyland Vehicles Ltd, 1976–78; Dir, British Leyland, 1976–78; Man. Dir, Plessey Telecommunications and Office Systems, 1978–83; Dir, Plessey Co., 1979–83; Dep. Chm. NW Water Gp, 1991– (Dir, 1990–). Mem., Northern Adv. Bd, Nat. Westminster Bank, 1989–. Dir, CEI, 1979; Pres., TEMA, 1981–83. Dep. Chm., Everton Football Club, 1990– (Dir, 1987–). Freeman, City of London, 1987. CBIM; FRIAS; Hon. FIDE; FRSA 1987. Knight, Order of St Hubert (Austria), 1991. *Publications:* Institution of Electrical Engineers Faraday Lectures, 1974–75; various lectures on social implications of computers and micro-electronics. *Recreations:* golf, music. *Address:* Onston Hall, Onston, Cheshire CW8 2RG. *T:* Weaverham (0606) 853176; Middle Dell, Bishopsgate Road, Englefield Green, Surrey. *T:* Egham (07844) 37645. *Clubs:* Brooks's, Royal Automobile; Royal Birkdale Golf; Royal Liverpool Golf; Moor Park Golf.

PITCHER, Prof. Wallace Spencer, PhD, DSc, DIC; George Herdman Professor of Geology, 1962–81, now Emeritus, and Leverhulme Emeritus Research Fellow, 1981–82, University of Liverpool; *b* 3 March 1919; *s* of Harry George and Irene Bertha Pitcher; *m* 1947, Stella Ann (*née* Scutt); two *s* two *d. Educ:* Acton Tech. Coll., Chelsea Coll. Asst Analytical Chemist, Geo. T. Holloway & Co., 1937–39. Served War, RAMC, 1939–44. Chelsea Coll., 1944–47; Imperial College: Demonstrator, 1947–48; Asst Lectr, 1948–50; Lectr, 1950–55; Reader in Geology, King's Coll., London, 1955–62. Geological Society London: Hon. Sec., 1970–73; Foreign Sec., 1974–75; Pres., 1976–77; Pres., Section C, British Assoc., 1979. Founder MIG; FIMM. Hon. MRIA 1977; Hon. Member: GA, 1972; Geol Soc. America, 1982. Hon. ScD Dublin, 1983. Lyell Fund, 1956, Bigsby Medal, 1963, Murchison Medal, 1979, Geol Soc. of London; Liverpool Geol Soc. Silver Medal, 1969; Aberconway Medal, Instn of Geologists, 1983. *Publications:* ed (with G. W. Flinn) Controls of Metamorphism, 1965; (with A. R. Berger) Geology of Donegal: a study of granite emplacement and unroofing, 1972; (with E. J. Cobbing) Geology of Western Cordillera of Northern Peru, 1981; (jtly) Magmatism at a Plate Edge: the Peruvian Andes, 1985; many papers on late Precambrian stratigraphy, tillites, Caledonian and Andean granites, structure of the Andes. *Address:* 14 Church Road, Upton, Wirral, Merseyside L49 6JZ. *T:* 051–677 6896.

PITCHERS, Christopher John; His Honour Judge Pitchers; a Circuit Judge, since 1986; *b* 2 Oct. 1942; *s* of Thomas and Melissa Pitchers; *m* 1965, Judith Stevenson; two *s. Educ:* Uppingham Sch.; Worcester Coll., Oxford. MA. Called to the Bar, Inner Temple, 1965; a Recorder, 1981–86. *Address:* The Crown Court, Wellington Street, Leicester.

PITCHFORD; *see* Watkins-Pitchford.

PITCHFORD, His Honour Charles Neville; a Circuit Judge, Wales and Chester Circuit, 1972–87. Called to the Bar, Middle Temple, 1948. *Address:* Llanynant, Kennel Lane, Coed Morgan, Abergavenny, Gwent.
See also C. J. Pitchford.

PITCHFORD, Christopher John; QC 1987; a Recorder, since 1987; *b* 28 March 1947; *s* of Charles Neville Pitchford, *qv; m* Rosalind (*née* Eaton); two *d. Educ:* Duffryn Comprehensive Sch., Newport, Gwent; Queen's Coll., Taunton, Somerset; Queen Mary Coll., London (LLB). Called to the Bar, Middle Temple, 1969. Practised London, 1969–72 and Cardiff, 1972–87; an Assistant Recorder, 1984–87. *Recreation:* fishing. *Address:* Garth Gynydd, Bedlinog, Mid Glam CF46 6TH. *Clubs:* Cardiff and County (Cardiff); Bedlinog Racing.

PITCHFORD, John Hereward, CBE 1971; FEng 1980; President, Ricardo Consulting Engineers Ltd, since 1976 (Chairman, 1962–76); *b* 30 Aug. 1904; *s* of John Pitchford and Elizabeth Anne Wilson; *m* 1930, Teresa Agnes Mary Pensotti; one *s* two *d. Educ:* Brighton Coll.; Christ's Coll., Cambridge (MA). FIMechE (Pres. 1962). Ricardo & Co. Engineers (1927) Ltd: Test Shop Asst, 1926; Asst Research Engr, 1929; Personal Asst to Man. Dir, 1935; Gen. Man., 1939; Dir and Gen. Man., 1941; Man. and Jt Techn. Dir, 1947; Chm. and Man. Dir, 1962; Chm. and Jt Man. Dir, 1965; Chm., 1967. Pres., Fédération Internationale des Sociétés d'Ingénieurs des Techniques de l'Automobile, 1961–63; Chm., Navy Dept Fuels and Lubricants Adv. Cttee, 1964–71. Hon. Mem., Associazione Tecnica Automobile, 1958. *Publications:* papers on all aspects of internal combustion engine. *Recreations:* music, sailing. *Address:* Byeways, Ditchling, East Sussex. *T:* Hassocks (07918) 2177. *Club:* Royal Automobile.
See also Sir J. H. G. Leahy.

PITCHFORD, John W.; *see* Watkins-Pitchford.

PITCHFORTH, Harry; General Manager, Home Grown Cereals Authority, 1974–78, retired; *b* 17 Jan. 1917; *s* of John William Pitchforth and Alice Hollas; *m* 1941, Edna May Blakebrough; one *s* one *d. Educ:* Heath Sch., Halifax; Queen's Coll., Oxford. 1st class Hons, School of Modern History, Oxford, 1939. Served War, 1940–45, Captain, RASC, and later Education Officer, 5 Guards Brigade. Ministry of Food, 1945; Principal Private Secretary, to Minister, Major G. Lloyd-George, 1952–54; seconded to National Coal Board, 1955–58; Ministry of Agriculture, Fisheries and Food: Regional Controller, 1957–61; Director of Establishments and Organisation, 1961–65; Under-Sec., HM Treasury, 1965–67; Controller of HM Stationery Office and the Queen's Printer of Acts of Parliament, 1967–69; Chief Executive, Metropolitan Water Bd, 1969–74. *Recreations:* walking, music. *Address:* 93 George V Avenue, Pinner, Mddx HA5 5SU. *T:* 081–863 1229.

PITFIELD, Hon. (Peter) Michael, CVO 1982; PC (Can.) 1984; QC (Can.) 1972; Senator, Canada, since Dec. 1982; *b* Montreal, 18 June 1937; *s* of Ward Chipman Pitfield and Grace Edith (*née* MacDougall); *m* 1971, Nancy Snow; one *s* two *d. Educ:* Lower Canada Coll., Montreal; Sedbergh Sch., Montebello; St Lawrence Univ. (BASc; Hon. DLitt 1979); McGill Univ. (BCL); Univ. of Ottawa (DESD). Lieut, RCNR. Read Law with Mathewson Lafleur & Brown, Montreal (associated with firm, 1958–59); called to Quebec Bar, 1962; QC (Fed.) 1972; Admin. Asst to Minister of Justice and Attorney-Gen. of Canada, 1959–61; Sec. and Exec. Dir, Royal Commn on Pubns, Ottawa, 1961–62; Attaché to Gov.-Gen. of Canada, 1962–65; Sec. and Res. Supervisor of Royal Commn on Taxation, 1963–66; entered Privy Council Office and Cabinet Secretariat of Govt of Canada, 1965; Asst Sec. to Cabinet, 1966; Dep. Sec. to Cabinet (Plans), and Dep. Clerk to Council, 1969; Dep. Minister, Consumer and Corporate Affairs, 1973; Clerk of Privy Council and Sec. to Cabinet, 1975–79 and 1980–Nov. 1982; Sen. Adviser to Privy Council Office, Nov.-Dec. 1982. Rep., UN Gen. Assembly, 1983; Chm., Senate Cttee on Security and Intelligence, 1983. Director: Power Corp., Montreal; Trust Co., LaPresse; Great West Life Assurance Co.; Investor's Gp Ltd, Winnipeg; Fellow, Harvard Univ., 1974; Mackenzie King Vis. Prof., Kennedy Sch. of Govt, Harvard, 1979–80. Member: Canadian, Quebec and Montreal Bar Assocs; Can. Inst. of Public Admin; Can. Hist. Assoc.; Can. Polit. Sci. Assoc.; Amer. Soc. Polit. and Social Sci.; Internat. Commn of Jurists; Beta Theta Pi. Trustee, Twentieth Century Fund, NY; Member Council: Canadian

Inst. for Advanced Res., Toronto; IISS. *Recreations:* squash, ski-ing, reading. *Address:* (office) The Senate, Ottawa, Ont K1A 0K4, Canada. *Clubs:* University, Mount Royal, Racket (Montreal).

PITMAN, Brian Ivor; Chief Executive and Director, Lloyds Bank Plc, since 1983; *b* 13 Dec. 1931; *s* of late Ronald Ivor Pitman and of Doris Ivy Pitman (*née* Short); *m* 1954, Barbara Mildred Ann (*née* Darby); two *s* one *d. Educ:* Cheltenham Grammar School. FIB. Entered Lloyds Bank, 1952, Jt Gen. Manager, 1975; Exec. Dir, Lloyds Bank International, 1976, Dep. Chief Exec., 1978; Dep. Group Chief Exec., Lloyds Bank Plc, 1982. Chm., Lloyds First Western Corp., 1983; Director: Lloyds Bank California, 1982–86; Nat. Bank of New Zealand Ltd, 1982–; Lloyds and Scottish Plc, 1983; Lloyds Bank International Ltd, 1985–87; Lloyds Merchant Bank Holdings Ltd, 1985–88; NBNZ Holdings Ltd, 1990–. *Recreations:* golf, cricket, music. *Address:* Lloyds Bank Plc, 71 Lombard Street, EC3P 3BS. *Clubs:* MCC, St George's Hill Golf.

PITMAN, David Christian; His Honour Judge Pitman; a Circuit Judge, since 1986; *b* 1 Dec. 1936; 3rd *s* of Sir (Isaac) James Pitman, KBE, and Hon. Margaret Beaufort Pitman (*née* Lawson-Johnston); *m* 1971, Christina Mary Malone-Lee; one *s* two *d. Educ:* Eton Coll.; Christ Church, Oxford (BA (PPE) 1961, MA 1964). Editorial role in publishing books in Initial Teaching Alphabet, 1960–63; called to Bar, Middle Temple,1963; commenced practice, 1964; a Recorder, 1986. National Service: 2nd Lieut, 60th Rifles, 1955–57; Territorial Army: Lieut Queen's Westminsters, KRRC, 1957–61; Captain, then Major, Queen's Royal Rifles (TA), 1961–67; Major, 5th (T) Bn RGJ, 1967–69. *Recreations:* music, the open air. *Address:* c/o The Crown Court, Snaresbrook, Hollybush Hill, E11 1QW.

PITMAN, Edwin James George, MA, DSc; FAA; Emeritus Professor of Mathematics, University of Tasmania (Professor, 1926; retired, Dec. 1962); *b* Melbourne, 29 Oct. 1897; of English parents; *s* of late Edwin Edward Major Pitman and Ann Ungley Pitman; *m* 1932, Edith Elinor Josephine, *y d* of late William Nevin Tatlow Hurst; two *s* two *d. Educ:* South Melbourne Coll.; Ormond Coll., University of Melbourne. Enlisted Australian Imperial Forces, 1918; returned from abroad, 1919; BA with First Class Honours, Dixson scholarship and Wyselaskie scholarship in Mathematics; acting-Professor of Mathematics at Canterbury Coll., University of New Zealand, 1922–23; Tutor in Mathematics and Physics at Trinity Coll. and Ormond Coll., University of Melbourne, 1924–25; Visiting Prof. of Mathematical Statistics at Columbia Univ., NY, Univ. of N Carolina, and Princeton Univ.,1948–49; Visiting Prof. of Statistics: Stanford Univ., Stanford, California, 1957; Johns Hopkins Univ., Baltimore, 1963–64; Chicago, 1968–69; Vis. Sen. Res. Fellow, Univ. of Dundee, 1973. Fellow, Inst. Math. Statistics, 1948; FAA 1954; Vice-Pres., 1960; Mem. International Statistical Institute, 1956; Pres., Australian Mathematical Soc., 1958–59; Hon. Fellow, Royal Statistical Soc., 1965; Hon. Life Member: Statistical Soc. of Australia, 1966 (first Pitman Medal, 1978, for contribs to theory of statistics and probability); Australian Mathematical Soc., 1968. Hon. DSc Tasmania, 1977. *Publication:* Some Basic Theory for Statistical Inference, 1979 (trans. Russian 1986). *Address:* Apt 206, Derwent Waters Retirement Club, Cadbury Road, Claremont, Tas 7011, Australia.

PITMAN, Jennifer Susan; professional racehorse trainer (National Hunt), since 1975; Director, Jenny Pitman Racing Ltd, since 1975; *b* 11 June 1946; *d* of George and Mary Harvey; *m* 1965, Richard Pitman (marr. diss.); two *s. Educ:* Sarson Secondary Girls' School. Training of major race winners includes: Midlands National, 1977 (Watafella); Massey Ferguson Gold Cup, Cheltenham, 1980 (Bueche Giorod); Welsh National, 1982 (Corbiere), 1983 (Burrough Hill Lad), 1986 (Stearsby); Grand National, 1983 (Corbiere); Cheltenham Gold Cup, 1984 (Burrough Hill Lad), 1991 (Garrison Savannah), 1991 (Smith's Cracker); Welsh Champion Hurdle, 1991 (Wonderman). King George VI Gold Cup, 1984 (Burrough Hill Lad); Hennessey Gold Cup, Newbury, 1984 (Burrough Hill Lad); Whitbread Trophy, 1985 (Smith's Man); Ritz Club National Hunt Handicap, Cheltenham, 1987 (Gainsay); Sporting Life Weekend Chase, Liverpool, 1987 (Gainsay); Philip Cornes Saddle of Gold Final, Newbury, 1988 (Crumpet Delite). Trainer of the Year,1983/84. *Publication:* Glorious Uncertainty (autobiog.),1984. *Address:* Weathercock House, Upper Lambourn, near Newbury, Berks. *T:* Lambourn (0488) 71714. *Club:* International Sporting.

PITOI, Sir Sere, Kt 1977; CBE 1975; MACE; Chairman, Public Services Commission of Papua New Guinea, since 1971; *b* Kapa Kapa Village, SE of Port Moresby, 11 Nov. 1935; *s* of Pitoi Sere and Laka Orira; *m* 1957, Daga Leva; two *s* three *d. Educ:* Sogeri (Teachers' Cert.); Queensland Univ. (Cert. in Diagnostic Testing and Remedial Teaching); Univ. of Birmingham, UK (Cert. for Headmasters and Administrators). Held a number of posts as teacher, 1955–57, and headmaster, 1958–68, in Port Moresby, the Gulf district of Papua, Eastern Highlands, New Britain. Apptd a District Inspector of Schools, 1968. Chm., Public Service Bd, Papua New Guinea, 1969–76. Fellow, PNG Inst. of Management. *Recreation:* fishing. *Address:* PO Box 6029, Boroko, Papua New Guinea. *Clubs:* Rotary (Port Moresby); Cheshire Home (PNG).

PITT, family name of **Baron Pitt of Hampstead.**

PITT OF HAMPSTEAD, Baron *cr* 1975 (Life Peer), of Hampstead, in Greater London and in Grenada; **David Thomas Pitt,** TC 1976; MB, ChB Edinburgh, DCH London; JP; DL; General Practitioner, London, since 1947; *b* St David's, Grenada, WI, 3 Oct. 1913; *m* 1943, Dorothy Elaine Alleyne; one *s* two *d. Educ:* St David's RC Sch., Grenada, WI; Grenada Boys' Secondary Sch.; Edinburgh Univ. First Junior Pres., Student Rep. Council, Edinburgh Univ., 1936–37. Dist Med. Officer, St Vincent, WI, 1938–39; Ho. Phys., San Fernando Hosp., Trinidad, 1939–41; GP, San Fernando, 1941–47; Mem. of San Fernando BC, 1941–47; Dep. Mayor, San Fernando, 1946–47; Pres., West Indian Nat. Party (Trinidad), 1943–47. Mem. LCC, 1961–64, GLC 1964–77, for Hackney (Dep. Chm., 1969–70; Chm. 1974–75). Mem. Nat. Cttee for Commonwealth Immigrants, 1965–67; Chm., Campaign Against Racial Discrimination, 1965; Dep. Chm., Community Relations Commn, 1968–77, Chm. 1977; Mem., Standing Adv. Council on Race Relations, 1977–79. Mem. (part time), PO Bd, 1975–77. Vice-Pres., Shelter, 1990– (Chm., 1979–90). Pres., BMA, 1985–86. JP 1966. Contested (Lab): Hampstead, 1959; Clapham (Wandsworth), 1970. Hon. DSc Univ. of West Indies, 1975; Hon. DLitt Bradford, 1977; Hon. LLD: Bristol, 1977; Hull, 1983; Shaw Univ., N Carolina, 1985. DL Greater London, 1988. *Recreations:* reading, watching television, watching cricket, listening to music, theatre. *Address:* 6 Heath Drive, NW3 7SY. *Clubs:* Commonwealth Trust, MCC.

PITT, Barrie (William Edward); author and editor of military histories; *b* Galway, 7 July 1918; *y s* of John Pitt and Ethel May Pitt (*née* Pennell); *m* 1st, 1943, Phyllis Kate (*née* Edwards); one *s* (decd); 2nd, 1953, Sonia Deirdre (*née* Hoskins) (marr. diss., 1971); 3rd, 1983, Frances Mary (*née* Moore). *Educ:* Portsmouth Southern Grammar Sch. Bank Clerk, 1935. Served War of 1939–45, in Army. Surveyor, 1946. Began writing, 1954. Information Officer, Atomic Energy Authority, 1961; Historical Consultant to BBC Series, The Great War, 1963; Editor, Purnell's History of the Second World War, 1964; Editor-in-Chief: Ballantine's Illustrated History of World War 2, 1967 (US Book Series); Ballantine's Illustrated History of the Violent Century, 1971; Editor: Purnell's History of the First World War, 1969; British History Illustrated, 1974–78; Consultant Editor, The

Military History of World War II, 1986. *Publications:* The Edge of Battle, 1958; Zeebrugge, St George's Day, 1918, 1958; Coronel and Falkland, 1960; 1918 The Last Act, 1962; The Battle of the Atlantic, 1977; The Crucible of War: Western Desert 1941, 1980; Churchill and the Generals, 1981; The Crucible of War: Year of Alamein 1942, 1982; Special Boat Squadron, 1983; (with Frances Pitt) The Chronological Atlas of World War II, 1989; contrib. to: Encyclopaedia Britannica; The Sunday Times. *Recreation:* golf. *Address:* FitzHead Court, Fitzhead, Taunton, Somerset TA4 3JP. *T:* Milverton (0823) 400923. *Club:* Savage.

PITT, Desmond Gordon; Commissioner of HM Customs and Excise, 1979–83; *b* 27 Dec. 1922; *s* of Archibald and Amy Pitt; *m* 1946, Barbara Irene; one *s* two *d. Educ:* Bournemouth Sch. FCCA, ACIS, AIB. Officer, HM Customs and Excise, 1947; Inspector, 1958; Asst Sec., 1973; Under Sec., 1979. Hon. Treasurer, Wessex Autistic Soc. *Recreations:* travel, sailing. *Address:* 4 Ken Road, Southbourne, Bournemouth, Dorset. *Club:* Thorpe Bay Yacht.

PITT, Rt. Rev. Mgr George Edward, CBE 1965; *b* 10 Oct. 1916; *s* of Francis Pitt and Anna Christina Oviedo. *Educ:* St Brendan's Coll., Bristol; Ven. English College, Rome. Priest, 1939; worked in Diocese of Clifton, 1940–43; joined Royal Navy as Chaplain, 1943; Principal Roman Catholic Chaplain, RN, 1963–69; Parish Priest, St Joseph's, Wroughton, Wilts, 1969–86. Nominated a Domestic Prelate, 1963. *Recreation:* music. *Address:* 5 West Mall, Bristol BS8 4BH. *T:* Bristol (0272) 733235.

PITT, Sir Harry (Raymond), Kt 1978; BA, PhD; FRS 1957; Vice-Chancellor, Reading University, 1964–79; *b* 3 June 1914; *s* of H. Pitt; *m* 1940, Clemency Catherine, *d* of H. C. E. Jacoby, MIEE; four *s. Educ:* King Edward's Sch., Stourbridge; Peterhouse, Cambridge. Bye-Fellow, Peterhouse, Cambridge, 1936–39; Choate Memorial Fellow, Harvard Univ., 1937–38; Univ. of Aberdeen, 1939–42. Air Min. and Min. of Aircraft Production, 1942–45. Prof. of Mathematics, Queen's Univ., Belfast, 1945–50; Deputy Vice-Chancellor, Univ. of Nottingham, 1959–62; Prof. of Pure Mathematics, Univ. of Nottingham, 1950–64. Visiting Prof., Yale Univ., 1962–63. Chm., Universities Central Council on Admissions, 1975–78. Pres., IMA, 1984–85. Hon. LLD: Aberdeen 1970; Nottingham 1970; Hon. DSc: Reading, 1978; Belfast, 1981. *Publications:* Tauberian Theorems, 1957; Measure, Integration and Probability, 1963; Measure and Integration for Use, 1986; mathematical papers in scientific journals. *Address:* 46 Shinfield Road, Reading, Berks RG2 7BW. *T:* Reading (0734) 872962.

PITT, Michael Edward, FICE; Chief Executive, Cheshire County Council, since 1990; *b* 2 Feb. 1949; *s* of Albert and Doris Joan Pitt; *m* 1969, Anna Maria Di Claudio; two *d. Educ:* University College London (first class Hons BSc Engrg). Civil Servant, 1970–72; motorway design and construction, 1972–75; transportation planner in private sector and local govt, 1975–80; Asst County Surveyor, Northumberland CC, 1980–84; Dep. Dir, Dir of Property Services and Dir of Tech. Services, Humberside CC, 1984–90. *Publications:* papers in technical jls. *Recreations:* family life, walking the Yorkshire moors. *Address:* County Hall, Chester CH1 1SF. *T:* Chester (0244) 602101.

PITT, William Henry; management consultant, construction industry; *b* 17 July 1937; *m* 1961, Janet Pitt (*née* Wearn); one *d. Educ:* Heath Clark Sch., Croydon; London Nautical Sch.; Polytechnic of South Bank; Polytechnic of N London (BA Philos./Classics). Lighting Engineer, 1955–75; Housing Officer, Lambeth Borough Council, 1975–81. Chm., Lambeth Br., NALGO, 1979–81. Joined Liberal Party, 1959; contested: (L) Croydon NW, Feb. and Oct. 1974, 1979, 1983; (L/Alliance) Thanet South, 1987. MP (L) Croydon NW, Oct. 1981–1983; first L and SDP Alliance cand. to be elected MP. *Recreations:* photography, choral singing, listening to music, reading, walking. *Address:* 10 Inverness Terrace, Broadstairs, Kent. *Club:* National Liberal.

PITTAM, Robert Raymond, MBE 1991; Assistant Under-Secretary of State, Home Office, 1972–79; *b* 14 June 1919; *e s* of Rev. R. G. Pittam and Elsie Emma Pittam (*née* Sale); *m* 1946, Gwendoline Lilian Brown; one *s* one *d. Educ:* Bootle Grammar Sch.; Pembroke Coll., Cambridge. MA; 1st Cl. Law Tripos. War of 1939–45: temp. Civil Servant, and service in RAOC, 1940–46. Home Office, 1946–66: Private Sec. to Home Secretary, 1955–57; Asst Sec., 1957; HM Treasury, 1966–68; CSD, 1968–72. Founder Chm., Home Office Retired Staff Assoc., 1982–. *Address:* 14 Devonshire Way, Shirley, Croydon, Surrey. *Club:* Civil Service.

PITTER, Ruth, CBE 1979; CLit 1974; poetess; *b* Ilford, Essex, 7 Nov. 1897; *d* of George Pitter, Elementary Schoolmaster. *Educ:* Elementary Sch.; Coborn Sch., Bow, E. Heinemann Foundation Award, 1954; Queen's Medal for Poetry, 1955. *Publications:* First Poems, 1920; First and Second Poems, 1927; Persephone in Hades (privately printed), 1931; A Mad Lady's Garland, 1934; A Trophy of Arms, 1936 (Hawthornden Prize, 1937); The Spirit Watches, 1939; The Rude Potato, 1941; The Bridge, 1945; Pitter on Cats, 1946; Urania, 1951; The Ermine, 1953; Still By Choice, 1966; Poems 1926–66, 1968; End of Drought, 1975. *Recreation:* gardening. *Address:* 71 Chilton Road, Long Crendon, near Aylesbury, Bucks. *T:* Long Crendon (0844) 208 373.

PITTS, Sir Cyril (Alfred), Kt 1968; Chairman of Governors, Polytechnic of Central London, since 1985 (Governor, since 1984); *b* 21 March 1916; *m* 1942, Barbara; two *s* one *d. Educ:* St Olave's; Jesus Coll., Cambridge. Chairman of ICI Companies in India, 1964–68; Chm., ICI (Export) Ltd and Gen. Manager, Internat. Coordination, ICI Ltd, 1968–78; Dir, ICI Americas Ltd, 1974–77; Dep. Chm., Ozalid Gp Holdings Ltd, 1975–77. Chairman: Process Plant EDC, 1979–83; Peter Brotherhood, 1980–83. President: Bengal Chamber of Commerce and Industry, and Associated Chambers of Commerce and Industry of India, 1967–68; British and S Asian Trade Assoc., 1978–83. Councillor, RIIA, 1968–77. *Address:* 11 Middle Avenue, Farnham, Surrey GU9 8JL. *T:* Farnham (0252) 715864. *Clubs:* Oriental; Bengal (Calcutta).

PITTS, John Kennedy; Chairman, Legal Aid Board, since 1988; *b* 6 Oct. 1925; *s* of Thomas Alwyn Pitts and Kathleen Margaret Pitts (*née* Kennedy); *m* 1957, Joan Iris Light (*d* 1986); *m* 1990, Julia Bentall. *Educ:* Bristol Univ. (BSc). Res. Officer, British Cotton Industry Res. Assoc., 1948–53; ICI, 1953–78; Dir, ICI Mond Div., 1969–71; Dep. Chm., ICI Agricl Div., 1972–77; Chairman: Richardsons Fertilizers, 1972–76; Hargreaves Fertilizers, 1975–77; Vice-Pres., Cie Neerlandaise de l'Azote, 1975–77. Chm. and Chief Exec., Tioxide Group, 1978–87. Mem., Tees and Hartlepool Port Authy, 1976–78; Vice-Chm., Shildon & Sedgefield Develt Agency, 1986–. Pres., Chem. Industries Assoc., 1984–86. *Address:* Legal Aid Board, Newspaper House, 8–16 Great New Street, EC4A 3BN. *Club:* Royal Automobile.

PITTS CRICK, R.; *see* Crick, Ronald P.

PITTS-TUCKER, Robert St John, CBE 1975; *b* 24 June 1909; *e s* of Walter Greame Pitts-Tucker, Solicitor, and Frances Elsie Wallace; *m* 1942, Joan Margery, *d* of Frank Furnivall, Civil Engineer, India, and Louisa Cameron Lees; three *s* one *d. Educ:* Haileybury (Schol.); Clare Coll., Cambridge (Schol.). 1st cl. Class. Tripos, Pts I and II, 1930 and 1931. Asst Master, Shrewsbury Sch., 1931–44; Headmaster, Pocklington Sch., 1945–66; Dep. Sec. to HMC and HMA, 1966–69, Sec., 1970–74. Mem., House of Laity, Church

Assembly, 1956–70; St Albans diocese: Reader; Vice-Pres. of Synod, 1976–79; Member: ER Yorks Educn Cttee, 1946–66; Herts Educn Cttee, 1974–85; Vice-Chm., Yorks Rural Community Council, 1949–65; Mem., Secondary Schools Examination Council, 1954–57. Governor: Mill Hill Sch.; Haileybury. Mem., GBA Exec. Cttee, 1975–80. *Recreations:* country walks, listening to music, gardening. *Address:* Hillside, Toms Hill Road, Aldbury, Tring, Herts HP23 5SA. *Clubs:* Commonwealth Trust, East India, Devonshire, Sports and Public Schools.

PIX WESTON, John; *see* Weston, J. P.

PIXLEY, Sir Neville (Drake), Kt 1976; MBE (mil.) 1944; VRD 1941; company director; *b* 21 Sept. 1905; *s* of Arthur and Florence Pixley; *m* 1938, Lorna, *d* of Llewellyn Stephens; three *d. Educ:* C of E Grammar Sch., Brisbane. FCIT. Served RANR, 1920–63; War Service, Comd Corvettes, 1939–46 (Comdr 1945). Macdonald, Hamilton & Co. (P&O agents), 1922–59, Managing Partner, 1949–59; Chm., P&O Lines of Australia, 1960–70; Director: Burns Philp & Co. Ltd, 1962–80; Mauri Brothers & Thomson Ltd, 1970–77; NSW Boards of Advice: Nat. Bank of Australasia Ltd, 1970–77; Elder Smith Goldsborough Mort Ltd, 1970–76. Chm. Australian Cttee, Lloyd's Register of Shipping, 1967–80. ADC to King George VI and to the Queen, 1951–54. Vice Chancellor, 1978–, and Receiver-Gen., 1963–, Order of St John in Australia; KStJ 1963; GCStJ 1984. Pres., Royal Humane Soc. of NSW. *Recreation:* tennis. *Address:* 23 Carlotta Road, Double Bay, Sydney, NSW 2028, Australia. *T:* 3275354. *Clubs:* Union, Australian (Sydney); Queensland (Qld).

See also N. S. Pixley.

PIXLEY, Norman Stewart, CMG 1970; MBE 1941; VRD 1927; retired company director; Dean of the Consular Corps of Queensland, 1965–72; Hon. Consul for the Netherlands, 1948–72; *b* Brisbane, 3 May 1898; 2nd *s* of Arthur and Florence Pixley; *m* 1931, Grace Josephine, *d* of Arthur and Grace Spencer; twin *s* one *d. Educ:* Bowen House Sch.; Brisbane Grammar School. Served in RANR, 1913–46; Comdr, RANR, retd. Councillor, National Trust of Queensland; Pres., Qld Lawn Tennis Assoc., 1948–52; Pres., Brisbane Chamber of Commerce, 1952–53; Leader of Aust. Delegn to British Commonwealth Chambers of Commerce Conf., 1951; founded Qld Div. of Navy League, 1953 (Pres. until 1969). FRHistSoc Qld 1965 (Pres. 1968–83). Kt, Order of Orange Nassau, 1964. *Publications:* papers on Australian history in Jl of Royal Hist. Soc. Qld, etc. *Recreations:* tennis, yachting, golf. *Address:* 1/16 Dovercourt Road, Toowong, Queensland 4066, Australia. *T:* 701150. *Clubs:* Queensland, United Service, Indooroopilly Golf (Qld).

See also Sir Neville Pixley.

PIZEY, Admiral Sir (Charles Thomas) Mark, GBE 1957 (KBE 1953); CB 1942; DSO 1942, and bar 1943; idc; RN retired; DL; *b* 1899; *s* of late Rev. C. E. Pizey, Mark and Huntspill, Somerset; *m* Phyllis, *d* of Alfred D'Angibau; two *d.* Served European War, 1914–18, Midshipman, Revenge, 1916–18; Lieut, 1920; HMS Danae Special Service Squadron World Cruise, 1921–22; Flag Lieut to Vice-Admiral Sir Howard Kelly, 2nd in command Mediterranean Fleet, 1929–30; Destroyer Commands Mediterranean and Home Fleets, 1930–39; War of 1939–45: Captain, 1939; Commanded HMS Ausonia, Atlantic Patrol and Convoys, 1939–40. Captain (D) 21st Destoyer Flotilla in HMS Campbell, Nore Command, Channel and North Sea Operations, 1940–42 (CB, DSO, despatches twice); commanded HMS Tyne and Chief Staff Officer to Rear-Admiral Destroyers, Home Fleet, Russian convoys, 1942–43 (bar to DSO); Director of Operations (Home) Admiralty Naval Staff, 1944–45; Chief of Staff to C-in-C Home Fleet, 1946; Imperial Defence Coll., 1947; Rear-Admiral, 1948; Chief of UK Services Liaison Staff, Australia, 1948–49; Flag Officer Commanding First Cruiser Squadron, 1950–51; Vice-Admiral, 1951; Chief of Naval Staff and Commander-in-Chief, Indian Navy, 1951–55; Admiral, 1954; Commander-in-Chief, Plymouth, 1955–58, retired. DL County of Somerset, 1962. *Address:* 1 St Ann's Drive, Burnham on Sea, Somerset.

PIZZEY, Erin Patria Margaret; *see* Shapiro, E. P. M.

PLACE, Rear-Adm. (Basil Charles) Godfrey, VC 1944; CB 1970; CVO 1991; DSC 1943; Lay Observer, 1975–78; *b* 19 July 1921; *s* of late Major C. G. M. Place, DSO, MC, and late Mrs Place; *m* 1943, Althea Annington, *d* of late Harry Tickler, Grimsby; one *s* two *d. Educ:* The Grange, Folkestone; RNC, Dartmouth. Midshipman, 1939; 10th and 12th submarine flotillas, 1941–43; Lieut, 1942; Comdr, 1952; HMS Glory (801 Sqn), 1952–53; Comdg HMS Tumult, 1955–56; Exec. Officer, HMS Theseus, 1956–57; HMS Corunna, 1957–58; Captain, 1958; Chief SO to Flag Officer Aircraft Carriers, 1958–60; Deputy Director of Air Warfare, 1960–62; HMS Rothesay and Captain (D), 25th Escort Squadron, 1962–63; HMS Ganges, 1963–65; HMS Albion, 1966–67; Adm. Comdg Reserves, and Dir-Gen., Naval Recruiting, 1968–70. Chm., VC and GC Assoc., 1971–. Polish Cross of Valour, 1941. *Address:* The Old Bakery, Corton Denham, Sherborne, Dorset.

PLAIDY, Jean; *see* Hibbert, Eleanor.

PLAISTOWE, (William) Ian (David), FCA; Director of Accounting and Audit for UK and Ireland, Arthur Andersen & Co., since 1987; *b* 18 Nov. 1942; *s* of David William Plaistowe and Julia (*née* Ross Smith); *m* 1968, Carolyn Anne Noble Wilson; two *s* one *d. Educ:* Marlborough Coll., Queens' Coll., Cambridge. Joined Arthur Andersen & Co., 1964; Partner, 1976; Head of Accounting and Audit practice, London, 1984–87. Institute of Chartered Accountants in England and Wales: Chairman: London Soc. of Chartered Accountants, 1981–82; Post Qualification Cttee, 1985–86; Practice Regulation Directorate, 1987–90; Mem. Council, 1985–; Vice-Pres., 1990–91; Dep. Pres., 1991–June 1992. *Publications:* articles in learned jls. *Recreations:* golf, tennis, squash, ski-ing, gardening. *Address:* Heybote, Ellesborough, Aylesbury, Bucks HP17 0XF. *T:* Aylesbury (0296) 622758. *Clubs:* Carlton; Moor Park Golf.

PLANT, Prof. Raymond, PhD; Professor of Politics, University of Southampton, since 1979; *b* 19 March 1945; *s* of Stanley and Marjorie Plant; *m* 1967, Katherine Sylvia Dixon; three *s. Educ:* Havelock Sch., Grimsby; King's Coll. London (BA); Hull Univ. (PhD 1971). Lectr, then Sen. Lectr in Philosophy, Univ. of Manchester, 1967–79. Lectures: Stevenson, Univ. of Glasgow, 1981; Agnes Cumming, UC Dublin, 1987; Stanton, Univ. of Cambridge, 1989–90 and 1990–91; Sarum, Univ. of Oxford, 1991. Chair, Labour Party Commn on Electoral Systems, 1991–. Times columnist, 1988–. *Publications:* Hegel, 1974, 2nd edn 1984; Community and Ideology, 1974; Political Philosophy and Social Welfare, 1981; Philosophy, Politics and Citizenship, 1984; Conservative Capitalism in Britain and the United States: a critical appraisal, 1988; Modern Political Thought, 1991. *Recreations:* music, opera, thinking about the garden, listening to my wife playing the piano, reading. *Address:* 6 Woodview Close, Bassett, Southampton SO2 3PZ. *T:* Southampton (0703) 769529.

PLASKETT, Maj.-Gen. Frederick Joseph, CB 1980; MBE 1966; FCIT; Director General and Chief Executive, Road Haulage Association, 1981–88; *b* 23 Oct. 1926; *s* of Frederick Joseph Plaskett and Grace Mary Plaskett; *m* 1st, 1950, Heather (*née* Kington) (*d* 1982); four *d*; 2nd, 1984, Mrs Patricia Joan Healy. Commnd infantry, 1946; RASC, 1951; RCT, 1965; regimental and staff appts, India, Korea, Nigeria, Malaya, Germany and UK; Student, Staff Coll., Camberley, 1958; Jt Services Staff Coll., 1964; Instr, Staff Coll., Camberley, 1966–68; Management Coll., Henley, 1969; RCDS, 1975; Dir of Movements (Army), 1975–78; Dir Gen., Transport and Movements (Army), 1978–81, retired. Col Comdt, RCT, 1981–91 (Rep. Col Comdt, 1989). Chm., British Railways Bd, London Midland Region, 1989– (Mem., 1986–88). Director: Foden Trucks (Paccar UK) (formerly Sandbach Engrg Co.), 1981–; RHA Insce Services Ltd, 1982–88; British Road Federation, 1982–88. Comr, Royal Hosp., Chelsea, 1985–88. *Recreations:* fishing, sailing, gardening. *Address:* c/o National Westminster Bank, The Commons, Shaftesbury, Dorset SP7 8JY. *Club:* Army and Navy.

PLASTOW, Sir David (Arnold Stuart), Kt 1986; Chief Executive, 1980–May 1992, and Chairman, 1987–May 1992, Vickers PLC (Director, 1975–92; Managing Director, 1980–86); Joint Deputy Chairman, Guinness PLC, since 1989 (Deputy Chairman, 1987–89); Chairman, Medical Research Council, since 1990; Deputy Chairman, TSB Group Plc, since 1991; *b* Grimsby, 9 May 1932; *s* of late James Stuart Plastow and Marie Plastow; *m* 1954, Barbara Ann May; one *s* one *d. Educ:* Culford Sch., Bury St Edmunds. Apprentice, Vauxhall Motors Ltd, 1950; joined Rolls-Royce Ltd, Motor Car Div., Crewe, Sept. 1958; apptd Marketing Dir, Motor Car Div., 1967; Managing Director: Motor Car Div., 1971; Rolls-Royce Motors Ltd, 1972 (Gp Man. Dir, 1974–80). Regional Dir, Lloyds Bank, 1974–76; non-executive Director: GKN, 1978–84; Legal & General Gp Plc, 1985–87. Chm., Royal Opera House Trust, 1992–. Mem., European Adv. Council, Tenneco, 1984–86; Bd Mem., Tenneco Inc. (Houston), 1985–. Vice-Pres., Inst. of Motor Industry, 1974–82; Pres., SMMT, 1976–77, 1977–78 (Dep. Pres., 1978–79, 1979–80); Pres., Motor Industry Res. Assoc., 1978–81; Chm., Grand Council, Motor and Cycle Trades Benevolent Fund, 1976–82. Patron, Coll. of Aeronautical and Automobile Engrg, 1972–79. Chm., Industrial Soc., 1983–87 (Mem., 1981); Dep. Chm., Listed Cos Adv. Cttee, 1987–90; Member: Council, CBI; BOTB, 1980–83; Engineering Council, 1980–83; Offshore Energy Technology Bd, 1985–86; Bd of Companions, BIM (Pres. S Cheshire Br.); Council, Regular Forces Employment Assoc. Patron, The Samaritans, 1987–; Chm., 40th Anniversary Appeal Cttee, Mental Health Foundn, 1988–; Gov., BUPA, 1990–. Chm. Governors, Culford Sch., 1979–. Pres., Crewe Alexandra FC, 1975–82. Liveryman, Worshipful Co. of Coachmakers & Coach Harness Makers. FRSA. Young Business Man of the Year Award, The Guardian, 1976. Hon. DSc Cranfield, 1978. *Recreations:* golf, music. *Address:* c/o Vickers PLC, Vickers House, Millbank Tower, Millbank, SW1P 4RA. *Clubs:* Buck's; Royal and Ancient (St Andrews); Royal St George's (Sandwich).

PLATER, Alan Frederick, FRSL 1985; freelance writer, since 1960; *b* 15 April 1935; *s* of Herbert Richard Plater and Isabella Scott Plater; *m* 1st, 1958, Shirley Johnson (marr. diss. 1985); two *s* one *d*; 2nd, 1986, Shirley Rubinstein; three step *s. Educ:* Pickering Road Jun. Sch., Hull; Kingston High Sch., Hull; King's Coll., Newcastle upon Tyne. ARIBA (now lapsed). Trained as architect and worked for short time in the profession before becoming full-time writer in 1960; has written extensively for radio, television, films and theatre; semi-regular contributor to Punch and has also written for The Guardian, Listener, New Statesman, etc. Co-chair, Writers' Guild of GB, 1986–87. FRSA 1991. Works include: *theatre:* A Smashing Day (also televised); Close the Coalhouse Door (Writers' Guild Radio Award, 1972); And a Little Love Besides; Swallows on the Water; Trinity Tales; The Fosdyke Saga; Fosdyke Two; On Your Way, Riley!; Skyhooks; A Foot on the Earth; Prez; Rent Party (musical); Sweet Sorrow; Going Home; I Thought I Heard a Rustling; *films:* The Virgin and the Gypsy; It Shouldn't Happen to a Vet; Priest of Love; *television:* plays: So Long Charlie; See the Pretty Lights; To See How Far It Is (trilogy); Land of Green Ginger; Willow Cabins; The Party of the First Part; The Blacktoft Diaries; Thank You, Mrs Clinkscales; biographies: The Crystal Spirit; Pride of our Alley; Edward Lear—at the edge of the sand; Coming Through; series and serials: Z Cars; Softly Softly; Shoulder to Shoulder; Trinity Tales; The Good Companions; The Consultant; Barchester Chronicles (adaptation of The Warden, and Barchester Towers, by Trollope); The Beiderbecke Affair; The Fortunes of War (adaptation of Balkan and Levant trilogies by Olivia Manning); A Very British Coup (International Emmy; Golden Fleece of Georgia (USSR); Best Series BAFTA Award; Best Series RTS Award; Best Series Broadcasting Press Guild Award; Best Series and Grand Prix, Banff Internat. TV Fest., Canada); The Beiderbecke Connection; Campion (adapted from Margery Allingham); A Day in Summer (adaptation of J. L. Carr novel); Misterioso; *radio:* The Journal of Vasilije Bogdanovic (Sony Radio Award, 1983). Hon. Fellow, Humberside Coll. of Higher Educn, 1983; Hon. DLitt Hull, 1985. RTS Writer's Award, 1984/85; Broadcasting Press Guild Award, 1987; Writer's Award, BAFTA, 1988; Northern Personality Award, Variety Club of GB, 1989. *Publications:* The Beiderbecke Affair, 1985; The Beiderbecke Tapes, 1986; Misterioso, 1987; The Beiderbecke Connection; plays and shorter pieces in various anthologies. *Recreations:* reading, theatre, snooker, jazz, dog-walking, talking and listening. *Address:* c/o Margaret Ramsay Ltd, 14A Goodwin's Court, St Martin's Lane, WC2N 4LL. *T:* 071–240 0691. *Clubs:* Dramatists', Ronnie Scott's.

PLATT, family name of **Baroness Platt of Writtle.**

PLATT OF WRITTLE, Baroness *cr* 1981 (Life Peer), of Writtle in the County of Essex; **Beryl Catherine Platt,** CBE 1978; FEng 1987; DL; Chairman, Equal Opportunities Commission, 1983–88; *b* 18 April 1923; *d* of Ernest and Dorothy Myatt; *m* 1949, Stewart Sydney Platt; one *s* one *d. Educ:* Westcliff High School; Girton Coll., Cambridge (MA; Fellow, 1988). CEng, FRAeS. Technical Assistant, Hawker Aircraft, 1943–46; BEA, 1946–49. Mem. Bd, British Gas, 1988–. Member: Engineering Council, 1981–90; Engrg Training Authy, 1990. Member, Chelmsford RDC, 1958–74. Member, Essex CC, 1965–85: Alderman, 1969–74; Vice-Chm., 1980–83; Chm., Education Cttee, 1971–80. Mem., H of L Select Cttee for Science and Technology, 1982–85 and 1990–. Mem., Adv. Cttee on Women's Employment, 1984–88. Vice-Chairman: Technician Education Council, 1979–81; London Regional Adv. Council for Technology Education, 1975–81. President: Chelmsford Engrg Soc., 1979–80; Cambridge Univ. Engrs Assoc., 1987–; Assoc. for Sci. Educn, 1988; Vice-President: UMIST, 1985–; Engrg Section, BAAS (Pres., 1988). Member: CNAA, 1973–79; Council, CGLI, 1974–; Cambridge Univ. Appointments Bd, 1975–79; ACC Education Cttee, 1974–80; Council, Careers Research and Adv. Centre, 1983–; Council, RSA, 1983–88; Member of Court: Essex Univ., 1964–; City Univ., 1969–78; Brunel Univ., 1985–; Cranfield Inst. of Technology, 1989–. Trustee, Homerton Coll., 1970–81. Liveryman, Engineers' Co., 1988. DL Essex 1983. Freeman, City of London, 1988. Fellow, 1987, Dir, 1989, Smallpeice Trust; Fellow, Manchester Polytechnic, 1989. FIGasE 1990; FRSA. Hon. FIMechE 1984; Hon. FITD 1984; Hon. FCP 1987; Hon. FIStructE 1991; Hon. FICE 1991; Hon. Fellow: Polytechnic of Wales, 1985; Women's Engrg Soc., 1988. Hon. DSc: City, 1984; Salford, 1984; Cranfield, 1985; DUniv: Open Univ., 1985; Essex, 1985; Hon. DEng Bradford, 1985; Hon. DTech Brunel, 1986; Hon. LLD Cantab, 1988. European Engr, FEANI, 1987; Insignia Award *hc*, CGLI, 1988. *Recreations:* cooking, reading. *Address:* House of Lords, SW1A 0PW. *Club:* United Oxford & Cambridge University.

PLATT, Anthony Michael Westlake, CBE 1991; Chief Executive, London Chamber of Commerce and Industry, 1984–91; *b* 28 Sept. 1928; *s* of late James Westlake Platt and

Veronica Norma Hope Platt (*née* Arnold); *m* 1st, 1952, Jennifer Susan Scott-Fox; three *s*; 2nd, 1984, Heather Mary Stubbs; one step *s* one step *d*; 3rd, 1987, Sarah Elizabeth Russell. *Educ:* Stowe School; Balliol College, Oxford (PPE 1951). 2nd Lieut RA, 1948–49; RAFVR 1950–51. Foreign Office, 1951, served Prague, 1953–54, NY, 1955–56; Shell Group of Cos: Switzerland, 1957; Guatemala, 1959; S Africa, 1961; Venezuela, 1963; London, 1969; The Hague, 1972; London, 1975–77 (Chm. and Chief Exec., Billiton UK); The Hague, 1977–78 (Vice-Pres. for Secondary Metals, Billiton Internat.); London, 1979–84 (Man. Dir, Consolidated Petroleum Co. and Area Co-ordinator, Shell Internat. Petroleum Co.). Chm., British-Mexican Businessmen's Cttee, 1989–91. *Recreations:* gliding, opera, languages.

See also C. P. S. Platt.

PLATT, Prof. Colin Peter Sherard; Professor of History, Southampton University, since 1983; *b* 11 Nov. 1934; twin *s* of late James Westlake Platt and Veronica Norma Hope Arnold; *m* 1963, Valerie Ashforth; two *s* two *d*. *Educ:* Collyers Grammar School, Horsham; Balliol College, Oxford (BA 1st cl., MA); Leeds University (PhD). Research Assistant in Medieval Archaeology, Leeds Univ., 1960–62, Lectr, 1962–64; Lectr, Sen. Lectr and Reader in History, Southampton Univ., 1964–83. *Publications:* The Monastic Grange in Medieval England, 1969; Medieval Southampton: the port and trading community AD 1000–1600, 1973; (with Richard Coleman-Smith) Excavations in Medieval Southampton 1953–1969, 2 vols, 1975; The English Medieval Town, 1976; Medieval England: a social history and archaeology from the Conquest to 1600 AD, 1978; The Atlas of Medieval Man, 1979; The Parish Churches of Medieval England, 1981; The Castle in Medieval England and Wales, 1982; The Abbeys and Priories of Medieval England, 1984; Medieval Britain from the Air, 1984; The Traveller's Guide to Medieval England, 1985; The National Trust Guide to late Medieval and Renaissance Britain, 1986; The Architecture of Medieval Britain: a social history (Wolfson History Award), 1990. *Recreations:* reading novels, visiting medieval antiquities. *Address:* Department of History, University of Southampton, Southampton SO9 5NH. *T:* Southampton (0703) 595000.

See also A. M. W. Platt.

PLATT, Eleanor Frances, QC 1982; a Recorder of the Crown Court, since 1982; *b* 6 May 1938; *er d* of late Dr Maurice Leon Platt and Sara Platt (*née* Stein), Hove, Sussex; *m* 1963; two *c*. *Educ:* Hove County School for Girls; University College London. LLB 1959. Called to the Bar, Gray's Inn, 1960. Mem., Matrimonial Causes Rule Cttee, 1986–90. Treas., Family Law Bar Assoc., 1990–. *Recreations:* the arts, travel, skiing. *Address:* 1 Garden Court, Temple EC4Y 9BJ. *T:* 071–353 5524.

PLATT, Sir (Frank) Lindsey, 2nd Bt *cr* 1958; *S* father, 1986; *m* 1951, Johanna Magdalena Elisabeth Laenger; one *d* (and one *d* decd). *Heir:* none.

PLATT, Margaret; Development Executive, The Law Society, since 1988; *b* 18 Oct. 1931; *d* of Harry Platt and Edith Baxter. *Educ:* Bedford College, Univ. of London (BA Hons 1st Cl., History). Called to the Bar, Gray's Inn, 1956. Estate Duty Officer, Inland Revenue, 1952–63; Inst. of Professional Civil Servants, 1963–87 (Dep. Gen. Sec., 1980–87); Gen. Sec., Clearing Bank Union, 1987–88. Mem., Industrial Disputes Panel, Jersey, 1989–. *Recreations:* renovating old houses, travel, reading. *Address:* 8 Lark Avenue, Moormede Park, Staines, Middx TW18 4RX. *T:* Staines (0784) 458723.

PLATT, Norman, OBE 1985; opera director and writer; Artistic Director of Kent Opera, 1969–89; *b* 29 Aug. 1920; *s* of Edward Turner Platt and Emily Jane Platt; *m* 1st, 1942, Diana Franklin Clay; one *s* one *d*; 2nd, 1963, Johanna Sigrid Bishop; one *s* two *d*. *Educ:* Bury Grammar Sch.; King's Coll., Cambridge (BA). Principal: Sadler's Wells Opera, 1946–48; English Opera Group, 1948; Mem. Deller Consort, and freelance singer, actor, teacher and producer in Britain and Western Europe; founded Kent Opera, 1969; co-founded Canterbury Theatre and Festival Trust, 1983. His many prodns for Kent Opera include: The Return of Ulysses; Agrippina; Dido and Aeneas; Peter Grimes. Hon. DCL Kent, 1981. *Publications:* translations of numerous songs and operas, incl. L'Incoronazione di Poppea, Don Giovanni and Fidelio; Editor, Opera in Performance series, 1991; articles on musical subjects. *Recreations:* reading, theatre, music. *Address:* Pembles Cross, Egerton, Ashford, Kent TN27 9EN. *T:* Egerton (023376) 237.

PLATT, Hon. Sir Peter, 2nd Bt *cr* 1959; Professor of Music, University of Sydney, 1975–89; *b* 6 July 1924; *s* of Baron Platt (Life Peer), and Margaret Irene (*d* 1987), *d* of Arthur Charles Cannon; *S* to baronetcy of father, 1978; *m* 1948, Jean Halliday, *d* of late Charles Philip Brentnall, MC; one *s* two *d*. *Educ:* Abbotsholme School, Derbyshire; Magdalen Coll., Oxford; Royal College of Music. BMus 1950, MA, BLitt 1954, Oxon; FGSM 1973. Lectr and Sen. Lectr in Music, Univ. of Sydney, 1952–57; Professor of Music, Univ. of Otago, NZ, 1957–75. Served War of 1939–45 with RNVR (despatches). *Heir:* *s* Martin Philip Platt [*b* 9 March 1952; *m* 1971, Frances Corinne Moana, *d* of Trevor Samuel Conley; two *s* two *d*]. *Address:* 1 Ellison Place, Pymble, NSW 2073, Australia.

PLATT, Stephen; Editor, New Statesman and Society, since 1991; *b* 29 Sept. 1954; *s* of Kenneth Norman Platt and Joyce (*née* Pritchard); *m*; one *d*. *Educ:* Longton High Sch., Stoke-on-Trent; Wade Deacon Sch., Widnes; LSE (BSc (Econ)). Teacher, Moss Brook Special Sch., Widnes, 1972–77; Dir, Self Help Housing Resource Library, Poly. of N London, 1977–80; Co-ordinator, Islington Community Housing, 1980–83; freelance writer and journalist, 1983–; News Editor, subseq. Acting Editor, New Society, 1986–91; columnist and writer, 1988. Editor, Enjoying the Countryside. *Publications:* various. *Recreations:* football, walking, countryside, gardening, breeding frogs, Paddington Bear. *Address:* 46 Tufnell Park Road, N7 0DT. *T:* 071–263 4185. *Clubs:* Red Rose; Port Vale.

PLATT, Terence Charles; Assistant Under-Secretary of State (Operations and Resources), Immigration and Nationality Department, Home Office, since 1986; Chief Inspector, Immigration Service, since 1991; *b* 22 Sept. 1936; *yr s* of Bertram Reginald Platt, QPM and Nina Platt; *m* 1959, Margaret Anne Cotmore; two *s*. *Educ:* St Olave's and St Saviour's Grammar School; Joint Services School for Linguists; Russian Interpreter. HM Immigration Officer, 1957; Asst Principal, Home Office, 1962; Principal, 1966; Cabinet Office, 1970; Principal Private Sec. to Sec. of State for NI (Rt Hon. William Whitelaw), 1972–73; Asst Sec., Home Office, 1973–81; Asst Under-Sec. of State and Princ. Estabt and Finance Officer, NI Office, 1981–82; Asst Under-Sec. of State and Dir of Regimes and Services, Prison Dept, Home Office, 1982–86. *Publication:* New Directions in Prison Design (Wkg Party Report), 1985. *Recreations:* growing roses, photography, butterflies. *Address:* c/o Home Office, 50 Queen Anne's Gate, SW1H 9AT.

PLATT, Rev. William James; General Secretary, British and Foreign Bible Society, 1948–60; Consultant, 1960–61; retired, 1961; *b* 2 May 1893; *s* of James and Mary Platt; *m* 1921, Hilda Waterhouse (*d* 1975); one *d*. *Educ:* Rivington Grammar School; Didsbury Theological College, Manchester. Methodist Missionary in West Africa, 1916–30; Chairman and General Superintendent, Methodist District of French West Africa, 1925–30; joined Bible Society Staff as Secretary for Equatorial Africa, 1930; since 1948 has travelled extensively as General Secretary of Bible Society. Chairman of Council, United Bible Societies, 1954–57. Hon. DD, Knox College, Toronto, Canada, 1954. Officer of the Order of Orange Nassau, 1954; Commander, National Order of the Ivory Coast Republic, 1985 (Officer, 1964). *Publications:* An African Prophet; From Fetish to Faith; Whose World?; Three Women in Central Asia; articles in religious and missionary publications. *Address:* Winton House, 51 Dedworth Road, Windsor, Berks SL4 5AZ. *T:* Windsor (0753) 840616. *Club:* Commonwealth Trust.

PLATTEN, Rev. Canon Stephen George; Archbishop of Canterbury's Secretary for Ecumenical Affairs, since 1990; *b* 17 May 1947; *s* of George Henry and Marjory Platten; *m* 1972, Rosslie Thompson; two *s*. *Educ:* Stationers' Company's Sch.; Univ. of London (BEd Hons 1972); Trinity Coll., Oxford (Dip. Theol. 1974); Cuddesdon Theol Coll. Deacon 1975, Priest 1976; Asst Curate, St Andrew, Headington, Oxford, 1975–78; Chaplain and Tutor, Lincoln Theol Coll., 1978–82; Diocesan Dir of Ordinands and Canon Residentiary, Portsmouth Cathedral, 1983–89; Dir, post-ordination trng and continuing ministerial educn, Dio. Portsmouth, 1984–89. Hon. Canon of Canterbury Cathedral, 1990–. Anglican Sec., Anglican-Roman Catholic Internat. Commn (II), 1990–. Chm., Soc. for Study of Christian Ethics, 1983–88. Minister Provincial, European Province, Third Order, SSF, 1991–. Dir, SCM Press, 1990–. Guestmaster, Nikaean Club, 1990–. *Publications:* (contrib.) Deacons in the Ministry of the Church, 1987; (series editor) Ethics and Our Choices, 1990–; (contrib.) Spirituality and Psychology, 1990; (contrib.) Say One for Me, 1991; contribs to theol and educnl jls. *Recreations:* walking, music, literature, Northumbria. *Address:* Lambeth Palace, SE1 7JU. *T:* 071–928 8282. *Clubs:* Athenæum.

PLATTS-MILLS, John Faithful Fortescue, QC 1964; Barrister; *b* 4 Oct. 1906; *s* of John F. W. Mills and Dr Daisy Platts-Mills, Karori, Wellington, NZ; *m* 1936, Janet Katherine Cree; six *s*. *Educ:* Nelson College and Victoria University, NZ; Balliol College, Oxford (Rhodes Scholar). LLM (NZ), MA (1st Cl.), BCL Oxon. MP (Lab) Finsbury, 1945–48, (Lab Ind) 1948–50. Pilot Officer, RAF, 1940; "Bevin Boy", 1944; collier, 1945. Bencher, Inner Temple, 1970. President: Haldane Soc.; Soc. for Cultural Relations with the USSR; Vice-Pres., Internat. Assoc. of Democratic Lawyers; Mem. TGWU. *Address:* Cloisters, Temple, EC4Y 7AA. *T:* 071–583 0303; Terrible Down Farm, Halland, E Sussex BN8 6PG. *T:* Halland (082584) 310. *Clubs:* Athenæum; Vincent's (Oxford); Leander (Henley-on-Thames).

PLAXTON, Ven. Cecil Andrew; Archdeacon of Wiltshire, 1951–74, now Archdeacon Emeritus of the Diocese of Salisbury; *b* 1902; *s* of Rev. J. W. Plaxton, Wells and Langport, Somerset; *m* 1929, Eleanor Joan Elisabeth Sowerby (*d* 1989); one *s* (and one *d* decd). *Educ:* Magdalen College School, Oxford; St Edmund Hall, Oxford; Cuddesdon Theological College. BA 1924, MA 1928, Oxford; Deacon, 1926; Priest, 1927; Curate of Chard, 1926–28; Curate of St Martin, Salisbury, 1928–32; Vicar of Southbroom, Devizes, 1932–37; Vicar of Holy Trinity, Weymouth, 1937–51; Rural Dean of Weymouth, 1941–51; Rector of Pewsey, 1951–65; Canon of Salisbury and Prebend of Netheravon, 1949. Officiating Chaplain to the Forces, 1932–51. *Publication:* The Treasure of Salisbury: Life and Death of St Edmund of Abingdon, 1971, repr. 1980. *Recreations:* archæology and travelling, music. *Address:* 12 Castle Court, St John's Street, Devizes, Wilts SN10 1DQ. *T:* Devizes (0380) 723391.

PLAYER, Dr David Arnott, FRCPE, FRCPsych, FFCM; District Medical Officer, South Birmingham Health Authority, since 1987; *b* 2 April 1927; *s* of John Player and Agnes Gray; *m* 1955, Anne Darragh; two *s*. *Educ:* Calder Street Sch.; Bellahouston Acad., Glasgow; Glasgow Univ. MB, ChB, DPH, DPM. House Surgeon, Dumfries and Galloway Royal Infirmary, 1950; Consultant in Dermatology and VD, RAMC (Far East), 1950–52; House Surgeon, Western Infirmary, Glasgow, 1952; House Physician, Bridge of Earn Hosp., 1952–53; House Surgeon (Obst., Gyn. and Paed.), Halifax Royal Infirmary, 1953–54; GP, W Cumberland and Dumfriesshire, 1954–59; Registrar (Infectious Diseases), Paisley Infectious Diseases Hosp., 1959–60; Asst MOH, Dumfriesshire, 1960–62; Registrar (Psychiatry), Crighton Royal Hosp., Dumfries, 1962–64; MOH, Dumfries Burgh, 1964–70; MO (Mental Health Div.), SHHD and Med. and Psych. Adviser to Sec. of State for Scotland on Scottish Prison and Borstal Service, 1970–73; Dir, Scottish Health Educn Group, 1973–82; Dir Gen., Health Educn Council, 1982–87. Hon. Vis. Prof., Dept of Clinical Epidemiology and Gen. Practice, Royal Free Hosp. Sch. of Medicine, 1983–. *Publications:* articles in Health Bulletin, Internat. Jl of Health Educn, Scottish Trade Union Review. *Recreations:* golf, cycling. *Address:* South Birmingham Health Authority, District Offices, Oak Tree Lane, Selly Oak, Birmingham B29 6JF.

PLAYER, Denis Sydney, CBE 1967; Hon. President, Newall Engineering Group, 1973 (Chairman 1962–73; Deputy Chairman, 1955); Chairman, Newall Machine Tool Co. Ltd, 1964–73; *b* 13 Nov. 1913; *s* of Sydney Player and Minnie Emma Rowe; *m* 1940, Phyllis Ethel Holmes Brown (*d* 1975); three *d*. *Educ:* England; Worcester Acad., Mass. Apprenticed to Newall Engrg Co. Ltd, 1930; spent a year with Federal Produce Corp., RI, before rejoining Newall Engrg on Sales side; Man. Dir, Optical Measuring Tools, 1940; formed Sales Div. for whole of Newall Engrg Gp, 1945. Joined Royal Artillery, 1939; invalided out, 1940. CEng, FIProdE, FRSA. High Sheriff of Rutland, 1970–71. *Recreations:* yachting, fishing, shooting. *Address:* c/o National Westminster Bank, 8 Bennetts Hill, Birmingham B2 5RT. *Clubs:* Royal Automobile, Royal Ocean Racing; Island Sailing (Cowes).

PLAYER, Gary (Jim); professional golfer, since 1953; *b* Johannesburg, 1 Nov. 1935; *s* of Francis Harry Audley Player and late Muriel Marie Ferguson; *m* 1957, Vivienne, *d* of Jacob Wynand Verwey; two *s* four *d*. *Educ:* King Edward Sch., Johannesburg. Won first, Dunlop tournament, 1956; major championship wins include: British Open, 1959, 1968, 1974; US Masters, 1961, 1974, 1978; US PGA, 1962, 1972; US Open, 1965; S African Open, thirteen times, 1956–81; S African PGA, 1959, 1960, 1969, 1979, 1982; Australian Open, seven times, 1958–74; Tooth Gold Coast Classic, Australia, 1981; Johnnie Walker Trophy, Spain, 1984; World Match Play Tournament, 1965, 1966, 1968, 1971, 1973. *Publication:* Golf Begins at 50 (with Desmond Tolhurst), 1988. *Address:* c/o IMG, 1 Erieview Plaza, Suite 1300, Cleveland, Ohio 44114, USA.

PLAYFAIR, Sir Edward (Wilder), KCB 1957 (CB 1949); *b* 17 May 1909; *s* of late Dr Ernest Playfair; *m* 1941, Dr Mary Lois Rae; three *d*. *Educ:* Eton; King's Coll., Cambridge (Hon. Fellow, 1986). Inland Revenue, 1931–34; HM Treasury, 1934–46 and 1947–56 (Control Office for Germany and Austria, 1946–47); Permanent Under-Secretary of State for War, 1956–59; Permanent Sec., Ministry of Defence, 1960–61. Chairman, International Computers and Tabulators Ltd, 1961–65; Director: National Westminster Bank Ltd, 1961–79; Glaxo Hldgs Ltd, 1961–79; Tunnel Holdings Ltd, 1966–80; Equity and Law Life Assce Soc. plc, 1968–83. Governor, Imperial Coll. of Science and Technology, 1958–83 (Fellow, 1972); College Cttee of UCL, 1961–77 (Hon. Fellow, UCL, 1969); Chm., National Gallery, 1972–74 (Trustee, 1967–74). Hon. FBCS. *Address:* 62 Coniger Road, Fulham, SW6 3TA. *T:* 071–736 3194. *Club:* Brooks's.

PLAYFORD, Jonathan Richard; QC 1982; a Recorder, since 1985; *b* 6 Aug. 1940; *s* of Cecil R. B. Playford and Euphrasia J. Playford; *m* 1978, Jill Margaret Dunlop; one *s* one *d*. *Educ:* Eton Coll.; London Univ. (LLB). Called to the Bar, Inner Temple, 1962.

Recreations: music, country pursuits, golf. *Address:* 2 Harcourt Buildings, Temple, EC4Y 9DB. *T:* 071–583 9020. *Clubs:* Garrick, Royal Automobile; Huntercombe Golf (Henley).

PLEASENCE, Donald; actor; *b* 5 Oct. 1919; *s* of late Thomas Stanley and of Alice Pleasence; *m* 1st, 1940, Miriam Raymond; two *d*; 2nd, 1959, Josephine Crombie (marr. diss. 1970); two *d*; 3rd, 1970, Meira Shore; one *d*; 4th, 1989, Linda Woollam. *Educ:* The Grammar School, Ecclesfield, Yorkshire. Made first stage appearance at the Playhouse Theatre, Jersey, CI, May 1939; first London appearance, Twelfth Night, Arts Theatre, 1942. Served with RAF, 1942–46 (Flt Lieut); shot down and taken prisoner, 1944. Returned to stage in The Brothers Karamazov, Lyric, Hammersmith, 1946; Huis Clos, Arts Theatre; Birmingham Repertory Theatre, 1948–50; Bristol Old Vic, 1951; Right Side Up, and Saint's Day, Arts Theatre, 1951; Ziegfeld Theatre, New York (with L. Olivier Co.), 1951; played in own play, Ebb Tide, Edinburgh Festival and Royal Court Theatre, 1952; Stratford-on-Avon season, 1953. *Other London Appearances:* Hobson's Choice, 1952; Antony and Cleopatra, 1953; The Rules of the Game, 1955; The Lark, 1956; Misalliance, 1957; Restless Heart, 1960; The Caretaker, London, 1960, New York, 1961; Poor Bitos, London and New York; The Man in the Glass Booth, St Martin's, 1967 (London Variety Award for Stage Actor of the Year, 1968), New York, 1968–69; Tea Party, The Basement, London, 1970; Reflections, Theatre Royal, Haymarket, 1980; 1970; Wise Child, NY, 1972; The Caretaker, 1990. Many television appearances, incl. The Barchester Chronicles, 1982, The Falklands Factor, 1983, Scoop, 1987. Named Actor of the Year, 1958. *Films include:* The Beachcomber, Heart of a Child, Manuela, The Great Escape, Doctor Crippen, The Caretaker, The Greatest Story Ever Told, The Hallelujah Trail, Fantastic Voyage, Cul-de-Sac, The Night of the Generals, Eye of the Devil, Will Penny, The Mad Woman of Chaillot, Sleep is Lovely, Arthur! Arthur?, THX 1138, Outback, Soldier Blue, The Pied Piper, The Jerusalem File, Kidnapped, Innocent Bystanders, Death Line, Henry VIII, Wedding in White, The Rainbow Boys, Malachi's Cove, Mutations, Tales From Beyond the Grave, The Black Windmill, Escape to Witch Mountain, I Don't Want to be Born, Journey Into Fear, Hearts of the West, Trial by Combat, The Last Tycoon, The Passover Plot, The Eagle has Landed, Golden Rod, The Devil's Men, Tomorrow Never Comes, Telefon, Sgt Pepper's Lonely Hearts Club Band, Halloween, Power Play, Dracula, Halloween II, The Monster Club, Escape from New York, Race for the Yankee Zephyr, Frankenstein's Great Aunt Tilly, A Rare Breed, Warrior of the Lost World, Creepers, The Ambassador, The Corsican Brothers, Master of the Game, Arch of Triumph, Phenomenon, Honour Thy Father, Nothing Underneath, The Rainbow Four, Into the Darkness, Nosferatu II, Ground Zero, Catacomb, Animale Metropolitani, Gila and Rick, The Return of Djiango, Fuja del'Inferno, Prince of Darkness, Imbalances, Hanna's War, Ground Zero, Commander Search and Destroy; Halloween IV, Paganini Horror, River of Blood, Murder on Safari, Buried Alive, Fall of the House of Usher, American Rickshaw, Casablanca Express, Halloween V, Women in Arms, Miliardi, Woody Allen Fall Project, Dien Bien Phu. *Recreation:* talking too much. *Address:* 219 The Plaza, 535 Kings Road, SW10 0SZ.

PLEETH, William, OBE 1989; FGSM; FRCM; Professor of 'Cello, Guildhall School of Music, 1948–78; *b* 12 Jan. 1916; *s* of John Pleeth and Edith Pleeth; *m* 1944, Margaret Good; one *s* one *d*. *Educ:* London until 1929; Leipzig Conservatoire, 1930–32. Internat. concert 'cellist in duos, trios, string quartets and concertos; début: Leipzig, 1931; London, 1933; broadcasting and recording, 1933–80; 'cello master classes in Europe, Canada, USA; frequent member, internat. music juries. *Publication:* Cello (Menuhin series), 1982. *Recreations:* gardening, reading, researching into old English furniture. *Address:* 19 Holly Park, N3 3JB. *T:* 081–346 0277.

PLENDER, Richard Owen; QC 1989; JSD, PhD; barrister; *b* 9 Oct. 1945; *s* of George Plender and Louise Mary (*née* Savage); *m* 1978, Patricia Clare (*née* Ward); two *d*. *Educ:* Dulwich Coll.; Queens' Coll., Cambridge (MA, LLB; Rebecca Squire Prize); Univ. of Illinois (LLM; JSD 1972; College of Law Prize); Univ. of Sheffield (PhD 1973). Called to the Bar, Inner Temple, 1972 (Berridale-Keith Prize); in practice at the Bar, 1974–. Consultant, UN Law and Population Programme, 1972–74; Consultant Legal Adviser, UN High Comr for Refugees, 1974–78; Legal Sec., Court of Justice of European Communities, 1980–83; Dir of Studies, 1987, Dir of Res., 1988, Hague Acad. of Internat. Law; Dir, Centre of European Law, KCL, 1988–91; Special Legal Advr to States of Jersey, 1988–. Leverhulme Fellow, Yale Law Sch., 1980; British Acad. Fellow, Soviet Acad. of Sciences, 1985; Sen. Mem., Robinson Coll., Cambridge, 1983–; Associate Prof., Univ. de Paris II (Univ. de Droit, d'Economie et des Sciences Sociales), 1989–90. *Publications:* International Migration Law, 1972, 2nd edn 1988; (ed and contrib.) Fundamental Rights, 1973; Cases and Materials on the Law of the European Communities, 1980 (with J. Usher), 2nd edn 1989; A Practical Introduction to European Community Law, 1980; (with J. Peres Santos) Introducción al Derecho Comunitario Europeo, 1984; (ed and contrib.) Legal History and Comparative Law: essays in honour of Albert Kiralfy, 1990; The European Contracts Convention: the Rome convention on the choice of law for contracts, 1991; contribs in English, French, German and Spanish to jls and encyclopedias. *Recreations:* writing light verse, classical music (especially late nineteenth century orchestral). *Address:* 3 Essex Court, Temple, EC4Y 9AL. *T:* 071–583 9294; Forrester & Norall, rue Joseph II No 30, Boîte 2, B-1040 Brussels, Belgium. *T:* 2 219 1620.

PLENDERLEITH, Harold James, CBE 1959; MC 1918; BSc, PhD; FRSE; FBA 1973; FSA; FMA; Director, International Centre for the Study of the Preservation and Restoration of Cultural Property (created by UNESCO), 1959–71, now Emeritus; Vice-President, International Institute for the Conservation of Museum Objects, 1958 (President, 1965–67, Hon. Fellow 1971); *b* 19 Sept. 1898; *s* of Robert James Plenderleith, FEIS; *m* 1926, Elizabeth K. S. Smyth (*d* 1982). *Educ:* Dundee Harris Acad.; St Andrews Univ. Scientific Asst, Dept of Scientific and Indust. Res., attached to British Museum, Bloomsbury, 1924; Asst Keeper, British Museum, 1927; Keeper, Research Lab., British Museum, 1949–59. Mem., Hon. Scientific Adv. Cttee, Nat. Gallery, 1935–81 (Chm., 1944–58); Professor of Chemistry, Royal Academy of Arts, London, 1936–58. Hon. Treas. Internat. Inst. for Conservation of Museum Objects, 1950–58; Hon. Mem., Internat. Council of Museums; Hon. Chm., Scottish Soc. for Conservation and Restoration, 1984. Rhind Lecturer (Edinburgh) 1954. Gold Medal, Society of Antiquaries of London, 1964; Gold Medal, Univ. of Young Nam, Tae Gu, Korea, 1970; Bronze Medal, UNESCO, 1971; Conservation Service Award, US Dept of the Interior, 1976; ICCROM International Oscar, Rome, 1979. Hon. LLD St Andrews. *Publications:* The Preservation of Antiquities, 1934; The Conservation of Prints, Drawings and Manuscripts, 1937; The Preservation of Leather Bookbindings, 1946; The Conservation of Antiquities and Works of Art, 1956 (2nd edn with A. E. A. Werner, 1971); papers on allied subjects and on technical examinations of museum specimens in museum and scientific journals. *Recreations:* art and music. *Address:* Riverside, 17 Rockfield Crescent, Dundee DD2 1JF. *T:* Dundee (0382) 641552. *Club:* Athenæum.

PLENDERLEITH, Ian; Associate Director, Bank of England, since 1990; Senior Broker to Commissioners for Reduction of National Debt, since 1989; *b* 27 Sept. 1943; *s* of Raymond William Plenderleith and Louise Helen Plenderleith (*née* Martin); *m* 1967, Kristina Mary Bentley; one *s* two *d*. *Educ:* King Edward's Sch., Birmingham; Christ Church, Oxford (MA); Columbia Business Sch., NY (MBA; Beta Gamma Sigma Medal, 1971). Joined Bank of England, 1965; seconded to IMF, Washington DC, 1972–74; Private Sec. to Governor, 1976–79; Alternate Dir, EIB, 1980–86; Hd of Gilt-Edged Div., 1982–90; Asst Dir, 1986–90. Mem., Stock Exchange Council, 1989–. Mem. Adv. Bd, Inst. of Archaeology Develt Trust, UCL, 1987–. Fellow, ACT, 1989. Liveryman, Innholders' Co., 1977. *Recreations:* archaeology, theatre, cricket. *Address:* Bank of England, EC2R 8AH. *T:* 071–601 4444. *Club:* Tillington Cricket.

PLENDERLEITH, Thomas Donald; Hon. Fellow, Royal Society of Painter-Etchers and Engravers, 1987 (RE 1961 (retd); ARE 1951); Senior Art Master, St Nicholas Grammar School, Northwood, 1956–85, retired; *b* 11 March 1921; *s* of James Plenderleith and Georgina Ellis; *m* 1949, Joyce Rogers; one *s*. *Educ:* St Clement Danes; Ealing Sch. of Art; Hornsey Sch. of Art. Pilot, Bomber Command, RAF, 1941–46. Art Master, Pinner County Grammar Sch., 1948–56. Art Teacher's Diploma, 1947. *Recreations:* cricket, badminton. *Address:* Homelea, Tresean, Cubert, Newquay, Cornwall TR8 5HN.

PLEVEN, René Jean; French Statesman; Compagnon de la Libération, 1943; Commandeur du Mérite Maritime, 1945; Député des Côtes-du-Nord, 1945–73; Président du Conseil Général des Côtes-du-Nord, 1949; Président du Conseil Régional de Bretagne, 1974; *b* 15 April 1901; *s* of Colonel Jules Pleven; *m* 1924, Anne Bompard (*d* 1966); two *d*. *Educ:* Faculté de Droit de Paris (LLD); Ecole Libre des Sciences Politiques. Company Director. Deputy chief of French Air Mission to USA, 1939. French National Committee and Comité Français de Libération Nationale (Finances, Colonies, Foreign Affairs), 1941–44; Minister: of Colonies (Provisional Government), 1944; of Finances, 1944–46; of Defence, Nov. 1949 and 1952–54; Président du Conseil, July 1950, Aug. 1951–Jan. 1952; Vice-Président du Conseil, Feb. 1951; Ministre des Affaires Etrangères, 1958; Délégué à l'Assemblée parlementaire européenne, and Chm., Liberal Gp of this Assembly, 1956–69; Ministre de la Justice, et Garde des Sceaux, 1969–73. Grand Officer Order of Leopold, 1945; Grand Cross: Le Million d'éléphants, 1949; Etoile Polaire, 1950; Orange-Nassau, 1950; Dannebrog, 1950; Nicham Alaouite, 1950; Vietnam, 1951; Order of Merit of the Republic of Italy, 1972; National Order of Ivory Coast, 1972; Order of Central African Republic, 1972; Hon GBE, 1972. *Publications:* Les Ouvriers de l'agriculture anglaise depuis la guerre, 1925; Avenir de la Bretagne, 1962. *Address:* 12 rue Chateaubriand, 22100 Dinan (Côtes d'Armor), France.

PLEYDELL-BOUVERIE, family name of **Earl of Radnor.**

PLIATZKY, Sir Leo, KCB 1977 (CB 1972); Civil Service, 1947–80; *b* 1919; *m* 1948, Marian Jean Elias (*d* 1979); one *s* one *d*. *Educ:* Manchester Grammar Sch.; City of London Sch.; Corpus Christi Coll., Oxford (Hon. Fellow, 1980). First Cl. Classical Honour Mods, 1939. Served in RAOC and REME, 1940–45 (despatches). First Cl. Philosophy, Politics and Economics, 1946. Research Sec., Fabian Soc., 1946–47; Min. of Food, 1947–50; HM Treasury, 1950–77; Under-Sec., 1967; Dep. Sec., 1971; Second Permanent Sec., 1976; Permanent Sec., Dept of Trade, 1977; retired 1979, retained for special duties, 1979–80. Mem., British Airways Bd, 1980–84 (Non-exec. Dir, 1984–85); Director: Associated Communications Corporation Ltd, 1980–82; Central Independent Television plc, 1981–89; Ultramar Co. plc, 1981–90. Chm., Industry Wkg Pty on Production of Television Commercials, 1986–89 (report published, 1987). Vis. Prof., City Univ., 1980–84; Associate Fellow, LSE, 1982–85; Sen. Res. Fellow, PSI, 1983–84. Trustee, History of Parliament Trust, 1982–, Treasurer 1983–. Hon. DLitt Salford, 1986. *Publications:* Getting and Spending, 1982, rev. edn 1984; Paying and Choosing, 1985; The Treasury under Mrs Thatcher, 1989. *Address:* 27 River Court, Upper Ground, SE1. *T:* 071–928 3667. *Club:* Reform.

PLOURDE, Most Rev. Joseph Aurèle; *see* Ottawa, Archbishop of, (RC).

PLOUVIEZ, Peter William; General Secretary, British Actors' Equity Association, 1974–91; *b* 30 July 1931; *s* of Charles and Emma Plouviez; *m* 1978, Alison Dorothy Macrae; two *d* (by previous marr.). *Educ:* Sir George Monoux Grammar Sch.; Hastings Grammar Sch. Greater London Organiser, NUBE, 1955–60; Asst Sec., Equity, 1960, Asst Gen. Sec., Equity, 1964. Contested (Lab), St Marylebone bye-election, 1963; Councillor, St Pancras, 1962–65. Chairman: Radio and Television Safeguards Cttee, 1974–; Festival of British Theatre Ltd, 1983–; Fedn of Theatre Unions, 1974–; Vice-President: Confedn of Entertainment Unions, 1974–; Internat. Fedn of Actors, 1987–; Member: Cinematograph Films Council, 1974; Cttee, Assoc. for Business Sponsorship of the Arts, 1977–; TUC Adv. Cttee on the Arts, Entertainment and Sports; British Screen Adv. Council, 1985–. Joint Secretary: London and Provincial Theatre Councils; Performers Alliance; Treasurer, Entertainment Charities Fund. Trustee: Theatres Trust, 1977–; Evelyn Norris Trust; Chm., Equity Trust Fund, 1991– (Dir, 1989–); Dir, Carl Rosa Trust Ltd. Bd Mem., Children's Film and TV Foundn. *Recreation:* contemplating retirement. *Address:* c/o Ann Maguire, Equity, 8 Harley Street, W1N 2AB. *Club:* Gerry's.

PLOWDEN, family name of **Baron Plowden.**

PLOWDEN, Baron, *cr* 1959, of Plowden (Life Peer); **Edwin Noel Plowden,** GBE 1987 (KBE 1946); KCB 1951; *b* 6 Jan. 1907; 4th *s* of late Roger H. Plowden; *m* 1933, Bridget Horatia (*see* Lady Plowden); two *s* two *d*. *Educ:* Switzerland; Pembroke College, Cambridge (Hon. Fellow, 1958). Temporary Civil Servant Ministry of Economic Warfare, 1939–40; Ministry of Aircraft Production, 1940–46; Chief Executive, and Member of Aircraft Supply Council, 1945–46; Vice-Chairman Temporary Council Cttee of NATO, 1951–52; Cabinet Office, 1947; Treasury, 1947–53, as Chief Planning Officer and Chairman of Economic Planning Board. Adviser on Atomic Energy Organization, 1953–54; Chairman, Atomic Energy Authority, 1954–59; Visiting Fellow, Nuffield College, 1956–64; Chm. Cttee of Enquiry: Treasury control of Public Expenditure, 1959–61; organisation of Representational Services Overseas, 1963–64; Aircraft Industry, 1964–65; Structure of Electricity Supply Industry in England and Wales, 1974–75; into CBI's aims and organisation, 1974–75; Dep. Chm., Cttee of Inquiry on Police, 1977–79; Chm., Police Complaints Bd, 1976–81; Independent Chm., Police Negotiating Bd, 1979–82; Chm., Top Salaries Review Body, 1981–89 (Mem., 1977–). Pres., TI Gp (formerly Tube Investments Ltd), 1976–90 (Chm., 1963–76); Director: Commercial Union Assurance Co. Ltd, 1946–78; National Westminster Bank Ltd, 1960–77; Chm., Equity Capital for Industry Ltd, 1976–82; Mem., Internat. Adv. Bd, Southeast Bank NA, 1982–86. Chm., CBI Companies Cttee, 1976–80; Vice-Chm., CBI Pres.'s Cttee, 1977–80. Pres., London Graduate Sch. of Business Studies, 1976–90 (Chm. 1964–76); Chm., Standing Adv. Cttee on Pay of Higher Civil Service, 1968–70; Member: Civil Service Coll. Adv. Council, 1970–76; Engineering Industries Council, 1976; Ford European Adv. Council, 1976–83. Hon. Fellow, London Business Sch., 1988. Hon. DSc: Pennsylvania State Univ., 1958; Univ. of Aston, 1972; Hon. DLitt, Loughborough, 1976. *Publication:* An Industrialist in the Treasury: the post war years (autobiog.), 1989. *Address:* Martels Manor, Dunmow, Essex CM6 1NB. *T:* Great Dunmow (0371) 872141; 11 Abingdon Gardens, Abingdon Villas, W8 6BY. *T:* 071–937 4238.

See also W. J. L. Plowden.

PLOWDEN, Lady, (Bridget Horatia), DBE 1972; Chairman: Independent Broadcasting Authority, 1975–80; Training Commission (formerly Manpower Services Commission) Area Manpower Board, North London, 1983–88; 2nd *d* of late Admiral Sir H. W. Richmond, KCB, and of Lady Richmond (Elsa, *née* Bell); *m* 1933, Baron Plowden, *qv*; two *s* two *d*. *Educ:* Downe House. Dir, Trust Houses Forte Ltd, 1961–72. A Governor and Vice-Chm., BBC, 1970–75. Chairman: Mary Feilding Guild (formerly Working Ladies Guild), 1945–88; Professional Classes Aid Council, 1958–73 (Pres., 1973–86); Central Adv. Council for Educn (England), 1963–66; Metropolitan Architectural Consortium for Educn, 1968–79; President: RELATE (formerly Nat. Marriage Guidance Council), 1983–; Adv. Cttee for Educn of Romany and other Travellers, 1983– (Chm., 1973–83); Voluntary Orgns Liaison Council for Under-Fives, 1985– (Founder and Chm., 1978); Nat. Inst. of Continuing Adult Educn, 1981–88; Coll. of Preceptors, 1987– (Vice-Pres., 1983; Hon. Fellow, 1973); Harding House Assoc.; Delves House, 1961–88 (formerly Chm.); Member: Nat. Theatre Bd, 1976–88; Drake Fellowship, 1981–87; Fairbridge/Drake Soc., 1988–89; (Co-opted) Educn Cttee, ILEA, 1967–73 (Vice-Chm., ILEA Schs Sub-Cttee, 1967–70); Houghton Inquiry into Pay of Teachers, 1974; Chairman: Governors, Philippa Fawcett Coll. of Educn, 1967–76; Robert Montefiore Comprehensive Sch., 1968–78. Liveryman, Goldsmiths' Co., 1979–. JP Inner London Area Juvenile Panel, 1962–71. FRTS 1980. Hon. LLD: Leicester, 1968; Reading, 1970; London, 1976; Hon. DLitt Loughborough, 1976; DUniv Open, 1974. *Address:* Martels Manor, Dunmow, Essex. *T:* Great Dunmow (0371) 872141; 11 Abingdon Gardens, Abingdon Villas, W8 6BY. *T:* 071–937 4238.
See also W. J. L. Plowden.

PLOWDEN, William Julius Lowthian, PhD; Senior Adviser, Harkness Fellowships, London, since 1991; *b* 7 Feb. 1935; *s* of Lord and Lady Plowden, *qqv*; *m* 1960, Veronica Gascoigne; two *s* two *d*. *Educ:* Eton; King's Coll., Cambridge (BA, PhD); Univ. of Calif, Berkeley. Staff Writer, Economist, 1959–60; BoT, 1960–65; Lectr in Govt, LSE, 1965–71; Central Policy Review Staff, Cabinet Office, 1971–77; Under Sec., Dept of Industry, 1977–78; Dir-Gen., RIPA, 1978–88; Exec. Dir, UK Harkness Fellowships, NY, 1988–91. Hon. Prof., Dept of Politics, Univ. of Warwick, 1977–82; Vis. Prof. in Govt, LSE, 1982–88. Mem., W Lambeth DHA, 1982–87. Trustee, CSV, 1984–. *Publications:* The Motor Car and Politics in Britain, 1971; (with Tessa Blackstone) Inside the Think Tank: advising the Cabinet 1971–1983, 1988. *Address:* 49 Stockwell Park Road, SW9 0DD. *T:* 071–274 4535.

PLOWDEN ROBERTS, Hugh Martin; Director: Argyll Group plc, since 1983; Lawson Mardon Group Ltd, since 1987; *b* 6 Aug. 1932; *s* of Stanley and Joan Plowden Roberts; *m* 1956, Susan Jane Patrick; two *d*. *Educ:* St Edward's School, Oxford; St Edmund Hall, Oxford. BA 1954, MA 1956. FIGD 1980. Payne & Son Meat Group, 1954–60 (Dir, 1958); Asst Gen. Manager (Meat Group), Co-operative Wholesale Society, 1960–67; Allied Suppliers Ltd, 1967–82: Dir, 1971; Dep. Man. Dir, 1974; Man. Dir, 1978; Chm., 1980–82; Dir, Cavenham Ltd, 1979, Chm., 1981–82; Dep. Chm., Argyll Stores Ltd, 1983–85; Chm., Dairy Crest Foods, subseq. Dairy Crest Ltd, 1985–88. Mem., MMB, 1983–89. *Recreations:* country pursuits. *Address:* Barn Cottage, Fulking, Henfield, W Sussex BN5 9NH. *T:* Poynings (0273) 857622. *Club:* Farmers'.

PLOWMAN, Sir (John) Anthony, Kt 1961; Judge of the High Court of Justice (Chancery Division), 1961–76, Vice-Chancellor, 1974–76; *b* 27 Dec. 1905; *e s* of late John Tharp Plowman (solicitor); *m* 1933, Vernon (*d* 1988), 3rd *d* of late A. O. Graham, Versailles; three *d*. *Educ:* Highgate School; Gonville and Caius Coll., Cambridge. Solicitors Final (John Mackrell Prize), 1927; LLB London, 1927; LLB Cantab (1st Cl.), 1929; LLM Cantab 1956. Called to Bar, Lincoln's Inn, 1931 (Tancred and Cholmeley studentships; Buchanan Prize); QC 1954; Bencher of Lincoln's Inn, 1961. Served, 1940–45, Squadron-Leader, RAF. Member of General Council of the Bar, 1956–60. *Address:* Treetop, Lane End, High Wycombe, Bucks.

PLOWMAN, Hon. Sir John (Robin), Kt 1979; CBE 1970 (OBE 1949); Member of the Legislative Council, later Senator, Bermuda, 1966–82, Government Leader in the Senate, 1968–82; Minister of Government and Commercial Services, Bermuda, 1980–82; *b* Bermuda, 18 Sept. 1908; *s* of Owen and Elizabeth Plowman; *m* 1936, Marjorie Hardwick (*d* 1990); two *s*. *Educ:* Bermuda and England. Member, Ealing Borough Council, 1931–35; returned to Bermuda, 1935; Bermuda Volunteer Engineers, 1939–42; Dep. Dir, Dir and later Chm. of Bermuda Supplies Commission, 1942–47; Man. Director of Holmes, Williams & Purvey Ltd, 1947–78, Chairman of Board, 1961–. Chm. or Mem. of various govt commns and bds, including Training and Employment, Ports Facilities, Transport Control and Civil Service; Minister of Organisation, 1968–77; Minister of Marine and Air Services, 1977–80. Attached to UK negotiating team for Bermuda II Civil Aviation agreement, 1977. Chm. Bd of Governors, Warwick Academy, 1946–73; Life Vice-Pres. Bermuda Olympic Assoc. and Bermuda Football Assoc. *Recreations:* golf, sports administration. *Address:* Chiswick, Paget, Bermuda. *Clubs:* Carlton; Royal Hamilton Dinghy and Mid-Ocean (Bermuda).

PLOWRIGHT, David Ernest; Chairman, Granada Television Ltd, since 1987 (Joint Managing Director, 1975–81, Managing Director, 1981–87); Director: Granada International, since 1975; Granada Group, since 1981; *b* 11 Dec. 1930; *s* of late William Ernest Plowright and of Daisy Margaret Plowright; *m* 1953, Brenda Mary (*née* Key); one *s* two *d*. *Educ:* Scunthorpe Grammar Sch.; on local weekly newspaper and during National Service, Germany. Reporter, Scunthorpe Star, 1950; freelance corresp. and sports writer, 1952; Reporter, Feature Writer and briefly Equestrian Corresp., Yorkshire Post, 1954; Granada Television: News Editor, 1957; Producer, Current Affairs, 1960; Editor, World in Action, 1966; Head of Current Affairs, 1968; Controller of Programmes, 1969–79. Chm., Network Programme Cttee, ITV, 1980–82. Chm., Independent Television Cos Assoc., 1984–86. Director: Superchannel, 1986–89; Merseyside Tourism Board, 1986–88; British Satellite Broadcasting, 1987–90; British Screen, 1988–; Tate Gall., Liverpool, 1988–. Vice Pres., RTS, 1982–; Member: Steering Cttee, European Film and TV Forum, 1988–; Internat. Council, Nat. Acad. for TV Arts and Scis, 1988–. Member: Civic Trust in the NW; Manchester Olympic Bid Cttee. Trustee, BAFTA. Gov., Manchester Polytechnic, 1988–90. Hon. DLitt Salford, 1989. *Recreations:* television, watching sport, messing about in a boat. *Address:* Granada TV Ltd, Manchester M60 9EA. *T:* 061–832 7211; Granada TV, 36 Golden Square, W1. *T:* 071–734 8080.
See also J. A. Plowright.

PLOWRIGHT, Joan Ann, (The Lady Olivier), CBE 1970; leading actress with the National Theatre, 1963–74; Member of the RADA Council; *b* 28 Oct. 1929; *d* of late William Ernest Plowright and of Daisy Margaret (*née* Burton); *m* 1st, 1953, Roger Gage (marr. diss.); 2nd, 1961, (as Sir Laurence Olivier) Baron Olivier, OM (*d* 1989); one *s* two *d*. *Educ:* Scunthorpe Grammar School; Laban Art of Movement Studio; Old Vic Theatre School. First stage appearance in If Four Walls Told, Croydon Rep. Theatre, 1948; Bristol Old Vic and Mem. Old Vic Co., S Africa tour, 1952; first London appearance in The Duenna, Westminster, 1954; Moby Dick, Duke of York's, 1955; season of leading parts, Nottingham Playhouse, 1955–56; English Stage Co., Royal Court, 1956; The Crucible, Don Juan, The Death of Satan, Cards of Identity, The Good Woman of Setzuan, The Country Wife (transferred to Adelphi, 1957); The Chairs, The Making of Moo, Royal Court, 1957; The Entertainer, Palace, 1957; The Chairs, The Lesson, Phoenix, NY, 1958; The Entertainer, Royale, NY, 1958; The Chairs, The Lesson, Major Barbara, Royal Court, 1958; Hook, Line and Sinker, Piccadilly, 1958; Roots, Royal Court, Duke of York's, 1959; Rhinoceros, Royal Court, 1960; A Taste of Honey, Lyceum, NY, 1960 (Best Actress Tony Award); Rosmersholm, Greenwich, 1973; Saturday, Sunday, Monday, Queen's, 1974–75; The Sea Gull, Lyric, 1975; The Bed Before Yesterday, Lyric, 1975 (Variety Club of GB Award, 1977); Filumena, Lyric, 1977 (Soc. of West End Theatre Award, 1978); Enjoy, Vaudeville, 1980; The Cherry Orchard, Haymarket, 1983; The House of Bernada Alba, Globe, 1986; Time and the Conways, Old Vic, 1990; Chichester Festival: Uncle Vanya, The Chances, 1962; St Joan (Best Actress Evening Standard Award), Uncle Vanya, 1963; The Doctor's Dilemma, The Taming of the Shrew, 1972; Cavell, 1982; The Way of the World, 1984; National Theatre: St Joan, Uncle Vanya, Hobson's Choice, opening season, 1963; The Master Builder, 1964; Much Ado About Nothing, 1967, 1968; Three Sisters, 1967, 1968; Tartuffe, 1967, 1968; The Advertisement, 1968; Love's Labour's Lost, 1968; The Merchant of Venice, 1970; A Woman Killed With Kindness, 1971; The Rules of the Game, 1971; Eden End, 1974; Mrs Warren's Profession, 1985. Produced, The Travails of Sancho Panza, 1969; directed: Rites, 1969; A Prayer for Wings, 1985; Married Love, 1988. *Films include:* The Entertainer, 1960; Three Sisters, 1970; Equus; Britannia Hospital, 1982; Wagner, Revolution, 1985; Drowning by Numbers, The Dressmaker, 1988; I Love You to Death, 1989; Avalon, 1991; *for TV:* The Merchant of Venice, Brimstone and Treacle, A Dedicated Man. Appears on TV; Daphne Laureola, 1976; The Birthday Party, 1987; The Importance of Being Earnest, 1988; And a Nightingale Sang, 1989. *Recreations:* reading, music, entertaining. *Address:* c/o Write On Cue, 10 Garrick Street, WC2E 9BH; ICM, 388 Oxford Street, W1N 9HE.
See also D. E. Plowright.

PLOWRIGHT, Rosalind Anne, (Mrs J. A. Kaye); soprano; *b* 21 May 1949; *d* of Robert Arthur Plowright and Celia Adelaide Plowright; *m* 1984, James Anthony Kaye; one *s* one *d*. *Educ:* Notre Dame High Sch., Wigan; Royal Northern Coll. of Music, Manchester. LRAM. London Opera Centre, 1974–75; Glyndebourne Chorus and Touring Co., début as Agathe in Der Freischutz, 1975; WNO, ENO, Kent Opera, 1975–78; Miss Jessel in Turn of the Screw, ENO, 1979 (SWET award); début at Covent Garden as Ortlinde in Die Walküre, 1980; with Bern Opera, 1980–81, Frankfurt Opera and Munich Opera, 1981; débuts: in USA (Philadelphia and San Diego), Paris, Madrid and Hamburg, 1982; at La Scala, Milan, Edinburgh Fest., San Francisco and New York (Carnegie Hall), 1983; in Berlin, 1984; in Houston, Pittsburgh and Verona, 1985; in Rome, Florence and Holland, 1986; in Tulsa, Buenos Aires, Santiago di Chile, Israel and Bonn, 1987; with NY Phil. and Paris Opera, 1987; in Lausanne, Geneva, Oviedo and Bilbao, 1988; in Zurich, Copenhagen and Lisbon, 1989; with Vienna State Opera, 1990. Principal rôles include: Ariadne; Aida; Amelia in Un Ballo in Maschera; Leonora in Il Trovatore; Leonora in La Forza del Destino; Desdemona in Otello; Violetta in La Traviata; Elena in I Vespri Siciliani; Abigaille in Nabucco; Elisabetta in Don Carlos; Lady Macbeth; Manon Lescaut; Giorgetta in Il Tabarro; Suor Angelica; Norma; Alceste; Médée; Maddalena in Andrea Chénier. Has given recitals and concerts in UK, USA and Europe, made opera and concert recordings, and opera telecasts. First prize, 7th Internat. Comp. for Opera Singers, Sofia, 1979; Prix Fondation Fanny Heldy, Acad. Nat. du Disque Lyrique, 1985. *Recreation:* fell walking. *Address:* c/o Kaye Artists Management Ltd, Barratt House, 7 Chertsey Road, Woking GU21 3AB. *T:* Guildford (0483) 776776, *Fax:* Guildford (0483) 747848.

PLOWRIGHT, Walter, CMG 1974; DVSc; FRS 1981; FRCVS; Head, Department of Microbiology, ARC Institute for Research on Animal Diseases, Compton, Berks, 1978–83; *b* 20 July 1923; 2nd *s* of Jonathan and Mahala Plowright, Holbeach, Lincs; *m* 1959, Dorothy Joy (*née* Bell). *Educ:* Moulton and Spalding Grammar Schs; Royal Veterinary Coll., London. DVSc (Pret.) 1964; MRCVS 1944; FRCVS 1977; FRVC 1987. Commissioned, RAVC, 1945–48; Colonial Service, 1950–64; Animal Virus Research Inst., Pirbright, 1964–71 (seconded E Africa, 1966–71); Prof. of Vet. Microbiology, RVC, 1971–78. Hon. Mem., Acad. Royale des Sciences d'Outre-Mer, Brussels, 1986. Hon. DSc: Univ. of Nairobi, 1984; Reading, 1986. J. T. Edwards Memorial Prize, 1964; R. B. Bennett Commonwealth Prize of RSA, 1972; Bledisloe Vet. Award, RASE, 1979; King Baudouin Internat. Develt Prize, 1984; Dalrymple-Champneys Cup, BVA, 1984; Gold Award, Office Internat. des Epizooties, Paris, 1988. *Publications:* numerous contribs to scientific jls relating to virus diseases of animals. *Recreations:* gardening, travel. *Address:* Whitehill Lodge, Goring-on-Thames, Reading RG8 0LL. *T:* Goring (0491) 872891.

PLUM, Patrick; *see* McConville, M. A.

PLUMB, family name of **Baron Plumb**.

PLUMB, Baron *cr* 1987 (Life Peer), of Coleshill in the County of Warwickshire; **Charles Henry Plumb;** Kt 1973; DL; Member (C) The Cotswolds, European Parliament, since 1979; *b* 27 March 1925; *s* of Charles and Louise Plumb; *m* 1947, Marjorie Dorothy Dunn; one *s* two *d*. *Educ:* King Edward VI School, Nuneaton. National Farmers Union: Member Council, 1959; Vice-President, 1964, 1965; Deputy-President, 1966, 1967, 1968, 1969; President, 1970–79. European Parliament: Chm., Agricl Cttee, 1979–82; Leader, EDG, 1982–87; Pres., 1987–89. Chm., British Agricl Council, 1975–79. Mem., Duke of Northumberland's Cttee of Enquiry on Foot and Mouth Disease, 1967–68; Member Council: CBI; Animal Health Trust. Chm., Internat. Agricl Trng Programme, 1987–. Pres., Royal Agric. Soc. of England, 1977, Dep. Pres. 1978; President: Internat. Fedn of Agricl Producers, 1979–82; Comité des Organisations Professionels Agricoles de la CEE (COPA), 1975–77. Pres., Nat. Fedn of Young Farmers' Clubs, 1976–; Patron, Warwicks Co. Fedn of YFC, 1974–; Hon. Pres., Ayrshire Cattle Soc. Director: United Biscuits Ltd; Lloyds Bank Ltd; Fisons Ltd. Liveryman, Farmers' Co. FRSA 1970; FRAgS 1974. DL Warwick 1977. Hon. DSc Cranfield, 1983. Order of Merit (FRG), 1979. *Recreations:* shooting, fishing. *Address:* The Dairy Farm, Maxstoke, Coleshill, Warwicks B46 2QJ. *T:* Coleshill (0675) 463133, *Fax:* Coleshill (0675) 464156; 2 Queen Anne's Gate, SW1H 9AA. *T:* 071–222 0411. *Clubs:* St Stephen's Constitutional, Farmers', Coleshill Rotary (Hon. Member).

PLUMB, Sir John (Harold), Kt 1982; FBA 1968; historian; Master of Christ's College, Cambridge, 1978–82; Professor of Modern English History, University of Cambridge, 1966–74, now Emeritus; *b* 20 Aug. 1911; 3rd *s* of late James Plumb, Leicester. *Educ:* Alderman Newton's Sch., Leicester; University Coll., Leicester; Christ's Coll., Cambridge. BA London, 1st Class Hons History, 1933; PhD Cambridge, 1936; LittD Cambridge, 1957. Ehrman Research Fellow, King's Coll., Cambridge, 1939–46; FO, 1940–45; Fellow of Christ's Coll., 1946–, Steward, 1948–50, Tutor, 1950–59. Vice-Master, 1964–68. Univ. Lectr in History, 1946–62; Reader in Modern English History, 1962–65; Chm. of History Faculty, 1966–68, Univ. of Cambridge. Trustee: National Portrait Gallery, 1961–82; Fitzwilliam Museum, 1985– (Syndic, 1960–77); Member: Wine Standards Bd, 1973–75; Council, British Acad., 1977–80; Chm., Centre of E Anglian Studies, 1979–82. FRHistS; FSA; FRSL 1969. Visiting Prof., Columbia Univ., 1960; Distinguished Vis. Prof., NYC Univ., 1971–72, 1976; Cecil and Ida Green Honors Chair, Texas Christian Univ., 1974;

Dist. Vis. Prof., Washington Univ., 1977; Lectures: Ford's, Oxford Univ., 1965–66; Saposnekov, City College, NY, 1968; Guy Stanton Ford, Univ. of Minnesota, 1969; Stenton, Reading, 1972; George Rogers Clark, Soc. of the Cincinnati, 1977. Chm., British Inst. of America, 1982–; Hon. For. Mem., Amer. Acad. for Arts and Sciences, 1970; Hon. Member: Soc. of Amer. Historians, 1976; Amer. Historical Assoc., 1981. Hon. DLitt: Leicester, 1968; East Anglia, 1973; Bowdoin Coll., 1974; S California, 1978; Westminster Coll., 1983; Washington Univ., St Louis, 1983; Bard Coll., NY, 1988. Editor, History of Human Society, 1959–; Sen. Editor to American Heritage Co. Historical Adviser, Penguin Books, 1960–; Editor, Pelican Social History of Britain, 1982–. *Publications:* England in the Eighteenth Century, 1950; (with C. Howard) West African Explorers, 1952; Chatham, 1953; (ed) Studies in Social History, 1955; Sir Robert Walpole, Vol. I, 1956, Vol. II, 1960, both vols repr. 1972; The First Four Georges, 1956; The Renaissance, 1961; Men and Places, 1962; Crisis in the Humanities, 1964; The Growth of Political Stability in England, 1675–1725, 1967; Death of the Past, 1969; In the Light of History, 1972; The Commercialisation of Leisure, 1974; Royal Heritage, 1977; New Light on the Tyrant, George III, 1978; Georgian Delights, 1980; Royal Heritage: The Reign of Elizabeth II, 1980; (with Neil McKendrick and John Brewer) The Birth of a Consumer Society, 1982; Collected Essays: Vol. I, The Making of a Historian, 1988; Vol. II, The American Experience, 1989; *contrib. to:* Man versus Society in Eighteenth Century Britain, 1968; Churchill Revised, 1969 (Churchill, the historian); *festschrift:* Historical Perspectives: Essays in Honour of J. H. Plumb, 1974. *Address:* Christ's College, Cambridge CB2 3BU. *T:* Cambridge (0223) 334900; The Old Rectory, Westhorpe, Stowmarket, Suffolk. *T:* Bacton (0449) 781235. *Club:* Brooks's.

PLUMBLY, Derek John, CMG 1991; HM Diplomatic Service; Deputy Head of Mission (formerly Head of Chancery and Political Counsellor), Riyadh, since 1988; *b* 15 May 1948; *s* of late John C. Plumbly and Jean Elizabeth (*née* Baker); *m* 1979, Nadia Gohar; two *s* one *d*. *Educ:* Brockenhurst Grammar Sch.; Magdalen Coll., Oxford (BA PPE). VSO, Pakistan, 1970; Third Sec., FCO, 1972; MECAS, 1973; Second Sec., Jedda, 1975; First Sec., Cairo, 1977; FCO, 1980; First Sec., Washington, 1984. *Address:* c/o Foreign and Commonwealth Office, King Charles Street, SW1A 2AL.

PLUME, John Trevor; Regional Chairman, Industrial Tribunals (London North), 1984–87; *b* 5 Oct. 1914; *s* of William Thomas and Gertrude Plume; *m* 1948, Christine Mary Wells; one *d*. *Educ:* City of London School; Inns of Court School of Law. Called to the Bar, Gray's Inn, 1936, Bencher, 1969. Legal Associate Mem., Town Planning Inst., 1939; served Royal Artillery, 1940–46 (Captain). Practiced at Bar, specialising in property law, 1936–76; Chm., Industrial Tribunals, 1976–87. Liveryman, Clockmakers' Co. *Recreations:* beekeeping, carpentry, gardening, fishing. *Address:* Mulberry Cottage, Forest Side, Epping, Essex CM16 4ED. *T:* Epping (0992) 72389.

PLUMLEY, Rev. Prof. Jack Martin; Herbert Thompson Professor of Egyptology, University of Cambridge, 1957–77; Priest-in-Charge, Longstowe, Cambs, since 1981; *b* 2 Sept. 1910; *e s* of Arthur Henry Plumley and Lily Plumley (*née* Martin); *m* 1st, 1938, Gwendolen Alice Darling (*d* 1984); three *s*; *m* 2nd, 1986, Ursula Clara Dowle. *Educ:* Merchant Taylors' Sch., London; St John's Coll., Durham (BA, Univ. Hebrew Schol., MLitt); King's Coll., Cambridge (MA). Deacon 1933; Priest 1934; Curacies, 1933–41; Vicar of Christ Church, Hoxton, 1942–45, of St Paul's, Tottenham, 1945–47; Rector and Vicar of All Saints', Milton, Cambridge, 1948–57. Acting Dean, Pembroke Coll., Cambridge, 1981–82. Associate Lectr in Coptic, Univ. of Cambridge, 1949–57; Fellow Selwyn Coll., 1957. Stephen Glanville Meml Lectr, Fitzwilliam Mus., Cambridge, 1982. Mem. Council of Senate, Cambridge, 1965–70. Dir of excavations on behalf of Egypt Exploration Soc. at Qasr Ibrim, Nubia, 1963, 1964, 1966, 1969, 1972, 1974, 1976; Chm., British Cttee of Internat. Critical Greek New Testament Project, 1963–87. Pres., Internat. Soc. for Nubian Studies, 1978–82, Patron, 1982–. FSA 1966; Fellow, Inst. of Coptic Studies, United Egyptian Repub., 1966; Corresp. Mem., German Inst. of Archaeology, 1966. *Recreations:* music, rowing, photography, travel. *Address:* Selwyn College, Cambridge; 13 Lyndewode Road, Cambridge. *T:* Cambridge (0223) 350328.

PLUMMER, family name of **Baron Plummer of St Marylebone.**

PLUMMER OF ST MARYLEBONE, Baron *cr* 1981 (Life Peer), of the City of Westminster; **(Arthur) Desmond (Herne) Plummer;** Kt 1971; TD 1950; JP; DL; President, Portman Building Society, since 1990 (Chairman, 1983–90); *b* 25 May 1914; *s* of late Arthur Herne Plummer and Janet (*née* McCormick); *m* 1941, Pat Holloway (Pres., Cons. Women's Adv. Cttee, Greater London Area, 1967–71); one *d*. *Educ:* Hurstpierpoint Coll.; Coll. of Estate Management. Served 1939–46, Royal Engineers. Member: TA Sports Bd, 1953–79; London Electricity Consultative Council, 1955–66; St Marylebone Borough Council, 1952–65 (Mayor, 1958–59); LCC, for St Marylebone, 1960–65; Inner London Educn Authority, 1964–76. Greater London Council: Mem. for Cities of London and Westminster, 1964–73, for St Marylebone, 1973–76; Leader of Opposition, 1966–67 and 1973–74; Leader of Council, 1967–73. Member: South Bank Theatre Board, 1967–74; Standing Conf. on SE Planning, 1967–74; Transport Co-ordinating Council for London, 1967–69; Local Authorities Conditions of Service Adv. Bd, 1967–71; Exec. Cttee, British Section of Internat. Union of Local Authorities, 1967–74; St John Council for London, 1971–; Exec. Cttee, Nat. Union Cons. and Unionist Assocs, 1967–76; Chm., St Marylebone Conservative Assoc., 1965–66. Chm., Horserace Betting Levy Bd, 1974–82; Dep. Chm., Nat. Employers' Mutual Gen. Insurance Assoc., 1973–86; Chm., Nat. Employers' Life Assce, 1983–89; Pres., Met. Assoc. of Bldg Socs, 1983–89. Member of Lloyd's. Mem. Court, Univ. of London, 1967–77. Chairman: Epsom and Walton Downs Trng Grounds Man. Bd, 1974–82; National Stud, 1975–82; President: London Anglers' Assoc., 1976–; Thames Angling Preservation Soc., 1970–. Liveryman, Worshipful Co. of Tin Plateworkers. FAI 1948; FRICS 1970; FRSA 1974; Hon. FFAS 1966. JP, Co. London, 1958; DL Greater London, 1970. KStJ 1986. *Publications:* Time for Change in Greater London, 1966; Report to London, 1970; Planning and Participation, 1973. *Recreations:* swimming (Capt. Otter Swimming Club, 1952–53); growing things, relaxing. *Address:* 4 The Lane, St Johns Wood, NW8 0PN. *Clubs:* Carlton (Chm., Political Cttee, 1979–84; Pres., 1984–), Royal Automobile, MCC.

PLUMMER, (Arthur) Christopher (Orme), CC (Canada) 1968; actor; *b* Toronto, 13 Dec. 1929; *m* 1st, 1956, Tammy Lee Grimes; one *d*; 2nd, 1962, Patricia Audrey Lewis (marr. diss. 1966); 3rd, 1970, Elaine Regina Taylor. *Educ:* public and private schs, Montreal. French and English radio, Canada, 1949–52; Ottawa Rep. Theatre; Broadway: Starcross Story, 1951–52; Home is the Hero, 1953; The Dark is Light Enough, 1954 (Theatre World Award); The Lark, 1955; J. B., 1958 (Tony nomination); Arturo Ui, 1963; Royal Hunt of the Sun, 1965–66; Stratford, Conn, 1955: Mark Antony, Ferdinand; leading actor, Stratford Festival, Canada, 1956–67: Henry V, The Bastard, Hamlet, Leontes, Mercutio, Macbeth, Cyrano de Bergerac, Benedic, Aguecheek, Antony; Royal Shakespeare Co., Stratford-on-Avon, 1961–62: Benedic, Richard III; London debut as Henry II in Becket, Aldwych and Globe, 1961 (Evening Standard Best Actor Award, 1961); National Theatre, 1971–72: Amphytrion 38, Danton's Death; Broadway musical, Cyrano, 1973 (Outer Critics Circle Award and Tony Award for Best Actor in a Musical, NY Drama Desk Award); The Good Doctor, NY, 1974; Iago in Othello, NY, 1982 (Drama Desk Award); Macbeth, NY, 1988. *Films:* Stage-Struck, 1956; Across the Everglades, 1957; The Fall of the Roman Empire, 1963; The Sound of Music, 1964 (Golden Badge of Honour, Austria); Daisy Clover, 1964; Triple Cross, 1966; Oedipus Rex, 1967; The Battle of Britain, 1968; Royal Hunt of the Sun, 1969; The Pyx, 1973; The Man Who Would Be King, 1975; Aces High, 1976; The Moneychangers, 1976 (Emmy Award); International Velvet, 1978; The Silent Partner, 1978; Hanover Street, 1979; Murder by Decree, 1980 (Genie Award, Canada); The Disappearance, 1981; The Janitor, 1981; The Amateur, 1982; Dreamscape, 1984; Playing for Keeps, 1985; Lily in Love, 1985; Souvenir, 1989; Where The Heart Is, 1990, and others. TV appearances, Britain, Denmark, and major N American networks, incl. Hamlet at Elsinore, BBC and Danish TV, 1964 (4 Emmy Award nominations). First entertainer to win Maple Leaf Award (Arts and Letters), 1982. *Recreations:* tennis, ski-ing, piano. *Clubs:* Hurlingham; Players, River (New York).

PLUMMER, Christopher; *see* Plummer, A. C. O.

PLUMMER, Maj.-Gen. Leo Heathcote, CBE 1974; retired 1979; *b* 11 June 1923; *s* of Lt-Col Edmund Waller Plummer and Mary Dorothy Brookesmith; *m* 1955, Judyth Ann Dolby; three *d*. *Educ:* Canford Sch.; Queens' Coll., Cambridge. Commnd RA, 1943; War Service, N Africa, Sicily, Italy, 1943–45 (mentioned in despatches, 1945); Adjt, TA, 1947–49; Staff Coll., Camberley, 1952, Directing Staff, 1961–63; Comdt, Sudan Staff Coll., 1963–65; CO, 20 Heavy Regt, 1965–67; Col, Gen. Staff, MoD, 1967; Brig., 1967; Comdr, 1st Artillery Bde, 1967–70; Dep. Dir Manning (Army), 1971–74; Asst Chief of Staff Ops, HQ Northern Army Gp, 1974–76; Chief, Jt Service Liaison Orgn, Bonn, 1976–78. ADC to HM The Queen, 1974–76; Col Comdt, RA, 1981–86. Chm., Civil Service Commn Selection Bd, 1983–91. *Recreation:* gardening. *Address:* Vivers Lodge, Old Road, Kirkby Moorside, York YO6 6BD. *Club:* Army and Navy.

PLUMMER, Peter Edward; Deputy Director, Department for National Savings, 1972–79; *b* 4 Nov. 1919; *s* of Arthur William John and Ethel May Plummer; *m* 1949, Pauline Wheelwright; one *s* one *d*. *Educ:* Watford Grammar Sch. Served War, REME, 1941–46. Customs and Excise, 1936–38; Dept for National Savings, 1938–79; Principal, 1956; Assistant Sec., 1964; seconded to Nat. Giro, 1970–71; Under-Sec., 1972. *Recreations:* gardening, photography. *Address:* Old Timbers, Farm Lane, Nutbourne, Chichester, W Sussex P018 8SA. *T:* Emsworth (0243) 77450.

PLUMPTON, Alan, CBE 1980; BSc, CEng, FIEE; FCIBSE; CBIM; FRSA; Chairman: Ewbank Preece Group, since 1986; Schlumberger Measurement and Systems, since 1988; Director, Schlumberger (UK), since 1986; Chairman, Manx Electricity Authority, since 1986; *b* 24 Nov. 1926; *s* of late John Plumpton and of Doris Plumpton; *m* 1950, Audrey Smith; one *s* one *d*. *Educ:* Sunderland Technical Sch.; Durham Univ. (BSc Elec. Eng). Pupil Engr, Sunderland Corp. Elec. Undertaking, 1942; various engrg and commercial appts, NEEB, 1948–61; Dist Manager, E Monmouthshire Dist, S Wales Electricity Bd, 1961–64. Admin. Staff Coll., Henley, 1963; Dep. Chief Commercial Engr, S Wales Elec. Bd, 1964–67; Chief Commercial Engr, S Wales Elec. Bd, 1967–72; Dep. Chm., London Elec. Bd, 1972–76, Chm., 1976–81; Dep. Chm., Electricity Council, 1981–86. MInstD 1986. Liveryman, Gardeners' Co. JP Mon, 1971–72. *Recreations:* golf, gardening. *Address:* Lockhill, Stubbs Wood, Amersham, Bucks HP6 6EX. *T:* Amersham (0494) 433791. *Clubs:* City Livery; Harewood Downs Golf.

PLUMPTRE, family name of **Baron Fitzwalter.**

PLUMSTEAD, Isobel Mary, (Mrs N. J. Coleman); District Judge, Principal Registry, Family Division of the High Court, since 1990; *b* 19 July 1947; *d* of John Archibald Plumstead, DFM, MA and Nancy Plumstead (*née* Drummond); *m* 1971, Nicholas John Coleman; one *s* two *d*. *Educ:* Norwich High Sch. for Girls (GPDST); St Hugh's College, Oxford (BA 1969; MA 1985); Inns of Court Sch. of Law. Blackstone Entrance Scholar, 1967, Colombos Prize for Internat. Law, 1970, Harmsworth Scholar, 1970–73, Middle Temple. Called to the Bar, Middle Temple, 1970; Registrar, Principal Registry, Family Div. of High Court, 1990. Trustee, New Parents' Infant Network (Newpin), 1989–. *Recreations:* family, food, fine and foul wines. *Address:* Principal Registry of Family Division, Somerset House, WC2R 1LP; Francis Taylor Building, Temple, EC4Y 7BY. *Club:* Aldeburgh Yacht.

PLUNKET, family name of **Baron Plunket.**

PLUNKET, 8th Baron *cr* 1827; **Robin Rathmore Plunket;** *b* 3 Dec. 1925; *s* of 6th Baron Plunket (*d* 1938) and Dorothé Mabel (*d* 1938), *d* of late Joseph Lewis and *widow* of Captain Jack Barnato, RAF; *S* brother, 1975; *m* 1951, Jennifer, *d* of late Bailey Southwell, Olivenhoutpoort, S Africa. *Educ:* Eton. Formerly Captain, Rifle Brigade. *Heir: b* Hon. Shaun Albert Frederick Sheridan Plunket [*b* 5 April 1931; *m* 1961, Judith Ann, *e d* of late G. P. Power; one *s* one *d*; *m* 1980, Mrs Elizabeth de Sancha (*d* 1986); *m* 1989, Mrs Andrea Reynolds]. *Address:* Rathmore, Chimanimani, Zimbabwe; 39 Lansdowne Gardens, SW8 2EL. *Club:* Boodle's.

PLUNKET GREENE, Mary, (Mrs Alexander Plunket Greene); *see* Quant, Mary.

PLUNKETT, family name of **Baron Dunsany,** and of **Baron Louth.**

PLUNKETT, William Joseph; Valuer and Estates Surveyor, Greater London Council, 1977–81; *b* 8 Nov. 1921; *s* of John Joseph Archer and Marjorie Martin Plunkett; *m* 1949, Gwendoline Innes Barron; two *s* five *d*. *Educ:* Finchley Catholic Grammar Sch.; Coll. of Estate Management. BSc(Est. Man.). FRICS. RN, 1941–46; commnd, 1942; Lt RNVR. Dep. County Valuer, Middlesex CC, 1962–65; Asst Valuer, Valuation and Estates Dept, GLC, 1965–73; Dep. Valuer and Estates Surveyor, GLC, 1973–74; Dir of Valuation and Estates Dept, GLC, 1974–77. Mem., South Bank Polytechnic Adv. Cttee on Estate Management, 1973–76; Chm., Covent Garden Officers' Steering Gp, 1977–81. Mem. General Council, RICS, 1978–80 (Pres. Planning and Develt Div., 1978–79; Chm., S London Br. Cttee, 1976–77); Pres., Assoc. of Local Authority Valuers and Estate Surveyors, 1980–81. *Publications:* articles on Compensation, Valuation and Development. *Address:* 63 Radnor Cliff, Folkestone, Kent CT20 2JL. *T:* Folkestone (0303) 48868.

PLYMOUTH, 3rd Earl of, *cr* 1905; **Other Robert Ivor Windsor-Clive;** Viscount Windsor (UK 1905); 15th Baron Windsor (England, *cr* 1529); DL; FRSA 1953; *b* 9 October 1923; *e s* of 2nd Earl and Lady Irene Charteris (*d* 1989), *d* of 11th Earl of Wemyss; *S* father, 1943; *m* 1950, Caroline Helen, *o d* of Edward Rice, Dane Court, Eastry, Kent; three *s* one *d*. *Educ:* Eton. Mem., Museums and Galls Commn (formerly Standing Commn on Museums and Galls), 1972–82; Chm., Reviewing Cttee on Export of Works of Art, 1982–85. DL County of Salop, 1961. *Heir: s* Viscount Windsor, *qv*. *Address:* Oakly Park, Ludlow, Salop.

See also Sir Alan Glyn.

PLYMOUTH, Bishop of, (RC), since 1986; **Rt. Rev. Mgr. Hugh Christopher Budd;** *b* 27 May 1937; *s* of John Alfred and Phyllis Mary Budd. *Educ:* St Mary's Primary School, Hornchurch, Essex; Salesian Coll., Chertsey, Surrey; Cotton Coll., North Staffs; English Coll., Rome. PhL; STD. Ordained Priest, 1962; post-ordination studies, 1963–65; Tutor,

English Coll., Rome, 1965–71; Lectr at Newman Coll., Birmingham and part-time Asst Priest, Northfield, Birmingham, 1971–76; Head of Training, Catholic Marriage Advisory Council, National HQ, London, 1976–79; Rector, St John's Seminary, Wonersh, Surrey, 1979–85; Administrator, Brentwood Cathedral, Essex, Nov. 1985–Jan. 1986. *Recreations:* walking, cricket (watching), music (listening). *Address:* Vescourt, Hartley Road, Plymouth PL3 5LR. *T:* Plymouth (0752) 772950.

PLYMOUTH, Bishop Suffragan of, since 1988; **Rt. Rev. Richard Stephen Hawkins;** *b* 2 April 1939; *s* of late Ven. Canon John Stanley Hawkins and of Elsie Hawkins (*née* Briggs); *m* 1966, Valerie Ann Herneman; one *s* one *d* (and one *s* one *d* decd). *Educ:* Exeter School; Exeter Coll., Oxford; St Stephen's House, Oxford. MA (Oxon); BPhil (Exeter Univ.); CQSW. Asst Curate, St Thomas, Exeter, 1963–66; Team Vicar of Clyst St Mary, Clyst Valley Team Ministry, 1966–78; Bishop's Officer for Ministry and Joint Director, Exeter-Truro Ministry Training Scheme, 1978–81; Team Vicar, Central Exeter Team Ministry, 1978–81; Diocesan Director of Ordinands, 1979–81; Priest-in-charge, Whitestone with Oldridge, 1981–87; Archdeacon of Totnes, 1981–88. *Address:* 31 Riverside Walk, Tamerton Foliot, Plymouth PL5 4AQ. *T:* Plymouth (0752) 769836.

PLYMOUTH, Archdeacon of; *see* Ellis, Ven. R. G.

POANANGA, Maj.-Gen. Brian Matauru, CB 1980; CBE 1977 (OBE 1967; MBE 1962); Chief of General Staff, New Zealand Army, 1978–81, retired; *b* 2 Dec. 1924; *s* of Henare and Atareta Poananga; *m* 1949, Doreen Mary Porter (formerly QAIMNS/R); two *s* one *d*. *Educ:* Royal Military College, Duntroon, Australia. Graduated RMC, 1946; served BCOF, Japan, 1947–48; Commonwealth Div., Korea, 1952–53; (mentioned in despatches, 1952); Staff Coll., Camberley, 1957; 28 Commonwealth Inf. Bde, Malaya, 1959–61; Jt Services Staff Coll., Latimer, 1964; CO 1RNZIR, Malaysia, 1965–67 (mentioned in despatches, Sarawak, 1966); Dir of Army Training, 1968–69; Dir of Services Intelligence, 1969–70; Comdr Army Training Gp, 1970–72; RCDS, 1973; Comdr 1st (NZ) Inf. Bde Gp, 1974; NZ High Commissioner to Papua New Guinea, 1974–76; Deputy Chief of General Staff, 1977–78. *Recreations:* golf and fishing. *Address:* PO Box 397, Taupo, New Zealand. *T:* Taupo 48296. *Club:* Taupo (NZ).

POCOCK, Air Vice-Marshal Donald Arthur, CBE 1975 (OBE 1957); Director, British Metallurgical Plant Constructors Association, 1980–85; *b* 5 July 1920; *s* of late A. Pocock and of E. Broad; *m* 1947, Dorothy Monica Griffiths; two *s* three *d*. *Educ:* Crouch End. Served War of 1939–45: commissioned, 1941; Middle East, 1941–48. Transport Command, 1948–50; commanded RAF Regt Sqdn, 1950–52; Staff Coll., 1953; Staff Officer, HQ 2nd Allied TAF, 1954–57; comd RAF Regt Wing, 1957–58; MoD, 1958–59; HQ Allied Air Forces Central Europe, 1959–62; Sen. Ground Defence SO, NEAF, 1962–63; MoD, 1963–66; Sen. Ground Defence SO, FEAF, 1966–68; ADC to the Queen, 1967; Commandant, RAF Catterick, 1968–69; Dir of Ground Defence, 1970–73; Comdt-Gen. RAF Regt, 1973–75. Gen. Man., Iran, British Aerospace Dynamics Gp, 1976–79. *Recreations:* shooting, equitation. *Address:* 16 Dence Park, Herne Bay, Kent CT6 6BQ. *T:* Herne Bay (0227) 374773. *Club:* Royal Air Force.

POCOCK, Gordon James; Director, Communications Educational Services Ltd, 1983–87; *b* 27 March 1933; *s* of late Leslie and Elizabeth Maud Pocock; *m* 1959, Audrey Singleton (*d* 1990). *Educ:* Royal Liberty Sch., Romford; Keble Coll., Oxford. Joined PO, 1954; Private Sec. to Dir Gen., 1958–59; Principal, 1960–68; Asst Sec., 1968–72; Dep. Dir, 1972–76; Dir, Ext. Telecommns, 1976–79; Dir, Telecommns Marketing, 1979, Sen. Dir, 1979–81; Chief Exec., Merlin Business Systems, BT, 1981–84. Fellow, Nolan Norton & Co., 1985–87. *Publications:* Corneille and Racine, 1973; Boileau and the Nature of Neo-Classicism, 1980; article on Nation, Community, Devolution and Sovereignty. *Recreations:* travel, theatre, local history. *Address:* Friars Lodge, Friars Lane, Richmond, Surrey TW9 1NL. *T:* 081–940 7118.

POCOCK, Kenneth Walter; *b* 20 June 1913; *s* of Walter Dunsdon Pocock and Emily Marion Pocock; *m* 1939, Anne Tidmarsh; one *s* one *d*. *Educ:* Canford School. United Dairies (London) Ltd, 1930; Armed Forces, 1942–46; Man. Dir, Edinburgh and Dumfriesshire Dairy Co. Ltd, 1946; Dir, United Dairies Ltd, 1948; Pres., Scottish Milk Trade Fedn, 1956–59; Dir, Unigate Ltd, 1959; Man. Dir, Unigate Ltd and United Dairies Ltd, 1963; Chm. of Milk Div., Unigate Ltd, 1968; Dep. Chm., Unigate Ltd, 1970–75; Pres., Unigate Long Service Corps (40 years), 1971–. Governor, Nat. Dairymen's Benevolent Instn (Chm., 1977–81). *Recreations:* motoring, shooting, photography, gardening. *Address:* Cedar Lodge, Marsham Lane, Gerrards Cross, Bucks SL9 8HD. *T:* Gerrards Cross (0753) 889278.

POCOCK, Leslie Frederick, CBE 1985; Chairman, Liverpool Health Authority, 1982–86; *b* 22 June 1918; *s* of Frederick Pocock and Alice Helena Pocock; *m* 1946, Eileen Horton; two *s*. *Educ:* Emanuel School. FCCA. Chief Accountant: London & Lancashire Insurance Co. Ltd, 1959; Royal Insurance Co. Ltd, 1966; Chief Accountant and Taxation Manager, 1971, Dep. Gp Comptroller, 1974, Royal Insurance Gp; retired 1981. Gen. Comr of Income Tax, 1982–. Pres., Assoc. of Certified Accountants, 1977–78. Mem., UK Central Council for Nursing, Midwifery and Health Visiting, 1983–87; Chm., Merseyside Residuary Body, 1985; Hon. Treas., Merseyside Improved Houses, 1986–. Chm. Governors, Sandown Coll., Liverpool, 1989–. *Recreations:* countryside, golf. *Address:* Farnley, Croft Drive West, Caldy, Wirral, Merseyside L48 2JQ. *T:* 051–625 5320.

PODDAR, Prof. Ramendra Kumar, PhD; Professor of Biophysics, Calcutta University, since 1973; Member of Parliament (Rajya Sabha), since 1985 (Vice-Chairman, 1987–89); *b* 9 Nov. 1930; *m* 1955, Srimati Jharna Poddar; two *s* one *d*. *Educ:* Univ. of Calcutta (BSc Hons Physics, MSc Physics; PhD Biophysics); Associateship Dip., Saha Inst. of Nuclear Physics. Progressively, Research Asst, Lecturer, Reader, Associate Prof., Biophysics Div., Saha Inst. of Nuclear Physics, 1953–73; Calcutta University: Pro-Vice-Chancellor (A), 1977–79; Vice-Chancellor, 1979–83. IAEA Advr to Govt of Mali, 1962. Study visits to Univ. of California, Berkeley, 1958–60, Cold Spring Harbor Biological Lab., 1960, Purdue Univ., 1960–61, California Inst. of Technology, 1970, CNRS, Paris, 1978. *Publications:* more than 50 research papers in the fields of biophysics, molecular biology and photobiology. *Address:* Department of Biophysics, Molecular Biology and Genetics, University College of Science, Calcutta 700009, India. *T:* (office) 36–6386/6396; (home) 56–9572/59–5260 (Calcutta); 3782193 (New Delhi).

PODMORE, Ian Laing; Chief Executive, Sheffield City Council, 1974–89; *b* 6 Oct. 1933; *s* of Harry Samuel Podmore and Annie Marion (*née* Laing); *m* 1961, Kathleen Margaret (*née* Langton); one *s* one *d*. *Educ:* Birkenhead School. Admitted Solicitor 1960. Asst Solicitor, Wallasey County Borough, 1960–63; Sen. Asst Solicitor, Southport Co. Borough, 1963–66; Deputy Town Clerk: Southport, 1966–70; Sheffield, 1970–74. *Recreations:* golf, gardening, watching football. *Address:* 55 Devonshire Road, Sheffield S17 3NU. *Club:* Abbeydale Golf.

PODRO, Prof. Michael Isaac, PhD; Professor, Department of Art History and Theory, University of Essex, since 1973; *b* 13 March 1931; *s* of Joshua Podro and Fanny Podro; *m* 1961, Charlotte Booth; two *d*. *Educ:* Berkhamsted Sch.; Jesus Coll., Cambridge (MA); University Coll. London (PhD). Hd of Dept of Art History, Camberwell Sch. of Art and Crafts, 1961–67; Lectr in the Philosophy of Art, Warburg Inst., Univ. of London, 1967–69; Reader, Dept of Art History and Theory, Univ. of Essex, 1969–73. Trustee, V&A Mus., 1987–. *Publications:* Manifold in Perception: theories of art from Kant to Hildebrand, 1972; Critical Historians of Art, 1982. *Address:* 1 Provost Road, NW3 4ST. *T:* 071–722 7435.

POETT, Gen. Sir (Joseph Howard) Nigel, KCB 1959 (CB 1952); DSO and Bar, 1945; idc; psc; *b* 20 Aug. 1907; *s* of late Maj.-General J. H. Poett, CB, CMG, CBE; *m* 1937, Julia, *d* of E. J. Herrick, Hawkes Bay, NZ; two *s* one *d*. *Educ:* Downside; RMC Sandhurst. 2nd Lieut, DLI, 1927; Operations, NW Frontier, 1930–31; Adjt 2nd Bn DLI, 1934–37; GSO2, 2nd Div., 1940; GSO1, War Office, 1941–42; Comd 11th Bn DLI, 1942–43; Comdr, 5th Parachute Bde, 1943–46; served North-West Europe, 1944–45; Far East, 1945–46; Director of Plans, War Office, 1946–48; idc 1948; Dep.-Commander, British Military Mission, Greece, 1949; Maj.-General, 1951; Chief of Staff, FARELF, 1950–52; GOC 3rd Infantry Division, Middle East Land Forces, 1952–54; Dir of Military Operations, War Office, 1954–56; Commandant, Staff Coll., Camberley, 1957–58; Lt-Gen., 1958; General Officer Commanding-in-Chief, Southern Command, 1958–61; Commander-in-Chief, Far East Land Forces, 1961–63; General, 1962. Colonel, The Durham Light Infantry, 1956–65. Dir, British Productivity Council, 1966–71. Silver Star, USA. *Address:* Swaynes Mead, Great Durnford, Salisbury, Wilts. *Club:* Army and Navy.

PÖHL, Karl Otto; Grosses Verdienstkreuz mit Stern und Schulterband des Verdienstordens der Bundesrepublik Deutschland; Governor, Deutsche Bundesbank and German Governor, International Monetary Fund and Bank for International Settlements, 1980–91; *b* 1 Dec. 1929; *m* 1974; two *s* two *d*. *Educ:* Göttingen Univ. (Econs; Diplom.-Volkswirt). Div. Chief for Econ. Res., IFO-Institut, Munich, 1955–60; econ. journalist, Bonn, 1961–67; Mem. Exec., Fed. Assoc. of German Bank, Cologne, 1968–69; Div. Chief in Fed. Min. of Econs, Bonn, 1970–71; Dept Chief in Fed. Chancellery (Head, Dept for Econ. and Fiscal Policy), Bonn, 1971–72; Sec. of State in Fed. Min. of Finance, 1972–77; Dep. Governor, Deutsche Bundesbank, 1977–79; Chairman: EEC Monetary Cttee, 1976–77; Deputies of Gp of Ten, 1978–80; Gp of Ten, 1983–89; Cttee of Governors, Central Banks of EC Member States, 1990–91. Hon. DHL Georgetown Univ., 1983; Hon. DEconSc Ruhr Univ., 1985; Hon. DPhil Tel Aviv, 1986; Hon. Dr of Laws, Univ. of Md, 1987. *Publications:* miscellaneous. *Address:* c/o Deutsche Bundesbank, Wilhelm-Epstein-strasse 14, 6000 Frankfurt 50, Federal Republic of Germany. *T:* Frankfurt 1581.

POITIER, Sidney, KBE (Hon.) 1974; actor, film and stage; director; *b* Miami, Florida, 20 Feb. 1927; *s* of Reginald Poitier and Evelyn (*née* Outten); *m* 1950, Juanita Hardy (marr. diss.); four *d*; *m* 1975, Joanna Shimkus; two *d*. *Educ:* private tutors; Western Senior High Sch., Nassau; Governor's High Sch., Nassau. Served War of 1941–45 with 1267th Medical Detachment, United States Army. Started acting with American Negro Theatre, 1946. *Plays include:* Anna Lucasta, Broadway, 1948; A Raisin in the Sun, Broadway, 1959; *films include:* Cry, the Beloved Country, 1952; Red Ball Express, 1952; Go, Man, Go, 1954; Blackboard Jungle, 1955; Goodbye, My Lady, 1956; Edge of the City, 1957; Band of Angels, 1957; Something of Value, 1957; The Mark of the Hawk, 1958; The Defiant Ones, 1958 (Silver Bear Award, Berlin Film Festival, and New York Critics Award, 1958); Porgy and Bess, 1959; A Raisin in the Sun, 1960; Paris Blues, 1960; Lilies of the Field, 1963 (award for Best Actor of 1963, Motion Picture Academy of Arts and Sciences); The Bedford Incident, 1965; The Slender Thread, 1966; A Patch of Blue, 1966; Duel at Diablo, 1966; To Sir With Love, 1967; In the Heat of the Night, 1967; Guess Who's Coming to Dinner, 1968; For Love of Ivy, 1968; They Call Me Mister Tibbs, 1971; The Organization, 1971; The Wilby Conspiracy, 1975; Deadly Pursuit, 1988; director and actor: Buck and the Preacher, 1972; A Warm December, 1973; Uptown Saturday Night, 1975; Let's Do It Again, 1976; A Piece of the Action, 1977; *director:* Stir Crazy, 1981; Hanky Panky, 1982. *Publication:* This Life (autobiography), 1980. *Address:* c/o Verdon Productions Ltd, 9350 Wilshire Boulevard, Beverly Hills, Calif 90212, USA.

POLAK, Cornelia Julia, OBE 1964 (MBE 1956); HM Diplomatic Service, retired; *b* 2 Dec. 1908; *d* of late Solomon Polak and late Georgina Polak (*née* Pozner). Foreign Office, 1925–38; Asst Archivist, British Embassy, Paris, 1938–40; Foreign Office, 1940–47; Vice-Consul, Bergen, 1947–49; Consul, Washington, 1949–51; Foreign Office, 1951–55; Consul, Paris, 1955–57; Consul, Brussels, 1957–60; Foreign Office, 1960–63; Head of Treaty and Nationality Department, Foreign Office, 1963–67; Consul General, Geneva, 1967–69, retired; re-employed at FCO, 1969–70. *Address:* 24 Belsize Court, NW3 5QJ.

POLAK, Prof. Julia Margaret, (Mrs Daniel Catovsky), FRCPath; Professor of Endocrine Pathology, Royal Postgraduate Medical School, London University, since 1984, and Deputy Director, Department of Histopathology, Hammersmith Hospital, since 1988; *b* 26 June 1939; *d* of Carlos and Rebeca Polak; *m* 1961, Daniel Catovsky; two *s* one *d*. *Educ:* Univ. of Buenos Aires (MD 1964; Dip Histopath. 1966); DSc London, 1980. Hospital appts, Buenos Aires, 1961–67; Royal Postgraduate Medical School, London: Research Assistant in Histochemistry, 1968–69; Asst Lectr, Lectr, and Sen. Lectr, 1970–82; Reader, 1982–84; Member: Exec. Cttee, Acad. Bd, 1990–; Med. Exec. Unit, Hammersmith Hosp., 1990–; Sub-Cttee in Biotech., London Univ., 1988–. Chm., British Endocrine Pathologists Gp, 1988–; Mem., Exec. Cttee of Council, Amer. Heart Assoc., 1989–. Mem., editl bds of med. jls. Benito de Udaondo Cardiology Prize, 1967; Medal, Soc. of Endocrinology, 1984; Sir Eric Sharpe Prize for Oncology, Cable and Wireless, 1986–87. *Publications:* contribs to Nature and numerous professional jls. *Address:* Department of Histochemistry, Royal Postgraduate Medical School, Du Cane Road, W12 0NN. *T:* 081–740 3231.

POLAND, Rear-Adm. Edmund Nicholas, CB 1967; CBE 1962; *b* 19 Feb. 1917; 2nd *s* of late Major Raymond A. Poland, RMLI; *m* 1941, Pauline Ruth Margaret Pechell; three *s* one *d* (and one *d* decd). *Educ:* Royal Naval Coll., Dartmouth. Served at sea during Abyssinian and Palestine crises, Spanish Civil War; War of 1939–45: convoy duties, Norwegian waters; Motor Torpedo Boats, Channel and Mediterranean; Torpedo Specialist, 1943; Staff Officer Ops to Naval Force Comdr, Burma; Sqdn T. Officer, HMS Royalist; HMS Hornet, 1946; Flotilla Torpedo and Anti-Submarine Officer of Third Submarine Flotilla, HMS Montclare; Air Warfare Div., Admiralty, 1950; British Naval Staff, Washington, 1953; jssc 1955; Directorate of Tactics and Ship Requirements, Admiralty; comd RN Air Station, Abbotsinch, 1956; Nato Standing Gp, Washington; Director of Under Sea Warfare (Naval), Ministry of Defence, 1962; Chief of Staff to C-in-C Home Fleet, 1965–68; retired. Commander, 1950; Capt., 1956; Rear-Adm., 1965. Vice-Pres., Internat. Prisoners' Aid Assoc., 1978, Chm. (UK), 1979; Vice-Pres., Scottish Assoc. for Care and Resettlement of Offenders, 1979 (Dir, 1974–79). *Recreations:* golf, fishing, gardening. *Address:* Yew Tree Lodge, 46 Shaftesbury Road, Wilton, Wilts SP2 0DR.

See also R. D. Poland.

POLAND, Richard Domville, CB 1973; *b* 22 Oct. 1914; *er s* of late Major R. A. Poland, RMLI, and late Mrs F. O. Bayly-Jones; *m* 1948, Rosalind Frances, *y d* of late Surgeon-Captain H. C. Devas; one *s* one *d*. *Educ:* RN Coll., Dartmouth. Traffic Trainee, Imperial

Airways, 1932; Traffic Clerk, British Continental Airways and North Eastern Airways, 1934–39. Ops Officer, Air Ministry, Civil Aviation Dept, 1939; Civil Aviation Dept Rep., W Africa, 1942–44; Private Secretary to Minister of Civil Aviation, 1944–48; Principal, 1946; Asst Secretary, 1953; Shipping Attaché, British Embassy, Washington, DC, 1957–60; Under-Secretary: Min. of Transport, 1964–70; DoE, 1970–74. Sec., Internat. Maritime Industry Forum, 1976–78. Chm., Kent Branch, CPRE, 1980. *Address:* 63 Alexandra Road, Kew, Surrey TW9 2BT. *T:* 081–948 5039.

See also Rear-Admiral E. N. Poland.

POLANI, Prof. Paul Emanuel, MD, DCH; FRCP; FRCOG; FRS 1973; Prince Philip Professor of Pædiatric Research in the University of London, 1960–80, now Professor Emeritus; Geneticist, Pædiatric Research Unit, Guy's Hospital, London, since 1983 (in Division of Medical and Molecular Genetics of United Medical and Dental Schools of Guy's and St Thomas's Hospitals); Children's Physician, and Consultant Emeritus, Guy's Hospital; Geneticist, Italian Hospital; Director, SE Thames Regional Genetics Centre, 1976–82; *b* 1 Jan. 1914; first *s* of Enrico Polani and Elsa Zennaro; *m* 1944, Nina Ester Sullam; no *c. Educ:* Trieste, Siena and Pisa (Scuola Normale Superiore, Italy). MD (Pisa) 1938; DCH 1945; MRCP (London) 1948; FRCP (London) 1961; FRCOG *ad eund* 1979. National Birthday Trust Fund Fellow in Pædiatric Research, 1948; Assistant to Director, Dept of Child Health, Guy's Hospital Medical School, 1950–55; Research Physician on Cerebral Palsy and Director, Medical Research Unit, National Spastic Society, 1955–60; Dir, Paediatric Res. Unit, Guy's Hosp. Med. Sch., 1960–83. Consultant to WHO (Regional Office for Europe) on Pregnancy Wastage, 1959; Consultant, Nat. Inst. Neurol. Disease and Blindness, Nat. Insts of Health, USA, 1959–61. Chm., Mutagenesis Cttee, UK, 1975–86. Vis. Prof. of Human Genetics and Develt, Columbia Univ., 1977–86. Hon. FRCPath 1985. Sanremo Internat. Award and Prize for Genetic Res., 1984; Baly Medal, RCP, 1985; Gold Medal, International Cerebral Palsy Society, 1988. Commendatore, Order of Merit of the Republic, Italy, 1981. *Publications:* chapters in books on human genetics, mental deficiency, psychiatry and pædiatrics; papers on human genetics, cytogenetics, experimental meiosis, congenital malformations and neurological disorders of children. *Recreations:* reading, riding, ski-ing. *Address:* Little Meadow, West Clandon, Surrey GU4 7TL. *T:* Guildford (0483) 222436. *Club:* Athenæum.

POLANYI, Prof. John Charles, CC (Canada) 1979 (OC 1974); FRS 1971; FRSC 1966 (Hon. FRSC 1991); University Professor, since 1974 and Professor of Chemistry, University of Toronto, since 1962; *b* 23 Jan. 1929; *m* 1958, Anne Ferrar Davidson; one *s* one *d. Educ:* Manchester Grammar Sch.; Victoria Univ., Manchester (BSc, PhD, DSc). Research Fellow: Nat. Research Council, Ottawa, 1952–54; Princeton Univ., 1954–56; Univ. of Toronto: Lectr, 1956; Asst Prof., 1957–60; Assoc. Prof., 1960–62. Mem., Scientific Adv. Bd, Max Planck Inst. for Quantum Optics, Garching, Germany, 1982–. Sloan Foundn Fellow, 1959–63; Guggenheim Meml Fellow, 1970–71, 1979–80; Sherman Fairchild Distinguished Scholar, CIT, 1982; Vis. Prof. of Chem., Texas A & M Univ., 1986; John W. Cowper Dist. Vis. Lectr, SUNY at Buffalo, 1986; Dist. Vis. Speaker, Univ. of Calgary, 1987; Consolidated Bathurst Vis. Lectr, Concordia Univ., 1988. Lectures: Centennial, Chem. Soc., 1965; Ohio State Univ., 1969 (and Mack Award); Reilly, Univ. of Notre Dame, 1970; Harkins Meml, Univ. of Chicago, 1971; Purves, McGill Univ., 1971; Killam Meml Schol., 1974, 1975; F. J. Toole, Univ. of New Brunswick, 1974; Philips, Haverford Coll., 1974; Kistiakowsky, Harvard Univ., 1975; Camille and Henry Dreyfus, Kansas, 1975; J. W. T. Spinks, Saskatchewan, 1976; Laird, Western Ontario, 1976; CIL Dist., Simon Fraser Univ., 1977; Gucker, Indiana Univ., 1977; Jacob Bronowski Meml, Toronto Univ., 1978; Hutchison, Rochester Univ., 1979; Priestley, Penn State Univ., 1980; Barré, Univ. of Montreal, 1982; Chute, Dalhousie, and Redman, McMaster, 1983; Wiegand, Toronto Univ., Condon, Colorado Univ., Allan, Alberta Univ., and Willard, Wisconsin Univ., 1984; Holmes, Lethbridge Univ., 1985; Walker-Ames, Univ. of Washington, 1986; Morino, Japan, J. T. Wilson, Ont Sci. Centre, Welsh, Univ. of Toronto, and Spiers Meml, Faraday Div., RSChem., 1987. Polanyi, IUPAC, W. B. Lewis, Atomic Energy of Canada Ltd, Priestman, Univ. of New Brunswick, Killam, Univ. of Windsor, Herzberg, Carleton Univ., and Falconbridge, Laurentian Univ., 1988; Dupont, Indiana Univ., and C. R. Mueller, Purdue Univ., 1989. Hon. FRSE 1988; Hon. For. Mem., Amer. Acad. of Arts and Sciences, 1976; For. Associate, Nat. Acad. of Sciences, USA, 1978; Mem., Pontifical Acad. of Scis, 1986. Hon. DSc: Waterloo, 1970; Memorial, 1976; McMaster, 1977; Carleton, 1981; Harvard, 1982; Rensselaer, Brock, 1984; Lethbridge, Victoria, Ottawa, Sherbrooke, 1987; Manchester, York, 1988; Acadia, Univ. de Montréal, and Weizmann Inst. of Science, Israel, 1989; Univ. of Bari, Italy, Univ. of BC, and McGill Univ., 1990; Hon. LLD: Trent, 1977; Dalhousie, 1983; St Francis Xavier, 1984; Concordia Univ., 1990. Marlow Medal, Faraday Soc., 1963; Steacie Prize for Natural Scis, 1965; Chem. Inst. Canada Medal, 1976 (Noranda Award, 1967); Chem. Soc. Award, 1970; Henry Marshall Tory Medal, RSC, 1977; Remsen Award, Amer. Chem. Soc., 1978; (jtly) Wolf Prize in Chemistry, Wolf Foundn, Israel, 1982; (jtly) Nobel Prize for Chemistry, 1986; Killam Meml Prize, Canada Council, 1988; Royal Medal, Royal Soc., 1989. *Film:* Concept in Reaction Dynamics, 1970. *Publications:* (with F. G. Griffiths) The Dangers of Nuclear War, 1979; papers in scientific jls, articles on science policy and on control of armaments. *Address:* 142 Collier Street, Toronto, Ont M4W 1M3, Canada.

POLE; *see* Carew Pole.

POLE; *see* Chandos-Pole.

POLE, Prof. Jack Richon, PhD; FBA 1985; FRHistS; Rhodes Professor of American History and Institutions, Oxford University, 1979–89; Fellow of St Catherine's College, since 1979; *b* 14 March 1922; *m* 1952, Marilyn Louise Mitchell (marr. diss. 1988); one *s* two *d. Educ:* Oxford Univ. (BA 1949); Princeton Univ. (PhD 1953). MA Cantab 1963. FRHistS 1970. Instr in History, Princeton Univ., 1952–53; Asst Lectr/Lectr in Amer. History, UCL, 1953–63; Cambridge University: Reader in Amer. History and Govt, 1963–79; Fellow, Churchill Coll., 1963–79 (Vice-Master, 1975–78); Mem., Council of Senate, 1970–74. Vis. Professor: Berkeley, 1960–61; Ghana, 1966; Chicago, 1969; Peking, 1984. Commonwealth Fund Amer. Studies Fellowship, 1956; Fellow, Center for Advanced Study in Behavioral Sciences, 1969–70; Guest Schol., Wilson Internat. Center, Washington, 1978–79; Golieb Fellow, NY Univ. Law Sch., 1990; Sen. Res. Fellow, Coll. of William & Mary, Va, 1991. Jefferson Meml Lectr, Berkeley, 1971; Richard B. Russell Lectr, Ga, 1981. Member: Council, Inst. for Early Amer. History and Culture, 1973–76; Acad. Européenne d'Histoire, 1981. Hon. Fellow, Hist. Soc. of Ghana. *Publications:* Abraham Lincoln and the Working Classes of Britain, 1959; Abraham Lincoln, 1964; Political Representation in England and the Origins of the American Republic, 1966 (also USA); (ed) The Advance of Democracy, USA 1967; The Seventeenth Century: the origins of legislative power, USA 1969; (ed) The Revolution in America: documents of the internal development of America in the revolutionary era, 1971 (also USA); (co-ed) The Meanings of American History, USA 1971; Foundations of American Independence, 1763–1815, 1973 (USA 1972); (Gen. Editor) American Historical Documents (ed, Slavery, Secession and Civil War), 1975; The Decision for American Independence, USA 1975; The Idea of Union, USA 1977; The Pursuit of Equality in American History, USA 1978; Paths to the American Past, 1979 (also USA); The Gift of Government: political responsibility from the English Restoration to American Independence, USA 1983; (co-ed) Colonial British America: essays in the new history of the early modern era, USA 1983; (ed) The American Constitution: For and Against: the Federalist and Anti-Federalist papers, USA 1987; (co-ed) The Blackwell Encyclopedia of the American Revolution, 1991 (also USA); articles in Amer. Hist. Rev., William and Mary Qly, and Jl of Southern Hist. *Recreations:* cricket, painting, drawing. *Address:* 20 Divinity Road, Oxford OX4 1LJ; St Catherine's College, Oxford OX1 3UJ. *Clubs:* MCC; Trojan Wanderers Cricket (Co-founder, 1957).

POLE, Sir Peter Van Notten, 5th Bt, *cr* 1791; FASA; ACIS; accountant, retired; *b* 6 Nov. 1921; *s* of late Arthur Chandos Pole and late Marjorie, *d* of late Charles Hargrave, Glen Forrest, W Australia; *S* kinsman, 1948; *m* 1949, Jean Emily, *d* of late Charles Douglas Stone, Borden, WA; one *s* one *d. Educ:* Guildford Grammar Sch. *Recreations:* reading, travel. *Heir: s* Peter John Chandos Pole [*b* 27 April 1952; *m* 1973, Suzanne Norah, BAppSc(MT), *d* of Harold Raymond and Gwendoline Maude Hughes; two *s* one *d*]. *Address:* 9 Yeovil Way, Karrinyup, WA 6018, Australia.

POLGE, Prof. (Ernest John) Christopher, FRS 1983; Scientific Director, Animal Biotechnology Cambridge Ltd, Animal Research Station, Cambridge, since 1986; Hon. Professor of Animal Reproductive Biotechnology, University of Cambridge, since 1989; Fellow, Wolfson College, Cambridge, since 1984; *b* 16 Aug. 1926; *s* of late Ernest Thomas Ella Polge and Joan Gillet Polge (*née* Thorne); *m* 1954, Olive Sylvia Kitson; two *s* two *d. Educ:* Bootham Sch., York; Reading Univ. (BSc Agric.); PhD London 1955. Dept of Agricl Econs, Bristol Univ., 1947–48; Nat. Inst. for Med. Res., London, 1948–54; ARC Unit of Reproductive Physiology and Biochem., later Animal Res. Station, 1954–86, Officer-in-Charge, 1979–86. Lalor Foundn Fellow, Worcester Foundn for Exptl Biol., Shrewsbury, Mass and Univ. of Illinois, 1967–68. Consultant: WHO, Geneva, 1965; FAO, Rome, 1983 and 1987. Member Committee: Soc. for Study of Fertility, 1955–64, 1976–83 (Sec., 1960–63; Chm., 1978–81); Soc. for Low Temp. Biol., 1974–79 (Chm., 1976–79). Chm., Journals of Reproduction and Fertility Ltd, 1982– (Mem., Council of Management and Exec. Cttee, 1972–79). Lectures: Sir John Hammond Meml, Soc. for Study of Fertility, 1974; Blackman, Oxford, 1979; Cameron-Gifford, Newcastle, 1984; E. H. W. Wilmott, Bristol, 1986; Clive Behrens, Leeds, 1988; Sir John Hammond Meml, British Soc. of Animal Production, 1989. Hon. FRASE 1984; Hon. ARCVS 1986. Hon. DSc Univ. of Illinois, 1990. (Jtly) John Scott Award, City of Philadelphia, 1969; Sir John Hammond Meml Prize, British Soc. of Animal Prodn, 1971; Pioneer Award, Internat. Embryo Transfer Soc., 1986; Marshall Medal, Soc. for Study of Fertility, 1988; Internat. Prize for Agriculture, Wolf Foundn, 1988. *Publications:* papers on reproduction in domestic animals and low temp. biol., in biological jls. *Recreations:* gardening, fishing. *Address:* The Willows, 137 Waterbeach Road, Landbeach, Cambridge CB4 4EA. *T:* Cambridge (0223) 860075.

POLIAKOFF, Stephen; playwright and film director; *s* of Alexander Poliakoff and Ina Montagu; *m* 1983, Sandy Welch; one *d. Educ:* Westminster Sch.; Cambridge Univ. *Plays:* Clever Soldiers, 1974; The Carnation Gang, 1974; Hitting Town, 1975; City Sugar, 1976; Strawberry Fields, NT, Shout Across the River, RSC, 1978; The Summer Party, 1980; Favourite Nights, 1981; Breaking the Silence, RSC, 1984; Coming in to Land, NT, 1987; Playing With Trains, RSC, 1989; *films:* Hidden City; Close My Eyes; *TV plays include:* Caught on a Train (BAFTA Award); She's Been Away (Venice Film Festival Prize). *Publications:* all plays; Plays One, 1989. *Recreations:* watching cricket, going to the cinema. *Address:* 33 Devonia Road, N1 8JQ. *T:* 071–354 2695.

POLKINGHORNE, Rev. John Charlton, FRS 1974; President, Queens' College, Cambridge, since 1989; *b* 16 Oct. 1930; *s* of George Baulkwill Polkinghorne and Dorothy Evelyn Polkinghorne (*née* Charlton); *m* 1955, Ruth Isobel Martin; two *s* one *d. Educ:* Elmhurst Grammar Sch.; Perse Sch.; Trinity Coll., Cambridge (MA 1956; PhD 1955; ScD 1974); Westcott House, Cambridge, 1979–81. Deacon, 1981; Priest, 1982. Fellow, Trinity Coll., Cambridge, 1954–86; Commonwealth Fund Fellow, California Institute of Technology, 1955–56; Lecturer in Mathematical Physics, Univ. of Edinburgh, 1956–58; Cambridge University: Lecturer in Applied Mathematics, 1958–65; Reader in Theoretical Physics, 1965–68; Prof. of Mathematical Physics, 1968–79; Fellow, Dean and Chaplain of Trinity Hall, Cambridge, 1986–89 (Hon. Fellow, 1989). Hon. Prof. of Theoretical Physics, Univ. of Kent at Canterbury, 1985. Curate: St Andrew's, Chesterton, 1981–82; St Michael's, Bedminster, 1982–84; Vicar of St Cosmus and St Damian in the Blean, 1984–86. Mem. SRC, 1975–79; Chairman: Nuclear Phys Bd, 1978–79; Cttee to Review the Research Use of Fetuses and Fetal Material, 1988–89. Member: C of E Doctrine Commn, 1989–; Gen. Synod of C of E, 1990–. Chm. of Governors, Perse Sch., 1972–81; Governor, SPCK, 1984–. Licensed Reader, Diocese of Ely, 1975. *Publications:* (jointly) The Analytic S-Matrix, 1966; The Particle Play, 1979; Models of High Energy Processes, 1980; The Way the World Is, 1983; The Quantum World, 1984; One World, 1986; Science and Creation, 1988; Science and Providence, 1989; Rochester Roundabout, 1989; Reason and Reality, 1991; many articles on elementary particle physics in learned journals. *Recreation:* gardening. *Address:* The President's Lodge, Queens' College, Cambridge CB3 9ET. *T:* Cambridge (0223) 335532. *Club:* United Oxford & Cambridge University.

POLLACK, Anita Jean; Member (Lab) London SW, European Parliament, since 1989; *b* NSW, Australia, 3 June 1946; *d* of John and Kathleen Pollack; *m* 1986, Philip Bradbury; one *d. Educ:* City of London Polytechnic (BA 1979); Birkbeck Coll., Univ. of London (MSc Polit. Sociology 1981). Advertising copy writer, Australia, 1963–69; book editor, 1970–75; student, 1976–79; Research Asst to Rt Hon. Barbara Castle, MEP, 1981–89. *Recreations:* family, cinema, rock music. *Address:* 139 Windsor Road, E7 0RA.

POLLARD, Maj.-Gen. Antony John Griffin, CBE 1985; General Officer Commanding, South West District, since 1990; *b* 8 April 1937; *s* of William Pollard and Anne Irene Griffin; *m* Marie-Luise; four *s. Educ:* Oakham Sch.; Jesus Coll., Cambridge. Commnd Royal Leics Regt, 1956; served Cyprus, Germany, Hong Kong, Borneo, Malta; Staff Coll., 1969; Staff 7 Armd Bde, 1970–72; Instr, Staff Coll., 1975–77; CO 1st Bn Royal Anglian Regt, 1977–79; (Norway, NI, Germany); QMG's Secretariat, 1980; Col, Tactical Doctrine, BAOR, 1981; Col, Ops and Tactical Doctrine, 1(BR) Corps, 1982; Comdr, British Forces, Belize, 1983–84; Comdt, Sch. of Infantry, 1984–87; Comdr, British Mil. Mission to Uganda, 1985–86; Dir Gen., Trng and Doctrine (Army), 1987–90. Dep. Col, Royal Anglian Regt, 1986; Colonel Commandant: SASC, 1987; Queen's Div., 1990. *Recreations:* fishing, gardening, ancient buildings. *Club:* Army and Navy.

POLLARD, Maj.-Gen. Barry; *see* Pollard, Maj.-Gen. C. B.

POLLARD, Bernard, CB 1988; Deputy Secretary and Director General (Technical), Board of Inland Revenue, 1985–88; *b* 24 Oct. 1927; *m* 1961, Regina (*née* Stone); one *s* one *d. Educ:* Tottenham Grammar Sch.; London Univ. (BSc Econ; Gladstone Meml Prize (Econs), 1949). Called to the Bar, Middle Temple, 1968. Served RAF (Flying Officer), 1949–53. Entered Tax Inspectorate, Inland Revenue, 1953; Principal Inspector of Taxes, 1969; Asst Sec., 1973; Under Sec., 1979; Dir of Counter Avoidance and Evasion Div., 1981–85. *Recreations:* reading biographies, watching cricket and National Hunt racing.

Address: 10 Merrows Close, Northwood, Mddx HA6 2RT. *T:* Northwood (09274) 24762.

POLLARD, Charles; QPM 1990; Chief Constable of Thames Valley Police, since 1991; *b* 4 Feb. 1945; *s* of Humphrey Charles Pollard and Margaret Isobel Pollard (*née* Philpott); *m* 1972, Erica Jane Allison Jack; two *s* one *d. Educ:* Oundle Sch.; Bristol Univ. (LLB). Metropolitan Police, 1964; Sussex Police, 1980; Asst Chief Constable, Thames Valley Police, 1985–88; Dep. Asst Comr, i/c No 5 (SW) Area of London, Metropolitan Police, 1988–91. *Recreations:* tennis, walking, family pursuits. *Address:* Thames Valley Police HQ, Kidlington, Oxon OX5 2NX. *T:* Kidlington (0865) 846000.

POLLARD, Maj.-Gen. (Charles) Barry; Chairman, Haig Homes, since 1987; *b* 20 April 1927; *s* of Leonard Charles Pollard and Rose Constance (*née* Fletcher); *m* 1954, Mary Heyes; three *d. Educ:* Ardingly Coll.; Selwyn Coll., Cambridge. Commnd, Corps of RE, 1947; served in ME, Korea and UK, 1947–58; Student, Staff Coll., Camberley, 1958; GSO 2 (Trng), HQ Eastern Comd, 1959–61; Liaison Officer, Ecole du Genie, France, 1961–63; OC 5 Field Sqdn, 1963–65; JSSC, 1965; Mil. Asst to DCOS, Allied Forces Central Europe, 1966; GSO 1 MoD, 1967; GSO 1 (DS), Staff Coll., Camberley, 1968; CRE 3 Div., 1969–71; Col GS 3 Div., 1971–72; CCRE 1st British Corps, 1972–74; RCDS, 1975; Chief Engr, BAOR, 1976–79. Col Comdt, RE, 1982–87. National Dir, Trident Trust, 1980–84; Gen. Man., Solent Business Fund, 1984–91. *Recreations:* sailing, golf. *Address:* Yateley, Coombe Road, Salisbury, Wilts.

POLLARD, Christopher Charles; Managing Editor, Gramophone, since 1986; *b* 30April 1957; *s* of Anthony Cecil and Margaret Noelle Pollard; *m* 1984, Margaret Ann Langlois; two *d. Educ:* Merchant Taylors' Sch., Northwood; Newland Park Coll. Joined Gramophone, 1981. Editor, The Good CD Guide, 1988–. *Recreations:* Rugby football, cricket, cars, music. *Address:* Beechcroft, Hotley Bottom, Great Missenden, Bucks HP16 9PL. *T:* Great Missenden (02406) 5964.

POLLARD, Eve, (Lady Lloyd); Editor, Sunday Express, since 1991; *d* of late Ivor and Mimi Pollard; *m* 1st, 1968, Barry Winkleman (marr. diss. 1979); one *d*; 2nd, 1979, Sir Nicholas Lloyd, *qv*; one *s*. Fashion Editor: Honey, 1967–68; Daily Mirror Magazine, 1968–69; Women's Editor: Observer Magazine, 1970–71; Sunday Mirror, 1971–81; Asst Ed., Sunday People, 1981–83; Features Ed. and presenter, TV-am, 1983–85; Editor: Elle USA (launched magazine in NY), 1985–86; Sunday magazine, News of the World, 1986; You magazine, Mail on Sunday, 1986–88; Sunday Mirror and Sunday Mirror Magazine, 1988–91. Formerly contributor to Sunday Times. *Publication:* Jackie: biography of Mrs J. K. Onassis, 1971. *Address:* Ludgate House, 245 Blackfriars Road, SE1 9UX. *T:* 071–928 8000.

POLLARD, Richard Frederick David; His Honour Judge Pollard; a Circuit Judge, since 1990; *b* 26 April 1941; *s* of William Pollard and Anne Irene Pollard (*née* Griffin), CBE; *m* 1964, Angela Susan Hardy; one *s* two *d. Educ:* Oakham School; Trinity College Dublin (BA); Univ. of Cambridge (Dip. Crim.). Called to the Bar, Gray's Inn, 1967. *Recreations:* walking, art nouveau, looking out of the window. *Address:* c/o Midland and Oxford Circuit, 2 Newton Street, Birmingham B4 7LU.

POLLARD, Prof. Sidney; Professor of Economic History, University of Bielefeld, 1980–90, Emeritus Professor since 1990; *b* 21 April 1925; *s* of Moses and Leontine Pollak; *m* 1st, 1949, Eileen Andrews; two *s* one *d*; 2nd, 1982, Helen Trippett. *Educ:* London School of Economics. University of Sheffield: Knoop Fellow, 1950–52; Asst Lecturer, 1952–55; Lecturer, 1955–60; Senior Lecturer, 1960–63; Prof. of Economic History, 1963–80. Corresp. Fellow, British Acad., 1989. *Publications:* Three Centuries of Sheffield Steel, 1954; A History of Labour in Sheffield 1850–1939, 1959; The Development of the British Economy 1914–1950, 1962, 3rd edn, 1914–1980, 1983; The Genesis of Modern Management, 1965; The Idea of Progress, 1968; (with D. W. Crossley) The Wealth of Britain, 1086–1966, 1968; (ed) The Gold Standard and Employment Policies between the Wars, 1970; (ed, with others) Aspects of Capital Investment in Great Britain, 1750–1850, 1971; (ed) The Trades Unions Commission: the Sheffield outrages, 1971; (ed with J. Salt) Robert Owen, prophet of the poor, 1971; (ed with C. Holmes) Documents of European Economic History, vol. 1, 1968, vols 2 and 3, 1972; The Economic Integration of Europe, 1815–1970, 1974; (ed with C. Holmes) Essays in the Economic and Social History of South Yorkshire, 1977; (with Paul Robertson) The British Shipbuilding Industry 1870–1914, 1979; Peaceful Conquest, 1981; The Wasting of the British Economy, 1982; (with C. H. Feinstein) Studies in Capital Formation in Great Britain, 1988; Britain's Prime and Britain's Decline, 1988; Wealth and Poverty, 1990; articles in learned journals in field of economics, economic history and history. *Recreations:* walking, music. *Address:* 34 Bents Road, Sheffield S11 9RJ. *T:* Sheffield (0742) 368543.

POLLEN, Sir John Michael Hungerford, 7th Bt of Redenham, Hampshire, *cr* 1795; *b* 6 April 1919; *s* of late Lieut-Commander John Francis Hungerford Pollen, RN; *S* kinsman, Sir John Lancelot Hungerford Pollen, 6th Bt, 1959; *m* 1st, 1941, Angela Mary Oriana Russi (marr. diss., 1956); one *s* one *d*; 2nd, 1957, Mrs Diana Jubb. *Educ:* Downside; Merton Coll., Oxford. Served War of 1939–45 (despatches). *Heir: s* Richard John Hungerford Pollen [*b* 3 Nov. 1946; *m* 1971, Christianne, *d* of Sir Godfrey Agnew, *qv*; four *s* two *d*]. *Address:* Manor House, Rodbourne, Malmesbury, Wiltshire; Lochportain, Isle of North Uist, Outer Hebrides.

POLLEN, Peregrine Michael Hungerford; Executive Deputy Chairman, 1975–77, Deputy Chairman, 1977–82, Sotheby Parke Bernet and Co.; *b* 24 Jan. 1931; *s* of late Sir Walter Michael Hungerford Pollen, MC, JP, and Lady Pollen; *m* 1958, Patricia Helen Barry; one *s* two *d. Educ:* Eton Coll.; Christ Church, Oxford. National Service, 1949–51. ADC to Sir Evelyn Baring, Governor of Kenya, 1955–57; Sotheby's, 1957–82: Dir, 1961; Pres., Sotheby Parke Bernet, New York, 1965–72. *Address:* Norton Hall, Mickleton, Glos GL55 6PU. *T:* Mickleton (0386) 218. *Clubs:* Brooks's, Beefsteak.

POLLINGTON, Viscount; John Andrew Bruce Savile; *b* 30 Nov. 1959; *s* and *heir* of 8th Earl of Mexborough, *qv*.

POLLOCK, family name of **Viscount Hanworth.**

POLLOCK, Alexander; Advocate, Scottish Bar; *b* 21 July 1944; *s* of Robert Faulds Pollock, OBE, and Margaret Findlay Pollock; *m* 1975, Verena Francesca Gertraud Alice Ursula Critchley; one *s* one *d. Educ:* Rutherglen Academy; Glasgow Academy; Brasenose Coll., Oxford (Domus Exhibnr; MA); Edinburgh Univ. (LLB); Perugia Univ. Solicitor, Bonar Mackenzie & Kermack, WS, 1970–73; passed advocate, 1973; Advocate Depute, 1990–. Contested (C) Moray, 1987. MP (C): Moray and Nairn, 1979–83; Moray, 1983–87. PPS to Sec. of State for Scotland, 1982–86, to Sec. of State for Defence, 1986–87. Mem., Commons Select Cttee on Scottish Affairs, 1979–82, 1986–87. Sec., British-Austrian Parly Gp, 1979–87. Mem., Queen's Body Guard for Scotland, Royal Co. of Archers, 1984–. *Recreations:* music, cycling. *Address:* Drumdarrach, Forres, Moray, Scotland IV36 0DW. *Clubs:* New (Edinburgh); Highland (Inverness).

POLLOCK, David John Frederick; Director, Action on Smoking and Health, since 1991; *b* 3 Feb. 1942; *s* of Leslie William Pollock and Dorothy Emily (*née* Holt); *m* 1976, Lois Jaques (marr. diss. 1991); one *s. Educ:* Beckenham and Penge Grammar Sch.; Keble Coll., Oxford (BA Lit. Hum. 1964); London Business Sch. British Coal Corporation, 1964–90: Head of Central Secretariat, 1972–78; Head of Staff Planning and Orgn, 1980–90. Mem., Hackney BC, 1974–78. Sec., Charity Law Reform Cttee, 1972–77. Chairman: British Humanist Assoc., 1970–72; Rationalist Press Assoc., 1989–. *Publications:* articles in Humanist and other jls. *Recreations:* theatre, gardening. *Address:* 13 Dunsmure Road, N16 5PU. *T:* 081–800 3542.

POLLOCK, Ellen Clara; actress and director; President, The Shaw Society; Professor at RADA and Webber Douglas School of Acting; *m* 1st, 1929, Lt-Col L. F. Hancock, OBE, RE (decd); one *s*; 2nd, 1945, James Proudfoot (*d* 1971). *Educ:* St Mary's College, W2; Convent of The Blessed Sacrament, Brighton. First appeared, Everyman, 1920, as page in Romeo and Juliet. Accompanied Lady Forbes-Robertson on her S. African tour, and later visited Australia as Moscovitch's leading lady. West End successes include: Hit the Deck, Hippodrome, 1927; Her First Affaire, Kingsway, and Duke of York's, 1930; The Good Companions, Her Majesty's, 1931; Too True to be Good, New, 1933; Finished Abroad, Savoy, 1934; French Salad, Westminster and Royalty, 1934; The Dominant Sex, Shaftesbury and Aldwych, 1935. Open Air Theatre: Lysistrata; As You Like It. Seasons of Shaw's plays: at Lyric, Hammersmith, 1944, and with late Sir Donald Wolfit at King's, Hammersmith, 1953; three seasons of Grand Guignol plays at The Irving and Granville, Walham Green; Six Characters in Search of an Author, New Mayfair Theatre, 1963; Lady Frederick, Vaudeville and Duke of York's, 1969–70; Ambassador, Her Majesty's, 1971; Pygmalion, Albery, 1974; Tales from the Vienna Woods, Nat. Theatre, 1976; The Dark Lady of the Sonnets, Nat. Theatre, 1977; The Woman I Love, Churchill, 1979; Country Life, Lyric, Hammersmith, 1980; Harlequinade, and Playbill, Nat. Theatre, 1980. Has acted in numerous films and TV, incl. Forsyte Saga, The Pallisers, World's End and The Nightingale Saga. *Productions include:* Summer in December, Comedy Theatre, 1949; Miss Turner's Husband, St Martin's, 1949; The Third Visitor, Duke of York's, 1949; Shavings, St Martin's, 1951; Mrs Warren's Profession, Royal Court, 1956; A Matter of Choice, Arts, 1967. *Recreations:* motoring, antiques and cooking. *Address:* 9 Tedworth Square, SW3. *T:* 071–352 5082.

POLLOCK, Sir George F(rederick), 5th Bt, *cr* 1866; Artist-Photographer since 1963; *b* 13 Aug. 1928; *s* of Sir (Frederick) John Pollock, 4th Bt and Alix l'Estom (*née* Soubiran); *S* father, 1963; *m* 1951, Doreen Mumford, *o d* of N. E. K. Nash, CMG; one *s* two *d. Educ:* Eton; Trinity Coll., Cambridge. BA 1953, MA 1957. 2nd Lieut, 17/21 Lancers, 1948–49. Admitted Solicitor, 1956, retd. Hon. FRPS (Past Pres.). FRSA. Past Chm., London Salon of Photography. *Recreation:* ski-ing. *Heir: s* David Frederick Pollock [*b* 13 April 1959; *m* 1985, Helena, *o d* of L. J. Tompsett]. *Address:* Netherwood, Stones Lane, Westcott, near Dorking, Surrey RH4 3QH. *T:* Dorking (0306) 885447. *Club:* DHO (Wengen).

POLLOCK, Sir Giles (Hampden) Montagu-, 5th Bt *cr* 1872; management consultant, since 1974; Associate of Korn/Ferry International Ltd, since 1989; *b* 19 Oct. 1928; *s* of Sir George Seymour Montagu-Pollock, 4th Bt, and Karen-Sofie (*d* 1991), *d* of Hans Ludwig Dedekam, Oslo; *S* father, 1985; *m* 1963, Caroline Veronica, *d* of Richard F. Russell; one *s* one *d. Educ:* Eton; de Havilland Aeronautical Technical School. de Havilland Enterprise, 1949–56; Bristol Aeroplane Co. Ltd, 1956–59; Bristol Siddeley Engines Ltd, 1959–61; Associate Dir, J. Walter Thompson Co. Ltd, 1961–69; Director: C. Vernon & Sons Ltd, 1969–71; Acumen Marketing Group Ltd, 1971–74; 119 Pall Mall Ltd, 1972–78; Associate, John Stork & Partners, subseq. John Stork Internat., 1980–89. *Recreations:* bicycling, water-skiing, walking. *Heir: s* Guy Maximilian Montagu-Pollock, *b* 27 Aug. 1966. *Address:* The White House, 7 Washington Road, SW13 9BG. *T:* 081–748 8491. *Club:* Institute of Directors.

POLLOCK, John Denton; General Secretary, Educational Institute of Scotland, 1975–88; a Forestry Commissioner, 1978–91; *b* 21 April 1926; *s* of John Pollock and Elizabeth (*née* Crawford); *m* 1961, Joyce Margaret Sharpe; one *s* one *d. Educ:* Ayr Academy; Royal Technical Coll., Glasgow; Glasgow Univ.; Jordanhill Coll. of Education. BSc (Pure Science). FEIS 1971. RE, 1945–48 (commnd). Teacher, Mauchline Secondary Sch., 1951–59; Head Teacher, Kilmaurs Secondary Sch., 1959–65; Rector, Mainholm Acad., 1965–74. Chm., Scottish Labour Party, 1959 and 1971. Vice-Chm., Scottish TUC, 1980–81, Chm., 1981–82 (Mem., Gen. Council, 1975–87). Member: (Annan) Cttee on Future of Broadcasting, 1974–77; Gen. Adv. Council, BBC, 1981–84; Broadcasting Council for Scotland, 1985–89; Manpower Services Cttee Scotland, 1977–88; Employment Appeal Tribunal, 1991–; Council for Tertiary Educn in Scotland, 1979–83; Exec. Bd, European Trade Union Cttee for Educn, 1980–90 (Vice-Pres., 1986–87 and 1989–90); Chm., European Cttee, World Conf. of Orgns of Teaching Profession, 1980–90; Mem. World Exec., World Conf. of Orgns of Teaching Profession, 1986–90. *Address:* 52 Douglas Road, Longniddry, East Lothian, Scotland EH32 0LJ. *T:* Longniddry (0875) 52082.

POLLOCK, Martin Rivers, FRS 1962; Professor of Biology, University of Edinburgh, 1965–76, now Emeritus; *b* 10 Dec. 1914; *s* of Hamilton Rivers Pollock and Eveline Morton Pollock (*née* Bell); *m* 1st, 1941, Jean Ilsley Paradise (marr. diss.); two *s* two *d*; 2nd, 1979, Janet Frances Machen. *Educ:* Winchester Coll., Trinity Coll., Cambridge; University College Hospital, London. BA Cantab, 1936; Senior Scholar, Trinity Coll., Cambridge, 1936; MRCS, LRCP 1939; MB, BCh Cantab 1940. House Appointments at UCH and Brompton Hospital, 1940–41; Bacteriologist, Emergency Public Health Laboratory Service, 1941–45; seconded to work on Infective Hepatitis with MRC Unit, 1943–45; apppointment to scientific staff, Medical Research Council, under Sir Paul Fildes, FRS, 1945–; Head of Division of Bacterial Physiology, Nat. Inst. for Medical Research, Mill Hill (MRC), 1949–65. *Publications:* (ed) Report of Conference on Common Denominators in Art and Science, 1983; articles in British Journal of Experimental Pathology, Biochemical Journal, Journal of General Microbiology, etc. *Recreation:* contemplating, planning and occasionally undertaking various forms of mildly adventurous travel, preferably through deserts, painting. *Address:* Marsh Farm House, Margaret Marsh, Shaftesbury, Dorset SP7 0AZ. *T:* Marnhull (0258) 820479.

POLLOCK, Adm. of the Fleet Sir Michael (Patrick), GCB 1971 (KCB 1969; CB 1966); LVO 1952; DSC 1944; *b* 19 Oct. 1916; *s* of late C. A. Pollock and Mrs G. Pollock; *m* 1st, 1940, Margaret Steacy (*d* 1951), Bermuda; two *s* one *d*; 2nd, 1954, Marjory Helen Reece (*née* Bisset); one step *d. Educ:* RNC Dartmouth. Entered Navy, 1930; specialised in Gunnery, 1941. Served War of 1939–45 in Warspite, Vanessa, Arethusa and Norfolk, N. Atlantic, Mediterranean and Indian Ocean. Captain, Plans Div. of Admiralty and Director of Surface Weapons; comd HMS Vigo and Portsmouth Sqdn, 1958–59; comd HMS Ark Royal, 1963–64; Asst Chief of Naval Staff, 1964–66; Flag Officer Second in Command, Home Fleet, 1966–67; Flag Officer Submarines and Nato Commander Submarines, Eastern Atlantic, 1967–69; Controller of the Navy, 1970–71; Chief of Naval Staff and First Sea Lord, 1971–74; First and Principal Naval Aide-de-Camp to the Queen, 1972–74. Comdr, 1950; Capt., 1955; Rear-Adm., 1964; Vice-Adm., 1968; Adm., 1970. Bath King of Arms, 1976–85. *Recreations:* sailing, shooting, travel. *Address:* c/o National Westminster Bank, Mardol Head, Shrewsbury, Shropshire SY1 1HE.

POLLOCK, Peter Brian; His Honour Judge Pollock; a Circuit Judge, since 1987; *b* 27 April 1936; *s* of Brian Treherne Pollock and Helen Evelyn Pollock (*née* Holt-Wilson); *m* 1st, 1966, Joan Maryon Leggett (marr. diss. 1981); two *s* (and one *s* decd); 2nd, 1988, Jeannette Mary Nightingale. *Educ:* St Lawrence College. Called to the Bar, Middle Temple, 1958. A Recorder of the Crown Court, 1986–87. *Recreations:* playing tennis, watching cricket, travel, walking, cooking, gardening. *Address:* 17 Gilpin Avenue, Sheen, SW14 8QX. *T:* 081-876 9704. *Clubs:* MCC, Roehampton.

POLLOCK, Sir William H. M.; see Montagu-Pollock.

POLTIMORE, 7th Baron *cr* 1831; **Mark Coplestone Bampfylde;** Bt 1641; Director, Christie's, since 1987 (Associate Director, 1984–87); *b* 8 June 1957; *s* of Captain the Hon. Anthony Gerard Hugh Bampfylde (*d* 1969) (*er s* of 6th Baron) and of Brita Yvonne (who *m* 2nd, 1975, Guy Elmes), *o d* of late Baron Rudolph Cederström; *S* grandfather, 1978; *m* 1982, Sally Anne, *d* of Dr Norman Miles; two *s* one *d*. *Publication:* (with Philip Hook) Popular Nineteenth Century Painting: a dictionary of European genre painters, 1986. *Heir:* *s* Hon. Henry Anthony Warwick Bampfylde, *b* 3 June 1985. *Address:* 55 Elsynge Road, SW18 2HR. *Club:* White's.

POLUNIN, Nicholas, CBE 1976; MS (Yale); MA, DPhil, DSc (Oxon.); FLS; FRGS; Editor (founding), Environmental Conservation, since 1974; Convener and General Editor, Environmental Monographs and Symposia, since 1979; Secretary-General and Editor, International Conferences on Environmental Future, since 1971; President: The Foundation for Environmental Conservation, since 1975; World Council for the Biosphere, since 1984; *b* Hammonds Farm, Checkendon, Oxon; *e s* of late Vladimir and Elizabeth Violet (*née* Hart) Polunin; *m* 1st, 1939, Helen Lovat Fraser (*d* 1973); one *s*; 2nd, 1948, Helen Eugenie Campbell; two *s* one *d*. *Educ:* The Hall, Weybridge; Latymer Upper and privately; Oxford, Yale and Harvard Univs. Open Scholar of Christ Church, Oxford, 1928–32; First Class Hons Nat. Sci. Final Examination, Botany and Ecology; Goldsmiths' Senior Studentship for Research, 1932–33; Botanical tutor in various Oxford Colls, 1932–47; Henry Fellowship at Pierson Coll., Yale Univ., USA, 1933–34 (Sigma Xi); Departmental Demonstrator in Botany 1934–35, and Senior (Research) Scholar of New Coll., Oxford, 1934–36; Dept of Scientific and Industrial Research, Senior Research Award, 1935–38; Rolleston Memorial Prize, 1938; DSIR Special Investigator, 1938; Research Associate, Gray Herbarium, Harvard Univ., USA, 1936–37, and subs. Foreign Research Associate: Fielding Curator and Keeper of the Univ. Herbaria, Oxford, and Univ. Demonstrator and Lectr in Botany, 1939–47; Oxford Univ. Botanical Moderator, 1941–45; Macdonald Prof. of Botany, McGill Univ., Canada, 1947–52 (Visiting Prof., 1946–47); Research Fellow, Harvard Univ., 1950–53; Lectr in Plant Science and Research Associate, Yale Univ., 1953–55; Project Dir, US Air Force, 1953–55, and Consultant to US Army Corps of Engineers; formerly Sen. Research Fell. and Lectr, New Coll., Oxford; Prof. of Plant Ecology and Taxonomy, Head of Dept of Botany, and Dir of Univ. Herbarium, etc., Baghdad, Iraq, Jan. 1956–58 (revolution); Founding Prof. of Botany and Head of Dept, Faculty of Science (which he established as Dean), Univ. of Ife, Nigeria, 1962–66 (revolutions, etc). Leverhulme Res. Award, 1941–43; Arctic Inst. Res. Fellowship, 1946–48; Guggenheim Mem. Fellowship, 1950–52. Haley Lectr, Acadia Univ., NS, 1950; Visiting Lectr and Adviser on Biology, Brandeis Univ., Waltham, Mass, 1953–54; Guest Prof., Univ. of Geneva, 1959–61 and 1975–76. FRHS; Fellow: AAAS, Arctic Inst. NA, American Geographical Soc. Member or Leader, numerous scientific expeditions from 1930, particularly in arctic or sub-arctic regions, including Spitsbergen (widely, including crossing alone), Lapland (3 times), Iceland, Greenland, Canadian Eastern Arctic (5 times, including confirmation of Spicer Islands in Foxe Basin north of Hudson Bay and discovery in 1946 of last major islands to be added to world map following their naming in 1949 as Prince Charles Is. and Air Force Is.), Labrador—Ungava (many times), Canadian Western Arctic (including Magnetic Pole), Alaska, summer and winter flights over geographical North Pole; subsequently in Middle East and West Africa; Ford Foundation Award, Scandinavia and USSR, 1966–67. International Botanical Congresses: VII (Stockholm, 1950); VIII (Paris, 1954); X (Edinburgh, 1964); XI (Seattle, 1969, symposium chm., etc.); XII (Leningrad, 1975, Conservation Section 1st chm., etc.); XIII (Sydney, 1981); International Congresses of Ecology: I (The Hague, 1974); II (Jerusalem, 1978); IV (Syracuse, NY, 1986, contrib. paper *in absentia* with E. P. Odum). Founding Editor: Biological Conservation, 1967–74; Plant Science Monographs, 1954–78; World Crops Books, 1954–69; Chm. Editl Bd, Cambridge Studies in Environmental Policy; Member, Advisory Board: The Environmentalist, 1981–; Environmental Awareness, 1989–, and other jls. Chm., Internat. Steering Cttee and Editor of Proceedings, 1st Internat. Conf. on Environmental Future, Finland, 1971, Secretary-General and Editor: 2nd Conf., Iceland, 1978; 3rd Conf., Edinburgh, 1987; 4th Conf., Budapest, 1990; Chm. (founding), Foundn for Environmental Conservation, 1973– (subsequently consolidated and placed under Geneva cantonal and Swiss federal surveillance). US Order of Polaris; Marie-Victorin Medal for services to Canadian botany; Ramdeo Medal for Environmental Scis, India, 1986; Internat. Sasakawa Environment Prize, 1987; Academia Sinica Medal, China, 1988; USSR Vernadsky Medal, 1988; Hungarian Acad. of Sciences' Founder's (Zéchenyi) Medal, 1990. UNEP Global 500. Officer, Order of Golden Ark (Netherlands), 1990. *Publications:* Russian Waters, 1931; The Isle of Auks, 1932; Botany of the Canadian Eastern Arctic, vol. I, Pteridophyta and Spermatophyta, 1940; (ed) vol. II, Thallophyta and Bryophyta, 1947; vol. III, Vegetation and Ecology, 1948; Arctic Unfolding, 1949; Circumpolar Arctic Flora, 1959; Introduction to Plant Geography, 1960 (subseq. Amer., Indonesian and other edns); Eléments de Géographie botanique, 1967; (ed) The Environmental Future, 1972; Growth Without Ecodisasters?, 1980; Ecosystem Theory and Application, 1986; (with Sir John Burnett) Maintenance of the Biosphere, 1990; papers chiefly on arctic and boreal flora, phytogeography, ecology, vegetation, aerobiology, and conservation; editor of International Industry, 1943–46, and founding editor of World Crops Books, 1954–76; contrib. Encyclopædia Britannica, Encyclopedia of the Biological Scis, etc., and some 600 other scientific papers, editorials, reviews, etc, to various jls. *Recreations:* travel and scientific exploration, nature conservation, stock-markets. *Address:* 7 Chemin Taverney, 1218 Grand-Saconnex, Geneva, Switzerland. *T:* (022) 7982383/4, *Fax:* (022) 7982344; c/o New College, Oxford. *Clubs:* Reform (life); Harvard (life), Torrey Botanical (New York City); New England Botanical (Boston); Canadian Field Naturalists' (Ottawa).

POLWARTH, 10th Lord, *cr* 1690 (Scot.); **Henry Alexander Hepburne-Scott,** TD; DL; Vice-Lord-Lieutenant, Borders Region (Roxburgh, Ettrick and Lauderdale), since 1975; Member, Royal Company of Archers; a Scots Representative Peer, 1945–63; Chartered Accountant; *b* 17 Nov. 1916; *s* of late Hon. Walter Thomas Hepburne-Scott (*d* 1942); *S* grandfather, 1944; *m* 1st, 1943, Caroline Margaret (marr. diss. 1969; she *d* 1982), 2nd *d* of late Captain R. A. Hay, Marlefield, Roxburghshire, and Helmsley, Yorks; one *s* three *d*; 2nd, 1969, Jean, *d* of late Adm. Sir Angus Cunninghame Graham of Gartmore, KBE, CB, and formerly wife of C. E. Jauncey, QC (now Rt Hon. Lord Jauncey); two step *s* one step *d*. *Educ:* Eton Coll.; King's Coll., Cambridge. Served War of

1939–45, Captain, Lothians and Border Yeomanry. Former Partner, firm of Chiene and Tait, CA, Edinburgh; Governor, Bank of Scotland, 1966–72, Director, 1950–72 and 1974–87; Chm., General Accident, Fire & Life Assurance Corp., 1968–72; Director: ICI Ltd, 1969–72, 1974–81; Halliburton Co., 1974–87; Canadian Pacific Ltd, 1975–86; Sun Life Assurance Co. of Canada, 1975–84. Minister of State, Scottish Office, 1972–74. Chm., later Pres., Scottish Council (Develt and Industry), 1955–72. Member: Franco-British Council, 1981–90; H of L Select Cttee on Trade, 1984–85. Chairman: Scottish Nat. Orchestra Soc., 1975–79; Scottish Forestry Trust, 1987–90. Murrayfield Hosp., 1982–90. Chancellor, Aberdeen Univ., 1966–86. Hon. LLD: St Andrews; Aberdeen; Hon. DLitt Heriot-Watt; DUniv Stirling. FRSE; FRSA; Hon. FRIAS. DL Roxburgh, 1962. *Heir:* *s* Master of Polwarth, *qv*. *Address:* Harden, Hawick, Roxburghshire TD9 7LP. *T:* Hawick (0450) 72069. *Clubs:* Pratt's, Army and Navy; New (Edinburgh).

See also Baron Moran.

POLWARTH, Master of; Hon. Andrew Walter Hepburne-Scott; *b* 30 Nov. 1947; *s* and heir of 10th Lord Polwarth, *qv*; *m* 1971, Isabel Anna, *e d* of Maj. J. F. H. Surtees, OBE, MC; two *s* two *d*. *Educ:* Eton; Trinity Hall, Cambridge. *Address:* 72 Cloncurry Street, SW6. *Clubs:* New (Edinburgh); Knickerbocker (New York).

POLYNESIA, Bishop in, since 1975; **Rt. Rev. Jabez Leslie Bryce;** *b* 25 Jan. 1935. *Educ:* St John's College, Auckland, NZ (LTh); St Andrew's Seminary, Manila, Phillipines (BTh). Deacon 1960, priest 1962, Polynesia; Curate of Suva, 1960–63; Priest-in-charge: Tonga, 1964; St Peter's Chinese Congregation, Manila, 1965–67; Archdeacon of Suva, 1967–69; Deputy Vicar-General, Holy Trinity Cathedral, Suva, 1967–72; Lectr, St John Baptist Theological Coll., Suva, 1967–69; Vicar of Viti Levu W, 1969–75; Archdeacon in Polynesia, 1969–75; Vicar-General of Polynesia, 1972–75. Chm., Pacific Conf. of Churches, 1976–86. *Recreations:* tennis, golf. *Address:* Bishop's House, PO Box 35, Suva, Fiji Islands. *T:* (office) 304716, (home) 302553, *Fax:* 302 152.

POMEROY, family name of **Viscount Harberton.**

PONCET, Jean André F.; see François-Poncet.

POND, Carole; see Tongue, C.

PONSONBY, family name of **Earl of Bessborough** and of **Barons de Mauley, Ponsonby of Shulbrede,** and **Sysonby.**

PONSONBY OF SHULBREDE, 4th Baron *cr* 1930, of Shulbrede; **Frederick Matthew Thomas Ponsonby;** *b* 27 Oct. 1958; *o s* of 3rd Baron and of Ursula Mary, *yr d* of Comdr Thomas Stanley Lane Fox-Pitt, OBE, RN; *S* father, 1990. *Educ:* Holland Park Comprehensive Sch.; University Coll., Cardiff; Imperial Coll., London. Councillor, London Borough of Wandsworth, 1990–. *Heir:* none. *Address:* 34 Dalby Road, SW18 1AW.

PONSONBY, Sir Ashley (Charles Gibbs), 2nd Bt *cr* 1956; MC 1945; Chairman, Colville Estate Ltd; Director, J. Henry Schroder, Wagg & Co. Ltd, 1962–80; Lord-Lieutenant of Oxfordshire, since 1980; *b* 21 Feb. 1921; *o s* of Col Sir Charles Edward Ponsonby, 1st Bt, TD, and Hon. Winifred (*d* 1984), *d* of 1st Baron Hunsdon; *S* father, 1976; *m* 1950, Lady Martha Butler, *yr d* of 6th Marquess of Ormonde, CVO, MC; four *s*. *Educ:* Eton; Balliol College, Oxford. 2nd Lieut Coldstream Guards, 1941; served war 1942–45 (North Africa and Italy, wounded); Captain 1943; on staff Bermuda Garrison, 1945–46. A Church Commissioner, 1963–80; Mem., Council of Duchy of Lancaster, 1977–. DL Oxon, 1974–80. *Heir:* *e s* Charles Ashley Ponsonby [*b* 10 June 1951; *m* 1983, Mary P., *yr d* of late A. R. Bromley Davenport and of Mrs A. R. Bromley Davenport, Over Peover, Knutsford, Cheshire; two *s* one *d*]. *Address:* Woodleys, Woodstock, Oxon OX7 1HJ. *T:* Woodstock (0993) 811422. *Club:* Pratt's.

PONSONBY, Myles Walter, CBE 1966; HM Diplomatic Service, retired; County Councillor, Idmiston Division, Wiltshire County Council, since 1988; Chairman, Fight for Sight Appeal, Wiltshire, since 1991; *b* 12 Sept. 1924; *s* of late Victor Coope Ponsonby, MC and Gladys Edith Ponsonby (*née* Walter); *m* 1951, Anne Veronica Theresa Maynard, *y d* of Brig. Francis Herbert Maynard, CB, DSO, MC, and of Ethel Maynard (*née* Bates); one *s* two *d*. *Educ:* St Aubyn's, Rottingdean; Eton College. HM Forces (Captain, KRRC), 1942–49. Entered foreign (subseq. Diplomatic) Service, 1951; served in: Egypt, 1951; Cyprus, 1952–53; Beirut, 1953–56; Djakarta, 1958–61; Nairobi, 1963–64; Hanoi (Consul-Gen.), 1964–65; FO, 1966–69; Rome, 1969–71; FCO, 1972–74; Ambassador to Mongolian People's Republic, 1974–77; FCO, 1977–80. *Recreation:* gardening. *Address:* The Old Vicarage, Porton, near Salisbury, Wilts SP4 0LH. *T:* Idmiston (0980) 610914. *Club:* Army and Navy.

PONSONBY, Robert Noel, CBE 1985; Administrator, Friends of the Musicians Benevolent Fund; Controller of Music, BBC, 1972–85; *b* 19 Dec. 1926; *o s* of late Noel Ponsonby, BMus, Organist Christ Church Cathedral, Oxford, and Mary White-Thomson; *m* 1st, 1957, Una Mary (marr. diss.), *er d* of late W. J. Kenny; 2nd, 1977, Lesley Margaret Black, *o d* of late G. T. Black. *Educ:* Eton; Trinity Coll., Oxford. MA Oxon, Eng. Litt. Commissioned Scots Guards, 1945–47. Organ Scholar, Trinity Coll., Oxford, 1948–50; staff of Glyndebourne Opera, 1951–55; Artistic Director of the Edinburgh International Festival, 1955–60; with Independent Television Authority, 1962–64; Gen. Administrator, Scottish Nat. Orchestra, 1964–72. Director: Commonwealth Arts Festival, Glasgow, 1965; Henry Wood Promenade Concerts, 1974–86; Artistic Dir, Canterbury Fest., 1987–88. Artistic Adviser to Internat. Arts Guild of Bahamas, 1960–72. Chm., London Choral Soc., 1990–. Mem., Music Adv. Panel, Arts Council of GB, 1986–89. Trustee, Young Concert Artists Trust, 1984–89. Governor, Purcell Sch., 1985–88. Hon. RAM 1975. FRSA 1979. *Publication:* Short History of Oxford University Opera Club, 1950. *Recreations:* fell-walking, English and Scottish painting, music. *Address:* 11 St Cuthbert's Road, NW2 3QJ.

PONTECORVO, Guido, FRS 1955; FRSE 1946; FLS 1971; PhD; DrAgr; *b* Pisa, Italy, 29 Nov. 1907; *s* of Massimo Pontecorvo and Maria (*née* Maroni); *m* 1939, Leonore Freyenmuth, Frauenfeld (*d* 1986), Switzerland; one *d*. *Educ:* Univ. of Pisa (DrAgr 1928); Univ. of Edinburgh (PhD 1941). Ispettorato Agrario per la Toscana, Florence, 1931–38; Inst. of Animal Genetics, Univ. of Edinburgh, 1938–40 and 1944–45; Dept of Zoology, Univ. of Glasgow, 1941–44; Dept of Genetics, Univ. of Glasgow, 1945–68 (Prof. 1956–68); Hon. Dir, MRC Unit of Cell Genetics, 1966–68; Mem. Res. Staff, Imperial Cancer Res. Fund, 1968–75; Hon. Consultant Geneticist, 1975–80. Jesup Lectr, Columbia Univ., 1956; Messenger Lectr, Cornell Univ., 1957; Visiting Prof., Albert Einstein Coll. Med., 1965, 1966; Vis. Lectr, Washington State Univ., 1967; Royal Society, Leverhulme Overseas Vis. Prof., Inst. of Biophysics, Rio de Janeiro, 1969 and Dept of Biology, Pahlavi Univ., 1974; Sloane Foundn Vis. Prof., Vermont, 1971; Visiting Professor: UCL, 1968–75; King's Coll., London, 1970–71; Biology Dept, Tehran Univ., 1975; Prof. Ospite Linceo, Scuola Normale Superiore, Pisa, 1976–81; L. C. Dunn Lectr, NY Blood Center, 1976; Raman Prof., Indian Acad. of Scis, 1982–83; J. Weigle Meml Lectr, CIT, 1984; Gandhi Meml Lectr, Raman Inst., 1983. Pres., Genetical Soc., 1964–66; Vice-Pres., Inst. of Biology, 1969–71. For. Hon. Member: Amer. Acad. Arts and Sciences, 1958;

Danish Royal Acad. Sci. and Letters, 1966; Peruvian Soc. of Medical Genetics, 1969; Indian National Science Acad., 1983; Indian Acad. of Scis, 1984; For. Associate, Nat. Acad. of Scis, USA, 1983. Hon. DSc: Leicester, 1968; Camerino, 1974; East Anglia, 1974; Hon. LLD Glasgow, 1978. Hansen Prize, Carlsberg Foundn, 1961; Darwin Medal, Royal Soc., 1978. Campano d'Oro, Pisa, 1979. *Publications:* Ricerche sull' economia montana dell' Appennino Toscano, 1933 (Florence); Trends in Genetic Analysis, 1958; Topics in Genetic Analysis, 1985; numerous papers on genetics and high mountain botany. *Recreation:* alpine plants photography. *Address:* 60 Thornhill Square, N1 1BE. *T:* 071–700 5320.

PONTEFRACT, Bishop Suffragan of, since 1971; **Rt. Rev. Thomas Richard Hare;** *b* 1922; *m* 1963, Sara, *d* of Lt-Col J. E. Spedding, OBE; one *s* two *d*. *Educ:* Marlborough; Trinity Coll., Oxford; Westcott House, Cambridge. RAF, 1942–45, Curate of Haltwhistle, 1950–52; Domestic Chaplain to Bishop of Manchester, 1952–59; Canon Residentiary of Carlisle Cathedral, 1959–65; Archdeacon of Westmorland and Furness, 1965–71; Vicar of St George with St Luke, Barrow-in-Furness, 1965–69; Vicar of Winster, 1969–71. *Address:* 306 Barnsley Road, Wakefield WF2 6AX. *T:* Wakefield (0924) 256935.

PONTEFRACT, Archdeacon of; *see* Unwin, Ven. K.

PONTI, Signora Carlo; *see* Loren, Sophia.

PONTIFEX, Brig. David More, CBE 1977 (OBE 1965; MBE 1956); General Secretary, Army Cadet Force Association and Secretary, Combined Cadet Force Association, 1977–87; *b* 16 Sept. 1922; *s* of Comdr John Weddall Pontifex, RN, and Monica Pontifex; *m* 1968, Kathleen Betsy (*née* Matheson); one *s* four *d*. *Educ:* Worth Preparatory Sch.; Downside Sch. Commnd The Rifle Brigade, 1942; served War, Italy (despatches); Staff Coll., Camberley, 1951; HQ Parachute Brigade, 1952–54; Kenya, 1954–56; War Office, 1956–58; Armed Forces Staff Coll., USA, 1958–59; Brigade Major, 63 Gurkha Brigade, 1961–62; CO 1st Bn Federal Regular Army, Aden, 1963–64; GSO1 2nd Div., BAOR, 1965–66; Col GS, Staff Coll., Camberley, 1967–69; Divisional Brig., The Light Div., 1969–73; Dep. Dir, Army Staff Duties, MoD, 1973–75; Dep. Comdr and COS, SE District, 1975–77, retired 1977. ADC to the Queen, 1975–77. *Address:* 68 Shortheath Road, Farnham, Surrey GU9 8SQ. *T:* Farnham (0252) 723284. *Club:* Naval and Military.

PONTIN, Sir Frederick William, (Sir Fred Pontin), Kt 1976; Founder: Pontin's Ltd, 1946; Pontinental Ltd, 1963; Chairman and Joint Managing Director of Pontin's Ltd, 1946–79 (Hon. President, since 1987), and Pontinental (HS) Ltd, 1972–79; Chairman, 1983–85, Deputy Chairman, 1985–87, Kunick Leisure; Chairman, Ponti's, 1988, retired; *b* 24 Oct. 1906; *m* Dorothy Beatrice Mortimer; one *d*. *Educ:* Sir George Monoux Grammar Sch., Walthamstow. Began career on London Stock Exchange, 1920. Catering and welfare work for Admiralty, Orkney Is, 1939–46. Acquired: Industrial Catering Bristol, 1946; Brean Sands Holiday Village, 1946. Chief Barker, Variety Club of GB (Raising £1,000,000 for charity), 1968; Mem. Exec. Bd, Variety Club, 1968–, Pres. 1969–75, formed 15 regional centres of club; Companion Mem., Grand Order of Water Rats. Prescot Band. Life Mem., BRCS (Hon. Vice Pres., Dorset Branch). Freeman of Christchurch, Dorset. *Recreations:* racing (owner of Specify, winner of 1971 Grand National, and Cala Mesquida, winner of 1971 Schweppes Gold Trophy); connected with Walthamstow Avenue FC for many years prior to 1939–45 war; interested in all sporting activities. *Address:* Flat 64, 3 Whitehall Court, SW1A 2EL. *T:* 071–839 5251. *Clubs:* Farmers', Lord's Taverners, Saints and Sinners, Institute of Directors, Variety of GB.

PONTIN, John Graham; Chairman: JT Group Ltd, since 1961; Country Club Hotels, since 1973; Dartington Hall Trust, since 1984 (Trustee, since 1980); *b* 2 June 1937; *s* of Charles Cyril Pontin and Phyllis (*née* Frieze); *m* 1st, 1966, Gillian Margaret Harris (marr. diss. 1971); one *s* one *d*; 2nd, 1977, Sylviane Marie-Louise Aubel. *Educ:* Bristol Tech. Sch. (Building). Founder, JT Group, 1961; acquired Ashton Court Gp, 1973, now trading as Country Club Hotels; Director: GWR Radio, 1979–; Avery's of Bristol, 1982–; Dartington & Co., 1986–; Chm., Dartington Glass, 1986–88. Trustee, Gtr Bristol Community Trust, 1987–. *Recreations:* gardening, walking. *Address:* 8 High Street, Chew Magna, Bristol BS18 8PW. *T:* Bristol (0272) 297127. *Club:* Reform.

POOLE, family name of **Baron Poole.**

POOLE, 1st Baron, *cr* 1958, of Aldgate; **Oliver Brian Sanderson Poole,** PC 1963; CBE 1945; TD; Member of Lloyd's; lately Director, S. Pearson & Son Ltd; *b* 11 Aug. 1911; *s* of late Donald Louis Poole of Lloyd's; *m* 1st, 1933, Betty Margaret Gilkison (marr. diss., 1951; she *d* 1988); one *s* three *d*; 2nd, 1952, Mrs Daphne Heber Percy (marr. diss., 1965); 3rd, 1966, Barbara Ann Taylor. *Educ:* Eton; Christ Church, Oxford. Life Guards, 1932–33; joined Warwickshire Yeomanry, 1934. Service in 1939–45 in Iraq, Syria, North Africa, Sicily and NW Europe (despatches thrice, MBE, OBE, CBE, US Legion of Merit, Order of Orange Nassau). MP (C) Oswestry Division of Salop, 1945–50. Conservative Party Organisation: Jt Hon. Treas., 1952–55; Chairman, 1955–57; Dep.-Chm., 1957–59; Jt Chm., May–Oct. 1963, Vice-Chm., Oct. 1963–Oct. 1964. Governor of Old Vic, 1948–63; a Trustee, Nat. Gallery, 1973–81. Hon. DSc City Univ., 1970. *Heir: s* Hon. David Charles Poole [*b* 6 Jan. 1945; *m* 1st, 1967, Fiona, *d* of John Donald, London SW6; one *s*; 2nd, 1975, Philippa, *d* of Mark Reeve]. *Address:* 24 Campden Hill Gate, Duchess of Bedford Walk, W8. *Clubs:* MCC, Buck's; Royal Yacht Squadron (Cowes).
See also Sir John Lucas-Tooth, Bt.

POOLE, Anthony Cecil James; Head of Administration Department, House of Commons, 1985–88, retired; *b* 9 Oct. 1927; *s* of Walter James Poole and Daisy Poole (*née* Voyle); *m* 1951, Amelia Keziah (*née* Pracy); one *d*. *Educ:* Headlands Grammar School, Swindon. Served RN, 1945–47; Department of Employment, 1947–76; Principal Establishments Officer, Manpower Services Commn, 1976–80; House of Commons, 1980, Head of Establishments Office, 1981. *Recreations:* golf, gardening.

POOLE, Mrs Avril Anne Barker; Chief Nursing Officer, Department of Health (formerly of Health and Social Security), 1982–June 1992; *b* 11 April 1934; *d* of Arthur George and Norah Heritage; *m* 1959, John Percy Poole. *Educ:* High Sch., Southampton. SRN 1955, SCM 1957, Health Visitors Cert., 1958. Asst Chief Nursing Officer, City of Westminster, 1967–69; Chief Nursing Officer, London Borough of Merton, 1969–73; Area Nursing Officer, Surrey AHA, 1974–81; Dep. Chief Nursing Officer, DHSS, 1981–82. CBIM 1984. *Address:* (until June 1992) Department of Health, Richmond House, 79 Whitehall, SW1A 2NF. *T:* 071–210 5597; Ancaster House, Church Hill, Merstham, Surrey.

POOLE, David Anthony; QC 1984; a Recorder of the Crown Court, since 1983; *b* 8 June 1938; *s* of William Joseph Poole and Lena (*née* Thomas); *m* 1974, Pauline Ann O'Flaherty; four *s*. *Educ:* Ampleforth; Jesus Coll., Oxford (Meyricke Exhibnr in Classics; MA); Univ. of Manchester Inst. of Science and Technology (DipTechSc). Called to the Bar, Middle Temple, 1968. Chm., Assoc. of Lawyers for the Defence of the Unborn, 1985–. *Address:* 1 Deans Court, Crown Square, Manchester. *T:* 061–834 4097; 1 Crown Office Row, Temple, EC4. *Clubs:* London Irish Rugby Football, Vincent's, The Wolfhounds, Northern Lawn Tennis.

POOLE, David Arthur Ramsay; Managing Director, Blue Circle Industries, 1987–89; *b* 30 Sept. 1935; *s* of Arthur Poole and late Viola Isbol (*née* Ramsay); *m* 1961, Jean Mary Male; three *d*. *Educ:* King's Sch., Canterbury; St Edmund Hall, Oxford (MA Jurisprudence). Nat. service, 2nd Lieut, RA, 1955–57. Baring Bros & Co., 1960–65; APCM Ltd (now BCI), 1965–70; Wm Brandts & Co., 1970–73; British Caledonian Gp, 1973–75; Blue Circle Industries, 1976–89. Freeman, City of London, 1976; Liveryman, Fanmakers' Co., 1976–. *Recreations:* shooting, ski-ing, travel. *Address:* Fairhaven, Fairmile Avenue, Cobham, Surrey KT11 2JA. *T:* Cobham (0932) 64830. *Club:* East India.

POOLE, David James, RP 1969; ARCA; artist; President, Royal Society of Portrait Painters, since 1983; *b* 5 June 1931; *s* of Thomas Herbert Poole and Catherine Poole; *m* 1958, Iris Mary Toomer; three *s*. *Educ:* Stoneleigh Secondary Sch.; Wimbledon Sch. of Art; Royal Coll. of Art. National Service, RE, 1949–51. Sen. Lectr in Painting and Drawing, Wimbledon Sch. of Art, 1962–77. One-man Exhibns, Zurich and London. Portraits include: The Queen, The Duke of Edinburgh, The Queen Mother, Prince Charles, Princess Anne, Princess Margaret, Earl Mountbatten of Burma and The Duke of Kent; also distinguished members of govt, industry, commerce, medicine, the academic and legal professions. Work in private collections of the Queen and the Duke of Edinburgh, and in Australia, S Africa, Bermuda, France, W Germany, Switzerland, Saudi Arabia and USA. *Recreations:* painting, drawing. *Address:* The Granary, Oxton Barns, Kenton, Exeter, Devon EX6 8EX. *T:* Starcross (0626) 891611; Studio 6, Burlington Lodge, Rigault Road, Fulham, SW6 4JJ. *T:* 071–736 9288.

POOLE, Isobel Anne; Sheriff of the Lothian and Borders, since 1979, at Edinburgh, since 1986; *b* 9 Dec. 1941; *d* of late John Cecil Findlay Poole, DM Oxon, and of Constance Mary (*née* Gilkes), SRN. *Educ:* Oxford High Sch. for Girls; Edinburgh Univ. (LLB). Admitted to Faculty of Advocates, 1964. Formerly Standing Jun. Counsel to Registrar Gen. for Scotland. Member: Sheriffs' Council, 1980–85; Scottish Lawyers European Gp, 1977–. *Recreations:* country, arts, houses, gardens, friends. *Address:* Sheriff's Chambers, Sheriff Court House, Lawnmarket, Edinburgh EH1 2NS. *Club:* Scottish Arts (Edinburgh).

POOLE, Richard John; Director, Defence Operational Analysis Establishment, Ministry of Defence, 1986–89, retired; *b* 20 Feb. 1929; *s* of Leonard Richard Poole and Merrie Wyn Poole; *m* 1953, Jean Doreena Poole (*née* Welch); two *d*. *Educ;* Univ. of Adelaide, SA (BEng 1st Cl. Hons). Long Range Weapons Estabt, Aust. Dept of Defence, 1951; Ministry of Defence, UK: Admiralty Signals and Radar Estabt, 1957; Head of Div., 1971; Scientific Adviser, 1980, Dir Gen. (Estabts), 1984. *Recreations:* radio, cars, photography. *Club:* Civil Service.

POOLE-WILSON, Prof. Philip Alexander, MD, FRCP; Simon Marks British Heart Foundation Professor of Cardiology, National Heart and Lung Institute (formerly Cardiothoracic Institute), University of London, since 1988; *b* 26 April 1943; *s* of Denis Smith Poole-Wilson, CBE, MCh, FRCS and Monique Michelle Poole-Wilson; *m* 1969, Mary Elizabeth, *d* of William Tattersall MD and Joan Tattersall; two *s* one *d*. *Educ:* Marlborough Coll.; Trinity Coll., Cambridge (Major Scholar; MA, MD); St Thomas's Hosp. Med. Sch. House appts, St Thomas' Hosp., Brompton Hosp., Hammersmith Hosp.; Lectr, St Thomas' Hosp.; British-American Travelling Fellowship from British Heart Foundn at UCLA, 1973–74; Cardiothoracic Institute, London University: Senior Lectr and Reader, 1976–83; Vice-Dean, 1981–84; apptd Prof. of Cardiology, 1983; Hon. Consultant Physician, Royal Brompton Nat. Heart and Lung Hosp. (formerly at Nat. Heart Hosp.), 1976–. Chm., Cardiac Muscle Research Group, 1984–87; Mem. Council, British Heart Foundn, 1985–; Sec., European Soc. of Cardiology, 1990– (Mem. Bd, 1988–90). Strickland-Goodall Lectr and Medal, British Cardiac Soc., 1983. *Publications:* articles and contribs to books on physiology and biochemistry of normal and diseased heart. *Recreations:* sailing, gardening. *Address:* 174 Burbage Road, SE21 7AG. *T:* 071–274 6742. *Clubs:* Athenæum; Parkstone Yacht.

POOLEY, Dr Derek; Managing Director, Nuclear Business Group, AEA Technology, since 1991; *b* 28 Oct. 1937; *s* of Richard Pike Pooley and Evelyn Pooley; *m* 1961; Jennifer Mary Davey; two *s* one *d*. *Educ:* Sir James Smith's Sch., Camelford, Cornwall; Birmingham Univ. (BSc 1958; PhD 1961). FInstP 1979; FInstE 1984. A. A. Noyes Res. Fellow, Calif Inst. of Technol., Pasadena, 1961–62; UKAEA, Harwell: Res. Scientist, 1962–68; Leader of Defects Gp, later of Physics Applications Gp, 1968–76; Head of Materials Develt Div., 1976–81; Dir of Non-nuclear Energy Res., 1981–83; Chief Scientist, Dept of Energy, 1983–86; Dep. Dir, 1986–89, Dir, 1989–90, Atomic Energy Estabt, later AEA Technol.; Chief Exec., AEA Thermal Reactor Services, 1990–91. *Publications:* Real Solids and Radiation, 1975; chapters in: Treatise on Materials Science and Technology, 1974; Radiation Damage Processes in Materials, 1975; Shaping Tomorrow, 1981; Energy and Feedstocks in the Chemical Industry, 1983. *Recreations:* photography, gardening, walking. *Address:* 11 Halls Close, Drayton, Abingdon, Oxon OX14 4LU.

POOLEY, Frederick Bernard, CBE 1968; PPRIBA; Architect to Greater London Council, 1978–80, Controller of Planning and Transportation, 1974–80, and Superintending Architect of Metropolitan Buildings, 1978–80; *b* 18 April 1916; *s* of George Pooley and Elizabeth Pawley; *m* 1944, Hilda Olive Williams; three *d*. *Educ:* West Ham Grammar Sch.; RIBA, FRICS, FRTPI, MIStructE, FCIArb. Served war, RE, 1940–45. Deputy Borough Architect and Planning Officer, County Borough of West Ham, 1949–51; Deputy City Architect and Planning Officer, Coventry, 1951–54; County Architect and Planning Officer, Bucks, 1954–74. Major projects include: public and sch. bldg programme; scheme for public acquisition of bldgs of arch. or hist. interest for preservation and resale; new methods for assembling and servicing land; early planning work for new Milton Keynes. RIBA: Mem. Council, 1962–; Treasurer, 1972; Pres., 1973–75. *Publications:* contribs on planning, transport and architecture. *Address:* Long Ridge, Whiteleaf, Aylesbury, Bucks HP17 0LZ. *T:* Princes Risborough (08444) 6151.

POOLEY, Peter; Deputy Director General for Development, European Commission, since 1989 (Deputy Director General, Agriculture, 1983–89); *b* 19 June 1936; *er* (twin) *s* of late W. M. Pooley, OBE, Truro, and of Grace Lidbury; *m* 1966, Janet Mary, *er d* of Jack Pearson, Banbury; one *s* one *d*. *Educ:* Brentwood Sch.; Clare Coll., Cambridge (BA); Royal Tank Regt. Joined MAFF as Asst Principal, 1959; seconded to: Diplomatic Service, 1961–63 (served in Brussels) and 1979–82 (Minister (Agric.), Office of UK Perm. Rep. to EEC, Brussels); CSD, 1977–79; Under-Sec., 1979, Fisheries Sec., 1982, MAFF. Chm., Bd of Management, British Sch. of Brussels. *Recreation:* playing cricket. *Address:* 53 Dereymaekerlaan, 3080 Tervuren, Belgium; Flat 2, 93 Cornwall Gardens, SW7.
See also R. Pooley.

POOLEY, Robin; Managing Director: Anglian Produce Ltd, since 1988; Anglian Potato Services Ltd, since 1988; Director: Butchers Co. Estates Ltd, since 1977; Solanex Ltd, since 1981; Member, British Agricultural Council, since 1981; *b* 19 June 1936; *yr* (twin) *s* of late W. Melville Pooley, OBE and of Grace M. Pooley (*née* Lidbury); *m* 1972, Margaret Anne, *yr d* of Jack Pearson, Banbury; one *d*. *Educ:* Brentwood School. Various posts, Towers & Co. Ltd, 1954–71; Gen. Manager, CWS Gp, 1971–76; Man. Dir, Buxted Poultry Ltd, 1976–81; Chief Exec., Potato Marketing Bd, 1981–88. Master, Worshipful Co. of Butchers, 1987. *Recreations:* country pursuits. *Address:* Barn Hill, Strumpshaw,

Norfolk NR13 4NS. *T:* Norwich (0603) 715992. *Clubs:* Farmers', City Livery.
See also P. Pooley.

POORE, Duncan; *see* Poore, M. E. D.

POORE, Sir Herbert Edward, 6th Bt, *cr* 1795; *b* April 1930; *s* of Sir Edward Poore, 5th Bt, and Amelia Guliemone; *S* father 1938. *Heir: u* Nasionceno Poore [*b* 1900; *m* Juana Borda (*d* 1943); three *s* three *d*]. *Address:* Curuzu Cuatia, Corrientes, Argentine Republic.

POORE, Dr (Martin Edward) Duncan, MA, PhD; FIBiol, FRGS; Senior Consultant (formerly Director), Forestry and Land Use Programme, International Institute for Environment and Development, and consultant in conservation and land use, since 1983; *b* 25 May 1925; *s* of T. E. D. Poore and Elizabeth McMartin; *m* 1948, Judith Ursula, *d* of Lt-Gen. Sir Treffry Thompson, KCSI, CB, CBE, and late Mary Emily, *d* of Rev. Canon Medd; two *s*. *Educ:* Trinity Coll., Glenalmond; Edinburgh Univ.; Clare Coll., Cambridge. MA, PhD Cantab.; MA Oxon. MICFor. Japanese interpreter, 1943–45. Nature Conservancy, 1953–56; Consultant Ecologist, Hunting Technical Services, 1956–59; Prof. of Botany, Univ. of Malaya, Kuala Lumpur, 1959–65; Dean of Science, Univ. of Malaya, 1964–65; Lectr, Forestry Dept, Oxford, 1965–66; Dir, Nature Conservancy, 1966–73; Scientific Dir, Internat. Union for Conservation of Nature and Natural Resources, Switzerland, 1974–78; Prof. of Forest Science and Dir, Commonwealth Forestry Inst., Oxford Univ., 1980–83; Fellow of St John's Coll., Oxford, 1980–83. Member: Thames Water Authority, 1981–83; Nature Conservancy Council, 1981–84. FRSA. *Publications:* The Vanishing Forest, 1986; No Timber without Trees, 1990; papers on ecology and land use in various jls and scientific periodicals. *Recreations:* hill walking, natural history, music, gardening, photography. *Address:* Balnacarn, Glenmoriston, Inverness-shire IV3 6YJ. *T:* Glenmoriston (0320) 40261. *Club:* Commonwealth Trust.

POOT, Anton, Hon. CBE 1989; Managing Director, 1984–88, Chairman, 1984–89, Philips Electronics & Associated Industries Ltd; Chairman, Philips UK Ltd, 1985–89; *b* 23 Nov. 1929; *m* 1983, Jesmond Masters; one *s* one *d* by a former marriage. *Educ:* High School in Holland; electronics and economics, Holland and Johannesburg. NV Philips' Gloeilampenfabrieken, Hilversum, Utrecht, Eindhoven, 1946–51; Philips S Africa, Fedn of Rhodesia and Nyasaland, 1951–63; NV Philips' Gloeilampenfabrieken, Eindhoven, 1963–66; Chairman and Man. Dir, Philips East Africa, 1967–71; Man. Dir, Ada (Halifax) Ltd and Philips Electrical Ltd UK, 1971–76; Man. Dir, NV Philips' Gloeilampenfabrieken, Eindhoven, 1976–78; Chm. and Man. Dir, Philips Appliances Div., 1978–83. A Dir, LSO, 1988–. Hon. Freeman, Co. of Information Technologists, 1988. CBIM; FRSA. Officer, Order of Oranje-Nassau (Netherlands), 1989. *Recreations:* music, golf, sailing, ski-ing. *Address:* Priors Corner, Priorsfield Road, Godalming, Surrey GU7 2RQ. *Clubs:* Buck's; Wimbledon Park.

POPA, Pretor; Order Star of Socialist Republic of Romania; Order of Labour and other medals; Deputy Foreign Trade Minister, Romania, since 1980; *b* 20 April 1922; *m* Ileana Popa. *Educ:* Academy for High Commercial and Industrial Studies, Bucharest. Director, Ministry for Oil Extraction and Processing, 1950–66; Gen. Director, Ministry for Foreign Trade, 1966–70; Deputy Minister, Ministry for Foreign Trade, and Vice-Chairman at Chamber of Commerce, 1970–73; Ambassador of Romania to the UK, 1973–80. *Address:* Ministry for Foreign Trade, 1 University Square, Bucharest, Romania.

POPE, His Holiness the; *see* John Paul II.

POPE, Andrew Lancelot, (Lance); CMG 1972; CVO 1965; OBE 1959; HM Diplomatic Service, retired; *b* 27 July 1912; *m* 1st, 1938 (marr. diss.); 2nd, 1948, Ilse Migliarina (*d* 1988); one step *d*. *Educ:* Harrow School. Served War of 1939–45 (despatches): Lieut, Royal Fusiliers, 1939; POW 1940–45. Served in Mil. Govt and Allied High Commn in Germany, 1945–56; entered Foreign (subseq. Diplomatic) Service, 1959; Counsellor, Bonn, 1962–72. Director: Conf. Bd, NY, 1972–80; Gerling Global General and Reinsurance Co. Ltd. Liveryman, Worshipful Co. of Grocers. Order of Merit (Germany), 1965; Order of Merit (Bavaria), 1970; Order of Merit (Lower Saxony), 1972. *Recreations:* shooting, gardening. *Address:* Goldhill Grove, Lower Bourne, Farnham, Surrey. *T:* Farnham (0252) 721662.

POPE, Cathryn Mary; soprano; *b* 6 July 1957; *m* 1982, Stuart Petersen. *Educ:* Royal College of Music (ARCM); National Opera Studio. Début, ENO: Sophie, in Werther, 1983; Anna, in Moses, 1986; Susanna, in Marriage of Figaro, 1987; Gretel, in Hansel and Gretel, 1987; Oksana, in Christmas Eve, 1988; Despina, in Così fan tutte, 1988; Pamina, in Die Zauberflöte, 1989; Amsterdam: début, Gretel, 1990; Mélisande, in Pelléas et Mélisande, 1991; Elvira, in Don Giovanni, and Susanna, 1991. Numerous recordings. *Address:* c/o Stafford Law Associates, 26 Mayfield Road, Weybridge, Surrey KT13 8XB.

POPE, Dudley Bernard Egerton; Naval historian and author; *b* 29 Dec. 1925; *s* of late Sydney Broughton Pope and late Alice Pope (*née* Meehan); *m* 1954, Kathleen Patricia Hall; one *d*. *Educ:* Ashford (Kent). Served War of 1939–45: Midshipman, MN, 1941–43 (wounded and invalided). The Evening News: naval and defence correspondent, 1944–57, Dep. Foreign Editor, 1957–59; resigned to take up full-time authorship, 1959. Counsellor, Navy Record Soc., 1964–68. Cruising trans-Atlantic and Caribbean in own yacht, doing naval historical research, 1965–87. Created: "Lt Ramage RN" series of historical novels covering life of naval officer in Nelson's day, 1965; series of novels portraying sea life of Yorke family, 1979. Hon. Mem., Mark Twain Soc., 1976. *Publications: non-fiction:* Flag 4, the Battle of Coastal Forces in the Mediterranean, 1954; The Battle of the River Plate, 1956, repr. 1987; 73 North, 1958; England Expects, 1959; At 12 Mr Byng was Shot, 1962, repr. 1987; The Black Ship, 1963; Guns, 1965; The Great Gamble, 1972; Harry Morgan's Way, 1977; Life in Nelson's Navy, 1981; The Devil Himself, 1987; *fiction: the Ramage series:* Ramage (Book Society Choice) 1965; Ramage and the Drum Beat (Book Society Alternative Choice), 1967; Ramage and the Freebooters (Book of the Month Club Alt. Choice), 1969; Governor Ramage, RN, 1973; Ramage's Prize, 1974; Ramage and the Guillotine, 1975; Ramage's Diamond, 1976; Ramage's Mutiny, 1977; Ramage and the Rebels, 1978; The Ramage Touch, 1979; Ramage's Signal, 1980; Ramage and the Renegades, 1981; Ramage's Devil, 1982; Ramage's Trial, 1984; Ramage's Challenge, 1985; Ramage at Trafalgar, 1986; Ramage and the Saracens, 1988; Ramage and the Dido, 1989; *the Yorke series:* Convoy (Book Club Associates' Choice), 1979; Buccaneer, 1981; Admiral, 1982; Decoy, (World Book Club Choice), 1983; Galleon, 1986; Corsair, 1987. *Recreations:* ocean cruising, skin-diving. *Address:* c/o Campbell Thomson & McLaughlin, 31 Newington Green, N16 9PU.

POPE, Sir Ernle; *see* Pope, Sir J. E.

POPE, Geoffrey George, CB 1986; PhD; FEng 1988; FRAeS; Deputy Chief Scientific Adviser, Ministry of Defence, since 1989; *b* 17 April 1934; *s* of Sir George Reginald Pope and of Susie (*née* Hendy); *m* 1961, Rosemary Frances Harnden (*d* 1989); two *s*; *m* 1991, Helen Vernom Brewis. *Educ:* Epsom Coll.; Imperial Coll., London. MSc (Eng) 1959, DIC 1959; PhD 1963; FRAeS 1970; FCGI 1982. Junior Technical Asst, Hawker Aircraft Ltd, 1952–53; Student, Imperial Coll., 1953–58; Royal Aircraft Establishment: Structures Dept, 1958–73 (Head, Research Div., 1969–73); Aerodynamics Dept, 1973–77 (Head, 1974–77); Gp Head, Aerodynamics, Structures and Materials Depts, 1978–79; Dep. Dir (Weapons), 1979–81; Asst Chief Scientific Advr (Projects), MoD, 1981–82; Dep. Controller and Adviser (Res. and Technol.), MoD, 1982–84; Dir, RAE, 1984–89. *Publications:* technical papers, mainly on structural mechanics and optimum design of structures, in ARC (R&M series) and various technical jls. *Recreations:* music, photography, walking. *Address:* Ministry of Defence, Main Building, Whitehall, SW1A 2HB.

POPE, Jeremy James Richard, OBE 1985; Managing Director, Eldridge, Pope & Co. plc, since 1988 (Joint Managing Director, 1982–88); *b* 15 July 1943; *s* of Philip William Rolph Pope and Joyce Winifred Harcourt Pope (*née* Slade); *m* 1969, Hon. Jacqueline Best; three *s*. *Educ:* Charterhouse; Trinity Coll., Cambridge. Law tripos, MA. Solicitor. Joined Eldridge, Pope & Co., 1969, Finance and Planning Dir, 1972–82. Chm., Smaller Firms Council, CBI, 1981–83; Member: NEDC, 1981–85; Top Salaries Review Body, 1986–; Exec. Cttee, Food and Drinks Fedn, 1986–89 (Dep. Pres., 1987–89). Mem., Royal Commn on Environmental Pollution, 1984–. Chm., Winterbourne Hosp. plc, 1981–89. Gov., Forres Sch., Swanage, 1984–. FRSA. *Recreations:* shooting, fishing, gardening, cooking the resultant produce. *Address:* (office) Dorchester Brewery, Dorchester, Dorset DT1 1QT. *T:* Dorchester (0305) 251251; (home) Field Cottage, West Compton, Dorchester, Dorset DT2 0EY. *T:* Maiden Newton 0300 20469.

POPE, Air Vice-Marshal John Clifford, CB 1963; CBE 1959; CEng, FIMechE; FRAeS; RAF (retired); *b* 27 April 1911; *s* of George Newcombe-Pope; *m* 1950, Christine Agnes (*d* 1982), *d* of Alfred Hames, Chichester; one *s* two *d*. *Educ:* Tiverton Boys' Middle Sch.; RAF Technical Training Sch., Halton (aircraft apprentice); RAF Coll., Cranwell (cadet; Sir Charles Wakefield Scholar). Graduated as pilot and commnd, 1932; served with No 3 Sqdn, 1933, Nos 27 and 39, on NW Frontier, 1933–36. War of 1939–45; Comd RAF Station, Cleave, 1940–42; served in Egypt and Palestine, 1943–46; Asst Dir Research and Develt, Min. of Supply, 1947–50; Dir of Engineering, RNZAF, 1951–53; Comd RAF Station, Stoke Heath, 1954–57; Sen. Tech. Staff Officer, No 3 Gp Bomber Comd, 1957–59 and Flying Trng Comd, 1960–61; AOC and Comdt, RAF Technical College, 1961–63; Senior Technical Staff Officer, Transport Command, 1963–66. Life Vice-Pres., RAF Boxing Assoc. *Recreation:* scale model steam engineering. *Address:* Dilston, 47 Oxford Road, Stone, near Aylesbury, Bucks. *T:* Aylesbury (0296) 748467. *Club:* Royal Air Force.

POPE, Vice-Adm. Sir (John) Ernle, KCB 1976; *b* 22 May 1921; *s* of Comdr R. K. C. Pope, Homme House, Herefordshire. *Educ:* RN Coll., Dartmouth. Royal Navy, 1935. Served throughout War of 1939–45, in Destroyers. CO, HMS Decoy, 1962–64; Dir, Naval Equipment, 1964–66; CO, HMS Eagle, 1966–68; Flag Officer, Western Fleet Flotillas, 1969–71; C of S to C-in-C Western Fleet, 1971–74; Comdr, Allied Naval Forces, S Europe, 1974–76; Rear-Adm. 1969; Vice-Adm. 1972. Dep. Pres., Royal Naval Assoc. *Recreations:* sailing, shooting. *Address:* Homme House, Much Marcle, Herefordshire. *Club:* Army and Navy.
See also Rear-Adm. M. D. Kyrle Pope.

POPE, Sir Joseph (Albert), Kt 1980; DSc, PhD (Belfast), WhSc; Director, since 1960, Consultant, since 1988, TQ International (formerly TecQuipment Group), Nottingham (Chairman, 1974–88); *b* 18 October 1914; *s* of Albert Henry and Mary Pope; *m* 1940, Evelyn Alice Gallagher; one *s* two *d*. *Educ:* School of Arts and Crafts, Cambridge; King's College, London. Apprentice, Boulton & Pauls, Norwich, 1930–35. Whitworth Scholarship, 1935. Assistant Lecturer in Engineering, Queen's Univ., Belfast, 1938–44; Assistant Lecturer in Engineering, Univ. of Manchester, 1944–45; Lecturer, then Senior Lecturer, Univ. of Sheffield, 1945–49; Professor of Mechanical Engineering, Nottingham University, 1949–60; Research Dir, Mirrlees Nat. Research Div., Stockport, and Dir, Mirrlees National Ltd 1960–69; Vice-Chancellor, Univ. of Aston in Birmingham, 1969–79. Director: John Brown & Co. Ltd, 1970–82; Midlands Electricity Bd, 1975–80; Royal Worcester Ltd, 1979–83; Chm., W Midlands Econ. Planning Council, 1977–79. Gen. Treasurer, British Assoc., 1975–82; Pres., Whitworth Soc., 1978–79; Chm., Birmingham Civic Soc., 1978–79. Hon. LLD Birmingham, 1979; Hon. DUniv Heriot-Watt, 1979; Hon. DSc: Aston, 1979; Belfast, 1980; Salford, 1980; Nottingham, 1987. *Publications:* papers on the impact of metals and metal fatigue published in Proc. of Inst. of Mech. Engineers and Jl of Iron and Steel Inst. *Address:* 3 Mapperley Hall Drive, Nottingham NG3 5EP. *T:* Nottingham (0602) 621146.

POPE, Lance; *see* Pope, A. L.

POPE, Rear-Adm. Michael Donald K.; *see* Kyrle Pope.

POPE, Very Rev. Robert William, OBE 1971; Dean of Gibraltar, 1977–82; *b* 20 May 1916; *s* of late Rev. Jonas George Pope and Marjorie Mary Pope (*née* Coates); *m* 1940, Elizabeth Beatrice Matilda (*née* Bressey); two *s* one *d*. *Educ:* English College, Temuco, Chile; Harvey Grammar Sch., Folkestone; Maidstone Grammar Sch.; St Augustine's Coll., Canterbury; Durham Univ. (LTh). Deacon 1939, priest, 1940, Rochester; Curate: Holy Trinity, Gravesend, 1939–41; St Nicholas, Guildford, 1942–43; Priest in charge, Peaslake, 1943–44; Chaplain, Royal Navy, 1944–71; Vicar of Whitchurch with Tufton and Litchfield, Dio. Winchester, 1971–77. Member of Sion College. Minister Provincial of European Province, 1985– and Minister Gen., 1987–, Third Order of Soc. of St Francis. *Address:* 5 Wreath Green, Tatworth, Chard, Somerset TA20 2SN. *T:* Chard (0460) 20987.

POPE-HENNESSY, Sir John (Wyndham), Kt 1971; CBE 1959 (MBE 1944); FBA 1955; FSA; FRSL; Professor of Fine Arts, New York University, since 1977; *b* 13 Dec. 1913; *er s* of late Major-General L. H. R. Pope-Hennessy, CB, DSO, and late Dame Una Pope-Hennessy, DBE. *Educ:* Downside School; Balliol Coll., Oxford (Hon. Fellow). Joined staff of Victoria and Albert Museum, 1938. Served Air Ministry, 1939–45. Victoria and Albert Museum: Keeper, Dept of Architecture and Sculpture, 1954–66; Dir and Sec., 1967–73; Dir, British Museum, 1974–76; Consultative Chm., Dept of European Paintings, Metropolitan Mus., NY, 1977–86. Slade Professor of Fine Art, Univ. of Oxford, 1956–57; Clark Professor of Art, Williams College, Mass., USA, 1961–62; Slade Professor of Fine Art, and Fellow of Peterhouse, University of Cambridge, 1964–65. Member: Arts Council, 1968–76; Ancient Monuments Bd for England, 1969–72; Dir, Royal Opera House, 1971–76. Fellow, Amer. Acad. of Arts and Scis, 1978; Corresponding Member: Accademia Senese degli Intronati; Bayerische Akademie der Wissenschaften; Hon. Academician, Accademia del Disegno, Florence; For. Mem., Amer. Philosophical Soc., 1974; Hon. Fellow, Pierpoint Morgan Library, 1975. Serena Medal of British Academy for Italian Studies, 1961; New York University Medal, 1965; Torch of Learning Award, Hebrew Univ., Jerusalem, 1977; Art Dealers Assoc. Award, 1984; Jerusalem Prize of Arts and Letters, 1984; Premio Galileo Galilei, 1986. Hon. LLD Aberdeen, 1972; Hon. Dr RCA, 1973. Hon. Citizen, Siena, 1982; Grande Ufficiale, Order of Merit of the Republic, Italy, 1988. Mangia d'Oro, 1982. *Publications:* Giovanni di Paolo, 1937; Sassetta, 1939; Sienese Quattrocento Painting, 1947; A Sienese Codex of the Divine Comedy, 1947; The Drawings of Domenichino at Windsor Castle, 1948; A Lecture on Nicholas Hilliard, 1949; Donatello's Ascension, 1949; The Virgin with the Laughing Child, 1949; edition of the Autobiography of Benvenuto Cellini, 1949; Paolo Uccello, 1950, rev. edn, 1972; Italian Gothic Sculpture in the Victoria and Albert Museum, 1952; Fra Angelico, 1952, rev. edn, 1974; Italian Gothic Sculpture, 1955, rev. edn 1985; Italian Renaissance Sculpture, 1958, rev. edn 1985; Italian High Renaissance and Baroque Sculpture, 1963, rev. edn 1985; Catalogue of Italian Sculpture in the Victoria and Albert Museum, 1964; Renaissance Bronzes in the Kress Collection, 1965; The Portrait in the Renaissance, 1967; Essays on Italian Sculpture, 1968; Catalogue of Sculpture in the Frick Collection, 1970; Raphael (Wrightsman lectures), 1970; (with others) Westminster Abbey, 1972; Luca della Robbia, 1980 (Mitchell Prize, 1981); The Study and Criticism of Italian Sculpture, 1980; Cellini, 1985; La Scultura Italiana del Rinascimento, 1986; The Robert Lehman Collection-1, Italian Paintings, 1987; Learning to Look (autobiog.), 1991; contribs to NY Rev. of Books, TLS, etc. *Recreation:* music. *Address:* 28 via de' Bardi, Florence 50125, Italy.

POPHAM, Maj.-Gen. Christopher John, CB 1982; Director, British Atlantic Committee, 1982–April 1992; *b* 2 April 1927; *s* of late Gordon F. B. Popham and Dorothy A. L. Popham (*née* Yull); *m* 1950, Heather Margaret, *y d* of late Lt-Col and Mrs H. R. W. Dawson; two *s*. *Educ:* Merchant Taylors' School. Commnd Royal Engineers, 1946; served with King George V's Own Bengal Sappers and Miners, RIE and Royal Pakistan Engineers, 1946–48; UK and Germany, 1948–57; Staff Coll., 1958; Cyprus, 1959–62; OC 4 Field Sqdn, 1963–65; JSSC 1965; Mil. Asst to QMG, 1966–68; CO 36 Engineer Regt, 1968–70; CRE 4 Div., 1971–73; Comd 12 Engineer Bde, 1973–75; BGS Intelligence and Security, HQ BAOR and ACOS G-2 HQ Northern Army Group, 1976–79; Asst Chief of Staff (Intell.), SHAPE, 1979–82. Col Comdt, RE, 1982–87. FBIM. *Recreations:* music, photography, railways. *Address:* c/o Barclays Bank, High Street, Andover, Hants.

POPHAM, Mervyn Reddaway, FBA 1988; FSA; Lecturer in Aegean Archaeology, Oxford, since 1972; *b* 14 July 1927; *s* of Richard and Lilly Popham. *Educ:* Exeter Sch.; Univ. of St Andrews (MA); Univ. of Oxford (DipArch). FSA 1960. Colonial Administrative Service, Cyprus, 1951–58 (Comr, Troodos Dist., 1955–56); Macmillan Student, 1961–63 and Asst Dir, 1963–70, British Sch. of Archaeology at Athens; Asst Prof., Univ. of Cincinnati, 1970–72. *Publications:* The Last Days of the Palace at Knossos, 1964; The Destruction of the Palace at Knossos, 1970; Lefkandi I: the iron age settlement and cemeteries, 1980; The Unexplored Mansion at Knossos, 1984; articles and excavation reports in learned jls. *Recreations:* music, photography. *Address:* 110 Woodstock Road, Oxford. *T:* Oxford (0865) 512605.

POPJÁK, George Joseph, DSc (London), MD; FRS 1961; FRSC; Professor of Biochemistry at University of California in Los Angeles, 1968–84, now Emeritus; *b* 5 May 1914; *s* of late George and Maria Popják, Szeged, Hungary; *m* 1941, Hasel Marjorie, *d* of Duncan and Mabel Hammond, Beckenham, Kent. *Educ:* Royal Hungarian Francis Joseph University, Szeged. Demonstrator at Department of Morbid Anatomy and Histology, University of Szeged, 1938–39; Br. Council Scholar, Postgraduate Med. School of London, 1939–41; Demonstrator in Pathology, Dept of Pathology, St Thomas's Hosp. Med. School, London, 1941–43; Beit Mem. Fellow for medical research at St Thomas's Hosp. Med. School, London, 1943–47; Member scientific staff of Med. Research Council at Nat. Inst. for Med. Research, 1947–53; Director of Medical Research Council Experimental Radiopathology Research Unit, Hammersmith Hosp., 1953–62; Jt Dir, Chemical Enzymology Lab., Shell Res. Ltd, 1962–68; Assoc. Prof. in Molecular Sciences, Warwick Univ., 1965–68. Foreign member of Belgian Roy. Flemish Acad. of Science, Literature and Fine Arts, 1955; Hon. Member: Amer. Soc. of Biological Chemists, 1968; Alpha-Omega-Alpha, 1970; Mem., Amer. Acad. of Arts and Sciences, 1971. (With Dr J. W. Cornforth, FRS) CIBA Medal of Biochemical Soc., 1965 (first award); Stouffer Prize, 1967; Davy Medal, Royal Soc., 1968; Award in Lipid Chem., Amer. Oil Chem. Soc., 1977; Distinguished Scientific Achievement award, Amer. Heart Assoc., 1978. *Publications:* Chemistry, Biochemistry and Isotopic Tracer Technique (Roy. Inst. of Chemistry monograph), 1955; (jtly) Lipids, Chemistry, Biochemistry and Nutrition, 1986; articles on fat metabolism in Jl Path. Bact., Jl Physiol., Biochemical Jl, etc. *Recreations:* music, modelling and gardening. *Address:* Departments of Medicine and Biological Chemistry, University of California at Los Angeles, Center for the Health Sciences 47–123 CHS, Los Angeles, Calif 90024, USA.

POPLE, John Anthony, FRS 1961; John Christian Warner University Professor of Natural Sciences (formerly Professor of Chemical Physics), Carnegie-Mellon University, Pittsburgh, USA, since 1964; *b* 31 Oct. 1925; *e s* of Herbert Keith Pople and Mary Frances Jones, Burnham-on-Sea, Som.; *m* 1952, Joy Cynthia Bowers; three *s* one *d*. *Educ:* Bristol Grammar School; Cambridge University, MA, PhD. Mayhew Prize, 1948, Smith Prize, 1950, Cambridge; Fellow, Trinity College, 1951–58, Lecturer in Mathematics, 1954–58, Cambridge; Superintendent of Basic Physics Division, National Physical Laboratory, 1958–64. Ford Visiting Professor, Carnegie Inst. of Technology, Pittsburgh, 1961–62. Fellow: Amer. Physical Soc., 1970; Amer. Acad. of Arts and Scis, 1971; AAAS, 1980. For. Associate, Nat. Acad. of Sci., 1977. Marlow Medal, Faraday Soc., 1958; ACS Pauling Award, 1977; Awards from American Chemical Society: Langmuir, 1970; Harrison Howe, 1971; Gilbert Newton Lewis, 1973; Pittsburgh, 1975. Sen. US Scientist Award, Alexander von Humboldt Foundn, 1981; G. Willard Wheland Award, Univ. of Chicago, 1981; Evans Award, Ohio State Univ., 1982; Oesper Award, Univ. of Cincinnati, 1984; Davy Medal, Royal Soc., 1988. *Publications:* High Resolution nuclear magnetic resonance, 1959; Approximate Molecular Orbital Theory, 1970; Ab initio Molecular Orbital Theory, 1986; scientific papers on molecular physics and theoretical chemistry. *Recreations:* music, travel. *Address:* Carnegie-Mellon University, 4400 Fifth Avenue, Pittsburgh, Pa 15213, USA; #7K, 1500 Sheridan Road, Wilmette, Ill 60091, USA.

POPOV, Viktor Ivanovich; Soviet Ambassador to the Court of St James's, 1980–86; *b* 19 May 1918; *m* Natalia Aleksandrovna Popova; two *s*. *Educ:* Moscow Inst. of History and Philosophy; Higher Diplomatic Sch. of USSR. Entered Min. of Foreign Affairs, 1954; Vietnam, 1960–61; Australia, 1967–68; UK, 1968; Ambassador on special assignments, UN and Unesco, and Rector, Diplomatic Acad. of USSR, 1968–80. Many Soviet and foreign awards. *Publications:* Anglo-Soviet Relations 1927–29; Anglo-Soviet Relations 1929–39; (jtly) History of Diplomacy series III. *Address:* c/o Ministry of Foreign Affairs, 32–34 Smolenskaya Sennaya Ploshchad, Moscow, USSR.

POPPER, Prof. Sir Karl (Raimund), CH 1982; Kt 1965; FRS 1976; FBA 1958; PhD (Vienna), MA (New Zealand), DLit (London); Professor of Logic and Scientific Method in the University of London (London School of Economics and Political Science), 1949–69; Emeritus Professor, 1969; Guest Professor in the Theory of Science, University of Vienna, since 1986; Senior Research Fellow, Hoover Institution, Stanford University, since 1986; *b* Vienna, 28 July 1902; *s* of Dr Simon Siegmund Carl Popper, Barrister, of Vienna, and of Jenny Popper (*née* Schiff); *m* 1930, Josefine Anna Henninger (*d* 1985); no *c*. *Educ:* University of Vienna. Senior Lecturer in Philosophy, Canterbury University College, Christchurch (Univ. of NZ), 1937–45; Reader in Logic and Scientific Method, LSE, Univ. of London, 1945–49. Fellow, Center for Advanced Study in the Behavioral Sciences, Stanford, Calif, 1956–57; Visiting Professor: Harvard (Wm James Lectures in Philosophy), 1950; Univ. of California Berkeley, 1962; Minnesota Center for Phil. of Science, 1962; Indiana Univ., 1963; Inst. for Advanced Studies, Vienna, 1964; Denver Univ., 1966; Vis. Fellow, The Salk Institute for Biological Studies, 1966–67; Kenan Univ. Prof., Emory Univ., 1969; Jacob Ziskind Vis. Prof. in Philosophy and the History of Thought, Brandeis Univ., 1969; William Evans Vis. Prof., Otago, 1973; Vis. Erskine Fellow, Canterbury, NZ, 1973; Lectures: Yale, Princeton, Chicago, Emory Univs, 1950, 1956; Eleanor Rathbone, Bristol, 1956; Annual Philos. to British Acad., 1960; Herbert Spencer, Oxford, 1961 and 1973; Shearman Meml, UCL, 1961; Farnum, Princeton, 1963; Arthur H. Compton Meml, Washington, 1965; Romanes, Oxford, 1972; Broadhead Meml, Canterbury NZ, 1973; First Darwin, Darwin Coll., Cambridge, 1977; Tanner, Ann Arbor, 1978; Frank Nelson Doubleday, Smithsonian Inst., 1979; first Morrell Meml, York, 1981; first Medawar, Royal Soc., 1986. Member: Editorial Bd: Foundations of Physics; British Jl Phil. of Science; Studi Internat. di Filosofia; Jl of Political Theory; Biologie et Logique; Board of Consulting Editors: Theory and Decision; Idea; Advisory Board: Medical Hypotheses; The Monist; Co-Editor: Ratio; Studies in the Foundations Methodology and Philosophy of Science; Methodology and Science; Rechtstheorie; Schriftenreihe Erfahrung und Denken; Library of Exact Philosophy; Ed. Correspond., Dialectica. Chairman, Phil. of Science Group, 1951–53; President: The Aristotelian Soc., 1958–59; British Society for the Phil. of Science, 1959–61; Mem. Council, Assoc. for Symb. Logic, 1951–55. Mem., Académie Internat. de Philosophie des Sciences, 1949; Hon. Mem., RSNZ, 1965; For. Hon. Mem., Amer. Acad. of Arts and Sciences, 1966; Correspondant de l'Institut de France, 1974–80; Associate Mem., Académie Royale de Belgique, 1976; Membre d'Honneur, Académie Internationale d'Histoire des Sciences, 1977; Hon. Mem., Deutsche Akademie für Sprache und Dichtung, 1979; Membre de l'Académie Européenne des Sciences, des Arts et des Lettres (Delegn of GB), 1980; Membre de l'Institut de France, 1980; Socio Straniero dell'Accademia Nazionale dei Lincei, 1981; Ehrenmitglied, Oesterreichische Akademie der Wissenschaften, 1982; Mem., Konrad Lorenz Inst., Altenberg, Austria, 1990. Hon. Mem., Harvard Chapter of Phi Beta Kappa, 1964; Hon. Fellow, LSE, 1972; Hon. Mem., Allgemeine Gesellschaft für Philosophie in Deutschland, 1979; Hon. Fellow, Darwin Coll., Cambridge, 1980; Hon. Research Fellow, Dept of History & Philosophy of Science, KCL, 1982; Hon. Mem., Gesellschaft der Ärzte, Vienna, 1986. Hon. Prof. of Econs, Vienna, 1986. Hon. LLD: Chicago, 1962; Denver, 1966; Hon. LittD: Warwick, 1971; Canterbury, NZ, 1973; Cantab, 1980; Hon. DLitt: Salford, 1976; City Univ., 1976; Guelph, Ontario, 1978; Oxon 1982; Hon. Dr.rer.nat, Vienna, 1978; Dr. phil *hc*: Mannheim, 1978; Salzburg, 1979; Eichstätt, 1991; Hon. Dr.rer.pol, Frankfurt, 1979; Hon. DSc: Gustavus Adolphus Coll., 1981; London, 1986. Prize of the City of Vienna for 'Geisteswissenschaften' (mental and moral sciences) 1965; Sonning Prize for merit in work that has furthered European civilization, Univ. of Copenhagen, 1973; Lippincott Award, Amer. Pol. Sci. Assoc., 1976; Dr Karl Renner Prize, Vienna, 1978; Dr Leopold Lucas Prize, Univ. of Tübingen, 1981; Alexis de Tocqueville Prize, Fondation Tocqueville, 1984; International Prize of Catalonia (1st recipient), 1989. Grand Decoration of Honour in Gold (Austria), 1976; Gold Medal for Disting. Service to Sci., Amer. Mus. of Nat. Hist., NY, 1979; Ehrenzeichen für Wissenschaft und Kunst (Austria), 1980; Order Pour le Mérite (German Fed. Rep.), 1980; Grand Cross with Star, Order of Merit (German Fed. Rep.), 1983; Ring of Honour, City of Vienna, 1983. *Publications:* (trans. into 26 languages): Logik der Forschung, 1934, rev. 2nd edn 1966, rev. 8th edn 1984; The Open Society and Its Enemies, 1945, 5th edn, rev. 1966, 14th impr. 1984; The Poverty of Historicism, 1957, 11th impr. 1984; The Logic of Scientific Discovery, 1959, 12th impr. 1985; On the Sources of Knowledge and of Ignorance, 1961; Conjectures and Refutations, 1963, 9th impr. 1984; Of Clouds and Clocks, 1966; Objective Knowledge, 1972, 7th impr. 1983; Unended Quest: An Intellectual Autobiography, 1976, 7th impr. 1985; (with Sir John Eccles) The Self and Its Brain, 1977, rev. pbk edn (UK), 1984, 3rd impr. rev. edn 1985; Die beiden Grundprobleme der Erkenntnistheorie, 1979, 2nd edn 1991; Postscript to The Logic of Scientific Discovery (ed W. W. Bartley), 3 vols, 1982–83 (vol. 1, Realism and the Aim of Science; vol. 2, The Open Universe; vol. 3, Quantum Theory and the Schism in Physics, 1982); (with F. Kreuzer) Offene Gesellschaft—Offenes Universum, 1982, 3rd edn 1983; A Pocket Popper (ed David Miller), 1983; Auf der Suche nach einer besseren Welt, 1984, 3rd edn 1988; (with Konrad Lorenz) Die Zukunft ist Offen, 1984, 2nd edn 1985; (ed David Miller) Popper Selections, 1985; A World of Propensities, 1990; contribs to: learned jls; anthologies; The Philosophy of Karl Popper, Library of Living Philosophers (ed P. A. Schilpp), 1974. *Recreation:* music. *Address:* c/o London School of Economics, Houghton Street, Aldwych, WC2A 2AE.

POPPLEWELL, Catharine Margaret, (Lady Popplewell); JP; Member, Independent Television Commission, since 1991; *b* 30 July 1929; *d* of Alfred John Storey and Gladys Mabel Storey; *m* 1954, Hon. Sir Oliver Bury Popplewell, *qv*; four *s* (and one *s* decd). *Educ:* Malvern Girls' College; Newnham College, Cambridge (MA Hons); Hughes Hall, Cambridge (PGCE). Mem., Bd of Visitors, Aylesbury Prison, 1974–79; Chm., Bucks County Probation Cttee, 1981–; Mem., Bucks County Council, 1977–85 (Chm., Educn Cttee, 1981–85). Mem., IBA, 1987–90. Chm., Oxford Dio. Council for the Deaf, 1987–91; Trustee, Bucks Historic Churches Trust, 1985–. Mem. Council, Open Univ., 1985–; Chm. Governors, Amersham Coll. of Further Educn, Art and Design, 1981–; School Governor: Godstowe; Winchester House; Ashfold; Alfriston. JP Bucks, 1968. FRSA. *Recreations:* sailing, theatre. *Address:* c/o Independent Television Commission, 70 Brompton Road, SW3 1EY.

POPPLEWELL, Hon. Sir Oliver (Bury), Kt 1983; **Hon. Mr Justice Popplewell;** Judge of the High Court of Justice, Queen's Bench Division, since 1983; *b* 15 Aug. 1927; *s* of late Frank and Nina Popplewell; *m* 1954, Catharine Margaret Storey (*see* C. M. Popplewell); four *s* (and one *s* decd). *Educ:* Charterhouse (Schol.); Queens' Coll., Cambridge (Class. exhibnr). BA 1950; LLB 1951; MA. CUCC, 1949–51. Called to the Bar, Inner Temple, 1951, Bencher, 1978; QC 1969. Recorder, Burton-on-Trent, 1970–71; Dep. Chm., Oxon QS, 1970–71; a Recorder of the Crown Court, 1972–82. Indep. Mem., Wages Councils, 1962–82, Chm. 1973–82; Mem., Home Office Adv. Bd on Restricted Patients, 1981–82; Vice-Chm., Parole Bd, 1986–87 (Mem., 1985–87); Mem., Parole Review Cttee, 1987–88; Chm., Inquiry into Crowd Safety and Control at sports grounds, 1985–86; Pres., Employment Appeal Tribunal, 1986–88 (Mem., 1984–85). MCC: Mem. Cttee, 1971–74, 1976–79, 1980–; Trustee, 1983–. Gov., Sutton's Hosp. in Charterhouse, 1986–88. *Recreations:* sailing, cricket, tennis. *Address:* Royal Courts of Justice, Strand, WC2. *Clubs:* MCC; Hawks (Cambridge), Blakeney Sailing.

PORCHER, Michael Somerville, CMG 1962; OBE 1960; Secretary (Operations Division), Royal National Life-Boat Institution, 1964–83, retired; *b* 9 March 1921; *s* of late Geoffrey Lionel Porcher and Marjorie Fownes Porcher (*née* Somerville); *m* 1955, Mary Lorraine Porcher (*née* Tweedy); two *s*. *Educ:* Cheltenham College; St Edmund Hall, Oxford. Military Service, 1941–42. Joined Colonial Admin. Service: Sierra Leone; Cadet, 1942; Asst Dist, Comr, 1945; Dist Comr, 1951; British Guiana: Dep. Colonial Sec., 1952; Governor's Sec. and Clerk Exec. Council, 1953; Dep. Chief Sec., 1956. British Honduras: Colonial Secretary, 1960; Chief Secretary, 1961; retired, 1964. *Recreation:* fishing. *Address:* Bladon, Worth Matravers, near Swanage, Dorset BH19 3LQ.

PORCHESTER, Lord; George Reginald Oliver Molyneux Herbert; *b* 10 Nov. 1956; *s* and *heir* of Earl of Carnarvon, *qv*; *m* 1989, Jayne, *d* of K. A. Wilby, Cheshire; one *d*. *Educ:* St John's Coll., Oxford (BA). A Page of Honour to the Queen, 1969–73. *Address:* Dairy Farm Cottage, Highclere Park, Newbury RG15 9RN. *Club:* Turf.

PORRITT, family name of **Baron Porritt.**

PORRITT, Baron *cr* 1973 (Life Peer), of Wanganui, NZ, and of Hampstead; **Arthur Espie Porritt,** GCMG 1967 (KCMG 1950); GCVO 1970 (KCVO 1957); CBE 1945 (OBE 1943); Bt 1963; Vice-President, African Medical and Research Foundation, 1981–89 (Chairman, 1973–81); President, Arthritis and Rheumatism Council, 1979–88 (Chairman, 1973–79); *b* 10 Aug. 1900; *e s* of late E. E. Porritt, VD, MD, FRCS, Wanganui, New Zealand; *m* 1st, 1926, Mary Frances Wynne, *d* of William Bond; 2nd, 1946, Kathleen Mary, 2nd *d* of late A. S. Peck and Mrs Windley, Spalding, Lincs; two *s* one *d*. *Educ:* Wanganui Collegiate School, NZ; Otago University, NZ; Magdalen College, Oxford (Rhodes Scholar); St Mary's Hospital, London. MA Oxon.; MCh Oxon. Surgeon; St Mary's Hosp.; Hosp. of St John and St Elizabeth; King Edward VII Hosp. for Officers; Royal Masonic Hosp.; Consulting Surgeon: Princess Louise Kensington Hosp. for Children; Paddington Hosps; Royal Chelsea Hosp.; Civil Consulting Surgeon to the Army, 1954–67, Emeritus, 1971; Brigadier, RAMC, 21 Army Group; Surgeon-in-Ordinary to the Duke of York; Surgeon to HM Household; a Surgeon to King George VI, 1946–52; Sergeant-Surgeon to the Queen, 1952–67; Governor-General of New Zealand, 1967–72. Dir, Sterling Winthrop, 1973–. Chairman: Medical Advisory Cttee, Ministry of Overseas Develt; Medical Services Review Cttee, 1958; Red Cross Comr for NZ in UK; Chapter-Gen., Order of St John; Hunterian Soc., 1934–39 (Past Pres.); President: RCS, 1960–63; BMA, 1960–61 (Gold Medallist, 1964); RSM, 1966–67; Assoc. of Surgeons of Gt Britain and Ireland; Patron, Med. Council on Alcoholism; Pres., Med. Commn on Accident Prevention, 1973–89; Master, Soc. of Apothecaries, 1964–66; Vice-Pres., Royal Commonwealth Soc.; Pres., OUAC, 1925–26; holder of 100 yards and 220 yards hurdles records at Oxford and 100 yards Oxford v. Cambridge (9 9/10 seconds); represented Oxford in Athletics, 1923–26; Finalist, Olympic 100 metres (Bronze Medallist), Paris, 1924; Captain NZ Olympic Team, Paris, 1924, Amsterdam, 1928, Manager Berlin, 1936; Mem., Internat. Olympic Cttee, British Olympic Council; Vice-Pres., British Empire and Commonwealth Games Federation. Olympic Order (1st cl.), 1985. FRCS (Eng.); Fellow: Amer. Surgical Assoc.; Amer. Soc. of Clinical Surgery; French Acad. of Surgery; Hon. FRACS; Hon. FRCS (Ed.); Hon. FACS; Hon. FRCS (Glas.); Hon. FRCS (Can.); Hon. FCS (SAf); Hon. FRCS (I); Hon. FRCP; Hon. FRACP; Hon FRCOG; Hon. FRACR; Hon. Fellow, Magdalen College, Oxford, 1961. Hon. LLD: St Andrews; Birmingham; New Zealand; Otago. Hon. MD Bristol; Hon. DSc Oxon. Legion of Merit (USA); KStJ. *Publications:* Athletics (with D. G. A. Lowe), 1929; Essentials of Modern Surgery (with R. M. Handfield-Jones), 1938, 6th edn 1956; various surgical articles in medical jls. *Recreations:* riding, golf, swimming; formerly athletics and Rugby football. *Heir* (to baronetcy only): *s* Hon. Jonathon Espie Porritt, *qv. Address:* 57 Hamilton Terrace, NW8 9RG. *Club:* Buck's.

PORRITT, Hon. Jonathon (Espie); freelance writer and broadcaster; Director, Friends of The Earth, 1984–90; *b* 6 July 1950; *s* and *heir* (to Baronetcy) of Baron Porritt, *qv.*; *m* 1986, Sarah, *d* of Malcolm Staniforth, Malvern; one *d*. *Educ:* Eton; Magdalen Coll., Oxford (BA (First Cl.) Modern Languages). ILEA Teacher, 1975–84: Head of English and Drama, Burlington Danes School, W12, 1980–84. Presenter, Where on earth are we going?, BBC TV, 1990. Ecology Party: candidate: General Elections, 79 and 1983; European Elections, 1979 and 1984; Local Elections, 1977, 1978, 1982; Party Council Member, 1978–80, 1982–84; Chairman, 1979–80, 1982–84. *Publications:* Seeing Green - the Politics of Ecology, 1984; Friends of the Earth Handbook, 1987; The Coming of the Greens, 1988; Where on Earth are We Going?, 1991. *Recreation:* walking. *Address:* 17A Laurier Road, NW5.

PORT ELIZABETH, Bishop of, since 1975; **Rt. Rev. Bruce Read Evans;** *b* 10 Nov. 1929; *s* of Roy Leslie and Lilia Evans; *m* 1955, Joan Vanda Erlangsen; two *s* one *d*. *Educ:* King Edward Sch., Johannesburg; Univ. of the Witwatersrand, Johannesburg; Oak Hill Theological Coll., London. ACIS 1952; DipTh 1958; Diploma of Journalism, 1964. Director of companies, 1952–54. Ordained into CofE, Southwark, 1957; Curate, Holy Trinity, Redhill, Surrey, 1957–59; Senior Curate, St Paul's, Portman Square, W1, and Chaplain to West End Business Houses in London, 1959–61; Curate-in-Charge: St Luke's, Diep River, Cape, 1962; Christ Church, Kenilworth, Cape, 1963–69; Rector of St John's, Wynberg, Cape, 1969–75. International speaker. *Publications:* (jointly): I Will Heal their Land, 1974; The Earth is the Lord's, 1975; Facing the New Challenges, 1978; The Church and the Alternative Society, 1979. *Recreations:* formerly boxing and hockey; now painting. *Address:* Bishop's House, 75 River Road, Walmer, Port Elizabeth, CP, 6070, South Africa. *T:* 51–4296. *Club:* Port Elizabeth.

PORT MORESBY, Archbishop of, (RC), since 1981; **Most Rev. Sir Peter Kurongku,** KBE 1986; DD; *b* 1932; *s* of Adam Mapa and Eve Kawa. *Educ:* Holy Spirit National Seminary. Ordained priest, 1966; consecrated Bishop, 1978. *Address:* PO Box 1032, Boroko, Papua New Guinea. *T:* (office) 251192, (home) 253126.

PORT OF SPAIN, Archbishop of, since 1968; **Most Rev. Anthony Pantin,** CSSp; *b* 27 Aug. 1929; *s* of Julian and Agnes Pantin, both of Trinidad. *Educ:* Sacred Heart Private Sch., Belmont Boys' Intermediate Sch., St Mary's Coll., Port of Spain; Seminary of Philosophy, Montreal; Holy Ghost Missionary Coll., Dublin. Ordained Dublin, 1955; Guadeloupe, French West Indies, 1956–59; Fatima College, Port of Spain, 1959–64; Superior, St Mary's Coll., Port of Spain, 1965–68. Member: Vatican Secretariat for Christian Unity, 1971–83; Vatican Congregation for Evangelisation of Peoples, 1989–. Vice-Pres., Antilles Episcopal Conference, 1990– (Pres., 1979–84). Hon. FCP 1982. *Address:* Archbishop's House, 27 Maraval Road, Port of Spain, Trinidad. *T:* 622–1103.

PORTAL, family name of **Baroness Portal of Hungerford.**

PORTAL, Sir Jonathan (Francis), 6th Bt *cr* 1901; ACA; Group Financial Controller, Henderson Administration Group plc, since 1989; *b* 13 Jan. 1953; *s* of Sir Francis Spencer Portal, 5th Bt, and of Jane Mary, *d* of late Albert Henry Williams, OBE; *S* father, 1984; *m* 1982, Louisa Caroline, *er d* of F. J. C. G. Hervey-Bathurst, Somborne Park, near Stockbridge, Hants; two *s*. *Educ:* Marlborough; Univ. of Edinburgh (BCom). ACA 1977. Chief Accountant, Internat. Press Distributors, 1986–89. Mem., Clothworkers' Co. *Heir:* *s* William Jonathan Francis Portal, *b* 1 Jan. 1987. *Address:* 37 Napier Avenue, SW6 3PS.

PORTARLINGTON, 7th Earl of, *cr* 1785; **George Lionel Yuill Seymour Dawson-Damer;** Baron Dawson 1770; Viscount Carlow 1776; *b* 10 Aug. 1938; *er s* of Air Commodore Viscount Carlow (killed on active service, 1944) and Peggy (who *m* 2nd, 1945, Peter Nugent; she *d* 1963), *yr d* of late Charles Cambie; *S* grandfather, 1959; *m* 1961, Davina, *e d* of Sir Edward Windley, KCMG, KCVO; three *s* one *d*. *Educ:* Eton. Page of Honour to the Queen, 1953–55. Director: G. S. Yuill & Co. Ltd, Sydney, 1964; Yuills Australia, Sydney, 1983–; John Swire & Sons Pty Ltd, Sydney, 1988–; Australian Stock Breeders Co. Ltd, Brisbane, 1966. *Heir:* *s* Viscount Carlow, *qv. Recreations:* fishing, ski-ing, books. *Address:* 19 Coolong Road, Vaucluse, NSW 2030, Australia. *T:* Sydney 337–3013. *Clubs:* Union, Australian (Sydney); Royal Sydney Golf.

PORTEN, Anthony Ralph; QC 1988; *b* 1 March 1947; *s* of late Ralph Charles Porten and of Joan Porten (*née* Edden); *m* 1970, Kathryn Mary (*née* Edwards); two *d*. *Educ:* Epsom Coll.; Emmanuel Coll., Cambridge (BA; Athletics Blue, 1967). Called to the Bar, Inner Temple, 1969; joined Lincoln's Inn (*ad eund.*), 1973. Practising mainly in town and country planning and local government work. *Recreations:* family, walking, motoring. *Address:* Clive Cottage, Claremont Drive, Esher, Surrey. *T:* Esher (0372) 467513; 8 New Square, Lincoln's Inn, WC2A 3QP. *T:* 071–242 4986. *Clubs:* Royal Automobile; Hawks (Cambridge).

PORTEOUS, Christopher, MA; Headmaster of Eltham College, 1959–83; *b* 2 April 1921; *e s* of late Rev. Gilbert Porteous; *m* 1944, Amy Clunis, *d* of Theodore J. Biggs; one *s* three *d*. *Educ:* Nottingham High Sch. (Foundation Scholar); Emmanuel Coll., Cambridge (Senior Scholar). First Classes, with distinction, in Classical Tripos. Master of Classical Sixth, Mill Hill Sch., 1947–55; Asst Director, HM Civil Service Commission, 1955–59. Mem., Admiralty Interview Bd, 1975–. *Publication:* Eltham College, Past and Present, 1992. *Recreations:* travel, the countryside. *Address:* Little Thatch, Edwardstone, Suffolk CO6 5PR.

PORTEOUS, Christopher Selwyn; Solicitor to Commissioner of Police for the Metropolis, since 1987; *b* 8 Nov. 1935; *s* of Selwyn Berkeley Porteous (*né* Potous) and Marjorie Irene Porteous; *m* 1960, Brenda Jacqueline Wallis; four *d*. *Educ:* Dulwich Coll.; Law Society Sch. of Law. Articled to Clerk to Malling RDC, 1954–60; qual. as solicitor, 1960; LCC, 1960–62; Legal Asst with Scotland Yard, 1962–68; Sen. Legal Asst, 1968–76; Asst Solicitor, 1976–87. Anglican Reader, 1958–; Mem., Pastoral Cttee, Rochester Dio., 1984–88. *Recreations:* reading, poetry, hymn writing, walking. *Address:* c/o Solicitor's Department, New Scotland Yard, Broadway, SW1H 0BG. *T:* 071–230 7353.

PORTEOUS, James, DL; FEng 1986; FIEE; FInstE; FSS; Chairman and Chief Executive, Yorkshire Electricity Group plc, since 1990; *b* 29 Dec. 1926; *e s* of James and Isabella Porteous; *m* 1960, Sheila Beatrice (*née* Klotz); two *d*. *Educ:* Jarrow Grammar School; King's College, Durham University. BSc Hons. NESCo Ltd, NE Electricity Bd, NE Div., BEA, 1945–62; Central Electricity Generating Board: Operations Dept, HQ, 1962–66; System Op. Eng., Midlands Region, 1966–70; Dir, Operational Planning, SE Region, 1970–72; NE Region, 1972–75; Dir-Gen., Midlands Region, 1975–84; Chm., Yorks Electricity Bd, 1984–90. Mem., Electricity Council, 1984–90; Director: Electricity Association Ltd, 1990–; National Grid Company (Holdings) plc, 1990–. Chm., BR (Eastern) Board, 1990– (Mem., 1986–90); Mem., E Midlands Economic Planning Council, 1976–79. Dir, Peter Peregrinus Ltd, 1981–. Hon. DSc Aston, 1990; Hon. DEng Bradford, 1991. CBIM. DL N Yorks, 1991. *Recreations:* highland life, railways. *Address:* c/o Yorkshire Electricity Group plc, Scarcroft, Leeds LS14 3HS. *T:* Leeds (0532) 895040. *Club:* Caledonian.

PORTEOUS, Rev. Norman Walker, MA Edinburgh et Oxon, BD Edinburgh, DD St Andrews; *b* Haddington, 9 Sept. 1898; *yr s* of late John Dow Porteous, MA, formerly Rector of Knox Memorial Inst, Haddington, and Agnes Paton Walker; *m* 1929, May Hadwen (*d* 1981), *y d* of late John Cook Robertson, Kirkcaldy; three *s* three *d*. *Educ:* Knox Memorial Institute, Haddington; Universities of Edinburgh, Oxford (Trinity College), Berlin, Tübingen and Münster; New Coll., Edinburgh. MA Edinburgh with 1st Class Honours in Classics; MA Oxon with 1st Class in Literæ Humaniores; BD Edinburgh with distinction in Old Testament; 1st Bursar at Edinburgh University, 1916; C. B. Black Scholar in New Testament Greek, 1920; John Edward Baxter Scholar in Classics, 1923; Ferguson Scholar in Classics, 1923; Senior Cunningham Fellow at New College and Kerr Travelling Scholar, 1927; served in army, 1917–19, commissioned 2nd Lieut, March 1918, served overseas with 13th Royal Scots; Ordained to Ministry of United Free Church of Scotland, 1929; Minister of Crossgates Church, Church of Scotland, 1929–31; Regius Professor of Hebrew and Oriental Languages in the University of St Andrews, 1931–35; Professor of Old Testament Language, Literature and Theology in the University of Edinburgh, 1935–37; Prof. of Hebrew and Semitic Languages, Univ. of Edinburgh, 1937–68; Principal of New Coll., and Dean of Faculty of Divinity, Univ. of Edinburgh, 1964–68; retd, 1968; now Emeritus Professor. Hon. DD St Andrews, 1944; Lectures: Stone, Princeton Theological Seminary, 1953; Montague Burton, Leeds, 1974. President, Soc. for Old Testament Study, 1954. *Publications:* Das Alte Testament Deutsch 23: Das Danielbuch, 1962, 4th edn 1985 (English edition, 1965, 2nd, 1979); Living the Mystery: Collected Essays, 1967; Old Testament and History, 5 lectures in Annual of Swedish Theological Inst., vol. VIII, 1970–71; contributions to: Theologische Aufsätze Karl Barth zum 50 Geburtstag, 1936; Record and Revelation, 1938; The Old Testament and Modern Study, 1951; Peake's Commentary on the Bible, 1962. *Address:* 3 Hermitage Gardens, Edinburgh EH10 6DL. *T:* 031–447 4632.

PORTEOUS, Colonel Patrick Anthony, VC 1942; RA, retired 1970; *b* 1 Jan. 1918; *s* of late Brig.-General C. McL. Porteous, 9th Ghurkas, and late Mrs Porteous, Fleet, Hampshire; *m* 1943, Lois Mary (*d* 1953), *d* of late Maj.-General Sir H. E. Roome, KCIE; one *s* one *d*; *m* 1955, Deirdre, *d* of late Eric King; three *d*. *Educ:* Wellington Coll.; Royal Military Acad., Woolwich. BEF France, Sept. 1939–May 1940, with 6th AA Regt, RA; Dieppe, Aug. 1942 (VC); No 4 Commando, Dec. 1940–Oct. 1944; BLA June-Sept. 1944; 1st Airborne Div. Dec. 1944–July 1945; 6th Airborne Div., July 1945–March 1946; Staff Coll., Camberley, May-Nov. 1946; 16 Airborne Div. TA, Jan. 1947–Feb. 1948; 33 Airborne Lt Regt, RA, Feb. 1948–April 1949; No 1 Regular Commission Board, 1949; Instructor, RMA, Sandhurst, July 1950–July 1953; GHQ, Far East Land Forces, Singapore, Sept. 1953–July 1955; 1st Singapore Regt, RA, July-Dec. 1955; 14 Field Regt, RA, 1956–58; RAF Staff Coll., Jan. 1958–Dec. 1958; AMS, HQ Southern Comd, 1959–60; Colonel Junior Leaders Regt, RA, 1960–63; Colonel, General Staff War Office, later Ministry of Defence, 1963–66; Comdr Rheindahlen Garrison, 1966–69. *Recreation:* sailing. *Address:* Christmas Cottage, Church Lane, Funtington, W Sussex PO18 9LQ. *T:* Bosham (0243) 575315.

PORTER, family name of **Baron Porter of Luddenham.**

PORTER OF LUDDENHAM, Baron *cr* 1990 (Life Peer), of Luddenham in the County of Kent; **George Porter,** OM 1989; Kt 1972; BSc (Leeds); MA, PhD, ScD (Cambridge); FRS 1960; Professor, since 1987, and Chairman of the Centre for Photochemistry and Photosynthesis, Imperial College of Science, Technology and Medicine, London, since 1990; Chancellor of Leicester University, since 1986; Emeritus Professor, Royal Institution, since 1988; *b* 6 Dec. 1920; *m* 1949, Stella Jean Brooke; two *s*. *Educ:* Thorne Grammar Sch.; Leeds Univ.; Emmanuel Coll., Cambridge. Ackroyd Scholar, Leeds Univ., 1938–41. Served RNVR, Radar Officer, in Western Approaches and Mediterranean, 1941–45. Cambridge: Demonstrator in Physical Chemistry, 1949–52, Fellow of Emmanuel Coll., 1952–54; Hon. Fellow, 1967; Asst Director of Research in Physical Chemistry, 1952–54; Asst Director of British Rayon Research Assoc., 1954–55; Prof. of Physical Chemistry, 1955–63, Firth Prof. of Chemistry, 1963–66, Univ. of Sheffield; Resident Prof. and Dir, Royal Institution of Great Britain, 1966–85, Hon. Mem., 1988–. Member: ARC, 1964–66; Adv. Scientific Cttee, Nat. Gall., 1966–68; BBC Sci. Consultative Gp, 1967–75; Open Univ. Council, 1969–75; Science Mus. Adv. Council, 1970–73; Council and Science Bd, SRC, 1976–80; ACOST, 1987–. Trustee, BM, 1972–74. President: Chemical Soc., 1970–72 (Pres. Faraday Div., 1973–74); Comité

Internat. de photobiologie, 1968–72; Nat. Assoc. for Gifted Children, 1975–80; R&D Soc., 1977–82; Assoc. for Science Educn, 1985; BAAS, 1985–86; Royal Soc., 1985–90; Internat. Youth Sci. Fortnight, 1987–89. Counsellor, Inst. for Molecular Sci., Okasaki, Japan, 1980–83. Fairchild Scholar, CIT, 1974; Hitchcock Prof., Univ. of Calif at Berkeley, 1978; Gresham Prof. of Astronomy, Gresham Coll., 1990–. Lectures: Bakerian, 1977, Humphry Davy, 1985, Royal Soc.; Romanes, Oxford, 1978; Dimbleby, 1988; many other named lectures. Foreign Associate: Nat. Acad. of Scis; Amer. Acad. of Arts and Scis; Amer. Philos. Soc.; Pontifical Acad.; Japan Acad.; Accad. dei Lincei; Indian Nat. Science Acad.; Indian Acad. of Scis; acads of Madrid, Lisbon, Göttingen, Leopoldina, Hungary and NY; Foreign Mem., USSR Acad. of Sciences, 1988. Hon. Professor: Univ. of Kent; Beijing Tech. Univ.; Chinese Acad. of Scis; Hon. Fellow: Emmanuel Coll., Cambridge; QMC; Imperial Coll., London; Hon. FRSE 1983; Hon. FRSC 1991. Hon. Doctorates: Utah, Sheffield, East Anglia, Durham, Leeds, Leicester, Heriot-Watt, City, Manchester, St Andrews, London, Kent, Oxon, Hull, Instituto Quimica de Sarria, Barcelona, Pennsylvania, Coimbra, Lille, Open, Surrey, Bristol, Notre Dame, Reading, Loughborough, Brunel, Bologna, Rio de Janeiro, Philippines, Córdoba, Liverpool. Royal Society of Chemistry: Corday-Morgan Medal, 1955; Tilden Medal, 1958; Liversidge Medal, 1970; Faraday Medal, 1980; Longstaff Medal, 1981; (jtly) Nobel Prize for Chemistry, 1967; Silvanus Thompson Medal, 1969; Royal Society: Davy Medal, 1971; Rumford Medal, 1978; Kalinga Prize, UNESCO, 1977; first Porter Medal for photochemistry, Eur., Japanese and Inter-Amer. Photochemical Socs, 1988. *Publications:* Chemistry for the Modern World, 1962; scientific papers in Proc. Royal Society, Trans. Faraday Society, etc. TV Series: Laws of Disorder, 1965–66; Young Scientist of the Year, 1966–81; Time Machines, 1969–70; Controversy, 1971–75; Natural History of a Sunbeam, 1976–77. *Recreation:* sailing. *Address:* Department of Biology, Imperial College, SW7 2BB.

PORTER, Alastair Robert Wilson, CBE 1985; Secretary and Registrar, Royal College of Veterinary Surgeons, 1966–91, retired; barrister; *b* 28 Sept. 1928; *s* of late James and Olivia Porter (*née* Duncan); *m* 1954, Jennifer Mary Priaulx Forman; two *s* one *d*. *Educ:* Irvine Royal Academy; Glasgow Academy; Merton Coll., Oxford (MA). Called to Bar, Gray's Inn, 1952. Resident Magistrate, N Rhodesia, 1954; Registrar of High Court of N Rhodesia, 1961; Permanent Secretary: Min. of Justice, N Rhodesia, 1964; Min. of Justice, Govt of Republic of Zambia, Oct. 1964. Mem., Fedn (formerly Liaison Cttee) of Veterinarians of the EEC, 1966–86, Sec.-Gen., 1973–79; Chm., EEC's Adv. Cttee on Veterinary Trng, 1986–87 (Vice-Chm., 1981–86). Lectures: Wooldridge Meml, BVA Congress, 1976; MacKellar Meml, Western Counties Veterinary Assoc., Tavistock, 1978; Weipers, Glasgow Univ., 1985; Keith Entwhistle Meml, Cambridge Univ., 1987. Hon. Mem., BVA, 1978; Hon. Associate, RCVS, 1979. Centenary Prize, 1981, and Victory Medal, 1991, Central Vet. Soc.; Akademische Ehrenbürger, Hannover Veterinary Sch., 1988. *Publication:* (jtly) An Anatomy of Veterinary Europe, 1972. *Address:* 4 Savill Road, Lindfield, Haywards Heath, West Sussex RH16 2NX. *T:* Lindfield (0444) 482001. *Club:* Caledonian.

PORTER, Prof. Arthur, OC 1983; MSc, PhD (Manchester); FIEE; FCAE; FRSC 1970; Professor of Industrial Engineering, and Chairman of Department, University of Toronto, Toronto, 1961–76, now Emeritus Professor; President, Arthur Porter Associates Ltd, since 1973; Associate, Institute for Environmental Studies, University of Toronto, since 1981; *b* 8 Dec. 1910; *s* of late John William Porter and Mary Anne Harris; *m* 1941, Phyllis Patricia Dixon; one *s*. *Educ:* The Grammar Sch., Ulverston; University of Manchester. Asst Lecturer, University of Manchester, 1936–37; Commonwealth Fund Fellow, Massachusetts Inst. of Technology, USA, 1937–39; Scientific Officer, Admiralty, 1939–45; Principal Scientific Officer, National Physical Laboratory, 1946; Prof. of Instrument Technology, Royal Military Coll. of Science, 1946–49; Head, Research Division, Ferranti Electric Ltd, Toronto, Canada, 1949–55; Professor of Light Electrical Engineering, Imperial College of Science and Technology, University of London, 1955–58; Dean of the College of Engineering, Saskatchewan Univ., Saskatoon, 1958; Acting Dir, Centre for Culture and Technology, Toronto Univ., 1967–68; Academic Comr, Univ. of W Ontario, 1969–71. Dir and Founding Chm., Scientists and Engineers for Energy and Environment Inc., 1981–84. Chairman: Canadian Environmental Adv. Council, 1972–75; Ontario Royal Commn on Electric Power Planning, 1975–80. *Publications:* An Introduction to Servomechanisms, 1950; Cybernetics Simplified, 1969; Towards a Community University, 1971; articles in Trans. Royal Society, Proc. Royal Society, Phil. Mag., Proc. Inst. Mech. Eng, Proc. IEE, Nature, etc. *Recreations:* tennis, travel, energy conservation. *Address:* PO Box GB-85, Alliston, Ont L0M 1A0, Canada. *T:* (705) 435–3988; (winter) Apt 603, Imperial Club, 3399 Gulf Shore Boulevard N, Naples, Fla 33940, USA. *T:* (813) 263–2540. *Clubs:* Athenæum; Arts and Letters, National (Toronto); Wyndemere (Naples, Florida).

PORTER, Arthur Thomas, MRSL 1979; MA, PhD; Vice-Chancellor, University of Sierra Leone, Freetown, Sierra Leone, 1974–84; *b* 26 Jan. 1924; *m* 1953, Rigmor Sondergaard (*née* Rasmussen); one *s* one *d*. *Educ:* Fourah Bay Coll. (BA Dunelm); Cambridge Univ. (BA (Hist Tripos), MA); Boston Univ. (PhD). Asst, Dept of Social Anthropology, Edinburgh Univ., UK, 1951–52. Prof. of History and Head of Dept of Hist., also Dir of Inst. of African Studies, Fourah Bay Coll., 1963–64; Principal, University Coll., Nairobi, Univ. of E Africa, 1964–70; UNESCO Field Staff Officer; Educl Planning Adviser, Min. of Educn, Kenya, 1970–74. Mem. Exec. Bd, UNESCO, 1976–80. Africanus Horton Meml Lectr, Edinburgh Univ., 1983; Fulbright Schol.-in-Residence, Bethany Coll., Kansas, 1986–87. Chm., Bd of Dirs, Sierra Leone Nat. Diamond Mining Co., 1976–85. Hon. LHD Boston 1969; Hon. LLD Royal Univ. of Malta 1969; Hon. DLitt Univ. of Sierra Leone, 1988. Phi Beta Kappa 1972. Symonds Medal, ACU, 1985. *Publications:* Creoledom, a Study of the Development of Freetown Society, 1963; contribs to The Times, Africa, African Affairs. *Recreation:* photography. *Address:* 26b Spur Road, Wilberforce, PO Box 1363, Freetown, Sierra Leone, West Africa. *T:* 31736; 81 Fitzjohn Avenue, Barnet, Herts EN5 2HN. *T:* 081–441 1551.

PORTER, Barry; *see* Porter, G. B.

PORTER, Rt. Rev. David Brownfield; *b* 10 May 1906; *s* of Sydney Lawrence Porter and Edith Alice Porter; *m* 1936, Violet Margaret Eliot (*d* 1956); one *s*; *m* 1961, Mrs Pamela Cecil (*née* Lightfoot) (*d* 1974), *widow* of Neil McNeill. *Educ:* Hertford Coll., Oxford. Curate of St Augustine's, Leeds, 1929; Tutor of Wycliffe Hall, Oxford, 1931; Chaplain, 1933; Chaplain of Wadham Coll., Oxford, 1934; Vicar of All Saints', Highfield, Oxford, 1935; Vicar of Darlington, 1943; Rector of St John's, Princes Street, Edinburgh, 1947–61; Dean of Edinburgh, 1954–61; Bishop Suffragan of Aston, 1962–72. Select Preacher, Oxford Univ., 1964. *Recreations:* fishing and painting. *Address:* Silver Leys, Brockhampton, near Cheltenham GL54 5TH. *T:* Cheltenham (0242) 820431.

PORTER, David John; MP (C) Waveney, since 1987; *b* 16 April 1948; *s* of late George Porter and of Margaret Porter; *m* 1978, Sarah Jane Shaw; two *s* two *d*. *Educ:* Lowestoft Grammar School; New College of Speech and Drama, London. Teacher, London, 1970–72; Dir and Co-Founder, Vivid Children's Theatre, 1972–78; Head of Drama, Benjamin Britten High School, Lowestoft, 1978–81; Conservative Party Agent: Eltham, 1982–83; Norwich North, 1983–84; Waveney, 1985–87. Mem., Select Cttee on Social Security, 1991–. *Recreations:* family, Waveney area—past, present and future. *Address:* House of Commons, Westminster, SW1A 0AA. *T:* 071–219 6235/3516.

PORTER, Dorothea Noelle Naomi, (Thea Porter); fashion designer, since 1967; *b* 24 Dec. 1927; *d* of Rev. Dr M. S. Seale and Renée Seale; *m* 1953, Robert S. Porter (marr. diss. 1967); one *d*. *Educ:* Lycée français, Damascus; Fernhill Manor; Royal Holloway Coll., London Univ. Embassy wife, Beirut; fashion designer, 1967–, interior and fabric designer. *Recreations:* cooking, travelling, music, painting, collecting antique Islamic fabrics and objets; consulting clairvoyants. *Address:* 13 Bolton Street, W1Y 7PA. *Club:* Colony Room.

PORTER, Eric (Richard); actor; *b* London, 8 April 1928; *s* of Richard John Porter and Phoebe Elizabeth (*née* Spall). *Educ:* LCC and Wimbledon Technical College. First professional appearance with Shakespeare Memorial Theatre Company, Arts, Cambridge, 1945; first appearance on London stage as Dunois' Page in Saint Joan with the travelling repertory company, King's, Hammersmith, 1946; Birmingham Repertory Theatre, 1948–50; under contract to H. M. Tennant, Ltd, 1951–53. *Plays include:* The Silver Box, Lyric, Hammersmith, 1951; The Three Sisters, Aldwych, 1951; Thor, With Angels, Lyric, Hammersmith, 1951; title role in Noah, Whitehall, 1951; The Same Sky, Lyric, Hammersmith, 1952; Under the Sycamore Tree, Aldwych, 1952; season at Lyric, Hammersmith, directed by John Gielgud, 1953–plays: Richard II, The Way of the World, Venice Preserved; with Bristol Old Vic Company, 1954, and again 1955–56; parts included title roles in King Lear, Uncle Vanya, Volpone; with Old Vic Company, 1954–55: parts included Jacques in As You Like It, title role in Henry IV, Bolingbroke in Richard II, Christopher Sly in The Taming of the Shrew; Romanoff and Juliet, Piccadilly, 1956; A Man of Distinction, Edinburgh Festival and Princes, 1957; Time and Again, British tour with the Lunts, 1957, and New York in The Visit, 1958; The Coast of Coromandel, English tour, 1959; Rosmersholm, Royal Court, 1959, Comedy, 1960. (Evening Standard Drama Award as Best Actor of 1959); under contract to Royal Shakespeare Company, 1960–65; parts: Malvolio in Twelfth Night, Stratford, 1960, Aldwych, 1961; Duke in The Two Gentlemen of Verona, Stratford, 1960; Leontes in The Winter's Tale, Stratford, 1960; Ulysses in Troilus and Cressida, Stratford, 1960; Ferdinand in The Duchess of Malfi, Stratford, 1960, Aldwych, 1961; Lord Chamberlain in Ondine, Aldwych, 1961; Buckingham in Richard III, Stratford, 1961; title role in Becket, Aldwych, 1961, Globe, 1962; title role in Macbeth, Stratford, 1962; Iachimo in Cymbeline, Stratford, 1962; Pope Pius XII in The Representative, Aldwych, 1963. Stratford Season, 1964; Bolingbroke in Richard II; Henry IV in Henry IV Parts I and II; Chorus in Henry V; Richmond in Richard III; Stratford Season, 1965: Barabas in The Jew of Malta; Shylock in The Merchant of Venice; Chorus in Henry V, Aldwych, 1965; Ossip in The Government Inspector, Aldwych, 1966; Stratford Season, 1968; Lear in King Lear; Faustus in Dr Faustus (US tour, 1969); Paul Thomsen in My Little Boy-My Big Girl (also directed), Fortune, 1969; The Protagonist, Brighton, 1971; Peter Pan, Coliseum, 1971; Malvolio, inaugural season, St George's Elizabethan Theatre, 1976; Big Daddy in Cat on a Hot Tin Roof, National, 1988 (Evening Standard Drama Award, Best Actor); title rôle in King Lear, Old Vic, 1989; Malvolio in Twelfth Night, Playhouse, 1991. *Films:* The Fall of the Roman Empire, 1964; The Pumpkin Eater, 1964; The Heroes of Telemark, 1965; Kaleidoscope, 1966; The Lost Continent, 1968; Hands of the Ripper, Nicholas and Alexandra, Antony and Cleopatra, 1971; Hitler: the last ten days, 1973; The Day of the Jackal, 1973; The Belstone Fox, 1973; Callan, 1974; Hennessy, 1975; The Thirty-Nine Steps, 1978; Little Lord Fauntleroy, 1980; *television parts include:* Soames Forsyte in The Forsyte Saga, BBC (Best Actor Award, Guild of TV Producers and Directors, 1967); Karenin, in Anna Karenina, BBC, 1977; Alanbrooke in Churchill and the Generals, BBC, 1979; Polonius in Hamlet, BBC, 1980; Dep. Governor Danforth in The Crucible, BBC, 1981; Neville Chamberlain in Winston Churchill: The Wilderness Years, Southern, 1981; Count Bronowsky in The Jewel in the Crown, 1983; Moriarty in Sherlock Holmes, 1984; Fagin in Oliver Twist, 1985. *Recreations:* walking, model railways. *Address:* c/o Duncan Heath Associates, 162 Wardour Street, W1.

PORTER, George Barrington, (Barry); MP (C) Wirral South, since 1983 (Bebington and Ellesmere Port, 1979–83); *b* 11 June 1939; *s* of Kenneth William Porter and Vera Porter; *m* 1965, Susan Carolyn James; two *s* three *d*. *Educ:* Birkenhead Sch.; University Coll., Oxford (BA Hons). Admitted solicitor, 1965. Councillor: Birkenhead County Bor. Council, 1967–74; Wirral Bor., 1975–79 (Chm., Housing Cttee, 1976–77, and Educn Cttee, 1977–79). Mem., Select Cttee on Trade and Industry; Sec., All Party Parly Solicitors Gp. *Recreations:* golf, Rugby Union football, watching cricket, real ale. *Address:* House of Commons, SW1A 0AA. *Clubs:* Royal Commonwealth Society, Royal Automobile; Oxton Conservative, Ellesmere Port Conservative; Birkenhead Park Football, Wirral Ladies Golf, Birkenhead Squash Racquets, Oxton Cricket.

PORTER, Ivor Forsyth, CMG 1963; OBE 1944; HM Diplomatic Service, retired; *b* 12 Nov. 1913; *s* of Herbert and Evelyn Porter; *m* 1951, Ann, *o d* of late Dr John Speares (marr. diss., 1961); *m* 1961, Katerina, *o c* of A. T. Cholerton; one *s* one *d*. *Educ:* Barrow Grammar Sch.; Leeds Univ. (BA, PhD). Lecturer at Bucharest Univ., 1939–40; Temp. Secretary, at Bucharest Legation, 1940–41; Raiding Forces, 1941–45 (Major). Joined Foreign (subseq. Diplomatic) Service, May 1946, as 2nd Secretary in Sen. Branch; 1st Secretary 1948; transferred to Washington, 1951; Foreign Office, 1953; UK Delegation to NATO Paris as Counsellor and Head of Chancery, 1956; Nicosia, 1959 (Deputy Head UK Mission), Deputy High Commissioner, 1961–62, Cyprus; Permanent Rep. to Council of Europe, Strasbourg, 1962–65 (with personal rank of Minister); Dep. High Commissioner, Eastern India, 1965–66; Ambassador, UK Delegn to Geneva Disarmament Conf., 1968–71 (Minister, 1967–68); Ambassador to Senegal, Guinea, Mali and Mauritania, 1971–73; later Dir, Atlantic Region, Research Dept, FCO, retired. *Publications:* (as Ivor Crane) The Think Trap (novel), 1972; Operation Autonomous: with SOE in wartime Roumania, 1989. *Recreations:* writing, walking. *Address:* 17 Redcliffe Road, SW10. *Clubs:* Travellers', PEN.

PORTER, James Forrest, CBE 1991; Director General (formerly Director) of the Commonwealth Institute, 1978–91; Leverhulme Research Fellow, and Visiting Fellow, London University Institute of Education, since 1991; *b* Frodsham, Cheshire, 2 Oct. 1928; *s* of Ernest Porter and Mary Violetta Porter; *m* 1952, Dymphna, *d* of Leo Francis Powell, London; two *d*. *Educ:* Salford Grammar Sch.; LSE (BSc Sociol.); Univ. of London Inst. of Educn (MA). Asst Master, St George in the East Sec. Sch., Stepney, 1948–50; Leverhulme Scholar, Univ. of London, 1950–55; Lectr in Sociol. and Educn, Worcester Coll., 1955–60; Head of Educn Dept, Chorley Coll., 1960–62; Dep. Principal, Coventry Coll., 1962–67; Principal, Bulmershe Coll. of Higher Educn, Reading, 1967–78. Director: bi-annual internat. courses on teacher educn, Brit. Council, 1975, 1977, 1979, on Museum Educn, 1982; Adult Literacy Support Services Fund, 1977–81. Consultant: Finland, 1976; Unesco, Paris, 1979–; Commonwealth Fellow, Australia, 1977. Chairman: World Educn Fellowship, 1979–82; Newsconcern Foundn, 1984–; Member: Nat. Cttee of Inquiry into Teacher Educn and Trng (James Cttee), 1971; Educn Cttee, UGC, 1970–78; Educnl Adv. Council, IBA, 1970–80; Nat. Council for Dance Educn, 1978; Exec. Cttee, Internat. Council of Museums, 1981–; Educn Council, BBC, 1987–; Pres., British Comparative

Educn Soc., 1983–84. Member: UK Delegn to Unesco, Geneva, 1975 (Vice-Pres., Commn on Changing Role of Teacher); Unesco Missions to Morocco and Senegal, 1982, to Jordan, 1983. Mem., Educn Council, Royal Opera House, Covent Garden, 1985–. Mem., Editorial Bd, Higher Education Review, 1974–; Chm., Editorial Bd, Commonwealth Today, 1985– (Mem., 1982). FRSA 1978; Hon. FCP 1978; FRGS 1984. *Publications:* (ed) Rural Development and the Changing Countries of the World, 1969; (with N. Goble) The Changing Role of the Teacher, Paris 1977. *Recreations:* writing, river watching. *Address:* House by the Water, Bolney Avenue, Shiplake, Oxon. *Clubs:* Athenæum, Commonwealth Trust.

PORTER, Air Vice-Marshal John Alan, OBE 1973; CEng, FRAeS, FIEE; Director, Science and Technology, Government Communications Headquarters, Cheltenham, since 1991; *b* 29 Sept. 1934; *s* of late Alan and Etta Porter. Educ: Lawrence Sheriff School, Rugby; Bristol Univ. (BSc); Southampton Univ. (Dip Soton). Commissioned in Engineer Branch, RAF, 1953; appts in UK, USA and Cyprus, 1953–79; Royal College of Defence Studies, 1980; Dep. Gen. Manager, NATO MRCA Develt and Production Agency (NAMMA), Munich, 1981–84; Dir-Gen. Aircraft 2, MoD(PE), 1984–88; Dir-Gen., Communications, Inf. Systems and Orgn (RAF), 1988–89; RAF retd, 1989. Dir, Communications-Electronics Security Gp, GCHQ, 1989–91. *Recreations:* music, horology. *Address:* c/o R3, Cox's and King's Branch, Lloyds Bank, 7 Pall Mall, SW1. *Club:* Royal Air Force.

PORTER, John Andrew, TD; JP; DL; Partner, Porter and Cobb, as Chartered Surveyor, 1940–81; *b* 18 May 1916; *s* of late Horace Augustus Porter, DFC, JP, and Vera Marion Porter; *m* 1941, Margaret Isobel Wisnom; two *d*. *Educ:* Radley Coll.; Sidney Sussex Coll., Cambridge (MA). Commissioned RA, TA, 1938; served War, 1939–46, Lt-Col. Director: Kent County Building Soc., 1947 (Chm., 1965–68); Hastings and Thanet Building Soc., 1968–78 (Chm., 1972–78); Anglia, Hastings and Thanet, later Anglia, Building Soc., 1978–87 (Chm., 1978–81). JP Gravesham PSD, 1952, Chm., Gravesham Div., 1976–83, Dep. Chm., 1983–. Pres., Gravesend Cons. Assoc., 1965–77. Chm., Bd of Govs, Cobham Hall Sch., 1987–. General Commissioner of Taxes, 1970–90. DL Kent, 1984. *Recreations:* cricket, reading, golf. *Address:* Leaders, Hodsoll Street, near Wrotham, Kent TN15 7LH. *T:* Fairseat (0732) 822260. *Clubs:* Royal Automobile, MCC; Hawks (Cambridge); Kent CC (Pres., 1985–86).

PORTER, Sir John Simon H.; *see* Horsbrugh-Porter.

PORTER, Prof. Rev. Canon (Joshua) Roy; Professor of Theology, University of Exeter, 1962–86 (Head of Department, 1962–85), now Professor Emeritus; *b* 7 May 1921; *s* of Joshua Porter and Bessie Evelyn (*née* Earlam). *Educ:* King's Sch., Macclesfield; Merton Coll., Oxford (Exhibnr); S Stephen's House, Oxford. BA: Mod. Hist. (Cl. I), Theology (Cl. I), MA Oxon. Liddon Student, 1942; Deacon 1945, Priest 1946; Curate of S Mary, Portsea, 1945–47; Resident Chaplain to Bp of Chichester, 1947–49; Hon. Chaplain, 1949–50; Examining Chaplain from 1950; Fellow, Chaplain and Lectr, Oriel Coll., Oxford, 1949–62; Tutor, 1950–62; Kennicott Hebrew Fellow, 1955; Sen. Denyer and Johnson Schol., 1958; Select Preacher: Univs of Oxford, 1953–55, Cambridge, 1957, TCD, 1958; Canon and Preb. of Wightring and Theol Lectr in Chichester Cath., 1965–88; Wiccamical Canon and Preb. of Exceit, 1988–; Vis. Prof., Southeastern Seminary, Wake Forest, N Carolina, 1967; Dean of Arts, Univ. of Exeter, 1968–71; Proctor in Convocation of Canterbury for dio. of Exeter, 1964–75; for Other Univs (Canterbury), 1975–; Examining Chaplain to Bps of Peterborough, 1973–86, of Truro, 1973–81, of London, 1981–, and of Gibraltar in Europe, 1989–. Ethel M. Wood Lectr, Univ. of London 1979; Michael Harrah Wood Lectr, Univ. of the South, Sewanee, Tenn, 1984; Lectr in Old Testament Studies, Holyrood Seminary, NY, 1987–. Member: Gen. Synod, 1970–90 (Panel of Chairmen, 1984–86); ACCM, 1975–86; Council of Management, Coll. of St Mark and St John, 1980–85; Vice-Pres., Folklore Soc., 1979– (Pres., 1976–79); President: Soc. for OT Study, 1983; Anglican Assoc., 1986–; Vice-Chm., Prayer Book Soc., 1987–. FAMS. *Publications:* World in the Heart, 1944; Moses and Monarchy, 1963; The Extended Family in the Old Testament, 1967; Proclamation and Presence, 1970, 2nd rev. edn, 1983; The Non-Juring Bishops, 1973; Leviticus, 1976, Japanese edn 1984; Animals in Folklore, 1978; The Crown and the Church, 1978; Folklore and the Old Testament, 1981; trans. C. Westermann, The Living Psalms, 1989; Synodical Government in the Church of England, 1990; *contributor to:* Promise and Fulfilment, 1963; A Source Book of the Bible for Teachers, 1970; The Journey to the Other World, 1975; Tradition and Interpretation, 1979; A Basic Introduction to the Old Testament, 1980; Divination and Oracles, 1981; Folklore Studies in the Twentieth Century, 1981; The Folklore of Ghosts, 1981; Israel's Prophetic Tradition, 1982; Tracts for Our Times, 1983; The Hero in Tradition and Folklore, 1984; Harper's Bible Dictionary, 1985; Arabia and the Gulf: from traditional society to modern states, 1986; Oxford Companion to the Bible, 1988; The Seer in Celtic and Other Traditions, 1989; Schöpfung und Befreiung, 1989; A Dictionary of Biblical Interpretation, 1990; Christianity and Conservatism, 1990; Oil of Gladness, 1991; numerous articles in learned jls and dictionaries. *Recreations:* theatre and opera, book-collecting, travel. *Address:* 36 Theberton Street, Barnsbury, N1 0QX. *T:* 071–354 5861; 68 Sand Street, Longbridge Deverill, near Warminster, Wilts BA12 7DS. *T:* Warminster (0985) 40311. *Club:* Royal Over-Seas League.

PORTER, Sir Leslie, Kt 1983; President, Tesco PLC, 1985–90 (Chairman, 1973–85; Deputy Chairman and Managing Director, 1972–73); *b* 10 July 1920; *s* of late Henry Alfred and Jane Porter; *m* 1949, Shirley Cohen (*see* Dame Shirley Porter); one *s* one *d*. *Educ:* Holloway County Sch. Joined family textile business (J. Porter & Co), 1938. Served War: Techn. Quartermaster Sergt, 1st Bn The Rangers, KRRC, in Egypt, Greece, Crete, Libya, Tunisia, Algeria, Italy, 1939–46. Re-joined J. Porter & Co, 1946; became Managing Dir, 1955. Joined Tesco Stores (Holdings) Ltd: Dir, 1959; Asst Managing Dir, 1964; Dep. Chm., 1970. Member of Lloyd's, 1964– (John Poland syndicate). Pres., Inst. of Grocery Distribution, 1977–80. Vice-President: Age Concern England; NPFA; Chm., Sports Aid Foundn, 1985–88 (Hon. Vice Pres., 1988–). Internat. Vice-Pres., Mus. of the Diaspora, 1984–. Hon. Chm., Bd of Governors, Tel Aviv Univ., 1989–; Governor, Hong Kong Baptist Coll.; Hon. PhD (Business Management), Tel Aviv Univ., 1973. *Recreations:* golf, yachting, bridge. *Clubs:* Royal Automobile, City Livery, Rugby; Dyrham Park County (Barnet, Herts); Coombe Hill Golf (Kingston Hill, Surrey); Frilford Heath Golf (Abingdon).

PORTER, Marguerite Ann, (Mrs Nicky Henson); Guest Artist, Royal Ballet Co., since 1986 (Senior Principal Dancer, 1976–85); *b* 30 Nov. 1948; *d* of William Albert and Mary Porter; *m* (marr. diss.); *m* 1986, Nicky Henson, *qv*; one *s*. *Educ:* Doncaster. Joined Royal Ballet School, 1964; graduated to Royal Ballet Co., 1966; soloist, 1972; Principal, 1976; favourite roles include: Juliet in Romeo and Juliet, Manon, Natalia in A Month in the Country. *Film:* Comrade Lady. *Publication:* Ballerina: a dancer's life, 1989. *Recreations:* my family, friends. *Address:* c/o Richard Jackson, 59 Knightsbridge, SW1X 7RA.

PORTER, Air Marshal Sir (Melvin) Kenneth (Drowley), KCB 1967 (CB 1959); CBE 1945 (OBE 1942); Royal Air Force, retired; *b* 19 Nov. 1912; *s* of late Flt Lieut Edward Ernest Porter, MBE, DCM and late Helen Porter; *m* 1940, Elena, *d* of F. W. Sinclair; two *s* one *d*. *Educ:* No. 1 School of Technical Training, Halton; RAF Coll., Cranwell. Commissioned, 1932; Army Co-operation Sqdn, Fleet Air Arm, 1933–36, as PO and FO; specialised on Signals, 1936–37, Flt-Lieut; Sqdn Leader, 1939. Served War of 1939–45 (despatches thrice, OBE, CBE, Legion of Merit, USA); Chief Signals Officer, Balloon Command, 1939; DCSO and CSO, HQ No. 11 Group, 1940–42; Temp. Wing Comdr, 1941; CSO, HQ 2nd TAF, 1943–45; Temp Gp Captain, 1943; Actg Air Commodore, 1944–45; CSO, HQ Bomber Command, 1945; Air Min. Tech. Plans, 1946–47, Gp Captain, 1946; Member Directing Staff, RAF Staff Coll., Andover, 1947–49; Senior Tech. Staff Officer, HQ No. 205 Group, 1950–52; Comdg Nos 1 and 2 Air Signallers Schools, 1952–54; CSO HQ 2nd ATAF, 1954–55; CSO, HQ Fighter Command, Actg Air Commodore, 1955–58, Air Cdr, 1958; Student Imperial Defence Coll., 1959; Commandant of No 4 School of Technical Training, RAF St Athan, Glamorgan, and Air Officer Wales, 1960–61; Actg Air Vice-Marshal, 1961; Air Vice-Marshal, 1962; Director-General: Ground Training, 1961–63; of Signals (Air), Ministry of Defence, 1964–66; AOC-in-C, Maintenance Command, 1966–70; Hd of RAF Engineer Branch, 1968–70; Actg Air Marshal, 1966; Air Marshal, 1967. Dir of Tech. Educn Projects, UC Cardiff, 1970–74. CEng 1966; FIEE; FRAeS; FBIM. *Recreation:* reading. *Address:* c/o Lloyds Bank, Redland Branch, 163 Whiteladies Road, Clifton, Bristol BS6 6XA.

PORTER, Hon. Sir Murray (Victor), Kt 1970; Agent-General for Victoria in London, 1970–76; *b* 20 Dec. 1909; *s* of late V. Porter, Pt Pirie, SA; *m* 1932, Edith Alice Johnston, *d* of late C. A. Johnston; two *d*. *Educ:* Brighton (Victoria) Grammar Sch., Australia. Served War, 2nd AIF, 1941–45. MLA (Liberal) Sandringham, Victoria, 1955–70; Govt Whip, 1955–56; Asst Minister, 1956–58; Minister for: Forests, 1958–59; Local Govt, 1959–64; Public Works, 1964–70. *Recreations:* golf, swimming. *Address:* Flat 7, The Point, 405 Beach Road, Beaumaris, Victoria 3193, Australia. *Clubs:* Melbourne Cricket, Royal Melbourne Golf, Royal Automobile Club of Victoria.

PORTER, Peter Neville Frederick, FRSL; freelance writer, poet; *b* Brisbane, 16 Feb. 1929; *s* of William Ronald Porter and Marion Main; *m* 1961, Jannice Henry (*d* 1974); two *d*. *Educ:* Church of England Grammar Sch., Brisbane; Toowoomba Grammar Sch. Worked as journalist in Brisbane before coming to England in 1951; clerk, bookseller and advertising writer, before becoming full-time poet, journalist, reviewer and broadcaster in 1968. Chief work done in poetry and English literature. Hon. DLitt: Melbourne, 1985; Loughborough, 1987. *Publications:* Once Bitten, Twice Bitten, 1961; Penguin Modern Poets No 2, 1962; Poems, Ancient and Modern, 1964; A Porter Folio, 1969; The Last of England, 1970; Preaching to the Converted, 1972; (trans.) After Martial, 1972; (with Arthur Boyd) Jonah, 1973; (with Arthur Boyd) The Lady and the Unicorn, 1975; Living in a Calm Country, 1975; (jt ed) New Poetry 1, 1975; The Cost of Seriousness, 1978; English Subtitles, 1981; Collected Poems, 1983 (Duff Cooper Prize); Fast Forward, 1984; (with Arthur Boyd) Narcissus, 1985; The Automatic Oracle, 1987 (Whitbread Poetry Award, 1988); (with Arthur Boyd) Mars, 1988; A Porter Selected, 1989; Possible Worlds, 1989. *Recreations:* buying records and listening to music; travelling in Italy. *Address:* 42 Cleveland Square, W2. *T:* 071–262 4289.

PORTER, Prof. Robert, DM, FRACP, FAA; Dean, Faculty of Medicine, Monash University, Victoria, since 1989; *b* 10 Sept. 1932; *s* of William John Porter and late Amy Porter (*née* Tottman); *m* 1961, Anne Dorothy Steell; two *s* two *d*. *Educ:* Univ. of Adelaide (BMedSc, DSc); Univ. of Oxford (MA, BCh, DM). Rhodes Scholarship, South Australia, 1954; Radcliffe Travelling Fellowship in Med. Sci., University Coll., Oxford, 1962; Lectr, Univ. Lab. of Physiology, Oxford, 1960–67; Fellow, St Catherine's Coll., and Medical Tutor, Oxford, 1963–67; Prof. of Physiology and Chm., Dept of Physiology, Monash Univ., 1967–79; Howard Florey Prof. of Med. Res., and Dir, John Curtin Sch. of Med. Res., ANU, 1980–89; Fogarty Scholar-in-Residence, NIH, 1986–87. Member: Bd of Dirs, Alfred Gp of Hosps and Monash Med. Centre, 1989–; Bd of Govs, Menzies Sch. of Health Res., Darwin, 1985–; Bd of Management, Baker Med. Res. Inst., 1980–. *Publications:* Cortico-Spinal Neurones: their role in movement (with C. G. Phillips), 1977; articles on neurophysiology and control of movement by the brain. *Recreations:* outdoor sports. *Address:* 7 Beach Street, Balnarring Beach, Vic 3926, Australia. *T:* (home) (059) 831518; (office) (03) 5654318.

PORTER, Rt. Rev. Robert George, OBE 1952; Bishop of The Murray, 1970–89; *b* 7 Jan. 1924; *s* of Herbert James and Eileen Kathleen Porter; *m* 1954, Elizabeth Mary Williams; two *d*. *Educ:* Canterbury Boys' High School; St John's Theological Coll., Morpeth, NSW; Moore College, Sydney (ThL Hons). Served with AIF, 1942–44. Deacon 1947, priest 1948; Assistant Curate, Christ Church Cathedral, Ballarat, Victoria, 1947–49; Assistant Curate, St Paul's, Burwood, Sydney, 1949–50; Priest in charge of Isivita and Agenehambo, Diocese of New Guinea, 1950–57; Archdeacon of Ballarat, 1957–70; Assistant Bishop of Ballarat, 1967–70. *Recreations:* gardening, reading. *Address:* 48 Eleanor Terrace, Murray Bridge, SA 5253, Australia. *T:* 32 2240.

PORTER, Robert Stanley, CB 1972; OBE 1959; Deputy Secretary (Chief Economist), Overseas Development Administration, Foreign and Commonwealth Office (formerly Ministry of Overseas Development), 1980–84; retired; *b* 17 Sept. 1924; *s* of S. R. Porter; *m* 1st, 1953, Dorothea Naomi (marr. diss. 1967), *d* of Rev. Morris Seale; one *d*; 2nd, 1967, Julia Karen, *d* of Edmund A. Davies. *Educ:* St Clement Danes, Holborn Estate, Grammar Sch.; New Coll., Oxford. Research Economist, US Economic Cooperation Administration Special Mission to the UK, 1949; British Middle East Development Division: Asst Statistical Adviser, Cairo, 1951; Statistical Adviser and Economist, Beirut, 1955; Min. of Overseas Development: Dir, Geographical Div., Economic Planning Staff, 1965; Dep. Dir-Gen. of Economic Planning, 1967; Dir-Gen. of Economic Planning, 1969. Vis. Prof., David Livingstone Inst. for Overseas Develt Studies, 1984–87. *Publications:* articles in Oxford Economic Papers, Kyklos, Review of Income and Wealth, ODI Development Policy Review. *Recreations:* music, theatre. *Address:* Lower Saunders, Cheriton Fitzpaine, Crediton, Devon EX17 4JA. *T:* Cheriton Fitzpaine (0363) 866645. *Club:* Athenæum.

PORTER, Rt. Hon. Sir Robert (Wilson), Kt 1971; PC (NI) 1969; QC (NI) 1965; County Court Judge, Northern Ireland, since 1978; *b* 23 Dec. 1923; *s* of late Joseph Wilson Porter and late Letitia Mary (*née* Wasson); *m* 1953, Margaret Adelaide, *y d* of late F. W. Lynas; one *s* one *d* (and one *d* decd). *Educ:* Model Sch. and Foyle Coll., Londonderry; Queen's Univ., Belfast. RAFVR, 1943–46; Royal Artillery (TA), 1950–56. Foundation Schol., Queen's Univ., 1947 and 1948; LLB 1949. Called to Bar: N Ireland, 1950; Ireland, 1975; Middle Temple, 1988. Lecturer in Contract and Sale of Goods, Queen's Univ., 1950–51; Jun. Crown Counsel, Co. Londonderry, 1960–63, Co. Down, 1964–65; Counsel to Attorney-General for N Ireland, 1963–64 and 1965; Recorder of Londonderry, 1979–81. Vice-Chairman, 1959–61, Chairman, 1961–66, War Pensions Appeal Tribunal for N Ireland. MP (U) Queen's Univ. of Belfast, 1966–69, Lagan Valley, 1969–73, Parlt of N Ireland; Minister of Health and Social Services, N Ireland, 1969; Parly Sec., Min. of Home Affairs, 1969; Minister of Home Affairs, Govt of NI, 1969–70. *Recreations:* gardening, golf. *Address:* Larch Hill, Ballylesson, Belfast, N Ireland BT8 8JX. *Club:* Royal Air Force.

PORTER, Rev. Canon Roy; *see* Porter, Rev. Canon J. R.

PORTER, Dame Shirley, (Lady Porter), DBE 1991; DL; Councillor, Hyde Park Ward, Westminster City Council, since 1974, Leader of the Council, 1983–91; Lord Mayor of Westminster, May 1991–92; *b* 29 Nov. 1930; *d* of late Sir John (Edward) Cohen and Lady (Sarah) Cohen; *m* 1949, Sir Leslie Porter, *qv*; one *s* one *d*. *Educ:* Warren Sch., Worthing, Sussex; La Ramée, Lausanne, Switzerland. Founded Designers' Guild, 1970; Sec., Porter Investments, 1970–; Dir, Capital Radio, 1982–88. Westminster City Council: Conservative Whip, 1974–77; Road Safety Cttee, 1974–82; Member: Co-ordinating Cttee, 1981–82; Chairman: Highways and Works Cttee, 1978–82 (Vice-Chm., 1977–78); Gen. Purposes Cttee, 1982–83; Policy Review Cttee, 1982–83; Policy and Resources Cttee, 1983–91. Chairman: (also Founder), WARS Campaign (Westminster Against Reckless Spending), 1981–84; Cleaner City Campaign, 1979–81; Vice-Pres., Cleaner London Campaign, 1979–81; Mem. Exec., Keep Britain Tidy Gp, 1977–81. Member: Bd, London Festival Ballet, 1988–89; Court, Guild of Cleaners, 1976–; Hon. Mem., London Community Cricket Assoc., 1989–. Governor, Tel Aviv Univ., 1982. JP Inner London, 1972–84; DL Greater London, 1988. FRSA 1989. *Recreations:* golf, tennis, ballet, promoting London. *Address:* Westminster City Hall, Victoria Street, SW1E 6QP. *T:* 071–828 8070. *Clubs:* Royal Automobile, Queen's, Racquets; Frilford Heath Golf (Oxford); Coombe Hill Golf, Dyrham Park Golf.

PORTER, Thea; *see* Porter, D. N. N.

PORTER, Walter Stanley, TD 1950; MA (Cantab); Headmaster of Framlingham College, 1955–71; *b* 28 Sept. 1909; *s* of late Walter Porter, Rugby; *m* 1937, Doreen, *o d* of B. Haynes, Rugby; one *d*. *Educ:* Rugby Sch.; Gonville and Caius Coll., Cambridge. Assistant Master and Officer Commanding Training Corps, Trent Coll., 1933–36; Felsted Sch., 1936–43; Radley Coll., 1944–55. FRSA 1968. *Recreations:* travel, amateur dramatics; formerly Rugby football, hockey. *Address:* The Hermitage, 29 Cumberland Street, Woodbridge, Suffolk IP12 4AH. *T:* Woodbridge (03943) 382340.

PORTERFIELD, Dr James Stuart; retired; Reader in Bacteriology, Sir William Dunn School of Pathology, Oxford University, and Senior Research Fellow, Wadham College, Oxford, 1977–89; now Emeritus Fellow; *b* 17 Jan. 1924; *yr s* of late Dr Samuel Porterfield and Mrs Lilian Porterfield, Widnes, Lancs, and Portstewart, Co. Londonderry, NI; *m* 1950, Betty Mary Burch; one *d* (one *s* decd). *Educ:* Wade Deacon Grammar Sch., Widnes; King's Sch., Chester; Liverpool Univ. MB, ChB 1947, MD 1949. Asst Lectr in Bacteriology, Univ. of Liverpool, 1947–49; Bacteriologist and Virologist, Common Cold Res. Unit, Salisbury, Wilts, 1949–51; Pathologist, RAF Inst. of Pathology and Tropical Med., Halton, Aylesbury, Bucks, 1952–53; seconded to W African Council for Med. Res. Labs, Lagos, Nigeria, 1953–57; Mem. Scientific Staff, Nat. Inst. for Med. Res., Mill Hill, 1949–77; WHO Regional Ref. Centre for Arthropod-borne Viruses, 1961–65; WHO Collaborating Lab., 1965–89; Ref. Expert on Arboviruses, Public Health Lab. Service, 1967–76. Chm., Arbovirus Study Gp, Internat. Cttee for Nomenclature of Viruses, 1968–78; Meetings Sec., Soc. for General Microbiology, 1972–77; Vice-Pres., Royal Soc. for Tropical Med. and Hygiene, 1980–81 (Councillor, 1973–76); Secretary and Vice-Pres., Royal Institution, 1973–78. *Publications:* (ed) Andrewes' Viruses of Vertebrates, 5th edn, 1989; contribs to medical and scientific jls. *Recreations:* fell-walking, gardening. *Address:* Green Valleys, Goodleigh, Barnstaple, Devon EX32 7NH.

PORTES, Prof. Richard David, DPhil; Professor of Economics, Birkbeck College, University of London, since 1972; Director, Centre for Economic Policy Research, since 1983; *b* 10 Dec. 1941; *s* of Herbert Portes and Abra Halperin Portes; *m* 1963, Barbara Diana Frank; one *s* one *d*. *Educ:* Yale Univ. (BA 1962 *summa cum laude* maths and philosophy); Balliol and Nuffield Colls, Oxford (Rhodes Schol., Woodrow Wilson Fellow, Danforth Fellow; MA 1965; DPhil 1969). Official Fellow and Tutor in Econs, Balliol Coll., Oxford, 1965–69; Asst Prof. of Econs and Internat. Affairs, Princeton Univ., 1969–72; Head, Dept of Econs, Birkbeck Coll., 1975–77 and 1980–83. Dir d'Etudes, Ecole des Hautes Etudes en Sciences Sociales, Paris, 1978–. Guggenheim Fellow, 1977–78; British Acad. Overseas Vis. Fellow, 1977–78; Res. Associate, Nat. Bureau of Econ. Res., Cambridge, Mass, 1980–; Vis. Prof., Harvard Univ., 1977–78. Vice-Chm., Econs Cttee, SSRC, 1981–84. Member: Bd of Dirs, Soc. for Econ. Analysis (Rev. of Econ. Studies), 1967–69, 1972–80 (Sec. 1974–77); RIIA, 1973– (Res. Cttee, 1982–); Council on Foreign Relations, 1978–; Hon. Degrees Cttee, Univ. of London, 1984–89. Fellow, Econometric Soc., 1983–; Mem. Council, Royal Econ. Soc., 1986– (Mem. Exec. Cttee, 1987–). Co-Chm., Bd of Governors, and Sen. Editor, Economic Policy, 1985–. *Publications:* (ed) Planning and Market Relations, 1971; The Polish Crisis, 1981; Deficits and Détente, 1983; (ed) Threats to International Financial Stability, 1987; (ed) Global Macroeconomics: policy conflict and cooperation, 1987; (ed) Blueprints for Exchange Rate Management, 1989; (ed) Macroeconomic Policies in an Interdependent World, 1989; (ed) Economic Transformation in Hungary and Poland, 1990; (ed) External Constraints on Macroeconomic Policy: the experience of Europe, 1991; contribs to many learned jls. *Recreation:* living beyond my means. *Address:* Centre for Economic Policy Research, 6 Duke of York Street, SW1Y 6LA. *T:* 071–930 7182. *Clubs:* YMCA, Groucho.

PORTILLO, Michael Denzil Xavier; MP (C) Enfield, Southgate, since December 1984; Minister of State, Department of the Environment, since 1990; *b* 26 May 1953; *s* of Luis Gabriel Portillo and Cora Waldegrave Blyth; *m* 1982, Carolyn Claire Eadie. *Educ:* Harrow County Boys' School; Peterhouse, Cambridge (1st cl. Hons MA History). Ocean Transport & Trading Co., 1975–76; Conservative Res. Dept., 1976–79; Special Advr, Sec. of State for Energy, 1979–81; Kerr McGee Oil (UK) Ltd, 1981–83; Special Adviser: to Sec. of State for Trade and Industry, 1983; to Chancellor of the Exchequer, 1983–84; an Asst Govt Whip, 1986–87; Parly Under Sec. of State, DHSS, 1987–88; Minister of State, Dept of Transport, 1988–90. *Address:* House of Commons, SW1A 0AA. *Club:* Carlton.

PORTLAND, 11th Earl of, *cr* 1689; **Henry Noel Bentinck;** Viscount Woodstock, Baron Cirencester, 1689; Count of the Holy Roman Empire; *b* 2 Oct. 1919; *s* of Capt. Count Robert Bentinck (*d* 1932) and Lady Norah Ida Emily Noel (*d* 1939), *d* of 3rd Earl of Gainsborough; *S* to Earldom of kinsman, 9th Duke of Portland, CMG, 1990; *m* 1st, 1940, Pauline (*d* 1967), *y d* of late Frederick William Mellowes; one *s* two *d*; 2nd, 1974, Jenifer, *d* of late Reginald Hopkins. *Heir:* *s* Viscount Woodstock, *qv*.

PORTMAN, family name of **Viscount Portman.**

PORTMAN, 9th Viscount, *cr* 1873; **Edward Henry Berkeley Portman;** Baron 1873; *b* 22 April 1934; *s* of late Hon. Michael Berkeley Portman (*d* 1959) (*yr s* of 7th Viscount), and June Charles (*d* 1947); *S* uncle, 1967; *m* 1st, 1956, Rosemary Farris (marr. diss., 1965); one *s* one *d*; 2nd, 1966, Penelope Allin; three *s* (and one *s* decd). *Educ:* Canford; Royal Agricultural College. Farmer. *Recreations:* shooting, fishing, music. *Heir:* *s* Hon. Christopher Edward Berkeley Portman [*b* 30 July 1958; *m* 1983, Caroline Steenson (marr. diss.); one *s*; *m* 1987, Patricia Martins Pim, *er d* of Senhor Bernardino Pim; one *s*]. *Address:* Clock Mill, Clifford, Herefordshire. *T:* Clifford (04973) 235. *Club:* White's.

PORTSMOUTH, 10th Earl of, *cr* 1743; **Quentin Gerard Carew Wallop;** Viscount Lymington, Baron Wallop, 1720; Hereditary Bailiff of Burley, New Forest; Director, Grainger Trust plc; *b* 25 July 1954; *s* of Oliver Kintzing Wallop (Viscount Lymington) (*d* 1984) and Ruth Violet (*d* 1978), *yr d* of Brig.-Gen. G. C. Sladen, CB, CMG, DSO, MC; *S* grandfather, 1984; *m* 1st, 1981, Candia (*née* McWilliam) (marr. diss. 1984), adopted *d* of Baron Strathcona and Mount Royal, *qv*; one *s* one *d*; 2nd, 1990, Annabel, *d* of Dr and Mrs Ian Fergusson; one *d*. *Educ:* Eton. *Heir:* *s* Viscount Lymington, *qv*. *Address:* Farleigh Wallop, Basingstoke, Hants.

PORTSMOUTH, Bishop of, since 1985; **Rt. Rev. Timothy John Bavin,** OGS; *b* 17 Sept. 1935; *s* of Edward Sydney Durrance and Marjorie Gwendoline Bavin. *Educ:* Brighton Coll.; Worcester Coll., Oxford (2nd Cl. Theol., MA); Cuddesdon Coll. Curate, St Alban's Cathedral Pretoria, 1961–64; Chaplain, St Alban's Coll., Pretoria, 1965–68; Curate of Uckfield, Sussex, 1969–71; Vicar of Good Shepherd, Brighton, 1971–73; Dean and Rector of Cathedral of St Mary the Virgin, Johannesburg, 1973–74; Bishop of Johannesburg, 1974–84. Mem., OGS, 1987–. ChStJ 1975. *Publication:* Deacons in the Ministry of the Church, 1987. *Recreations:* music, theatre, walking, gardening. *Address:* Bishopswood, Fareham, Hants PO14 1NT. *Clubs:* Athenæum; Royal Naval (Portsmouth); Royal Yacht Squadron (Cowes).

PORTSMOUTH, Bishop of, (RC), since 1988; **Rt. Rev. (Roger Francis) Crispian Hollis;** *b* 17 Nov. 1936; *s* of Christopher and Madeleine Hollis. *Educ:* Stonyhurst College; Balliol Coll., Oxford (MA); Venerable English College, Rome (STL). National Service as 2nd Lt, Somerset Light Infantry, 1954–56. Ordained priest, 1965; Assistant in Amesbury, 1966–67; RC Chaplain, Oxford Univ., 1967–77; RC Assistant to Head of Religious Broadcasting, BBC, 1977–81; Administrator, Clifton Cathedral, Bristol, 1981–87; Auxiliary Bishop of Birmingham (Bishop in Oxfordshire), 1987–88. *Recreations:* occasional golf, walking, cricket watching. *Address:* Bishop's House, Edinburgh Road, Portsmouth PO1 3HG.

PORTSMOUTH, Archdeacon of; *see* Crowder, Ven. N. H.

PORTSMOUTH, Provost of; *see* Stancliffe, Very Rev. D. S.

POSKITT, Prof. Trevor John, DSc, PhD; Professor of Civil Engineering, Queen Mary and Westfield College (formerly Queen Mary College), University of London, since 1972; *b* 26 May 1934; *s* of late William Albert Poskitt, Worthing, and Mrs D. M. Poskitt, Lincoln; *m* 1968, Gillian Mary, *d* of L. S. Martin, MBE, Romiley, Cheshire; one *s* one *d*. *Educ:* Corby Technical Sch.; Huddersfield Technical Coll.; Univ. of Leeds; Univ. of Cambridge. HND (Mech. Eng.); BSc Leeds, PhD Cambridge, DSc Manchester; FICE, FIStructE. Apprentice Engineer to Thos. Broadbent & Sons, Huddersfield, 1949–53; Graduate Assistant, English Electric Co. Ltd, 1958–60; Whitworth Fellow, 1960–63; Lectr, 1963–71, Senior Lectr, 1971–72, in Civil Engineering, Univ. of Manchester. *Publications:* numerous on civil engineering topics. *Recreations:* tennis, music. *Address:* Queen Mary and Westfield College, Mile End Road, E1 4NS. *T:* 081–980 4811.

POSNER, Michael Vivian, CBE 1983; Secretary-General, European Science Foundation, since 1986; *b* 25 Aug. 1931; *s* of Jack Posner; *m* 1953, Rebecca Posner, *qv*; one *s* one *d*. *Educ:* Whitgift Sch.; Balliol Coll., Oxford. Research Officer, Oxford Inst. of Statistics, 1953–57; University of Cambridge: Asst Lecturer, Lecturer, then Reader in Economics, 1958–79; Fellow, Pembroke Coll., 1960–83; Chm., Faculty Bd of Economics, 1974–75. Vis. Prof., Brookings Instn, Washington, 1971–72. Director of Economics, Ministry of Power, 1966–67; Economic Adviser to Treasury, 1967–69; Economic Consultant to Treasury, 1969–71; Consultant to IMF, 1971–72; Energy Adviser, NEDO, 1973–74; Econ. Adviser, Dept of Energy, 1974–75; Dep. Chief Econ. Adviser, HM Treasury, 1975–76. Chm., SSRC, 1979–83; Econ. Dir, NEDO, 1984–86. Member: BRB, 1976–84; Post Office Bd, 1978–79; Member: Adv. Council for Energy Conservation, 1974–82; Standing Commn on Energy and the Environment, 1978–81. Mem. Council, PSI, 1978–83 (Senior Res. Fellow, 1983–84). DEd (*hc*) CNAA, 1989. *Publications:* (co-author) Italian Public Enterprise, 1966; Fuel Policy: a study in applied economics, 1973; (ed) Resource Allocation in the Public Sector, 1977; (ed) Demand Management, 1978; (co-author) Energy Economics, 1981; (ed) Problems of International Money 1972–1985, 1986; books and articles on economics. *Recreation:* country life. *Address:* Rushwood, Jack Straw's Lane, Oxford OX3 0DN. *T:* Oxford (0865) 63578; European Science Foundation, 1 Quai Lezay-Marnésia, Strasbourg, France. *Club:* United Oxford & Cambridge University.

POSNER, Prof. Rebecca; Professor of the Romance Languages, University of Oxford, since 1978; Fellow, St Hugh's College, Oxford, since 1978; *b* 17 Aug. 1929; *d* of William and Rebecca Reynolds; *m* 1953, Michael Vivian Posner, *qv*; one *s* one *d*. *Educ:* Somerville Coll., Oxford. MA, DPhil (Oxon); PhD (Cantab). Fellow, Girton Coll., Cambridge, 1960–63; Prof. of French Studies, Univ. of Ghana, 1963–65; Reader in Language, Univ. of York, 1965–78. Vis. Prof. of Romance Philology, Columbia Univ., NY, 1971–72; Vis. Senior Fellow, Princeton Univ., 1983. *Publications:* Consonantal Dissimilation in the Romance Languages, 1961; The Romance Languages, 1966; (with J. Orr and I. Iordan) Introduction to Romance Linguistics, 1970; (ed with J. N. Green) Trends in Romance Linguistics and Philology, 4 vols, 1980–82, vol. 5 1991; (contrib.) Legacy of Latin, ed R. Jenkyns, 1991; numerous articles. *Recreations:* walking, gardening, theatre, music. *Address:* St Hugh's College, Oxford OX2 6LE. *T:* Oxford (0865) 274995 and 270488; Rushwood, Jack Straw's Lane, Oxford OX3 0DN. *T:* Oxford (0865) 63578.

POSNETT, Sir Richard (Neil), KBE 1980 (OBE 1963); CMG 1976; HM Diplomatic Service, retired; *b* 19 July 1919; *s* of Rev. Charles Walker Posnett, K-i-H, Medak, S India, and Phyllis (*née* Barker); *m* 1st; two *s* one *d*; 2nd, 1959, Shirley Margaret Hudson; two *s* one *d*. *Educ:* Kingswood; St John's Coll., Cambridge (won 120 yards hurdles for Cambridge *v* Oxford, 1940). BA 1940, MA 1947. Called to the Bar, Gray's Inn, 1951. HM Colonial Administrative Service in Uganda, 1941; Chm., Uganda Olympic Cttee, 1956; Colonial Office, London, 1958; Judicial Adviser, Buganda, 1960; Perm. Sec. for External Affairs, Uganda, 1962; Perm. Sec. for Trade and Industry, 1963; joined Foreign (subseq. Diplomatic) Service, 1964; FO, 1964; served on UK Mission to UN, NY, 1967–70; briefly HM Comr in Anguilla, 1969; Head of W Indian Dept, FCO, 1970–71; Governor and C-in-C of Belize, 1972–76; Special Mission to Ocean Island, 1977; Dependent Territories Adviser, FCO, 1977–79; British High Comr, Kampala, 1979. UK Comr, British Phosphate Comrs, 1978–81. Governor and C-in-C, Bermuda, 1981–83. Mem., Lord Chancellor's Panel of Ind. Inspectors, 1983–89. First ascent of South Portal Peak on Ruwenzori, 1942. Member: RIIA; Royal Forestry Soc.; Royal African Soc. President: Kingswood Assoc., 1980; Godalming Joigny Friendship Assoc., 1987– (Chm., 1984–87); Kingswood Sch., 1985–. KStJ 1972. *Publications:* articles in Uganda Journal, World Today. *Recreations:* ski-ing, golf, trees. *Address:* Timbers, Northway, Godalming, Surrey. *Clubs:* Commonwealth Trust, Achilles; West Surrey Golf; Mid-Ocean Golf; Privateers Hockey.

POSNETTE, Prof. Adrian Frank, CBE 1976; FRS 1971; VMH 1982; Director, East Malling Research Station, Kent, 1972–79 (Deputy Director, 1969–72, and Head of Plant

Pathology Section, 1957–72); *b* 11 Jan. 1914; *e s* of late Frank William Posnette and Edith (*née* Webber), Cheltenham; *m* 1937, Isabelle, *d* of Dr Montgomery La Roche, New York; one *s* two *d*. *Educ:* Cheltenham Grammar Sch.; Christ's Coll., Cambridge. MA, ScD Cantab; PhD London; AICTA Trinidad; FIBiol. Research at Imperial Coll. of Tropical Agriculture, Trinidad, 1936–37; Colonial Agric. Service, Gold Coast, 1937; Head of Botany and Plant Pathology Dept, W African Cacao Research Inst., 1944; research at East Malling Research Stn, 1949–. Vis. Prof. in Plant Sciences, Wye Coll., Univ. of London, 1971–78. *Publications:* Virus Diseases of Apples and Pears, 1963; numerous research papers in Annals of Applied Biology, Jl of Horticultural Science, Nature, Tropical Agriculture. *Recreations:* ornithology, sailing, gardening. *Address:* Walnut Tree, East Sutton, Maidstone, Kent ME17 3DR. *T:* Maidstone (0622) 843282. *Clubs:* Farmers'; Hawks (Cambridge).

POST, Herschel; Chief Operating Officer, Lehman Brothers International Ltd and Lehman Brothers Securities Ltd, since 1990; President and Director: Shearson Lehman Global Asset Management, since 1984; Posthorn Global Asset Management, since 1984; Deputy Chairman, London Stock Exchange (formerly International Stock Exchange), since 1989 (Member of Council, since 1988); *b* 9 Oct. 1939; *s* of Herschel E. and Marie C. Post; *m* 1963, Peggy Mayne; one *s* three *d*. *Educ:* Yale Univ. (AB); Oxford Univ. (BA, MA); Harvard Law Sch. (LLB). Associate, Davis Polk & Wardwell, attorneys, 1966–69; Exec. Dir, Parks Council of NY, 1969–72; Dep. Adminr and Comr, Parks, Recreation and Cultural Affairs Admin, NYC, 1973; Vice-Pres., Morgan Guaranty Trust Co., 1974–83. Trustee, Earthwatch Europe, 1988–. *Address:* One Broadgate, EC2M 7HA. *T:* 071–260 2613.

POST, Col Kenneth Graham, CBE 1945; TD; *b* 21 Jan. 1908; *s* of Donnell Post and Hon. Mrs Post; *m* 1st, 1944, Stephanie Bonté Wood (marr. diss., 1963); one *s* two *d*; 2nd, 1963, Diane Allen; two *s*. *Educ:* Winchester; Magdalen, Oxford. London Stock Exchange, 1929–37; 2nd Lieut, RA (TA) 1937; Norway, 1940; War Office, 1941–42; Ministry of Supply, 1943–44; Ministry of Works, 1945–47; Ministry of Housing, 1956–57; Ministry of Defence, 1957–59. Member Corby New Town Development Corporation, 1955–62; Director, Civic Trust, 1957–63. *Address:* 3 Shepherds Walk, Pembury Road, Tunbridge Wells, Kent. *T:* Tunbridge Wells (0892) 548560. *Club:* Pratt's.

POSTGATE, Prof. John Raymond, FRS 1977; FIBiol; Director, AFRC Unit of Nitrogen Fixation, 1980–87 (Assistant Director, 1963–80), and Professor of Microbiology, University of Sussex, 1965–87, now Emeritus; *b* 24 June 1922; *s* of Raymond William Postgate and Daisy Postgate (*née* Lansbury); *m* 1948, Mary Stewart; three *d*. *Educ:* Woodstock Sch., Golders Green; Kingsbury County Sch., Mddx; Balliol Coll., Oxford. BA, MA, DPhil, DSc. Research in chemical microbiology: with D. D. Woods on action of sulfonamide drugs, 1946–48, with K. R. Butlin on sulphate-reducing bacteria, 1948–59. Research on bacterial death, 1959–63, incl. Visiting Professor: Univ. of Illinois, 1962–63, working on sulphate-reducing bacteria; Oregon State Univ., 1977–78. President: Inst. of Biology, 1982–84; Soc. for Gen. Microbiology, 1984–87. Hon. DSc Bath, 1990. *Publications:* Microbes and Man, 1969, 2nd edn 1986; Biological Nitrogen Fixation, 1972; Nitrogen Fixation, 1978; The Sulphate-Reducing Bacteria, 1979, 2nd edn 1984; The Fundamentals of Nitrogen Fixation, 1982; A Plain Man's Guide to Jazz, 1973; ed, 4 scientific symposia; regular columnist in Jazz Monthly, 1952–72; numerous scientific papers in microbiol/biochem. jls; many jazz record reviews in specialist magazines; articles on jazz. *Recreations:* listening to jazz and attempting to play it. *Address:* 1 Houndean Rise, Lewes, Sussex BN7 1EG. *T:* Lewes (0273) 472675.

POSTGATE, Richmond Seymour, MA; FCP; formerly consultant, education and broadcasting; *b* 31 Dec. 1908; *s* of Prof. J. P. Postgate, FBA and Edith Postgate; *m* 1949, Audrey Winifred Jones; one *s* two *d*. *Educ:* St George's Sch., Harpenden, Herts; Clare Coll., Cambridge. Editorial staff, Manchester Guardian newspaper; teaching in Public and Elementary Schools; County LEA Administration; RAFVR. In BBC: Head of School Broadcasting, etc; Director-General, Nigerian Broadcasting Corporation, 1959–61; Controller, Educnl Broadcasting, BBC, 1965–72. FCP 1973. *Recreation:* walking. *Address:* 3 Stanford Road, Faringdon, Oxon. *T:* Faringdon (0367) 240172.

POSWILLO, Prof. David Ernest, CBE 1989; FDSRCS, FRACDS, FIBiol, FRCPath; Professor of Oral and Maxillofacial Surgery, United Medical and Dental Schools of Guy's and St Thomas' Hospitals, University of London, since 1983; *b* 1 Jan. 1927; *s* of Ernest and Amelia Poswillo, Gisborne, NZ; *m* 1956, Elizabeth Alison, *d* of Whitworth and Alice Russell, Nelson, NZ; two *s* two *d*. *Educ:* Gisborne Boys' High, NZ; Univ. of Otago. BDS 1948, DDS 1962, DSc 1975, Westminster Hosp.; FDSRCS 1952, FRACDS 1966, FIBiol 1974, FRCPath 1981. OC S District Hosp., RNZDC, 1949–51; Hill End Hosp., St Albans, 1952; Dir of Oral Surgery, Christchurch Hosp., NZ, 1953–68; Prof. of Teratology, RCS, 1969–77; Consultant Oral Surgeon, Queen Victoria Hosp., East Grinstead, 1969–77; Prof. of Oral Path. and Oral Surgery, Univ. of Adelaide, and Sen. Oral and Maxillofacial Surgeon, Royal Adelaide and Childrens' Hosps, 1977–79; Prof. of Oral Surgery, and Mem. Council, Royal Dental Hosp., London, 1977–83. Consultant Adviser to Chief MO, DHSS, 1979–86; Mem., Bd of Faculty of Dental Surgery, RCS, 1981–89; Medical Defence Union: Vice-Pres. and Council Mem., 1983–; Chm., Dental Cttee, 1983–88; Sec. Gen., Internat. Assoc. of Oral and Maxill. Surgeons, 1983–89; President: BAOMS, 1990–91; Section of Odontology, RSM, 1989–90. Trustee, Tobacco Products Research Trust, 1980–; Human Task Force, WHO, 1976–78. Mem. Council of Govs, UMDS of Guy's and St Thomas's Hosps, 1983–89. Hunterian Prof., RCS, 1968, 1976; Regents' Prof., Univ. of California, 1987. Lectures: Arnott Demonstrator, 1972; Erasmus Wilson, 1973; Darwin-Lincoln, Johns Hopkins, 1975; Waldron, Harvard, 1976; Richardson, Harvard, 1981; Tomes, RCS, 1982; President's, BAOMS, 1985; Friel Meml, European Orthodontic Soc., 1987; Sarnat, UCLA, 1989; William Guy, RCSE, 1990. Hon. FFDRCSI, 1984; Hon. FIMFT, 1985. Hon. MD Zürich, 1983. RNZADC Prize, 1948; Tomes Prize, 1966; Down Medal, 1973; Kay-Kilner Prize, 1975; ASOMS Research Award, 1976; Hunter Medal and Triennial Prize, 1976; 2nd Orthog. Surg. Award, Univ. of Texas, 1982; Edison Award, Univ. of Michigan, 1987; Colyer Gold Medal, RCS, 1990. *Publications:* (with C. L. Berry) Teratology, 1975; (with B. Cohen and D. K. Mason) Oral Surgery and Pathology, 1978; (with B. Cohen and D. K. Mason) Oral Medicine and Diagnosis, 1978; (with D. J. Simpson and D. David) The Craniosynostoses, 1982; (with D. Henderson) Atlas of Orthognathic Surgery, 1984; (jtly) Dental, Oral and Maxillofacial Surgery, 1986; (jtly) The Effects of Smoking on the Foetus, Neonate and Child, 1991; papers on surgery, pathology and teratology in dental, medical and sci jls. *Recreations:* art, reading, gardening. *Address:* Ferndale, Oldfield Road, Bickley BR1 2LE *T:* 081–467 1578.

POTTER, Prof. Allen Meyers, PhD; James Bryce Professor of Politics, University of Glasgow, 1970–84, retired; *b* 7 March 1924; *s* of Maurice A. and Irene M. Potter; *m* 1949, Joan Elizabeth Yeo; two *d*. *Educ:* Wesleyan Univ., Conn (BA 1947, MA 1948); Columbia Univ., NY (PhD 1955). FSS 1967. Instructor, College of William and Mary, 1949–51; Lectr/Sen. Lectr, Univ. of Manchester, 1951–62; Vis. Professor, Univ. of Texas, 1960; Professor: Univ. of Strathclyde, 1963–65; Univ. of Essex, 1965–70; Pro-Vice-Chancellor, Univ. of Essex, 1969–70. Vice-Principal, Univ. of Glasgow, 1979–82. Member, US-UK Educational Commn, 1979–84. Governor, Glasgow Sch. of Art, 1979–82. *Publications:* American Government and Politics, 1955, 2nd edn 1978; Organised Groups in British National Politics, 1961; articles in American and British social science jls. *Recreations:* inventing table games, bridge. *Address:* 14 Severn Drive, Malvern, Worcs WR14 2SZ. *T:* Malvern (0684) 569315.

POTTER, Arthur Kingscote, CMG 1957; CBE (mil.) 1946; *b* 7 April 1905; *s* of late Richard Ellis Potter, Ridgewood, Almondsbury, Glos and Harriott Isabel Potter (*née* Kingscote, of Kingscote, Glos); *m* 1950, Hilda, *d* of late W. A. Butterfield, OBE; one *d*. *Educ:* Charterhouse; New Coll., Oxford (BA). Entered Indian CS, 1928; posted to Burma; in charge of Pegu earthquake relief, 1930–31; District Comr, 1934; Controller of Finance ('reserved' subjects), 1937; Financial Adviser, Army in Burma, 1942 (despatches); Finance Secretary, Government of Burma (in Simla), 1942–43; Financial Adviser (Brigadier), 11th Army Group, 1943, and Allied Land Forces, South-East Asia, 1943–44; Chief Financial Officer (Brig.), Military Administration of Burma, 1944–47; HM Treasury Representative in India, Pakistan and Burma, 1947–50; Asst Secretary, HM Treasury, 1950–56; Counsellor, UK Delegation to NATO, Paris, 1956–65. *Address:* Lower House Barns, Bepton, Midhurst, W Sussex GU29 0JB.

POTTER, Dennis (Christopher George); playwright, author and journalist (freelance since 1964); *b* 17 May 1935; *e s* of Walter and Margaret Potter; *m* 1959, Margaret Morgan; one *s* two *d*. *Educ:* Bell's Grammar Sch., Coleford, Glos; St Clement Danes Grammar Sch.; New Coll., Oxford (Hon. Fellow, 1987). Editor, Isis, 1958; BA (Hons) in PPE Oxon, 1959. BBC TV (current affairs), 1959–61; Daily Herald, feature writer, then TV critic, 1961–64; contested (Lab) East Herts, 1964; Leader writer, The Sun, Sept.-Oct. 1964, then resigned; TV Critic, Sunday Times, 1976–78. First television play, 1965. NFT retrospective, 1980. *Television plays:* Vote Vote Vote for Nigel Barton (also at Bristol Old Vic, 1968; SFTA Award, 1966); Stand Up Nigel Barton; Where the Buffalo Roam; A Beast with Two Backs; Son of Man; Traitor; Paper Roses; Casanova; Follow the Yellow Brick Road; Only Make Believe; Joe's Ark; Schmoedipus; (adapted from novel by Angus Wilson) Late Call, 1975; Brimstone and Treacle, 1976 (transmitted, 1987); Double Dare, 1976; Where Adam Stood, 1976; Pennies from Heaven (sextet), 1978 (BAFTA award, 1978); Blue Remembered Hills, 1979 (BAFTA award, 1980); Blade on the Feather, Rain on the Roof, Cream in my Coffee, 1980 (Prix Italia, 1982); Tender is the Night (sextet, from Scott Fitzgerald), 1985; The Singing Detective (sextet), 1986; Visitors, 1987; Christabel (quartet, from The Past Is Myself, by Christabel Bielenberg), 1988; Blackeyes (quartet), 1989; *screenplays:* Pennies from Heaven, 1981; Brimstone and Treacle, 1982; Gorky Park, 1983; Dreamchild, 1985; Track 29, 1988; Blackeyes, 1990; *stage play:* Sufficient Carbohydrate, 1983. *Publications:* The Glittering Coffin, 1960; The Changing Forest, 1962; *plays:* The Nigel Barton Plays (paperback, 1968); Son of Man, 1970; Brimstone and Treacle, 1979; Sufficient Carbohydrate, 1983; Waiting for the Boat (3 plays), 1984; *novels:* Hide and Seek, 1973; Pennies from Heaven, 1982; Ticket to Ride, 1986; Blackeyes, 1987. *Recreations:* nothing unusual, *ie* the usual personal pleasures, sought with immoderate fervour. *Address:* Morecambe Lodge, Duxmere, Ross-on-Wye, Herefordshire HR9 5BB.

POTTER, Donald Charles, QC 1972; *b* 24 May 1922; *s* of late Charles Potter, Shortlands, Kent. *Educ:* St Dunstan's Coll.; London Sch. of Economics. RAC (Westminster Dragoons), 1942–46 (Lieut); served England, NW Europe (D-day), Germany; mentioned in despatches; Croix de Guerre (France). LLB London 1947; called to Bar, Middle Temple, 1948; Bencher, Lincoln's Inn, 1979. Asst Lectr in Law, LSE, 1947–49; practised at Bar, 1950–. Chm., Revenue Bar Assoc., 1978–88. Special Comr of Income Tax (part-time), 1986–; Chm. (part-time), VAT Tribunal, 1986–. *Publication:* (with H. H. Monroe) Tax Planning with Precedents, 1954. *Recreations:* farming, travel, theatre, reading. *Address:* 27 Old Buildings, Lincoln's Inn, WC2A 3UJ; Compass Cottage, East Portlemouth, Devon TQ8 8PE. *Club:* Garrick.

POTTER, Ernest Frank; Director, Finance, 1979–87 (Director of Finance and Corporate Planning, 1977–79), Cable & Wireless plc; Chairman, Themes International PLC, since 1991; Director: Telephone Corporation Ltd, since 1988; Cable Corporation Ltd, since 1989; Micrelec Group, since 1989; *b* 29 April 1923; *s* of Frank William and Edith Mary Potter; *m* 1945, Madge (*née* Arrowsmith) (*d* 1990); one *s*. *Educ:* Dr Challoner's Grammar Sch., Amersham. FCMA, FCIS, MIMC. Commissioned Pilot and Navigator, RAF, 1941–49. Chief Accountant, Bulmer & Lumb Ltd, 1950–58; Director, Management Consulting, Coopers & Lybrand, 1959–71; British Steel Corporation, Cammell Laird Shipbuilders Ltd, 1972–77; Director (non-executive): Cable & Wireless (West Indies) Ltd, 1977–87; Bahrain Telecommunications Corp., 1982–89; Cable & Wireless North America Inc, 1980–87; Cable & Wireless Hongkong Ltd, 1982–87; Cable & Wireless (Leasing) Ltd, 1982–87; Bahrain Telecommunications Corp., 1982–89; Cable & Wireless Marine Ltd, 1984–87; Mercury Communications Ltd, 1985–87; Cable & Wireless (Bermuda) Ltd, 1986–87; General Hybrid Ltd, 1987–91. Chairman: Clebern Internat. Ltd, 1988–89; Holmes Protection Inc., 1990–. Mem., Accounting Standards Cttee, 1985–. *Recreation:* golf. *Address:* Long Meadow, Gorse Hill Road, Virginia Water, Surrey GU25 4AS. *T:* Wentworth (09904) 2178. *Clubs:* Royal Air Force; Wentworth (Surrey).

POTTER, Francis Malcolm; His Honour Judge Malcolm Potter; a Circuit Judge, since 1978; *b* 28 July 1932; *s* of Francis Martin Potter and Zilpah Jane Potter; *m* 1970, Bertha Villamil; one *s* one *d*. *Educ:* Rugby Sch.; Jesus Coll., Oxford. Called to Bar, Lincoln's Inn, 1956. A Recorder of the Crown Court, 1974–78. *Recreation:* painting. *Address:* Queen Elizabeth II Law Courts, Newton Street, Birmingham B4 6NE. *Club:* Army and Navy.

POTTER, Sir Ian; *see* Potter, Sir W. I.

POTTER, Jeremy; *see* Potter, R. J.

POTTER, Jeremy Patrick L.; *see* Lee-Potter.

POTTER, Maj.-Gen. Sir John, KBE 1968 (CBE 1963; OBE 1951); CB 1966; Chairman, Traffic Commissioners and Licensing Authority, Western Traffic Area, 1973–83; *b* 18 April 1913; *s* of late Major Benjamin Henry Potter, OBE, MC; *m* 1st, 1943, Vivienne Madge (*d* 1973), *d* of late Captain Henry D'Arcy Medlicott Cooke; one *s* one *d*; 2nd, 1974, Mrs D. Ella Purkis; one step *s* one step *d*. Served War of 1939–45. Major-General, 1962; Colonel Comdt: RAOC, 1965–69; RCT, 1968–73. Director of Supplies and Transport, 1963–65; Transport Officer in Chief (Army), 1965–66; Dir of Movements (Army), MoD, 1966–68; retired. *Address:* Orchard Cottage, The Orchard, Freshford, Bath, Avon BA3 6EW.

POTTER, John Herbert, MBE 1974; HM Diplomatic Service, retired; *b* 11 Jan. 1928; *s* of Herbert George and Winifred Eva Potter; *m* 1953, Winifred Susan Florence Hall; one *d*. *Educ:* elementary education at various state schools. Electrical Engineering jobs, 1942–45; served HM Forces, 1945–48; GPO, 1948–53; Foreign Office, 1953–55; Commercial Attaché, Bangkok, 1955–57; FO, 1957–60; Istanbul, 1960; Ankara, 1960–64; Second Secretary, Information, 1962; Second Sec., Information, Addis Ababa, 1964; Vice-Consul, Information, Johannesburg, 1964–66; DSAO, later FCO, 1966–70; First Sec. (Administration): Brussels, 1970–74; Warsaw, 1974–76; FCO (Inspectorate), 1976–80; Counsellor (Admin.) and Consul-Gen., Moscow, 1980–81; Counsellor

(Administration), Bonn, 1981–82. *Recreations:* reading, languages, walking, gardening. *Address:* Newlands, Westcourt Drive, Bexhill-on-Sea, E Sussex TN39 3NA.

POTTER, John McEwen, DM, FRCS; Director of Postgraduate Medical Education and Training, University of Oxford, 1972–87; Emeritus Fellow and Dean of Degrees, Wadham College, Oxford, since 1987; *b* 28 Feb. 1920; *er s* of Alistair Richardson Potter and Mairi Chalmers Potter (*née* Dick); *m* 1943, Kathleen Gerrard; three *s*. *Educ:* Clifton Coll.; Emmanuel Coll., Cambridge; St Bartholomew's Hosp. BA, MB, BChir Cantab, 1943; MA 1945; FRCS 1951; MA, BM, BCh Oxon, 1963, DM 1964. Active service (Captain, RAMC), Europe, India and Burma, 1944–47. Lectr in Physiol. and Jun. Chief Asst, Surg. Professorial Unit, St Bart's Hosp., 1948–51; Graduate Asst to Nuffield Prof. of Surgery, Oxford, 1951–56; E. G. Fearnsides Scholar, Cambridge, 1954–56; Hunterian Prof., 1955; Cons. Neurosurgeon: Manchester Royal Infirmary, 1956–61; Radcliffe Infirm., Oxford, 1961–72; Hon. Cons. Neurosurgeon, Oxford RHA and Oxfordshire HA, 1972–87. Vis. Prof., UCLA, 1967; University of Oxford: Clin. Lectr in Neurosurgery, 1962–68; Univ. Lectr, 1968–87; Mem., Gen. Bd of Faculties, 1975–83; Hebdomadal Council, 1983–89; Fellow: Linacre Coll., 1967–69; Wadham Coll., 1969–87 (Professorial Fellow, 1974–87; Sub-Warden, 1978–81). Governor, United Oxford Hosps, 1973. Cairns Lectr, Adelaide, 1974. Examr for Final BM, BCh Oxon; Ext. Examr, Med. Sciences Tripos Pt II, Cambridge Univ. FRSM (Pres., Sect. of Neurol., 1975–76); Member: GMC, 1973–89 (Chm., Registration Cttee, 1979–89); Oxfordshire HA, 1982–89; Soc. of British Neurol Surgeons (Archivist; formerly Hon. Sec.); Vice-Pres., 4th Internat. Congress of Neurol Surgery. Corres. Member: Amer. Assoc. of Neurol Surgeons; Deutsche Gesellschaft für Neurochirurgie; Sociedad Luso-Espanhola de Neurocirurgia; Hon. Mem., Egyptian Soc. of Neurol Surgeons. *Publications:* The Practical Management of Head Injuries, 1961, 4th edn 1984; contrib. to books and jls on subjects relating mostly to neurology and med. educn. *Recreation:* fishing. *Address:* 47 Park Town, Oxford OX2 6SL. *T:* Oxford (0865) 57875; Myredykes, Newcastleton, Roxburghshire TD9 0SR.
See also R. J. Potter.

POTTER, Sir (Joseph) Raymond (Lynden), Kt 1978; Chairman, Halifax Building Society, 1974–83; *b* 21 April 1916; *s* of Rev. Henry Lynden and Mabel Boulton Potter; *m* 1939, Daphne Marguerite, *d* of Sir Crawford Douglas-Jones, CMG; three *s* one *d*. *Educ:* Haileybury Coll.; Clare Coll., Cambridge (MA). War Service, 1939–46, Queen's Own Royal W Kent Regt, England and Middle East; GSO2 Staff Duties, GHQ, MEF; AQMG War Office. Sec., Royal Inst. of Internat. Affairs, 1947–51; joined Halifax Building Soc., 1951; Gen. Man. 1956; Chief Gen. Man., 1960–74; Dir, 1968–83. Mem., Board, Warrington and Runcorn (formerly Warrington) New Town Develt Corp., 1969–86. Vice Pres., Building Socs Assoc., 1981– (Mem. Council, 1965–81; Chm., 1975–77). Freeman, City of London, 1981. Life Governor, Haileybury Coll. *Recreation:* music. *Address:* Oakwood, Chilbolton, Stockbridge, Hampshire SO20 6BE. *T:* Chilbolton (0264) 860523. *Club:* Hawks (Cambridge).

POTTER, Malcolm; *see* Potter, F. M.

POTTER, Hon. Sir Mark Howard, Kt 1988; **Hon. Mr Justice Potter;** a Judge of the High Court of Justice, Queen's Bench Division, since 1988; *b* 27 Aug. 1937; *s* of Prof. Harold Potter, LLD, PhD, and Beatrice Spencer Potter (*née* Crowder); *m* 1962, Undine Amanda Fay, *d* of Major James Miller, 5/6th Rajputana Rifles, and Bunty Miller, painter; two *s*. *Educ:* Perse Sch., Cambridge; Gonville and Caius Coll., Cambridge (Schol.; BA (Law Tripos) 1960, MA 1963). National Service, 15 Med. Regt RA, 1955–57 (commnd 1956); Territorial Army, 289 Lt Parachute Regt RHA(TA), 1958–64. Asst Supervisor, Legal Studies, Gonville and Caius, Queens' and Sidney Sussex Colls, 1961–68; called to Bar, Gray's Inn, 1961, Bencher, 1987; in practice, 1962–88; QC 1980; a Recorder, 1986–88. Member: Supreme Ct Rule Cttee, 1980–84; Lord Chancellor's Civil Justice Review Cttee, 1985–88; Chm., Bar Public Affairs Cttee, 1987; Vice-Chm., Council of Legal Educn, 1989–. *Recreations:* family and sporting. *Address:* Royal Courts of Justice, Strand, WC2A 2LL. *Club:* Garrick.

POTTER, Rev. Philip Alford; Chaplain to University of West Indies and Lecturer, United Theological College of West Indies, since 1985; *b* 19 Aug. 1921; *s* of Clement Potter and Violet Peters, Roseau, Dominica, Windward Is, WI; *m* 1st, 1956, Ethel Olive Doreen Cousins (*d* 1980), Jamaica, WI; 2nd, 1984, Rev. Barbel von Wartenberg, FRG. *Educ:* Dominica Grammar Sch.; United Theological Coll., Jamaica; London Univ. BD, MTh. Methodist Minister. Overseas Sec., British SCM, 1948–50; Superintendent, Cap Haitien Circuit, Methodist Church, Haiti, 1950–54; Sec., later Dir, Youth Dept, WCC, 1954–60; Sec. for WI and W Africa, Methodist Missionary Society, London, 1961–66; Dir, Commn on World Mission and Evangelism, and Associate Gen. Sec., WCC, 1967–72; Gen. Sec., WCC, 1972–84. Mem., then Chm., Youth Dept Cttee, WCC, 1948–54; Chm., World Student Christian Fedn, 1960–68. Editor: Internat. Review of Mission, 1967–72; Ecumenical Rev., 1972–84. Hon. Doctor of Theology: Hamburg Univ., Germany, 1971; Geneva, 1976; Theol Inst. of Rumanian Orthodox Church, 1977; Humboldt Univ., Berlin (GDR), 1982; Uppsala, 1984; Hon. LLD W Indies, 1974; Hon. DD Birmingham, 1985. Niwano Peace Prize, Japan, 1986. *Publications:* (with Prof. Hendrik Berkhof) Key Words of the Gospel, 1964; The Love of Power or the Power of Love, 1974; Life in all its Fullness, 1981; chapter in Explosives Lateinamerika (ed by T. Tschuy), 1969; essays in various symposia; contrib. various jls, incl. Ecumenical Rev., Internat. Rev. of Mission, Student World. *Recreations:* swimming, hiking, music, geology. *Address:* United Theological College of the West Indies, PO Box 136, Golding Avenue, Kingston 7, Jamaica, WI.

POTTER, Sir Raymond; *see* Potter, Sir J. R. L.

POTTER, Raymond, CB 1990; Deputy Secretary (Courts and Legal Services), since 1986, and Deputy Clerk of the Crown in Chancery, since 1989, Lord Chancellor's Department; *b* 26 March 1933; *s* of William Thomas Potter and Elsie May Potter; *m* 1959, Jennifer Mary Quicke; one *s*. *Educ:* Henry Thornton Grammar School. Called to the Bar, Inner Temple, 1971, Bencher, 1989. Central Office, Royal Courts of Justice, 1950; Western Circuit, 1963; Chief Clerk, Bristol Crown Court, 1972; Dep. Circuit Administrator, Western Circuit, 1976; Circuit Administrator, Northern Circuit, 1982–86. *Recreation:* painting. *Address:* Trevelyan House, Great Peter Street, SW1P 2BY. *Club:* Athenæum.

POTTER, (Ronald) Jeremy; Director: LWT (Holdings) plc, since 1979; Constable & Co. (Publishers), since 1980; *b* 25 April 1922; *s* of Alistair Richardson Potter and Mairi Chalmers (*née* Dick); *m* 1950, Margaret, *d* of Bernard Newman; one *s* one *d*. *Educ:* Clifton Coll.; Queen's Coll., Oxford (Neale Exhibnr, MA). Served War, Intell. Officer, Indian Army. Manager, subseq. Man. Dir, Dep. Chm., New Statesman, 1951–69; Man. Dir, Independent Television Publications Ltd, 1970–79; Chm., Independent Television Books Ltd, 1971–79; Chm., Hutchinson Ltd, 1982–84 (Dir, 1978–84; Dep. Chm., 1980–82); Dir, Page and Moy (Holdings) plc, 1979–88. Pres., Periodical Publishers Assoc., 1978–79; Appeals Chm., Newsvendors' Benevolent Instn, 1979; Chairman: Twickenham Arts Council, 1967–68; Richard III Soc., 1971–89; Oxford Playhouse Trust, 1990–. FRSA. Captain, Hampstead Hockey Club, 1954–57; World Amateur over 60s Champion, Real tennis, 1986–88. *Publications:* Good King Richard?, 1983; Pretenders, 1986; Independent Television in Britain, Vol. 3: Politics and Control 1968–80, 1989, Vol. 4: Companies and Programmes 1968–80, 1990; *novels:* Hazard Chase, 1964; Death in Office, 1965; Foul Play, 1967; The Dance of Death, 1968; A Trail of Blood, 1970; Going West, 1972; Disgrace and Favour, 1975; Death in the Forest, 1977. *Recreations:* reading, writing, Real tennis. *Address:* The Old Pottery, Larkins Lane, Headington, Oxford OX3 9DW. *Clubs:* Garrick, MCC, Puritans Hockey.
See also J. McE. Potter.

POTTER, Ronald Stanley James; Director of Social Services, Surrey County Council, 1970–81; *b* 29 April 1921; *e s* of late Stanley Potter and Gertrude Mary Keable, Chelmsford; *m* 1954, Ann (Louisa Eleanor) Burnett; one *s* one *d*. *Educ:* King Edward VI Grammar Sch., Chelmsford. MISW. Territorial Army, 1939, War Service, 1939–47; commnd RA, 1942; Captain 1946. Area Welfare Officer, Essex CC, 1953–61; Dep. Co. Welfare Officer, Lindsey CC, 1962; County Welfare Officer: Lindsey CC, 1962–64; Herts CC, 1964–70. Dir, Watford Sheltered Workshop Ltd, 1964–70. Mem. Cttee of Enquiry into Voluntary Workers in Social Services, 1966–69; Dir, Industrial Advisers to Blind Ltd, 1969–74; Vice Pres., SE Regional Assoc. for Deaf, 1984–88 (Vice-Chm., 1968–76; Chm., 1976–84); Member: Council of Management, RNID, 1968–71, 1976–84; Nat. Jt Council for Workshops for the Blind, 1970–81; Adv. Council, Nat. Corp. for Care of Old People, 1974–77; Local Authorities Adv. Cttee on Conditions of Service of Blind Workers, 1974–81; Exec. Council, RNIB, 1975–81; Nat. Adv. Council on Employment of Disabled People, 1978–81; Dir, Remploy Ltd, 1974–86. *Recreations:* walking, swimming, caravanning, bowls. *Address:* Ridge Cottage, 16 Howard Ridge, Burpham Lane, Guildford, Surrey GU4 7LY. *T:* Guildford (0483) 504272.

POTTER, Maj.-Gen. Sir Wilfrid John; *see* Potter, Maj.-Gen. Sir John.

POTTER, Sir (William) Ian, Kt 1962; FAA; Stockbroker, Melbourne, Australia; *b* 25 Aug. 1902; *s* of James William Potter and Maria Louisa (*née* McWhinnie); *m* 1975, Primrose Catherine Dunlop, AO, JP, CLJ; two *d* of former *m*. *Educ:* University of Sydney (BEc). Economist to Federal Treas., 1935–36; Commonwealth Rep. Rural Debt Adjustment Cttee, 1936; founded Ian Potter & Co., 1937; Principal Partner, 1937–67. Mem., Internat. Adv. Bd, Chemical Bank, USA, 1967–77. Served RANVR, 1939–44. Member: Cttee Stock Exchange of Melbourne, 1945–62; Melbourne University Council, 1947–71; Commonwealth Immigration Planning Council, 1956–62; Victorian Arts Centre Building Cttee, 1960–78. President, Australian Elizabethan Theatre Trust, 1964–66 and 1983– (Chairman 1968–83); Vice-Pres., Howard Florey Inst., Melbourne. Hon. Life Member: Aust. Ballet; Aust. Opera; Nat. Gall. of Vic. Hon. LLD Melbourne. Kt 1st Cl., Order of the Star of the North (Sweden). *Publications:* contrib. articles on financial and economic subjects to learned journals and press. *Recreations:* yachting, tennis, golfing. *Address:* 99 Spring Street, Melbourne, Victoria 3000, Australia. *Clubs:* Melbourne, Australian, Royal Automobile of Victoria, Royal Melbourne Golf (Melbourne); Australian (Sydney); The Links (NY).

POTTERTON, Homan, FSA; art historian and writer; Director, National Gallery of Ireland, 1980–88; *b* 9 May 1946; sixth *s* of late Thomas Edward Potterton and Eileen Potterton (*née* Tong). *Educ:* Kilkenny Coll.; Trinity Coll., Dublin (BA 1968, MA 1973); Edinburgh Univ. (Dip. Hist. Art 1971). FSA 1981. Cataloguer, National Gall. of Ireland, 1971–73; Asst Keeper, National Gall., London, 1974–80. Mem. Bd, GPA Dublin Internat. Piano Competition, 1987–. HRHA 1982. Mem. Editl Bd, Irish Arts Rev., 1990–. *Publications:* Irish Church Monuments 1570–1880, 1975; A Guide to the National Gallery, 1976, rev. edn 1980 (German, French, Italian and Japanese edns 1977); The National Gallery, London, 1977; Reynolds and Gainsborough: themes and painters in the National Gallery, 1976; Pageant and Panorama: the elegant world of Canaletto, 1978; (jtly) Irish Art and Architecture, 1978; Venetian Seventeenth Century Painting (National Gallery Exhibn Catalogue), 1979; introd. to National Gallery of Ireland Illustrated Summary Catalogue of Paintings, 1981; (jtly) National Gallery of Ireland, 50 Pictures, 1981; Dutch 17th and 18th Century Paintings in the National Gallery of Ireland: a complete catalogue, 1986; contrib. Burlington Mag., Apollo, Connoisseur, FT and Country Life. *Recreations:* America, Italy. *Address:* 119 West 71st Street, New York, NY 10023, USA. *T:* (212) 721 0510.

POTTINGER, (William) George; *b* 11 June 1916; *e s* of late Rev. William Pottinger, MA, Orkney, and Janet Woodcock; *m* 1946, Margaret Rutherfurd Clark McGregor; one *s*. *Educ:* George Watson's; High School of Glasgow; Edinburgh Univ.; Heidelberg; Queens' Coll., Cambridge (Major Scholar). Entered Scottish Home Dept, as Assistant Principal, 1939. Served War of 1939–45, RFA; France, N Africa, Italy (despatches), Lieut-Col RA. Principal, 1945; Private Secretary to successive Secretaries of State for Scotland, 1950–52; Asst Secretary, Scottish Home Dept, 1952; Secretary, Royal Commn on Scottish Affairs, 1952–54; Under-Secretary: Scottish Home Dept, 1959–62; Scottish Home and Health Dept, 1962–63; Scottish Development Dept, 1963–64; Scottish Office, 1964–68; Dept of Agriculture and Fisheries for Scotland, 1968–71; Secretary, Dept of Agriculture and Fisheries for Scotland, 1971. *Publications:* The Winning Counter, 1971; Muirfield and the Honourable Company, 1972; St Moritz: an Alpine caprice, 1972; The Court of the Medici, 1977; The Secretaries of State for Scotland 1926–76, 1979; Whisky Sour, 1979; The Afghan Connection, 1983; Mayo, Disraeli's Viceroy, 1990; papers and reviews. *Recreations:* real tennis, golf, fishing. *Address:* West Lodge, Balsham, Cambridge CB1 6EP. *T:* Cambridge (0223) 892958. *Club:* Savile.

POTTS, Archibold; Director, Bewick Press, since 1989; *b* 27 Jan. 1932; *s* of late Ernest W. Potts and Ellen Potts; *m* 1957, Marguerite Elsie (*née* Elliott) (*d* 1983); one *s* one *d*. *Educ:* Monkwearmouth Central Sch., Sunderland; Ruskin and Oriel Colls, Oxford (Dip. Econ. and Pol. Sci., 1958; BA PPE 2nd cl. hons, 1960); ext. postgrad. student, London Univ. (Postgrad. CertEd 1964) and Durham Univ. (MEd 1969). Nat. Service, RAF, 1950–53. Railway Clerk, 1947–50 and 1953–56. Lecturer: N Oxfordshire Tech. Coll., 1961; York Tech. Coll., 1962–65; Rutherford Coll. of Technology and Newcastle upon Tyne Polytechnic, 1965–80; Head of Sch. of Business Admin, 1980–87, Associate Dean, Faculty of Business and Professional Studies, 1988, Newcastle upon Tyne Polytechnic. Tyne and Wear County Council: Councillor, 1979–86; Vice-Chm., Planning Cttee, 1981–86; Vice-Chm., Council, 1983–84; Chm., Council, 1984–85. Contested (Lab) Westmorland, 1979. Chm., NE Labour History Soc., 1990–; Mem., Exec. Cttee, Soc. for Study of Labour History, 1987–. *Publications:* Stand True, 1976; Bibliography of Northern Labour History, 1982–; (ed) Shipbuilders and Engineers, 1987; Jack Casey, the Sunderland Assassin, 1991; contribs to Dictionary of Labour Biography, vol. 2 1974, vol. 4 1977, vol. 5 1979; articles on economics and history. *Recreations:* local history, military modelling. *Address:* 41 Kenton Avenue, Kenton Park, Newcastle upon Tyne NE3 4SE. *T:* 091–285 6361. *Club:* Victory Service.

POTTS, Hon. Sir (Francis) Humphrey, Kt 1986; **Hon. Mr Justice Potts;** a Judge of the High Court of Justice, Queen's Bench Division, since 1986; *b* 18 Aug. 1931; *er s* of late Francis William Potts and Elizabeth Hannah (*née* Humphrey), Penshaw, Co. Durham; *m* 1971, Philippa Margaret Campbell, *d* of the late J. C. H. Le B. Croke and Mrs J. F. G. Downes; two *s* and two step-*s*. *Educ:* Royal Grammar Sch., Newcastle upon Tyne; St

Catherine's Society, Oxford. BCL 1954, MA 1957. Barrister-at-Law, Lincoln's Inn, 1955 (Tancred Student, 1953; Cholmeley Scholar, 1954), Bencher, 1979; North Eastern Circuit, 1955; practised in Newcastle upon Tyne, 1955–71; QC 1971; a Recorder, 1972–86; admitted to Hong Kong Bar, 1984; Presiding Judge, NE Circuit, 1988–91. Member: Mental Health Review Tribunal, 1984–86; Criminal Injuries Compensation Bd, 1985–86. *Address:* Royal Courts of Justice, Strand, WC2A 2LL.

POTTS, Peter; JP; General Secretary, General Federation of Trade Unions, since 1977; *b* 29 June 1935; *s* of late John Peter Potts and of Margaret (*née* Combs); *m* 1st, 1956, Mary Longden (*d* 1972); two *s* one *d*; 2nd, 1974, Angela Elouise van Lieshout (*née* Liddelow); one step *s* one step *d*. *Educ:* Chorlton High Sch., Manchester; Ruskin Coll., Oxford; Oxford Univ. (Dip. in Econs and Pol. Science). Served RAF, 1953–55. USDAW, 1951–65; Res. Officer, Union of Tailors and Garment Workers, 1965–74; National Officer, Clerical and Supervisory Staffs, 1974–77. Member: Clothing EDC, 1970–77 (Trade Union Advisor, 1966–70); Jt Textile Cttee, NEDO, 1970–77; Trade Union Unit Trust Investors Cttee, 1977– (Chm., 1984–); Trade Union Res. Unit, 1975–; Trade Union Internat. Res. and Educn Gp, 1979–; Press Council, 1987–90; Governing Council, Ruskin Coll., 1977– (Mem. Exec. Cttee, 1977–; Vice-Chm., 1984–). JP N Beds, 1983. *Recreations:* tennis, do-it-yourself hobbies, art, listening to jazz. *Address:* 3 Tadmere, Two Mile Ash, Milton Keynes, Bucks.

POTTS, Robin, QC 1982; barrister; *b* 2 July 1944; *s* of William and Elaine Potts; *m*; one *s*; *m* Helen Elizabeth Sharp; one *s* one *d*. *Educ:* Wolstanton Grammar Sch.; Magdalen Coll., Oxford (BA, BCL). Called to the Bar, Gray's Inn, 1968. *Publication:* (contrib.) Gore-Browne on Companies, 43rd edn. *Address:* The Grange, Church Lane, Pinner, Mddx HA5 3AB. *T:* 081–866 9013.

POTTS, Thomas Edmund, ERD 1957; Company Director, retired; *b* 23 March 1908; *s* of late T. E. Potts, Leeds; *m* 1932, Phyllis Margaret, *d* of late J. S. Gebbie, Douglas, Isle of Man; one *s*. *Educ:* Leeds Modern School. Joined The British Oxygen Co. Ltd, 1928. Commissioned RE, Supp. R of O, 1938; served War of 1939–45, Madras Sappers and Miners in India, Eritrea, Western Desert, Tunisia, with 4th and 5th Indian Divs (despatches, 1942 and 1943; Major); CRE 31st Indian Armoured Div., 9th Army (Lt-Col); released from active service and transferred to RARO (resigned Commission, RE, 1950). Rejoined British Oxygen Co. Ltd, London, 1945; Managing Director, African Oxygen Ltd, Johannesburg, 1947; Director, British Oxygen Co. Ltd, 1955; Group Managing Director, The British Oxygen Co. Ltd, 1958–63; UK Atomic Energy Authority: Consultant, 1968–78, a Dir, 1971–78, Radiochemical Centre; Dir, Amersham Corp., Chicago, 1968–78. Pres. South African Instn of Welding, 1951; Vice-Pres., Inst. of Welding, 1963–64. CBIM 1979. *Recreations:* golf, gardening. *Address:* Cleeve, Brayfield Road, Bray-on-Thames, Berks SL6 2BW. *T:* Maidenhead (0628) 26887. *Clubs:* Rand (Johannesburg); Temple Golf.

POULTER, Brian Henry; Secretary, Northern Ireland Audit Office, since 1989; *b* 1 Sept. 1941; *s* of William Henry Poulter, PhC, MPS, and Marjorie Elizabeth Everett McBride; *m* 1968, Margaret Ann Dodds; one *s* twin *d*. *Educ:* Regent House Grammar Sch., Newtownards. Qual. as certified accountant, 1966. Hill, Vellacott and Bailey, Chartered Accountants, 1959–62; entered NICS, 1962; Min. of Health and Local Govt, 1962–65; Min. of Health and Social Services, 1965–71; Deputy Principal: Local Enterprise Develt Unit, 1971–74; Dept of Commerce, 1974–75; Chief Auditor 1975–81, Dep. Dir 1981–82, Dir 1982–87, Exchequer and Audit Dept; Dir, NI Audit Office, 1987–88. *Recreations:* reading, walking, cricket. *Address:* Northern Ireland Audit Office, Rosepark House, Upper Newtownards Road, Belfast BT4 3NS. *T:* Dundonald (02318) 4567.

POULTON, Richard Christopher, MA; Head Master, Christ's Hospital, Horsham, since 1987; *b* 21 June 1938; *e s* of Rev. Christopher Poulton and Aileen (*née* Sparrow); *m* 1965, Zara, *o d* of Prof. P. and Mrs J. Crossley-Holland; two *s* one *d*. *Educ:* King's Coll., Taunton; Wesleyan Univ., Middletown, Conn, USA; Pembroke Coll., Cambridge (BA 1961, CertEd 1962, MA 1965). Asst Master: Bedford Sch., 1962–63; Beckenham and Penge Grammar Sch., 1963–66; Bryanston School: Asst Master, 1966–80; Head of History Dept, 1971–76; Housemaster, 1972–80; Headmaster, Wycliffe Coll., 1980–86. Gov., Oxford and Cambridge Examinations Bd, 1987–90. JP S Glos, 1985–86. Freeman, City of London, 1987; Yeoman, Co. of Ironmongers, 1990. *Publications:* Victoria, Queen of a Changing Land, 1975; Kings and Commoners, 1977; A History of the Modern World, 1980. *Recreations:* writing, hill walking, choral music. *Address:* The Head Master's House, Christ's Hospital, Horsham, W Sussex RH13 7LS. *T:* Horsham (0403) 52547.

POUNCEY, Denys Duncan Rivers, MA, MusB Cantab; FRCO; Organist and Master of the Choristers, Wells Cathedral, 1936–70; Conductor of Wells Cathedral Oratorio Chorus and Orchestra, 1946–66; Hon. Diocesan Choirmaster, Bath and Wells Choral Association, 1946–70; *b* 23 Dec. 1906; *s* of late Rev. George Ernest Pouncey and late Madeline Mary Roberts; *m* 1937, Evelyn Cottier. *Educ:* Marlborough College; Queens' College, Cambridge. Asst to Dr Cyril Rootham, Organist and Choirmaster of St John's Coll., Cambridge, 1928–34; Organist and Choirmaster, St Matthew's, Northampton, 1934–36; Founder Conductor of Northampton Bach Choir. *Address:* Waverley Hotel, 10 Tregonwell Road, Minehead, Somerset TA24 5DJ. *T:* Minehead (0643) 704764.

POUND, Sir John David, 5th Bt *cr* 1905; *b* 1 Nov. 1946; *s* of Sir Derek Allen Pound, 4th Bt; *S* father, 1980; *m* 1st, 1968 (marr. diss.); one *s*; 2nd, 1978, Penelope Ann, *er d* of Grahame Arthur Rayden, Bramhall, Cheshire; two *s*. Liveryman, Leathersellers' Co. *Heir:* *s* Robert John Pound, *b* 12 Feb. 1973.

POUND, Ven. Keith Salisbury; Chaplain-General and Archdeacon to the Prison Service, since 1986; a Chaplain to the Queen since 1988; *b* 3 April 1933; *s* of Percy Salisbury Pound and Annie Florence Pound. *Educ:* Roan School, Blackheath; St Catharine's Coll., Cambridge (BA 1954, MA 1958); Cuddesdon Coll., Oxford. Curate, St Peter, St Helier, Dio. Southwark, 1957–61; Training Officer, Hollowford Training and Conference Centre, Sheffield, 1961–64, Warden 1964–67; Rector of Holy Trinity, Southwark, with St Matthew, Newington, 1968–78; RD, Southwark and Newington, 1973–78; Rector of Thamesmead, 1978–86; Sub-Dean of Woolwich, 1984–86; Dean of Greenwich, 1985–86. Hon. Canon of Southwark Cathedral, 1985. *Publication:* Creeds and Controversies, 1976. *Recreations:* theatre, music, books, crosswords. *Address:* Prison Service Chaplaincy, Cleland House, Page Street, SW1P 4LN. *T:* 071–217 6266. *Club:* Civil Service.

POUNDS, Maj.-Gen. Edgar George Derek, CB 1975; Chairman, Royal Marines Officers' Widows Pension Funds, since 1987; *b* 13 Oct. 1922; *s* of Edgar Henry Pounds, MBE, MSM, and Caroline Beatrice Pounds; *m* 1944, Barbara Winifred May Evans; one *s* one *d*. *Educ:* Reading Sch. War of 1939–45: enlisted, RM, 1940 (King's Badge, trng); HMS Kent, 1941–42 (Atlantic); commissioned as Reg. Off., Sept. 1942 (sword for dist., trng); HMS Berwick, 1943–44 (Atlantic and Russia). Co. Comdr, RM, 1945–51: Far East, Palestine, Malta, UK (Sniping Wing), Korea (US Bronze Star, 1950); Captain 1952. Instr, RM Officers' Trng Wing, UK, 1952–54; Adjt, 45 Commando, RM, 1954–57, Malta, Cyprus (despatches), Suez; RAF Staff Coll., Bracknell, 1958; Staff Captain, Dept of CGRM, London, 1959–60; Major 1960; Amphibious Ops Officer, HMS Bulwark, 1961–62, Kuwait, Aden, E Africa, Borneo; Corps Drafting Off., UK, 1962–64; 40 Commando RM: 2nd in Comd, 1964–65, Borneo, and CO, 1966–67, Borneo and Far East; CO, 43 Commando, RM, 1967–68, UK based; GSO1 Dept CGRM, 1969–70; Col 1970; Naval Staff, MoD, 1970–72; Comdt Commando Trng Centre, RM, 1972–73; Actg Maj.-Gen. 1973; Maj.-Gen., RM, 1974; Commanding Commando Forces, RM, 1973–76, retired. Chief Exec., British Friesian Cattle Soc., 1976–87. Agricl Cons. (Europe), 1987. *Publications:* articles on strategy, amphibious warfare, and tactics in professional jls, and cattle breeding and dairying in farming jls. *Recreations:* target rifle shooting, gardening, reading. *Clubs:* Army and Navy, Farmers'.

POUNDS, Prof. Kenneth Alwyne, CBE 1984; FRS 1981; Professor of Space Physics, and Director, X-ray Astronomy Group, since 1973, and Head of Department of Physics and Astronomy, since 1986, University of Leicester; *b* 17 Nov. 1934; *s* of Harry and Dorothy Pounds; *m* 1st, 1961, Margaret Mary (*née* Connell); two *s* one *d*; 2nd, 1982, Joan Mary (*née* Millit); one *s* one *d*. *Educ:* Salt Sch., Shipley, Yorkshire; University Coll. London (BSc, PhD). Department of Physics, University of Leicester: Asst Lectr, 1960; Lecturer, 1961; Sen. Lectr, 1969. Member: SERC, 1980–84 (Chm., Astronomy, Space and Radio Bd); Management Bd, British Nat. Space Centre, 1986–88; Pres., RAS, 1990–. DUniv York, 1984. Gold Medal, RAS, 1989. *Publications:* many, in Monthly Notices, Nature, Astrophysical Jl, etc. *Recreations:* cricket, music. *Address:* 12 Swale Close, Oadby, Leicester LE2 4GF. *T:* Leicester (0533) 719370.

POUNTAIN, Sir Eric (John), Kt 1985; DL; Group Chief Executive, since 1979, and Chairman, since 1983, Tarmac PLC; Chairman: James Beattie PLC, since 1987 (Deputy Chairman, 1985–87; Director, since 1984); IMI PLC, since 1989 (Director, since 1988); Director, Midland Bank, since 1986; *b* 5 Aug. 1933; *s* of Horace Pountain and Elsie Pountain; *m* 1960, Joan Patricia Sutton; one *s* one *d*. *Educ:* Queen Mary Grammar Sch., Walsall. CBIM; FFB, FIHE, FCIB; FRSA. Joined F. Maitland Selwyn & Co., auctioneers and estate agents, 1956, joint principal, 1959; founded Midland & General Develts, 1964, acquired by John McLean & Sons Ltd, 1969; Chief Exec., John McLean & Sons, 1969, acquired by Tarmac PLC, 1974; Chief Exec., newly formed Tarmac Housing Div., until 1979. Dir, Tarmac PLC, 1977–. Member: Financial Develt Bd, NSPCC, 1985–; Adv. Council, Prince's Youth Business Trust, 1988–; President's Appeal Cttee, Age Concern, 1991–. President: Haflinger Soc. of GB; Shropshire Enterprise Trust; Midlands Industrial Council, 1988–; Patron, Staffs Agricl Soc. DL Stafford, 1985. *Recreations:* golf, shooting, tennis. *Address:* Edial House, Edial, Lichfield.

POUNTNEY, David Willoughby; Director of Productions, English National Opera, since 1982; Artistic Director, Contemporary Opera Studio, since 1990; *b* 10 Sept. 1947; *s* of Dorothy and Willoughby Pountney; *m* 1980, Jane Henderson; one *s* one *d*. *Educ:* St John's College Choir School, Cambridge; Radley College; St John's College, Cambridge (MA). Joined Scottish Opera, 1970; 1st major production Katya Kabanova (Janacek), Wexford Fest., 1972; Dir of Productions, Scottish Opera, 1976–80; individual guest productions for all British Opera companies, also USA, Aust., Italy, Germany, The Netherlands; productions for ENO include: Rusalka (Dvorak); Osud (Janacek); Dr Faust (Busoni); Lady Macbeth of Mtsensk (Shostakovich); Wozzeck (Berg); Pelléas and Mélisande (Debussy). *Publications:* numerous trans. of opera, esp. Czech and Russian repertoire. *Recreations:* croquet, food and wine. *Address:* 35 Brookfield, Highgate West Hill, N6 6AT. *T:* 081–342 8900. *Club:* Garrick.

POUT, Harry Wilfrid, CB 1978; OBE 1959; CEng, FIEE; Marconi Underwater Systems Ltd, 1982–86, Defence Consultant, since 1986; *b* 11 April 1920; British; *m* 1949, Margaret Elizabeth (*née* Nelson); three *d*. *Educ:* East Ham Grammar Sch.; Imperial Coll., London. BSc (Eng); ACGI 1940. RN Scientific Service, 1940; Admty Signal Estab. (later Admty Signal and Radar Estab.), 1940–54; Dept of Operational Research, Admty, 1954–59; idc 1959; Head of Guided Weapon Projects, Admty, 1960–65; Asst Chief Scientific Adviser (Projects), MoD, 1965–69; Dir, Admiralty Surface Weapons Estabt, 1969–72; Dep. Controller, Guided Weapons, 1973, Guided Weapons and Electronics, 1973–75, Air Systems, 1975–79, Aircraft Weapons and Electronics, 1979–80, MoD. Defence consultant, 1980–82. FCGI 1972; FBIM. *Publications:* (jtly) The New Scientists, 1971; classified books; contribs to jls of IEE, RAeS, RUSI, Jl of Naval Sci., etc. *Recreations:* mountaineering, gardening and do-it-yourself activities, amateur geology. *Address:* Oakmead, Fox Corner, Worplesdon, near Guildford, Surrey GU3 3PP. *T:* Worplesdon (0483) 232223.

POVER, Alan John, CMG 1990; HM Diplomatic Service; High Commissioner to the Republic of Gambia, since 1990; *b* 16 Dec. 1933; *s* of John Pover and Anne (*née* Hession); *m* 1964, Doreen Elizabeth Dawson; one *s* two *d*. *Educ:* Salesian College, Thornleigh, Bolton. Served HM Forces, 1953–55; Min. of Pensions and Nat. Insce, 1955–61; Commonwealth Relations Office, 1961; Second Secretary: Lagos, 1962–66; Tel Aviv, 1966–69; Second, later First, Sec., Karachi/Islamabad, 1969–73; First Sec., FCO, 1973–76; Consul, Cape Town, 1976–80; Counsellor, Diplomatic Service Inspector, 1983–86; Counsellor and Consul-Gen., Washington, 1986–90. *Recreations:* cricket, golf, gardening. *Address:* c/o Foreign and Commonwealth Office, SW1; 6 Wetherby Close, Emmer Green, Reading, Berks. *T:* Reading (0734) 477037. *Club:* Commonwealth Trust.

POWDITCH, Alan (Cecil Robert), MC 1944; JP; District Administrator, NW District, Kensington and Chelsea and Westminster Area Health Authority, 1974–77, retired; *b* 14 April 1912; *s* of Cecil John and Annis Maudie Powditch; *m* 1942, Barbara Leggat; one *s* one *d*. *Educ:* Mercers School. Entered Hospital Service, 1933; Accountant, St Mary's Hospital, W2, 1938. Served War of 1939–45, with 51st Royal Tank Regt, 1941–46. Dep. House Governor, St Mary's Hospital, 1947–50, Sec. to Bd of Governors, 1950–74. Mem. Nat. Staff Cttee (Min. of Health) 1964–72; Chm., Juvenile Panel, Gore Div., 1973–76. Mem. Council, Sue Ryder Foundn, 1977–85; Mem. Magistrates' Courts Cttee, 1979–81. JP Co. Middlesex 1965, supp. List 1982. *Recreations:* golf; interested in gardening when necessary. *Address:* 27 Gateway Close, Northwood, Mddx HA6 2RW.

POWELL; *see* Baden-Powell.

POWELL, Albert Edward, JP; General President of Society of Graphical and Allied Trades, 1973–82, of SOGAT '82 1982–83; *b* 20 May 1927; *s* of Albert and Mary Powell; *m* 1947, Margaret Neville; one *s* two *d*. *Educ:* Holy Family Elementary Sch., Morden. FIWSP. London Organiser, SOGAT, 1957, Organising Secretary, 1967. Has served on various Committees and Boards, including: past Chairman, Croydon College of Art, past Governor, London College of Printing. Chairman, Paper & Paper Products Industry Trng Bd, 1975– (Mem. Central Arbitration Cttee, 1976–); Member: TUC Printing Industries Cttee, 1971–; NEDO Printing Industries Sector Working Party, 1980–; Methods-Time Measurement Assoc., 1966–. Member: Industrial Tribunal, 1983–; Social Security Appeal Tribunal, 1984–; Parole Bd, 1986–. JP: Wimbledon, 1961–75; Southend-on-Sea, 1975–80; Bexley, 1980–. Queen's Silver Jubilee Medal, 1977. *Recreations:* gardening reading (science fiction), music. *Address:* 31 Red House Lane, Bexleyheath, Kent DA6 8JF. *T:* 081–304 7480.

POWELL, Anthony Dymoke, CH 1988; CBE 1956; *b* 21 Dec. 1905; *o s* of late Lt-Col P. L. W. Powell, CBE, DSO; *m* 1934, Lady Violet Pakenham, 3rd *d* of 5th Earl of

Longford, KP; two *s*. *Educ*: Eton; Balliol College, Oxford. MA; Hon. Fellow, 1974. Served War of 1939–45, Welch Regt and Intelligence Corps, Major. A Trustee, National Portrait Gallery, 1962–76. Hon. Mem., Amer. Acad. of Arts and Letters, 1977; Hon. Fellow, Mod. Lang. Assoc. of Amer., 1981. Hon. DLitt: Sussex, 1971; Leicester, 1976; Kent, 1976; Oxon, 1980; Bristol, 1982. Hudson Review Bennett Prize, 1984; T. S. Eliot Prize for Creative Lit., Ingersoll Foundn, 1984. Orders of: the White Lion (Czechoslovakia); the Oaken Crown and Croix de Guerre (Luxembourg); Leopold II (Belgium). *Publications*: Afternoon Men, 1931; Venusberg, 1932; From a View to a Death, 1933; Agents and Patients, 1936; What's become of Waring, 1939; John Aubrey and His Friends, 1948, rev. edn 1988; Selections from John Aubrey, 1949; A Dance to the Music of Time, 12 vol. sequence, 1951–75: A Question of Upbringing, 1951; A Buyer's Market, 1952; The Acceptance World, 1955; At Lady Molly's, 1957 (James Tait Black Memorial Prize); Casanova's Chinese Restaurant, 1960; The Kindly Ones, 1962; The Valley of Bones, 1964; The Soldier's Art, 1966; The Military Philosophers, 1968; Books do Furnish a Room, 1971; Temporary Kings, 1973 (W. H. Smith Prize, 1974); Hearing Secret Harmonies, 1975; O, How The Wheel Becomes It!, 1983; The Fisher King, 1986; The Album of Anthony Powell's Dance to the Music of Time (ed. V. Powell), 1987; Miscellaneous Verdicts (criticism), 1990; Under Review (criticism), 1992; *memoirs*: To Keep the Ball Rolling, 4 vols, 1976–82 (abridged one vol. edn 1983): Infants of the Spring, 1976; Messengers of Day, 1978; Faces In My Time, 1980; The Strangers All are Gone, 1982; *plays*: Afternoon Men (adapted by Riccardo Aragno), Arts Theatre Club, 1963; The Garden God, 1971; The Rest I'll Whistle, 1971. *Address*: The Chantry, near Frome, Somerset BA11 3LJ. *T*: Frome (0373) 836314. *Clubs*: Travellers', Pratt's.

POWELL, Sir Arnold Joseph Philip; *see* Powell, Sir Philip.

POWELL, Arthur Barrington, CMG 1967; *b* 24 April 1918; *er s* of late Thomas and Dorothy Powell, Maesteg, Glam; *m* 1945, Jane, *d* of late Gen. Sir George Weir, KCB, CMG, DSO; four *s* one *d*. *Educ*: Cowbridge; Jesus Coll. Oxford. Indian Civil Service, 1939–47; served in Province of Bihar. Asst Princ., Min. of Fuel and Power, 1947; Princ. Private Sec. to Minister, 1949–51; Asst Sec., 1955; Petroleum Div., 1957–68; Petroleum Attaché, HM Embassy, Washington, 1962–64; Gas Div., 1968–72; Reg. Finance Div., DoI, 1972–76; Exec. Dir, Welsh Develt Agency, 1976–83. *Address*: The Folly, Newchurch West, Chepstow, Gwent NP6 6AU. *Clubs*: United Oxford & Cambridge University; Royal Porthcawl Golf; St Pierre Golf & Country (Chepstow).

POWELL, Sir Charles (David), KCMG 1990; Private Secretary to the Prime Minister, 1984–91; Director: Matheson & Co., since 1991; National Westminster Bank, since 1991; *b* 6 July 1941; *s* of Air Vice Marshal John Frederick Powell, *qv*; *m* 1964, Carla Bonardi; two *s*. *Educ*: King's Sch., Canterbury; New Coll., Oxford (BA). Entered Diplomatic Service, 1963; Third Sec., FO, 1963–65; Second Sec., Helsinki, 1965–67; FCO, 1968–71; First Sec. and Private Sec. to HM Ambassador, Washington, 1971–74; First Sec., Bonn, 1974–77; FCO, 1977–80 (Counsellor, 1979; Special Counsellor for Rhodesia negotiations, 1979–80); Counsellor, UK Perm. Repn to European Communities, 1980–84. *Recreation*: walking. *Address*: c/o Matheson & Co., 3 Lombard Street, EC3V 9AQ. *Clubs*: Turf, Royal Automobile.

POWELL, Gen. Colin Luther; Legion of Merit, Bronze Star, Air Medal, Purple Heart; Chairman, Joint Chiefs of Staff, USA, since 1989; *b* 5 April 1937; *s* of late Luther Powell and Maud Ariel Powell (*née* McKoy); *m* 1962, Alma V. Johnson; one *s* two *d*. *Educ*: City Univ. of New York (BS Geology); George Washington Univ. (MBA). Commissioned 2nd Lieut, US Army, 1958; White House Fellow, 1972–73; Comdr, 2nd Brigade, 101st Airborne Div., 1976–77; exec. asst to Sec. of Energy, 1979; sen. mil. asst to Dep. Sec. of Defense, 1979–81; Asst Div. Comdr, 4th Inf. Div., Fort Carson, 1981–83; sen. mil. asst to Sec. of Defense, 1983–86; US V Corps, Europe, 1986–87; dep. asst to President 1987, asst 1987–89, for Nat. Security Affairs; General 1989; C-in-C, US Forces Command, Fort McPherson, April–Sept. 1989. *Recreations*: racquetball, restoring old Volvos. *Address*: Chairman, Joint Chiefs of Staff, Washington, DC 20318–0001, USA. *T*: (703) 697–9121.

POWELL, David; *b* 1914; *s* of Edward Churton Powell and Margaret (*née* Nesfield); *m* 1941, Joan Boileau (Henderson); one *s* four *d*. *Educ*: Charterhouse. Served 1939–46: Lt, Kent Yeomanry RA; Captain and Major on Staff. Qualified as Chartered Accountant, 1939, admitted, 1943; in practice, 1946–47; joined Booker McConnell Ltd, 1947; Finance Dir, 1952; Dep. Chm. 1957; Man. Dir, 1966; Chm. and Chief Exec., 1967, retired 1971. *Recreations*: golf, English water-colours, fishing, reading. *Address*: The Cottage, 20 Coldharbour Lane, Hildenborough, Kent TN11 9JT. *T*: Hildenborough (0732) 833103.

POWELL, Dewi Watkin, JP; **His Honour Judge Watkin Powell;** a Circuit Judge, and Official Referee for Wales, since 1972; *b* Aberdare, 29 July 1920; *o s* of W. H. Powell, AMICE and of M. A. Powell, Radyr, Glam; *m* 1951, Alice, *e d* of William and Mary Williams, Nantmor, Caerns; one *d*. *Educ*: Penarth Grammar Sch.; Jesus Coll., Oxford (MA). Called to Bar, Inner Temple, 1949. Dep. Chm., Merioneth and Cardigan QS, 1966–71; Dep. Recorder of Cardiff, Birkenhead, Merthyr Tydfil and Swansea, 1965–71; Junior, Wales and Chester Circuit, 1968; Liaison Judge for Dyfed, 1974–84, for Mid Glamorgan, 1984–; Vice-Pres., South and Mid Glamorgan and Gwynedd branches of Magistrates' Assoc. Mem. Exec. Cttee, Plaid Cymru, 1943–55, Chm., Constitutional Cttee, 1967–71; Mem. Council, Hon. Soc. of Cymmrodorion, 1965– (Chm., 1978–84). Member, Court and Council: Univ. of Wales; Univ. of Wales Coll. of Cardiff (Vice Pres. and Vice Chm. of Council); Univ. of Wales Coll. of Medicine. Hon. Mem., Gorsedd of Bards. Pres., Cymdeithas Theatr Cymru, 1984–89. JP Mid Glamorgan. *Recreations*: gardening, reading theology, Welsh history and literature. *Address*: Crown Court, Law Courts, Cathays Park, Cardiff.

POWELL, (Elizabeth) Dilys, CBE 1974; FRSL; Film Critic, Punch, since 1979; *b* 20 July 1901; *yr d* of late Thomas and Mary Powell; *m* 1st, 1926, Humfry Payne, later Director of the British School of Archæology at Athens (*d* 1936); 2nd, 1943, Leonard Russell (*d* 1974); no *c*. *Educ*: Bournemouth High School; Somerville College, Oxford. Editorial Staff, Sunday Times, 1928–31 and 1936–41; Film Critic, 1939–79, Films on TV notes, 1976–. Lived and travelled extensively in Greece, 1931–36. Member: Bd of Governors of British Film Institute, 1948–52 (Fellow, BFI, 1986); Independent Television Authority, 1954–57; Cinematograph Films Council, 1965–69; President, Classical Association, 1966–67. Hon. Mem., ACTT. Award of Honour, BAFTA, 1984. *Publications*: Descent from Parnassus, 1934; Remember Greece, 1941; The Traveller's Journey is Done, 1943; Coco, 1952; An Affair of the Heart, 1957; The Villa Ariadne, 1973; The Golden Screen (collected reviews), 1989. *Address*: 14 Albion Street, Hyde Park, W2 2AS. *T*: 071–723 9807.

POWELL, Rt. Hon. Enoch; *see* Powell, Rt Hon. J. E.

POWELL, Francis Turner, MBE 1945; Chairman, Laing & Cruickshank, Stockbrokers, 1978–80; *b* 15 April 1914; *s* of Francis Arthur and Dorothy May Powell; *m* 1940, Joan Audrey Bartlett; one *s* one *d*. *Educ*: Lancing College. Served War, Queen's Royal Regt (TA), 1939–45 (Major). Joined L. Powell Sons & Co. (Stockbrokers), 1932, Partner, 1939; merged with Laing & Cruickshank, 1976. Mem. Council, Stock Exchange, 1963–78 (Dep. Chm., 1976–78). *Recreations*: golf, gardening. *Address*: Tanglewood, Oak Grange Road, West Clandon, Surrey. *T*: Guildford (0483) 222698.

POWELL, Geoffrey; *see* Powell, J. G.

POWELL, Geoffry Charles Hamilton; Founding Partner, Chamberlin, Powell & Bon, 1952–85, retired; Consultant, Chamberlin, Powell, Bon and Woods, since 1985; *b* 7 Nov. 1920; *s* of late Col D. H. Powell and Violet (*née* Timins); *m* 1st, Philippa Cooper; two *d*; 2nd, Dorothy Grenfell Williams (head, African Service, BBC); one *s*. *Educ*: Wellington College; AA School of Architecture. RIBA; AA Dipl. Asst to Frederick Gibberd, 1944, to Brian O'Rorke, 1946; teaching at Kingston School of Art (School of Architecture), 1949. Work includes: Golden Lane Estate; expansion of Leeds Univ.; schools, houses, commercial buildings; Barbican. Member: Council, Architectural Assoc., 1969–75; SE Economic Planning Council, 1967–69. *Recreations*: travel, painting. *Address*: Glen Cottage, River Lane, Petersham, Surrey TW10 7AG. *T*: 081–940 6286.

POWELL, Harry Allan Rose, (Tim Powell), MBE 1944; TD 1973; Chairman, Massey-Ferguson Holdings Ltd, 1970–80 (Managing Director, 1962–78); Director, Holland and Holland Holdings Ltd, 1960–89 (Chairman, 1982–87); *b* 15 Feb. 1912; *er s* of late William Allan Powell and Marjorie (*née* Mitchell); *m* 1936, Elizabeth North Hickley (*d* 1990); two *d*. *Educ*: Winchester; Pembroke Coll., Cambridge (MA). Joined Corn Products Ltd, 1934. Commissioned Hertfordshire Yeomanry, 1938; Staff Coll., 1942; War Office 1942; Joint Planning Staff, 1943; seconded to War Cabinet Secretariat, 1943–44; Head of Secretariat, Supreme Allied Commander, South East Asia, 1944–45 (Col). Mitchells & Butlers Ltd, 1946–49; Gallaher Ltd, 1949–52. Joined Harry Ferguson Ltd, 1952. British Inst. of Management: Fellow, 1963; Vice-Chm., 1970–77. Governor, St Thomas' Hosp., 1971–74. *Recreations*: fishing, lapidary, arguing. *Address*: Ready Token, near Cirencester, Glos GL7 5SX. *T*: Bibury (028574) 219; 12 Shafto Mews, Cadogan Square, SW1. *T*: 071–235 2707. *Clubs*: Buck's, MCC.

POWELL, John Alfred, MA, DPhil, CEng, FIEE, FRSE; consultant; *b* 4 Nov. 1923; *s* of Algernon Powell and Constance Elsie (*née* Honour); *m* 1949, Zena Beatrice (*née* Steventon); one *s* one *d*. *Educ*: Bicester County Sch.; The Queen's Coll., Oxford. No 1 Sch. of Technical Trng, RAF Halton, 1940–42. The Queen's Coll., Oxford, 1945–48. DPhil, Clarendon Lab., Oxford, 1948–51; Post-Doctorate Research Fellowship, Nat. Research Council, Ottawa, Canada, 1952–54; Marconi Research Labs, 1954–57; Texas Instruments Ltd: joined, 1957; Gen. Manager, 1959; Man. Dir, 1963; Asst Vice-Pres., TI Inc. (US), 1968; EMI Ltd: Main Bd Dir, Group Tech. Dir, 1971; Dir, Commercial Electronics, 1972; Dep. Man. Dir, 1973; Gp Man. Dir, 1974–78; Vice Chm., 1978–79. Mem., Honeywell Adv. Council, 1978–82. Faraday Lectr, 1978–79. CBIM (FBIM 1974); FRSA 1975; SMIEE (US). Member: Electronic Components Bd, 1968–71; Court of Cranfield Coll. of Technology, 1968–72; Electronics Research Council, 1972–74; Cttee of Inquiry into Engrg Profession, 1977–80; Physical Scis Sub-Cttee, UGC, 1980–85. Hon. Mem., BIR, 1980. *Recreations*: arts, sports, the rural scene. *Address*: Kym House, 21 Buccleuch Road, Branksome Park, Poole, Dorset BH13 6LF.

POWELL, Rt. Hon. (John) Enoch, PC 1960; MBE 1943; MA (Cantab); *b* 16 June 1912; *s* of Albert Enoch Powell and Ellen Mary Breese; *m* 1952, Margaret Pamela, *d* of Lt-Col L. E. Wilson, IA; two *d*. *Educ*: King Edwards, Birmingham; Trinity College, Cambridge. Craven Scholar, 1931; First Chancellor's Classical Medallist; Porson Prizeman; Browne Medallist, 1932; BA (Cantab); Craven Travelling Student, 1933; Fellow of Trinity College, Cambridge, 1934–38; MA (Cantab) 1937; Professor of Greek in the University of Sydney, NSW, 1937–39; Pte and L/Cpl R Warwickshire Regt, 1939–40; 2nd Lieut General List, 1940; Captain, General Staff, 1940–41; Major, General Staff, 1941; Lieut-Col, GS, 1942; Col, GS, 1944; Brig. 1944; Diploma in Oriental and African Studies. Contested (UU) South Down, 1987. MP: (C) Wolverhampton SW, 1950–Feb. 1974; (UU) Down South Oct. 1974–83, South Down, 1983–87 (resigned seat Dec. 1985 in protest against Anglo-Irish Agreement; re-elected Jan. 1986). Parly Sec., Ministry of Housing and Local Government, Dec. 1955–Jan. 1957; Financial Secretary to the Treasury, 1957–58; Minister of Health, July 1960–Oct. 1963. *Publications*: The Rendel Harris Papyri, 1936; First Poems, 1937; A Lexicon to Herodotus, 1938; The History of Herodotus, 1939; Casting-off, and other poems, 1939; Herodotus, Book VIII, 1939; Llyfr Blegywryd, 1942; Thucydidis Historia, 1942; Herodotus (translation), 1949; Dancer's End and The Wedding Gift (poems), 1951; The Social Services; Needs and Means, 1952; (jointly) One Nation, 1950; Change is our Ally, 1954; Biography of a Nation (with Angus Maude), 1955, 2nd edn 1970; Great Parliamentary Occasions, 1960; Saving in a Free Society, 1960; A Nation not Afraid, 1965; Medicine and Politics, 1966, rev. edn 1976; The House of Lords in the Middle Ages (with Keith Wallis), 1968; Freedom and Reality, 1969; Common Market: the case against, 1971; Still to Decide, 1972; Common Market: renegotiate or come out, 1973; No Easy Answers, 1973; Wrestling with the Angel, 1977; Joseph Chamberlain, 1977; A Nation or No Nation (ed R. Ritchie), 1978; Enoch Powell on 1992 (ed R. Ritchie), 1989; Collected Poems, 1990; numerous political pamphlets. *Address*: 33 South Eaton Place, SW1. *T*: 071–730 0988. *Club*: Athenæum.

POWELL, Air Vice-Marshal John Frederick, OBE 1956; Warden and Director of Studies, Moor Park College, 1972–77; *b* 12 June 1915; *y s* of Rev. Morgan Powell, Limpley Stoke, Bath; *m* 1939, Geraldine Ysolda, *e d* of late Sir John Fitzgerald Moylan, CB, CBE; four *s*. *Educ*: Lancing; King's Coll., Cambridge (MA). Joined RAF Educnl Service, 1937; Lectr, RAF College, 1938–39; RAFVR (Admin. and Special Duties) ops room duties, Coastal Comd, 1939–45 (despatches); RAF Educn Br., 1946; Sen. Instructor in History, RAF Coll., 1946–49; RAF Staff Coll., 1950; Air Min., 1951–53; Sen. Tutor, RAF Coll., 1953–59; Educn Staff, HQ FEAF, 1959–62; MoD, 1962–64; Comd Educn Officer, HQ Bomber Comd, 1964–66; OC, RAF Sch. of Educn, 1966–67; Dir of Educational Services, RAF, 1967–72; Air Commodore, 1967; Air Vice-Marshal, 1968. *Recreations*: choral music, tennis, gardening. *Address*: Barker's Hill Cottage, Donhead St Andrew, Shaftesbury, Dorest SP7 9EB. *T*: Donhead (074788) 505. *Club*: Royal Air Force.
See also Sir C. D. Powell.

POWELL, (John) Geoffrey, CBE 1987; Deputy Chairman, Local Government Boundary Commission for England, 1984–90; *b* 13 Jan. 1928; *s* of H. W. J. and W. A. S. Powell. *Educ*: Shrewsbury. FRICS; FSVA; ACIArb. Lieut, Welsh Guards, 1945–48. Chm., Property Adv. Gp, DoE, 1982–86 (Chm., New Towns Sub-Gp, 1982–86); Member: Skelmersdale New Town Corp., 1978–85; Review Cttee of Govt Valuation Services, 1982; British Rail Property Board, 1985–91; NCB Pension Fund Adv. Panel, 1985–90. Sec.-Gen., European Group of Valuers of Fixed Assets, 1982–87; European Rep., Internat. Assets Valuation Standards Cttee, 1984–87. Chm., RICS Cttees, 1960–83, incl. Assets

Valuation Standards Cttee, 1981–83. External Examr, Reading Univ., 1986–88; Member: Liverpool Univ. Dept. of Civic Design Adv. Cttee, 1986–90; Adv. Panel, Law Center, USC, 1987–. Mem. Editl Bd, Rent Review and Lease Renewal, 1985–89. *Address:* Whites Farmhouse, Mickleton, near Chipping Campden, Glos GL55 6PU. *T:* Mickleton (0386) 438146.

POWELL, John Lewis; QC 1990; *b* 14 Sept. 1950; *s* of Gwyn Powell and Lilian Mary (*née* Griffiths); *m* 1973, Eva Zofia Lomnicka; one *s* two *d. Educ:* Christ Coll., Brecon; Amman Valley Grammar Sch.; Trinity Hall, Cambridge (MA, LLB). Called to the Bar, Middle Temple, 1974 (Harmsworth Schol.). In practice, 1974–. Contested (Lab) Cardigan, 1979. *Publications:* (with R. Jackson) Professional Negligence, 1982, 2nd edn 1987; (with Eva Lomnicka) Encyclopedia of Financial Services Law, 1987; (ed jtly) Palmer's Company Law, 27th edn 1987; Issues and Offers of Company Securities: the new regimes, 1988. *Recreations:* travel, walking. *Address:* 2 Crown Office Row, Temple, EC4Y 7HJ. *T:* 071–583 8155.

POWELL, Jonathan Leslie; Controller, BBC1, since 1988; *b* 25 April 1947; *s* of James Dawson Powell and Phyllis Nora Sylvester (*née* Doubleday). *Educ:* Sherborne; University of East Anglia. BA Hons (English and American Studies). Script editor and producer of drama, Granada TV, 1970–77; BBC TV: Producer, drama serials, 1977–83; Hd of Drama Series and Serials, 1983–87; Hd of Drama, 1987. *TV serials include:* Testament of Youth, 1979 (BAFTA award); Tinker Tailor Soldier Spy, 1979; Pride and Prejudice, 1980; Thérèse Raquin, 1980; The Bell, 1982; Smiley's People, 1982 (Peabody Medal, USA); The Old Men at the Zoo, 1983; Bleak House, 1985; Tender is the Night, 1985; A Perfect Spy, 1987. Royal Television Soc. Silver Award for outstanding achievement, 1979–80. *Address:* c/o Television Centre, Wood Lane, W12 7RJ. *T:* 081–743 8000.

POWELL, Prof. Lawrie William, AC 1990; MD, PhD; FRCP, FRACP; Professor of Medicine, University of Queensland, since 1975; Director, Queensland Institute of Medical Research, since 1990; *b* 4 Dec. 1934; *s* of Victor Alexander Powell and Ellen Evelyn (*née* Davidson); *m* 1958, Margaret Emily Ingram; two *s* three *d. Educ:* Univ. of Queensland (MB BS 1958; PhD 1973); Univ. of London (MD 1965); Harvard Medical Sch. FRCP 1991. FRACP 1975. Hon. Lectr, Royal Free Hosp. and Univ. of London, 1963–65; Vis. Prof., Harvard Medical Sch., 1972–73. *Publications:* Metals and the Liver, 1978; Fundamentals of Gastroenterology, 1975, 5th edn 1991. *Recreations:* music, chess, bushwalking. *Address:* 22 Paten Road, The Gap, Brisbane, Qld 4061, Australia.

POWELL, Lewis Franklin, Jr; Associate Justice of US Supreme Court, 1971–87, retired; *b* Suffolk, Va, USA, 19 Sept. 1907; *s* of Lewis Franklin Powell and Mary Lewis (*née* Gwathmey); *m* 1936, Josephine Pierce Rucker; one *s* three *d. Educ:* McGuire's Univ. Sch., Richmond, Va; Washington and Lee Univ., Lexington, Va (BS *magnum cum laude,* LLB); Harvard Law Sch. (LLM). Admitted to practice, Bar of Virginia, 1931; subseq. practised law; partner in firm of Hunton, Williams, Gay, Powell and Gibson, in Richmond, 1938–71. Served War, May 1942–Feb. 1946, USAAF, overseas, to rank Col; subseq. Col. US Reserve. Legion of Merit and Bronze Star (US), also Croix de Guerre with Palms (France). Member: Nat. Commn on Law Enforcement and Admin of Justice, 1965–67; Blue Ribbon Defence Panel, 1969–70. Chairman or Dir of companies. Pres., Virginia State Bd of Educn; Past Chm. and Trustee, Colonial Williamsburg Foundn; Trustee, Washington and Lee Univ., etc. Mem., Amer. Bar Assoc. (Pres. 1964–65); Fellow, Amer. Bar Foundn (Pres. 1969–71); Pres. or Mem. various Bar Assocs and other legal and social instns; Hon. Bencher, Lincoln's Inn. Holds several hon. degrees. Phi Beta Kappa. Is a Democrat. *Publications:* contribs to legal periodicals, etc. *Address:* c/o Supreme Court Building, Washington, DC 20543, USA. *Club:* University (NYC).

POWELL, Prof. Michael James David, FRS 1983; John Humphrey Plummer Professor of Applied Numerical Analysis, University of Cambridge, since 1976; Professorial Fellow of Pembroke College, Cambridge, since 1978; *b* 29 July 1936; *s* of William James David Powell and Beatrice Margaret (*née* Page); *m* 1959, Caroline Mary Henderson; two *d* (one *s* decd). *Educ:* Eastbourne Coll.; Peterhouse, Cambridge (Schol.; BA 1959; ScD 1979). Mathematician at Atomic Energy Research Estabt, Harwell, 1959–76; special merit research appt to banded level, 1969, and to senior level, 1975. George B. Dantzig prize in Mathematical Programming, 1982; Naylor Prize, London Math. Soc., 1983. *Publications:* Approximation Theory and Methods, 1981; papers on numerical mathematics, especially approximation and optimization calculations. *Recreations:* canals, golf, walking. *Address:* 134 Milton Road, Cambridge.

POWELL, Sir Nicholas (Folliott Douglas), 4th Bt *cr* 1897; Company Director; *b* 17 July 1935; *s* of Sir Richard George Douglas Powell, 3rd Bt, MC, and Elizabeth Josephine (*d* 1979), *d* of late Lt-Col O. R. McMullen, CMG; *S* father, 1980; *m* 1st, 1960, Daphne Jean (marr. diss. 1987), 2nd *d* of G. H. Errington, MC; one *s* one *d*; 2nd, 1987, Davina Allsopp; two *s. Educ:* Gordonstoun. Lieut Welsh Guards, 1953–57. *Heir: s* James Richard Douglas Powell, *b* 17 Oct. 1962. *Address:* Hillside Estate, Bromley, Zimbabwe.

POWELL, Prof. Percival Hugh, MA, DLitt, Dr Phil.; Professor of German, Indiana University, 1970–83, now Emeritus; *b* 4 Sept. 1912; 3rd *s* of late Thomas Powell and late Marie Sophia Roeser; *m* 1944, Dorothy Mavis Pattison (*née* Donald) (marr. diss. 1964); two *s* one adopted *d*; *m* 1966, Mary Kathleen (*née* Wilson); one *s. Educ:* University College, Cardiff (Fellow 1981); Univs of Rostock, Zürich, Bonn. 1st Class Hons German (Wales), 1933; Univ. Teachers' Diploma in Education, 1934; MA (Wales) Dist. 1936; Research Fellow of Univ. of Wales, 1936–38; Modern Languages Master, Towyn School, 1934–36; Dr Phil. (Rostock) 1938; Lektor in English, Univ. of Bonn, 1938–39; Asst Lectr, Univ. Coll., Cardiff, 1939–40; War Service, 1940–46 (Capt. Intelligence Corps); Lecturer in German, Univ. Coll., Leicester, 1946, Head of Department of German, 1954; Prof. of German, Univ. of Leicester, 1958–69. Barclay Acheson Prof. of Internat. Studies at Macalester Coll., Minn., USA, 1965–66. DLitt (Wales) 1962. British Academy award, 1963; Fritz Thyssen Foundation Award, 1964; Leverhulme Trust Award, 1968. *Publications:* Pierre Corneilles Dramen in Deutschen Bearbeitungen, 1939; critical editions of dramas of Andreas Gryphius, 1955–72; critical edn of J. G. Schoch's Comœdia vom Studentenleben, 1976; Trammels of Tradition, 1988; articles and reviews in English and foreign literary jls. *Recreation:* music. *Address:* c/o Department of Germanic Studies, Ballantine Hall, Indiana University, Bloomington, Indiana 47405, USA.

POWELL, Sir Philip, CH 1984; Kt 1975; OBE 1957; RA 1977 (ARA 1972); FRIBA; Partner of Powell and Moya, Architects, since 1946, and Powell, Moya and Partners, since 1976; *b* 15 March 1921; *yr s* of late Canon A. C. Powell and late Mary Winnifred (*née* Walker), Epsom and Chichester; *m* 1953, Philippa, *d* of Lt-Col C. C. Eccles, Tunbridge Wells; one *s* one *d. Educ:* Epsom Coll.; AA Sch. of Architecture (Hons Diploma). *Works include:* Churchill Gdns flats, Westminster, 1948–62 (won in open competition); houses and flats at Gospel Oak, St Pancras, 1954, Vauxhall Park, Lambeth, 1972, Covent Garden, 1983; houses at: Chichester, 1950; Toys Hill, 1954; Oxshott, 1954; Baughurst, Hants, 1954; Skylon for Fest. of Britain, 1951 (won in open competition); British Pavilion, Expo 70, Osaka, Japan, 1970; Mayfield Sch., Putney, 1955; Plumstead Manor Sch., Woolwich, 1970; Dining Rooms at Bath Acad. of Art, Corsham, 1970, and Eton Coll., 1974; extensions, Brasenose Coll., Oxford, 1961, and Corpus Christi Coll., Oxford, 1969;

picture gall. and undergrad. rooms, Christ Church, Oxford, 1967; Wolfson Coll., Oxford, 1974; Cripps Building, St John's Coll., Cambridge, 1967; Cripps Court, Queens' Coll., Cambridge, 1976; Chichester Fest. Theatre, 1961; Swimming Baths, Putney, 1967; Hosps at Swindon, Slough, High Wycombe, Wythenshawe, Woolwich, Maidstone, Hastings; Museum of London, 1976; London and Manchester Assurance HQ, near Exeter, 1978; Sch. for Advanced Urban Studies, Bristol Univ., 1981; NatWest Bank, Shaftesbury Ave, London, 1982; labs etc, and Queen's Building, RHBNC, Egham, 1986; Queen Elizabeth II Conf. Centre, Westminster, 1986. Has won numerous medals and awards for architectural work, inc. Royal Gold Medal for Architecture, RIBA, 1974. Mem. Royal Fine Art Commn, 1969–; Treas. RA, 1985–. *Recreations:* travel, listening to music. *Address:* 16 The Little Boltons, SW10 9LP. *T:* 071–373 8620; 21 Upper Cheyne Row, SW3 5JW. *T:* 071–351 3881.

POWELL, Raymond; MP (Lab) Ogmore, since 1979; *b* 19 June 1928; *s* of Albert and Lucy Powell; *m* 1950, Marion Grace Evans; one *s* one *d. Educ:* Pentre Grammar Sch.; National Council of Labour Colls; London School of Economics. British Rail, 1945–50; Shop Manager, 1950–66; Secretary/Agent to Walter Padley, MP, 1967–69, voluntarily, 1969–79; Sen. Administrative Officer, Welsh Water Authority, 1969–79. Welsh Regl Opposition Whip, Opposition Pairing Whip. Member: Select Cttee, Employment, 1979–82; Welsh Select Cttee, 1982–85; Select Cttee, H of C Services, 1987–; Cttee of Selection, 1987–; Chm., Parly New Building Cttee, 1987–. Chairman: Labour Party Wales, 1977–78; S Wales Euro-Constituency Labour Party, 1979–. Secretary: Welsh PLP, 1984–; Welsh Parly Party; Anglo-Bulgarian All Party Gp, 1984–; Treas., Anglo-Romanian All Party Gp, 1984–; Vice-Chm., Parly Agric. Cttee, 1987. *Recreations:* gardening, sport, music. *Address:* 8 Brynteg Gardens, Bridgend, Mid-Glam. *T:* Bridgend (0656) 652159. *Club:* Ogmore Constituency Labour Party Social.

POWELL, Sir Richard (Royle), GCB 1967 (KCB 1961; CB 1951); KBE 1954; CMG 1946; Deputy Chairman, Permanent Committee on Invisible Exports, 1968–76; Chairman, Alusuisse (UK) Ltd and subsidiary companies, 1969–84; *b* 30 July 1909; *er s* of Ernest Hartley and Florence Powell; unmarried. *Educ:* Queen Mary's Grammar Sch., Walsall; Sidney Sussex Coll., Cambridge (Hon. Fellow, 1972). Entered Civil Service, 1931 and apptd to Admiralty; Private Sec. to First Lord, 1934–37; Member of British Admiralty Technical Mission, Canada, and of British Merchant Shipbuilding Mission, and later of British Merchant Shipping Mission in USA, 1940–44; Civil Adviser to Commander-in-Chief, British Pacific Fleet, 1944–45; Under-Secretary, Ministry of Defence, 1946–48. Dep. Sec., Admiralty, 1948–50; Dep. Sec., Min. of Defence, 1950–56; Permanent Secretary, Board of Trade, 1960–68 (Min. of Defence, 1956–59). Dir, Philip Hill Investment Trust, 1968–81; Director: Whessoe Ltd, 1968–88; Sandoz Gp of Cos, 1972–87 (Chm.); Clerical, Medical and General Life Assurance Soc., 1972–85; BPB Industries PLC, 1973–83; Ladbroke Gp, 1980–86; Bridgewater Paper Co. Ltd, 1984–90. Pres., Inst. for Fiscal Studies, 1970–78. *Address:* 56 Montagu Square, W1H 1TG. *T:* 071–262 0911. *Club:* Athenæum.

POWELL, Robert Lane B.; *see* Bayne-Powell.

POWELL, Robert William; Headmaster of Sherborne, 1950–70; retired; *b* 29 October 1909; *s* of late William Powell and Agnes Emma Powell; *m* 1938, Charity Rosamond Collard; one *s. Educ:* Bristol Grammar School; Christ Church, Oxford. Assistant Master, Repton, May-Dec. 1934; Assistant Master, Charterhouse, 1935. Served War of 1939–45, 1940–45. Housemaster of Gownboys, Charterhouse, 1946–50. *Recreations:* fishing, music. *Address:* Manor Farm House, Child Okeford, near Blandford, Dorset DT11 8EE. *T:* Child Okeford (0258) 860648.

POWELL, Sally Jane, (Mrs Jonathan Powell); *see* Brampton, S. J.

POWELL, Tim; *see* Powell, H. A. R.

POWELL, Victor George Edward; Senior Partner, Victor G. Powell Associates, Management Consultants, 1963–88; Professor of Management, ILO International Centre for Advanced Training, 1982–88; Director, Mosscare Housing Association Ltd, 1974–88; retired; *b* London, 1 Jan. 1929; *s* of George Richard Powell and Kate Hughes Powell, London; *m* 1956, Patricia Copeland Allen; three *s* one *d. Educ:* Beckenham Grammar Sch.; Univs of Durham and Manchester. BA 1st cl. hons Econs 1954, MA Econ. Studies 1957, Dunelm; PhD Manchester 1963. RN Engrg Apprentice, 1944–48. Central Work Study Dept, ICI, London, 1954–56; Chief Work Study Engr, Ind Coope Ltd, 1956–58; Lectr in Industrial Administration, Manchester Univ., 1959, Hon. Lectr 1959–63; Asst Gen. Manager, Louis C. Edwards & Sons Ltd, 1959–63; Chm., Food Production & Processing Ltd, 1971–74. Sen. Advr, 1976, Dir and Chief Advr, 1977–82, ILO. Gen. Sec., 1970–72, Dir, 1972–73, War on Want. MBIM 1957; Mem. Inst. Management Consultants, 1968. *Publications:* Economics of Plant Investment and Replacement Decisions, 1964; Techniques for Improving Distribution Management, 1968; Warehousing, 1976; Improving the Performance of Public Enterprises, 1986; various articles. *Recreations:* music, walking. *Address:* Knowles House, Hollin Lane, Sutton, Macclesfield, Cheshire SK11 0HR. *T:* Sutton (02605) 2334.

POWELL, William Rhys; MP (C) Corby, since 1983; *b* 3 Aug. 1948; *s* of Rev. Canon Edward Powell and Anne Powell; *m* 1973, Elizabeth Vaudin; three *d. Educ:* Lancing College; Emmanuel College, Cambridge. BA 1970, MA 1973. Called to the Bar, Lincoln's Inn, 1971; Barrister, South Eastern Circuit, 1971–87. PPS to Minister for Overseas Develt, 1985–86, to Sec. of State for the Envmt, 1990–. Member: Select Cttee on Procedure, 1987–90; Select Cttee on Foreign Affairs, 1990–91; Jt Parly Ecclesiastical Cttee, 1987–; Joint Secretary: Cons. Back-bench for. Affairs Cttee, 1985 and 1987–90; Cons. Back-bench Defence Cttee, 1988–90. Mem. Council, British Atlantic Cttee, 1985–90. As Private Mem. piloted Copyright (Computer Software) Amendment Act, 1985. *Address:* House of Commons, SW1A 0AA. *Club:* Corby Conservative.

POWELL-COTTON, Christopher, CMG 1961; MBE 1951; MC 1945; JP; Uganda CS, retired; *b* 23 Feb. 1918; *s* of Major P. H. G. Powell-Cotton and Mrs H. B. Powell-Cotton (*née* Slater); unmarried. *Educ:* Harrow School; Trinity College, Cambridge. Army Service, 1939–45: commissioned Buffs, 1940; seconded KAR, Oct. 1940; T/Major, 1943. Apptd to Uganda Administration, 1940, and released for Mil. Service. District Commissioner, 1950; Provincial Commissioner, 1955; Minister of Security and External Relations, 1961. Landowner in SE Kent. Dir, Powell-Cotton Museum of Nat. History and Ethnography. *Address:* Quex Park, Birchington, Kent. *T:* Thanet (0843) 41836. *Club:* MCC.

POWELL-JONES, John Ernest, CMG 1974; HM Diplomatic Service, retired; Ambassador to Switzerland, 1982–85; *b* 14 April 1925; *s* of late Walter James Powell-Jones and Gladys Margaret (*née* Taylor); *m* 1st, 1949, Ann Murray (marr. diss. 1967); two *s* one *d*; 2nd, 1968, Pamela Sale. *Educ:* Charterhouse; University Coll., Oxford (1st cl. Modern Hist.). Served with Rifle Bde, 1943–46. HM Foreign (now Diplomatic) Service, 1949; 3rd Sec. and Vice-Consul, Bogota, 1950–52; Eastern and later Levant Dept, FO, 1952–55; 2nd, later 1st Sec., Athens, 1955–59; News Dept, FO, 1959–60; 1st Sec., Leopoldville, 1961–62; UN Dept, FO, 1963–67; ndc Canada 1967–68; Counsellor,

Political Adviser's Office, Singapore, 1968–69; Counsellor and Consul-General, Athens, 1970–73; Ambassador at Phnom Penh, 1973–75; RCDS 1975; Ambassador to Senegal, Guinea, Mali, Mauritania and Guinea-Bissau, 1976–79, to Cape Verde, 1977–79; Ambassador and Perm. Rep., UN Conf. on Law of the Sea, 1979–82. Chm., Inter Counsel UK Ltd, 1986–. Mem., Waverley BC, 1987–. Member: Bd, Surrey Historic Bldgs Trust, 1989–; Council, SE England Agricl Soc., 1991–. *Recreations:* gardening, walking. *Address:* Gascons, Gaston Gate, Cranleigh, Surrey GU6 8QY. *T:* Cranleigh (0483) 274313. *Club:* Travellers'.

See also M. E. P. Jones.

POWER, Sir Alastair John Cecil, 4th Bt *cr* 1924, of Newlands Manor; *b* 15 Aug. 1958; *s* of Sir John Patrick McLannahan Power, 3rd Bt and of Melanie, *d* of Hon. Alastair Erskine; *S* father, 1984. *Heir: b* Adam Patrick Cecil Power, *b* 22 March 1963.

POWER, Mrs Brian St Quentin; *see* Stack, (Ann) Prunella.

POWER, Eugene Barnum, Hon. KBE 1977; microphotographer, retired 1970; business executive; *b* Traverse City, Mich, 4 June 1905; *s* of Glenn Warren Power and Annette (*née* Barnum); *m* 1929, Sadye L. Harwick; one *s*. *Educ:* Univ. of Mich (AB 1927, MBA 1930). With Edwards Bros, Inc., Ann Arbor, Mich, 1930–38; engaged in expts with methods and uses of microfilm technique for reprodn of materials for res., 1935; Founder: Univ. Microfilms (merged with Xerox Corp. 1962), 1938; Univ. Microfilms, Ltd London, 1952; Dir, Xerox Corp., 1962–68. Organized: 1st large microfilming proj. for libraries, copying all books printed in England before 1640; Microfilms, Inc., as distbn agency, using microfilm as reprodn medium for scientific and technical materials, 1942–62; Projected Books, Inc. (non-profit corp.), for distbn of reading and entertainment materials in photog. form to physically incapacitated, 1944–70; Eskimo Art, Inc. (non-profit corp.). During War 1939–45, dir. large-scale copying of important Brit. MSS in public and private archives, also enemy documents. Pres. and Chm., Power Foundn, 1968–; Mem. Bd of Dirs, Domino's Pizza Inc., Ann Arbor, 1978–. Special Rep. Co-ordinator of Inf. and of Library of Congress, London 1942, Office of Strategic Services, 1943–45. President: Internat. Micrographic Congress, 1964–65; Nat. Microfilm Assoc., 1946–54. Chm., Mich Co-ordinating Council for State Higher Educn; Regent, Univ. of Michigan, 1956–66. Chm., Ann Arbor Summer Festival Inc., 1978–88 (Trustee, 1978–). Member: Council of Nat. Endowment for the Humanities, 1968–74; Amer. Philos. Soc., 1975. Fellow, Nat. Microfilm Assoc., 1963 (Award of Merit, 1956); Fellow of Merit, Internat. Micrographic Congress, 1978; Paul Harris Fellow, Rotary Internat., 1979. Hon. Fellow: Magdalene Coll., Cambridge, 1967; Northwestern Mich Coll., 1967. Hon. LHD: St John's Univ., 1966; Univ. of Michigan, 1971. First Alumni Achievement Award, Univ. of Michigan Business Sch., 1990. *Publications:* numerous articles on techniques and uses of microfilm. *Recreations:* swimming, sailing, fishing, hunting, music. *Address:* (home) 989 Forest Road, Barton Hills, Ann Arbor, Mich 48105, USA. *T:* (313) 662–2886; (office) 2929 Plymouth Road, Ann Arbor, Mich 48105, USA. *T:* (313) 769–8424. *Clubs:* American; Rotary (Ann Arbor).

POWER, Michael George; Director, Greenwich Hospital, 1982–87; *b* 2 April 1924; *s* of Admiral of the Fleet Sir Arthur Power, GCB, GBE, CVO, and Amy Isabel (*née* Bingham); *m* 1954, Kathleen Maeve (*née* McCaul); one *s* two *d* and two step *d*. *Educ:* Rugby Sch.; Corpus Christi Coll., Cambridge. Served War, Rifle Bde, 1942–46 (Captain); ME Centre of Arab Studies (Jerusalem), 1946–47; Colonial Admin. Service, 1947–63: District Officer: Kenya, 1948–53; Malaya, 1953–57; Kenya, 1957–63; Home Civil Service, 1963–81; Under-Sec., MoD, 1973–81. Almoner, Christ's Hosp., 1983–88. *Recreations:* carpentry, gardening. *Address:* Wancom Way, Puttenham Heath Road, Compton, Guildford. *T:* Guildford (0483) 810470.

POWER, Hon. Noel Plunkett; Hon. Mr Justice Power; a Justice of Appeal of the Supreme Court of Hong Kong, since 1987 (a Judge of the Supreme Court, 1979–87); *b* 4 Dec. 1929; *s* of John Joseph Power and Hilda Power; *m* 1965, Irma Maroya; two *s* one *d*. *Educ:* Downlands Coll.; Univ. of Queensland (BA, LLB). Called to the Bar, Supreme Court of Queensland and High Court of Australia, 1955; Magistrate, Hong Kong, 1965–76; Pres., Lands Tribunal, Hong Kong, 1976–79. *Publications:* (ed) Lands Tribunal Law Reports, 1976–79. *Recreations:* travel, cooking, reading, tennis. *Address:* 76 G Peak Road, Hong Kong. *T:* 5–8496798. *Clubs:* Hong Kong (Hong Kong); Queensland (Brisbane).

POWERSCOURT, 10th Viscount *cr* 1743; **Mervyn Niall Wingfield;** Baron Wingfield, 1743; Baron Powerscourt (UK), 1885; *b* 3 Sept. 1935; *s* of 9th Viscount Powerscourt and of Sheila Claude, *d* of late Lt-Col Claude Beddington; *S* father, 1973; *m* 1962, Wendy Ann Pauline (marr. diss. 1974), *d* of R. C. G. Slazenger; one *s* one *d*; *m* 1978, Pauline, *d* of W. P. Vann, San Francisco. *Educ:* Stowe; Trinity Coll., Cambridge. Formerly Irish Guards. *Heir: s* Hon. Mervyn Anthony Wingfield, *b* 21 Aug. 1963.

See also Sir H. R. H. Langrishe, Bt.

POWIS, 7th Earl of, *cr* 1804; **George William Herbert;** Baron Clive (Ire.) 1762; Baron Clive (GB) 1794; Viscount Clive, Baron Herbert of Chirbury, Baron Powis 1804; *b* 4 June 1925; *s* of Rt Rev. Percy Mark Herbert, KCVO (*d* 1968), former Bishop of Norwich, and Hon. Elaine Letitia Algitha (*d* 1984), *d* of 5th Baron Bolton; *S* cousin, 1988; *m* 1949, Hon. Katherine Odeyne de Grey, *d* of 8th Baron Walsingham, DSO, OBE; four *s* two adopted *d*. *Educ:* Eton; Trinity Coll., Cambridge (MA). FRICS. Served War with Rifle Brigade, 1943–46. Resident Land Agent, 1949–70. *Recreations:* agriculture, genealogy, local history. *Heir: s* Viscount Clive, *qv*. *Address:* Marrington Hall, Chirbury, Montgomery, Powys SY15 6DR. *T:* Chirbury (093872) 256.

POWLES, Sir Guy (Richardson), ONZ 1990; KBE 1961; CMG 1954; ED 1944; first Ombudsman of New Zealand, 1962–75, Chief Ombudsman, 1975–77; *b* 5 April 1905; *s* of late Colonel C. G. Powles, CMG, DSO, New Zealand Staff Corps; *m* 1931, Eileen, *d* of A. J. Nicholls; two *s*. *Educ:* Wellington Coll., NZ; Victoria Univ. (LLB). Barrister, Supreme Court, New Zealand, 1929; served War of 1939–45 with NZ Military Forces, to rank of Colonel; Counsellor, NZ Legation, Washington, DC, USA, 1946–48; High Comr, Western Samoa, 1949–60, for NZ in India, 1960–62, Ceylon, 1960–62, and Ambassador of NZ to Nepal, 1960–62. President, NZ Inst. of Internat. Affairs, 1967–71. NZ Comr, Commn of the Churches on Internat. Affairs, World Council of Churches, 1971–80; Comr, Internat. Commn of Jurists, Geneva, 1975–. Race Relations Conciliator, 1971–73. Patron: Amnesty International (NZ); NZ-India Soc.; Environmental Defence Soc. Hon. LLD Victoria Univ. of Wellington, 1969. *Publications:* articles and speeches on international affairs, administrative law and race relations. *Address:* 34 Wesley Road, Wellington, NZ.

POWLETT; *see* Orde-Powlett.

POWLEY, John Albert; Enquiry Officer, Post Office; *b* 3 Aug. 1936; *s* of Albert and Evelyn Powley; *m* 1957, Jill (*née* Palmer); two *s* one *d*. *Educ:* Cambridge Grammar Sch.; Cambridgeshire Coll. of Arts and Technology. Apprenticeship, Pye Ltd, 1952–57; RAF, 1957–59; retail shop selling and servicing radio, television and electrical goods, 1960–84. Cambs CC, 1967–77; Cambridge City Council, 1967–79; Leader, Cons. Group, 1973–79; Chm., Housing Cttee, 1972–74, 1976–79; Leader of Council, 1976–79. Contested (C): Harlow, 1979; Norwich S, 1987. MP (C) Norwich S, 1983–87. Sec./Manager, Wensum Valley Golf Club, Taverham, Norfolk. *Recreations:* golf, cricket, football. *Address:* Kyte End, 70A Brook Street, Soham, Ely, Cambs CB7 5AE.

POWNALL, Henry Charles; QC 1979; **His Honour Judge Pownall;** a Circuit Judge, since 1984; *b* 25 Feb. 1927; *er s* of late John Cecil Glossop Pownall, CB, and of Margaret Nina Pownall (*née* Jesson); *m* 1955, Sarah Bettine, *d* of late Major John Deverell; one *s* one *d* (and one *d* decd). *Educ:* Rugby Sch.; Trinity Coll., Cambridge; BA 1950, MA 1963; LLB 1951. Served War, Royal Navy, 1945–48. Called to Bar, Inner Temple, 1954, Bencher, 1976; joined South-Eastern Circuit, 1954. Junior Prosecuting Counsel to the Crown at the Central Criminal Court, 1964–71; a Sen., subseq. 2nd, Prosecuting Counsel, 1971–79; a Recorder of the Crown Court, 1972–84; Sen. Resident Judge, Knightsbridge Crown Court, 1984–88; a Judge, Courts of Appeal of Jersey and Guernsey, 1980–86. Mem. Cttee: Orders and Medals Research Soc., 1961–69, and 1970– (Pres., 1971–75, 1977–81); Nat. Benevolent Instn, 1964–. Hon. Legal Advr, ABA, 1976–89. Freeman, City of London, 1989. *Publication:* Korean Campaign Medals, 1950–53, 1957. *Recreations:* travel; medals and medal ribbons. *Address:* Central Criminal Court, Old Bailey, EC4M 7EH. *Clubs:* Pratt's; Ebury Court.

See also J. L. Pownall, Sir D. M. Mountain.

POWNALL, John Harvey; Director, DTI-North West, since 1988; *b* 24 Oct. 1933; *s* of Eric Pownall and Gladys M. Pownall (*née* Baily); *m* 1958, Pauline M. Marsden, *o d* of William Denton Marsden; one *s* two *d*. *Educ:* Tonbridge School; Imperial College, London (BSc Eng Met). ARSM, MIMM, CEng. Scientific Officer, Atomic Energy Research Estab., Harwell, 1955–59; Warren Spring Lab., DSIR, 1959–64; Dept of Economic Affairs, 1964–66; Board of Trade/Dept of Trade and Industry, 1966–83; Dir-Gen., Council of Mechanical and Metal Trade Assocs, 1983–85; Hd of Electricity Div., Dept of Energy, 1985–87; Under Sec., DTI, 1987, on secondment to CEGB, 1987–88. *Publications:* papers in professional jls. *Address:* c/o Department of Trade and Industry, Sunley Tower, Piccadilly Plaza, Manchester M1 4BA. *T:* 061–838 5500. *Clubs:* Athenæum; St James's (Manchester).

POWNALL, Brig. John Lionel, OBE 1972; Deputy Chairman, Police Complaints Authority, since 1986 (Member, since 1985); *b* 10 May 1929; *yr s* of late John Cecil Glossop Pownall, CB and of Margaret Nina Pownall (*née* Jesson); *m* 1962, Sylvia Joan Cameron Conn, *d* of late J. Cameron Conn, WS and Florence Conn (*née* Lennox); two *s*. *Educ:* Rugby School; RMA Sandhurst. Commissioned 16th/5th Lancers, 1949; served Egypt, Cyrenaica, Tripolitania, BAOR, Hong Kong, Cyprus; psc, jssc; Comd 16th/5th The Queen's Royal Lancers, 1969–71; Adjutant-Gen.'s Secretariat, 1971–72; Officer i/c RAC Manning and Records, 1973–75; Col, GS Near East Land Forces/Land Forces Cyprus, 1975–78; Asst Dir, Defence Policy Staff, MoD, 1978–79; Brig. RAC, UKLF, 1979–82; Brig. GS, MoD, 1982–84; retired 1984. Col, 16th/5th The Queen's Royal Lancers, 1985–90. *Recreations:* country pursuits, arts. *Address:* c/o Coutts & Co., 440 Strand, WC2R 0QS. *Club:* Cavalry and Guards.

See also H. C. Pownall.

POWNALL, Leslie Leigh, MA, PhD; Chairman, NSW Planning and Environment Commission, 1974–77, retired; *b* 1 Nov. 1921; *y s* of A. de S. Pownall, Wanganui, New Zealand; *m* 1943, Judith, *d* of late Harold Whittaker, Palmerston North. *Educ:* Palmerston North Boys' High Sch.; Victoria University College, University of Canterbury, University of Wisconsin. Asst Master, Christchurch Boys' High Sch., 1941–46; Lecturer in Geography: Christchurch Teachers' Coll., 1946–47; Ardmore Teachers' Coll., 1948–49; Auckland University College, 1949–51; Senior Lecturer in Geography, 1951–60, Prof. of Geography, 1960–61, Vice-Chancellor and Rector, 1961–66, University of Canterbury; Clerk of the University Senate, Univ. of London, 1966–74. Consultant, Inter-University Council for Higher Educn Overseas, London, 1963; Consultant to Chm. of Working Party on Higher Educn in E Africa, 1968–69. Member Meeting, Council on World Tensions on Social and Economic Development (S Asia and Pacific), Kuala Lumpur, Malaysia, 1964; Governor, Internat. Students Trust, London, 1967–74; Member: Central Governing Body, City Parochial Foundation, London, 1967–74 (Mem., Grants Sub-Cttee; Chm., Finance and Gen. Purposes Cttee); UK Commonwealth Scholarship Commn, 1979–80. *Publications:* New Zealand, 1951 (New York); geographic contrib. in academic journals of America, Netherlands and New Zealand. *Recreations:* music, literature. *Clubs:* Canterbury, University (Christchurch, NZ).

POWYS, family name of **Baron Lilford.**

POYNTON, Sir (Arthur) Hilton, GCMG 1964 (KCMG 1949; CMG 1946); *b* 20 April 1905; *y s* of late Arthur Blackburne Poynton, formerly Master of University College, Oxford; *m* 1946, Elisabeth Joan, *d* of late Rev. Edmund Williams; two *s* one *d*. *Educ:* Marlborough Coll.; Brasenose Coll., Oxford (Hon. Fellow 1964). Entered Civil Service, Department of Scientific and Industrial Research, 1927; transferred to Colonial Office, 1929; Private Secretary to Minister of Supply and Minister of Production 1941–43; reverted to Colonial Office, 1943; Permanent Under-Secretary of State, CO, 1959–66. Mem. Governing Body, SPCK, 1967–72. Mem., Ct of Governors, London Sch. Hygiene and Tropical Med., 1965–77; Treas., Soc. Promotion Roman Studies, 1967–76; Dir, Overseas Branch, St John Ambulance, 1968–75. KStJ 1968. *Recreations:* music, travel. *Address:* Craigmillar, 47 Stanhope Road, Croydon CR0 5NS. *T:* 081–688 3729.

POYNTON, (John) Orde, CMG 1961; MD; Consulting Bibliographer, University of Melbourne, 1962–74; Fellow of Graduate House, University of Melbourne, 1971–84; *b* 9 April 1906; *o s* of Frederick John Poynton, MD, FRCP, and Alice Constance, *d* of Sir John William Powlett Campbell-Orde, 3rd Bt, of Kilmory; *m* 1965, Lola, *widow* of Group Captain T. S. Horry, DFC, AFC. *Educ:* Marlborough Coll.; Gonville and Caius Coll., Cambridge; Charing Cross Hospital (Univ. Schol. 1927–30). MA, MD (Cambridge); MD (Adelaide) 1948; MRCS, LRCP; Horton-Smith prize, University of Cambridge, 1940. Sen. Resident MO, Charing Cross Hosp., 1932–33; Health Officer, Fed. Malay States, 1936–37; Res. Officer Inst. for Med. Research, FMS, 1937–38, Pathologist, 1938–46; Lectr in Pathology, Univ. of Adelaide, 1947–50; Pathologist, Inst. of Med. and Veterinary Science, S Australia, 1948–50, Director, 1950–61. Dir, Commercial Finance Co., 1960–70. Hon. LLD Melbourne, 1977. *Publications:* monographs and papers relating to medicine and bibliography. *Recreation:* bibliognostics. *Address:* 8 Seymour Avenue, Mount Eliza, Victoria 3930, Australia. *Club:* MCC.

POYNTZ, Rt. Rev. Samuel Greenfield; *see* Connor, Bishop of.

PRACY, Robert, FRCS; Dean of the Institute of Laryngology and Otology, University of London, 1981–85, retired; a Medical Chairman, Pensions Appeal Tribunals, since 1984 (Medical Member, since 1982); *b* 19 Sept. 1921; *s* of Douglas Sherrin Pracy and Gwendoline Blanche Power; *m* 1946, Elizabeth Patricia Spicer; one *s* two *d* (and one *s* decd). *Educ:* Berkhamsted Sch.; St Bartholomew's Hosp. Med. Coll. (MB BS 1945); MPhil (Lond.) 1984. LRCP 1944; MRCS, FRCS 1953. Former Captain, RAMC. House Surgeon appts, St Bartholomew's Hosp.; formerly: Registrar, Royal Nat. Throat, Nose and Ear Hosp.; Consultant Surgeon: Liverpool Regional Board, 1954; United Liverpool Hosps, 1959; Alder Hey Childrens' Hosp., 1960; Royal Nat. Throat, Nose and Ear Hosp.; Hosp. for Sick Children, Gt Ormond St; Dir, Dept of Otolaryngology, Liverpool Univ. Mem. Ct of Examnrs, RCS and RCSI. Lectures: Yearsley, 1976; Joshi, 1978; Wilde, 1979; Semon, London Univ., 1980. Pres., British Assoc. of Otolaryngologists; FRSocMed (Pres., Sect. of Laryngology, 1982–83). Hon. FRCSI 1982; Hon. Fellow: Irish Otolaryngol Assoc.; Assoc. of Otolaryngologists of India; Polish Otolaryngological Assoc. *Publications:* (jtly) Short Textbook: Ear, Nose and Throat, 1970, 2nd edn 1974 (trans. Italian, Portuguese, Spanish); (jtly) Ear, Nose and Throat Surgery and Nursing, 1977; contribs to learned jls. *Recreations:* cabinet making, painting, engraving, reading, theatre. *Address:* Wardens Post, Moor Lane, South Newington, near Banbury, Oxon OX15 4JQ. *T:* Banbury (0295) 720433.

PRAG, (Andrew) John (Nicholas Warburg), MA, DPhil; FSA; Keeper of Archaeology, Manchester Museum, University of Manchester, since 1969; *b* 28 Aug. 1941; *s* of Adolf Prag and Frede Charlotte (*née* Warburg); *m* 1969, Kay (*née* Wright); one *s* one *d. Educ:* Westminster Sch. (Queen's Scholar); Brasenose Coll., Oxford (Domus Exhibnr 1960; Hon. Scholar 1962; BA 1964; Dip. Classical Archaeol. 1966; Sen. Hulme Scholar, 1967; MA 1967; DPhil 1975). FSA 1977. Temp. Asst Keeper, Ashmolean Museum, Oxford, 1966–67; Hon. Lectr, Dept of History, 1977–83, Dept of Archaeology, 1984–, Univ. of Manchester. Vis. Prof. of Classics, McMaster Univ., 1978. Editor, Archaeological Reports, 1975–87. *Publications:* The Oresteia: iconographic and narrative tradition, 1975; articles on Greek art and archaeology in learned jls. *Recreations:* travel, walking, cooking, music. *Address:* 9 Prince's Road, Heaton Moor, Stockport, Cheshire SK4 3NQ. *T:* 061–432 2459.

PRAG, Derek; Member (C) Hertfordshire, European Parliament, since 1979; *b* 6 Aug. 1923; *s* of Abraham J. Prag and Edith Prag; *m* 1948, Dora Weiner; three *s. Educ:* Bolton Sch.; Emmanuel Coll., Univ. of Cambridge (MA; Cert. of Competent Knowledge in Russian). Served War, Intelligence Corps, England, Egypt, Italy, Austria, 1942–47. Economic journalist with Reuters News Agency in London, Brussels and Madrid, 1950–55; Information Service of High Authority, European Coal and Steel Community, 1955–59; Head of Division, Jt Information Service of European Communities, 1959–65; Director, London Information Office of European Communities, 1965–73; ran own consultancy company on relations with EEC, 1973–79. Mem., 1982–, Dep. Chm., 1989–, Institutional Cttee (Europ. Democratic Gp spokesman, 1982–84 and 1987–); Political spokesman for European Democratic (Cons.) Group, 1984–87; Chm., European Parlt All-Party Disablement Gp, 1980–. Associate Mem., RIIA, 1973–. Hon. Dir, EEC Commn, 1974. Silver Medal of European Merit, Fondation du Mérite Européen, 1974. *Publications:* Businessman's Guide to the Common Market, 1973; various reports on Europe's internat. role, and booklets and articles on European integration. *Recreations:* reading, theatre, music, walking, swimming, gardening. *Address:* 47 New Road, Digswell, Welwyn, Herts AL6 0AQ. *Clubs:* Carlton; Royal Automobile (Brussels).

PRAG, John; *see* Prag, A. J. N. W.

PRAGNELL, Anthony William, CBE 1982 (OBE 1960); DFC 1944; Deputy Director-General, Independent Broadcasting Authority (formerly Independent Television Authority), 1961–83; Director, Channel Four Television, 1983–88; *b* 15 Feb. 1921; *s* of William Hendley Pragnell and Silvia Pragnell; *m* 1955, Teresa Mary (*d* 1988), *d* of Leo and Anne Monaghan, Maidstone; one *s* one *d. Educ:* Cardinal Vaughan Sch., London. Asst Examiner, Estate Duty Office, 1939. Served RAF, 1942–46. Examiner, Estate Duty Office, 1946. LLB London Univ., 1949. Asst Principal, General Post Office, 1950; Asst Secretary, ITA, 1954; Secretary, ITA, 1955. Vis. Fellow, European Inst. for the Media, Univ. of Manchester, 1983. Fellow, Royal Television Soc., 1980. Emile Noël European Prize, 1987. *Publication:* Television in Europe: quality and values in a time of change, 1985. *Recreations:* reading, music. *Address:* Ashley, Grassy Lane, Sevenoaks, Kent TN13 1PL. *T:* Sevenoaks (0732) 451463. *Club:* Royal Air Force.

PRAIS, Prof. Sigbert Jon, FBA 1985; Senior Research Fellow, National Institute of Economic and Social Research, London, since 1970; Visiting Professor of Economics, City University, since 1975; *b* 19 Dec. 1928; *s* of Samuel and Bertha Prais; *m* 1971, Vivien Hennessy, LLM, solicitor; one *s* three *d. Educ:* King Edward's School, Birmingham; Univ. of Birmingham (MCom); Univ. of Cambridge (PhD, ScD); Univ. of Chicago. Dept of Applied Economics, Cambridge, 1950–57; research officer, NIESR, 1953–59; UN Tech. Assistance Orgn, 1959–60; IMF Washington, 1960–61; Finance Dir, Elbief Co., 1961–70. Mem. Council, Royal Economic Soc., 1979–83. Mem. Council, City Univ., 1990. Hon. DLitt City Univ., 1989. *Publications:* Analysis of Family Budgets (jtly), 1955, 2nd edn 1971; Evolution of Giant Firms in Britain, 1976, 2nd edn 1981; Productivity and Industrial Structure, 1981; articles in economic and statistical jls, esp. on influence of educn on economic progress. *Address:* 83 West Heath Road, NW3 7TN. *T:* 081–458 4428; (office) 071–222 7665.

PRANCE, Prof. Ghillean Tolmie, DPhil; FLS, FIBiol; FRGS; Director, Royal Botanic Gardens, Kew, since 1988; *b* 13 July 1937; *s* of Basil Camden Prance, CIE, OBE and Margaret Hope Prance (*née* Tolmie); *m* 1961, Anne Elizabeth Hay; two *d. Educ:* Malvern Coll.; Keble Coll., Oxford (BA, MA, DPhil). FLS 1961; FIBiol 1988. New York Botanical Garden: Res. Asst, 1963–66; Associate Curator, 1966–68; B. A. Krukoff Curator of Amazonian Botany, 1968–75; Dir of Research, 1975–81; Vice-Pres., 1977–81; Senior Vice-Pres., 1981–88. Adjunct Prof., City Univ. of NY, 1968–; Vis. Prof. in Tropical Studies, Yale, 1983–89; Vis. Prof., Reading Univ., 1988–; Dir of Graduate Studies, Instituto Nacional de Pesquisas da Amazônia, Manaus, Brazil, 1973–75; 14 botanical expedns to Amazonia. President: Assoc. of Tropical Biol., 1979–80; Amer. Assoc. of Plant Taxonomists, 1984–85; Systematics Assoc., 1989–91; Mem. Council, RHS, 1990–. FRGS 1989; Fellow, AAAS, 1990; Corresp. Mem., Brazilian Acad. of Scis, 1976; Foreign Member: Royal Danish Acad. of Scis and Letters, 1988; Royal Swedish Acad. of Scis, 1989. Fil Dr *hc* Univ. Göteborgs, Sweden, 1983. Linnean Medal, 1990. *Publications:* Arvores de Manaus, 1975; Algumas Flores da Amazonia, 1976; Extinction is Forever, 1977; Biological Diversification in the Tropics, 1981; Amazonia: key environments, 1985; Leaves, 1986; Manual de Botânica Econômica do Maranhão, 1988; Flowers for all Seasons, 1989. *Recreations:* squash, flower stamp collecting, bird watching. *Address:* 49 Kew Green, Richmond, Surrey TW9 3AA. *T:* 081–940 1171. *Club:* Explorers (New York) (Fellow).

PRANKERD, Thomas Arthur John, FRCP; Professor of Clinical Haematology, 1965–79 and Dean, 1972–77, University College Hospital Medical School; Hon. Consultant Physician: University College Hospital; Whittington Hospital; *b* 11 Sept. 1924; *s* of late H. A. Prankerd, Barrister-at-Law, and J. D. Shorthose; *m* 1950, Margaret Vera Harrison Cripps; two *s* (and one *s* one *d* decd). *Educ:* Charterhouse Sch.; St Bartholomew's Hospital Med. Sch. MD (London) Gold Medal 1949; FRCP 1962. Jnr med. appts, St Bart's and University Coll. Hosp., 1947–60. Major, RAMC, 1948–50. Univ. Travelling Fellow, USA, 1953–54; Consultant Physician, University Coll. Hosp., 1960–65. Goulstonian Lectr, RCP, 1963; Examr, RCP, and various univs. Vis. Prof.,

Univ. of Perth, WA, 1972. Mem., NE Thames RHA, 1976–79. Mem. Bd of Governors, UCH, 1972–74. *Publications:* The Red Cell, 1961; Haematology in Medical Practice, 1968; articles in med. jls. *Recreations:* fishing, gardening, music. *Address:* Milton Lake, Milton Abbas, Blandford, Dorset DT11 0BJ. *T:* Milton Abbas (0822) 880278.

PRASADA, Krishna, CIE 1943; JP; ICS retired; Director-General, Posts and Telegraphs, New Delhi, 1945–53; *b* 4 Aug. 1894; *s* of Pandit Het Ram, CIE, *m* 1911, Bishan Devi (*d* 1950); three *s. Educ:* Bareilly; New Coll., Oxford. Joined ICS 1921; Joint Magistrate and subsequently a District Magistrate in UP. Services borrowed by Government of India in 1934, when he was appointed as Postmaster-General. Led Government of India deputations to International Tele-communications Conference, Cairo, 1938, Buenos Aires, 1952, and to International Postal Congress, Paris, 1947. Retired, 1954. Director, Rotary International, 1961–63. *Recreation:* tennis, Oxford Tennis Blue (1921) and played for India in the Davis Cup in 1927 and 1932. Won All India Tennis Championships. *Address:* D/152, East of Kailash, New Delhi 24, 65 India.

PRASASVINITCHAI, Sudhee; Kt Grand Cordon, Order of the Crown of Thailand, 1982; Kt Grand Cordon, Order of the White Elephant, 1986; Ambassador of Thailand to the Court of St James's, 1986–91; *b* 17 March 1931; *s* of Phra and Nang Prasasvinitchai; *m* 1964, Ponglak (*née* Sriyanonda); one *s* two *d. Educ:* Thammasat Univ., Bangkok (LLB); Magdalene Coll., Cambridge (MA, LLB); Univ. of Paris (DUP); National Defence Coll., Thailand. Joined Min. of Foreign Affairs, Thailand, 1950; Chief of S Asia Div., Political Dept, 1966; First Sec., Jakarta, 1968–70; Chief of Legal Div., Treaty and Legal Dept, 1970; Dep. Dir-Gen., Political Dept, 1973; Minister-Counsellor, Washington, DC, 1974–75; Ambassador and Perm. Rep. to UN, Geneva, 1976; Ambassador to Fed. Republic of Germany, 1979–82; Dir-Gen., Political Dept, 1982–84; Dep. Perm. Sec., Min. of Foreign Affairs, 1984–86. Chakrabarti Mala Medal, 1975. *Address:* c/o Royal Thai Embassy, 30 Queen's Gate, SW7 5JB. *T:* 071–589 2853. *Clubs:* Travellers', Hurlingham.

PRASHAR, Usha Kumari, (Mrs V. K. Sharma); Director, National Council for Voluntary Organisations, 1986–91; a part-time Civil Service Commissioner, since 1990; *b* 29 June 1948; *d* of Nauhria Lal Prashar and Durga Devi Prashar; *m* 1973, Vijay Kumar Sharma. *Educ:* Duchess of Gloucester Sch., Nairobi; Wakefield Girls' High Sch. (Head Girl, 1966–67); Univ. of Leeds (BA Hons Pol. Studies); Univ. of Glasgow (postgrad. Dip. Social Admin). Race Relations Bd, 1971–75; Asst Dir, Runnymede Trust, 1976–77, Dir, 1977–84; Res. Fellow, PSI, 1984–86. Vice-Chm., British Refugee Council, 1987–. Member: Arts Council of GB, 1979–81; Study Commn on the Family, 1980–83; Social Security Adv. Cttee, 1980–83; Exec. Cttee, Child Poverty Action Gp, 1984–85; GLAA, 1984–86; London Food Commn, 1984–90; BBC Educnl Broadcasting Council, 1987–89; Adv. Council, Open College, 1987–89; Solicitors' Complaints Bureau, 1989–; Lord Chancellor's Adv. Cttee on Legal Educn and Conduct, 1991–. Hon. Vice-Pres., Council for Overseas Student Affairs, 1986–. Trustee: Thames Help Trust, 1984–86; Charities Aid Foundn, 1986; Independent Broadcasting Telethon Trust, 1987–; Acad. of Indian Dance, 1987–; Chm., English Adv. Cttee, Nat. AIDS Trust, 1988–89; Patron: Sickle Cell Soc., 1986–; Elfrida Rathbone Soc., 1988–. FRSA. *Publications:* contributed to: Britain's Black Population, 1980; The System: a study of Lambeth Borough Council's race relations unit, 1981; Scarman and After, 1984; Sickle Cell Anaemia, Who Cares? a survey of screening, counselling, training and educational facilities in England, 1985; Routes or Road Blocks, a study of consultation arrangements between local authorities and local communities, 1985; Acheson and After: primary health care in the inner city, 1986. *Recreations:* painting, reading, country walks, squash, music.

PRATLEY, Alan Sawyer; Deputy Financial Controller, Commission of the European Communities, since 1990 (Director, Financial Control, 1986–90); *b* 25 Nov. 1933; *s* of Frederick Pratley and Hannah Pratley (*née* Sawyer); *m* 1st, 1960, Dorothea Rohland (marr. diss. 1979); two *d*; 2nd, 1979, Josette Kairis; one *d. Educ:* Latymer Upper School; Sidney Sussex Coll., Cambridge. BA Modern Languages (German, Russian). Head, German Dept, Stratford Grammar Sch., West Ham, 1958–60; Asst Dir, Examinations, Civil Service Commn, 1960–68; Home Office, 1968–73; Commission of the European Communities: Head, Individual Rights Div., 1973–79; Dep. Chef de cabinet to Christopher Tugendhat, 1979–80; Adviser to Michael O'Kennedy, 1980–81; Dir of Admin, 1981–86. *Recreations:* tennis, gardening. *Address:* Avenue de l'Abbaye d'Affligem 3, 1300 Wavre, Belgium. *T:* Wavre 22.66.06. *Club:* Travellers'.

PRATLEY, Clive William; Under Secretary, Lord Chancellor's Department, 1976–85; Circuit Administrator: Midland and Oxford Circuit, 1976–82; North-Eastern Circuit, 1982–85; a Reference Secretary (reserve panel), Monopolies and Mergers Commn, since 1990; *b* 23 Jan. 1929; *s* of late F. W. Pratley and late Minnie Pratley (*née* Hood); *m* 1962, Eva, *d* of Nils and Kerstin Kellgren, Stockholm; one *s* one *d. Educ:* RMA Sandhurst; and after retirement from Army, at Univs of Stockholm, 1961–62, and Hull, 1962–65 (LLB Hons). Commissioned into Royal Tank Regt, 1949; active list, 1949–61; Adjt, 2nd RTR, 1959–61; reserve list, 1961–79; Hon. Captain, 1979–. Entered Administrative Class of Home Civil Service as Principal, 1966; Lord Chancellor's Department: Sen. Principal, 1971; Asst Sec., 1974; Under Sec., 1976. *Recreations:* offshore sailing (RYA coastal skipper), the countryside, badminton, music. *Address:* The Old Chapel, Aldfield, near Ripon, North Yorkshire HG4 3BE. *T:* Ripon (0765) 620277. *Club:* Army and Navy.

PRATLEY, David Illingworth; Arts consultant, since 1986; Managing Director, Trinity College of Music, since 1988; *b* 24 Dec. 1948; *s* of Arthur George Pratley and Olive Constance Illingworth. *Educ:* Westminster Abbey Choir Sch.; Westminster Sch.; Univ. of Bristol (LLB). PRO, Thorndike Theatre, Leatherhead, 1970–71; Gen. Asst, Queen's Univ. Festival, Belfast, 1971–73; Dep. Dir, Merseyside Arts Assoc., 1973–76; Dir, Greater London Arts Assoc., 1976–81; Regl Dir, Arts Council of GB, 1981–86; Chief Exec., Royal Liverpool Philharmonic Soc., 1987–88. Chm., Alliance Arts Panel, 1987–88; Council Mem., Nat. Campaign for the Arts, 1986– (Chm., 1988–); Dir, Dance Umbrella Ltd, 1986–. FRSA. *Publications:* (co-ed) Culture for All, 1981; reports: The Pursuit of Competence—the Arts and the European Community, 1987; Cumbria County Arts Strategy, 1987. *Recreations:* music, theatre, art, countryside, travel. *Address:* (office) Mandeville Place, W1M 6AQ; 13 St James Street, W6 9RW. *Club:* Athenæum.

PRATT, family name of **Marquess Camden.**

PRATT, Anthony Malcolm G.; *see* Galliers-Pratt.

PRATT, (Arthur) Geoffrey, CBE 1981; Hon. Secretary, Institution of Gas Engineers, 1982–87; *b* 19 Aug. 1922; *s* of William Pratt, Willington, Co. Durham; *m* 1946, Ethel Luck; two *s* twin *d. Educ:* King James I Grammar Sch., Bishop Auckland. CEng, FIGasE. Joined E Mids Gas Bd, 1951: Chief Engr, 1964; Dir of Engrg, 1967; Dep. Chm., S Eastern Gas Bd, 1970–72; Chm., SE Gas Region, 1972–81; part-time Mem., British Gas Corp., 1981–82. Chm., Metrogas Building Soc., 1977. Pres., IGasE, 1974–75. *Recreations:* golf, squash, swimming, bridge. *Address:* c/o Institution of Gas Engineers, 17 Grosvenor Crescent, SW1.

PRATT, Christopher Leslie; Metropolitan Stipendiary Magistrate, since 1990; *b* 15 Dec. 1947; *s* of Leslie Arthur Cottrell Pratt and Phyllis Elizabeth Eleanor Pratt; *m* 1973, Jill

Rosemary Hodges; two *s. Educ:* Highgate Sch. Admitted Solicitor, 1972. Court Clerk, Hendon, Harrow and Uxbridge Courts, 1967–72; Dep. Clerk to the Justices, Wimbledon and Uxbridge, 1972–76; Clerk to the Justices, Highgate, Barnet and S Mimms, 1976–90; Clerk to Barnet Magistrates' Courts Cttee and Trng Officer, Justices and staff, 1986–90. Mem. Council, Justices' Clerks' Soc., 1983–90 (Chm., Parly Cttee, Chm., Conf. and Social Cttee). *Recreation:* conjuring (Hon. Sec., The Magic Circle). *Address:* Highbury Corner Magistrates' Court, 51 Holloway Road, N7. *T:* 071–607 6757. *Club:* Magic Circle.

PRATT, (Ewart) George, CVO 1986; Trustee: The Prince's Trust, since 1976 (Chairman, 1978–86; Hon. Administrator, 1976–78); react, since 1990; *b* 10 Oct. 1917; *s* of George William Pratt and Florence (*née* Redding); *m* 1948, Margaret Heath; two *s. Educ:* an independent sch.; London Sch. of Economics and Political Science (Dip. Social Sci. and Public Admin). Successively, probation officer, sen. probation officer, asst chief and, from 1970, dep. chief probation officer, Inner London Probation Service, 1949–81. Mem. numerous govtl, professional and charitable adv. gps, including: Cttee on the Voluntary Worker in the Social Services, 1966–69; Home Office Working Party on Community Service by Offenders, 1971–72; Social Responsibility Cttees of the Baptist Union and BCC, and Sec., a church-related housing assoc., 1964–81. Chm., Assoc. of Social Workers, 1959–70; Founder-Gov., Nat. Inst. for Social Work, 1961–71; Treas., BASW, 1970–73. Elder, URC. Silver Jubilee Medal, 1977. *Publications:* essays and articles on issues relating to field of criminal justice and treatment of offenders. *Recreations:* music, theatre, travel, lecturing and talking about The Prince's Trust and the needs of disadvantaged young people. *Address:* 14 The Squirrels, The Avenue, Branksome Park, Poole BH13 6AF. *T:* Poole (0202) 767552. *Club:* Royal Automobile.

PRATT, His Honour Hugh MacDonald; a Circuit Judge (formerly County Court Judge) 1947–72; *b* 15 Sept. 1900; *o c* of late Sir John William Pratt; *m* 1928, Ingeborg, *e d* of late Consul Johannes Sundfőr, MBE, Haugesund, Norway; one *s. Educ:* Hillhead High Sch., Glasgow; Aske's Haberdashers' Sch., London; Balliol Coll., Oxford. Called to Bar, Inner Temple, 1924; practised London and Western Circuit; member General Council of the Bar; President, Hardwicke Society; contested Drake Div. of Plymouth, 1929; Dep. President War Damage (Valuation Appeals) Panel, 1946. Chairman, Devon Quarter Sessions, 1958–64. Hon. LLD Exeter, 1972. *Publications:* English trans. of Professor Axel Möller's International Law (Vol. I, 1931, Vol. II, 1935); trans. of various articles in Norwegian, Danish and Swedish on commercial and international law. *Recreations:* reading, gardening. *Address:* New Pond Farm, New Pond Road, Compton, Surrey GU3 1HY. *T:* Godalming (04868) 6049.

PRATT, Very Rev. John Francis Isaac, MA; Provost Emeritus, since 1978; *b* 30 June 1913; *s* of late Rev. J. W. J. Pratt, Churchill, Somerset; *m* 1939, Norah Elizabeth (*d* 1981), *y d* of late F. W. Corfield, Sandford, Somerset; two *d. Educ:* Keble Coll., Oxford; Wells Theological Coll. Priest, 1937. CF, 1st KSLI, 1941–46; (despatches, 1943); SCF, Cyprus, 1946. Vicar of: Rastrick, 1946–49; Wendover, 1949–59; Reading S Mary's (with All Saints, S Saviour's, S Mark's and S Matthew's), 1959–61; Vicar of Chilton with Dorton, 1961–70; Archdeacon of Buckingham, 1961–70; Provost of Southwell, 1970–78; Priest-in-charge, Edingley with Halam, 1975–78. RD of Wendover, 1955–59; Chaplain to High Sheriff of Bucks, 1956, 1962; Examining Chaplain to Bishop of Southwell, 1971–78. *Address:* Manormead, Tilford Road, Hindhead, Surrey GU26 6RA.

PRATT, Michael John; QC 1976; a Recorder of the Crown Court, since 1974; *b* 23 May 1933; *o s* of W. Brownlow Pratt; *m* 1960, Elizabeth Jean Hendry; two *s* three *d. Educ:* West House Sch., Edgbaston; Malvern Coll. LLB (Birmingham). Army service, 2nd Lieut, 3rd Carabiniers (Prince of Wales's Dragoon Guards); Staff Captain. Called to the Bar, Middle Temple, 1954, Bencher, 1986. *Recreations:* music, theatre, sport generally. *Address:* 9 Moorland Road, Edgbaston, Birmingham B16 9JP. *T:* 021–454 1071. *Clubs:* Cavalry and Guards; Birmingham Conservative.

PRATT, Prof. Peter Lynn, PhD; FInstP; CEng, FIM; FACerS; Professor of Crystal Physics, Imperial College of Science and Technology, London University, since 1963; *b* 10 March 1927; *s* of late William Lynn Pratt and Margery Florence Pratt; *m* 1951, Lydia Elizabeth Anne, *y d* of late G. A. Lyon Hatton, Edgbaston; two *s. Educ:* Cheltenham Coll.; Birmingham Univ. (BSc 1948); Pembroke Coll., Cambridge (PhD 1952). FInstP 1967; FIM 1980; FACerS 1987. Res. Fellow, AERE, 1951–53; Lectr, Univ. of Birmingham, 1953–58; Reader in Physical Metallurgy, Imperial Coll., 1959–63; Dean, Royal Sch. of Mines, and Mem. Governing Body, Imperial Coll., 1977–80; Dir of Continuing Educn, Imperial Coll., 1981–86. Vis. Scientist, N Amer. Aviation Centre, 1963; Vis. Prof., Univ. of Stanford, 1964; Eshbach Soc. Disting. Vis. Schol., Technol Inst. of Northwestern Univ., 1989; Vis. Prof., Univ. of British Columbia, 1991. Consultant at various times to: AERE; DoE; DTI; MoD; Commonwealth Trans-Antarctic Expedn; Commonwealth Develt Corp.; indust. firms and publishing houses. Dir, London Centre for Marine Technol., 1981–. Chm., Adv. Cttee on Trng and Qualification of Patent Agents, 1972–73; Member: Continuing Educn and Trng Cttee, Engrg Council, 1986–90; Visitors' Panel, BRE, 1988–; Tech. Adv. Cttee, Marine Technol. Directorate Ltd, 1989–. Pres., RSM Assoc., 1984–85; Mem. Council and Exec. Cttee, Inst. of Metals, 1987–91. Sir George Beilby Gold Medal and Prize, Institute of Metals, 1964; A. A. Griffith Medal and Prize, Inst. of Metals, 1990. *Publications:* (ed) Fracture, 1969; technical appendix to Longbow (by Robert Hardy), 1976; articles on materials science and engrg in learned jls. *Recreations:* toxophily (esp. the English longbow), sailing, music, motor racing. *Address:* 20 Westfield Road, Beaconsfield, Bucks HP9 1EF. *T:* Beaconsfield (0494) 673392.

PRATT, Timothy Jean Geoffrey; Deputy Treasury Solicitor, since 1990; *b* 25 Nov. 1934; *s* of Geoffrey Cheeseborough Pratt and Elinor Jean (*née* Thomson); *m* 1963, Pamela Ann Blake; two *d. Educ:* Brighton College; Trinity Hall, Cambridge (MA). Called to the Bar, Middle Temple, 1959; in practice, 1959–61; joined Treasury Solicitor's Dept, 1961; Law Officers' Dept, 1972; DTI, 1974; Legal Advr to Dir-Gen. of Fair Trading, 1979, to Cabinet Office (European Secretariat), 1985. *Address:* Treasury Solicitor's Department, Queen Anne's Chambers, 28 Broadway, SW1H 9JS. *T:* 071–210 3129. *Club:* United Oxford & Cambridge University.

PRAWER, Prof. Siegbert Salomon, FBA 1981; Taylor Professor of German Language and Literature, University of Oxford, 1969–86, now Professor Emeritus; Professorial Fellow, 1969–86, Supernumerary Fellow, 1986–90, Hon. Fellow, 1990, The Queen's College, Oxford (Dean of Degrees, since 1978); *b* 15 Feb. 1925; *s* of Marcus and Eleonora Prawer; *m* 1949, Helga Alice (*née* Schaefer); one *s* two *d* (and one *s* decd). *Educ:* King Henry VIII Sch., Coventry; Jesus Coll. (Schol.) and Christ's Coll., Cambridge. Charles Oldham Shakespeare Scholar, 1945, MA 1950, LittD 1962, Cantab; PhD Birmingham, 1953; MA 1969, DLitt 1969, Oxon. Adelaide Stoll Res. Student, Christ's Coll., Cambridge, 1947–48; Asst Lecturer, Lecturer, Sen. Lecturer, University of Birmingham, 1948–63; Prof. of German, Westfield Coll., London Univ., 1964–69. Visiting Professor: City Coll., NY, 1956–57; University of Chicago, 1963–64; Harvard Univ., 1968; Hamburg Univ., 1969; Univ. of Calif, Irvine, 1975; Otago Univ., 1976; Pittsburgh Univ., 1977; Visiting Fellow: Knox Coll., Dunedin, 1976; Humanities Research Centre, ANU, 1980; Tauber Inst., Brandeis Univ., 1981–82; Russell Sage Foundn, NY, 1988. Hon. Director, London Univ. Inst. of Germanic Studies, 1966–68. President: British Comp. Lit. Assoc., 1984–87 (Hon. Fellow, 1989); English Goethe Soc., 1990–. Hon. Fellow, London Univ. Inst. Germanic Studies, 1987. Hon. Mem., Modern Language Assoc. of America, 1986. Hon. Dr. phil. Cologne, 1984; Hon. DLitt Birmingham, 1988. Goethe Medal, 1973; Friedrich Gundolf Prize, 1986. Co-editor: Oxford German Studies, 1971–75; Anglica Germanica, 1973–79. *Publications:* German Lyric Poetry, 1952; Mörike und seine Leser, 1960; Heine's Buch der Lieder: A Critical Study, 1960; Heine: The Tragic Satirist, 1962; The Penguin Book of Lieder, 1964; The Uncanny in Literature (inaug. lect.), 1965; (ed, with R. H. Thomas and L. W. Forster) Essays in German Language, Culture and Society, 1969; (ed) The Romantic Period in Germany, 1970; Heine's Shakespeare, a Study in Contexts (inaug. lect.), 1970; (ed) Seventeen Modern German Poets, 1971; Comparative Literary Studies: an Introduction, 1973; Karl Marx and World Literature, 1976 (Isaac Deutscher Meml Prize, 1977); Caligari's Children: the film as tale of terror, 1980; Heine's Jewish Comedy: a study of his portraits of Jews and Judaism, 1983; A. N. Stencl: poet of Whitechapel (Stencl Meml Lect.), 1984; Coalsmoke and Englishmen (Bithell Meml Lecture), 1984; Frankenstein's Island: England and the English in the writings of Heinrich Heine, 1986; Israel at Vanity Fair: Jews and Judaism in the writings of W. M. Thackeray, 1991; articles on German, English and comparative literature in many specialist periodicals and symposia. *Recreation:* portrait drawing. *Address:* 9 Hawkswell Gardens, Oxford OX2 7EX.

See also Mrs R. P. Jhabvala.

PRAWER JHABVALA, Mrs Ruth; *see* Jhabvala.

PREBBLE, David Lawrence; Master, Queen's Bench Division, Supreme Court of Justice, since 1981; *b* 21 Aug. 1932; *s* of late George Wilson Prebble and of Margaret Jessie Prebble (*née* Cuthbertson); *m* 1959, Fiona W. Melville; three *d. Educ:* Cranleigh; Christ Church, Oxford. MA. National Service, 1950–52; commissioned in 3rd Carabiniers (Prince of Wales's Dragoon Guards); served TA, 1952–61, City of London Yeomanry (Rough Riders) TA (Captain). Called to the Bar, Middle Temple, 1957; practised at Bar, 1957–81. *Recreations:* reading; operetta; wine and food; hounds and dogs; friends' horses; own wife and family; (not necessarily in foregoing order as to precedence). *Address:* 16 Wool Road, Wimbledon, SW20 0HW. *T:* 081–946 1804. *Club:* Royal Wimbledon Golf.

PREBBLE, John Edward Curtis, FRSL; Writer; *b* 23 June 1915; *o s* of late John William Prebble, Petty Officer, RN, and Florence (*née* Wood); *m* 1936, Betty, *d* of late Ernest Golby; two *s* one *d. Educ:* Sutherland Public Sch., Saskatchewan; Latymer Upper Sch., London. Entered journalism, 1934; in ranks with RA, 1940–45; Sergeant-reporter with No 1 British Army Newspaper Unit (Hamburg), 1945–46; reporter, columnist and feature-writer for British newspapers and magazines, 1946–60; novelist, historian, film-writer and author of many plays and dramatised documentaries for radio and TV. *Publications: novels:* Where the Sea Breaks, 1944; The Edge of Darkness, 1948; Age Without Pity, 1950; The Mather Story, 1954; The Brute Streets, 1954; The Buffalo Soldiers, 1959; *short stories:* My Great Aunt Appearing Day, 1958; Spanish Stirrup, 1972; *biography:* (with J. A. Jordan) Mongaso, 1956; *history:* The High Girders, 1956; Culloden, 1961; The Highland Clearances, 1963; Glencoe, 1966; The Darien Disaster, 1968; The Lion in the North, 1971; Mutiny: Highland Regiments in Revolt, 1975; John Prebble's Scotland, 1984; The King's Jaunt: George IV in Edinburgh, 1988. *Recreation:* serendipity. *Address:* Hill View, The Glade, Kingswood, Surrey KT20 6LL. *T:* Mogador (0737) 832142.

PRELOG, Prof. Dr Vladimir; Professor of Organic Chemistry, Swiss Federal Institute of Technology, 1950–76, retired; *b* 23 July 1906; *m* 1933, Kamila Vitek; one *s. Educ:* Inst. of Technology, Prague. Chemist, Prague, 1929–34; Lecturer and Professor, University of Zagreb, 1935–41. Privatdozent, Swiss Federal Inst. of Technology, Zürich, 1941; Associate Professor, 1947, Full Professor, 1950. Mem. Bd, CIBA-GEIGY Ltd, Basel, 1960–78. Vis. Prof. of Chemistry, Univ. of Cambridge, 1974. Mem. Leopoldina, Halle/Saale, 1963; Hon. Member: American Acad. of Arts and Sciences, 1960; Chem. Society, 1960; Nat. Acad. of Sciences, Washington, 1961; Royal Irish Acad., Dublin, 1971; Foreign Member: Royal Society, 1962; Acad. of Sciences, USSR, 1966; Acad. dei Lincei, Roma 1965; Istituto Lombardo, Milano, 1964; Royal Danish Acad. of Sciences, 1971; Amer. Philosophical Soc. Philadelphia, 1976; Acad. Sciences, Paris, 1981; Mem., Papal Acad. of Science, 1986–. Dr *hc:* Universities of: Zagreb, 1954; Liverpool, 1963; Paris, 1963; Bruxelles, 1969; Weizmann Inst., Rehovot, 1985. Hon. DSc: Cambridge, 1969; Manchester, 1977; Inst. Quimico Sarria, Barcelona, 1978; Edvard Kardelj Univ. of Ljubljana, 1989; Univ. of Osijek, 1989. Davy Medal, Royal Society, 1967; A. W. Hofmann Medal, Gesell. deutscher Chem., 1967; Marcel Benoist Prize, 1965; Roger Adams Award, 1969; (jtly) Nobel Prize for Chemistry, 1975. Order of Rising Sun, Japan, 1977; Order of Yugoslav Star, 1977; Order of Yugoslav Banner with Golden Wreath, 1986. *Publications:* numerous scientific papers, mainly in Helvetica chimica acta. *Address:* (office) Laboratorium für organische Chemie, ETH-Zentrum, Universitätstrasse 16, CH-8092 Zürich, Switzerland; (home) Bellariastr. 33, 8002 Zürich. *T:* CH 01 202 17 81.

PREMADASA, Hon. Ranasinghe; President of Sri Lanka, since 1989; Minister of Defence, Finance, Local Government, Housing and Construction, Highways, and the Emergency Civil Administration; *b* 23 June 1924; *m* 1964, Hema Wickrematunga; one *s* one *d. Educ:* Lorenz Coll., Colombo; St Joseph's Coll., Colombo. Member, Colombo Municipal Council, 1950; Dep. Mayor of Colombo, 1955. Joined United Nat. Party and contested Ruvanwella, 1956; MHR (Colombo Central), 1960, 1965–88; Chief Whip, Govt Parly Gp, 1965; Parly Sec. to Minister of Information and Broadcasting, also to Minister of Local Govt, 1965; Minister of Local Govt, 1968–70; Chief Whip, Opp. Parly Gp, 1970–77; Leader, Nat. State Assembly, 1977–88; Prime Minister, 1978–88; Dep. Leader, United Nat. Party, 1976. Delegate to: Buddha Sangayana, Burma, 1955; China, Soviet Union, 1959; Commonwealth Parly Conf., Canberra, 1970; Commonwealth Heads of Govt meetings, Lusaka, 1979, Aust., 1981; 35th Session, UN Gen. Assembly, 1980; 4th Session, 1980–11th Session, 1988, UN Commn (formerly conf.) on Human Settlements; 40th Anniv. Session of UN, NY, 1985; Internat. Shelter Seminar, MIT, 1986; 8th Summit of Hds of State of Non-Aligned Nations, Harare, 1986. *Publications:* numerous books in Sinhalese language. *Address:* President's House, Colombo, Republic of Sri Lanka.

PRENDERGAST, (Christopher) Anthony, CBE 1981; DL; Chairman, Dolphin Square Trust Ltd, since 1967; Director General, Location of Industry Bureau Ltd, since 1983; an Underwriting Member of Lloyd's; *b* 4 May 1931; *s* of Maurice Prendergast, AINA, and Winifred Mary Prendergast, Falmouth; *m* 1959, Simone Ruth Laski (*see* Dame S. R. Prendergast); one *s. Educ:* Falmouth Grammar School. Westminster City Council: Mem., 1959–90; Chairman: Housing Cttee, 1962–65; Health Cttee, 1965–68; Town Planning Cttee, 1972–75, 1976–78; Gen. Purposes Cttee, 1978–80; Management Services, 1981–83; Licensing Sub Cttee, 1983–90; Lord Mayor and Dep. High Steward of Westminster, 1968–69; High Sheriff of Greater London, 1980. Additional Mem., GLC (Covent Garden Cttee), 1971–75; Member: London Boroughs Trng Cttee, 1965–68; Docklands Develt Cttee, 1974; AMA Cttee, 1976–89; Nat Jt Council (Manual Workers), 1978–82, 1983–89; Conf. of Regl and Local Auths of Europe, 1983–89. Chairman:

Location of Offices Bureau, 1971–79; LACSAB, 1983–89; Joint Negotiating Cttee for Chief Execs of Local Authorities, 1984–89, for Chief Officers of Local Authorities, 1984–89; Gen. Purposes Cttee, London Boroughs Assoc., 1986–90. Mem., LEB, 1983–89; Dir, LE plc, 1990–. Governor, Westminster Sch., 1974–. Master, Pattenmakers' Co., 1983–84. DL Greater London, 1988. FRSA 1984. *Recreations:* fishing, shooting, photography. *Address:* 52 Warwick Square, SW1V 2AJ. *T:* 071-821 7653. *Clubs:* Carlton, Brooks's, Irish; MCC.

PRENDERGAST, Sir John (Vincent), KBE 1977 (CBE 1960); CMG 1968; GM 1955; CPM 1955; QPM 1963; retired; Deputy Commissioner and Director of Operations, Independent Commission Against Corruption, Hong Kong, 1973–77; *b* 11 Feb. 1912; *y s* of late John and Margaret Prendergast; *m* 1943, Enid Sonia, *yr d* of Percy Speed; one *s* one *d. Educ:* in Ireland; London Univ. (External). Local Government, London, 1930–39. War Service, 1939–46 (Major). Asst District Comr, Palestine Administration, 1946–47; Colonial Police Service, Palestine and Gold Coast, 1947–52; seconded Army, Canal Zone, on special duties, 1952–53; Colonial Police Service, Kenya, 1953–58 (Director of Intelligence and Security, 1955–58); Chief of Intelligence, Cyprus, 1958–60; Director, Special Branch, Hong Kong (retired as Dep. Comr of Police), 1960–66. Director of Intelligence, Aden, 1966–67. Dir, G. Heywood Hill Ltd, 1983–. *Recreations:* racing, collecting first editions. *Address:* 20 Westbourne Terrace, W2 3UP. *T:* 071–262 9514. *Clubs:* East India; Hong Kong, Royal Hong Kong Jockey (Hong Kong).

PRENDERGAST, Robert James Christie Vereker; His Honour Judge Prendergast; a Circuit Judge, since 1989; *b* 21 Oct. 1941; *s* of Richard Henry Prendergast and Jean (*née* Christie); *m* 1971, Berit, (Bibi), Thauland; one *d. Educ:* Downside; Trinity Coll., Cambridge (BA (Hons) Law; MA). Called to the Bar, Middle Temple, 1964; Harmsworth Law Schol.; S Eastern Circuit, 1964–89; an Asst Recorder, 1984–87; a Recorder, 1987–89. Chm., NE London Crown Court Liaison Cttee, 1984–89. Mem., S Eastern Circuit Wine Cttee, 1987–89. *Recreations:* most gentle pursuits. *Address:* 9 King's Bench Walk, Temple, EC4Y 7DX. *T:* 071–353 5638.

PRENDERGAST, Dame Simone (Ruth), DBE 1986 (OBE 1981); JP, DL; *b* 2 July 1930; *d* of late Mrs Neville Blond, OBE and late Norman Laski; *m* 1st, 1953, Albert Kaplan (marr. diss. 1957); 2nd, 1959, Christopher Anthony Prendergast, *qv*; one *s. Educ:* Queen's College; Cheltenham Ladies' College. Lady Mayoress of Westminster, 1968–69; Member: Lord Chancellor's Adv. Cttee for Inner London, 1981–91; Solicitors' Disciplinary Tribunal, 1986–; E London and Bethnal Green Housing Assoc., 1988–; Chairman: Greater London Area Nat. Union of Conservative Assocs, 1984–87; Blond McIndoe Centre for Med. Research, 1986–; Westminster Children's Soc., 1980–90; Jewish Refugees Cttee, 1980–; Vice-Chm., Age Concern, Westminster, 1989–; Mem. Council, Central British Fund for World Jewish Relief, 1969–. Mem. Court of Patrons, RCS, 1987. FRSA 1988. JP Inner London 1971; DL Greater London 1982. Associate CStJ 1982. *Recreation:* gardening. *Address:* 52 Warwick Square, SW1V 2AJ. *T:* 071–821 7653.

PRENDERGAST, (Walter) Kieran, CMG 1990; HM Diplomatic Service; High Commissioner to Zimbabwe, since 1989; *b* 2 July 1942; *s* of late Lt-Comdr J. H. Prendergast and Mai Hennessy; *m* 1967, Joan Reynolds; two *s* two *d. Educ:* St Patrick's College, Strathfield, Sydney, NSW; Salesian College, Chertsey; St Edmund Hall, Oxford. Turkish language student Istanbul, 1964; Ankara, 1965; FO (later FCO), 1967; 2nd Sec. Nicosia, 1969; Civil Service Coll., 1972; 1st Sec. FCO, 1972; The Hague, 1973; Asst Private Sec. to Foreign and Commonwealth Sec. (Rt Hon. Anthony Crosland, Rt Hon. Dr David Owen), 1976; UK Mission to UN, NY, 1979 (detached for duty Jan.-March 1980 at Govt House, Salisbury); Counsellor, Tel Aviv, 1982; Head of Southern African Dept, FCO, 1986–89. Rhodesia Medal, 1980; Zimbabwe Independence Medal, 1980. *Recreations:* family, walking, reading, sport, wine. *Address:* c/o Foreign and Commonwealth Office, SW1A 2AH. *Clubs:* Travellers', Beefsteak.

PRENTICE, Prof. Daniel David; Allen & Overy Professor of Corporate Law, Oxford University, since 1991; Fellow of Pembroke College, Oxford; *b* 7 Aug. 1941; *s* of Thomas James Prentice and Agnes Prentice (*née* Fox); *m* 1965, Judith Mary Keane; one *s* one *d. Educ:* St Malachy's Coll., Belfast; Queen's Univ., Belfast (LLB); Univ. of Chicago (JD); MA Oxford (by special resolution). Called to the Bar, Lincoln's Inn, 1982. Associate Prof., Univ. of Ontario, 1966–68; Lectr, UCL, 1968–73; Lectr, 1973–90, Reader, 1991, Univ. of Oxford. Vis. Prof., various univs. Asst. Editor, Law Qly Rev., 1988–. *Publication:* (ed) Chitty, Law of Contracts, 25th edn 1983, 26th edn 1989. *Recreation:* squash. *Address:* Pembroke College, Oxford OX1 1DW. *T:* Oxford (0865) 276438.

PRENTICE, (Hubert Archibald) John, CEng; FInstP; consultant on manufacturing and management strategies to several UK and USA companies; *b* 5 Feb. 1920; *s* of Charles Herbert Prentice and Rose Prentice; *m* 1947, Sylvia Doreen Elias; one *s. Educ:* Woolwich Polytechnic, London; Salford Univ. (BSc, MSc). CEng; MRAeS 1962; FInstP 1967. Min. of Supply, 1939–56; R&D posts, res. estabts and prodn, MoD, 1956–60; Space Dept, RAE, Min. of Aviation, 1960–67; Head, Road User Characteristics Res., 1967–70, and Head, Driver Aids and Abilities Res., 1970–72, MoT; Head, Road User Dynamics Res., DoE, 1972–75; Counsellor (Sci. and Technol.), British Embassy, Tokyo, 1975–80. *Recreations:* walking, climbing. *Address:* 5 Foxhill Crescent, Camberley, Surrey GU15 1PR. *T:* Camberley (0276) 66373.

PRENTICE, Rt. Hon. Sir Reginald (Ernest), (Sir Reg), Kt 1987; PC; JP; company director and public affairs consultant; *b* 16 July 1923; *s* of Ernest George and Elizabeth Prentice; *m* 1948, Joan Godwin; one *d. Educ:* Whitgift Sch.; London School of Economics. Temporary Civil Servant, 1940–42; RA, 1942–46; commissioned 1943; served in Italy and Austria, 1944–46. Student at LSE, 1946–49. BSc (Econ). Member staff of Transport and General Workers' Union, Asst to Legal Secretary; in charge of Union's Advice and Service Bureau, 1950–57. MP (Lab): E Ham N, May 1957–1974, Newham NE, 1974–Oct. 1977; MP (C): Newham NE, Oct. 1977–1979; Daventry, 1979–87; Minister of State, Department of Education and Science, 1964–66; Minister of Public Building and Works, 1966–67; Minister of Overseas Develt, 1967–69; Opposition Spokesman on Employment, 1972–74; Sec. of State for Educn and Science, 1974–75; Minister for Overseas Develt, 1975–76; Minister of State (Minister for Social Security), DHSS, 1979–81. Exec. Mem. Cttee, Nat. Union of Cons. Assocs, 1988–90. Alderman, GLC, 1970–71. JP County Borough of Croydon, 1961. *Publications:* (jt) Social Welfare and the Citizen, 1957; Right Turn, 1978. *Recreations:* walking, golf. *Address:* Wansdyke, Church Lane, Mildenhall, Marlborough, Wilts SN8 2LU. *Club:* Marlborough Golf.

PRENTICE, Thomas, MC 1945; Life President, Harrisons & Crosfield plc, since 1988 (Chairman, 1977–88); *b* 14 Oct. 1919; *s* of Alexander and Jean Young Prentice; *m* 1949, Peggy Ann Lloyd; two *s* two *d. Educ:* McLaren High Sch., Callander, Perthshire. Served Army, 1939–46. Harrisons & Crosfield (Sabah) Sdn. Bhd., Malaysia, 1947–67; Harrisons & Crosfield plc, 1967–. *Recreations:* golf, gardening. *Address:* Harrisons & Crosfield plc, 1/4 Great Tower Street, EC3. *Club:* East India, Devonshire, Sports and Public Schools.

PRENTICE, Hon. Sir William (Thomas), Kt 1977; MBE 1945; Senior Member, Administrative Appeals Tribunal, Australia, 1981–87; *b* 1 June 1919; *s* of Claud Stanley

and Pauline Prentice; *m* 1946, Mary Elizabeth, *d* of F. B. Dignam; three *s* one *d. Educ:* St Joseph's College, Hunters Hill; Sydney Univ. (BA, LLB). AIF, Middle East and New Guinea, 2–33 Inf. Bn and Staff Captain 25 Aust. Inf. Bde, Owen Stanleys and Lae Ramu campaigns; Staff Course, Duntroon, 1944; Staff Captain, 7 Aust. Inf. Bde, Bougainville campaign, 1944–45. Resumed law studies, 1946; admitted Bar, NSW, 1947; Judge, Supreme Court, PNG, 1970; Senior Puisne Judge, 1975; Deputy Chief Justice on independence, PNG, 1975, Chief Justice 1978–80. *Recreations:* bush walking, swimming, reading. *Address:* 16 Olympia Road, Naremburn, NSW 2065, Australia. *Clubs:* Tattersall's, Cricketers' (Sydney).

PRENTICE, Dame Winifred (Eva), DBE 1977 (OBE 1972); SRN; President, Royal College of Nursing, 1972–76; *b* 2 Dec. 1910; *d* of Percy John Prentice and Anna Eva Prentice. *Educ:* Northgate Sch. for Girls, Ipswich; E Suffolk and Ipswich Hosp. (SRN); W Mddx Hosp. (SCM Pt I); Queen Elizabeth Coll., London Univ. (RNT); Dip. in Nursing, London Univ. Ward Sister: E Suffolk and Ipswich Hosp., 1936–39; Essex County Hosp., 1941–43; Nurse Tutor, King's Lynn Hosp., 1944–46; Principal Tutor, Stracathro Hosp., Brechin, Angus, 1947–61, Matron, 1961–72. *Publications:* articles in Nursing Times and Nursing Mirror. *Recreations:* music, amateur dramatics, gardening. *Address:* Marleish, 4 Duke Street, Brechin, Angus. *T:* Brechin (03562) 2606. *Club:* New Cavendish.

PRESCOTT, Prof. John Herbert Dudley, PhD; FIBiol; FRAgS; Principal, Wye College, University of London, since 1988; *b* 21 Feb. 1937; *s* of Herbert Prescott and Edith Vera Prescott; *m* 1960, Diana Margaret Mullock; two *s* two *d. Educ:* Haileybury; Univ. of Nottingham (BSc (Agric), PhD). FIBiol 1983; FRAgS 1986. Lectr in Animal Prodn, Univ. of Newcastle upon Tyne, 1963–72; Animal Prodn Officer in Argentina, FAO, UN, 1972–74; Head of Animal Prodn Advisory and Develt, E of Scotland Coll. of Agric., 1974–78; Prof. of Animal Prodn, 1978–84, and Head of Animal Div., 1978–84, Sch. of Agric., Univ. of Edinburgh; Dir, Grassland, later Animal and Grassland, Res. Inst., 1984–86; Dir, Grassland and Animal Prodn Res., AFRC, 1986–88. Vis. Prof., Univ. of Reading, 1985–88; Vis. Prof., UCW, Aberystwyth, 1988. *Publications:* scientific papers in Animal Prodn and Agricultural Science; technical articles. *Recreations:* farming, walking, wildlife, the countryside. *Address:* Wye College, University of London, Wye, Ashford, Kent TN25 5AH.

PRESCOTT, John Leslie; MP (Lab) Hull East, since 1983 (Kingston upon Hull (East), 1970–83); *b* 31 May 1938; *s* of John Herbert Prescott, JP, and Phyllis Prescott; *m* 1961, Pauline Tilston; two *s. Educ:* Ellesmere Port Secondary Modern Sch.; WEA; correspondence courses; Ruskin Coll., Oxford (DipEcon/Pol Oxon); Hull Univ. (BSc Econ). Trainee Chef, 1953–55; Steward, Passenger Lines, Merchant Navy, 1955–63; Ruskin Coll., Oxford, 1963–65; Recruitment Officer, General and Municipal Workers Union (temp.), 1965; Hull Univ., 1965–68. Contested (Lab) Southport, 1966; Full-time Official, National Union of Seamen, 1968–70. PPS to Sec. of State for Trade, 1974–76; opposition spokesman on Transport, 1979–81; opposition front bench spokesman on Regional Affairs and Devolution, 1981–83, on Transport, 1983–84 and 1988–, on Employment, 1984–87, on Energy, 1987–88; Mem., Shadow Cabinet, 1983–. Member: Select Cttee Nationalized Industries, 1973–79; Council of Europe, 1972–75; European Parlt, 1975–79 (Leader, Labour Party Delegn, 1976–79). Mem., NEC, Labour Party, 1989–. *Publication:* Not Wanted on Voyage, 1966. *Address:* 365 Saltshouse Road, Sutton-on-Hull, North Humberside HU8 9HS.

PRESCOTT, Sir Mark, 3rd Bt, *cr* 1938, of Godmanchester; Racehorse Trainer, in Newmarket; *b* 3 March 1948; *s* of late Major W. R. Stanley Prescott (MP for Darwen Div., 1943–51; 2nd *s* of Colonel Sir William Prescott, 1st Bt) and of Gwendolen (who *m* 2nd, 1952, Daniel Orme (*d* 1972)), *o c* of late Leonard Aldridge, CBE; *S* uncle, Sir Richard Stanley Prescott, 2nd Bt, 1965. *Educ:* Harrow. *Address:* Heath House, Moulton Road, Newmarket, Suffolk CB8 8DU. *T:* Newmarket (0638) 662117.

PRESCOTT, Brig. Peter George Addington, MC 1944; Secretary, National Rifle Association, 1980–88; *b* 22 Sept. 1924; *s* of Col and Mrs John Prescott; *m* 1953, June Marian Louise Wendell; one *s* one *d. Educ:* Eton Coll.; Staff Coll. (psc 1957); Royal Coll. of Defence Studies (rcds 1973). Commnd Grenadier Guards, 1943; 2nd Armoured Bn Gren. Gds, 1944–45; comd 2nd Bn Gren. Gds, 1966–69; Comdr 51st Inf. Bde, 1970–72; Dep. Comdr NE Dist, 1974–77; Dep. Dir of Army Trng, 1977–79, retd. Chevalier, Royal Order of the Sword, Sweden, 1954. *Recreations:* sailing, painting, gardening. *Address:* The Bourne, Church Lane, Holybourne, Alton, Hants.

PRESCOTT, Peter John; Director, Arts Division, British Council, since 1990; *b* 6 April 1936; *s* of Wentworth James Prescott and Ellen Marie (*née* Burrows); *m* 1971, Gillian Eileen Lowe. *Educ:* Windsor Grammar School; Pembroke College, Oxford (MA). Joined British Council, 1963; Asst Cultural Attaché, Egypt, 1963–67; London, 1967–70; Sussex Univ., 1970–71; France, 1971–75; London, 1975–79; on secondment to Dept of Education and Science, 1979–81; Australia, 1981–84; Rep., France, and Cultural Counsellor, British Embassy, Paris, 1984–90. *Recreations:* reading, music, walking, swimming. *Address:* British Council, 10 Spring Gardens, SW1A 2BN. *T:* 071–930 8466.

PRESCOTT, Peter Richard Kyle; QC 1990; *b* 23 Jan. 1943; *s* of Richard Stanley Prescott and Sarah Aitchison Shand; *m* 1967, Frances Rosemary Bland; two *s* one *d. Educ:* St George's Coll., Argentina; Dulwich Coll.; University Coll. London (BSc); Queen Mary Coll., London (MSc). Called to the Bar, Lincoln's Inn, 1970. *Publication:* The Modern Law of Copyright (with Hugh Laddie, QC, and Mary Vitoria), 1980. *Recreations:* classical music, jazz, flying, reading. *Address:* Francis Taylor Building, Temple, EC4. *T:* 071–353 5657.

PRESCOTT, Westby William P.; *see* Percival-Prescott.

PRESLAND, John David; Executive Vice-Chairman, Port of London Authority, 1978–82; *b* 3 July 1930; *s* of Leslie and Winifred Presland; *m* 1969, Margaret Brewin. *Educ:* St Albans Sch.; London Sch. of Economics. BScEcon. FCA, IPFA, MBCS. Knox Cropper & Co., Chartered Accountants, 1950–58; Pfizer Ltd (various financial posts), 1958–64; Berk Ltd: Chief Accountant, 1964–67; Financial Controller, 1967–68; Dir and Financial Controller, 1968–71; Port of London Authority: Financial Controller, 1971–73; Asst Dir-Gen. (Finance), 1973–76; Exec. Dir (Finance), 1976–78. Freeman of City of London; Freeman of Company of Watermen and Lightermen of River Thames. *Recreations:* history, natural history, music. *Address:* c/o Pilots' National Pension Fund, New Premier House, 150 Southampton Row, WC1B 5AL. *Club:* Oriental.

PRESS, John Bryant, FRSL; author and poet; *b* 11 Jan. 1920; *s* of late Edward Kenneth Press and late Gladys (*née* Cooper); *m* 1947, Janet Crompton; one *s* one *d. Educ:* King Edward VI Sch., Norwich; Corpus Christi Coll., Cambridge, 1938–40 and 1945–46. Served War of 1939–45: RA, 1940–45. British Council, 1946–79: Athens, 1946–47; Salonika, 1947–50; Madras, 1950–51; Colombo, 1951–52; Birmingham, 1952–54; Cambridge, 1955–62; London, 1962–65; Paris, 1966–71 (also Cultural Attaché, British Embassy); Regional Dir, Oxford, 1972–78; Literature Advr, London, 1978–79. Mem. Council, RSL, 1961–88. Gave George Elliston Poetry Foundation Lectures at Univ. of Cincinnati, 1962; Vis. Prof., Univ. of Paris, 1981–82. *Publications:* The Fire and the

Fountain, 1955; Uncertainties, 1956; (ed) Poetic Heritage, 1957; The Chequer'd Shade, 1958 (RSL Heinemann Award); Andrew Marvell, 1958; Guy Fawkes Night, 1959; Herrick, 1961; Rule and Energy, 1963; Louis MacNeice, 1964; (ed) Palgrave's Golden Treasury, Book V, 1964; A Map of Modern English Verse, 1969; The Lengthening Shadows, 1971; John Betjeman, 1974; Spring at St Clair, 1974; Aspects of Paris, (with illus by Gordon Bradshaw), 1975; (with Edward Lowbury and Michael Riviere) Troika, 1977; Poets of World War I, 1983; Poets of World War II, 1984; A Girl with Beehive Hair, 1986. Libretto, new version of Bluebeard's Castle, for Michael Powell's colour television film of Bartok's opera, 1963. *Recreations*: travel (especially in France), theatre, opera, concerts, cinema; architecture and visual arts; watching football and cricket. *Address*: 5 South Parade, Frome BA11 1EJ. *T*: Frome (0373) 61142.

PRESSMAN, Mrs J. J.; *see* Colbert, Claudette.

PRESTON; *see* Campbell-Preston.

PRESTON, family name of **Viscount Gormanston**.

PRESTON, F(rederick) Leslie, FRIBA; AADip; formerly Senior Partner in firm of Easton Robertson Preston and Partners, Architects; *b* 27 Nov. 1903; *m* 1927, Rita Lillian (*d* 1982), *d* of late T. H. J. Washbourne; one *d*. *Educ*: Dulwich Coll.; Architectural Association Sch., London. Henry Jarvis Student, 1924; joined firm of Easton & Robertson, 1925, and engaged on: in London: Royal Horticultural Society's New Hall; Royal Bank of Canada; Metropolitan Water Board's Laboratories; in Cambridge: reconstruction of Old Library; Zoological laboratories; School of Anatomy; Gonville and Caius new buildings; in New York: British Pavilion, World's Fair, 1939. Hon. Citizen of City of New York, 1939. Served War of 1939-45, RAF, Wing Comdr, Airfield Construction Branch (despatches). *Principal works*: laboratories for Brewing Industry Research Foundation; laboratories for Coal Research Establishment, NCB, Cheltenham; Bank of England, Bristol; offices for Lloyds Bank, Plymouth; Birmingham; plans for development of Reading University: Faculty of Letters, Library, Windsor Hall, Depts of Physics and Sedimentology, Dept of Mathematics. Applied Physical Science Building, Palmer Building, Whiteknights House, Students Union, Animal Biology and Plant Sciences Buildings; additions to St Patrick's Hall and to Depts of Horticulture and Dairying, Reading Univ.; Buildings for Dulwich Coll.; office building for Salters' Co., London; Laboratories and Aquarium for Marine Biological Association, Plymouth; offices for Friends' Provident & Century Life Office, Dorking; Research Laboratories for Messrs Arthur Guinness Son & Co. (Park Royal) Ltd; University of Keele, Library; Midland Hotel, Manchester, alterations; University of Kent at Canterbury, Chemistry Laboratories, Biology Laboratories, Physics 11; Bank of England Printing Works Extension, Debden; Eagle Star Insurance Head Office, City; Plans for Aquarium, Rangoon Zoological Gardens. Member of RIBA Practice Cttee, 1951-55; Member Council of Architects' Registration Council of the UK, 1954-60; Pres., Surveyors' Club, 1962. Governor of Westminster Technical College, 1957-67. Hon. DLitt, Reading, 1964. *Recreations*: seeing friends and places of interest, reading. *Address*: Wintershaw, Westcott, Surrey RH4 3NU. *T*: Dorking (0306) 885472. *Clubs*: Athenæum, Reform.

PRESTON, Geoffrey Averill; Assistant Counsel to Chairman of Committees, House of Lords, 1982-89; *b* 19 May 1924; *s* of George and Winifred Preston; *m* 1953, Catherine Wright. *Educ*: St Marylebone Grammar Sch. Barrister-at-Law. Served, RNVR, 1942-46. Called to Bar, Gray's Inn, 1950. Treasury Solicitor's Dept, 1952-71; Solicitor's Department: Dept of Environment, 1971-74; Dept of Trade, 1974-75; Under-Sec. (Legal), Dept of Trade, 1975-82. *Recreations*: gardening, carpentry, chess. *Address*: Ledsham, Glaziers Lane, Normandy, Surrey. *T*: Guildford (0483) 811250.

PRESTON, Dr Ian Mathieson Hamilton, FEng 1982; FIEE; Chief Executive, Scottish Power, since 1990; *b* 18 July 1932; *s* of John Hamilton Preston and Edna Irene Paul; *m* 1958, Sheila Hope Pringle; two *s*. *Educ*: Univ. of Glasgow (BSc 1st cl. Hons; PhD). MInstP. Asst Lectr, Univ. of Glasgow, 1959-65; joined SSEB, 1965, Chief Engineer, Generator Design and Construction, 1972-77; Dir Gen., Generation Develt and Construction Div., CEGB, 1977-83; Dep. Chm., SSEB, 1983-90. *Recreations*: fishing, gardening. *Address*: Scottish Power, Cathcart House, Spean Street, Glasgow G44 4BE. *T*: 041-637 7177. *Club*: Royal Automobile (Glasgow).

PRESTON, Jeffrey William, CB 1989; Deputy Director General, Office of Fair Trading, since 1990; *b* 28 Jan. 1940; *s* of William and Sybil Grace Preston (*née* Lawson). *Educ*: Liverpool Collegiate Sch.; Hertford Coll., Oxford (MA 1966). Asst Principal, Min. of Aviation, 1963; Private Sec. to Permanent Sec., BoT, 1966; Principal: BoT, 1967; HM Treasury, 1970; DTI, 1973; Asst Sec., Dept of Trade, 1975-82; Under Sec. and Regional Dir, Yorks and Humberside Region, DTI, 1982-85; Dep. Sec., Industrial and Economic Affairs, Welsh Office, 1985-90. Chm., Hertford Soc., 1987-. *Recreations*: motoring, opera, swimming. *Address*: Office of Fair Trading, Field House, Bream's Buildings, EC4A 1PR. *T*: 071-269 8921. *Clubs*: United Oxford & Cambridge University.

PRESTON, Sir Kenneth (Huson), Kt 1959; *b* 19 May 1901; *e s* of late Sir Walter Preston, Tetbury, Glos; *m* 1st, 1922, Beryl Wilmot (decd), *d* of Sir William Wilkinson; one *s* one *d*; 2nd, 1984, Mrs V. E. Dumont. *Educ*: Rugby; Trinity Coll., Oxford. Dir, J. Stone & Co, 1925; Chm. Platt Bros, 1946; Chm. Stone-Platt Industries, 1958-67; Dir, Midland Bank Ltd, 1945-76. Mem. S Area Bd, BR. Mem. British Olympic Yachting team, 1936 and 1952, Captain 1960. *Recreations*: yachting, hunting. *Address*: Court Lodge, Avening, Tetbury, Glos GL8 8NX. *T*: Nailsworth (045383) 4402. *Clubs*: Royal Thames Yacht (Vice-Cdre, 1953-56); Royal Yacht Squadron (Vice-Cdre, 1965-71).

PRESTON, Leslie; *see* Preston, F. L.

PRESTON, Michael Richard, ATD; FCSD; consultant designer; *b* 15 Oct. 1927; *s* of Major Frederick Allan Preston, MC and Winifred Gertrude (*née* Archer); *m* 1st, 1955, Anne Gillespie Smith; 2nd, 1980, Judith Gaye James. *Educ*: Whitgift Sch.; Guildford Sch. of Art; Goldsmiths' Coll., London Univ. (NDD 1953; ATD 1954); Dip. in Humanities (London) 1964. FCSD (FSIAD 1972; MSIAD 1953). Served HM Forces, Queen's Royal Regt, 1944-48, Queen's Royal Regt, TA & HAC, 1948-61. Asst Art Master, Whitgift Sch., 1954-55; Drawing Master, Dulwich Coll., 1955-64; Science Mus., 1964-87; Head of Design, 1964-86; Keeper, Dept of Museum Services, 1987; designed exhibitions, including: Centenary of Charles Babbage, 1971; A Word to the Mermaids, 1973; Tower Bridge Observed, 1974; The Breath of Life, 1974; Nat. Rly Mus., York, 1975; Sci. and Technol. of Islam, 1976; Nat. Mus. of Photography, Bradford, 1977-83; Stanley Spencer in the Shipyard, 1979; Wellcome Mus. of Hist. of Medicine, 1980; Sci. and Technol. of India, 1982; The Great Cover-up Show, 1982; Beads of Glass, 1983; Louis Pasteur and Rabies, 1985. Advisory Assignments on Museum Projects: Iran, 1976-79; Spain, 1977-80; Germany, 1978-79; Canada, 1979-82, 1984-86; Trinidad, 1982-83; Turkey, 1984-; Hong Kong, 1985; consultant to: Dean and Chapter of Canterbury, 1987-; Wellcome Foundn, 1987-; TAVRA Greater London, 1988-; Mus. of Far Eastern Antiquities, Bath, 1988-; Design Expo '89, Nagoya; Bank of England Museum, 1989; Norwich Tourism Agency, 1989-; Tricycle Theatre, 1989-90; Nat. Theatre, 1989-90; Scottish Office, 1990; English Heritage, 1990; Richmond Theatre, 1990; Accademia Italiana, 1990-.

Mem., BTEC Validation Panel, 1986-. Chm., Greenwich Soc., 1961-64. Society of Industrial Artists and Designers: Vice-Pres., 1976, 1979-81; Chm., Membership Bd, 1976-79; Chm., Design Management Panel, 1976-80. Mem., ICOM, 1964-. Trustee, Vivat Trust, 1989-. Vis. Prof., NID, Ahmedabad, 1989. Guild of Glass Engravers: Hon. FGGE 1980; Pres., 1986-. FRSA 1955-68. *Recreations*: travel, food, conversation, jazz. *Address*: 37 Walham Grove, SW6 1QR. *T*: 071-381 4363. *Club*: Arts.

PRESTON, Myles Park; HM Diplomatic Service, retired; *b* 4 April 1927; *s* of Robert and Marie Preston; *m* 1st, 1951, Ann Betten (marr. diss.); one *s* one *d*; 2nd, 1981, Joy Moore (*née* Fisher). *Educ*: Sudley Road Council Sch.; Liverpool Inst. High Sch.; Clare Coll., Cambridge. Instructor Lieut, RN, 1948-51; Asst Principal, Admty, 1951-53; CRO, 1953-54; 2nd Sec., British High Commn, New Delhi, 1954-56; 1st Sec., CRO, 1956-59; 1st Sec., Governor-General's Office and British High Commn, Lagos, 1959-62; CRO, 1962-64; 1st Sec., British High Commn, Kampala, 1964-67; Commonwealth Office and FCO, 1967-69; Counsellor and Consul-Gen., Djakarta, 1969-72; Canadian Nat. Defence Coll., 1972-73; FCO, 1973-77; Dep. Governor, Solomon Islands, 1977-78; Consul-Gen., Vancouver, 1978-79. *Address*: 20 Prince Edwards Road, Lewes, East Sussex BN7 1BE. *T*: Lewes (0273) 475809.

PRESTON, Peter John; Editor, The Guardian, since 1975; *b* 23 May 1938; *s* of John Whittle Preston and Kathlyn (*née* Chell); *m* 1962, Jean Mary Burrell; two *s* two *d*. *Educ*: Loughborough Grammar Sch.; St John's Coll., Oxford (MA EngLit). Editorial trainee, Liverpool Daily Post, 1960-63; Guardian: Political Reporter, 1963-64; Education Correspondent, 1965-66; Diary Editor, 1966-68; Features Editor, 1968-72; Production Editor, 1972-75. British Exec. Chm. and European Vice-Chm., IPI. Hon. DLitt Loughborough, 1982. *Recreations*: football, films; four children. *Address*: The Guardian, 119 Farringdon Road, EC1R 3ER.

PRESTON, Sir Peter (Sansome), KCB 1978 (CB 1973); Permanent Secretary, Overseas Development Administration, Foreign and Commonwealth Office (formerly Ministry of Overseas Development), 1976-82; *b* Nottingham, 18 Jan. 1922; *s* of Charles Guy Preston, Solicitor; *m* 1951, Marjory Harrison; two *s* three *d*. *Educ*: Nottingham High School. War Service, RAF, 1942-46; Board of Trade: Exec. Officer, 1947; Higher Exec. Off., 1950; Asst Principal, 1951; Principal, 1953; Trade Comr, New Delhi, 1959; Asst Sec., 1964; idc 1968; Under-Sec., BoT later DTI, 1969-72; Dep. Sec., Dept of Trade, 1972-76. Mem., BOTB, 1975-76. Dir, Wellcome Internat. Trading Co. Ltd, 1985-; Dep. Chm., CARE Britain, 1985-; Mem. Council, Overseas Develt Inst. *Address*: 5 Greville Park Avenue, Ashtead, Surrey KT21 2QS. *T*: Ashtead (0372) 272099.

PRESTON, Prof. Reginald Dawson, FRS 1954; retired; Professor of Plant Biophysics, 1953-73 (now Professor Emeritus), and Head, Astbury Department of Biophysics, 1962-73, University of Leeds; Chairman, School of Biological Sciences, 1970-73; Dean of the Faculty of Science, 1955-58; *b* 21 July 1908; *s* of late Walter C. Preston, builder, and late Eliza Preston; *m* 1935, Sarah J. Pollard (decd); two *d* (one *s* decd); *m* 1963, Dr Eva Frei. *Educ*: Leeds University; Cornell University, USA. BSc (Hons Physics, Class I), 1929; PhD (Botany), 1931; 1851 Exhibition Fellowship, 1932-35; Rockefeller Foundation Fellowship, 1935-36. Lecturer, Botany Dept, Univ. of Leeds, 1936-46; Sen. Lectr, 1946-49; Reader, 1949-53. Vis. Prof. of Botany, Imperial Coll., London, 1976-79. Mem. NY Acad. Sci., 1960. Hon. Mem., Internat. Assoc. of Wood Anatomists, 1981. DSc 1943; CPhys (FInstP 1944); FLS 1958; FIWSc 1960; FIAWS 1973. Anselme Payen Award, Amer. Chem. Soc., 1983; Disting. Service Medal, Leeds Phil. Lit. Soc., 1983. Editor: Proc. Leeds Phil. Soc. Sci. Sec., 1950-74; Advances in Botanical Research, 1968-77; Associate Editor, Jl Exp. Bot., 1950-77. *Publications*: Molecular Architecture of Plant Cell Walls, 1952; Physical Biology of Plant Cell Walls, 1974; about 180 articles in Proc. Roy. Soc., Nature, Ann. Bot., Biochem. Biophys Acta, Jl Exp. Bot., etc. *Recreations*: walking, climbing, music. *Address*: 117 St Anne's Road, Leeds, West Yorks LS6 3NZ. *T*: Leeds (0532) 785248.

PRESTON, Sir Ronald (Douglas Hildebrand), 7th Bt *cr* 1815; country landowner and journalist; *b* 9 Oct. 1916; *s* of Sir Thomas Hildebrand Preston, 6th Bt, OBE, and Ella Henrietta (*d* 1989), *d* of F. von Schickendantz; *S* father, 1976; *m* 1st, 1954, Smilya Stefanovic (marr. diss.); 2nd, 1972, Pauleen Jane, *d* of late Paul Lurcott. *Educ*: Westminster School; Trinity Coll., Cambridge (Hons History and Economics, MA); Ecole des Sciences Politiques, Paris. Served War, 1940-46, in Intelligence Corps, reaching rank of Major: Western Desert, Middle East, Italy, Austria, Allied Control Commn, Bulgaria. Reuter's Correspondent, Belgrade, Yugoslavia, 1948-53; The Times Correspondent: Vienna and E Europe, 1953-60; Tokyo and Far East, 1960-63. HM Diplomatic Service, 1963-76; retired, 1976. *Recreations*: shooting, tennis, picture frame making. *Heir*: cousin Philip Charles Henry Hulton Preston [*b* 31 Aug. 1946; *m* 1980, Kirsi Sylvi Annikk, *d* of late Eino Yrjö Pullinen; one *s* two *d*]. *Address*: Beeston Hall, Beeston St Lawrence, Norwich NR12 8YS. *T*: Horning (0692) 630771. *Clubs*: Travellers'; Norfolk (Norwich); Tokyo (Tokyo).

PRESTON, Rev. Prof. Ronald Haydn, DD; Professor of Social and Pastoral Theology in the University of Manchester, 1970-80, now Emeritus; *b* 12 March 1913; *o s* of Haydn and Eleanor Jane Preston; *m* 1948, Edith Mary Lindley; one *s* two *d*. *Educ*: London School of Economics, University of London; St Catherine's Coll., Oxford. BSc (Econ.) 1935, Cl. II, Div. I; Industrial Secretary of Student Christian Movement, 1935-38; BA Cl. I Theology, 1940; MA 1944; MA Manchester 1974; BD, DD Oxon 1983. Curate, St John, Park, Sheffield, 1940-43; Study Secretary, Student Christian Movement, 1943-48; Warden of St Anselm Hall, University of Manchester, 1948-63; Lectr in Christian Ethics, Univ. of Manchester, 1948-70; Examining Chaplain to Bishop of Manchester, 1948-; to Bishop of Sheffield, 1971-80; Canon Residentiary of Manchester Cathedral, 1957-71, Sub-Dean 1970-71, Hon. Canon 1971, Canon Emeritus, 1980. Editor, The Student Movement, 1943-48. *Publications*: (jointly) Christians in Society, 1939; (jointly) The Revelation of St John the Divine, 1949; Technology and Social Justice, 1971; (ed) Industrial Conflicts and their Place in Modern Society, 1974; (ed) Perspectives on Strikes, 1975; (ed) Theology and Change, 1975; Religion and the Persistence of Capitalism, 1979; (ed jtly) The Crisis in British Penology, 1980; Explorations in Theology, No 9, 1981; Church and Society in the late Twentieth Century, 1983; The Future of Christian Ethics, 1987; Religion and the Ambiguities of Capitalism, 1991; reviews, etc in The Guardian, Theology, etc. *Address*: 161 Old Hall Lane, Manchester M14 6HJ. *T*: 061-225 3291.

PRESTON, Simon John; Organist and Master of the Choristers, Westminster Abbey, 1981-87; *b* 4 Aug. 1938. *Educ*: Canford Sch.; King's Coll., Cambridge (Dr Mann Organ Student). BA 1961, MusB 1962, MA 1964. ARCM, FRAM. Sub Organist, Westminster Abbey, 1962-67; Acting Organist, St Albans Abbey, 1968-69; Organist and Lecturer in Music, Christ Church, Oxford, 1970-81. Conductor, Oxford Bach Choir, 1971-74. FRSA. Hon. FRCO 1975; Hon. FRCCO 1986; Hon. FRCM 1986. Edison Award, 1971; Grand Prix du Disque, 1979; Performer of the Year Award, NY Chapter, Amer. Guild of Organists, 1987. *Recreations*: croquet, theatre. *Address*: Little Hardwick, Langton Green, Tunbridge Wells, Kent TN3 0EY. *T*: Tunbridge Wells (0892) 862042.

PRESTON, Timothy William; QC 1982; a Recorder of the Crown Court, since 1979; *b* 3 Nov. 1935; *s* of Charles Frank Preston, LDS, RCS and Frances Mary, *o d* of Captain W. Peters, 5th Lancers; *m* 1965, Barbara Mary Haygarth. *Educ:* Haileybury; Jesus Coll., Oxford (BA 1960). 2/Lieut 16/5 Lancers, 1955; Captain, Staffs Yeomanry, retd. Called to the Bar, Inner Temple, 1964. *Recreations:* hunting, golf. *Address:* 2 Temple Gardens, EC4Y 9AY. *T:* 071–583 6041. *Club:* Cavalry and Guards.

PRESTON, Walter James, FRICS; Partner, Jones Lang Wootton, 1957–87, Consultant since 1987; *b* 20 March 1925; *s* of Walter Ronald and Agnes Ann McNeil Preston; *m* 1956, Joy Dorothea Ashton; two *s* one *d*. *Educ:* Dollar Academy, Perthshire. Served Royal Engineers, 1943–47. Jones Lang Wootton, 1948–, Staff, 1948–57. Dir (non-exec.), Lynton Property and Reversionary plc, 1985–88. *Recreation:* golf. *Address:* Barry Lodge, Pond Road, Hook Heath, Woking, Surrey GU22 0JY. *T:* Woking (0483) 63420. *Clubs:* Carlton; Phyllis Court (Henley); Woking Golf; Trevose Golf and Country (North Cornwall).

PRESTT, His Honour Arthur Miller, QC 1970; a Circuit Judge (formerly Judge of County Courts), 1971–90; Hon. Recorder of Manchester and Senior Circuit Judge, Manchester, 1982–90; *b* 23 April 1925; *s* of Arthur Prestt and Jessie (*née* Miller), Wigan; *m* 1949, Jill Mary, *d* of late Graham Dawbarn, CBE, FRIBA, FRAeS, and of Olive Dawbarn (*née* Topham); one *s* one *d*. *Educ:* Bootham Sch., York; Trinity Hall, Cambridge (MA). Served 13th Bn Parachute Regt, France, Belgium, India, Malaya, Java, 1944–46; Major Legal Staff and War Crimes Prosecutor, 1946–47. Called to Bar, Middle Temple, 1949. Chm., Mental Health Review Tribunal, 1963–70; Dep. Chm., Cumberland QS, 1966–69, Chm., 1970–71. Has held various appts in Scout Assoc. (Silver Acorn, 1970). Pres., SW Lancs Parachute Regt Assoc., 1980–91. JP Cumberland, 1966. 5 years Medal, Ampleforth Lourdes Hospitalite, 1976. *Recreations:* gardening, golf. *Address:* 10 Heigham Grove, Norwich NR2 3DQ.
See also I. Prestt.

PRESTT, Ian, CBE 1986; Director General (formerly Director), Royal Society for the Protection of Birds, since 1975; *b* 26 June 1929; *s* of Arthur Prestt and Jessie Prestt (*née* Miller); *m* 1956, Jennifer Ann Wagstaffe; two *d* (one *s* decd). *Educ:* Bootham School, York; Sch. of Architecture, Liverpool; Univ. of Liverpool (BSc, MSc). FIBiol. 2nd Lt, RA, 1947–49. Joined staff of Nature Conservancy, 1956; Asst Regional Officer (SW England), 1956–59; Asst to Dir-Gen. and Ornithological Officer (GB, HQ), 1959–61; Dep. Regional Officer (N England), 1961–63; PSO, Monks Wood Experimental Station, 1963–70; Dep. Dir, Central Unit on Environmental Pollution, Cabinet Office and DoE, 1970–74; Dep. Dir, Nature Conservancy Council, 1974–75. Member: Council and Exec. Cttee, Wildfowl Trust, 1976–90; Adv. Cttee on Birds, Nature Conservancy Council, 1981–; Vice Pres., Internat. Council for Bird Preservation, 1990– (Mem., 1979–90, Chm., 1982–90, Exec. Cttee); Pres., Cambridge Branch, CPRE, 1990– (Chm., Huntingdon Div., 1975–90). *Publications:* scientific papers in ecol and ornithol jls. *Recreations:* sketching, architecture, reading. *Address:* Eastfield House, Tuddenham Road, Barton Mills, Suffolk IP28 6AG. *T:* Mildenhall (0638) 715139. *Club:* Athenæum.
See also A. M. Prestt.

PRESTWICH, Prof. Michael Charles, FRHistS; FSA; Professor of History, University of Durham, since 1986; *b* 30 Jan. 1943; *s* of John Oswald Prestwich and late Menna Prestwich; *m* 1973, Margaret Joan Daniel; two *s* one *d*. *Educ:* Charterhouse; Magdalen Coll., Oxford (MA, DPhil). FSA 1980. Res. Lectr, Christ Church, Oxford, 1965–69; Lectr in Mediaeval History, Univ. of St Andrews, 1969–79; Reader in Medieval History, Univ. of Durham, 1979–86. *Publications:* War, Politics and Finance under Edward I, 1972; The Three Edwards: war and state in England 1272–1377, 1980; Documents illustrating the Crisis of 1297–98 in England, 1980; Edward I, 1988; English Politics in the Thirteenth Century, 1990; articles in learned jls. *Recreation:* ski-ing. *Address:* 46 Albert Street, Western Hill, Durham DH1 4RJ. *T:* Durham (091) 3862539.

PRESTWOOD, Viscount; John Richard Attlee; *b* 3 Oct. 1956; *s* and *heir* of 2nd Earl Attlee, *qv*.

PRETORIA, Bishop of, since 1982; **Rt. Rev. Richard Austin Kraft;** *b* 3 June 1936; *s* of Arthur Austin Kraft and Mary Roberta Hudson Kraft; *m* 1958, Phyllis Marie Schaffer; three *s* one *d*. *Educ:* Ripon Coll., Ripon, Wisconsin, USA (BA); General Theolog. Seminary, New York (MDiv; Hon. DD 1983). Deacon then priest, 1961; Asst priest, St Alphege's, Scottsville, dio. Natal, 1961–63; Asst priest and Rector, St Chad's Mission, Klip River, 1963–67; Dir of Christian Education, Diocese of Zululand, 1968–76; Rector, All Saints Parish, Melmoth, 1974–76; Dir of Education Dept, Church of Province of S Africa, 1977–79; Dean and Rector, St Alban's Cathedral, Diocese of Pretoria, 1979–82. Canon, Dio. of Zululand, 1971; Canon Emeritus, 1977. *Recreation:* woodwork. *Address:* Bishop's House, 264 Celliers Street, Muckleneuk, Pretoria, 0002, S Africa. *T:* (home) (012) 443163, (office) (012) 3222218.

PRETTY, Dr Katharine Bridget; Principal, Homerton College, Cambridge, since 1991; *b* 18 Oct. 1945; *d* of M. W. and B. E. W. Hughes; *m* 1988, Prof. Tjeerd Hendrik van Andel. *Educ:* King Edward VI High Sch. for Girls, Birmingham; New Hall, Cambridge (MA, PhD). New Hall, Cambridge: College Lectr and Fellow in Archaeology, 1972–91; Admissions Tutor, 1979–85; Sen. Tutor, 1985–91. Member: Council of Senate, Univ. of Cambridge, 1981–89; Financial Bd, Univ. of Cambridge, 1986–. *Recreations:* archaeology, botany, Arctic travel. *Address:* Homerton College, Cambridge CB2 2PH. *T:* Cambridge (0223) 411141.

PREVIN, André (George); conductor and composer; Composer Laureate, London Symphony Orchestra, since 1991; *b* Berlin, Germany, 6 April 1929; *s* of Jack Previn and Charlotte Epstein; *m* 1970; three *s* (inc. twin *s*), three *d*; *m* 1982, Heather, *d* of Robert Sneddon; one *s*. *Educ:* Berlin and Paris Conservatoires; private study with Pierre Monteux, Castelnuovo-Tedesco. Composer of film scores, 1950–62 (four Academy Awards). Music Dir, Houston Symphony Orchestra, 1967–69; Principal Conductor, London Symphony Orchestra, 1968–79, Conductor Emeritus, 1979; Music Director: Pittsburgh Symphony Orchestra, 1976–84; Los Angeles Phil. Orch., 1986–89; Music Dir, 1985–86, Prin. Conductor, 1987–91, RPO; Guest Conductor, most major orchestras, US and Europe, Covent Garden Opera, Salzburg Festival, Edinburgh Festival, Osaka Festival; Music Dir, London South Bank Summer Festival, 1972–74. Member: Composers Guild of GB; Amer. Composers League; Dramatists League. Recording artist. Principal compositions: Cello Concerto; Guitar Concerto; Wind Quintet; Serenades for Violin; piano preludes; Piano Concerto, 1984; Symphony for Strings; overtures; Principals, Reflections (for orchestra); Every Good Boy Deserves Favour (text by Tom Stoppard); Six Songs Mezzo-Soprano (text by Philip Larkin). Annual TV series: specials for BBC; PBS (USA). *Publications:* Music Face to Face, 1971; (ed) Orchestra, 1979; André Previn's Guide to Music, 1983; *relevant publications:* André Previn, by Edward Greenfield, 1973; Previn, by H. Ruttencutter, 1985. *Address:* c/o Harrison/Parrott Ltd, 12 Penzance Place, W11 4PA. *Club:* Garrick.

PREVOST, Sir Christopher (Gerald), 6th Bt *cr* 1805; Chairman and Managing Director, Mailtronic Ltd, since 1977; *b* 25 July 1935; *s* of Sir George James Augustine Prevost, 5th Bt and Muriel Emily (*d* 1939), *d* of late Lewis William Oram; *S* father, 1985; *m* 1964, Dolores Nelly, *o d* of Dezo Hoffmann; one *s* one *d*. *Educ:* Cranleigh School. Served 60th Regt (formed by Prevost family) and Rifle Bde; Kenya Service Medal, 1955. IBM, 1955–61; Pitney-Bowes, 1963–76; founder of Mailtronic Ltd, manufacturers and suppliers of mailroom equipment, 1977. Mem., Business Equipment Trade Assoc., 1983–. Lord of the Manor, Stinchcombe, Glos. *Recreations:* squash; skiing (Member of British Jetski Assoc. and Team sponsor). *Heir:* *s* Nicholas Marc Prevost, *b* 13 March 1971. *Address:* Highway Cottage, Berrygrove Lane, Watford, Herts WD2 8AE. *Club:* Cloisters Wood (Stanmore, Middx).

PREY, Hermann; baritone; *b* Berlin, 11 July 1929; *s* of Hermann Prey; *m* Barbara Pniok; one *s* two *d*. *Educ:* Humanistisches Gymnasium, Berlin; Staatliche Musikhochschule, Berlin. With State Opera, Wiesbaden, 1952; appearances in Germany, Vienna, (La Scala) Milan, (Metropolitan Opera) New York, Buenos Aires, San Francisco, Covent Garden, etc. Festivals include: Salzburg, Bayreuth, Edinburgh, Vienna, Tokyo, Aix-en-Provence, Perugia, Berlin. *Address:* D-8033 Krailling vor München, Fichtenstrasse 14, Federal Republic of Germany; c/o Lies Askonas, 186 Drury Lane, WC2B 5QD.

PRICA, Srdja; Member: Council of the Federation of Yugoslavia, 1972; Council for Foreign Affairs of the Presidency of the Republic of Yugoslavia, 1971; *b* 20 Sept. 1905; *m* 1956, Vukica Tomanović-Prica. *Educ:* University of Zagreb, Yugoslavia. Newspaperman until 1946; Director of Department, Foreign Office, Belgrade, 1947–49; Asst Min., FO, Belgrade, 1949–51; Ambassador of Yugoslavia, Paris, 1951–55; Under-Sec. of State for Foreign Affairs, Belgrade, 1955–60; Ambassador: to Court of St James's, 1960–65; to Italy, 1967–71; to Malta, 1968–72. Grand Officier, Légion d'Honneur (France); Egyptian, Italian, Norwegian, Austrian and Greek Orders.

PRICE, (Alan) Anthony; author and journalist; Editor, The Oxford Times, 1972–88; *b* 16 Aug. 1928; *s* of Walter Longsdon Price and Kathleen Price (*née* Lawrence); *m* 1953, Yvonne Ann Stone; two *s* one *d*. *Educ:* King's Sch., Canterbury; Merton Coll., Oxford (Exbnr; MA). Oxford & County Newspapers, 1952–88. *Publications:* The Labyrinth Makers, 1970 (CWA Silver Dagger); The Alamut Ambush, 1971; Colonel Butler's Wolf, 1972; October Men, 1973; Other Paths to Glory, 1974 (CWA Gold Dagger, 1974; Swedish Acad. of Detection Prize, 1978); Our Man in Camelot, 1975; War Game, 1976; The '44 Vintage, 1978; Tomorrow's Ghost, 1979; The Hour of the Donkey, 1980; Soldier No More, 1981; The Old Vengeful, 1982; Gunner Kelly, 1983; Sion Crossing, 1984; Here Be Monsters, 1985; For the Good of the State, 1986; A New Kind of War, 1987; A Prospect of Vengeance, 1988; The Memory Trap, 1989; Eyes of the Fleet, 1990. *Recreation:* military history. *Address:* Wayside Cottage, Horton-cum-Studley, Oxford OX9 1AW. *T:* Stanton St John (086735) 326.

PRICE, (Arthur) Leolin; QC 1968; *b* 11 May 1924; 3rd *s* of late Evan Price and Ceridwen Price (*née* Price), Hawkhurst, Kent; *m* 1963, Hon. Rosalind Helen Penrose Lewis, *er d* of 1st Baron Brecon, PC, and of Mabel, Baroness Brecon, CBE, JP; two *s* two *d*. *Educ:* Judd Sch., Tonbridge; Keble Coll., Oxford (Schol.; MA). War service, 1943–46 with Army: Capt., RA; Adjt, Indian Mountain Artillery Trng Centre and Depot, Ambala, Punjab, 1946. Treas., Oxford Union, 1948; Pres., Oxford Univ. Conserv. Assoc., 1948. Tutor (part-time), Keble Coll., Oxford, 1951–59. Called to Bar, Middle Temple, 1949, Bencher, 1970–, Treas. 1990; Barrister of Lincoln's Inn, 1959. QC (Bahamas) 1969; QC (NSW) 1987. Member: Editorial Cttee, Modern Law Review, 1954–65; Bar Council Law Reform Cttee, 1969–75; Cttee, Soc. of Cons. Lawyers, 1971– (Vice-Chm., 1987–90); Cttee of Management, Inst. of Child Health, 1972– (Chm., 1976–). Director: Thornton Pan-European Investment Trust (formerly Child Health Res. Investment Trust), 1980– (Chm., 1987–); Marine Adventure Sailing Trust plc, 1981–89; Thornton Asian Emerging Markets Investment Trust plc, 1989–. Governor, Gt Ormond St Hosp. for Sick Children, 1972–; Mem., Falkland Islands Cttee, 1972–. Governor, Christ Coll., Brecon, 1977–. Chancellor, Diocese of Swansea and Brecon, 1982–. *Publications:* articles and notes in legal jls. *Address:* 32 Hampstead Grove, NW3 6SR. *T:* 071–435 9843; 10 Old Square, Lincoln's Inn, WC2A 3SU. *T:* 071–405 0758; Moor Park, Llanbedr, near Crickhowell, Powys NP8 1SS. *T:* Crickhowell (0873) 810443; Selborne Chambers, 174 Phillip Street, Sydney, NSW 2000, Australia. *T:* 612 233 5188. *Club:* Carlton.
See also V. W. C. Price.

PRICE, Barry; *see* Price, W. F. B.

PRICE, Barry David Keith, CBE 1991; QPM 1981; Co-ordinator, National Drugs Intelligence Unit, since 1987; *b* 28 June 1933; *s* of John Leslie Price and Lena Price; *m* 1953, Evelyne Jean Horlick; three *d*. *Educ:* Southall Grammar Sch. FBIM 1975. Metropolitan Police, 1954–75: Constable, uniform and CID, then through ranks to Det. Chief Supt; Asst Chief Constable, Northumbria Police, 1975–78; Dep. Chief Constable, Essex Police, 1978–80; Chief Constable, Cumbria Constabulary, 1980–87. Member: Adv. Council on the Misuse of Drugs, 1982–87; Drugs Intelligence Steering Gp, 1987–; Advr to ACPO Crime Cttee on drugs matters, 1985–88 (past Chm. and Sec.). President: English Police Golf Assoc., 1981–; Northern Police Cricket League, 1983–87; Patron, NW Counties Schoolboys ABA, 1980–87. SBStJ 1982 (County Dir, St John Amb. Assoc., 1981–87). Police Long Service and Good Conduct Medal, 1976. *Publications:* various articles in law enforcement and med. pubns. *Recreations:* golf, painting, gardening. *Address:* National Drugs Intelligence Unit, New Scotland Yard, Broadway, SW1H 0BG.

PRICE, (Benjamin) Terence; Secretary-General, Uranium Institute, 1974–86; *b* 7 January 1921; *er s* of Benjamin and Nellie Price; *m* 1947, Jean Stella Vidal; one *s* one *d*. *Educ:* Crypt School, Gloucester; Queens' College, Cambridge. Naval electronics res., 1942–46; Atomic Energy Research Establishment, Harwell (Nuclear Physics Division), 1947–59; Head of Reactor Development Division, Atomic Energy Estabt, Winfrith, 1959; Chief Scientific Officer, Ministry of Defence, 1960–63; Assistant Chief Scientific Adviser (Studies), Ministry of Defence, 1963–65; Director, Defence Operational Analysis Establishment, MoD, 1965–68; Chief Scientific Adviser, Min. of Transport, 1968–71; Dir of Planning and Development, Vickers Ltd, 1971–73. Chm., NEDO Mechanical Handling Sector Working Party, 1976–80. Reviewer, CET, 1984–85. *Publications:* Radiation Shielding, 1957; Political Electricity, 1990. *Recreations:* flying, ski-ing, making music. *Address:* Seers Bough, Wilton Lane, Jordans, Beaconsfield, Bucks HP9 2RG. *T:* Chalfont St Giles (02407) 4589. *Club:* Athenæum.

PRICE, Bernard Albert; County Clerk and Chief Executive, Staffordshire County Council, and Clerk to the Lieutenancy, since 1983; *b* 6 Jan. 1944; *s* of Albert and Doris Price; *m* 1966, Christine Mary, *d* of Roy William Henry Combes; two *s* one *d*. *Educ:* Whitchurch Grammar Sch., Salop; King's Sch., Rochester, Kent; Merton Coll., Oxford (BA 1965, MA 1970). DMS, Wolverhampton Polytechnic, 1972. Articled, later Asst Solicitor, Worcs CC, 1966–70; Asst Solicitor, subseq. Dep. Dir of Admin, Staffs CC, 1970–80; Sen. Dep. Clerk, Staffs CC, 1980–83. *Recreations:* sailing, walking. *Address:* The Cottage, Yeatsall Lane, Abbots Bromley, Rugeley, Staffs WS15 3DY. *T:* Burton on Trent (0283) 840269.

PRICE, Rear-Adm. Cecil Ernest, CB 1978; AFC 1953; Deputy Assistant Chief of Staff (Operations), SHAPE, 1976–80, retired; *b* 29 Oct. 1921; *s* of Ernest C. Price and Phyllis M. Price; *m* 1946, Megan Morgan; one *s* one *d*. *Educ:* Bungay Grammar Sch. Joined Royal Navy, 1941; Captain 1966; idc 1970; Director: Naval Air Warfare, 1971–72; Naval Operational Requirements, 1972–73; CO RNAS, Culdrose, 1973–75; Rear-Adm. 1976. *Recreations:* golf, fishing, gardening. *Address:* Low Farm, Mendham, Harleston, Norfolk. *T:* Harleston (0379) 852676.

PRICE, Hon. Charles H., II; Chairman of Board, President, and Chief Executive Officer, Ameribanc, Inc., since 1989; non-executive Director, since 1989: British Airways PLC; Hanson PLC; New York Times Co.; Texaco Inc.; United Telecommunications Inc.; *b* 1 April 1931; *s* of Charles Harry Price and Virginia (*née* Ogden); *m* 1969, Carol Ann Swanson; two *s* three *d*. *Educ:* University of Missouri. Chairman: Price Candy Co., 1969–81; American Bancorpn, 1973–81; American Bank & Trust Co., 1973–81; American Mortgage Co., 1973–81; Ambassador: to Belgium, 1981–83; to UK, 1983–89. Chm., Midwest Res. Inst., 1990– (Vice-Chm. and Mem. Exec. Cttee, 1978–81); Mem. Bd of Dirs, Civic Council, Greater Kansas City, 1979–80. Member: Young Presidents Orgn; IISS; World Business Council. Hon. Fellow, Regent's Coll., London, 1986. Hon. Dr Westminster Coll., Missouri, 1984; Hon. Dr of Laws Missouri, 1988. Salvation Army's William Booth Award, 1985; Kansas City Mayor's World Citizen of the Year, 1985, Trustee Citation Award, Midwest Res. Inst., 1987; Distinguished Service Award, Internat. Relations Council, 1989; Mankind Award, Cystic Fibrosis Foundn, 1990; Gold Good Citizen Award, Sons of the American Revolution, 1991. *Recreations:* tennis, golf, shooting. *Address:* 1 West Armour Boulevard, Ste 300, Kansas City, Mo 64111, USA. *Clubs:* White's, Mark's; Swinley Forest Golf; Metropolitan (Washington); Eldorado Country (Palm Springs); Castle Pines Country (Denver); Kansas City Country, River (Kansas City); Mill Reef (Antigua).

PRICE, Sir Charles (Keith Napier) Rugge-, 9th Bt *cr* 1804; Senior Management Consultant, City of Edmonton, since 1982; *b* 7 August, 1936; *s* of Lt-Col Sir Charles James Napier Rugge-Price, 8th Bt, and of Lady (Maeve Marguerite) Rugge-Price (*née* de la Peña); *S* father, 1966; *m* 1965, Jacqueline Mary (*née* Loranger); two *s*. *Educ:* Middleton College, Eire. 5th Regt Royal Horse Artillery, Germany and Wales, 1954–59. Actuarial Dept, William Mercers Ltd, Canada, 1959–60; Alexander and Alexander Services Ltd, Montreal, Canada, 1960–67; with Domtar Ltd, 1968–71; Manager, Tomenson Alexander Ltd, Toronto, 1971–76; Supervisor, Compensation, City of Edmonton, 1976–81. *Heir:* *s* James Keith Peter Rugge-Price, *b* 8 April 1967. *Address:* 23 Lambert Crescent, St Albert, Alberta T8N 1M1, Canada.

PRICE, Christopher; Director, Leeds Polytechnic, since 1986; freelance journalist and broadcaster; *b* 26 Jan. 1932; *s* of Stanley Price; *m* 1956, Annie Grierson Ross; two *s* one *d*. *Educ:* Leeds Grammar School; Queen's College, Oxford. Sec., Oxford Univ. Labour Club, 1953; Chm., Nat. Assoc. of Labour Student Organisations, 1955–56. Sheffield City Councillor, 1962–66; Dep. Chm., Sheffield Educn Cttee, 1963–66. Contested (Lab): Shipley, 1964; Birmingham, Perry Barr, 1970; Lewisham W, 1983. MP (Lab): Perry Barr Division of Birmingham, 1966–70; Lewisham W, Feb. 1974–1983; PPS to Secretary of State for Education and Science, 1966–67 and 1975–76; Chm., H of C Select Cttee on Educn, Science and the Arts, 1980–83. Mem., European Parlt, 1977–78. Dir, London Internat. Festival of Theatre Ltd, 1982–86; Pro-Asst Dir, The Polytechnic of the South Bank, 1983–86; Dir, New Statesman Nation Publishing, 1991–. Chm., Council, Nat. Youth Bureau, 1977–80; Mem. Bd, Phoenix House Ltd (Britain's largest gp of drug rehabilitation houses), 1986– (Chm., 1980–86); Member: Council, Inst. for Study of Drug Dependence, 1984–86; Delegacy, Univ. of London Goldsmiths' Coll., 1981–86; Court, Polytechnic of Central London, 1982–86; London Centre for Biotechnology Trust, 1984–86; Fellow, Internat. Inst. of Biotechnology, 1984. FRSA 1988. Editor, New Education, 1967–68; Educn corresp., New Statesman, 1969–74; Columnist, TES, 1983–85. *Publications:* (contrib.) A Radical Future, 1967; Crisis in the Classroom, 1968; (ed) Your Child and School, 1968; Which Way?, 1969; (contrib.) Life and Death of the Schools Council, 1985; (contrib.) Police, the Constitution and the Community, 1985. *Address:* Leeds Polytechnic, Calverley Street, Leeds LS1 3HE; Churchwood, Beckett Park, Leeds LS6 3QS. *Club:* Athenæum.

PRICE, Maj.-Gen. David; *see* Price, Maj.-Gen. M. D.

PRICE, Sir David (Ernest Campbell), Kt 1980; DL; MP (C) Eastleigh Division of Hampshire, since 1955; *b* 20 Nov. 1924; *o s* of Major Villiers Price; *m* 1960, Rosemary Eugénie Evelyn, *o d* of late Cyril F. Johnston, OBE; one *d*. *Educ:* Eton; Trinity College, Cambridge; Yale University, USA; Rosebery Schol., Eton; Open History Schol., Trinity College, Cambridge. Served with 1st Battalion Scots Guards, CMF; subsequently Staff Captain (Intelligence) HQ, 56 London Div., Trieste, 1942–46. Trin. Coll., Cambridge, BA Hons, MA. Pres. Cambridge Union; Vice-Pres. Fedn of Univ. Conservative and Unionist Assocs, 1946–48; Henry Fellow of Yale Univ., USA, 1948–49. Industrial Consultant. Held various appts in Imperial Chemical Industries Ltd, 1949–62. Parly Sec., Board of Trade, 1962–64; Opposition Front-Bench spokesman on Science and Technology, 1964–70; Parly Sec., Min. of Technology, June-Oct. 1970; Parly Sec., Min. of Aviation Supply, 1970–71; Parly Under-Sec. of State, Aerospace, DTI, 1971–72. Member: Public Accounts Cttee, 1974–75; Select Cttee on Transport, 1979–83; Select Cttee on Social Services, 1983–90; Select Cttee on Health, 1990–; Vice-Pres., Parly and Scientific Cttee, 1975–79 and 1982–86 (Vice-Chm., 1965–70, Chm., 1973–75 and 1979–82). Vice-Chm., Cons. Arts and Heritage Cttee, 1979–81 and 1983–87; Chm., Cons. Shipping and Ship-Building Cttee, 1985–; Pres., Wessex Area Cons. and Unionist Party, 1986–. British Representative to Consultative Assembly of the Council of Europe, 1958–61. Dir, Assoc. British Maltsters, 1966–70. Gen. Cons. to IIM (formerly IWM), 1973–; Cons. to Union International Ltd. Vice-Pres., IIM, 1980–. Pres., Wessex Rehabilitation Soc., 1990–. Governor, Middlesex Hospital, 1956–60. DL Hants, 1982. *Recreations:* swimming, arts and heritage, history, ornithology, wine, cooking, gardening. *Address:* 16 Laxford House, Cundy Street, SW1. *T:* 071–730 3326; Forest Lodge, Moonhills Lane, Beaulieu, Brockenhurst, Hampshire. *T:* Beaulieu (0590) 612537. *Club:* Beefsteak.

PRICE, Eric Hardiman Mockford; Under Secretary, Head of Economics and Statistics Division, and Chief Economic Adviser, Department of Energy, since 1980; Director, Robinson Brothers (Ryders Green) Ltd, since 1985; *b* 14 Nov. 1931; *s* of Frederick H. Price and Florence N. H. Price (*née* Mockford); *m* 1963, Diana M. S. Robinson; one *s* three *d*. *Educ:* St Marylebone Grammar Sch.; Christ's Coll., Cambridge. Econs Tripos, 1955; MA 1958. FREconS, 1956; FSS 1958. Army service, 1950–52; HAC, 1952–57. Supply Dept, Esso Petroleum Co. Ltd, 1955–56; Economist: Central Electricity Authority, 1956–57; Electricity Council, 1957–58; British Iron & Steel Fedn, 1958–62; Chief Economist, Port of London Authority, 1962–67; Sen. Econ. Adviser, Min. of Transport, 1966–69; Chief Econ. Adviser, Min. of Transport, 1969–71; Dir of Econs, 1971–75, Under Sec., 1972–76, Dir of Econs and Stats, 1975–76, DoE; Under Sec., Econs and Stats Div., Depts of Industry, Trade and Consumer Protection, 1977–80. Member: Soc. of Business Economists, 1961; Expert Adv. Gp on Entry into Freight Transport Market, EEC, 1973–75; Northern Regional Strategy Steering Gp, 1976–77; Expert Gp on Venture Capital for Industrial Innovation, EEC, 1978–79; Soc. of Strategic and Long-range Planning, 1980–; Council, Internat. Assoc. of Energy Economists, 1981–85; Energy Panel, SSRC, 1980–83; Council, British Inst. of Energy Economics, 1986 (Mem., 1980–; Vice-Chm., 1981–82 and 1988–89; Chm., 1982–85); Steering Cttee, Jt Energy Programme, RIIA, 1981–89, Steering Cttee, Energy and Envmtl Prog., 1989–; Adv. Council, Energy Econs Centre, Univ. of Surrey, 1989–. UK rep., Econ. Res. Cttee, European Council of Ministers of Transport, 1968–76; UK rep. on Six Nations' Prog. on Govt Policies towards Technological Innovation in Industry, 1977–80; World Bank's Groupe des Sages on Econs of Global Warming, 1990–. Member, Advisory Board: Transport Studies Unit, Oxford Univ., 1973–75; Centre for Res. in Industrial, Business and Admin Studies, Univ. of Warwick, 1977–80. FInstD 1990. *Publications:* various articles in learned jls on transport and industrial economics, energy and energy efficiency, investment, public sector industries, technological innovation in industry, regional planning, environmental abatement policies, and East European energy issues. *Recreations:* tennis, squash, local history. *Address:* Batchworth Heath Farm, London Road, Rickmansworth, Herts WD3 1QB. *Clubs:* Moor Park Golf; Northwood Squash.

PRICE, Sir Francis (Caradoc Rose), 7th Bt *cr* 1815; barrister and solicitor; *b* 9 Sept. 1950; *s* of Sir Rose Francis Price, 6th Bt and of Kathleen June, *d* of late Norman W. Hutchinson, Melbourne; *S* father, 1979; *m* 1975, Marguerite Jean Trussler, Justice, Court of Queen's Bench, Alberta, *d* of Roy S. Trussler, Victoria, BC; three *d*. *Educ:* Eton; Trinity College, Melbourne Univ. (Sen. Student 1971, LLB Hons 1973); Univ. of Alberta (LLM 1975); Canadian Petroleum Law Foundn Fellow, 1974–75. Admitted Province of Alberta 1976, Northwest Territories 1978, Canada; Bencher, Law Soc. of Alberta, 1990. Lectr, 1979–89, and Course Head, 1983–89, Alberta Bar Admission Course. *Publications:* Pipelines in Western Canada, 1975; Mortgage Actions in Alberta, 1985; contribs to Alberta and Melbourne Univ. Law Revs, etc. *Recreations:* cricket, skiing, opera, running, theatre. *Heir:* *b* Norman William Rose Price, [*b* 17 March 1953; *m* 1987, Charlotte Louise, *yr d* of R. R. B. Baker]. *Address:* 9677 95th Avenue, Edmonton, Alberta T6C 2A3, Canada. *Clubs:* Centre, Faculty (Edmonton).

PRICE, Sir Frank (Leslie), Kt 1966; DL; Chairman, Sir Frank Price Associates SA, since 1986; *b* 26 July 1922; *s* of G. F. Price; marr. diss.; one *s*; *m* Daphne Ling. *Educ:* St Matthias Church Sch., Birmingham; Vittoria Street Arts Sch. Elected to Birmingham City Council, 1949; Alderman, 1958–74; Lord Mayor, 1964–65. Member: Council, Town and Country Planning Assoc., 1958–74; W Midlands Economic Planning Council, 1965–72; Nat. Water Council, 1975–79; Chm., British Waterways Bd, 1968–84. Founder/Chm., Midlands Art Centre for Young People, 1960–71; Chairman: W Midlands Sports Council, 1965–69; Telford Development Corporation, 1968–71; Dir, National Exhibn Centre, 1968–74. Member: Minister of Transport's Cttee of Inquiry into Major Ports, 1961; English Tourist Board, 1976–83; Pres., BAIE, 1979–83. Livery Co. of Basketmakers. FSVA; FCIT; Mem., Fédn Internat. des Professions Immobilières. FRSA. DL: Warwicks, 1970–77; West Midlands, 1974–77; Herefordshire and Worcestershire, 1977–84. Freeman, City of London. *Publications:* various pamphlets and articles on town planning, transport and public affairs. *Recreations:* painting, cruising. *Address:* Apartado 534, Mojacar Playa, Mojacar, Almeria 04638, Spain. *Club:* Reform.

PRICE, Gareth; Controller of Broadcasting, Thomson Foundation, since 1990; *b* 30 Aug. 1939; *s* of Rowena and Morgan Price; *m* 1962, Mari Griffiths; two *s* one *d*. *Educ:* Aberaeron Grammar School and Ardwyn Grammar School, Aberystwyth; University College of Wales, Aberystwyth (BA Econ; Hon. Fellow, 1987). Asst Lectr in Economics, Queen's Univ., Belfast, 1962–64; BBC Wales: Radio Producer, Current Affairs, 1964–66; Television Producer, Features and Documentaries, 1966–74; Dep. Head of Programmes, 1974–81; Head of Programmes, 1981–85; Controller, 1986–90. Pres., Old Students' Assoc., UCW, Aberystwyth, 1989–90. *Publication:* David Lloyd George (with Emyr Price and Bryn Parry), 1981. *Recreations:* all sports and restaurants. *Address:* 98 Pencisely Road, Llandaff, Cardiff, South Glamorgan. *T:* Cardiff (0222) 568332. *Club:* Cardiff and County (Cardiff).

PRICE, Geoffrey Alan, IPFA, CBIM; Chief Executive and County Treasurer, Hereford and Worcester County Council. Formerly County Treasurer, Hants CC; previous appts in: Gloucester CC; Southend-on-Sea; Cheshire CC; West Sussex CC. *Address:* County Hall, Spetchley Road, Worcester WR5 2NP.

PRICE, Rt. Hon. George (Cadle), PC 1982; Prime Minister of Belize, 1981–84, and since 1989 (Premier from 1964 until Independence, 1981); *b* 15 Jan. 1919; *s* of William Cadle Price and Irene Cecilia Escalante de Price. *Educ:* Holy Redeemer Primary Sch., Belize City; St John's Coll., Belize City. Private Sec. to late Robert S. Turton; entered politics, 1944; City Councillor, 1947–65 (Mayor of Belize City several times); founding Mem., People's United Party, 1950; Party Sec., 1950–56; became Leader, 1956; elected to National Assembly, 1954; under 1961 Ministerial System, led People's United Party to 100% victory at polls and became First Minister; under 1964 Self-Govt Constitution, title changed to Premier; has led delegns to Central American and Caribbean countries; spearheaded internationalization of Belize problem at internat. forums; addressed UN's Fourth Cttee, 1975, paving way for overwhelming victory at UN when majority of nations voted in favour of Belize's right to self-determination and territorial integrity. *Address:* Office of the Prime Minister, Belmopan, Belize.

PRICE, Geraint; *see* Price, W. G.

PRICE, Very Rev. Hilary Martin Connop; Rector and Provost of Chelmsford, 1967–77, now Provost Emeritus; *b* 1912; *s* of late Rev. Connop Lewis Price and late Shirley (*née* Lewis); *m* 1939, Dorothea (*née* Beaty-Pownall); one *s* two *d*. *Educ:* Cheltenham Coll.; Queens' Coll., Cambridge (MA); Ridley Hall, Cambridge. Asst Curate, St Peter's, Hersham, Surrey, 1936–40; Sen. Chaplain, Portsmouth Cathedral, 1940–41; Asst Curate, Holy Trinity, Cambridge, 1941–46; Chaplain, RAFVR, 1943–46; Vicar, St Gabriel's, Bishopwearmouth, 1946–56; Rector and Rural Dean, Newcastle-under-Lyme, 1956–67. Prebendary of Lichfield, 1964–67. Proctor in Convocation: of York for Durham Dio., 1954–56; of Canterbury for Lichfield Dio., 1962–67. Mem., General Synod, 1970–75. *Address:* 98 St James Street, Shaftesbury, Dorset SP7 8HF. *T:* Shaftesbury (0747) 52118.

PRICE, Sir (James) Robert, KBE 1976; FAA 1959; Chairman of the Executive, Commonwealth Scientific and Industrial Research Organization, 1970–77; *b* 25 March 1912; *s* of Edgar James Price and Mary Katherine Price (*née* Hughes); *m* 1940, Joyce Ethel (*née* Brooke); one *s* two *d*. *Educ:* St Peter's Coll., Adelaide; Univ. of Adelaide (BSc Hons, MSc, DSc); Univ. of Oxford (DPhil). Head, Chemistry Section, John Innes Horticultural Inst., London, 1937–40; (UK) Min. of Supply, 1941–45; Div. of Industrial Chemistry, Council for Scientific and Industrial Research (CSIR), Australia, from 1945; CSIRO: Officer-in-Charge, Organic Chem. Section, 1960, subseq. Chief of Div. of Organic Chem.; Mem., Executive, 1966. Pres., Royal Aust. Chemical Inst., 1963–64. *Publications:* numerous scientific papers in learned jls. *Recreations:* squash; growing Australian native plants. *Address:* Yangoora, 2 Ocean View Avenue, Red Hill South, Victoria 3937, Australia. *Club:* Sciences (Melb.).

PRICE, John Alan, QC 1980; a Recorder of the Crown Court, since 1980; a Deputy Circuit Judge, since 1975; *b* 11 Sept. 1938; *s* of Frederick Leslie Price and Gertrude Davilda Alice Price; *m* 1964, Elizabeth Myra (*née* Priest) (marr. diss. 1982); one *s* one *d*; *m* 1984, Alison Elizabeth Curran (*née* Ward); two step *d*. *Educ:* Stretford Grammar Sch.; Manchester Univ. (LLB Hons 1959). Called to the Bar, Gray's Inn, 1961; in practice on Northern Circuit; Head of 60 King St Chambers, Manchester, 1978–80. *Recreations:* tennis, squash, football, golf. *Address:* 5 Essex Court, Temple, EC4Y 9AH; 25 Byrom Street, Manchester. *Club:* Wilmslow Rugby Union Football.

PRICE, John Lister Willis, CVO 1965; HM Diplomatic Service, retired; *b* 25 July 1915; *s* of Canon John Willis Price, Croughton, Brackley, Northants; *m* 1940, Frances Holland (marr. diss.); one *s* one *d*. *Educ:* Bradfield; New College, Oxford. Military Service, 1940–46 (despatches). Joined Foreign Office News Dept, 1946; apptd First Secretary, Paris, 1950; transf. to FO, 1952; to Sofia, 1956; FO, 1959; Counsellor, Head of British Information Services, Bonn, 1962–66; IDC 1967; seconded as Dir of Information, NATO, 1967–72; retired 1972. Dir, Merseyside Develt Office in London, 1972–79. *Recreations:* mountains, hill walking. *Address:* c/o National Westminster Bank, Hove Palmeira Branch, 64 Western Road, Hove, E Sussex BN3 2JR. *Club:* Ski Club of Great Britain (Invitation Life Mem.).

PRICE, J(ohn) Maurice; QC 1976; *b* 4 May 1922; second *s* of Edward Samuel Price and Hilda M. Price, JP; *m* 1945, Mary, *d* of Dr Horace Gibson, DSO and bar, Perth, WA; two *s*. *Educ:* Grove Park Sch., Wrexham; Trinity Coll., Cambridge (MA). Served in Royal Navy, 1941–46 (Submarines, 1943–46), Lieut RNVR. Called to Bar, Gray's Inn, 1949 (Holt Scholar, Holker Sen. Scholar; Bencher 1981), and to Lincoln's Inn (*ad eundem*), 1980; called to Singapore Bar, 1977. Mem., Senate of Inns of Court and the Bar, 1975–78. *Recreations:* fishing, opera. *Address:* Bowzell Place, Weald, Sevenoaks, Kent TN14 6NF; (chambers) 2 New Square, Lincoln's Inn, WC2A 3RU. *T:* 071–242 6201. *Club:* Flyfishers'.

PRICE, Air Vice-Marshal John Walter, CBE 1979 (OBE 1973); joined Clyde Petroleum, 1984, Manager, External Affairs, since 1986; *b* Birmingham, 26 Jan. 1930; *s* of late Henry Walter Price and Myrza Price (*née* Griffiths); *m* 1956, Margaret Sinclair McIntyre (*d* 1989), Sydney, Aust. *Educ:* Solihull Sch.; RAF Coll., Cranwell. MRAeS 1971, FBIM 1979. Joined RAF, 1948; Adjutant, No 11 (Vampire) Sqn, 1950–52; No 77 (Meteor) Sqn, RAAF, Korea, 1952–53 (mentioned in despatches, 1953); No 98 Sqn (Venoms and Vampires), 1953–54; No 2 (F) Op. Trng Unit (Vampires) and No 75 (F) Sqn (Meteors), RAAF, 1954–56; Cadet Wing Adjutant, RAF Tech. Coll., Henlow, 1956–60; RAF Staff Coll., 1960; Air Ministry (Ops Overseas), 1961–64; Comd No 110 Sqn (Sycamore and Whirlwind), 1964–66; Directing Staff, RAF Staff Coll., 1966–68; PSO to Chief of Air Staff, 1968–70; Comd No 72 (Wessex) Sqn, 1970–72; Air Warfare Course, 1973; Dep. Dir Ops (Offensive Support and Jt Warfare), MoD (Air), 1973–75; sowc 1975–76; Comd RAF Laarbruch, 1976–78; Gp Capt. Ops, HQ Strike Comd, 1979; Dir of Ops (Strike), MoD (Air), 1980–82; ACAS (Ops), 1982–84, retd. Governor, Solihull Sch., 1979–, Chm., 1983–. *Recreations:* motorcycling, golf, cabinet making. *Address:* 2 Palace Yard, Hereford. *Club:* Royal Air Force.

PRICE, Leolin; *see* Price, A. L.

PRICE, Leonard Sidney, OBE 1974; HM Diplomatic Service, retired 1981; *b* 19 Oct. 1922; *s* of late William Price and late Dorothy Price; *m* 1958, Adrienne Mary (*née* Wilkinson); two *s* one *d*. *Educ:* Central Foundation Sch., EC1. Served War, 1942–45. Foreign Office, 1939–42 and 1945–48; Chungking, later Vice-Consul, 1948; Mexico City, 1950; Rome, 1953; Vice-Consul, later Second Sec., Katmandu, 1954; FO, 1957; Consul, Split, 1960; Consul and First Sec., Copenhagen, 1963; FO, later FCO, 1967; First Sec. i/c, Kuching, 1970; Suva, 1972; Parly Clerk, FCO, 1975; Counsellor (Admin), Canberra, 1977–81. Dep. Dir, St John Ambulance Assoc., Somerset, 1982–84; Hon. Treas., Council of Order of St John, Somerset, 1983–88. *Recreation:* reading ancient, medieval and military history. *Address:* 5 Staplegrove Manor, Taunton, Somerset TA2 6EG. *T:* Taunton (0823) 337093. *Club:* Civil Service.

PRICE, Leontyne; Opera Prima Donna (Soprano), United States; *b* 10 Feb. 1927. *Educ:* Public Schools, Laurel, Mississippi; Central State College, Wilberforce, Ohio (BA); Juilliard Sch. of Music, NY. Four Saints, 1952; Porgy and Bess, 1952–54. Operatic Debut on TV, 1955, as Tosca; Concerts in America, England, Australia, Europe. Operatic debut as Madame Lidouine in Dialogues of Carmelites, San Francisco, 1957; Covent Garden, Verona Arena, Vienna Staatsoper, 1958; five roles, inc. Leonora in Il Trovatore, Madame Butterfly, Donna Anna in Don Giovanni, Metropolitan, 1960–61; Salzburg debut singing soprano lead in Missa Solemnis, 1959; Aida in Aida, Liu in Turandot, La Scala, 1960; opened season at Metropolitan in 1961 as Minnie in Fanciulla del West; opened new Metropolitan Opera House, 1966, as Cleopatra in world premiere of Samuel Barber's Antony and Cleopatra; debut Teatre Dell'Opera, Rome, in Aida, 1967; debut Paris Opera, in Aida, 1968; debut Teatro Colon, Buenos Aires, as Leonora in Il Trovatore, 1969; opened season at Metropolitan Opera, in Aida, 1969. Numerous recordings. Vice-Chm., Nat. Inst. for Music Theatre. Member: Metropolitan Opera Assoc.; Bd of Dirs, Dance Theatre of Harlem; Bd of Trustees, NY Univ. Life Mem., NAACP. Fellow, Amer. Acad. of Arts and Sciences. Hon. Dr of Music: Howard Univ., Washington, DC, 1962; Central State Coll., Wilberforce, Ohio, 1968; Hon. DHL, Dartmouth Univ., 1962; Hon. Dr of Humanities, Rust Coll., Holly Springs, Miss, 1968; Hon. Dr of Humane Letters, Fordham Univ., New York, 1969. Hon. Mem. Bd of Dirs, Campfire Girls, 1966. Presidential Medal of Freedom, 1965; Spingarn Medal, NAACP, 1965; Nat. Medal of Arts, 1985; 18 Grammy Awards, Nat. Acad. Recording Arts and Scis. Order of Merit (Italy), 1966; Commandeur, Ordre des Arts et des Lettres (France), 1986. *Recreations:* cooking, dancing, shopping for clothes, etc, antiques for homes in Rome and New York. *Address:* c/o Columbia Artists Management Inc., 165 W 57th Street, New York, NY 10019, USA.

PRICE, Sir Leslie Victor, Kt 1976; OBE 1971; former Chairman, Australian Wheat Board; retired; *b* Toowoomba, Qld, 30 Oct. 1920; *s* of late H. V. L. Price; *m* Lorna Collins; one *s* two *d*. President: Queensland Graingrowers Assoc., 1966–77; Australian Wheatgrowers Fedn, 1970–72; Mem., Queensland State Wheat Bd, 1968–77. *Recreation:* clay target shooting. *Address:* 6 Alayne Court, Toowoomba, Qld 4350, Australia. *Clubs:* Queensland; Melbourne.

PRICE, (Llewelyn) Ralph, CBE 1972; Director, Honeywell, since 1971 (Chairman, 1971–81); Chairman, Enborne Foods Ltd, since 1988; *b* 23 Oct. 1912; *s* of late L. D. Price, schoolmaster, and late Lena Elizabeth (*née* Dixon); *m* 1939, Vera Patricia Harrison; one *s* two *d*. *Educ:* Quarry Bank Sch., Liverpool. Chartered Accountant, 1935; Sec. to Honeywell Ltd, 1936; Cost Investigator, Min. of Supply, 1943–46; Dir of Manufacturing (Scotland), Honeywell Ltd, 1947; Financial Dir, Honeywell Europe, 1957; Dir, Computer Div., Honeywell, 1960; Managing Dir, Honeywell Ltd, 1965; Chm., Honeywell UK Adv. Council, 1981–. Chm., ML Hldgs Ltd, 1976–87. Pres., British Industrial, Measuring & Control Apparatus Manufrs Assoc., 1971–76. CBIM. *Recreations:* golf, bridge, music. *Address:* Nascot, Pinkneys Drive, Pinkneys Green, Maidenhead, Berks. *T:* Maidenhead (0628) 28270. *Clubs:* Royal Automobile; Temple Golf (Maidenhead).

PRICE, Margaret Berenice, CBE 1982; opera singer; *b* Tredeger, Wales, 13 April 1941; *d* of late Thomas Glyn Price and of Lilian Myfanwy Richards. *Educ:* Pontllanfraith Secondary Sch.; Trinity Coll. of Music, London. Debut as Cherubino in Marriage of Figaro, Welsh Nat. Opera Co., 1962; debut, in same rôle, at Royal Opera House, Covent Garden, 1963; has subseq. sung many principal rôles at Glyndebourne, San Francisco Opera Co., Cologne Opera House, Munich State Opera, Hamburg State Opera, Vienna State Opera, Lyric Opera, Chicago, Paris Opera; La Scala, Milan; Metropolitan Opera House, NY. Major rôles include: Countess in Marriage of Figaro; Pamina in The Magic Flute; Fiordiligi in Cosi Fan Tutte; Donna Anna in Don Giovanni; Konstanze in Die Entführung; Amelia in Simone Boccanegra; Agathe in Freischütz; Desdemona in Otello; Elisabetta in Don Carlo; Amelia in Un Ballo In Maschera; title rôles in Aida, Norma and Ariadne auf Naxos. BBC recitals and concerts, also TV appearances. Has made recordings. Hon. FTCL; Hon. DMus Wales, 1983. Elisabeth Schumann Prize for Lieder; Ricordi Prize for Opera; Silver Medal, Worshipful Co. of Musicians; Bayerische Kammersängerin. *Recreations:* cooking, driving, reading, walking, swimming. *Address:* c/o Bayerische Staatsoper München, Max Josef Platz 2, 8000 München 22, Germany.

PRICE, Maj.-Gen. (Maurice) David, CB 1970; OBE 1956; *b* 13 Feb. 1915; *s* of Edward Allan Price and Edna Marion Price (*née* Turner); *m* 1st, 1938, Ella Lacy (*d* 1971), *d* of late H. L. Day; two *s* two *d*; 2nd, 1972, Mrs Olga Marion Oclee (*d* 1989). *Educ:* Marlborough; RMA, Woolwich. 2nd Lt R Signals, 1935; Vice-Quartermaster-Gen., MoD (Army), 1967–70, retired. Col Comdt, Royal Corps of Signals, 1967–74. *Recreation:* fishing. *Address:* The Cross, Chilmark, Salisbury, Wiltshire SP3 5AR. *T:* Teffont (0722) 716212.

PRICE, Sir Norman (Charles), KCB 1975 (CB 1969); Member, European Court of Auditors, 1977–83; Chairman, Board of Inland Revenue, 1973–76 (Deputy Chairman, 1968–73); *b* 5 Jan. 1915; *s* of Charles William and Ethel Mary Price; *m* 1940, Kathleen Beatrice (*née* Elston); two *d*. *Educ:* Plaistow Grammar School. Entered Civil Service as Executive Officer, Customs and Excise, 1933; Inspector of Taxes, Inland Revenue, 1939; Secretaries' Office, Inland Revenue, 1951; Board of Inland Revenue, 1965. *Recreations:* music, history. *Address:* 73 Linkswood, Compton Place Road, Eastbourne BN21 1EF. *T:* Eastbourne (0323) 25941.

PRICE, Rev. Canon Peter Bryan; General Secretary, United Society for the Propagation of the Gospel, since 1991; *b* 17 May 1944; *s* of Alec Henry Price and Phyllis Evelyn Mary Price; *m* 1967, Edith Margaret Burns; four *s*. *Educ:* Redland Coll., Bristol (Cert Ed 1966); Oak Hill Theol Coll. (Dip. in Pastoral Studies, 1974). Asst Master, Ashton Park Sch., Bristol, 1966–70; Tutor, Lindley Lodge, Nuneaton, 1970; Head of Religious Studies, Cordeaux Sch., Louth, 1970–72; ordained, 1974; Community Chaplain, Crookhorn, Portsmouth and Asst Curate, Christ Church, Portsdown, 1974–78; Chaplain, Scargill House, Kettlewell, 1978–80; Vicar, St Mary Magdalene, Addiscombe, Croydon, 1980–88; Canon Residentiary and Chancellor, Southwark Cathedral, 1988–91. *Publication:* The Church as Kingdom, 1987. *Recreations:* painting, swimming, walking, conversation. *Address:* 14 Oakwood Road, SW20 0PW. *T:* 081–946 3814.

PRICE, Peter Nicholas; Member (C) London South East, since 1984 (Lancashire West, 1979–84), European Parliament; *b* 19 Feb. 1942; *s* of Rev. Dewi Emlyn Price and Kate Mary Price (*née* Thomas). *Educ:* Worcester Royal Grammar Sch.; Aberdare Boys' Grammar Sch.; Univ. of Southampton (BA (Law)); Coll. of Law, Guildford. Solicitor. Interviewer and current affairs freelance broadcaster, 1962–67; Asst Solicitor, Glamorgan CC, 1967–68; solicitor in private practice, 1966–67 and 1968–85. Contested (C) Gen. Elecs: Aberdare 1964, 1966; Caerphilly 1970; Nat. Vice-Chm., Young Conservatives, 1971–72; Mem., Nat. Union Exec. Cttee, 1969–72 and 1978–79; Vice-Chm., Cons. Pol. Centre Nat. Cttee, 1978–79; Hon. Sec., For. Affairs Forum, 1977–79; Vice-Chm., Cons. Gp for Europe, 1979–81; Mem. Council, Europ. Movement, 1971–81. Chm., European Parliament: Budgetary Control Cttee, 1989– (Vice-Chm., 1979–84, and its Rapporteur for series of 4 major reports on Community finances, 1985–86); spokesman for Europ. Democratic Gp: Legal Affairs Cttee, 1984–87; Budgets Cttee, 1986–89; Mem., ACP/EEC Jt Assembly, 1981–. Fellow, Industry and Parlt Trust, 1981–82; Vice-Pres., UK Cttee, Europ. Year of Small and Med.-sized Enterprises, 1983. Vice-Pres., Llangollen Internat. Eisteddfod, 1981–. *Publications:* misc. pol. pamplets and newspaper articles. *Recreations:* theatre, music, photography. *Address:* 60 Marlings Park Avenue, Chislehurst, Kent BR7 6RD. *T:* Orpington (0689) 820681, *Fax:* Orpington (0689) 890622.

PRICE, Rev. Peter Owen, CBE 1983; BA; FPhS; RN retired; Minister of Blantyre Old Parish Church, Glasgow, since 1985; *b* Swansea, 18 April 1930; *e s* of late Idwal Price and Florence Price; *m* 1957, Margaret Trevan (*d* 1977); three *d*. *Educ:* Wyggeston Sch., Leicester; Didsbury Theol Coll., Bristol. BA Open Univ. Ordained, 1960, Methodist Minister, Birmingham; commnd RN as Chaplain, 1960; served: HMS Collingwood, 1960; RM, 1963–64; Staff of C-in-C Med., 1964–68; RNAS Brawdy, 1968–69; RM, 1970–73; HMS Raleigh, 1973; HMS Drake, 1974–78; BRNC Dartmouth, 1978–80; Principal Chaplain, Church of Scotland and Free Churches (Naval), MoD, 1981–84. Hon. Chaplain to the Queen, 1981–84. *Recreations:* warm water sailing, music. *Address:* The Manse of Blantyre Old, High Blantyre, Glasgow G72 9UA.

PRICE, Peter S.; *see* Stanley Price.

PRICE, Ralph; *see* Price, L. R.

PRICE, Sir Robert; *see* Price, Sir J. R.

PRICE, Air Vice-Marshal Robert George, CB 1983; *b* 18 July 1928; *s* of Charles and Agnes Price, Hale, Cheshire; *m* 1st, 1958, Celia Anne Mary Talamo (*d* 1987); one *s* four *d*; 2nd, 1989, Edith Barbara Dye. *Educ:* Oundle Sch.; RAF Coll., Cranwell. 74 Sqn, 1950; Central Flying Sch., 1952; 60 Sqn, 1956; Guided Weapons Trials Sqn, 1958; Staff Coll., 1960; Bomber Comd, 1961; JSSC 1964; CO 31 Sqn, 1965; PSO to Dep. SACEUR, 1968; CO RAF Linton-on-Ouse, 1970; RCDS 1973; Dep. Dir Operations, 1974; Group Captain Flying Trng, Support Comd, 1978; Dep. Chief of Staff, Support HQ, 2nd Allied Tactical Air Force, 1979; AOA, RAF Germany, 1980; AOA, HQ Strike Comd, 1981–83. *Recreations:* golf, ski-ing, bridge. *Address:* c/o Barclays Bank, Easingwold, Yorkshire. *Club:* Royal Air Force.

PRICE, Sir Robert (John) G.; *see* Green-Price.

PRICE, Brig. Rollo Edward Crwys, CBE 1967; DSO 1961; *b* 6 April 1916; *s* of Eardley Edward Carnac Price, CIE; *m* 1945, Diana Budden; three *d*. *Educ:* Canford; RMC Sandhurst. Commissioned 2nd Lt in S Wales Borderers, 1936; War Service, Middle East and Italy, 1939–45; Lt-Col and seconded for service with Queen's Own Nigeria Regt, 1959–61; Col 1962; Comdr 160 Inf. Bde, 1964–67; Brig. 1966; Comdr, British Troops, Malta, 1968–69, retired. *Address:* Elsford, Netherton, near Yeovil, Somerset. *T:* Yetminster (0935) 872377.

PRICE, Roy Kenneth, CB 1980; Under-Secretary (Legal), in office of HM Treasury Solicitor, 1972–81; *b* 16 May 1916; *s* of Ernest Price and Margaret Chapman Price (*née* Scott); *m* 1948, Martha (*née* Dannhauser); one *s* one *d*. *Educ:* Eltham Coll. Qualified as

Solicitor, 1937. Town Clerk, Borough of Pembroke, and Clerk to Castlemartin Justices, 1939–40. Served War, Army, 1940–46. Officer in Charge, Legal Aid (Welfare), Northern Command, 1946 (Lt-Col). Joined HM Treasury Solicitor, as Legal Asst, 1946; Sen. Legal Asst, 1950; Asst Solicitor, 1962. Mem. Exec. Council, RNIB, 1981–; Pres., Richmond Assoc., Nat. Trust, 1985–; Vice Chm., Friends of Museum of Richmond, 1988–; Trustee, Richmond Almshouse Charities, 1987–; Chm., Portcullis Trust, 1980–90. *Recreations:* gardening, theatre, travel. *Address:* 6 Old Palace Lane, Richmond, Surrey TW9 1PG. *T:* 081–940 6685. *Club:* Law Society.

PRICE, Terence; *see* Price, B. T.

PRICE, Vivian William Cecil; QC 1972; *b* 14 April 1926; 4th *s* of late Evan Price, Hawkhurst, Kent; *m* 1961, Elizabeth Anne, *o c* of late Arthur Rawlins and Georgina (*née* Guinness); three *s* two *d*. *Educ:* Judd Sch., Tonbridge, Kent; Trinity Coll., Cambridge (BA); Balliol Coll., Oxford (BA). Royal Navy, 1946–49, Instructor Lieut. Called to the Bar: Middle Temple, 1954 (Bencher, 1979); Hong Kong, 1975; Singapore, 1979. Dep. High Court Judge (Chancery Div.), 1975–85; a Recorder of the Crown Court, 1984. Sec., Lord Denning's Cttee on Legal Educn for Students from Africa, 1960; Junior Counsel (Patents) to the Board of Trade, 1967–72; Mem., Patents Procedure Cttee, 1973. Mem., Incorporated Council of Law Reporting for England and Wales, 1980–85. *Address:* Redwall Farmhouse, Linton, Kent. *T:* Maidstone (0622) 743682. *Club:* Travellers'.
See also A. L. Price.

PRICE, Prof. William Charles, FRS 1959; Wheatstone Professor of Physics, University of London, at King's College, 1955–76, now Emeritus; *b* 1 April 1909; *s* of Richard Price and Florence Margaret (*née* Charles); *m* 1939, Nest Myra Davies; one *s* one *d*. *Educ:* Swansea Grammar Sch.; University of Wales, Swansea (Hon. Fellow, 1985); Johns Hopkins University, Baltimore; Trinity Coll., Cambridge, BSc (Wales) 1930; Commonwealth Fellow, 1932; PhD (Johns Hopkins), 1934; Cambridge: Senior 1851 Exhibitioner, 1935, University Demonstrator, 1937–43, PhD (Cantab) 1937. Prize Fellow, Trinity Coll., 1938; ScD (Cantab) 1949; Meldola Medal of Inst. of Chem., 1938; Senior Spectroscopist, ICI (Billingham Div.), 1943–48; Research Associate, University of Chicago, 1946–47; Reader in Physics, University of London (King's Coll.) 1948. FKC 1970. FRIC 1944; FIP 1950. Co-editor, British Bulletin of Spectroscopy, 1950–. Hon. DSc Wales, 1970. *Publications:* research and review articles on physics and chemistry in scientific journals. *Address:* 38 Cross Way, Orpington, Kent BR5 1PE. *T:* Orpington (0689) 828815.

PRICE, (William Frederick) Barry, OBE 1977; HM Diplomatic Service, retired; Consul-General, Amsterdam, 1983–85; Hon. Secretary, William and Mary Tercentenary Trust, since 1989 (Secretary, 1986–89); *b* 12 Feb. 1925; *s* of William Thomas and Vera Price; *m* 1948, Lorraine Elisabeth Suzanne Hoather; three *s* two *d*. *Educ:* Worcester Royal Grammar Sch.; St Paul's Training Coll., Cheltenham. Served War: Armed Forces, 1944–47: commissioned Royal Warwicks, 1945; demobilised, 1947. Primary Sch. Teacher, 1948. Joined Bd of Trade, 1950; Asst Trade Comr: in Delhi, 1954; in Nairobi, 1957; Trade Commissioner, Accra, 1963; transferred to HM Diplomatic Service, 1966; 1st Sec., Sofia, 1967; seconded to East European Trade Council, 1971; Consul-Gen., Rotterdam, 1973–77; Consul, Houston, 1978–81; Counsellor (Commercial and Economic), Bangkok, 1981–82; Kuala Lumpur, 1982. Chm., Anglo-Netherlands Soc., 1989–. Comdr, Order of Orange-Nassau (Netherlands), 1989. *Recreation:* Open University student. *Address:* 46 Finchley Park, N12 9JL. *T:* 081–445 4642. *Club:* Oriental.

PRICE, William George; *b* 15 June 1934; *s* of George and Lillian Price; *m* 1963, Joy Thomas (marr. diss. 1978); two *s*. *Educ:* Forest of Dene Technical Coll.; Gloucester Technical Coll. Staff Journalist: Three Forest Newspapers, Cinderford, until 1959; Coventry Evening Telegraph, 1959–62; Birmingham Post & Mail, 1962–66. Consultant, Nat. Fedn of Licensed Victuallers, 1979. MP (Lab) Rugby, Warks, 1966–79; PPS: to Sec. of State for Educn and Science, 1968–70; to Dep. Leader, Labour Party, 1972–74; Parliamentary Secretary: ODM, March-Oct. 1974; Privy Council Office, 1974–79. Contested (Lab): Rugby, 1979; Dudley W, 1983. *Recreation:* sport. *Address:* 53 West Heath Court, Northend Road, NW11.

PRICE, Prof. (William) Geraint, FRS 1988; FEng 1986; FIMechE; FRINA; Professor of Ship Science, Department of Ship Science, University of Southampton, since 1990; *b* 1 Aug. 1943; *s* of Thomas Price and Ursula Maude Price (*née* Roberts); *m* 1967, Jennifer Mary Whitten; two *d*. *Educ:* Merthyr Tydfil County Grammar Sch.; University Coll. Cardiff (Univ. of Wales) (G. H. Latham Open Sci. Scholar; BSc, PhD); Univ. of London (DSc(Eng)). FRINA 1980; FIMechE 1989. Res. Asst, later Lectr, UCL, 1969–81; Reader in Applied Mechanics, Univ. of London, 1981–82; Prof. of Applied Mechanics, Brunel Univ., 1982–90. Fellow, Japan Soc. for Promotion of Science, 1987. *Publications:* Probabilistic Theory of Ship Dynamics, 1974; Hydroelasticity of Ships, 1979. *Recreations:* walking, sailing, rugby, squash, barbecueing. *Address:* Tŷ Gwyn, 45 Palmerston Way, Alverstoke, Gosport, Hants PO12 2LY. *T:* Gosport (0705) 581164.

PRICE, William John R.; *see* Rea Price.

PRICE, Winford Hugh Protheroe, OBE 1983; FCA; City Treasurer, Cardiff City Council, 1975–83; *b* 5 Feb. 1926; *s* of Martin Price and Doris Blanche Price. *Educ:* Cardiff High Sch. IPFA 1952; FCA 1954. Served War, RAFVR, 1944–48. City Treasurer's and Controller's Dept, Cardiff, 1942; Dep. City Treasurer, Cardiff, 1973–75. Public Works Loan Comr, 1979–83. Treasurer and Financial Adviser, Council for the Principality, 1975–83; Financial Adviser, Assoc. of Dist Councils Cttee for Wales, 1975–83; Treasurer: The Queen's Silver Jubilee Trust (S Glam), 1976–83; Royal National Eisteddfod of Wales (Cardiff), 1978. Occasional lectr on local govt topics. *Publications:* contrib. to jls. *Recreation:* chess. *Address:* 3 Oakfield Street, Roath, Cardiff CF2 3RD. *T:* Cardiff (0222) 494635.

PRICE EVANS, David Alan; *see* Evans.

PRICHARD, Mathew Caradoc Thomas; Chairman: Agatha Christie Ltd, since 1971; Booker Entertainment (formerly Authors' Division, Booker McConnell PLC), since 1985; *b* 21 Sept. 1943; *s* of late Major H. de B. Prichard and of Rosalind Hicks; *m* 1967, Angela Caroline Maples; one *s* two *d*. *Educ:* Eton College; New College, Oxford. BA (PPE). Penguin Books, 1965–69; Advisory Local Dir, Barclays Bank plc, 1977–. Pres., Welsh Group of Artists, 1974–; Member: Court of Governors and Council, Nat. Museum of Wales, 1975–; Welsh Arts Council, 1980– (Vice-Chm., 1983–86; Chm., 1986–); Arts Council of GB, 1983–. High Sheriff, Glamorgan, 1972–73. *Recreations:* golf, cricket, bridge. *Address:* Pwllywrach, Cowbridge, South Glamorgan CF7 7NJ. *T:* Cowbridge (0446) 772256. *Clubs:* Boodle's, MCC; Cardiff and County; Royal & Ancient Golf (St Andrews); Royal Porthcawl Golf.

PRICHARD, Air Vice-Marshal Richard Augustin R.; *see* Riseley-Prichard.

PRICHARD, Air Commodore Richard Julian Paget, CB 1963; CBE 1958; DFC 1942; AFC 1941; *b* 4 Oct. 1915; *o s* of Major W. O. Prichard, 24th Regt; unmarried. *Educ:* Harrow; St Catharine's Coll., Cambridge. Entered RAF, 1937; Air Armament Sch., Eastchurch and Manby, 1937–39; Flying Instructor, South Cerney, 1939–41; No. 21 (LB) Squadron, 1942–43; Staff Coll. (psa), 1943; AEAF, 1943–45; Chief Intelligence Officer, Burma and FEAF, 1946–47; Chief Flying Instructor, RAF Coll., Cranwell, 1947–49; Ministry of Defence, 1949–52; Instructor, RAF Staff Coll., 1953–55; Station Comdr, RAF Tengah, Singapore, 1956–58. IDC, 1959; Director Air Plans, Air Ministry, 1960–63; AOC No 13 Scottish Sector, Fighter Command, 1963–64; AOC Northern Sector of Fighter Command, 1965–66; retired, 1966. US Legion of Merit, 1944. *Recreations:* tennis, fishing. *Club:* Royal Air Force.

PRICHARD-JONES, Sir John, 2nd Bt, *cr* 1910; barrister; farmer and bloodstock breeder; *b* 20 Jan. 1913; *s* of 1st Bt and Marie, *y d* of late Charles Read, solicitor; *S* father, 1917; *m* 1937, Heather, (from whom he obtained a divorce, 1950), *er d* of late Sir Walter Nugent, 4th Bt; one *s*; *m* 1959, Helen Marie Thérèse, *e d* of J. F. Liddy, dental surgeon, 20 Laurence Street, Drogheda; one *d*. *Educ:* Eton; Christ Church, Oxford (BA Hons; MA). Called to Bar, Gray's Inn, 1936. Commnd, Queen's Bays, 1939, and served throughout War. *Heir: s* David John Walter Prichard-Jones, BA (Hons) Oxon, *b* 14 March 1943. *Address:* Allenswood House, Lucan, Co. Dublin.

PRICKETT, Prof. (Alexander Thomas) Stephen, PhD; Regius Professor of English Language and Literature, University of Glasgow, since 1990; *b* 4 June 1939; *s* of Rev. William Ewart Prickett and Barbara Browning (*née* Lyne); *m* 1st, 1967, Diana Joan Mabbutt; one *s* one *d*; 2nd, 1983, Maria Angelica Alvarez. *Educ:* Kent Coll., Canterbury; Trinity Hall, Cambridge (BA 1961; PhD 1968); University Coll., Oxford (DipEd). FAHA 1986. English teacher, Uzuakoli, E Nigeria, 1962–64; Asst Lectr, Lectr, and Reader, Univ. of Sussex, 1967–82; Prof. of English, ANU, Canberra, 1983–89. Vis. Lectr, Smith Coll., Mass, USA, 1970–71; Vis. Fulbright Prof., Univ. of Minnesota, 1979–80. *Publications:* Do It Yourself Doom, 1962; Coleridge and Wordsworth: the poetry of growth, 1970, 2nd edn 1980; Romanticism and Religion, 1976; Victorian Fantasy, 1979, 2nd edn 1982; Words and the Word: language poetics and biblical interpretation, 1986, 2nd edn 1988; England and the French Revolution, 1988; Reading the Text: biblical criticism and literary theory, 1991. *Recreations:* walking, ski-ing, drama. *Address:* Department of English, University of Glasgow, Glasgow G12 8QQ.

PRICKETT, Air Chief Marshal Sir Thomas (Other), KCB 1965 (CB 1957); DSO 1943; DFC 1942; RAF retired; *b* 31 July 1913; *s* of late E. G. Prickett; *m* 1st, 1942, Elizabeth Gratian, (*d* 1984), *d* of late William Galbally, Laguna Beach, Calif, USA; one *s* one *d*; 2nd, 1985, Shirley Westerman. *Educ:* Stubbington House Sch.; Haileybury Coll. Joined RAF, 1937; commanded RAF Tangmere, 1949–51; Group Captain operations, HQ Middle East Air Force, 1951–54; commanded RAF Jever, 1954–55; attended Imperial Defence Coll., 1956; Chief of Staff Air Task Force, 1956; Director of Policy, Air Ministry, 1957–58; SASO, HQ No 1 Group, 1958–60; ACAS (Ops) Air Ministry, 1960–63; ACAS (Policy and Planning) Air Ministry, 1963–64; AOC-in-C, NEAF, Comdr British Forces Near East, and Administrator, Sovereign Base Area, 1964–66; AOC-in-C, RAF Air Support Command, 1967–68; Air Mem. for Supply and Organisation, MoD, 1968–70. *Recreations:* polo, sailing, golf. *Address:* 46 Kingston Hill Place, Kingston upon Thames KT2 7LX. *Club:* Royal Air Force.

PRICKMAN, Air Cdre Thomas Bain, CB 1953; CBE 1945; *b* 1902; *m* 1st, Ethel Serica (*d* 1949), *d* of John Cubbon, Douglas, IOM; 2nd, 1952, Dorothy (who *m* 1946, Group Captain F. C. Read, *d* 1949), *d* of John Charles Clarke. *Educ:* Blundell's Sch. Joined RAF, 1923. Served War of 1939–45, with Fighter Command; RAF Liaison staff in Australia, 1946–48; AOA, Home Command, 1950–54; retired, 1954. *Address:* Tilsmore Cottage, Cross-in-Hand, Heathfield, Sussex TN21 0LS.

PRIDAY, Christopher Bruton; QC 1986; *b* 7 Aug. 1926; *s* of Arthur Kenneth Priday and Rosemary Priday; *m* 1953, Jill Holroyd Sergeant, *o d* of John Holroyd Sergeant and Kathleen Sergeant; two *s*. *Educ:* Radley College; University College, Oxford (MA). Called to the Bar, Gray's Inn, 1951, Bencher, 1991; Hon. *ad eundem* Mem., Middle Temple, 1985. Associate, RICS 1987. Hon. Mem., CAAV, 1988. *Publications:* jt editor, publications on law of landlord and tenant. *Recreations:* opera, golf at St Enodoc. *Address:* 61 Chiddingstone Street, SW6 4QT. *T:* 071–736 4681. *Club:* St Enodoc Golf.

PRIDDLE, Robert John; Deputy Secretary, Department of Energy, since 1989; *b* 9 Sept. 1938; *s* of Albert Leslie Priddle and Alberta Edith Priddle; *m* 1962, Janice Elizabeth Gorham; two *s*. *Educ:* King's Coll. Sch., Wimbledon; Peterhouse, Cambridge (MA). Asst Principal, Min. of Aviation, 1960, Principal 1965; Private Sec. to Minister for Aerospace, 1971–73; Asst Sec., DTI, 1973, and Dept of Energy, 1974; Under Sec., Dept of Energy, 1977–85; Under Sec., DTI, 1985–89. Pres., Conf. of European Posts and Telecommunications Administrations, 1987–89. *Publication:* Victoriana, 1959, 2nd edn 1963. *Address:* Department of Energy, 1 Palace Street, SW1E 5AG.

PRIDEAUX, Sir Humphrey (Povah Treverbian), Kt 1971; OBE 1945; DL; Chairman, Morland & Co., since 1983 (Director, 1981; Vice Chairman, 1982); Chairman, Lord Wandsworth Foundation, since 1966; *b* 13 Dec. 1915; 3rd *s* of Walter Treverbian Prideaux and Marion Fenn (*née* Arbuthnot); *m* 1939, Cynthia, *er d* of late Lt-Col H. Birch Reynardson, CMG; four *s*. *Educ:* St Aubyns, Rottingdean; Eton; Trinity Coll., Oxford (MA). Commissioned 3rd Carabiniers (Prince of Wales's Dragoon Guards) 1936; DAQMG Guards Armd Div., 1941; Instructor, Staff Coll., 1942; AQMG 21 Army Gp, 1943; AA QMG Guards Armd Div., 1944; Joint Planning Staff, War Office, 1945; Naval Staff Coll., 1948; Commandant School of Administration, 1948; Chiefs of Staff Secretariat, 1950; retired, 1953. Director, NAAFI, 1956–73 (Man. Dir, 1961–65; Chm., 1963–73); Dir, London Life Association Ltd, 1964–88 (Vice-Pres., 1965–72; Pres., 1973–84); Chm., Brooke Bond Liebig Ltd, 1972–80 (Dir, 1968; Dep. Chm., 1969–71); Vice-Chm., W. H. Smith & Son Ltd, 1977–81 (Dir, 1969–77); Dir, Grindlays, 1982–85. DL Hants 1983. *Recreations:* country pursuits. *Address:* Summers Farm, Long Sutton, Basingstoke, Hants RG25 1TQ. *T:* Basingstoke (0256) 862295. *Club:* Cavalry and Guards.
See also Sir J. F. Prideaux, J. H. Prideaux, W. A. Prideaux.

PRIDEAUX, John Denys Charles Anstice, PhD; Managing Director, InterCity, British Railways Board, since 1991 (Director, 1986–91); *b* 8 Aug. 1944; *s* of Denys Robert Anstice-Prideaux and Frances Hester Dorothy Anstice-Prideaux (*née* Glaze); *m* 1972, Philippa Mary (*née* Morgan); one *s* one *d*. *Educ:* St Paul's; Univ. of Nottingham (BSc, PhD). Operational Research, BR, 1965; Area Manager, Newton Abbot, 1972; Strategic Planning Officer, 1974; Divl Manager, Birmingham, 1980; Dir, Policy Unit, 1983–86. Member: Adv. Cttee on Trunk Road Assessment, 1977; Transport Cttee, SERC and ESRC, 1982; Planning and Envmt Cttee, ESRC, 1985. Mem, Council, Manchester Business School, 1987. *Publications:* railway histories, papers on management and transport. *Recreations:* riding, hunting, shooting, sailing, ski-ing, design. *Address:* British Railways Board, Euston House, 24 Eversholt Street, NW1 1DZ.

PRIDEAUX, Sir John (Francis), Kt 1974; OBE 1945; DL; *b* 30 Dec. 1911; 2nd *s* of Walter Treverbian Prideaux and Marion Fenn (*née* Arbuthnot); *m* 1934, Joan, *er d* of late Captain Gordon Hargreaves Brown, MC, and Lady Pigott Brown; two *s* one *d*. *Educ:* St Aubyns, Rottingdean; Eton. Middlesex Yeomanry, 1933; served War of 1939–45,

Colonel Q, 2nd Army, 1944. Joined Arbuthnot Latham & Co. Ltd, Merchant Bankers, 1930, Dir, 1936–69, Chm., 1964–69. Mem., London Adv. Bd, Bank of NSW, 1948–74; Director: Westminster Bank Ltd, later National Westminster Bank Ltd, 1955–81 (Chm., 1971–77); Westminster Foreign Bank Ltd, later Internat. Westminster Bank Ltd, 1955–81 (Chm., 1969–77). Chm., Cttee of London Clearing Bankers, 1974–76; Vice-Pres., British Bankers' Assoc., 1972–77. Pres., Inst. of Bankers, 1974–76. Mem., Wilson Cttee to review functioning of financial instns in the City, 1977–80. Dep. Chm., Commonwealth Develt Corp., 1960–70; Chm., Victoria League for Commonwealth Friendship, 1977–81. Mem., Lambeth, Southwark and Lewisham AHA(T), 1974–82 (Commissioner, Aug. 1979–March 1980); Treasurer and Chm., Bd of Governors, St Thomas' Hosp., 1964–74; Chm., Special Trustees, St Thomas' Hosp., 1974–88. Prime Warden, Goldsmiths' Company, 1972. DL Surrey 1976. Legion of Merit, USA, 1945. *Address:* Elderslie, Ockley, Surrey. *T:* Dorking (0306) 711263. *Clubs:* Brooks's, Overseas Bankers (Pres. 1976–77).

See also Sir H. P. T. Prideaux, W. A. Prideaux.

PRIDEAUX, Julian Humphrey; Chief Agent, National Trust, since 1987; *b* 19 June 1942; 2nd *s* of Sir Humphrey Povah Treverbian Prideaux, *qv*; *m* 1967, Jill, 3rd *d* of R. P. Roney-Dougal; two *s*. *Educ:* St Aubyns, Rottingdean; Eton; Royal Agricultural Coll. (Dip. Estate Management). ARICS 1966, FRICS 1974. Land Agent with Burd & Evans, Shrewsbury, 1964–67; Agent to Col Hon. C. G. Cubitt and others, 1967–69; Land Agent, Cornwall Region, NT, 1969–77; Dir, Thames and Chilterns Region, NT, 1978–86. *Recreations:* walking, fishing. *Address:* Steps House, West Wycombe, High Wycombe, Bucks HP14 3AG. *T:* High Wycombe (0494) 443319. *Club:* Farmers'.

PRIDEAUX, Walter Arbuthnot, CBE 1973; MC 1945; TD 1948; *b* 4 Jan. 1910; *e s* of Walter Treverbian Prideaux and Marion Fenn (*née* Arbuthnot); *m* 1937, Anne, *d* of Francis Stewart Cokayne; two *s* two *d*. *Educ:* Eton; Trinity Coll., Cambridge. Solicitor, 1934. Assistant Clerk of the Goldsmiths' Company, 1939–53, Clerk 1953–75. Chm., City Parochial Foundn, 1972–80. Kent Yeomanry, 1936–48. *Recreation:* rowed for Cambridge, 1930, 1931. *Address:* 16 Tanbridge Place, Horsham, West Sussex RH12 1RY. *T:* Horsham (0403) 58891.

See also Sir H. P. T. Prideaux, Sir J. F. Prideaux.

PRIDHAM, Brian Robert; HM Diplomatic Service, retired; Research Fellow, since 1983, and Director, 1985–86 and since 1987, Centre for Arab Gulf Studies (Deputy Director, 1984–85), and Lecturer in Arabic, Department of Arabic and Islamic Studies, 1984–87, University of Exeter; *b* 22 Feb. 1934; *s* of Reginald Buller Pridham and Emily Pridham (*née* Winser); *m* 1954, Fay Coles; three *s*. *Educ:* Hele's Sch., Exeter. MA Exon, 1984. RWAFF (Nigeria Regt), 1952–54; Foreign Office, 1954–57; MECAS, 1957–59; Bahrain, 1959; Vice-Consul, Muscat, 1959–62; Foreign Office, 1962–64; 2nd Sec., Algiers, 1964–66, 1st Sec., 1966–67; Foreign Office, 1967–70; Head of Chancery: La Paz, 1970–73; Abu Dhabi, 1973–75; Dir of MECAS, Shemlan, Lebanon, 1975–76; Counsellor, Khartoum, 1976–79; Head of Communications Ops Dept, FCO, 1979–81. *Publications:* (ed) Contemporary Yemen: politics and historical background, 1984; (ed) Economy, Society and Culture in Contemporary Yemen, 1984; (ed) The Arab Gulf and the West, 1985; (ed) Oman: economic, social and strategic developments, 1986; The Arab Gulf and the Arab World, 1987. *Recreations:* sailing, old roses. *Address:* c/o Barclays Bank, Exeter.

PRIDHAM, Kenneth Robert Comyn, CMG 1976; HM Diplomatic Service, retired; *b* 28 July 1922; *s* of late Colonel G. R. Pridham, CBE, DSO, and Mignonne, *d* of late Charles Cumming, ICS; *m* 1965, Ann Rosalind, *d* of late E. Gilbert Woodward, Metropolitan Magistrate, and of Mrs Woodward. *Educ:* Winchester; Oriel Coll., Oxford. Lieut, 60th Rifles, 1942–46; served North Africa, Italy, Middle East (despatches). Entered Foreign (subseq. Diplomatic) Service, 1946; served at Berlin, Washington, Belgrade and Khartoum, and at the Foreign Office; Counsellor: Copenhagen, 1968–72; FCO, 1972–74; Asst Under Sec. of State, FCO, 1974–78; Ambassador to Poland, 1978–81. Vis. Res. Fellow, RIIA, 1981–82. *Address:* c/o Lloyds Bank, 16 St James's Street, SW1. *Club:* Travellers'.

PRIEST, Rear-Adm. Colin Herbert Dickinson C.; *see* Cooke-Priest.

PRIEST, Prof. Robert George, MD, FRCPsych; Professor of Psychiatry, University of London and Head of Department of Psychiatry at St Mary's Hospital Medical School, Imperial College of Science, Technology and Medicine, since 1973; Hon. Consultant Psychiatrist, St Mary's Hospital, London, since 1973; *b* 28 Sept. 1933; *er s* of late James Priest and of Phoebe Priest; *m* 1955, Marilyn, *er d* of late Baden Roberts Baker and of Evelyn Baker; two *s*. *Educ:* University Coll., London and University Coll. Hosp. Med. Sch. MB, BS 1956; DPM 1963; MRCPE 1964; MD 1970; MRCPsych 1971 (Foundn Mem.); FRCPE 1974; FRCPsych 1974. Lectr in Psychiatry, Univ. of Edinburgh, 1964–67; Exchange Lectr, Univ. of Chicago, 1966; Consultant, Illinois State Psychiatric Inst., Chicago, 1966; Sen. Lectr, St George's Hosp. Med. Sch., London, 1967–73; Hon. Consultant: St George's Hosp., London, 1967–73; Springfield Hosp., London, 1967–73. University of London: Recognised Teacher, 1968–; Mem., Bd of Studies in Medicine, 1968– (Chm., 1987–89); Mem., Academic Adv. Bd in Medicine, 1987–90; Mem. Senate, 1989–; Mem., Academic Council, 1989–. Examiner in Psychiatry, NUI, 1975–78, 1980–83. Chm., Psychiatric Adv. Sub-Cttee, NW Thames RHA, 1976–79 (Vice-Chm., Reg. Manpower Cttee, 1980–83). Member: Council (Chm. Membership Cttee), British Assoc. for Psychopharmacology, 1977–81; World Psychiatric Assoc., 1980– (Mem. Cttee, 1985–, Mem. Council, 1989–); Central Cttee for Hosp. Med. Services, 1983–89 (Chm., Psych. Sub-Cttee, 1983–87); Pres., Soc. for Psychosomatic Res., 1980–81 (Vice-Pres., 1978–80); Chm., Mental Health Gp Cttee, BMA, 1982–85 (Mem. 1978–85, 1990–); Internat. Coll. of Psychosomatic Medicine: Fellow, 1977; Mem. Gov. Body and UK Delegate, 1978–81; Treasurer, 1981–83; Secretary, 1981–85; Vice-Pres., 1985–87; Royal Coll. of Psychiatrists: Mem., Public Policy Cttee, 1972–80, 1983– (Chm., 1983–88); Mem. Council, 1982–; Registrar, 1983–88; Chm., Gen. Psych. Cttee, 1985–89; Mem., Court of Electors, 1983–88 (Chm., Fellowship Sub-Cttee, 1984–88). A. E. Bennett Award, Soc. for Biol Psychiatry, USA (jtly), 1965; Doris Odlum Prize (BMA), 1968; Gutheil Von Domarus Award, Assoc. for Advancement of Psychotherapy and Amer. Jl of Psychotherapy, NY, 1970. *Publications:* Insanity: A Study of Major Psychiatric Disorders, 1977; (ed jtly) Sleep Research, 1979; (ed jtly) Benzodiazepines Today and Tomorrow, 1980; (ed) Psychiatry in Medical Practice, 1982; Anxiety and Depression, 1983; (ed) Sleep, 1984; (ed) Psychological Disorders in Obstetrics and Gynaecology, 1985; (jtly) Minski's Handbook of Psychiatry, 7th edn, 1978, 8th edn as Handbook of Psychiatry, 1986; (jtly) Sleepless Nights, 1990; chapters in: Current Themes in Psychiatry, 1978; Mental Illness in Pregnancy and the Puerperium, 1978; Psychiatry in General Practice, 1981; Modern Emergency Department Practice, 1983; The Scientific Basis of Psychiatry, 1983; The Psychosomatic Approach: contemporary practice of wholeperson care, 1986; articles in BMJ, Brit. Jl of Psychiatry, Amer. Jl of Psychotherapy and other learned jls. *Recreations:* squash, tennis, foreign languages, nature study. *Address:* Woodeaves, 29 Old Slade Lane, Richings Park, Iver, Bucks SL0 9DY. *T:* Iver (0753) 653178.

PRIESTLEY, Prof. Charles Henry Brian, AO 1976; FAA 1954; FRS 1967; Professor of Meteorology, Monash University, Australia, 1978–80; *b* 8 July 1915; *s* of late T. G. Priestley; *m* 1946, Constance, *d* of H. Tweedy; one *s* two *d*. *Educ:* Mill Hill Sch.; St John's Coll., Cambridge. MA 1942, ScD 1953. Served in Meteorological Office, Air Ministry, 1939–46; subseq. with CSIRO, Australia; Chief of Div. of Meteorological Physics, 1946–71; Chm., Environmental Physics Res., 1971–78. David Syme Prize, University of Melbourne, 1956. Member Exec. Cttee, International Assoc. of Meteorology, 1954–60, Vice-Pres., 1967–75; Vice-Pres., Australian Acad. of Science, 1959–60; Mem., Adv. Cttee, World Meteorological Organisation, 1964–68 (Chm., 1967; Internat. Met. Orgn Prize, 1973). FRMetSoc (Hon. Life Fellow, 1978; Buchan Prize, 1950 and Symons Medal, 1967, of Society); FInstP. Hon. Mem., Amer. Met. Soc., 1978 (Rossby Medal, 1975). Hon. DSc Monash, 1981. *Publications:* Turbulent Transfer in the Lower Atmosphere, 1959; about 60 papers in scientific journals. *Recreation:* golf. *Address:* Unit 7, 4 Fraser Street, Malvern, Vic 3144, Australia.

PRIESTLEY, Clive, CB 1983; management consultant; *b* 12 July 1935; *s* of late Albert Ernest and Annie May Priestley; *m* 1st, 1961, Barbara Anne (marr. diss. 1984), *d* of George Gerard and Ann Doris Wells; two *d*; 2nd, 1985, Daphne June Challis Loasby, JP, *o d* of late W. Challis and Dorothy Franks. *Educ:* Loughborough Grammar Sch.; Nottingham Univ. BA 1956; MA 1958. Nat. Service, 1958–60. Joined HM Home Civil Service, 1960; Min. of Educn, later DES, 1960–65; Schools Council, 1965–67; Harkness Commonwealth Fund Fellow, Harvard Univ., 1967–68; CSD, 1969–79; Prime Minister's Office, 1979–83 (Chief of Staff to Sir Derek Rayner); Under Sec., 1979–83; MPO, 1982–83; Dir, British Telecom plc, 1983–88. Consultant: Corp. of London, 1988–90; Metropolitan Police Comr, 1989–; LDDC, 1990–91. Member: Council, Univ. of Reading, 1984–86; Philharmonia Trust, 1985–87; Univ. of Cambridge Careers Service Syndicate, 1986–90; Adv. Council, Buxton Festival, 1987–; Council, St Bartholomew's Hosp. Med. Coll., 1990–; Arts Council, 1991–; Chm., London Arts Bd, 1991–. Governor, Royal Shakespeare Co., 1984–. Wandsman, St Paul's Cathedral, 1983–. Freeman, City of London, 1989; Liveryman, Worshipful Co. of Glaziers and Painters of Glass, 1989. *Publications:* financial scrutinies of the Royal Opera House, Covent Garden Ltd, and of the Royal Shakespeare Co., 1984. *Address:* 80 Thomas More House, Barbican, EC2Y 8BU. *T:* 071-628 9424. *Club:* Army and Navy.

PRIESTLEY, Mrs J. B.; *see* Hawkes, Jacquetta.

PRIESTLEY, Rev. John Christopher; Vicar of Christ Church, Colne, since 1975; Chaplain to the Queen, since 1990; *b* 23 May 1939; *s* of Ronald Edmund Priestley and Winifred Mary Priestley (*née* Hughes); *m* 1964, Margaret Ida Machan; one *s* one *d*. *Educ:* William Hulme Grammar Sch.; Trinity Coll., Oxford (MA); Wells Theol Coll. Asst Master, St James Sch., Clitheroe, 1961–64; Dep. Headmaster, Green Sch., Padiham, 1964–70; ordained, Blackburn Cathedral, 1968; Asst Curate: All Saints, Habergham, Burnley, 1968–70; St Leonard's, Padiham, 1970–75. Convenor, Pastoral Auxiliaries, Dio. Blackburn, 1987–91; Rural Dean of Pendle, 1991–. *Publications:* contribs to Church Times, Church of England Newspaper. *Recreation:* music, reading, long-distance walking. *Address:* Christ Church Vicarage, Colne, Lancs BB8 7HF. *T:* Colne (0282) 863511.

PRIESTLEY, Leslie William, TD 1974; FCIB; CBIM; FCIM; Board Member, Civil Aviation Authority, since 1990; *b* 22 Sept. 1933; *s* of Winifred and George Priestley; *m* 1960, Audrey Elizabeth (*née* Humber); one *s* one *d*. *Educ:* Shooters Hill Grammar School. Head of Marketing, Barclaycard, 1966–73; Asst Gen. Manager, Barclays Bank, 1974–77, Local Dir, 1978–79; Sec. Gen., Cttee of London Clearing Bankers, 1979–83; Dir, Bankers' Automated Clearing Services, 1979–83; Man. Dir, Barclays Insurance Services Co., 1983–84; Regional Gen. Manager, Barclays Bank, 1984–85; Dir and Chief Exec., TSB England & Wales plc (formerly TSB England and Wales and Central Trustee Savings Bank), 1985–89; Director: TSB Gp plc, 1986–89; Hill Samuel Bank, 1988–89; Pearce Gp Hldgs, 1989–. Director: London Electricity plc (formerly London Electricity Board), 1984–; Pinnacle Insurance. Mem., Monopolies and Mergers Commn, 1990–. Member of Council: Chartered Inst. of Bankers, 1988–89; Assoc. for Payment Clearing Services, 1988–89. Vis. Fellow, UCNW, 1989–. Consultant Editor, Bankers' Magazine, 1972–81. FCIM (FInstM 1987). FRSA. *Publication:* (ed) Bank Lending with Management Accounts, 1981. *Recreations:* reading, gardening, swimming. *Address:* CAA House, 45–59 Kingsway, WC2B 6TE. *Clubs:* Royal Automobile, Wig and Pen.

PRIESTLEY, Prof. Maurice Bertram, MA, PhD; Professor of Statistics, University of Manchester Institute of Science and Technology, since 1970 and Head of Department of Mathematics, 1973–75, 1977–78, 1980–85 and 1987–89; *b* 15 March 1933; *s* of Jack and Rose Priestley; *m* 1959, Nancy, *d* of late Ralph and Hilda Nelson; one *s* one *d*. *Educ:* Manchester Grammar Sch.; Jesus Coll., Cambridge. BA (Wrangler, 1954), MA, DipMathStat (Cambridge); PhD (Manchester). Scientific Officer, RAE, 1955–56; Asst Lectr, Univ. of Manchester, 1957–60, Lectr, 1960–65; Vis. Professor, Princeton and Stanford Univs, USA, 1961–62; Sen. Lectr, UMIST, 1965–70; Dir, Manchester-Sheffield Sch. of Probability and Stats, and Hon. Prof. of Probability and Stats, Sheffield Univ., 1976–79, 1988–89. Mem. Court and Council, UMIST, 1971–74 and 1989–. FIMS; FSS; Member Council: Royal Statistical Soc., 1971–75; Manchester Statistical Soc., 1986–; Mem., ISI. Editor-in-chief, Jl of Time Series Analysis, 1980–. *Publications:* Spectral Analysis and Time Series, Vols I and II, 1981; Non-linear and non-stationary time series analysis, 1988; papers and articles in Jl RSS, Biometrika, Technom., Automatica, Jl of Sound and Vibration. *Recreations:* music, hi-fi and audio, golf. *Address:* Department of Mathematics, University of Manchester Institute of Science and Technology, PO Box 88, Manchester M60 1QD. *T:* 061-236 3311.

PRIESTLEY, Philip John; HM Diplomatic Service; Fellow, Center for International Affairs, Harvard University, since 1991; *b* 29 Aug. 1946; *s* of late Frederick Priestley and Caroline (*née* Rolfe); *m* 1972, Christine Rainforth; one *s* one *d*. *Educ:* Boston Grammar Sch.; Univ. of East Anglia (BA Hons). FCO 1969; served Sofia and Kinshasa; First Sec., FCO, 1976; Wellington, 1979–83; FCO, 1984–87; Commercial Counsellor and Dep. Head of Mission, Manila, 1987–90; Ambassador to Gabon, 1990–91. *Recreations:* golf, tennis, bridge, Rotary, theatre. *Address:* c/o Foreign and Commonwealth Office, King Charles Street, SW1A 2AH.

PRIESTLEY, Dr Robert Henry, CBiol, FIBiol; General Secretary, Institute of Biology, since 1989; *b* 19 March 1946; *s* of Henry Benjamin Priestley, MA, BSc and Margaret Alice (*née* Lambert); *m* 1970, Penelope Ann Fox, BSc; two *d*. *Educ:* Brunts Grammar Sch., Mansfield; Univ. of Southampton (BSc 1967); Univ. of Exeter (PhD 1972). FIBiol 1988. Plant Pathologist, Lord Rank Res. Centre, Rank Hovis McDougall, 1970–73; National Institute of Agricultural Botany: Cereal Pathologist, 1973–78; Head of Cereal Path. Section, 1978–82; Head of Plant Path. Dept, 1982–88. Sec., UK Cereal Pathogen Virulence Survey, 1974–82; Member: Council Fedn of British Plant Pathologists, 1980–81; Internat. Soc. for Plant Path., 1988–; Treasurer, British Soc. for Plant Path., 1981–87; Member: British Nat. Cttee for Microbiology, 1982–89; Cttee of Management, Biol. Council, 1989–; Bd, CSTI, 1989–; Parly and Sci. Cttee, 1989–; UK rep., European Communities Biol. Assoc., 1989–. *Publications:* papers on diseases of crops; articles in Biologist. *Recreation:* music, gardening, collecting, football, swimming. *Address:* Institute of Biology, 20 Queensberry Place, SW7 2DZ. *T:* 071-581 8333.

PRIESTMAN, Jane, OBE 1991; FCSD; Director, Architecture and Design, British Railways Board, since 1986; *b* 7 April 1930; *d* of late Reuben Stanley Herbert and Mary Elizabeth Herbert (*née* Ramply); *m* 1954, Arthur Martin Priestman (marr. diss. 1986); two *s*. *Educ:* Northwood College; Liverpool Coll. of Art (NDD, ATD). Design practice, 1954–75; Design Manager, Gen. Manager, Architecture and Design, BAA, 1975–86. Member: Jaguar Styling Panel; Design Management Gp, CSD; Council, Arch. Assoc.; Percentage for Art Steering Gp, Arts Council. Governor: Commonwealth Inst.; Kingston Polytechnic. Hon. FRIBA; FRSA. *Recreations:* textiles, city architecture, opera, travel. *Address:* 30 Duncan Terrace, N1 8BS. *T:* 071–837 4525. *Club:* Architecture.

PRIESTMAN, John David; Clerk of the Parliamentary Assembly of the Council of Europe, 1971–86; *b* 29 March 1926; *s* of Bernard Priestman and Hermine Bréal; *m* 1951, Nada Valić; two *s* two *d*. *Educ:* private sch. in Paris; Westminster Sch.; Merton Coll. and Christ Church, Oxford (Hon. Mods, Lit. Hum.). Served Coldstream Guards, 1944–47, Temp. Captain. Third, subseq. Second, Sec., Belgrade, 1949–53; Asst Private Sec. to Rt Hon. Anthony Eden, 1953–55; joined Secretariat, Council of Europe, 1955; Head of Sec. Gen's Private Office, 1961; Sec., Cttee of Ministers, 1966; Dep. Clerk of Parly Assembly, 1968–71. Hon. Life Mem., Assoc. of Secretaries General of Parlt, 1986. *Recreations:* off-piste Alpine ski-ing, music, competition bridge, gastronomic research. *Address:* 13 chemin de la Colle, 06160 Antibes, France. *T:* 93–617724; 6 rue Adolphe Wurtz, 67000 Strasbourg, France. *T:* 88–354049.

PRIGOGINE, Vicomte Ilya; Grand-Croix de l'Ordre de Léopold II, Belgium; Professor, Université Libre de Bruxelles, 1951–87, now Emeritus; Director, Instituts Internationaux de Physique et de Chimie, since 1959; Director, Ilya Prigogine Center of Statistical Mechanics, Thermodynamics and Complex Systems, since 1967 and Ashbel Smith Regental Professor, since 1984, University of Texas at Austin; *b* Moscow, 25 Jan. 1917; created Viscount, 1989; *m* 1961, Marina Prokopowicz; two *s*. *Educ:* Univ. of Brussels (Lic. Sc. Physiques, 1939; (Dr en Sciences Chimiques, 1941). Prof., Dept of Chemistry, Enrico Fermi Inst. for Nuclear Studies, and Inst. for Study of Metals, Univ. of Chicago, 1961–66. Associate Dir of Studies, l'Ecole des Hautes Etudes en Sciences Sociales, France, 1987; Hon. Prof., Banaras Hindu Univ., Varanasi, 1988; RGK Foundn Centennial Fellow, Univ. of Texas, 1989–90. President: Internat. Soc. for Gen. Systems Res., Louisville, Ky, USA, 1987; l'Institut Européen pour la Co-opération Est-Ouest, UNESCO, 1990. Mem. Sci. Adv. Bd, Internat. Acad. for Biomedical Drug Res., 1990. Hon. Pres., Université Philosophique Européenne, Paris; Member: Académie Royale de Belgique, 1958; Royal Soc. of Sciences, Uppsala, Sweden, 1967; German Acad. Naturforscher Leopoldina, GDR, 1970; Acad. Internat. de Philosophie des Sciences, 1973; Acad. Européenne des Scis, des Arts et des Lettres, Paris, 1980 (Vice-Pres., 1980); Accademia Mediterranea delle Scienze, Catania, 1982; Internat. Acad. of Social Perspective, Geneva, 1983; Haut Conseil de la Francophonie, Paris, 1984; Max-Planck Foundn, Fed. Republic of Germany, 1984; Hon. Member: Amer. Acad. of Arts and Sciences, 1960; Chem. Soc., Warsaw, 1971; Soc. for Studies on Entropy, Japan, 1983; Biophys. Soc., China, 1986; Royal Soc. of Chemistry, Belgium, 1987. Fellow: Acad. of Sciences, New York, 1962; World Acad. of Art and Science, 1986; Centennial Foreign Fellow, Amer. Chem. Soc., 1976; Foreign Fellow: Indian Nat. Sci. Acad., 1979; Acad. das Ciencias de Lisbõa; Foreign Associate, Nat. Acad. of Sciences, USA, 1967; Foreign Member: Akad. der Wissenschaften der DDR, Berlin, 1980; USSR Acad. of Scis, 1982; Corresponding Member: Acad. of Romania, 1965; Soc. Royale des Sciences, Liège, 1967; Section of Phys. and Math., Akad. der Wissenschaften, Göttingen, 1970; Akad. der Wissenschaften, Vienna, 1971; Rheinish-Westfählische Akad. der Wissenschaften, Düsseldorf, 1980; Archives de Psychologie, Univ. of Geneva, 1982. Dr (*hc*): Newcastle upon Tyne, 1966; Poitiers, 1966; Chicago, 1969; Bordeaux, 1972; Uppsala, 1977; Liège, 1978; Aix-Marseille, 1979; Georgetown, 1980; Rio de Janeiro, 1981; Cracow, 1981; Stevens Inst. of Technology, Hoboken, 1981; Tours, France, 1984; Heriot-Watt, 1985; Universidad Nacional de Educación a Distancia, Madrid, 1985; Nanking Univ., China, 1986; Peking Univ., China, 1986; Buenos Aires, 1989; Facolta di Magistero, Cagliari Univ., 1990; Univ. of Siena, 1990; Nice, France, 1991; Univ. of the Philippines, 1991. Prizes: Van Laar, Société Chimique de Belgique, 1947; A. Wetrems 1950, and Annual (jtly) 1952, Acad. Royale de Belgique; Francqui, 1955; E. J. Solvay, 1965; Nobel Prize for Chemistry, 1977; Southwest Science Forum, New York Acad. of Science; Honda, Honda Foundn, Tokyo, 1983; Umberto Biancamano, Pavia, Italy, 1987; (jtly) Gravity Res. Foundn Award, 1988. Gold Medals: Swante Arrhenius, Royal Acad. of Sciences, Sweden, 1969; Cothenius, German Acad. Naturforscher Leopoldina, 1975; Rumford, Royal Soc., 1976; Ostend, 1987. Bourke Medal, Chem. Soc., 1972; Medal, Assoc. for the Advancement of Sciences, Paris, 1975; Karcher Medal, Amer. Crystallographic Assoc., 1978; Descartes Medal, Univ. Descartes, Paris, 1979; Médaille d'Or de la Ville de Pavie, 1987; Médaille d'Or de la Ville d'Ostende, 1987; Médaille d'Or de l'Université de Padoue, 1988; Distinguished Service Medal, Austin, Texas, 1989. Hon. Citizen: Dallas, USA, 1983; Montpellier, France, 1983; Uccle, Belgium, 1987. Commandeur, l'Ordre du Mérite, France; Commandeur, l'Ordre des Arts et des Lettres, France, 1984; Commandeur de la Légion d'Honneur, France, 1989. *Publications:* (with R. Defay) Traité de Thermodynamique, conformément aux méthodes de Gibbs et de Donder: Vol. I, Thermodynamique Chimique, 1944 (Eng. trans. 1954); Vol. II, Tension Superficielle et Adsorption, 1951 (Eng. trans. 1965); Etude Thermodynamique des Phénomènes Irreversibles, 1947; Introduction to Thermodynamics of Irreversible Processes, New York 1954 (3rd edn 1967); (with A. Bellemans and V. Mathot) The Molecular Theory of Solutions, Amsterdam 1957; Non. Equilibrium Statistical Mechanics, 1962 (also New York); (with R. Herman) Kinetic Theory of Vehicular Traffic, New York 1971; (with P. Glansdorff) Thermodynamic Theory of Structure, Stability and Fluctuations, London and New York 1971 (also French edn); (with G. Nicolis) Self-Organization in Non Equilibrium Systems, 1977 (also New York); From Being to Becoming: time and complexity in the physical sciences, 1980 (also French, German, Japanese, Russian, Italian and Chinese edns); (with I. Stengers) La Nouvelle Alliance: les métamorphoses de la science, 1981 (Prix du Haut Comité de la langue française, Paris, 1981) (also English, German, Italian, Yugoslavian, Spanish, Rumanian, Swedish, Dutch, Danish, Portuguese, Russian, Japanese, Chinese, Bulgarian, Korean and Polish edns); (with I. Stengers) Entre le temps et l'éternité, 1988 (also Dutch, Italian, Portuguese and Spanish edns); (with G. Nicolis) Exploring Complexity, 1989 (also German, Chinese, Russian and Italian edns). *Recreations:* art, music. *Address:* avenue Fond'Roy 67, 1180 Bruxelles, Belgium. *T:* 02/3742952.

PRIMAROLO, Dawn; MP (Lab) Bristol South, since 1987; *b* 2 May 1954; *m*; one *s*. *Educ:* Thomas Bennett Comprehensive Sch., Crawley; Bristol Poly.; Bristol Univ. Mem., Avon CC, 1985–87. Sec., Bristol SE Constit. Lab. Party; Chm., Bristol Dist Lab. Party; Mem., Nat. Labour Women's Cttee. *Address:* House of Commons, SW1A 0AA; (office) 272 St John's Lane, Bristol BS3 5AU. *T:* Bristol (0272) 635948.

PRIME, Prof. Henry Ashworth, CEng, FIEE; Professor of Electronic and Electrical Engineering, University of Birmingham, 1963–86, now Professor Emeritus; *b* 11 March 1921; *s* of late E. V. Prime and Elsie (*née* Ashworth); *m* 1943, Ella Stewart Reid; one *s* one *d*. *Educ:* N Manchester High Sch.; Manchester Univ. (MSc). CEng, FIEE 1964. Scientific Officer, Admiralty Signal and Radar Estab., 1942–46; Lectr, Univ. of Liverpool, 1946–50; Sen. Lectr, Univ. of Adelaide, 1950–55; Chief Electronic Engr and Manager Control Div., Brush Elec. Engrg Co., 1955–63. Pro-Vice-Chancellor, Univ. of Birmingham, 1978–82. Vis. Professor: Univ. of Teheran, 1971; Univ. of Hanover, 1978; Univ. of Cape Town, 1984. Chm., IFAC Technical Cttee on Terminology, 1987–. Member: CNAA Elec. Engrg Bd, 1970–74; Naval Educn Adv. Cttee, 1973–79 (Chm., 1978–79). Mem. Council, IEE, 1974–77, 1980–84, 1985–88; Chm., Computing and Control Divl Bd, IEE, 1982–83. *Publications:* (contrib.) Telecommunication Satellites, ed Gatland, 1964; Modern Concepts in Control Theory, 1970; papers in scientific jls on electrical discharges, microwave interaction with ionised gases, and control systems. *Recreation:* golf. *Address:* 2 Oakdene Drive, Birmingham B45 8LQ. *T:* 021–445 2545.

PRIMROSE, family name of **Earl of Rosebery.**

PRIMROSE, Sir John Ure, 5th Bt *cr* 1903, of Redholme, Dumbreck, Govan; *b* 28 May 1960; *s* of Sir Alasdair Neil Primrose, 4th Bt and of Elaine Noreen, *d* of Edmund Cecil Lowndes, Buenos Aires; *S* father, 1986; *m* 1983, Marion Cecilia, *d* of Hans Otto Altgelt; two *d*. *Heir: b* Andrew Richard Primrose, *b* 19 Jan. 1966. *Educ:* St Peter's School and Military Acad. BA.

PRIMUS, The; *see* Henderson, Rt Rev. G. K. B.

PRINCE, (Celestino) Anthony; solicitor; Taxing Master of the Supreme Court, since 1983; *b* 20 Aug. 1921; *s* of Charles Prince and Amelia (*née* Daubenspeck); *m* 1950, Margaret (*née* Walker) (rep., 200 metres, GB in Olympic Games, 1948 and England in British Empire Games, 1950); one *s* one *d*. *Educ:* Finchley Grammar Sch. Served War, RN, 1939–45: Western Mediterranean in HMS Antelope; Atlantic, Indian Ocean and Pacific in HMS Arbiter; commnd Sub-Lt, 1944. Articled to Kenneth George Rigden of Beaumont Son & Rigden, Fleet Street, 1939; admitted solicitor, 1947; founded firm of C. Anthony Prince & Co., Ealing, 1952; retd as Sen. Partner, 1981. Mem., No 1 (London), later No 14, Legal Aid Area Cttee, 1966–71. Founder Chm., Ealing Family Housing Assoc., 1963. Hon. Sec., Bucks CCC, 1954–69 (played in Minor Counties Comp., 1946–49); Captain, W Mddx Golf Club, 1970–71. *Recreations:* cricket, golf, sailing (Mem., Australian Sardinia Cup team, 1978; Fastnet Race, 1981). *Address:* Royal Courts of Justice, Strand, WC2A 2LL. *Clubs:* MCC; West Middlesex Golf; Pevero Golf (Sardinia).

PRINCE, Prof. Frank Templeton, MA (Oxon); *b* Kimberley, South Africa, 13 Sept. 1912; 2nd *s* of late H. Prince and Margaret Templeton (*née* Hetherington); *m* 1943, Pauline Elizabeth, *d* of late H. F. Bush; two *d*. *Educ:* Christian Brothers' Coll., Kimberley, South Africa; Balliol Coll., Oxford. Visiting Fellow, Graduate Coll., Princeton, NJ, 1935–36. Study Groups Department, Chatham House, 1937–40. Served Army, Intelligence Corps, 1940–46. Department of English, 1946–57, Prof. of English, 1957–74, Southampton Univ.; Prof. of English, Univ. of WI, Jamaica, 1975–78. Hurst Vis. Prof., Brandeis Univ., 1978–80; Vis. Prof., Washington Univ., St Louis, 1980–81, Sana'a Univ., N Yemen, 1981–83; Visiting Fellow, All Souls Coll., 1968–69. Clark Lectr, Cambridge, 1972–73. Pres., English Assoc., 1985–86. Hon. DLitt Southampton, 1981; DUniv York, 1982. *Publications:* Poems, 1938; Soldiers Bathing (poems), 1954; The Italian Element in Milton's Verse, 1954; The Doors of Stone (poems), 1963; Memoirs in Oxford (verse), 1970; Drypoints of the Hasidim (verse), 1975; Collected Poems, 1979; Later On (poems), 1983; Walks in Rome (verse), 1987; Collected Poems, 1991. *Recreations:* music, etc. *Address:* 32 Brookvale Road, Southampton SO2 1QR. *T:* Southampton (0703) 555457.

PRINCE, Harold Smith; theatrical director/producer; *b* NYC, 30 Jan. 1928; *s* of Milton A. Prince and Blanche (*née* Stern); *m* 1962, Judith Chaplin; two *d*. *Educ:* Univ. of Pennsylvania (AB 1948). Co-Producer: The Pajama Game, 1954–56 (co-prod film, 1957); Damn Yankees, 1955–57 (co-prod film, 1958); New Girl in Town, 1957–58; West Side Story, 1957–59; Fiorello!, 1959–61 (Pulitzer Prize); Tenderloin, 1960–61; A Call on Kuprin, 1961; They Might Be Giants, London 1961; Side By Side By Sondheim, 1977–78. Producer: Take Her She's Mine, 1961–62; A Funny Thing Happened on the Way to the Forum, 1962–64; Fiddler on the Roof, 1964–72; Poor Bitos, 1964; Flora the Red Menace, 1965. Director-Producer: She Loves Me, 1963–64, London 1964; Superman, 1966; Cabaret, 1966–69, London 1968, tour and NY, 1987; Zorba, 1968–69; Company, 1970–72, London 1972; A Little Night Music, 1973–74, London 1975 (dir. film, 1977); Pacific Overtures, 1976. Director: A Family Affair, 1962; Baker Street, 1965; Something For Everyone (film), 1970; New Phoenix Rep. prodns of Great God Brown, 1972–73, The Visit, 1973–74, and Love for Love, 1974–75; Some of my Best Friends, 1977; On the Twentieth Century, 1978; Evita, London 1978, USA 1979–83, Australia, Vienna, 1980, Mexico City, 1981; Sweeney Todd, 1979, London 1980; Girl of the Golden West, San Francisco Op., 1979; world première, Willie Stark, Houston Grand Opera, 1981; Merrily We Roll Along (musical) 1981; A Doll's Life (musical), 1982; Madame Butterfly, Chicago Lyric Op., 1982; Turandot, Vienna state Op., 1983; Play Memory, 1984; End of the World, 1984; Diamonds, 1985; The Phantom of the Opera, London, 1986, NY, 1988, Los Angeles, 1989, Canada, 1989; Roza, USA, 1987; Cabaret (20th anniversary revival), tour and Broadway, 1987; Kiss of the Spider Woman, 1990. Directed for NY City Opera: Ashmedai, 1976; Kurt Weill's Silverlake, 1980; Candide, 1982; Don Giovanni, 1989; Faust, Metropolitan Opera, 1990; co-Director-Producer, Follies, 1971–72; co-Producer-Director: Candide, 1974–75; Merrily We Roll Along, 1981; A Doll's Life, 1982; Grind (musical), 1985. Antoinette Perry Awards for: The Pajama Game; Damn Yankees; Fiorello!; A Funny Thing Happened on the Way to the Forum; Fiddler on the Roof; Cabaret; Company; A Little Night Music; Candide; Sweeney Todd; Evita; The Phantom of the Opera; SWET award: Evita, 1977–78. Member: League of New York Theatres (Pres., 1964–65); Council for National Endowment for the Arts. Hon. DLit, Emerson College, 1971; Hon. Dr of Fine Arts, Univ. of Pennsylvania, 1971. Drama Critics' Circle Awards; Best Musical Award, London Evening Standard, 1955–58, 1972. *Publication:* Contradictions: notes on twenty-six years in the theatre, 1974. *Recreation:* tennis. *Address:* Suite 1009, 10 Rockefeller Plaza, New York, NY 10020, USA. *T:* 212–399–0960.

PRINCE, Maj.-Gen. Hugh Anthony, CBE 1960; retired as Chief, Military Planning Office, SEATO, Bangkok; *b* 11 Aug. 1911; *s* of H. T. Prince, FRCS, LRCP; *m* 1st, 1938, Elizabeth (*d* 1959), *d* of Dr Walter Bapty, Victoria, BC; two *s*; 2nd, 1959, Claude-Andrée, *d* of André Romanet, Château-de-Tholot, Beaujeu, Rhône; one *s*. *Educ:* Eastbourne Coll.; RMC, Sandhurst. Commissioned, 1931; served in 6th Gurkha Rifles until 1947; The King's Regt (Liverpool), 1947. *Recreations:* golf, gardening, antiques. *Address:* 36 Route de la Crau, 13280 Raphèle-les-Arles, France. *T:* 90.98.46.93.

PRINCE-SMITH, Sir (William) Richard, 4th Bt, *cr* 1911; *b* 27 Dec. 1928; *s* of Sir William Prince-Smith, 3rd Bt, OBE, MC, and Marjorie, Lady Prince-Smith (*d* 1970); *S* father, 1964; *m* 1st, 1955, Margaret Ann Carter; one *s* one *d*; 2nd, 1975, Ann Christina Faulds. *Educ:* Charterhouse; Clare Coll., Cambridge (MA). BA (Agric.) 1951. *Recreations:* music, photography, travel. *Heir: s* James William Prince-Smith, Capt. 13th/18th Royal Hussars (QMO), *b* 2 July 1959. *Address:* 40–735 Paxton Drive, Rancho Mirage, Calif 92270, USA. *T:* (619) 321–1975. *Clubs:* Thunderbird, Springs Country (Rancho Mirage).

PRING, Prof. Richard Anthony; Professor of Educational Studies, University of Oxford, since 1989; Fellow of Green College, Oxford, since 1989; *b* 20 April 1938; *s* of Joseph Edwin and Anne-Marie Pring; *m* 1970, Helen Faye Evans; three *d*. *Educ:* Gregorian Univ. and English College, Rome (PhL); University Coll. London (BA Hons Philosophy); Univ. of London Inst. of Education (PhD); College of St Mark and St John (PGCE). Asst Principal, Dept of Educn and Science, 1962–64; teacher in London comprehensive schools, 1965–67, 1973–78; Lectr in Education: Goldsmiths' Coll., 1967–70; Univ. of London Inst. of Educn, 1972–78; Prof. of Educn, Univ. of Exeter, 1978–89. Editor, British Jl of Educational Studies, 1986–. *Publications:* Knowledge and Schooling, 1976; Personal and Social Education, 1984; The New Curriculum, 1989. *Recreations:* running half marathons, gardening, writing, fell walking, campaigning for comprehensive schools. *Address:* Green College, Oxford.

PRING-MILL, Robert Duguid Forrest, DLitt; FBA 1988; Fellow of St Catherine's College, Oxford, since 1965; *b* 11 Sept. 1924; *o s* of late Major Richard Pring-Mill, RA and Nellie (*née* Duguid); *m* 1950, Maria Brigitte Heinsheimer; one *s* one *d*. *Educ:* Colegio de Montesión, Palma de Mallorca; New Coll., Oxford (BA 1st cl. Mod. Langs, 1949; DLitt 1986). Enlisted, 1941; commnd The Black Watch, RHR, 1942; temp. Capt., 1945; despatches, 1947. Oxford University: Sen. Demy, Magdalen Coll., 1950–52; Univ. Lectr in Spanish, 1952–88; Lectr, New Coll., 1956–88, Exeter Coll., 1963–81; Tutor, St Catherine's Coll., 1965–88. English Editor: Romanistisches Jahrbuch, 1953–; Estudios Lulianos, 1957–; Commissió Editora Lul·liana, 1960–. Magister, Maioricensis Schola Lullistica, 1957; Corresp. Mem., Inst. d'Estudis Catalans, 1966. Premi Pompeu Fabra, 1956; Premi Ciutat de Palma, 1979; Premi Catalònia, 1991. Cross of St George (Generalitat de Catalunya), 1990; Commander, Order of Isabel la Católica (Spain), 1990. *Publications:* Chinese Triad Societies, 1946; (ed) Lope de Vega: Five Plays, 1961; El Microcosmos Lul·lià, 1961; Ramón Llull y el Número Primitivo de las Dignidades, 1963; (with N. Tarn) The Heights of Macchu Picchu, 1966; (with Katya Kohn) Neruda Poems, 1969; (ed) Raymundus Lullus, Quattuor Libri Principiorum, 1969; Neruda: A Basic Anthology, 1975; Cardenal: Marilyn Monroe & Other Poems, 1975; The Scope of Spanish-American Committed Poetry, 1977; (with Donald Walsh) Cardenal: Apocalypse and Other Poems, 1977; Spanish American Committed Poetry: canciones de lucha y esperanza, 1978; (ed jtly) Studies in Honour of P. E. Russell, 1981; (ed jtly) Hacia Calderón, 1982; Cantas-Canto-Cantemos, 1983; Gracias a la vida: the power and poetry of song, 1990; articles in learned jls, Encyc. Britannica, etc, on Ramón Llull, Calderón, modern poetry and Spanish-American protest song. *Recreations:* glass engraving; travel, photography and field recording in Latin America. *Address:* 11 North Hills, Brill, Bucks HP18 9TH. *T:* Brill (0844) 237481.

PRINGLE, Air Marshal Sir Charles (Norman Seton), KBE 1973 (CBE 1967); MA, FEng; CBIM; Director, FR Group plc, 1985–89; *b* 6 June 1919; *s* of late Seton Pringle, OBE, FRCSI, Dublin; *m* 1946, Margaret, *d* of late B. Sharp, Baildon, Yorkshire; one *s*. *Educ:* Repton; St John's Coll., Cambridge. Commissioned, RAF, 1941; served India and Ceylon, 1942–46. Air Ministry, 1946–48; RAE, Farnborough, 1949–50; attached to USAF, 1950–52; appts in UK, 1952–60; STSO No 3 Group, Bomber Comd, 1960–62, and Air Forces Middle East, 1962–64; Comdt RAF St Athan and Air Officer Wales, 1964–66; MoD, 1967; IDC, 1968. Dir-Gen. of Engineering (RAF) MoD, 1969–70; Air Officer Engineering, Strike Command, 1970–73; Dir-Gen. Engineering (RAF), 1973; Controller, Engrg and Supply (RAF), 1973–76; Sen. Exec., Rolls Royce Ltd, 1976–78; Dir, Hunting Engineering Ltd, 1976–78; Dir and Chief Exec., SBAC, 1979–84. Pres., RAeS, 1975–76; Vice-Chm., 1976–77, Chm., 1977–78, CEI. Mem. Council, RSA, 1978–83 and 1986–. Chm. Governors, Repton Sch., 1985–. Hon. FRAeS, 1989. *Recreations:* photography, ornithology, motor sport. *Address:* Appleyards, Fordingbridge, Hants SP6 3BP. *T:* Fordingbridge (0425) 652357; K9 Sloane Avenue Mansions, SW3 3JP. *T:* 071–584 3432. *Clubs:* Royal Air Force, Buck's.

PRINGLE, Dr Derek Hair, CBE 1980; BSc, PhD, DSc; FRSE; CPhys; FInstP; Chairman: Borders Health Board, since 1989; SEEL Ltd, since 1980; *b* 8 Jan. 1926; *s* of Robert Pringle and Lillias Dalgleish Hair; *m* 1949, Anne Collier Caw; three *s* one *d*. *Educ:* George Heriot's Sch., Edinburgh; Edinburgh Univ. (BSc 1948, PhD 1954). FInstP 1957; FRSE 1970. Res. Physicist, Ferranti Ltd, Edinburgh, 1948–59; Nuclear Enterprises Ltd: Technical Dir, 1960–76; Man. Dir, 1976–78; Chm., 1978–80; Chm., Bioscot, 1983–86; Director: Amersham Internat., 1978–87; Creative Capital Nominees Ltd, 1982–90; Melville Street Investments PLC, 1983–. Chm., Scottish Health Service Cttee on Non-Surgical Management of Cancer in Scotland, 1990–91. Member: Nat. Radiol Protection Bd, Harwell, 1969–81; Council for Applied Science in Scotland, 1981–86; CNAA, 1982–85. Vice-Pres., RSE, 1985–88 (Mem. Council, 1982–88); Member: Council, Scottish Museums Adv. Bd, 1984–85; Bd of Trustees, Nat. Museums of Scotland, 1985–. Mem., Court, Heriot-Watt Univ., 1968–77. Pres., Edinburgh Chamber of Commerce and Manufactures, 1979–81; Chm., Assoc. of Scottish Chambers of Commerce, 1985–87; Mem. Council, Assoc. of British Chambers of Commerce, 1986–87; Vice-Chm. (Scotland), Industry Matters, 1987–88. Faraday Lectr, 1978–79. Hon. FRCSE, 1988. Hon. DSc Heriot Watt Univ., 1981. *Publications:* papers on microwave engrg, gas discharge physics and nuclear science in scientific jls. *Recreations:* golf, gardening. *Address:* Earlyvale, Eddleston, Peeblesshire EH45 8QX. *T:* Eddleston (07213) 231. *Clubs:* Royal Over-Seas League, English-Speaking Union.

See also R. W. Pringle.

PRINGLE, John Martin Douglas; *b* 1912; *s* of late J. Douglas Pringle, Hawick, Scotland; *m* 1936, Celia, *d* of E. A. Carroll; one *s* two *d*. *Educ:* Shrewsbury Sch.; Lincoln Coll., Oxford. First Class Literae Humaniores, 1934. Editorial Staff of Manchester Guardian, 1934–39. Served War of 1939–45 with King's Own Scottish Borderers, 1940–44; Assistant Editor, Manchester Guardian, 1944–48; Special Writer on The Times, 1948–52; Editor of The Sydney Morning Herald, 1952–57; Deputy Editor of The Observer, 1958–63; Managing Editor, Canberra Times, 1964–65; Editor, Sydney Morning Herald, 1965–70. *Publications:* China Struggles for Unity, 1938; Australian Accent, 1958; Australian Painting Today, 1963; On Second Thoughts, 1971; Have Pen, Will Travel, 1973; The Last Shenachie, 1976; The Shorebirds of Australia, 1987. *Address:* 8/105A Darling Point Road, Darling Point, NSW 2027, Australia.

PRINGLE, Margaret Ann; Head of Holland Park School, since 1986; *b* 28 Sept. 1946. *Educ:* Holton Park Girls' Grammar Sch.; Somerville College, Oxford (MA, BLitt English Lang. and Lit.). English Teacher, Selhurst High School, Croydon, 1972–76; Head of English, Thomas Calton School, Peckham, 1976–81; Dep. Head, George Green's School, Isle of Dogs, 1981–86. *Recreations:* all food, all music, most dancing, and occasionally not thinking about education. *Address:* Holland Park School, Airlie Gardens, Campden Hill Road, W8 7AF.

PRINGLE, Dr Robert William, OBE 1967; BSc, PhD; CPhys; FRSE; FRS(Can); President, Nuclear Enterprises Ltd, Edinburgh, since 1976; *b* 2 May 1920; *s* of late Robert Pringle and late Lillias Dalgleish Hair; *m* 1948, Carol Stokes; three *s* one *d*. *Educ:* George Heriot's Sch., Edinburgh; Edinburgh Univ. (Vans Dunlop Scholar in Natural Philosophy). Lecturer, Natural Philosophy, Edinburgh, 1945; Associate Professor of Physics, Manitoba, 1949; Prof. and Chairman of Physics, Manitoba, 1953–56; Chm. and Man. Dir, Nuclear Enterprises Ltd, 1956–76 (Queen's Award to Industry, 1966, 1979); Dir, N Sea Assets Ltd, 1977–78. Member: Scottish Council, CBI (Cttee), 1966–72; Scottish Univs Industry Liaison Cttee, 1968–75; Bd, Royal Observatory (Edinburgh), 1968–79; Council, SRC, 1972–76; Bd, Astronomy, Space and Radio (SRC), 1970–72; Bd, Nuclear Physics (SRC), 1972–76; Economic Council for Scotland, 1971–75; Bd, Scottish Sch. Business Studies, 1972–83. University of Edinburgh: Mem. Court, 1967–75; Mem., Finance Cttee, 1967–75; Mem. Bd, Centre for Indust. Liaison and Consultancy, 1968–84; Mem., Press Cttee, 1977–78. Trustee: Scottish Hospitals Endowments Res. Trust, 1976–88; Scottish Trust for the Physically Disabled, 1977–84. Hon. Adviser, Nat. Museum of Antiquities of Scotland, 1969–. FInstP 1948; Fellow, American Inst. Physics, 1950; FRS(Can) 1955; FRSE 1964; Hon. Fellow, Royal Scottish Soc. Arts, 1972; CPhys 1985. *Publications:* (with James Douglas) 20th Century Scottish Banknotes, Vol. II, 1986; papers on nuclear spectroscopy and nuclear geophysics in UK and US scientific journals. *Recreations:* golf, book-collecting, Rugby (Edinburgh, Edinburgh and Glasgow, Rest of Scotland, 1945–48; organiser, first Monte Carlo Internat. Rugby Sevens, 1987). *Address:* 27 avenue Princesse Grace, Monaco. *Clubs:* Athenæum; New (Edinburgh); Yacht Club de Monaco, Golf de Monte Carlo.

See also D. H. Pringle.

PRINGLE, Lt-Gen. Sir Steuart (Robert), 10th Bt, *cr* 1683, Stichill, Roxburghshire; KCB 1982; Commandant General Royal Marines 1981–84; Chairman and Chief Executive, Chatham Historic Dockyard Trust, 1984–91; *b* 21 July 1928; *s* of Sir Norman H. Pringle, 9th Bt and Lady (Oonagh) Pringle (*née* Curran) (*d* 1975); *S* father, 1961; *m* 1953, Jacqueline Marie Gladwell; two *s* two *d*. *Educ:* Sherborne. Royal Marines: 2nd Lieut, 1946; 42 Commando, 1950–52; 40 Commando, 1957–59; Chief Instructor, Signal Trng Wing, RM, 1959–61; Bde Signal Officer, 3 Commando Bde, RM, 1961–63; Defence Planning Staff, 1964–67; Chief Signal Officer, RM, 1967–69; 40 Commando, Far East, 1969–71; CO 45 Commando Group, 1971–74; HQ Commando Forces, 1974–76; RCDS, 1977; Maj.-Gen. RM Commando Forces, 1978–79; Chief of Staff to Comdt Gen., RM, 1979–81. Col Comdt, RM, 1989–90, Representative Col Comdt, 1991–92. Pres., St Loye's Coll. for the Disabled, 1984–; Vice-Pres., Officers Pensions Assoc., 1984–; Mem. Council, Union Jack Club, 1982–85; Vice-Patron, Royal Naval Benevolent Trust, 1984–. CBIM. Liveryman, Plaisterers' Co., 1984. Hon. DSc City, 1982. Hon. Admiral, Texas Navy; Hon. Mem., Co. of Bear Tamers. *Publications:* (contrib) Peace and the Bomb, 1982; The Future of British Seapower, 1984; contribs to RUSI Jl, Navy International, etc. *Heir:* *s* Simon Robert Pringle, *b* 6 Jan. 1959. *Address:* 76 South Croxted Road, Dulwich, SE21. *Clubs:* Army and Navy; Royal Thames Yacht, MCC.

PRIOR, family name of **Baron Prior.**

PRIOR, Baron *cr* 1987 (Life Peer), of Brampton in the County of Suffolk; **James Michael Leathes Prior;** PC 1970; Chairman, The General Electric Company plc, since 1984; *b* 11 Oct. 1927; 2nd *s* of late C. B. L. and A. S. M. Prior, Norwich; *m* 1954, Jane Primrose Gifford, 2nd *d* of late Air Vice-Marshal O. G. Lywood, CB, CBE; three *s* one *d*. *Educ:* Charterhouse; Pembroke College, Cambridge. 1st class degree in Estate Management, 1950; commissioned in Royal Norfolk Regt, 1946; served in India and Germany; farmer and land agent in Norfolk and Suffolk. MP (C): Lowestoft, Suffolk, 1959–83; Waveney, 1983–87. PPS to Pres. of Bd of Trade, 1963, to Minister of Power, 1963–64, to Mr Edward Heath, Leader of the Opposition, 1965–70; Minister of Agriculture, Fisheries and Food, 1970–72; Lord Pres. of Council and Leader of House of Commons, 1972–74; Opposition front bench spokesman on Employment, 1974–79; Sec. of State for Employment, 1979–81; Sec. of State for NI, 1981–84. A Dep. Chm., Cons. Party, 1972–74 (Vice-Chm., 1965). Chm., Allders, 1989–; Director: United Biscuits (Holdings), 1984–; Barclays Bank, 1984–89; Barclays International, 1984–89; J. Sainsbury, 1984–; Member: Tenneco European Adv. Bd, 1986–; Internat. Adv. Bd, Amer. Internat. Gp, 1988–. Chairman: Council of Industry and Higher Educn, 1986–; Archibishops' Commn on Rural Areas, 1988–; Great Ormond Street Wishing Well Appeal, 1985–89; Royal Veterinary Coll., 1990–; Trustee, Internat. Centre for Child Studies, 1987–. *Publications:* (jtly) The Right Approach to the Economy, 1977; A Balance of Power, 1986. *Recreations:* cricket, tennis, golf, gardening. *Address:* Old Hall, Brampton, Beccles, Suffolk. *T:* Brampton (050279) 278; 36 Morpeth Mansions, SW1. *T:* 071–834 5543. *Clubs:* MCC; Butterflies Cricket.

PRIOR, Ven. Christopher, CB 1968; Archdeacon of Portsmouth, 1969–77, Archdeacon Emeritus since 1977; *b* 2 July 1912; *s* of late Ven. W. H. Prior; *m* 1945, Althea Stafford (*née* Coode); two *d*. *Educ:* King's Coll., Taunton; Keble Coll., Oxford; Cuddesdon Coll. Curate of Hornsea, 1938–41; Chaplain RN from 1941, Chaplain of the Fleet, 1966–69. Served in: HMS Royal Arthur, 1941; HMHS Maine, 1941–43; HMS Scylla, 1943–44; HMS Owl, 1944–46; various ships, 1946–58; Britannia RNC, Dartmouth, 1958–61; HMS Blake, 1961–62; HM Dockyard, Portsmouth, 1963–66; QHC, 1966–69. *Recreation:* walking. *Address:* Ponies End, West Melbury, Shaftesbury, Dorset SP7 0LY. *T:* Shaftesbury (0747) 811239.

PRIOR, Peter James, CBE 1980; DL; Chairman, H. P. Bulmer Holdings PLC, 1977–82 (Director, 1977–85; Managing Director, H. P. Bulmer Ltd, 1966–77); *b* 1 Sept. 1919; *s* of Percy Prior; *m* 1957, Prinia Mary, *d* of late R. E. Moreau, Berrick Prior, Oxon; two *s*. *Educ:* Royal Grammar Sch., High Wycombe; London Univ. BSc(Econ). FCA, FIMC, CBIM, FIIM, FRSA. Royal Berks Regt, 1939; Intell. Corps, 1944–46 (Captain) (Croix-de-Guerre 1944). Company Sec., Saunders-Roe (Anglesey) Ltd, 1948; Consultant, Urwick, Orr & Partners, 1951; Financial Dir, International Chemical Co., 1956; Financial Dir, British Aluminium Co., 1961; Dep. Chm., Holden Hydroman, 1984–88; Dir, Trebor, 1982–86. Member: English Tourist Bd, 1969–75; Midlands Electricity Bd, 1973–83; Chairman: Inquiry into Potato Processing Industry, 1971; Motorway Service Area Inquiry, 1977–78; Home Office Deptl Inquiry into Prison Discipline, 1984–85. Pres., Incorp. Soc. of British Advertisers' Council, 1980–83; Mem. Council, BIM, 1974–82. Chm. Trustees, Leadership Trust, 1975–79; Member: Council, Regular Forces Employment Assoc., 1981–86; Council, Operation Raleigh, 1984–89. DL Hereford and Worcester, 1983. Communicator of the Year Award, British Assoc. of Industrial Editors, 1982. *Publications:* Leadership is not a Bowler Hat, 1977; articles on management and leadership. *Recreations:* free-fall parachuting (UK record for longest delayed drop (civilian), 1981), flying (Vice Chm., Hereford Air Sports Centre, 1979–84), motor-cycling, sub-aqua swimming. *Address:* Rathays, Sutton Saint Nicholas, Herefordshire HR1 3AY. *T:* Sutton Saint Nicholas (043272) 313. *Clubs:* Army and Navy, Special Forces.

PRIOR, William Johnson, CBE 1979; CEng, FIEE; Chairman, Manx Electricity Authority, 1984–85; retired; *b* 28 Jan. 1924; *s* of Ernest Stanley and Lilian Prior; *m* 1945, Mariel (*née* Irving); two *s* one *d*. *Educ:* Goole and Barnsley Grammar Schs. Barugh, Mexborough, Stuart Street (Manchester) and Stockport Power Stations, 1944–52; Keadby, 1952–56, Supt, 1954–56; Supt, Berkeley, 1957–58; Supt, Hinkley Point Generating Station, 1959–66; CEGB and predecessors: Asst Reg. Dir (Generation), NW Region, 1967–70; Dir (Generation), SW Region, 1970–72; Dir-Gen., SE Region, 1972–76; Mem., Electricity Council, 1976–79; Chm., Yorks Electricity Bd, 1979–84. Member: NCB,

1977–83; Adv. Cttee on Safety of Nuclear Installations, 1980–87. *Recreation:* country walking. *Address:* Highfield House, Lime Kiln Lane, Kirk Deighton, Wetherby, W Yorks LS22 4EA. *T:* Wetherby (0937) 584434.

PRITCHARD, family name of **Baron Pritchard.**

PRITCHARD, Baron *cr* 1975 (Life Peer), of West Haddon, Northamptonshire; **Derek Wilbraham Pritchard;** Kt 1968; DL; *b* 8 June 1910; *s* of Frank Wheelton Pritchard and Ethel Annie Pritchard (*née* Cheetham); *m* 1941, Denise Arfor Pritchard (*née* Huntbach); two *d. Educ:* Clifton College, Bristol. Took over family business of E. Halliday & Son, Wine Merchants, 1929, Man. Dir, 1930–51, Chm., 1947. Called up in TA and served War of 1939–45; demob. as Col and joined Bd of E. K. Cole, Ltd, 1946. Joined Ind Coope Ltd, as Man. Dir of Grants of St James's Ltd, 1949, Chm., 1960–69; Chm., Victoria Wine Co. Ltd, 1959–64. Director: Ind Coope Ltd, 1951; Ind Coope Tetley Ansell Ltd on merger of those companies, 1961, subseq. renamed Allied Breweries Ltd, 1961–80 (Chm., 1968–70); Allied Breweries Investments Ltd, 1961–80; Licences & General Assurance Ltd, 1952–56, subseq. merged with Guardian Assurance Ltd, 1956–80; Guardian Royal Exchange Assurance Ltd, 1956–80; George Sandeman Sons & Co. Ltd, 1952–80; J. & W. Nicholson (Holdings), 1962–82; Carreras Ltd, 1970–72 (Chm.); Dorchester Hotel Ltd, 1976–80 (Chm.); Rothmans of Pall Mall Canada Ltd, 1972–77; Rothmans of Pall Mall (Australia) Ltd, 1972–77; Rothmans of Pall Mall (Malaysia) Berhad, 1972–77; Rothmans of Pall Mall (Singapore) Ltd, 1972–77; Deltec International, 1975–77; London-American Finance Corp., 1976–78; Midland Bank Ltd, 1968–85; Samuel Montagu Ltd, 1969–86; Adelaide Associates Ltd, 1970–; Rothmans International Ltd, 1972–86 (Chm., 1972–75); Rothmans Group Services SA, 1972–86; Rothmans of Pall Mall (London) Ltd, 1972–86; Rothmans Tobacco Hldgs Ltd, 1972–86; Carreras Group (Jamaica) Ltd, 1972–86; Paterson, Zochonis & Co. Ltd, 1977–89; Philips Electronic & Associated Industries Ltd, 1978–85; Lyford Cay Property Owners Assoc. Ltd, 1980–; Tiedmann-Goodnow Internat. Capital Corp., 1980–89 (Chm., 1980–86); Matterhorn Investment Co. Ltd (Chm., 1980–85); Thoroughbred Holdings Internat. Ltd, 1982– (Chm.); Euro-Canadian Bank Inc., 1984–89; Templeton Foundn Adv. Bd, 1980– (Chm., 1984–85); Templeton, Galbraith & Hansberger Ltd, 1987–; Templeton Investments Management Ltd, 1980–; Best Investments Inc.; Chalk International Airlines, 1984–; Equator Hldgs, 1985–; Equator Bank, 1985–; Dextra Bank & Trust Co., 1986–89 (Chm.). Chairman: Dorchester Hotel Bd of Trustees, 1976–87; Dorchester Pension Fund, 1976–86; Rothmans Internat. Adv. Bd, 1986–89; Mem., Salomon Bros Adv. Bd, USA, 1980–83; Dep Chm., British National Export Council, 1965–66, Chm. 1966–68; Member: Nat. Inds Appts Bd, 1973–82; Top Salaries Review Body, 1975–78; House of Lords EEC Cttee, 1975–79, EEC Sub-Cttee A, 1975–80; Cttee, British Foundn for Age Research, 1975–84; British Overseas Trade Adv. Council, 1976–84; Fund Raising Cttee, RCS, 1976–87; Chancellor of the Duchy of Lancaster's Cttee on Business Sponsorship of the Arts, 1980–87; Amer. European Community Assoc., 1981–88; President: British Export Houses Assoc., 1976–83; Northants Co. Branch, Royal Agricl Benevolent Instn, 1981–87; Patron: Northants British Red Cross Soc., 1982– (Pres., 1975–83); Inst. of Directors, 1966– (Pres., 1968–74); Vice-President: Inst. of Export, 1976– (Pres., 1974–76); Wine and Spirit Assoc. of GB, 1964– (Pres., 1962–64); Northants Youth Club Assoc., 1965–; East of England Agricl Soc., 1974–; Co-Chm., UK-Jamaica Cttee, 1981–87; Trustee: Age Action Trust, 1975–80; St Giles Church, Northampton, 1976–86; Patron: Northampton and County Chamber of Commerce, 1978–; Three Shires Indept Hosp., 1978–; Abbeyfield Soc. for the Aged, 1979– (Pres., 1970–79); Governor: Clifton Coll., Bristol; Nene Coll., Northampton. DL Northants, 1974. *Recreations:* farming, tennis, golf, hunting. *Address:* West Haddon Hall, Northampton NN6 7AU. *T:* West Haddon (078887) 210.

PRITCHARD, Arthur Alan, CB 1979; JP; formerly Deputy Under Secretary of State, Ministry of Defence; *b* 3 March 1922; *s* of Arthur Henry Standfast Pritchard and Sarah Bessie Myra Pritchard (*née* Mundy); *m* 1949, Betty Rona Nevard (*née* Little); two *s* one *d. Educ:* Wanstead High Sch., Essex. Board of Trade, 1939. RAFVR Pilot, 1941–52. Joined Admiralty, 1952; Asst Sec., 1964; Royal College of Defence Studies, 1972; Asst Under-Sec. of State, Naval Personnel and Op. Requirements, MoD, 1972–76; seconded as Dep. Sec., NI Office, 1976–78; Secretary to the Admiralty Bd, 1978–81. Management consultant, 1984–89. Chm., Fordingbridge and Dist Community Assoc., 1990–. JP Ringwood, 1986 (Totton and New Forest, 1981–86; Chm., Ringwood Bench, 1991–). *Recreations:* caravanning, walking. *Address:* Courtlands, Manor Farm Road, Fordingbridge, Hants. *Club:* Royal Air Force.

PRITCHARD, Rear-Adm. Gwynedd Idris, CB 1981; *b* 18 June 1924; *s* of Cyril Idris Pritchard and Lily Pritchard; *m* 1975, Mary Thérèsa (*née* Curtin); three *s* (by previous marriage). *Educ:* Wyggeston Sch., Leicester. FBIM, MNI. Joined Royal Navy, 1942; Sub-Lieut 1944; Lieut 1946; Lt-Comdr 1954; Comdr 1959; Captain 1967; Rear-Adm. 1976; Flag Officer Sea Training, 1976–78; Flag Officer Gibraltar, 1979–81; retired list, 1981. Mem., Dorset CC, 1985–. *Recreations:* riding, caravanning. *Address:* Hoofprints, Beach Road, Burton Bradstock, Dorset.

PRITCHARD, Gwynn; *see* Pritchard, I. G.

PRITCHARD, Hugh Wentworth, CBE 1969; Member of Council of Law Society, 1947–66; *b* 15 March 1903; *s* of late Sir Harry G. Pritchard; *m* 1934, Barbara Stableforth (*d* 1987); two *s. Educ:* Charterhouse; Balliol College, Oxford. Admitted a solicitor, 1927; partner in Sharpe Pritchard & Co., 1928–80. Pres. Soc. of Parliamentary Agents, 1952–55; Member: Statute Law Committee, 1954–81; Committee on Administrative Tribunals and Enquiries, 1955; Council on Tribunals, 1958–70. Lay Reader, 1947. Served War of 1939–45, in England, France, Belgium and Germany; joined The Queen's as a private; commissioned in RAOC, attaining rank of Lt-Col. *Recreation:* golf. *Address:* 128 Foxley Lane, Purley, Surrey CR8 3NE. *T:* 081–660 9029.

PRITCHARD, (Iorwerth) Gwynn; Senior Commissioning Editor for Education, Channel Four Television, since 1989; *b* 1 Feb. 1946; *s* of Rev. Islwyn Pritchard and Megan Mair Pritchard; *m* 1970, Marilyn Bartholomew; two *s* one *d. Educ:* King's Coll., Cambridge (MA). Producer: BBC Television, London, 1969–78; BBC Wales, 1979–81; HTV Wales, 1982–85; Commissioning Editor, Channel 4, 1985–. UK Rep., INPUT Internat. Bd, 1988–. Trustee: Broadcasting Support Services, 1990–; Nat. Inst. for Adult and Continuing Educn, 1990–; Welsh Writers Trust, 1990–. Winston Churchill Fellow, 1973; Huw Weldon Fellow, 1990–91. Chevalier, l'ordre des Arts et des Lettres, (France), 1990. *Recreations:* swimming, walking, cinema. *Address:* Channel Four Television, 60 Charlotte Street, W1P 2AX. *T:* 071–631 4444.

PRITCHARD, Kenneth John, CB 1982; Director, Greenwich Hospital, since 1987; *b* 18 March 1926; *s* of William Edward Pritchard and Ethel Mary Pritchard (*née* Cornfield); *m* 1st, 1949, Elizabeth Margaret Bradshaw (*d* 1978); two *d*; 2nd, 1979, Angela Madeleine Palmer; one *s* two *d. Educ:* Newport High Sch.; St Catherine's Coll., Oxford (MA 1951). Served Army, 1944–48; Indian Mil. Acad., Dehra Dun, 1945; served with 8th/12th Frontier Force Regt and 2nd Royal W Kent Regt. Asst Principal, Admiralty, 1951; Private Sec. to Sec. of State for Wales, 1964; Asst Sec., Min. of Aviation, 1966; RCDS, 1972; Principal Supply and Transport Officer (Naval), Portsmouth, 1978, Exec. Dir 1980; Dir Gen. of Supplies and Transport (Naval), MoD, 1981–86, retd. FInstPS 1986. *Recreations:* squash, tennis. *Address:* Pickford House, Beckington, Som BA3 6SJ. *T:* Frome (0373) 830329. *Club:* Bath and County (Bath).

PRITCHARD, Kenneth William; Secretary of the Law Society of Scotland, since 1976; *b* 14 Nov. 1933; *s* of Dr Kenneth Pritchard, MB, BS, DPH, and Isobel Pritchard, LDS (*née* Broom); *m* 1962, Gretta (*née* Murray); two *s* one *d. Educ:* Dundee High Sch.; Fettes Coll.; St Andrews Univ. (BL). National Service, Argyll and Sutherland Highlanders, 1955–57; commnd 2nd Lieut, 1956; TA 1957–62 (Captain). Joined J. & J. Scrimgeour, Solicitors, Dundee, 1957, Sen. Partner, 1970–76. Hon. Sheriff, Dundee, 1978–. Member: Sheriff Court Rules Council, 1973–76; Lord Dunpark's Cttee Considering Reparation upon Criminal Conviction, 1973–77; Secretary, Scottish Council of Law Reporting, 1976. Governor, Moray House Coll. of Educn, 1982–84; Mem. Ct, Univ. of Dundee, 1990–. Mem., National Trust for Scotland Jubilee Appeal Cttee, 1980–82. Pres., Dundee High Sch. Old Boys Club, 1975–76; Captain of the School's RFC, 1959–62. Hon. Prof. of Law, Strathclyde Univ., 1986–. *Recreation:* golf. *Address:* 36 Ravelston Dykes, Edinburgh EH4 3EB. *T:* 031–332 8584. *Clubs:* New, Bruntsfield Links Golfing Association (Edinburgh); Hon. Company of Edinburgh Golfers (Muirfield).

PRITCHARD, Sir Neil, KCMG 1962 (CMG 1952); HM Diplomatic Service, retired; Ambassador in Bangkok, 1967–70; *b* 14 January 1911; *s* of late Joseph and Lillian Pritchard; *m* 1943, Mary Burroughes (*d* 1988), Pretoria, S Africa; one *s. Educ:* Liverpool Coll.; Worcester Coll., Oxford. Dominions Office, 1933; Private Secretary to Permanent Under-Sec., 1936–38; Assistant Secretary, Rhodesia-Nyasaland Royal Commission, 1938; Secretary, Office of UK High Commissioner, Pretoria, 1941–45; Principal Secretary, Office of UK Representative, Dublin, 1948–49; Assistant Under-Secretary of State, Commonwealth Relations Office, 1951–54; Dep. UK High Commissioner: Canada, 1954–57; Australia, 1957–60; Actg Dep. Under-Sec. of State, CRO, 1961; British High Comr in Tanganyika, 1961–63; Deputy Under-Secretary of State, Commonwealth Office (formerly CRO), 1963–67. *Recreation:* golf. *Address:* Little Garth, Daglingworth, Cirencester, Glos GL7 7AQ.

PRITCHARD, Prof. Thomas Owen, JP; Director for Wales, Nature Conservancy Council, 1973–91; Hon. Professor, Institute of Earth Studies, University of Wales, Aberystwyth; *b* 13 May 1932; *s* of late Owen and Mary Pritchard; *m* 1957, Enyd Ashton; one *s* one *d. Educ:* Botwnnog Grammar Sch.; Univ. of Wales (BSc Hons Botany and Agric. Botany); Univ. of Leeds (PhD Genetics). Vis. Prof., Dept of Forestry and Resource Management, Univ. of California, Berkeley, 1981–. Dir, CTF Training Ltd, 1982–; Chairman: Coed Cymru Ltd, 1983–; Bangor Centre for Envtl Strategy, 1986–; Bardsey Island Trust, 1987–; former Chm. and Mem., conservation and envtl bodies, nat. and internat.; Trustee, Caernarvon Harbour Trust, 1989–. Member: Genetical Soc.; British Ecological Soc. Member: Ct of Govs and Council: UC, Bangor, 1981–; Nat. Museum of Wales, 1981–; Gov., Normal Coll., Bangor, 1990–. Member: Gorsedd of Bards, Royal Nat. Eisteddfod; Hon. Soc. of Cymmrodorion. FRSA. JP Bangor, 1978. *Publications:* Cynefin y Cymro, 1989; numerous contribs to sci. and educn jls. *Recreation:* sailing. *Address:* Graig Lwyd, 134 Ffordd Penrhos, Bangor, Gwynedd LL57 2BX. *T:* Bangor (0248) 370401.

PRITCHETT, Sir Victor (Sawdon), Kt 1975; CBE 1968; CLit 1988; author and critic; *b* 16 Dec. 1900; *s* of Sawdon Pritchett and Beatrice Martin; *m* Dorothy, *d* of Richard Samuel Roberts, Welshpool, Montgomeryshire; one *s* one *d. Educ:* Alleyn's School. Christian Gauss Lectr, Princeton Univ., 1953; Beckman Prof., Univ. California, Berkeley, 1962; Writer-in-Residence, Smith Coll., Mass, 1966; Vanderbilt Univ., Tenn., 1981; Visiting Professor: Brandeis Univ., Mass; Columbia Univ.; Clark Lectr, 1969. Foreign Member: Amer. Acad. and Inst., 1971; Amer. Acad. Arts and Sciences, 1971. Pres., Internat. PEN, 1974–76; Soc. of Authors, 1977–. Hon. LittD Leeds, 1972; Hon. DLitt: Columbia, 1978; Sussex, 1980; Harvard, 1985. *Publications:* Marching Spain, 1928, repr. 1988; Clare Drummer, 1929; The Spanish Virgin, 1930; Shirley Sanz, 1932; Nothing Like Leather, 1935; Dead Man Leading, 1937; You Make Your Own Life, 1938; In My Good Books, 1942; It May Never Happen, 1946; The Living Novel, 1946; Why Do I Write?, 1948; Mr Beluncle, 1951; Books in General, 1953; The Spanish Temper, 1954; Collected Stories, 1956; When My Girl Comes Home, 1961; London Perceived, 1962; The Key to My Heart, 1963; Foreign Faces, 1964; New York Proclaimed, 1965; The Working Novelist, 1965; Dublin: A Portrait, 1967; A Cab at the Door (autobiog.), 1968 (RSL Award); Blind Love, 1969; George Meredith and English Comedy, 1970; Midnight Oil (autobiog.), 1971; Balzac, 1973; The Camberwell Beauty, 1974; The Gentle Barbarian, 1977; Selected Stories, 1978; The Myth Makers, 1979; On the Edge of the Cliff, 1980; The Tale Bearers, 1980; (ed) The Oxford Book of Short Stories, 1981; (with Reynolds Stone) The Turn of the Years, 1982; Collected Stories, 1982; More Collected Stories, 1983; The Other Side of a Frontier, 1984; Man of Letters, 1985; Chekhov, 1988; A Careless Widow and Other Stories, 1989; At Home and Abroad, 1990; The Complete Short Stories, 1990; Lasting Impressions, 1990. *Address:* 12 Regent's Park Terrace, NW1. *Clubs:* Savile, Beefsteak.

PRITTIE, family name of **Baron Dunalley.**

PROBERT, David Henry, FCIS, FCMA, FCCA; Chairman, W. Canning plc, since 1986 (Director, 1976; Chief Executive, 1979–86); Chairman, Crown Agents for Oversea Governments and Administrations, since 1990 (Deputy Chairman, 1985–90; Crown Agent since 1981); Crown Agent for Holdings and Realisation Board, since 1981; *b* 11 April 1938; *s* of William David Thomas Probert and Doris Mabel Probert; *m* 1968, Sandra Mary Prince; one *s* one *d. Educ:* Bromsgrove High School. Director: BSA Ltd, 1971–73; Mills and Allen International Ltd, 1974–76; HB Electronics plc, 1977–86; British Hallmarking Council, 1983–91; Linread Public Limited Company, 1983–90; ASD plc, 1985–90; Sandvik Ltd, 1985–90; Rockwool Ltd, 1988–90; Private Patients Plan Ltd, 1988–; Richard Burbridge Ltd, 1990–. CBIM. *Recreations:* theatre, music, sport. *Address:* 4 Blakes Field Drive, Barnt Green, Worcs B45 8JT. *Clubs:* Royal Automobile, City Livery, Lord's Taverners.

PROBERT, (William) Ronald; Managing Director, Gas Supply and Strategy, since 1989, Member of the Board, since 1985, Group Executive Member, since 1989, British Gas plc (formerly British Gas Corporation); *b* 11 Aug. 1934; *s* of William and Florence Probert; *m* 1957, Jean (*née* Howard); three *s. Educ:* Grammar Sch., Ashton-under-Lyne; Univ. of Leeds (BA). FIGasE; CBIM. Entered gas industry, 1957; various marketing appts in E Midlands Gas Bd, 1957–67; Conversion Manager, 1967, Service Manager, 1971, Marketing Dir, 1973, E Midlands Gas Bd; Asst Dir of Marketing, 1975, Dir of Sales, 1977, British Gas Corp.; Man. Dir Marketing, British Gas, 1982–89. *Recreations:* narrowboats, music, winemaking. *Address:* British Gas plc, Rivermill House, 152 Grosvenor Road, SW1V 3JL. *T:* 071–821 1444.

PROBINE, Dr Mervyn Charles, CB 1986; FRSNZ; FInstP; FNZIM; company director and consultant, since 1986; *b* 30 April 1924; *s* of Frederick Charles and Ann Kathleen Probine; *m* 1949, Marjorie Walker; one *s* one *d. Educ:* Univ. of Auckland (BSc); Victoria Univ. of Wellington (MSc); Univ. of Leeds (PhD). Physicist, DSIR, 1946–67; Dir, Physics and Engineering Lab., 1967–77; Asst Dir-Gen., DSIR, 1977–79; State Services Commission: Comr, 1979–80; Dep. Chm., 1980–81; Chm., 1981–86, retired. *Publications:* numerous scientific research papers and papers on application of science in industry. *Recreations:* bridge, sailing, angling. *Address:* 24 Bloomfield Terrace, Lower Hutt, New Zealand. *T:* (04) 663492. *Club:* Wellington (Wellington, NZ).

PROBY, Sir Peter, 2nd Bt *cr* 1952; FRICS; Lord-Lieutenant of Cambridgeshire, 1981–85; *b* 4 Dec. 1911; *s* of Sir Richard George Proby, 1st Bt, MC, and Betty Monica (*d* 1967), *d* of A. H. Hallam Murray; *S* father, 1979; *m* 1944, Blanche Harrison, *o d* of Col Henry Harrison Cripps, DSO; one *s* three *d* (and one *s* decd). *Educ:* Eton; Trinity College, Oxford. BA 1934. Served War of 1939–45, Captain, Irish Guards. Bursar of Eton College, 1953–71. *Heir: s* William Henry Proby, MA, FCA [*b* 13 June 1949; *m* 1974, Meredyth Anne Brentnall; four *d. Educ:* Eton; Lincoln Coll., Oxford (MA)]. *Address:* Pottle Green, Elton, Peterborough PE8 6SG. *T:* Oundle (0832) 280434.

PROBYN, Air Commodore Harold Melsome, CB 1944; CBE 1943; DSO 1917; *b* 8 Dec. 1891; *s* of late William Probyn; *m* 1920, Marjory (*d* 1961), *d* of late Francis Evance Savory. Served European War, 1914–17 (despatches, DSO); commanded: 208 (AC) Squadron, Egypt; No 2 (AC), Squadron, Manston; 25 (Fighter) Squadron at Hawkinge; RAF School of Photography, 1932; No 22 Group, RAF, 1932–34; Senior Personnel Staff Officer, Middle East, Cairo, 1934–35; Senior Engineer Staff Officer, Middle East, Cairo, 1935–37; No 12 (Fighter) Group Royal Air Force, Hucknall, Notts, 1937; served War of 1939–45 (despatches); SASO, No 11 Fighter Group, Uxbridge, 1939–40; commanded RAF Station, Cranwell, 1940–44; retired, 1944. *Recreations:* flying, fishing, golf. *Club:* Naval and Military.

PROCKTOR, Patrick, RWS 1981; RE 1991; painter since 1962; *b* 12 March 1936; 2nd *s* of Eric Christopher Procktor and Barbara Winifred (*née* Hopkins); *m* 1973, Kirsten Bo (*née* Andersen) (*d* 1984); one *s. Educ:* Highgate; Slade Sch. (Diploma). Many one-man exhibns, Redfern Gallery, from 1963. Designed windows for AIDS Recreation Centre, St Stephen's Hosp., Fulham, 1988. Retrospective tour, England and Wales, 1990. *Publications:* One Window in Venice, 1974; Coleridge's Rime of the Ancient Mariner (new illustrated edn), 1976; A Chinese Journey (aquatint landscapes), 1980; (illustrated) Sailing through China, by Paul Theroux, 1983; Patrick Procktor Prints 1959–85 (catalogue raisonné), 1985; A Shropshire Lad, by A. E. Housman (new illustrated edn), 1986; *relevant publication:* Patrick Procktor (monograph by Patrick Kinmonth), 1985. *Recreation:* Russian ballet. *Address:* 26 Manchester Street, W1M 5PG. *T:* 071–486 1763. *Club:* Garrick.

PROCTER, Norma; Contralto Singer; *b* Cleethorpes, Lincolnshire, 1928. Studied under Roy Henderson and Alec Redshaw. Made first London appearance at Southwark Cathedral; debut at Covent Garden, in Gluck's Orpheus, 1961. Has sung at major British music and European festivals. Numerous concerts and recitals throughout Europe; frequent broadcasts in Britain, Holland and Germany; has made many recordings. Hon. RAM 1974. *Address:* 194 Clee Road, Grimsby, Lincolnshire.

PROCTER, Robert John Dudley; Chief Executive, Lincolnshire County Council, since 1983; *b* 19 Oct. 1935; *s* of Luther Donald Procter and Edith Muriel Procter; *m* 1962, Adrienne Allen; one *s* one *d. Educ:* Cheltenham Grammar School. Admitted Solicitor, 1961. Articled Clerk, Glos CC, 1956–61; Assistant Solicitor: Bath City, 1961–63; Cumberland CC, 1963–65; Lindsey County Council: Sen. Asst Solicitor, 1965–69; Asst Clerk, 1969–71; Dep. Clerk, Kesteven CC, 1971–73; Dir of Personnel, 1973–77, Dir of Admin, 1977–83, Lincolnshire CC. *Recreations:* horse racing, swimming, keyboard playing, freemasonry. *Address:* Pas Seul, The Paddock, Sudbrooke, Lincoln LN2 2QS. *T:* Lincoln (0522) 750313.

PROCTER, Sidney, CBE 1986; FCIB; Commissioner, Building Societies Commission, since 1986; company director; *b* 10 March 1925; *s* of Robert and Georgina Margaret Procter; *m* 1952, Isabel (*née* Simmons); one *d. Educ:* Ormskirk Grammar School. Served RAF, 1943–47. Entered former Williams Deacon's Bank, 1941; Asst General Manager, 1969; Dep. Dir, Williams & Glyn's Bank, 1970; Divl Dir, 1975; Exec. Dir, 1976–85; Asst Chief Executive, 1976; Dep. Chief Executive, 1977; Chief Exec., 1978–82; Dep. Gp Man. Dir, Royal Bank of Scotland Gp, 1979–82; Gp Chief Exec., 1982–85; Vice Chm., 1986; Director: Royal Bank of Scotland, 1978–86 (Vice Chm., 1986); Provincial Insurance Co., 1985–86; Dep. Chm., Provincial Group, 1991– (Dir, 1986–); Chm., Exeter Bank, 1991–; Adviser to Governor, Bank of England, 1985–87. Chm., Exeter Trust, 1986– (Dir, 1985–). *Address:* The Piece House, Bourton-on-the-Water, Glos GL54 2AZ. *T:* Cotswold (0451) 20425.

PROCTOR, Anthony James; His Honour Judge Proctor; a Circuit Judge, since 1988; *b* 18 Sept. 1931; *s* of James Proctor and Savina Maud (*née* Horsfield); *m* 1964, Patricia Mary Bryan; one *d. Educ:* Mexborough Grammar Sch., Yorkshire; St Catharine's Coll., Cambridge (MA, LLM). Articled to Sir Bernard Kenyon, County Hall, Wakefield, 1955–58; admitted Solicitor 1958. Sen. Prosecuting Solicitor, Sheffield Corp., 1959–64; Partner, Broomhead & Neals, Solicitors, Sheffield, 1964–74; Dist Registrar and County Court Registrar, Barrow in Furness, Lancaster, Preston, 1974–88; a Recorder, 1985. Pres., Assoc. of Dist and Court Registrars, 1985–86. *Recreations:* fell walking, travel, genealogy. *Address:* Manchester Crown Court, Crown Square, Manchester M3 3FL. *T:* 061–832 8393.

PROCTOR, David Victor; Research Associate and Consultant, National Maritime Museum, since 1989; *b* 1 March 1930; *s* of Comdr Victor William Lake Proctor, RN and Marjorie Proctor (*née* Weeks); *m* 1st, 1959, Margaret Graham (marr. diss. 1984); three *s*; 2nd, 1984, Marion Clara Calver; one step *s* five step *d. Educ:* Dauntsey's Sch.; Clare Coll., Cambridge (MA; DipEd 1955); Imperial Coll., London (DIC). Shipbroking, 1953–54; Teacher: Lycée de Brest, France, 1955–56; Clifton Coll., Bristol, 1956–62; National Maritime Museum: Educn Officer, 1962–72; Sec. and Educn Officer, 1972–74; Head of Educn and Res. Facilities, 1974–76; Head of Printed Books and Manuscripts Dept, 1976–87; Head of Printed, Manuscript and Technical Records Dept, 1987–89. Internat. Congress of Maritime Museums: Sec. Gen., 1972–78; Mem. Exec. Council, 1978–81; Vice-Pres., 1981–84; Trustee, 1984–. Chm., Gp for Educnl Services in Museums, 1971–75; Mem., Adv. Council, Internat. Council of Museums, 1983–; Vice Pres., Internat. Commn for Maritime Hist., 1990– (Sec. Gen., 1980–85; Mem., Exec. Council, 1985–90); Trustee: Madeleine Mainstone Trust, 1980–; Jane Austen Centre. Fellow, Huguenot Soc. of London, 1986–. *Publications:* Child of War, 1972; contribs to jls on museums, museum educn and hist. of science. *Recreations:* sailing, piano, walking, travel, DIY. *Address:* 6 Vange Mews, Rochester, Kent ME1 1RA. *T:* Medway (0634) 849592. *Clubs:* Royal Cruising; Rochester Cruising.

PROCTOR, Harvey; *see* Proctor, K. H.

PROCTOR, Ian Douglas Ben, RDI 1969; FCSD (FSIAD 1969); FRSA 1972; Chairman, Ian Proctor Metal Masts Ltd, 1959–76 and 1981–86 (Director, 1959–86); freelance industrial designer since 1950; *b* 12 July 1918; *s* of Douglas McIntyre Proctor and Mary Albina Louise Proctor (*née* Tredwen); *m* 1943, Elizabeth Anne Gifford Lywood, *d* of Air Vice-Marshal O. G. Lywood, CB, CBE; three *s* one *d. Educ:* Gresham's Sch., Holt; London University. RAFVR (Flying Officer), 1942–46. Man. Dir, Gosport Yacht Co., 1947–48; Joint Editor Yachtsman Magazine, 1948–50; Daily Telegraph Yachting Correspondent, 1950–64. Yachtsman of the Year, 1965; Council of Industrial Design Award, 1967; Design Council Awards, 1977, 1980. *Publications:* Racing Dinghy Handling, 1948; Racing Dinghy Maintenance, 1949; Sailing: Wind and Current, 1950; Boats for Sailing, 1968; Sailing Strategy, 1977. *Recreation:* sailing. *Address:* Ferry House, Duncannon, Stoke Gabriel, near Totnes, Devon TQ9 6QY. *Club:* Stoke Gabriel Boating Assoc.

PROCTOR, Ven. Jesse Heighton, MA (London); Archdeacon of Warwick, 1958–74, now Emeritus; Vicar of Sherbourne, Warwick, 1958–69; *b* 26 May 1908; *s* of Thomas and Sophia Proctor, Melton Mowbray; *m* 1938, Helena Mary Wood, *d* of John Thomas and Jessie Wood, Melton Mowbray; one *s* two *d. Educ:* County Grammar Sch. of King Edward VII, Melton Mowbray; Coll. of St Mark and St John, Chelsea, Univ. of London; St Andrew's Theological Training House, Whittlesford. Asst Master, Winterbourne Sch., Croydon, 1929–32; Sen. History Master, Melton Mowbray Gram. Sch., 1932–35; Deacon 1935, Priest 1936; Chap. and Tutor, St Andrew's, Whittlesford, 1935–38; Curate, St Philip's, Leicester, 1938–39; Vicar, Glen Parva and South Wigston, and Chap., Glen Parva Barracks, Leicester, 1939–46; Precentor of Coventry Cath., 1946–58; Hon. Canon of Coventry, 1947; Chaplain, Gulson Hosp., 1953–58; Sen. Examining Chap. to Bishop of Coventry, 1947–65; Canon Theologian of Coventry, 1954–59; Vice-Pres. CMS. Governor: Univ. of Warwick, 1966–68; City of Coventry Coll. of Educn, 1966–70. Barnabas of Coventry Evening Telegraph, 1955–75. *Publication:* contrib. to Neville Gorton (SPCK), 1957. *Recreations:* study of theology and history; the countryside. *Address:* Dilkusha, 22 Bank Crescent, Ledbury, Herefordshire HR8 1AA. *T:* Ledbury (0531) 2241.

PROCTOR, (Keith) Harvey; Director, Proctor's Shirts and Ties; Vice-President, Richmond Chamber of Commerce; *b* 16 Jan. 1947; *s* of Albert Proctor and Hilda Tegerdine. *Educ:* High School for Boys, Scarborough; Univ. of York. BA History Hons, 1969. Asst Director, Monday Club, 1969–71; Research Officer, Conservative 1970s Parliamentary Gp, 1971–72; Exec. Director, Parliamentary Digest Ltd, 1972–74; British Paper & Board Industry Federation: Asst Sec., 1974–78; Secretary, 1978–79; Consultant, 1979. MP (C): Basildon, 1979–83; Billericay, 1983–87. Mem., Exec. Council, Monday Club, 1983–87. *Publication:* Billericay in Old Picture Postcards, 1985. *Recreations:* tennis, collecting British contemporary art. *Address:* 11 Brewers Lane, Richmond Upon Thames, Surrey TW9 1HH. *T:* 081–332 1099.

PROCTOR, Sir Roderick (Consett), Kt 1978; MBE 1946; FCA; company director; *b* 28 July 1914; *s* of Frederick William Proctor and Ethel May (*née* Christmas); *m* 1st, 1943, Kathleen Mary (*née* Murphy; *d* 1978); four *s*; 2nd, 1980, Janice Marlene (*née* Pryor). *Educ:* Hale Sch., Perth, WA; Melbourne C of E Grammar Sch., Vic. FCA 1958. Served War, 1939–45. Commenced career as chartered accountant, 1931, as Jun. Clerk with R. Goyne Miller, Perth; joined Clarke & Son, Chartered Accountants, Brisbane, Qld, 1937; Partner, 1950, Sen. Partner, 1966 (firm merged with Aust. national firm, Hungerfords, 1960); retd as Partner, 1976. *Recreations:* surfing, boating. *Address:* 18 Captains Court, Raby Bay, Qld 4163, Australia. *Clubs:* Queensland, Brisbane, United Service (Brisbane); Brisbane Polo; Southport Yacht, Royal Queensland Yacht.

PROCTOR-BEAUCHAMP, Sir Christopher Radstock P.; *see* Beauchamp.

PROFUMO, John Dennis, CBE 1975 (OBE (mil.) 1944); 5th Baron of the former United Kingdom of Italy; *b* 30 Jan. 1915; *e s* of late Baron Albert Profumo, KC; *m* 1954, Valerie Hobson, *qv*; one *s. Educ:* Harrow; Brasenose College, Oxford. 1st Northamptonshire Yeomanry, 1939 (despatches); Brigadier, Chief of Staff UK Mission in Japan, 1945. MP (C) Kettering Division, Northamptonshire, 1940–45; MP (C) Stratford-on-Avon Division of Warwickshire, 1950–63; Parliamentary Secretary, Ministry of Transport and Civil Aviation, Nov. 1952–Jan. 1957; Parliamentary Under-Secretary of State for the Colonies, 1957–58; Parliamentary Under-Sec. of State, Foreign Affairs, Nov. 1958–Jan. 1959; Minister of State for Foreign Affairs, 1959–60; Secretary of State for War, July 1960–June 1963. Dir, Provident Life Assoc. of London, 1975– (Dep. Chm., 1978–82). Mem., Bd of Visitors, HM Prison, Grendon, 1968–75. Chm., Toynbee Hall, 1982–85, Pres. 1985–. *Recreations:* fishing, gardening, DIY. *Heir: s* David Profumo [*b* 30 Oct. 1955; *m* 1980, Helen, *o d* of Alasdair Fraser; two *s*]. *Club:* Boodle's.

PROKHOROV, Prof. Alexander Mikhailovich; Hero of Socialist Labour, 1969, 1986; Order of Lenin (five-fold); Physicist; Director, General Physics Institute, Academy of Sciences of the USSR, Moscow, since 1983; Editor-in-Chief, Bolshaya Sovetskaya Encyclopedia Publishing House, since 1970; *b* Atherton, Australia, 11 July 1916; *s* of Mikhail Prokhorov; *m* 1941, Galina Alexeyevna (*née* Shelepina); one *s. Educ:* Leningrad State University; Lebedev Inst. of Physics. Corresp. Mem., Academy of Sciences of the USSR (Department of General Physics and Astronomy), 1960–66, Full Mem., 1966–, Mem. Presidial Body, 1970, Academician-Secretary, 1973–. Chm., Nat. Commn of Soviet Physicists, 1973–. Professor, Moscow University, 1958–. Hon. Professor: Delhi Univ.; Bucharest Univ., 1971; Cluz Univ., 1977; Praha Politechnical Inst., 1980. Member: European Phys. Soc., 1977; European Acad. of Scis, Art and Literature, 1986; Hon. Member: Amer. Acad. of Arts and Sciences, 1972; Acad. of Sciences of Hungary, 1976; Acad. of Sciences, German Democratic Republic, 1977; Acad. of Scis of Czechoslavakia, 1982; Acad. of Scis Leopoldina, 1984. Member, Communist Party of the Soviet Union, 1950–. Awarded Lenin Prize, 1959; Nobel Prize for Physics (jointly with Prof. N. G. Basov and Prof. C. H. Townes), 1964. *Publications:* contributions on non-linear oscillations, radiospectroscopy and quantum radio-physics. *Address:* General Physics Institute, Academy of Sciences of the USSR, Vavilov Street 38, 117942, GSP-1 Moscow, USSR.

PROKHOROVA, Violetta; *see* Elvin, V.

PROOM, Major William Arthur, TD 1953; *b* 18 Dec. 1916; *s* of Arthur Henry Proom and Nesta Proom; *m* 1941, Nellie Lister; one *s* one *d. Educ:* Richmond Sch., Yorks; Keighley Technical Coll. Commnd TA, 1/6 Bn Duke of Wellington's Regt, 1938; served War: Iceland, 1940–42; REME/IEME, India and Burma, 1943–46; Major, retd. Mayor of Keighley, 1973; Member: W Yorks Metropolitan CC, 1974–81 (Chm., 1979–80); City of Bradford Metrop. Dist Council, 1975–79. Chm., NE Gas Consumers' Council, 1973–77. *Recreations:* gardening, reading. *Address:* 15 The Hawthorns, Sutton-in-Craven, Keighley, W Yorks BD20 8BP.

PROOPS, Mrs Marjorie, OBE 1969; journalist; *d* of Alfred and Martha Rayle; *m* 1935; one *s. Educ:* Dalston Secondary Sch. Daily Mirror, 1939–45; Daily Herald, 1945–54; Daily Mirror, 1954–. Broadcaster, Television, 1960–. Member: Royal Commn on Gambling, 1976–78; Council for One Parent Families. Woman Journalist of the Year, 1969. *Publications:* Pride, Prejudice & Proops, 1975; Dear Marje, 1976. *Address:* 9 Sherwood Close, SW13.

PROPHET, Prof. Arthur Shelley, CBE 1980; DDS; DpBact; FDSRCS; FFDRCSI; Professor of Dental Surgery, University of London, 1956–83, now Emeritus; *b* 11 Jan. 1918; *s* of Eric Prophet and Mabel Wightman; *m* 1942, Vivienne Mary Bell; two *s. Educ:*

Sedbergh School; University of Manchester. BDS Hons (Preston Prize and Medal), 1940; Diploma in Bacteriology (Manchester), 1948; DDS (Manchester) 1950; FDSRCS 1958; FFDRCS Ireland, 1964. RNVR (Dental Branch), 1941–46; Nuffield Dental Fellow, 1946–48; Lecturer in Dental Bacteriology, University of Manchester, 1948–54; Lecturer in Dental Surgery, QUB, 1954–56; Dir of Dental Studies, 1956–74, Dean of Dental Studies, 1974–77, UCH Dental Sch.; Dean, UCH Medical Sch., 1977–80; Dean, 1980–82, Vice-Dean, 1982–83, Faculty of Clinical Scis, UCL. Lectures: Charles Tomes, RCS, 1977; Wilkinson, Univ. of Manchester, 1978; Elwood, QUB, 1979; Shefford, UCL, 1983. Rep. of University of London on Gen. Dental Council, 1964–84. Elected Mem. Bd, Faculty of Dental Surgery, RCS, 1964–80 (Vice-Dean, 1972–73); Member: Cttee of Management, Inst. of Dental Surgery, 1963–83; Dental Sub-Cttee, UGC, 1968–78; Bd of Governors, UCH, 1957–74; Camden and Islington AHA(T), 1974–82; Bloomsbury HA, 1982–83. WHO Consultant, 1966; Consultant Dental Advr, DHSS, 1977–83. DSc *hc* Malta, 1987. *Publications:* contrib. to medical and dental journals. *Recreations:* golf, gardening. *Address:* Little Orchard, Minstead, Lyndhurst, Hants SO43 7FW. *T:* Southampton (0703) 814003.

PROPHET, John; Regional Chairman of Industrial Tribunals, Yorkshire and Humberside, since 1988; *b* 19 Nov. 1931; *s* of Benjamin and Elsie Prophet; *m* 1961, Pauline Newby; three *d*. *Educ:* Trinity Coll., Cambridge (MA). Called to the Bar, Lincoln's Inn, 1956; Shell International, 1956–60; private practice at the Bar, 1960–; Sen. Lectr, Law Faculty, Leeds Univ., 1968–76; full-time Chm. of Industrial Tribunals, 1976–88. Consultant, Nat. Assoc. of Local Councils, 1968–89. *Publications:* The Structure of Government, 1968; The Parish Councillor's Guide, 1974, 15th edn 1988; Fair Rents, 1976. *Recreations:* tennis, chess, gardening.

PROPHIT, Prof. Penny Pauline; Professor and Head of Department of Nursing Studies, University of Edinburgh, since 1983; *b* 7 Feb. 1939; *d* of C. Alston Prophit and Hortense Callahan. *Educ:* Marillac Coll., St Louis Univ., USA (BSN); Catholic Univ. of America (MSN, BNSc, PhD). Asst Prof., Catholic Univ. of America, 1975; Associate Professor: Univ. of Southern Mississippi, 1975; Louisiana State Univ. Med. Center, 1975; Cons., WHO, Europ. Office, Copenhagen, 1977–; Prof., Katholieke Univ., Leuven, Belgium, 1977. Mental Welfare Comr for Scotland, 1985–; Mem., UK Central Council for Nursing, Midwifery and Health Visiting, 1988–. Delta Epsilon Sigma, Nat. Catholic Scholastic Honor Soc., 1966; Sigma Theta Tau, Internat. Nursing Scholastic Honor Soc., 1970; Sigma Epsilon Phi, Catholic Univ. of Amer. Honor Soc., 1975. *Publications:* Understanding/Responding, 1982; res. articles on nursing care of the elderly, stress in nursing, interdisciplinary collaboration, etc. *Recreations:* jogging, reading and writing poetry and short stories, playing piano and listening to music of all kinds. *Address:* 2 Garvald Grange Cottages, Haddington, East Lothian EH41 4LL. *T:* Garvald (062083) 222.

PROPPER, Arthur, CMG 1965; MBE 1945; *b* 3 Aug. 1910; 2nd *s* of late I. Propper; *m* 1941, Erica Mayer; one *d*. *Educ:* Owen's Sch.; Peterhouse, Cambridge (schol.). 1st class, Hist. Tripos, Pt 2. With W. S. Crawford Ltd (Advertising Agents), 1933–38, and the J. Walter Thompson Co. Ltd, 1939; Min. of Economic Warfare, 1940; transf. to Min. of Food, 1946 (subseq. to Min. of Agric., Fisheries and Food); established in Home Civil Service, 1949; Asst Sec., 1952; Mem. UK Delegn at Common Market negotiations, with rank of Under-Sec., 1962–63; seconded to Foreign Office, 1963; Counsellor (Agric.), UK Delegn to the European Communities, Brussels, and HM Embassy, Bonn, 1963–64; Under-Sec., Min. of Agriculture, Fisheries and Food, 1964–70; Common Mkt Advr, Unigate Ltd, 1970–73; Sec., Food Panel, Price Commn, 1973–76. *Recreations:* the theatre, music, buying books, visiting Scotland. *Address:* 3 Hill House, Stanmore Hill, Stanmore, Mddx HA7 3EW. *T:* 081–954 1242. *Club:* United Oxford & Cambridge University.

PROSSER, Hon. Lord; William David Prosser; a Senator of the College of Justice in Scotland and Lord of Session, since 1986; *b* 23 Nov. 1934; *yr s* of David G. Prosser, MC, WS, Edinburgh; *m* 1964, Vanessa, *er d* of Sir William O'Brien Lindsay, KBE, Nairobi; two *s* two *d*. *Educ:* Edinburgh Academy; Corpus Christi Coll., Oxford (MA); Edinburgh Univ. (LLB). Advocate, 1962; QC (Scotland) 1974; Standing Junior Counsel in Scotland, Board of Inland Revenue, 1969–74; Advocate-Depute, 1978–79; Vice-Dean, Faculty of Advocates, 1979–83; Dean of Faculty, 1983–86. Mem., Scottish Cttee, Council on Tribunals, 1977–84. Chm., Royal Fine Art Commn for Scotland, 1990–. Chairman: Royal Lyceum Theatre Co., 1987–; Scottish Historic Buildings Trust, 1988–. *Address:* 7 Randolph Crescent, Edinburgh EH3 7TH. *T:* 031–225 2709; Netherfoodie, Dairsie, Fife. *T:* Balmullo (0334) 870438. *Clubs:* New, Scottish Arts (Edinburgh).

PROSSER, (Elvet) John; QC 1978; **His Honour Judge Prosser;** a Circuit Judge, since 1988; *b* 10 July 1932; *s* of David and Hannah Prosser; *m* 1957, Mary Louise Cowdry; two *d*. *Educ:* Pontypridd Grammar Sch.; King's Coll., London Univ. LLB. Flt Lt, RAF, 1957–59. Called to the Bar, Gray's Inn, 1956, Bencher, 1986; Mem., Senate of Inns of Court and the Bar, 1980–87; a Recorder, 1972–88; Leader, Wales and Chester Circuit, 1984–87. Part-time Chm. of Industrial Tribunals, 1975–81. An Asst Boundary Comr for Wales, 1977–. *Recreations:* watching cricket and television. *Address:* 78 Marsham Court, Westminster, SW1. *T:* 071–834 9779; Hillcroft, Mill Road, Lisvane, Cardiff CF4 5XJ. *T:* Cardiff (0222) 752380. *Clubs:* East India, Devonshire, Sports and Public Schools; Cardiff and County (Cardiff).

PROSSER, Ian Maurice Gray, FCA; Chairman and Chief Executive, Bass PLC, since 1987 (Vice Chairman, 1982–87; Group Managing Director, 1984–87); *b* 5 July 1943; *s* of Maurice and Freda Prosser; *m* 1964, Elizabeth Herman; two *d*. *Educ:* King Edward's School, Bath; Watford Grammar School; Birmingham Univ. (BComm). Coopers & Lybrand, 1964–69; Bass Charrington Ltd, later Bass PLC, 1969–; Financial Dir, 1978. Director: Boots Co., 1984–; Lloyds Bank, 1988–. Dir, Brewers' Soc., 1983–. *Recreations:* bridge, gardening. *Address:* Bass PLC, 66 Chiltern Street, W1M 1PR. *T:* 071–486 4440. *Club:* Royal Automobile.

PROSSER, Margaret Theresa; National Secretary, Transport and General Workers' Union, since 1984; *b* 22 Aug. 1937; *d* of Frederick James and Lillian (*née* Barry); *m* (marr. diss.); one *s* two *d*. *Educ:* St Philomena's Convent, Carshalton; North East London Polytechnic (Post Grad. Dip. in Advice and Inf. Studies, 1977). Associate Mem., Inst. of Legal Execs, 1982. Advice Centre Organiser, Southwark Community Develt Project, 1974–76; Advr, Southwark Law Project, 1976–83; Trade Union Official, 1983–. Mem., Equal Opportunities Commn, 1987–. *Recreations:* walking, gardening, reading. *Address:* 154 Moffat Road, Thornton Heath, Surrey CR4 8PX. *T:* 081–771 5487.

PROSSER, Raymond Frederick, CB 1973; MC 1942; *b* 12 Sept. 1919; *s* of Frederick Charles Prosser and Jane Prosser (*née* Lawless); *m* 1949, Fay Newmarch Holmes; two *s* three *d*. *Educ:* Wimbledon Coll.; The Queen's Coll., Oxford (1938–39 and 1946). Served Royal Artillery (Field), 1939–45 (MC, despatches): service in Egypt, Libya, India and Burma; Temp. Major. Asst Principal, Min. of Civil Aviation, 1947; Sec., Air Transport Advisory Council, 1952–57; Private Sec. to Minister of Transport and Civil Aviation, 1959, and to Minister of Aviation, 1959–61; Counsellor (Civil Aviation), HM Embassy, Washington, DC, 1965–68; Under-Sec., Marine Div., BoT, later DTI, 1968–72; Deputy Sec., Regional Industrial Organisation and Policy, DTI, later DoI, 1972–77; Principal Estabt and Finance Officer, Depts of Industry, Trade, and Prices and Consumer Protection, 1977–79, retired. Dir, European Investment Bank, 1973–77. Mem. (part-time), CAA, 1980–85. *Address:* Juniper House, Shalford Common, Shalford, Guildford, Surrey GU4 8DF. *T:* Guildford (0483) 66498.

PROSSER, William David; *see* Prosser, Hon. Lord.

PROTHEROE, Alan Hackford, CBE (mil.) 1991 (MBE (mil.) 1980); TD 1981; journalist, broadcaster, writer and media consultant; Managing Director, Services Sound and Vision Corporation, since 1988; *b* 10 Jan. 1934; *s* of Rev. B. P. Protheroe and R. C. M. Protheroe; *m* 1956, Anne Miller; two *s*. *Educ:* Maesteg Grammar Sch., Glamorgan. FBIM; MIPR. Nat. Service, 2nd Lieut The Welch Regt, 1954–56; Lt-Col, Royal Regt of Wales (TA), 1979–84; Col, 1984–90. Reporter, Glamorgan Gazette, 1951–53; BBC Wales: Reporter, 1957–59; Industrial Correspondent, 1959–64; Editor, News and Current Affairs, 1964–70; BBC TV News: Asst Editor, 1970–72; Dep. Editor, 1972–77; Editor, 1977–80; Asst Dir, BBC News and Current Affairs, 1980–82; Asst Dir Gen., BBC, 1982–87. During BBC career wrote, produced, directed and presented films and radio programmes, reported wars, and travelled widely; seconded to Greek Govt to assist in reorganisation of Greek TV, 1973. Mem., Steering Cttee, EBU News Gp, 1977–87; Director: Visnews Ltd, 1982–87; Defence Public Affairs Consultants Ltd, 1987–; Europac Gp Ltd, 1989–; Chm., CHALTEC. Mem. Council, RUSI, 1984–87; Association of British Editors: Founder Mem., 1984–; Dep. Chm., 1984–87; Chm., 1987. Dep. Chm., Eastern Wessex Reserve Forces Assoc., 1990–. St James Vice Pres. (Hon. Consultant), Royal British Legion. Hon. Col, TA Information Officers, 1991–. *Publications:* contribs to newspapers and specialist jls on industrial, media and defence affairs. *Recreations:* pistol and rifle shooting. *Address:* Amberleigh House, 60 Chapman Lane, Flackwell Heath, Bucks HP10 9BD. *T:* Bourne End (06285) 28492. *Club:* Savile.

PROUD, Air Cdre Harold John Granville Ellis, CBE 1946; *b* 23 Aug. 1906; *s* of late Ralph Henry Proud, Glasgow; *m* 1937, Jenefer Angela Margaret, *d* of late Lt-Col J. Bruce, OBE, 19th Lancers; two *d*. HAC (Inf.), 1924–26; commissioned RAF, pilot, 1926; Staff Coll., 1936; served in: Mediterranean (FAA), 1928; India, 1937 and 1942 (Inspector Gen. Indian Air Force, 1942–43; AOA Air HQ, 1943–45); Dir of Ground Def., Air Min., 1945–47; served in Singapore, 1949; AOC 67 (NI) Gp and Senior Air Force Officer N Ire., 1951–54; Provost Marshal and Chief of Air Force Police, 1954; retired 1956; in business, 1957–71; now domiciled in Switzerland; Mem. Council, British Residents Assoc. of Switzerland, 1973–77, Chm., 1974–75. *Address:* Appt 10, Les Libellules, 1837 Château d'Oex, Switzerland. *T:* (029) 46223. *Club:* Royal Air Force.

PROUD, Sir John (Seymour), Kt 1978; mining engineer; director and chairman of companies; *b* 9 Aug. 1907; *s* of William James Proud and Hannah Seymour; *m* 1964, Laurine, *d* of M. Ferran. *Educ:* Univ. of Sydney (Bachelor of Engrg, Mining and Metallurgy). CEng, FIMM, FIE(Aust), F(Aus)IMM. Chm., Newcastle Wallsend Coal Co., which merged with Peko Mines NL, 1960; Chm., Peko-Wallsend Investments Ltd, then Chm., Peko-Wallsend Ltd; retd from chair, 1978; Dir/Consultant, 1978–82. Chairman: Electrical Equipment Ltd (Group), 1978–82 (Dir, 1943–83); Oil Search Ltd, 1978–88 (Dir, 1974–); Oil Co. of Australia NL, 1979–83; Dir, CSR Ltd, 1974–79. Fellow of Senate, Univ. of Sydney, 1974–83. Chm. Trustees, Lizard Island Reef Res. Foundn, 1978–87; Trustee, Aust. Museum, 1971–77. Hon. DEng Sydney, 1984. *Recreations:* yachting, pastoral activity. *Address:* 9 Finlay Road, Turramurra, NSW 2074, Australia. *Clubs:* Union, Royal Sydney Yacht Squadron, Royal Prince Alfred Yacht, American (Sydney).

PROUDFOOT, Bruce; *see* Proudfoot, V. B.

PROUDFOOT, Bruce Falconer; Publicity Officer, Ulster Savings Committee, 1963–69; Editor, Northern Whig and Belfast Post, 1943–63; *b* 1903; 2nd *s* of G. A. Proudfoot, Edinburgh; *m* 1928, Cecilia, *er d* of V. T. T. Thompson, Newcastle on Tyne; twin *s*. *Educ:* Edinburgh Education Authority's Primary and Secondary Schools. Served with Edinburgh Evening Dispatch, Galloway Gazette (Newton-Stewart) and Newcastle Daily Chronicle before joining Northern Whig, 1925. *Address:* Westgate, Wardlaw Gardens, St Andrews, Fife KY16 9DW. *T:* St Andrews (0334) 73293.

See also V. B. Proudfoot.

PROUDFOOT, (George) Wilfred; owner, self-service stores; consultant in distribution; professional hypnotist and hypnotherapist, Master Practitioner of Neuro-Linguistic Programming; owner, Proudfoot School of Hypnosis and Hypnotherapy; *b* 19 December 1921; *m* 1950, Margaret Mary, *d* of Percy Clifford Jackson, Pontefract, Yorks; two *s* one *d*. *Educ:* Crook Council Sch.; Scarborough Coll. Served War of 1939–45, NCO Fitter in RAF, 1940–46. Served Scarborough Town Council, 1950–58 (Chm. Health Cttee, 1952–58). MP (C) Cleveland Division of Yorkshire, Oct. 1959–Sept. 1964; PPS to Minister of State, Board of Trade, Apr.-July 1962, to Minister of Housing and Local Govt and Minister for Welsh Affairs (Rt Hon. Sir Keith Joseph, Bt, MP), 1962–64; MP (C) Brighouse and Spenborough, 1970–Feb. 1974; Minister of State, Dept of Employment, 1970; contested (C) Brighouse and Spenborough, Oct. 1974. Man. Dir, Radio 270, 1965–. Chm., Scarborough Cons. Assoc., 1978–80; Chm., Cleveland European Constituency Cons. Assoc., 1979–. Professional hypnotist; face lifted by Dr John Williams, USA, 1978. Chm., British Council of Hypnotist Examiners, 1983–. *Publication:* The Two Factor Nation, or How to make the people rich, 1977. *Recreations:* reading, photography, caravanning, travel, walking, skiing, jogging. *Address:* 278 Scalby Road, Scarborough, North Yorkshire YO12 6EA. *T:* Scarborough (0723) 367027.

PROUDFOOT, Prof. (Vincent) Bruce, FSA 1963; FRSE 1979; FRSGS; Professor of Geography, University of St Andrews, since 1974; *b* 24 Sept. 1930; *s* of Bruce Falconer Proudfoot, *qv*; *m* 1961, Edwina Valmai Windram Field; two *s*. *Educ:* Royal Belfast Academical Instn; Queen's Univ., Belfast (BA, PhD). Research Officer, Nuffield Quaternary Research Unit, QUB, 1954–58; Lectr in Geography, QUB, 1958–59, Durham Univ., 1959–67; Tutor, 1960–63, Librarian, 1963–65, Hatfield Coll., Durham; Visiting Fellow, Univ. of Auckland, NZ, and Commonwealth Vis. Fellow, Australia, 1966; Associate Prof., 1967–70, Prof., 1970–74, Univ. of Alberta, Edmonton, Canada; Acting Chm., Dept of Geography, Univ. of Alberta, 1970–71; Co-ordinator, Socio-Economic Opportunity Studies, and Staff Consultant, Alberta Human Resources Research Council, 1971–72. Trustee, Nat. Mus. of Antiquities of Scotland, 1982–85. Chairman: Rural Geog. Study Gp, Inst. of British Geographers, 1980–84; Soc. for Landscape Studies, 1979–83. Vice-President: RSE, 1985–88 (Mem. Council, 1982–85 and 1990–91); Soc. of Antiquaries of Scotland, 1982–85; Pres., Section H (Anthrop. and Archaeol.), BAAS, 1985; Hon. Pres., Scottish Assoc. of Geography Teachers, 1982–84. Lectures: Lister, BAAS, 1964; Annual, Soc. for Landscape Studies, 1983; Estyn Evans, QUB, 1985. FRSGS 1991 (Hon. Editor, 1979–). *Publications:* The Downpatrick Gold Find, 1955; (with R. G. Ironside *et al*) Frontier Settlement Studies, 1974; (ed) Site, Environment and Economy, 1983; numerous papers in geographical, archaeological and soils jls. *Recreation:* gardening. *Address:* Westgate, Wardlaw Gardens, St Andrews, Scotland KY16 9DW. *T:* St Andrews (0334) 73293.

PROUDFOOT, Wilfred; *see* Proudfoot, G. W.

PROUT, Sir Christopher (James), Kt 1990; TD 1987; QC 1988; Member (C) Shropshire and Stafford, European Parliament, since 1979; Leader, European Democratic Group, since 1987; barrister-at-law; *b* 1 Jan. 1942; *s* of late Frank Yabsley Prout, MC and bar, and Doris Lucy Prout (*née* Osborne). *Educ:* Sevenoaks Sch.; Manchester Univ. (BA); The Queen's Coll., Oxford (Scholar; BPhil, DPhil). TA Officer (Major): OU OTC, 1966–74; 16/5 The Queen's Royal Lancers, 1974–82; 3rd Armoured Div., 1982–88. Called to the Bar, Middle Temple, 1972. English-Speaking Union Fellow, Columbia Univ., NYC, 1963–64; Staff Mem., IBRD (UN), Washington DC, 1966–69; Leverhulme Fellow and Lectr in Law, Sussex Univ., 1969–79. Dep. Whip, 1979–82, Chief Whip, 1983–87, EDG; Chairman: Parlt Cttee on Electoral Disputes, 1982–83; Parlt Cttee on Legal Affairs, 1987. Gen. Rapporteur, Fourteenth FIDE Congress, 1990. Grande Médaille de la Ville de Paris, 1988. *Publications:* Market Socialism in Yugoslavia, 1985; (contrib.) vols 51 and 52, Halsbury's Laws of England, 1986. *Recreations:* riding, sailing. *Address:* 2 Queen Anne's Gate, SW1H 9AA. *T:* 071–222 1720; 4 Breams Buildings, EC4A 1AQ. *T:* 071–353 5835. *Clubs:* Pratt's, Beefsteak, Royal Ocean Racing.

PROVAN, James Lyal Clark; Executive Director, Scottish Financial Enterprise, since 1990; European affairs consultant; farmer; Chairman: McIntosh Donald Ltd, since 1989; James McIntosh & Co. Ltd, since 1990; *b* 19 Dec. 1936; *s* of John Provan and Jean (*née* Clark); *m* 1960, Roweena Adele Lewis; twin *s* one *d*. *Educ:* Ardvreck Sch., Crieff; Oundle Sch., Northants; Royal Agricultural Coll., Cirencester. Member: Tayside Regional Council, 1978–82; Tay River Purification Bd, 1978–82. MEP (C) NE Scotland, 1979–89; Quaestor, 1987–89; Member: Agriculture and Fisheries Cttee, 1979–89 (EDG spokesman on agricl and fisheries affairs, 1982–87); Environment, Consumer Affairs and Public Health Cttee, 1979–89. Mem., AFRC, 1990–. Area President, Scottish NFU, 1965 and 1971; Manager, Scottish Farming News, 1966–68; Founder Vice-Chm., East of Scotland Grassland Soc. (Chm., 1973–75). Treasurer, Perth and E Perthshire Conservative Assoc., 1975–77; Member, Lord Lieutenant's Queen's Jubilee Appeal Cttee, 1977. *Publication:* The European Community: an ever closer union?, 1989. *Recreations:* country pursuits, sailing, flying, musical appreciation, travel. *Address:* Wallacetown, Bridge of Earn, Perth, Scotland PH2 8QA. *T:* Bridge of Earn (0738) 812243, *Fax:* Bridge of Earn (0738) 812944. *Clubs:* Farmers', East India; Royal Perth Golfing Society.

PROVAN, Marie; *see* Staunton, M.

PROWSE, Florence Irene; *see* Calvert, F. I.

PRUDE, Mrs Walter F.; *see* de Mille, Agnes George.

PRYCE, (George) Terry; Chairman: Solway Foods Ltd, 1990; Horticulture Research International (formerly British Society for Horticultural Research), since 1990; *b* 26 March 1934; *s* of Edwin Pryce and Hilda Florence (*née* Price); *m* 1957, Thurza Elizabeth Tatham; two *s* one *d*. *Educ:* Welshpool Grammar Sch.; National Coll. of Food Technol. MFC, FIFST, CBIM. Dir, various food cos in THF Gp, 1965–70; Asst Man. Dir, Dalgety (UK) Ltd, 1970–72; Man. Dir, Dalgety (UK) and Dir, DPIC, 1972–78; Man. Dir, 1978–81, Chief Exec., 1981–89, Dalgety PLC. Dir, H. P. Bulmer Holdings, 1984–. Council Member: AFRC, 1986–; UK Food and Drink Fedn, 1987–89; Mem. Adv. Bd, Inst. of Food Res., 1988. Chairman: Board for Food Sci. and Technol., Reading Univ., 1984; UK Food Assoc., 1986–88. *Recreations:* sport, esp. golf; reading. *Address:* 89 Brookmans Avenue, Brookmans Park, Hatfield, Herts AL9 7QG. *T:* Hatfield (0707) 42039. *Club:* Athenæum.

PRYCE, Rt. Rev. James Taylor; a Suffragan Bishop of Toronto (Area Bishop of York-Simcoe), since 1985; *b* 3 May 1936; *s* of James Pryce and Florence Jane (*née* Taylor); *m* 1962, Marie Louise Connor; two *s* one *d* (and one *s* decd). *Educ:* Bishop's Univ., Lennoxville, Quebec (BA, LST). Ordained Deacon, 1962, priest, 1963; Asst Curate, Church of the Ascension, Don Mills, 1962–65; Incumbent: St Thomas' Church, Brooklin, Ont, 1965–70; St Paul's, Lorne Park, 1970–75; Christ Church, Scarborough, 1975–81; St Leonard's, North Toronto, 1981–85. Hon. DD, Wycliffe Coll., 1986. *Address:* 8 Pinehurst Court, Aurora, Ontario L4G 6B2, Canada. *T:* 1–416–727–7863.

PRYCE, Jonathan; actor; *b* 1 June 1947. *Educ:* RADA. *Theatre includes:* The Comedians, Nottingham Old Vic, 1975, NY 1976 (Tony Award); title rôle, Hamlet, Royal Court, 1980 (Olivier Award); The Caretaker, Nat. Th., 1981; Accidental Death of an Anarchist, Broadway, 1984; The Seagull, Queen's, 1985; title rôle, Macbeth, RSC, 1986; Uncle Vanya, Vaudeville, 1988; Miss Saigon, Drury Lane, 1989 (Olivier Award and Variety Club Award, NY, 1991 (Tony Award for Best Actor in Musical); *television includes:* Roger Doesn't Live Here Anymore (series), 1981; Timon of Athens, 1981; Martin Luther, 1983; Praying Mantis, 1983; Whose Line Is It Anyway?, 1988–; The Man from the Pru, 1990; Selling Hitler, 1991; *films include:* Something wicked this way comes, 1982; The Ploughman's Lunch, 1983; Brazil, 1985; The Doctor and the Devils, 1986; Haunted Honeymoon, 1986; Jumpin' Jack Flash, 1987; Consuming Passions, 1988; The Adventures of Baron Munchausen, 1988; The Rachel Papers, 1989. *Address:* c/o James Sharkey Associates Ltd, 15 Golden Square, W1R 3AG; c/o J. Michael Bloom Associates, 233 Park Avenue South, Floor 10, New York, NY 10003, USA.

PRYCE, Maurice Henry Lecorney, FRS 1951; Professor of Physics, University of British Columbia, 1968–78, now Emeritus Professor; *b* 24 Jan. 1913; *e s* of William John Pryce and Hortense Lecorney; *m* 1939, Susanne Margarete Born (marr. diss., 1959); one *s* three *d*; *m* 1961, Freda Mary Kinsey. *Educ:* Royal Grammar Sch., Guildford; Trinity Coll., Cambridge. Commonwealth Fund Fellow at Princeton, NJ, USA, 1935–37; Fellow of Trinity Coll., Cambridge, and Faculty Asst Lecturer, University of Cambridge, 1937–39; Reader in Theoretical Physics, University of Liverpool, 1939–45. Engaged on Radar research with Admiralty Signal Establishment, 1941–44, and on Atomic Energy Research with National Research Council of Canada, Montreal, 1944–45. University Lecturer in Mathematics and Fellow of Trinity Coll., Cambridge, 1945–46; Wykeham Professor of Physics, University of Oxford, 1946–54; Henry Overton Wills Professor of Physics, University of Bristol, 1954–64; Prof. of Physics, University of Southern California, 1964–68. Visiting Professor: Princeton Univ., NJ, USA, 1950–51; Duke Univ., NC, USA, 1958; Univ. of Sussex, 1976–77. Mem., Technical Adv. Cttee to Atomic Energy of Canada Ltd on Nuclear Fuel Waste Management Program, 1979–. *Publications:* various on Theoretical Physics, in learned journals. *Recreations:* theoretical scientific research, reading, music. *Address:* 4754 West 6th Avenue, Vancouver, BC V6T 1C5, Canada; Physics Department, University of British Columbia, 6224 Agriculture Road, Vancouver, BC V6T 2A6, Canada. *Club:* Athenæum.

PRYCE, Prof. Roy; Director, Federal Trust for Education and Research, 1983–90, Senior Research Fellow, since 1990; *b* 4 Oct. 1928; *s* of Thomas and Madeleine Pryce; *m* 1954, Sheila Rose, *d* of Rt Hon. James Griffiths, CH; three *d*. *Educ:* Grammar Sch., Burton-on-Trent; Emmanuel Coll., Cambridge (MA, PhD). MA Oxon. Research Fellow: Emmanuel Coll., Cambridge, 1953–55; St Antony's Coll., Oxford, 1955–57; Head of London Information Office of High Authority of European Coal and Steel Community, 1957–60; Head of London Inf. Office, Jt Inf. Service of European Communities, 1960–64; Rockefeller Foundn Res. Fellow, 1964–65; Dir, Centre for Contemp. European Studies, Univ. of Sussex, 1965–73; Directorate General for Information, Commission of the European Communities: Dir, 1973–78; Sen. Advr for Direct Elections, 1978–79; Chief Advr for Programming, 1979–81. Vis. Professorial Fellow, Centre for Contemporary European Studies, Univ. of Sussex, 1973–81; Vis. Professor: Coll. of Europe, Bruges, 1965–72; Eur. Univ. Inst., Florence, 1981–83; Eur. Inst. for Public Admin, Maastricht, 1983–88. *Publications:* The Italian Local Elections 1956, 1957; The Political Future of the European Community, 1962; (with John Pinder) Europe After de Gaulle, 1969, German and Ital. edns 1970; The Politics of the European Community, 1973; (ed) The Dynamics of European Union, 1987; contrib. Encyl. Brit., Jl Common Market Studies, etc. *Recreations:* gardening, collecting water colours and prints.

PRYCE, Terry; *see* Pryce, G. T.

PRYCE-JONES, Alan Payan, TD; book critic, author and journalist; *b* 18 Nov. 1908; *s* of late Colonel Henry Morris Pryce-Jones, CB; *m* 1934, Thérèse (*d* 1953), *d* of late Baron Fould-Springer and of Mrs Frank Wooster, Paris; one *s*; *m* 1968, Mrs Mary Jean Kempner Thorne (*d* 1969), *d* of late Daniel Kempner. *Educ:* Eton; Magdalen Coll., Oxford. Formerly Asst Editor, The London Mercury, 1928–32; subseq. Times Literary Supplement; Editor, Times Literary Supplement, 1948–59; Book critic: New York Herald Tribune, 1963–66; World Journal Tribune, 1967–68; Newsday, 1969–71; Theatre Critic, Theatre Arts, 1963–. Trustee, National Portrait Gallery, 1950–61; Director, Old Vic Trust, 1950–61; Member Council, Royal College of Music, 1956–61; Program Associate, The Humanities and Arts Program, Ford Foundation, NY, 1961–63. Served War of 1939–45, France, Italy, Austria; Lieut-Colonel, 1945. *Publications:* The Spring Journey, 1931; People in the South, 1932; Beethoven, 1933; 27 Poems, 1935; Private Opinion, 1936; Nelson, an opera, 1954; Vanity Fair, a musical play (with Robin Miller and Julian Slade), 1962; The Bonus of Laughter (autobiog.), 1987. *Recreations:* music, travelling. *Address:* 46 John Street, Newport, RI 02840, USA. *Clubs:* Travellers', Garrick, Beefsteak, Pratt's; Knickerbocker, Century (New York); Artillery (Galveston, Texas).

PRYER, (Eric) John, CB 1986; Chief Land Registrar, 1983–90; Assistant Secretary, Council for Licensed Conveyancers, since 1991; *b* 5 Sept. 1929; *s* of late Edward John and Edith Blanche Pryer; *m* 1962, Moyra Helena Cross; one *s* one *d*. *Educ:* Beckenham and Penge County Grammar Sch.; Birkbeck Coll., London Univ. (BA Hons). Called to the Bar, Gray's Inn, 1957. Exec. Officer, Treasury Solicitor's Dept, 1948; Legal Asst, HM Land Registry, 1959; Asst Land Registrar, 1965; Dist Land Registrar, Durham, 1976; Dep. Chief Land Registrar, 1981–83. Associate Mem., RICS, 1986. *Publications:* (ed) Ruoff and Roper, The Law and Practice of Registered Conveyancing, 5th edn 1986; Land Registration Handbook, 1990; official pubns; articles in jls. *Recreation:* reading.

PRYKE, Sir David Dudley, 3rd Bt *cr* 1926; *b* 16 July 1912; *s* of Sir William Robert Dudley Pryke, 2nd Bt; *S* father 1959; *m* 1945, Doreen Winifred, *er d* of late Ralph Bernard Wilkins; two *d*. *Educ:* St Lawrence Coll., Ramsgate. Liveryman Turners' Company, 1961 (Master, 1985–86). *Heir: b* William Dudley Pryke [*b* 18 Nov. 1914; *m* 1940, Lucy Irene, *d* of late Frank Madgett; one *s* one *d*]. *Address:* Flatholme, Brabant Road, North Fambridge, Chelmsford, Essex. *T:* Maldon (0621) 740227.

PRYKE, Roy Thomas; Director of Education Services, Kent County Council, since 1989; *b* 30 Nov. 1940; *s* of Thomas George and Nellie Matilda Pryke; *m* 1962, Susan Pauline Andrew; one *s* three *d*. *Educ:* Univ. of Wales (BA Hons); Univ. of Manchester (PGCE). Teacher, Manchester, 1963–71; Education Officer, Devon, 1971–79; Deputy Chief Education Officer: Somerset, 1980–82; Devon, 1983–87; Dep. Chief Educn Officer and Head of Operations, Cambridgeshire, 1987–89. FRSA 1988. *Publications:* contributor to: Open Plan Schools, 1978; The Head's Legal Guide, 1984; The Revolution in Education and Training, 1986; articles in Education Jl on curriculum and on education management. *Recreations:* foreign travel and languages, photography, tennis, running. *Address:* South House, Lambden Thorne, Pluckley, Kent TN27 0RB. *T:* Pluckley (023384) 720.

PRYN, Maj.-Gen. William John, OBE 1973; MB, BS; FRCS, FRCSEd; Director of Army Surgery, and Consulting Surgeon to the Army, 1982–86, retired; *b* 25 Jan. 1928; *s* of late Col Richard Harold Cotter Pryn, FRCS, late RAMC and Una St George Ormsby (*née* Roe); *m* 1st, 1952, Alison Lynette (marr. diss.), 2nd *d* of Captain Norman Arthur Cyril Hardy, RN; two *s* one *d*; 2nd, 1982, June de Medina, *d* of Surg. Comdr Norman Bernard de Medina Greenstreet, RN; one step *s* one step *d*. *Educ:* Malvern Coll.; Guy's Hosp. Med. Sch., London Univ. (MB, BS 1951). MRCS, LRCP 1951; FRCS 1958; FRCSEd 1984. Trooper, 21st SAS Regt (Artists Rifles), TA, 1948–50. House appts, Gen. Hosp., Ramsgate and Royal Berks Hosp., Reading, 1951–52; commnd into RAMC, 1952; Regtl MO to No 9 Training Regt RE, 1952–53; surg. appts in mil. hosps in UK, Cyprus and N Africa, 1953–58; seconded as Surg. Registrar, Royal Postgrad. Med. Sch., Hammersmith Hosp., 1958–59; Officer i/c Surg. Div. and Consultant Surgeon to mil. hosps, Malaya, Singapore, N Borneo and UK, 1959–69; CO BMH Dhekelia, 1969–72; Sen. Consultant Surgeon in mil. hosps, UK and NI, 1972–77; Consulting Surgeon to BAOR, 1977–82; Consultant in Surgery to Royal Hosp., Chelsea, 1982–86; Hon. Consultant to S Dist, Kensington and Chelsea and Westminster AHA (T), 1981. Member: EUROMED Gp on Emergency Medicine, 1980–86; Specialty Bd in Surgery, and Reg. Trng Cttee in Gen. Surgery, Defence Medical Services, 1982–86; Med. Cttee, Defence Scientific Adv. Council, 1982–86; BMA, 1950–; Wessex Surgeons Club, 1976–. Member Council: RAMC, 1982–86; Mil. Surgical Soc., 1982–. Fellow, Assoc. of Surgeons of GB and Ireland, 1960 (Mem., Educn Adv. Cttee, 1982–86). QHS 1981–86. OStJ 1984. Mem., Editorial Bd, Injury, 1982–86. *Publications:* (contrib.) Field Surgery Pocket Book, 1981; original articles in the Lancet and British Jl of Surgery. *Recreations:* fishing, shooting and other country pursuits, golf, tennis, sailing, gardening, joinery, house maintenance.

PRYOR, Arthur John, PhD; Director General, British National Space Centre, since 1988; *b* 7 March 1939; *s* of Quinton Arthur Pryor, FRICS and Elsie Margaret (*née* Luscombe); *m* 1964, Marilyn Kay Petley; one *s* one *d*. *Educ:* Harrow County Grammar Sch.; Downing Coll., Cambridge (MA; PhD). Asst Lectr, then Lectr, in Spanish and Portuguese, UC Cardiff, 1963–66; Asst Principal, BoT and ECGD, 1966–69; Principal, DTI, 1970–73; First Sec., British Embassy, Washington, 1973–75; Principal, Dept of Trade, 1975–77; Assistant Secretary: Shipping Policy Div., Dept of Trade, 1977–80; Air Div., DoI, 1980–83; Department of Trade and Industry: Asst Sec., Internat. Trade Policy Div., 1984–85; Under Sec. and Regional Dir, W Midlands Region, 1985–88. *Publications:* contribs to modern lang. jls. *Recreations:* tennis, golf, book collecting. *Address:* British National Space Centre, Dean Bradley House, 52 Horseferry Road, SW1P 2AG. *T:* 071–276 2688.

PRYOR, Brian Hugh; QC 1982; **His Honour Judge Brian Pryor;** a Circuit Judge, since 1986; *b* 11 March 1931; *s* of Lt-Col Ronald Ernest Pryor, Royal Sussex Regt, and Violet Kathleen Pryor (*née* Steele); *m* 1955, Jane Mary Smith; one *s* two *d*. *Educ:* Chichester High Sch.; University Coll., Oxford (Open Exhibnr Mod. History; BA Jurisprudence). Called to the Bar, Lincoln's Inn, 1956; Sir Thomas More Bursary, Lincoln's Inn, 1958. Member: SE Circuit Bar Mess, 1957; Kent County Bar Mess, 1957; Chm.,

Kent Bar Mess, 1979–82; Mem., SE Circuit Bar Mess Wine Cttee, 1979–82. A Recorder, 1981–86. *Recreation:* gardening.

PRYOR, John Pembro, MS; FRCS; Consultant Urological Surgeon to King's College Hospital and St Peter's Hospital, since 1975; Dean, Institute of Urology, London University, 1978–85; *b* 25 Aug. 1937; *s* of William Benjamin Pryor and Kathleen Pryor; *m* 1959, Marion Hopkins; four *s*. *Educ:* Reading Sch.; King's Coll. and King's Coll. Hosp. Med. Sch. (MB, BS). AKC 1961; FRCS 1967; MS London 1971. Training appointments: Doncaster Royal Infirm., 1965–66; Univ. of Calif, San Francisco, 1968–69; King's Coll. Hosp. and St Paul's Hosp., 1971–72. Hunterian Prof., RCS, 1971. Chm. (first), British Andrology Soc., 1979–84. *Publications:* articles on urology and andrology in scientific jls. *Address:* Andrology Unit, Lister Hospital, Chelsea Bridge Road, SW1W 8RH. *T:* 071–730 3417.

PRYOR, Robert Charles, QC 1983; a Recorder, since 1989; *b* 10 Dec. 1938; *s* of Charles Selwyn Pryor and Olive Woodall Pryor; *m* 1969, Virginia Sykes; one *s* one *d*. *Educ:* Eton; Trinity Coll., Cambridge (BA). National Service, KRRC, 2nd Lieut 1958. Called to the Bar, Inner Temple, 1963. Director, Sun Life Assurance plc, 1977–. *Recreations:* fishing, shooting. *Address:* Chitterne House, Warminster, Wilts BA12 0LG. *T:* Warminster (0985) 50255.

PRYS-DAVIES, family name of **Baron Prys-Davies.**

PRYS-DAVIES, Baron *cr* 1982 (Life Peer), of Llanegryn in the County of Gwynedd; **Gwilym Prys Prys-Davies;** Partner, Morgan Bruce & Nicholas, Solicitors, Cardiff, Pontypridd and Porth, since 1957; *b* 8 Dec. 1923; *s* of William and Mary Matilda Davies; *m* 1951, Llinos Evans; three *d*. *Educ:* Towyn Sch., Towyn, Merioneth; University College of Wales, Aberystwyth. Served RN, 1942–46. Faculty of Law, UCW, Aberystwyth, 1946–52; President of Debates, Union UCW, 1949; President Students' Rep. Council, 1950; LLB 1949; LLM 1952. Admitted Solicitor, 1956. Contested (Lab) Carmarthen, 1966. Special Adviser to Sec. of State for Wales, 1974–78. Official opposition spokesman: on health, 1983–89; on N Ireland, 1985–; on legal affairs, 1990–. Member: H of L Select Cttee on Parochial Charities Bill and Small Charities Bill, 1983–84; H of L Select Cttee on murder and life imprisonment, 1988–89; British-Irish Inter-Parly Body, 1990–. Chm., Welsh Hosps Bd, 1968–74; Member: Welsh Council, 1967–69; Welsh Adv. Cttee, ITA, 1966–69; Working Party on 4th TV Service in Wales, Home Office and Welsh Office, 1975–; Adv. Gp, Use of Fetuses and Fetal Material for Res., DHSS and Welsh Office, 1972; Econ. and Social Cttee, EEC, 1978–82. Vice-Pres., Coleg Harlech, 1989–. OStJ. *Publications:* A Central Welsh Council, 1963; Y Ffermwr a'r Gyfraith, 1967. *Address:* Lluest, 78 Church Road, Tonteg, Pontypridd, Mid Glam. *T:* Newtown Llantwit (0443) 2462.

PUDDEPHATT, Andrew Charles; General Secretary, National Council for Civil Liberties, since 1989; *b* 2 April 1950; *s* of Andrew Ross Puddephatt and Margaret McGuire; two *d*. *Educ:* Sidney Sussex College, Cambridge (BA 1971). Worked as teacher in 1970s; computer programmer, 1978–81. Councillor, Hackney Council, 1982–90 (Leader, 1986–89). *Recreations:* literature, music. *Address:* National Council for Civil Liberties, 21 Tabard Street, SE1 4LA. *T:* 071–403 3888.

PUGH, Alastair Tarrant, CBE 1986; Consultant, Goldman Sachs International Ltd, since 1988; Executive Vice Chairman/Director of Strategy, British Caledonian Group plc, 1985–88; *b* 16 Sept. 1928; *s* of Sqdn Leader Rev. Herbert Cecil Pugh, GC, MA, and Amy Lilian Pugh; *m* 1957, Sylvia Victoria Marlow; two *s* one *d*. *Educ:* Tettenhall Coll., Staffs; De Havilland Aeronautical Tech. Sch. FRAeS; FCIT; FIFF; CBIM. Design Dept, De Havilland Aircraft Co., 1949–52; Sen. Designer, H. M. Hobson, 1952–55; journalist, Flight, 1955–61; Channel Air Bridge, 1961–63; British United Airways, 1963–70: Planning Dir, 1968; British Caledonian Airways: Dir, R&D, 1970; Production Dir, 1973–74; Corporate Planning Dir, 1974–77; Dep. Chief Exec., 1977–78; Man. Dir, 1978–85. President: Inst. of Freight Forwarders, 1981–82; CIT, 1988–89. *Recreation:* the chain-driven Frazer Nash. *Address:* England's Cottage, Sidlow Bridge, Reigate, Surrey. *T:* Reigate (0737) 43456.

PUGH, Andrew Cartwright; QC 1988; a Recorder, since 1990; *b* 6 June 1937; *s* of late Lewis Gordon Pugh and of Erica Pugh; *m* 1984, Chantal Hélène Langevin; two *d*. *Educ:* Tonbridge; New Coll. Oxford (MA). Served Royal Sussex Regt, 1956–57. Bigelow Teaching Fellow, Law Sch., Univ. of Chicago, 1960–61. Called to the Bar, Inner Temple, 1961, Bencher, 1989. *Recreations:* gardening, reading, tennis. *Address:* 2 Hare Court, Temple, EC4. *T:* 071–583 1770. *Club:* United Oxford & Cambridge University.

PUGH, Charles Edward, (Ted Pugh), CBE 1988; Managing Director, National Nuclear Corporation Ltd, 1984–87; *b* 17 Sept. 1922; *s* of Gwilym Arthur and Elsie Doris Pugh; *m* 1945, Edna Wilkinson; two *s* and *d*. *Educ:* Bolton and Salford Technical Colleges. CEng, MIMechE; FInstE 1987. Lancashire Electric Power Co., 1941–48; CEGB Project Manager responsible for construction of 6 power stations, 1951–71; Chief Electrical and Control and Instrumentation Engineer, CEGB, Barnwood, 1971–73; Special Services, CEGB, 1973–76; Dir of Projects, CEGB, 1976–82; PWR Project Dir, NNC, 1982–84. Pres., Inst. of Energy, 1988–89. Hon. FINucE 1984. *Recreations:* power stations, sculpture, painting, music, gardening and walking.

PUGH, Harold Valentine, CBE 1964; Chairman, Northern Ireland Joint Electricity Authority, 1967–70, retired; *b* 18 Oct. 1899; *s* of Henry John Valentine Pugh and Martha (*née* Bott); *m* 1934, Elizabeth Mary (*née* Harwood); two *s* one *d*. *Educ:* The High Sch., Murree, India; Manchester College of Technology. Trained Metropolitan-Vickers (asst engineer erection, 1925–30). Chief Engineer, Cory Bros, 1930–35; Deputy Superintendent and later Superintendent, Upper Boat Power Station, 1935–43; Generation Engineer, South Wales Power Company, 1943–44; Deputy Chief Engineer, Manchester Corporation Electricity Dept, 1944–48; Controller, British Electricity Authority, South Wales Division, 1948; Controller, British (later Central) Electricity Authority, London Division, 1951; Chairman: Eastern Electricity Board, 1957–63; South-Eastern Electricity Board, 1963–66. Director: Aberdare Holdings, 1966–70. AMCT; FIEE; FIMechE. *Recreations:* gardening, golf. *Address:* Clontaff, Doggetts Wood Lane, Chalfont St Giles, Bucks HP8 4TH. *T:* Little Chalfont (0494) 2330.

PUGH, Sir Idwal (Vaughan), KCB 1972 (CB 1967); Chairman, Chartered Trust Ltd, 1979–88; Director: Standard Chartered Bank, 1979–88; Halifax Building Society, 1979–88; *b* 10 Feb. 1918; *s* of late Rhys Pugh and Elizabeth Pugh; *m* 1946, Mair Lewis (*d* 1985); one *s* one *d*. *Educ:* Cowbridge Grammar Sch.; St John's Coll., Oxford (Hon. Fellow, 1979). Army Service, 1940–46. Entered Min. of Civil Aviation, 1946; Alternate UK Rep. at International Civil Aviation Organisation, Montreal, 1950–53; Asst Secretary, 1956; Civil Air Attaché, Washington, 1957–59; Under Secretary, Min. of Transport, 1959; Min. of Housing and Local Govt, 1961; Dep. Sec., Min. of Housing and Local Govt, 1966–69; Permanent Sec., Welsh Office, 1969–71; Second Permanent Sec., DoE, 1971–76. Parly Comr for Administration and Health Service Comr for England, Wales and Scotland, 1976–79. Chm., Develt Corp. of Wales, 1980–83. Chm., RNCM, 1988–; Vice-Pres, UC Swansea, 1988–; Pres., Coleg Harlech, 1990–. Hon. LLD Wales, 1988. *Address:* Flat 1, The Old House, Cathedral Green, Llandaff, Cardiff CF5 2EB. *Club:* Brooks's.

PUGH, John Arthur, OBE 1968; HM Diplomatic Service, retired; British High Commissioner to Seychelles, 1976–80; *b* 17 July 1920; *er s* of late Thomas Pugh and Dorothy Baker Pugh; unmarried. *Educ:* Brecon Grammar Sch.; Bristol Univ. RN, 1941–45. Home CS, 1950–54; Gold Coast Admin. Service, 1955–58; Adviser to Ghana Govt, 1958–60; First Sec., British High Commn, Lagos, 1962–65; First Sec. (Economic), Bangkok, and British Perm. Rep. to Economic Commn for Asia and Far East, 1965–68; British Dep. High Comr, Ibadan, 1971–73; Diplomatic Service Inspector, 1973–76. *Publications:* editorial and other contributions to jls etc on political affairs, travel and history. *Recreations:* Oriental ceramics, anthropology, the sea. *Address:* Pennybrin, Hay on Wye, Hereford HR3 5RS. *T:* Hay on Wye (0497) 820695. *Club:* Commonwealth Trust.

PUGH, John Stanley; Editor, Liverpool Echo, 1978–82; *b* 9 Dec. 1927; *s* of John Albert and Winifred Lloyd Pugh; *m* 1953, Kathleen Mary; two *s* one *d*. *Educ:* Wallasey Grammar School. Editor, Liverpool Daily Post, 1969–78. *Recreation:* golf. *Address:* 26 Westwood Road, Noctorum, Birkenhead, Merseyside L43 9RQ. *Club:* Royal Liverpool (Hoylake).

PUGH, Lionel Roger Price, CBE 1975; VRD 1953; Executive Member, British Steel Corporation, 1972–77; *b* 9 May 1916; *s* of late Henry George Pugh, Cardiff; *m* 1942, Joyce Norma Nash; one *s* one *d*. *Educ:* Clifton. FCA. Supply Officer, RNVR, 1938–60; war service mainly in Mediterranean, 1939–46; retired as Lt Comdr, RNR, 1960. With Deloitte & Co., 1933–47; joined Guest Keen & Bladwins Iron & Steel Co. Ltd, 1947; Dir 1955; Man. Dir 1960; Chm. 1962; Jt Man. Dir, GKN Steel, 1964. Dir, Product Co-ordination, British Steel Corp., 1967; Dep. Commercial Man. Dir, 1969; Man. Dir, Ops and Supplies, 1970; Mem., Corporate Finance and Planning, 1972; Chairman: BSC (UK) Ltd, 1974–77; BSC Chemicals Ltd, 1974–77; Redpath Dorman Long Ltd, 1974–77. Dir, 1973, Dep. Chm., 1977–86, Bridon plc; Dir, Ryan Internat., 1979–85. Pres., Iron and Steel Inst., 1973; Hon. Member: American Iron and Steel Inst. 1973; Metals Soc., 1976; Inst. of Metals, 1985. Mem., Civil Aviation Council for Wales, 1962–66; part-time Mem., S Wales Electricity Bd, 1963–67. DL S Glamorgan (formerly Glamorgan), 1963–78. Gold Cross of Merit (Poland), 1942. *Address:* Brook Cottage, Bournes Green, Oakridge, Glos GL6 7NL. *T:* Gloucester (0452) 770554. *Clubs:* Naval and Military; Cardiff and County; Royal Porthcawl Golf, Cirencester Golf.

PUGH, Surg. Rear-Adm. Patterson David Gordon, OBE 1968; surgeon and author; *b* 19 Dec. 1920; *o s* of late W. T. Gordon Pugh, MD, FRCS, Carshalton, and Elaine V. A. Pugh (*née* Hobson), Fort Beaufort, S Africa; *m* 1st, 1948, Margaret Sheena Fraser; three *s* one *d*; 2nd, 1967, Eleanor Margery Jones; one *s* one *d*. *Educ:* Lancing Coll.; Jesus Coll., Cambridge; Middlesex Hosp. Med. Sch. MA (Cantab), MB, BChir; FRCS, LRCP. Ho. Surg., North Middlesex Hosp., 1944. RNVR, 1945; served, HMS Glasgow and HMS Jamaica, 1945–47; perm. commn, 1950; served, HMS Narvik, 1952, HMS Warrior, 1956; Consultant in Orthopaedics, RN Hospitals: Malta, 1960; Haslar, 1962; Plymouth, 1968; Sen. MO (Admin.), RN Hosp., Plymouth, 1973; MO i/c, RN Hosp., Malta, 1974–75; Surgeon Rear-Adm. (Naval Hosps), 1975–78. QHS, 1975–78. MO, Home Office Prison Dept, 1978–80. Fellow, British Orthopaedic Assoc.; FRSA; Mem., Soc. of Authors. CStJ 1976. *Publications:* Practical Nursing, 16th edn 1945, to 21st edn 1969; Nelson and his Surgeons, 1968; Staffordshire Portrait Figures and Allied Subjects of the Victorian Era, 1970, enlarged edn 1981; Naval Ceramics, 1971; Heraldic China Mementos of the First World War, 1972; Pugh of Carshalton, 1973. *Recreation:* travel. *Address:* 3 Chilworth Road, Camps Bay, Cape Town, 8001, Republic of South Africa. *T:* 021–4381122.

PUGH, Peter David S.; *see* Storie-Pugh.

PUGH, Roger Courtenay Beckwith, MD; Pathologist to St Peter's Hospitals and the Institute of Urology, London, 1955–82; *b* 23 July 1917; *y s* of late Dr Robert Pugh, Talgarth, Breconshire, and of late Margaret Louise Pugh (*née* Gough); *m* 1942, Winifred Dorothy, *yr d* of late Alfred Cooper and late Margaret Cooper (*née* Evans); one *s* one *d*. *Educ:* Gresham's Sch., Holt; St Mary's Hospital (University of London). MRCS, LRCP 1940; MB, BS, 1941; MD 1948; MCPath 1964, FRCPath 1967; FRCS 1983. House Surgeon, St Mary's Hospital and Sector Hospitals, 1940–42; War Service in RAF (Mediterranean theatre), 1942–46, Sqdn Leader; Registrar, Department of Pathology, St Mary's Hospital, 1946–48; Asst Pathologist and Lecturer in Pathology, St Mary's Hospital, 1948–51; Asst Morbid Anatomist, The Hospital for Sick Children, Great Ormond Street, 1951–54. Erasmus Wilson Demonstrator, RCS, 1959, 1961; Member: Board of Governors, St Peter's Hospitals, 1961–82; Pathological Society of Great Britain and Ireland; Assoc. of Clin. Pathologists (Marshall Medal, 1982); Internat. Society of Urology; Internat. Acad. of Pathology (former Pres., British Div.); Hon. Member British Assoc. of Urological Surgeons (St Peter's Medal, 1981); FRSocMed (former Pres., Sect. of Urology). *Publications:* (ed) Pathology of the Testis, 1976; various contributions to Pathological, Urological and Paediatric Journals. *Recreations:* gardening, photography. *Address:* 3 Waldron Gardens, Shortlands Road, Bromley, Kent BR2 0JR. *T:* 081–464 4240.

PUGH, Ted; *see* Pugh, C. E.

PUGH, William David, CBE 1965; FIM; CBIM; FIIM; JP; Deputy Chairman, English Steel Corporation Ltd, 1965–67 (Managing Director, 1955–65); Director of Personnel, British Steel Corporation (Midland Group), 1967–70; *b* 21 Nov. 1904; *s* of late Sir Arthur and Lady Pugh; *m* 1936, Mary Dorothea Barber; one *d*. *Educ:* Regent Street Polytechnic; Sheffield Univ. Joined Research Dept, Vickers Ltd, Sheffield, 1926, Director, Vickers Ltd, 1962–67; Chairman: The Darlington Forge Ltd, 1957–66; Taylor Bros & Co. Ltd, 1959–66; Director: (and alternate Chairman), Firth Vickers Stainless Steels Ltd, 1948–67; High Speed Steel Alloys Ltd, 1953–68; Industrial Training Council Service, 1960–67; British Iron and Steel Corp. Ltd, 1962–67; Sheffield Boy Scouts Holdings Ltd, 1965–85 (Scout Silver Wolf, 1983); Sheffield Centre for Environmental Research Ltd. Associate of Metallurgy (Sheffield University; Mappin Medallist). Hon. DMet (Sheffield), 1966. Hon. Fellow, Sheffield Poly., 1969. *Recreations:* gardening, golf, reading, voluntary work, drystone-walling. *Address:* Rigel, Church View Drive, Baslow, Derbyshire DE4 1RA. *T:* Baslow (0246) 2386. *Club:* Sheffield (Sheffield).

PUGSLEY, Sir Alfred Grenvile, Kt 1956; OBE 1944; DSc; FRS 1952; FEng; Professor of Civil Engineering, University of Bristol, 1944–68, now Emeritus; Pro-Vice-Chancellor, 1961–64; *b* May 1903; *s* of H. W. Pugsley, BA, FLS, London; *m* 1928, Kathleen M. Warner (*d* 1974); no *c*. *Educ:* Rutlish Sch.; London Univ. Civil Engineering Apprenticeship at Royal Arsenal, Woolwich, 1923–26; Technical Officer, at the Royal Airship Works, Cardington, 1926–31; Member scientific and technical staff at Royal Aircraft Establishment, Farnborough, 1931–45, being Head of Structural and Mechanical Engineering Dept there, 1941–45. Visiting Lecturer on aircraft structures at Imperial Coll., London, 1938–40. Chairman of Aeronautical Research Council, 1952–57; Member: Advisory Council on Scientific Policy, 1956–59; Tribunal of Inquiry on Ronan Point, 1968; Member of various scientific and professional institutions and cttees; President: IStructE, 1957–58; Section G, British Assoc. for Advancement of Science, 1960; a Vice-

Pres., ICE, 1971–73. Emeritus Mem., Smeatonian Soc. of Civil Engrs, 1989. Hon. FRAeS 1963; Hon. FICE 1981. Hon. Fellow, Bristol Univ., 1986. Hon. DSc: Belfast, 1965; Cranfield, 1978; Birmingham, 1982; Hon. DUniv Surrey, 1968. Structural Engineers' Gold Medal, 1968; Civil Engineers' Ewing Gold Medal, 1979. *Publications:* The Theory of Suspension Bridges, 1957 (2nd edn 1968); The Safety of Structures, 1966; (ed and contrib.) The Works of Isambard Kingdom Brunel, 1976; numerous Reports and Memoranda of Aeronautical Research Council; papers in scientific journals and publications of professional engineering bodies; articles and reviews in engineering press. *Address:* 4 Harley Court, Clifton Down, Bristol BS8 3JU. *Club:* Athenæum.

PUGSLEY, David Philip; Chairman of Industrial Tribunals, Birmingham Region, since 1985; a Recorder, since 1991; *b* 11 Dec. 1944; *s* of Rev. Clement Pugsley and Edith (*née* Schofield); *m* 1966, Judith Mary Mappin; two *d. Educ:* Shebbear College; St Catharine's College, Cambridge (MA). Called to the Bar, Middle Temple, 1968; practised Midland and Oxford Circuit until 1985. *Publication:* (jtly) Industrial Tribunals Compensation for Loss of Pension Rights, 1990. *Recreations:* golf, fly fishing, theatre. *Address:* 41 Pilkington Avenue, Sutton Coldfield, West Midlands B72 1LA. *T:* 021–354 1464.

PUIG DE LA BELLACASA, José Joaquín, Hon. GCVO 1986; Grand Cross of Isabel la Católica; Grand Cross of Merito Naval; Encomienda de Numero de Carlos III; Spanish Ambassador to Lisbon, since 1991; *b* 5 June 1931; *s* of José Maria Puig de la Bellacasa and Consuelo de Urdampilleta; *m* 1960, Paz de Aznar Ybarra; four *s* two *d. Educ:* Areneros Jesuit Coll., Madrid; Madrid Univ. Barrister-at-law. Entered Diplomatic Service, 1959; Dirección General Politica Exterior, 1961–62; Minister's Cabinet, 1962–69; Counsellor, Spanish Embassy, London, 1971–74; Private Sec. to Prince of Spain, 1974–75, to HM King Juan Carlos, 1975–76; Director-General: Co-op. Tecnica Internacional, 1976; Servicio Exterior, 1977–78; Under-Sec. of State for Foreign Affairs, 1978–80; Ambassador to Holy See, 1980–83; Ambassador to UK, 1983–90; Sec.-Gen., Spanish Royal Household, 1990–91. Hon. Fellow, QMC, 1987. Holds several foreign decorations. *Address:* Palacio de Palhavã, Plaza de España, 1000 Lisboa, Portugal; Felipe IV 7, Madrid 14, Spain. *Clubs:* Beefsteak, White's; Nuevo, Golf de Puerta de Hierro (Madrid).

PULFORD, Richard Charles; General Director (Administration), South Bank Centre, since 1986; *b* 14 July 1944; *s* of late Charles Edgar Pulford and Grace Mary Pulford (*née* Vickors). *Educ:* Royal Grammar Sch., Newcastle upon Tyne; St Catherine's Coll., Oxford (BA Jurisprudence). Voluntary service in the Sudan, 1966–67; Home Civil Service, 1967–79: Department of Education and Science: Asst Principal, 1967–72, Principal, 1972–75; HM Treasury, 1975–77; Asst Secretary, DES, 1977–79. Arts Council of GB: Dep. Sec.-Gen., 1979–85; South Bank Planning Dir, 1985–86. Bd Mem., Internat. Soc. of Performing Arts Administrators, 1988– (Pres., 1990–91); Member: South Bank Theatre Bd, 1985–; Council and Exec. Cttee, English Stage Co., 1989–; Vice Pres., Mid-Northumberland Arts Gp, 1985–; Mem., W Midlands Arts Trust, 1985–. *Recreations:* leaving at intervals, complaining in restaurants, primary smoking. *Address:* 905 Beatty House, Dolphin Square, SW1V 3PN. *T:* 071–798 8308.

PULLAN, Prof. Brian Sebastian, PhD; FBA 1985; Professor of Modern History, University of Manchester, since 1973; *b* 10 Dec. 1935; *s* of Horace William Virgo Pullan and Ella Lister Pullan; *m* 1962, Janet Elizabeth Maltby; two *s. Educ:* Epsom Coll.; Trinity Coll., Cambridge (MA, PhD); MA Manchester. Nat. Service, RA, 1954–56. Cambridge University: Res. Fellow, Trinity Coll., 1961–63; Official Fellow, Queens' Coll., 1963–72; Univ. Asst Lectr in History, 1964–67; Lectr, 1967–72; Dean, Faculty of Arts, Manchester Univ., 1982–84. Feoffee of Chetham's Hosp. and Library, Manchester, 1981–. Corresp. Fellow, Ateneo Veneto, 1986. *Publications:* (ed) Sources for the History of Medieval Europe, 1966; (ed) Crisis and Change in the Venetian Economy in the Sixteenth and Seventeenth Centuries, 1968; Rich and Poor in Renaissance Venice, 1971; A History of Early Renaissance Italy, 1973; The Jews of Europe and the Inquisition of Venice, 1983; (ed with Susan Reynolds) Towns and Townspeople in Medieval and Renaissance Europe: essays in memory of Kenneth Hyde, 1990; articles and reviews in learned jls and collections. *Recreations:* dogs, theatre. *Address:* 30 Sandhurst Road, Didsbury, Manchester M20 0LR. *T:* 061–445 3665.

PULLAN, John Marshall, MChir, FRCS; Hon. Surgeon, St Thomas' Hospital, London; late of King Edward VII Hospital, Bolingbroke Hospital, London and Royal Masonic Hospital, London; *b* 1 Aug. 1915; *e s* of late William Greaves Pullan and Kathleen, *d* of Alfred Marshall, Otley, Yorkshire; *m* 1940, Leila Diana, *d* of H. C. Craven-Veitch, Surgeon; one *s* three *d. Educ:* Shrewsbury; King's Coll., Cambridge; St Thomas' Hospital, London. MA Cantab (1st Cl. Nat. Sc. Tripos) 1937; MB, BChir 1940; FRCS, 1942; MChir 1945. Teacher in Surgery, Univ. of London; Examiner in Surgery, Univs of: London, 1956; Cambridge. Member: Court of Examiners, RCS, 1964; Board of Governors, St Thomas' Hospital. *Publications:* Section on Diseases of the Liver, Gall Bladder and Bile Ducts, in Textbook of British Surgery, ed Sir Henry Souttar, 1956; articles in surgical journals. *Address:* Palings, Warboys Road, Kingston Hill, Surrey KT2 7LS. *T:* 081–546 5310. *Clubs:* White's, Flyfishers', Boodle's.

PULLÉE, Ernest Edward, CBE 1967; ARCA, ACSD, FSAE, NEAC; painter; Chief Officer, National Council for Diplomas in Art and Design, 1967–74; retired; *b* 19 Feb. 1907; *s* of Ernest and Caroline Elizabeth Pullée; *m* 1933, Margaret Fisher, ARCA, NEAC; one *s. Educ:* St Martin's Sch., Dover; Royal Coll. of Art, London. Principal: Gloucester Coll. of Art, 1934–39; Portsmouth Coll. of Art, 1939–45; Leeds Coll. of Art, 1945–56; Leicester Coll. of Art and Design, 1956–67. Regular exhibitor, RA summer exhibns and at London and provincial galls. Pres., Nat. Soc. for Art Educn, 1945, 1959; Chm., Assoc. of Art Instns, 1959; Mem., Nat. Adv. Coun. for Art Educn, 1959; Mem., Nat. Coun. for Diplomas in Art and Design, 1961. FRSA 1952. Hon. Life Mem., NEAC, 1986. Hon. Fellow: Portsmouth Polytechnic, 1976; Leicester Polytechnic, 1977. Hon. DA (Manchester), 1961. *Publications:* contribs to professional and academic jls. *Recreation:* travel. *Address:* 3 March Square, The Drive, Summersdale, Chichester, W Sussex PO19 4AN. *Club:* Chelsea Arts.

PULLEIN-THOMPSON, Denis; *see* Cannan, D.

PULLEN, Sir (William) Reginald (James), KCVO 1987 (CVO 1975; MVO 1966); LLB; FCIS; JP; Clerk to the Trustees, United Westminster Almshouses, since 1987; Receiver-General, 1959–87, and Chapter Clerk 1963–87, Westminster Abbey; *b* 17 Feb. 1922; *er s* of late William Pullen and Lillian Pullen (*née* Chinn), Falmouth; *m* 1948, Doreen Angela Hebron; two *d. Educ:* Falmouth Gram. School; King's College, London; private study. Served War of 1939–45; Flt Lt, RAFVR (admin and special duties) SE Asia. Asst to Chief Accountant, Westminster Abbey, 1947; Dep. Registrar, 1951; Registrar, 1964–84; Sec. Westminster Abbey Appeal, 1953. Westminster City Council, 1962–65. Jt. Hon. Treas., CCJ, 1988–. Trustee: The Passage (RC) Day Centre for Homeless People, 1983–; St Marylebone Almshouses (representing Westminster CC), 1988–; Abbey Community Centre, 1990–. JP Inner London, 1967. Liveryman, Worshipful Co. of Fishmongers; Freeman, Worshipful Co. of Wax Chandlers. KStJ 1987 (CStJ 1981; OStJ 1969). *Publication:* contrib. A House of Kings, 1966. *Recreations:* travel, dogwalking, gerentology. *Address:* 42 Rochester Row, SW1P 1BU. *T:* 071–828 3210. *Clubs:* Royal Air Force, MCC.

PULLEYBLANK, Prof. Edwin George, PhD; FRSC; Professor of Chinese, University of British Columbia, 1966–87, now Emeritus; *b* Calgary, Alberta, 7 Aug. 1922; *s* of W. G. E. Pulleyblank, Calgary; *m* 1945, Winona Ruth Relyea (decd), Arnprior, Ont; one *s* two *d. Educ:* Central High School, Calgary; University of Alberta; University of London. BA Hons Classics, Univ. of Alberta, 1942; Nat. Research Council of Canada, 1943–46. School of Oriental and African Studies, Univ. of London: Chinese Govt Schol., 1946; Lectr in Classical Chinese, 1948; PhD in Classical Chinese, 1951; Lectr in Far Eastern History, 1952; Professor of Chinese, University of Cambridge, 1953; Head, Dept of Asian Studies, Univ. of British Columbia, 1968–75. Fellow of Downing Coll., Cambridge, 1955–66. *Publications:* The Background of the Rebellion of An Lu-Shan, 1955; Middle Chinese, 1984; Lexicon of Reconstructed Pronunciation in Early Middle Chinese, Late Middle Chinese and Early Mandarin, 1991; articles in Asia Major, Bulletin of School of Oriental and African Studies, etc. *Address:* c/o Department of Asian Studies, University of British Columbia, Vancouver, BC V6T 1W5, Canada.

PULLINGER, Sir (Francis) Alan, Kt 1977; CBE 1970; DL; Chairman, Haden Carrier Ltd, 1961–79; *b* 22 May 1913; *s* of William Pullinger; *m* 1st, 1946, Felicity Charmian Gotch Hobson (decd); two *s* one *d;* 2nd, 1966, Jacqueline Louise Anne Durin. *Educ:* Marlborough Coll.; Balliol Coll., Oxford (MA). Pres., IHVE, 1972–73. Chm., Hertfordshire Scouts, 1976–91. Vice Chm. Council, Benenden Sch., 1980–. Hon. FCIBSE, 1977. DL Herts, 1982. *Recreations:* mountaineering, sailing, beagling. *Address:* Barnhorn, Meadway, Berkhamsted, Herts HP4 2PL. *T:* Berkhamsted (0442) 863206. *Clubs:* Alpine, Travellers'.

PULLINGER, John Elphick; His Honour Judge Pullinger; a Circuit Judge, since 1982; *b* 27 Aug. 1930; *s* of late Reginald Edward Pullinger and of Elsie Florence Pullinger; *m* 1956, Carette Maureen, *d* of late Flt Lieut and late Mrs E. D. Stephens; one *s* one *d. Educ:* Friern Barnet Grammar Sch.; Quintin Sch.; London Sch. of Econs and Pol. Science (LLB 1955). Called to the Bar, Lincoln's Inn, 1958; Sir Thomas More Bursary, 1958. Legal Sec. to Lord Shrewsbury's Commn of Enquiry into the Infantile Paralysis Fellowship, 1958–59; Dep. Judge Advocate, 1965; AJAG, 1972–82; Judge Advocate to NZ Force SE Asia, 1973–75; served on JAG's staff in Germany, Mediterranean, Near East and Far East. Member: NSRA, 1977–; NRA, 1979–; Historical Breechloading Smallarms Assoc., 1984–; Internat. Soc. for Military Law and the Law of War, UK Gp, 1988–; HAC, 1950–. *Publication:* The Position of the British Serviceman under the Army and Air Force Acts 1955, 1975. *Recreations:* shottist, bibliophile. *Address:* 1 Essex Court, Temple, EC4Y 9AR.

PULVERTAFT, Rear-Adm. David Martin, CB 1990; Director General Procurement and Support Organisation (Navy), since 1990; *b* 26 March 1938; *s* of late Captain William Godfrey Pulvertaft, OBE, RN and Annie Joan Pulvertaft (*née* Martin); *m* 1961, Mary Rose Jeacock; one *s* two *d. Educ:* Canford Sch., Dorset; Britannia RN Coll., Dartmouth; RN Engineering Coll., Manadon. BSc (Eng) 1962. FIMechE 1989 (MIMechE 1974). HMS Ceylon, 1958–59; HMS Anchorite, Singapore, 1963–66; HMS Dreadnought, 1967–71; 10th Submarine Sqdn, 1971–72; HM Dockyard, Devonport, 1973–75; Nat. Defence Coll., Latimer, 1975–76; MoD 1976–78; HM Dockyard, Devonport, 1979–82; RCDS, 1983; MoD, 1984–87; Dir Gen. Aircraft (Navy), 1987–90. FBIM 1990. *Recreations:* genealogy, printing, bookbinding. *Address:* c/o Naval Secretary, Ministry of Defence (Navy), Whitehall, SW1A 2BL. *Club:* Naval.

PULZER, Prof. Peter George Julius, PhD; FRHistS; Gladstone Professor of Government and Public Administration, University of Oxford, since Jan. 1985; Fellow of All Souls College, since 1985; *b* 20 May 1929; *s* of Felix and Margaret Pulzer; *m* 1962, Gillian Mary Marshall; two *s. Educ:* Surbiton County Grammar Sch.; King's Coll., Cambridge (1st Cl. Hons Historical Tripos 1950; PhD 1960); London Univ. (1st Cl. Hons BSc Econ 1954). FRHistS 1971. Lectr in Politics, Magdalen Coll. and Christ Church, Oxford, 1957–62; University Lectr in Politics, Oxford, 1960–84; Official Student and Tutor in Politics, Christ Church 1962–84. Vis. Professor: Univ. of Wisconsin, 1965; Sch. of Advanced Internat. Studies, Johns Hopkins Univ., 1972; Univ. of Calif, LA, 1972; Eric Voegelin Vis. Prof., Munich Univ., 1988. *Publications:* The Rise of Political Anti-Semitism in Germany and Austria, 1964, 2nd edn 1988 (German edn 1966); Political Representation and Elections in Britain, 1967, 3rd edn 1975; Jews and the State in Modern Germany, 1991; contrib. to jls, year books and symposia. *Recreations:* opera, walking. *Address:* All Souls College, Oxford OX1 4AL. *T:* Oxford (0865) 279348.

PUMFREY, Nicholas Richard; QC 1990; *b* 22 May 1951; *s* of Peter and Maureen Pumfrey. *Educ:* St Edward's Sch., Oxford; St Edmund Hall, Oxford (BA Physics, 1972, Law, 1974). Called to the Bar, Middle Temple, 1975; Jun. Counsel to HM Treasury (Patents), 1987–90. *Recreation:* cycling. *Address:* 11 South Square, Gray's Inn, WC1R 5EU.

PUMPHREY, Sir (John) Laurence, KCMG 1973 (CMG 1963); HM Diplomatic Service, retired; Ambassador to Pakistan (formerly High Commissioner), 1971–76; *b* 22 July 1916; *s* of late Charles Ernest Pumphrey and Iris Mary (*née* Moberly-Bell); *m* 1945, Jean, *e d* of Sir Walter Buchanan Riddell, 12th Bt; four *s* one *d. Educ:* Winchester; New College, Oxford. Served War of 1939–45 in Army. Foreign Service from 1945. Head of Establishment and Organisation Department, Foreign Office, 1955–60; Counsellor, Staff of British Commissioner-General for SE Asia, Singapore, 1960–63; Counsellor, HM Embassy, Belgrade, 1963–65; Deputy High Commissioner, Nairobi, 1965–67; British High Comr, Zambia, 1967–71. Military Cross, 3rd Class (Greece), 1941. *Address:* Caistron, Thropton, Morpeth, Northumberland NE65 7LG.

PUNGAN, Vasile; Minister of Foreign Trade and International Economic Co-operation, Romania, 1982–86; *b* 2 Nov. 1926; *m* 1952, Liliana Niţă (*d* 1973); one *d. Educ:* Inst. of Econs, Bucharest. Dr in Econ. Scis and Univ. Prof.; Dean of Faculty, Agronomical Inst., Bucharest, 1954; Gen. Dir, Min. of Agric. and Forestry, 1955–58; Counsellor, Romanian Embassy, Washington, 1959–62; Dir and Mem. College, Min. of Foreign Affairs, 1963–66; Ambassador of Socialist Republic of Romania to Court of St James's, 1966–72; Counsellor to Pres. of Romania, 1973–78 and 1979–82; Minister and Sec. of State, State Council, 1979–82. Mem., Central Cttee of Romanian Communist Party, 1972 (Alternate Mem. 1969); Mem., Grand National Assembly, 1975. Holds orders and medals of Socialist Republic of Romania and several foreign countries. *Address:* c/o Ministry of Foreign Affairs, Bucharest, Romania.

PURCELL, Prof. Edward Mills, PhD; Gerhard Gade University Professor, Harvard University, 1960–80, now Emeritus; *b* 30 Aug. 1912; *s* of Edward A. Purcell and Mary Elizabeth Mills; *m* 1937, Beth C. Busser; two *s. Educ:* Purdue University; Harvard University. PhD Harvard, 1938. Instructor in Physics, Harvard, 1938–40; Radiation Laboratory, Mass. Inst. of Technology, 1940–45; Associate Professor of Physics, Harvard, 1945–49; Professor of Physics, 1949–60. Senior Fellow, Society of Fellows, Harvard, 1950–71. Halley Lectr, Oxford Univ., 1982. Foreign Mem., Royal Soc., 1989. Hon. DEng

Purdue, 1953; Hon. DSci Washington Univ., St Louis, 1963. (Jointly) Nobel Prize in Physics, 1952; Nat. Medal of Science, 1979. *Publications:* Principles of Microwave Circuits, 1948; Physics for Students of Science and Engineering, 1952; Electricity and Magnetism, 1965; papers in Physical Review, Astrophys. Jl, Biophys. Jl. *Address:* 5 Wright Street, Cambridge, Mass 02138, USA. *T:* 547–9317.

PURCELL, Harry, CBE 1982; Member (C) for Chaddesley Corbett, Hereford and Worcester County Council, since 1974 (Vice-Chairman, 1989–90); *b* 2 Dec. 1919; *s* of Charles and Lucy Purcell; *m* 1941, Eunice Mary Price; three *s* one *d*. *Educ:* Bewdley C of E Sch.; Kidderminster Coll. Joined TA, 1938; served War, 1939–46, Queen's Own Worcester Hussars; Transport Officer, Berlin, 1946–48. Carpet industry, 1949–60; self-employed, 1961. Formerly Mem., Kidderminster Bor. Council; Mayor of Kidderminster, 1967–68. Chairman: West Mercia Police Authority, 1979–82; Police Cttee, National Assoc. of County Councils, 1977–; Chm., National Police Negotiating Bd, 1978–82; Vice-Chm., ACC, 1982–85. *Recreations:* theatre, tennis, public service. *Address:* Meadowsmead, Woodrow, Chaddesley Corbett, near Kidderminster, Worcs. *T:* Chaddesley Corbett (056283) 347. *Club:* Carlton.

PURCELL, (Robert) Michael, CMG 1983; HM Diplomatic Service, retired; Adviser and Secretary, East Africa Association, 1984–87; *b* 22 Oct. 1923; *s* of late Lt-Col Walter Purcell and Constance (*née* Fendick); *m* 1965, Julia Evelyn, *o d* of late Brig. Edward Marsh-Kellett; two *d*. *Educ:* Ampleforth Coll. Commnd 60th Rifles (Greenjackets), 1943–47. Colonial Service, later HMOCS, Uganda, 1949–62, retd; 1st Sec., CRO, later FCO, 1964–68; 1st Sec. (Commercial/Economic), Colombo, 1968–69; FCO, 1969–71; 1st Sec. (Aid), Singapore, 1971–73; Head of Chancery, HM Legation to the Holy See, 1973–76; Counsellor and Dep. High Comr, Malta, 1977–80; Ambassador to Somali Democratic Republic, 1980–83. KCSG 1976. *Recreations:* country life, painting. *Address:* French Mill Cottage, Shaftesbury, Dorset SP7 0LT. *T:* Shaftesbury (0747) 53615. *Club:* Naval and Military.

PURCELL, Rev. Canon William Ernest; author and broadcaster; Residentiary Canon of Worcester Cathedral, 1966–76; *b* 25 May 1909; *s* of Will and Gwladys Purcell; *m* 1939, Margaret Clegg; two *s* one *d*. *Educ:* Keble Coll., Oxford (MA); Univ. of Wales (BA); Queens Coll., Birmingham. Curate: St. John's Church, Keighley, 1938; Dover Parish Church, 1939–43; Vicar: St. Peter's, Maidstone, 1944–47; Sutton Valence, 1947–53; Chaplain, HM Borstal Instn, East Sutton, 1947–53; Religious Broadcasting Organiser, BBC Midlands, 1953–66. *Publications:* These Thy Gods, 1950; Pilgrim's Programme, 1957; Onward Christian Soldier (biog. of S. Baring Gould), 1957; A Plain Man Looks At Himself, 1962; Woodbine Willie (biog. of G. Studdert Kennedy), 1962; This Is My Story, 1963; The Plain Man Looks At The Commandments, 1966; Fisher of Lambeth (biog. of Archbp of Canterbury), 1969; Portrait of Soper (biog. of Lord Soper), 1972; British Police in a Changing Society, 1974; A Time to Die, 1979; Pilgrim's England, 1981; The Christian in Retirement, 1982; Martyrs of Our Time, 1983; Seekers and Finders, 1985; The Anglican Spiritual Tradition, 1988. *Address:* 14 Conifer Close, Cumnor Hill, Oxford OX2 9HP. *Club:* National Liberal.

PURCELL, Ven. William Henry Samuel, MA; Archdeacon of Dorking, 1968–82; *b* 22 Jan. 1912; *m* 1941, Kathleen Clough, Leeds; one *s* (and one *s* decd). *Educ:* King Edward VI School, Norwich; Fitzwilliam House, Cambridge (MA). Asst Curate, St Michael's, Headingley, Leeds, 1937; Minor Canon of Ripon Cathedral, 1940; Vicar: St Matthew, Holbeck, Leeds, 1943; St Matthew, Chapel Allerton, Leeds, 1947; St Martin's, Epsom, 1963. Rural Dean of Epsom, 1965. Hon. Canon of Ripon Cathedral, 1962; Hon. Canon of Guildford Cathedral, 1968, Canon Emeritus, 1982. *Recreations:* walking, travel. *Address:* 55 Windfield, Epsom Road, Leatherhead, Surrey KT22 8UQ. *T:* Leatherhead (0372) 375708.

PURCHAS, Christopher Patrick Brooks; QC 1990; a Recorder, since 1986; *b* 20 June 1943; *s* of Rt Hon. Sir Francis Purchas, *qv*; *m* 1974, Bronwen Mary Vaughan; two *d*. *Educ:* Summerfield Sch.; Marlborough Coll.; Trinity Coll., Cambridge (MA). Called to the Bar, Inner Temple, 1966. *Recreations:* tennis, shooting. *Address:* 2 Crown Office Row, Temple, EC4. *T:* 071–353 9337.

See also R. M. Purchas.

PURCHAS, Rt. Hon. Sir Francis (Brooks), Kt 1974; PC 1982; **Rt. Hon. Lord Justice Purchas;** a Lord Justice of Appeal, since 1982; *b* 19 June 1919; *s* of late Captain Francis Purchas, 5th Royal Irish Lancers and late Millicent Purchas (*née* Brooks); *m* 1942, Patricia Mona Kathleen, *d* of Lieut Milburn; two *s*. *Educ:* Summerfields Sch., Oxford; Marlborough Coll.; Trinity Coll., Cambridge. Served RE, 1940–46: North Africa, 1943 (despatches); Hon. Lt-Col retd (Africa Star, Italy Star, 1939–45 Medal; Defence Medal). Allied Mil. Commission, Vienna. Called to Bar, Inner Temple, 1948, QC 1965, Bencher, 1972; practised at Bar, 1948–74; Leader, SE Circuit, 1972–74; Dep. Chm., E Sussex QS, 1966–71; Recorder of Canterbury, 1969–71 (Hon. Recorder of Canterbury, 1972–74); Recorder of the Crown Court, 1972–74; a Judge of the High Court of Justice, Family Div., 1974–82; Presiding Judge, SE Circuit, 1977–82. Comr, Central Criminal Court, 1970–71. Mem., Bar Council, 1966–68, 1969–71, 1972–74. Mem. of Livery, Worshipful Co. of Broderers, 1962. *Recreations:* shooting, golf, fishing. *Address:* Parkhurst House, near Haslemere, Surrey GU27 3BY. *T:* North Chapel (042878) 280; 1 Temple Gardens, Temple, EC4Y 9BB. *T:* 071–353 5124. *Club:* Hawks (Cambridge).

See also C. P. B. Purchas, R. M. Purchas.

PURCHAS, Robin Michael; QC 1987; a Recorder, since 1989; *b* 12 June 1946; *s* of Rt Hon. Sir Francis Brooks Purchas, *qv*; *m* 1970, Denise Anne Kerr Finlay; one *s* one *d*. *Educ:* Summerfields; Marlborough College; Trinity College, Cambridge (MA). Called to the Bar, Inner Temple, 1968; practised principally in local govt, administrative and parliamentary work, 1969–; Assistant Recorder, 1985. *Recreations:* opera, music, theatre, tennis, swimming, ski-ing, sailing, shooting, golf. *Address:* (chambers) 2 Harcourt Buildings, Temple, EC4Y 9DB. *T:* 071–353 8415. *Clubs:* Lansdowne, Queen's; Royal West Norfolk Golf; Royal Worlington and Newmarket Golf; Brancaster Staithe Sailing.

See also C. P. B. Purchas.

PURDEN, Roma Laurette, (Laurie Purden; Mrs J. K. Kotch), MBE 1973; journalist and writer; *b* 30 Sept. 1928; *d* of George Cecil Arnold Purden and Constance Mary Sheppard; *m* 1957, John Keith Kotch (*d* 1979); two *d*. *Educ:* Harecroft Sch., Tunbridge Wells. Fiction Editor, Home Notes, 1948–51; Asst Editor, Home Notes, 1951–52; Asst Editor, Woman's Own, 1952; Sen. Asst Editor, Girl, 1952–54; Editor of: Housewife, 1954–57; Home, 1957–62; House Beautiful, 1963–65; Good Housekeeping, 1965–73; Editor-in-Chief: Good Housekeeping, and Womancraft, 1973–77; Woman's Journal, 1978–88; Woman & Home, 1982–83. Dir, Brickfield Publications Ltd, 1978–80. Magazine Editor of the Year, 1979, British Soc. of Magazine Editors; Consumer Magazine of the Year awarded by Periodical Publishers Assoc. to Woman's Journal, 1985. *Address:* 174 Pavilion Road, SW1X 0AW. *T:* 071–730 4021.

PURDON, Maj.-Gen. Corran William Brooke, CBE 1970; MC 1945; CPM 1982; *b* 4 May 1921; *s* of Maj.-Gen. William Brooke Purdon, DSO, OBE, MC, KHS, and Dorothy Myrtle Coates; *m* 1945, Maureen Patricia, *d* of Major J. F. Petrie, Guides Infantry, IA; two *s* one *d*. *Educ:* Rokeby, Wimbledon; Campbell Coll., Belfast; RMC Sandhurst. MBIM. Commnd into Royal Ulster Rifles, 1939; service with Army Commandos, France and Germany, 1940–45 (wounded; MC); 1st Bn RU Rifles, Palestine, 1945–46; GHQ MELF, 1949–51; psc 1955; Staff, Malayan Emergency, 1956–58; Co. Comdr, 1 RU Rifles, Cyprus Emergency, 1958; CO, 1st Bn RU Rifles, BAOR and Borneo War, 1962–64; GSO1 and Chief Instructor, Sch. of Infantry, Warminster, 1965–67; Comdr, Sultan's Armed Forces, Oman, and Dir of Ops, Dhofar War, 1967–70 (Sultan's Bravery Medal, 1968 and Distinguished Service Medal for Gallantry, 1969, Oman; CBE); Commandant: Sch. of Infantry, Warminster, 1970–72; Small Arms Sch. Corps, 1970–72; GOC, NW Dist, 1972–74; GOC Near East Land Forces, 1974–76, retired. Dep. Comr, Royal Hong Kong Police Force, 1978–81; Comdr, St John Ambulance, Wilts, 1981–84 (Mem. Council, 1981–86). Hon. Colonel: Queen's Univ. Belfast OTC, 1975–78; D (London Irish Rifles) Co., 4th (V) Bn, Royal Irish Rangers, 1986–. Pres., Army Gymnastic Union, 1973–76; Patron, Small Arms Sch. Corps Assoc., 1985–90; Governor, Royal Humane Soc., 1985–. KStJ 1983. *Publications:* List the Bugle, 1990; articles in military jls. *Recreations:* physical training, swimming, dogs. *Address:* Old Park House, Devizes, Wilts SN10 5JR. *Clubs:* Army and Navy; Hong Kong.

PURDY, Robert John, CMG 1963; OBE 1954; Bursar, Gresham's School, Holt, 1965–81; retired from HM Overseas Civil Service, 1963; *b* 2 March 1916; 2nd *s* of late Lt-Col T. W. Purdy, Woodgate House, Aylsham, Norfolk; *m* 1957, Elizabeth (*née* Sharp); two *s* one *d*. *Educ:* Haileybury College; Jesus College, Cambridge (BA). Served 1940–46 with 81 West African Division Reconnaissance Regt, 3rd and 4th Burma Campaigns (despatches, Major). Appointed to Colonial Administrative Service, Northern Nigeria, 1939; promoted Resident, 1956; Senior Resident, Staff Grade, 1957. Resident, Adamawa Province, 1956; Senior Resident, Plateau Province, 1958–61; Senior Resident, Sokoto Province, 1961–63, retd. *Recreations:* shooting, fishing, gardening. *Address:* Spratt's Green House, Aylsham, Norwich NR11 6TX. *T:* Aylsham (0263) 732147.

PURKIS, Dr Andrew James; Director, Council for the Protection of Rural England, since 1987; *b* 24 Jan. 1949; *s* of Clifford Henry Purkis and Mildred Jeannie Purkis; *m* 1980, Jennifer Harwood Smith; one *s* one *d*. *Educ:* Highgate Sch.; Corpus Christi Coll., Oxford; St Antony's Coll., Oxford. 1st class Hons MA Mod. Hist. 1970; DPhil 1978. Home Civil Service, N Ireland Office, 1974; Private Sec. to Perm. Under-Sec. of State, NI Office, 1976–77; Head of Policy Unit, Nat. Council for Voluntary Organisations, 1980; Asst Dir, NCVO, 1986. Mem. Bd, Contact a Family (charity), 1986–. *Publications:* (with Paul Hodson) Housing and Community Care, 1982; (with Rosemary Allen) Health in the Round, 1983. *Recreations:* walking, surf-riding, bird-watching, music, theatre. *Address:* 38 Endlesham Road, Balham, SW12 8JL. *T:* 081–675 2439.

PURLE, Charles Lambert; QC 1989; *b* 9 Feb. 1947; *s* of Robert Herbert Purle and Doreen Florence (*née* Button); *m* 1st, 1969, Lorna Barbara Brown (marr. diss. 1990); one *s* one *d*; 2nd, 1991, Virginia Dabney Hopkins Rylatt. *Educ:* Nottingham Univ. (LLB 1969); Worcester Coll., Oxford (BCL 1971). Called to the Bar, Gray's Inn, 1970; in practice, 1972–. *Recreations:* opera, music, my children. *Address:* 12 New Square, Lincoln's Inn, WC2A 3SW. *T:* 071–405 3808.

PURNELL, Nicholas Robert; QC 1985; a Recorder, since 1986; *b* 29 Jan. 1944; *s* of late Oliver Cuthbert Purnell and of Pauline Purnell; *m* 1970, Melanie Jill Stanway; four *s*. *Educ:* Oratory Sch.; King's Coll. Cambridge (Open Exhibnr; MA). Called to the Bar, Middle Temple, 1968 (Astbury Schol.), Bencher 1990; Junior of Central Criminal Court Bar Mess, 1972–75; Prosecuting Counsel to Inland Revenue, 1977–79; Jun. Treasury Counsel, 1979–85. Mem., Bar Council and Senate, 1973–77, 1982–85, 1989–91 (Chm., Legal Aid Fees Cttee, 1989–90); Member: Lord Chancellor's and Home Secretary's Working Party on the Training of the Judiciary, 1975–78; Crown Court Rules Cttee, 1982–88; Lord Chancellor's Adv. Cttee on Educn and Conduct, 1991–; Chm., Criminal Bar Assoc., 1990–91. *Recreations:* living in France as much as possible, watching Wimbledon FC. *Address:* 36 Essex Street, WC2R 3AS. *T:* 071–413 0353.

See also P. O. Purnell.

PURNELL, Paul Oliver; QC 1982; a Recorder, since 1985; *b* 13 July 1936; *s* of Oliver Cuthbert Purnell and Pauline (*née* Brailli); *m* 1966, Celia Consuelo Ocampo; one *s* two *d*. *Educ:* The Oratory Sch.; Jesus Coll., Oxford (MA). Served 4th/7th Royal Dragoon Guards, 1958–62. Called to the Bar, Inner Temple, 1962. Jun. Treasury Counsel at Central Criminal Court, 1976–82. *Recreations:* windsurfing, tennis. *Address:* 1 Crown Office Row, Temple, EC4Y 7HH. *T:* 071–583 3724. *Club:* Cavalry and Guards.

See also N. R. Purnell.

PURSE, Hugh Robert Leslie; Legal Adviser, Department of Employment and Principal Assistant Treasury Solicitor, since 1988; *b* 22 Oct. 1940; *s* of Robert Purse and Elsie Purse (*née* Kemp). *Educ:* St Peter's School, York; King's College London (LLB). Called to the Bar, Gray's Inn, 1964 (Atkin Scholar). Legal Asst, Dept of Employment, 1969; Legal Adviser to Price Commission, 1978–79; Govt legal service, 1979–. *Address:* Department of Employment, Caxton House, Tothill Street, SW1H 9NF. *T:* 071–273 5849.

PURSEGLOVE, John William, CMG 1973; Tropical Crops Specialist, Overseas Development Administration at East Malling Research Station, Kent, 1967–75; *b* 11 Aug. 1912; *s* of late Robert and Kate Purseglove; *m* 1947, Phyllis Agnes Adèle, *d* of late George and Mary Turner, Falkland Is; one *s* (one *d* decd). *Educ:* Lady Manners Sch., Bakewell; Manchester Univ. (BSc Hons Botany); Gonville and Caius Coll, Cambridge; Imperial Coll. of Tropical Agriculture, Trinidad (AICTA). Agricultural and Sen. Agricl Officer, Uganda, 1936–52; Lectr in Tropical Agriculture, Univ. of Cambridge, 1952–54; Dir, Botanic Gardens, Singapore, 1954–57; Prof. of Botany, Imperial Coll. of Tropical Agriculture and Univ. of the West Indies, Trinidad, 1957–67. Pres., Assoc. for Tropical Biology, 1962–65. FLS 1945; FIBiol 1970; Hon. Mem., Trop. Agric. Assoc., 1984. *Publications:* Tobacco in Uganda, 1951; Tropical Crops, Dicotyledons, 2 vols, 1968; Tropical Crops, Monocotyledons, 2 vols, 1972; (with E. G. Brown, C. L. Green and S. R. J. Robbins) Spices, 2 vols, 1981, Japanese edn 1985; papers on land use, ethnobotany, etc, in scientific jls and symposia vols. *Recreations:* gardening, natural history. *Address:* Walnut Trees, Sissinghurst, Cranbrook, Kent TN17 2JL. *T:* Cranbrook (0580) 712836.

PURSSELL, Anthony John Richard; Chairman, Thames Valley and South Midlands Regional Board, Lloyds Bank plc, 1989–91 (Regional Director, 1982–91); *b* 5 July 1926; *m* 1952, Ann Margaret Batchelor; two *s* one *d*. *Educ:* Oriel Coll., Oxford (MA Hons Chemistry). Managing Director: Arthur Guinness Son & Co. (Park Royal) Ltd, 1968; Arthur Guinness Son & Co. (Dublin) Ltd, 1973; Arthur Guinness & Sons plc, 1975–81; Jt Dep. Chm., 1981–83. Member: IBA, 1976–81; Bd, CAA, 1984–90. Trustee and Hon. Treas., Oxfam, 1985–. *Recreations:* travel, golf, sailing, books. *Address:* Allendale, Bulstrode Way, Gerrards Cross, Bucks SL9 7QT. *Club:* Leander (Henley).

PURVES, Dame Daphne (Helen), DBE 1979; Senior Lecturer in French, Dunedin Teachers College, 1967–73, retired (Lecturer, 1963–66); *b* 8 Nov. 1908; *d* of Irvine Watson Cowie and Helen Jean Cowie; *m* 1939, Herbert Dudley Purves; one *s* two *d*.

Educ: Otago Girls' High Sch., Dunedin, NZ; Univ. of Otago, Dunedin (MA 1st Cl. Hons English and French). Secondary sch. teacher, 1931–40 and 1957–63. Pres., NZ Fedn of University Women, 1962–64; Internat. Fedn of University Women: Mem., Cultural Relations Cttee, 1965–68, Convener, 1968–71; 3rd Vice-Pres., 1971–74; 1st Vice-Pres., 1974–77; Pres., 1977–80. Chm., National Theme Cttee, The Child in the World, NZ Nat. Commn for Internat. Year of the Child, 1978–80; Mem., Internat. Year of the Child Telethon Trust, 1978–81; Exec. Mem., NZ Cttee for Children (IYC) Inc., 1980–82. Mem., NZ Nat. Commn, Unesco, 1964–68. Vice-Pres. for Women, Global Cooperation Soc. Club, 1980; Pres., Friends of Olveston Inc., 1986–88. Mem., Theomin Gall. Management Cttee, 1986–. *Recreations:* reading, croquet, bridge, travel, public speaking, heraldry. *Address:* 12 Grendon Court, 36 Drivers Road, Dunedin, New Zealand. *T:* Dunedin 4675 105. *Club:* Punga Croquet (Pres., 1988–90).

PURVES, Elizabeth Mary, (Libby), (Mrs Paul Heiney); writer and broadcaster; *b* 2 Feb. 1950; *d* of late James Grant Purves, CMG; *m* 1980, Paul Heiney; one *s* one *d*. *Educ:* Convent of the Sacred Heart, Tunbridge Wells; St Anne's Coll., Oxford (1st Cl. Hons Eng. Lang. and Lit.). BBC Local Radio (Oxford), 1972–76; Today, Radio 4: Reporter, 1976–79; Presenter, 1979–81; freelance writer, broadcaster; BBC TV Choices, 1982, Midweek (Presenter, 1984–), documentaries; writer for The Times, Sunday Times, Sunday Express, Good Housekeeping, *et al*; Editor, Tatler, March-Oct. 1983, resigned. *Publications:* (ed) The Happy Unicorns, 1971; (ed) Adventures Under Sail, H. W. Tilman, 1982; Britain At Play, 1982; Sailing Weekend Book, 1985; How Not to be a Perfect Mother, 1986; Where Did You Leave the Admiral, 1987; (jtly) The English and their Horses, 1988; The Hurricane Tree, 1988; One Summer's Grace, 1989; How Not to Raise a Perfect Child, 1991. *Recreations:* sailing, walking, writing, radio. *Address:* c/o A. P. Watt Ltd, 20 John Street, WC1N 2DL. *Clubs:* Royal Thames Yacht, Royal Cruising.

PURVES, William, CBE 1988; DSO 1951; Chairman and Chief Executive: Hongkong and Shanghai Banking Corporation Ltd, since 1986; HSBC Holdings plc, since 1990; Chairman, British Bank of the Middle East, since 1986; *b* 27 Dec. 1931; *s* of Andrew and Ida Purves; *m* 1st, 1958, Diana Troutbeck Richardson (marr. diss. 1988); two *s* two *d*; 2nd, 1989, Rebecca Jane Lewellen. Educ: Kelso High School. AIBScot; FCIB. National Service, with Commonwealth Div. in Korea (Subaltern; DSO). National Bank of Scotland, 1948–54; Hongkong and Shanghai Banking Corporation: Germany, Hong Kong, Malaysia, Singapore, Sri Lanka, Japan, 1954–70; Chief Accountant, Hong Kong, 1970; Manager, Tokyo, 1974; Sen. Manager Overseas Operations, 1976; Asst General Manager, Overseas Operations, 1978; General Manager, 1979; Executive Director, 1982; Dep. Chm., 1984. Director: Marine Midland Banks Inc., 1982–; Midland Bank Plc, 1987–. Hon. Dr Stirling, 1987. *Recreations:* golf, Rugby. *Address:* 19 Middle Gap Road, Hong Kong. *T:* 5–8496134. *Clubs:* New (Edinburgh); Royal Hong Kong Jockey, Royal Hong Kong Golf, Shek-o Country, Hong Kong, Rugby Union (Hong Kong).

PURVIS, Air Vice-Marshal Henry R.; *see* Reed-Purvis.

PURVIS, John Robert, CBE 1990; Managing Director, Gilmerton Management Services Ltd, since 1973; Senior Partner, Purvis & Co., since 1986; *b* 6 July 1938; *s* of Lt-Col R. W. B. Purvis, MC, JP, and Mrs R. W. B. Purvis, JP; *m* 1962, Louise S. Durham; one *s* two *d*. *Educ:* Cargilfield, Barnton, Edinburgh; Trinity Coll., Glenalmond, Perthshire; St Salvator's Coll., Univ. of St Andrews (MA Hons). National Service, Lieut Scots Guards, 1956–58. First National City Bank, New York, 1962–69: London, 1962–63; New York, 1963–65; Milan, 1965–69; Treasurer, Noble Grossart Ltd, Edinburgh, 1969–73. Mem. (C) Mid-Scotland and Fife, European Parlt, 1979–84, contested same seat, 1984; European Democratic Group, European Parliament: whip, 1980–82; spokesman on energy, research and technology, 1982–84. Vice Pres., Scottish Cons. and Unionist Assoc., 1987–89 (Chm., Industry Cttee, 1986–); Mem., IBA, 1985–89 (Chm., Scottish Adv. Cttee, 1985–89); Mem., Scottish Adv. Cttee on Telecommunications, 1990–. *Publication:* (section 'Money') in Power and Manoeuvrability, 1978. *Address:* Gilmerton, Dunino, St Andrews, Fife, Scotland KY16 8NB. *T:* St Andrews (0334) 73275. *Clubs:* Cavalry and Guards, Farmers'; New (Edinburgh); Royal and Ancient (St Andrews).

PURVIS, Vice-Adm. Neville; Chief of Fleet Support, since 1991; *b* 8 May 1936; *s* of Charles Geoffrey and Sylvia Rose Purvis; *m* 1970, Alice Margaret (*née* Hill); two *s*. *Educ:* Chaterhouse; Selwyn College, Cambridge (MA). BRNC Dartmouth, 1953; reading engineering at Cambridge, 1954–57; joined submarine service, 1959; served in HM Ships Turpin, 1960, Dreadnought, 1963, Repulse, 1967; Naval Staff, 1970; Sqdn Engineer Officer, 3rd Submarine Sqdn, 1973; Staff of Flag Officer, Submarines, 1975; RCDS 1980; in Command, HMS Collingwood, 1985–87; Dir Gen., Future Material Projects (Naval), 1987–88; Dir Gen., Naval Manpower and Trng, 1988–90. *Recreations:* gardening, chess. *Address:* Ministry of Defency (Navy), London. *Clubs:* Commonwealth Trust, Institute of Directors.

PURVIS, Stewart Peter; Editor, Independent Television News, since 1989; *b* 28 Oct. 1947; *s* of Peter and Lydia Purvis; *m* 1972, Mary Presnail; one *d*. *Educ:* Dulwich Coll.; Univ. of Exeter (BA). BBC News trainee, 1969; ITN journalist, 1972; Programme Editor, News At Ten, 1980; Editor, Channel Four News, ITN, 1983; Dep. Editor, ITN, 1988. FRTS 1991. *Address:* ITN House, 200 Gray's Inn Road, WC1. *Club:* Lansdowne (Walton-on-Thames).

PUSACK, George Williams, MS; Chief Executive, Mobil Oil Australia Ltd, 1980–85, retired; *b* 26 Sept. 1920; *s* of George F. Pusack and Winifred (*née* Williams); *m* 1942, Marian Preston; two *s* one *d*. *Educ:* Univ. of Michigan; Univ. of Pennsylvania. BSE (AeroEng), BSE (Eng.Math), MS (MechEng). Aero Engr, US Navy, 1942–45; Corporal, US Air Force, 1945–46; Mobil Oil Corp.: Tech. Service and Research Manager, USA, 1946–53; Product Engrg Manager, USA, 1953–59; International Supply Manager, USA, 1959–69; Vice-Pres., N Amer. Div., USA, 1969–73; Regional Exec., Mobil Europe, London, 1973–76; Chm. and Chief Exec, Mobil Oil Co. Ltd, 1976–80. Pres., County Hospice, York, SC, 1989–91. Trustee, Victorian State Opera Foundn. Teacher, layreader, vestryman and warden of Episcopal Church. *Recreations:* golf, travel. *Address:* 23 Hickory Nut Lane, Clover, SC 29710, USA. *T:* 803–831–7628. *Clubs:* River Hills Country (Pres., 1991) (Clover, USA); Australian, Royal Melbourne Golf (Melbourne).

PUSEY, Nathan Marsh, PhD; President Emeritus, Harvard University; *b* Council Bluffs, Iowa, 4 April 1907; *s* of John Marsh Pusey and Rosa Pusey (*née* Drake); *m* 1936, Anne Woodward; two *s* one *d*. *Educ:* Harvard University, USA. AB 1928, AM 1932, PhD, 1937. Assistant, Harvard, 1933–34; Sophomore tutor, Lawrence Coll., 1935–38; Asst Prof., history and literature, Scripps Coll., Claremont, Calif., 1938–40; Wesleyan Univ.: Asst Prof., Classics, 1940–43, Assoc. Prof., 1943–44; President: Lawrence Coll., Appleton, Wisconsin, 1944–53; Harvard Univ., 1953–71; Andrew Mellon Foundn, 1971–75. Pres., United Bd for Christian Higher Educn in Asia, 1979–83. Holds many hon. degrees from Universities and colleges in USA and other countries. Officier de la Légion d'Honneur, 1958. *Publications:* The Age of the Scholar, 1963; American Higher Education 1945–1970, 1978. *Address:* 200 East 66th Street, New York, NY 10021, USA.

PUSINELLI, (Frederick) Nigel (Molière), CMG 1966; OBE 1963; MC 1940; HM Overseas Civil Service, retired; *b* 28 April 1919; second *s* of late S. Jacques and T. May Pusinelli, Frettenham, Norfolk and Fowey, Cornwall; *m* 1941, Joan Mary Chaloner, *d* of late Cuthbert B. and Mildred H. Smith, Cromer, Norfolk and Bexhill-on-Sea, Sussex; one *s* one *d*. *Educ:* Aldenham School; Pembroke College, Cambridge (BA Hons in law). Commissioned RA 1939; served BEF, 1940; India/Burma, 1942–45; Major, 1942; Staff College, Quetta, 1945. Administrative officer, Gilbert and Ellice Islands Colony, 1946–57. Transferred to Aden, 1958; Dep. Financial Sec. and frequently Actg Financial Sec. till 1962; Director of Establishments, 1962–68, and Assistant High Commissioner, 1963–68, Aden and Federation of South Arabia. Member E African Currency Board, 1960–62. Salaries Commissioner various territories in West Indies, 1968–70. Chm., Overseas Service Pensioners' Assoc., 1978–. Chairman: Chichester Harbour Conservancy, 1987–90 (Vice-Chm., 1985–87; Mem., Adv. Cttee, 1971–); RYA Southern Region, 1979–; Chichester Harbour Fedn of sailing clubs and yachting orgns, 1980–87. *Publication:* Report on Census of Population of Gilbert and Ellice Islands Colony, 1947. *Recreation:* dinghy racing. *Address:* Routledge Cottage, Westbourne, Emsworth, Hants PO10 8SE. *T:* Emsworth (0243) 372915. *Clubs:* Commonwealth Trust; Royal Yachting Assoc., Cambridge University Cruising, Emsworth Sailing.

PUTT, S(amuel) Gorley, OBE 1966; MA; Fellow, Christ's College, Cambridge, since 1968 (Senior Tutor, 1968–78; Praelector, 1976–80); *b* 9 June 1913; *o c* of late Poole Putt and late Ellen Blake Gorley, Brixham. *Educ:* Torquay Grammar School; Christ's College, Cambridge; Yale University. 1st Class English Tripos Pts I and II, MA 1937, Cambridge; Commonwealth Fund Fellow, MA 1936, Yale. BBC Talks Dept, 1936–38; Warden and Sec., Appts Cttee, Queen's Univ. of Belfast, 1939–40; RNVR, 1940–46, Lieut-Comdr; Warden and Tutor to Overseas Students and Director International Summer School, Univ. Coll., Exeter, 1946–49; Warden of Harkness House, 1949–68 and Director, Div. of International Fellowships, The Commonwealth Fund, 1966–68. Chm., 1964–72, Vice-Pres., 1972–78, English Assoc. Visiting Professor: Univ. of Massachusetts, 1968; Univ. of the South, Sewanee, 1976; Univ. of Pisa, 1979; Texas Christian Univ., 1985. Member: English-Speaking Union, London Cttee, 1952–57; UK-US Educational Commn: Travel Grants Cttee, 1955–64; Cttee of Management, Inst. of US Studies, London Univ., 1965–69. Contested (L) Torquay, 1945. FRSL 1952. Cavaliere, Order of Merit of Italy, 1980. *Publications:* Men Dressed As Seamen, 1943; View from Atlantis, 1955; (ed) Cousins and Strangers, 1956; Coastline, 1959; Scholars of the Heart, 1962; (ed) Essays and Studies, 1963; A Reader's Guide to Henry James, 1966; The Golden Age of English Drama, 1981; A Preface to Henry James, 1986; Wings of a Man's Life, 1990. *Address:* Christ's College, Cambridge. *T:* Cambridge (0223) 334900. *Club:* Athenæum.

PUTTICK, Richard George; Chairman, 1974–85 and Chief Executive, 1978–85, Taylor Woodrow plc, retired; *b* Kingston, Surrey, 16 March 1916; *e s* of late George Frederick Puttick and Dorothea (*née* Bowerman); *m* 1943, Betty Grace Folbigg; two *s*. *Educ:* St Mark's, Teddington. Joined Taylor Woodrow Construction Ltd, 1940 (the Taylor Woodrow Group's largest contracting subsidiary co.); Dir, 1955; Asst Managing Dir, 1968; Dir, Taylor Woodrow Ltd, 1969; Jt Dep. Chm., 1972. Mem. Council, CBI, July 1967–Dec. 1969; Pres., NW Mddx Branch, BIM, 1976–85. FCIOB; CBIM. Liveryman, Worshipful Co. of Joiners and Ceilers. *Recreations:* music, reading, gardening, supporting sports. *Address:* Woodlawn, Hanger Hill, Weybridge, Surrey KT13 9XU. *T:* Weybridge (0932) 845131.

PUTTNAM, David Terence, CBE 1983; film producer; Chairman, Enigma Productions Ltd, since 1978; *b* 25 Feb. 1941; *s* of Leonard Arthur Puttnam and Marie Beatrix Puttnam; *m* 1961, Patricia Mary (*née* Jones); one *s* one *d*. *Educ:* Minchenden Grammar Sch., London. Advertising, 1958–66; photography, 1966–68; film prodn, 1968–. Producer of feature films including: Bugsy Malone, 1976 (four BAFTA awards); The Duellists, 1977 (Jury Prize, Cannes); Midnight Express, 1978 (two Acad. Awards, three BAFTA Awards); Chariots of Fire, 1981 (four Acad. Awards, three BAFTA Awards); Local Hero, 1982 (two BAFTA Awards); Cal, 1984 (Acting Prize, Cannes); The Killing Fields, 1985 (three Acad. Awards, eight BAFTA Awards incl. Best Film); The Mission, 1986 (Palme d'Or, Cannes, 1986, one Acad. Award, three BAFTA awards, 1987); Memphis Belle, 1990; Meeting Venus, 1991. Chm. and Chief Exec. Officer, Columbia Pictures, 1986–88. Producer of films and series for television. Vis. Industrial Prof., Drama Dept, Bristol Univ., 1986–. Director: National Film Finance Corp., 1980–85; Anglia Television Gp, 1982–; Survival Anglia, 1989–; Chm., Internat. Television Enterprises Ltd, 1988–; Governor, National Film and Television Sch., 1974–, Chm., 1988–. Pres., CPRE, 1985–. Trustee, Tate Gall., 1986–. FRGS; FRSA; FRPS. Hon. Fellow, Manchester Polytechnic, 1990; Hon. FCSD, 1990. Michael Balcon Award for outstanding contribn to British Film Industry, BAFTA, 1982. Hon. LLD Bristol, 1983; Hon. DLitt Leicester, 1986. Chevalier, l'Ordre des Arts et des Lettres, France, 1986. *Recreations:* watching cricket, going to the cinema. *Club:* MCC.

PUXON, (Christine) Margaret, (Mrs Margaret Williams); QC 1982; MD, FRCOG; practising barrister, since 1954; *b* 25 July 1915; *d* of Reginald Wood Hale and Clara Lilian Hale; *m* 1955, F. Morris Williams (*d* 1986), MBE; two *s* one *d*. *Educ:* Abbey Sch., Malvern Wells; Birmingham Univ. (MB, ChB; MD Obstetrics 1944). MRCS, LRCP 1942; FRCOG 1976. Gynaecological Registrar, Queen Elizabeth Hosp., Birmingham, and later Consultant Gynaecologist, Essex CC, 1942–49. Called to the Bar, Inner Temple, 1954. A Dep. Circuit Judge, 1970–86; a Recorder, 1986–88. Privy Council Member, Council of Royal Pharmaceutical Soc., 1971–90; Member: Genetic Manipulation Adv. Gp, 1979–84; Ethical Cttee, RCGP, 1981–. Liveryman, Worshipful Soc. of Apothecaries, 1982–. *Publications:* The Family and the Law, 1963, 2nd edn 1971; contrib. to Progress in Obstetrics and Gynaecology, 1983; contrib. to In Vitro Fertilisation: Past, Present and Future, 1986; contrib. to Gynaecology (ed Shaw, Souter and Stauton), 1991; contrib. med. and legal jls, incl. Proc. RSM, Practitioner, New Law Jl and Solicitors' Jl. *Recreations:* cooking, travel, opera, gardening. *Address:* Francis Taylor Building, Temple, EC4Y 7BY. *T:* 071–353 9942; 19 Clarence Gate Gardens, Glentworth Street, NW1 6AY. *T:* 071–723 7922.

PYATT, Rt. Rev. William Allan, CBE 1985; MA; formerly Bishop of Christchurch, retired; *b* Gisborne, NZ, 4 Nov. 1916; *e s* of A. E. Pyatt; *m* 1942, Mary Lilian Carey; two *s* one *d*. *Educ:* Gisborne High Sch.; Auckland Univ.; St John's Coll., Auckland; Westcott House, Cambridge. BA 1938 (Senior Schol. in Hist.); MA 1939. Served War of 1939–45: combatant service with 2 NZEF; Major, 2 IC 20 NZ Armd Regt 1945. Ordained, 1946; Curate, Cannock, Staffs, 1946–48; Vicar: Brooklyn, Wellington, NZ, 1948–52; Hawera, 1952–58; St Peter's, Wellington, 1958–62; Dean of Christchurch, 1962–66; Bishop of Christchurch, 1966–83. *Publications:* contribs to NZ Jl of Theology. *Recreations:* Rugby referee; political comment on radio; golf, wood turning, caravanning; lecturing on current affairs, study of Maori language and racial issues in New Zealand. *Address:* 55a Celia Street, Christchurch 8, New Zealand.

PYBUS, William Michael; Chairman, AAH Holdings plc, since 1968; *b* 7 May 1923; *s* of Sydney James Pybus and Evelyn Mary (*née* Wood); *m* 1959, Elizabeth Janet Whitley; two *s* two *d*. *Educ:* Bedford Sch.; New College, Oxford (1st cl. hons Jurisprudence).

Served War, 1942–46: commissioned 1st King's Dragoon Guards; Lieut attached XIth Hussars in Normandy (wounded); King's Dragoon Guards, Egypt, Palestine, Syria, Lebanon; Prosecutor, Mil. Courts, Palestine, 1946 (Major). Admitted Solicitor (Scott Schol.), 1950; Partner, Herbert Oppenheimer, Nathan & Vandyk, Solicitors, 1953–88. Consultant, Denton Hall Burgin & Warrens, 1988–. Chairman: Siebe (formerly Siebe Gorman Hldgs), 1980–90 (Dir, 1972–); Leigh Interests, 1982–89; British Fuel Co., 1968–87; Inter-Continental Fuels Ltd, 1975–88; Overseas Coal Developments Ltd, 1979–88; Ashdown House School Trust Ltd, 1975–88; Vestric Ltd, 1985–; Homeowners Friendly Soc., 1991– (Dir, 1980–); Dep. Chm., R. Mansell Ltd, 1980–85; Director: National Westminster Bank (Outer London Region), 1977–88; Cornhill Insurance PLC, 1977–; Bradford & Bingley Building Soc., 1983–. Part-time Member: British Railways (London Midland) Bd, 1974; British Railways (Midlands and West) Bd, 1975–77; Chm., BR (London Midland) Bd, 1977–89. Dir, Coal Trade Benevolent Assoc., 1969–; Vice-Pres., Coal Industry Soc., 1981– (Pres., 1976–81). Governor, Harpur Trust, 1979–87. Master, Pattenmakers' Co., 1972–73. CBIM 1974; FInstM 1974; FRSA 1984. *Recreation:* fishing. *Address:* 5 Chancery Lane, Clifford's Inn, EC4A 1BU. *T:* 071–242 1212. *Clubs:* Cavalry and Guards, MCC; Yorkshire CC.

PYE, Prof. John David, FLS; Professor of Zoology, Queen Mary and Westfield College (formerly Queen Mary College), University of London, 1973–91, now Emeritus; *b* 14 May 1932; *s* of Wilfred Frank Pye and Gwenllian Pye (*née* Davies); *m* 1958, Dr Ade Pye (*née* Kuku), Sen. Lectr, UCL. *Educ:* Queen Elizabeth's Grammar School for Boys, Mansfield; University Coll. of Wales, Aberystwyth (BSc 1954, Hons 1955); Bedford Coll., London Univ. (PhD 1961). Research Asst, Inst. of Laryngology and Otology, London Univ., 1958–64; Lectr in Zoology, 1964–70, Reader, 1970–73, King's Coll. London; Head of Dept of Zoology and Comparative Physiology, Queen Mary Coll., 1977–82. A founder Dir, QMC Instruments Ltd, 1976–89. Linnean Society: Editor, Zoological Jl, 1981–85; Editl Sec. and Mem. Council, 1985–91; Vice-Pres., 1987–90; Mem., IEE Professional Gp Cttee E15, Radar, Sonar, Navigation and Avionics, 1983–86. Mem., RHS, 1988–. Member Editorial Boards: Zoolog. Soc., 1972–77, 1978–83, 1985–90; Jl of Exper. Biol., 1974–78; Jl of Comp. Physiol. A, 1978–; Bioacoustics, 1987–. Associate Mem., Royal Instn, 1979– (delivered Friday discourses 1979, 1983, and televised Christmas Lects for Children, 1985–86. *Publications:* Bats, 1968; (with G. D. Sales) Ultrasonic Communication by Animals, 1974; (ed with R. J. Bench and A. Pye) Sound Reception in Mammals, 1975; articles and research papers. *Recreations:* viticulture and vinification, travelling in warm climates. *Address:* Woodside, 24 St Mary's Avenue, Finchley, N3 1SN. *T:* 081–346 6869; (office) 071–975 5555.

PYE, Prof. Norman; Professor of Geography, University of Leicester, 1954–79, now Emeritus; Pro-Vice-Chancellor, 1963–66; Dean, Faculty of Science, 1957–60; Chairman of Convocation, 1982–85; *b* 2 Nov. 1913; *s* of John Whittaker Pye and Hilda Constance (*née* Platt); *m* 1940, Isabella Jane (*née* Currie); two *s*. *Educ:* Wigan Grammar School; Manchester University. Manchester University: BA Hons Geography Class I, 1935, Diploma in Education Class I, 1936. Asst Lecturer in Geography, Manchester Univ., 1936–37 and 1938–46; Mem., Cambridge Univ. Spitsbergen Expedn, 1938. Seconded to Hydrographic Dept, Admiralty, for War Service, 1940–46; pt-time lectr, Univ. of Bristol Cttee on Educn in HM Forces, 1941–45. Lecturer in Geography, 1946–53, Sen. Lecturer, 1953–54, Manchester Univ; Mem. Expedn to US Sonora and Mojave Deserts, 1952. Chm., Conf. of Heads of Depts of Geography in British Univs, 1968–70. Vis. Professor: Univ. of Ghana, 1958, 1960; Univ. of BC, 1964, 1983; Univ. of Alberta, Edmonton, 1967, 1968, 1969, 1973, 1974, 1975, 1978; External Examnr: Univ. of E Africa, 1964–67; Univ. of Guyana, 1974–78. Editor, "Geography", 1965–80. Member Corby Development Corp., 1965–80. Governor, Up Holland Grammar Sch., 1953–74; Member: Northants CC Educn Cttee, 1956–74; Court, Nottingham Univ., 1964–79; Standing Conf. on Univ. Entrance, 1966–79; Schools Council, 1967–78. Member: Council, RMetS, 1953–56; Council, Inst. of Brit. Geographers, 1954, 1955; Council, RGS, 1967–70 (Hon. Fellow, 1991); Council for Urban Studies Centres, 1974–81; Brit. Nat. Cttee for Geography, 1970–75; Civic Trust Educn Gp (formerly Heritage Educn Gp), 1976–90; Young Enterprise Leics Area Bd, 1983–; Hon. Mem., Geographical Assoc., 1983– (Mem. Council, 1965–83; Hon. Vice-Pres., 1979–83). *Publications:* Leicester and its Region (ed and contrib.), 1972; research papers and articles in learned journals. *Recreations:* travel, oenology, music, gardening. *Address:* 127 Spencefield Lane, Evington, Leicester LE5 6GG. *T:* Leicester (0533) 415167. *Club:* Geographical.

PYKE, David Alan, CBE 1986; MD, FRCP; Registrar, Royal College of Physicians of London, since 1975; Physician-in-charge, Diabetic Department, King's College Hospital, London, 1971–86; *b* 16 May 1921; *s* of Geoffrey and Margaret Pyke; *m* 1948, Janet, *d* of Dr J. Gough Stewart; one *s* two *d*. *Educ:* Leighton Park Sch., Reading; Cambridge Univ.; University Coll. Hosp. Med. Sch., London. MD Cantab; FRCP. Junior med. appts in London and Oxford, 1945–59. Service in RAMC, 1946–48. Apptd to staff of King's Coll. Hosp., 1959. Hon. Sec.: Assoc. of Physicians of GB and Ire., 1968–73; Royal Soc. of Med., 1972–74. *Publications:* (jt ed) Clinical Diabetes and its Biochemical Basis, 1968; (ed) Clinics in Endocrinology and Metabolism, Vol. 1, No 3, 1972; (jtly) Diabetes and its Management, 1973, 3rd edn 1978; articles in med. and sci. jls. *Recreations:* golf, opera. *Address:* 17 College Road, SE21 7BG. *T:* 081–693 2313.

PYKE, Magnus, OBE 1978; PhD, CChem, FRSC, FInstBiol, FIFST, FRSE; *b* 29 Dec. 1908; *s* of Robert Bond Pyke and Clara Hannah Pyke (*née* Lewis); *m* 1937, Dorothea Mina Vaughan (*d* 1986); one *s* one *d*. *Educ:* St Paul's Sch., London; McGill Univ., Montreal; University Coll. London (Fellow, 1984–). BSc, PhD. Scientific Adviser's Div., Min. of Food, London, 1941–45; Nutritional Adviser, Allied Commn for Austria, Vienna, 1945–46; Principal Scientific Officer (Nutrition), Min. of Food, London, 1946–48; Distillers Co. Ltd: Dep. Manager, Yeast Research Outstation, 1949–55; Manager, Glenochil Research Station, 1955–73; Sec. and Chm. of Council, British Assoc. for the Advancement of Science, 1973–77 (Mem. Council, 1968–77; Pres. Section X, 1965). Member: (Vice-Pres.) Soc. for Analytical Chemistry, 1959–61; Council, Royal Inst. of Chemistry, 1953–56, 1962–65; Council, Royal Soc. of Edinburgh, 1961–64; Council, Soc. of Chemical Industry, 1967–69; (Chm.) Scottish Section, Nutrition Soc., 1954–55; (Vice-Pres.) Assoc. for Liberal Education, 1964–81; (Pres.) Inst. of Food Science and Technology of the UK, 1969–71; Participated in Don't Ask Me, 1974–78, Don't Just Sit There, 1979–80, Yorkshire TV. FInstBiol (Mem. Council, Scottish Sect., 1959–62). Hon. Fellow: Australian IFST, 1973; NZ IFST, 1979. Hon. Senior Mem., Sen. Common Room, Darwin Coll., Univ. of Kent, 1979. DUniv Stirling, 1974; Hon. DSc: Lancaster, 1976; McGill, 1981. Silver Medal, RSA, 1972; Pye Colour TV Award: the most promising newcomer to television, 1975; BBC Multi-Coloured Swap Shop Star Award (Expert of the Year), 1977–78. *Publications:* Manual of Nutrition, 1945; Industrial Nutrition, 1950; Townsman's Food, 1952; Automation, Its Purpose and Future, 1956; Nothing Like Science, 1957; Slaves Unaware, 1959; The Boundaries of Science, 1961; Nutrition, 1962; The Science Myth, 1962; Food Science and Technology, 1964; The Science Century, 1967; Food and Society, 1968; Man and Food, 1970; Synthetic Food, 1970; Technological Eating, 1972; Catering Science and Technology, 1973; Success in Nutrition, 1975; Butter-side Up, 1976; There and Back, 1978; Food for all the Family, 1980; Long Life, 1980; Our Future, 1980; (with P. Moore) Everyman's Scientific Facts and Feats, 1981; Six Lives of Pyke, 1981; Curiouser and Curiouser, 1983; Red Rag to a Bull, 1983; (contrib.) Diet and Health in Modern Britain, ed D. J. Oddy and D. S. Miller, 1985; (contrib.) The World's Food Supply, ed J. Asimov, 1985; Dr Magnus Pyke's 101 Inventions, 1986. *Recreation:* Until he was 75 he wrote a page a day and savoured the consequences. *Address:* Elmbank, 38 Carlton Drive, SW15. *T:* 081–780 9027. *Club:* Savage.

PYLE, Cyril Alfred; Head Master, South East London School, 1970–80; *s* of Alfred John Pyle and Nellie Blanche Pyle; *m* 1940, Jean Alice Cotten; one *s* one *d*. *Educ:* Shooters Hill Grammar Sch.; Univ. of London, Goldsmiths' Coll. Dep. Headmaster, Woolwich Polytechnic Secondary Sch., 1940–66; Headmaster, Bow Sch., 1966–70. Pres., London Teachers' Assoc., 1962; Chm., Council for Educnl Advance, 1964–76; Sec., Conference of London Comprehensive School Heads, 1973–79. *Recreations:* Rotary Club, motoring, gardening. *Address:* Barleyfields, Hartlip, Sittingbourne, Kent ME9 7TH. *T:* Newington (0795) 842719.

PYM, family name of **Baron Pym.**

PYM, Baron *cr* 1987 (Life Peer), of Sandy in the County of Bedfordshire; **Francis Leslie Pym;** PC 1970; MC 1945; DL; *b* 13 Feb. 1922; *s* of late Leslie Ruthven Pym, MP, and Iris, *d* of Charles Orde; *m* 1949, Valerie Fortune Daglish; two *s* two *d*. *Educ:* Eton; Magdalene Coll., Cambridge (Hon. Fellow 1979). Served War of 1939–45 (despatches, 1944 and 1945, MC): 9th Lancers, 1942–46; African and Italian campaigns. Contested (C) Rhondda West, 1959; MP (C): Cambridgeshire, 1961–83; Cambridgeshire South East, 1983–87. Asst Govt Whip (unpaid), Oct. 1962–64; Opposition Whip, 1964–67; Opposition Dep. Chief Whip, 1967–70; Parly Sec. to the Treasury and Govt Chief Whip, 1970–73; Sec. of State for NI, 1973–74; Opposition spokesman on: agriculture, 1974–76; H of C affairs and devolution, 1976–78; Foreign and Commonwealth affairs, 1978–79; Sec. of State for Defence, 1979–81; Chancellor of the Duchy of Lancaster and Paymaster Gen., and Leader of the House of Commons, 1981; Lord Pres. of the Council and Leader of the House of Commons, 1981–82; Sec. of State for Foreign and Commonwealth Affairs, 1982–83. Chairman: CableVision Communications, 1990–; Philip N. Christie & Co., 1990–. Pres., Atlantic Treaty Assoc., 1985–87. Chm., E-SU, 1987–. Mem. Herefordshire County Council, 1958–61. DL Cambs, 1973. *Publication:* The Politics of Consent, 1984. *Recreations:* gardens, plants. *Address:* Everton Park, Sandy, Beds. *Clubs:* Buck's, Cavalry and Guards.

PYMAN, Lancelot Frank Lee, CMG 1961; HM Diplomatic Service, retired; *b* 8 August 1910; *s* of late Dr F. L. Pyman, FRS, and of Mrs I. C. Pyman; *m* 1936, Sarah Woods Gamble (*d* 1981). *Educ:* Dover College; King's College, Cambridge (Exhibitioner). Entered Levant Consular Service, 1933; various posts in Persia, 1933–38; Consul, Cernauti, Roumania, 1939–40; Vice-Consul, Beirut, Lebanon, 1940–41. Served with HM Forces in Levant States, 1941. Asst Oriental Secretary, HM Embassy, Tehran, Dec. 1941–44; Foreign Office, 1944–48; Consul, St Louis, Missouri, Dec. 1948–49; Oriental Counsellor, Tehran, Dec. 1949–Sept. 1952; Counsellor, British Embassy, Rio de Janeiro, 1952–53; Consul-General, Tetuan, 1953–56; Counsellor, British Embassy, Rabat, 1956–57; HM Consul-General: Zagreb, 1957–61; Basra, March-Dec. 1961; Ambassador to the Somali Republic, 1961–63; Consul-General, San Francisco, 1963–66. *Recreations:* listening to music, duplicate bridge. *Address:* Knockroe, Delgany, Co. Wicklow, Ireland.

PYPER, Mark Christopher Spring-Rice; Headmaster, Gordonstoun School, since 1990; *b* 13 Aug. 1947; *s* of Arthur Spring-Rice Pyper and Rosemary Isabel Pyper; *m* 1979, Jennifer Lindsay Gilderson; one *s* two *d*. *Educ:* Winchester College; Balliol College, Oxford (BA Mod. Hist.). Asst Master, Stoke Brunswick Sch., East Grinstead, 1966–68; Asst Master, then Joint Headmaster, St Wilfrid's Sch., Seaford, 1969–79; Registrar, Housemaster, then Dep. Headmaster, Sevenoaks Sch., 1979–90. Dir, Sevenoaks Summer Festival, 1979–90. *Address:* Headmaster's House, Gordonstoun School, Elgin, Moray IV30 2RF. *T:* Hopeman (0343) 830445. *Club:* MCC.

PYRAH, Prof. Leslie Norman, CBE 1963; retired as Senior Consultant Surgeon, Department of Urology, Leeds General Infirmary (1950–64); Hon. Director, Medical Research Council Unit, Leeds General Infirmary, 1956–64; Professor of Urological Surgery, Leeds University, 1956–64, now Emeritus; *b* 11 April 1899; *s* of Arthur Pyrah; *m* 1934, Mary Christopher Batley (*d* 1990); one *s* one *d* (and one *s* decd). *Educ:* University of Leeds; School of Medicine, Leeds. Hon. Asst Surgeon, Leeds Gen. Infirmary, 1934; Hon. Consultant Surgeon, Dewsbury Infirmary, Leeds Public Dispensary, Goole Hosp., and Lecturer in Surgery, Univ. of Leeds, 1934; Hon. Cons. Surgeon, St James' Hosp., Leeds, 1941; Surgeon with charge of Out-patients, Leeds Infirmary, 1944; Weild Lectr, Royal Faculty Physicians and Surgeons, Glasgow, 1955; Ramon Guiteras Lectr, Amer. Urological Assoc., Pittsburgh, USA, 1957; Pres., Section of Urology, Royal Soc. Med., 1958; Litchfield Lectr, Univ. of Oxford, 1959; Hunterian Orator, RCS, 1969. Chm., Specialist Adv. Cttee in Urology, Jt Royal Colls of Surgeons of GB and Ireland, 1968–72. Pres., British Assoc. of Urological Surgeons, 1961, 1962; Pres. Leeds and W Riding Medico-Chirurgical Soc., 1959. Mem. Council (elected), Royal College of Surgeons of England, 1960–68. Hon. Mem. Soc. Belge de Chirurgie, 1958; Corresponding Member: Amer. Assoc. of Genito-Urinary Surgeons, 1962; Amer. Soc. of Pelvic Surgeons, 1962; Australasian Soc. of Urology, 1963. St Peter's Medal (British Assoc. of Urological Surgeons) for outstanding contributions to urology, 1959; Honorary Medal, RCS, 1975. DSc (*hc*) Leeds, 1965; Hon. FRSM, 1978. *Publications:* Renal Calculus, 1979; (contrib.) British Surgical Progress, 1956; numerous contribs to British Journal of Surgery, British Journal of Urology, Proc. Royal Soc. Med., Lancet, BMJ. *Recreations:* tennis, music. *Address:* Fieldhead, Weetwood Lane, Leeds LS16 5NP. *T:* Leeds (0532) 752777.

PYTCHES, Rt. Rev. (George Edward) David; Vicar of St Andrew's, Chorleywood, Rickmansworth, since 1977; *b* 9 Jan. 1931; 9th *c* and 6th *s* of late Rev. Thomas Arthur Pytches and late Eirene Mildred Pytches (*née* Welldon); *m* 1958, Mary Trevisick; four *d*. *Educ:* Old Buckenham Hall, Norfolk; Framlingham Coll., Suffolk; Univ. of Bristol (BA); Trinity Coll., Bristol. MPhil Nottingham, 1984. Deacon 1955, priest 1956; Asst Curate, St Ebbe's, Oxford, 1955–58; Asst Curate, Holy Trinity, Wallington, 1958–59; Missionary Priest in Chol Chol, Chile, 1959–62; in Valparaiso, Chile, 1962–68; Rural Dean, Valparaiso, 1966–70; Diocese of Chile, Bolivia and Peru: Asst Bishop, 1970–72; Vicar General, 1971–72; Bishop, 1972–77. *Publications:* Come Holy Spirit, 1985; Does God Speak Today?, 1989; Some Said It Thundered, 1990; (jtly) New Wineskins, 1991. *Recreations:* collecting semi-precious stones, walking. *Address:* The Vicarage, Quickley Lane, Chorleywood, Rickmansworth, Herts WD3 5AE. *T:* Chorleywood (09278) 2391.

Q

QUANT, Mary, (Mrs A. Plunket Greene), OBE 1966; RDI 1969; Director of Mary Quant Group of companies since 1955; *b* 11 Feb. 1934; *d* of Jack and Mildred Quant; *m* 1957, Alexander Plunket Greene (*d* 1990); one *s*. *Educ:* 13 schools; Goldsmiths' College of Art. Fashion Designer. Mem., Design Council, 1971–74. Member: British/USA Bicentennial Liaison Cttee, 1973; Adv. Council, V&A Museum, 1976–78. Exhibition, Mary Quant's London, London Museum, 1973–74. FCSD (FSIA 1967). Maison Blanche Rex Award (US), 1964; Sunday Times Internat. Award, 1964; Piavola d'Oro Award (Italy), 1966; Annual Design Medal, Inst. of Industrial Artists and Designers, 1966; Hall of Fame Award, British Fashion Council, 1990. *Publication:* Quant by Quant, 1966. *Address:* 3 Ives Street, SW3 2NE. *T:* 071–584 8781.

QUANTRILL, Prof. Malcolm, RIBA; architect, author and critic; Distinguished Professor of Architecture, Texas A&M University, since 1986; *b* Norwich, Norfolk, 25 May 1931; *s* of Arthur William Quantrill and Alice May Newstead; *m* 1971, Esther Maeve, *d* of James Brignell Dand and Winifred Dand, Chester; two *s* two *d*. *Educ:* City of Norwich Sch.; Liverpool Univ. (BArch); Univ. of Pennsylvania (MArch); Univ. of Wroclaw (Doc. Ing Arch). RIBA 1961. Fulbright Scholar and Albert Kahn Meml Fellow, Univ. of Pennsylvania, 1954–55; Asst Prof., Louisiana State Univ., 1955–60; Lecturer: Univ. of Wales, Cardiff, 1962–65; UCL, 1965–66; Asst to Dir, Architectural Assoc., 1966–67, Dir, 1967–69; Lectr, Univ. of Liverpool, 1970–73; Dean, Sch. of Environmental Design, Polytechnic of N London, 1973–80; Prof. of Architecture and Urban Design, Univ. of Jordan, Amman-Jordan, 1980–83. Vis. Professor: Univ. of Illinois, Chicago, 1973–75; Carleton Univ., Ottawa, 1978; Gastprofessor, Technische Universität, Wien, 1975–77; Fellow, Graham Foundn for Advanced Studies in the Fine Arts, Chicago, 1984. Sir William Dobell Meml Lectr in Modern Art, Sydney, NSW, 1978. Plays performed: Honeymoon, 1968; Life Class, 1968 (TV); radio plays include: The Fence, 1964; Let's Get This Straight, 1977; Immortal Bite, 1982. *Publications:* The Gotobed Trilogy (novels), 1962–64; Ritual and Response in Architecture, 1974; Monuments of Another Age, 1975; On the Home Front (novel), 1977; The Art of Government and the Government of Art, 1978; Alvar Aalto—a critical study, 1983; Reima Pietilä—architecture, context and modernism, 1985; The Environmental Memory, 1987; Reima Pietilä: one man's odyssey in search of Finnish architecture, 1988; articles in RIBA Jl, Arch. Assoc. Qly, Arch. Design, and Art Internat. *Address:* 18 Causton Road, Highgate, N6. *T:* 081–348 1064; School of Architecture, Texas A&M University, College Station, Texas 77843–3137, USA. *Club:* Garrick.

QUANTRILL, William Ernest; HM Diplomatic Service; Ambassador to the Republic of Cameroon, since 1991, and concurrently to the Central African Republic, to the Republic of Chad, and to Equatorial Guinea; *b* 4 May 1939; *s* of late Ronald Frederick Quantrill and Norah Elsie Quantrill (*née* Matthews); *m* 1964, Rowena Mary Collins; three *s* one *d*. *Educ:* Colston's Sch., Bristol; Hatfield Coll., Univ. of Durham (BA Hons French). Entered FO, 1962; served Brussels, Havana, Manila, Lagos, 1964–80; Head of Training Dept, FCO, 1980–81; Dep. Head of Personnel Ops Dept, FCO, 1981–84; Counsellor and Hd of Chancery, Caracas, 1984–88; Dep. Gov., Gibraltar, 1988–90. *Recreations:* wild life, travel. *Address:* c/o Foreign and Commonwealth Office, SW1A 2AH. *T:* 071–270 3000.

QU'APPELLE, Bishop of, since 1986; **Rt. Rev. Eric Bays;** *b* 10 Aug. 1932; *s* of Rev. Canon P. C. Bays and Hilda (*née* Harper); *m* 1967, Patricia Ann Earle; one *s* one *d*. *Educ:* Univ. of Manitoba (BSc 1955); Univ. of Saskatchewan (BA 1959): Univ. of Emmanuel College (LTh 1959); Christian Theological Seminary (MMin 1974). Flight Lieut, RCAF (Reserve), 1955. Asst Curate, All Saints', Winnipeg, 1959–61; Lecturer, Emmanuel Coll., 1961–62; Priest-in-charge: Burns Lake, BC, 1962–63; Masset, BC, 1963–64; Novice, Community of the Resurrection, Yorks, 1964–65; Vicar, St Saviour's, Winnipeg with Bird's Hill, 1965–68; Rector, All Saints', Winnipeg, 1968–76; Professor, Coll. of Emmanuel and St Chad, 1976–86, Vice-Principal 1981–86. Canon of St John's Cathedral, Winnipeg, 1971–86. Hon. DD Coll. of Emmanuel and St Chad, 1987. *Recreations:* golf, curling. *Address:* Bishop's Court, 1701 College Avenue, Regina, Saskatchewan S4P 1B8, Canada. *T:* (306) 522 8898.

QUARMBY, David Anthony, MA, PhD; FCIT; FILDM; CBIM; Joint Managing Director, J. Sainsbury plc, since 1988 (Director, since 1984); *b* 22 July 1941; *s* of Frank Reginald and Dorothy Margaret Quarmby; *m* 1968, Hilmary Hunter; four *d*. *Educ:* Shrewsbury Sch.; King's Coll., Cambridge (MA); Leeds Univ. (PhD, Dip. Industrial Management). Asst Lectr, then Lectr, Dept of Management Studies, Leeds Univ., 1963; Economic Adviser, Economic Planning Directorate, Min. of Transport, 1966; London Transport Executive: Dir of Operational Research, 1970; Chief Commercial and Planning Officer, 1974; Mem., 1975–84; Man. Dir (Buses), 1978–84; Mem., London Regional Transport, 1984; Director: Homebase Ltd, 1987–89; Shaw's Supermarkets Inc., 1987–. Vice-President: Bus and Coach Council, 1981–84; CIT, 1987–; Mem., Nat. Council, Freight Transport Assoc., 1985–88. Member: Southwark Diocesan Synod, 1982–85; London Adv. Bd, Salvation Army, 1982–87. Dir, and Chm. Develt Cttee, Blackheath Concert Halls, 1990–. Gov., 1987–, Chm., Finance Cttee, 1991–, James Allen's Girls' Sch., London. FRSA. *Publications:* Factors Affecting Commuter Travel Behaviour (PhD Thesis, Leeds), 1967; contribs to Jl of Transport Economics and Policy, Regional Studies, Enterprise Management, and to books on transport, distribution, economics and operational research. *Recreations:* music, singing. *Address:* 13 Shooters Hill Road, Blackheath, SE3 7AR. *T:* 081–858 7371, 3962.

QUARREN EVANS, (John) Kerry; His Honour Judge Quarren Evans; a Circuit Judge, on South Eastern circuit, since 1980; *b* 4 July 1926; *s* of late Hubert Royston Quarren Evans, MC and of Violet Soule Quarren Evans; *m* 1958, Janet Shaw Lawson; one *s* one *d*. *Educ:* King Edward VIII Sch., Coventry; Cardiff High Sch.; Trinity Hall, Cambridge, 1948–51 (MA, LLM). 21st Glam. (Cardiff) Bn Home Guard, 1943–44; enlisted, Grenadier Gds, 1944; commnd Royal Welch Fusiliers, 1946, from OTS Bangalore; att. 2nd Bn The Welch Regt, Burma, 1946–47; Captain 1947. Admitted solicitor, 1953; Partner: Lyndon Moore & Co., Newport, 1954–71; T. S. Edwards & Son, Newport, 1971–80; Recorder, Wales and Chester Circuit, 1974–80. Clerk to Gen. Comrs of Income Tax, Dinas Powis Div., 1960–80; Chm., Newport Nat. Insurance Local Tribunal, 1968–71. *Recreations:* golf, Rugby football, oenology, staurologosophy, old things. *Address:* 2 Mount Park Crescent, Ealing, W5 2RN. *Clubs:* Denham Golf, Newport Golf, Royal Porthcawl Golf, Crawshay's Welsh Rugby Football.

QUARTANO, Ralph Nicholas, CBE 1987; CEng, MIChemE; Chairman, PosTel Investment Management Ltd, 1987–91 (Chief Executive, 1983–87); Director: 3i Group plc (formerly Investors in Industry Group), since 1986; Clerical Medical Investment Group, since 1987; Booker plc, since 1988; British Maritime Technology Ltd, since 1988; Deputy Chairman, Securities and Investments Board, since 1987 (Director, since 1985); Governor, BUPA, since 1987; *b* 3 Aug. 1927; *s* of late Charles and Vivienne Mary Quartano; *m* 1954, Cornelia Johanna de Gunst; two *d*. *Educ:* Sherborne Sch.; Pembroke Coll., Cambridge (MA). Bataafsche Petroleum Mij, 1952–58; The Lummus Co, 1958–59; Temple Press, 1959–65; Man. Director: Heywood Temple Industrial Publications, 1965–68; Engineering Chemical and Marine Press, 1968–70. The Post Office, 1971–74; Sen. Dir, Central Finance, 1973–74; Chief Exec., Post Office Staff Superannuation Fund, 1974–83. Director: London American Energy NV, 1981–88; Britoil plc, 1982–88; John Lewis Partnership Pensions Trust, 1986–89; Enterprise Oil, 1991–. Member: Engrg Council, 1981–83; City Capital Markets Cttee, 1985–; City Adv. Gp to Dir-Gen., CBI, 1985–; Investment Cttee, Pensioen Fonds PGGM, Netherlands, 1986–; Financial Reporting Council, 1990–. Sloan Fellow of London Business School. Trustee, Monteverdi Trust, 1986–. *Address:* 20 Oakcroft Road, SE13 7ED. *T:* 081–852 1607.

QUAYLE, James Danforth, (Dan), JD; Vice-President of the United States of America, since 1989; *b* 4 Feb. 1947; *m* 1972, Marilyn Tucker; two *s* one *d*. *Educ:* DePauw Univ. (BS 1969); Indiana Univ. (JD 1974). Admitted to Indiana Bar, 1974. Court reporter, 1965–69, Associate Publisher and Gen. Manager, 1974–76, Huntington Herald Press; Mem., Consumer Protection Div., Office of the Attorney General, Indiana, 1970–71; Admin. Assistant to Gov. of Indiana, 1971–73; Dir, Inheritance Tax Div., Indiana, 1973–74; teacher of business law, Huntington Coll., 1975. Mem. of Congress, 1976–80; Mem. for Indiana, US Senate, 1981–88. *Address:* The White House, Washington DC 20501, USA.

QUAYLE, Prof. John Rodney, PhD; FRS 1978; Vice-Chancellor, University of Bath, 1983–Aug. 1992; *b* 18 Nov. 1926; *s* of John Martin Quayle and Mary Doris Quayle (*née* Thorp); *m* 1951, Yvonne Mabel (*née* Sanderson); one *s* one *d*. *Educ:* Alun Grammar Sch., Mold; University Coll. of North Wales, Bangor (BSc, PhD); Univ. of Cambridge (PhD); MA Oxon. Res. Fellow, Radiation Lab., Univ. of California, 1953–55; Sen. Scientific Officer, Tropical Products Institute, London, 1955–56; Mem. Scientific Staff, MRC Cell Metabolism Res. Unit, Univ. of Oxford, 1956–63; Lectr, Oriel Coll., Oxford, 1957–63; Sen. Lectr in Biochemistry, 1963–65, West Riding Prof. of Microbiol., 1965–83, Sheffield Univ. Vis. Res. Prof. of Gesellschaft für Strahlen und Umweltforschung, Institut für Mikrobiologie, Universität Göttingen, 1973–74; Walker-Ames Vis. Prof., Univ. of Washington, Seattle, 1981. Chm., British Nat. Cttee for Microbiol., 1985–90; Member: AFRC, 1982–84; Adv. Council, RMCS, 1983–; Council, Royal Soc., 1982–84; Biol Sciences Cttee, SERC, 1981–84; Pres., Soc. for General Microbiology, 1990–. Trustee, Bath Festival Soc., 1984–89. Korrespondierendes Mitglied, Akademie der Wissenschaften, Göttingen, 1976. Hon. Dr *rer. nat.*, Göttingen, 1989. Ciba Medal, Biochem. Soc., 1978. *Publications:* articles in scientific jls. *Recreations:* hill-walking, gardening, bread-making. *Address:* (until Aug. 1992) The Lodge, North Road, Claverton Down, Bath BA2 6HE; (from Aug. 1992) The Coach House, Vicarage Lane, Compton Dando, Bristol BS18 4LB. *T:* Compton Dando (0761) 490399. *Club:* Athenæum.

QUAYLE, Maj.-Gen. Thomas David Graham, CB 1990; Ombudsman for Corporate Estate Agents, since 1990; *b* 7 April 1936; *s* of Thomas Quayle and Phyllis Gwendolen Johnson; *m* 1962, Susan Jean Bradford; three *d*. *Educ:* Repton; Trinity College, Oxford. Commissioned RA 1958; Student, Indian Staff Coll., 1968; Comdr, The Chestnut Troop, 1971–72; Instructor, Staff Coll., Camberley, 1974–76; Comdr, 40 Field Regt (The Lowland Gunners), 1976–79; Comdr Artillery, 4th Armoured Div., 1981–83; Defence Attaché, Bonn, 1983–86; Comdr Artillery, 1st British Corps, 1987–90, retd. *Recreations:* shooting, fishing, bridge. *Address:* c/o National Westminster Bank, Salisbury, Wilts.

QUEBEC, Archbishop of, (RC), and Primate of Canada, since 1981; **His Eminence Cardinal Louis-Albert Vachon,** CC (Canada) 1969; OQ 1985; FRSC 1974; Officier de l'Ordre de la fidélité française, 1963; *b* 4 Feb. 1912; *s* of Napoléon Vachon and Alexandrine Gilbert. *Educ:* Laval Univ. (PhD Philosophy, 1947); PhD Theology, Angelicum, Rome, 1949. Ordained priest, 1938; Prof. of Philosophy, 1941–47, Prof. of Theology, 1949–55, Laval Univ. Superior, Grand Séminaire de Québec, 1955–59; Superior General, 1960–77; Auxiliary Bishop of Quebec, 1977–81; Cardinal, 1985. Vice-Rector of Laval Univ., 1959–60, Rector, 1960–72. Mem., Royal Canadian Soc. of Arts. Hon. FRCP&S (Canada), 1972. Hon. doctorates: Montreal, McGill and Victoria, 1964; Guelph, 1966; Moncton, 1967; Queen's, Bishop's and Strasbourg, 1968; Notre-Dame (Indiana), 1971; Carleton, 1972; Laval, 1982. Centennial Medal, 1967. KHS 1985; KM 1987. *Publications:* Espérance et Présomption, 1958; Vérité et Liberté, 1962; Unité de l'Université, 1962; Apostolat de l'universitaire catholique, 1963; Mémorial, 1963; Communauté universitaire, 1963; Progrès de l'université et consentement populaire, 1964; Responsabilité collective des universitaires, 1964; Les humanités aujourd'hui, 1966; Excellence et loyauté des universitaires, 1969; Pastoral Letters, 1981. *Recreations:* reading, beaux arts. *Address:* (home) 2 Port-Dauphin, PO Box 459, Quebec G1R 4R6, Canada. *T:* 692–3935; (office) 1073 boulevard St Cyrille ouest, Sillery, Quebec G1S 4R5, Canada. *T:* 688–1211.

QUEBEC, Bishop of, since 1991; **Rt Rev. Alexander Bruce Stavert;** *b* 1 April 1940; *s* of Ewart and Kathleen Stavert; *m* 1982, Diana Greig; one *s* two *d. Educ:* Lower Canada Coll., Montreal; Bishop's Univ., Lennoxville, PQ (BA 1961): Trinity Coll., Univ. of Toronto (STB 1964; MTh, 1976). Incumbent of Schefferville, Quebec, 1964–69; Fellow, 1969–70, Chaplain, 1970–76, Trinity Coll., Univ. of Toronto; Incumbent, St Clement's Mission East, St Paul's River, PQ, 1976–81; Chaplain, Bishop's Univ., Lennoxville, 1981–84; Dean and Rector, St Alban's Cathedral, Prince Albert, Sask., 1984–91. Hon. DD Toronto, 1986. *Recreations:* swimming, ski-ing. *Address:* 36 rue des Jardins, Québec, PQ G1R 4L5, Canada. *T:* (418) 692–3858. *Club:* University (Montreal).

QUEENSBERRY, 12th Marquess of, *cr* 1682; **David Harrington Angus Douglas;** late Royal Horse Guards; Viscount Drumlanrig and Baron Douglas, 1628; Earl of Queensberry, 1633; Bt (Nova Scotia), 1668; Professor of Ceramics, Royal College of Art, 1959–83; Partner, Queensberry Hunt design group; *b* 19 Dec. 1929; *s* of 11th Marquess of Queensberry and late Cathleen Mann; *S* father, 1954; *m* 1st, 1956, Mrs Ann Radford; two *d*; 2nd, 1969, Alexandra (marr. diss. 1986), *d* of Guy Wyndham Sich; three *s* one *d. Educ:* Eton. Mem. Council, Crafts Council; Pres., Design and Industries Assoc., 1976–78. FCSD. *Heir: s* Viscount Drumlanrig, *qv.*

QUEENSLAND, NORTH, Bishop of, since 1971; **Rt. Rev. Hurtle John Lewis,** AM 1989; *b* 2 Jan. 1926; *s* of late Hurtle John Lewis and late Hilda Lewis. *Educ:* Prince Alfred Coll.; London Univ. (BD). ThL of ACT. Royal Australian Navy, 1943–46; Student, St Michael's House, S Aust., 1946–51; Member, SSM, 1951–; Provincial Australia, SSM, 1962–68; Prior, Kobe Priory, Japan, 1969–71. *Recreations:* rowing, horse riding. *Address:* Box 1244, Townsville, Queensland 4810, Australia. *T:* 71–2297.

QUEGUINER, Jean; Légion d'Honneur, 1970; Administrateur Général des Affaires Maritimes, France; maritime consultant, since 1985; *b* 2 June 1921; *s* of Etienne Quéguiner and Anne Trehin; *m* 1952, Marguerite Gaillard; one *s* one *d. Educ:* Lycée Buffon, Collège Stanislas and Faculté de Droit, Paris; Coll. of Administration of Maritime Affairs, St Malo. Docteur en Droit (maritime), Bordeaux. Head of Maritime Dist of Caen, 1953; Dep. Head of Coll. of Admin. of Maritime Affairs, 1955; Head of Safety of Navigation Section, 1963; Vice-Chm. of Maritime Safety Cttee, 1965–68, Dep. Sec.-Gen., 1968–77, IMCO; Chm., Chantiers Navals de l'Esterel, 1981–85. Maritime expert to the Courts, 1986–. *Publications:* Législation et réglementation maritime, 1955; Le code de la mer, 1965; La croisière cotière, 1967; Le code fluvial à l'usage des plaisanciers, 1970. *Recreation:* sailing. *Address:* 13 rue de l'Horizon, 17480 Le Château d'Oléron, France.

QUENINGTON, Viscount; Michael Henry Hicks Beach; *b* 7 Feb. 1950; *s* and *heir* of 2nd Earl St Aldwyn, *qv*; *m* 1982, Gilda Maria, *o d* of Barão Saavedra, Copacabana, Rio de Janeiro; two *d. Educ:* Eton; Christ Church, Oxford. MA. *Address:* 17 Hale House, 34 De Vere Gardens W8 5AQ. *T:* 071–937 6223.

QUENNELL, Joan Mary, MBE 1958; *b* 23 Dec. 1923; *o c* of late Walter Quennell, Dangstein, Rogate. *Educ:* Dunhurst and Bedales Schools. War Service, WLA and BRCS. Vice-Chairman, Horsham Division Cons. Assoc., 1949 (Chairman, 1958–61); W Sussex CC, 1951–61. Served on Finance, Local Government, Selection and Education Cttees, etc; also as Governor various schools and colleges; Governor, Crawley Coll., Further Education, 1956–69; Member: Southern Reg. Council for Further Education, 1959–61; Reg. Adv. Council, Technological Education (London and Home Counties), 1959–61. MP (C) Petersfield, 1960–Sept. 1974; PPS to the Minister of Transport, 1962–64; Member: Select Cttee on Public Accounts, 1970–74; Speaker's Panel of Temporary Chairmen of House of Commons, 1970–74; Cttee of Selection, House of Commons, 1970–74; Select Cttee on European Secondary Legislation, 1973–74. Chm., EUW, Hampshire, 1978–80. JP W Sussex, 1959–80. *Recreations:* reading, gardening. *Address:* Dangstein, Rogate, near Petersfield, Hants GU31 5BZ.

QUENNELL, Peter, CBE 1973; *b* March 1905; *s* of late Marjorie and C. H. B. Quennell. *Educ:* Berkhamsted Grammar Sch.; Balliol Coll., Oxford. Editor, History To-day, 1951–79; edited The Cornhill Magazine, 1944–51. *Publications:* Poems, 1926; Baudelaire and the Symbolists, 1929, 2nd edn 1954; A Superficial Journey through Tokyo and Peking, 1932, 2nd edn 1934; Sympathy, and Other Stories, 1933; Byron, 1934; Byron: the years of fame, 1935, 3rd edn 1967; Victorian Panorama: a survey of life and fashion from contemporary photographs, 1937; Caroline of England, 1939; Byron in Italy, 1941; Four Portraits, 1945, 2nd edn 1965; John Ruskin, 1949; The Singular Preference, 1952; Spring in Sicily, 1952; Hogarth's Progress, 1955; The Sign of the Fish, 1960; Shakespeare: the poet and his background, 1964; Alexander Pope: the education of Genius 1688–1728, 1968; Romantic England, 1970; Casanova in London and other essays, 1971; Samuel Johnson: his friends and enemies, 1972; The Marble Foot (autobiog.), 1976; The Wanton Chase (autobiog.), 1980; Customs and Characters, 1982; The Pursuit of Happiness, 1988; *edited:* Aspects of Seventeenth Century Verse, 1933, 2nd edn 1936; The Private Letters of Princess Lieven to Prince Metternich, 1820–1826, 1948; Byron: selected letters and journals, 1949; H. Mayhew, Mayhew's Characters, 1951; Diversions of History, 1954; H. Mayhew, Mayhew's London, 1954; George Borrow, The Bible in Spain, 1959; H. Mayhew, London's Underworld, 1960; G. G. N. Byron, Lord Byron, Byronic Thoughts, 1960; H. de Montherlant, Selected Essays, 1960; W. Hickey, Memoirs, 1960; T. Moore, The Journal of Thomas Moore, 1964; H. Mayhew, Mayhew's Characters, 1967; Marcel Proust, 1871–1922: a centenary volume, 1971; (with H. Johnson) A History of English Literature, 1973; Vladimir Nabokov, his Life, his Work, his World, 1979; A Lonely Business: a self-portrait of James Pope-Hennessy, 1981.

QUEREJAZU CALVO, Roberto; Cross of the Chaco and Award of Military Merit (Bolivia); Bolivian Ambassador to the Court of St James's 1966–70, and to the Court of The Hague, 1966–70; *b* 24 Nov. 1913; *m* 1944, Dorothy Allman-Lewis; one *s* one *d. Educ:* Sucre Univ., Bolivia. Director of Minister's Cabinet, Legal Dept, and Political Dept, Bolivian Foreign Service, 1939–42; First Secretary, Embassy in Brazil, 1943; Secretary-General, Bolivian Delegn to UN, 1946; Bolivian Embassy, London: Counsellor, 1947; Chargé d'Affaires, 1948–52; Bolivian Rep.: to UN Conference on Tin, 1951; to Interamerican Conference for De-Nuclearization of Latin America, Mexico, 1964; Bolivian Delegate: XX UN General Assembly, 1965; 2nd Interamerican Conference Extraord., Rio de Janeiro, 1965; Under-Secretary of State for Foreign Affairs, Bolivia, 1966. Holds foreign awards. *Publications:* Masamaclay (history of Chaco War), 1966; Bolivia and the English, 1973; Llallagua (history of a mountain), 1976; Guano, Salitre, Sangre (history of the Pacific War), 1979; Adolfo Costa du Rels (biography of a diplomat and writer), 1981; Chuquisaca 1539–1825 (colonial history of the capital of Bolivia), 1987. *Address:* Casilla 4243, Cochabamba, Bolivia.

QUICK, Anthony Oliver Hebert; Headmaster of Bradfield College, 1971–85, retired; *b* 26 May 1924; *er s* of late Canon O. C. Quick, sometime Regius Prof. of Divinity at Oxford, and late Mrs F. W. Quick; *m* 1955, Eva Jean, *er d* of late W. C. Sellar and of Mrs Hope Sellar; three *s* one *d. Educ:* Shrewsbury Sch.; Corpus Christi Coll., Oxford; Sch. of Oriental and African Studies, Univ. of London (Govt Schol.). 2nd cl. hons Mod. History, Oxford. Lieut, RNVR, serving mainly on East Indies Stn, 1943–46. Asst Master, Charterhouse, 1949–61; Headmaster, Rendcomb Coll., Cirencester, 1961–71. *Publications:* (jtly) Britain 1714–1851, 1961; Britain 1851–1945, 1967; Twentieth Century Britain, 1968; Charterhouse: a history of the school, 1990. *Recreations:* walking, gardening, sailing, fishing. *Address:* Corbin, Scorriton, Buckfastleigh, Devon TQ11 0HU.

QUICK, Dorothy, (Mrs Charles Denis Scanlan); Metropolitan Stipendiary Magistrate, since 1986; *b* 10 Dec. 1944; *d* of Frederick and Doris Quick; *m* 1971, Charles Denis Scanlan; two *s. Educ:* Glanafan Grammar Sch., Port Talbot; University Coll. London (LLB). Called to the Bar, Inner Temple, 1969; barrister-at-law, 1969–86. Mem., British Acad. of Forensic Sciences, 1987–. *Recreations:* gardening, theatre, books. *Address:* 5 Essex Court, Temple, EC4Y 9AH.

QUICK, Norman, CBE 1984; DL; Chairman, Quicks Group (formerly H. & J. Quick Group) plc, since 1965 (Managing Director, 1965–84); *b* 19 Nov. 1922; *s* of James and Jessie Quick; *m* 1949, Maureen Cynthia Chancellor; four *d. Educ:* Arnold Sch., Blackpool. FIMI. H. & J. Quick Ltd to H. & J. Quick Group plc, 1939–; served RNVR, Lieut 1941–46 (despatches Mediterranean, 1943); Non Executive Director: Williams & Glyn's Bank, 1979–85; Royal Bank of Scotland, 1985–90; Dir, Piccadilly Radio (formerly Greater Manchester Independent Radio), 1972–89 (Chm., 1980–88). Mem., NW Indust. Council. Pres., Stretford Cons. Assoc., 1974– (formerly Chm.). Mem., Lancs CC, 1954–57. Treasurer, 1975–80, Chm., 1980–83, Univ. of Manchester Council; Mem., Bd of Governors, Arnold Sch. Ltd, Blackpool, 1980–. DL Greater Manchester, 1987, High Sheriff, 1990. Hon. MA Manchester, 1977; Hon. LLD Manchester, 1984. *Recreations:* golf, Rugby. *Address:* Birkin House, Ashley, Altrincham, Cheshire WA14 3QL. *T:* Bucklow Hill (0565) 830175. *Clubs:* Royal Automobile; St James's (Manchester).

QUICKE, Sir John (Godolphin), Kt 1988; CBE 1978; DL; *b* 20 April 1922; *s* of Captain Noel Arthur Godolphin Quicke and Constance May Quicke; *m* 1953, Prudence Tinné Berthon, *d* of Rear-Adm. (E) C. P. E. Berthon; three *s* three *d. Educ:* Eton; New Coll., Oxford. Vice-Chm., North Devon Meat, 1982–86; Mem., SW Reg. Bd, National Westminster Bank, 1974–. Chairman: Minister of Agriculture's SW Regional Panel, 1972–75; Agricl EDC, NEDO, 1983–88, Agricl Sector Gp, 1988–; RURAL, 1983–; Estates Panel, NT, 1984–; Member: Consultative Bd for R&D in Food and Agric., 1981–84; Severn Barrage Cttee, 1978–80; Countryside Commn, 1981–88 (Chm., Countryside Policy Review Panel, 1986–87); Properties Cttee, NT, 1984–. President: CLA, 1975–77; Royal Bath & West of England Soc., 1989–90. Mem. Bd of Governors, Polytechnic SW, 1989–. DL Devon, 1985. Hon. FRASE, 1989. Hon. DSc: Exeter, 1989; Polytechnic South West, 1991. Bledisloe Gold Medal for Landowners, RASE, 1985. *Recreations:* reading, music, trees, gardening. *Address:* Sherwood, Newton St Cyres, near Exeter, Devon EX5 5BT. *T:* Exeter (0392) 851216. *Club:* Boodle's.

QUIGLEY, Anthony Leslie Coupland, CEng, FIEE; Director, Strategic Defence Initiative Participation Office, Ministry of Defence, since 1990; *b* 14 July 1946; *s* of late Leslie Quigley and of Vera Barbara Rodaway (*née* Martin); *m* 1968, Monica Dean; one *s* two *d. Educ:* Apsley Grammar Sch.; Queen Mary Coll., Univ. of London (BSc Eng). Computer Systems Div., SO, Computer Div., and PSO, Command and Control Div., ASWE, 1967–81 (Exchange Scientist, US Naval Surface Weapons Center, 1976–79); Supt, Command and Control Div., 1981–84, Hd, Command, Control and Assessment Gp, 1984–87, RARDE; Dep. Head, Science and Technology Assessment Office, Cabinet Office, 1987–90. *Publications:* technical papers on radar tracking and command and control. *Recreations:* playing and umpiring cricket, golf, flying models. *Address:* Ministry of Defence, Northumberland House, Northumberland Avenue, WC2N 5BP. *T:* 071–218 4239.

QUIGLEY, George; *see* Quigley, W. G. H.

QUIGLEY, Johanna Mary, (Mrs D. F. C. Quigley); *see* Foley, J. M.

QUIGLEY, (William) George (Henry), CB 1982; PhD; Chairman, Ulster Bank Ltd, since 1989 (Deputy Chairman, 1988–89); Director, National Westminster Bank, since 1990; *b* 26 Nov. 1929; *s* of William George Cunningham Quigley and Sarah Hanson Martin; *m* 1971, Moyra Alice Munn, LLB. *Educ:* Ballymena Academy; Queen's Univ., Belfast, BA (1st Cl. Hons), 1951; PhD, 1955. Apptd Asst Principal, Northern Ireland Civil Service, 1955; Permanent Secretary: Dept of Manpower Services, NI, 1974–76; Dept of Commerce, NI, 1976–79; Dept of Finance, NI, 1979–82; Dept of Finance and Personnel, NI, 1982–88. Director: Irish-American Partnership, 1989–; Short Brothers, 1989–; Chm., NI Div., Inst. of Dirs, 1990–; Member: Fair Employment Commn for NI, 1989–; Council, NI Chamber of Commerce and Industry, 1989–. Professorial Fellow, QUB, 1988; Fellow, Inst. of Bankers in Ireland, 1989. CBIM. *Publication:* (ed with E. F. D. Roberts) Registrum Iohannis Mey: The Register of John Mey, Archbishop of Armagh, 1443–1456, 1972. *Recreations:* historical research, reading, music, gardening. *Address:* Ulster Bank Ltd, 47 Donegall Place, Belfast BT1 5AU.

QUILLEY, Denis Clifford; actor; *b* 26 Dec. 1927; *s* of Clifford Charles Quilley and Ada Winifred (*née* Stanley); *m* 1949, Stella Chapman; one *s* two *d. Educ:* Bancroft's, Woodford, Essex. First appearance, Birmingham Rep. Theatre, 1945; The Lady's not for Burning, Globe, 1949; Old Vic and Young Vic Cos, 1950–51: parts included: Fabian in Twelfth Night (on tour, Italy), Gratiano in Merchant of Venice; Revue, Airs on a Shoe String (exceeded 700 perfs), Royal Court, 1953; first leading rôle in West End as Geoffrey Morris in Wild Thyme, Duke of York's, 1955; subseq. parts incl.: Tom Wilson in Grab Me a Gondola (over 600 perfs), Lyric; Captain Brassbound, and Orlando, Bristol Old Vic; Candide, Saville; Benedick in Much Ado about Nothing, Open Air Th.; Archie Rice in The Entertainer, Nottingham Playhouse; Krogstad in A Doll's House, Brighton; Nat. Theatre, 1971–76: Aufidius (Coriolanus); Macbeth; Bolingbroke (Richard II); Caliban (The Tempest); Lopakin (Cherry Orchard); Jamie (Long Day's Journey into Night); Claudius (Hamlet); Hector (Troilus and Cressida); Bajazeth (Tamburlaine); Privates on Parade, Aldwych, 1977, Piccadilly, 1978 (SWET award, 1977); Morell in Candida, Albery Theatre, 1977; Deathtrap, Garrick, 1978; title rôle in Sweeney Todd, Theatre Royal Drury Lane (SWET award), 1980; Molokov in Chess, Barbican, 1985; Antony, in Antony and Cleopatra, Chichester, 1985; Fatal Attraction, Haymarket, 1985; La Cage aux Folles, Palladium, 1986; Pizarro in Royal Hunt of the Sun, UK tour, 1989; The School for Scandal, NT, 1990; Brachiano, The White Devil, NT, 1991; has played in NY, Melbourne and Sydney. *Films:* Life at the Top, Anne of the Thousand Days, Murder on the Orient Express, The Antagonists, Evil Under the Sun, Privates on Parade, King David, Mr Johnson, The Shell-seekers, A Dangerous Man, 1991. *TV plays and series* incl.: Merchant of Venice; The Father; Henry IV (Pirandello); Murder in the Cathedral; Time Slip; Contrabandits (Aust.); Clayhanger; The Serpent Son; The Crucible; Gladstone, in No 10; Masada; Anno Domini; Murder of a Moderate Man; Rich Tea and Sympathy. *Recreations:* playing the piano, flute and cello, walking. *Address:* 22 Willow Road, Hampstead, NW3 1TL. *T:* 071–435 5976.

QUILLIAM, Hon. Sir (James) Peter, Kt 1988; **Hon. Mr Justice Quilliam;** Judge of the High Court and Court of Appeal, Cook Islands, since 1988; New Zealand Police Complaints Authority, since 1989; *b* 23 March 1920; *s* of Ronald Henry Quilliam, CBE and Gwendoline Minnie Quilliam; *m* 1945, Ellison Jean Gill; two *s* one *d*. *Educ:* Wanganui Collegiate Sch.; Victoria Univ. of Wellington (LLB). Private practice as barrister and solicitor, 1945–69; Crown Prosecutor, New Plymouth, NZ, 1955–69; Judge, High Court of NZ, 1969–88, and Senior Puisne Judge, 1985–88. Pres., Taranaki Dist Law Soc., 1965–67. *Recreations:* golf, fishing, gardening, reading. *Address:* 9 Puketiro Avenue, Northland, Wellington 5, New Zealand. *T:* Wellington 758166. *Clubs:* Wellington, Wellington Golf (NZ).

QUILLIAM, Prof. Juan Pete, (Peter), OBE 1986; DSc; FRCP; Professor of Pharmacology, University of London, at St Bartholomew's Hospital Medical College, 1962–83, now Emeritus; Hon. Clinical Assistant, St Bartholomew's Hospital; Chairman of Convocation of the University of London, 1973–90; *b* 20 Nov. 1915; *e s* of late Thomas Quilliam, Peel, IoM and Maude (*née* Pavitt); *m* 1st, 1946, Melita Kelly (*d* 1957); one *s* one *d*; 2nd, 1958, Barbara Lucy Marion, *y d* of late Rev. William Kelly, Pelynt, Cornwall. *Educ:* University Coll. Sch.; UCL (exhibnr); UCH Med. Sch. MSc 1938, MB BS 1941; DSc 1969; FRCP 1975. Vice-Pres., London Univ. Athletic Union, 1938; Pres., London Univ. Boat Club, 1939–40 (rowing purple 1938). Sharpey Physiol Schol., UCL, 1939–41; House Phys. and House Surg., UCH, 1941; House Phys., Brompton Hosp. for Diseases of Chest, 1941–42; Asst TB Officer, Chelsea, 1941–42; Exptl Officer, Min. of Supply, 1942–43; served RAFVR Med. Br. (Central Fighter Estabt), 1943–46; Lectr in Pharmacol., KCL, 1945–55; London Univ. Travelling Fellow, 1949–50; Fellow, Johns Hopkins Hosp. Med. Sch., 1949–50; Sen. Lectr and Head of Pharmacol. Dept, 1956, Reader, 1958, St Bartholomew's Hosp. Med. Coll. Gresham Prof. of Physic, 1967–68. London University Convocation: Mem. Standing Cttee, 1966–74; Senator, Medicine, 1968–74; Chm., Trust, 1973–90; Mem. Ct and Senate, London Univ. Examiner in Pharmacol. and Clinical Pharmacol. to Univs of London, Edinburgh, Cambridge, Dundee, Liverpool, Manchester and Cardiff, also to Fac. of Anaesthetists and Apothecaries Soc. Mem., 1960–88, Dep. Chm., 1975–88, Gen. Optical Council; Gen. Sec., British Pharmacol Soc., 1968–71; British Medical Association: Mem. Council, 1971–; Chairman: Med. Academic Staff Cttee, 1978, 1980, 1982; Bd of Sci. and Educn, 1982–85; Fellow, 1981; Vice-Pres., 1988. Member: IBA Advertising Adv. Cttee, 1984–; Joint BBC/IBA Central Appeals Adv. Cttee, 1987–. Crouch Harbour Authority: Mem., 1987; Vice-Chm., 1988; Chm., 1989; Mem., 1974, Chm., 1987, Crouch Area Yachting Fedn.Trustee: City Parochial Foundn, 1977–89; Trust for London, 1986–89; Trustee and Co-Chm., Help the Hospices Trust, 1984–. Press Editor, British Jl of Pharmacol., 1957–60. *Publications: jointly:* Medical Effects of Nuclear War, 1983; Boxing, 1984; Young People and Alcohol, 1986; Long term environment effects of nuclear war, 1986; Alternative Therapy, 1986; The Torture Report, 1986; papers on visual purple, blood/acqueous humour barrier permability, intra-ocular fluid, DFP and synaptic transmission in heart and muscle, action drugs on the iris, the ocular critical flicker fusion frequency, the auditory flutter fusion frequency, the electro-pharmacology of sedatives, general anaesthetics on autonomic ganglia as a model of brain synapses, GABA-like actions on lobster muscle, effects of staphylococcal α-toxin on intestine, the ultrastructural effects in autonomic ganglia in the presence of chemical substances, World Medicine, University "Cuts" 1983. *Recreations:* work, sailing. *Address:* Hornbeams, 34 Totteridge Common, Totteridge, N20 8NE. *Club:* United Hospitals Sailing (Burnham-on-Crouch) (Cdre, 1974–).

QUILLIAM, Hon. Sir Peter; *see* Quilliam, Hon. Sir J. P.

QUILLIAM, Peter; *see* Quilliam, J. P.

QUILTER, Sir Anthony (Raymond Leopold Cuthbert), 4th Bt, *cr* 1897; landowner since 1959; *b* 25 March 1937; *s* of Sir (John) Raymond (Cuthbert) Quilter, 3rd Bt and Margery Marianne (*née* Cooke); *S* father 1959; *m* 1964, Mary Elise, *er d* of late Colonel Brian (Sherlock) Gooch, DSO, TD; one *s* one *d*. *Educ:* Harrow. Is engaged in farming. *Recreations:* shooting, golf. *Heir: s* Guy Raymond Cuthbert Quilter, *b* 13 April 1967. *Address:* Sutton Hall, Sutton, Woodbridge, Suffolk IP12 3EQ. *T:* Shottisham (0394) 411246.

QUILTER, David (Cuthbert) Tudway; Vice Lord-Lieutenant of Somerset, since 1978; Local Director, Barclays Bank, Bristol, 1962–84 (Director, Barclays Bank UK Ltd, 1971–81); Director, Bristol Evening Post, since 1982; *b* 26 March 1921; *o s* of Percy Cuthbert Quilter and Clare Tudway; *m* 1953, Elizabeth Mary, *er d* of Sir John Carew Pole, Bt, *qv*; one *s* two *d*. *Educ:* Eton. Served War of 1939–45, Coldstream Guards, 1940–46. JP London Juvenile Courts, 1959–62. Mayor of Wells, 1974–75; Chm. of Trustees, Wells Cathedral Preservation Trust, 1976–; Treasurer, Bristol Univ., 1976–88; Governor, Wells Cathedral Sch., 1968–; Member: Council, Outward Bound Trust, 1959–; Garden Soc., 1973–; Life Trustee, Carnegie UK Trust, 1981–. Master, Soc. of Merchant Venturers, 1984–85. DL 1970, High Sheriff 1974–75, Somerset. Hon. LLD Bristol, 1989. *Publications:* No Dishonourable Name, 1947; A History of Wells Cathedral School, 1985. *Recreations:* gardening, music, tennis, golf, shooting. *Address:* Milton Lodge, Wells, Somerset BA5 3AQ. *T:* Wells (0749) 72168. *Clubs:* Boodle's, Pratt's.

QUIN; *see* Wyndham-Quin, family name of **Earl of Dunraven.**

QUIN, Joyce Gwendolen; MP (Lab) Gateshead East, since 1987; *b* 26 Nov. 1944; *d* of Basil Godfrey Quin and Ida (*née* Ritson). *Educ:* Univ. of Newcastle upon Tyne (BA French, 1st Cl. Hons); Univ. of London (MSc Internat. Relns). Research Asst, Internat. Dept, Labour Party Headquarters, Transport House, 1969–72; Lecturer in French, Univ. of Bath, 1972–76; Resident Tutor, St Mary's Coll., and Lectr in French and Politics, Univ. of Durham, 1977–79. Mem. (Lab) European Parliament, S Tyne and Wear, 1979–84, Tyne and Wear, 1984–89. Opposition front bench spokesman on trade and industry, 1989–. Mem., Select Cttee on Treasury and Civil Service, 1987–89. Hon. Fellow, Sunderland Polytechnic, 1986. *Publications:* various articles in newspapers and journals. *Recreations:* North-East local history (Newcastle upon Tyne City Guide), music, theatre, walking, cycling. *Address:* House of Commons, SW1A 0AA; (office) Old Bank, Swinburne Street, Gateshead, Tyne & Wear NE8 1AN. *T:* 091–490 0117.

QUINCE, Peter; *see* Thompson, John W. McW.

QUINE, Prof. Willard Van Orman; American author; Professor of Philosophy, 1948, and Edgar Pierce Professor of Philosophy, 1956–78, Harvard University, now Emeritus Professor; *b* Akron, Ohio, 25 June 1908; *s* of Cloyd Robert and Hattie Van Orman Quine; *m* 1st, 1930, Naomi Clayton; two *d*; 2nd, 1948, Marjorie Boynton; one *s* one *d*. *Educ:* Oberlin Coll., Ohio (AB); Harvard Univ. (AM, PhD). Harvard: Sheldon Travelling Fellow, 1932–33 (Vienna, Prague, Warsaw); Jun. Fellow, Society of Fellows, 1933–36 (Sen. Fellow, 1949–78, Chairman, 1957–58); Instructor and Tutor in Philosophy, 1936–41; Assoc. Professor of Philosophy, 1941–48; Chairman, Dept of Philosophy, 1952–53. Visiting Professor, Universidade de São Paulo, Brazil, 1942. Lieut, then Lieut-Commander, USNR, active duty, 1942–46. Consulting editor, Journal of Symbolic Logic, 1936–52; Vice-President, Association for Symbolic Logic, 1938–40; President, 1953–55; Vice-President, Eastern Division, American Philosophical Assoc., 1950, President, 1957; Member: Amer. Philos. Soc., 1957– (Councillor, 1966–68, 1982–); Acad. Internat. de Philosophie de Science, 1960; Institut International de Philosophie, 1983–. FAAAS, 1945– (Councillor, 1950–53); Fellow, Nat. Acad. of Sciences, 1977–. Corres. Member: Instituto Brasileiro de Filosofia, 1963–; Institut de France, 1978–; Corres. Fellow: British Acad., 1959–; Norwegian Acad. of Scis, 1979–; Trustee, Institute for Unity of Science, 1949–56; Syndic, Harvard University Press: 1951–53; 1954–56, 1959–60, 1962–66. George Eastman Visiting Prof., Oxford Univ., 1953–54; Vis. Professor: Univ. of Tokyo, 1959; Rockefeller Univ., 1968; Collège de France, 1969. A. T. Shearman Lecturer, University of London, 1954; Gavin David Young Lectr in Philosophy, Univ. of Adelaide, 1959; John Dewey Lectr, Columbia Univ., 1968; Paul Carus Lectr, Amer. Philos. Assoc., 1971; Hägerström Lectr, Uppsala, 1973; Vis. Lectr, Calcutta, 1983. Member Institute for Advanced Study, Princeton, USA, 1956–57. Fellow: Centre for Advanced Study in the Behavioural Sciences, Palo Alto, California, 1958–59; Centre for Advanced Studies, Wesleyan Univ., Conn, 1965; Sir Henry Saville Fellow, Merton Coll., Oxford, 1973–74. Hon. degrees: MA Oxon, 1953; DLitt Oxon, 1970; LittD: Oberlin, 1955; Akron, 1965; Washington, 1966; Temple, 1970; Cambridge, 1978; Ripon, 1983; LLD: Ohio State, 1957; Harvard, 1979; DèsL Lille, 1965; LHD: Chicago, 1967; Syracuse, 1981; DPh: Uppsala, 1980; Berne, 1982; Granada, 1986. N. M. Butler Gold Medal, 1970. *Publications:* A System of Logistic, 1934; Mathematical Logic, 1940, rev. edn 1951; Elementary Logic, 1941, rev. edn 1965; O sentido da nova logica, 1944 (São Paulo); Methods of Logic, 1950, rev. edn 1982; From a Logical Point of View, 1953, rev. edn 1961; Word and Object, 1960; Set Theory and its Logic, 1963, revised edn 1969; Ways of Paradox and Other Essays, 1966, rev. edn 1976; Selected Logic Papers, 1966; Ontological Relativity and Other Essays, 1969; Philosophy of Logic, 1970; (with J. S. Ullian) The Web of Belief, 1970; The Roots of Reference, 1974; Theories and Things, 1981; The Time of My Life, 1985; (jtly) The Philosophy of W. V. Quine, 1986; La Scienza e i Dati di Senso, 1987; Quiddities, 1987; Pursuit of Truth, 1989; (jtly) Perspectives on Quine, 1989; The Logic of Sequences, 1990; contribs to Journal of Symbolic Logic; Journal of Philosophy; Philosophical Review; Mind; Rivista di Filosofia; Scientific American; NY Review of Books; Library of Living Philosophers. *Recreation:* travel. *Address:* 38 Chestnut Street, Boston, Mass 02108, USA. *T:* 723–6754.

QUINLAN, Rt. Rev. Alan Geoffrey; A Bishop Suffragan, Diocese of Cape Town, since 1988; *b* 20 Aug. 1933; *s* of late Robert Quinlan and of Eileen Beatrice Quinlan; *m* 1963, Rosalind Arlen Sallie (*née* Reed); three *s* one *d*. *Educ:* Kelham Theological College. RAF, 1952–54. Deacon 1958, Priest 1959; Asst Curate, St Thomas's, Leigh, Lancs, 1958–61; Rector: St Margaret's, Bloemfontein, 1962–68; St Michael and All Angels, Sasolburg, OFS, 1968–72; Warden, Community of Resurrection, Grahamstown and Chaplain, Grahamstown Training Coll., 1972–76; Priest-in-Charge of Training in Ministries and Discipleship, Cape Town Diocese, 1976–80; Rector, All Saints, Plumstead, Cape Town, 1980–88. Canon, St George's Cathedral, Cape Town, 1980. *Recreations:* chess, reading, bird-watching, computers. *Address:* 79 Kildare Road, Newlands, Cape Town, 7700, South Africa. *T:* Cape Town 642–444.

QUINLAN, Maj.-Gen. Henry, CB 1960; *b* 5 Jan. 1906; *s* of Dr Denis Quinlan, LRCP, LRCS (Edinburgh), of Castletownroche, Co. Cork; *m* 1936, Euphemia Nancy, *d* of John Tallents Wynyard Brooke of Shanghai, and Altrincham, Cheshire; two *s* two *d*. *Educ:* Clongowes Wood Coll., Sallins, Co. Kildare. BDS 1926; FFD RCS (I) 1964. Royal Army Dental Corps; Lieut, 1927; Captain, Dec. 1930; Major, 1937; Lieut-Colonel, Dec. 1947; Colonel, 1953; Maj.-General, Oct. 1958; Director Army Dental Service, 1958–63; QHDS 1954–64, retired; Colonel Comdt Royal Army Dental Corps, 1964–71. Officer OStJ 1958. *Address:* White Bridges, Redlands Lane, Crondall, Hants. *T:* Aldershot 850239.

QUINLAN, Sir Michael (Edward), GCB 1991 (KCB 1985; CB 1980); Permanent Under Secretary of State, Ministry of Defence, 1988–April 1992; Director, Ditchley Foundation, from August 1992; *b* 11 Aug. 1930; *s* of late Gerald and Roseanne Quinlan; *m* 1965, Margaret Mary Finlay; two *s* two *d*. *Educ:* Wimbledon Coll.; Merton Coll., Oxford. (1st Cl. Hon. Mods, 1st Cl. LitHum; MA; Hon. Fellow, 1989). RAF, 1952–54. Asst Principal, Air Ministry, 1954; Private Sec. to Parly Under-Sec. of State for Air, 1956–58; Principal, Air Min., 1958; Private Sec. to Chief of Air Staff, 1962–65; Asst Sec., MoD, 1968; Defence Counsellor, UK Delegn to NATO, 1970–73; Under-Sec., Cabinet Office, 1974–77; Dep. Under-Sec. of State, MoD, 1977–81; Dep. Sec., HM Treasury, 1981–82; Perm. Sec., Dept of Employment, 1983–88. Chm., Civil Service Sports Council, 1985–89. Governor, Henley Management Coll., 1983–88. CBIM 1983. *Publications:* articles on defence and public service ethics. *Recreations:* squash, watching cricket, listening to music. *Address:* (until April 1992) c/o Ministry of Defence, Main Building, Whitehall, SW1A 2HB; (from Aug. 1992) Ditchley Foundation, Ditchley Park, Oxford OX7 4ER. *Club:* Royal Air Force.

QUINN, Brian; Executive Director, Bank of England, since 1988; *b* 18 Nov. 1936; *s* of Thomas Quinn and Margaret (*née* Cairns); *m* 1961, Mary Bradley; two *s* one *d*. *Educ:* Glasgow Univ. (MA Hons); Manchester Univ. (MA Econs); Cornell Univ. (PhD). Economist, African Dept, IMF, 1964–70, Rep., Sierra Leone, 1966–68; joined Bank of England, 1970; Economic Div., 1970–74; Chief Cashier's Dept, 1974–77; Head of Information Div., 1977–82; Asst Dir, 1982–88; Head of Banking Supervision, 1986–88. FRSA. *Publications:* (contrib.) Surveys of African Economies, vol. 4, 1971; (contrib.) The New Inflation, 1976; articles in learned jls. *Recreations:* fishing, golf. *Club:* Overseas Bankers'.

QUINN, Brian; *see* Quinn, J. S. B.

QUINN, Prof. David Beers, DLit (QUB), PhD (London), MRIA, FRHistS; Andrew Geddes and John Rankin Professor of Modern History, University of Liverpool, 1957–76; *b* 24 April 1909; *o s* of late David Quinn, Omagh and Belfast, and Albertina Devine, Cork; *m* 1937, Alison Moffat Robertson, MA, *d* of late John Ireland Robertson, Edinburgh; two *s* one *d*. *Educ:* Clara (Offaly) No 2 National Sch.; Royal Belfast Academical Institution; Queen's Univ., Belfast; King's Coll., University of London. University Schol., QUB, 1928–31 (1st Class Hons in Medieval and Modern History, 1931); PhD London, 1934. Asst Lecturer, 1934, and Lecturer, 1937, University College, Southampton; Lecturer in History, QUB, 1939–44; seconded to BBC European Service, 1943; Prof. of History, University College, Swansea, 1944–57; DLit (QUB), 1958. Secretary, Ulster Society for Irish Historical Studies, 1939–44; Member: Council of Hakluyt Society, 1950–54, 1957–60 (Vice-Pres., 1960–82, 1987–, Pres., 1982–87); Council of Royal Historical Society, 1951–55, 1956–60 (Vice-Pres., 1964–68, Hon. Vice-Pres., 1983); Fellow, Folger Shakespeare Lib. (Washington, DC), 1957, 1959, 1963–64; Fellow, John Carter Brown Lib., 1970, 1982; Leverhulme Res. Fellow, 1963; British Council Visiting Scholar, NZ, 1967; Hungary, 1972; Fellow, Huntington Library, 1980; Fellow, Nat. Inst. for the Humanities, 1983; Fulbright Fortieth Anniversary Dist. Fellow, 1986–87; Harrison Vis. Prof., Coll. of William and Mary, Williamsburg, Va, 1969–70; Visiting Professor: St Mary's Coll., St Mary's City, Md, 1976–78, 1980–82, 1984; Michigan Univ., 1979. Hon. Mem. American Historical Assoc., 1986. Hon. FBA 1984. Hon. DLitt: Newfoundland, 1964; New Univ. of Ulster, 1975; NUI, 1981; Hon. DHL

St Mary's Coll., 1978; Hon. LLD Univ. of N Carolina, 1980. Hon. Phi Beta Kappa, 1984. *Publications:* The Port Books or Petty Customs Accounts of Southampton for the Reign of Edward IV, 2 vols, 1937–38; The Voyages and Colonising Enterprises of Sir Humphrey Gilbert, 2 vols, 1940; Raleigh and the British Empire, 1947; The Roanoke Voyages, 1584–90, 2 vols, 1955; (with Paul Hulton) The American Drawings of John White, 1577–1590, 1964; (with R. A. Skelton) R. Hakluyt's Principall Navigations (1589), 1965; The Elizabethans and the Irish, 1966; Richard Hakluyt, Editor, 1967; North American Discovery, 1971; (with W. P. Cumming and R. A. Skelton) The Discovery of North America, 1972; (with N. M. Cheshire) The New Found Land of Stephen Parmenius, 1972; (with A. M. Quinn) Virginia Voyages from Hakluyt, 1973; England and the Discovery of America 1481–1620, 1974; The Hakluyt Handbook, 2 vols, 1974; (with W. P. Cumming, S. E. Hillier and G. Williams) The Exploration of North America, 1630–1776, 1974; The Last Voyage of Thomas Cavendish, 1975; North America from First Discovery to Early Settlements, 1977; (with A. M. Quinn and S. Hillier) New American World, 5 vols, 1979; Early Maryland and a Wider World, 1982; (with A. M. Quinn) The First Settlers, 1982; (with A. M. Quinn) English New England Voyages 1602–1608, 1983; (with A. N. Ryan) England's Sea Empire, 1550–1642, 1983; Set Fair for Roanoke, 1985; (ed) John Derricke, The Image of Ireland, 1986; contrib. to A New History of Ireland, vol. 2, ed A. Cosgrove, 1987; Raleigh and Quinn: the explorer and his Boswell, ed H. G. Jones, 1988; Explorers and Colonies: America 1500–1625, 1990; contribs on Irish history and the discovery and settlement of N America in historical journals. *Address:* 9 Knowsley Road, Cressington Park, Liverpool L19 0PF. *T:* 051–427 2041.

QUINN, Hon. James Aiden O'Brien; Chief Justice of Botswana, 1981–87; *b* 3 Jan. 1932; *s* of late William Patrick Quinn (Comr, Gárda Siochána) and Helen Mary (*née* Walshe); *m* 1960, Christel Tyner; two *s* one *d.* *Educ:* Presentation Coll., Bray, Co. Wicklow, Ireland; University Coll., Dublin, NUI (BA, LLB Hons). Called to the Bar: Kings' Inns, Dublin, 1957; Inner Temple, 1967. National City Bank, Dublin, 1949–53; in practice at the Bar, under Colonial Office Scheme, 1958–60; Crown Counsel and Actg Sen. Crown Counsel, Nyasaland, 1960–64; Asst Attorney Gen. and Actg Attorney Gen., West Cameroon, 1964–66; Procureur Général, West Cameroon, and Avocat Général, Fed. Republic of Cameroon, 1966–68; Fed. Republic of Cameroon, 1968–72: Conseiller, Cour Fédérale de Justice; Judge, W Cameroon Supreme Court; Conseiller Technique (Harmonisation des Lois), Ministère de la Justice, Yaoundé; Président, Tribunal Administratif, Cameroun Occidental; Chargé de Cours, Ecole Nationale de l'Administration et de la Magistrature, Yaoundé; Republic of Seychelles: Attorney Gen., also of British Indian Ocean Territory, 1972–76; MLC, MEC and Mem. Parlt, 1972–76; QC 1973; Chief Justice, 1976–77; Actg Dep. Governor, 1974; Mem., Official Delegn on Self-Govt, 1975, and on Independence Constitutions, 1976; collab. with Prof. A. G. Chloros on translation and up-dating of Code Napoleon, 1975–76; Chm., Judicial Service Commn, 1976–77; Gilbert Islands (Kiribati): Chief Justice, 1977–81; Chm., Judicial Service Commn, 1977–81; set up new Courts' system, 1978; Mem., Council of State, 1979–81; Judge, High Court of Solomon Is, 1977–79; Chm., Judicial Service Commn Botswana, 1981–87; Special Prosecutor, Falkland Is, 1981. Mem., Panel of Experts of UN on Prevention of Crime and Treatment of Offenders, 1985–. Chevalier, Ordre de la Valeur, Republic of Cameroon, 1967; Kiribati Independence Medal, 1979. *Publications:* Magistrates' Courts Handbook: West Cameroon, 1968; Kiribati, 1979; edited: West Cameroon Law Reports, 1961–68; Gilbert Islands Law Reports, 1977–79; Kiribati Law Reports, 1977–79; articles in Commonwealth Law Jl, The Magistrate, etc. *Recreations:* languages, travel, reading, swimming. *Address:* 9 Lorane Court, Langley Road, Watford, Herts WD1 3LZ. *Clubs:* Commonwealth Trust, Challoner; Lions' International.

QUINN, James Charles Frederick; film producer and exhibitor; Chairman, The Minema, since 1984; *b* 23 Aug. 1919; *y s* of Rev. Chancellor James Quinn and Muriel Alice May (*née* MaGuire); *m* 1942, Hannah, 2nd *d* of Rev. R. M. Gwynn, BD (Sen. Fellow and Vice-Provost, TCD), and Dr Eileen Gwynn; one *s* one *d.* *Educ:* Shrewsbury Sch.; TCD (Classical Exhibnr); Christ Church, Oxford (MA; Dip. in Econ. and Polit. Sci.). Served War, Irish Guards, Italy, NW Europe; British Army Staff, France, and Town Major, Paris, 1945–46. Courtaulds Ltd, 1949–55. Dir, BFI, 1955–64: National Film Theatre built, London Film Festival inaugurated, 1st Univ. Lectureship in Film Studies in UK estabd at Slade Sch. of Fine Art, University Coll., London and BFI's terms of ref. enld to incl. television. Council of Europe Fellowship, 1966. Chairman: Internat. Short Film Conf., 1971–78 (Life Pres., 1979); National Panel for Film Festivals, 1974–83. Member: Gen. Adv. Council, BBC, 1960–64; Bd, Gardner Arts Centre, Sussex Univ., 1968–71; British Council Film Television and Video Adv. Cttee, 1983–90. Trustee: Imperial War Museum, 1968–78; Grierson Meml Trust, 1975–; Nat. Life Story Collection, 1986–. Invited to stand by New Ulster Movement as Indep. Unionist Parly candidate, S Down, 1968. Foreign Leader Award, US State Dept, 1962. Films: co-producer, Herostratus, 1966; Producer, Overlord, 1975. Silver Bear Award, Berlin Internat. Film Festival, 1975; Special Award, London Evening News British Film Awards, 1976. Chevalier de l'Ordre des Arts et des Lettres, France, 1979. *Publications:* Outside London, 1965; The Film and Television as an Aspect of European Culture, 1968; contrib. Chambers's Encyclopaedia (cinema), 1956–59. *Recreations:* lawn tennis; formerly Eton Fives. *Address:* Crescent Cottage, 108 Marine Parade, Brighton, E Sussex BN2 1AT. *Clubs:* Cavalry and Guards; Vincent's (Oxford).

QUINN, (James Steven) Brian; Director, since 1985, Chief Executive, since 1989, Digital Computer Services; *b* 16 June 1936; *s* of James and Elizabeth Quinn; *m* 1962, Blanche Cecilia James; two *s* one *d.* *Educ:* St Mary's Coll., Crosby; Waterpark Coll., Ireland; University Coll., Dublin (BCL, LLB). Kings Inn, Dublin. Director: Johnson Radley, 1966–68; United Glass Containers, 1968–69; Head of Industrial Activities, Prices and Incomes Board, 1969–71; Dir, M. L. H. Consultants, 1971–79; Corporate Develt Advr, Midland Bank Internat., 1977–80; Chief Industrial Advr, Price Commn, 1977–78. Chairman: BrightStar Communications, 1983–85; BAJ Holdings, 1985–87; Harmer Holbrook, 1987–88; Man. Dir, Visnews, 1980–86; Dir, Telematique Services, 1985–. British Institute of Management: FBIM 1978; CBIM 1985; Mem. Council, 1981–87, 1990–; Mem. Finance Cttee, 1981–; Chm., City of London Branch, 1981–83; Vice Pres., 1983–; Chm., Gtr London Regl Council, 1990–. International Institute of Communications: Trustee, 1982–88, 1992–; Chm., Exec. Cttee, 1984–88; Pres., 1988–91. Mem., Exec. Cttee, Inst. of European Trade and Technology, 1983–. Trustee: Internat. Centre of Communications, San Diego State Univ., 1990–. Chm., Finance Cttee, Great Japan Exhbn, 1979–82. *Recreations:* golf, reading, veteran vehicles. *Address:* Craiglea House, Austenwood Lane, Gerrards Cross, Bucks SL9 9DA. *Club:* Athenæum.

QUINN, Dame Sheila (Margaret Imelda), DBE 1987 (CBE 1978); FHSM; FRCN; President, Royal College of Nursing, 1982–86; *b* 16 Sept. 1920; *d* of late Wilfred Amos Quinn and Ada Mazella (*née* Bottomley). *Educ:* Convent of Holy Child, Blackpool; London Univ. (BScEcon Hons); Royal Lancaster Infirmary (SRN 1947); Birmingham (SCM); Royal Coll. of Nursing, London (RNT). FHSM 1971; FRCN 1978. Admin. Sister, then Principal Sister Tutor, Prince of Wales' Gen. Hosp., London, 1950–61; Internat. Council of Nurses, Geneva: Dir, Social and Econ. Welfare Div., 1961–66; Exec. Dir, 1967–70; Chief Nursing Officer, Southampton Univ. Hosps, 1970–74; Area Nursing Officer, Hampshire AHA (Teaching), 1974–78; Regional Nursing Officer, Wessex RHA, 1978–83. Member: E Dorset DHA, 1987–90; Dorset FHSA, 1990–. Nursing Advr, BRCS, 1983–88. Pres., Standing Cttee of Nurses of EEC, 1983–91; Member: Council, Royal Coll. of Nursing, 1971–79 (Chm. Council, 1974–79; Dep. Pres., 1980–82); Bd of Dirs, Internat. Council of Nurses, 1977–85 (first Vice-Pres., 1981–85); Mem., EEC Adv. Cttee on Trng in Nursing, 1978–90. Hon. DSc (Social Sciences) Southampton, 1986. *Publications:* Nursing in The European Community, 1980; Caring for the Carers, 1981; ICN Past and Present, 1989; articles, mainly on internat. nursing and EEC, in national and internat. jls. *Recreations:* travel, gardening. *Address:* 31 Albany Park Court, Winn Road, Southampton SO2 1EN. *T:* Southampton (0703) 676592. *Clubs:* New Cavendish, St John's House, Royal Society of Medicine.

QUINNEN, Peter John; Chairman, Frew Dale Macmaster, since 1990; *b* 4 April 1945; *s* of John Norman Quinnen and Mabel Elisabeth Clark; *m* 1972, Pammy Urquhart; two *s.* *Educ:* St Benedict's School, Ealing; Christ Church, Oxford (MA Jurisp). FCA. Peat, Marwick, Mitchell & Co., 1966–72; James Capel & Co., 1972–90, Dir, 1982, Chm., and Chief Exec., 1986–90. *Recreations:* golf, opera, music, ballet, sport. *Clubs:* Royal Automobile; Royal Mid-Surrey Golf, St George's Hill Golf, Wednesday Golf.

QUINTON, family name of **Baron Quinton.**

QUINTON, Baron *cr* 1982 (Life Peer), of Holywell in the City of Oxford and County of Oxfordshire; **Anthony Meredith Quinton,** FBA 1977; Chairman of the Board, British Library, 1985–90; *b* 25 March 1925; *s* of late Richard Frith Quinton, Surgeon Captain, RN, and late Gwenllyan Letitia Quinton; *m* 1952, Marcelle Wegier; one *s* one *d.* *Educ:* Stowe Sch.; Christ Church, Oxford (St Cyres Scholar; BA 1st Cl. Hons PPE 1948). Served War, RAF, 1943–46: flying officer and navigator. Fellow: All Souls Coll., Oxford, 1949–55; New Coll., Oxford, 1955–78 (Emeritus Fellow, 1980); Pres., Trinity Coll., Oxford, 1978–87 (Hon. Fellow, 1987). Delegate, OUP, 1970–76. Mem., Arts Council, 1979–81; Vice Pres., British Acad., 1985–86. Vis. Professor: Swarthmore Coll., Pa, 1960; Stanford Univ., Calif, 1964; New Sch. for Social Res., New York, 1976–77. Lecturer: Dawes Hicks, British Acad., 1971; Gregynog, Univ. of Wales, Aberystwyth, 1973; T. S. Eliot, Univ. of Kent, Canterbury, 1976; Robbins, Univ. of Stirling, 1987; Hobhouse, LSE, 1988; Tanner, Warsaw, 1988; R. M. Jones, QUB, 1988; Carter, Lancaster, 1989. President: Aristotelian Soc., 1975–76; Soc. for Applied Philosophy, 1988–; Royal Inst. of Philosophy, 1990–. Chm., Kennedy Meml Trust, 1990–. Governor, Stowe Sch., 1963–84 (Chm. Governors, 1969–75); Fellow, Winchester Coll., 1970–85. DHumLit NY Univ., 1987; DHum Ball State Univ., 1990. Order of Leopold II, Belgium, 1984. *Publications:* Political Philosophy (ed), 1967; The Nature of Things, 1973; Utilitarian Ethics, 1973; (trans.) K. Ajdukiewicz (with H. Skolimowski) Problems and Theories of Philosophy, 1973; The Politics of Imperfection, 1978; Francis Bacon, 1980; Thoughts and Thinkers, 1982; From Wodehouse to Wittgenstein, 1992. *Recreations:* sedentary pursuits. *Address:* A11 Albany, Piccadilly, W1V 9RP; Mill House, Turville, Henley-on-Thames, Oxford RG9 6QL. *Clubs:* Garrick, Beefsteak, United Oxford & Cambridge University.

QUINTON, Sir John (Grand), Kt 1990; Chairman, Barclays Bank PLC, since 1987 (Deputy Chairman, 1985–87); *b* 21 Dec. 1929; *s* of William Grand Quinton and Norah May (*née* Nunn); *m* 1954, Jean Margaret Chastney; one *s* one *d.* *Educ:* Norwich Sch.; St John's Coll., Cambridge (MA 1954); FCIB (FIB 1964). Joined Barclays Bank, 1953: Asst Manager, Piccadilly, 1961; Dep. Principal, Staff Trng Centre, 1963; Manager, King's Cross, 1965; seconded to Min. of Health as Principal, Internat. Div. and UK Deleg., World Health Assembly, 1966; Asst Gen. Manager, 1968; Local Dir, Nottingham, 1969; Reg. Gen. Manager, 1971; Gen. Manager, 1975; Dir and Sen. Gen. Man., 1982–84; Vice-Chm., 1985. Dep. Chm., Mercantile Credit Co. Ltd, 1975–79. Chairman: Chief Exec. Officers, Cttee of London Clearing Bankers, 1982–83; Adv. Council, London Enterprise Agency, 1986–90; Office of the Banking Ombudsman, 1987–; Cttee of London and Scottish Bankers, 1989–91. Member: City Capital Markets Cttee, 1981–86; NE Thames RHA, 1974–87; Accounting Standards Cttee, 1982–85; Econ. and Financial Policy Cttee, CBI, 1985–88 (Chm., 1987–88). Chm., Motability Finance Ltd, 1978–85; Treasurer, Chartered Inst. of Bankers, 1980–86 (Pres., 1989–90); Hon. Treas. and Bd Mem., Business in the Community, 1986–91. Chm., British Olympic Appeal, 1988. Trustee, Royal Acad. Trust, 1987–; Chm. Bd of Trustees, Botanic Gdns Conservation Secretariat. Governor: Motability, 1985–; Ditchley Foundn, 1987–; Member: Court of Governors, Royal Shakespeare Theatre, 1986–; Court, Henley Coll., 1987–. FRSA 1988. *Recreations:* gardening, music, occasional golf. *Address:* c/o Barclays Bank PLC, 4 Royal Mint Court, EC3N 4HJ. *Club:* Reform.

QUIRK, Prof. Sir (Charles) Randolph, Kt 1985; CBE 1976; FBA 1975; President, British Academy, 1985–89; Fellow of University College London; *b* 12 July 1920; *s* of late Thomas and Amy Randolph Quirk, Lambfell, Isle of Man; *m* 1st, 1946, Jean (marr. diss. 1979), *d* of Ellis Gauntlett Williams; two *s*; 2nd, 1984, Gabriele, *d* of Judge Helmut Stein. *Educ:* Cronk y Voddy Sch.; Douglas High Sch., IOM; University College London. MA, PhD, DLit London. Served RAF, 1940–45. Lecturer in English, University College London, 1947–54; Commonwealth Fund Fellow, Yale Univ. and University of Michigan, 1951–52; Reader in English Language and Literature, University of Durham, 1954–58; Professor of English Language in the University of Durham, 1958–60, in the University of London, 1960–68; Quain Prof. of English Language and Literature, University Coll. London, 1968–81; Vice-Chancellor, Univ. of London, 1981–85. Dir, Survey of English Usage, 1959–81. Member: Senate, Univ. of London, 1970–75 (Chm., Acad. Council, 1972–75); Ct, Univ. of London, 1972–75; Bd, British Council, 1983–; BBC Archives Cttee, 1975–81; RADA Council, 1985–. President: Inst. of Linguists, 1982–85; Coll. of Speech Therapists, 1987–; North of England Educn Conf., 1989; Vice-Pres., Foundn for Science and Technology, 1986–90; Governor: British Inst. of Recorded Sound, 1975–80; E-SU, 1980–85; Amer. Internat. Coll. of London, 1981–. Chairman: Cttee of Enquiry into Speech Therapy Services, 1969–72; Hornby Educnl Trust, 1979–; Anglo-Spanish Foundn, 1983–85; British Library Adv. Cttee, 1984–. Trustee: Wolfson Foundn, 1987–; American Sch. in London, 1987–89. Mem., Academia Europaea, 1988. Foreign Fellow: Royal Belgian Acad. of Scis, 1975; Royal Swedish Acad., 1987. Hon. FCST; Hon. FIL; Hon. Fellow: Imperial Coll., 1985; QMC, 1986; Goldsmiths' Coll., 1987; King's Coll., 1990; RHBNC, 1990. Hon. Bencher, Gray's Inn, 1982. Hon. Fil. Dr Lund and Uppsala; Hon. DU: Essex; Bar Ilan; Brunel; DUniv Open; Hon. DHC: Liège; Paris; Hon. DLitt: Reading; Newcastle upon Tyne; Durham; Bath; Salford; California; Sheffield; Glasgow; Nijmegen; Hon. DCL CNAA; Hon. LLD Leicester. Jubilee Medal, Inst. of Linguists, 1973. *Publications:* The Concessive Relation in Old English Poetry, 1954; Studies in Communication (with A. J. Ayer and others), 1955; An Old English Grammar (with C. L. Wrenn), 1955, revised edn, 1958; Charles Dickens and Appropriate Language, 1959; The Teaching of English (with A. H. Smith), 1959, revised edn, 1964; The Study of the Mother-Tongue, 1961; The Use of English (with Supplements by A. C. Gimson and J. Warburg), 1962, enlarged edn, 1968; Prosodic and Paralinguistic Features in English (with D. Crystal), 1964; A Common Language (with A. H. Marckwardt), 1964; Investigating Linguistic Acceptability (with J. Svartvik), 1966; Essays on the English

Language—Mediaeval and Modern, 1968; (with S. Greenbaum) Elicitation Experiments in English, 1970; (with S. Greenbaum, G. Leech, J. Svartvik) A Grammar of Contemporary English, 1972; The English Language and Images of Matter, 1972; (with S. Greenbaum) A University Grammar of English, 1973; The Linguist and the English Language, 1974; (with V. Adams, D. Davy) Old English Literature: a practical introduction, 1975; (with J. Svartvik) A Corpus of English Conversation, 1980; Style and Communication in the English Language, 1982; (with S. Greenbaum, G. Leech, J. Svartvik) A Comprehensive Grammar of the English Language, 1985; (with H. Widdowson) English in the World, 1985; Words at Work: lectures on textual structure, 1986; (with G. Stein) English in Use, 1990; (with S. Greenbaum) A Student's Grammar of the English Language, 1990; contrib. to: conf. proceedings and volumes of studies; papers in linguistic and literary journals. *Address:* University College London, Gower Street, WC1E 6BT. *Club:* Athenæum.

QUIRK, John Stanton S.; *see* Shirley-Quirk.

R

RABAN, Jonathan, FRSL; novelist, travel writer and critic; *b* 14 June 1942; *s* of Rev. Peter J. C. P. Raban and Monica (*née* Sandison); *m* 1985, Caroline Cuthbert (separated). *Educ:* Univ. of Hull (BA Hons English). FRSL 1975. Lecturer in English and American Literature: UCW, Aberystwyth, 1965–67; Univ. of E Anglia, 1967–69; professional writer, 1969–. *Publications:* The Technique of Modern Fiction, 1969; Mark Twain: Huckleberry Finn, 1969; The Society of the Poem, 1971; Soft City, 1973; Arabia Through the Looking Glass, 1979; Old Glory, 1981 (Heinemann Award, RSL, 1982; Thomas Cook Award, 1982); Foreign Land, 1985; Coasting, 1986; For Love and Money, 1987; God, Man & Mrs Thatcher, 1989; Hunting Mister Heartbreak, 1990; (ed) The Oxford Book of the Sea, 1992. *Recreation:* sailing. *Address:* c/o Aitken & Stone Ltd, 29 Fernshaw Road, SW10 0TG. *Clubs:* Groucho, Cruising Association; Shilshole Bay Yacht (Seattle).

RABBI, The Chief; *see* Sacks, Rabbi Dr J. H.

RABBITTS, Dr Terence Howard, FRS 1987; Member, Scientific Staff, MRC Laboratory of Molecular Biology, Cambridge, since 1973; *b* 17 June 1946; *s* of Joan and Frederick Rabbitts; *m* 1984, Pamela Gage; one *d. Educ:* John Ruskin Grammar School; Univ. of East Anglia (BSc). Nat. Inst. for Medical Research (PhD). Research Fellow, Dept of Genetics, Univ. of Edinburgh, 1971–73. Colworth Medal, Biochemical Soc., 1981. *Publications:* papers in scientific jls. *Address:* MRC Laboratory of Molecular Biology, Hills Road, Cambridge CB2 2QH. *T:* Cambridge (0223) 248011.

RABIN, Prof. Brian Robert; Professor of Biochemistry, since 1988, Fellow since 1984, University College, London; *b* 4 Nov. 1927; *s* of Emanuel and Sophia Rabin, both British; *m* 1954; one *s* one *d. Educ:* Latymer Sch., Edmonton; University Coll., London. BSc 1951, MSc 1952, PhD 1956. University College, London: Asst Lectr, 1954–57; Lectr, 1957–63; Reader, 1963–67; Prof. of Enzymology, 1967–70; Hd of Dept of Biochemistry, 1970–88. Rockefeller Fellow, Univ. of California, 1956–57. Founder Dir, London Biotechnology Ltd, 1985–. *Publications:* numerous in Biochem. Jl, European Jl of Biochem., Nature, Proc. Nat. Acad. Sciences US, etc. *Recreations:* travel, listening to music, carpentry. *Address:* 34 Grangewood, Potters Bar, Herts EN6 1SL. *T:* Potters Bar (0707) 54576. *Club:* Athenæum.

RABINOVITCH, Prof. Benton Seymour, FRS 1987; Professor of Chemistry, University of Washington, Seattle, 1957–86, now Emeritus; *b* 19 Feb. 1919; *s* of Samuel Rabinovitch and Rachel Schachter; *m* 1st, 1949, Marilyn Werby; two *s* two *d*; 2nd, 1980, Flora Reitman. *Educ:* McGill Univ. (BSc, PhD). Served Canadian Army overseas, Captain, 1942–46. Milton Fellow, Harvard Univ., 1946–48; University of Washington: Asst Prof., 1948–53; Associate Prof., 1953–57. Guggenheim Fellow, 1961–62. Sigma Xi Dist. Res. Award, 1981; Peter Debye Award, ACS, 1984; Michael Polanyi Medal, RSC, 1984. *Publications:* Physical Chemistry, 1964; Antique Silver Servers, 1990; (ed) annual reviews Phys. Chem., 1975–85; over 200 contribs to jls. *Recreation:* silversmithing. *Address:* Department of Chemistry BG–10, University of Washington, Seattle, Wash 98195, USA. *T:* 206–543–1636.

RABINOWITZ, Harry, MBE 1977; freelance conductor and composer; *b* 26 March 1916; *s* of Israel and Eva Rabinowitz; *m* 1944, Lorna Thurlow Anderson; one *s* two *d. Educ:* Athlone High Sch., S Africa; Witwatersrand Univ.; Guildhall Sch. of Music. Conductor, BBC Radio, 1953–60; Musical Dir, BBC TV Light Entertainment, 1960–68; Head of Music, LWT, 1968–77; freelance film, TV, radio and disc activities, 1977–. Conductor: Cats, New London Th., 1981; Song and Dance, Palace Th., 1982; Hollywood Bowl Concerts, 1983 and 1984; Boston "Pops" concerts, 1985, 1986, 1988, 1989, 1990, 1991; concerts with RPO, LSO and London Concert Orch.; *films:* conductor: La Dentellière, 1977; Mon Oncle d'Amérique, 1980; The Time Bandits, 1980; Chariots of Fire, 1981; Heat and Dust, 1982; The Missionary, 1983; Electric Dreams (actor/conductor), 1984; The Bostonians, 1984; Return to Oz, Lady Jane Grey, and Revolution—1776, 1985; F/X, and Manhattan Project, 1986; Masters of the Universe, Maurice, 1987; Simon Wiesenthal, Camille Claudet, 1988; Shirley Valentine (jt composer/conductor), Queen of Hearts, 1989; Music Box, Lord of the Flies, La Fille des Collines, 1990; Jalousie, La Tribu, Jesuit Joe, Iran Day of Crisis, Ballad of the Sad Café, 1991; *television:* composer-conductor: Agatha Christie Hour, 1982; Reilly Ace of Spies, 1983; Glorious Day, 1985; Land of the Eagle, 1990. Gold Badge of Merit, British Acad. of Songwriters, Composers and Authors, 1985; award for lifetime contribution to Allmusic, 1990. *Recreations:* listening to others making music, gathering edible fungi, wine tasting. *Address:* Yellow Cottage, Walking Bottom, Peaslake, Surrey GU5 9RR. *T:* Dorking (0306) 730605.

RABUKAWAQA, Sir Josua Rasilau, KBE 1977 (CBE 1974; MBE 1968); MVO 1970; Ambassador-at-Large for Fiji and Chief of Protocol, Fiji, 1977–80; *b* 2 Dec. 1917; *s* of Dr Aisea Rasilau and Adi Mereoni Dimaicakau, Bau, Fiji; *m* 1944, Mei Tolanivutu; three *s* two *d. Educ:* Suva Methodist Boys' Sch.; Queen Victoria Sch.; Teachers' Trng Coll., Auckland. Diploma in Public and Social Admin. 1958. Teaching in schools throughout Fiji, 1938–52; Co-operatives Inspector, 1952. Joined Fiji Mil. Forces, 1953; attached Gloucester Regt at Warminster Sch. of Infantry and Support Weapons Wing, Netheravon; comd Mortar Platoon, Malaya, 1954–55. Subseq. Econ. Develt Officer, Fiji, 1957; District Officer, Fiji Admin. Service, 1961; Comr, Central Div., 1968. MLC, Fiji, 1964–66; Delegate, Constitutional Conf., London, 1965; (first) High Comr for Fiji in London, 1970–76. Active worker for Scouts, Red Cross and Methodist Church Choir. Formed Phoenix Choir. Compiled manual of singing in Fijian language, 1956, and guide for Fijian pronunciation for use by Fiji Broadcasting Commn, 1967; Chm., Fijian Adv. Cttee of Fiji Broadcasting Commn, 1965–70; Chm. Bd of Examrs for High Standard Fijian and Interpreters Exams, 1965–70; Mem., Housing Authority; Mem., Educn Adv. Council. *Recreations:* cricket, Rugby football (toured NZ as player/manager for Fiji, 1967). *Address:* 6 Vunivivi Hill, Nausori, Fiji. *Clubs:* Commonwealth Trust; Defence, Union (Fiji).

RACE, (Denys Alan) Reg; management and policy consultant; *b* 23 June 1947; *s* of Denys and Elsie Race. *Educ:* Sale Grammar School; Univ. of Kent. BA (Politics and Sociology), PhD (Politics). Senior Research Officer, National Union of Public Employees, 1972. MP (Lab) Haringey, Wood Green, 1979–83; Head of Programme Office, GLC, 1983–86; Special Res. Officer, ACTT, 1986; County Dir, Derbys County Council, 1988. Advr, Health Policy Adv. Unit, 1989. *Publications:* The Challenge Now (report on management and organisation of ACTT), 1986; numerous pamphlets and articles in Labour Movement press.

RACE, Ruth Ann; *see* Sanger, Dr R. A.

RACE, Steve, (Stephen Russell Race); broadcaster, musician and author; *b* Lincoln, 1 April 1921; *s* of Russell Tinniswood Race and Robina Race (*née* Hurley); *m* 1st, Marjorie Clair Leng (*d* 1969); one *d*; 2nd, Léonie Rebecca Govier Mather. *Educ:* Lincoln Sch. (now Christ's Hospital Sch.); Royal Academy of Music. FRAM 1978. Served War, RAF, 1941–46; free-lance pianist, arranger and composer, 1946–55; Light Music Adviser to Associated-Rediffusion Ltd, 1955–60; conductor for many TV series incl. Tony Hancock and Peter Sellers Shows. Appearances in radio and TV shows include: My Music, A Good Read, Jazz in Perspective, Any Questions?, Music Now, Music Weekly, Kaleidoscope, Musician at Large, Captain Pepper's Autograph Album, Jazz Revisited, With Great Pleasure, Desert Island Discs, Steve Race Presents the Radio Orchestra Show, Gershwin Among Friends, Irving Berlin Among Friends; radio reviews in The Listener, 1975–80; long-playing records and commentary for Nat. Gall., London, Glasgow Art Gall. and Nat. Mus. of Wales, 1977–80. Dep. Chm., PRS, 1973–76. Member: Council, Royal Albert Hall of Arts and Scis, 1976–; Exec. Council, Musicians' Benevolent Fund, 1985–. FRSA 1975. Freeman, City of London, 1982. Governor of Tokyo Metropolis Prize for Radio, 1979; Wavendon Allmusic Media Personality of the Year, 1987; Radio Prog. of the Year, TV and Radio Industries Club Awards, 1988. *Principal compositions:* Nicola (Ivor Novello Award); Faraway Music; The Pied Piper; incidental music for Richard The Third, Cyrano de Bergerac, Twelfth Night (BBC); Cantatas: Song of King David; The Day of the Donkey; Song of Praise; My Music—My Songs; misc. works incl. ITV advertising sound-tracks (Venice Award, 1962; Cannes Award, 1963); film scores include: Calling Paul Temple, Three Roads to Rome, Against The Tide, Land of Three Rivers. *Publications:* Musician at Large: an autobiography, 1979; My Music, 1979; Dear Music Lover, 1981; Steve Race's Music Quiz, 1983; The Illustrated Counties of England, 1984; You Can't be Serious, 1985; The Penguin Masterquiz, 1985; With Great Pleasure, 1986; The Two Worlds of Joseph Race, 1988; contribs to DNB, Punch, Literary Review, Times, Daily Telegraph, Daily Mail, Independent, Listener, Country Living. *Recreations:* reading about the past, looking at paintings, the open air. *Address:* Martins End Lane, Great Missenden, Bucks HP16 9HS.

RACZYNSKI, Count Edward, Dr Juris; Chairman, Polish Cultural Foundation, since 1970; Hon. President, The Polish Institute and Sikorski Museum, since 1977 (Chairman, 1966–77); Polish President-in-exile, 1979–86; *b* 19 Dec. 1891; *s* of Count Edouard Raczynski and Countess Rose Potocka; *m* 1st, 1925, Joyous (*d* 1930), *d* of Sir Arthur Basil Markham, 1st Bt, and Lucy, CBE, *d* of Captain A. B. Cunningham, late RA; 2nd, 1932, Cecile (*d* 1962), *d* of Edward Jaroszynski and Wanda Countess Sierakowska; three *d. Educ:* Universities of Krakow and Leipzig; London School of Economics and Political Science. Entered Polish Ministry of Foreign Affairs, 1919; served in Copenhagen, London, and Warsaw; Delegate to Disarmament Conference, Geneva, 1932–34; Polish Minister accredited to the League of Nations, 1932–34; Polish Ambassador to the Court of St James's, 1934–45; Acting Polish Minister for Foreign Affairs, 1941–42; Minister of State in charge of Foreign Affairs, Cabinet of Gen. Sikorski, 1942–43; Chief Polish Rep. on Interim Treasury Cttee for Polish Questions, 1945–47; Hon. Chief Polish Adviser, Ministry of Labour and National Service, 1952–Dec. 1956; Chairman: Polish Research Centre, London, 1940–67. Grand Officier of the Order of Polonia Restituta, Order of White Eagle, Poland, Grand Cross of the Crown of Rumania, etc. *Publications:* In Allied London: Diary 1939–45 (in Polish); In Allied London: (Wartime Diaries), (in English), 1963; Rogalin and its Inhabitants (in Polish), 1963; Pani Róża (in Polish), 1969; Book of Verse (in Polish), 1960; Memoirs of Viridianne Fiszer (translated from French to Polish), 1975; From Narcyz Kulikowski to Winston Churchill (in Polish), 1976; From Geneva to Yalta: discussion of Count Raczynski with Tadeusz Zenczykowski (in Polish), 1988; A Time of Great Change: conversations with Krzysztof Muszkowski (in Polish), 1990. *Recreations:* tennis, golf, skating, ski-ing. *Address:* 8 Lennox Gardens, SW1X 0DG; 5 Krakowskie Przedmieście, Warsaw, Poland.

RADCLIFFE, Anthony Frank; Keeper Emeritus, Victoria and Albert Museum, since 1990; *b* Wivenhoe, Essex, 23 Feb. 1933; *s* of Dr Walter Radcliffe and Murielle Laure Radcliffe (*née* Brée); *m* 1960, Enid Clair Cawkwell; two *s. Educ:* Oundle Sch.; Gonville and Caius Coll., Cambridge (MA). Victoria and Albert Museum: joined Dept of Circulation, 1958; transferred to Dept of Architecture and Sculpture, 1960; Res. Asst, Dept of Circulation, 1961–67; Asst to Dir, 1967–74; Asst Keeper, Dept of Architecture and Sculpture, 1974–79; Keeper of Sculpture, 1979–89; Head of Res., 1989–90. Mellon Sen. Vis. Curator, Nat. Gall. of Art, Washington, 1990; Guest Scholar, J. Paul Getty Mus., 1991. Medal, Accademia delle Arti del Disegno, Florence, 1986. *Publications:* European Bronze Statuettes, 1966; Jean-Baptiste Carpeaux, 1968; (with J. Pope-Hennessy and T. Hodgkinson) The Frick Collection: an illustrated catalogue, III, IV, 1970; (with C. Avery) Giambologna, sculptor to the Medici, 1978; The Thyssen-Bornemisza Collection: Italian renaissance and baroque sculpture and bronzes, 1991; contribs to Burlington Mag., Apollo, Connoisseur, etc. *Address:* c/o Victoria and Albert Museum, SW7 2RL.

RADCLIFFE, Francis Charles Joseph; *b* 23 Oct. 1939; *s* of Charles Joseph Basil Nicholas Radcliffe and Norah Radcliffe (*née* Percy); *m* 1968, Nicolette, *e d* of Eugene Randag; one *s* two *d.* *Educ:* Ampleforth Coll.; Gonville and Caius Coll., Cambridge (MA). Called to the Bar, Gray's Inn, 1962; a Recorder of the Crown Court, 1979. Mem., Assoc. of Lawyers for the Defence of the Unborn. Contested (Christian: stop abortion candidate) York, 1979; founded York Christian Party, 1981. *Recreations:* shooting, beagling, gardening, etc. *Address:* 11 King's Bench Walk, Temple, EC4Y 7EQ.

RADCLIFFE, Hugh John Reginald Joseph, MBE 1944; Chairman, Dun and Bradstreet Ltd, 1974–76; *b* 3 March 1911; 2nd *s* of Sir Everard Radcliffe, 5th Bt; *m* 1937, Marie Therese, *d* of late Maj.-Gen. Sir Cecil Pereira, KCB, CMG; five *s* one *d.* *Educ:* Downside. Dep. Chm., London Stock Exchange, 1967–70. Kt Comdr St Silvester (Papal), 1965; Kt of St Gregory (Papal), 1984. *Address:* The White House, Stoke, Andover, Hants SP11 0LU.

See also Sir S. E. Radcliffe, Bt, Very Rev. T. P. J. Radcliffe.

RADCLIFFE, Percy, CBE 1985; farmer; Chairman, Isle of Man Government Executive Council (Manx Cabinet), 1981–85; *b* 14 Nov. 1916; *s* of Arthur and Annie Radcliffe; *m* 1942, Barbara Frances Crowe; two *s* one *d.* *Educ:* Ramsey Grammar Sch., Isle of Man. Member (Ind.) Isle of Man Govt, 1963, re-elected 1966, 1971, 1976; elected by House of Keys to be Mem. Legislative Council, 1980; Chairman: IOM Local Govt Board, 1966–76; Finance Board, 1976–81; elected by Tynwald (Govt of IOM) first Chm. of Manx Cabinet, 1981. Pres., Riding/Driving for Disabled, IOM Gp, 1985–; Member: Isle of Man Agricultural Marketing Soc., 1945–75; British Horse Driving Soc., 1979–. Silver Jubilee Medal, 1977. *Address:* Kellaway, Sulby, Isle of Man. *T:* Sulby (062489) 7257.

RADCLIFFE, Sir Sebastian Everard, 7th Bt *cr* 1813; *b* 8 June 1972; *s* of Sir Joseph Benedict Everard Henry Radcliffe, 6th Bt, MC and of Marcia Anne Helen (who *m* 1988, H. M. S. Tanner), *y d* of Major David Turville Constable Maxwell, Bosworth Hall, Husbands Bosworth, Rugby; *S* father, 1975. *Heir: uncle* Hugh John Reginald Joseph Radcliffe, *qv.* *Address:* Le Château de Cheseaux, 1033 Cheseaux, Vaud, Switzerland.

RADCLIFFE, Very Rev. Timothy Peter Joseph, OP; Provincial of the English Province of the Order of Preachers (Dominicans), since 1988; *b* 22 Aug. 1945; 3rd *s* of Hugh John Reginald Joseph Radcliffe, *qv.* *Educ:* Downside; St John's College, Oxford (MA). Entered Dominican Order, 1965; Chaplain to Imperial Coll., 1976–78; taught theology at Blackfriars, Oxford, 1978–88; Prior of Blackfriars, 1982–88; Faculty of Theology, Oxford Univ., 1985–88. John Toohey Schol. in Residence, Sydney Univ., 1984. Pres., Conf. of Major Religious Superiors, 1991–. Chm., New Blackfriars, 1983–88. *Publications:* articles in books and periodicals. *Recreations:* walking and talking with friends, reading Dickens. *Address:* St Dominic's Priory, Southampton Road, NW5 4LB. *T:* 071–485 2760.

RADCLYFFE, Sir Charles Edward M.; *see* Mott-Radclyffe.

RADDA, Prof. George K., MA, DPhil; FRS 1980; British Heart Foundation Professor of Molecular Cardiology, University of Oxford, since 1984; Professorial Fellow, Merton College, Oxford, since 1984; Hon. Director, Medical Research Council Unit of Biochemical and Clinical Magnetic Resonance, since 1988; *b* 9 June 1936; *s* of Dr Gyula Radda and Dr Anna Bernolak; *m* 1961, Mary O'Brien; two *s* one *d.* *Educ:* Pannonhalma, Hungary; Eötvös Univ., Budapest, Hungary; Merton Coll., Oxford (BA Cl. 1, Chem., 1960; DPhil 1962). Res. Associate, Univ. of California, 1962–63; Lectr in Organic Chemistry, St John's Coll., Oxford, 1963–64; Fellow and Tutor in Organic Chem., Merton Coll., Oxford, 1964–84; University Lectr in Biochem., Oxford Univ., 1966–84. Vis. Prof., Cleveland Clinic, 1987. Medical Research Council: Mem. Council, 1988–; Chm., Cell Biology and Disorders Bd, 1988–. Council, Royal Soc., 1990–; Council, ICRF, 1991–. Mem., various Editorial Bds of scientific jls including: Editor, Biochemical and Biophysical Research Communications, 1977–85; Man. Editor, Biochimica et Biophysica Acta, 1977– (Chm. Editl Bd, 1989–). Founder Mem., Oxford Enzyme Gp, 1970–86; Pres., Soc. for Magnetic Resonance in Medicine, 1985–86. Mem., Fachbeirat, Max Planck Inst. für Systemphysiologie, Dortmund, 1987–. Hon. FRCR 1985; Hon. MRCP 1987; Hon. Fellow, Amer. Heart Assoc., 1988. Hon. DM Bern, 1985; Hon. MD London, 1991. Colworth Medal, Biochem. Soc., 1969; Feldberg Prize, Feldberg Foundn, 1982; British Heart Foundn Prize and Gold Medal for cardiovascular research, 1982; CIBA Medal and Prize, Biochem. Soc., 1983; Gold Medal, Soc. for Magnetic Resonance in Medicine, 1984; Buchanan Medal, Royal Soc., 1987; Internat. Lectr and Citation, Amer. Heart Assoc., 1987; Skinner Lecture and Medal, RCR, 1989; Rank Prize in Nutrition, 1991. *Publications:* articles in books and in jls of biochemistry and medicine. *Recreations:* opera, swimming, jazz. *Address:* Merton College, Oxford; Department of Biochemistry, Oxford University, South Parks Road, Oxford OX1 3QU. *T:* Oxford (0865) 275272.

RADFORD, (Courtenay Arthur) Ralegh, FBA 1956; *b* 7 Nov. 1900; *o s* of late Arthur Lock and Ada M. Radford; unmarried. *Educ:* St George's School, Harpenden; Exeter College, Oxford. BA 1921; MA 1937; Inspector of Ancient Monuments in Wales and Monmouthshire, 1929–34; Director of the British School at Rome, 1936–39; Member of Royal Commission on Ancient Monuments in Wales and Monmouthshire, 1935–46; Member of Royal Commission on Historical Monuments (England), 1953–76; supervised excavations at Tintagel, Ditchley, Castle Dore, the Hurlers, Whithorn, Glastonbury, Birsay and elsewhere; FSA 1928 (Vice-Pres. 1954–58; Gold Medal, 1972); FRHistS 1930; President: Prehistoric Soc., 1954–58; Roy. Archæological Inst., 1960–63; Cambrian Archæological Assoc., 1961; Soc. of Medieval Archæology, 1969–71. Hon. DLitt Glasgow, 1963; Univ. of Wales, 1963; Exeter, 1973; *Publications:* Reports on the Excavations at Tintagel, Ditchley, Whithorn, etc.; various articles on archæological subjects. *Address:* Culmcott, Uffculme, Devon EX15 3AT. *Club:* Athenæum.

RADFORD, Joseph; Public Trustee, 1978–80; *b* 7 April 1918; *s* of Thomas Radford and Elizabeth Ann Radford (*née* Sanders); *m* 1976, Rosemary Ellen Murphy. *Educ:* Herbert Strutt, Belper; Nottingham Univ. Admitted solicitor, 1940. First Cl. Hons, Law Soc. Intermediate, 1937; Dist., Law Soc. Final, 1940. Served War, 1940–47, RA; 41st (5th North Staffordshire) RA; 1st Maritime Regt, RA; Staff, MELF (Major). Joined Public Trustee Office, 1949; Chief Admin. Officer, 1973–75; Asst Public Trustee, 1975–78. Mem., Law Soc., 1945– (Hon. Auditor, 1963–65). Freeman, City of London, 1983. Silver Jubilee Medal, 1977. *Address:* 80 Cunningham Park, Harrow, Mddx HA1 4QJ.

RADFORD, Ralegh; *see* Radford, C. A. R.

RADFORD, Robert Edwin, CB 1979; Assistant Director General, St John Ambulance Association, 1981–84; Deputy Secretary and Principal Finance Officer, Department of Health and Social Security, 1977–81; *b* 1 April 1921; *s* of late Richard James Radford and late May Eleanor Radford (*née* Briant); *m* 1945, Eleanor Margaret, *d* of late John Idwal Jones; one *s* one *d.* *Educ:* Royal Grammar Sch., Guildford. Board of Educn, 1938. Served War, Lieut, RNVR, 1940–46. Colonial Office: Asst Principal, 1947; Private Sec. to Permanent Under-Sec. of State for the Colonies, 1950–51; Principal, 1951; First Sec., UK Commn, Singapore, 1961–63; Asst Sec., Dept of Techn. Co-op., 1963; transferred to ODM, 1964; Counsellor, British Embassy, Washington, and UK Alternate Exec. Dir, IBRD, 1965–67; Under Secretary: FCO (ODA), 1973; DHSS, 1974–76. Mem., SW Surrey HA, 1982–89. *Recreations:* walking, reading. *Address:* 10 Edgeborough Court, Upper Edgeborough Road, Guildford, Surrey GU1 2BL. *T:* Guildford (0483) 61822.

RADFORD, Sir Ronald (Walter), KCB 1976 (CB 1971); MBE 1947; Hon. Secretary-General, Customs Co-operation Council, since 1983 (Secretary-General, 1978–83); *b* 28 Feb. 1916; *er s* of late George Leonard Radford and Ethel Mary Radford; *m* 1949, Jean Alison Dunlop Strange; one *s* one *d.* *Educ:* Southend-on-Sea High Sch.; St John's Coll., Cambridge (Schol., Wrangler, MA). Joined ICS, 1939; Dist Magistrate and Collector, Shahabad, Bihar, 1945; on leave, prep. to retirement from ICS, 1947; Admin. Class, Home CS, and posted to HM Customs and Excise, 1947; Asst Sec., 1953; Comr, 1965; Dep. Chm., 1970; Chm., 1973–77. Mem. Management Cttee, RNLI, 1977– (Vice-Chm., 1986–). *Address:* 4 Thomas Close, Brentwood, Essex CM15 8BS. *T:* Brentwood (0277) 211567. *Clubs:* Reform, Civil Service, City Livery; MCC.

RADICE, Edward Albert, CBE 1946; *b* 2 Jan. 1907; *s* of C. A. Radice, ICS and Alice Effie (*née* Murray), DSc (Econ); *m* 1936, Joan Keeling (*d* 1991); one *s* one *d.* *Educ:* Winchester Coll.; Magdalen Coll., Oxford (1st in Maths Mods; 1st in Lit. Hum.; DPhil). Commonwealth Fund Fellow, Columbia Univ., New York, 1933–35; Assistant Professor of Economics, Wesleyan University, Middletown, Conn., 1937–39; League of Nations Secretariat, 1939; Ministry of Economic Warfare, 1940–44; HM Foreign Service, 1945–53; Min. of Defence, 1953–70 (Dir of Economic Intelligence, 1966–70); Senior Research Fellow, St Antony's Coll., Oxford, 1970–73. *Publications:* (jt) An American Experiment, 1936; Fundamental Issues in the United States, 1936; Savings in Great Britain, 1922–35, 1939; (contrib.) Communist Power in Europe 1944–1949, 1977; (jtly, also co-ed) The Economic History of Eastern Europe 1919–1975, Vols I and II, 1986; papers in Econometrica, Oxford Economic Papers, Economic History Review. *Address:* 2 Talbot Road, Oxford OX2 8LL. *T:* Oxford (0865) 515573.

See also I. de L. Radice.

RADICE, Giles Heneage; MP (Lab) Durham North, since 1983 (Chester-le-Street, March 1973–1983); *b* 4 Oct. 1936. *Educ:* Winchester; Magdalen Coll., Oxford. Head of Research Dept, General and Municipal Workers' Union (GMWU), 1966–73. Front Bench Spokesman on foreign affairs, 1981, on employment, 1981–83, on education, 1983–87; Mem., Treasury and Civil Service Select Cttee, 1987–. Mem., Council, Policy Studies Inst., 1978–83. *Publications:* Democratic Socialism, 1965; (ed jointly) More Power to People, 1968; (co-author) Will Thorne, 1974; The Industrial Democrats, 1978; (co-author) Socialists in Recession, 1986; Labour's Path to Power: the new revisionism, 1989. *Recreations:* reading, tennis. *Address:* 58A Dartmouth Park Road, NW5.

RADICE, Italo de Lisle, CB 1969; Appointed Member, Royal Patriotic Fund Corporation, 1969–91; *b* 2 March 1911; *s* of Charles Albert Radice, ICS, and Alice Effie (*née* Murray); *m* 1935, Betty Dawson (*d* 1985); three *s* (and one *d* decd). *Educ:* Blundell's School; Magdalen College, Oxford (demy). Admitted Solicitor, 1938; Public Trustee Office, 1939; Military Government East and North Africa, Italy, and Germany, 1941–46; Treasury, 1946, Under-Secretary, 1961–68; Sec. and Comptroller General, Nat. Debt Office, 1969–76. Dir, Central Trustee Savings Bank Ltd, 1976–80. Comr for Income Tax, City of London, 1972–86. Cavaliere Ufficiale dell'Ordine al Merito (Italy), 1981. *Address:* 2A Windmill Hill, NW3 6RU. *T:* 071–794 8983.

See also E. A. Radice.

RADJI, Parviz Camran; diplomat; Ambassador of Iran to the Court of St James's, 1976–79; *b* 1936; *m* 1986, Golgoun Partovi. *Educ:* Trinity Hall, Cambridge (MA Econs). National Iranian Oil Co., 1959–62; Private Sec. to Minister of Foreign Affairs, 1962–65; Private Sec. to Prime Minister, subseq. Personal Asst, 1965–72; Special Adviser to Prime Minister, 1972–76. *Publication:* In the Service of the Peacock Throne: the diaries of the Shah's last Ambassador to London, 1983. *Address:* 21 Pembroke Gardens, W8 6HT.

RADLEY-SMITH, Eric John, MS; FRCS; Surgeon: Royal Free Hospital, London; Brentford Hospital; Epsom Hospital; Neurosurgeon, Royal National Throat, Nose and Ear Hospital. *Educ:* Paston; King's College, London; King's College Hospital. MB, BS (Hons, Distinction in Medicine, Surgery, Forensic Medicine and Hygiene), 1933; MS, London, 1936; LRCP, 1933; FRCS 1935 (MRCS 1933). Served War of 1939–45, Wing Comdr i/c Surgical Div. RAFVR. Formerly: Surgical Registrar, King's Coll. Hosp.; House Surgeon, National Hosp. for Nervous Diseases, Queen Square. Examnr in Surgery, Univs of London and West Indies. Mem. Court, RCS. Mem. Assoc. of British Neurosurgeons; Fellow, Assoc. of Surgeons of Great Britain. *Publications:* papers in medical journals. *Recreations:* football and farming.

RADNOR, 8th Earl of, *cr* 1765; **Jacob Pleydell-Bouverie;** Bt 1713–14; Viscount Folkestone, Baron Longford, 1747; Baron Pleydell-Bouverie, 1765; *b* 10 Nov. 1927; *e s* of 7th Earl of Radnor, KG, KCVO, and Helen Olivia, *d* of late Charles R. W. Adeane, CB; *S* father, 1968; *m* 1st, 1953, Anne (marr. diss. 1962), *d* of Donald Seth-Smith, Njoro, Kenya and Whitsbury Cross, near Fordingbridge, Hants; two *s*; 2nd, 1963, Margaret Robin (marr. diss. 1985), *d* of late Robin Fleming, Catter House, Drymen; four *d*; 3rd, 1986, Mary Jillean Gwenellan Pettit. *Educ:* Harrow; Trinity Coll., Cambridge (BA Agriculture). *Heir: s* Viscount Folkestone, *qv.* *Address:* Longford Castle, Salisbury, Wilts SP5 4EF. *T:* Salisbury (0722) 411515.

RADZINOWICZ, Sir Leon, Kt 1970; MA, LLD; FBA 1973; Fellow of Trinity College, Cambridge, since 1948; Wolfson Professor of Criminology, University of Cambridge, 1959–73, and Director of the Institute of Criminology, 1960–72; Associate Fellow, Silliman College, Yale, since 1966; Adjunct Professor of Law and Criminology, Columbia Law School, 1966–75; *b* Poland, 15 Aug. 1906; *m* 1st, 1933, Irene Szereszewski (marr. diss., 1955); 2nd, 1958, Mary Ann (marr. diss. 1979), *d* of Gen. Nevins, Gettysburg, Pa, USA; one *s* one *d*; 3rd, 1979, Isolde Klarmann, *d* of late Prof. Emil and Elfriede Doernenburg, and widow of Prof. Adolf Klarmann, Philadelphia; naturalised British subject, 1947. *Educ:* Cracow, Paris, Geneva and Rome. University of Paris, 1924–25; Licencié en Droit, Univ. of Geneva, 1927; Doctor of Law, Rome, 1928; LLD Cambridge, 1951. Lectr, Univ. of Geneva, 1928–31; Doctor of Law, Cracow, 1929; Reported on working of penal system in Belgium, 1930; Lectr, Free Univ. of Warsaw, 1932–36. Came to England on behalf of Polish Ministry of Justice to report on working of English penal system, 1938; Asst Dir of Research, Univ. of Cambridge, 1946–49; Dir, Dept of Criminal Science, Univ. of Cambridge, 1949–59; Walter E. Meyer Research Prof. of Law, Yale Law Sch., 1962–63; Adj. Prof. in Law of Criminology, Columbia Law Sch, 1964–74; Visiting Professor: Virginia Law Sch., 1968–75; Univ. of Pennsylvania, 1970–73; Benjamin Cardozo Law Sch., Yeshiva Univ., 1979–81; Overseer, Pennsylvania Law Sch. and Associate Trustee, Pennsylvania Univ., 1978–82. Mem., Conseil de Direction de l'Assoc. Intern. de Droit Pénal, Paris, 1947–; Vice-Pres. Internat. Soc. of Social Defence, 1956–; Head of Social Defence Section, UN, New York, 1947–48. Member: Roy. Commn on Capital Punishment, 1949–53; Advisory Council on the Treatment of Offenders, Home Office, 1950–63; Adv. Council on the Penal System, Home Office, 1966–74; Jt Chm., Second UN Congress on Crime, 1955; Chief Rapporteur, 4th UN Congress on Crime, Kyoto, 1970; Chm. Sub-Cttee on Maximum Security in Prisons, 1967–68; Mem. Advisory Coun. on the Penal System, 1966–74; first Pres., Brit. Acad. of

Forensic Sciences, 1960–61, Hon. Vice-Pres., 1961–; First Chm. Council of Europe Sci. Cttee, Problems of Crime, 1963–70; Mem. Royal Commn on Penal System in Eng. and Wales, 1964–66; Consultant: Ford Foundn and Bar Assoc., NYC, on teaching and res. in criminol., 1964–65; President's Nat. Commn on Violence, Washington, 1968–69; Min. of Justice, NSW, and Nat. Inst. of Criminology, Canberra, 1973; Hon. Vice-Chm., Fifth UN Congress on Crime, Geneva, 1975; Hon. Vice-Pres., British Soc. of Criminology, 1978. For. Hon. Mem., Amer. Acad. of Arts and Sciences, 1973; Hon. Mem., Amer. Law Inst., 1981; Hon. Fellow, Imperial Police Coll., 1968. Hon. LLD: Leicester, 1965; Edinburgh, 1988. James Barr Ames Prize and Medal, Faculty of Harvard Law School, 1950; Bruce Smith Sr award, Amer. Acad. Criminal Justice Sciences, 1976; Sellin-Glueck Award, Amer. Assoc. of Criminology, 1976. Coronation Medal, 1953. Chevalier de l'Ordre de Léopold, Belgium, 1930. *Publications:* Sir James Fitzjames Stephen (Selden Soc. Lect.), 1957; In Search of Criminology, 1961 (Italian edn 1965; French edn 1965; Spanish edn 1971); The Need for Criminology, 1965; Ideology and Crime (Carpentier Lectures), 1966, (Italian edn 1968); The Dangerous Offender (Frank Newsam Memorial Lecture), 1968; History of English Criminal Law, Vol. I, 1948 (under auspices of Pilgrim Trust), Vols II and III, 1956, Vol. IV, 1968 (under auspices of Rockefeller Foundation), Vol. V (with R. Hood), 1986 (under auspices of Home Office and MacArthur Foundn); (ed with Prof. M. E. Wolfgang) Crime and Justice, 3 vols, 1971, 2nd edn 1977; (with Joan King) The Growth of Crime, 1977 (trans. Italian, 1981); (with R. Hood) Criminology and the Administration of Criminal Justice: a Bibliography (Joseph L. Andrews Award, Amer. Assoc. of Law Libraries 1977), 1976; The Cambridge Institute of Criminology: the background and scope, 1988; The Roots of the International Association of Criminal Law and their Significance, 1991; (ed) English Studies in Criminal Science, now Cambridge Studies in Criminology, 52 vols (Vols I–VII with J. W. C. Turner); numerous articles in English and foreign periodicals. *Address:* Trinity College, Cambridge CB2 1TQ; Rittenhouse Claridge, Apt 2416, Rittenhouse Square, Philadelphia, Pa 19103, USA. *Club:* Athenæum.

RAE, Allan Alexander Sinclair, CBE 1973; Chairman, CIBA-GEIGY PLC, 1972–90; *b* 26 Nov. 1925; *s* of John Rae and Rachel Margaret Sinclair; *m* 1st, 1955, Sheila Grace (*née* Saunders) (*d* 1985); two *s* one *d*; 2nd, 1986, Gertrud (*née* Dollinger). *Educ:* Ayr Acad.; Glasgow Univ. LLB. Admitted Solicitor, 1948. Served Army, RA then JAG's Dept (Staff Captain), 1944–47. Partner, 1950, Sen. Partner, 1959, Crawford Bayley & Co., Bombay (Solicitors); Dir and Hd of Legal and Patents Dept, CIBA Ltd, Basle, 1964, Mem. Management Cttee, 1969; Mem. Exec. Cttee, CIBA-GEIGY Ltd, Basle and Chm., CIBA-GEIGY Gp of Cos in UK, 1972; Chm., Ilford Ltd, 1972–88; Vice Chm., BIAC, 1987–; Director: The Clayton Aniline Co. Ltd, 1965– (Chm., 1965–87); CIBA–GEIGY Chemicals Ltd, 1965–90 (Chm., 1965–87); Gretag Ltd (formerly Gretag-CX Ltd), 1978–89 (Chm. 1978–87); ABB Power Ltd (formerly British Brown-Boveri Ltd), 1973–89; T & N plc (formerly Turner & Newall PLC), 1979–; Brown Boveri Kent (Hldgs) Ltd, 1980–; Mettler Instruments Ltd, 1985–89; Riggs AP Bank Ltd (formerly AP Bank Ltd), 1986–. Internat. Consultant, Loxleys, Solicitors, 1990–. Member of Council: Chemical Industries Assoc., 1976– (Pres., 1986–88); CBI, 1980–; British Swiss Chamber of Commerce, 1965– (Pres., 1969–72). Vice-Chm., Business and Industry Adv. Cttee to OECD, 1986–. *Recreations:* sailing, golf, ski-ing. *Address:* Bryn Dulas House, Llanddulas, Clwyd LL22 8NA. *Clubs:* Buck's; Royal Thames Yacht, Sunningdale Golf Club.

RAE, Henry Edward Grant, JP; Lord Provost, City of Aberdeen, 1984–88; Lord Lieutenant, City of Aberdeen, 1984–88; *b* 17 Aug. 1925; *s* of late James and Rachel Rae; *m* 1955, Margaret Raffan Burns; one *d*. *Educ:* Queen's Cross School, Aberdeen; Ruthrieston School, Aberdeen. Chairman: Aberdeen Dist Cttee, TGWU, 1969–82; Grampian and Northern Isles Dist Cttee, 1982–85. Councillor, Aberdeen City Council, 1974– (Convener, Libraries Cttee, 1977–80, Manpower Cttee, 1980–84). JP Aberdeen 1984 (Chm., Justices' Cttee). OStJ 1987. *Address:* 76 Whitehouse Street, Aberdeen AB1 1QH. *T:* Aberdeen (0224) 640425; (office) Town House, Aberdeen AB9 1LP. *T:* Aberdeen (0224) 642121.

RAE, Dr John; Chief Executive, AEA Environment & Energy, since 1990; *b* 29 Sept. 1942; *s* of late John Rae and of Marion Rae (*née* Dow); *m* 1968, Irene (*née* Cassells); one *s* one *d*. *Educ:* Rutherglen Academy; University of Glasgow (BSc 1964, PhD 1967). FInstE 1987. Lecturing and research in physics: Univ. of Glasgow, 1967–68; Univ. of Texas, 1968–70; Univ. Libre, Brussels, 1970–72; Queen Mary College London, 1972–74; Theoretical Physics Div., Harwell: Industrial Fellow, 1974–76; Leader, Theory of Fluids Group, 1976–85; Acting Div. Head, 1985; Chief Scientist, Dept of Energy, 1986–89. Member: SERC, 1986–89; NERC, 1986–89. *Publications:* scientific papers in professional jls. *Recreations:* music, especially singing; gardening, astronomy. *Address:* AEA Environment & Energy, B 551 Harwell Laboratory, Oxfordshire OX11 0RA. *T:* Didcot (0235) 432986.

RAE, Dr John (Malcolm); Director: Portman Group, since 1989; The Observer Ltd, since 1986; *b* 20 March 1931; *s* of late Dr L. John Rae, radiologist, London Hospital, and Blodwen Rae; *m* 1955, Daphné Ray Simpson, *d* of John Phimester Simpson; two *s* four *d*. *Educ:* Bishop's Stortford Coll.; Sidney Sussex Coll., Cambridge. MA Cantab 1958; PhD 1965. 2nd Lieut Royal Fusiliers, 1950–51. Asst Master, Harrow School, 1955–66; Dept of War Studies, King's Coll., London, 1962–65; Headmaster: Taunton School, 1966–70; Westminster School, 1970–86; Dir, Laura Ashley Foundn, 1986–89. Gresham Prof. of Rhetoric, 1988–90. Chairman: HMC, 1977; Council for Educn in World Citizenship, 1983–87. Member: Council, Nat. Cttee for Electoral Reform; Council, King's Coll. London, 1981–84. Trustee: Children's Film Unit, 1979–; Imperial War Mus., 1980–85. Gov. Highgate Sch., 1989–. JP Middlesex, 1961–66. Hon. FCP 1982. FRSA. *Publications:* The Custard Boys, 1960 (filmed 1979); (jtly, film) Reach for Glory (UN Award); Conscience and Politics, 1970; The Golden Crucifix, 1974; The Treasure of Westminster Abbey, 1975; Christmas is Coming, 1976; Return to the Winter Palace, 1978; The Third Twin: a ghost story, 1980; The Public School Revolution: Britain's independent schools, 1964–1979, 1981; Letters from School, 1987; Too Little, Too Late?, 1989; articles in The Times, Encounter; columnist in Times Ed. Supp. *Recreations:* writing, swimming, children, cinema. *Address:* The Portman Group, 2d Wimpole Street, W1M 7AA. *T:* 071–499 1010; 101 Millbank Court, 24 John Islip Street, Westminster, SW1P 4LG. *T:* 071–828 1842. *Clubs:* Royal Automobile; Hawks (Cambridge).

RAE, Hon. Robert Keith; MPP for York South, Ontario, since 1982; Premier of Ontario, since 1990; *b* 2 Aug. 1948; *s* of Saul Rae and Lois (*née* George); *m* 1980, Arlene Perly; three *d*. *Educ:* Ecole Internationale, Geneva; Univ. of Toronto (BA Hons 1969; LLB 1977); Balliol Coll., Oxford (BPhil 1971). MP for Broadview-Greenwood, Ontario, 1978–82; Finance Critic, New Democratic Party, 1979–82; Leader, Ontario New Democrats, 1982–; Leader, Official Opposition, Ontario legislature, 1987–90. *Recreations:* tennis, golf, ski-ing, fishing, reading. *Address:* Legislative Building, Queen's Park, Toronto, Ont M7A 1A1, Canada. *T:* (416) 965–1941.

RAE, Robert Wright; Civil Service, retired; Clerk to the General Commissioners of Income Tax, Blackheath Division, 1977–88 (Clerk, Bromley Division, 1977–85); *b* 27 March 1914; *s* of Walter Rae and Rachel Scott; *m* 1st, 1945, Joan McKenzie (*d* 1966); two *s*; 2nd, 1977, Marjorie Ann Collyer. *Educ:* George Heriot's Sch., Edinburgh; Edinburgh Univ. MA 1st cl. hons. Asst Inspector of Taxes, 1936; Dep. Chief Inspector of Taxes, 1973–75; Dir Personnel, Inland Revenue, 1975–77. *Recreations:* gardening, walking. *Address:* Oak Lodge, Blackbrook Lane, Bickley, Bromley BR1 2LP. *T:* 081–467 2377.

RAE, Air Vice-Marshal Ronald Arthur R.; *see* Ramsay Rae.

RAE, Hon. Sir Wallace (Alexander Ramsay), Kt 1976; Agent-General for Queensland, in London, 1974–80; Hon. Chairman, Brisbane Forest Park Advisory Board, since 1981; grazier, Ramsay Park, Blackall, Queensland; *b* 31 March 1914; *s* of George Ramsay Rae and Alice Ramsay Rae. *Educ:* Sydney, Australia. Served War: RAAF Coastal Command, 1939; Pilot, Flt Lt, UK, then OC Test Flight, Amberley, Qld. Mem., Legislative Assembly (Nat. Party of Australia) for Gregory, Qld, 1957–74; Minister for: Local Govt and Electricity, 1969–74; Lands and Forestry, Qld, 1974. Founder Pres., Pony Club Assoc. of Queensland. *Recreations:* bowls, golf. *Address:* 6 Ondine Street, Mermaid Waters, Gold Coast, Qld 4218, Australia. *Clubs:* Queensland, Tattersall's (Brisbane); Longreach (Longreach).

See also Air Vice-Marshal R. A. Ramsay Rae.

RAE SMITH, David Douglas, CBE 1976; MC 1946; MA; FCA; Senior Partner, Deloitte Haskins & Sells, Chartered Accountants, 1973–82 (Partner, 1954); *b* 15 Nov. 1919; *s* of Sir Alan Rae Smith, KBE, and Lady (Mabel Grace) Rae Smith; *m* 1947, Margaret Alison Watson, *d* of James Watson; three *s* one *d*. *Educ:* Radley Coll.; Christ Church, Oxford (MA). FCA 1959. Served War, RA, 1939–46: ME, N Africa and NW Europe; Captain; MC and mentioned in despatches. Chartered accountant, 1950. Hon. Treasurer, RIIA, 1961–81. Director: Thomas Tilling Ltd, 1982–83; Sandoz Products Ltd, 1983–; Dep. Chm., Bankers Trustee Co., 1984–. Member: Licensed Dealers Tribunal, 1974–88; Council, Radley Coll., 1966– (Chm., 1976–). *Recreations:* horse racing, golf, travel. *Address:* Oakdale, Crockham Hill, Edenbridge, Kent TN8 6RL. *T:* Edenbridge (0732) 866220. *Club:* Gresham.

RAEBURN, David Antony; Grammatikos (tutor in Ancient Greek Language), Faculty of Literae Humaniores, University of Oxford, since 1991; *b* 22 May 1927; *e s* of late Walter Augustus Leopold Raeburn, QC; *m* 1961, Mary Faith, *d* of Arthur Hubbard, Salisbury, Rhodesia; two *s* one *d*. *Educ:* Charterhouse; Christ Church, Oxford (Schol., MA). 1st cl. hons Hon. Mods, 2nd in Greats. Nat. Service, 1949–51: Temp. Captain, RAEC. Asst Master: Bristol Grammar Sch., 1951–54; Bradfield Coll., 1955–58 (prod. Greek Play, 1955 and 1958); Senior Classics Master, Alleyn's Sch., Dulwich, 1958–62; Headmaster: Beckenham and Penge Grammar Sch., 1963–70 (school's name changed to Langley Park School for Boys, Beckenham in 1969); Whitgift Sch., Croydon, 1970–91. Schoolteacher Fellow-Commoner, Jesus Coll., Cambridge, 1980. Chm. Classics Cttee, Schs Council, 1974–80; Pres., Jt Assoc. of Classical Teachers, 1983–85; Treas., HMC, 1984–89. FRSA 1969. *Publications:* articles on Greek play production. *Recreation:* play production (produced Cambridge Greek Play, 1980, 1983). *Address:* 13A St Anne's Road, Eastbourne, Sussex BN21 2AJ. *T:* Eastbourne (0323) 24696; Christ Church, Oxford OX1 1DP.

RAEBURN, Maj.-Gen. Sir Digby; *see* Raeburn, Maj.-Gen. Sir W. D. M.

RAEBURN, Prof. John Ross, CBE 1972; BSc (Agric.), PhD, MS; FRSE; FIBiol; Strathcona-Fordyce Professor of Agriculture, Aberdeen University, 1959–78; Principal, North of Scotland College of Agriculture, 1963–78; *b* 20 Nov. 1912; *s* of late Charles Raeburn and Margaret (*née* Ross); *m* 1941, Mary, *o d* of Alfred and Kathrine Roberts; one *s* three *d*. *Educ:* Manchester Grammar School; Edinburgh and Cornell Universities. Professor of Agricultural Economics, Nanking University, 1936–37; Research Officer, Oxford University, 1938–39; Ministry of Food Divisional statistician, 1939–41, Head Agricultural Plans Branch, 1941–46; Senior research officer, Oxford University, 1946–49; Reader in Agricultural Economics, London University, 1949–59. Visiting Professor: Cornell, 1950; Wuhan, 1983. Consultant to UN. Member: Agricultural Mission to Yugoslavia, 1951; Mission of Enquiry into Rubber Industry, Malaya, 1954; Colonial Economic Research Committee, 1949–61; Scottish Agricultural Improvement Council, 1960–71; Scottish Agricultural Develt Council, 1971–76; Verdon-Smith Committee, 1962–64; Council, Scottish Agricultural Colls, 1974–78. Hon. MA Oxford, 1946. FRSE 1961; FIBiol 1968. Vice-President, International Association of Agricultural Economists, 1964–70 (Hon. Life Mem., 1976–); President, Agric. Econ. Society, 1966–67 (Hon. Life Mem., 1981–). *Publications:* Preliminary economic survey of the Northern Territories of the Gold Coast, 1950; (jtly) Problems in the mechanisation of native agriculture in tropical African Territories, 1950; Agriculture: foundations, principles and development, 1984; (jtly) History of the IAAE, 1990; research bulletins and contributions to agricultural economic journals. *Recreation:* gardening. *Address:* 30 Morningfield Road, Aberdeen AB2 4AQ.

RAEBURN, Michael Edward Norman; (4th Bt, *cr* 1923, but does not use the title); *b* 12 Nov. 1954; *s* of Sir Edward Alfred Raeburn, 3rd Bt, and of Joan, *d* of Frederick Hill; *S* father, 1977; *m* 1979, Penelope Henrietta Theodora, *d* of Alfred Louis Penn; two *s* two *d*. *Heir:* *s* Christopher Edward Alfred Raeburn, *b* 4 Dec. 1981. *Address:* 1 Spring Cottages, Fletching Street, Mayfield, E Sussex TN20 6TN.

RAEBURN, Maj.-Gen. Sir (William) Digby (Manifold), KCVO 1979; CB 1966; DSO 1945; MBE 1941; Major and Resident Governor, HM Tower of London, and Keeper of the Jewel House, 1971–79; *b* 6 Aug. 1915; *s* of late Sir Ernest Manifold Raeburn, KBE, and Lady Raeburn; *m* 1960, Adeline Margaret (*née* Pryor). *Educ:* Winchester; Magdalene College, Cambridge (MA). Commnd into Scots Guards, 1936; comd 2nd Bn Scots Guards, 1953; Lieut-Col Comdg Scots Guards, 1958; Comdr, 1st Guards Bde Group, 1959; Comdr, 51st Infty Bde Group, 1960; Director of Combat Development (Army), 1963–65; Chief of Staff to C-in-C, Allied Forces, N Europe, 1965–68; Chief Instructor (Army), Imperial Defence College, 1968–70. Freeman of City of London, 1972. *Recreations:* ski-ing, shooting, sailing. *Address:* c/o Lloyds Bank, 6 Pall Mall, SW1. *Clubs:* Pratt's, Cavalry and Guards; Royal Yacht Squadron.

RAFAEL, Gideon; Ambassador of Israel, retired 1978; *b* Berlin, 5 March 1913; *s* of Max Rafael; *m* 1940, Nurit Weissberg; one *s* one *d*. *Educ:* Berlin Univ. Went to Israel, 1934; Member, kibbutz, 1934–43; Jewish Agency Polit. Dept, 1943; in charge of prep. of Jewish case for JA Polit. Dept, Nuremberg War Crimes Trial, 1945–46; Member: JA Commn to Anglo-American Commn of Enquiry, 1946, and of JA Mission to UN Special Commn for Palestine, 1947; Israel Perm. Deleg. to UN, 1951–52; Alt. Rep. to UN, 1953; Rep. at UN Gen. Assemblies, 1947–67; Counsellor in charge of ME and UN Affairs, Min. for Foreign Affairs, 1953–57; Ambassador to Belgium and Luxembourg, 1957–60, and to the European Economic Community, 1959; Head, Israel Delegn to 2nd Geneva Conf. on Maritime Law, 1960; Dep. Dir-Gen., Min. of Foreign Affairs, 1960–65; Perm. Rep. to UN and Internat. Organizations in Geneva, Sept. 1965–April 1966; Special Ambassador and Adviser to Foreign Minister, 1966–67; Perm. Rep. to UN, 1967; Dir-Gen., Min. for Foreign Affairs, 1967–71; Head, Israel Delegn to UNCTAD III, 1972; Sen. Polit. Adviser,

Foreign Ministry, 1972–73; Ambassador to the Court of St James's, 1973–77, and non-resident Ambassador to Ireland, 1975–77; Sen. Advr to Foreign Minister, 1977–78. Vis. Prof., Woodrow Wilson Sch., Princeton Univ., 1988. Bd Mem., Israel Cancer Soc., 1985–. *Publications:* Destination Peace: three decades of Israeli foreign policy, 1981; articles on foreign affairs in Israel and internat. periodicals. *Address:* Ministry for Foreign Affairs, Jerusalem, Israel.

RAFF, Prof. Martin Charles, FRS 1985; Professor of Biology, University College London, since 1979; *b* 15 Jan. 1938; *s* of David and Reba Raff; *m* 1979, Carol Winter; two *s* one *d*. *Educ:* McGill Univ. (BSc; MD; CM). House Officer, Royal Victoria Hosp., Montreal, 1963–65; Resident in Neurology, Massachusetts General Hosp., 1965–68; Postdoctoral Fellow, Nat. Inst. for Med. Res., 1968–71; Co-director, MRC Develtl Neurobiology Programme, 1971–. *Publications:* (jtly) T and B Lymphocytes, 1973; (jtly) Molecular Biology of the Cell, 1983, 2nd edn 1989. *Address:* 67 Upper Park Road, NW3 2UL. *T:* 071–722 5610.

RAFFAN, Keith William Twort; MP (C) Delyn, since 1983; *b* 21 June 1949; *s* of A. W. Raffan, TD, MB, ChB, FFARCS. *Educ:* Robert Gordon's Coll., Aberdeen; Trinity Coll., Glenalmond; Corpus Christi Coll., Cambridge. BA 1971, MA 1977. Parly Correspondent, Daily Express, 1981–83. Candidate's Parly Aide, by-elections of: Cynon Valley, 1984; Brecon and Radnor, 1985. Mem., Select Cttee on Welsh Affairs, 1983–. Introduced Controlled Drugs (Penalties) Act (Private Member's Bill, 1985). Vice-Chm., Cons. Party Orgn Cttee, 1985–89; President: Wales Cons. Trade Unionists, 1984–87; Wales Young Conservatives, 1987–90 (Vice-Pres., 1984). Nat. Chm., PEST, 1970–74; Vice-President: Clwyd Pre-School Playgroups Assoc., 1983–; Delyn and Deeside Multiple Sclerosis Soc. Contested (C) Dulwich, Feb. 1974, and East Aberdeenshire, Oct. 1974. Mem. NUJ, 1976–. *Address:* House of Commons, SW1A 0AA. *T:* 071–219 3000. *Clubs:* Carlton, Chelsea Arts, Royal Automobile; Flint Conservative; Prestatyn Conservative.

RAFFERTY, Anne Judith, (Mrs B. J. Barker); QC 1990; a Recorder, South Eastern Circuit, since 1991; *m* 1977, Brian John Barker, *qv*; three *d* (and one *d* decd). *Educ:* Univ. of Sheffield (LLB). Criminal Bar Association: Mem. Cttee, 1986–91; Sec., 1989–91; Chm., Bar Conf., 1992. Mem., Royal Commn on Criminal Justice, 1991–. Member: SE Circuit Wine Cttee, 1987–90; Pigot Cttee, 1988–89; Circuit Cttee, SE Circuit, 1991–. *Address:* 4 Brick Court, Temple, EC4Y 9AD. *T:* 071–583 8455. *Club:* Roehampton.

RAFFERTY, Hon. Joseph Anstice, BA; FAIM, FID; JP; Agent General for Victoria in London, 1979–83; investor and primary producer, Australia, since 1983; *s* of late Col Rupert A. Rafferty, DSO, and Rose Sarah Anne Rafferty; *m* 1st, 1940, Miriam K. (decd), *d* of late Frank Richards, Devonport, Tas; two *s*; 2nd, 1973, Lyn, *d* of Grace Jones, Brisbane, Qld. *Educ:* Christ Coll., Univ. of Tas (BA); Univ. of Melbourne. FAIM 1954; FID 1960. Commonwealth Public Service, 1934–45; Personnel Manager, Australian National Airways, 1945–53; Personnel Management and Indust. Relations Consultant, 1953–70 (own practice; co. dir). MP (Lib) for: Caulfield, Vic, 1955–58; Ormond, Vic, 1958–67; Glenhuntly, Vic, 1967–79; Chm. Cttees and Dep. Speaker, Victorian Legislative Assembly, 1961–65; Parly Sec. for Cabinet, 1965–70; Minister for Labour and Industry, 1970–76; Asst Minister for Educn, 1970–72; Minister for Consumer Affairs, 1972–76; Minister for Fed. Affairs, 1974–76; Minister for Transport, 1976–78; Chief Sec., 1978–79; Leader, Aust. Delegn to ILO Conf., Geneva, 1974. Pres., Melbourne Jun. Chamber of Commerce, 1950; Treasurer, Nat. Assoc. of Jun. Chambers of Commerce of Australia, 1951; Councillor: Melbourne Chamber of Commerce, 1950–76; Victorian Employers' Fedn, 1952–65. Dep. Leader, Aust. Delegn, 5th World Congress, Jun. Chamber of Commerce, Manila, 1950; Aust. Delegate, 6th World Congress, Jun. Chamber of Industry, Montreal, 1951; Delegate, 17th Triennial Congress, British Empire Chambers of Commerce, London, 1951. Mem. Council, La Trobe Univ., Vic, 1964–70; Trustee, Caulfield Racecourse Reserve, 1965–. JP Victoria, 1970. *Recreations:* golf, swimming, walking, travel. *Address:* 8 Matlock Court, Caulfield North, Vic 3161, Australia. *T:* Melbourne (03) 500 0282. *Clubs:* Royal Wimbledon Golf; Athenæum, Metropolitan Golf, MCC (Melbourne).

RAFFERTY, Rt. Rev. Mgr. Kevin Lawrence; Titular Bishop of Ausuaga and Bishop Auxiliary to Archbishop of St Andrews and Edinburgh, since 1990; Parish Priest of SS John Cantius and Nicholas, Broxburn, since 1986; *b* 24 June 1933; *s* of John Rafferty and Catherine Quigg. *Educ:* Lisnascreaghog and St Adamnan's primary schs; St Columb's Coll., Derry; St Kieran's Coll., Kilkenny. Priest 1957; Assistant Priest: Linlithgow, 1957–67; St David's, Dalkieth, 1967–77; Chaplain, St David's High Sch., Dalkieth, 1967–73; Parish priest, Our Lady, Star of the Sea, North Berwick, 1977–86; Dean of Midlothian and East Lothian, 1982–86; Mem., Coll. of Consultors of archdio., 1984; Vicar-General, archdio. St Andrews and Edinburgh, 1989–. Prelate of Honour to the Pope, 1989. *Recreations:* golf, football, music, reading. *Address:* SS John Cantius and Nicholas, 34 West Main Street, Broxburn, West Lothian EH52 5RJ. *T:* Broxburn (0506) 852040.

RAFFERTY, Kevin Robert; Managing Editor, International Media Partners, New York, since 1989; *b* 5 Nov. 1944; *s* of Leo and Thérèse Rafferty; *m* 1985, Michelle Misquitta. *Educ:* Marist Coll., Kingston upon Hull; Queen's Coll., Oxford (MA). Journalistic training, The Guardian, Sun, 1966–69; Financial Times, 1970–76; Founder Editor, Business Times Malaysia, 1976–77; Consultant Editor, Indian Express Gp, 1978–79; Foreign Correspondent, Financial Times, 1980; Asia Pacific Editor, Institutional Investor, 1981–87; Ed., The Universe, 1987–88. Founder Editor, then Associate Editor, Asia and Pacific Review, Saffron Walden, 1980–. *Publication:* City on the Rocks: Hong Kong's uncertain future, 1989. *Recreations:* travelling, meeting ordinary people, reading. *Address:* International Media Partners, The Cable Building, 611 Broadway, Suite 322, New York, NY 10012, USA. *T:* (212) 995 9595. *Clubs:* United Oxford & Cambridge University; Foreign Correspondents (Hong Kong).

RAFFO, Carlos; Minister for Industry, Peru, 1989–90; *b* 23 Aug. 1927; *s* of Carlos Raffo and Maria Julia Dasso de Raffo; *m* 1953, Araceli Quintana de Raffo; one *s* two *d*. *Educ:* Univ. Nacional Mayor de San Marcos; Univ. Católica, Peru (Law and Humanities). Dir, Banco Industrial, 1960–66; Founder, Inst. Peruano de Admin. de Empresas, 1963; Ambassador to UK, 1986–89. Grand Cross, Peruvian Orders: El Sol del Perú, 1986; Al Mérito por Serviciós Distinguidos, 1990; Officer, Al Mérito Agrícola, 1969; Comdr, Swedish Order of Vassa, 1974. *Recreation:* golf. *Address:* Camino Real #456, Torre Real, Piso 5, San Isidro, Lima 27, Peru. *Clubs:* Beefsteak; Royal and Ancient (St Andrews); Sunningdale Golf; Nacional (Lima); Lima Golf.

RAFTERY, Peter Albert, CVO 1984 (MVO 1979); MBE 1972; HM Diplomatic Service, retired; *b* 8 June 1929; *s* of John Raftery and Mary (*née* Glynn); *m* 1st, 1949, Margaret Frances Hulse (decd); four *d*; 2nd, 1975, Fenella Jones. *Educ:* St Ignatius Coll., London. Nat. Service, 1947–49. India Office, 1946; CRO, 1949; New Delhi, 1950; Peshawar, 1956; Cape Town, 1959; Kuala Lumpur, 1963; Nairobi, 1964; Asst Political Agent, Bahrain, 1968; First Sec., FCO, 1973; Head of Chancery, Gaborone, 1976; Asst Head, E Africa Dept, FCO, 1980; Counsellor and Consul Gen., Amman, 1982–85; High Comr to Botswana, 1986–89. *Recreation:* tennis. *Address:* PO Box 170, Gaborone, Botswana.

RAGG, Rt. Rev. Theodore David Butler, DD; *b* 23 Nov. 1919; *s* of late Rt Rev. Harry Richard Ragg and Winifred Mary Ragg (*née* Groves); *m* 1945, Dorothy Mary Lee; one *s* two *d*. *Educ:* Univ. of Manitoba; Trinity Coll., Univ. of Toronto (BA, LTh); General Synod (BD). Deacon, 1949; priest, 1950; Asst Curate, St Michael and All Angels, Toronto, 1949; Rector: Nokomis, 1951; Wolseley, 1953; St Clement's N Vancouver, 1955; St Luke's, Victoria, 1957; Bishop Cronyn Memorial, London, 1962; St George's, Owen Sound, 1967. Examining Chaplain to Bishop of Huron, 1964–67; Archdeacon of Saugeen, 1967; elected Suffragan Bishop of Huron, 1973; Bishop of Huron, 1974–84, retired. Hon. DD: Huron Coll., London, Ont., 1975; Trinity Coll., Toronto, Ont., 1975. *Recreations:* woodworking, golf. *Address:* 1771 McRae Avenue, Victoria, BC V8P 1J2, Canada.

RAGLAN, 5th Baron, *cr* 1852; **FitzRoy John Somerset;** JP; DL; Chairman, Cwmbran New Town Development Corporation, 1970–83; *b* 8 Nov. 1927; *er s* of 4th Baron and Hon. Julia Hamilton, CStJ (*d* 1971), *d* of 11th Baron Belhaven and Stenton, CIE; *S* father, 1964; *m* 1973, Alice Baily (marr. diss. 1981), *yr d* of Peter Baily, Great Whittington, Northumberland. *Educ:* Westminster; Magdalen College, Oxford; Royal Agricultural College, Cirencester. Captain, Welsh Guards, RARO. Crown Estate Comr, 1970–74. Mem., Agriculture and Consumer Affairs sub-cttee, House of Lords Select Cttee on the European Community, 1974– (Chm., 1975–77). Pres., UK Housing Trust, 1983– (Chm., S Wales Region, 1976–89). Pres., Pre Retirement Assoc., 1970–77, Vice-Pres. 1977–, Hon. Treas., 1987–. Chairman: Bath Preservation Trust, 1975–77; The Bath Soc., 1977–; Bugatti Owners' Club, 1988–. President: Gwent Foundn Concert Soc.; Usk Civic Soc.; Usk Farmers Club; Bath Centre of Nat. Trust; S Wales Reg., RSMHCA, 1971–; Mem., Distinguished Members Panel, National Secular Soc.; Patron, The Raglan Baroque Players. JP 1958, DL 1971, Gwent (formerly Monmouthshire). Farms 600 acres at Usk. *Recreation:* being mechanic to a Bugatti. *Heir:* *b* Hon. Geoffrey Somerset [*b* 29 Aug. 1932; *m* 1956, Caroline Rachel, *d* of Col E. R. Hill, *qv*; one *s* two *d*]. *Address:* Cefntilla, Usk, Gwent. *T:* Usk (02913) 2050. *Clubs:* Beefsteak, Vintage Sports Car; Usk Farmers'.

RAHTZ, Prof. Philip Arthur; Professor of Archaeology, University of York, 1978–86; *b* 11 March 1921; *s* of Frederick John Rahtz and Ethel May Rahtz; *m* 1st, 1940, Wendy Hewgill Smith (*d* 1977); three *s* two *d*; 2nd, 1978, Lorna Rosemary Jane Watts. *Educ:* Bristol Grammar Sch. MA Bristol 1964. FSA. Served RAF, 1941–46. Articled to accountant, 1937–41; photographer (Studio Rahtz), 1946–49; schoolteacher, 1950–53; archaeological consultant, 1953–63; Univ. of Birmingham: Lectr, 1963–75; Sen. Lectr, later Reader, 1975–78. Pres., Council for British Archaeology, 1986–89. *Publications:* Rescue Archaeology, 1973; Chew Valley Lake Excavations, 1978; Saxon and Medieval Palaces at Cheddar, 1979; Invitation to Archaeology, 1985; Tamworth Saxon Watermills, 1991; contrib. nat. and regional jls in England, W Africa and Poland. *Recreations:* swimming, sunbathing, music, travel. *Address:* Old School, Harome, Helmsley, North Yorkshire. *T:* Helmsley (0439) 70862.

RAIKES, Vice-Adm. Sir Iwan (Geoffrey), KCB 1976; CBE 1967; DSC 1943; DL; Flag Officer Submarines, and Commander Submarines, Eastern Atlantic Area, 1974–76; retired 1977; *b* 21 April 1921; *s* of late Adm. Sir Robert Henry Taunton Raikes, KCB, CVO, DSO, and Lady (Ida Guinevere) Raikes; *m* 1947, Cecilla Primrose Hunt; one *s* one *d*. *Educ:* RNC Dartmouth. Entered Royal Navy, 1935; specialised in Submarines, 1941; comd HM Submarines: H43, 1943; Varne, 1944; Virtue, 1946; Talent, 1948–49; Aeneas, 1952; comd HM Ships: Loch Insh, 1961; Kent, 1968; Exec. Officer, HMS Newcastle, 1955–57; Dep. Dir, Undersurface Warfare, 1962–64; Dir, Plans & Operations, Staff of C-in-C Far East, 1965–66; JSSC, 1957; IDC, 1967. Rear-Adm., 1970; Naval Sec., 1970–72; Vice-Adm., 1973; Flag Officer, First Flotilla, 1973–74. Mem., Governing Body, Church in Wales, 1979–. DL Powys, 1983. *Recreations:* shooting, fishing, sailing, skiing, tennis, gardening. *Address:* Aberyscir Court, Brecon, Powys. *Club:* Naval and Military.

RAILTON, Brig. Dame Mary, DBE 1956 (CBE 1953); *b* 28 May 1906; *d* of late James and Margery Railton. *Educ:* privately. Joined FANY, 1938; commissioned in ATS, 1940; WRAC 1949; Director WRAC, 1954–57; Deputy Controller Commandant, 1961–67. *Address:* 1 Ilsom House, Tetbury, Glos GL8 8RX.

RAILTON, Dame Ruth, DBE 1966 (OBE 1954); Founder and Musical Director of the National Youth Orchestra and National Junior Music School, 1947–65; *b* 14 Dec. 1915; *m* 1962, Cecil Harmsworth King (*d* 1987). Educ: St Mary's School, Wantage; Royal Academy of Music, London. Director of Music or Choral work for many schools and societies, 1937–49; Adjudicator, Fedn of Music Festivals, 1946–74; Pres., Ulster Coll. of Music, 1960–; Governor, Royal Ballet School, 1966–74. Founder and Pres., Irish Children's Theatre, 1978–; Vice-Pres., Cork Internat. Fest., 1975–85; Mem., Bd of Dirs, Nat. Concert Hall, Dublin, 1981–86; Advr, Nat. Children's Orchestra, 1985–. Hon. Professor: Chopin Conservatoire, Warsaw, 1960; Conservatoire of Azores, 1972. FRAM 1956; Hon. RMCM 1959; Hon. FRCM 1965; Hon. FTCL 1969. Hon. LLD Aberdeen Univ., 1960. Harriet Cohen Medal for Bach, 1955. *Recreations:* interested in everything. *Address:* 54 Ardoyne House, Pembroke Park, Dublin 4. *T:* Dublin 617262.

RAINBOW, (James) Conrad (Douglas), CBE 1979; Chairman, Sovereign Country House Ltd, since 1979; *b* 25 Sept. 1926; *s* of Jack Conrad Rainbow and Winifred Edna (*née* Mears); *m* 1974, Kathleen Margaret (*née* Holmes); one *s* one *d*. *Educ:* William Ellis Sch., Highgate; Selwyn Coll., Cambridge (MA). Asst Master, St Paul's Sch., London, 1951–60; HM Inspector of Schools, 1960–69; Dep. Chief Educn Officer, Lancashire, 1969–74, Chief Educn Officer, 1974–79. Vis. Prof., Univ. of Wisconsin, 1979. Education Consultant: ICI, 1980–85; Shell Petroleum Co. Ltd, 1980–; Advr to H of C Select Cttee on Educn, 1980–82. Mem., Exec. Cttee, Council of British Internat. Schs in EEC, 1975–. Mem., Inst. of Dirs. Chm. of Governors, Northcliffe Sch., Hants, 1984–. *Publications:* various articles in educnl jls. *Recreations:* rowing (now as an observer), music, reading. *Address:* Freefolk House, Laverstoke, Whitchurch, Hants RG28 7PB. *T:* Whitchurch (0256) 892634. *Clubs:* Commonwealth Trust; Leander.

RAINE, Craig Anthony; poet; Fellow of New College, Oxford, since 1991; *b* 3 Dec. 1944; *s* of Norman Edward Raine and Olive Marie Raine; *m* 1972, Ann Pasternak Slater; one *d* three *s*. *Educ:* Barnard Castle Sch.; Exeter Coll., Oxford (BA Hons in English; BPhil). College Lecturer, Oxford University: Exeter Coll., 1971–72; Lincoln Coll., 1974–75; Exeter Coll., 1975–76; Christ Church, 1976–79. Books Editor, New Review, 1977–78; Editor, Quarto, 1979–80; Poetry Editor: New Statesman, 1981; Faber & Faber, 1981–91. Cholmondeley Poetry Award, 1983. *Publications:* The Onion, Memory, 1978, 5th edn 1986; A Martian Sends a Postcard Home, 1979, 5th edn 1983; A Free Translation, 1981, 2nd edn 1981; Rich, 1984, 2nd edn 1984; The Electrification of the Soviet Union, 1986; (ed) A Choice of Kipling's Prose, 1987; The Prophetic Book, 1988; '1953', 1990; Hadyn and the Valve Trumpet (essays), 1990. *Recreation:* music. *Address:* c/o New College, Oxford OX1 3BN.

RAINE, (Harcourt) Neale, CBE 1986; Chairman, Business and Technician Education Council, 1983–86 (of Technician Education Council, 1976–83); *b* 5 May 1923; *s* of late

Harold Raine and Gertrude Maude Healey; *m* 1947, Eileen Daphne, *d* of A. A. Hooper; one *s*. *Educ:* Dulwich and London. MSc (Eng) London; CEng, FIProdE, MICE, FIMC. Various appts as professional civil engr, 1947–52; Industrial Management Consultant with Production Engrg Ltd, 1953–59; Jt Man. Dir, Mycalex & TIM Ltd, 1959–63; Chief Exec., Car Div., Wilmot Breedon Ltd, 1963; Management Consultancy in assoc. with Production Engrg Ltd, 1964–65; Dep. Man. Dir, 1965, later Chm. and Man. Dir, Brico Engrg Ltd (Associated Engrg Gp); Chm., Coventry Radiator & Presswork Co. Ltd (Associated Engrg Gp), 1968–70; Man. Dir, Alfred Herbert Ltd, 1970–75. Dir, Associated Engineering Ltd and Man.-Dir of Gen. Div., 1968–70; Dir, Stothert & Pitt Ltd, 1978–86. Nat. Chm., IProdE, 1987–89. Pres., Coventry and District Engrg Employers' Assoc., 1975–77. Governor, Lanchester Polytechnic, Coventry and Rugby, 1970–80. *Address:* Penn Lea, The Avenue, Charlton Kings, Cheltenham, Glos GL53 9BJ. *T:* Cheltenham (0242) 526185.

RAINE, John Stephen; County Director, Derbyshire County Council, since 1989; *b* 13 April 1941; *s* of Alan and Ruby Raine; *m* 1961, Josephine Marlow; two *s*. *Educ:* Sir Joseph Williamson's Mathematical School, Rochester. MIPR. Journalist; Kent Messenger, Sheffield Morning Telegraph, Sheffield Star, Raymond's News Agency, 1957–70; Derbyshire County Council: County Public Relations Officer, 1973–79; Asst to Clerk and Chief Exec., 1979–81; Asst Chief Exec., 1981–88; Dep. County Dir, 1988–89. *Recreations:* walking, travel, smallholding. *Address:* Far Hill Farm, Far Hill, Ashover, Chesterfield, Derbyshire S45 0BB. *T:* Chesterfield (0246) 590501.

RAINE, Kathleen Jessie, (Mrs Madge), FRSL; poet; *b* 1908; *o d* of late George Raine, schoolmaster, and Jessie Raine; *m* Charles Madge (marr. diss.); one *s* one *d*. *Educ:* Girton College, Cambridge. Hon. DLitt: Leicester, 1974; Durham, 1979; Caen, 1987. *Publications:* Stone and Flower, 1943; Living in Time, 1946; The Pythoness, 1949; The Year One, 1952; Collected Poems, 1956; The Hollow Hill (poems), 1965; Defending Ancient Springs (criticism), 1967, 1985; Blake and Tradition (Andrew Mellon Lectures, Washington, 1962), Princeton 1968, London 1969 (abridged version, Blake and Antiquity, Princeton 1978, London 1979, trans. Japanese, 1988); (with George Mills Harper) Selected Writings of Thomas Taylor the Platonist, Princeton and London, 1969; William Blake, 1970; The Lost Country (verse), 1971 (W. H. Smith & Son Award, 1972); On a Deserted Shore (verse), 1973; Yeats, the Tarot and The Golden Dawn (criticism), 1973; Faces of Day and Night, 1973; Farewell Happy Fields (autobiog.), 1973 (French trans. as Adieu prairies heureuses, 1978; Prix du meilleur livre étranger); Death in Life and Life in Death (criticism), 1974; The Land Unknown (autobiog.), 1975 (French trans. as Le royaume inconnu, 1978), The Oval Portrait (verse), 1977; The Lion's Mouth (autobiography), 1977 (French trans. as La Gueul du Lion, 1987); David Jones and the Actually Loved and Known (criticism), 1978; From Blake to a Vision (criticism), 1979; The Oracle in the Heart, (verse), 1979; Blake and the New Age (criticism), 1979; Collected Poems, 1981; The Human Face of God, 1982; The Inner Journey of the Poet and other papers (criticism), 1982; L'Imagination Créatrice de William Blake; Yeats the Initiate, 1986; The Presence (verse), 1988; Selected Poems, 1988; Visages du Jour et de la Nuit, 1989; India Seen Afar, 1990; Golgonooza, City of the Imagination, 1991; French trans. of verse: Isis errante, 1978; Sur un rivage désert, 1978; Le Premier Jour, 1980; Le Royaume Invisible, 1991; Spanish trans.: En una desierta orilla, 1980; Swedish trans.: Den Ösedda Rosen (selected poetry), 1988; Editor, Temenos, a bi-annual Review devoted to the Arts of the Imagination, 1982– (Jt Editor, 1981–82) (10th issue 1989); contributions to literary journals. *Address:* 47 Paultons Square, SW3. *Club:* University Women's.

RAINE, Neale; *see* Raine, H. N.

RAINER, Luise; actress and painter; *b* Vienna, 12 Jan.; *d* of Heinz Rainer; *m* 1937, Clifford Odets (from whom she obtained a divorce, 1940; he *d* 1963); *m* 1945, Robert (*d* 1989), *s* of late John Knittel; one *d*. *Educ:* Austria, France, Switzerland and Italy. Started stage career at age of sixteen under Max Reinhardt in Vienna; later was discovered by Metro-Goldwyn-Mayer talent scout in Vienna; came to Hollywood; starred in: Escapade, The Great Ziegfeld, The Good Earth, Emperor's Candlesticks, Big City, Toy Wife (Frou Frou), The Great Waltz, Dramatic School; received Motion Picture Academy of Arts and Sciences Award for the best feminine performance in 1936 and 1937. One-man exhibn of paintings at Patrick Seale Gallery, SW1, 1978. US Tour in dramatised recitation of Tennyson's Enoch Arden with music by Richard Strauss, 1981–82, 1983. George Eastman Award, George Eastman Inst., Rochester, NY, 1982. Grand Cross 1st class, Order of Merit (Federal Republic of Germany), 1985. *Recreation:* mountain climbing. *Address:* Casa Isola, Vico Morcote, Lake Lugano, CH 6911, Switzerland. *T:* (091) 692201.

RAINGER, Peter, CBE 1978; FRS 1982; FEng; Deputy Director of Engineering, British Broadcasting Corporation, 1978–84, retired; *b* 17 May 1924; *s* of Cyril and Ethel Rainger; *m* 1st, 1953, Josephine Campbell (decd); two *s*; 2nd, 1972, Barbara Gibson. *Educ:* Northampton Engrg Coll.; London Univ. (BSc(Eng)). CEng, FIEE; FEng 1979. British Broadcasting Corporation: Head of Designs Dept, 1968–71; Head of Research Dept, 1971–76; Asst Dir of Engrg, 1976–78. Chairman: Professional Gp E14, IEE, 1973–76; various working parties, EBU, 1971–84. Fellow, Royal Television Soc., 1969. Geoffrey Parr Award, Royal TV Soc., 1964; J. J. Thompson Premium, IEE, 1966; TV Acad. Award, Nat. Acad. of Arts and Scis, 1968; David Sarnoff Gold Medal, SMPTE, 1972. *Publications:* Satellite Broadcasting, 1985; technical papers in IEE, Royal TV Soc. and SMPTE jls. *Recreations:* sailing, model engineering. *Address:* 22 Mill Meadow, Milford on Sea, Hants SO41 0UG.

RAINS, Prof. Anthony John Harding, CBE 1986; MS, FRCS; Hon. Librarian, since 1984, and Hunterian Trustee, since 1982, Royal College of Surgeons of England; *b* 5 Nov. 1920; *s* of late Dr Robert Harding Rains and Mrs Florence Harding Rains; *m* 1943, Mary Adelaide Lillywhite; three *d*. *Educ:* Christ's Hospital School, Horsham; St Mary's Hospital, London. MB, BS London 1943; MS London 1952; MRCS; LRCP 1943; FRCS 1948. Ho. Surg. and Ho. Phys. St Mary's, 1943. RAF, 1944–47. Ex-Service Registrar to Mr Handfield-Jones and Lord Porritt, 1947–48; Res. Surgical Officer, Bedford County Hosp., 1948–50; Lectr in Surgery, Univ. of Birmingham, 1950–54, Sen. Lectr, 1955–59; Prof. of Surgery, Charing Cross Hosp. Medical Sch., Univ. of London, and Hon. Consultant Surgeon, Charing Cross Hosp., 1959–81; Asst Dir, BPMF, Univ. of London, and Postgraduate Dean, SW Thames RHA, 1981–85. Hon. Consulting Surgeon, United Birmingham Hospitals, 1954–59; Hon. Consultant Surgeon to the Army, 1972–82. Royal College of Surgeons of England: Mem. Court of Examiners, 1968–74; Mem. Council, 1972–84; Dean, Inst. of Basic Med. Scis, 1976–82; Vice-President, 1983–84. Chm., Med. Commn on Accident Prevention, 1974–83. Pres., Nat. Assoc. of Theatre Nurses, 1979–81. Sir Arthur Keith medal, RCS. Editor: Annals of RCS; Jl of RSocMed, 1985–. *Publications:* (ed with Dr P. B. Kunkler) The Treatment of Cancer in Clinical Practice, 1959; Gallstones: Causes and Treatment, 1964; (ed) Bailey and Love's Short Practice of Surgery, 13th edn (ed with W. M. Capper), 1965, 20th edn (ed with C. V. Mann), 1988; Edward Jenner and Vaccination, 1975; Emergency and Acute Care, 1976; Lister and Antisepsis, 1977; 1,001 Multiple Choice Questions and Answers in Surgery, 1978, 3rd edn 1991; articles on the surgery of the gall bladder, on the formation of gall stones, inguinal hernia and arterial disease. *Recreations:* rough work, painting. *Address:* Target Cottage, West Strand, West Wittering, Chichester, W Sussex PO20 8AU. *T:* Birdham (0243) 513353.

RAINSFORD, Surg. Rear-Adm. (retd) Seymour Grome, CB 1955; FRCPath 1964; ARC Research Fellow, Bone and Joint Research Unit, London Hospital Medical College, since 1975; Hon. Consultant in Coagulation Disorders, Wessex Regional Hospital Board, since 1975; *b* 24 April 1900; *s* of Frederick Edward Rainsford, MD, Palmerstown Hse, Co. Dublin; *m* 1st, 1929, Violet Helen (*née* Thomas) (decd); 2nd, 1972, Caroline Mary Herschel, *d* of late Sir Denis Hill, FRCP, FRCPsych; twin *s*. *Educ:* St Columba's College, Co. Dublin; Trinity College, Dublin. MD 1932; ScD 1939; DPH 1937; FRCPath 1964; FRCP 1977. Joined RN as Surg. Lieut, 1922. North Persian Forces Memorial Medal, for research on Mediterranean Fever, 1933; Gilbert Blane Gold Medal for research on Typhoid Fever, 1938; Chadwick Gold Medal and Prize for research on typhoid vaccine and on blood transfusion in the Royal Navy, 1939. Surgeon Rear-Adm. 1952; Deputy Medical Director-General of the Royal Navy, 1952–55. Chevalier de la Légion d'Honneur, 1948; CStJ 1955. *Publications:* papers on typhoid fever and other tropical diseases, haematology, blood transfusion, blood clotting disorders and physiological problems concerned in diving and submarine escape, in Jl Hygiene, Lancet, BMJ, British Jl of Haematology, Jl Clin. Pathology, Thrombosis et Diathesis and Journal RN Med. Serv. *Recreations:* shooting, golf. *Address:* The Ashes, 25 Colletts Close, Corfe Castle, Wareham, Dorset BH20 5HG. *Club:* Army and Navy.

RAIS, Tan Sri Abdul J.; *see* Jamil Rais.

RAISMAN, John Michael, CBE 1983; Deputy Chairman, British Telecom, 1987–91 (Government Director, 1984–87); *b* 12 Feb. 1929; *er s* of Sir Jeremy Raisman, GCMG, GCIE, KCSI, and late Renee Mary Raisman; *m* 1953, Evelyn Anne, *d* of Brig. J. I. Muirhead, CIE, MC; one *s* three *d*. *Educ:* Dragon Sch., Oxford; Rugby Sch.; The Queen's Coll., Oxford (Jodrell Schol., MA Lit Hum). CBIM 1980. Joined Royal Dutch/Shell Group, 1953; served in Brazil, 1954–60; General Manager, Shell Panama, 1961–62; Asst to Exploration and Production Coordinator, The Hague, 1963–65; Gen. Man., Shell Co. of Turkey, 1966–69; President, Shell Sekiyu K. K. Japan, 1970–73; Head, European Supply and Marketing, 1974–77; Man. Dir, Shell UK Oil, 1977–78; Regional Coordinator, UK and Eire, Shell Internat. Pet. Co. Ltd, 1978–85; Shell UK Ltd: Dep. Chm., 1978–79; Chief Exec., 1978–85; Chm., 1979–85. Director: Vickers PLC, 1981–90; Glaxo Hldgs PLC, 1982–90; Lloyds Bank Plc, 1985–; Lloyds Merchant Bank Hldgs Ltd, 1985–87; Candover Investments PLC, 1990–. Chairman: Adv. Council, London Enterprise Agency, 1979–85; UK Oil Industry Emergency Cttee, 1980–85; Council of Industry for Management Educn, 1981–85; Investment Bd, Electra-Candover Partners, 1985–. Member: Council, CBI, 1979– (Chm., CBI Europe Cttee, 1980–88; Mem., President's Cttee, 1980–88); Council, Inst. of Petroleum, 1979–81; Council, Inst. for Fiscal Studies, 1982–; Governing Council, Business in the Community, 1982–85; Council, UK Centre for Econ. and Environmental Develt, 1985–89; Royal Commn on Environmental Pollution, 1986–87; Chm., Electronics Industry EDC, 1986–87. Mem., Council for Charitable Support, 1986–; Chm., RA Trust, 1987–, Trustee, RA, 1983–; Governor, National Inst. of Econ. and Social Res., 1983–; Pro-Chancellor, Aston Univ., 1987–. DUniv Stirling, 1983; Hon. LLD: Aberdeen, 1985; Manchester, 1986. *Recreations:* golf, skiing, music, theatre, travel. *Clubs:* Brooks's; Royal Mid-Surrey; Sunningdale Golf.

RAISON, Dr John Charles Anthony, MA, MD; FFPHM; Consultant in Public Health Medicine, Wessex Regional Health Authority, 1982–91, retired; *b* 13 May 1926; *s* of late Cyril A. Raison, FRCS, Edgbaston, Birmingham, and of Ceres Raison; *m* 1st, 1951 (marr. diss. 1982); one *s* two *d*; 2nd, 1983, Ann Alexander, *d* of Captain and Mrs J. H. R. Faulkner, Southampton; three step *d*. *Educ:* Malvern Coll.; Trinity Hall, Cambridge; Birmingham Univ. Consultant Clinical Physiologist in Cardiac Surgery, Birmingham Reg. Hosp. Bd, 1962; Hon. Associate Consultant Clinical Physiologist, United Birmingham Hosps, 1963; Sen. Physiologist, Dir of Clinical Res. and Chief Planner, Heart Research Inst., Presbyterian-Pacific Medical Center, San Francisco, 1966; Chief Scientific Officer and Sen. Princ. Medical Officer, Scientific Services, DHSS, 1974–78; Dep. Dir, Nat. Radiological Protection Bd, 1978–81. Vis. Consultant, Civic Hosps, Lisbon (Gulbenkian Foundn), 1962; Arris and Gale Lectr, Royal College of Surgeons, 1965. Councillor, Southam RDC, 1955–59. *Publications:* chapters in books, and papers in medical jls on open-heart surgery, extracorporeal circulation, intensive care, scientific services in health care, and computers in medicine. *Recreations:* tennis, gardening, theatre, sailing. *Address:* Broom Cottage, Easton, near Winchester, Hants SO21 1EF. *T:* Itchen Abbas (096278) 723.

RAISON, Rt. Hon. Sir Timothy (Hugh Francis), Kt 1991; PC 1982; MP (C) Aylesbury since 1970; Chairman, Advertising Standards Authority, since 1991; *b* 3 Nov. 1929; *s* of Maxwell and late Celia Raison; *m* 1956, Veldes Julia Charrington; one *s* three *d*. *Educ:* Dragon Sch., Oxford; Eton (King's Schol.); Christ Church, Oxford (Open History Schol.). Editorial Staff: Picture Post, 1953–56; New Scientist, 1956–61; Editor: Crossbow, 1958–60; New Society, 1962–68. Member: Youth Service Develt Council, 1960–63; Central Adv. Council for Educn, 1963–66; Adv. Cttee on Drug Dependence, 1966–70; Home Office Adv, Council on Penal System, 1970–74; (co-opted) Inner London Educn Authority Educn Cttee, 1967–70; Richmond upon Thames Council, 1967–71. PPS to Sec. of State for N Ireland, 1972–73; Parly Under-Sec. of State, DES, 1973–74; Opposition spokesman on the Environment, 1975–76; Minister of State, Home Office, 1979–83; Minister of State, FCO, and Minister for Overseas Develt, 1983–86. Chm., Select Cttee on Educn, Science and the Arts, 1987–89. Sen. Fellow, Centre for Studies in Soc. Policy, 1974–77; Mem. Council, PSI, 1978–79; Vice-Chm. Bd, British Council, 1987–. Nansen Medal (for share in originating World Refugee Year), 1960. *Publications:* Why Conservative?, 1964; (ed) Youth in New Society, 1966; (ed) Founding Fathers of Social Science, 1969; Power and Parliament, 1979; Tories and the Welfare State, 1990; various political pamphlets. *Recreations:* golf, gardening. *Address:* House of Commons, SW1A 0AA. *Clubs:* Beefsteak, MCC.

RAITZ, Vladimir Gavrilovich; travel consultant; *b* 23 May 1922; *s* of Dr Gavril Raitz and Cecilia Raitz; *m* 1954, Helen Antonia (*née* Corkrey); three *d*. *Educ:* Mill Hill Sch.; London University. BSc(Econ.), Econ. History, 1942. British United Press, 1942–43; Reuters, 1943–48; Chm., Horizon Holidays, 1949–74. Member: NEDC for Hotels and Catering Industry, 1968–74; Cinematograph Films Council, 1969–74; Ct of Governors, LSE, 1971–. Cavaliere Ufficiale, Order of Merit (Italy), 1971. *Recreations:* reading, skiing. *Address:* 32 Dudley Court, Upper Berkeley Street, W1. *T:* 071–262 2592; The Coach House, Oakdale Road, Tunbridge Wells, Kent. *T:* Tunbridge Wells (0892) 547619. *Club:* Reform.

RAJ, Prof. Kakkadan Nandanath; Hon. Emeritus Fellow, Centre for Development Studies, Trivandrum, Kerala State, since 1983 (Fellow, 1973–84); *b* 13 May 1924; *s* of K. N. Gopalan and Karthiayani Gopalan; *m* 1957, Dr Sarasamma Narayanan; two *s*. *Educ:* Madras Christian Coll., Tambaram (BA (Hons), MA, in Economics); London Sch. of Economics (PhD (Econ); Hon. Fellow, 1982). Asst Editor, Associated Newspapers of Ceylon, Nov. 1947–July 1948; Research Officer, Dept of Research, Reserve Bank of India,

Aug. 1948–Feb. 1950; Asst Chief, Economic Div., Planning Commn, Govt of India, 1950–53; Prof. of Economics, Delhi Sch. of Economics, Univ. of Delhi, 1953–73 (Vice-Chancellor, Univ. of Delhi, 1969–70; Nat. Fellow in Economics, 1971–73; Jawaharlal Nehru Fellow, 1987–88). Mem., Economic Adv. Council to Prime Minister of India, 1983–91. Visiting Prof., Johns Hopkins Univ., Jan.-June, 1958; Vis. Fellow, Nuffield Coll., Oxford, Jan.-June, 1960; Corresp. Fellow, British Academy, 1972. Hon. Fellow, Amer. Economic Assoc. *Publications:* The Monetary Policy of the Reserve Bank of India, 1948; Employment Aspects of Planning in Underdeveloped Economies, 1956; Some Economic Aspects of the Bhakra-Nangal Project, 1960; Indian Economic Growth-Performance and Prospects, 1964; India, Pakistan and China-Economic Growth and Outlook, 1966; Investment in Livestock in Agrarian Economies, 1969; (ed jtly) Essays on the Commercialization of Indian Agriculture, 1985; Organizational Issues in Indian Agriculture, 1990; also articles in Economic Weekly, Economic and Political Weekly, Indian Economic Review, Oxford Economic Papers. *Address:* 'Nandavan', Kumarapuram, Trivandrum 695011, Kerala State, India. *T:* (home) 73309, (office) 8881–8884, 8412.

RAJAH, Arumugam Ponnu; a Judge of the Supreme Court, Singapore, 1976–90; *b* Negri Sembilan, Malaysia, 23 July 1911; *m* Vijaya Lakshmi; one *s* one *d*. *Educ:* St Paul's Inst., Seremban; Raffles Instn and Raffles Coll., Singapore; Lincoln Coll., Oxford Univ. (BA). Barrister-at-law, Lincoln's Inn. City Councillor, Singapore: nominated, 1947–49; elected, 1949–57; MLA for Farrer Park, Singapore, 1959–66, Chm., Public Accounts Cttee, 1959–63, Speaker, 1964–66; first High Comr for Singapore to UK, 1966–71; High Comr to Australia, 1971–73; practised law, Tan Rajah & Cheah, Singapore, 1973–76. Mem. Bd of Trustees, Singapore Improvement Trust, 1949–57; Mem., Raffles Coll. Council and Univ. of Malaya Council, 1955–63; Chm., Inst. of SE Asian Studies, 1975–84; Pro-Chancellor, Nat. Univ. of Singapore, 1975–. Hon. Dr Laws Nat. Univ. of Singapore, 1984. *Address:* 7–D Balmoral Road, Singapore 1025.

RALEIGH, Dr Jean Margaret Macdonald C.; *see* Curtis-Raleigh.

RALLI, Sir Godfrey (Victor), 3rd Bt, *cr* 1912; TD; *b* 9 Sept. 1915; *s* of Sir Strati Ralli, 2nd Bt, MC; *S* father 1964; *m* 1st, 1937, Nora Margaret Forman (marriage dissolved, 1947); one *s* two *d*; 2nd, 1949, Jean, *er d* of late Keith Barlow. *Educ:* Eton. Joined Ralli Bros Ltd, 1936. Served War of 1939–45 (despatches), Captain, Berkshire Yeomanry RA. Director and Vice-Chairman, Ralli Bros Ltd, 1946–62; Chm., Greater London Fund for the Blind, 1962–82. *Recreations:* fishing, golf. *Heir: s* David Charles Ralli [*b* 5 April 1946; *m* 1975, Jacqueline Cecilia, *d* of late David Smith; one *s* one *d*]. *Address:* Great Walton, Eastry, Sandwich, Kent CT13 0DN. *T:* Sandwich (0304) 611355. *Clubs:* White's, Naval and Military.

RALLING, (Antony) Christopher, FRGS; freelance writer/director; *b* 12 April 1929; *s* of Harold St George Ralling and Dorothy Blanche Ralling; *m* 1963, Angela Norma (*née* Gardner); one *d*. *Educ:* Charterhouse; Wadham Coll., Oxford (BA 2nd Cl. Hons English). Joined BBC External Services, Scriptwriter, 1955; British Meml Foundn Fellowship to Australia, 1959; Dep. Editor, Panorama, BBC TV, 1964; joined BBC TV Documentaries, 1966; directed The Search for the Nile, 1972 (Amer. Acad. Award, 1972; Peabody Award, 1972); Mem., British Everest Expedn, 1975; produced The Voyage of Charles Darwin, 1978 (British Acad. Award, 1978; Desmond Davies British Acad. Award, 1978; RTS Silver Medal, 1979); Hd of Documentaries, BBC TV, 1980; left BBC to start Dolphin Productions, 1982; directed: The History of Africa, 1984; Chasing a Rainbow (Josephine Baker), 1986 (Amer. Acad. Award, 1986); Prince Charles at Forty, LWT, 1988. FRGS 1978. *Publications:* Muggeridge Through the Microphone, 1967; The Voyage of Charles Darwin, 1978; Shackleton, 1983; The Kon-Tiki Man, 1990. *Recreations:* tennis, ski-ing. *Address:* The Coach House, Tankerville, Kingston Hill, Surrey KT2 7JH. *Club:* Alpine.

RALPH, Colin John, MPhil; RGN; DN; Registrar and Chief Executive, United Kingdom Central Council for Nursing, Midwifery and Health Visiting, since 1987; *b* 16 June 1951; *s* of Harold Ernest Ralph and Vining Bromley. *Educ:* Royal West Sussex Hosp. (RGN); RCN/Univ. of London (DN); Brunel Univ. (MPhil). Staff Nurse and Student, Nat. Heart Hosp., 1974; Charge Nurse, Royal Free Hosp., 1974–77; Nursing Officer, London Hosp., 1978–83; Dir of Nursing, Westminster Hosp. and Westminster Children's Hosp., 1983–86; Chief Nursing Adviser, Gloucester HA, 1986–87. British Red Cross Society: Mem., Nat. Exec. Cttee, 1974–76; Nursing Adviser, 1975–. Member: Standing Nursing and Midwifery Adv. Cttee, 1986–; Professional Services Cttee, RCN, 1986–87; EC Adv. Cttee on Trng in Nursing, 1990–; Internat. Cttee, RCN, 1991–; National Florence Nightingale Memorial Committee: Florence Nightingale Scholar, 1981; Mem., Council of Management, 1983–. *Publications:* contribs to nursing profession jls and books. *Recreations:* friends, the arts, travel. *Address:* 23 Portland Place, W1N 3AF. *T:* 071–637 7181.

RALPHS, Enid Mary, (Lady Ralphs), CBE 1984; JP; DL; Chairman of the Council, Magistrates' Association, 1981–84; *b* 20 Jan. 1915; *d* of Percy William Cowlin and Annie Louise Cowlin (*née* Willoughby); *m* 1938, Sir (Frederick) Lincoln Ralphs, Kt 1973 (*d* 1978); one *s* two *d*. *Educ:* Camborne Grammar Sch.; University Coll., Exeter (BA); DipEd Cambridge. Pres., Guild of Undergrads, Exeter, 1936–37; Vice-Pres., NUS, 1937–38. Teacher, Penzance Grammar Sch., 1937–38; Staff Tutor, Oxford Univ. Tutorial Classes Cttee, 1942–44; pt-time Sen. Lectr, Keswick Hall Coll. of Educn, 1948–80. Member: Working Party on Children and Young Persons Act 1969, 1977–78; Steering Cttee on Community Alternatives for Young Offenders, NACRO, 1979–82; Consultative Cttee on Educn in Norwich Prison, 1982–87; Home Office Adv. Bd on Restricted Patients, 1985–. Member: Religious Adv. Council, BBC Midland Reg., 1963–66; Guide Council for GB, 1965–68. President: Norwich and Dist Br., UNA, 1973–; Norfolk Girl Guides, 1987–. Governor: Norwich Sch.; Culford Sch.; Wymondham Coll. Trustee, Norfolk Children's Projects, 1982–. JP Norwich 1958; Chairman: Norwich Juvenile Panel, 1964–79; Norwich Bench, 1977–85; former Mem., Licensing Cttee; Mem., Domestic Panel, 1981–85; Chm., Norfolk Br., Magistrates' Assoc.; Dep. Chm., Norfolk Magistrates' Courts Cttee, 1978–85 (Chm., Trng Sub-Cttee); Mem., Central Council, Magistrates' Courts Cttees, 1974–81. DL Norfolk 1981. Hon. DCL East Anglia, 1989. *Publications:* contribs to various jls. *Recreations:* (jtly) The Magistrate as Chairman, 1987; gardening, travel. *Address:* Jesselton, 218 Unthank Road, Norwich NR2 2AH. *T:* Norwich (0603) 53382. *Club:* Royal Over-Seas League.

RAMA RAU, Santha; free-lance writer since 1945; English teacher at Sarah Lawrence College, Bronxville, NY, since 1971; *b* Madras, India, 24 Jan. 1923; *d* of late Sir Benegal Rama Rau, CIE and Lady Dhanvanthi Rama Rau; *m* 1st, 1951, Faubion Bowers (marr. diss. 1966); one *s*; 2nd, Gurdon W. Wattles. *Educ:* St Paul's Girls' School, London, England; Wellesley College, Mass., USA. Feature writer for the Office of War Information, New York, USA, during vacations from college, 1942–45. Hon. doctorate: Bates College, USA, 1961; Russell Sage College, 1965; Phi Beta Kappa, Wellesley College, 1960. Screenplay: A Passage to India, 1985. *Publications:* Home to India, 1945; East of Home, 1950; This is India, 1953; Remember the House, 1955; View to the South-East, 1957; My Russian Journey, 1959; A Passage to India (dramatization), 1962; Gifts of Passage, 1962; The Adventuress, 1971; Cooking of India, 1971 (2 vols); A Princess Remembers (with Maharani Gayatri Devi of Jaipur), 1976; An Inheritance (with Dhanvanthi Rama Rau), 1977; many articles and short stories in New Yorker, Art News, Horizon, Saturday Evening Post, Reader's Digest, etc. *Address:* RR1, Box 200, Amenia, NY 12501, USA.

RAMACHANDRAN, Prof. Gopalasamudram Narayana, FRS 1977; Indian National Science Academy Albert Einstein National Professor, 1984, retired; specialist in molecular biology, biophysics and mathematical logic; *b* 8 Oct. 1922; *s* of G. R. Narayana Iyer and Lakshmi Ammal; *m* 1945, Rajalakshmi Sankaran; two *s* one *d*. *Educ:* Maharaja's Coll., Ernakulam, Cochin; Indian Inst. of Science; Univ. of Madras (MA, MSc, DSc); Univ. of Cambridge (PhD). Lectr in Physics, Indian Inst. of Science, 1946–47, Asst Prof., 1949–52; 1851 Exhibn Scholar, Univ. of Cambridge, 1947–49; Prof., Univ. of Madras, 1952–70 (Dean, Faculty of Science, 1964–67); Indian Institute of Science: Prof. of Biophysics, 1970–78; Prof. of Mathematical Philosophy, 1978–81; Hon. Fellow, 1984; Dist. Scientist, Centre for Cellular and Molecular Biology, Hyderabad, 1981–83. Dir, Univ. Grants Commn Centre of Advanced Study in Biophysics, 1962–70; part-time Prof. of Biophysics, Univ. of Chicago, 1967–78. Member: Physical Res. Cttee, 1959–69; Nat. Cttee for Biophysics, 1961–; Bd of Sci. and Ind. Res., India, 1962–65; Council, Internat. Union of Pure and Applied Biophysics, 1969–72; Commn on Macromolecular Biophysics, 1969; Chm., Nat. Cttee for Crystallography, 1963–70; Senior Vis. Prof., Univ. of Michigan, 1965–66; Jawaharlal Nehru Fellow, 1968–70; Fogarty Internat. Schol., NIH, 1977–78. Fellow, Indian Acad. of Sciences, 1950 (Mem. Council, 1953–70; Sec., 1956–58; Vice-Pres., 1962–64); Fellow, Indian Nat. Sci. Acad., 1963; FRSA 1971. Hon. Mem., Amer. Soc. of Molecular Biology, 1965; Hon. Foreign Mem., Amer. Acad. of Arts and Scis; Founder Member: Indian Acad. of Yoga, 1980; Third World Acad., Rome, 1982. Hon. DSc: Roorkee, 1979; Indian Inst. Technology, Madras, 1985; Hyderabad, 1989; Banaras Hindu, 1991. Bhatnagar Meml Prize, 1961; Watumull Prize, 1964; John Arthur Wilson Award, 1967; Ramanujan Medal, 1971; Maghnad Saha Medal, 1971; J. C. Bose Gold Medal and Prize of Bose Inst., 1975; Fogarty Medal, 1978; Distinguished Alumni Award, Indian Inst. of Sci., 1978; C. V. Raman Award, 1982; Birla Award for Medical Science, 1984. Editor: Current Science, 1950–58; Jl Indian Inst. of Sci., 1973–77; Member Editorial Board: Jl Molecular Biol., 1959–66; Biochimica et Biophysica Acta, 1965–72; Indian Jl Pure and Applied Physics, 1963–80; Internat. Jl Peptide and Protein Res., 1969–82; Indian Jl Biochem. and Biophys., 1970–78; Connective Tissue Research 1972–84; Biopolymers, 1973–86; Jl Biomolecular Structure and Dynamics, 1984–. *Publications:* Crystal Optics, in Handbuch der Physik, vol. 25; Molecular Structure of Collagen, in Internat. Review of Connective Tissue Research, vol. 1; Conformation of Polypeptides and Proteins, in Advances in Protein Chemistry, vol. 23; Conformation Polypeptide Chains, in Annual Reviews in Biochemistry, vol. 39; Fourier Methods in Crystallography, 1970; (ed) Advanced Methods of Crystallography; (ed) Aspects of Protein Structure; (ed) Treatise on Collagen, 2 vols, 1967; (ed) Conformation of Biopolymers, vols 1 and 2, 1967; (ed) Crystallography and Crystal Perfection; (ed) Biochemistry of Collagen. *Recreations:* Indian and Western music; detective fiction. *Address:* Gita, 5, 10–A Main Road, Malleswaram West, Bangalore 560055, India. *T:* 340362.

RAMADHANI, Most Rev. John Acland; *see* Tanzania, Archbishop of.

RAMAGE, (James) Granville (William), CMG 1975; HM Diplomatic Service, retired; *b* 19 Nov. 1919; *s* of late Rev. George Granville Ramage and Helen Marion (*née* Middlemass); *m* 1947, Eileen Mary Smith; one *s* two *d*. *Educ:* Glasgow Acad.; Glasgow University. Served in HM Forces, 1940–46 (despatches). Entered HM Foreign Service, 1947; seconded for service at Bombay, 1947–49; transf. to Foreign Office, 1950; First Sec. and Consul at Manila, 1952–56; South-East Asia Dept, FO, 1956–58; Consul at Atlanta, Ga, 1958–62; Gen. Dept, FO, 1962–63; Consul-General, Tangier, 1963–67; High Comr in The Gambia, 1968–71; Ambassador, People's Democratic Republic of Yemen, 1972–75; Consul General at Boston, Massachusetts, 1975–77. *Recreations:* music, golf. *Address:* 4 Merton Hall Road, Wimbledon, SW19 3PP. *T:* 081–542 5492.

RAMBAHADUR LIMBU, Captain, VC 1966; MVO 1984; HM the Queen's Gurkha Orderly Officer, 1983–84; employed in Sultanate of Negara Brunei Darussalam, since 1985; *b* Nov. 1939; *s* of late Tekbir Limbu; *m* 1st, 1960, Tikamaya Limbuni (*d* 1966); two *s*; 2nd, 1967, Purnimaya Limbuni; three *s*. Army Cert. of Educn 1st cl. Enlisted 10th Princess Mary's Own Gurkha Rifles, 1957; served on ops in Borneo (VC); promoted Sergeant, 1971; WOII, 1976; commissioned, 1977. Hon. Captain (Gurkha Commnd Officer), 1985. *Publication:* My Life Story, 1978. *Recreations:* football, volley-ball, badminton, basketball. *Address:* Gurkha Reserve Unit, Sungai Akar Camp, Post Box No 420, Negara Brunei Darussalam; Ward No 13 Damak, Nagar Palika, PO Box Damak, District Jhapa, Mechi Zone, East Nepal. *Clubs:* VC and GC Association, Royal Society of St George (England).

RAMELSON, Baruch, (Bert); Member, Editorial Board, World Marxist Review, published in Prague, and Editor of the English edition, 1977–90, retired; *b* 22 March 1910; *s* of Jacob and Liuba Mendelson; *m* 1st, 1939, Marion Jessop (*d* 1967); 2nd, 1970, Joan Dorothy Smith; one step *s* two step *d*. *Educ:* Univ. of Alberta. 1st cl. hons LLB. Barrister and Solicitor, Edmonton, Alta, 1934–35; Internat. Bde, Mackenzie-Pappinard Bn, Spanish Civil War, 1937–39; Adjt, Canadian Bn of Internat. Bde; Tank Driver, Royal Tank Corps, 1941; captured, Tobruk, 1941; escaped Prison Camp, Italy, 1943; OCTU, Catterick, 1944–45, commnd RA 1945; served in India, 1945–46 (Actg Staff Captain Legal). Communist Party of GB: full-time Sec., Leeds, 1946–53; Sec., Yorks, 1953–65; Mem. Nat. Exec., 1953–78; Mem. Polit. Cttee, 1954–78; National Industrial Organiser, 1965–77. *Publications:* The Case for an Alternative Policy, 1977; Consensus or Socialism, 1987; various pamphlets and booklets; contrib. Communist (Moscow), Marxism Today, World Marxist Review. *Recreations:* travel, reading. *Address:* 160A Conisborough Crescent, Catford, SE6 2SF. *T:* 081–698 0738.

RAMIN, Mme Manfred; *see* Cotrubas, I.

RAMM, Rev. Canon (Norwyn) MacDonald; Vicar of St Michael at North Gate with St Martin and All Saints, Oxford, 1961–88 (Curate, 1957–61); City Rector, Oxford, 1961–89; Chaplain to the Queen, since 1985; *b* 8 June 1924; *s* of Rev. Ezra Edward and Dorothy Mary Ramm; *m* 1962, Ruth Ellen, *d* of late Robert James Kirton, CBE, FIA; two *s* one *d*. *Educ:* Berkhamsted School; St Peter's Theological College, Jamaica; Lincoln College, Oxford. Jamaica appointments: Curate, St James, 1951–53, deacon 1951, priest, 1952; Master, Cornwall College; Rector, Stony Hill with Mount James, 1953–57; Master, Wolmers Girls' School; Chaplain to Approved Sch., Stony Hill; Priest in charge, St Martin and All Saints, Oxford, 1961–71; Hon. Canon, Christ Church Cathedral, Oxford, 1985–88, now Emeritus. Chaplain to: HM Prison, Oxford, 1975–88; British Fire Services Assoc., 1980–; The Sea Cadets, RAF Assoc., RTR, Para Regtl Assoc., Desert Forces (all Oxford branches), Oxford City Police Assoc. Pres., Isis Dist Scout Assoc., 1984–; Chm. Council, Headington Sch., 1984–; Founder and Pres., Samaritans of Oxford, 1963–. *Recreations:* ski-ing, gardening, collecting Graces. *Address:* Fairlawn, Church Lane,

Harwell, Abingdon, Oxon OX11 0EZ. *T:* Abingdon (0235) 835454. *Clubs:* Clarendon, Frewen (Oxford), Oxford Rotary.

RAMPAL, Jean-Pierre Louis; Commandeur de la Légion d'Honneur et de l'Ordre National du Mérite; Officier des Arts et Lettres; musician, concert flautist, conductor; *b* Marseilles, 7 Jan. 1922; *s* of Joseph Rampal and Andrée Roggero; *m* 1947, Françoise Bacqueyrisse; one *s* one *d. Educ:* Lycée Thiers; Facultés des Sciences et de Médecine, Marseilles; Conservatoire Nat. Sup. de Musique, Paris. Flute Prizes, Marseilles and Paris. Professional flautist, 1945–; numerous internat. festivals, world wide tours; Prof. of Flute, Conservatoire Nat. Sup. de Musique, 1969–82; research in ancient music; conducting début, French Provinces, 1948, Paris, 1967; conducting career mostly in USA, parallel to soloist performances. Prix Edison, Prix Léonie Sonning, 1978; Prix d'Honneur de Montreux, 1980. *Publication:* Music, My Love, 1989. *Recreations:* amateur cinema, tennis, diving. *Address:* (home) 15 avenue Mozart, 75016 Paris, France; (business) Bureau de Concerts de Valmalete, 75008 Paris, France.

RAMPHAL, Sir Shridath Surendranath, OE 1983; GCMG 1990 (CMG 1966); OM (Jamaica) 1990; ONZ 1990; AC 1982; Kt 1970; QC (Guyana) 1965, SC 1966; Chairman, West Indian Commission; Executive President, Willy Brandt International Foundation; President, World Conservation Union (IUCN); Secretary-General of the Commonwealth, 1975–90; *b* 1928; *m. Educ:* King's Coll., London (LLM 1952). FKC 1975; Fellow, London Sch. of Econs, 1979. Called to the Bar, Gray's Inn, 1951 (Hon. Bencher 1981). Colonial Legal Probationer, 1951; Arden and Atkin Prize, 1952; John Simon Guggenheim Fellow, Harvard Law Sch., 1962. Crown Counsel, British Guiana, 1953–54; Asst to Attorney-Gen., 1954–56; Legal Draftsman, 1956–58; First Legal Draftsman, West Indies, 1958–59; Solicitor-Gen., British Guiana, 1959–61; Asst Attorney-Gen., West Indies, 1961–62, Attorney-Gen., Guyana, 1965–73; Minister of State for External Affairs, Guyana, 1967–72; Foreign Minister and Attorney General, Guyana, 1972–73; Minister, Foreign Affairs and Justice, 1973–75; Mem., National Assembly, Guyana, 1965–75. Member: Hon. Adv. Cttee, Center for Internat. Studies, NY Univ., 1966–; Internat. Commn of Jurists, 1970–; Bd, Vienna Inst. of Develt, 1973–; Internat. Hon. Cttee, Dag Hammarskjold Foundn, 1977–; Independent (Brandt) Commn on International Development Issues, 1977–; Ind. (Palme) Commn on Disarmament and Security Issues, 1980–89; Ind. Commn on Internat. Humanitarian Issues, 1983–; World Commn on Environment and Develt, 1984–; Indep. Commn of the South on Develt Issues, 1987–; Brandt Conf. Wkg Gp, 1990; Council, Television Trust for the Environment, 1984–; Internat. Bd, United World Colls, 1984–; Bd of Governors, World Maritime Univ., Oslo, 1984–; Commonwealth of Learning, 1988–. Vice Pres., Royal Over-Seas League. Chairman: Selection Cttee, Third World Prize, 1979–; UN Cttee on Develt Planning, 1984–87; W Indian Commn, 1990–. Vice-Chm., Centre for Research on New Internat. Econ. Order, Oxford, 1977–; Chancellor: Univ. of Guyana, 1988; Univ. of Warwick, 1989; Univ. of WI, 1989. Visiting Professor: Exeter Univ., 1988; Faculty of Laws, KCL, 1988. FRSA 1981; CBIM 1986. Hon. Fellow, Magdalen Coll., Oxford, 1982; Hon. LLD: Panjab, 1975; Southampton, 1976; St Francis Xavier, NS, 1978; Univ. of WI, 1978; Aberdeen, 1979; Cape Coast, Ghana, 1980; London, 1981; Benin, Nigeria, 1982; Hull, 1983; Yale, 1985; Cambridge, 1985; Warwick, 1988; York, Ont, 1988; Malta, 1989; Otago, 1990; DUniv: Surrey, 1979; Essex, 1980; Hon. DHL: Simmons Coll., Boston, 1982; Duke Univ., 1985; Hon. DCL: Oxon, 1982; E Anglia, 1983; Durham, 1985; Hon. DLitt: Bradford, 1985; Indira Gandhi Nat. Open Univ., New Delhi, 1989; Hon. DSc Cranfield Inst. of Technology, 1987. Albert Medal, RSA, 1988; Internat. Educn Award, Richmond Coll., 1988. *Publications:* One World to Share: selected speeches of the Commonwealth Secretary-General 1975–79, 1979; Nkrumah and the Eighties: Kwame Nkrumah Memorial Lectures, 1980; Sovereignty and Solidarity: Callander Memorial Lectures, 1981; Some in Light and Some in Darkness: the long shadow of slavery (Wilberforce Lecture), 1983; The Message not the Messenger (STC Communication Lecture), 1985; The Trampling of the Grass (Economic Commn for Africa Silver Jubilee Lecture), 1985; Inseparable Humanity: an anthology of reflections of Shridath Ramphal (ed Ron Sanders), 1988; An End to Otherness (eight speeches by the Commonwealth Secretary-General), 1990; contrib. various political, legal and other jls incl. International and Comparative Law Qly, Caribbean Qly, Public Law, Guyana Jl, Round Table, Foreign Policy, Third World Qly, RSA Jl Internat. Affairs. *Address:* 31 St Matthew's Lodge, 50 Oakley Square, NW1 1NL. *Clubs:* Athenæum, Royal Automobile, Travellers'.

RAMPHUL, Sir Indurduth, Kt 1991; Governor, Bank of Mauritius, since 1982; *b* 10 Oct. 1931; *m* 1962, Taramatee Seedoyal; one *s* one *d. Educ:* Univ. of Exeter (Dip. Public Admin). Asst Sec., Min. of Finance, 1966–67; Bank of Mauritius: Manager, 1967; Chief Manager, 1970; Man. Dir, 1973. Alternate Governor, IMF for Mauritius. *Recreations:* reading, swimming. *Address:* (home) 9 Buswell Avenue, Quatre Bornes, Mauritius. *T:* 454–1643; (office) Bank of Mauritius, Sir William Newton Street, Port Louis, Mauritius. *T:* 208–4164 and 212–6127. *Club:* Mauritius Turf.

RAMPTON, Sir Jack (Leslie), KCB 1973 (CB 1969); Director, London Atlantic Investment Trust, since 1981; *b* 10 July 1920; *s* of late Leonard Wilfrid Rampton and of Sylvia (*née* Davies); *m* 1950, Eileen Joan (*née* Hart); one *s* one *d. Educ:* Tonbridge Sch.; Trinity Coll., Oxford. MA. Treasury, 1941; Asst Priv. Sec. to successive Chancellors of the Exchequer, 1942–43; Priv. Sec. to Financial Sec., 1945–46; Economic and Financial Adv. to Comr-Gen. for SE Asia and to British High Comr, Malaya, 1959–61; Under-Secretary, HM Treasury, 1964–68; Dep. Sec., Min. of Technology (formerly Min. of Power), 1968–70; Dep. Sec., DTI, 1970–72; Second Permanent Sec. and Sec. (Industrial Develt), DTI, 1972–74; Perm. Under-Sec. of State, Dept of Energy, 1974–80. Dep. Chm., Sheerness Steel Co., 1985–87 (Dir, 1982–87); Special Adviser: North Sea Sun Oil Co., 1982–87; Sun Exploration and Development Co. Inc., 1982–87; Magnet Gp, WA, 1981–84; Director: ENO Co., 1982–88; Flextech plc, 1985–. Member: Oxford Energy Policy Club, 1978–; Honeywell UK Adv. Council, 1981–; Energy Industries Club, 1985–. Mem., British Library of Tape Recordings Adv. Council, 1977–88; Council Member: Victoria League, 1981– (Dep. Chm. 1985–); Cook Soc., 1978– (Chm., 1986–87; Dep. Chm., 1988–89); Britain-Australia Soc., 1986– (Hon. Sec., 1986–; Vice-Chm., 1988; Chm., 1992–); Commonwealth Trust, 1988– (Gov., 1988–; Vice Chm., 1989–); London House for Overseas Graduates (Gov., 1989–); Advr, Sir Robert Menzies Meml Trust, 1990–. CBIM; CIGasE; FInstPet 1982. Hon. DSc Aston, 1979. *Recreations:* gardening, games, photography, travel; Oxford Squash V (Capt.) 1939–40; Authentic, 1940. *Address:* 17 The Ridgeway, Tonbridge, Kent TN10 4NQ. *T:* Tonbridge (0732) 352117. *Clubs:* Pilgrims, Britain Australia Society, Tuesday; Vincent's (Oxford).

RAMSAY, family name of **Earl of Dalhousie.**

RAMSAY, Lord; James Hubert Ramsay; Director, Jamestown Investments Ltd, since 1987; *b* 17 Jan. 1948; *er s* and *heir* of 16th Earl of Dalhousie, *qv*; *m* 1973, Marilyn, *yr d* of Major Sir David Butter, *qv*; one *s* two *d. Educ:* Ampleforth. 2nd Bn Coldstream Guards, commnd 1968–71, RARO 1971. Director: Hambros Bank Ltd, 1981–82; (exec.) Enskilda Securities, 1982–87; Capel-Cure Myers Capital Management Ltd, 1988–. Mem., Royal Co. of Archers (The Queen's Body Guard for Scotland), 1979–. President: British Deer Soc., 1987–; Caledonian Club. *Heir: s* Hon. Simon David Ramsay, *b* 18 April 1981. *Address:* Dalhousie Lodge, Edzell, Angus; 3 Vicarage Gardens, W8. *Clubs:* White's, Pratt's, Turf.

RAMSAY, Sir Alexander William Burnett, 7th Bt, *cr* 1806, of Balmain (also *heir-pres* to Btcy of Burnett, *cr* 1626 (Nova Scotia), of Leys, Kincardineshire, which became dormant, 1959, on death of Sir Alexander Edwin Burnett of Leys, and was not claimed by Sir Alexander Burnett Ramsay, 6th Bt, of Balmain); *b* 4 Aug. 1938; *s* of Sir Alexander Burnett Ramsay, 6th Bt and Isabel Ellice, *e d* of late William Whitney, Woodstock, New South Wales; *S* father, 1965; *m* 1963, Neryl Eileen, *d* of J. C. Smith Thornton, Trangie, NSW; three *s. Heir: s* Alexander David Ramsay, *b* 20 Aug. 1966. *Address:* Bulbah, Warren, NSW 2824, Australia.

RAMSAY, Allan John (Heppel Ramsay), CMG 1989; HM Diplomatic Service; Ambassador to Sudan, since 1990; *b* 19 Oct. 1937; *s* of Norman Ramsay Ramsay and Faith Evelyn Sorel-Cameron; *m* 1966, Pauline Therese Lescher; two *s* one *d. Educ:* Bedford Sch.; RMA Sandhurst; Durham Univ. Served Army, 1957–70: Somerset Light Infantry, 1957–65; DLI, 1965–70. Entered FCO, 1970; Ambassador to Lebanon, 1988–90. *Address:* c/o Foreign and Commonwealth Office, SW1A 2AH. *Club:* Brooks's.

RAMSAY, Maj.-Gen. Charles Alexander, CB 1989; OBE 1979; landowner and farmer; Chief Executive, Caledonian Eagle, 1991; *b* 12 Oct. 1936; *s* of Adm. Sir Bertram Home Ramsay, KCB, KBE, MVO, Allied Naval C-in-C, Invasion of Europe, 1944 (killed on active service, 1945), and Helen Margaret Menzies; *m* 1967, Hon. Mary MacAndrew, *d* of 1st Baron MacAndrew, PC, TD; two *s* two *d. Educ:* Eton; Sandhurst. Commissioned Royal Scots Greys, 1956; attended Canadian Army Staff Coll., 1967–68; served abroad in Germany, Middle East and Far East; Mil. Asst to VCDS, 1974–77; commanded Royal Scots Dragoon Guards, 1977–79; Colonel General Staff, MoD, 1979–80; Comdr 12th Armoured Bde, BAOR and Osnabrück Garrison, 1980–82; Dep. Dir of Mil. Ops, MoD, 1983–84; GOC Eastern District, 1984–87; Dir Gen., Army Orgn and TA, 1987–89; resigned from Army. Chm., Eagle Enterprises, 1991; Dir, John Menzies plc, 1990. Member, Queen's Body Guard for Scotland, Royal Company of Archers. *Recreations:* field sports, equitation, travel, motoring, aviation. *Address:* Bughtrig, Coldstream, Berwickshire TD12 4JP. *T:* Leitholm (089084) 221; Chesthill, Glenlyon, Perthshire. *T:* Glenlyon (08877) 224. *Clubs:* Boodle's, Cavalry and Guards, Farmers', Pratt's; New (Edinburgh).

RAMSAY, Donald Allan, ScD; FRS 1978, FRSC 1966; Principal Research Officer, National Research Council of Canada, 1968–87; *b* 11 July 1922; *s* of Norman Ramsay and Thirza Elizabeth Beckley; *m* 1946, Nancy Brayshaw; four *d. Educ:* Latymer Upper Sch.; St Catharine's Coll., Cambridge. BA 1943, MA 1947, PhD 1947, ScD 1976 (all Cantab). Research Scientist (Div. of Chemistry, 1947, Div. of Physics, 1949, Herzberg Inst. of Astrophysics, 1975), Nat. Research Council of Canada. Fellow, Amer. Phys. Soc., 1964; FCIC 1970; Vice-Pres., Acad. of Science, 1975–76; Hon. Treas., RSC, 1976–79, 1988–91, Centennial Medal, RSC, 1982. Dr *hc* Reims, 1969; Fil.Hed. Stockholm, 1982. Queen Elizabeth II Silver Jubilee Medal, 1977. *Publications:* numerous articles on molecular spectroscopy and molecular structure, espec. free radicals. *Recreations:* sailing, fishing, organ playing. *Address:* 1578 Drake Avenue, Ottawa, Ontario K1G 0L8, Canada. *T:* 613–733–8899. *Club:* Leander (Henley).

RAMSAY, Henry Thomas, CBE 1960; Director, Safety in Mines Research Establishment, Ministry of Technology (formerly Ministry of Power), Sheffield, 1954–70, retired; *b* 7 Dec. 1907; *s* of Henry Thomas and Florence Emily Ramsay, Gravesend, Kent; *m* 1953, Dora Gwenllian Burgoyne Davies (*d* 1979); one *s* one *d*; *m* 1983, Vivian Ducatel Prague, Bay St Louis, Miss. *Educ:* Gravesend Junior Techn. Sch.; thereafter by evening study. On scientific staff, Research Labs, GEC, 1928–48; RAE, 1948–54. Chartered engineer; FInstP; FIMinE; Pres., Midland Inst. Mining Engrs, 1970–71. *Publications:* contrib. to: Trans of Instn of Electrical Engrs; Jl of Inst. of Mining Engrs; other technical jls. *Recreations:* reading, walking.

RAMSAY, Prof. John Graham, FRS 1973; Professor of Geology, Eidgenössische Technische Hochschule and University of Zürich, since 1977; *b* 17 June 1931; *s* of Robert William Ramsay and Kathleen May Ramsay; *m* 1st, 1952, Sylvia Hiorns (marr. diss. 1957); 2nd, 1960, Christine Marden (marr. diss. 1987); three *d* (and one *d* decd); 3rd, 1990, Dorothee Dietrich. *Educ:* Edmonton County Grammar Sch.; Imperial Coll., London. DSc, PhD, DIC, BSc, ARCS, FGS. Musician, Corps of Royal Engineers, 1955–57; academic staff Imperial Coll., London, 1957–73: Prof. of Geology, 1966–73; Prof. of Earth Sciences, Leeds Univ., 1973–76. Mem., NERC, 1989–. Vice-Pres., Société Géologique de France, 1973. For. Associate, US Nat. Acad. of Scis, 1985. Dr *hc* Rennes, 1978. *Publications:* Folding and Fracturing of Rocks, 1967; The Techniques of Modern Structural Geology, 1983. *Recreations:* chamber music, mountaineering, ski-ing. *Address:* Eidgenössische Technische Hochschule Zürich, ETH Zentrum, CH 8092 Zürich, Switzerland.

RAMSAY, Norman James Gemmill; Sheriff of South Strathclyde, Dumfries and Galloway at Kirkcudbright, Stranraer and Dumfries (formerly Dumfries and Galloway, Western Division), 1971–85, now Hon. Sheriff; *b* 26 Aug. 1916; *s* of late James Ramsay and late Mrs Christina Emma Ramsay; *m* 1952, Rachael Mary Berkeley Cox, *d* of late Sir Herbert Charles Fahie Cox; two *s. Educ:* Merchiston Castle Sch.; Edinburgh Univ. (MA, LLB). Writer to the Signet, 1939; Advocate, Scotland, 1956. War Service, RN, 1940–46; Lt (S), RNVR. Colonial Legal Service, Northern Rhodesia: Administrator-General, 1947; Resident Magistrate, 1956; Sen. Resident Magistrate, 1958; Puisne Judge of High Court, Northern Rhodesia, later Zambia, 1964–68. Mem., Victoria Falls Trust, 1950–58. *Address:* Mill of Borgue, Kirkcudbright DG6 4SY.

RAMSAY, Patrick George Alexander; Controller, BBC Scotland, 1979–83; retired; *b* 14 April 1926; *yr s* of late Rt Rev. Ronald Erskine Ramsay, sometime Bishop of Malmesbury, and Winifred Constance Ramsay (*née* Partridge); *m* 1948, Hope Seymour Dorothy, *y d* of late Rt Rev. Algernon Markham, sometime Bishop of Grantham, and Winifred Edith Markham (*née* Barne); two *s. Educ:* Marlborough Coll.; Jesus Coll., Cambridge (MA). Served War, Royal Navy (Fleet Air Arm), 1944–46. Joined BBC as Report Writer, Eastern European Desk, Monitoring Service, 1949; Liaison Officer, US Foreign Broadcasts Information Service, Cyprus, 1951–52; Asst, Appts Dept, 1953–56; Sen. Admin. Asst, External Broadcasting, 1956–58; Admin. Officer News and Head of News Administration, 1958–64; Planning Manager, Television Programme Planning, 1964–66; Asst Controller: Programme Services, 1966–69; Programme Planning, 1969–72; Controller, Programme Services, 1972–79. General Managerial Advr, Oman Broadcasting Service, 1984–85. A Dir, Windsor Festival Soc., 1973–76. Councillor and Alderman, Royal Borough of New Windsor, 1962–67; Chm., Windsor and Eton Soc., 1971–76. FRSA. *Recreations:* fellwalking, gardening, foreign travel, history, looking in junk shops, thwarting bureaucrats. *Address:* Abcott Manor, Clungunford, Shropshire.

RAMSAY, Richard Alexander McGregor; Director, since 1988, Managing Director, Corporate Finance Division, since 1991, Barclays De Zoete Wedd Ltd; *b* 27 Dec. 1949; *s* of Alexander John McGregor Ramsay and Beatrice Kent Lanauze; *m* 1975, Elizabeth

Catherine Margaret Blackwood; one s one d. *Educ:* Dalhousie Sch.; Trinity Coll., Glenalmond; Aberdeen Univ. (MA Hons in Politics and Sociology). ACA 1975; FCA. Price Waterhouse & Co., 1972–75; Grindlay Brandts, 1976–78; Hill Samuel & Co. Ltd, 1979–87 (Dir, 1984–87); on secondment as Dir, Industrial Develt Unit, DTI, 1984–86. *Recreations:* hill walking, ski-ing, classic cars, gardening. *Address:* The Little Priory, Sandy Lane, South Nutfield, Surrey RH1 4EJ. *T:* Nutfield Ridge (0737) 822329.

RAMSAY, Thomas Anderson; retired; *b* 9 Feb. 1920; *s* of David Mitchell Ramsay and Ruth Bramfitt Ramsay; *m* 1949, Margaret Lilian Leggat Donald; one *s* two *d*. *Educ:* Glasgow Univ. BSc, MB, ChB. FRCSGlas; FFCM; FRSH; FRCP. Surg. Lieut, RNVR, 1945–47. Various posts in general and clinical hospital practice (mainly paediatric and orthopaedic surg.), 1943–56; Asst, later Dep. Sen. Admin. Med. Officer, NI Hospitals Authority, 1957–58; Dep. Sen., later Sen. Admin. Med. Officer, NE Metropolitan Reg. Hospital Bd, 1958–72; Post-Grad. Dean and Prof. of Post-Grad. Med., Univ. of Aberdeen, 1972–76; Dir of Post-Grad. Med. Educn, NE Region (Scotland), 1972–76; Regl Med. Officer, W Midlands RHA, 1976–79; Prof. of Post Graduate Med. Educn, Univ. of Warwick, 1980–83; Dir, Post Graduate Med. Educn, Coventry AHA, Warwicks Post Graduate Med. Centre, 1980–85. Vis. Prof. of Health Services Admin, London Sch. of Hygiene and Tropical Medicine, 1971–72; Vis. Prof., Health Services Admin., Univ. of Aston, 1979–. Mem. Bd, Faculty of Community Medicine, 1972–. Governor, London Hosp., 1965–72. *Publications:* several papers in learned jls regarding post-graduate medical educn and community medicine. *Recreations:* travel, photography. *Address:* 1 Vallum Close, Carlisle, Cumbria. *T:* Carlisle (0228) 33870.

RAMSAY, Sir Thomas (Meek), Kt 1972; CMG 1965; Chairman: The Kiwi International Company Ltd, Melbourne, 1967–80; joined The Kiwi Polish Co. Pty Ltd, Melbourne, 1926, Managing Director, 1956–72 (Joint Managing Director, 1945); *b* Essendon, Victoria, 24 Nov. 1907; *s* of late William Ramsay, Scotland; *m* 1941, Catherine Anne, *d* of John William Richardson, Adelaide, SA; four *s* one *d*. *Educ:* Malvern Grammar; Scotch Coll.; Melbourne Univ. (BSc). CMF, 1940–41 (Lieut); Asst Controller, Min. of Munitions, 1941–45. Chairman: Norwich Union Life Insurance Soc. (Aust. Bd) 1968–79; Collie (Aust.) Ltd Group, 1977–79; Industrial Design Council of Australia, 1969–76; ANZAC Fellowship Selection Cttee, 1971–78; Director: Australian Consolidated Industries Ltd Group, 1965–79; Alex Harvey Industries Group, NZ. President: Associated Chambers of Manufrs of Australia, 1962–63; Victorian Chamber of Manufrs, 1962–64; Mem., Selection Cttee (Industrial) Sir Winston Churchill Fellowships. FRHistS of Queensland, 1964; FRHistS of Victoria, 1965; FAIM; FSAScot; FBIM; Fellow, Mus. of Victoria (formerly Hon. Sen. Fellow). *Recreations:* gardening, Australian historical research. *Address:* 23 Airlie Street, South Yarra, Victoria 3141, Australia. *T:* 03 266 1751. *Clubs:* Athenæum, Australian, Melbourne (Melbourne).

RAMSAY-FAIRFAX-LUCY, Sir Edmund J. W. H. C.; *see* Fairfax-Lucy.

RAMSAY RAE, Air Vice-Marshal Ronald Arthur, CB 1960; OBE 1947; *b* 9 Oct. 1910; *s* of late George Ramsay Rae, Lindfield, NSW, and Alice Ramsay Rae (*née* Haselden); *m* 1939, Rosemary Gough Howell, *d* of late Charles Gough Howell, KC, Attorney General, Singapore; one *s* one *d*. *Educ:* Sydney, New South Wales, Australia. Served Australian Citizen Force and then as Cadet, RAAF, at Point Cook, 1930–31; transf. to RAF, 1932; flying duties in UK and Middle East with Nos 33 and 142 Sqdns until 1936; Advanced Armament Course; Armament officer in Far East, 1938–42; then Comdr RAF Tengah, Singapore; POW, 1943–45; Gp Captain in comd Central Gunnery Sch., Leconfield, Yorks, 1946; despatches, 1946. RAF Staff Coll., Andover, 1948; Dep. Dir Organisation (Estabt), Middle East; in comd RAF North Luffenham and then RAF Oakington (206 Advanced Flying Sch.); Commandant, Aircraft and Armament Exptl Estabt, Boscombe Down, 1955–57; Dep. Air Sec., Air Min., 1957–59; AOC No 224 Group, RAF, 1959–62, retd. Gen. Sec., NPFA, 1963–71. AFRAeS 1956. *Recreations:* cricket, golf, tennis, winter sports (Cresta Run and ski-ing; Pres., St Moritz Tobogganing Club, 1978–84). *Address:* Commonwealth Bank of Australia, 8 Old Jewry, EC2R 8ED; Little Wakestone, Bedham, Fittleworth, W Sussex. *Club:* Royal Air Force.

See also Hon. Sir Wallace A. R. Rae.

RAMSBOTHAM, family name of **Viscount Soulbury.**

RAMSBOTHAM, Gen. Sir David (John), KCB 1987; CBE 1980 (OBE 1974); Adjutant General, since 1990; Aide-de-Camp General to the Queen, since 1990; *b* 6 Nov. 1934; *s* of Rt Rev. J. A. Ramsbotham; *m* 1958, Susan Caroline (*née* Dickinson); two *s*. *Educ:* Haileybury Coll.; Corpus Christi Coll., Cambridge (BA 1957, MA 1973). Nat. Service, 1952–54; Rifle Bde, UK and BAOR, 1958–62; seconded to KAR, 1962–63; Staff Coll., 1964; Rifle Bde, Far East, 1965; Staff, 7 Armoured Bde, 1966–68; 3 and 2 Green Jackets (BAOR), 1968–71; MA to CGS (Lt-Col), 1971–73; CO, 2 RGJ, 1974–76; Staff, 4 Armd Div., BAOR, 1976–78; Comd, 39 Infantry Bde, 1978–80; RCDS, 1981; Dir of Public Relns (Army), 1982–84; Comdr, 3 Armd Div., 1984–87; Comdr, UK Field Army and Inspector Gen., TA, 1987–90. Col Comdt, 2nd Battalion, The Royal Green Jackets, 1987–. Hon. Col, Cambridge Univ. OTC, 1987–. *Recreations:* sailing, shooting, gardening. *Address:* c/o Lloyds Bank, Grey Street, Newcastle upon Tyne NE99 1SL. *Club:* MCC.

RAMSBOTHAM, Hon. Sir Peter (Edward), GCMG 1978 (KCMG 1972; CMG 1964); GCVO 1976; HM Diplomatic Service, retired; *b* 8 Oct. 1919; *yr s* of 1st Viscount Soulbury, PC, GCMG, GCVO, OBE, MC; *b* and *heir pres.* to 2nd Viscount Soulbury, *qv*; *m* 1st, 1941, Frances Blomfield (*d* 1982); two *s* one *d*; 2nd, 1985, Dr Zaida Hall, *widow* of Ruthven Hall. *Educ:* Eton College; Magdalen College, Oxford. HM Forces, 1943–46 (despatches; Croix de Guerre, 1945). Control Office for Germany and Austria from 1947; Regional Political Officer in Hamburg; entered Foreign Service, Oct. 1948; Political Division of Allied Control Commission, Berlin, Nov. 1948; transferred to Foreign Office, 1950; 1st Secretary, 1950; Head of Chancery, UK Delegation, New York, 1953; Foreign Office, 1957; Counsellor, 1961, Head of Western Organisations and Planning Dept; Head of Chancery, British Embassy, Paris, 1963–67; Foreign Office, 1967–69 (Sabbatical year, Inst. of Strategic Studies, 1968); High Comr, Nicosia, 1969–71; Ambassador to Iran, 1971–74; Ambassador to the United States, 1974–77; Governor and C-in-C of Bermuda, 1977–80. Director: Lloyds Bank, 1981–90; Lloyds Bank Internat., 1981–83; Southern Regl Bd, Lloyds Bank, 1981–90 (Chm., 1983–90); Commercial Union Assurance Co., 1981–90. Trustee, Leonard Cheshire Foundn, 1981–; Chm., Ryder-Cheshire Mission for the Relief of Suffering, 1982–; Governor, King's Sch., Canterbury, 1981–90. Hon. LLD: Akron Univ., 1975; Coll. of William and Mary, 1975; Maryland Univ., 1976; Yale Univ., 1977. KStJ 1976. *Recreations:* gardening, fishing. *Address:* East Lane, Ovington, near Alresford, Hants SO24 0RA. *T:* Alresford (0962) 2515. *Clubs:* Garrick; Metropolitan (Washington).

RAMSBURY, Area Bishop of, since 1989; **Rt. Rev. Peter St George Vaughan;** *b* 27 Nov. 1930; *s* of late Dr Victor St George Vaughan and Dorothy Marguerite Vaughan; *m* 1961, Elisabeth Fielding Parker; one *s* two *d*. *Educ:* Charterhouse; Selwyn Coll., Cambridge (MA Theology); Ridley Hall, Cambridge. Deacon 1957, priest 1958; Asst Curate, Birmingham Parish Church, 1957–62; Chaplain to Oxford Pastorate, 1963–67; Asst Chaplain, Brasenose Coll., Oxford, 1963–67; Vicar of Christ Church, Galle Face,

Colombo, 1967–72; Precentor of Holy Trinity Cathedral, Auckland, NZ, 1972–75; Principal of Crowther Hall, CMS Training Coll., Selly Oak Colleges, Birmingham, 1975–83; Archdeacon of Westmorland and Furness, 1983–89. Hon. Canon, Salisbury Cathedral, 1989–. Commisary for Bishop of Colombo. MA Oxon (By Incorporation). *Recreations:* gardening, reading, people. *Address:* Bishop's House, High Street, Urchfont, Devizes, Wilts SN10 4QH. *T:* Devizes (0380) 840373.

RAMSDEN, Prof. Herbert, MA, Dr en Filosofía y Letras; Professor of Spanish Language and Literature, University of Manchester, 1961–82, now Emeritus; *b* 20 April 1927; *s* of Herbert and Ann Ramsden; *m* 1953, Joyce Robina Hall, SRN, ONC, CMB; three *s* (incl. twin *s*) twin *d*. *Educ:* Sale Grammar Sch.; Univs of Manchester, Strasbourg, Madrid and Sorbonne. National Service, Inf. and Intell. Corps, 1949–51 (commnd). Travel, study and research abroad (Kemsley Travelling Fellow, etc), 1951–54; University of Manchester: Asst Lectr in Spanish, 1954–57; Lectr in Spanish, 1957–61; Pres., Philological Club, 1966–68. British Hispanists' rep., Nat. Council for Modern Languages, 1972–73; British rep., Asociación Europea de Profesores de Español, 1975–80. *Publications:* An Essential Course in Modern Spanish, 1959; Weak-Pronoun Position in the Early Romance Languages, 1963; (ed with critical study) Azorín, La ruta de Don Quijote, 1966; Angel Ganivet's Idearium español: A Critical Study, 1967; The Spanish Generation of 1898, 1974; The 1898 Movement in Spain, 1974; (ed with critical study) Lorca, Bodas de sangre, 1980; Pío Baroja: La busca, 1982; Pío Baroja: La busca 1903 to La busca 1904, 1982; (ed with critical study) Lorca, La casa de Bernarda Alba, 1983; Lorca's Romancero gitano, 1988; (ed, with critical study) Lorca, Romancero gitano, 1988; articles in Bulletin of Hispanic Studies, Modern Language Review, Modern Languages, etc. *Recreations:* family, hill-walking, foreign travel. *Address:* 7 Burford Avenue, Bramhall, Stockport, Cheshire SK7 1BL. *T:* 061–439 4306.

RAMSDEN, Rt. Hon. James Edward, PC 1963; Director: Prudential Assurance Co. Ltd, 1972–91 (Deputy Chairman, 1976–82); Prudential Corporation Ltd, 1979–91 (Deputy Chairman, 1979–82); *b* 1 Nov. 1923; *s* of late Capt. Edward Ramsden, MC, and Geraldine Ramsden, OBE, Breckamore Hall, Ripon; *m* 1949, Juliet Barbara Anna, *y d* of late Col Sir Charles Ponsonby, 1st Bt, TD, and Hon. Lady Ponsonby, *d* of 1st Baron Hunsdon; three *s* two *d*. *Educ:* Eton; Trinity College, Oxford (MA). Commnd KRRC, 1942; served North-West Europe with Rifle Brigade, 1944–45. MP (C) Harrogate, WR Yorks, March 1954–Feb. 1974; PPS to Home Secretary, Nov. 1959–Oct. 1960; Under-Sec. and Financial Sec., War Office, Oct. 1960–Oct. 1963; Sec. of State for War, 1963–64; Minister of Defence for the Army, April-Oct. 1964. Director: UK Board, Colonial Mutual Life Assurance Society, 1966–72; Standard Telephones and Cables, 1971–81. Chm., London Clinic, 1984– (Dir, 1973–). Mem., Historic Buildings Council for England, 1971–72. *Address:* Old Sleningford Hall, Ripon, North Yorks HG4 3JD. *T:* Ripon (0765) 85229. *Club:* Pratt's.

RAMSDEN, Sir John (Charles Josslyn), 9th Bt *cr* 1689, of Byrom, Yorks; HM Diplomatic Service; Counsellor and Deputy Head of Mission, Berlin, since 1991; *b* 19 Aug. 1950; *s* of Sir Caryl Oliver Imbert Ramsden, 8th Bt, CMG, CVO, and of Anne, *d* of Sir Charles Wickham, KCMG, KBE, DSO; *S* father, 1987; *m* 1985, (Jennifer) Jane Bevan; two *d*. *Educ:* Eton; Trinity Coll., Cambridge (MA). With merchant bank, Dawnay, Day & Co. Ltd, 1972–74. Entered FCO, 1975; 2nd Sec., Dakar, 1976; 1st Sec., MBFR, Vienna, 1978; 1st Sec., Head of Chancery and Consul, Hanoi, 1980; FCO, 1982–90; Counsellor, E Berlin, 1990. *Address:* c/o Foreign and Commonwealth Office, King Charles Street, SW1.

RAMSDEN, (John) Michael; Editor of Publications, Royal Aeronautical Society, since 1989; *b* 2 Oct. 1928; *s* of John Leonard Ramsden and Edith Alexandra Ramsden; *m* 1953, Angela Mary Mortimer; one *s* one *d*. *Educ:* Bedford Sch.; de Havilland Aeronautical Tech. Sch. CEng, FRAeS. With de Havilland Aircraft Co. Ltd, 1946–55; Flight, 1955–89: Air Transport Editor, 1961–64; Editor, 1964–81; Editor-in-Chief, Flight International, 1981–89. Chm., Press and Broadcasting Side, Defence Press and Broadcasting Cttee, 1983–89. Dir, de Havilland Aircraft Mus., 1970–. Queen's Silver Jubilee Medal, 1977. *Publications:* The Safe Airline, 1976, 2nd edn 1978; Caring for the Mature Jet, 1981. *Recreations:* light-aircraft flying, water-colour painting. *Club:* London School of Flying (Elstree).

RAMSDEN, Michael; *see* Ramsden, J. M.

RAMSDEN, Sally, OBE 1981; Director, North East Broadcasting Co. Ltd (Metro Radio), 1973–81; *d* of John Parkin and Hannah Bentley; *m* 1948, Allan Ramsden. *Educ:* Ryhope Grammar Sch.; Neville's Cross Coll., Durham (Teaching Diploma). Teacher, 1930–47; Headmistress, 1947–69; Asst. Group Officer (part time), Nat. Fire Service, 1941–45; Hon. Organiser, Citizens' Advice Bureau, 1971–73; Pres., UK Fedn of Business and Professional Women, 1972–75 (Hon. Mem., NE Div., 1988–); Member: Women's Nat. Commn, 1972–75; Women's Internat. Year Cttee, 1974–75; VAT Tribunals, 1973–84; Royal Commn on Legal Services, 1976–79; Durham Posts and Telecom Adv. Cttee, 1980–. *Recreations:* fly fishing, gardening, reading. *Address:* 1 Westcott Drive, Durham Moor, Durham City DH1 5AG. *T:* Durham (091) 3842989.

RAMSEY, Sir Alfred (Ernest), Kt 1967; *b* Dagenham, 1920; *m* 1951, Victoria Phyllis Answorth, *d* of William Welch. *Educ:* Becontree Heath School. Started playing for Southampton and was an International with them; transferred to Tottenham Hotspur, 1949; with Spurs (right back), 1949–51; they won the 2nd and 1st Division titles in successive seasons. Manager of Ipswich Town Football Club, which rose from 3rd Division to Championship of the League, 1955–63; Manager, FA World Cup Team, 1963–74. Played 31 times for England. *Address:* 41 Valley Road, Ipswich, Suffolk IP1 4EE.

RAMSEY, Basil Albert Rowland; Editor, The Musical Times, since 1990; *b* 26 April 1929; *s* of Florence Lily Ramsey (*née* Childs) and Alfred John Rowland Ramsey; *m* 1953, Violet Mary Simpson; one *s* two *d*. *Educ:* State schools. ARCO. Novello & Co.: Music Editor, 1949; Head of Publishing, 1963; established own publishing Co., 1976; Serious Music Publishing Consultant, Filmtrax plc, 1987–90. Editor: Organists' Review, 1972–84; Music & Musicians, 1989–90. *Publications:* articles and reviews in Musical Times, 1955–. *Recreations:* walking, reading, calligraphy. *Address:* 604 Rayleigh Road, Eastwood, Leigh-on-Sea, Essex SS9 5HU. *T:* Southend-on-Sea (0702) 524305.

RAMSEY, Brig. Gael Kathleen, MBE 1976; Director, Women's Royal Army Corps, since 1989; *b* 8 June 1942; *d* of William and Kathleen Hammond; *m* 1977, Col Michael Gordon Ramsey; two step *d*. *Educ:* 16 schools world wide. Commissioned, WRAC, 1968; ADC to the Queen, 1989. *Recreations:* domestic pursuits, reading, cycling. *Address:* c/o Barclays Bank, 139/142 North Street, Brighton BN1 1RU. *Club:* Queen's.

RAMSEY, Prof. Norman Foster; Higgins Professor of Physics, Harvard University, since 1947; Senior Fellow, Harvard Society of Fellows, since 1971; *b* 27 Aug. 1915; *s* of Brig.-Gen. and Mrs Norman F. Ramsey; *m* 1940, Elinor Stedman Jameson (*d* 1983); four *d*; *m* 1985, Ellie A. Welch. *Educ:* Columbia Univ.; Cambridge Univ. (England). Carnegie Fellow, Carnegie Instn of Washington, 1939–40; Assoc., Univ. of Ill, 1940–42; Asst Prof., Columbia Univ., 1942–45; Research Assoc., MIT Radiation Laboratory, 1940–43; Cons.

to Nat. Defense Research Cttee, 1940–45; Expert Consultant to Sec. of War, 1942–45; Grp Leader and Assoc. Div. Head, Los Alamos Lab. of Atomic Energy Project, 1943–45; Chief Scientist of Atomic Energy Lab. at Tinian, 1945; Assoc. Prof., Columbia Univ., 1945–47; Head of Physics Dept, Brookhaven Nat. Lab., 1946–47; Assoc. Prof., Harvard Univ., 1947–50; John Simon Guggenheim Fell., Oxford Univ., 1953–54; George Eastman Vis. Prof., Oxford Univ., 1973–74; Luce Prof. of Cosmology, Mt Holyoke, 1982–83; Prof., Univ. of Virginia, 1983–84. Dir Harvard Nuclear Lab., 1948–50, 1952; Chm., Harvard Nuclear Physics Cttee, 1948–60; Science Adviser, NATO, 1958–59; Fell. Amer. Phys. Soc. and Amer. Acad. of Arts and Sciences; Nat. Acad. of Sciences; Amer. Philos. Soc.; Foreign Associate, French Acad. of Science; Sigma Xi; Phi Beta Kappa; Amer. Assoc. for Advancement of Science, 1940– (Chm., Phys. Sect., 1976). Bd of Directors, Varian Associates, 1964–66; Bd of Trustees: Associated Univs; Brookhaven Nat. Lab., 1952–55; Carnegie Endowment for Internat. Peace; Univ. Research Assoc. (Pres., 1966–81, Pres. Emeritus 1981–); Rockefeller Univ., 1976–; Air Force Sci. Adv. Bd, 1948–54; Dept of Defense Panel on Atomic Energy, 1953–59; Bd of Editors of Review of Modern Physics, 1953–56; Chm. Exec. Cttee for Camb. Electron Accelerator, 1956–63; Coun. Amer. Phys. Soc., 1956–60 (Vice-Pres., 1977; Pres., 1978); Chm., Bd of Governors, Amer. Inst. of Physics, 1980–86. Gen. Adv. Cttee, Atomic Energy Commn, 1960–72. Chm., High Energy Accelerator Panel of President's Sci. Adv. Cttee and AEC, 1963. Chm. Bd, Physics and Astronomy Nat. Res. Council, 1986–89. Pres., Phi Beta Kappa, 1985 (Vice-Pres., 1982). Presidential Certificate of Merit, 1947; E. O. Lawrence Award, 1960; Davisson-Germer Prize, 1974; Award for Excellence, Columbia Univ. Graduate Alumni, 1980; Medal of Honor, IEEE, 1984; Rabi Prize, Frequency Control Symposium, IEEE, 1985; Monie Ferst Prize, Sigma Xi, 1985; Compton Award, Amer. Inst. of Physics, 1985; Rumford Premium, Amer. Acad. of Arts and Scis, 1985; Oersted Medal, Amer. Assoc. of Physics Teachers, 1988; Nat. Medal of Science, 1988; (jtly) Nobel Prize for Physics, 1989. Hon. MA Harvard, 1947; Hon. ScD Cambridge, 1953; Hon. DSc: Case Western Reserve, 1968; Middlebury Coll., 1969; Oxford, 1973; Rockefeller Univ., 1986; Chicago, 1989; Hon. DCL Oxford, 1990. *Publications:* Experimental Nuclear Physics, 1952; Nuclear Moments, 1953; Molecular Beams, 1956; Quick Calculus, 1965; and numerous articles in Physical Review and other scientific jls. *Recreations:* tennis, ski-ing, walking, sailing, etc. *Address:* 21 Monmouth Court, Brookline, Mass 02146, USA. *T:* 617–277–2313.

RAMSEY, Waldo Emerson W.; *see* Waldron-Ramsey.

RANASINGHE, Hon. K. A. Parinda; Hon. Mr Justice Ranasinghe; Chief Justice of Sri Lanka, since 1988; *b* 20 Aug. 1926; *s* of Solomon Ranasinghe and Somawathie Ranasinghe; *m* 1956, Chitra; one *s* three *d.* *Educ:* Royal Coll., Colombo. Advocate of the Supreme Court; appointed Magistrate, 1958; District Judge, 1966–74; High Court Judge, 1974–78; Judge, Court of Appeal, 1978–82, Pres. 1982; Judge, Supreme Court, 1982–88. *Recreation:* walking. *Address:* 306 Galle Road, Colombo 4, Sri Lanka. *T:* Colombo 581309.

RANCE, Gerald Francis, OBE 1985 (MBE 1968); HM Diplomatic Service, retired; *b* 20 Feb. 1927; *s* of Cecil Henry and Jane Carmel Rance; *m* 1949, Dorothy (*née* Keegan); one *d.* *Educ:* Brompton Oratory. HM Forces (RCMP), 1945–48; joined Foreign Service, 1948; Foreign Office, 1948–51; served Belgrade, Rome, Bucharest, Istanbul, Munich, Kabul, New York and Dallas; Inspectorate, FCO, 1973–77; Head of Chancery, Mbabane, 1977–79; First Sec. (Comm.), Nicosia, 1980–83; High Comr to Tonga, 1984–87. *Recreations:* golf, tennis, reading. *Address:* 1 Bruton Close, Chislehurst, Kent. *Clubs:* Commonwealth Trust; Chislehurst Golf.

RANCHHODLAL, Sir Chinubhai Madhowlal, 3rd Bt *cr* 1913, of Shahpur, Ahmedabad, India; *b* 25 July 1929; *s* of 2nd Bt and Tanumati (*d* 1970), *d* of Javerilal Mehta; *S* father, 1990; grandfather, 1st Bt, was only member of Hindu Community to receive a baronetcy; *m* 1953, Muneera Khodad Fozdar; one *s* three *d.* Arjuna Award, 1972. *Heir:* *s* Prashant Ranchhodlal [*b* 15 Dec. 1955; *m* 1977, Swati Hrishikesh Mehta; three *d*]. *Address:* Shantikunj, Shahibaug, Ahmedabad-380004, India. *T:* 387531. *Clubs:* Willingdon, Cricket Club of India (Bombay).

RANDALL, Col Charles Richard, OBE 1969; TD 1947; Vice Lord-Lieutenant for the County of Bedfordshire, since 1978; *b* 21 Jan. 1920; *s* of Charles Randall and Elizabeth Brierley; *m* 1945, Peggy Dennis; one *s* one *d.* *Educ:* Bedford Sch. Served War, 1939–45: commissioned Bedfordshire Yeomanry, 1939. High Sheriff, Bedfordshire, 1974–75. *Recreations:* shooting, fishing, gardening. *Address:* The Rookery, Aspley Guise, Milton Keynes MK17 8HP. *T:* Milton Keynes (0908) 582188. *Clubs:* Naval and Military, MCC.

RANDALL, Rev. Edmund Laurence, AM 1980; Warden, St Barnabas' Theological College, 1964–85, retired; Scholar in Residence, Diocese of Wangaratta, since 1986; *b* 2 June 1920; *s* of Robert Leonard Randall and Grace Annie Randall (*née* Young); unmarried. *Educ:* Dulwich College; Corpus Christi College, Cambridge. BA 1941. MA 1947. Served War, 1940–45, with Royal Artillery (AA). Corpus Christi Coll., 1938–40 and 1945–47. Wells Theological College, 1947–49. Deacon, 1949; Priest, 1950. Assistant Curate at St Luke's, Bournemouth, 1949–52; Fellow of Selwyn College, Cambridge, 1952–57; Chaplain, 1953–57; Residentiary Canon of Ely and Principal of Ely Theological Coll., 1957–59; Chaplain, St Francis Theological Coll., Brisbane, 1960–64; Hon. Canon of Adelaide, 1979–86, of Wangaratta, 1989–. Vis Lectr, St Barnabas' Theol Coll., and Lectr in Theology, Flinders Univ. of SA, Feb–July 1990. *Recreations:* travel, motoring, *Address:* 44 Mackay Street, Wangaratta, Vic 3677, Australia. *T:* 057 219007.

RANDALL, Stuart; MP (Lab) Kingston upon Hull West, since 1983; *b* 22 June 1938; *m* 1963, Gillian Michael; three *d.* *Educ:* University Coll., Cardiff (BSc Elect. Engrg). English Electric Computers and Radio Corp. of America, USA, 1963–66; Marconi Automation, 1966–68; Inter-Bank Res. Orgn, 1968–71; BSC, 1971–76; BL, 1976–80; Nexos Office Systems, 1980–81; Plessey Communications Systems, 1981–83. PPS to Shadow Chancellor of the Exchequer, 1984–85; Opposition front bench spokesman on Agricl, Food and Fisheries Affairs, 1985–87, on home affairs, 1987–. *Recreation:* sailing. *Address:* House of Commons, SW1A 0AA. *T:* 071–219 3000.

RANDALL, William Edward, CBE 1978; DFC 1944; AFC 1945; Chairman, Chubb & Son Ltd, 1981–84 (Managing Director, 1971–81, Deputy Chairman, 1976–81); *b* 15 Dec. 1920; *s* of William George Randall and Jane Longdon (*née* Pannell); *m* 1st, 1943, Joan Dorothea Way; two *s* one *d*; 2nd, 1975, Iris Joyce Roads. *Educ:* Tollington Sch., London. FRSA. Served RAF, Flt Lieut, 1941–46. Commercial Union Assce Co., 1946–50; Chubb & Sons Lock and Safe Co., 1950, Man. Dir, 1965; Dir, Chubb & Son Ltd, 1965; Dir, Metal Closures Gp, 1976–86. Member: Home Office Standing Cttee on Crime Prevention, 1967–85; Exec. Cttee, British Digestive Foundn, 1982–86; Chairman: Council, British Security Industry Assoc., 1981–85; Airport Export Gp, NEDO, 1983. *Recreations:* reading, playing bridge. *Address:* Flat 8, Woodhouse, 10 The Avenue, Branksome Park, Poole, Dorset.

RANDELL, Peter Neil; Head of Finance and Administration, Institute of Metals, 1984–89; *b* 18 Nov. 1933; *s* of Donald Randell and Dorothy (*née* Anthonisz); *m* 1962, Anne Loraine Mudie; one *s* one *d.* *Educ:* Bradfield Coll.; Wye Coll., Univ. of London (BSc (Agric) Hons). FCIS. Farming and other employments, Rhodesia, 1955–61; Asst to Sec., British Insulated Callenders Cables Ltd, 1962–65; Asst Sec., NRDC, 1965–73, Sec. 1973–83, Board Member 1980–81; Sec. Admin and Personnel, British Technology Gp (NRDC and NEB), 1981–83. *Recreations:* the outdoors, reading. *Address:* Wood Dene, Golf Club Road, Hook Heath, Woking, Surrey. *T:* Woking (0483) 763824.

RANDLE, Prof. Sir Philip (John), Kt 1985; MD, FRCP; FRS 1983; Professor of Clinical Biochemistry, University of Oxford, since 1975; Fellow of Hertford College, Oxford, since 1975; *b* 16 July 1926; *s* of Alfred John and Nora Anne Randle; *m* 1952, Elizabeth Ann Harrison; three *d* (one *s* decd). *Educ:* King Edward VI Grammar Sch., Nuneaton; Sidney Sussex Coll., Cambridge (MA, PhD, MD); UCH, London (Fellow, UCL, 1990). Med. and Surg. Officer, UCH, 1951; Res. Fellow in Biochem., Cambridge, 1952–55; Univ. Lectr, Biochem., Cambridge, 1955–64; Fellow of Trinity Hall and Dir of Med. Studies, 1957–64 (Hon. Fellow, Trinity Hall, 1988); Prof. of Biochem., Univ. of Bristol, 1964–75. Member: Board of Governors, United Cambridge Hospitals, 1960–64; Clinical Endocrinology Cttee, MRC, 1957–64; Chm., Grants Cttee, MRC, 1975–77; Pres., European Assoc. for Study of Diabetes, 1977–80; Chairman, Research Committee: British Diabetic Assoc., 1971–78; British Heart Foundn, 1987–. DHSS: Mem. Cttee on Med. Aspects Food Policy, 1981–89; Chm., COMA Panel on Diet and Cardiovascular Disease, 1981–84; Consultant Adviser in Biochemistry to CMO, 1981–89. Member: General Medical Council, 1967–75; Gen. Dental Council, 1971–75; Council, Royal Soc., 1987–89 (Vice Pres., 1988–89). Lectures: Banting, British Diabetic Assoc., 1965; Minkowski, European Assoc. for Study of Diabetes, 1966; Copp, La Jolla, 1972; Humphry Davy Rolleston, RCP, 1983; Ciba Medal and Lectr, Biochem. Soc., 1984. Corresp. Mem. of many foreign medical and scientific bodies. *Publications:* numerous contribs to books and med. sci. jls on diabetes mellitus, control of metabolism and related topics. *Recreations:* travel, swimming, bricklaying. *Address:* John Radcliffe Hospital, Headington, Oxford OX3 9DU; 11 Fitzherbert Close, Iffley, Oxford OX4 4EN.

RANDOLPH, Denys, BSc; CEng, MRAeS, FIProdE, FInstD, CBIM; Chairman: Woodrush Investments Ltd, since 1980; Poitires Eyots Ltd, since 1972; *b* 6 Feb. 1926; *s* of late Harry Beckham Randolph and Margaret Isabel Randolph; *m* 1951, Marjorie Hales; two *d.* *Educ:* St Paul's School: Queen's Univ., Belfast (BSc). Served Royal Engineers, 1944–48 (Captain). Queen's Univ., Belfast, 1948–52; post-grad. apprenticeship, Short Bros & Harland, 1952–55; Wilkinson Sword Ltd: Prod. Engr/Prod. Dir, Graviner Div., 1955–66; Man. Dir, Hand Tools Div., 1966–69; Chm., Graviner Div., 1969–79; Chm., 1972–79; Pres., 1980–85; Wilkinson Match Ltd: Dir, 1974–80; Chm., 1976–79. Institute of Directors: Chm., 1976–79; Vice-Pres., 1979–. Past Master: Worshipful Co. of Scientific Instrument Makers, 1977; Cutlers' Co., 1986. Mem. Council, Brunel Univ., 1986–91; Governor, Henley Admin. Staff Coll., 1979–91. FRSA (Manufactures and Commerce). *Publication:* From Rapiers to Razor Blades—The Development of the Light Metals Industry (paper, RSA). *Recreations:* yachting, golf, viticulture. *Address:* Clapcot House, Rush Court, Wallingford OX10 8LJ. *T:* Wallingford (0491) 36586. *Clubs:* Army and Navy, Royal Automobile, City Livery, Little Ship.

RANDOLPH, His Honour John Hugh Edward; a Circuit Judge, 1972–87; *b* 14 Oct. 1913; *s* of late Charles Edward Randolph and Phyllis Randolph; *m* 1959, Anna Marjorie (*née* Thomson). *Educ:* Bradford Grammar Sch.; Leeds University. RAF, 1940–46. Called to Bar, Middle Temple, 1946; practised on NE Circuit until 1965; Stipendiary Magistrate of Leeds, 1965–71. Deputy Chairman: E Riding QS, 1958–63; W Riding QS, 1963–71. *Recreation:* golf. *Address:* Crown Court, Leeds. *Club:* Leeds (Leeds).

RANDOLPH, Rev. Michael Richard Spencer; Local Non-Stipendiary Minister, Biddenden and Smarden, since 1990; Editor-in-Chief, Reader's Digest (British Edition), 1957–88; *b* 2 Jan. 1925; *s* of late Leslie Richard Randolph and late Gladys (*née* Keen); *m* 1952, Jenefer Scawen Blunt; two *s* two *d.* *Educ:* Merchant Taylors' Sch.; New Rochelle High Sch., NY, USA; Queen's Coll., Oxford; Canterbury Sch. of Ministry. Served RNVR, Intell. Staff Eastern Fleet, 1944–46, Sub-Lieut. Editorial staff, Amalgamated Press, 1948–52; Odham's Press, 1952–56; Reader's Digest, 1956–88. Press Mem., Press Council, 1975–88; Chm., Soc. of Magazine Editors, 1973. Ordained deacon, 1990. Pres., Weald of Kent Preservation Soc., 1988–. Mem. Smarden Parish Council, 1987–. FRSA 1962. *Recreation:* grandparenthood. *Address:* Little Smarden House, Smarden, Kent TN27 8NB. *Club:* Savile.

RANELAGH, John O'B.; *see* O'Beirne Ranelagh.

RANFURLY, 7th Earl of, *cr* 1831 (Ire.); **Gerald François Needham Knox;** Baron Welles 1781; Viscount Northland 1791; Baron Ranfurly (UK) 1826; Chairman, Brewin Dolphin & Co. Ltd, since 1987; *b* 4 Jan. 1929; *s* of Captain John Needham Knox, RN (*d* 1967) (*g g g s* of 1st Earl) and Monica B. H. (*d* 1975), *d* of Maj.-Gen. Sir Gerald Kitson, KCVO, CB, CMG; *S* cousin, 1988; *m* 1955, Rosemary, *o d* of Air Vice-Marshal Felton Vesey Holt, CMG, DSO; two *s* two *d.* *Educ:* Wellington College. Served RN, 1947–60; retired as Lieut Comdr. Member of Stock Exchange, 1964; Partner in Brewin & Co., 1965; Senior Partner, Brewin Dolphin & Co., 1982. *Recreation:* foxhunting. *Heir:* *s* Edward John Knox, *b* 21 May 1957. *Address:* Maltings Chase, Nayland, Colchester, Essex.

RANG, Prof. Humphrey Peter, DPhil; FRS 1980; Director, Sandoz Institute for Medical Research, University College London, since 1983; *b* 13 June 1936; *s* of Charles Rang and Sybil Rang; *m* 1960, Elizabeth Harvey Clapham; one *s* three *d.* *Educ:* University Coll. Sch.; University Coll. London (MSc 1960); UCH Med. Sch. (MB, BS 1961); Balliol Coll., Oxford (DPhil 1965). J. H. Burn Res. Fellow, Dept of Pharmacol., Oxford, 1961–65; Vis. Res. Associate, Albert Einstein Coll. of Medicine, NY, 1966–67; Univ. Lectr in Pharmacol., Oxford, 1966–72; Fellow and Tutor in Physiol., Lincoln Coll., Oxford, 1967–72; Prof. of Pharmacology: Univ. of Southampton, 1972–74; St George's Hosp. Med. Sch., London, 1974–79; Prof. of Pharmacol., 1979–83, Fellow and Vis. Prof., 1983–, UCL. *Publications:* Drug Receptors, 1973; Pharmacology, 1987. *Recreations:* sailing, music. *Address:* 1 Belvedere Drive, SW19 7BX. *T:* 081–947 7603.

RANGER, Sir Douglas, Kt 1978; FRCS; Otolaryngologist, The Middlesex Hospital, 1950–82; Dean, The Middlesex Hospital Medical School, 1974–83; Hon. Civil Consultant in Otolaryngology, RAF, since 1983; *b* 5 Oct. 1916; *s* of William and Hatton Thomasina Ranger; *m* 1943, Betty, *d* of Captain Sydney Harold Draper and Elsie Draper; two *s.* *Educ:* Church of England Grammar Sch., Brisbane; The Middlesex Hosp. Med. Sch. MB BS 1941, FRCS 1943. Surgical Registrar, The Mddx Hosp., 1942–44. Served War, Temp. Maj. RAMC and Surgical Specialist, 1945–48 (SEAC and MELF). Otolaryngologist, Mount Vernon Hosp., 1958–74; Hon. Sec., Brit. Assoc. of Otolaryngologists, 1965–71. RCS: Mem. Court of Examiners, 1966–72; Mem. Council, 1967–72; Pres., Assoc. of Head and Neck Oncologists of GB, 1974–77. Civil Consultant in Otolaryngology, RAF, 1965–83. Dir, Ferens Inst. of Otolaryngology, 1965–83; Cons. Adviser in Otolaryngology, DHSS, 1971–82. *Publications:* The Middlesex Hospital Medical School, Centenary to Sesquicentenary, 1985; papers and lectures on otolaryngological subjects, esp. with ref. to malignant disease. *Address:* The Tile House, The Street, Chipperfield, King's Langley, Herts WD4 9BH. *T:* King's Langley (0923) 268910.

RANGER, Prof. Terence Osborn, DPhil; FBA 1988; Rhodes Professor of Race Relations, and Fellow of St Antony's College, University of Oxford, since 1987; *b* 29 Nov. 1929; *s* of Leslie and Anna Ranger; *m* 1954, Shelagh Campbell Clark; three *d. Educ:* Highgate Sch.; Univ. of Oxford (BA, MA; DPhil 1960). Lecturer: RNC, Dartmouth, 1955–56; Coll. of Rhodesia and Nyasaland, 1957–63; Prof. of History, Univ. of Dar es Salaam, 1963–69; Prof. of African History, Univ. of Calif, LA, 1969–74; Prof. of Modern History, Univ. of Manchester, 1974–87; Chm., Oxford Univ. Cttee on African Studies, 1987–. Chm., Jl of Southern African Studies, 1976–; Vice-Chm., Past and Present, 1987–. *Publications:* Revolt in Southern Rhodesia 1896–7, 1967; The African Voice in Southern Rhodesia 1898–1930, 1970; Dance and Society in Eastern Africa, 1975; Peasant Consciousness and Guerrilla War in Zimbabwe, 1985. *Recreations:* theatre, opera, walking. *Address:* St Antony's College, Oxford OX2 6JF. *Club:* Commonwealth Trust.

RANK, Sir Benjamin (Keith), Kt 1972; CMG 1955; MS, FRCS; FRACS; FACS; Consulting Plastic Surgeon, Royal Melbourne Hospital, Repatriation Department, Victoria Eye and Ear Hospital; *b* 14 Jan. 1911; *s* of Wreghitt Rank and Bessie Rank (*née* Smith); *m* 1938, Barbara Lyle Facy; one *s* three *d. Educ:* Scotch College, Melbourne; Ormond College, University of Melbourne. MB, BS Melbourne, 1934; Resident Medical Officer, Royal Melbourne Hospital, 1935–36; MS (Melb.), 1937; MRCS, LRCP 1938; Resident Surgical Officer, London County Council, 1938–39 (St James' Hospital, Balham); FRCS 1938; Assistant Plastic Surgeon (EMS) at Hill End (Bart's), 1939–40; AAMC, 1940–45; Officer i/c AIF Plastic Surgery Unit in Egypt, and later at Heidelberg Military Hospital, Victoria, Australia (Lt-Col); Hon. Plastic Surgeon, Royal Melbourne Hosp., 1946–66. Carnegie Fellow, 1947. Member: Dental Board of Victoria 1949–73, Joske Orator 1974; BMA State Council, 1950–60; Chm. Exec. Cttee, RACS (Pres., 1966–68); Chm., Cttee of Management, Victorian Plastic Surgery Unit (Preston Hosp.), 1966–85; Member: Bd of Management, Royal Melbourne Hosp., 1976–82 (Vice-Pres., 1979–82); Motor Accident Bd, Victoria, 1972–82. Chm., Consult. Council on Casualty Services, Victoria Health Council; Pres., St John's Ambulance Council, Victoria, 1983–88 (Chm. 1978–83). Sir Arthur Sims Commonwealth Travelling Prof., RCS, 1958; Moynihan Lectr, 1972; Vis. Prof., Harvard Med. Sch., 1976. Syme Orator, RACS, 1976; Stawell Orator, 1977. 87th Mem., James IV Assoc. of Surgeons; Pres., British Assoc. of Plastic Surgeons, 1965. Pres., 5th Internat. Congress of Plastic Surgery, Melbourne, 1971. FRACS 1943; Hon. FACST 1952; Hon. FRCS Canada; Hon. FRCSE 1973; Hon. FACS. Hon. DSc Punjabi Univ., 1970; Hon. Member: Société Française de Chirurgie Plastique; Indian Association of Surgeons. KStJ 1988 (CStJ 1982). *Publications:* (jointly) Surgery of Repair as applied to Hand Injuries, 1953; Jerry Moore, 1975; Head and Hands, 1987; papers in British, American and Australian Surgical Jls. *Recreations:* golf, gardening, painting. *Address:* 12 Jerula Avenue, Mount Eliza, Victoria 3930, Australia. *Clubs:* Melbourne (Melbourne); Peninsula Golf.

RANK, Joseph McArthur; President, Ranks Hovis McDougall Ltd, since 1981; *b* 24 April 1918; *s* of late Rowland Rank and of Margaret McArthur; *m* 1946, Hon. Moira (who *m* 1940, Peter Anthony Stanley Woodwark, killed in action, 1943; one *d*), *d* of 3rd Baron Southborough; one *s* one *d. Educ:* Loretto. Joined Mark Mayhew Ltd, 1936. Served RAF, 1940–46. Personal Pilot to Air C-in-C, SEAC, 1945; Jt Man. Dir, Joseph Rank Ltd, 1955–65; Dep. Chm. and Chief Exec., Ranks Hovis McDougall Ltd, 1965–69, Chm., 1969–81. Pres., Nat. Assoc. of British and Irish Millers, 1957–58, Centenary Pres., 1978. Chm., Millers Mutual Assoc., 1969–; Chm. Council, British Nutrition Foundation, 1968–69; Dir, Royal Alexandra and Albert Sch., 1952–, Chm., Governing Body, 1975–84; Friend of the Royal Coll. of Physicians, 1967–; Council, Royal Warrant Holders Assoc., 1968–71. Mem., Shrievalty Assoc., 1974. First High Sheriff of East Sussex, 1974. Hon. FRCP, 1978. *Recreations:* boating, travelling. *Address:* Landhurst, Hartfield, East Sussex. *T:* Hartfield (089277) 293. *Clubs:* Royal Air Force; Sussex.

RANKEILLOUR, 4th Baron *cr* 1932, of Buxted; **Peter St Thomas More Henry Hope;** farmer and landowner; *b* 29 May 1935; *s* of 3rd Baron Rankeillour and Mary Sibyl, *d* of late Col Wilfrid Ricardo, DSO; *S* father, 1967; unmarried. *Educ:* Ampleforth College; privately. *Recreations:* shooting, architecture, large-scale landscaping; agricultural equipment inventor. *Heir: cousin* Michael Richard Hope [*b* 21 Oct. 1940; *m* 1964, Elizabeth Rosemary, *e d* of Col F. H. Fuller; one *s* two *d*]. *Address:* Achaderry House, Roy Bridge, West Inverness-shire. *T:* Spean Bridge (039781) 206.

RANKIN, Alick Michael, CBE 1987; Chairman, Scottish & Newcastle plc (formerly Scottish & Newcastle Breweries), since 1989 (Chief Executive, 1983–91); *b* 23 Jan. 1935; *s* of late Lt-Col (Arthur) Niall (Talbot) Rankin, FRPS, FRGS and of Lady Jean Rankin, *qv*; *m* 1st, 1958, Susan Margaret Dewhurst (marr. diss. 1976); one *s* three *d*: 2nd, 1976, Suzetta Barber (*née* Nelson). *Educ:* Ludgrove; Eton College. Scots Guards, 1954–56. Wood Gundy & Co., Investment Dealers, Toronto, 1956–59; Scottish & Newcastle Breweries: joined, 1960; Dir, Retail, Scottish Brewers, 1965–69; Chm. and Man. Dir, Waverley Vintners, 1969–76; Director, 1974; Marketing Dir, 1977–82; Chm., Scottish Brewers, 1982–83; Dep. Chm., 1987–89. Non-Executive Director: Christian Salvesen, 1986–; Edinburgh's Capital Ltd, 1986–; Bank of Scotland plc, 1987–; High Gosforth Park plc, 1988–. Chm., The Brewers' Soc., 1989–90. *Recreations:* fishing, shooting, golf, tennis, ornithology, oenology. *Address:* 3 Saxe-Coburg Place, Edinburgh EH3 5BR. *T:* 031–332 3684; 49 Pont Street, SW1X 0BD. *T:* 071–581 1086. *Clubs:* Boodle's; New (Edinburgh); Hon. Co. of Edinburgh Golfers (Muirfield), Royal and Ancient Golf (St Andrews); I Zingari, Eton Ramblers Cricket.
See also Sir I. N. Rankin, Bt.

RANKIN, Andrew, QC 1968; a Recorder of the Crown Court, since 1972; *b* 3 Aug. 1924; *s* of William Locke Rankin and Mary Ann McArdle, Edinburgh; *m* 1st, 1944, Winifred (marr. diss. 1963), *d* of Frank McAdam, Edinburgh; two *s* two *d* (and one *s* decd); 2nd, 1964, Veronica (*d* 1990), *d* of George Aloysius Martin, Liverpool; 3rd, 1991, Jenifer Margaret, *d* of Alfred George Hodges Bebington, Wirral. *Educ:* Royal High Sch., Edinburgh; Univ. of Edinburgh; Downing Coll., Cambridge. Served War of 1939–45: Sub-Lt, RNVR, 1943. BL (Edin.) 1946; BA, 1st cl. hons Law Tripos (Cantab), 1948. Royal Commonwealth Soc. Medal, 1942; Cecil Peace Prize, 1946; Lord Justice Holker Exhibn, Gray's Inn, 1947–50; Lord Justice Holker Schol., Gray's Inn, 1950–53; Univ. Blue, Edin., 1943 and 1946 and Camb., 1948. Lectr in Law, Univ. of Liverpool, 1948–52. Called to Bar, Gray's Inn, 1950. *Publications:* (ed, 4th edn) Levie's Law of Bankruptcy in Scotland, 1950; various articles in UK and foreign legal jls. *Recreations:* swimming, travel by sea, racing (both codes), watching soccer (especially Liverpool FC). *Address:* Chelwood, Pine Walks, Prenton, Birkenhead, Merseyside L42 8LQ. *T:* 051–608 2987; 69 Cliffords Inn, EC4 1BX. *T:* 071–405 2932; Strand Chambers, 218 Strand, WC2R 1AP. *T:* 071–353 7825.

RANKIN, Sir Ian (Niall), 4th Bt *cr* 1898, of Bryngwyn, Much Dewchurch, Co. Hereford; Chairman, I. N. Rankin Oil Ltd, since 1981; *b* 19 Dec. 1932; *s* of Lt-Col Arthur Niall Rankin (*d* 1965) (*yr s* of 2nd Bt) and of Lady Jean Rankin, *qv*; *S* uncle, 1988; *m* 1st, 1959, Alexandra (marr. diss.), *d* of Adm. Sir Laurence Durlacher, KCB, OBE, DSC; one *s* one *d*; 2nd, 1980, Mrs June Norman, *d* of late Captain Thomas Marsham-Townshend; one *s*. *Educ:* Eton College; Christ Church, Oxford (MA). Chairman, I. N. Rankin Sales Ltd, 1961–; Director: Lindsay and Williams Ltd, 1973; Bayfine Ltd and subsidiaries, 1974–85 (Jt Chm., 1974–81); Highgate Optical and Industrial Co. Ltd and subsidiary, 1976–84 (Jt Chm., 1976–81); New Arcadia Explorations Ltd, 1987–; R. F. Recovery Systems Inc., 1987–. *Recreations:* tennis, ski-ing, chess. *Heir: s* Gavin Niall Rankin, *b* 19 May 1962. *Address:* 63 Marlborough Place, NW8 0PT. *T:* (office) 071–286 0251, (home) 071–625 5330. *Clubs:* White's, Beefsteak, Pratt's; Royal Yacht Squadron.
See also A. M. Rankin.

RANKIN, James Deans, CBE 1983; PhD; Chief Inspector, Cruelty to Animals Act (1876), Home Office, 1976–83; *b* 17 Jan. 1918; *s* of late Andrew Christian Fleming Rankin and Catherine Sutherland (*née* Russell); *m* 1950, Hilary Jacqueline Bradshaw; two *d*. *Educ:* Hamilton Acad.; Glasgow Veterinary Coll. (MRCVS); Reading Univ. (PhD Microbiology). FIBiol. Gen. practice, 1941; Res. Officer, Min. of Agriculture and Fisheries, 1942; Principal Res. Officer, ARC, 1952; Inspector, Home Office, 1969. *Publications:* scientific contribs in standard works and in med. and veterinary jls. *Club:* Farmers'.

RANKIN, Lady Jean (Margaret), DCVO 1969 (CVO 1957); Woman of the Bedchamber to Queen Elizabeth The Queen Mother, 1947–81, Extra Woman of the Bedchamber, since 1982; *b* 15 Aug. 1905; *d* of 12th Earl of Stair; *m* 1931, Niall Rankin (*d* 1965), *s* of Sir Reginald Rankin, 2nd Bt; two *s*. Governor: Thomas Coram Foundation; Magdalen Hosp. Trust. *Address:* House of Treshnish, Dervaig, Isle of Mull. *T:* Dervaig (06884) 249; 3 Catherine Wheel Yard, SW1. *T:* 071–493 9072.
See also A. M. Rankin, Sir I. N. Rankin, Bt.

RANKIN, Prof. Robert Alexander, MA, PhD, ScD; FRSE, FRSAMD; Professor Emeritus, Glasgow University, since 1982 (Professor of Mathematics, 1954–82; Clerk of the Senate, 1971–78; Dean of Faculties, 1986–88); *b* 27 Oct. 1915; *s* of late Rev. Prof. Oliver Shaw Rankin, DD, and late Olivia Theresa Shaw; *m* 1942, Mary Ferrier Llewellyn, *d* of late W. M. Llewellyn and late K. F. Llewellyn, JP; one *s* three *d*. *Educ:* Fettes; Clare Coll., Cambridge. Wrangler, 1936; Fellow of Clare College, 1939–51; Vis. Fellow, Clare Hall, 1971. Ministry of Supply (work on rockets), 1940–45; Faculty Asst Lecturer, Cambridge Univ., 1945–48; Univ. Lecturer, Cambridge, 1948–51; Asst Tutor, Clare Coll., 1947–51; Praelector, Clare Coll., 1949–51; Mason Professor of Pure Mathematics at Birmingham University, 1951–54. Mathematical Sec. and Editor of Proceedings of Cambridge Philosophical Soc., 1947–51; Hon. Pres. Glasgow Gaelic Soc., 1957–; Pres. Edinburgh Mathematical Soc., 1957–58, 1978–79; Mem., Special Cttee, Advisory Coun. on Educn in Scotland, 1959–61; Vis. Prof., Indiana Univ., 1963–64; Vice-Pres. Roy. Soc. of Edinburgh, 1960–63; Vice-Pres., Scottish Gaelic Texts Soc., 1967–; Founder Mem., and Chm., Scottish Mathematical Council, 1967–73; Chm., Clyde Estuary Amenity Council, 1969–82. Hon. Mem., Edinburgh Mathematical Soc., 1990. Keith Prize, RSE, 1961–63; Senior Whitehead Prize, London Mathematical Soc., 1987. *Publications:* Matematicheskaya Teorija Dvizhenija Neupravljaemykh Raket, 1951; An Introduction to Mathematical Analysis, 1963; The Modular Group and its Subgroups, 1969; Modular Forms and Functions, 1977; (ed) Modular Forms, 1985; papers on the Theory of Numbers, Theory of Functions, Rocket Ballistics and Gaelic Subjects in various journals. *Recreations:* hill-walking, Gaelic studies, organ music. *Address:* 98 Kelvin Court, Glasgow G12 0AH. *T:* 041–339 2641.

RANKIN, Robert Craig McPherson, CompICE; Chairman, BKR Financial Ltd, since 1988; Chief Executive, Lilley PLC, since 1988; Director, British Shipbuilders, since 1985; *b* 15 Aug. 1937; *s* of Robert Craig Rankin and Julia Rankin (*née* Duff); *m* 1963, Alison Barbara Black Douglas; one *s* one *d*. *Educ:* The Academy, Ayr; Royal College of Science and Technology, Glasgow. CompICE 1987; CBIM 1987. Dir, Balfour Beatty Construction (Scotland) Ltd, 1973–74; Dir 1974–83, Exec. Dir 1983–85, Balfour Beatty Construction Ltd; Balfour Beatty Ltd: Dir, 1983–85; Dep. Man. Dir, 1985–86; Man. Dir, 1986–87; Chief Exec., 1986–88; Dir, BICC PLC, 1987–88; Non-executive Director: London & Edinburgh Trust PLC, 1988–; LDDC, 1989–. *Recreations:* opera, music, golf, field sports. *Club:* Wentworth Golf.

RANKINE, Jean Morag; Deputy Director of the British Museum, since 1983; *b* 5 Sept. 1941; *d* of Alan Rankine and Margaret Mary Sloan Rankine (*née* Reid). *Educ:* Central Newcastle High Sch.; University College London (BA, MPhil); Univ. of Copenhagen. Grad. Assistant, Durham Univ. Library, 1966–67; British Museum: Res. Assistant, Dept of Printed Books, 1967–73; Asst Keeper, Director's Office, 1973–78; Dep. Keeper, Public Services, 1978–83. *Recreations:* sculling, ski-ing, fell-walking, opera, motorcycling. *Address:* British Museum, WC1B 3DG. *Clubs:* Thames Rowing; Clydesdale Amateur Rowing (Glasgow).

RANKING, His Honour Robert Duncan; a Circuit Judge (formerly County Court Judge), 1968–88; Judge of the Mayors and City of London Court, 1980–88; *b* 24 Oct. 1915; *yr s* of Dr R. M. Ranking, Tunbridge Wells, Kent; *m* 1949, Evelyn Mary Tagart (*née* Walker); one *d*. *Educ:* Cheltenham Coll.; Pembroke Coll., Cambridge (MA). Called to Bar, 1939. Served in Queen's Own Royal W Kent Regt, 1939–46. Dep. Chm. E Sussex QS, 1962–71; Dep. Chm., Agricultural Land Tribunal (S Eastern Area), 1963. *Address:* 4 Arundel Road, Seaford, E Sussex. *T:* Seaford (0323) 892557.

RANNIE, Prof. Ian; FRCPath 1964; FIBiol 1964; Professor of Pathology (Dental School), University of Newcastle upon Tyne, 1960–81, Professor Emeritus 1981; *b* 29 Oct. 1915; *o s* of James Rannie, MA, and Nicholas Denniston McMeekan; *m* 1943, Flora Welch; two *s*. *Educ:* Ayr Academy; Glasgow University. BSc (Glas), 1935; MB, ChB (Glas), 1938; BSc Hons Pathology and Bacteriology (Glas), 1939; Hutcheson Research Schol. (Pathology), 1940. Assistant to Professor of Bacteriology, Glasgow, 1940–42; Lecturer in Pathology, 1942–60, King's College, Univ. of Durham. Consultant Pathologist, United Newcastle upon Tyne Hospitals, 1948–81, Hon. Consultant 1981–. Pres., International Soc. of Geographical Pathology, 1969–72; Vice-President: Assoc. of Clinical Pathologists, 1978–80; Internat. Union of Angiology. Hon. Mem., Hungarian Arteriosclerosis Res. Soc. *Publications:* papers on various subjects in medical journals. *Recreation:* golf. *Address:* 5 Osborne Villas, Newcastle upon Tyne NE2 1JU. *T:* Tyneside 091–281 3163. *Clubs:* East India, Royal Over-Seas League.

RANT, James William, QC 1980; **His Honour Judge Rant;** a Circuit Judge, since 1984, at Central Criminal Court, since 1986; Judge Advocate General of the Army and Royal Air Force, since 1991; *b* 16 April 1936; *s* of late Harry George Rant, FZS and Barbara Rant; *m* 1963, Helen Rant (*née* Adnams), BA; two *s* two *d*. *Educ:* Stowe Sch.; Selwyn Coll., Cambridge (MA, LLM). Called to the Bar, Gray's Inn, 1961; pupillage with late James N. Dunlop, 1962–63; a Dep. Circuit Judge, 1975–79; a Recorder, 1979–84. Freeman: City of London, 1986; Clockmakers' Co., 1989. *Recreations:* cookery, music, family life. *Address:* 3 Temple Gardens, Middle Temple Lane, EC4Y 9AA.

RANTZEN, Esther Louise, (Mrs Desmond Wilcox), OBE 1991; Television Producer/Presenter, since 1968; *b* 22 June 1940; *d* of Harry and Katherine Rantzen; *m* 1977, Desmond Wilcox, *qv*; one *s* two *d*. *Educ:* North London Collegiate Sch.; Somerville Coll., Oxford (MA). Studio manager making dramatic sound effects, BBC Radio, 1963; BBC TV: Researcher, 1965; Dir, 1967; Reporter, Braden's Week, 1968–72; Producer/

Presenter, That's Life, 1973–, scriptwriter, 1976–; Producer, documentary series, The Big Time, 1976; Presenter: Esther Interviews ..., 1988; Hearts of Gold, 1988; Presenter, Drugwatch, Childwatch, and Producer/Presenter, The Lost Babies and other progs on social issues; reporter/producer, various documentaries, religious and current affairs TV progs. Member: Nat. Consumer Council, 1981–90; Health Educn Authority, 1989–. Chm., Childline; Pres., Meet-a-Mum Assoc.; a Vice-President: ASBAH; Health Visitors' Assoc.; Spastics Soc.; Patron: Addenbrookes Kidney Patients Assoc.; Contact-a-Family (families of disabled children); DEMAND (furniture for the disabled); Downs Children's Assoc.; Trustee, Ben Hardwick Meml Fund. Hon. Mem., NSPCC, 1989. Personality of 1974, RTS award; BBC TV Personality of 1975, Variety Club of GB; European Soc. for Organ Transplant Award, 1985; Richard Dimbleby Award, BAFTA, 1988. *Publications:* (with Desmond Wilcox): Kill the Chocolate Biscuit, 1981; Baby Love, 1985; (with Shaun Woodward) Ben: the story of Ben Hardwick, 1985. *Recreations:* family life, the countryside, appearing in pantomime. *Address:* BBC TV, Lime Grove Studios, Lime Grove, W12. *T:* 081–743 8000; Noel Gay Artists, 24 Denmark Street, WC2. *T:* 071–836 3941.

RAO, Calyampudi Radhakrishna, FRS 1967; Eberly Professor of Statistics, Penn State University, since 1988; Adjunct Professor, University of Pittsburgh, since 1988 (University Professor, 1979); National Professor, India, since 1987; *b* 10 Sept. 1920; *s* of C. D. Naidu and A. Laksmikantamma; *m* 1948, C. Bhargavi Rao; one *s* one *d*. *Educ:* Andhra Univ. (MA, 1st Class Maths); Calcutta Univ. (MA, 1st Class Statistics; Gold Medal); PhD, ScD, Cambridge (Hon. Fellow, King's Coll., Cambridge, 1975). Indian Statistical Institute: Superintending Statistician, 1943–49; Professor and Head of Division of Theoretical Research and Training, 1949–64; Dir, Res. and Training Sch., 1964–76 (Sec., 1972–76); Jawaharlal Nehru Professor, 1976–84. Co-editor, Sankhya, Indian Jl of Statistics, 1964–72, Editor, 1972–. Member, Internat. Statistical Inst., 1951 (Mem. Statistical Educn Cttee, 1958–; Treasurer, 1962–65; Pres.-elect, 1975–77, Pres., 1977–79, Hon. Mem. 1982); Chm., Indian Nat. Cttee for Statistics, 1962–; President: Biometric Soc., 1973–75 (Hon. Life Mem., 1986); Indian Econometric Soc., 1971–76; Forum for Interdisciplinary Mathematics, 1982–84. Fellow: Indian Nat. Sci. Acad., 1953 (Vice-Pres., 1973, 1974); Inst. of Math. Statistics, USA, 1958 (Pres., 1976–77); Amer. Statistical Assoc., 1972; Econometric Soc., 1972; Indian Acad. of Sciences, 1974; Founder Fellow, Third World Science Acad., 1983. Hon. Fellow: Royal Stat. Soc., 1969; Amer. Acad. of Arts and Sciences, 1975; Calcutta Stat. Assoc., 1985; Biometric Soc., 1986. Shanti Swarup Bhatnagar Memorial Award, 1963; Guy Medal in Silver, Royal Stat. Soc., 1965; Padma Bhushan, 1968; Meghnad Saha Medal, 1969; J. C. Bose Gold Medal, 1979; S. S. Wilkes Meml Medal. Hon. DSc: Andhra; Leningrad; Athens; Osmania; Ohio State; Philippines; Tampere; Neuchatel; Poznan; Indian Statistical Inst.; Colorado State; Hyderabad; Hon. DLitt Delhi. Hon. Prof., Univ. of San Marcos, Lima. *Publications:* (with Mahalanobis and Majumdar) Anthropometric Survey of the United Provinces, 1941, a statistical study, 1949; Advanced Statistical Methods in Biometric Research, 1952; (with Mukherjee and Trevor) The Ancient Inhabitants of Jebal Moya, 1955; (with Majumdar) Bengal Anthropometric Survey, 1945, a statistical study, 1959; Linear Statistical Inference and its Applications, 1965; (with A. Matthai and S. K. Mitra) Formulae and Tables for Statistical Work, 1966; Computers and the Future of Human Society, 1968; (with S. K. Mitra) The Generalised Inverse of Matrices and its Applications, 1971; (with A. M. Kagan and Yu. V. Linnik) Characterization Problems of Mathematical Statistics, 1973; (with J. Kleffe) Estimation of Variance Components and its Applications, 1988; Statistics and Truth, 1989. *Address:* Department of Statistics, 121 Pond Laboratory, Penn State University, University Park, Pa 16802, USA.

RAO, Prof. Chintamani Nagesa Ramachandra, Padma Shri, 1974; Padma Vibhushan, 1985; FRS 1982; CChem, FRSC; Director, since 1984, Professor of Chemical Sciences, since 1976, Indian Institute of Science, Bangalore, India; *b* 30 June 1934; *s* of H. Nagesa Rao; *m* 1960, Indumati; one *s* one *d*. *Educ:* Univ. of Mysore (DSc); Univ. of Purdue, USA (PhD). Research Chemist, Univ. of California, Berkeley, 1958–59; Lectr, Indian Inst. of Science, 1959–63; Prof., Indian Inst. of Technology, Kanpur, 1963–76, Head of Chemistry Dept, 1964–68, Dean of Research, 1969–72; Jawaharlal Nehru Fellow, 1973–75; Commonwealth Vis. Prof., Univ. of Oxford, and Fellow, St Catherine's Coll., 1974–75; Jawaharlal Nehru Vis. Prof., Univ. of Cambridge, and Professorial Fellow, Kings' Coll., Cambridge, 1983–84. Chm., Solid State and Structural Chemistry Unit and Materials Res. Laboratory, Indian Inst. of Science, Bangalore, 1976–84; President: INSA, 1985–87; IUPAC, 1985–87. Member: First Nat. Cttee of Science and Technology, Govt of India, 1971–74; Science Adv. Cttee to Union Cabinet of India, 1981–86; Chm., Science Adv. Council to Prime Minister, 1986–90. Hon. DSc: Purdue, 1982; Bordeaux, 1983; Sri Venkateswara, 1984; Roorkee, 1985; Banaras, Osmania, Mangalore and Manipur, 1987; Anna, Mysore, Burdwan, 1988; Wroclaw, 1989. Fellow, Indian Acad. of Scis; Foreign Member: Slovenian Acad. of Scis, 1983; Serbian Acad. of Scis, 1986; Amer. Acad. of Arts and Scis, 1986; USSR Acad. of Scis, 1988; Czechoslovak Acad. of Scis, 1988; Polish Acad. of Scis, 1988; Founder Mem., Third World Acad. Sci.; many awards and medals, incl.: Marlow Medal of Faraday Soc. (London), 1967; Royal Soc. of Chemistry (London) Medal, 1981; Centennial For. Fellowship of Amer. Chemical Soc., 1976. *Publications:* Ultraviolet and Visible Spectroscopy, 1960, 3rd edn 1975; Chemical Applications of Infrared Spectroscopy, 1964; Spectroscopy in Inorganic Chemistry, 1970; Modern Aspects of Solid State Chemistry, 1970; University General Chemistry, 1973; Solid State Chemistry, 1974; Phase Transitions in Solids, 1978; Preparation and Characterization of Materials, 1981; The Metallic and the Non-metallic States of Matter, 1985; New Directions in Solid State Chemistry, 1986; Chemistry of Oxide Superconductors, 1988; Chemical and Structural Aspects of High Temperature Oxide Superconductors, 1988; Bismuth and Thallium Superconductors, 1989; 600 research papers. *Recreations:* gourmet cooking, gardening. *Address:* Indian Institute of Science, Bangalore-560012, India. *T:* 341690.

RAO, P. V. Narasimha; Prime Minister of India and Leader of the Congress (I) Party, since 1991; *b* Karimnagar, Andhra Pradesh, 28 June 1921; widower; three *s* five *d*. *Educ:* Osmania Univ., Hyderabad; Bombay Univ.; Nagpur Univ. (BSc, LLB). Career as leader, writer, poet, agriculturalist, advocate and administrator. Member, Andhra Pradesh Legislative Assembly, 1957–77; Minister in Andhra Pradesh Govt, 1962–71; Chief Minister of the State, 1971–73. Chm., Telugu Academy, Andhra Pradesh, 1968–74; Vice-Pres., Dakshin Bharat Hindi Prachar Sabha, Madras, 1972; Gen. Sec., All India Congress Cttee, 1975–76. Elected to Lok Sabha (from Hanamkonda, Andhra Pradesh) 1972, 1977 and 1980, (from Ramtek) 1984; Minister: for External Affairs, 1980–84; for Home Affairs, 1984; of Defence, 1985; of Human Resources Develt, 1985–88; of Health and Family Welfare, 1986–88; of External Affairs, 1988–89. Chairman: Public Accounts Cttee, 1978–79; Bharatiya Vidya Bhavan's Andhra Centre. Has lectured on political matters in univs in USA and Federal Republic of Germany, and has visited many countries. *Publications:* many, including Sahasra Phan (Hindi trans.). *Recreations:* music, cinema, theatre. *Address:* Prime Minister's Office, South Block, New Delhi 110011, India; Vangara Post, Karimnagar District, Andhra Pradesh, India.

RAPER, (Alfred) Graham, CBE 1988; PhD; FEng; Chairman, Projecta, consulting engineers; Chief Executive and Deputy Chairman, Davy Corporation, 1985–87; *b* 15 May 1932; *s* of Hilda and Alfred William Raper; *m* 1st, Elizabeth Williams (marr. diss. 1975); two *s* one *d*; 2nd, Valerie Benson; one *s*. *Educ:* Lady Manners School, Bakewell; Univ. of Sheffield (BScTech Hons, PhD). FIChemE, FIM. Research Engineer, Head Wrightson Co., 1957–59; Technical Manager, Davy United Engineering, 1959–65; Steel Plant Manager, Highveld Steel & Vanadium, S Africa, 1965–69; joined Davy Corp., 1969. *Publications:* articles in jls of Iron & Steel Institute and British Association. *Recreations:* golf, gardening. *Address:* 54 Golf Links Road, Ferndown, Wimborne, Dorset BH22 8BZ. *T:* Wimborne (0202) 873512.

RAPHAEL, Adam Eliot Geoffrey; Executive Editor, The Observer, since 1988; *b* 22 April 1938; *s* of Geoffrey George Raphael and Nancy Raphael (*née* Rose); *m* 1970, Caroline Rayner Ellis; one *s* one *d*. *Educ:* Arnold House, Charterhouse; Oriel Coll., Oxford (BA Hons History). 2nd Lieut Royal Artillery, 1956–58. Copy Boy, Washington Post, USA, 1961; Swindon Evening Advertiser, 1962–63; Film Critic, Bath Evening Chronicle, 1963–64; The Guardian: Reporter, 1965; Motoring Correspondent, 1967–68; Foreign Correspondent, Washington and S Africa, 1969–73; Consumer Affairs Columnist, 1974–76; Political Correspondent, The Observer, 1976–81, Political Editor, 1981–86; Presenter, Newsnight, BBC TV, 1987–88; an Asst Editor, The Observer, 1988. Awards include: Granada Investigative Journalist of the Year, 1973; British Press Awards, Journalist of the Year, 1973. *Publication:* My Learned Friends, 1989. *Recreations:* tennis, ski-ing. *Address:* 50 Addison Avenue, W11 4QP. *T:* 071–603 9133. *Clubs:* Hurlingham, Royal Automobile, Ski Club of Great Britain.

RAPHAEL, Chaim, CBE 1965 (OBE 1951); *b* Middlesbrough, 14 July 1908; *s* of Rev. David Rabinovitch and Rachel Rabinovitch (name Hebraised by deed poll 1936); *m* 1934, Diana Rose (marr. diss. 1964); one *s* one *d*. *Educ:* Portsmouth Grammar Sch.; University Coll., Oxford. PPE 1930. James Mew Post-Grad. Schol. in Hebrew, 1931. Kennicott Fellowship, 1933–36. Cowley Lectr in Post-Biblical Hebrew, 1932–39. Liaison Officer for Internment Camps: UK 1940; Canada 1941. Adviser, British Information Services, NY, 1942–45; Dir (Economics), 1945–57; Dep. Head of Information Div., HM Treasury, 1957–59; Head of Information Division: HM Treasury, 1959–68; Civil Service Dept, 1968–69. Research Fellow, Univ. of Sussex, 1969–75. *Publications:* Memoirs of a Special Case, 1962; The Walls of Jerusalem, 1968; A Feast of History, 1972; A Coat of Many Colours, 1979; The Springs of Jewish Life, 1982 (jtly, Wingate Prize, 1983); The Road from Babylon: the story of Sephardi and Oriental Jews, 1985, repr. as The Sephardic Story, 1991; A Jewish Book of Common Prayer, 1986; The Festivals: a history of Jewish celebration, 1990; *novels:* (under pseudonym Jocelyn Davey): The Undoubted Deed, 1956; The Naked Villany, 1958; A Touch of Stagefright, 1960; A Killing in Hats, 1964; A Treasury Alarm, 1976; Murder in Paradise, 1982; A Dangerous Liaison, 1987. *Recreation:* America. *Address:* 40 St John's Court, Finchley Road, NW3 6LL. *T:* 071–625 8489. *Club:* Reform.

RAPHAEL, Prof. David Daiches, DPhil, MA; Emeritus Professor of Philosophy, University of London, since 1983; *b* 25 Jan. 1916; 2nd *s* of late Jacob Raphael and Sarah Warshawsky, Liverpool; *m* 1942, Sylvia, *er d* of late Rabbi Dr Salis Daiches and Flora Levin, Edinburgh; two *d*. *Educ:* Liverpool Collegiate School; University College, Oxford (scholar). 1st Class, Classical Moderations, 1936; Hall-Houghton Junior Septuagint Prizeman, 1937; 1st Class, Literae Humaniores, 1938; Robinson Senior Scholar of Oriel College, Oxford, 1938–40; Passmore Edwards Scholar, 1939. Served in Army, 1940–41. Temporary Assistant Principal, Ministry of Labour and National Service, 1941–44; temp. Principal, 1944–46. Professor of Philosophy, University of Otago, Dunedin, NZ, 1946–49; Lecturer in Moral Philosophy, Univ. of Glasgow, 1949–51; Senior Lecturer, 1951–60; Edward Caird Prof. of Political and Social Philosophy, Univ. of Glasgow, 1960–70; Prof. of Philosophy, Univ. of Reading, 1970–73; Prof. of Philosophy, Imperial Coll., Univ. of London, 1973–83 (Acad. Dir of Associated Studies, 1973–80; Head of Dept of Humanities, 1980–83; Hon. Fellow 1987). Visiting Professor of Philosophy, Hamilton Coll., Clinton, NY (under Chauncey S. Truax Foundation), and Univ. of Southern California, 1959; Mahlon Powell Lectr, Indiana Univ., 1959; Vis. Fellow, All Souls Coll., Oxford, 1967–68; John Hinkley Vis. Prof. of Political Sci., Johns Hopkins Univ., 1984. Independent Member: Cttee on Teaching Profession in Scotland (Wheatley Cttee), 1961–63; Scottish Agricultural Wages Board, 1962–84; Agricultural Wages Bd for England and Wales, 1972–78. Mem. Academic Adv. Cttee, Heriot-Watt Univ., Edinburgh, 1964–71; Mem. Cttee on Distribution of Teachers in Scotland (Roberts Cttee), 1965–66; Independent Member Police Advisory Board for Scotland, 1965–70; Member Social Sciences Adv. Cttee, UK Nat. Commission, UNESCO, 1966–74; Vice-Pres., Internat. Assoc. Philosophy of Law and Social Philosophy, 1971–87; Pres., Aristotelian Soc., 1974–75. Academic Mem., Bd of Governors, Hebrew Univ. of Jerusalem, 1969–81, Hon. Governor 1981–. *Publications:* The Moral Sense, 1947; Edition of Richard Price's Review of Morals, 1948; Moral Judgement, 1955; The Paradox of Tragedy, 1960; Political Theory and the Rights of Man, 1967; British Moralists 1650–1800, 1969; Problems of Political Philosophy, 1970; (ed jtly) Adam Smith's Theory of Moral Sentiments, 1976; Hobbes: Morals and Politics, 1977; (ed jtly) Adam Smith's Lectures on Jurisprudence, 1978; (ed jtly) Adam Smith's Essays on Philosophical Subjects, 1980; Justice and Liberty, 1980; Moral Philosophy, 1981; (trans. jtly with Sylvia Raphael) Richard Price as Moral Philosopher and Political Theorist, by Henri Laboucheix, 1982; Adam Smith, 1985; articles in jls of philosophy and of political studies. *Address:* Imperial College of Science, Technology and Medicine, SW7 2AZ.

RAPHAEL, Frederic Michael; author; *b* 14 Aug. 1931; *s* of late Cedric Michael Raphael and of Irene Rose (*née* Mauser); *m* 1955, Sylvia Betty Glatt; two *s* one *d*. *Educ:* Charterhouse; St John's Coll., Cambridge (MA (Hons)). FRSL 1964. *Publications: novels:* Obbligato, 1956; The Earlsdon Way, 1958; The Limits of Love, 1960; A Wild Surmise, 1961; The Graduate Wife, 1962; The Trouble with England, 1962; Lindmann, 1963; Orchestra and Beginners, 1967; Like Men Betrayed, 1970; Who Were You With Last Night?, 1971; April, June and November, 1972; Richard's Things, 1973; California Time, 1975; The Glittering Prizes, 1976; Heaven and Earth, 1985; After the War, 1988 (adapted for television, 1989); The Hidden I, 1990; *short stories:* Sleeps Six, 1979; Oxbridge Blues, 1980 (also pubd as scripts of TV plays, 1984); Think of England, 1986; *biography:* Somerset Maugham and his World, 1977; Byron, 1982; *essays:* Bookmarks (ed), 1975; Cracks in the Ice, 1979; *screenplays:* Nothing but the Best, 1964; Darling, 1965 (Academy Award); Two For The Road, 1967; Far From the Madding Crowd, 1967; A Severed Head, 1972; Daisy Miller, 1974; The Glittering Prizes, 1976 (sequence of TV plays) (Writer of the Year 1976, Royal TV Soc.); Rogue Male, 1976; (and directed) Something's Wrong (TV), 1978; School Play (TV), 1979; The Best of Friends (TV), 1979; Richard's Things, 1981; After the War (TV series), 1989; *plays:* From The Greek, Arts, Cambridge, 1979; The Daedalus Dimension (radio), 1982; The Thought of Lydia (radio), 1988; *translations:* (with Kenneth McLeish): Poems of Catullus, 1976; The Oresteia, 1978 (televised as The Serpent Son, BBC, 1979); The complete plays of Aeschylus, 1991. *Recreation:* tennis. *Address:* The Wick, Langham, Colchester, Essex CO4 5PE. *Clubs:* Savile, The Queen's.

RAPHAEL, Prof. Ralph Alexander, CBE 1982; PhD, DSc (London), ARCS, DIC; FRS 1962; FRSE, FRSC; Fellow of Christ's College, Professor of Organic Chemistry, and Head of Department of Organic and Inorganic Chemistry, Cambridge University, 1972–88, now Hon. Fellow and Professor Emeritus; *b* 1 Jan. 1921; *s* of Jack Raphael; *m* 1944, Prudence Marguerite Anne, *d* of Col P. J. Gaffikin, MC, MD; one *s* one *d*. *Educ:* Wesley College, Dublin; Tottenham County School; Imperial College of Science and Technology (FIC 1991). Chemist, May & Baker Ltd, 1943–46. ICI Research Fellow, Univ. of London, 1946–49; Lecturer in Organic Chemistry, Univ. of Glasgow, 1949–54; Professor of Organic Chemistry, Queen's University, Belfast, 1954–57; Regius Prof. of Chemistry, Glasgow Univ., 1957–72. Tilden Lectr, Chem. Soc., 1960, Corday-Morgan Vis. Lectr, 1963; Roy. Soc. Vis. Prof., 1967; Pedler Lectr, Chem. Soc., 1973; Pacific Coast Lectr, West Coast Univs tour from LA to Vancouver, 1979; Lady Davis Vis. Prof., Hebrew Univ. of Jerusalem, 1980; Sandin Lectr, Univ. of Alberta, 1985; Andrews Lectr, Univ. of NSW, 1985; Royal Soc. Kan Tong-Po Vis. Prof., Hong Kong Univ., 1989; Emilio Noelting Vis. Prof., Univ. de Haute Alsace, 1990. Vice-Pres. Chemical Soc., 1967–70; Mem., Academic Adv. Bd, Warwick Univ. Hon. MRIA 1987. DUniv Stirling, 1982; Hon. DSc: East Anglia, 1986; QUB, 1989. Meldola Medallist, RIC, 1948; Chem. Soc. Ciba-Geigy Award for Synthetic Chemistry, 1975; Davy Medal, Royal Soc., 1981. *Publications:* Chemistry of Carbon Compounds, Vol. IIA, 1953; Acetylenic Compounds in Organic Synthesis, 1955; papers in Journal of Chemical Society. *Recreations:* music, bridge. *Address:* University Chemical Laboratory, Lensfield Road, Cambridge CB2 1EW. *T:* Cambridge (0223) 336328; 4 Ivy Field, High Street, Barton, Cambs CB3 7BJ. *Club:* Athenæum.

RAPHAEL, Ven. Timothy John; Archdeacon of Middlesex, since 1983; *b* 26 Sept. 1929; *s* of Hector and Alix Raphael; *m* 1957, Anne Elizabeth Shepherd; one *s* two *d*. *Educ:* Christ's College, Christchurch, NZ; Leeds Univ. (BA). Asst Curate, St Stephen, Westminster, 1955–60; Vicar of St Mary, Welling, Kent, 1960–63; Vicar of St Michael, Christchurch, NZ, 1963–65; Dean of Dunedin, 1965–73; Vicar, St John's Wood, London, 1973–83. *Recreations:* contemporary poetry, theatre, beach-combing. *Address:* 12 St Ann's Villas, W11 4RS. *T:* 071–603 0856.

RAPHOE, Bishop of, (RC), since 1982; **Most Rev. Séamus Hegarty;** *b* 26 Jan. 1940; *s* of James Hegarty and Mary O'Donnell. *Educ:* Kilcar National School; St Eunan's Coll., Letterkenny; St Patrick's Coll., Maynooth; University Coll., Dublin. Priest, 1966; post-grad. studies, University Coll., Dublin, 1966–67; Dean of Studies 1967–71, President 1971–82, Holy Cross College, Falcarragh. *Publication:* contribs to works on school administration and student assessment. *Recreations:* bridge, fishing. *Address:* Ard Adhamhnain, Letterkenny, Co. Donegal, Ireland. *T:* Letterkenny (74) 21208.

RASCH, Sir Richard Guy Carne, 3rd Bt, *cr* 1903; a Member of HM Body Guard, Honourable Corps of Gentlemen-at-Arms, 1968–88; *b* 10 Oct. 1918; *s* of Brigadier G. E. C. Rasch, CVO, DSO (*d* 1955); *S* uncle, 1963; *m* 1st, 1947, Anne Mary (*d* 1989), *d* of late Major J. H. Dent-Brocklehurst; one *s* one *d*; 2nd, 1961, Fiona Mary, *d* of Robert Douglas Shaw. *Educ:* Eton; RMC, Sandhurst. Major, late Grenadier Guards. Served War of 1939–45; retired, 1951. *Recreations:* shooting, fishing. *Heir:* *s* Simon Anthony Carne Rasch [*b* 26 Feb. 1948; *m* 1987, Julia, *er d* of Major Michael Stourton; one *d*. *Educ:* Eton; Royal Agric. Coll., Cirencester]. *Address:* 30 Ovington Square, SW3 1LR. *T:* 071–589 9973; The Manor House, Lower Woodford, near Salisbury, Wilts. *Clubs:* White's, Pratt's, Cavalry and Guards.

RASHLEIGH, Sir Richard (Harry), 6th Bt *cr* 1831; Management Accountant, United Biscuits PLC, since 1985; *b* 8 July 1958; *s* of Sir Harry Evelyn Battie Rashleigh, 5th Bt and Honora Elizabeth (*d* 1987), *d* of George Stuart Sneyd; *S* father, 1984. *Educ:* Allhallows School, Dorset. Management Accountant with Arthur Guinness Son & Co., 1980–82; Dexion-Comino International Ltd, 1982–84. *Recreation:* sailing. *Heir:* none. *Address:* Stowford Grange, Lewdown, near Okehampton, Devon. *T:* Lewdown (0566) 237. *Club:* Naval.

RASHLEIGH BELCHER, John; *see* Belcher, J. R.

RASMINSKY, Louis, CC (Canada), 1968; CBE 1946; Governor, Bank of Canada, 1961–73; *b* 1 Feb. 1908; *s* of David and Etta Rasminsky; *m* 1930, Lyla Rotenberg; one *s* one *d*. *Educ:* University of Toronto; London School of Economics. Financial Section, League of Nations, 1930–39; Chairman, Foreign Exchange Control Board, Canada, 1940–51; Deputy Governor, Bank of Canada, 1956–61. Executive Director: IMF, 1946–62; International Bank, 1950–62; Alternate Governor for Canada, IMF, 1969–73. Chm., Bd of Governors, Internat. Develt Res. Centre, 1973–78. Hon. Fellow, LSE, 1960. Hon. LLD: Univ. of Toronto, 1953; Queen's Univ., 1967; Bishop's Univ., 1968; McMaster Univ., 1969; Yeshiva Univ., 1970; Trent Univ., 1972; Concordia Univ., 1975; Univ. of Western Ontario, 1978; Univ. of British Columbia, 1979; Carleton Univ., 1987; Hon. DHL Hebrew Union Coll., 1963. Outstanding Achievement Award of Public Service of Canada, 1968; Vanier Medal, Inst. of Public Admin, 1974. *Recreations:* golf, fishing. *Address:* 20 Driveway, Apt 1006, Ottawa, Ont K2P 1C8, Canada. *T:* 613–594–0150. *Clubs:* Rideau, Cercle Universitaire d'Ottawa (Ottawa); Five Lakes (Wakefield, PQ).

RATCLIFF, Antony Robin Napier; Director, Eagle Star Holdings plc, since 1980; Deputy Chairman and Chief Executive, Eagle Star Insurance, 1985–87; Visiting Professor, City University Business School, since 1987; *b* 26 Sept. 1925; *m* 1956, Helga Belohlawek, Vienna; one *s*. FIA 1953; ASA. Nat. Correspondent for England, Internat. Actuarial Assoc., 1965–70; Mem. Council, Assoc. of British Insurers (formerly British Insurance Assoc.), 1969–87. Pres., Inst. of Actuaries, 1980–82; Vice-Pres., London Insce Inst., 1964–87. Vice-Pres., Assoc. internat. pour l'Etude de l'Economie de l'Assurance, 1986–90. Corresponding Member: Deutsche Gesellschaft für Versicherungsmathematik; Verein zur Förderung der Versicherungswirtschaft. FRSA. Hon. Treasurer, German Christ Church, London. Messenger and Brown Prize-Winner, Inst. of Actuaries, 1963. Hon. DLitt City, 1986. *Publications:* (jtly) Lessons from Central Forecasting, 1965; (jtly) Strategic Planning for Financial Institutions, 1974; (jtly) A House in Town, 1984; contribs to Jl of Inst. of Actuaries, Trans of Internat. Congress of Actuaries, Jl London Insce Inst., Jl Chartered Insce Inst., Blätter der Deutschen Gesellschaft für Versicherungsmathematik. *Address:* 60 St Mary Axe, EC3A 8BA. *T:* 071–929 1111. *Clubs:* Actuaries, Roehampton, Anglo-Austrian Society.

RATCLIFFE, Frederick William, MA, PhD; JP; University Librarian, University of Cambridge, since 1980; Fellow, Corpus Christi College, Cambridge, since 1980; *b* 28 May 1927; *y s* of late Sydney and Dora Ratcliffe, Leek, Staffs; *m* 1952, Joyce Brierley; two *s* one *d*. *Educ:* Leek High Sch., Staffs; Manchester Univ. (MA, PhD); MA Cantab. Served in N Staffs Regt, 1945–48. Manchester University: Graduate Res. Scholarship, 1951; Res. Studentship in Arts, 1952; Asst Cataloguer and Cataloguer, 1954–62; Sub-Librarian, Glasgow Univ., 1962–63; Dep. Librarian, Univ. of Newcastle upon Tyne, 1963–65; University Librarian, 1965–80, Dir, John Rylands University Library, 1972–80, Manchester University. Trustee, St Deiniol's Library, Hawarden, 1975–. Hon. Lectr in Historical Bibliography, Manchester Univ., 1970–80; External Prof., Dept of Library and Inf. Studies, Loughborough Univ., 1981–86; Hon. Res. Fellow, Dept of Library, Archive and Inf. Studies, UCL, 1987–; Sandars Reader in Bibliography, Cambridge Univ., 1988–89. Chm., Library Panel, The Wellcome Trust, 1988–. Fellow, Chapter of Woodard Schools (Eastern Div.), 1981–. Chm., Adv. Cttee, Nat. Preservation Office, 1984–. Hon. FLA 1986. JP Stockport, 1972–80, Cambridge, 1981. Comendador de la Orden del Merito Civil (Spain), 1988. *Publications:* Preservation Policies and Conservation in British Libraries, 1984; many articles in learned journals. *Recreations:* book collecting, hand printing, cricket. *Address:* 84 Church Lane, Girton, Cambs CB3 0JP. *T:* Cambridge (0223) 277512; Ridge House, The Street, Rickinghall Superior, Diss, Norfolk IP22 1DY. *T:* Diss (0379) 898232.

RATCLIFFE, (John) Michael; Literary Editor, The Observer, since 1989; *b* 15 June 1935; *s* of Donald Ratcliffe and Joyce Lilian Dilks. *Educ:* Cheadle Hulme Sch.; Christ's Coll., Cambridge (MA). Trainee journalist, Sheffield Telegraph, 1959–61; Asst Literary and Arts Editor, Sunday Times, 1962–67; Literary Editor, 1967–72, chief book reviewer, 1972–82, The Times; freelance writer, 1982–83; theatre critic, Observer, 1984–89. Commended Critic of the Year, British Press Awards, 1989. *Publications:* The Novel Today, 1968; The Bodley Head 1887–1987 (completed for J. W. Lambert), 1987. *Recreations:* music, travel, architecture, walking, gardening. *Address:* 4 Elia Street, N1 8DE. *T:* 071–837 1687.

RATFORD, David John Edward, CMG 1984; CVO 1979; HM Diplomatic Service; Ambassador to Norway, since 1990; *b* 22 April 1934; *s* of George Ratford and Lilian (*née* Jones); *m* 1960, Ulla Monica, *d* of Oskar and Gurli Jerneck, Stockholm; two *d*. *Educ:* Whitgift Middle Sch.; Selwyn Coll., Cambridge (1st Cl. Hons Mod. and Med. Langs). National Service (Intell. Corps), 1953–55. Exchequer and Audit Dept, 1952; FO, 1955; 3rd Sec., Prague, 1959–61; 2nd Sec., Mogadishu, 1961–63; 2nd, later 1st Sec., FO, 1963–68; 1st Sec. (Commercial), Moscow, 1968–71; FCO, 1971–74; Counsellor (Agric. and Econ.), Paris, 1974–78; Counsellor, Copenhagen, 1978–82; Minister, Moscow, 1983–85; Asst Under-Sec., of State (Europe), 1986–90, and Dep. Political Dir, 1987–90, FCO; UK Rep., Permanent Council of WEU, 1986–90. Comdr, Order of the Dannebrog, Denmark, 1979. *Recreations:* music, tennis. *Address:* c/o Foreign and Commonwealth Office, SW1. *Club:* Travellers'.

RATHBONE, John Francis Warre, CBE 1966; TD 1950; Secretary of National Trust for Places of Historic Interest or Natural Beauty, 1949–68; President, London Centre of the National Trust, since 1968; *b* 18 July 1909; *e s* of Francis Warre Rathbone and Edith Bertha Hampshire, Allerton Beeches, Liverpool. *Educ:* Marlborough; New College, Oxford. Solicitor, 1934. Served War of 1939–45; AA Comd and staff (Col 1945). Dir Ministry of Justice Control Branch, CCG (British Element), 1946–49. Mem. Management Cttee, Country Houses Assoc. Ltd; Cttee, Friends of UCH; Mem. Council, Over Forty Assoc. *Recreations:* music, travel. *Address:* 2 Chartwell House, 12 Ladbroke Terrace, W11 3PG. *T:* 071–792 3529. *Club:* Travellers'.

RATHBONE, John Rankin, (Tim Rathbone); MP (C) Lewes since Feb. 1974; *b* 17 March 1933; *s* of J. R. Rathbone, MP (killed in action 1940) and Lady Wright (*see* Beatrice Wright); *m* 1st, 1960, Margarita Sanchez y Sanchez (marr. diss. 1981); two *s* one *d*; 2nd, 1982, Mrs Susan Jenkin Stopford Sackville. *Educ:* Eton; Christ Church, Oxford; Harvard Business School. 2nd Lieut KRRC, 1951–53. Robert Benson Lonsdale & Co., Merchant Bankers, 1956–58; Trainee to Vice-Pres., Ogilvy & Mather Inc., NY, 1958–66; Chief Publicity and Public Relations Officer, Conservative Central Office, 1966–68; Director: Charles Barker Group, 1968–87; Ayer Barker Ltd, 1971–87 (Man. Dir 1971–73; Dep. Chm., 1973–79); Charles Barker City, 1981–87; Charles Barker Manchester, 1983–87 (Chm., 1983–86). PPS to Minister of Health, 1979–82, to Minister for Trade (Consumer Affairs), 1982–83, to Minister for the Arts, 1985. Vice-Chm., All Party British–Japanese Gp; Founder Member: All Party Parly Drugs Misuse Gp, 1984 (Chm., 1987–); Parly Engrg Develt Gp, 1987; Conservatives for Fundamental Change in South Africa, 1986; All Party Groups: British-Amer.; British-S Amer.; British Southern Africa; European Movt; Sane Planning. Deleg. to Council of Europe and WEU, 1987–. Chm., Adv. Cttee, Inst. of Management Resources, 1987–; Member Council: Nat. Cttee for Electoral Reform; RSA, 1985–88. FRSA 1979. *Publication:* pamphlet on nursery schooling. *Recreation:* family. *Address:* House of Commons, SW1A 0AA. *T:* 071–219 3460. *Clubs:* Brooks's, Pratt's; Sussex; Society of Sussex Downsmen.

RATHBONE, Very Rev. Norman Stanley; Dean of Hereford, 1969–82, now Dean Emeritus; *b* 8 Sept. 1914; *er s* of Stanley George and Helen Rathbone; *m* 1952, Christine Olive Gooderson; three *s* two *d*. *Educ:* Lawrence Sheriff Sch., Rugby; Christ's Coll., Cambridge; Westcott House, Cambridge. BA 1936, MA 1939. St Mary Magdalen's, Coventry: Curate, 1938; Vicar, 1945; Examining Chaplain to Bp of Coventry, 1944; Canon Theologian, Coventry Cathedral, 1954; Canon Residentiary and Chancellor, Lincoln Cathedral, 1959. *Address:* The Daren, Newton St Margarets, Herefordshire. *T:* Michaelchurch (098123) 623.

RATHBONE, Tim; *see* Rathbone, J. R.

RATHCAVAN, 2nd Baron *cr* 1953, of The Braid, Co. Antrim; **Phelim Robert Hugh O'Neill;** Bt 1929; PC (N Ireland) 1969; Major, late RA; *b* 2 Nov. 1909; *s* of 1st Baron Rathcavan, PC and Sylvia (*d* 1972), *d* of Walter A. Sandeman; *S* father, 1982; *m* 1st, 1934, Clare Désirée (from whom he obtained a divorce, 1944), *d* of late Detmar Blow; one *s* one *d*; 2nd, 1953, Mrs B. D. Edwards-Moss, *d* of late Major Hon. Richard Coke; three *d* (and one *d* decd). *Educ:* Eton. MP (UU) for North Antrim (UK Parliament), 1952–59; MP (U) North Antrim, Parliament of N Ireland, 1959–72; Minister, N Ireland: Education, 1969; Agriculture, 1969–71. *Heir:* *s* Hon. Hugh Detmar Torrens O'Neill, *qv*. *Address:* The Lodge, Killala, Co. Mayo, Ireland. *T:* Ballina 32252.

RATHCREEDAN, 3rd Baron *cr* 1916; **Christopher John Norton;** Partner, Norton & Brooksbank, Pedigree Livestock Auctioneers, since 1983; *b* 3 June 1949; *er s* of 2nd Baron Rathcreedan, TD and of Ann Pauline, *d* of late Surg.-Capt. William Bastian, RN; *S* father, 1990; *m* 1978, Lavinia Anne Ross, *d* of A. G. R. Ormiston; two *d*. *Educ:* Wellington Coll.; RAC Cirencester. Partner, Hobsons, Pedigree Livestock Auctioneers; founded Norton & Brooksbank, 1983. *Recreations:* horse racing, gardening. *Heir:* *b* Hon. Adam Gregory Norton [*b* 2 April 1952; *m* 1980, Hilary Shelton, *d* of Edmond Ryan; two *d*.]. *Address:* Waterton Farm House, Ampney Crucis, Cirencester, Glos GL7 5RR. *T:* Cirencester (0285) 654282. *Club:* Turf.

RATHDONNELL, 5th Baron, *cr* 1868; **Thomas Benjamin McClintock Bunbury;** *b* 17 Sept. 1938; *o s* of William, 4th Baron Rathdonnell and Pamela (*d* 1989), *e d* of late John Malcolm Drew; *S* father 1959; *m* 1965, Jessica Harriet, *d* of George Gilbert Butler, Scatorish, Bennettsbridge, Co. Kilkenny; three *s* one *d*. *Educ:* Charterhouse; Royal Naval College, Dartmouth. Lieutenant RN. *Heir:* *s* Hon. William Leopold McClintock Bunbury, *b* 6 July 1966. *Address:* Lisnavagh, Rathvilly, County Carlow, Ireland. *T:* Carlow 61104.

RATLEDGE, Prof. Colin, PhD; CChem, FRSC; CBiol, FIBiol; Professor of Microbial Biochemistry, University of Hull, since 1983; *b* 9 Oct. 1936; *s* of Fred Ratledge and Freda Smith Ratledge (*née* Proudlock); *m* 1961, Janet Vivien Bottomley; one *s* two *d*. *Educ:* Bury High Sch.; Manchester Univ. (BSc Tech, PhD). AMCST; CChem, FRSC 1970; CBiol, FIBiol 1982. Res. Fellowship, MRC Ireland, 1960–64; Res. Scientist, Unilever plc,

1964–67; Hull University, 1967–: Lectr, 1967–73; Sen. Lectr, 1973–77; Reader, 1977–83; Head of Dept of Biochemistry, 1986–88. Mem., AFRC Food Res. Cttee, 1989–; Chairman: AFRC Food Res. Grants Bd, 1989–; Brit. Co-ordinating Cttee for Biotechnology, 1989–91; Soc. of Chemical Ind. Biotechnology Gp, 1990–91; Inst. of Biol Biotechnology Gp, 1990–; Sec., Internat. Cttee of Envmtl and Applied Microbiology, 1991–; Mem., Biotechnology Cttee, Internat. Union of Biochemistry, 1984–. Editor-in-Chief, World Jl of Microbiol. and Biotechnol., 1987–; Exec. Editor, Biotechnology Techniques, 1988–. *Publications:* The Mycobacteria, 1977; Co-Editor: Microbial Technology: current state, future prospects, 1979; The Biology of the Mycobacteria, vol. 1 1982, vol. 2 1983, vol. 3 1989; Biotechnology for the Oils and Fats Industry, 1984; Microbial Technology in the Developing World, 1987; Microbial Lipids, vol. 1 1988, vol. 2 1989; Microbial Physiology and Manufacturing Industry, 1988; Biotechnology: social and economic impact, 1991; numerous scientific papers in biol science jls. *Recreations:* walking, gardening. *Address:* Department of Applied Biology, University of Hull, Hull HU6 7RX; 49 Church Drive, Leven, Beverley, E Yorks HU17 5LH. *T:* Hornsea (0964) 542690.

RATNER, Gerald Irving; Chairman since 1986, and Managing Director since 1984, Ratners Group; *b* 1 Nov. 1949; *s* of Leslie and Rachelle Ratner; *m* 1st (marr. diss. 1989); two *d;* 2nd, 1989, Moira Day; one *s* one *d. Educ:* Town and Country School, London NW3. Present company from school. *Recreations:* keeping fit, art, chess. *Address:* (office) 15 Stratton Street, W1X 5FD.

RATTEE, Hon. Sir Donald (Keith), Kt 1989; **Hon. Mr Justice Rattee;** a Judge of the High Court of Justice, Family Division, since 1989; Liaison Judge, Family Division (North Eastern Circuit), since 1990; *b* 9 March 1937; *s* of Charles Ronald and Dorothy Rattee; *m* 1964, Diana Mary, *d* of John Leslie and Florence Elizabeth Howl; four *d. Educ:* Clacton County High School; Trinity Hall, Cambridge (MA, LLB). Called to Bar, Lincoln's Inn, 1962, Bencher, 1985; Second Junior Counsel to the Inland Revenue (Chancery), 1972–77; QC 1977; Attorney Gen. of the Duchy of Lancaster, 1986–89; a Recorder, 1989. Mem., Gen. Council of the Bar, 1970–74. *Recreations:* golf, music, gardening. *Address:* Royal Courts of Justice, Strand, WC2A 2LL. *Clubs:* Royal Automobile; Banstead Downs Golf (Banstead).

RATTLE, Simon, CBE 1987; Principal Conductor, City of Birmingham Symphony Orchestra since Sept. 1980; Principal Guest Conductor, Los Angeles Philharmonic, since 1981; *b* Liverpool, 1955; *m* 1980, Elise Ross, American soprano; one *s.* Won Bournemouth John Player Internat. Conducting Comp., when aged 19. Has conducted: Bournemouth Sinfonietta; Philharmonia; Northern Sinfonia; London Philharmonic; London Sinfonietta; Berlin Philharmonic; Boston Symphony; Chicago Symphony; Cleveland Symphony; Concertgebouw; Stockholm Philharmonic; Toronto Symphony, etc. Festival Hall début, 1976. Royal Albert Hall (Proms. etc.), 1976–; Asst Conductor, BBC Scottish Symphony Orch., 1977–80; Associate Conductor, Royal Liverpool Philharmonic Soc., 1977–80; Glyndebourne début, 1977; Principal Conductor, London Choral Soc., 1979–84; Artistic Dir, South Bank Summer Music, 1981–83; Principal Guest Conductor, Rotterdam Philharmonic, 1981–84. Exclusive contract with EMI Records. *Address:* c/o Harold Holt Ltd, 31 Sinclair Road, W14 0NS. *T:* 071–603 4600.

RAU, Santha Rama; *see* Rama Rau, S.

RAVEN, Prof. John Albert, FRS 1990; FRSE; Professor of Biology (Personal Chair), University of Dundee, since 1980; *b* 25 June 1941; *s* of John Harold Edward Raven and Evelyn Raven; *m* 1985, Linda Lea Handley. *Educ:* Wimbish County Primary Sch.; Friends' Sch., Saffron Walden; St John's College, Cambridge (MA, PhD). FRSE 1981. University of Cambridge: Research Fellow, and Official Fellow, St John's Coll., 1966–71; Univ. Demonstrator in Botany, 1968–71; Lectr, and Reader, Dept of Biol Scis, Univ. of Dundee, 1971–80. *Publications:* Energetics and Transport in Aquatic Plants, 1984; numerous papers in learned jls and chapters in multi-author vols. *Recreations:* aviation, jogging, literature. *Address:* Spital Beag, Inverbay, Invergowrie, Dundee DD2 5DQ. *T:* Dundee (0382) 562292.

RAVEN, John Armstrong, CBE 1982; Director-General, International Express Carriers' Conference, since 1991; Consultant, World Bank, since 1983; Chairman, Aleph Systems Ltd, since 1983; *b* 23 April 1920; *s* of late John Colbeck Raven; *m* 1st, 1945, Megan Humphreys (*d* 1963); one *s* one *d;* 2nd, 1965, Joy Nesbitt (*d* 1983); one step *d. Educ:* High Sch., Cardiff; Downing Coll., Cambridge (MA). Called to Bar, Gray's Inn, 1955. Dir, British Coal Exporters' Fedn, 1947–68; Section Head, Nat. Economic Develt Office, 1968–70. Dir-Gen., Assoc. of British Chambers of Commerce, 1972–74; Vice-Chm., SITPRO, 1974–82. *Recreation:* wondering. *Address:* 4 rue des Arènes, 89100 Sens, France. *T:* 86 65 6333. *Club:* United Oxford & Cambridge University.

RAVEN, Dame Kathleen, (Dame Kathleen Annie Ingram), DBE 1968; FRCN 1986; SRN 1936; SCM 1938; Chief Nursing Officer in the Department of Health and Social Security (formerly Ministry of Health), 1958–72; *b* 9 Nov. 1910; *o d* of late Fredric William Raven and late Annie Williams Raven (*née* Mason); *m* 1959, Prof. John Thornton Ingram, MD, FRCP (*d* 1972). *Educ:* Ulverston Grammar School; privately; St Bartholomew's Hosp., London; City of London Maternity Hospital. St Bartholomew's Hospital: Night Superintendent, Ward Sister, Administrative Sister, Assistant Matron, 1936–49; Matron, Gen. Infirmary, Leeds, 1949–57; Dep. Chief Nursing Officer, Min. of Health, 1957–58. Mem. Gen. Nursing Council for England and Wales, 1950–57; Mem. Council and Chm. Yorkshire Br., Roy. Coll. of Nursing, 1950–57; Mem. Central Area Advisory Bd for Secondary Education, Leeds, 1953–57; Area Nursing Officer, Order of St John, 1953–57; Mem. Exec. Cttee Assoc. of Hospital Matrons for England and Wales, 1955–57; Mem. Advisory Cttee for Sister Tutor's Diploma, Univ. of Hull, 1955–57; Internal Examr for Diploma of Nursing, Univ. of Leeds, 1950–57; Member: Area Nurse Trg Cttee, 1951–57; Area Cttee Nat. Hosp. Service Reserve, 1950–57; Central Health Services Council, 1957–58; Council and Nursing Advisory Bd, British Red Cross Soc., 1958–72; Cttee of St John Ambulance Assoc., 1958–72; National Florence Nightingale Memorial Cttee of Great Britain and Northern Ireland, 1958–72; WHO Expert Advisory Panel on Nursing, 1961–79; WHO Fellow, 1960; a Vice-Pres., Royal Coll. of Nursing, 1972–. Civil Service Comr, 1972–80. Chief Nursing Adviser, Allied Med. Gp, 1974–. Nursing missions to Saudi Arabia and Egypt, 1972–. Mem., Council, Distressed Gentlefolk's Aid Assoc., 1974–89 (Chm., F and GP Cttee 1981–87). Founder Gov., Aylesbury GS, 1985. Freedom, City of London, 1986. Hon. Freewoman, Worshipful Co. of Barbers, 1981. FRSA 1970. Officer (Sister) Order of St John, 1963. *Recreations:* painting, reading, travel. *Address:* Jesmond, Burcott, Wing, Leighton Buzzard, Bedfordshire LU7 0JU. *T:* Aylesbury (0296) 688244; 29 Harley Street, W1. *T:* 071–580 3765. *Club:* Commonwealth Trust.

See also R. W. Raven.

RAVEN, Ronald William, OBE (mil.) 1946; TD 1953; FRCS 1931; Consulting Surgeon, Westminster Hospital and Royal Marsden Hospital, since 1969; Surgeon, French Hospital, London, 1936–69; Cons. Surgeon (General Surgeon) Eversfield Chest Hospital 1937–48; Cons. Surgeon, Royal Star and Garter Home for Disabled Sailors, Soldiers and Airmen 1948–69; *b* 28 July 1904; *e s* of late Fredric William Raven and Annie Williams Raven (*née* Mason), Coniston. *Educ:* Ulverston Grammar School; St Bartholomew's Hospital Medical College, Univ. of London. St Bart's Hosp.: gained various prizes and Brackenbury surgical schol.; resident surgical appts, 1928–29; Demonstrator in Pathology, St Bart's Hosp., 1929–31; Registrar Statistics Nat. Radium Commn, 1931–34; jun. surgical appts, 1931–35; Asst Surg. Gordon Hosp., 1935; Asst Surg. Roy. Cancer Hosp., 1939–46, Surg. 1946–62; Jt Lectr in Surgery, Westminster Med. Sch., Univ. of London, 1951–69; Surgeon, Westminster (Gordon) Hosp., 1947–69; Sen. Surgeon, Royal Marsden Hosp. and Inst. of Cancer Research, Royal Cancer Hosp., 1962–69. Lectr, RIPH&H, 1965–85. Member: DHSS Standing Sub-Cttee on Cancer; DHSS Adv. Cttee on Cancer Registration; Chairman: Jt Nat. Cancer Survey Cttee; Cancer Rehabilitation and Continuing Care Cttee, UICC, 1982–90. Fellow Assoc. of Surg. of GB; Hon. FRSM 1987 (PP, Section of Proctology, PP, Section of Oncology); Mem. Council, 1968–76, Mem. Court of Patrons, 1976–, RCS; (Founder) Pres., British Assoc. of Surgical Oncology, 1973–77; (Founder) Pres., Assoc. of Head and Neck Oncologists of GB, 1968–71; formerly Member: European Soc. Surgical Oncology: Internat. Soc. of Surgery; President: Marie Curie Meml Foundn, 1990– (Chm. Council, 1961–90; Chm. Exec. Cttee, 1948–61); Epsom Coll., 1990– (Vice-Pres. and Chm., Council, 1954–); late Chm., Conjoint Cttee; late Mem. Bd of Governors Royal Marsden Hosp.; formerly Mem. Council of Queen's Institute of District Nursing; Mem. (late Chm.), Cttee of Management Med. Insurance Agency; formerly Mem. Council, Imperial Cancer Res. Fund; Life Pres., Hellenic Soc. of Oncology, 1990; Vice-President: John Grooms Assoc. for the Disabled, 1958–; Malta Meml District Nursing Assoc., 1982–. Surg. EMS, 1939; joined RAMC, 1941, and served in N Africa, Italy and Malta (despatches); o/c Surg. Div. (Lt-Col); and o/c Gen. Hosp. (Col), 1946; Lt-Col RAMC (TA); o/c Surg. Div. Gen. Hosp., 1947–53; Col RAMC (TA); o/c No 57 (Middlesex) General Hospital (TA), 1953–59; Colonel TARO, 1959–62; Hon. Colonel RAMC. OStJ 1946. Hon. Professor National Univ. of Colombia, 1949; Hon. MD Cartagena, 1949; Corresponding Foreign Member: Soc. of Head and Neck Surgeons of USA; Roman Surg. Soc.; Soc. Surg. of Bogotà; Société de Chirurgie de Lyon; Acad. of Athens, 1983; Member: Nat. Acad. Med. of Colombia; NY Acad. of Sciences; Soc. of Surgeons of Colombia; Italian Soc. Thoracic Surg.; Czechoslovak Soc. of J. E. Purkyne; Hon. Mem., Indian Assoc. of Oncology, 1983; Diploma de Socio Honorario, Soc. de Cancerologia de El Salvador, 1983. Diploma de Honor al Merito, Liga Nacional de El Salvador, 1983. Lectures: Arris and Gale, 1933; Erasmus Wilson, 1935, 1946, 1947; Malcolm Morris Meml, 1954; Blair Bell Meml, 1960; Elizabeth Matthai Endowment, Madras Univ., 1965; First W. Emory Burnett Honor, Temple Univ., USA, 1966; Edith A. Ward Meml, 1966; Gerald Townsley Meml, 1974; Bradshaw, RCS, 1975; Ernest Miles Meml, 1980; Honor, Amer. Soc. of Surg. Oncology, 1981; Honor, 1st Congress, Eur. Soc. of Surg. Oncology, Athens, 1982; Honor-Centenary, George N. Papanicolaou, Athens, 1983; First Kitty Cookson Meml, Royal Free Hosp., 1985. Hunterian Prof., RCS, 1948; Vis. Prof. of Surgery: Ein-Shams University, Cairo, 1961; Cancer Inst., Madras, 1965; Maadi Hosp., Cairo, 1974. Surgical missions to: Colombia, 1949; Saudi Arabia, 1961, 1962, 1975, 1976; United Arab Emirates, 1975, 1985. Consulting Editor, Clinical Oncology, 1979–82. FRSA, 1987. Mem. Court, 1973–, Master, 1980–81, Worshipful Co. of Barbers; Mem., Livery Consultative Cttee, 1981–86. Freeman, City of London, 1956. Furnished Ronald William Raven Room, Mus. of Royal Crown Derby Porcelain Co., 1987; Ronald Raven Chair in Clinical Oncology, Royal Free Hosp. Sch. of Medicine (London Univ.), established 1990. Hon. Life Mem., Derby Porcelain Internat. Soc., 1988. G. Paparicolaou Gold Medal, 1990. Chevalier de la Légion d'Honneur, 1952. *Publications:* Treatment of Shock, 1942 (trans. Russian); Surgical Care, 1942, 2nd edn 1952; Cancer in General Practice (jointly), 1952; Surgical Instruments and Appliances (jointly), 1952; War Wounds and Injuries (jt editor and contrib.). 1940; chapters on Shock and Malignant Disease in Encyclopædia British Medical Practice, 1952, 1955, 1962–69, and Medical Progress, 1970–71; Handbook on Cancer for Nurses and Health Visitors, 1953; Cancer and Allied Diseases, 1955; contrib. chapters in Operative Surgery (Rob and Rodney Smith), 1956–57; Editor and contrib. Cancer (7 vols), 1957–60; Cancer of the Pharynx, Larynx and Oesophagus and its Surgical Treatment, 1958; (ed) Cancer Progress, 1960 and 1963; (ed jtly) The Prevention of Cancer, 1967; (ed) Modern Trends in Oncology 1, part 1, Research Progress, part 2, Clinical Progress, 1973; (ed and contrib.) The Dying Patient, 1975 (trans. Japanese and Dutch); (ed and contrib.) Principles of Surgical Oncology, 1977; (ed and contrib.) Foundations of Medicine, 1978; Rehabilitation and Continuing Care in Cancer, 1986; (jtly) Cancer Care—an international survey, 1986; The Gospel of St John, 1987; The Theory and Practice of Oncology: its historical evolution and present principles, 1990; Death Into Life, 1990; Rehabilitation Oncology, 1991; papers on surgical subjects, especially relating to Cancer in British and foreign journals. *Recreations:* philately (medallist Internat. Stamp Exhibn, London, 1950), music, ceramics and pictures, travel. *Address:* 29 Harley Street, W1N 1DA. *T:* 071–580 3765; Manor Lodge, Wingrave, Aylesbury, Bucks. *T:* Aylesbury (0296) 681287. *Clubs:* MCC, Pilgrims.

See also Dame Kathleen Raven.

RAVEN, Simon (Arthur Noël); author, critic and dramatist since 1957; *b* 28 Dec. 1927; *s* of Arthur Godart Raven and Esther Kate Raven (*née* Christmas); *m* 1951, Susan Mandeville Kilner (marriage dissolved); one *s. Educ:* Charterhouse; King's Coll., Cambridge (MA). Research, 1951–52; regular commn, King's Shropshire Light Inf., 1953–57 (Capt.): served in Kenya; resigned, 1957. Member, Horatian Society. *Publications: novels:* The Feathers of Death, 1959; Brother Cain, 1959; Doctors Wear Scarlet, 1960; Close of Play, 1962; The Roses of Picardie, 1980; An Inch of Fortune, 1980; September Castle, 1983. The Alms for Oblivion sequence: The Rich Pay Late, 1964; Friends in Low Places, 1965; The Sabre Squadron, 1966; Fielding Gray, 1967; The Judas Boy, 1968; Places Where They Sing, 1970; Sound the Retreat, 1971; Come like Shadows, 1972; Bring Forth the Body, 1974; The Survivors, 1976; The First-born of Egypt sequence: Morning Star, 1984; The Face of the Waters, 1985; Before the Cock Crow, 1986; New Seed for Old, 1988; Blood of My Bone, 1989; In the Image of God, 1990; *short stories:* The Fortunes of Fingel, 1976; *memoirs:* Shadows on the Grass, 1982; The Old School, 1986; The Old Gang, 1988; Bird of Ill Omen, 1989; Is There Anybody There? Said the Traveller: memories of a private nuisance, 1991; *general:* The English Gentleman, 1961; Boys Will be Boys, 1963; Royal Foundation and Other Plays, 1965; contribs to Observer, Spectator, Punch, etc. *Plays and dramatisations for broadcasting:* BBC TV: Royal Foundation, 1961; The Scapegoat, 1964; Sir Jocelyn, 1965; Huxley's Point Counter-Point, 1968; Trollope's The Way We Live Now, 1969; The Pallisers, a serial in 26 episodes based on the six Palliser novels of Anthony Trollope, 1974; Iris Murdoch's An Unofficial Rose, 1975; Sexton Blake, 1978; ABC TV: The Gaming Book, 1965; Thames TV: Edward and Mrs Simpson, a serial based on Edward VIII by Frances Donaldson, 1978; Love in a Cold Climate, a dramatisation of Nancy Mitford's Pursuit of Love and Love in a Cold Climate, 1980; BBC Radio: Triad, a trilogy loosely based on Thucydides' History of the Peloponnesian War, 1965–68. *Recreations:* cricket, travel, reading, the turf. *Address:* c/o Curtis Brown Ltd, 162–168 Regent Street, W1R 5TB. *Clubs:* MCC, Butterflies Cricket, Trogs' Cricket.

RAVENSCROFT, John Robert Parker, (John Peel); broadcaster/journalist, since 1961; *b* 30 Aug. 1939; *s* of Robert Leslie and Joan Mary Ravenscroft; *m* 1974, Sheila

Mary Gilhooly; two *s* two *d*. *Educ:* Woodlands Sch., Deganwy, N Wales; Shrewsbury. National Service, Royal Artillery (B2 Radar Operator), 1957–59. Mill operative, Rochdale, 1959–60; office boy, Dallas, Texas, 1960–65; part-time disc-jockey, 1961–; computer programmer, 1965; Pirate Radio, London, 1967; BBC Radio 1, 1967–. Hon. MA East Anglia, 1989. *Recreations:* making plans to go and live in France, staring out of the window. *Address:* c/o BBC Radio 1, W1A 4DJ. *T:* 071–580 4468. *Clubs:* Liverpool Supporters; Eddie Grundy Fan (Sutton).

RAVENSCROFT, Ven. Raymond Lockwood; Archdeacon of Cornwall and Canon Librarian of Truro Cathedral, since 1988; *b* 15 Sept. 1931; *s* of Cecil and Amy Ravenscroft; *m* 1957, Ann (*née* Stockwell); one *s* one *d*. *Educ:* Sea Point Boys' High School, Cape Town, SA; Leeds Univ. (BA Gen. 1953); College of the Resurrection, Mirfield. Assistant Curate: St Alban's, Goodwood, Cape, SA, 1955–58; St John's Pro-Cathedral, Bulawayo, S Rhodesia, 1958–59; Rector of Francistown, Bechuanaland, 1959–62; Asst Curate, St Ives, Cornwall, 1962–64; Vicar: All Saints, Falmouth, 1964–68; St Stephen by Launceston with St Thomas, 1968–74; Team Rector of Probus Team Ministry, 1974–88; RD of Powder, 1977–81; Hon. Canon of Truro Cathedral, 1982–88. *Recreations:* walking, reading, local history. *Address:* Archdeacon's House, Knights Hill, Kenwyn, Truro, Cornwall TR1 3UY. *T:* Truro (0872) 72866.

RAVENSDALE, 3rd Baron *cr* 1911; **Nicholas Mosley,** MC 1944; Bt 1781; *b* 25 June 1923; *e s* of Sir Oswald Mosley, 6th Bt (*d* 1980) and Lady Cynthia (*d* 1933), *d* of 1st Marquess Curzon of Kedleston; *S* to barony of aunt, who was also Baroness Ravensdale of Kedleston (Life Peer), 1966, and to baronetcy of father, 1980; *m* 1st, 1947, Rosemary Laura Salmond (marr. diss. 1974; she *d* 1991); three *s* one *d*; 2nd, 1974, Mrs Verity Bailey; one *s*. *Educ:* Eton; Balliol College, Oxford. Served in the Rifle Brigade, Captain, 1942–46. *Publications:* (as Nicholas Mosley): Spaces of the Dark, 1951; The Rainbearers, 1955; Corruption, 1957; African Switchback, 1958; The Life of Raymond Raynes, 1961; Meeting Place, 1962; Accident, 1964; Experience and Religion, 1964; Assassins, 1966; Impossible Object, 1968; Natalie Natalia, 1971; The Assassination of Trotsky, 1972; Julian Grenfell: His Life and the Times of his Death, 1888–1915, 1976; The Rules of the Game: Sir Oswald and Lady Cynthia Mosley 1896–1933, 1982; Beyond the Pale: Sir Oswald Mosley 1933–1980, 1983; *novels* (series): Catastrophe Practice, 1979; Imago Bird, 1980; Serpent, 1981; Judith, 1986; Hopeful Monsters (Whitbread Prize), 1990. *Heir: s* Hon. Shaun Nicholas Mosley [*b* 5 August 1949; *m* 1978, Theresa Clifford; three *s*]. *Address:* 2 Gloucester Crescent, NW1 7DS. *T:* 071–485 4514.

RAVENSWORTH, 8th Baron *cr* 1821; **Arthur Waller Liddell,** Bt 1642; JP; *b* 25 July 1924; *s* of late Hon. Cyril Arthur Liddell (2nd *s* of 5th Baron) and Dorothy L., *d* of William Brown, Slinfold, Sussex; *S* cousin 1950; *m* 1950, Wendy, *d* of J. S. Bell, Cookham, Berks; one *s* one *d*. *Educ:* Harrow. Radio Engineer, BBC, 1944–50. JP Northumberland, 1959. *Heir: s* Hon. Thomas Arthur Hamish Liddell [*b* 27 Oct. 1954; *m* 1983, Linda, *d* of H. Thompson; one *s* one *d*]. *Address:* Eslington Park, Whittingham, Alnwick, Northumberland. *T:* Whittingham (066574) 239.

RAWBONE, Rear-Adm. Alfred Raymond, CB 1976; AFC 1951; *b* 19 April 1923; *s* of A. Rawbone and Mrs E. D. Rawbone (*née* Wall); *m* 1943, Iris Alicia (*née* Willshaw); one *s* one *d*. *Educ:* Saltley Grammar Sch., Birmingham. Joined RN, 1942; 809 Sqdn War Service, 1943; CO 736 Sqdn, 1953; CO 897 Sqdn, 1955; CO Loch Killisport, 1959–60; Comdr (Air) Lossiemouth and HMS Ark Royal, 1961–63; Chief Staff Officer to Flag Officer Naval Air Comd, 1965–67; CO HMS Dido, 1968–69; CO RNAS Yeovilton, 1970–72; CO HMS Kent, 1972–73; Dep. ACOS (Operations), SHAPE, 1974–76. Comdr 1958; Captain 1964; Rear-Adm. 1974. Director: Vincents of Yeovil, 1983–86; Vindata, 1984–86; Vincents (Bridgewater) Ltd, 1984–86. *Address:* Halstock Leigh, Halstock, near Yeovil, Somerset BA22 9QU.

RAWCLIFFE, Rt. Rev. Derek Alec, OBE 1971; Assistant Bishop, Diocese of Ripon, since 1991; *b* 8 July 1921; *s* of James Alec and Gwendoline Rawcliffe; *m* 1977, Susan Speight (*d* 1987). *Educ:* Sir Thomas Rich's School, Gloucester; Univ. of Leeds (BA, 1st cl. Hons English); College of the Resurrection, Mirfield. Deacon 1944, priest 1945, Worcester; Assistant Priest, Claines St George, Worcester, 1944–47; Asst master, All Hallows School, Pawa, Solomon Islands, 1947–53; Headmaster, 1953–56; Headmaster, S Mary's School, Maravovo, Solomon Is, 1956–58; Archdeacon of Southern Melanesia, New Hebrides, 1959–74; Assistant Bishop, Diocese of Melanesia, 1974–75; First Bishop of the New Hebrides, 1975–80; Bishop of Glasgow and Galloway, 1981–91. New Hebrides Medal, 1980; Vanuatu Independence Medal, 1980. *Recreations:* music, poetry, numismatics. *Address:* Kitkatts, Wetherby Road, Bardsey, Leeds LS17 9BB. *T:* Wetherby (0937) 572201.

RAWES, Francis Roderick, MBE 1944; MA; *b* 28 Jan. 1916; *e s* of late Prescott Rawes and Susanna May Dockery; *m* 1940, Dorothy Joyce, *d* of E. M. Hundley, Oswestry; two *s* one *d*. *Educ:* Charterhouse; St Edmund Hall, Oxford. Served in Intelligence Corps, 1940–46; GSO3(I) 13 Corps; GSO1 (I) HQ 15 Army Group and MI14 WO. Asst Master at Westminster School, 1938–40 and 1946–64; Housemaster, 1947–64; Headmaster, St Edmund's School, Canterbury, 1964–78. Chm. Governing Body, Westonbirt Sch., 1983– (Governor, 1979–). *Address:* Peyton House, Chipping Campden, Glos.

RAWLEY, Alan David, QC 1977; a Recorder of the Crown Court, since 1972; *b* 28 Sept. 1934; *er s* of late Cecil David Rawley and of Theresa Rawley (*née* Pack); *m* 1964, Ione Jane Ellis; two *s* one *d*. *Educ:* Wimbledon Coll.; Brasenose Coll., Oxford. Nat. Service, 1956–58; commnd Royal Tank Regt. Called to the Bar, Middle Temple, 1958; Bencher, 1985. Dep. Chairman, Cornwall Quarter Sessions, 1971. *Address:* Lamb Building, Temple, EC4Y 7AS. *T:* 071–353 6381. *Clubs:* Garrick, Pilgrims, MCC; Hampshire (Winchester).

RAWLINGS, Margaret; actress; *b* Osaka, Japan, 5 June 1906; *d* of Rev. G. W. Rawlings and Lilian Boddington; *m* 1st, 1927, Gabriel Toyne, actor (marr. diss. 1938); no *c*; 2nd, 1942, Robert Barlow (knighted 1943; *d* 1976); one *d*. *Educ:* Oxford High School for Girls; Lady Margaret Hall, Oxford. Left Oxford after one year, and joined the Macdona Players Bernard Shaw Repertory Company on tour, 1927; played Jennifer in the Doctor's Dilemma and many other parts; toured Canada with Maurice Colbourne, 1929; First London engagement Bianca Capello in The Venetian at Little Theatre in 1931, followed by New York; played Elizabeth Barrett Browning, in The Barretts of Wimpole Street in Australia and New Zealand; Oscar Wilde's Salome at Gate Theatre; Liza Kingdom, The Old Folks at Home, Queen's; Mary Fitton in This Side Idolatry, Lyric; Jean in The Greeks had a word for it, Liza Doolittle in Pygmalion and Ann in Man and Superman, Cambridge Theatre, 1935; Katie O'Shea in Parnell, Ethel Barrymore Theatre, New York 1935, later at New, London; Lady Macbeth for OUDS 1936; Mary and Lily in Black Limelight, St James's and Duke of York's, 1937–38; Helen in Trojan Women, Karen Selby in The Flashing Stream, Lyric, 1938–39, and in New York; Revival of Liza in Pygmalion, Haymarket, 1939; You of all People, Apollo, 1939; A House in the Square, St Martin's, 1940; Mrs Dearth in Dear Brutus, 1941–42; Gwendolen Fairfax in the Importance of Being Earnest, Royal Command Perf., Haymarket, 1946; Titania in Purcell's Fairy Queen, Covent Garden, 1946; Vittoria Corombona in Webster's The White Devil, Duchess, 1947; Marceline in Jean-Jacques Bernard's The Unquiet Spirit, Arts, 1949; Germaine in A Woman in Love, tour and Embassy, 1949; The Purple Fig Tree, Piccadilly, 1950; Lady Macbeth, Arts, 1950; Spring at Marino, Arts, 1951; Zabina in Tamburlaine, Old Vic, 1951–52; Lysistrata in The Apple Cart, Haymarket, 1953; Countess in The Dark is Light Enough, Salisbury and Windsor Repertory, 1955; Paulina and Mistress Ford, Old Vic, 1955–56; Title Rôle in Racine's Phèdre, Theatre in the Round, London and tour, 1957–58; Sappho in Sappho, Lyceum, Edinburgh, 1961; Ask Me No More, Windsor, 1962; Title role in Racine's Phèdre, Cambridge Arts, 1963; Ella Rentheim in John Gabriel Borkman, Duchess, 1963; Jocasta in Œdipus, Playhouse (Nottingham), 1964; Gertrude in Hamlet, Ludlow Festival, 1965; Madame Torpe in Torpe's Hotel, Yvonne Arnaud Theatre, Guildford, 1965; Mrs Bridgenorth, in Getting Married, Strand, 1967; Carlotta, in A Song at Twilight, Windsor, 1968; Cats Play, Greenwich, 1973; Mixed Economy, King's Head Islington, 1977; Lord Arthur Saville's Crime, Malvern Fest. and tour, 1980; Uncle Vanya, Haymarket, 1982. One-woman performance, Empress Eugénie, May Fair, London, transf. to Vaudeville, UK tour and Dublin Fest., 1979; repeated at King's Lynn Fest., Riverside Theatre, London, New Univ. of Ulster, 1980; Cologne, Horsham, MacRobert Arts Centre, Stirling, Pitlochry Fest., New Univ. of Ulster, 1981; Spoleto Fest., Charleston, SC, 1983. *Films:* Roman Holiday; Beautiful Stranger; No Road Back; Hands of the Ripper; Dr Jekyll and Mr Hyde, 1989. *Television:* Criss Cross Quiz; Somerset Maugham Hour; Sunday Break; Compact; Maigret; Planemakers; solo performance, Black Limelight, Armchair Theatre, 1969; Wives and Daughters, 1971; Folio, 1983. Innumerable radio broadcasts, incl. We Beg to Differ, Brains Trust, Desert Island Discs (an early castaway), plays (Tumbledown Dick, 1986; Golovliovo, 1988; Crown House (serial), 1988; poetry recitals; recordings of: Keats, Gerard Manley Hopkins, Alice in Wonderland; (Marlowe Soc.) King Lear, Pericles; New English Bible Gospels. *Publication:* (trans.) Racine's Phèdre, 1961, (US, 1962). *Recreation:* poetry. *Address:* Rocketer, Wendover, Aylesbury, Bucks HP22 6PR. *T:* Wendover (0296) 622234.

RAWLINGS, Patricia Elizabeth; Member (C) Essex South West, European Parliament, since 1989; *b* 27 Jan. 1939; *d* of Louis Rawlings and Mary (*née* Boas de Winter); *m* 1962, David Wolfson (*see* Baron Wolfson of Sunningdale) (marr. diss. 1967). *Educ:* Oak Hall, Haslemere, Surrey; Le Manoir, Lausanne; Florence Univ.; University Coll. London (BA Hons); London School of Economics (post grad. diploma course, Internat. Relns). Children's Care Cttee, LCC, 1959–61; WNHR Nursing, Westminster Hosp., until 1968. European Parliament: Dep. Whip, EDG; Vice-Pres., Albanian, Bulgarian and Rumania Delegn; Youth, Sport and Culture, Educn, Media and Political Affairs Cttees. British Red Cross Society: Mem., 1964–; Chm., Appeals, London Br., until 1988; Nat. Badge of Honour, 1981, Hon. Vice Pres., 1988. Member Council: British Bd of Video Classification; Peace through NATO; Special Advr to Ministry on Inner Cities, DoE, 1987–88. Member: IISS; RIIA; EUW; Cons. Women's Nat. Cttee. Dir, English Chamber Orch. and Music Soc. Contested (C): Sheffield Central, 1983; Doncaster Central, 1987. *Recreations:* music, art, golf, ski-ing, travel. *Address:* 97–113 Rue Belliard, 1040 Brussels. *T:* 234211; European Parliament, Palais de l'Europe, 67006 Strasbourg, France. *T:* 88374001. *Club:* Queen's.

RAWLINS, Colin Guy Champion, OBE 1965; DFC 1941; Director of Zoos and Chief Executive Officer, Zoological Society of London, 1966–84; *b* 5 June 1919; *s* of R. S. C. Rawlins and Yvonne Blanche Andrews; *m* 1946, Rosemary Jensen; two *s* one *d*. *Educ:* Prince of Wales Sch., Nairobi; Charterhouse; Queen's Coll., Oxford (MA). Served with RAF, 1939–46: Bomber Comd, NW Europe; POW, 1941–45; Sqdn-Leader. HM Overseas Civil Service, 1946–66: Administrative Officer, Northern Rhodesia (later Zambia); appointments at Headquarters and in field; Provincial Commissioner, Resident Secretary. Mem., Pearce Commn on Rhodesian Opinion, 1972. Past Pres., Internat. Union of Dirs of Zool. Gardens. FCIS 1967. *Recreations:* aviation, travel, gardening. *Address:* Birchgrove, Earl Howe Road, Holmer Green, Bucks HP15 6QT.

RAWLINS, Brig. Gordon John, OBE 1986; Deputy Secretary, Institution of Electrical Engineers, since 1991; *b* 22 April 1944; *s* of Arthur and Joyce Rawlins; *m* 1st, 1965, Ann Beard (*d* 1986); one *s*; 2nd, 1986, Margaret Anne Ravenscroft; one step *s* one step *d*. *Educ:* Peter Symond's, Winchester; Welbeck College; RMA Sandhurst; RMCS Shrivenham (BSc Eng). CEng, FIProdE, MRAeS, FIIM, psc. Commissioned REME, 1964; served Aden, Oman, Jordan, Hong Kong, BAOR, UK, 1964–77; Staff Coll., 1978; MoD 1978–80; 2 i/c 5 Armd Wksp, REME, BAOR, 1981–82; CO 7 Armd Wksp, REME, BAOR, 1982–84; MoD, 1984–87 (Sec. to COS Cttee, 1987); Comd Maint., 1 (BR) Corps, BAOR, 1988. Sec., Instn of Production, subseq. Manufacturing, Engrs, 1988–91. *Recreations:* opera, blues music, Rugby, cricket. *Address:* c/o Royal Bank of Scotland, Holt's Farnborough Branch, Victoria Road, Farnborough, Hants GU14 7NR. *Club:* Army & Navy.

RAWLINS, Surg. Vice-Adm. Sir John (Stuart Pepys), KBE 1978 (OBE 1960; MBE 1956); *b* 12 May 1922; *s* of Col S. W. H. Rawlins, CB, CMG, DSO and Dorothy Pepys Cockerell; *m* 1944, Diana Colbeck; one *s* three *d*. *Educ:* Wellington Coll.; University Coll., Oxford (Hon. Fellow, 1991); St Bartholomew's Hospital. BM, BCh 1945; MA, FRCP, FFCM, FRAeS. Surg. Lieut RNVR, HMS Triumph, 1947; Surg. Lieut RN, RAF Inst. Aviation Med., 1951; RN Physiol Lab., 1957; Surg. Comdr RAF Inst., Aviation Med., 1961; HMS Ark Royal, 1964; US Navy Medical Research Inst., 1967; Surg. Captain 1969; Surg. Cdre, Dir of Health and Research (Naval), 1973; Surg. Rear-Adm. 1975; Dean of Naval Medicine and MO i/c, Inst. of Naval Medicine, 1975–77; Actg Surg. Vice-Adm. 1977; Medical Dir-Gen. (Navy), 1977–80. QHP 1975. Chairman: Deep Ocean Engineering Inc., 1983–89; Medical Express Ltd, 1984–; Trident Underwater Engrg (Systems) Ltd, 1985–; General Offshore Corp. (UK) Ltd, 1988–91; Director: Diving Unlimited International Ltd, 1980–; Deep Ocean Technology Inc., 1989– (Chm., 1983–89); Deep Ocean Engrg, 1989–. Pres., Soc. for Underwater Technology, 1980–84 (Hon. Fellow, 1986); Vice-Pres., Underseas Med. Soc.; Hon. Life Mem., British Sub-Aqua Club, 1983; Founder-Mem. European Underseas Biomed. Soc.; Fellow Aerospace Med. Soc. (Armstrong Lectr, 1980); FRAeS 1973; FRSM. Hon. Fellow, Lancaster Univ., 1986. Erroll-Eldridge Prize 1967; Sec. of US Navy's Commendation 1971; Gilbert Blane Medal 1971; Tuttle Meml Award 1973; Chadwick Medal and Prize 1975; Nobel Award, Inst. of Explosives Engrs, 1987; Man of the Year, British Council for Rehabilitation of the Disabled, 1964. *Publications:* papers in fields of aviation and diving medicine. *Recreations:* diving, fishing, stalking, riding. *Address:* Little Cross, Holme, Newton Abbot, S Devon TQ13 7RS. *T:* Poundsgate (03643) 249, *Fax:* Poundsgate (03643) 400. *Club:* Vincent's (Oxford).

RAWLINS, Prof. Michael David, MD; FRCP, FRCPE, FFPM; Ruth and Lionel Jacobson Professor of Clinical Pharmacology, since 1973, and Public Orator, since 1990, University of Newcastle upon Tyne; *b* 28 March 1941; *s* of Rev. Jack and Evelyn Daphne Rawlins; *m* 1963, Elizabeth Cadbury Hambly; three *d*. *Educ:* St Thomas's Hosp. Med. Sch., London (BSc 1962; MB BS 1965); MD London 1973. FRCP 1977; FRCPE 1987; FFPM 1989. Lectr in Medicine, St Thomas's Hosp., London, 1967–71; Sen. Registrar, Hammersmith Hosp., London, 1971–72; Vis. Res. Fellow, Karolinska Inst., Stockholm, Sweden, 1972–73. Pres., NE Council on Addictions, 1991–; Vice-Chm., Northern RHA, 1990–; Member:

Nat. Cttee on Pharmacology, 1977–83; Cttee on the Safety of Medicines, 1980–; Cttee on Toxicity, 1989–. Chm., Newcastle SDP, 1981–84. Bradshaw Lectr, RCP, 1986. FRSM 1972. *Publications:* Variability in Human Drug Response, 1973; articles on clinical pharmacology in med. and scientific jls. *Recreations:* music, golf. *Address:* 29 The Grove, Gosforth, Newcastle upon Tyne NE3 1NE. *T:* 091–285 5581; Shoreston House, Shoreston, near Seahouses, Northumberland NE68 7SX. *T:* Seahouses (0665) 720203. *Clubs:* Royal Society of Medicine; Bamburgh Castle Golf.

RAWLINS, Peter Jonathan, FCA; Chief Executive, London (formerly International) Stock Exchange, since 1989; *b* 30 April 1951; *e s* of late Kenneth Raymond Ivan Rawlins and Constance Amande Rawlins (*née* Malzy); *m* 1973, Louise Langton; one *s* one *d. Educ:* Arnold House Sch.; St Edward's Sch., Oxford; Keble Coll., Oxford (Hons English Lang. and Lit.; MA). Arthur Andersen & Co., 1972–85: Audit Manager, 1977; Partner, 1983; UK Practice Develt Partner, 1984; full-time secondment to Lloyd's of London as PA to Chief Exec. and Dep, Chm., 1983–84; Dir, Sturge Holdings, and Man. Dir, R. W. Sturge & Co., 1985–89; Director: Sturge Lloyd's Agencies, 1986–89; Wise Speke Holdings, 1987–89; non-exec. Dir, Lloyd-Roberts & Gilkes, 1989–. Mem., Cttee, Lloyd's Underwriting Agents Assoc., 1986–89 (Treasurer, 1986–87; Dep. Chm., 1988); Mem., standing cttees, Council of Lloyd's, 1985–89. Director: London Sinfonietta Trust, 1985–88; Half Moon Theatre, 1986–88; Mem. Council and Co. Sec., Assoc. for Business Sponsorship of the Arts, 1982–; Dir and Trustee, London City Ballet Trust, 1986–. *Recreations:* family, performing arts, tennis, squash, clay pigeon shooting, travelling. *Address:* London Stock Exchange, EC2N 1HP. *T:* 071–588 2355. *Clubs:* City of London, MCC.

RAWLINSON, family name of **Baron Rawlinson of Ewell.**

RAWLINSON OF EWELL, Baron *cr* 1978 (Life Peer), of Ewell in the County of Surrey; **Peter Anthony Grayson Rawlinson,** PC 1964; Kt 1962; QC 1959; QC (NI) 1972; *b* 26 June 1919; *o surv. s* of late Lt-Col A. R. Rawlinson, OBE, and Ailsa, *e d* of Sir Henry Mulleneux Grayson, Bt, KBE; *m* 1st, 1940, Haidee Kavanagh; three *d*; 2nd, 1954, Elaine Dominguez, Newport, Rhode Island, USA; two *s* one *d. Educ:* Downside; Christ's Coll., Cambridge (Exhibitioner 1938, Hon. Fellow 1980). Officer Cadet Sandhurst, 1939; served in Irish Guards, 1940–46; N Africa, 1943 (despatches); demobilized with rank of Major, 1946. Called to Bar, Inner Temple, 1946, Bencher, 1962, Reader, 1983, Treas., 1984; Recorder of Salisbury, 1961–62; called to Bar, Northern Ireland, 1972; Recorder of Kingston upon Thames, 1975–85; Leader, Western Circuit, 1975–82; retired from practice at the Bar, 1986. Contested (C) Hackney South, 1951; MP(C) Surrey, Epsom, 1955–74, Epsom and Ewell, 1974–78. Solicitor-General, July 1962–Oct. 1964; Opposition Spokesman: for Law, 1964–65, 1968–70; for Broadcasting, 1965; Attorney-General, 1970–74; Attorney-General for NI, 1972–74. Chm., Parly Legal Cttee, 1967–70. Member of Council, Justice, 1960–62, 1964; Trustee of Amnesty, 1960–62; Member, Bar Council, 1966–68; Mem. Senate, Inns of Court, 1968, Vice-Chm., 1974; Vice-Chm., Bar, 1974–75; Chairman of the Bar and Senate, 1975–76; Pres., Senate of Inns of Court and Bar, 1986–87; Chm., Enquiry into Constitution of the Senate, 1985–86. Chm. of Stewards, RAC, 1985–. Director: Pioneer International (formerly Pioneer Concrete Services) Ltd, Sydney, 1985– (Chm., UK subsidiary); Daily Telegraph plc, 1985–; STC plc, 1986–91; Mem., London Adv. Cttee, Hongkong and Shanghai Banking Corp., 1984–90. Hon. Fellow, Amer. Coll. of Trial Lawyers, 1973; Hon. Mem., Amer. Bar Assoc., 1976. SMO Malta. *Publications:* War Poems and Poetry today, 1943; Public Duty and Personal Faith—the example of Thomas More, 1978; A Price Too High (autobiog.), 1989; The Jesuit Factor, 1990; articles and essays in law jls. *Recreations:* the theatre and painting. *Address:* 9 Priory Walk, SW10 9SP. *Clubs:* White's, Pratt's, Royal Automobile, MCC.

RAWLINSON, Sir Anthony Henry John, 5th Bt *cr* 1891; photographer and inventor; *b* 1 May 1936; *s* of Sir Alfred Frederick Rawlinson, 4th Bt and of Bessie Ford Taylor, *d* of Frank Raymond Emmatt, Harrogate; *S* father, 1969; *m* 1st, 1960, Penelope Byng Noel (marr. diss. 1967), 2nd *d* of Rear-Adm. G. J. B. Noel, RN; one *s* one *d*; 2nd, 1967, Pauline Strickland (marr. diss. 1976), *d* of J. H. Hardy, Sydney; one *s*; 3rd, 1977, Helen Leone (separated), *d* of T. M. Kennedy, Scotland; one *s. Educ:* Millfield School. Coldstream Guards, 1954–56. *Recreations:* tennis, sailing. *Heir: s* Alexander Noel Rawlinson, *b* 15 July 1964. *Address:* Heath Farm, Guist, Dereham, Norfolk.

RAWLINSON, Charles Frederick Melville; Senior Adviser, Morgan Grenfell Group plc, since 1988; *b* 18 March 1934; *s* of Rowland Henry Rawlinson and Olivia Melville Rawlinson; *m* 1962, Jill Rosalind Wesley; three *d. Educ:* Canford Sch.; Jesus Coll., Cambridge (MA). FCA, FCT. With A. E. Limehouse & Co., Chartered Accts, 1955–58; Peat Marwick Mitchell & Co., 1958–62; Morgan Grenfell & Co. Ltd, Bankers, 1962–87: Dir, 1970–87; Jt Chm., 1985–87; Morgan Grenfell Group PLC: Dir, 1985–88; Vice-Chm., 1987–88; seconded as Man. Dir, Investment Bank of Ireland Ltd, Dublin, 1966–68; Director: Associated Paper Industries plc, 1972–91 (Chm., 1979–91); Willis Faber plc, 1981–89. Cambridge Symphony Orch., 1988–. Joint Hon. Treas., 1983–, Dep. Chm., 1989–, Nat. Assoc. of Boys' Clubs. Chm., Peache Trustees, 1980–. *Recreations:* music, sailing, shooting, walking in the hills. *Address:* (office) 23 Great Winchester Street, EC2P 2AX; (home) The Old Forge, Arkesden, Saffron Walden, Essex CB11 4EX. *Clubs:* Brooks's; Leander (Henley-on-Thames).

See also under Royal Family.

RAWLINSON, Dennis George Fielding, OBE 1978; JP; FCIT; Member, Transport Tribunal, since 1986; Company Director, since 1964; *b* 3 Sept. 1919; *s* of George and Mary Jane Rawlinson; *m* 1943, Lilian Mary; one *s* one *d. Educ:* Grocers' Co.'s Sch. Army, 1939–46. Various progressive positions in omnibus industry. JP Darlington, 1971. *Recreations:* theatre, music, golf and various lesser sports. *Address:* 62 Cleveland Avenue, Darlington, Co. Durham DL3 7HG. *T:* Darlington (0325) 461254. *Club:* Army and Navy.

RAWNSLEY, Prof. Kenneth, CBE 1984; FRCP, FRCPsych, DPM; Professor and Head of Department of Psychological Medicine, University of Wales College of Medicine (formerly Welsh National School of Medicine), 1964–85, now Emeritus; *b* 1926; *m* Dr Elinor Kapp; one *s* one *d* (two *s* one *d* by previous marr.). *Educ:* Burnley Grammar Sch.; Univ. of Manchester Med. Sch. MB ChB Manchester 1948; MRCP 1951; DPM Manchester 1954; FRCP 1967; FRCPsych 1971. Member, Scientific Staff of Medical Research Council, 1954–64; Registrar, Bethlem Royal and Maudsley Hosps; Pres., Royal College of Psychiatrists, 1981–84 (Dean, 1972–77); Vice-Provost, Welsh Nat. Sch. of Medicine, 1979–80; Hon. Consultant Psychiatrist, S Glam. AHA(T), 1960–85; Postgrad. Organiser and Clinical Tutor in Psychiatry, S Glam., 1968–85. Chm., Management Cttee, Nat. Counselling Service for Sick Doctors. Hon MD Wales, 1989. *Publications:* contribs to Brit. Jl Psych., Postgrad. Med. Jl, Jl Psychosom. Res., etc. *Address:* 46 Cathedral Road, Cardiff. *T:* Cardiff (0222) 397850. *Club:* Athenæum.

RAWSON, Christopher Selwyn Priestley; JP; an Underwriting Member of Lloyd's; *b* 25 March 1928; *e s* of late Comdr Selwyn Gerald Caygill Rawson, OBE, RN (retd) and late Dr Doris Rawson, MB, ChB (*née* Brown); *m* 1959, Rosemary Ann Focke; two *d. Educ:* The Elms Sch., Colwall, near Malvern, Worcs; The Nautical College, Pangbourne,

Berks. Navigating Apprentice, Merchant Service, T. & J. Brocklebank Ltd, 1945–48. Sheriff of the City of London, 1961–62; Member of Court of Common Council (Ward of Bread Street), 1963–72; Alderman, City of London, (Ward of Lime Street), 1972–83; one of HM Lieutenants of City of London, 1980–83. A Younger Brother of Trinity House, 1988–. Chairman: Governors, The Elms Sch., Colwall, near Malvern, Worcs, 1965–84; Port and City of London Health Cttee, 1967–70; Billingsgate and Leadenhall Mkt Cttee, 1972–75. Silver Medal for Woollen and Worsted Raw Materials, City and Guilds of London Institute, 1951; Livery of Clothworkers' Company, 1952 (Mem. Court of Assistants, 1977; Master, 1988–89); Freeman, Company of Watermen and Lightermen, 1966 (Mem. Ct of Assts, 1974, Master, 1982–84). President: Lime St Ward Club, 1973–83 (Hon. Patron, 1983–91); Sowerby St Peter's Cricket Club, 1975–. Hon. Mem., London Metal Exchange, 1979. ATI 1953; AIMarE 1962. CStJ 1985. JP City of London, 1967. Commander: National Order of Senegal, 1961; Order of the Ivory Coast, 1962; Star of Africa, Liberia, 1962. *Recreations:* shooting, sailing. *Address:* 56 Ovington Street, SW3. *T:* 071–589 3136; Prince Rupert House, 64 Queen Street, EC4R 1AD. *T:* 071–236 1471. *Clubs:* Garrick, Royal London Yacht (Cdre, 1990–), City Livery Yacht (Cdre, 1987–90).

RAWSON, Jessica Mary, FBA 1990; Keeper, Department of Oriental Antiquities, British Museum, since 1987; *b* 20 Jan. 1943; *d* of Roger Nathaniel Quirk and Paula Quirk; *m* 1968, John Rawson; one *d. Educ:* New Hall, Cambridge (BA Hons History); London Univ. (BA Hons Chinese Lang. and Lit.). Asst Principal, Min. of Health, 1965–67; Department of Oriental Antiquities, British Museum: Asst Keeper II, 1967–71; Asst Keeper I, 1971–76; Dep. Keeper, 1976–87. *Publications:* Chinese Jade Throughout the Ages (with John Ayers), 1975; Animals in Art, 1977; Ancient China, Art and Archaeology, 1980; Chinese Ornament: the lotus and the dragon, 1984; Chinese Bronzes: art and ritual, 1987; The Bella and P. P. Chiu Collection of Ancient Chinese Bronzes, 1988; Western Zhou Ritual Bronzes from the Arthur M. Sackler Collections, 1990; (with Emma Bunker) Ancient Chinese and Ordos Bronzes. *Recreation:* fell walking. *Address:* 3 Downshire Hill, NW3 1NR. *T:* 071–794 4002.

RAWSON, Prof. Kenneth John, MSc; FEng; RCNC; consultant; Professor and Head of Department of Design and Technology, 1983–89, Dean of Education and Design, 1983–89, Brunel University; *b* 27 Oct. 1926; *s* of late Arthur William Rawson and Beatrice Anne Rawson; *m* 1950, Rhona Florence Gill; two *s* one *d. Educ:* Northern Grammar Sch., Portsmouth; HM Dockyard Technical Coll., Portsmouth; RN Colls, Keyham and Greenwich. RCNC; FEng 1984; FRINA; FCSD. WhSch. At sea, 1950–51; Naval Construction Res. Estabt, Dunfermline, 1951–53; Ship Design, Admiralty, 1953–57; Lloyd's Register of Shipping, 1957–59; Ship and Weapons Design, MoD, Bath, 1959–69; Naval Staff, London, 1969–72; Prof. of Naval Architecture, University Coll., Univ. of London, 1972–77; Ministry of Defence, Bath: Head of Forward Design, Ship Dept, 1977–79; Dep. Dir, Ship Design and Chief Naval Architect (Under Sec.), 1979–83. FRSA. *Publications:* Photoelasticity and the Engineer, 1953; (with E. C. Tupper) Basic Ship Theory, 1968, 3rd edn 1983; contrib. numerous technical publications. *Recreations:* cabinet making, wine making, gardening, walking. *Address:* Moorlands, The Street, Chilcompton, Bath BA3 4HB. *T:* Stratton-on-the-Fosse (0761) 232793.

RAWSTHORNE, Anthony Robert; Assistant Under-Secretary, Equal Opportunities and General Department, Home Office, since 1991; *b* 25 Jan. 1943; *s* of Frederic Leslie and Nora Rawsthorne; *m* 1967, Beverley Jean Osborne; one *s* two *d. Educ:* Ampleforth College; Wadham College, Oxford (MA). Home Office, 1966; Asst Sec., 1977; Crime Policy Planning Unit, 1977–79; Establishment Dept, 1979–82; Sec., Falkland Islands Review Cttee, 1982; Principal Private Sec., 1983; Immigration and Nationality Dept, 1983–86; Asst Under-Sec., Establishment Dept, 1986. *Recreations:* bridge, cycling, squash, holidays in France. *Address:* c/o Home Office, Queen Anne's Gate, SW1H 9AT.

RAWSTHORNE, Rt. Rev. John; Titular Bishop of Rotdon and an Auxiliary Bishop of Liverpool, (RC), since 1981; President, St Joseph's College, since 1982; *b* Crosby, Merseyside, 12 Nov. 1936. Priest, 1962. Administrator, St Mary's, Highfield, 1982. *Address:* 7 Lancaster Court, Lancaster Lane, Parbold, Wigan WN8 7HT.

RAY, Hon. Ajit Nath; Chief Justice of India, Supreme Court of India, 1973–77; *b* Calcutta, 29 Jan. 1912; *s* of Sati Nath Ray and Kali Kumari Debi; *m* 1944, Himani Mukherjee; one *s. Educ:* Presidency Coll., Calcutta; Calcutta Univ. (Hindu Coll. Foundn Schol., MA); Oriel College, Oxford (MA; Hon. Fellow, 1975). Called to Bar, Gray's Inn, 1939; practised at Calcutta High Court, 1940–57; Judge, Calcutta High Court, 1957–69; Judge, Supreme Court of India, 1969–73. Pres., Governing Body, Presidency Coll., Calcutta, 1959–70; Vice-President: Asiatic Soc., 1963–65 (Hon. Treas. 1960–63); Internat. Law Assoc., 1977– (Pres., 1974–76; Pres., Indian Br., 1973–77); Indian Law Inst., New Delhi, 1973–77; Ramakrishna Mission Inst. of Culture, 1981–; Mem., Internat. Court of Arbitration, 1976–; Pres., Soc. for Welfare of Blind, Narendrapur, 1959–80; Member: Karma Samiti (Exec. Council), 1963–67 and 1969–72, and Samsad (Court), 1967–71, Visva-Bharati Univ., Santiniketan. *Address:* 15 Panditia Place, Calcutta 700029, India. *T:* Calcutta 75–5213. *Club:* Calcutta (Calcutta).

RAY, Cyril; *b* 16 March 1908; *e s* of Albert Benson Ray (who changed the family name from Rotenberg, 1913), and Rita Ray; *m* 1953, Elizabeth Mary, JP, *o d* of late Rev. H. C. Brocklehurst; one *s. Educ:* elementary sch., Bury, Lancs; Manchester Gr. Sch. (Foundation schol.); Jesus Coll., Oxford (open schol.). Manchester Guardian and BBC war correspondent: 5th Destroyer Flotilla, 1940 (Hon. Mem. HMS Kelly Reunion); N African landings, 1942; 8th Army, Italy (despatches); US 82nd Airborne Div. (US Army citation, Nijmegen), and 3rd Army, 1944–45. UNESCO missions, Italy, Greece, East, Central and S Africa, 1945–50. Sunday Times, 1949–56 (Moscow Correspondent, 1950–52); Editor, The Compleat Imbiber, 1956–71, 1986–89, 1992– (Wine and Food Soc.'s first André Simon Prize, 1964); Asst Editor, The Spectator, 1958–62; Wine Correspondent: The Director, 1958–76; The Observer, 1959–73; Punch, 1978–84; Chief Consltnt, The Good Food Guide, 1968–74; Founder and past President, Circle of Wine Writers. Trustee, Albany, 1967– (Chm. Trustees, 1981–86). Much occasional broadcasting, 1940–62 (The Critics, 1958–62), Southern TV, 1958–59. Hon. Life Mem., NUJ; Mem., Punch Table (old regime). Glenfiddich Wine and Food Writer of the Year, 1979; Special Glenfiddich Award, 1985. Freeman, City of London; Liveryman, Fan-Makers Co. Mem. Labour Party. Commendatore, Italian Order of Merit, 1981 (Cavaliere 1972); Chevalier, French Order of Merit, 1985 (Mérite Agricole, 1974). *Publications:* (ed) Scenes and Characters from Surtees, 1948; From Algiers to Austria: The History of 78 Division, 1952; The Pageant of London, 1958; Merry England, 1960; Regiment of the Line: The Story of the Lancashire Fusiliers, 1963; (ed) The Gourmet's Companion, 1963; (ed) Morton Shand's Book of French Wines, 1964; (ed) Best Murder Stories, 1965; The Wines of Italy, 1966 (Bologna Trophy, 1967); In a Glass Lightly, 1967; Lafite: The Story of Château Lafite-Rothschild, 1968, rev. edn 1985; Bollinger: the story of a champagne, 1971, rev. edn 1982; Cognac, 1973, rev. edn 1985; Mouton: the story of Mouton-Rothschild, 1974; (with Elizabeth Ray) Wine with Food, 1975; The Wines of France, 1976; The Wines of Germany, 1977; The Complete Book of Spirits and Liqueurs, 1978; The Saint Michael Guide to Wine, 1978; Ruffino: the story of a Chianti, 1979; Lickerish Limericks, with Filthy Pictures by Charles Mozley, 1979; Ray on Wine (Glenfiddich Wine Book of the

Year), 1979; The New Book of Italian Wines, 1982; (ed) Vintage Tales, 1984; Robert Mondavi of the Napa Valley, 1984; Bollinger—Tradition of a Champagne Family, 1988. *Recreation:* formerly riding, now The Times crossword. *Address:* Albany, Piccadilly, W1V 9RQ. *T:* 071–734 0270. *Clubs:* Athenæum, Brooks's, MCC, Special Forces; Puffin's (Edinburgh) (Hon. Life Mem.); Civil Service Riding (Hon. Life Mem.).

RAY, Edward Ernest, CBE 1988; Senior Partner, Spicer and Pegler, Chartered Accountants, 1984–88 (Partner, 1957); *b* 6 Nov. 1924; *s* of Walter James Ray and Cecilia May Ray; *m* 1949, Margaret Elizabeth, *d* of George Bull; two *s. Educ:* Holloway Co. Sch.; London Univ. (External) (BCom). Served RN, 1943–46. Qualified, Inst. of Chartered Accountants: Mem., 1950; FCA 1955; Council Mem., 1973; Vice Pres., 1980; Dep. Pres., 1981; Pres., 1982, 1983. Chm., London Chartered Accountants, 1972–73. Dir, SIB, 1985–90; Chm., Investors' Compensation Scheme Ltd, 1988–91; Member: City Capital Markets Cttee, 1984–88; Marketing of Investments Bd Organising Cttee, 1984–88. *Publications:* Partnership Taxation, 1972, 3rd edn 1987; (jtly) VAT for Accountants and Businessmen, 1972; contrib. accountancy magazines. *Recreations:* walking, birdwatching, golf. *Address:* 1 Brooklands Court, Bush Hill, N21 2BZ. *T:* 081–360 0028. *Club:* City of London.

RAY, Philip Bicknell, CMG 1969; Ministry of Defence 1947–76, retired; *b* 10 July 1917; *s* of late Basil Ray and Clare (*née* Everett); *m* 1946, Bridget Mary Robertson (decd); two *s* one *d. Educ:* Felsted Sch.; Selwyn Coll., Cambridge (MA). Indian Police, 1939–47. *Address:* The Cottage, Little Shoddesden, Andover, Hants SP11 9LW.

RAY, Hon. Robert Francis; Senator for Victoria, since 1981; Minister for Defence, and Manager of Government Business in the Senate, Australia, since 1990; *b* Melbourne, 8 April 1947; *m* Jane. *Educ:* Monash Univ.; Rusden State Coll. Former technical sch. teacher. Australian Labor Party: Mem., 1966–; Deleg., Vic. State Conf., 1970–; Mem., Nat. Exec., 1983–; Minister for Home Affairs and Dep. Manager of Govt Business in the Senate, 1987; Minister assisting the Minister for Transport and Communications, 1988; Minister for Immigration, Local Govt and Ethnic Affairs, 1988–90. *Address:* Parliament House, Canberra, ACT 2600, Australia.

RAY, Robin; freelance broadcaster and writer; *s* of Ted Ray and Sybil (*née* Olden); *m* 1960, Susan Stranks; one *s. Educ:* Highgate Sch. West End Stage debut, The Changeling, 1960. Chief Technical Instructor, RADA, 1961–65; Associate Dir, Meadowbrook Theatre, Detroit, USA, 1965–66. As writer and broadcaster, over 1000 progs for radio and television, mainly music and arts, including: Music Now; The Lively Arts; Face the Music; Film Buff of the Year, etc, 1966–85. Deviser, Tomfoolery, Criterion Theatre, 1980; author, Café Puccini, Wyndham's Theatre, 1986; reviewer of classical records for Capital Radio, 1979–84; Drama Critic, Punch, 1986–87; for BBC Radio: Revolutions In Sound, Robin Ray's Waxworks, 1988–89; The Tingle Factor, Screenplay, Robin Ray on Record, 1989–91. Artistic Dir, Classic FM Radio, 1988–91. *Publications:* Time For Lovers (anthology), 1975; Robin Ray's Music Quiz, 1978; Favourite Hymns and Carols, 1982; Words on Music, 1984. *Recreations:* music, cinema, reading, shopping. *Address:* c/o David Wilkinson Associates, 115 Hazlebury Road, SW6 2LX. *T:* 071–371 5188.

RAY, Satyajit; Padma Shree, 1957; Padma Bhushan, 1964; Padma Bibhushan, 1976; Indian film producer and film director since 1953; *b* 2 May 1921; *s* of late Sukumar and Suprabha Ray (*née* Das); *m* 1949, Bijoya (*née* Das); one *s. Educ:* Ballygunge Govt School; Presidency College, Calcutta. Joined British advertising firm, D. J. Keymer & Co., as visualiser, 1943; Art Director, 1950. In 1952, started first feature film, Pather Panchali, finished in 1955 (Cannes Special Award, 1956, San Francisco, best film, 1957). Left advertising for whole-time film-making, 1956. Other films: Aparajito, 1957 (Venice Grand Prix, 1957, San Francisco, best direction); Jalsaghar, 1958; Devi, 1959; Apur Sansar, 1959 (Selznick Award and Sutherland Trophy 1960); Teen Kanya (Two Daughters), 1961; Kanchanjangha, 1962; Mahanagar, 1963; Charulata, 1964; The Coward and The Holy Man (Kapurush-O-Mahapurush), 1965; The Hero (Nayak), 1965; Goopy Gyne and Bagha Byne, 1969; Days and Nights in the Forest, 1970; Pratidwandi (The Adversary), 1970; Company Limited, 1971; Distant Thunder, 1973 (Golden Bear, Berlin Film Festival, 1973); The Golden Fortress, 1974; The Middleman, 1975; The Chess Players, 1977; The Elephant God, 1979; The Kingdom of Diamonds, 1980; Pikoo, Deliverance, 1981; Ghare Baire (The Home and the World), 1984; Ganashatru (Public Enemy), 1989; Shakha-Proshakha (Branches of a Tree), 1990. Founded first Film Society in Calcutta, 1947. Composes background music for own films. Fellow, BFI, 1983. Hon. DLitt Oxon, 1978; Légion d'Honneur, 1989. *Publications:* Our Films, Their Films, 1976; Stories, 1987; The Chess Players and other screenplays, 1989; film articles in Sight and Sound, Sequence; (Editor, 1961–) children's magazine Sandesh, with contributions of stories, poems. *Recreations:* listening to Indian and Western classical music, and reading science-fiction. *Address:* Flat 8, 1–1 Bishop Lefroy Road, Calcutta 20, India. *T:* 447–8747.

RAYLEIGH, 6th Baron *cr* 1821; **John Gerald Strutt;** Company Chairman, since 1988; *b* 4 June 1960; *s* of Hon. Charles Richard Strutt (*d* 1981) (2nd *s* of 4th Baron) and of Hon. Jean Elizabeth, *d* of 1st Viscount Davidson, PC, GCVO, CH, CB; *S* uncle, 1988; *m* 1991, Annabel Kate, *d* of W. G. Patterson. *Educ:* Eton College; Royal Agricultural College, Cirencester. Lieut, Welsh Guards, 1980–84. Chairman, Lord Rayleigh's Farms Inc., 1988–; Director: Strutt and Parker Farms Ltd, 1987–; Bridge Farm Dairies Ltd, 1987–. MRI. *Recreations:* cricket, gardening, shooting, silviculture. *Heir: uncle* Hon. Hedley Vicars Strutt, *b* 19 Feb. 1915. *Address:* Terling Place, Chelmsford, Essex CM3 2PJ. *T:* Terling (024533) 436. *Clubs:* Brooks's, Turf, Lansdowne, MCC; Constitutional (Witham).

RAYMER, Michael Robert, OBE 1951; Assistant Secretary, Royal Hospital, Chelsea, 1975–82; *b* 22 July 1917; surv. *s* of late Rev. W. H. Raymer, MA; *m* 1948, Joyce Marion Scott; two *s* one *d. Educ:* Marlborough College (Foundation Scholar); Jesus College, Cambridge (Rustat Schol.). BA (Hons) 1939. Administrative Officer, Nigeria, 1940–49 and 1952–55. Served in Royal W African Frontier Force, 1940–43. Colonial Sec. to Govt of the Falkland Islands, 1949–52; Prin. Estab. Officer, N Nigeria, 1954; Controller of Organisation and Establishments, to Government of Fiji, 1955–62; retired, 1962; Principal, MoD, 1962–75. *Recreation:* gardening. *Address:* The Stable House, Manor Farm, Apethorpe, Northants PE8 5DG.

RAYMOND, William Francis, CBE 1978; FRSC; Agricultural Science Consultant; *b* 25 Feb. 1922; *m* 1949, Amy Elizabeth Kelk; three *s* one *d. Educ:* Bristol Grammar Sch.; The Queen's Coll., Oxford (MA). Research Officer, MRC, 1943–45; Head of Animal Science Div. and later Asst Dir, Grassland Research Inst., Hurley, 1945–72; Dep. Chief Scientist, 1972–81, Chief Scientist (Agriculture and Horticulture), 1981–82, MAFF. Mem., ARC, 1981–82. Sec., 8th Internat. Grassland Congress, 1960; President: Brit. Grassland Soc., 1974–75; Brit. Soc. Animal Production, 1981–82. Vis. Prof. in Agriculture, Wye Coll., 1978–83. Chm., Stapledon Meml Trust, 1983–; Hon. Treas., RURAL, 1984–. *Publications:* (with Shepperson and Waltham) Forage Conservation and Feeding, 1972, 4th edn (with Redman and Waltham), 1986; EEC Agricultural Research Framework Programme, 1983; Research in Support of Agricultural Policies in Europe, FAO Regional Conf., Reykjavik, 1984; over 160 papers in scientific jls. *Recreation:* gardening. *Address:* Periwinkle Cottage, Christmas Common, Watlington OX9 5HR. *T:* Watlington (049161) 2942. *Club:* Farmers'.

RAYNE, family name of **Baron Rayne.**

RAYNE, Baron *cr* 1976 (Life Peer), of Prince's Meadow in Greater London; **Max Rayne,** Kt 1969; Chairman, London Merchant Securities plc, since 1960; *b* 8 Feb. 1918; *er s* of Phillip and Deborah Rayne; *m* 1st, 1941, Margaret Marco (marr. diss., 1960); one *s* two *d*; 2nd, 1965, Lady Jane Antonia Frances Vane-Tempest-Stewart, *er d* of 8th Marquess of Londonderry; two *s* two *d. Educ:* Central Foundation Sch. and University Coll., London. Served RAF 1940–45. Chm., Westpool Investment Trust plc, 1980–; Dep. Chm., First Leisure Corp. plc, 1984–; British Lion Films, 1967–72; Dir, other companies. Governor: Royal Ballet Sch., 1966–79; Yehudi Menuhin Sch., 1966–87 (Vice Pres., 1987–); Malvern Coll., 1966–; Centre for Environmental Studies, 1967–73; Special Trustee, St Thomas' Hosp., 1974– (Governor, 1962–74); Member: Gen. Council, King Edward VII's Hosp. Fund for London, 1966–; Council, St Thomas's Hospital Medical School, 1965–82; RADA Council, 1973–; South Bank Bd, 1986–; Council of Governors, United Med. Schs of Guy's and St Thomas's Hosps, 1982–89. Hon. Vice-Pres., Jewish Care, 1966–; Chairman: London Festival Ballet Trust, 1967–75; Nat. Theatre Board, 1971–88; Founder Patron, The Rayne Foundation, 1962–. Hon. Fellow: Darwin Coll., Cambridge, 1966; UCL, 1966; LSE 1974; King's Coll. Hosp. Med. Sch., 1980; UC, Oxford, 1982; King's Coll. London, 1983; Westminster Sch., 1989. Hon. FRCPsych, 1977. Hon. LLD London, 1968. Officier, Légion d'Honneur, 1987 (Chevalier 1973). *Address:* 33 Robert Adam Street, W1M 5AH. *T:* 071–935 3555.

RAYNE, Sir Edward, Kt 1988; CVO 1977; Chairman and Managing Director of H. & M. Rayne Ltd, 1951–87; Executive Chairman, Harvey Nichols, 1979–86; *b* 19 Aug. 1922; *s* of Joseph Edward Rayne and Meta Elizabeth Reddish (American); *m* 1952, Phyllis Cort; two *s. Educ:* Harrow. Pres., 1961–72, Exec. Chm., 1972–86, Rayne-Delman Shoes Inc.; Dir, Debenhams Ltd, 1975–88; Pres., Debenhams Inc., 1976–86; Chairman: Fashion Multiple Div., Debenhams Ltd, 1978–86; Harvey Nichols Ltd, 1978–88; Lotus Ltd, 1978–86. Member: Export Council for Europe, 1962–71; European Trade Cttee, 1972–84; Bd of Governors, Genesco Inc., 1967–73; Franco British Council, 1980–89. Chairman: Incorp. Soc. of London Fashion Designers, 1960–; British Fashion Council, 1985–90; Pres., Royal Warrant Holders' Assoc., 1964, Hon. Treas. 1974–91; President: British Footwear Manufacturers' Fedn, 1965; British Boot and Shoe Instn, 1972–79; Clothing and Footwear Inst., 1979–80. Master, Worshipful Co. of Pattenmakers, 1981. FRSA 1971. Harper's Bazaar Trophy, 1963. Chevalier, l'Ordre Nat. du Mérite, France, 1984. *Recreations:* golf and bridge (Mem., winning British team, European Bridge Championship, 1948, 1949). *Address:* 29 Hartfield Road, Cooden Beach, E Sussex TN39 3EA. *T:* Cooden (04243) 2175. *Clubs:* Portland, White's.

RAYNER, family name of **Baron Rayner.**

RAYNER, Baron *cr* 1983 (Life Peer), of Crowborough in the County of East Sussex; **Derek George Rayner;** Kt 1973; Chairman, 1984–91, Joint Managing Director, 1973–91, Marks and Spencer plc; *b* 30 March 1926; *o s* of George William Rayner and Hilda Jane (*née* Rant); unmarried. *Educ:* City Coll., Norwich; Selwyn Coll., Cambridge (Hon. Fellow 1983). Fellow, Inst. Purchasing and Supply, 1970. Nat. Service, commnd RAF Regt, 1946–48. Joined Marks & Spencer, 1953; Dir, 1967; Chief Exec., 1983–88. Special Adviser to HM Govt, 1970; Chief Exec., Procurement Executive, MoD, 1971–72. Mem., UK Permanent Security Commn, 1977–80. Dep. Chm., Civil Service Pay Bd, 1978–80. Member: Design Council, 1973–75; Council RCA, 1973–76. Adviser to Prime Minister on improving efficiency and eliminating waste in Government, 1979–83. Chm., Coronary Artery Disease Res. Assoc. (CORDA), 1985–. Pres., St Bartholomew's Hosp. Med. Coll., 1988–. *Recreations:* music, food, travel. *Address:* c/o Michael House, 47 Baker Street, W1A 1DN.

RAYNER, Bryan Roy, CB 1987; Deputy Secretary, Department of Health (formerly of Health and Social Security), 1984–91; *b* 29 Jan. 1932; *s* of Harold and Florence Rayner; *m* 1957, Eleanora Whittaker; one *d. Educ:* Stationers' Company's School, N8. Clerical Officer, Customs and Excise, 1948; Asst Private Sec. to Minister of Health, 1960–62; Principal, 1965, Asst Sec., 1970, Under Sec., 1975, DHSS. *Recreations:* listening to music, photography. *Club:* Royal Over-Seas League.

RAYNER, Claire Berenice; writer and broadcaster; *b* 22 Jan. 1931; *m* 1957, Desmond Rayner; two *s* one *d. Educ:* City of London Sch. for Girls; Royal Northern Hosp. Sch. of Nursing, London (Gold Medal; SRN 1954); Guy's Hosp. (midwifery). Formerly: Nurse, Royal Free Hosp.; Sister, Paediatric Dept, Whittington Hosp. Woman's Own: Med. Correspondent, as Ruth Martin, 1966–75, as Claire Rayner, 1975–87; advice column: The Sun, 1973–80; The Sunday Mirror, 1980–88; Today, 1988–91; columnist, Woman, 1988–. Radio and television broadcasts include: family advice, Pebble Mill at One, BBC, 1972–74; (co-presenter) Kitchen Garden, ITV, 1974–77; Contact, BBC Radio, Wales, 1974–77; Claire Rayner's Casebook (series), BBC, 1980, 1983, 1984; TV-am Advice Spot, 1985–; A Problem Shared, Sky TV Series, 1989. FRSM. Pres., Gingerbread; Patron: Terrence Higgins Trust; Turning Point; Royal Philanthropic Soc.; Down's Assoc., and others. Hon. Fellow, Polytechnic of N London, 1988. Freeman, City of London, 1981. Med. Journalist of the Year, 1987; Best Specialist Consumer Columnist Award, 1988. *Publications:* Mothers and Midwives, 1962; What Happens in Hospital, 1963; The Calendar of Childhood, 1964; Your Baby, 1965; Careers with Children, 1966; Essentials of Out-Patient Nursing, 1967; For Children, 1967; Shall I be a Nurse, 1967; 101 Facts an Expectant Mother should know, 1967; 101 Key Facts of Practical Baby Care, 1967; Housework - The Easy Way, 1967; Home Nursing and Family Health, 1967; A Parent's Guide to Sex Education, 1968; People in Love, 1968 (subseq. publd as About Sex, 1972); Protecting Your Baby, 1971; Woman's Medical Dictionary, 1971; When to Call the Doctor - What to Do Whilst Waiting, 1972; The Shy Person's Book, 1973; Childcare Made Simple, 1973; Where Do I Come From?, 1975; (ed and contrib.) Atlas of the Body and Mind, 1976; (with Keith Fordyce) Kitchen Garden, 1976; (with Keith Fordyce) More Kitchen Garden, 1977; Family Feelings, 1977; Claire Rayner answers your 100 Questions on Pregnancy, 1977; (with Keith Fordyce) Claire and Keith's Kitchen Garden, 1978; The Body Book, 1978; Related to Sex, 1979; (with Keith Fordyce) Greenhouse Gardening, 1979; Everything your Doctor would Tell You if He Had the Time, 1980; Claire Rayner's Lifeguide, 1980; Baby and Young Child Care, 1981; Growing Pains, 1984; Claire Rayner's Marriage Guide, 1984; The Getting Better Book, 1985; Woman, 1986; When I Grow Up, 1986; Safe Sex, 1987; The Don't Spoil Your Body Book, 1989; *fiction:* Shilling a Pound Pears, 1964; The House on the Fen, 1967; Starch of Aprons, 1967 (subseq. publd as The Hive, 1968); Lady Mislaid, 1968; Death on the Table, 1969; The Meddlers, 1970; A Time to Heal, 1972; The Burning Summer, 1972; Sisters, 1978; Reprise, 1980; The Running Years, 1981; Family Chorus, 1984; The Virus Man, 1985; Lunching at Laura's, 1986; Maddie, 1988; Clinical Judgements, 1989; Postscripts, 1990; The Performers: Book 1, Gower Street, 1973; Book 2, The Haymarket, 1974; Book 3, Paddington Green, 1975; Book 4, Soho Square, 1976; Book 5, Bedford Row, 1977; Book 6, Long Acre, 1978; Book 7, Charing Cross, 1979; Book 8, The Strand, 1980; Book 9,

Chelsea Reach, 1982; Book 10, Shaftesbury Avenue, 1983; Book 11, Piccadilly, 1985; Book 12, Seven Dials, 1986; Poppy Chronicle: Book 1, Jubilee, 1987; Book 2, Flanders, 1988; Book 3, Flapper, 1989; Book 4, Blitz, 1990; *as Sheila Brandon: fiction:* The Final Year, 1962; Cottage Hospital, 1963; Children's Ward, 1964; The Lonely One, 1965; The Doctors of Downlands, 1968; The Private Wing, 1971; Nurse in the Sun, 1972; *as Ann Lynton:* Mothercraft, 1967; contrib. Lancet, Med. World, Nursing Times, Nursing Mirror, and national newspapers and magazines, incl. Design. *Recreations:* talking, cooking, party-giving, theatre-going. *Address:* Holly Wood House, Roxborough Avenue, Harrow-on-the-Hill, Mddx HA1 3BU.

RAYNER, David Edward, FCIT; Member, since 1987, and Managing Director, Engineering and Operations, since 1989, British Railways Board; *b* 26 Jan. 1940; *s* of Marjory and Gilbert Rayner; *m* 1966, Enid Cutty; two *d. Educ:* St Peter's School, York; Durham University (BSc Hons). Joined British Railways, 1963; Passenger Marketing Manager, BR Board, 1982; Dep. Gen. Manager, BR, London Midland Region, 1984–86; Gen. Manager, BR, Eastern Region, 1986–87; Jt Man. Dir, BR Board, 1987–89. *Recreation:* collector.

RAYNER, Edward John, CBE 1990; Controller, Europe (formerly Europe and North Asia) Division, British Council, 1986–89; *b* 27 Feb. 1936; *s* of Edward Harold Rayner and Edith Rayner; *m* 1960, Valerie Anne Billon; one *s* one *d. Educ:* Slough Grammar Sch.; London Univ. (BSc Econs). British Council: Asst Regional Rep., Lahore, Pakistan, 1959–62; Asst Rep., Lagos, Nigeria, 1962–65; Inspector, Complements Unit, 1965–67; Head, Overseas Careers, Personnel Dept, 1967–70; Dep. Rep., Pakistan, 1970–71; Regional Dir, Sao Paulo, Brazil, 1972–75; Controller, Estabts Div., 1975–78; Secretary, 1978–82; Rep., Brazil, 1983–86. *Recreations:* sport, theatre, music.

RAYNER, Most Rev. Keith; see Melbourne, Archbishop of.

RAYNES, Prof. Edward Peter, FRS 1987; Deputy Chief Scientific Officer, Royal Signals and Radar Establishment, Malvern, since 1988; *b* 4 July 1945; *s* of Edward Gordon and Ethel Mary Raynes; *m* 1970, Madeline Ord; two *s. Educ:* St Peter's School, York; Gonville and Caius College, Cambridge (MA, PhD). CPhys, FInstP. Royal Signals and Radar Establishment, 1971–; SPSO, 1981. Hon. Prof., Sch. of Chemistry, Univ. of Hull, 1990. Rank Prize for Opto-electronics, 1980; Paterson Medal, Inst. of Physics, 1986; Special Recognition Award, Soc. for Information Display, 1987. *Publications:* (ed jtly) Liquid Crystals: their physics, chemistry and applications, 1983; numerous scientific papers and patents. *Recreation:* choral and solo singing. *Address:* 23 Leadon Road, Malvern, Worcs WR14 2XF. *T:* Malvern (0684) 565497.

RAYNHAM, Viscount; Charles George Townshend; *b* 26 Sept. 1945; *s* and *heir* of 7th Marquess Townshend, *qv; m* 1st, 1975, Hermione (*d* 1985), *d* of Lt-Cdr R. M. D. Ponsonby and Mrs Dorothy Ponsonby; one *s* one *d;* 2nd, 1990, Mrs Alison Marshall, *yr d* of Sir Willis Combs, *qv. Educ:* Eton; Royal Agricultural College, Cirencester. Chm. and Dir, AIMS Ltd, 1977–87; Man. Dir, Raynham Workshops Ltd, 1986–; Dir, Pera International, 1988– (Vice-Chm., 1990–). Member Council: Design Gp Great Britain Ltd, 1984–90 (Chm., 1988); RASE, 1982–. *Heir: s* Hon. Thomas Charles Townshend, *b* 2 Nov. 1977. *Address:* Pattesley House, Fakenham, Norfolk NR21 7HT. *T:* Fakenham (0328) 701818. *Club:* White's.

RAYNSFORD, Nick; see Raynsford, W. R. N.

RAYNSFORD, Wyvill Richard Nicolls, (Nick); Partner, Raynsford and Morris, consultants, since 1987; *b* 28 Jan. 1945; *s* of Wyvill Raynsford and Patricia Raynsford (*née* Dunn); *m* 1968, Anne Raynsford (*née* Jelley); three *d. Educ:* Repton Sch.; Sidney Sussex Coll., Cambridge (MA); Chelsea Sch. of Art (DipAD). Market research, A. C. Nielsen Co. Ltd, 1966–68; Gen. Sec., Soc. for Co-operative Dwellings, 1972–73; SHAC: Emergency Officer, 1973–74; Research Officer, 1974–76; Dir, 1976–86. Councillor (Lab) London Borough of Hammersmith & Fulham, 1971–75 (Chm., Leisure and Recreation Cttee, 1972–74). Contested (Lab) Fulham, 1987. MP (Lab) Fulham, April 1986–1987. Prospective Parly Candidate (Lab) Greenwich, 1990–. *Publication:* A Guide to Housing Benefit, 1982, 7th edn 1986. *Recreations:* running, walking, sleeping. *Address:* 31 Cranbury Road, Fulham, SW6 2NS. *T:* 071–731 0675.

RAZ, Prof. Joseph, FBA 1987; Professor of the Philosophy of Law, Oxford, since 1985, and Fellow of Balliol College, Oxford; *b* 21 March 1939. *Educ:* Hebrew University, Jerusalem (MJur 1963); University Coll., Oxford (DPhil 1967). Lectr, Hebrew Univ., Jerusalem, 1967–70; Research Fellow, Nuffield Coll., Oxford, 1970–72; Tutorial Fellow, Balliol Coll., Oxford, 1972–85. *Publications:* The Concept of a Legal System, 1970, 2nd edn 1980; Practical Reason and Norms, 1975, 2nd edn 1990; The Authority of Law, 1979; The Morality of Freedom, 1986. *Address:* Balliol College, Oxford OX1 3BJ. *T:* Oxford (0865) 277721.

RAZZALL, Leonard Humphrey; a Master of the Supreme Court (Taxing), 1954–81; *b* 13 Nov. 1912; *s* of Horace Razzall and Sarah Thompson, Scarborough; *m* 1936, Muriel (*d* 1968), *yr d* of late Pearson Knowles; two *s. Educ:* Scarborough High Sch. Admitted solicitor, 1935; founded firm Humphrey Razzall & Co., 1938. Served in Royal Marines, 1941–46, Staff Captain; Staff Coll., Camberley (jsc). Contested (L) Scarborough and Whitby Division, 1945. Sometime Examr in High Court practice and procedure for solicitors final examination. *Publications:* A Man of Law's Tale, 1982; Law, Love and Laughter, 1984. *Recreations:* travel, cricket, book-collecting and book-selling, writing letters to The Times. *Address:* 6 Malthouse Passage, Barnes, SW13 0AQ. *T:* 081–876 8478. *Clubs:* National Liberal, English-Speaking Union.

REA, family name of **Baron Rea.**

REA, 3rd Baron *cr* 1937, of Eskdale; **John Nicolas Rea,** MD; Bt 1935; General Medical Practitioner in James Wigg Group Practice, Kentish Town Health Centre, NW5, since 1968; *b* 6 June 1928; *s* of Hon. James Russell Rea (*d* 1954) (2nd *s* of 1st Baron) and Betty Marion (*d* 1965), *d* of Arthur Bevan, MD; *S* uncle, 1981; *m* 1951, Elizabeth Anne, *d* of late William Hensman Robinson; four *s. Educ:* Dartington Hall School; Belmont Hill School, Mass, USA; Dauntsey's School; Christ's Coll., Cambridge Univ.; UCH Medical School. MA, MD (Cantab); MRCGP; DPH, DCH, DObstRCOG. Research Fellow in Paediatrics, Lagos, Nigeria, 1962–65; Lecturer in Social Medicine, St Thomas's Hosp. Medical School, 1966–68. Vice-Chm., Nat. Forum for Prevention of Coronary Heart Disease, 1985–. FRSocMed (Pres., Section of Gen. Practice, 1985–86). *Publications:* Interactions of Infection and Nutrition (MD Thesis, Cambridge Univ.), 1969; (jtly) Learning Teaching—an evaluation of a course for GP Teachers, 1980; articles on epidemiology and medical education in various journals. *Recreations:* music (bassoon), fishing, sailing, foreign travel, walking. *Heir: s* Hon. Matthew James Rea, *b* 28 March 1956. *Address:* 11 Anson Road, N7 0RB. *T:* 071–607 0546.

REA, Rev. Ernest; Head of Religious Broadcasting, BBC, since 1989; *b* 6 Sept. 1945; *s* of Ernest Rea and Mary Wylie (*née* Blue); *m* 1973, Kathleen (Kay) Kilpatrick; two *s. Educ:* Methodist Coll., Belfast; Queen's Univ., Belfast; Union Theological Coll., Belfast. Asst

Minister, Woodvale Park Presb. Ch., Belfast, 1971–74; Minister, Bannside Presb. Ch., Banbridge, Co. Down, 1974–79; Religious Broadcasting Producer, BBC Belfast, 1979–84; Sen. Religious Broadcasting Producer, BBC S and W, 1984–88; Editor, Network Radio, BBC S and W, 1988–89. *Recreations:* reading, watching cricket, playing tennis, theatre, music. *Address:* 8 Bannett's Tree Crescent, Alveston, Bristol BS12 2LY. *T:* Thornbury (0454) 415127.

REA, James Taylor, CMG 1958; HM Overseas Civil Service, retired; *b* 19 Oct. 1907; *s* of Rev. Martin Rea, Presbyterian Minister, and Mary Rea (*née* Fisher); *m* 1934, Catharine (*d* 1990), *d* of Dr W. H. Bleakney, Whitman College, Walla Walla, Washington, USA; one *s* one *d. Educ:* Royal School, Dungannon; Queen's University, Belfast (BA); St John's College, Cambridge (MA). HM Colonial Administrative Service (now known as HM Overseas Civil Service) serving throughout in Malaya and Singapore, 1931–58; Principal offices held: Asst Sec., Chinese Affairs, Fedn of Malaya, 1948; Dep. Comr for Labour, Fedn of Malaya, 1949; Dep. Malayan Establishment Officer, 1950; Dep. Pres., 1952–55, Pres., 1955–58, City Council, Singapore. Retired, 1958. Chairman: Hotel Grants Adv. Cttee, NI, 1963–75; NI Training Exec., 1972–75; Down District Cttee, Eastern Health and Social Services Bd, 1974–78; Mem., NI Housing Trust, 1959–71, Vice Chm., 1970–71. Indep. Mem.: Catering Wages Council, N Ireland, 1965–82; Retail Bespoke Tailoring Wages Council, 1965–82; Laundry Wages Council, 1965–82; Shirtmaking Wages Council, 1965–82. Nominated Member General Dental Council, under Dentist Act, 1957, 1961–79. Mem. Downpatrick HMC, 1966–73, Chm., 1971–73. *Address:* Craigduff, 29 Downpatrick Road, Clough, Downpatrick, N Ireland BT30 8NL. *T:* Seaforde (039687) 258.

REA, Dr John Rowland, FBA 1981; Lecturer in Documentary Papyrology, University of Oxford, since 1965; Senior Research Fellow, Balliol College, Oxford, since 1969; *b* 28 Oct. 1933; *s* of Thomas Arthur Rea and Elsie Rea (*née* Ward); *m* 1959, Mary Ogden. *Educ:* Methodist Coll., Belfast; Queen's Univ., Belfast (BA); University Coll. London (PhD). Asst Keeper, Public Record Office, 1957–61; Res. Lectr, Christ Church, Oxford, 1961–65. *Publications:* The Oxyrhynchus Papyri, Vol. XL, 1972, Vol. XLVI, 1978, Vol. LI, 1984, Vol LV, 1988, Vol. LVIII, 1991, also contribs to Vols XXVII, XXXI, XXXIII, XXXIV, XXXVI, XLI, XLIII, XLIX, L; (with P. J. Sijpesteijn) Corpus Papyrorum Raineri V, 1976; articles in classical jls. *Address:* Balliol College, Oxford.

REA, Rupert Lascelles P.; see Pennant-Rea.

REA PRICE, (William) John, OBE 1991; Director, National Children's Bureau, since 1991; *b* 15 March 1937; *s* of late John Caxton Rea Price and of Mary Hilda Rea Price; *m* 1962, Maryrose Wingate Miller; two *s* one *d. Educ:* University College Sch.; Corpus Christi Coll., Cambridge (MA); LSE (DSA; Cert. Applied Social Studies). London Probation Service, 1962–65; London Borough of Islington Children's Dept, 1965–68; Nat. Inst. for Social Work, 1968–69; Home Office, Community Develt Project, 1969–72; Dir of Social Services, London Borough of Islington, 1972–90. Pres., Assoc. of Dirs of Social Services, 1989–90. *Recreations:* cycling, archaeology, history of landscape. *Address:* National Children's Bureau, 8 Wakley Street, EC1V 7QE. *T:* 071–278 9441.

READ, Miss; see Saint, D. J.

READ, Prof. Alan Ernest Alfred, CBE 1989; MD, FRCP; Professor of Medicine and Director of Medical Professorial Unit, University of Bristol, since 1969; *b* 15 Nov. 1926; *s* of Ernest Read and Annie Lydia; *m* 1952, Enid Malein; one *s* two *d. Educ:* Wembley County Sch.; St Mary's Hosp. Med. Sch., London. House Phys., St Mary's Hosp., 1950; Med. Registrar, Royal Masonic Hosp., 1951; Mil. Service Med. Specialist, Trieste, 1952–54; Registrar and Sen. Registrar, Central Mddx and Hammersmith Hosps, 1954–60; University of Bristol: Lectr in Medicine and Cons. Phys., 1961; Reader in Medicine, 1966; Dean of Faculty of Medicine, 1983–85; Pro-Vice-Chancellor, 1987–90. Sen. Censor and Sen. Vice-Pres., RCP, 1986–87. Associate Prof. of Medicine, Univ. of Rochester, USA, 1967. *Publications:* Clinical Apprentice (jtly), 1948, 6th edn 1989; (jtly) Basic Gastroenterology, 1965, 3rd edn 1980; (jtly) Modern Medicine, 1975, 3rd edn 1984. *Recreations:* boating, fishing, golf, riding. *Address:* Riverbank, 77 Nore Road, Portishead, Bristol BS20 9JZ.

READ, Rt. Rev. Allan Alexander; see Ontario, Bishop of.

READ, Gen. Sir Antony; see Read, Gen. Sir J. A. J.

READ, Air Marshal Sir Charles (Frederick), KBE 1976 (CBE 1964); CB 1972; DFC 1942; AFC 1958; Chief of the Air Staff, RAAF, 1972–75, retired; *b* Sydney, NSW, 9 Oct. 1918; *s* of J. F. Read, Bristol, England; *m* 1946, Betty E., *d* of A. V. Bradshaw; three *s. Educ:* Sydney Grammar Sch. Former posts include: OC, RAAF Base, Point Cook, Vic., 1965–68; OC, RAAF, Richmond, NSW, 1968–70; Dep. Chief of Air Staff, 1969–72. *Recreation:* yachting. *Address:* 2007 Pittwater Road, Bayview, NSW 2104, Australia. *T:* 997–1686.

READ, Rev. David Haxton Carswell, MA, DD; Minister of Madison Avenue Presbyterian Church, New York City, USA, 1956–89, now Minister Emeritus; regular broadcaster on National Radio Pulpit; *b* Cupar, Fife, 2 Jan. 1910; *s* of John Alexander Read and Catherine Haxton Carswell; *m* 1936, Dorothy Florence Patricia Gilbert; one *s. Educ:* Daniel Stewart's College, Edinburgh; Edinburgh Univ.; Univs of Montpellier, Strasbourg, Paris, and Marburg; New Coll., Edinburgh. MA Edin. (first class Hons in Lit.) 1932; BD (dist. in Dogmatics) 1936. Ordained Minister of the Church of Scotland, 1936; Minister of Coldstream West Church, 1936–39. CF, 1939–45 (despatches; POW, 1940–45, Germany). Minister of Greenbank Parish, Edinburgh, 1939–49; first Chaplain, Univ. of Edinburgh, 1949–55; Chaplain to the Queen in Scotland, 1952–55. Pres., Japan Internat. Christian Univ. Foundn. Guest Lectr and Preacher in USA, Scotland, Canada, Australia. Hon. DD: Edinburgh, 1956; Yale, 1959; Lafayette Coll., 1965; Hope Coll., 1969; Knox Coll., Canada, 1979; Hon. LHD: Hobart Coll., 1972; Trinity Univ., 1972; Hon. LittD Coll. of Wooster, 1966; Hon. DHL: Japan Internat. Christian Univ., 1979; Rockford Coll., 1982. *Publications:* The Spirit of Life, 1939; The Church to Come (trans. from German), 1939; Prisoners' Quest, Lectures on Christian doctrine in a POW Camp, 1944; The Communication of The Gospel, Warrack Lectures, 1952; The Christian Faith, 1955 (NY 1956); I am Persuaded, 1961 (NY 1962); Sons of Anak, 1964 (NY); God's Mobile Family, 1966 (NY); Whose God is Dead?, 1966 (Cin); Holy Common Sense, 1966 (Tenn); The Pattern of Christ, 1967 (NY); The Presence of Christ, 1968 (NJ); Christian Ethics, 1968 (NY 1969); Virginia Woolfe Meets Charlie Brown, 1968 (Mich); Giants Cut Down To Size, 1970; Religion Without Wrappings, 1970; Overheard, 1971; Curious Christians, 1972; Sent from God, 1974; Good News in the Letters of Paul, 1975; Go and make Disciples, 1978; Unfinished Easter, 1978; The Faith is Still There, 1980; Preaching About the Needs of Real People, 1988; *autobiography:* This Grace Given, 1984; Grace Thus Far, 1986; articles and sermons in Atlantic Monthly, Scottish Jl of Theology, Expository Times, etc. *Recreations:* languages; drama; travel, especially in France. *Address:* 750 Columbus Avenue, New York, NY 10025, USA. *Clubs:* Pilgrims of the US, The Century (New York).

READ, Prof. David John, PhD; FRS 1990; Professor of Plant Science, Sheffield University, since 1990; *b* 20 Jan. 1939; *s* of O. Read; *m* (marr. diss.); one *s*. *Educ:* Sexey's Sch., Bruton, Som; Hull Univ. (BSc 1960; PhD 1963). Sheffield University: Jun. Res. Fellow, 1963–66; Asst Lectr, 1966–69; Lectr, 1969–79; Sen. Lectr, 1979–81; Reader in Plant Sci., 1981–90. *Publications:* editor of numerous books and author of papers in learned jls mostly on subject of symbiosis, specifically the mycorrhizal symbiosis between plant roots and fungi. *Recreations:* walking, botany. *Address:* Minestone Cottage, Youlgrave, Bakewell, Derbys DE4 1WD. *T:* Bakewell (0629) 636360.

READ, Prof. Frank Henry, FRS 1984; Professor of Physics, Victoria University of Manchester, since 1975; *b* 6 Oct. 1934; *s* of late Frank Charles Read and Florence Louise (*née* Wright); *m* 1961, Anne Stuart (*née* Wallace); two *s* two *d*. *Educ:* Haberdashers' Aske's Hampstead Sch. (Foundn Scholar, 1946); Royal Coll. of Science, Univ. of London (Royal Scholar, 1952; ARCS 1955; BSc 1955). PhD 1959, DSc 1975, Victoria Univ. of Manchester. FInstP 1968; MIEE 1982; CEng; CPhys. Univ. of Manchester: Lectr, 1959; Sen. Lectr, 1969; Reader, 1974. Vis. Scientist: Univ. of Paris, 1974; Univ. of Colorado, 1974–75; Inst. for Atomic and Molecular Physics, Amsterdam, 1979–80. Consultant to industry, 1976–. Vice Pres., Inst. of Physics, 1985–89 (Chm., IOP Publishing Ltd, 1985–89); Member: Science Bd, SERC, 1987–90; Council, Royal Soc., 1987–89. Hon. Editor, Jl of Physics B, Atomic and Molecular Physics, 1980–84. *Publications:* (with E. Harting) Electrostatic Lenses, 1976; Electromagnetic Radiation, 1980; papers in physics jls. *Recreations:* stone-masonry, farming. *Address:* Hardingland Farm, Macclesfield Forest, Cheshire SK11 0ND. *T:* Macclesfield (0625) 425759.

READ, Harry; British Commissioner, Salvation Army, 1987–90; Editor, Words of Life, since 1990; *b* 17 May 1924; *s* of Robert and Florence Read; *m* 1950, Winifred Humphries; one *s* one *d*. *Educ:* Sir William Worsley Sch., Grange Town, Middlesbrough. Served RCS, 1942–47 (6th Airborne Div., 1943–45). Commnd Salvation Army Officer, 1948; pastoral work, 1948–54; Lectr, Internat. Training Coll., 1954–62; pastoral work, 1962–64; Divl Youth Sec., 1964–66; Lectr, Internat. Training Coll., 1966–72; Dir, Information Services, 1972–75; Divl Comdr, 1975–78; Principal, Internat. Training Coll., 1978–81; Chief Sec., Canada Territory, 1981–84; Territorial Comdr, Australia Eastern Territory, 1984–87. *Recreations:* writing, hymns, poetry. *Address:* 5 Kingates Court, 43 Wickham Road, Beckenham, Kent BR3 2NB. *T:* 081–650 4187.

See also J. L. Read.

READ, Imelda Mary, (Mel); Member (Lab) Leicester, European Parliament, since 1989; *b* Hillingdon, 8 Jan. 1939; *d* of Robert Alan Hocking and Teresa Mary Hocking; *m*; one *s* one *d*, and one step *s*. *Educ:* Bishopshalt Sch., Hillingdon, Mddx; Nottingham Univ. (BA Hons 1977). Laboratory technician, Plessey, 1963–74; researcher, Trent Polytechnic, 1977–80; Lectr, Trent Polytechnic and other instns, 1980–84; Employment Officer, Nottingham Community Relations Council, 1984–89. Chair, British Labour Gp, Eur. Parlt, 1990–. Contested (Lab): Melton, 1979; Leicestershire NW, 1983. Member: Nat Exec. Council, ASTMS, 1975; NEC, MSF; TUC Women's Adv. Cttee; Chair, Regl TUC Women's Cttee. *Recreations:* beekeeping, gardening. *Address:* 81 Great Central Street, Leicester LE1 4ND.

READ, Gen. Sir (John) Antony (Jervis), GCB 1972 (KCB 1967; CB 1965); CBE 1959 (OBE 1957); DSO 1945; MC 1941; Governor of Royal Hospital, Chelsea, 1975–81; *b* 10 Sept. 1913; *e s* of late John Dale Read, Heathfield, Sussex; *m* 1947, Sheila, *e d* of late F. G. C. Morris, London, NW8; three *d*. *Educ:* Winchester; Sandhurst. Commissioned Oxford and Bucks Lt Inf., 1934; seconded to Gold Coast Regt, RWAFF, 1936; comd 81 (WA) Div. Reconnaissance Regt, 1943; comd 1 Gambia Regt, 1944; war service Kenya, Abyssinia, Somaliland, Burma; DAMS, War Office, 1947–49; Company Comd RMA Sandhurst, 1949–52; AA&QMG 11 Armd Div., 1953–54; comd 1 Oxford and Bucks Lt Inf., 1955–57; comd 3 Inf. Bde Gp, 1957–59; Comdt School of Infantry, 1959–62; GOC Northumbrian Area and 50 (Northumbrian) Division (TA), 1962–64; Vice-Quarter-Master-General, Min. of Defence, 1964–66; GOC-in-C, Western Comd, 1966–69; Quartermaster-General, 1969–72; Comdt, Royal Coll. of Defence Studies, 1973. ADC (Gen.) to the Queen, 1971–73. Colonel Commandant: Army Catering Corps, 1966–76; The Light Division, 1968–73; Small Arms School Corps, 1969–74; Hon. Col, Oxfordshire Royal Green Jackets Bn ACF, 1983. President: TA Rifle Assoc., 1972–90; Ex-Services Fellowship Centres, 1975–; ACF Assoc., 1982– (Chm., 1973–82). Treas., Lord Kitchener Nat. Meml Fund, 1980–87. Governor: Royal Sch. for Daughters of Officers of the Army, 1966–83 (Chm., 1975–81); St Edward's Sch., Oxford, 1972–86; Special Comr, Duke of York's Royal Mil. Sch., 1974–90. FBIM 1972. *Address:* Brackles, Little Chesterton, near Bicester, Oxon. *T:* Bicester (0869) 252189. *Club:* Army and Navy.

READ, Sir John (Emms), Kt 1976; FCA 1947; Chairman, Charities Aid Foundation, since 1990 (Trustee, since 1985); Chairman: TSB Group plc, 1986–88; Trustee Savings Banks Central Board, 1980–88; Deputy Chairman, Thames Television Ltd, 1981–88 (Director, since 1973); *b* 29 March 1918; *s* of late William Emms Read and of Daysie Elizabeth (*née* Cooper); *m* 1942, Dorothy Millicent Berry; two *s*. *Educ:* Brighton, Hove and Sussex Grammar Sch. Served Royal Navy, 1939–46 (rank of Comdr (S) RNVR); Admiral's Secretary: to Asst Chief of Naval Staff, Admty, 1942–45; to Brit. Admty Technical Mission, Ottawa, Canada, 1945–46. Ford Motor Co. Ltd, 1946–64 (Admin. Staff Coll., Henley, 1952), Dir of Sales, 1961–64; Dir, Electric and Musical Industries Ltd, 1965–87; EMI Group: Jt Man. Dir, 1967; Chief Exec., 1969–79; Dep. Chm., 1973–74; Chm., 1974–79; Thorn EMI: Dep. Chm., 1979–81, Dir, 1981–87. Director: Capitol Industries-EMI Inc., 1970–83; Group Five Management Ltd, 1984–; Dunlop Holdings Ltd, 1971–84; Wonderworld plc, 1984–; Hill Samuel Gp, 1987–88; Cafman Ltd, 1990–; NCVO Ltd, 1990–; Chairman: CBI Finance & GP Cttee, 1978–84; TSB Holdings Ltd, 1980–86; Central TSB Ltd, 1983–86; TSB England and Wales, 1983–86; UDT, 1981–85; Target Gp plc, 1987–88; FI Group plc, 1989–. Chm., EDC for Electronics Industry, 1977–80. Member: (part time), PO Bd, 1975–77; Engineering Industries Council, 1975–80; BOTB, 1976–79; Armed Forces Pay Review Body, 1976–83; Nat. Electronics Council, 1977–80; Groupe des Présidents des Grandes Enterprises Européennes, 1977–80. Vice-Pres., Inst. of Bankers, 1982–89. Member: RN Film Corp., 1975–83; Brighton Festival Soc. Council of Management, 1977–82; CBI Council, 1977–90 (Mem., Presidents' Cttee, 1977–84); White Ensign Assoc. Council of Management, 1979–; Council, The Prince's Youth Business Trust, 1987–89; Nat. Theatre Develt Council, 1987–90; Court, Surrey Univ., 1986–; Governing Body and F&GP Cttee, BPMF, London Univ., 1982– (Dep. Chm., 1987–); Governing Council, Business in the Community, 1985–89; Council, British Heart Foundn, 1986–89; Chm., Inst. of Neurology Council of Management, 1980–; Trustee: Westminster Abbey Trust, 1978–85; Brain Res. Trust, 1982– (Chm., 1986–); Dir and Trustee, Brighton Fest. Trust, 1977–; President: Sussex Assoc. of Boys' Clubs, 1982–; Cheshire Homes, Seven Rivers, Essex, 1979–85; Governor, Admin. Staff Coll., Henley, 1974–. CBIM (FBIM 1974); CompIERE 1974; FRSA 1974; FIB 1982. DUniv. Surrey, 1989. *Recreations:* music, arts, sports. *Address:* Muster House, 12 Muster Green North, Haywards Heath, W Sussex RH16 4AG. *Clubs:* Royal Over-Seas League, MCC.

READ, John Leslie, FCA; Chairman, LEP Group plc, since 1982; *b* 21 March 1935; *s* of Robert and Florence Read; *m* 1958, Eugenie Ida (*née* Knight); one *s* one *d*. *Educ:* Sir William Turner's School. Partner, Price Waterhouse & Co., 1966–75; Finance Dir, then Jt Chief Exec., Unigate plc, 1975–80; Chm., Macarthy plc, 1989– (Dir, 1986–); Director: MB Group (formerly Metal Box) plc, 1979–; Equity Law Life Assurance Soc. plc, 1980–87; Border and Southern Stockholders Investment Trust, now Govett Strategic Investment Trust, 1985–. Chm., Audit Commn for Local Authorities in England and Wales, 1983–86. *Recreations:* music, sport, reading, photography. *Address:* LEP Group, LEP House, 87 East Street, Epsom, Surrey KT17 1DT. *T:* Epsom (03727) 29595. *Club:* Royal Automobile.

See also H. Read

READ, Leonard Ernest, (Nipper), QPM 1976; National Security Adviser to the Museums and Galleries Commission, 1978–86; *b* 31 March 1925; *m* 1st, 1951, Marion Alexandra Millar (marr. diss. 1979); one *d*; 2nd, 1980, Patricia Margaret Allen. *Educ:* elementary schools. Worked at Players Tobacco factory, Nottingham, 1939–43; Petty Officer, RN, 1943–46; joined Metropolitan Police, 1947; served in all ranks of CID; Det. Chief Supt on Murder Squad, 1967; Asst Chief Constable, Notts Combined Constabulary, 1970; National Co-ordinator of Regional Crime Squads for England and Wales, 1972–76. Vice-President: British Boxing Bd of Control, 1991– (Mem. Council, 1976–; Vice-Chm., 1988); World Boxing Assoc., 1989–. Freeman, City of London, 1983. *Publication:* Nipper, 1991. *Recreations:* home computing, playing the keyboard. *Address:* 23 North Barn, Broxbourne, Herts EN10 6RR.

READ, Lionel Frank, QC 1973; a Recorder of the Crown Court, since 1974; a General Commissioner of Income Tax, Gray's Inn Division, 1986–90; *b* 7 Sept. 1929; *s* of late F. W. C. Read and Lilian (*née* Chatwin); *m* 1956, Shirley Greenhalgh; two *s* one *d*. *Educ:* Oundle Sch.; St John's Coll., Cambridge (MA). Mons OCS Stick of Honour; commnd 4 RHA, 1949. Called to Bar, Gray's Inn, 1954; Bencher, 1981; Mem., Senate of the Inns of Court and the Bar, 1974–77. Chm., Local Government and Planning Bar Assoc., 1990– (Vice-Chm., 1986–90); Member: Bar Council, 1990–; Mem., Council on Tribunals, 1990–. *Recreations:* golf, gardening. *Address:* Cedarwood, Church Road, Ham Common, Surrey TW10 5HG. *T:* 081–940 5247. *Club:* Garrick.

READ, Mel; *see* Read, I. M.

READ, Piers Paul, FRSL; author; *b* 7 March 1941; 3rd *s* of Sir Herbert Read, DSO, MC and Margaret Read, Stonegrave, York; *m* 1967, Emily Albertine, *o d* of Evelyn Basil Boothby, CMG and of Susan Asquith; two *s* two *d*. *Educ:* Ampleforth Coll.; St John's Coll., Cambridge (MA). Artist-in-residence, Ford Foundn, Berlin, 1963–64; Sub-Editor, Times Literary Supplement, 1965; Harkness Fellow, Commonwealth Fund, NY, 1967–68. Member: Council, Inst. of Contemporary Arts, 1971–75; Cttee of Management, Soc. of Authors, 1973–76; Literature Panel, Arts Council, 1975–77. Adjunct Prof. of Writing, Columbia Univ., NY, 1980. Bd Mem., Aid to the Church in Need, 1988–. Governor, Cardinal Manning Boys' Sch., 1985–91. TV plays: Coincidence, 1968; The House on Highbury Hill, 1972; The Childhood Friend, 1974; radio play: The Family Firm, 1970. *Publications: novels:* Game in Heaven with Tussy Marx, 1966; The Junkers, 1968 (Sir Geoffrey Faber Meml Prize); Monk Dawson, 1969 (Hawthornden Prize and Somerset Maugham Award); The Professor's Daughter, 1971; The Upstart, 1973; Polonaise, 1976; A Married Man, 1979 (televised 1983); The Villa Golitsyn, 1981; The Free Frenchman, 1986 (televised 1989); A Season in the West, 1988 (James Tait Black Meml Prize); On the Third Day, 1990; *non-fiction:* Alive, 1974; The Train Robbers, 1978. *Address:* 50 Portland Road, W11 4LG.

READE, Brian Anthony; HM Diplomatic Service; Counsellor, Foreign and Commonwealth Office, since 1986; *b* 5 Feb. 1940; *s* of Stanley Robert Reade and Emily Doris (*née* Lee); *m* 1964, Averille van Eugen; one *s* one *d*. *Educ:* King Henry VIII Sch., Coventry; Univ. of Leeds (BA Hons 1963). Interlang Ltd, 1963–64; Lectr, City of Westminster Coll., 1964–65; 2nd Sec., FCO, 1965–69; 2nd Sec., Bangkok, 1970–71, 1st Sec., 1971–74; FCO, 1974–77; Consul (Econ.), Consulate-General, Düsseldorf, 1977–81; FCO, 1981–82; 1st Sec., Bangkok, 1982–84; Counsellor (ESCAP), Bangkok, 1984–86. *Recreations:* watching sport, conversation, reading. *Address:* c/o Foreign and Commonwealth Office, SW1. *Clubs:* Coventry Rugby Football; Royal Bangkok Sports (Thailand).

READE, Sir Clyde Nixon, 12th Bt *cr* 1661; *b* 1906; *s* of Sir George Reade, 10th Bt; *S* brother, Sir John Reade, 11th Bt, 1958; *m* 1930, Trilby (*d* 1958), *d* of Charles McCarthy. Is a Royal Arch Mason.

READER HARRIS, Dame (Muriel) Diana, DBE 1972; Headmistress, Sherborne School for Girls, Dorset, 1950–75; *b* Hong Kong, 11 Oct. 1912; *er d* of late Montgomery Reader Harris. *Educ:* Sherborne School for Girls; University of London (external student). BA 1st Class Honours (English), 1934. Asst Mistress, Sherborne School for Girls, 1934, and House Mistress, 1938. Organised Public Schools and Clubs Camps for Girls, 1937–39; in charge of group evacuated from Sherborne to Canada, 1940; joined staff of National Association of Girls' Clubs, 1943; Chm. Christian Consultative Cttee Nat. Assoc. of Mixed Clubs and Girls' Clubs, 1952–68, Vice-Pres., 1968; Chm. Outward Bound Girls' Courses, 1954–59; Mem. Council, Outward Bound Trust, 1956–64. Member: Women's Consultative Cttee, Min. of Labour, 1958–77; Women's Nat. Commn, 1976–78. Member: Dorset Educn Cttee, 1952–70; Exec. Cttee, Assoc. of Headmistresses, 1953–58, 1960 (Pres., 1964–66); Pres., Assoc. of Headmistresses of Boarding Schs, 1960–62; Member: Cttee on Agricl Colls, Min. of Agric., 1961–64; Schs Council, 1966–75. Member: Archbishop's Council on Evangelism, 1966–68; Panel on Broadcasting, Synod of C of E, 1975–86; Bd, Christian Aid, 1976–83 (Chm., 1978–83); Exec. Cttee and Assembly, BCC, 1977–83. Pres., CMS, 1969–82 (Mem., 1953–82, Chm., 1960–63, Exec. Cttee). Lay Canon, Salisbury Cathedral, 1987–. King George's Jubilee Trust: Mem., Standing Res. and Adv. Cttee, 1949; Mem., Admin. Council, 1955–67. Member: Council, 1951–62, Exec. and Council, 1976–79, Nat. Youth Orch. of GB; ITA, 1956–60; Council, Westminster Abbey Choir Sch., 1976–88; Court, Royal Foundn of St Katharine, 1979–90 (Chm., 1981–88). Patron, Jt Educational Trust, 1986– (Chm., 1982–84, Trustee, 1975–86); President: Sch. Mistresses and Governesses Benevolent Instn, 1980–89; Time and Talents Assoc., 1981–; British and For. Sch. Soc., 1982–91; Churches' Commn on Overseas Students, 1984–91. Governor: Godolphin Sch., Salisbury, 1975–86; St Michael's Sch., Limpsfield, 1975–83 (Chm., 1977–83). FRSA 1964 (Mem. Council, RSA, 1975–89; Chm., 1979–81; Vice-Pres., 1981–89; Vice-Pres. Emerita, 1989–); Mem., The Pilgrims, 1979–. Hon. FCP 1975. *Address:* 35 The Close, Salisbury, Wilts SP1 2EL. *T:* Salisbury (0722) 26889.

READING, 4th Marquess of, *cr* 1926; **Simon Charles Henry Rufus Isaacs;** Baron 1914; Viscount 1916; Earl 1917; Viscount Erleigh 1917; Joint Chief Executive: Abbey Hickman Ltd; Abbey Corporate Events Ltd, since 1989; Director, Shephard Insurance Holdings Ltd, since 1987; Chairman, Glentronic International Inc., since 1985; *b* 18 May 1942; *e s* of 3rd Marquess of Reading, MBE, MC, and of Margot Irene, *yr d* of late Percy Duke, OBE; *S* father, 1980; *m* 1979, Melinda Victoria, *yr d* of Richard Dewar, Hay Hedge, Bisley, Glos; one *s* two *d*. *Educ:* Eton. Short service commission, 1st Queen's Dragoon Guards, 1961–64. Member of Stock Exchange, 1970–74. Chm. of Govs, Dean

Close Sch., 1990–. Hon. Dr Soka, Tokyo, 1989. *Heir:* *s* Viscount Erleigh, *qv*. *Address:* Jaynes Court, Bisley, Glos GL6 7BE. *Clubs:* Cavalry and Guards, MCC, Queen's, All England Lawn Tennis and Croquet.

READING, Area Bishop of, since 1989; **Rt. Rev. John Frank Ewan Bone;** *b* 28 Aug. 1930; *s* of Jack and Herberta Blanche Bone; *m* 1954, Ruth Margaret Crudgington; two *s* two *d* and one adopted *s*. *Educ:* Monkton Combe School, Bath; St Peter's Coll., Oxford (MA); Ely Theological Coll.; Whitelands Coll. of Education (Grad. Cert. in Education). Ordained, 1956; Assistant Curate: St Gabriel's, Warwick Square, 1956–60; St Mary's, Henley on Thames, 1960–63; Vicar of Datchet, 1963–76; Rector of Slough, 1976–78; Rural Dean of Burnham, 1974–77; Archdeacon of Buckingham, 1978–89. Mem. of General Synod, 1980–85. *Recreations:* collecting antique maps and prints, classical music, coarse gardening, walking. *Address:* Greenbanks, Old Bath Road, Sonning, Reading RG4 0SY.

READWIN, Edgar Seeley, CBE 1971; retired; *b* 7 Nov. 1915; *s* of Ernest Readwin, Master Mariner and Edith Elizabeth Readwin; *m* 1940, Lesley Margaret (*née* Barker); two *s* one *d*. *Educ:* Bracondale Sch., Norwich. FCA. Articled Clerk, Harman & Gowen, Norwich, 1932–37; Asst Auditor, Bengal & North Western Railway, 1938–40; commnd service 14th Punjab Regt, 1941–45, PoW Far East, Singapore, Siam-Burma Railway, 1942–45; Indian Railway Accounts Service, 1945–49. Booker Group of Companies in Guyana: Asst to Accounts Controller, 1950; Finance Dir, 1951–56; Dep. Chm., 1956–62; Chm., 1962–71. Dir, West Indies Sugar Assoc., 1962–71; Finance Dir, Indonesia Sugar Study, 1971–72; Chm., Minvielle & Chastenet Ltd, St Lucia, 1973–76. Hon. Treas., Guyana Lawn Tennis Assoc., 1951–67, Pres., 1968–70, Hon. Life Vice-Pres., 1971–. *Recreations:* lawn tennis, golf, gardening, chess, bridge. *Address:* Puxholt, 2 Halliwick Gardens, Felpham, Bognor Regis, West Sussex PO22 7JE. *Clubs:* Veterans' Lawn Tennis of Great Britain; Bognor Tennis; Littlehampton Golf.

REAGAN, Ronald, Hon. GCB 1989; President of the United States of America, 1981–89; *b* Tampico, Ill, 6 Feb. 1911; *m* 1st, 1940, Jane Wyman (marr. diss. 1948); one *s* one *d*; 2nd, 1952, Nancy Davis; one *s* one *d*. *Educ:* public schools in Tampico, Monmouth, Galesburg, and Dixon, Ill; Eureka Coll., Ill (AB). Sports Announcer, WHO, Des Moines, 1932–37; actor, films and television, 1937–66; Host and Program Superviser, Gen. Electric Theater (TV), 1954–62; Host, Death Valley Days (TV), 1962–65. Pres., Screen Actors' Guild, 1947–52, 1959–60; Chm., Motion Picture Industry Council, 1949. Served with USAAF, 1942–45. Governor, State of California, 1967–74; Chairman, State Governors' Assoc., 1969. Republican Candidate for nomination for the Presidency, 1976. Operates horsebreeding and cattle ranch. *Publications:* Where's the Rest of Me? (autobiog.), 1965 (repr. 1981 as My Early Life); Abortion and the Conscience of the Nation, 1984; An American Life (autobiog.), 1990. *Address:* 668 St Cloud Road, Bel Air, Los Angeles, Calif 90077, USA.

REARDON, Rev. John Patrick; General Secretary, Council of Churches for Britain and Ireland, since 1990; *b* 15 June 1933; *s* of John Samuel Reardon and Ivy Hilda Reardon; *m* 1957, Molly Pamela Young; four *s* one *d*. *Educ:* Gravesend Grammar Sch. for Boys; University College London (BA Hons English); King's College London (postgraduate Cert. in Educn). Teacher, London and Gravesend, 1958–61; Minister, Horsham Congregational Church, 1961–68 (Chm., Sussex Congregational Union, 1967); Minister, Trinity Congregational Church, St Albans, 1968–72 (Chm., Herts Congregational Union, 1971–72); Sec., Church and Society Dept, 1972–90, and Dep. Gen. Sec., 1983–90, URC. *Publications:* More Everyday Prayers (contrib.), 1982; (ed) Leaves from the Tree of Peace, 1986; (ed) Threads of Creation, 1989. *Recreations:* modern literature, photography, philately, travel. *Address:* Inter-Church House, 35–41 Lower Marsh, SE1 7RL. *T:* 071–620 4444.

REARDON, Rev. Canon Martin Alan; General Secretary, Churches Together in England, since 1990; *b* 3 Oct. 1932; *s* of Ernest William Reardon, CBE and Gertrude Mary; *m* 1964, Ruth Maxim Slade; one *s* one *d*. *Educ:* Cumnor House Sch.; St Edward's Sch., Oxford; Selwyn Coll., Cambridge (MA); Cuddesdon Coll., Oxford; Univ. of Geneva; Univ. of Louvain. Asst Curate, Rugby Parish Church, 1958–61; Sec., Sheffield Council of Churches, 1962–71; Sub-Warden, Lincoln Theol Coll., 1971–78; Sec., Bd for Mission and Unity, Gen. Synod of C of E, 1978–89; Rector, Plumpton with East Chiltington, 1989–90. *Publications:* Christian Unity in Sheffield, 1967; (with Kenneth Greet) Social Questions, 1964; What on Earth is the Church For?, 1985; contribs to One in Christ, Theology, Clergy Review, etc. *Recreations:* walking, sketching. *Address:* Inter-Church House, 35–41 Lower Marsh, SE1 7RL.

REARDON-SMITH, Sir William; *see* Smith.

REAY, 14th Lord, *cr* 1628, of Reay, Caithness; **Hugh William Mackay;** Bt of Nova Scotia, 1627; Baron Mackay of Ophemert and Zennewijnen, Holland; Chief of Clan Mackay; Minister of State, Department of Trade and Industry, since 1991; *b* 19 July 1937; *s* of 13th Lord Reay and Charlotte Mary Younger; *S* father, 1963; *m* 1st, 1964, Hon. Annabel Thérèse Fraser (marr. diss. 1978; she *m* 1985, Henry Neville Lindley Keswick, *qv*), *y d* of 17th Baron Lovat, *qv*; two *s* one *d*; 2nd, 1980, Hon. Victoria Isabella Warrender, *d* of Baron Bruntisfield, *qv*; two *d*. *Educ:* Eton; Christ Church. Mem., European Parlt, 1973–79 (Vice-Chm., Cons. Gp); Delegate, Council of Europe and WEU, 1979–86. Lord in Waiting (Govt Whip), 1989–91. *Heir:* *s* The Master of Reay, *qv*. *Address:* House of Lords, SW1A 0PW.

REAY, Master of; Aeneas Simon Mackay, *b* 20 March 1965; *s* and *heir* of 14th Lord Reay, *qv*. *Educ:* Westminster School; Brown Univ., USA. *Recreations:* most sports, especially football, cricket and shooting.

REAY, Lt-Gen. Sir Alan; *see* Reay, Lt-Gen. Sir H. A. J.

REAY, David William, CEng, FIEE; CPhys, FInstP; Chief Executive, Tyne Tees Television Holdings PLC, since 1991; *b* 28 May 1940; *s* of Stanley Reay and of late Madge Reay (*née* Hall); *m* 1964, Constance Susan Gibney; two *d*. *Educ:* Monkwearmouth Grammar School, Sunderland; Newcastle upon Tyne Polytechnic. Independent Television Authority, 1960–62; Alpha Television (ATV and ABC) Services Ltd, 1962–64; Tyne Tees Television Ltd, 1964–72; HTV Ltd: Engineering Manager, 1972–75; Chief Engineer, 1975–79; Dir of Engineering, 1979–84; Man. Dir, Tyne Tees Television Hldgs, 1984–91. Chairman: Hadrian Television Ltd, 1988–; Legend Television Ltd, 1989–; Director: Tyne Tees Television Ltd, 1984–; Tyne Tees Music, 1984–; Tyne Tees Enterprises, 1984–; ITCA, now ITVA, 1984–; Independent Television Publications, 1984–89; Tube Productions, 1986–; ITN, 1990–; Tyne and Wear Develt Corp., 1986–88; The Wearside Opportunity Ltd, 1988. Mem. Council, Univ. of Newcastle upon Tyne, 1989–. CBIM 1987; FRTS 1984. *Recreations:* walking, reading, music, watching soccer (particularly Sunderland AFC). *Address:* Warreners House, Northgate, Morpeth, Northumberland NE61 3BX. *Club:* Savile.

REAY, Lt-Gen. Sir (Hubert) Alan (John), KBE 1981; FRCP, FRCP(Edin); Chief Hon. Steward, Westminster Abbey, since 1985; Director General, Army Medical Services, 1981–85; *b* 19 March 1925; *s* of Rev. John Reay; *m* 1960, Ferelith Haslewood Deane; two *s* two *d* (and one *s* decd). *Educ:* Lancing College; Edinburgh Univ. MB, DTM&H, DCH. Field Medical Services, Malaya, 1949–52 (despatches); Exchange Physician, Brooke Hosp., San Antonio, Texas, 1957; Command Paediatrician: Far East, 1962; BAOR, 1965; Adviser in Paediatrics, MoD (Army), 1968; Hon. Out-patient Consultant, Great Ormond Street Hosp., 1975–79, 1985–87; QHP 1976–85; Postgraduate Dean and Comdt, Royal Army Med. Coll., 1977–79; DMS, HQ BAOR, 1979–81. Hon. Col, 217 (London) General Hosp. RAMC (Volunteers) TA, 1986–90. Chm., Med. Cttee, Royal Star and Garter Home, 1986–. Member Council: SSAFA, 1986–; RSocMed, 1987– (Pres., Paediatric Section, 1984–85). Trustee, Children's Hospice for Eastern Reg., Cambridge, 1988–. Inaugural Lectr, Soc. of Armed Forces Med. Consultants, Univ. of Health Scis, Bethesda, 1984. Hon. Mem., BPA, 1988. Hon. FRCGP 1985. CStJ 1981 (OStJ 1979). *Publications:* paediatric articles in med. jls. *Address:* c/o National Westminster Bank, 7–9 Dean Bradley Street, SW1P 3EP.

REAY, Dr John Sinclair Shewan; Director, Warren Spring Laboratory, Department of Trade and Industry, since 1985; *b* Aberdeen, 8 June 1932; *s* of late George Reay, CBE and Tina (*née* Shewan); *m* 1958, Rhoda Donald Robertson; two *s* one *d*. *Educ:* Robert Gordon's College, Aberdeen; Univ. of Aberdeen; Imperial College, London (Beit Fellow). BSc, PhD, DIC. CChem, FRSC. Joined Scottish Agricultural Industries, 1958; Warren Spring Lab., Min of Technology, 1968; Head of Air Pollution Div., DoI, 1972–77; Head, Policy and Perspectives Unit, DTI, 1977–79; Head of Branch, Research Technology Div., DoI, 1979–81; Dep. Dir, Warren Spring Lab., 1981–85. *Publications:* papers on surface chemistry and air pollution. *Recreations:* playing violin, listening to music. *Address:* 13 Grange Hill, Welwyn, Herts Al6 9RH. *T:* Welwyn (043871) 5587.

REBBECK, Dr Denis, CBE 1952; JP, DL; MA, MSc, PhD, BLitt; FEng, FICE, FIMechE, FRINA, FIMarE, FCIT; *b* 22 Jan. 1914; *er s* of late Sir Frederick Ernest Rebbeck, KBE; *m* 1938, Rosamond Annette Kathleen, *e d* of late Henry Jameson, Bangor, Co. Down; four *s*. *Educ:* Campbell Coll., Belfast; Pembroke Coll., Cambridge. BA (Hons) Mech. Sciences Tripos, 1935; MA (Cantab) 1939; MA (Dublin) 1945; BLitt (Dublin) 1946; MSc (Belfast) 1946; PhD (Belfast) 1950; Part-time Post-grad. Research. Harland & Wolff, Ltd: Director, 1946–70; Dep. Man. Director, 1953; Man. Dir, 1962–70; Chm., 1965–66. Chm., 1972–84, Dir, 1950–84, Iron Trades Employers' Insurance Association Ltd and Iron Trades Mutual Insurance Co. Ltd (Vice-Chm., 1969–72); Director: Nat. Shipbuilders Security Ltd, 1952–58; Colvilles Ltd, 1963–67; Brown Brothers & Co. Ltd, 1967–68; Shipbuilding Corporation Ltd, 1963–73; National Commercial Bank of Scotland Ltd, 1965–69; Royal Bank of Scotland Ltd, 1969–84; Belships Co. Ltd, 1970–76 (Chm., 1972–76); John Kelly Ltd, 1968–79 (Dep. Chm., 1968; Chm., 1969–79); Howdens Ltd, 1977–79; Norman Canning Ltd, 1977–79; Nationwide Building Soc., 1980–87; Nationwide Anglia Building Soc., 1987–89; General Underwriting Agencies Ltd, 1984– (Chm. 1984–); Nordic Business Forum for Northern Britain Ltd, 1980–84. Special Consultant, Swan Hunter Group Ltd, 1970–79; Consultant, Ellerman Travel, 1979–84. Belfast Harbour Commissioner, 1962–85. Member Research Council, and Chairman, Design Main Committee, British Ship Research Association, 1965–73; Pres., Shipbuilding Employers' Fedn, 1962–63; Past Chm. Warship Gp., Shipbuilding Conf.; NI Economic Council, 1965–70; Lloyd's Register of Shipping General Cttee, 1962–85 and Technical Cttee, 1964–76; Management Board: Engineering Employers Fedn, 1963–75; Shipbuilders & Repairers Nat. Assoc., 1966–71; Council, RINA, 1964–72; Council for Scientific R&D in NI, 1948–59; Member Inst. of Engineers and Shipbuilders in Scotland; Past Chm. and Trustee, Belfast Savings Bank; Cambridge Univ. Engineers' Assoc.; Science Masters' Assoc. (Pres. NI Branch, 1954–55); NI Grammar Schools Careers Assoc. (Pres., 1964–65); Life Mem. Brit. Assoc. for the Advancement of Science; National Playing Fields Assoc. (NI Exec. Cttee), 1952–77; Chairman: Adv. Cttee on Marine Pilotage, 1977–79; Pilotage Commn, 1979–83; Member: Drummond Technical Investigation Cttee, 1955–56; Lord Coleraine's Committee to enquire into Youth Employment Services in NI, 1957–58; Sir John Lockwood's Cttee on Univ. and Higher Techn. Educn in Northern Ireland, 1963–64; Queen's Univ., Better Equipment Fund Exec. Cttee, 1951–82; Hon. Life Mem., Irish Port Authorities Assoc., 1985; Vice-Pres. of Belfast Savings Council; Visitor, Linen Industry Research Assoc., DSIR, 1954–57; President: Belfast Assoc. of Engineers, 1947–48; NI Society of Incorporated Secretaries, 1955–70; Glencraig Curative Schools, NI, 1953–70; World Ship Soc., 1978–81 (Vice Pres., 1956); Past Mem. Council IMechE; IMarE; Chm. NI Assoc., ICE, 1952–53; FEng 1979. Member: Smeatonian Soc. of Civil Engrs; Incorp. of Hammermen of Glasgow. Liveryman, Worshipful Company of Shipwrights, 1952– (Prime Warden, 1980–81). Hon. Mem., BUPA, 1984. Vice-Pres., Queen's Univ. Guild, 1951–65; Board Governors Campbell Coll., Belfast, 1952–60 (Vice-Chm. 1957–60); Member of Court, New Univ. of Ulster. Mem., T&AFA for Belfast, 1947–65; Dep.-Chm. NI Festival of Britain, 1948–51; papers read before British Association, ICE, etc; Akroyd Stuart Award, IMarE, 1943. JP County Borough of Belfast, 1949; DL County of the City of Belfast, 1960. *Recreations:* sailing, worldwide travel. *Address:* The White House, Craigavad, Holywood, County Down, N Ireland BT18 0HE. *T:* Holywood (02317) 2294. *Clubs:* Royal Yacht Squadron, Royal Automobile, City Livery, Den Norske; Cambridge Union; Shippingklubben (Oslo); Royal Norwegian Yacht; Royal North of Ireland Yacht (Cultra, Co. Down).

RECKITT, Lt-Col Basil Norman, TD 1946; Director, Reckitt and Colman Ltd, retired 1972 (Chairman, 1966–70); *b* 12 Aug. 1905; *s* of Frank Norman Reckitt, Architect, and Beatrice Margaret Hewett; *m* 1st, 1928, Virginia Carre-Smith (*d* 1961); three *d*; 2nd, 1966, Mary Holmes (*née* Peirce), *widow* of Paul Holmes, Malham Tarn, near Settle. *Educ:* Uppingham; King's Coll., Cambridge (MA). Joined Reckitt & Sons Ltd, 1927; Dir, Reckitt & Colman Ltd, 1938. 2nd Lieut, 62nd HAA Regt (TA), 1939; Bde Major, 39th AA Brigade, 1940; CO 141 HAA (M) Regt, 1942; Military Government, Germany, 1944–45. Chm. Council, 1971–80, and Pro-Chancellor, 1971–, Hull Univ. Sheriff of Hull, 1970–71. Chm., Friends of Abbot Hall Art Gall. and Museums, Kendal, 1982–87; Vice-Chm., YMCA Nat. Centre, Lakeside, Windermere, 1982–87. Hon. LLD, Hull University, 1967. *Publications:* History of Reckitt & Sons Ltd, 1951; Charles I and Hull, 1952; The Lindley Affair, 1972; Diary of Military Government in Germany, 1989; The Journeys of William Reckitt, 1989. *Recreations:* riding, walking. *Address:* Haverbrack, Milnthorpe, Cumbria LA7 7AH. *T:* Milnthorpe (05395) 63142.

REDDAWAY, Brian; *see* Reddaway, W. B.

REDDAWAY, (George Frank) Norman, CBE 1965 (MBE 1946); HM Diplomatic Service, retired; *b* 2 May 1918; *s* of late William Fiddian Reddaway and late Kate Waterland Reddaway (*née* Sills); *m* 1944, Jean Brett, OBE; two *s* three *d*. *Educ:* Oundle School; King's College, Cambridge. Scholar Modern Langs, 1935; 1st Class Hons Mod. Langs Tripos Parts 1 and 2, 1937 and 1939. Served in Army, 1939–46; psc Camberley, 1944. Foreign Office, 1946; Private Sec. to Parly Under Sec. of State, 1947–49; Rome, 1949; Ottawa, 1952; Foreign Office, 1955; Imperial Defence College, 1960; Counsellor, Beirut, 1961; Counsellor, Office of the Political Adviser to the C-in-C, Far East, Singapore, 1965–66; Counsellor (Commercial), Khartoum, 1967–69; Asst Under-Sec. of State, FCO, 1970–74; Ambassador to Poland, 1974–78. Chm., International House (formerly English

International), 1978–; Dir, Catalytic International, 1978–89; Consultant, Badger Catalytic; Trustee, Thomson Foundn, 1978–. Commander, Order of Merit, Polish People's Republic, 1985. *Recreations:* international affairs, gardening, family history. *Address:* 51 Carlton Hill, NW8 0EL. *T:* 071–624 9238. *Clubs:* Athenæum, United Oxford & Cambridge University, Commonwealth Trust.

REDDAWAY, Norman; *see* Reddaway, G. F. N.

REDDAWAY, Prof. (William) Brian, CBE 1971; FBA 1967; Professor of Political Economy, University of Cambridge, 1969–80; Fellow of Clare College, Cambridge, since 1938; Economic Consultant to the World Bank, since 1966; *b* 8 Jan. 1913; *s* of late William Fiddian Reddaway and late Kate Waterland Reddaway (*née* Sills); *m* 1938, Barbara Augusta Bennett; three *s* one *d*. *Educ:* Oundle Sch.; King's Coll., Cambridge; Maj. schol. natural science; 1st cl. Maths tripos, part I, 1st cl. 1st div. Economics tripos, part II; Adam Smith Prize; MA. Assistant, Bank of England, 1934–35; Research Fellow in Economics, University of Melbourne, 1936–37; Statistics Division, Board of Trade (final rank Chief Statistician), 1940–47; University Lectr in Economics, 1939–55, Reader in Applied Economics, 1957–65, Dir of Dept of Applied Economics, 1955–69, Univ. of Cambridge. Economic Adviser to OEEC, 1951–52; Visiting Economist, Center for International Studies, New Delhi, 1959–60; Vis. Lectr, Economic Develt Inst. (Washington), 1966–67; Consultant, Harvard Develt Adv. Service (in Ghana), 1967; Vis. Prof., Bangladesh Inst. of Develt Studies, 1974–75. Economic Consultant to CBI, 1972–83. Regional Adviser, Economic Commn for Western Asia, 1979–80; Consultant to World Bank on Nigerian economy, 1983–87. Member: Royal Commn on the Press, 1961–62; NBPI, 1967–71; Chm., Inquiry into Consulting Engineering Firms' Costs and Earnings, 1971–72. Editor, Economic Jl, 1971–76. *Publications:* Russian Financial System, 1935; Economics of a Declining Population, 1939; (with C. F. Carter, Richard Stone) Measurement of Production Movements, 1948; The Development of the Indian Economy, 1962; Effects of UK Direct Investment Overseas, Interim Report, 1967, Final Report, 1968; Effects of the Selective Employment Tax, First Report, 1970, Final Report, 1973; (with G. C. Fiegehen) Companies, Incentives and Senior Managers, 1981; Some Key Issues for the Development of the Economy of Papua New Guinea, 1986; articles in numerous economic journals. *Recreations:* skating, walking. *Address:* 12 Manor Court, Grange Road, Cambridge CB3 9BE. *T:* Cambridge (0223) 350041.

REDDINGTON, (Clifford) Michael; Chief Executive, Liverpool City Council, 1986–88; *b* 14 Sept. 1932; *s* of Thomas Reddington and Gertrude (*née* Kenny); *m* 1968 Ursula Moor. *Educ:* St Michael's Coll., Leeds; St Edward's Coll., Liverpool; Liverpool Univ. BCom 1953; IPFA 1958; MBCS 1964. Served RAF, 1958–60. City Treasury, Liverpool, 1953–58 and 1960–86; Dep. City Treasurer, 1974, City Treasurer, 1982–86. Mem., Indep. Inquiry into Capital Market Activities of London Borough of Hammersmith and Fulham, 1990. Trust Fund Manager, Hillsborough Disaster Appeal Fund, 1989–. *Recreations:* fell-walking, choral singing, cooking. *Address:* Entwood, Westwood Road, Noctorum, Birkenhead L43 9RQ. *T:* 051–652 6081. *Club:* Athenæum (Liverpool).

REDDISH, Prof. Vincent Cartledge, OBE 1974; Professor Emeritus, Edinburgh University, 1980; *b* 28 April 1926; *s* of William H. M. Reddish and Evelyn Reddish; *m* 1951, Elizabeth Waltho; two *s*. *Educ:* Wigan Techn. Coll.; London Univ. BSc Hons, PhD, DSc. Lectr in Astronomy, Edinburgh Univ., 1954; Lectr in Radio Astronomy, Manchester Univ., 1959; Royal Observatory, Edinburgh: Principal Scientific Officer, 1962; Sen. Principal Sci. Off., 1966; Dep. Chief Sci. Off., 1974; Regius Prof. of Astronomy, Edinburgh Univ., Dir, Royal Observatory, Edinburgh, and Astronomer Royal for Scotland, 1975–80. Governor, Rannoch Sch., 1981–. *Publications:* Evolution of the Galaxies, 1967; The Physics of Stellar Interiors, 1974; Stellar Formation, 1978; numerous sci. papers in Monthly Notices RAS, Nature and other jls. *Recreations:* hill walking, sailing, ornithology, do-it-yourself. *Address:* 11 Greenhill Terrace, Edinburgh EH10 4BS. *T:* 031–447 8935.

REDDY, (Neelam) Sanjiva; farmer and lemon grower; President of India, 1977–82; *b* 13 May 1913; *m* Nagaratnamma; one *s* three *d*. *Educ:* Adyar Arts Coll., Anantapur. Andhra Provincial Congress: Sec., Congress Cttee, 1936–46; Pres., 1951–; Leader, Congress Legislature Party, 1953–; Mem. and Sec., Madras Legislative Assembly, 1946; Mem., Indian Constituent Assembly, 1947; Minister for Prohibition, Housing and Forests, Madras Govt, 1949–51; Mem., Rajya Sabha, 1952–53; Andhra Pradesh: Mem., Legislative Assembly, 1953–64; Dep. Chief Minister, 1953–56; Chief Minister, 1956–57 and 1962–64; Pres., All-India Congress Party, 1960–62; Member: Rajya Sabha, 1964–67; Lok Sabha, 1967–71, and 1977; Minister: of Steel and Mines, 1964–65; of Transport, Aviation, Shipping and Tourism, 1966–67; Speaker of Lok Sabha, 1967–69, 1977. *Address:* Illure, Anantapur, Andhra Pradesh, India.

REDESDALE, 6th Baron *cr* 1902; **Rupert Bertram Mitford;** *b* 18 July 1967; *s* of 5th Baron and of Sarah Georgina Cranstoun, *d* of Brig. Alston Cranstoun Todd, OBE; *S* father, 1991. *Educ:* Highgate Sch.; Newcastle Univ. (BA Hons Archaeology). Outdoor instructor, Fernwood Adventure Centre, South Africa, 1990–91. *Recreations:* caving, climbing, ski-ing. *Address:* 2 St Mark's Square, NW1 7TP. *T:* 071–722 1965. *Club:* Newcastle University Caving.

REDFERN, Philip, CB 1983; Deputy Director, Office of Population Censuses and Surveys, 1970–82; *b* 14 Dec. 1922; *m* 1951, Gwendoline Mary Phillips; three *d*. *Educ:* Bemrose Sch., Derby; St John's Coll., Cambridge. Wrangler, Mathematical Tripos, Cambridge, 1942. Asst Statistician, Central Statistical Office, 1947; Chief Statistician, Min. of Education, 1960; Dir of Statistics and Jt Head of Planning Branch, Dept of Educn and Science, 1967.

REDFORD, (Charles) Robert; American actor and director; *b* 18 Aug. 1937; *s* of Charles Redford and Martha (*née* Hart); *m* 1958, Lola Jean Van Wagenen; one *s* two *d*. *Educ:* Van Nuys High Sch.; Univ. of Colorado; Pratt Inst., Brooklyn; Amer. Acad. of Dramatic Arts. *Theatre:* appearances include: Tall Story, Broadway, 1959; Sunday in New York, Broadway, 1961–62; Barefoot in the Park, Biltmore, NY, 1963–64; *television:* appearances include, The Iceman Cometh, 1960; *films* include: as actor: War Hunt, 1962; Inside Daisy Clover, 1965; Barefoot in the Park, 1967; Butch Cassidy and the Sundance Kid, 1969; The Candidate, 1972; The Way We Were, 1973; The Sting, 1973; The Great Gatsby, 1974; All the President's Men, 1976; The Electric Horseman, 1979; The Natural, 1984; Out of Africa, 1985; Legal Eagles, 1986; Havana, 1990; as director: Ordinary People, 1980 (Acad. Award for Best Dir, 1981); Milagro Beanfield War (also prod.), 1988. *Publication:* The Outlaw Trail, 1978. *Address:* c/o Wildwood Enterprises, 1101 Montana Avenue, Suite E, Santa Monica, Calif 90403, USA.

REDFORD, Donald Kirkman, CBE 1980; DL; President, The Manchester Ship Canal Company, since 1986 (Managing Director, 1970–80; Chairman, 1972–86); *b* 18 Feb. 1919; *er s* of T. J. and S. A. Redford; *m* 1942, Mabel (*née* Wilkinson), Humberstone, Lincs; one *s* one *d*. *Educ:* Culford Sch.; King's Coll., Univ. of London (LLB). Served, 1937–39, and War until 1945, in RAFVR (retd as Wing Comdr). Practice at the Bar until end of 1946, when joined The Manchester Ship Canal Company, with which Company has since remained. Chairman, Nat. Assoc. of Port Employers, 1972–74; Dep. Chm., British Ports Assoc., 1973–74, Chm. 1974–78. Member: Cttee of Management, RNLI, 1977– (Chm., Search and Research Cttee, 1984–89); Court and Council, Manchester Univ., 1977– (Dep. Treas., 1980–82, Treas., 1982–83, Chm. of Council, 1983–87). CBIM, FRSA. DL Lancs 1983. Hon. LLD Manchester, 1988. *Recreations:* reading, history, sailing, golf. *Address:* North Cotes, 8 Harrod Drive, Birkdale, Southport PR8 2HA. *T:* Southport (0704) 67406; The Manchester Ship Canal Co., Dock Office, Trafford Road, Manchester M5 2XB. *T:* 061–872 2411. *Clubs:* Oriental; Union (Southport).

REDFORD, Robert; *see* Redford, C. R.

REDGRAVE, Lynn; actress; *b* 8 March 1943; *d* of late Sir Michael Redgrave, CBE, and of Rachel Kempson, *qv*; *m* 1967, John Clark; one *s* two *d*. *Educ:* Queensgate Sch.; Central Sch. of Speech and Drama. Nat. Theatre of GB, 1963–66 (Tulip Tree, Mother Courage, Andorra, Hay Fever, etc); Black Comedy, Broadway 1967; The Two of Us, Slag, Zoo Zoo Widdershins Zoo, Born Yesterday, London 1968–71; A Better Place, Dublin 1972; My Fat Friend, Knock Knock, Mrs Warren's Profession, Broadway 1973–76; The Two of Us, California Suite, Hellzapoppin, US tours 1976–77; Saint Joan, Chicago and NY 1977; Twelfth Night, Amer. Shakespeare Festival, Conn, 1978; Les dames du jeudi, LA, 1981; Sister Mary Ignatius Explains It All For You, LA, 1983; The King and I, N American Tour, 1983; Three Sisters, Queen's, 1990. *Films include:* Tom Jones, Girl with Green Eyes, Georgy Girl (NY Film Critics, Golden Globe and IFIDA awards, Academy nomination Best Actress), Deadly Affair, Smashing Time, Virgin Soldiers, Last of the Mobile Hotshots, Every Little Crook and Nanny, National Health, Happy Hooker, Everything You Always Wanted to Know about Sex, The Big Bus, Sunday Lovers. *Television includes:* USA: Co-host of nationally televised talk-show, Not For Women Only, appearances in documentaries, plays, The Muppets, Centennial, Beggarman Thief, The Seduction of Miss Leona, Rehearsal for Murder, and series: Housecalls (CBS); Teachers Only (NBC); BBC: A Woman Alone, 1988; Death of a Son, 1989. *Recreations:* cooking, gardening, horse riding. *Address:* PO Box 1207, Topanga, Calif 90290, USA. *T:* (213) 455–1334.

REDGRAVE, Rachel, (Lady Redgrave); *see* Kempson, R.

REDGRAVE, Maj.-Gen. Sir Roy Michael Frederick, KBE 1979; MC 1945; FRGS; *b* 16 Sept. 1925; *s* of late Robin Roy Redgrave and Michelene Jean Capsa; *m* 1953, Caroline Margaret Valerie, *d* of Major Arthur Wellesley; two *s*. *Educ:* Sherborne Sch. Served War of 1939–45: enlisted Trooper, Royal Horse Guards, 1943; Lieut, 1st Household Cavalry Regt, NW Europe, 1944–45. GSO III Intell., HQ Rhine Army, 1950; Canadian Army Staff Coll., 1955; GSO II Ops HQ, London Dist, 1956; Recce, Sqn Ldr, Cyprus, 1959 (despatches); Mil. Assistant to Dep. SACEUR, Paris, 1960–62; JSSC 1962; Comd Household Cavalry Regt (Mounted), 1963–64; Comd Royal Horse Guards (The Blues), 1965–67; AAG PS12, MoD, 1967–68; Chief of Staff, HQ 2nd Div., 1968–70; Comdr, Royal Armoured Corps, 3rd Div., 1970–72; Nat. Defence Coll., Canada, 1973; Comdt Royal Armoured Corps Centre, 1974–75; British Comdt, Berlin, 1975–78; Comdr, British Forces, Hong Kong, and Maj.-Gen. Brigade of Gurkhas, 1978–80. Hon. Col 31st (RR) Signal Regt (V), 1983–88. Dir Gen., Winston Churchill Meml Trust, 1980–82. Member: Council, Charing Cross and Westminster Med. Sch., 1981–; Hammersmith SHA, 1981–85; Council, Victoria League for Commonwealth Friendship; Britain Nepal Soc., 1982–. Chairman: Hammersmith and Fulham HA, 1981–85; Lambrook Appeal, 1984–85; Charing Cross and West London Hosps, 1984– (Special Trustee, 1981–87); Trustee: Westminster and Roehampton Hosps, 1988–; Governor General's Horse Guards, Canada, 1987–; Governor, Commonwealth Trust, 1989–. *Recreations:* walking, archaeology, philately. *Address:* c/o Lloyds Bank, Wareham, Dorset BH20 4LX. *Club:* Cavalry and Guards.

REDGRAVE, Vanessa, CBE 1967; Actress since 1957; *b* 30 Jan. 1937; *d* of late Sir Michael Redgrave, CBE, and of Rachel Kempson, *qv*; *m* 1962, Tony Richardson, *qv* (marr. diss., 1967); two *d*. *Educ:* Queensgate School; Central School of Speech and Drama. Frinton Summer Repertory, 1957; Touch of the Sun, Saville, 1958; Midsummer Night's Dream, Stratford, 1959; Look on Tempests, 1960; The Tiger and the Horse, 1960; Lady from the Sea, 1960; Royal Shakespeare Theatre Company: As You Like It, 1961, Taming of the Shrew, 1961, Cymbeline, 1962; The Seagull, 1964; The Prime of Miss Jean Brodie, Wyndham's, 1966; Daniel Deronda, 1969; Cato Street, 1971; The Threepenny Opera, Prince of Wales, 1972; Twelfth Night, Shaw Theatre, 1972; Antony and Cleopatra, Bankside Globe, 1973; Design for Living, Phoenix, 1973; Macbeth, LA, 1974; Lady from the Sea, NY, 1976, Roundhouse, 1979; The Aspern Papers, Haymarket, 1984; The Seagull, Queen's, 1985; Chekhov's Women, Lyric, 1985; The Taming of the Shrew and Antony and Cleopatra, Haymarket, 1986; Ghosts, Young Vic, transf. Wyndham's, 1986; Touch of the Poet, Young Vic, transf. Comedy, 1988; Orpheus Descending, Haymarket, 1988, NY, 1989; A Madhouse in Goa, Lyric, Hammersmith, 1989; Three Sisters, Queen's, 1990; When She Danced, Globe, 1991. *Films:* Morgan—A Suitable Case for Treatment, 1966 (Cannes Fest. Award, Best Actress 1966); The Sailor from Gibraltar, 1967; Blow-Up, 1967; Camelot, 1967; Red White and Zero, 1967; Charge of the Light Brigade, 1968; Isadora, 1968; A Quiet Place in the Country, 1968; The Seagull, 1969; Drop-Out, 1970; La Vacanza, 1970; The Trojan Women, 1971; The Devils, 1971; Mary, Queen of Scots, 1972; Murder on the Orient Express, 1974; Out of Season, 1975; Seven Per Cent Solution, 1975; Julia, 1976 (Academy Award, 1977; Golden Globe Award); Agatha, 1978; Yanks, 1978; Bear Island, 1978; Playing for Time, 1980; My Body, My Child, 1981; Wagner, 1983; The Bostonians, 1984; Wetherby, 1985; Steaming, 1985; Comrades, 1987; Prick Up Your Ears, 1987; Consuming Passions, 1988; A Man For All Seasons, 1988; Orpheus Descending, 1990; Young Catherine, 1990; Whatever Happened to Baby Jane, 1990; The Ballad of the Sad Café, 1991. Has appeared on TV. *Publication:* Pussies and Tigers (anthology of writings of school children), 1963. *Address:* c/o James Sharkey Associates, 15 Golden Square, W1R 3AG.

See also N. J. Richardson.

REDGROVE, Peter William, FRSL; poet, analytical psychologist; Resident Author, Falmouth School of Art, 1966–83; *b* 2 Jan. 1932; *s* of late Gordon James Redgrove and Nancy Lena Cestrilli-Bell; *m* Penelope Shuttle, *qv*; one *d*; (two *s* one *d* by former marr.). *Educ:* Taunton Sch.; Queens' Coll., Cambridge. Scientific journalist and copywriter, 1954–61; Visiting Poet, Buffalo Univ., NY, 1961–62; Gregory Fellow in Poetry, Leeds Univ., 1962–65; study with John Layard, 1968–69. O'Connor Prof. of Literature, Colgate Univ., NY, 1974–75; Leverhulme Emeritus Fellow, 1985–87; Writer at large, N Cornwall Arts, 1988. George Rylands' Verse-speaking Prize, 1954; Fulbright Award, 1961; Poetry Book Society Choices, 1961, 1966, 1979, 1981; Arts Council Awards, 1969, 1970, 1973, 1975, 1977, 1982; Guardian Fiction Prize, 1973; Prudence Farmer Poetry Award, 1977; Cholmondeley Award, 1985. FRSL 1982. *Publications: poetry:* The Collector, 1960; The Nature of Cold Weather, 1961; At the White Monument, 1963; The Force, 1966; Penguin Modern Poets 11, 1968; Work in Progress, 1969; Dr Faust's Sea-Spiral Spirit, 1972; Three Pieces for Voices, 1972; The Hermaphrodite Album (with Penelope Shuttle), 1973; Sons of My Skin: Selected Poems, 1975; From Every Chink of the Ark, 1977; Ten Poems, 1977; The Weddings at Nether Powers, 1979; The Apple-

Broadcast, 1981; The Working of Water, 1984; The Man Named East, 1985; The Mudlark Poems and Grand Buveur, 1986; In the Hall of the Saurians, 1987; The Moon Disposes, 1987; Poems 1954–1987, 1989; The First Earthquake, 1989; Dressed as for a Tarot Pack, 1990; *novels*: In the Country of the Skin, 1973; The Terrors of Dr Treviles (with Penelope Shuttle), 1974; The Glass Cottage, 1976; The Sleep of the Great Hypnotist, 1979; The God of Glass, 1979; The Beekeepers, 1980; The Facilitators, 1982; The One Who Set out to Study Fear, 1989; *plays*: Miss Carstairs Dressed for Blooding (play-book containing several dramatic pieces), 1976; (for radio): In the Country of the Skin, 1973; The Holy Sinner, 1975; Dance the Putrefact, 1975; The God of Glass, 1977 (Imperial Tobacco Award 1978); Martyr of the Hives, 1980 (Giles Cooper Award 1981); Florent and the Tuxedo Millions, 1982 (Prix Italia); The Sin-Doctor, 1983; Dracula in White, 1984; The Scientists of the Strange, 1984; Time for the Cat-Scene, 1985; Trelamia, 1986; Six Tales from Grimm, 1987; Six Views to a Haunt, 1991; (for television): The Sermon, 1963; Jack Be Nimble, 1980; *non-fiction*: The Wise Wound (with Penelope Shuttle), 1978, rev. edn 1986; The Black Goddess and the Sixth Sense, 1987. *Recreations*: work, photography, judo (1st Kyu Judo: Otani and Brit. Judo Assoc.), yoga. *Address*: c/o David Higham Associates, 5–8 Lower John Street, Golden Square, W1R 4HA.

REDHEAD, Brian; Presenter, Today programme, BBC Radio, since 1975; *b* 28 Dec. 1929; *s* of Leonard Redhead and Janet Fairley; *m* 1954, Jean, (Jenni), Salmon; two *s* one *d* (and one *s* decd). *Educ*: Royal Grammar Sch., Newcastle upon Tyne; Downing Coll., Cambridge. Northern Editor, The Guardian, 1965–69; Editor, Manchester Evening News, 1969–75. BBC Radio, Presenter: A Word in Edgeways; Workforce; The Good Book, 1986; The Pillars of Islam, 1987; The Christian Centuries, 1988; The Wandering Scholar, 1989. Dir, World Wide Pictures, 1980. Former Pres., Council for Nat. Parks; President: Trinity–the Hospice in the Fylde; Cat Action Trust. *Publications*: (with F. Gumley) The Good Book, 1987; (with S. Gooddie) The Summers of Shotton, 1987; A Love of the Lakes, 1988; The National Parks of England and Wales, 1988; (with F. Gumley) The Christian Centuries, 1989. *Address*: 71 Thomas More House, Barbican, EC2Y 8AB. *T*: 071–638 5111. *Club*: Garrick.

REDHEAD, Prof. Michael Logan Gonne, FBA 1991; Professor and Head of Department of History and Philosophy of Science, Cambridge University, since 1987; Fellow of Wolfson College, Cambridge, since 1988; *b* 30 Dec. 1929; *s* of Robert Arthur Redhead and Christabel Lucy Gonne Browning; *m* 1964, Jennifer Anne Hill; three *s*. *Educ*: Westminster Sch.; University College London (BSc 1st Cl. Hons Physics 1950; PhD Mathematical Phys. 1970). FInstP 1982. Dir, Redhead Properties Ltd, 1962; Partner, Galveston Estates, 1970; Lectr, Sen. Lectr in Philosophy of Science, 1981–84, Prof., Philosophy of Physics, 1984–85, Chelsea Coll., Univ. of London; Prof. of Philosophy of Physics, King's College London, 1985–87. Tarner Lectr, Trinity Coll., Cambridge, 1991–. Pres., British Soc. for Philos. of Sci., 1989–91. Lakatos Award in Philosophy of Science, 1988. *Publications*: Incompleteness, Nonlocality and Realism, 1987; papers in learned jls. *Recreations*: tennis, poetry, music. *Address*: 1 Orchard Court, Orchard Street, Cambridge CB1 1PR. *T*: Cambridge (0223) 321226. *Clubs*: Hurlingham, Queen's.

REDMAN, Maj.-Gen. Denis Arthur Kay, CB 1963; OBE 1942; retired; Colonel Commandant, REME, 1963–68; Director, Electrical and Mechanical Engineering, War Office, 1960–63; *b* 8 April 1910; *s* of late Brig. A. S. Redman, CB; *m* 1943, Penelope, *d* of A. S. Kay; one *s* one *d*. *Educ*: Wellington Coll.; London Univ. BSc (Eng) 1st class Hons (London); FCGI, MIMechE, AMIEE. Commissioned in RAOC, 1934; served in Middle East, 1936–43; transferred to REME, 1942; Temp. Brig., 1944; DDME 1st Corps, 1951; Comdt REME Training Centre 1957–59. Graduate of Staff Coll., Joint Services Staff Coll. and Imperial Defence Coll. *Recreations*: normal. *Club*: Army and Navy.

REDMAN, Maurice; Chairman, Scottish Region, British Gas Corporation, 1974–82 (Deputy Chairman, 1970–74); *b* 30 Aug. 1922; *s* of Herbert Redman and Olive (*née* Dyson); *m* 1960, Dorothy (*née* Appleton); two *d*. *Educ*: Hulme Grammar Sch., Oldham; Manchester Univ. BSc(Tech), 1st cl. Hons. Joined staff of Co. Borough of Oldham Gas Dept, 1943; Asst, later Dep. Production Engr, North Western Gas Bd, 1951; Chief Develt Engr, NW Gas Bd, 1957; Chief Engr, Southern Gas Bd, 1966; Dir of Engrg, Southern Gas Bd, 1970. Mem., Internat. Gas Union Cttee on Manufactured Gases, 1961–82. *Publications*: papers to Instn of Gas Engrs, Inst. of Fuel, various overseas conferences, etc. *Recreations*: gardening, music, photography. *Address*: Avington, 3 Cramond Regis, Edinburgh EH4 6LW. *T*: 031–312 6178. *Club*: New (Edinburgh).

REDMAN, Sydney, CB 1961; *b* 12 Feb. 1914; *s* of John Barritt Redman and Annie Meech; *m* 1939, Barbara Mary Grey; one *s* two *d*. *Educ*: Manchester Gram. Sch.; Corpus Christi Coll., Oxford. Asst Principal, WO, 1936; Principal Private Sec. to Secretary of State for War, 1942–44; Asst Under-Sec. of State: War Office, 1957–63; Ministry of Defence, 1963–64; Dep. Under-Sec. of State, MoD, 1964–73. Dir-Gen., Timber Trade Fedn, 1973–82. *Address*: Littlehurst, Birch Avenue, Haywards Heath, West Sussex. *T*: Haywards Heath (0444) 413738.

REDMAYNE, Clive; aeronautical engineering consultant; *b* 27 July 1927; *s* of late Procter Hubert Redmayne and Emma (*née* Torkington) *m* 1952, Vera Muriel, *d* of late Wilfred Toplis and Elsie Maud Toplis; one *s* one *d*. *Educ*: Stockport Sch. BSc (Hons Maths) London External. CEng, MIMechE; FRAeS. Fairey Aviation Co.: apprentice, 1944–48; Stress Office, 1948–50; English Electric Co., Warton: Stress Office, 1950–51; A. V. Roe & Co., Chadderton: Stress Office, 1951–55; A. V. Roe & Co., Weapons Research Div., Woodford: Head of Structural Analysis, 1955–62; Structures Dept, RAE, 1962–67; Asst Director, Project Time and Cost Analysis, Min. of Technology, 1967–70; Sen. Officers' War Course, RNC, Greenwich, 1970; Asst Dir, MRCA, MoD(PE), 1970–74; Division Leader, Systems Engrg, NATO MRCA Management Agency (NAMMA), Munich, 1974–76; Chief Supt, A&AEE, Boscombe Down, 1976–78; Dir, Harrier Projects, MoD(PE), 1978–80; Director General, Future Projects, MoD(PE), 1980–81; Dir Gen. Aircraft 3, Procurement Exec., MoD, 1981–84. *Recreations*: reading, chess, ski-ing, squash, sailing, caravanning. *Address*: Bowstones, 5 Westbrook View, Stottingway Street, Upwey, Weymouth, Dorset DT3 5QA. *T*: Weymouth (0305) 814691.

REDMAYNE, Hon. Sir Nicholas (John), 2nd Bt *cr* 1964; Chairman and Managing Director, Kleinwort Benson Securities; Director: Kleinwort Benson Ltd, since 1987; Kleinwort Benson Group, since 1989; *b* 1 Feb. 1938; *s* of Baron Redmayne, DSO, PC (Life Peer) and Anne (*d* 1982), *d* of John Griffiths; *S* to baronetcy of father, 1983; *m* 1st, 1963, Ann Saunders (marr. diss. 1976; she *d* 1985); one *s* one *d*; 2nd, 1978, Christine Diane Wood Hewitt (*née* Fazakerley); two step *s*. *Educ*: Radley College; RMA Sandhurst. Grenadier Guards, 1957–62. Joined Grieveson, Grant, later Kleinwort Benson Securities, 1963. *Recreations*: shooting, skiing. *Heir*: *s* Giles Martin Redmayne, *b* 1 Dec. 1968. *Address*: Walcote Lodge, Walcote, Lutterworth, Leics LE17 4JR.

REDMOND, Sir James, Kt 1979; FEng, FIEE; Director of Engineering, BBC, 1968–78; *b* 8 Nov. 1918; *s* of Patrick and Marion Redmond; *m* 1942, Joan Morris; one *s* one *d*. *Educ*: Graeme High Sch., Falkirk. Radio Officer, Merchant Navy, 1935–37 and 1939–45; BBC Television, Alexandra Palace, 1937–39; BBC: Installation Engr, 1949; Supt Engr Television Recording, 1960; Sen. Supt Engr TV, 1963; Asst Dir of Engrg, 1967. Pres., Soc. of Electronic and Radio Technicians, 1970–75; Pres., IEE, 1978–79. Mem. Bd, Services Sound and Vision Corporation, 1983–. Member: Council, Brunel Univ., 1980–88; Council, Open Univ., 1981–. Hon. FIEE, 1989. Hon. DTech Brunel, 1991. *Recreation*: golf. *Address*: 43 Cholmeley Crescent, Highgate, N6. *T*: 081–340 1611. *Club*: Athenæum.

REDMOND, Martin; MP (Lab) Don Valley, since 1983; *b* 15 Aug. 1937. *Educ*: Woodlands RC Sch.; Sheffield Univ. Mem., Doncaster Borough Council, 1975–; Chm. of Labour Gp and Leader of Council, 1982–. Vice-Chm., Doncaster AHA. Mem., NUM. *Address*: House of Commons, SW1A 0AA.

REDMOND, Robert Spencer, TD 1953; Director and Chief Executive, National Federation of Clay Industries, 1976–84; *b* 10 Sept. 1919; *m* 1949, Marjorie Helen Heyes; one *s*. *Educ*: Liverpool Coll. Served War, Army, 1939–46: commissioned The Liverpool Scottish, 1938; transferred, RASC, 1941; Middle East, Junior Staff Sch., 1943; DAQMG, HQ Special Ops (Mediterranean), 1943–45; released, rank of Major, 1946. Conservative Agent, 1947–56 (Wigan, 1947–49, Knutsford, 1949–56). Managing Dir, Heyes & Co. Ltd, Wigan, 1956–66; Ashley Associates Ltd: Commercial Manager, 1966–69; Managing Dir, 1969–70; Dir, 1970–72. Dir, Manchester Chamber of Commerce, 1969–74. MP (C) Bolton West, 1970–Sept. 1974; Vice-Chm., Cons. Parly Employment Cttee, 1972–74 (Sec., 1971–72). Pres., Alderley Edge Royal British Legion, 1968–76; Chairman: Knutsford and Dist Royal British Legion, 1990–; (and Founder), NW Export Club, 1958–60. *Publication*: How to Recruit Good Managers, 1989. *Address*: 194 Grove Park, Knutsford, Cheshire WA16 8QE. *T*: Knutsford (0565) 632657. *Club*: Army and Navy.

REDPATH, John Thomas, CB 1969; MBE 1944; FRIBA; Deputy Chief Executive, Property Services Agency, Department of the Environment, 1972–75; architect in private practice, 1977–87; *b* 24 Jan. 1915; *m* 1st, 1939, Kate (*née* Francis) (*d* 1949); one *d*; 2nd, 1949, Claesina (*née* van der Vlerk); three *s* one *d*. *Educ*: Price's Sch.; Southern Coll. of Art. Served with RE, 1940–47. Asst Architect: Kent CC, 1936–38; Oxford City Coun., 1938–40; Princ. Asst Architect, Herts, CC, 1948–55; Dep. County Architect, Somerset CC, 1955–59; Chief Architect (Abroad), War Office, 1959–63; MPBW later DoE: Dir of Development, 1963–67; Dir Gen. of Research and Development, 1967–71; Dir Gen. of Develt, 1971–72; Man. Dir, Millbank Technical Services Educn Ltd, 1975–77. *Publications*: various articles in architectural jls. *Recreation*: golf. *Address*: Pines Edge, Sandy Lane, Cobham, Surrey. *Club*: Arts.

REDSHAW, Peter Robert Gransden; HM Diplomatic Service; Counsellor, Kuala Lumpur, since 1988; *b* 16 April 1942; *s* of Robert Henry Gransden Redshaw and Audrey Nita Redshaw (*née* Ward); *m* 1970, Margaret Shaun (*née* Mizon); one *s* two *d*. *Educ*: Boxgrove School; Charterhouse; Trinity College, Cambridge (MA). ACA. Price Waterhouse, 1964–67; FCO, 1968; Kampala, 1970–73; 1st Sec., 1971; FCO, 1973; Lagos, 1982–85; Counsellor, 1985; FCO, 1985–88. *Recreations*: books, sailing, models, travel. *Address*: c/o Foreign and Commonwealth Office, SW1A 2AH. *Clubs*: Bosham Sailing; Kampala, Royal Lake (Kuala Lumpur).

REDSHAW, Emeritus Prof. Seymour Cunningham, DSc (Wales), PhD (London), FICE, FIStructE, FRAeS; Beale Professor and Head of Civil Engineering Department, University of Birmingham, 1950–69; Dean of Faculty of Science, 1955–57; Member of Aeronautical Research Council, 1955; a Governor of Coll. of Aeronautics, 1951–69; *b* 20 March 1906; *s* of Walter James Redshaw and Edith Marion Cunningham; *m* 1935, Mary Elizabeth Jarrold; three *s*. *Educ*: Blundell's School; University of Wales. Technical Assistant, Bristol Aeroplane Co. Ltd, 1927–31; Asst Designer General Aircraft Ltd, 1931–32; Member of Staff: Imperial College, London, 1933–35; Building Research Station, 1936–40; Boulton Paul Aircraft Ltd, 1940–50: Chief Engineer, 1945; Director, 1949. Mem. Adv. Cttee on Building Research, 1965–67; Mem. Council, Univ. of Aston, 1966–67; Chm., Acad. Adv. Cttee, and Mem. Council, Univ. of Bath, 1966. Hon. DSc: Bath, 1966; Cranfield, 1976. *Publications*: numerous papers in scientific and engineering journals. *Address*: 22 Newport Street, Brewood, Staffs ST19 9DT. *T*: Brewood (0902) 850274.

REDWOOD, John Alan, DPhil; MP (C) Wokingham, since 1987; Minister of State (Minister for Corporate Affairs), Department of Trade and Industry, since 1990; *b* 15 June 1951; *s* of William Charles Redwood and Amy Emma Redwood (*née* Champion); *m* 1974, Gail Felicity Chippington; one *s* one *d*. *Educ*: Kent Coll., Canterbury; Magdalen and St Antony's Colls, Oxford. MA, DPhil Oxon. Fellow, All Souls Coll., 1972–87. Investment Adviser, Robert Fleming & Co., 1973–77; Investment Manager and Dir, N. M. Rothschild & Sons, 1977–87; Norcros plc: Dir, 1985–89; Jt Dep. Chm., 1986–87; non-exec. Chm., 1987–89. Adviser, Treasury and Civil Service Select Cttee, 1981; Head of PM's Policy Unit, 1983–85. Councillor, Oxfordshire CC, 1973–77. Parly Under Sec. of State, DTI, 1989–90. Governor of various schools, 1974–83. *Publications*: Reason, Ridicule and Religion, 1976; Public Enterprise in Crisis, 1980; (with John Hatch) Value for Money Audits, 1981; (with John Hatch) Controlling Public Industries, 1982; Going for Broke, 1984; Equity for Everyman, 1986; Popular Capitalism, 1988. *Recreations*: water sports, village cricket. *Address*: House of Commons, SW1A 0AA. *T*: 071–219 4205.

REDWOOD, Sir Peter (Boverton), 3rd Bt *cr* 1911; Colonel, late King's Own Scottish Borderers, retired 1987; *b* 1 Dec. 1937; *o s* of Sir Thomas Boverton Redwood, 2nd Bt, TD, and Ruth Mary Redwood (*née* Creighton, then Blair); *S* father, 1974; *m* 1964, Gilian, *o d* of John Lee Waddington Wood, Limuru, Kenya; three *d*. *Educ*: Gordonstoun. National Service, 1956–58, 2nd Lieut, Seaforth Highlanders; regular commn, KOSB, 1959; served in UK (despatches 1972), BAOR, Netherlands, ME, Africa and Far East; Staff Coll., Camberley, 1970; Nat. Defence Coll., Latimer, 1978–79. Mem., Queen's Body Guard for Scotland (Royal Co. of Archers). Liveryman, Goldsmiths' Co. *Heir*: *half-b* Robert Boverton Redwood [*b* 24 June 1953; *m* 1978, Mary Elizabeth Wright; one *s* one *d*]. *Recreations*: shooting, silver and silversmithing. *Address*: c/o National Westminster Bank, 7 Dean Bradley Street, SW1P 3EP. *Club*: Army and Navy.

REECE, Sir Charles (Hugh), Kt 1988; Research and Technology Director, Imperial Chemical Industries, 1979–89; *b* 2 Jan. 1927; *s* of Charles Hugh Reece and Helen Youlle; *m* 1951, Betty Linford; two *d*. *Educ*: Pocklington Sch., E Riding; Huddersfield Coll.; Leeds Univ. (PhD, BSc Hons). FRSC. ICI: joined Dyestuffs Div., 1949; Head of Medicinal Process Develt Dept, Dyestuffs Div., 1959; Manager, Works R&D Dept, 1965; Jt Research Manager, Mond Div., 1967; Dir, R&D, Mond Div., 1969; Dep. Chm., Mond Div., 1972; Chm., Plant Protection Div., 1975. Dir, Finnish Chemicals, 1971–75; Chm., Teijin Agricultural Chemicals, 1975–78; non-executive Director: APV plc (formerly APV Holdings), 1984–; British Biotechnology Gp, 1989–. Chm., Univ. of Surrey Robens Inst. of Indust. and Envtl Health and Safety Cttee, 1985; Member: ACARD, 1983–87, ACOST, 1987–89; Adv. Cttee on Industry, Cttee of Vice-Chancellors and Principals, 1983–; Council, RSC, 1985–; SERC, 1985–89; ABRC, 1989–; UFC, 1989–; Royal Instn of GB, 1979– (Mem. Council, 1985–88); SCI; Parly and Sci. Cttee, 1979– (Vice-Chm., 1986–). Hon. DSc: St Andrews, 1986; Queen's, 1988; Bristol, 1989; DUniv Surrey, 1989.

FRSA 1988. *Publications:* reports and papers in learned jls. *Recreations:* sailing, gardening. *Address:* Heath Ridge, Graffham, Petworth, W Sussex GU28 0PT.

REECE, (Edward Vans) Paynter; His Honour Judge Paynter Reece; a Circuit Judge, since 1982; *b* 17 May 1936; *s* of Clifford Mansel Reece and Catherine Barbara Reece (*née* Hathorn); *m* 1967, Rosamund Mary Reece (*née* Roberts); three *s* one *d*. *Educ:* Blundell's Sch.; Magdalene Coll., Cambridge (MA). Called to the Bar, Inner Temple, 1960; a Recorder of the Crown Court, 1980–82. *Recreation:* fishing.

REECE, Sir (James) Gordon, Kt 1986; public affairs consultant, since 1985; *b* 1930; *m* (marr. diss.); six *c*. *Educ:* Ratcliffe Coll.; Downing Coll., Cambridge (Associate Fellow, 1986). Formerly: reporter, Liverpool Daily Post and Echo, then Sunday Express; television producer, ITV, 1960–70; Jt Man. Dir, RM EMI Ltd, 1970–74; Advr to Rt Hon. Margaret Thatcher, 1975–79; Dir of Publicity, Cons. Central Office, 1978–80; a Vice-Pres., Occidental Petroleum Corp., 1980–85. *Recreations:* racing, bridge, books. *Address:* c/o Wells Fargo Bank, 10850 Wilshire Boulevard, Los Angeles, Calif 90025, USA. *Clubs:* Portland, Garrick, Buck's; California (Los Angeles); Beach (Santa Monica).

REECE, Paynter; *see* Reece, E. V. P.

REED, Adrian Harbottle, CMG 1981; HM Diplomatic Service, retired; Consul-General, Munich, 1973–80; *b* 5 Jan. 1921; *s* of Harbottle Reed, MBE, FRIBA, and Winifred Reed (*née* Rowland); *m* 1st, 1947, Doris Davidson Duthie (marr. diss. 1975); one *s* one *d*; 2nd, 1975, Maria-Louise, *d* of Dr and Mrs A. J. Boekelman, Zeist, Netherlands. *Educ:* Hele's Sch., Exeter; Emmanuel Coll., Cambridge. Royal Artillery, 1941–47. India Office, 1947; Commonwealth Relations Office, 1947; served in UK High Commission: Pakistan, 1948–50; Fedn of Rhodesia and Nyasaland, 1953–56; British Embassy, Dublin, 1960–62; Commonwealth Office, 1962–68; Counsellor (Commercial), and Consul-Gen., Helsinki, 1968–70; Economic Counsellor, Pretoria, 1971–73. Chm., Devon and Exeter Instn, 1989–. Bavarian Order of Merit, 1980. *Recreations:* maritime history, the English countryside. *Address:* Old Bridge House, Uffculme, Cullompton, Devon EX15 3AX. *T:* Craddock (0884) 840595.

REED, Alec Edward; Founder, Chairman and Chief Executive, Reed Executive; *b* 16 Feb. 1934; *s* of Leonard Reed and Anne Underwood; *m* 1961, Adrianne Mary Eyre; two *s* one *d*. *Educ:* Grammar School. FCMA, FCIS, FECI. Divl Financial Accountant, Gillette Industries, 1956–60; founded: Reed Executive, 1960; Medicare Ltd; Inter-Company Comparison Ltd (now ICC); Reed College of Accountancy. President: Inst. of Employment Consultants, 1974–78; Internat. Confedn of Private Employment Agency Assocs, 1978–81; Company Dr, Hon. Chm. and Chief Exec., Andrews & Partners, 1985–89 (charity-owned); Council, CIMA, 1991–. Member: Overseas Cttee, Help the Aged, 1985–; Bd of Trustees, Womankind Worldwide, 1988– (founder); Bd of Trustees, Ethiopiaid, 1989– (founder); Oxfam Fundraising Cttee, 1989–. Mem. Council, RHC, 1979–85 (Chm., Finance and Investment Cttees, 1982–85). Fellow, RHBNC, 1988. *Publication:* Returning to Work, 1989. *Recreations:* family, theatre, cinema, tennis, riding, animals. *Address:* Reed Executive, 114 Peascod Street, Windsor, Berks SL4 1AY. *Club:* Royal Over-Seas League.

REED, Air Cdre April Anne, RRC 1981; Director of RAF Nursing Services, 1984–85, retired; *b* 25 Jan. 1930; *d* of Captain Basil Duck Reed, RN, and Nancy Mignon Ethel Reed. *Educ:* Channing Sch., Highgate. SRN, SCM. SRN training, Middlesex Hosp., 1948–52; midwifery training, Royal Maternity Hosp., Belfast, 1953; joined Royal Air Force, 1954; Dep. Matron, 1970; Sen. Matron, 1976; Principal Matron, 1981; Matron in Chief (Director), 1984. *Recreations:* sailing, ornithology, antiques, gardening, interest in oriental carpets. *Address:* 3 Edieham Cottages, Angle Lane, Shepreth, Royston, Herts SG8 6QJ. *T:* Royston (0763) 261329. *Club:* Royal Air Force.

REED, Barry St George Austin, CBE 1988; MC 1951; DL; Chairman, Austin Reed Group PLC, since 1973; Director, UK Advisory Board, since 1990, and Chairman, Eastern Regional Advisory Board, since 1987, National Westminster Bank PLC; *b* 5 May 1931; *s* of late Douglas Austin Reed and Mary Ellen (*née* Philpott); *m* 1956, Patricia (*née* Bristow), JP; one *s* one *d*. *Educ:* Rugby Sch. Commnd Middlesex Regt (DCO), 1950; served Korea, 1950–51; TA, 1951–60. Joined Austin Reed Group, 1953; Dir, 1958–; Man. Dir, 1966–85. National Westminster Bank: Dir, City and West End Regions, 1980–87; Dir, 1987–90. Pres., Menswear Assoc. of Britain, 1966–67; Chairman: Retail Alliance, 1967–70; British Knitting and Clothing Export Council, 1985–89; Member: Bd, Retail Trading-Standards Assoc., 1964–78; Consumer Protection Adv. Cttee, 1973–79; European Trade Cttee, 1975–84; Cttee, Fleming American Exempt Fund, 1979–; Council, Royal Warrant Holders Assoc., 1980– (Pres., 1990). Freeman, City of London, 1963; Liveryman: Glovers' Co., 1963– (Master 1980–81); Guild of Freemen, 1983. DL Greater London, 1977. FRSA; CBIM. *Publications:* papers in clothing, textile and banking jls. *Recreations:* travel, gardens, reading. *Address:* Crakehall House, Crakehall, Bedale, North Yorks DL8 1HS. *T:* Bedale (0677) 422743; 103 Regent Street, W1A 2AJ. *T:* 071–734 6789. *Clubs:* Naval and Military, Pilgrims, MCC.

See also L. D. Reed.

REED, David; Director of Corporate Communications, Whitbread plc, since 1990; *b* 24 April 1945; *s* of Wilfred Reed and Elsie Swindon; *m* 1973, Susan Garrett, MA Oxon, MScEcon. *Educ:* West Hartlepool Grammar Sch. Former journalist and public relations adviser to Investors in Industry, Rank Xerox, Ernst & Whinney, Hewlett-Packard. Dir and Hd of Corporate and Financial PR, Ogilvy and Mather. MP (Lab) Sedgefield, Co. Durham, 1970–Feb. 1974. *Publications:* many articles in national newspapers and other jls. *Recreations:* theatre, music, walking the dog. *Address:* St Luke's Cottage, Stonor, Oxon RG9 6HE.

REED, Edward John; Clerk to the Clothworkers' Company of the City of London, 1963–78; *b* 2 Sept. 1913; *o c* of late Edward Reed; *m* 1939, Rita Isabel Venus Cheston-Porter; one *s* one *d*. *Educ:* St Paul's School. Admitted Solicitor, 1938. Territorial Service with HAC; commnd 1940; served BEF and BAOR with 63 (WR) Medium Regt RA; Capt. 1942. Clerk to Governors of Mary Datchelor Girls' Sch., 1963–78. Vice Pres., Metropolitan Soc. for the Blind, 1979– (Chm., 1965–79); Chm., Indigent Blind Visiting Society, 1965–79; Vice-Pres., N London District, St John Ambulance, 1969–81. Chm., City Side, Joint Grand Gresham Cttee, 1984. Member: Court of Common Council, City of London, for Tower Ward, 1978–86; Lloyds, 1979–. Clothworkers' Co.: Liveryman, 1964; Sen. Warden, 1981; Mem., Ct of Assistants, 1982–. Governor: Christ's Hosp., 1981–86; City of London Freemen's Sch., 1982–86. Hon. MA Leeds, 1979. CStJ 1968. Chevalier, Order of Leopold with Palm, and Croix de Guerre with Palm, Belgium, 1944. *Recreations:* sailing, photography. *Address:* 54 Hillcrest Gardens, Hinchley Wood, Esher, Surrey KT10 0BX. *T:* 081–398 3904. *Club:* City Livery.

REED, Gavin Barras; Group Vice Chairman, Scottish & Newcastle plc, since 1991; Chairman, Scottish & Newcastle Breweries Ltd, since 1991; *b* 13 Nov. 1934; *s* of Lt-Col Edward Reed and Greta Milburn (*née* Pybus); *m* 1957, Muriel Joyce Rowlands; one *s* three *d*. *Educ:* Eton; Trinity Coll., Cambridge (BA). National Service, Fleet Air Arm Pilot, 1953–55. Joined Newcastle Breweries Ltd, 1958; took charge of Scottish & Newcastle Breweries Gp Hotels, 1963, Man. Dir, Thistle Hotels, 1965; Dir, Scottish & Newcastle Breweries Ltd, and Chm., Thistle Hotels, 1970; Man. Dir (Develt and Retail), 1974, Man. Dir, 1988–91, S&NB; Chairman: Newcastle Breweries, 1982; McEwan Younger, 1983; Matthew Brown Ltd (acquired by S&NB), 1987. Chm., N Region, CBI, 1987–88. *Recreations:* shooting, tennis. *Address:* Whitehill, Aberdour, Burntisland, Fife KY3 0RW. *Clubs:* Naval; New (Edinburgh).

REED, Jane Barbara; Director of Corporate Relations, News International plc, since 1989; 2nd *d* of late William and Gwendoline Reed, Letchworth, Herts. *Educ:* Royal Masonic Sch.; sundry further educational establishments. Worked on numerous magazines; returned to Woman's Own, 1965; Editor, 1970–79; Publisher, IPC Women's Monthly Group, 1979–81; Editor-in-Chief, Woman magazine, 1981–82; IPC Magazines: Asst Man. Dir, Specialist Educn and Leisure Gp, 1983; Man. Dir, Holborn Publishing Gp, 1983–85; Man. Editor (Features), Today, News (UK) Ltd, 1985–86; Man. Editor, Today, 1986–89. Chm., Publicity Cttee, Birthright, 1979–; Mem., Royal Soc.'s Cttee for the Public Understanding of Science, 1986–. FRSA 1991. *Publications:* Girl About Town, 1964; (jtly) Kitchen Sink—or Swim?, 1982. *Address:* 1 Virginia Street, E1 9XY.

REED, Dr John Langdale, FRCP, FRCPsych; Senior Principal Medical Officer, Mental Health, The Elderly and Disability Division, Department of Health (formerly of Health and Social Security), since 1986; *b* 16 Sept. 1931; *s* of John Thompson Reed and Elsie May Abbott; *m* 1959, Hilary Allin; one *s* one *d*. *Educ:* Oundle Sch.; Cambridge Univ.; Guy's Hosp. Med. Sch. FRCP 1974; FRCPsych 1974. Maudsley Hosp., 1960–67; Consultant Psychiatrist and Sen. Lectr in Psychol Medicine, St Bartholomew's Hosp., 1967–. QHP 1990–. *Publications:* (with G. Lomas) Psychiatric Services in the Community, 1984; papers on psychiatric services in the community and on drug abuse. *Recreations:* genealogy, opera, bridge, walking (preferably in the Lake District). *Address:* Department of Health, Wellington House, 133–135 Waterloo Road, SE1 8UG.

REED, Laurance Douglas; *b* 4 Dec. 1937; *s* of late Douglas Austin Reed and Mary Ellen Reed (*née* Philpott). *Educ:* Gresham's Sch., Holt; University Coll., Oxford (MA). Nat. Service, RN, 1956–58; worked and studied on Continent (Brussels, Bruges, Leyden, Luxembourg, Strasbourg, Paris, Rome, Bologna, Geneva), 1963–66; Public Sector Research Unit, 1967–69. MP (C) Bolton East, 1970–Feb. 1974; PPS to Chancellor of Duchy of Lancaster, 1973–74. Jt Sec., Parly and Scientific Cttee, 1971–74; Member: Soc. for Underwater Technology; Select Cttee on Science and Technology, 1971–74. *Publications:* Europe in a Shrinking World, 1967; An Ocean of Waste, 1972; Political Consequences of North Sea Oil, 1973; The Soay of Our Forefathers, 1986. *Recreations:* gardening, painting. *Address:* 1 Disraeli Park, Beaconsfield, Bucks HP9 2QE. *T:* Beaconsfield (0494) 673153. *Club:* Carlton.

See also B. St G. A. Reed.

REED, Leslie Edwin, PhD; CEng, MIMechE, FInstE; Chief Industrial Air Pollution Inspector, Health and Safety Executive, 1981–85; *b* 6 Feb. 1925; *s* of Edwin George and Maud Gladys Reed; *m* 1947, Ruby; two *s*. *Educ:* Sir George Monoux Grammar Sch., Walthamstow; University Coll. London (BScEng, MScEng, PhD). Engineering Officer, RNVR, 1945–47; Fuel Research Station, 1950–58; Warren Spring Laboratory, 1958–70; Central Unit on Environmental Pollution, DoE, 1970–79; Head, Air and Noise Div., DoE, 1979–81. *Address:* 20 Deards Wood, Knebworth, Herts SG3 6PG. *T:* Stevenage (0438) 813272.

REED, Sir Nigel (Vernon), Kt 1970; CBE 1967 (MBE (mil.) 1945); TD 1950; Chief Justice of the Northern States of Nigeria, 1968–75; *b* 31 Oct. 1913; *s* of Vernon Herbert Reed, formerly MP and MLC New Zealand, and of Eila Mabel Reed; *m* 1945, Ellen Elizabeth Langstaff; one *s* two *d*. *Educ:* Wanganui Collegiate School, NZ; Victoria University College, NZ; Jesus College, Cambridge. LLB (NZ) and LLB (Cantab). Called to the Bar, Lincoln's Inn, 1939. Military Service, 1939–45, Lt-Col 1944. Appointed to Colonial Legal Service, 1946; Magistrate, Nigeria, 1946; Chief Magistrate, Nigeria, 1951; Chief Registrar, High Court of the Northern Region of Nigeria, 1955; Judge, High Court of the Northern Region of Nigeria, 1956; Sen. Puisne Judge, High Court of Northern Nigeria, 1964. Comr for Law Revision in States of N Nigeria, 1988–. *Address:* Old Farm Cottage, Corton, Warminster, Wilts BA12 0SZ.

REED, Oliver; *see* Reed, R. O.

REED, (Robert) Oliver; actor; *b* 13 Feb. 1938; *s* of Peter and Marcia Reed; one *s* one *d*; *m* 1985, Josephine Burge. *Educ:* Ewel Castle. Films include: Oliver, 1967; Women In Love, 1969; The Devils, 1971; Three Musketeers, 1974; Tommy, 1975; The Prince and the Pauper, 1977; Lion of the Desert, Condorman, 1981; Venom, The Sting II, 1982; Second Chance, 1983; Captive, Castaway, 1986; The Adventures of Baron Munchausen, 1989; The Return of the Musketeers, 1989; Treasure Island, 1990. *Publication:* Reed All About Me, 1979. *Recreations:* rugby, racing. *Address:* c/o Maddens, 500 Reigate Road, Tadworth, Surrey KT20 5PF. *T:* Tadworth (0737) 360460.

REED, Stanley William; Director, British Film Institute, 1964–72, Consultant on Regional Development, 1972–76; *b* 21 Jan. 1911; *s* of Sidney James Reed and Ellen Maria Patient; *m* 1937, Alicia Mary Chapman; three *d*. *Educ:* Stratford Grammar Sch.; Coll. of St Mark and St John, Chelsea. Teacher in E London schools, 1931–39. In charge of school evacuation parties, 1939–45. Teacher and Visual Aids Officer, West Ham Education Cttee, 1939–50. British Film Institute: Educn Officer, 1950–56; Sec., 1956–64. *Publications:* The Cinema, 1952; How Films are Made, 1955; A Guide to Good Viewing, 1961. Neighbourhood 15 (film, also Dir). *Recreations:* opera and exploring London's suburbs. *Address:* 54 Felstead Road, Wanstead, E11. *T:* 081–989 6021.

REED, Prof. Terence James, FBA 1987; Taylor Professor of the German Language and Literature, and Fellow, Queen's College, Oxford, since 1989; *b* 16 April 1937; *s* of William Reed and Ellen (*née* Silcox); *m* 1960, Ann Macpherson; one *s* one *d*. *Educ:* Shooters' Hill Grammar Sch., Woolwich; Brasenose Coll., Oxford (MA). Sen. Scholar, Christ Church, Oxford, 1960–61; Jun. Res. Fellow, Brasenose Coll., Oxford, 1961–63; Fellow and Tutor in Mod. Langs, St John's Coll., Oxford, 1963–88. Co-founder and Editor, Oxford German Studies, 1965–; Editor, Oxford Magazine, 1985–. *Publications:* (ed) Death in Venice, 1972, German edn 1983; Thomas Mann, The Uses of Tradition, 1974; The Classical Centre: Goethe and Weimar 1775–1832, 1980, German edn 1982; Goethe, 1984; (trans.) Heinrich Heine: Deutschland, a not so sentimental journey, 1986; Schiller, 1991. *Recreation:* hill walking. *Address:* 14 Crick Road, Oxford. *T:* Oxford (0865) 58511.

REED, Most Rev. Thomas Thornton, CBE 1980; MA, DLitt, ThD; *b* Eastwood, South Australia, 9 Sept. 1902; *s* of Alfred Ernest Reed, Avoca, Vic; *m* 1932, Audrey Airlie, *d* of Major Harry Lort Spencer Balfour-Ogilvy, MBE, DCM, Tannadice, Renmark, South Australia; two *d* (and one *d* decd). *Educ:* Collegiate Sch. of St Peter, Adelaide; Trinity College, University of Melbourne (Hon. Schol., BA, MA); St Barnabas' Theol. Coll., Adelaide. ThL, ATC, 1st cl. hons. Fred Johns Schol. for Biography, Univ. of Adelaide, 1950. Deacon, 1926; Priest, 1927; Curate, St Augustine's, Unley, 1926–28; Priest in Charge, Berri Mission, 1928–29; Resident Tutor, St Mark's Coll., Univ. of Adelaide, and

Area Padre, Toc H, 1929–31; Asst Chaplain, Melbourne Grammar Sch., 1932–36; Rector, St Michael's, Henley Beach, 1936–44; Rector, St Theodore's, Rose Park, 1944–54; Chaplain, Australian Mil. Forces, 1939–57; Chaplain, AIF with HQ, New Guinea Force, 1944–45; Asst Tutor, St Barnabas' Coll., 1940–46; Senior Chaplain, RAAChD, HQ, C Command, South Australia, 1953–56; Editor, Adelaide Church Guardian, 1940–44; Rural Dean, Western Suburbs, 1944; Priest Comr, Adelaide Dio. Centenary, 1947; Canon of Adelaide, 1947–49; Archdeacon of Adelaide, 1949–53; Dean of Adelaide, 1953–57; Bishop of Adelaide, 1957–73; Archbishop of Adelaide, and Metropolitan of S Australia, 1973–75. Pres., Toc H, S Aust., 1960; Pres., St Mark's Coll., Univ. of Adelaide, 1961–74, Hon. Fellow, 1973. Hon. ThD, Australian Coll. of Theology, 1955; DLitt, Univ. of Adelaide, 1954. Chaplain and Sub Prelate of Venerable Order of St John of Jerusalem, 1965. *Publications:* Henry Kendall: A Critical Appreciation, 1960; Sonnets and Songs, 1962; (ed) The Poetical Works of Henry Kendall, 1966; A History of the Cathedral Church of St Peter, Adelaide, 1969; Historic Churches of Australia, 1978. *Recreations:* golf, research on Australian literature, heraldry, and genealogy. *Address:* 44 Jeffcott Street, North Adelaide, SA 5006, Australia. *T:* 2674841; PO Box 130, North Adelaide, SA 5006, Australia. *Clubs:* Adelaide, Naval, Military and Air Force, Royal Adelaide Golf (Adelaide).

REED-PURVIS, Air Vice-Marshal Henry, CB 1982; OBE 1972; Sales Director, British Aerospace Dynamics Group, 1983–89; *b* 1 July 1928; *s* of late Henry Reed and of Nancy Reed-Purvis; *m* 1951, Isabel Price; three *d.* *Educ:* King James I School, Durham; Durham Univ. BSc Hons 1950. Entered RAF, 1950; various Op. Sqdns, 1951–58; Instr, Jt Nuclear Biological and Chemical Sch., 1958–60; RMCS Shrivenham (Nuclear Sci. and Tech.), 1961; MoD Staff, 1962–64; OC No 63 Sqdn, RAF Regt, Malaya, 1964–66; Exchange Duties, USAF, 1966–69; USAF War Coll., 1969–70; OC No 5 Wing RAF Regt, 1970–72; Gp Capt. Regt, HQ Strike Comd, 1972–74, HQ RAF Germany, 1974–76; ADC to the Queen, 1974–76; Dir, RAF Regt, 1976–79; Comdt Gen. RAF Regt and Dir Gen. of Security (RAF) 1979–83. Mem. Exec. Cttee, Forces Help Soc. and Lord Roberts Workshops, 1986–; Vice Pres., Council for Cadet Rifle Shooting, 1985–. *Recreations:* golf, bridge and music. *Address:* Cobb House, Bampton, Oxon OX18 2LW. *T:* Bampton Castle (0993) 851032. *Club:* Royal Air Force.

REEDER, John; QC 1989; a Recorder, since 1991; *b* 18 Jan. 1949; *s* of Frederick and Barbara Reeder; *m* 1971, Barbara Kotlarz. *Educ:* Catholic Coll., Preston; University Coll. London (LLM); PhD Birmingham 1976. Called to the Bar, Gray's Inn, 1971, NSW 1986. Lectr in Law, Univ. of Birmingham, 1971–76; commenced practice, 1976; Junior Counsel to the Treasury (Admiralty), 1981–89. Lawyer, PNG, 1984. *Recreations:* sailing, travel. *Address:* 5 Perrymead Street, SW6 3SW. *T:* 071–736 4667. *Club:* Royal Corinthian Yacht.

REEDY, Norris John, (Jack); Senior National and Regional Officer, Independent Television Commission (formerly Independent Broadcasting Authority), since 1988 (Regional Officer, Midlands, 1983–88); editorial consultant; *b* 1934; *s* of John Reedy; *m* 1964, Sheila Campbell McGregor; one *d.* *Educ:* Chorlton High Sch., Manchester; Univ. of Sheffield. Sheffield Telegraph, 1956; Sunday Times, 1961; Lancashire Evening Telegraph, 1962; Guardian, 1964; Birmingham Post, 1964–82 (Editor, 1974–82). Former Chm. and Nat. Vice-Pres., W Midlands Region, Guild of British Newspaper Editors; Secretary: Birmingham Press Club Ltd; Midlands Centre, Royal Television Soc.; Council Mem., Rotary Club of Birmingham. Chm., Recruitment and Publicity, TA & VRA. *Recreations:* astronomy, natural history, painting, photography. *Address:* The Old Manor, Rowington, near Warwick. *T:* Lapworth (05643) 3129.

REEKIE, Henry Enfield; Headmaster of Felsted School, 1951–68; *b* Hayfield, Derbyshire, 17 Oct. 1907; *s* of John Albert Reekie and Edith Dowson; *m* 1936, Pauline Rosalind, *d* of Eric W. Seeman; one *s* three *d.* *Educ:* Oundle; Clare College, Cambridge. Asst Master, Felsted School, 1929, Housemaster, 1933, Senior Science Master, 1945; Headmaster, St Bees School, 1946. *Recreations:* ski-ing, gardening, travel. *Address:* Tarn House, Mark Cross, Crowborough, East Sussex TN6 3NT. *T:* Mayfield (0435) 873100. *Club:* East India, Devonshire, Sports and Public Schools.

REES, family name of **Baron Rees.**

REES, Baron *cr* 1987 (Life Peer), of Goytre in the County of Gwent; **Peter Wynford Innes Rees;** PC 1983; QC 1969; Deputy Chairman, Leopold Joseph Holdings Plc, since 1985; Chairman, LASMO (formerly London and Scottish Marine Oil) plc, since 1988; director of companies; *b* 9 Dec. 1926; *s* of late Maj.-Gen. T. W. Rees, Indian Army, Goytre Hall, Abergavenny; *m* 1969, Mrs Anthea Wendell, *d* of late Major H. J. M. Hyslop, Argyll and Sutherland Highlanders. *Educ:* Stowe; Christ Church, Oxford. Served Scots Guards, 1945–48. Called to the Bar, 1953, Bencher, Inner Temple, 1976; Oxford Circuit. Contested (C): Abertillery, 1964 and 1965; Liverpool, West Derby, 1966. MP (C): Dover, 1970–74 and 1983–87; Dover and Deal, 1974–83; PPS to Solicitor General, 1972; Minister of State, HM Treasury, 1979–81; Minister for Trade, 1981–83; Chief Sec. to HM Treasury, 1983–85. Director: James Finlay, 1986–; Fleming Mercantile Investment Trust, 1987–; General Cable, 1990–; Chm., Economic Forestry Group, 1989–. Chm., Duty Free Confedn, 1987–. Member: Council and Court of Governors, Museum of Wales, 1987–; Museums and Galleries Commn, 1988–. *Address:* 39 Headfort Place, SW1; Goytre Hall, Abergavenny, Gwent. *Clubs:* Boodle's, Beefsteak, White's.

REES, Anthony John David; Head Master, Blundell's School, Tiverton, Devon, since 1980; *b* 20 July 1943; *s* of Richard Frederick and Betty Rees; *m* 1967, Carol Stubbens; one *s* one *d* (and one *d* decd). *Educ:* Newcastle Royal Grammar Sch.; Clare Coll., Cambridge (Exhibr; BA 2nd Cl. Hons Geog.); PGCE 1966. Head of Economics, Harrow Sch., 1966–80. Established Notting Dale Urban Study Centre, 1972; Vis. Tutor, London Inst. of Education, 1973–. Member Executive Committee: Queen's Silver Jubilee Appeal, 1976–82; and Admin. Council, Royal Jubilee Trusts, 1978–82; Chairman: Prince's Trust for Devon, 1981–83; Youth Clubs UK, 1987–89; Founder Dir, Mid Devon Enterprise Agency, 1984–; Member: CoSIRA Cttee for Devon, 1981–83; Council, Drake Fellowship, 1981–; Cttee, HMC, 1986–; Bd, Youth Business Initiatives, 1984–; Prince of Wales Community Venture, 1985–; Bd, Devon and Cornwall Prince's Youth Business Trust. *Publications:* articles on economics and community service in many jls incl. Economics, Youth in Society, etc. *Recreations:* hill walking, family and friends. *Address:* Blundell's School, Tiverton, Devon. *T:* Tiverton (0884) 252543.

REES, Arthur Morgan, CBE 1974 (OBE 1963); QPM 1970; DL; Chairman, St John's Staffordshire, since 1974; *b* 20 Nov. 1912; *s* of Thomas and Jane Rees, The Limes, Llangadog; *m* 1943, Dorothy Webb (*d* 1988); one *d.* *Educ:* Llandovery Coll.; St Catharine's Coll., Cambridge. BA 1935, MA 1939. Metropolitan Police, 1935–41; RAF (Pilot), 1941–46 (Subst. Sqdn Ldr; Actg Wing Comdr); Metropolitan Police, 1946–57; Chief Constable: Denbighshire, 1957–64; Staffordshire, 1964–77. Consultant Director: for Wales, Britannia Building Soc., 1983–88; Inter-Globe Security Services Ltd, 1986–88. Chm. (Founder), EPIC, ExPolice in Industry and Commerce, 1978–. Life Mem., Midlands Sports Adv. Cttee, 1981; Chm., Queen's Silver Jubilee Appeal (Sport), 1976–; Mem., King George's Jubilee Trust Council, 1973–; Chm., The Prince's Trust Cttee (Sport and Leisure), 1981–88. Chm., British Karate Fedn, 1982–; President: Welsh Karate Fedn; Staffs Playing Fields Assoc., 1985–; Dep. Pres., Staffs Assoc. of Boys' Clubs, 1975–; Chm., Staffs St John Ambulance Brigade, 1970. Trustee and Board of Governors, Llandovery College; Mem. Court, Univ. of Keele, 1981–84. Founder Pres., Eccleshall Rugby Football Club, 1980–; Founder and Life Pres., EPIC (Ex Police in Industry and Commerce), 1988. DL Staffs, 1967. KStJ 1977 (CStJ 1969). *Recreations:* former Rugby International for Wales (14 caps), Cambridge Rugby Blue, 1933 and 1934; played Welsh Schs Hockey Internationals, 1930; Chm., Crawshays Welsh Rugby XV, 1960–. *Address:* National Westminster Bank, Eccleshall, near Stafford ST21 6BP. *Clubs:* Royal Air Force; Hawks (Cambridge) (Vice-Chm. 1985, Chm. 1986).

REES, Brian, MA Cantab; Director, Argentine-British Conference; Headmaster, Rugby School, 1981–84; *b* 20 Aug. 1929; *s* of late Frederick T. Rees; *m* 1st, 1959, Julia (*d* 1978), *d* of Sir Robert Birley, KCMG; two *s* three *d*; 2nd, 1987, Juliet Akehurst. *Educ:* Bede Grammar Sch., Sunderland; Trinity Coll., Cambridge (Scholar). 1st cl. Historical Tripos, Part I, 1951; Part II, 1952. Eton College: Asst Master, 1952–65; Housemaster, 1963–65; Headmaster: Merchant Taylors' Sch., 1965–73; Charterhouse, 1973–81. Pres., Conference for Independent Further Education, 1973–82; Chm., ISIS, 1982–84. Res. Fellow, City Univ., 1989–90. Patron, UC of Buckingham, 1973–. Liveryman, Merchant Taylors' Co., 1981. *Publications:* A Musical Peacemaker: biography of Sir Edward German, 1987; (ed) History and Idealism: essays, addresses and letters, by Sir Robert Birley, 1990. *Recreations:* music, painting. *Address:* 52 Spring Lane, Flore, Northants NN7 4LS. *T:* Weedon (0327) 41330.

REES, Prof. Brinley Roderick, MA Oxon; PhD, Hon. LLD Wales; Principal, Saint David's University College, Lampeter, 1975–80; *b* 27 Dec. 1919; *s* of John David Rees and Mary Ann (*née* Roderick); *m* 1951, Zena Muriel Stella Mayall; two *s.* *Educ:* Christ Coll., Brecon; Merton Coll., Oxford (Postmaster). 1st Cl., Class. Hons Mods and Hon. Mention, Craven and Ireland Schols, 1946. Welch Regt, 1940–45. Asst Classics Master, Christ Coll., Brecon, 1947; Cardiff High Sch., 1947–48; Asst Lectr in Classics, University Coll. of Wales Aberystwyth, 1948–49; Lectr 1949–56; Sen. Lectr in Greek, Univ. of Manchester, 1956–58; UC Cardiff: Prof. of Greek, 1958–70; Dean of Faculty of Arts, 1963–65; Dean of Students, 1967–68; Hon. Lectr, 1980–88; Prof. Emeritus, 1981; Vice-Pres., 1986–88; University of Birmingham: Prof. of Greek, 1970–75; Dean of Faculty of Arts, 1973–75; Hon. Life Mem. of Court, 1983. Welsh Supernumerary Fellow, Jesus Coll., Oxford, 1975–76; Leverhulme Emeritus Fellow, 1984–86. Hon. Secretary, Classical Association, 1963–69, Vice-Pres., 1969–78, 1979–, Pres., 1978–79. Hon. LLD Wales, 1981. *Publications:* The Merton Papyri, Vol. II (with H. I. Bell and J. W. B. Barns), 1959; The Use of Greek, 1961; Papyri from Hermopolis and other Byzantine Documents, 1964; (with M. E. Jervis) Lampas: a new approach to Greek, 1970; Classics: an outline for intending students, 1970; Aristotle's Theory and Milton's Practice, 1972; Strength in What Remains, 1980; Pelagius: a reluctant heretic, 1988; Letters of Pelagius and his Followers, 1991; articles and reviews in various classical and other jls. *Address:* 31 Stephenson Court, Wordsworth Avenue, Cardiff CF2 1AX. *T:* Cardiff (0222) 472058.

REES, Prof. Charles Wayne, DSc; FRS 1974; FRSC; Hofmann Professor of Organic Chemistry, Imperial College, London, since 1978; *b* 15 Oct. 1927; *s* of Percival Charles Rees and Daisy Alice Beck; *m* 1953, Patricia Mary Francis; three *s.* *Educ:* Farnham Grammar Sch.; University Coll., Southampton (BSc, PhD). Lectr in Organic Chem.: Birkbeck Coll., Univ. of London, 1955–57; King's Coll., Univ. of London, 1957–63, Reader, 1963–65; Prof. of Organic Chem., Univ. of Leicester, 1965–69; Prof. of Organic Chem., 1969–77, Heath Harrison Prof. of Organic Chem., 1977–78, Univ. of Liverpool. Visiting Prof., Univ. of Würzburg, 1968; Royal Society of Chemistry (formerly Chemical Society): Tilden Lectr, 1973–74; Award in Heterocyclic Chem., 1980; Pres., Perkin Div., 1981–83; Pedler Lectr, 1984–85; Pres. Elect, 1991–June 1992. Pres., Chemistry Sect., BAAS, 1984. *Publications:* Organic Reaction Mechanism (8 annual vols), 1965–72; Carbenes, Nitrenes, Arynes, 1969; (ed jtly) Comprehensive Heterocyclic Chemistry (8 vols), 1984; about 300 research papers and reviews, mostly in jls of Chemical Soc. *Recreations:* music, wine. *Address:* Department of Chemistry, Imperial College of Science, Technology and Medicine, South Kensington, SW7 2AY. *T:* 071–225 8334.

REES, Sir (Charles William) Stanley, Kt 1962; TD 1949; DL; Judge of High Court of Justice, Family Division (formerly Probate, Divorce and Admiralty Division), 1962–77; *b* 30 Nov. 1907; *s* of Dr David Charles Rees, MRCS, LRCP, and Myrtle May (*née* Dolley); *m* 1934, Jean Isabel Munro Wheildon (*d* 1985); one *s.* *Educ:* St Andrew's College, Grahamstown, S Africa; University College, Oxford. BA, BCL (Oxon). Called to the Bar, 1931; Bencher, Inner Temple, 1962. 2nd Lt 99th Regt AA RA (London Welsh), 1939; JAG's office in Home Commands, 1940–43; Lt-Col in charge JAG's Branch, HQ Palestine Command, 1944–45; released from military service as Hon. Lt-Col, 1945. QC 1957; Recorder of Croydon, 1961–62; Commissioner of Assize, Stafford, Dec. 1961; Dep. Chm., 1959–64, Chm., 1964–71, E Sussex QS. DL E Sussex (formerly Sussex), 1968. Chm., Statutory Cttee, Pharmaceutical Soc. of GB, 1980–81. Governor, Brighton College, 1954–83 (Pres., 1973–83; Vice Patron, 1983). *Recreation:* mountain walking. *Address:* Lark Rise, Lyoth Lane, Lindfield, Haywards Heath, W Sussex RH16 2QA. *Clubs:* United Oxford & Cambridge University, Sussex.

See also Harland Rees.

REES, Prof. David, FRS 1968; Emeritus Professor of Pure Mathematics, University of Exeter (Professor, 1958–83); *b* 29 May 1918; *s* of David and Florence Gertrude Rees; *m* 1952, Joan Sybil Cushen; four *d.* *Educ:* King Henry VIII Grammar School, Abergavenny; Sidney Sussex College, Cambridge. Manchester University: Assistant Lecturer, 1945–46, Lecturer, 1946–49; Cambridge University: Lecturer, 1949–58; Fellow of Downing College, Cambridge, 1950–58, Hon. Fellow, 1970–. Mem. Council, Royal Soc., 1979–81. *Publications:* papers on Algebraic topics in British and foreign mathematical journals. *Recreations:* reading and listening to music. *Address:* 6 Hillcrest Park, Exeter EX4 4SH. *T:* Exeter (0392) 59398.

REES, Dr David Allan, BSc, PhD, DSc; FRS 1981; FRSC, FIBiol; Secretary, Medical Research Council, since 1987; *b* 28 April 1936; *s* of James Allan Rees and Elsie Bolam; *m* 1959, Myfanwy Margaret Parry Owen; two *s* one *d.* *Educ:* Hawarden Grammar Sch., Clwyd; University Coll. of N Wales, Bangor, Gwynedd (BSc 1956; PhD 1959; Hon. Fellow, 1988). DSc Edinburgh, 1970. DSIR Res. Fellow, University Coll., Bangor, 1959, and Univ. of Edinburgh, 1960; Asst Lectr in Chem., 1961, Lectr, 1962–70, Univ. of Edinburgh; Section Manager, 1970–72, Principal Scientist, 1972–82, and Sci. Policy Exec., 1978–82, Unilever Res., Colworth Lab.; Chm., Science Policy Gp for Unilever Res., 1979–82. Associate Dir (pt-time), MRC Unit for Cell Biophysics, KCL, 1980–82; Dir, Nat. Inst. for Med. Res., Mill Hill, 1982–87. Vis. Professorial Fellow, University Coll., Cardiff, 1972–77. Philips Lecture, Royal Soc., 1984. Member: MRC, 1984–; Council, Royal Soc., 1985–87. FKC 1989. Hon. FRCP 1986. Hon. DSc Edinburgh, 1989. Colworth Medal, Biochemical Soc., 1970; Carbohydrate Award, Chemical Soc., 1970. *Publications:* various, on carbohydrate chem. and biochem. and cell biology. *Recreations:* river boats, reading, listening to music.

REES, Dr (Florence) Gwendolen, FRS 1971; FIBiol; a Professor of Zoology, University of Wales, at University College of Wales, Aberystwyth, 1971–73, now Emeritus; *b* 3 July 1906; *yr d* of late E. and E. A. Rees; unmarried. *Educ*: Girls' Grammar Sch., Aberdare; UCW Cardiff. BSc 1927; PhD 1930; DSc 1942. FIBiol 1971. UCW, Aberystwyth: Lectr in Zoology, 1930–46; Sen. Lectr, 1946–66; Reader, 1966–71. Vis. Scientist, Univ. of Ghana, 1961. Research grants from Royal Soc., SRC, Shell Grants Cttee, Nat. Research Council, USA. Hon. Member: Amer. Soc. of Parasitologists, 1975; British Soc. for Parasitology, 1976. Linnean Medal for services to zoology, Linnean Soc., 1990. *Publications*: numerous papers on parasitology (helminthology) in scientific jls. *Recreations*: riding, amateur dramatics, the arts. *Address*: Grey Mist, North Road, Aberystwyth, Dyfed. *T*: Aberystwyth (0970) 612389.

REES, Gwendolen; see Rees, F. G.

REES, Harland, MA, MCh, FRCS; Hon. Consultant Urological Surgeon, King's College Hospital; Hon. Consultant Surgeon and Urological Surgeon, Royal Free Hospital; *b* 21 Sept. 1909; *yr s* of Dr David Charles Rees, MRCS, LRCP, and Myrtle May (*née* Dolley); *m* 1950, Helen Marie Tarver; two *s* (one *d* decd). *Educ*: St Andrew's Coll., Grahamstown, S Africa; University Coll., Oxford; Charing Cross Hospital. Rhodes Scholar, Oxford University. Served RAMC, 1942–46; OC Surgical Div. 53, Indian General Hospital. Adviser in Surgery, Siam (Thailand). Examiner in Surgery, University of Cambridge, 1963–73; Councillor (C), S Beds DC, 1978– (Chm., 1986–87). *Publications*: articles and chapters in various books and journals, 1952–63. *Recreations*: walking, cultivation of trees; Rugby football, Oxford *v* Cambridge, 1932–33. *Address*: Kensworth Gorse, Kensworth, near Dunstable, Beds LU6 3RF. *T*: Whipsnade (0582) 872411. *Club*: Vincent's (Oxford).
  See also Hon. Sir C. W. S. Rees.

REES, Haydn; see Rees, T. M. H.

REES, Prof. Hubert, DFC 1945; PhD, DSc; FRS 1976; Professor of Agricultural Botany, University College of Wales, Aberystwyth, since 1968; *b* 2 Oct. 1923; *s* of Owen Rees and Tugela Rees, Llangennech, Carmarthenshire; *m* 1946, Mavis Hill; two *s* two *d*. *Educ*: Llandovery and Llanelli Grammar Schs; University Coll. of Wales, Aberystwyth (BSc). PhD, DSc Birmingham. Served RAF, 1942–46. Student, Aberystwyth, 1946–50; Lectr in Cytology, Univ. of Birmingham, 1950–58; Sen. Lectr in Agric. Botany, University Coll. of Wales, Aberystwyth, 1958, Reader 1966. *Publications*: Chromosome Genetics, 1977; B Chromosomes, 1982; articles on genetic control of chromosomes and on evolutionary changes in chromosome organisation. *Recreation*: fishing. *Address*: Irfon, Llanbadarn Road, Aberystwyth, Dyfed SY23 1EY. *T*: Aberystwyth (0970) 623668.

REES, Hugh; see Rees, J. E. H.

REES, Hugh Francis E.; see Ellis-Rees.

REES, Rt. Rev. Ivor; see Rees, Rt Rev. J. I.

REES, John Charles; QC 1991; *b* 22 May 1949; *s* of Ronald Leslie Rees and Martha Therese Rees; *m* 1970, Dianne Elizabeth Kirby; three *s* one *d*. *Educ*: St Illtyd's College, Cardiff; Jesus College, Cambridge (double first class Hons; BA (Law), LLB (Internat. Law), MA, LLM; repr. Univ. in boxing and Association Football; boxing Blue). Called to the Bar, Lincoln's Inn, 1972. Trustee and Governor, St John's College, Cardiff, 1987–. Representative Steward, and Chm., Welsh Area Council, BBB of C. *Recreations*: all sport, esp. boxing and Association Football; theatre. *Address*: 96 Pencisely Road, Llandaff, Cardiff; 30 Park Place, Cardiff CF1 3BA. *T*: Cardiff (0222) 564151. *Club*: Hawks (Cambridge).

REES, (John Edward) Hugh; Chartered Surveyor; *b* 8 Jan. 1928; *s* of David Emlyn Rees, Swansea; *m* 1961, Gillian Dian Milo-Jones (decd); two *s*. MP (C) Swansea, West Division, Oct. 1959–64; Assistant Government Whip, 1962–64. UK Rep., Econ. and Soc. Cttee, EEC, 1972–78. Dir, Abbey National plc (formerly Abbey National Building Soc.), 1976–; Chm., Abbey Housing Association Ltd., 1980–. Mem., Welsh Develt Agency, 1980–86. Trustee, Ffynone House Sch. Trust, 1973– (Chm. 1977–85). Governor, Nat. Mus. of Wales. FRICS, FRVA. *Address*: Sherwood, 35 Caswell Road, Newton, Mumbles, Swansea, W Glamorgan.

REES, Rt. Rev. (John) Ivor; see St Davids, Bishop of.

REES, John Samuel; editorial consultant; Editor, Western Mail, 1981–87; *b* 23 Oct. 1931; *s* of John Richard Rees and Mary Jane Rees; *m* 1957, Ruth Jewell; one *s* one *d*. *Educ*: Cyfarthfa Castle Grammar Sch., Merthyr Tydfil. Nat. Service, Welch Regt and RAEC, 1950–52. Reporter, 1948–50, Sports Editor, 1952–54, Merthyr Express; The Star, Sheffield: Reporter, 1954–56; Sub Editor, 1956–58; Dep. Chief Sub Editor, 1958–59; Dep. Sports Editor, 1959–61; Asst Editor, 1961–66; Dep. Editor, Evening Echo, Hemel Hempstead, 1966–69; Editor: Evening Mail, Slough and Hounslow, 1969–72; The Journal, Newcastle upon Tyne, 1972–76; Evening Post-Echo, Hemel Hempstead, 1976–79, Asst Man. Dir, Evening Post-Echo Ltd, 1979–81. *Recreations*: marquetry, watching cricket and rugby, walking, gardening. *Address*: Timbertops, St Andrew's Road, Dinas Powys, S Glam CF6 4HB. *T*: Cardiff (0222) 513254.

REES, Prof. Lesley Howard, FRCP; FRCPath; Professor of Chemical Endocrinology, since 1978, Dean since 1989, St Bartholomew's Hospital Medical College; *b* 17 Nov. 1942; *d* of Howard Leslie Davis and Charlotte Patricia Siegrid Young; *m* 1969, Gareth Mervyn Rees. *Educ*: Pates Girls' Grammar Sch., Cheltenham; Malvern Girls' Coll. MSc, MD London. Editor, Clinical Endocrinology, 1979–84; Subdean, St Bartholomew's Hosp. Med. Coll., 1983–88; Public Orator, London Univ., 1984–86. Chm., Soc. for Endocrinology, 1984–87; Sec.-Gen., Internat. Soc. of Endocrinology, 1984–. Mem., Press Complaints Commn, 1991–. *Recreations*: music, poetry, reading, ski-ing, administrative gardening. *Address*: 23 Church Row, Hampstead, NW3 6UP. *T*: 071–794 4936. *Club*: Mosimann's.

REES, Rt. Rev. Leslie Lloyd; Assistant Bishop, Diocese of Winchester, since 1987; *b* 14 April 1919; *s* of Rees Thomas and Elizabeth Rees; *m* 1944, Rosamond Smith (*d* 1989); two *s*. *Educ*: Pontardawe Grammar Sch.; Kelham Theological College. Asst Curate, St Saviour, Roath, 1942; Asst Chaplain, HM Prison, Cardiff, 1942; Chaplain, HM Prison, Durham, 1945; Dartmoor, 1948; Vicar of Princetown, 1948; Chaplain, HM Prison, Winchester, 1955; Chaplain General of Prisons, Home Office Prison Dept, 1962–80; Bishop Suffragan of Shrewsbury, 1980–86. Chaplain to the Queen, 1971–80. Hon. Canon of Canterbury, 1966–80, of Lichfield, 1980–. Freeman, City of London. ChStJ. *Recreation*: music. *Address*: Kingfisher Lodge, Arle Gardens, Alresford, Hants SO24 9BA.

REES, Linford; see Rees, W. L. L.

REES, Llewellyn; see Rees, (Walter) L.

REES, Prof. Martin John, FRS 1979; Plumian Professor of Astronomy and Experimental Philosophy, Cambridge University, since 1973; Director, Institute of Astronomy, Cambridge, 1977–82 and since 1987; Fellow of King's College, since 1973 (and 1969–72);

b 23 June 1942; *s* of Reginald J. and Joan Rees; *m* 1986, Dr Caroline Humphrey, *d* of late Prof. C. H. Waddington. *Educ*: Shrewsbury Sch.; Trinity Coll., Cambridge. MA, PhD (Cantab). Fellow, Jesus Coll., Cambridge, 1967–69; Research Associate, California Inst. of Technology, 1967–68 and 1971; Mem., Inst. for Advanced Study, Princeton, 1969–70; Visiting Prof., Harvard Univ., 1972 and 1986–88; Prof., Univ. of Sussex, 1972–73; Vis. Prof., Inst. for Advanced Studies, Princeton, 1982; Regents Fellow of Smithsonian Instn, Washington, 1984–88; Fairchild Vis. Scholar, CIT, 1992. Chm., Science Adv. Cttee, ESA, 1976–78; Mem. Council, Royal Soc., 1983–85. Lectures: H. P. Robertson Meml, US Nat. Acad. Sci, 1975; George Darwin, Royal Astron. Soc., 1976; Halley, Oxford, 1978; Milne, Oxford, 1980; Loeb, Harvard, 1980; Bakerian, Royal Soc., 1982; Danz, Univ. of Washington, 1984; Lauritsen, CIT, 1987. Member: Academia Europaea, 1989; Pontifical Acad. of Sci., 1990; For. Hon. Mem., Amer. Acad. of Arts and Sciences, 1975; Foreign Associate, Nat. Acad. of Sciences, USA, 1982. Hon. Fellow, Indian Acad. of Sci., 1990. Hon. DSc Sussex, 1990. Hopkins Prize, Cambridge Phil. Soc., 1982; Heinemann Prize, Amer. Inst. Physics, 1984; Bappu Award, Indian Nat. Science Acad., 1986; Gold Medal, RAS, 1987; Guthrie Medal and Prize, Inst. of Physics, 1989; Balzan Prize, Balzan Foundn, 1989; Schwarzschild Medal, Astron. ges., 1989; Robinson Prize for Cosmology, Univ. of Newcastle upon Tyne, 1990. *Publications*: mainly articles and reviews in scientific jls. *Address*: c/o King's College, Cambridge CB2 1ST. *T*: Cambridge (0223) 350411; (office) Cambridge (0223) 337548.

REES, Rt. Hon. Merlyn, PC 1974; MP (Lab) Morley and Leeds South, since 1983 (South Leeds, June 1963–83); *b* Cilfynydd, South Wales, 18 Dec. 1920; *s* of late L. D. and E. M. Rees; *m* 1949, Colleen Faith (*née* Cleveley); three *s*. *Educ*: Elementary Schools, S Wales and Wembley, Middx; Harrow Weald Grammar School; London School of Economics; London Univ. Institute of Education. Nottingham Univ. Air Sqdn; Served RAF, 1941–46; demobilised as Sqdn Ldr. Teacher in Economics and History, Harrow Weald Grammar School, 1949–60. Organised Festival of Labour, 1960–62. Lecturer in Economics, Luton Coll. of Technology, 1962–63; contested (Lab) Harrow East, Gen. Elections 1955 and 1959 and by-election, 1959; PPS to Chancellor of the Exchequer, 1964; Parly Under-Sec. of State, MoD (Army), 1965–66; MoD (RAF), 1966–68; Home Office, 1968–70; Mem., Shadow Cabinet, 1972–74; Opposition spokesman on NI affairs, 1972–74; Sec. of State for NI, 1974–76; Home Sec., 1976–79; Shadow Home Sec., 1979–80; Opposition spokesman on Energy, 1980–83. Member: Cttee to examine operation of Section 2 of Official Secrets Act, 1971; Falkland Is Inquiry Cttee, 1982. Chm., South Leeds Groundwork Trust, 1987– (Mem. Bd, Groundwork Foundn, 1990–). Hon. Fellow, Goldsmiths' Coll., London Univ., 1984. Hon. LLD Wales, 1987. *Publications*: The Public Sector in the Mixed Economy, 1973; Northern Ireland: a personal perspective, 1985. *Recreation*: reading. *Address*: House of Commons, SW1.

REES, Meuric; see Rees, R. E. M.

REES, Rev. Canon Michael; see Rees, Rev. Canon R. M.

REES, Owen, CB 1991; Under Secretary, Welsh Office, since 1977, and Head of Agriculture Department, since 1990; *b* 26 Dec. 1934; *s* of late John Trevor and Esther Rees, Trimsaran, Dyfed; *m* 1958, Elizabeth Gosby; one *s* two *d*. *Educ*: Llanelli Grammar Sch.; Univ. of Manchester. BA(Econ). Bank of London and South America, 1957; regional development work in Cardiff, Birmingham and London, BoT, 1959–69; Cabinet Office, 1969–71; Welsh Office, 1971–; Asst Sec. (European Div.), 1972; Sec. for Welsh Educn, 1977–78; Dir, Industry Dept, 1980–85; Head, Economic and Regl Policy Gp, 1985–90. *Address*: 4 Llandennis Green, Cyncoed, Cardiff CF2 6JX. *T*: Cardiff (0222) 759712.

REES, Peter Magnall; a Senior Clerk, House of Lords, 1981–84; *b* 17 March 1921; *s* of late Edward Saunders Rees and Gertrude Rees (*née* Magnall); *m* 1949, Moya Mildred Carroll. *Educ*: Manchester Grammar Sch.; Jesus Coll., Oxford. Served War, RA, 1941–46 (SE Asia, 1942–45). HM Overseas Service, Nigeria, 1948; Dep. Govt Statistician, Kenya, 1956; Dir of Economics and Statistics, Kenya, 1961; HM Treasury, 1964; Chief Statistician, 1966; Under-Sec., DTI later Dept of Industry, 1973–81. Consultant, OECD, 1981. *Publications*: articles in statistical jls. *Recreations*: choral singing, music, studying architecture. *Address*: The Old Orchard, Sandford Orcas, Sherborne, Dorset DT9 4RP. *T*: Corton Denham (096322) 244. *Club*: Commonwealth Trust.

REES, Peter Wynne, RIBA; FRTPI; City Planning Officer, Corporation of London, since 1987; *b* 26 Sept. 1948; *s* of Gwynne Rees, MM, CEng, MIMechE, FMES, and late Elizabeth Rodda Rees (*née* Hynam). *Educ*: Pontardawe Grammar Sch.; Whitchurch Grammar Sch., Cardiff; Bartlett Sch. of Architecture, UCL (BSc Hons); Welsh Sch. of Architecture, Univ. of Wales (BArch); Polytechnic of the South Bank (BTP). Architectural Asst, Historic Bldgs Div., GLC, 1971–72; Asst to Gordon Cullen, CBE, RDI, FSIA, 1973–75; Architect, Historic Areas Conservation, DoE, 1975–79; UK Rep., Council of Europe Wkg Parties studying New Uses for Historic Buildings and The Economics of Building Conservation, 1977–78; Asst Chief Planning Officer, London Bor. of Lambeth, 1979–85; Controller of Planning, Corp. of London, 1985–87. Trustee, Building Conservation Trust, 1985–. Founder Mem. and Dir, British Council for Offices, 1989. London Rep., European Working Party on Technological Impact on Future Urban Change, 1989–. FRSA 1988. *Publications*: City of London Local Plan, 1989; contribs to professional studies and jls. *Recreations*: swimming, playing the viola, music, tidying. *Address*: City Planning Officer, Guildhall, EC2P 2EJ. *T*: 071–260 1700. *Clubs*: Guildhall; Cottons.

REES, Philip; a Recorder of the Crown Court, since 1983; *b* 1 Dec. 1941; *s* of John Trevor Rees and Olwen Muriel Rees; *m* 1969, Catherine Good; one *s* one *d*. *Educ*: Monmouth Sch.; Bristol Univ. (LLB Hons). Called to the Bar, Middle Temple, 1965. *Recreations*: music, sport. *Address*: 34 Park Place, Cardiff CF1 3BA. *T*: Cardiff (0222) 382731. *Club*: Cardiff and Counties (Cardiff).

REES, Prof. Ray; Professor of Economics, University of Guelph, Ontario, since 1987; *b* 19 Sept. 1943; *s* of Gwyn Rees and Violet May (*née* Powell); *m* 1976, Denise Sylvia (*née* Stinson); two *s*. *Educ*: Dyffryn Grammar Sch., Port Talbot; London School of Economics and Political Science (MScEcon). Lectr 1966–76, Reader 1976–78, Queen Mary Coll., Univ. of London; Economic Advr, HM Treasury (on secondment), 1968–72; Prof. of Econs, UC, Cardiff, 1978–87. Member (part-time), Monopolies and Mergers Commn, 1985–87. *Publications*: A Dictionary of Economics, 1968, 3rd edn 1984; Public Enterprise Economics, 1975, 3rd edn 1992; Microeconomics, 1981, 2nd edn 1992; Economics: a mathematical introduction, 1991; The Theory of Principal and Agent, 1992; Introduction to Game Theory, 1992; articles in Economic Jl, Amer. Econ. Rev., Jl of Public Econs, Economica, and others. *Recreations*: playing the guitar, losing chess games, learning German. *Address*: 14 Dean Avenue, Guelph, Ontario N1G 1K5, Canada. *T*: (519) 7635078.

REES, (Richard Ellis) Meuric, CBE 1982; JP; FRAgS; Lord Lieutenant for Gwynedd, since 1990; Member: Countryside Commission, since 1981 (Chairman, Committee for Wales); Agriculture Training Board, since 1974 (Chairman, Committee for Wales); Vice

Chairman, Hill Farming Advisory Committee (Chairman, Committee for Wales); *b* Pantydwr, Radnorshire, 1924; *m*; three *d*. President: YFC in Wales, 1961; Merioneth Agricl Soc., 1972; Royal Welsh Agricl Show, 1978; former Chm., Welsh Council of NFU; Mem., CLA. Governor: Welsh Agricl Coll., Aberystwyth; Coleg Meirionnydd, Dolgellau. Mem., Tywyn UDC, 1967–73. Chm., N Wales Police Authority, 1982–84. JP Tywyn, 1957 (Chm. of Bench, 1974–); High Sheriff of Gwynedd, 1982–83; DL Gwynedd, 1988. FRAgS 1973. *Address:* Escuan Hall, Tywyn, Gwynedd.

REES, Dr Richard John William, CMG 1979; FRCP, FRCPath; Grant holder, Division of Communicable Diseases, Clinical Research Centre, Harrow; Head, Laboratory for Leprosy and Mycobacterial Research, and WHO Collaborating Centre for Reference and Research on *M. leprae*, National Institute for Medical Research, London, 1969–82; *b* 11 Aug. 1917; *s* of William and Gertrude Rees; *m* 1942, Kathleen Harris; three *d*. *Educ:* East Sheen County Sch., London; Guy's Hosp., London (BSc 1939; MB, BS 1942). MRCS, LRCP 1941, FRCP 1983; MRCPath 1963, FRCPath 1964. Served War, 1942–46: Captain, RAMC Army Blood Transfusion Service, N Africa and Italy campaigns. House Surg. and Phys., Southern Hosp., Kent, 1941–42; Asst Clin. Pathologist, Guy's Hosp., 1946–49; Mem. of Scientific Staff, NIMR, 1949–69. Sec., MRC Leprosy Cttee, 1959–88; Consultant, US Japanese Co-op. Scientific Prog. on Leprosy, 1969–73. Chairman: LEPRA Med. Adv. Bd, 1963–87 (Mem. Exec. Cttee, 1964–87; Vice-Pres., 1987–); Acid Fast Club, 1960; Pres., Section of Comparative Medicine, RSM, 1975. Vice-Pres., Internat. Leprosy Assoc., 1988– (Mem. Council, 1963–88). Member: Trop. Medicine Res. Bd, 1968–72; 3rd WHO Expert Cttee on Leprosy, 1965; WHO IMMLEP Steering Cttee, 1974–; WHO THELEP Steering Cttee, 1977–82. Almoth Wright Lectr, 1971; Erasmus Wilson Demonstration, RCS, 1973; 1st Clayton Meml Lectr, 1974; BMA Film, Silver Award, Leprosy, 1974. Mem. Editorial Boards: Leprosy Review; Internat. Jl of Leprosy. Hon. Mem., RSM Comparative Medicine Section, 1982. Manson Medal, 1980. *Publications:* scientific papers on basic and applied studies in animals and man relevant to pathogenesis, immunology and chemotherapy of leprosy and tuberculosis. *Address:* Highfield, Highwood Hill, Mill Hill, NW7 4EU. *T:* 081–959 2021; Division of Communicable Diseases, Clinical Research Centre, Harrow, Mddx HA1 3OJ. *T:* 081–864 3232.

REES, Rev. Canon (Richard) Michael; Residentiary Canon, Chester Cathedral, and Canon Missioner, Diocese of Chester, since 1990; *b* 31 July 1935; *s* of Richard and Margaret Rees; *m* 1958, Yoma Patricia; one *s* one *d*. *Educ:* Brighton College; St Peter's College, Oxford (MA Theol); Tyndale Hall, Bristol. Curate: Crowborough, 1959–62; Christ Church, Clifton, Bristol, 1962–64; Vicar: Christ Church, Clevedon, 1964–72; Holy Trinity, Cambridge, 1972–84; Proctor, General Synod for Ely Diocese, 1975–85; Chief Sec., Church Army, 1984–90. BCC, 1983–90 (Moderator, Evangelism Cttee, 1986–90). Editor, Missionary Mandate, 1955–68. *Recreations:* photography, filling waste paper baskets. *Address:* 5 Abbey Green, Chester CH1 2JH.

REES, Sir Stanley; *see* Rees, Sir C. W. S.

REES, (Thomas Morgan) Haydn, CBE 1975; JP; DL; Chairman, Welsh Water Authority, 1977–82; Member: National Water Council, 1977–82; Water Space Amenity Commission, 1977–82; *b* 22 May 1915; *y s* of late Thomas Rees and Mary Rees, Gorseinon, Swansea; *m* 1941, Marion, *y d* of A. B. Beer, Mumbles, Swansea; one *d*. *Educ:* Swansea Business Coll. Served War, 1939–45. Admitted solicitor, 1946; Sen. Asst Solicitor, Caernarvonshire CC, 1947; Flints County Council, 1948–65: Dep. Clerk, Dep. Clerk of the Peace, Police Authority, Magistrates Courts Cttee, and of Probation Cttee; 1966–74: Chief Exec.; Clerk of Peace (until office abolished, 1971); Clerk, Flints Police Authority (until merger with N Wales Police Authority, 1967); Clerk of Probation, Magistrates Courts, and of Justices Adv. Cttees; Clerk to Lieutenancy; Chief Exec., Clwyd CC, and Clerk, Magistrates Courts Cttee, 1974–77; Clerk to Lieutenancy and of Justices Adv. Cttee, Clwyd, 1974–77. Clerk, N Wales Police Authority, 1967–77; Secretary: Welsh Counties Cttee, 1968–77; (Corresp.) Rep. Body (Ombudsman) Cttee for Wales, 1974–77; Mem., Severn Barrage Cttee, 1978–81. Asst Comr, Royal Commn on Constitution, 1969–73. Chm., New Jobs Team, Shotton Steelworks, 1977–82; part-time Mem. Bd, BSC (Industry) Ltd, 1979–83. Chm., N Wales Arts Assoc., 1981–. Member: Lord Chancellor's Circuit Cttee for Wales and Chester Circuit, 1972–77; Welsh Council, 1968–79; Welsh Arts Council, 1968–77 (Mem. Regional Cttee 1981–); Gorsedd, Royal National Eisteddfod for Wales; Prince of Wales Cttee, 1976–79; Welsh Political Archive Adv. Cttee, Nat. Library of Wales, 1989–; N Wales Music Festival Cttee, 1983–. Clerk, 1974–77, Mem., 1983–, Theatr Clwyd Governors. Chairman: Govt Quality of Life Experiment in Clwyd, 1974–76; Deeside Enterprise Trust Ltd, 1982–89; President: Clwyd Voluntary Services Council, 1980–; Clwyd Pre-Retirement Assoc., 1986–. DL Flints 1969, Clwyd 1974; JP Mold, 1977 (Dep. Chm., 1978–84; Chm., 1985). *Recreations:* the arts, golf. *Address:* Cefn Bryn, Gwernaffield Road, Mold, Clwyd CH7 1RQ. *T:* Mold (0352) 2421. *Club:* Mold Golf.

REES, (Walter) Llewellyn, MA; Actor and Theatre Administrator; Hon. Life Member: British Actors' Equity Association, 1981 (General Secretary, 1940–46); Theatrical Management Association, 1985; Honorary President of International Theatre Institute since 1951; *b* 18 June 1901; *s* of Walter Francis Rees and Mary Gwendoline Naden; *m* 1961, Madeleine Newbury; one *s* one *d*. *Educ:* King Edward's School, Birmingham; Keble College, Oxford. Private Tutor, 1923–26; studied at RADA, 1926–28; Actor, 1928–40; Jt Secretary: London Theatre Council, 1940–46, Prov. Theatre Council, 1942–46; Sec. of Fed. of Theatre Unions, 1944–46; Governor of the Old Vic, 1945–47; Drama Director, Arts Council of Great Britain, 1947–49; Administrator of the Old Vic, 1949–51; Administrator of Arts Theatre, 1951–52; General Administrator, Donald Wolfit's Company, 1952–58; Chairman Executive Committee of International Theatre Institute, 1948–51; Hon. Counsellor to Council of Repertory Theatres, 1951–77. Returned to West End Stage, 1956, as Bishop of Buenos Aires in The Strong are Lonely, Theatre Royal, Haymarket; Olmeda in The Master of Santiago, Lyric Theatre, Hammersmith, 1957; Polonius in Hamlet, Bristol Old Vic, 1958; Dean of College in My Friend Judas, Arts Theatre, 1959; Mr Brandy in Settled out of Court, Strand Theatre, 1960–61; Justice Worthy in Lock Up Your Daughters, Mermaid Theatre and Her Majesty's, 1962–63; Sir Henry James in the Right Honourable Gentleman, Her Majesty's, 1964–65; Father Ambrose in The Servants and the Snow, Greenwich, 1970; Duncan in Macbeth, Greenwich, 1971; Mr Justice Millhouse in Whose Life Is It Anyway?, Savoy, 1978–79. Many film and television appearances. *Recreation:* travel. *Address:* 6 Byfeld Gardens, Barnes, SW13 9HP.

REES, William Howard Guest, CB 1988; Chief Veterinary Officer, State Veterinary Service, 1980–88; *b* 21 May 1928; *s* of Walter Guest Rees and Margaret Elizabeth Rees; *m* 1952, Charlotte Mollie (*née* Collins); three *s* one *d*. *Educ:* Llanelli Grammar Sch.; Royal Veterinary Coll., London (BSc). MRCVS; DVSM. Private practice, Deal, Kent, 1952–53; joined MAFF as Veterinary Officer, 1953; stationed Stafford, 1953–66; Divl Vet. Officer, Vet. Service HQ, Tolworth, 1966–69; Divl Vet. Officer, Berks, 1969–71; Dep. Regional Vet. Officer, SE Reg., 1971–73; Regional Vet. Officer, Tolworth, 1973–76, Asst Chief Vet. Officer, 1976–80. Mem., AFRC, 1980–88. FRASE, 1988. Bledisloe Award, RASE, 1988. *Recreations:* Rugby and cricket follower, golf.

REES, William Hurst; Member of Lands Tribunal, 1973–89; *b* 12 April 1917; *s* of Richard and Florence A. Rees; *m* 1941, Elizabeth Mary Wight; two *s* one *d*. *Educ:* College of Estate Management, Univ. of London (BSc (Est. Man.)). FRICS. Served War, RA and RE (SO2), 1940–46; Liaison Officer, Belgian Army Engrs. Head of Valuation Dept, Coll. of Estate Management, 1948–51. Principal in Private Practice as Chartered Surveyor: City of London, Richard Ellis & Son, 1951–61; East Grinstead, Sx, Turner, Rudge & Turner, 1961–73. Gov., Coll. of Estate Management, 1965–72; Mem. Council, RICS, 1967–70; Chm. Bd of Studies in Estate Management, Univ. of London, 1970–74; Chm., Surveying Bd, CNAA, 1976–77; Hon. Mem., Rating Surveyors Assoc. Pres., BSc (Estate Management) Club, 1961–62; Chm., Exams Bd, Incorporated Soc. of Valuers and Auctioneers, 1984–. Hon. FSVA, 1987. *Publications:* Modern Methods of Valuation, 1943, (jointly) 6th edn 1971; (ed) Valuations: Principles into Practice, 1980, 3rd edn 1988. *Recreation:* music, mainly opera. *Address:* Brendon, Carlton Road, South Godstone, Godstone, Surrey RH9 8LD. *T:* South Godstone (0342) 892109.

REES, (William) Linford (Llewelyn), CBE 1978; FRCP; FRCPsych; Emeritus Professor of Psychiatry, University of London, 1980; Consulting Physician, St Bartholomew's Hospital, since 1981; Lecturer in Psychological Medicine, St Bartholomew's Medical College, since 1958; Recognised Clinical Teacher in Mental Diseases, Institute of Psychiatry, University of London, since 1956; Chairman: University of London Teachers of Psychiatry Committee; Armed Services Consultant Advisory Board in Psychiatry, since 1979; *b* 24 Oct. 1914; *e s* of late Edward Parry Rees and Mary Rees, Llanelly, Carmathenshire; *m* 1940, Catherine, *y d* of late David Thomas, and of Angharad Thomas, Alltwen, Glam; two *s* two *d*. *Educ:* Llanelly Grammar School; University Coll., Cardiff; Welsh Nat. Sch. of Medicine; The Maudsley Hosp.; Univ. of London. BSc 1935; MB, BCh 1938; DPM 1940; DSc London, 1978; MRCP 1942; MD 1943; FRCP 1950; FRCPsych 1971 (Pres., 1975–78); Hon. FRCPsych 1978. David Hepburn Medal and Alfred Hughes Medal in Anatomy, 1935; John Maclean Medal and Prize in Obstetrics and Gynaecology, 1937, etc. Specialist, EMS, 1942; Dep. Med. Supt, Mill Hill Emergency Hosp., 1945; Asst Physician and Postgrad. Teacher in Clinical Psychiatry, The Maudsley Hosp., 1946; Dep. Physician Supt, Whitchurch Hosp., 1947; Regional Psychiatrist for Wales and Mon, 1948; Consultant Physician, The Bethlem Royal Hosp. and The Maudsley Hosp., 1954–66; Med. Dir, Charter Clinic, London, 1980–; Chief Psychiatrist and Exec. Med. Dir, Charter Medical, 1984–; Dir and Med. Advr, Huntercombe Manor Hosp., and Rehabilitation Gp Ltd, 1989–. Consultant Advisor in Psychiatry to RAF; WHO Consultant to Sri Lanka, 1973; Hon. Consultant, Royal Sch. for Deaf Children. Lectures to Univs and Learned Socs in Europe, USA, Asia, Australia and S America. Examiner: Diploma Psychological Medicine, RCP, 1964–69; MRCP, RCP, RCPE and RCPGlas, 1969–; MB and DPM, Univ. of Leeds, 1969–. President: Soc. for Psychosomatic Research, 1957–58; Royal Coll. of Psychiatrists, 1975–78 (Vice-Pres., 1972–75; Chm., E Anglian Region); Section of Psychiatry, RSM, 1971–72 (Vice-Pres., 1968; Hon. Mem., 1982); BMA, 1978– (Fellow, 1981); Vice-President: Stress Foundn, 1984–; Psychiatric Rehabilitation Assoc., 1988–; Chm., Medico-Pharmaceutical Forum, 1982 (Vice-Chm., 1981). Treasurer, World Psychiatric Assoc., 1966– (Hon. Mem., 1982). Member: Clinical Psychiatry Cttee, MRC, 1959–; Council, Royal Medico-Psychological Assoc. (Chm., Research and Clinical Section, 1957–63); Soc. for Study of Human Biology; Asthma Research Council; Cttee on Safety of Medicines (also Toxicity and Clinical Trials Sub-Cttee), 1971–; Psychological Medicine Group, BMA, 1967–; Bd of Advanced Med. Studies, Univ. of London, 1966–69; Higher Degrees Cttee, Univ. of London; Acad. Council Standing Sub-Cttee in Medicine, Univ. of London; Cttee of Management, Inst. of Psychiatry, Maudsley Hosp., 1968–; Council and Exec. Cttee, St Bartholomew's Hosp. Med. Coll., 1972–; Jt Policy Cttee, QMC, St Bartholomew's Hosp. and London Hosp., 1973–; Cttee on Review of Medicines (Chm., Psychotropic Drugs Sub-Cttee); Central Health Services Council; Standing Medical Adv. Cttee; Jt Consultants Cttee; Conference of Presidents of Royal Colls; GMC, 1980–84 (Mem., Educn Cttee, Preliminary Health Cttee and Prof. Conduct Cttee). Founder Mem., Internat. Coll. of Neuro-psychopharmacology. Hon. Mem. Learned Socs in USA, Sweden, Venezuela, East Germany, Spain and Greece. FRSM; Fellow: Eugenics Soc.; and Vice-Pres., Internat. Coll. of Psychosomatic Medicine, 1973; University Coll., Cardiff, 1980 (Governor, 1984–); Distinguished Fellow, Amer. Psychiatric Assoc., 1968; Hon. Fellow: Amer. Soc. of Physician Analysts; Amer. Coll. Psychiatrists; Hon. Member: Biological Psychiatry Assoc., USA; Hong Kong Psychiatric Soc., 1982. Chm. Bd of Trustees, Stress Syndrome Foundn, 1981– (Chm., Scientific Adv. Council). Governor: The Bethlem Royal Hosp. and The Maudsley Hosp.; Med. Coll. of St Bartholomew's Hosp., 1980–. President: Extend, 1976; Golden Jubilee Appeal, Welsh Nat. Sch. of Med., 1980. Co-Editor, Jl of Psychosomatic Research. Liveryman: Barber Surgeons; Apothecaries. Hon. LLD Wales, 1981. Bard of Welsh Gorsedd. *Publications:* (with Eysenck and Himmelweit) Dimensions of Personality, 1947; Short Textbook of Psychiatry, 1967. Chapters in: Modern Treatment in General Practice, 1947; Recent Progress in Psychiatry, 1950; Schizophrenia: Somatic Aspects, 1957; Psychoendocrinology, 1958; Recent Progress in Psychosomatic Research, 1960; Stress and Psychiatric Disorders, 1960. Papers in: Nature, BMJ, Jl of Mental Sci., Jl of Psychosomatic Research, Eugenics Review, etc. Contribs to Med. Annual, 1958–68. *Recreations:* swimming, photography, amusing grandchildren. *Address:* Penbryn, 62 Oakwood Avenue, Purley, Surrey. *Club:* Athenæum.

REES-DAVIES, William Rupert, QC 1973; Barrister-at-law; *b* 19 Nov. 1916; *o s* of late Sir William Rees-Davies, KC, DL, JP, formerly Chief Justice of Hong Kong and Liberal MP for Pembroke and of late Lady Rees-Davies; *m* 1st, 1959, Jane (marr. diss. 1981), *d* of Mr and Mrs Henry Mander; two *d*; 2nd, 1982, Sharlie Kingsley. *Educ:* Eton; Trinity Coll., Cambridge; Eton Soc., Eton XI, 1934–35; Eton Victor Ludorum; Cambridge Cricket XI, 1938; Honours in History and Law. Called to Bar, Inner Temple, 1939. Commissioned HM Welsh Guards, 1939; served War of 1939–45 (discharged disabled with loss of arm, 1943). Contested (C) South Nottingham in 1950 and 1951. MP (C) Isle of Thanet, March 1953–1974, Thanet W, 1974–83; Cons. Leader, Select Cttee on Health and the Social Services, 1980–83; Chm., Cons. Cttee on Tourism. *Recreations:* racing, collecting pictures and antiques. *Address:* 5 Lord North Street, SW1. *Clubs:* Turf, Guards' Polo, MCC; Hawks, University Pitt (Cambridge).

REES-JONES, Geoffrey Rippon, MA Oxon; Principal, King William's College, Isle of Man, 1958–79; *b* 8 July 1914; *er s* of W. Rees-Jones, BA, Ipswich; *m* 1950, Unity Margaret McConnell (*d* 1982), *d* of Major P. M. Sanders, Hampstead; one *s* one *d*. *Educ:* Ipswich School (scholar); University College, Oxford (open scholar). Assistant Master, Eastbourne College, 1936–38, Marlborough College, 1938–54 (Housemaster, C2, 1946–54); Headmaster, Bembridge School, 1954–58. Served War mainly in Commandos, 1940–45; Commandant, Commando Mountain Warfare School, 1943; Staff College, Camberley, 1944 (sc); Brigade Major, 4 Commando Bde, 1944–45 (despatches). *Recreations:* sailing, cricket, golf, fives; Oxford Rugby blue, 1933–35, Wales XV, 1934–36. *Address:* Red Lion Cottage, Braaid, Isle of Man. *T:* Castletown (0624) 851360.

REES-MOGG, family name of **Baron Rees-Mogg**.

REES-MOGG, Baron *cr* 1988 (Life Peer), of Hinton Blewitt in the County of Avon; **William Rees-Mogg;** Kt 1981; Chairman and Proprietor, Pickering & Chatto Ltd, since 1981; Director, General Electric Co., since 1981; Chairman, Broadcasting Standards Council, since 1988; *b* 14 July 1928; *s* of late Edmund Fletcher Rees-Mogg and late Beatrice Rees-Mogg (*née* Warren), Temple Cloud, Somerset; *m* 1962, Gillian Shakespeare Morris, *d* of T. R. Morris; two *s* three *d. Educ:* Charterhouse; Balliol Coll., Oxford (Brackenbury Scholar). President, Oxford Union, 1951. Financial Times, 1952–60, Chief Leader Writer, 1955–60; Asst Editor, 1957–60; Sunday Times, City Editor, 1960–61; Political and Economic Editor, 1961–63; Deputy Editor, 1964–67; Editor, The Times, 1967–81; Mem., Exec. Bd, Times Newspapers Ltd, 1968–81; Director: The Times Ltd, 1968–81; Times Newspapers Ltd, 1978–81. Chm., Sidgwick & Jackson, 1985–89. Vice-Chm., Bd of Governors, BBC, 1981–86; Chm., Arts Council of GB, 1982–89. Contested (C) Chester-le-Street, Co. Durham, By-election 1956; General Election, 1959. Treasurer, Institute of Journalists, 1960–63, 1966–68, Pres., 1963–64; Vice-Chm. Cons. Party's Nat. Advisory Cttee on Political Education, 1961–63. Pres., English Assoc., 1983–84. Mem., Internat. Cttee, Pontifical Council for Culture, 1983–87. Vis. Fellow, Nuffield Coll., Oxford, 1968–72. High Sheriff, Somerset, 1978. Hon. LLD Bath, 1977. *Publications:* The Reigning Error: the crisis of world inflation, 1974; An Humbler Heaven, 1977; How to Buy Rare Books, 1985; (with James Dale Davidson) Blood in the Streets, 1988. *Recreation:* collecting. *Address:* 3 Smith Square, SW1; The Old Rectory, Hinton Blewitt, near Bristol, Avon. *Club:* Garrick.

REES-WILLIAMS, family name of **Baron Ogmore.**

REESE, Prof. Colin Bernard, PhD, ScD; FRS 1981; FRSC; Daniell Professor of Chemistry, King's College, London, University of London, since 1973; *b* 29 July 1930; *s* of Joseph and Emily Reese; *m* 1968, Susanne Bird; one *s* one *d. Educ:* Dartington Hall Sch.; Clare Coll., Cambridge (BA 1953, PhD 1956, MA 1957, ScD 1972). 1851 Sen. Student, 1956–58; Research Fellow: Clare Coll., Cambridge, 1956–59; Harvard Univ., 1957–58; Official Fellow and Dir of Studies in Chem., Clare Coll., 1959–73; Cambridge University: Univ. Demonstrator in Chem., 1959–63; Asst Dir of Res., 1963–64; Univ. Lectr in Chem., 1964–73. FKC 1989. *Publications:* scientific papers, mainly in chemical jls. *Address:* Department of Chemistry, King's College, London, Strand, WC2R 2LS. *T:* 071–873 2260.

REESE, Colin Edward; QC 1987; *b* 28 March 1950; *s* of Robert Edward Reese and Katharine Reese (*née* Moore); *m* 1978, Diana Janet Anderson; two *s* one *d. Educ:* Hawarden Grammar School; King Edward VI School, Southampton; Fitzwilliam College, Cambridge (BA 1972; MA 1976). Called to the Bar, Gray's Inn, 1973 (Mould Schol., 1974); admitted, *ad eund.*, Lincoln's Inn, 1976; in practice, 1975–. Pres., Cambridge Univ. Law Soc., 1971–72. *Address:* 1 Atkin Building, Gray's Inn, WC1R 5BQ. *T:* 071–404 0102.

REESE, Surg. Rear-Adm. (John) Mansel, CB 1962; OBE 1953; *b* 3 July 1906; *s* of late Dr D. W. Reese, and late Mrs A. M. Reese; *m* 1946, Beryl (*née* Dunn) (*d* 1973); two *d* (and one *s* decd). *Educ:* Epsom Coll.; St Mary's Hosp. Med. Sch., London University. MRCS, LRCP 1930; DPH 1934. Entered Royal Navy, Jan. 1931; Naval Medical Officer of Health, Orkney and Shetland Comd, 1942–44; Naval MOH, Ceylon, 1944–46; Admiralty, 1947–53; Medical Officer-in-Charge RN Hospital, Plymouth, 1960–63; QHP 1960–63. Surgeon Comdr, 1943; Surgeon Captain, 1954; Surgeon Rear-Adm., 1960; retd 1963. FRSTM&H. Sir Gilbert Blane Gold Medal, 1939. Member Gray's Inn, 1953. CStJ 1961. *Address:* 4 Meldon Court, East Budleigh Road, Budleigh Salterton, Devon EX9 6HE.

REESE, (John) Terence; bridge expert, author and journalist; *b* 28 Aug. 1913; *s* of John and Anne Reese; *m* 1970, Alwyn Sherrington. *Educ:* Bilton Grange; Bradfield Coll. (top scholar); New Coll., Oxford (top class. scholar). Worked at Harrods, 1935–36; left to follow career as bridge expert and journalist. Became bridge correspondent of the Evening News, 1948, the Observer, 1950, the Lady, 1954, and the Standard, 1981. Winner of numerous British, European and World Championships. *Publications:* The Elements of Contract, 1938; Reese on Play, 1948; The Expert Game, 1958; Play Bridge with Reese, 1960; Story of an Accusation, 1966; Precision Bidding and Precision Play, 1972; Play These Hands With Me, 1976; Bridge at the Top (autobiog.), 1977; (jtly) Squeeze Play is Easy, 1980 (reprinted as Squeeze Play Made Easy, 1988); (with Julian Pottage) Positive Declarer's Play, 1986; *with Albert Dormer:* The Acol System Today, 1961; The Play of the Cards, 1967; Bridge for Tournament Players, 1969; The Complete Book of Bridge, 1973; *with Roger Trézel:* Safety Plans, 1976; The Mistakes You Make in Bridge, 1984; *with David Bird:* Miracles of Card Play, 1982; Tricks of the Trade, 1989; and many others. *Recreations:* golf, backgammon. *Address:* 23 Adelaide Crescent, Hove, Sussex BN3 2JG. *T:* Brighton (0273) 722187.

REESE, Mansel; *see* Reese, J. M.

REEVE, Anthony, CMG 1986; HM Diplomatic Service; Ambassador to South Africa, since 1991; *b* 20 Oct. 1938; *s* of Sidney Reeve and Dorothy (*née* Mitchell); *m* 1964, Pamela Margaret Angus (marr. diss. 1988); one *s* two *d. Educ:* Queen Elizabeth Grammar Sch., Wakefield; Marling Sch., Stroud; Merton Coll., Oxford (MA). Lever Brothers & Associates, 1962–65; joined HM Diplomatic Service, 1965; Middle East Centre for Arab Studies, 1966–68; Asst Political Agent, Abu Dhabi, 1968–70; First Secretary, FCO, 1970–73; First Sec., later Counsellor, Washington, 1973–78; Head of Arms Control and Disarmament Dept, FCO, 1979–81; Counsellor, Cairo, 1981–84; Head of Southern Africa Dept, FCO, 1984–86; Asst Under Sec. of State (Africa), FCO, 1986–87; Ambassador to Jordan, 1988–91. *Recreations:* writing, music. *Address:* c/o Foreign and Commonwealth Office, SW1A 2AH. *Clubs:* United Oxford & Cambridge University; Leander (Henley-on-Thames).

REEVE, Sir (Charles) Trevor, Kt 1973; a Judge of the High Court of Justice, Family Division, 1973–88; *b* 4 July 1915; *o s* of William George Reeve and Elsie (*née* Bowring), Wokingham; *m* 1941, Marjorie (*d* 1990), *d* of Charles Evelyn Browne, Eccles, Lancs. *Educ:* Winchester College; Trinity College, Oxford. Commissioned 10th Royal Hussars (PWO) 1940; served BEF, CMF (Major) 1940–44 (despatches); Staff College, Camberley, 1945. Called to Bar, Inner Temple, 1946, Bencher, 1965; Mem., Bar Council, 1950–54. QC 1965; County Court Judge, 1968; Circuit Judge, 1972. Mem., Appeals Tribunal for E Africa in respect of Commonwealth Immigration Act, 1968. *Recreations:* golf, dancing. *Address:* 95 Abingdon Road, Kensington, W8 6QU. *T:* 071–937 7530. *Clubs:* Garrick; Royal North Devon Golf (Westward Ho!); Sunningdale Golf.

REEVE, James Ernest, CMG 1982; HM Diplomatic Service, retired; Secretariat, International Primary Aluminium Institute, London, since 1985; *b* 8 June 1926; *s* of Ernest and Anthea Reeve; *m* 1947, Lillian Irene Watkins; one *s* one *d. Educ:* Bishop's Stortford Coll. Vice-Consul, Ahwaz and Khorramshahr, Iran, 1949–51; UN General Assembly, Paris, 1951; Asst Private Sec. to Rt Hon. Selwyn Lloyd, Foreign Office, 1951–53; 2nd Secretary: Brit. Embassy, Washington, 1953–57; Brit. Embassy, Bangkok, 1957–59; FO, 1959–61; HM Consul, Frankfurt, 1961–65; 1st Secretary: Brit. Embassy in Libya, 1965–69; Brit. Embassy, Budapest, 1970–72; Chargé d'Affaires, Budapest, 1972; Counsellor (Commercial), East Berlin, 1973–75; Consul-Gen., Zurich and Principality of Liechtenstein, 1975–80; HM Minister and Consul-Gen., Milan, 1980–83. Dir, Sprester Investments Ltd, 1986–. *Recreations:* theatre, tennis, skiing, travel. *Address:* 20 Glenmore House, Richmond Hill, Surrey; Sultan's Gate, 10 Montpellier Parade, Cheltenham, Glos. *Club:* Royal Automobile.

REEVE, John; Managing Director, Sun Life Corporation plc, since 1990; *b* 13 July 1944; *s* of Clifford Alfred Reeve and Irene Mary Turnidge Reeve; *m* 1st, 1968, Patricia Mary Tomkins (marr. diss. 1973); 2nd, 1974, Sally Diane Welton; one *d. Educ:* Westcliff High School (Grammar). FCA; CBIM. Selbey Smith & Earle, 1962–67; Peat Marwick McLintock, 1967–68; Vickers, Roneo Vickers Group: Commercial Dir, Furniture & Systems Div., subseq. Manager, Group Financial Evaluation & Planning, 1968–76; Dir, Accounting Services, Wilkinson Match, 1976–77; Amalgamated Metal Corp.: Controller, Physical Trading Div., subseq. Corporate Controller, 1977–80; Group Finance Director: British Aluminium Co., 1980–83; Mercantile House Holdings, 1983–87; Group Man. Dir, 1987, Asst Man. Dir, 1988–89, Man. Dir, 1989–, Sun Life Assurance Soc. Director: The English Concert, 1987–; HMC Group plc, 1988–. Dep. Pres., Inst. of Business Ethics, 1991–. Gov., Res. into Ageing, 1991–. *Recreations:* yachting, music, theatre. *Address:* Starvelarks, 85 Warren Road, Leigh-on-Sea, Essex SS9 3TT. *T:* Southend-on-Sea (0702) 556769. *Club:* Essex Yacht.

REEVE, Mrs Marjorie Frances, CBE 1944; TD 1950; JP; *d* of late Charles Fry, Bedford; *m* 1st, Lieutenant-Commander J. K. Laughton, Royal Navy (*d* 1925); (one *s* decd); 2nd, Major-General C. M. Wagstaff, CB, CMG, CIE, DSO (*d* 1934); 3rd, 1950, Major-General J. T. W. Reeve, CB, CBE, DSO (*d* 1983). Joined ATS, 1938; served with BEF, and in Middle East and BAOR; late Controller ATS. Was i/c Public Welfare Section of Control Commission for Germany (BE); Principal in Board of Trade (Overseas) till 1950; Swedish Red Cross Medal in Silver, 1950; County Director, BRCS, 1953–57; Dep. Pres. Suffolk BRCS, 1957, Hon. Vice-Pres., 1977. Badge of Honour (2nd Class) BRCS, 1970. JP (W Suffolk), 1954. *Address:* Moorhouse Nursing Home, Hindhead, Surrey GU26 6RA. *T:* Hindhead (042873) 5313.

REEVE, Prof. Michael David, FBA 1984; Kennedy Professor of Latin, and Fellow of Pembroke College, University of Cambridge, since 1984; *b* 11 Jan. 1943; *s* of Arthur Reeve and Edith Mary Barrett; *m* 1970, Elizabeth Klingaman; two *s* one *d. Educ:* King Edward's Sch., Birmingham; Balliol Coll., Oxford (MA). Harmsworth Senior Scholar, Merton Coll., Oxford, 1964–65; Woodhouse Research Fellow, St John's Coll., Oxford, 1965–66; Tutorial Fellow, Exeter Coll., Oxford, 1966–84, now Emeritus Fellow. Visiting Professor: Univ. of Hamburg, 1976; McMaster Univ., 1979; Univ. of Toronto, 1982–83. Corresp. Mem., Akademie der Wissenschaften, Göttingen, 1990. Editor, Classical Quarterly, 1981–86. *Publications:* Longus, Daphnis and Chloe, 1982; contribs to Texts and Transmission, ed L. D. Reynolds, 1983; articles in European and transatlantic jls. *Recreations:* chess, music, gardening, mountain walking. *Address:* Pembroke College, Cambridge CB2 1RF.

REEVE, Robin Martin, MA; Head Master, King's College School, Wimbledon, since 1980; *b* 22 Nov. 1934; *s* of Percy Martin Reeve and Cicely Nora Parker; *m* 1959, Brianne Ruth Hall; one *s* two *d. Educ:* Hampton Sch.; Gonville and Caius Coll., Cambridge (Foundation Schol.; BA cl. 1 Hist. Tripos, 1957; MA). Asst Master, King's Coll. Sch., Wimbledon, 1958–62; Head of History Dept, 1962–80, and Dir of Studies, 1975–80, Lancing Coll. Chm., Governors, Rosemead Sch., Littlehampton, 1983–. *Publication:* The Industrial Revolution 1750–1850, 1971. *Recreations:* English history and architecture, gardening. *Address:* 20 Burghley Road, SW19 5BH; The Old Rectory, Coombes, Lancing, W Sussex BN15 0RS. *Club:* East India, Devonshire, Sports and Public Schools.

REEVE, Suzanne Elizabeth, (Mrs Norman Warner); Personal Adviser to Deputy Chairman, British Telecommunications plc, since 1991; *b* 12 Aug. 1942; *d* of Charles Clifford Reeder and Elizabeth Joan Armstrong Reeder; *m* 1st, 1967, Jonathan Reeve (marr. diss. 1980); one *s*; 2nd, 1990, Norman Reginald Warner, *qv*; one *s. Educ:* Badminton Sch., Bristol; Univ. of Sussex (BA Hons History); Univ. of Cambridge (Dip. Criminology). Home Office Res. Unit, 1966–67; Personal Assistant to Sec. of State for Social Services, DHSS, 1968–70; Principal, DHSS, 1970–73; Central Policy Review Staff, 1973–74; Asst Sec., DHSS, 1979–85; Sec., 1985–88, Actg Chm., 1987–88, ESRC; Exec. Dir, Food from Britain, 1988–90; Chief Exec., Foundn for Educn Business Partnerships, 1990–91. *Recreations:* family life, cooking, gardening, reading, films. *Address:* 8 College Gardens, Dulwich, SE21 7BE.

REEVE, Hon. Sir Trevor; *see* Reeve, Hon. Sir C. T.

REEVES, Christopher Reginald; Vice Chairman, Merrill Lynch International Ltd, since 1989; Group Chief Executive, 1980–87, and Deputy Chairman, 1984–87, Morgan Grenfell Group PLC; Joint Chairman, Morgan Grenfell & Co. Ltd, 1984–87; *b* 14 Jan. 1936; *s* of Reginald and Dora Reeves; *m* 1965, Stella, *d* of Patrick and Maria Whinney; three *s. Educ:* Malvern College. National Service, Rifle Bde, 1955–57. Bank of England, 1958–63; Hill Samuel & Co. Ltd, 1963–67; joined Morgan Grenfell & Co. Ltd, 1968; Dir, 1970. Sen. Advr to Pres., Merrill Lynch, 1988–89. Director: London Board, Westpac Banking Corp. (formerly Commercial Bank of Australia Ltd) 1972–90 (Chm., 1976–82, Dep. Chm., 1982–89); Midland and International Banks Ltd, 1976–83; BICC, 1982–; Andrew Weir & Co., 1982–; Allianz Internat. Insurance Co. Ltd, 1983–; Oman Internat. Bank, 1984–; International Freehold Properties SARL, 1988–. Member: Adv. Panel, City University Business Sch., 1972–81 (Chm., 1979–81); Council, City Univ. Business Sch., 1986–; Council, Inst. for Fiscal Studies, 1982–87; Governor: Stowe Sch., 1976–81; Dulwich College Prep. Sch., 1977–; Mermaid Theatre Trust, 1981–85. *Recreations:* sailing, shooting, ski-ing. *Address:* 64 Flood Street, SW3 5TE. *Clubs:* Boodle's; Royal Southern Yacht (Southampton).

REEVES, Rev. Donald St John; Rector, St James's Church, Piccadilly, since 1980; *b* 18 May 1934; *s* of Henry and Barbara Reeves. *Educ:* Sherborne; Queens' Coll., Cambridge (BA Hons 1957); Cuddesdon Theol Coll. 2nd Lieut, Royal Sussex Regt, 1952–54. Lectr, British Council, Beirut, 1957–60; Tutor, Brasted Theol Coll., 1960–61; Cuddesdon Theol Coll., 1961–63; deacon, 1963, priest, 1964; Curate, All Saints, Maidstone, 1963–65; Chaplain to Bishop of Southwark, 1965–68; Vicar of St Peter's, Morden, 1969–80. Mem., Gen. Synod of C of E, 1990–. *Publications:* (ed) Church and State, 1984; For God's Sake, 1988; Making Sense of Religion, 1989. *Recreations:* playing the organ, bee-keeping, watching TV soap operas. *Address:* St James's Church, Piccadilly, W1V 9LF. *T:* 071–734 4511. *Clubs:* Arts (Hon.), Royal Automobile.

REEVES, Gordon; *see* Reeves, W. G.

REEVES, Helen May, OBE 1986; Director, National Association of Victims Support Schemes, since 1980; *b* 22 Aug. 1945; *d* of Leslie Percival William Reeves and Helen Edith Reeves (*née* Brown). *Educ:* Dartford Grammar School for Girls; Nottingham University (BA Hons Social Admin. 1966). Probation Officer, Inner London Probation Service, 1967–79 (Senior Probation Officer, 1975–79). Mem., Religious Society of Friends.

Recreations: social and local history and architecture, food, gardens. *Address:* Cranmer House, 39 Brixton Road, SW9 6DZ. *T:* 071–735 9166.

REEVES, Marjorie Ethel, MA (Oxon), PhD (London), DLitt (Oxon); FRHistS; FBA 1974; Vice-Principal, St Anne's College, Oxford, 1951–62, 1964–67; *b* 17 July 1905; *d* of Robert J. W. Reeves and Edith Saffery Whitaker. *Educ:* The High School for Girls, Trowbridge, Wilts; St Hugh's Coll., Oxford; Westfield Coll., London. Asst Mistress, Roan School, Greenwich, 1927–29; Research Fellow, Westfield Coll., London, 1929–31; Lecturer, St Gabriel's Trng Coll., London, 1931–38; Tutor, later Fellow of St Anne's College, 1938–72, Hon. Fellow, 1973. Member: Central Advisory Council, Min. of Educn, 1947–61; Academic Planning Bd, Univ. of Kent; Academic Advisory Cttee, University of Surrey; formerly Member: Educn Council, ITA; British Council of Churches; School Broadcasting Council. Corresp. Fellow, Medieval Acad. of America, 1979. *Publications:* Growing Up in a Modern Society, 1946; (ed, with L. Tondelli, B. Hirsch-Reich) Il Libro delle Figure dell'Abate Gioachino da Fiore, 1953; Three Questions in Higher Education (Hazen Foundation, USA), 1955; Moral Education in a Changing Society (ed W. Niblett), 1963; ed, Eighteen Plus: Unity and Diversity in Higher Education, 1965; The Influence of Prophecy in the later Middle Ages: a study in Joachimism, 1969; Higher Education: demand and response (ed W. R. Niblett), 1969; (with B. Hirsch-Reich) The Figurae of Joachim of Fiore, 1972; Joachim of Fiore and the Prophetic Future, 1976; Sheep Bell and Ploughshare, 1978; Why History, 1980; (with W. Gould) Joachim of Fiore and the Myth of the Eternal Evangel in the Nineteenth Century, 1987; Competence, Delight and the Common Good: reflections on the crisis in higher education, 1988; (with J. Morrison) The Diaries of Jeffery Whitaker, 1989; (ed) Prophetic Rome in the High Renaissance period, 1991; Then and There Series: The Medieval Town, 1954, The Medieval Village, 1954, Elizabethan Court, 1956, The Medieval Monastery, 1957, The Norman Conquest, 1958, Alfred and the Danes, 1959; The Medieval Castle, 1960, Elizabethan Citizen, 1961; A Medieval King Governs, 1971; Explorers of the Elizabethan Age, 1977; Elizabethan Country House, 1984; The Spanish Armada, 1988; contributions on history in Speculum, Medieval and Renaissance Studies, Traditio, Sophia, Recherches de Théologie, etc, and on education in Times Educational Supplement, New Era, etc. *Recreations:* music, gardening, bird-watching. *Address:* 38 Norham Road, Oxford. *T:* Oxford (0865) 57039. *Club:* University Women's.

REEVES, Prof. Nigel Barrie Reginald, OBE 1987; DPhil; FIL; Professor of German and Head of Department of Modern Languages, Aston University, since 1990; *b* 9 Nov. 1939; *s* of Reginald Arthur Reeves and Marjorie Joyce Reeves; *m* 1982, Minou (*née* Samimi); one *s* one *d. Educ:* Merchant Taylors' Sch.; Worcester Coll., Oxford (MA); St John's Coll., Oxford (DPhil 1970). FIL 1981. Lectr in English, Univ. of Lund, Sweden, 1964–66; Lectr in German, Univ. of Reading, 1968–74; Alexander von Humboldt Fellow, Univ. of Tübingen, 1974–75; University of Surrey: Prof. of German, 1975–90; Hd of Dept of Linguistic and Internat. Studies, 1979–90; Dean, Faculty of Human Studies, 1986–90. Guest Prof. of German, Royal Holloway Coll., London Univ., 1976; Vis. Prof., European Business Sch., 1981–; Sen. Alexander von Humboldt Fellow, Univ. of Hamburg, 1986. Chairman: Council, Inst. of Linguists, 1985–88; Nat. Congress on Langs in Educn, 1986–90; Vice-Chm., Conf. of Univ. Teachers of German, 1988–91; President: Nat. Assoc. of Language Advisers, 1986–91; Assoc. of Teachers of German, 1988–89. Gov., Germanic Inst., Univ. of London, 1989–. FRSA 1986; CIEx 1987. Goethe Medal, Goethe Inst., Munich, 1989. *Publications:* Merkantil-Tekniska Stilar, 2 Vols, 1965–66; Heinrich Heine: poetry and politics, 1974; (with K. Dewhurst) Friedrich Schiller: medicine, psychology and literature, 1978; (with D. Liston) Business Studies, Languages and Overseas Trade, 1985; (jtly) Making Your Mark: effective business communication in Germany, 1988; (with D. Liston) The Invisible Economy: a profile of Britain's invisible exports, 1988; (jtly) Franc Exchange, effective business communication in France, 1990; over 40 articles in learned jls on language, language educn, literature and overseas trade. *Recreations:* gardening, walking. *Address:* Department of Modern Languages, Aston University, Aston Triangle, Birmingham, B4 7ET.

REEVES, Most Rev. Sir Paul Alfred, GCMG 1985; GCVO 1986; QSO 1990; Kt 1985; Representative of Anglican Consultative Council at the United Nations, since 1991; Assisting Bishop, Episcopal Diocese of New York, since 1991; *b* 6 Dec. 1932; 2nd *s* of D'Arcy Lionel and Hilda Mary Reeves; *m* 1959, Beverley Gwendolen Watkins; three *d. Educ:* Wellington Coll., New Zealand; Victoria Univ. of Wellington (MA); St John's Theol. Coll., Auckland (LTh); St Peter's Coll., Univ. of Oxford (MA; Hon. Fellow, 1980). Deacon, 1958; Priest, 1960; Curate: Tokoroa, NZ, 1958–59; St Mary the Virgin, Oxford, 1959–61; Kirkley St Peter, Lowestoft, 1961–63; Vicar, St Paul, Okato, NZ, 1964–66; Lectr in Church History, St John's Coll., Auckland, NZ, 1966–69; Dir of Christian Educn, Dio. Auckland, 1969–71; Bishop of Waiapu, 1971–79; Bishop of Auckland, 1979–85; Primate and Archbishop of New Zealand, 1980–85; Governor-General, NZ, 1985–90. Chm., Environmental Council, 1974–76. KStJ 1986. Hon. DCL Oxford, 1985; Hon LLD Wellington, 1989. *Recreations:* jogging, sailing, swimming. *Address:* The General Theological Seminary, 175 Ninth Avenue, New York, NY 10011, USA.

REEVES, Philip Thomas Langford, RSA 1976 (ARSA 1971); artist in etching and other mediums; Senior Lecturer, Glasgow School of Art, 1973–91; *b* 7 July 1931; *s* of Herbert Reeves and Lilian; *m* 1964, Christine MacLaren; one *d. Educ:* Naunton Park Sch., Cheltenham. Student, Cheltenham Sch. of Art, 1947–49. Army service, 4th/7th Royal Dragoon Guards, Middle East, 1949–51. RCA, 1951–54 (ARCA 1st Cl.); Lectr, Glasgow Sch. of Art, 1954–73. Associate, Royal Soc. of Painter Etchers, 1954, Fellow 1964; RSW 1962; RGI 1981. Works in permanent collections: Arts Council; V&A; Gall. of Modern Art, Edinburgh; Glasgow Art Gall.; Glasgow Univ. Print Collection; Hunterian Art Gall., Glasgow; Manchester City Art Gall.; Royal Scottish Acad.; Aberdeen Art Gall.; Paisley Art Gall.; Inverness Art Gall.; Milngavie Art Gall.; Dept of the Environment; Dundee Art Gall.; Scottish Develt Agency; Stirling and Strathclyde Univs; Contemporary Art Soc. *Recreation:* walking. *Address:* 13 Hamilton Drive, Glasgow G12 8DN. *Club:* Traverse (Edinburgh).

REEVES, William Desmond; Under Secretary, Cabinet Office, since 1989; *b* 26 May 1937; *s* of late Thomas Norman and of Anne Reeves; *m* 1967, Aase Birte Christensen; two *d. Educ:* Darwen Grammar Sch.; King's Coll., Cambridge (BA Hist.). National service, RAEC, 1959–61. Joined Admiralty as Asst Principal, 1961; MoD, 1964; Asst Sec., 1973; seconded to Pay Board, 1973–74; Asst Under Sec. of State, Air, MoD (PE), 1982–84, Resources and Progs, MoD, 1984, Systems, Office of Management and Budget, MoD, 1985–88. *Address:* Cabinet Office, 70 Whitehall, SW1A 2AS.

REEVES, Dr (William) Gordon, FRCP, FRCPath; Medical Editor and Consultant, Communicable Diease Surveillance Centre, Public Health Laboratory Service, since 1991; *b* 9 July 1938; *s* of Rev. W. H. and Mrs E. L. Reeves; *m* 1970, Elizabeth Susan, *d* of Surg.-Comdr L. A. and Mrs P. Moules; one *s* one *d. Educ:* Perse Sch., Cambridge; Guy's Hosp. Med. Sch. (BSc, MB BS). MRCS, LRCP 1964; MRCP 1966; FRCP 1978; FRCPath 1985. Editor, Guy's Hosp. Gazette, 1962–63. HO and Med. Registrar appts at Guy's, Central Middx, Brompton, National, Middx, and University Coll. Hosps, 1964–68; Lecturer: Clinical Pharmacology, Guy's Hosp. Med. Sch., 1968–71; Immunology and Medicine, Royal Postgrad. Med. Sch., 1971–73; Consultant Immunologist, Nottingham HA, 1973–88; Nottingham University: Sen. Lectr, 1975–85; Prof. of Immunology, 1985–88; Editor, The Lancet, 1989–90. Chm. Cttee, British Soc. for Immunology, 1984–85; Member: Research Cttee, British Diabetic Assoc., 1985–88; Specialty Adv. Cttee on Immunology, RCPath, 1986–88; Hon. Sec., Cttee on Clinical Immunology and Allergy, RCP, 1986–88. *Publications:* (with E. J. Holborow) Immunology in Medicine: a comprehensive guide to clinical immunology, 1977, 2nd edn 1983; Lecture Notes on Immunology, 1987, 2nd edn 1991; contribs to med. and scientific books and jls on immunology and infectious diseases. *Recreations:* cathedrals, cottages, cricket. *Address:* Saxons, Little Gaddesden, Herts HP4 1PE. *T:* Hemel Hempstead (0442) 842441. *Club:* Royal Society of Medicine.

REFFELL, Adm. Sir Derek (Roy), KCB 1984; Governor and Commander-in-Chief, Gibraltar, since 1989; *b* 6 Oct. 1928; *s* of late Edward (Roy) and Murielle Reffell; *m* 1956, Janne Gronow Davis; one *s* one *d. Educ:* Culford Sch., Suffolk; Royal Naval Coll., Dartmouth. FNI; CBIM. Various ships at Home, Mediterranean, West Indies and Far East, 1946–63; qualified Navigating Officer, 1954; Comdr 1963; Comd HMS Sirius, 1966–67; Comdr BRNC Dartmouth, 1968–69; Captain 1970; Chief Staff Officer Plans Far East, 1970–71; Naval Staff, 1971–74; Comd HMS Hermes, 1974–76; Director Naval Warfare, 1976–78; Commodore Amphibious Warfare, 1978–79; Asst Chief of Naval Staff (Policy), 1979–82; Flag Officer Third Flotilla and Comdr Anti-Submarine Group Two, March 1982–Aug. 1983; Flag Officer, Naval Air Comd, 1983–84; Controller of the Navy, 1984–89, retd. Assistant, Coachmakers Company, 1986–. KStJ 1989. *Recreations:* golf, wine-making. *Address:* The Convent, Gibraltar, BFPO 52.

REFSHAUGE, Maj.-Gen. Sir William (Dudley), AC 1980; Kt 1966; CBE 1959 (OBE 1944); ED 1965; Secretary-General, World Medical Association, 1973–76; Hon. Consultant to Australian Foundation on Alcoholism and Drugs of Dependence, since 1979; *b* 3 April 1913; *s* of late F. C. Refshauge, Melbourne; *m* 1942, Helen Elizabeth, *d* of late R. E. Allwright, Tasmania; four *s* one *d. Educ:* Hampton High Sch.; Scotch Coll., Melbourne; Melbourne University. MB, BS (Melbourne) 1938; FRCOG 1961; FRACS 1962; FRACP 1963; Hon. FRSH 1967; FACMA 1967; FRACOG 1978. Served with AIF, 1939–46; Lt-Col, RAAMC (despatches four times). Medical Supt, Royal Women's Hosp., Melbourne, 1948–51; Col, and Dep. DGAMS, Aust., 1951–55; Maj.-Gen., and DGAMS, Aust., 1955–60; QHP, 1955–64. Commonwealth Dir-Gen. of Health, Australia, 1960–73. Chairman: Council, Aust. Coll. of Nursing, 1958–60 (Chm. Educn Cttee, 1951–58); Nat. Health and MRC, 1960–73; Nat. Fitness Council, 1960–; Nat. Tuberculosis Adv. Council, 1960–; Prog. and Budget Cttee, 15th World Health Assembly, 1962; Admin., Fin. and Legal Cttee 19th World Health Assembly (Pres., 24th Assembly, 1971); Exec. Bd, WHO, 1969–70 (Mem., 1967–70). Member: Council, Aust. Red Cross Soc., 1954–60; Mem. Nat. Blood Transfusion Cttee, ARCS 1955–60; Nat. Trustee, Returned Services League Aust., 1961–73, 1976–; Mem. Bd of Management, Canberra Grammar Sch., 1963–68; Mem. Bd of Trustees, Walter and Eliza Hall Inst. of Med. Res., Melbourne, 1977–86 (Chm., Ethics Cttee, 1983–); Chm., Governing Bd, Menzies Sch. of Health Research, Darwin, 1983–87. Chm., ACT Cttee, Mem., Nat. Cttee and Mem. Nat. Exec., Sir Robert Menzies Foundn, 1979–84; Chm., Australian-Hellenic Meml Cttee, 1986–88. Hon. Life Mem., Australian Dental Assoc., 1966. Patron: Australian Sports Medicine Assoc., 1971–; ACT Br., Aust. Sports Medicine Fedn, 1980–; Totally and Permanently Incapacitated Assoc., ACT, 1982–; 2/2 (2nd AIF) Field Regtl Assoc., 1984–; Medical Assoc. for Prevention of War (MAPW), 1989–. Leader, Commemorative Tour of Europe for 60th anniversary, RSL. Nat. Pres., 1st Pan Pacific Conf. on alcohol and drugs, 1980. Hon MD Sydney, 1988. Anzac Peace Prize, RSL, 1990. *Publications:* contribs to Australian Med. Jl, NZ Med. Jl, etc. *Recreations:* bowls, rug-making, gardening. *Address:* 26 Birdwood Street, Hughes, Canberra, ACT 2605, Australia. *Clubs:* Royal Society of Medicine (London); Naval and Military, Cricket (Melbourne); Commonwealth (Canberra); Bowling (Canberra); Royal Automobile (Victoria).

REGAN, Charles Maurice; Clerk to the Trustees, Hampstead Wells and Campden Trust, since 1985; Under-Secretary, Department of Health and Social Security, 1972–79 and 1981–85; *b* 31 Oct. 1925; *m* 1961, Susan (*née* Littmann) (*d* 1972); one *s* one *d. Educ:* Taunton Sch.; London Sch. of Economics and Political Science (BSc(Econ)). Academic research, 1950–52. Asst Principal, Min. of National Insurance, 1952; Principal Private Sec. to Minister of Pensions and National Insurance, 1962–64; Asst Sec., 1964; Treasury/Civil Service Dept, 1967–70; Under-Sec., DES, 1979–81. *Recreations:* walking, travel. *Address:* 35 Crediton Hill, NW6 1HS. *T:* 071–794 6404.

REGAN, Hon. Donald Thomas; financier, author; President, Regdon Associates, since 1987; Chief of Staff to the President of the United States, 1985–87; *b* 21 Dec. 1918; *s* of late William F. Regan and Kathleen A. Regan; *m* 1942, Ann Gordon Buchanan; two *s* two *d. Educ:* Cambridge Latin Sch.; Harvard Univ. (BA). Served War, US Marine Corps, 1940–46; retd as Lt Col, Marine Corps Reserve. Merrill Lynch, Pierce, Fenner & Smith Inc., 1946–81: Vice Pres., 1959–64; Exec. Vice Pres., 1964–68; Pres., 1968–71; Chm. of Bd, 1971–80; Chm. of Bd, Merrill Lynch & Co., Inc., 1973–81; Sec. of the Treasury, US Treasury Dept, 1981–85. Hon. LLD: Hahnemann Med. Coll. and Hosp., 1968; Tri-State Coll., 1969; Univ. of Penn., 1972; Hon. Dr of Commercial Science, Pace Univ., 1973; Hon DHL Colgate Univ., 1984. Fortune magazine's Hall of Fame for business leadership, 1981. Legion of Honour, 1982. *Publications:* A View from the Street, 1972; For the Record: from Wall Street to Washington, 1988. *Recreations:* golf, reading, boating. *Address:* 11 Canal Center Plaza, Suite 301, Alexandria, Va 22314, USA. *Clubs:* Metropolitan, Army-Navy (Washington, DC); Burning Tree (Bethesda, Md).

REGAN, Hon. Gerald Augustine, PC (Can.) 1980; QC (Can.) 1970; President, Hawthorne Developments, since 1984; lawyer; *b* Windsor, NS, 13 Feb. 1929; *s* of Walter E. Regan and Rose M. Greene; *m* 1956, A. Carole, *d* of John H. Harrison; three *s* three *d. Educ:* Windsor Academy; St Mary's and Dalhousie Univs, Canada; Dalhousie Law Sch. (LLB). Called to Bar of Nova Scotia, 1954. Liberal candidate in Provincial gen. elecs, 1956 and 1960, and in Fed. gen. elec., 1962. MP for Halifax, NS, House of Commons of Canada, 1963–65; Leader, Liberal Party of Nova Scotia, 1965–80; MLA for Halifax-Needham, Provincial gen. elec., 1967, re-elected, 1970–74 and 1978; Premier of Nova Scotia, 1970–78, Leader of the Opposition 1978–80; Minister of Labour, Govt of Canada, 1980–81, Minister responsible for Fitness and Amateur Sport 1980–82; Secretary of State for Canada, 1981–82; Minister for International Trade, 1982–84; Minister of Energy, Mines and Resources, June–Sept. 1984. Mem., NS Barristers Soc.; Chm. Exec. Cttee, Commonwealth Parly Assoc., 1973–76; Mem., Canadian Delegn, UN, 1965. Director: United Financial Management; Canadian Surety Co.; Air Atlantic; Urban Transport Develt Corp.; Sceptre Resources; Roman Corp.; Provigo Inc.; Sovereign Life Insce Co. Governor, Olympic Trust of Canada. *Recreations:* tennis, ski-ing. *Address:* PO Box 828 Station B, Ottawa, Ontario K1P 5P9, Canada; (home) 2332 Georgina Drive, Ottawa, K2B 7M4, Canada. *Club:* Halifax (Halifax, NS).

REGINA, Archbishop of, (RC), since 1973; **Most Rev. Charles A. Halpin;** *b* 30 Aug. 1930; *s* of John S. Halpin and Marie Anne Gervais. *Educ:* St Boniface Coll. (BA); St

Boniface Seminary (BTh); Gregorian Univ., Rome (JCL). Priest, 1956; Vice-Chancellor of Archdiocese of Winnipeg and Secretary to Archbishop, 1960; Officialis of Archdiocesan Matrimonial Tribunal, 1962; Chaplain to the Holy Father with title of Monsignor, 1969; ordained Bishop, Nov. 1973; installed as Archbishop of Regina, Dec. 1973. *Address:* 445 Broad Street North, Regina, Saskatchewan S4R 2X8, Canada.

REGO, (Maria) Paula (Figueiroa), (Mrs Victor Willing); artist; *b* 26 Jan. 1935; *d* of José Fernandes Figueiroa Rego and Maria de S José Pavva Figueiroa Rego; *m* 1959, Victor Willing; one *s* two *d*. *Educ:* St Julian's Sch., Carcavelos, Portugal; Slade School of Fine Art, UCL. Attached to Nat. Gall., Jan.–Dec. 1990. Selected solo exhibitions: (1st at) Soc. Nat. de Belas Artes, Lisbon, 1965; Gal. S Mamede, Lisbon, 1971; Gal. Modulo, Porto, 1977; Gal. III, Lisbon, 1978; Air Gall., London, 1981; Edward Totah Gall., 1982, 1985, 1987; Arnolfini, 1983; Art Palace, NY, 1985; Gulbenkian Foundn (retrospective), 1988; Serpentine Gall. (retrospective), 1988; Marlborough Graphics (nursery rhymes), 1989. Many collective shows include: ICA, 1965; S Paulo Biennale, 1969, 1985; British Art Show, 1985; also in Japan, Australia, all over Europe. Sen. Fellow, RCA, 1989–. *Recreations:* going to the movies, plays. *Address:* c/o Marlborough Fine Art, 6 Albemarle Street, W1X 4BY. *T:* 071–629 5161.

REHNQUIST, William H.; Chief Justice of the United States, since 1986; *b* 1 Oct. 1924; *s* of William Benjamin and Margery Peck Rehnquist; *m* 1953, Natalie Cornell; one *s* two *d*. *Educ:* Stanford and Harvard Univs. BA, MA 1948, LLB 1952, Stanford; MA Harvard 1949. Law Clerk for Mr Justice Robert H. Jackson, 1952–53; Partner, Phoenix, Ariz: Evans, Kitchell & Jenckes, 1953–55; Ragan & Rehnquist, 1956–57; Cunningham, Carson & Messenger, 1957–60; Powers & Rehnquist, 1960–69; Asst Attorney-Gen., Office of Legal Counsel, Dept of Justice, 1969–72; Associate Justice, Supreme Court, 1972–86. Phi Beta Kappa; Order of the Coif. *Publications:* contrib. US News and World Report, Jl of Amer. Bar Assoc., Arizona Law Review. *Recreations:* swimming, tennis, reading, hiking. *Address:* Supreme Court of the United States, Washington, DC 20543, USA. *Club:* National Lawyers (Washington, DC).

REIACH, Alan, OBE 1965; RSA 1986; architect; Senior Partner, Reiach and Hall, 1964–75, retired; *b* 2 March 1910; *s* of Herbert L. Reiach and Marie Barbara Fredenson; *m* 1940, Julie Dittmar; *m* 1949, Patricia Anne Duncan; one *s* one *d*. *Educ:* Edinburgh Acad.; Edinburgh Coll. of Art, 1928–35. Lorimer & Matthew, Edinburgh, 1928–33; Sch. of Architecture, Coll. of Art, 1933–35; Travelling Schol., USA and Europe, 1935–36; worked for Robert Atkinson and Partners, London, 1936–38; Andrew Grant Fellow, Edinburgh, 1938–40; Asst Sec., Scottish Housing Adv. Cttee, Dept of Health, Scottish Office, 1940–44; Planning Asst, Clyde Valley Planning Authy, 1944–46; established own practice, 1949, and joined with Eric Hall and Partners, 1964. *Publication:* Building Scotland (with Robert Hurd), 1940, 2nd edn 1944. *Recreation:* watercolour painting. *Address:* 3 Winton Loan, Edinburgh EH10 7AN. *T:* 031–445 1006. *Clubs:* New, Scottish Arts (Edinburgh).

REICH, Peter Gordon; Assistant Chief Scientist (G), Royal Air Force, 1984–85; *b* 16 Sept. 1926; *s* of Douglas Gordon Reich and Josephine Grace Reich; *m* 1948, Kathleen, *d* of Alan and Florence Lessiter, Banstead; three *d*. *Educ:* Sutton Grammar Sch.; London Univ. (BSc). FRIN 1967 (Bronze Medal, 1967). Served RN, 1944–47. Entered Civil Service as Scientific Officer, 1952; Armament Res. Estab., 1952–54; Opl Res. Br., Min. of Transport and Civil Aviation, 1955–60; RAE, 1960–68; Asst Dir of Electronics Res. and Develt (2), Min. of Technol., 1968–70; Asst Dir of Res. (Avionics, Space and Air Traffic), Min. of Aviation Supply, 1971–73; Supt, Def. Opl Analysis Estab., MoD, 1973–76; Mem., Reliability and Costing Study Gp, MoD, 1976–79; Counsellor (Defence Res.), Canberra, and Head of British Defence Res. and Supply Staffs, Australia, 1979–83. *Publications:* papers in Jl of Inst. of Nav., and Jl of Opl Res. Soc. *Recreations:* racquet games, walking, aural pleasures.

REICHSTEIN, Prof. Tadeus, Dr ing chem; Ordentlicher Professor, Head of Department of Organic Chemistry, University of Basel, 1946–60, now Emeritus; *b* Wloclawek, Poland, 20 July 1897; *s* of Isidor Reichstein and Gustava Brockmann; *m* 1927, Henriette Louise Quarles van Ufford; two *d*. *Educ:* Oberrealschule and Eidgenössische Technische Hochschule, Department of Chemistry, Zürich. Assistant, ETH, Zürich, 1922–34; professor of organic chemistry, ETH, Zürich, 1934; head of department of pharmacy, University of Basel, 1938. Dr *hc* Sorbonne, Paris, 1947, Basel 1951, Geneva, 1967, ETH, Zürich, 1967, Abidjan 1967, London 1968, Leeds 1970. Marcel Benoît Prize, 1948; (jointly) Nobel Prize for Medicine, 1950; Cameron Prize, 1951; Copley Medal, Royal Soc., 1968; Dale Medal, Soc. for Endocrinology, 1975. Foreign Member: Royal Society, 1952; Linnean Society, 1974. Hon. Member: British Pteridological Soc., 1967; Amer. Fern Soc., 1974; Deutsche Botanische Gesellschaft, 1976; Schweizerische Botanische Gesellschaft, 1977. *Publications:* numerous papers. *Recreations:* botany (ferns), devoted gardener, mountain-climber. *Address:* Institut für Organische Chemie der Universität, St Johanns-Ring 19, CH 4056 Basel, Switzerland. *T:* (061) 322 6060.

REID, Sir Alexander (James), 3rd Bt *cr* 1897; JP; DL; *b* 6 Dec. 1932; *s* of Sir Edward James Reid, 2nd Bt, KBE, and of Tatiana, *d* of Col Alexander Fenoult, formerly of Russian Imperial Guard; *S* father, 1972; *m* 1955, Michaela Ann, *d* of late Olaf Kier, CBE; one *s* three *d*. *Educ:* Eton; Magdalene Coll., Cambridge. Nat. Certificate Agriculture (NCA). 2nd Lieut, 1st Bn Gordon Highlanders, 1951; served Malaya; Captain, 3rd Bn Gordon Highlanders (TA), retired 1964. Director: Ellon Castle Estates Co. Ltd, 1965–; Cristina Securities Ltd, 1970–; Cytozyme (UK) Ltd, 1985–. Governor, Heath Mount Prep. Sch., Hertford, 1970, Chm., 1976. JP Cambridgeshire and Isle of Ely, 1971, DL 1973; High Sheriff, Cambridgeshire, 1987–88. *Recreation:* shooting. *Heir:* *s* Charles Edward James Reid, *b* 24 June 1956. *Address:* Kingston Wood Manor, Arrington, Royston, Herts SG8 0AP. *T:* Caxton (0954) 719231. *Club:* Caledonian.

REID, Andrew Milton; Deputy Chairman, Imperial Group, 1986–89; *b* 21 July 1929; *s* of late Rev. A. R. R. Reid, DD and of Lilias Symington Tindal; *m* 1953, Norma Mackenzie Davidson; two *s*. *Educ:* Glasgow Academy; Jesus Coll., Oxford. Imperial Tobacco Management Pupil, 1952; Asst Managing Director, John Player & Sons, 1975; Director Imperial Group Ltd, 1978; Chm., Imperial Tobacco Ltd, 1979–86. Director: Trade Indemnity plc, 1982–; Renold PLC, 1983–. Member, Tobacco Adv. Council, 1977–86. Member: Bath and Wells Diocesan Synod, 1986–; Council, RSCM, 1987–89; Court and Council, Bristol Univ., 1986–; Board, Bristol Develt Corp., 1989–. Chm. Governors, Colston's Sch., 1986–. High Sheriff of Avon, 1991. *Recreations:* sailing, golf, fishing. *Address:* Parsonage Farm, Publow, Pensford, near Bristol BS18 4JD. *Clubs:* United Oxford & Cambridge University; Clifton (Bristol).

REID, Archibald Cameron, CMG 1963; CVO 1970; retired 1971; *b* 7 Aug. 1915; *s* of William Reid; *m* 1941, Joan Raymond Charlton; two *s* two *d*. *Educ:* Fettes; Queens' College, Cambridge. Apptd Admin. Officer, Class II, in Colony of Fiji, 1938; Admin. Officer, Class I, 1954; British Agent and Consul, Tonga, 1957–59; Sec. for Fijian Affairs, 1959–65; British Comr and Consul, Tonga, 1965–70; Dep. High Comr, Tonga, 1970–71. Engaged in Pacific History research. *Publications:* Tovata I and II. *Recreations:* walking, painting. *Address:* 37 Kevin Avenue, Avalon Beach, NSW 2107, Australia. *T:* 918 9759.

REID, Beryl, OBE 1986; actress; *b* 17 June 1920. *Educ:* Lady Barne House Sch.; Withington High Sch.; Levenshulme High Sch., Manchester. First stage appearance, Bridlington, 1936; on London stage, 1951; appeared in variety, numerous sketches, revues and pantomimes, 1951–64. *Plays:* The Killing of Sister George, Duke of York's, 1965, NY, 1966 (Tony Award for Best Actress); Blithe Spirit, Globe, 1970; Entertaining Mr Sloane, Royal Court, Duke of York's, 1975; National Theatre: Spring Awakening, Romeo and Juliet, 1974; Il Campiello, Counting the Ways, 1976; The Way of the World, RSC, Aldwych, 1978; Born in the Gardens, Bristol Old Vic, 1979, Globe (SWET Award), 1980; The School for Scandal, Haymarket, and Duke of York's, 1983; A Little Bit on the Side, Yvonne Arnaud, Guildford, 1983; Gigi, Lyric, 1985. *Films include:* The Belles of St Trinians, Star, The Killing of Sister George, Entertaining Mr Sloane, No Sex Please—We're British!, Joseph Andrews, Carry On Emmanuelle, Yellowbeard, The Doctor and the Devils, Comic Strip: Didn't You Kill My Brother? Frequent television and radio performances, including This is Your Life, and her own series on several occasions; Best TV actress award, BAFTA, 1983 (for Smiley's People). *Publications:* So Much Love (autobiog.), 1984; (with Eric Braun) The Cats Whiskers, 1986; (with Eric Braun) Beryl, Food and Friends, 1987; The Kingfisher Jump, 1991. *Recreations:* gardening, cooking. *Address:* Robert Luff, 294 Earls Court Road, SW5. *T:* 071–373 7003; James Sharkey Associates, 3rd Floor, 15 Golden Square, W1.

REID, Dougal Gordon, CMG 1983; HM Diplomatic Service, retired; Director of Studies, Royal Institute of Public Administration International Services, since 1985; *b* Hong Kong, 31 Dec. 1925; *e s* of late Douglas Reid and Catherine Jean (*née* Lowson), Forfar; *m* 1950, Georgina Elizabeth Johnston; one *s* (and one *s* decd). *Educ:* Sedbergh Sch.; Trinity Hall, Cambridge; LSE. Served in Royal Marines, 1944–46. Cadet, Colonial Admin. Service (later HMOCS), Sierra Leone, 1949; District Comr 1956; retd as Perm. Sec., Min. of Natural Resources, 1962. Arthur Guinness Son & Co. Ltd, 1962–63. Entered CRO, later FCO, 1963; served in: Accra, 1964–65; CO, 1966; Accra, 1966–68 (concurrently Lomé, 1967–68); Seoul, 1968–71; FCO, 1971–74; Kinshasa (and concurrently at Brazzaville, Bujumbura and Kigali), 1974–77; New Delhi, 1977–78; Singapore, 1979–80; Ambassador to Liberia, 1980–85. Mem., Internat. Cttee, Leonard Cheshire Foundn, 1985–. *Recreations:* golf, jazz, watching sport. *Clubs:* Travellers', Commonwealth Trust, MCC; London Scottish Football; Sadan Pubin (Seoul).

REID, Very Rev. Douglas William John; Dean of Glasgow and Galloway, since 1987; Rector of St Ninian's Episcopal Church, Glasgow, since 1973; *b* 15 Feb. 1934; *s* of Thomas Wood Reid and Catherine Henrietta Reid (*née* Ramsay); *m* 1964, Janet Cicely Nash; two *s*. *Educ:* Trinity Academy, Edinburgh; Episcopal Theological Coll., Edinburgh. Solicitor's clerk, Edinburgh, 1950–53; Army, 1953–55; industrial banking, 1956–60; theol coll., 1960–63; Asst Curate, Holy Trinity, Ayr, 1963–68; Rector, St James, Glasgow, 1968–73. *Recreations:* gardening, hill-walking, steam railways, reading. *Address:* St Ninian's Rectory, 32 Glencairn Drive, Glasgow G41 4PW. *T:* 041–423 1247.

REID, George Newlands; Director (International Promotion), International Red Cross and Red Crescent Movement, since 1990; *b* 4 June 1939; *s* of late George Reid, company director, and of Margaret Forsyth; *m* 1968, Daphne Ann MacColl; two *d*. *Educ:* Tullibody Sch.; Dollar Academy; Univ. of St Andrews (MA Hons). Pres., Students' Representative Council. Features Writer, Scottish Daily Express, 1962; Reporter, Scottish Television, 1964; Producer, Granada Television, 1965; Head of News and Current Affairs (Scottish Television), 1968; freelance broadcaster and journalist, 1972–84; presenter, political and documentary progs, BBC. Head of Inf., 1984–86, Dir of Public Affairs, 1986–90, League of Red Cross and Red Crescent Socs, Geneva. MP (SNP) Stirlingshire E and Clackmannan, Feb. 1974–1979; Member, Select Committee on: Assistance to Private Members, 1975–76; Direct Elections to European Assembly, 1976–77; Mem., British Parly Delegn to Council of Europe and WEU, 1977–79. Dir, Scottish Council Res. Inst., 1974–77. Chief Red Cross deleg. to Armenia, Dec. 1988–Jan. 1989 (awarded Pirogov Gold Medal of Soviet Red Cross). *Address:* 23 Avenue du Bouchet, 1209 Petit Saconnex, Geneva, Switzerland. *T:* 734–6705.

REID, Hon. Sir George Oswald, Kt 1972; QC (Vic) 1971; Attorney-General, Victoria, Australia, 1967–73; Barrister and Solicitor; *b* Hawthorn, Vic, 22 July 1903; *s* of late George Watson Reid and Lillias Margaret Reid (*née* Easton); *m* 1st, 1930, Beatrix Waring McCay, LLM (*d* 1972), *d* of Lt-Gen. Hon. Sir James McCay; one *d*; 2nd, 1973, Dorothy, *d* of late C. W. F. Ruttledge. *Educ:* Camberwell Grammar Sch. and Scotch Coll., Melbourne; Melbourne Univ. (LLB). Admitted to practice as Barrister and Solicitor, Supreme Ct of Vic., 1926. Has practised as Solicitor in Melbourne, 1929–. Served War, RAAF, 1940–46, Wing Comdr. MLA (Liberal) for Box Hill, 1947–52, and 1955–73. Government of Victoria: Minister without Portfolio, 1955–56; Minister of Labour and Industry and Electrical Undertakings, 1956–65; Minister: for Fuel and Power, 1965–67; of Immigration, 1967–70; Chief Secretary, March 9–Apr. 27, 1971. *Recreations:* golf, reading. *Address:* Southern Cross Homes, Broadford Crescent, Macleod, Vic 3085, Australia. *Clubs:* Melbourne, Savage, Melbourne Cricket (Melbourne).

REID, Graham Livingstone, CB 1991; Deputy Secretary, Industrial Relations and International Directorate, Department of Employment, since 1990; *b* 30 June 1937; *s* of late William L. Reid and of Louise M. Reid; *m* 1st, 1973, Eileen M. Loudfoot (marr. diss. 1983); 2nd, 1985, Sheila Rothwell. *Educ:* Univ. of St Andrews (MA); Queen's Univ., Kingston, Canada (MA). Dept of Social and Economic Res., Univ. of Glasgow: Asst Lectr in Applied Economics, 1960, Lectr 1963, Sen. Lectr 1968, Reader 1971; Sen. Econ. Adviser and Head of Econs and Statistics Unit, Scottish Office, 1973–75; Dir, Manpower Intelligence and Planning Div., MSC, 1975–84; Department of Employment: Chief Economic Adviser and Hd, Economic and Social Div., 1984–88 and Dir, Enterprise and Deregulation Unit, 1987; Dep. Sec., Manpower Policy, 1988–90, Resources and Strategy, 1990. Vis. Associate Prof., Mich State Univ., 1967; Vis. Res. Fellow, Queen's Univ., Canada, 1969. *Publications:* Fringe Benefits, Labour Costs and Social Security (ed with D. J. Robertson), 1965; (with K. J. Allen) Nationalised Industries, 1970 (3rd edn 1975); (with L. C. Hunter and D. Boddy) Labour Problems of Technological Change, 1970; (with K. J. Allen and D. J. Harris) The Nationalised Fuel Industries, 1973; contrib. to Econ. Jl, Brit. Jl of Indust. Relations, Scot. Jl of Polit. Econ., Indust & Lab. Relns Rev. *Recreations:* golf, music. *Address:* Department of Employment, Caxton House, Tothill Street, SW1H 9NF. *Club:* Commonwealth Trust.

REID, Sir (Harold) Martin (Smith), KBE 1987; CMG 1978; HM Diplomatic Service, retired; Hon. Secretary, Friends of the Student Christian Movement, since 1989; *b* 27 Aug. 1928; *s* of late Marcus Reid and late Winifred Mary Reid (*née* Stephens); *m* 1956, Jane Elizabeth Harwood; one *s* three *d*. *Educ:* Merchant Taylors' Sch.; Brasenose Coll., Oxford (Open Scholar). RN, 1947–49. Entered HM Foreign Service, 1953; served in: FO, 1953–54; Paris, 1954–57; Rangoon, 1958–61; FO, 1961–65; Georgetown, 1965–68; Bucharest, 1968–70; Dep. High Comr, Malawi, 1970–73; Private Sec. to successive Secs of State for NI, 1973–74; Head of Central and Southern Africa Dept, FCO, 1974–78; Minister, British Embassy, Pretoria/Cape Town, 1979–82; Resident Chm. (Dip. Service) CS Selection Bd, 1983–84; High Comr to Jamaica, and Ambassador (non-resident) to Haiti, 1984–87; Research Advr, FCO, 1987–88. One-man exhibitions: London, 1983;

Kingston, Jamaica, 1987; Dulwich, 1989, 1991. *Recreation:* painting. *Address:* 43 Carson Road, SE21 8HT. *T:* 081–670 6151.
See also M. H. M. Reid.

REID, Sir Hugh, 3rd Bt *cr* 1922; farmer; *b* 27 Nov. 1933; *s* of Sir Douglas Neilson Reid, 2nd Bt, and of Margaret Brighton Young, *d* of Robert Young Maxtone, MBE, JP; *S* father, 1971. *Educ:* Loretto. Royal Air Force, 1952–56; RAFVR, 1956–78 (Flying Officer, Training Branch, 1965–78). *Recreations:* skiing, travel. *Heir:* none. *Address:* Caheronaun Park, Loughrea, Co. Galway.

REID, Iain; Director, Arts Co-ordination, Arts Council, since 1989; *b* 27 March 1942; *s* of Jean Reid (*née* Money) and George Aitken Reid; *m* 1st, 1968, Judith Coke; 2nd, 1982, Kay Barlow; one *s* one *d*. *Educ:* Uppingham; RADA; Lancaster Univ. (MA). Actor, 1963–73; theatre administrator, 1973–77; Drama Officer, Greater London Arts, 1977–82; Dir of Arts, Calouste Gulbenkian Foundn (UK), 1982–89. *Recreations:* skating, sailing. *Address:* Arts Council, 14 Great Peter Street, SW1P 3NQ.

REID, Ian George; Director, Centre for European Agricultural Studies, Wye College, University of London, 1974–86; *b* 12 May 1921; 2nd *s* of James John Reid and Margaret Jane Reid; *m* 1946, Peggy Eileen Bridgman. *Educ:* Merchant Taylors' Sch.; London Sch. of Econs (BScEcon); Christ's Coll., Cambridge (Dip. Agric.). Lectr, Reading Univ., 1945–53; Lectr, 1953–63, and Sen. Lectr, 1963–86, Wye Coll. Pres., Agricultural Econs Soc., 1981–82. *Recreations:* enjoying music, gardening, art. *Address:* 20 Bridge Street, Wye, Ashford, Kent TN25 5EA. *T:* Wye (Kent) (0233) 812388. *Club:* Farmers'.

REID, Col Ivo; *see* Reid, Col P. F. I.

REID, James, OBE (mil.) 1968; VRD 1967; Director, Investments and Loans, Commission of European Communities, 1973–76; *b* 23 Nov. 1921; *s* of William Reid, MBE, and Dora Louisa Reid (*née* Smith); *m* 1949, Margaret James (*d* 1987); two *d*. *Educ:* City of London Sch.; Emmanuel Coll., Cambridge (MA). Served War, RN: RNVR (Sub. Lieut), 1942–45. Served RNVR and RNR (Comdr), 1953–72. Entered Northern Ireland Civil Service, 1948 (Asst Principal); Min. of Finance, 1948–61 and 1963–73; Min. of Commerce, 1961–63; Principal, 1953; Asst Sec., 1963; Sen. Asst Sec., 1971; Dep. Sec., 1972. *Recreations:* reading, music. *Address:* 4 Old School Court, King's Lynn, Norfolk PE30 1ET. *Club:* United Oxford & Cambridge University.

REID, James Robert; QC 1980; a Recorder, since 1985; *b* 23 Jan. 1943; *s* of late Judge J. A. Reid, MC and of Jean Ethel Reid; *m* 1974, Anne Prudence Wakefield; two *s* one *d*. *Educ:* Marlborough Coll.; New Coll., Oxford (MA). Called to the Bar, Lincoln's Inn, 1965, Bencher, 1988. Mem., Senate of Inns of Court and the Bar, 1977–80; Mem., Gen. Council of the Bar, 1990–. Hon. Jt Treas., Barristers Benevolent Assoc., 1986–. *Recreations:* fencing, cricket. *Address:* 9 Old Square, Lincoln's Inn, WC2.

REID, Dr John; MP (Lab) Motherwell North, since 1987; *b* 8 May 1947; *s* of late Thomas Reid and of Mary Reid; *m* 1969, Catherine (*née* McGowan); two *s*. *Educ:* St Patrick's Senior Secondary Sch., Coatbridge; Stirling Univ. (BA History, PhD Economic History). Scottish Research Officer, Labour Party, 1979–83; Political Adviser to Rt Hon. Neil Kinnock, 1983–85; Scottish Organiser, Trades Unionists for Labour, 1985–87. Opposition spokesman on children, 1989–90, on defence, 1990–. Mem., Public Accounts Cttee, 1988–89. *Recreations:* football, reading, crossword puzzles. *Address:* House of Commons, SW1A 0AA; (office) 114 Manse Road, Newmains, Strathclyde ML1 9BD. *T:* Cambusnethan (0698) 383866, *Fax:* Cambusnethan (0698) 381243.

REID, John Boyd, AO 1980; LLB; FAIM; Chairman, James Hardie Industries Ltd, since 1973; *b* 27 Dec. 1929; *s* of Sir John Thyne Reid, CMG. *Educ:* Scotch College; Melbourne Univ. Chm., Comsteel Vickers Ltd, 1983–86; Vice-Chm., Qantas Airways, 1981–86 (Dir, 1977–86); Director: Broken Hill Pty Co., 1972–; Barclays Internat. Australia, 1982–85; Bell Resources Ltd, 1987–88; Peregrine Capital Australia Ltd, 1991. Chm., Australian Bicentennial Authy, 1979–85; Dir, World Expo 88, 1986–89; Member: Admin. Review Cttee, 1975–76; Indep. Inquiry into Commonwealth Serum Labs, 1978; Australian Japan Business Co-operation Cttee, 1978–; Patron, Australia Indonesia Business Co-operation Cttee, 1979–88 (Pres., 1973–79); Mem., Internat. Adv. Bd, Swiss Banking Corp., 1986–; Chm., Review of Commonwealth Admin, 1981–82. Trustee and Internat. Counsellor, Conference Bd USA; Internat. Council, Stanford Res. Inst., USA. Chairman: NSW Educn and Trng Foundn, 1989–; Cttee, Aust. Scout Educn and Trng Foundn, 1991. Chm. Council, Pymble Ladies Coll., 1975–82 (Mem., 1965–75); Governor, Ian Clunies Ross Meml Foundn, 1975–; Member: Sydney Adv. Cttee, Salvation Army, 1985–; Nat. Council, Aust. Opera; Inst. of Company Dirs. Life Governor, AIM (Sydney Div.). Melbourne Univ. Graduate Sch. of Business Admin Award, 1983; John Storey Medal, AIM, 1985. *Address:* c/o James Hardie Industries Ltd, GPO Box 3935, Sydney, NSW 2001, Australia. *Clubs:* Australian (Sydney); Royal Sydney Yacht Squadron.

REID, Sir John (James Andrew), KCMG 1985; CB 1975; TD 1958; MD, FRCP, FRCPE; Consultant Adviser on International Health, Department of Health (formerly of Health and Social Security), 1986–91; Hon. Consultant in Community Medicine to the Army, 1971–90; Chairman, Review Board for Overseas Qualified Practitioners, since 1990 (Deputy Chairman, 1986–90); *b* 21 Jan. 1925; *s* of Alexander Scott Reid and Mary Cullen Reid (*née* Andrew); *m* 1949, Marjorie Reid (*née* Crumpton), MB, ChB (*d* 1990); one *s* four *d*. *Educ:* Bell-Baxter Sch.; Univ. of St Andrews. BSc 1944; MB, ChB 1947; DPH 1952; MD 1961; Hon. DSc 1979; FRCP (Edin.) 1970; FRCP 1971; FFCM 1972; FRCP (Glas) 1980. Lt-Col RAMC (TA). Hospital, Army (Nat. Service) and junior Public Health posts, 1947–55; Lectr in Public Health and Social Medicine, Univ. of St Andrews, 1955–59; Dep. County MOH, Northamptonshire, 1959–62; County MOH, Northamptonshire, 1962–67; County MOH, Buckinghamshire, 1967–72; Dep. Chief MO, DHSS, 1972–77, Chief MO, SHHD, 1977–85. Member: GMC (Crown Nominee), 1973–81, 1985; Council for Post-grad. Med. Educn, 1973–77; Scottish Council for Post-grad. Med. Educn, 1977–85; Scottish Health Service Planning Council, 1977–85; Exec. Bd, WHO, 1973–75, 1976–79, 1980–83, 1984–87 (Vice Chm., 1977–78; Chm., 1978–79; consultant); MRC, 1977–85; EC Adv. Cttee on Med. Training, 1976–85. WHO Fellow, 1962; Mem., Standing Med. Adv. Cttee, DHSS, 1966–72; Chm., Jt Sub-Cttee on Health and Welfare Services for People with Epilepsy (Report, People with Epilepsy, 1969); Chm., Jt Working Party for Health Services in Milton Keynes, 1968–74; Dep. Co-Chm., UK/USSR Cttee on Health Care, 1975–77; Jt Chm., Scottish/Finnish Health Agreement, 1978–85; Mem., Working Party on Medical Administrators (Report, 1972); Public Health Lab. Service Bd, 1974–77; Hospital Management Committees: St Crispins, 1959–69; Northampton, 1962–67; St Johns, 1967–72. Vis. Prof. in Health Services Admin, London Sch. of Hygiene and Tropical Medicine, 1973–78 (Governor and Mem., 1977–, Chm., 1989–, Bd of Management); Vis. Lectr and Examr, univs in UK and abroad; Vice-Pres., Liverpool Sch. of Tropical Medicine, 1987–; Governor, United Oxford Hosps, 1962–66. Hon. LLD Dundee, 1985. Léon Bernard Foundn Prize, 1987. *Publications:* papers on public and international health, community medicine, diabetes, epilepsy, etc, in BMJ, Lancet, etc. *Address:* The Manor House, Manor Road, Oving, Aylesbury, Bucks HP22 4HW.

REID, Rev. Prof. John Kelman Sutherland, CBE 1970; TD 1961; Professor of Christian Dogmatics, 1961–70, of Systematic Theology 1970–76, University of Aberdeen; *b* 31 March 1910; *y s* of late Reverend Dr David Reid, Calcutta and Leith, and of late Mrs G. T. Reid (*née* Stuart); *m* 1950, Margaret Winifrid Brookes (*d* 1989). *Educ:* George Watson's Boys' College, Edinburgh; Universities of Edinburgh (MA and BD), Heidelberg, Marburg, Basel, and Strasbourg. MA 1st Cl. Hons Philosophy, 1933. Prof. of Philosophy in Scottish Church Coll., Univ. of Calcutta, 1935–37; BD (dist. in Theol.), 1938, and Cunningham Fellow. Ordained into Church of Scotland and inducted into Parish of Craigmillar Park, Edinburgh, 1939. CF, chiefly with Parachute Regt, 1942–46. Jt Ed. Scot. Jl Theol. since inception, 1947; Hon. Sec. Jt Cttee on New Translation of the Bible, 1949–82; Prof. of Theology and Head of Department of Theology, University of Leeds, 1952–61. Hon. DD (Edinburgh), 1957. *Publications:* The Authority of Scripture, 1957; Our Life in Christ, 1963; Christian Apologetics, 1969. Translation of: Oscar Cullmann's The Earliest Christian Confessions, 1949; Baptism in the New Testament, 1952; Calvin's Theological Treatises, ed and trans. 1954; Jean Bosc's The Kingly Office of the Lord Jesus Christ, 1959; Calvin's Concerning the Eternal Pre-destination of God, ed and trans., 1961, repr. 1982. *Address:* 8 Abbotsford Court, 18 Colinton Road, Edinburgh EH10 5EH. *Club:* Mortonhall Golf (Edinburgh).

REID, Prof. John Low, DM; Regius Professor of Medicine and Therapeutics, University of Glasgow, since 1989; *b* 1 Oct. 1943; *s* of Dr James Reid and Irene M. Dale; *m* 1964, Randa Pharaon; one *s* one *d*. *Educ:* Fettes Coll., Edinburgh; Magdalen Coll., Oxford. MA; DM; FRCP, FRCPGlas. House Officer, Radcliffe Infirmary, Oxford, and Brompton Hosp., 1967–70; Res. Fellow, RPMS, 1970–73; Vis. Fellow, Nat. Inst. of Mental Health, USA, 1973–74; Royal Postgraduate Medical School: Sen. Lectr in Clin. Pharmacol., and Consultant Physician, 1975–77; Reader in Clin. Pharmacol., 1977–78; Regius Prof. of Materia Medica, Univ. of Glasgow, 1978–89. *Publications:* Central Action of Drugs in Regulation of Blood Pressure, 1975; Lecture Notes in Clinical Pharmacology, 1982; Handbook of Hypertension, 1983; papers on cardiovascular and neurological diseases in clinical and pharmacological journals. *Recreations:* books, gardening, the outdoors. *Address:* Department of Medicine, Western Infirmary, Glasgow G11 6NT. *T:* 041–339 8822.

REID, Rt. Rev. John Robert; Bishop of South Sydney since 1983 (Assistant Bishop, Diocese of Sydney, since 1972); *b* 15 July 1928; *s* of John and Edna Reid; *m* 1955, Alison Gertrude Dunn; two *s* four *d*. *Educ:* Melbourne Univ. (BA); Moore Coll., Sydney (ThL). Deacon 1955, Priest 1955; Curate, Manly, 1955–56; Rector, Christ Church, Gladesville, NSW, 1956–69; Archdeacon of Cumberland, NSW, 1969–72. *Recreation:* walking. *Address:* 33 Fairfax Road, Bellevue Hill, NSW 2023, Australia. *T:* 327–3320.

REID, John (Robson); DL; architect and consultant designer; Partner, John and Sylvia Reid, since 1951; Pageantmaster to the Lord Mayors of London, since 1972; *b* 1 Dec. 1925; *m* 1948, Sylvia Reid (*née* Payne), Dip. Arch., RIBA, FCSD; one *s* twin *d*. *Educ:* Wellingborough Grammar Sch.; Sch. of Architecture, The Polytechnic, WI (Dip. in Architecture with dist.). RIBA, PPCSD, FCIBS. Capt., Green Howards, 1944–47; Mem. HAC, 1980. *Architectural work includes:* hotels, showrooms, museums, houses and pubs: Civic Suite, Wandsworth Town Hall; Savile Room, Merton Coll., Oxford; Great Room, Grosvenor House; Dunhill Res. Lab., Inst. of Dermatology; Westminster Theatre; Lawson House, ICI, Runcorn; Heatherside Shopping Centre; Savoy Grill; Exec. Suite, British Telecoms HQ; Barbican Exhibition Halls, Corporation of City of London; Sherlock Holmes Mus., Meiringen, Switzerland; *industrial design work includes:* furniture, lighting fittings, road and rail transport, carpets, textiles, civic regalia; lighting consultant for Coventry Cathedral; some-time design consultant to Thorn, Rotaflex, Stag, CMC, BR, N General Transport, PO; UNIDO consultant on industrial design in India, Pakistan, Egypt and Turkey, 1977–79; British Council tour, India, 1985. *Exhibitions:* 350th Anniversary Celebration, Jamestown, Virginia, USA, 1957; various exhibns for BR, Cardiff Corp., City of London, etc. Leader, British delegn of design educn in Soviet Union, Anglo-Soviet Cultural Exchange Treaty, 1967. Dean of Art and Design, Middx Polytechnic, 1975–78; some-time mem. of adv. cttees, Central Sch. of Art and Design, Leeds Coll. of Art and Design, Newcastle-upon-Tyne Sch. of Art and Design, Carleton Univ., Ottawa; Governor, Hornsey Coll. of Art; Trustee, Geffrye Mus., 1990. Lectured in Canada, Czechoslovakia, Eire, Hungary, Japan, Poland, USA, USSR. PSIAD, 1965–66; Pres., Internat. Council of Socs of Ind. Design, 1969–71; Vice-Pres., Illuminating Engrg Soc., 1969–71. RIBA Mem., Bd of Nat. Inspection Council for Electrical Installation Contracting (Chm., 1972–73). Master, Worshipful Co. of Furniture Makers, 1989–90; Inaugural Master, Worshipful Co. of Chartered Architects, 1988–89. DL Gtr London, 1991. Four CoID Awards; Silver Medals of 12th and 13th Milan Internat. Triennales. *Publications:* International Code of Professional Conduct, 1969; A Guide to Conditions of Contract for Industrial Design, 1971; Industrial Design in India, Pakistan, Egypt and Turkey, 1978; various articles in professional jls. *Recreations:* music, gardening. *Address:* Arnoside House, The Green, Old Southgate, N14 7EG. *T:* 081–882 1083.

REID, Leslie, CBE 1978; HM Diplomatic Service, retired; Director General, The Association of British Mining Equipment Companies, 1980–83; *b* 24 May 1919; *s* of late Frederick Sharples and Mary Reid; *m* 1942, Norah Moorcroft; three *d*. *Educ:* King George V Sch., Southport, Lancs. Served War of 1939–45, W Europe and SEAC, Major, XX The Lancashire Fusiliers. Board of Trade, 1947–49; Asst Trade Commissioner: Salisbury, Rhodesia, 1949–55; Edmonton, Alberta, 1955–56; Trade Comr, Vancouver, 1956–60; Principal, BoT, 1960–62; Trade Comr and Economic Advisor, British High Commn, Cyprus, 1962–64; BoT, 1964–66; 1st Sec., FCO, 1966–68; Sen. Commercial Sec., British High Commn, Jamaica, and 1st Sec., British Embassy, Port-au-Prince, Haiti, 1968–70; Commercial and Economic Counsellor, Ghana, 1970–73; Consul Gen., Cleveland, Ohio, 1973–79. *Recreations:* golf, reading. *Address:* Abbotswood, Guildford, Surrey GU1 1UY.

REID, Prof. Lynne McArthur; S. Burt Wolbach Professor of Pathology, Harvard Medical School, since 1976; Chairman, Department of Pathology, Children's Hospital Medical Center, Boston, since 1976; *b* Melbourne, 12 Nov. 1923; *er d* of Robert Muir Reid and Violet Annie Reid (*née* McArthur). *Educ:* Wimbledon Girls' Sch. (GPDST); Janet Clarke Hall, Trinity Coll., Melbourne Univ.; Royal Melbourne Hosp. MB, BS Melb. 1946; MRACP 1950; MRCP 1951; FRACP, MRCPath (Foundn Mem.) 1964; FRCPath 1966; FRCP 1969; MD Melb. 1969. House Staff, Royal Melb. Hosp., 1946–49; Res. Fellow, Nat. Health and MRC, Royal Melb. Hosp. and Eliza Hall, 1949–51; Res. Asst, Inst. Diseases of Chest, 1951–55; Sen. Lectr founding Res. Dept of Path., Inst. Diseases of Chest, 1955; Reader in Exper. Path., London Univ., 1964; Prof. of Exper. Path., Inst. of Diseases of Chest (later Cardiothoracic Inst.), 1967–76; Hon. Lectr, UC Med. Sch., 1971–76; Hon. Consultant in Exper. Path., Brompton Hosp., 1963–76; Dean, Cardiothoracic Inst. (British Postgrad. Med. Fedn), 1973–76. 1st Hastings Vis. Prof. in Path., Univ. of California, 1965; Holme Lectr, UC Med. Sch., 1969; Walker-Ames Prof., Univ. of Washington, 1971; Neuhauser Lectr, 1976; Fleischner Lectr, 1976; Waring Prof., Stanford and Denver, 1977; Amberson Lectr, Amer. Thoracic Soc., 1978. Mem. Fleischner Soc., 1971 (Pres., 1977); 1st Hon. Fellow, Canadian Thoracic Soc., 1973; Chm., Cystic Fibrosis Res. Trust, 1974 (Mem. Med. Adv. Cttee 1964); Royal Soc. Medicine (Sect. Pathology): Vice-Pres. 1974; Standing Liaison Cttee on Sci. Aspects of Smoking and Health, 1971; Commn of European Cttees (Industrial Safety and Medicine), 1972; Mem. Bd of Governors, Nat. Heart and Chest Hosps, 1974; Manager, Royal Instn of Gt Britain, 1973 (Vice-Pres. 1974); Mem. Gov. Body, British Postgrad. Med. Fedn, 1974. *Publications:* The Pathology of Emphysema, 1967; numerous papers in sci. jls. *Recreations:* music, travel, reading. *Address:* 75 Montrose Court, Princes Gate, SW7; Children's Hospital Medical Center, Harvard Medical School, 300 Longwood Avenue, Boston, Mass 02115, USA. *Clubs:* University Women's; Harvard (Boston).

REID, Malcolm Herbert Marcus; Director, Mercury Life Assurance Co. Ltd, since 1989; *b* 2 March 1927; *s* of late Marcus Reid and Winifred Stephens; *m* 1st, 1956, Eleanor (*d* 1974), *d* of late H. G. Evans, MC; four *s*; 2nd, 1975, Daphne, *e d* of Sir John Griffin, *qv*. *Educ:* Merchant Taylors' Sch.; St John's Coll., Oxford. Served in Navy, 1945–48 and in RNVR, 1949–53. Entered Board of Trade, 1951; Private Secretary to Permanent Secretary, 1954–57; Trade Comr in Ottawa, 1957–60; Board of Trade, 1960–63; Private Secretary to successive Prime Ministers, 1963–66; Commercial Counsellor, Madrid, 1967–71; Asst Sec., DTI, 1972–74; Under Sec., Dept of Industry, 1974–78, of Trade, 1978–83, DTI, 1983–84; Registrar, Registry of Life Assurance Commn, 1984–86; Chief Exec., Lautro, 1986–89. Mem., Appeal Cttee, ICAEW, 1990–. *Recreation:* National Hunt racing. *Address:* 7 Church Street, St Ives, Cambs PE17 4DG. *T:* St Ives (0480) 69753. *Club:* United Oxford & Cambridge University.
See also Sir H. M. S. Reid.

REID, Sir Martin; *see* Reid, Sir H. M. S.

REID, Sir Norman (Robert), Kt 1970; DA (Edinburgh); FMA; FIIC; Director, the Tate Gallery, 1964–79; *b* 27 December 1915; *o s* of Edward Daniel Reid and Blanche, *d* of Richard Drouet; *m* 1941, Jean Lindsay Bertram; one *s* one *d*. *Educ:* Wilson's Grammar School; Edinburgh Coll. of Art; Edinburgh Univ. Served War of 1939–46, Major, Argyll and Sutherland Highlanders. Joined staff of Tate Gallery, 1946; Deputy Director, 1954; Keeper, 1959. Fellow, International Institute for Conservation (IIC) (Secretary General, 1963–65; Vice-Chm., 1966); British Rep. Internat. Committee on Museums and Galleries of Modern Art, 1963–79; President, Penwith Society of Arts; Member: Council, Friends of the Tate Gall., 1958–79 (Founder Mem.); Arts Council Art Panel, 1964–74; Inst. of Contemporary Arts Adv. Panel, 1965–; Contemporary Art Soc. Cttee, 1965–72, 1973–77; "Paintings in Hospitals" Adv. Cttee, 1965–69; British Council Fine Arts Cttee, 1965–77 (Chm. 1968–75); Culture Adv. Cttee of UK Nat. Commn for Unesco, 1966–70; Univ. of London, Bd of Studies in History of Art, 1968; Cttee, The Rome Centre, 1969–77 (Pres. 1975–77); Adv. Council, Paul Mellon Centre, 1971–78; Council of Management, Inst. of Contemp. Prints, 1972–78; Council, RCA, 1974–77. Mem. Bd, Burlington Magazine, 1971–75. Trustee, Graham and Kathleen Sutherland Foundn, 1980–85. Hon. LittD East Anglia, 1970. Officer of the Mexican Order of the Aztec Eagle. *Address:* 50 Brabourne Rise, Park Langley, Beckenham, Kent BR3 2SH. *Club:* Arts.

REID, Col (Percy Fergus) Ivo, OBE 1953; DL; *b* 2 Nov. 1911; *er s* of Col Percy Lester Reid, CBE, DL, JP; *m* 1940, Mary Armida, *d* of Col James Douglas Macindoe, MC; two *s* one *d*. *Educ:* Stowe; Pembroke Coll., Oxford. Joined Irish Guards, 1933; Egypt, 1936–38; served in 2nd World War, Guards Armd Div., Europe (Despatches); Staff Coll., 1945; Comdt, Guards Depot, 1950–53; Lt Col 1951; comd Irish Guards and Regt District, 1955–59; Col 1955; retd 1959. Mem., HM Bodyguard of Hon. Corps of Gentlemen at Arms, 1961–81; Harbinger, 1979–81. Northamptonshire: High Sheriff 1967; DL 1969. *Recreations:* hunting, shooting. *Address:* The Glebe House, Marston St Lawrence, Banbury, Oxon OX17 2DA. *T:* Banbury (0295) 710300. *Club:* White's.

REID, Maj.-Gen. Peter Daer, CB 1981; Associate Member, Burdeshaw Associates Ltd (USA), 1982; Defence Consultant, Vickers Defence Systems Ltd; *b* 5 Aug. 1925; *s* of Col S. D. Reid and Dorothy Hungerford (*née* Jackson) *m* 1958, Catherine Fleetwood (*née* Boodle); two *s* two *d*. *Educ:* Cheltenham College; Wadham Coll., Oxford. Commissioned into Coldstream Guards, 1945; transferred Royal Dragoons, 1947; served: Germany, Egypt, Malaya, Gibraltar, Morocco; Staff Coll., 1959; Comdg Officer, The Royal Dragoons, 1965–68; student, Royal College of Defence Studies, 1973; Commander RAC, 3rd Div., 1974–76; Dir, RAC, 1976–78; Chief Exec., Main Battle Tank 80 Proj., 1979–80; Dir, Armoured Warfare Studies, 1981; Defence Advr, GKN, 1983–88; Mil. Advr, Howden Airdynamics, 1982–88. *Recreations:* sailing, ski-ing, fishing, bird watching. *Address:* The Border House, Cholderton, near Salisbury, Wilts. *Clubs:* Army and Navy; Royal Western Yacht; Kandahar Ski.

REID, Philip; *see under* Ingrams, R. R.

REID, Sir Robert (Basil), Kt 1985; CBE 1980; FCIT; Chairman, British Railways Board, 1983–90; Chairman, West Lambeth Health Authority, since 1990; *b* 7 Feb. 1921; *s* of Sir Robert Niel Reid, KCSI, KCIE, ICS and Lady (A. H.) Reid (*née* Disney); *m* 1951, Isobel Jean McLachlan (*d* 1976); one *s* one *d*. *Educ:* Malvern Coll.; Brasenose Coll., Oxford (MA; Hon. Fellow, 1985). Commnd Royal Tank Regt, 1941, Captain 1945. Traffic Apprentice, LNER, 1947; Goods Agent, York, 1958; Asst Dist Goods Manager, Glasgow, 1960, Dist Passenger Man., 1961, Divl Commercial Man., 1963; Planning Man., Scottish Region, 1967; Divl Man., Doncaster, 1968; Dep. Gen. Man., Eastern Region, York, 1972; Gen. Manager, Southern Reg., BR, 1974–76; British Railways Board: Exec. Mem. for Marketing, 1977–80; Chief Exec. (Railways), 1980–83; a Vice-Chm., 1983. Dir, British Transport Hotels Ltd, 1977–83; Chm., Freightliner Co. Ltd, 1978–80. Chm., Nat. Industries Chairmen's Gp, 1987–88; Pres., European Community Rlys Dirs General, 1988–89. President: CIT, 1982–83; Inst. of Administrative Management, 1989–. FCIM; CBIM. CStJ 1985. Freeman, City of London. Master, Carmen's Co., 1990–91. Hon. DBA Buckingham Internat. Management Centre, 1988; Hon. DEng Bristol, 1990. Hon. Col, 275 Railway Sqn, RCT(V), 1989–91. *Recreations:* fishing, shooting. *Address:* St Thomas' Hospital, Lambeth Palace Road, SE1 7EH. *T:* 071–928 9292. *Club:* Naval and Military.

REID, Sir Robert Paul, (Sir Bob), Kt 1990; Chairman, British Railways Board, since 1990; *b* 1 May 1934; *m* 1958, Joan Mary; three *s*. *Educ:* St Andrews Univ. (MA Pol. Econ. and Mod. Hist.). Joined Shell, 1956; Sarawak Oilfields and Brunei, 1956–59; Nigeria 1959–67 (Head of Personnel); Africa and S Asia Regional Orgn, 1967–68; PA and Planning Adviser to Chairman, Shell & BP Services, Kenya, 1968–70; Man. Dir, Nigeria, 1970–74; Man. Dir, Thailand, 1974–78; Vice-Pres., Internat. Aviation and Products Trading, 1978–80; Exec. Dir, Downstream Oil, Shell Co. of Australia, 1980–83; Co-Ordinator for Supply and Marketing, London, 1983; Dir, Shell International Petroleum Co., 1984–90; Chm. and Chief Exec., Shell UK, 1985–90. Chairman: Foundn for Management Educn, 1986–; BIM, 1988–90; Council, London Enterprise Agency, 1990–. Trustee, Science Museum, 1987–. Hon. LLD: St Andrews, 1987; Aberdeen, 1988. *Recreations:* golf, sailing. *Clubs:* MCC; Royal and Ancient Golf; Royal Melbourne (Melbourne); Frilford Heath Golf. *Address:* British Railways Board, Euston House, 24 Eversholt Street, NW1 1DZ. *T:* 071–928 5751.

REID, Seona Elizabeth; Director, Scottish Arts Council, since 1990; *b* 21 Jan. 1950; *d* of George Robert Hall and Isobel Margaret Reid. *Educ:* Park Sch., Glasgow; Strathclyde Univ. (BA Hons Sociology); Liverpool Univ. (DBA). Business Manager, Lincoln Theatre Royal, 1972–73; Press and Publicity Officer, Northern Dance Theatre, 1973–76; Press and PRO, Ballet Rambert, 1976–79; freelance Arts consultant, 1979–80; Dir, Shape, 1980–87; Asst Dir, Strategy and Regl Develt, Greater London Arts, 1987–90. FRSA 1991. *Recreations:* walking, food, arts. *Address:* Scottish Arts Council, 12 Manor Place, Edinburgh EH3 7DD. *T:* 031–226 6051.

REID, Whitelaw; President, Reid Enterprises; *b* 26 July 1913; *s* of late Ogden M. Reid and Mrs Ogden M. Reid; *m* 1st, 1948, Joan Brandon (marr. diss., 1959); two *s*; 2nd, 1959, Elizabeth Ann Brooks; one *s* one *d*. *Educ:* Lincoln Sch., NYC; St Paul's Sch., Concord, New Hampshire; Yale Univ. (BA). New York Herald Tribune: in various departments, 1938–40; foreign correspondent, England, 1940; Assistant to Editor, 1946; Editor, 1947–55; Pres., 1953–55; Chm. of Bd, 1955–58; Director, 1946–65; Dir, 1946–65, Pres., 1946–62, Herald Tribune Fresh Air Fund. Served War of 1939–45, 1st Lieut naval aviator, USNR. Formerly Director: Farfield Foundn; Freedom House; Golden's Bridge Hounds Inc., 1970–83; Dir, Yale Westchester Alumni Assoc. Chm., NY State Cttee on Public Employee Security Procedures, 1956–57. Ambassador to inauguration of President Ponce, Ecuador, 1956. Member: Nat. Commn for Unesco, 1955–60; President's Citizen Advisers on the Mutual Security Program, 1956–57; Yale Alumni Board (Vice-Chm., 1962–64), Yale Univ. Council (Chm., Publications Cttee, 1965–70; Sec., Class of Yale 1936, 1986–91); Council on Foreign Relations; Nat. Inst. of Social Sciences. District Comr, Purchase Pony Club, 1964–70; Pres., New York State Horse Council (formerly Empire State Horsemen's Assoc.), 1975–80. Fellow, Pierson Coll., Yale, 1949–. *Address:* (home and office) Reid Enterprises, Ophir Farm North, 73 West Patent Road, Bedford Hills, NY 10507, USA. *Clubs:* Century, Overseas Press, Silurians, Pilgrims, Amateur Ski (New York); Metropolitan (Washington); Windermere Island (Eleuthera, Bahamas); Bedford Golf and Tennis; St Regis Yacht.

REID, Flight Lt William, VC 1943; agricultural consultant; Agriculture Adviser, The MacRobert Trust, Douneside, Tarland, Aberdeenshire, since 1950; *b* 21 Dec. 1921; *s* of late William Reid, Baillieston, Glasgow; *m* 1952, Violet Gallagher, 11 Dryburgh Gdns, Glasgow, NW1; one *s* one *d*. *Educ:* Coatbridge Secondary Sch.; Glasgow Univ.; West of Scotland Coll. of Agriculture. Student of Metallurgy, Sept. 1940; BSc (Agric.), 1949; Post-Graduate World Travelling Scholarship for 6 months, to study Agric. and Installations in India, Australia, NZ, USA and Canada, 1949–50. Joined RAF 1941; trained in Lancaster, Calif, USA. Won VC during a trip to Düsseldorf, 3 Nov. 1943, when member of 61 Squadron; pilot RAFVR, 617 Squadron (prisoner); demobilised, 1946; recalled to RAF for 3 months, Dec. 1951. Joined RAFVR, commissioned Jan. 1949, 103 Reserve Centre, Perth. Nat. Cattle and Sheep Advr, Spillers Ltd, 1959–81. Freedom of City of London, 1988. *Recreations:* golf, shooting, fishing, etc. *Address:* Cranford, Ferntower Place, Crieff, Perthshire PH7 3DD. *T:* Crieff (0764) 2462. *Club:* Royal Air Force.

REID, William, CBE 1987; FSA; Director, National Army Museum, 1970–87; Consultative Director, The Herald Museum, since 1988; *b* Glasgow, 8 Nov. 1926; *o s* of Colin Colquhoun Reid and Mary Evelyn Bingham; *m* 1958, Nina Frances Brigden. *Educ:* Glasgow and Oxford. Commnd RAF Regt, 1946–48. Joined staff of Armouries, Tower of London, 1956. Organising Sec., 3rd Internat. Congress of Museums of Arms and Military History, London, Glasgow and Edinburgh, 1963; Sec.-Gen., Internat. Assoc. of Museums of Arms and Military History, 1969–81, Pres., 1981–87, Hon. Life Pres., 1987; Member: British Nat. Cttee, ICOM, 1973–88; Council, Chelsea Soc., 1979–85; Founding Council, Army Records Soc., 1983–88. FSA 1965 (Mem. Council, 1975–76); FMA 1974–88, resigned. Trustee: The Tank Museum, 1970–87; RAEC Museum, 1985–; Museum of Richmond, 1987–; Florence Nightingale Museum Trust, 1987–; Royal Hants Regt Mus., 1990–; Mem., Conservative Adv. Cttee on the Arts and Heritage, 1988–. Hon. Life Mem., Friends of the Nat. Army Mus., 1987; Hon. Member: Amer. Soc. of Arms Collectors, 1975; Indian Army Assoc., 1981. Freeman, Scriveners' Co., 1989 (Liveryman, 1990); Freeman, City of London, 1989. *Publications:* (with A. R. Dufty) European Armour in the Tower of London, 1968; The Lore of Arms, 1976 (Military Book Society choice) (also trans. French, German, Danish, Italian and Swedish); contribs to British and foreign jls. *Recreations:* the study of armour and arms, military history, music, bird-watching. *Address:* 66 Ennerdale Road, Richmond, Surrey TW9 2DL. *T:* 081–940 0904. *Club:* Athenæum.

REID, Rev. William Gordon; Chaplain of St Peter and St Sigfrid's Church, Stockholm, since 1989; *b* 28 Jan. 1943; *s* of William Albert Reid and Elizabeth Jean Inglis. *Educ:* Galashiels Academy; Edinburgh Univ. (MA); Keble Coll., Oxford (MA); Cuddesdon College. Deacon 1967, priest 1968; Curate, St Salvador's, Edinburgh, 1967–69; Chaplain and Tutor, Salisbury Theological Coll., 1969–72; Rector, St Michael and All Saints, Edinburgh, 1972–84; Provost of St Andrew's Cathedral, Inverness, 1984–88; Chaplain of St Nicolas, Ankara, 1988–89. Councillor, Lothian Regional Council, 1974–84; Chm., Lothian and Borders Police Bd, 1982–84. *Recreations:* travel and languages, Church and politics. *Address:* Styrmansgatan 1, 114 54 Stockholm, Sweden. *T:* 08663 82 48. *Club:* New (Edinburgh).

REID, William Kennedy, CB 1981; Parliamentary Commissioner for Administration, and Health Service Commissioner for England, Scotland and Wales, since 1990; *b* 15 Feb. 1931; 3rd *s* of late James and Elspet Reid; *m* 1959, Ann, *d* of Rev. Donald Campbell; two *s* one *d*. *Educ:* Robert Gordon's Coll.; George Watson's Coll.; Univ. of Edinburgh; Trinity Coll., Cambridge. MA 1st cl. Classics Edinburgh and Cantab. Ferguson scholar 1952; Craven scholar 1956. Nat. service, 1952–54. Min. of Educn, 1956; Cabinet Office, 1964; Private Sec. to Sec. of Cabinet, 1965–67; Sec., Council for Scientific Policy, 1967–72; Under Sec., 1974–78, Accountant-General, 1976–78, DES; Dep. Sec. (Central Services), Scottish Office, 1978–84; Sec., SHHD, 1984–90. Chm. of Govs, Scottish Police Coll., 1984–90. Mem., Council on Tribunals, 1990–. *Recreation:* hill walking. *Address:* Church House, Great Smith Street, SW1P 3BW; 11 Inverleith Terrace, Edinburgh EH3 5NS. *Club:* New (Edinburgh).

REID, William Macpherson; Sheriff of Tayside, Central and Fife, since 1983; *b* 6 April 1938; *s* of William Andrew Reid and Mabel McLeod; *m* 1971, Vivien Anne Eddy; three *d*. *Educ:* Elgin Academy; Aberdeen Univ.; Edinburgh Univ. MA; LLB. Admitted Advocate, 1963; Sheriff of: Lothian and Borders, 1978; Glasgow and Strathkelvin, 1978–83. *Address:* Sheriffs' Chambers, Sheriff Court House, Carnegie Drive, Dunfermline KY12 7HJ.

REID BANKS, Lynne; *see* Banks.

REIDHAVEN, Viscount, (Master of Seafield); James Andrew Ogilvie-Grant; *b* 30 Nov. 1963; *s* and *heir* of Earl of Seafield, *qv*.

REIGATE, Baron *cr* 1970 (Life Peer), of Outwood, Surrey; **John Kenyon Vaughan-Morgan;** Bt 1960; PC 1961; *b* 2 Feb. 1905; *yr s* of late Sir Kenyon Vaughan-Morgan, DL, OBE, MP and late Lady Vaughan-Morgan; *m* 1940, Emily, *d* of late Mr and Mrs W. Redmond Cross, New York City; two *d*. *Educ:* Eton; Christ Church, Oxford. Mem. Chelsea Borough Council, 1928; Member of London County Council for Chelsea, 1946–52; Chm. East Fulham Conservative and Unionist Assoc., 1935–38 (Pres. 1945);

MP (C) Reigate Div. of Surrey, 1950–70. Parly Sec., Min. of Health, 1957; Minister of State, BoT, 1957–59. Dir, Morgan Crucible Co. Ltd, now retired. Chm. Bd of Govs, Westminster Hosp., 1963–74 (Mem., 1960). Pres., Royal Philanthropic Sch., Redhill. Dep. Chm., South Westminster Justices, now retired. Mem., Court of Assistants, Merchant Taylors Co. (Master 1970). Hon. Freeman, Borough of Reigate, 1971. Served War of 1939–45; Welsh Guards, 1940; GSO2, War Office; GSO1, HQ 21 Army Group (despatches). *Address:* 36 Eaton Square, SW1. *T:* 071–235 6506. *Clubs:* Brooks's, Beefsteak, Hurlingham.

REIGATE, Archdeacon of; *see* Coombs, Ven. P. B.

REIHER, Frederick Bernard Carl, CMG 1982; Director, Harrisons & Crosfield (PNG) Ltd, since 1982; Chairman, Harcos Trading, since 1982; Manager, Protocol and Overseas Service Hospitality (POSH); *b* 7 Feb. 1945; *s* of William and Ruth Reiher; *m* 1974, Helen Perpetua; one *s* two *d. Educ:* Holy Spirit National Seminary; Univ. of Papua New Guinea (BD). Private Sec. to Minister for Finance, PNG, 1973–76. Joined Diplomatic Service, 1976; established Diplomatic Mission for PNG in London, 1977; High Comr for PNG in London, 1978–80; Sec. to Prime Minister of PNG, and accredited Ambassador to FRG, Belgium, EEC, Israel, and Turkey, 1980–82. *Address:* PO Box 7500, Boroko, Papua New Guinea. *Clubs:* Commonwealth Trust, Travellers' (Hon.); Aviat Social & Sporting, South Pacific Motor Sports, PNG Pistol.

REILLY, Sir (D'Arcy) Patrick, GCMG 1968 (KCMG 1957; CMG 1949); OBE 1942; Chairman, Banque Nationale de Paris Ltd (formerly British and French Bank), 1969–80; *b* 17 March 1909; *s* of late Sir D'Arcy Reilly, Indian Civil Service; *m* 1st, 1938, Rachel Mary (*d* 1984), *d* of late Brigadier-General Sir Percy Sykes, KCIE, CB, CMG; two *d*; 2nd, 1987, Ruth, *widow* of Sir Arthur Novrington. *Educ:* Winchester; New Coll., Oxford. (1st class Hon. Mods, 1930, Lit Hum 1932), Hon. Fellow 1972. Laming Travelling Fellow, Queen's College, 1932; Fellow of All Souls College, 1932–39, 1969–; Diplomatic Service, 1933; Third Secretary, Tehran, 1935–38; Ministry of Economic Warfare, 1939–42; First Secretary, Algiers, 1943; Paris, 1944; Athens, 1945. Counsellor, HM Foreign Service, 1947; Counsellor at Athens, 1947–48; Imperial Defence College, 1949; Assistant Under-Secretary of State, Foreign Office, 1950–53; Minister in Paris, 1953–56; Dep. Under-Sec. of State, Foreign Office, Oct. 1956; Ambassador to the USSR, 1957–60; Dep. Under-Sec. of State, Foreign Office, 1960–64; Official Head of UK Delegation to UN Conference on Trade and Development, 1964; Ambassador to France, 1965–68. Pres., 1972–75, Vice-Pres., 1975–, London Chamber of Commerce and Industry. Chairman: London Chamber of Commerce Standing Cttee for Common Market countries, 1969–72; Overseas Policy Cttee, Assoc. of British Chambers of Commerce, 1970–72; London Univ. Management Cttee, British Inst. in Paris, 1970–79; Council, Bedford Coll., London Univ., 1970–75. Hon. DLitt Bath, 1982. Comdr Légion d'Honneur, 1979. *Address:* 75 Warrington Crescent, W9 1EH. *T:* 071–289 5384; 12 Lansdown Crescent, Bath BA1 5EX. *T:* Bath (0225) 311412. *Club:* Athenæum.

REILLY, Lt-Gen. Sir Jeremy (Calcott), KCB 1987; DSO 1973; Commander Training and Arms Directors, 1986–89, retired; *b* 7 April 1934; *s* of late Lt-Col J. F. C. Reilly and of E. N. Reilly (*née* Moreton); *m* 1960, Julia Elizabeth (*née* Forrester); two *d* (and one *d* decd). *Educ:* Uppingham; RMA Sandhurst. Commissioned Royal Warwickshire Regt, 1954; served Egypt, Cyprus (Despatches), Ireland, Hong Kong, Germany, Borneo, BJSM Washington DC; psc 1965; Brigade Major, BAOR, 1967–69; Chief Instructor, RMA, 1969–71; CO 2nd Bn Royal Regt of Fusiliers, 1971–73 (DSO); Instructor, Staff Coll., 1974–75; Col GS (Army Deployment), MoD, 1975–77; PSO to Field Marshal Lord Carver and attached FCO (Rhodesia), 1977–79; Comdr 6 Field Force and UK Mobile Force, 1979–81; Comdr 4th Armoured Div., BAOR, 1981–83; Dir Battle Develt, MoD, 1983–84; ACDS (Concepts), MoD, 1985–86. Dep. Col, RRF (Warwickshire), 1981–86; Col, RRF, 1986–; Col Comdt, The Queen's Div., 1988–90. *Publications:* minor articles in various jls. *Address:* RHQ RRF, HM Tower of London, EC3N 4AB.

REILLY, Sir Patrick; *see* Reilly, Sir D. P.

REIMAN, Dr Donald Henry; Editor, Shelley and his Circle, Carl H. Pforzheimer Collection, New York Public Library, since 1986; *b* 17 May 1934; *s* of Mildred A. (Pearce) Reiman and Henry Ward Reiman; *m* 1st, 1958, Mary A. Warner (marr. diss. 1974); one *d*; 2nd, 1975, Hélène Dworzan. *Educ:* Coll. of Wooster, Ohio (BA 1956; Hon. LittD 1981); Univ. of Illinois (MA 1957; PhD 1960). Instructor, 1960–62, Asst Prof. 1962–64, Duke Univ.; Associate Prof., Univ. of Wisconsin, Milwaukee, 1964–65; Editor, Shelley and his Circle, Carl H. Pforzheimer Liby, 1965–86. James P. R. Lyell Reader in Bibliography, Oxford Univ., 1988–89. Gen. Editor, Manuscripts of the Younger Romantics, 1984–; Editor-in-Chief, Bodleian Shelley MSS, 1984–. *Publications:* Shelley's The Triumph of Life, 1965; Percy Bysshe Shelley, 1969, rev. edn 1990; (ed) The Romantics Reviewed, 9 Vols, 1972; (ed) Shelley and his Circle, vols V–VI, 1973, Vols VII–VIII, 1986; (with D. D. Fischer) Byron on the Continent, 1974; (ed with S. B. Powers) Shelley's Poetry and Prose, 1977; (ed) The Romantic Context: Poetry, 128 vols, 1976–79; (ed jtly) The Evidence of the Imagination, 1978; English Romantic Poetry 1800–1835, 1979; Romantic Texts and Contexts, 1987; Intervals of Inspiration, 1988; contribs to reviews and learned jls. *Address:* Room 226, New York Public Library, Fifth Avenue at 42nd Street, New York, NY 10018, USA. *T:* (212) 764–0655.

REINERS, William Joseph; Director of Research Policy, Departments of the Environment and Transport, 1977–78, retired 1978; *b* 19 May 1923; *s* of late William and Hannah Reiners; *m* 1952, Catharine Anne Palmer; three *s* one *d. Educ:* Liverpool Collegiate Sch.; Liverpool Univ. RAE Farnborough, 1944–46; Min. of Works, 1946–50; Head, Building Operations and Economics Div., Building Research Station, 1950–63; Dir of Research and Information, MPBW, 1963–71; Dir of Research Requirements, DoE, 1971–77. *Publications:* various on building operations and economics. *Address:* Valais, Berks Hill, Chorleywood, Herts. *T:* Chorleywood (09278) 3293.

REINHARDT, Max; Chairman: Reinhardt Books Ltd (formerly HFL (Publishers) Ltd), since 1947; The Nonesuch Press Ltd, since 1986; *b* 30 Nov. 1915; *s* of Ernest Reinhardt and Frieda Reinhardt (*née* Darr); *m* 1st, 1947, Margaret Leighton, CBE (marr. diss. 1955; she *d* 1976); 2nd, 1957, Joan, *d* of Carlisle and Dorothy MacDonald, New York City; two *d. Educ:* English High Sch. for Boys, Istanbul; Ecole des Hautes Etudes Commerciales, Paris; London School of Economics. Acquired HFL (Publishers) Ltd, 1947; founded Max Reinhardt Ltd, 1948, which bought: The Bodley Head Ltd, 1956 (Man. Dir, 1957–81; Chm., 1981–87); Putnam & Co., 1963; Jt Chm., Chatto, Bodley Head and Jonathan Cape Ltd, 1973–87. Mem. Council: Publishers' Assoc., 1963–69; Royal Academy of Dramatic Art, 1965–. *Recreations:* reading for pleasure, swimming, bridge. *Address:* Flat 2, 43 Onslow Square, SW7 3LR. *T:* 071–589 5527. *Clubs:* Beefsteak, Garrick, Savile, Royal Automobile.

REISS, John Henry, OBE 1972; British Ambassador to Liberia, 1973–78, retired; *b* 26 March 1918; *s* of late Rev. Leopold Reiss and Dora Lillian (*née* Twisden-Bedford); *m* 1943, Dora Lily (*née* York); one *s* two *d. Educ:* Bradfield Coll.; St Thomas' Hosp. Served War, Army, 1939–42. Kenya Govt, 1945–59; Dir of Information, 1954–59; Commonwealth Office, 1959; Dir of Information Services: Johannesburg, 1961–63; Wellington, New Zealand, 1963–65. Foreign and Commonwealth Office, 1966–69; Dep. British Govt Representative, Antigua/St Kitts, 1969–73. *Recreations:* bridge, computing. *Address:* 1 Manor Crescent, Tytherington, Macclesfield, Cheshire SK10 2EN.

REISZ, Karel; film director; *b* 21 July 1926; *s* of Joseph Reisz and Frederika; *m* 1963, Betsy Blair; three *s. Educ:* Leighton Park Sch., Reading; Emmanuel Coll., Cambridge (BA). Formerly: co-ed with Lindsay Anderson, film magazine, Sequence; worked for BFI; first Programme Dir, National Film Theatre. Co-directed, with Tony Richardson, Momma Don't Allow, 1956; produced: Every Day Except Christmas, 1957; This Sporting Life, 1960; directed: We Are the Lambeth Boys, 1958; Saturday Night and Sunday Morning, 1959; Night Must Fall, 1963; Morgan, a Suitable Case for Treatment, 1965; Isadora, 1967; The Gambler, 1975; Dog Soldiers, 1978; The French Lieutenant's Woman, 1981; Sweet Dreams, 1986; Everybody Wins, 1991. *Publication:* The Technique of Film Editing (also ed), 1953.

REITH, Barony of (*cr* 1940); title disclaimed by 2nd Baron; *see under* Reith, Christopher John.

REITH, Christopher John; farmer; *b* 27 May 1928; *s* of 1st Baron Reith, KT, PC, GCVO, GBE, CB, TD, of Stonehaven, and Muriel Katharine, *y d* of late John Lynch Odhams; *S* father, 1971, as 2nd Baron Reith, but disclaimed his peerage for life, 1972; *m* 1969, Penelope Margaret Ann, *er d* of late H. R. Morris; one *s* one *d. Educ:* Eton; Worcester College, Oxford (MA Agriculture). Served in Royal Navy, 1946–48; farming thereafter. *Recreations:* fishing, gardening, forestry. *Heir (to disclaimed peerage): s* Hon. James Harry John Reith, *b* 2 June 1971. *Address:* Whitebank Farm, Methven, Perthshire. *T:* Methven (073884) 333.

REITH, Douglas, QC (Scotland) 1957; a Social Security (formerly National Insurance) Commissioner, since 1960; *b* 29 June 1919; *s* of William Reith and Jessie McAllan; *m* 1949, Elizabeth Archer Stewart; one *s* one *d. Educ:* Aberdeen Grammar School; Aberdeen University (MA, LLB). Became Member of Faculty of Advocates in Scotland, 1946. Served in Royal Signals, 1939–46. Standing Junior Counsel in Scotland to Customs and Excise, 1949–51; Advocate-Depute, Crown Office, Scotland, 1953–57; Pres., Pensions Appeal Tribunal (Scotland), 1958–64; Chm., Nat. Health Service Tribunal (Scotland), 1963–65. *Address:* 2 Ravelston Court, Ravelston Dykes, Edinburgh EH12 6HQ. *T:* 031–337 0332. *Club:* New (Edinburgh).

REITH, Martin; HM Diplomatic Service, retired; *b* 6 Dec. 1935; *s* of late James Reith and of Christian (*née* Innes); *m* 1964, Ann Purves; four *s. Educ:* Royal High Sch. of Edinburgh. Served: India (Calcutta), 1957–59; Uganda, 1962–66; Scottish Office, Edinburgh, 1966–68; Australia (Canberra), 1969–72; Asst Head of Central and Southern Africa Dept, FCO, 1974–77; Commercial Sec., Beirut, 1977–78; UN Dept, FCO, 1979; Counsellor, NATO Def. Coll., Rome, 1980; Dep. High Comr, Malta, 1980–83; High Comr, Swaziland, 1983–87; Ambassador, Republic of Cameroon, 1987–91. *Recreations:* hill-walking, bridge, Scottish literature. *Address:* Solway Cottage, Broughton, Peeblesshire ML12 6HQ.

RELLIE, Alastair James Carl Euan, CMG 1987; HM Diplomatic Service; Counsellor, Foreign and Commonwealth Office, since 1979; *b* 5 April 1935; *s* of William and Lucy Rellie; *m* 1961, Annalisa (*née* Modin); one *s* two *d. Educ:* Michaelhouse, SA; Harvard Univ., USA (BA). Rifle Bde, 1958–60. Second Sec., FCO, 1963–64; Vice-Consul, Geneva, 1964–67; First Secretary: FCO, 1967–68; (Commercial), Cairo, 1968–70; Kinshasa, 1970–72; FCO, 1972–74; (and later Counsellor), UK Mission to UN, New York, 1974–79. *Recreations:* travel, talk, newspapers. *Address:* c/o Foreign and Commonwealth Office, King Charles Street, SW1A 2AH. *Clubs:* Brooks's, Greenjackets.

RELLY, Gavin Walter Hamilton; Chairman: Anglo American Corporation of South Africa Ltd, 1983–90 (Deputy Chairman, 1977–82); AECI Ltd, since 1983; *b* 6 Feb. 1926; *s* of Cullis Hamilton Relly and Helen Relly; *m* 1951, Jane Margaret Glenton; one *s* two *d. Educ:* Diocesan Coll., Cape Town; Trinity Coll., Oxford (MA). Joined Anglo American Corp., 1949 (Sec. to H. F. Oppenheimer and then to Sir Ernest Oppenheimer); Manager, Chm.'s Office, 1958; elected to Bd of Corp., 1965; Exec. Dir, 1966; Chm., Exec. Cttee, 1978; Mem. Bd, Anglo American Industrial Corp., 1973–90 (Chm., 1973–83). Dir, Minerals & Resources Corp. Ltd, 1974–. Member: South Africa Foundn, 1975– (Pres., 1981–82); Bd of Governors, Urban Foundn, 1985. Chm., Bd of Trustees, SA Nature Foundn, 1987–; Trustee: Univ. of S Africa Foundn, 1975–; Univ. of the Witwatersrand Foundn, 1984–. *Recreations:* fishing, golf. *Address:* PO Box 61587, Marshalltown, 2107, South Africa. *T:* 638–3234. *Clubs:* Rand, Country (Johannesburg).

RELPH, Michael Leighton George; film producer, director, designer, writer; *s* of late George Relph and Deborah Relph (later Harker); *m* 1st, 1939, Doris Gosden (marr. diss.); one *s*; 2nd, 1950, Maria Barry; one *d. Educ:* Bembridge Sch. Stage designer, 1940–50: West-end prodns include: Indoor Fireworks; The Doctor's Dilemma; Up and Doing; Watch on the Rhine; The Man Who Came to Dinner; Frieda; Saloon Bar; Old Acquaintance; Quiet Week-end; Heartbreak House; Relative Values; A Month in the Country; The Last of Summer; Love in Idleness; The White Carnation; The Petrified Forest; The Banbury Nose; They Came to a City. Began film career as apprentice, then Asst Art Dir, Gaumont British Studios; Art Dir, Warner Brothers Studios; Art Dir, Ealing Studios, 1942–45: prodns include: The Bells Go Down; Dead of Night; Champagne Charley; Nicholas Nickleby; Saraband for Dead Lovers (nominated Hollywood Oscar); Associate Producer to Michael Balcon, 1945; subseq. Producer with Basil Dearden as Dir until Dearden's death, 1972: prodns include: The Captive Heart; Kind Hearts and Coronets; The Blue Lamp (Best British Film Award, Brit. Film Acad.); Frieda; Saraband for Dead Lovers; I Believe in You (co-author); The Ship that Died of Shame; The Rainbow Jacket; The Square Ring; The Gentle Gunman; Cage of Gold; Pool of London. Director: Davy, 1957; Rockets Galore, 1958; Producer: Violent Playground; Sapphire (Best British Film Award, Brit. Film Acad.); All Night Long; The Smallest Show on Earth. Founder Dir, Allied Film Makers: produced: League of Gentlemen; Victim; Man in the Moon (co-author); Life for Ruth; The Mind Benders; Woman of Straw; Masquerade (co-author); The Assassination Bureau (also author and designer); The Man Who Haunted Himself (co-author); in charge of production, Boyd's Company, 1978–82: Scum (exec. producer), 1979; An Unsuitable Job for a Woman (co-producer), 1982; Treasure Houses of Britain (TV; exec. producer), 1985; Heavenly Pursuits, 1986; The Torrents of Spring, 1988 (production consultant). Chm., Film Prodn Assoc. of GB, 1971–76; Mem., Cinematograph Films Council, 1971–76; Governor, BFI, 1972–79 (Chm., Prodn Bd, 1972–79). *Recreations:* reading, theatre going, painting. *Address:* The Lodge, Primrose Hill Studios, Fitzroy Road, NW1 8JP. *T:* 071–586 0249.

See also S. G. M. Relph.

RELPH, Simon George Michael; independent film producer, Skreba and Greenpoint Films; *b* 13 April 1940; *s* of Michael Leighton George Relph, *qv*; *m* 1963, Amanda, *d* of Anthony Grinling, MC; one *s* one *d. Educ:* Bryanston School; King's College, Cambridge (MA Mech. Scis). Asst Dir, Feature Films, 1961–73; Production Administrator, Nat.

Theatre, 1974–78; Chief Exec., British Screen Finance Ltd, 1985–90. *Films* include: Production Executive: Yanks, 1978; Reds, 1980; Producer/Co-Producer: The Return of the Soldier, 1981; Privates on Parade, 1982; Ploughman's Lunch, 1983; Secret Places, 1984; Wetherby, 1985; Comrades, 1986. *Recreations:* gardening, photography, golf. *Address:* 338 Liverpool Road, N7 8PZ.

RELTON, Stanley; HM Diplomatic Service, retired; Counsellor (Administration), British Embassy, Brussels, 1978–83; *b* 19 May 1923; *m* 1953, José Shakespeare; four *d.* Army, 1942–47. Joined HM Diplomatic Service, 1948: Haifa, 1949; Seoul, 1950; Tokyo, 1951; FCO, 1952–53; Vice-Consul, Stuttgart, 1954–57; Bremen, 1957–59; Consul, Rotterdam, 1959–61; Budapest, 1961–64; Second Sec., Buenos Aires, 1964–68; First Sec., Algiers, 1968–71; FCO, 1971–75; First Sec., Blantyre, Malaŵi, 1975–78. *Recreations:* music, chess. *Address:* 20A Waldegrave Park, Twickenham, Mddx.

REMEDIOS, Alberto Telisforo, CBE 1981; opera and concert singer; *b* 27 Feb. 1935; *s* of Albert and Ida Remedios; *m* 1965, Judith Annette Hosken; two *s* one *d. Educ:* studied with Edwin Francis, Liverpool. Début with Sadler's Wells Opera, 1956; sings regularly: English Nat. Opera; Royal Opera House, Covent Garden; Welsh Nat. Opera; Metropolitan NY, San Francisco, San Diego, Seattle, Australia, NZ, S Africa, Frankfurt, Bonn, France, Spain; sang Peter Grimes, Teatro Colon, Buenos Aires, 1979; also with major English orchestras. Recordings include Wagner's Ring; Tippett: A Midsummer Marriage. Queen's Prize, RCM, 1958; 1st prize, Union of Bulgarian Composers, 1963. *Recreations:* soccer, motoring, record collecting. *Address:* c/o Ibbs & Tillett Ltd, 18b Pindock Mews, W9.

REMEZ, Aharon; sculptor; *b* 8 May 1919; *m* 1952, Rita (*née* Levy); one *s* three *d. Educ:* Herzliah Grammar Sch., Tel Aviv; New Sch. for Social Res., NY; Business Sch., Harvard Univ.; Woodrow Wilson Sch. of Public and Internat. Affairs, Princeton Univ. Volunteered for service with RAF, and served as fighter pilot in Gt Brit. and in European theatre of war; after end of war with British Occupation forces in Germany. Mem., kibbutz Kfar Blum, 1947–. Dir Planning and of Ops and subseq. Chief of Staff, and C-in-C Israel Air Force (rank Brig.-Gen.), 1948–51; Head of Min. of Defence Purchasing Mission, USA, 1951–53; Aviation Adviser to Minister of Def., 1953–54; Mem. Bd of Dirs, Solel Boneh Ltd, and Exec. Dir, Koor Industries Ltd, 1954–59; MP (Israel Lab Party) for Mapai, 1956–57; Admin. Dir, Weizmann Inst. of Science, Rehovot, 1959–60. Dir, Internat. Co-op. Dept, Min. for Foreign Affairs, Jerusalem, 1960; Adviser on Internat. Co-operation to Min. for Foreign Affairs, also Consultant to OECD, 1964–65; Ambassador of Israel to the Court of St James's, 1965–70. Dir Gen., Israel Ports Authority, 1970–77. Chairman: Nat. Council for Civil Aviation, 1960–65; Bd of Dirs, Airports Authority, 1977–81. *Recreations:* handicrafts, sculpture. *Address:* San Martin Street, Cottage 11, Jerusalem 93341, Israel.

REMNANT, family name of **Baron Remnant.**

REMNANT, 3rd Baron *cr* 1928, of Wenhaston; **James Wogan Remnant,** Bt 1917; CVO 1979; FCA; Chairman, National Provident Institution, since 1990 (Director, since 1963); Vice-Chairman, Société Générale Touche Remnant, since 1989; *b* 23 October 1930; *s* of 2nd Baron and Dowager Lady Remnant (*d* 1990); *S* father, 1967; *m* 1953, Serena Jane Loehnis, *o d* of Sir Clive Loehnis, *qv*; three *s* one *d. Educ:* Eton. Partner, Touche Ross & Co., 1958–70; Man. Dir, 1970–80, Chm., 1981–89, Touche, Remnant & Co.; Chairman: TR City of London Trust, 1978–90 (Dir, 1973–); TR Pacific Investment Trust, 1987–. Dep. Chm., Ultramar, 1981– (Dir, 1970–); Director: Australia and New Zealand Banking Group, 1968–81 (Mem., Internat. Bd of Advice, 1987–91); Union Discount Co. of London, 1968– (Dep. Chm., 1970–86); Bank of Scotland, 1989– (Dir, 1973–, Chm., 1979–, London Bd), and other cos. Chm., Assoc. of Investment Trust Cos, 1977–79. A Church Comr, 1976–84. Trustee, Royal Jubilee Trusts, 1980– (Hon. Treasurer, 1972–80; Chm., 1980–89); Pres., Nat. Council of YMCAs, 1983–. FCA 1955. *Heir: s* Hon. Philip John Remnant [*b* 20 December 1954; *m* 1977, Caroline Elizabeth Clare, *yr d* of late Godfrey H. R. Cavendish; one *s* two *d*]. *Address:* Bear Ash, Hare Hatch, Reading RG10 9XR.

RENALS, Sir Stanley, 4th Bt, *cr* 1895; formerly in the Merchant Navy; *b* 20 May 1923; 2nd *s* of Sir James Herbert Renals, 2nd Bt; *S* brother, Sir Herbert Renals, 3rd Bt, 1961; *m* 1957, Maria Dolores Rodriguez Pinto, *d* of late José Rodriguez Ruiz; one *s. Educ:* City of London Freemen's School. *Heir: s* Stanley Michael Renals, BSc, CEng, MIMechE, MIProdE [*b* 14 January 1958; *m* 1982, Jacqueline Riley; one *s* one *d*]. *Address:* 52 North Lane, Portslade, Sussex BN4 2HG.

RENAUD, Madeleine, (Mme Jean-Louis Barrault); Officier de la Légion d'Honneur; actress; formed Madeleine Renaud-Jean-Louis Barrault Company, 1946, Co-director and player leading parts; *b* Paris, 21 Feb. 1903; *d* of Prof. Jean Renaud; *m*; one *s*; *m* 1940, Jean-Louis Barrault, *qv. Educ:* Lycée Racine; Conservatoire de Paris (Ier Prix de Comédie). Pensionnaire, Comédie Française, 1921–46. Jt Founder, Madeleine Renaud-Jean-Louis Barrault Company, 1947. Has appeared in classical and modern plays, and in films. Mem., Conseil d'administration, ORTF, 1967–68. Grand Officier de l'ordre national du Mérite; Commandeur des Arts et Lettres. *Publications:* novels, short stories, plays. *Address:* 18 Avenue du Président Wilson, 75116 Paris, France.

RENDALL, Peter Godfrey; Headmaster, Bembridge School, Isle of Wight, 1959–74; *b* 25 April 1909; *s* of Godfrey A. H. Rendall and Mary Whishaw Rendall (*née* Wilson); *m* 1944, Ann McKnight Kauffer; two *s* one *d. Educ:* Rugby School; Corpus Christi College, Oxford. Assistant Master: Felsted School, Essex, 1931–34; Upper Canada College, Toronto, 1934–35; Felsted School, Essex, 1935–43. Served War of 1939–45, RAF, 1943–46, Flight-Lieut. Second Master, St Bees School, Cumberland, 1946–48; Headmaster Achimota School, Gold Coast, 1949–54; Assistant Master, Lancing College, 1954–59. Clerk to Burford Town Council, 1977–85. Coronation Medal, 1953. *Recreations:* reading, gardening, carpentry, painting. *Address:* Chippings, The Hill, Burford, Oxon OX18 4RE. *T:* Burford (099382) 2459. *Clubs:* Commonwealth Trust; Oxford Union Society.

RENDELL, Ruth Barbara; crime novelist, since 1964; *b* 17 Feb. 1930; *d* of Arthur Grasemann and Ebba Kruse; *m* 1950, Donald Rendell; marr. diss. 1975; remarried Donald Rendell, 1977; one *s. Educ:* Loughton County High School. FRSL. Arts Council National Book Award for Genre Fiction, 1981. *Publications:* From Doon with Death, 1964; To Fear a Painted Devil, 1965; Vanity Dies Hard, 1966; A New Lease of Death, 1967; Wolf to the Slaughter, 1967 (televised 1987); The Secret House of Death, 1968; The Best Man to Die, 1969; A Guilty Thing Surprised, 1970; One Across Two Down, 1971; No More Dying Then, 1971; Murder Being Once Done, 1972; Some Lie and Some Die, 1973; The Face of Trespass, 1974 (televised, as An Affair in Mind, 1988); Shake Hands for Ever, 1975; A Demon in my View, 1976; A Judgement in Stone, 1977; A Sleeping Life, 1978; Make Death Love Me, 1979; The Lake of Darkness, 1980 (televised, as Dead Lucky, 1988); Put on by Cunning, 1981; Master of the Moor, 1982; The Speaker of Mandarin, 1983; The Killing Doll, 1984; The Tree of Hands, 1984 (film 1989); An Unkindness of Ravens, 1985; Live Flesh, 1986; Heartstones, 1987; Talking to Strange Men, 1987; (ed) A Warning to the Curious—The Ghost Stories of M. R. James, 1987; The Veiled One, 1988 (televised 1989); The Bridesmaid, 1989; Ruth Rendell's Suffolk, 1989; (with Colin Ward) Undermining the Central Line, 1989; Going Wrong, 1990; *short stories:* The Fallen Curtain, 1976; Means of Evil, 1979; The Fever Tree, 1982; The New Girl Friend, 1985; Collected Short Stories, 1987; The Copper Peacock, 1991; (as Barbara Vine): A Dark-Adapted Eye, 1986; A Fatal Inversion, 1987; The House of Stairs, 1988; Gallowglass, 1990. *Recreations:* reading, walking, opera. *Address:* Nussteads, Polstead, Suffolk; 26 Cornwall Terrace Mews, NW1 5LL. *Clubs:* Groucho, Detection.

RENDELL, Sir William, Kt 1967; General Manager, Commonwealth Development Corporation, 1953–73, retired; *b* 25 Jan. 1908; *s* of William Reginald Rendell and Hon. Janet Marion Rendell; *m* 1950, Annie Henriette Maria (*née* Thorsen). *Educ:* Winchester; Trinity Coll., Cambridge. FCA. Partner, Whinney Murray & Co., 1947–52. *Recreations:* fishing, gardening. *Address:* 10 Montpelier Place, SW7 1HJ. *T:* 071–584 8232.

RENDLE, Michael Russel; Managing Director, British Petroleum plc, 1981–86; Deputy Chairman, British-Borneo Petroleum Syndicate plc, since 1986; Director: Willis Corroon (formerly Willis Faber) plc, since 1985; Forestry Investment Management Ltd, since 1989; *b* 20 Feb. 1931; *s* of late H. C. R. Rendle and Valerie Patricia (*née* Gleeson); *m* 1957, Heather, *d* of J. W. J. Rinkel; two *s* two *d. Educ:* Marlborough; New College, Oxford. MA. Joined Anglo-Iranian Oil Co. (now BP), 1954; Man. Dir, BP Trinidad, 1967–70; Man. Dir, BP Australia, 1974–78; Dir, BP Trading Ltd, 1978–81; Chairman: BP Chemicals Int., 1981–83; BP Coal, 1983–86; BP Nutrition, 1981–86. Dep. Chm., Imperial Continental Gas Assoc., 1986–87; Director: London Adv. Bd, Westpac Banking Corp. (formerly Commercial Bank of Australia), 1978–89; Petrofina SA, 1986–87. Mem. BOTB, 1982–86; Chm., European Trade Cttee, 1982–86. Chm. Social Affairs Cttee, UNICE, 1984–87; Mem. Internat. Council and UK Adv. Bd, INSEAD, 1984–86. Mem. Council, Marlborough Coll., 1987–. *Recreations:* golf, music, outdoor sports, gardening. *Address:* c/o Willis Corroon plc, 10 Trinity Square, EC3P 3AX. *T:* 071–481 7152. *Clubs:* Vincent's (Oxford); Australian, Royal Melbourne Golf (Melbourne).

RENDLE, Peter Critchfield; Under-Secretary (Principal Finance Officer), Scottish Office, 1978–80, retired; *b* Truro, 31 July 1919; *s* of late Martyn and Florence Rendle; *m* 1944, Helen Barbara Moyes; three *s. Educ:* Queen Elizabeth's Sch., Hartlebury. Clerical Officer, Min. of Transport, 1936–49. Served War, Royal Navy, 1940–46 (Lieut RNVR). Min. of Town and Country Planning, 1949; Dept of Health for Scotland, 1950–59 (Sec., Guest Cttee on Bldg Legislation in Scotland); Scottish Home and Health Dept, 1959–63 and 1972–73; Scottish Educn Dept, 1963–72; Under Sec., Housing, Scottish Development Dept, 1973–78. Member: Legal Aid Central Cttee for Scotland, 1980–87; Scottish Is Councils Cttee of Inquiry, 1982–84; Scottish Legal Aid Bd, 1987–89. *Publication:* Rayner Report, Scrutiny of HM Inspectors of Schools in Scotland, 1981. *Recreations:* hockey, taking photographs. *Address:* 3/6 Caithness Place, Clark Road, Edinburgh EH5 3AE. *T:* 031–552 8024. *Club:* Scottish Arts (Edinburgh).

RENDLESHAM, 8th Baron, *cr* 1806; **Charles Anthony Hugh Thellusson;** Royal Corps of Signals; *b* 15 March 1915; *s* of Lt-Col Hon. Hugh Edmund Thellusson, DSO (3rd *s* of 5th Baron); *S* uncle, 1943; *m* 1st, 1940, Margaret Elizabeth (marr. diss. 1947; she *m* 1962, Patrick P. C. Barthropp), *d* of Lt-Col Robin Rome, Monk's Hall, Glemsford; one *d*; 2nd, 1947, Clare (*d* 1987), *d* of Lt-Col D. H. G. McCririck; one *s* three *d. Educ:* Eton. *Heir: s* Hon. Charles William Brooke Thellusson [*b* 10 Jan. 1954; *m* 1983, Susan Fielding]. *Address:* 498 King's Road, SW10 0LE.

See also Sir William Goring, Bt.

RENÉ, (France) Albert; barrister-at-law; President of the Republic of Seychelles since 1977 (elected, 1979, 1984); Minister of Administration, Finance and Industries, Planning and External Relations, since 1984; Minister of Defence, since 1986; *b* Mahé, Seychelles, 16 Nov. 1935; *s* of Price René and Louisa Morgan; *m* 1st, 1956, Karen Handlay; one *d*; 2nd, 1975, Geva Adam; one *s. Educ:* St Louis Coll., Seychelles; St Moritz, Switzerland; St Mary's Coll., Southampton, England; King's Coll., Univ. of London; Council of Legal Educn, 1956; LSE, 1961. Called to Bar, 1957. Leader, Founder, Pres., 1964–78, Seychelles People's United Party (first effective political party and liberation movement in Seychelles); MP, 1965; Mem. in Governing Council, 1967; Mem., Legal Assembly, 1970 and 1974; Minister of Works and Land Development, 1975; Prime Minister, 1976–77; Minister of Transport, 1984–86. Founder, Leader and Sec.-Gen., Seychelles People's Progressive Front, 1978. Advocates positive non-alignment, the development of a Seychellois-socialist society and the promotion of the Indian Ocean as a zone of peace. Order of the Golden Ark (1st cl.), 1982. *Address:* President's Office, State House, Republic of Seychelles.

RENFREW, family name of **Baron Renfrew of Kaimsthorn.**

RENFREW OF KAIMSTHORN, Baron *cr* 1991 (Life Peer), of Hurlet in the District of Renfrew; **Andrew Colin Renfrew,** FBA 1980; Disney Professor of Archaeology, University of Cambridge, since 1981; Master of Jesus College, Cambridge, since 1986; *b* 25 July 1937; *s* of late Archibald Renfrew and Helena Douglas Renfrew (*née* Savage); *m* 1965, Jane Margaret, *d* of Ven. Walter F. Ewbank, *qv*; two *s* one *d. Educ:* St Albans Sch.; St John's Coll., Cambridge (Exhibr); British Sch. of Archaeology, Athens. Pt I Nat. Scis Tripos 1960; BA 1st cl. hons Archaeol. and Anthrop. Tripos 1962; MA 1964; PhD 1965; ScD 1976. Pres., Cambridge Union Soc., 1961; Sir Joseph Larmor Award 1961. Nat. Service, Flying Officer (Signals), RAF, 1956–58. Res. Fellow, St John's Coll., Cambridge, 1965, Professorial Fellow, 1981–86; Bulgarian Govt Schol., 1966; Univ. of Sheffield: Lectr in Prehistory and Archaeol., 1965–70; Sen. Lectr, 1970–72; Reader, 1972; Prof. of Archaeology, Southampton Univ., 1972–81. Vis. Lectr, Univ. of Calif at Los Angeles, 1967. Contested (C) Sheffield Brightside, 1968; Chm., Sheffield Brightside Conserv. Assoc., 1968–72. Member: Ancient Monuments Bd for England, 1974–84; Royal Commn on Historical Monuments (England), 1977–87; Historic Buildings and Monuments Commn for England, 1984–86; Ancient Monuments Adv. Cttee, 1984–; UK Nat. Commn for UNESCO, 1984–86 (Mem. Culture Adv. Cttee, 1984–86); Trustee, Antiquity Trust, 1974–; Chm., Hants Archaeol Cttee, 1974–81; a Vice-Pres., RAI, 1982–85. Chm., Governors, The Leys, 1984–. Lectures: Dalrymple in Archaeol., Univ. of Glasgow, 1975; George Grant MacCurdy, Harvard, 1977; Patten, Indiana Univ., 1982; Harvey, New Mexico Univ., 1982; Hill, Univ. of Minnesota, 1987. Excavations: Saliagos near Antiparos, 1964–65; Sitagroi, Macedonia, 1968–70; Phylakopi in Melos, 1974–76; Quanterness, Orkney, 1972–74; Maes Howe, 1973–74; Ring of Brodgar, 1974; Liddle Farm, 1973–74. Rivers Meml Medal, RAI, 1979. FSA 1968 (Vice-Pres., 1987–); FSAScot 1970. Hon. LittD Sheffield, 1987. *Publications:* (with J. D. Evans) Excavations at Saliagos near Antiparos, 1968; The Emergence of Civilisation, 1972; (ed) The Explanation of Culture Change, 1973; Before Civilisation, 1973; (ed) British Prehistory, a New Outline, 1974; Investigations in Orkney, 1979; (ed) Transformations: Mathematical Approaches to Culture Change, 1979; Problems in European Prehistory, 1979; (with J. M. Wagstaff) An Island Polity, 1982; (ed) Theory and Explanation in Archaeology, 1982; Approaches to Social Archaeology, 1984; The Prehistory of Orkney, 1985; The Archaeology of Cult, 1985; Archaeology and Language, 1987; (with G. Daniel) The Idea of Prehistory, 1988; The Cycladic Spirit, 1991; (with P. Bahn) Archaeology, 1991; articles in archaeol jls. *Recreations:* modern art, numismatics, travel. *Address:* Master's Lodge, Jesus College,

Cambridge CB5 8BL. *T:* Cambridge (0223) 323934; Department of Archaeology, Downing Street, Cambridge CB2 3DZ. *T:* Cambridge (0223) 333520. *Clubs:* Athenæum, United Oxford & Cambridge University.

RENFREW, Rt. Rev. Charles McDonald; Titular Bishop of Abula and Auxiliary to the Archbishop of Glasgow, (RC), since 1977; Vicar General of Archdiocese of Glasgow, since 1974; *b* 21 June 1929; *s* of Alexander Renfrew and Mary (*née* Dougherty). *Educ:* St Aloysius College, Glasgow; Scots College, Rome. PhL, STL (Gregorian). Ordained Rome, 1953; Assistant at Immaculate Conception, Glasgow, 1953–56; Professor and Procurator, Blairs Coll., Aberdeen, 1956–61; First Rector and founder of St Vincent's Coll., Langbank, 1961–74. Sound and television broadcasts for BBC and STV. Comdr, Order of Merit (Republic of Italy), 1982. *Publications:* St Vincent's Prayer Book, 1971; Rambling Through Life, 1975; Ripples of Life, 1975; Pageant of Holiness, 1975; pamphlets and articles in newspapers and magazines. *Recreation:* music, especially grand and light opera. *Address:* St Joseph's, 38 Mansionhouse Road, Glasgow G41 3DN. *T:* 041–649 2228.

RENFREW, Glen McGarvie; Managing Director and Chief Executive, Reuters Ltd, 1981–91; *b* 15 Sept. 1928; *s* of Robert Renfrew and Jane Grey Watson; *m* 1954, Daphne Ann Hailey; one *s* two *d* (and one *d* decd). *Educ:* Sydney Univ., NSW, Australia (BA). Joined Reuters, London, 1952; reporting and/or management assignments in Asia, Africa and Europe, 1956–64; London management posts in computer and economic information services, 1964–70; Manager, Reuters N America, 1971–80. *Recreation:* sailing. *Address:* c/o Reuters, 85 Fleet Street, EC4. *T:* 071–250 1122. *Clubs:* Manhasset Bay Yacht (Long Island, NY), National Press (Washington).

RENFREY, Rt. Rev. Lionel Edward William; Dean of Adelaide, since 1966; Assistant Bishop of Adelaide, 1969–89; *b* Adelaide, SA, 26 March 1916; *s* of late Alfred Cyril Marinus Renfrey and Catherine Elizabeth Rose Frerichs (*née* Dickson); *m* 1948, Joan Anne, *d* of Donald Smith, Cooke's Plains, SA; one *s* five *d*. *Educ:* Unley High School; St Mark's Coll., Univ. of Adelaide; St Barnabas' Theological Coll., Adelaide. BA (First Cl. Hons English), ThL (ACT) (Second Cl. Hons). Deacon 1940, priest 1941, Dio. Adelaide; Curate, St Cuthbert's, Prospect, 1940–43; Mission Chaplain, Mid Yorke Peninsula, 1943–44; Warden, Brotherhood of St John Baptist, 1944–47; Priest-in-charge: Berri-Barmera, 1948–50; Kensington Gardens, 1950–57; Rector, St James', Mile End, 1957–63; Rural Dean, Western Suburbs, 1962–63; Organising Chaplain, Bishop's Home Mission Soc., 1963–66; Editor, Adelaide Church Guardian, 1961–66; Archdeacon of Adelaide, 1965–66; Examining Chaplain to Bishop of Adelaide, 1965–85; Administrator (*sede vacante*), Diocese of Adelaide, 1974–75; Rector, Mallala and Two Wells, 1981–88. Patron, Prayer Book Soc. in Australia, 1980. OStJ 1981 (SBStJ 1969). *Publications:* Father Wise: a Memoir, 1951; Short History of St Barnabas' Theological College, 1965; What Mean Ye By This Service?, 1978; (ed) Catholic Prayers, 1980; (ed) SS Peter and Paul Prayer Book, 1982; Arthur Nutter Thomas, Bishop of Adelaide 1906–1940, 1988. *Recreations:* reading, golf, motoring. *Address:* The Deanery, 13 Northcote Terrace, Medindie, SA 5081, Australia. *Clubs:* Adelaide, Royal Adelaide Golf (Adelaide).

RENNELL, 3rd Baron *cr* 1933, of Rodd, Herefordshire; **John Adrian Tremayne Rodd;** *b* 28 June 1935; *s* of Hon. Gustaf Guthrie Rennell Rodd (*d* 1974) (*yr s* of 1st Baron) and Yvonne Mary Rodd (*d* 1982), *d* of late Sir Charles Murray Marling, GCMG, CB; *S* uncle, 1978; *m* 1977, Phyllis, *d* of T. D. Neill; one *s* two *d*. *Educ:* Downside; RNC, Dartmouth. Served Royal Navy, 1952–62. With Morgan Grenfell & Co. Ltd, 1963–66; free-lance journalist, 1966–67; Marks of Distinction Ltd, 1968–79; Dir, Tremayne Ltd, 1980–. *Recreations:* Scotland Rugby XV, 1958–65; golf, Real tennis. *Heir: s* Hon. James Roderick David Tremayne Rodd, *b* 9 March 1978. *Clubs:* White's, Queen's; Sunningdale (Ascot).

RENNIE, Alexander Allan, CBE 1980; QPM 1971; Chief Constable, West Mercia Constabulary, 1975–81, retired; *b* 13 June 1917; *s* of Charles Rennie and Susan Parsons Rennie; *m* 1941, Lucy Brunt; one *s* one *d*. *Educ:* Ellon Acad., Aberdeenshire. Armed Services, 1941–45: commnd 30 Corps Royal Northumberland Fusiliers; active service in Europe (mentioned in despatches, 1945). Joined Durham County Constab., 1937; Chief Supt, 1963; Dep. Chief Constable, Shropshire, 1963–67; Dir, Sen. Comd Course, Police Coll., Bramshill, 1967–69; Asst Chief Constable, West Mercia, 1969–72, Dep. Chief Constable, 1973–75. OStJ 1975. *Recreations:* golf, hill walking. *Address:* 14 Minter Avenue, St Andrews Gardens, Droitwich, Worcs WR9 8RP.

RENNIE, Archibald Louden, CB 1980; Secretary, Scottish Home and Health Department, 1977–84, retired; *b* 4 June 1924; *s* of John and Isabella Rennie; *m* 1950, Kathleen Harkess; four *s*. *Educ:* Madras Coll.; St Andrews University. Minesweeping Res. Div., Admty, 1944–47; Dept of Health for Scotland, 1947–62; Private Sec. to Sec. of State for Scotland, 1962–63; Registrar Gen. for Scotland, 1969–73; Under-Sec., Scottish Office, 1973–77. Member: Scottish Records Adv. Council, 1985–; Council on Tribunals, 1987–88. Gen. Council Assessor, St Andrews Univ. Court, 1984–85; Chancellor's Assessor and Finance Convener, 1985–89; Vice-Chm., Adv. Cttee on Distinction Awards for Consultants, 1985–; Chm., Disciplined Services Pay Review Cttee, Hong Kong, 1988. Trustee, Lockerbie Air Disaster Trust, 1988–. Vice-Cdre, Elie and Earlsferry Sailing Club, 1989–. Hon. LLD St Andrews, 1990. *Recreations:* Scottish literature, sailing, gardening. *Address:* Baldinnie, Park Place, Elie, Fife KY9 1DH. *T:* Elie (0333) 330741. *Club:* Scottish Arts (Edinburgh).

RENNIE, James Douglas Milne, CB 1986; Parliamentary Counsel, since 1976; *b* 2 Nov. 1931; *s* of Douglas Frederick Milne Rennie and Margaret Wilson Fleming Rennie (*née* Keanie); *m* 1962, Patricia Margaret Calhoun Watson; one *s* one *d*. *Educ:* Charterhouse; New Coll., Oxford (Schol.). 1st cl. Hon. Mods 1953; 2nd cl. Lit. Hum. 1955; 2nd cl. Jurisprudence 1957; MA. Called to Bar, Lincoln's Inn, 1958 (Cholmeley Schol.). Asst Lectr, UCW Aberystwyth, 1957; practised at Chancery Bar, 1958–65; Asst Parly Counsel, HM Treasury, 1965; Sen. Asst Parly Counsel, 1972; Dep. Parly Counsel, 1973–75. *Recreations:* opera, travel. *Address:* 8 Wellesley Road, W4 4BL. *T:* 081–994 6627.

RENNIE, John Chalmers; Town Clerk of Aberdeen, 1946–68; retired; *b* 16 April 1907; *s* of late John Chalmers Rennie, Pharmacist, Wishaw; *m* 1937, Georgina Stoddart, *d* of late Henry Bell, Engineer and Ironfounder, Wishaw; one *s*. *Educ:* University of Glasgow (BL). Admitted solicitor, 1929. Town Clerk Depute, Motherwell and Wishaw, 1929–43; Town Clerk Depute, Aberdeen, 1943–46. Dep. Controller, Civil Defence Servs, Motherwell and Wishaw, 1939–43; Secretary: Aberdeen Harbour Bd, 1946–60; NE Fire Area Jt Bd, 1948–68. Mem. Council, Law Soc. of Scotland, 1958–61. Hon. Solicitor (Scotland), NALGO, 1949–64. *Recreation:* surviving. *Address:* 34 Morningfield Road, Aberdeen AB2 4AQ. *T:* Aberdeen (0224) 316904.

RENNIE, Sir John Shaw, GCMG 1968 (KCMG 1962; CMG 1958); OBE 1955; Commissioner-General, United Nations Relief and Works Agency for Palestine Refugees, 1971–77 (Deputy Commissioner-General, 1968–71); *b* 12 Jan. 1917; *s* of late John Shaw Rennie, Saskatoon, Sask, Canada; *m* 1946, Mary Winifred Macalpine Robertson; one *s*. *Educ:* Hillhead High School; Glasgow University; Balliol College, Oxford. Cadet, Tanganyika, 1940; Asst District Officer, 1942; District Officer, 1949; Deputy Colonial Secretary, Mauritius, 1951; British Resident Comr, New Hebrides, 1955–62; Governor and C-in-C of Mauritius, 1962–March 1968, Governor-General, March-Aug. 1968. Hon. LLD Glasgow, 1972. *Address:* 26 College Cross, N1 1PR; via Roma 33, 06050 Collazzone (PG), Italy. *Club:* Commonwealth Trust.

RENOUF, Sir Francis (Henry), Kt 1987; Chairman, Renouf Group, since 1960; *b* 31 July 1918; *s* of Francis Charles Renouf and Mary Ellen (*née* Avery); *m* 1954, Ann, *d* of Eamon Harkin; one *s* three *d*. *Educ:* Victoria Univ. of Wellington (MCom 1940); Oxford Univ. (DipEcon 1949). Stockbroker, 1950–87; Chairman: NZ United Corp. Ltd, 1960–83; Renouf Corp. Ltd, 1983–87. Officer's Cross, Order of Merit, Federal Republic of Germany, 1986. *Recreation:* lawn tennis. *Address:* 37 Eaton Square, SW1W 9DH. *T:* 071–235 1124. *Club:* Cavalry and Guards.

RENOWDEN, Very Rev. Charles Raymond; Dean of St Asaph since 1971; *b* 27 Oct. 1923; *s* of Rev. Canon Charles Renowden; *m* 1951, Ruth Cecil Mary Collis; one *s* two *d*. *Educ:* Llandysil Grammar Sch.; St David's Univ. Coll., Lampeter; Selwyn Coll., Cambridge. BA (Hons Philosophy, cl. I), Lampeter; BA, MA (Hons Theology, cl. I), Cambridge. Served War, Army, Intelligence Corps, in India and Japan, 1944–47. Cambridge Ordination Course; Deacon, 1951, Priest, 1952, Wales. Asst Curate, Hubberston, Milford Haven, 1951–55. St David's Univ. Coll., Lampeter: Lectr in Philosophy and Theology, 1955–57; Head of Dept of Philosophy, 1957–69; Sen. Lectr in Philosophy and Theology, 1969–71. *Publications:* (monograph) The Idea of Unity, 1965; New Patterns of Ministry, 1973; The Rôle of a Cathedral Today and Tomorrow, 1974; contributor to: Theology, The Modern Churchman, Church Quarterly Review, Trivium, Province. *Recreations:* music, gardening, ornithology. *Address:* The Deanery, St Asaph, Clwyd LL17 0RL. *T:* St Asaph (0745) 583597.

RENOWDEN, Rev. Canon Glyndwr Rhys, CB 1987; Chaplain in Chief, Royal Air Force, 1983–88; *b* 13 Aug. 1929; *s* of Charles and Mary Elizabeth Renowden; *m* 1956, Mary Kinsey-Jones; one *d*. *Educ:* Llanelli Grammar Sch.; St David's Coll., Lampeter (BA, LTh). Curate: St Mary's, Tenby, 1952–55; St Mary's, Chepstow, 1955–58; Chaplain, RAF, 1958–88; Asst Chaplain in Chief, 1975–83. QHC, 1980–88. *Recreations:* Rugby football, bridge. *Address:* Red Cedars, Kenystyle, Penally, near Tenby, Dyfed SA70 7RJ.

RENSHAW, Sir (Charles) Maurice (Bine), 3rd Bt *cr* 1903; *b* 7 Oct. 1912; *s* of Sir (Charles) Stephen (Bine) Renshaw, 2nd Bt and of Edith Mary, *d* of Rear-Adm. Sir Edward Chichester, 9th Bt, CB, CMG; *S* father, 1976; *m* 1942, Isabel Bassett (marr. diss. 1947), *d* of late Rev. John L. T. Popkin; one *s* one *d* (and one *s* decd); *m* 2nd, Winifred May, *d* of H. F. Gliddon, Ashwater, Devon, and formerly wife of James H. T. Sheldon; three *s* three *d*. *Educ:* Eton. Served as Flying Officer, RAF (invalided). *Heir: s* John David Renshaw [*b* 9 Oct. 1945; *m* 1970, Jennifer (marr. diss. 1988), *d* of Group Captain F. Murray, RAF; one *s* two *d*]. *Address:* Tam-na-Marghaidh, Balquhidder, Perthshire; Linwood, Instow, N Devon.

RENTON, family name of **Baron Renton.**

RENTON, Baron *cr* 1979 (Life Peer), of Huntingdon in the County of Cambridgeshire; **David Lockhart-Mure Renton,** KBE 1964; TD; PC 1962; QC 1954; MA; BCL; DL; a Deputy Speaker of the House of Lords, 1982–88; *b* 12 Aug. 1908; *s* of late Dr Maurice Waugh Renton, The Bridge House, Dartford, Kent, and Eszma Olivia, *d* of late Allen Walter Borman, Alexandria; *m* 1947, Claire Cicely Duncan (*d* 1986); three *d*. *Educ:* Stubbington; Oundle; University College, Oxford (BA (Hons Jurisprudence), 1930; BCL, 1931; MA; Hon. Fellow, 1990). Called to Bar, Lincoln's Inn, 1933; South-Eastern Circuit; elected to General Council of the Bar, 1939; Bencher, Lincoln's Inn, 1962, Treasurer, 1979. Commnd RE (TA), 1938; transferred to RA 1940; served throughout War of 1939–45; Capt. 1941; Major, 1943; served in Egypt and Libya, 1942–45. MP (Nat L) 1945–50, (Nat L and C) 1950–68, (C) 1968–79, Huntingdonshire; Parly Sec., Min. of Fuel and Power, 1955–57, Ministry of Power, 1957–58; Joint Parly Under-Sec. of State, Home Office, 1958–61; Minister of State, Home Office, 1961–62; Chm., Select Cttee for Revision of Standing Orders, House of Commons, 1963 and 1970; Dep. Chm., Select Cttee on H of C Procedure, 1976–78; Mem., Cttee of Privileges, 1973–79. Recorder of Rochester, 1963–68, of Guildford, 1968–71; Vice-Chm., Council of Legal Educn, 1968–70, 1971–73. Member: Senate of Inns of Court, 1967–69, 1970–71, 1975–79; Commn on the Constitution, 1971–73; Chm., Cttee on Preparation of Legislation, 1973–75. Pres., Statute Law Soc., 1980–. Pres., Royal Soc. for Mentally Handicapped Children, 1982–88 (Hon. Treas., 1976–78; Chm., 1978–82). President: Conservation Soc., 1970–71; Nat. Council for Civil Protection (formerly Nat. Council for Civil Defence), 1980–; Jt Pres., All Party Arts and Heritage Gp, 1989–. Patron: Nat. Law Library, 1979–; Huntingdonshire Conservative Assoc., 1979–; Ravenswood Foundn, 1979–; Gtr London Assoc. for the Disabled, 1986–; DEMAND (Design and Manufacture for Disablement), 1986–. DL Huntingdonshire, 1962, Huntingdon and Peterborough, 1964, Cambs, 1974. Coronation and Jubilee Medals. *Recreations:* outdoor sports and games, gardening. *Address:* Moat House, Abbots Ripton, Huntingdon, Cambs PE17 2PE. *T:* Abbots Ripton (04873) 227; 16 Old Buildings, Lincoln's Inn, WC2A 3TL. *T:* 071–242 8986. *Clubs:* Carlton, Pratt's.

RENTON, Gordon Pearson; Chairman, R & D Communications Ltd, since 1990; Director, Mediajet Ltd, since 1987; Assistant Under-Secretary of State, Department of Trade and Industry, 1983–84; *b* 12 Dec. 1928; *s* of Herbert Renton and Annie (*née* Pearson); *m* 1st, 1952, Joan Mary Lucas (marr. diss. 1971); two *s*; 2nd, 1978, Sylvia Jones. *Educ:* King Edward VII Sch., Sheffield; Lincoln Coll., Oxford (Scholar, BA Lit. Hum.). Served Royal Signals, 1951–53. Teacher, W Riding, 1953–54; Asst Principal, Home Office, 1954; Asst Private Sec. to Home Sec. and Lord Privy Seal, 1959–60; Principal, 1960; Asst Sec., 1967; Asst Under-Sec. of State, 1978. Mem., Parole Bd, 1985–88. *Recreations:* music, gardening, sailing. *Address:* Ship Cottage, Pwll Du, Bishopston, Swansea SA3 2AU. *T:* Bishopston (044128) 3796. *Clubs:* Reform; Bristol Channel Yacht.

RENTON, Air Cdre Helen Ferguson, CB 1982; Director, Women's Royal Air Force, 1980–86; *b* 13 March 1931; *d* of late John Paul Renton and Sarah Graham Renton (*née* Cook). *Educ:* Stirling High Sch.; Glasgow Univ. (MA). Joined WRAF, 1954; commnd, 1955; served in UK, 1955–60; Cyprus, 1960–62; HQ Staff, Germany, 1967; MoD Staff, 1968–71; NEAF, 1971–73; Training Comd, 1973–76; MoD Staff, 1976–78. Hon. LLD Glasgow, 1981. *Publications:* (jtly) Service Women, 1977. *Recreations:* needlework, travel, reading. *Club:* Royal Air Force.

RENTON, Rt. Hon. Ronald Timothy, PC 1989; MP (C) Mid-Sussex since Feb. 1974; Minister of State, Privy Council Office (Minister for the Arts), since 1990; *b* 28 May 1932; *yr s* of R. K. D. Renton, CBE, and Mrs Renton, MBE; *m* 1960, Alice Fergusson of Kilkerran, Ayrshire; two *s* three *d*. *Educ:* Eton Coll. (King's Schol.); Magdalen Coll., Oxford (Roberts Gawen Schol.). First cl. degree in History, MA Oxon. Joined C. Tennant Sons & Co. Ltd, London, 1954; with Tennants' subsidiaries in Canada, 1957–62; Dir, C. Tennant Sons & Co. Ltd and Managing Dir of Tennant Trading Ltd, 1964–73; Director: Silvermines Ltd, 1967–84; Australia & New Zealand Banking Group, 1967–76; J. H. Vavasseur & Co. Ltd, 1971–74. Mem., BBC Gen. Adv. Council, 1982–84. Contested (C)

Sheffield Park Div., 1970; PPS to Rt Hon. John Biffen, MP, 1979–81, to Rt Hon. Geoffrey Howe, MP, 1983–84; Parly Under Sec. of State, FCO, 1984–85; Minister of State: FCO, 1985–87; Home Office, 1987–89; Parly Sec. to HM Treasury and Govt Chief Whip, 1989–90. Mem., Select Cttee on Nationalised Industries, 1974–79; Vice-Chm., Cons. Parly Trade Cttee, 1974–79; Chm., Cons. Foreign and Commonwealth Council, 1982–84; Vice-Pres., 1978–80, Pres., 1980–84, Cons. Trade Unionists; Fellow, Industry and Parlt Trust, 1977–79. Mem., APEX. Mem. Council, Roedean Sch., 1982–. Trustee, Mental Health Foundn, 1985–89. *Recreations:* gardening, tennis, mucking about in boats, listening to opera. *Address:* House of Commons, SW1. *Club:* Garrick.

RENWICK, family name of **Baron Renwick.**

RENWICK, 2nd Baron *cr* 1964, of Coombe; **Harry Andrew Renwick;** Bt 1927; *b* 10 Oct. 1935; *s* of 1st Baron Renwick, KBE, and of Mrs John Ormiston, Miserden House, Stroud, *er d* of late Major Harold Parkes, Alveston, Stratford-on-Avon; *S* father, 1973; *m* 1st, 1965, Susan Jane (marr. diss. 1989), *d* of late Captain Kenneth S. B. Lucking and of Mrs Moir P. Stormonth-Darling, Lednathie, Glen Prosen, Angus; two *s*; 2nd, 1989, Mrs Homayoun Mazandi, *d* of late Col Mahmoud Yazdanparst Pakzad. *Educ:* Eton. Grenadier Guards (National Service), 1955–56. Partner, W. Greenwell & Co., 1964–80. Dir, General Technology Systems Ltd, 1975–. Vice-Pres., British Dyslexia Assoc., 1982– (Chm., 1977–82); Chm., Dyslexia Educnl Trust, 1986–. *Heir:* *s* Hon. Robert James Renwick, *b* 19 Aug. 1966. *Address:* House of Lords, SW1A 0PW. *Clubs:* White's, Turf.

RENWICK, Prof. James Harrison, DSc; FRCP, FRCPath; Professor of Human Genetics and Teratology, University of London, 1979–91, now Emeritus; *b* 4 Feb. 1926; *s* of late Raymond Renwick and of Edith Helen Renwick; *m* 1st, 1959, Helena Verheyden (marr. diss. 1979); one *s* one *d*; 2nd, 1981, Kathleen Salafia; two *s*. *Educ:* Sedbergh School; Univ. of St Andrews; MB ChB (commend), 1948; University Coll. London; PhD 1956, DSc 1970; FRCP 1972, MFCM 1972; FRCPath 1982. Captain RAMC, Korean war; research on genetical effects of atomic bomb, Hiroshima, 1951–53. Univ. of Glasgow, 1959, Prof. of Human Genetics, 1967–68; London Sch. of Hygiene and Tropical Medicine, 1968, Head of Preventive Teratology Unit, 1977–91. Mem., Med. Res. Club. Hon. Treasurer, Genetical Soc., 1960–65, Hon. Auditor, 1965–72; Hon. Pres., Develtl Pathology Soc., 1989–91. FRSocMed. Freeman, Co. of Stationers and Newspaper Makers. *Publications:* numerous scientific articles on mapping of genes on human chromosomes and on prevention of human congenital malformations. *Recreations:* walking, music. *Address:* Rue des Coteaux 17, Bruxelles 1030, Belgium. *T:* (2) 218 7668.

RENWICK, Sir Richard Eustace, 4th Bt *cr* 1921; *b* 13 Jan. 1938; *er s* of Sir Eustace Deuchar Renwick, 3rd Bt, and of Diana Mary, *e d* of Colonel Bernard Cruddas, DSO; *S* father, 1973; *m* 1966, Caroline Anne, *er d* of Major Rupert Milburn; three *s*. *Educ:* Eton. *Heir:* *s* Charles Richard Renwick, *b* 10 April 1967. *Address:* Whalton House, Whalton, Morpeth, Northumberland NE61 3UZ. *T:* Whalton (067075) 383. *Club:* Northern Counties (Newcastle).

RENWICK, Sir Robin (William), KCMG 1989 (CMG 1980); HM Diplomatic Service; Ambassador to Washington, since 1991; *b* 13 Dec. 1937; *s* of Richard Renwick, Edinburgh, and the late Clarice Henderson; *m* 1965, Annie Colette Giudicelli; one *s* one *d*. *Educ:* St Paul's Sch.; Jesus Coll., Cambridge (1st Cl. Hons History Tripos; Newling Prize); Univ. of Paris (Sorbonne). Army, 1956–58. Entered Foreign Service, 1963; Dakar, 1963–64; FO, 1964–66; New Delhi, 1966–69; Private Sec. to Minister of State, FCO, 1970–72; First Sec., Paris, 1972–76; Counsellor, Cabinet Office, 1976–78; Head, Rhodesia Dept, FCO, 1978–80; Political Adviser to Governor of Rhodesia, 1980; Vis. Fellow, Center for Internat. Affairs, Harvard, 1980–81; Head of Chancery, Washington, 1981–84; Asst Under Sec. of State, FCO, 1984–87; Ambassador to S Africa, 1987–91. Hon. LLD Wits Univ. *Publication:* Economic Sanctions, 1981. *Recreations:* tennis, trout fishing. *Address:* c/o Foreign and Commonwealth Office, SW1A 2AH. *Clubs:* Hurlingham, Travellers'.

REPORTER, Sir Shapoor (Ardeshirji), KBE 1973 (OBE 1969); Consultant on Economic and Political Matters concerning Iran, since 1962; *b* 26 Feb. 1921; *s* of Ardeshirji Reporter and Shirin Reporter; *m* 1952, Assia Alexandra; one *s* one *d*. *Educ:* Zoroastrian Public Sch., Teheran; matriculated in Bombay (specially designed course in Political Science under Cambridge Univ. Tutors, UK). PRO, British Legation, Teheran, 1941–43; in charge of Persian Unit of All India Radio, New Delhi, 1943–45; Teaching English, Imperial Staff Coll., Teheran, 1945–48; Political Adviser, US Embassy, Teheran, 1948–54; Free-lance Correspondent, 1954–62; Economic Consultant to major British interests in Iran, 1962–73. *Publications:* English-Persian Phrases, 1945 (Delhi); Dictionary of English-Persian Idioms, 1956 (Teheran); Dictionary of Persian-English Idioms, 1972 (Teheran Univ.). *Recreations:* tennis, walking, travelling.

REPP, Richard Cooper, DPhil; Master, St Cross College, Oxford, since 1987; *b* 1 April 1936; *s* of Robert Mathias Repp, Jun., and Martha Repp (*née* Cooper); *m* 1972, Catherine Ross MacLennan; one *s* one *d*. *Educ:* Shady Side Acad., Pittsburgh; Williams Coll., Mass (BA); Worcester Coll., Oxford (1st Cl. Hons Oriental Studies, MA, DPhil; Hon. Fellow 1989). Instr in Humanities, Robert Coll., Istanbul, 1959–62; Oxford University: Univ. Lectr in Turkish History, 1963–; Sen. Proctor, 1979–80; Vice-Chm., Staff Cttee, 1982–84; Mem., Gen. Bd of the Faculties, 1982–84, 1985–89; Linacre College: Fellow, 1964–87, Hon. Fellow, 1987; Sen. Tutor, 1985–87. *Publications:* The Müfti of Istanbul, 1986; various articles on Ottoman history. *Recreations:* gardening, music. *Address:* St Cross College, Oxford OX1 3LZ. *T:* Oxford (0865) 278493. *Clubs:* United Oxford & Cambridge University; Williams (New York).

REPTON, Bishop Suffragan of, since 1986; **Rt. Rev. Francis Henry Arthur Richmond,** MA; *b* 6 Jan. 1936; *s* of Frank and Lena Richmond; *m* 1966, Caroline Mary Berent; two *s* one *d*. *Educ:* Portora Royal School, Enniskillen; Trinity Coll., Dublin (MA); Univ. of Strasbourg (BTh); Linacre Coll., Oxford (MLitt); Wycliffe Hall, Oxford. Deacon, 1963; Priest, 1964; Asst Curate, Woodlands, Doncaster, 1963–66; Sir Henry Stephenson Research Fellow, Sheffield Univ. and Chaplain, Sheffield Cathedral, 1966–69; Vicar, St George's, Sheffield, 1969–77; Anglican Chaplain to Sheffield Univ. and Mem. Sheffield Chaplaincy for Higher Education, 1974–77; Warden, Lincoln Theolog. Coll., and Canon and Prebendary of Lincoln Cathedral, 1977–86. Examng Chaplain to Bishop of Lincoln; Proctor in Convocation for Lincoln, 1980. Select Preacher, Univ. of Oxford, 1985. *Recreations:* listening to classical music, reading, theatre, walking, gardening. *Address:* Repton House, Lea, Matlock, Derbys DE4 5JP. *T:* Dethick (0629) 534644.

RESNAIS, Alain; French film director; *b* Vannes, 3 June 1922; *s* of Pierre Resnais and Jeanne (*née* Gachet); *m* 1969, Florence Mairaux. *Educ:* Collège St François-Xavier, Vannes; Institut des hautes études cinématographiques. Assistant to Nicole Védrée for film Paris 1900, 1947–48; has directed his own films (many of which have won prizes), since 1948. Short films, 1948–59, include: Van Gogh, 1948; Guernica (jtly with Robert Hessens), 1950; Les statues meurent aussi (jtly with Chris Marker), 1952; Nuit et brouillard, 1955. Full length films include: Hiroshima mon amour, 1959; L'année dernière à Marienbad, 1961; Muriel, 1963; La guerre est finie, 1966; Je t'aime, je t'aime, 1968; Stavisky, 1974; Providence, 1977; Mon Oncle d'Amérique, 1980; La vie est un roman, 1983; L'amour à Mort, 1984. *Address:* Artmedia, 10 Avenue George V, 75008 Paris, France.

RESO, Sidney Joseph; Executive Vice President, since 1986, President, since 1988, Exxon Co. International; *b* 12 Feb. 1935; *s* of late James A. Reso and of J. Agnes Reso; *m* 1955, Patricia M. Armond; two *s* three *d*. *Educ:* Louisiana State Univ. (BS Petroleum Engrg). Joined Humble Oil & Refining Co., Houston, Texas (now Exxon Co., USA), as engineer, 1957; USA and Australia: engrg assignments, 1961–66; managerial assignments, 1967–71; Dir, Esso Australia Ltd, Sydney, 1972; managerial assignments, USA, 1973–74; Vice-Pres., Esso Europe Inc. and Managing Dir, Esso Petroleum Co., 1975–78; Vice-Pres., Exxon Corp., 1978–80; Exxon Co. USA: Vice-Pres., 1980–81; Sen. Vice-Pres., 1981–85; Exec. Vice-Pres., 1985–86. *Recreations:* golf, tennis, photography, reading. *Address:* 200 Park Avenue, Florham Park, NJ 07932–1002, USA. *Club:* River Oaks Country (Houston).

RESTIEAUX, Rt. Rev. Cyril Edward; *b* 25 Feb. 1910; *s* of Joseph and Edith Restieaux. *Educ:* English Coll., Rome; Gregorian University. Ordained, 1932; Curate at Nottingham, 1933; Parish Priest at Matlock, 1936; Hon. Canon of Nottingham, 1948; Vicar-General of Nottingham, 1951; Provost and Domestic Prelate to HH Pope Pius XII, 1955; Bishop of Plymouth, 1955–86. *Publication:* Dedicated to Christ, 1989. *Address:* Stoodley Knowle, Anstey's Cove Road, Torquay TQ1 2JB.

RESTREPO-LONDOÑO, Andrés; Order of Boyacá, Colombia; Colombian Ambassador to the Court of St James's, 1981–82; President, Empresa Colombiana de Petróleos-ECOPETROL, since 1988; *b* 20 Jan. 1942; *m* 1968, Ghislaine Ibiza; one *s* three *d*. *Educ:* Universidad de Antioquia; Université de Paris (postgraduate courses, 1966). Professor and Head of Economic Dept., Univ. de Antioquia, 1967–68; Gen. Man., La Primavera chain of stores, 1969–76; Finance Man., Empresas Públicas de Medellín, 1976–79; Gen. Man., Carbones de Colombia (Colombian Coal Bd), 1979–80; Minister for Economic Develt, May 1980–March 1981. Chm., Proban SA (Banana Exporting Co.), 1983–84; Pres., Industrias e Inversiones Samper SA (Cement Co.), 1985–88. Order Sol of Perú; Order Cruzeiro do Sul, Brazil. *Publications:* Carbones Térmicos en Colombia, Bases para una Política Contractual, 1981; several articles in El Colombiano, daily newspaper of Medellín, Colombia. *Recreations:* fishing, tennis. *Address:* Calle 136A No 57B-17, Bogotá, DE, Colombia. *Club:* Lagartos (Bogotá).

RETTIE, (James) Philip, CBE 1987; TD 1962; farmer, since 1964; Partner, Crossley and Rettie, since 1989; Director, Edinburgh and Glasgow Investment Co., since 1989; *b* 7 Dec. 1926; *s* of James Rettie and Rachel Buist; *m* 1st, 1955, Helen Grant; two *s* one *d*; 2nd, 1980, Mrs Diana Harvey (*née* Ballantyne). *Educ:* Trinity College, Glenalmond. Royal Engineers, 1945–48; RE (TA), 1949–65. Wm Low & Co. plc, 1948–85 (Chm., 1980–85); Mem., TSB Scotland Area Bd, 1983–88. Chm., Sea Fish Industry Authority, 1981–87. Trustee, Scottish Civic Trust, 1983–. Hon. Colonel: 117 (Highland) Field Support Squadron, RE, TAVR, 1982–87; 277 Airfield Damage Repair Sqdn, RE(T), 1984–89. FRSA. *Recreations:* shooting, gardening, hill-walking. *Address:* Hill House, Ballindean, Inchture, Perthshire PH14 9QS. *T:* Inchture (0828) 86337. *Club:* Caledonian.

REUPKE, Michael; *b* Potsdam, Germany, 20 Nov. 1936; *s* of Dr Willm Reupke and Dr Frances G. Reupke (*née* Kinnear); *m* 1963, (Helen) Elizabeth Restrick; one *s* two *d*. *Educ:* Latymer Upper Sch., London; Jesus Coll., Cambridge (MA Mod. Langs); Collège d'Europe, Bruges. Joined Reuters, 1962; reporter, France, Switzerland, Guinea and West Germany, 1962–69; Asst European Manager, Gen. News Div., 1970–72; Chief Rep., West Germany, 1973–74; Manager, Latin America and the Caribbean, 1975–77; Editor-in-Chief, 1978–89; Gen. Manager, 1989. Dir, Visnews, 1985–89; Trustee, Reuter Foundn, 1982–89. *Recreation:* sailing. *Address:* Tippings, The Common, Stokenchurch, Bucks HP14 3UD. *T:* High Wycombe (0494) 482341. *Clubs:* Royal Automobile; Leander (Henley-on-Thames).

REUTER, Edzard; Chairman of Executive Board, Daimler-Benz AG, since 1987; *b* 16 Feb. 1928; *m* 1972, Helga Roeder. *Educ:* Univs of Berlin and Göttingen (maths and physics); Free Univ. of Berlin (law). Research Asst, Free Univ. of Berlin Law Faculty, 1954–56; Universum Film, 1957–62; Manager, TV prod. section, Bertelsmann Group, Munich, 1962–64; exec., finance dept, Daimler-Benz, 1964; responsible for management planning and organization, 1971; Dep. Mem., Bd, 1973; Full Mem., Exec. Bd, 1976. *Publication:* Vom Geist der Wirtschaft, 1986. *Recreations:* riding, ski-ing, sailing, tennis. *Address:* Daimler-Benz AG, PO Box 80 02 30, 7000 Stuttgart 80, Germany. *T:* 0711/17–94333.

REUTER, Prof. Gerd Edzard Harry, MA Cantab; Professor of Mathematics, Imperial College of Science and Technology, London, 1965–83, now Emeritus; *b* 21 Nov. 1921; *s* of Ernst Rudolf Johannes Reuter and Gertrud Charlotte Reuter (*née* Scholz); *m* 1945, Eileen Grace Legard; one *s* three *d*. *Educ:* The Leys School and Trinity College, Cambridge. Mem. of Dept of Mathematics, Univ. of Manchester, 1946–58; Professor of Pure Mathematics, Univ. of Durham, 1959–65. *Publications:* Elementary Differential Equations and Operators, 1958; articles in various mathematical and scientific jls. *Address:* 47 Madingley Road, Cambridge CB3 0EL.

REVANS, Prof. Reginald William, PhD; MIMinE; Founder, Action Learning Trust, 1977; Professorial Fellow in Action Learning, University of Manchester, since 1986; *b* 14 May 1907; *s* of Thomas William Revans, Principal Ship Surveyor, Board of Trade; *m* 1st, 1932, Annida Aquist, Gothenburg (marriage dissolved, 1947); three *d*; 2nd, 1955, Norah Mary Merritt, Chelmsford; one *s*. *Educ:* Battersea Grammar School; University Coll., London; Emmanuel Coll., Cambridge. BSc London, PhD Cantab. Commonwealth Fund Fellow, Univ. of Michigan, 1930–32; Research Fellow, Emmanuel Coll., Cambridge, 1932–35; Dep. Chief Education Officer, Essex CC, 1935–45; Dir of Education, Mining Assoc. of Gt Britain, 1945–47 and NCB, 1947–50; Research on management of coalmines, 1950–55; Prof., Industrial Admin., Univ. of Manchester, 1955–65; Res. Fellow, Guy's Hosp. Med. Sch., 1965–68; External Prof., Management Studies, Leeds Univ., 1976–78. Dist. Vis. Scholar, Southern Methodist Univ., USA, 1972. Pres., European Assoc. of Univ. Management Centres, 1962–64. Hon. DSc Bath, 1969. Chevalier, Order of Leopold, Belgium, 1971. *Publications:* Report on Education for Mining Industry, 1945; Education of the Young Worker, 1949; Standards for Morale, 1964; Science and the Manager, 1965; The Theory and Practice of Management, 1965; Developing Effective Managers, 1971; (ed) Hospitals, Communication, Choice and Change, 1972; Workers' Attitudes and Motivation (OECD Report), 1972; Childhood and Maturity, 1973; Action Learning in Hospitals, 1976; The ABC of Action Learning, 1978; Action Learning, 1979; The Origins and Growth of Action Learning, 1982; various in professional magazines upon application of analytical methods to understanding of industrial morale. *Recreations:* British Olympic Team, 1928; holder of Cambridge undergraduate long jump record, 1929–62. *Address:* 8 Higher Downs, Altrincham, Cheshire. *Club:* National Liberal.

REVELL, Surg. Rear-Adm. Anthony Leslie, QHS 1989; FFARCS; Surgeon Rear-Admiral, Operational Medical Services, since 1991; *b* 26 April 1935; *s* of Leslie Frederick Revell and Florence Mabel (*née* Styles). *Educ:* King's Coll. Sch., Wimbledon; Ashford and Eastbourne Grammar Schs; Univ. of Birmingham Med. Sch. (MB, ChB); DA 1968.

FFARCS 1969; FRSM 1970. Joined RN, 1960; HMS Troubridge, 1960–62; HMS Dampier, 1962; HMS Loch Fada and 5th Frigate Sqdn, 1963; Anæsthetist, RN Hosp., Plymouth, 1964–65; HMS Eagle, 1965–67; Clin. Assistant, Radcliffe Infy, Oxford, Alder Hey Children's Hosp., Liverpool, and various courses, 1967–69; Anæsthetist, RN Hosp., Plymouth, 1969–70; RAF Hosps Nocton Hall and Akrotiri, Cyprus, 1970–72; ANZUK Mil. Hosp., Singapore, 1972–74; Cons. Anæsthetist, RN Hosp., Haslar, 1974–79; *ndc*, Latimer, 1979–80; Recruiter, MoD, 1980; Dir of Studies, Inst. of Naval Medicine, 1980–82; on staff, Surg. Rear-Adm. (Naval Hosps), 1982–84; Dir, Med. Personnel, 1984–86; RCDS, 1986; MO i/c, RN Hosp., Plymouth, 1987–88; on staff, C-in-C Fleet, 1988–90; Dir, Clinical Services, Defence Med. Directorate, 1990–91. OStJ 1984. *Publications:* Haslar: the Royal Hospital, 1979; (ed jtly) Proc. World Assoc. Anæsthetists, 1970. *Recreation:* choral music. *Address:* 29 Little Green, Alverstoke, Gosport, Hants PO12 2EX. *Club:* Naval and Military.

REVELSTOKE, 4th Baron *cr* 1885; **Rupert Baring;** *b* 8 Feb. 1911; *o s* of 3rd Baron and Maude (*d* 1922), *d* of late Pierre Lorillard; *S* father, 1934; *m* 1934, Flora (who obtained a divorce 1944; she *d* 1971), 2nd *d* of 1st Baron Hesketh; two *s*. *Educ:* Eton. 2nd Lt Royal Armoured Corps (TA). *Heir: s* Hon. John Baring, *b* 2 Dec. 1934. *Address:* Lambay Island, Rush, Co. Dublin, Ireland.

REVERDIN, Prof. Olivier, DrLitt; Professor of Greek, University of Geneva, 1958–83 (Hon. Professor, since 1983); Member, Consultative Assembly of Council of Europe, 1963–74 (President, 1969–72); Deputy (Liberal) for Geneva, Swiss National Council, 1955–71, Council of States (Senate), 1971–79; *b* 15 July 1913; *m* 1936, Renée Chaponnière; two *s* one *d*. *Educ:* Geneva, Paris and Athens. LicLitt 1935; DrLitt Geneva, 1945. Foreign Mem., French Sch. of Archaeology, Athens, 1936–38; Attaché Swiss Legation, Service of Foreign Interests, Rome, 1941–43; Privatdocent of Greek, Univ. of Geneva, 1945–57; Parly Redactor, 1945–54; Chief Editor 1954–59, Manager 1954–67, Pres., 1972–79, Journal de Genève. Mem. 1963–80, Pres. 1968–80, Swiss National Research Council; Mem., Swiss Science Council, 1958–80; Président: Fondation Hardt pour l'étude de l'antiquité classique, Geneva, 1959–; Fondation Archives Jean Piaget, 1973–87; Vice-Pres., European Science Foundn, 1974–77, Mem. Exec. Council, 1977–80; Chm., Collections Baur, Geneva, 1984–. *Publications:* La religion de la cité platonicienne, 1945; La guerre du Sonderbund, 1947, 2nd edn 1987; La Crète, berceau de la civilisation occidentale, 1960; Connaissance de la Suisse, 1966; Les premiers cours de Grec au Collège de France, 1984. *Address:* 8 rue des Granges, 1204 Geneva, Switzerland. *T:* 022–21–51–91.

REX, Prof. John Arderne; Research Professor on Ethnic Relations, 1984–90, now Emeritus, and Associate Director, Centre for Research in Ethnic Relations, 1974–90, University of Warwick; *b* 5 March 1925; *s* of Frederick Edward George Rex and Winifred Natalie Rex; *m* 1st, 1949, Pamela Margaret Rutherford (marr. diss. 1963); two *d*; 2nd, 1965, Margaret Ellen Biggs; two *s*. *Educ:* Grey Institute High Sch. and Rhodes University Coll., S Africa. BA (S Africa), PhD (Leeds). Served War, Royal Navy (Able Seaman), 1943–45. Graduated, 1948; Lecturer: Univ. of Leeds, 1949–62; Birmingham, 1962–64; Prof. of Social Theory and Institutions, Durham, 1964–70; Prof. of Sociology, Univ. of Warwick, 1970–79; Dir, SSRC Research Unit on Ethnic Relations, Univ. of Aston in Birmingham, 1979–84. Vis. Prof., Univ. of Toronto, 1974–75. *Publications:* Key Problems of Sociological Theory, 1961; (with Robert Moore) Race Community and Conflict, 1967, 2nd edn 1973; Race Relations in Sociological Theory, 1970; Discovering Sociology, 1973; Race, Colonialism and the City, 1974; (ed) Approaches to Sociology, 1974; Sociology and the Demystification of the Modern World, 1974; (with Sally Tomlinson) Colonial Immigrants in a British City, 1979; Social Conflict, 1980; (ed) Apartheid and Social Research, 1981; Race and Ethnicity, 1986; The Ghetto and the Underclass, 1988. *Recreations:* politics, race relations work. *Address:* 33 Arlington Avenue, Leamington Spa, Warwicks CV32 5UD.

REX, Hon. Sir Robert (Richmond), KBE 1984 (OBE 1973); CMG 1978; Prime Minister of Niue, since 1974; Representative of Alofi South on the Niue Island Council, since 1952; *b* 25 Jan. 1909; *s* of Leslie Lucas Richmond Rex and Monomono Paea; *m* 1941, Tuagatagaloa Patricia Vatolo; two *s* two *d*. *Educ:* Tufukia Technical Sch., Niue. Engrg Apprentice, Rakiraki Sugar-mills, Fiji Islands, 1926; Employee, NZ Steamship Union Co., 1927; farmer, Niue, 1930; Businessman (retailing), R. R. Rex & Sons Ltd, 1952. Clerk and Official Interpreter (Jack-of-all-trades), Niue Govt, 1934; Mem. Exec. Cttee, Niue Island Assembly, 1960; Leader of Govt Business, 1966; is known as the longest-serving statesman in the Pacific. Mem., Commonwealth Parly Assoc. *Recreations:* cricket, Rugby, fishing, planting, billiards. *Address:* Alofi South, Niue Island, New Zealand. *T:* 275. *Club:* Niue Sports.

REYES, Narciso G., Bintang Mahaputera, 1964; Order of Diplomatic Service Merit, 1972; President, Philippine Council for Foreign Relations, 1986–87; *b* Manila, 6 Feb. 1914; *m*. *Educ:* Univ. of Sto Tomas (AB). Mem., English Faculty, Univ. of Sto Tomas, 1935–36; Assoc. Ed., Philippines Commonweal, 1935–41; Nat. Language Faculty, Ateneo de Manila, 1939–41; Assoc. Ed., Manila Post, 1945–47; Assoc. News Ed., Evening News, Manila, 1947–48; Man. Ed., Philippine Newspaper Guild Organ, 1947–48; Dir, Philippine Information Agency, 1954–55; Minister-Counsellor, Bangkok, 1956; Public Relations Dir, SEATO, 1956–58; Minister, later Amb., Burma, 1958–62; Ambassador to: Indonesia, 1962–67; London, Stockholm, Oslo, Copenhagen, 1967–70; Permanent Rep. to UN, 1970–77; Philippine Ambassador to People's Republic of China, 1977–80; Sec. Gen., ASEAN, 1980–82. Mem. various delegns and missions, incl. sessions of UN; Philippine Rep. to UN Commn for Social Devt, 1967–72 (Vice-Chm., 1967; Chm., 1968); Special UN Rep. on Social Develt, 1968; Rep. to UN Human Rights Commn, 1970–72; Chairman: UNICEF Exec. Bd, 1972–74; UN Gen. Assembly Finance and Economic Cttee, 1971; Pres., UNDP Governing Council, 1974; Vice-Pres., UN Environment Governing Council, 1975. Chm., External Educn Plans, 1988–89. Vice-Chm., Philippine Futuristics Soc. Editor, Foreign Relations Jl, 1986–. Outstanding Alumnus, Univ. of Sto Tomas, 1969. Dr of Laws (*hc*), Philippine Women's Univ., 1977. *Publications:* essays, poems and short stories. *Address:* 8 Lipa Road, Philamlife Homes, Quezon City, Manila, Philippines.

REYNOLD, Frederic; QC 1982; *b* 7 Jan. 1936; *s* of late Henry and Regina Reynold. *Educ:* Battersea Grammar School; Magdalen College, Oxford. BA Hons Jurisprudence. Called to the Bar, Gray's Inn, 1960; commenced practice, 1963. *Publication:* The Judge as Lawmaker, 1967. *Recreations:* music, the arts, association croquet, dining out among friends. *Address:* 5 Hillcrest, 51 Ladbroke Grove, W11. *T:* 071–229 3848. *Club:* Sussex County Croquet.

REYNOLDS, Alan (Munro); painter, maker of reliefs, and printmaker; *b* 27 April 1926; *m* 1957, Vona Darby. *Educ:* Woolwich Polytechnic Art School; Royal College of Art (Scholarship and Medal). One man exhibitions: Redfern Gall., 1952, 1953, 1954, 1956, 1960, 1962, 1964, 1966, 1970, 1972, 1974; Durlacher Gall., New York, 1954, 1959; Leicester Galleries, 1958; Aldeburgh, Suffolk, 1965; Arnolfini Gall., Bristol, 1971 (graphics); Annely Juda Fine Art, 1978, 1991; Juda Rowan Gall., 1982, 1986; Thomas Agnew, Albemarle Street Gall., 1982; Gall. Wack, Kaiserslautern, 1986, 1990; Galarie Lalumière, Paris, 1990. Work in exhibitions: Carnegie (Pittsburgh) Internat., USA, 1952, 1955, 1958, 1961; Internat. Exhibn, Rome, (awarded one of the three equal prizes), subsequently Musée d'Art Moderne, Paris, and Brussels; British Council Exhibn, Oslo and Copenhagen, 1956; Redfern Gall., 1971; Spectrum, Arts Council of GB, 1971; British Painting 1952–77, Royal Academy, 1977; Galerie Loyse Oppenheim, Nyon, Switzerland, 1977; Galerie Renée Ziegler, Zürich, 1981; group exhibitions: Scottish Nat. Gall. of Modern Art, Edinburgh, 1984; Annely Juda Fine Art and Juda Rowan Gall., London, 1985; Galeries Renée Ziegler, Zürich, 1985–86; Annely Juda Fine Art, 1986; Wilhelm-Hack Mus., Ludwigshafen am Rhein, 1987. Works acquired by: Tate Gall.; V&A; National Galleries of: S Aust.; Felton Bequest, Vic., Aust.; NZ; Canada; City Art Galleries of: Birmingham; Bristol; Manchester; Wakefield; Mus. of Modern Art, NY; Contemporary Art Soc.; British Council; Arts Council of GB; Rothschild Foundn; The Graves Art Gall., Sheffield; Nottingham Castle Mus.; Fitzwilliam Mus., Cambridge; Mus. of Modern Art, São Paulo, Brazil; Leeds Art Gall.; Toledo Art Gall., Ohio, USA; Oriel Coll., Oxford; Warwick Univ.; Mus. and Art Galls, Brighton and Plymouth; Texas Univ., Austin, USA; Berlin Nat. Gall.; McCrory Corp., NY; Wilhelm-Hack Mus., Ludwigshafen am Rhein; Louisiana Mus., Denmark; Tel Aviv Mus., Israel; Musée des Beaux Arts de Grenoble; Mus. Pfalzgalerie, Kaiserslautern, W Germany. CoID Award, 1965; Arts Council of GB Purchase Award, 1967. *Relevant Publication:* The Painter, Alan Reynolds, by J. P. Hodin, 1962. *Address:* Briar Cottage, High Street, Cranbrook, Kent TN17 3EN.

REYNOLDS, Albert; Member of the Dáil (TD) (FF), since 1977; Minister for Finance, Republic of Ireland, since 1988; Vice President, Fianna Fáil, since 1983; *b* Rooskey, Co. Roscommon, Nov. 1932; *m* Kathleen Coen; two *s* five *d*. *Educ:* Summerhill Coll., Sligo. Minister: for Posts and Telegraphs, and for Transport, 1979–81; for Industry and Energy, March–Dec. 1982; Opposition spokesperson: for Industry and Employment, 1983–84; for Energy, 1984–87; Minister for Industry and Commerce, 1987–88. Mem., Oireachtas Jt Cttee on Commercial State-Sponsored Bodies, 1983–87. Member: Longford CC, 1974–79; Longford County Cttee of Agric., 1974–79; Longford Health Cttee, 1974–79. Pres., Longford Chamber of Commerce, 1974–78; Chm., Longford Recreational Develt Centre. *Address:* Department of Finance, Government Buildings, Upper Merrion Street, Dublin 2, Ireland. *T:* Dublin 767571.

REYNOLDS, (Arthur) Graham, OBE 1984; Keeper of the Department of Prints and Drawings, 1961–74 (of Engraving, Illustration and Design, 1959–61), and of Paintings, Victoria and Albert Museum, 1959–74; *b* Highgate, 10 Jan. 1914; *o s* of late Arthur T. Reynolds and Eva Mullins; *m* 1943, Daphne, *d* of late Thomas Dent, Huddersfield. *Educ:* Highgate School; Queens' College, Cambridge. Joined staff of Victoria and Albert Museum, 1937. Seconded to Ministry of Home Security, 1939–45. Member: Adv. Council, Paul Mellon Centre for Studies in British Art, 1977–84; Reviewing Cttee on the Export of Works of Art, 1984–90. Trustee, William Morris Gallery, Walthamstow, 1972–75; Chm., Gainsborough's House Soc., Sudbury, 1977–79. Leverhulme Emeritus Fellowship, 1980–81. *Publications:* Twentieth Century Drawings, 1946; Nicholas Hilliard and Isaac Oliver, 1947, 2nd edn 1971; Van Gogh, 1947; Nineteenth Century Drawings, 1949; Thomas Bewick, 1949; An Introduction to English Water-Colour Painting, 1950, rev. edn 1988; Gastronomic Pleasures, 1950; Elizabethan and Jacobean Costume, 1951; English Portrait Miniatures, 1952, rev. edn 1988; Painters of the Victorian Scene, 1953; Catalogue of the Constable Collection, Victoria and Albert Museum, 1960, rev. edn 1973; Constable, the Natural Painter, 1965; Victorian Painting, 1966, 2nd edn 1987; Turner, 1969; A Concise History of Water Colour Painting, 1972; Catalogue of Portrait Miniatures, Wallace Collection, 1980; Constable's England, 1983; The Later Paintings and Drawings of John Constable, 2 vols, 1984 (Mitchell Prize); Editor of series English Masters of Black and White; contribs to Burlington Magazine, Apollo, etc. *Address:* The Old Manse, Bradfield St George, Bury St Edmunds, Suffolk IP30 0AZ. *T:* Sicklesmere (0284) 386610. *Club:* Athenæum.

REYNOLDS, Barbara, MA Cantab; BA (Hons), PhD London; author, lexicographer; Reader in Italian Studies, University of Nottingham, 1966–78; *b* 13 June 1914; *d* of late Alfred Charles Reynolds; *m* 1st, 1939, Prof. Lewis Thorpe (*d* 1977); one *s* one *d*; 2nd, 1982, Kenneth Imeson, *qv*. *Educ:* St Paul's Girls' Sch.; UCL. Asst Lectr in Italian, LSE 1937–40. Chief Exec. and Gen. Editor, The Cambridge Italian Dictionary, 1948–81; Man. Editor, Seven, an Anglo-American Literary Review, 1980–89. Mem. Coun. Senate, Cambridge Univ., 1961–62. University Lecturer in Italian Literature and Language, Cambridge, 1945–62 (Faculty Assistant Lecturer, 1940–45); Warden of Willoughby Hall, Univ. of Nottingham, 1963–69. Vis. Professor: Univ. of Calif., Berkeley, 1974–75; Wheaton Coll., Illinois, 1977–78, 1982; Trinity Coll., Dublin, 1980, 1981; Hope Coll., Mich., 1982. Hon. Reader in Italian, Univ. of Warwick, 1975–80. Chm., Dorothy L. Sayers Soc., 1986–. Hon. DLitt: Wheaton Coll., Illinois, 1979; Hope Coll., Mich., 1982. Silver Medal for Services to Italian culture (Italian Govt), 1964; Edmund Gardner Prize, 1964; Silver Medal for services to Anglo-Veneto cultural relations, Prov. Admin of Vicenza, 1971; Cavaliere Ufficiale al Merito della Repubblica Italiana, 1978. *Publications:* (with K. T. Butler) Tredici Novelle Moderne, 1947; The Linguistic Writings of Alessandro Manzoni: a Textual and Chronological Reconstruction, 1950; rev. edn with introd., Dante and the Early Astronomers, by M. A. Orr, 1956; The Cambridge Italian Dictionary, Vol. I, Italian-English, 1962, Vol. II, English-Italian, 1981; (with Dorothy L. Sayers) Paradise: a translation into English triple rhyme, from the Italian of Dante Alighieri, 1962; (with Lewis Thorpe) Guido Farina, Painter of Verona, 1967; La Vita Nuova (Poems of Youth); trans. of Dante's Vita Nuova, 1969; Concise Cambridge Italian Dictionary, 1975; Orlando Furioso, trans. into rhymed octaves of Ariosto's epic, Vol. I, 1975 (Internat. Literary Prize, Monselice, Italy, 1976) Vol. II, 1977; (ed) Cambridge-Signorelli Dizionario Italiano-Inglese, Inglese-Italiano, 1986; (ed jtly) The Translator's Art, 1987; The Passionate Intellect: Dorothy L. Sayers' encounter with Dante, 1989; numerous articles on Italian literature in learned jls. *Address:* 220 Milton Road, Cambridge CB4 1LQ. *T:* Cambridge (0223) 424894. *Clubs:* University Women's (Chm., 1988–90), Authors'.

See also A. C. Thorpe.

REYNOLDS, Sir David James, 3rd Bt, *cr* 1923; Member of Lloyd's Insurance; *b* 26 Jan. 1924; *er s* of Sir John Francis Roskell Reynolds, 2nd Bt, MBE, JP and Milicent (*d* 1931), *d* of late Major James Orr-Ewing and late Lady Margaret Orr-Ewing, *d* of 7th Duke of Roxburghe; *S* father 1956; *m* 1966, Charlotte Baumgartner; one *s* two *d*. *Educ:* Downside. Active service in Army, 1942–47, Italy, etc; on demobilisation, Captain 15/19 Hussars. *Recreation:* sport. *Heir: s* James Francis Reynolds, *b* 10 July 1971. *Address:* Blanche Pierre House, St Lawrence, Jersey, CI.

REYNOLDS, Eric Vincent, TD 1948; MA; Headmaster of Stowe, 1949–58, retired; *b* 30 April 1904; *o s* of late Arthur John and Lily Reynolds; unmarried. *Educ:* Haileybury College; St John's College, Cambridge. Modern and Mediæval languages Tripos, Parts 1 and 2; Lector in English at University of Leipzig, 1926–27; MA 1930. Assistant Master: Rugby School, 1927–31; Upper Canada College, Toronto, 1931–32; Rugby School, 1932–49 (Housemaster, 1944–49). CO, Rugby School JTC, 1938–44. *Recreations:* ski-ing and mountaineering. *Address:* 48 Lemsford Road, St Albans, Herts AL1 3PR. *T:* St Albans (0727) 53599.

REYNOLDS, Eva Mary Barbara; *see* Reynolds, Barbara.

REYNOLDS, Francis Martin Baillie, DCL; FBA 1988; Reader in Law, University of Oxford, since 1977; Fellow of Worcester College, Oxford, since 1960; *b* 11 Nov. 1932; *s* of Eustace Baillie Reynolds and Emma Margaret Hanby Reynolds (*née* Holmes); *m* 1965, Susan Claire Shillito; two *s* one *d. Educ:* Winchester Coll.; Worcester Coll., Oxford (BA 1956; BCL 1957; MA 1960; DCL 1986). Bigelow Teaching Fellow, Chicago Univ., 1957–58. Called to the Bar, Inner Temple, 1960, Hon. Bencher 1979. Visiting Professor: Nat. Univ. of Singapore, 1984, 1986, 1988, 1990; UCL, 1986–89; Vis. Lectr, Univ. of Auckland, 1971, 1977. Gen. Editor, Lloyd's Maritime and Commercial Law Qly, 1983–87; Editor, Law Qly Review, 1987–. *Publications:* (ed jtly) Chitty on Contracts, 24th edn 1977, to 26th edn 1989; (ed jtly) Benjamin's Sale of Goods, 1974, 3rd edn 1987; Bowstead on Agency, (ed jtly) 13th edn 1968, 14th edn 1976, (ed) 15th edn 1985; contribs to legal jls. *Recreations:* music, walking. *Address:* Worcester College, Oxford OX1 2HB. *T:* Oxford (0865) 278300.

REYNOLDS, Frank Arrowsmith, OBE 1974; LLB; HM Diplomatic Service, retired; *b* 30 March 1916; *s* of late Sydney Edward Clyde Reynolds and Bessie (*née* Foster); *m* 1938, Joan Marion Lockyer; one *s* two *d. Educ:* Addey and Stanhope Sch.; London University. Army, 1941–46 (Lieut, RE). District Officer, Tanganyika, 1950; Commonwealth Relations Office, 1962–63; First Secretary, Bombay, 1964–67; CO, later FCO, 1967–69; Consul-Gen., Seville, 1969–71; Head of Chancery, Maseru, 1971–75. *Publication:* Guide to Super-8 Photography, 1981. *Recreations:* music, sailing, photography. *Address:* 26 Nelson Street, Brightlingsea, Essex CO7 0DZ. *Clubs:* Royal Bombay Yacht; Colne Yacht.

REYNOLDS, Gillian; Radio Critic, The Daily Telegraph, since 1975; *b* 15 Nov. 1935; *d* of Charles Morton and Ada (*née* Kelly); *m* 1958, Stanley Reynolds (marr. diss. 1982); three *s. Educ:* St Anne's Coll., Oxford (BA); Mount Holyoke Coll., South Hadley, Mass, USA. TV journalist, 1964–; Radio Critic, The Guardian, 1967–74; Programme Controller, Radio City, Liverpool, 1974–75. Fellow (first to be apptd), Radio Acad., 1990. *Recreation:* listening to the radio. *Address:* Flat 3, 1 Linden Gardens, W2 4HA. *T:* 071–229 1893. *Club:* University Women's.

REYNOLDS, Graham; *see* Reynolds, A. G.

REYNOLDS, Guy Edwin K.; *see* King-Reynolds.

REYNOLDS, Maj.-Gen. Jack Raymond, CB 1971; OBE 1945; ERD 1948; DL; Director of Movements (Army), Ministry of Defence, 1968–71, retired; *b* 10 June 1916; *s* of Walter Reynolds and Evelyn Marion (*née* Burrows); *m* 1940, Joan Howe Taylor; one *s* one *d. Educ:* Haberdashers' Aske's. Student Apprentice, AEC Ltd, 1934. Commissioned RASC (SR), 1936. Served War of 1939–45, France, Middle East and Italy (despatches). CRASC 7th Armoured Div., 1955–57; GSO 1 War Office, 1958–60; Col GS; UK Delegn to NATO Standing Group, Washington, DC, 1960–62; DDST, Southern Command, 1962–64; Commandant, RASC Training Centre, 1964–65; Imperial Defence College, 1966; Dep. Quarter-Master-General, BAOR, 1967–68. Col Comdt, Royal Corps of Transport, 1972–78. Dir-Gen., BHS, 1971–75; Dir-Gen., 1975–85, Pres., 1985–88, BEF. FCIT. DL Northants, 1984. *Recreation:* fishing. *Address:* Old Mill House, Hellidon, near Daventry, Northants NN11 6LG.

REYNOLDS, James; Judge of the High Court, Eastern Region of Nigeria, 1956–63; *b* Belfast, May, 1908; *yr s* of late James Reynolds and late Agnes Forde (*née* Cully); *m* 1946, Alexandra Mary Erskine Strain; two *s* two *d. Educ:* Belfast Roy. Acad.; Queen's Univ., Belfast. Called to Bar of N Ire., 1931; practised at N Ire Bar, 1931–40. Colonial Legal Service as Crown Counsel in Hong Kong, 1940. Prisoner-of-war in Japanese hands, 1941–45. Returned to Hong Kong, 1946; apptd District Judge, 1953. Chairman: Local Tribunal under Nat. Insce Acts, 1964–83; Industrial Tribunal, 1969–81. *Address:* 10 Church Road, Helen's Bay, Co. Down, Northern Ireland.

REYNOLDS, Joyce Maire, FBA 1982; Fellow of Newnham College, 1951–84, now Hon. Fellow, and Reader in Roman Historical Epigraphy, 1983–84, University of Cambridge; *b* 18 Dec. 1918; *d* of late William Howe Reynolds and Nellie Farmer Reynolds. *Educ:* Walthamstow County High Sch. for Girls; St Paul's Girls' Sch., Hammersmith; Somerville Coll., Oxford (Hon. Fellow, 1988). Temp. Civil Servant, BoT, 1941–46; Rome Scholar, British Sch. at Rome, 1946–48; Lectr in Ancient History, King's Coll., Newcastle upon Tyne, 1948–51; Cambridge University: Asst Lectr in Classics, 1952–57; Univ. Lectr 1957–83; Dir of Studies in Classics, 1951–79 and Lectr in Classics, 1951–84, Newnham Coll. Woolley Travelling Fellow, Somerville Coll., Oxford, 1961; Mem., Inst. for Advanced Study, Princeton, USA, 1984–85; Vis. Prof., Univ. of Calif at Berkeley, 1987. President: Soc. for Libyan Studies, 1981–86; Soc. for the Promotion of Roman Studies, 1986–89. Corresp. Mem., German Archaeol Inst., 1971–. Hon. DLitt Newcastle upon Tyne, 1984. *Publications:* (with J. B. Ward Perkins) The Inscriptions of Roman Tripolitania, 1952; Aphrodisias and Rome, 1982; (with R. Tannenbaum) Jews and Godfearers at Aphrodisias, 1987; articles on Roman history and epigraphy in jls, 1951–. *Recreation:* walking. *Address:* Newnham College, Cambridge CB3 9DF. *T:* Cambridge (0223) 335700.

REYNOLDS, Leighton Durham, FBA 1987; Fellow and Tutor in Classics, Brasenose College, Oxford, since 1957; *b* 11 Feb. 1930; *s* of Edgar James Reynolds and Hester Ann Reynolds (*née* Hale); *m* 1962, Susan Mary Buchanan, *d* of Prof. Sir Colin Buchanan, *qv*; one *s* two *d. Educ:* Caerphilly Grammar Sch.; University Coll., Cardiff (BA 1st cl. Hons 1950); St John's Coll., Cambridge (BA 1st cl. Hons 1952; Craven Student, 1952; MA 1956); MA Oxon 1956. Flying Officer, RAF, 1952–54. Jun. Res. Fellow, Queen's Coll., Oxford, 1954–57. Visiting Professor: Cornell Univ., 1960, 1971; Univ. of Texas at Austin, 1967. Mem., Inst. for Advanced Study, Princeton, 1965, 1987. Editor, Classical Review, 1975–87. *Publications:* The Medieval Tradition of Seneca's Letters, 1965; (ed) Seneca, Epistulae Morales, 1965; (with N. G. Wilson) Scribes and Scholars, 1968, 3rd edn 1991; (ed) Seneca, Dialogi, 1977; (ed) Texts and Transmission: a survey of the Latin classics, 1983; (ed) Sallust, 1991. *Recreations:* walking, camping, gardening, plant-hunting. *Address:* Winterslow Cottage, Lincombe Lane, Boars Hill, Oxford OX1 5DZ. *T:* Oxford (0865) 735741.

REYNOLDS, Dr Martin Richard Finch; Consultant in Public Health Medicine, Hull Health Authority, since 1989 (Specialist in Community Medicine, 1986–89); *b* 26 July 1943; 2nd *s* of Gerald Finch Reynolds and Frances Bertha (*née* Locke); *m* 1965, Shelagh (*née* Gray); two *d. Educ:* Newton Abbot Grammar Sch.; Univ. of Bristol. MB ChB, DPH; FFPHM. House posts in medicine, surgery, infectious diseases and paediatrics, 1966–67; Dep. Med. Officer, Glos CC, 1967–70; Sen. Dep. Med. Officer, Bristol City and Asst Sen. Med. Officer, SW Regional Hosp. Bd, 1970–74; Dist Community Physician, Southmead Dist of Avon AHA (Teaching) and Med. Officer for Environmental Health, Northavon Dist Council, 1974–79; Area Med. Officer, Wilts AHA, 1979–80; Regional MO/Chief Med. Advr, South Western RHA, 1980–86. *Publications:* contrib. various articles in professional jls on subjects in community medicine. *Address:* Knights Garth, Callas, Bishop Burton, Beverley, N Humberside HU17 8QL.

REYNOLDS, Michael Emanuel, CBE 1977; Founder/Owner, Susan Reynolds Books Ltd, 1977–84; *b* 22 April 1931; *s* of Isaac Mark and Henrietta Rosenberg; *m* 1964, Susan Geraldine Yates; two *d. Educ:* Haberdashers' Aske's (HSC). Marks & Spencer Ltd, 1951–61; Food Controller, British Home Stores Ltd, 1961–64; Spar (UK) Ltd, 1964–77: Trading Controller, 1964–67; Chm. and Managing Dir, 1967–77; BV Intergroup Trading (IGT), 1974–77: Founder Mem., Bd of Admin.; Dir, 1974–75; Chm. and Dir, 1975–77. FRSA. *Recreations:* tennis, squash, bridge. *Address:* 55 Newlands Terrace, 155 Queenstown Road, SW8 3RN. *T:* 071–627 5862.

REYNOLDS, Maj.-Gen. Michael Frank, CB 1983; Assistant Director, International Military Staff, HQ NATO (Plans and Policy), 1983–86; *b* 3 June 1930; *s* of Frank Reynolds and Gwendolyn Reynolds (*née* Griffiths); *m* 1955, Anne Bernice (*née* Truman); three *d. Educ:* Cranleigh; RMA, Sandhurst. Commnd Queen's Royal Regt, 1950; served Germany, Korea, Cyprus, Canada, Persian Gulf, Netherlands, Belgium; psc 1960; GSO 1 Ops, HQ AFCENT, 1970–71; comd 2 Queen's, BAOR and Ulster, 1971–73; GSO 1 Ops, N Ireland, 1973–74; comd 12 Mech Bde BAOR, 1974–76; RCDS, 1977; Dep. Adjt Gen., BAOR, 1978–80; Comdr, Allied Command Europe Mobile Force (Land), 1980–83. Col Comdt, Queen's Division, 1984–86; Col, The Queen's Regt, 1989–. *Recreations:* military history (especially Battle of the Ardennes, 1944), gardening.

REYNOLDS, Sir Peter (William John), Kt 1985; CBE 1975; Deputy Chairman, Ranks Hovis McDougall plc, since 1989 (Chairman, 1981–89); Director: Boots Co. plc, since 1986; Guardian Royal Exchange plc, since 1986; Avis Europe Ltd, since 1988; Cilva Holdings plc, since 1989; Nationwide Anglia Building Society, since 1990; *b* 10 Sept. 1929; *s* of Harry and Gladys Victoria Reynolds; *m* 1955, Barbara Anne, *d* of Vincent Kenneth Johnson, OBE; two *s. Educ:* Haileybury Coll., Herts. National Service, 2nd Lieut, RA, 1948–50. Unilever Ltd, 1950–70: Trainee; Managing Dir, then Chm., Walls (Meat & Handy Foods) Ltd. Asst Gp Managing Dir, Ranks Hovis McDougall Ltd, 1971, Gp Man. Dir, 1972–81. Director: Guardian Royal Exchange Assurance plc, 1986–; The Royal Exchange Assurance, 1986–; Guardian Assurance plc, 1986–; Pioneer Concrete (Hldgs), 1990–. Chairman: EDC Employment and Trng Cttee, 1982–87; Resources Cttee, Food and Drink Fedn (formerly Food and Drink Industries Council), 1983–86; Member: EDC for Food and Drink Manufg Industry, 1976–87; Consultative Bd for Resources Develt in Agriculture, 1982–84; Covent Garden Market Authority, 1989–; Dir, Industrial Develt Bd for NI, 1982–89; Mem., Peacock Cttee on Financing the BBC, 1985–86. High Sheriff, Bucks, 1990–91. *Recreations:* gardening, beagling. *Address:* Rignall Farm, Rignall Road, Great Missenden, Bucks HP16 9PE. *T:* Great Missenden (02406) 4714. *Club:* Naval and Military.

REYNOLDS, Prof. Philip Alan, CBE 1986; DL; Vice-Chancellor, University of Lancaster, 1980–85; *b* 15 May 1920; *s* of Harry Reynolds and Ethel (*née* Scott); *m* 1946, Mollie Patricia (*née* Horton); two *s* one *d. Educ:* Worthing High Sch.; Queen's Coll., Oxford (BA 1940, 1st Cl. Mod. Hist.; MA 1950). Served War, 1940–46: HAA and Staff, UK, ME and Greece; Major 1945. Asst Lectr, then Lectr in Internat. History, LSE, 1946–50; Woodrow Wilson Prof. of Internat. Politics, UCW Aberystwyth, 1950–64 (Vice-Principal, 1961–63); Prof. of Politics and Pro-Vice-Chancellor, Univ. of Lancaster, 1964–80. Vis. Professor: in Internat. Relations, Toronto, 1953; in Commonwealth History and Instns, Indian Sch. of Internat. Studies, New Delhi, 1958; Anspach Fellow, Univ. of Pa, 1971; Vis. Res. Fellow, ANU Canberra, 1977. Vice-Chm., Cttee of Vice-Chancellors and Principals, 1984–85; Chm., Brit. Internat. Studies Assoc., 1976, Hon. Pres., 1981–84; Mem. Council, RIIA, 1975–80. DL Lancs, 1982. Hon. DLitt Lancaster, 1985. *Publications:* War in the Twentieth Century, 1951; Die Britische Aussenpolitik zwischen den beiden Weltkriegen, 1952 (rev. edn, 1954, as British Foreign Policy in the Inter-War Years); An Introduction to International Relations, 1971, rev. edn 1980 (Japanese edn 1977, Spanish edn 1978); (with E. J. Hughes) The Historian as Diplomat: Charles Kingsley Webster and the United Nations 1939–46, 1976; contrib. New Cambridge Mod. Hist., History, Slavonic Rev., Pol. Qly, Pol. Studies, Internat. Jl, Internat. Studies, Brit. Jl of Internat. Studies, Educn Policy Bulletin, Higher Educn, Univs Qly, Minerva. *Recreations:* music, bridge, eating and drinking. *Address:* Lattice Cottage, Borwick, Carnforth, Lancs. *T:* Carnforth (0524) 732518.

REYNOLDS, William Oliver, OBE 1973 (MBE 1944); *b* 2 Nov. 1915; General Manager, Eastern Region, British Rail, 1973–76; *s* of Edgar Ernest Reynolds and Elizabeth Wilson Biesterfield; *m* 1944, Eleanor Gill; two *s. Educ:* Royal Grammar Sch., Newcastle upon Tyne. LNER Traffic apprentice, 1936. Served War, with Royal Engineers, 1940–46: despatches, 1942 and 1944; Lt-Col, 1944. Lt-Col, Engineer and Railway Staff Corps, RE (T&AVR IV), 1971–. Divisional Manager, London Midland, BR, 1960; Asst Gen. Manager, Scottish Region, 1964; Chief Operating Manager, BR Bd, 1968; Exec. Dir, BR Bd, 1969. Mem., Adv. Council, Science Mus. 1975–84; Chm., Friends of Nat. Railway Mus. 1984–. FCIT. *Recreations:* fishing, golf, gardening. *Address:* Oak House, Follifoot, Harrogate, N Yorks HG3 1DR. *Club:* Oriental.

REYNTIENS, Nicholas Patrick, OBE 1976; Head of Fine Art, Central School of Art and Design, London, 1976–86; *b* 11 Dec. 1925; *s* of Nicholas Serge Reyntiens, OBE, and Janet MacRae; *m* 1953, Anne Bruce; two *s* two *d. Educ:* Ampleforth; Edinburgh Coll. of Art (DA). Served Scots Guards, 1943–47. St Marylebone Sch. of Art, 1947–50; Edinburgh Coll. of Art, 1950–51. Founder (with wife, Anne Bruce, the painter), Reyntiens Trust, which ran art sch., Burleighfield, where pupils from UK, Ireland, France, Germany, Japan, Canada, Australia, New Zealand, US and Iceland learned art of stained glass, and which had facilities for tapestry design and teaching, a printing house for editioning in lithography, etching and silkscreen, as well as workshops for stained glass, ceramics, drawing and painting. Has lectured in USA, Spain, Mexico, France and Switzerland. Many commissions, including glass for Liverpool RC Metropolitan Cathedral; for 35 years, interpreted painters' designs into stained glass, as well as own commissions for stained glass, 1953–, including baptistery window, Coventry Cathedral, Eton Coll. Chapel, Robinson Coll., Cambridge, St Margaret's Westminster (all with John Piper), Derby Cathedral and Liverpool Metropolitan Cathedral (with Ceri Richards), All Saints Basingstoke (with Cecil Collins); completed glazing of Christ Church Hall, Oxford, 1980–84. Member: Court, RCA; Adv. Cttee in Decoration, Brompton Oratory; Adv. Cttee in Decoration, Westminster Cathedral; Adv. Cttee, Westminster Abbey, 1981–. Art Critic, The Tablet. *Publications:* Technique of Stained Glass, 1967, 2nd edn 1977; The Beauty of Stained Glass, 1990; has written for architectural, art, literary and political magazines and on cooking for Harpers & Queen. *Address:* Ilford Bridges Farm, Close Stocklinch, Ilminster, Som TA19 9HZ. *T:* Ilminster (0460) 52241, *Fax:* Ilminster (0460) 57150.

RHEA, Alexander Dodson, III; *b* 10 May 1919; *s* of Alexander D. Rhea, Jr and Annie Rhea; *m* 1945, Suzanne Menocal; one *s. Educ:* Princeton Univ. BA Econs and Social Instns. Active service as Lt-Comdr USNR, 1941–45. Vice-Pres., Govt Employees Ins. Corp., Washington, DC, 1946–48; Treas. and Man. Dir, General Motors de Venezuela,

Caracas, 1949–55; Vice-Pres., General Motors Overseas Corp., 1960–68; Regional Gp Dir, NY, 1960–66, Staff Man., 1966–67, General Motors Overseas Operations; Chm. and Man. Dir, General Motors-Holden's, Melbourne, 1968–70; Chm. and Man. Dir., Vauxhall Motors Ltd, 1970–74; Chm., General Motors Corp. European Adv. Council, 1974–77; Exec. Vice-Pres. and Dir, General Motors Overseas Corp., 1974–77. *Recreations:* reading, golf. *Address:* 580 Park Avenue, New York, NY 10021, USA. *Clubs:* Knickerbocker, Princeton, Colony (New York); Fort Worth, River Crest Country (Fort Worth, Texas); Melbourne (Melbourne); Greenbrier Golf and Tennis (White Sulphur Springs, West Virginia).

RHIND, Prof. David William; Director General and Chief Executive, Ordnance Survey, since 1992; *b* 29 Nov. 1943; *s* of late William Rhind and of Christina Rhind; *m* 1966, Christine Young; one *s* two *d*. *Educ:* Berwick Grammar School; Bristol Univ. (BSc); Edinburgh Univ. (PhD). FRGS; FRICS 1991. Research Fellow, Royal College of Art, 1969–73; Lectr then Reader, Univ. of Durham, 1973–81; Birkbeck College, London University: Prof. of Geography, 1982–91; Dean, Faculty of Economics, 1984–86; Co-ordinator for IT, 1985–88; Governor, 1986–90; Head, Resources Centre for Economics, Geography and Statistics, 1987–91, also for Computer Science and Maths, 1989–91. Visiting Fellow: Internat. Trng Centre, Netherlands, 1975; ANU, 1979. Vice-Pres., Internat. Cartographic Assoc., 1984–91; Mem., Govt Cttee on Enquiry into handling of geographic inf., 1985–87; Advisor, H of L Select Cttee on Sci. and Tech., 1983–84; Chairman: Bloomsbury Computing Consortium Management Cttee, 1988–; Royal Soc. Ordnance Survey Scientific Cttee, 1989–. Hon. Sec., RGS, 1988–. *Publications:* (jtly) Land Use, 1980; The Census User's Handbook, 1983; (jtly) Atlas of EEC Affairs, 1984; (jtly) Geographical Information Systems, 1991; numerous papers on map-making and computerised databases. *Recreations:* travelling, home decorating. *Address:* Ordnance Survey, Romsey Road, Maybush, Southampton SO9 4DH. *T:* Southampton (0703) 79200. *Club:* Athenæum.

RHODES, Col Sir Basil (Edward), Kt 1987; CBE 1981 (OBE (mil.) 1945; MBE (mil.) 1944); TD 1946; DL; Partner, Gichard & Co., solicitors, since 1946; *b* Rotherham, 8 Dec. 1915; *s* of late Col Harry Rhodes and of Astri Rhodes (*née* Natvig); *m* 1962, Joëlle, *er d* of Robert Vilgard, Paris; one *s*. *Educ:* St Edward's Sch., Oxford. Served War of 1939–45, Western Desert, Greece, Crete and Burma (wounded; mentioned in despatches). Admitted solicitor, 1946. Director: Carlton Main Brickworks, 1972–; Duncan Millar & Associates; S. H. Ward & Co.; Wessex Fare; Yorkshire Merchant Securities. Mem. (C) Town Council, Rotherham, 1949–74, Mayor, 1970–71; Chm., 1949–75, Pres., 1975–, Rotherham Cons. Assoc.; Chm., S Yorks Cons. Fedn, 1964–; Treas., Cons. Central Office Yorks Area, 1983–84. DL 1975, High Sheriff, 1982–83, S Yorks. *Recreations:* fieldsports, ski-ing, gardening. *Address:* Bubnell Hall, Baslow, Bakewell, Derbys. *T:* Baslow (024688) 3266. *Clubs:* Cavalry and Guards; Sheffield (Sheffield).

RHODES, George Harold Lancashire, TD 1946; Regional Chairman of Industrial Tribunals: Manchester, 1985–88; Liverpool, 1987–88; *b* 29 Feb. 1916; *er s* of Judge Harold and Ena Rhodes of Bowdon, Cheshire. *Educ:* Shrewsbury School; The Queen's College, Oxford (MA 1941). Commissioned 52nd Field Regt RA TA, 1938; war service, BEF, 1940, Middle East, 1942, Italy, 1943–46 (Major). Called to the Bar, Gray's Inn, 1947; practised on N Circuit; the Junior, 1948; Office of Judge Advocate General (Army and RAF), 1953; Asst Judge Advocate General, 1967; Chm., Industrial Tribunals (Manchester), 1974, Dep. Regional Chm., 1975. *Recreations:* walking, golf. *Address:* 8 Newington Court, The Firs, Bowdon, Cheshire WA14 2UA. *T:* 061–928 1200.

RHODES, John Andrew, FCIT; Director General, West Yorkshire Passenger Transport Executive, since 1988; *b* 22 May 1949; *s* of George and Elsie Rhodes; *m* 1985, Marie Catherine Carleton. *Educ:* Queen Elizabeth Sch., Barnet; Wadham Coll., Oxford (MA Mod. History). Civil Service: various posts in DoE, Cabinet Office, Dept of Transport, 1971–87. *Recreations:* music, squash. *Address:* 10 Gilstead Way, Middleton, Ilkley, West Yorkshire LS29 0AE. *T:* Ilkley (0943) 603497.

See also P. J. Rhodes.

RHODES, Sir John (Christopher Douglas), 4th Bt, *cr* 1919; *b* 24 May 1946; *s* of Sir Christopher Rhodes, 3rd Bt, and of Mary Florence, *d* of late Dr Douglas Wardleworth; *S* father, 1964. *Heir:* *b* Michael Philip James Rhodes [*b* 3 April 1948; *m* 1973, Susan, *d* of Patrick Roney-Dougal; one *d*].

RHODES, John Ivor McKinnon, CMG 1971; *b* 6 March 1914; *s* of late Joseph Thomas Rhodes and late Hilda (*née* McKinnon); *m* 1939, Eden Annetta Clark (*d* 1990); one *s* one *d*. *Educ:* Leeds Modern School. Exec. Officer, WO, 1933; Financial Adviser's Office, HQ British Forces in Palestine, 1938; Major 1940; Asst Comd Sec., Southern Comd, 1944; Financial Adviser, London District, 1946; Principal 1947, Asst Sec. 1959, HM Treasury; Minister, UK Mission to UN, 1966–74. Member: UN Pension Board, 1966–71; UN Cttee on Contributions, 1966–71, 1975–77; Chm., UN Adv. Cttee on Admin. and Budgetary Questions, 1971–74; Senior Adviser (Asst Sec.-Gen.) to Administrator, UNDP, 1979–80. *Recreations:* gardening, playing the electronic organ. *Address:* Quintins, Watersfield, Pulborough, W Sussex RH20 1NE. *T:* Bury (0798) 831634.

RHODES, Marion, RE 1953 (ARE 1941); etcher, painter in water colour and oils; *b* Huddersfield, Yorks, 1907; *d* of Samuel Rhodes and Mary Jane Mallinson. *Educ:* Greenhead High School, Huddersfield; Huddersfield Art School; Leeds College of Art; The Central School of Arts and Crafts, London. Art Teachers' Certificate (Univ. of Oxford), 1930; teaching posts, 1930–67; pt-time lecturer in Art at Berridge House Training Coll., 1947–55. SGA 1936, Hon. Life Mem., 1969; FRSA 1944; Member, Manchester Acad. of Fine Art, 1955–81; Paris Salon: Honourable Mention, 1952; Bronze Medal, 1956; Silver Medal 1961; Gold Medal, 1967. Exhibited from 1934 at: Royal Academy, Royal Scottish Academy, Mall Gall., The Paris Salon, Walker Art Gall., Towner Art Gall., Atkinson Art Gall., Southport, Brighton, Bradford, Leeds, Manchester and other provincial Art Galls, also USA and S Africa. Etching of Jordans' Hostel and drawing of The Meeting House purchased by Contemporary Art Soc. and presented to British Museum; other works in the Print Room, BM, and Print Room, V&A; work also purchased by Bradford Corp. Art Gall., Brighouse Art Gall., Huddersfield Art Gall., Stoke-on-Trent Educn Cttee's Loan Scheme, and South London (Camberwell) Library Committee; works reproduced. Fellow, Ancient Monuments Soc.; Associate, Artistes Français, 1971–79; Hon. Mem., Tommasso Campanella Acad., Rome (Silver Medal, 1970). Cert. of Merit, Dictionary of Internat. Biography, 1972. Mem., Accademia delle Arti e de Lavoro (Parma), 1979–82; Academic of Italy with Gold Medal, 1979. *Publication:* illustrations for Robert Harding's Snettisham, 1982. *Recreations:* gardening and geology. *Address:* 2 Goodwyn Avenue, Mill Hill, NW7 3RG. *T:* 081–959 2280. *Club:* English-Speaking Union.

RHODES, Sir Peregrine (Alexander), KCMG 1984 (CMG 1976); HM Diplomatic Service, retired; Director-General, British Property Federation, since 1986; *b* 14 May 1925; *s* of Cyril Edmunds Rhodes and Elizabeth Jocelyn Rhodes; *m* 1st, 1951, Jane Marion Hassell (marr. diss.); two *s* one *d*; 2nd, 1969, Margaret Rosemary Page. *Educ:* Winchester Coll.; New Coll., Oxford (BA Lit. Hum. (1st cl)). Served with Coldstream Guards, 1944–47. Joined FO, 1950; 2nd Sec., Rangoon, 1953–56; Private Sec. to Minister of State, 1956–59; 1st Sec., Vienna, 1959–62; 1st Sec., Helsinki, 1962–65; FCO, 1965–68, Counsellor 1967; Inst. for Study of Internat. Organisation, Sussex Univ., 1968–69; Counsellor, Rome, 1970–73; Chargé d'Affaires, E Berlin, 1973–75; on secondment as Under Sec., Cabinet Office (Chief of Assessments Staff), 1975–78; High Comr, Cyprus, 1979–82; Ambassador, Greece, 1982–85. Chm., Anglo-Hellenic League, 1986–90; Vice-Pres. British Sch., Athens, 1982–. FRSA 1988. *Recreations:* photography, reading. *Address:* Pond House, Thorpe Morieux, Bury St Edmunds, Suffolk. *Club:* Travellers'.

RHODES, Prof. Peter John, FBA 1987; Professor of Ancient History, University of Durham, since 1983; *b* 10 Aug. 1940; *s* of George Thomas Rhodes and Elsie Leonora Rhodes (*née* Pugh); *m* 1971, Jan Teresa Adamson. *Educ:* Queen Elizabeth's Boys' Grammar Sch., Barnet; Wadham Coll., Oxford (minor schol.; BA (1st cl. Mods, 1st cl. Greats); MA; DPhil). Harmsworth Schol., Merton Coll., Oxford, 1963–65; Craven Fellow, Oxford Univ., 1963–65; Lectr in Classics and Ancient History, 1965, Sen. Lectr, 1977, Durham Univ. Fellow, Center for Hellenic Studies, Washington, DC, 1978–79; Visiting Fellow: Wolfson Coll., Oxford, 1984; Univ. of New England, Aust., 1988. Mem., Inst. for Advanced Study, Princeton, USA, 1988–89. *Publications:* The Athenian Boule, 1972; Greek Historical Inscriptions 359–323 BC, 1972; Commentary on the Aristotelian Athenaion Politeia, 1981; (trans.) Aristotle: the Athenian Constitution, 1984; The Athenian Empire, 1985; The Greek City States: a source book, 1986; (ed) Thucydides Book II, 1988; articles and reviews in jls. *Recreations:* music, typography, travel. *Address:* Department of Classics, University of Durham, 38 North Bailey, Durham, DH1 3EU. *T:* Durham (091) 374 2073.

See also J. A. Rhodes.

RHODES, Philip, FRCS, FRCOG, FRACMA, FFOM; Regional Postgraduate Dean of Medical Studies, and Professor of Postgraduate Medical Education, Southampton University, 1980–87, retired; *b* 2 May 1922; *s* of Sydney Rhodes, Dore, Sheffield; *m* 1946, Mary Elizabeth Worley, Barrowden, Rutland; three *s* two *d*. *Educ:* King Edward VII Sch., Sheffield; Clare Coll., Cambridge; St Thomas's Hospital Medical School. BA(Cantab) 1943, MB, BChir(Cantab) 1946; FRCS 1953; MRCOG 1956; FRCOG 1964; FRACMA 1976; FFOM 1990. Major RAMC, 1948–50. Medical appointments held in St Thomas' Hosp., Folkestone, Harrogate, Chelsea Hosp. for Women, Queen Charlotte's Hosp., 1946–58; Consultant Obstetric Physician, St Thomas' Hosp., 1958–63; Prof. of Obstetrics and Gynæcol., St Thomas's Hosp. Med. Sch., Univ. of London, 1964–74, Dean, 1968–74; Dean, Faculty of Medicine, Univ. of Adelaide, 1975–77; Postgrad. Dean and Dir, Regional Postgrad. Inst. for Med. and Dentistry, Newcastle Univ., 1977–80. Member: SW Metropolitan Regional Hosp. Board, 1967–74; SE Thames Reg. Health Authority, 1974; GMC, 1979–89 (Educn Cttee, 1984–89). Mem. Steering Cttee of DHSS on management of NHS, 1971–72. Mem., Adv. Cttee, Nat. Inst. of Medical Hist., Australia, 1976. Chm., Educn Cttee, King Edward's Hosp. Fund for London, 1981–87; Member: UGC Working Party on Continuing Educn, 1983; Council for Postgrad. Med. Educn in England and Wales, 1984–87. Governor: Dulwich Coll., 1966–74; St Thomas' Hosp., 1969–74; Pembroke Sch., Adelaide, 1976–77. FRSA 1989. *Publications:* Fluid Balance in Obstetrics, 1960; Introduction to Gynæcology and Obstetrics, 1967; Reproductive Physiology for Medical Students, 1969; Woman: A Biological Study, 1969; The Value of Medicine, 1976; Dr John Leake's Hospital, 1978; Letters to a Young Doctor, 1983; An Outline History of Medicine, 1985; Associate Editor, The Oxford Companion to Medicine, 1986; articles in Jl of Obstetrics and Gynæcology of the British Empire, Lancet, Brit. Med. Jl, Med. Jl of Australia. *Recreations:* reading, gardening, photography. *Address:* 1 Wakerley Court, Wakerley, Oakham, Leics LE15 8PA. *T:* Morcott (057287) 665.

RHODES, Reginald Paul; Chairman, Southern Gas Region, 1975–83; *b* 10 April 1918; *s* of Edwin Rhodes and Dorothy Lena Molyneux; *m* 1940, Margaret Frances Fish; two *s* three *d*. *Educ:* Merchant Taylors Sch., Northwood. Joined Gas Light & Coke Co., 1937; North Thames Gas, 1948 (Dep. Chm., 1972). Deputy Chairman: Southampton Industrial Therapy Organisation, 1980–89; Solent Productivity Assoc., 1983–; Chm., Solent Business Fund, 1983–; Member: Wessex RHA, 1984–; Shaw Trust, 1984–. Mem., Co. of Pikemen, Honourable Artillery Company. FIGasE. *Recreations:* music, gardening. *Address:* 9 The Paddock, Brockenhurst, Hants SO42 7QU. *T:* Lymington (0590) 22399.

RHODES, Richard David Walton, JP; Headmaster, Rossall School, since 1987; *b* 20 April 1942; *er s* of Harry Walton Rhodes and Dorothy Rhodes (*née* Fairhurst); *m* 1966, Stephanie Heyes, 2nd *d* of Frederic William Heyes and Catherine Heyes; two *d*. *Educ:* Rossall Sch.; St John's Coll., Durham (BA 1963). Asst Master, St John's Sch., Leatherhead, 1964–75 (Founder Housemaster, Montgomery House, 1973–75); Deputy Headmaster, Arnold Sch., Blackpool, 1975–79, Headmaster, 1979–87. Chm., NW Div., HMC, 1987. Member Council: Univ. of Salford, 1987–; Lawrence Hse Sch., Lytham St Annes, 1988–; Gov., Terra Nova Sch., Jodrell Bank, 1989–. JP Fylde, 1978. *Recreations:* photography, sports, motoring, gardening in the Lake District. *Address:* The Hall, Rossall School, Fleetwood, Lancs FY7 8JW. *T:* Fleetwood (0253) 774201. *Club:* East India, Devonshire, Sports and Public Schools.

RHODES, Robert Elliott; QC 1989; a Recorder, since 1987; *b* 2 Aug. 1945; *s* of late Gilbert G. Rhodes, FCA and of Elly, who *m* 2nd, Leopold Brook, *qv*; *m* 1971, Georgina Caroline, *d* of J. G. Clarfelt, *qv*; two *s* one *d*. *Educ:* St Paul's School; Pembroke Coll., Oxford. MA. Called to the Bar, Inner Temple, 1968. Second Prosecuting Counsel to Inland Revenue at Central Criminal Court and Inner London Crown Courts, 1979, First Prosecuting Counsel, 1981–89. *Recreations:* opera, reading, cricket, real tennis, fishing. *Address:* 2 Crown Office Row, Temple, EC4. *T:* 071–583 2681. *Club:* MCC.

RHODES, Zandra Lindsey, RDI 1977; DesRCA, FCSD; Managing Director, Zandra Rhodes (UK) Ltd and Zandra Rhodes (Shops) Ltd, since 1975; *b* 19 Sept. 1940; *d* of Albert James Rhodes and Beatrice Ellen (*née* Twigg). *Educ:* Medway Technical Sch. for Girls, Chatham; Medway Coll. of Art; Royal Coll. of Art (DesRCA 1964). FSIAD 1982. With Alexander MacIntyre, set up print factory and studio, 1965; sold designs (and converted them on to cloth) to Foale and Tuffin and Roger Nelson; formed partnership with Sylvia Ayton and began producing dresses using her own prints, 1966; opened Fulham Road Clothes Shop, designing dresses as well as prints, first in partnership, 1967–68, then (Fulham Road shop closed) alone, producing first clothes range in which she revolutionised use of prints in clothes by cutting round patterns to make shapes never before used; took collection to USA, 1969; sold to Fortnum and Mason, London, through Anne Knight, 1969, then to Piero de Monzi, 1971; began building up name and business in USA (known for her annual spectacular Fantasy Shows); also started designing in jersey and revolutionised its treatment with lettuce edges and seams on the outside; with Anne Knight and Ronnie Stirling founded Zandra Rhodes (UK) Ltd and Zandra Rhodes (Shops) Ltd, 1975–86; opening first shop in London, 1975; others opened in Bloomingdales NY, Marshall Field, Chicago, and Harrods, London, 1976; new factory premises opened in Hammersmith, London, 1984. Licensees: Wamsutta, USA, 1976 (sheets and pillowcases); CVP Designs, 1977 (patterns for the interior); Regal Rugs, USA, 1977 (rugs); Baar and Beard Inc., USA, 1978 (scarves); Sari Fabrics, 1979 (kitchen accessories); Wagner Furs, 1979 (furs); Sabrina Coats, 1979 (coats); Jack Mulqueen, USA, 1980 (printed silk dresses and blouses); Green and Makofsky, USA, 1980 (coats); Senko, Japan, 1980 (rugs and bathroom accessories); Suffola, USA, 1980 (sheets and bed accessories); Falmers, 1981 (jeans and T-shirts); Seibu, Japan, 1981 (blouses); Courtaulds, 1981 (knitted silk lingerie); Zandra Rhodes Sportswear, 1982; Lyle & Scott, 1982 (cashmere knitwear); Zandra Rhodes 'Designs on Legs' Jambetex, 1984 (hosiery); Universal Leather, 1984 (handbags); Japan Feather Bedding Co., Japan, 1984 (bedlinen, cushions and bedroom accessories); Zandra Rhodes Shoes for Pentland Industries, 1984; Monitor Designs, 1985 (bedlinen); Kyoai, Japan, 1986 (handbags and belts); Fusuke, Japan, 1986 (hosiery collection); Philip Hockley, 1986 (furs); Swarovski, 1987 (jewellery); Hilmet Ltd, 1988 (silk and wool scarf and shawl collection); Albany Fine China Ltd, 1988 (limited edn of fine china figurines); Osborne & Little Plc, 1988 (printed furnishing fabric and wallpapers); Fifth Avenue Ltd, 1988 (catalogue suits, dresses and co-ordinates); Dyansen Galleries, USA, 1988 (artworks and prints). Launched: Zandra Rhodes Ready-to-Wear, Australia, 1979; Zandra Rhodes II Ready-to-Wear, UK, 1984; personally introduced authentic Zandra Rhodes Indian Sarees and Shalwar Chamise (tunic and trouser outfits), 1987. One-man exhibitions: Oriel, Cardiff (Welsh Arts Council), 1978; Texas Gall., Houston, 1981; Otis Parsons, Los Angeles, 1981; La Jolla Museum of Contemporary Art, San Diego, 1982; ADITI Creative Power, Barbican Centre, 1982; Sch. of Art Inst., Chicago, 1982; Parsons Sch. of Design, NY, 1982; Art Museum of Santa Cruz Co., Calif, 1983; retrospective exhibition of 'Works of Art' with textiles, Museum of Art, El Paso, Texas, 1984; retrospective of Garments & Textiles (also Lead Speaker for Art to Wear exhibn), Columbus, Ohio, 1987; retrospective for Seibu Seed Hall, Seibu, Tokyo, 1987. Work represented in major costume collections: UK: V&A; City Mus. and Art Gall., Stoke-on-Trent; Bath Mus.; Royal Pavilion Brighton Mus.; Platt Fields Costume Mus., Manchester; City Art Gall., Leeds; overseas: Metropolitan Mus., NY; Chicago Historical Soc.; Smithsonian Instn; Royal Ontario Mus.; Mus. of Applied Arts and Scis, Sydney; Nat. Mus. of Victoria, Melbourne; La Jolla Mus. of Contemp. Art. Opening speaker, Famous Women of Fashion, Smithsonian Inst., Washington, 1978. Hon. DFA Internat. Fine Arts Coll, Miami, Florida, 1986; Hon. Dr RCA, 1986; Hon. DD CNAA, 1987. Designer of the Year, English Fashion Trade UK, 1972; Emmy Award for Best Costume Designs in Romeo and Juliet on Ice, CBS TV, 1984; Woman of Distinction award, Northwood Inst., Dallas, 1986; citations and commendations from USA estabs. *Publications:* The Art of Zandra Rhodes, 1984, US edn 1985; The Zandra Rhodes Collection by Brother, 1988; *relevant publications:* in English Vogue, 1978 and 1982; Architectural Digest, 1978; The Connoisseur, 1981; comment and illus. in numerous books and articles since 1971. *Recreations:* travelling, drawing. *Address:* (factory) 87 Richford Street, Hammersmith, W6 7HJ. *T:* (business) 081–749 9561.

RHODES JAMES, Sir Robert (Vidal), Kt 1991; MP (C) Cambridge, since Dec. 1976; Chairman, History of Parliament Trust, since 1983; *b* 10 April 1933; *y s* of late Lieut-Col W. R. James, OBE, MC; *m* 1956, Angela Margaret Robertson, *er d* of late R. M. Robertson; four *d*. *Educ:* private schs in India; Sedbergh Sch.; Worcester Coll., Oxford. Asst Clerk, House of Commons, 1955–61; Senior Clerk, 1961–64. Fellow of All Souls Coll., Oxford, 1965–68, 1979–81; Dir, Inst. for Study of Internat. Organisation, Univ. of Sussex, 1968–73; Principal Officer, Exec. Office of Sec.-Gen. of UN, 1973–76. Kratter Prof. of European History, Stanford Univ., Calif., 1968. Consultant to UN Conf. on Human Environment, 1971–72; UK Mem., UN Sub-Commn on Prevention of Discrimination and Protection of Minorities, 1972–73. PPS, FCO, 1979–82; Mem., Chairmen's Panel, H of C, 1987–. Conservative Party Liaison Officer: for Higher Educn, 1979–85 and 1986–87; for Higher and Further Educn, 1987–88; Chm., Conservative Friends of Israel, 1989–. Vice-Pres., Anglo-Israel Assoc., 1990–. FRSL 1964; NATO Fellow, 1965; FRHistS 1973; Professorial Fellow, Univ. of Sussex, 1973. Hon. DLitt Westminster Coll., Fulton, Missouri, 1986. *Publications:* Lord Randolph Churchill, 1959; An Introduction to the House of Commons, 1961 (John Llewelyn Rhys Memorial Prize); Rosebery, 1963 (Royal Society Lit. Award); Gallipoli, 1965; Standardization and Production of Military Equipment in NATO, 1967; Churchill: a study in failure, 1900–39, 1970; Ambitions and Realities: British politics 1964–70, 1972; Victor Cazalet: a portrait, 1976; The British Revolution 1880–1939, vol. I, 1976, vol. II, 1977, 1 Vol. edn, 1978; Albert, Prince Consort, 1983; Anthony Eden, 1986; Bob Boothby: a portrait, 1991; *edited:* Chips: The Diaries of Sir Henry Channon, 1967; Memoirs of a Conservative: J. C. C. Davidson's Memoirs and Papers, 1969; The Czechoslovak Crisis 1968, 1969; The Complete Speeches of Sir Winston Churchill, 1897–1963, 1974; contrib. to: Suez Ten Years After, 1967; Essays From Divers Hands, 1967; Churchill: four faces and the man, 1969; International Administration, 1971; The Prime Ministers, vol. II, 1975. *Address:* The Stone House, Great Gransden, near Sandy, Beds. *T:* Great Gransden (07677) 7025. *Clubs:* Travellers', Pratt's, Grillion's.

RHYMES, Rev. Canon Douglas Alfred; Canon Residentiary and Librarian, Southwark Cathedral, 1962–69, Hon. Canon, 1969, Canon Emeritus since 1984; Lecturer in Ethics, Chichester Theological College, since 1984; *b* 26 March 1914; *s* of Peter Alfred and Jessie Rhymes; unmarried. *Educ:* King Edward VI School, Birmingham; Birmingham Univ.; Ripon Hall Theological College, Oxford. BA (2nd Cl. Hons 1st Div.) Philosophy 1939. Asst Curate, Dovercourt, Essex, 1940–43; Chaplain to the Forces, 1943–46; Asst Curate, Romford, Essex (in charge of St George's, Romford and St Thomas', Noak Hill), 1946–49; Priest-in-charge, Ascension, Chelmsford, 1949–50; Sacrist, Southwark Cathedral, 1950–54; Vicar, All Saints, New Eltham, SE9, 1954–62; Director of Lay Training, Diocese of Southwark, 1962–68; Vicar of St Giles, Camberwell, 1968–76; Parish Priest of Woldingham, 1976–84. Proctor in Convocation and Mem. of Gen. Synod, 1975–85. *Publications:* (jtly) Crisis Booklets, Christianity and Communism, 1952; (jtly) Layman's Church, 1963; No New Morality, 1964; Prayer in the Secular City, 1967; Through Prayer to Reality, 1974; (jtly) Dropping the Bomb, 1985. *Recreations:* theatre, conversation, country walks. *Address:* Chillington Cottage, 7 Dukes Road, Fontwell, W Sussex BN18 0SP. *T:* Eastergate (0243) 543268.

RHYS, family name of **Baron Dynevor.**

RHYS JONES, Griffith; actor, writer and producer; *b* 16 Nov. 1953; *s* of Elwyn Rhys Jones and Gwyneth Margaret Jones; *m* 1981, Joanna Frances Harris; one *s* one *d*. *Educ:* Brentwood Sch.; Emmanuel Coll., Cambridge. BBC Radio Producer, 1976–79; *television:* Not the Nine O'Clock News (also co-writer), 1979–81; Alas Smith and Jones (also co-writer), 1982–87; Porterhouse Blue (serial), 1987; The World according to Smith and Jones, 1987; A View of Harry Clark, 1989; *theatre:* Charley's Aunt, 1983; Trumpets and Raspberries, 1985; The Alchemist, 1985; Arturo Ui, 1987; Small Doses (series of short plays) (writer, Boat People), 1989; Smith & Jones (also co-writer), 1989–; The Wind in the Willows, Royal Nat. Th., 1990; dir, Twelfth Night, RSC, 1991; *films:* Morons from Outer Space, 1985; Wilt, 1989; *opera:* Die Fledermaus, Royal Opera Covent Garden, 1989. Director: Talkback, Advertising and Production; Playback, 1987–; Smith Jones Brown & Cassie, 1988–. *Publications:* Janet Lives with Mel and Griff, 1988; The Lavishly Tooled Smith & Jones. *Recreation:* playing Circus Tavern, Purfleet. *Address:* c/o Talkback, 33 Percy Street, W1P 9FG. *T:* 071–631 3940.

RHYS WILLIAMS, Sir (Arthur) Gareth (Ludovic Emrys), 3rd Bt *cr* 1918, of Miskin, Parish of Llantrisant, Co. Glamorgan; Managing Director, NFI Electronics, since 1990; *b* 9 Nov. 1961; *s* of Sir Brandon Rhys Williams, 2nd Bt, MP and of Caroline Susan, *e d* of L. A. Foster; *S* father, 1988. *Educ:* Eton; Durham Univ. (BSc Hons Eng); Insead (MBA). MIProdE; MBPICS. Systems Analyst, STC Components, 1983–85; Lucas CAV: Optimised Prodn Technol. Analyst, 1986–87; Materials Manager, 1987–88. *Recreations:* Territorial Army (Captain); shooting, travel, chess. *Heir:* none. *Address:* 32 Rawlings Street, SW3 2LT.

RIABOUCHINSKA, Tatiana, (Mme Lichine); Ballerina of Russian Ballet; owns and operates the Lichine Ballet Academy, Beverly Hills; *b* 23 May 1916; *d* of Michael P. Riabouchinsky, Moscow (Banker), and Tatiana Riabouchinska (*d* 1935), Dancer of Moscow Imperial School of Dance; *m* 1942, David Lichine (*d* 1972); one *d*. *Educ:* Cour Fénelon, Paris. Trained first by her mother; then by Volinine (dancer of the Moscow Imperial Grand Theatre); then by Mathilde Kchesinska. First appeared as child dancer with Balieff's Chauve Souris in London, 1931; joined new Russian Ballet (de-Basil), 1932, and danced with them in nearly all countries of Western Europe, Australia and N and S America. Contribution to books on dancing by: Andre Levinson, Arnold L. Haskell, Irving Deakin, Rayner Heppenstall, Kay Ambrose, Prince Peter Lieven, Cyril W. Beaumont, Cyril Brahms, Adrian Stokes, A. V. Coton, Ninette de Valois, etc. Citizen of Honor, Beverly Hills, 1990. *Publication:* (contrib.) Garcia-Marquez, The Ballets Russes: Colonel de Basil's Ballets Russe de Monte Carlo 1932–52, 1991. *Address:* 965 Oakmont Drive, Los Angeles, Calif 90049, USA.

RIBBANS, Prof. Geoffrey Wilfrid, MA; Kenan University Professor of Hispanic Studies, Brown University, USA, since 1978; *b* 15 April 1927; *o s* of late Wilfrid Henry Ribbans and Rose Matilda Burton; *m* 1956, Magdalena Cumming (*née* Willmann), Cologne; one *s* two *d*. *Educ:* Sir George Monoux Grammar Sch., Walthamstow; King's Coll., Univ. of London. BA Hons Spanish 1st cl., 1948; MA 1953. Asst Lectr, Queen's Univ., Belfast, 1951–52; Asst, St Salvator's Coll., Univ. of St Andrews, 1952–53; Univ. of Sheffield: Asst Lectr, 1953–55; Lectr, 1955–61; Sen. Lectr, 1961–63; Gilmour Prof. of Spanish, Univ. of Liverpool, 1963–78; First Director, Centre for Latin-American Studies, 1966–70; Dean, Faculty of Arts, 1977–78; Chm., Dept of Hispanic and Italian Studies, Brown Univ., USA, 1981–84. Andrew Mellon Vis. Prof., Univ. of Pittsburgh, 1970–71; Leverhulme Res. Fellow, 1975; NEH Univ. Fellowship, 1991. Lectures: Fundación Juan March, Madrid, 1984; Norman Maccoll, Univ. of Cambridge, 1985; Fordham Cervantes, NY, 1988. Vice-Pres., Internat. Assoc. of Hispanists, 1974–80 (Pres., Local Organising Cttee, 8th Congress, Brown Univ., 1983); Pres., Anglo-Catalan Soc., 1976–78. Dir, Liverpool Playhouse, 1974–78. Editor, Bulletin of Hispanic Studies, 1964–78. Hon. Fellow, Inst. of Linguists, 1972. Corresp. Member: Real Academia de Buenas Letras, Barcelona, 1978; Hispanic Soc. of Amer., 1981. MA *ad eund.* Brown Univ., 1979. *Publications:* Catalunya i València vistes pels viatgers anglesos del segle XVIIIè, 1955; Niebla y Soledad: aspectos de Unamuno y Machado, 1971; ed, Soledades, Galerias, otros poemas, by Antonio Machado, 1975, 5th edn 1988; Antonio Machado (1875–1939): poetry and integrity, 1975; B. Pérez Galdós: Fortunata y Jacinta, a critical guide, 1977 (trans. Spanish 1989); (ed) Campos de Castilla, by Antonio Machado, 1989; numerous articles on Spanish and Catalan literature in specialised publications. *Recreations:* travel, fine art. *Address:* c/o Department of Hispanic Studies, Box 1961, Brown University, Providence, Rhode Island 02912, USA.

RICE; *see* Spring Rice, family name of Baron Monteagle of Brandon.

RICE, Dennis George, PhD; Social Security (formerly National Insurance) Commissioner, since 1979; a Recorder, since 1991; *b* 27 Nov. 1927; *s* of George Henry Rice and Ethel Emily Rice; *m* 1959, Jean Beryl Wakefield; one *s*. *Educ:* City of London Sch.; King's Coll., Cambridge (Scholar and Prizeman; 1st Cl. Classical Tripos Pt I, Law Tripos Pt II; BA 1950, LLB 1951, MA 1955); London Sch. of Econs (PhD 1956). Called to the Bar, Lincoln's Inn, 1952. Served RAF, 1946–48. Entered J. Thorn and Sons Ltd, 1952; Dir, 1955; Man. Dir, 1956; Chm. and Man. Dir, 1958–69; in practice at Chancery Bar, 1970–79. Member: Cttee of Timber Bldg Manufrs Assoc., 1967–69; Cttee of Joinery and Woodwork Employers Fedn, 1968–69. *Publications:* Rockingham Ornamental Porcelain, 1965; Illustrated Guide to Rockingham Pottery and Porcelain, 1971; Derby Porcelain: the golden years, 1750–1770, 1983; English Porcelain Animals of the Nineteenth Century, 1989; articles on company law in legal jls and on Rockingham porcelain in art magazines. *Recreations:* history of English porcelain, gardening. *Address:* c/o Office of the Social Security Commissioners, Harp House, 83 Farringdon Street, EC4A 4DH. *Club:* Reform.

RICE, Maj.-Gen. Sir Desmond (Hind Garrett), KCVO 1989 (CVO 1985); CBE 1976 (OBE 1970); Vice Adjutant General, 1978–79; *b* 1 Dec. 1924; *s* of Arthur Garrett Rice and Alice Constance (*née* Henman); *m* 1954, Denise Ann (*née* Ravenscroft); one *d*. *Educ:* Marlborough College. Commissioned into The Queen's Bays, 1944; psc 1954; 1st The Queen's Dragoon Guards, 1958; jssc 1963; First Comdg Officer, The Royal Yeomanry, 1967–69; Col GS 4 Div., 1970–73; BGS (MO) MoD, 1973–75; rcds 1976; Director of Manning (Army), 1977–78. Col, 1st The Queen's Dragoon Guards, 1980–86. Sec., Central Chancery of Orders of Knighthood, 1980–89. An Extra Gentleman Usher to the Queen, 1989–. *Recreations:* field sports, skiing, gardening. *Address:* Fairway, Malacca Farm, West Clandon, Surrey GU4 7UQ. *T:* Guildford (0483) 222677. *Club:* Cavalry and Guards.

RICE, Gordon Kenneth; His Honour Judge Rice; a Circuit Judge, since 1980; *b* 16 April 1927; *m* 1967. *Educ:* Brasenose Coll., Oxford (MA). Called to the Bar, Middle Temple, 1957. *Address:* 83 Beach Avenue, Leigh-on-Sea, Essex.

RICE, Peter Anthony Morrish; stage designer; *b* 13 Sept. 1928; *s* of Cecil Morrish Rice and Ethel (*née* Blacklaw); *m* 1954, Patricia Albeck; one *s*. *Educ:* St Dunstan's Coll., Surrey; Royal Coll. of Art (ARCA 1951). Designed first professional prodn, Sex and the Seraphim, Watergate Theatre, London, 1951, followed by The Seraglio, Sadler's Wells Opera, 1952, and Arlecchino, Glyndebourne, 1954; subsequently has designed over 100 plays, operas and ballets, including: *plays:* Time Remembered, 1954; The Winter's Tale, and Much Ado About Nothing, Old Vic, 1956; Living for Pleasure, 1956; A Day in the Life of . . ., 1958; The Lord Chamberlain Regrets, and Toad of Toad Hall, 1961; The Farmer's Wife, The Italian Straw Hat, and Heartbreak House, Chichester, 1966; Flint, and Arms and the Man, 1970; Happy Birthday, 1977; Private Lives, Greenwich and West End, 1980; Present Laughter, Greenwich and West End, 1981; Cavell, and Goodbye Mr Chips, Chichester, 1982; The Sleeping Prince, Chichester and West End, 1983; Forty Years On, Chichester and West End, 1984; Thursday's Ladies, Apollo, 1987; Hay Fever, Chichester, and Re: Joyce!, Fortune, 1988; Don't Dress for Dinner, Apollo, 1990; *operas:* Count Ory, Sadler's Wells, 1962; Arabella, Royal Opera, 1964, Paris Opera, 1981, Chicago, 1984, and Covent Garden, 1986; The Thieving Magpie, and The Violins of St Jacques, Sadler's Wells, 1967; La Bohème, Scottish Opera, 1970; The Magic Flute, Ottawa, 1974; Tosca, Scottish Opera, 1980; The Secret Marriage, Buxton Fest., 1981; The Count of Luxembourg, Sadler's Wells, 1982, 1987; Death in Venice, Antwerp, and Die Fledermaus, St Louis, USA, 1983; Manon, Covent Garden, 1987; Così Fan Tutte, Ottawa, 1990; *ballets:* Romeo and Juliet, Royal Danish Ballet, 1955, and London Festival Ballet, 1985; Sinfonietta, Royal Ballet, 1966; The Four Seasons, Royal Ballet, 1974. Theatre interiors: Vaudeville Theatre, London; Grand Theatre, Blackpool; His Majesty's Theatre, Aberdeen;

Minerva Studio Theatre, Chichester. *Publications*: The Clothes Children Wore, 1973; Farming, 1974; Narrow Boats, 1976. *Recreation*: ancient films. *Address*: 4 Western Terrace, W6 9TX. *T*: 081–748 3990. *Club*: Garrick.

RICE, Peter D.; see Davis-Rice.

RICE, Timothy Miles Bindon; writer and broadcaster; *b* 10 Nov. 1944; *s* of late Hugh Gordon Rice and of Joan Odette Rice; *m* 1974, Jane Artereta McIntosh; one *s* one *d*. *Educ*: Lancing Coll. EMI Records, 1966–68; Norrie Paramor Org., 1968–69. Lyrics for musicals (with music by Andrew Lloyd Webber): Joseph and the Amazing Technicolor Dreamcoat, 1968 (rev. 1973); Jesus Christ Superstar, 1970; Evita, 1976 (rev. 1978); Cricket, 1986; (with music by Stephen Oliver) Blondel, 1983; (with music by Benny Andersson and Björn Ulvaeus) Chess, 1984 (rev. 1986); (with music by Michel Berger and book by Luc Plamondon) Starmania, 1991. Producer, Anything Goes, Prince Edward Theatre, 1989. Lyrics for songs, 1975–, with other composers, incl. Marvin Hamlisch, Elton John, Rick Wakeman, Vangelis, Paul McCartney, Mike Batt, Francis Lai, John Barry and Freddie Mercury. Awards include gold and platinum records in over 20 countries, 2 Tony Awards and 2 Grammy Awards. Founder and Director: GRRR Books, 1978–; Pavilion Books, 1981–. TV includes: Lyrics by Tim Rice; Three More Men in a Boat; Musical Triangles (series); Tim Rice (series); radio incls: numerous quiz shows from Just a Minute downwards; script for 15-part series on hist. of Western popular music for BBC World Service Broadcasts to China. Film début as actor in insultingly small rôle, The Survivor, 1980. Chairman: Stars Organization for Spastics, 1983–85; Shaftesbury Avenue Centenary Cttee, 1984–86; Foundn for Sport and the Arts, 1991–; Pres., Lord's Taverners, 1988–90. *Publications*: Heartaches Cricketers' Almanack, yearly, 1975–; (ed) Lord's Taverners Sticky Wicket Book, 1979; Treasures of Lord's, 1989; (with Andrew Lloyd Webber): Evita, 1978; Joseph and the Amazing Technicolour Dreamcoat, 1982; (jtly) Guinness Books of British Hit Singles and Albums and associated pubns, 1977–, 22nd bk in series, 1991. *Recreations*: cricket, history of popular music. *Address*: 196 Shaftesbury Avenue, WC2H 8JL. *T*: 071–240 5617. *Clubs*: Garrick, MCC (Mem., Arts and Liby Sub-cttee, 1986–), Dramatists', Saints and Sinners (Chm., 1990); Fonograf (Budapest).

RICE-OXLEY, James Keith, CBE 1981; Chairman, Merchant Navy Training Board, since 1981; *b* 15 Aug. 1920; *o s* of late Montague Keith Rice-Oxley and Margery Hyacinth Rice-Oxley (*née* Burrell), Kensington; *m* 1949, Barbara, *yr d* of late Frederick Parsons, Gerrards Cross; two *d*. *Educ*: Marlborough Coll.; Trinity Coll., Oxford. MA(Law). Served War of 1939–45: Wiltshire Regt, Royal West Kents (wounded El Alamein); GSO III, HQ 3 Corps; GSO II, HQ Land Forces, Greece (despatches). Joined Shipping Fedn, 1947, Dir, 1965–75; Dir, Internat. Shipping Fedn, 1970–80; Dir, Gen. Council of British Shipping, 1975–80. Chm., Nat. Sea Training Trust, 1965–80; Mem. Nat. Maritime Bd, 1965–80; Mem., Merchant Navy Welfare Bd, 1965–80; Internat. Shipowners' Chm. and British Shipowners' Rep. on Jt Maritime Commn of ILO, 1970–80; Chm., Shipowners' Gp at Internat. Labour (Maritime) Confs, 1969, 1970, 1975, 1976; a Vice-Pres., IMCO/ILO Maritime Conf., 1978. Chm., Maritime Studies Cttee, BTEC, 1980–87; Mem. Industrial Tribunals (England and Wales), 1981–88; General Comr of Income Tax, 1986–. Barnardo's: Mem. Council and Exec. Cttee, 1981–; Vice-Chm. Council, 1988–89; Chm., Shaftesbury Civic Soc., 1982–85; Mem. Council, King George's Fund for Sailors, 1965–82; UK Mem., Bd of Governors, World Maritime Univ., Malmö, 1983–89. *Recreations*: squash, ceramics. *Address*: Ox House, Bimport, Shaftesbury SP7 8AX. *T*: Shaftesbury (0747) 52741.

RICH, John Rowland, CMG 1978; HM Diplomatic Service, retired; *b* 29 June 1928; *s* of late Rowland William Rich, Winchester, and of Phyllis Mary, *e d* of Charles Linstead Chambers, Southgate; *m* 1956, Rosemary Ann, *yr d* of late Bertram Evan Williams, Ferndown, Dorset; two *s* one *d*. *Educ*: Sedbergh; Clare Coll., Cambridge (Foundn Exhibnr 1948). BA 1949, MA 1954. HM Forces, 1949–51; FO, 1951–53; 3rd, later 2nd Sec., Addis Ababa, 1953–56; 2nd, later 1st Sec., Stockholm, 1956–59; FO, 1959–63; 1st Sec. (Economic) and Head of Chancery, Bahrain (Political Residency), 1963–66; FCO, 1966–69; Counsellor and Head of Chancery, Prague, 1969–72; Diplomatic Service Inspector, 1972–74; Commercial Counsellor, Bonn, 1974–78; Consul-Gen., Montreal, 1978–80; Ambassador: to Czechoslovakia, 1980–85; to Switzerland, 1985–88. *Recreations*: walking, wild orchids, steam locomotives. *Address*: 23 Embercourt Road, Thames Ditton, Surrey KT7 0LH. *T*: 081–398 1205. *Club*: Travellers'.

RICH, Michael Anthony; Regional Chairman, Industrial Tribunals, Southampton, since 1987; *b* 16 March 1931; *s* of Joseph and Kate Alexandra Rich; *m* 1959, Helen Kit Marston, MB, BS; one *s* one *d*. *Educ*: Kimbolton Sch., Hunts. Admitted Solicitor, 1954. Army Legal Aid, 1954–56; Partner, Rich and Carr, Leicester, 1960–76; Part-time Chm., 1972, Permanent Chm., 1976, Industrial Tribunals. Pres., Leicester Law Soc., 1976–77. Trustee, Ulverscroft Foundn, 1972–. *Recreations*: railway modelling, France, wine. *Address*: 4 Hickory Drive, Harestock, Winchester, Hants SO22 6NJ.

RICH, Michael Samuel, QC 1980; a Recorder, since 1986; *b* 18 Aug. 1933; *s* of late Sidney Frank Rich, OBE and of Erna Babette; *m* 1963, Janice Sarita Benedictus; three *s* one *d*. *Educ*: Dulwich Coll.; Wadham Coll., Oxford (MA, 1st Class Hons PPE). Called to the Bar, Middle Temple, 1958, Bencher, 1985. Medal of Merit, Boy Scouts Assoc., 1970. *Publication*: (jtly) Hill's Law of Town and Country Planning, 5th edn, 1968. *Recreations*: "prog-nosed" activities. *Address*: 2 Paper Buildings, Temple, EC4. *T*: 071–353 5835; 18 Dulwich Village, SE21. *T*: 081–693 1957. *Club*: Garrick.

RICH, Nigel Mervyn Sutherland; Managing Director, Jardine Matheson Holdings Ltd, since 1989; *b* 30 Oct. 1945; *s* of Charles Albert Rich and Mina Mackintosh Rich; *m* 1970, Cynthia Elizabeth (*née* Davies); two *s* two *d*. *Educ*: Sedbergh Sch.; New Coll., Oxford (MA). FCA. Deloitte, Plender Griffiths, London, 1967–71; Deloitte, Haskins & Sells, New York, 1971–73; Jardine Matheson, 1974–; served in varying positions in Hong Kong, Johannesburg (Rennies Consolidated Holdings) and Manila (Jardine Davies); seconded to Hongkong Land, 1983–88. Liveryman, Tobacco Pipemakers and Tobacco Blenders Co.; Freeman, City of London, 1970. *Recreations*: tennis, golf, windsurfing. *Address*: 11 Shek O, Hong Kong. *Clubs*: MCC, Hurlingham, Army and Navy; Royal and Ancient Golf; Shek O, American, Royal Hong Kong Golf (Hong Kong).

RICHARD, family name of **Baron Richard**.

RICHARD, Baron *cr* 1990 (Life Peer), of Ammanford in the County of Dyfed; **Ivor Seward Richard**; QC 1971; *b* 30 May 1932; *s* of Seward Thomas Richard, mining and electrical engineer, and Isabella Irene Richard; *m* (marr. diss.); two *s* one *d*; *m* 1989, Janet Jones; one *s*. *Educ*: St Michael's Sch., Bryn, Llanelly; Cheltenham Coll.; Pembroke Coll., Oxford (Wightwick Scholar; Hon Fellow, 1981). BA Oxon (Jurisprudence) 1953; MA 1970; called to Bar, Inner Temple, 1955, Bencher, 1985. Practised in chambers, London, 1955–74. UK Perm. Representative to UN, 1974–79; Mem., Commn of EEC, 1981–84; Chm., Rhodesia Conf., Geneva, 1976. Parly Candidate, S Kensington, 1959; MP (Lab) Barons Court, 1964–Feb. 1974. Delegate: Assembly, Council of Europe, 1965–68; Western European Union, 1965–68; Vice-Chm., Legal Cttee, Council of Europe, 1966–67; PPS, Sec. of State for Defence, 1966–69; Parly Under-Sec. (Army), Min. of

---

Defence, 1969–70; Opposition Spokesman, Broadcasting, Posts and Telecommunications, 1970–71; Dep. Spokesman, Foreign Affairs, 1971–74. Chm., World Trade Centre Wales Ltd (Cardiff), 1985–. Member: Fabian Society; Society of Labour Lawyers; Inst. of Strategic Studies; Royal Inst. of Internat. Affairs. *Publications*: (jt) Europe or the Open Sea, 1971; We, the British, 1983 (USA); articles in various political jls. *Recreations*: playing piano, watching football matches, talking. *Address*: 11 South Square, Gray's Inn, WC2.

RICHARD, Cliff, OBE 1980; singer, actor; *b* 14 Oct. 1940; *s* of Rodger Webb and Dorothy Webb. *Educ*: Riversmead Sch., Cheshunt. Awarded 13 Gold Discs for records: Living Doll, 1959; The Young Ones, 1962; Bachelor Boy, 1962; Lucky Lips, 1963; Congratulations, 1968; Power to all Our Friends, 1973; Devil Woman, 1976; We Don't Talk Anymore, 1979; Wired for Sound, 1981; Daddy's Home, 1981; Living Doll (with The Young Ones), 1986; All I Ask of You (with Sarah Brightman), 1986; Mistletoe and Wine, 1988; also 35 Silver Discs and 2 Platinum Discs (Daddy's Home, 1981; All I Ask of You, 1986). Films: Serious Charge, 1959; Expresso Bongo, 1960; The Young Ones, 1962; Summer Holiday, 1963; Wonderful Life, 1964; Finders Keepers, 1966; Two a Penny, 1968; His Land, 1970; Take Me High, 1973. Own TV series, ATV and BBC. Stage: rep. and variety seasons; Time, Dominion, 1986–87. Top Box Office Star of GB, 1962–63 and 1963–64. *Publications*: Questions, 1970; The Way I See It, 1972; The Way I See It Now, 1975; Which One's Cliff, 1977; Happy Christmas from Cliff, 1980; You, Me and Jesus, 1983; Mine to Share, 1984; Jesus, Me and You, 1985; Single-minded, 1988; Mine Forever, 1989. *Recreations*: swimming, tennis. *Address*: c/o PO Box 46C, Esher, Surrey KT10 9AA. *T*: Esher (0372) 467752.

RICHARDS, family name of **Baron Milverton**.

RICHARDS, Alun; see Richards, R. A.

RICHARDS, Archibald Banks, CA; retired; *b* 29 March 1911; *s* of late Charles Richards and Margaret Pollock Richards; *m* 1st, 1941, Edith Janet Sinclair (*d* 1987); one *s* one *d*; 2nd, 1990, Constance Mary Fleming Mason. *Educ*: Daniel Stewart's Coll., Edinburgh. Partner, A. T. Niven & Co., Chartered Accountants, Edinburgh, 1939–69, Touche Ross & Co., Chartered Accountants, 1964–78. Inst. of Chartered Accountants of Scotland: Mem., 1934; Mem. Council, 1968–73; Vice Pres., 1974–76; Pres., 1976–77. *Address*: 7 Midmar Gardens, Edinburgh EH10 6DY. *T*: 031–447 1942.

RICHARDS, Arthur Cyril, FIA; consultant; *b* 7 April 1921; *s* of Ernest Arthur Richards and Kate Richards (*née* Cooper); *m* 1st, 1944, Joyce Bertha Brooke (marr. diss. 1974); two *s* two *d*; 2nd, 1975, Els Stoyle (*née* van der Stoel); two step *s* one step *d*. *Educ*: Tollington Sch., London. FIA 1949; FSVA 1962. Insurance, 1937–41. Served RAF, 1941–46. Insurance, consulting actuary, steel manufacture, investment banking, internat. property develt, 1946–64; Advr, Samuel Montagu & Co. Ltd, 1965–67; Gp Finance Dir, Bovis Ltd, 1967–71; United Dominions Trust Ltd: Gp Finance Dir, 1971–76; Gp Man. Dir, 1976–80; Chief Exec., 1981–83; Dir, 1978–88, Chm., 1983–88, Blackwood Hodge plc. Chm., Federated Land, 1982; Director: MSL Gp Internat., 1970–81; TSB Trust Co., 1981–88; Combined Lease Finance PLC, 1985–89. *Recreations*: sailing, windsurfing, antiques. *Address*: Caboose, Tilt Meadow, Cobham, Surrey KT11 3AJ.

RICHARDS, Bertrand; see Richards, E. B. B.

RICHARDS, Brian Henry, CEng, FIEE; Chief Executive, Atomic Weapons Establishment, since 1990; *b* 19 July 1938; *s* of Alfred Edward Richards and Lilian Maud Richards (*née* Bennett); *m* 1961, Jane Wilkins; one *s* one *d*. *Educ*: Buckhurst Hill County Grammar Sch.; St John's College, Cambridge (Mech. Sci. Tripos, 1st Class Hons 1959, BA 1960; MA 1965). GEC Electronics, later Marconi Defence Systems, 1960–87: Guided Weapons Division: develt, systems, project management appts, 1960–76; Business Develt Manager, 1977; Manager, 1978; Asst Gen. Manager and Manager, 1982; Dir, Guided Weapons, 1985; RCDS, 1986; Asst Man. Dir, 1987; Technical Dir, Hunting Engineering, 1988–90. *Recreations*: golf, listening to music, water colour painting, DIY, gardening. *Address*: Atomic Weapons Establishment, Aldermaston, Reading RG7 4PR.

RICHARDS, Dr Brian Mansel, CBE 1990; Chairman, British Bio-technology Group, since 1989; *b* 19 Sept. 1932; *s* of Cyril Mansel Richards and Gwendolyn Hyde Richards; *m* 1952, Joan Lambert Breese; one *s* one *d*. *Educ*: Lewis Sch., Pengam, Glam; University Coll. of Wales, Aberystwyth (BSc); King's College London (PhD). British Empire Cancer Fellowship, 1955–57; Nuffield Fellowship, 1957; MRC Biophysics Research Unit, 1957–64; Reader in Biology, Univ. of London, 1964–66; Research Div., G. D. Searle & Co., 1966–86; Vice-Pres., UK Preclinical R&D, 1980–86; Chm., British Bio-technology Ltd, 1986–89. Chm., Biotechnology Working Party, CBI, 1988; Mem., Res. and Manufg Cttee, CBI, 1988; Mem., Sci. Bd, SERC, 1987; Chm., Biotechnology Jt Adv. Bd, SERC/DTI, 1989; Mem., Adv. Cttee for Genetic Modification (previously Manipulation), HSE, 1984; Consultant on Biotechnology, OECD, 1987. *Publications*: papers in sci. jls. *Recreations*: collecting Jaguar cars, photography, deprecating ball games. *Address*: British Bio-technology Group, Watlington Road, Cowley, Oxford OX4 5LY. *T*: Oxford (0865) 748747.

RICHARDS, Sir Brooks; see Richards, Sir F. B.

RICHARDS, Catherine Margaret; Secretary and Registrar, Institute of Mathematics and its Applications, since 1987; *b* 12 May 1940; *d* of John Phillips Richards and Edna Vivian (*née* Thomas). *Educ*: Newport High Sch. for Girls, Gwent; Bedford Coll., Univ. of London (BSc 1962). Information Officer, British Oxygen Co., 1962–63; Chemistry Mistress, St Joseph's Convent Grammar Sch., Abbeywood, 1963–65; Asst Editor, Soc. for Analytical Chemistry, 1965–70; Dep. Sec., IMA, 1970–87. *Recreation*: reading. *Address*: Institute of Mathematics and its Applications, 16 Nelson Street, Southend-on-Sea, Essex SS1 1EF. *T*: Southend-on-Sea (0702) 354020. *Clubs*: University Women's, Wig and Pen.

RICHARDS, Charles Anthony Langdon, CMG 1958; *b* 18 April 1911; *s* of T. L. Richards, Bristol, Musician; *m* 1937, Mary Edith Warren-Codrington; two *s*. *Educ*: Clifton Coll.; Brasenose Coll., Oxford. Appointed Colonial CS, Uganda, 1934; Major, 7th King's African Rifles, 1939–41: duties in Mauritius, 1941–46; District Officer, Uganda, 1946–50; Commissioner for Social Development, Tanganyika, 1950–53; Commissioner for Community Development, Uganda, 1953–54; Resident, Buganda, Oct. 1954–60; Minister of Local Government, Uganda, 1960–61. *Recreation*: gardening. *Address*: The Wall House, Oak Drive, Highworth, Wilts SN6 7BP.

RICHARDS, David Gordon, CBE 1989; FCA; Non-Executive Chairman, Walker Greenbank plc, since 1990 (Director, since 1988); *b* 25 Aug. 1928; *s* of late Gordon Charles Richards and Vera Amy (*née* Barrow); *m* 1960, Stephanie, *er d* of late E. Gilbert Woodward, Metropolitan Magistrate and of Mrs Woodward; one *s* two *d*. *Educ*: Highgate Sch. FCA 1961. Articled to Harmood Banner & Co., 1945; served, 8th Royal Tank Regt, 1947–49; Partner: Harmood Banner & Co., 1955–74; Deloitte Haskins & Sells, 1974–84. Admitted Associate Mem. Inst. of Chartered Accountants in England and Wales, 1951 (Council, 1970–87; Vice-Pres., 1977–78; Dep. Pres., 1978–79; Centenary Pres., 1979–80; Mem., Gen. Purposes and Finance Cttee, 1977–83; Chm., Internat. Affairs Cttee,

1980–83); Mem., Cttee of London Soc. of Chartered Accountants, 1966–70, 1981–82 (Chm., 1969–70); Chm., Cons. Cttee of Accountancy Bodies, 1979–80; UK and Ireland rep. on Council, Internat. Fedn of Accountants, 1981–83. Dep. Chm., Monopolies and Mergers Commn, 1983–90; Member: Cttees of Investigation under Agricultural Marketing Act (1958), 1972–88; Council for Securities Industry, 1979–80; Panel on Take Overs and Mergers, 1979–80; Review Body on Doctors' and Dentists' Remuneration, 1984–90; Chm., Disciplinary Bd, BPsS, 1988–. Governor, Highgate Sch., 1982– (Chm. 1983–); Trustee: The Bob Champion Cancer Trust, 1983–; Royal Acad. of Music Foundn, 1985–; Prince's Youth Business Trust, 1986–. Pres., Old Cholmeleian Soc., 1988–89. Master, Worshipful Co. of Chartered Accountants in England and Wales, 1986–87. *Publications:* numerous contribs to professional press and lectures on professional topics given internationally. *Recreations:* golf, lawn tennis, sailing, shooting, silviculture, music. *Address:* Eastleach House, Eastleach, Glos GL7 3NW. *T:* Southrop (036785) 416.

RICHARDS, Denis Edward, CMG 1981; HM Diplomatic Service, retired; Ambassador to the United Republic of Cameroon and the Republic of Equatorial Guinea, 1979–81; *b* 25 May 1923; *m* 1947, Nancy Beryl Brown; two *d. Educ:* Wilson's Grammar Sch., London; St Peter's Coll., Oxford. Lieut RNVR, 1941–46; Colonial Service (HMOCS), 1948–60: District Admin. and Min. of Finance, Ghana (Gold Coast); HM Diplomatic Service, 1960–81: CRO, 1960; Karachi, 1961–63; FO (News Dept), 1964–68; Brussels (NATO), 1969; Brussels (UK Negotiating Delegn), 1970–72; Counsellor, Kinshasa, 1972–74; Consul-Gen., Philadelphia, 1974–79. *Recreations:* music, watching cricket. *Address:* Tresco House, Spencer Road, Birchington, Kent CT7 9EY. *T:* Thanet (0843) 45637.

RICHARDS, Denis George, OBE 1990; author; *b* 10 Sept. 1910; *s* of late George Richards and Frances Amelia Gosland; *m* 1940, Barbara, *d* of J. H. Smethurst, Heaton, Bolton; four *d. Educ:* Owen's Sch.; Trinity Hall, Cambridge (Scholar). BA 1931 (1st Cl. in both Parts of Historical Tripos); MA 1935; Asst Master, Manchester Grammar School, 1931–39; Senior History and English Master, Bradfield Coll., 1939–41; Narrator in Air Ministry Historical Branch, writing confidential studies on various aspects of the air war, 1942–43; Sen. Narrator, 1943–47; Hon. Sqdn Ldr RAFVR, 1943–47; engaged in writing, under Air Min. auspices, an official History of the Royal Air Force in the Second World War, 1947–49; was established in Admin. Civil Service, Principal, Department of Permanent Under Secretary of State for Air, 1949–50; Principal, Morley College, 1950–65; Longman Fellow in Univ. of Sussex, 1965–68. Chm., Women's League of Health and Beauty, 1966–88; Vice-Pres., Purcell Sch. for Young Musicians, 1984–. *Publications:* An Illustrated History of Modern Europe, 1938; Modern Europe (1919–39 section for revised edn of work by Sydney Herbert), 1940; (with J. W. Hunt) An Illustrated History of Modern Britain, 1950; (with late Hilary St G. Saunders) Royal Air Force 1939–45–an officially commissioned history in 3 volumes, 1953–54 (awarded C. P. Robertson Memorial Trophy, 1954); (with J. Evan Cruikshank) The Modern Age, 1955; Britain under the Tudors and Stuarts, 1958; Offspring of the Vic: a History of Morley College, 1958; (with Anthony Quick) Britain 1714–1851, 1961; (with J. A. Bolton) Britain and the Ancient World, 1963; (with Anthony Quick) Britain, 1851–1945, 1967; (with Anthony Quick) Twentieth Century Britain, 1968; (with A. W. Ellis) Medieval Britain, 1973; Portal of Hungerford, 1978; (with Richard Hough) The Battle of Britain: the Jubilee history, 1989; (ed) The Few and the Many, 1990. *Recreations:* music, pictures, golf, travel in the more civilized parts of Europe, the lighter tasks in the garden. *Address:* 16 Broadlands Road, N6 4AN. *T:* 081–340 5259. *Clubs:* Arts, Garrick, PEN.

See also W. P. Shovelton.

RICHARDS, His Honour (Edmund) Bertrand (Bamford); a Circuit Judge, 1972–86; *b* 14 Feb. 1913; *s* of Rev. Edmund Milo Richards, Llewesog Hall, Denbigh; *m* 2nd, 1966, Jane, *widow* of Edward Stephen Porter. *Educ:* Lancing Coll.; Corpus Christi Coll., Oxford. Served War, RA, 1940–46. Called to Bar, Inner Temple, 1941. Dep. Chm., Denbighshire QS, 1964–71. Hon. Recorder of Ipswich, 1975. *Address:* Melton Hall, near Woodbridge, Suffolk.

RICHARDS, Prof. Elfyn John, OBE 1958; FEng; FRAeS; FIMechE; Research Professor, Southampton University, and Acoustical Consultant, 1975–84, now Emeritus. *b* Barry, Glamorgan, South Wales, 28 Dec. 1914; *s* of Edward James Richards, Barry, schoolmaster, and of Catherine Richards; *m* 1941, Eluned Gwenddydd Jones (*d* 1978), Aberporth, Cardigan; three *d*; *m* 1986, Olive Meakin (*d* 1989); *m* 1990, Miriam Davidson, Romsey, Hants. *Educ:* Barry County School; Univ. Coll. of Wales, Aberystwyth (BSc); St John's Coll., Cambridge (MA). DSc (Wales), 1959. Research Asst, Bristol Aeroplane Company, 1938–39; Scientific Officer, National Physical Laboratory, Teddington, 1939–45, and Secretary, various Aeronautical Research Council sub-cttees; Chief Aerodynamicist and Asst Chief-Designer, Vickers Armstrong, Ltd, Weybridge, 1945–50; Prof. of Aeronautical Engineering, 1950–64, and Founder Dir, Inst. of Sound and Vibration Research, 1963–67, Univ. of Southampton, also Aeronautical Engineering Consultant; Vice-Chancellor, Loughborough Univ., 1967–75. Res. Prof., Florida Atlantic Univ., 1983. Member: SRC, 1970–74; Noise Adv. Council; Noise Research Council, ARC, 1968–71; Construction Research and Adv. Council, 1968–71; Inland Transport and Develt Council, 1968–71; Gen. Adv. Council of BBC (Chm. Midlands Adv. Council, 1968–71); Cttee of Scientific Advisory Council; Wilson Cttee on Problems of Noise; Planning and Transport Res. Adv. Council, 1971–. Chm., Univs Council for Adult Educn; President: British Acoustical Soc., 1968–70; Soc. of Environmental Engrs, 1971–73. Mem. Leics CC. Hon. LLD Wales, 1973; Hon. DSc: Southampton, 1973; Heriot-Watt, 1983; Hon. DTech Loughborough, 1975. Hon. FIOA 1978; Hon. Fellow Acoustical Soc. of America, 1980. Taylor Gold Medal, RAeS, 1949; James Watt Medal, ICE, 1963; Silver Medal, RSA, 1971. *Publications:* books and research papers (250) in acoustics, aviation, education. *Address:* 53 The Harrage, Romsey, Hants.

RICHARDS, Sir (Francis) Brooks, KCMG 1976 (CMG 1963); DSC and Bar, 1943; *b* 18 July 1918; *s* of Francis Bartlett Richards; *m* 1941, Hazel Myfanwy, *d* of Lt-Col Stanley Price Williams, CIE; one *s* one *d. Educ:* Stowe School; Magdalene College, Cambridge. Served with RN, 1939–44 (Lieut-Comdr RNVR). HM Embassy: Paris, 1944–48; Athens, 1952–54; First Sec. and Head of Chancery, Political Residency, Persian Gulf, 1954–57; Assistant Private Secretary to Foreign Secretary, 1958–59; Counsellor (Information), HM Embassy, Paris, 1959–64; Head of Information Policy Dept, 1964, and of Jt Inf. Policy and Guidance Dept, FO/CRO, 1964–65; seconded to Cabinet Office, 1965–69; HM Minister, Bonn, 1969–71; HM Ambassador, Saigon, 1972–74; HM Ambassador, Greece, 1974–78; Dep. Sec., Cabinet Office, 1978–80; NI Office, 1980–81. Chm., CSM Parliamentary Consultants Ltd, 1984–. Vice-pres., Friends of Imperial War Museum, 1991– (Chm., 1989–91); Chm., Paintings in Hosps, 1990–; Anglo Hellenic League, 1990–. Mem., RIIA. Chevalier, Légion d'Honneur and Croix de Guerre (France), 1944. *Recreations:* collecting, gardening, travelling. *Address:* The Ranger's House, Farnham, Surrey GU9 0AB. *T:* Farnham (0252) 716764. *Clubs:* Travellers', Special Forces, Royal Ocean Racing.

See also F. N. Richards.

RICHARDS, Francis Neville; HM Diplomatic Service; High Commissioner in Windhoek, since 1990; *s* of Sir Francis Brooks Richards, *qv*; *m* 1971, Gillian Bruce Nevill, *d* of late I. S. Nevill, MC and of Dr L. M. B. Dawson; one *s* one *d. Educ:* Eton; King's Coll., Cambridge (MA). Royal Green Jackets, 1967 (invalided, 1969). FCO, 1969; Moscow, 1971; UK Delegn to MBFR negotiations, Vienna, 1973; FCO, 1976–85 (Asst Private Sec. to Sec. of State, 1981–82); Economic and Commercial Counsellor, New Delhi, 1985–88; FCO, 1988–90 (Head, S Asian Dept). *Recreations:* walking, travelling, riding. *Address:* c/o Foreign and Commonwealth Office, SW1A 2AH. *Clubs:* Travellers'; President's Estate Polo (New Delhi).

RICHARDS, Very Rev. Gwynfryn; Dean of Bangor, 1962–71; Archdeacon of Bangor, 1957–62; Rector of Llandudno, 1956–62; *b* 10 Sept. 1902; *er s* of Joshua and Elizabeth Ann Richards, Nantyffyllon, Glam; *m* 1935, Margery Phyllis Evans; one *s* one *d. Educ:* Universities of Wales, Oxford and Boston. Scholar, Univ. Coll., Cardiff, 1918–21; BSc (Wales), 1921; Jesus Coll., Oxford, 1921–23; Certificate, School of Geography, Oxford, 1922; BA 1st Cl. Hons School of Natural Science, 1923; MA 1928. In industry (USA), 1923–25. Boston Univ. Sch. of Theology, 1926–28; STB First Cl., 1928; Scholar and Travelling Fellow, 1928–29; Oxford, 1928–29; St Michael's Coll., Llandaff, 1929–30; deacon, 1930; priest, 1931. Curate of: Llanrhos, 1930–34; Aberystwyth, St Michael, 1934–38; Rector of Llanllyfni, 1938–49; Vicar of Conway with Gyffin, 1949–56. Canon of Bangor Cathedral, 1943–62, Treas., 1943–57; Examining Chaplain to Bp of Bangor, 1944–71; Rural Dean of Arllechwedd, 1953–57. Pantyfedwen Lectr, Univ. Coll., Aberystwyth, 1967. *Publications:* Ffurfiau Ordeinio Holl Eglwysi Cymru, 1943; Yr Hen Fam, 1952; Ein Hymraniadau Annedwydd, 1963; Gwir a Diogel Obaith, 1972; Ar Lawer Trywydd, 1973; A Fynn Esgyn, Mynn Ysgol, 1980; contrib. to Journal of the Historical Society of the Church in Wales, Nat. Library of Wales Jl, Trans of Caernarvonshire Hist. Soc. *Recreations:* gardening, photography, local history. *Address:* Llain Werdd, Llandegfan, Menai Bridge, Gwynedd LL59 5LY. *T:* Menai Bridge (0248) 713429.

RICHARDS, (Isaac) Vivian (Alexander); cricketer; Captain, West Indies Cricket Team, since 1985; *b* St Johns, Antigua, 7 March 1952; *s* of Malcolm Richards; *m* Miriam Lewis; one *s* one *d. Educ:* Antigua Grammar School. First class débuts, Leeward Islands, 1971, India (for WI), 1974; played for: Somerset, 1974–86; Queensland, 1976–77; Rishton, Lancs League, 1987; Glamorgan, 1990–; played in 100th Test Match, 1988; scored 100th first class century, 1988; 100th Test Match catch, 1988; highest Test score, 291, *v* England, Oval, 1976; highest first class score, 322, *v* Warwicks, Taunton, 1985; fastest Test century *v* England, Antigua, 1986; highest number of Test runs by a West Indian batsman, 1991. Hon. DLitt Exeter, 1986. *Publications:* (with David Foot) Viv Richards (autobiog.), 1982; (with Patrick Murphy) Cricket Masterclass, 1988; (with Michael Middles) Hitting across the Line (autobiog.), 1991. *Recreations:* tennis, music, football. *Address:* c/o David Copp Management, PO Box 19, Sherborne, Dorset DT9 3EF. *T:* Sherborne (0935) 816011.

RICHARDS, James Alan, OBE 1979; Agent-General for Western Australia in London, 1975–78, retired; *b* 8 Oct. 1913; *s* of James Percival Richards and Alice Pearl Richards (*née* Bullock) Adelaide; *m* 1939, Mabel Joyce, *d* of R. H. Cooper, Riverton, S Austr.; three *s* one *d. Educ:* Unley High Sch.; Coll. of Business Admin, Univ. of Hawaii. Served War of 1939–45, 2nd AIF. Ampol Petroleum Ltd, 1946–75: Sales Man., South Australia, 1952–53; State Man., Western Australia, 1954–75. *Recreation:* bowls. *Address:* 98/7 Harman Road, Sorrento, WA 6020, Australia.

RICHARDS, Sir James (Maude), Kt 1972; CBE 1959; FSA 1980; architectural writer, critic and historian; Editor, Architectural Review, 1937–71; Editor, Architects' Journal, 1947–49 (editorial board, 1949–61); Architectural Correspondent, The Times, 1947–71; *b* 13 Aug. 1907; 2nd *s* of late Louis Saurin Richards and Lucy Denes (*née* Clarence); *m* 1st, 1936, Margaret (marr. diss., 1948), *d* of late David Angus; (one *s* decd) one *d*; 2nd, 1954, Kathleen Margaret (Kit), *widow* of late Morland Lewis and 2nd *d* of late Henry Bryan Godfrey-Faussett-Osborne, Queendown Warren, Sittingbourne, Kent; one *s* decd. *Educ:* Gresham's School, Holt; AA School of Architecture. ARIBA, AADipl 1930. Studied and practised architecture in Canada and USA, 1930–31, London and Dublin, 1931–33; Asst Editor, The Architects' Jl, 1933; The Architectural Review, 1935; Editor, Publications Div., 1942, Director of Publications, Middle East, Cairo, 1943–46, MOI; Gen. Editor, The Architectural Press, 1946. Hoffman Wood Prof. of Architecture, Leeds Univ., 1957–59. Editor, European Heritage, 1973–75. Member: exec. cttee Modern Architectural Research Gp, 1946–54; AA Council, 1948–51, 1958–61, 1973–74; Advisory Council, Inst. of Contemporary Arts, 1947–68; Architecture Council, Festival of Britain, 1949–51; British Cttee, Internat. Union of Architects, 1950–66; Royal Fine Art Commn, 1951–66; Fine Art Cttee, Brit. Council, 1954–78; Council of Industrial Design, 1955–61; Min. of Transport (Worboys) Cttee on traffic signs, 1962–63; World Soc. of Ekistics, 1965–86; Council, Victorian Soc., 1965–; National Trust, 1977–83; Vice-Pres. Nat. Council on Inland Transport, 1963–; Exec. Cttee, Venice in Peril Fund, 1969–; Chm., Arts Council inquiry into provision for the arts in Ireland, 1974–76; British Cttee, Icomos, 1975–88. Broadcaster, television and sound (regular member, BBC Critics panel, 1948–68). FRSA 1970; Hon. AILA, 1955; Hon. FAIA, 1985. Chevalier (First Class), 1960, Comdr, 1985, Order of White Rose of Finland; Gold Medal, Mexican Institute of Architects, 1963; Bicentenary Medal, RSA, 1971. *Publications:* Miniature History of the English House, 1938; (with late Eric Ravilious) High Street, 1938; Introduction to Modern Architecture, 1940, new edn 1970 (trans. seven langs); (with John Summerson) The Bombed Buildings of Britain, 1942; Edward Bawden, 1946; The Castles on the Ground, 1946, new enl. edn 1973; The Functional Tradition in Early Industrial Buildings, 1958; (ed) New Building in the Commonwealth, 1961; An Architectural Journey in Japan, 1963; Guide to Finnish Architecture, 1966; A Critic's View, 1970; (ed, with late Nikolaus Pevsner) The Anti-Rationalists, 1972; Planning and Redevelopment in London's Entertainment Area, 1973 (Arts Council report); The Professions: Architecture, 1974; (ed) Who's Who in Architecture: from 1400 to the present day, 1977; 800 Years of Finnish Architecture, 1978; Memoirs of an Unjust Fella (autobio.), 1980; The National Trust Book of English Architecture, 1981; Goa, 1982; The National Trust Book of Bridges, 1984. *Recreations:* travel and topography. *Address:* 29 Fawcett Street, SW10 9AY. *T:* 071–352 9874. *Clubs:* Athenæum, Beefsteak.

RICHARDS, Ven. John; Archdeacon of Exeter and Canon Residentiary of Exeter Cathedral, since 1981; *b* 4 Oct. 1933; *s* of William and Ethel Mary Richards; *m* 1958, Ruth Haynes; two *s* three *d. Educ:* Reading School; Wyggeston Grammar School, Leicester; Sidney Sussex Coll., Cambridge (MA); Ely Theological Coll. Asst Curate, St Thomas, Exeter, 1959–64; Rector of Holsworthy with Hollacombe and Cookbury, 1964–74; RD of Holsworthy, 1970–74; Rector of Heavitree with St Paul's, Exeter, 1974–81; RD of Exeter, 1978–81. Chm. of House of Clergy, Exeter Diocesan Synod, 1979–82; Mem. Gen. Synod, 1985–. Mem., C of E Pensions Bd, 1989–. A Church Commissioner, 1988–. *Recreations:* gardening, fishing, walking. *Address:* 12 The Close, Exeter. *T:* Exeter (0392) 75745.

RICHARDS, John Arthur; Under-Secretary, Department of Education and Science, 1973–77; *b* 23 June 1918; *s* of late Alderman A. J. Richards and Mrs Annie Richards, Dulwich; *m* 1946, Sheelagh, *d* of late Patrick McWalter and Katherine McWalter, Balla, Co. Mayo; two *s* one *d. Educ:* Brockley Sch.; King's Coll., London. BA, AKC, Dip. in

Educn. Hon. Sec., King's Coll. Union Soc., 1939. Served War: Captain RA; Directorate of Personnel Selection, War Office, 1945–46. Temp. Third Sec., Foreign Office, 1946; Staff, Hackney Downs Grammar Sch., 1948; Ministry of Education: Asst Principal and Principal, 1949 (Jt Sec., Secondary Schs Examinations Council, 1956–57); Asst Sec. (also Dept of Educn and Science), 1963–73. *Publications:* occasional verse and contribs to journals. *Recreations:* journalism, writing verse. *Address:* 14 Blacksmiths Hill, Sanderstead, Surrey CR2 9AY. *T:* 081–657 1275.

RICHARDS, Lt-Gen. Sir John (Charles Chisholm), KCB 1980; KCVO 1991; HM Marshal of the Diplomatic Corps, 1982–March 1992; *b* 21 Feb. 1927; *s* of Charles C. Richards and Alice Milner; *m* 1953, Audrey Hidson; two *s* one *d. Educ:* Worksop Coll., Notts. Joined Royal Marines, 1945; 45 Commando, Malaya, 1950–52; Instructor, Officers' Sch., 1953–55; HMS Birmingham, 1955–56; Canadian Army Staff Coll., 1959–61; Adjt and Company Comdr, 43 Commando, 1962–63; Naval staff, 1963–64; Instructor, Staff Coll., Camberley, 1965–67; 45 Commando: 2nd in Comd, Aden, 1967; CO, 1968–69; GSO1 Plymouth Gp, 1969; CO 42 Commando, 1970–72; Chief of Staff, Brit. Def. Staff, Washington DC, UN Deleg., and Mem. Mil. Staff Cttee, 1972–74; Comdr 3rd Commando Bde, 1975–76; Commandant General, Royal Marines, 1977–81. Col Comdt, RM, 1987–88, Representative Col Comdt, 1989–90. CBIM 1980. Freeman, City of London, 1982. *Recreations:* golf, gardening. *Address:* (until April 1992) St James's Palace, SW1; (from April 1992) c/o National Westminster Bank, 36 St James's Street, SW1. *Club:* Army and Navy.

RICHARDS, John Deacon, CBE 1978; RSA 1989 (ARSA 1974); RIBA; PPRIAS; architect; Senior Consultant, Robert Matthew, Johnson-Marshall and Partners, since 1986 (Partner, 1964–86, Chairman, 1983–86); *b* 7 May 1931; *s* of late William John Richards and Ethel Richards; *m* 1958, Margaret Brown, RIBA, ARIAS; one *s* three *d. Educ:* Geelong Grammar Sch., Vic.; Cranleigh Sch.; Architect. Assoc. Sch. of Arch., London (Dipl. 1954). RIBA 1955; FRIAS 1968 (PRIAS, 1983–85). RE, 1955–57. Buildings include: Stirling Univ., 1965–; Royal Commonwealth Pool, Edinburgh, 1970. Member: Royal Fine Art Commn for Scotland, 1975–89; Bd, Housing Corp., 1982–89 (Chm., Scottish Cttee, 1982–89); Bd, Scottish Homes, 1988– (Dep. Chm., 1989–). Mem., Agrément Bd, 1980–83. Trustee, Nat. Galleries of Scotland, 1986–90. Hon. DUniv Stirling, 1976. Gold Medallist, RSA, 1972. *Recreation:* country life. *Address:* Lady's Field, Whitekirk, Dunbar, East Lothian EH42 1XS. *T:* Whitekirk (062087) 206. *Club:* Athenæum.

RICHARDS, Michael; Director, Samuel Montagu & Co. Ltd, 1960–85; *b* 4 Oct. 1915; *s* of Frank Richards and Jenny Charlotte (*née* Levinsen); *m* 1942, Lucy Helen Quirey; three *d.* Qualified Solicitor, 1936. Partner, Ashurst, Morris Crisp & Co., Solicitors, City of London, 1936–54; Chm. and Man. Dir, Hart, Son & Co. Ltd, Merchant Bankers, 1954–60. Chm., Wood Hall Trust Ltd, 1950–82. *Recreations:* work, farming, collecting works of art. *Address:* Wood Hall, Shenley, Herts WD7 9AY. *T:* Radlett (0923) 856624.

RICHARDS, Michael Anthony, CBiol, FIBiol 1985; MRCVS; Chief Inspector, Animals (Scientific Procedures) Act 1986 (formerly Cruelty to Animals Act (1876)), Home Office, 1982–87, retired; *b* 12 Oct. 1926; *s* of Edward Albert Richards and Clara Muriel (*née* Webb); *m* 1956, Sylvia Rosemary, *d* of Geoffrey Charles Pain, JP; two *d. Educ:* St Albans Coll., St George's Coll., and J. M. Estrada Coll., all in Buenos Aires; Royal Vet. Coll., London Univ. MRCVS 1953. Served Army, Intell. Corps, 1945–47. In general practice, 1953; Lectr in Vet. Medicine, Univ. of London, 1963–67; Lectr in Vet. Pathology, Univ. of Edinburgh, 1967–69; Home Office, 1969–87. *Publications:* scientific contribs to standard works and med. and vet. jls. *Recreation:* philately. *Address:* Hillview, Back Row, Charleston, by Glamis, Forfar, Angus DD8 1UG. *T:* Glamis (030784) 231. *Club:* Civil Service.

RICHARDS, Prof. Peter; Dean and Professor of Medicine, since 1979, St Mary's Hospital Medical School (part of Imperial College of Science, Technology and Medicine, since 1988), University of London; Pro-Rector (Medicine), Imperial College, since 1988; *b* 25 May 1936; *s* of William and Barbara Richards; *m* 1st, 1959, Anne Marie Larsen (marr. diss. 1986); one *s* three *d*; 2nd, 1987, Dr Carol Ann Seymour. *Educ:* Monkton Combe Sch.; Emmanuel Coll., Cambridge (BA 1957; MB BChir 1960; MA 1961; MD 1971); St George's Hosp. Medical Sch.; Royal Postgraduate Medical Sch. (PhD 1966); FRCP 1976. Consultant Physician, St Peter's Hosp., Chertsey and Hon. Sen. Lectr in Medicine, St Mary's Hosp. Med. Sch., 1970–73; Sen. Lectr in Medicine, St George's Hosp. Med. Sch., 1973–79. *Publications:* The Medieval Leper, 1977; (ed jtly) Clinical Medicine and Therapeutics, Vol. I, 1977, Vol. II, 1979; Understanding Water, Electrolyte and Acid/Base Metabolism, 1983; Learning Medicine, 1983, 6th edn 1989; Living Medicine, 1990; scientific papers esp. concerning kidney disease and criteria for selection of medical students in Lancet, BMJ, etc. *Recreations:* walking, listening to music, Finland, social history. *Address:* St Mary's Hospital Medical School, Paddington, W2 1PG. *Club:* Garrick.

RICHARDS, Sir Rex (Edward), Kt 1977; DSc Oxon 1970; FRS 1959; FRSC; Director, The Leverhulme Trust, since 1985; Chancellor, Exeter University, since 1982; *b* 28 Oct. 1922; *s* of H. W. and E. N. Richards; *m* 1948, Eva Edith Vago; two *d. Educ:* Colyton Grammar School, Devon; St John's College, Oxford. Senior Demy, Magdalen College, Oxford, 1946; MA; DPhil; Fellow, Lincoln College, Oxford, 1947–64, Hon. Fellow, 1968; Research Fellow, Harvard University, 1955; Dr Lee's Prof. of Chemistry, Oxford, 1964–70; Fellow, Exeter College, 1964–69; Warden, Merton Coll., Oxford, 1969–84, Hon. Fellow, 1984; Vice-Chancellor, Oxford Univ., 1977–81; Hon. Fellow, St John's Coll., Oxford, 1968; Associate Fellow, Morse Coll., Yale, 1974–79. Director: IBM-UK Ltd, 1978–83; Oxford Instruments Group, 1982–91. Chm., BPMF, 1986–; Member: Chemical Society Council, 1957, 1987–; Faraday Society Council, 1963; Royal Soc. Council, 1973–75; Scientific Adv. Cttee, Nat. Gall., 1978–; ABRC, 1980–83; ACARD, 1984–87; Comr, Royal Comm for the Exhibition of 1851, 1984–; Pres., Royal Soc. of Chemistry, 1990–July 1992; Trustee: CIBA Foundn, 1978–; Nat. Heritage Memorial Fund, 1980–84; Tate Gall., 1982–88; Nat. Gall., 1982–; Henry Moore Foundn, 1989–. Tilden Lectr, 1962. Corday-Morgan Medal of Chemical Soc., 1954; Davy Medal, Royal Soc., 1976; Award in Theoretical Chemistry and Spectroscopy, Chem. Soc., 1977; Educn in Partnership with Industry or Commerce Award, DTI, 1982; Medal of Honour, Rheinische Friedrich-Wilhelms Univ., Bonn, 1983; Royal Medal, Royal Soc., 1986. FRIC 1970. Hon. FRCP 1987; Hon. FBA 1990. Hon. DSc: East Anglia, 1971; Exeter, 1975; Leicester, 1978; Salford, 1979; Edinburgh, 1981; Leeds, 1984; Hon. LLD Dundee, 1977; Hon. ScD Cambridge, 1987. *Publications:* various contributions to scientific journals. *Recreation:* 20th century painting and sculpture. *Address:* 13 Woodstock Close, Oxford OX2 8DB. *T:* Oxford (0865) 513621; 214 The Colonnades, Porchester Square, W2 6AS. *T:* 071–402 2955; The Leverhulme Trust, Lintas House, New Fetter Lane, EC4A 1NR. *T:* 071–822 6938.

RICHARDS, (Richard) Alun; Welsh Secretary in charge of Welsh Office Agriculture Department, 1978–81, retired; *b* 2 Jan. 1920; *s* of Sylvanus and Gwladys Richards, Llanbrynmair, Powys; *m* 1944, Ann Elonwy Mary (Nansi) Price, Morriston, Swansea; two *s. Educ:* Machynlleth County Sch.; Liverpool Univ. (BVSc, MRCVS, 1942). Veterinary Officer with State Vet. Service, Caernarfon and Glamorgan, 1943–57; Divl Vet. Officer, HQ Tolworth and in Warwick, 1957–65; Dep. Reg. Vet. Officer (Wales), 1965–67; seconded to NZ Govt to advise on control of Foot and Mouth disease, 1967–68; Reg. Vet. Officer, HQ Tolworth, 1968–71; Asst Chief Vet. Officer, 1971–77; Asst Sec., Welsh Dept, MAFF, 1977–78; Under-Sec., 1978. *Publications:* contrib. to vet. jls. *Recreations:* beekeeping, fishing, shooting. *Address:* Isfryn, Llandre, Aberystwyth, Dyfed SY24 5BS. *T:* Aberystwyth (0970) 828246.

RICHARDS, Lt-Comdr Richard Meredyth, JP, DL; RN; Vice Lord-Lieutenant of Gwynedd, since 1985; *b* 27 Dec. 1920; *s* of late Major H. M. Richards, OBE, JP, VL and Mrs Mary Richards, MBE, MSc; *m* 1945, Pamela Watson; three *s* (one *d* decd). *Educ:* RNC, Dartmouth (Naval Cadet). Midshipman, 1939; Sub-Lt 1940; Lieut 1942; Lt-Comdr 1950; served in FAA, 1941–49; returned to gen. service, 1949; retd 1954 (to take over family estate). High Sheriff, Merioneth, 1960; DL Merioneth, 1967; JP Tal-y-Bont (Dolgellau), 1969. *Recreations:* fishing, shooting, sailing, ski-ing. *Address:* Caerynwch, Dolgellau, Gwynedd LL40 2RF. *T:* Dolgellau (0341) 422263.

RICHARDS, Rt. Rev. Ronald Edwin, MA, ThD (*jure dig*); *b* Ballarat, Vic., 25 Oct. 1908; *s* of Edward and Margaret Elizabeth Richards, Ballarat; *m* 1937, Nancy, *d* of W. E. Lloyd Green; one *d. Educ:* Ballarat High Sch.; Trinity Coll., Melbourne Univ. BA 2nd Cl. Hons Phil., 1932, MA 1937; Asst Master, Ballarat C of E Gram. Sch., 1926, Malvern C of E Gram. Sch., 1927–28; deacon, 1932; priest, 1933; Curate of Rokewood, 1932–33, Priest-in-charge, 1934; Priest-in-charge, Lismore, 1934–41 and 1945–46; Chaplain AIF, 1941–45; Vicar of Warrnambool, 1946–50; Archdeacon of Ballarat, and Examining Chapl. to Bp of Ballarat, 1950–57; Vicar-Gen., 1952–57; Bishop of Bendigo, 1957–74. *Address:* Madron, 119 Dare Street, Ocean Grove, Victoria 3226, Australia. *Clubs:* Royal Automobile of Victoria (Melbourne); Barwon Heads Golf.

RICHARDS, Vivian; *see* Richards, I. V. A.

RICHARDSON, family name of **Barons Richardson** and **Richardson of Duntisbourne.**

RICHARDSON, Baron *cr* 1979 (Life Peer), of Lee in the County of Devon; **John Samuel Richardson,** 1st Bt, *cr* 1963; Kt 1960; LVO 1943; MD, FRCP; retired; President, General Medical Council, 1973–80; Hon. Consulting Physician: St Thomas' Hospital; King Edward VII's Hospital for Officers; Consultant Emeritus to the Army; Consulting Physician: Metropolitan Police, 1957–80; London Transport Board, since 1964; *b* 16 June 1910; *s* of Major John Watson Richardson, solicitor, and Elizabeth Blakeney, *d* of Sir Samuel Roberts, 1st Bt, both of Sheffield; *m* 1933, Sybil Angela Stephanie (*d* 1991), *d* of A. Ronald Trist, Stanmore; two *d. Educ:* Charterhouse; Trinity Coll., Cambridge (Hon. Fellow, 1979); St Thomas' Hosp. (Bristowe Medal; Hadden Prize, 1936; Perkins Fellowship, 1938). MB BChir 1936, MD 1940; MRCP 1937, FRCP 1948; FRCPE 1975. Major, RAMC (temp.), 1939; Lt-Col, RAMC (temp.), 1942. 1st asst, Med. Professorial Unit, St Thomas' Hosp., 1946; Physician to St Thomas' Hosp., 1947–75. Examiner to Univs of Cambridge, London, Manchester, NUI, RCP London and Edinburgh Conjoint Bd. President: Internat. Soc. of Internal Medicine, 1966–70 (Hon. Pres. 1970); Royal Soc. of Medicine, 1969–71 (Hon. Librarian, 1957–63; Pres., Med. Educn Sect., 1967–68); BMA, 1970–71; 2nd Congress, Assoc. Européene de Médicine Interne d'Ensemble, Bad-Godesberg, 1973 (Hon. Mem. 1974); Assoc. for the Study of Med. Educn, 1978–80 (Vice-Pres., 1974–78, Hon. Mem., 1980); Vice-President: Med. Soc. of London, 1961–63 (Hon. Fellow, 1981); Royal Coll. of Nursing, 1972–; Chairman: Jt Consultants Cttee, 1967–72; Council for Postgrad. Med. Educn in England and Wales, 1972–80; Medico-Pharmaceutical Forum, 1973–76; Armed Forces Med. Adv. Bd, MoD, 1975–80. Mem., Bd of Governors, St Thomas's Hosp., 1953–59, 1964–74. Mem. Ct, Soc. of Apothecaries, 1960–85 (Master, 1971–72). Lectures: Lettsomian, Med. Soc. of London, 1963; Scott Heron, Royal Victoria Hosp., Belfast, 1969; Maudsley, RCPsych, 1971; Wilkinson Meml, Inst. of Dental Surgeons, London Univ., 1976; Harveian Oration, RCP, 1978; Orator, Med. Soc. of London, 1981. Hon. Fellow: Swedish Soc. Med. Scis, 1970; RSocMed 1973; Heberden Soc., 1973; Osler Club of London, 1973; Hon. Mem., Assoc. of Clinical Tutors of GB, 1980; Hon. FPS, 1974; Hon. FRCPI 1975; Hon. FFCM 1977; Hon. FRCPsych 1979; Hon. FRCS 1980; Hon. FRCPSG 1980; Hon. FRCPE 1981. Hon. Bencher, Gray's Inn, 1974. Hon. DSc: NUI, 1975; Hull, 1981; Hon. DCL Newcastle, 1980; Hon. LLD: Nottingham, 1981, Liverpool, 1983. CStJ 1970. Baron de Lancey Law Prize, RSM, 1978; Gold Medal, BMA, 1982; Guthrie Medal, RAMC, 1982. Editor-in-Chief, British Encylopaedia of Medical Practice, 1970–74. *Publications:* The Practice of Medicine, 2nd edn 1960; Connective Tissue Disorders, 1963; Anticoagulant Prophylaxis and Treatment (jointly), 1965. *Heir* to baronetcy: none. *Address:* Windcutter, Lee, near Ilfracombe, North Devon EX34 8LW. *T:* Ilfracombe (0271) 63198.

RICHARDSON OF DUNTISBOURNE, Baron *cr* 1983 (Life Peer), of Duntisbourne in the County of Gloucestershire; **Gordon William Humphreys Richardson,** KG 1983; MBE 1944; TD 1979; PC 1976; DL; Chairman, Morgan Stanley International Inc., since 1986; Governor, Bank of England, 1973–83, Member, Court of the Bank of England, 1967–83; *b* 25 Nov. 1915; *er s* of John Robert and Nellie Richardson; *m* 1941, Margaret Alison, *er d* of Canon H. R. L. Sheppard; one *s* one *d. Educ:* Nottingham High School; Gonville and Caius College, Cambridge (BA, LLB). Commnd S Notts Hussars Yeomanry, 1939; Staff Coll., Camberley, 1941; served until 1946. Called to Bar, Gray's Inn, 1946 (Hon. Bencher, 1973); Mem. Bar Council, 1951–55; ceased practice at Bar, Aug. 1955. Industrial and Commercial Finance Corp. Ltd, 1955–57; Director: J. Henry Schroder & Co., 1957; Lloyds Bank Ltd, 1960–67 (Vice-Chm., 1962–66); Legal and General Assurance Soc., Ltd, 1956–70 (Vice-Chm. 1959–70); Director: Rolls Royce (1971) Ltd, 1971–73; ICI Ltd, 1972–73; Chairman: J. Henry Schroder Wagg & Co. Ltd, 1962–72; Schroders Ltd, 1966–73; Schroders Inc. (NY), 1968–73. Chm., Industrial Develt Adv. Bd, 1972–73. Mem. Company Law Amendment Committee (Jenkins Committee), 1959–62; Chm. Cttee on Turnover Taxation, 1963. Member: Court of London University, 1962–65; NEDC, 1971–73, 1980–83; Trustee, National Gallery, 1971–73, Chm., Pilgrim Trust, 1984–89. One of HM Lieutenants, City of London, 1974–; High Steward of Westminster, 1985–89; DL Glos, 1983. Deputy High Steward, Univ. of Cambridge, 1982–; Hon. Fellow: Gonville and Caius Coll., 1977; Wolfson Coll., Cambridge, 1977. Hon. LLD Cambridge, 1979; Hon. DSc: City Univ., 1976; Aston, 1979; Hon. DCL East Anglia, 1984. Benjamin Franklin Medal, RSA, 1984. *Address:* c/o Morgan Stanley International, Kingsley House, 1A Wimpole Street, W1M 7AA. *Clubs:* Athenæum, Brooks's.

See also Sir John Riddell, Bt.

RICHARDSON, Anthony; *see* Richardson, H. A.

RICHARDSON, Sir Anthony (Lewis), 3rd Bt *cr* 1924; *b* 5 Aug. 1950; *s* of Sir Leslie Lewis Richardson, 2nd Bt, and of Joy Patricia, Lady Richardson, *d* of P. J. Rillstone, Johannesburg; *S* father, 1985; *m* 1985, Honor Gillian Dauney; one *d. Educ:* Diocesan College, Cape Town, S Africa. Stockbroker with L. Messel & Co., London, 1973–75; Insurance Broker with C. T. Bowring, London and Johannesburg, 1975–76; Stockbroker with Fergusson Bros, Hall, Stewart & Co., Johannesburg and Cape Town, 1976–78; Stockbroker with W. Greenwell & Co., London, 1979–81; with Rowe & Pitman, subseq.

S. G. Warburg Securities, London, 1981– (Dir, 1986–), seconded to S. G. Warburg Securities/Potter Partners Joint Venture, 1986–89. *Recreations:* various sports, photography. *Heir: b* Charles John Richardson, *b* 8 Dec. 1955. *Address:* 7 Westover Road, SW18 2RE. *Clubs:* Boodle's, Hurlingham.

RICHARDSON, Gen. Sir Charles (Leslie), GCB 1967 (KCB 1962; CB 1957); CBE 1945; DSO 1943; Member of the Army Board (Quartermaster General to the Forces, then Master-General of the Ordnance), 1965–71; *s* of late Lieutenant-Colonel C. W. Richardson, RA, and Mrs Richardson; *m* 1947, Audrey Styles (*née* Jorgensen); one *s* one *d* and one step *d. Educ:* Wellington College; Royal Military Acad., Woolwich (King's Medal); Cambridge Univ. (BA). Commissioned Royal Engineers, 1928; Exhibitioner, Clare College, Cambridge, 1930, 1st Cl. Hons Mech Sciences Tripos. Served France and Belgium, 1939–40; GSO1 Plans HQ, Eighth Army, 1942; BGS Eighth Army, 1943; Deputy Chief of Staff Fifth US Army, 1943; BGS Plans, 21st Army Group, 1944; Brigade Commander, 1953–54; Commandant, Royal Military College of Science, 1955–58; General Officer Commanding Singapore District, 1958–60; Director of Combat Development, War Office, 1960–61; Director-General of Military Training, 1961–63; General Officer Commanding-in-Chief, Northern Command, 1963–65; ADC (General) to the Queen, 1967–70; Chief Royal Engr, 1972–77. Col Comdt, RAOC, 1967–71. Consultant, International Computers Ltd, 1971–76. Treasurer, Kitchener Nat. Meml Fund, 1971–81; Chm., Gordon Boy's Sch., 1977–87. Legion of Merit (US), 1944. *Publications:* Flashback: a soldier's story, 1985; Send for Freddie, 1987; From Churchill's Secret Circle to the BBC: the biography of Gen. Sir Ian Jacob, 1991; contrib. to DNB. *Address:* The Stables, Betchworth, Surrey RH3 7AA. *Club:* Army and Navy.

See also J. B. W. McDonnell.

RICHARDSON, Brigadier (retd) Charles Walter Philipps, DSO and Bar 1945; *b* 8 Jan. 1905; *s* of W. J. Richardson and E. C. Philipps; *m* 1st, 1932, Joan Kathleen Constance Lang (from whom he obtained a divorce, 1946); one *s*; 2nd, 1946, Hon. Mrs Averil Diana Going; one *s. Educ:* RNC Osborne and Dartmouth; RMC Sandhurst. 2nd Lieut KOSB, 1924; served in Egypt, China and India; Bde Maj. 52nd (Lowland) Div., 1942; Comdr 6th Bn KOSB 15th (Scottish) Div., 1944–46; Colonel 1946; Comdt, Tactical Wing, School of Infantry, Warminster, 1947–48; GSO(1) Singapore District, 1948–49 (despatches, Malaya, 1948); Deputy Comdt Malay Regt, 1949; Dir Amphibious Warfare Trg, 1951; Comdr 158 Inf. Bde (TA), 1952; Brig. 1952; Dep. Comdr Lowland District, 1955–57. Retired 1957. Order of Leopold and Belgian Croix de Guerre, 1945; King Haakon Victory Medal, 1945. *Recreations:* fishing. *Address:* Quintans, Steventon, Hants. *T:* Dummer (0256) 473.

RICHARDSON, David; Director, London Office, International Labour Organisation, since 1982; *b* 24 April 1928; *s* of Harold George Richardson and Madeleine Raphaële Richardson (*née* Lebret); *m* 1951, Frances Joan Pring; three *s* one *d. Educ:* Wimbledon Coll.; King's Coll., London (BA Hons). FIPM 1986. RAF, 1949. Unilever, 1951. Inland Revenue, 1953; Min. of Labour, 1956; Sec., Construction Industry Training Bd, 1964; Chm., Central Youth Employment Exec., 1969; Royal Coll. of Defence Studies, 1971; Under Sec., Dept of Employment, 1972; Dir, Safety and Gen. Gp, Health and Safety Exec., 1975; Dir and Sec., ACAS, 1977. Director: The Tablet, 1985–; Industrial Training Service Ltd, 1987–. *Recreations:* music, walking, landscape gardening. *Address:* 183 Banstead Road, Carshalton, Surrey SM5 4DP. *T:* 081–642 1052. *Club:* Royal Air Force.

RICHARDSON, Air Marshal Sir (David) William, KBE 1986; Chief Engineer, Royal Air Force, 1986–88, retired; Director, Aero and Industrial Technology Ltd, since 1989; *b* 10 Feb. 1932; *s* of Herbert Cyril Richardson and Emily Lydia Richardson; *m* 1954, Mary Winifred Parker; two *s* one *d. Educ:* Southend Grammar Sch.; Birmingham Univ. (BSc Maths); Cranfield Inst. of Technology (MSc Eng). CEng, FIMechE, FRAeS. Joined RAF from Univ. Air Sqdn, 1953 and completed flying and technical trng; served in Fighter Comd before attending Staff Coll. 1964; Staff: HQ Middle East, 1965–67; HQ RAF Germany, 1969–71; CO, RAF Colerne, 1971–74; RCDS, 1974; AO Engrg and Supply, HQ NEAF, 1975; Dir, Engrg and Supply Policy, 1976–78; AO Engrg and Supply, HQ RAF Germany, 1978–81; AOC Maintenance Gp, RAF Support Comd, 1981–83; AO Engrg, RAF Strike Comd, 1983–86. Trustee, MONITOR Charity for Motor Neurone Disease sufferers, 1989–. *Publications:* contrib. RUSI Jl. *Recreation:* formerly sailing (past Cdre, RAF Sailing Assoc; past Pres., Assoc. of Service Yacht Clubs). *Club:* Royal Air Force.

RICHARDSON, Sir Egerton (Rudolf), OJ 1975; Kt 1968; CMG 1959; Permanent Representative of Jamaica to the United Nations, New York, 1981–84; *b* 15 Aug. 1912; *s* of James Neil Richardson and Doris Adel (*née* Burton); *m*; one *s* one *d. Educ:* Calabar High School, Kingston, Jamaica; Oxford University. Entered Civil Service, 1933; Secretary Land Policy Co-ordinating Committee, 1943–53; Permanent Sec., Min. of Agric. and Lands, 1953–54; Under-Sec. Finance, 1954–56; on secondment, CO, London, 1953–54; Financial Secretary, Jamaica, 1956–62; Ambassador: and Permanent Representative at UN, 1962–67; to USA, 1967–72; to Mexico, 1967–75; Permanent Sec., Min. of the Public Service, 1973–75. *Recreations:* swimming, golf, astronomy. *Address:* c/o Ministry of Foreign Affairs, 85 Knutsford Boulevard, Kingston 5, Jamaica.

RICHARDSON, Elliot Lee; Partner, Milbank, Tweed, Hadley & McCloy, Washington DC, since 1980; *b* 20 July 1920; *s* of Dr Edward P. and Clara Lee Richardson; *m* 1952, Anne F. Hazard; two *s* one *d. Educ:* Harvard Coll.; Harvard Law Sch. BA 1941, LLB 1947, *cum laude.* Served with US Army, 1942–45 (Lieut): litter-bearer platoon ldr, 4th Inf. Div., Normandy Landing (Bronze Star, Purple Heart). Law clerk, 1947–49; Assoc., Ropes, Gray, Best, Coolidge and Rugg, lawyers, Boston, 1949–53 and 1955–56; Asst to Senator Saltonstall, Washington, 1953 and 1954; Asst Sec. for Legislation of Dept of Health, Educn and Welfare, 1957–59 (Actg Sec., April-July 1958); US Attorney for Massachusetts, 1959–61; Special Asst to Attorney General of US, 1961; Partner, Ropes & Gray, 1961–62 and 1963–64; Lieut Governor of Mass, 1964; Attorney General of Mass, 1966; Under Sec. of State, 1969–70; Sec. of Health, Educn and Welfare, 1970–73; Sec. of Defense, Jan.-May 1973; Attorney General of US, May-Oct. 1973, resigned; Ambassador to UK, 1975–76; Sec. of Commerce, 1976–77; Ambassador-at-large and Special Rep. of the US Pres. to the Law of the Sea Conf., 1977–80. Special Rep. of Pres. for multilateral assistance initiative for the Philippines, 1989–; Personal Rep. of UN Sec. for monitoring electoral process in Nicaragua, 1989–90. Fellow, Woodrow Wilson Internat. Center for Scholars, 1973–74. Holds numerous hon. degrees. *Publications:* The Creative Balance, 1976; numerous articles on law, social services and govt policy. *Address:* 1100 Crest Lane, McLean, Va 22101, USA.

RICHARDSON, Sir Eric; *see* Richardson, Sir J. E.

RICHARDSON, Maj.-Gen. Frank McLean, CB 1960; DSO 1941; OBE 1945; MD; FRCPE; Director Medical Services, BAOR, 1956–61; *b* 3 March 1904; *s* of late Col Hugh Richardson, DSO, and of Elizabeth Richardson; *m* 1944, Sylvia Innes, *d* of Col S. A. Innes, DSO; two *s* one *d. Educ:* Glenalmond; Edinburgh Univ. MB, ChB 1926. MD 1938. FRCPE 1986. Joined RAMC, 1927; Captain 1930; Major 1936; Lt-Col 1945; Col 1949; Brig. 1956; Maj.-Gen. 1957. Honorary Surgeon to the Queen, 1957–61. Hon. Col 51 (H) Div. Dist RAMC, TA, 1963–67. *Publications:* Napoleon: Bisexual Emperor, 1972; Napoleon's Death: An Inquest, 1974; Fighting Spirit: psychological factors in war, 1978; The Public and the Bomb, 1981; Mars without Venus: a study of some homosexual Generals, 1981; (with S. MacNeill) Piobaireachd and its Interpretation, 1987. *Address:* c/o Royal Bank of Scotland, Kirkland House, SW1; 4B Barnton Avenue West, Edinburgh EH4 6DE.

RICHARDSON, George Barclay, CBE 1978; Warden, Keble College, Oxford, since 1989; Pro-Vice-Chancellor, Oxford University, since 1988; *b* 19 Sept. 1924; *s* of George and Christina Richardson; *m* 1957, Isabel Alison Chalk; two *s. Educ:* Aberdeen Central Secondary Sch. and other schs in Scotland; Aberdeen Univ.; Corpus Christi Coll., Oxford (Hon. Fellow, 1987). BSc Physics and Maths, 1944 (Aberdeen); MA (Oxon) PPE 1949. Admty Scientific Res. Dept, 1944; Lieut, RNVR, 1945. Intell. Officer, HQ Intell. Div. BAOR, 1946–47; Third Sec., HM Foreign Service, 1949; Student, Nuffield Coll., Oxford, 1950; Fellow, St John's Coll., Oxford, 1951–89, Hon. Fellow, 1989; University Reader in Economics, Oxford, 1969–73; Sec. to Delegates and Chief Exec., OUP, 1974–88 (Deleg., 1971–74). Economic Advr, UKAEA, 1968–74. Member: Economic Develt Cttee for Electrical Engineering Industry, 1964–73; Monopolies Commn, 1969–74; Royal Commn on Environmental Pollution, 1973–74; Council, Publishers Assoc., 1981–87. Mem., UK Delegation, CSCE Cultural Forum, 1985. Hon. DCL Oxon, 1988. *Publications:* Information and Investment, 1960, 2nd edn 1991; Economic Theory, 1964; articles in academic jls. *Address:* Warden's Lodgings, Keble College, Oxford OX1 3PG. *Club:* United Oxford & Cambridge University.

RICHARDSON, George Taylor; President, James Richardson & Sons, Limited, Winnipeg, Canada, since 1966 (Vice-President 1954); Chairman, Richardson Greenshields of Canada Ltd; *b* 22 Sept. 1924; *s* of late James Armstrong Richardson and Muriel (*née* Sprague); *m* 1948, Tannis Maree Thorlakson; two *s* one *d. Educ:* Grosvenor Sch. and Ravenscourt Sch. Winnipeg; Univ. of Manitoba (BComm). Joined family firm of James Richardson & Sons Ltd, 1946. Dir of cos owned by James Richardson & Sons Ltd; Director: Inco Ltd; United Canadian Shares Ltd; Du Pont Canada Inc. Member: Chicago Bd of Trade; Chicago Mercantile Exchange; Bd of Trade, Kansas City; Winnipeg Commodity Exchange. Hon. Dir, Canada's Aviation Hall of Fame. Hon. LLD: Manitoba; Winnipeg. *Recreations:* hunting, helicopter flying. *Address:* (business) James Richardson & Sons, Limited, Richardson Building, One Lombard Place, Winnipeg, Manitoba R3B 0Y1, Canada. *T:* 934–5811. *Clubs:* Manitoba, St Charles (Winnipeg); Vancouver (Vancouver); Toronto (Toronto).

RICHARDSON, Graham Edmund; Rector, Dollar Academy, Clackmannanshire, 1962–75; *b* 16 July 1913; *s* of H. W. Richardson, BSc, MIEE, AMIMechE, Studland, Dorset; *m* 1939, Eileen Cynthia, *d* of Lewis Beesly, FRCSE, Brightwalton, Newbury, Berks; one *s* one *d. Educ:* Tonbridge School; Strasbourg University; Queen's College, Oxford. Asst Master, Fettes College, Edinburgh, 1935–55; Housemaster, 1946–55; Headmaster, Melville College, Edinburgh, 1955–62. Mem., Scottish Adv. Cttee, IBA, 1968–73. *Recreations:* sailing, fishing, natural history. *Address:* Sunnyholme, Studland, Dorset.

RICHARDSON, (Henry) Anthony; a Recorder of the Crown Court, since 1978; a Deputy Traffic Commissioner and a Deputy Licensing Authority, North Eastern Traffic Area, since 1989; barrister; *b* 28 Dec. 1925; *er s* of late Thomas Ewan Richardson and Jessie (*née* Preston), Batley, W Yorks; *m* 1954, Georgina (*née* Lawford), *d* of Rosamond Bedford and step *d* of Gp Captain G. R. Bedford, MB, ChB, RAF retd. *Educ:* Giggleswick Sch.; Leeds Univ. (LLB 1950, LLM 1956). Called to the Bar, Lincoln's Inn, 1951; North-Eastern Circuit; Dep. Circuit Judge, 1972–78. Chm., a Police Disciplinary Appeal Tribunal, 1983. *Publications:* articles in legal periodicals. *Recreations:* walking, gardening, listening to music. *Address:* (home) Grey Thatch, Wetherby Road, Scarcroft, Leeds LS14 3BB. *T:* Leeds (0532) 892555; (chambers) 38 Park Square, Leeds LS1 2PA. *T:* Leeds (0532) 439422.

RICHARDSON, Horace Vincent, OBE 1968; HM Diplomatic Service, retired; *b* 28 Oct. 1913; *s* of late Arthur John Alfred Richardson and late Mrs Margaret Helena Jane Richardson (*née* Hooson); *m* 1942, Margery Tebbutt; two *s* one *d* (and one *d* decd). *Educ:* Abergele Grammar Sch.; King's Coll., London (LLB). Served with Army, 1940–45. LCC, 1931–35; Supreme Court of Judicature, 1935–47; FO, 1947–48; British Vice-Consul, Shanghai, 1948–50; Washington, 1950–53; 2nd Sec., Rome, 1953–56; FO, 1956–61; Consul, Philadelphia, 1961–63; FO, 1963–66; Consul, Cairo, 1966–68; 1st Sec., Washington, 1968–70; Head of Nationality and Treaty Dept, FCO, 1970–73. Rep. HM Govt at 9th and 10th Sessions of Hague Conf. of Private Internat. Law. *Recreations:* golf, gardening, tennis. *Address:* 34 Friern Barnet Lane, N11. *T:* 081–368 1983. *Clubs:* MCC, Civil Service; Turf (Cairo); Highgate Golf.

RICHARDSON, Hugh Edward, CIE 1947; OBE 1944; *b* 22 Dec. 1905; *s* of Hugh Richardson, DSO, MD, and Elizabeth (*née* McLean); *m* 1951, Huldah (*née* Walker), *widow* of Maj.-Gen. T. G. Rennie, Black Watch, killed in action 1945. *Educ:* Trinity College, Glenalmond; Keble College, Oxford (Hon. Fellow, 1981). Entered Indian Civil Service, 1930; SDO, Tamluk, Midnapore Dist, Bengal, 1932–34; entered Foreign and Political Service of Govt of India, 1934; APA Loralai, Baluchistan, 1934–35; British Trade Agent, Gyantse, and O-in-C British Mission, Lhasa, 1936–40; service in NWFP, 1940–42; 1st Sec. Indian Agency-General in China, Chungking, 1942–43; Dep. Sec. to Govt of India, EA Dept, 1944–45; British Trade Agent, Gyantse, and O-in-C, British Mission, Lhasa, 1946–47; Indian Trade Agent, Gyantse and Officer-in-charge, Indian Mission, Lhasa, 1947–50. Retd from ICS, 1950. Hon. FBA 1986. Hon. DLitt St Andrews, 1985. *Publications:* Tibet and its History, 1962; (with D. L. Snellgrove) A Cultural History of Tibet, 1968; A Corpus of Early Tibetan Inscriptions, 1985. *Recreation:* golf. *Address:* c/o Grindlay's Bank, 13 St James's Square, SW1. *Club:* Royal and Ancient Golf (St Andrews).

RICHARDSON, Ian William, CBE 1989; actor; *b* 7 April 1934; *s* of John Richardson and Margaret Drummond; *m* 1961, Maroussia Frank; two *s. Educ:* Tynecastle; Edinburgh; Univ. of Glasgow. Studied for stage at Coll. of Dramatic Art, Glasgow (James Bridie Gold Medal, 1957). FRSAMD 1971. Joined Birmingham Repertory Theatre Co. 1958 (leading parts incl. Hamlet); joined Shakespeare Meml Theatre Co. (later RSC), 1960; rôles, Stratford and Aldwych, 1960–: Arragon in Merchant of Venice; Sir Andrew Aguecheek, 1960; Malatesti in Duchess of Malfi, 1960; Oberon in A Midsummer Night's Dream, 1961; Tranio in Taming of the Shrew, 1961; the Doctor in The Representative, 1963; Edmund in King Lear, 1964; Antipholus of Ephesus in Comedy of Errors, 1964; Herald and Marat in Marat/Sade, 1964, 1965; Ithamore, The Jew of Malta, 1964; Ford, Merry Wives of Windsor, 1964, 1966, 1969; Antipholus of Syracuse in Comedy of Errors, 1965; Chorus, Henry V, 1965; Vindice, The Revengers Tragedy, 1965, 1969; Coriolanus, 1966; Bertram, All's Well That Ends Well, 1966; Malcolm, Macbeth, 1966; Cassius, Julius Caesar, 1968; Pericles, 1969; Angelo, Measure for Measure, 1970; Buckingham, Richard III, 1970; Proteus, Two Gentlemen of Verona, 1970; Prospero, The Tempest, 1970; Richard II/Bolingbroke, Richard II, 1973; Berowne, Love's Labour's Lost, 1973; Iachimo, Cymbeline, 1974; Shalimov, Summer Folk, 1974; Ford, Merry Wives of Windsor, 1975;

Richard III, 1975; tours with RSC: Europe and USSR, NY, 1964; NY, 1965; USSR, 1966; Japan, 1970; NY, 1974, 1975; Tom Wrench in musical Trelawny, Sadler's Wells, 1971–72; Professor Higgins, My Fair Lady, Broadway, 1976 (Drama Desk Award, 1976); Jack Tanner, in Man and Superman, and Doctor in The Millionairess, Shaw Festival Theatre, Niagara, Ont; The Government Inspector, Old Vic, 1979; Romeo and Juliet, Old Vic, 1979; Lolita, Broadway, 1981. *Films:* Captain Fitzroy in The Darwin Adventure, 1971; Priest in Man of la Mancha, 1972; Montgomery in Ike—the War Years, 1978; Charlie Muffin, 1979; The Sign of Four, 1982; Hound of the Baskervilles, 1982; Brazil, 1984; Whoops Apocalypse, 1987; The Fourth Protocol, 1987; Burning Secret, 1989. *Television: plays:* Danton's Death, 1978; Churchill and the Generals, 1979; A Cotswold Death, Passing Through, 1981; Russian Night, Kisch-Kisch, Beauty and the Beast, Salad Days, 1982; Slimming Down, 1984; Star Quality, 1985; The Devil's Disciple, 1987; The Winslow Boy, 1989; *films:* Monsignor Quixote, 1985; Blunt, 1987; Rosencrantz and Guildenstern Are Dead, 1990; *serials and series:* Eyeless in Gaza, 1971; Tinker, Tailor, Soldier, Spy, 1979; Private Schulz, 1981; The Woman in White, 1982; Ramsay Macdonald, in Number 10, 1982; The Master of Ballantrae, 1984; Six Centuries of Verse, 1984; Mistral's Daughter, 1985; Nehru, in Mountbatten—the last Viceroy, 1986; Porterhouse Blue, 1987; Troubles, 1988; Twist of Fate, 1989; Under a Dark Angel's Eye, 1989; Phanton of the Opera, 1990; The Plot to Kill Hitler, 1990; The Gravy Train, 1990; House of Cards, 1990 (BAFTA Best Actor Award, 1991). RTS Award, 1982. *Publication:* Preface to Cymbeline (Folio Soc.), 1976. *Recreations:* music, exploring churches and castles. *Address:* c/o London Management, Regent House, 235–241 Regent Street, W1R 7AG. *T:* 071–493 1610. *Club:* Garrick.

RICHARDSON, Rt. Hon. Sir Ivor (Lloyd Morgan), Kt 1986; PC 1978; SJD; **Rt. Hon. Mr Justice Richardson;** Judge, Court of Appeal of New Zealand, since 1977; *b* 24 May 1930; *s* of W. T. Richardson; *m* 1955, Jane, *d* of I. J. Krchma; three *d. Educ:* Canterbury Univ. (LLB); Univ. of Mich (LLM, SJD). Partner, Macalister Bros, Invercargill, 1957–63; Crown Counsel, Crown Law Office, Wellington, 1963–66; Prof. of Law, Victoria Univ. of Wellington, 1967–73 (Dean of Law Faculty, 1968–71; Pro-Chancellor, 1979–84; Chancellor, 1984–86); Partner, Watts & Patterson, Wellington, 1973–77. Chm., Cttees of Inquiry into Inflation Accounting, 1975–76, into Solicitors Nominee Cos, 1983. Chairman: Council of Legal Educn, 1983–; Royal Commn on Social Policy, 1986–88. Hon. LLD: Canterbury, 1987; Victoria, 1989. *Publications:* books and articles on legal subjects. *Address:* 29 Duthie Street, Wellington 5, New Zealand. *T:* 4769–310. *Club:* Wellington (Wellington, NZ).

RICHARDSON, Hon. James Armstrong, PC (Can.); *b* Winnipeg, Manitoba, 28 March 1922; *s* of James Armstrong Richardson and Muriel Sprague; *m* 1949, Shirley Anne, *d* of John Rooper, Shamley Green, Surrey, England; two *s* three *d. Educ:* St John's-Ravenscourt, Winnipeg; Queen's Univ., Kingston, Ont. (BA). Pilot with No 10 BR Sqdn, before entering family firm of James Richardson & Sons, Ltd, Winnipeg, Oct. 1945; he was Chm. and Chief Exec. Officer of this company, but resigned to enter public life, 1968. MP (L), June 1968 (re-elected Oct. 1972, July 1974); Minister, Canadian Federal Cabinet, July 1968; Minister of Supply and Services, May 1969; Minister of Nat. Defence, 1972–76; resigned from Federal Cabinet over constitutional language issue, Oct. 1976; crossed floor of House to sit as an Independent MP, 27 June 1978. Chm., Westmead Ltd; Pres., Jarco Ltd; Director: James Richardson & Sons Ltd; Lombard Place Ltd. Director: Max Bell Foundn; Canada's America's Cup Challenge; Hon. Pres., Commonwealth Games Assoc. of Canada, Inc. *Address:* 5209 Roblin Boulevard, Winnipeg, Manitoba R3R 0G8, Canada.
See also G. T. Richardson.

RICHARDSON, Rev. Canon James John; Executive Director, Council of Christians and Jews, since 1988; *b* 28 March 1941; *s* of late James John Richardson and of Gladys May (*née* Evans); *m* 1966, Janet Rosemary Welstand; two *s* one *d. Educ:* Catford Central Sch.; Hull Univ. (BA); Sheffield Univ. (DipEd); Cuddesdon Coll., Oxford. Assistant Master, Westfield Comp. Sch., Sheffield, 1964–66; Curate, St Peter's Collegiate Church, Wolverhampton, 1969–72; Priest i/c, All Saints, Hanley, Stoke-on-Trent, 1972–75; Rector of Nantwich, 1975–82; Vicar of Leeds, 1982–88. Hon. Canon, 1982–88, Canon Emeritus, 1988–, Ripon Cathedral. Chm., Racial Harrassment Commn, Leeds, 1986–87; N of England Vice-Pres., UN Year of Peace, 1986–87. Mem. Court, Leeds Univ., 1986–88; Chairman of Governors: Abbey Grange High Sch., Leeds, 1982–86; Leeds Grammar Sch., 1983–88; Governor: Leeds Girls' High Sch., 1982–88; Leeds Music Fest., 1982–88. FRSA 1991. *Publications:* (contrib.) Four Score Years; contrib. Yorkshire Post, 1982–90. *Recreations:* leading pilgrimages to Israel, biography—especially life and times of Rupert Brooke. *Address:* (office) 1 Dennington Park Road, NW6 1AX. *T:* 071–794 8178; 27 Strawberry Hill, Berrydale, Northampton NN9 5HL. *T:* Northampton (0604) 405183.

RICHARDSON, Joanna, MA Oxon; FRSL; author; *o d* of late Frederick Richardson and late Charlotte Elsa (*née* Benjamin). *Educ:* The Downs School, Seaford; St Anne's College, Oxford. Contributions to BBC include: translated plays; interviews; numerous features for Radios 3 and 4. Mem. Council, Royal Soc. of Literature, 1961–86. Chevalier de l'Ordre des Arts et des Lettres, 1987. *Publications include:* Fanny Brawne: a biography, 1952; Théophile Gautier: his Life and Times, 1958; Edward FitzGerald, 1960; (ed) FitzGerald: Selected Works, 1962; The Pre-Eminent Victorian: a study of Tennyson, 1962; The Everlasting Spell: a study of Keats and his Friends, 1963; (ed) Essays by Divers Hands (trans. Royal Soc. Lit.), 1963; introd. to Victor Hugo: Choses Vues (The Oxford Lib. of French Classics), 1964; Edward Lear, 1965; George IV: a Portrait, 1966; Creevey and Greville, 1967; Princess Mathilde, 1969; Verlaine, 1971; Enid Starkie, 1973; (ed and trans.) Verlaine, Poems, 1974; Stendhal: a critical biography, 1974; (ed and trans.) Baudelaire, Poems, 1975; Victor Hugo, 1976; Zola, 1978; Keats and his Circle: an album of portraits, 1980; (trans.) Gautier, Mademoiselle de Maupin, 1981; The Life and Letters of John Keats, 1981; Letters from Lambeth: the correspondence of the Reynolds family with John Freeman Milward Dovaston 1808–1815, 1981; Colette, 1983; Judith Gautier, 1987 (trans. French 1989; Prix Goncourt for Biography); Portrait of a Bonaparte: the life and times of Joseph-Napoleon Primoli 1851–1927, 1987; has contributed to The Times, The Times Literary Supplement, Sunday Times, Spectator, New Statesman, New York Times Book Review, The Washington Post, French Studies, French Studies Bulletin, Modern Language Review, Keats-Shelley Memorial Bulletin, etc. *Recreations:* antique-collecting, sketching. *Address:* 55 Flask Walk, NW3 1EY. *T:* 071–435 5156.

RICHARDSON, John David Benbow, CBE 1988; MC 1942, and Bar 1943; President, Northern Rent Assessment Panel, since 1979 (Vice-President, 1968–79); *b* 6 April 1919; *s* of His Honour Judge Thomas Richardson, OBE, and Winifred Ernestine (*née* Templer); *m* 1946, Kathleen Mildred (*née* Price-Turner); four *s. Educ:* Harrow; Clare Coll., Cambridge. Called to Bar, Middle Temple, 1947. Served War of 1939–45, as Captain in King's Dragoon Guards (wounded; MC and Bar). ADC to Governor of South Australia (Lt-Gen. Sir Willoughby Norrie, later Lord Norrie), 1946–47. Dep. Chm., Durham County Quarter Sessions, 1964–71, and Recorder, 1972–73. Mem., Police Complaints Bd, 1977–82. *Recreations:* fishing, gardening, golf. *Address:* The Old Vicarage, Nine Banks, Whitfield, near Hexham, Northumberland NE47 8DB. *T:* Whitfield (04985) 217. *Clubs:* MCC; York County Stand; Northern Counties (Newcastle upon Tyne).

RICHARDSON, Sir (John) Eric, Kt 1967; CBE 1962; PhD, DSc, BEng, CEng, FIEE, MIMechE, FBHI, FBOA, FPS; FRSA; Director, The Polytechnic of Central London, 1969–70; *b* 30 June 1905; *e surv. s* of late William and Mary Elizabeth Richardson, Birkenhead; *m* 1941, Alice May, *d* of H. M. Wilson, Hull; one *s* two *d* (and one *d* decd). *Educ:* Birkenhead Higher Elementary Sch.; Liverpool Univ. BEng 1st Cl. Hons, 1931, PhD 1933, Liverpool. Chief Lectr in Electrical Engineering, 1933–37, Head of Engineering Dept, 1937–41, Hull Municipal Technical Coll.; Principal: Oldham Municipal Technical Coll., 1942–44; Royal Technical Coll., Salford, 1944–47; Northampton Polytechnic, London, EC1, 1947–56; Dir Nat. Coll. of Horology and Instrument Technology, 1947–56; Dir of Educn, Regent Street Polytechnic, W1, 1957–69. Hon. Sec., Assoc. of Technical Insts, 1957–67, Chm., 1967–68; Pres. Assoc. of Principals of Technical Instns, 1961–62; Dep. Chm., Council for Overseas Colls of Arts, Science and Technology, 1949–62; Member: Council for Tech. Educn and Trng in Overseas Countries, 1962–73 (Chm. Technical Educn Cttee, 1971–73); and Vice-Chm. Council and Cttees, London and Home Counties Regional Adv. Council for Technol Educn, 1972–84; Chm., Adv. Cttee on Educn for Management, 1961–66; Pres. and Chm., CICRIS, 1972–89; Member: Governing Council of Nigerian Coll. of Art, Science and Technology, 1953–61; Council, Univ. Coll., Nairobi, 1961–70; Provisional Council, Univ. of East Africa, 1961–63; Governing Body, College of Aeronautics, Cranfield, 1956–59; Council of British Horological Institute, 1951–56; Gen. Optical Council, 1959–78 (Chm., 1975–78); Assoc. of Optical Practitioners (Vice-Pres., 1983–84; Pres., 1984–); Science and Technol Cttee of CNAA, 1965–71; Electrical Engrg Bd of CNAA (Chm.); Industrial Trg Bd for Electricity Supply Industry, 1965–71; Univ. and Polytechnic Grants Cttee, Hong Kong, 1972–77; Council, RSA, 1968–78 (Chm. Exams Cttee, 1969–78, Hon. Treasurer, 1974–78); Council and Exec. Cttee, Leprosy Mission, 1970–84 (Chm., 1974–84; Vice-Pres., 1984–); Council and Exec. Cttee, City and Guilds of London Inst., 1969–80 (Chm. Policy and Overseas Cttees; Vice-Chm. Technical Educn Cttee; Jt Hon. Sec., 1970–80; Vice-Pres., 1979–82; Hon. FCGI 1981); Chm., Ealing Civic Soc., 1972–76. Chairman: Africa Evangelical Fellowship (SAGM), 1950–70; Nat. Young Life Campaign, 1949–64; Council, Inter-Varsity Fellowship of Evangelical Unions, 1966–69; President: Crusaders Union, 1972–86; Governors of London Bible Coll., 1968– (Chm., 1970–77; Pres., 1978–90); Chm., Governors, Clarendon Sch., Abergele, 1971–75. *Publications:* paper in IEE Jl (Instn Prize); various papers on higher technological education in UK and Nigeria. *Recreations:* gardening, photography. *Address:* 73 Delamere Road, Ealing, W5 3JP. *T:* 081–567 1588.

RICHARDSON, John Eric, MS; FRCS; Surgeon: The London Hospital, 1949–81; The Royal Masonic Hospital, 1960–81; King Edward VII's Hospital for Officers, 1960–81; Prince of Wales Hospital, Tottenham, N15, 1958–65; former Consultant Surgeon to the Navy; *b* Loughborough, 24 February 1916; *s* of late C. G. Richardson, MD, FRCS; *m* 1943, Elisabeth Jean, *d* of late Rev. John Webster; one *s* one *d. Educ:* Clifton College; London Hospital. MB, BS London (Hons and Distinction, Pathology), 1939; MRCS, LRCP 1939. Andrew Clarke Prize, London Hosp., 1939. Resident Appointments, London Hospital and Poplar Hospital, 1939–41; Surgeon Lieut RNVR, HMS Prince of Wales (Surgical Specialist), 1941–46; Surgical Registrar, London Hosp., 1946–47; Rockefeller Travelling Fellow, 1947–48; Research Fellow in Surgery, Harvard Univ., 1947–48; Fellow in Clinical Surgery, Massachusetts Gen. Hosp., Boston, Mass, 1947–48. Surgeon, St Andrews Hosp., Dollis Hill, 1965–73. Mem., Med. Appeal Tribunal, 1980–88. Hunterian Prof., RCS, 1953; Lettsomian Lectr, Med. Soc. of London, 1973. Pres., Med. Soc. of London, 1974–75. Examr in Surgery to Soc. of Apothecaries, London, 1959–67 and Univ. of London, 1962–63, 1965–66. Mem., Bd of Governors, London Hosp., 1964–73. *Publications:* contrib. to Lancet, BMJ and Brit. Jl of Surgery on gastro-enterology and endocrine disease. *Address:* Allen's Barn, Swin Lane, Swinbrook, Burford, Oxfordshire OX18 4EA. *T:* Burford (099382) 2456.

RICHARDSON, John Flint; Chairman of Tyne and Wear County Council, 1976–77; *b* 5 May 1906; *s* of Robert Flint Richardson and Jane Lavinia; *m* 1932, Alexandra Graham; two *s. Educ:* Cone Street, South Shields. Councillor, 1938, Alderman, 1954, Mayor, 1960–61, South Shields; Freeman, South Shields, 1973. *Recreations:* serving people, reading.

RICHARDSON, John Francis; Director and Chief Executive, National & Provincial Building Society, 1985–86; *b* 16 June 1934; *s* of Francis and Stella Richardson; *m* 1960, Jacqueline Mary Crosby; two *d. Educ:* Wadham College, Oxford (PPE). FCBSI. Burnley Building Society, 1959–82; Chief General Manager, 1980–82; Dep. Chief Executive, National & Provincial Building Society, 1983–85. Pres., CBSI, 1985. *Recreations:* golf, gardening, military history. *Address:* Low Gables, Spofforth Hill, Wetherby, West Yorks LS22 4SF. *Club:* Pannal Golf.

RICHARDSON, Very Rev. John Stephen; Provost of Bradford Cathedral, since 1990; *b* 2 April 1950; *s* of James Geoffrey and Myra Richardson; *m* 1972, Elizabeth Susan Wiltshire; one *s* two *d* (and one *s* decd). *Educ:* Haslingden Grammar Sch.; Univ. of Southampton (BA Hons Theology); St John's Theological Coll., Nottingham. Deacon 1974, priest 1975; Asst Curate, St Michael's, Bramcote, 1974–77; Priest-in-Charge, Emmanuel Church, Radipole and Melcombe Regis, 1977–80; Asst Diocesan Missioner and Lay Trainer Adviser, dio. of Salisbury and Priest-in-Charge of Stinsford, Winterborne Monkton and Winterborne Came with Witcombe, 1980–83; Vicar of Christ Church, Nailsea, 1983–90; Adviser in Evangelism, dio. of Bath and Wells, 1985–90. Trustee: Acorn Healing Trust, 1990–; Spennithorne Hall, 1990–. Council Mem., St John's Theological Coll., Nottingham, 1988–; Gov., Bradford Grammar Sch., 1990–. *Publication:* Ten Rural Churches, 1988. *Recreations:* football, cricket, North Western Municipal Bus Operators, walking, writing, broadcasting. *Address:* The Provost's House, 1 Cathedral Close, Bradford BD1 4EG. *T:* Bradford (0274) 732023, *Fax:* Bradford (0274) 722898. *Clubs:* Commonwealth Trust; Bradford.

RICHARDSON, Josephine, (Jo Richardson); MP (Lab) Barking, since Feb. 1974. Opposition spokesperson on women's rights, 1983–. Mem., Labour Party NEC, 1979–; a Vice President, Campaign for Nuclear Disarmament; Chairperson, Tribune Group, 1978–79 (Secretary, 1948–78; formerly Keep Left Group, then Bevan Group); Member: MSF; APEX. *Recreations:* politics, cooking. *Address:* House of Commons, SW1A 0AA. *T:* 071–219 5028.

RICHARDSON, Rev. Kathleen Margaret; President of the Methodist Conference, June 1992–93; *b* 24 Feb. 1938; *d* of Francis and Margaret Fountain; *m* 1964, Ian David Godfrey Richardson; three *d. Educ:* St Helena Sch., Chesterfield; Stockwell Coll. (Cert Ed); Deaconess Coll., Ilkley; Wesley House, Cambridge. School teacher, 1958–61. Wesley Deaconess, Champness Hall, Rochdale, 1961–64; Lay Worker, Team Ministry, Stevenage, 1973–77; Minister, Denby Dale and Clayton West Circuit, 1979–87; ordained presbyter, 1980; Chm., West Yorks Dist, 1987–. *Recreations:* reading, needlework, homemaking. *Address:* 4 Lyndhurst Avenue, Brighouse, West Yorks HD6 3RY. *T:* Brighouse (0484) 719993.

RICHARDSON, Kenneth Albert; QC 1985; **His Honour Judge Richardson;** a Circuit Judge, since 1988; *b* 28 July 1926; *s* of Albert Robert Richardson and Ida Elizabeth

Richardson (*née* Williams); *m* 1956, Dr Eileen Mary O'Cleary, Galway; two *s* one *d* (and one *s* decd). *Educ:* Ruthin Sch.; Merton Coll., Oxford. MA (in English and Jurisprudence). Called to the Bar, Middle Temple, 1952 (Harmsworth Scholar; Bencher, 1975). Commissioned RWF, 1945 (attached 8th Punjab Regt). Junior Prosecuting Counsel to the Crown, 1967–73; Senior Prosecuting Counsel to the Crown, 1973–81; First Sen. Prosecuting Counsel to the Crown at CCC, 1981–85; a Recorder of the Crown Court, 1980–88. Mem., Bar Council, 1972; Senate of the Inns and Bar, 1974–80. Chm., British Suzuki Inst., 1980–84; Pres., Porters Park Golf Club, 1980–82. *Recreations:* ski-ing, golf, sailing, music. *Clubs:* Garrick; Vincent's (Oxford).

RICHARDSON, Kenneth Augustus, CBE 1989; JP; Secretary to the Cabinet, Bermuda, since 1984; *b* 13 Feb. 1939; *s* of Augustus J. Richardson; *m* 1966, Brenda Joyce (*née* Smith); one *s* one *d*. *Educ:* Howard Univ., Washington DC (BSc); Manchester Polytechnic (Dip. Personnel Admin and Labour Relations). Teacher, Sandys Secondary School, Bermuda, 1964; Admin. Cadet, Colonial Sec.'s Office, 1967; Training and Recruitment Officer, Bermuda Govt, 1969; Perm. Sec., Labour and Home Affairs, 1974. MIPM 1973; MInstD. JP 1984. *Recreations:* sport (soccer, tennis). *Address:* Cabinet Office, 105 Front Street, Hamilton HM 12, Bermuda. *T:* (809) 292 5501, *Fax:* (809) 292 8397; Mahogany, 19 Trimingham Hill, Paget, Bermuda; PO Box HM 1703, Hamilton HM GX, Bermuda. *T:* (809) 236 1788.

RICHARDSON, Sir Michael (John de Rougemont), Kt 1990; Vice Chairman, N. M. Rothschild & Sons Ltd, since 1990 (Managing Director, 1981–90); Chairman, Smith New Court plc, since 1990; *b* 9 April 1925; *s* of Arthur Wray Richardson and Audrey de Rougemont; *m* 1949, Octavia Mayhew; one *s* two *d*. *Educ:* Harrow; Kent Sch., Conn, USA. Captain, Irish Guards, 1943–49. Drayton Gp, 1949–52; Partner: Panmure Gordon & Co., 1952–71; Cazenove & Co., 1971–81. *Recreations:* fox hunting, sailing. *Address:* (office) Smith New Court House, 20 Farringdon Road, EC1M 3NH. *Clubs:* Island Sailing, Bembridge Sailing (IoW).

RICHARDSON, Group Captain Michael Oborne, RAF, retired; *b* Holmfirth, Yorks, 13 May 1908; *s* of Rev. Canon G. L. Richardson, MA, BD, and Edith Maria (*née* Ellison); *m* 1st, 1935, Nellie Marguerita (*d* 1974), *d* of Walter Ross Somervell, Elizavetgrad, Russia; one *s* one *d*; 2nd, 1979, Gwendolyn Oenone Jane Bevan, *e d* of William Stuart Rashleigh, JP, Menabilly and Stoketon, Cornwall. *Educ:* Lancing Coll.; Keble Coll., Oxford; Guy's Hospital. BA 1929; MRCS, LRCP 1938; DPH 1955; MA Oxon 1963; DPhysMed 1964. Oxford House, Bethnal Green, 1930. Commissioned RAF, 1939; served at Kenley; War Service included HQ Fighter Comd (Unit), S Africa, Western Desert, Malta, Sicily, Italy (despatches). Post-war service in Germany and Aden and comdt various hosps and Medical Rehabilitation Units; Commandant, Royal Star and Garter Home for Disabled Sailors, Soldiers and Airmen, 1967–73. OStJ 1965. *Recreation:* the countryside. *Address:* Tremethek, Penscott Lane, Tregorrick, St Austell, Cornwall PL26 7AH. *T:* St Austell (0726) 63768. *Clubs:* Royal Air Force; Webbe.

RICHARDSON, Miranda; actress; *b* 3 March 1958; *d* of William Alan Richardson and Marian Georgina Townsend. *Educ:* St Wyburn, Southport, Merseyside; Southport High Sch. for Girls; Bristol Old Vic Theatre Sch. Repertory: Manchester Library Theatre, 1979–80; Derby Playhouse, Duke's Playhouse, Lancaster, Bristol Old Vic and Leicester Haymarket, 1982–83; West End début, Moving, Queen's, 1980–81; Royal Court: Edmund, 1985; A Lie of the Mind, 1987; Etta Jenks, 1990; National Theatre: The Changeling, and Mountain Language, 1988. *Television:* series include: Agony; Sorrell and Son; Blackadder II and III; Die Kinder, 1990; plays include: The Master Builder; The Demon Lover; After Pilkington; Sweet as You Are (RTS Award, 1987–88); Ball-trap on the Côte Sauvage, 1989; *films:* Dance with a Stranger (role, Ruth Ellis) (City Limits Best Film Actress, 1985); Underworld; Death of the Heart; Empire of the Sun; The Mad Monkey; Dr Grasler. Evening Standard Best Actress, 1985; Variety Club Most Promising Artiste, 1985. *Recreations:* reading, walking, softball, gardening, music, junkshops, occasional art, animals. *Address:* c/o Kerry Gardner Management, 15 High Street, Kensington, W8. *T:* 071–603 1142.

RICHARDSON, Natasha Jane; actress; *b* 11 May 1963; *d* of Tony Richardson, *qv* and Vanessa Redgrave, *qv*; *m* 1990, Robert Fox. *Educ:* Lycée Française de Londres; St Paul's Girls' Sch.; Central Sch. of Speech and Drama. Season at Leeds Playhouse; A Midsummer Night's Dream, New Shakespeare Co.; Ophelia in Hamlet, Young Vic; The Seagull, Lyric Hammersmith, tour and Queen's, 1985; China, Bush Th., 1986; High Society, Leicester Haymarket and Victoria Palace, 1986; Anna Christie, Young Vic, 1990. *Films:* Every Picture Tells a Story, 1985; Gothic, 1987; A Month in the Country, 1987; Patty Hearst, 1988; Fat Man and Little Boy, 1989; The Handmaid's Tale, 1990; The Comfort of Strangers, 1990; The Favor, the Watch and the Very Big Fish; Past Midnight. *Television:* In a Secret State, 1985; Ghosts, 1986. Most Promising Newcomer Award, Plays and Players, 1986; Best Actress: Evening Standard Film Awards, 1990; London Theatre Critics, 1990; Plays and Players, 1990.

RICHARDSON, Prof. Peter Damian, FRS 1986; Professor of Engineering and Physiology, Brown University, USA, since 1984; *b* West Wickham, Kent, 22 Aug. 1935; *s* of Reginald William Merrells Richardson and late Marie Stuart Naomi (*née* Ouseley). *Educ:* Imperial College, Univ. of London (BSc (Eng) 1955; PhD 1958; DSc (Eng) 1974; ACGI 1955; DIC 1958; DSc 1983); MA Brown Univ. 1965. Demonstrator, Imperial Coll., 1955–58; Brown University: Vis. Lectr, 1958–59; Research Associate, 1959–60; Asst Prof. of Engrg, 1960–65; Associate Prof. of Engrg, 1965–68; Prof. of Engrg, 1968–84; Chair, University Faculty, 1987– (Vice-Chair, 1986–87). Sen. Vis. Fellow, Univ. of London, 1967; Prof. d'échange, Univ. of Paris, 1968; leave at Orta Doğu Teknik Univ., Ankara, 1969. FASME 1983. Humboldt-Preis, A. von Humboldt Sen. Scientist Award, 1976; Laureate in Medicine, Ernst Jung Foundn, 1987. *Publications:* numerous articles in learned jls. *Recreations:* photography, travel, country life. *Address:* Box D, Brown University, Providence, Rhode Island 02912, USA. *T:* 010–1–401–863–2687.

RICHARDSON, Robert Augustus; HM Chief Inspector of Schools, Department of Education and Science, 1968–72; *b* 2 Aug. 1912; *s* of late Ferdinand Augustus Richardson and Muriel Emma Richardson; *m* 1936, Elizabeth Gertrude Williamson; one *d*. *Educ:* Royal College of Art. Schoolmaster, 1934; Headmaster, Sidcup School of Art, 1937. Served in Royal Navy, 1941–46. Principal: Folkestone Sch. of Art, 1946; Maidstone Coll. of Art, 1948. Dept of Education and Science: HM Inspector of Schools, 1958; HM Staff Inspector, 1966. ARCA 1934. *Recreations:* theatre, music. *Address:* Amber Cottage, Sigglesthorne, Hull, North Humberside HU11 5QA. *T:* Hornsea (0964) 534596.

RICHARDSON, Lt-Gen. Sir Robert (Francis), KCB 1982; CVO 1978; CBE 1975 (OBE 1971; MBE 1965); Administrator, MacRobert Trusts, since 1985; *b* 2 March 1929; *s* of late Robert Buchan Richardson and Anne (*née* Smith); *m* 1st, 1956, Maureen Anne Robinson (*d* 1986); three *s* one *d*; 2nd, 1988, Alexandra Inglis (*née* Bomford); two step *s*. *Educ:* George Heriot's Sch., Edinburgh; RMA Sandhurst. Commnd into The Royal Scots, 1949; served in BAOR, Korea, and Middle East with 1st Bn The Royal Scots until 1960; Defence Services Staff Coll., India, 1960–61; psc 1961; GSO II MO4, MoD, 1961–64; jssc 1964; Brigade Major Aden Bde, 1967 (Despatches); GSO II ACDS (Ops), MoD, 1968–69; CO 1st Bn The Royal Scots, 1969–71; Col Gen. Staff, Staff Coll. Camberley, 1971–74; Comdr 39 Infantry Bde, Northern Ireland, 1974–75; Deputy Adjutant General, HQ BAOR, 1975–78; GOC Berlin (British Sector), 1978–80; Vice Adjutant Gen. and Dir of Army Manning, 1980–82; GOC NI, 1982–85. Col, The Royal Scots (The Royal Regt), 1980–90. *Recreations:* golf and other outdoor sports, gardening. *Address:* c/o Bank of Scotland, London Chief Office, 38 Threadneedle Street, EC2P 2EH. *Clubs:* Royal Scots (Edinburgh); Hon. Co. of Edinburgh Golfers (Muirfield).

RICHARDSON, Ronald Frederick, CBE 1973 (MBE 1945); Deputy Chairman, Electricity Council, 1972–76; *b* 1913; *s* of Albert F. Richardson and Elizabeth Jane (*née* Sayer); *m* 1946, Anne Elizabeth McArdle; two *s*. *Educ:* Coopers' Company's School; Northampton Engineering Inst.; Polytechnic Inst.; Administrative Staff College. Served War of 1939–45: Major, Field Park Company RE, 1942–46. Callenders Cables, 1929–36; Central London Electricity, 1936–39, 1946–48; London Electricity Board, 1948–52; British Electricity Authority, 1952–57; South Western Electricity Board, 1957–63; Chm., North Western Electricity Board, 1964–71. Chm., Nat. Inspection Council for Electrical Installation Contracting, 1969–70; Dep. Chm., NW Regional Council, CBI, 1971; Member: North West Economic Planning Council, 1965–70; Adv. Council on Energy Conservation, 1974–76; (part-time): NCB, 1975–77; Electricity Council, 1976; Price Commn, 1977–79. Member: Court of Manchester Univ., 1969–71; Council, 1970–71, Court, 1970–, Salford Univ., 1970–74; Governor, William Temple Coll., 1971–74. *Recreations:* music, the open air.

RICHARDSON, Hon. Ruth Margaret; MP (Nat. Party) Selwyn, New Zealand, since 1981; Minister of Finance, since 1990; *b* 13 Dec. 1950; *d* of Ross Pearce Richardson and Rita Joan Richardson; *m* 1975, Andrew Evan Wright; one *s* one *d*. *Educ:* Canterbury Univ., NZ (LLB Hons 1971). Admitted to the Bar, 1973; Legal Adviser: Law Reform Div., Dept of Justice, 1972–75; Federated Farmers of NZ, 1975–80. Opposition spokesman: on Education and on Youth Issues, 1984–87; on Finance, 1987–90. *Recreations:* running, swimming, gardening. *Address:* Parliament House, Wellington, New Zealand. *T:* 04–719–330.

RICHARDSON, Prof. Sam Scruton, AO 1980; CBE 1965 (OBE 1960); Commissioner for Law Revision, Northern States of Nigeria, since 1987; Foundation Principal, Canberra College of Advanced Education (subsequently University of Canberra), 1969–84, Emeritus Fellow, 1984–90, Emeritus Professor, since 1990; *b* 31 Dec. 1919; *s* of Samuel and Gladys Richardson; *m* 1949, Sylvia May McNeil; two *s* one *d*. *Educ:* Magnus Sch., Newark-on-Trent; Trinity Coll., Oxford (State Scholarship, 1937; BA PPE, 1940; MA 1946); Sch. of Oriental and African Studies, Univ. of London. Called to the Bar, Lincoln's Inn, 1958. Served War, 1940–46: commnd Royal Marines; Commando Bdes, Europe and Far East (despatches); demob., Major, 1946. Dist Comr, Sudan Polit. Service, 1946–54 (served in Kordofan and Darfur, 1946–53; Resident, Dar Masalit, 1953–54); HMOCS, Nigeria, 1954–67: Dist Comr, Bornu Prov., 1954–58; Comr for Local Courts in Attorney Gen.'s Chambers, N Nigeria, 1958–60; Dir, Inst. of Admin, Zaria, 1960–67; Dep. Vice-Chancellor, Ahmadu Bello Univ., Nigeria, 1962–67; Prof. of Public Admin, 1967–68, and Acting Vice-Chancellor, 1968, Univ. of Mauritius; occasional Lectr in Islamic Law, ANU, 1971–82; Vis. Prof., Ahmadu Bello Univ., Nigeria, 1986. Consultant: Aust. Law Reform Commn, 1980–; Museum of Australia, 1985–. Chm., Aust. Conf. of Principals, 1979–80; Pres., Internat. Assoc. of Schs and Insts of Admin, 1982–89; Member: Council, Inst. of Admin, Papua New Guinea, 1970–84; Immigration Adv. Council, 1971–74; Nat. Standing Control Cttee on Drugs of Dependence, 1974–84; Australian Council on Overseas Prof. Qualifications, 1975–; Adv. Council, Aust. Jt Services Staff Coll., 1977–84; Academic Adv. Council, RAN Coll., Jervis Bay, 1978–; Council, ANU, 1981–84; Exec. Cttee, Internat. Inst. of Admin. Scis, 1982–90. Mem., Bd of Management, Aust. Inst. of Sport, 1980–84. Governor, Portsmouth Polytechnic, 1989– (Hon. Fellow, 1984). Nat. Pres., Australia Britain Soc., 1980–84; Vice-Pres., Britain Australia Soc., 1984–. Freeman, City of London, 1989–; Mem., Guild of Freeman, 1989–. Hon. LLD Ahmadu Bello, 1967; Hon. Dr Canberra, 1990. *Publications:* Notes on the Penal Code of N Nigeria, 1959, 4th edn 1987; (with T. H. Williams) The Criminal Procedure Code of N Nigeria, 1963; (with E. A. Keay) The Native and Customary Courts of Nigeria, 1965; Parity of Esteem—the Canberra College of Advanced Education 1968–78, 1979; regular book revs in Canberra Times, 1970–; articles on public admin, customary law and higher educn in learned jls. *Recreations:* travel, reading, community service. *Address:* The Malt House, Wylye, Warminster, Wilts BA12 0QP. *T:* Wylye (09856) 348. *Clubs:* United Oxford & Cambridge University; University House (ANU, Canberra).

RICHARDSON, Sir Simon Alaisdair S.; *see* Stewart-Richardson.

RICHARDSON, Maj.-Gen. Thomas Anthony, (Tony), CB 1976; MBE 1960; Secretary: British Christmas Tree Growers Association, since 1980; Christmas Tree Growers Association of Western Europe, since 1989; *b* 9 Aug. 1922; *s* of late Maj.-Gen. T. W. Richardson, Eaton Cottage, Unthank Road, Norwich, and late Mrs J. H. Boothby, Camberley; *m* 1st, 1945, Katharine Joanna Ruxton Roberts (*d* 1988), Woodland Place, Bath; one *s* one *d*; 2nd, 1991, Anthea Rachel Fry, Wimbledon. *Educ:* Wellington Coll., Berks. Technical Staff Course, psc, Fixed Wing Pilot, Rotary Wing Pilot, Parachutist. War of 1939–45: enlisted, Feb. 1941; commissioned, RA, March 1942; Essex Yeomanry (France and Germany), 1942–45; Air Observation Post, 1945–46. Tech. Staff/G Staff, 1949–52, 1954–55, 1959–60, 1963–64; Regt duty, 1942–45, 1952–54, 1957–58, 1961–62. Instr, Mil. Coll. Science, 1955–56; CO, 7th Para, RHA, 1965–67; CRA, 2 Div., 1967–69; Dir, Operational Requirements (Army), 1969–71; Dir, Army Aviation, 1971–74; Defence and Military Advr, India, 1974–77. Col Comdt, RA, 1978–83. Asst Sec., 1978–80, Sec. 1980–84, Timber Growers England and Wales Ltd; Dep. Chm., 1984–86, Chm., 1986–88, Tree Council. *Recreations:* sailing, skiing, fishing, shooting. *Address:* 12 Lauriston Road, Wimbledon, SW19 4TQ. *Club:* Army and Navy.

RICHARDSON, Thomas Legh, CMG 1991; HM Diplomatic Service; UK Deputy Permanent Representative to UN, with personal rank of Ambassador, since 1989; *b* 6 Feb. 1941; *s* of Arthur Legh Turnour Richardson and Penelope Margaret Richardson; *m* 1979, Alexandra Frazier Wasiqullah (*née* Ratcliff). *Educ:* Westminster Sch.; Christ Church, Oxford. MA (Hist.). Joined Foreign Office, 1962; seconded to Univ. of Ghana, 1962–63; FO, 1963–65; Third Sec., Dar-Es-Salaam, 1965–66; Vice-Consul (Commercial), Milan, 1967–70; seconded to N. M. Rothschild & Sons, 1970; FCO, 1971–74; First Sec., UK Mission to UN, 1974–78; FCO, 1978–80; seconded to Central Policy Review Staff, Cabinet Office, 1980–81; Head of Chancery, Rome, 1982–86; Head of Economic Relns Dept, FCO, 1986–89. *Recreations:* reading, walking, travel, music. *Address:* c/o Foreign and Commonwealth Office, SW1. *Club:* United Oxford & Cambridge University.

RICHARDSON, Maj.-Gen. Tony; *see* Richardson, Maj.-Gen. Thomas A.

RICHARDSON, Tony; Director, Woodfall Film Productions Ltd, since 1958; *b* 5 June 1928; *s* of Clarence Albert and Elsie Evans Richardson; *m* 1962, Vanessa Redgrave, *qv* (marr. diss., 1967); two *d*; one *d*. *Educ:* Wadham College, Oxford. Associate Artistic Dir, English Stage Co., Royal Court Theatre, 1956–64. *Plays* directed or produced: Look Back in Anger, 1956; The Chairs, 1957; Pericles and Othello (Stratford), 1958; The Entertainer,

1958; A Taste of Honey, NY, 1961; Luther, 1961; Semi-Detached, 1962; Arturo Ui, 1963; Natural Affection, 1963; The Milk Train Doesn't Stop Here Any More, 1963; The Seagull, 1964; St Joan of the Stockyards, 1964; Hamlet, 1968; The Threepenny Opera, Prince of Wales, 1972; I Claudius, Queen's, 1972; Antony and Cleopatra, Bankside Globe, 1973; Lady from the Sea, New York, 1977; As You Like It, Los Angeles, 1979. *Films* directed or produced: Look Back in Anger, 1958; The Entertainer, 1959; Saturday Night and Sunday Morning (prod), 1960; Taste of Honey, 1961; The Loneliness of the Long Distance Runner (prod and dir.), 1962; Tom Jones (dir.), 1962; Girl with Green Eyes (prod), 1964; The Loved One (dir.), 1965; Mademoiselle (dir.), 1965; The Sailor from Gibraltar (dir.), 1965; Red and Blue (dir.) 1966; The Charge of the Light Brigade (dir.), 1968; Laughter in the Dark (dir.), 1969; Hamlet (dir.), 1969; Ned Kelly (dir.), 1969; A Delicate Balance, 1972; Dead Cert, 1974; Joseph Andrews, 1977; A Death in Canaan, 1978; The Border, 1981; The Hotel New Hampshire, 1983. *Films for television*: Penalty Phase, 1986; Shadow on the Sun, 1988; Phantom of the Opera, 1989; Hills Like White Elephants, 1989; Blue Sky, 1990. *Recreations*: travel, tennis, birds, directing plays and films. *Address*: 1478 North King's Road, Los Angeles, Calif 90069, USA.

RICHARDSON, Air Marshal Sir William; *see* Richardson, Air Marshal Sir D. W.

RICHARDSON, William, CBE 1981; DL; CEng; FRINA; retired, 1983; Chairman: Vickers Shipbuilding and Engineering Ltd, 1976–83 (Managing Director, 1969–76); Vosper Thornycroft (UK) Ltd, 1978–83; Barclay Curle Ltd, 1978–83; Brook Marine Ltd, 1981–83; Member Board, British Shipbuilders (from incorporation), 1977–83, Deputy Chairman 1981–83; Director, Vickers Cockatoo Dockyard Pty Ltd, Australia, 1977–84; *b* 15 Aug. 1916; *s* of Edwin Richardson, marine engr, and Hannah (*née* Remington); *m* 1941, Beatrice Marjorie Iliffe; one *s* one *d*. *Educ*: Ocean Road Boys' Sch., Walney Is, Barrow-in-Furness; Jun. Techn. and Techn. Colls, Barrow-in-Furness (part-time). HNC (Dist.) Naval Architecture; HNC (1st Cl.) Mech. Engrg. CBIM 1981 (FBIM 1977); FInstD 1977–83. Vickers Ltd, Barrow-in-Furness: Shipbldg Apprentice, 1933–38; Techn. Dept, 1938–39; Admiralty Directorate of Aircraft Maintenance and Repair, UK and Far East, 1939–46; Vickers Ltd Barrow Shipyard: Techn. Depts, 1946–51; Asst Shipyard Manager, 1951–60; Dockside Outfitting Man., 1960–61; Dep. Shipyard Man., 1961–63; Shipyard Man., 1963–64; Dir and Gen. Man., 1964–66; Dir and Gen. Man., Vickers Ltd Naval Shipyard, Newcastle upon Tyne, 1966–68; Dep. Man. Dir, Swan Hunter & Tyne Shipbldrs Ltd, 1968–69. Director: Slingsby Sailplanes, 1969–70 (co. then incorp. into Vickers Ltd); Vickers Oceanics, 1972–77; Chm., Clark & Standfield (subsid. of Vickers Gp), 1976–83; Dir, Vosper Shiprepairers, 1978–82. Dir of Trustees, 1976–, Mem. Res. Council and Office Bearer, 1976–78, BSRA; Mem. Exec. Council, 1969–77, Chm. Management Bd, 1976–78, SRNA; Pres. Brit. Productivity Assoc., Barrow and Dist, 1969–72; Shipbldg Ind. Rep., DIQAP, 1972–82; Mem., Shipbuilding Industry Trng Bd, 1979–82; Mem., NE Coast IES, 1967–. FRINA 1970 (ARINA 1950, MRINA 1955). Liveryman, Shipwrights' Co., 1978. DL Cumbria, 1982. Queen's Silver Jubilee Medal, 1977. *Publications*: papers on various aspects of UK shipbldg industry; contribs to techn. jls. *Recreations*: sailing, small-bore shooting, golf, fishing. *Address*: Sequoia, Sunbrick Lane, Baycliff, Ulverston, Cumbria LA12 9RQ. *T*: Ulverston (0229) 869434. *Club*: National Small-Bore Rifle Association.

RICHARDSON, William Eric, CEng, FIEE, FBIM; Chairman, South Wales Electricity Board, 1968–77; Member, Electricity Council, 1968–77; retired 1977; *b* 21 May 1915; *o s* of William Pryor and Elizabeth Jane Richardson, Hove, Sussex; *m* (she *d* 1975); one *s*; *m* 1976, Barbara Mary Leech. *Educ*: Royal Masonic Sch., Bushey. Engineer with Brighton Corp., 1934–37; Southampton Corp., 1937–39; Norwich Corp., 1939–46; Distribution Engr with Newport (Mon) Corp., 1946–48; Area Engr with S Wales Electricity Bd, 1948–57; Area Manager, 1957–65; Chief Commercial Engr, 1965–67; Dep. Chm., 1967–68. *Recreations*: sailing, golf, gardening. *Address*: 57 Allt-yr-Yn View, Newport, Gwent NP9 5DN. *T*: Newport (Gwent) (0633) 264388.

RICHARDSON-BUNBURY, Sir (Richard David) Michael, *see* Bunbury.

RICHES, Sir Derek (Martin Hurry), KCMG 1963 (CMG 1958); Ambassador to Lebanon, 1963–67, retired; *b* 26 July 1912; *s* of late Claud Riches and Flora Martin; *m* 1942, Helen Barkley Hayes (*d* 1989), Poughkeepsie, NY, USA; one *d*. *Educ*: University College School; University College, London. Appointed Probationer Vice-Consul, Beirut, Dec. 1934. Subsequently promoted and held various appts, Ethiopia and Cairo; Foreign Office, 1944; promoted one of HM Consuls serving in FO, 1945. Kabul, 1948 (in charge, 1948 and 1949); Consul at Jedda, 1951 (Chargé d'Affaires, 1952); Officer Grade 6, Branch A, Foreign Service and apptd Trade Comr, Khartoum, 1953. Attached to Imperial Defence College, 1955; returned to Foreign Office, 1955; Counsellor in the Foreign Office, Head of Eastern Department, 1955; British Ambassador in Libya, 1959–61; British Ambassador to the Congo, 1961–63. *Address*: 48 The Avenue, Kew Gardens, Surrey.

RICHES, General Sir Ian (Hurry), KCB 1960 (CB 1959); DSO 1945; *b* 27 Sept. 1908; *s* of C. W. H. Riches; *m* 1936, Winifred Eleanor Layton; two *s*. *Educ*: Univ. Coll. Sch., London. Joined Royal Marines, 1927; Major, 1946; Lt-Colonel, 1949; Colonel, 1953; Maj.-Gen., 1957; Lt-Gen., 1959; General, 1961. Maj.-Gen., RM, Portsmouth Group, 1957–59; Commandant-General, Royal Marines, 1959–62; Regional Dir of Civil Defence, 1964–68; Representative Col Comdt, 1967–68. *T*: Winchester (0962) 854067.

RICHES, Rt. Rev. Kenneth, DD, STD; Assistant Bishop of Louisiana, USA, 1976–77; *b* 20 Sept. 1908; *s* of Capt. A. G. Riches; *m* 1942, Kathleen Mary Dixon, JP 1964; two *s* one *d*. *Educ*: Royal Gram. Sch., Colchester; Corpus Christi Coll., Cambridge. Curate of St Mary's, Portsea, 1932–35; St John's, East Dulwich, 1935–36; Chaplain and Librarian, Sidney Sussex Coll., Cambridge, 1936–42; Examining Chaplain to Bishops of Bradford and Wakefield, 1936; Editorial Sec., Cambridgeshire Syllabus, 1935; Editor, Cambridge Review, 1941–42; Rector of Bredfield with Boulge, Suffolk, and Dir of Service Ordination Candidates, 1942–45; Principal of Cuddesdon Theological Coll., Oxford, and Vicar of Cuddesdon, 1945–52; Hon. Canon of Portsmouth Cathedral, 1950–52; Bishop Suffragan of Dorchester, Archdeacon of Oxford and Canon of Christ Church, 1952–56; Bishop of Lincoln, 1956–74. Select Preacher: University of Cambridge, 1941, 1948, 1961, and 1963; University of Oxford, 1954–55. Mem. Archbishops' Commission on Training for the Ministry, 1942; Sec. of Theol. Commn on the Church of Faith and Order Movement. Visiting Lecturer the General Theological Seminary, New York, 1956 and 1962. Hon. Fellow: Sidney Sussex Coll., Cambridge, 1958; Lincoln Coll., Oxford, 1974; Corpus Christi Coll., Cambridge, 1975. Chm., Central Advisory Council for the Ministry, 1959–65. *Recreations*: gardening, antiques, and country life. *Address*: Little Dingle, Dunwich, Saxmundham, Suffolk IP17 3EA. *T*: Westleton (072873) 316.

RICHINGS, Lewis David George; *b* 22 April 1920; *s* of Lewis Vincent Richings and Jessie Helen (*née* Clements); *m* 1944, Margaret Alice Hume; three *d*. *Educ*: Battersea Grammar Sch.; Devonport High Sch.; Darlington Grammar Sch.; London Sch. of Econs and Polit. Science (part-time). Served War, Army, 1939–46: commnd 2 Lieut Inf., 1940; attached 8 DLI, 1940–41; seconded 11 KAR, 1941–45; Actg Major, 1945; various postings, UK, 1945–46. MAFF, 1937–58; attached MoD, 1958; Gen. Administrator, AWRE, 1958–65; Health and Safety Br., UKAEA, 1965–70; Sec., Nat. Radiol Protection Bd, 1970–79, Dep. Dir, 1978–80. Mem., Radiol Protection and Public Health Cttee, Nuclear Energy Agency, OECD, 1966–80 (Chm., 1972–74). FRSA. *Publications*: articles in press and jls on admin and technical matters relating to common land, rural electrification, earthquakes, and radiol protection. *Recreation*: boats. *Address*: 31 Kennedy Street, Blairgowrie, Vic 3942, Australia; 26 Three Acre Road, Newbury, Berks.

RICHLER, Mordecai; author; *b* 27 Jan. 1931; *s* of late Moses Isaac Richler and Lily Rosenberg; *m* 1960, Florence Wood; three *s* two *d*. *Educ*: Sir George Williams Univ., Montreal (left without degree). Writer-in-residence, Sir George Williams Univ., 1968–69; Vis. Prof., English Dept, Carleton Univ., Ottawa, 1972–74. Edit. Bd, Book-of-the-Month Club, NY. Canada Council Senior Arts Fellowship, 1960; Guggenheim Fellowship, Creative Writing, 1961; Governor-General's Award for Literature, 1969 and 1972; Paris Review Humour Prize, 1969; Commonwealth Writers Prize, 1990. *Publications*: *novels*: The Acrobats, 1954; A Choice of Enemies, 1955; Son of a Smaller Hero, 1957; The Apprenticeship of Duddy Kravitz, 1959, repr. 1972 (filmed, Golden Bear Award, Berlin Film Fest., 1974; Writers Guild of America Annual Award, 1974; Academy Award nomination, 1974); The Incomparable Atuk, 1963; Cocksure, 1968; St Urbain's Horseman, 1971; Joshua Then and Now, 1980 (filmed, 1985); Solomon Gursky Was Here, 1990; *essays*: Hunting Tigers Under Glass, 1969; Shovelling Trouble, 1973; Home Sweet Home, 1984; Broadsides, 1991; *autobiography*: The Street, 1972; *children's books*: Jacob Two-Two Meets the Hooded Fang, 1975; Jacob Two-Two and the Dinosaur, 1987; *anthology*: (ed) The Best of Modern Humour, 1983; (ed) Writers on World War II, 1991; contrib. Encounter, Commentary, New York Review of Books, etc. *Recreations*: poker, snooker. *Address*: Apt 80C, 1321 Sherbrooke Street W, Montreal, Quebec H3G 1J4, Canada. *T*: 514–288–2008.

RICHMAN, Stella; television producer; *b* 9 Nov. 1922; *d* of Jacob Richman and Leoni Richman; *m* 1st, Alec Clunes; 2nd, 1953, Victor Brusa (*d* 1965); one *s* one *d*. *Educ*: Clapton County Secondary Sch. for Girls. Started TV career at ATV, running Script Dept 1960; created and produced Love Story, 1963; joined Rediffusion, 1964; Exec. Head of Series (prod The Informer); Exec. Prod., award-winning Man of Our Times, Half Hour Story and Blackmail; prod first 6 plays, Company of Five, for newly formed London Weekend Television, 1968; Man. Dir, London Weekend Internat., 1969, and Controller of Programmes, London Weekend Television, 1970–71 (first woman to sit on bd of a television co.); in partnership with David Frost formed Stella Richman Productions (first independent TV co.), 1972–78: resp. for Miss Nightingale, Jennie, Clayhanger, Bill Brand, Just William. Chm. and owner, White Elephant Club, 1960–88. FRTS 1982. *Publications*: The White Elephant Cook Books, 1973, 1979. *Recreations*: travel, wine collecting, herb cultivation, reading biographies, watching TV and theatre. *Address*: Garden Flat, 5 Hill Road, NW8 9QE.

RICHMOND, 10th Duke of, *cr* 1675, **AND GORDON,** 5th Duke of, *cr* 1876; **Charles Henry Gordon-Lennox;** Baron Settrington, Earl of March, 1675; Lord of Torboulton, Earl of Darnley, Duke of Lennox (Scot.) 1675; Earl of Kinrara, 1876; Duc d'Aubigny (France), 1684; Hereditary Constable of Inverness Castle; Lord-Lieutenant of West Sussex, since 1990; *b* 19 Sept. 1929; *s* of 9th Duke of Richmond and Gordon, and of Elizabeth Grace, *y d* of late Rev. T. W. Hudson; *S* father, 1989; *m* 1951, Susan Monica, *o d* of late Colonel C. E. Grenville-Grey, CBE, Hall Barn, Blewbury, Berks; one *s* four *d*. *Educ*: Eton; William Temple Coll. 2nd Lieut, 60th Rifles, 1949–50. Chartered Accountant, 1956. Dir of Industrial Studies, William Temple Coll., 1964–68; Chancellor, Univ. of Sussex, 1985– (Treasurer, 1979–82). Church Commissioner, 1963–76; Mem. Gen. Synod of Church of England, formerly Church Assembly, 1960–80 (Chm., Bd for Mission and Unity, 1967–77); Mem., Central and Exec. Cttees, World Council of Churches, 1968–75; Chairman: Christian Orgn Res. and Adv. Trust, 1965–87; House of Laity, Chichester Diocesan Synod, 1976–79; Vice-Chm., Archbishop's Commn on Church and State, 1966–70; Pres., Voluntary and Christian Service, 1982–. Mem., W Midlands Regional Economic Planning Council, 1965–68; Chairman: Goodwood Group of Cos, 1969–; Ajax Insurance (Holdings) Ltd, 1987–89; Director: Radio Victory Ltd, 1982–87; John Wiley and Sons Ltd, 1984–. Historic Houses Association: Hon. Treas., 1975–82; Chm., SE Region, 1975–78; Dep. Pres., 1982–86; President: Sussex Rural Community Council, 1973–; British Horse Soc., 1976–78; South of England Agricultural Soc., 1981–82; SE England Tourist Bd, 1990– (Vice-Pres., 1974–90); Chm., Assoc. of Internat. Dressage Event Organisers, 1987–; Chairman: Rugby Council of Social Service, 1961–68; Dunfold Coll., (YMCA), 1969–82; Dir, Country Gentlemen's Assoc. Ltd, 1975–89. Chairman: of Trustees, Sussex Heritage Trust, 1978–; Planning for Economic Prosperity in Chichester and Arun, 1984–89; Chichester Cathedral Develt Trust, 1985–91; President: Chichester Festivities, 1975–; Sussex CCC, 1991–. DL W Sussex, 1975–90. CBIM 1982. Hon LLD Sussex, 1986. Medal of Honour, British Equestrian Fedn, 1983. *Heir*: *s* Earl of March and Kinrara, *qv*. *Address*: Goodwood House, Chichester, W Sussex. *T*: (office) Chichester (0243) 774107; (home) Chichester (0243) 774760.

See also Lord N. C. Gordon Lennox.

RICHMOND, Archdeacon of; *see* McDermid, Ven. N. G. L. R.

RICHMOND, Sir Alan (James), Kt 1969; engineering consultant, expert witness and arbitrator; *b* 12 Oct. 1919; *m* 1951, Sally Palmer (*née* Pain); one step *s* one step *d*. *Educ*: Berlin; Gland près Nyon, Switzerland; Wimbledon Tech. Coll.; Acton Tech. Coll.; Northampton Polytechnic, London. Trained and employed Engineering Industry, 1938–45; London Univ., BSc(Eng) 1945, PhD 1954; Lecturer, Battersea Polytechnic, 1946–55; Head of Engineering Dept, Welsh Coll. of Advanced Technology, 1955–58; Principal, Lanchester College of Technology, Coventry, 1959–69; Director, Lanchester Polytechnic, 1970–72; Principal, Strode Coll., Street, 1972–81; Associate Tutor, Further Education Staff Coll., Blagdon, Bristol, 1982–85. Chairman: Coventry Productivity Assoc., 1964–67; CNAA Mech./Prodn Engrg Subject Bd, 1965–68; CNAA Cttees for Sci. and Technology, 1968–72; Founder Chm., Cttee of Dirs of Polytechnics, 1970–72; Member: Home Office Deptl Cttee of Enquiry into Fire Service in GB, 1967–70; Open Univ. Planning Cttee, 1967–69; Open Univ. Council, 1969–71. FIMechE; FCIArb. Hon. DSc CNAA, 1972. *Publications*: (with W. J. Peck) Applied Thermodynamics Problems for Engineers, 1950; Problems in Heat Engines, 1957; various lectures, reviews and articles. *Recreations*: gardening, reading. *Address*: 5 The Orchard, Westfield Park South, Bath BA1 3HT. *T*: Bath (0225) 333393. *Club*: Commonwealth Trust.

RICHMOND, Rear-Adm. Andrew John, CB 1987; Chief Executive (formerly Executive Director), Royal Society for the Prevention of Cruelty to Animals, 1987–91; *b* 5 Nov. 1931; *s* of Albert George Richmond and Emily Margaret (*née* Denbee); *m* 1957, Jane Annette (*née* Ley); one *s* two *d*. *Educ*: King's School, Bruton; Nautical College, Pangbourne. Joined RN 1950; staff of C-in-C East Indies, 1953; flying training, 1955; Cyprus 847 Sqdn, 1956; HMS Victorious 824 Sqdn, 1958; staff of FO Arabian Sea, 1960; BRNC Dartmouth, 1963; Sec., FO Carriers and Amphibious Ships, 1968; Supply School, HMS Pembroke, 1970; Fleet Supply Officer, 1974; Asst Dir Naval Manpower, 1976; Sec., C-in-C Naval Home Comd, 1977; Captain, HMS Cochrane, 1979; Dir, Naval Logistic Planning, 1982; ADC 1984; ACDS (Logistics), 1985, and Chief Naval Supply and Secretariat Officer, 1986. FRSA. *Recreations*: home, gardening, golf. *Address*: c/o

Royal Bank of Scotland, South Street, Chichester, West Sussex. *Clubs:* Royal Over-Seas League; Goodwood Golf.

RICHMOND, Rt. Hon. Sir Clifford (Parris), PC 1973; KBE 1977; Kt 1972; Judge of the Court of Appeal of New Zealand, 1972–81, President, 1976–81; *b* 23 June 1914; *s* of Howard Parris Richmond, QC, and Elsie Wilhelmina (*née* MacTavish); *m* 1938, Valerie Jean Hamilton; two *s* one *d*. *Educ:* Wanganui Collegiate Sch.; Victoria and Auckland Univs. LLM (1st cl. Hons). Served War of 1939–45: 4 Field Regt 2NZEF, North Africa and Italy, 1942–45 (despatches, 1944). Partner, legal firm, Buddle Richmond & Co., Auckland, 1946–60. Judge of the Supreme Court of New Zealand, 1960–71. *Recreations:* golf, fishing. *Address:* 16 Glanville Terrace, Parnell, Auckland, New Zealand. *T:* 3077–104. *Club:* Northern (Auckland).

RICHMOND, Rt. Rev. Francis Henry Arthur; *see* Repton, Bishop Suffragan of.

RICHMOND, Prof. John, MD, FRCP, FRCPE; President, Royal College of Physicians of Edinburgh, 1988–91; Emeritus Professor of Medicine, University of Sheffield, since 1989; *b* 30 May 1926; *er s* of late Hugh Richmond and Janet Hyslop Brown; *m* 1951, Jenny Nicol, 2nd *d* of T. Nicol; two *s* one *d*. *Educ:* Doncaster Grammar Sch.; Univ. of Edinburgh. MB, ChB 1948 (with Distinction in Medicine); MD 1963. FRCPE 1963; FRCP 1970; FRCPS 1989; FRCPI 1990; FCPS (Pak) 1990; FRCSE 1991; Hon. FACP 1990; Hon. FFPM 1990; Hon. FRACP 1991; Hon. FCP(SoAf) 1991; Hon. FFPHM 1991. House Officer, in Edinburgh hosps and Northants, 1948–49, 1952–54; RAMC, Military Mission to Ethiopia, Captain 1st Bn King's African Rifles, N Rhodesia, 1949–50; Rural Gen. Practice, Galloway, Scotland, 1950–52; Res. Fellow, Meml Sloan Kettering Cancer Center, New York, 1958–59; Sen. Lectr, later Reader in Medicine, Univ. of Edinburgh, 1963–73; University of Sheffield: Prof. of Medicine, 1973–89; Chm., Academic Div. of Medicine, 1978–85; Hon. Dir of Cancer Res., 1983–88; Dean of Medicine and Dentistry, 1985–88. Censor, 1981–82, Sen. Vice-Pres. and Sen. Censor, 1984–85, RCP; Mem. Council, RCPE, 1987–88. Chm., MRCP (UK) Part 2 Examining Bd, 1985–89. Member: Sheffield HA, 1982–84; Clin. Standards Adv. Gp, Dept of Health, 1991–; Bd of Advrs, London Univ., 1984–; External Advr, Chinese Univ. of Hong Kong, 1984–. Mem. Council of Management, Yorkshire Cancer Res. Campaign, 1989–. High Constables of Edinburgh, 1961–70. *Publications:* Mem. Editorial Bd and contribs, A Companion to Medical Studies, ed R. Passmore and J. S. Robson, vols I-III; contribs: Davidson's Principles and Practice of Medicine, ed J. G. Macleod; Abdominal Operations, ed Rodney Maingot; (jtly) The Spleen, 1973; papers in med. jls mainly on haematology and oncology. *Recreations:* gardening, photography. *Address:* 15 Church Hill, Edinburgh EH10 4BG; Royal College of Physicians, 9 Queen Street, Edinburgh EH2 1JQ. *T:* 031–225 7324. *Club:* New (Edinburgh).

RICHMOND, Sir John (Frederick), 2nd Bt, *cr* 1929; *b* 12 Aug. 1924; *s* of Sir Frederick Henry Richmond, 1st Bt (formerly Chm. Debenham's Ltd and Harvey Nichols & Co. Ltd), and Dorothy Agnes (*d* 1982), *d* of Frances Joseph Sheppard; *S* father 1953; *m* 1965, Mrs Anne Moreen Bentley; one *d*. *Educ:* Eton; Jesus Coll., Cambridge. Lt 10th Roy. Hussars; seconded Provost Br., 1944–47. *Address:* Shimpling Park Farm, Bury St Edmunds, Suffolk. *Club:* MCC.

RICHMOND, Sir Mark (Henry), Kt 1986; PhD, ScD; FRCPath; FRS 1980; Chairman, Science and Engineering Research Council, since 1990; *b* 1 Feb. 1931; *s* of Harold Sylvester Richmond and Dorothy Plaistowe Richmond; *m* 1958, Shirley Jean Townrow; one *s* one *d* (and one *d* decd). *Educ:* Epsom College; Clare Coll., Cambridge. BA, PhD, ScD. Scientific Staff, MRC, 1958–65; Reader in Molecular Biology, Univ. of Edinburgh, 1965–68; Prof. of Bacteriology, Univ. of Bristol, 1968–81; Vice-Chancellor, and Prof. of Molecular Microbiol., Victoria Univ. of Manchester, 1981–90. Member: Bd, PHLS, 1976–85; Fulbright Commn, 1980–84; SERC, 1981–85; Chairman: British Nat. Cttee for Microbiol., 1980–85; CVCP, 1987–89; Cttee on Microbiological Food Safety, 1989–91; Member: Genetic Manipulation Adv. Gp 1976–84; Adv. Cttee on Genetic Manipulation, 1984–85. Member: IBM Academic Adv. Bd, 1984–90; Knox Fellowship Cttee, 1984–87; CIBA-Geigy Fellowship Trust, 1984–91; Jarrett Cttee for University Efficiency, 1985; Governing Body, Lister Inst., 1987–90; Council, ACU, 1988–90; Council, Royal Northern Coll. of Music, 1990–. *Publications:* several in microbiology and biochemistry jls. *Recreation:* hill-walking. *Address:* Science and Engineering Research Council, Polaris House, North Star Avenue, Swindon SN2 1ET. *Club:* Athenæum.

RICHMOND, Prof. Peter, PhD; CPhys, FInstP; Director, AFRC Institute of Food Research, Norwich Laboratory, since 1986; *b* 4 March 1943; *s* of John Eric Richmond and Nellie (*née* Scholey); *m* 1967, Christine M. Jackson; one *s* one *d*. *Educ:* Whitcliffe Mount Grammar Sch., Cleckheaton; Queen Mary Coll., London (BSc, PhD); London Univ. (DSc). MRSC. ICI Res. Fellow, Univ. of Kent, 1967–69; Univ. of NSW, 1969–71; Queen Elizabeth II Res. Fellow, Inst. of Advanced Studies, ANU, 1971–73; Unilever Res., 1973–82; Hd, Process Physics, AFRC Food Res. Inst., Norwich, 1982–86; Industrial Prof., Univ. of Loughborough, 1985–88; Prof., Univ. of E Anglia, 1986–. Mem., MAFF/DoH Adv. Cttee on novel foods and processes, 1988–. *Publications:* (with R. D. Bee and J. Mingins) Food Colloids, 1989; contribs to learned jls. *Recreations:* music, talking, stock markets, badminton. *Address:* AFRC Institute of Food Research, Norwich Research Park, Colney, Norwich NR4 7UA. *T:* Norwich (0603) 56122. *Club:* Athenæum.

RICHNELL, Donovan Thomas, CBE 1973; Director General, British Library Reference Division, 1974–79; *b* 3 Aug. 1911; *o s* of Thomas Hodgson Richnell and Constance Margaret Richnell (*née* Allen); *m* 1957, Renée Norma Hilton; one *s* one *d*. *Educ:* St Paul's School; Corpus Christi Coll., Cambridge; University Coll., London (Fellow 1975). BA, FLA. Sub-Librarian, Royal Soc. Med., 1946–49; Dep. Librarian, London Univ. Library, 1949–60; Librarian, Univ. of Reading, 1960–67; Dir, and Goldsmiths' Librarian, Univ. of London Library, 1967–74. Library Association: Mem. Council, 1962–71; President 1970; Hon. Fellow 1979; Chm. of Council, Aslib, 1968–70. Member: Library Adv. Council for England, 1966–71, 1974–77; British Library Organising Cttee, 1971–73; Adv. Cttee for Scientific and Technical Information, 1970–74; British Library Bd, 1974–79; Chm., Standing Conf. of Nat. and Univ. Libraries, 1973–75. Hon. DLitt Loughborough, 1977. *Address:* 2 Queen Anne's Gardens, Bedford Park, W4.

RICHTER, Prof. Burton; Paul Pigott Professor in the Physical Sciences, Stanford University, USA, since 1980 (Professor of Physics, since 1967), and Director, Stanford Linear Accelerator Center, since 1984 (Technical Director, 1982–84); *b* 22 March 1931; *s* of Abraham Richter and Fannie Pollack; *m* 1960, Laurose Becker; one *s* one *d*. *Educ:* Massachusetts Inst. of Technology. BS 1952, PhD (Physics) 1956. Stanford University: Research Associate, Physics, High Energy Physics Lab., 1956–60; Asst Prof., 1960–63; Associate Prof., 1963–67; full Prof., 1967. Member: Nat. Acad. of Scis; Amer. Acad. of Arts and Scis. E. O. Lawrence Award, 1975; Nobel Prize for Physics (jointly), 1976. *Publications:* over 200 articles in various scientific journals. *Address:* Stanford Linear Accelerator Center, PO Box 4349, Stanford University, Stanford, California 94309, USA.

RICHTER, Sviatoslav; Hero of Socialist Labour, 1975; pianist; *b* Zhitomir, Ukraine, 20 March 1915; *m* Nina Dorliak. *Educ:* Moscow State Conservatoire. Gave first piano recital at age of nineteen and began to give concerts on a wide scale in 1942. Appeared at the Royal Albert Hall and the Royal Festival Hall, London, 1961; Royal Festival Hall, 1963, 1966, 1977, 1979, 1989. Was recently awarded Lenin Prize, and also holds the title of "Peoples' Artist of the USSR"; Order of Lenin, 1965. *Recreations:* walking, ski-ing and painting.

RICKARD, Dr John Hellyar; Under Secretary, Public Expenditure Economics Division, HM Treasury, since 1991; *b* 27 Jan. 1940; *s* of Peter John Rickard and Irene Eleanor (*née* Hales); *m* 1963, Christine Dorothy Hudson; one *s* two *d*. *Educ:* Ilford County High Sch.; St John's Coll., Oxford (MA 1966; DPhil 1976); Univ. of Aston in Birmingham (MSc 1969). Lectr, Univ. of Aston, 1967–70; Economist, Programmes Analysis Unit, AEA, Harwell, 1970–72; Res. Associate, and Dep. Head, Health Services Evaluation Gp, Dept of Regius Prof. of Medicine, Univ. of Oxford, 1972–74; Econ. Adviser, Dept of Health, 1974–76; Sen. Econ. Adviser: Dept of Prices and Consumer Protection, 1976–78; Central Policy Review Staff, Cabinet Office, 1978–82; HM Treasury, 1982–84; Econ. Adviser, State of Bahrain, 1984–87; Chief Economic Advr, Dept of Transport, 1987–91. *Publications:* (with D. Aston) Macro-Economics: a critical introduction, 1970; articles in books and learned jls. *Recreations:* sailing, music. *Address:* 24 Condray Place, Battersea, SW11 3PE. *T:* 071–223 8359. *Club:* Civil Service Sailing Association.

RICKARD, Prof. Peter, DPhil, PhD, LittD; Drapers Professor of French, University of Cambridge, 1980–82, Emeritus since 1983; Fellow of Emmanuel College, Cambridge, 1953, Professorial Fellow, 1980, Life Fellow, since 1983; *b* 20 Sept. 1922; *yr s* of Norman Ernest Rickard and Elizabeth Jane (*née* Hosking); unmarried. *Educ:* Redruth County Grammar Sch., Cornwall; Exeter Coll., Oxford (Pt I Hons Mod. Langs (French and German), Cl. I, 1942; Final Hons Cl. I, 1948; MA 1948). DPhil Oxon 1952; PhD Cantab 1952; LittD Cambridge 1982. Served War, 1st Bn Seaforth Highlanders and Intell. Corps, India, 1942–46. Heath Harrison Travelling Scholar (French), 1948; Amelia Jackson Sen. Scholar, Exeter Coll., Oxford, 1948–49; Lectr in Mod. Langs, Trinity Coll., Oxford, 1949–52; Univ. of Cambridge: Asst Lectr in French, 1952–57, Lectr, 1957–74; Reader in French Lang., 1974–80; Mem., St John's Coll., 1952–; Tutor, Emmanuel Coll., 1954–65. *Publications:* Britain in Medieval French Literature, 1956; La langue française au XVIe siècle, 1968; (ed with T. G. S. Combe) The French Language: studies presented to Lewis Charles Harmer, 1970; (ed and trans.) Fernando Pessoa, Selected Poems, 1971; A History of the French Language, 1974; Chrestomathie de la langue française au XVe siècle, 1976; (ed with T. G. S. Combe) L. C. Harmer, Uncertainties in French Grammar, 1979; The Embarrassments of Irregularity, 1981; articles in Romania, Trans Phil Soc., Neuphilologische Mitteilungen, Cahiers de Lexicologie, and Zeitschrift für Romanische Philologie. *Recreations:* travel, music. *Address:* Emmanuel College, Cambridge CB2 3AP. *T:* Cambridge (0223) 334223; Upper Rosevine, Portscatho, Cornwall. *T:* Portscatho (087258) 582.

RICKARDS, Dr (Richard) Barrie, CGeol, FGS; Reader in Palaeobiology, University of Cambridge, since 1990; Curator, Sedgwick Museum of Geology, since 1969; Fellow, Emmanuel College, Cambridge, since 1977; *b* 12 June 1938; *s* of Robert Rickards and Eva (*née* Sudborough); *m* 1960, Christine Townsley; one *s*. *Educ:* Goole Grammar Sch.; Univ. of Hull (BSc; PhD 1963; DSc 1990). MA Cantab, 1969; ScD Cantab, 1976. FGS 1960; Founder MIFM 1969; CGeol 1990. Reckitt Scholar, Univ. of Hull, 1960–63; Curator, Garwood Library, UCL, 1963; Asst in Research, Univ. of Cambridge, 1964–66; SSO, BM (Natural History), 1967; Lecturer: TCD, 1967–69; Univ. of Cambridge, 1969–90; Official Lectr, Emmanuel Coll., Cambridge, 1977–. Founder and first Sec., Pike Anglers' Club; Founding Mem., Nat. Anglers' Council; Deleg, E Reg., 1987–, Mem., Gen. Purposes Cttee, 1989–, Nat. Fedn of Anglers; Mem. Council, Waterbeach Angling Club, 1980–84; first Fishery Manager, Leland Water, 1982–83. Murchison Fund, Geol Soc., 1982; John Phillips Medal, Yorks Geol Soc., 1988. *Publications: angling:* (with R. Webb) Fishing for Big Pike, 1971, (sole author) 3rd edn, as Big Pike, 1986; Perch, 1974; (with R. Webb) Fishing for Big Tench, 1976, 2nd edn 1986; Pike, 1976; (with K. Whitehead) Plugs and Plug Fishing, 1976, and Spinners, Spoons and Wobbled Baits, 1977, rev. edn of both titles as A Textbook of Spinning, 1987; (with N. Fickling) Zander, 1979, 2nd edn 1990; (with K. Whitehead) Fishing Tackle, 1981; (with K. Whitehead) A Fishery of Your Own, 1984; Angling: fundamental principles, 1986; (with M. Gay) A Technical Manual of Pike Fishing, 1986; (ed) River Piking, 1987; (ed) Best of Pikelines, 1988; (with M. Gay) Pike, 1989; (with M. Bannister) The Ten Greatest Pike Anglers, 1991; *geology:* Graptolites: writing in the rocks, 1991; upwards of 160 scientific articles and monographs in internat. jls, mostly on fossils (graptolites) and evolution. *Recreations:* angling, marathon running, angling administration (from local to national). *Address:* Emmanuel College, Cambridge CB2 3AP. *T:* Cambridge (0223) 334282.

RICKETS, Brig. Reginald Anthony Scott, (Tony); Managing Director, Irvine Development Corporation, since 1981; Director, Ayrshire Chamber of Industries, since 1981 (Vice-President, 1985; President, 1986); *b* 13 Dec. 1929; *s* of Captain R. H. Rickets and Mrs V. C. Rickets (*née* Morgan) *m* 1952, Elizabeth Ann Serjeant; one *s* one *d*. *Educ:* St George's Coll., Weybridge; RMA Sandhurst. 2nd Lieut, RE, 1949; served with airborne, armoured and field engrs in UK, Cyrenaica, Egypt, Malaya, Borneo, Hong Kong and BAOR; special employment military forces Malaya, 1955–59; Staff Coll., Camberley, 1962; BM Engr Gp, BAOR, 1963–66; OC 67 Gurkha Indep. Field Sqn, 1966–68; DS Staff Coll., 1968–70; Comdt Gurkha Engrs/CRE Hong Kong, 1970–73; COS British Sector, Berlin, 1973–77; Col GS RSME, 1977–78; Chief Engr UKLF, 1978–81. Pres., Ayrshire Chamber of Industry and Commerce, 1989–; Exec. Bd, Scottish Council (Develt and Industry), 1990–; Cons. Cttee, Scottish Develt Agency, 1981–; Dir, Enterprise Ayrshire, 1990–; Patron, Galloway Training, 1989–; Dir, Ex-Services Mentally Handicapped Disabled Welfare Soc., 1986–. *Recreation:* sailing (DTI Ocean skipper and RYA coach/examiner). *Address:* Irvine Development Corporation, Perceton House, Irvine, Ayrshire KA11 2AL. *Club:* Royal Engineer Yacht (Commodore, 1979–81).

RICKETT, Sir Denis Hubert Fletcher, KCMG 1956 (CMG 1947); CB 1951; Director: Schroder International, 1974–79; De La Rue Co., 1974–77; Adviser, J. Henry Schroder Wagg & Co., 1974–79; *b* 27 July 1907; *s* of late Hubert Cecil Rickett, OBE, JP; *m* 1946, Ruth Pauline (MB, BS, MRCS, LRCP), *d* of late William Anderson Armstrong, JP; two *s* one *d*. *Educ:* Rugby School; Balliol College, Oxford (Schol. 1925; Jenkyns Exhibnr 1929; 1st cl. Hon. Mods 1927; 1st cl. Lit.Hum. 1929). Fellow of All Souls College, Oxford, 1929–49. Joined staff of Economic Advisory Council, 1931; Offices of War Cabinet, 1939; Principal Private Secretary to Right Honourable Oliver Lyttelton, when Minister of Production, 1943–45; Personal Assistant (for work on Atomic Energy) to Rt Hon. Sir John Anderson, when Chancellor of the Exchequer, 1945; transferred to Treasury, 1947; Principal Private Secretary to the Rt Hon. C. R. Attlee, when Prime Minister, 1950–51; Economic Minister, British Embassy, Washington, and Head of UK Treasury and Supply Delegation, 1951–54; Third Secretary, HM Treasury, 1955–60, Second Secretary, 1960–68. Vice-Pres., World Bank, 1968–74. *Recreations:* music, travel. *Address:* 9 The Close, Salisbury, Wilts SP1 2EB. *T:* Salisbury (0722) 20125.*Clubs:* Athenæum, Brooks's. *See also W. F. S. Rickett.*

RICKETT, Sir Raymond (Mildmay Wilson), Kt 1990; CBE 1984; BSc, PhD, CChem, FRSC; Director, Middlesex Polytechnic, 1972–91, retired; *b* 17 March 1927; *s* of

Mildmay Louis Rickett and Winifred Georgina Rickett; *m* 1958, Naomi Nishida; one *s* two *d*. *Educ:* Faversham Grammar Sch.; Medway Coll. of Technology (BSc London); Illinois Inst. of Technology (PhD). Royal Navy, 1946–48; Medway Coll. of Technology, 1953–55; Illinois Inst. of Technology, 1955–59; Plymouth Coll. of Technology, 1959; Lectr, Liverpool Coll. of Technology, 1960–62; Senr Lectr/Principal Lectr, West Ham Coll. of Technology, 1962–64; Head of Dept, Wolverhampton Coll. of Technology, 1965–66; Vice-Principal, Sir John Cass Coll., 1967–69; Vice-Provost, City of London Polytechnic, 1969–72. Chairman: Cttee of Dirs of Polytechnics, 1980–82 and 1986–88; UK Nat. Commn for UNESCO Educn Adv. Cttee, 1983–85; IUPC, 1988–; Cttee for Internat. Co-operation in Higher Educn, 1988–; UK Erasmus Students Grants Council, 1988–; CNAA, 1991–; Member: Oakes Cttee, 1977–78; Higher Educn Review Group for NI, 1978–82; NAB Bd, 1981–87; Open Univ. Council, 1983–; Council for Industry and Higher Educn, 1985–; British Council Bd, 1988–; Erasmus (EEC) Adv. Cttee, 1988–90. Governor, Yehudi Menuhin Live Music Now Scheme, 1977–. Officer's Cross, Order of Merit (FRG), 1988. *Publications:* Experiments in Physical Chemistry (jtly), 1962, new edn 1968; 2 chapters in The Use of the Chemical Literature, 1962, new edn 1969; articles on Polytechnics in the national press and contribs to learned jls. *Recreations:* cricket, theatre-going, opera. *Address:* 1 The Barn, Pontus Farm, Knockwood Lane, Molash, near Canterbury, Kent CT4 8HW. *Club:* Athenæum.

RICKETT, William Francis Sebastian; Director General, Energy Efficiency Office, Department of Energy, since 1990; *b* 23 Feb. 1953; *s* of Sir Denis Rickett, *qv*; *m* 1979, Lucy Caroline Clark; one *s* one *d*. *Educ:* Eton; Trinity Coll., Cambridge (BA 1974). Joined Department of Energy, 1975; Private Sec. to Perm. Under Sec. of State, 1977; Principal, 1978; Private Sec. to Prime Minister, 1981–83; seconded to Kleinwort Benson Ltd, 1983–85; Asst Sec., Oil Div., Dept of Energy, 1985; Asst Sec., Electricity Privatisation, 1987; Grade 4, Electricity Div., 1989; Under Sec., 1990. *Recreations:* playing with my children, painting, sports. *Address:* Department of Energy, 1 Palace Street, SW1E 5HE. *T:* 071–238 3000.

RICKETTS, Maj.-Gen. Abdy Henry Gough, CBE 1952; DSO 1945; *b* 8 Dec. 1905; *s* of Lt-Col P. E. Ricketts, DSO, MVO, and L. C. Ricketts (*née* Morant); *m* 1932, Joan Warre, *d* of E. T. Close, Camberley; one *s* one *d*. *Educ:* Winchester. Sandhurst, 1924; Durham LI, 1925; Shanghai Defence Force, 1927; NW Frontier, India (medal and clasp), 1930; Burma "Chindit" campaign, 1944–45; Gen. Service Medal and clasp, Malaya, 1950; comd British Brigade, Korea, 1952; Comdr (temp. Maj.-Gen.), Cyprus District, 1955–56. Col, Durham LI, 1965–68; Dep. Col, The Light Infantry (Durham), 1968–70. DL Somerset, 1968–90. Officer, Legion of Merit (USA), 1953. *Address:* The Old Rectory, Pylle, Shepton Mallet, Som BA4 6TE. *T:* Ditcheat (074986) 248.

RICKETTS, (Anne) Theresa, (Lady Ricketts), CBE 1983; Chairman, National Association of Citizens' Advice Bureaux, 1979–84; *b* 12 April 1919; *d* of late Rt Hon. Sir (Richard) Stafford Cripps, CH, FRS, QC, and Dame Isobel Cripps, GBE; *m* 1945, Sir Robert Ricketts, Bt, *qv*; two *s* two *d*. *Educ:* Oxford University. Second Officer, WRNS, War of 1939–45. Joined Citizens' Advice Bureaux Service, 1962. Member: Electricity Consumers' Council, 1977–90; Council, Direct Mail Services Standards Board, 1983–. *Recreations:* gardening, field botany. *Address:* Forwood House, Minchinhampton, Stroud, Glos GL6 9AB. *T:* Brimscombe (0453) 882160. *Club:* Commonwealth Trust.

See also Sir J. S. Cripps.

RICKETTS, Michael Rodney, MA; Headmaster, Sutton Valence School, 1967–80; *b* 29 Sept. 1923; *er s* of late Rt Rev. C. M. Ricketts, Bishop of Dunwich, and Dorothy Ricketts; *m* 1958, Judith Anne Caroline Corry; two *s* two *d*. *Educ:* Sherborne; Trinity Coll., Oxford. Served War of 1939–45: in 8th Army, Africa, Italy, with 60th Rifles, 1942–47. Trinity Coll., Oxford, 1947–50; Asst Master and Housemaster, Bradfield Coll., 1950–67. Dir, ISIS (Eastern England), 1980–; Nat. ISIS Management Cttee, 1981–. Member: HMC Cttee, 1976–79 (Chm., HMC/SHA Services Cttee, 1975–80); British Atlantic Cttee, 1974–, Council, 1979–; Chairman: British Atlantic Educn Cttee, 1984–87 (Mem., 1974–); Atlantic Educn Cttee, 1986–. Governor: Gresham's Sch.; Orwell Park; Vinehall. Fellow, Woodard Corp. *Recreations:* cricket, shooting, country activities. *Address:* Church Farm, Saxlingham, Holt, Norfolk NR25 7JY. *T:* Binham (032875) 307. *Clubs:* East India, Devonshire, Sports and Public Schools, Free Foresters, Harlequins, I Zingari, MCC; Vincent's (Oxford).

RICKETTS, Sir Robert (Cornwallis Gerald St Leger), 7th Bt, *cr* 1828; retired Solicitor; *b* 8 Nov. 1917; *s* of Sir Claude Albert Frederick Ricketts, 6th Bt, and Lilian Helen Gwendoline (*d* 1955), *o d* of Arthur M. Hill, late 5th Fusiliers; *S* father 1937; *m* 1945, Anne Theresa Cripps (*see* A. T. Ricketts); two *s* two *d*. *Educ:* Haileybury; Magdalene College, Cambridge (2nd Cl. Hons in History and Law, BA 1939, MA 1943). Served War of 1939–45 (Captain, Devon Regiment); Personal Assistant to Chief of Staff, Gibraltar, 1942–45; ADC to Lieutenant-Governor of Jersey, 1945–46. Formerly Partner in Wellington and Clifford. FRSA. Hon. Citizen, Mobile, USA, 1970. *Heir:* *s* Robert Tristram Ricketts [*b* 17 April 1946; *m* 1969, Ann, *yr d* of late E. W. C. Lewis, CB; one *s* one *d*]. *Address:* Forwood House, Minchinhampton, Stroud, Glos GL6 9AB. *TA* and *T:* Brimscombe (0453) 882160.

See also G. F. P. Mason.

RICKETTS, Theresa; *see* Ricketts, A. T.

RICKFORD, Jonathan Braithwaite Keevil; Director of Government Relations, British Telecommunications plc, since 1989; *b* 7 Dec. 1944; *s* of R. B. K. Rickford, MD, FRCS, FRCOG and of Dorothy Rickford (*née* Lathan); *m* 1968, Dora R. Sargant; one *s* two *d*. *Educ:* Sherborne School; Magdalen College, Oxford (BA (Jurisp.); BCL). Barrister, 1970–85; Solicitor, 1985–. Teaching Associate, Univ. of California Sch. of Law, 1968–69; Lectr in Law, LSE, 1969–72; Legal Asst, Dept of Trade, 1972–73; Senior Legal Assistant: Dept of Prices and Consumer Protection, 1974–76; Law Officers' Dept, Attorney General's Chambers, 1976–79; Dept of Trade and Industry (formerly Dept of Trade): Asst Solicitor (Company Law), 1979–82; Under Sec. (Legal), 1982–85; Solicitor, 1985–87; Solicitor and Chief Legal Advr, British Telecom, 1987–89. *Publications:* articles in learned jls. *Recreation:* sailing. *T:* (office) 071–356 5100. *Clubs:* Reform; Royal Dart Yacht.

RICKMAN, Prof. Geoffrey Edwin, FBA 1989; Professor of Roman History, University of St Andrews, since 1981; *b* 9 Oct. 1932; *s* of Charles Edwin Rickman and Ethel Ruth Mary (*née* Hill); *m* 1959, Ann Rosemary Wilson; one *s* one *d*. *Educ:* Peter Symonds' Sch., Winchester; Brasenose Coll., Oxford (MA, DipClassArchaeol, DPhil). FSA 1966. Henry Francis Pelham Student, British Sch. at Rome, 1958–59; Jun. Res. Fellow, The Queen's Coll., Oxford, 1959–62; University of St Andrews: Lectr in Ancient History, 1962–68; Sen. Lectr, 1968–81. Vis. Fellow, Brasenose Coll., Oxford, 1981; Mem., Faculty of Archaeol., History and Letters, British Sch. at Rome, 1979–87 (Chm., 1983–87). *Publications:* Roman Granaries and Storebuildings, 1971; The Corn Supply of Ancient Rome, 1980. *Recreations:* opera, swimming, walking beside the sea. *Address:* 56 Hepburn Gardens, St Andrews, Fife KY16 9DG. *T:* St Andrews (0334) 72063.

RICKS, Prof. Christopher Bruce, FBA 1975; Professor of English, Boston University, since 1986; *b* 18 Sept. 1933; *s* of James Bruce Ricks and Gabrielle Roszak; *m* 1st, 1956, Kirsten Jensen (marr. diss.); two *s* two *d*; 2nd, 1977, Judith Aronson; one *s* two *d*. *Educ:* King Alfred's Sch., Wantage; Balliol Coll., Oxford (Hon. Fellow, 1989). 2nd Lieut, Green Howards, 1952. BA 1956, BLitt 1958, MA 1960, Oxon. Andrew Bradley Jun. Res. Fellow, Balliol Coll., Oxford, 1957; Fellow of Worcester Coll., Oxford, 1958–68 (Hon. Fellow, 1990); Prof. of English, Bristol Univ., 1968–75; University of Cambridge: Prof. of English, 1975–82; King Edward VII Prof. of English Lit., 1982–86; Fellow, Christ's Coll., 1975–86. Visiting Professor: Berkeley and Stanford, 1965; Smith Coll., 1967; Harvard, 1971; Wesleyan, 1974; Brandeis, 1977, 1981, 1984. Lectures: Lord Northcliffe, UCL, 1972; Alexander, Univ. of Toronto, 1987; T. S. Eliot, Univ. of Kent, 1988; Clarendon, Univ. of Oxford, 1990; Clark, Trinity Coll., Cambridge, 1991. A Vice-Pres., Tennyson Soc. Co-editor, Essays in Criticism. Fellow, American Acad. of Arts and Scis, 1991. George Orwell Meml Prize, 1979; Beefeater Club Prize for Literature, 1980. *Publications:* Milton's Grand Style, 1963; (ed) The Poems of Tennyson, 1969, rev. edn 1987; Tennyson, 1972, rev. edn 1989; Keats and Embarrassment, 1974; (ed with Leonard Michaels) The State of the Language, 1980, new edn 1990; The Force of Poetry, 1984; (ed) The New Oxford Book of Victorian Verse, 1987; (ed) A. E. Housman: Collected Poems and Selected Prose, 1988; T. S. Eliot and Prejudice, 1988. *Address:* 39 Martin Street, Cambridge, Mass 02138, USA. *T:* 617–354–7887; Lasborough Cottage, Lasborough Park, near Tetbury, Glos GL8 8UF. *T:* Leighterton (0666) 7890252.

RICKS, David Trulock, OBE 1981; British Council Director, France, and Cultural Counsellor, British Embassy, Paris, since 1990; *b* 28 June 1936; *s* of Percival Trulock Ricks and Annetta Helen (*née* Hood); *m* 1960, Nicole Estelle Aimée Chupeau; two *s*. *Educ:* Kilburn Grammar Sch.; Royal Acad. of Music; Merton Coll., Oxford (MA); Univ. of London Inst. of Educn; Univ. of Lille (LèsL). Teaching in Britain, 1960–67; joined British Council, 1967: Rabat, 1967–70; Univ. of Essex, 1970–71; Jaipur, 1971–74, New Delhi, 1974; Dar Es Salaam, 1974–76; Tehran, 1976–80; London, 1980–85; Rep., Italy, and Cultural Counsellor, British Embassy, Rome, 1985–90. FRSA 1989. *Publication:* (jtly) Penguin French Reader, 1967. *Recreations:* music, playing the piano, ski-ing. *Address:* c/o The British Council, 10 Spring Gardens, SW1A 2BN. *T:* 071–930 8466. *Club:* United Oxford & Cambridge University.

RICKS, Sir John (Plowman), Kt 1964; Solicitor to the Post Office, 1953–72; *b* 3 April 1910; *s* of late James Young Ricks; *m* 1st, 1936, May Celia (*d* 1975), *d* of late Robert William Chubb; three *s*; 2nd, 1976, Mrs Doreen Ilsley. *Educ:* Christ's Hosp.; Jesus Coll., Oxford. Admitted Solicitor, 1935; entered Post Office Solicitor's Department, 1935; Assistant Solicitor, Post Office, 1951. *Address:* 8 Sunset View, Barnet, Herts EN5 4LB. *T:* 081–449 6114.

See also R. N. Ricks.

RICKS, Robert Neville; Legal Adviser, Department of Education and Science, since 1990; *b* 29 June 1942; *s* of Sir John Plowman Ricks, *qv*. *Educ:* Highgate Sch.; Worcester Coll., Oxford (MA). Admitted Solicitor, 1967. Entered Treasury Solicitor's Dept as Legal Asst, 1969; Sen. Legal Asst, 1973; Asst Solicitor, 1981; Prin. Asst Solicitor, 1986. *Recreations:* collecting original cartoons, wine. *Address:* 2 Eaton Terrace, Aberavon Road, E3 5AJ. *T:* 081–981 3722. *Club:* United Oxford & Cambridge University.

RICKUS, Gwenneth Margaret, CBE 1981; Director of Education, London Borough of Brent, 1971–84; *b* 1925; *d* of Leonard William Ernest and Florence Rickus. *Educ:* Latymer Sch., Edmonton; King's Coll., Univ. of London. BA, PGCE. Teaching, 1948–53; Asst Sec., AAM, 1953–61; Education Administration: Mddx CC, 1961–65; London Borough of Brent, 1965–84. Cllr, New Forest DC, 1991–. Co-opted Mem. Educn Cttee, Hampshire CC, 1985–. Comr for Racial Equality, 1977–80. *Recreations:* walking, reading, crafts, gardening, music, politics.

RIDD, John William Gregory; HM Diplomatic Service; Foreign and Commonwealth Office, 1978–91; *b* 4 June 1931; *s* of William John and Lilian Gregory Cooke; adoptive *s* of Philip and Elizabeth Anne Ridd; *m* 1956, Mary Elizabeth Choat; three *s* one *d*. *Educ:* Lewis' Sch., Pengam; Wallington County Grammar Sch.; St Edmund Hall, Oxford (BA Hons 1954). National Service, 1949–51 (Army). Foreign Office, 1954; Buenos Aires, 1957–61; First Sec., Cairo, 1963–66, Prague, 1968–70, Brasilia, 1974–77; First Sec., later Counsellor, FCO, 1978–91. *Recreations:* books, distance running, allotment gardening, travel, music, singing.

RIDDELL, Sir John (Charles Buchanan), 13th Bt, *cr* 1628; CVO 1990; CA; DL; Extra Equerry to HRH the Prince of Wales, since 1990; Deputy Chairman, Credit Suisse First Boston Ltd, since 1990 (Director, 1978–85); *b* 3 Jan. 1934; *o s* of Sir Walter Buchanan Riddell, 12th Bt, and Hon. Rachel Beatrice Lyttelton (*d* 1965), *y d* of 8th Viscount Cobham; *S* father 1934; *m* 1969, Hon. Sarah, *o d* of Baron Richardson of Duntisbourne, *qv*; three *s*. *Educ:* Eton; Christ Church, Oxford. 2nd Lieut Rifle Bde, 1952–54. With IBRD, Washington DC, 1969–71; Associate, First Boston Corp., 1972–75; Director: First Boston (Europe) Ltd, 1975–78; UK Provident Instn, 1975–85; Northern Rock Bldg Soc., 1981–85, 1990–. Dep Chm., IBA, 1981–85; Private Sec., 1985–90, and Treasurer, 1986–90, to TRH the Prince and Princess of Wales; Member, Prince's Council, 1985–90. Contested (C): Durham NW, Feb. 1974; Sunderland S, Oct. 1974. Mem., Bloomsbury DHA, 1982–85; Trustee, Buttle Trust, 1981–87. FRSA 1990. DL Northumberland, 1990. *Heir:* *s* Walter John Buchanan Riddell, *b* 10 June 1974. *Address:* Hepple, Morpeth, Northumberland. *TA:* Hepple; 49 Campden Hill Square, W8 7JR. *Clubs:* Garrick; Northern Counties (Newcastle upon Tyne).

See also R. L. Ollard, Sir J. L. Pumphrey.

RIDDELL-WEBSTER, John Alexander, MC 1943; farmer; Member (C) Tayside Regional Council, since 1986; *b* 17 July 1921; *s* of Gen. Sir Thomas Riddell-Webster, GCB, DSO; *m* 1960, Ruth, *d* of late S. P. L. A. Lithgow; two *s* one *d*. *Educ:* Harrow; Pembroke Coll., Cambridge. Seaforth Highlanders (Major), 1940–46. Joined Anglo-Iranian Oil Co., 1946; served in Iran, Iraq, Bahrain, Aden; Vice-Pres. Marketing, BP Canada, 1959; Dir, Shell-Mex and BP, 1965, Man. Dir, Marketing, 1971–75; Dir, BP Oil Ltd, 1975–82 (Dep. Man. Dir, 1976–80); Dir, Public Affairs, Scotland, BP, 1979–81. Mem. Cttee, AA, 1980–90; Mem. Exec. Cttee, Scottish Council (Develt and Industry), 1981–84; Member of Council: Advertising Assoc., 1974–80; Inc. Soc. of British Advertisers, 1968–80; for Vehicle Servicing and Repair, 1972–80 (Chm., 1975); Royal Warrant Holders' Assoc. (Vice-Pres., 1979; Pres., 1980); British Road Fedn, 1971–80; Chm., Transport Action Scotland, 1982–; Pres., Oil Industries Club, 1977–78. CBIM. *Recreations:* shooting, fishing, gardening. *Address:* Lintrose, Coupar Angus, Perthshire. *T:* Coupar Angus (0828) 27472. *Clubs:* New (Edinburgh); Royal Perth Golfing Society.

RIDDELSDELL, Dame Mildred, DCB 1972; CBE 1958; Second Permanent Secretary, Department of Health and Social Security, 1971–73; (Deputy Secretary, 1966–71); *b* 1 Dec. 1913; 2nd *d* of Rev. H. J. Riddelsdell. *Educ:* St Mary's Hall, Brighton; Bedford Coll., London. Entered Min. of Labour, 1936; Asst Sec., Min. of National Insurance, 1945; Under Secretary, 1950; On loan to United Nations, 1953–56; Secretary, National Incomes Commission, 1962–65; Ministry of Pensions and National Insurance, 1965,

Social Security, 1966. Chm., CS Retirement Fellowship, 1974–77. *Recreation:* gardening. *Address:* 26A New Yatt Road, Witney, Oxon.

RIDDICK, Graham Edward Galloway; MP (C) Colne Valley, since 1987; *b* 26 Aug. 1955; *s* of John Julian Riddick and late Cecilia Margaret Riddick (*née* Ruggles-Brise); *m* 1988, Sarah Northcroft; one *s*. *Educ:* Stowe Sch., Buckingham; Univ. of Warwick (Chm., Warwick Univ. Cons. Assoc.). Sales management with Procter & Gamble, 1977–82; Coca-Cola, 1982–87. PPS to Financial Sec. to HM Treasury, 1990–. Secretary: Cons. Employment Cttee, 1988–90; All Party Textiles Gp, 1988–. Chm., Angola Study Gp, 1988–; Mem. Nat. Council, Freedom Assoc, 1988–. First Cons. MP in Colne Valley for 102 years. *Recreations:* people, fishing, shooting, sports. *Address:* House of Commons, SW1A 0AA. *T:* 071–219 4215. *Clubs:* Carlton; Yorkshire Cricket.

RIDDLE, Hugh Joseph, (Huseph), RP 1960; Artist; Portrait Painter; *b* 24 May 1912; *s* of late Hugh Howard Riddle and late Christine Simons Brown; *m* 1936, Joan Claudia Johnson; one *s* two *d*. *Educ:* Harrow; Magdalen, Oxford; Slade School of Art; Byam Shaw School of Art and others. *Recreations:* sailing, ski-ing, swimming, tennis, golf. *Address:* 18 Boulevard Verdi, Domaine du château de Tournon, Montauroux 83440, France.

RIDEOUT, Prof. Roger William; Professor of Labour Law, University College, London, since 1973; *b* 9 Jan. 1935; *s* of Sidney and Hilda Rideout; *m* 1st, 1959, Marjorie Roberts (marr. diss. 1976); one *d*; 2nd, 1977, Gillian Margaret Lynch. *Educ:* Bedford School; University Coll., London (LLB, PhD). Called to the Bar, Gray's Inn, 1964. National Service, 1958–60; 2nd Lt RAEC, Educn Officer, 1st Bn Coldstream Guards. Lecturer: Univ. of Sheffield, 1960–63; Univ. of Bristol, 1963–64. University Coll., London: Sen. Lectr, 1964–65; Reader, 1965–73; Dean of Faculty of Laws, 1975–77. Dep. Chairman: Central Arbitration Cttee; Industrial Tribunals. ACAS panel arbitrator, 1981–; Vice-Pres., Industrial Law Society. Mem., Zool Soc. of London. Jt Editor, Current Legal Problems, 1975–; Gen. Editor, Federation News, 1989–. *Publications:* The Right to Membership of a Trade Union, 1962; The Practice and Procedure of the NIRC, 1973; Trade Unions and the Law, 1973; Principles of Labour Law, 1972, 5th edn 1989. *Address:* 255 Chipstead Way, Woodmansterne, Surrey. *T:* Downland (0737) 552033. *Club:* MCC.

RIDGE, Anthony Hubert; Director-General, International Bureau, Universal Postal Union, Bern, 1973–74 (Deputy Director-General, 1964–73); *b* 5 Oct. 1913; *s* of Timothy Leopold Ridge and Magdalen (*née* Hernig); *m* 1938, Marjory Joan Sage; three *s* one *d*. *Educ:* Christ's Hospital; Jesus College, Cambridge. Entered GPO, 1937; seconded to Min. Home Security, 1940; GPO Personnel Dept, 1944; PPS to Postmaster General, 1947; Dep. Dir, London Postal Region, 1949; Asst Sec., Overseas Mails, 1951, Personnel, 1954, Overseas Mails, 1956; Director of Clerical Mechanization and Buildings, and Member of Post Office Board, GPO, 1960–63. Mem., Postling Parish Council, 1979–87. Governor, Christ's Hosp. *Recreations:* music, languages, transport, gardening, two donkeys. *Address:* Staple, Postling, Hythe, Kent CT21 4HA. *T:* Lyminge (0303) 862315. *Clubs:* Christ's Hospital, United Oxford & Cambridge University, Cambridge Society.

RIDGERS, John Nalton Sharpe; Deputy Chairman and Treasurer, Lloyd's Register of Shipping, 1973–78; Director: Smit International (UK) Ltd, 1974–84; *b* 10 June 1910; 4th *c* and *o s* of Sharpe Ridgers; *m* 1936, Barbara Mary, *o d* of Robert Cobb; five *d*. *Educ:* Wellington College. Entered Lloyd's, 1928; underwriting member, 1932. Member Cttee Lloyd's Underwriters' Association, 1951–61, 1964–69, Chm. 1961; Member Joint Hull Cttee, 1957–69, Dep. Chm., 1968, Chm., 1969. Mem. Cttee of Lloyd's, 1957–60, 1962–65, Dep. Chm., 1962, Chm., 1963. Director: London Trust Co. Ltd, 1963–80; Arbuthnot Insurance Services Ltd, 1974–80; Danae Investment Trust Ltd, 1975–80. *Recreations:* snooker, carpentry. *Address:* Little Watlynge, 4 Chestnut Lane, Sevenoaks, Kent TN13 3AR.

RIDGWAY, Gen. Matthew Bunker, DSC (with Oak Leaf Cluster); DSM (with 3rd Oak Leaf Cluster); Silver Star (with Oak Leaf Cluster); Legion of Merit; Bronze Star Medal V (with Oak Leaf Cluster); Purple Heart; Hon. KCB 1955 (Hon. CB 1945); Chairman of The Mellon Institute of Industrial Research 1955–60, retired; *b* 3 March 1895; *s* of Thomas Ridgway and Ruth Starbuck Bunker; *m* 1st, 1917; two *d*; 2nd, 1930; one *d*; 3rd, 1947, Mary Anthony; (one *s* decd). *Educ:* United States Military Academy, 1913–17. Inf. School (Company Officers' Course), 1924–25; Mem. Am. Electoral Commn, Nicaragua, 1927–28; Mem. Commn on Bolivian-Paraguayan boundary dispute, 1929; Inf. School (Advanced Course), 1929–30; Liaison Officer to Govt in Philippine Is, Tech. Adviser to Gov.-Gen., 1932–33; Comd and Gen. Staff School, 1933–35; Asst Chief of Staff, 6th Corps Area, 1935–36; Dep. Chief of Staff, Second Army, 1936; Army War College, 1936–37; Assistant Chief of Staff, Fourth Army, 1937–39; accompanied Gen. Marshall on special mission to Brazil, 1939; War Plans Div., War Department Gen. Staff, 1939–42; Asst Div. Comdr, 82nd Inf. Div., 1942; Comdr 1942; Comdg Gen. 82nd Airborne Div., Sicily, Italy, Normandy, 1942–44; Comdr 18th Airborne Corps, Belgium, France, Germany, 1944–45; Comdr Luzon Area Command, 1945; Comdr Medit. Theater, and Dep. Supreme Allied Comdr, Medit., 1945–46; Senior US Army Member Military Staff Cttee, UN, 1946–48; Chm. Inter-Am. Defense Bd, 1946–48; C-in-C Caribbean Command, 1948–49; Dep. Army Chief of Staff for Admin., 1949–50 (and Chm. Inter-Am. Defense Bd, 1950); Comdg Gen. Eighth Army in Korea, 1950–51; Comdr UN Comd in Far East, C-in-C of Far East Comd and Supreme Comdr for Allied Powers in Japan, 1951–52; Supreme Allied Comdr, Europe, 1952–53; Chief of Staff, United States Army, 1953–55, retired. Holds many American and foreign decorations.

RIDLER, Anne (Barbara); author; *b* 30 July 1912; *o d* of late H. C. Bradby, housemaster of Rugby School, and Violet Milford; *m* 1938, Vivian Ridler, *qv*; two *s* two *d*. *Educ:* Downe House School; King's College, London; and in Florence and Rome. *Publications: poems:* Poems, 1939; A Dream Observed, 1941; The Nine Bright Shiners, 1943; The Golden Bird, 1951; A Matter of Life and Death, 1959; Selected Poems (New York), 1961; Some Time After, 1972; (contrib.) Ten Oxford Poets, 1978; New and Selected Poems, 1988; *plays:* Cain, 1943; The Shadow Factory, 1946; Henry Bly and other plays, 1950; The Trial of Thomas Cranmer, 1956; Who is my Neighbour?, 1963; The Jesse Tree (libretto), 1972; The King of the Golden River (libretto), 1975; The Lambton Worm (libretto), 1978; *translations:* Italian opera libretti: Rosinda, 1973; Orfeo, 1975; Eritrea, 1975; Return of Ulysses, 1978; Orontea, 1979; Agrippina, 1981; Calisto, 1984; Così fan Tutte, 1986; Don Giovanni, 1990; Marriage of Figaro, 1991; *biography:* Olive Willis and Downe House, 1967; *edited:* Shakespeare Criticism, 1919–35; A Little Book of Modern Verse, 1941; Best Ghost Stories, 1945; Supplement to Faber Book of Modern Verse, 1951; The Image of the City and other essays by Charles Williams, 1958; Shakespeare Criticism 1935–60, 1963; Poems of James Thomson, 1963; Thomas Traherne, 1966; (with Christopher Bradby) Best Stories of Church and Clergy, 1966; Selected Poems of George Darley, 1979; Poems of William Austin, 1983; A Victorian Family Postbag, 1988; (jtly) Profitable Wonders: aspects of Traherne, 1989; A Measure of English Poetry, 1991. *Recreations:* music; the theatre; the cinema. *Address:* 14 Stanley Road, Oxford OX4 1QZ. *T:* Oxford (0865) 247595.

RIDLER, Vivian Hughes, CBE 1971; MA Oxon 1958 (by decree; Corpus Christi College); Printer to the University of Oxford, 1958–78; *b* 2 Oct. 1913; *s* of Bertram Hughes Ridler and Elizabeth Emmeline (*née* Best); *m* 1938, Anne Barbara Bradby (*see* A. B. Ridler); two *s* two *d*. *Educ:* Bristol Gram. Sch. Appren. E. S. & A. Robinson, Ltd, 1931–36. Works Manager University Press, Oxford, 1948; Assistant Printer, 1949–58. Pres., British Federation of Master Printers, 1968–69. Professorial Fellow, St Edmund Hall, 1966, Emeritus Fellow, 1978. *Recreations:* printing, theatre, cinema, cinematography. *Address:* 14 Stanley Road, Oxford OX4 1QZ. *T:* Oxford (0865) 247595.

RIDLEY, family name of **Viscount Ridley.**

RIDLEY, 4th Viscount, *cr* 1900; **Matthew White Ridley,** TD 1960; JP; DL; Baron Wensleydale, *cr* 1900; Bt 1756; Lord-Lieutenant and Custos Rotulorum of Northumberland, since 1984; Chancellor, University of Newcastle, since 1989; Lord Steward of HM Household, since 1989; *b* 29 July 1925; *e s* of 3rd Viscount Ridley; *S* father, 1964; *m* 1953, Lady Anne Lumley, 3rd *d* of 11th Earl of Scarbrough, KG, PC, GCSI, GCIE, GCVO; one *s* three *d*. *Educ:* Eton; Balliol College, Oxford. ARICS 1951. Coldstream Guards (NW Europe), 1943–46, Captain, 1946; Second Northumberland Hussars, 1947–64 (Lt-Col 1961, Bt Col 1964); Bt-Col Northumberland Hussars (TA); Hon. Colonel: Northumberland Hussars Sqdn, Queen's Own Yeomanry, 1979–86; Queen's Own Yeomanry RAC TA, 1984–86; Northumbrian Univs OTC, 1986–90; Col Comdt, Yeomanry RAC TA, 1982–86. Chm., Northern Rock Building Soc., 1987–; Dir, Municipal Mutual Insurance; formerly Director: Tyne Tees Television; Barclays Bank (NE) Ltd. Pres., British Deer Soc., 1970–73. Member: Layfield Cttee of Enquiry into Local Govt Finance, 1974–; Commonwealth War Graves Commn, 1991–. Chm., N of England TA Assoc., 1980–84; Pres., TA & VRA Council, 1984–. Chm., Newcastle Univ. Develt. Trust, 1981–84; Hon. Fellow, Newcastle upon Tyne Polytechnic, 1980; Hon. FRHS 1986; Hon. FRICS 1986. JP 1957, CC 1958, CA 1963, DL 1968, Northumberland; Chm., Northumberland CC, 1967–74, Chm., new Northumberland CC, 1974–79; Pres., ACC, 1979–84. KStJ 1984; Hon. DCL Newcastle, 1989. Order of Merit, West Germany, 1974. *Heir: s* Hon. Matthew White Ridley, *b* 7 Feb. 1958; *m* 1989, Dr Anya Hurlbert, *d* of Dr Robert Hurlbert, Houston, Texas. *Address:* Blagdon, Seaton Burn, Newcastle upon Tyne NE13 6DD. *T:* Stannington 789236. *Clubs:* Turf, Pratt's; Northern Counties (Newcastle upon Tyne).

See also Rt Hon. Nicholas Ridley.

RIDLEY, Sir Adam (Nicholas), Kt 1985; Executive Director, Hambros Bank PLC, since 1985; *b* 14 May 1942; *s* of Jasper Maurice Alexander Ridley and Helen Cressida Ridley (*née* Bonham Carter); *m* 1981, Margaret Anne Passmore; three *s* (inc. twin *s*). *Educ:* Eton Coll.; Balliol Coll., Oxford (1st cl. hons PPE 1965); Univ. of California, Berkeley. Foreign Office, 1965, seconded to DEA, 1965–68; Harkness Fellow, Univ. of California, Berkeley, 1968–69; HM Treasury, 1970–71, seconded to CPRS, 1971–74; Economic Advr to shadow cabinet and Asst Dir, Cons. Res. Dept, 1974–79; Special Advr to Chancellor of the Exchequer, 1979–84, to Chancellor of the Duchy of Lancaster, 1985. *Publications:* articles on regional policy, public spending, international economics. *Recreations:* music, painting, travel. *Address:* c/o Hambros Bank, 41 Bishopsgate, EC2P 2AA. *Club:* Garrick.

RIDLEY, Dame Betty; *see* Ridley, Dame M. B.

RIDLEY, Edward Alexander Keane, CB 1963; Principal Assistant Solicitor, Treasury Solicitor's Department, 1956–69, retired; *b* 16 April 1904; *s* of late Major Edward Keane Ridley, Dudswell House, near Berkhamsted, Herts, and late Ethel Janet Ridley, *d* of Alexander Forbes Tweedie; unmarried. *Educ:* Wellington College; Keble College, Oxford. Admitted Solicitor, 1928. Entered Treasury Solicitor's Department, 1934. Hon. RCM 1977. *Publications:* Wind Instruments of European Art Music, 1975; Catalogue of Wind Instruments in the Museum of the Royal College of Music, 1982. *Recreation:* music. *Address:* c/o Coutts & Co., 440 Strand, WC2.

RIDLEY, Prof. Frederick Fernand, OBE 1978; PhD; Professor of Political Theory and Institutions, University of Liverpool, since 1965; *b* 11 Aug. 1928; *s* of late J. and G. A. Ridley; *m* 1967, Paula Frances Cooper Ridley, *qv*; two *s* one *d*. *Educ:* The Hall, Hampstead; Highgate Sch.; LSE (BScEcon, PhD); Univs of Paris and Berlin. Lectr, Univ. of Liverpool, 1958–65. Vis. Professor: Graduate Sch. of Public Affairs, Univ. of Pittsburgh, 1968; Coll. of Europe, Bruges, 1975–83. Manpower Services Commission, Merseyside: Chm., Job Creation Prog., 1975–77; Vice-Chm., 1978–87, Chm., 1987–88, Area Manpower Bd. Member: Jt Univ. Council for Social and Public Admin, 1964– (Chm., 1972–74); Exec., Polit. Studies Assoc., 1967–75; Council, Hansard Soc., 1970–; Polit. Science Cttee, SSRC, 1972–76; Cttee, European Gp on Public Admin, 1973–; Public and Social Admin Bd, CNAA, 1975–82; Social Studies Res. Cttee, CNAA, 1980–83 (Chm.); Academic Cttee, Assoc. Internat. de la Fonction Publique, 1988–; Vice Pres., Rencontres Européennes des Fonctions Publiques, 1990–. Member: Res. Adv. Gp, Arts Council, 1979–82; Exec., Merseyside Arts (RAA), 1979–84; Adv. Council, Granada Foundn, 1984–; Trustee, Friends of Merseyside Museums and Galleries, 1977–85. Hon. Pres., Politics Assoc., 1976–81. Editor: Political Studies, 1969–75; Parliamentary Affairs, 1975–. *Publications:* Public Administration in France, 1964; (ed) Specialists and Generalists, 1968; Revolutionary Syndicalism in France, 1970; The Study of Government, 1975; (ed) Studies in Politics, 1975; (ed) Government and Administration in W Europe, 1979; (ed) Policies and Politics in W Europe, 1984; numerous articles on political sci. and public admin. *Address:* Riversdale House, Grassendale Park, Liverpool L19 0LR. *T:* 051–427 1630.

RIDLEY, Gordon, OBE 1980; MA; FICE, FIHT; retired; Director of Planning and Transportation, Greater London Council, 1978–80; *b* 1 Nov. 1921; *s* of Timothy Ridley and Lallah Sarah Ridley; *m* 1952, Doreen May Browning; one *s* one *d*. *Educ:* Selwyn Coll., Cambridge (MA). FICE 1965; FIMunE 1964; FInstHE 1966. Served War, Admiralty Signals Estab., 1941–46. Engrg appts, various local authorities, 1946–55; Bridges Br., MoT, 1955–58; AEA, 1958–63; LCC, 1963–65; engrg appts, GLC, 1965–78. *Publications:* papers on engrg topics presented to learned instns. *Recreations:* words, walking, photography. *Address:* 26 Greenacres, Preston Park Avenue, Brighton BN1 6HR. *T:* Brighton (0273) 559951.

RIDLEY, Harold; *see* Ridley, N. H. L.

RIDLEY, Jasper Godwin; author; *b* 25 May 1920; *s* of Geoffrey Ridley and Ursula (*née* King); *m* 1949, Vera, *d* of Emil Pollak; two *s* one *d*. *Educ:* Felcourt Sch.; Sorbonne, Paris; Magdalen Coll., Oxford. Certif. of Honour, Bar Finals. Called to Bar, Inner Temple, 1945. St Pancras Borough Council, 1945–49. Pres., Hardwicke Soc., 1954–55. Contested (Lab): Winchester, 1955; Westbury, 1959. Vice-Pres. for life, English Centre of Internat. PEN, 1985. Mem. Ct of Assts, Carpenters' Co. (Master, 1988–89, 1990–91). Has written many radio scripts on historical subjects. FRSL 1963. *Publications:* Nicholas Ridley, 1957; The Law of Carriage of Goods, 1957; Thomas Cranmer, 1962; John Knox, 1968; Lord Palmerston, 1970 (James Tait Black Meml Prize, 1970); Mary Tudor, 1973; Garibaldi, 1974; The Roundheads, 1976; Napoleon III and Eugénie, 1979; History of England, 1981; The Statesman and the Fanatic: Thomas Wolsey and Thomas More, 1982; Henry VIII, 1984; Elizabeth I, 1987; The Tudor Age, 1988; The Love Letters of Henry VIII,

1989. *Recreations:* walking, tennis, chess. *Address:* 6 Oakdale Road, Tunbridge Wells, Kent TN4 8DS. *T:* Tunbridge Wells (0892) 522460.

RIDLEY, Michael; *see* Ridley, R. M.

RIDLEY, Michael Kershaw; Clerk of the Council, Duchy of Lancaster, since 1981; *b* 7 Dec. 1937; *s* of George K. and Mary Ridley; *m* 1968, Diana Loraine McLernon; two *s*. *Educ:* Stowe; Magdalene College, Cambridge. MA. FRICS. Grosvenor Estate, Canada and USA, 1965–69, London, 1969–72; Property Manager, British & Commonwealth Shipping Co., 1972–81. A Gen. Comr of Income Tax, 1984–. Mem., Adv. Panel, Greenwich Hosp., 1978–. Mem. Court, Lancaster Univ., 1981–. *Recreation:* golf. *Address:* Duchy of Lancaster Office, 1 Lancaster Place, Strand, WC2E 7ED. *Club:* Royal Mid-Surrey Golf.

RIDLEY, Dame (Mildred) Betty, DBE 1975; MA (Lambeth) 1958; Third Church Estates Commissioner, 1972–81; a Church Commissioner, 1959–81; *b* 10 Sept. 1909; *d* of late Rt Rev. Henry Mosley, sometime Bishop of Southwell; *m* 1929, Rev. Michael Ridley (*d* 1953), Rector of Finchley; three *s* one *d*. *Educ:* North London Collegiate School; Cheltenham Ladies' College. Member: General Synod of Church of England, 1970–81, and its Standing Cttee, 1971–81; Central Board of Finance, 1955–79; Mem., Faculty Jurisdiction Commn, 1980–83; Vice-Pres. British Council of Churches, 1954–56. Governor, King Alfred's Coll., Winchester, 1985–. FRSA 1981. *Recreation:* listening to music. *Address:* 6 Lions Hall, St Swithun Street, Winchester SO23 9HW. *T:* Winchester (0962) 855009. *Club:* Reform.

RIDLEY, Rt. Hon. Nicholas, PC 1983; MP (C) Cirencester and Tewkesbury Division of Gloucestershire, since 1959; *b* 17 Feb. 1929; *yr s* of 3rd Viscount Ridley, CBE, TD; *m* 1st, 1950, Hon. Clayre Campbell (marr. diss. 1974), 2nd *d* of 4th Baron Stratheden and Campbell, CBE; three *d*; 2nd, 1979, Judy Kendall. *Educ:* Eton; Balliol College, Oxford. Civil Engineering Contractor, Brims & Co. Ltd, Newcastle upon Tyne, 1950–59, Director, 1954–70; Director: Heenan Group Ltd, 1961–68; Ausonia Finance, 1973–79; Marshall Andrew Ltd, 1975–79. Contested (C) Blyth, Gen. Election, 1955; PPS to Minister of Education, 1962–64; Delegate to Council of Europe and WEU, 1962–66; Parly Sec., Min. of Technology, June-Oct. 1970; Parly Under-Sec. of State, DTI, 1970–72; Minister of State, FCO, 1979–81; Financial Sec. to HM Treasury, 1981–83; Secretary of State: for Transport, 1983–86; for the Envmt, 1986–89; for Trade and Industry, 1989–90. Mem., Royal Commn on Historical Manuscripts, 1967–79. *Publication:* My Style of Government: the Thatcher years, 1991. *Recreations:* painting, architecture, gardening, fishing. *Address:* Old Rectory, Naunton, Cheltenham, Glos GL54 3AT; House of Commons, SW1A 0AA.

RIDLEY, (Nicholas) Harold (Lloyd), MD; FRCS; FRS 1986; Hon. Consultant Surgeon, Moorfields Eye Hospital, 1971 (Surgeon, 1938–71); Hon. Consultant Surgeon, Ophthalmic Department, St Thomas' Hospital, 1971 (Ophthalmic Surgeon, 1946–71); *b* 10 July 1906; *s* of late N. C. Ridley, MB (London), FRCS, Royal Navy retired, Leicester; *m* 1941, Elisabeth Jane, *d* of late H. B. Wetherill, CIE; two *s* one *d*. *Educ:* Charterhouse; Pembroke Coll., Cambridge; St Thomas' Hospital, London. MB 1931, MD 1946, Cambridge; FRCS 1932; Hon. FCOphth 1989. Originator in 1949 of intraocular implants. Late Hon. Ophthalmic Surgeon, Royal Buckinghamshire Hospital. Temp. Major, RAMC. Hon. Cons. in Ophthalmology to Min. of Defence (Army), 1964–71; Life Pres., Internat. Intraocular Implants Club, 1972; late Vice-Pres., Ophthalmological Soc. of UK; Mem. Advisory Panel, WHO, 1966–71; Hon. Mem., Oxford Ophthalmological Congress. Hon. Fellow International College of Surgeons, Chicago, 1952; Hon. FRSM 1986; Hon. Member: Peruvian Ophthalmic Society, 1957; Ophthalmological Society of Australia, 1963; Irish Ophthalmological Society; Ophthalmological Soc. of UK, 1984; Amer. Intraocular Implants Soc., 1974; European Intra-Ocular Implantlens Council, 1983. Hon. LHD Med. Univ. of SC, 1989. Galen Medal, Apothecaries' Soc., 1986; Lord Crook Gold Medal, Spectacle Makers' Co., 1987. *Publications:* Monograph on Ocular Onchocerciasis; numerous contrib. in textbooks and medical journals on intraocular implant surgery and other subjects. *Recreation:* fly-fishing. *Address:* Keeper's Cottage, Stapleford, Salisbury, Wilts SP3 4LT. *T:* Salisbury (0722) 790209. *Club:* Flyfishers'.

RIDLEY, Paula Frances Cooper, JP; DL; MA; Associate Editor, Granada Action; Consultant, BAT Industries Small Businesses Ltd; Trustee, Tate Gallery, since 1988; *b* 27 Sept. 1944; *d* of Ondrej Clyne and Ellen (*née* Cooper); *m* 1967, Frederick Fernand Ridley, *qv*; two *s* one *d*. *Educ:* Kendal High Sch., Westmorland; Univ. of Liverpool. BA, MA; Lady Pres., Guild of Undergraduates. Standing Cttee of Convocation, Univ. of Liverpool, 1966–74 (Clerk of Convocation, 1972–74); Mem., Univ. Court, 1972–. Lectr in Politics and Public Admin., Liverpool Polytechnic, 1966–71; Proj. Coordinator, Regeneration Projects Ltd, 1981–84; Director: Community Initiatives Res. Trust, 1983–90; New Enterprise Workshops (Toxteth) Ltd, 1984–; Associate, CEI Consultants, 1984–88. Mem., IBA for Radio in Liverpool, 1975–78; Authority Mem., IBA, 1982–88. Chm., Tate Gall. Liverpool Adv. Cttee, 1988–; Member: Governing Body, Stocktonwood County Primary Sch., 1970–81 (Chm., 1976–79); Liverpool Heritage Bureau, 1971–88; Management Cttee, Liverpool Victoria Settlement, 1971–86 (Vice-Chm., 1977–86); Barnardo's Intermediate Treatment Adv. Gp in Liverpool, 1980–86; Council, Liverpool and Huyton Colls, 1979– (Life Governor); Cttee of Friends of Merseyside Maritime Mus., 1980–82; Merseyside Enterprise Forum, 1986–89; Mersey Partnership, 1989–; Granada Telethon Trust, 1988–. Merseyside Civic Society: Hon. Sec., 1971–82; Vice-Chm., 1982–86; Chm., 1986–. JP Liverpool, 1977; Juvenile Panel, 1979–; Jt Cttee, Juv. Panel and Educn and Social Services Cttees, Liverpool City Council, 1981–88. DL Merseyside, 1989. FRSA. *Address:* Riversdale House, Grassendale Park, Liverpool L19 0LR. *T:* 051–427 1630.

RIDLEY, Philip Waller, CB 1978; CBE 1969; Director, Fingerscan Developments Ltd, since 1986; consultant to other companies; *b* 25 March 1921; *s* of Basil White Ridley and Frida (*née* Gutknecht); *m* 1942, Foye Robins; two *s* one *d*. *Educ:* Lewes County Grammar Sch.; Trinity Coll., Cambridge. Intelligence Corps, 1941–47 (Major); German Section, FO, 1948–51; Min. of Supply, 1951–55; BoT, 1955–56 and 1960–66; Atomic Energy Office, 1956–60; Counsellor (Commercial), British Embassy, Washington, 1966–70; Under-Sec., 1971–75, Dep. Sec., 1975–80, Dept of Industry. Dir, Avon Rubber Co., 1980–89. *Recreations:* music, gardening, ski-ing, walking. *Address:* Old Chimneys, Plumpton Green, Lewes, East Sussex BN8 4EN. *T:* Plumpton (0273) 890342.

RIDLEY, (Robert) Michael; Principal, Royal Belfast Academical Institution, since 1990; *b* 8 Jan. 1947; *s* of Maurice Roy Ridley and Jean Evelyn Lawther (*née* Carlisle); *m* 1985, Jennifer Mary Pearson; two *d*. *Educ:* Clifton Coll.; St Edmund Hall, Oxford (MA, Cert Ed). Wellington Coll., Berks, 1970–82 (Housemaster, 1975–82); Hd of English, Merchiston Castle Sch., Edinburgh, 1982–86; Headmaster, Denstone Coll., 1986–90. *Recreations:* cricket (Oxford Blue, 1968–70), golf, reading, travel. *Address:* The Royal Belfast Academical Institution College Square East, Belfast BT1 6DL. *T:* Belfast (0232) 240461. *Clubs:* East India; Vincent's (Oxford).

RIDLEY, Sir Sidney, Kt 1953; Emeritus Fellow, St John's College, Oxford, 1969 (Fellow, 1962); Indian Civil Service, retired; *b* 26 March 1902; *s* of John William and Elizabeth Janet Ridley; *m* 1929, Dorothy Hoole (*d* 1987); three *d*. *Educ:* Lancaster Royal Grammar Sch.; Sidney Sussex Coll., Cambridge. MA Cantab, MA Oxon. Joined ICS, 1926; Finance Secretary, Govt of Sind, 1936; Secretary to the Agent-General for India in South Africa, 1936–40; Chief Secretary, Govt of Sind, 1944; Commissioner: Northern Division, Ahmedabad, 1946; Central Div., Poona, 1947; Revenue Commissioner in Sind and Secretary to Government, 1947–54. Representative of W Africa Cttee in Ghana, Sierra Leone and the Gambia, 1957–60; Domestic Bursar, St John's Coll., Oxford, 1960–68. *Recreation:* golf. *Address:* Lambrook Cottage, Waytown, Bridport, Dorset DT6 5LF. *T:* Netherbury (030888) 337.

RIDLEY, Prof. Tony Melville, CBE 1986; PhD; CEng, FICE; FCIT; Rees Jeffreys Professor of Transport Engineering, Imperial College of Science, Technology and Medicine, since 1991; *b* 10 Nov. 1933; *s* of late John Edward and of Olive Ridley; *m* 1959, Jane (*née* Dickinson); two *s* one *d*. *Educ:* Durham Sch.; King's Coll. Newcastle, Univ. of Durham (BSc); Northwestern Univ., Ill (MS); Univ. of California, Berkeley (PhD); Stanford Univ., Calif (Sen. Exec. Prog.). Nuclear Power Group, 1957–62; Univ. of California, 1962–65; Chief Research Officer, Highways and Transportation, GLC, 1965–69; Director General, Tyne and Wear Passenger Transport Exec., 1969–75; Man. Dir, Hong Kong Mass Transit Rly Corp., 1975–80; Bd Mem., 1980–88, Man. Dir (Rlys), 1980–85, LTE, then LRT; Chm., 1985–88, Man. Dir, 1985–88, Chief Exec., 1988, London Underground Ltd; Man. Dir-Project, Eurotunnel, 1989–90 (Dir, 1987–90). Chm., Docklands Light Railway Ltd, 1987–88; Director: Halcrow Fox and Associates, 1980–; London Transport Internat., 1982–88. Pres., Light Rail Transit Assoc., 1974–; Vice-Pres., CIT, 1987–; Mem. Council, ICE (Chm., Transport Bd). Freeman, City of London, 1982. FHKIE, MITE. Highways Award, Instn of Highways and Transportn, 1988. *Publications:* articles in transport, engrg and other jls. *Recreations:* theatre, music, international affairs, rejuvenation of Britain. *Address:* Department of Civil Engineering, Imperial College, SW7 2BU. *T:* 071–589 5111, *Fax:* 071–823 7659. *Clubs:* Hong Kong, Jockey (Hong Kong).

RIDLEY, Rear-Adm. William Terence Colborne, CB 1968; OBE 1954; Admiral Superintendent/Port Admiral, Rosyth, 1966–72; Chairman, Ex-Services Mental Welfare Society, 1973–83; *b* 9 March 1915; *s* of late Capt. W. H. W. Ridley, RN and late Vera Constance (*née* Walker); *m* 1938, Barbara Allen; one *s*. *Educ:* Emsworth House; RNC, Dartmouth (Robert Roxburgh Prize); RNEC, Keyham. HMS Exeter, 1936; HMS Valiant, 1939; HMS Firedrake, 1940 (despatches twice); E-in-C Dept Admty, 1941; HMS Indefatigable, 1944; Admty Fuel Experimental Stn, 1947; Seaslug Project Officer, RAE Farnborough, 1950; HMS Ark Royal, 1956; E-in-C Dept Admty, Dreadnought Project Team, 1958; CO, RNEC, 1962; Staff of C-in-C Portsmouth, 1964. Lt-Comdr 1944; Comdr 1947; Capt. 1957; Rear-Adm. 1966. *Recreations:* gardening, do-it-yourself. *Address:* 12 New King Street, Bath, Avon BA1 2BL. *T:* Bath (0225) 318371.

RIDLEY-THOMAS, Roger; Managing Director, Thomson Regional Newspapers Ltd, since 1989; Chairman, Thomson Free Newspapers, since 1989; *b* 14 July 1939; *s* of late John Montague Ridley-Thomas, MB, ChB, FRCSE, Norwich, and Christina Anne (*née* Seex); *m* 1962, Sandra Grace McBeth Young; two *s* two *d*. *Educ:* Gresham's Sch. Served Royal Norfolk Regt, 1958–60. Newspaper Publisher: Eastern Counties Newspapers, 1960–65; Thomson Regional Newspapers, 1965– (Dir, 1985–); Managing Director: Aberdeen Journals, 1980–84; Scotsman Publications, 1984–89; Director: Caledonian Offset, 1979–; Radio Forth, 1978–81; TRN Viewdata, 1978–89; Thomson Scottish Organisation, 1984–89; Northfield Newspapers, 1984–89; The Scotsman Communications, 1984–; The Scotsman Publications, 1984–; Central Publications, 1984–; Aberdeen Journals, 1980–84, 1990–; Barwell Gurney Advertising, 1990–; Belfast Telegraph Newspapers, 1990–; Chester Chronicle, 1990–; Newcastle Chronical & Journal, 1990–; North Western Newspaper Co., 1990–; Thames Valley Newspapers, 1990–; Western Mail & Echo, 1990–; Regional Daily Advertising Council, 1989–; Aberdeen Chamber of Commerce, 1981–84; Scottish Business in the Community, 1984–89; Scottish Business Achievement Award Trust, 1985–; Edinburgh Ch. of Commerce and Manufrs, 1985–88. Pres., Scottish Daily Newspaper Soc., 1983–85; Mem. Council, CBI, 1983–86; Mem., Scottish Wildlife Appeal Cttee, 1985–88. *Recreations:* vegetable growing, shooting, fishing, golf, tennis, travel. *Address:* (office) Hannay House, 39 Clarendon Road, Watford, Herts WD1 1JA; Copse Hill House, Flaunden Lane, near Bovingdon, Herts HP3 0PA. *T:* Hemel Hempstead (0442) 834052. *Clubs:* Caledonian; New (Edinburgh).

RIDSDALE, Sir Julian (Errington), Kt 1981; CBE 1977; MP (C) Harwich Division of Essex, since Feb. 1954; *b* 8 June 1915; *m* 1942, Victoire Evelyn Patricia Bennett (*see* V. E. P. Ridsdale); one *d*. *Educ:* Tonbridge; Sandhurst. 2nd Lieutenant, Royal Norfolk Regiment, 1935; attached British Embassy, Tokyo, 1938–39; served War of 1939–45: Royal Norfolk Regt, Royal Scots, and Somerset Light Infantry; Asst Mil. Attaché, Japan, 1940; GSO3, Far Eastern Sect., War Office, 1941; GSO2, Joint Staff Mission, Washington, 1944–45; retired from Army with rank of Major, 1946. Contested SW Islington (C), LCC, 1949, N Paddington (C), Gen. Elec., 1951. PPS to Parly Under-Sec. of State for Colonies, 1957–58; PPS to Minister of State for Foreign Affairs, 1958–60; Parly Under-Sec. of State: for Air and Vice-President of the Air Council, 1962–64; for Defence for the Royal Air Force, Ministry of Defence, April-Oct. 1964. Chairman: British Japanese Parly Group, 1964–; Parly Gp for Engrg Develt, 1985–; Vice-Chm., UN Parly Assoc., 1966–82; Mem., Select Cttee of Public Accounts, 1970–74. Leader, Parly Delegns to Japan, 1973, 1975, annually 1977–82, 1988. Member: Trilateral Commn, EEC, USA and Japan, 1973–; North Atlantic Assembly, 1979– (Vice-Pres., Political Cttee, 1983–87). Dep. Chm., Internat. Triangle, USA, Japan and Europe, 1981–85. Chm., Japan Soc., London, 1976–79. British Comr Gen., British Garden Expo 90, Osaka, Japan, 1990. Master, Skinners' Co., 1970–71. Order of the Sacred Treasure, Japan, 1967, Grand Cordon, 1990. *Recreations:* tennis, chess, gardening, travelling, and sailing. *Address:* 12 The Boltons, SW10 9TD. *T:* 071–373 6159; Fiddan, St Osyth, Essex. *T:* St Osyth 367. *Clubs:* Carlton, MCC, Hurlingham; Frinton Tennis.

See also P. H. Newall.

RIDSDALE, Victoire Evelyn Patricia, (Paddy), (Lady Ridsdale), DBE 1991; *b* 11 Oct. 1921; *d* of Col J. and Edith Marion Bennett; *m* 1942, Sir Julian Ridsdale, *qv*; one *d*. *Educ:* Sorbonne. Sec., DNI, 1939–42; Sec. to her husband, 1953–. Chm., Conservative MP's Wives, 1978–91. *Address:* 12 The Boltons, SW10 9TD. *T:* 071–373 6159.

RIE, Dame Lucie, DBE 1991 (CBE 1981; OBE 1968); studio potter since 1927; *b* 16 March 1902; *d* of Prof. Dr Benjamin and Gisela Gomperz. *Educ:* Vienna Gymnasium (matriculate); Kunstgewerbe Schule. Pottery workshop: Vienna, 1927; London, 1939. Work included in V&A Museum, Fitzwilliam Museum, Cambridge Museum, Boymans-van Beuningen Museum, Stedelijk Museum, Museum of Modern Art, NY, Aust. Nat. Gall., Canberra, and other public collections in England and abroad. Exhibitions include: Arts Council retrospective, 1967; (with Hans Coper) Boymans-van Beuningen Museum, 1967; Expo '70, Osaka, 1970; (with Hans Coper) Museum of Art and Crafts, Hamburg,

1972; Hetjens Museum, Düsseldorf, 1978; retrospective, Sainsbury Centre and V&A Mus, 1981–82; one-woman, Sogetsu-Kai Foundn, Tokyo, 1989; (with Hans Coper and pupils) Sainsbury Centre, 1990, Fitzwilliam Mus., Cambridge, 1991. Gold medals: Internat. Exhibn, Brussels, 1935; Trienniale, Milan, 1936, 1954; Internat. Exhib., Munich, 1964. Hon. Doctor, Royal College of Art, 1969. *Relevant Publications:* Lucie Rie (ed by John Houston), 1981; Lucie Rie (biography by Tony Birks), 1987.

RIESCO, Germán; Chilean Ambassador to the Court of St James's, since 1990; *b* 17 Aug. 1941; *s* of Ignacio Riesco and Eliana Zañartu de Riesco; *m* 1974, Jacqueline Cassel; four *s* two *d. Educ:* Colegio San Ignacio, Santiago; Univ. of California, Davis (agric. degree; Special Award); Univ. of California, Berkeley (Economics). MP Nuble (National Party), 1969–73; Pres., Cttee on Economy, Chamber of Deputies; Dir, Agric. Planning Office, 1976–78. National Party: Vice-Pres., 1983–88; Pres., for No Vote, 1988; Pres., PAC-Centre Alliance Party, 1988–90. Board Mem., Fundación Chile, 1983–90. Pres., Nat. Agric. Soc., Chile, 1979–81, 1981–83. Negotiator at FAO, World Bank and other internat. orgns. *Publications:* papers on Chilean agric. and econs. *Recreations:* music, theatre, tennis, ski-ing. *Address:* 12 Devonshire Street, W1N 2DS. *T:* 071–580 6392; 92 Eaton Place, SW1X 8LW. *T:* 071–235 1047. *Clubs:* Chile, De La Union, Los Leones Country (Santiago, Chile).

RIFKIND, Rt. Hon. Malcolm (Leslie), PC 1986; QC (Scot.) 1985; MP (C) Edinburgh, Pentlands, since Feb. 1974; Secretary of State for Transport, since 1990; *b* 21 June 1946; *yr s* of late E. Rifkind, Edinburgh; *m* 1970, Edith Amalia Rifkind (*née* Steinberg); one *s* one *d. Educ:* George Watson's Coll.; Edinburgh Univ. LLB, MSc. Lectured at Univ. of Rhodesia, 1967–68. Called to Scottish Bar, 1970. Contested (C) Edinburgh, Central, 1970. Opposition front-bench spokesman on Scottish Affairs, 1975–76; Parly Under Sec. of State, Scottish Office, 1979–82, FCO, 1982–83; Minister of State, FCO, 1983–86; Sec. of State for Scotland, 1986–90. Jt Sec., Cons. Foreign and Commonwealth Affairs Cttee, 1978; Member: Select Cttee on Europ. Secondary Legislation, 1975–76; Select Cttee on Overseas Develt, 1978–79. Hon. Pres., Scottish Young Conservatives, 1975–76. *Address:* House of Commons, SW1A 0AA. *Club:* New (Edinburgh).

RIGBY, Bryan; Managing Director, UK, Ireland and Scandinavia, BASF Group, since 1987; *b* 9 Jan. 1933; *s* of William George Rigby and Lily Rigby; *m* 1978, Marian Rosamund; one *s* one *d* of a former marriage, and one step *s* one step *d. Educ:* Wigan Grammar Sch.; King's Coll., London (BSc Special Chemistry, Dip. Chem. Engrg). UKAEA Industrial Gp, Capenhurst, 1955–60; Beecham Gp, London and Amsterdam, 1960–64; Laporte Industries (Holdings) Ltd, 1964–78; Dep. Dir-Gen., CBI, 1978–83; Man. Dir, UK Ops, BASF Gp, 1984–87. *Recreations:* music, golf, gardening. *Address:* Cluny, 61 Penn Road, Beaconsfield, Bucks HP9 2LW. *T:* Beaconsfield (0494) 673206. *Club:* Reform.

RIGBY, Lt-Col Sir (Hugh) John (Macbeth), 2nd Bt, *cr* 1929; ERD and 2 clasps; Director, Executors of James Mills Ltd, retired 1977; *b* 1 Sept. 1914; *s* of Sir Hugh Mallinson Rigby, 1st Bt, and Flora (*d* 1970), *d* of Norman Macbeth; *S* father, 1944; *m* 1946, Mary Patricia Erskine Leacock (*d* 1988); four *s. Educ:* Rugby; Magdalene Coll., Cambridge. Lt-Col RCT, retd, 1967. *Heir: s* Anthony John Rigby [*b* 3 Oct. 1946; *m* 1978, Mary, *e d* of R. G. Oliver, Park Moor Cottage, Pott Shrigley, Macclesfield; three *s* one *d*]. *Address:* 5 Park Street, Macclesfield, Cheshire SK11 6SR. *T:* Macclesfield (0625) 613959; Casa das Palmeiras, 8365 Armação de Pẽra, Alcantarilha, Algarve, Portugal. *T:* (82) 312548.

RIGBY, Jean Prescott, (Mrs Jamie Hayes); mezzo-soprano; Principal, English National Opera, 1982–90; *d* of late Thomas Boulton Rigby and of Margaret Annie Rigby; *m* 1987, Jamie Hayes; two *s. Educ:* Birmingham and Midland Inst. Sch. of Music (ABSM 1976); Royal Acad. of Music (Dip.RAM; Hon. ARAM 1984; Hon. FRAM 1989). ARCM 1979. Début: Royal Opera House, Covent Garden, 1983; Glyndebourne Festival Opera, 1984. Several TV performances. *Recreations:* British heritage, sport, cooking. *Address:* c/o John Coast, Manfield House, 376–379 Strand, WC2R 0LR.

RIGBY, Sir John; *see* Rigby, Sir H. J. M.

RIGBY, Norman Leslie; company chairman, retired; *b* 27 June 1920; *s* of Leslie Rigby and Elsie Lester Wright; *m* 1950, Mary Josephine Calderhead; two *d* (one *s* decd). *Educ:* Cowley Sch., St Helens. Served War, RAF, 1939–45, Intell. Officer to Free French Air Force. Management Trainee, Simon Engineering Group, 1946–48; Marketing Exec., Procter & Gamble Ltd, 1948–55; Marketing Dir, Macleans Ltd (Beecham Group), 1955–59; Nabisco Ltd: Marketing Dir 1959; Man. Dir 1960; Vice-Chm. 1962; Chm. 1964; Industrial Adviser, 1968–70, Co-ordinator of Industrial Advisers, HM Govt, 1969–70; Dir, Spillers Ltd, 1970–80 (Divl Man. Dir, 1977–80); Chm., Allan H. Williams Ltd and associated cos, 1981–82. *Recreations:* gardening, golf. *Address:* 38 West Common Way, Harpenden, Herts AL5 2LG. *T:* Harpenden (0582) 715448.

RIGBY, Peter William Jack, PhD; Head, Genes and Cellular Controls Group and Laboratory of Eukaryotic Molecular Genetics, MRC National Institute for Medical Research since 1986; *b* 7 July 1947; *s* of Jack and Lorna Rigby; *m* 1st, 1971, Paula Webb (marr. diss. 1983; 2nd, 1985, Julia Maidment. *Educ:* Lower Sch., John Lyon, Harrow; Jesus Coll., Cambridge (BA, PhD). MRC Lab. of Molecular Biol., Cambridge, 1971–73; Helen Hay Whitney Foundn Fellow, Stanford Univ. Med. Sch., 1973–76; Imperial College London: then Sen. Lectr in Biochem., 1976–83; Reader in Tumour Virology, 1983–86; Vis. Prof., 1986–. Member: EMBO, 1979; Science Council, Celltech Ltd, 1982–; Scientific Cttee, Cancer Res. Campaign, 1983–88; MRC Cell Board, 1988–. European Editor, Cell, 1984–. *Publications:* papers on molecular biology in sci. jls. *Recreations:* narrow boats, listening to music, sunbathing. *Address:* National Institute for Medical Research, The Ridgway, Mill Hill, NW7 1AA. *T:* 081–959 3666.

RIGBY, Reginald Francis, TD 1950 and Clasp 1952; a Recorder of the Crown Court, 1977–83; *b* Rudyard, Staffs, 22 June 1919; *s* of Reginald Rigby, FRIBA, FRICS, and Beatrice May Rigby, *d* of John Frederick Green, Woodbridge, Suffolk; *m* 1949, Joan Edwina, *d* of Samuel E. M. Simpson, Newcastle-under-Lyme, and of Dorothy C. Simpson; one *s* (and one *s* decd). *Educ:* Manchester Grammar Sch.; Victoria Univ., Manchester. Solicitor, 1947 (Hons; John Peacock and George Hadfield Prizeman, Law Society Art Prize, 1962); practised Newcastle-under-Lyme; retired as Sen. Partner, Rigby Rowley Cooper & Co., 1984. Served War: commissioned 2nd Lieut 41 Bn, Royal Tank Corps, TA, 1939; served AFV Sch.; volunteered for maritime service: Captain in RASC motor boat companies in home coastal waters, India, Burma, Malaya and its Archipelago; demob. 1946; Major, QORR, The Staffordshire Yeomanry. Mem., Market Drayton RDC, 1966–71; Chm., Woore Parish Council, 1971–79; Hon. Sec., North Staffs Forces Help Soc., 1964–84; Mem., Staffs War Pensions Cttee; Member: 1745 Assoc. and Mil. Hist. Soc.; Pres., Uttoxeter Flyfishing Club, 1975–77; Trustee, Birdsgrove Flyfishing Club, Ashbourne. Life Mem., Clan Morrison Soc. Member, Military and Hospitaller Order of St Lazarus of Jerusalem. *Recreation:* fishing. *Address:* The Rookery, Woore, Salop CW3 9RG. *T:* Pipe Gate (063081) 414. *Clubs:* Army and Navy, Flyfishers'.

RIGG, Diana, CBE 1988; actress; Director, United British Artists, since 1982; *b* Doncaster, Yorks, 20 July 1938; *d* of Louis Rigg and Beryl Helliwell; *m* 1982, Archibald Stirling; one *d. Educ:* Fulneck Girls' Sch., Pudsey. Trained for the stage at Royal Academy of Dramatic Art. First appearance on stage in RADA prod. in York Festival, at Theatre Royal, York, summer, 1957 (Natella Abashwili in The Caucasian Chalk Circle); after appearing in repertory in Chesterfield and in York she joined the Royal Shakespeare Company, Stratford-upon-Avon, 1959; first appearance in London, Aldwych Theatre, 1961 (2nd Ondine, Violanta and Princess Berthe in Ondine); at same theatre, in repertory (The Devils, Becket, The Taming of the Shrew), 1961; (Madame de Tourvel, The Art of Seduction), 1962; Royal Shakespeare, Stratford-upon-Avon, Apr. 1962 (Helena in A Midsummer Night's Dream, Bianca in The Taming of the Shrew, Lady Macduff in Macbeth, Adriana in The Comedy of Errors, Cordelia in King Lear); subseq. appeared in the last production at the Aldwych, Dec. 1962, followed by Adriana in The Comedy of Errors and Monica Stettler in The Physicists, 1963. Toured the provinces, spring, 1963, in A Midsummer Night's Dream; subseq. appeared at the Royal Shakespeare, Stratford, and at the Aldwych, in Comedy of Errors, Dec. 1963; again played Cordelia in King Lear, 1964, prior to touring with both plays for the British Council, in Europe, the USSR, and the US; during this tour she first appeared in New York (State Theatre), 1964, in same plays; Viola in Twelfth Night, Stratford, June 1966; Heloise in Abelard and Heloise, Wyndham's, 1970, also at the Atkinson, New York, 1971; joined The National Theatre, 1972: in Jumpers, 'Tis Pity She's a Whore and Lady Macbeth in Macbeth, 1972; The Misanthrope, 1973, Washington and NY, 1975; Phaedra Britannica, 1975 (Plays and Players Award for Best Actress); The Guardsman, 1978; Pygmalion, Albery, 1974; Night and Day, Phoenix, 1978 (Plays and Players award, 1979); Colette, USA, 1982; Heartbreak House, Haymarket, 1983; Little Eyolf, Lyric, Hammersmith, 1985; Antony and Cleopatra, Chichester, 1985; Wildfire, Phoenix, 1986; Follies, Shaftesbury, 1987; All for Love, Almeida, 1991; *films include:* A Midsummer Night's Dream, Assassination Bureau, On Her Majesty's Secret Service, Julius Caesar, The Hospital, Theatre of Blood, A Little Night Music, The Great Muppet Caper, Evil Under the Sun (Film Actress of the Year Award, Variety Club, 1983); *TV appearances include:* Sentimental Agent, The Comedy of Errors, The Avengers, Married Alive, Diana (US series), In This House of Brede (US), Three Piece Suite, The Serpent Son, Hedda Gabler, The Marquise, Little Eyolf, King Lear, Witness of the Prosecution, Bleak House, Mother Love (BAFTA award), and others. A Vice-Pres., Baby Life Support Systems (BLISS), 1984–. *Publication:* No Turn Unstoned, 1982. *Recreations:* reading and trying to get organized. *Address:* c/o London Management, 235 Regent Street, W1A 2JT.

RIGNEY, Howard Ernest; HM Diplomatic Service, retired; Consul-General, Lyons, 1977–82; *b* 22 June 1922; *o s* of late Wilbert Ernest and Minnie Rigney; *m* 1950, Margaret Grayling Benn; one *s. Educ:* Univs of Western Ontario, Toronto and Paris. BA Western Ont. 1945, MA Toronto 1947. Lectr, Univ. of British Columbia, 1946–48; grad. studies, Paris Univ., 1948–50; COI, 1953–56; CRO, 1956; Regional Information Officer, Dacca, 1957–60, Montreal, 1960–63; CRO, 1963–65; FO/CO, 1965–67; Consul (Information), Chicago, 1967–69; Dep. Consul-Gen., Chicago, 1969–71; Head of Chancery and Consul, Rangoon, 1971–73; Head of Migration and Visa Dept, FCO, 1973–77. Hon DLitt, Winston Churchill Coll., Ill, 1971. *Recreations:* opera, book-collecting, gardening, golf. *Address:* c/o Lloyds Bank, 125 High Street, Sittingbourne, Kent. *Clubs:* Cercle de l'Union (Lyon), Golf Club de Lyon.

RIKANOVIC, Svetozar; Yugoslav Ambassador to the Court of St James's, since 1989; *b* 6 April 1938; *s* of Ilija and Jelisaveta Rikanovic; *m* 1964, Darinka; two *s. Educ:* Faculty of Economics, Univ. of Belgrade. Chm., City Cttee, People's Youth of Belgrade, and several other political functions, 1959–66; Pres., Socialist Alliance of Working People—Municipality of Stari Grad, 1966–68; Manager, Publishing Dept of Savremena Administracija, Belgrade, 1968–70; Asst Man., Planning Authorities of City of Belgrade, 1970–73; Sec. for Economic Develt, nd Mem., Exec. Council, City Assembly of Belgrade, 1973–75; Pres., Beobanka, 1975–82; Vice-Pres., Govt of Serbia, 1982–86; Fed. Sec. for Finance, and Mem., Fed. Govt, 1986–89; Fed. Secretariat for For. Affairs, 1989–. Awarded a number of Yugoslav decorations. *Address:* 25 Hyde Park Gate, SW7. *T:* 071–581 2140. *Club:* Athenæum.

RILEY, Bridget Louise, CBE 1972; Artist; *b* 24 April 1931; *d* of John Riley and late Louise (*née* Gladstone). *Educ:* Cheltenham Ladies' College; Goldsmiths' School of Art; Royal College of Art. ARCA 1955. AICA critics Prize, 1963; Stuyvesant Bursary, 1964; Ohara Mus. Prize, Tokyo, 1972; Gold Medal, Grafik Biennale, Norway, 1980. Mem., RSA. One-man shows: London, 1962, 1963, 1969, 1971 (retrospective, at Hayward Gall.), 1976, 1981, 1983, 1987, 1989; New York, Los Angeles, 1965; New York, 1967, 1975, 1978, 1986, 1990; Hanover, 1970; Turin, Düsseldorf, Berne, Prague, 1971; Basle, 1975; Sydney, 1976; Tokyo, 1977, 1983, 1990; Stockholm and Zurich, 1987; touring retrospective, USA, Aust. and Japan, 1978–80. Exhibited in group shows: England, France, Israel, America, Germany, Italy. Represented Britain: Paris Biennale, 1965; Venice Biennale, 1968 (awarded Chief internat. painting prize). Public collections include: Tate Gallery, Victoria and Albert Museum, Arts Council, British Council, Museum of Modern Art, New York', Australian Nat. Gallery, Canberra, Museum of Modern Art, Pasadena, Ferens Art Gallery, Hull, Allbright Knox, Buffalo, USA, Museum of Contemporary Art, Chicago, Ulster Museum, Ireland, Stedelijk Museum, Berne Kunsthalle. Designed Colour Moves, for Ballet Rambert, 1983. Trustee, Nat. Gallery, 1981–88. Hon. DLit: Manchester, 1976; Ulster, 1986.

RILEY, Christopher John; Under Secretary, HM Treasury, since 1988; *b* 20 Jan. 1947; *s* of Bernard Francis Riley and Phyllis (*née* Wigley); *m* 1982, Helen Marion Mynett; two *s. Educ:* Ratcliffe Coll., Leicester; Wadham Coll., Oxford (MA Maths); Univ. of East Anglia (MA Econs). Economist, HM Treasury, 1969–77; Res. Fellow, Nuffield Coll., Oxford, 1977–78; Sen. Economic Advr, HM Treasury, 1978–88. *Publications:* various articles in books and learned jls. *Recreation:* music, especially choral singing. *Address:* c/o HM Treasury, Parliament Street, SW1P 3AG. *T:* 071–270 4439.

RILEY, Major John Roland Christopher; Chairman, Channel Islands Communications (TV) Group (formerly Channel Television), since 1982; *b* 4 July 1925; *s* of Christopher John Molesworth Riley and Bridget Maisie Hanbury; *m* 1956, Penelope Ann Harrison (*d* 1978); two *d. Educ:* Winchester College. Commissioned Coldstream Guards, 1943; served NW Europe, Palestine, Malaya; Instructor, Army Staff Coll., 1960–62; retired 1962; Elected Deputy, States of Jersey, 1963, Senator, 1975; retired from Govt, 1981. Director: Air UK, 1963–91; Jersey Gas Co., 1970–; Chase Bank and Trust Co. (CI), 1975–91; Fuel Supplies CI, 1976–; Servisair Jersey, 1976–; Royal Trust Asset Management (CI) Ltd, 1980–; Royal Trust Fund Management (CI) Ltd, 1984–. Seigneur de la Trinité. *Recreations:* horse riding (Master Jersey Drag Hunt), yachting. *Address:* Trinity Manor, Jersey, Channel Islands JE3 5DD. *T:* Jersey (0534) 61026, *Fax:* Jersey (0534) 64526. *Clubs:* Cavalry and Guards, Royal Yacht Squadron.

RILEY, Sir Ralph, Kt 1984; DSc; FRS 1967; Deputy Chairman, 1983–85, Secretary, 1978–85, Agricultural and Food Research Council; *b* 23 Oct. 1924; *y c* of Ralph and Clara Riley; *m* 1949, Joan Elizabeth Norrington; two *d. Educ:* Audenshaw Gram. Sch.; Univ.

of Sheffield. Infantry Soldier, 1943–47; Univ. of Sheffield, 1947–52; Research worker, Plant Breeding Inst., Cambridge, 1952–78; Head of Cytogenetics Dept, 1954–72; Dir, 1971–78. National Research Council/Nuffield Foundn Lectr at Canadian Univs, 1966; Special Prof. of Botany, Univ. of Nottingham, 1970–78. Fellow of Wolfson Coll., Cambridge, 1967–91. Lectures: Sir Henry Tizard Meml, 1973; Holden, Univ. of Nottingham, 1975; Woodhull, Royal Instn, 1976; Bewley, Glasshouse Crops Res. Inst., 1980; Bernal, Birkbeck Coll., 1983. Sec., Internat. Genetics Fedn, 1973–78; Board Member: Internat. Rice Res. Inst., Manila, 1974–77; Internat. Centre Agricl Res. Dry Areas, Aleppo, 1989–; Chairman: Rothamsted Experimental Station, 1990–; Adv. Cttee, Prog. Rice Biotech., Rockefeller Foundn, 1985–; UGC Working Pty on Vet. Educn., 1987–89. President: Genetical Soc., 1973–75; Sect. K, BAAS, 1979; Hon. Vice-Pres., 16th Internat. Congress of Genetics, Toronto, 1988. For. Fellow, INSA, 1976; For. Correspondent, Acad. d'Agriculture de France, 1981; For. Associate, Nat. Acad. Scis, USA, 1982. Hon. FRASE, 1980. Hon. DSc: Edinburgh, 1976; Hull, 1982; Cranfield, 1985; Hon. LLD Sheffield, 1984. William Bate Hardy Prize, Cambridge Phil. Soc., 1969; Royal Medal, Royal Soc., 1981; Wolf Foundn Prize in Agriculture, 1986. *Publications:* scientific papers and articles on genetics of chromosome behaviour, plant cytogenetics and evolution and breeding of crop plants especially wheat. *Address:* 16 Gog Magog Way, Stapleford, Cambridge CB2 5BQ. *T:* Cambridge (0223) 843845, *Fax:* Cambridge (0223) 845825. *Club:* Athenæum.

RILEY-SMITH, Prof. Jonathan Simon Christopher, FRHistS; Professor of History, University of London, since 1978, at Royal Holloway and Bedford New College, since 1985 (at Royal Holloway College, 1978–85); *b* 27 June 1938; *s* of late William Henry Douglas Riley-Smith and Elspeth Agnes Mary Riley-Smith (*née* Craik Henderson); *m* 1968, Marie-Louise Jeannetta, *d* of Wilfred John Sutcliffe Field; one *s* two *d*. *Educ:* Eton College; Trinity College, Cambridge (MA, PhD). Dept of Mediaeval History, University of St Andrews: Asst Lectr, 1964–65; Lectr, 1966–72; Faculty of History, Cambridge: Asst Lectr, 1972–75; Lectr, 1975–78; Queens' College, Cambridge: Fellow and Dir of Studies in History, 1972–78; Praelector, 1973–75; Librarian, 1973, 1977–78; Head of Dept of History, RHBNC, 1984–90. Chairman: Bd of Management, Inst. of Historical Res., 1988–; Victoria County Hist. Cttee, 1989–; Pres., Soc. for the Study of the Crusades and the Latin East, 1990–. KStJ 1969 (Librarian of Priory of Scotland, 1966–78, of Grand Priory, 1982–); KM 1971 (Officer of Merit, 1985). Prix Schlumberger, Acad. des Inscriptions et Belles-Lettres, Paris, 1988. *Publications:* The Knights of St John in Jerusalem and Cyprus, 1967; (with U. and M. C. Lyons) Ayyubids, Mamlukes and Crusaders, 1971; The Feudal Nobility and the Kingdom of Jerusalem, 1973; What were the Crusades?, 1977; (with L. Riley-Smith) The Crusades: idea and reality, 1981; The First Crusade and the Idea of Crusading, 1986; The Crusades: a short history, 1987 (trans. French, 1990); (ed) The Atlas of the Crusades, 1991; articles in learned jls. *Recreation:* the past and present of own family. *Address:* Department of History, Royal Holloway and Bedford New College, Egham Hill, Egham, Surrey TW20 0EX. *T:* Egham (0784) 34455.

RIMBAULT, Brig. Geoffrey Acworth, CBE 1954; DSO 1945; MC 1936; DL; Director, Army Sport Control Board, 1961–73; *b* 17 April 1908; *s* of late Arthur Henry Rimbault, London; *m* 1933, Joan (*d* 1991), *d* of late Thomas Hallet-Fry, Beckenham, Kent; one *s*. *Educ:* Dulwich College. 2nd Lieut, The Loyal Regt (N Lancs), 1930; served: India, Waziristan, 1931–36; Palestine, 1937; Staff Coll., Camberley; N Africa, Anzio, Italy and Palestine, 1939–46; Chief Instructor, RMA Sandhurst, 1950–51; Chief of Staff, E Africa, 1952–54; comd 131 Inf. Bde, 1955–57; comd Aldershot Garrison, 1958–61. Colonel, The Loyal Regt, 1959–70. Life Vice-Pres., Surrey CCC (Pres., 1982–83). Liveryman, Mercers' Co., 1961, Master, 1970–71. DL Surrey, 1971. *Recreations:* cricket, tennis, golf, shooting. *Address:* 10 Clarke Place, Elmbridge, Cranleigh, Surrey GU6 8TH. *T:* Cranleigh (0483) 271207. *Clubs:* Army and Navy, MCC.

RIMER, Colin Percy Farquharson; QC 1988; *b* 30 Jan. 1944; *s* of Kenneth Rowland Rimer and Maria Eugenia Rimer (*née* Farquharson); *m* 1970, Penelope Ann Gibbs; two *s* one *d*. *Educ:* Dulwich Coll.; Trinity Hall, Cambridge (MA, LLB). Legal Assistant, Inst. of Comparative Law, Paris, 1967–68; called to the Bar, Lincoln's Inn, 1968; in practice, 1969–. *Recreations:* music, photography, novels, walking. *Address:* 13 Old Square, Lincoln's Inn, WC2A 3UA. *T:* 071–404 4800.

RIMINGTON, Claude, FRS 1954, MA, PhD Cantab, DSc London; Emeritus Professor of Chemical Pathology, University of London; Head of Department of Chemical Pathology, University College Hospital Medical School, 1945–67; *b* 17 Nov. 1902; *s* of George Garthwaite Rimington, Newcastle upon Tyne; *m* 1929, Soffi, *d* of Clemet Andersen, Askerøy, Lyngør, Norway; one *d*. *Educ:* Emmanuel College, Cambridge. Benn W. Levy Research Scholar, Univ. of Cambridge, 1926–28; Biochemist, Wool Industries Research Association, Leeds, 1928–30; Empire Marketing Board Senior Research Fellow, then Scientific Research Officer, Division of Veterinary Services, Govt of Union of South Africa, at Onderstepoort Veterinary Research Laboratory, Pretoria, 1931–37; Biochemist, National Institute for Medical Research, Medical Research Council, London, 1937–45. Guest Res. Worker, Inst. for Cancer Res., Norwegian Radium Hosp., Oslo, 1985–. Mem., Norwegian Acad. of Sci. and Letters, 1988. Hon. FRCP Edinburgh, 1967; Hon. Mem. Brit. Assoc. of Dermatology, 1967. Graham Gold Medal, Univ. of London, 1967. Knight (1st Class), Royal Norwegian Order of Merit, 1989. *Publications:* (with A. Goldberg), Diseases of Porphyrin Metabolism, 1962; (with M. R. Moore, K. E. L. McColl and Sir Abraham Goldberg) Disorders of Porphyrin Metabolism, 1987; numerous biochemical and scientific papers. *Recreations:* sailing, languages, Scandinavian literature. *Address:* Askerøy, Per Vestre Sandøy 4915, Norway.

RIMINGTON, John David, CB 1987; Director-General, Health and Safety Executive, since 1984; *b* 27 June 1935; *s* of John William Rimington and Mabel Dorrington; *m* 1963; two *d*. *Educ:* Nottingham High Sch.; Jesus Coll., Cambridge (Cl. I Hons History, MA). Nat. Service Commn, RA, 1954–56. Joined BoT, 1959; seconded HM Treasury (work on decimal currency), 1961; Principal, Tariff Div., BoT, 1963; 1st Sec. (Economic), New Delhi, 1965; Mergers Div., DTI, 1969; Dept of Employment, 1970; Asst Sec. 1972 (Employment Policy and Manpower); Counsellor, Social and Regional Policy, UK perm. representation to EEC, Brussels, 1974; MSC, 1977–81; Under Sec. 1978; Dir, Safety Policy Div., HSE, 1981–83; Dep. Sec., 1984. *Publications:* contrib. to RIPA Jl, New Asia Review. *Recreations:* walking, gardening, watching cricket. *Address:* Health and Safety Executive, Baynards House, Chepstow Place, W2 4TF.

RIMMER, Prof. Frederick William, CBE 1980; MA (Cantab), BMus (Dunelm); FRCO; FRSAMD; Gardiner Professor of Music, University of Glasgow, 1966–80, now Emeritus Professor; Director of Scottish Music Archive, 1968–80; *b* 21 Feb. 1914; 2nd *s* of William Rimmer and Amy Graham McMillan, Liverpool; *m* 1941, Joan Doreen, *d* of Major Alexander Hume Graham and Beatrice Cecilia Myles; two *s* one *d*. *Educ:* Quarry Bank High Sch., Liverpool. FRCO (Harding Prize), 1934; BMus (Dunelm), 1939. Served War: 11th Bn, The Lancashire Fusiliers, Middle East, 1941–45 (Maj. 1944). Selwyn Coll., Cambridge (Organ Scholar), 1946–48; Sen. Lectr in Music, Homerton Coll., Cambridge, 1948–51; Cramb Lectr in Music, Univ. of Glasgow, 1951–56; Sen. Lectr, 1956–66, and Organist to the Univ., 1954–66. Henrietta Harvey Vis. Prof., Memorial Univ. of Newfoundland, 1977. A Dir of Scottish Opera, 1966–80; Chm., BBC's Scottish Music Adv. Cttee, 1972–77; Mem., Music Adv. Cttee, British Council, 1973–82, Scottish Adv. Cttee, 1979–82. Hon. Fellow, Selwyn Coll., Cambridge, 1982. Hon. DMus Durham, 1991. Special Award for services to contemp. music in Scotland, Composers' Guild of GB, 1975. *Publications:* contrib. to: A History of Scottish Music, 1973; Companion to Scottish Culture, 1981; articles on 20th century music, in: Tempo; Music Review; Organists' Review; compositions for solo organ: Five Preludes on Scottish Psalm Tunes, Pastorale and Toccata, Invenzione e Passacaglia Capricciosa, Ostinato Mesto, Fugato Giocoso; for choir and organ: Sing we merrily; Christus natus est alleluia; O Lord, we beseech thee; O Blessed God in Trinity; Five carols of the Nativity; Magnificat and Nunc Dimittis; for solo soprano and organ: Of a Rose; Born is the Babe. *Recreations:* travel, reading and gardening. *Address:* Manor Farmhouse, 6 Mill Way, Grantchester, Cambridge CB3 9NB. *T:* Cambridge (0223) 840716.

RINFRET, Hon. Gabriel-Edouard, OC 1983; PC (Canada) 1949; Chief Justice of Québec, 1977–80, retired; *b* St-Jérôme, PQ, 12 May 1905; *s* of Rt Hon. Thibaudeau Rinfret, Chief Justice of Canada, and Georgine, *d* of S. J. B. Rolland; *m* 1929; two *s*; *m* 1982. *Educ:* Collège Notre-Dame, Côte des Neiges, PQ; Petit Séminaire, Montréal; Collège Ste-Marie (BA with distinction); McGill Univ., Montréal (LLM with distinction); pupil of Hon. J. L. Perron. Admitted to practice, 1928; joined law office of Campbell, McMaster, Couture, Kerry and Bruneau; partner, Campbell, Weldon, MacFarlane and Rinfret, 1945. KC 1943. Sec. or Legal Adviser to various provincial govt commns of enquiry, 1934–45. Pres., Jeunesse Libérale de Montréal, 1934; Co-founder and 1st Pres., Assoc. de la Jeunesse Libérale de la Province de Québec, 1934–35; MP (L) Outremont, 1945–49, Outremont-St Jean 1949–52, House of Commons of Canada; Postmaster General in St Laurent Cabinet. A Judge of the Court of Appeal of Québec, 1952–80. Pres. or Director: Concerts Symphoniques de Montréal; Inst. Internat. de Musique; Grands Ballets Canadiens; Dominion Drama Festival (organised Montréal Festival, 1961; Pres., W Québec Region, and Mem., Nat. Exec. Cttee, 1962–68; Canadian Drama Award, 1969); Vice Pres., Conservatoire Lassalle, 1967–. Hon. LLD, Univ. of British Columbia, 1979. *Publications:* Répertoire du théâtre canadien d'expression française, vol. 1, 1975, vol. 2, 1976, vol. 3, 1977, vol. 4, 1978; Histoire du Barreau de Montréal, 1989. *Recreations:* cabinet-work, Canadian paintings; formerly baseball, lacrosse, tennis, hockey, ski-ing. *Address:* 121 Melbourne Avenue, Town of Mount Royal, Québec, H3P 1G3, Canada.

RING, Prof. James, CBE 1983; Emeritus Professor of Physics, Imperial College of Science, Technology and Medicine, since 1984; Member, Independent Television Commission, since 1991; *b* 22 Aug. 1927; *s* of James and Florence Ring; *m* 1949, Patricia, *d* of Major H. J. Smith, MBE; two *s*. *Educ:* Univ. of Manchester (BSc, PhD). FInstP, FRAS. Reader in Spectrometry, Univ. of Manchester, 1957; Prof. of Applied Physics, Hull Univ., 1962; Prof. of Physics, 1962, and Associate Hd of Physics Dept, 1979, Imperial Coll. of Sci. and Technol. Director: Queensgate Instruments, 1979–; Infrared Engrg, 1970–91; IC Optical Systems, 1970–. Member: IBA, 1974–81; Inquiry into Cable Expansion and Broadcasting Policy, 1982; Dep. Chm., Cable Authority, 1984–90. *Publications:* numerous papers and articles in learned jls. *Recreations:* stargazing, dinghy sailing. *Address:* 1 Mude Gardens, Mudeford, Dorset BH23 4AR.

RING, Sir Lindsay (Roberts), GBE 1975; JP; Chairman, Ring & Brymer (Birchs) Ltd; Lord Mayor of London for 1975–76; *b* 1 May 1914; *y s* of George Arthur Ring and Helen Rhoda Mason Ring (*née* Stedman); *m* 1940, Hazel Doris, *d* of A. Trevor Nichols, CBE; two *s* one *d*. *Educ:* Dulwich Coll.; Mecklenburg, Germany. Served 1939–45, Europe and Middle East, Major RASC. Underwriting Member of Lloyd's, 1964. Fellow, Hotel and Catering Inst.; Chm., Hotel and Catering Trades Benevolent Assoc., 1962–71; Member: Bd of Verge of Royal Palaces, 1977–84; Gaming Bd for GB, 1977–83; NI Develt Agency, 1977–81. Chm., City of London (Arizona) Corp., 1981–84. Chancellor, City Univ., 1975–76. Governor, Farringtons Sch. Freeman, City of London, 1935; Member, Court of Assistants: Armourers' and Brasiers' Co. (Master 1972); Chartered Secretaries' and Administrators' Co. Common Councilman, City of London (Ward of Bishopsgate), 1964–68; Alderman (Ward of Vintry), 1968–84; Sheriff, City of London, 1967–68; Governor, Hon. Irish Soc., 1980–84. HM Lieut for City of London; JP Inner London, 1964. Hon. Col, 151 (Greater London) Regt, RCT(V). Hon. Burgess, Borough of Coleraine, NI. KStJ 1976. FCIS 1976. Hon. DSc City Univ., 1976; Hon. DLitt Ulster, 1976. Comdr, Legion of Honour, 1976; Order of Rio Branca (Brazil), 1976. *Address:* Chalvedune, Wilderness Road, Chislehurst, Kent, BR7 5EY. *Club:* City Livery.

RINGADOO, Hon. Sir Veerasamy, GCMG 1986; Kt 1975; QC 1983; Officier de l'Ordre National Malgache 1969; Governor-General and Commander-in-Chief of Mauritius, since 1986; *b* 1920; *s* of Nagaya Ringadoo; *m* 1954, Lydie Vadamootoo; one *s* one *d*. *Educ:* Port Louis Grammar Sch.; LSE Eng. (LLB; Hon. Fellow, 1976). Called to Bar, 1949. Municipal Councillor, Port Louis, 1956; MLC for Moka-Flacq, 1951–67; Minister: Labour and Social Security, 1959–63; Education, 1964–67; Agriculture and Natural Resources, 1967–68; Finance, 1968–82; attended London Constitutional Conf., 1965; first MLA (Lab) for Quartier Militaire and Moka, 1967, re-elected 1976. Governor, IMF and African Develt Bank, 1970–82; Chm., Bd of Governors, African Development Bank and African Development Fund, 1977–78. Hon. DCL Mauritius, 1976; Hon. DLit Andhra, 1978; Dr *hc*: Bordeaux Univ., 1988; Bharatidasan Univ., Tiruchirapalli, 1988. Médaille de l'Assemblée Nat. Française, 1971. *Address:* Government House, Le Réduit, Mauritius.

RINGEN, Prof. Stein; Professor of Sociology and Social Policy, and Fellow of Green College, University of Oxford, since 1990; *b* 5 July 1945; *s* of John Ringen and Anna Ringen (*née* Simengard). *Educ:* Univ. of Oslo (MA, dr. philos.). Broadcasting reporter, Norwegian Broadcasting Corp., 1970–71; Fellow, Internat. Peace Res. Inst., Oslo, 1971–72; Head of Secretariat, Norwegian Level of Living Study, 1972–76; Fellow, Inst. for Social Res., Oslo, 1976–78; Head of Res., Min. of Consumer Affairs and Govt Admin, Oslo, 1978–83; Prof. of Welfare Studies, Univ. of Stockholm, 1983–86; Sen. Res. Scientist, Central Bureau of Statistics, Oslo, 1986–88; Asst Dir Gen., Min. of Justice, Oslo, 1988–90. *Publication:* The Possibility of Politics, 1987. *Address:* University of Oxford, Department of Applied Social Studies and Social Research, Barnett House, Wellington Square, Oxford OX1 2ER. *T:* Oxford (0865) 270325.

RINGROSE, Prof. John Robert, FRS 1977; FRSE; Professor of Pure Mathematics, since 1964, and a Pro-Vice-Chancellor, 1983–88, University of Newcastle upon Tyne; *b* 21 Dec. 1932; *s* of Albert Frederick Ringrose and Elsie Lilian Ringrose (*née* Roberts); *m* 1956, Jean Margaret Bates; three *s*. *Educ:* Buckhurst Hill County High School, Chigwell, Essex; St John's Coll., Cambridge (MA, PhD). Lecturer in Mathematics: King's Coll., Newcastle upon Tyne, 1957–61; Univ. of Cambridge (also Fellow of St John's Coll.), 1961–63; Sen. Lectr in Mathematics, Univ. of Newcastle upon Tyne, 1963–64. *Publications:* Compact Non-self-adjoint Operators, 1971; (with R. V. Kadison) Fundamentals of the Theory of Operator Algebras, 1983; mathematical papers in various research jls. *Address:* Department of Mathematics and Statistics, The University, Newcastle upon Tyne NE1 7RU. *T:* 091–222 6000.

RINGWOOD, Prof. Alfred Edward, FAA 1966; FRS 1972; Professor of Geochemistry, Australian National University, since 1967; *b* 19 April 1930; *s* of Alfred Edward Ringwood and Wilhelmena Grace Bruce Ringwood (*née* Robertson); *m* 1960, Gun Ivor Carlsson, Halsingborg, Sweden; one *s* one *d*. *Educ:* Hawthorn Central Sch., Melbourne; Geelong Grammar Sch.; Melbourne Univ. BSc 1950, MSc 1953, PhD 1956, Melbourne. Research Fellow, Geochemistry, Harvard Univ., 1957–58; Australian National University: Sen. Res. Fellow, 1959; Sen. Fellow, 1960; Personal Prof., 1963; Dir, Res. Sch. of Earth Scis, 1978–84. Lectures: Clark Meml, Royal Soc., NSW, 1969; William Smith, Geol Soc. of London, 1973; Vernadsky, USSR Acad. of Scis, 1975; Centenary, Chem. Soc., London, 1977 (also Medal); Foster Hewitt, Lehigh Univ., Penn, USA, 1978; Matthew Flinders, Australian Acad. of Sci., 1978; Pawsey Meml, Aust. Inst. of Physics, 1980; Sir Maurice Mawby Meml, Min. Soc., Vic, 1981; Hallimond, Mineralogical Soc. of GB, 1983; Bakerian, Royal Soc., 1983; Alix G. Mautner Meml, UCLA, 1990. Commonwealth and Foreign Mem., Geol Soc., London, 1967; Fellow, Amer. Geophysical Union, 1969; Vice-Pres., Australian Acad. of Science, 1971. For. Associate, Nat. Acad. of Scis of Amer., 1975; Hon. Mem., All-Union Mineralog. Soc., USSR, 1976. Hon. DSc Göttingen, 1987. Internat. Co-operation Year Medal, Govt of Canada, 1965; Mineralogical Soc. of America Award, 1967; Britannica Australia Award for Science, 1969; Rosentiel Award, AAAS, 1971; Werner Medaille, German Mineralogical Soc., 1972; Bowie Medal, American Geophysical Union, 1974; Day Medal, Geological Soc. of America, 1974; Mueller Medal, Aust. and NZ Assoc. for Advancement of Sci., 1975; Holmes Medal, European Union of Geosciences, 1985; Gold Medal for Research, Royal Soc., Vic, 1985; Wollaston Medal, Geol Soc. Lond., 1988; Ingerson Award, Internat. Assoc. Cosmochem., Geochem., 1988. *Publications:* Composition and Petrology of the Earth's Mantle, 1975; Safe Disposal of High Level Nuclear Reactor Wastes: a new strategy, 1978; Origin of Earth and Moon, 1979; numerous papers in learned jls dealing with nature of earth's interior, phase transformations under high pressures, origin and evolution of earth, moon, planets and meteorites, and safe immobilization of high level nuclear reactor wastes. *Recreations:* music, travel. *Address:* 3 Vancouver Street, Red Hill, Canberra, ACT 2603, Australia. *T:* Canberra 062–953635.

RINK, Margaret Joan; *see* Suttill, Dr. M. J.

RIPA DI MEANA, Carlo; Member for Italy, Commission of the European Communities, since 1985; *b* 15 Aug. 1929; *m* 1982, Marina Punturieri. Editor, Il Lavoro (Ital. Gen. Conf. of Labour weekly newspaper), and Editor, foreign dept, Unita (Ital. Communist Party daily paper), 1950–53; rep. of Italy on UIE, Prague, 1953–56; founded jointly Nuova Generazione, 1956; left Ital. Communist Party, 1957; founded jointly Passato e Presente, 1957 (chief editor); joined Italian Socialist Party (PSI), 1958; worked in publishing until 1966; Councillor for Lombardy (PSI), 1970–74 (Chm., Constitutional Cttee); leader, PSI Group, regional council; head, international relations PSI, 1979–80; Mem., European Parlt, 1979–84. Pres., Inst. for Internat. Economic Cooperation and Develt Problems, 1983; Sec.-Gen., Club Turati, Milan, 1967–76; Mem. Board, Scala Theatre, Milan, 1970–74; Mem. Council, Venice Biennale 1974–82 (Chm., 1974–79); founder Mem., Crocodile Club; Pres., Fernando Santi Inst.; Pres., Unitary Fedn, Italian Press abroad; Vice-Chm., Internat. Cttee for Solidarity with Afghan People. *Publications:* Un viaggio in Viet-Nam (A Voyage to Vietnam), 1956; A tribute to Raymond Roussel and his Impressions of Africa, 1965; Il governo audiovisivo (Audiovisual Government), 1973. *Recreations:* horse riding, sailing. *Address:* 200 Rue de la Loi, 1049 Brussels, Belgium.

RIPLEY, Prof. Brian David, PhD; FRSE; Professor of Applied Statistics, and Fellow of St Peter's College, University of Oxford, since 1990; *b* 29 April 1952; *s* of Eric Lewis Ripley and Sylvia May (*née* Gould); *m* 1973, Ruth Mary Appleton. *Educ:* Farnborough Grammar Sch.; Churchill Coll., Cambridge (MA, PhD). FIMS 1987; FRSE 1990. Lectr in Statistics, Imperial Coll., London, 1976–80; Reader, Univ. of London, 1980–83; Prof. of Statistics, Univ. of Strathclyde, 1983–90. Mem., Internat. Statistical Inst., 1982. Adams Prize, Univ. of Cambridge, 1987. *Publications:* Spatial Statistics, 1981; Stochastic Simulation, 1987; Statistical Inference for Spatial Processes, 1988; numerous papers on statistics and applications in biology, chemistry and earth sciences. *Recreation:* natural history. *Address:* 1 South Parks Road, Oxford OX1 3TG. *T:* Oxford (0865) 272861.

RIPLEY, Dillon; *see* Ripley, S. D.

RIPLEY, Sir Hugh, 4th Bt, *cr* 1880; former Director, John Walker & Sons Ltd, Scotch Whisky Distillers, retired 1981; *b* 26 May 1916; *s* of Sir Henry William Alfred Ripley, 3rd Bt, and Dorothy (*d* 1964), *e d* of late Robert William Daker Harley; *S* father 1956; *m* 1st, 1946, Dorothy Mary Dunlop Bruce-Jones (marr. diss. 1971); one *s* one *d*; 2nd, 1972, Susan, *d* of W. Parker, Leics; one *d*. *Educ:* Eton. Served in Africa and Italy with 1st Bn KSLI (despatches twice, American Silver Star); retired regular Major. *Recreations:* golf, fishing, shooting. *Heir:* *s* William Hugh Ripley, *b* 13 April 1950. *Address:* 20 Abingdon Villas, W8 6BX; The Oak, Bedstone, Bucknell, Salop. *Club:* Boodle's.

RIPLEY, (Sidney) Dillon, II, Hon. KBE 1979; PhD; Secretary, Smithsonian Institution, 1964–84, now Secretary Emeritus; *b* 20 Sept. 1913; *s* of Louis Arthur Ripley and Constance Baillie (*née* Rose); *m* 1949, Mary Moncrieffe Livingston; three *d*. *Educ:* St Paul's Sch., Concord, NH; Yale Univ. (BA 1936); Harvard Univ. (PhD 1943). Staff, Acad. of Natural Sciences, Philadelphia, 1936–39; Volunteer Asst, Amer. Museum of Natural History, New York, 1939–40; Teaching Asst, Harvard Univ., 1941–42; Asst Curator of Birds, Smithsonian Instn, 1942; OSS, 1942–45; Lectr, Curator, Associate Prof. of Zool. and Prof. of Biol., Yale Univ., 1946–64; Dir, Peabody Museum of Nat. Hist., 1959–64. Dir, Riggs Nat. Corp., Washington, 1984. Chm. (US), E-SU, 1984. Pres., 1958–82, Pres. Emeritus, 1982–, ICBP. Benjamin Franklin Fellow, RSA, 1968. Member: Amer. Acad. of Arts and Scis, 1984; Nat. Acad. of Sci., 1968; Hon. Mem., Amer. Inst. of Architects, 1975–. Hon. MA Yale Univ., 1961; Hon DHL: Marlboro Coll., 1965; Williams Coll., 1972; Johns Hopkins, 1984; Washington Coll., 1986; Hon. DSc: George Washington Univ., 1966; Catholic Univ., 1968; Univ. of Md, 1970; Cambridge Univ., 1974; Brown Univ., 1975; Trinity Coll., 1977; Hon. LLD: Dickinson Coll., 1967; Hofstra Univ., 1968; Yale Univ., 1975; Gallaudet Coll., 1981; Harvard, 1984; Hon. DE Stevens Inst. of Technol., 1977. Order of White Elephant, Thailand, 1949; Order of the Sacred Treasure, 2nd Cl., Japan, 1982; Officer: l'Ordre des Arts et des Lettres, France, 1975; Order of Leopold, Belgium, 1981; Légion d'Honneur, France, 1985; Commander: Order of Golden Ark, Netherlands, 1976; Order of Merit, State Council of Polish People's Republic, 1979; Order of Orange-Nassau, Netherlands, 1982; Comdr's Cross, Order of the Dannebrog, Denmark, 1976; Caballero Gran Cruz, Orden del Merito Civil, Spain, 1976; Order of James Smithson, Smithsonian Instn, 1984; Padma Bhushan, India, 1986. Freedom Medal, Thailand, 1949; President's Medal of Freedom, USA, 1985; Gold Medal: New York Zool Soc., 1966; Royal Zool Soc. of Antwerp, 1970; Thomas Jefferson Award, Amer. Soc. of Interior Designers, 1974; Medal for Distinguished Achievement, Holland Soc. of New York, 1977; F. K. Hutchinson Medal, Garden Club of America, 1979; Medal of Honor, National Soc. of Daughters of Amer. Revolution, 1981; Delacour Medal, ICBP, 1982; Henry Shaw Medal, St Louis Botannical Garden, 1982; Gold Medal, Acad. of Soc. Sci., New York, 1982; Addison Emery Verrill Medal, Peabody Mus., Yale Univ., 1984; Olympia Prize, Onassis Foundn, 1984; Medal of Distinction, Barnard Coll., 1985; Cosmos Club Award, Washington, 1988; Bishop Mus. Medal, Hawaii, 1990. *Publications:* The Trail of the Money Bird, 1942 (Sweden, 1945; UK 1947); Search for the Spiny Babbler, 1952, re-issued as A Naturalist's Adventure in Nepal, 1978; A Paddling of Ducks, 1957 (UK 1959); A Synopsis of the Birds of India and Pakistan, 1961, rev. edn 1982; (ed with Lynette L. Scribner) Ornithological Books in the Yale University Library, 1961; The Land and Wildlife of Tropical Asia, 1964, rev. edns 1971 and 1974; (with H. G. Deignan and R. A. Paynter, Jr) Check-list of Birds of the World, Vol. X (continuation of work of James L. Peters), 1964; The Sacred Grove, 1969; The Paradox of the Human Condition, 1975; Rails of the World, 1977; (with Sálim Ali) Handbook of the Birds of India and Pakistan: Vol. I, 1968, rev. edn 1978; Vol. II, 1969, rev. edn 1979; Vol. III, 1969, rev. edn 1981; Vol. IV, 1970, rev. edn 1984; Vol. V, 1972, rev. edn 1987; Vol. VI, 1971; Vol. VII, 1972; Vol. VIII, 1973; Vol. IX, 1973; Vol. X, 1974; (with Sálim Ali) A Pictorial Guide to Birds of the Indian Subcontinent, 1983, rev. edn 1988. *Recreation:* watching ducks. *Address:* 2324 Massachusetts Avenue, NW, Washington, DC 20008, USA. *T:* (202) 232–3131; Paddling Ponds, Litchfield, Conn 06759, USA. *T:* (203) 567–8208. *Clubs:* English-Speaking Union; Alliance Française, Pilgrims of the US, Knickerbocker, Century Association, Yale (New York); Cosmos, Society of Cincinnati, Alibi, Metropolitan (Washington, DC); Himalayan (New Delhi).

RIPON, Bishop of, since 1977; **Rt. Rev. David Nigel de Lorentz Young;** *b* 2 Sept. 1931; *s* of late Brig. K. de L. Young, CIE, MC; *m* 1962, Rachel Melverley Lewis (*d* 1966); one *s* one *d*; *m* 1967, Jane Havill Collison; three *s*. *Educ:* Wellington Coll.; Balliol Coll., Oxford (MA). Director, Dept of Buddhist Studies, Theological Coll. of Lanka, 1964; Lecturer in Comparative Religion, Manchester Univ., 1967; Vicar of Burwell, Cambridge, 1970–75; Archdeacon of Huntingdon, 1975–77; Vicar of Great with Little and Steeple Gidding, 1975–77; Rector of Hemingford Abbots, 1977; Hon. Canon of Ely Cathedral, 1975–77. Mem., Doctrine Commn, 1978–81; Chairman: Partnership for World Mission, 1978–86; Governing Body, SPCK, 1979–88; Anglican Interfaith Consultants, 1981–; Scargill Council, 1984–90. *Publications:* contribs to Religious Studies. *Recreations:* tennis, sailing. *Address:* Bishop Mount, Ripon, N Yorks HG4 5DP. *Club:* Commonwealth Trust.

RIPON, Dean of; *see* Campling, Very Rev. C. R.

RIPPENGAL, Derek, CB 1982; QC 1980; Counsel to Chairman of Committees, House of Lords, since 1977; *b* 8 Sept. 1928; *s* of William Thomas Rippengal and Margaret Mary Rippengal (*née* Parry); *m* 1963, Elizabeth Melrose (*d* 1973); one *s* one *d*. *Educ:* Hampton Grammar Sch.; St Catharine's Coll., Cambridge (Scholar; MA). Called to Bar, Middle Temple, 1953 (Harmsworth schol.). Entered Treasury Solicitor's Office, 1958, after Chancery Bar and univ. posts; Sen. Legal Asst, 1961; Asst Treasury Solicitor, 1967; Principal Asst Treasury Solicitor, 1971; Solicitor to DTI, 1972–73; Dep. Parly Counsel, 1973–74, Parly Counsel, 1974–76, Law Commn. *Recreations:* music, fishing. *Address:* Wychwood, Bell Lane, Little Chalfont, Amersham, Bucks HP6 6PF. *Club:* Athenæum.

RIPPON, family name of **Baron Rippon of Hexham**.

RIPPON OF HEXHAM, Baron *cr* 1987 (Life Peer), of Hesleyside in the county of Northumberland; **(Aubrey) Geoffrey (Frederick) Rippon;** PC 1962; QC 1964; *b* 28 May 1924; *o s* of late A. E. S. Rippon; *m* 1946, Ann Leyland, OBE 1984, *d* of Donald Yorke, MC, Prenton, Birkenhead, Cheshire; one *s* three *d*. *Educ:* King's College, Taunton; Brasenose College, Oxford (Hulme Open Exhibitioner; MA), Hon. Fellow, 1972. Secretary and Librarian of the Oxford Union, 1942; Pres. Oxford University Conservative Assoc., 1942; Chm., Federation of University Conservative Associations, 1943. Called to the Bar, Middle Temple, 1948 (Robert Garraway Rice Pupillage Prizeman), Bencher, 1979. Member Surbiton Borough Council, 1945–54; Alderman, 1949–54; Mayor, 1951–52; Member: LCC (Chelsea), 1952–61 (Leader of Conserv. Party on LCC, 1957–59); Court, Univ. of London, 1958–; Chairman: British Section (individual members) of the Council of European Municipalities; British Sect., European League for Economic Co-operation; President: London Mayors' Assoc., 1968–71; Surrey Mayors' Assoc., 1974–76; Assoc. of District Councils, 1986–; Town and Country Planning Assoc., 1988–; Admiral of the Manx Herring Fleet, 1971–74. Chm. Conservative National Advisory Committee on Local Government, 1957–59, Pres., 1972–74; Vice-Pres., Council of Europe's Local Government Conference, 1957 and 1958; Contested (C) Shoreditch and Finsbury, General Elections, 1950 and 1951; MP (C): Norwich South, 1955–64; Hexham, 1966–87. PPS, Min. of Housing and Local Govt, 1956–57, Min. of Defence, 1957–59; Parly Sec., Min. of Aviation, 1959–61; Jt Parly Sec., Min. of Housing and Local Govt, Oct. 1961–July 1962; Minister of Public Building and Works, 1962–64 (Cabinet, 1963–64); Chief Opposition Spokesman on housing, local govt and land, 1966–68, on defence, 1968–70; Minister of Technology (incorporating Mins of Industry, Fuel and Power, Aviation and Supply), 1970; Chancellor of the Duchy of Lancaster, 1970–72 (resp. for negotiating Britain's entry into the EEC); Sec. of State for the Environment (incorporating Mins of Trans., Housing, Land, Local Govt, Public Bldg and Works), 1972–74; Chief Opposition Spokesman on Foreign and Commonwealth Affairs, 1974–75. Chm., Parly Foreign and Commonwealth Affairs Cttee, 1979–81; Leader: Cons. Party Delegn to Council of Europe and WEU, 1967–70; Cons. Gp, European Parlt, 1977–79; Chm., Council of Ministers, EFTA, 1970–72. Chairman: Dun and Bradstreet Ltd, 1976–; Britannia Arrow Hldgs, subseq. Invesco MIM, 1977–89 (Pres., 1989–); Brassey's Defence Publishers, 1977–; Singer & Friedlander Hldgs, 1984–87; Robert Fraser and Partners, 1985–; Michael Page Plc, 1987–; UniChem, 1990–; Holland, Hannen & Cubitts, 1965–69; Dep. Chm., Drake & Gorham, 1969–70; Director: Fairey Co. Ltd, 1965–70; Bristol Aeroplane Co., 1965–69; Hotung Estates, 1974–75; Groupe Bruxelles Lambert, 1982–90; Maxwell Communications Corp., 1986–; Acer Group Ltd, 1991–. Chm., Univ. of London Ct, 1991–. FCIArb; Hon. Mem., Rating and Valuation Assoc. Hon. LLD London, 1989. Knight Grand Cross, Royal Order of North Star (Sweden); Grand Cross, Order of Merit (Liechtenstein). *Publications:* (co-author) Forward from Victory, 1943; The Rent Act, 1957; various pamphlets and articles on foreign affairs, local government and legal subjects. *Recreations:* watching cricket, travel. *Address:* The Old Vicarage, Broomfield, near Bridgwater, Somerset; 1 Essex Court, Temple, EC4Y 9AR; 2 Paper Buildings, Temple, EC4Y 7ET. *T:* 071–353 5835. *Clubs:* Whites, Pratt's, MCC.

RISELEY-PRICHARD, Air Vice-Marshal Richard Augustin; Principal Medical Officer, Royal Air Force Support Command, 1980–85, retired; Associate Member, Swindon District Health Authority, since 1990 (Member, 1988–90); *b* 19 Feb. 1925; *s* of late Dr J. A. Prichard and Elizabeth (*née* Riseley); *m* 1953, Alannah *d* of late Air Cdre C. W. Busk, CB, MC, AFC; four *d*. *Educ:* Beaudesert Park; Radley Coll.; Trinity Coll., Oxford (MA, BM, BCh); St Bartholomew's Hosp., London. FFCM. Commnd RAF Med. Br., 1951; pilot trng, 1951–52; served at RAF Coll., Cranwell, 1953–56; Dep. Principal Med. Officer (Flying), HQ Transport Comd and HQ RAF Germany, 1956–63; RAF Staff Coll., 1964; SMO, British Forces, Aden, 1967; Dep. Principal Med. Officer, HQ Strike Comd, 1970–73; Commanding Officer: RAF Hosp. Wegberg, Germany, 1973–76; Princess Alexandra Hosp., Wroughton, 1977–80. QHS 1980–85. Hon. Air Cdre, No 4626, RAuxAF Sqn, 1986–. Gen. Comr of Income Tax, 1987–. Mem., Armed Forces Cttee, BMA, 1989–. Governor: Dauntsey's Sch., 1982– (Vice-Chm., 1985–86, Chm., 1986–); BUPA Medical Foundn, 1990–. CStJ. *Recreations:* tennis, squash, bridge, gardening. *Address:* The Little House, Allington, Devizes, Wilts SN10 3NN. *T:* Devizes (0380) 860662. *Clubs:* Royal Air Force; All England Lawn Tennis.

RISK, Douglas James; Sheriff of Grampian, Highland and Islands, at Aberdeen and Stonehaven, since 1979; *b* 23 Jan. 1941; *s* of James Risk and Isobel Katherine Taylor Risk (*née* Dow); *m* 1967, Jennifer Hood Davidson; three *s* one *d*. *Educ:* Glasgow Academy; Gonville and Caius Coll., Cambridge (BA 1963, MA 1967); Glasgow Univ. (LLB 1965). Admitted to Faculty of Advocates, 1966; Standing Junior Counsel, Scottish Education Dept, 1975; Sheriff of Lothian and Borders at Edinburgh, 1977–79. Hon. Lectr, Faculty of Law, Univ. of Aberdeen, 1981–. *Address:* Sheriffs Chambers, Sheriff Court House, Exchequer Row, Aberdeen AB9 1AP. *T:* Aberdeen (0224) 572780. *Club:* Royal Northern and University (Aberdeen).

RISK, Sir Thomas (Neilson), Kt 1984; FRSE; Governor of the Bank of Scotland, 1981–91; (Director, 1971; Deputy Governor, 1977–81); *b* 13 Sept. 1922; *s* of late Ralph Risk, CBE, MC, and Margaret Nelson Robertson; *m* 1949, Suzanne Eiloart; three *s* (and one *s* decd). *Educ:* Kelvinside Academy; Glasgow Univ. (BL). Flight Lieut, RAF, 1941–46; RAFVR, 1946–53. Partner, Maclay Murray & Spens, Solicitors, 1950–81; Director: Standard Life Assurance Co., 1965–88 (Chm., 1969–77); British Linen Bank, 1968–91 (Governor, 1977–86); Howden Group, 1971–87; Merchants Trust, 1973–; MSA (Britain) Ltd, 1958–; Shell UK Ltd, 1982–; Barclays Bank, 1983–85; Bank of Wales, 1986–91; Chm., Scottish Financial Enterprise, 1986–89. Member: Scottish Industrial Develt Bd, 1972–75; Scottish Econ. Council, 1983–; NEDC, 1987–91. Trustee, Hamilton Bequest. FRSE 1988. Hon. LLD Glasgow, 1985; Dr *hc* Edinburgh, 1990. *Address:* 10 Belford Place, Edinburgh EH4 3DH. *T:* 031–332 9425. *Clubs:* Royal Air Force; New (Edinburgh).

RISK, William Symington, CA; Chairman, Fleming and Ferguson Ltd, 1980–87; *b* 15 Sept. 1909; *er s* of late William Risk and Agnes Hetherington Symington, Glasgow; *m* 1937, Isobel Brown McLay; one *s* one *d*. *Educ:* Glasgow Academy; Glasgow Univ.; Edinburgh Univ. (BCom). FCMA 1944, JDipMA 1969. Served War, with Admiralty, on torpedo production at RN Torpedo Factory, at Greenock and elsewhere, 1940–45. Partner, Robson, Morrow & Co., 1945–53; Managing Director: H. W. Nevill Ltd (Nevill's Bread), 1953; Aerated Bread Co. Ltd, 1956; Chm., The London Multiple Bakers' Alliance, 1958–59; Regional Dir for Southern England, British Bakeries Ltd, 1960; Industrial Consultant, Hambros Bank Ltd, 1963; Chm., Martin-Black Ltd, 1976–79. Inst. of Chartered Accountants of Scotland: Mem. Exam. Bd, 1951–55; Mem. Council, 1963–68; Pres., 1974–75; Jt Dip. in Management Accounting Services, and First Chm. of Bd, 1966; Inst. of Cost and Management Accountants: Mem. Council, 1952–70; Pres. of Inst., 1960–61; Gold Medal of Inst., for services to the Inst. and the profession, 1965. Mem. Bd of Governors, Queen Charlotte's Hosp., 1970–80. *Publications:* technical papers on Accountancy and Management subjects; papers to internat. Congress of Accountants (London, 1952, Paris, 1967). *Recreation:* reading. *Address:* Craigowrie, Strathspey Drive, Grantown on Spey, Morayshire PH26 3EY. *T:* Grantown on Spey (0479) 3001. *Clubs:* Caledonian; New (Edinburgh); Royal Scottish Automobile (Glasgow).

RISNESS, Eric John, CBE 1982; FEng 1990; FIEE; Managing Director, STC Technology Ltd, 1987–90; *b* 27 July 1927; *s* of Kristen Riisnaes and Ethel Agnes (*née* Weeks); *m* 1952, Colleen Edwina Armstrong; two *s* two *d*. *Educ:* Stratford Grammar School, London; Corpus Christi College, Cambridge (MA, PhD). RN Scientific Service, Admiralty Research Lab., 1954; Naval Staff Coll., 1959; Admiralty Underwater Weapons Estabt, 1961; RCDS 1970; Ministry of Defence: Defence Science, 1974; Underwater Research, 1975; Sting Ray Torpedo Project, 1977; Underwater Weapons Projects, 1979; Admiralty Surface Weapons Estabt, 1980; Dir of Naval Analysis, 1982; Dir-Gen., Surface Weapons Projects, 1983; Man. Dir, Admiralty Res. Estabt, Portland, 1984–87. *Recreations:* music, genealogy, golf. *Address:* 8 Orchard Road, Shalford, Guildford, Surrey GU4 8ER. *T:* Guildford (0483) 34581.

RISSON, Maj.-Gen. Sir Robert Joseph Henry, Kt 1970; CB 1958; CBE 1945 (OBE 1942); DSO 1942; ED 1948; Chairman Melbourne and Metropolitan Tramways Board, 1949–70; Chairman, National Fitness Council of Victoria, 1961–71; *b* 20 April 1901; *s* of late Robert Risson; *m* 1934, Gwendolyn, *d* of late C. A. Spurgin; no *c*. *Educ:* Gatton High Sch.; Univ. of Queensland. BE (Civil); FICE; FIEAust; FAIM. Served AIF, War of 1939–45: GOC 3 Div. (Australian), 1953–56; Citizen Military Forces Member Australian Military Board, 1957–58. Chief Commissioner, Boy Scouts, Victoria, 1958–63; Pres., Instn Engineers, Australia, 1962–63. OStJ 1966. *Address:* 39 Somers Street, Burwood, Victoria 3125, Australia. *Clubs:* Australian (Melbourne); Naval and Military (Melbourne); United Service (Brisbane).

RIST, Prof. John Michael, FRSC; Professor of Classics and Philosophy, University of Toronto, since 1983; *b* 6 July 1936; *s* of Robert Ward Rist and Phoebe May (*née* Mansfield) *m* 1960, Anna Thérèse (*née* Vogler); two *s* two *d* *Educ:* Trinity Coll., Cambridge (BA 1959, MA 1963). FRSC 1976. Univ. of Toronto: firstly Lectr, finally Prof. of Classics, 1959–80; Chm., Grad. Dept of Classics, 1971–75; Regius Prof. of Classics, Aberdeen Univ., 1980–83. *Publications:* Eros and Psyche, Canada 1964; Plotinus: the road to reality, 1967; Stoic Philosophy, 1969; Epicurus: an introduction, 1972; (ed) The Stoics, USA 1978; On the Independence of Matthew and Mark, 1978; Human Value, 1982; Platonism and its Christian Heritage, 1985; The Mind of Aristotle, 1989; contrib. classical and phil jls. *Recreations:* travel, swimming, hill-walking. *Address:* University of Toronto, 16 Hart House Circle, Toronto, Ontario M5S 1A1, Canada.

RITBLAT, John Henry, FSVA; Chairman and Managing Director, The British Land Co. plc, since 1970; Chairman and Chief Executive, The British Land Corporation, since 1991; *b* 3 Oct. 1935; *m* 1st, 1960, Isabel Paja (*d* 1979); two *s* one *d*; 2nd, 1986, Jill Zilkha (*née* Slotover). *Educ:* Dulwich Coll.; London Univ. College of Estate Management. Articles with West End firm of Surveyors and Valuers, 1952–58. Founder Partner, Conrad Ritblat & Co., Consultant Surveyors and Valuers, 1958; Man. Dir, Union Property Holdings (London) Ltd, 1969. Comr, Crown Estate Paving Commn, 1969–. Hon. Surveyor, King George's Fund for Sailors, 1979. Member: Council, Business in the Community, 1987–; Prince of Wales' Royal Parks Tree Appeal Cttee, 1987–; British Olympic Assoc., 1979; Olympic Appeal Cttee, 1984 and 1988; Patrons of British Art, Tate Gall.; English Heritage; Royal Horticultural Soc.; Architecture Club; SPAB; Royal Acad. (Mem. Cttee); Nat. Art-Collections Fund; Life Member: Nat. Trust; Zool Soc. of London; Georgian Gp; RGS; Trollope Soc. Trustee, Zool Soc. of London Develt Trust, 1986–89. Patron, London Fedn of Boys' Clubs Centenary Appeal; Founder Sponsor, Young Explorers Trust; Sponsor: RGS, 1982–85; (sole), British Nat. Ski Championships, 1978–91; Vice-Pres., British Ski Fedn, 1984–89. Dep. Chm. Governors, Hall Sch. FRGS 1982; CBIM; Life FRSA. *Recreations:* antiquarian books and libraries, old buildings and the countryside, bees, squash, golf, skiing. *Address:* 10 Cornwall Terrace, Regent's Park, NW1 4QP. *T:* 071–486 4466. *Clubs:* Royal Automobile, MCC, The Pilgrims; Cresta (St Moritz).

RITCHESON, Prof. Charles Ray; University Professor of History and University Librarian Emeritus, since 1991; *b* 26 Feb. 1925; *s* of Charles Frederick and Jewell Vaughn Ritcheson; *m* 1st, 1953, Shirley Spackman (marr. diss. 1964); two *s*; 2nd, 1965, Alice Luethi; four *s*. *Educ:* Univs of Harvard, Zürich, Oklahoma and Oxford. DPhil (Oxon). FRHistS. Prof. and Chm. of History, Kenyon Coll., 1953–65; Chm. and Dir, Graduate Studies, Southern Methodist Univ., 1965–70; Lovell Prof. of History, Univ. of Southern Calif., 1971–74; Cultural Attaché, US Embassy, 1974–77; University of Southern California: Lovell Distinguished Prof. of History, 1977–84; Lovell Univ. Prof., Univ. Librarian, Dean and Special Asst. to Pres., 1984–91. Chm., British Inst. of the US, 1979–81. Vice-Pres., Board of Dirs, Amer. Friends of Covent Garden, 1978–84; Member: National Council for the Humanities, 1983–87 and 1988–91; US Bd of Foreign Scholarships, 1987–88; Adv. Council, Ditchley Foundn, 1977–; Adv. Council, Univ. of Buckingham (formerly UC Buckingham), 1977–. Hon. DLitt Leicester, 1976. *Publications:* British Politics and the American Revolution, 1954; Aftermath of Revolution: British policy toward the United States 1783–1795, 1969 (paperback, 1971); The American Revolution: the Anglo-American relation, 1969; (with E. Wright) A Tug of Loyalties, 1971. *Recreations:* horseback riding, swimming, opera. *Address:* 3605 Lowell Street, NW, Washington, DC 20016, USA. *Clubs:* Beefsteak, Brooks's; California (Los Angeles); Cosmos (Washington).

RITCHIE, family name of **Baron Ritchie of Dundee.**

RITCHIE OF DUNDEE, 5th Baron *cr* 1905; **Harold Malcolm Ritchie;** English and Drama Teacher, Bedgebury School, Kent, retired 1984; Social and Liberal Democrat (formerly Liberal) spokesman on education, House of Lords, since 1985; *b* 29 Aug. 1919; 4th *s* of 2nd Baron Ritchie of Dundee and Sarah Ruth (*d* 1950), *d* of J. L. Jennings, MP; *S* brother, 1978; *m* 1948, Anne, *d* of late Col C. G. Johnstone, MC; one *s* one *d*. *Educ:* Stowe School; Trinity College, Oxford. MA 1940. Served in Middle East, Italy and Greece, Captain KRRC, 1940–46. Assistant Headmaster, Brickwall House School, Northiam, Sussex, 1952–65; Headmaster, 1965–72. *Recreations:* gardening, drama, music. *Heir:* *s* Hon. Charles Rupert Rendall Ritchie [*b* 15 March 1958; *m* 1984, Tara Van Tuyl Koch]. *Address:* House of Lords, SW1. *Club:* Commonwealth Trust.

RITCHIE, Albert Edgar, CC 1975; Canadian Diplomat, retired Nov. 1981; *b* 20 Dec. 1916; *m*; two *s* two *d*. *Educ:* Mount Allison Univ., New Brunswick (BA 1938); Queen's College, Oxford (Rhodes Scholar, 1940; BA). Officer, Econ. Affairs Dept, UN, and Secretariat of Gen. Agreement on Tariffs and Trade, 1946–48; Counsellor, Office of Canadian High Comr, London, UK, 1948–52; Deputy Under-Secretary of State for External Affairs, Canada, 1964–66; Canadian Ambassador to USA, 1966–70; Under-Sec. of State for External Affairs, Canada, 1970–74; Special Advisor to Privy Council Office, Canada, 1974–76; Canadian Ambassador to Republic of Ireland, 1976–81. Hon. LLD: Mount Allison Univ., 1966; St Thomas Univ., 1968; Carleton Univ., 1985. *Address:* 336 Frost Avenue, Ottawa, Ont K1H 5J2, Canada. *Club:* Rideau (Ottawa).

RITCHIE, Alexander James Otway; Chairman, Union Discount Co. of London plc, 1970–90; *b* 5 May 1928; *s* of Charles Henry Ritchie and Marjorie Alice Ritchie (*née* Stewart); *m* 1953, Joanna Willink Fletcher; two *s* (one *d* decd). *Educ:* Stowe; St John's Coll., Cambridge (MA). Joined Glyn, Mills and Co., 1951 (Dir, 1964); Exec. Dir, Williams & Glyn's Bank, 1970; resigned Williams & Glyn's Bank, 1977; Dep. Chm., Grindlays Bank plc, 1977–83, Chief Exec. 1980–83; Dep. Chm., Grindlays Holdings, 1978–83; Chairman: Grindlays Bank, 1984–87; ANZ Hldgs (UK), 1985–87; Dep. Chm., Italian Internat. Bank, 1989– (Dir, 1986–). Director: Australian and New Zealand Banking Gp, 1984–87; European Investment Bank, 1986–; Debenham Tewson & Chinnocks Holdings plc, 1987–. Mem., London Cttee, Ottoman Bank, 1966–; Mem., Export Guarantees Adv. Council, 1977–82 (Dep. Chm., 1980–81). *Address:* 54 Sydney Buildings, Bath, Avon BA2 6DB.

RITCHIE, Anthony Elliot, CBE 1978; MA, BSc, MD; FRSE; Secretary and Treasurer, 1969–86, Trustee, since 1987, Carnegie Trust for the Universities of Scotland; *b* 30 March 1915; *s* of late Prof. James Ritchie; *m* 1941, Elizabeth Lambie Knox, MB, ChB, *y d* of John Knox, Dunfermline; one *s* three *d*. *Educ:* Edinburgh Academy; Aberdeen and Edinburgh Universities. MA (Aber), 1933; BSc 1936, with Hunter Memorial Prize. MB, ChB (Edin.) 1940. Carnegie Research Scholar, Physiology Dept, Edin. Univ., 1940–41; Asst Lectr 1941; Lectr 1942. Ellis Prize in Physiology, 1941; Gunning Victoria Jubilee Prize, 1943; MD (Edin.) with Gold Medal Thesis, 1945; senior lecturer grade, 1946. Lecturer in Electrotherapy, Edin. Royal Infirmary, 1943–48, 1972–; Chandos Prof. of Physiology, Univ. of St Andrews, 1948–69; Dean, Faculty of Science, 1961–66. Hon. Physiologist Gogarburn Nerve Injuries Hospital, 1941–46; Honeyman Gillespie Lecturer, 1944; Hon. Consultant in Electrotherapy, Scot. E Regional Hospital Board, 1950–69; Fellow Royal Soc. of Edinburgh, 1951 (Council RSE 1957–60, 1979–80; Secretary to Ordinary Meetings, 1960–65, Vice-President, 1965–66 and 1976–79; General Secretary, 1966–76); Scientific Adviser, Civil Defence, 1961–80; Adv. Cttee on Med. Research, Scotland, 1961–, Vice-Chm., 1967–69; Chairman: Scottish Cttee on Science Educn, 1970–78; Blood Transfusion Adv. Gp, 1970–80; Scottish Universities Entrance Bd, 1963–69; St Leonard's Sch., St Andrews, 1968–69; Mem., Council for Applied Science in Scotland, 1978–86; Mem., British Library Bd, 1973–80; Trustee, Nat. Library of Scotland. Mem., Cttee of Inquiry into Teachers' Pay. Examiner, Chartered Soc. of Physiotherapy, Pharmaceutical Soc. of Great Britain, and RCSE. RAMC (TA) commission, 1942–44. Hon. FCSP 1970; Hon. FRCPE 1986. Hon. DSc St Andrews, 1972; Hon. LLD Strathclyde, 1985. Bicentary Medal, RSE, 1983. *Publications:* (with J. Lenman) Clinical Electromyography, 1976, 4th edn 1987; medical and scientific papers on nerve injury diagnosis and medical electronics. *Recreations:* reading, mountaineering, motor cars. *Address:* 12 Ravelston Park, Edinburgh EH4 3DX. *T:* 031–332 6560. *Clubs:* Caledonian; New (Edinburgh).

RITCHIE, Charles Stewart Almon, CC 1972; FRSL 1982; *b* 23 Sept. 1906; *s* of William Bruce Almon Ritchie, KC and Lilian Constance Harriette Ritchie (*née* Stewart), both of Halifax, Nova Scotia; *m* 1948, Sylvia Catherine Beatrice Smellie; no *c*. *Educ:* University of King's College; Ecole Libre des Sciences Politiques, Paris. BA, MA Oxford 1929, MA Harvard, 1930. Joined Dept of External Affairs, 3rd Sec. Ottawa, 1934; 3rd Sec., Washington, 1936; 2nd Sec., London, 1939; 1st Sec., London, 1943; 1st Sec., Ottawa, 1945; Counsellor, Paris, 1947; Asst Under-Secretary of State for External Affairs, Ottawa, 1950, Deputy Under-Secretary of State for External Affairs, 1952; Ambassador to Federal Republic of Germany, Bonn, and Head of Military Mission, Berlin, 1954; Permanent Rep. to UN, New York 1958; Ambassador of Canada to the United States, 1962; Ambassador and Permanent Representative of Canada to the North Atlantic Council, 1966–67; Canadian High Comr in London, 1967–71; Special Adviser to Privy Council, Canada, 1971–73. Hon. DCL: Univ. of King's College, Halifax, NS; McGill Univ., Montreal. Hon. Fellow, Pembroke College, Oxford. *Publications:* 4 vols of diaries: The Siren Years: undiplomatic diaries 1937–1945, 1974; An Appetite for Life: the education of a young diplomat, 1978; Diplomatic Passport, 1981; Storm Signals, 1983; My Grandfather's House, 1987. *Address:* Apt 10, 216 Metcalfe Street, Ottawa K2P 1R1, Canada. *Clubs:* Brooks's, Beefsteak; Rideau (Ottawa).

RITCHIE, David Robert; Regional Director, West Midlands Regional Office, Departments of the Environment and Transport, since 1989; *b* 10 March 1948; *s* of late

James Ritchie and of Edith Ritchie (*née* Watts); *m* 1989, Joan Gibbons. *Educ:* Manchester Grammar School; St John's College, Cambridge (BA, MA). Min. of Transport, 1970; DoE, 1970–. *Recreations:* fell-walking, cooking. *Address:* Five Ways Tower, Frederick Road, Edgbaston, Birmingham B15 1SJ. *T:* 021–626 2570.

RITCHIE, Douglas Malcolm; Managing Director, Chief Executive Officer, British Alcan Aluminium, since 1986; *b* Parry Sound, Ont., 8 Jan. 1941; *s* of Ian David Ritchie and Helen Mary Ritchie (*née* Jamieson); *m* 1965, Cydney Ann Brown; three *s*. *Educ:* McGill University (BSc 1962, MBA 1966). Alcan Group Cos, 1966–73; Vice-Pres. Gen. Manager, 1973–75, Exec. Vice-Pres., 1975–78, Alcan Canada Products; Corp. Vice-Pres., Aluminium Co. Can., 1978–80; Exec. Vice-Pres., 1980–82, Pres., 1982–86, Alcan Smelters & Chems; Dir and Exec. Vice-Pres., Alcan Aluminium, Cleveland, 1985–86. Non-executive Director: Laurentian Gp Corp., Montreal, 1988–; Laurentian Financial Group plc (formerly Laurentian Life), 1989–. *Address:* Chalfont Park, Gerrards Cross, Bucks SL9 0QB.

RITCHIE, Rear-Adm. George Stephen, CB 1967; DSC 1942; writer; retired hydrographer; *b* 30 Oct. 1914; *s* of Sir (John) Douglas Ritchie, MC and late Margaret Stephen, OBE 1946, JP, Officer of the Order of Orange-Nassau, *d* of James Allan, Methlick, Aberdeenshire; *m* 1942, Mrs Disa Elizabeth Smith (*née* Beveridge); three *s* one *d*. *Educ:* RNC, Dartmouth. Joined RN Surveying Service, 1936; attached Eighth Army, 1942–43; served in HM Survey Ship Scott for invasion of Europe, 1944; comd HMS Challenger on scientific voyage round world, 1950–51; comd HM New Zealand Survey Ship Lachlan and NZ Surveying Service, 1953–56; comd HM Surveying Ship Dalrymple, Persian Gulf, 1959; comd HM Surveying Ship Vidal, West Indies and Western Europe, 1963–65; ADC to the Queen, 1965; Hydrographer of the Navy, 1966–71; Vis. Research Fellow, Southampton Univ., 1971–72; Pres., Directing Cttee, Internat. Hydrographic Bureau, Monaco, 1972–82; Founder Pres., 1972–73, Emeritus Mem., 1988–, Hydrographic Soc. Founder's Medal, RGS, 1972; Prix Manley-Bendall, Académie de Marine, Paris, 1977; Gold Medal, Royal Inst. of Navigation, 1978. *Publications:* Challenger, 1957; The Admiralty Chart, 1967; papers on navigation and oceanography in various jls, including Developments in British Hydrography since days of Captain Cook (RSA Silver Medal, 1970). *Recreations:* conserving Collieston, boules, sea-fishing. *Address:* Sea View, Collieston, Ellon, Aberdeenshire AB41 8RS. *Clubs:* Reform; Royal Northern and University (Aberdeen); Collieston Boules (Pres.); Monte Carlo (Emeritus Mem.), Bouliste Monegasque.

RITCHIE, Horace David; Professor of Surgery, University of London, 1964–85, now Emeritus; Director of the Surgical Unit at The London Hospital, 1964–85; *b* 24 Sept. 1920; *m*; three *s*. *Educ:* Universities of Glasgow, Cambridge and Edinburgh. Dean, London Hosp. Med. Coll. and Dental Sch., 1982–83. *Publications:* contribs to various scientific journals. *Club:* Athenæum.

RITCHIE, Ian Carl, RIBA; Principal, Ian Ritchie Architects, since 1981; Consultant, Rice Francis Ritchie, since 1987; *b* 25 May 1947; *s* of Christopher Charles Ritchie and Mabel Berenice (*née* Long); *m* 1972, Jocelyne van den Bossche; one *s*. *Educ:* Varndean, Brighton; Liverpool and Polytechnic of Central London Schs of Architecture (Dip. Arch. distinction). MCSD. With Foster Associates, 1972–76; in private practice in France, 1976–78; Partner, Chrysalis Architects, 1979–81; Director: Rice, Francis Ritchie, 1981–87; Lhermitte-Ritchie, 1987–90. Tableau de l'Ordre des Architectes Français, 1982. *Recreations:* art, swimming, reading, writing, film making, lecturing on concept design. *Address:* 14 Garford Street, E14 9JG. *T:* 071–515 4989.

RITCHIE, (James) Martin; Chairman: British Enkalon Ltd, 1975–83; Haymills Holdings Ltd, 1977–83; Director, Sun Alliance and London Insurance Ltd, 1970–87; *b* 29 May 1917; *s* of late Sir James Ritchie, CBE and Lady Ritchie (*née* Gemmell); *m* 1939, Noreen Mary Louise Johnston; three *s*. *Educ:* Strathallan Sch., Perthshire. Joined Andrew Ritchie & Son Ltd, Glasgow, corrugated fibre container manufrs, 1934; Dir, 1938. TA Officer, 1938; served War of 1939–45: HAA Regt; Capt. 1941; psc 1943; DAA&QMG, MEF, Middle East, 1944–45 (Maj.). Rejoined Andrew Ritchie & Son Ltd, then part of Eburite Organisation; Man. Dir, 1950; Gen. Man., Bowater-Eburite Ltd, on merger with Bowater Organisation, 1956; Bowater Paper Corp. Ltd: Dir, 1959; Man. Dir, 1964; Dep. Chm. and Man. Dir, 1967; Chm. 1969–72. FBIM 1971; FRSA 1971. *Recreations:* golf, fishing. *Address:* Tilehouse, Scotswood Close, Beaconsfield, Bucks HP9 2LJ. *T:* Beaconsfield (0494) 676517. *Clubs:* Caledonian; Denham Golf.

RITCHIE, James Walter, MC; Director, Inchcape & Co. Ltd, 1972–84, retired; *b* 12 Jan. 1920; *m* 1951, Penelope June (*née* Forbes); two *s* two *d*. *Educ:* Ampleforth Coll.; Clare Coll., Cambridge. Gordon Highlanders. *Recreations:* hunting, fishing, golf. *Address:* Lockeridge Down, Lockeridge, near Marlborough, Wilts. *T:* Lockeridge (067286) 244. *Clubs:* Oriental; Muthaiga Country (Nairobi).

RITCHIE, Dr John Hindle, MBE 1985; architect; Chief Executive and Member, Merseyside Development Corporation, since 1985; *b* 4 June 1937; *s* of Charles A. Ritchie; *m* 1963, Anne Leyland; two *d*. *Educ:* Royal Grammar School, Newcastle upon Tyne; Univ. of Liverpool (BArch Hons); Univ. of Sheffield (PhD Building Science). Science Research Council, 1963–66; Liverpool City Council, 1966–69; Rowntree Housing Trust, Univ. of Liverpool, 1969–72; Cheshire County Council, 1972–74; Merseyside CC, 1974–80; Dir of Develt, Merseyside Develt Corp., 1980–85. Chm., Merseyside Educn Training Enterprise Ltd, 1986–; Mem., Merseyside Tourism Bd, 1986–88. FBIM. *Publications:* scientific and planning papers on urban environment and obsolescence. *Address:* c/o Merseyside Development Corporation, Royal Liver Building, Pierhead, Liverpool L3 1JH. *T:* 051–236 6090.

RITCHIE, Prof. J(oseph) Murdoch, PhD, DSc; FRS 1976; Eugene Higgins Professor of Pharmacology, Yale University, since 1968; *b* 10 June 1925; *s* of Alexander Farquharson Ritchie and Agnes Jane (*née* Bremner); *m* 1951, Brenda Rachel (*née* Bigland); one *s* one *d*. *Educ:* Aberdeen Central Secondary Sch.; Aberdeen Univ. (BSc Maths); UCL (BSc Physiol., PhD, DSc; Fellow 1978). MInstP. Res. in Radar, Telecommunications Res. Estabt, Malvern, 1944–46; University Coll. London: Hon. Res. Asst, Biophysics Res. Unit, 1946–49; Lectr in Physiol., 1949–51; Mem. staff, Nat. Inst. for Med. Res., Mill Hill, 1951–55; Asst Prof. of Pharmacology, 1956–57, Associate Prof., 1958–63 and Prof., 1963–68, Albert Einstein Coll. of Medicine, NY; Overseas Fellow, Churchill Coll., Cambridge, 1964–65; Chm., Dept of Pharmacol., 1968–74, Dir, Div. of Biol Scis, 1975–78, Yale Univ. Hon. MA Yale, 1968; Hon. DSc Aberdeen, 1987. *Publications:* papers on nerve and muscle physiol. and biophysics in Jl of Physiol. *Recreations:* skiing, chess. *Address:* 47 Deepwood Drive, Hamden, Conn 06517, USA. *T:* (home) (203) 777–0420; (office) (203) 785–4567. *Club:* Yale (NYC).

RITCHIE, Kenneth Gordon, CMG 1968; HM Diplomatic Service, retired; *b* 19 Aug. 1921; *s* of Walter Ritchie, Arbroath; *m* 1951, Esme Stronsa Nash. *Educ:* Arbroath High Sch.; St Andrews Univ. (MA). Joined FO, 1944; Embassy, Ankara, 1944–47; Foreign Office, 1947–49; Khorramshahr, 1949–50; Tehran, 1950–52; Djakarta, 1952–55; Foreign Office, 1955–57; Peking, 1957–62; Santiago, 1962–64; Elisabethville, 1965–66; Dep. High Commissioner, Lusaka, 1966–67; High Commissioner, Guyana, 1967–70; Head of Perm. Under-Sec.'s Dept, FCO, 1970–73; High Comr, Malaŵi, 1973–77. *Recreations:* cinephotography, model railways. *Address:* Dalforbie, North Esk Road, Edzell, Angus DD9 7TW.

RITCHIE, Margaret Claire; Headmistress of Queen Mary School, Lytham, since 1981; *b* 18 Sept. 1937; *d* of Roderick M. Ritchie, Edinburgh. *Educ:* Leeds Girls' High Sch.; Univ. of Leeds (BSc). Postgraduate Certificate in Education, Univ. of London. Asst Mistress, St Leonards Sch., St Andrews, 1960–64; Head of Science Dept, Wycombe Abbey Sch., High Wycombe, 1964–71; Headmistress, Queenswood Sch., 1972–81. *Address:* Queen Mary School, Clifton Drive South, Lytham St Annes, Lancs FY8 1DS.

RITCHIE, Martin; *see* Ritchie, J. M.

RITCHIE, Robert Blackwood; grazier running family sheep and cattle property, Western Victoria, since 1958; Director, Amskan Ltd, since 1986; *b* 6 April 1937; *s* of Alan Blackwood Ritchie and Margaret Louise (*née* Whitcomb); *m* 1965, Eda Natalie Sandford Beggs; two *s* one *d*. *Educ:* Geelong Grammar Sch.; Corpus Christi Coll., Cambridge (MA; Rowing Blue, 1958). Dir, Agricl Investments Australia, 1968–89 (Chm., 1968–85). Exec. Mem., Graziers Assoc. of Vic, 1968–72; Mem., National Rural Adv. Council, 1974–75; Chm., Exotic Animal Diseases Preparedness Consultative Council, 1990–. Dir-Gen., Min. for Economic Develt, Vic, 1981–83. Geelong Grammar School: Mem. Council, 1966–78 (Chm., 1973–78); Chief Exec., 1979–80 (during period between Head Masters). *Recreation:* sailing. *Address:* Blackwood, Penshurst, Vic 3289, Australia. *T:* (055) 765432. *Club:* Melbourne (Melbourne).

RITCHIE, Shirley Anne, (Mrs R. H. C. Anwyl), QC 1979; a Recorder of the Crown Court, since 1981; *b* 10 Dec. 1940; *d* of James Ritchie and Helen Sutherland Ritchie; *m* 1969, Robin Hamilton Corson Anwyl; two *s*. *Educ:* St Mary's Diocesan Sch. for Girls, Pretoria; Rhodes Univ., S Africa (BA, LLB). Called to the South African Bar, 1963; called to the Bar, Inner Temple, 1966, Bencher, 1985. Member: Senate of Inns of Court and Bar, 1978–81; Gen. Council of the Bar, 1987; Criminal Injuries Compensation Bd, 1980–; Mental Health Review Tribunal, 1983–. Chm., Barristers' Benevolent Assoc., 1989–. FRSA 1989. *Recreations:* theatre, sailing. *Address:* 4 Paper Buildings, Temple, EC4Y 7EX. *T:* 071–353 3420. *Club:* Academy.

RITTNER, Luke Philip Hardwick; Secretary General, the Arts Council of Great Britain, 1983–90; *b* 24 May 1947; *s* of late George Stephen Hardwick Rittner and of Joane (*née* Thunder); *m* 1974, Corinna Frances Edholm; one *d*. *Educ:* Blackfriars School, Laxton; City of Bath Technical Coll.; Dartington Coll. of Arts; London Acad. of Music and Dramatic Art. Asst Administrator, Bath Festival, 1968–71, Jt Administrator, 1971–74, Administrative Director, 1974–76; Dir, Assoc. for Business Sponsorship of the Arts, 1976–83. Chm., English Shakespeare Co., 1990–. Member: Adv. Council, V&A Museum, 1980–83; Music Panel, British Council, 1979–83. Trustee: Bath Preservation Trust, 1968–73; Theatre Royal, Bath, 1979–82; Foundn Trustee, Holburne Museum, Bath, 1981–; Governor, Urchfont Manor, Wiltshire Adult Educn Centre, 1982–83. *Recreations:* the arts, people, travel. *Address:* 29 Kelso Place, W8 5QG.

RIVERDALE, 2nd Baron, *cr* 1935; **Robert Arthur Balfour,** Bt 1929; DL; President, Balfour Darwins Ltd, 1969–75 (Chairman, 1961–69); *b* Sheffield, 1 Sept. 1901; *er s* of 1st Baron Riverdale, GBE; *S* father, 1957; *m* 1st, 1926, Nancy Marguerite (*d* 1928), *d* of late Rear-Adm. Mark Rundle, DSO; one *s*; 2nd, 1933, Christian Mary (*d* 1991), *er d* of late Major Rowland Hill; one *s* one *d*. *Educ:* Aysgarth; Oundle. MRINA. Served with RNVR, 1940–45, attaining rank of Lt-Comdr. Joined Arthur Balfour & Co. Ltd, 1918; Dir, 1924; Man. Dir, 1949; Chm. and Man. Dir, 1957–61; Exec. Chm., 1961–69. Director: National Provincial Bank, Main Central Bd, 1964–69 (Local Bd, 1949–69); National Westminster Bank, E Region, 1969–71; Light Trades House Ltd, 1956–65; Yorkshire Television, 1967–73. The Association of British Chambers of Commerce: Mem. Exec. Council, 1950–; Vice-Pres., 1952–54; Dep. Pres., 1954–57; Pres., 1957–58; Chm., Overseas Cttee, 1953–57. President: Nat. Fedn of Engineers' Tool Manufacturers, 1951–57 (Hon. Vice-Pres., 1957–; Representative on Gauge and Tool Adv. Council, 1946–64); Sheffield Chamber of Commerce, 1950 (Jt Hon. Sec., 1957–); Milling Cutter and Reamer Trade Assoc., 1936–54 (Vice-Pres., 1954–57); Twist Drill Traders' Assoc., 1946–55; Chm., British Council, Aust. Assoc. of British Manufacturers, 1954–57 (Vice-Chm., 1957–65; Hon. Mem., 1965–); Member: Management and Tech. Cttee, High Speed Steel Assoc., 1947–65; British Nat. Cttee of Internat. Chamber of Commerce Adv. Cttee, 1957–58; Nat. Production Adv. Cttee, 1957–58; Consultative Cttee for Industry, 1957–58; Standing Cttee, Crucible and High Speed Steel Conf., 1951–64; Western Hemisphere Exports Council (formerly Dollar Exports Council), 1957–61; Governor, Sheffield Savings Bank, 1948–58 (Patron, 1958–); Master Cutler, 1946; Trustee, Sheffield Town Trust, 1958–; Town Collector, Sheffield, 1974–; Guardian of Standard of Wrought Plate within City of Sheffield, 1948–; Belgian Consul for Sheffield area, 1945–. JP, City of Sheffield, 1950–66 (Pres., S Yorks Br. Magistrates' Assoc., 1971–); DL, S Yorks (formerly WR Yorks and City and County of York), 1959–. Pres., Derwent Fly Fishing Club. Is a Churchman and a Conservative. Chevalier of Order of the Crown, Belgium, 1956; La Médaille Civique de première classe; Officier de l'Ordre de Leopold II, 1971. *Recreations:* yachting, yacht designing, shooting, stalking, fishing. *Heir: s* Hon. Mark Robin Balfour, *qv*. *Address:* Ropes, Grindleford, via Sheffield S30 1HX. *T:* Hope Valley (0433) 30408. *Clubs:* Royal Cruising; Sheffield (Sheffield).

RIVERINA, Bishop of, since 1971; **Rt. Rev. Barry Russell Hunter;** *b* Brisbane, Queensland, 15 Aug. 1927; *s* of late John Hunter; *m* 1961, Dorothy Nancy, *d* of B. P. Sanders, Brisbane; three *d*. *Educ:* Toowoomba Grammar Sch.; St Francis' Theological Coll., Brisbane; Univ. of Queensland (BA, ThL). Assistant Curate, St Matthew's, Sherwood, 1953–56; Member, Bush Brotherhood of St Paul, Cunnamulla, Queensland, 1956–61; Rector, St Cecilia's, Chinchilla, 1961–66; Rector, St Gabriel's, Biloela, 1966–71; Archdeacon of the East, Diocese of Rockhampton, 1969–71. *Recreation:* music. *Address:* Bishop's Lodge, 127 Audley Street, Narrandera, NSW 2700, Australia. *T:* Narrandera (069) 59 1177. *Club:* Griffith Aero (Griffith).

RIVET, Prof. Albert Lionel Frederick, FBA 1981; Professor of Roman Provincial Studies, University of Keele, 1974–81, now Emeritus; *b* 30 Nov. 1915; *s* of Albert Robert Rivet, MBE and Rose Mary Rivet (*née* Bulow); *m* 1947, Audrey Catherine Webb; one *s* one *d*. *Educ:* Felsted Sch. (schol.); Oriel Coll., Oxford. BA 1938, MA 1946. FSA 1953; FSAScot 1959. Schoolmaster, 1938–39; ARP, 1939–40; mil. service, mainly in E Africa, 1940–46 (Major, Royal Signals); bookseller, 1946–51; Asst Archaeology Officer, Ordnance Survey, 1951–64; Keele University: Lectr in Classics, 1964–67; Reader in Romano-British Studies, 1967–74. Member: Royal Commn on Historical Monuments (England), 1979–85; Exec. Cttee, British Sch. at Rome, 1974–83. Pres., Soc. for Promotion of Roman Studies, 1977–80. Corresp. Mem., German Archaeol Inst., 1960–. Editor, Procs of Soc. of Antiquaries of Scotland, 1961–64. *Publications:* Town and Country in Roman Britain, 1958, 2nd edn 1964; (ed) The Iron Age in Northern Britain, 1966; (ed) The Roman Villa in Britain, 1969; (with C. C. Smith) The Place-Names of Roman Britain,

1979; Gallia Narbonensis, 1988; contribs to books, atlases, encyclopaedias and learned journals. *Recreation:* conversation. *Address:* 7 Springpool, Keele, Staffs ST5 5BN.

RIVETT, Dr Geoffrey Christopher; Senior Principal Medical Officer, Department of Health (formerly of Health and Social Security), since 1985; *b* 11 Aug. 1932; *s* of Frank Andrew James Rivett and Catherine Mary Rivett; *m* 1976, Elizabeth Barbara Hartman; two *s* by previous marr. *Educ:* Manchester Grammar Sch.; Brasenose Coll., Oxford (MA 1st Cl. Hons Animal Physiol.); University Coll. Hosp. (BM, BCh); FRCGP, DObst RCOG. House Officer, Radcliffe Inf., Oxford, 1957; House Phys., London Chest Hosp., 1958; RAMC, 1958–60; GP, Milton Keynes, 1960–72; DHSS, 1972–. Liveryman, Soc. of Apothecaries, 1981–; Mem., Barbers' Co, 1989–. ARPS 1971. *Publication:* The Development of the London Hospital System 1823–1982, 1986. *Recreations:* photography, house conversion. *Address:* 50 Andrewes House, Barbican, EC2Y 8AX. *T:* 071–628 5682; Shilling Orchard, Shilling Street, Lavenham, Suffolk CO10 9RH. *T:* Lavenham (0787) 247808. *Clubs:* Wig and Pen, Royal Society of Medicine.

RIVETT-CARNAC, Miles James; Deputy Chairman, Barings plc, since 1988; Chairman, Baring Asset Management Ltd, since 1989; *b* 7 Feb. 1933; *s* of Vice-Adm. James William Rivett-Carnac, CB, CBE, DSC (2nd *s* of 6th Bt) (*d* 1970), and Isla Nesta Rivett-Carnac (*d* 1974), *d* of Harry Officer Blackwood; *heir-pres.* to brother, Rev. Canon Sir Nicholas Rivett-Carnac, Bt, *qv*; *m* 1958, April Sally Villar; two *s* one *d*. *Educ:* Royal Naval College, Dartmouth, RN, 1950–70 (despatches 1965); Commander, 1965; US Staff Coll., 1966; Commanded HMS Dainty, 1967–68; MoD, 1968–70. Joined Barings, 1971; Dir. Baring Bros & Co., 1976; Pres., Baring Bros Inc., 1978; Managing Dir, Baring Bros & Co., 1981. Chairman: Tribune Investment Trust, 1985–; Hampshire Boys' Clubs, 1982–. *Recreations:* tennis, golf, shooting, philately (FRPS). *Address:* Martyr Worthy Manor, Winchester, Hants SO21 1DY. *T:* Itchen Abbas (096278) 311. *Clubs:* White's, Naval and Military; Links, Racquet (NY).

RIVETT-CARNAC, Rev. Canon Sir (Thomas) Nicholas, 8th Bt *cr* 1836; Pastor, Kingdom Faith Ministries, Roffey Place, Horsham, since 1989; Hon. Canon of Southwark Cathedral, since 1980; *b* 3 June 1927; *s* of Vice-Admiral James William Rivett-Carnac, CB, CBE, DSC (2nd *s* of 6th Bt) (*d* 1970), and of Isla Nesta Rivett-Carnac (*d* 1974), *d* of Harry Officer Blackwood; *S* uncle, 1972; *m* 1977, Susan Marigold MacTier Copeland, *d* of late Harold and Adeline Copeland. *Educ:* Marlborough College. Scots Guards, 1945–55. Probation Service, 1957–59. Ordained, 1963; Curate: Holy Trinity, Rotherhithe, 1963–68; Holy Trinity, Brompton, 1968–72; Vicar, St Mark's, Kennington, 1972–89; Rural Dean of Lambeth, 1978–82. *Heir: b* Miles James Rivett-Carnac, *qv*. *Address:* 23 Heather Close, Horsham, W Sussex RH12 4XD.

RIVETT-DRAKE, Brig. Dame Jean (Elizabeth), DBE 1964 (MBE 1947); JP; DL; Member, Hove Borough Council, 1966–84; Mayor of Hove, 1977–78; Lay Member, Press Council, 1973–78; Director, Women's Royal Army Corps, 1961–64, retd; *b* 13 July 1909; *d* of Comdr Bertram Gregory Drake and of late Dora Rivett-Drake. Served War of 1939–45 (despatches, 1946). Hon. ADC to the Queen, 1961–64. Mem., East Sussex CC, 1973–77 (Mem. Educn and Social Services Cttees, AHA). JP 1965; DL E Sussex, 1983. *Address:* 9 Kestrel Close, Hove, East Sussex BN3 6NS. *T:* Brighton (0273) 505839; c/o Barclays Bank, 92 Church Road, Hove, East Sussex. *Club:* English-Speaking Union.

RIVLIN, Geoffrey, QC 1979; **His Honour Judge Rivlin;** a Circuit Judge, since 1989; *b* 28 Nov. 1940; *s* of late M. Allenby Rivlin and late May Rivlin; *m* 1974, Maureen Smith, violinist; two *d*. *Educ:* Bootham Sch.; Leeds Univ. (LLB). Called to the Bar, Middle Temple, 1963 (Colombos Prize, Internat. Law); Bencher, 1987. NE Circuit Junior 1967; a Recorder, 1978–89. Mem., Senate of Inns of Court and the Bar, 1976–79. Gov., St Christopher's Sch., Hampstead, 1990–. *Address:* 4 Paper Buildings, Temple, EC4Y 7EX.

RIX, Bernard Anthony, QC 1981; a Recorder, since 1990; *b* 8 Dec. 1944; *s* of Otto Rix and Sadie Silverberg; *m* 1983, Hon. Karen Debra, *er d* of Baron Young of Graffham, *qv*; twin *s* one *d*. *Educ:* St Paul's School, London; New College, Oxford (BA: Lit.Hum. 1966, Jur. 1968; MA); Harvard Law School (Kennedy Scholar 1968; LLM 1969). Called to Bar, Inner Temple, 1970, Bencher, 1990. Member: Senate, Inns of Court and Bar, 1981–83; Bar Council, 1981–83. Dir, London Philharmonic Orchestra, 1986–. Chm., British Friends of Bar-Ilan Univ., 1987–; Mem. Bd of Trustees, Bar-Ilan Univ., 1988–. *Recreations:* music, opera, Italy, formerly fencing. *Address:* 3 Essex Court, Temple, EC4. *T:* 071–583 9294.

RIX, Sir Brian (Norman Roger), Kt 1986; CBE 1977; actor-manager, 1948–77; Chairman: Mencap (Royal Society for Mentally Handicapped Children and Adults), since 1988 (Secretary-General, 1980–87); Mencap City Foundation, since 1988 (Founder and Governor, 1984); Vice Lord-Lieutenant of Greater London, since 1988; *b* 27 Jan. 1924; *s* of late Herbert and Fanny Rix; *m* 1949, Elspet Jeans Macgregor-Gray; two *s* two *d*. *Educ:* Bootham Sch., York. Stage career: joined Donald Wolfit, 1942; first West End appearance, Sebastian in Twelfth Night, St James's, 1943; White Rose Players, Harrogate, 1943–44. Served War of 1939–45, RAF and Bevin Boy. Became actor-manager, 1948; ran repertory cos at Ilkley, Bridlington and Margate, 1948–50; toured Reluctant Heroes and brought to Whitehall Theatre, 1950–54; Dry Rot, 1954–58; Simple Spymen, 1958–61; One For the Pot, 1961–64; Chase Me Comrade, 1964–66; went to Garrick Theatre, 1967, with repertoire of farce: Stand By Your Bedouin; Uproar in the House; Let Sleeping Wives Lie; after 6 months went over to latter, only, which ran till 1969; then followed: She's Done It Again, 1969–70; Don't Just Lie There, Say Something!, 1971–73 (filmed 1973); New Theatre, Cardiff, Robinson Crusoe, 1973; Cambridge Theatre, A Bit Between The Teeth, 1974; Fringe Benefits, Whitehall Theatre, 1976; returned to theatre 1988; Dry Rot, Lyric Theatre, 1989; dir., You'll Do For Me!, tour, 1989. Entered films, 1951: subsequently made eleven, including Reluctant Heroes, 1951, Dry Rot, 1956. BBC TV contract to present farces on TV, 1956–72; first ITV series Men of Affairs, 1973; A Roof Over My Head, BBC TV series, 1977. Presenter, Let's Go ..., BBC TV series (first ever for mentally handicapped), 1978–83; Disc Jockey (for first time) BBC Radio 2 series, 1978–80. Dir and Theatre Controller, Cooney-Marsh Group, 1977–80; Trustee, Theatre of Comedy, 1983–; Arts Council: Mem., 1986–; Chairman: Drama Panel, 1986–; Monitoring Cttee, Arts and Disabled People; Indep. Develt Council for People with Mental Handicap, 1981–86; Friends of Normansfield; Libertas. Gov., ESU, 1987–. DL Greater London, 1987. Hon. MA: Hull, 1981; Open, 1983; DUniv Essex, 1984; Hon. LLD Manchester, 1986; Hon. DSc Nottingham, 1987. Hon. Fellow, Humberside Coll. of Higher Educn, 1984. *Publications:* My Farce from My Elbow: an autobiography, 1975; Farce about Face (autobiog.), 1989. *Recreations:* cricket, amateur radio (G2DQU; Hon. Vice-Pres., Radio Soc. of GB, 1979). *Address:* 3 St Mary's Grove, Barnes Common, SW13 0JA. *T:* 081–785 9626. *Clubs:* Garrick, Lord's Taverners (Pres. 1970), MCC; Yorkshire County Cricket.

RIX, Sir John, Kt 1977; MBE 1955; DL; FEng 1979; Chairman, Seahorse International Ltd, 1986–89; Deputy Chairman, The Victorian Cruise Line Ltd, since 1987; Director, Chilworth Centre Ltd, since 1986; *b* 1917; *s* of Reginald Arthur Rix; *m* 1953, Sylvia Gene Howe; two *s* one *d*. *Educ:* Southampton Univ. FRINA; FIMarE. Chm. and Chief Exec., Vosper Thornycroft (UK) Ltd, 1970–78; Chm. and Dir, Vosper PLC, 1958–85; Chairman: Vosper Shiprepairers Ltd, 1977–78; David Brown Vosper (Offshore) Ltd, 1978–85; Vosper Hovermarine Ltd, 1980–85; David Brown Gear Industries Ltd, 1980–85; Mainwork Ltd, 1980–85; Director: Vosper Private Ltd, 1966–77 and 1978–85; Charismarine Ltd, 1976–88; Southampton Cable Ltd, 1986–88. DL Hants 1985. *Recreations:* sailing, tennis, golf, walking. *Address:* Lower Baybridge House, Owslebury, Winchester, Hants SO21 1JN. *T:* Owslebury (0962) 777306. *Club:* Royal Thames Yacht.

RIX, Timothy John; Chairman, Longman Group Ltd, 1984–90 (Chief Executive, 1976–89); *b* 4 Jan. 1934; *s* of late Howard Terrell Rix and Marguerite Selman Rix; *m* 1st, 1960, Wendy Elizabeth Wright (marr. diss. 1967); one *d*; 2nd, 1967, Gillian Diana Mary Greenwood; one *s* one *d*. *Educ:* Radley Coll.; Clare Coll., Cambridge (BA); Yale Univ., USA. Sub-Lieut, RNVR, 1952–54. Mellon Fellow, Yale, 1957–58; joined Longmans, Green & Co. Ltd, subseq. Longman Gp, 1958; Overseas Educnl Publisher, 1958–61; Publishing Manager, Far East and SE Asia, 1961–63; Head of English Language Teaching Publishing, 1964–68; Divl Man. Dir, 1968–72; Jt Man. Dir, 1972–76. Director: Pearson Longman Ltd, 1979–83; Goldcrest Television, 1981–83; Yale Univ. Press, London, 1984–; ECIC (Management) Ltd, 1990–; Blackie and Son Ltd, 1990–; B. H. Blackwell Ltd, 1990–; Chm., Book Marketing Ltd, 1990–; Sen. Consultant, Pofcher Co., 1990–. Chm., Pitman Examns Inst., 1987–90. Publishers Association: Chm., Trng Cttee, 1974–78; Chm., Book Develt Council, 1979–81; Vice-Pres., 1980–81 and 1983–84; Pres., 1981–83. Chairman: Book Trust, 1986–88; Book House Training Centre, 1986–89; British Library Centre for the Book, 1990–; Society of Bookmen, 1990–. Member: Exec. Cttee, NBL, 1979–86 (Dep. Chm., 1984–86); Publishers Adv. Panel, British Council, 1978–; Arts Council Literature Panel, 1983–86; British Library Adv. Council, 1982–86; British Library Bd, 1986–; British Council Bd, 1988–. Gov., Bell Educnl Trust, 1990–. CBIM 1981; FRSA 1986. *Publications:* articles on publishing in trade jls. *Recreations:* reading, landscape, wine. *Address:* Top Flat, 27 Wolseley Road, N8 8RS. *T:* 081–348 4143. *Club:* Garrick.

RIZA, Alper Ali; QC 1991; *b* 16 March 1948; *s* of Ali Riza and Elli Liasides; *m* 1981, Vanessa Hall-Smith; two *d*. *Educ:* American Academy, Larnaca, Cyprus; English Sch., Nicosia. Called to the Bar, Gray's Inn, 1973. Pupillage, 1974–75; Turnpike Lane Law and Advice, 1975–77; Appeals Lawyer, Jt Council for Welfare of Immigrants, 1977–82; private practice, 1982–. *Publication:* (ed jtly) Butterworth's Immigration Law Service, 1991. *Recreations:* chess, music. *Address:* 2 Paper Buildings, Temple, EC4. *T:* 071–936 2611.

RIZK, Waheeb, CBE 1984 (OBE 1977); MA, PhD; FEng, FIMechE; Engineering Consultant, W R Associates, since 1986; Deputy President, British Standards Institution, since 1985 (Chairman of Board, 1982–85); *b* 11 Nov. 1921; *s* of Dr and Mrs I. Rizk; *m* 1952, Vivien Moyle, MA (Cantab); one *s* one *d* (and one *d* decd). *Educ:* Emmanuel College, Cambridge. MA, PhD. Joined English Electric Co., 1954, Chief Engineer, Gas Turbine Div., 1957, Gen. Manager, new div., combining gas turbines and industrial steam turbines, 1967; after merger with GEC became Man. Dir, GEC Gas Turbines Ltd, 1971; Chairman: GEC-Ruston Gas Turbines Ltd, 1983–86; GEC Diesels Ltd, 1983–86. Pres., IMechE, 1984–85 (Mem. Council, 1978–89); Mem. Council, Fellowship of Engrg, 1982–85. Pres., Internat Council on Combustion Engines (CIMAC), 1973–77. Mem. Council, Cranfield Inst. of Technology, 1985–; Mem. Court, Brunel Univ., 1986–. Liveryman and Mem. Ct of Assistants, Worshipful Co. of Engineers. Gold Medal, CIMAC, 1983. *Publications:* technical papers to IMechE, Amer. Soc. of Mech. Engineers and CIMAC. *Recreations:* intelligent tinkering with any mechanism, photography, old motor cycles. *Address:* 231 Hillmorton Road, Rugby CV22 5BD. *T:* Rugby (0788) 565093. *Club:* Athenæum.

RIZZELLO, Michael Gaspard, OBE 1977; PPRBS; FCSD; sculptor and coin designer; *b* 2 April 1926; *s* of Arthur Rizzello and Maria Rizzello (*née* D'Angelo); *m* 1950, Sheila Semple Maguire; one *d*. *Educ:* Oratory Central Boys Sch., SW3; Royal College of Art. Military Service, 1944–48; served in India and Far East; commissioned 1945. Major Travelling Scholarship (Sculpture) and Drawing Prize, RCA, 1950. ARCA 1950; ARBS 1955, FRBS 1961, PRBS 1976–86; FCSD (FSIAD 1978). Pres., Soc. of Portrait Sculptors, 1968. Prix de Rome (Sculpture), 1951. Sir Otto Beit Medal for Sculpture, 1961. Sculptor: National Memorial to David Lloyd George, Cardiff; Official Medals for Investiture of HRH Prince of Wales, 1969; 900th Anniversary of Westminster Abbey, 1965; Churchill Centenary Trust, 1974; Sir Thomas Beecham bust, Royal Opera House, 1979, and Royal Festival Hall, 1986; sculptures at Nat. Postal Mus., 1972 and London Docklands, 1988 and 1990. Designer and Sculptor of coinages for over 90 countries. *Recreation:* people. *Address:* Melrose Studio, 7 Melrose Road, SW18 1ND. *T:* 081–870 8561. *Club:* Reform.

ROACH, Prof. Gary Francis, FRSE; Professor of Mathematics, University of Strathclyde, since 1979; *b* 8 Oct. 1933; *s* of John Francis Roach and Bertha Mary Ann Roach (*née* Walters); *m* 1960, Isabella Grace Willins Nicol. *Educ:* University Coll. of S Wales and Monmouthshire (BSc); Univ. of London (MSc); Univ. of Manchester (PhD, DSc). FRAS, FIMA. RAF (Educn Branch), Flying Officer, 1955–58; Research Mathematician, BP, 1958–61; Lectr, UMIST, 1961–66; Vis. Prof., Univ. of British Columbia, 1966–67; University of Strathclyde: Lectr, 1967; Sen Lectr, 1970; Reader, 1971; Prof., 1979; Dean, Faculty of Science, 1982–. Mem., Edinburgh Mathematical Soc. (Past Pres.). *Publications:* Green's Functions, 1970, 2nd edn 1982; articles in learned jls. *Recreations:* mountaineering, photography, philately, gardening, music. *Address:* 11 Menzies Avenue, Fintry, Glasgow G63 0YE. *T:* Fintry (036086) 335.

ROADS, Dr Christopher Herbert; Director, National Sound Archive, since 1983; consultant in museums and audio visual archives; *b* 3 Jan. 1934; *s* of late Herbert Clifford Roads and Vera Iris Roads; *m* 1976, Charlotte Alicia Dorothy Mary Lothian; one *d*. *Educ:* Cambridge and County Sch.; Trinity Hall, Cambridge (MA; PhD 1961). Adviser to WO on Disposal of Amnesty Arms, 1961–62; Imperial War Museum: Keeper of Dept of Records, 1962–70; Dep. Dir-Gen. at Main Building, Southwark, 1964–79, at Duxford, Cambridge, 1976–79, HMS Belfast, Pool of London, 1978–79. Dir, Museums & Archives Develt Associates Ltd, 1977–85. UNESCO consultant designing major audio visual archives or museums in Philippines, Panama, Bolivia, Kuwait, Jordan and Saudi Arabia, 1976–. Founder and Dir, Cambridge Coral/Starfish Res. Gp, 1968–; Director: Nat. Discography Ltd, 1986–; Historic Cable Ship John W. Mackay, 1986–; AVT Communications Ltd, 1988–; Cedar Audio Ltd, 1989–. Chm., Coral Conservation Trust, 1972–; President: Historical Breechloading Small Arms Assoc., 1973–; Internat. Film and TV Council (UNESCO Category A), 1990– (Pres., Archives Commn, 1970–); Vice President: World Expeditionary Assoc., 1971–; Duxford Aviation Soc., 1974–; English Eight Club, 1980–; Cambridge Univ. Rifle Assoc., 1987 (Mem. Council, 1955–87); Mem. Council, Scientific Exploration Soc., 1971–82; Sec., Nat. Archives Cttee, Internat. Assoc. of Sound Archives; Hon. Sec., Cambridge Univ. Long Range Rifle Club, 1979–. Trustee: HMS Belfast Trust, 1970–78; Nat. Life Stories Collection, 1986–; NSA Wild Life Sound Trust, 1986–. Adjt, English VIII, 1964–. Churchill Fellowship, 1970; Vis. Fellow, Centre of Internat. Studies, Univ. of Cambridge, 1983–84. FRGS. Order of Independence, 2nd cl. (Jordan), 1977. *Publications:* The British Soldier's Firearm, 1850–1864, 1964; (jtly) New Studies on the Crown of Thorns Starfish, 1970; The Story of the Gun, 1978. *Recreations:* rifle shooting, marine and submarine exploration, wind surfing, motorcycling, cine and still photography. *Address:* The White House, 90 High Street, Melbourn, near Royston, Herts SG8 6AL. *T:* Royston (0763) 260866. *Clubs:* United Oxford & Cambridge University; Hawks (Cambridge).

ROADS, Peter George, MD; FFCM; Regional Medical Officer, South West Thames Regional Health Authority, 1973–82, retired; *b* 14 Nov. 1917; *s* of Frank George Roads and Mary Dee Hill (*née* Bury); *m* 1949, Evelyn Clara (*née* Daniel); one *s* one *d*. *Educ:* Bedford Sch.; Univ. of London (St Mary's Hosp. Med. Sch.); Hon. Society of Inner Temple. MD (London); FFCM, Royal Colls of Physicians. Served War, in China, 1944–46. MRC, Pneumoconiosis Unit, 1949–50; Dep. MOH, etc, City and Co. of Bristol, 1956–59; MOH, Principal Sch. Med. Officer and Port Med. Officer for City and Port of Portsmouth, 1959–73; Med. Referee to Portchester Crematorium, 1959–73. Mem., Central Midwives Bd, 1964–76; Adviser on Health Services, Assoc. of Municipal Corporations, 1966–74. FRSocMed; Fellow, Soc. of Public Health (formerly of Community Medicine) (Pres., 1988–89). Chairman: Bucks Br., Historical Assoc., 1987–; Bucks Family History Soc., 1990–. *Publications:* Care of Elderly in Portsmouth, 1970; Medical Importance of Open Air Recreation (Proc. 1st Internat. Congress on Leisure and Touring), 1966. *Recreations:* open air, walking, forestry, history, touring. *Address:* Pasture Cottage, School Lane, Dinton, near Aylesbury, Bucks HP17 8UG. *T:* Aylesbury (0296) 748504.

ROARK, Helen Wills; *b* California, 1905; *d* of Dr Clarence A. Wills (surgeon) and Catherine A. Wills; *m* 1st, 1929, Frederick Schander Moody (marr. diss. 1937); 2nd, 1939, Aidan Roark. *Educ:* Anna Head School, Berkeley, California; University of California; Phi Beta Kappa (Scholarship Society). *Publications:* three books on tennis; Mystery Book, 1939; articles in various magazines and periodicals. *Recreations:* American Lawn Tennis Championship, 1923–24–25–27–28–29 and 1931; English Lawn Tennis Championship, 1927–28–29–30–32–33–35–38; French, 1927–28–29–30; has held exhibitions of drawing and paintings at Cooling Galleries, London, 1929 (drawings); Grand Central Art Galleries, New York, 1930 (drawings), 1936 (flower paintings in oil); Berheim-Jenne Galleries, Paris, 1932 (etchings). *Clubs:* All England Lawn Tennis; Colony, West Side Lawn Tennis (New York); Burlingame Country (California).

ROB, Prof. Charles Granville, MC 1943; Professor of Surgery, Uniformed Services University of the Health Sciences, Bethesda, Maryland, since 1983; *b* 4 May 1913; *s* of Joseph William Rob, OBE, MD; *m* 1941, Mary Dorothy Elaine Beazley; two *s* two *d*. *Educ:* Oundle School; Cambridge Univ.; St Thomas's Hospital. FRCS 1939; MChir Cantab, 1941. Lt-Col RAMC Surgeon, St Thomas' Hospital, 1948; Professor of Surgery, London University, 1950–60; Professor and Chm. Dept of Surgery, Univ. of Rochester, NY, 1960–78; Prof. of Surg., E Carolina Univ., 1978–83. Formerly Surgeon and Director of the Surgical Professorial Unit, St Mary's Hospital; Consultant Vascular Surgeon to the Army. *Publications:* (ed, with Rodney Smith) Operative Surgery (8 vols), 1956–57, (14 vols), 1968–69; various surgical. *Recreations:* mountaineering, ski-ing. *Address:* Uniformed Services University of the Health Sciences, Bethesda, Md 20814, USA. *Club:* Alpine.

ROBARTS, (Anthony) Julian; Managing Director, Coutts & Co., since 1986; *b* 6 May 1937; *s* of late Lt-Col Anthony V. C. Robarts, DL and of Grizel Mary Robarts (Grant); *m* 1961, Edwina Beryl Hobson; two *s* one *d*. *Educ:* Eton College. National Service, 11th Hussars (PAO), 1955–57; joined Coutts & Co., 1958, Dir, 1963, Dep. Man. Dir, 1976–86; Director: Coutts Finance Co., 1967–; F. Bolton Group, 1970–; International Fund for Institutions Inc., USA, 1983–; Regional Dir, Nat. Westminster Bank, 1971–. Hon. Treasurer, Union Jack Club. *Recreations:* shooting, gardening, opera. *Address:* c/o Coutts & Co., 440 Strand, WC2R 0QS. *T:* 071–753 1447. *Club:* MCC.

ROBARTS, Basil; Director, 1964–85, and Chief General Manager, 1963–75, Norwich Union Insurance Group; *b* 13 Jan. 1915; *s* of late Henry Ernest Robarts and Beatrice Katie (*née* Stevens); *m* 1941, Sheila Margaret Cooper Thwaites; one *s* one *d*. *Educ:* Gresham's Sch., Holt. Served Army, 1939–45 (Lt-Col, RA). Joined Norwich Union Life Insce Soc., 1934; Gen. Man. and Actuary, 1953. Institute of Actuaries: Fellow (FIA), 1939; Treas., 1965–67; Gen. Commissioner of Income Tax, 1958–90; Chm., British Insce Assoc., 1969–71. Trustee, Charities Official Investment Fund, 1977–85. *Recreation:* music. *Address:* 466B Unthank Road, Norwich NR4 7QJ. *T:* Norwich (0603) 51135. *Club:* Naval and Military.

ROBARTS, Eric Kirkby; *b* 20 Jan. 1908; *s* of Charles Martin Robarts and Flora Robarts (*née* Kirkby); *m* 1930, Iris Lucy Swan; five *d*. *Educ:* Bishops Stortford Coll.; Herts Inst. of Agriculture. Ran family business, C. M. Robarts & Son, until Aug. 1942. Joined Express Dairy Co. Ltd, 1942: Dir, 1947–73; Man. Dir, 1960–73; Dep. Chm., 1966; Chm., 1967–73. FRSA; FBIM. *Recreations:* hunting, shooting. *Address:* Frithcote, Watford Road, Northwood, Middx. *T:* Northwood (09274) 22533. *Club:* Farmers'.

ROBARTS, Julian; *see* Robarts, A. J.

ROBB, Prof. James Christie; Professor of Physical Chemistry, 1957–84, and Head of Department of Chemistry, 1981–84, University of Birmingham; *b* 23 April 1924; *s* of James M. Robb, Rocklands, The House of Daviot, Inverurie, Aberdeenshire; *m* 1951, Joyce Irene Morley; three *d*. *Educ:* Daviot School; Inverurie Academy; Aberdeen University (BSc Hons, 1945, PhD 1948); DSc Birmingham, 1954. DSIR Senior Research Award, Aberdeen, 1948–50. ICI Fellow, Birmingham Univ., 1950–51; on Birmingham Univ. staff, 1951–84. A Guardian of Birmingham Assay Office, 1980–. Mem. Council, Birmingham Civic Soc., 1981–. Pres., Birmingham Rotary Club, 1982–83. *Publications:* scientific contrib. to Proc. Royal Soc., Trans. Faraday Soc., etc. *Recreations:* motoring, photography, computing. *Address:* 32 Coleshill Close, Hunt End, Redditch, Worcs B97 5UN.

ROBB, John Weddell; Chief Executive, Wellcome Plc, since 1990 (Deputy Chief Executive, 1989–90); *b* 27 April 1936; *s* of John and Isabella Robb; *m* 1965, Janet Teanby; two *s* one *d*. *Educ:* Daniel Stewart's College, Edinburgh. Market Research Exec., H. J. Heinz, 1952; Product Manager, Associated Fisheries, 1960; Marketing Exec., Young & Rubicam, 1965; Beecham Group: Marketing Exec., Toiletry Div., Beecham Products, 1966; Man. Dir, Beecham (Far East), Kuala Lumpur, 1971; Vice-Pres., W. Hemisphere Div., Beecham Products, USA, 1974; Man. Dir, Food and Drink Div., Beecham Products, 1976; Group Board, 1980; Chm., Food and Drink Div., 1980; Chm., Beecham Products, 1984–85; Gp Man. Dir, 1985–88. Non-Exec. Dep. Chm., NFC, 1990– (Non-Exec. Dir, 1983–); Non-Exec. Dir, STC, 1985–88. *Recreations:* golf, gardening, racing. *Club:* Sunningdale.

ROBBE-GRILLET, Alain, literary consultant, writer and cinéaste; Editions de Minuit, Paris, since 1955; *b* 18 Aug. 1922; *s* of Gaston Robbe-Grillet and Yvonne Canu; *m* 1957, Catherine Rstakian. *Educ:* Lycée Buffon, Paris; Lycée St Louis, Paris; Institut National Agronomique, Paris. Engineer: Institut National de la Statistique, 1945–49; Institut des Fruits et Agrumes Coloniaux, 1949–51. *Films:* L'Immortelle, 1963; Trans-Europ-Express, 1967; L'Homme qui ment, 1968; L'Eden et après, 1970; Glissements progressifs du plaisir, 1974; Le jeu avec le feu, 1975; La belle captive, 1983. *Publications:* Les Gommes, 1953 (The Erasers, 1966); Le Voyeur, 1955 (The Voyeur, 1959); La Jalousie, 1957 (Jealousy, 1960); Dans le labyrinthe, 1959 (In the Labyrinth, 1967); L'Année dernière à Marienbad, 1961 (Last Year in Marienbad, 1962); Instantanés, 1962 (Snapshots, and, Towards a New Novel, 1965); L'Immortelle, 1963 (The Immortal One, 1971); Pour un nouveau roman, 1964; La Maison de rendezvous, 1965 (The House of Assignation, 1968); Projet pour une révolution à New York, 1970 (Project for a Revolution in New York, 1972); Glissements progressifs du plaisir, 1974; Topologie d'une cité fantôme, 1976 (Topology of a Phantom City, 1978); La Belle captive, 1976; Souvenirs du Triangle d'or, 1978 (Recollections of the Golden Triangle, 1985); Un Régicide, 1978; Djinn, 1981; Le Miroir qui revient (autobiog.), 1985 (Ghosts in the Mirror, 1988); Angélique ou l'enchantement (autobiog.), 1988. *Address:* 18 Boulevard Maillot, 92200 Neuilly-sur-Seine, France. *T:* (1) 47 22 31 22.

ROBBINS, Prof. Frederick C., MD; Bronze Star (US Army), 1945; President, Institute of Medicine, National Academy of Sciences, Washington, DC, 1980–85; University Professor, Case Western Reserve University, 1985, Emeritus, since 1986 (Professor of Pediatrics, School of Medicine, 1952–80, Dean, 1966–80, now Emeritus); *b* 25 Aug. 1916; *s* of William J. Robbins and Christine Chapman Robbins; *m* 1948, Alice Havemeyer Northrop; two *d*. *Educ:* University of Missouri (AB); University of Missouri Medical School (BS); Harvard Medical School (MD). US Army, 1942–46; rank on discharge, Major. Various posts in the Children's Hospital, Boston, from 1940, finishing as Chief Resident in Medicine, 1948; Sen. Fellow in Virus Diseases, National Research Council, 1948–50; Research Fellow in Pediatrics, Harvard Med. Sch., 1948–50; Instr in Ped., 1950–51, Associate in Ped., 1951–52, at Harvard Medical School; Dir, Department of Pediatrics, Cleveland Metropolitan General Hospital, 1952–66. Associate, Research Div. of Infectious Diseases, the Children's Medical Center, Boston, 1950–52; Research Fellow in Ped., the Boston Lying-in Hospital, Boston, Mass, 1950–52; Asst to Children's Medical Service, Mass Gen. Hosp., Boston, 1950–52. Visiting Scientist, Donner Lab., Univ. of California, 1963–64. President: Soc. for Pediatric Research, 1961–62; Amer. Pediatric Soc., 1973–74. Member: Nat. Acad. of Sciences, 1972 (Co-Chm., Forum on Human Experimentation, 1974); Amer. Philosophical Soc., 1972; Adv. Cttee, Office of Technol. Assessment for Congress, 1973; Adv. Cttee on Med. Research, Pan American Health Organization, WHO, 1981–. First Mead Johnson Award, 1953; Nobel Prize in Physiology or Medicine, 1954; Award for Distinguished Achievement (Modern Medicine), 1963; Med. Mutual Honor Award for 1969. Hon. Dr of Science: John Carroll University, 1955; Missouri, 1958; North Carolina, 1979; Tufts, 1983; Med. Coll. of Ohio, 1983; Albert Einstein Coll. of Medicine, 1984; Med. Coll. of Wisconsin, 1984; Hon. Dr of Laws, New Mexico, 1968; Hon. Dr Med. Sci., Med. Coll. of Pa, 1984. *Publications:* numerous in various jls, primarily on subject of viruses and infectious diseases. *Recreations:* music, tennis, sailing. *Address:* 2626 West Park Boulevard, Shaker Heights, Ohio 44120, USA; (office) CWRU School of Medicine, 2119 Abington Road, Cleveland, Ohio 44106, USA.

ROBBINS, Harold; writer; *m* Grace; one *d*. *Educ:* New York. Formerly sugar exporter, film publicist, film impresario, etc. *Publications:* The Dream Merchants, 1949; 79 Park Avenue, 1955; A Stone for Danny Fisher, 1955; Never Leave Me, 1956; Never Love a Stranger, 1958; Stiletto, 1960; The Carpetbaggers, 1961; Where Love Has Gone, 1964; The Adventurers, 1966; The Inheritors, 1969; The Betsy, 1971 (filmed 1978); The Pirate, 1974; The Lonely Lady, 1976; Dreams Die First, 1977; Memories of Another Day, 1979; Goodbye, Janette, 1981; Spellbinder, 1982; Descent from Xanadu, 1984; The Storyteller, 1985; The Piranhas, 1991. *Address:* c/o New English Library, 47 Bedford Square, WC1B 3DP.

ROBBINS, Jerome; Choreographer and Director; Co-Ballet Master in Chief, New York City Ballet, since 1983 (Ballet Master, 1969–83; Associate Artistic Director, 1949–59); Founder Director, Ballets: USA, 1958–61; *b* New York, 11 Oct. 1918; *s* of Harry and Lena Robbins. *Educ:* Woodrow Wilson High School, Weehawken, NJ; New York University. Studied ballet with Antony Tudor and Eugene Loring, and Modern, Spanish and oriental dance. First stage experience with Sandor-Sorel Dance Center, New York, 1937; dancer in chorus of American musicals, 1938–40; Ballet Theatre, 1940–44 (soloist 1941), London season, 1946; formed own company, Ballets: USA, 1958. Member: NY State Council on the Arts/Dance Panel, 1973–77; Nat. Council on the Arts, 1974–80. City of Paris Award, 1971; Handel Medallion, NYC, 1976; Kennedy Center Honoree, 1981, and many other awards. Hon. Degrees from Ohio Univ., 1974, City Univ. of NY, 1980. Chevalier, Order of Arts and Letters (France), 1964. *Ballets include:* (for Ballet Theater) Fancy Free, 1944; (for Concert Varieties) Interplay, 1945; (for New York City Ballet) Age of Anxiety, 1950; The Cage, 1951; Afternoon of a Faun, 1953; Fanfare, 1953; The Concert, 1956; (for American Ballet Theater) Les Noces, 1965; Dances at a Gathering, 1969; In the Night, 1970; The Goldberg Variations, 1971; Watermill, 1972; Requiem Canticles, 1972; An Evening's Waltzes, 1973; Dybbuk (later The Dybbuk Variations, then renamed Suite of Dances), 1974; Concerto in G (later in G Major), 1975; Ma Mère l'Oye (later Mother Goose), 1975; Chansons Madécasses, 1975; The Four Seasons, 1979; Opus 19, The Dreamer, 1979; Rondo, 1981; Piano Pieces, 1981; The Gershwin Concerto, 1982; Four Chamber Works, 1982; Glass Pieces, 1983; I'm Old Fashioned, 1983; Antique Epigraphs, 1984; (with Twyla Tharp) Brahms/Handel, 1984; Eight Lines, 1985; In Memory Of, 1985; Quiet City, 1986; Piccolo Balleto, 1986; Ives, Songs, 1988; Jerome Robbins Broadway, NY, 1989; (for Ballets: USA) NY Export: Opus Jazz, 1958; Moves, 1959; (for Star Spangled Gala) Other Dances, 1976. *Musicals include:* On the Town, 1945; Billion Dollar Baby, 1946 (Donaldson award); High Button Shoes, 1947 (Donaldson and Tony awards); Miss Liberty, 1949; Call Me Madam, 1950; The King and I, 1951 (Donaldson award); Two's Company, 1952 (Donaldson award); Peter Pan, 1954; Bells Are Ringing, 1956; West Side Story, 1957 (Tony, Evening Standard, Laurel and two Academy awards); Gypsy, 1959; Fiddler on the Roof, 1964 (two Tony awards and Drama Critics' award). Has directed and choreographed films, drama and TV (inc. Peter Pan with Mary Martin, 1955 (Emmy award)). Hon. Mem., AAIL, 1985. Hon. Dr Fine Arts, NY Univ., 1985. *Address:* c/o New York City Ballet, New York State Theater, Lincoln Center, New York, NY 10023, USA.

ROBBINS, Prof. Keith Gilbert; Principal, St David's University College, Lampeter, since 1992; *b* 9 April 1940; *s* of Gilbert Henry John and Edith Mary Robbins; *m* 1963, Janet Carey Thomson; three *s* one *d*. *Educ:* Bristol Grammar Sch.; Magdalen and St Antony's Colls, Oxford. MA, DPhil (Oxon); DLitt (Glas.). FRSE 1991. University of York: Asst Lectr in History, 1963; Lectr in Hist., 1964; Prof. of History, 1971–79, Dean of Faculty of Arts, 1977–79, UCNW, Bangor. Vis. Prof., British Columbia Univ., 1983; Lectures: Enid Muir, Newcastle Univ., 1981; A. H. Dodd, UCNW, Bangor, 1984; Raleigh, British Acad., 1984; Ford, Oxford Univ., 1986–87. Winston Churchill Travelling Fellow, 1990. Pres., Historical Assoc., 1988–91. Editor, History, 1977–86; Editorial Bd, Jl of Ecclesiastical History, 1978–; Prof. of Modern Hist., Glasgow Univ., 1980–91. *Publications:* Munich 1938, 1968; Sir Edward Grey, 1971; The Abolition of War: The British Peace Movement 1914–1919, 1976; John Bright, 1979; The Eclipse of a Great Power: Modern Britain 1870–1975, 1983; The First World War, 1984; Nineteenth-Century Britain: integration and diversity, 1988; Appeasement, 1988; (ed) Blackwell

Biographical Dictionary of British Political Life in the Twentieth Century, 1990; (ed) Protestant Evangelicalism, 1991; articles in Historical Jl, Internat. Affairs, Jl of Contemporary Hist., Jl of Ecclesiastical Hist., Jl of Commonwealth and Imperial Hist., etc. *Recreations:* music, gardening, walking. *Address:* St David's University College, Lampeter, Dyfed SA48 7ED. *T:* Lampeter (0570) 422351.

ROBBINS, Michael; *see* Robbins, Raymond F. M.

ROBBINS, Michael; *see* Robbins, Richard M.

ROBBINS, Dr (Raymond Frank) Michael, CBE 1987; higher education consultant; Director, Polytechnic South West (formerly Plymouth Polytechnic), 1974–89, Hon. Fellow, 1989; *b* 15 Feb. 1928; *s* of Harold and Elsie Robbins; *m* 1955, Eirian Meredith Edwards; two *d. Educ:* Grove Park Grammar Sch., Wrexham; UCW Aberystwyth. PhD 1954; FRIC 1962. Research Chemist, Monsanto Chemicals Ltd, 1954–55; Research Fellow, Univ. of Exeter, 1955–56; Lectr, Nottingham Coll. of Technology, 1956–59; Sen. Lectr, Hatfield Coll. of Technology, 1960–61; Head of Dept of Chem. Sciences, Hatfield Polytechnic, 1961–70; Dep. Dir, Plymouth Polytechnic, 1970–74. Chm., Sci. Prog. Adv. Gp, PCFC, 1989–; Mem., British Accreditation Council, 1984–. *Publications:* papers on organic chemistry in chem. jls, various reviews and articles in sci. and educnl press. *Recreations:* hill walking, creative gardening. *Address:* Lent Hill Cottage, Ashburton, Devon TQ13 7NW.

ROBBINS, (Richard) Michael, CBE 1976; *b* 7 Sept. 1915; *er s* of late Alfred Gordon Robbins and Josephine, *d* of R. L. Capell, Northampton; *m* 1939, Rose Margaret Elspeth, *er d* of late Sir Robert Reid Bannatyne, CB, Lindfield, Sussex; one *s* two *d. Educ:* Westminster Sch. (King's Schol.); Christ Church, Oxford (Westminster Schol.; MA); Univ. of Vienna. Joined London Passenger Transport Board, 1939. War service, RE (Transportation), 1939–46: Persia and Iraq, 1941–43; GHQ, MEF, 1943–44; Major, AML (Greece), 1944–45. Rejoined London Transport, 1946; Sec. to Chm., 1947–50; Sec., London Transp. Exec., 1950–55; Sec. and Chief Public Relations Off., 1955–60; Chief Commercial and Pub. Rel. Off., 1960–65; Mem., London Transport Exec., 1965–80 (Man. Dir, Rlys, 1971–78). Chm., Transport Adv. Cttee, Transport and Road Res. Lab., 1977–81. Pres., Inst. of Transport, 1975–76 (Mem. Council, 1957–60 and 1962–64; Chm., Metrop. Sect., 1962–63; Chm., Educn and Trg Cttee, 1969–72; Vice-Pres., 1972–75); Pres., Omnibus Soc., 1965; Chairman: Middx Victoria County History Council, 1963–76; Middx Local History Council, 1958–65; Internat. Metrop. Rlys Cttee, Internat. Union of Public Transport, 1976–81; Victorian Soc., 1978–81; President: London and Middx Archæol. Soc., 1965–71 (Mem. Council, 1951–56 and 1960–65); Greater London Industrial Archæol. Soc., 1969–; Rly Students Assoc., 1967–68; St Marylebone Soc., 1971–74; Mem., Ancient Monuments Adv. Cttee, English Heritage, 1986–91. Dunhill lectr on industrial design, Australia, 1974. FSA 1957; Pres., Soc. of Antiquaries, 1987–91 (Mem. Council, 1965–67, 1970–71; Treas., 1971–87); Chm., Museum of London, 1979–90 (Governor, 1968–); Vice Chm., Greater Manchester Museum of Science and Industry, 1987–90 (Trustee, 1982–90); Trustee, London Museum, 1970–75. Hon. DLitt City Univ., 1987. *Publications:* The North London Railway, 1937; 190 in Persia, 1951; The Isle of Wight Railways, 1953; Middlesex, 1953; (ed) Middlesex Parish Churches, 1955; The Railway Age, 1962; (with T. C. Barker) History of London Transport, vol. 1, 1963, vol. 2, 1974; George and Robert Stephenson, 1966, rev. edn 1981; Points and Signals, 1967; A Public Transport Century, 1985; Joint Editor, Journal of Transport History, 1953–65; contribs to transport and historical jls. *Recreations:* exploring cities and suburbs; travelling abroad and in branch railway trains; concert-going. *Address:* 7 Courthope Villas, Wimbledon, SW19 4EH. *T:* 081–946 7308. *Club:* Athenæum.

ROBENS, family name of **Baron Robens of Woldingham.**

ROBENS OF WOLDINGHAM, Baron *cr* 1961, of Woldingham (Life Peer); **Alfred Robens,** PC 1951; President, Snamprogetti, since 1988 (Chairman, 1980–88); Chairman, Alfred Robens Associates, since 1984; a Director: Times Newspapers Holdings Ltd, 1980–83 (Times Newspapers Ltd, 1967–80); AAH, since 1971; AMI (Europe) Ltd, since 1981; Chairman, Engineering Industries Council, since 1976; *b* 18 Dec. 1910; *s* of George and Edith Robens; *m* 1937, Eva, *d* of Fred and late Elizabeth Powell. *Educ:* Manchester Secondary Sch. Official of Union of Distributive and Allied Workers, 1935–45; Manchester City Councillor, 1942–45. MP (Lab) Wansbeck Div. of Northumberland, 1945–50, and for Blyth, 1950–60. Parliamentary Private Secretary to Minister of Transport, 1945–47; Parliamentary Secretary, Ministry of Fuel and Power, 1947–51; Minister of Labour and National Service, April-Oct. 1951. Chairman: National Coal Bd, 1961–71; Vickers Ltd, 1971–79; St Regis Internat., 1976–81; MLH Consultants, 1971–81; Johnson Matthey PLC, 1971–83 (Hon. Pres., 1983–); St Regis Newspapers, Bolton, 1975–80 (Dir, 1976); a Director: Bank of England, 1966–81; St Regis Paper Co. (NY), 1976–80; Trust House Forte Ltd, 1971–86; British Fuel Co., 1967–87. Chairman: Foundation on Automation and Employment, 1962; Engrg Industries Council, 1976–80; Member: NEDC, 1962–71; Royal Commn on Trade Unions and Employers' Assocs, 1965–68. President: Advertising Assoc., 1963–68; Incorporated Soc. of British Advertisers, 1973–76; Chairman: Jt Steering Cttee for Malta, 1967; Jt Econ. Mission to Malta, 1967. Member: Council of Manchester Business School, 1964–79 (Dep. Chm., 1964–70; Chm., 1970–79); Court of Governors, LSE, 1965; Chancellor, Univ. of Surrey, 1966–77. Governor, Queen Elizabeth Training Coll. for the Disabled, 1951–80; Chairman: Bd of Govs, Guy's Hosp., 1965–74; Guy's Hosp. Medical and Dental Sch., 1974–82; Cttee on Safety and Health of people at their place of work, 1970–72; Fellow, Manchester Coll. of Science and Technology, 1965–; Hon. FRCR, 1975. Hon. DCL: Univ. of Newcastle upon Tyne, 1964; Manchester Univ., 1974; Hon. LLD: Leicester, 1966; London, 1971. Hon. MInstM, 1968; Hon. FIOB, 1974. Mackintosh Medal, Advertising Assoc., 1970; Albert Medal, RSA, 1977. *Publications:* Engineering and Economic Progress, 1965; Industry and Government, 1970; Human Engineering, 1970; Ten Year Stint, 1972; sundry articles to magazines, journals and newspapers. *Address:* House of Lords, SW1.

ROBERGE, Guy, QC (Can.); Counsel, McCarthy Tétrault, Ottawa (formerly Clarkson Tétrault), Barristers and Solicitors, since 1982; *b* 26 Jan. 1915; *s* of P. A. Roberge and Irène Duchesneau; *m* 1957, Marie Raymond; one *s* one *d. Educ:* Laval Univ., Quebec. Called to Bar, 1937; Mem., Quebec Legislative Assembly, 1944–48; Mem., Restrictive Trade Practices Commn of Canada, 1955–57; Chm. and Chief Exec. Officer, Nat. Film Bd of Canada, 1957–66; Agent-General for Govt of PQ in UK, 1966–71; Vice-Pres. (Law), Canadian Transport Commn, 1971–81. Hon. DCL, Bishop's Univ., 1967; Hon. doctorat d'université, Laval Univ., 1975. *Address:* 555 Wilbrod, Ottawa, Ontario K1N 5R4, Canada. *Club:* Rideau (Ottawa).

ROBERTS, family name of **Baron Clwyd.**

ROBERTS, Prof. Adam; *see* Roberts, E. A.

ROBERTS, Albert, JP; DL; *b* 14 May 1908; *s* of Albert Roberts and Annie Roberts (*née* Ward); *m* 1932, Alice Ashton (*d* 1989); one *s* one *d. Educ:* Woodlesford School; Normanton and Whitwood Technical College, Yorks. Sec., Woodlesford Br., Yorks Miners Assoc., 1935–41; Safety Board, Mines Inspector, 1941–51. Mem., Rothwell UDC, 1937–52. MP (Lab) Normanton, 1951–83; Exec. Mem., British Group, Inter-Parly Union, 1955–83 (Chm., 1968–70). Exec. Mem., Yorkshire Area Heart Foundn; Vice-Pres., Yorkshire Soc. JP 1946, DL 1967, W Yorks. Order of Isabela la Católica (Spain), 1967; Diplomatic Order of Merit, Korean Republic, 1979. *Publication:* One of a Family (autobiog.), 1988. *Recreations:* cricket, bowls. *Address:* Cordoba, 14 Aberford Road, Oulton-Woodlesford, near Leeds LS26 8JR. *T:* Leeds (0532) 822303.

ROBERTS, Dr Albert, MSc, PhD; CEng; Head of Department of Mining Engineering, University of Nevada, 1969–75, retired 1975; *b* 25 April 1911; British; *m* 1938, May Taberner; two *s* one *d. Educ:* Wigan Mining and Techn. College. Mining Engr, Wigan Coal Corp., 1931–35, 1938–40; Ashanti Goldfields Corp., 1935–38; Lectr: Sunderland Techn. Coll., 1940–45; Nottingham Univ., 1945–55; Sheffield Univ., 1955; Dir, Postgraduate Sch. of Mining, Sheffield Univ., 1956–69. Ed., Internat. Jl of Rock Mechanics and Mining Sciences, 1964–68. *Publications:* Geological Structures, 1946; Underground Lighting, 1959; Mine Ventilation, 1959; Mineral Processing, 1965; Geotechnology, 1977; Applied Geotechnology, 1981. *Recreation:* music.

ROBERTS, Allan Deverell; Under-Secretary (Principal Assistant Solicitor), Solicitor's Office, Departments of Health and of Social Security, since 1989; *b* 14 July 1950; *s* of Irfon Roberts and Patricia Mary (*née* Allan). *Educ:* Eton Coll.; Magdalen Coll., Oxford (MA). Solicitor in private practice, 1974–76; Solicitor's Office, DHSS, 1976–. *Recreations:* hill walking, tegestology, football, listening to music. *Address:* (office) New Court, 48 Carey Street, WC2A 2LS. *T:* 071–972 2000.

ROBERTS, Alwyn; Vice Principal, since 1985, and Director of Extra Mural Studies, since 1979, University College of North Wales, Bangor; *b* 26 Aug. 1933; *s* of late Rev. Howell Roberts and Buddug Roberts; *m* 1960, Mair Rowlands Williams; one *s. Educ:* Penygroes Grammar Sch.; Univ. of Wales, Aberystwyth and Bangor (BA, LLB); Univ. of Cambridge (MA). Tutor, Westminster Coll., Cambridge, 1959; Principal, Pachhunga Meml Govt Coll., Aijal, Assam, India, 1960–67; Lectr in Social Admin, University Coll., Swansea, 1967–70; Lectr, subseq. Sen. Lectr, Dept of Social Theory and Instns, UCNW, Bangor, 1970–79. BBC National Governor for Wales, 1979–86; Chm., Broadcasting Council for Wales, 1979–86 (Mem., 1974–78); Member: Welsh Fourth TV Channel Auth., 1981–86; Gwynedd CC, 1973–81 (Chm., Social Services Cttee, 1977–81); Gwynedd AHA, 1973–80; Royal Commn on Legal Services, 1976–79; Parole Bd, 1987–90. Chm., Royal National Eisteddfod of Wales, 1989– (Vice-Chm., 1987–89; Mem. Council, 1979–); Mem. Bd, Cwmni Theatr Cymru, 1982–86. *Address:* Brithdir, 43 Talycae, Tregarth, Bangor, Gwynedd. *T:* Bangor (0248) 600007.

ROBERTS, Air Vice-Marshal Andrew Lyle, CBE 1983; AFC 1969; Assistant Chief of Defence Staff (Concepts), since 1989; *b* 19 May 1938; *s* of Ronald and Norah Roberts; *m* 1962, Marcia Isabella Ward, *d* of Lt-Col C. L. C. Ward; three *d. Educ:* Cranbrook Sch.; RAF Coll., Cranwell. Commnd RAF, 1958; ADC to AOC No 18 Gp, 1965–66; Flight Comdr, 201 Sqdn, 1967–68 (AFC); RNSC, 1969; Personal Air Sec. to Parly Under-Sec. of State (RAF), MoD, 1970–71; i/c 236 Operational Conversion Unit, 1972–74; US Armed Forces Staff Coll., 1974; staff, SACLANT, 1975–77; i/c RAF Kinloss, 1977–79; Gp Capt. Ops, HQ Strike Command, 1980–82 (CBE); RCDS, 1983; Dir, Air Plans, MoD, 1984–86; C of S, HQ No 18 Gp, 1987–89. MBIM. *Recreations:* cross-country and hill walking, natural history, classical music, church organ, choral singing, off-shore sailing. *Address:* c/o Midland Bank, 61 High Street, Staines, Middx TW18 4QW. *Club:* Royal Air Force.

ROBERTS, Angus Thomas; Director of Litigation and Prosecution, Post Office Solicitor's Office (formerly Principal Assistant Solicitor to General Post Office), 1965–74; *b* 28 March 1913; *s* of late Edward Roberts and late Margaret (*née* Murray); *m* 1940, Frances Monica, *d* of late Frederick and late Agnes Bertha Cane; two *s. Educ:* Felsted School. Admitted Solicitor, 1936. Entered Post Office Solicitor's Dept, 1939. Served in Royal Navy, 1941–46 (Lieut, RNVR). Asst Solicitor to GPO, 1951. *Recreations:* golf, fishing, gardening. *Address:* 1 The Mulberries, The Inner Silk Mill, Malmesbury, Wilts SN16 9LP. *T:* Malmesbury (0666) 824981.

ROBERTS, Ann; *see* Clwyd, Ann.

ROBERTS, (Anthony) John, CBE 1991; Managing Director, Post Office Counters Ltd (formerly Counter Services), and Board Member, The Post Office, since 1985; *b* 26 Aug. 1944; *s* of Douglas and Margaret Roberts; *m* 1970, Diana June (*née* Lamdin); two *s. Educ:* Hampton Sch.; Exeter Univ. (BA Hons). CBIM. Open Entrant, Administrative Class Civil Service, The Post Office, 1967; PA to Dep. Chairman and Chief Executive, 1969–71; Principal, Long Range Planning, 1971–74; Controller Personnel and Finance, North Western Postal Board, 1974–76; Principal Private Sec. to Chairman, 1976–77; Director, Chairman's Office, 1977–80; Secretary Designate, 1980–81, Sec., 1981–82; Dir, Counter Services, 1981–85. Chm., South Thames TEC, 1989–. Freeman, City of London, 1983; Liveryman, Gardeners' Co., 1988. *Recreations:* squash, golf, gardening, music. *Address:* Post Office Counters Ltd, Drury House, 1/16 Blackfriars Road, SE1 9UA. *T:* 071–922 1101. *Clubs:* Oxshott Squash Rackets, Betchworth Park Golf.

ROBERTS, Arthur Loten, OBE 1971; Emeritus Professor, formerly Livesey Professor of Coal Gas and Fuel Industries, 1947–71, and Chairman of the Houldsworth School of Applied Science, 1956–70, University of Leeds; Pro-Vice-Chancellor, 1967–69; *b* 1 April 1906; *s* of Arthur James Roberts, Hull, and Alice Maude Loten, Hornsea, E Yorks; *m* 1941, Katherine Mary Hargrove; one *s* one *d. Educ:* Christ's Hospital; Univ. of Leeds. BSc 1928, PhD 1930, Assistant Lecturer, Lecturer, Senior Lecturer, Leeds Univ. Part-time mem. North-Eastern Area Gas Board, 1950–71; Mem. Gas Corp. Res. Cttee (formerly Gas Council Research Cttee), 1951–79; Hon. Sec. Advisory Research Cttee of Gas Council and University, 1947–71; Chm., former Joint Refractories Cttee of British Ceramic Research Assoc. and the Gas Corporation; Pres. British Ceramic Society, 1957–58; Member of Technology Sub-Cttee, UGC, 1960–69. FRIC, FInstF, Hon. Fellow Inst. Ceram., Hon. FInstGasE, Hon. FIChemE. *Publications:* numerous contributions to chemical, ceramic and fuel jls. *Recreations:* painting, pianoforte, garden. *Address:* Hillside, 6 King's Road, Bramhope, Leeds, W Yorks. *T:* Leeds (0532) 674977.

ROBERTS, Barbara Haig; *see* MacGibbon, B. H.

ROBERTS, Prof. Benjamin Charles, MA Oxon; Professor of Industrial Relations, London School of Economics, University of London, 1962–84, now Emeritus; *b* 1 Aug. 1917; *s* of Walter Whitfield Roberts and Mabel Frances Roberts; *m* 1945, Veronica Lilian, *d* of George Frederick and Vera Lilian Vine-Lott; two *s. Educ:* LSE (Hon. Fellow, 1988); New Coll., Oxford. Research Student, Nuffield Coll., Oxford, 1948–49; Part-time Lectr, Ruskin Coll., Oxford, 1948–49; London Sch. of Economics: Lectr in Trade Union Studies, 1949–56; Reader in Industrial Relations, 1956–62; Mem. Ct of Govs, 1964–69, 1979–83. Vis. Prof: Princeton Univ., 1958; MIT 1959; Univ. of Calif., Berkeley, 1965. Assoc., Internat. Inst. of Labour Studies, Geneva, 1966; Member: Council, Inst. Manpower Studies; British-N American Cttee; Nat. Reference Tribunal of Coal Mining Industry, 1970–; Council, ACAS, 1979–86; Bruges Gp, 1990–. Editor, British Jl of Industrial

Relations, 1963–89, Hon. Editor, 1990–. Pres., British Univs Industrial Relations Assoc., 1965–68; Pres., Internat. Industrial Relations Assoc., 1967–73. Consultant to EEC, 1976–79. Chm., Economists' Bookshop, 1979–87. Wincott Lecture, IEA, 1987. *Publications:* Trade Unions in the New Era, 1947; Trade Union Government and Administration in Great Britain, 1956; National Wages Policy in War and Peace, 1958; The Trades Union Congress, 1868–1921, 1958; Trade Unions in a Free Society, 1959; (ed) Industrial Relations: Contemporary Problems and Perspectives, 1962; Labour in the Tropical Territories of the Commonwealth, 1964; (ed) Manpower Planning and Employment Trends 1966; (with L. Greyfié de Bellecombe) Collective Bargaining in African Countries, 1967; (ed) Industrial Relations: Contemporary Issues, 1968; (with John Lovell) A Short History of the TUC, 1968; (with R. O. Clarke and D. J. Fatchet) Workers' Participation in Management in Britain, 1972; (with R. Loveridge and J. Gennard) Reluctant Militants: a study of industrial technicians, 1972; (with H. Okomoto and G. Lodge) Collective Bargaining and Employee Participation in Western Europe, North America and Japan, 1979; also Evidence to Royal Commn on Trade Unions, 1966, and Report to ILO on Labour and Automation: Manpower Adjustment Programmes in the United Kingdom, 1967; Industrial Relations in Europe: the imperatives of change, 1985; (with T. Kochan and N. Meltz) New Departures in Industrial Relations: developments in USA, the UK and Canada, 1988; Europe—Uniformity or Freedom?: the real EC questions, 1991. *Address:* 28 Temple Fortune Lane, NW11 7UD. *T:* 081–458 1421. *Clubs:* Reform, Political Economy.

ROBERTS, Bertie; Director, Department of the Environment (Property Services Agency), 1971–79; *b* 4 June 1919; *y s* of late Thomas and Louisa Roberts, Blaengarw, S Wales; *m* 1st, 1946, Dr Peggy Clark; one *s*; 2nd, 1962, Catherine Matthew. *Educ:* Garw Grammar School. Entered Civil Service, 1936; HM Forces, 1942–46, Captain RAOC; leader of study on feasibility of using computers in Min. of Public Bldg and Works, 1958; formed and directed operational computer orgn, 1962; Comptroller of Accounts, 1963; Dir of Computer Services, 1967; Head of Organisation and Methods, 1969; Dir of Estate Management Overseas, Dept of the Environment (with FCO), 1971; Reg. Dir, DoE (Maj.-Gen.), British Forces Germany, 1976–79. Mem., Community Health Council (Hastings Health Dist), 1982–90. *Recreations:* travel, music. *Address:* Fairmount, 41 Hollington Park Road, St Leonards on Sea, E Sussex TN38 0SE. *T:* Hastings 714177. *Club:* Rotary of St Leonard's-on-Sea.

ROBERTS, Brian Stanley; HM Diplomatic Service, retired; Head of Art History, Putney High School, since 1989; *b* 1 Feb. 1936; *s* of Stanley Victor Roberts and Flora May (*née* McInnes); *m* 1st, 1961, Phyllis Hazel Barber (marr. diss. 1976); two *s*; 2nd, 1985, Jane Catharine Chisholm; one *d*. *Educ:* Liverpool Collegiate Sch., Christ's Coll., Cambridge (MA); Courtauld Institute, London (MA). Served Royal Navy, 1955–57. Staff, Edinburgh Univ., 1960–62; Lecturer in Art History, Goldsmiths' Coll., London, 1962–69; entered FCO, 1970: First Secretary, Capetown/Pretoria, 1972; FCO, 1974; attached to Hong Kong Govt, 1977; FCO, 1980; Counsellor, Stockholm, 1983–87; Cabinet Office, 1987. Teacher, Art Hist., Cheltenham Ladies' Coll., 1988–89. *Recreations:* walking, looking at pictures. *Clubs:* United Oxford & Cambridge University, Lansdowne.

ROBERTS, Sir Bryan Clieve, KCMG 1973 (CMG 1964); QC; JP; a Metropolitan Stipendiary Magistrate, since 1982; Chairman, Commonwealth Magistrates' and Judges' Association (formerly Commonwealth Magistrates' Association), since 1979; *b* 22 March 1923; *s* of late Herbert Roberts, MA, and Doris Evelyn Clieve; *m* 1st, 1958, Pamela Dorothy Campbell (marr. diss.); 2nd, 1976, Brigitte Patricia Reilly-Morrison (marr. diss.); 3rd, 1985, Barbara Forter. *Educ:* Whitgift School; Magdalen Coll., Oxford (MA). Served War of 1939–45: commissioned in RA and RHA, 1941–46; active service in Normandy, Belgium, Holland and Germany, 1944–45. Called to Bar, Gray's Inn, 1950; in chambers in Temple, 1950–51; Treasury Solicitor's Dept, 1951–53. Crown Counsel, N Rhodesia, 1953–60; Dir of Public Prosecutions, N Rhodesia, 1960–61; QC (Fedn of Rhodesia and Nyasaland) 1961; Nyasaland: Solicitor-General, 1961–64; Minister of Justice, 1962–63; Mem., Legislative Council, 1961–63; Attorney-Gen. of Malawi, 1964–72; Perm. Sec. to Office of the President, Sec. to the Cabinet, and Head of Malawi Civil Service, 1965–72; Chairman: Malawi Army Council; Nat. Security and Intell. Council; Nat. Develt and Planning Council, 1966–72. Lord Chancellor's Office, 1973–82 (Under Sec., 1977–82). JP Inner London, 1975 (Dep. Chm., South Westminster Bench, 1977–82). Officer of the Order of Menelik II of Ethiopia, 1965; Comdr, Nat. Order of Republic of Malagasy, 1969. *Address:* 3 Caroline Place, W2; Stonebarrow Lodge, Charmouth, Dorset. *Club:* Oriental.

ROBERTS, Dr Brynley Francis, FSA; Librarian, National Library of Wales, since 1985; Hon. Professor, Department of Welsh, University College of Wales, Aberystwyth, since 1986; *b* 3 Feb. 1931; *s* of Robert F. Roberts and Laura Jane Roberts (*née* Williams); *m* 1957, Rhiannon Campbell; twin *s*. *Educ:* Grammar School, Aberdare; University College of Wales, Aberystwyth (BA Hons Welsh, MA, PhD). Fellow, Univ. of Wales, 1956–57; Lectr, Sen. Lectr, Reader, Dept of Welsh, University Coll. of Wales, Aberystwyth, 1957–78; Prof. of Welsh Language and Literature, University Coll. Swansea, 1978–85. Sir John Rhys Fellow, Jesus Coll., Oxford, 1973–74. Chairman: United Theological Coll., Aberystwyth, 1977–; Gwasg Pantycelyn, Caernarfon, 1977–. Pres., Welsh Library Assoc., 1985–; Chm., Welsh Books Council, 1989– (Vice-Chm., 1986–89). FRSA. *Publications:* Gwasanaeth Meir, 1961; Brut y Brenhinedd, 1971, 2nd edn 1984; Cyfranc Lludd a Llefelys, 1975; Brut Tysilio, 1980; Edward Lhuyd: the making of a scientist, 1980; Gerald of Wales, 1982; Itinerary through Wales, 1989; Tales and Romances, 1991; articles in learned jls. *Recreations:* walking, music. *Address:* Hengwrt, Llanbadarn Road, Aberystwyth. *T:* Aberystwyth (0970) 623577.

ROBERTS, Rear-Adm. Cedric Kenelm, CB 1970; DSO 1952; *b* 19 April 1918; *s* of F. A. Roberts; *m* 1940, Audrey, *d* of T. M. Elias; four *s*. *Educ:* King Edward's Sch., Birmingham. Joined RN as Naval Airman 2nd Cl., 1940; commnd Temp. Sub-Lt (A), RNVR, 1940; sunk in HMS Manchester, 1942, Malta Convoy; interned in Sahara; released, Nov. 1942; Personal Pilot to Vice-Adm. Sir Arthur Lyster, 1943; HMS Trumpeter, Russian Convoys, 1944; perm. commn as Lt RN, HMS Vindex, Pacific, 1945; CO 813 Sqdn, 1948; Naval Staff Coll., 1949; CO 767 Sqdn, 1950–51; CO 825 Sqdn, 1951–52: served Korean War; shot down, rescued by US Forces; lent to RAN as Dep. Dir, Air Warfare, 1953–55; CO, RNAS Eglinton, 1958–59; Chief Staff Officer: FONFT, 1959–61; FOAC, 1961–62; Capt., HMS Osprey, 1962–64; Capt., RNAS Culdrose, 1964–65; Chief Staff Officer (Ops), Far East Fleet, 1966–67; Flag Officer, Naval Flying Training, 1968–71; retired 1971; farmed in Somerset, 1971–79; emigrated to Australia, 1979. Comdr 1952; Capt. 1958; Rear-Adm. 1968. *Recreations:* sitting in the sun, drinking plonk, and watching the sheilas go by. *Address:* 11 Collins Street, Merimbula, NSW 2548, Australia. *T:* Merimbula 951754.

ROBERTS, Christopher William, CB 1986; Deputy Secretary, Department of Trade and Industry, since 1983; *b* 4 Nov. 1937; *s* of Frank Roberts and Evelyn Dorothy Roberts. *Educ:* Rugby Sch.; Magdalen Coll., Oxford (MA). Lectr in Classics, Pembroke Coll., Oxford, 1959–60; Asst Principal, BoT, 1960; Second Sec. (Commercial), British High Commn, New Delhi, 1962–64; Asst Private Sec. to Pres. of BoT, 1964–65; Principal, 1965; Cabinet Office, 1966–68; Private Sec. to Prime Minister, 1970–73; Asst Sec., 1972; Dept of Trade, 1973–77; Under Secretary: Dept of Prices and Consumer Protection, 1977–79; Dept of Trade, 1979–82; Chief Exec., BOTB, 1983–87. *Recreations:* travel, cricket, opera. *Clubs:* United Oxford & Cambridge University, MCC.

ROBERTS, David Ewart; His Honour Judge David Roberts; a Circuit Judge, since 1982; *b* 18 Feb. 1921; *s* of John Hobson Roberts and Dorothy Roberts. *Educ:* Abingdon Sch.; St John's Coll., Cambridge. MA, LLB. Served War, 1941–46; commnd RA (Field); service in Middle East, North Africa, Italy, Yugoslavia and Germany. Called to Bar, Middle Temple, 1948. Asst Recorder, Coventry QS, 1966–71; a Recorder of the Crown Court, 1978–82. *Recreations:* travel, photography. *Address:* 4 Greville Drive, Birmingham B15 2UU. *T:* 021–440 3231.

ROBERTS, David Francis; Deputy Director General, Agriculture, European Commission, since 1990; *b* 28 Aug. 1941; *s* of Arthur Roberts and Mary Roberts; *m* 1974, Astrid Suhr Henriksen; two *s* one *d*. *Educ:* Priory Grammar School, Shrewsbury; Worcester College, Oxford (MA). Joined MAFF, 1964; seconded to FCO as First Sec. (Agric.), Copenhagen, 1971–74; Principal Private Sec. to Minister of Agriculture, 1975–76; seconded to HM Treasury as Head of Agric. Div., 1979–80; Under Sec., 1985, seconded to FCO as Minister (Agric.), UK Repn to the European Communities, Brussels, 1985–90. *Recreations:* sailing, squash. *Address:* Directorate-General VI, Commission of the European Communities, 120 rue de la Loi, 1049 Brussels, Belgium.

ROBERTS, (David) Gwilym (Morris), CBE 1987; FEng 1986; Chairman: Acer Group Ltd, since 1987; Acer-ICF Ltd, since 1990; *b* 24 July 1925; *er s* of late Edward and Edith Roberts of Crosby; *m* 1st, 1960, Rosemary Elizabeth Emily (*d* 1973), *d* of late J. E. Giles of Tavistock; one *s* one *d*; 2nd, 1978, Wendy Ann, *d* of late Dr J. K. Moore of Beckenham and Alfriston. *Educ:* Merchant Taylors' School, Crosby; Sidney Sussex College, Cambridge (Minor Scholar, MA). FICE, FIMechE, FIWEM. Engineering Officer, RNVR, 1945–47; Lieut Comdr RNR, retired 1961. Asst Engineer, 1947–55, Partner, 1956–90 (Sen. Partner, 1981–90), John Taylor & Sons; principally development of water and wastewater projects, UK towns and regions, and Abu Dhabi, Bahrain, Egypt, Iraq, Kuwait, Mauritius, Qatar, Saudi Arabia and Thailand. Director: Acer Gp Ltd, 1987–; various transportation projects in UK and abroad. Vis. Prof., Loughborough Univ., 1991–. Chairman: BGS Programme Bd, 1989–; Football Stadia Adv. Design Council, 1990–; 2nd Severn Crossing Technical Adjudication Panel, 1991–; Member: UK Cttee, IAWPRC, 1967–83; Bd of Control, AMBRIC (American British Consultants), 1978–; (Construction Industry) Group of Eight, 1983–85, 1987–88; President: IPHE, 1968–69 (IPHE Silver Medal 1974; Gold Medal 1987); ICE, 1986–87 (Vice-Pres., 1983–86; Overseas Premium, 1978; Halcrow Premium, 1985; George Stephenson Medal, 1986). Council Member: Brighton Polytechnic, 1983–86; NERC, 1987–; CIRIA, 1988–. Member: Exec. Cttee, British Egyptian Soc., 1991–; Nat. Cttee, British-Arab Univ. Assoc., 1991–. Governor: Chailey Sch., 1988–; Roedean Sch., 1989–. Freeman, City of London, 1977; Liveryman: Engineers' Co., 1985; Constructors' Co., 1990. *Publications:* (co-author) Civil Engineering Procedure, 3rd edn, 1979; papers to Royal Soc., Arab League, ICE, IPHE. *Recreations:* tennis, walking, local history, engineering archaeology in Middle East. *Address:* (office) Acer House, Medawar Road, Surrey Research Park, Guildford, Surrey. *T:* Guildford (0483) 35000; North America Farm, Hundred Acre Lane, Westmeston, Hassocks, Sussex BN6 8SH. *T:* Plumpton (0273) 890324. *Clubs:* St Stephen's Constitutional, United Oxford & Cambridge University, MCC.

ROBERTS, Rt. Rev. (David) John; Abbot of Downside, 1974–90; *b* 31 March 1919; *s* of Albert Edward and Elizabeth Minnith Roberts. *Educ:* Downside School; Trinity Coll., Cambridge (MA). Royal Sussex Regt, Oct. 1939–Nov. 1945 (POW Germany, May 1940–April 1945). Entered monastery, Feb. 1946; ordained, 1951. House Master, Downside School, 1953–62; Novice Master, 1962–66; Prior 1966–74. *Address:* Downside Abbey, Stratton-on-the-Fosse, Bath BA3 4RH.

ROBERTS, Maj.-Gen. David Michael, MD; FRCP, FRCPE; equestrian centre proprietor; *b* 9 Sept. 1931; *s* of James Henry and Agnes Louise Roberts; *m* 1964, Angela Louise Squire; one *s* two *d*. *Educ:* Emanuel Sch., London; Royal Free Hospital School of Medicine (MB, BS). Qualified in medicine, 1954; commissioned RAMC, 1955; service in field units, BAOR, 1955–59; Hon. Registrar in Medicine, Radcliffe Infirmary, Oxford, 1960; various medical specialty appts in military hosps in UK, BAOR and Hong Kong, 1960–75; graded consultant physician, 1968; Joint Professor of Military Medicine, RAMC and RCP, London, 1975–81; Command Cons. Physician, BAOR, 1981–84; Dir of Army Medicine and Cons. Physician to the Army, 1984–88, retired. Consulting Physician, Royal Hosp., Chelsea, 1984–88; MO (Res.), MoD, 1988–90. Lectr in Tropical Medicine, Mddx Hosp. Medical Sch., 1976–81; Examiner in Tropical Medicine for RCP, 1981–88. Mem., British Soc. of Gastroenterology, 1973–90. QHP 1984–88. *Publications:* many articles on gastroenterological subjects. *Recreations:* mixing concrete, building things.

ROBERTS, Denis Edwin, CBE 1974 (MBE 1945); Managing Director, Posts, 1977–80; *b* 6 Jan. 1917; *s* of late Edwin and Alice G. Roberts; *m* 1940, Edith (*née* Whitehead); two *s*. *Educ:* Holgate Grammar Sch., Barnsley. Served War of 1939–45, Royal Signals, France, N Africa, Italy and Austria. Entered Post Office, Barnsley, 1933; various appts, 1933–71; Dir Postal Ops, 1971–75; Sen. Dir, Postal Services, 1975–77. Mem., Industrial Tribunal, 1982–86. Chm., British Philatelic Trust, 1981–85. Liveryman, Gardeners' Co. *Address:* 302 Gilbert House, Barbican, EC2Y 8BD. *T:* 071–638 0881. *Clubs:* City of London, City Livery.

ROBERTS, Hon. Sir Denys (Tudor Emil), KBE 1975 (CBE 1970; OBE 1960); SPMB; **Hon. Mr Justice Roberts;** Chief Justice of Negara Brunei Darussalam, since 1979; President, Court of Appeal, Bermuda, since 1988; *b* 19 Jan. 1923; *s* of William David and Dorothy Elizabeth Roberts; *m* 1st, 1949, Brenda Marsh (marr. diss. 1973); one *s* one *d*; 2nd, 1985, Anna Fiona Dollar Alexander; one *s*. *Educ:* Aldenham; Wadham Coll., Oxford, 1942 and 1946–49 (MA 1948, BCL 1949; Hon. Fellow, 1984); served with Royal Artillery, 1943–46, France, Belgium, Holland, Germany, India (Captain). English Bar, 1950–53; Crown Counsel, Nyasaland, 1953–59; QC Gibraltar 1960; QC Hong Kong 1964; Attorney-General, Gibraltar, 1960–62; Solicitor-General, Hong Kong, 1962–66; Attorney-General, Hong Kong, 1966–73; Chief Secretary, Hong Kong, 1973–78; Chief Justice, Hong Kong, 1979–88. Hon. Bencher, Lincoln's Inn, 1978. SPMB (Negara Brunei Darussalam), 1984. *Publications:* Smuggler's Circuit, 1954; Beds and Roses, 1956; The Elwood Wager, 1958; The Bones of the Wajingas, 1960; How to Dispense with Lawyers, 1964. *Recreations:* cricket, walking, writing. *Address:* The Supreme Court, Bandar Seri Begawan, Brunei; PO Box 338, Paphos, Cyprus. *Clubs:* Garrick, MCC (Pres., 1989–90); Hong Kong (Hong Kong).

ROBERTS, Derek Franklyn, FCII, FCBSI; Director and Chief Executive, Yorkshire Building Society, since 1987; Chairman, Yorkshire Building Society Estate Agents Ltd, since 1988; *b* 16 Oct. 1942; *s* of Frank Roberts, MBE, and May Evelyn Roberts; *m* 1969, Jacqueline (*née* Velho); two *s* one *d*. *Educ:* Park High Grammar Sch., Birkenhead; Liverpool Coll. of Commerce; Harvard Business Sch. (AMP (Grad.)). Royal Insurance

Co. Ltd, 1961–72; Huddersfield Building Society: Insce Services Man., 1972; apptd to Executive, as Business Develt Man., 1975; Develt Man., 1979; on formation of Yorkshire Building Soc., 1982, apptd Asst Gen. Man. (Marketing). Dir, BWD Securities PLC, 1988–. Pres., Huddersfield Dist Centre CBSI, 1988–. *Recreations:* golf, gardening, walking. *Address:* Lower Snow Lea Farm, Lamb Hall Road, Longwood, Huddersfield, West Yorks HD3 3TH. *T:* Huddersfield (0484) 533504. *Clubs:* Huddersfield Golf, Royal Liverpool Golf; Huddersfield Rugby Union FC.

ROBERTS, Derek Harry, CBE 1983; FRS 1980, FEng, FInstP; Provost of University College London, since 1989; *b* 28 March 1932; *s* of Harry and Alice Roberts; *m* 1958, Winifred (*née* Short); one *s* one *d*. *Educ:* Manchester Central High Sch.; Manchester Univ. (BSc). MIEE. Joined Plessey Co.'s Caswell Res. Lab., 1953; Gen. Man., Plessey Semiconductors, 1967; Dir, Allen Clark Res. Centre, 1969; Man. Dir, Plessey Microelectronics Div., 1973; Technical Dir, 1983–85, Jt Dep. Man. Dir (Technical), 1985–88, GEC. Hon. DSc: Bath, 1982; Loughborough, 1984; City, 1985; Lancaster, 1986; Manchester, 1987; Salford, Essex, London, 1988; DUniv Open, 1984. *Publications:* about 20 pubns in scientific and technical jls. *Recreations:* reading, gardening. *Address:* University College London, Gower Street, WC1E 6BT. *T:* 071–380 7234.

ROBERTS, Prof. (Edward) Adam, FBA 1990; Montague Burton Professor of International Relations and Fellow of Balliol College, Oxford, since 1986; *b* 29 Aug. 1940; *s* of Michael Roberts and Janet Roberts (*see* Janet Adam Smith); *m* 1966, Frances P. Dunn; one *s* one *d*. *Educ:* Westminster School; Magdalen College, Oxford (BA 1962, MA 1981). Asst Editor, Peace News Ltd, 1962–65; Noel Buxton Student in Internat. Relations, LSE, 1965–68; Lectr in Internat. Relations, LSE, 1968–81; Alastair Buchan Reader in Internat. Relations, Oxford, and Professorial Fellow, St Antony's Coll., Oxford, 1981–86. Mem., Council, RIIA, 1985–91. *Publications:* (ed) The Strategy of Civilian Defence, 1967; (jtly) Czechoslovakia 1968, 1969; Nations in Arms, 1976, 2nd edn, 1986; (ed jtly) Documents on the Laws of War, 1982, 2nd edn 1989; (ed jtly) United Nations, Divided World, 1988; (ed jtly) Hugo Grotius and International Relations, 1990. *Recreations:* rock climbing, mountaineering, running. *Address:* Balliol College, Oxford OX1 3BJ. *T:* Oxford (0865) 277777. *Club:* Alpine.

ROBERTS, Rev. Canon Edward Eric, JP; Canon Emeritus of Southwell, since 1980; *b* 29 April 1911; *o s* of late Edward Thomas Roberts and Mrs Charlotte Roberts, Liverpool; *m* 1938, Sybil Mary (*née* Curren); two *d*. *Educ:* Univ. of Liverpool; St Augustine's Coll., Canterbury. Youth Officer: City of Oxford LEA, 1938–43; Wallasey CB, LEA, 1943–44; Training Officer, Church of England Youth Council, 1944–52; Southwell Diocesan Director: of Further Educn, 1952–61; of Educn, 1961–68. Canon, 1964; Canon Residentiary, Vice-Provost of Southwell Cathedral and Personal Chaplain to Bishop of Southwell, 1969–79; Ecumenical Officer, Diocese of Southwell, 1973–79. Sec., Nottingham Council of Churches, 1980–84. JP, City of Nottingham, 1958–. *Recreation:* photography. *Address:* 24 Manor Close, Southwell, Nottinghamshire NG25 0AP. *T:* Southwell (0636) 813246.

ROBERTS, Sir (Edward Fergus) Sidney, Kt 1978; CBE 1972; former Federal President, Australian Country Party; grazier and manager of companies; *b* 19 April 1901; *s* of late E. J. Roberts. *Educ:* Scots Coll., Sydney. Gen. Manager, Ungra, Brisbane, 1957–70; owner, Boolaroo Downs, Clermont, Qld, 1928–63. United Graziers' Assoc., Qld: Mem. Council, 1948–76; Vice-Pres., 1950–52. Aust. Road Fedn: Mem., 1954–63; Nat. Pres., 1962–63. Mem. Bd, Queensland Country Life Newspaper, 1969–77; Pres., Aust. Country Party, Qld, 1967; Chm., Federal Council, ACP, 1969–74. Knighthood awarded for distinguished service to Primary Industry, Australia. *Address:* 53 Eldernell Avenue, Hamilton, Queensland 4007, Australia. *Club:* Queensland (Brisbane).

ROBERTS, Rt. Rev. Edward James Keymer; *b* 18 April 1908; *s* of Rev. Arthur Henry Roberts; *m* 1st, 1941, Dorothy Frances (*d* 1982), *d* of Canon Edwin David Bowser, Deal; three *s* one *d*; 2nd, 1984, Diana, *widow* of Dr Christopher Grey. *Educ:* Marlborough; Corpus Christi Coll., Cambridge; Cuddesdon Theological Coll. BA 2nd class Theological Tripos, 1930; MA 1935; DD (*hc*) Cambridge, 1965. FRSCM 1977. Deacon, 1931; priest, 1932; Curate of All Saints, Margaret Street, 1931–35; Vice-Principal Cuddesdon Coll., 1935–39; Examining Chaplain to Bishop of Portsmouth and Commissary, Johannesburg, 1936–39; Vicar of St Matthew, Southsea, 1940–45; Curate-in-charge of St Bartholomew, Southsea, 1941–45; Examining Chaplain to Bishop of Portsmouth, 1942–56; Proctor in Convocation, Portsmouth, 1944–49; Commissary, Northern Rhodesia, 1946–51; Hon. Canon of Portsmouth, 1947–49; Archdeacon of Isle of Wight, Vicar of Brading, Rector of Yaverland, 1949–52; Archdeacon of Portsmouth, 1952–56; Suffragan Bishop of Malmesbury, 1956–62; Examining Chaplain to Bishop of Bristol, 1959–62; Suffragan Bishop of Kensington, 1962–64; Bishop of Ely, 1964–77. Episcopal Commissary, Portsmouth, 1984–85. Hon. Fellow, Corpus Christi Coll., Cambridge, 1964–. Select Preacher, University of Cambridge, 1966, 1978. *Recreation:* shoe cleaning. *Address:* The House on the Marsh, Quay Lane, Brading, IoW. *T:* Isle of Wight (0983) 407434.

See also Hon. P. J. S. Roberts.

ROBERTS, Eirlys Rhiwen Cadwaladr, CBE 1977 (OBE 1971); Deputy Director, Consumers' Association (Which?), 1973–77 (Head of Research and Editorial Division, 1958–73); *b* 3 Jan. 1911; *d* of Dr Ellis James Roberts and Jane Tennant Macaulay; *m* 1941, John Cullen (marr. diss.); no *c*. *Educ:* Clapham High School; Girton College, Cambridge. BA (Hons) Classics. Sub-editor in Amalgamated Press; Military, then Political Intelligence, 1943–44 and 1944–45; Public Relations in UNRRA, Albanian Mission, 1945–47; Information Division of the Treasury, 1947–57. Chief Exec., Bureau of European Consumer Orgns, 1973–78. Mem., Royal Commn on the Press, 1974–77. Mem., Economic and Social Cttee of EEC, 1973–82 (Chm., Environment and Consumer Protection section, 1978–82); Chm., European Res. into Consumer Affairs, 1978–. *Publication:* Consumers, 1966. *Recreations:* walking, reading detective novels. *Address:* 8 Lloyd Square, WC1X 9BA. *T:* 071–837 2492.

ROBERTS, Rt. Rev. Eric Matthias; *b* 18 Feb. 1914; *s* of Richard and Jane Roberts; *m* 1944, Nancy Jane Roberts (*née* Davies); two *s*. *Educ:* Friars Sch., Bangor; University Coll., Bangor; St Edmund Hall, Oxon (MA); St Michael's Coll., Llandaff. Curate, Penmaenmawr, 1938–40; Sub-Warden, St Michael's Coll., Llandaff, 1940–47; Vicar: Port Talbot, 1947–56; Roath, 1956–65; Archdeacon of Margam, 1965–71; Bishop of St David's, 1971–81. ChStJ 1973. *Address:* 2 Tudor Close, Westbourne Road, Penarth, South Glamorgan CF6 2BR.

ROBERTS, Ernest Alfred Cecil; *b* 20 April 1912; *s* of Alfred and Florence Roberts; *m* 1953, Joyce Longley; one *s* two *d*. *Educ:* St Chad's Boys' Elementary Sch., Shrewsbury. Engineer, 1925–57; Assistant General Secretary, AUEW, 1957–77. MP (Lab) Hackney North and Stoke Newington, 1979–87. Former Chairman: PLP Health and Social Security Cttee; Lab. Party Parly Assoc. Tom Mann Gold Medal for services to trade unionism, 1943. *Publication:* Workers' Control, 1973. *Recreations:* work and politics, reading. *Address:* 9 Scotsdale Close, Petts Wood, Orpington, Kent.

ROBERTS, Sir Frank (Kenyon), GCMG 1963 (KCMG 1953; CMG 1946); GCVO 1965; Director, Hoechst (UK); Mercedes-Benz (UK); Vice-President: European Atlantic Group, since 1983 (Chairman, 1970–73; President, 1973–83); Atlantic Treaty Association, since 1973 (President, 1969–73); British Atlantic Committee, since 1982 (President, 1968–81); *b* Buenos Aires, 27 Oct. 1907; *s* of Henry George Roberts, Preston, and Gertrude Kenyon, Blackburn; *m* 1937, Celeste Leila Beatrix (*d* 1990), *d* of late Sir Said Shoucair Pasha, Cairo, Financial Adviser to Sudan Government; no *c*. *Educ:* Bedales; Rugby; Trinity College, Cambridge (Scholar). Entered Foreign Office, 1930; served HM Embassy, Paris, 1932–35 and at HM Embassy, Cairo, 1935–37; Foreign Office, 1937–45; Chargé d'Affaires to Czechoslovak Govt, 1943; British Minister in Moscow, 1945–47; Principal Private Secretary to Secretary of State for Foreign Affairs, 1947–49; Deputy High Commr (UK) in India, 1949–51; Deputy-Under Secretary of State, Foreign Office, 1951–54; HM Ambassador to Yugoslavia, 1954–57; United Kingdom Permanent Representative on the North Atlantic Council, 1957–60; Ambassador: to the USSR, 1960–62; to the Federal Republic of Germany, 1963–68. Vice-Pres., German Chamber of Commerce in UK, 1974– (Pres., 1971–74); Dep. Chm., British Nat. Cttee, Internat. Chamber of Commerce, 1978–81. Mem., FCO Review Cttee on Overseas Representation, 1968–69. Pres., Anglo-German Assoc.; Vice-Pres., GB-USSR Assoc. Grand Cross, German Order of Merit, 1965. *Publication:* Dealing with Dictators, 1991. *Address:* 25 Kensington Court Gardens, W8 5QF. *Clubs:* Brooks's, Royal Automobile.

ROBERTS, Prof. Gareth Gwyn, FRS 1984; Vice-Chancellor, University of Sheffield, since 1991; Visiting Professor of Electronic Engineering, Department of Engineering Science and Fellow, Brasenose College, Oxford University, since 1985; *b* 16 May 1940; *s* of Edwin and Meri Roberts; *m* 1962, Charlotte Standen; two *s* one *d*. *Educ:* UCNW, Bangor (BSc, PhD, DSc); MA Oxon 1987. Lectr in Physics, Univ. of Wales, 1963–66; Res. Physicist, Xerox Corp., USA, 1966–68; Sen. Lectr, Reader, and Professor of Physics, NUU, 1968–76; Prof. of Applied Physics and Head, Dept of Applied Physics and Electronics, Univ. of Durham, 1976–85; Dir of Research, 1986–90, Thorn EMI plc (Chief Scientist, 1985). BBC/Royal Instn Christmas Lectures, 1988. Mem., UFC, 1989–. Holweck Gold Medal and Prize, Inst. of Physics, 1986. *Publications:* Insulating Films on Semiconductors, 1979; Langmuir-Blodgett Films, 1990; many publications and patents on physics of semiconductor devices and molecular electronics. *Recreations:* soccer, duplicate bridge, classical music. *Address:* Snaithing Croft, Snaithing Lane, Sheffield S10 3LF. *T:* Sheffield (0742) 306297.

ROBERTS, Prof. Geoffrey Frank Ingleson, CBE 1978; FEng 1978; Chairman, British Pipe Coaters Ltd, 1978–88; Professor of Gas Engineering, University of Salford, 1983–89, Professorial Fellow, 1989–91; *b* 9 May 1926; *s* of late Arthur and Laura Roberts; *m* 1949, Veronica, *d* of late Captain J. Busby, Hartlepool; two *d*. *Educ:* Cathedral Sch., and High Sch. for Boys, Hereford; Leeds Univ. (BSc hons). FIChemE; FInstE. Pupil engr, Gas Light & Coke Co., and North Thames Gas Bd, 1947–50; North Thames Gas Board: Asst Engr, 1950–59; Stn Engr, Slough, 1959–61; Dept. Stn Engr, Southall Stn, 1961–66; Group Engr, Slough Group, 1966–68; Dep. Dir (Ops) Gas Council, 1968–71; Mem. for Production and Supply, Gas Council, later British Gas Corp., 1972–78; Mem. for External Affairs, British Gas Corp., 1979–81, retired. President: IGasE, 1980–81 (Hon. FIGasE); Inst. of Energy, 1983–84. *Recreations:* gardening, reading. *Address:* Ranmoor, St Nicholas Road, Middleton, Ilkley, West Yorks LS29 0AN. *T:* Ilkley (0943) 608915. *Club:* Royal Automobile.

ROBERTS, Air Cdre Sir Geoffrey Newland, Kt 1973; CBE 1946; AFC 1942; Hon. FRAeS; Company Director, retired; *b* Inglewood, Taranaki, New Zealand, 8 Dec. 1906; *s* of Charles Oxford Roberts, England, and Hilda Marion Newland, New Zealand; *m* 1934, Phyllis Hamilton Bird; one *s* one *d*. *Educ:* New Plymouth Boys' High Sch., New Plymouth, Taranaki, NZ. In commerce, NZ, 1924–28; RAF, England/India, 1928–34; commerce, UK, 1935–36; commerce, NZ, 1936–39. Served War: RNZAF, NZ and Pacific (final rank Air Cdre), 1939–46. Air New Zealand, General Manager, 1946–58; Dir, 1958–65; Chm., 1965–75. Chairman: Lion Breweries Ltd Mimiwhangata Farm Park Trust Board, 1975–86; Kaipara Edible Oils Refinery Ltd, 1978–82; Director: MFL Mutual Fund Ltd, 1971–86; Saudi NZ Capital Corp., 1980–84. Patron: Soc. of Licensed Aircraft Engrs and Technologists, 1964–86; Internat. Fedn of Airworthiness, 1976–84. Hon. FRAeS 1990 (FRAeS 1970). US Legion of Merit, 1944. *Relevant publication:* To Fly a Desk, by Noel Holmes, 1982. *Address:* Puketiro, No 2: RD, Wellsford, North Auckland, New Zealand. *T:* Wellsford 7219. *Clubs:* Northern, Auckland (Auckland, NZ); Probus (Warkworth, NZ).

ROBERTS, Brig. Sir Geoffrey P. H.; *see* Hardy-Roberts.

ROBERTS, George Arnott; Head of Administration Department, House of Commons, 1988–91; *b* 16 April 1930; *s* of David Roberts and Doris (*née* Sykes); *m* 1956, Georgina (*née* Gower); two *s* one *d*. *Educ:* Rastrick Grammar Sch.; London Univ. (extra-mural). Min. of Labour, then Dept of Employment, 1947–74; Advisory, Conciliation and Arbitration Service, 1974–85: Sec., Central Arbitration Cttee, 1978–80; Dir of Administration, 1980–83; Dir, London Region, 1983–85; House of Commons, 1985–91: Hd of Establishment Office, 1985–88. *Recreations:* golf, gardening. *Club:* Sonning Golf.

ROBERTS, Maj.-Gen. (George) Philip (Bradley), CB 1945; DSO 1942; MC 1941; late RTR; *b* 5 Nov. 1906; *m* 1st, 1936, Désirée (*d* 1979), *d* of Major A. B. Godfray, Jersey; two *s* two *d*; 2nd, 1980, Annie Cornelia, *d* of Lt-Col F. E. W. Toussieng, Kt of Dannebrog, and *widow* of Brig. J. K. Greenwood, OBE. *Educ:* Marlborough; RMC, Sandhurst. 2nd Lieut Royal Tank Corps, 1926; served War of 1939–45 (MC, DSO and two Bars, CB, despatches thrice); Officier Légion d'Honneur; Croix de Guerre avec palmes. Adjt 6 RTR 1939; DAQMG 7th Armed Div., Bde Maj. 4th Armed Bde, GSO II 7th Armed Div., AQMG 30 Corps, CO 3 RTR 1939–41; Comd 22nd Armed Bde, Comd 26th Armed Bde, Comd 30th Armed Bde, 1941–43; Commander 11th Armoured Div., 1943–46; Comdr 7th Armoured Div., 1947–48; Dir, Royal Armoured Corps, War Office, 1948–49; retired pay, 1949. Hon. Col Kent and County of London Yeomanry Squadron, The Royal Yeomanry Regt, T&AVR, 1963–70. JP County of Kent, 1960–70. *Publication:* From the Desert to the Baltic, 1987. *Address:* Greenbank, West Street, Mayfield, E Sussex TN20 6DS; c/o Royal Bank of Scotland, Kirkland House, Whitehall, SW1. *Club:* Army and Navy.

See also Sir R. M. H. Vickers.

ROBERTS, Sir Gilbert (Howland Rookehurst), 7th Bt *cr* 1809; *b* 31 May 1934; *s* of Sir Thomas Langdon Howland Roberts, 6th Bt, CBE, and of Evelyn Margaret, *o d* of late H. Fielding-Hall; *S* father, 1979; *m* 1958, Ines, *o d* of late A. Labunski; one *s* one *d*. *Educ:* Rugby; Gonville and Caius Coll., Cambridge (BA 1957). CEng, MIMechE. *Recreation:* hang gliding. *Heir:* *s* Howland Langdon Roberts, *b* 19 Aug. 1961. *Address:* 3340 Cliff Drive, Santa Barbara, Calif 93109, USA.

ROBERTS, Gillian Frances; Academic Registrar, University of London, since 1983; *b* 3 Nov. 1944; *d* of late Frank Murray and of Mabel Murray; *m* 1969, Andrew Clive Roberts. *Educ:* Sydenham High Sch.; Southampton Univ. (BA Hist., 1966). Academic

Dept, London Univ., 1967–83. *Address:* Senate House, University of London, Malet Street, WC1E 7HU. *T:* 071–636 8000.

ROBERTS, Sir Gordon (James), Kt 1984; CBE 1975; JP; DL; Chairman, Oxford Regional Health Authority, 1978–90; Member, Commission for the New Towns, since 1978 (Deputy Chairman, 1978–82); *b* 30 Jan. 1921; *s* of Archie and Lily Roberts; *m* 1944, Barbara Leach; one *s* one *d. Educ:* Deanshanger Sch., Northants. Chairman: Northants AHA, 1973–78; Supervisory Bd, NHS Management Adv. Service, 1982–85; NHS Computer Policy Cttee, 1981–85; RHA Chairmen, 1982–84; Member: Oxford Reg. Hosp. Bd, 1968–74; St Crispin Hosp. Management Cttee, 1965–74; Northants Exec. Council, NHS, 1954–74; E Midlands Econ. Planning Council, 1975–79; Bd, Northampton Develt Corp., 1976–85 (Dep. Chm., 1985). Contested (Lab) S Northants, 1970, Mem., Towcester RDC, 1953–56; Mem., Northants CC, 1954–77 (Leader, 1973–77). JP Northants, 1952; Chm., Towcester Bench, 1977–83. DL Northants, 1984, High Sheriff, 1989. FRSA 1985. *Publication:* (with Dr O. F. Brown) Passenham—the history of a forest village, 1975. *Recreations:* music, reading, walking, local history. *Address:* 114 Ridgmont, Deanshanger, Milton Keynes, Bucks MK19 6JG. *T:* Milton Keynes (0908) 562605.

ROBERTS, Gwilym; see Roberts, D. G. M.

ROBERTS, Gwilym Edffrwd, PhD; FIS; *b* 7 Aug. 1928; *s* of William and Jane Ann Roberts; *m* 1954, Mair Griffiths; no *c. Educ:* Brynrefail Gram. Sch.; UCW (Bangor); City Univ. BSc. Industrial Management, 1952–57; Lecturer (Polytechnic and University), 1957–66, 1970–74. MP (Lab): South Bedfordshire, 1966–70; Cannock, Feb. 1974–1983; PPS, DoI, 1976–79. Contested (Lab): Ormskirk, 1959; Conway, 1964; S Beds, 1970; Cannock and Burntwood, 1983, 1987. Business Analyst, Economic Forecasting, Market and Operational Research, 1957–. Institute of Statisticians: Vice-Pres., 1978–; Hon. Officer, 1983–84; Editor, Newsletter, 1967–78. FBIM. *Publications:* many articles on technical, political, parliamentary and European matters. *Recreations:* cricket, table tennis. *Address:* 60 Swasedale Road, Luton, Beds. *T:* Luton (0582) 573893; 8 Main Road, Brereton, Rugeley, Staffs. *T:* Rugeley (0889) 583601.

ROBERTS, (Herbert) John, CMG 1965; a Director, Rural Development Corporation of Zambia, since 1980; *b* 22 Nov. 1919; *m* 1946, Margaret Pollard; three *s* one *d. Educ:* Holy Trinity, Weymouth; Milton, Bulawayo. Served War of 1939–45; Somaliland, Ethiopia, Burma. Elected MLC, 1954; Leader of Northern Rhodesia United Federal Party, 1959–63; Founder of National Progress Party, 1963; MP Zambia, Nat. Progress Party 1964–66, Ind. 1967–69; Min. of Labour and Mines, 1959–61; Leader of Opposition (NR) 1961–64; Leader of Opposition (Zambia), 1964–65; disbanded Nat. Progress Party, 1966. *Address:* Chanyanya Ranch, PO Box 32037, Lusaka, Zambia.

ROBERTS, Hugh Eifion Pritchard, QC 1971; DL; **His Honour Judge Eifion Roberts;** a Circuit Judge, since 1977; *b* 22 Nov. 1927; *er s* of late Rev. and Mrs E. P. Roberts, Anglesey; *m* 1958, Buddug Williams; one *s* two *d. Educ:* Beaumaris Grammar Sch.; University Coll. of Wales, Aberystwyth (LLB); Exeter Coll., Oxford (BCL). Called to Bar, Gray's Inn, 1953; practised as a Junior Counsel on Wales and Chester Circuit, Sept. 1953–April 1971. Dep. Chairman: Anglesey QS, 1966–71; Denbighshire QS, 1970–71; a Recorder of the Crown Court, 1972–77. Formerly Asst Parly Boundary Comr for Wales; Mem. for Wales of the Crawford Cttee on Broadcasting Coverage. DL Clwyd, 1988. *Recreation:* gardening. *Address:* Maes-y-Rhedyn, Gresford Road, Llay, Wrexham, Clwyd. *T:* Wrexham (0978) 852292.

ROBERTS, Hugh Martin P.; see Plowden Roberts.

ROBERTS, Ian White; HM Diplomatic Service, retired; Hon. Visiting Fellow, School of Slavonic and East European Studies, University of London, 1985; *b* 29 March 1927; *s* of George Dodd Roberts and Jessie Dickson Roberts (*née* White); *m* 1956, Pamela Johnston; one *d. Educ:* Royal Masonic Sch., Bushey, Herts; Gonville and Caius Coll., Cambridge (MA 1st Cl. Hons Mod. Langs). Served Royal Air Force (Pilot Officer), 1948–50; postgrad. student, Cambridge (Scarbrough Award), 1950. Joined Foreign Office, 1951–; Klagenfurt, 1952; Munich, 1954; Berlin, 1955; FCO, 1957–61; Second (later First) Secretary, Budapest, 1961–63; FCO, 1963; Bujumbura, 1965; FCO, 1965–66; Buenos Aires, 1966; FCO, 1969–74; Oslo, 1974–76; FCO, 1976–84; Counsellor, 1976. *Publications:* Nicholas I and the Russian Intervention in Hungary, 1991; articles in philatelic jls. *Recreations:* music, reading, philately (Mem., Royal Philatelic Soc.). *Address:* c/o Lloyds Bank, 1 Butler Place, SW1H 0PR. *Club:* Travellers'.

ROBERTS, Rt. Hon. Sir (Ieuan) Wyn (Pritchard), Kt 1990; PC 1991; MP (C) Conwy, since 1983 (Conway, 1970–83); Minister of State, Welsh Office, since 1987; *b* 10 July 1930; *s* of late Rev. E. P. Roberts and Margaret Ann; *m* 1956, Enid Grace Williams; three *s. Educ:* Harrow; University Coll., Oxford. Sub-editor, Liverpool Daily Post, 1952–54; News Asst, BBC, 1954–57; TWW Ltd: News, Special Events and Welsh Language Programmes Producer, 1957–59; Production Controller, 1959–60; Exec. Producer, 1960–68; Welsh Controller, 1964–68; Programme Exec., Harlech TV, 1969. PPS to Sec. of State for Wales, 1970–74; Opposition Front-Bench Spokesman on Welsh Affairs, 1974–79; Parly Under Sec of State, Welsh Office, 1979–87. Vice-Pres., Assoc. of District Councils, 1975–79. Mem. of Gorsedd, Royal National Eisteddfod of Wales, 1966. Member, Court of Governors: Nat. Library of Wales; Nat. Museum of Wales; University Coll. of Wales, Aberystwyth, 1970–. *Recreation:* gardening. *Address:* Tan y Gwalia, Conway, Gwynedd. *T:* Tyn y Groes (0492) 650371. *Clubs:* Savile; Cardiff and County (Cardiff).

ROBERTS, Ivor Anthony; HM Diplomatic Service; Minister and Deputy Head of Mission, Madrid, since 1989; *b* 24 Sept. 1946; *s* of late Leonard Moore Roberts and of Rosa Maria Roberts (*née* Fusco); *m* 1974, Elizabeth Bray Bernard Smith; two *s* one *d. Educ:* St Mary's Coll., Crosby; Keble Coll., Oxford (schol.; MA). Entered HM Diplomatic Service, 1968; MECAS, 1969; Third, later Second Sec., Paris, 1970–73; Second, later First Sec., FCO, 1973–78; First Sec., Canberra, 1978–82; Dep. Head of News Dept, FCO, 1982–86; Head, Security Co-ordination Dept, FCO, 1986–88. *Recreations:* opera, ski-ing, golf, squash. *Address:* c/o Foreign and Commonwealth Office, King Charles Street, SW1A 2AH. *Clubs:* United Oxford & Cambridge University; Downhill Only (Wengen).

ROBERTS, Hon. Jane; see Roberts, Hon. P. J. S.

ROBERTS, Jeremy Michael Graham; QC 1982; Barrister; a Recorder of the Crown Court, since 1981; *b* 26 April 1941; *s* of late Lt-Col J. M. H. Roberts and E. D. Roberts; *m* 1964, Sally Priscilla Johnson. *Educ:* Winchester; Brasenose Coll., Oxford. BA. Called to the Bar, Inner Temple, 1965. *Recreations:* racing, reading, theatre, opera. *Address:* 2 Dr Johnson's Buildings, Temple, EC4Y 7AY. *T:* 071–353 5371.

ROBERTS, John; see Roberts, A. J.

ROBERTS, Rt. Rev. John; see Roberts, Rt Rev. D. J.

ROBERTS, John; see Roberts, H. J.

ROBERTS, John Anthony; QC 1988; a Recorder of the Crown Court, since 1987; *b* Sierra Leone, 17 May 1928; *s* of late John Anthony Roberts of Brazil and Regina Roberts of Sierra Leone; *m* 1961, Eulette Valerie; one *s. Educ:* St Edward's RC Secondary Sch., Sierra Leone; Inns of Court Sch. of Law. FCIArb. Costs Clerk, Taylor Woodrow W Africa Ltd; Civil Servant, Sierra Leone; RAF 1952–62 (GSM), served UK, Europe, Near East, Far East, S Pacific; qualified Air Traffic Control Officer, 1962–64; Civil Service, UK, 1964–69, incl. Inland Revenue; part time law student; called to the Bar, Gray's Inn, 1969; Head of Chambers, 1975; Asst Recorder, 1983–87. First person of African ancestry to be appointed QC at the English Bar; called to the Bar in: Jamaica, 1973; Sierra Leone, 1975; Trinidad and Tobago, 1978; Bahamas, 1984; St Kitts and Nevis, 1988. *Recreations:* music; singing in a choir (Latin Mass and Gregorian Chant), flying light aircraft (qualified pilot), playing piano, organ and guitar, reading. *Address:* 2 Stone Buildings, Lincoln's Inn, WC2A 3TA. *T:* 071–405 4232. *Club:* West Indian Ex-Servicemen's Association.

ROBERTS, John Arthur, CEng, FIEE; Under-Secretary, Department of Energy, 1974–77; *b* 21 Dec. 1917; *s* of late John Richard and Emily Roberts; *m* 1st, 1944, Winifred Wilks Scott (*d* 1976); two *s* one *d*; 2nd, 1977, Rosetta Mabel Price. *Educ:* Liverpool Institute; Liverpool Univ. (BEng). Apprentice, Metropolitan-Vickers Electrical Co Ltd, 1939. Served War, Royal Signals, 1940–46, Major. Sen. Lectr, Applied Science, RMA, Sandhurst, 1947–49; SSO and PSO, RAE, Farnborough, 1949–59; Head, Control and Computers Section, Applications Br., Central Electricity Generating Bd, 1959–62; Project Ldr, Automatic Control, CEGB, 1962–67; DCSO, Min. of Tech. and DTI, 1967–72; Under-Sec., DTI, 1972–74. *Address:* 27 Ashcombe Court, Ilminster, Somerset TA19 0ED. *T:* Ilminster (0460) 57749.

ROBERTS, John Charles Quentin; Director, Great Britain-USSR Association, since 1974; *b* 4 April 1933; *s* of Hubert and Emilie Roberts; *m* 1st, 1959, Dinah Webster-Williams (marr. diss.); one *s* one *d*; 2nd, 1982, Elizabeth Roberts (Pres., Cooper Estates Inc., LA, Calif.), *y d* of late W. H. Gough-Cooper, Farningham, Kent. *Educ:* King's Coll., Taunton (open scholar); Merton Coll., Oxford (MA). MIL 1972. Royal Air Force CSC Interpreter, 1953; Russian Language Tutor, SSEES, Univ. of London, 1953; Shell International Petroleum Co. Ltd, 1956; Shell Co. of E Africa Ltd: Representative, Zanzibar and S Tanganyika, 1957, Kenya Highlands, 1958; PA to Man. Dir, Shell Austria AG Vienna, 1960; Pressed Steel Co. Ltd, Oxford, 1961; Asst Master, Marlborough Coll., 1963. Chairman: Organising Cttee for British Week in Siberia, 1978; Steering Cttee, British Month in USSR (Kiev), 1990. Member: Council, SSEES, Univ. of London, 1981–; Internat. Adv. Bd, State Library of Foreign Literature, Moscow, 1991; Vice Pres., Assoc. of Teachers of Russian, 1984–89; Governor, Cobham Hall, 1984–88. *Recreations:* family, choral singing, walking, gardening. *Address:* 52 Paultons Square, SW3 5DT. *T:* 071–352 3882. *Clubs:* Athenæum, Special Forces.

ROBERTS, John Eric, DSc (Leeds); CPhys; FInstP; Emeritus Professor of Physics, University of London, 1969; Physicist to Middlesex Hospital, W1, 1946–70; Consultant Adviser in Physics, Department of Health and Social Security, 1960–71; *b* Leeds, 1907; *e s* of late James J. Roberts, Normanton, Yorks; *m* Sarah, *o d* of late Thomas Raybould, Normanton, Yorks; two *d. Educ:* Normanton Grammar School; University of Leeds (Brown Scholar; BSc (Physics Hons) 1928; Univ. Res. Schol., 1928; PhD 1930; DSc 1944). FInstP 1938; CPhys 1985. Research Assistant in Physics, University of Leeds, 1930; Assistant Physicist, Royal Cancer Hospital, 1932; Senior Asst Physicist, Middlesex Hosp., 1937; Joel Prof. of Physics Applied to Medicine, Univ. of London, 1946–69; Regional Adviser, ME, Internat. Atomic Energy Agency, 1963–64. Pres., British Inst. of Radiology, 1951–52; Pres. Hospital Physicists Assoc., 1950–51; Editor, Physics in Medicine and Biology, 1956–60; Editor, British Jl of Radiology, 1964–67. Hon. Mem., Royal Coll. of Radiologists. Hon. FIPSM 1989. *Publications:* Nuclear War and Peace, 1956; What Must I Believe?, 1989; scientific papers in various journals. *Address:* 41 The Maltings, Station Street, Tewkesbury, Glos GL20 5NN. *T:* Tewkesbury (0684) 295511.

ROBERTS, Air Vice-Marshal John Frederick, CB 1967; CBE 1960 (OBE 1954); *b* 24 Feb. 1913; *y s* of late W. J. Roberts, Pontardawe; *m* 1st, 1942, Mary Winifred (*d* 1968), *d* of late J. E. Newns; one *s*; 2nd, 1976, Mrs P. J. Hull, *d* of A. Stiles. *Educ:* Pontardawe Gram. Sch., Glam. Chartered Accountant, 1936. Joined RAF, 1938; service in Middle East, 1942–45 (despatches); Mem. Directing Staff, RAF Staff Coll., Bracknell, 1954–56; SASO, RAF Record Office, 1958–60; Dep. Comptroller, Allied Forces Central Europe, 1960–62; Stn Comdr RAF Uxbridge, 1963; Dir of Personal Services I, Min. of Def. (Air), 1964–65; Dir-Gen. of Ground Training (RAF), 1966–68; retd, 1968. With Deloitte & Co., Chartered Accountants, Swansea, 1969–78. *Recreations:* cricket, golf, cabinet-making. *Address:* 1 Lon Cadog, Sketty, Swansea SA2 0TS. *T:* Swansea (0792) 203763. *Clubs:* Royal Air Force, MCC; Pontardawe Golf (Pres., 1978–88).

ROBERTS, John Harvey Polmear; His Honour Judge John Roberts; a Circuit Judge, since 1991; *b* 11 June 1935; *s* of George Edward Polmear Roberts and Mary Harvey Roberts (*née* Sara); *m* 1961, Mary Patricia Gamble; two *s* two *d. Educ:* Blundell's Sch., Tiverton; College of Law. Admitted Solicitor with Hons, 1957; Managing Partner, Winter Taylors, 1984–91. HM Coroner, S Bucks, 1980–91; Regional Chm., Mental Health Review Tribunals, Oxford and Wessex Regions, 1981–. *Recreations:* golf, football, reading. *Address:* Badgers Hill, Speen, Aylesbury, Bucks HP17 0SP. *T:* High Wycombe (0494) 488289. *Clubs:* Oriental, Wig and Pen.

ROBERTS, John Herbert; Director, Compliance and Collection Division, Inland Revenue, since 1988; *b* 18 Aug. 1933; *s* of late John Emanuel Roberts and Hilda Mary Roberts; *m* 1965, Patricia Iris; one *s* three *d. Educ:* Canton High Sch.; London School of Economics (BScEcon Hons). Entered Civil Service by Open Competition as Inspector of Taxes, 1954; National Service, commnd RASC, 1955–57; returned to Inland Revenue, 1957; Principal Inspector, 1974; Sen. Principal Inspector, 1979; Under Secretary, 1981; Director of Operations, 1981–85; Dir, Technical Div. 2, 1985–88. *Recreations:* music, walking, Welsh Springers. *Address:* Somerset House, WC2R 1LB. *T:* 071–438 7649.

ROBERTS, Dr John Laing; Director, Adhealth, since 1989; Regional Adviser in Health Services, World Health Organisation Office for Europe, Copenhagen, since 1990; Hon. Senior Research Fellow, University of Manchester, since 1990; *b* 26 Dec. 1939; *s* of Charles F. Roberts and May Roberts; *m* 1st, 1963, Meriel F. Dawes (marr. diss. 1980); three *d*; 2nd, 1981, Judith Mary Hare. *Educ:* Latymer Upper School; Univ. of Birmingham. PhD, BSocSc. FHA. NHS Nat. Administrative Trainee, 1962–63; Senior Administrative Asst, United Birmingham Hosps, 1964–66; Sen. Res. Associate, Dept of Social Medicine, Univ. of Birmingham, 1966–69; Dep. Dir, Res. Div., Health Education Council, 1969–74; Operational Services Gen. Administrator, S Glamorgan AHA (T), 1974–77; Regional Gen. Administrator, W Midlands RHA, 1977–82; Regional Administrator, 1983–85, Regl Prevention Manager, 1985–89, N Western RHA. *Publications:* papers on health education, health service administration, economics and health; PhD thesis, Studies of Information Systems for Health Service Resource Planning and Control. *Recreations:* swimming, hill walking. *Address:* Island West, Steep, near Petersfield, Hants; Ehlersvej 21, 2900 Hellerup, Copenhagen, Denmark.

ROBERTS, John Lewis, CMG 1987; Assistant Under-Secretary of State (Equipment Collaboration), Ministry of Defence, 1985–88; *b* 21 April 1928; *s* of Thomas Hubert and Meudwen Roberts; *m* 1952, Maureen Jocelyn (*née* Moriarty); two *s*. *Educ:* Pontardawe Grammar Sch.; Trinity Hall, Cambridge. BA (Hons) History. Joined Min. of Civil Aviation, 1950; Private Sec. to the Parly Sec., 1953; Principal: in Railways, then in Sea Transport; branches of MoT and Civil Aviation, 1954–59; Civil Air Attaché, Bonn Embassy, 1959–62; Defence Supply Counsellor, Paris Embassy, 1966–69; Ministry of Defence: Asst Sec., Internat. Policy Div., 1971–74; Assistant Under-Secretary of State: Air MoD PE, 1974–76; Sales, 1976–77; Personnel, (Air), 1977–80; Supply and Organisation, (Air), 1980–82; Internat. and Industrial Policy, PE, 1982–85. FRSA 1988. *Recreations:* angling, sailing.

ROBERTS, Dr John Morris; Warden, Merton College, Oxford, since 1984; a Governor of the BBC, since 1988; *b* 14 April 1928; *s* of late Edward Henry Roberts and late Dorothy Julia Roberts, Bath, Som.; *m* 1964, Judith Cecilia Mary, *e d* of late Rev. James Armitage and Monica Armitage; one *s* two *d*. *Educ:* Taunton Sch.; Keble Coll., Oxford (Schol.; Hon. Fellow, 1981). National Service, 1949–50; Prize Fellow, Magdalen Coll., Oxford, 1951–53; Commonwealth Fund Fellow, Princeton and Yale, 1953–54; Merton College, Oxford: Fellow and Tutor, 1953–79 (Hon. Fellow, 1980–84); acting Warden, 1969–70, 1977–79; Sen. Proctor, Oxford Univ., 1967–68; Vice-Chancellor and Prof., Southampton Univ., 1979–85. Mem., Inst. for Advanced Study, Princeton, 1960–61; Vis. Prof., Univ. of S Carolina, 1961; Sec. of Harmsworth Trust, 1962–68; Member: Council, European Univ. Inst., 1980–88; US/UK Educn Commn, 1981–88; Gen. Cttee, Royal Literary Fund, 1975–; Bd, British Council, 1991–. Trustee, Nat. Portrait Gall., 1984–; Rhodes Trustee, 1988–. Editor, English Historical Review, 1967–77. Pres. Council, Taunton Sch., 1978–89. Presenter, TV series, The Triumph of the West, 1985. Hon. DLitt Southampton, 1987. Cavalier, Order of Merit (Italy), 1991. *Publications:* French Revolution Documents, 1966; Europe 1880–1945, 1967; The Mythology of the Secret Societies, 1972; The Paris Commune from the Right, 1973; Revolution and Improvement: the Western World 1775–1847, 1976; History of the World, 1976; The French Revolution, 1978; The Triumph of the West, 1985; General Editor: Purnell's History of the 20th Century; The New Oxford History of England; articles and reviews in learned jls. *Recreation:* music. *Address:* Merton College, Oxford OX1 4JD. *Club:* United Oxford & Cambridge University.

ROBERTS, Rear-Adm. John Oliver, CB 1976; MNI; Managing Director, Demak Ltd, International Consultants, since 1983; *b* 4 April 1924; *er s* of J. V. and M. C. Roberts; *m* 1st, 1950, Lady Hermione Mary Morton Stuart (marr. diss. 1960; she *d* 1969); one *d*; 2nd, 1963, Honor Marigold Gordon Gray (marr. diss 1987); one *s* one *d*; 3rd, 1987, Sheila Violet Mary Traub (*née* Barker). *Educ:* RN Coll., Dartmouth. Served War: Midshipman, HM Ships Renown and Tartar, 1941–43; Sub-Lt, HMS Serapis, 1943–44; Lieut, 1945; Pilot Trg, 1944–46. HMS Triumph, 1947–49; RNAS, Lossiemouth, 1949–51; Flag-Lt to FOGT, 1952; Lt-Comdr, 1953; HMAS Vengeance and Sydney, 1953–54; RNVR, Southern Air Div., 1954–56; CO, No 803 Sqdn, HMS Eagle, 1957–58; Comdr, 1958; RNAS, Brawdy, 1958–60; CO, HMS St Bride's Bay, 1960–61; Naval Staff, 1962–64; Captain, 1964; CSO, Flag Officer Aircraft Carriers, 1964–66; CO, HMS Galatea, 1966–68; Naval Staff, 1968–70; CO, HMS Ark Royal, 1971–72; Rear-Adm., 1972; Flag Officer Sea Training, 1972–74; COS to C-in-C Fleet, 1974–76; Flag Officer, Naval Air Command, 1976–78. Non-exec. Dir, Aeronautical & General Instruments Ltd, 1981–82 (Head of Marketing and Sales, Defence Systems Div., 1980–81); Dir Gen., British Printing Industries Fedn, 1981–82. FRSA. *Recreations:* Rugby football, cricket, athletics, sailing, skiing. *Address:* Priory House, Blakesley, Northants. *Club:* East India, Devonshire, Sports and Public Schools.

ROBERTS, Julian; *see* Roberts, R. J.

ROBERTS, Prof. Lewis Edward John, CBE 1978; FRS 1982; Wolfson Professor of Environmental Risk Assessment, University of East Anglia, 1986–90; Emeritus Professor, since 1990; *b* 31 Jan. 1922; *s* of William Edward Roberts and Lilian Lewis Roberts; *m* 1947, Eleanor Mary Luscombe; one *s*. *Educ:* Swansea Grammar Sch.; Jesus Coll., Oxford (MA, DPhil). Clarendon Laboratory, Oxford, 1944; Scientific Officer, Chalk River Res. Estabt, Ont, Canada, 1946–47; AERE, Harwell, 1947, Principal Scientific Officer, 1952; Commonwealth Fund Fellow, Univ. of Calif, Berkeley, 1954–55; Dep. Head, Chemistry Div., 1966, Asst Dir, 1967, Dir, 1975–86, AERE. Mem., UKAEA, 1979–86. Pres., British Nuclear Energy Soc., 1985–87. R. M. Jones Lectr, QUB, 1981. Governor, Abingdon Sch., 1978–86. *Publications:* Nuclear Power and Public Responsibility, 1984; Power Generation and the Environment, 1990; papers in qly revs and in scientific journals and IAEA pubns. *Recreations:* reading, gardening. *Address:* Penfold Wick, Chilton, Didcot OX11 0SH. *T:* Abingdon (0235) 834309. *Club:* Commonwealth Trust.

ROBERTS, Prof. Michael, FBA 1960; Director, Institute for Social and Economic Research, Rhodes University, 1974–76; Professor of Modern History, The Queen's University, Belfast, 1954–73; Dean of the Faculty of Arts, 1957–60; *b* 21 May 1908; *s* of Arthur Roberts and Hannah Elizabeth Landless; *m* 1941, Ann McKinnon Morton; one *d*. *Educ:* Brighton Coll.; Worcester Coll., Oxford. Gladstone Meml Prizeman, 1931; A. M. P. Read Scholar (Oxford), 1932. Procter Vis. Fell., Princeton Univ., USA, 1931–32; Lectr, Merton Coll., Oxford, 1932–34; Asst Lectr, Univ. of Liverpool, 1934–35; DPhil, Oxford, 1935; Prof. of Modern History, Rhodes Univ., S Africa, 1935–53. Lieut, SA Int. Corps, 1942–44. British Council Representative, Stockholm, 1944–46. Public Orator, Rhodes Univ., 1951–53; Hugh Le May Vis. Fellow, Rhodes Univ., 1960–61; Lectures: A. L. Smith, Balliol Coll., Oxford, 1962; Enid Muir Meml, Univ. of Newcastle upon Tyne, 1965; Creighton in History, Univ. of London, 1965; Stenton, Univ. of Reading, 1969; James Ford special, Oxford Univ., 1973; Wiles, QUB, 1977. Hon. Fellow, Worcester Coll., Oxford, 1966; Vis. Fellow, All Souls Coll., Oxford, 1968–69; Leverhulme Faculty Fellow in European Studies, 1973; Vis. Fellow, Pomona Coll., Claremont, Calif, 1978. Vis. Fellow, Trevelyan Coll., Univ. of Durham, 1981. MRIA 1968. For. Member: Roy. Swedish Acad. of Letters, History and Antiquities; Royal Swedish Academy of Science; Hon. Mem. Samfundet för utgivande av handskrifter rörande Skandinaviens historia. FRHistS; Fil dr (*hc*) (Stockholm), 1960; Hon. DLit QUB, 1977; Hon. DLitt Rhodes, 1988. Kungens medalj i Serafimerband (Sweden), 1981. Chevalier, Order of North Star (Sweden), 1954. *Publications:* The Whig Party, 1807–1812, 1939; (with A. E. G. Trollip) The South African Opposition, 1939–1945, 1947; Gustavus Adolphus: A History of Sweden, 1611–1632, Vol. I, 1953, Vol. II, 1958; Essays in Swedish History, 1967; The Early Vasas: A History of Sweden 1523–1611, 1968; Sweden as a Great Power 1611–1697, 1968; Sverige och Europa, 1969; Gustav Vasa, 1970; Gustavus Adolphus and the Rise of Sweden, 1973; (ed) Sweden's Age of Greatness, 1973; Macartney in Russia, 1974; The Swedish Imperial Experience 1560–1718, 1979; British Diplomacy and Swedish Politics, 1758–1773, 1980; Sverige som Stormakt, 1980; The Age of Liberty: Sweden 1719–1772, 1986; (ed and trans.) Swedish Diplomats at Cromwell's Court, 1988; From Axel Oxenstierna to Charles XII, four studies, 1991; trans. from Swedish of works by Nils Ahnlund, F. G. Bengtsson, Gunnar Wennerberg (Gluntarne), Birger Sjöberg (Fridas bok), Carl Michael Bellman (Epistles and Songs, I-III), Anna Maria Lenngren; articles in New Cambridge Mod. Hist., EHR, History, Historical Jl, Past and Present, Scandia, Karolinska Förbundets Årsbok, South African Archives Yearbook, etc. *Recreation:* music. *Address:* 1 Allen Street, Grahamstown, CP 6140, South Africa. *T:* Grahamstown 24855.

ROBERTS, Norman Stafford, MA, DPA; Headmaster, Taunton School, 1970–87, educational consultant to School Fees Insurance Agency; *b* 15 Feb. 1926; *s* of late Walter S. Roberts, LLM and Florence E. Roberts (*née* Phythian), Calderstones, Liverpool; *m* 1965, Beatrice, *o d* of late George and Winifred Best, Donaghadee, Co. Down; one *s* two *d*. *Educ:* Quarry Bank High Sch., Liverpool; Hertford Coll., Oxford (Open Exhibnr, History). Served in RA, Egypt and Palestine, 1945–47 (Lieut). 2nd cl. hons PPE 1950; DipEd Oxford 1951; DPA London 1951. Asst Master, Berkhamsted Junior Sch., 1951–55; House Master, Sixth Form Master, Berkhamsted Sch., 1955–59; Walter Hines Page Scholar to USA, 1959, 1980; Senior History Master, CO CCF (Hon. Major 1965), Monkton Combe Sch., 1959–65, Housemaster 1962–65; Schoolmaster Student, Merton Coll., Oxford, 1964; Headmaster, Sexey's Sch., Bruton, 1965–70. Chm., Bath and Wells Diocese, Church Urban Fund, 1987–90. Chm. of Govs, St Audries Sch., Som, 1987–. Governor: Wycliffe Coll., 1988–; King Edward Sch., Witley 1988–. *Recreations:* foreign travel, bridge, hockey, tennis. *Address:* 23 Mount Street, Taunton, Somerset TA1 3QF. *T:* Taunton (0823) 331623. *Club:* Commonwealth Trust.

ROBERTS, Patrick John; Director of Corporate Affairs, Edelman Public Relations Worldwide, since 1990 (Director of European Affairs, 1989–90); *b* 21 Oct. 1942; *s* of Frank and Hilda Mary Roberts; *m* 1978, Alison Mary Taylor; one *s* one *d*. *Educ:* Rotherham Grammar Sch.; Lincoln Coll., Oxford (BA Hons Modern Langs). Foreign Office, 1965; Bangkok, 1966; FCO, 1970; First Sec., Lagos, 1971; FCO, 1974; UK Repn to EEC, Brussels, 1977; FCO, 1980; Counsellor (Inf.), Paris, 1984. *Recreations:* shooting, swimming, cooking. *Address:* Daniel J. Edelman Ltd, 536 Kings Road, SW10 0TE. *T:* 071–835 1222.

ROBERTS, Prof. Paul Harry, PhD, ScD; FRS 1979; FRAS; Professor of Mathematics, University of California at Los Angeles, since 1986; *b* 13 Sept. 1929; *s* of Percy Harry Roberts and Ethel Frances (*née* Mann); *m* 1989, Maureen (*née* Tabrett). *Educ:* Ardwyn Grammar Sch., Aberystwyth; University Coll. of Wales, Aberystwyth; Gonville and Caius Coll., Cambridge (George Green Student; BA, MA, PhD, ScD). FRAS 1955. Res. Associate, Univ. of Chicago, 1954–55; Scientific Officer, AWRE, 1955–56; ICI Fellow in Physics, 1956–59, Lectr in Phys, 1959–61, Univ. of Newcastle upon Tyne; Associate Prof. of Astronomy, Univ. of Chicago, 1961–63; Prof. of Applied Maths, Univ. of Newcastle upon Tyne, 1963–85. Editor, Geophysical and Astrophysical Fluid Dynamics, 1976–. *Publications:* An Introduction to Magnetohydrodynamics, 1967; contrib. to Geophys. and Astrophys. Fluid Dyn., Jl Low Temp. Phys., Astrophys. Jl, Jl Fluid Mech., and Jl Phys. Soc. *Recreations:* playing bassoon, chess. *Address:* 2642 Cordelia Street, Los Angeles, Calif 90049, USA. *T:* 213–471–5491; Department of Mathematics or Institute of Geophysics and Planetary Physics UCLA, Los Angeles, Calif 90024, USA. *T:* 213–825–7764; 213–206–2707.

ROBERTS, Percy Charles; Chairman and Chief Executive, Mirror Group Newspapers Ltd, 1977–80; *b* 30 July 1920; *s* of late Herbert Bramwell Roberts and Alice (*née* Lang); *m* 1st 1946, Constance Teresa Violet Butler (marr. diss. 1977); two *s*; 2nd, 1978, Pauline Moore. *Educ:* Brighton Hove and Sussex Grammar Sch. Reporter, Sussex Daily News, 1936–39. Served War of 1939–45: Sussex Yeomanry, in France and ME (Captain). Sub-Editor, Egyptian Mail, Cairo, 1946; Reporter, Mid-East Mail, Palestine, 1947; Sub-Editor: Sussex Daily News, 1948; Liverpool Daily Post, 1949; Editor, Nigerian Citizen, 1949–51; Editorial Adviser, Gen. Manager, Managing Dir, Nigerian Daily Times, 1951–60; Managing Dir, Mirror Gp Newspapers in Caribbean, 1960–62; Gen. Manager, Mirror Newspapers in Manchester, 1962–66; Dir, 1964–80, Managing Dir, 1966–80, Daily Mirror Newspapers Ltd; Vice-Chm., West of England Newspapers Ltd, 1965–69; Managing Dir, IPC Newspapers Ltd, 1968–75; Dir, Scottish Daily Record & Sunday Mail Ltd, 1969–74; Chm., Overseas Newspapers Ltd, 1969–75; Dep. Chm. and Chief Exec., Mirror Gp Newspapers Ltd, 1975–77. Dir, Reed Publishing Holdings Ltd, 1975–80; Mem., Reed Internat. UK Cttee, 1975–80. Mem., CBI Employment Policy Cttee, 1975–78. Mem. Council, CPU, 1979–83. CBIM. *Address:* Magnolia Cottage, Bromsash, Ross-on-Wye, Herefordshire HR9 7PR. *T:* Lea (098981) 706. *Clubs:* MCC, Royal Automobile; Ross Rotary.

ROBERTS, Maj.-Gen. Philip; *see* Roberts, Maj.-Gen. G. P. B.

ROBERTS, Philip Bedlington; a Recorder of the Crown Court, since 1982; Consultant, Scholfield Roberts & Hill, since 1990; *b* 15 Dec. 1921; *s* of late R. J. S. Roberts, solicitor and A. M. Roberts; *m* 1944, Olive Margaret, *d* of E. R. Payne, Mugswell, Chipstead, Surrey; one *s* one *d*. *Educ:* Dawson Court, Kensington; St Matthew's Sch., Bayswater. RAFVR, 1940–46. Admitted solicitor, 1949; in private practice with Scholfield Roberts & Hill, 1950–75; part-time Chm. of Industrial Tribunals, 1966–75, Chm., 1975–84, Regional Chm. (Bristol), 1984–90, retd. Chairman: Nat. Insce Tribunals, 1959–75; Compensation Appeals Tribunal, 1962. Solicitor, Somerset British Legion, 1960–75. *Publications:* contribs to professional jls. *Recreation:* gardening. *Address:* Charlynch House, Spaxton, Bridgwater, Somerset TA5 1BY. *T:* Spaxton (027867) 356. *Club:* Royal Air Force.

ROBERTS, Phyllida Katharine S.; *see* Stewart-Roberts.

ROBERTS, Hon. (Priscilla) Jane (Stephanie), (Hon. Mrs Roberts), MVO 1985; Curator of the Print Room, Royal Library, Windsor Castle, since 1975; *b* 4 Sept. 1949; *d* of Baron Aldington, *qv*; *m* 1975, Hugh Ashley Roberts (Dep. Surveyor of the Queen's Works of Art), *s* of Rt Rev. Edward James Keymer Roberts, *qv*; two *d*. *Educ:* Cranborne Chase School; Westfield College, Univ. of London (BA Hons); Courtauld Inst., Univ. of London (MA). *Publications:* Holbein, 1979; Leonardo: Codex Hammer, 1981; Master Drawings in the Royal Collection, 1985; Royal Artists, 1987; (jtly) Leonardo da Vinci, 1989; articles in Burlington Magazine, Report of Soc. of Friends of St George's. *Recreations:* singing, sewing. *Address:* Salisbury Tower, Windsor Castle, Berks. *T:* Windsor (0753) 855581.

ROBERTS, Ven. Raymond Harcourt, CB 1984; Chairman, Customer Service Committee for Wales, Office of Water Services, since 1990; Hon. Chaplain of Llandaff Cathedral, since 1991; *b* 14 April 1931; *s* of Thomas Roberts and Carrie Maud Roberts. *Educ:* St Edmund Hall, Oxford (MA English); St Michael's Theol Coll., Llandaff. Nat. Service, RN, 1949–51. Deacon 1956, priest 1957, dio. of Monmouth (Curate of Bassaleg); Chaplain RNVR, 1958, RN, 1959; Destroyers and Frigates, Far East, 1959; HMS Pembroke, 1962; Dartmouth Trng Sqdn, 1963; RM Commando Course, 1965; 45 Commando, S. Arabia, 1965; RN Engrg Coll., 1967; HMS Bulwark, 1968; BRNC Dartmouth, 1970; HMS Ark Royal, 1974; Commando Trng Centre, RM, 1975; HMS Drake and HM Naval Base, Plymouth, 1979; Chaplain of the Fleet and Archdeacon for RN, 1980–84, Archdeacon Emeritus, 1985–; QHC, 1980–84; Hon. Canon, Cathedral of Holy Trinity, Gibraltar, 1980–84; Gen. Sec., Jerusalem and ME Church Assoc., 1985–89;

licensed, dio. of Guildford, 1986–91. *Address:* 1 Woolmer Close, Danescourt, Llandaff, Cardiff CF5 2QY. *T:* Cardiff (0222) 564804.

ROBERTS, Richard (David Hallam); freelance academic and writer, yachtmaster, bookbinder's mate, semi-trained househusband, gardener, woodman, antiquarian cyclist; *b* 27 July 1931; *s* of Arthur Hallam Roberts, Barrister-at-law, sometime Attorney-General, Zanzibar, and Ruvé Constance Jessie Roberts; *m* 1960, Wendy Ewen Mount; three *s*. *Educ:* King's Sch., Canterbury; Jesus Coll., Cambridge. Commissioned into RA 6th Field Regt, 1952. Asst Master, King's Sch., Canterbury, 1956; Housemaster, 1957; Head of Modern Language Dept, 1961; Senior Housemaster, 1965; Headmaster: Wycliffe Coll., Stonehouse, 1967–80; King Edward's Sch., Witley, 1980–85. *Address:* Smithy Cottage, Orford, Suffolk IP12 2NW. *Club:* Orford Sailing.

ROBERTS, Rear-Adm. Richard Douglas, CB 1971; CEng; FIMechE; Rear-Admiral Engineering on staff Flag Officer Naval Air Command, 1969–72; *b* 7 Nov. 1916; *s* of Rear-Adm. E. W. Roberts and Mrs R. E. Roberts (*née* Cox); *m* 1943, Mary Norma Wright; one *s* one *d*. *Educ:* RNC Dartmouth; RNEC Keyham. Frobisher, 1934; RNEC Keyham, 1935–38 (qual. Marine Eng); HM Ships: Kent, 1938–40; Exeter, 1941; Bermuda, 1942; Mauritius, 1943–45; RNEC Manadon, 1945 (qual. Aero Eng); RNAY Donibristle, 1946 (AMIMechE); RNAS Worthy Down, 1947; RNAS Yeovilton, 1948–49; Staff of Rear-Adm. Reserve Aircraft, 1949–50; Comdr, 1950; RN Staff Coll., 1951; RNAY Fleetlands, 1952–53 (Production Man.); HMS Newfoundland, 1954–56 (Engr Officer); Engr-in-Chief's Dept, Bath, 1956–60; Captain 1960; RNAY Belfast, 1961–62 (Supt); idc, 1963 (MIMechE); Dir, Fleet Maintenance, 1964–66; Dir, Naval Officer Appts (E), 1966–68; Naval ADC to the Queen, 1968; Rear-Adm. 1969. FBIM 1982. *Recreations:* sailing (RNSA, 1936), fishing; light railways; Vice Pres., Axe Vale Conservation Soc. *Club:* Army and Navy.

ROBERTS, Rev. Richard Frederick Anthony, CBE 1985; Assistant Priest, St Barnabas Anglican Church, Nassau, Bahamas, since 1988; *b* 12 May 1932; *s* of Enoch Pedro Roberts and Gladys Raine Roberts (*née* Archer); *m* 1960, Melvern Hollis Bain; one *s* two *d*. *Educ:* St John's College; Mercer Theol Sch.; Gen. Theol Seminary, USA. Ordained deacon, 1987, priest, 1988. Personnel Officer, Bahamas Airways, 1963–67; Exec. Dir and Partner, Venn, Livingstone, Roberts (Public Relns), 1967–68; Personnel Dir, New Providence Develt Co. Ltd (Land Develt), March-Oct. 1968; MP Centreville, 1968–77; Parly Sec.: Min. of Finance, 1969–72; Min. of Agric., 1971–72; Minister of Agric. and Fisheries, Oct. 1972–Feb. 1973; Minister of Home Affairs, March-Dec. 1973; Minister of Agric., Fisheries and Local Govt, 1974–77; High Comr for Commonwealth of Bahamas in London, 1977–84. Pres., Airline Workers Union; Sec. Gen., Amalgamated Building Constructional Engrg Trade Union; Asst Gen. Sec., Bahamas Fedn of Labour; Pres. and Gen. Sec., Bahamas TUC. Progressive Liberal Party: Asst Gen. Sec.; first Vice-Chm.; Mem., Nat. Gen. Council. Mem., Adv. Cttee to Labour Bd; Chm., Maritime Bd; Mem., Broadcasting and TV Commn; Vice-Chm., Bahamas Agricl Corp. Sec., Methodist Preachers' Cttee. Asst Scout Master; Lt, Boys Brigade. Mem. Internat. Cultural Exchange. *Recreations:* fishing, reading, sports, religion. *Address:* Carmichael Road, PO Box 565, Nassau, Bahamas. *Clubs:* Royal Automobile, Hurlingham.

ROBERTS, (Richard) Julian, FSA; Deputy Librarian, since 1986, and Keeper of Printed Books, since 1974, Bodleian Library, Oxford; Fellow of Wolfson College, Oxford, since 1975; *b* 18 May 1930; *s* of A. R. and K. M. Roberts; *m* 1957, Anne Ducé; one *s* one *d*. *Educ:* King Edward's Sch., Birmingham; Magdalen Coll., Oxford. ALA 1956; FSA 1983. Asst Keeper, BM, 1958–74. Vicegerent, Wolfson Coll., Oxford, 1983–85. Regents' Prof., UCLA, 1991. Pres., Bibliographical Soc., 1986–88. *Publications:* (ed) Beawty in Raggs: poems by Cardell Goodman, 1985; John Dee's Library Catalogue, 1990; contrib. to Library, Book Collector, Jl of Librarianship, etc. *Recreations:* walking, antiquarianism. *Address:* St John's Farm House, Tackley, Oxford OX5 3AT. *T:* Tackley (086983) 249.

ROBERTS, Robert Evan, CBE 1976; National General Secretary, National Council of YMCAs, 1965–75; *b* 16 July 1912; *s* of late Robert Thomas Roberts, Llanilar, Denbighshire; *m* 1939, Rhoda, *d* of late William Driver, Burnley, Lancs; one *s* one *d*. *Educ:* Cilcain, Flintshire; Liverpool. YMCA: Asst Sec.: Central YMCA Liverpool, 1933; Hornsey (N London), 1935; Asst Div. Sec., Lancs/Cheshire, 1937; Div. Sec., NW Div., 1939; Dep. Dir, YMCA Welfare Services, NW Europe, 1944–46 (despatches); Mem. 21st Army Gp, Council of Voluntary Welfare Work, 1944–46. Nat. Sec., Ireland, 1946; Sec., Personnel Dept, Nat. Council of YMCAs, London, 1948; Nat. Sec., Nat. Council of YMCAs, Wales, 1956–65; Hon. Sec/Treasurer, Assoc. of Secs of YMCAs of Gt Brit. and Ireland, 1963–65; Dep. Chm., Welsh Standing Conf. of Nat. Vol. Youth Orgs. 1963–65. Past Member: Welsh Nat. Council of Social Service; Welsh Jt Educn Cttee; Nat. Inst. of Adult Educn. Member: Nat. Council of Social Service, 1965–75; Brit. Council of Churches (and its Exec.), 1965–74; Council of Voluntary Welfare Work, 1965–75; World Council of YMCAs (and its Finance Cttee), 1965–75; Vice-Pres., Welsh Nat. Council of YMCAs, 1975; Chm., Job Creation Programme, Barrow and S Lakeland, 1976–80; Exec. Member: SE Cumbria Community Health Council, 1977–82; S Lakeland Voluntary Action, 1978–85; S Cumbria Community Health Council, 1982– (Vice-Chm., 1986–); S Cumbria DHA Ethics of Research Cttee, 1983–; Cumbria FHSA, 1990–; CHC Observer, Cumbria FPC, 1984–90. Trustee, Framlington Trust, 1973–. Age Concern: Mem., 1976–82, Vice Chm., 1981–82, Exec. Cttee, Cumbria; Chm., S Lakeland, 1977–82; Exec. Mem. and Trustee, Kendal and Ulveston. Dist Judge, Cumbria Best Kept Village, 1977–85; Warden, Lakeland Horticultural Soc. Gardens, 1977–. Fellow, Royal Commonwealth Soc., 1974. Silver Jubilee Medal, 1977. *Recreations:* fell-walking, gardening. *Address:* 5 Priory Crescent, Kents Bank, Grange over Sands, Cumbria LA11 7BL. *T:* Grange over Sands (05395) 32161.

ROBERTS, Prof. Ronald John, PhD; FRCPath, FIBiol; FRSE; Professor of Aquatic Pathobiology and Director, Institute of Aquaculture, University of Stirling, since 1971; *b* 28 March 1941; *s* of Ronald George Roberts and Marjorie Kneale; *m* 1964, Helen, *d* of Gordon Gregor Macgregor; two *s*. *Educ:* Campbeltown Grammar Sch., Argyll; Univ. of Glasgow Vet. Sch. (PhD, BVMS). MRCVS; FRSE 1978. Univ. of Glasgow: Asst in Microbiology, 1964–66; Lectr in Vet. Pathology, 1966–71. Consultant in Fish Diseases: Dept Agric. and Fisheries for Scotland, 1968–71; ODA, 1974–; FAO, Rome, 1978–83; World Bank, 1989. Dir, Machrihanish Marine Envmtl Res. Lab., 1991–. Editor: Jl Fish Diseases, 1978–; Aquaculture and Fisheries Management, 1978–. Chm., Stirling Aquaculture, 1987; Director: Stirling Salmon, 1987–; Tarbert Fyne Foods, 1987–90; Stirling Aquatic Technology, 1987–90. Buckland Prof. and Medallist, 1985–86; C-Vet Award, BVA, 1989; Dalrymple-Champneys Cup and Medal, BVA, 1990. *Publications:* (with C. J. Shepherd) Handbook of Salmon and Trout Diseases, 1974; Fish Pathology, 1978, 2nd edn 1989; various scientific publications on histopathology of fishes. *Recreations:* arboriculture, rhododendron culture, golf, squash, admiring and conserving the Scottish natural environment, travelling in SE Asia. *Address:* 9 Alexander Drive, Bridge of Allan, Stirling. *T:* Stirling (0786) 833078; Ardnacross Shorelands, by Campbeltown, Argyll. *T:* Campbeltown (0586) 54417. *Clubs:* Commonwealth Trust, Royal Society of Medicine; Machrihanish Golf (Kintyre).

ROBERTS, Roy Ernest James, CBE 1986; FEng, FIMechE, FIProdE; AMIBF; Chairman: Simon Engineering plc, since 1987; Dowty Group PLC, since 1991 (Deputy Chairman, 1986–91); *b* 14 Dec. 1928; *s* of Douglas Henry Roberts and Elsie Florence (*née* Rice); *m* 1950, Winson Madge Smith; two *s*. *Educ:* Farnham Grammar Sch.; Royal Aircraft Estabt, Farnborough (student apprentice). Management trainee, Guest, Keen and Nettlefolds, 1951–55; Asst to Directors, C. & B. Smith Ltd, 1956–57, Works Director, 1958–66, Dir and Gen. Manager, 1966–70 (C. & B. Smith was acquired by GKN, 1966); Managing Director: GKN Cwmbran Ltd, 1970–72; GKN Engineering Ltd, 1972–74; GKN Gp, 1980–87; Dep. Chm., GKN Gp, 1987–88; Chairman, GKN Engineering Ltd and GKN Building Supplies & Services Ltd, 1974–77; Member, main board of GKN, 1975–88; Group Director, GKN, with special responsibilities for engrg and construction services activities, also for interests in India, Pakistan, S Africa and the Middle East, 1977–79. Mem. (pt-time), UKAEA, 1981–88. Instn of Mechanical Engineers: Pres., 1989–90 (Vice Pres., 1986–89); Chm. Bd, Manufg Industries Div., 1983–86; Mem. Council, 1983–; Instn of Production Engineers: Vice Pres., 1983–89; Mem., Exec. Policy Bd, 1983–89. Chm., Standing Conf. on Schools' Science and Technol., 1988–; Mem. Exec. Cttee, SMMT, 1983–87; Vice-Pres., Engrg Employers' Fedn, 1988–. Member: Council, Cranfield Inst. of Technol., 1983–89; Engineering Council, 1986–88. CBIM 1979; FInstD 1980; FRSA 1980. *Recreations:* field sports, music. *Address:* Simon Engineering plc, Buchanan House, 3 St James's Square, SW1Y 4JU. *T:* 071–925 0666. *Club:* Royal Automobile.

ROBERTS, Sir Samuel, 4th Bt *cr* 1919, of Ecclesall and Queen's Tower, City of Sheffield; Chairman, Cleyfield Properties Ltd, since 1984; *b* 16 April 1948; *s* of Sir Peter Geoffrey Roberts, 3rd Bt, and of Judith Randell, *d* of late Randell G. Hempson; *S* father, 1985; *m* 1977, Georgina Ann, *yr d* of David Cory; one *s* three *d*. *Educ:* Harrow School; Sheffield Univ. (LLB); Manchester Business School. Called to the Bar, Inner Temple, 1972. Director: Wombwell Management Co. Ltd, 1974–84; Curzon Steels Ltd, 1978–84; Sterling Silverware Ltd, 1978–84; Wellman plc, 1981–84. *Heir: s* Samuel Roberts, *b* 12 Aug. 1989. *Address:* Cockley Cley Hall, Swaffham, Norfolk PE37 8AG. *T:* Swaffham (0760) 721308.

ROBERTS, Dame Shelagh (Marjorie), DBE 1981; former Industrial Relations Consultant; *b* 13 Oct. 1924; *d* of Glyn and Cecelia Roberts, Ystalyfera. *Educ:* St Wyburn Sch., Birkdale, Lancs. Member: Kensington and Chelsea Borough Council, 1953–71; GLC, 1970–81 (Leader, Planning and Communications Policy Cttee, 1977–79); MEP (C) London SW, Sept. 1979–1989: Vice Chm., Transport Cttee, 1979–84; Chm., Cttee on External Econ. Relations, 1984–87; Dep. Chm., Cons. Gp, 1987–89; contested (C) London SW, European Parly Elecn, 1989. Member: Bd of Basildon Development Corp., 1971–75; Occupational Pensions Bd, 1973–79; Race Relations Bd, 1973–77; Panel of Industrial Tribunals, 1973–79; PLA, 1976–79. Chairman: London Tourist Bd and Convention Bureau, 1989–; Payroll Giving Assoc., 1989–. Chm., National Women's Advisory Cttee of Conservative Party, 1972–75; Pres., Nat. Union of Conservative Party, 1988–89 (Chm., 1976–77). Co-Chm., Jt Cttee Against Racialism, 1978–80. *Publications:* (co-author) Fair Share for the Fair Sex, 1969; More Help for the Cities, 1974. *Recreation:* enjoying the sun and fresh air. *Address:* 47 Shrewsbury House, Cheyne Walk, SW3 5LW. *T:* 071–352 3711. *Clubs:* Hurlingham, St Stephen's Constitutional.

ROBERTS, Sir Sidney; *see* Roberts, Sir E. F. S.

ROBERTS, Sir Stephen (James Leake), Kt 1981; Chairman, Milk Marketing Board, 1977–87; *b* 13 April 1915; *s* of Frank Roberts and Annie Leake; *m* 1940, Muriel Hobbins; two *s* two *d*. *Educ:* Wellington Grammar Sch. Farmer; founded Wrekin Farmers Ltd, 1960 (Chm., 1960–77); Shropshire delegate to NFU Council, 1962–70; Member: MMB for W Midland Region, 1966–87 (Vice-Chm., 1975–77); Food from Britain Council, 1983–87. *Recreation:* football (now spectator). *Address:* Littleworth, Little Wenlock, Wellington, Telford, Shropshire TF6 5AX. *T:* Telford (0952) 504569. *Club:* Farmers'.

ROBERTS, Stephen Pritchard; baritone; professional singer, since 1972; *b* 8 Feb. 1949; *s* of Edward Henry Roberts and Violet Pritchard. *Educ:* Royal College of Music (schol.). ARCM 1969; GRSM 1971. Professional Lay-Cleric, Westminster Cathedral Choir, 1972–76; now sings regularly in London, UK and Europe, with all major orchs and choral socs; has also sung in USA, Canada, Israel, Hong Kong, Singapore and S America. *Opera* rôles include: Count, in Marriage of Figaro; Falke, in Die Fledermaus; Ubalde, in Armide; Ramiro, in Ravel's L'Heure Espagnole; Aeneas, in Dido and Aeneas; Don Quixote, in Master Peter's Puppet Show; Mittenhofer, in Elegy for Young Lovers; *television* appearances include: Britten's War Requiem; Weill's Seven Deadly Sins; Delius' Sea Drift; Handel's Jeptha; Handel's Judas Maccabaeus; Penderecki's St Luke Passion, 1983 Proms; Walton's Belshazar's Feast, 1984 Proms; *recordings* include: Tippett's King Priam; Birtwistle's Punch and Judy; Gluck's Armide; Orff's Carmina Burana; Vaughan Williams' Five Mystical Songs, Epithalamion, Sea Symphony, Fantasia on Christmas Carols, and Hodie; Elgar's Apostles; Penderechi's St Luke Passion; Fauré's Requiem; and works by J. S. Bach, C. P. E. Bach and Duruflé. *Address:* 144 Gleneagle Road, SW16 6BA. *T:* 081–769 1512.

ROBERTS, Thomas Somerville, JP; FCIT; Chairman, Milford Haven Conservancy Board, 1976–82; *b* Ruabon, N Wales, 10 Dec. 1911; *s* of Joseph Richard Roberts, Rhosllanerchrugog and Lily Agnes (*née* Caldwell); *m* 1st, 1938, Ruth Moira Teasdale; two *s*; 2nd, 1950, Margaret Peggy Anderson, Sunderland. *Educ:* Roath Park Elem. Sch., Cardiff; Cardiff High Sch.; Balliol Coll., Oxford (Domus Exhibnr). Traffic Apprentice, LNER, 1933; Docks Manager, Middlesbrough and Hartlepool, 1949; Chief Docks Manager: Hull, 1959; S Wales, 1962; Port Dir, S Wales Ports, 1970–75. Chm., S Wales Port Employers, 1962–75; Member: Nat. Jt Council for Port Transport Industry, 1962–75; Nat. Dock Labour Bd, 1970–75; Race Relations Bd, 1968–76. Dir, Develt Corp. for Wales, 1965–80, Vice-Pres. 1979–83; Dep. Chm., Welsh Develt Agency, 1976–80. Member: Court, Univ. of Wales; Pwyllgor Tywysog Cymru (Prince of Wales' Cttee), 1977–81; Exec. Cttee, Welsh Environment Foundn, 1977–. Hon. Fellow and Life Governor, Univ. of Wales Coll. Cardiff (formerly University Coll., Cardiff and UWIST). JP City of Cardiff, 1966. *Recreation:* TV. *Address:* Marcross Lodge, 9 Ely Road, Llandaff, Cardiff CF5 2JE. *T:* Cardiff (0222) 561153.

ROBERTS, Sir William (James Denby), 3rd Bt *cr* 1909; *b* 10 Aug. 1936; *s* of Sir James Denby Roberts, 2nd Bt, OBE, and of Irene Charlotte D'Orsey, *yr d* of late William Dunn, MB, CM; *S* father, 1973. *Educ:* Rugby; Royal Agricultural Coll., Cirencester. MRAC, FRICS. Farms at Strathallan Castle, and Combwell Priory, Flimwell, Wadhurst, Sussex. Founder, 1969, and owner 1969–81, Strathallan Aircraft Collection. *Recreations:* swimming and flying. *Heir: b* Andrew Denby Roberts, *b* 21 May 1938. *Address:* Strathallan Castle, Auchterarder, Perthshire PH3 1JZ. *T:* Auchterarder (0764) 62131.

ROBERTS, Rt. Hon. Sir Wyn; *see* Roberts, Rt Hon. Sir I. W. P.

ROBERTS-JONES, Ivor, CBE 1975; RA 1973 (ARA 1969); sculptor; Teacher of sculpture, Goldsmiths' College School of Art, 1946–68; *b* 2 Nov. 1913; *s* of William and Florence Robert-Jones; *m* 1940, Monica Florence Booth; one *d* (one *s* decd). *Educ:*

Oswestry Grammar Sch.; Worksop Coll.; Goldsmiths' Coll. Art Sch.; Royal Academy Schs. Served in RA, 1939–46; active service in Arakan, Burma. One-man Exhibitions of Sculpture: Beaux Arts Gall., 1957; Oriel, Welsh Arts Council Gall., Cardiff 1978; Eisteddfod, 1983. Works purchased by: Tate Gall.; National Portrait Gall.; Arts Council of Gt Brit.; Welsh Arts Council; Beaverbrook Foundation, New Brunswick; Nat. Mus. of Wales. Public commissions: Winston Churchill, Parliament Square; Augustus John Memorial, Fordingbridge; Saint Francis, Lady Chapel, Ardleigh, Essex; Apsley Cherry Garrard, Wheathampstead; Winston Churchill, Oslo, 1975; Winston Churchill, New Orleans, 1977; Earl Attlee, Members' Lobby, House of Commons, 1979; Janus Rider (equestrian group), Harlech Castle, 1982; Rupert Brooke memorial, Rugby, 1988; Field Marshal Lord Slim, Whitehall, 1990. Exhibited at: The John Moore, Leicester Galls, Royal Academy, Arts Council travelling exhibitions, Jubilee Exhibn of Modern British Sculpture, Battersea Park, 1977, etc. Work is in many private collections. Best known portraits include: Paul Claudel, Somerset Maugham, Yehudi Menuhin, The Duke of Edinburgh, Geraint Evans, Speaker George Thomas, Sir James Callaghan. Hon. LLD Wales, 1983. *Publications:* poetry published in Welsh Review, Poets of the Forties, etc. Sculpture illustr. in British Art since 1900 by John Rothenstein; British Sculptors, 1947; Architectural Review, etc. *Address:* The Bridles, Hall Lane, Shimpling, near Diss, Norfolk IP21 4UH. *T:* Diss (0379) 740204.

ROBERTS-WEST, Lt-Col George Arthur Alston-; *see* West.

ROBERTSON, family name of **Baron Robertson of Oakridge** and **Baroness Wharton.**

ROBERTSON, Hon. Lord; Ian Macdonald Robertson, TD 1946; a Senator of the College of Justice in Scotland, 1966–87; *b* 30 Oct. 1912; *s* of late James Robertson and Margaret Eva Wilson, Broughty Ferry, Angus, and Edinburgh; *m* 1938, Anna Love Glen, *d* of late Judge James Fulton Glen, Tampa, Florida, USA; one *s* two *d. Educ:* Merchiston Castle School; Balliol College, Oxford; Edinburgh University. BA Oxford (Mod. Greats), 1934; LLB Edinburgh 1937; Vans Dunlop Schol. in Law, Edinburgh 1937. Member Faculty of Advocates, 1939; Advocate-Depute, 1949–51; QC (Scot.), 1954; Sheriff of Ayr and Bute, 1961–66; Sheriff of Perth and Angus, 1966. Chairman: Medical Appeals Tribunal, 1957–63; Scottish Jt Council for Teachers' Salaries, 1965–81; Scottish Valuation Adv. Council, 1977–86; Member Court of Session Rules Council; UK Rep., Central Council, Internat. Union of Judges, 1974–87. Formerly, External Examiner in law subjects, Aberdeen, Glasgow, Edinburgh and St Andrews Universities; Member Committee on Conflicts of Jurisdiction affecting Children, 1958; Governor of Merchiston Castle School, 1954, Chm., 1970–; Assessor on Court of Edinburgh Univ., 1967–81. Chairman: Edinburgh Centre of Rural Economy, 1967–85; Edinburgh Centre for Tropical Veterinary Medicine. Served War of 1939–45, 8th Bn The Royal Scots (The Royal Regt); commd 1939; SO (Capt.), 44th Lowland Brigade (15th Scottish Division), Normandy and NW Europe (despatches). *Publication:* From Normandy to the Baltic, 1945. *Recreation:* golf. *Address:* 13 Moray Place, Edinburgh EH3 6DT. *T:* 031–225 6637. *Clubs:* New, Honourable Company of Edinburgh Golfers (Captain 1970–72).

ROBERTSON OF OAKRIDGE, 2nd Baron *cr* 1961; **William Ronald Robertson;** Bt 1919; Member of the London Stock Exchange, since 1973; *b* 8 Dec. 1930; *s* of General Lord Robertson of Oakridge, GCB, GBE, KCMG, KCVO, DSO, MC, and Edith (*d* 1982), *d* of late J. B. Macindoe; *S* father, 1974; *m* 1972, Celia Jane, *d* of William R. Elworthy; one *s. Educ:* Hilton Coll., Natal; Charterhouse; Staff Coll., Camberley (psc). Served The Royal Scots Greys, 1949–69. Mem. Salters' Co (Master, 1985–86). *Heir: s* Hon. William Brian Elworthy Robertson, *b* 15 Nov. 1975. *Club:* Anglo-German Association.

ROBERTSON, Dr Alan, CBE 1982; PhD; CChem, FRSC; Chairman, Council of Management, National Waterways Museum Trust, since 1989; *b* 15 Aug. 1920; *s* of William Arthur Robertson and Clarice Firby Robertson; *m* 1948, Dorothy Eileen Freeman; two *s* one *d. Educ:* Middlesbrough High Sch.; BSc London; University Coll., Durham (PhD); Balliol Coll., Oxford (PhD 1947). CChem, FRSC 1970. ICI, 1936–82: variety of posts in research and works management; served on Boards of Dyestuffs Div., Mond Div., ICI Australia and ICI USA; Dep. Chm., Organics Div., 1965–73; Chm., Plant Protection Div., 1973–75; Main Bd Dir, 1975–82 (Agricl Product Dir, Management Services Dir, and Territorial Dir, Pacific and Far East). Chm., Agricultural Genetics Co., 1983–89. Vice-Chm., British Waterways Bd, 1983–89; Dir, First Step Housing Co. Ltd, 1990–. Royal Society of Chemistry: Mem. Council, 1978–81; Chm., Environment Gp, 1978–81; Chm., Indust. Div., 1978–81; Industrial Medal, 1982. Chairman: Eur. Chemical Industry Ecology and Toxicology Centre, 1978–83; British Nutrition Foundn, 1981–83; Member: NEDC for Paper and Paper Bd Industry, 1964–67; Teijin Agrochemicals Bd, 1975–82; British Industrial Biol Res. Assoc. Council, 1980–82; London Bd, Halifax Bldg Soc., 1980–83; Kao Atlas Bd, 1975–82; Pestalozzi Children's Village Trust Council, 1977–; Indust. Cttee, C of E Bd for Social Responsibility, 1980–86; Council, China Soc., 1985–; Vice-Pres., Heulwen Trust, 1986–; Mem. Court and Dep. Chm. of Council, UMIST, 1968–73; Governor, Lister Inst. of Preventive Medicine, 1985–. *Publications:* scientific papers in learned jls. *Recreations:* most sports (now non-active), gardening, industrial archaeology, biographical history, all matters oriental, children's and old people's welfare. *Address:* Woodlands, Tennyson's Lane, Haslemere, Surrey GU27 3AF. *T:* Haslemere (0428) 4196. *Clubs:* Oriental, Farmers'.

ROBERTSON, Prof. Anne Strachan, DLitt; FRSE, FSA, FSAScot; Titular Professor of Roman Archaeology, Glasgow University, 1974–75, retired; *d* of John Anderson Robertson and Margaret Purden. *Educ:* Hillhead High Sch.; Glasgow High Sch. for Girls; Glasgow Univ. (MA, DLitt); London Univ. (MA). FRSE 1975; FMA 1958; FRNS 1937; FSA 1958; FSAScot 1941. Glasgow University: Dalrymple Lectr in Archaeol., 1939; Under-Keeper, Hunterian Museum and Curator, Hunter Coin Cabinet, 1952; Reader in Roman Archaeol., Keeper of Cultural Collections and of Hunter Coin Cabinet, Hunterian Museum, 1964; Keeper of Roman Collections and of Hunter Coin Cabinet, 1974. Hon. Mem., Internat. Numismatic Commn, 1986. Silver Medal, RNS, 1964; Silver Huntington Medal, Amer. Numismatic Soc., 1970. *Publications:* An Antonine Fort: Golden Hill, Duntocher, 1957; The Antonine Wall, 1960, 4th edn 1990; Sylloge of Anglo-Saxon Coins in the Hunter Coin Cabinet, 1961; Catalogue of Roman Imperial Coins in the Hunter Coin Cabinet: Vol. 1, 1962; Vol. 2, 1971; Vol. 3, 1977; Vol. 4, 1978; Vol. 5, 1982; The Roman Fort at Castledykes, 1964; Birrens (Blatobulgium), 1975; contrib. to Britannia, Numismatic Chron., Proc. Soc. of Antiquaries of Scotland. *Recreations:* reading, writing, photography, walking, gardening. *Address:* 31 Upper Glenburn Road, Bearsden, Glasgow G61 4BN. *T:* 041–942 1136.

ROBERTSON, Bryan Charles Francis, OBE 1961; author, broadcasting and television, etc; regular contributor to The Spectator; *b* 1 April 1925; *yr s* of A. F. Robertson and Ellen Dorothy Black; unmarried. *Educ:* Battersea Grammar School. Worked and studied in France and Germany, 1947–48; Director: Heffer Gallery, Cambridge, 1949–51; Whitechapel Art Gallery, London, 1952–68. Mem. Arts Council Art Panel, 1958–61, 1980–84; Mem. Contemporary Art Soc. Cttee, 1958–73. US Embassy Grant to visit United States, 1956; Lectr on art, Royal Ballet School, 1958; Ford Foundn Grant for research for writing, 1961; British Council Lecture Tour, SE Asia and Australian State Galleries, 1960. Dir, State Univ. of NY Museum, 1970–75. Since 1953 has organized major exhibitions at Whitechapel, including Turner, Hepworth, Moore, Stubbs, John Martin, Rowlandson and Gillray, Bellotto, Mondrian, de Stäel, Nolan, Davie, Smith, Malevich, Pollock, Richards, Australian Painting, Rothko, Tobey, Vaughan, Guston, Poliakof, Caro, Medley, etc. *Publications:* Jackson Pollock, a monograph, 1960; Sidney Nolan, a monograph, 1961; (jtly) Private View, 1965; (with H. Tatlock Miller) Loudon Sainthill, 1973; Edward Burra, 1978; contribs (art criticism) to London Magazine, Art News (US), Spectator, Harpers & Queen, Twentieth Century, Listener, Cambridge Review, Museums Jl, etc. *Address:* 73 Barnsbury Street, N1 1EJ. *Club:* Athenæum.

ROBERTSON, Rev. Charles; Parish Minister, Canongate (The Kirk of Holyroodhouse), since 1978; *b* 22 Oct. 1940; *s* of late Thomas Robertson and late Elizabeth Halley; *m* 1965, Alison Margaret Malloch; one *s* two *d. Educ:* Camphill School, Paisley; Edinburgh Univ. (MA); New College, Edinburgh. Asst Minister, North Morningside, Edinburgh, 1964–65; Parish Minister, Kiltearn, Ross-shire, 1965–78. Chaplain to Lord High Comr, 1990–. Sec., Gen. Assembly's Panel on Worship, 1982–; C of S rep. on Joint Liturgical Group, 1984–. Mem., Broadcasting Standards Council, 1988–. Chaplain: Clan Donnachaidh Soc., 1981–; New Club, Edinburgh, 1986–; Moray House Coll. of Educn, 1986–; No 2 (City of Edinburgh) Maritime HQ Unit, RAAF, 1987–. Lectr, St Colm's Coll., 1980–. Mem., Historic Buildings Council for Scotland, 1990–. Chm., Bd of Queensberry House Hosp., 1985–; Gov., St Columba's Hospice, 1986–; Trustee: Edinburgh Old Town Trust, 1987–; Church Hymnary Trust, 1987–; Pres., Church Service Soc., 1988–. JP Edinburgh, 1980–. Sec. of cttees which compiled Hymns for a Day, 1983 and Songs of God's People, 1988. *Publications:* (ed) Singing the Faith, 1990; contribs to Record of the Church Service Soc. *Recreations:* Scottish and Edinburgh history and literature, hymnody, collecting Canongate miscellanea. *Address:* Manse of Canongate, Edinburgh EH8 8BR. *T:* 031–556 3515. *Clubs:* Athenæum; New (Edinburgh).

ROBERTSON, Prof. Charles Martin; FBA 1967; Lincoln Professor of Classical Archæology and Art, University of Oxford, 1961–78; *b* 11 Sept. 1911; *s* of late Professor Donald Struan Robertson, FBA, FSA, and Petica Coursolles Jones; *m* 1st, 1942, Theodosia Cecil Spring Rice (*d* 1984); four *s* two *d*; 2nd, 1988, Louise Berge (*née* Holstein). *Educ:* Leys School, Cambridge; Trinity College, Cambridge (Hon. Fellow, 1987). BA Cambridge, 1934, MA 1947; student at British School of Archæology, Athens, 1934–36; Asst Keeper, Dept of Greek and Roman Antiquities, British Museum, 1936–48 (released for service, War of 1939–45, 1940–46); Yates Professor of Classical Art and Archæology in the Univ. of London (Univ. Coll.), 1948–61. Corresp. Mem., German Archæological Inst., 1953; Ordinary Mem., 1953; Chm., Man. Cttee, British School at Athens, 1958–68. Mem., Inst. for Advanced Study, Princeton, 1968–69. Guest Schol., J. Paul Getty Museum, Malibu, 1980 and 1988. Hon. Fellow: Lincoln Coll., Oxford, 1980; UCL, 1980. For. Hon. Mem., Archaeological Inst. of America, 1985. Hon. DLit QUB, 1978. Kenyon Medal, British Acad., 1987. *Publications:* Why Study Greek Art? (Inaugural Lecture), 1949; Greek Painting, 1959; The Visual Arts of the Greeks (in The Greeks), 1962; Between Archæology and Art History (Inaugural Lecture), 1963; Crooked Connections (poems), 1970; indexes and editorial work in late Sir John Beazley's Paralipomena, 1971; For Rachel (poems), 1972; A History of Greek Art, 1975; (with Alison Frantz) The Parthenon Frieze, 1975; A Hot Bath at Bedtime (poems), 1977; The Sleeping Beauty's Prince (poem), 1977; (with John Boardman) Corpus Vasorum Antiquorum, Castle Ashby, 1978; A Shorter History of Greek Art, 1981; The Attic Black-figure and Red-figure Pottery, in Karageorghis, Excavations at Kition IV, 1981; (contrib.) Greek Religion and Society (ed P. E. Easterling and J. V. Muir), 1985; Catalogue of Greek, Etruscan and Roman Vases in the Lady Lever Art Gallery, 1987; The Art of Vase-painting in Classical Athens, 1991; articles, notes and reviews since 1935, in British and foreign periodicals. *Address:* 7a Parker Street, Cambridge CB1 1JL. *T:* Cambridge (0223) 311913.

ROBERTSON, Charles Robert Suttie; Member, Management Committee of The Distillers Company plc, 1970–82, retired; chartered accountant; *b* 23 Nov. 1920; *s* of late David Young McLellan Robertson and Doris May Beaumont; *m* 1949, Shona MacGregor Riddel (*d* 1985), *d* of late Robert Riddel, MC, and Phyllis Mary Stewart; one *s. Educ:* Dollar Academy. Joined DCL group, 1949; appointed: Managing Director, Scottish Malt Distillers, 1960; Sec., DCL, 1966, Finance Director, 1967. *Recreation:* hill walking. *Address:* The Arch, Edzell, Angus DD9 7TF. *T:* Edzell (03564) 484.

ROBERTSON, Sheriff Daphne Jean Black, WS; Sheriff of Glasgow and Strathkelvin, since 1979; *b* 31 March 1937; *d* of Rev. Robert Black Kincaid and Ann Parker Collins; *m* 1965, Donald Buchanan Robertson, *qv. Educ:* Hillhead High Sch.; Greenock Acad.; Edinburgh Univ. (MA); Glasgow Univ. (LLB). Admitted solicitor, 1961; WS 1977. *Address:* Sheriff Court House, Glasgow G5 9DA.

ROBERTSON, David Lars Manwaring, CVO 1990; Director, Kleinwort Benson Group plc, 1970–87; *b* 29 Jan. 1917; *m* 1939, Pamela Lauderdale Meares; three *s. Educ:* Rugby; University Coll., Oxford. Served Welsh Guards, 1940–45. Man. Dir, Charterhouse Finance Corp. Ltd, 1945–55; joined Kleinwort, Sons & Co. Ltd, 1955; Dir, Kleinwort, Benson Ltd, 1955–81; Chairman: MK Electric Group plc, 1975–87; Provident Mutual Life Assurance Assoc., 1973–89; Provident Mutual Managed Pensions Funds Ltd, 1974–89; Dir, Berry Bros and Rudd. JP Crowborough, 1971–87. *Recreations:* skiing, golf, fishing, shooting. *Address:* 12 Lennox Gardens Mews, SW1 0DP. *Clubs:* Boodle's, MCC.

ROBERTSON, Donald Buchanan, QC (Scot.) 1973; *b* 29 March 1932; *s* of Donald Robertson, yachtbuilder, Sandbank, Argyll, and Jean Dunsmore Buchanan; *m* 1st, 1955, Louise Charlotte, *d* of Dr J. Linthorst-Homan; one *s* one *d*; 2nd, 1965, Daphne Jean Black Kincaid (*see* D. J. B. Robertson). *Educ:* Dunoon Grammar Sch.; Glasgow Univ. (LLB). Admitted Solicitor, 1954; Royal Air Force (National Service), 1954–56. Passed Advocate, 1960; Standing Junior to Registrar of Restrictive Practices, 1970–73. Member: Sheriff Court Rules Council, 1972–76; Royal Commn on Legal Services in Scotland, 1976–80; Legal Aid Central Cttee, 1982–85; Criminal Injuries Compensation Bd, 1986–; Chm., VAT Tribunal, 1978–85. Hon. Sheriff, Lothian and Peebles, 1982–. FSA (Scot.) 1982. *Recreations:* shooting, numismatics, riding. *Address:* 11 Grosvenor Crescent, Edinburgh EH12 5ED. *T:* 031–337 5544; Cranshaws Castle, By Duns, Berwickshire. *T:* Longformacus (03617) 268. *Clubs:* New (Edinburgh); RNVR (Glasgow).

ROBERTSON, Douglas William, CMG 1947; DSO 1918; MC 1918; *b* 30 Nov. 1898; 2nd surv. *s* of late Rev. J. A. Robertson, MA; *m* 1924, Mary Eagland (*d* 1968), *y d* of late W. E. Longbottom, Adelaide; no *c. Educ:* George Watson's College, Edinburgh. 2nd Lt KRRC, 1917; France, 1918 (wounded, MC, DSO, despatches); Administrative Service, Uganda, 1921–50; Resident of Buganda, 1945; Secretary for African Affairs, Uganda, 1947–50, retired, 1950. *Address:* 3a Ravelston Park, Edinburgh EH4 3DX. *Club:* East India, Devonshire, Sports and Public Schools.

ROBERTSON, Francis Calder F.; *see* Ford-Robertson.

ROBERTSON, Geoffrey Ronald; QC 1988; barrister; author; *b* 30 Sept. 1946; *s* of Francis Albert Robertson and Bernice Joy (*née* Beattie); *m* 1990, Kathy Lette; one *s. Educ:*

Epping Boys' High Sch.; Univ. of Sydney (BA 1966; LLB Hons 1970); University Coll., Oxford (BCL 1972; Rhodes Schol.). Called to the Bar, Middle Temple, 1973; Supreme Court of NSW, 1977. Visiting Fellow: Univ. of NSW, 1977; Warwick Univ., 1980–81. Consultant on Human Rights to Attorney Gen. of Australia, 1983. Chm., Inquiry into Press Council, 1982–83. Member: BFI Wkg Party on New Technologies, 1984; Exec. Council, ICA, 1987–; Freedom of Inf. Campaign, 1987–. *Television:* Moderator, Hypotheticals, 1981–; writer and presenter, Tree of Liberty, 1982; Chm., The World This Week, 1987. Editor, legal column, The Guardian, 1980–85. *Publications:* The Trials of Oz (play), 1973; Whose Conspiracy?, 1974; Reluctant Judas, 1976; Obscenity, 1979; People Against the Press, 1983; (with A. Nicol) Media Law, 1984, 2nd edn 1990; Hypotheticals, 1986; Does Dracula have Aids?, 1987; Freedom, the Individual and the Law, 6th edn 1989; contribs to anthologies and learned jls. *Recreations:* tennis, opera, fishing. *Address:* 11 Doughty Street, WC1N 2PG. *T:* 071–404 1313.

ROBERTSON, George Islay Macneill; MP (Lab) Hamilton, since 1978; *b* 12 April 1946; *s* of George Phillip Robertson and Marion I. Robertson; *m* 1970, Sandra Wallace; two *s* one *d. Educ:* Dunoon Grammar Sch.; Univ. of Dundee (MA Hons 1968). Res. Asst, Tayside Study, 1968–69; Scottish Res. Officer, G&MWU, 1969–70, Scottish Organiser, 1970–78. PPS to Sec. of State for Social Services, 1979; opposition spokesman on Scottish Affairs, 1979–80, on Defence, 1980–81, on Foreign and Commonwealth Affairs, 1981–; principal spokesman on European Affairs, 1984–. Chm., Scottish Council of Labour Party, 1977–78; Mem., Scottish Exec. of Lab. Party, 1973–79; Sec., Manifesto Gp of PLP, 1979–84. Vice Chairman: Bd, British Council, 1985–; Prince's Trust Community Venture, Blantyre, 1990–; Vice-Pres., Operation Raleigh, 1982–; Member: Bd, Scottish Develt Agency, 1975–78; Bd, Scottish Tourist Bd, 1974–76; Council, National Trust for Scotland, 1976–82 and 1983–85; Police Adv. Bd for Scotland, 1974–78; Council, British Atlantic Cttee, 1981–; Governing Body, GB/E Europe Centre, 1983– (Vice Chm., 1990–); Steering Cttee, annual British-German Königswinter Conference, 1983–; Council, RIIA, 1984–; Steering Cttee, Atlantic Conf., 1987–; Council, GB/USSR Assoc., 1986–; Bd, British/Amer. Project for Successor Generation, 1986–; Council, BESO, 1991–. Editorial Bd, European Business Jl, 1988–. Chm., Seatbelt Survivors Club, 1981–. Governor, Ditchley Foundn, 1989–. *Recreations:* photography, golf. *Address:* House of Commons, SW1A 0AA. *T:* 071–219 3000; 3 Argyle Park, Dunblane, Central Scotland.

ROBERTSON, Air Vice-Marshal Graeme Alan, CBE 1988 (OBE 1985); Deputy Commander in Chief, Royal Air Force, Germany, since 1991; *b* 22 Feb. 1945; *s* of Ronald James Harold Robertson and Constance Rosemary (*née* Freeman); *m* 1972, Barbara Ellen (*née* Mardon); one *d. Educ:* Bancroft's Sch.; RAF Coll., Cranwell. BA Open Univ. Pilot: 8 Sqn, 1968–69; 6 Sqn, 1970–72; 228 OCU, 1972–73; Flight Commander: 550 TFTS, USAF, 1973–76; 56 Sqn, 1976–77; RAF Staff Coll., 1977–78; OR/Air Plans Staff, MoD, 1978–82; Commanding Officer: 92 Sqn, 1982–84; 23 Sqn, 1984–85; RAF Wattisham, 1985–87; ADC to the Queen, 1985–87; Dir of Air Staff Briefing and Co-ordination, MoD, 1987–88; RCDS, 1989; Dir of Defence Programmes, MoD, 1990–91. QCVSA 1973. *Recreations:* shooting, golf, winter sports. *Address:* c/o National Westminster Bank, Sleaford, Lincs NG34 7BJ. *Clubs:* Royal Air Force, MCC.

ROBERTSON, Hamish, MBE 1964; Under Secretary, Scottish Office Education Department (formerly Scottish Education Department), since 1987; *b* 6 April 1931; *s* of James and Elizabeth Robertson, Huntly; *m* 1955, Barbara Suzanne Taylor, *d* of late Dr G. C. Taylor, Peterhead; two *s* two *d. Educ:* The Gordon Schs, Huntly; Aberdeen Univ. (MA); St John's Coll., Cambridge. RA, 1952–54. Joined Colonial Admin. Service; Nyasaland, 1954–64; HMOCS, Malawi, 1964–67; Scottish Office: Principal, 1967; Asst Sec., 1973. *Recreations:* country pursuits. *Address:* 14 Harviestoun Road, Dollar FK14 7HG. *T:* Dollar (0259) 42374. *Club:* Commonwealth Trust.

ROBERTSON, (Harold) Rocke, CC (Canada) 1969; MD, CM, FRCS(C), FRCSE, FACS, FRSC; Principal and Vice-Chancellor of McGill University, 1962–70; *b* 4 Aug. 1912; *s* of Harold Bruce Robertson and Helen McGregor Rogers; *m* 1937, Beatrice Roslyn Arnold; three *s* one *d. Educ:* St Michael's Sch., Victoria, BC; Ecole Nouvelle, Switzerland; Brentwood College, Victoria, BC; McGill University. Montreal Gen. Hospital: rotating, 1936; pathology, 1937–38; Clin. Asst in Surg., Roy. Infirmary, Edinburgh, 1938–39; Demonstr in Anat., Middx Hosp. Med. Sch., 1939; Jun. Asst in Surg., Montreal Gen. Hosp., 1939–40; RCAMC, 1940–45; Chief of Surgery: Shaughnessy Hosp., DVA, Vancouver, 1945–59 (Prof. of Surg., Univ. of BC, 1950–59); Vancouver Gen. Hosp., 1950–59; Montreal Gen. Hosp., 1959–62 (Prof. of Surg., McGill University, 1959–62). Member: Nat. Research Coun., 1964; Science Council of Canada, 1976–82. Pres., Traffic Injury Res. Foundn, 1969–72, 1977–79; Hon. Pres., Mont St Hilaire Nature Conservation Centre, 1974–. Hon. DCL, Bishop's Univ., 1963; Hon. LLD: Manitoba, 1964; Toronto, 1964; Victoria, 1964; Glasgow, 1965; Michigan, 1967; Dartmouth, 1967; Sir George Williams, 1970; McGill, 1970; Hon. DSc: Brit. Columbia, 1964; Memorial, 1968; Jefferson Med. Coll., 1969; Dr de l'Univ., Montreal, 1965. FRSA 1963. *Publications:* article on wounds, Encyclopædia Britannica; numerous contribs to scientific journals and text books. *Recreations:* tennis, fishing, gardening, golf. *Address:* RR2, Mountain, Ontario K0E 1S0, Canada. *T:* 613–989–2967.

ROBERTSON, Iain Samuel, CA; Group Finance Director, County Natwest, since 1990; *b* 27 Dec. 1945: *s* of Alfred and Kathleen Robertson; *m* 1972, Morag; two *s* two *d. Educ:* Jordanhill College Sch.; Glasgow Univ. (LLB). Industry and professional practice 1966–72; Civil Servant, 1972–83. Director: Scottish Development Finance, 1983–90; Locate in Scotland, 1983–86; Selective Assets Trust plc, 1988–; Chief Exec., SDA, 1987–90. *Recreations:* golf, reading. *Address:* 135 Bishopsgate, EC2M 3UR. *T:* 071–375 5000.

ROBERTSON of Brackla, Maj.-Gen. Ian Argyll, CB 1968; MBE 1947; MA; DL; Vice-Lord-Lieutenant, Highland Region (Nairn), 1980–88; Representative in Scotland of Messrs Spink & Son, 1969–76; Chairman, Royal British Legion, Scotland, 1974–77 (Vice-Chairman, 1971–74); *b* 17 July 1913; 2nd *s* of John Argyll Robertson and Sarah Lilian Pitt Healing; *m* 1939, Marjorie Violet Isobel Duncan; two *d. Educ:* Winchester Coll.; Trinity Coll., Oxford. Commnd Seaforth Highlanders, 1934; Brigade Major: 152 Highland Bde, 1943; 231 Infantry Bde, 1944; GSO2, Staff College, Camberley, 1944–45; AAG, 15 Indian Corps, 1945–46; GSO1, 51 Highland Div., 1952–54; Comdg 1st Bn Seaforth Highlanders, 1954–57; Comdg Support Weapons Wing, 1957–59; Comdg 127 (East Lancs) Inf. Bde, TA, 1959–61; Nat. Defence College, Delhi, 1962–63; Comdg School of Infantry, 1963–64; Commanding 51st Highland Division, 1964–66; Director of Army Equipment Policy, Ministry of Defence, 1966–68; retd. Mem. Council, Nat. Trust for Scotland, 1972–75. DL Nairn 1973. *Recreations:* various in a minor way. *Address:* Brackla House, Nairn. *T:* Cawdor (06677) 220. *Clubs:* Army and Navy, MCC; Vincent's (Oxford).

ROBERTSON, Rear-Adm. Ian George William, CB 1974; DSC 1944; *b* 21 Oct. 1922; *s* of late W. H. Robertson, MC, and Mrs A. M. Robertson; *m* 1947, Barbara Irène Holdsworth; one *s* one *d. Educ:* Radley College. Joined RNVR, 1941; qual. Pilot; Sub-Lt 1943; air strike ops against enemy shipping and attacks against German battleship Tirpitz, 1944 (DSC); Lieut, RN, 1945; flying and instructional appts, 1944–53; Comdr (Air): RNAS Culdrose, 1956; HMS Albion, 1958; in comd: HMS Keppel, 1960; HMS Mohawk, 1963; RNAS Culdrose, 1965; HMS Eagle, 1970; Admiral Comdg Reserves, 1972–74; retd 1974. Comdr 1954; Captain 1963; Rear-Adm. 1972; idc 1968. Dir-Gen., Navy League, 1975–76; Scoutreach Resources Organiser, Scout Assoc., 1976–79. *Recreations:* golf, sailing, fishing. *Address:* Moons Oast, Barcombe Road, Piltdown, Sussex TN22 3XG. *T:* Newick (082572) 2279. *Clubs:* Naval; Piltdown Golf.

ROBERTSON, Ian Macbeth, CB 1976; LVO 1956; JP; Secretary of Commissions for Scotland, 1978–83; *b* 1 Feb. 1918; *s* of late Sheriff-Substitute J. A. T. Robertson and Brenda Lewis; *m* 1947, Anne Stewart Marshall. *Educ:* Melville College; Edinburgh University. Served War of 1939–45 in Middle East and Italy; Royal Artillery and London Scottish, Captain. Entered Dept of Health for Scotland, 1946. Private Secretary to Minister of State, Scottish Office, 1951–52 and to Secretary of State for Scotland, 1952–55. Asst Secretary, Dept of Health for Scotland, 1955; Assistant Under-Secretary of State, Scottish Office, 1963–64; Under-Secretary: Scottish Development Department, 1964–65; Scottish Educn Dept, 1966–78. Mem., Williams Cttee on Nat. Museums and Galls in Scotland, 1979–81. Chm. of Governors, Edinburgh Coll. of Art, 1981–88. JP Edinburgh 1978. HRSA 1987. Hon. DLitt Heriot-Watt, 1988. *Address:* Napier House, 8 Colinton Road, Edinburgh EH10 5DS. *T:* 031–447 4636. *Club:* New (Edinburgh).

ROBERTSON, Ian Macdonald; *see* Robertson, Hon. Lord.

ROBERTSON, Maj.-Gen. James Alexander Rowland, CB 1958; CBE 1956 (OBE 1949; MBE 1942); DSO 1944 (Bar 1945); DL; *b* 23 March 1910; *s* of Colonel James Currie Robertson, CIE, CMG, CBE, IMS, and Catherine Rowland Jones; *m* 1st, 1949, Ann Madeline Tosswill (*d* 1949); 2nd, Joan Wills (*née* Abercromby), *widow* of R. L. Wills, CBE, MC. *Educ:* Aysgarth School; Epsom College, RMC, Sandhurst. Commissioned 2 Lieutenant IA, 1930, attached 1st KOYLI; posted 6th Gurkha Rifles, 1931; Instructor Sch. of Physical Training, 1936–37; Staff Coll., Quetta, July-Dec. 1941; Bde Major 1 (Maymyo) Bde, Jan.-June, 1942; Bde Major, 106 I Inf. Bde, 1942–44; Comdr 1/7 Gurkha Rifles, 1944–45; Comdr 48 Ind. Inf. Bde, 1945–47; GSO 1, Instr Staff Coll., Quetta, June-Nov., 1947; Comdr 1/6th Gurkha Rifles, 1947–48; GSO 1 Gurkha Planning Staff, March-June, 1948; GSO 1 Malaya comd, June-Nov. 1948; BGS 1948–49. GSO 1, War Office, 1950–52; Col GS, 1 Corps, Germany, 1952–54; Comdr 51 Indep. Bde, 1955–57; Commander 17 Gurkha Division Overseas Commonwealth Land Forces, and Maj.-Gen. Brigade of Gurkhas, 1958–61; GOC Land Forces, Middle East Command, 1961–63; Gurkha Liaison Officer, War Office, 1963–64, retd. Personnel Dir, NAAFI, 1964–69. Colonel, 6th Queen Elizabeth's Own Gurkha Rifles, 1961–69; Chm., 1968–80, Pres., 1980–87, Life Vice-Pres., 1987–, Gurkha Brigade Assoc. DL Greater London, 1977. *Recreations:* fishing, sculpture, an outdoor life.

ROBERTSON, James Downie, RSA 1989 (ARSA 1974); RSW 1962; RGI; Senior Lecturer in Fine Art (Drawing and Painting), Glasgow School of Art, since 1975; *b* 2 Nov. 1931; *s* of Thomas Robertson and Mary Welsh; *m* 1970, Ursula Orr Crawford; two step *s* one step *d. Educ:* Hillhead High Sch., Glasgow; Glasgow Sch. of Art. DA Glasgow. RGI 1980. Taught at Keith Grammar Sch., 1957–58; Glasgow School of Art: part time Lectr, 1959; Lectr in Drawing and Painting, 1967. Vis. Lectr, Art Schools and Univs, Scotland, England and overseas; one-man exhibns, 1961–, UK, Spain, USA, incl. Christopher Hull Gallery, London, 1984, 1987, 1989; numerous group exhibns; annual exhibns at RSA, RSW, RGI, RA; works in public collections of arts socs, art galleries (incl. RSA), corporations, banks, univs and in many private collections. Awards: RGI, 1971, 1982, 1990; RSW, 1976, 1981, 1987; Shell Exploration and Production Award, 1985. *Recreations:* drawing, painting. *Address:* Carruthmuir, by Kilbarchan,. Renfrewshire PA10 2QA. *T:* Bridge of Weir (0505) 613592. *Club:* Glasgow Art.

ROBERTSON, James Geddes, CMG 1961; formerly Under-Secretary, Department of the Environment, and Chairman, Northern Economic Planning Board, 1965–71, retired 1971; *b* 29 Nov. 1910; *s* of late Captain A. M. Robertson, Portsoy, Banffshire; *m* 1939, Marion Mitchell Black; one *s* one *d. Educ:* Fordyce Academy, Banffshire; George Watson's College, Edinburgh; Edinburgh University. Kitchener Schol., 1928–32, MA 1st cl. Hons History (Edinburgh), 1932. Entered Ministry of Labour as Third Class Officer, 1933; Principal, 1943; on exchange to Commonwealth Dept of Labour and Nat. Service, Australia, 1947–49; Asst Sec., Min of Labour, 1956; Member of Government Delegations to Governing Body and Conference of ILO, 1956–60, and Social Cttee, Council of Europe, 1953–61; Safety and Health Dept, 1961–63; Training Department, Ministry of Labour, 1963–65. Member: Industrial Tribunals Panel, 1971–73; Northern Rent Scrutiny Bd, 1973–74; Rent Assessment Panel for Scotland, 1975–81. Served War of 1939–45, RAF 1942–45. *Address:* 1/1 Wyvern Park, The Grange, Edinburgh EH9 2JY. *T:* 031–662 4367.

ROBERTSON, Rev. Canon James Smith, OBE 1984; Canon Emeritus, Zambia, 1965; Secretary, United Society for the Propagation of the Gospel, 1973–83; a Chaplain to the Queen, 1980–87; *b* 4 Sept. 1917; *s* of Stuart Robertson and Elizabeth Mann Smith, Forfar; *m* 1950, Margaret Isabel Mina Mounsey; one *d. Educ:* Glasgow Univ.; Edinburgh Theol Coll.; London Univ. MA Glasgow 1938; PCE London 1953. Curate, St Salvador's, Edinburgh, 1940–45; Mission Priest, UMCA, N Rhodesia, 1945–50; St Mark's Coll., Mapanza, 1950–55; Chalimbana Trng Coll., Lusaka, 1955–65, Principal 1958–65; Head, Educn Dept, Bede Coll., Durham, 1965–68; Sec., Church Colls of Educn, Gen. Synod Bd of Educn, 1968–73; Sec., USPG, 1973–83. British Council of Churches: Chm., Conf. for World Mission, 1977–81; Vice-Pres., 1984–87. *Publications:* contributed to: Education in South Africa, 1970; The Training of Teachers, 1972; Values and Moral Development in Higher Education, 1974; Grow or Die, 1981; A Dictionary of Religious Education, 1984; Stepping Stones, 1987. *Recreations:* music, electronics, philosophy. *Address:* 13 Onslow Avenue Mansions, Onslow Avenue, Richmond, Surrey TW10 6QD. *T:* 081–940 8574.

ROBERTSON, Jean, CBE 1986; RRC 1981; Matron-in-Chief, Queen Alexandra's Royal Naval Nursing Service, 1983–86; Director of Defence Nursing Services, Ministry of Defence, and Director of Royal Naval Nursing Services, 1985–86; working voluntarily for Help the Aged, since 1987; *b* 21 Sept. 1928; *d* of late Alexander Robertson and Jean Robertson (*née* McCartney). *Educ:* Mary Erskine's School for Girls, Edinburgh. Registered Sick Children's Nurse, 1948, General Nurse, 1951; Ward Sister, Edinburgh Sick Children's Hospital, 1953; QARNNS 1955; QHNS, 1983–86. SSStJ 1981. *Recreations:* gardening, reading. *Address:* 14 The Haven, Alverstoke, Hants PO12 2BD. *T:* Gosport (0705) 582301.

ROBERTSON, Maj.-Gen. John Carnegie; Director of Army Legal Services, Ministry of Defence, 1973–76; *b* 24 Nov. 1917; *s* of late Sir William C. F. Robertson, KCMG and Dora (*née* Whelan); *m* 1961, Teresa Mary Louise, *d* of Cecil T. Porter. *Educ:* Cheltenham Coll.; RMC, Sandhurst. Served War of 1939–45: Officer in Gloucestershire Regt (PoW, Germany, 1940). Called to the Bar, Gray's Inn, 1949. Joined Judge Advocate's Dept, 1948; served subseq. in Middle East, BAOR, East Africa and the Far East. Dep. Dir, Army Legal Services, HQ, BAOR, 1971–73. *Address:* Berry House, Nuffield, Henley-on-Thames, Oxon RG9 5SS. *T:* Nettlebed (0491) 641740. *Club:* Huntercombe Golf.

ROBERTSON, John David H.; *see* Home Robertson.

ROBERTSON, Rear Adm. John Keith, CB 1983; FIEE; consultant; *b* 16 July 1926; *s* of G. M. and J. L. Robertson; *m* 1951, Kathleen (*née* Bayntun); one *s* three *d*. *Educ:* RNC Dartmouth; Clare Coll., Cambridge (BA 1949). FIEE 1981; FBIM 1980. RNC Dartmouth, 1940–43; served, 1943–83 (Clare Coll., Cambridge, 1946–49): HM Ships Queen Elizabeth, Zest, Gabbard, Aisne and Decoy; Staff, RNC Dartmouth; Grad. Recruiting; Weapon Engr Officer, HMS Centaur; Comdr, RNEC Manadon; RCDS; Captain Technical Intell. (Navy), 1974–76; Captain Fleet Maintenance, Portsmouth, 1976–78; Dir, Naval Recruiting, 1978–79; Dir, Management and Support of Intelligence, MoD, 1980–82; ACDS (Intelligence), 1982–83. *Recreations:* hockey, tennis, golf, wood carving. *Address:* Alpina, Kingsdown, Corsham, Wilts SN14 9BJ. *Club:* Corkscrew (Bath).

ROBERTSON, John Windeler; Senior Partner, Wedd Durlacher Mordaunt, 1979–86; *b* 9 May 1934; *s* of late John Bruce Robertson and Evelyn Windeler Robertson; *m* 1st 1959, Jennifer-Ann Gourdou (marr. diss.); one *s* one *d*; 2nd 1987, Rosemary Helen Jane Banks. *Educ:* Winchester Coll. National Service, RNVR, 1953–55. Joined Wedd Jefferson & Co. (Members of Stock Exchange), 1955; Partner, 1961. Dep. Chm., Barclays de Zoete Wedd Securities Ltd (BZW), 1986–88. Dep. Chm., Stock Exchange, 1976–79 (Mem. Council, 1966–86); Dir, Securities Assoc., 1986–88. Mem., City Capital Markets' Cttee, 1981–88. *Recreations:* golf, deer stalking, motor boating. *Address:* Eckensfield Barn, Compton, near Chichester, West Sussex PO18 9NT. *T:* Compton (0705) 631239. *Club:* City of London.

ROBERTSON, Julia Ann; *see* Burdus, J. A.

ROBERTSON, Sir Lewis, Kt 1991; CBE 1969; FRSE; industrialist and administrator; Chairman: Lilley plc (formerly F. J. C. Lilley), since 1986; Havelock Europa plc, since 1989; Stakis plc, since 1991; *b* 28 Nov. 1922; *s* of John Farquharson Robertson and Margaret Arthur; *m* 1950, Elspeth Badenoch; three *s* one *d*. *Educ:* Trinity Coll., Glenalmond. Accountancy training; RAF Intelligence. Chm., 1968–70, and Man. Dir, 1965–70, Scott & Robertson Ltd; Chief Executive, 1971–76, and Dep. Chm., 1973–76, Grampian Holdings Ltd; Director: Scottish and Newcastle Breweries plc, 1975–87; Whitman (International) SA (formerly IC Industries (International) SA), Geneva, 1987–90; Aristuein, 1990–; EFM Income Trust plc, 1991–; Scottish Financial Enterprise, 1991–; Chairman: Girobank Scotland, 1984–90; Borthwicks (formerly Thomas Borthwick & Sons plc), 1985–89; Triplex Lloyd, 1987–90 (F. H. Lloyd Hldgs, 1982–87; Triplex, 1983–87). Mem, 1975–76, Dep. Chm. and Chief Exec., Scottish Develt Agency, 1976–81. Chairman: Eastern Regional Hosp. Bd (Scotland), 1960–70; Carnegie Trust for Univs of Scotland, 1990– (Trustee, Exec. Cttee, 1963–); Member: Provincial Synod, Episcopal Church of Scotland, 1963–83 (Chm. Policy Cttee, 1974–76); (Sainsbury) Cttee of Enquiry, Pharmaceutical Industry, 1965–67; Court (Finance Convener), Univ. of Dundee, 1967–70; Monopolies and Mergers Commn, 1969–76; Arts Council of GB (and Chm., Scottish Arts Council), 1970–71; Scottish Economic Council, 1977–83; Scottish Post Office Bd, 1984–90; British Council (Chm., Scottish Adv. Cttee), 1978–87; Council, Scottish Business School, 1978–82; Restrictive Practices Court, 1983–; Edinburgh Univ. Press Cttee, 1985–88; Bd, Friends of Royal Scottish Acad., 1986–; Chm., Bd for Scotland, BIM, 1981–83. Mem., Adv. Bd, critical edn of Waverley novels, 1984–. Trustee, Foundn for Study of Christianity and Society, 1980–88. FRSE 1978; FRSA 1981; CBIM 1976. Hon. LLD Dundee, 1971. *Recreations:* work, foreign travel, computer use, music, reading, things Italian. *Address:* 32 Saxe Coburg Place, Edinburgh EH3 5BP. *T:* 031–332 5221. *Clubs:* Athenæum; New (Edinburgh).

ROBERTSON, Commandant Dame Nancy (Margaret), DBE 1957 (CBE 1953; OBE 1946); retired as Director of Women's Royal Naval Service (Dec. 1954–April 1958); *b* 1 March 1909; *er d* of Rev. William Cowper Robertson and Jessie Katharine (*née* McGregor). *Educ:* Esdaile School, Edinburgh; Paris. Secretarial work, London and Paris, 1928–39; WRNS, 1939. *Recreations:* needlework, gardening. *Address:* 14 Osborne Way, Wigginton, Tring, Herts HP23 6EN. *T:* Tring (044282) 2560.

ROBERTSON, Prof. Noel Farnie, CBE 1978; BSc Edinburgh; MA Cantab; PhD Edinburgh; FRSE; Professor of Agriculture and Rural Economy, University of Edinburgh, and Principal, East of Scotland College of Agriculture, 1969–83; *b* 24 Dec. 1923; *o s* of late James Robertson and Catherine Landles Robertson (*née* Brown); *m* 1948, Doreen Colina Gardner; two *s* two *d*. *Educ:* Trinity Academy, Edinburgh; University of Edinburgh; Trinity College, Cambridge. Plant Pathologist, West African Cacao Research Institute, 1946–48; Lecturer in Botany, University of Cambridge, 1948–59; Prof. of Botany, Univ. of Hull, 1959–69. Pres., British Mycol Soc., 1965; Trustee, Royal Botanic Garden, Edinburgh, 1986–. Chm. of Governors, Scottish Crop Res. Inst., 1983–89 (Governor, 1973–). *Publication:* (with I. J. Fleming) Britain's First Chair of Agriculture at the University of Edinburgh 1790–1990, 1990. *Address:* Woodend, Juniper Bank, Walkerburn, Peeblesshire. *T:* Walkerburn (089687) 523. *Club:* Farmers'

ROBERTSON, Prof. Norman Robert Ean, CBE 1991; FDSRCPSGlas; Professor of Orthodontics, since 1970, Dean of the Dental School, 1985–89 and since 1989, University of Wales College of Medicine; Hon. Consultant in Orthodontics with South Glamorgan Health Authority, since 1970; *b* 13 March 1931; *s* of late Robert Robertson and of Jean Robertson (*née* Dunbar); *m* 1954, Morag Wyllie, *d* of George McNicol, MA; three *s* two *d*. *Educ:* Hamilton Acad.; Glasgow Univ. (BDS); Manchester Univ. (MDS 1962; DDS 1989). FDSRCPSGlas 1967. Registrar, then Sen. Registrar in Orthodontics, Glasgow Dental Hosp., 1957–59; Lectr in Orthodontics, 1960–62, Sen. Lectr in Orthodontics, 1962–70, Manchester Univ. Member: GDC, 1985–; Standing Dental Adv. Cttee, 1989; S Glamorgan HA, 1976. *Publications:* Oral Orthopaedics and Orthodontics for Cleft Lip and Palate, 1983; articles in dental and med. jls. *Recreations:* sailing in summertime, walking in wintertime. *Address:* 51 Heol y Coed, Rhiwbina, Cardiff CF4 6HQ. *T:* Cardiff (0222) 613439; University of Wales College of Medicine, Dental School, Heath Park, Cardiff CF4 4XY. *Club:* Cruising Association.

ROBERTSON, Patrick Allan Pearson, CMG 1956; *b* 11 Aug. 1913; *s* of A. N. McI. Robertson; *m* 1st, 1939, Penelope Margaret Gaskell (*d* 1966); one *s* two *d*; 2nd, 1975, Lady Stewart-Richardson. *Educ:* Sedbergh School; King's College, Cambridge. Cadet, Tanganyika, 1936; Asst Dist Officer, 1938; Clerk of Exec. and Legislative Councils, 1945–46; Dist Officer, 1948; Principal Asst Sec., 1949; Financial Sec., Aden, 1951; Asst Sec., Colonial Office, 1956–57; Chief Sec., Zanzibar, 1958; Civil Sec., Zanzibar, 1961–64; Deputy British Resident, Zanzibar, 1963–64; retired, 1964. Associate Member, Commonwealth Parliamentary Association. Freeman, City of London. *Recreations:* golf, tennis, fishing. *Address:* Lynedale, Longcross, Chertsey, Surrey KT16 0DP. *T:* Ottershaw (0932) 872329. *Club:* Commonwealth Trust.

See also Sir Simon Stewart-Richardson, Bt.

ROBERTSON, (Richard) Ross, RSA, FRBS; DA; sculptor; *b* Aberdeen, 10 Sept. 1914; *s* of Rev. R. R. Robertson; *m* Kathleen May Matts; two *d*. *Educ:* Glasgow School of Art; Gray's School of Art, Aberdeen (DA). Lectr, Gray's Sch. of Art, 1946–79. FRBS 1963 (ARBS 1951); RSA 1977 (ARSA 1969). *Recreation:* study of art. *Address:* Creaguir, Woodlands Road, Rosemount, Blairgowrie, Perthshire.

ROBERTSON, Robert, CBE 1967; JP; Member, Strathclyde Regional Council, 1974–86; *b* 15 Aug. 1909; *s* of late Rev. William Robertson, MA; *m* 1938, Jean, *d* of late James Moffatt, MA, Invermay, Broomhill, Glasgow; one *s* one *d*. *Educ:* Forres Academy; Royal Technical Coll., Glasgow. Civil Engr, retd 1969. Mem., Eastwood Dist Council, 1952–58; Chm., Renfrewshire Educn Cttee, 1962–73; Convener, Renfrewshire County Council, 1973–75 (Mem., 1958); Mem., Convention of Scottish Local Authorities, 1975–86. Chm., Sec. of State's Cttee on Supply and Trng of Teachers for Further Educn, 1962–78; Chm., Nat. Cttee for Inservice Trng of Teachers, 1965–78. Mem. Scottish Council for: Research in Educn, 1962–80; Commercial Admin. and Professional Educn, 1960–69; Development of Industry, 1973–75. Chm., Sch. of Further Educn for training of teachers in Scotland, 1969–83. Governor: Jordanhill Coll. of Educn, 1966–83; Watt Memorial and Reid Kerr Colls, 1966–75, 1977–86. Member: Scottish Nat. School Camps Assoc., 1975–80; Scottish Assoc. of Young Farmers' Clubs, 1975–83; Glasgow Educnl Trust, 1978–86; Hutchison Educnl Trust, 1978–86; Council, Glasgow Coll. of Bldg and Printing, 1978–86. Fellow, Educnl Inst. of Scotland (FEIS), at Stirling Univ., 1970; Hon. Warden, Co. of Renfrew, Ont., Canada, 1970. JP Renfrewshire, 1958. *Publications:* Robertson Report on: The Training of Teachers in Further Education (HMSO), 1965. *Recreations:* fishing, painting. *Address:* 24 Broadwood Park, Alloway, Ayrshire. *T:* Alloway (0292) 43820; Castlehill, Maybole, Ayrshire. *T:* Dunure (029250) 337. *Clubs:* RNVR (Scotland); SV Carrick (Glasgow).

ROBERTSON, Robert Alexander; Lord Provost, City of Aberdeen, since 1988; *b* 17 June 1922; *m* 1946, Susie Gladys Ivy Edmondson. Hon. LLD Aberdeen, 1991. *Address:* 49 Hopetoun Avenue, Bucksburn, Aberdeen AB2 9QU. *T:* Aberdeen (0224) 713882.

ROBERTSON, Robert Henry; Ambassador of Australia to Argentina, Uruguay and Paraguay, since 1989; *b* 23 Dec. 1929; *s* of James Rowland Robertson and Hester Mary (*née* Kay); *m*; 2nd, 1958, Jill Bryant Uther (marr. diss. 1982); two *s* one *d*; 3rd, 1986, Isabelle Costa de Beauregard, *d* of Comte and Comtesse René Costa de Beauregard. *Educ:* Geelong Church of England Grammar Sch.; Trinity Coll., Univ. of Melbourne (LLB). Third Secretary, Australian High Commn, Karachi, 1954–56; Second Sec., Mission to UN, New York, 1958–61; First Sec., later Counsellor, Washington, 1964–67; Ambassador to Jugoslavia, Romania and Bulgaria, 1971–73; Asst Sec., Personnel Br., Dept of Foreign Affairs, Canberra, 1974–75; First Asst Sec., Western Div., 1975–76, Management and Foreign Service Div., 1976–77; Ambassador to Italy, 1977–81; Dep. High Comr in London, 1981–84; Perm. Rep. to UN in Geneva, 1984–88. Chm., Exec. Cttee, UN High Comr for Refugees, 1987–88. *Address:* Zabala 1900, 1426 Buenos Aires, Argentina. *T:* 804–1018. *Club:* Commonwealth (Canberra).

ROBERTSON, Ross; *see* Robertson, R. R.

ROBERTSON, Prof. Sir Rutherford (Ness), AC 1980; Kt 1972; CMG 1968; DSc; PhD; FRS 1961; FAA; Emeritus Professor; *b* 29 Sept. 1913; *o c* of Rev. J. Robertson, MA, and Josephine Robertson; *m* 1937, Mary Helen Bruce Rogerson; one *s*. *Educ:* St Andrew's Coll., NZ; Univ. of Sydney; St John's Coll., Cambridge (Hon. Fellow 1973). DSc Sydney 1961; FAA 1954. Sydney Univ. Science Res. Schol., 1934–35, Linnean Macleay Fell., 1935–36. Exhibn of 1851 Res. Schol., 1936–39; Res. at Botany Sch., Cambridge, in plant physiology, 1936–39, PhD 1939; Asst Lectr, later Lectr, Botany Sch., Univ. of Sydney, 1939–46; Sen. Res. Offr, later Chief Res. Offr, Div. of Food Preservation, CSIRO, 1946–59 (res. in plant physiol. and biochem.); Sydney University: jointly in charge of Plant Physiol. Unit, 1952–59, Hon. Res. Associate, 1954–59; Hon. Vis., Sch. of Biol. Scis, 1979–87; Visiting Prof., Univ. of Calif, Los Angeles, 1958–59; Kerney Foundn Lectr, Univ. of Calif, Berkeley, 1959; Mem. Exec., CSIRO 1959–62; Prof. of Botany, Univ. of Adelaide, 1962–69, now Emeritus; Dir, Res. Sch. of Biol Scis, ANU, 1973–78, now Emeritus Professor (Master, University House, 1969–72); Pro-Chancellor, ANU, 1984–86. Chm., Aust. Res. Grants Cttee, 1965–69; Dep. Chm., Aust. Sci. and Tech. Council, 1977–81. Pres. Linnean Soc. of NSW, 1949; Hon. Sec. Austr. Nat. Res. Council, 1951–55; President: Australian Academy of Science, 1970–74 (Sec. Biological Sciences, 1957–58); Aust. and NZ Assoc. for the Advancement of Science, 1964–66; XIII Internat. Botanical Congress, Sydney, 1981; Corresp. Mem., Amer. Soc. of Plant Physiologists, 1953; For. Associate, US Nat. Acad. of Scis, 1962; Hon. Mem., Royal Soc. of NZ, 1971; Hon. FRSE 1983; For. Mem., Amer. Philosophical Soc., 1971; For. Hon. Mem., Amer. Acad. of Arts and Scis, 1973. Three Societies Lecture, 1988. Hon. DSc: Tasmania, 1965; Monash, 1970; ANU, 1979; Hon ScD Cambridge, 1969. Clarke Meml Medal, Royal Soc. of NSW, 1955; Farrer Meml Medal, 1963; ANZAAS Medal, 1968; Mueller Medal, 1970; Burnet Medal, 1975. *Publications:* (with G. E. Briggs, FRS, and A. B. Hope) Electrolytes and Plant Cells, 1961; Protons, Electrons, Phosphorylation and Active Transport, 1968; The Lively Membranes, 1983; various scientific papers on plant physiology and biochemistry. *Recreations:* reading, water colours. *Address:* PO Box 9, Binalong, NSW 2584, Australia. *Club:* Union (Sydney).

ROBERTSON, Brig. Sidney Park, MBE 1962; TD 1967; JP; Vice Lord-Lieutenant of Orkney, since 1987; Director, S. & J. D. Robertson Group Ltd (Chairman, 1965–79); *b* 12 March 1914; *s* of John Davie Manson Robertson and Elizabeth Park Sinclair; *m* 1940, Elsa Miller Croy; one *s* one *d*. *Educ:* Kirkwall Grammar Sch.; Edinburgh Univ. (BCom 1939). MIBS 1936. Served War; commnd RA, 1940 (despatches, NW Europe, 1945). Managerial posts, Anglo-Iranian Oil Co., ME, 1946–51; Manager, Operation/Sales, Southern Div., Shell Mex and BP, 1951–54; founded Robertson firm, 1954. Chm., Orkney Hosps Bd of Management/Orkney Health Bd, 1965–79. Maj. comdg 861 (Ind.) LAA Batt., RA (Orkney and Zetland) TA, 1956–61; Lt-Col comdg Lovat Scouts, TA, 1962–65; CRA 51st Highland Div., TA, 1966–67 (Brig.); Hon. Col, 102 (Ulster and Scottish) Light Air Defence Regt, RA (TA), 1975–80; Hon. Col Comdt, RA, 1977–80; Chm., RA Council of Scotland, 1980–84; Vice Pres., Nat. Artillery Assoc., 1977–; Hon. Vice Pres., Royal British Legion, Orkney, 1975–; Hon. Pres., Orkney Bn, Boys' Bde, 1972–; Vice-Pres., RNLI, 1985–. DL Orkney, 1968; Hon. Sheriff, Grampian, Highlands and Islands, 1969–. Freedom of Orkney, 1990. *Recreations:* travel, hill walking, angling. *Address:* Daisybank, Kirkwall, Orkney KW15 1LX. *T:* Kirkwall (0856) 2085. *Clubs:* Army and Navy, Caledonian; New (Edinburgh).

ROBERTSON, Toby, (Sholto David Maurice Robertson), OBE 1978; director and actor, theatre, opera and television; Director, Theatr Clwyd, Mold, since 1985; *s* of David Lambert Robertson and Felicity Douglas (*née* Tomlin); *m* 1963, Teresa Jane McCulloch (marr. diss. 1981); two *s* two *d*. *Educ:* Stowe; Trinity Coll., Cambridge (BA 1952, MA 1981). Formerly an actor. Dir. first prof. prodn, The Iceman Cometh, New Shakespeare, Liverpool, 1958. Dir. plays, London, Pitlochry and Richmond, Yorks, and for RSC, 1959–63. Member: Bd, Prospect Productions Ltd, 1964– (Artistic Dir, Prospect Theatre Co., 1964–79); Bd, Cambridge Theatre Co., 1970–74; Director: Old Vic Theatre, 1977–80, Old Vic Co., 1979–80; Acting Co., Kennedy Centre, Washington, 1983; Associate Dir, Circle Rep., New York, 1983–84. Drama Advr, Argo Records, 1979–; Prof. of Theatre, Brooklyn Coll., City Univ. NY, 1981–82; Hon. Prof. of Drama,

1987–90, Hon. Prof. of English, 1990–92, UCNW. Lectures: Wilson Meml, Cambridge Univ., 1974; Hamlet, Athens Univ., 1978; Rikstheatre, Stockholm, 1980; Hamlet, Gulbenkian Foundn, Lisbon, 1987. Director of over 40 prodns for *Prospect Theatre Co.*, many staged in London and Edinburgh, 1964–79, including: The Soldier's Fortune; You Never Can Tell; The Confederacy; The Importance of Being Earnest; The Square; Howard's End; The Man of Mode; Macbeth; The Tempest; The Gamecock; A Murder of No Importance; A Room with a View; No Man's Land; The Beggar's Opera; The Servant of Two Masters; Edward II; Much Ado About Nothing; Boswell's Life of Johnson; Venice Preserved; King Lear and Love's Labour's Lost (Australian tour); Alice in Wonderland; Richard III; Ivanov; The Grand Tour; Twelfth Night, Pericles and The Royal Hunt of the Sun (internat. fests, Moscow, Leningrad and Hong Kong); The Pilgrim's Progress; A Month in the Country (Chichester Fest.); directed for *Old Vic Co.*: War Music; Antony and Cleopatra; Smith of Smiths; Buster; The Lunatic, The Lover and The Poet; Romeo and Juliet; The Government Inspector; The Padlock; Ivanov; Hamlet (Elsinore, and first visit by a British co., China, 1980); directed for *Theatr Clwyd*: Medea (also Young Vic), 1986; Barnaby and the Old Boys, 1987 (also Vaudeville, 1989); Edward III (jtly adapted, attrib. William Shakespeare) (also Cambridge and Taormina Fests), 1987; Captain Carvallo, 1988, transf. Greenwich; Revenger's Tragedy, 1988; The Old Devils, 1989; Othello, 1989; The Importance of Being Earnest, 1990; Enemy of the People, 1991, transf. Lyric Hammersmith; The Cherry Orchard, 1991 (also Brighton Festival); directed *other productions*, including: Next Time I'll Sing to You, Greenwich, 1980; Beggar's Opera, Lyric, Hammersmith, 1980; Measure for Measure, People's Arts Theatre, Peking, 1981; Pericles, NY, 1981 (Obie award, 1982); Night and Day (opening prodn), 1982 and The Taming of the Shrew, 1983, Huntingdon Theatre Co., Boston; The Tempest (opening prodn), New Cleveland Playhouse, 1983; Love's Labour's Lost, Shakespeare Workshop, 1983, Circle Rep., 1984, NYC; York Cycle of Mystery Plays, York Fest., 1984; Midsummer Night's Dream, Open Air Theatre, Regent's Park, 1985; (jt dir) Antony and Cleopatra, The Taming of the Shrew, Haymarket, 1986; Coriolanus, festivals in Spain, 1986; You Never Can Tell, Haymarket, 1988; Richard II, Folger Theatre, Washington. *Opera*: for Scottish Opera, incl.: A Midsummer Night's Dream, 1972; Hermiston, 1975; Marriage of Figaro, 1977; for Opera Co. of Philadelphia: Elisir d'Amore (with Pavarotti and winner of Pavarotti competition), Dido and Aeneas, Oedipus Rex, 1982; Faust, 1984; Wiesbaden: A Midsummer Night's Dream, 1984; NY City Opera: Barber of Seville, 1984; Wexford Opera: The Kiss, 1984. Asst Dir, Lord of the Flies (film), 1961. Dir of more than 25 television prodns, incl.: The Beggar's Opera; Richard II; Edward II. *Recreations*: painting, sailing. *Address*: 210 Brixton Road, SW9. *Club*: Garrick.

ROBERTSON, Vernon Colin, OBE 1977; self employed consultant, specialising in environmental issues in developing countries; *b* 19 July 1922; *s* of Colin John Trevelyan Robertson and Agnes Muriel Robertson (*née* Dolphin). *Educ*: Imperial Service College, Windsor; Univ. of Edinburgh (BSc Agr subs. Forestry); Univ. of Cambridge (Dip Agr 1950; MA). Joined Home Guard, 1940; enlisted RA, 1941, commissioned 1942; served 12th HAC Regt RHA, N Africa, Italy, Austria, 1942–45 (despatches 1945); with 1st Regt RHA, Italy, 1945–46 (Adjutant). Staff, Sch. of Agric., Cambridge, 1950; joined Hunting Aerosurveys Ltd, 1953, as ecologist heading new natural resources survey dept; developed this into overseas land and water resource consultancy, renamed Hunting Technical Services Ltd (Managing Director, 1959–77; after retirement continuing as Director and Consultant until 1987), development planning in Africa, Asia and Latin America. Director: Hunting Surveys and Consultants Ltd, 1962–77; Groundwater Development Consultants (International) Ltd, 1975–85; Vice-Chm. and acting Chm., Environmental Planning Commn, Internat. Union for Conservation of Nature, 1972–78; Chm., Trop. Agric. Assoc. (UK), 1981–85; Mem. Bd, Commonwealth Develt Corp., 1982–90. *Publications*: articles in learned jls. *Recreations*: natural history, esp. plants and birds, gardening, painting, photography, music, sailing. *Address*: Brickfield, Quay Lane, Kirby-le-Soken, Essex CO13 0DP. *T*: Frinton-on-Sea (0255) 674585. *Clubs*: Honourable Artillery Company, Farmers'.

ROBERTSON, Prof. William Bruce, MD, FRCPath; Professor of Histopathology, St George's Hospital Medical School, 1968–84, now Emeritus; Director of Studies, Royal College of Pathologists, since 1984; *b* 17 Jan. 1923; *s* of late William Bruce Robertson and Jessie Robertson (*née* McLean); *m* 1948, Mary Patricia Burrows two *d*. *Educ*: The Academy, Forfar; Univ. of St Andrews. BSc 1944, MB ChB 1947, MD 1959; MRCPath 1963, FRCPath 1969. Junior appts, Cumberland Infirm., Carlisle, 1947–48; RAMC, E Africa, 1948–50; Registrar Pathology, Cumberland Infirm., 1950–53; Demonstr Pathology, Royal Victoria Infirm., Newcastle upon Tyne, 1953–56; Sen. Lectr Pathology, Univ. of the West Indies, Jamaica, 1956–64; Reader in Morbid Anatomy, St George's Hosp. Med. Sch., Univ. of London, 1964–68. Visiting Professor: Louisiana State Univ., New Orleans, USA, 1961–62; Katholieke Universiteit te Leuven, Belgium, 1972–73. *Publications*: scientific papers and book chapters in various med. jls and publns. *Address*: 3 Cambisgate, Church Road, Wimbledon, SW19 5AL. *T*: 081–947 6731.

ROBERTSON, Air Cdre William Duncan, CBE 1968; Royal Air Force, retired; Senior Air Staff Officer, HQ 38 Group, Royal Air Force, 1975–77; *b* 24 June 1922; *s* of William and Helen Robertson, Aberdeen; *m* 1st, 1952, Doreen Mary (*d* 1963), *d* of late Comdr G. A. C. Sharp, DSC, RN (retd); one *s* one *d*; 2nd, 1968, Ute, *d* of late Dr R. Koenig, Wesel, West Germany; one *d*. *Educ*: Robert Gordon's Coll., Aberdeen. Sqdn Comdr, No 101 Sqdn, 1953–55, No 207 Sqdn, 1959–61. Gp Dir, RAF Staff Coll., 1962–65; Station Comdr, RAF Wildenrath, 1965–67; Dep. Dir, Administrative Plans, 1967; Dir of Ops (Plans), 1968; Dir of Ops Air Defence and Overseas, 1969–71; RCDS, 1971–72; SASO RAF Germany, 1972–74; SASO 46 Group, 1975. *Recreations*: golf, tennis. *Address*: Parkhouse Farm, Leigh, Surrey. *Club*: Royal Air Force.

ROBEY, Douglas John Brett, CMG 1960; HM Diplomatic Service, retired; *b* 7 Aug. 1914; *s* of late E. J. B. and Margaret Robey; *m* 1943, Elizabeth, *d* of late Col David D. Barrett, US Army; two *s* one *d*. *Educ*: Cranleigh School; St John's College, Oxford; Ecole des Sciences Politiques, Paris. BA (History); Editor of The Cherwell. Joined HM Foreign Service, 1937. Served in China, USA, Paris, Berlin, Baghdad; Consul-Gen., Chicago, 1966–69; Ambassador and Permanent UK Representative, Council of Europe, Strasbourg, 1969–74. *Publication*: The Innovator, 1945. *Recreations*: reading, writing, and the Niebelung Ring. *Address*: Allan Down House, Rotherfield, East Sussex TN6 3RT. *T*: Rotherfield (089285) 2329. *Club*: Cercle Européen de Strasbourg (Hon. Life Pres.).

ROBIN, Dr Gordon de Quetteville; Director, 1958–82, Senior Associate, since 1982, Scott Polar Research Institute, University of Cambridge; Fellow since 1964 and Vice-Master, 1974–78, Darwin College, Cambridge; *b* Melbourne, 17 Jan. 1921; *s* of Reginald James Robin and Emily Mabel Robin; *m* 1953, Jean Margaret Fortt, Bath; two *d*. *Educ*: Wesley Coll., Melbourne; Melbourne Univ. ScD Cantab, MSc Melbourne, PhD Birmingham; FInstP. War service, RANVR: anti-submarine, 1942–44; submarine, RN, 1944–45 (Lieut). Physics Dept, Birmingham Univ.: research student, lectr, ICI Research Fellow, 1945–56; Sen. Fellow, Geophysics Dept, ANU, 1957–58. Meteorologist and Officer i/c Signy Is, South Orkneys, with Falkland Is Dependencies Survey, 1947–48; Physicist and Sen. British Mem. of Norwegian-British-Swedish Antarctic Expedn, 1949–52 (made first effective measurements of Antarctic ice thickness); further researches in Antarctic in 1959, 1967, 1969, 1974, and in Arctic, 1964, 1966, 1973; Sec., 1958–70, Pres., 1970–74, and Hon. Member: Scientific Cttee on Antarctic Research of Internat. Council of Scientific Unions; Adv. Bd, Geophysical Inst., Univ. of Alaska, 1974–81. President: Antarctic Club, 1974; Arctic Club, 1986. Hon. DPhil Stockholm, 1978. Kongens Fortjensmedalje, Norway, 1952; Back Grant, RGS, 1953; Bruce Medal, RSE, 1953; Polar Medal, 1956; Patrons Medal, RGS, 1974; Seligman Crystal, Internat. Glaciological Soc., 1986. *Publications*: scientific reports of Norwegian-British-Swedish Antarctic Expedition (Glaciology III, 1958; Upper Winds, 1972); (ed) Annals of the IGY, Vol. 41, Glaciology, 1967; (ed and contrib.) The Climatic Record in Polar Ice Sheets, 1983; papers and articles on polar glaciology in scientific jls. *Recreations*: Mallorca, walking. *Address*: 10 Melbourne Place, Cambridge CB1 1EQ. *T*: Cambridge (0223) 358463.

ROBIN, Ian (Gibson), FRCS; *b* 22 May 1909; *s* of Dr Arthur Robin, Edinburgh, and Elizabeth Parker; *m* 1939, Shelagh Marian (*d* 1978), *d* of late Colonel C. M. Croft; one *s* two *d*. *Educ*: Merchiston Castle School; Clare College, Cambridge. MA, MB, BCh Cantab 1933; LRCP 1933; FRCS 1935. Guy's Hosp.; late House Phys.; Sen. Science Schol., 1930; Treasurer's Gold Medals in Clinical Surgery and Medicine, 1933; Arthur Durham Travelling Schol., 1933; Charles Oldham Prize in Ophthalmology, 1933; Registrar and Chief Clin. Asst, ENT Dept, 1935–36; late Consulting ENT Surgeon: Royal Chest Hosp., 1939–44; Royal Northern Hosp., 1937–74; St Mary's Hosp., Paddington, 1948–74; Princess Louise (Kensington) Hosp. for Children, 1948–69; Paddington Green Children's Hosp., 1969–74; Surgeon EMS, Sector III London Area, 1939–45. Late Vice-Chm., Royal Nat. Institute for the Deaf. Member Hunterian Soc.; Council of Nat. Deaf Children's Soc.; Past Pres., Brit. Assoc. of Otolaryngologists, 1971–72; Past Pres., Laryng. Section, RSM, 1967–68; Vice-Pres., Otolog. Section, RSM, 1967–68, 1969; late Examiner for DLO of RCS of England. Lectures: Yearsley, 1968; Jobson Horne, 1969. Mem., Royal Water-Colour Soc. *Publications*: (jt) Diseases of Ear, Nose and Throat (Synopsis Series), 1957; papers in various med. treatises, jls, etc. *Recreations*: golf, gardening, sketching; formerly athletics and Rugby. *Address*: Stowe House, 3 North End, Hampstead, NW3 7HH. *T*: 081–458 2292; 86 Harley Street, W1. *T*: 071–580 3625. *Clubs*: Hawks (Cambridge); Achilles (Great Britain); Hampstead Golf.

ROBINS, Group Captain Leonard Edward, CBE (mil.) 1979; AE 1958 (and 2 clasps); DL; on Lord Mayor of London's personal staff, since 1986; Representative DL, Borough of Wandsworth, since 1979; Inspector, Royal Auxiliary Air Force, 1973–83; *b* 2 Nov 1921; *yr s* of late Joseph Robins, Bandmaster RM, and late Louisa Josephine (*née* Kent); *m* 1949, Jean Ethelwynne (Headteacher) (*d* 1985), *d* of late Roy and Bessie Searle, Ryde, IoW. *Educ*: Singlegate, Mitcham, Surrey; City Day Continuation School, EC. Entered Civil Service, GPO, 1936; War service RAF, UK, SEAC, Ceylon, India, 1941–46; resumed with GPO, 1946; Min. of Health, 1948; Min. of Housing and Local Govt, 1962; DoE, 1970–80, retired. Airman, No 3700 (Co. of London) Radar Reporting Unit RAuxAF, 1950; Commissioned 1953, radar branch; transf. to No 1 (Co. of Hertford) Maritime HQ Unit RAuxAF, intelligence duties, 1960; OC No 1 Maritime Headquarters Unit, RAuxAF, 1969–73; Gp Capt., Inspector RAuxAF, 1973. ADC to the Queen, 1974–83. Selected Air Force Mem., Greater London TAVRA, 1973–83 and City of London TAVRA, 1980–84. Lord Mayor of London's personal staff, 1977–78, 1980–81 and 1982–83. Pres., Wandsworth Victim Support Scheme, 1980–87. Trustee, Royal Foundn of Greycoat Hosp., 1983–88. Freeman, City of London, 1976. Coronation Medal, 1953; Silver Jubilee Medal, 1977. Officer of Merit with Swords, SMO Malta, 1986. DL Greater London, 1978–. FBIM. *Recreations*: naval, military and aviation history; book hunting; kipping; speech writing. *Address*: 16 Summit Way, Upper Norwood, SE19 2PU. *T*: 081–653 3173; Higher Bosigran Cottage, Pendeen, Penzance, Cornwall TR20 8YX. *T*: Penzance (0736) 796884. *Club*: Royal Air Force.

ROBINS, Malcolm Owen, CBE 1978; Learned Societies Officer, Royal Society/British Academy, 1979–81; a Director, Science Research Council, 1972–78; *b* 25 Feb. 1918; *s* of late Owen Wilfred Robins and Amelia Ada (*née* Wheelwright); *m* 1944, Frances Mary, *d* of late William and Frances Hand; one *s* one *d*. *Educ*: King Edward's Sch., Stourbridge; The Queen's Coll., Oxford (Open Scholar in Science). MA (Oxon) 1943. On scientific staff of Royal Aircraft Establishment, 1940–57; a Div. Supt in Guided Weapons Dept, RAE, 1955–57; Asst Dir, Guided Weapons, Min. of Supply, London, 1957–58; UK Project Manager for jt UK/USA Space Research programme, and hon. Research Associate, University Coll. London, 1958–62; a Dep. Chief Scientific Officer and Head of Space Research Management Unit, Office of Minister for Science (later Dept of Educn and Science), 1962–65; Head of Astronomy, Space and Radio Div., SRC, 1965–68; a Research Planning post in Min. of Technology (later Dept of Trade and Industry), 1968–72. Vis. Prof., University Coll., London, 1974–77. FInstP 1945; FRAS 1974. *Publications*: (with Sir Harrie Massey) History of British Space Science, 1986; (with K. Proust and S. C. B. Gascoigne) The Creation of the Anglo-Australian Observatory, 1990; papers on space research in scientific jls. *Recreations*: gardening, golf. *Address*: Wychbury, Gorse Lane, Farnham, Surrey GU10 4SD. *T*: Farnham (0252) 723186.

ROBINS, Sir Ralph (Harry), Kt 1988; FEng 1988; FRAeS; Deputy Chairman, since 1989, and Chief Executive, since 1990, Rolls Royce plc; *b* 16 June 1932; *s* of Leonard Haddon and Maud Lillian Robins; *m* 1962, Patricia Maureen Grimes; two *d*. *Educ*: Imperial Coll., Univ. of London (BSc, ACGI). MIMechE; FRAeS 1990. Development Engr, Rolls-Royce, Derby, 1955–66; Exec. Vice-Pres., Rolls-Royce Inc., 1971; Man. Dir, RR Industrial & Marine Div., 1973; Commercial Dir, RR Ltd, 1978; Chm., International Aero Engines AG, 1983–84; Man. Dir, Rolls-Royce plc, 1984–89. Chm., Defence Industries Council, 1986–; Dep. Pres., Soc. of British Aerospace Companies, 1987–88 (Pres., 1986–87). *Recreations*: tennis, golf, music. *Address*: Rolls-Royce plc, 65 Buckingham Gate, SW1E 6AT.

ROBINS, Prof. Robert Henry, FBA 1986; Professor of General Linguistics, 1966–86, now Emeritus, and Dean, Faculty of Arts, 1984–86, University of London; Head of Department of Phonetics and Linguistics, School of Oriental and African Studies, University of London, 1970–85; *b* 1 July 1921; *s* of John Norman Robins, medical practitioner, and Muriel Winifred (*née* Porter); *m* 1953, Sheila Marie Fynn (*d* 1983). *Educ*: Tonbridge Sch.; New Coll., Oxford, 1940–41 and 1945–48, MA 1948; DLit London 1968. Served war, RAF Intelligence, 1942–45. Lectr in Linguistics, Sch. of Oriental and African Studies, London, 1948–55; Reader in General Linguistics, Univ. of London, 1955–65. Mem. Senate, Univ. of London, 1980–85. Research Fellow, Univ. of California, 1951; Vis. Professor: Washington, 1963; Hawaii, 1968; Minnesota, 1971; Florida, 1975; Salzburg, 1977, 1979; Leverhulme Emeritus Fellow, 1990–91. President: Societas Linguistica Europaea, 1974; CIPL, 1977– (British Rep., 1970–77); Philological Soc., 1988–May 1992 (Hon. Sec., 1961–88). Mem., Academia Europaea, 1991. Hon. Mem., Linguistic Soc. of Amer., 1981–. *Publications*: Ancient and Mediaeval Grammatical Theory in Europe, 1951; The Yurok Language, 1958; General Linguistics: an introductory survey, 1964; A Short History of Linguistics, 1967; Diversions of Bloomsbury, 1970;

Ideen- und Problemgeschichte der Sprachwissenschaft, 1973; System and Structure in Sundanese, 1983; articles in Language, TPS, BSOAS, Lingua, Foundations of Language, Man, etc. *Recreations:* gardening, travel. *Address:* 65 Dome Hill, Caterham, Surrey CR3 6EF. *T:* Caterham (0883) 343778. *Clubs:* Athenæum, Commonwealth Trust.

ROBINS, William Edward Charles; Metropolitan Stipendiary Magistrate, 1971–89; solicitor; *b* 13 March 1924; *s* of late E. T. and late L. R. Robins; *m* 1946, Jean Elizabeth, *yr d* of Bruce and Flora Forsyth, Carlyle, Saskatchewan, Canada; one *s* one *d. Educ:* St Alban's Sch. Served War: commissioned as Navigator, RAF, 1943–47. Admitted as a Solicitor, 1948; joined Metropolitan Magistrates' Courts' service, 1950; Dep. Chief Clerk, 1951–60; Chief Clerk, 1960–67; Sen. Chief Clerk, Thames Petty Sessional Div., 1968–71. Sec., London Magistrates' Clerks' Assoc., 1953–60 (Chm. 1965–71). Member, Home Office working parties, on: Magistrates' Courts' Rules; Legal Aid; Motor Vehicle Licences; Fines and Maintenance Orders Enforcement, 1968–71; Member: Lord Chancellor's Sub-Cttee on Magistrates' Courts' Rules, 1969–70; Adv. Council on Misuse of Drugs, 1973–86. Fellow Commoner, Corpus Christi Coll., Cambridge, Michaelmas 1975. *Recreations:* touring off the beaten track, music, theatre.

ROBINSON, family name of **Baron Martonmere.**

ROBINSON, Alastair; *see* Robinson, F. A. L.

ROBINSON, Sir Albert (Edward Phineas), Kt 1962; Director, E. Oppenheimer and Son (Pty) Ltd, since 1963; *b* 30 December 1915; *s* of late Charles Phineas Robinson (formerly MP Durban, S Africa) and of late Mabel V. Robinson; *m* 1st, 1944, Mary Judith Bertish (*d* 1973); four *d*; 2nd, 1975, Mrs M. L. Royston-Piggot (*née* Barrett). *Educ:* Durban High School; Universities of Stellenbosch, London, Cambridge (Trinity Coll.) and Leiden; MA (Cantab). Pres., Footlights Club, Cambridge, 1937. Barrister, Lincoln's Inn. Served War of 1939–45, in Imperial Light Horse, Western Desert, N Africa, 1940–43. Member Johannesburg City Council, 1945–48 (Leader United Party in Council, 1946–47); MP (United Party), S African Parlt, 1947–53; became permanent resident in Rhodesia, 1953. Dep. Chm., General Mining and Finance Corp. Ltd, 1963–71; Chairman: Johannesburg Consolidated Investment Co., 1971–80; Rustenburg Platinum Mines, 1971–80; Australian Anglo American Ltd, 1980–85; Director: Anglo American Corp., Zimbabwe Ltd, 1964–86; Founders Bldg Soc., 1954–86; Rand Mines Ltd, 1965–71; Anglo American Corp. of SA Ltd, 1965–88; Johannesburg Consolidated Investment Co., 1965–85; Standard Bank Investment Corp., 1972–86; Director, in Zimbabwe and South Africa, of various Mining, Financial and Industrial Companies. Chm. Central African Airways Corp., 1957–61. Member, Monckton Commission, 1960; High Commissioner in the UK for the Federation of Rhodesia and Nyasaland, 1961–63. Chancellor, Univ. of Bophuthatswana, 1981–91. Hon. DComm Bophuthatswana, 1990. *Recreations:* people, music and conversation. *Address:* 36 Smits Road, Dunkeld, Johannesburg 2196, South Africa. *Clubs:* Carlton (London); City (Capetown).

ROBINSON, Alwyn Arnold; Managing Director, Daily Mail, 1975–89; *b* 15 Nov. 1929. Mem., Press Council, 1977–87 (Jt Vice-Chm., 1982–83).

ROBINSON, Dr Ann; Head of Policy Unit, Institute of Directors, since 1989; *b* 28 Jan. 1937; *d* of Edwin Samuel James and Dora (*née* Thorne); *m* 1961, Michael Finlay Robinson; two *s. Educ:* St Anne's Coll., Oxford (MA); McGill Univ. (MA, PhD). Financial journalist, Beaverbrook Newspapers, 1959–61; University Lecturer: Durham, 1962–63; Bristol, 1970–72; Bath, 1972–75; Cardiff, 1972–89 (Sen. Lectr, 1987–89). Member: Equal Opportunities Commn, 1980–85; Econ. and Social Cttee, EEC, 1986– (Chm., Ind. Section, 1990–); Welsh Arts Council, 1991–. *Publications:* Parliament and Public Spending, 1978; (jtly) Tax Policy Making in the United Kingdom, 1984; articles in acad. jls and chapters on public expenditure control by Parliament. *Recreations:* Alpine sports, summer and winter, gardening. *Address:* Institute of Directors, 116 Pall Mall, SW1Y 5ED.

ROBINSON, Arthur Alexander; Director of Computing Centre, University of Wales College of Cardiff (formerly at University of Wales Institute of Science and Technology), since 1976; *b* 5 Aug. 1924; *o s* of Arthur Robinson and Elizabeth (*née* Thompson); *m* 1956, Sylvia Joyce Wagstaff; two *s* one *d. Educ:* Epsom Coll.; Clare Coll., Cambridge (MA); Univ. of Manchester (PhD). English Electric Co. Ltd, 1944; Ferranti Ltd, 1950; Dir and Gen. Man., Univ. of London Atlas Computing Service, 1962; Dir, Univ. of London Computer Centre, 1968; Dir, National Computing Centre Ltd, 1969–74. *Publications:* papers in Proc. IEE. *Recreation:* gardening. *Address:* 6 Portland Close, Penarth, S Glamorgan CF6 2DY.

ROBINSON, (Arthur) Geoffrey, CBE 1978; Chairman, Medway Ports Authority, 1978–87; *b* 22 Aug. 1917; *s* of Arthur Robinson and Frances M. Robinson; *m* 1st, 1943, Patricia MacAllister (*d* 1971); three *s* one *d*; 2nd, 1973, Hon. Mrs Treves, *d* of Rt Hon. Lord Salmon, *qv*; three step *s* one step *d. Educ:* Lincoln Sch.; Jesus Coll., Cambridge (MA); Sch. of Oriental and African Studies, London Univ. Served War, RA, 1939–46. Solicitor, 1948; Treasury Solicitor's Dept, 1954–62; PLA, 1962–66; Man. Dir, Tees and Hartlepool Port Authority, 1966–77; Chm., English Indust. Estates Corp., 1977–83. Member: National Dock Labour Bd, 1972–77; National Ports Council, 1980–81; Chm., British Ports Assoc., 1983–85. *Publications:* Hedingham Harvest, 1977; various articles. *Recreation:* music. *Address:* Salts End, Goss Hall Lane, Ash, Canterbury, Kent CT3 2AN. *T:* Ash (0304) 812366; La Baume, Uzès, 30700 Gard, France. *T:* 66.22.55.44. *Club:* United Oxford & Cambridge University.

See also P. H. Robinson.

ROBINSON, Hon. (Arthur Napoleon) Raymond; barrister; Prime Minister, Trinidad and Tobago, since 1986; Leader, National Alliance for Reconstruction, Trinidad and Tobago, since 1986; *b* 16 Dec. 1926; *s* of late James Alexander Andrew Robinson, Headmaster, and Emily Isabella Robinson; *m* 1961, Patricia Rawlins; one *s* one *d. Educ:* Bishop's High Sch., Tobago; St John's Coll., Oxford (Hon. Fellow 1988). LLB (London); MA (PPE) Oxon. Called to Bar, Inner Temple; in practice, 1956–61. Treas., People's Nat. Movt (governing Party) 1956; Mem. Federal Parlt, 1958; MHR for Tobago East, 1961–71 and 1976–80; Minister of Finance, 1961–66; Dep. Political Leader of Party, 1966; Actg Prime Minister (during his absence), April and Aug. 1967; Minister of External Affairs, Trinidad and Tobago, 1967–68; Chm., Democratic Action Congress, 1971–86; Chm., Tobago House of Assembly, 1980–86. Member: Legal Commn on US Leased Areas under 1941 Agreement, 1959; Industrial Develt Corp., 1960; Council, Univ. of West Indies, 1960–62. Consultant, Foundn for establishment of an Internat. Criminal Court, 1972–75, Exec. Dir, 1976–77. Mem., UN Expert Gp on Crime and the Abuse of Power, 1979. Dist. Internat. Criminal Law Award, Internat. Criminal Court Foundn, 1977. Gran Cordon, Orden de El Libertador (Venezuela), 1990. *Publications:* The New Frontier and the New Africa, 1961; Fiscal Reform in Trinidad and Tobago, 1966; The Path of Progress, 1967; The Teacher and Nationalism, 1967; The Mechanics of Independence, 1971; Caribbean Man, 1986; articles and addresses. *Address:* Office of the Prime Minister, Central Bank Tower, Eric Williams Plaza, Port of Spain, Trinidad and Tobago.

ROBINSON, Sir Austin; *see* Robinson, Sir E. A. G.

ROBINSON, Basil William, FBA 1981; retired; *b* 20 June 1912; *o c* of William Robinson and Rebecca Frances Mabel, *d* of Rev. George Gilbanks; *m* 1st, 1945, Ailsa Mary Stewart (*d* 1954); 2nd, 1958, Oriel Hermione Steel; one *s* one *d. Educ:* Winchester (Exhibitioner); CCC Oxford. BA 1935; MA, BLitt, 1938. Asst Keeper, Victoria and Albert Museum, 1939. Min. of Home Security, 1939–40. Served as Captain, 2nd Punjab Regt, India, Burma, Malaya, 1943–46. Deputy Keeper, V&A Museum, 1954, Keeper, Dept of Metalwork, 1966–72, Keeper Emeritus, 1972–76. Pres., Royal Asiatic Soc., 1970–73; Vice-Pres., Arms and Armour Soc., 1953; Hon. Pres., Tō-ken Soc. of Great Britain, 1967. FSA 1974. *Publications:* A Primer of Japanese Sword-blades, 1955; Persian Miniatures, 1957; Japanese Landscape Prints of the 19th Century, 1957; A Descriptive Catalogue of the Persian Paintings in the Bodleian Library, 1958; Kuniyoshi, 1961; The Arts of the Japanese Sword, 1961, 2nd edn, 1971; Persian Drawings, 1965; part-author, vols 2 and 3, Catalogue of Persian MSS and Miniatures in the Chester Beatty Library, 3 vols, 1958–62; Persian Miniature Painting, 1967; Persian Paintings in the India Office Library, 1976; (ed. and jt author) Islamic painting in the Keir Collection, 1976; Japanese Sword-fittings in the Baur Collection, 1980; Persian Paintings in the John Rylands Library, 1980; Kuniyoshi: the Warrior Prints, 1982 (Uchiyama Meml Prize, Japan Ukiyoe Soc.); Persian Painting and the National Epic (Hertz Lecture, British Acad.), 1983; (jtly) The Aldrich Book of Catches, 1989; numerous booklets, articles and reviews on Persian and Japanese art. *Recreations:* catch singing (founder and Chairman, Aldrich Catch Club); cats. *Address:* 41 Redcliffe Gardens, SW10 9JH. *T:* 071–352 1290. *Club:* Hurlingham.

ROBINSON, Bill; *see* Robinson, P. W.

ROBINSON, Air Vice-Marshal Brian Lewis; Senior Partner, Belmont Consultants, advising construction industry on military works worldwide; *b* 2 July 1936; *s* of Frederick Lewis Robinson and Ida (*née* Croft); *m* 1962, Ann Faithfull; one *s* one *d. Educ:* Bradford Grammar Sch. Served, 1956–76: 74 Sqn; Oxford Univ. Air Sqn; 73 Sqn; Canberra Trials and Tactical Evaluation Unit; Directorate of Flight Safety, MoD; RAF Staff Coll.; RAF Valley; 2 ATAF Germany; Canadian Forces Comd and Staff Coll., and Air Reserve Sqn, Toronto; Chief Instr, 4 Flying Trg Sch., 1976–78, OC, 1978–80, RAF Valley; Internat. Mil. Staff HQ, NATO, Brussels, 1980–82; Defence and Air Attaché, Moscow, 1983–86; Dir of Orgn and Quartering, RAF, MoD, 1986–88; RAF Long-term Deployment Study, 1988; AO Admin, HQ Strike Command, 1989–91. Editor, Flight Safety section, Air Clues, 1967–69. Mem., RAF and British Bobsleigh teams, 1967–74. *Recreations:* viticulture, beekeeping. *Address:* c/o Lloyds Bank, 122 East Street, South Molton, Devon. *Club:* Royal Air Force.

ROBINSON, Air Vice-Marshal Bruce, CB 1968; CBE 1953; Air Officer Commanding No 24 Gp, RAF, 1965–67; retired, 1967; *b* 19 Jan. 1912; *s* of late Dr G. Burton Robinson, Cannington, Somerset; *m* 1940, Elizabeth Ann Compton, *d* of Air Commodore D. F. Lucking; one *s* one *d. Educ:* King's School, Bruton. Commissioned in SR of O, The Somerset Light Infty, 1931–33; Commissioned in RAF, 1933; No 16 (Army Co-op. Sqdn), 1934–37; Specialist Engineer course, 1937–39. Served War of 1939–45: Technical duties in Fighter and Bomber Commands, UK Senior Technical Staff Officer, Rhodesian Air Training Group, 1946–48; on loan to Indian Air Force (Director of Technical Services), 1951–53; Commandant, No 1 Radio School, RAF Locking, 1953–55; Sen. RAF Officer at Wright Patterson Air Force Base, Dayton, Ohio, 1958–60; Commandant No 1 Sch. of Technical Training, RAF Halton, Bucks, 1961–63. Director of RAF Aircraft Development, Min. of Aviation, 1963–65. *Recreations:* golf, sailing, painting, writing.

ROBINSON, Christopher John, LVO 1986; Organist, Director of Music, and Fellow, St John's College, Cambridge, since 1991; *b* 20 April 1936; *s* of late Prebendary John Robinson, Malvern, Worcs; *m* 1962, Shirley Ann, *d* of H. F. Churchman, Sawston, Cambs; one *s* one *d. Educ:* St Michael's Coll., Tenbury; Rugby; Christ Church, Oxford. MA, BMus; FRCO; Hon. RAM. Assistant Organist of Christ Church, Oxford, 1955–58; Assistant Organist of New College, Oxford, 1957–58; Music Master at Oundle School, 1959–62; Assistant Organist of Worcester Cathedral, 1962–63; Organist and Master of Choristers: Worcester Cathedral, 1963–74; St George's Chapel, Windsor Castle, 1975–91. Conductor: City of Birmingham Choir, 1963–; Oxford Bach Choir, 1977–; Leith Hill Musical Festival, 1977–80. Pres., RCO, 1982–84. Hon. Fellow, Birmingham Polytechnic, 1990. Hon. MMus Birmingham, 1987. *Recreations:* watching cricket, motoring. *Address:* St John's College, Cambridge CB2 1TP. *Club:* MCC.

ROBINSON, Sir Christopher Philipse, 8th Bt *cr* 1854, of Toronto; *b* 10 Nov. 1938; *s* of Christopher Robinson, QC (*d* 1974) (*g s* of 1st Bt) and of Neville Taylor, *d* of Rear-Adm. Walter Rockwell Gherardi, USN; *S* kinsman, Sir John Beverley Robinson, 7th Bt, 1988; *m* 1962, Barbara Judith, *d* of late Richard Duncan; two *s* (and one *s* decd). *Heir: s* Peter Duncan Robinson, *b* 31 July 1967.

ROBINSON, Mrs Clare; *see* Panter-Downes, M. P.

ROBINSON, Clifton Eugene Bancroft, CBE 1985 (OBE 1973); JP; a Deputy-Chairman, Commission for Racial Equality, 1977–85; *b* 5 Oct. 1926; *s* of Theodore Emanuel and Lafrance Robinson; *m* (marr. diss.); one *s* three *d*; *m* 1977, Margaret Ann Ennever. *Educ:* Kingston Technical Coll., Jamaica; Birmingham Univ.; Leicester Univ.; Lancaster Coll. of Educn. BA, DipEd. Served War, RAF, 1944–49. Teacher: Mellor Sch., Leicester, 1951–61; i/c Special Educn Unit, St Peter's Sch., Leicester, 1961–64; Dep. Headteacher, Charnwood Sch., Leicester, 1964–68; Headteacher: St Peter's Sch., Leicester, 1968–70; Uplands Sch., Leicester, 1970–77. A Vice-Pres., Internat. Friendship League; President: Leicester United Caribbean Assoc.; Roots Coll. JP Leicester, 1974. *Recreations:* music (mainly classical), walking; when there is time, gardening. *Address:* 80 Numa Court, Justin Close, Brentford, Middlesex TW8 8QF.

ROBINSON, (David) Duncan; Director, Yale Center for British Art, New Haven, Connecticut, Chief Executive, Paul Mellon Centre for Studies in British Art, London, and Adjunct Professor of the History of Art, Yale University, since 1981; Fellow, Berkeley College, Yale University, since 1981 (Acting Master 1986); *b* 27 June 1943; *s* of Tom and Ann Robinson; *m* 1967, Elizabeth Anne Sutton; one *s* two *d. Educ:* King Edward VI Sch., Macclesfield; Clare Coll., Cambridge (MA); Yale Univ. (Mellon Fellow, 1965–67; MA). Asst Keeper of Paintings and Drawings, 1970–76, Keeper, 1976–81, Fitzwilliam Museum, Cambridge; Fellow and Coll. Lectr, Clare Coll., Cambridge, 1975–81. Mem. Cttee of Management, and Chm., Exhibns Cttee, Kettle's Yard, Cambridge Univ., 1970–81. Member: Art Panel, Eastern Arts Assoc., 1973–81 (Chm., 1979–81); Arts Council of GB, 1981 (Mem., 1978–81, Vice-Chm., 1981, Art Panel); Assoc. of Art Mus. Dirs (USA), 1982–88; Bd of Managers, Lewis Walpole Library, Farmington Ct, USA, 1982–; Council of Management, The William Blake Trust, 1983–; Vis. Cttee, Dept of Paintings Conservation, Metropolitan Museum of Art, NY, 1984–; Walpole Soc., 1983– (Mem. Council, 1985–87); Art and Artifacts Indemnity Adv. Panel (USA), 1991–. Gov., Yale Univ. Press, 1987–; Trustee: Yale Univ. Press, London, 1990–; Charleston Trust (USA), 1990–. FRSA 1990. Organised Arts Council exhibitions: Stanley Spencer, 1975; William Nicholson, 1980. *Publications:* Companion Volume to the Kelmscott Chaucer, 1975, re-issued as Morris, Burne-Jones and the Kelmscott Chaucer, 1982; Stanley Spencer, 1979, rev. edn 1990; (with Stephen Wildman) Morris & Company in Cambridge, 1980; Town,

Country, Shore & Sea: English Watercolours from van Dyck to Paul Nash, 1982; catalogues; articles and reviews in Apollo, Burlington Magazine, etc. *Address:* 142 Huntington Street, New Haven, Conn 06511, USA. *T:* (203) 787 7199. *Clubs:* Athenæum; Century, Yale (NY); Mory's (New Haven).

ROBINSON, David Julien; Film Critic, The Times, since 1974; *b* 6 Aug. 1930; *s* of Edward Robinson and Dorothy Evelyn (*née* Overton). *Educ:* Lincoln Sch.; King's Coll., Cambridge (BA Hons). Associate Editor, Sight and Sound, and Editor, Monthly Film Bulletin, 1956–58; Programme Dir, NFT, 1959; Film Critic, Financial Times, 1959–74; Editor, Contrast, 1962–63. Vis. Prof. of Film, Westfield Coll., Univ. of London. Director: Garrett Robinson Co., 1987–88; The Davids Film Co., 1988–. Guest Dir, Edinburgh Film Fest., 1989–91. Films produced and directed: Hetty King — Performer, 1969; (Co-dir) Keeping Love Alive, 1987; (Co-dir) Sophisticated Lady, 1989. *Publications:* Hollywood in the Twenties, 1969; Buster Keaton, 1969; The Great Funnies, 1972; World Cinema, 1973, 2nd edn 1980 (US edn The History of World Cinema, 1974, 1980); Chaplin: the mirror of opinion, 1983; Chaplin: his life and art, 1985; (ed and trans.) Luis Buñuel (J. F. Aranda); (ed and trans.) Cinema in Revolution (anthology); (ed jtly) The Illustrated History of the Cinema, 1986. *Recreations:* collecting optical toys, model theatres. *Address:* 96–100 New Cavendish Street, W1M 7FA. *T:* 071–580 4959; 1 Winifreds Dale, Cavendish Road, Bath. *T:* Bath (0225) 420305.

ROBINSON, Derek, CBE 1979; Fellow of Magdalen College, Oxford, since 1969; Senior Research Officer, Oxford Institute of Economics and Statistics; *b* 9 Feb. 1932; *s* of Benjamin and Mary Robinson; *m* 1956, Jean Evelyn (*née* Lynch); one *s* one *d*. *Educ:* Barnsley Holgate Grammar Sch.; Ruskin Coll., Oxford; Lincoln Coll., Oxford. MA (Oxon), DipEcPolSci (Oxon). Civil Service, 1948–55. Sheffield Univ., 1959–60; Senior Research Officer, Oxford Inst. of Economics and Statistics, 1961–. Economic Adviser, Nat. Bd for Prices and Incomes, 1965–67; Sen. Economic Adviser, Dept of Employment and Productivity, 1968–70; Dep. Chm., Pay Bd, 1973–74; Chm., SSRC, 1975–78. Mem., British Library Bd, 1979–82. Visiting Professor: Cornell Univ., 1983; Univ. of Hawaii, 1983. Chairman: Oxfordshire Dist Manpower Cttee, 1980–83 (Oxf. and S Bucks, 1975–79); Cttee of Inquiry into the remuneration of members of local authorities, 1977; Chilterns Area Bd, Manpower Services Commn Special Programmes, 1978–79. Inter-regional Adviser on Wage Policy, ILO, 1986–88. *Publications:* Non-Wage Incomes and Prices Policy, 1966; Wage Drift, Fringe Benefits and Manpower Distribution, 1968; Workers' Negotiated Savings Plans for Capital Formation, 1970; (ed) Local Labour Markets and Wage Structures, 1970; Prices and Incomes Policy: the Austrian Experience (with H. Suppanz), 1972; Incomes Policy and Capital Sharing in Europe, 1973; (with J. Vincens) Research into Labour Market Behaviour, 1974; (with K. Mayhew *et al*) Pay Policies for the Future, 1983; Introduction to Economics, 1986; Monetarism and the Labour Market, 1986; Civil Service Pay in Africa, 1990; contributor to Bulletin of Oxford Univ. Inst. of Economics and Statistics; Industrial Relations Jl, etc. *Address:* 56 Lonsdale Road, Oxford. *T:* Oxford (0865) 52276. *Club:* Reform.

ROBINSON, Derek Anthony, DPhil; Head of Science Group (formerly Keeper, Department of Physical Sciences), Science Museum, London, since 1987; *b* 21 April 1942; *s* of late Charles Frederick Robinson and of Mary Margaret Robinson; *m* 1965, Susan Gibson; two *s*. *Educ:* Hymers Coll., Hull; The Queen's Coll., Oxford (BA 1963; MA, DPhil 1967). Post-doctoral Res. Fellow, Dept of Chemistry, Univ. of Reading, 1967–69; Mem. scientific staff, Molecular Pharmacology Unit of MRC, Cambridge, 1969–72; Sen. Asst in Res., Dept of Haematol Medicine, Cambridge Univ. Med. Sch., 1972–74; Science Museum: Asst Keeper I, Dept of Chem., 1974–77; Dep. Keeper (formerly Asst Keeper I), Wellcome Mus. of History of Medicine, and Sec. of Adv. Council, 1977–78; Keeper, Dept of Museum Services, 1978–87. Mem., British Nat. Cttee for History of Sci., Medicine and Technology, 1987–88; Mem., CGLI, 1984–; Dir, Bd, Mus. Documentation Assoc., 1989–. *Publications:* (contrib.) 2nd edn Acridines, ed R. M. Acheson, 1973; (contrib.) Vol. VI, The History of Technology, ed T. I. Williams, 1978; (contrib.) Cambridge General Encyclopaedia, ed D. Crystal, 1990; papers on heterocyclic chemistry, molecular pharmacol., and leukaemia chemotherapy, in Jl Chem. Soc., Brit. Jl Pharmacol., and Biochem. Trans. *Recreations:* cricket, junior rugby, travel, walking. *Address:* 3 Broadwater Avenue, Letchworth, Herts SG6 3HE. *T:* Letchworth (0462) 686961, (office) 071–938 8040.

ROBINSON, Most Rev. Donald William Bradley; *see* Sydney, Archbishop of.

ROBINSON, Duncan; *see* Robinson, David D.

ROBINSON, Prof. Sir (Edward) Austin (Gossage), Kt 1975; CMG 1947; OBE 1944; FBA 1955; Emeritus Professor of Economics, Cambridge University since 1966 (Professor, 1950–65); Fellow of Sidney Sussex College, Cambridge, since 1931; Secretary of Royal Economic Society, 1945–70; *b* 20 Nov. 1897; *s* of late Rev. Canon Albert Gossage Robinson; *m* 1926, Joan (*d* 1983), *d* of late Major-General Sir Frederick Maurice, KCMG, CB; two *d*. *Educ:* Marlborough College (Scholar); Christ's College, Cambridge (Scholar). BA 1921; MA 1923; RNAS and RAF (Pilot), 1917–19; Fellow of Corpus Christi Coll., Cambridge, 1923–26; Tutor to HH The Maharaja of Gwalior, 1926–28; University Lecturer, Cambridge, 1929–49; Asst Editor of Economic Journal, 1934–44, Joint Editor, 1944–70; Member of Economic Section, War Cabinet Office, 1939–42; Economic Adviser and Head of Programmes Division, Ministry of Production, 1942–45; Member of British Reparations Mission, Moscow and Berlin, 1945; Economic Adviser to Board of Trade, 1946; returned to Cambridge, Sept. 1946. Mem. of Economic Planning Staff, 1947–48; Treasurer of International Economic Association, 1950–59, President 1959–62; Mem. Council, DSIR, 1954–59; Dir of Economics, Min. of Power, 1967–68. Chairman: Council Nat. Inst. of Economic and Social Research, 1949–62; European Energy Advisory Commn, OEEC, 1957–60; Exec. Cttee, Overseas Develt Inst. *Publications:* The Structure of Competitive Industry, 1931; Monopoly, 1941; Economic Consequences of the Size of Nations, 1960; Economic Development of Africa South of the Sahara, 1964; Problems in Economic Development, 1965; The Economics of Education (with J. E. Vaizey), 1966; Backward Areas in Advanced Countries, 1969; Economic Development in South Asia, 1970; (ed jtly) The Economic Development of Bangladesh within a Socialist Framework, 1974; (ed jtly) Employment Policy in a Developing Country, 1983; contributor to: Modern Industry and the African, 1933; Lord Hailey's African Survey, 1938; articles in Economic Journal, etc. *Address:* Sidney Sussex College, Cambridge. *T:* Cambridge (0223) 357548. *Club:* Reform.

ROBINSON, Eric Embleton; Director, Lancashire Polytechnic (formerly Preston Polytechnic), 1982–90; *b* 12 March 1927; *s* of Cyril Robinson and Florence Mary Embleton. *Educ:* local authority schools, Nelson and Colne, Lancs; London Univ. (MSc). Teaching, Prescot Grammar Sch., 1948, Acton Tech. Coll., 1949–56, Brunel Coll., 1956–62, Enfield Coll., 1962–70; Dep. Dir, NE London Polytechnic, 1970–73; Principal, Bradford Coll., 1973–82. Pres., Assoc. of Teachers in Tech. Instns, 1962; Exec. Mem., Nat. Union of Teachers, 1961–67; Member: Burnham Cttees, 1961–67; Nat. Council for Training and Supply of Teachers, 1964–66; Minister's Working Party on Polytechnics, 1965–66; Equal Opportunities Commn, 1976–81; CNAA, 1976–82; UNESCO Nat. Commn, 1975–78. Vice Pres., Socialist Educn Assoc. Hon. Advr, Peking Inst. of Business; Hon. Vis. Prof., Wolverhampton Polytechnic; Hon. Fellow, Sheffield City Polytechnic, 1990. Hon. DEd CNAA, 1990. *Publications:* The New Polytechnics, 1968; numerous articles and papers. *Address:* 5 Millfield Road, Chorley, Lancs PR7 1RF. *T:* Chorley (0257) 262213. *Club:* Savile.

ROBINSON, (Francis) Alastair (Lavie); Executive Director, Barclays Bank, since 1990; *b* 19 Sept. 1937; *s* of Stephen and Patricia Robinson; *m* 1961, Lavinia Elizabeth Napier; two *d*. *Educ:* Eton. Nat Service, 4th/7th Royal Dragoon Guards, 1956–58 (2nd Lieut). Mercantile Credit: management trainee, 1959; Gen. Manager, 1971; Mem. Board, 1978; Chief Exec. Officer and Pres., Barclays American, USA, 1981; Regional Gen. Manager, Asia-Barclays International, 1984; Dir Personnel, Barclays Bank, 1987, Exec. Dir, UK Ops, 1990. *Recreations:* music, opera, gardening, fishing, shooting. *Address:* Easby House, Great Chesterford, Essex CB10 1PL. *T:* Saffron Walden (0799) 30473. *Clubs:* Cavalry and Guards, City of London.

ROBINSON, Geoffrey; *see* Robinson, A. G.

ROBINSON, Geoffrey; MP (Lab) Coventry North-West, since March 1976; *b* 25 May 1938; *s* of Robert Norman Robinson and Dorothy Jane Robinson (*née* Skelly); *m* 1967, Marie Elena Giorgio; one *s* one *d*. *Educ:* Emanuel School; Cambridge and Yale Univs. Labour Party Research Assistant, 1965–68; Senior Executive, Industrial Reorganisation Corporation, 1968–70; Financial Controller, British Leyland, 1971–72; Managing Director, Leyland Innocenti, Milan, 1972–73; Chief Exec., Jaguar Cars, Coventry, 1973–75; Chief Exec. (unpaid), Meriden Motor Cycle Workers' Co-op, 1978–80 (Dir, 1980–82). Opposition spokesman on science, 1982–83, on regional affairs and industry, 1983–87. Dir, W Midlands Enterprise Bd, 1980–84. *Recreations:* reading, architecture, gardens. *Address:* House of Commons, SW1A 0AA. *T:* 071–219 3000.

ROBINSON, Harold George Robert, OBE 1961; FRAeS; CEng, MIEE; Director-General Research (General), Ministry of Defence (Procurement Executive), and Assistant Chief Scientific Adviser (Research), Ministry of Defence, 1981–84, retired; Senior Consultant, General Technology Systems Ltd, since 1984; *b* 2 April 1924; *s* of Harold Arthur Robinson and Winifred Margaret (*née* Ballard); *m* 1955, Sonja (*née* Lapthorn); two *s*. *Educ:* Portsmouth Northern Grammar Sch.; Imperial Coll., London Univ.; California Inst. of Technology. WhSch 1944; BSc 1948; FCGI 1970. Joined RAE as Scientific Officer, 1948; Head of Satellite Launcher Div., Space Dept, RAE, 1961; Head of Avionics Dept, RAE, 1965–69; Head of Research Planning Div., Min. of Technology, 1969–71; Dir Gen., Aerospace Assessment and Res., DTI, 1971–74; Under-Sec., Space and Air Res., DoI, 1974–76; a Dep. Dir, RAE, 1976–81, Acting Dir, 1981. Pres., Astronautics Commn, FAI, 1969–70 (Paul Tissandier Diploma, 1971); FRAeS 1981 (Bronze Medal, 1961). Pres., Whitworth Soc., 1982–83. *Publications:* various scientific and technical papers, contribs to books, primarily on rocket and space research. *Recreations:* bowls, photography. *Address:* 39 Crosby Hill Drive, Camberley, Surrey. *T:* Camberley (0276) 23771.

ROBINSON, Jancis Mary, (Mrs N. L. Lander), MW; wine writer and broadcaster; *b* 22 April 1950; *d* of Thomas Edward Robinson and Ann Sheelagh Margaret Robinson (*née* Conacher); *m* 1981, Nicholas Laurence Lander; one *s* two *d*. *Educ:* Carlisle and County High Sch. for Girls; St Anne's Coll., Oxford (MA). Editor, Wine & Spirit, 1976–80; Founder and Editor, Drinker's Digest (now Which? Wine Monthly), 1977–82; Editor, Which? Wine Guide, 1980–82; Sunday Times Wine Corresp., 1980–86; Evening Standard Wine Corresp., 1987–88; Financial Times Wine Columnist, 1989–; freelance journalism, particularly on wine, food and people, 1980–; freelance television and radio broadcasting, on various subjects, 1983–; Writer/Presenter: The Wine Programme, 1983 (Glenfiddich Trophy), 1985, 1987; Jancis Robinson Meets . . ., 1987; Matters of Taste, 1989, 1991; wine judging and lecturing, 1983–. *Publications:* The Wine Book, 1979, rev. edn 1983; The Great Wine Book, 1982 (Glenfiddich Award); Masterglass, 1983, rev. edn 1987; How to Choose and Enjoy Wine, 1984; Vines, Grapes and Wines, 1986 (André Simon Meml Prize, Wine Guild Award, Clicquot Book of the Year); Jancis Robinson's Adventures with Food and Wine, 1987; Jancis Robinson on the Demon Drink, 1988; Vintage Timecharts, 1989. *Recreations:* wine, food and words. *Address:* c/o A. P. Watt, 20 John Street, WC1N 2DR.

ROBINSON, John Armstrong, CMG 1969; HM Diplomatic Service, retired; Ambassador to Israel, 1980–81; *b* 18 Dec. 1925; *m* 1952, Marianne Berger; one *s* one *d*. HM Forces, 1944–46; Foreign Office, 1949–50; Second Secretary, Delhi, 1950–52; Foreign Office, 1952–53; Helsinki, 1953–56; Second later First Secretary, Paris, 1956–58; Foreign Office, 1958–61; First Secretary in UK Delegation to European Communities, Brussels, 1962–67; Counsellor, Foreign Office, 1967; Head of European Economic Integration Dept, FCO, 1968–70; appointed Member of team of nine officials for negotiations on British entry into the Common Market, Brussels, 1970–71; Asst Under-Sec. of State, FCO, 1971–73; Ambassador to Algeria, 1974–77; Minister, Washington, 1977–80. *Address:* La Sirgarié, St Martin Laguépie, 81170 Cordes, Tarn, France.

ROBINSON, Sir John (James Michael Laud), 11th Bt *cr* 1660; DL; *b* 19 Jan. 1943; *s* of Michael Frederick Laud Robinson (*d* 1971) and Elizabeth (*née* Bridge); *S* grandfather, 1975; *m* 1968, Gayle Elizabeth (*née* Keyes); two *s* one *d*. *Educ:* Eton; Trinity Coll., Dublin (MA, Economics and Political Science). Chartered Financial Analyst. Chm., St Andrews Hosp., Northampton, 1984–. DL Northants, 1984. *Heir:* *s* Mark Christopher Michael Villiers Robinson, *b* 23 April 1972. *Address:* Cranford Hall, Cranford, Kettering, Northants.

ROBINSON, Rev. Canon Joseph, MTh, FKC; Master of the Temple since 1980; *b* 23 Feb. 1927; *er s* of Thomas and Maggie Robinson; *m* 1953, Anne Antrobus; two *s* two *d*. *Educ:* Upholland Grammar Sch., Lancs; King's Coll., London. BD (1st cl. Hons); AKC (1st cl.) 1951; MTh 1958; FKC 1973. Deacon, 1952; Priest, 1953; Curate, All Hallows, Tottenham, 1952–55; Minor Canon of St Paul's Cathedral, 1956–68; Sacrist, 1958–68; Lectr in Hebrew and Old Testament Studies, King's Coll., London, 1959–68; Canon Residentiary, Canterbury Cathedral, 1968–80, now Canon Emeritus; Librarian, 1968–73; Treasurer, 1972–80; Exam. Chaplain to Archbishop of Canterbury, 1968–80. Golden Lectr, 1963; St Antholin Lectr, 1964–67. Chaplain, Worshipful Co. of Cutlers, 1963–; Sub Chaplain, Order of St John of Jerusalem, 1965–. *Publications:* The Cambridge Bible Commentary on 1 Kings, 1972, 2 Kings, 1976; articles in: Church Quarterly Review, Expository Times, Church Times; many reviews in various jls. *Recreations:* reading, gardening. *Address:* The Master's House, The Temple, EC4Y 7BB. *T:* 071–353 8559. *Club:* Athenæum.

ROBINSON, Kathleen Marian, (Mrs Vincent F. Sherry; Kathleen M. Sherry); FRCS, FRCOG, MD; retired; Hon. Obstetrician, and Hon. Gynæcologist, Royal Free Hospital; Hon. Obstetrician, Queen Charlotte's Hospital; *b* 25 May 1911; *d* of late James Robinson and Ruth Robinson (*née* Edmeston); *m* 1946, Vincent Francis Sherry; one *s* one *d* (and one *d* decd). *Educ:* Penrhos College, Colwyn Bay; Royal Free Hospital School of Medicine, London University. MB, BS, 1936; MRCS, LRCP 1936; MD London 1940;

FRCS 1940; MRCOG 1941; FRCOG 1953. House Surgeon: Royal Free Hospital; Samaritan Hospital, Royal Marsden Hospital, Queen Charlotte's Hospital. Resident Obstetrician, Queen Charlotte's Hospital. Recognised Teacher of the London University. FRSM; FRHS. *Publications:* contributor to Queen Charlotte's Text Book of Obstetrics, also to Practical Motherhood and Parentcraft. *Recreations:* gardening, cooking, travel. *Address:* 17 Herondale Avenue, SW18 3JN. *T:* 081–874 8588.

ROBINSON, Keith; *see* Robinson, L. K.

ROBINSON, Rt. Hon. Sir Kenneth, Kt 1983; PC 1964; Hon. DLitt; FCIT; Chairman, Arts Council of Great Britain, 1977–82; *b* Warrington, Lancs, 19 March 1911; *s* of late Clarence Robinson, MRCS, LRCP; *m* 1941, Helen Elizabeth Edwards; one *d. Educ:* Oundle Sch. Insurance Broker at Lloyd's, 1927–40. Served War of 1939–45, RN 1941–46; Ord. Seaman, 1941; commissioned, 1942; Lieut-Comdr RNVR, 1944; served Home Fleet, Mediterranean, Far East and Pacific. Company Secretary, 1946–49. MP (Lab) St Pancras N, 1949–70; Asst Whip (unpaid), 1950–51, an Opposition Whip, 1951–54; Minister of Health, 1964–68; Minister for Planning and Land, Min. of Housing and Local Govt, 1968–69. Dir, Social Policy, 1970–72, Man. Dir (Personnel and Social Policy Div.), 1972–74, British Steel Corp.; Chm., LTE, 1975–78. Chairman: English National Opera, 1972–77; Young Concert Artists Trust, 1983–90; Carnegie Council Arts and Disabled People, 1985–87; Jt Treas., RSA, 1983–88. Trustee, Imperial War Mus., 1978–84. Hon. FRCGP; Hon. MRCP 1989; Hon. DLitt Liverpool, 1980. *Publications:* Wilkie Collins, a Biography, 1951; Policy for Mental Health, 1958; Patterns of Care, 1961; Look at Parliament, 1962. *Recreations:* looking at paintings, reading, listening to music. *Address:* 12 Grove Terrace, NW5.

ROBINSON, Kenneth Ernest, CBE 1971; MA, FRHistS; *b* 9 March 1914; *o s* of late Ernest and Isabel Robinson, Plumstead, Kent; *m* 1938, Stephanie, *o d* of late William Wilson, Westminster; one *s* one *d. Educ:* Monoux Grammar School, Walthamstow; Hertford College, Oxford (Scholar, 1st Cl. PPE; 1st Cl. Mod. Hist.; Beit Senior Schol. in Colonial History); London School of Economics. Colonial Office, 1936; Asst Sec. 1946; resigned 1948. Fellow of Nuffield Coll. (Hon. Fellow, 1984) and Reader in Commonwealth Govt, Oxford, 1948–57; Dir, Inst. of Commonwealth Studies and Prof. of Commonwealth Affairs, Univ. of London, 1957–65 (Hon. Life Mem., 1980–); Vice-Chancellor, Univ. of Hong Kong, 1965–72; Hallsworth Res. Fellow, Univ. of Manchester, 1972–74; Dir, Commonwealth Studies Resources Survey, Univ. of London, 1974–76. Leverhulme Res. Fellow, 1952–53; Vis. Lectr, Sch. of Advanced Internat. Studies, Johns Hopkins Univ., 1954; Carnegie Travel Grant, East, Central and S Africa, 1960; Reid Lectr, Acadia Univ., 1963; Vis. Prof., Duke Univ., NC, 1963; Callander Lectr, Aberdeen, 1979. Editor, Jl of Commonwealth Political Studies, 1961–65; Special Commonwealth Award, ODM, 1965. Member: (part-time) Directing Staff, Civil Service Selection Bd, 1951–56, Assessor Panel, 1973–77; Colonial Economic Res. Cttee, 1949–62; Colonial SSRC, 1958–62; Inter-Univ. Council for Higher Educn Overseas, 1973–79; Mem. Council: Overseas Develt Inst. 1960–65; RIIA, 1962–65; Internat. African Inst., 1960–65; African Studies Assoc., UK, 1963–65, 1978–81; ACU, 1967–68; Hong Kong Management Assoc., 1965–72; Chinese Univ. of Hong Kong, 1965–72; Univ. of Cape Coast, 1972–74; Royal Commonwealth Soc., 1974–87 (Vice Pres., 1984–); Royal African Soc., 1983–89 (Pres., 1989–); Life Mem. Ct, Univ. of Hong Kong, 1972. Governor, LSE, 1959–65. Corresp. Mem., Académie des Sciences d'Outre-Mer, Paris. Hon. LLD Chinese Univ. of Hong Kong, 1969; Hon. DLitt, Univ. of Hong Kong, 1972; DUniv Open, 1978. JP Hong Kong, 1967–72. *Publications:* (with W. J. M. Mackenzie) Five Elections in Africa, 1960; (with A. F. Madden) Essays in Imperial Government presented to Margery Perham, 1963; The Dilemmas of Trusteeship, 1965; (with W. B. Hamilton & C. D. Goodwin) A Decade of the Commonwealth 1955–64 (USA), 1966. Contrib. to Africa Today (USA), 1955; Africa in the Modern World (USA), 1955; University Cooperation and Asian Development (USA), 1967; L'Europe du XIXe et du XXe Siècle, Vol. 7 (Italy), 1968; Experts in Africa, 1980; Perspectives on Imperialism and Decolonisation, 1984; papers in learned jls. *Address:* The Old Rectory, Church Westcote, Oxon. *T:* Shipton under Wychwood (0993) 830586. *Clubs:* Commonwealth Trust, United Oxford & Cambridge University, Lansdowne; Hong Kong.

ROBINSON, Lee Fisher, CEng; Chief Executive and Deputy Chairman, Turriff Construction Corporation Ltd, since 1970; Chairman, Biotechna Ltd, since 1982; Consultant, International Management Consultants, since 1972; Director and Vice-President, RTL SA, since 1977; Director and Chief Executive, RTR SA, since 1977; Director and Chairman, Ingeco Laing Ltd (UK), since 1977; *b* 17 July 1923; *m* 1st, 1944; three *d*; 2nd, 1976, June Edna Hopkins. *Educ:* Howard Sch.; Cardiff Tech. College. MICE; ACIArb. Royal Engrs, Sappers and Miners, IE, 1942–45. Turriff Const. Corp. Ltd, HBM (BCC), 1963; Man. Dir, Power Gas Corp. Ltd, 1964; Director: Davy-Ashmore Ltd, 1970; Combustion Systems (NRDC), 1972– (Chm., 1978); Redwood Internat. (UK) Ltd, 1972; Altech SA, 1976–; Protech SA, 1976–; Altech of Canada, 1976–; Danks Gowerton, 1976–; Hewlee Ltd, 1976–; BCS Ltd, 1976–; Charterhouse Strategic Development Ltd, 1976–80 (Gp Indust. Adviser, Charterhouse Gp); Altech (Canada) Ltd, 1976–; Ingeco Laing SA, 1977–; RTR (Oil Sands) Alberta, 1977–; RTR Canada Ltd, 1977–; SPO Minerals Co. Ltd, 1980–81; Thalassa (North Sea) Ltd, 1980–; Marcent Natural Resources Ltd (Man. Dir), 1980–; WGI Engineering Ltd, 1980–; Hydromet Mineral Co., 1983–; Solvex Corp., 1988–; Chairman: Graesser (Contractors) Ltd; HMC Technology Ltd. Chm., Warren Spring Adv. Bd, 1969–72; Mem. Adv. Council for Technology, 1968–69. *Publications:* Cost and Financing of Fertiliser Projects in India, 1967; various articles. *Recreations:* badminton, sailing. *Address:* Flat 3, Athenaeum Hall, Vale-of-Health, NW3 1AP. *Club:* Wig and Pen.

ROBINSON, (Leonard) Keith, CBE 1981; DL; management consultant, 1985–87; County Chief Executive, Hampshire County Council, 1973–85; Clerk of Lieutenancy, 1973–85; *b* 2 July 1920; *m* 1948, Susan May Tomkinson; two *s* two *d. Educ:* Queen Elizabeth's Grammar Sch., Blackburn; Victoria Univ. of Manchester (LLB). Solicitor. RAFVR, 1940–46 (Navigator, Sqdn-Ldr). Asst Solicitor, City and County of Bristol, 1948–55; Dep. Town Clerk, Birkenhead Co. Borough Council, 1955–66; Town Clerk, Stoke-on-Trent City Council, 1966–73. Association of County Councils: Mem., Officers Adv. Gp, 1974–83 (Chm., 1977–82); Adviser, Policy Cttee, 1975–82; Adviser, Local Govt Finance Cttee, 1976–85; Chm., Assoc. of County Chief Execs, 1975–77. Member: W Mids Econ. Planning Council, 1967–73; Keele Univ. Council, 1968–73; Central Cttee for Reclamation of Derelict Land, 1971–74; Quality Assce Council, BSI, 1973–77; Job Creation Programme Action Cttee for London and SE, 1976–77; District Manpower Cttee, 1980–83; Adv. Council for Energy Conservation, 1982–84; Local Authorities' Mutual Investment Trust, 1982–83; Hillier Arboretum Management Cttee, 1985– (Sec., 1977–85); Southern Arts, 1985–; Exec. Cttee, Hampshire Develt Assoc., 1985–91; Vice-Chm., Nuffield Theatre Bd, 1985–; Asst Comr, Local Govt Boundary Commn, 1986–. Trustee, New Theatre Royal (Portsmouth) Ltd, 1976–; Mem. Exec. Cttee, Hampshire Gardens Trust, 1985–; Dir, Salisbury Playhouse, 1979–. DL Hants, 1985. Knight, Hon. Soc. of Knights of the Round Table, 1984–. *Publications:* contrib. local govt and legal jls. *Recreations:* fly-fishing, theatre, photography, gardening. *Address:* Bransbury Mill Cottage, Bransbury, Barton Stacey, Winchester, Hants SO21 3QJ. *Club:* MCC.

ROBINSON, Lloyd; *see* Robinson, T. L.

ROBINSON, Group Captain Marcus, CB 1956; AFC 1941 and Bar 1944; AE 1942; DL; Chairman, Robinson, Dunn & Co. Ltd and subsidiary companies, 1966–77, retired; *b* 27 May 1912; *s* of Wilson and Eileen Robinson; *m* 1st, 1941, Mrs Mary Playfair (marr. diss. 1951); 2nd, 1953, Mrs Joan E. G. O. Weatherlake (*née* Carter); one *s* one *d. Educ:* Rossall. Commissioned AAF, 602 Sqdn, 1934; Squadron Ldr, 1940, commanding 616 Squadron; Wing Comdr, 1942; Group Capt., 1945; re-formed 602 Squadron, 1946; Member Air Advisory Council, Air Ministry, 1952–56; Chairman Glasgow TA and AFA, 1953–56; Chairman Glasgow Rating Valuation Appeals Cttee, 1963–74 (Dep. Chm., 1958–63). A Vice-Pres., Earl Haig Fund, Scotland, 1978– (Chm., 1974–78). DL Glasgow, 1953. Silver Jubilee Medal, 1977. *Recreations:* ski-ing, sailing. *Address:* Rockfort, Helensburgh, Dunbartonshire G84 7BA. *Club:* Royal Northern and Clyde Yacht (Rhu).

ROBINSON, Mark Noel Foster; Director, Leopold Joseph & Sons Ltd, since 1988 (Consultant, since 1987); *b* 26 Dec. 1946; *s* of late John Foster Robinson, CBE, TD and Margaret Eve Hannah Paterson; *m* 1982, Vivien Radclyffe (*née* Pilkington); one *s* one *d. Educ:* Harrow School; Christ Church, Oxford. MA Hons Modern History. Called to the Bar, Middle Temple, 1975. Research Assistant to Patrick Cormack, 1970–71; Special Asst to US Congressman Hon. F. Bradford Morse, 1971–72; Special Asst to Chief of UN Emergency Operation in Bangladesh, 1972–73; Second Officer, Exec. Office, UN Secretary-General, 1974–77; Asst Dir, Commonwealth Secretariat, 1977–83. Contested (C) Newport West, 1987; Prospective Parly Candidate (C) Somerton and Frome, 1989–. MP (C) Newport West, 1983–87. PPS to Sec. of State for Wales, 1984–85; Parly Under Sec. of State, Welsh Office, 1985–87. Mem., Foreign Affairs Select Cttee, 1983–84. Hon. Sec., UN Parly Gp, 1983–85. Mem., Commonwealth Develt Corp., 1988–. Fellow, Industry and Parlt Trust, 1985. Member: RUSI, 1984; RIIA, 1984. FBIM 1983; FRSA 1990. *Recreations:* include the countryside and fishing. *Address:* 33 Clarendon Road, W11 4JB. *Club:* Travellers'.

ROBINSON, Mary; President of Ireland, since 1990; *b* 21 May 1944; *d* of Aubrey and Tessa Bourke; *m* 1970, Nicholas Robinson; two *s* one *d. Educ:* Trinity Coll. Dublin (BA; LLB 1967); Harvard Law Sch. (LLM). Called to the Bar, King's Inn, Dublin, 1967, Middle Temple, 1973 (Hon. Bencher, 1991); SC 1980. Reid Prof. of Constitutional and Criminal Law, TCD, 1969–75. Mem., Irish Senate, 1969–89 (Chm., Social Affairs Sub-Cttee, 1977–87, Chm., Legal Affairs Cttee, 1987–89, Parly Jt Cttee). Former Member: Adv. Bd, Common Market Law Review; Internat. Commn of Jurists; European Air Law Assoc. Pres., Cherish, 1973–90. *Address:* Aras an Uachtaráin, Phoenix Park, Dublin 8, Ireland.

ROBINSON, Air Vice-Marshal Michael Maurice Jeffries, CB 1982; *b* 11 Feb. 1927; *s* of Dr Maurice Robinson and Muriel (*née* Jeffries); *m* 1952, Drusilla Dallas Bush; one *s* two *d. Educ:* King's Sch., Bruton; Queen's Coll., Oxford; RAF Coll., Cranwell. psa 1961, jssc 1965. Commnd, 1948; 45 Sqdn, Malaya, 1948–51; CFS, 1953–55; OC 100 Sqdn, 1962–64; Comd, RAF Lossiemouth, 1972–74; Asst Comdt, RAF Coll., Cranwell, 1974–77; SASO No 1 Gp, 1977–79; Dir Gen. of Organisation (RAF), 1979–82, retd. Wing Comdr 1961, Gp Captain 1970, Air Cdre 1976, Air Vice-Marshal 1980. Sec. (Welfare), RAF Benevolent Fund, 1982–87. Chairman: Trustees, Housing Assoc., Officers' Families; SSAFA, Somerset. Governor: King's Sch., Bruton, 1980–; Duke of Kent Sch. (RAF Benevolent Fund), 1982–; Gordon's Sch., 1986–. *Recreations:* golf, gardening, going to the opera. *Address:* Midland Bank, 1 Market Place, Wells, Somerset BA5 2RN. *Club:* Royal Air Force.

ROBINSON, Moureen Ann, (Mrs Peter Robinson); Director of Policy and Planning Benefits Agency, Department of Social Security, since 1990; *d* of William and Winifred Flatley; *m* 1961, Peter Crawford Robinson. DHSS, 1969–74; Central Policy Review Staff, 1974–77; nurses and midwives pay, educn and professional matters, 1981–85; liaison with Health Authorities, NHS planning and review, 1985–86; social security operations, 1986–. *Recreations:* walking, fine wine, bridge, fun tennis and badminton. *Address:* 1 Heathfield Road, Maidstone, Kent; 29 Upper Berkeley Street, W1H 7PG.

ROBINSON, Ven. Neil; Archdeacon of Suffolk, since 1987; *b* 28 Feb. 1929; *s* of James and Alice Robinson; *m* 1956, Kathlyn Williams; two *s* two *d. Educ:* Penistone Grammar School; Univ. of Durham (BA, DipTh). Curate of Holy Trinity Church, Hull, 1954–58; Vicar of St Thomas, South Wigston, Leicester, 1958–69; Rector and RD of Market Bosworth, Leicester, 1969–83; Residentiary Canon of Worcester Cathedral, 1983–87. *Recreation:* hill walking. *Address:* 38 Saxmundham Road, Aldeburgh, Suffolk IP15 5JE. *T:* Aldeburgh (0728) 454034.

ROBINSON, Sir Niall B. L.; *see* Lynch-Robinson.

ROBINSON, Oliver John; Editor, Good Housekeeping, 1947–65, Editor-in-Chief, 1965–67; *b* 7 April 1908; *s* of late W. Heath and Josephine Constance Robinson; *m* 1933, Evelyn Anne Laidler. *Educ:* Cranleigh Sch. Art Editor, Good Housekeeping, 1930; Art Editor, Nash's, 1933. Temporary commission, Queen's Royal Regt, 1941; Camouflage Development and Training Centre, 1942; Staff Officer, War Office, 1944. *Address:* 92 Charlbert Court, Eamont Street, NW8 7DA. *T:* 071–722 0723. *Club:* Savage.

ROBINSON, Oswald Horsley, CMG 1983; OBE 1977; HM Diplomatic Service, retired; Director, RCC Pilotage Foundation, since 1985; *b* 24 Aug. 1926; *s* of Sir Edward Stanley Gotch Robinson, CBE, FSA, FBA, and Pamela, *d* of Sir Victor Horsley, CB, FRS; *m* 1954, Helena Faith, *d* of Dr F. R. Seymour; two *s* one *d. Educ:* Bedales Sch.; King's Coll., Cambridge. Served RE, 1943–48. Joined FO, 1951; served: Rangoon and Maymyo, 1954; FO, 1958; Mexico and Guatemala, 1961; Quito and Bogotá, 1963; FO (later FCO), 1965; Georgetown, Guyana, 1973; Bangkok, 1976; FCO, 1979–84. *Publications:* (ed) Atlantic Spain and Portugal, 1988; (ed) Ports and Anchorages of the Antilles, 1991; (ed) North Africa, 1991. *Recreation:* sailing. *Clubs:* Royal Cruising; Ocean Cruising; West Mersea Yacht.

ROBINSON, Dr Patrick William, (Bill); Director, Institute for Fiscal Studies, since 1986; Economic Columnist, The Independent, since 1989; *b* 6 Jan. 1943; *s* of Harold Desmond Robinson and Joyce Grover; *m* 1966, Heather Jackson; two *s* one *d. Educ:* Bryanston Sch.; St Edmund Hall, Oxford; DPhil Sussex 1969; MSc LSE 1971. Economic Asst, 10 Downing Street, 1969–70; Cabinet Office, 1970–71; Economic Adviser, HM Treasury, 1971–74; Head of Div., European Commn, 1974–78; Sen. Res. Fellow, London Business Sch., 1979–86; Adviser, Treasury and Civil Service Cttee, 1981–86; Special Adviser to the Chancellor, 1991–. Mem., Retail Prices Index Adv. Cttee, 1988–. Editor: Exchange Rate Outlook, LBS, 1979–86; Economic Outlook, LBS, 1980–86; IFS Green Budget, 1987–. *Publications:* Medium Term Exchange Rate Guidelines for Business Planning, 1983; numerous articles. *Recreations:* bassoon playing, opera, ski-ing, sailboarding. *Address:* Institute for Fiscal Studies, 7 Ridgmount Street, WC1E 7AE. *T:* 071–636 3784.

ROBINSON, Peter; Director, Tootal Ltd, 1973–91; *b* 18 Jan. 1922; *s* of Harold Robinson and Jane Elizabeth Robinson; *m* Lesley Anne, step-*d* of Major J. M. May, TD; two *s* two *d. Educ:* Prince Henry's Sch., Otley; Leeds Coll. of Technology (Diploma in Printing). Mem., Inst. of Printing; CBIM. Management Trainee, 1940–41; flying duties, RAFVR, 1942–46; Leeds Coll. of Technol., 1946–49; Asst Manager, Robinson & Sons Ltd, Chesterfield, 1949–53; Works Dir and Man. Dir, Taylowe Ltd, 1953–62; Director: Hazell Sun, 1964; British Printing Corp., 1966–81, Man. Dir 1969–75; Chm. and Chief Exec., BPC Ltd (formerly British Printing Corp.), 1976–81. Formerly Council Mem., PIRA. *Recreations:* military history, cricket, golf. *Address:* 20 Links Road, Flackwell Heath, High Wycombe, Bucks HP10 9LY.

ROBINSON, Peter Damian, CB 1983; Deputy Secretary, Lord Chancellor's Department, 1980–86; *b* 11 July 1926; *s* of late John Robinson and Jill Clegg (*née* Easten); *m* 1st, 1956, Mary Katinka Bonner (*d* 1978), Peterborough; two *d*; 2nd, 1985, Mrs Sheila Suzanne Gibbins (*née* Guille). *Educ:* Corby Sch., Sunderland; Lincoln Coll., Oxford. MA. Royal Marine Commandos, 1944–46. Called to Bar, Middle Temple, 1951; practised common law, 1952–59; Clerk of Assize, NE Circuit, 1959–70; Administrator, NE Circuit, 1970–74; Circuit Administrator, SE Circuit, 1974–80; Dep. Clerk of the Crown in Chancery, Lord Chancellor's Dept, 1982–86. Advr on Hong Kong Judiciary, 1986. Member, Home Office Departmental Cttee on Legal Aid in Criminal Proceedings (the Widgery Cttee), 1964–66; Chm., Interdeptl Cttee on Conciliation, 1982–83. *Recreations:* reading, the countryside, world travel, photography. *Address:* 15 Birklands Park, St Albans AL1 1TS. *Club:* Athenæum.

ROBINSON, Peter David; MP (DemU) Belfast East, since 1979 (resigned seat Dec. 1985 in protest against Anglo-Irish Agreement; re-elected Jan. 1986); *b* 29 Dec. 1948; *s* of David McCrea Robinson and Sheliah Robinson; *m* 1970, Iris Collins; two *s* one *d*. *Educ:* Annadale Grammar School; Castlereagh Further Education College. Gen. Secretary, Ulster Democratic Unionist Party, 1975–79, Dep. Leader, 1980–87. Mem. (DemU) Belfast E, NI Assembly, 1982–86; Member, Castlereagh Borough Council, 1977; Deputy Mayor, 1978; Mayor of Castlereagh, 1986. *Publications:* (jtly) Ulster—the facts, 1982; booklets: The North Answers Back, 1970; Capital Punishment for Capital Crime, 1978; Self Inflicted, 1981; Ulster in Peril, 1981; Savagery and Suffering, 1981; Their Cry Was "No Surrender", 1989. *Address:* 51 Gransha Road, Dundonald, Northern Ireland.

ROBINSON, Prof. Peter Michael; Professor of Econometrics, London School of Economics and Political Science, since 1984; *b* 20 April 1947; *s* of Maurice Allan Robinson and Brenda Margaret (*née* Ponsford); *m* 1981, Wendy Rhea Brandmark; one *d*. *Educ:* Brockenhurst Grammar Sch.; University Coll. London (BSc); London School of Economics (MSc); Australian National Univ. (PhD). Lectr, LSE, 1969–70; Asst Prof. 1973–77, Associate Prof. 1977–79, Harvard Univ.; Associate Prof., Univ. of British Columbia, 1979–80; Prof., Univ. of Surrey, 1980–84. Fellow, Econometric Soc., 1989. Co-Editor, Econometrica, 1991–. *Publications:* articles in books, and in learned jls, incl. Econometrica, Annals of Statistics. *Recreation:* walking. *Address:* Department of Economics, London School of Economics and Political Science, Houghton Street, WC2A 2AE. *T:* 071–405 7686.

ROBINSON, Philip; Director of Finance, City of Bradford Metropolitan Council, since 1987; *b* 2 March 1949; *s* of late Clifford Robinson and of Vera Robinson; *m* 1974, Irene Langdale. *Educ:* Grange Grammar Sch., Bradford. IPFA, IRRV. Principal Accountant 1982, Asst Dir of Finance 1985, City of Bradford Metropolitan Council. *Recreations:* sport, music, live theatre. *Address:* City of Bradford Metropolitan Council, Directorate of Finance, Britannia House, Hall Ings, Bradford BD1 1HX. *T:* Bradford (0274) 752700.

ROBINSON, Philip Henry; Chairman, Sunbury Investment Co. Ltd, since 1985; *b* 4 Jan. 1926; *s* of Arthur Robinson and Frances M. Robinson; *m* 1st, 1959, Helen Wharton (marr. diss. 1979); one *s* one *d*; 2nd, 1985, Mrs A. L. D. Baring; two step *s*. *Educ:* Lincoln Sch.; Jesus Coll., Cambridge (Exhibr, MA); Sch. of Oriental and African Studies, London Univ.; NY Univ. Graduate Sch. of Business Admin. Member, Gray's Inn. Royal Navy, 1944–47; N. M. Rothschild & Sons, 1950–54; Actg Sec., British Newfoundland Corp., Montreal, 1954–56; Asst Vice-Pres., J. Henry Schroder Banking Corp., New York, 1956–61; J. Henry Schroder Wagg & Co. Ltd, 1961; Director: J. Henry Schroder Wagg & Co. Ltd, 1966–85; Siemens Ltd, 1967–86; Schroders & Chartered Ltd Hong Kong, 1971–85; Exec. Vice-Pres., Schroder International Ltd, 1977–85 (Dir, 1973–85); Chairman: Schroder Leasing Ltd, 1979–85; Berkertex Hldgs Ltd, 1987–88; Dir, Standard Chartered PLC, 1986–91 (Chm., Audit Cttee, 1989–91). Managing Trustee, Municipal Mutual Insurance Ltd, 1977–. Mem., Nat. Coal Board, 1973–77. Hon. Treasurer, Nat. Council for One Parent Families, 1977–79. *Publications:* contrib. Investor's Chronicle. *Recreations:* music, tennis. *Address:* Stone Hall, Great Mongeham, Deal, Kent. *Club:* Brooks's.

See also A. G. Robinson.

ROBINSON, Hon. Raymond; *see* Robinson, Hon. A. N. R.

ROBINSON, Robert Henry; writer and broadcaster; *b* 17 Dec. 1927; *o s* of Ernest Redfern Robinson and Johanna Hogan; *m* 1958, Josephine Mary Richard; one *s* two *d*. *Educ:* Raynes Park Grammar Sch.; Exeter Coll., Oxford (MA). Editor of Isis, 1950. TV columnist, Sunday Chronicle, 1952; film and theatre columnist, Sunday Graphic, and radio critic, Sunday Times, 1956; editor Atticus, Sunday Times, 1960; weekly column, Private View, Sunday Times, 1962; film critic, Sunday Telegraph, 1965. Writer and presenter of TV programmes: Picture Parade, 1959; Points of View, 1961; Divided We Stand, 1964; The Look of the Week, 1966; Reason to Believe?, The Fifties, 1969; Chm., Call My Bluff, Ask The Family, 1967; The Book Programme, Vital Statistics, 1974; Word for Word, 1978; The Book Game, 1983 and 1985; Behind The Headlines, 1989; films for TV: Robinson's Travels - the Pioneer Trail West, 1977; B. Traven: a mystery solved, 1978; From Shepherd's Bush to Simla, 1979; Robinson Cruising, 1981; The Auden Landscape, 1982; Robinson Country, 1983, 1987; In Trust—Houses and Heritage, 1986; The Magic Rectangle, 1986; presenter of: BBC radio current affairs programme Today, 1971–74; Chm., Brain of Britain, 1973–; Chm., Stop the Week, 1974–; Ad Lib, 1989–. Mem., Kingman Cttee on the teaching of the English Language, 1987–88. Pres., Johnson Soc. of Lichfield, 1982. Radio Personality of the Year: Radio Industries Club, 1973; Variety Club of GB, 1980. *Publications:* (ed) Poetry from Oxford, 1951; Landscape with Dead Dons, 1956; Inside Robert Robinson (essays), 1965; (contrib.) To Nevill Coghill from Friends, 1966; The Conspiracy, 1968; The Dog Chairman, 1982; (ed) The Everyman Book of Light Verse, 1984; Bad Dreams, 1989; Prescriptions of a Pox Doctor's Clerk, 1990; contrib. The Times, Punch, Listener, etc. *Address:* 16 Cheyne Row, SW3; Laurel Cottage, Buckland St Mary, Somerset. *Club:* Garrick.

ROBINSON, Prof. Roger James, FRCP; Professor of Paediatrics, United Medical and Dental Schools of Guy's and St Thomas's Hospitals (formerly Guy's Hospital Medical School), University of London, 1975–90, now Emeritus; *b* 17 May 1932; *s* of Albert Edward and Leonora Sarah Robinson; *m* 1962, Jane Hippisley Packham; two *s* one *d*. *Educ:* Poole Grammar Sch.; Balliol Coll., Oxford (Brackenbury schol.; MA, DPhil, BM, BCh). Lectr of Christ Church, Oxford, 1953; appts at Radcliffe Infirmary, Oxford, National Hosp., Queen Square, and Hammersmith Hosp., 1960–66; Visiting Fellow, Harvard, 1967; Sen. Lectr, Inst. of Child Health, Hammersmith Hosp., 1967; Cons. Paediatrician, Guy's Hosp., 1971. *Publications:* Brain and Early Behaviour: development in the fetus and infant, 1969; (jtly) Medical Care of Newborn Babies, 1972; papers on paediatrics and child neurology. *Recreations:* literature (especially poetry), theatre, walking, canoeing. *Address:* 60 Madeley Road, Ealing, W5 2LU.

ROBINSON, Prof. Ronald Edward, CBE 1970; DFC 1944; Beit Professor of the History of the British Commonwealth, and Fellow of Balliol College, Oxford University, 1971–87; Director, University of Oxford Development Records Project, 1978–87; *b* 3 Sept. 1920; *e s* of William Edward and Ada Theresa Robinson, Clapham; *m* 1948, Alice Josephine Denny; two *s* two *d*. *Educ:* Battersea Grammar Sch.; St John's Coll., Cambridge. Major Scholar in History, St John's Coll., 1939; BA 1946, PhD 1949, Cantab. F/Lt, 58 Bomber Sqn, RAF, 1942–45. Research Officer, African Studies Branch, Colonial Office, 1947–49; Lectr in History, 1953–66, Smuts Reader in History of the British Commonwealth, 1966–71, Univ. of Cambridge; Tutor 1961–66, Fellow 1949–71, St John's Coll., Cambridge; Chm., Faculty Bd of Modern Hist., Oxford, 1974–76, Vice-Chm., 1979–87. Inst. for Advanced Studies, Princeton, 1959–60. Mem., Bridges Cttee on Trng in Public Administration, 1961–62; Chm., Cambridge Confs on Problems of Developing Countries, 1961–70. UK observer, Zimbabwe election, 1980. *Publications:* Africa and the Victorians, 1961; Developing the Third World, 1971; articles in Cambridge History of the British Empire, Vol. III, 1959, and The New Cambridge Modern History, Vol. XI, 1963; reports on Problems of Developing Countries, 1963–71; articles and reviews in learned jls. *Recreation:* room cricket. *Address:* c/o Balliol College, Oxford. *Clubs:* Commonwealth Trust; Hawks (Cambridge); Gridiron (Oxford).

ROBINSON, Stanley Scott, MBE 1944; TD 1950; BL; SSC; Sheriff of Grampian, Highland and Islands (formerly Inverness (including Western Isles), Ross, Cromarty, Moray and Nairn), 1973–83; retired; *b* 27 March 1913; *s* of late William Scott Robinson, Engineer, and of Christina Douglas Robinson; *m* 1937, Helen Annan Hardie; three *s*. *Educ:* Boroughmuir Sch., Edinburgh; Edinburgh Univ. Admitted as solicitor, 1935; Solicitor in the Supreme Courts. Commissioned in TA, 1935. Served War: France and Belgium, 1939–40, Captain RA; France, Holland and Germany, 1944–45 (despatches twice); Major, RA, 1943; Lt-Col, 1948. Solicitor in gen. practice in Montrose, Angus, 1935–72 (except during war service). Hon. Sheriff: of Perth and Angus, 1970–72; of Inverness, 1984. Mem. Council of Law Society of Scotland, 1963–72 (Vice-Pres., 1971–72); Dean, Soc. of Solicitors of Angus, 1970–72. *Publications:* The Law of Interdict, 1987; The Law of Game and Fishing in Scotland, 1989; contribs to Stair Memorial Encyclopaedia and Jl of Law Society of Scotland. *Recreations:* golf, bowling, military history. *Address:* Flat 3, Drumallin House, Drummond Road, Inverness. *T:* Inverness (0463) 233488. *Club:* Highland (Inverness).

ROBINSON, Stephen Joseph, OBE 1971; FRS 1976; FEng, FIEE; FInstP; Director, Royal Signals and Radar Establishment, Ministry of Defence, since 1989 (Deputy Director, 1985–89); *b* 6 Aug. 1931; *s* of Joseph Allan Robinson and Ethel (*née* Bunting); *m* 1957, Monica Mabs Scott; one *s* one *d*. *Educ:* Sebright Sch., Wolverley; Jesus Coll., Cambridge (MA Natural Sciences). RAF, 1950–51. Mullard Res. Labs, 1954–72; MEL Div., Philips Industries (formerly MEL Equipment Co. Ltd), 1972–79; Product Dir, 1973–79; Man. Dir, Pye TVT Ltd, 1980–84. Vis. Prof., Birmingham Univ., 1990–. Mem. Council, Royal Soc., 1982–. *Recreations:* sailing, ski-ing.

ROBINSON, Rev. Thomas Hugh, CBE 1989; Team Rector, Cleethorpes, since 1990; *b* Murree, India, 11 June 1934; *s* of Lt-Col James Arthur Robinson, OBE and Maud Loney Robinson; *m* 1959, Mary Elizabeth Doreen Clingan; two *s* one *d*. *Educ:* Bishop Foy School, Waterford; Trinity Coll., Dublin (BA 1955, MA 1971). Pres., Univ. Philosophical Soc., 1955–56. Deacon 1957, priest 1958; Curate, St Clement's, Belfast, 1957–60; Chaplain, Missions to Seamen, Mombasa, 1961–64; Rector of Youghal, Diocese of Cork, 1964–66; CF, 1966–89; DACG, 2 Armoured Div., 1977–80; Senior Chaplain: RMCS, 1980–82; Eastern Dist, 1982–84; 1st British Corps, 1984–85; BAOR, 1985–86; Dep. Chaplain Gen. to the Forces, 1986–89. QHC 1985–89. *Recreations:* gardening, social golf, wine making. *Address:* St Peter's Rectory, 42 Queens Parade, Cleethorpes, S Humberside DN35 0DG. *T:* Cleethorpes (0472) 693234.

ROBINSON, Thomas Lloyd, TD; Honorary President, The Dickinson Robinson Group Ltd, since 1988 (Chairman, 1974–77, Deputy Chairman, 1968); *b* 21 Dec. 1912; *s* of late Thomas Rosser Robinson and Rebe Francis-Watkins; *m* 1939, Pamela Rosemary Foster; one *s* two *d*. *Educ:* Wycliffe Coll. Served War, 1939–45: Royal Warwickshire Regt, 61 Div., and SHAEF; Staff Coll., Camberley. Director, E. S. & A. Robinson Ltd, 1952; Jt Managing Dir, 1958; Dep. Chm., E. S. & A. Robinson (Holdings) Ltd, 1963; Director: Bristol Waterworks Co., 1978–84; Van Leer Groep, Holland, 1977–81; Legal & General Assurance Society (now Legal & General Group plc), 1970–83 (Vice-Chm., 1978–83); Chm., Legal & General South and Western Advisory Bd, 1972–84. Chm., Council of Governors, Wycliffe Coll., 1970–83, Pres., 1988–; Mem. Council, Univ. of Bristol, 1977–, Pro-Chancellor, 1983–. Master, Soc. of Merchant Venturers, Bristol, 1977–78. High Sheriff, Avon, 1979–80; President: Glos CCC, 1980–83; Warwicks Old County Cricketers Assoc., 1989. Hon. LLD Bristol, 1985. *Recreations:* music, golf. *Address:* Lechlade, 23 Druid Stoke Avenue, Stoke Bishop, Bristol BS9 1DB. *T:* Bristol (0272) 681957. *Clubs:* Army & Navy, MCC; Royal and Ancient (St Andrews); Clifton (Bristol).

ROBINSON, Victor, CEng, FIChemE; non-executive Director, Davy International Projects (concerned with major multi-discipline overseas projects); *b* 31 July 1925; *s* of Arthur Worsley Robinson and Nellie (*née* Halliwell); *m* 1948, Sadie Monica (*née* Grut); one *s* five *d*. *Educ:* Manchester Grammar Sch.; Cambridge Univ. (MA); Admin. Staff Coll., Henley. CEng, FIChemE 1960. Simon Carves Ltd: R&D Proj. Engrg, 1945; Technical Dir, 1961; Dir, 1964; Man. Dir Overseas Ops and Dir, Sim-Chem Ltd and subsid. cos, 1966; Man. Dir, Turriff Taylor Ltd, 1974–76; Industrial Adviser, Dept of Trade (on secondment from Davy Corp. Ltd), 1978–81. *Recreation:* fell and alpine walking. *Address:* 15 Adams Close, Surbiton, Surrey KT5 8LB.

ROBINSON, Vivian; QC 1986; a Recorder, since 1986; *b* 29 July 1944; *s* of late William and of Ann Robinson; *m* 1975, Louise Marriner; one *s* two *d*. *Educ:* Queen Elizabeth Grammar School, Wakefield; The Leys School, Cambridge; Sidney Sussex College, Cambridge (BA). Called to the Bar, Inner Temple, 1967 (Bencher, 1991). Liveryman, Gardeners' Co. *Address:* Queen Elizabeth Building, Temple, EC4Y 9BS. *Clubs:* Garrick, MCC.

ROBINSON, Sir Wilfred (Henry Frederick), 3rd Bt, *cr* 1908; Finance Officer, Society of Genealogists, since 1980; Staff, Diocesan College School, Rondebosch, South Africa, 1950–77, Vice-Principal, 1969–77; *b* 24 Dec. 1917; *s* of Wilfred Henry Robinson (*d* 1922) (3rd *s* of 1st Bt), and Eileen (*d* 1963), *d* of Frederick St Leger, Claremont, SA; *S* uncle, Sir Joseph Benjamin Robinson, 2nd Bt, 1954; *m* 1946, Margaret Alison Kathleen, *d* of late Frank Mellish, MC, Cape Town, SA; one *s* two *d*. *Educ:* Diocesan Coll., Rondebosch; St John's Coll., Cambridge, MA 1944. Served War of 1939–45, Devonshire Regt and Parachute Regt, Major. *Heir:* *s* Peter Frank Robinson, [*b* 23 June 1949; *m* 1988, Alison Jane, *e d* of D. Bradley, Rochester, Kent]. *Address:* 24 Ennismore Gardens, SW7 1AB.

ROBINSON, Ven. William David; Archdeacon of Blackburn, since 1986; *b* 15 March 1931; *s* of William and Margaret Robinson; *m* 1955, Carol Averil Roma Hamm; one *s* one *d*. *Educ:* Queen Elizabeth's Grammar School, Blackburn; Durham Univ. (MA, DipTh). Curate: Standish, 1958–61; Lancaster Priory (i/c St George), 1961–63; Vicar, St James, Blackburn, 1963–73; Diocesan Stewardship Adviser, Blackburn, and Priest-in-charge, St James, Shireshead, 1973–86; Hon. Canon, Blackburn Cathedral, 1975–86; Vicar of Balderstone, 1986–87. *Recreation:* fell walking. *Address:* 7 Billinge Close, Blackburn BB2 6SB. *T:* Blackburn (0254) 53442.

ROBINSON, William Good; Deputy Secretary, Department of the Civil Service, Northern Ireland, 1978–80, retired; *b* 20 May 1919; *s* of William Robinson and Elizabeth Ann (*née* Good); *m* 1947, Wilhelmina Vaughan; two *d*. *Educ:* Clones High Sch.; Queen's Univ. of Belfast (BScEcon, BA). Served War, RAF, 1941–46 (Flt Lieut, Navigator). Entered NI Civil Service, 1938; Min. of Labour and National Insurance, NI, 1946–63; Principal, Min. of Home Affairs, NI, 1963; Asst Sec., 1967; Sen. Asst Sec., NI Office, 1973. *Recreations:* do-it-yourself, reading history. *Address:* Stormochree, 47 Castlehill Road, Belfast BT4 3GN. *T:* Belfast (0232) 763646.

ROBINSON, Rt. Rev. William James; *b* 8 Sept. 1916; *s* of Thomas Albert Robinson and Harriet Mills; *m* 1946, Isobel Morton; one *s* three *d*. *Educ:* Bishop's Univ., Lennoxville, PQ. BA in Theology; DCL (*hc*) 1973. Deacon, 1939; Priest, 1940; Asst Curate in Trenton, 1939–41; Rector of: Tweed and Madoc, 1941–46, Tweed and N Addington, 1946–47; Napanee, 1948–53; St Thomas' Church, Belleville, 1953–55; St John's Church, Ottawa, 1955–62; Church of Ascension, Hamilton, 1962–67; St George's Church, Guelph, 1967–70. Canon of Christ Church Cathedral, Hamilton, 1964–68; Archdeacon of Trafalgar (Niagara Diocese), 1968–70; Bishop of Ottawa, 1970–81; retired. *Recreations:* woodworking and gardening. *Address:* 168 Inverness Crescent, Kingston, Ont K7M 6N7, Canada. *T:* (613) 549–7599.

ROBINSON, William Rhys Brunel; Under Secretary, Overseas Division, Department of Employment, 1980–89; *b* 12 July 1930; *s* of late William Robinson and Elizabeth Myfanwy Robinson (*née* Owen); *m* 1988, Pamela Mary Hall. *Educ:* Chepstow Secondary Grammar Sch.; St Catherine's Soc., Oxford (MA,BLitt). Entered Min. of Labour, 1954; Asst Private Sec. to Minister, 1958–59; Principal, Min. of Labour, 1959; Asst Sec., 1966; London Sch. of Economics, 1972–73 (MSc Industrial Relations, 1973); Asst Sec., Trng Services Agency, 1973–75; Dep. Chief Exec., Employment Service Agency, 1975–77; Under-Sec. and Dir of Establishments, Dept of Employment, 1977–80. Chm., Governing Body, ILO, 1986–87. FSA 1978; FRHistS 1991. *Publications:* articles in historical jls. *Recreation:* historical research. *Address:* 7 Shere Avenue, Cheam, Surrey SM2 7JU. *T:* 081-393 3019.

ROBLES, Marisa, FRCM; harpist; Professor of Harp, Royal College of Music, since 1971; *b* 4 May 1937; *d* of Cristobal Robles and Maria Bonilla; *m* 1985, David Bean; two *s* one *d* by previous marriage. *Educ:* Madrid National Sch.; Royal Madrid Conservatoire. Prof. of Harp, Royal Madrid Conservatoire, 1958–60. Recitals and solo appearances with major orchestras in UK, Europe, Africa, Canada, USA, South America, Japan, China and Australia. Mem., UK Harp Assoc. Recordings include concerti by Handel, Dittersdorf, Boildieu, Debussy, Rodrigo, Moreno-Buendia, solo repertoire by Beethoven, Mozart, Fauré, Hasselmans, Tournier, Guridi and others, and chamber music by Alwyn, Roussel, Britten, Ravel, Debussy and others. Hon. Royal Madrid Conservatoire 1958; Hon. RCM 1973; FRCM 1983. *Recreations:* theatre, gardening, indoor plants, family life in general. *Address:* 38 Luttrell Avenue, Putney, SW15 6PE. *T:* 081–785 2204. *Clubs:* Anglo-Spanish, Royal Over-Seas League.

ROBLIN, Ven. Graham Henry, OBE 1983; Archdeacon to the Army, since 1990; Deputy Chaplain General to the Forces, since 1989; Hon. Chaplain to the Queen, since 1987; *b* 18 Aug. 1937; *s* of Ewart and Marjorie Roblin; *m* 1964, Penelope Ann Cumberlege; one *s* one *d*. *Educ:* Cathedral Sch., Exeter; King's Coll., Taunton; King's Coll., London (AKC). Deacon, 1962; priest, 1963; Curate of St Helier, Southwark, 1962–66; joined Army Chaplaincy Service, 1966; Dep. Asst Chaplain Gen., Hong Kong, 1979–81; Dep. Asst Chaplain Gen., 2nd Armd Div., 1981–83; Warden, RAChD Centre, Bagshot Park, 1983–86; Senior Chaplain: 1st British Corps, 1986–87; BAOR, 1987–89. Mem., Gen. Synod of C of E, 1990–. *Recreation:* writing. *Address:* Ministry of Defence Chaplains, Bagshot Park, Bagshot, Surrey. *T:* Bagshot (0276) 71717.

ROBOROUGH, 2nd Baron, *cr* 1938, of Maristow; **Massey Henry Edgcumbe Lopes;** Bt, *cr* 1805; JP; Brevet Major Reserve of Officers Royal Scots Greys; Lord-Lieutenant and Custos Rotulorum of Devon, 1958–78; *b* 4 Oct. 1903; *o s* of 1st Baron and Lady Albertha Louisa Florence Edgcumbe (*d* 1941), *d* of 4th Earl of Mount Edgcumbe; *S* father 1938; *m* 1936, Helen, *o d* of late Colonel E. A. F. Dawson, Launde Abbey, Leicestershire; two *s* (and one *d* decd). *Educ:* Eton Coll.; Christ Church, Oxford (BA). Served in Royal Scots Greys, 1925–38; served again 1939–45 (twice wounded). ADC to Earl of Clarendon, when Governor of Union of South Africa, 1936–37. CA Devon, 1956–74; DL 1946; Vice-Lieutenant of Devon, 1951; Member of Duchy of Cornwall Council, 1958–68; High Steward of Barnstaple. Chairman: Dartmoor National Park, 1965–74; SW Devon Div. Educn Cttee, 1954–74; Devon Outward Bound, 1960–75; President: SW Reg., YMCA, 1958–67; Devon British Legion, 1958–68; Devon Conservation Forum, 1972–78; President, Devon, 1958–78: Magistrates Cttee; Council of St John; CPRE; Trust for Nature Conservation; Boy Scouts Assoc.; Football Assoc.; Assoc. of Youth Clubs. Governor: Exeter Univ.; Seale-Hayne, Kelly, Plymouth and Exeter Colls. Hon. Col, Devon Army Cadet Force, 1967–78. Hon. LLD Exeter, 1969. KStJ. *Heir: s* Hon. Henry Massey Lopes [*b* 2 Feb. 1940; *m* 1968, Robyn, *e d* of John Bromwich, Melbourne, Aust.; two *s* two *d*; *m* 1986, Sarah Anne Pipon, second *d* of Colin Baker; two *d*]. *Address:* Bickham Barton, Roborough, Plymouth, Devon PL6 7BL. *T:* Yelverton (0822) 852478. *Club:* Cavalry and Guards.

ROBOTHAM, Sir Lascelles (Lister), Kt 1987; Chief Justice, Eastern Caribbean Supreme Court, since 1984; *b* 22 Oct. 1923; *s* of Vivian Constantine Robotham and Ethline Blanche Robotham; *m* 1949, Gloria Angela Stiebel; one *s* one *d*. *Educ:* Calabar Coll., Jamaica. Called to the Bar, Lincoln's Inn, 1955, Hon. Bencher, 1988. Crown Counsel, Jamaica, 1955–58; Dep. Dir of Public Prosecutions, 1958–62; Resident Magistrate, 1962–64; Puisne Judge, 1964–76; Justice of Appeal, Jamaica, 1976–79; Justice of Appeal, Eastern Caribbean Supreme Court, 1979–84; Pres., Eastern Caribbean Court of Appeal, 1984–. *Recreations:* reading, gardening, cricket. *Address:* Chief Justice's Chambers, PO Box 1093, Castries, St Lucia, West Indies. *T:* (office) 809–45–22574; (home) 809–45–28566.

ROBSON, family name of **Baroness Robson of Kiddington.**

ROBSON OF KIDDINGTON, Baroness *cr* 1974 (Life Peer), of Kiddington; **Inga-Stina Robson,** JP; Chairman, South-West Thames Regional Health Authority, 1974–82; *b* 20 Aug. 1919; *d* of Erik R. Arvidsson and Lilly A. Arvidsson (*née* Danielson); *m* 1940, Sir Lawrence W. Robson (*d* 1982); one *s* two *d*. *Educ:* Stockholm, Sweden. Swedish Foreign Office, 1939–40; Min. of Information, 1942–43. Contested (L) Eye Div., 1955 and 1959, Gloucester City, 1964 and 1966. President: Women's Liberal Fedn, 1968–69 and 1969–70; Liberal Party Org., 1970–71; Chm., Liberal Party Environment Panel, 1971–77. Chairman: Bd of Governors, Queen Charlotte's and Chelsea Hosps, 1970–84; Midwife Teachers Training Coll.; Nat. Assoc. of Leagues of Hosp. Friends, 1985–; Member: Bd of Governors, University Coll. Hosp., 1966–74; Council, Surrey Univ., 1974. Chm., Anglo-Swedish Soc., 1983–. JP Oxfordshire, 1955. *Recreations:* sailing, skiing. *Address:* Kiddington Hall, Woodstock, Oxon OX7 1BU.

ROBSON, Brian Ewart, CB 1985; Deputy Under-Secretary of State (Personnel and Logistics), Ministry of Defence, 1984–86; *b* 25 July 1926; 2nd *s* of late Walter Ewart Robson; *m* 1962, Cynthia Margaret, *o d* of late William James Scott, Recife, Brazil; two *d*. *Educ:* Steyning Grammar Sch.; Varndean Sch., Brighton; The Queen's Coll., Oxford (BA Modern History). Royal Sussex Regt and Kumaon Regt, Indian Army, 1944–47. Air Min., 1950; Asst Private Sec. to Sec. of State for Air, 1953–55; Principal, 1955; Asst Sec., 1965; Imperial Defence Coll., 1970; Ecole Nationale d'Administration, Paris, 1975; Asst Under-Sec. of State, MoD, 1976–82; Dep. Under-Sec. of State (Army), 1982–84. Mem., Central Finance Bd of C of E, 1985–. Comr, Royal Hosp., 1982–85; Member Council: Soc. for Army Historical Res., 1977–; Army Records Soc., 1984–89. Nat. Army Museum, 1982–; Trustee, Imperial War Museum, 1984–86. Governor, Whitelands Coll., 1988–. *Publications:* Swords of the British Army, 1975; The Road to Kabul: the Second Afghan War 1878–1880, 1986; numerous articles on weapons and military history. *Recreations:* military history, cricket, travel. *Address:* 17 Woodlands, Hove, East Sussex BN3 6TJ. *T:* Brighton (0273) 505803. *Club:* Oxford Union.

ROBSON, David Ernest Henry, QC 1980; a Recorder of the Crown Court (NE Circuit), since 1979; *b* 1 March 1940; *s* of late Joseph Robson and of Caroline Robson. *Educ:* Robert Richardson Grammar Sch., Ryhope; Christ Church, Oxford (MA). Called to the Bar, Inner Temple, 1965 (Profumo Prize, 1963), Bencher, 1988. NE Circuit, 1965–. Artistic Dir, Royalty Studio Theatre, Sunderland, 1986–88. Pres., Herrington Burn YMCA, Sunderland 1987–. *Recreations:* acting, Italy. *Address:* Whitton Grange, Whitton, Rothbury, Northumberland NE65 7RL. *T:* Rothbury (0669) 20929. *Club:* County (Durham).

ROBSON, Prof. Elizabeth Browel; Galton Professor of Human Genetics and Head of Department of Genetics and Biometry, University College London, since 1978; *b* 10 Nov. 1928; *d* of Thomas Robson and Isabella (*née* Stoker); *m* 1955, George MacBeth, *qv* (marr. diss. 1975). *Educ:* Bishop Auckland Girls' Grammar Sch.; King's Coll., Newcastle upon Tyne. BSc Dunelm; PhD London. Rockefeller Fellowship, Columbia Univ., New York City, 1954–55; external scientific staff of MRC (London Hosp. Med. Coll. and King's Coll. London), 1955–62; Member and later Asst Director, MRC Human Biochemical Genetics Unit, University Coll. London, 1962–78. Visiting Professor: Second Univ. of Rome, 1986–; Univ. of Calabria, 1988–. Founding Councillor, Human Genome Orgn, 1988; Vice-Pres., Genetical Soc. of GB, 1989–. Member, Board of Trustees, Royal Botanic Gardens, Kew, 1984–. Jt Editor, Annals of Human Genetics, 1978–. *Publications:* papers on biochemical human genetics and gene mapping in scientific jls. *Address:* 44 Sheen Road, Richmond, Surrey TW9 1AW.

ROBSON, Frank Elms, OBE 1991; Senior Partner, Winckworth and Pemberton, Solicitors, Oxford and Westminster, since 1990 (Partner, 1962); Registrar: Diocese of Oxford, since 1970; Province of Canterbury, since 1982; *b* 14 Dec. 1931; *s* of Joseph A. Robson and Barbara Robson; *m* 1958, Helen (*née* Jackson) four *s* one *d*. *Educ:* King Edward VI Grammar Sch., Morpeth; Selwyn Coll., Cambridge (MA). Admitted solicitor, 1954. DCL Lambeth, 1991. *Recreations:* fell-walking, clocks, following Oxford United. *Address:* 2 Simms Close, Stanton St John, Oxford OX9 1HB. *T:* Stanton St John (086735) 393.

ROBSON, Godfrey; Under Secretary, Fisheries, Scottish Office, since 1989; *b* 5 Nov. 1946; *s* of late William James Robson and of Mary Finn; *m* 1969, Agnes Wight (separated 1989); one *s*. *Educ:* St Joseph's Coll., Dumfries; Edinburgh Univ. (MA). Joined Scottish Office, 1970; Pvte Sec. to Parly Under-Sec. of State, 1973–74, to Minister of State, 1974; Prin. Pvte Sec. to Sec. of State for Scotland, 1979–81; Assistant Secretary: Roads and Transport, 1981–86; Local Govt Finance, 1986–89. *Recreations:* walking, travel by other means, reading history. *Address:* 50 East Trinity Road, Edinburgh EH5 3EN. *T:* 031–552 9519. *Club:* National Liberal.

ROBSON, Prof. Sir (James) Gordon, Kt 1982; CBE 1977; MB, ChB; FRCS; FFARCS; Professor of Anaesthetics, University of London, Royal Postgraduate Medical School and Hon. Consultant, Hammersmith Hospital, 1964–86, retired; Chairman, Advisory Committee on Distinction Awards, since 1984; *b* Stirling, Scot., 18 March 1921; *o s* of late James Cyril Robson and Freda Elizabeth Howard; *m* 1st, 1945, Dr Martha Graham Kennedy (*d* 1975); one *s*; 2nd, 1984, Jennifer Kilpatrick. *Educ:* High Sch. of Stirling; Univ. of Glasgow. FRCS 1977. RAMC, 1945–48 (Captain). Sen. Registrar in Anaesthesia, Western Inf., Glasgow, 1948–52; First Asst, Dept of Anaesthetics, Univ. of Durham, 1952–54; Cons. Anaesth., Royal Inf., Edinburgh, 1954–56; Wellcome Res. Prof. of Anaesth., McGill Univ., Montreal, 1956–64. Consultant Advr in Anaesthetics to DHSS, 1975–84; Hon. Consultant in Anaesthetics to the Army, 1983–88. Royal College of Surgeons: Master, Hunterian Inst., 1982–88. Mem. Bd of Faculty of Anaesthetists, 1968–85 (Dean of Faculty, 1973–76); Mem. Council, 1973–81, 1982–88 (a Vice-Pres., 1977–79); Chm., Jt Cttee on Higher Trng of Anaesthetists, 1973–76; Member: AHA, Ealing, Hammersmith and Hounslow, 1974–77 (NW Met. RHB, 1971–74); Chief Scientists' Res. Cttee and Panel on Med. Res., DHSS, 1973–77; Neurosciences Bd, MRC, 1974–77; Clin. Res. Bd, MRC (Chm. Grants Cttee II), 1969–71; Mem. Council, RPMS (Vice-Chm. Academic Bd, 1973–76; Chm. 1976–80); Mem., Rock Carling Fellowship Panel, 1976–78; Vice-Chm., Jt Consultants' Cttee, 1974–79. Special Trustee, Hammersmith Hosp., 1974–77; Chm., Cttee of Management, Inst. of Basic Med. Scis, 1982–85; Hon. Sec., Conf. of Med. Royal Colls and Their Faculties, UK, 1976–82; Examiner, Primary FFARCS, 1967–73; Member: Editorial Bd (and Cons. Editor), British Jl of Anaesthesia, 1965–85; Edit. Bd, Psychopharmacology; Council, Assoc. of Anaesths of GB and Ire., 1973–84; Physiol. Soc., 1966–; Cttee of AA, 1979–91; Hon. Mem., Assoc. of Univ. Anaesths (USA), 1963–; President: Scottish Soc. of Anaesthetists, 1985–86; RSocMed, 1986–88. Cttee of Management, RNLI, 1988–; Chm., Med. and Survival Cttee, RNLI, 1988–91; Sir Arthur Sims Commonwealth Trav. Prof., 1968; Visiting Prof. to many med. centres, USA and Canada; Lectures: Wesley Bourne, McGill Univ., 1965; First Gillies Meml, Dundee, 1978; 2nd Gilmartin, Faculty of Anaesthetists, RCSI, 1986; Morrell Mackenzie, Inst. of Laryngology, 1989. Joseph Clover Medal and Dudley Buxton Prize, Fac. of Anaesths, RCS, 1972; John Snow Medal, Assoc. of Anaesthetists of GB and Ireland, 1986. Hon. FFARACS 1968; Hon. FFARCSI 1980; Hon. FDSRCS 1979; Hon. FRCP(C) 1988; Hon. FRSM 1989. Hon. DSc McGill, 1984. *Publications:* on neurophysiol., anaesthesia, pain and central nervous system mechanisms of respiration, in learned jls. *Recreations:* golf, wet fly fishing. *Club:* Denham Golf.

ROBSON, Prof. James Scott, MD; FRCP, FRCPE; Professor of Medicine, University of Edinburgh, 1977–86, now Emeritus; Consultant Physician, and Physician in charge,

Medical Renal Unit, Royal Infirmary, Edinburgh, 1959–86; *b* 19 May 1921; *s* of William Scott Robson, FSA and Elizabeth Hannah Watt; *m* 1948, Mary Kynoch MacDonald, MB ChB, FRCP, *d* of late Alexander MacDonald, Perth; two *s*. *Educ:* Edinburgh Univ. (Mouat Schol.). MB ChB (Hons) 1945, MD 1946; FRCPE 1960, FRCP 1977. Captain, RAMC, India, Palestine and Egypt, 1945–48. Rockefeller Student, NY Univ., 1942–44; Rockefeller Res. Fellow, Harvard Univ., 1949–50. Edinburgh University: Sen. Lectr in Therapeutics, 1959; Reader, 1961; Reader in Medicine, 1968. Hon. Associate Prof., Harvard Univ., 1962; Merck Sharp & Dohme Vis. Prof., Australia, 1968. External examnr in medicine to several univs in UK and overseas. Mem., Biomed. Res. Cttee, SHHD, 1979–84; Chm., Sub-cttee in Medicine, Nat. Med. Consultative Cttee, 1983–85. Pres., Renal Assoc., London, 1977–80. Hon. Mem., Australasian Soc. of Nephrology. Sometime Mem. Editl Bd, and Dep. Chm., Clinical Science, 1969–73, and other med. jls. *Publications:* (ed with R. Passmore) Companion to Medical Studies, vol. 1, 1968, 3rd edn 1985; vol. 2, 1970, 2nd edn 1980; vol. 3, 1974; contribs on renal physiology and disease to med. books, symposia and jls. *Recreations:* gardening, theatre, reading, writing. *Address:* 1 Grant Avenue, Edinburgh EH13 0DS. *T:* 031–441 3508. *Clubs:* New, University Staff (Edinburgh).

ROBSON, Sir John (Adam), KCMG 1990 (CMG 1983); HM Diplomatic Service, retired; Ambassador to Norway, 1987–90; *b* 16 April 1930; *yr s* of Air Vice-Marshal Adam Henry Robson, CB, OBE, MC; *m* 1958, Maureen Molly, *er d* of E. H. S. Bullen; three *d*. *Educ:* Charterhouse; Gonville and Caius Coll., Cambridge (Major Scholar). BA 1952, MA 1955, PhD 1958. Fellow, Gonville and Caius Coll., 1954–58; Asst Lectr, University Coll. London, 1958–60. HM Foreign Service (later Diplomatic Service), 1961; Second Sec., British Embassy, Bonn, 1962–64; Second, later First, Secretary, Lima, 1964–66; First Sec., British High Commn, Madras, 1966–69; Asst Head, Latin American Dept, FCO, 1969–73; Head of Chancery, Lusaka, 1973–74; RCDS, 1975; Counsellor, Oslo, 1976–78; Head of E African Dept, FCO, and Comr for British Indian Ocean Territory, 1979–82; Ambassador to Colombia, 1982–87. Leader, UK Delegn, Conf. on Human Dimension, CSCE, 1990–91. Mem. Ct, Kent Univ., 1990–. Royal Order of Merit (Norway), 1988. *Publications:* Wyclif and the Oxford Schools, 1961; articles in historical jls. *Recreation:* gardening. *Address:* Biggenden Oast, Paddock Wood, Tonbridge, Kent TN12 6ND. *Club:* United Oxford & Cambridge University.

ROBSON, Rev. John Phillips; Chaplain of the Queen's Chapel of the Savoy and Chaplain of the Royal Victorian Order, since 1989; *b* 22 July 1932; *s* of Thomas Herbert and Nellie Julia Robson. *Educ:* Hele's School, Exeter; Brentwood School; St Edmund Hall, Oxford (Liddon Exhibnr 1954); King's College London (AKC 1958). Deacon 1959, priest 1960; Curate, Huddersfield Parish Church, 1959–62; Asst Chaplain 1962–65, Senior Chaplain 1965–80, Christ's Hospital, Horsham; Senior Chaplain of Wellington College, Berks, 1980–89. *Recreations:* golf, cinema, theatre. *Address:* The Queen's Chapel of the Savoy, Savoy Hill, Strand, WC2R 0DA. *T:* 071–836 7221. *Club:* Liphook Golf.

ROBSON, Lawrence Fendick; Member, Electricity Council, 1972–76; *b* 23 Jan. 1916; *s* of (William) Bertram Robson and Annie (*née* Fendick); *m* 1945, Lorna Winifred Jagger, Shafton, Yorks; two *s* one *d*. *Educ:* Rotherham Grammar Sch.; Clare Coll., Cambridge (BA). FIEE. North Eastern Electric Supply Co. Ltd, 1937; Royal Corps of Signals, 1939–45; various positions with NE and London Electricity Bds, 1948–65; Commercial Adviser, Electricity Council, 1965–72. *Recreations:* music, open air. *Address:* Millers Hill, Priestman's Lane, Thornton Dale, N Yorks.

ROBSON, Nigel John; Chairman, London Committee, Ottoman Bank, since 1987 (Deputy Chairman, 1983–87; Member, since 1959); Member, Board of Banking Supervision, since 1986; London Adviser to Bank of Tokyo Group, since 1984; Vice-Chairman, Automobile Association, since 1990 (Treasurer, 1986–89); *b* 25 Dec. 1926; *s* of late Col the Hon. Harold Burge Robson, TD, DL, JP, Pinewood Hill, Wormley, Surrey, and late Iris Robson (*née* Abel Smith); *m* 1957, Anne Gladstone, *yr d* of late Stephen Deiniol Gladstone and late Clair Gladstone; three *s*. *Educ:* Eton. Grenadier Guards, 1945–48. Joined Arbuthnot Latham & Co. Ltd, Merchant Bankers, 1949, a Director, 1953, Chm., 1969–75; Dir, Arbuthnot Latham Holdings Ltd, 1969–81; Dir, Grindlays Bank plc, 1969–83, Dep. Chm., 1975–76, Chm. 1977–83; Director: British Sugar plc, 1982–86; Central Trustee Savings Bank, 1984–86; TSB Gp, 1985–; Royal Trustco Ltd, Toronto, 1985–89; Chairman: Alexander Howden Underwriting, subseq. Alexander Howden & Beck Ltd, 1984–88; Royal Trust Co. of Canada, subseq. Royal Trust Bank, 1984–89; TSB England & Wales, 1986–89. Mem. Council, British Heart Foundn, 1984– (Chm., F & GP Cttee, 1984–89; Hon. Treas., 1985–89); Mem., 250th Anniv. Cttee, Royal London Hosp., 1989–91; Treas., Univ. of Surrey, 1987–. Gov., King Edward's Sch., Witley, 1975–. *Recreations:* tennis, music. *Address:* Pinewood Hill, Wormley, Godalming, Surrey GU8 5UD. *Clubs:* Brooks's, City of London, MCC.

See also W. M. Robson.

ROBSON, Prof. Peter Neville, OBE 1983; FRS 1987; FEng 1983; Professor of Electronic and Electrical Engineering, University of Sheffield, since 1968; *b* 23 Nov. 1930; *s* of Thomas Murton and Edith Robson; *m* 1957, Anne Ross Miller Semple; one *d*. *Educ:* Cambridge Univ. (BA); PhD Sheffield. FIEE, FIEEE. Res. Engr, Metropolitan Vickers Electrical Co., Manchester, 1954–57; Lectr 1957–63, Sen. Lectr 1963–66, Sheffield Univ.; Res. Fellow, Stanford Univ., USA, 1966–67; Reader, University Coll. London, 1967–68. *Publications:* Vacuum and Solid State Electronics, 1963; numerous papers on semiconductor devices and electromagnetic theory. *Address:* Department of Electronic and Electrical Engineering, Sheffield University, Mappin Street, Sheffield S1 3JD. *T:* Sheffield (0742) 768555, ext. 5131.

ROBSON, Air Vice-Marshal Robert Michael, OBE 1971; sheep farmer; *b* 22 April 1935; *s* of Dr John Alexander and Edith Robson; *m* 1959, Brenda Margaret (*née* Croysdill); one *s* two *d*. *Educ:* Sherborne; RMA Sandhurst. Commissioned 1955; RAF Regt, 1958; Navigator Training, 1959; Strike Squadrons, 1965; Sqdn Comdr, RAF Coll., 1968; Defence Adviser to British High Comr, Sri Lanka, 1972; Nat. Defence Coll., 1973; CO 27 Sqdn, 1974–75; MoD staff duties, 1978; CO RAF Gatow, 1978–80; ADC to the Queen, 1979–80; RCDS 1981; Dir of Initial Officer Training, RAF Coll., 1982–84; Dir of Public Relations, RAF, 1984–87; Hd, RAF Study of Officers' Terms of Service, 1987; retired. Chm., Aerotech Alloys Ltd, 1990–. *Recreations:* fly fishing, photography. *Club:* Royal Air Force.

ROBSON, Robert William, CBE 1991; Manager, PSV Eindhoven, Netherlands, since 1990; *b* 18 Feb. 1933; *s* of Philip and Lilian Robson; *m* 1955, Elsie Mary Gray; three *s*. *Educ:* Langley Park Primary Sch.; Waterhouses Secondary Mod. Sch., Co. Durham. Professional footballer: Fulham FC, 1950–56 and 1962–67; West Bromwich Albion FC, 1956–62; twenty appearances for England; Manager: Vancouver FC, 1967–68; Fulham FC, 1968–69; Ipswich Town FC, 1969–82; England Assoc. Football Team, and Nat. Coach, 1982–90. *Publications:* Time on the Grass (autobiog.), 1982; (with Bob Harris) So Near and Yet So Far: Bobby Robson's World Cup diary, 1986; (with Bob Harris) Against The Odds, 1990. *Recreations:* golf, squash, reading, gardening. *Address:* c/o PSV Eindhoven, Frederiklaan 10a, NL 5616 NH Eindhoven, Netherlands.

ROBSON, Stephen Arthur, PhD: Under Secretary, Public Enterprises and Privatisation Group, HM Treasury, since 1990; *b* 30 Sept. 1943; *s* of Arthur Cyril Robson and Lilian Marianne (*née* Peabody); *m* 1974, Meredith Hilary Lancashire; two *s*. *Educ:* Pocklington Sch.; St John's Coll., Cambridge (MA, PhD); Stanford Univ., USA (MA). Joined Civil Service (HM Treasury), 1969; Private Sec. to Chancellor of the Exchequer, 1974–76; seconded to Investors in Industry plc, 1976–78; Under Sec., Treasury Defence Policy and Material Gp, 1987–89. *Recreation:* sailing. *Address:* c/o HM Treasury, Parliament Street, SW1P 3AG. *Club:* Bosham Sailing.

ROBSON, Thomas Snowdon, CBE 1986 (OBE 1970; MBE 1964); FEng 1989; FIEE; Director of Engineering, Independent Broadcasting Authority, 1978–86; *b* 6 Aug. 1922; *s* of Thomas Henry Robson and Annie Jessie (*née* Snowdon); *m* 1951, Ruth Bramley; one *s* one *d*. *Educ:* Portsmouth Grammar Sch. BBC, 1941–42; RAF Techn. Br., 1942–46; EMI Research Labs, 1947–57; ITA: Engr in Charge, Black Hill, 1957–58; Sen. Engr, Planning and Construction, 1958–67; Head of Station Design and Construction, 1967–69; Asst Dir of Engrg, 1969–73; IBA, Dep. Dir of Engrg, 1973–77. FRTS 1976; Hon. FBKSTS 1986. Eduard Rhein Prize, Eduard Rhein Foundn, Berlin, 1984. *Recreations:* home computing, racket-ball, study of history. *Address:* 3 Sleepers Hill Gardens, Winchester, Hants SO22 4NT. *T:* Winchester (0962) 68540.

ROBSON, William Michael; Deputy Chairman, The Standard Bank Ltd, 1965–83 (Director, 1960–83); Member of Lloyd's, since 1937; *b* 31 Dec. 1912; *e s* of late Col the Hon. Harold Burge Robson, TD, DL, JP, Pinewood Hill, Witley, Surrey and late Ysolt Robson (*née* Leroy-Lewis); *m* 1st, 1939, Audrey Isobel Wales (*d* 1964), *d* of late Maj. William Dick, Low Gosforth Hall, Northumberland; two *s* one *d*; 2nd, 1965, Frances Mary Wyville, *d* of late James Anderson Ramage Dawson, Balado House, Kinross, and *widow* of Andrew Alexander Nigel Buchanan (he *d* 1960). *Educ:* Eton; New College, Oxford. Served War of 1939–45: with Grenadier Guards (Maj. 1944), England and Europe BAOR. A Vice-Chm., Victoria League for Commonwealth Friendship, 1962–65. Director: Booker McConnell Ltd, 1955–78 (Chm., Booker Pensions, 1957–78); United Rum Merchants Ltd, 1965–78; British South Africa Co., 1961–66 (Vice-Chm., Jt East & Central African Bd, 1956–63); Antony Gibbs & Sons (Insurance) Ltd, 1946–48, 1973–76; Antony Gibbs (Insurance Holdings), 1976–80; Antony Gibbs, Sage Ltd, 1976–80; Anton Underwriting Agencies Ltd, 1977–82; Chm., Standard Bank Finance & Develt Corp. Ltd, 1966–73; Deputy Chairman: The Chartered Bank, 1974–83; Standard and Chartered Banking Gp Ltd, 1974–83 (Dir, 1970–83). Mem., BNEC, Africa, 1965–71 (Dep. Chm., 1970–71). High Sheriff of Kent, 1970. Liveryman, Vintners Co., 1953. Mem. Council of The Shrievalty Assoc., 1971–76. *Club:* Brooks's.

See also N. J. Robson.

ROBSON, Prof. William Wallace, FRSE; Masson Professor of English Literature, University of Edinburgh, 1972–90, now Emeritus; *b* 20 June 1923; *o s* of late W. Robson, LLB, barrister, and Kathleen Ryan; *m* 1962, Anne-Varna Moses, MA; two *s*. *Educ:* Leeds Modern School; New College, Oxford (R. C. Sherriff Scholar; BA 1944, MA 1948). Asst Lectr, King's College London, 1944–46; Lectr, Lincoln College, Oxford, 1946–48, Fellow, 1948–70; Prof. of English, Univ. of Sussex, 1970–72. Visiting Lecturer: Univ. of S California, 1953; Univ. of Adelaide, 1956; Vis. Prof., Univ. of Delaware, 1963–64; Elizabeth Drew Prof., Smith Coll., USA, 1969–70; Vis. Fellow: All Souls Coll., Oxford, 1982; New Coll., Oxford, 1985. FRSE 1988. *Publications:* Critical Essays, 1966; The Signs Among Us, 1968; Modern English Literature, 1970, 5th edn 1984; The Definition of Literature, 1982; A Prologue to English Literature, 1986. *Address:* Department of English Literature, The University, Edinburgh EH8 9YL. *T:* 031–667 1011.

ROCARD, Michel Louis Léon; Prime Minister of France, 1988–91; Mayor of Conflans-Sainte-Honorine, since 1977; *b* 23 Aug. 1930; *s* of Yves Rocard and Renée (*née* Favre); *m* 1st; one *s* one *d*; 2nd, 1972, Michèle Legendre; two *s*. *Educ:* Lycée Louis-le-Grand, Paris; Univ. of Paris (Nat. Sec., Association des étudiants socialistes, 1953–55); Ecole Nationale d'Administration, 1956–58. Inspecteur des Finances, 1958; Econ. and Financial Studies Service, 1962; Head of Budget Div., Forecasting Office, 1965; Sec.-Gen., Nat. Accounts and Budget Commn, 1965. Nat. Sec., Parti Socialiste Unifié, 1967–73; candidate for Presidency of France, 1969; Deputy for Yvelines, 1969–73, 1978–81, re-elected 1986; Minister of Planning and Regl Devel, 1981–83; Minister of Agriculture, 1983–85. Joined Parti Socialiste, 1974: Mem., Exec. Bureau, 1975–81 and 1986–; Nat. Sec. in charge of public sector, 1975–79. *Publications:* Le PSU et l'avenir socialiste de la France, 1969; Des militants du PSU présentés par Michel Rocard, 1971; Questions à l'Etat socialiste, 1972; Un député, pour quoi faire?, 1973; (jtly) Le Marché commun contre l'Europe, 1973; (jtly) L'Inflation au cœur, 1975; Parler vrai, 1979; A l'épreuve des faits: textes politiques 1979–85, 1986; Le coeur à l'ouvrage, 1987; Un pays comme le nôtre, 1989. *Address:* Assemblée Nationale, 75355 Paris, France.

ROCH, Hon. Sir John (Ormond), Kt 1985; **Hon. Mr Justice Roch;** a Judge of the High Court of Justice, Queen's Bench Division, since 1985; *b* 19 April 1934; *s* of Frederick Ormond Roch and Vera Elizabeth (*née* Chamberlain); *m* 1967, Anne Elizabeth Greany; three *d*. *Educ:* Wrekin Coll.; Clare Coll., Cambridge (BA, LLB). Called to Bar, Gray's Inn, 1961, Bencher, 1985; QC 1976; a Recorder, 1975–85; Presiding Judge, Wales and Chester Circuit, 1986–90. *Recreations:* sailing, music. *Address:* c/o Royal Courts of Justice, Strand, WC2. *Clubs:* Dale Yacht, Bar Yacht.

ROCH, Muriel Elizabeth Sutcliffe, BA; Headmistress, School of S Mary and S Anne, Abbots Bromley, Staffs, 1953–77; *b* 7 Sept. 1916; *d* of late Rev. Sydney John Roch, MA Cantab, Pembroke and Manchester. *Educ:* Manchester High Sch.; Bedford Coll., London; Hughes Hall, Cambridge. Teaching appointments at: Devonport High School, 1939–41; Lady Manners, Bakewell, 1941–44; Howells School, Denbigh, 1944–47; Talbot Heath, Bournemouth, 1947–53. *Recreations:* music, travel. *Address:* Northdown Cottage, Lamphey, Dyfed SA71 5PL. *T:* Lamphey (0646) 672577.

ROCHDALE, 1st Viscount *cr* 1960; 2nd Baron 1913; **John Durival Kemp,** OBE 1945; TD; DL; *b* 5 June 1906; *s* of 1st Baron and Lady Beatrice Egerton, 3rd *d* of 3rd Earl of Ellesmere; *S* father, 1945; *m* 1931, Elinor Dorothea Pease (CBE 1964; JP); one *s* (one *d* decd). *Educ:* Eton; Trin. Coll., Cambridge. Hons degree Nat. Science Tripos. Served War of 1939–45 (despatches); attached USA forces in Pacific with rank of Col, 1944; Temp. Brig., 1945. Hon. Col 251 (Westmorland and Cumberland Yeomanry) Field Regiment, RA, TA, later 851 (W&CY) Field Bty, RA, 1959–67. Joined Kelsall & Kemp Ltd, 1928, Chm., 1952–71; Director: Consett Iron Co. Ltd, 1957–67; Geigy (Hldgs) Ltd, 1959–64; Williams Deacon's Bank Ltd, 1960–70; Nat. and Commercial Banking Gp Ltd, 1971–77; Deputy Chairman: West Riding Worsted & Woollen Mills, 1969–72; Williams & Glyn's Bank Ltd, 1973–77; Chm., Harland & Wolff, 1971–75. Mem., H of L Select Cttee on European Affairs (Chm., sub cttee B), 1981–86. President: National Union of Manufacturers, 1953–56; NW Industrial Develt Assoc., 1974–84; Economic League, 1964–67; Member: Dollar Exports Council, 1953–61; Central Transport Consultative Cttee for GB, 1953–57; Western Hemisphere Exports Council, 1961–64; Chairman: Cotton Board, 1957–62; Docks and Harbours Committee of Inquiry, 1961; National Ports Council, 1963–67; Cttee of Inquiry into Shipping, 1967–70. A Governor of the

BBC, 1954–59. Dir, Cumbria Rural Enterprise Agency, 1986–91. Chm., Rosehill Arts Trust, 1970–83. Pres., British Legion, NW Area, 1955–61. Companion, Textile Inst. 1959; MInstT 1964. Upper Bailiff, Weavers' Co., 1949–50, 1956–57. DL Cumberland, 1948–84. Medal, Textile Inst., 1986 *Recreations:* gardening, forestry, music. *Heir: s* Hon. St John Durival Kemp [*b* 15 Jan. 1938; *m* 1st, 1960, Serena Jane Clark-Hall (marr. diss. 1974); two *s* two *d*; 2nd, 1976, Elizabeth Anderton]. *Address:* Lingholm, Keswick, Cumbria CA12 5UA. *T:* Keswick (07687) 72003. *Club:* Lansdowne.
See also Sir J. K. Barlow, Bt, Duke of Sutherland.

ROCHDALE, Archdeacon of; *see* Dalby, Ven. J. M. M.

ROCHE, family name of **Baron Fermoy.**

ROCHE, Sir David (O'Grady), 5th Bt *cr* 1838 of Carass, Limerick; FCA; Chairman: Echo Hotel plc; Roche & Co. Ltd; Carass Property Ltd; *b* 21 Sept. 1947; *s* of Sir Standish O'Grady Roche, 4th Bt, DSO, and of Evelyn Laura, *d* of Major William Andon; *S* father, 1977; *m* 1971, Hon. (Helen) Alexandra Briscoe Frewen, *d* of 3rd Viscount Selby; one *s* one *d* (and one *s* decd). *Educ:* Wellington Coll., Berks; Trinity Coll., Dublin. Liveryman, Worshipful Co. of Saddlers, 1970. *Heir: s* David Alexander O'Grady Roche, *b* 28 Jan. 1976. *Address:* Bridge House, Starbotton, Skipton, N Yorks BD23 5HY. *T:* Skipton (0756) 76863; 36 Coniger Road, SW6. *T:* 071–736 0382. *Clubs:* Buck's; Kildare Street and University (Dublin); Royal Yacht Squadron.

ROCHE, Frederick Lloyd, CBE 1985; Deputy Chairman, Conran Roche, since 1981; *b* 11 March 1931; *s* of John Francis Roche and Margaret Roche. *Educ:* Regent Street Polytechnic. DipArch, ARIBA. Architect (Schools), City of Coventry, 1958–62; Principal Develt Architect, Midlands Housing Consortium, 1962–64; Chief Architect and Planning Officer, Runcorn Develt Corp., 1964–70; Gen. Manager, Milton Keynes Develt Corp., 1970–80. Vice-Pres., RIBA, 1983. *Publications:* numerous technical articles. *Address:* Conran Roche, Nutmeg House, 60 Gainsford Street, SE1 2NY. *T:* 071–403 8899.

ROCHE, Hon. Thomas Gabriel, QC 1955; Recorder of the City of Worcester, 1959–71; *b* 1909; *yr s* of late Baron Roche, PC. *Educ:* Rugby; Wadham Coll., Oxford. Called to the Bar, Inner Temple, 1932. Served War of 1939–45 (Lt-Col 1944, despatches). Church Commissioner, 1961–65; Member, Monopolies Commission, 1966–69. *Address:* Chadlington, Oxford. *Club:* United Oxford & Cambridge University.

ROCHESTER, 2nd Baron, of the 4th creation, *cr* 1931, of Rochester in the County of Kent; **Foster Charles Lowry Lamb,** DL; *b* 7 June 1916; *s* of 1st Baron Rochester, CMG, and Rosa Dorothea (*née* Hurst); *S* father 1955; *m* 1942, Mary Carlisle, *yr d* of T. B. Wheeler, CBE; two *s* one *d* (and one *d* decd). *Educ:* Mill Hill; Jesus College, Cambridge. MA. Served War of 1939–45: Captain 23rd Hussars; France, 1944. Joined ICI Ltd, 1946: Labour Manager, Alkali Div., 1955–63; Personnel Manager, Mond Div., 1964–72. Pro-Chancellor, Univ. of Keele, 1976–86. Chairman: Cheshire Scout Assoc., 1974–81; Governors of Chester Coll., 1974–83. DL Cheshire, 1979. DUniv Keele, 1986. *Heir: s* Hon. David Charles Lamb [*b* 8 Sept. 1944; *m* 1969, Jacqueline Stamp; two *s*. *Educ:* Shrewsbury Sch.; Univ. of Sussex]. *Address:* The Hollies, Hartford, Cheshire CW8 1PG. *T:* Northwich (0606) 74733. *Clubs:* Reform, MCC.
See also Hon. K. H. L. Lamb.

ROCHESTER, Bishop of, since 1988; **Rt. Rev. Michael Turnbull;** *b* 27 Dec. 1935; *s* of George Ernest Turnbull and Adeline Turbull (*née* Awty); *m* 1963, Brenda Susan Merchant; one *s* two *d*. *Educ:* Ilkley Grammar Sch.; Keble Coll., Oxford (MA); St John's Coll., Durham (DipTh). Deacon, 1960; priest, 1961; Curate: Middleton, 1960–61; Luton, 1961–65; Domestic Chaplain to Archibishop of York, 1965–69; Rector of Heslington and Chaplain, York Univ., 1969–76; Chief Secretary, Church Army, 1976–84; Archdeacon of Rochester, also Canon Residentiary of Rochester Cathedral and Chm., Dio. Bd for Mission and Unity, 1984–88. Mem., General Synod, C of E, 1970–75, 1987–; Vice-Chm., Central Bd of Finance, C of E, 1990–; Mem. Bd, Church Commissioners, 1989– (Vice-Chm., Houses Cttee, 1989–). Chairman: Coll. of Preachers, 1990–; Bible Reading Fellowship, 1990–; Partnership for World Mission, 1991–. Examining Chaplain to Bishop of Norwich, 1982–84. *Publications:* (contrib.) Unity: the next step?, 1972; God's Front Line, 1979; Parish Evangelism, 1980; Learning to Pray, 1981. *Recreations:* cricket, family life. *Address:* Bishopscourt, Rochester, Kent ME1 1TS. *T:* Medway (0634) 842721. *Clubs:* Athenæum, MCC.

ROCHESTER, Dean of; *see* Shotter, Very Rev. E. F.

ROCHESTER, Archdeacon of; *see* Warren, Ven. N. L.

ROCHESTER, Prof. George Dixon, FRS 1958; FInstP; Professor of Physics, University of Durham, 1955–73, now Professor Emeritus; *b* 4 Feb. 1908; *s* of Thomas and Ellen Rochester; *m* 1938, Idaline, *o d* of Rev. J. B. Bayliffe; one *s* one *d*. *Educ:* Wallsend Secondary Sch. and Technical Inst.; Universities of Durham, Stockholm and California. BSc, MSc, PhD (Dunelm). Earl Grey Memorial Scholar, Armstrong College, Durham University, 1926–29; Earl Grey Fellow, at Stockholm Univ., 1934–35; Commonwealth Fund Fellow at California Univ., 1935–37; Manchester University: Asst Lectr, 1937–46; Lectr, 1946–49; Sen. Lectr, 1949–53; Reader, 1953–55. Scientific Adviser in Civil Defence for NW Region, 1952–55. (Jt) C. V. Boys Prizeman of the Physical Society of London, 1956; Symons Memorial Lecturer of the Royal Meteorological Soc., 1962. Member: Council CNAA, 1964–74; Council, British Assoc. for Advancement of Science, 1971–72; Council, Royal Soc., 1972–74; Chm., NE Branch, Inst. of Physics, 1972–74. Second Pro-Vice-Chancellor, Univ. of Durham, 1967–69, Pro-Vice-Chancellor, 1969–70. Hon. DSc: Newcastle upon Tyne, 1973; CNAA, 1975; Hon. Fellow, Newcastle upon Tyne Polytechnic, 1977. Methodist. *Publications:* (with J. G. Wilson) Cloud Chamber Photographs of the Cosmic Radiation, 1952; scientific papers on spectroscopy, cosmic rays and history of the strange particles. *Recreations:* outdoor activities, history of physics and astronomy. *Address:* 18 Dryburn Road, Durham DH1 5AJ. *T:* Durham (091) 3864796.

ROCHETA, Dr Manuel Farrajota; Military Order of Christ of Portugal; Ambassador for Portugal in Madrid, 1968–74, retired; *b* 6 Aug. 1906; *s* of Manuel and Rosa Rocheta; *m* 1933, Maria Luiza Belmarco Rocheta; one *d*. *Educ:* Lisbon University. Entered Diplomatic Service, 1931; Assistant Consul Hamburg, 1934; Consul Copenhagen, 1935–39; First Sec. and Chargé d'Affaires *ai*, Bucarest, 1943–45; First Sec. and Chargé d'Affaires *ai*, Dublin, 1945; First Secretary, Washington, 1946, Counsellor, 1947, Minister-Counsellor, 1950 (Chargé d'Affaires, 1 Nov. 1946–31 March 1947 and 11 Feb. 1950–6 June 1950); Asst Dir-Gen. of Political Dept, Foreign Affairs Ministry, Lisbon, 1951; Minister-Plen. and Dir-Gen. of Political Dept, Foreign Ministry, Lisbon, 1954; Minister in Bonn, 1956, Ambassador, 1956–58; Ambassador: to Rio de Janeiro, 1958–61; to the Court of St James's, 1961–68. Doctor in Law, Univ. of Bahia, Brazil. Knight Grand Cross of Royal Victorian Order, Gt Brit. (Hon. GCVO) 1955, and holds Grand Cross of several foreign orders. *Recreations:* walking and swimming. *Address:* c/o Ministry of Foreign Affairs, Lisbon, Portugal.

ROCK, Prof. Paul Elliot; Professor of Sociology, London School of Economics and Political Science, since 1986; *b* 4 Aug. 1943; *s* of Ashley Rock and Charlotte (*née* Dickson); *m* 1965, Barbara David; two *s*. *Educ:* London School of Economics (BScSoc); Nuffield Coll., Oxford (DPhil). London School of Economics: Asst Lectr, 1967; Lectr, 1970; Sen. Lectr, 1976; Reader in Sociology, 1980; Reader in Social Institutions, 1981. Vis. Prof., Princeton Univ., 1974–75; Vis. Schol., Ministry of Solicitor Gen. of Canada, 1981–82. *Publications:* Making People Pay, 1973; Deviant Behaviour, 1973; The Making of Symbolic Interactionism, 1979; (with D. Downes) Understanding Deviance, 1982, 2nd edn 1988; A View from the Shadows, 1986; Helping Victims of Crime, 1990. *Recreation:* stained glass. *Address:* London School of Economics and Political Science, Houghton Street, Aldwych, WC2A 2AE. *T:* 071–955 7296.

ROCKE, John Roy Mansfield; Vice-Chairman, J. Bibby & Sons, 1975–82, retired; *b* 13 April 1918; *s* of late Frederick Gilbert Rocke and late Mary Susan Rocke; *m* 1948, Pauline Diane Berry; no *c*. *Educ:* Charterhouse; Trinity Coll., Cambridge (BA). War Service, Grenadier Guards, 1940–46 (Maj.). Orme & Eykyn (Stockbrokers), 1946–50; Booker McConnell Ltd, 1950–70, Dir, 1954, Vice-Chm., 1962–70. Mem., BNEC, and Chm., BNEC (Caribbean), 1965–68; Chm., Nat. Econ. Development Cttee for the Food Manufacturing Industry, 1967–71. *Address:* Pendomer Manor, Pendomer, near Yeovil, Somerset BA22 9PH. *Club:* Cavalry and Guards.

ROCKEFELLER, David; banker; *b* New York City, 12 June 1915; *s* of John Davison Rockefeller, Jr and Abby Greene (Aldrich) Rockefeller; *m* 1940, Margaret, *d* of Francis Sims McGrath, Mount Kisco, NY; two *s* four *d*. *Educ:* Lincoln School of Columbia University's Teachers College; Harvard Univ. (BS); London School of Economics; Univ. of Chicago (PhD). Sec. to Mayor Fiorello H. LaGuardia, 1940–41; Asst Regional Dir, US Office of Defense Health and Welfare Services, 1941. Served in US Army, N Africa and France, 1942–45 (Captain). Joined Chase National Bank, NYC, 1946; Asst Manager, Foreign Dept, 1946–47; Asst Cashier, 1947–48; Second Vice-Pres., 1948–49; Vice-Pres., 1949–51; Senior Vice-Pres., 1951–55; Chase Manhattan Bank (merger of Chase Nat. Bank and Bank of Manhattan Co.): Exec. Vice Pres., 1955–57; Dir, 1955–81; Vice-Chm., 1957–61; Pres. and Chm., Exec. Cttee, 1961–69; Chm. of Bd, 1969–81; Chief Exec. Officer, 1969–80; Chairman: Chase Internat. Investment Corp., 1961–81; Chase Internat. Adv. Cttee, 1980–; Rockefeller Brothers Fund Inc., 1981–87 (Vice Chm., 1968–80); The Rockefeller Group Inc., 1987. Director: Internat. Exec. Service Corps (Chm., 1964–68); NY Clearing House, 1971–78; Center for Inter-American Relations (Chm. 1966–70); Overseas Develt Council; US-USSR Trade and Econ. Council, Inc.; Chairman: Americas Soc.; Council on Foreign Relations; NY Chamber of Commerce and Industry; Exec. Cttee, Rockefeller Univ., 1950–75; NYC Partnership, 1979–88; US Business Cttee on Jamaica, 1980–; N America Chm., Trilateral Commn; Member: Exec. Cttee, Museum of Modern Art (Chm., 1962–72); Harvard Coll. Bd of Overseers, 1954–60, 1962–68; Urban Develt Corp., NY State, Business Adv. Council, 1968–72; US Adv. Cttee on Reform of Internat. Monetary System, 1973–; Sen. Adv. Gp, Bilderberg Meetings; US Exec. Cttee, Dartmouth Conf.; Bd, Inst. of Internat. Economics. Director: Downtown-Lower Manhattan Assoc., Inc. (Chm., 1958–65); Internat. House, NY, 1940–63; Morningside Heights, 1947–70 (Pres., 1947–57, Chm., 1957–65); B. F. Goodrich Co., 1956—64; Equitable Life Assce Soc. of US, 1960–65. Trustee: Univ. of Chicago, 1947–62 (Life Trustee, 1966); Carnegie Endowment for Internat. Peace, 1947–60; Council of the Americas (Chm., 1965–70); Sleepy Hollow Restorations, 1981–. Member: American Friends of LSE; US Hon. Fellows, LSE; Founding Mem., Business Cttee for the Arts; Hon. Mem., Commn on White House Fellows, 1964–65; Hon. Chm., Japan Soc. World Brotherhood Award, Jewish Theol Seminary, 1953; Gold Medal, Nat. Inst. Social Sciences, 1967; Medal of Honor for city planning, Amer. Inst. Architects, 1968; C. Walter Nichols Award, NY Univ., 1970; Reg. Planning Assoc. Award, 1971. Hon. LLD: Columbia Univ., 1954; Bowdoin Coll., 1958; Jewish Theol Seminary, 1958; Williams Coll., 1966; Wagner Coll., 1967; Harvard, 1969; Pace Coll., 1970; St John's Univ., 1971; Middlebury, 1974; Univ. of Liberia, 1979; Rockefeller Univ., 1980; Hon. DEng: Colorado Sch. of Mines, 1974; Univ. of Notre Dame, 1987. Holds civic awards. Officer, Legion of Honour, France, 1955; Order of Merit of the Republic, Italy; Order of the Southern Cross, Brazil; Order of the White Elephant and Order of the Crown, Thailand; Order of the Cedar, Lebanon; Order of the Sun, Peru; Order of Humane African Redemption, Liberia; Order of the Crown, Belgium; National Order of Ivory Coast. *Publications:* Unused Resources and Economic Waste, 1940; Creative Management in Banking, 1964. *Recreation:* sailing. *Address:* 30 Rockefeller Plaza, New York, NY 10112, USA. *Clubs:* Century, Harvard, River, Knickerbocker, Links, University, Recess (New York); New York Yacht.
See also L. S. Rockefeller.

ROCKEFELLER, James Stillman; President and Director, Indian Spring Land Co.; Vice-President and Director, Indian Rock Corp.; *b* New York, 8 June 1902; *s* of William Goodsell Rockefeller and Elsie (*née* Stillman); *m* 1925, Nancy Carnegie; two *s* two *d*. *Educ:* Yale University (BA). With Brown Bros & Co., NYC, 1924–30; joined National City Bank of New York (later First Nat. City Bank; now Citibank, NA), 1930; Asst Cashier, 1931; Asst Vice-Pres. 1933; Vice-Pres., 1940–48; Sen. Vice-Pres., 1948–52; Exec. Vice-Pres., 1952; Pres. and Director, 1952–59; Chairman, 1959–67. Rep. Greenwich (Conn.) Town Meeting, 1933–42. Served as Lieutenant-Colonel in US Army, 1942–46. Member Board of Overseers, Memorial Hospital for Cancer and Allied Diseases, NY; Trustee of Estate of William Rockefeller; Trustee American Museum of National History. Hon. Dir, NCR Corp. *Address:* Room 2900, 399 Park Avenue, New York, NY 10043, USA. *Clubs:* Down Town Assoc., Union League, University (New York); Metropolitan (Washington, DC); Field, Round Hill (Greenwich, Conn).

ROCKEFELLER, Laurance Spelman, OBE (Hon.) 1971; conservationist and business executive; Director, Rockefeller Center Inc., 1936–78 (Chairman, 1953–56, 1958–66); *b* New York, 26 May 1910; *s* of John Davison Rockefeller, Jr, FRS and Abby Greene Aldrich; *m* 1934, Mary French; one *s* three *d*. *Educ:* Lincoln School of Teachers College; Princeton University (BA). War service, Lt-Comdr, USNR, 1942–45. Chairman: Citizens' Adv. Cttee on Environmental Quality, 1969–73 (Mem., 1973–79); Meml Sloan-Kettering Cancer Center, 1960–82 (Hon. Chm., 1982–); NY Zool Soc., 1970–75 (Hon. Chm., 1975–); Jackson Hole Preserve Inc.; Woodstock Resort Corp.; Director: Eastern Air Lines, 1938–60, 1977–81, Adv. Dir, 1981–87; Readers' Digest Assoc., 1973–; Pres., Palisades Interstate Park Commn, 1970–77 (Comr Emeritus, 1978–); Adv. Trustee, Rockefeller Bros Fund, 1982–85 (Chm., 1958–80; Vice-Chm., 1980–82); Charter Trustee, Princeton Univ.; Trustee: Alfred P. Sloan Foundn, 1950–82; Greenacre Foundn; Sleepy Hollow Restorations, 1975– (Chm., 1981–85); Hon. Trustee, Nat. Geog. Soc.; Life Mem., Mass Inst. of Technology; Dir, Community Blood Council of Gtr NY; Mem., Nat. Cancer Adv. Bd, 1977–79; Chairman: Outdoor Recreation Resources Review Commn, 1958–65; Hudson River Valley Commn, 1956–66; 1965 White House Conf. on Nat. Beauty; Delegate UN Conf. on Human Environment, 1972. Holds numerous awards, medals and hon. degrees. Comdr, Royal Order of the Lion, Belgium, 1950; US Medal of Freedom, 1969. *Address:* Room 5600, 30 Rockefeller Plaza, New York, NY 10112, USA. *Clubs:* Boone and Crockett, River, Princeton, Lotos, University, Brook,

New York Yacht, Links, Knickerbocker (New York City).
See also David Rockefeller.

ROCKHAMPTON, Bishop of, since 1981; **Rt. Rev. George Arthur Hearn;** *b* 17 Nov. 1935; *s* of Albert Frederick and Edith Maxham Hearn; *m* 1957, Adele Taylor; two *s* one *d*. *Educ:* Northcote High School; University High School; Latrobe Univ., Melbourne. BA, ThL 1965, DipRE, ThSchol Aust. Coll. of Theology; MACE. Deacon 1964, priest 1965, Diocese of Gippsland; Curate of Traralgon, 1964–66; Vicar of Omeo, 1966–69; Rector of Wonthaggi, 1969–73; Rector of Kyabram, dio. Bendigo, 1973–77; Field Officer, Dept of Christian Education, Diocese of Melbourne, 1977–79; Dir, Gen. Bd of Religious Education, 1978–81. *Recreations:* gardening, reading, golf and music. *Address:* PO Box 116, Rockhampton, Queensland 4700, Australia. *T:* (079) 27 3188.

ROCKLEY, 3rd Baron *cr* 1934; **James Hugh Cecil;** Vice-Chairman, Kleinwort Benson Group, since 1988; Director: Equity and Law plc, since 1980; Christies International, since 1989; FR Group, since 1990; Abbey National, since 1990; Foreign and Colonial Investment Trust, since 1991; *b* 5 April 1934; *s* of 2nd Baron Rockley, and Anne Margaret (*d* 1980), *d* of late Adm. Hon. Sir Herbert Meade-Featherstonhaugh, GCVO, CB, DSO; *S* father, 1976; *m* 1958, Lady Sarah Primrose Beatrix, *e d* of 7th Earl Cadogan, *qv*; one *s* two *d*. *Educ:* Eton; New Coll., Oxford. Wood Gundy & Co. Ltd, 1957–62; Kleinwort Benson Ltd, 1962–. Mem., Design Council, 1987–; Trustee, Nat. Portrait Gall., 1981–88. *Heir: s* Hon. Anthony Robert Cecil [*b* 29 July 1961; *m* 1988, Katherine Jane, *d* of G. A. Whalley]. *Address:* Lytchett Heath, Poole, Dorset. *T:* Lytchett Minster (0202) 622228.

ROCKLIN, David Samuel; Chairman, Norton Opax, 1973–89; *b* 15 Aug. 1931; *s* of Alfred Rocklin and Ada Rebecca Rocklin; *m* 1955, Dorothy Ann; two *s* two *d*. *Educ:* Heles School, Exeter. Managing Director, Norton Opax, 1969–73. *Recreations:* books, travel, music, painting, good food and conversation.

RODD, family name of **Baron Rennell.**

RODDICK, (George) Winston; QC 1986; a Recorder, since 1987; *b* Caernarfon, 2 Oct. 1940; *s* of William and Aelwen Roddick; *m* 1966, Cennin Parry; one *s* one *d*. *Educ:* University Coll. London (LLB, LLM). Called to the Bar, Gray's Inn, 1968; Contested: (L) Anglesey, 1970; (L) Cardiff S and Penarth, 1983; (L/Alliance) Newport W, 1987. Chm., Alliance in Wales, 1985–87; Chm., 1982–84, Pres., 1987–88, Welsh Liberal Party. Chm., Lloyd George Soc., 1985–89. Mem., Welsh Language Bd, 1988–; Dir and Trustee, Wales Diabetes Res. Trust, 1987–. *Recreation:* walking the countryside. *Address:* 17 Llandennis Avenue, Cyncoed, Cardiff CF2 6JD. *T:* Cardiff (0222) 759376. *Clubs:* National Liberal; Cardiff and County (Cardiff); Caernarfon Sailing.

RODDIE, Prof. Ian Campbell, CBE 1988; TD 1967; FRCPI; Medical Director and Head of Medical Education, King Khalid National Guard Hospital, Jeddah, since 1990; Dunville Professor of Physiology, Queen's University, Belfast, 1964–87, now Emeritus; *b* 1 Dec. 1928; *s* of Rev. J. R. Wesley Roddie and Mary Hill Wilson; *m* 1st, 1958, Elizabeth Ann Gillon Honeyman (decd); one *s* three *d*; 2nd, 1974, Katherine Ann O'Hara (marr. diss.); one *s* one *d*; 3rd, 1987, Janet Doreen Saville (*née* Lennon). *Educ:* Methodist Coll., Belfast; Queen's Univ., Belfast. Malcolm Exhibnr, 1951, McQuitty Schol., 1953; BSc (1st cl. Hons Physiol.), MB BCh, BAO, MD (with gold medal), DSc; MRCPI; MRIA. Major RAMC (T&AVR); OC Med. Sub-unit, QUB OTC, retd 1968. Resident MO, Royal Victoria Hosp., Belfast, 1953–54; Queen's University, Belfast: Lectr in Physiology, 1954–60; Sen. Lectr, 1961–62; Reader, 1962–64; Dep. Dean, 1975–76, Dean, 1976–81, Faculty of Medicine; Pro-Vice-Chancellor, 1983–87. Consultant Physiologist: NI Hosps Authority, 1962–72; Eastern Health Bd, NI, 1972–88. Staff Consultant, Asian Develt Bank, Manila, 1987–88. Harkness Commonwealth Fund Fellow, Washington Univ., 1960–61; Visiting Professor: Univ. of NSW, 1983–84; Chinese Univ. of Hong Kong, 1988–90; Res. Fellow, Japan Soc. for Promotion of Science, Matsumoto, Japan, 1984. External Examiner: Univs of Aberdeen, Baghdad, Benghazi, Birmingham, Bristol, Glasgow, Ireland, Jos, Leeds, London, Sheffield, Southampton, Zimbabwe; RCS, RCSE, RCPGlas, RCSI. Chief Reg. Sci. Advr for Home Defence, NI, 1977–88; Member: Home Defence Sci. Adv. Conf., 1977–88; Eastern Area Health and Social Services Bd, NI, 1976–81; Physiol Systems Bd, MRC, 1974–76; Med. Adv. Cttee, Cttee of Vice-Chancellors and Principals, 1976–81; GMC, 1979–81; GDC, 1979–81. President: Royal Acad. of Medicine in Ireland, 1985–88; Biol Scis Sect., Royal Acad. of Medicine in Ireland, 1964–66; Ulster Biomed. Engrg Soc., 1979–; Chm. Cttee, Physiol Soc., 1985–88 (Mem. Cttee, 1966–69; Hon. Mem., 1989). Arris and Gale Lectr, RCS, 1962. Conway Bronze Medal, Royal Acad. of Medicine in Ireland, 1977. *Publications:* Physiology for Practitioners, 1971, 2nd edn 1975; Multiple Choice Questions in Human Physiology, 1971, 3rd edn 1984; The Physiology of Disease, 1975; papers on physiology and pharmacology of vascular, sudorific and lymphatic systems. *Address:* Department of Medical Education, King Khalid National Guard Hospital, PO Box 9515, Jeddah 21423, Saudi Arabia. *T:* 665 6200, *Telex:* 605422, *Fax:* 665 3031.

RODECK, Prof. Charles Henry, DSc, FRCOG; Professor of Obstetrics and Gynaecology, University College and Middlesex School of Medicine, since 1990; *b* 23 Aug. 1944; *s* of Heinz and Charlotte Rodeck; *m* 1971, Elisabeth (*née* Rampton); one *s* one *d*. *Educ:* University College London (BSc Anatomy 1966); UCH Med. Sch. (MB BS 1969); DSc (Med) London 1991. MRCOG 1975; FRCOG 1987. House appts to 1975; King's College Hospital Medical School: Registrar, 1975; Lectr, 1976; Sen. Lectr/Consultant, 1978; Dir, Harris Birthright Res. Centre for Fetal Medicine, 1983–86; Prof., Inst. of Obstetrics and Gynaecol., RPMS, Queen Charlotte's and Chelsea Hosp., 1986–90. Mem. Council: Obst. and Gyn. Sect., RSocMed; British Assoc. of Perinatal Med.; Chm., Subspeciality Bd, RCOG, 1989–; Mem., Working Party on Antenatal Diagnosis, RCP, 1986–89; Chm., Steering Gp for Tissue Bank, MRC, 1989–; Mem., EEC Working Party on Chorion Villus Sampling, 1983–85. Examr, RCOG and Univs of Brussels, London, Oxford, Reading, Singapore; Vis. Prof., USA Univs. Mem. or Hon. Mem., med. socs Europe and USA. Mem., editl bds of professional jls, UK and overseas; Associate Editor, Prenatal Diagnosis, 1985–. *Publications:* (ed) Prenatal Diagnosis, 1984; (ed) Fetal Diagnosis of Genetic Defects, 1987; (ed) Fetal Medicine, 1989; articles on prenatal diagnosis and fetal medicine. *Recreation:* stroking the cat. *Address:* Department of Obstetrics and Gynaecology, University College and Middlesex School of Medicine, 86–96 Chenies Mews, WC1E 6HX. *T:* 071–387 2389. *Club:* Athenæum.

RODEN, 9th Earl of, *cr* 1771; **Robert William Jocelyn;** Baron Newport, 1743; Viscount Jocelyn, 1755; a baronet of England, 1665; Captain Royal Navy; retired; *b* 4 Dec. 1909; *S* father 1956; *m* 1937, Clodagh (*d* 1989), *d* of late Edward Kennedy, Bishopscourt, Co. Kildare; three *s*. Retired 1960. *Address:* 75 Bryansford Village, Newcastle, Co. Down BT33 0PT. *T:* Newcastle (03967) 23469.

RODERICK, Caerwyn Eifion; Councillor, South Glamorgan County Council, since 1980; *b* 15 July 1927; *m* 1952, Eirlys Mary Lewis; one *s* two *d*. *Educ:* Maes-y-Dderwen County Sch., Ystradgynlais; University Coll. of North Wales, Bangor. Asst Master, Caterham Sch., Surrey, 1949–52; Sen. Master, Chartesey Sch., LCC, 1952–54; Sen. Maths Master, Boys' Grammar Sch., Brecon, 1954–57; Method Study Engineer, NCB, 1957–60; Sen. Maths Master, Hartridge High Sch., Newport, Mon, 1960–69; Lecturer, Coll. of Educn, Cardiff, 1969–70. MP (Lab) Brecon and Radnor, 1970–79; PPS to Rt Hon. Michael Foot. Mem. Council: UC, Cardiff; formerly Mem. Council, RCVS. *Address:* 29 Charlotte Square, Rhiwbina, Cardiff CF4 6NE. *T:* Cardiff (0222) 628269.

RODERICK, Rev. Charles Edward Morys; Chaplain to the Queen, 1962–80; Rector of Longparish and Hurstbourne Priors, 1971–80; *b* 18 June 1910; *s* of Edward Thomas and Marion Petronella Roderick; *m* 1940, Betty Margaret Arrowsmith; two *s*. *Educ:* Christ's College, Brecon; Trinity College, Oxford (MA). Schoolmaster, 1932–38; training for ordination, 1938–39; ordained, 1939; Curate, St Luke's Parish Church of Chelsea, 1939–46; Chaplain to the Forces, 1940–45; Rector of Denham, Bucks, 1946–53. Vicar of St Michael's, Chester Square, London, 1953–71. HCF. *Address:* 135 Little Ann, Abbotts Ann, Andover, Hants SP11 7NW.

RODGER, Alan Ferguson; QC(Scot) 1985; FBA 1991; Solicitor-General for Scotland, since 1989; *b* 18 Sept. 1944; *er s* of Prof. Thomas Ferguson Rodger and Jean Margaret Smith Chalmers. *Educ:* Kelvinside Acad., Glasgow; Glasgow Univ. (MA, LLB); New Coll., Oxford (MA (by decree), DPhil; DCL). Dyke Jun. Res. Fellow, Balliol Coll., Oxford, 1969–70; Fellow, New Coll., Oxford, 1970–72; Mem., Faculty of Advocates, 1974; Clerk of Faculty, 1976–79; Advocate Depute, 1985–88, Home Advocate Depute, 1986–88. Member: Mental Welfare Commn for Scotland, 1981–84; UK Delegn to CCBE, 1984–89. Maccabaean Lectr, British Acad., 1991. *Publications:* Owners and Neighbours in Roman Law, 1972 (asst editor) Gloag and Henderson's Introduction to the Law of Scotland, 9th edn, 1987; articles mainly on Roman Law. *Recreation:* walking. *Address:* Crown Office, 5/7 Regent Road, Edinburgh EH7 5BL. *T:* 031–557 3800. *Club:* Athenæum.

RODGER, Allan George, OBE 1944; Under-Secretary, Scottish Education Department, 1959–63, retired; *b* Kirkcaldy, 7 Jan. 1902; *s* of Allan Rodger, Schoolmaster, and Annie Venters; *m* 1930, Barbara Melville Simpson; one *s* one *d*. *Educ:* Pathhead Primary School, Kirkcaldy; Kirkcaldy High School; Edinburgh University (MA (Hons) Maths, BSc, MEd, Dip Geog). Teacher, Viewforth School, Kirkcaldy, 1926–29; Lecturer, Moray House Training Coll. and Univ. Dept of Educ. (Edinburgh), 1929–35; HM Inspector of Schools, 1935–45, with special duties in regard to geography, special schools, and training colleges (seconded to special administrative duties in Education Dept, 1939–45); Asst Secretary, Scottish Educ. Dept, 1945–59. Served on Educational Commission for Govts of Uganda and Kenya, 1961. Chairman of various Govt Cttees on Scottish Educ. matters. *Publications:* contrib. to Jl of Educational Psychology and other educational journals. *Recreations:* reading, music. *Address:* 9 Viewpark, Milngavie, Glasgow. *T:* 041–956 6114.

RODGER, Rt. Rev. Patrick Campbell; an Assistant Bishop, Diocese of Edinburgh, since 1986; *b* 28 Nov. 1920; *s* of Patrick Wylie and Edith Ann Rodger; *m* 1952, Margaret Menzies Menzies, MBE (*d* 1989); one *s* (and one *s* decd). *Educ:* Cargilfield; Rugby; Christ Church, Oxford (Hon. Student, 1990); Theological College, Westcott House, Cambridge; Deacon, 1949; Priest, 1950. Asst Curate, St John's Church, Edinburgh, 1949–51, and Chaplain to Anglican Students in Edinburgh, 1951–54. Study Secretary, SCM of Gt Brit. and Ire., 1955–58; Rector, St Fillan's, Kilmacolm, with St Mary's Bridge of Weir, 1958–61; Exec. Sec. for Faith and Order, World Council of Churches, 1961–66; Vice-Provost, St Mary's Cathedral, Edinburgh, 1966–67; Provost, 1967–70; Bishop of Manchester, 1970–78; Bishop of Oxford, 1978–86; Mem., House of Lords, 1974–86. Chm., Churches' Unity Commn, 1974–78; Pres., Conf. of European Churches, 1974–86. *Publications:* The Fourth World Conference on Faith and Order, Montreal (ed), 1964; Songs in a Strange Land, 1989. *Recreations:* music and walking. *Address:* 12 Warrender Park Terrace, Edinburgh EH9 1EG. *T:* 031–229 5075. *Clubs:* Commonwealth Trust; New (Edinburgh).

RODGERS, (Andrew) Piers (Wingate); Secretary, Royal Academy of Arts, London, since 1982; *b* 24 Oct. 1944; second *s* of Sir John Rodgers, Bt, *qv*; *m* 1979, Marie Agathe Houette; two *s*. *Educ:* Eton Coll.; Merton Coll., Oxford (BA 1st Cl. Honour Mods, Prox. acc. Hertford and De Paravicini Prizes). J. Henry Schroder Wagg & Co. Ltd, London, 1967–73: Personal Asst to Chairman, 1971–73; Director, International Council on Monuments and Sites (ICOMOS), Paris, 1973–79; Consultant, UNESCO, Paris, 1979–80; Member, Technical Review Team, Aga Khan Award for Architecture, 1980, 1983; Secretary, UK Committee of ICOMOS, 1981. FRSA 1973. Mem., Court of Assts, Masons' Co., 1982–. Chevalier de l'Ordre des Arts et des Lettres (France), 1987. *Publications:* articles on protection of cultural heritage. *Recreations:* music, Islamic art. *Address:* 18 Hertford Street, W1. *T:* 071–409 3110. *Clubs:* Brooks's, Pratt's, MCC.

RODGERS, Mrs Barbara Noel, OBE 1975; Reader in Social Administration, Manchester University, 1965–73, retired; *b* 1912; *d* of F. S. Stancliffe, Wilmslow, Cheshire; *m* 1950, Brian Rodgers (*d* 1987); no *c*. *Educ:* Wycombe Abbey Sch.; (Exhibitioner) Somerville Coll., Oxford (MA). Social work and travel, 1935–39; Jt appt with Manch. and Salford Council of Social Service and Manchester Univ. (practical work Tutor and special Lectr), 1939–45; Lectr 1945, Sen. Lectr, 1955, Manchester Univ.; Teaching Fellowship in Grad. Sch. of Social Work, Toronto Univ., 1948–49; Sen. Res. Fellow, Centre for Studies in Social Policy, 1973–75. Member: various wages councils and Industrial Tribunal Panel, 1950–85; National Assistance Bd, 1965; Supplementary Benefits Commn, 1966–76. Served and serving on numerous voluntary welfare organisations. *Publications:* (co-author) Till We Build Again, 1948; (with Julia Dixon) Portrait of Social Work, 1960; A Follow Up Study of Manchester Social Administration Students, 1940–60, 1963; Careers of Social Studies Graduates, 1964; (co-author) Comparative Social Administration, 1968; (with June Stevenson) A New Portrait of Social Work, 1973; chapter on Comparative Studies in Social Administration, in Foundations of Social Administration (ed H. Heisler), 1977; The Study of Social Policy: a comparative approach, 1979; numerous articles in learned jls mainly on social security and social services in America, France and Canada. *Recreations:* walking, bird watching, travel. *Address:* 19 High Street, Great Budworth, Cheshire CW9 6HF. *T:* Comberbach (0606) 892068.

RODGERS, George; Library Officer, Labour Party Headquarters, 1988–90; *b* 7 Nov. 1925; *s* of George and Lettitia Georgina Rodgers; *m* 1952, Joan, *d* of James Patrick and Elizabeth Graham; one *s* two *d*. *Educ:* St Margaret's and Holy Trinity, Liverpool; St Michael's, Sylvester, Rupert Road and Longview, Huyton. Co-operative Soc., Whiston, Lancs, 1939–43. Served War, RN, 1943–46 (War Medals, France, Germany Star). White's, Engrs, Widnes, 1946–50; with Civil Engineers: Eave's, Blackpool, 1950–53; Costain, Liverpool, 1953–54; Brit. Insulated Callender Cables, 1954–74. Sales Organiser, 1980, Circulation and Promotion Manager, 1980–87, Labour Weekly; Campaigns Officer, PLP, 1988. Mem., Huyton UDC, 1964–74 (Chm., Educn Cttee, 1969–73; Chm., Local Authority, 1973–74); Mem. Liverpool Regional Hosp. Bd, 1967–74. MP (Lab) Chorley, Feb. 1974–1979; Chm., NW Region Lab MPs, 1975–79. Contested (Lab) Pendle, 1983. *Publication:* (with Ivor Clemitson) A Life to Live: beyond full employment, 1981. *Recreations:* cycling, political history, amateur boxing (spectator). *Address:* 32 Willoughby Road, Huyton, Liverpool L14 6XB. *T:* 051–489 1913. *Club:* Labour (Huyton).

RODGERS, Prof. Harold William, OBE 1943; FRCS 1933; Professor of Surgery, Queen's University of Belfast, 1947–73; Professor Emeritus, 1973; *b* 1 Dec. 1907; *s* of Major R. T. Rodgers; *m* 1938, Margaret Boycott; one *s* three *d*. *Educ:* King's College School; St Bartholomew's Hospital. St Bartholomew's Hospital: House Surgeon, Demonstrator in Anatomy, Chief Asst, Casualty Surgeon, Senior Asst Surgeon. Served War of 1939–45, RAMC, North Africa, Italy, France; Hon. Lt-Col. Prof. of Surgery and Head of Div. of Hosp. Care, Univ. of Ife, Nigeria, 1974–77, retd. Nuffield Medical Visitor to African Territories; WHO Vis. Prof. to India; Vice-Pres. Intervarsity Fellowship; Past President: Section of Surgery, RSM; British Society of Gastro-enterology; Christian Medical Fellowship; British Surgical Research Soc.; YMCA (Belfast); Past Chairman, Ct of Examiners of RCS; Pres., Hibernian CMS. District Surgeon, St John's Ambulance Brigade. Mem., RIIA, 1947–. Hon. Fellow, Polish Soc. of Surgeons, 1972. Hon. MD QUB, 1981. OStJ 1968. *Publications:* Gastroscopy, 1937; general articles in surgical and medical journals. *Recreations:* painting, travel, gardening, poetry. *Address:* 47 Fordington Road, N6 4TH.

RODGERS, Sir John (Charles), 1st Bt, *cr* 1964; DL; *b* 5 Oct. 1906; *o s* of Charles and Maud Mary Rodgers; *m* Betsy, JP, East Sussex, *y d* of Francis W. Aikin-Sneath, JP, and of Louisa, *d* of Col W. Langworthy Baker; two *s*. *Educ:* St Peter's, York; Ecole des Roches, France; Keble College, Oxford (scholar). MA. Sub-Warden, Mary Ward Settlement, 1929; Lectr and Administrative Asst, Univ. of Hull, 1930; FO, 1938–39 and 1944–45; Special Mission to Portugal, December 1945; Dir, Commercial Relations Div., MOI, 1939–41; Dir, Post-War Export Trade Develt, Dept of Overseas Trade, 1941–42; Head Industrial Inf. Div., Min. of Production, 1942–44; Foundation Gov. of Administrative Staff Coll.; Exec. Council Member, Foundation for Management Education, 1959–; BBC General Advisory Council, 1946–52; Hon. Secretary Smuts Memorial Committee, 1953; Chm. Cttee on Litter in Royal Parks, 1954; Exec. Cttee of British Council, 1957–58; Governor, British Film Institute, 1958; Member Tucker Cttee on Proceedings before Examining Justices, 1957; Leader, Parliamentary Panel, and on Exec. and Coun., Inst. of Dirs, 1955–58; Vice-Chm. Exec. Cttee Political and Economic Planning (PEP), 1962–68; Mem. Exec., London Library, 1963–71. MP (C) Sevenoaks, Kent, 1950–79 (where Winston Churchill was one of his constituents); PPS to Rt Hon. Viscount Eccles (at Ministries of Works, Education and Board of Trade), 1951–57; Parliamentary Sec., Bd of Trade, and Minister for regional development and employment, 1958–60. UK Delegate and Leader of the Conservatives to Parly Assembly, Council of Europe, and Vice-Pres., WEU, 1969–79; Chm., Independent Gp, Council of Europe, 1974–79; Chm., Political Affairs Cttee, 1976–79; Vice-Pres., European League for Econ. Co-operation, 1970–79; Hon. Treasurer, Europe-Atlantic Gp, 1975–; Mem., UK Cttee, European Cultural Foundn, 1982–. President: Centre Européen de Documentation et Information, 1963–66; Friends of Free China, 1969–. Dep. Chm., J. Walter Thompson Co. Ltd, 1931–70; Chairman: Cocoa Merchants Ltd, 1959–81; British Market Research Bureau Ltd, 1933–54; New English Library, 1961–70; Radio Luxembourg London, 1979–83 (Hon. Pres., 1983–); dir of Comweld Ltd and other cos. Mem. Council, Nat. Trust, 1978–83; Vice-Chm., Heritage of London Trust, 1980–. Mem. Court: City Univ., 1969–; Brunel Univ., 1981–84. President: Inst. of Practitioners in Advertising, 1967–69; Soc. for Individual Freedom, 1970–73; Inst. of Statisticians, 1971–77; Master, Worshipful Company of Masons, 1968–69; Freeman of the City of London. DL Kent 1973. CBIM; FSS; FIS; FRSA. Knight Grand Cross, Order of Civil Merit (Spain), 1965; Grand Cross of Liechtenstein, 1970; Comdr, Order of Dom Infante Henrique (Portugal), 1972; Grand Officier, Order of Leopold II (Belgium), 1978; Order of Brilliant Star (China), 1979; Kt Comdr, 1st cl., Royal Order of North Star, Sweden, 1980; Comdr, 1st cl., Order of Lion of Finland, 1980; Medal of Merit, Council of Europe, 1980; Grand Officer, Order of Merit of Grand Duchy of Luxembourg, 1983. *Publications:* Mary Ward Settlement: a history, 1930; The Old Public Schools of England, 1938; The English Woodland, 1941; (jtly) Industry looks at the New Order, 1941; English Rivers, 1948; (jtly) One Nation, 1950; York, 1951; (ed) Thomas Gray, 1953; (jtly) Change is our Ally, 1954; (jtly) Capitalism—Strength and Stress, 1958; One Nation at Work, 1976; and other pamphlets. *Recreations:* travel, theatre. *Heir:* *s* John Fairlie Tobias Rodgers, *b* 2 July 1940. *Address:* The Dower House, Groombridge, Kent. *T:* Groombridge (089276) 213. *Clubs:* Brooks's, Pratt's, Beefsteak, Royal Thames Yacht.

See also A. P. W. Rodgers.

RODGERS, Dr Patricia Elaine Joan; High Commissioner of the Commonwealth of the Bahamas to the United Kingdom, since 1988; also Ambassador (non-resident) to: Federal Republic of Germany, and Belgium, since 1988; European Community, and France, since 1989; Permanent Representative to the International Maritime Organization, since 1991; *b* 13 July 1948; *d* of late Dr Kenneth V. A. Rodgers, OBE and Anatol C. Rodgers, MBE. *Educ:* Univ. of Aberdeen (MA Hons English, 1970); Inst. of Internat. Relations, St Augustine, Trinidad (Dip. in Internat. Relns (Hons) 1972); Inst. Univ. des Hautes Etudes Internationales, Geneva (PhD 1977). Joined Ministry of Foreign Affairs, Nassau, Bahamas, 1970; Minister-Counsellor, Washington, 1978–83; Actg High Comr to Canada, 1983–86, High Comr, 1986–88. *Publication:* Mid-Ocean Archipelagos and International Law: a study of the progressive development of international law, 1981. *Recreations:* folk painting, gourmet cooking, theatre. *Address:* c/o Bahamas High Commission, 10 Chesterfield Street, W1X 8AH. *T:* 071–408 4488.

RODGERS, Piers; *see* Rodgers, A. P. W.

RODGERS, Rt. Hon. William Thomas, PC 1975; Director-General, Royal Institute of British Architects, since 1987; *b* 28 Oct. 1928; *s* of William Arthur and Gertrude Helen Rodgers; *m* 1955, Silvia, *d* of Hirsch Szulman; three *d*. *Educ:* Sudley Road Council Sch.; Quarry Bank High School, Liverpool; Magdalen College, Oxford. General Secretary, Fabian Society, 1953–60. Contested: (Lab) Bristol West, March 1957; (SDP) Stockton N, 1983; (SDP/Alliance) Milton Keynes, 1987. MP (Lab 1962–81, SDP 1981–83) Stockton-on-Tees, 1962–74, Teesside, Stockton, 1974–83; Parly Under-Sec. of State: Dept of Econ. Affairs, 1964–67, Foreign Office, 1967–68; Leader, UK delegn to Council of Europe and Assembly of WEU, 1967–68; Minister of State: BoT, 1968–69; Treasury, 1969–70; MoD, 1974–76; Sec. of State for Transport, 1976–79. Chm., Expenditure Cttee on Trade and Industry, 1971–74. Vice-Pres., SDP, 1982–87. Borough Councillor, St Marylebone, 1958–62. *Publications:* Hugh Gaitskell, 1906–1963 (ed), 1964; (jt) The People into Parliament, 1966; The Politics of Change, 1982; (ed) Government and Industry, 1986; pamphlets, etc. *Address:* 48 Patshull Road, NW5 2LD. *T:* 071–485 9997. *Club:* Garrick.

RODNEY, family name of **Baron Rodney.**

RODNEY, 9th Baron *cr* 1782; **John Francis Rodney;** Bt 1764; *b* 28 June 1920; *s* of 8th Lord Rodney and Lady Marjorie Lowther (*d* 1968), *d* of 6th Earl of Lonsdale; *S* father, 1973; *m* 1952, Régine, *d* of late Chevalier Pangaert d'Opdorp, Belgium, and the late Baronne Pangaert d'Opdorp; one *s* one *d*. *Educ:* Stowe Sch., Buckingham; McGill Univ., Montreal. Served War of 1939–45 with Commandos, Burma, 1943–45 (despatches). Alternate Delegate to Council of Europe and WEU, 1986– (Member: Science and Technology Cttee; Agricl Cttee, Council of Europe); Mem., Standing Cttee on Drug Abuse, 1986–; Chm., All Party Gp on Pseudo Religious Cults, 1985–. Past Chm. and Council Mem., British Fedn of Printing Machinery and Supplies; Chm., Printing Equipment Educnl Trust, 1986–. *Recreations:* sailing, shooting, gardening, travelling round the world (not all recreation). *Heir:* *s* Hon. George Brydges Rodney, *b* 3 Jan. 1953. *Address:* 38 Pembroke Road, W8 6NU. *T:* 071–602 4391. *Clubs:* White's; Royal Yacht Squadron.

RODRIGUES, Sir Alberto, Kt 1966; CBE 1964 (OBE 1960; MBE (mil.) 1948); ED; General Medical Practitioner, Hong Kong; Senior Unofficial Member Executive Council 1964–74; Pro-Chancellor and Chairman of Executive Council, University of Hong Kong; *b* 5 November 1911; *s* of late Luiz Gonzaga Rodrigues and late Giovanina Remedios; *m* 1940, Cynthia Maria da Silva; one *s* two *d*. *Educ:* St Joseph's College and University of Hong Kong. MB BS Univ. of Hong Kong, 1934; FRCPE 1988. Post graduate work, London and Lisbon, 1935–36; Medical Practitioner, 1937–40; also Medical Officer in Hong Kong Defence Force. POW, 1940–45. Medical Practitioner, 1945–50; Post graduate work, New York, 1951–52; Resident, Winnipeg Maternity Hosp. (Canada), 1952–53; General Medical Practitioner, 1953–. Member: Urban Council (Hong Kong), 1940–41; 1947–50; Legislative Council, 1953–60; Executive Council, 1960–74. Med. Superintendent, St Paul's Hospital, 1953–. Director: Jardine Strategic Hldgs (formerly Jardine Securities), 1969–; Lap Heng Co. Ltd, 1970–; HK & Shanghai Hotels Ltd, 1969–; Peak Tramways Co. Ltd, 1971–; Li & Fung Ltd, 1973; HK Commercial Broadcasting Co. Ltd, 1974–; Hong Kong and Shanghai Banking Corporation, 1974–76. Officer, Ordem de Cristo (Portugal), 1949; Chevalier, Légion d'Honneur (France), 1962; Knight Grand Cross, Order of St Sylvester (Vatican), 1966. *Recreations:* cricket, hockey, tennis, swimming, badminton. *Address:* St Paul's Hospital Annexe, Causeway Bay, Hong Kong. *T:* 760017. *Clubs:* Royal Hong Kong Jockey, Hong Kong Country, Lusitano, Recreio (all Hong Kong).

RODWELL, Daniel Alfred Hunter; QC 1982; **His Honour Judge Rodwell;** a Circuit Judge, since 1986; *b* 3 Jan. 1936; *s* of late Brig. R. M. Rodwell, AFC, and Nellie Barbara Rodwell (*née* D'Costa); *m* 1967, Veronica Ann Cecil; two *s* one *d*. *Educ:* Munro Coll., Jamaica; Worcester Coll., Oxford, 1956–59 (BA Law). National service, 1954–56; 2/Lieut 1st West Yorks, PWO, 1955; TA, 1956–67: Captain and Adjt 3 PWO, 1964–67. Called to Bar, Inner Temple, 1960. A Deputy Circuit Judge, 1977; a Recorder, 1980–86. *Recreations:* hunting, gardening, sailing. *Address:* Luton Crown Court, 7 George Street, Luton LU1 2AA. *T:* Luton (0582) 488488.

ROE, Anthony Maitland, DPhil; CChem, FRSC; Executive Secretary, Council of Science and Technology Institutes, since 1987; *b* 13 Dec. 1929; *s* of late Percy Alex Roe and Flora Sara Roe (*née* Kisch); *m* 1958, Maureen, *d* of late William James Curtayne and of Kathleen (*née* Wigfull); two *s* one *d*. *Educ:* Harrow Sch.; Oriel Coll., Oxford (BA, MA, DPhil). ARIC 1955; FRSC, CChem 1976. Commnd Intell. Corps, 1955–57. Univ. of Rochester, NY, 1957–59; Sen. Chemist, Smith Kline & French Res. Inst., 1959–65; Hd of Chemistry Gp, Smith Kline & French Labs Ltd, 1965–78; Dir of Chemistry, Smith Kline & French Res. Ltd, 1978–86. Royal Society of Chemistry: Mem. Council, 1982–85, 1987–91; Vice-Pres., Perkin Div., 1986–88; Chm., Heterocyclic Gp, 1986–88; Chm., 'Chemistry in Britain' Management Cttee, 1987–91. Founder Cttee Mem., Soc. for Drug Res., 1966–77; Mem., Bd for Science, BTEC, 1985–88. *Publications:* research papers, patents and reviews in field of organic and medicinal chem. *Recreations:* listening to music, walking, good food and wine. *Address:* 10 Lodge Drive, Hatfield, Herts AL9 5HN. *T:* Hatfield (Herts) (0707) 265075.

ROE, Geoffrey Eric; Director-General Defence Contracts, Ministry of Defence, since 1991; *b* 20 July 1944; *s* of Herbert William Roe and Florence Roe (*née* Gordon); *m* 1968, Elizabeth Anne Ponton; one *s* one *d*. *Educ:* Tottenham Grammar School. Min. of Aviation, 1963; Asst Private Sec. to Sir Ronald Melville, 1967–69; Exports and Internat. Relations Div., Min. of Technology, 1969–74; Guided Weapons Contracts Branch, 1974–76; seconded British Aerospace, 1976–78; Rocket Motor Exec., 1978–81; Asst Dir Contracts (Air), 1981–86; Dir of Contracts (Underwater Weapons), 1986–89; Head, Material Co-ord. (Naval), 1989–90; Principal Dir, Navy and Nuclear Contracts, 1990–91. *Recreations:* ski-ing, fell-walking, sailing, private flying. *Adddress:* Ministry of Defence, Whitehall, SW1A 2HB.

ROE, Marion Audrey; MP (C) Broxbourne, since 1983; *b* 15 July 1936; *d* of William Keyte and Grace Mary (*née* Bocking); *m* 1958, James Kenneth Roe; one *s* two *d*. *Educ:* Bromley High Sch. (GPDST); Croydon High Sch. (GPDST); English Sch. of Languages, Vevey. Member: London Adv. Cttee, IBA, 1978–81; Gatwick Airport Consultative Cttee, 1979–81; SE Thames RHA, 1980–83. Member (C): Bromley Borough Council, 1975–78; for Ilford N, GLC, 1977–86 (Cons. Dep. Chief Whip, 1978–82). Contested (C) Barking, 1979. Parly Private Secretary to: Parly Under-Secs of State for Transport, 1985; Minister of State for Transport, 1986; Sec. of State for Transport, 1987; Parly Under Sec. of State, DoE, 1987–88. Member: Agriculture Select Cttee, 1984–85; Social Services Select Cttee, 1988–89; Chm., Cons. Backbench Horticulture and Markets Sub-Cttee, 1989–; Jt. Chm., All-Party Fairs and Showgrounds Gp, 1989–; Vice-Chm., Cons. Backbench Social Security Cttee, 1988–; Secretary: Cons. Backbench Horticulture Cttee, 1983–85; Cons. Backbench Party Orgn Cttee, 1985; All-Party Hospices Gp, 1990–; Mem., Adv. Cttee on Women's Employment, Dept of Employment, 1989–; Substitute Mem., UK Delegn to Council of Europe and WEU, 1989–. Vice-Pres., Women's Nat. Cancer Control Campaign, 1985–; Patron, UK Nat. Cttee for UN Develt Fund for Women, 1985–87; Gov., Research into Ageing Trust, 1988–. *Recreations:* ballet, opera. *Address:* House of Commons, SW1A 0AA. *Club:* Carlton (Associate Member).

ROE, Dame Raigh (Edith), DBE 1980 (CBE 1975); JP; Director, Airlines of Western Australia, since 1981; World President, Associated Country Women of the World, 1977–80; *b* 12 Dec. 1922; *d* of Alwyn and Laura Kurts; *m* 1941, James Arthur Roe; three *s*. *Educ:* Perth Girls' Sch., Australia. Country Women's Association: State Pres., 1967–70; National Pres., 1969–71. World Ambassador, WA Council, 1978–; Hon. Ambassador, State of Louisiana, USA, 1979–. Comr, ABC, 1978–83; Nat. Dir (Aust.), Queen Elizabeth II Silver Jubilee Trust for Young Australians, 1978–. JP Western Australia, 1966. Australian of the Year, 1977; Brooch of Merit, Deutscher Landfrauenverband, Fed. Republic of Germany, 1980. *Address:* 76 Regency Drive, Crestwood, Thornlie, WA 6108, Australia. *T:* 4598765.

ROE, Air Chief Marshal Sir Rex (David), GCB 1981 (KCB 1977; CB 1974); AFC; retired 1981; *b* 1925; *m* 1948, Helen Sophie (*née* Nairn) (*d* 1981); one *s* two *d*. *Educ:* City of London Sch.; London University. Joined RAF 1943; trained in Canada; served with Metropolitan Fighter Sector, No 11 Group, 203 Sqn, 1950–51; Sch. of Maritime Reconnaissance, 1951–53; Central Flying School and Flying Training Units, 1953–55; Commanded RNZAF Central Flying School, 1956–58; RAF Staff College, 1959; Commanded No 204 Sqn, 1960–62; College of Air Warfare, 1962–64; SASO No 18 (Maritime) Gp, 1964–67; Stn Comdr RAF Syerston, 1967–69; Director of Flying Trng, 1969–71; RCDS, 1971; Deputy Controller Aircraft (C), MoD (Procurement Executive), 1972–74; SASO HQ Near East Air Force, 1974–76; AOC-in-C Training Comd, 1976–77; AOC-in-C, Support Command, 1977–78; Air Mem. for Supply and

Organisation, 1978–81. *Recreations:* reading, Rugby football. *Address:* c/o Lloyds Bank, 7 Pall Mall, SW1. *Club:* Royal Air Force.

ROE, Rt. Rev. William Gordon; *see* Huntingdon, Bishop Suffragan of.

ROEBUCK, Roy Delville; Barrister-at-law; *b* Manchester, 25 Sept. 1929; *m* 1957, Dr Mary Ogilvy Adams; one *s. Educ:* various newspapers. Called to the Bar, Gray's Inn, 1974. Served RAF (National Service), 1948–50 (FEAF). Journalist, Stockport Advertiser, Northern Daily Telegraph, Yorkshire Evening News, Manchester Evening Chronicle, News Chronicle, Daily Express, Daily Mirror and Daily Herald, 1950–66; freelance, 1966–. MP (Lab) Harrow East, 1966–70; PA to Rt Hon. George Wigg, Paymaster-Gen., 1966–67; Advr to Lord Wigg, Pres. of Betting Office Licensees Assoc., 1975–83. Contested (Lab): Altrincham and Sale, 1964 and Feb. 1965; Leek, Feb. 1974. Member: Islington CHC, 1988–; Bd of Governors, Moorfields Eye Hospital, 1984–88; Governor, Thornhill Sch., Islington, 1986–88. *Recreations:* tennis, ski-ing, music, reading Hansard. *Address:* 12 Brooksby Street, N1 1HA. *T:* 071–607 7057; Bell Yard Chambers, 16 Bell Yard, WC2A 2JR. *T:* 071–306 9292. *Club:* Royal Automobile.

ROEG, Nicolas Jack; film director; *b* 15 Aug. 1928; *s* of Jack Roeg and Gertrude Silk; *m* 1st, 1957, Susan (marr. diss.), *d* of Major F. W. Stephen, MC; four *s*; 2nd, Theresa Russell; two *s. Educ:* Mercers' Sch. Original story of Prize of Arms; Cinematographer: The Caretaker; Masque of the Red Death; Nothing But the Best; Petulia; A Funny Thing Happened on the Way to the Forum; Fahrenheit 451; Far From the Madding Crowd, etc; 2nd Unit Director and Cinematographer: Judith; Lawrence of Arabia; Co-Dir, Performance; Director: Walkabout; Don't Look Now; The Man who Fell to Earth; Bad Timing; Eureka, 1983; Insignificance, 1985; Castaway, 1986; Track 29, 1987; Aria, 1987; Sweet Bird of Youth, 1989; Witches, 1990; Cold Heaven, 1991; Exec. Producer, Without You I'm Nothing, 1989. *Address:* c/o Hatton & Baker, 18 Jermyn Street, SW1Y 6HN.

ROFF, Derek Michael, OBE 1972; HM Diplomatic Service; Counsellor, Foreign and Commonwealth Office, since 1981; *b* 1 Aug. 1932; *m* 1957, Diana Susette Barrow; three *s. Educ:* Royal Grammar Sch., Guildford; St Edmund Hall, Oxford (BA). National Service with The Cameronians (Scottish Rifles) and King's African Rifles, 1952–54. ICI Ltd, 1958–67; entered Foreign Office, 1967; Consul (Economic), Frankfurt, 1968; First Sec., UK Delegn to the European Communities, Brussels, 1970; Consul (Economic), Düsseldorf, 1973; First Sec., FCO, 1977. *Address:* c/o Foreign and Commonwealth Office, SW1A 2AH. *Club:* Commonwealth Trust.

ROFFEY, Harry Norman, CMG 1971; Assistant Secretary, Department of Health and Social Security, 1954–72, retired; *b* 2 March 1911; *s* of Henry Roffey and Ella Leggatt; *m* 1964, Florence Dickie; no *c. Educ:* Brighton Grammar Sch.; St Catharine's Coll., Cambridge (BA Hons, MA); Inst. of Education, London Univ. (Teacher's Dip.). Teaching (languages), 1935–40. Air Ministry and Foreign Office, 1940–45 (left as Wing Comdr); Min. of Health (Principal), 1946–54; Dept of Health and Social Security, 1954–72 (as Asst Sec. i/c Internat. Affairs, on the Health side). *Recreations:* travel, music, etc. *Address:* 2 Sunnyside Place, Wimbledon, SW19 4SJ. *T:* 081–946 4991.

ROGAN, Rev. Canon John; Canon Residentiary, since 1983 and Chancellor, since 1989, Bristol Cathedral (Precentor, 1983–89); Bishop's Adviser in Social Responsibility, since 1983; *b* 20 May 1928; *s* of William and Jane Rogan; *m* 1953, Dorothy Margaret Williams; one *s* one *d. Educ:* Manchester Central High School; St John's Coll., Univ. of Durham. BA 1949, MA 1951; DipTheol with distinction, 1954; BPhil 1981. Education Officer, RAF, 1949–52. Asst Curate, St Michael and All Angels, Ashton-under-Lyne, 1954–57; Chaplain, Sheffield Industrial Mission, 1957–61; Secretary, Church of England Industrial Cttee, 1961–66; Asst Secretary, Board for Social Responsibility, 1962–66; Vicar of Leigh, Lancs, 1966–78; Sec., Diocesan Bd for Social Responsibility, 1967–74, Chm. 1974–78; Rural Dean of Leigh, 1971–78; Hon. Canon of Manchester, 1975–78; Provost, St Paul's Cathedral, Dundee, 1978–83. *Publication:* (ed jtly) Principles of Church Reform: Thomas Arnold, 1962. *Recreations:* Roman history, walking, music. *Address:* 84 Concorde Drive, Bristol BS10 6PX.

ROGERS, Rt. Rev. Alan Francis Bright, MA; an Hon. Assistant Bishop, Diocese of London (Kensington Area), since 1985; Hon. Assistant Curate, St Mary's, Twickenham, since 1985; *b* 12 Sept. 1907; *s* of Thomas and Alice Rogers, London, W9; *m* 1st, 1932, Millicent Boarder (*d* 1984); two *s*; 2nd, 1985, Barbara Gower. *Educ:* Westminster City Sch.; King's Coll., London; Leeds Univ.; Bishop's Coll., Cheshunt (Kitchener Schol., 1926–30). Curate of St Stephen's, Shepherds Bush, 1930–32; Holy Trinity, Twickenham, 1932–34; Civil Chaplain, Mauritius, 1934–49; Archdeacon of Mauritius, 1946–49; Commissary to Bishop of Mauritius, 1949–59; Vicar of Twickenham, 1949–54; Proctor in Convocation, 1951–59; Vicar of Hampstead, 1954–59; Rural Dean of Hampstead, 1955–59; Bishop of Mauritius, 1959–66; Suffragan Bishop of Fulham, 1966–70; Suffragan Bishop of Edmonton, 1970–75; Priest-in-Charge: Wappenham, 1977–80; Abthorpe with Slapton, 1977–83. An Hon. Asst Bishop of Peterborough, 1975–84. Chm., Archbishops' Bd of Examiners, USPG, 1972–83. MA Lambeth 1959. *Publications:* Threads of Friendship (autobiog.), 1989; Walking with God as a Friend, 1990. *Recreations:* swimming, crosswords, theatre-going, travel. *Address:* 20 River Way, Twickenham, Middx TW2 5JP. *T:* 081–894 2031. *Club:* Royal Over-Seas League.

ROGERS, Allan Ralph, FGS; MP (Lab) Rhondda, since 1983; *b* 24 Oct. 1932; *s* of John Henry Rogers and Madeleine Rogers (*née* Smith); *m* 1955, Ceridwen James; one *s* three *d. Educ:* University College of Swansea (BSc Hons Geology). Geologist, UK, Canada, USA, Australia, 1956–63; Teacher, 1963–65; Tutor-organiser, WEA, 1965–70, District Sec., 1970–79. Opposition spokesman on defence, 1987–. European Parliament: Mem. (Lab) SE Wales, 1979–84; Vice-Pres., 1979–82. *Recreation:* all sports. *Address:* House of Commons, SW1A 0AA. *Club:* Workmen's (Treorchy).

ROGERS, General Bernard William; General, United States Army, retired; Supreme Allied Commander, Europe, 1979–87; *b* 16 July 1921; *s* of late Mr and Mrs W. H. Rogers; *m* 1944, Ann Ellen Jones; one *s* two *d. Educ:* Kansas State Coll.; US Mil. Acad. (BS); Oxford Univ. (Rhodes Scholar; BA, MA); US Army Comd Staff Coll., Fort Leavenworth, Kansas; US Army War Coll., Carlisle Barracks, Pa. CO 3rd Bn, 9th Inf. Regt, 2nd Inf. Div., Korea, 1952–53; Bn Comdr 1st Bn, 23rd Inf., 2nd Inf. Div., Fort Lewis, Washington, 1955–56; Comdr, 1st Battle Gp, 19th Inf., Div. COS, 24th Inf. Div., Augsburg, Germany, 1960–61; Exec. Officer to Chm., Jt Chiefs of Staff, Washington, DC, 1962–66; Asst Div. Comdr, 1st Inf. Div., Republic of Vietnam, 1966–67; Comdt of Cadets, US Mil. Acad., 1967–69; Comdg Gen., 5th Inf. Div., Fort Carson, Colo, 1969–70; Chief of Legislative Liaison, Office of Sec. to the Army, Washington, DC, 1971–72; Dep. Chief of Staff for Personnel, Dept of the Army, Washington, DC, 1972–74; Comdg Gen., US Army Forces Comd, Fort McPherson, Ga, 1974–76; Chief of Staff, US Army, Washington, DC, 1976–79. Mem., Council on Foreign Relations, 1983–. Hon. Fellow, University Coll., Oxford, 1979. Hon. LLD: Akron, 1978; Boston, 1981; Hon. DCL Oxon, 1983. *Publications:* Cedar Falls-Junction City: a Turning Point, 1974; contribs to: Foreign Affairs, RUSI, 1982; Strategic Review, NATO's Sixteen Nations, 1983; Europa Archiv, Defense, NATO Review, 1984; Europäische Wehrkunde, Rivista Militaire, 1985; The Adelphi Papers, 1986; Soldat und Technik, 1987. *Recreations:* golf, reading. *Address:* 1467 Hampton Ridge Drive, McLean, Va 22101, USA.

ROGERS, Surgeon Rear-Adm. (D) Brian Frederick, CB 1980; Director of Naval Dental Services, 1977–80; *b* 27 Feb. 1923; *s* of Frederick Reginald Rogers, MIMechE, MIMarE, and Rosa Jane Rogers; *m* 1946, Mavis Elizabeth (*née* Scott); one *s* two *d. Educ:* Rock Ferry High Sch.; Liverpool Univ. (LDS 1945). House Surgeon, Liverpool Dental Hosp., 1945; joined RNVR, 1946; transf. to RN, 1954; served HMS Ocean, 1954–56 and HMS Eagle, 1964–66; Fleet Dental Surg. on staff of C-in-C Fleet, 1974–77; Comd Dental Surg. to C-in-C Naval Home Comd, 1977. QHDS 1977. *Recreations:* European touring, photography, DIY. *Address:* 22 Trerieve, Downderry, Torpoint, Cornwall PL11 3LY. *T:* Downderry (05035) 526; Montana roja, Lanzarote, Canary Islands.

ROGERS, Prof. C(laude) Ambrose, FRS 1959; Astor Professor of Mathematics, University College, London, 1958–86, now Emeritus; *b* 1 Nov. 1920; *s* of late Sir Leonard Rogers, KCSI, CIE, FRS; *m* 1952, Mrs J. M. Gordon, *widow* of W. G. Gordon, and *d* of F. W. G. North; two *d. Educ:* Berkhamsted School; University Coll., London; Birkbeck Coll., London. BSc, PhD, DSc (London, 1941, 1949, 1952). Experimental officer, Ministry of Supply, 1940–45; lecturer and reader, University College, London, 1946–54; Prof. of Pure Mathematics, Univ. of Birmingham, 1954–58. Mem. Council, Royal Soc., 1966–68 and 1983–84; Pres., London Mathematical Soc., 1970–72; Chm., Jt Mathematical Council, 1982–84. *Publications:* Packing and Covering, 1964; Hausdorff Measures, 1970; articles in various mathematical journals. *Recreation:* string figures. *Address:* Department of Statistical Science, University College, WC1E 6BT; 8 Grey Close, NW11 6QG. *T:* 081–455 8027.

ROGERS, Ven. David Arthur; Archdeacon of Craven, 1977–86; *b* 12 March 1921; *s* of Rev. Canon Thomas Godfrey Rogers and Doris Mary Cleaver Rogers (*née* Steele); *m* 1951, Joan Malkin; one *s* three *d. Educ:* Saint Edward's School, Oxford (scholar); Christ's College, Cambridge (exhibitioner). BA 1947, MA 1952. War service with Green Howards and RAC, 1940–45; Christ's Coll. and Ridley Hall, Cambridge, 1945–49; Asst Curate, St George's, Stockport, 1949–53; Rector, St Peter's, Levenshulme, Manchester, 1953–59; Vicar of Sedbergh, Cautley and Garsdale, 1959–79; Rural Dean of Sedbergh and then of Ewecross, 1959–77; Hon. Canon of Bradford Cathedral, 1967. *Address:* Borrens, Leck, via Carnforth, Lancs LA6 2JG. *T:* Kirkby Lonsdale (05242) 71616.

ROGERS, David Bryan, CB 1984; Deputy Secretary and Director General, Board of Inland Revenue, 1981–89; *b* 8 Sept. 1929; *s* of Frank Rogers and Louisa Rogers; *m* 1955, Marjory Geraldine Gilmour Horribine; one *s* two *d. Educ:* Grove Park, Wrexham; University Coll., London (BA Classics). Inspector of Taxes, 1953; Principal Inspector, 1968; Sen. Principal Inspector, 1976; Under Sec. and Dir of Operations, Bd of Inland Revenue, 1978–81. Mem. Council, UCL, 1983–. *Recreations:* piano, organ, singing, reading.

ROGERS, Rev. Edward; General Secretary, Methodist Division of Social Responsibility (formerly Christian Citizenship Department), 1950–75; *b* 4 Jan. 1909; *s* of Capt. E. E. Rogers, Fleetwood; *m* 1st, 1937, Edith May, *o d* of A. L. Sutton, Plaistow; 2nd, 1979, Lucy Eveline Howlett. *Educ:* Baines's Poulton-Le-Fylde Grammar School; Manchester University; Hartley Methodist Coll. Kitchener Scholar, Shuttleworth Scholar, Hulme Hall, Manchester. MA (Econ. and Pol.) 1931, BD, 1933, Manchester Univ. Methodist Circuit Minister: East London Mission, Bakewell, Birmingham (Sutton Park), Southport, 1933–50. Lectures: Fernley, 1951; Ainslie, 1952; Beckly, 1957; Peake 1971. Editorial Dir, Methodist Newspaper Co., 1949–; Organising Dir, Methodist Relief Fund, 1953–75; Chairman, Inter-Church Aid and Refugee Service, British Council of Churches, 1960–64; Pres., Methodist Conf., 1960; Moderator, Free Church Federal Council, 1968 (Chm., Exec., 1974–80); Vice-Pres., British Council of Churches, 1971–74. Chairman: Standing Commn on Migration, 1964–70; Churches Cttee on Gambling Legislation, 1967–73; Exec. Council, UK Immigrants Adv. Service, 1970; Community and Race Relations Unit, 1971–75; Avec Board, 1977–89; Select Committee on Cruelty to Animals, 1963. *Publications:* First Easter, 1948; A Commentary on Communism, 1951; Programme for Peace, 1954; God's Business, 1957; That They Might Have Life, 1958; The Christian Approach to the Communist, 1959; Church Government, 1964; Living Standards, 1964; Law, Morality and Gospel, 1969; Search for Security, 1973; Plundered Planet, 1973; Money, 1976; Thinking About Human Rights, 1978; Changing Humanity: genetic engineering, 1989. *Recreations:* travel, indiscriminate reading. *Address:* 49 Fernhurst Road, Croydon, Surrey CR0 7OJ. *T:* 081–656 1729.

ROGERS, Eric William Evan, DSc(Eng); FRAeS; aeronautical research consultant; Deputy Director (A), Royal Aircraft Establishment, Farnborough, Hants, 1978–85; *b* 12 April 1925; *o s* of late W. P. Rogers, Southgate, N London; *m* 1950, Dorothy Joyce Loveless; two *s* one *d. Educ:* Southgate County Grammar Sch.; Imperial Coll., London. FCGI, DIC. Aerodynamics Div., NPL, 1945–70 (Head of Hypersonic Research, 1961); Aerodynamics Dept, RAE, 1970 (Head, 1972). *Publications:* various papers on aerodynamics and on industrial aerodynamics, in ARC (R and M series), RAeS jls and elsewhere. *Recreations:* music, history. *Address:* 64 Thetford Road, New Malden, Surrey KT3 5DT. *T:* 081–942 7452.

ROGERS, Sir Frank (Jarvis), Kt 1988; Deputy Chairman: Argyll Investments Ltd, 1982–90; Daily Telegraph plc, since 1986 (Director, since 1985); Director, EMAP plc (formerly East Midland Allied Press), 1971–91 (Chairman, 1973–90); *b* 24 Feb. 1920; *s* of Percy Rogers, Stoke-on-Trent; *m* 1949, Esma Holland; two *d. Educ:* Wolstanton Grammar School. Journalist, 1937–49; Military Service, 1940–46; Gen. Man., Nigerian Daily Times, 1949–52; Manager, Argus, Melbourne, 1952–55; Man. Dir, Overseas Newspapers, 1958–60; Dir, Daily Mirror, 1960–65; Man. Dir, IPC, 1965–70. Chairman: Nat. Newspaper Steering Gp, 1970–72; Newspaper Publishers Assoc., 1990– (Vice-Chm., 1968–69; Dir, 1971–73). Adviser on Corporate Affairs, The Plessey Co. Ltd, 1973–81. Trustee, Reuters Founders Share Co., 1989–. Mem., British Exec. Cttee, Internat. Press Inst., 1988– (Chm., 1978–88). Mem. Council and Chm., Exec. Cttee, Industrial Soc., 1976–79; Chm. Council, Industry and Parliament Trust, 1979–81; Mem. Council, Advertising Standards Authority, 1985–90. *Recreations:* motoring, golf. *Address:* Greensleeves, Loudwater Drive, Rickmansworth, Herts.

ROGERS, George Theodore; retired; Under-Secretary, Department of Trade, 1974–79; *b* 26 Feb. 1919; *s* of George James and late Margaret Lilian Rogers; *m* 1944, Mary Katherine Stedman; three *s* two *d. Educ:* Portsmouth Grammar Sch.; Keble Coll., Oxford (Open Schol. in Classics). Served War, Indian Infy, Burma, 1939–45. Resumed univ. educn (PPE), 1945–48; NATO Defence Coll., 1953–54. Min. of Supply/Min. of Aviation, 1948–65; Univ. Grants Cttee, 1965–68; Min. of Technology, 1968–70; DTI, 1970–74; Under-Sec., 1973. *Recreations:* gardening, travel, aviation. *Address:* 39 Sandy Lane, Cheam, Surrey SM2 7PQ. *T:* 081–642 6428.

ROGERS, Henry Augustus, OBE 1976 (MBE 1967); HM Diplomatic Service, retired; *b* 11 Dec. 1918; *s* of Henry Augustus Rogers and Evelyn Mary Rogers (*née* Casey); *m* 1947,

Margaret May Stainsby; three *s. Educ:* The Fox Sch.; West Kensington Central Sch., London, W. With Solicitors, Wedlake Letts & Birds, Temple, prior to war. Joined RNVR, 1938; served war, 1939–45. Joined Foreign Office, 1945; Buenos Aires, 1946; Havana, 1953; Vice-Consul, Guatemala City, 1954; Vice-Consul, Los Angeles, 1958; Second Sec., Belgrade, 1961; FO, 1963; Second Sec., Kaduna, 1965; First Sec., Head of Chancery and Consul, Tegucigalpa, 1967; FCO, 1971; Consul, Luanda, Angola, 1973; Consul-Gen., Brisbane, 1976–77; FCO, 1978. *Recreations:* reading, classical literature and modern history, art (the Impressionists), music. *Address:* 18 Carew Views, Carew Road, Eastbourne, East Sussex BN21 2JL. *T:* Eastbourne (0323) 30915.

ROGERS, Dr (John) Michael, FSA; FBA 1988; Khalili Professor of Islamic Art, School of Oriental and African Studies, University of London, since 1991; *b* 25 Jan. 1935. *Educ:* Ulverston Grammar Sch.; Corpus Christi Coll., Oxford (MA, DPhil). FSA 1974. Robinson Sen. Student, Oriel Coll., Oxford, 1958–61; Tutor in Philosophy, Pembroke and Wadham Colls, Oxford, 1961–65; Asst, then Associate, Prof. of Islamic Art and Archaeol., Center for Arabic Studies, Amer. Univ. in Cairo, 1965–77; Dep. Keeper, Dept of Oriental Antiquities, BM, 1977–91. Vis. Sen. Res. Fellow, Merton Coll., Oxford, 1971–72. Corresp. Mem., Deutsches Archäologisches Inst., Berlin, 1988. Order of the Egyptian Republic, 2nd cl., 1969. *Publications:* The Spread of Islam, 1976; Islamic Art and Design 1500–1700, 1983; (with R. M. Ward) Süleyman the Magnificent, 1988; numerous articles on hist. and archaeol. of Islamic Turkey, Egypt, Syria, Iran and Central Asia. *Recreations:* walking, music, botany. *Address:* School of Oriental and African Studies, Thornhaugh Street, Russell Square, WC1H 0XG. *Club:* Beefsteak.

ROGERS, John Michael Thomas; QC 1979; barrister-at-law; a Recorder of the Crown Court, since 1976; *b* 13 May 1938; *s* of Harold Stuart Rogers and Sarah Joan Thomas; *m* 1971, Jennifer Ruth Platt (marr. diss. 1984); one *d. Educ:* Rydal Sch.; Birkenhead Sch.; Fitzwilliam House, Cambridge (MA, LLB). Schoolmaster, 1962–64; called to Bar, Gray's Inn, 1963, Bencher 1991. Leader, Wales and Chester Circuit, 1990–. Chancellor, Dio. of St Asaph, 1983–. *Recreations:* farming, gardening. *Address:* Treanna, Dwyran, Anglesey. *T:* Brynsiencyn (0248430) 814; 2 Dr Johnson's Building, Temple, EC4. *T:* 071–353 5371. *Clubs:* Reform; Pragmatists (Wirral); Ruthin Rugby Football.

ROGERS, Air Chief Marshal Sir John (Robson), KCB 1982; CBE 1971; FRAeS; Executive Chairman, Motor Sports Association, since 1989; Vice-Chairman, Royal Automobile Club, since 1990; Director, First Technology Group, since 1986; *b* 11 Jan. 1928; *s* of B. R. Rogers; *m* 1955, Gytha Elspeth Campbell; two *s* two *d. Educ:* Brentwood Sch.; No 1 Radio Sch., Cranwell; Royal Air Force Coll., Cranwell. OC 56(F) Sqdn, 1960–61; Gp Captain, 1967; OC RAF Coningsby, 1967–69; Air Commodore, 1971; Dir of Operational Requirements (RAF), 1971–73; Dep. Comdt, RAF Coll., 1973–75; RCDS, 1976; Air Vice-Marshal, 1977; Dir-Gen. of Organisation, RAF, 1977–79; AOC Training Units, RAF Support Comd, 1979–81; Air Mem. for Supply and Organisation, MoD, 1981–83; Controller Aircraft, MoD PE, 1983–86, retired. FRAeS 1983. *Recreation:* motor racing. *Address:* c/o Lloyds Bank, 27 High Street, Colchester, Essex. *Clubs:* Royal Automobile, Royal Air Force.

ROGERS, John Willis; QC 1975; a Recorder of the Crown Court, since 1974; *b* 7 Nov. 1929; *s* of late Reginald John Rogers and late Joan Daisy Alexandra Rogers (*née* Willis); *m* 1952, Sheila Elizabeth Cann; one *s* one *d. Educ:* Sevenoaks Sch.; Fitzwilliam House, Cambridge (MA). Called to Bar, Lincoln's Inn, 1955 (Cholmeley Schol.); Bencher, 1984. 1st Prosecuting Counsel to Inland Revenue, SE Circuit, 1969–75. Hon. Recorder, City of Canterbury, 1985. Chm., Adv. Cttee on Conscientious Objectors, 1991–. *Recreations:* cricket, gardening, change ringing. *Address:* 3 Serjeants' Inn, Temple, EC4Y 1BQ. *T:* 071–353 5537. *Clubs:* Garrick, MCC, Band of Brothers.

ROGERS, Malcolm Austin, DPhil; FSA; Deputy Director since 1983, and Keeper since 1985, National Portrait Gallery (Deputy Keeper, 1983–85); *b* 3 Oct. 1948; *s* of late James Eric Rogers and Frances Anne (*née* Elsey). *Educ:* Oakham School; Magdalen College, Oxford (Open Exhbr); Christ Church, Oxford (Senior Scholar). MA 1973; DPhil 1976. Assistant Keeper, National Portrait Gallery, 1974. *Publications:* Dictionary of British Portraiture, 4 vols (ed jtly), 1979–81; Museums and Galleries of London, 1983, 3rd edn 1991; William Dobson, 1983; John and John Baptist Closterman: a catalogue of their works, 1983; Elizabeth II: portraits of sixty years, 1986; Camera Portraits, 1989; Montacute House, 1991; (with Sir David Piper) Companion Guide to London, 1992; (ed) The English Face, by Sir David Piper, 1992; articles and reviews in Burlington Magazine, Apollo, Connoisseur, TLS. *Recreations:* food and wine, opera, travel. *Address:* 76A Ashley Gardens, Thirleby Road, SW1P 1HG. *T:* 071–828 5304. *Club:* Beefsteak.

ROGERS, Martin Hartley Guy; HM Diplomatic Service, retired; *b* 11 June 1925; *s* of late Rev. Canon T. Guy Rogers and Marguerite Inez Rogers; *m* 1959, Jean Beresford Chinn; one *s* three *d. Educ:* Marlborough Coll.; Jesus Coll., Cambridge. CRO, 1949; 2nd Sec., Karachi, 1951–53; CRO, 1953–56 and 1958–60; seconded to Govt of Fedn of Nigeria, 1956–57; ndc 1960–61; 1st Sec., Ottawa, 1961–62; Adviser to Jamaican Min. of External Affairs, 1963; CRO, later Commonwealth Office, 1963–68; Dep. High Comr, Bombay, 1968–71, Kaduna, 1972–75; High Comr, The Gambia, 1975–79; on loan to CSSB as Asst Dir, 1979–85. *Recreations:* golf, bridge. *Address:* Croftside, Harrow Road East, Dorking, Surrey RH4 2AX. *T:* Dorking (0306) 883789.

ROGERS, Martin John Wyndham; Director, Farmington Institute for Christian Studies, and Fellow, Manchester College, Oxford, since 1991; *b* 9 April 1931; *s* of late John Frederick Rogers and Grace Mary Rogers; *m* 1957, Jane Cook; two *s* one *d. Educ:* Oundle Sch.; Heidelberg Univ.; Trinity Hall, Cambridge (MA). Henry Wiggin & Co., 1953–55; Westminster School: Asst Master, 1955–60; Sen. Chemistry Master, 1960–64; Housemaster, 1964–66; Under Master and Master of the Queen's Scholars, 1967–71; Headmaster of Malvern Coll., 1971–82; Chief Master, King Edward's Sch., Birmingham, Headmaster of the Schs of King Edward VIth in Birmingham, 1982–91. Seconded as Nuffield Research Fellow (O-level Chemistry Project), 1962–64; Salter's Company Fellow, Dept of Chemical Engrg and Chemical Technology, Imperial Coll., London, 1969. Chairman: Curriculum Cttee of HMC, GSA and IAPS, 1979–86; HMC, 1987. Mem., Council, Birmingham Univ., 1985–. Gov., Oundle Sch., 1988–. *Publications:* John Dalton and the Atomic Theory, 1965; Chemistry and Energy, 1968; (Editor) Foreground Chemistry Series, 1968; Gas Syringe Experiments, 1970; (co-author) Chemistry: facts, patterns and principles, 1972. *Address:* Manchester College, Oxford OX1 3TD. *Club:* East India, Devonshire, Sports and Public Schools.

ROGERS, Maurice Arthur Thorold; Secretary, Royal Institution, 1968–73; Joint Head, Head Office Research and Development Department, ICI, 1962–72; *b* 8 June 1911; *s* of A. G. L. Rogers; *g s* of Prof. J. E. Thorold Rogers; *m* 1947, Margaret Joan (*née* Craven) one *s* two *d. Educ:* Dragon Sch.; Westminster Sch.; University Coll., London. 1st Class hons BSc (Chem.) UCL 1932, PhD (Chem.) 1934. Chemist, ICI Dyestuffs Div., 1934–45; Head of Academic Relations Dept, 1946–58; Head of Head Office Research Dept, ICI, 1958–62. *Publications:* numerous papers in: Jl of Chem. Soc.; Nature; etc. *Recreations:* climbing, gardening, china restoration, conservation of countryside. *Address:* Mount Skippet, Ramsden, Oxford OX7 3AP. *T:* Ramsden (0993) 868253.

ROGERS, Michael; *see* Rogers, J. M.

ROGERS, Nigel David; free-lance singer, conductor and teacher; Professor of Singing, Royal College of Music, since 1979; *b* 21 March 1935; *m* 1961, Frederica Bement Lord (marr. diss. 1974); one *d. Educ:* Wellington Grammar Sch.; King's Coll., Cambridge (MA). Studied in Italy and Germany. Professional singer, 1961–; began singing career in Munich with group Studio der frühen Musik. Is a leading specialist in field of Baroque music, of which he has made about 70 recordings; gives concerts, recitals, lectures and master classes in many parts of world; most acclaimed role in opera as Monteverdi's Orfeo. Formed vocal ensemble Chiaroscuro, to perform vast repertory of Italian Baroque music, 1979, later extended to include Chiaroscuro Chamber Ensemble and Chiaroscuro Baroque Orch. Has lectured and taught at Schola Cantorum Basiliensis, Basle, Switzerland. Hon. RCM 1981. *Publications:* chapter on Voice, Companion to Baroque Music (ed J. A. Sadic), 1991; articles on early Baroque performance practice in various periodicals in different countries. *Recreations:* oenology, country pursuits, travel, especially Italy. *Address:* Chestnut Cottage, East End, East Woodhay, near Newbury, Berks. *T:* Highclere (0635) 253319.

ROGERS, Maj.-Gen. Norman Charles, FRCS 1949; civilian consultant surgeon, retired; *b* 14 Oct. 1916; *s* of Wing Comdr Charles William Rogers, RAF, and Edith Minnie Rogers (*née* Weaver); *m* 1954, Pamela Marion (*née* Rose); two *s* one *d. Educ:* Imperial Service Coll.; St Bartholomew's Hosp. MB, BS London; MRCS, LRCP 1939. Emergency Commn, Lieut RAMC, Oct. 1939; 131 Field Amb. RAMC, Dunkirk (despatches); RMO, 4th Royal Tank Regt, N Africa, 1941–42; Italy, 1942–43 (POW); RMO 1st Black Watch, NW Europe, 1944–45 (wounded, despatches twice). Ho. Surg., St Bartholomew's Hosp., 1946–47; Registrar (Surgical) Appts, Norwich, 1948–52; Sen. Registrar Appts, Birmingham, 1952–56; granted permanent commn, RAMC, 1956; surgical appts in mil. hospitals: Chester, Dhekelia (Cyprus), Catterick, Iserlohn (BAOR), 1956–67; Command Consultant Surgeon, BAOR, 1967–69; Dir, Army Surgery, 1969–73; QHS, 1969–73. Clin. Supt, 1975–80, and Consultant, 1973–81, Accident and Emergency Dept, Guy's Hosp; Civilian Consultant Surgeon: BMH Iserlohn, 1983–86; BMH Munster, 1986. *Publications:* contribs on surgical subjects. *Address:* 29 Ponsonby Terrace, SW1.

ROGERS, Mrs P. E.; *see* Box, B. E.

ROGERS, Parry; see Rogers, T. G. P.

ROGERS, Paul; actor; *b* Plympton, Devon, 22 March 1917; *s* of Edwin and Dulcie Myrtle Rogers; *m* 1st, 1939, Jocelyn Wynne (marr. diss. 1955); two *s*; 2nd, 1955, Rosalind Boxall; two *d. Educ:* Newton Abbot Grammar School, Devon. Michael Chekhov Theatre Studio, 1936–38. First appearance on stage as Charles Dickens in Bird's Eye of Valour, Scala, 1938; Stratford-upon-Avon Shakespeare Memorial Theatre, 1939; Concert Party and Colchester Rep. Co. until 1940. Served Royal Navy, 1940–46. Colchester Rep. Co. and Arts Council Tour and London Season, Tess of the D'Urbervilles, 1946–47; Bristol Old Vic, 1947–49; London Old Vic (incl. tour S Africa and Southern Rhodesia), 1949–53; also at Edinburgh, London and in USA, 1954–57; London, 1958; tour to Moscow, Leningrad and Warsaw, 1960. Roles with Old Vic include numerous Shakespearean leads; Gloucester, in King Lear, 1989. Other parts include: Sir Claude Mulhammer in The Confidential Clerk, Edinburgh Festival and Lyric, London, 1953; Lord Claverton in The Elder Statesman, Edinburgh Fest. and Cambridge Theatre, London, 1958; Mr Fox in Mr Fox of Venice, Piccadilly, 1959; Johnny Condell in One More River, Duke of York's and Westminster, 1959; Nickles in JB, Phœnix, 1961; Reginald Kinsale in Photo Finish, Saville, 1962; The Seagull, Queen's, 1964; Season of Goodwill, Queen's, 1964; The Homecoming, Aldwych, 1965; Timon of Athens, Stratford-upon-Avon, 1965; The Government Inspector, Aldwych, 1966; Henry IV, Stratford-upon-Avon, 1966; Max in The Homecoming, New York, 1967 (Tony Award and Whitbread Anglo-American Award); Plaza Suite, Lyric, 1969; The Happy Apple, Apollo, 1970; Sleuth, St Martin's, 1970, NY, 1971 and 1974; Othello, Nat. Theatre Co., Old Vic, 1974; Heartbreak House, Nat. Theatre, 1975; The Marrying of Ann Leete, Aldwych, 1975; The Return of A. J. Raffles, Aldwych, 1975; The Zykovs, Aldwych, 1976; Volpone, The Madras House, Nat. Theatre, 1977; Eclipse, Royal Court, 1978; You Never Can Tell, Lyric, Hammersmith, 1979; The Dresser, New York, 1981, 1982; The Importance of Being Earnest, A Kind of Alaska, Nat. Theatre, 1982; The Apple Cart, Theatre Royal, Haymarket, 1986; Danger: Memory!, Hampstead, 1988; Other People's Money, Lyric, 1990. Appears in films and television. *Publication:* a Preface to Folio Soc. edition of Shakespeare's Love's Labour's Lost, 1959. *Recreations:* gardening, carpentry, books. *Address:* 9 Hillside Gardens, Highgate, N6 5SU. *T:* 081–340 2656. *Club:* Naval.

ROGERS, Rev. Percival Hallewell, MBE 1945; Headmaster, Portora Royal School, Enniskillen, 1954–73; *b* 13 Sept. 1912; *m* 1940, Annie Mary Stuart, 2nd *d* of Lt-Col James Morwood; two *s* one *d. Educ:* Brentwood School; St Edmund Hall, Oxford. BA Class II, Hons English, Oxford, 1935; Diploma in Education, 1936; MA 1946. Two terms of teaching, Westminster School; Master in charge of English, Haileybury, 1936; served War, 1940–45 (despatches twice, MBE): RA, Major; DAA QMG; Bishop's College, Cheshunt, 1946; ordained, 1947; Asst Chaplain and English Master, Haileybury, 1947; Chaplain and English Master, 1949; student, Internat. Acad. for Continuous Educn, Sherborne, 1973–74; Chaplain, Gresham's Sch., Holt, 1974–75; Dean, Internat. Acad. for Continuous Educn, 1975–76; Asst Priest, Trinity Episcopal Church, New Orleans, 1976–80; Dir of Ordinands, Warden of Lay Readers, Dio. of Clogher, 1982–84; Priest-in-Charge, Sandford-on-Thames, 1985–86. *Publications:* The Needs of the Whole Man, Systematics, 1971; Editor and contrib. to A Guide to Divinity Teaching (SPCK), 1962. *Address:* 7 Eyot Place, Iffley Fields, Oxford OX4 1SA. *T:* Oxford (0865) 244976. *Club:* East India, Devonshire, Sports and Public Schools.

ROGERS, Peter Brian; Deputy Chief Executive and Director of Finance, Independent Television Commission, since 1991; Director, Channel Four Television Company Ltd, since 1982; *b* 8 April 1941; *s* of late William Patrick Rogers and Margaret Elizabeth Rogers; *m* 1966, Jean Mary Bailey; one *s* two *d. Educ:* De La Salle Grammar Sch., Liverpool; Manchester Univ. (1st Cl. Hons BAEcon; Cobden Prize); London Sch. of Econs and Pol. Science, London Univ. (MSc Econs). Tax Officer, Inland Revenue, 1959–67; Res. Associate, Manchester Univ., 1967–68; Econ. Adviser, HM Treasury, 1968–73; Sen. Econ. Adviser, Central Policy Review Staff, Cabinet Office, 1973–74; Dir of Econ. Planning, Tyne and Wear CC (on secondment from Central Govt), 1974–76; Sen. Econ. Adviser, DoE, 1976–79; Dep. Chief Exec., Housing Corp., 1979–82; Dir of Finance, IBA, 1982–90. *Recreations:* woodwork, windsurfing. *Address:* Riverhead Cottage, Kilmeston Road, Cheriton, Alresford, Hants SO24 0NJ. *T:* Bramdean (0962) 771790.

ROGERS, Sir Philip (James), Kt 1961; CBE 1952; Chairman, Tobacco Research Council, 1963–71; *b* 1908; *s* of late James Henry Rogers; *m* 1939, Brenda Mary Sharp, CBE, *d* of late Ernest Thompson Sharp. *Educ:* Blundell's Sch. Served War (RWAFF and Intell. Corps), 1940–44. MLC, Nigeria, 1947–51; MLC, Kenya, 1957–62; Elected Representative, Kenya, East African Legislative Assembly, 1962 and 1963. President: Nigerian Chamber of Commerce, 1948 and 1950 (Vice-Pres. 1947 and 1949); Nairobi Chamber of Commerce, 1957 (Vice-Pres. 1956); AAA of Nigeria, 1951; Dir, Nigerian Elec. Corp., 1951; Governor, Nigeria Coll. of Technology, 1951; Member: Nigerian

Exec. Cttee, Rd Transport Bd, 1948–51; Central Council Red Cross Soc. of W Africa, 1950–51; Trades Adv. Cttee, Nigeria, 1950 and 1951–; Wages Adv. Bd, Kenya, 1955–61; EA Industrial Council, 1954–63; EA Air Licensing Appeals Trib., 1958–60; EA Air Adv. Council, 1956–60; Kenya Road Authority, 1957–61; Provl Council, Univ. of E Africa, 1961–63; Gov. Council, Roy. Tech. Coll. of E Africa, 1957–58 (Chm. 1958/59/60). Chairman: East African Tobacco Co. Ltd, 1951–63; Rift Valley Cigarette Co. Ltd, 1956–63; EA Rd Fedn, 1954–56; Kenya Cttee on Study and Trg in USA, 1958–63; Bd of Govs, Coll. of Social Studies, 1960–63; Nairobi Special Loans Cttee, 1960–63; African Teachers' Service Bd, 1956–63; Council, Royal College (now University Coll., Nairobi), 1961–63; Fedn of Sussex Amenity Socs, 1968–; Trustee, Outward Bound Trust of Kenya, 1959–63; Rep. of Assoc. Chambers of Commerce & Indust. of Eastern Africa; Mem. of Industrial Tribunals, England and Wales, 1966–80. Governor, Plumpton Agric. Coll., 1967–76. Member: E Sussex Educn Cttee, 1969–75; Finance Cttee, UCL, 1972–79; Indep. Schools Careers Orgn, 1972–79; Chairman: Fedn of Sussex Amenity Socs, 1968–80; Age Concern, East Sussex, 1974–80. *Address:* Church Close, Newick, East Sussex BN8 4JZ. *T:* Newick (082572) 2210.

ROGERS, Sir Richard (George), Kt 1991; RA 1984 (ARA 1978); MArch; RIBA; architect; Chairman, Richard Rogers Architects Ltd, London, Tokyo and Berlin; Director: River CADS Ltd; River Cafe, Thames Wharf Studios, London; *b* 23 July 1933; *s* of Dada Geiringer and Nino Rogers; *m*; three *s*; *m* 1973, Ruth Elias; two *s*. *Educ:* Architectural Assoc. (AA Dipl.); Yale Univ. (MArch; Fulbright, Edward D. Stone, and Yale Scholar); Royal Inst. of British Architects. Winner: of internat. competition for Centre Pompidou, 1971–77 (Internat. Union of Architects August Perret Prize for most outstanding internat. work, 1975–78); of Lloyd's internat. comp. for HQ in City of London, 1978 (FT Architecture at Work Award, 1987; Civic Trust Award, 1987; RIBA Regional Award, 1988; PA Award for innovation in bldg design and construction, 1988). *Other major projects include:* Creek Vean House, Cornwall (RIBA Award for work of outstanding quality, 1969); Reliance Controls, Swindon, 1967 (FT Award for most outstanding indust. bldg, 1966–67); B&B factory, Como, Italy, 1972–73; HQ and Labs, Universal Oil Products, 1973–74 (BSC Award, 1975; RIBA Regional Award (Commendation), 1975); Res. Labs, PA Technology, Melbourn, Herts, 1975–83 (FT Indust. Arch. Award, 1975; RIBA Commendation, 1975); Music Res. Centre for Pierre Boulez and Min. of Cultural Affairs, IRCAM, Paris, 1977; Fleetguard Manufg and Distribn Centre, Quimper, France, 1979–81 (Premier Award for most exceptional steel structure); Inmos Microprocessor factory, Newport, S Wales, 1982 (UK Steel Design Award, 1982; FT Architecture at Work Award (Commendation), 1983); apptd by City of Florence to revitalise banks of River Arno, 1983; PA Technology, Princeton, NJ, USA, 1984; Linn hi-fi equipment, Glasgow, 1985; appt master plan architects for office develt, Royal Victoria Docks, London, 1985; Reuters Docklands Bldg, 1988; Billingsgate redevelt, London, 1989. *Current projects:* European Court of Human Rights, Strasbourg; airport masterplanning and extension, Marseille; office develt, World Trade Centre, St Katharine Docks, London; masterplanning, King's Dock, Liverpool; masterplanning, Dunkirk and Nice; Channel 4 HQ, London; Daiwa Europe HQ, London; office develts, Kabuchi-cho and Iikura, Tokyo; commercial develt, Brau und Brunnen, Berlin; masterplanning, Potsdamer Platz, Berlin. *Exhibitions:* ICA; Royal Acad.; Mus. of Modern Art, NY; Graham Foundn, Chicago; UCLA; Mus. of Mod. Art, Warsaw; Deutsches Architekturmuseum, Frankfurt; Magasins d'Usines, Centre Pompidou, Paris; Louvre Mus. of Decorative Arts, Paris; AIA San Francisco; Berlin Aedes Gall.; Venice Biennale, 1991. *Taught at:* AA, London; Cambridge Univ.; Yale, Princeton, Harvard and Cornell Univs, and Univ. of Calif, LA and Berkeley; McGill Univ., Canada; Aachen Univ., Germany; Eero Saarinem Prof. of Arch., Yale, 1985. Chm. Bd of Trustees, Tate Gall., 1984–88; Member: UN Architects Cttee; Council and Policy Cttees, RIBA, Hon. FAIA; Hon. Fellow, Royal Acad. of Art, The Hague; Hon. Dr RCA. Royal Gold Medal for Arch., 1985. Chevalier de la Légion d'Honneur, France. Subject of several television documentaries on architecture. *Publications:* Richard Rogers + Architects, 1985; Richard Rogers 1978–1988, 1988; Architecture: a modern view, 1990; *relevant publication:* Richard Rogers, a biography, by Bryan Appleyard, 1986. *Recreations:* friends, food, art, architecture, travel. *Address:* (office) Thames Wharf, Rainville Road, W6 9HA. *T:* 071–385 1235.

ROGERS, Thomas Edward, CMG 1960; MBE 1945; HM Diplomatic Service, retired; *b* 28 Dec. 1912; *s* of T. E. Rogers and Lucy Jane Browne; *m* 1950, Eileen Mary, *d* of R. J. Speechley; no *c*. *Educ:* Bedford Sch.; Emmanuel Coll., Cambridge (Exhibnr); School of Oriental Studies, London. Selected for Indian Civil Service, 1936, and for Indian Political Service, 1941. Served in Bengal, 1937–41; in Persia and Persian Gulf, 1941–45; Political Agent, Quetta, 1947; Dep. Sec. (Cabinet Secretariat), Pakistan Govt, 1947–48. Entered Foreign Service, 1948: FO, 1948–50; Bogotá, 1950–53; jssc, 1953–54; Coun. (Comm.), Madrid, 1954–58; Coun. (Econ.), Belgrade, 1958–62; Minister (Econ.), Buenos Aires, 1963–66; Dep. UK High Comr, Canada, 1966–70, Actg High Comr, 1967–68; Ambassador to Colombia, 1970–73. Chm., Anglo-Colombian Soc., 1981–88. Great Cross of St Carlos, Colombia, 1974. *Recreation:* travel. *Address:* Chintens, Firway, Grayshott, Hindhead, Surrey GU26 6JQ. *Club:* United Oxford & Cambridge University.

ROGERS, (Thomas Gordon) Parry, CBE 1991; Chairman: Business and Technician Education Council, since 1986; Salisbury Health Authority, since 1986; Percom Ltd, since 1984; PRIMA Europe Ltd, since 1987; Future Perfect (counselling) Ltd, since 1989; ECCTIS 2000 Ltd, since 1989; *b* 7 Aug. 1924; *s* of late Victor Francis Rogers and Ella (*née* May); *m* 1st, 1947, Pamela Mary (*née* Greene) (marr. diss. 1973); one *s* seven *d*; 2nd, 1973, Patricia Juliet (*née* Curtis); one *s* one *d*. *Educ:* West Hartlepool Grammar Sch.; St Edmund Hall, Oxford. MA; CIPM, CBIM; FRSA; FInstD. Procter & Gamble Ltd, 1948–54; Mars Ltd, 1954–56; Hardy Spicer Ltd, 1956–61; IBM United Kingdom Ltd, 1961–74 (Dir, 1964–74); The Plessey Co. plc, 1974–86 (Dir, 1976–86); Director: MSL Gp Internat. Ltd, 1970–78; ICL plc, 1977–79; Hobsons Publishing plc, 1985–90; Ocean Gp plc; Butler Cox plc; BNB Resources plc; Norman Broadbent Internat. Ltd, 1985–90; Careers Res. Adv. Centre, 1965– (Mem. Council); CBI Educn Foundn, 1985–89. Vice-Pres., Inst of Dirs, 1988– (Chm., 1985–88); ISCO, 1990–; Third Age Network Ltd, 1990–; Member: Inst. of Manpower Studies, 1970–86; Industrial Participation Assoc., 1972–86; CBI/BIM Panel on Management Educn, 1968–78; Employment Appeal Tribunal, 1978–87; Standing Commn on Pay Comparability, 1980–81; Management Bd, EEF, 1980–86; E European Trade Council, 1982–85; Econ. League, 1982–86; Nat. Steering Gp, Technical and Vocational Educn Initiative, MSC, 1983–86; IT Skill Shortages Cttee, DTI, 1984; IT Skills Agency, 1985–; Review Team, Children and Young Persons Benefits, DHSS, 1984–85; Oxford Univ. Appts Cttee, 1972–87; CBI Employment Policy Cttee, 1980–86; Pres., Inst. of Personnel Management, 1975–77; Chairman: Cttee on Charitable Fund Raising, NCSS, 1970–76; Salisbury HA, 1986–90. Chm., SW London Coll. HEC, 1989–; Governor: Ashridge Management Coll., 1985–; Warminster Sch., 1989–; St Mary's Sch., Shaftesbury, 1991–. Mem., Information Technologists' Co., 1987–. *Publications:* The Recruitment and Training of Graduates, 1970; contribs to: The Director's Handbook, Management and the Working Environment, and various newspapers and jls. *Recreations:* birdwatching, golf, tennis. *Address:* St Edward's Chantry, Bimport, Shaftesbury, Dorset SP7 8BA. *T:* Shaftesbury (0747) 52789; 32 Romulus Court, Brentford Dock, Mddx. *T:* 081–568 6060. *Clubs:* Savile; Sherborne Golf.

ROGERS, William Pierce; Partner, law firm of Rogers & Wells, since 1973 (of Royall, Koegel, Rogers and Wells, 1961–69); *b* 23 June 1913; *s* of Harrison A. and Myra Beswick Rogers; *m* 1937, Adele Langston; three *s* one *d*. *Educ:* Canton High School, Canton, New York; Colgate University; Cornell Law School. Law firm of Cadwalader, Wickersham and Taft, NY City, 1937; an Asst District Attorney in NY County, 1938; US Navy, 1942–46; Dist Attorney's Office in New York, 1946; Chief Counsel, Senate Investigating Cttee, 1947; Counsel, Senate Permanent Investigating Cttee, 1949; law firm of Dwight, Royall, Harris, Koegel and Caskey, offices in New York and Washington, 1950; Dep. Attorney-General, 1953; Attorney-General of the US, 1957–61; Secretary of State, USA, 1969–73. Holds several hon. degrees in Law, from Univs and Colls in the USA, 1956–60. Mem. Bar Assocs in the USA. US Representative: to 20th Session of UN General Assembly, 1965; on UN Ad Hoc Cttee on SW Africa, 1967; Mem., President's Commn on Law Enforcement and Administration of Justice, 1965–67. *Recreations:* golf, tennis, swimming. *Address:* Rogers & Wells, 200 Park Avenue, New York, NY 10166, USA. *Clubs:* Metropolitan (Washington); Burning Tree (Bethesda); Racquet and Tennis, The Sky (NYC); Chevy Chase (Chevy Chase).

ROGERSON, Rt. Rev. Barry; *see* Bristol, Bishop of.

ROGERSON, Nicolas; Chairman, Dewe Rogerson International, since 1985; Chief Executive, Dewe Rogerson Group, since 1969 (Deputy Chairman, 1969–88); *b* 21 May 1943; *s* of Hugh and Olivia Rogerson; *m* 1972, Elizabeth, Baroness Rummel; two step *s*. *Educ:* Cheam Sch.; Winchester Coll.; Magdalene Coll., Cambridge. Staff Journalist, Investors Chronicle, 1964–65; Executive, Angel Court Consultants, 1966–68; formed Dewe Rogerson, 1969. Appeals Chm., King George's Fund for Sailors. *Recreations:* sailing, ski-ing, Real tennis, field sports, languages and European history. *Address:* 12 Redcliffe Road, SW10 9NR. *T:* 071–352 4454. *Clubs:* City of London, Turf; Pitt (Cambridge); Racquet (New York).

ROGERSON, Susan, (Mrs T. S. Rogerson); *see* Darling, S.

ROGG, Lionel; organist and composer; Professor of Organ and Improvisation, Geneva Conservatoire de Musique, since 1961; *b* 1936; *m* Claudine Effront; three *s*. *Educ:* Conservatoire de Musique, Geneva (1st prize for piano and organ). Concerts or organ recitals on the five continents. Records include works by Alain, Buxtehude (complete organ works; Deutscher Schallplatten Preis, 1980), Couperin and Martin; also complete works of J. S. Bach (Grand Prix du Disque, 1970, for The Art of the Fugue). *Compositions:* Acclamations, 1964; Chorale Preludes, 1971; Partita, 1975; Variations on Psalm 91, 1983; Cantata "Geburt der Venus", 1984; Introduction, Ricerare and Toccata, 1985; Two Etudes, 1986; Monodies, 1986; Psalm 92, 1986; Piece for Clarinette, 1986; Face-à-face for two pianos, 1987; Organ Concerto, 1991. DèsL Univ. de Genève, 1989. *Publication:* Eléments de Contrepoint, 1969. *Address:* Conservatoire de Musique, Place Neuve, Geneva, Switzerland; 38A rte de Troinex, CH–1234 Vessy-Genève, Switzerland.

ROH, Tae Woo, Hon. GCMG 1989; President of Republic of Korea, since 1988; *b* 4 Dec. 1932; *m* 1959, Kim-Ok-Sook; one *s* one *d*. *Educ:* Korean Military Academy; Republic of Korea War College. Commander, Capital Security, 1978, Defence Security, 1980; retd as Army General; Minister of State for Nat. Security and Foreign Affairs, 1981; Minister of Sports, and of Home Affairs, 1982; President: Seoul Olympic Organizing Cttee, 1983; Asian Games Organizing Cttee, 1983; Korean Olympic Cttee, 1984. Mem., Nat. Assembly and Pres., Ruling Democratic Justice Party, 1985. Hon. Dr George Washington Univ., 1989. Order of Nat. Security Merit (Sam Il Medal) (Korea), 1967; Grand Order of Mugunghwa (Korea), 1988; foreign decorations, incl. France, Germany, Kenya, Paraguay. *Publications:* Widaehan pot'ongsaram ui shidae (A great era of the ordinary people), 1987, trans. Japanese, 1988; Korea: A Nation Transformed, 1990. *Recreations:* tennis, swimming, golf, music, reading. *Address:* Chong Wa Dae, #1 Sejongno, Chongno-gu, Seoul 110–050, Korea.

ROHMER, Eric, (Maurice Henri Joseph Schérer); French film director and writer; *b* 21 March 1920; *s* of Désiré Schérer and Jeanne Monzat; *m* 1957, Thérèse Barbet. *Educ:* Paris. Teacher, 1942–55; journalist, 1951–55. Film critic, Revue du cinéma, Arts, Temps Modernes, La Parisienne, 1949–63; Jt Founder, La Gazette du cinéma (also former Jt Editor). Dir of educnl films for French television, 1964–70. Co-Dir, Société des Films du Losange, 1964–. Films include (director and writer): Charlotte et son steak (short film), 1951; Le signe du lion, 1959; La boulangère de Monceau (short film), 1962; La collectionneuse, 1966; Ma nuit chez Maud, 1969 (prix Max Ophüls, 1970); Le genou de Claire, 1970 (prix Louis-Delluc, prix Méliès, 1971); L'amour l'après-midi, 1972; La Marquise d'O, 1976; Perceval le Gallois, 1978; Le beau mariage, 1982; Pauline à la plage, 1982; Les nuits de la pleine lune, 1984; Le rayon vert (Lion d'or, Venice Film Fest., prix de la critique internationale), 1986; L'ami de mon amie, 1988. Best Dir Award, Berlin Film Fest., 1983. *Publications:* Alfred Hitchcock, 1957; Charlie Chaplin, 1973; Six contes moraux, 1974; L'organisation de l'espace dans le "Faust" de Murnau, 1977. *Address:* Les Films du Losange, 26 avenue Pierre 1er de Serbie, 75116 Paris, France.

ROHRER, Dr Heinrich; IBM Research Division, Zurich Research Laboratory, since 1963, and IBM Fellow, since 1986; *b* 6 June 1933; *s* of Henrich and Katharina Rohrer; *m* 1961, Rose-Marie Egger; two *d*. *Educ:* Federal Inst. of Technology, ETH, Zürich (Dr. sc. nat); PhD 1960. Post-doctoral Fellow, Rutgers Univ., 1961–63; joined IBM Res. Div. as Res. Staff Mem., 1963; then various managerial posts. Vis. Scientist, Univ. of Calif. at Santa Barbara, 1974–75. Mem., Swiss Acad. of Technical Scis, 1988; For. Associate, US Acad. of Sci., 1988; Hon. Mem., Swiss Physical Soc., 1990. Hon. Fellow, RMS, 1988. Hon. Dr: Rutgers, 1987; Marseille, 1988; Madrid, 1988. (Jtly) King Faisal Internat. Prize for Science, 1984; Hewlett Packard Europhysics Prize, 1984; (jtly) Nobel Prize in Physics, 1986; (jtly) Cresson Medal, Franklin Inst., Philadelphia, 1987. *Recreations:* ski-ing, hiking, gardening. *Address:* IBM Research Division, Zürich Research Laboratory, CH-8803 Rüschlikon, Switzerland. *T:* 41–1–724 81 11.

ROITH, Oscar, CB 1987; FEng, FIMechE; Chief Engineer and Scientist, Department of Trade and Industry, 1982–87; *b* London, 14 May 1927; *s* of late Leon Roith and Leah Roith; *m* 1950, Irene Bullock; one *d*. *Educ:* Gonville and Caius Coll., Cambridge (minor schol.; Mech. Scis Tripos; MA). FIMechE 1967; FEng 1983; Eur Ing 1988. CBIM. FRSA. Research Dept, Courtaulds, 1948; Distillers Co. Ltd: Central Engrg Dept, 1952; Engrg Manager, Hull Works, 1962; Works Manager, 1968, Works Gen. Manager, 1969, BP Chemicals, Hull; General Manager: Engrg and Technical, BP Chemicals, 1974; Engrg Dept, BP Trading, 1977; Chief Exec. (Engrg), BP Internat., 1981. Director: Trueland Ltd, 1987–; British Maritime Technology, 1987–. Mem., Yorks and Humberside Economic Planning Council, 1972–74. Comr, Royal Commn for Exhibition of 1851, 1988–. Chm., Mech. and Electrical Engrg Requirements Bd, 1981–82; Member: Mech. Engrg and Machine Tools Requirements Bd, 1977–81; (non-exec.) Res. Cttee. British Gas, 1987–; ACORD, 1982–87; ACARD, 1982–87; Process Plant EDC, NEDO, 1979–82; SERC, 1982–87; NERC, 1982–87; Bd (part-time), LRT, 1988–; Chm., Res. Adv. Gp, PCFC. Pres., IMechE, 1987–88 (Dep. Pres., 1985–87; Mem. Council, 1981–; Mem., Process Engrg Gp Cttee, 1962–68); Dep. Chm. Council, Foundn for Science and Technol., 1988–; Hon. Sec., Mech. Engrg, Council of Fellowship of Engrg, 1988–. Gov.,

Brighton Polytechnic, 1988–. *Recreations:* cricket, gardening, walking. *Address:* 20 Wraymill House, Wraymill Park, Batts Hill, Reigate, Surrey RH2 0LQ.

ROITT, Prof. Ivan Maurice, FRS 1983; Professor, since 1968 and Head of Department of Immunology, since 1968 and of Rheumatology Research, since 1984, University College and Middlesex School of Medicine (formerly Middlesex Hospital Medical School); *b* 30 Sept. 1927; *e s* of Harry Roitt; *m* 1953, Margaret Auralie Louise, *d* of F. Haigh; three *d. Educ:* King Edward's Sch., Birmingham; Balliol Coll., Oxford (exhibnr; BSc 1950; MA 1953; DPhil 1953; DSc 1968). FRCPath 1973. Res. Fellow, 1953, Reader in Immunopathol., 1965–68, Middlesex Hosp. Med. Sch. Chm., WHO Cttee on Immunolog. Control of Fertility, 1976–79; Mem., Biol. Sub-Cttee, UGC. Mem., Harrow Borough Council, 1963–65; Chm., Harrow Central Lib. Assoc., 1965–67. Florey Meml Lectr, Adelaide Univ., 1982. Hon. MRCP (London). (Jtly) Van Meter Prize, Amer. Thyroid Assoc., 1957; Gairdner Foundn Award, Toronto, 1964. *Publications:* Essential Immunology, 1971, 6th edn 1988; (jtly) Immunology of Oral Diseases, 1979; (jtly) Immunology, 1989; 240 contribs to learned scientific jls. *Address:* Department of Immunology, University College and Middlesex School of Medicine, Arthur Stanley House, 40–50 Tottenham Street, W1P 9PG.

ROKISON, Kenneth Stuart; QC 1976; a Recorder, since 1989; *b* 13 April 1937; *s of* late Frank Edward and late Kitty Winifred Rokison; *m* 1973, Rosalind Julia (*née* Mitchell); one *s* two *d. Educ:* Whitgift School, Croydon; Magdalene College, Cambridge (BA 1960). Called to the Bar, Gray's Inn, 1961, Bencher, 1985. *Recreation:* acting. *Address:* Ashcroft Farm, Gadbrook, Betchworth, Surrey. *T:* Dawes Green (030678) 244.

ROLAND, Nicholas; *see* Walmsley, Arnold Robert.

ROLF, Percy Henry; a Recorder of the Crown Court, 1978–87; Consultant, Robinson Jarvis & Rolf, Solicitors, Isle of Wight, since 1986 (Partner 1948; Senior Partner, 1964); *b* 25 Dec. 1915; *s of* Percy Algernon Rolf and Lydia Kate (*née* Arnold); *m* 1939, Cecilia Florence Cooper; one *s* one *d. Educ:* Sandown Grammar Sch.; London Univ. (LLB). Solicitor. Served War, RAF, 1940–46: Wing Comdr; Sen. Air Traffic Control Officer, Transport Comd, 1945–46. Member: Eastbourne Br., Hour of Revival Assoc., 1959– (Chm., 1987–); Holly Soc. of America Inc., 1986–. *Recreations:* golf, gardening. *Address:* Ashlake Water, Fishbourne, Isle of Wight PO33 4EY. *T:* Wootton Bridge (0983) 882513. *Club:* Shanklin–Sandown Golf (Hon. Pres., 1990–).

ROLFE, Rear-Adm. Henry Cuthbert Norris, CB 1959; *b* 1908; *s* of Benedict Hugh Rolfe, MA Oxon; *m* 1931, Mary Monica Fox; one *s* two *d. Educ:* Pangbourne Nautical College. Joined Royal Navy, 1925. Served War of 1939–45: HMS Hermes, 1939; South-East Asia, 1944; Staff of Director of Air Warfare, Admiralty, 1947; commanded HMS Veryan Bay, 1948; service with Royal Canadian Navy, 1949; commanded: HMS Vengeance, 1952; RN Air Station, Culdrose, 1952; HMS Centaur, 1954–56; RN Air Station, Ford, 1956–57; Asst Chief of Naval Staff (Warfare) 1957–60; Regional Director, Northern Region, Commonwealth Graves Commission, 1961–64, retd. Naval ADC to the Queen, 1957; Rear-Admiral, 1957. Liveryman, Worshipful Company of Coachmakers and Coach Harnessmakers, 1962. *Address:* 43 Nuns Road, Winchester, Hants SO23 7EF.

ROLFE, Hume B.; *see* Boggis-Rolfe.

ROLFE, Marianne Teresa N.; *see* Neville-Rolfe.

ROLFE, William David Ian, PhD; FRSE, FGS, FMA; Keeper of Geology, National Museums of Scotland, since 1986; *b* 24 Jan. 1936; *s* of late William Ambrose Rolfe and Greta Olwen Jones; *m* 1960, Julia Mary Margaret, *d* of late Capt. G. H. G. S. Rayer, OBE; two *d. Educ:* Royal Liberty Grammar Sch., Romford; Birmingham Univ. (BSc 1957; PhD 1960). FGS 1960; FMA 1972; FRSE 1983. Demonstrator in Geol., UC of N Staffs, 1960; Fulbright Schol., and Asst Curator, Mus. of Comparative Zool., Harvard Coll., Cambridge, Mass, 1961–62; Geol. Curator, Univ. Lectr, then Sen. Lectr in Geol., Hunterian Mus., Univ. of Glasgow, 1962–81; Dep. Dir, 1981–86. Vis. Scientist, Field Mus. of Natural Hist., Chicago, 1981. Mem., Trng Awards Cttee, NERC, 1980–83. Vice-President: Palaeontol Assoc., 1974–76; Soc. Hist. Natural Hist., 1987. Geological Society of Glasgow: Ed., Scottish Jl of Geol., 1967–72; Pres., 1973–76; Geological Society: Editl Chm., Journal, 1973–76; Chm., Conservation Cttee, 1980–85; Murchison Fund, 1978; Tyrrell Res. Fund, 1982; Coke Medal, 1984; Pres., Edinburgh Geological Soc., 1989–91. FRSA 1985. *Publications:* (ed) Phylogeny and Evolution of Crustacea, 1963; Treatise on Invertebrate Paleontology, part R, 1969; Geological Howlers, 1980; papers on fossil phyllocarid crustaceans and palaeontol., esp. other arthropods, and hist. of 18th century natural sci. illustration. *Recreations:* visual arts, walking, swimming, music. *Address:* 4A Randolph Crescent, Edinburgh EH3 7TH. *T:* 031–226 2094. *Clubs:* Geological; University Staff (Edinburgh).

ROLL, family name of **Baron Roll of Ipsden**.

ROLL OF IPSDEN, Baron *cr* 1977 (Life Peer), of Ipsden in the County of Oxfordshire; **Eric Roll**, KCMG 1962 (CMG 1949); CB 1956; Director of the Bank of England, 1968–77; Chancellor, University of Southampton, 1974–84; Joint Chairman, S. G. Warburg & Co. Ltd, 1983–87 (Chairman, 1974–83; Deputy Chairman, 1967–74); President: S. G. Warburg Group Plc, since 1987; *b* 1 Dec. 1907; *yr s* of Mathias and Fany Roll; *m* 1934, Winifred, *o d* of Elliott and Sophia Taylor; two *d. Educ:* on the Continent; Univ. of Birmingham. BCom 1928; PhD 1930; Gladstone Memorial Prize, 1928; Univ. Research Scholarship, 1929. Prof. of Economics and Commerce, Univ. Coll. of Hull, 1935–46 (leave of absence 1939–46). Special Rockefeller Foundation Fellow, USA, 1939–41. Member, later Dep. Head, British Food Mission to N America, 1941–46; UK Dep. Member and UK Exec. Officer, Combined Food Board, Washington, until 1946; Asst Sec., Ministry of Food, 1946–47; Under-Secretary, HM Treasury (Central Economic Planning Staff), 1948; Minister, UK Delegation to OEEC, 1949. Deputy Head, United Kingdom Delegation to North Atlantic Treaty Organization, Paris, 1952; Under Secretary Ministry of Agriculture, Fisheries and Food, 1953–57; Executive Dir, International Sugar Council, 1957–59; Chm., United Nations Sugar Conf., 1958; Deputy Secretary, Ministry of Agriculture, Fisheries and Food, 1959–61; Deputy Leader, UK Delegation for negotiations with the European Economic Community, 1961–63; Economic Minister and Head of UK Treasury Delegation, Washington, 1963–64, also Exec. Dir for the UK International Monetary Fund and International Bank for Reconstruction and Development; Permanent Under-Sec. of State, Dept of Economic Affairs, 1964–66. Chm., subseq. Hon. Chm., Book Development Council, 1967–. Independent Mem., NEDC, 1971–80. Director: Times Newspapers Ltd, 1967–80; Times Newspapers Holdings Ltd, 1980–83; also other Directorships; President: Mercury Securities Ltd, 1985–87 (Chm., 1974–84); Mercury Internat. Gp, 1985–87. Hon. DSc Hull, 1967; Hon. DSocSci Birmingham, 1967; Hon. LLD Southampton, 1974. Grosses Goldene Ehrenzeichen mit Stern (Austria), 1979; Comdr 1st Cl., Order of the Dannebrog (Denmark), 1981; Officier, Légion d' Honneur, 1984. *Publications:* An Early Experiment in Industrial Organization, 1930; Spotlight on Germany, 1933; About Money, 1934; Elements of Economic Theory, 1935; Organized Labour (collaborated), 1938; The British Commonwealth at War (collaborated), 1943; A History of Economic Thought, 1954,

new edn, 1973; The Combined Food Board, 1957; The World After Keynes, 1968; The Uses and Abuses of Economics, 1978; (ed) The Mixed Economy, 1982; Crowded Hours (autobiog.), 1985; articles in Economic Jl, Economica, American Economic Review, etc. *Recreation:* reading. *Address:* D2 Albany, Piccadilly, W1V 9RG. *Club:* Brooks's.

ROLL, Rev. Sir James (William Cecil), 4th Bt, *cr* 1921; Vicar of St John's, Becontree, 1958–83, retired; *b* 1 June 1912; *s* of Sir Cecil Ernest Roll, 3rd Bt, and Mildred Kate (*d* 1926), *d* of William Wells, Snaresbrook; *S* father, 1938; unmarried. *Educ:* Chigwell School, Essex; Pembroke College, Oxford; Chichester Theological College. Deacon, 1937. Curate East Ham Parish Church, 1944–58. *Heir:* none. *Address:* 82 Leighcliff Road, Leigh on Sea, Essex SS9 1DN.

ROLLAND, Lawrence Anderson Lyon, PPRIBA; PPRIAS; FRSE; Senior Partner: L. A. Rolland & Partners, since 1959; The Hurd Rolland Partnership (formerly Robert Hurd and Partners), since 1965; President of Royal Institute of British Architects, 1985–87; *b* 6 Nov. 1937; *s* of Lawrence Anderson Rolland and Winifred Anne Lyon; *m* 1960, Mairi Melville; two *s* two *d. Educ:* George Watson Boys' College, Edinburgh; Duncan of Jordanstone College of Art. Diploma of Art (Architecture) 1959; ARIBA 1960; FRIAS 1965 (Pres., RIAS, 1979–81); FRSE 1989. Founder Mem., Scottish Construction Industry Group, 1979–81; Mem., Bldg EDC, NEDC, 1982–88. Architect for: The Queen's Hall, concert hall, Edinburgh; restoration and redesign of Bank of Scotland Head Office (original Architect, Sibbald, Reid & Crighton, 1805 and later, Bryce, 1870); much housing in Fife's royal burghs; British Golf Museum, St Andrews. Gen. Trustee, Church of Scotland. Gov., Duncan of Jordanstone Coll. of Art, 1990–. FRSA 1988. Winner of more than 20 awards and commendations from Saltire Soc., Stone Fedn, Concrete Soc., Civic Trust, Europa Nostra and Times Conservation Award. *Recreations:* music, fishing, food, wine, cars. *Address:* Rossend Castle, Burntisland, Fife KY3 0DF. *T:* Burntisland (0592) 873535. *Clubs:* Reform; Scottish Arts (Edinburgh).

ROLLO, family name of **Lord Rollo**.

ROLLO, 13th Lord *cr* 1651; **Eric John Stapylton Rollo**; Baron Dunning, 1869; JP; *b* 3 Dec. 1915; *s* of 12th Lord and Helen Maud (*d* 1928), *o c* of Frederick Chetwynd Stapylton of Hatton Hill, Windlesham, Surrey; *S* father, 1947; *m* 1938, Suzanne Hatton; two *s* one *d. Educ:* Eton. Served War of 1939–45, Grenadier Guards, retiring with rank of Captain. JP Perthshire, 1962. *Heir: s* Master of Rollo, *qv. Address:* Pitcairns, Dunning, Perthshire PH2 9BX. *T:* Dunning (076484) 202.

ROLLO, Master of; Hon. David Eric Howard Rollo; *b* 31 March 1943; *s* and *heir* of 13th Lord Rollo, *qv; m* 1971, Felicity Anne Christian, *o d* of Lt-Comdr J. B. Lamb; three *s. Educ:* Eton. Late Captain Grenadier Guards. *Address:* 20 Draycott Avenue, SW3. *Clubs:* Cavalry and Guards, Turf.

ROLO, Cyril Felix, CMG 1975; OBE 1959; HM Diplomatic Service, retired; *b* 13 Feb. 1918; *s* of late I. J. Rolo and Linda (*née* Suares); *m* 1948, Marie Luise Christine (*née* Baeurle); one *s. Educ:* Charterhouse; Oriel Coll., Oxford (MA). Served with Armed Forces, 1940–46 (Major): Oxf. and Bucks LI, later on Gen. Staff; Western Desert, E Africa, Italy, Austria. Joined HM Foreign (subseq. Diplomatic) Service, 1946: Allied Commn for Austria, 1947–48; 2nd Sec., Rome, 1948–50; Political Adviser's Office, Berlin, 1950–52; FO, 1952–57; 1st Sec., Vienna, 1957–62; FO (subseq. FCO), 1962–76; Counsellor, 1971. *Recreations:* travel, golf, reading. *Address:* 32 Roxburghe Mansions, Kensington Court, W8 5BQ. *T:* 071–937 4696. *Clubs:* Travellers'; Sunningdale Golf.

ROLPH, C. H., (Cecil Rolph Hewitt); *b* London, 23 Aug. 1901; *s* of Frederick Thompson Hewitt and Edith Mary Speed; *m* 1st, 1926, Audrey Mary Buttery (marr. diss., 1946; she *d* 1982); one *d*; 2nd, 1947, Jenifer Wayne (*d* 1982), author and scriptwriter; one *s* two *d. Educ:* State schools. City of London Police, 1921–46 (Chief Inspector); editorial staff, New Statesman, 1947–70; editor, The Author, 1956–60; Dir, New Statesman, 1965–80. Mem., Parole Bd, 1967–69; Mem. Council, Soc. of Authors. *Publications:* A Licensing Handbook, 1947; Crime and Punishment, 1950; Towards My Neighbour, 1950; On Gambling, 1951; Personal Identity, 1956; (ed) The Human Sum, 1957; Mental Disorder, 1958; Commonsense About Crime and Punishment, 1961; The Trial of Lady Chatterley, 1961; (with Arthur Koestler) Hanged by the Neck, 1961; All Those in Favour? (The ETU Trial), 1962; The Police and The Public, 1962; Law and the Common Man, 1967; Books in the Dock, 1969; Kingsley, 1973; Believe What You Like, 1973; Living Twice (autobiog.), 1974; Mr Prone, 1977; The Queen's Pardon, 1978; London Particulars (autobiog.), 1980; The Police (child's history), 1980; As I Was Saying, 1985; Further Particulars (autobiog.), 1987; contributor to The Encyclopædia Britannica, Chambers's Encyclopædia, Punch, The Week-End Book, The New Law Journal, The Times Literary Supplement, The Author, The Nation (NY), daily and weekly press. *Recreations:* music, reading, and the contemplation of work. *Address:* 33 Hitherwood, Cranleigh, Surrey GU6 8BW. *T:* Guildford (0483) 272793.

ROMAIN, Roderick Jessel Anidjar; Metropolitan Stipendiary Magistrate, 1972–83; *b* 2 Dec. 1916; *s* of late Artom A. Romain and Winifred (*née* Rodrigues); *m* 1947, Miriam, *d* of late Semtob Sequerra; one *s* one *d. Educ:* Malvern Coll.; Sidney Sussex Coll., Cambridge. Called to the Bar, Middle Temple, 1939. Commissioned from HAC to 27th Field Regt, RA, 1940. Served War of 1939–45; France and Belgium, also N Africa and Italy, JAG Staff, 1943–45; JA at Neuengamme War Crimes Trial. Admitted a Solicitor, 1949, in practice as Partner, in Freke Palmer, Romain & Gassman, until 1972; recalled to Bar, 1973; a Dep. Circuit Judge, 1975–78. *Club:* Garrick.

ROMANES, Professor George John, CBE 1971; PhD; Professor of Anatomy, 1954–84, and Dean of Faculty of Medicine, 1979–83, Edinburgh University; Professor of Anatomy, Royal Scottish Academy, since 1983; *b* 2 Dec. 1916; *s* of George Romanes, BSc, AMICE, and Isabella Elizabeth Burn Smith; *m* 1945, Muriel Grace Adam, Edinburgh; four *d. Educ:* Edinburgh Academy; Christ's College, Cambridge (BA, PhD); Edinburgh University (MB, ChB). Marmaduke Sheild Scholar in Human Anatomy, 1938–40; Demonstrator in Anatomy, Cambridge, 1939; Beit Memorial Fellow for Medical Research, Cambridge, 1944–46; Lectr in Neuroanatomy, Edinburgh, 1946; Prof. of Anatomy, Edinburgh, 1954. Commonwealth Fund Fell., Columbia Univ., NY, 1949–50. Chm., Bd of Management, Edinburgh Royal Infirmary, 1959–74. Mem. Anatomical Soc. of Gt Brit. and Ireland; Mem. Amer. Assoc. of Anatomists; Assoc. Mem. Amer. Neurological Assoc. FRSE 1955; FRCSE 1958. Hon. DSc Glasgow, 1983. *Publications:* (ed) Cunningham's Textbook and Manuals of Anatomy; various papers on the anatomy and development of the nervous system in Jl of Anatomy and Jl of Comparative Neurology. *Recreations:* angling and curling. *Address:* Camus na Feannag, Kishorn, Strathcarron, Ross-shire IV54 8XA. *T:* Kishorn (05203) 273.

ROMER, Mark Lemon Robert; a Metropolitan Stipendiary Magistrate since 1972; *b* 12 July 1927; *s* of late Rt Hon. Sir Charles Romer, OBE, and Hon. Lady Romer; *m* 1953, Philippa Maynard Tomson (marr. diss. 1991); one *s* two *d. Educ:* Bryanston; Trinity Hall, Cambridge (MA, LLM). Called to Bar, Lincoln's Inn, 1952; practised privately until 1958 when joined Govt Legal Service. *Recreations:* bird-watching, reading, music. *Address:*

Gillings Hill, Arkesden Road, Clavering, Essex CB11 4QU. *T:* Saffron Walden (0799) 550792.

ROMNEY, 7th Earl of, *cr* 1801; **Michael Henry Marsham;** Bt 1663; Baron of Romney, 1716; Viscount Marsham, 1801; *b* 22 Nov. 1910; *s* of Lt-Col the Hon. Reginald Hastings Marsham, OBE (*d* 1922) (2nd *s* of 4th Earl) and Dora Hermione (*d* 1923), *d* of late Charles North; *S* cousin, 1975; *m* 1939, Frances Aileen, *o d* of late Lt-Col James Russell Landale, IA. *Educ:* Sherborne. Served War of 1939–45, Major RA. *Heir: cousin* Julian Charles Marsham [*b* 28 March 1948; *m* 1975, Catriona Ann, *d* of Lt-Col Robert Christie Stewart, *qv*; two *s* one *d*]. *Address:* Wensum Farm, West Rudham, King's Lynn, Norfolk PE31 8SZ. *T:* East Rudham (048522) 249.

ROMSEY, Lord; Norton Louis Philip Knatchbull; *b* 8 Oct. 1947; *s* and *heir* of Baron Brabourne, *qv* and of Countess Mountbatten of Burma, *qv*; *m* 1979, Penelope Meredith Eastwood; one *s* two *d*. *Educ:* Dragon School, Oxford; Gordonstoun; University of Kent (BA Politics). *Heir: s* Hon. Nicholas Louis Charles Norton Knatchbull, *b* 15 May 1981. *Address:* Broadlands, Romsey, Hants SO51 9ZD. *T:* Romsey (0794) 517888.

RONALD, Edith, (Mrs Edmund Ronald); *see* Templeton, Mrs Edith.

RONALDSHAY, Earl of; Robin Lawrence Dundas; Director: Redcar Race Co., since 1989; Catterick Racecourse Co., since 1988; *b* 5 March 1965; *s* and *heir* of Marquess of Zetland, *qv*. *Educ:* Harrow; Royal Agricl Coll., Cirencester. *Recreations:* shooting, ski-ing, tennis. *Address:* 7 Hasker Street, SW3 2LE. *Club:* Slainte Mhah.

RONAY, Egon; Founder of the Egon Ronay hotel and restaurant guides (taken over by the Automobile Association, 1985, and purchased by Alfresco plc, 1990); *m* 1967, Barbara Greenslade; one *s*, and two *d* of previous marr. *Educ:* School of Piarist Order, Budapest; Univ. of Budapest (LLD); Academy of Commerce, Budapest. Dip. Restaurateurs' Guild, Budapest; FHCIMA. After univ. degree, trained in kitchens of family catering concern; continued training abroad, finishing at Dorchester Hotel, London; progressed to management within family concern of 5 restaurants, of which eventually he took charge; emigrated from Hungary, 1946; Gen. Manager, Princes Restaurant, Piccadilly, then Society Restaurant, Jermyn Street, followed by 96 Restaurant, Piccadilly; opened own restaurant, The Marquee, SW1, 1952–55; started eating-out and general food, wine and tourism weekly column in Daily Telegraph and later Sunday Telegraph, 1954–60, also eating-out guide, 1957; weekly dining out column in Evening News, 1968–74. Mem. l'Académie des Gastronomes, France, 1979; Vice Pres., Internat. Acad. of Gastronomy, 1985. Médaille de la Ville de Paris, 1983; Chevalier de l'Ordre du Mérite Agricole, 1987. *Publications:* Egon Ronay's Guide to Hotels and Restaurants, annually, 1956–85; Egon Ronay's Just A Bite, annually, 1979–85; Egon Ronay's Pub Guide, annually, 1980–85; Egon Ronay's Guide to 500 Good Restaurants in Europe's main cities, annually, 1983–85; The Unforgettable Dishes of My Life, 1989; various other tourist guides to Britain, to ski resorts in Europe, to Scandinavian hotels and restaurants and to eating places in Greece.

RONSON, Gerald Maurice; Chairman and Chief Executive, Heron Corporation PLC and Heron International PLC; *b* 27 May 1939; *s* of Henry and Sarah Ronson; *m* 1967, Gail; four *d*. Chief Executive, 1976–, Chairman, 1979–, Heron Corp. PLC; Chm. and Chief Exec., Heron International PLC, 1983–. *Recreations:* yachting, shooting. *Address:* Heron House, 19 Marylebone Road, NW1 5JL. *T:* 071–486 4477. *Clubs:* Marylebone Rifle and Pistol; Royal Southern Yacht (Southampton).

ROOK, Peter Francis Grosvenor; QC 1991; *b* 19 Sept. 1949; *s* of Dr Arthur James Rook and Frances Jane Elizabeth Rook (*née* Knott); *m* 1978, Susanna Marian Tewson; one *s* two *d*. *Educ:* Charterhouse; Trinity College, Cambridge (Open Exhibnr; MA Hist.); Bristol Univ. (Dip. Soc. Studies). Called to the Bar, Gray's Inn, 1973; 2nd Standing Counsel to Inland Revenue at Central Criminal Court and Inner London Courts, 1981, 1st Standing Counsel, 1989; Asst Recorder, 1990. *Publication:* Rook and Ward on Sexual Offences, 1990. *Recreations:* tennis, squash, cricket, theatre, growing tropical plants. *Address:* 5 King's Bench Walk, Temple, EC4Y 7DN. *T:* 071–353 4713. *Club:* Coolhurst Lawn Tennis and Squash.

ROOKE, Daphne Marie; author; *b* 6 March 1914; *d* of Robert Pizzey and Marie Knevitt; *m* 1937, Irvin Rooke; one *d*. *Educ:* Durban, S Africa. *Publications:* A Grove of Fever Trees, 1950, repr. 1989; Mittee, 1951, repr. 1987; Ratoons, 1953; The South African Twins, 1953; The Australian Twins, 1954; Wizards' Country; The New Zealand Twins, 1957; Beti, 1959; A Lover for Estelle, 1961; The Greyling, 1962; Diamond Jo, 1965; Boy on the Mountain, 1969; Double Ex!, 1970; Margaretha de la Porte, 1974; A Horse of his Own, 1976. *Recreation:* bushwalking. *Address:* 34 Bent Street, Fingal Bay, NSW 2315, Australia.

ROOKE, Sir Denis (Eric), Kt 1977; CBE 1970; BSc (Eng.); FRS 1978; FEng 1977; Chairman, British Gas plc (formerly British Gas Corporation and earlier, The Gas Council), 1976–89 (Deputy Chairman, 1972–76); Chancellor, Loughborough University of Technology, since 1989; *b* 2 April 1924; *yr s* of F. G. Rooke; *m* 1949, Elizabeth Brenda, *d* of D. D. Evans, Ystradgynlais, Brecon; one *d*. *Educ:* Westminster City Sch.; Addey and Stanhope Sch.; University Coll., London (Fellow, 1972). Served with REME, UK and India, 1944–49 (Major). Joined staff of S Eastern Gas Bd as Asst Mechanical Engr in coal-tar by-products works, 1949; Dep. Man. of works, 1954; seconded to N Thames Gas Bd, 1957, for work in UK and USA on liquefied natural gas; mem. technical team which sailed in Methane Pioneer on first voyage bringing liquefied natural gas to UK, 1959; S Eastern Gas Bd's Development Engr, 1959; Development Engr, Gas Council, 1960; Mem. for Production and Supplies, 1966–71. Chm., CNAA, 1978–83; Member: Adv. Council for R&D, 1972–77; Adv. Council for Energy Conservation, 1974–77; Offshore Energy Technology Bd, 1975–78; BNOC, 1976–82; NEDC, 1976–80; Energy Commn, 1977–79. President: IGasE, 1975; Assoc. for Science Educn, 1981; Fellowship of Engineering, 1986–91; BAAS, 1990; Inst. of Quality Assce, 1990–June 1992. Foreign Associate, NAE, 1987. Trustee, Science Museum, 1984–; Comr, Royal Commn for Exhibn of 1851, 1984–. Hon. DSc: Salford, 1978; Leeds, 1980; City, 1985; Durham, 1986; Cranfield Inst. of Technol., 1987; Hon. DTech CNAA, 1986; Hon. LLD Bath, 1987; Hon. DEng Bradford, 1989; DUniv Surrey, 1990. KStJ 1989. Rumford Medal, Royal Soc., 1986. *Publications:* papers to Instn of Gas Engrs, World Power Conf., World Petroleum Conf., etc. *Recreations:* photography, listening to music. *Address:* 23 Hardy Road, Blackheath, SE3 7NS. *Clubs:* Athenæum, English-Speaking Union.

ROOKE, Giles Hugh, TD 1963; QC 1979; **His Honour Judge Rooke;** a Circuit Judge, since 1981; *b* 28 Oct. 1930; *s* of late Charles Eustace Rooke, CMG, and Irene Phyllis Rooke; *m* 1968, Anne Bernadette Seymour, *d* of His Honour John Perrett, *qv*; four *s* one *d*. *Educ:* Stowe; Exeter Coll., Oxford (MA). Kent Yeomanry, 1951–61, Kent and County of London Yeomanry, 1961–65 (TA), Major. Called to Bar, Lincoln's Inn, 1957; practised SE Circuit, 1957–81; a Recorder of the Crown Court, 1975–81. Hon. Recorder of Margate, 1980–. *Address:* St Stephen's Cottage, Bridge, Canterbury CT4 5AH. *T:* Canterbury (0227) 830298.

ROOKE, James Smith, CMG 1961; OBE 1949; Grand Decoration of Honour in Gold, of the Austrian Republic, 1981; Chief Executive, British Overseas Trade Board, 1972–75; HM Diplomatic Service, retired; now lecturer, Diplomatic Academy, Vienna; *b* 6 July 1916; *s* of Joseph Nelson Rooke and Adeline Mounser (*née* Woodgate); *m* 1938, Maria Theresa Rebrec, Vienna; one *s* two *d*. *Educ:* Workington Grammar Sch.; University College, London; Vienna Univ. Apptd to Dept of Overseas Trade, 1938. Military service, 1940–45, KRRC and AEC. Second Secretary (Commercial), British Embassy, Bogotá, 1946; UK Delegation to ITO Conf., Havana, 1947; Dep. UK Commercial Rep., Frankfurt, 1948; First Secretary (Commercial), British Embassy, Rome, 1951; Consul (Commercial), Milan, 1954; Deputy Consul-General (Commercial), New York, 1955–59; HM Counsellor (Commercial) British Embassy, Berne, 1959–63, Rome, 1963–66; Minister (Commercial), British High Commn, Canberra, 1966–68; Minister (Economic), British Embassy, Paris, 1968–72. *Recreations:* climbing, tennis, ski-ing. *Address:* c/o Diplomatische Akademie, Favoritenstrasse 15, A1040 Vienna, Austria. *Club:* East India, Devonshire, Sports and Public Schools.

ROOKE, Brig. Vera Margaret, CB 1984; CBE 1980; RRC 1973; Matron-in-Chief (Army) and Director of Army Nursing Services, 1981–84; *b* 21 Dec. 1924; *d* of late William James Rooke and Lily Amelia Rooke (*née* Cole). *Educ:* Girls' County Sch., Hove, Sussex. Addenbrooke's Hosp., Cambridge (SRN); Royal Alexandra Children's Hosp., Brighton (RSCN); St Helier Hosp., Carshalton (Midwifery). Joined Queen Alexandra's Royal Army Nursing Corps, 1951; appointments include: service in military hospitals, UK, Egypt, Malta, Singapore; Staff Officer in Work Study; Liaison Officer, QARANC, MoD, 1973–74; Assistant Director of Army Nursing Services and Matron: Military Hosp., Hong Kong, 1975; Royal Herbert Hosp. and Queen Elizabeth Military Hosp., Woolwich, 1976–78; Dep. Dir, Army Nursing Services, HQ UKLF, 1979–80. QHNS, 1981–84. Lt-Col 1972, Col 1975, Brig. 1981. *Recreations:* gardening, walking, cookery, opera. *Address:* c/o Lloyds Bank, 208 Portland Road, Hove, Sussex.

ROOKER, Jeffrey William, CEng; MP (Lab) Birmingham, Perry Barr, since Feb. 1974; *b* 5 June 1941; *m* 1972, Angela. *Educ:* Handsworth Tech. Sch.; Handsworth Tech. Coll.; Warwick Univ. (MA); Aston Univ. (BScEng). CEng, FIProdE; MBIM. Apprentice toolmaker, King's Heath Engrg Co. Ltd, Birmingham, 1957–63; student apprentice, BLMC, 1963–64; Asst to Works Manager, Geo. Salter & Co., West Bromwich, 1964–65, Assembly Manager, 1965–67; Prodn Manager, Rola Celestion Ltd, Thames Ditton and Ipswich, 1967–70; Industrial Relations and Safety Officer, Metro-Cammell, Birmingham, 1971; Lectr, Lanchester Polytechnic, Coventry, 1972–74. Opposition spokesman on social services, 1979–80, on social security, 1980–83, on treasury and economic affairs, 1983–84, on housing, 1984–87, on local government, 1987–88, on health and social services, 1990–; Mem., Public Accounts Cttee, 1989–91. Chair, Labour Campaign for Electoral Reform, 1989–. Mem. Council, Instn of Prodn Engrs, 1975–81. *Recreation:* full-time MP. *Address:* House of Commons, SW1. *T:* (home) 021–350 6186.

ROOLEY, Anthony; lutenist; Artistic Director, The Consort of Musicke, since 1969; *b* 10 June 1944; *s* of Madge and Henry Rooley; *m* 1967, Carla Morris; three *d*; one *s* by Emma Kirkby, *qv*. *Educ:* Royal Acad. of Music. LRAM (Performers). Recitals in Europe, USA, Middle East, Japan, S America, New Zealand, Australia; radio and TV in UK and Europe; numerous recordings, British and German. Hon. FRAM 1990. *Publications:* Penguin Book of Early Music. 1982; Performance—revealing the Orpheus within, 1990. *Recreations:* food, wine, gardening, philosophy. *Address:* 54A Leamington Road Villas, W11.

ROOME, Maj. Gen. Oliver McCrea, CBE 1973; Vice Lord-Lieutenant, Isle of Wight, since 1987; *b* 9 March 1921; *s* of late Maj. Gen. Sir Horace Roome, KCIE, CB, CBE, MC, DL, late Royal Engineers; *m* 1947, Isobel Anstis, *d* of Rev. A. B. Jordan; two *s* one *d*. *Educ:* Wellington Coll. Commissioned in Royal Engineers, 1940. Served War: UK, Western Desert, Sicily, Italy, 1939–45. Various appts, UK, Far and Middle East, Berlin, 1946–68; IDC, 1969; Director of Army Recruiting, 1970–73; Chief, Jt Services Liaison Organisation, Bonn, 1973–76; retired. Col Comdt, RE, 1979–84. County Comr, Scouts, Isle of Wight, 1977–85. DL Isle of Wight, 1981; High Sheriff of the Isle of Wight, 1983–84. *Recreations:* sailing, maritime and military history. *Address:* Lloyds Bank, PO Box 1190, 7 Pall Mall, SW1. *Clubs:* Army and Navy, Royal Ocean Racing, Royal Cruising; Royal Yacht Squadron.

ROONEY, Denis Michael Hall, CBE 1977; FEng, FIMechE, FIEE; CBIM; industrial consultant; *b* 9 Aug. 1919; *s* of late Frederick and Ivy Rooney; *m* 1st, 1942, Ruby Teresa (*née* Lamb) (*d* 1984); three *s* three *d*; 2nd, 1986, Muriel Franklin; one step *d*. *Educ:* Stonyhurst Coll.; Downing Coll., Cambridge (MA). Served War, Royal Navy, 1941–46 (Lieut Engr). Various appts with BICC Ltd, 1946–69; Balfour Beatty Ltd: Dep. Managing Dir, 1969–72; Man. Dir, 1973–77; Chm., 1975–80; BICC Ltd: Exec. Dir, 1973–80; Exec. Vice-Chm., 1978–80; Chm., BICC Internat., 1978–80; Dep. Chm., Metal Manufactures Ltd, Australia, 1978–80; Chm., Nat. Nuclear Corp., 1980–81; Consultant, Goddard, Kay, Rogers, 1983–85; Chm., Laserfix Ltd, 1984–86. Chm., SE Asia Trade Adv. Gp, BOTB, 1975–79; Member: British Overseas Trade Adv. Council, 1976–80; Overseas Projects Bd, BOTB, 1976–79; BOTB, 1979–80; Council: Export Gp for Construction Industries, 1964–80; Christian Assoc. of Business Execs, 1979–; Inst. of Business Ethics; W London Cttee for Protection of Children; Batti Wallahs Soc. Liveryman, Worshipful Company of Turners of London. USSR Jubilee Medal, 1988. *Publication:* contrib. (Brazilian Rlwy Electrification) IEE Jl. *Recreation:* golf. *Address:* 36 Edwardes Square, W8 6HH. *T:* 071–603 9971. *Clubs:* Roehampton, Institute of Directors.

ROONEY, Michael John, RA 1991 (ARA 1990); Lecturer in Painting, Royal Academy Schools, since 1991; *b* 5 March 1944; *s* of Elisabeth and John Rooney; *m* 1st, 1967, Patricia Anne Lavender (marr. diss. 1984); one *s* one *d*; 2nd, 1988, Alexandra Grascher, Vienna; one *s*. *Educ:* primary and secondary schools; Sutton Sch. of Art; Wimbledon Sch. of Art (NDD); Royal Coll. of Art (MA RCA, ARCA); British Sch. at Rome (Austin Abbey Award). Part-time lectr, various art colls; artist-in-residence, Towner Art Gall., Eastbourne, 1983; one man exhibns in Holland, London, Edinburgh and other UK locations; work in public collections: Sussex; Birmingham; Punta del Este, Uruguay; London. Prizes include: Calouste Gulbenkian Printmakers' Award, 1984; John Player Portrait Award, Nat. Portrait Gallery, 1985; RA Summer Exhibn Awards, 1986, 1988, 1989. *Recreation:* cooking. *Address:* The Old Sorting House, 19 Alder Road, Mortlake, SW14 8ER. *T:* 081–876 0459. *Clubs:* Arts, Chelsea Arts.

ROONEY, Terence Henry; MP (Lab) Bradford North, since Nov. 1990; *b* 11 Nov. 1950; *s* of Eric and Frances Rooney; *m* 1969, Susanne; one *s* two *d*. *Educ:* Buttershaw Comprehensive Sch.; Bradford Coll. Formerly: commercial insurance broker; Welfare Rights Advice Worker, Bierley Community Centre. Councillor, Bradford City, 1983–90 (Dep. Leader, 1990). *Address:* c/o House of Commons, SW1A 0AA.

ROOSE-EVANS, James Humphrey; freelance theatre director and author; non-stipendiary Anglican priest; *b* 11 Nov. 1927; *s* of Jack Roose-Evans and Catharina Primrose Morgan. *Educ:* Univ. of Oxford (MA). Started career in repertory, as an actor; Artistic Dir, Maddermarket Theatre, Norwich, 1954–55 (dir. English première of The

Language of Flowers, 1955); Faculty of Julliard Sch. of Music, NY, 1955–56; on staff of RADA, 1956–; founded Hampstead Theatre, 1959; Resident Dir, Belgrade Theatre, Coventry, 1961. Regularly tours USA, lecturing and leading workshops. Productions directed include: *Hampstead Theatre*: The Square, 1963; The Little Clay Cart (also adapted), 1964; Adventures in the Skin Trade, world première, The Two Character Play, world première, Letters from an Eastern Front (also adapted), 1966; An Evening with Malcolm Muggeridge (also devised), 1966; *West End*: Cider with Rosie (also adapted), Private Lives, 1963; An Ideal Husband, 1966; The Happy Apple, 1967; 84 Charing Cross Road (also adapted), 1981 (Best Dir, Drama award), NY 1982 (awards for Best Play and Best Dir); Seven Year Itch, 1986; The Best of Friends, 1988 (also prod Comédie des Champs-Elysées, Paris, 1989); Temptation, 1990. Consultant, Theatre Mus. Founder and Chm., Bleddfa Trust-Centre for Caring and the Arts, Powys, 1974–. Columnist (Something Extra), Woman, 1986–88. *Publications*: adaptation of The Little Clay Cart, by King Sudraka, 1965; Directing a Play, 1968; Experimental Theatre, 1970, 4th revd edn, 1988; London Theatre, 1977; play version of 84 Charing Cross Road, by Helen Hanff, 1983; Inner Journey, Outer Journey, 1987 (US as The Inner Stage, 1990); (introd. and ed) Darling Ma: the letters of Joyce Grenfell, 1988; The Tale of Beatrix Potter, 1988; (with Maureen Lipman) Re:Joyce!, 1988; (introd and ed) The Time of My Life: wartime journals of Joyce Grenfell, 1989; (trans.) Obey, On the Edge of Midnight, 1989; *for children*: The Adventures of Odd and Elsewhere, 1971; The Secret of the Seven Bright Shiners, 1972; Odd and the Great Bear, 1973; Elsewhere and the Gathering of the Clowns, 1974; The Return of the Great Bear, 1975; The Secret of Tippity-Witchit, 1975; The Lost Treasure of Wales, 1977. *Recreations*: the Bleddfa Trust-Centre for Caring and the Arts, otherwise work! *Address*: c/o David Higham Associates, 5–8 Lower John Street, Golden Square, W1. *Club*: Garrick.

ROOT, Rev. Canon Howard Eugene; Director of the Anglican Centre, Rome, 1981–91; St Augustine Canon of Canterbury Cathedral, 1980–91, now Canon Emeritus; *b* 13 April 1926; *s* of Dr Howard Root and Flora Hoskins; *m* 1952, Celia, *e d* of Col R. T. Holland, CBE, DSO, MC; two *s* two *d*. *Educ*: Univ. of Southern California; St Catherine's Coll. and Magdalen Coll., Oxford; Ripon Hall, Oxford. BA S Calif 1945; BA Oxon 1951; MA Oxon 1970; MA Cantab 1953. Teaching Fellow, 1945–47; Instructor, American Univ., Cairo, 1947–49; Sen. Demy, Magdalen Coll., Oxford, and Liddon Student, 1951–53. Deacon, 1953; Priest, 1954. Curate of Trumpington, 1953; Asst Lectr in Divinity, Cambridge, 1953–57; Lectr, 1957–66; Fellow, Emmanuel Coll., Cambridge, 1954–66, Chaplain, 1954–56, Dean, 1956–66; Prof. of Theology, Univ. of Southampton, 1966–81. Wilde Lectr, Oxford Univ., 1957–60; Senior Denyer and Johnson Scholar, Oxford, 1963–64; Bampton Lectr, Univ. of Oxford, 1972; Pope Adrian VI Chair, Univ. of Louvain, 1979; Vis. Prof., Pontificial Gregorian Univ., Rome, 1984–91. Exam. Chaplain to Bishops of Ripon, 1959–76, Southwark, 1964–81, Bristol, 1965–81, Winchester, 1971–81, and Wakefield, 1977–81; Commissary to Bishop in Jerusalem, 1976–. Official Anglican Observer at Second Vatican Council, 1963–65; Consultant, Lambeth Conf., 1968 and 1988; Counsellor on Vatican affairs to Archbishop of Canterbury, 1981–91. Chm., Archbishops' Commn on Marriage, 1968–71; Member: Academic Council, Ecumenical Inst., Jerusalem, 1966–81; Anglican-RC Preparatory Commn, 1967–68; Archbishops' Commn on Christian Doctrine, 1967–74; Anglican-Roman Catholic Internat. Commn, 1969–81. Hon. Chaplain, Winchester Cathedral, 1966–67; Canon Theologian of Winchester, 1967–80. Mem., BBC Central Religious Adv. Cttee, 1971–75. Jt Editor, Jl of Theol Studies, 1969–74. *Recreations*: music, silence. *Address*: c/o Barclays Bank, Old Bank, PO Box 333, Oxford OX1 3HS. *Club*: Brooks's.

ROOTES, family name of **Baron Rootes.**

ROOTES, 2nd Baron *cr* 1959; **William Geoffrey Rootes**; Chairman, 1967–73, Chrysler United Kingdom (lately Rootes Motors Ltd); *b* 14 June 1917; *er s* of 1st Baron Rootes, GBE; *S* father, 1964; *m* 1946, Marian, *widow* of Wing Comdr J. H. Slater, AFC, and *d* of late Lt-Col H. R. Hayter, DSO; one *s* one *d*. *Educ*: Harrow; Christ Church, Oxford. Served War of 1939–45 in RASC (France, E Africa, Western Desert, Libya, Tunisia and Italy), demobilised, Actg Major, 1946. Rejoined Rootes Group, 1946: Man. Dir, 1962–67; Dep. Chm., 1965–67; Chm. 1967–70. Director: Rank Hovis McDougall, 1973–84; Joseph Lucas Industries Ltd, 1973–85. President: SMMT, 1960–61 (Hon. Officer, 1958–62, Chm. Exec. Cttee, 1972–73); Motor & Cycle Trades Benevolent Fund, 1968–70; Motor Ind. Research Assoc., 1970–71; Inst. of Motor Industry, 1973–75. Member: Nat. Adv. Council, Motor Manufrg Industry, 1964–71; Nat. Economic Development Cttee, Motor Manufacturing Industry, 1968–73; BNEC (Chm., American Cttee, 1969–71); Council, CBI, 1967–74, Europe Cttee CBI, 1972–76; Council, Inst. of Dirs, 1953–78; Council, Warwick Univ., 1968–74 (Chm., Careers Adv. Bd); Council, Game Conservancy (Chm., 1975–79); Vice-Pres., British Field Sports Soc., 1978–; Mem. Council, WWF UK, 1983– (Trustee, 1983–88; Chm., Educnl Adv. Council, 1984–88). County Pres., St John Ambulance, Berks, 1983–88; KStJ 1988 (CStJ 1983). FRSA; FBIM; FIMI; FIPE. *Recreations*: shooting, fishing. *Heir*: *s* Hon. Nicholas Geoffrey Rootes [*b* 12 July 1951; *m* 1976, Dorothy Anne Burn-Forti, *d* of Cyril Wood]. *Address*: North Standen House, Hungerford, Berks RG17 0QZ. *Clubs*: Buck's, Flyfishers'.

ROOTS, Guy Robert Godfrey; QC 1989; *b* 26 Aug. 1946; *s* of William Lloyd Roots and Elizabeth Colquhoun Gow (*née* Gray); *m* 1975, Caroline (*née* Clarkson); three *s*. *Educ*: Winchester College; Brasenose College, Oxford (MA). Called to the Bar, Middle Temple, 1969; Harmsworth Scholar, 1970. Liveryman, Drapers' Co., 1972. *Publication*: (ed) Ryde on Rating, 1986. *Recreations*: sailing, fishing, ski-ing, photography, woodworking. *Address*: 2 Mitre Court Buildings, Temple, EC4Y 7BX. *T*: 071–583 1380. *Club*: Itchenor Sailing.

ROOTS, Paul John; Director of Industrial Relations, Ford Motor Co. Ltd, 1981–86, retired; *b* 16 Oct. 1929; *s* of John Earl and Helen Roots; *m* 1951, Anna Theresa Pateman; two *s* two *d*. *Educ*: Dormers Wells Sch.; London Sch. of Economics. Cert. in Personnel Admin. CIPM; CBIM. RN, 1947–54: service in Korean War. Personnel Officer, Brush Gp, 1955; Labour Officer, UKAEA, 1956, Labour Manager, 1959; Ford Motor Co. Ltd: Personnel Manager, Halewood, 1962; Forward Planning Manager, 1966; Labour Relations Manager, 1969; Dir of Employee Relations, 1974. Vice-Pres., IPM, 1981–83. Chairman: CBI Health and Safety Policy Cttee, 1984–; CBI Health and Safety Consultative Cttee, 1984–; Member: Council of Management, CBI Educn Foundn, 1981–; CBI Working Party on the Employment of Disabled People, 1981–; CBI Employment Policy Cttee, 1983–; CBI Council, 1984–; Engrg Industry Training Bd, 1985–. *Publications*: (jtly) Communication in Practice, 1981; (jtly) Corporate Personnel Management, 1986; Financial Incentives for Employees, 1988; articles in personnel management jls. *Recreations*: riding, theatre, music.

ROPER; *see* Trevor-Roper.

ROPER, Hon. Sir Clinton Marcus, Kt 1985; Chief Justice, High Court of the Cook Islands, since 1988; Acting Judge, High Court of New Zealand, since 1989; *b* Christchurch, 19 June 1921; *s* of Wilfred Marcus Roper; *m* 1947, Joan Elsa Turnbull; one *s* one *d*. *Educ*: Christchurch West High Sch.; Canterbury Univ.; Victoria Univ. of Wellington. LLB. Served War of 1939–45, Pacific, Italy and Japan (Lieut). Crown Solicitor, Christchurch, 1961–68; Judge: High Court of NZ, 1968–85; Court of Appeal, Fiji, 1985–87; High Court, Cook Islands, 1985–88; Tongan Privy Council Court, 1986–90; Tongan Court of Appeal, 1990–. Chairman: Prisons Parole Bd, 1970–85; Prisons Rev. Cttee, 1987–89; Cttee of Inquiry into Violence, 1985–87. *Address*: 15 Allister Avenue, Christchurch, New Zealand.

ROPER, John Charles Abercromby, CMG 1969; MC; HM Diplomatic Service, retired; *b* 8 June 1915; *s* of late Charles Roper, MD, and of Mrs Roper; *m* 1st, 1945, Valerie Armstrong-MacDonnell (marr. diss.); two *d*; 2nd, 1960, Kathryn (*d* 1984), *d* of late Edgar Bibas, New York; 3rd, 1986, Phoebe, *d* of late R. B. Foster, London and New York. *Educ*: Harrow; Universities of Cambridge and Princeton (Commonwealth Fellow). Served 1939–46, Scots Guards and Special Forces, Major (MC). HM Diplomatic Service, 1946; Athens, 1947–51; Foreign Office, 1951–54; Washington, 1954–59. Seconded to Min. of Defence and apptd Dep. Commandant (Civil) of NATO Defence College, Paris, 1960–62; Asst Sec., Cabinet Office, 1962–64; Counsellor, UK Delegn to OECD, 1964–70; Ambassador to Luxembourg, 1970–75. *Address*: Tenuta di Monteverdi, 58048 Paganico, Provincia di Grosseto, Italy. *Club*: Special Forces.

ROPER, John (Francis Hodgess); Head of Western European Union Institute for Security Studies, Paris, since 1990; *b* 10 Sept. 1935; *e s* of Rev. Frederick Mabor Hodgess Roper and Ellen Frances (*née* Brockway); *m* 1959, Valerie Hope, *er d* of late Rt Hon. L. John Edwards, PC, OBE, MP, and late Mrs D. M. Edwards; one *d*. *Educ*: William Hulme's Grammar Sch., Manchester; Reading Sch.; Magdalen Coll., Oxford; Univ. of Chicago. Nat. Service, commnd RNVR, 1954–56; studied PPE, Oxford, 1956–59 (Pres. UN Student Assoc., 1957; organised Univ. referendum on Nuclear Disarmament); Harkness Fellow, Commonwealth Fund, 1959–61; Research Fellow in Economic Statistics, Univ. of Manchester, 1961; Asst Lectr in Econs, 1962–64, Lectr 1964–70, Faculty Tutor 1968–70; RIIA, 1983–90: Editor of International Affairs, 1983–88; Head of Internat. Security Programme, 1985–88, and 1989–90; Dir of Studies, 1988–89. Contested: (Lab) High Peak (Derbys), 1964; (SDP) Worsley, 1983. MP (Lab and Co-op 1970–81, SDP 1981–83) Farnworth, 1970–83; PPS to Minister of State, DoI, 1978–79; opposition front bench spokesman on defence, 1979–81; Social Democrat Chief Whip, 1981–83. Vice-Chairman: Anglo-German Parly Gp, 1974–83; Anglo-Benelux Parly Gp, 1979–83; Chm., British-Atlantic Gp of Young Politicians, 1974–75. Council of Europe: Consultant, 1965–66; Mem., Consultative Assembly, 1973–80; Chm., Cttee on Culture and Educn, 1979–80; Mem., WEU Assembly, 1973–80; Chm., Cttee on Defence Questions and Armaments, WEU, 1977–80. Hon. Treasurer, Fabian Soc., 1976–81; Chairman: Labour Cttee for Europe, 1976–80; GB/East Europe Centre, 1987–90; Council on Christian Approaches to Defence and Disarmament, 1983–89. Research Adviser (part-time), DEA in NW, 1967–69. Director: Co-op. Wholesale Soc., 1969–74; Co-op Insurance Soc., 1973–74. Pres., Gen. Council, UNA, 1972–78; Mem. Council, Inst. for Fiscal Studies, 1975–90; Mem. Gen. Adv. Council, IBA, 1974–79. Vice-Pres., Manchester Statistical Soc., 1971–. Trustee, Hist. of Parlt Trust, 1974–84. *Publications*: (with Lloyd Harrison) Towards Regional Co-operatives, 1967; The Teaching of Economics at University Level, 1970; The Future of British Defence Policy, 1985; (ed with Karl Kaiser) British–German Defence Co-operation, 1988; (ed with Yves Boyer) Franco-British Defence Co-operation, 1988. *Recreations*: reading, travel. *Address*: 12 rue de Bassano, 75116 Paris, France. *T*: 47.23.53.57. *Club*: United Oxford & Cambridge University.

ROPER, Michael, FRHistS; Keeper of Public Records, 1988–Aug. 1992; *b* 19 Aug. 1932; *s* of Jack Roper and Mona Roper (*née* Nettleton); *m* 1957, Joan Barbara Earnshaw; one *s* one *d*. *Educ*: Heath Grammar Sch., Halifax; Univ. of Manchester (BA, MA; Langton Fellow). Registered Mem., Soc. of Archivists, 1987. Public Record Office: Asst Keeper, 1959–70; Principal Asst Keeper, 1970–82; Records Admin Officer, 1982–85; Dep. Keeper of Public Records, 1985–88. Sec., Adv. Council on Public Records, 1963–68; Lectr (part time) in Archive Studies, UCL, 1972–87, Hon. Res. Fellow, 1988–. Pres., Soc. of Archivists, 1989– (Vice-Chm., 1983–84, Chm., 1985–86); Vice-President: British Records Soc., 1988–; RHistS, 1989– (Hon. Treas., 1974–80); Sec.-Gen., Internat. Council on Archives, 1988– (Sec. for Standardization, 1984–88). Ext. Examr, Nat. Univ. of Ireland, 1982–86, Univ. of Liverpool, 1986–89. Chm., Judy Segal Trust, 1990–. Hon. DLitt Bradford, 1991. *Publications*: Yorkshire Fines 1300–1314, 1965; Records of the Foreign Office 1782–1939, 1969; (with J. A. Keene) Planning, Equipping and Staffing a Document Reprographic Service, 1984; Guidelines for the Preservation of Microforms, 1986; Directory of National Standards Relating to Archives Administration and Records Management, 1986; Planning, Equipping and Staffing an Archival Preservation and Conservation Service, 1989; contribs to learned jls. *Recreations*: listening to music, gardening, walking the dog. *Address*: 157B Fairfax Road, Teddington, Middx TW11 9BU. *T*: 081–977 4642.

ROPER, Robert Burnell, CB 1978; Chief Land Registrar, 1975–83 (Deputy Chief Land Registrar, 1973–75); *b* 23 Nov. 1921; *s* of late Allen George and Winifred Roper; *m* 1948, Mary Brookes; two *s*. *Educ*: King's College Sch., Wimbledon; King's Coll., London. LLB (Hons) 1941. Called to Bar, Gray's Inn, 1948. Served War, RAF, 1942–46. Miners' Welfare Commn, 1946–48; Nat. Coal Bd, 1948–49; Treasury Solicitor's Dept, 1949–50; HM Land Registry, 1950–83. *Publications*: (Ruoff and Roper) The Law and Practice of Registered Conveyancing, 3rd edn 1972, to 6th edn 1991; Consulting Editor on Land Registration matters for Encyclopaedia of Forms and Precedents (4th edn). *Recreations*: gardening, watching sport. *Address*: 11 Dukes Road, Lindfield, Haywards Heath, West Sussex RH16 2JH.

ROPER, Prof. Warren Richard, FRS 1989; FRSNZ 1984; Professor of Chemistry, University of Auckland, New Zealand, since 1984; *b* 27 Nov. 1938; *m* 1961, Judith Delcie Catherine Miller; two *s* one *d*. *Educ*: Nelson Coll., Nelson, NZ; Univ. of Canterbury, Christchurch, NZ (MSc, PhD). FNZIC. Postdoctoral Res. Associate, Univ. of N Carolina, 1963–65; Lectr in Chemistry, Univ. of Auckland, 1966. Vis. Lectr, Univ. of Bristol, 1972; Pacific W Coast Inorganic Lectr, 1982; Brotherton Vis. Res. Prof., Univ. of Leeds, 1983; Visiting Professor: Univ. de Rennes, 1984, 1985; Stanford Univ., 1988. Mellor Lectr, NZ Inst. of Chemistry, 1985; Centenary Lectr and Medallist, RSC, 1988. RSC Award in Organometallic Chemistry, 1983; ICI Medal, NZ Inst. of Chemistry, 1984. *Publications*: over 100 sci. papers in internat. jls. *Recreations*: music, espec. opera, walking. *Address*: 26 Beulah Road, Auckland 10, New Zealand. *T*: (09) 478 6940.

ROPER-CURZON, family name of **Baron Teynham.**

ROPNER, David; *see* Ropner, W. G. D.

ROPNER, Sir John (Bruce Woollacott), 2nd Bt *cr* 1952; Director, Ropner PLC; *b* 16 April 1937; *s* of Sir Leonard Ropner, 1st Bt, MC, TD, and of Esmé, *y d* of late Bruce Robertson; *S* father, 1977; *m* 1st, 1961, Anne Melicent (marr. diss. 1970), *d* of late Sir Ralph Delmé-Radcliffe; two *d*; 2nd, 1970, Auriol, *d* of late Captain Graham Lawrie Mackeson-Sandbach, Caerllo, Llangernyw; one *s* two *d*. *Educ*: Eton; St Paul's School, USA. High Sheriff, N Yorks, 1991. *Recreation*: field sports. *Heir*: *s* Henry John William

Ropner, *b* 24 Oct. 1981. *Address:* Thorp Perrow, Bedale, Yorks DL8 2PR. *Club:* Brooks's. *See also Viscount Knutsford.*

ROPNER, John Raymond; Consultant, Ropner PLC, and other companies; *b* 8 May 1903; *s* of William Ropner; *m* 1928, Joan Redhead; two *s* one *d*. *Educ:* Harrow; Clare College, Cambridge (BAEcon 1925). Durham Heavy Bde, RA (TA), 1922–28; joined Sir R. Ropner & Co. Ltd, 1925; Ministry of War Transport, North Western Europe, 1944–45. High Sheriff of Durham, 1958. Member, Shipping Advisory Panel, 1962. Order of Oranje-Nassau, 1947. *Recreations:* gardening, fishing; formerly golf (Cambridge blue, 1925). *Address:* The Limes, Dalton, Richmond, N Yorkshire DL11 7XJ. *T:* Teesdale (0833) 21447.

ROPNER, Sir Robert Douglas, 4th Bt, *cr* 1904; *b* 1 Dec. 1921; *o s* of Sir (E. H. O.) Robert Ropner, 3rd Bt; *S* father, 1962; *m* 1943, Patricia Kathleen, *d* of W. E. Scofield, W. Malling, Kent; one *s* one *d*. *Educ:* Harrow. Formerly Captain, RA. *Heir: s* Robert Clinton Ropner, *b* 6 Feb. 1949.

ROPNER, (William Guy) David; Director, Ropner PLC, since 1953 (Chairman, 1973–85); *b* 3 April 1924; *s* of late Sir William Guy Ropner and Lady (Margarita) Ropner; *m* 1st, 1955, Mildred Malise Hare Armitage (marr. diss. 1978); one *d* three *s*; 2nd, 1985, Hon. Mrs Charlotte M. Taddei; one *s*. *Educ:* Harrow. FICS 1953. Served War, 1942–47: 2nd Lieut RA, Essex Yeomanry; Captain 3rd Regt, RHA. Joined Sir R. Ropner and Co. Ltd, 1947; dir of various Ropner PLC gp cos, 1953–. Member: Lloyd's, 1952–; Gen. Cttee, Lloyd's Register of Shipping, 1961–; Pres., Gen. Council of British Shipping, 1979–80; Chairman: Deep Sea Tramp Section, Chamber of Shipping, 1970–72; Lights Adv. Cttee, GCBS, 1978–87; Merchant Navy Welfare Bd, 1980–; Cleveland & Durham Industrial Council, 1980–; Dir, British Shipowners Assoc., 1954–89. Dir, Guidehouse Expansion Management, 1984–. *Recreations:* country and garden pursuits. *Address:* 1 Sunningdale Gardens, Stratford Road, W8 6PX. *T:* 071–937 3862. *Club:* St Moritz Tobogganing.

ROQUES, (David) John (Seymour); Managing Partner and Chief Executive, Touche Ross & Co., since 1990; Member, Executive Committee, DRT International, since 1990; *b* 14 Oct. 1938; *s* of late Frank Davy Seymour Roques and of Marjorie Mabel Hudson; *m* 1963, Elizabeth Anne Mallender; two *s* one *d*. *Educ:* St Albans Sch. Mem., Inst. of Chartered Accountants of Scotland, 1962. Touche Ross & Co.: Partner, 1967; Partner in charge, Midlands region, 1973; Partner in charge, Scottish region, 1978; Partner in charge, London office, 1984. Dir (non-exec.), British Nuclear Fuels, 1990–. Mem., Financial Reporting Review Panel. FRSA. *Recreations:* Rugby football, racing, opera, gardening. *Address:* Peterborough Court, 133 Fleet Street, EC4A 2TR. *T:* 071–936 3000. *Clubs:* Edgbaston Golf (Edgbaston); Wasps Football (Sudbury).

RORKE, Prof. John, CBE 1979; PhD; FRSE; FIMechE; Professor of Mechanical Engineering, 1980–88, and Vice-Principal, 1984–88, Heriot-Watt University, now Professor Emeritus; Chairman: Orkney Water Test Centre Ltd, since 1987; Environment and Resource Technology Ltd, since 1991; *b* 2 Sept. 1923; *s* of John and Janet Rorke; *m* 1948, Jane Craig Buchanan; two *d*. *Educ:* Dumbarton Acad.; Univ. of Strathclyde (BSc, PhD). Lectr, Strathclyde Univ., 1946–51; Asst to Engrg Dir, Alexander Stephen & Sons Ltd, 1951–56; Technical Manager, subseq. Gen. Man., and Engrg Dir, Wm Denny & Bros Ltd, 1956–63; Tech. Dir, subseq. Sales Dir, Man. Dir, and Chm., Brown Bros & Co. Ltd (subsid. of Vickers Ltd), 1963–78; Man. Dir, Vickers Offshore Engrg Gp, 1978; Dir of Planning, Vickers Ltd, 1979–80. Pres., Instn of Engineers and Shipbuilders in Scotland, 1985–87. *Recreations:* golf, bridge. *Address:* 3 Barnton Park Grove, Edinburgh EH4 6HG. *T:* 031–336 3044. *Club:* Bruntsfield Links Golfing Society (Edinburgh).

ROSCOE, (John) Gareth; Legal Adviser to the BBC, since 1989; Director, BBC Enterprises Ltd; *b* 28 Jan. 1948; *s* of late John Roscoe and Ann (*née* Jones); *m* 1st, 1970, Helen Jane Taylor (marr. diss. 1979); one *d*; 2nd, 1980, Alexis Fayrer Brett-Holt; one *s* one *d*. *Educ:* Manchester Warehousemen and Clerks' Orphan Schools (now Cheadle Hulme Sch.); Stretford Tech. Coll.; London Sch. of Economics and Political Science (LLB). Called to the Bar, Gray's Inn, 1972; in practice, 1972–75; Legal Asst 1975–79, Sen. Legal Asst 1979, DoE; Law Officers' Dept, Attorney-General's Chambers, 1979–83; Asst Solicitor, 1983–87, Dep. Solicitor, 1987–89, DoE. Mem., Gen. Council of the Bar, 1987–90. Mem., Adv. Cttee, Centre for Communications and Information Law, UCL. *Recreations:* music, horology. *Address:* BBC, Broadcasting House, W1A 1AA. *T:* 071–580 4468. *Club:* Athenæum.

ROSCOE, Sir Robert Bell, KBE 1981; FASA, ABIA, ABINZ; Director, Chase-NBA Group Ltd (Australia and New Zealand), 1969–80; Chairman: Melbourne Underground Rail Loop Authority, 1971–81; First Federation Discount Co. Ltd, 1975–84; *b* 7 August 1906; *s* of T. B. Roscoe; *m* 1931, Daphne, *d* of G. Maxwell; one *d*. *Educ:* Central Tech. Coll., Brisbane. Liquidator, Qld Nat. Bank Ltd, 1949; State Manager, Qld, 1951–54; Nat. Bank of Australasia: State Manager, Victoria, 1954–60; Chief Inspector, 1960–65; Sen. Chief Inspector, 1965–66; Asst Chief Manager, 1966–69. Director: Hoechst Australia Ltd, 1970–; All States Commercial Bills Ltd; Oceania Capital Corp. Ltd. *Address:* 833 Burwood Road, Hawthorn East, Victoria 3123, Australia. *Club:* Australian (Melbourne).

ROSE, Andrew; *see* Rose, W. A.

ROSE, (Arthur) James; HM Chief Inspector for Primary Education, Department of Education and Science, since 1986; *m* 1960, Pauline; one *d*. *Educ:* Kesteven College; Leicester University. Formerly Headteacher of Shaftesbury Junior School and Shenton Primary School, Leicester. *Address:* Department of Education and Science, Sanctuary Buildings, Great Smith Street, SW1P 3BT.

ROSE, Barry, MBE 1981; editor and publisher; Chairman, own group of companies, since 1970; *b* 17 July 1923; *s* of late William George Rose and Beatrice Mary (*née* Castle); *m* 1963, Dorothy Jean Colthrup, *d* of Lt-Col W.R. Bowden; one *d*. Editor: Justice of the Peace and Local Government Review, 1944–72; Justice of the Peace, 1972–74; Local Government Review, 1972–76; law and local govt oriented periodicals. Member: Chichester RDC, 1951–61; West Sussex CC, 1952–73 (Leader, Cons. Group, 1967–72; Alderman, 1972); Pagham Parish Council, 1952–62; Bognor Regis UDC, 1964–68; Hon. Editor, Rural District Review, 1959–63; Mem., RDCA, 1960–63, CCA 1968–72; Chm., SE Area Cons. Local Govt Adv. Cttee, 1969–73; Pres., Assoc. of Councillors, 1975–86 (Treasurer, 1960–69; Chm., Exec. Cttee, 1969–75); posts in Cons. Party, 1945–74, incl. Constituency Chm., Chichester, 1961–69; Pres., Chichester Div., Young Conservatives, 1959–69. Publisher, Centre for Policy Studies, 1974–76. Member: Parly All-Party Penal Affairs Gp; Magistrates' Assoc.; NACRO; Council for Science and Society. Liveryman, Stationers' Co., 1974. FRSA 1960. Hon. Life Mem., Justices' Clerks' Soc., 1985. *Publications:* Change of Fortune (play), 1950; Funny Business (play), 1951; England Looks at Maud, 1970; A Councillor's Work, 1971. *Recreations:* entertaining and being entertained. *Address:* Courtney Lodge, Sylvan Way, Bognor Regis, West Sussex. *T:* Bognor Regis (0243) 829902. *Clubs:* Athenæum, Garrick, MCC, United Oxford & Cambridge University; West Sussex County (Chichester).

ROSE, Barry Michael, FRSCM; FRAM; Master of the Music, St Albans Abbey, since 1988; *b* 24 May 1934; *s* of late Stanley George Rose and Gladys Mildred Rose; *m* 1965, Elizabeth Mary Ware; one *s* two *d*. *Educ:* Sir George Monoux Grammar Sch., Walthamstow; Royal Acad. of Music (ARAM). FRSCM 1973; FRAM 1989. First Organist and Master of the Choristers, new Guildford Cathedral, 1960–74; Sub-Organist, St Paul's Cath., 1974–77; Master of the Choir, 1977–84; Master of the Choirs, The King's School, Canterbury, 1985–88. Music Adviser to Head of Religious Broadcasting, BBC, 1970–90. *Recreation:* running a record company (Guild Records, founded 1967). *Address:* 31 Abbey Mill Lane, St Albans, Herts AL3 4HA. *T and Fax:* St Albans (0727) 51810.

ROSE, Bernard William George, OBE 1980; MusB Cantab 1938, MA Oxon, Cantab 1944, DMus Oxon 1955, FRCO; Fellow, Organist, Informator Choristarum, Magdalen College, Oxford, 1957–81, Vice-President, 1973 and 1974, Emeritus Fellow since 1981; University Lecturer in Music, 1950–81; Choragus in the University, 1958–63; *b* Little Hallingbury, Herts, 9 May 1916; *s* of William and Jessie Rose; *m* 1939, Molly Daphne, OBE, JP, DL, 5th *d* of D. G. Marshall, MBE, Cambridge; three *s*. *Educ:* Salisbury Cathedral Sch.; Royal Coll. of Music; St Catharine's Coll., Cambridge. Organ Scholar, St Catharine's, Cambridge, 1935–39; Stewart of Rannoch Scholar in Sacred Music, Cambridge, 1935–39; Organist, and Conductor of the Eaglesfield Musical Soc., The Queen's Coll., Oxford, 1939–57, Fellow, 1949. Served with 4th Co. of London Yeomanry (Sharpshooters), 1941–44, Adjutant 1942 (PoW 1943–44). Conductor, Oxford Orchestral Soc., 1971–74. Mem. Council, Royal Coll. of Organists (Pres. 1974–76). *Publications:* contrib. Proc. Roy. Mus. Assoc., 1955; various church music compositions and edns of church music; edns of Anthems of Thomas Tomkins; (ed) Early English Church Music, Vols 5, 9, 14, 27 and 37; Hallische Händel Ausgabe, 'Susanna'; reviews in Music and Letters, articles in Musical Times. *Recreations:* DIY, bowls. *Address:* Bampton House, Bampton, Oxford OX18 2JX. *T:* Bampton Castle (0993) 850135.

ROSE, Brian; HM Diplomatic Service, retired; *b* 26 Jan. 1930; *s* of Edwin and Emily Rose; *m* 1952, Audrey Barnes; one *d*. *Educ:* Canford Sch., Dorset. MIL 1983. Intelligence Corps, 1948–50. Min. of Food, 1950–54; CRO, 1954; Peshawar, 1955–56; Ottawa, 1958–61; Kingston, Jamaica, 1962–65; Rome, 1966; Zagreb, 1966–68; Zomba, Malawi, 1968–71; FCO, 1971–74; Düsseldorf, 1974–77; E Berlin, 1977–78; Zürich, 1978–82; Consul-Gen., Stuttgart, 1982–85; Commercial and Econ. Counsellor, Helsinki, 1985–88. *Recreations:* tennis, squash. *Club:* Travellers'.

ROSE, Major Charles Frederick, CBE 1988 (MBE 1968); CEng, FICE, MCIT; independent consultant in railway engineering and safety, since 1989; *b* 9 July 1926; *s* of Charles James Rose and Ida Marguerite Chollet; *m* 1956, Huguette Primerose Lecoultre; one *s* one *d*. *Educ:* Xaverian Coll., Brighton; Royal School of Military Engineering, 1951–52 and 1957–59. Student engineer, Southern Railway Co., 1942–46; commnd RE, 1947; service with mil. railways, Palestine and Egypt, 1947–51; with a Field Sqdn in Germany, 1952–53; Engr SO, Korea, 1953–54; Instructor: Mons Officer Cadet Sch., 1954–57; Transportation Centre, Longmoor, 1959–62; OC a Field Sqdn, Germany, 1962–64; Instr, Royal Sch. of Mil. Engrg, 1964–66; Engr, RE road construction project, Thailand, 1966–68; Inspecting Officer of Railways, MoT, 1968–82; Chief Inspecting Officer of Railways, Dept of Transport, 1982–88. Chm., Anglo-French Channel Tunnel Safety Authy, 1987–89. *Recreations:* cycling, walking, music, reading. *Address:* Hollybank, Shadyhanger, Godalming, Surrey GU7 2HR. *T:* Godalming (04868) 6429.

ROSE, Christine Brooke; *see* Brooke-Rose.

ROSE, Hon. Sir Christopher (Dudley Roger), Kt 1985; **Hon. Mr Justice Rose;** a Judge of the High Court, Queen's Bench Division, since 1985; *b* 10 Feb. 1937; *s* of late Roger Rose and Hilda Rose, Morecambe; *m* 1964, Judith, *d* of late George and Charlotte Brand, Didsbury; one *s* one *d*. *Educ:* Morecambe Grammar Sch.; Repton; Leeds Univ.; Wadham Coll., Oxford. LLB and Hughes Prize, Leeds, 1957; 1st cl. hons BCL 1959, Eldon Scholar 1959, Oxon. Lectr in Law, Wadham Coll., Oxford, 1959–60; called to Bar, Middle Temple, 1960 (Bencher, 1983); Bigelow Teaching Fellow, Law Sch., Univ. of Chicago, 1960–61; Harmsworth Scholar, 1961; joined Northern Circuit, 1961; QC 1974; a Recorder, 1978–85; Presiding Judge, 1987–90. Mem., Senate of Inns of Court and Bar, 1983–85. *Recreations:* playing the piano, listening to music, golf, travel. *Address:* Royal Courts of Justice, Strand, WC2A 2LL.

ROSE, Clifford; *see* Rose, F.C.

ROSE, Sir Clive (Martin), GCMG 1981 (KCMG 1976; CMG 1967); HM Diplomatic Service, retired; Consultant, Control Risks Group, since 1983; Director: Control Risks Information Services Ltd, since 1986; *b* 15 Sept. 1921; *s* of late Rt Rev. Alfred Carey Wollaston Rose and Lois Juliet (*née* Garton); *m* 1946, Elisabeth Mackenzie, *d* of late Rev. Cyril Lewis, Gilston; two *s* three *d*. *Educ:* Marlborough College; Christ Church, Oxford (MA). Rifle Bde, 1941–46 (Maj.; despatches): served in Europe, 1944–45; India, 1945; Iraq, 1945–46. CRO, 1948; Office of Deputy High Comr, Madras, 1948–49; Foreign Office, 1950–53; UK High Commn, Germany, 1953–54; British Embassy, Bonn, 1955; FO, 1956–59; 1st Sec. and HM Consul, Montevideo, 1959–62; FO, 1962–65; Commercial Counsellor, Paris, 1965–67; Imp. Defence Coll., 1968; Counsellor, British Embassy, Washington, 1969–71; Asst Under-Sec. of State, FCO, 1971–73; Head, British Delegn to Negotiations on Mutual Reduction of Forces and Armaments and Associated Measures in Central Europe, 1973–76; Dep. Secretary, Cabinet Office, 1976–79; UK Permanent Rep. on North Atlantic Council, 1979–82. Lectr to RCDS, 1979–87 (Mem., Adv. Bd, 1985–). Chm., Internat. Commn on Violence in the Basque Country, 1985–86; Pres., Assoc. of Civil Defence and Emergency Planning Officers, 1987–; Vice-Pres., RUSI, 1986– (Chm. Council, 1983–86). Vice-Pres., Suffolk Preservation Soc., 1988– (Chm., 1985–88). FRSA 1982; Hon. FICD 1989. *Publications:* Campaigns Against Western Defence: NATO's adversaries and critics, 1985, 2nd edn 1986; The Soviet Propaganda Network, 1988; articles on defence and arms control. *Recreations:* gardening, reading Trollope, family history. *Address:* Chimney House, Lavenham, Suffolk CO10 9QT. *Club:* Army and Navy.

ROSE, David Edward; Head of Drama, Channel Four Television, 1988–90; *b* 22 Nov. 1924; *s* of Alvan Edward Rose and Gladys Frances Rose; *m* 1st, 1952, Valerie Edwards (*d* 1966); three *s* three *d*; 2nd, 1966, Sarah Reid; one *d*, and one step *s* one step *d* adopted. *Educ:* Kingswood Sch., Bath; Guildhall Sch. of Music and Drama. Repertory Theatre, 1952; Ballets Jooss, and Sadler's Wells Theatre Ballet, 1954; BBC Television, 1954–81 (in production and direction; Head of Television Training, 1969; Head of Regional Television Drama, 1971–81); Sen. Commng Editor (Fiction), Channel Four TV, 1981–88. Mem., BAFTA. Prix Italia TV Award (for film Medico), 1959; BAFTA Producer and Director's Award, (for Z Cars (prod original series)), 1963; BFI Award (for Film on Four and work of new writers and directors), 1985; Desmond Davies Award, BAFTA, 1987; Prix Roberto Rossellini (for Channel Four Television), Cannes Film Fest., 1987; Critics Circle Special Film Award, 1987; Gold Medal, RTS, 1988.

ROSE, Donald Henry Gair, LVO 1982; HM Diplomatic Service, retired; Consul-General, Jedda, 1983–86; *b* 24 Sept. 1926; *m* 1950, Sheila Munro; three *s*. HM Forces,

1944–48; Scottish Office, 1948–66; Commonwealth Office, 1966; Nairobi, 1967; Tripoli, 1971; First Sec., Cairo, 1974–77; FCO, 1977–79; High Comr, Kiribati, 1979–83. *Address:* 11 Buckstone Gardens, Edinburgh EH10 6QD.

ROSE, Eliot Joseph Benn, (Jim Rose), CBE 1979; Chairman, Penguin Books, 1973–80; Director, Pearson Longman, 1974–81; *b* 7 June 1909; *s* of late Colonel E. A. Rose, CBE, and Dula, *e d* of Eliot Lewis, JP; *m* 1946, Susan Pamela Gibson; one *s* one *d*. *Educ:* Rugby; New College, Oxford. Served War of 1939–45, RAF, Wing-Comdr. Literary Editor, The Observer, 1948–51; Director: International Press Institute, Zürich, 1951–62; Survey of Race Relations in Britain, 1963–69; Editorial Dir, Westminster Press Ltd, 1970–74. Chm., Inter-Action Trust, 1968–84; Co-founder, Runnymede Trust; Mem., Cttee of Inquiry into educn of children from ethnic minority groups, 1979–81; Special Consultant to Unicef, 1981. Trustee, Writers and Scholars Educnl Trust. Sidney Ball Meml Lectr, Oxford, 1970. Legion of Merit (US). *Publication:* (with Nicholas Deakin) Colour and Citizenship, 1969. *Address:* 37 Pembroke Square, W8 6PE. *T:* 071–937 3772; Rocks Farm, Groombridge, Tunbridge Wells, Kent. *T:* Tunbridge Wells (0892) 864223. *Club:* Garrick.

ROSE, Dr Frank Clifford, FRCP; Director, London Neurological Centre, and Consulting Neurologist, Charing Cross Hospital; Secretary-Treasurer General, World Federation of Neurology, since 1989; Principal Medical Officer, Allied Dunbar Assurance Co. (formerly Hambro Life Assurance Co.), since 1970; *b* 29 Aug. 1926; *s* of James and Clare Rose; *m* 1963, Angela Juliet Halsted; three *s*. *Educ:* King's Coll., London; Westminster Hosp. Med. Sch.; Univ. of California, San Francisco; Hôpital de la Salpêtrière, Paris. MB BS London; DCH; MRCS; FRCP 1971 (LRCP 1949, MRCP 1954). Medical Registrar, Westminster Hosp., 1955; Resident MO, National Hosp., Queen Square, 1957; Sen. Registrar, Dept of Neurology, St George's Hosp., 1960; Consultant Neurologist: Medical Ophthalmology Unit, St Thomas' Hosp., 1963–85; Moor House Sch. for Speech Disorders, 1965–70; Physician i/c, Dept. of Neurology, Regl Neuroscis Centre, Charing Cross Hosp., 1965–91; Dir, Academic Unit of Neuroscis., Charing Cross and Westminster Med. Sch., 1985–91. Chairman: European Stroke Prevention Study, 1981–88; Res. Adv. Cttee, Assoc. for Res. in Multiple Sclerosis, 1987–; Internat. Amyotrophic Lateral Sclerosis/Motor Neurone Disease Res. Foundn, 1987–90; Motor Neurone Disease Assoc., 1988–90 (Scientific Advr, 1990–); President: Med. Soc. London, 1983–84 (Treas., 1984–89); Assurance Med. Soc., 1983–85; Section of Neurology, RSM, 1990–91; Medical Patron, Motor Neurone Disease Assoc., 1978–90; Trustee: Migraine Trust (Chm., 1988–); The Way Ahead Appeal, 1986–. Examr in Clinical Pharmacology and Therapeutics, Univ. of London. Lettsomian Lectr, Med. Soc. London, 1979; Guest Lectr, Scandinavian Migraine Soc., 1983. Harold Wolff Award, 1981 and 1984, and Distinguished Clinician Award, 1986, Amer. Assoc. for the Study of Headache. Editor, Neuroepidemiology, 1984–90 (Dep. Editor, 1982–83). *Publications:* (jtly) Hypoglycaemia, 1965, 2nd edn, 1981; (jtly) Basic Neurology of Speech, 1970, 3rd edn 1983; (ed) Physiological Aspects of Clinical Neurology, 1976; (ed) Medical Ophthalmology, 1976; (ed) Motor Neurone Disease, 1977; (ed) Clinical Neuroimmunology, 1978; (ed) Paediatric Neurology, 1979; (jtly) Optic Neuritis and its Differential Diagnosis, 1979; (ed jtly) Progress in Stroke Research 1, 1979; (ed jtly) Progress in Neurological Research, 1979; (ed jtly) Migraine: the facts, 1979; (ed) Clinical Neuroepidemiology, 1980; (ed) Animal Models of Neurological Disorders, 1980; (ed jtly) Research Progress in Parkinson's Disease, 1981; (ed) Metabolic Disorders of the Nervous System, 1981; (ed jtly) Progress in Migraine Research 1, 1981; (jtly) Stroke: The Facts, 1981; (ed jtly) Historical Aspects of the Neurosciences, 1982; Cerebral Hypoxia in the Pathogenesis of Migraine, 1982; Advances in Stroke Therapy, 1982; (ed) Advances in Migraine Research and Therapy, 1982; (ed) Research Progress in Epilepsy, 1982; (ed jtly) Immunology of Nervous System Infections, 1983; (ed) The Eye in General Disease, 1983; (ed jtly) Progress in Stroke Research 2, 1983; (ed) Research Progress in Motor Neurone Disease, 1984; (ed) Progress in Migraine Research 2, 1984; (ed) Progress in Aphasiology, 1985; (ed) Modern Approaches to the Dementias (2 vols), 1985; (ed jtly) Neuro-oncology, 1985; (ed) Migraine: clinical and research advances, 1985; Handbook of Clinical Neurology: headache, 1986; Stroke: epidemiological, therapeutic and socio-economic aspects, 1986; (ed jtly) Multiple Sclerosis: diagnostic, immunological and therapeutic aspects, 1987; (ed) Advances in Headache Research, 1987; (ed) Parkinson's Disease: clinical and research advances, 1987; (ed jtly) Physiological Aspects of Clinical Neuro-ophthalmology, 1987; (jtly) Answers to Migraine, 1987; (ed jtly) Aphasia, 1988; (ed) The Management of Headache, 1988; (ed jtly) Neuromuscular Stimulation, 1989; (ed) James Parkinson, his life and times, 1989; (ed) Control of the Hypothalamic-Pituitary-Adrenal Axis, 1989; (ed) New Advances in Headache Research, 1989; (ed) Neuroscience across the Centuries, 1989; (ed jtly) Amyotrophic Lateral Sclerosis: new advances in toxicology and epidemiology, 1990; papers in neurological and gen. med. jls. *Recreations:* travel, reading. *Address:* London Neurological Centre, 110 Harley Street, W1N 1AF. *T:* 071–935 3546, *Fax:* 071–935 4172. *Club:* Royal Society of Medicine.

ROSE, Prof. Geoffrey Arthur, CBE 1991; DM; FRCP, FRCGP, FFPHM; Emeritus Professor of Epidemiology, University of London, since 1991; *b* 19 April 1926; *s* of Rev. Arthur Norman Rose and Mary (*née* Wadsworth); *m* 1949, Ceridwen (*née* Coates); two *s* one *d*. *Educ:* Kingswood Sch.; Queen's Coll., Oxford (MA); St Mary's Hosp. Med. Sch. DM Oxford, 1958; FRCP 1970; FRCGP 1988; FFPHM (FFCM 1974). Professor of Epidemiology: St Mary's Hosp. Med. Sch., 1970–77; London Sch. of Hygiene and Tropical Medicine, 1977–91. Hon. Consultant Physician, St Mary's Hosp., 1964–91. Chairman: WHO Expert Cttees on Heart Disease Prevention, 1982, 1984; Council on Epidemiology and Prevention, Internat. Soc. and Fedn of Cardiology, 1982–86. Hon. Mem., Med. Acad. of Catalonia and Balearic Is, 1981. Hon. DSc Meml Univ. of Newfoundland, 1983; Hon. MD Univ. of Kuopio, Finland, 1991. Purkinje Medal, Czechoslovak Med. Soc., 1978; Duodecim Medal, Finnish Med. Soc., 1989. *Publications:* (with Prof. Blackburn) Cardiovascular Survey Methods, 1968, 2nd edn 1982; (with Prof. D. J. P. Barker) Epidemiology in Medical Practice, 1976, 4th edn 1990; (with Prof. D. J. P. Barker) Epidemiology for the Uninitiated, 1986; The Strategy of Preventive Medicine, 1992. *Recreations:* lay preaching, rural pursuits. *Address:* Trevalley, Penfold Lane, Holmer Green, High Wycombe, Bucks HP15 6XS.

ROSE, Gerald Gershon, PhD; CChem, FRSC; Director, Thornton Research Centre, Shell Research Ltd, 1975–80; *b* 4 May 1921; *m* 1945, Olive Sylvia; one *s* two *d*. *Educ:* Hendon County Grammar Sch.; Imperial Coll. of Science and Technology (BSc, ARCS, DIC, PhD). Joined Shell Group, 1944; served in refineries, Stanlow, Trinidad, Singapore and South Africa; General Manager, Shell/BP South Africa Petroleum Refineries, 1963; Manufacturing and Supply Director, Shell/BP Service Co., 1968; Manager, Teesport Refinery, 1971. *Recreations:* golf, tennis, gardening. *Address:* The Tithe Barn, Great Barrow, Chester, Cheshire CH3 7HW. *T:* Tarvin (0829) 40623.

ROSE, Graham John; gardening correspondent, Sunday Times, since 1978; *b* 28 Jan. 1928; *s* of Herbert Trower Whitfield Rose and Grace Rose (*née* Cain); *m* 1st, 1953, Catherine Marie Louise Degrais; 2nd, 1967, Elizabeth Dorothy Goldbach (*née* Dodd). *Educ:* Dame Allan's School, Newcastle-upon-Tyne; King's College, Durham Univ. (BSc Hons); Gonville and Caius College, Cambridge. Entomologist, ICI (India), Calcutta, 1950–51; Universal Crop Protection, 1951–53; Technical Dir, Micron Sprayers, 1953–57; Consultant: Micron Sprayers, Britten Norman, SDC Pesticides, Opico (UK), 1957–68; agricultural corresp., Sunday Times, 1968–78. *Publications:* Crop Protection, 1955; Landscape with Weeds, 1980; The Low Maintenance Garden, 1983; (with Peter King) Green Words, 1986; Gardener's Almanac, 1986; The Small Garden Planner, 1987; (jtly) Gardening with Style, 1988; The Romantic Garden, 1988; Woodland and Wildflower Gardening, 1988; The Traditional Garden Book, 1989; (with Peter King) The Good Gardens Guide, 1990, 2nd edn 1991; (with Peter King) The Love of Roses, 1990. *Recreations:* garden designing, building. *Address:* 58 Hugh Street, SW1V 4ER. *T:* 071–821 9378.

ROSE, Prof. Harold Bertram; Professor of Finance, London Graduate School of Business Studies, since 1965 (Esmée Fairbairn Chair until 1975, then Visiting Professor); *b* 9 Aug. 1923; *s* of late Isaac Rose and Rose Rose (*née* Barnett); *m* 1st, 1949, Valerie Frances Anne Chubb (marr. diss. 1974); three *s* one *d*; 2nd, 1974, Diana Mary Campbell Scarlett; one *s* one *d*. *Educ:* Davenant Foundn Sch.; LSE (BCom). Served with RA in Britain, India and Burma, 1942–45 (Captain). Head of Econ. Intell. Dept, Prudential Assce Co., Ltd, 1948–58; Sen. Lectr, then Reader, in Business Finance, LSE, 1958–65; Member: Council, Consumers' Assoc., 1958–63; Central Adv. Council on Primary Educn (Plowden Cttee), 1963–65; Business Studies Cttee, SSRC, 1967–68, and Univ. Grants Cttee, 1968–69; Reserve Pension Bd, 1973–75; HM Treasury Inquiry into Value of Pensions, 1980; Special Adviser to: H of C Treasury and Civil Service Cttee, 1980–81; DoI, 1980–81. Gp Economic Advr, Barclays Bank, 1975–88. Director: Economist Newspaper, 1969–71; Abbey National Building Soc., 1975–83. Mem., Retail Prices Adv. Cttee, 1985–89. Trustee, IEA, 1975–. Gov., The Hall Sch., 1987–. *Publications:* The Economic Background to Investment, 1959; Disclosure in Company Accounts, 1963; Management Education in the 1970's, 1970; various papers in econ. and financial jls. *Address:* 33 Dartmouth Park Avenue, NW5 1JL. *T:* 071–485 7315.

ROSE, Maj.-Gen. Hugh Michael, CBE 1986; QGM 1981; Commandant, Staff College, since 1991; *b* 5 Jan. 1940; *s* of Lt-Col Hugh Vincent Rose, IA, retd and Mrs Barbara Phoebe Masters (*née* Allcard); *m* 1968, Angela Raye Shaw; two *s*. *Educ:* Cheltenham College; St Edmund Hall, Oxford (2nd Cl. Hons PPE); Staff College; RCDS. Commissioned Gloucestershire Regt, TAVR, 1959; RAFVR, 1962; Coldstream Guards, 1964; served Germany, Aden, Malaysia, Gulf States, Dhofar, N Ireland (despatches), Falkland Is (despatches); BM16 Para. Bde, 1973–75; CO 22 SAS Regt, 1979–82; Comd 39 Inf. Bde, 1983–85; Comdt, Sch. of Infantry, 1987–88; DSF, 1988–89; GOC NE Dist and Comdr 2nd Inf. Div., 1989–91. Chm., Army Parachute Assoc., Cdre, Army Sailing Assoc. *Recreations:* sailing, ski-ing. *Address:* c/o Regimental HQ Coldstream Guards, Wellington Barracks, Birdcage Walk, SW1E 6HQ. *Club:* Cavalry and Guards.

ROSE, Jack, CMG 1963; MBE 1954; DFC 1942; *b* 18 Jan. 1917; *s* of late Charles Thomas Rose; *m* 1st, 1940, Margaret Valerie (*d* 1966), 2nd *d* of late Alec Stuart Budd; two *s*; 2nd, 1967, Beryl Elizabeth, 4th *d* of late A. S. Budd. *Educ:* Shooters Hill School; London University. Served RAF, 1938–46 (Wing Commander); served in fighter, fighter/bomber and rocket firing sqdns; France, 1940 and 1944; Battle of Britain; Burma, 1944–45. Joined Colonial Administrative Service, N Rhodesia, 1947; Private Secretary to Governor of Northern Rhodesia, 1950–53; seconded to Colonial Office, 1954–56; Administrative posts, Northern Rhodesia, 1956–60; Administrator, Cayman Islands (seconded), 1960–63; Assistant to Governor, British Guiana, 1963–64 (Actg Governor and Dep. Governor for periods). Member: Professional and Technical 'A' Whitley Council for Health Services, 1965–75 (Chm., 1973–75); Gen. Whitley Council for Health Services, 1973–75. Secretary: Chartered Soc. of Physiotherapy, 1965–75; Salmon and Trout Assoc., 1975–79 (Vice-Pres., 1980–). *Recreation:* writing. *Address:* The Little House, The Hill, Burford, Oxon OX18 4QY. *T:* Burford (0993) 822553.

ROSE, James; *see* Rose, A. J.

ROSE, Jeffrey David, CBE 1991; Chairman of the Royal Automobile Club, since 1981 (Deputy Chairman, 1979–81); *b* 2 July 1931; *s* of late Samuel and Daisy Rose; *m* 1958, Joyce (*née* Clompus) (separated 1990); one *s* two *d*. *Educ:* Southend High Sch.; London Sch. of Econs and Pol. Science. Nat. Service, RA, 1950–52, Lieut. Chm., RAC Motoring Services, 1980–; Vice Chm., British Road Fedn, 1982–; Vice Pres., Fédn Internationale de l'Automobile, 1983–; Chm., Commonwealth Motoring Conf., 1988–; Member: Management Cttee, Alliance Internationale de Tourisme, 1982–; Council, Inst. of Advanced Motorists, 1987–. Trustee, Brooklands Mus., 1991–. FIMI 1989. Liveryman, Worshipful Co. of Coachmakers and Coach Harness Makers, 1981–. *Recreations:* walking, dining, music. *Address:* Royal Automobile Club, 89–91 Pall Mall, SW1Y 5HS. *Clubs:* Royal Automobile, Brooks's, MCC.

ROSE, Jim; *see* Rose, E. J. B.

ROSE, John Raymond; Clerk of Standing Committees, House of Commons, 1987–91; *b* 22 April 1934; *s* of late Arthur Raymond Rose and of Edith Mary Rose, Minehead, Somerset; *m* 1st, 1961, Vivienne (marr. diss.), *d* of late Charles Dillon Seabrooke, IoW; one *s* one *d*; 2nd, 1991, Betty Webb, *d* of late Ernest Julian Webb, Statesville, NC, USA. *Educ:* Marlborough; Trinity Hall, Cambridge (Major Scholar in Classics; Law Tripos 1st Cl. Hons, Pts I and II). 2nd Lieut DCLI, Belize and Jamaica, 1953–55. Clerk's Department, House of Commons, 1958–: Clerk of Select Cttees on Estimates (Sub-Cttee), Public Accounts, Violence in the Family, Race Relations, Abortion, European Community Secondary Legislation, Foreign Affairs, 1959–87. Vis. Kenan Prof., Meredith Coll., NC, USA, 1981. Fellow, Industry and Parlt Trust, 1987. Freeman, City of London, 1959; Liveryman, Salters' Co., 1959. *Recreations:* travel, walking, cycling, gardening, country pursuits, Scottish dancing. *Address:* 220 Hillcrest Road, Raleigh, NC 26705, USA. *T:* 919–828–3443.

ROSE, Joyce Dora Hester, CBE 1981; JP, DL; Chairman, Council and Executive, Magistrates' Association, since 1990; *b* 14 Aug. 1929; *d* of late Abraham (Arthur) Woolf and Rebecca Woolf (*née* Simpson); *m* 1953, Cyril Rose; two *s* one *d*. *Educ:* King Alfred Sch., London; Queen's Coll., London; in N America. Chm., Watford Magistrates' Court, 1990– (Dep. Chm., Juvenile Panel, 1968–, Domestic Panel, 1982– (Chm., 1979–82)); Member: Herts Magistrates' Courts Cttee, 1973–; Herts Probation Cttee, 1971–. Pres., 1979–80, Chm., 1982–83, Liberal Party; Pres. and Chm., Women's Liberal Fedn, 1972, 1973. Mem., Women's Nat. Commn, 1981–87 (Mem. Exec., 1985–87); former Mem., Nat. Exec., UK Cttee, UNICEF (Vice-Chm., 1968–70). JP Herts, 1963; DL Herts, 1990. *Address:* 38 Main Avenue, Moor Park, Northwood, Middx HA6 2LQ. *T:* Northwood (0923) 821385. *Club:* National Liberal.

ROSE, Sir Julian (Day), 4th Bt *cr* 1909, of Hardwick House, and 5th Bt *cr* 1872, of Montreal; *b* 3 March 1947; 3rd and *o* surv. *s* of Sir Charles Henry Rose, 3rd Bt and of Phoebe, *d* of 2nd Baron Phillimore (*d* 1947); *S* father, 1966, and cousin, Sir Francis Cyril Rose, 4th Bt, 1979; *m* 1976, Elizabeth Goode Johnson, Columbus, Ohio, USA; one *s* one *d*. *Educ:* Stanbridge School. Actor/asst dir, Players' Theatre of New England, 1973–79; Co-founder, Inst. for Creative Develt, Antwerp, 1978–83. Co-ordinator, Organic Farming practice, Hardwick Estate, 1984–. Member: Council, Soil Assoc., 1984–; Agricl Panel, Intermediate Technology Develt Gp, 1984–; Bd, UK Register of Organic Food Standards, Food From Britain, 1987–; BBC Rural and Agricl Affairs Adv. Cttee, 1991–. *Heir: s* Lawrence Michael Rose, *b* 6 Oct. 1986. *Address:* Hardwick House, Whitchurch-on-Thames, Oxfordshire RG8 7RB.

ROSE, Kenneth Vivian, FRSL; writer; *b* 15 Nov. 1924; *s* of Dr J. Rose, MB, ChB. *Educ:* Repton Sch.; New Coll., Oxford (scholar; MA). Served Welsh Guards, 1943–46; attached Phantom, 1945. Asst master, Eton Coll., 1948; Editorial Staff, Daily Telegraph, 1952–60; founder and writer of Albany column, Sunday Telegraph, 1961–. *Publications:* Superior Person: a portrait of Curzon and his circle in late Victorian England, 1969; The Later Cecils, 1975; William Harvey: a monograph, 1978; King George V, 1983 (Wolfson Award for History, 1983; Whitbread Award for Biography, 1983; Yorkshire Post Biography of the Year Award, 1984); Kings, Queens and Courtiers: intimate portraits of the Royal House of Windsor, 1985; contribs to Dictionary of National Biography. *Address:* 38 Brunswick Gardens, W8 4AL. *T:* 071–221 4783. *Clubs:* Beefsteak, Pratt's.

ROSE, Paul (Bernard); HM Coroner, London Southern District, since 1988; *b* 26 Dec. 1935; *s* of Arthur and Norah Rose; *m* 1957, Eve Marie-Thérèse; two *s* one *d*. *Educ:* Bury Gram. Sch.; Manchester Univ.; Gray's Inn. LLB (Hons) Manch., 1956; Barrister-at-Law, 1957. Legal and Secretarial Dept, Co-op. Union Ltd, 1957–60; Lectureship, Dept of Liberal Studies, Royal Coll. of Advanced Technology, Salford, 1961–63; Barrister-at-Law, 1963–88; Asst Recorder (formerly Dep. Circuit Judge), 1974–88; Immigration Adjudicator (part-time), Hardmondsworth, 1987–. MP (Lab) Manchester, Blackley, 1964–79; PPS to Minister of Transport, 1967–68; Opposition Front Bench Spokesman, Dept of Employment, 1970–72. Chairman: Parly Labour Home Office Group, 1968–70; Parly Labour Employment Group, 1974–79; Campaign for Democracy in Ulster, 1965–73. Delegate to Council of Europe and WEU, 1968–69; Vice-Chm., Labour Cttee for Europe, 1977–79. Mem., Campaign for Electoral Reform, 1975–. Founder Mem., SDP (Brent Area Sec., 1981–82). Chm., NW Regional Sports Council, 1966–68. Member: Coroners' Soc.; Medico-Legal Soc. AIL. *Publications:* Handbook to Industrial and Provident Societies Act, 1960; Guide to Weights and Measures Act 1963, 1965; The Manchester Martyrs, 1970; Backbencher's Dilemma, 1981; The Moonies' Unmasked, 1981; (jt) A History of the Fenian Movement in Britain, 1982; contrib. to many periodicals on political and legal topics. *Recreations:* sport, theatre, languages, travel. *Address:* Coroner's Court, Barclay Road, Croydon CR9 3NE.

ROSE, Prof. Richard; Director and Professor of Public Policy, Centre for the Study of Public Policy, Strathclyde University, since 1976; *b* 9 April 1933; *o s* of Charles Imse and late Mary Conely Rose, St Louis, Mo, USA; *m* 1956, Rosemary J., *o d* of late James Kenny, Whitstable, Kent; two *s* one *d*. *Educ:* Clayton High Sch., Mo; Johns Hopkins Univ., BA (Double distinction, Phi Beta Kappa) comparative drama, 1953; London Sch. of Economics, 1953–54; Oxford University, 1957–60, DPhil (Lincoln and Nuffield Colls). Political public relations, Mississippi Valley, 1954–55; Reporter, St Louis Post-Dispatch, 1955–57; Lecturer in Govt, Univ. of Manchester, 1961–66; Prof. of Politics, Strathclyde Univ., 1966–82. Consultant Psephologist, The Times, Independent Television, Daily Telegraph, STV, UTV etc., 1964–. American SSRC Fellow, Stanford Univ., 1967; Vis. Lectr in Political Sociology, Cambridge Univ., 1967; Dir, ISSC European Summer Sch., 1973. Sec., Cttee on Political Sociology, Internat. Sociological Assoc., 1970–85; Founding Mem., European Consortium for Political Res., 1970; Member: US/UK Fulbright Commn, 1971–75; Eisenhower Fellowship Programme, 1971. Guggenheim Foundn Fellow, 1974; Visiting Scholar: Woodrow Wilson Internat. Centre, Washington DC, 1974; Brookings Inst., Washington DC, 1976; Amer. Enterprise Inst., Washington, 1980; Fiscal Affairs Dept, IMF, Washington, 1984; Vis. Prof., European Univ. Inst., Florence, 1977, 1978; Visitor, Japan Foundn, 1984; Hinkley Prof., Johns Hopkins Univ., 1987; Guest Prof., Wissenschaftzentrum, Berlin, 1988–; Ransone Lectr, Univ. of Alabama, 1990. Consultant Chm., NI Constitutional Convention, 1976; Home Office Working Party on Electoral Register, 1975–77. BBC Radio 3: Man of Action, 1974. Co-Founder, British Politics Gp, 1974–; Convenor, Work Gp on UK Politics, Political Studies Assoc., 1976–88; Mem. Council, Internat. Political Science Assoc., 1976–82; Keynote Speaker, Aust. Inst. of Political Science, Canberra, 1978; Technical Consultant, OECD; Dir, ESRC (formerly SSRC) Res. Programme, Growth of Govt, 1982–86; UNDP Cons. to Pres. of Colombia, 1990. Hon. Vice-Pres., Political Studies Assoc., UK, 1986. Editor, Jl of Public Policy, 1985–. Foreign Mem., Finnish Acad. of Science and Letters, 1985. *Publications:* The British General Election of 1959 (with D. E. Butler), 1960; Must Labour Lose? (with Mark Abrams), 1960; Politics in England, 1964, 5th edn 1989; (ed) Studies in British Politics, 1966, 3rd edn 1976; Influencing Voters, 1967; (ed) Policy Making in Britain, 1969; People in Politics, 1970; (ed, with M. Dogan) European Politics, 1971; Governing Without Consensus: an Irish perspective, 1971; (with T. Mackie) International Almanack of Electoral History, 1974, 3rd edn 1991; (ed) Electoral Behavior: a comparative handbook, 1974; (ed) Lessons from America, 1974; The Problem of Party Government, 1974; (ed) The Management of Urban Change in Britain and Germany, 1974; Northern Ireland: a time of choice, 1976; Managing Presidential Objectives, 1976; (ed) The Dynamics of Public Policy, 1976; (ed, with D. Kavanagh) New Trends in British Politics, 1977; (ed with J. Wiatr) Comparing Public Policies, 1977; What is Governing?: Purpose and Policy in Washington, 1978; (ed, with G. Hermet and A. Rouquié) Elections without Choice, 1978; (with B. G. Peters) Can Government Go Bankrupt?, 1978; (ed with W. B. Gwyn) Britain: progress and decline, 1980; Do Parties Make a Difference?, 1980, 2nd edn 1984; (ed) Challenge to Governance, 1980; (ed) Electoral Participation, 1980; (ed with E. Suleiman) Presidents and Prime Ministers, 1980; Understanding the United Kingdom, 1982; (with I. McAllister) United Kingdom Facts, 1982; (ed with P. Madgwick) The Territorial Dimension in United Kingdom Politics, 1982; (ed with E. Page) Fiscal Stress in Cities, 1982; Understanding Big Government, 1984; (with I. McAllister) The Nationwide Competition for Votes, 1984; Public Employment in Western Nations, 1985; (with I. McAllister) Voters Begin to Choose, 1986; (with D. Van Mechelen) Patterns of Parliamentary Legislation, 1986; (ed with R. Shiratori) The Welfare State East and West, 1986; Ministers and Ministries, 1987; (with T. Karran) Taxation by Political Inertia, 1987; The Post-Modern President: the White House meets the world, 1988; Ordinary People in Public Policy, 1989; (with I. McAllister) The Loyalty of Voters: a lifetime learning model, 1990; Lesson-Drawing Across Time and Space, 1990; contribs to academic journals in Europe and America; trans. into twelve foreign languages; broadcasts on British, Irish and American politics and public policy. *Recreations:* architecture (historical, Britain; modern, America), music, writing. *Address:* Centre for the Study of Public Policy, Livingstone Tower, Glasgow G1 1XH. *T:* 041–552 4400, *Fax:* 041–552 4711; Bennochy, 1 East Abercromby Street, Helensburgh, Dunbartonshire G84 7SP. *T:* Helensburgh (0436) 72164, *Fax:* Helensburgh (0436) 73125; 7430 Byron Place, St Louis Co., Mo 63105, USA. *Clubs:* Reform; Cosmos (Washington DC).

ROSE, (Thomas) Stuart, CBE 1974; PPCSD; Design Adviser, The Post Office, 1968–76; *b* 2 Oct. 1911; *s* of Thomas and Nellie Rose; *m* 1940, Dorothea Winifred, *d* of F. G. Ebsworth, Petrograd; two *d*. *Educ:* Choral Scholar, Magdalen College Sch., Oxford; Central Sch. of Arts and Crafts. Designer, Crawfords Advertising, 1934–39; free-lance graphics designer and typographer, 1946–68; Typographer, Cement and Concrete Assoc., 1946–51; Print Consultant, Fedn of British Industries, 1947–68; Art Editor, Design Magazine, 1947–53; Typographic Adviser to Postmaster General, 1962–68; Associate, Design Research Unit, industrial design partnership, 1964–68. Member: Industrial Design Cttee, FBI, 1948–65 (Chm. 1965–68); CoID Stamp Adv. Cttee, 1960–62; Post Office Stamp Adv. Cttee, 1968–76. Mem., Soc. of Industrial Artists and Designers, 1936, Pres. 1965. Governor, Central Sch. of Art and Design, 1965–74 (Vice-Chm., 1971–74). FRSA 1970. Phillips Gold Medal for Stamp Design, 1974. *Publication:* Royal Mail Stamps, 1980. *Recreations:* drawing, music, the country. *Address:* Walpole House, East Street, Coggeshall, Colchester, Essex CO6 1SH. *T:* Coggeshall (0376) 562409. *Club:* Arts (Chairman 1982–85).

ROSE, (Wilfred) Andrew; agriculturist, diplomat, industrialist, banker; Hon. chartered surveyor (Estate Management); Chairman and Managing Director, Photo-Scan International of South America Ltd; Chairman: Trinidad and Tobago Oil Co. Ltd; Eagle Enterprises, Trinidad; President and Chairman, Trinidad Co-operative Bank Ltd; Deputy Chairman, National Energy Corporation of Trinidad and Tobago; Director: Interstate Investment (Management) Ltd; Guyana and Trinidad Mutual Fire Insurance Co. Ltd; *b* 4 Oct. 1916; *s* of James Emmanuel Rose and Eleanora Rose; *m* 1944, Pamphylia Marcano; one *s*. *Educ:* Tranquility Boys' Intermediate Sch.; Queen's Royal Coll.; Imperial Coll. of Tropical Agriculture, Trinidad (DipAgr); Coll. of Estate Management, London; London University. FRICS. Agric. Technologist, Food Control Dept, during War of 1939–45. Subseq. Cane Farmers' Superintendent; Estate Manager; Housing Manager, Planning and Housing Commission, Trinidad and Tobago. Editor, Jl of Agricl Soc. of Trinidad and Tobago. Dir, Assoc. of Professional Agrologists of Trinidad and Tobago; Pres., Professional Valuation and Land Economy Surveyors of Trinidad and Tobago; Member: Roy. Soc. of Health; Agricl Soc. of Trinidad and Tobago (Life); W India Cttee (Life); West Indies National Party; People's National Movement (several cttees). Chm., Commn of Enquiry on Road Passenger Transport. Elected Member for St Ann's, Trinidad, Federal Elections of the West Indies, 1958. Minister of Communications and Works, Federal Govt, West Indies, 1958–62 (twice acted as Dep. Prime Minister); High Commissioner for Trinidad and Tobago: in Canada, 1962–64; in UK, 1964–69, Ambassador to EEC, 1965–69, and Ambassador to UN Agencies, Europe, and Permanent Representative to GATT, 1965–68; Ambassador to Brazil, 1969–72; led West Indies delegn to various confs; Rep. of Govt, frequently abroad. Chm., Commonwealth Rhodesia Sanctions Cttee, 1968–69; Vice-Chm., UNCTAD II, New Delhi, 1968; Member: Commonwealth Telecommunications Bd, 1964–68; Commonwealth Telecommunications Council, 1968. Chm., Nat. Museum Task Force. Freeman, City of London, 1967. *Publications:* articles on agriculture in the Trinidad Press, 1942–45. *Recreations:* agriculture, horse-riding, golf. *Address:* PO Box 1041, Port of Spain, Trinidad, WI. *Clubs:* Commonwealth Trust; Union (Trinidad).

ROSEBERY, 7th Earl of, *cr* 1703; **Neil Archibald Primrose,** DL; Bt 1651; Viscount of Rosebery, Baron Primrose and Dalmeny, 1700; Viscount of Inverkeithing, Baron Dalmeny and Primrose, 1703; Baron Rosebery (UK), 1828; Earl of Midlothian, Viscount Mentmore, Baron Epsom, 1911; *b* 11 Feb. 1929; *o* surv. *s* of 6th Earl of Rosebery, KT, PC, DSO, MC, and Eva Isabel Marian (Eva Countess of Rosebery, DBE) (*d* 1987), *d* of 2nd Baron Aberdare; *S* father, 1974; *m* 1955, Alison Mary Deirdre, *d* of late Ronald William Reid, MS, FRCS; one *s* four *d*. *Educ:* Stowe; New Coll., Oxford. DL Midlothian, 1960. *Heir: s* Lord Dalmeny, *qv*. *Address:* Dalmeny House, South Queensferry, West Lothian.

ROSEHILL, Lord; David John MacRae Carnegie; estate manager/owner; *b* 3 Nov. 1954; *s* and *heir* of 13th Earl of Northesk, *qv*; *m* 1979, Jacqueline Reid, *d* of Mrs Elizabeth Reid, Sarasota, Florida, USA; one *s* three *d*. *Educ:* West Hill Park, Titchfield; Eton; Brooke House, Market Harborough; UCL. *Heir: s* Hon. Alexander Robert MacRae Carnegie, *b* 16 Nov. 1980. *Address:* Fair Oak, Rogate, Petersfield, Hants GU31 5HR. *T:* Rogate (0730) 821508.

ROSEN, Charles; pianist; Professor of Music, State University of New York at Stony Brook; *b* New York, 5 May 1927; *s* of Irwin Rosen and Anita Gerber. *Educ:* studied piano with Mr and Mrs Moriz Rosenthal; Princeton Univ. (PhD). Début, NY, 1951. His many recordings include: first complete recording of Debussy Etudes, 1951; late keyboard works of Bach, 1969; last six Beethoven Sonatas, 1970; Schumann piano works; Diabelli Variations; also works by Liszt, Elliott Carter, Boulez, etc. Eliot Norton Prof. of Poetry, Harvard Univ., 1980; George Eastman Vis. Prof., Oxford Univ., 1987–88. Hon. MusD Trinity Coll., Dublin, 1976; Hon. DMus Durham, 1980. *Publications:* The Classical Style, 1971; Schoenberg, 1976; Sonata Forms, 1980; (with H. Zerner) Romanticism and Realism: the mythology of nineteenth century art, 1984. *Recreations:* music, books. *Address:* c/o Basil Douglas Ltd, 8 St George's Terrace, NW1 8XJ. *T:* 071–722 7142.

ROSEN, Rabbi Jeremy, PhD; Minister, Marble Arch Western Synagogue, London, since 1985; *b* 11 Sept. 1942; *s* of Rabbi Kopul Rosen and Bella Rosen; *m* 1st, 1971, Vera Giuditta Zippel (marr. diss. 1987); two *s* two *d*; 2nd, 1988, Suzanne Kaszirer. *Educ:* Carmel Coll.; Pembroke Coll., Cambridge (MA); Mir Academy, Jerusalem. Minister, Bulawayo Hebrew Congregation, Rhodesia, 1966; Minister, Giffnock Hebrew Congregation, Scotland, 1968–71; Headmaster, 1971–84, Principal, 1983–84, Carmel Coll. Pt-time Prof. of Jewish Studies, Faculty for Comparative Study of Religions, Antwerp, 1991–. Chief Rabbi's Rep. on Inter-Faith Affairs, 1987–91. *Address:* 20 Bryanston Mansions, York Street, W1H 1DA.

ROSEN, Prof. Michael, CBE 1990; FFARCS; FRCOG; Consultant Anaesthetist, South Glamorgan Health Authority, since 1961; Hon. Professor, University of Wales College of Medicine, since 1986; President, College of Anaesthetists, 1988–91 (Dean of the Faculty of Anaesthetists, Royal College of Surgeons, 1988); *b* 17 Oct. 1927; *s* of Israel Rosen and Lily Hyman; *m* 1955, Sally Cohen; two *s* one *d*. *Educ:* Dundee High Sch. (Dux, 1944); St Andrews Univ. (MB ChB 1949). FFARCS 1957; FRCOG 1989. House appts, Bolton, Portsmouth and Bradford, 1949–52; served RAMC, 1952–54; Registrar Anaesthetist, Royal Victoria Infirmary, Newcastle upon Tyne, 1954–57; Sen. Registrar, Cardiff, 1957–60; Fellow, Case Western Reserve Univ., Ohio, 1960–61. Member: GMC, 1989–; Clinical Standards Adv. Gp, 1991–. Mem., Bd, College (formerly Faculty) of Anaesthetists, RCS, 1978–; Pres., Assoc. of Anaesthetists of GB and Ire, 1986–88 (Mem. Council, 1972–; formerly Sec. and Treasurer); Founder Academician, European Acad. of Anaesthesiol., 1972 (Treas., 1985–); Chm., Obstetric Anaesthesia Cttee, World Fedn of Socs of Anaesthesia, 1980–88. Hon. Mem., French and Australian Socs of Anaesthetists; Hon. Fellow, Acad. of Medicine, Malaysia, 1989. *Publications:* Percutaneous Cannulation of Great Veins, 1981; Obstetric Anaesthesia and Analgesia: safer practice, 1982; Patient-Controlled Analgesia, 1984; Tracheal Intubation, 1985; Awareness and Pain in General Anaesthesia, 1987; Ambulatory Anaesthesia, 1991. *Recreations:* family, reading, opera. *Address:* 45 Hollybush Road, Cardiff CF2 6SZ. *T:* Cardiff (0222) 753893.

ROSENBERG, Richard Morris; Chairman and Chief Executive Officer, BankAmerica Corporation and Bank of America NT&SA, since 1990; *b* 21 April 1930; *s* of Charles Rosenberg and Betty (*née* Peck); *m* 1956, Barbara C. Cohen; two *s*. *Educ:* Suffolk Univ.

(BS 1956); Golden Gate Univ. (MBA 1962; LLB 1966). Served from Ensign to Lieut, USNR, 1953–59. Publicity Assistant, Crocker-Anglo Bank, San Francisco, 1959–62; Wells Fargo Bank: Banking Services Officer, 1962–65; Asst Vice Pres., 1965–68; Vice Pres., Marketing Dept, 1968; Vice Pres., Dir of Marketing, 1969; Sen. Vice Pres., Marketing and Advertising Div., 1970–75; Exec. Vice Pres., 1975–80; Vice Chm., 1980–83; Vice Chm., Crocker Nat. Corp., 1983–85; Pres., Chief Op. Officer and Dir, Seafirst Corp., 1986–87; Pres. and Chief Op. Officer, Seattle-First Nat. Bank, 1985–87; Vice Chm., BankAmerica Corp., 1987–90. Director: Airborne Express; Visa; Chm., Mastercard Internat. Member: Bd of Dirs, Marin Ecumenical Housing Assoc.; Bd, Regents Sch. of Bank Marketing, Colorado Univ. Member: Amer. Bankers Assoc. (Exec. Cttee, Marketing; Savings Div.); Bank Marketing Assoc. (Dir); State Bar of Calif. Jewish. *Recreations:* tennis, avid reader, history. *Address:* BankAmerica Corporation, 555 California Street, 40th Floor, San Francisco, Calif 94104, USA. *T:* (415) 953–7963. *Clubs:* Rainier (Seattle); Hillcrest (Los Angeles).

ROSENBLUM, Prof. Robert; Professor of Fine Arts, New York University, USA, since 1967; *b* 24 July 1927; *m* 1977, Jane Kaplowitz; one *s* one *d. Educ:* Queens Coll., Flushing, NY (BA); Yale Univ. (MA); New York Univ. (PhD); Oxford Univ. (MA). Prof. of Art and Archaeology, Princeton Univ., USA, 1956–66; Slade Prof. of Fine Art, Oxford Univ., 1971–72. Fellow, Amer. Acad. of Arts and Scis, 1984. Frank Jewett Mather Award for Art Criticism, 1981. *Publications:* Cubism and Twentieth-Century Art, 1960; Transformations in Late Eighteenth Century Art, 1967; Jean-Auguste-Dominique Ingres, 1967; Frank Stella, 1971; Modern Painting and the Northern Romantic Tradition: Friedrich to Rothko, 1975; French Painting, 1774–1830 (exhibn catalogue), 1975; Andy Warhol: Portraits of the Seventies, 1979; (with H. W. Janson) Nineteenth Century Art, 1984; The Dog in Art from Rococo to Post-Modernism, 1988; The Romantic Child from Runge to Sendak, 1988; Paintings in the Musée d'Orsay, 1989; articles in learned jls: Art Bulletin; Burlington Magazine; Jl of the Warburg and Courtauld Institutes; La Revue de l'Art, etc. *Address:* Department of Fine Arts, New York University, New York, NY 10003, USA. *T:* (212)–998–8180.

ROSENBROCK, Prof. Howard Harry, DSc, FEng; FRS 1976; FIEE, FIChemE; FInstMC; Professor of Control Engineering, 1966–87, now Emeritus, Vice-Principal, 1977–79, University of Manchester Institute of Science and Technology, (UMIST); Science Research Council Senior Fellow, 1979–83; *b* 16 Dec. 1920; *s* of Henry Frederick Rosenbrock and Harriett Emily (*née* Gleed); *m* 1950, Cathryn June (*née* Press); one *s* two *d. Educ:* Slough Grammar Sch.; University Coll. London. BSc, PhD; Fellow 1978. Served War, RAFVR, 1941–46. GEC, 1947–48; Electrical Research Assoc., 1949–51; John Brown & Co., 1951–54; Constructors John Brown Ltd, 1954–62 (latterly Research Manager); ADR, Cambridge Univ., 1962–66. Mem. Council, IEE, 1966–70, Vice-Pres., 1977–78; Pres., Inst. of Measurement and Control, 1972–73; Member: Computer Bd, 1972–76; SRC Engineering Bd, 1976–78; SERC/ESRC Jt Cttee, 1981–85. Hon. DSc Salford, 1987. *Publications:* (with C. Storey) Computational Techniques for Chemical Engineers, 1966; (with C. Storey) Mathematics of Dynamical Systems, 1970; State-space and Multivariable Theory, 1970; Computer-aided Control System Design, 1974; (ed) Designing Human-centred Technology, 1989; Machines with a Purpose, 1990; contribs Proc. IEE, Trans IChemE, Proc. IEEE, Automatica, Internat. Jl Control, etc. *Recreations:* microscopy, photography, 17th and 18th Century literature. *Address:* Linden, Walford Road, Ross-on-Wye, Herefordshire HR9 5PQ. *T:* Ross-on-Wye (0989) 65372.

ROSENFELD, Alfred John, CB 1981; Chairman, Shoreham Port Authority, since 1990 (Member, since 1983; Deputy Chairman, 1984–89); Deputy Secretary, 1979–82, and Principal Finance Officer, 1976–82, Department of Transport; *b* 27 Feb. 1922; *s* of late Ernest Rosenfeld and late Annie Jeanette Rosenfeld (*née* Samson); *m* 1955, Mary Elisabeth (*née* Prudence); two *s* one *d. Educ:* Leyton County High Sch. Entered Public Trustee Office, 1938. Served War, Fleet Air Arm, 1942–46. Min. of Civil Aviation, 1947 (later, Min. of Transport, and Dept of Environment); Private Sec. to Jt Parliamentary Sec., 1958–59; Asst Sec., 1967; Under-Sec., 1972. *Recreations:* chess, bridge, gardening. *Address:* 33 Elmfield Road, Chingford, E4 7HT. *T:* 081–529 8160.

ROSENTHAL, Jack Morris; writer; *b* 8 Sept. 1931; *s* of Samuel and Leah Rosenthal; *m* 1973, Maureen Lipman, *qv*; one *s* one *d. Educ:* Colne Grammar School; Sheffield Univ. (BA Eng. Lit. and Lang). *Television:* writer of over 250 productions, incl. That Was the Week That Was, 1963; 150 episodes of Coronation Street, 1961–69; The Evacuees, 1975; Bar Mitzvah Boy, 1976; Ready When You Are, Mr McGill, 1976; Spend Spend Spend, 1977; The Knowledge, 1979; P'tang Yang Kipperbang, 1982; Mrs Capper's Birthday, 1985; London's Burning, 1986; Fools on the Hill, 1986; Day to Remember, 1986; And a Nightingale Sang, 1989; Sleeping Sickness, 1991; Bag Lady, 1989; *stage:* five plays, incl. Smash!, 1981; *films:* six feature films including: Lucky Star, 1980; Yentl, 1983 (co-written with Barbra Streisand); The Chain, 1985. BAFTA Writer's Award, 1976; RTS Writer's Award, 1976. *Publications:* (contrib.) The Television Dramatist, 1973; (anthology) First Love, 1984; numerous TV plays. *Recreations:* work, frying fish, polishing almost anything tarnished, playing the violin in enforced privacy, remembering how Manchester United used to play, collecting models of rhinoceri and tortoisi. *Address:* c/o Margaret Ramsay Ltd, 14A Goodwin's Court, St Martin's Lane, WC2N 4LL. *T:* 071–240 0691. *Clubs:* Dramatists', Academy.

ROSENTHAL, Maureen Diane, (Mrs J. M. Rosenthal); *see* Lipman, M. D.

ROSENTHAL, Norman Leon; Exhibitions Secretary, Royal Academy of Arts, since 1977; *b* 8 Nov. 1944; *s* of Paul Rosenthal and Kate Zucker; *m* 1989, Manuela Beatriz Mena Marques, *d* of Francisco Mena and Manuela Marques de Mena, Madrid; one *d. Educ:* Westminster City Grammar School; University of Leicester. BA Hons History. Librarian, Thomas Agnew & Sons, 1966–68; Exhibitions Officer, Brighton Museum and Art Gallery, 1970–71; Exhibition Organiser, ICA, 1974–76; organiser of many exhibns including: Art into Society, ICA, 1974; A New Spirit in Painting, RA, 1981; Zeitgeist, West Berlin, 1982; German Art of the Twentieth Century, Royal Acad., London and Staatsgalerie, Stuttgart, 1985–86; Italian Art of the Twentieth Century, RA, 1989; Metropolis, Berlin, 1991. TV and radio broadcasts on contemporary art. Hon. Fellow RCA, 1987. Chevalier, l'Ordre des Arts et des Lettres, 1987. *Recreations:* music, especially opera. *Address:* The Royal Academy of Arts, Burlington House, W1V 0DS. *T:* 071–439 7438.

ROSENTHAL, Thomas Gabriel; publisher, critic and broadcaster; Chairman and Managing Director, André Deutsch Ltd (joined as Joint Chairman and Joint Managing Director, 1984); Chairman, Frew McKenzie (Antiquarian Booksellers), since 1985; *b* 16 July 1935; *o s* of late Dr Erwin I. J. Rosenthal; *m* Ann Judith Warnford-Davis; two *s. Educ:* Perse Sch., Cambridge; Pembroke Coll., Cambridge (Exhibnr, MA). Served RA, 1954–56, 2nd Lieut; subseq. Lieut Cambridgeshire Regt (TA). Joined Thames and Hudson Ltd, 1959; Man. Dir, Thames & Hudson Internat., 1966; joined Martin Secker & Warburg Ltd as Man. Dir, 1971; Dir, Heinemann Gp of Publishers, 1972–84; Man. Dir, William Heinemann International Ltd, 1979–84; Chairman: World's Work Ltd, 1979–84; Heinemann Zsolnay Ltd, 1979–84; William Heinemann Ltd, 1980–84; Martin Secker & Warburg Ltd, 1980–84; Kaye & Ward Ltd, 1980–84; William Heinemann, Australia and SA, 1981–82; Pres., Heinemann Inc., 1981–84. Art Critic of The Listener, 1963–66. Chm., Soc. of Young Publishers, 1961–62; Member: Cambridge Univ. Appts Bd, 1967–71; Exec. Cttee, NBL, 1971–74; Trans. Panel, Arts Council, 1988–; Cttee of Management, Amateur Dramatic Club, Cambridge (also Trustee); Council, RCA, 1982–87; exec. Council, ICA, 1987–; Trustee, Phoenix Trust. Mem. Editl Bd, Logos, 1989–. *Publications:* Monograph on Jack B. Yeats, 1964; (with Alan Bowness) Monograph on Ivon Hitchens, 1973; (with Ursula Hoff) Monograph on Arthur Boyd, 1986; A Reader's Guide to European Art History, 1962; A Reader's Guide to Modern American Fiction, 1963; introdns to paperback edns of Theodore Dreiser's The Financier, The Titan and Jennie Gerhardt; articles in The Times, Guardian, TLS, London Magazine, Encounter, New Statesman, Jl of Brit. Assoc. for Amer. Studies, Studio Internat., DNB, Bookseller, Nature, etc. *Recreations:* opera, bibliomania, looking at pictures, reading other publishers' books. *Address:* c/o André Deutsch Ltd, 105–106 Great Russell Street, WC1B 3LJ. *T:* 071–580 2746. *Clubs:* Garrick, MCC.

ROSEVEARE, Robert William, CBE 1977; retired; Board Member, Community Industry Ltd, since 1983; Secretary, 1967–83, and Managing Director, Policy Co-ordination, 1973–83, British Steel Corporation; *b* Mandalay, Burma, 23 Aug. 1924; *s* of late William Leonard Roseveare, MC and of Marjory C. Roseveare; *m* 1954, Patricia Elizabeth, *d* of Guy L. Thompson, FRCS, Scarborough; one *s* three *d. Educ:* Gresham's Sch., Holt; St John's Coll., Cambridge (MA). Served in Fleet Air Arm, 1943–46. Home Civil Service, Admin. Class, 1949. Asst Private Sec. to Minister of Fuel and Power, 1952–54; seconded to Cabinet Office, 1958–60; British Embassy, Washington, 1960–62; Asst Sec., Ministry of Power, 1964. Special Asst to Chm. of Organising Cttee for British Steel Corporation (Lord Melchett), 1966; seconded to British Steel Corporation on its formation, 1967; Dir, Admin. Services, 1969; Man. Dir, Corporate Administration, 1971. *Recreations:* hill-walking, bird-watching, singing. *Address:* Old Pasture, Hillfield Drive, Ledbury, Herefordshire HR8 1BH. *T:* Ledbury (0531) 2913.

ROSEWARN, John; Secretary, Royal Institution of Naval Architects, since 1989; *b* 14 Jan. 1940; *s* of Ernest and Frances Beatrice Rosewarn; *m* 1963, Josephine Rita Mullis; two *s. Educ:* Westminster City Sch. Royal Institution of Naval Architects, 1958–: Administrator, 1958–65; Chief Clerk, 1965–75; Asst Sec., 1975–84; Sen. Asst. Sec., 1984–89. Freeman, City of London, 1976. *Recreations:* sailing, DIY, reading. *Address:* c/o Royal Institution of Naval Architects, 10 Upper Belgrave Street, SW1X 8BQ. *T:* 071–235 4622.

ROSIER, Air Chief Marshal Sir Frederick (Ernest), GCB 1972 (KCB 1966; CB 1961); CBE 1955 (OBE 1943); DSO 1942; RAF, retired; *b* 13 Oct. 1915; *s* of E. G. Rosier; *m* 1939, Hettie Denise Blackwell; three *s* one *d. Educ:* Grove Park School, Wrexham. Commissioned RAF, 1935; 43 (F) Sqdn, 1936–39. Served War of 1939–45 in France, UK, Western Desert and Europe. OC Horsham St Faith, 1947; exchange duties with USAF, 1948–50; Instructor at Jt Services Staff College, 1950–52; Gp Capt. Operations at Central Fighter Establishment, 1952–54; Gp Capt. Plans at Fighter Command, 1955–56; ADC to the Queen, 1956–58; idc 1957; Director of Joint Plans, Air Ministry, 1958; Chm. Joint Planning Staff, 1959–61; AOC Air Forces Middle East, 1961–63; Senior Air Staff Officer, HQ Transport Command, 1964–66; Air Officer C-in-C, RAF, Fighter Command, 1966–68; UK Mem., Permanent Military Deputies Group, Central Treaty Organisation, Ankara, 1968–70; Dep. C-in-C, Allied Forces Central Europe, 1970–73. Air ADC to the Queen, 1972–73. Mil. Advr and Dir, British Aircraft Corp. (Preston) Ltd, 1973–77; Director i/c BAC Ltd, Saudi Arabia, 1977–80. Commander: Order of Orange Nassau, 1947; Order of Polonia Restituta, 1985. *Address:* Ty Haul, Sun Bank, Llangollen, N Wales LL20 7UH. *T:* Llangollen (0978) 861068; Flat 286, Latymer Court, Hammersmith, W6 7LD. *T:* 081–741 0765. *Club:* Royal Air Force.

ROSIER, Rt. Rev. Stanley Bruce, AM 1987; Rector of St Oswald's, Parkside, diocese of Adelaide, since 1987; *b* 18 Nov. 1928; *s* of S. C. and A. Rosier; *m* 1954, Faith Margaret Alice Norwood; one *s* three *d. Educ:* Univ. of WA; Christ Church, Oxford. Asst Curate, Ecclesall, Dio. of Sheffield, 1954; Rector of: Wyalkatchem, Dio. of Perth, 1957; Kellerberrin Dio. of Perth, 1964; Auxiliary Bishop in Diocese of Perth, Western Australia, 1967–70; Bishop of Willochra, 1970–87. *Recreation:* natural history. *Address:* St Oswald's Rectory, 7 St Ann's Place, Parkside, SA 5063, Australia. *T:* (08) 271 3254.

ROSKELL, Prof. John Smith, MA, DPhil; FBA 1968; Professor of Medieval History, University of Manchester, 1962–79, now Professor Emeritus; *b* Norden, Rochdale, 2 July 1913; *s* of John Edmund and Lucy A. Roskell; *m* 1942, Evelyn Liddle (*d* 1989); one *s* one *d. Educ:* Rochdale Municipal Secondary School; Accrington Grammar Sch.; University of Manchester; Balliol College, Oxford. Asst Lecturer in History, Manchester University, 1938; Lecturer, 1945; Senior Lecturer, 1950–52; Professor of Medieval History, University of Nottingham, 1952–62. President: Lancashire Parish Register Soc., 1962–84; Chetham Soc., 1972–84; Feoffee, Chetham's Hosp. and Libr., Manchester, 1963–90. Royal Navy, 1940–45; Lieut RNVR, 1942–45. *Publications:* The Knights of the Shire of the County Palatine of Lancaster (1377–1460), Chetham Society, 1937; The Commons in the Parliament of 1422, 1954; The Commons and their Speakers in English Parliaments, 1376–1523, 1965; (ed with F. Taylor) Gesta Henrici Quinti, 1975; Parliament and Politics in Late Medieval England, (3 vols), 1981–83; The Impeachment of Michael de la Pole, Earl of Suffolk, in 1386, 1984. *Recreation:* cricket. *Address:* 42 Barcheston Road, Cheadle, Cheshire SK8 1LL. *T:* 061–428 4630.

ROSKILL, family name of **Baron Roskill.**

ROSKILL, Baron *cr* 1980 (Life Peer), of Newtown in the County of Hampshire; **Eustace Wentworth Roskill;** Kt 1962; PC 1971; DL; a Lord of Appeal in Ordinary 1980–86; *b* 6 Feb. 1911; *y s* of late John Roskill, KC and of late Sybil Mary Wentworth, *d* of Ashton Wentworth Dilke, MP; *m* 1947, Elisabeth Wallace Jackson, 3rd *d* of late Thomas Frame Jackson, Buenos Aires; one *s* two *d. Educ:* Winchester College (exhibnr; Fellow, 1981–86); Exeter Coll., Oxford (exhibnr). 1st Cl. hons, Hon. Sch. of Mod. Hist. Oxford, BA 1932; MA 1936; Harmsworth Law Schol. Middle Temple, 1932; called to Bar, Middle Temple, 1933, Bencher 1961, Reader 1978, Dep. Treasurer 1979, Treasurer 1980; Hon. Bencher of The Inner Temple, 1980. Worked at Ministries of Shipping and War Transport, 1939–45. QC 1953. Dep. Chm. Hants QS, 1951–60, Chm. 1960–71; Comr of Assize (Birmingham), 1961; Judge of the High Court of Justice, Queen's Bench Division, 1962–71; a Lord Justice of Appeal, 1971–80. Vice-Chm., Parole Bd, 1967–69; Chm., Commn on Third London Airport, 1968–70. Pres., Senate of Four Inns of Court, 1972–74; Hon. Mem., 1974; Life Mem., Canadian Bar Assoc., 1974. Chairman: Average Adjusters Assoc., 1977–78; London Internat. Arbitration Trust, 1981–; Fraud Trials Cttee, 1983–85; Take-over Panel Appeal Cttee, 1987–. Hon. Fellow, Exeter College, Oxford, 1963. Hampshire: JP 1950; DL 1972. *Recreations:* music, swimming, gardening. *Address:* Heatherfield, Newtown, Newbury, Berks RG15 9DB. *T:* Newbury (0635) 40606; New Court, Temple, EC4. *T:* 071–353 8870; House of Lords, SW1. *Club:* Reform.

See also Sir Patrick Dean, Sir A. W. Roskill, O. W. Roskill.

ROSKILL, Oliver Wentworth, CChem, FRSC, CEng, FIChemE, CIMechE, SFInstE, CBIM, FIMC; Senior Partner, O. W. Roskill Industrial Consultants, 1930–74; Chairman: O. W. Roskill & Co (Reports) Ltd, 1957–74; Roskill Information Services Ltd, 1971–74; Life President, Exhibition Audience Audits Ltd, 1985; *b* 28 April 1906; *s* of John Roskill, KC, and Sibyl Mary Wentworth, *d* of Ashton Wentworth Dilke, MP. *Educ:* Oundle Sch.; Lincoln Coll., Oxford (scholar). MA, BSc (Oxon) (1st Cl. Hons). Captain, Oxford Univ. Rugby Fives Club, 1927. Imperial Chemical Industries Ltd, 1928–30. Min. of Economic Warfare, Dep. Head, Enemy Countries Intell., 1939–41. Mem. Exec. Cttee of Political and Economic Planning (now Policy Studies Inst.), 1931, Vice-Pres., 1975; Founder Mem. Council, British Inst. of Management, 1947–53 (Chm. Inf. and Research Cttee); Mem. British Nat. Export Council, Caribbean Cttee, 1965–69; Mem. Council, Inst. of Management Consultants, 1963–74 (Pres., 1970–71). Consultant on industrial development projects to Govts of Iran, Pakistan, Malta, Fed. Govt of Rhodesia, Windward Is, and others. *Publications:* Founder and part author of 'Who Owns Whom' series of directories; part author of Fifty Years of Political and Economic Planning; author of monographs on economics of metals and minerals (incl. tungsten, titanium, chromium, fluorspar); contributor to many jls of learned societies (incl. Chemical Engr, Inst. Fuel, RIBA, Town Planning Inst.). *Recreations:* mountain walking, playing chamber music, choral singing, real tennis, gardening. *Address:* The Priory, Beech Hill, Reading, Berks RG7 2AY. *T:* Reading (0734) 883146. *Clubs:* Brooks's; Woodmen of Arden; Hampton Court Tennis, Holyport Tennis.
See also Baron Roskill.

ROSLING, Derek Norman, CBE 1988; FCA; Vice-Chairman, Hanson PLC, since 1973; *b* 21 Nov. 1930; *s* of Norman and Jean Rosling; *m* (marr. diss. 1982); two *s* one *d*. *Educ:* Shrewsbury Sch. ACA 1955, FCA 1962. Professional practice, 1956–65; Hanson PLC, 1965–. FRSA 1990. *Recreations:* golf, sailing, theatre. *Address:* 388 Via Las Palmas, Palm Springs, Calif 92262, USA. *T:* 619 320 8065. *Clubs:* Roehampton; Royal Guernsey Golf, Royal Channel Island Yacht (Guernsey); Palm Valley Country (Palm Springs).

ROSLING, Peter Edward, CMG 1987; LVO 1972; HM Diplomatic Service, retired; *b* 17 June 1929; *s* of Peregrine Starr and Jessie Rosling; *m* 1950, Kathleen Nuell; three *s*. *Educ:* grammar school. Served Royal Navy, 1948–50. HM Diplomatic Service, 1946; Belgrade, Innsbruck, Cape Town, Rome (NATO Defence College), FCO; Consul-Gen., Zagreb, 1980–83; High Comr, Lesotho, 1984–88. Mem. Council, British Commonwealth Ex-Services League, 1988–. *Recreations:* walking, bird-watching, bridge. *Address:* Southernhay, Vaughan Way, Dorking, Surrey RH4 3DR. *Club:* Commonwealth Trust.

ROSOMAN, Leonard Henry, OBE 1981; RA 1969 (ARA 1960); FSA; Tutor, Royal College of Art, 1957–78; *b* 27 Oct. 1913; *s* of Henry Rosoman; *m* 1963, Jocelyn (marr. diss. 1969), *d* of Bertie Rickards, Melbourne, Australia. *Educ:* Deacons Sch., Peterborough; Durham Univ. Teacher of Drawing and Painting, Reimann Sch. of Art, London, 1938–39; Official War Artist to Admiralty, 1943–45; Teacher: Camberwell Sch. of Art, London, 1947–48; (Mural Painting) Edinburgh Coll. of Art, 1948–56; Chelsea School of Art, 1956–57. One Man Shows: St George's Gallery, London, 1946 and 1949; Roland, Browse and Delbanco Gallery, London, 1954, 1957, 1959, 1965 and 1969; Fine Art Soc., 1974, 1978, 1983. Works bought by: HM Govt, Arts Council, British Council, York Art Gall., Contemporary Art Soc., Adelaide Art Gallery, V&A Museum, Lincoln Center, NY. Executed large mural paintings for: Festival of Britain, 1951; British Pavilion, Brussels World Fair, 1958; Harewood House, 1959; Lambeth Palace Chapel, 1988. Hon. ARCA; HRSW. *Recreation:* travelling as much as possible. *Address:* 7 Pembroke Studios, Pembroke Gardens, W8. *T:* 071–603 3638. *Club:* Arts.

ROSPIGLIOSI, family name of **Earl of Newburgh.**

ROSS, family name of **Baron Ross of Newport.**

ROSS, Rt. Hon. Lord; Rt. Hon. Lord Justice-Clerk; Donald MacArthur Ross, PC 1985; a Senator of the College of Justice, Scotland, and Lord of Session, since 1977; Lord Justice-Clerk, since 1985; Lord High Commissioner, General Assembly, Church of Scotland, 1990 and 1991; *b* 29 March 1927; *s* of late John Ross, solicitor, Dundee; *m* 1958, Dorothy Margaret, *d* of late William Annand, Kirriemuir; two *d*. *Educ:* Dundee High School; Edinburgh University. MA (Edinburgh) 1947; LLB with distinction (Edinburgh) 1951. National Service with The Black Watch (RHR), 2nd Lt, 1947–49. Territorial Service, 1949–58, Captain. Advocate, 1952; QC (Scotland) 1964; Vice-Dean, Faculty of Advocates of Scotland, 1967–73; Dean, 1973–76; Sheriff Principal of Ayr and Bute, 1972–73. Dep. Chm., Boundary Commn for Scotland, 1977–85. Member: Scottish Cttee of Council on Tribunals, 1970–76; Cttee on Privacy, 1970. Mem. Court, Heriot-Watt Univ., 1978– (Chm., 1984–90). FRSE 1988. Hon. LLD: Edinburgh, 1987; Dundee, 1991; DUniv Heriot-Watt, 1988. *Recreation:* gardening. *Address:* 33 Lauder Road, Edinburgh EH9 2JG. *T:* 031–667 5731. *Club:* New (Edinburgh).

ROSS OF NEWPORT, Baron *cr* 1987 (Life Peer), of Newport in the county of the Isle of Wight; **Stephen Sherlock Ross,** FRICS; *b* 6 July 1926; *s* of Reginald Sherlock Ross and Florence Beryl (*née* Weston); *m* 1949, Brenda Marie Hughes; two *s* two *d*. *Educ:* Bedford Sch. Served War of 1939–45, RN, 1944–48. Articled Nock & Joseland, Kidderminster, 1948–51; Assistant: Heywood & Sons, Stone, Staffs, 1951–53; Sir Francis Pittis & Son, Newport, IoW, 1953–57 (Partner, 1958–73). County Councillor, IoW CC, 1967–74 and 1981–85 (Chm. Policy and Resources Cttee, 1973–74 and 1981–83). MP (L) Isle of Wight, Feb. 1974–1987. Chm., Nat. Housing Forum and Wildlife Link, 1990–. *Recreations:* cricket; antique porcelain collector. *Address:* Herb Cottage, Skyborry Green, Knighton, Powys LD7 1TW. *T:* Knighton (0547) 528229.

ROSS, Alan, CBE 1982; author, publisher and journalist; Editor of London Magazine; Managing Director, London Magazine Editions (Publishers), since 1965; *b* Calcutta, 6 May 1922; *o s* of John Brackenridge Ross, CBE and Clare, *d* of Captain Patrick Fitzpatrick, Indian Army; *m* 1949, Jennifer, *d* of Sir Geoffrey Fry, 1st and last Bt, KCB, CVO; one *s*. *Educ:* Haileybury; St John's College, Oxford. RN 1942–47; general service, Arctic and North Seas, 1942–44; Asst Staff Officer, Intelligence, 16th Destroyer Flotilla, 1944; on staff of Flag Officer, Western Germany, 1945, and Interpreter to British Naval Commander-in-Chief, Germany, 1946. British Council, 1947–50; on staff of The Observer 1950–71. Toured Australia as correspondent, with MCC, 1954–55, 1962–63; toured South Africa, 1956–57, 1964–65; toured West Indies, 1960, 1968. Atlantic Award for Literature (Rockefeller Foundation), 1946. FRSL 1971. *Publications:* The Derelict Day, 1947; Time Was Away, 1948, repr. 1989; The Forties, 1950; The Gulf of Pleasure, 1951; The Bandit on the Billiard Table, 1954 (revised edition South to Sardinia, 1960), repr. 1989; Something of the Sea, 1954; Australia 55, 1956, repr. 1985; Abroad (ed), 1957; Cape Summer and the Australians in England, 1957, repr. 1986; To Whom It May Concern, 1958; The Onion Man, 1959; Through the Caribbean, 1960; The Cricketer's Companion (ed), 1960; Danger on Glass Island, 1960; African Negatives, 1962; Australia 63, 1963; West Indies at Lord's, 1963, 2nd edn 1986; North from Sicily, 1965; Poems 1942–67, 1968; Tropical Ice, 1972; The Taj Express, 1973; (ed) London Magazine Stories 1–11, 1964–80; (ed) Living in London, 1974; Open Sea, 1975; (ed) Selected Poems of Lawrence Durrell, 1977; Death Valley and Other Poems, 1980; (ed) The Turf, 1982; Colours of War, 1983; Ranji, 1983; (ed) Living out of London, 1984; Blindfold Games (autobiog.), 1986; (ed) London Magazine 1961–85, 1986; The Emissary, 1986; Coastwise Lights (autobiog.), 1988; several trans and introductions; contrib. to various jls in England and America. *Recreations:* travel, sport (played cricket and squash for Oxford University and Royal Navy), racing. *Address:* 4 Elm Park Lane, SW3 6DB. *Clubs:* Garrick, MCC; Vincent's (Oxford).

ROSS, Sir Alexander, Kt 1971; Chairman: United Dominions Trust Ltd, 1963–74 (Director, 1955; Vice-Chairman, 1962); Australia and New Zealand Banking Group Ltd, 1970–75; Deputy Chairman: Eagle Star Insurance Co. Ltd, 1963–82; Eagle Star Holdings Ltd, retired 1982; *b* 2 Sept. 1907; *s* of William Alexander Ross and Kathleen Ross; *m* 1st, 1933, Nora Bethia Burgess (*d* 1974); two *s* two *d*; 2nd, 1975, Cynthia Alice Barton. *Educ:* Mount Albert Grammar Sch.; Auckland University (Dip. Banking). Joined Nat. Bank of NZ, 1927, and Reserve Bank of NZ on its establishment in 1934; Dep. Gov., 1948–55. Director: Whitbread Investment Trust Ltd, 1972–83; Drayton Far Eastern Trust Ltd (formerly British Aust. Investment Trust Ltd), 1975–82; Power Components Ltd, 1976–82; Chairman: East Coast Stereo FM Ltd, 1985–; Asiaciti Investment Hldgs, 1986–; Penhallurick Hldgs Pty Ltd, 1986–; Scott Street Developments Pty Ltd, 1986–; Criterion Capital Management, 1986–. Rep. NZ on numerous occasions overseas, including Commonwealth Finance Ministers' Conf. in Australia, 1954. Rep. NZ in rowing, at Empire Games, 1930; Manager, NZ team to Commonwealth Games, Vancouver, 1954; NZ rowing selector for Olympic and Commonwealth Games, NZ; Chairman: Commonwealth Games Fedn, 1968–82 (Vice Chm., 1966–68); Cttee for British Exports to NZ, 1965–67; East European Trade Council, 1967–69; British Aust. Soc., 1970–75; Queensland Community Foundn, 1986–; Vice-Pres., British Export Houses Assoc., 1968–71; Dir, NRDC, 1966–74; Mem., BNEC, 1967–69. Member: New Zealand Soc. (Past Pres.); Council, Dominion Students' Hall Trust; Pres., Friends of Bond Univ., 1988–; Governor, Royal Caledonian Schs, 1964–69; Trustee, Aust. Musical Soc. Foundn; a past Governor, E-SU. Pres., Fellowship of British Motor Industry, 1971–73. Dep. Chm., Central Council, Royal Over-Seas League, 1979–82, Life Vice Pres., 1982. Chm. Ct of Advisers, St Paul's Cathedral, 1981–82. Qld Pres., St John's Ambulance, 1982–; Patron, Gold Coast Heart Foundn. Life Vice-Pres., Commonwealth Games Fedn. Freeman, City of London. Hon. Mem., NUR. *Recreations:* walking, writing. *Address:* 20 Compass Way, Tweed Heads West, NSW 2485, Australia. *T:* (075) 36 7430.

ROSS, Rev. Dr Andrew Christian; Senior Lecturer in Ecclesiastical History, University of Edinburgh, since 1966; Principal of New College and Dean of the Faculty of Divinity, 1978–84; *b* 10 May 1931; *s* of George Adams Ross and Christian Glen Walton; *m* 1953, Isabella Joyce Elder; four *s* (one *d* decd). *Educ:* Dalkeith High Sch.; Univ. of Edinburgh (MA, BD, PhD); Union Theol Seminary, New York (STM). Served Royal Air Force, Pilot Officer, then FO, 1952–54. Ordained Minister of Church of Scotland, 1958; Minister, Church of Central Africa Presbyterian (Malâwi), 1958–65; Chm., Lands Tribunal of Nyasaland, then Malâwi Govt, 1963–65; Vice-Chm., Nat. Tenders Bd of Nyasaland, then Malâwi, 1963–65. Sen. Studentship in African History, Univ. of Edinburgh, 1965–66; Mem. Court of Univ. of Edinburgh, 1971–73, Chm. Student Affairs Cttee of the Court, 1977–83. Kerr Lectr, Glasgow Univ., 1984; Vis. Prof., Univ. of Witwatersrand, 1984; Coll. Lectr, Assembly's Coll., Belfast, 1985. *Publications:* chapter in: The Zambesian Past, 1965; Religion in Africa, 1965; Witchcraft and Healing, 1969; David Livingstone and Africa, 1973; Malâwi, Past and Present, 1974; introd. and ed for micro film-prodn: Life and Work in Central Africa 1885–1914, 1969; The Records of the UMCA 1859–1914, 1971; John Philip: missions, race and politics in South Africa, 1986; contribs to Union Qly Rev., New Left Rev., Scottish Historical Rev. *Recreation:* playing and watching soccer. *Address:* 27 Colinton Road, Edinburgh EH10 5DR. *T:* 031–447 5987. *Club:* University of Edinburgh Staff.

ROSS, Sir Archibald (David Manisty), KCMG 1961 (CMG 1953); HM Diplomatic Service, retired; *b* 12 Oct. 1911; *s* of late J. A. Ross, Indian Civil Service, and Dorothea, *e d* of late G. Eldon Manisty, Indian Civil Service; *m* 1939, Mary Melville, *d* of Melville Macfadyen; one *s* one *d* (and one *s* decd). *Educ:* Winchester; New College, Oxford (MA). 1st Class Hon. Mods 1932, Lit. Hum. 1934; Gaisford Greek Verse Prize, 1932; Laming Travelling Fellow, Queen's College, 1934–35. Diplomatic Service, 1936; Berlin, 1939, Stockholm, 1939–44; Foreign Office, 1944–47, Tehran, 1947–50; Counsellor, Foreign Office, 1950–53; HM Minister, Rome, 1953–56; Assistant Under Secretary of State for Foreign Affairs, 1956–60; Ambassador to Portugal, 1961–66; Ambassador to Sweden, 1966–71. Chairman: Alfa-Laval Co., 1972–82; Saab (GB), 1972–82; Scania (GB), 1972–82; Ericsson Information Systems, 1981–86. Mem. Council, RASE, 1980–85. Grand Cross, Order of the North Star, Sweden, 1981. *Address:* 17 Ennismore Gardens, SW7. *Clubs:* Travellers'; Leander.

ROSS, (Claud) Richard, CB 1973; British financial executive and economist; Vice-President, and Vice-Chairman Board of Directors, European Investment Bank, 1978–89; *b* 24 March 1924; *o s* of late Claud Frederick Ross and Frances Muriel Ross, Steyning, Sussex; *m* 1954, Leslie Beatrice, *d* of Oliver Arnell and late Dr H. M. Arnell, Kitale, Kenya; two *d*. *Educ:* Ardingly Coll.; Hertford Coll., Oxford (Open Schol., Mod. Hist.). 1st cl. PPE, 1950; MA. Fellow of Hertford Coll., 1951–63; Lectr in Economics, Oxford Univ., 1951–52 and 1955–63; Economic Advr to HM Treasury, 1952–55; Junior Proctor, Oxford Univ., 1958–59; Bursar, Hertford Coll., 1959–63; Prof. of Economics and Dean, School of Social Studies, Univ. of East Anglia, 1963–68 (Pro-Vice-Chancellor, 1964–68); Special Consultant, OECD, Paris, 1968–71; Dep. Sec., Central Policy Review Staff, Cabinet Office, 1971–78. Adviser, Bankers' Mission to India and Pakistan, 1960. Represented HM Treasury on OECD Working Party on Policies for Economic Growth, 1961–68. Leader, British Economic Mission to Tanzania, 1965; Member: East Anglia Regional Economic Planning Council, 1966–69 (Dep. Chm., 1967–69); Jt Mission for Malta, 1967. *Publications:* Financial and Physical Problems of Development in the Gold Coast (with D. Seers), 1952; articles on economics. *Address:* 2a Oliver's Wharf, 64 Wapping High Street, E1.

ROSS, Donald MacArthur; *see* Ross, Hon. Lord.

ROSS, Donald Nixon, FRCS; Consultant Cardiac Surgeon, National Heart Hospital, since 1963; *b* 4 Oct. 1922; *m* 1956, Dorothy Curtis; one *d*. *Educ:* Boys' High Sch., Kimberley, S Africa; Univ. of Capetown (BSc, MB, ChB 1st Cl. Hons, 1946). FRCS 1949; FACC 1973; FACS 1976. Sen. Registrar in Thoracic Surgery, Bristol, 1952; Guy's Hospital: Res. Fellow, 1953; Sen. Thoracic Registrar, 1954; Cons. Thoracic Surg., 1958; Cons. Surg., National Heart Hosp., 1963, Sen. Surg., 1967; Dir, Dept of Surgery, Inst. of Cardiology, 1970. Hon. FRCSI 1984; Hon. FRCS Thailand, 1987. Hon. DSc CNAA, 1982. Clement Price Thomas Award, RCS, 1983. Order of Cedar of Lebanon, 1975; Order of Merit (1st cl.), West Germany, 1981. *Publications:* A Surgeon's Guide to Cardiac Diagnosis, 1962; (jtly) Medical and Surgical Cardiology, 1968; (jtly) Biological Tissue in Heart Valve Replacement, 1972; contrib. BMJ, Lancet, Proc. RSM, Annals Royal Coll. Surg., Amer. Jl Cardiol. *Recreations:* Arabian horse breeding, horseriding, gardening. *Address:* 69 Gloucester Crescent, NW1 7EG. *T:* 071–935 8805. *Clubs:* Garrick; Kimberley (SA).

ROSS, Duncan Alexander, CEng, FIEE; Chairman, Southern Electric plc (formerly Southern Electricity Board), since 1984; *b* 25 Sept. 1928; *s* of William Duncan Ross and Mary Ross; *m* 1958, Mary Buchanan Clarke Parsons; one *s* one *d*. *Educ:* Dingwall Academy; Glasgow Univ. (BSc Elec. Engrg). CBIM. Various engineering posts, South of Scotland Electricity Board, 1952–57; engineering, commercial and management posts, Midlands Electricity Board, 1957–72; Area Manager, South Staffs Area, 1972–75, Chief Engineer, 1975–77; Dep. Chm., 1977–81, Chm., 1981–84, South Wales Electricity Bd. Mem., Electricity Council, 1981–90. *Recreations:* golf, ski-ing. *Address:* Holly House, Canon Hill Way, Bray, Maidenhead, Berks SL6 2EX. *T:* Maidenhead (0628) 782753.

ROSS, Ernest; MP (Lab) Dundee West, since 1979; *b* Dundee, July 1942; *m*; two *s* one *d*. *Educ:* St John's Jun. Secondary Sch. Quality Control Engineer, Timex Ltd. Mem., MSF (formerly AUEW (TASS)). *Address:* House of Commons, SW1.

ROSS, Rear-Adm. George Campbell, CB 1952; CBE 1945; FRGS; CEng, MIMechE; MRAeS; retired; *b* 9 Aug. 1900; *s* of late Sir Archibald Ross, KBE; *m* 1st, 1929, Alice Behrens; 2nd, 1950, Lucia Boer (marr. diss. 1969); two *d*; 3rd, 1975, Manolita Harris (*d* 1988). *Educ:* Royal Naval Colleges, Osborne and Dartmouth. Served European War, 1914–18, Grand Fleet (HM Ships Warspite, P59, Vendetta). Engineering Courses at RN College, Greenwich, and RNE College, Keyham, 1919–21; HMS Hawkins, Flagship China Station, 1921–24; RNE Coll., Lecturer in Marine Engineering, 1924–27; HMS Effingham, Flagship East Indies Station, 1927–29; HM Dockyard, Chatham, 1929–31; HMS Rodney, Atlantic Fleet, 1931–33 (incl. Invergordon Mutiny); Comdr 1933; Asst Naval Attaché, Embassy, Tokyo, 1933–36; Liaison Officer to Japanese Flagship Asigara, Coronation Review, 1937; introduced the Oerlikon 20mm gun to the Royal Navy, 1937 (adopted in 1939 largely owing to Lord Mountbatten and the First Sea Lord, Sir Roger Backhouse); HMS Manchester, E Indies Station, 1937–39; Engineer-in-Chief's Dept, Admiralty, 1939–41; Engineer Officer, HMS Nelson, and Staff Engineer Officer to Flag Officer, Force "H", Malta Convoy, N Africa and Sicily, 1941–Aug. 1943; Capt. 1943; HMS St Angelo, Malta, as Staff Engineer Officer (D), on staff of Captain (D), Force "H", Aug. 1943–Dec. 1943 (first officer to go aboard flagship of Italian Fleet after its surrender); Aircraft Maintenance and Repair Dept, Admiralty, 1943–47; ADC to the King, 1948–49; Chief of Staff to Rear-Admiral Reserve Aircraft, 1948–49; Rear-Adm. (E) 1949; Director of Aircraft Maintenance and Repair, Admiralty, 1949–53; retd, Oct. 1953. Joined Hawker Siddeley group, Nov. 1953, and retd Sept. 1965. Consultant to Grieveson Grant, Stockbrokers (1965–79), and other cos. Chairman, Combined Services Winter Sports Assoc., 1951–67. Freeman, City of London, 1955. *Recreations:* fishing, travel, painting, writing. *Address:* Alexander House, 23 Courtfield Gardens, SW5. *Club:* Hurlingham.

ROSS, His Honour James; QC 1966; a Senior Circuit Judge, 1985–87 (a Circuit Judge (formerly a Judge of County Courts), 1971–87); *b* 22 March 1913; *s* of John Stuart Ross, FRCSE; *m* 1939, Clare Margaret, *d* of Alderman Robert Cort-Cox, Stratford-on-Avon; one *d*. *Educ:* Glenalmond; Exeter Coll., Oxford. BA Oxon 1934. Admitted Solicitor, 1938; called to Bar, Gray's Inn, 1945. Legal Member, Mental Health Review Tribunal, Birmingham Region, 1962; Deputy Chairman, Agricultural Land Tribunal, East Midland Area, 1963; Dep. Chm. QS, Parts of Lindsey, 1968–71; Recorder of Coventry, 1968–71; Mem., Parole Bd, 1974–76. Hon. Recorder: Coventry, 1978–85; City of Birmingham, 1985–87. *Address:* 2 Dr Johnson's Buildings, Temple, EC4. *T:* 071–353 5371. *Club:* Bar Yacht.

ROSS, James Alexander, MBE (mil.) 1944; MD, FRCSEd, FRCSGlas; Professor of Anatomy, King Saud University, Riyadh, 1983–84, retired; *b* 25 June 1911; *s* of James McMath Ross and Bessie Hopper Flint; *m* 1940, Catherine Elizabeth (*d* 1988), *d* of Clark Booth Curtis; one *s* two *d* (and one *d* decd). *Educ:* Merchiston Castle Sch.; Edinburgh Univ. MB ChB Ed 1934, MD Ed 1947; FRCSEd 1938, FRCSGlas 1965. Served War: RAMC, 1939–45: France, ME, Europe; then Lt-Col RAMC, RARO, 1953–55. Surgeon, Leith Hosp., 1946–61, and Royal Infirmary, Edinburgh, 1947–61; Surgeon, Eastern Gen. Hosp., 1961–76 and Edenhall Hosp., 1970–76. Hon. Sec., Royal Coll. of Surgeons of Edinburgh, 1960–68; Vice-Pres., 1971–73; Pres., RCSEd, 1973–76; Pres., Edinburgh Harveian Soc., 1977–78; Vice-Pres., Internat. Fedn of Surgical Colls, 1975–81. Hon. Cons. Surgeon to Army in Scotland, 1970–76. Lectures: McCombe, RCSE, 1977; Mason Brown Meml, RCSE, 1978; Hutchinson, Edinburgh Univ., 1979; Mitchiner Meml, RAMC, 1979; Douglas Guthrie Hist. of Medicine, RCSE, 1983. Hon. FRCSI, 1976; Hon. FRACS, 1977; Hon. FDSRCSE, 1983; Hon. Fellow: Pakistan Coll., P and S, 1976; Sri Lanka Coll. of Surgeons, 1976; Hong Kong Surgical Soc., 1976. Governor, Merchiston Castle Sch., 1964–76. Guthrie Medallist, RAMC, 1976; Farquharson Award (teaching of anatomy and surgery), RCSE, 1986. *Publications:* Memoirs of an Army Surgeon, 1948; (jtly) Manual of Surgical Anatomy, 1964; (jtly) Behaviour of the Human Ureter, in Health and Disease, 1972; The Edinburgh School of Surgery after Lister, 1978; Memoirs of an Edinburgh Surgeon, 1988. *Recreations:* walking, swimming, watching cricket. *Address:* 3 Mansewood Court, 52B/3 Morningside Park, Edinburgh EH10 5HA.

ROSS, Sir (James) Keith, 2nd Bt *cr* 1960; RD 1967; MS, FRCS; FRCSE; Consultant Cardiac Surgeon, King Edward VII Hospital, Midhurst, since 1978; *b* 9 May 1927; *s* of Sir James Paterson Ross, 1st Bt, KCVO, FRCS, and Marjorie Burton Townsend (*d* 1978); *S* father, 1980; *m* 1956, Jacqueline Annella Clarke; one *s* three *d*. *Educ:* St Paul's School; Middlesex Hospital. MB BS 1950; MS 1965; FRCS 1956; FRCSE 1989. House Surgeon, Registrar, Sen. Registrar, Middlesex Hosp., 1950–67. Surgn Lieut, RNVR, 1952–54; Surg. Lt Comdr, RNR, retd 1972. Heller Fellowship, San Francisco, 1959; Registrar, Brompton Hosp., 1958, 1960. Consultant Thoracic Surgeon, Harefield and Central Middx Hosps, 1964–67; Consultant Surgeon, Nat. Heart Hosp., 1967–72; Consultant Cardiac Surgeon, Wessex Region, 1972–90. Hunterian Prof., 1961, Mem. Council, 1986–, RCS; Pres., Soc. of Cardiothoracic Surgeons, 1988. Hallet Prize, RCS, 1952; Bruce Medal, RCSE, 1989. *Publications:* on cardiac surgery in appropriate medical jls. *Recreations:* fly fishing, sailing, painting. *Heir:* *s* Andrew Charles Paterson Ross, *b* 18 June 1966. *Address:* Moonhills Gate, Exbury Road, Beaulieu, Brockenhurst, Hants SO42 7YS. *T:* Beaulieu (0590) 612104. *Clubs:* Army and Navy, MCC; Royal Lymington Yacht.

ROSS, Leonard Q.; *see* Rosten, L. C.

ROSS, Malcolm Keir; Headmaster of Crown Woods School, London, 1957–71; *b* 8 June 1910; *m* 1937, Isabel Munkley (*d* 1983); two *d*. *Educ:* Grangefield Grammar Sch., Stockton-on-Tees; Keble Coll., Oxford. Schoolmaster: Gordonstoun, 1933–34; Haverfordwest Grammar Sch., 1934–36; Bromley Grammar Sch., 1936–40; war service with RAF, 1940–45; Warden of Village Coll., Sawston, Cambs, 1945–57. Mem., Cttee of Enquiry into conditions of service life for young servicemen, 1969. Governor, Rachel McMillan Coll. of Education. Book reviewer for The Times Educational Supplement. FRSA. *Recreations:* gardening, reading. *Address:* 45 Winn Road, SE12 9EX.

ROSS, Rear-Adm. Maurice James, CB 1962; DSC 1940; retired; *b* 31 Oct. 1908; *s* of Basil James Ross and Avis Mary (*née* Wilkinson); *m* 1946, Helen Matheson McCall; one *d*. *Educ:* Charterhouse. Entered Royal Navy, 1927; specialised in gunnery, 1935; Comdr, 1943; Captain, 1951; Rear-Adm., 1960. Master, Gardeners' Company, 1983. *Publication:* Ross in the Antarctic 1839–1843, 1982. *Address:* The School House, Chippenham, Ely, Cambs CB7 5PP. *Club:* Army and Navy.

ROSS, Mrs Nicholas; *see* Phillpotts, M. Adelaide Eden.

ROSS, Norman Stilliard; Assistant Under-Secretary of State, Fire Department, Home Office, 1976–79; *b* 10 April 1919; *s* of late James Ross and Mary Jane Elizabeth Ross; *m* 1946, Sarah Cahill; one *s* two *d*. *Educ:* Solihull Sch., Warwickshire; Birmingham Univ. (BA). Served in local govt, City of Birmingham, 1935–39. War service, Army, RAMC and RAOC, in France, Belgium, Kenya, Ceylon, Burma and India, 1939–46 (despatches, France and Belgium, 1940). Asst Principal, Min. of Fuel and Power, 1949; Home Office, 1950; Asst Private Sec. to Sec. of State, 1950–52; Principal, 1952; Asst Sec., 1963; Asst Under-Sec. of State, 1976. *Recreations:* walking, music, reading. *Address:* 27 Detillens Lane, Limpsfield, Oxted, Surrey RH8 0DH. *T:* Oxted (0883) 712579.

ROSS, Richard; Professor of Film (formerly of Film and Television), Royal College of Art, since 1980; *b* 22 Dec. 1935; *s* of Lawrence Sebley Ross and Muriel Ross; *m* 1957, Phyllis Ellen Hamilton; one *s* one *d*. *Educ:* Westland High School, Hokitika, NZ; Canterbury University College, NZ. Exchange Telegraph, 1958–60; Visnews Ltd, 1960–65; BBC TV News, 1965–80. Consultant: Univ. Sains, Penang, Malaysia, 1984–; Calouste Gulbenkian Foundn, Lisbon, 1983–85. Chm., Educn Cttee, British Film Year, 1985–86. Consultant Dir, Film Educn, 1986–; Dir, Nat. Youth Film Foundn, 1988–. Fellow in Fine Arts, Trent Polytechnic, 1970–72. Fellow, RCA, 1981. *Recreations:* walking in London, eating in France, talking and drinking anywhere. *Address:* Royal College of Art, Kensington Gore, SW7 2EU; 51 Hanbury Street, E1.

ROSS, Richard; *see* Ross, C. R.

ROSS, Robert, MA, FLS; Keeper of Botany, British Museum (Natural History), 1966–77; *b* 14 Aug. 1912; *e s* of Robert Ross, Pinner, Middx; *m* 1939, Margaret Helen Steadman; one *s* three *d*. *Educ:* St Paul's Sch.; St John's Coll., Cambridge. Asst Keeper, British Museum (Natural History), 1936; Principal Scientific Officer, 1950; Deputy Keeper, 1962. Royal Microscopical Society: Hon. Librarian, 1947–51; Hon. Editor, 1953–71; Vice-Pres., 1959–60. Administrator of Finances, Internat. Assoc. of Plant Taxonomy, 1964–69; Sec., Gen. Cttee for Plant Nomenclature, 1964–69, Chm., 1969–81. President: British Phycological Soc., 1969–71; Quekett Microscopical Club, 1974–76. *Publications:* various papers in scientific jls on botanical subjects. *Recreations:* morris dancing (Bagman, Morris Ring, 1946–50); walking; gardening. *Address:* The Garden House, Evesbatch, Bishop's Frome, Worcester. *T:* Bosbury (053186) 366.

ROSS, Maj.-Gen. Robert Jeremy, OBE 1978; Major General Royal Marines Commando Forces, since 1990; *b* 28 Nov. 1939; *s* of Gerald and Margaret Ross; *m* 1965, Sara (*née* Curtis); one *s* one *d*. *Educ:* Wellington Coll.; Corpus Christi Coll., Cambridge (MPhil). Entered RM, 1957; Commando and Sea Service, 1959–69; Army Staff Coll., 1970; Commando Service, 1971–78; Instr, Army Staff Coll., 1978–79; CO 40 Commando RM, 1979–81; RCDS 1982; MoD, 1984–86; Comdr 3 Commando Bde, 1986–88; Maj.-Gen. RM Trng, Reserve and Special Forces, 1988–90. *Recreations:* ski-ing, shooting, fishing, walking. *Address:* c/o Barclays Bank, 50 Jewry Street, Winchester, Hampshire. *Club:* United Oxford & Cambridge University.

ROSS, Comdr Ronald Douglas, OBE 1984; RN; *b* 30 July 1920; *o s* of Captain James Ross, FRGS, Scottish Horse of Chengtu, Szechwan Province, China; *m* 1952, Elizabeth Mary, *er d* of Canon S. J. S. Groves; one *d*. *Educ:* Cargilfield; Sedbergh; RN Staff Coll. Joined Accountant Br. of RN and went to sea, 1937; war service in HM Ships Exeter, Devonshire and Tartar. Called to Bar, Middle Temple, 1950; called to the Bar, Supreme Court of Hong Kong, 1963; officiated frequently as Judge Advocate; Admiralty Prize Medal for Naval History, 1957; retired list, 1967. Clerk, Vintners' Co., 1969–84. Mem., Wine Standards Bd, 1973–84. Chevalier du Sacavin d'Anjou, 1974; Citizen and Vintner, 1975. *Publications:* contribs to The Times, Scotsman, New York Times, Investors' Chronicle, Brassey's Naval Annual, etc. *Recreation:* scripophily. *Address:* The Limes, Ashley Close, Sevenoaks, Kent TN13 3AP. *T:* Sevenoaks (0732) 455678.

ROSS, Sophie, (Mrs R. P. Ross); *see* Mirman, S.

ROSS, Timothy David M.; *see* Melville-Ross.

ROSS, Victor; management consultant; Chairman, Reader's Digest Association Ltd, 1978–84; *b* 1 Oct. 1919; *s* of Valentin and Eva Rosenfeld; *m* 1st, 1944, Romola Wallace; two *s*; 2nd, 1970, Hildegard Paiser. *Educ:* schs in Austria, Germany and France; London Sch. of Economics. Served in Army, 1942–45. Journalist and writer, 1945–55; joined Reader's Digest, 1955; Man. Dir and Chief Exec., 1972–81. Dir, Folio Soc., 1985–89. Pres., Assoc. of Mail Order Publishers, 1979–80, 1983–84; Mem., Data Protection Tribunal, 1985–. Mackintosh Medal for Advertising, Advertising Assoc., 1989. *Publications:* A Stranger in my Midst, 1948; Tightrope, 1952; Basic British, 1956. *Recreations:* collecting signed books, fishing. *Address:* Worten Mill, Great Chart, Kent TN23 3BS.

ROSS, Lt-Col Walter Hugh Malcolm, OBE 1988; Comptroller, Lord Chamberlain's Office, since 1991 (Assistant Comptroller, 1987–91); Secretary, Central Chancery of the Orders of Knighthood, 1989–91; *b* 27 Oct. 1943; *s* of Col Walter Ross and Josephine (*née* Cross); *m* 1969, Susie, *d* of Gen. Sir Michael Gow, *qv*; one *s* two *d*. *Educ:* Eton Coll.; Royal Military Acad., Sandhurst. Served in Scots Guards, 1964–87; Management Auditor, The Royal Household, 1987–89. An Extra Equerry to the Queen, 1988–. Mem., Queen's Body Guard for Scotland, Royal Company of Archers, 1981–. *Address:* Netherhall, Bridge-of-Dee, Castle-Douglas, Kirkcudbrightshire. *Clubs:* Pratt's; New (Edinburgh).

ROSS, William; MP (UU) Londonderry East, since 1983 (Londonderry, Feb. 1974–1983), resigned seat Dec. 1985 in protest against Anglo-Irish Agreement; re-elected Jan. 1986; *b* 4 Feb. 1936; *m* 1974, Christine; three *s* one *d*. *Recreations:* fishing, shooting. *Address:* Hillquarter, Turmeel, Dungiven, Northern Ireland. *T:* Dungiven (05047) 41428. *Club:* Northern Counties (Londonderry).

ROSS, William Mackie, CBE 1987; TD 1969; DL; MD; FRCS; FRCR; retired; Consultant Radiotherapist, Northern Regional Health Authority, 1953–87; Lecturer in Radiotherapy, University of Newcastle upon Tyne, 1973–87; *b* 14 Dec. 1922; *s* of Harry Caithness Ross and Catherine Ross; *m* 1948, Mary Burt; one *s* two *d*. *Educ:* Durham and Newcastle. MB, BS 1945, MD 1953; FRCS 1956, FRCR 1960. Trainee in Radiotherapy, 1945–51; National Service, 1951–53; RAMC TA, 1953–72; Col, CO 201 Gen. Hosp., 1967–72, Hon. Col, 1977–82. President: Section of Radiology, RSM, 1978; British Inst. of Radiology, 1979; North of England Surgical Soc., 1983; Royal Coll. of Radiologists, 1983–86. Hon. FACR, 1986. DL Northumberland, 1971–74, Tyne and Wear, 1974. *Publications:* articles on cancer, its causation and treatment. *Address:* 62 Archery Rise, Durham City DH1 4LA. *T:* Durham (091) 3869256.

ROSS-MUNRO, Colin William Gordon, QC 1972; *b* 12 Feb. 1928; *s* of late William Ross-Munro and of Adela Chirgwin; *m* 1958, Janice Jill Pedrana; one step *d*. *Educ:* Lycée

Français de Londres; Harrow Sch.; King's Coll., Cambridge. Served in Scots Guards and in Army Education Corps. Called to the Bar, Middle Temple, 1951 (Master of the Bench, 1983). *Recreations:* tennis and travel. *Address:* (home) 36 Roland Way, SW7 3RE; 2 Hare Court, Temple EC4Y 7BH.

ROSS RUSSELL, Graham; Chairman, EMAP plc, since 1990 (non-executive Director, since 1971); President, C.C.F. Holdings Ltd, since 1989; *b* 3 Jan. 1933; *s* of Robert Ross Russell and Elizabeth Ross Russell (*née* Hendry); *m* 1963, Jean Margaret Symington; three *s* one *d.* *Educ:* Loretto; Trinity Hall, Cambridge (BA); Harvard Business School (MBA; Frank Knox Fellow, 1958–60). Sub Lieut, RNVR, 1951–53 (Mediterranean Fleet). Merchant banking: Morgan Grenfell & Co. and Baring Brothers, 1956–58; Philip Hill Higginson Erlanger, 1960–63; Stockbroker, Laurence Prust & Co., 1963–90, Partner, 1965; Chm., Laurence Prust & Co. Ltd, 1986–88. Chm., Braham Miller Group, 1981–84; non-exec. Director: Fordath, 1971–84; Barlow Rand International, 1984–; CCF Foster Braithwaite, 1988–. Dir, SIB, 1989–. Mem. Council, Internat. Stock Exchange, subseq. London Stock Exchange, 1973–91 (Dep. Chm., 1984–88; Chairman: Pre-emption Gp, 1987–91; Rev. Cttee on Initial Public Offers, 1989–90). Comr, Public Works Loan Bd, 1980–; Chm., Domestic Promotions Cttee, British Invisible Exports Council, 1987–91. Gov., Sutton's Hosp., Charterhouse, 1988–. *Publications:* occasional articles in esoteric financial and fiscal jls. *Recreations:* tennis, reading. *Address:* 30 Ladbroke Square, W11 3NB. *T:* 071–727 5017. *Clubs:* Athenæum; Hawks (Cambridge); Woodpeckers (Oxford and Cambridge).

ROSSE, 7th Earl of, *cr* 1806; **William Brendan Parsons;** Bt 1677; Baron Oxmantown 1792; Member, Advisory Council on Development Co-operation, 1984–89, and Director, Agency for Personal Service Overseas, 1986–90, Government of Ireland; *b* 21 Oct. 1936; *s* of 6th Earl of Rosse, KBE, and of Anne, *o d* of Lt-Col Leonard Messel, OBE; *S* father, 1979; *m* 1966, Alison Margaret, *er d* of Major J. D. Cooke-Hurle, Startforth Hall, Barnard Castle, Co. Durham; two *s* one *d.* *Educ:* Eton; Grenoble Univ.; Christ Church, Oxford. BA 1961, MA 1964. 2nd Lieut, Irish Guards, 1955–57. UN Official 1963–80, appointed successively to Accra, Cotonou, New York, Teheran, Dacca and Algiers, in posts ranging from Area Officer to Dep. Resident Rep., with specific responsibility for directing the first teams of UN volunteers (in Iran) and co-ordinating disaster relief (in Bangladesh). Director: Historic Irish Tourist Houses and Gardens Assoc., 1980–; Sch. of Internat. Educn, 1988–; Trustee, Edward de Bono Foundn, 1984–. Lord of the Manor: Towton, and Womersley, W Yorks; Newtown, and Parsonstown, Ireland. FRAS. *Heir:* *s* Lord Oxmantown, *qv.* *Address:* (home) Birr Castle, Co. Offaly, Ireland. *T:* 353.509.20023.
See also Earl of Snowdon.

ROSSER, Sir Melvyn (Wynne), Kt 1974; DL; FCA; Chairman: HTV Group, 1986–91; Manpower Services Committee for Wales, 1980–88; Member (part-time), British Coal (formerly NCB), 1983–89; Director, West Midlands and Wales Regional Board, National Westminster Bank, 1986–89; *b* 11 Nov. 1926; *s* of late David John and of Anita Rosser; *m* 1957, Margaret; one *s* two *d.* *Educ:* Glanmor Sch., Swansea; Bishop Gore Grammar Sch., Swansea. Chartered Accountant, qual. 1949; joined staff Deloitte Plender Griffiths & Co. (later Deloitte, Haskins & Sells), Swansea, 1950, Partner 1961; practised in Swansea, 1961–68, in Cardiff, 1968–80, in London, 1980–85, retired. Director: Develt Corp. for Wales, 1965–80; Nat. Bus Co., 1969–72; Wales and Marches Telecom. Bd, 1970–80; Welsh Regional Council, CBI, 1970–80; BSC, 1972–80. Member: Welsh Econ. Council, 1965–68; Welsh Council, 1968–80 (Chm., 1971–80); Royal Commn on Standards of Conduct in Public Life, 1974; Prime Minister's Adv. Cttee on Outside Business Appts, 1976–83; Nat. Trng Task Force, 1989–91 (Chm., Trng Enterprise and Educn Adv. Gp for Wales, 1989–91). Pres., UCW, Aberystwyth, 1986– (Vice-Pres., 1977–86). Mem. Gorsedd of Bards, Royal Nat. Eisteddfod of Wales. DL West Glamorgan, 1986. Hon. LLD Wales, 1987. *Recreations:* music, gardening. *Address:* Corlan, 53 Birchgrove Road, Lonlas, Swansea SA7 9JR. *T:* Swansea (0792) 812286. *Clubs:* Royal Automobile; Cardiff and County (Cardiff); Bristol Channel Yacht.

ROSSER, Prof. Rachel Mary, FRCP, FRCPsych; Professor and Head of Department of Psychiatry, University College and Middlesex School of Medicine, London, since 1984; *d* of late John Rosser and of Madge Rosser; *m* 1967, Vincent Challacombe Watts; one *s* one *d.* *Educ:* King's High Sch., Warwick; Newnham Coll., Cambridge (MA); St Thomas's Hosp. Med. Sch. (MB, BChir). PhD London. Res. Registrar, Dept of Medicine, Guy's Hosp., 1969–71; Registrar, Maudsley Hosp., 1971–74; Sen. Registrar, Maudsley and Hammersmith Hosps, 1974–76; Sen. Lectr 1976–82, Reader 1983–84, Charing Cross Hosp. Pres., Soc. for Psychosomatic Research, 1984–86; Treas., Internat. Coll. of Psychosomatic Medicine, 1983–. *Publications:* (jtly) Health Care Priorities, 1980; Mind Made Disease, 1981; (jtly) Quality of Life: assessment and application, 1988; sci. papers on psychotherapy, psychosomatics, disaster aftermath. *Address:* Department of Psychiatry, Middlesex Hospital, Mortimer Street, W1. *T:* 071–380 9468. *Club:* United Oxford & Cambridge University.

ROSSER, Richard Andrew, JP; General Secretary, Transport Salaried Staffs' Association, since 1989; *b* 5 Oct. 1944; *s* of Gordon William Rosser and Kathleen Mary (*née* Moon); *m* 1973, Sheena Margaret (*née* Denoon); two *s* one *d.* *Educ:* St Nicholas Grammar Sch., Northwood. BScEcon London (external degree), 1970. MCIT 1968. Clerk, London Transport, 1962–65; PA to Operating Man. (Railways), LTE, 1965–66; joined full staff of TSSA, 1966: Res. Officer, 1966–74; Asst, London Midland Div. Sec., 1974–76; Finance and Organising Officer, 1976–77; London Midland Region Div. Sec., 1977–82; Asst Gen. Sec., 1982–89. Councillor, London Bor. of Hillingdon, 1971–78 (Chm., Finance Cttee, 1974–78); contested (Lab) Croydon Central, Feb. 1974. Mem., NEC, Labour Party, 1988–. JP Middlesex, 1978. *Recreations:* walking, music, reading The Guardian, and hoping for success for Watford FC. *Address:* Transport Salaried Staffs' Association, Walkden House, 10 Melton Street, NW1 2EJ. *T:* 071–387 2101.

ROSSI, Sir Hugh (Alexis Louis), Kt 1983; MP (C) Hornsey and Wood Green, since 1983 (Hornsey, 1966–83); *b* 21 June 1927; *m* 1955, Philomena Elizabeth Jennings; one *s* four *d.* *Educ:* Finchley Catholic Gram. Sch.; King's Coll., Univ. of London (LLB; FKC 1986). Solicitor with Hons, 1950; consultant in environmental law with Simmons and Simmons. Member: Hornsey Borough Coun., 1956–65; Haringey Council, 1965–68; Middlesex CC, 1961–65. Govt Whip, Oct. 1970–April 1972; Europe Whip, Oct. 1971–1973; a Lord Comr, HM Treasury, 1972–74; Parly Under-Sec. of State, DoE, 1974; opposition spokesman on housing and land, 1974–79; Minister of State: NI Office, 1979–81; for Social Security and the Disabled, DHSS, 1981–83. Chm., Select Cttee on the Environment, 1983–. Dep. Leader, UK Delegn to Council of Europe and WEU, 1972–73 (Mem., 1970–73). Chm., Italian Hosp., London, 1988–89. Knight of Holy Sepulchre, 1966; KCSG 1985. *Publications:* Guide to the Rent Act, 1974; Guide to Community Land Act, 1975; Guide to Rent (Agriculture) Act, 1976; Guide to Landlord and Tenant Act, 1987; Guide to Local Government Acts 1987 and 1988, 1988. *Address:* House of Commons, SW1.

ROSSITER, Rt. Rev. (Anthony) Francis, OSB; Abbot President of the English Benedictine Congregation, since 1985 (Second Assistant, 1976–85); *b* 26 April 1931; *s* of Leslie and Winifred Rossiter. *Educ:* St Benedict's, Ealing; Sant Anselmo, Rome (LCL). Priest, 1955; Second Master, St Benedict's School, 1960–67; Abbot of Ealing, 1967–91; Vicar for Religious, Archdiocese of Westminster, 1969–88; Pres., Conf. of Major Religious Superiors of England and Wales, 1970–74. Hon. DD St Vincent Coll., Pa, 1988. *Address:* Ealing Abbey, W5 2DY. *T:* 081–998 2158.

ROSSLYN, 7th Earl of, *cr* 1801; **Peter St Clair-Erskine;** Bt 1666; Baron Loughborough, 1795; *b* 31 March 1958; *s* of 6th Earl of Rosslyn, and of Athenais de Mortemart, *o d* of late Duc de Vivonne; *S* father, 1977; *m* 1982, Helen, *e d* of Mr and Mrs C. R. Watters, Christ's Hospital, Sussex; one *s* one *d.* *Educ:* Eton; Bristol Univ. Metropolitan Police, 1980–. Trustee, Dunimarle Museum. *Recreations:* opera, church music, piano. *Heir:* *s* Lord Loughborough, *qv.* *Club:* White's.

ROSSMORE, 7th Baron, *cr* 1796; **William Warner Westenra;** *b* 14 Feb. 1931; *o s* of 6th Baron and Dolores Cecil (*d* 1981), *d* of late Lieut-Col James Alban Wilson, DSO, West Burton, Yorks; *S* father, 1958; *m* 1982, Valerie Marion, *d* of Brian Tobin; one *s.* *Educ:* Eton; Trinity Coll., Cambridge (BA). 2nd Lieut, Somerset LI. Co-founder, Coolemine Therapeutic Community, Dublin. *Recreations:* drawing, painting. *Heir:* *s* Hon. Benedict William Westenra, *b* 6 March 1983. *Address:* Rossmore Park, Co. Monaghan, Eire. *T:* Monaghan 81947.

ROSSWALL, Prof. Thomas; Professor, Department of Water and Environmental Studies, University of Linköping, Sweden, since 1984; Executive Director, International Geosphere-Biosphere Programme, since 1986; *b* 20 Dec. 1941; *s* of Axel Rosswall and Britta (*née* Lindroth). *Educ:* Univ. of Uppsala (BSc 1966). Asst, Dept of Biochemistry, Univ. of Uppsala, 1967–70; Res. Asst, Dept of Microbiol., Swedish Univ. of Agricl Scis, 1970–76; Programme Officer, Swedish Council for Planning and Co-ordination of Research, 1976–80; Researcher, 1980–82, Asst Prof., 1982–84, Associate Prof., 1984, Dept of Microbiol., Swedish Univ. of Agricl Research. Mem., Academia Europaea, 1989; Fellow, Royal Swedish Acad. of Scis, 1989. *Publications:* edited: Systems Analysis in Northern Coniferous Forests, 1971; (jtly) IBP Tundra Biome Proc. 4th International Meeting on Biological Productivity of Tundra, 1971; Modern Methods in the Study of Microbial Ecology, 1973; (jtly) Structure and Function of Tundra Ecosystems, 1975; Processer i kvävets kretslopp, 1979; Nitrogen Cycling in West African Ecosystems, 1980; (jtly) Terrestrial Nitrogen Cycles: processes, ecosystems strategies and management impacts, 1981; (jtly) Nitrogen Cycling in South-East Asian Wet Monsoonal Ecosystems, 1981; (jtly) The Nitrogen Cycle, 1982; (jtly) Nitrogen Cycling in Ecosystems of Latin America and the Caribbean, 1982; (jtly) Scales and Global Change: spatial and temporal variability of biospheric and geospheric processes, 1988; (jtly) Ecoloygy of Arable Land: the role of organism in carbon and nitrogen cycling, 1989; 100 papers in scientific jls. *Address:* International Geosphere-Biosphere Progamme Secretariat, The Royal Swedish Academy of Sciences, Box 50005, S-104 05 Stockholm, Sweden. *T:* 46–8–166448.

ROST, Peter Lewis; MP (C) Erewash, since 1983 (Derbyshire South-East, 1970–83); *b* 19 Sept. 1930; *s* of Frederick Rosenstiel and Elisabeth Merz; *m* 1961, Hilary Mayo; two *s* two *d.* *Educ:* various primary schs; Aylesbury Grammar Sch. National Service, RAF, 1948–50; Birmingham Univ. (BA Hons Geog.), 1950–53. Investment Analyst and Financial Journalist with Investors Chronicle, 1953–58; firstly Investment Advisor, 1958, and then, 1962, Mem. London Stock Exchange, resigned 1977. Secretary: Cons. Parly Trade and Industry Cttee, 1972–73; Cons. Parly Energy Cttee, 1974–77; Select Cttee on Energy, 1979. Treasurer, Anglo-German Parly Gp, 1974–; Jt Chm., Alternative and Complementary Medicine Parly Gp, 1989–. FRGS (Mem. Council, 1980–83); Fellow, Industry and Parlt Trust, 1987. Grand Cross, Order of Merit, Germany, 1979. *Recreations:* tennis, ski-ing, gardening, antique map collecting. *Address:* Norcott Court, Berkhamsted, Herts. *T:* Berkhamsted (0442) 6123.

ROSTEN, Leo C., (pseudonym: **Leonard Q. Ross);** author and social scientist; *b* 11 April 1908; *s* of Samuel C. and Ida F. Rosten; *m* 1st, 1935, Priscilla Ann Mead (decd); one *s* two *d*; 2nd, 1960, Gertrude Zimmerman. *Educ:* University of Chicago (PhD); London School of Economics (Hon. Fellow, 1975). Research Assistant, Political Science Dept, Univ. of Chicago, 1933–35; Fellow, Social Science Research Council, 1934–36; Grants from Rockefeller Foundation and Carnegie Corporation, 1938–40. Dir, Motion Picture Research Project, 1939–41. Spec. Consultant, Nat. Defense Advisory Commn, Washington, 1939; Chief, Motion Picture Div., Office of Facts and Figures, Washington, 1941–42; Dep. Dir, Office of War Information, Washington, 1942–45; Special Consultant, Sec. of War, Washington, 1945; special mission to France, Germany, England, 1945. Faculty Associate, Columbia Univ., 1953–; Lectr in Political Science, Yale Univ., 1955, New School for Social Research, NY, 1959. Ford Vis. Prof. in Pol. Sci., Univ. of California (Berkeley), USA, 1960–61. Wrote film screenplays: Sleep, My Love; The Velvet Touch; Walk East on Beacon; The Dark Corner, etc. Member: Amer. Acad. of Political and Social Science; Amer. Assoc. for Advancement of Science; Nat. Acad. of Lit. and the Arts; Authors League of America; Authors Guild of America; Educnl Policies Cttee of Nat. Educnl Assoc. Phi Beta Kappa, 1929; Freedom Foundation's Award, 1955; George Polk Meml Award, 1955; Distinguished Alumnus Award, Univ. of Chicago, 1970. Hon. DHL: Univ. of Rochester, 1973; Hebrew Union Theol Coll., 1980. *Publications:* The Education of H*y*m*a*n K*a*p*l*a*n, 1937; The Washington Correspondents, 1937; The Strangest Places, 1939; Hollywood: The Movie Colony, The Movie Makers, 1941; The Dark Corner, 1945; (ed) Guide To The Religions of America, 1957; The Return of H*y*m*a*n K*a*p*l*a*n, 1959; Captain Newman, MD, 1961; The Story Behind the Painting, 1961; The Many Worlds of Leo Rosten; The Leo Rosten Bedside Book, 1965; A Most Private Intrigue, 1967; The Joys of Yiddish, 1968; A Trumpet for Reason, 1970; People I have Loved, Known or Admired, 1970; Rome Wasn't Burned in a Day, 1971; Leo Rosten's Treasury of Jewish Quotations, 1973; Dear "Herm", 1974; (ed) The Look Book, 1975; The 3.10 to Anywhere, 1976; O Kaplan! My Kaplan!, 1976; The Power of Positive Nonsense, 1977; Passions and Prejudices, 1978; (ed) Infinite Riches: Gems from a Lifetime of Reading, 1979; Silky!, 1979; King Silky!, 1980; Hooray for Yiddish!, 1983; Leo Rosten's Giant Book of Laughter, 1985; The Joys of Yinglish, 1989; contrib. learned journals. *Recreations:* photography, travel. *Address:* 36 Sutton Place South, NY 10022, USA. *Clubs:* Savile, Reform, Garrick (London); Cosmos (Washington); Chaos, Round Table (New York).

ROSTOW, Prof. Eugene Victor; Sterling Professor of Law, Yale University, 1938–84, now Emeritus; Distinguished Fellow, US Institute of Peace, since 1990; *b* 25 Aug. 1913; *s* of Victor A. and Lillian H. Rostow; *m* 1933, Edna B. Greenberg; two *s* one *d.* *Educ:* Yale Coll.; King's Coll., Cambridge (LLD 1962); Yale Law Sch. Practised law, New York, 1937–38; Yale Law Faculty, 1938–; Prof. of Law, 1944–84; Dean of Law Sch., 1955–65. Dist. Vis. Res. Prof. of Law and Diplomacy, Nat. Defense Univ., Washington, 1984–90. Asst to Asst Sec. of State Acheson, 1942–44; Asst to Exec. Sec., Econ. Commn for Europe, UN, Geneva, 1949–50; Under-Sec. of State for Political Affairs, 1966–69. Dir, Arms Control and Disarmament Agency, 1981–83. Pres., Atlantic Treaty Assoc., 1973–76. Pitt Prof., Cambridge, 1959–60; Eastman Prof., Oxford, 1970–71. Dir, American Jewish Cttee, 1972–74; Chm. Exec. Cttee, Cttee on the Present Danger (Washington), 1976–81, 1987–. Hon. LLD Boston, 1976. Dist. Civilian Service Medal, US Army. Chevalier,

Legion of Honour (France), 1960; Grand Cross, Order of the Crown (Belgium), 1969. *Publications:* A National Policy for the Oil Industry, 1948; Planning for Freedom, 1959; The Sovereign Prerogative, 1962; Law, Power and the Pursuit of Peace, 1968; (ed) Is Law Dead?, 1971; Peace in the Balance, 1972; The Ideal in Law, 1978; contribs to legal and economic jls. *Address:* Peru, Vermont 05152, USA. *T:* 802–824–6627; 1315 4th Street SW, Washington, DC 20024, USA. *Clubs:* Century (New York); Elizabethan, Lawn (New Haven); Cosmos (Washington).

See also W. W. Rostow.

ROSTOW, Walt Whitman; Professor of Economics and of History, University of Texas at Austin, Texas, since 1969; *b* 7 Oct. 1916; 2nd *s* of Victor and Lillian Rostow; *m* 1947, Elspeth, *o d* of Milton J. and Harriet Vaughan Davies; one *s* one *d. Educ:* Yale (BA 1936; PhD 1940); Oxford (Rhodes Scholar). Social Science Research Council Fellow, 1939–40; Instructor, Columbia Univ., 1940–41; Office Strategic Services, 1941–45 (Army of the United States, 1943–45, Major; Legion of Merit; Hon. OBE); Assistant Chief Division German-Austrian Economic Affairs, Department of State, 1945–46; Harmsworth Professor American History, Oxford, 1946–47; Special Assistant to Executive Secretary, Economic Commission for Europe, 1947–49; Pitt Professor of American History, Cambridge, 1949–50; Professor of Economic History, Massachusetts Institute of Technology, 1950–61. Deputy Special Assistant to the President (USA) for National Security Affairs, Jan. 1961–Dec. 1961; Counselor and Chairman, Policy Planning Council, Department of State, 1961–66; US Mem., Inter-Amer. Cttee on Alliance for Progress, 1964–66; Special Assistant to the President, The White House, 1966–69. Member: Royal Economic Society, England; American Academy of Arts and Sciences, 1957; Amer. Philos. Soc.; Massachusetts Historical Soc. Hon. LLD: Carnegie Inst. of Tech., Pittsburgh, 1962; Univ. Miami, 1965; Univ. Notre Dame, 1966; Middlebury Coll., 1967; Jacksonville Univ., 1974. Presidential Medal of Freedom, with distinction, 1969. *Publications:* The American Diplomatic Revolution, 1947; Essays on the British Economy of the Nineteenth Century, 1948; The Process of Economic Growth, 1952; (with A. D. Gayer and A. J. Schwartz) The Growth and Fluctuation of the British Economy, 1790–1850, 1953, new edn 1975; (with A. Levin and others) The Dynamics of Soviet Society, 1953; (with others) The Prospects for Communist China, 1954; (with R. W. Hatch) An American Policy in Asia, 1955; (with M. F. Millikan) A Proposal: Key to An Effective Foreign Policy, 1957; The Stages of Economic Growth, 1960, 2nd edn 1971; The United States in the World Arena, 1960; The Economics of Take-off into Sustained Growth (ed), 1963; View from the Seventh Floor, 1964; A Design for Asian Development, 1965; Politics and the Stages of Growth, 1971; The Diffusion of Power, 1972; How It All Began: origins of the modern economy, 1975; The World Economy: history and prospect, 1978; Getting from Here to There, 1978; Why the Poor Get Richer and the Rich Slow Down, 1980; Pre-Invasion Bombing Strategy: General Eisenhower's Decision of March 25, 1944, 1981; The Division of Europe after World War II: 1946, 1981; British Trade Fluctuations 1868–1896: a chronicle and a commentary, 1981; Europe after Stalin: Eisenhower's Three Decisions of March 11, 1953, 1982; Open Skies: Eisenhower's proposal of July 21, 1955, 1982; The Barbaric Counter-Revolution, 1983; Eisenhower, Kennedy and Foreign Aid, 1985; The United States and the Regional Organization of Asia and the Pacific 1965–85, 1985; Rich Countries and Poor Countries: reflections from the past, lessons for the future, 1987; Essays on a Half Century: ideas, policies and action, 1988; History, Policy and Theory: essays in interaction, 1989; Theorists of Economic Growth from David Hume to the Present, with a Perspective on the Next Century, 1990; various articles contributed to: The Economist, Economic Journal, Economic History Review, Journal of Econ. History, American Econ. Review, etc. *Address:* 1 Wild Wind Point, Austin, Texas 78746, USA. *Clubs:* Elizabethan (New Haven, Conn, USA); Cosmos (Washington, DC).

See also E. V. Rostow.

ROSTROPOVICH, Mstislav, Hon. KBE 1987; 'cellist; Music Director and Conductor, National Symphony Orchestra, Washington, since 1977; *b* 1927; *m* 1955, Galina Vishnevskaya, *qv*; two *d. Educ:* State Conservatoire, Moscow. Has played in many concerts in Russia and abroad from 1942; first performance of Shostakovich's 'cello concerto (dedicated to him), Edinburgh Festival, 1960. Series of concerts with London Symphony Orchestra under Gennadi Rozhdestvensky, Festival Hall, 1965 (Gold Medal); first perf. Britten's third cello suite, Aldeburgh, 1974. An Artistic Dir, Aldeburgh Festival, 1977–. Mem. Union of Soviet Composers, 1950–78. Lenin Prize, 1964. Holds over 30 honorary degrees including Hon. MusD: St Andrews, 1968; Cambridge, 1975; Harvard, 1976; Yale, 1976; Oxon, 1980. US Presidential Medal of Freedom, 1987; Commandeur de la Légion d'Honneur (France), 1987. *Address:* c/o National Symphony Orchestra, J. F. Kennedy Center for the Performing Arts, Washington, DC 20566, USA.

ROTBLAT, Prof. Joseph, CBE 1965; MA, DSc (Warsaw); PhD (Liverpool); DSc (London); FInstP; Professor of Physics in the University of London, at St Bartholomew's Hospital Medical College, 1950–76, now Emeritus; Physicist to St Bartholomew's Hospital, 1950–76; President, Pugwash Conferences on Science and World Affairs, since 1988; *b* 4 Nov. 1908; *e s* of late Z. Rotblat, Warsaw. *Educ:* University of Warsaw, Poland. Research Fellow of Radiological Laboratory of Scientific Society of Warsaw, 1933–39; Asst Director of Atomic Physics Institute of Free Univ. of Poland, 1937–39; Oliver Lodge Fellow of Univ. of Liverpool, 1939–40; Lecturer and afterwards Senior Lecturer in Dept of Physics, Liverpool Univ., 1940–49; Director of Research in nuclear physics at Liverpool Univ., 1945–49; work on atomic energy at Liverpool Univ. and Los Alamos, New Mexico. Treasurer, St Bartholomew's Hosp. Med. Coll., 1974–76; Vice-Dean, Faculty of Sci., London Univ., 1974–76. Mem., Adv. Cttee on Med. Res., WHO, 1972–75; Mem., WHO Management Gp, 1984–90. Ed., Physics in Medicine and Biol., 1960–72. Sec.-Gen., Pugwash Confs on Science and World Affairs, 1957–73; Chm., British Pugwash, 1978–88. Pres., Hosp. Physicists' Assoc, 1969–70; Pres., British Inst. of Radiology, 1971–72. Mem. Governing Body of Stockholm Internat. Peace Res. Inst., 1966–71. Pres., Internat. Youth Sci. Fortnight, 1972–74. Vis. Prof. of Internat. Relations, Univ. of Edinburgh, 1975–76. Member, Polish Academy of Sciences, 1966; Hon. For. Mem., Amer. Acad. of Arts and Sciences, 1972; For. Mem., Czechoslovak Acad. of Scis, 1988. Hon. Fellow, UMIST, 1985. Hon. DSc: Bradford, 1973; Liverpool, 1989; Dr *hc* Moscow, 1988. Bertrand Russell Soc. Award, 1983; Gold Medal, Czechoslovak Acad. of Sciences, 1988. Commander, Order of Merit (Polish People's Republic), 1987; Order of Cyril and Methodius (1st Cl.) (Bulgaria), 1988; Kt Commander's Cross, OM (FRG), 1989. *Publications:* Progress in Nuclear Physics, 1950; (with Chadwick) Radio-activity and Radioactive Substances, 1953; Atomic Energy, a Survey, 1954; Atoms and the Universe, 1956; Science and World Affairs, 1962; Aspects of Medical Physics, 1966; Pugwash, the First Ten Years, 1967; Scientists in the Quest for Peace, 1972; Nuclear Reactors: to breed or not to breed, 1977; Nuclear Energy and Nuclear Weapon Proliferation, 1979; Nuclear Radiation in Warfare, 1981; Scientists, The Arms Race and Disarmament, 1982; The Arms Race at a Time of Decision, 1984; Nuclear Strategy and World Security, 1985; World Peace and the Developing Countries, 1986; Strategic Defence and the Future of the Arms Race, 1987; Coexistence, Co-operation and Common Security, 1988; Verification of Arms Reductions, 1989; Nuclear Proliferation: technical and economic aspects, 1990; Global Problems and Common Security, 1990; Towards a Secure World in the 21st Century; papers on nuclear physics and radiation biology in Proceedings of Royal Society, Radiation Research, Nature, etc. *Recreations:* recorded music, travel. *Address:* 8 Asmara Road, West Hampstead, NW2 3ST. *T:* 071–435 1471. *Club:* Athenæum.

ROTH, Andrew; Political Correspondent, New Statesman, since 1984; Director, Parliamentary Profiles, since 1955; *b* NY, 23 April 1919; *s* of Emil and Bertha Roth; *m* 1949, Mathilda Anna Friederich (marr. diss. 1984); one *s* one *d. Educ:* City Coll. of NY (BSS); Columbia Univ. (MA); Harvard Univ. Reader, City Coll., 1939; Res. Associate, Inst. of Pacific Relations, 1940; US Naval Intell., 1941–45 (Lieut, SG); Editorial Writer, The Nation, 1945–46; Foreign Corresp., Toronto Star Weekly, 1946–50; London Corresp., France Observateur, Sekai, Singapore Standard, 1950–60; Political Corresp., Manchester Evening News, 1972–84. *Publications:* Japan Strikes South, 1941; French Interests and Policies in the Far East, 1942; Dilemma in Japan, 1945 (UK 1946); The Business Background of MPs, 1959, 7th edn 1980; The MPs' Chart, 1967, 5th edn 1979; Enoch Powell: Tory Tribune, 1970; Can Parliament Decide . . ., 1971; Heath and the Heathmen, 1972; Lord on the Board, 1972; The Prime Ministers, Vol. II (Heath chapter), 1975; Sir Harold Wilson: Yorkshire Walter Mitty, 1977; Parliamentary Profiles: Vol. I, A–D, 1984, 2nd edn 1988; Vol. II, E–K, 1984, 2nd edn 1989; Vol. III, L–R, 1985, 2nd edn 1990; Vol. IV, S–Z, 1985. *Recreations:* sketching, jazz-dancing. *Address:* 34 Somali Road, NW2 3RL. *T:* 071–435 6673; 2 Queen Anne's Gate Buildings, Dartmouth Street, SW1H 9BP. *T:* 071–222 5884, *Fax:* 071–222 5889.

ROTH, Prof. Klaus Friedrich, FRS 1960; Emeritus Professor, University of London; Visiting Professor in Department of Mathematics, Imperial College of Science, Technology and Medicine, since 1988; *b* 29 Oct. 1925; *s* of late Dr Franz Roth and Mathilde Roth (*née* Liebrecht); *m* 1955, Melek Khairy, BSc, PhD. *Educ:* St Paul's Sch.; Peterhouse, Cambridge (Hon. Fellow, 1989); Univ. College, London (Fellow, 1979). BA (Cambridge, 1945); MSc, PhD (London, 1948, 1950). Asst Master, Gordonstoun School, 1945–46. Member of Dept of Mathematics, University College, London, 1948–66; title of Professor in the University of London conferred 1961; Prof. of Pure Maths (Theory of Numbers), Imperial College, London, 1966–88. Visiting Lecturer, 1956–57, Vis. Prof., 1965–66, at Mass Inst. of Techn., USA. Foreign Hon. Mem., Amer. Acad. of Arts and Scis, 1966. Fields Medal awarded at International Congress of Mathematicians, 1958; De Morgan Medal, London Math. Soc., 1983. *Publications:* papers in various mathematical jls. *Recreations:* chess, cinema, ballroom dancing. *Address:* Department of Mathematics, Imperial College, 180 Queen's Gate, SW7 2BZ; 24 Burnsall Street, SW3 3ST. *T:* 071–352 1363; Colbost, 16A Drummond Road, Inverness IV2 4NB. *T:* Inverness (0463) 712595.

ROTH, Prof. Sir Martin, Kt 1972; MD; FRCP; FRCPsych; DPM; Professor of Psychiatry, University of Cambridge, 1977–85, now Emeritus; Fellow, Trinity College, Cambridge, since 1977; *b* Budapest, 6 Nov. 1917; *s* of late Samuel Simon and Regina Roth; *m* 1945, Constance Heller; three *d. Educ:* University of London, St Mary's Hospital. FRCP 1958. MA Cantab; MD Cantab 1984. Formerly: Senior Registrar, Maida Vale, and Maudsley Hosps; Physician, Crichton Royal Hosp., Dumfries; Director of Clinical Research, Graylingwell Hosp.; Prof. of Psychological Medicine, Univ. of Newcastle upon Tyne, 1956–77. Visiting Assistant Professor, in the Department of Psychiatry, McGill University, Montreal, 1954; Consultant, WHO Expert Cttee on Mental Health Problems of Ageing and the Aged, 1958; Member: Med. Cons. Cttee, Nuffield Provincial Hosp. Trust, 1962; Central Health Services Council, Standing Med. Adv. Cttee, Standing Mental Health Adv. Cttee, DHSS, 1966–75; Scientific Adv. Cttee, CIBA Foundn, 1970–; Syndic of Cambridge Univ. Press, 1980–87. Mayne Vis. Prof., Univ. of Queensland, 1968; Albert Sterne Vis. Prof., Univ. of Indiana, 1976; first Andrew Woods Vis. Prof., Univ. of Iowa, 1976. Adolf Meyer Lectr, Amer. Psychiatric Assoc., 1971; Linacre Lectr, St John's Coll., Cambridge, 1984. Pres., Section of Psychiatry, RSM, 1968–69; Member: MRC, 1964–68; Clinical Research Board, MRC, 1964–70; Hon. Dir, MRC Group for study of relationship between functional and organic mental disorders, 1962–68. FRCPsych (Foundn Fellow; Pres., 1971–75; Hon. Fellow, 1975); Distinguished Fellow, Amer. Psychiatric Assoc., 1972; Hon. FRCPSGlas. Corresp. Mem., Deutsche Gesellschaft für Psychiatrie und Nervenheilkunde; Hon. Mem., Société Royale de Médecine Mentale de Belgique. Hon. Fellow: Amer. Coll. Neuropsychopharmacology; Australian and New Zealand College of Psychiatry; Canadian Psychiatric Assoc., 1972. Hon. ScD TCD, 1977. Burlingame Prize, Royal Medico Psychol Assoc., 1951; First Prize, Anna Monika Foundn, 1977; Paul Hoch Prize, Amer. Psychopathological Assoc., 1979; Gold Florin, City of Florence, 1979; Gold Medal, Soc. of Biological Psychiatry, 1980; Kesten Prize, Univ. of Southern Calif, 1983; Sandoz Prize, Internat. Assoc. of Gerontology, 1985; Gold Medal, Max-Planck Inst., 1986. Hon. Citizen, Salamanca, Spain, 1975. Co-Editor: British Jl of Psychiatry, 1967; Psychiatric Developments, 1983–. *Publications:* (with Mayer-Gross and Slater) Clinical Psychiatry, 1954, (with Slater) rev. 3rd edn 1977 (trans. Spanish, Italian, Portuguese, Chinese); (with L. Iversen) Alzheimer's Disease and Related Disorders, 1986; (with J. Kroll) The Reality of Mental Illness, 1986; (jtly) CAMDEX: the Cambridge examination for mental disorders of the elderly, 1988; (ed jtly) Handbook of Anxiety, Vols I and II, 1988; papers on psychiatric aspects of ageing, depressive illness, anxiety states, in various psychiatric and medical journals. *Recreations:* music, literature, conversation, travel. *Address:* Trinity College, Cambridge.

ROTH, Philip; novelist; *b* 19 March 1933; *s* of Herman Roth and Bess Finkel; *m* 1990, Claire Bloom, *qv. Educ:* Bucknell Univ. (AB); Univ. of Chicago (MA). Member of Faculty: Univ. of Chicago, 1956–58; Univ. of Iowa, 1960–62; Princeton Univ., 1962–64; Univ. of Pennsylvania, 1965–78; Hunter Coll. of the City Univ. of New York, 1988–. Hon. degrees: Bucknell, 1979; Bard Coll., 1985; Rutgers, 1987; Columbia, 1987; Hartford, 1989; Brandeis, 1991. *Publications:* Goodbye Columbus, 1959; Letting Go, 1962; When She Was Good, 1967; Portnoy's Complaint, 1969; Our Gang, 1971; The Breast, 1972; The Great American Novel, 1973; My Life as a Man, 1974; Reading Myself and Others, 1975; The Professor of Desire, 1977; The Ghost Writer, 1979; A Philip Roth Reader, 1980; Zuckerman Unbound, 1981; The Anatomy Lesson, 1983; Zuckerman Bound, 1985; The Counterlife, 1987; The Facts, 1988; Deception, 1990; Patrimony, 1991. *Address:* c/o Wylie, Aitken & Stone, 250 W 57th Street, New York, NY 10107, USA..

ROTHENSTEIN, Sir John (Knewstub Maurice), Kt 1952; CBE 1948; KCStG 1977; PhD (London 1931); Hon. LLD (New Brunswick 1961; St Andrews 1964); writer; Director of the Tate Gallery, 1938–64; Hon. Fellow: Worcester College, Oxford, 1963; University College London, 1976; Member: Architectural and Art Advisory Committee, Westminster Cathedral, since 1979 (of Advisory Committee on Decoration, 1953–79); Council, Friends of the Tate Gallery, since 1958; President: Friends of the Bradford City Art Gallery and Museums, since 1973; Friends of the Stanley Spencer Gallery, Cookham, since 1981; *b* London, 11 July 1901; *er s* of Sir William Rothenstein and Alice Mary, *e c* of Walter John Knewstub, of Chelsea; *m* 1929, Elizabeth Kennard Whittington, 2nd *d* of Charles Judson Smith, of Lexington, Kentucky; one *d. Educ:* Bedales School; Worcester College, Oxford (MA); University College, London (PhD). Assistant Professor: of Art History in the University of Kentucky, 1927–28; Department of Fine Arts, University of

Pittsburgh, 1928–29; Director: City Art Gallery, Leeds, 1932–34; City Art Galleries and Ruskin Museum, Sheffield, 1933–38; Member: Executive Committee, Contemporary Art Society, 1938–65; British Council, 1938–64; Art Panel, Arts Council of Great Britain, 1943–56. Rector, University of St Andrews, 1964–67. Visiting Professor: Dept of Fine Arts, Fordham Univ., USA, 1967–68; of History of Art, Agnes Scott Coll., Ga, USA, 1969–70; Distinguished Prof., City Univ. of NY, at Brooklyn Coll., 1971, 1972; Regents' Lectr, Univ. of Calif at Irvine, 1973. Pres., Friends of the Stanley Spencer Gall., 1980–87. Editor, The Masters, 1965–67; Hon. Editor, Museums Jl, 1959–61. Knight Commander, Mexican Order of the Aztec Eagle, 1953. *Publications:* The Portrait Drawings of William Rothenstein, 1889–1925, 1926; Eric Gill, 1927; The Artists of the 1890's, 1928; Morning Sorrow: a novel, 1930; British Artists and the War, 1931; Nineteenth Century Painting, 1932; An Introduction to English Painting, 1933; The Life and Death of Conder, 1938; Augustus John (Phaidon British Artists), 1944; Edward Burra (Penguin Modern Painters), 1945; Manet, 1945; Modern Foreign Pictures in the Tate Gallery, 1949; Turner, 1949; London's River, 1951 (with Father Vincent Turner, SJ); Modern English Painters, vol. I, Sickert to Smith, 1952, vol. II, Lewis to Moore, 1956, vol. III, Wood to Hockney, 1973, new enl. edn, as Modern English Painters: Sickert to Hockney, 1984; The Tate Gallery, 1958 (new edn 1962); Turner, 1960; British Art since 1900: an Anthology, 1962; Sickert, 1961; Paul Nash, 1961; Augustus John, 1962; Matthew Smith, 1962; Turner (with Martin Butlin), 1963; Francis Bacon (with Ronald Alley), 1964; Edward Burra, 1973; Victor Hammer: artist and craftsman, 1978; (ed) Sixteen Letters from Oscar Wilde, 1930; (ed) Stanley Spencer the Man: Correspondence and Reminiscences, 1979; John Nash, 1984; Stanley Spencer, 1989; *autobiography:* Summer's Lease (I), 1965; Brave Day, Hideous Night (II), 1966; Time's Thievish Progress (III), 1970; contribs to DNB. *Television:* Churchill the Painter, COI, 1968; Collection and Recollection, BBC, 1968. *Address:* Beauforest House, Newington, Dorchester-on-Thames, Oxon OX9 8AG. *Clubs:* Athenæum (Hon. Mem.), Chelsea Arts (Hon. Mem.).

See also Baron Dynevor.

ROTHENSTEIN, Michael, RA 1983 (ARA 1977); Hon. RE; painter and print-maker; *b* 1908; *yr s* of late Sir William Rothenstein; *m* 1936, Betty Desmond Fitz-Gerald (marr. diss. 1957); one *s* one *d*; *m* 1958, Diana, 2nd *d* of late Comdr H. C. Arnold-Forster, CMG. *Works* acquired by: Museum of Modern Art, New York; Tate Gallery; British Museum; Victoria and Albert Museum; *exhibitions:* Ljubljana Biennale of Graphic Art; Albertina, Vienna; Tokyo Internat. Print Exhibn, and many others; *retrospective exhibitions:* Kunstnernes Hus, Oslo, 1969; Stoke-on-Trent, 1989; *one-man shows:* The Early Years, Redfern Gall., 1986; Prints of the '50s a nd '60s, Redfern Gall., 1987; Angela Flowers Gall., 1988. *Publications:* Frontiers of Printmaking, 1966; Relief Printing, 1970; Suns and Moons, 1972; Seven Colours (with Edward Lucie Smith), 1975; Song of Songs (folio), 1979. *Address:* Columbia House, Stisted, Braintree, Essex. *T:* Braintree (0376) 25444.

ROTHERHAM, Air Vice-Marshal John Kevitt, CB 1962; CBE 1960; Director-General (Engineering), RAF, 1967–69; retired; *b* 28 Dec. 1910; *s* of Colonel Ewan Rotherham; *m* 1st, 1936, Joan Catherine Penrose (*d* 1940); one *d*; 2nd, 1941, Margot Susan Hayter. *Educ:* Uppingham; Exeter College, Oxford. Joined RAF with Univ. perm. commn, 1933; 17 (F) Sqdn, 1934; 605 (B) Sqdn, 1936; School of Aeronautical Engineering, Henlow, 1936; post-grad. course, Imperial Coll., 1938; 43 (M) Group, 1939; Kidbrooke, 1940; MAP 1941; 41 (M) Group, 1942; HQ Flying Training Comd, 1946; exchange posting with USAF, 1947; Air Ministry, 1948; Joint Services Staff Coll., 1951; No 205 Group, Middle East, 1952; Air Ministry, 1954; seconded to Pakistan Air Force, 1957; Senior Technical Staff Officer, Transport Command, RAF, 1960–63; AOC No 24 (Training) Group, Technical Training Command, RAF, 1963–65; Senior Tech. Staff Officer, Bomber Command, 1965–67. AFRAeS 1949, FRAeS 1967. *Recreation:* fishing. *Address:* Herons, Westbrook Field, Bosham, Chichester, Sussex PO18 8JP. *T:* Bosham (0243) 573346. *Clubs:* Royal Air Force; Bosham Sailing.

ROTHERHAM, Leonard, CBE 1970; DSc; FRS 1963; FEng, FIEE, SFInstE, FIM, FInstP; Hon. Professor, Bath University, since 1985 (Vice-Chancellor, 1969–76); *b* 31 Aug. 1913; *m* 1937, Nora Mary Thompson (*d* 1991); one *s* two *d*. *Educ:* Strutt School, Belper; University College, London. Physicist, Brown Firth Research Laboratories, 1935–46; Head of Metallurgy Dept, RAE Farnborough, 1946–50; Dir, R&D, UKAEA, Industrial Group, Risley, 1950–58. Mem. for Research, Central Electricity Generating Bd, 1958–69; Head of Research, Electricity Supply Industry and Electricity Council, 1965–69. Chm., Adv. Cttee for Scientific and Technical Information, 1970–74. Member: Defence Scientific Adv. Council, 1967–77 (Chm., 1974–77); Central Adv. Council for Science and Technology, 1968–70; Adv. Council for Energy Conservation, 1974–79; Adv. Council for Applied R&D, 1976–81. Governor, Imperial Coll., 1977–89. Hon. LLD Bristol, 1972; Hon. DSc Bath, 1976. Fellow UCL, 1959; FIC 1987; Hon. Fellow, Inst. of Welding, 1965; Hon. Life Mem., American Society of Mechanical Engineers, 1963; President, Instn of Metallurgists, 1964; Inst. of Metals, 1965; Member of Council, Royal Society, 1965–66. Founder Fellow, Fellowship of Engineering, 1976 (Mem. Exec. Council, 1978–80). *Publications:* Creep of Metals, 1951; Research and Innovation, 1984; various scientific and technical papers; also lectures: Hatfield Memorial, 1961; Coal Science, 1961; Calvin Rice (of Amer. Soc. of Mech. Engrs), 1963; 2nd Metallurgical Engineering, Inst. of Metals, 1963. *Address:* Westhanger, Horningsham, Warminster, Wilts. *Club:* Athenæum.

ROTHERMERE, 3rd Viscount *cr* 1919, of Hemsted; **Vere Harold Esmond Harmsworth;** Bt 1910; Baron 1914; Chairman: Daily Mail and General Trust plc, since 1978; Associated Newspapers Holdings Ltd, since 1970; *b* 27 Aug. 1925; *s* of 2nd Viscount Rothermere and of Margaret Hunam, *d* of late William Redhead; *S* father, 1978; *m* 1957, Mrs Patricia Evelyn Beverley Brooks, *d* of John William Matthews, FIAS; one *s* two *d* (and one step *d*). *Educ:* Eton; Kent Sch., Conn, USA. With Anglo Canadian Paper Mills, Quebec, 1948–50; Associated Newspapers Ltd, 1951–; launched: New Daily Mail, 1971; Mail on Sunday, 1982. Trustee, Reuters; Dir, Power Corp., Canada. Pres., Euromoney Publications plc. Pres., Commonwealth Press Union, 1983–89 (Chm., UK Section, 1976); Pres., London Press Club, 1976–81; Patron, London Sch. of Journalism, 1980–. FRSA, FBIM. Commander: Order of Merit (Italy); Order of Lion (Finland). *Recreations:* painting, sailing, reading. *Heir:* *s* Hon. Harold Jonathan Esmond Vere Harmsworth, *b* 3 Dec. 1967. *Address:* 36 rue du Sentier, Paris, France. *Clubs:* Boodle's, Beefsteak; Royal Yacht Squadron; Brook (New York City); Travellers' (Paris).

See also Lord Ogilvy.

ROTHERWICK, 2nd Baron *cr* 1939; **Herbert Robin Cayzer;** Bt 1924; *b* 5 Dec. 1912; *s* of 1st Baron Rotherwick; *S* father 1958; *m* 1952, Sarah-Jane (*d* 1978), *o d* of Sir Michael Nial Slade, 6th Bt; three *s* one *d*. *Educ:* Eton; Christ Church, Oxford (BA). Supplementary Reserve Royal Scots Greys, 1938; served War of 1939–45 with them in Middle East. Former Deputy Chairman British & Commonwealth Shipping Co. Ltd, and Director of other and associated companies. *Heir:* *s* Hon. (Herbert) Robin Cayzer, Lt Life Guards (T&AVR) [*b* 12 March 1954; *m* 1982, Sara, *o d* of R. J. McAlpine, Swettenham Hall, Cheshire; one *s* one *d*]. *Address:* Cornbury Park, Charlbury, Oxfordshire. *T:* Charlbury (0608) 311. *Club:* White's.

ROTHES, 21st Earl of, *cr* before 1457; **Ian Lionel Malcolm Leslie;** Lord Leslie 1445; Baron Ballenbreich 1457; *b* 10 May 1932; *o s* of 20th Earl of Rothes and of Beryl, *o d* of J. Lionel Dugdale; *S* father, 1975; *m* 1955, Marigold, *o d* of Sir David M. Evans Bevan, 1st Bt; two *s*. *Educ:* Eton. Sub-Lt RNVR, 1953. *Heir:* *s* Lord Leslie, *qv*. *Address:* Tanglewood, West Tytherley, Salisbury, Wilts.

ROTHMAN, Sydney; Chairman of Rothmans Tobacco (Holdings) Ltd, 1953–79 (Chairman and Managing Director, Rothmans Ltd, 1929–53); *b* 2 December 1897; *s* of Louis and Jane Rothman; *m* 1929, Jeannette Tropp; one *s* one *d*. *Educ:* Highgate School. Joined L. Rothman & Company, 1919, Partner, 1923, Rothmans Ltd. Ministry of Supply, 1941–45. *Recreation:* golf. *Address:* Barclays Bank, Box 8, St Helier, Jersey.

ROTHNIE, Sir Alan (Keir), KCVO 1980; CMG 1967; HM Diplomatic Service, retired; Chairman, Newsbrief Ltd, since 1985; *b* 2 May 1920; *s* of late John and Dora Rothnie, Aberdeen; *m* 1953, Anne Cadogan Harris, *d* of late Euan Cadogan Harris; two *s* one *d*. *Educ:* Montrose Acad.; St Andrews University. Served RNVR, 1939–45. Entered Diplomatic Service, Nov. 1945; Foreign Office, 1945–46; 3rd Sec., HM Legation, Vienna, 1946–48; 2nd Sec., HM Embassy, Bangkok, 1949–50; FO 1951–53; 1st Sec. HM Embassy, Madrid, 1953–55; Asst Political Agent, Kuwait, 1956–58; FO, 1958–60; Middle East Centre for Arab Studies, Shemlan, 1960–62 (Chargé d'Affaires, HM Embassy, Kuwait, 1961); Commercial Counsellor: HM Embassy, Baghdad, 1963–64; HM Embassy, Moscow, 1965–68; Consul-Gen., Chicago, 1969–72; Ambassador to Saudi Arabia, 1972–76, to Switzerland, 1976–80. Hon. LLD St Andrews, 1981. *Recreations:* rural. *Address:* Little Job's Cross, Rolvenden Layne, Kent TN17 4PP. *T:* Cranbrook (0580) 241350. *Club:* White's.

ROTHSCHILD, family name of **Baron Rothschild.**

ROTHSCHILD, 4th Baron, *cr* 1885; **Nathaniel Charles Jacob Rothschild;** Bt 1847; Chairman: St James's Place Capital plc (formerly J. Rothschild Holdings plc), since 1971; Five Arrows Ltd, since 1980; *b* 29 April 1936; *e s* of 3rd Baron Rothschild, GBE, GM, FRS and Barbara, *o d* of St John Hutchinson, KC; *S* father, 1990; *m* 1961, Serena Mary, *er d* of late Sir Philip Gordon Dunn, 2nd Bt; one *s* three *d*. *Educ:* Eton; Christ Church, Oxford. BA 1st cl. hons History. Chm., Bd of Trustees, National Gallery, 1985–91. Mem. Council, RCA, 1986–. Comdr, Order of Henry the Navigator (Portugal), 1985. *Heir:* *s* Hon. Nathaniel Victor James Rothschild, *b* 12 July 1971. *Address:* 15 St James's Place, SW1A 1NW. *T:* 071–493 8111.

See also E. Rothschild.

ROTHSCHILD, Edmund Leopold de, TD; Director, N. M. Rothschild & Sons, since 1975 (Partner since 1946, Senior Partner, 1960–70, Chairman, 1970–75); Chairman, A. U. R. Hydropower Ltd, since 1980; *b* 2 Jan. 1916; *s* of late Lionel Nathan de Rothschild and Marie Louise Beer; *m* 1st, 1948, Elizabeth Edith Lentner (*d* 1980); two *s* two *d*; 2nd, 1982, Anne, JP, *widow* of J. Malcolm Harrison, OBE. *Educ:* Harrow Sch.; Trinity Coll., Cambridge. Major, RA (TA). Served France, North Africa and Italy, 1939–46 (wounded). Dep. Chairman: Brit. Newfoundland Corp. Ltd, 1963–69; Churchill Falls (Labrador) Corp. Ltd, 1966–69. Mem., Asia Cttee, BNEC, 1970–71, Chm., 1971. Trustee, Queen's Nursing Inst.; Mem. Council, Royal Nat. Pension Fund for Nurses; Pres., Assoc. of Jewish Ex-Servicemen and Women; Vice-Pres., Council of Christians and Jews. Governor, Tech. Univ. of Nova Scotia. Hon. LLD Memorial Univ. of Newfoundland, 1961; Hon. DSc Salford, 1983. Order of the Sacred Treasure, 1st Class (Japan), 1973. *Publication:* Window on the World, 1949. *Recreations:* gardening, fishing, shooting, cine-photography, hunting butterflies. *Address:* New Court, St Swithin's Lane, EC4P 4DU. *T:* 071–280 5000; Exbury House, Exbury, Southampton SO4 1AF. *Clubs:* White's, Portland; Mount Royal (Montreal).

See also L. D. de Rothschild.

ROTHSCHILD, Emma; Senior Research Fellow, King's College, Cambridge, since 1988; *b* 16 May 1948; *d* of 3rd Baron Rothschild, GBE, GM, FRS and of Lady Rothschild, MBE (*née* Teresa Mayor); *m* 1991, Prof. Amartya Kumar Sen, *qv*. *Educ:* Somerville Coll., Oxford (MA); Massachusetts Inst. of Technology (Kennedy Schol. in Econs). Associate Professor: of Humanities, MIT, 1978–80; of Science, Technology and Society, MIT, 1979–88; Dir de Recherches Invité, Ecole des Hautes Etudes en Sciences Sociales, Paris, 1981–82; Res. Advr, World Inst. for Develt Econs Res., 1989–. Mem., OECD Gp of Experts on Science and Technology in the New Socio-Economic Context, 1976–80; OECD Sci. Examiner, Aust., 1984–85. Member: Govg Bd, Stockholm Internat. Peace Res. Inst., 1983–; Govg Bd, Stockholm Envmt Inst., 1989–; Bd, Olof Palme Meml Fund (Stockholm), 1986–; Royal Commn on Environmental Pollution, 1986–. Trustee, Inst. for Public Policy Res., 1988–. Mem., Bd of Dirs, Bull. of the Atomic Scientists, 1983–89. *Publications:* Paradise Lost: the Decline of the Auto-Industrial Age, 1973; articles in learned and other jls. *Address:* King's College, Cambridge CB2 1ST.

ROTHSCHILD, Sir Evelyn de, Kt 1989; Chairman, N. M. Rothschild & Sons Ltd; *b* 29 Aug. 1931; *s* of late Anthony Gustav de Rothschild; *m* 1973, Victoria Schott; two *s* one *d*. *Educ:* Harrow; Trinity Coll., Cambridge. Chairman: Economist Newspaper, 1972–89; United Racecourses Ltd, 1977–. Chm., British Merchant Banking and Securities Houses Assoc. (formerly Accepting Houses Cttee), 1985–89. *Recreations:* art, racing.

ROTHSCHILD, Baron Guy (Edouard Alphonse Paul) de; Officier de la Légion d'Honneur, 1959; Director: Centro Asegurador SA, Madrid; Rothschild Inc., New York; *b* 21 May 1909; *s* of late Baron Edouard de Rothschild and late Baronne de Rothschild (*née* Germaine Halphen); *m* 1st, 1937, Baronne Alix Schey de Koromla (marriage dissolved, 1956; she *d* 1982); one *s*; 2nd, 1957, Baronne Marie-Hélène de Zuylen de Nyevelt (who *m* 1st, Comte François de Nicolay); one *s* and one step *s*. *Educ:* Lycées Condorcet et Louis le Grand, Facultés de Droit et des Lettres (Licencié en Droit). Served War of 1939–45 (Croix de Guerre). Chevalier du Mérite Agricole, 1948. Associé de MM de Rothschild Frères, 1936–67; President: Compagnie du Chemin de Fer du Nord, 1949–68; Banque Rothschild, 1968–78; Société Imétal, 1975–79. Mem., Société d'Encouragement. *Publication:* The Whims of Fortune (autobiog.), 1985. *Recreation:* haras et écurie de courses, golf. *Address:* 2 rue Saint-Louis-en-l'Isle, 75008 Paris, France. *Clubs:* Nouveau Cercle, Automobile Club de France.

ROTHSCHILD, Leopold David de, CBE 1985; Director, N. M. Rothschild & Sons Ltd, since 1970 (Partner, 1956–70); *b* 12 May 1927; *yr s* of Lionel de Rothschild and Marie Louise Beer. *Educ:* Bishops Coll. Sch., Canada; Harrow; Trinity Coll., Cambridge. Director of Bank of England, 1970–83. Chairman: Anglo Venezuelan Soc., 1975–78; English Chamber Orchestra and Music Soc. Ltd, 1963; Bach Choir, 1976; Music Adv. Cttee, British Council, 1986–; Council, RCM, 1988– (FRCM 1977). Trustee, Science Mus., 1987–; Mem. Council, Winston Churchill Meml Trust, 1990–. Order of Francisco de Miranda, 1st cl. (Venezuela), 1978. *Recreations:* music, sailing. *Address:* New Court, St Swithin's Lane, EC4. *T:* 071–280 5000. *Clubs:* Brooks's; Royal Yacht Squadron.

See also E. L. de Rothschild.

ROTHSCHILD, Hon. Miriam Louisa, (Hon. Mrs Miriam Lane), CBE 1982; FRS 1985; *b* 5 Aug. 1908; *e d* of Hon. N. C. Rothschild, 2nd *s* of 1st Baron Rothschild and

Rozsika de Wertheimstein; *m* 1943, Capt. George Lane, MC (marriage dissolved, 1957); one *s* three *d* (and one *s* one *d* decd). *Educ:* home. Member: Zoological and Entomological Research Coun.; Marine Biological Assoc.; Royal Entomological Soc.; Systematics Assoc.; Soc. for Promotion of Nature Reserves, etc.; Ed., Novitates Zoologica, 1938–41; Mem., Publications Cttee, Zoological Soc.; Foreign Office, 1940–42; Trustee, British Museum of Natural History, 1967–75. Mem., Amer. Acad. of Arts and Scis. Vis. Prof. in Biology, Royal Free Hosp. Romanes Lectr, Oxford, 1985. Hon. Fellow, St Hugh's Coll., Oxford. Hon. DSc: Oxford, 1968; Gothenburg, 1983; Hull, 1984; Northwestern Univ., 1986; Leicester, 1987; Open Univ., 1989. VMH 1990. Defence Medal (1940–45). *Publications:* Catalogue Rothschild Collection of Fleas (British Museum): vol. I 1953, vol. II 1956, vol. III 1962,vol. IV 1966, vol. V 1971, vol. VI 1983; (with Theresa Clay) Fleas, Flukes and Cuckoos, 1952; (with Clive Farrell) The Butterfly Gardener, 1983; Dear Lord Rothschild (biog.), 1983; (with Prof. Schlein and Prof. Ito) Atlas of Insect Tissue, 1985; Animals & Man, 1986; Butterfly Cooing Like a Dove, 1990; 300 contribs to scientific jls. *Recreation:* watching butterflies. *Address:* Ashton, Peterborough. *Clubs:* Queen's, Entomological.

ROTHSCHILD, Baron Robert, KCMG (Hon.) 1963; Grand Officier de l'Ordre de Leopold (Belgium); Belgian Ambassador to the Court of St James's, 1973–76; *b* 16 Dec. 1911; *s* of Bernard Rothschild and Marianne von Rynveld; one *d*. *Educ:* Univ. of Brussels (DrRerPol). Entered Belgian Foreign Office: Brussels, 1937; Lisbon, 1942; Chungking, China, 1944; Shanghai, 1946, Washington, USA, 1950; Paris, NATO, 1952; Brussels, 1954; Ambassador to Yugoslavia, 1958; Head of Mission, Katanga, Congo, 1960; Brussels, 1960; Ambassador to: Switzerland, 1964; France, 1966. *Publications:* La Chute de Chiang Kai-Shek, 1973 (Paris); Les Chemins de Munich, 1988 (Paris). *Recreations:* gardening, travel. *Address:* 43 Ranelagh Grove, SW1; 1 Rue E. Dereume, Rixensart 1330, Belgium.

ROTHSTEIN, Saul; Solicitor to the Post Office, 1976–81; *b* 4 July 1920; *s* of late Simon Rothstein and late Zelda Rothstein; *m* 1949, Judith Noemi (*née* Katz); two *d*. *Educ:* Church Institute Sch., Bolton; Manchester Univ (LLB). Admitted solicitor, 1947. War service, RAF, 1941–46 (Flt-Lt). Entered Solicitor's Dept, General Post Office, 1949, Asst Solicitor, 1963; Director, Advisory Dept, Solicitor's Office, Post Office, 1972–76. *Recreations:* chamber music, walking, travel. *Address:* 9 Templars Crescent, Finchley, N3 3QR. *T:* 081–346 3701.

ROTHWELL, Margaret Irene; HM Diplomatic Service; Ambassador to Côte d'Ivoire, since 1990, and concurrently to the Republic of Niger and the People's Democratic Republic of Burkina; *b* 25 Aug. 1938; *d* of Harry Rothwell and Martha (*née* Goedecke). *Educ:* Southampton Grammar School for Girls; Lady Margaret Hall, Oxford (BA LitHum). Foreign Office, 1961; Third, later Second Secretary, UK Delegn to Council of Europe, Strasbourg, 1964; FO, 1966; Second Sec. (Private Sec. to Special Representative in Africa), Nairobi, 1967; Second, later First Sec., Washington, 1968; FCO, 1972; First Sec. and Head of Chancery, Helsinki, 1976; FCO, 1980; Counsellor and Hd of Trng Dept, FCO, 1981–83; Counsellor, Consul-Gen. and Head of Chancery, Jakarta, 1984–87; Overseas Inspectorate, FCO, 1987–90. *Recreations:* gardening, cooking, tennis. *Address:* c/o Foreign and Commonwealth Office, SW1A 2AH.

ROTHWELL, Sheila Gwendoline; Director, Centre for Employment Policy Studies, Henley Administrative Staff College, since 1979; *b* 22 Aug. 1935; *d* of Reginald Herbert Paine and Joyce Margaret Paine; *m* 1958, Miles Rothwell (marr. diss. 1968); one *s* one *d*; *m* 1985, Graham L. Reid. *Educ:* Wyggeston Sch., Leicester; Westfield Coll., Univ. of London (BA Hons History, 1956); LSE (MScEcon Indust. Relations, 1972). Teaching and res., London, Trinidad and Barbados, 1958–68; Res. Officer/Lectr, Indust. Relations Dept, LSE, 1969–75; Asst Sec. (Negotiations), National Union of Bank Employees, 1975–76; Asst Chief Exec., Equal Opportunities Commn, 1976–78. Res. Sec. to House of Lords Select Cttee on Anti-Discrimination Bill, 1972–73. Member: Williams Cttee on Obscenity and Film Censorship, 1978–79; ACAS Panel of Arbitrators, 1988– (ACAS Indep. Expert on Equal Pay, 1984–87). Chm. Governors, Henley (Tertiary) Coll., 1989–. *Publications:* Labour Turnover, 1980; (ed) Strategic Planning for Human Resources, 1991; contrib. Internat. Labour Rev., and Brit. Jl of Indust. Relations. *Recreations:* cinema, theatre, walking, dressmaking, cycling. *Address:* 4 The Gardens, Fingest, Henley, Oxon RG9 6QF.

ROUGIER, Maj.-Gen. Charles Jeremy, CB 1986; FICE; Director, Royal Horticultural Society's Garden, Rosemoor, since 1988; *b* 23 Feb. 1933; *s* of late Lt-Col and Mrs C. L. Rougier; *m* 1964, Judith Cawood Ellis; three *s* one *d*. *Educ:* Marlborough Coll.; Pembroke Coll., Cambridge (MA). FICE 1986. Aden, 1960; Instructor, RMA Sandhurst, 1961–62; psc 1963; MA to MGO, 1964–66; comd 11 Engineer Sqn, Commonwealth Bde, 1966–68; jssc 1968; Company Comd, RMA Sandhurst, 1969–70; Directing Staff, Staff Coll., Camberley, 1970–72; CO 21 Engineer Regt, BAOR, 1972–74; Staff of Chief of Defence Staff, 1974–77; Commandant, Royal Sch. of Military Engineering, 1977–79; RCDS 1980; COS, Headquarters Northern Ireland, 1981; Asst Chief of General Staff (Trng), 1982–83; Dir of Army Training, 1983–84; Chm., Review of Officer Training and Educn Study, 1985; Engr-in-Chief (Army), 1985–88, retd. Col Comdt, RE, 1987–. *Recreations:* squash, hill walking, DIY, gardening. *Address:* c/o Lloyds Bank Plc, 2 Fore Street, Torrington, Devon EX38 8HJ. *Club:* Army and Navy.

ROUGIER, Hon. Sir Richard George, Kt 1986; **Hon. Mr Justice Rougier;** Judge of the High Court of Justice, Queen's Bench Division, since 1986; *b* 12 Feb. 1932; *s* of late George Ronald Rougier, CBE, QC, and Georgette Heyer, novelist; *m* 1962, Susanna Allen Flint (*née* Whitworth); one *s*. *Educ:* Marlborough Coll.; Pembroke Coll., Cambridge (Exhibr, BA). Called to Bar, Inner Temple, 1956, Bencher 1979. QC 1972; a Recorder, 1973–86. *Recreations:* fishing, golf, bridge. *Address:* Royal Courts of Justice, WC2A 2LL. *Clubs:* Garrick; Rye Golf.

ROUND, Prof. Nicholas Grenville; Stevenson Professor of Hispanic Studies, in the University of Glasgow, since 1972; *b* 6 June 1938; *s* of Isaac Eric Round and Laura Christabel (*née* Poole); *m* 1966, Ann Le Vin; one *d*. *Educ:* Boyton CP Sch., Cornwall; Launceston Coll.; Pembroke Coll., Oxford. BA (1st cl. Hons, Spanish and French) 1959; MA 1963; DPhil 1967. Lecturer in Spanish, Queen's Univ. of Belfast, 1962–71, Reader, 1971–72; Warden, Alanbrooke Hall, QUB, 1970–72. Mem., Exec. Cttee, Strathclyde Region Labour Party, 1986–. Officer, Order of Isabel the Catholic (Spain), 1990. *Publications:* Unamuno: Abel Sánchez: a critical guide, 1974; The Greatest Man Uncrowned: a study of the fall of Alvaro de Luna, 1986; trans., Tirso de Molina, Damned for Despair, 1986; (ed) Re-reading Unamuno, 1989; contribs to: Mod. Lang. Review, Bulletin Hispanic Studies, Proc. Royal Irish Academy, etc. *Recreations:* reading, music, all aspects of Cornwall. *Address:* Department of Hispanic Studies, The University, Glasgow G12 8QQ. *T:* 041–339 8855. *Club:* (Hon. Life Mem.) Students' Union (Belfast).

ROUNTREE, Peter Charles Robert; His Honour Judge Rountree; a Circuit Judge, since 1986; *b* 28 April 1936; *s* of late Francis Robert George Rountree and Mary Felicity Patricia Rountree (*née* Wilson); *m* 1968, Nicola Mary (*née* Norman-Butler); one *s* one step *d*. *Educ:* Uppingham School; St John's College, Cambridge (MA). Called to the Bar, Inner Temple, 1961; a Recorder, April–July 1986. *Recreations:* sailing, golf, tennis. *Address:* c/o Lloyds Bank plc, 112/114 Kensington High Street, W8. *Clubs:* Royal Automobile, Royal Yacht Squadron, Royal London Yacht; New Zealand Golf.

ROUS, family name of **Earl of Stradbroke.**

ROUS, Lt-Gen. Hon. William Edward, OBE 1981 (MBE 1974); Military Secretary, Ministry of Defence, since 1991; *b* 22 Feb. 1939; *s* of 5th Earl of Stradbroke, and Pamela Catherine Mabell, *d* of Captain Hon. Edward James Kay-Shuttleworth; *m* 1970, Judith Rosemary Persse; two *s*. *Educ:* Harrow; Royal Military Academy, Sandhurst. Commissioned Coldstream Guards, 1959; Comd 2nd Bn Coldstream Guards, 1979–81, Comd 1st Inf. Brigade, 1983–84; Dir of Public Relations (Army), 1985–87; GOC 4th Armoured Div., BAOR, 1987–89; Comdt, Staff Coll., Camberley, 1989–91. *Address:* RHQ Coldstream Guards, Wellington Barracks, SW1E 6HQ.

ROUSE, Sir Anthony (Gerald Roderick), KCMG 1969 (CMG 1961); OBE 1945; HM Diplomatic Service, retired; *b* 9 April 1911; *s* of late Lt-Col Maxwell Rouse and of Mrs Rouse, Eastbourne; *m* 1935, Beatrice Catherine Ellis. *Educ:* Harrow; Heidelberg Univ. Joined HAC 1935; RA (T) 1938; 2 Lt 1940; transf. to Intelligence Corps; served MEF and CMF on staff of 3rd Corps (commendation); Lt-Col 1944. Entered Foreign Service, 1946; First Secretary (Information), Athens, 1946; Foreign Office, 1949. British Embassy, Moscow, 1952–54; Counsellor, 1955; Office of UK High Commissioner, Canberra, 1955–57; HM Inspector of Foreign Service Establishments, 1957–59; Counsellor (Information) British Embassy, Bonn, 1959–62; British Deputy Commandant, Berlin, 1962–64; HM Minister, British Embassy, Rome, 1964–66; Consul-General, New York, 1966–71. *Address:* St Ritas, Paradise Drive, Eastbourne, E Sussex.

ROUSE, E(dward) Clive, MBE 1946; Medieval Archæologist, retired; Specialist in Mural and Panel Paintings; Lecturer; *b* 15 October 1901; *s* of late Edward Foxwell Rouse (Stroud, Gloucestershire and Acton, Middlesex) and late Frances Sarah Rouse (*née* Sams). *Educ:* Gresham's School; St Martin's School of Art. On leaving school studied art and medieval antiquities, 1920–21; FSA London, 1937 (Mem. of Council, 1943–44); FRSA 1968. President: Royal Archæological Institute, 1969–72 (Vice-Pres., 1965); Bucks Archaeological Soc., 1969–79. Liveryman, Fishmongers' Company, 1962. Served War of 1939–45, RAFVR (Intelligence); Flight-Lt, 1941–45; MBE for special services at Central Interpretation Unit, Medmenham. Hon. MA Oxon, 1969; Hon. DLitt Sussex, 1983. *Publications:* The Old Towns of England, 1936 (twice reprinted); Discovering Wall Paintings, 1968 (reprinted); (jointly) Guide to Buckinghamshire, 1935; contributor to: The Beauty of Britain, 1935; Collins' Guide to English Parish Churches, 1958. Papers in Archæologia, Antiquaries' Journal, Archæological Journal, and publications of many County Archæological Societies. *Recreations:* reading, bird watching. *Address:* Oakfield, North Park, Gerrards Cross, Bucks SL9 8JR. *T:* Gerrards Cross (0753) 882595.

ROUSSEAU, Paul Emile; Agent General in London for Saskatchewan, since 1986; *b* 20 Dec. 1929; *m* 1952, Janine Ducharme; five *d* (and one *d* decd). *Educ:* Fort Frances, Ont, Canada. Pres., Melville Motors, Melville, Sask, 1958–60; Gen. Man., Neil Motors, Regina, Sask, 1960–68; Pres. and Chief Exec. Officer, Crest View Chrysler Ltd, Regina, 1968–77; Mem., Sask Legislature, 1978–86; Minister: of Econ. Develt and Trade, Sask, 1982–83; of Revenue and Financial Services, Sask, 1983–86. *Recreation:* golf. *Address:* Flat 3, 2 Avenue Road, NW8 7PU. *T:* 071–586 0830. *Clubs:* East India, Royal Automobile, Royal Over-Seas League.

ROUSSEL, (Philip) Lyon, OBE 1974; Controller, Arts Division, British Council, 1979–83; retired; *b* 17 Oct. 1923; *s* of late Paul Marie Roussel and Beatrice (*née* Cuthbert; later Lady Murray); *m* 1959, Elisabeth Mary, *d* of Kenneth and Kathleen Bennett; one *s* one *d*. *Educ:* Hurstpierpoint Coll.; St Edmund Hall, Oxford (MA, Cert. Public and Social Admin); Chelsea Sch. of Art. Served Indian Army in Parachute Regt, 1942–46 (Major); Parachute Regt (TA), 1946–50. Sudan Political Service, 1950–55; Principal, War Office, 1955–56; Associated Newspapers, 1956–57; British Council, 1960–83: India, 1960–67 (Regional Rep., Western and Central India, 1964–67); Dir, Scholarships, 1967–71; Rep. and Cultural Attaché, British Embassy, Belgium and Luxembourg, 1971–76; Europalia-Great Britain Festival Cttee, 1973; Cultural Attaché (Counsellor), British Embassy, Washington, 1976–79. Sponsorship Consultant, National Theatre, 1983–84. Member: Fest. of India Cttee, 1981–82; British Adv. Cttee, Britain Salutes New York, 1981–83; Bd, The Hanover Band, 1984–87; Common Room, Wolfson Coll., Oxford, 1988. FRGS 1981; FRSA 1979. *Recreations:* painting, looking at pictures, travel, tennis and a barn in France. *Address:* 26 High Street, Woodstock, Oxford OX7 1TG. *Clubs:* Athenæum; Oxford Union; Probus (Woodstock); Woodstock Tennis.

ROUSSOS, Stavros G.; Secretary General, Ministry of Foreign Affairs, Greece, 1980–82, retired; *b* 1918; *m*; two *s* one *d*. *Educ:* Univ. of Lyons (LèsL); Univ. of Paris (LèsL, LèsScPol, LLD). Entered Greek Diplomatic Service as Attaché, Min. of Foreign Affairs, 1946; Mem., Greek Delegn to Gen. Assembly of UN, 1948 and 1954–55; Sec. to Permanent Mission of Greece to UN in New York, 1950; Consul, Alexandria, 1955; i/c Greek Consulate General, Cairo, 1956; Counsellor, 1959; Min. of Foreign Affairs, 1959–61; Mem., Perm. Delegn of Greece to EEC, Brussels, 1962; Perm. Rep. to EEC, 1969; Dir-Gen., Econ. and Commercial Affairs, Min. of Foreign Affairs, 1972; Ambassador of Greece to UK, 1974–79; Alternate Sec. Gen., Min. of Foreign Affairs, 1979–80. Grand Comdr, Order of Phoenix; Commander: Order of Belgian Crown; Order of Merit of Egypt. *Publication:* The Status of Dodecanese Islands in International Law, 1940 (Paris). *Address:* 5 Loukianou Street, Athens 10675, Greece.

ROUT, Owen Howard, FCIB; Executive Director (UK Operations), Barclays PLC and Barclays Bank PLC, 1987–90; Chairman: Barclays Financial Services Ltd, 1988–90; Mercantile Group, since 1989; Starmin PLC, since 1990; *b* 16 April 1930; *s* of Frederick Owen and Marion Rout; *m* 1954, Jean (*née* Greetham); two *d*. *Educ:* Grey High Sch., Port Elizabeth, SA. ACIS. Dir, Barclays Bank UK Ltd, 1977–87; Gen. Man., Barclays PLC and Barclays Bank PLC, 1982–87. Chairman: Barclays Insurance Services Co. Ltd, 1982–85; Barclays Insurance Brokers International Ltd, 1982–85; Director: Spreadeagle Insurance Co. Ltd, 1983–85; Baric Ltd, 1982–84; Albaraka Internat. Bank, 1990–. Chartered Institute of Bankers: Mem. Council, 1985–90; Treas., 1986–90. Mem., Supervisory Bd, Banking World Magazine, 1986–90. *Recreations:* watching sport—Rugby and cricket, playing golf, listening to music, gardening. *Address:* Mercantile Group, PO Box No 200, Churchill Plaza, Churchill Way, Basingstoke, Hants RG1 1GH. *Clubs:* Headingley Taverners (Leeds); Pannal Golf (Harrogate); Saffron Walden Golf.

ROUTH, Donald Thomas; Under Secretary, Department of the Environment, 1978–90; *b* 22 May 1936; *s* of Thomas and Flora Routh; *m* 1961, Janet Hilda Allum. *Educ:* Leeds Modern Sch. Entered WO, Northern Comd, York, as Exec. Officer, 1954; Nat. Service, RN, 1954–56; Higher Exec. Officer, Comd Secretariat, Kenya, 1961–64; Asst Principal, Min. of Housing and Local Govt, 1964–66; Asst Private Sec. to Minister, 1966–67; Principal, 1967; on loan to Civil Service Selection Bd, 1971; Asst Sec., DoE, 1972; Under Sec., 1978; Regional Dir, West Midlands, 1978–81; Hd of Construction Industries Directorate, 1981–85; Dir of Senior Staff Management, 1985–86; Controller, The Crown Suppliers, 1986.

ROUTLEDGE, Alan, CBE 1979; *b* 12 May 1919; *s* of George and Rose Routledge, Wallasey, Cheshire; *m* 1949, Irene Hendry, Falkirk, Stirlingshire; one *s* (and one *s* decd). *Educ:* Liscard High Sch., Wallasey. Served Army, Cheshire (Earl of Chester's) Yeomanry, 1939–46. Control Commn for Germany, 1946–51; Diplomatic Wireless Service of FO (now Foreign and Commonwealth Office), 1951–79: Head, Cypher and Signals Branch, 1962; Head, Commns Planning Staff, 1973; Head, Commns Ops Dept, 1979; retired FCO, 1979. *Recreations:* English history, cricket, golf. *Address:* 15 Ilford Court, Elmbridge, Cranleigh, Surrey GU6 8TJ. *T:* Cranleigh (0483) 276669. *Clubs:* Civil Service; Old Liscardians.

ROUTLEDGE, (Katherine) Patricia; actress; *b* 17 Feb. 1929; *d* of Isaac Edgar Routledge and Catherine (*née* Perry). *Educ:* Birkenhead High Sch.; Univ. of Liverpool; Bristol Old Vic Theatre Sch.; Guildhall Sch. of Music. *Theatre* appearances include: A Midsummer's Night Dream, Liverpool Playhouse, 1952; The Duenna, Westminster, 1954; musical version, The Comedy of Errors, Arts, 1956; The Love Doctor, Piccadilly, 1959; revue, Out of My Mind, Lyric, Hammersmith, 1961; Little Mary Sunshine, Comedy, 1962; Virtue in Danger, Mermaid, transf. Strand, 1963; How's the World Treating You?, Hampstead Theatre Club, 1965, New Arts, transf. Wyndham's, Comedy and Broadway, 1966; Darling of the Day, George Abbott, NY, 1967 (Antoinette Perry Award); The Caucasian Chalk Circle, The Country Wife, and The Magistrate, Chichester Fest., 1969; Cowardy Custard, Mermaid, 1972; Dandy Dick, Chichester Fest., transf. Garrick, 1973; 1600 Pennsylvania Avenue, Mark Hellinger, NY, 1976; Pirates of Penzance, NY, 1980; Noises Off, Savoy, 1981; When the Wind Blows, Whitehall, 1983; Richard III, RSC, 1984–85; Candide, Old Vic, 1988–89 (Laurence Olivier Award); Come for the Ride (one-woman show), Playhouse, 1989; *television* appearances include: Doris and Doreen, 1978; A Woman of No Importance, 1982; Victoria Wood As Seen on TV, 1983–86; Marjorie and Men, 1985; A Lady of Letters, 1988; Keeping Up Appearances; many radio plays. *Address:* c/o Marmont Management Ltd, Langham House, 308 Regent Street, W1R 5AL.

ROUX, Michel André; Director and Chef de Cuisine, since 1967; *b* 19 April 1941; *s* of late Henry Roux and of Germaine Triger; *m* 1984, Robyn (Margaret Joyce); one *s* two *d* by previous marr. *Educ:* Ecole Primaire, Saint Mande; Brevet de Maîtrise (Pâtisserie). Apprenticeship, Pâtisserie Loyal, Paris, 1955–57; Commis Pâtissier-Cuisinier, British Embassy, Paris, 1957–59; Commis de Cuisine with Miss Cécile de Rothschild, Paris, 1959–60; Military service, 1960–62, at Versailles and Colomb Bechar, Sahara; Chef with Miss Cécile de Rothschild, 1962–67; came to England, 1967; restaurants opened: Le Gavroche, 1967; Le Poulbot, 1969; Waterside Inn, 1972; Gavvers, 1981. Mem., UK Br., Académie Culinaire de France, 1984–. TV series, At Home with the Roux Brothers, 1988. Numerous French and British prizes and awards, including: Médaille d'Or, Cuisiniers Français, 1972; Restaurateur of the Year, Caterer & Hotelkeeper, 1985; Personnalité de l'Année, Gastronomie dans le Monde, Paris, 1985; Culinary Trophy, Assoc. of Maîtres-Pâtissiers La Saint Michel, 1986; Men of the Year (Radar), 1989. Chevalier, National Order of Merit (France), 1987; Officer, Order of Agricultural Merit (France), 1987; Chevalier, Order of Arts and of Letters (France), 1990. *Publications:* (all with Albert Roux): New Classic Cuisine, 1983 (French edn, 1985); The Roux Brothers on Pâtisserie, 1986; At Home with the Roux Brothers, 1988; French Country Cooking, 1989; Cooking for Two, 1991. *Recreations:* shooting, walking, skiing. *Address:* The Waterside Inn, Ferry Road, Bray, Berks SL6 2AT. *T:* Maidenhead (0628) 20691; River Cottage, Ferry Road, Bray, Berks. *Club:* The Benedicts.

ROW, Hon. Sir John Alfred, Kt 1974; Sugar Cane Farmer since 1926; retd as Minister for Primary Industries, Queensland, Australia, 1963–72; *b* Hamleigh, Ingham, Qld, Aust., 1 Jan. 1905; *s* of Charles Edward and Emily Harriet Row; *m* 1st, 1929, Gladys M. (decd), *d* of late H. E. Hollins; one *d*; 2nd, 1966, Irene, *d* of late F. C. Gough. *Educ:* Toowoomba Grammar Sch., Qld; Trebonne State Sch., Qld. Mem. for Hinchinbrook, Qld Legislative Assembly, 1960–72. Mem. Victoria Mill Suppliers Cttee and Herbert River Cane Growers Exec., 1932–60. Rep. Local Cane Prices Bd, 1948–60; Dir, Co-op Cane Growers Store, 1955–60; Councillor, Hinchinbrook Shire, and Rep. on Townsville Regional Electricity Bd, 1952–63; Life Mem.: Aust. Sugar Producers' Assoc.; Herbert River Pastoral and Agricultural Assoc. *Recreations:* bowls (past Pres. and Trustee of Ingham Bowls Club), gardening. *Address:* 10 Gort Street, Ingham, Queensland 4850, Australia. *T:* (077) 761671.

ROWALLAN, 3rd Baron *cr* 1911; **Arthur Cameron Corbett;** *b* 17 Dec. 1919; *s* of 2nd Baron Rowallan, KT, KBE, MC, TD, and Gwyn Mervyn (*d* 1971), *d* of J. B. Grimond, St Andrews; *S* father, 1977; *m* 1st, 1945, Eleanor Mary (marr. diss. 1962), *o d* of late Captain George Boyle, The Royal Scots Fusiliers; one *s* three *d*; 2nd, 1963, April Ashley (marr. annulled, 1970). *Educ:* Eton; Balliol College, Oxford. Served War of 1939–45. Croix de Guerre (France), 1944. *Heir: s* Hon. John Polson Cameron Corbett [*b* 8 March 1947; *m* 1st, 1970, Susan Jane Dianne Green (marr. diss. 1983); one *s* one *d*; 2nd, 1984, Sandrew Filomena, *d* of William Bryson; one *s* one *d*]. *Address:* c/o Hon. John Corbett, Meiklemosside, Fenwick, Ayrshire KA3 6AY.

ROWAN, Carl Thomas; Syndicated columnist, correspondent, Chicago Sun-Times; radio and TV commentator, Post-Newsweek Broadcasting; Roving Editor, Reader's Digest; *b* 11 August 1925; *s* of Thomas D. and Johnnie B. Rowan; *m* 1950, Vivien Murphy; two *s* one *d*. *Educ:* Tennessee State University; Washburn University; Oberlin Coll.; University of Minnesota. Mem. Staff of Minneapolis Tribune, 1948–61; Dept of State, 1961–63; US Ambassador to Finland, 1963–64; Director, United States Information Agency, Washington, DC, 1964–65. Hon. DLitt: Simpson Coll., 1957; Hamline Univ., 1958; Oberlin Coll., 1962; Dr of Humane Letters: Washburn Univ., 1964; Talladega Coll., 1965; St Olaf Coll., 1966; Knoxville Coll., 1966; Rhode Island Coll., 1970; Maine Univ., 1971; American Univ., 1980; Dr of Laws: Howard Univ., 1964; Alfred Univ., 1964; Temple Univ., 1964; Atlanta Univ., 1965; Allegheny Coll., 1966; Colby Coll., 1968; Clark Univ., 1971; Notre Dame, 1973; Dr of Public Admin., Morgan State Coll., 1964; Dr of Letters: Wooster Coll., 1968; Miami Univ., 1982; Drexel Inst. of Technology; Dr of Science Georgetown Med. Sch., 1982. *Publications:* South of Freedom, 1953; The Pitiful and the Proud, 1956; Go South to Sorrow, 1957; Wait Till Next Year, 1960; Between Us Blacks, 1974. *Recreations:* tennis, golf and bowling, singing and dancing. *Address:* 3116 Fessenden Street North-West, Washington, DC 20008, USA. *Clubs:* Federal City, Indian Spring, (Washington, DC).

ROWAN, Patricia Adrienne, (Mrs Ivan Rowan); journalist; Editor, The Times Educational Supplement, since 1989; *d* of late Henry Matthew Talintyre and of Gladys Talintyre; *m* 1960, Ivan Settle Harris Rowan; one *s*. *Educ:* Harrow County Grammar School for Girls. Time & Tide, 1952–56; Sunday Express, 1956–57; Daily Sketch, 1957–58; News Chronicle, 1958–60; Granada Television, 1961–62; Sunday Times, 1962–66; TES, 1972–. FRSA 1989. *Publications:* What Sort of Life?, 1980; (contrib.) Education—the Wasted Years?, 1988. *Recreations:* cookery, gardening. *Address:* The Times Educational Supplement, Priory House, St John's Lane, EC1M 4BX. *T:* 071–253 3000. *Club:* Reform.

See also D. G. Talintyre.

ROWAN-LEGG, Allan Aubrey; President, Edcom Ltd, Canada, since 1985 (Vice President, Western Region, 1976–85); *b* 19 May 1912; *m* 1944, Daphne M. Ker; three *d*. Dir, Vice-Pres. and Gen. Sales Man., Interlake Fuel Oil Ltd, and Interlake Steel Products, 1955–57; Pres. and Dir, Superior Propane Ltd, Northern Propane Gas Co., 1957–63; Dir, Vice-Pres. and Gen. Man., Garlock of Canada Ltd, and Yale Rubber Mfg Co. of Canada Ltd, 1963–64; Regional Dir for Ont., Canadian Corp. for 1967 World Exhibn, 1964–67; Agent General for Ontario in UK, 1967–72; Man. Dir, Canada Permanent Mortgage Corp. and Canada Permanent Trust Co., 1973–75; Director: Strata Council, 1989–; Wedgewood Estates, 1989–. Chm. and Pres., Art Gallery of Greater Victoria, BC, 1980, then ex officio, 1980–83. Liveryman, Painter Stainers Co., 1969–. Freeman of City of London, 1969. Canada Centennial Medal. *Recreations:* swimming, travelling. *Address:* #9–2200 Arbutus Cove Lane 477–0017, Victoria, British Columbia V8N 6J9, Canada. *Clubs:* Union, Victoria, Harbourside Rotary (Hon. Director and Hon. Mem.; Pioneer Rotarian, 1988) (Victoria, BC).

ROWE, Prof. Adrian Harold Redfern, FDSRCS; Professor of Conservative Dentistry, University of London, at Guy's Hospital, 1971–91; Dean of Dental Studies, 1985–89, Dean of Dental Sch., 1989–91, and Head of Department of Conservative Dental Surgery, 1967–91, United Medical and Dental Schools of Guy's and St Thomas' Hospitals; *b* 30 Dec. 1925; *y s* of late Harold Ridges Rowe and Emma Eliza (*née* Matthews), Lymington, Hants; *m* 1951, Patricia Mary Flett; three *s*. *Educ:* King Edward VI Sch., Southampton; Guy's Hosp. Dental Sch. (BDS 1948, distinguished in Surgery, Op. Dental Surgery, Dental Surgery and Orthodontics; distinguished in Dental Anatomy, 2nd BDS, 1946); MDS London, 1965. FDSRCS 1954; MCCD RCS, 1989. Nat. Service, RADC, 1949–50. Guy's Hospital Dental School: part-time practice and teaching, 1950–63; Sen. Lectr, 1963–67; Hon. Consultant, 1966–; Univ. Reader, 1967–71; London University: Chm., Bd of Studies in Dentistry, 1980–83; Mem., Senate, 1981–83. Member: Lewisham and N Southwark DHA, 1986–90; Special HA, 1986–90. Member: Dental Sub-Cttee, UGC, 1974–83; Council, Medical Defence Union, 1977–; Specialist Adv. Cttee in Restorative Dentistry, 1979–85; Bd, Faculty in Dental Surgery, RCS, 1980– (Vice Dean, 1987); Faculty Advr for SE Thames reg., RCS, 1983–89; President: British Endodontic Soc., 1964 (Hon. Mem., 1974); British Soc. for Restorative Dentistry, 1978. Past or present examiner in dental surgery in Univs of Belfast, Birmingham, Cardiff, Colombo, Dublin, Dundee, Edinburgh, Lagos, London, Malaysia, Malta, Manchester, Nairobi, Newcastle and Singapore; Statutory Exam. of GDC; Examnr for Licence and Fellowship exams of RCS and for Fellowship of RCSI. Dir, Medical Sickness Annuity and Life Assce Soc., 1987–91. Governor: UMDS of Guy's and St Thomas' Hosps, 1985–; Eastman Dental Hosp., 1986–90. Freeman, City of London, 1990; Mem., Soc. of Apothecaries. *Publications:* Companion to Dental Studies, vol. I: Book I, Anatomy, Biochemistry and Physiology, 1982; Book II, Dental Anatomy and Embryology, 1981; vol. II, Clinical Methods, Medicine, Pathology and Pharmacology, 1988; vol. III, Clinical Dentistry, 1986; contrib. to British and foreign dental jls. *Recreations:* golf, DIY, gardening. *Address:* 137 Sydenham Hill, SE23 3PH. *T:* 081–693 2990.

See also O. J. T. Rowe.

ROWE, Andrew; MP (C) Mid Kent, since 1983; *b* 11 Sept. 1935; *s* of John Douglas Rowe and Mary Katharine Storr; *m* 1st, 1960, Alison Boyd (marr. diss.); one *s*; 2nd, 1983, Sheila L. Finkle, PhD; two step *d*. *Educ:* Eton Coll.; Merton Coll., Oxford (MA). Sub Lt RNVR, 1954–56. Schoolmaster, 1959–62; Principal, Scottish Office, 1962–67; Lectr, Edinburgh Univ., 1967–74; Consultant to Voluntary Services Unit, Home Office, 1974; Dir, Community Affairs, Cons. Central Office, 1975–79; self-employed consultant and journalist, 1979–83. Chm., Parly Panel for Personal Social Services, 1986–. *Publications:* Democracy Renewed, 1975; pamphlets and articles incl. Somewhere to Start. *Recreations:* photography, reading, theatre. *Address:* Tudor Milgate, Milgate Park, Ashford Road, Thurnham, Maidstone ME14 4NN. *T:* Maidstone (0622) 36809. *Club:* Maidstone.

ROWE, Bridget; Editor, Sunday Mirror, since 1991; *b* 16 March 1950; *d* of Peter and Myrtle Rowe. *Educ:* St Michael's School, Limpsfield. Editor, Look Now, 1971–76; Editor, Woman's World, 1976–81; Asst Editor, The Sun, 1981–82; Editor: Sunday Magazine, 1982–86; Woman's Own, 1986–90; TV Times, 1990–91. *Recreations:* equestrian sports, travelling. *Address:* Sunday Mirror, Mirror Group Newspapers, Holborn Circus, EC1P 1DQ.

ROWE, Helen, (Mrs Brian Rowe); *see* Cresswell, H.

ROWE, Sir Henry (Peter), KCB 1978 (CB 1971); QC 1978; First Parliamentary Counsel, 1977–81; *b* 18 Aug. 1916; 3rd *s* of late Dr Richard Röhr and Olga Röhr, Vienna; *m* 1947, Patricia, *yr d* of R. W. King, London; two *s* one *d*. *Educ:* Vienna; Gonville and Caius Coll., Cambridge. War service, Pioneer Corps, RAC, Military Govt, British Troops, Berlin, 1941–46. Called to Bar, Gray's Inn, 1947. Joined Parliamentary Counsel Office, 1947; Jt Second Parly Counsel, 1973–76. Commonwealth Fund Travelling Fellowship in US, 1955; with Law Commn, 1966–68. *Recreations:* music, reading, walking. *Address:* 19 Paxton Gardens, Woking, Surrey GU21 5TR. *T:* Byfleet (0932) 343816.

ROWE, Sir Jeremy, Kt 1991; CBE 1980; Deputy Chairman, Abbey National plc (formerly Abbey National Building Society), 1978–89; Chairman: Peterborough Development Corporation, 1981–88; Family Assurance Society, since 1986; Occupational Pensions Board, since 1987; *b* 31 Oct. 1928; *s* of Charles William Dell Rowe and Alison (*née* Barford); *m* 1957, Susan Mary (*née* Johnstone); four *d*. *Educ:* Wellesley House Sch.; Uppingham Sch.; Trinity Coll., Cambridge (MA (Hons) Hist.). English-Speaking Union Scholarship to USA, 1952. Joined London Brick Co. Ltd as trainee, 1952: Personal Asst to Chm., 1954; Dir and Sales Manager, 1963–67; Man. Dir, 1967–70; Dep. Chm. and Man. Dir, 1970–79; Man. Dir, 1979–82 and Chm., 1979–84; Director: West End Bd, Sun Alliance Insce Co. Ltd, 1978–; John Maunders Group plc, 1984–; Telephone Rentals plc, 1984–89. *Recreations:* tennis, shooting, reading, music. *Address:* 23 Devonshire Place, W1. *T:* 071–935 4902; Woodside, Peasmarsh, near Rye, Sussex TN31 6YD. *Clubs:* Buck's; All England Lawn Tennis, Rye Golf.

ROWE, John Jermyn, QC 1982; Barrister; a Recorder of the Crown Court, since 1978; *b* 23 March 1936; *er s* of John Rowe and late Olga Brookes Rowe; *m* 1966, Susan, *d* of Wing Comdr Walter Dring, DSO, DFC (killed in action, 1945) and of Sheila Mary Patricia (who *m* 2nd, His Honour B. H. Gerrard, *qv*); two *d*. *Educ:* Manchester Grammar School; Brasenose Coll., Oxford (MA). 2nd Lieut RA, 1954–56. Called to the Bar, Middle Temple, 1960 (Harmsworth Schol.; Blackstone Schol.; Bencher, 1985); practice on Northern Circuit; Junior, 1961; Hon. Sec., Exec. Cttee, 1970–76; Prosecuting Counsel to the Inland Revenue, Northern Circuit, 1980–82; called to Irish Bar, Kings Inns, 1986; Leader, Northern Circuit, 1988–. Member: Gen. Council of the Bar, 1970–74, 1987–; Bar Representative, Senate of the Inns of Court and the Bar, 1978–81; Mem., Rawlinson Cttee on Constitution of Senate, 1985–86. Mem., Parole Bd, 1987–90. *Publication:* contrib. Bullen and Leake and Jacob on Precedents and Pleadings, 13th edn, 1991. *Address:* The Cottage, 77 Stamford Road, Bowdon, Altrincham, Cheshire WA14 2JJ; 2 Pump Court, Temple, EC4. *Clubs:* United Oxford & Cambridge University; Tennis and Racquet (Manchester); County (Carlisle).

ROWE, Norbert Edward, CBE 1944; FEng 1976; Hon. FRAeS, 1962; FIMechE; Vice-President, Engineering De Havilland Aircraft of Canada, 1962–66, retired, 1966; *b* 18 June 1898; *s* of Harold Arthur and Jane Rowe, Plymouth, Devon; *m* 1929, Cecilia Brown; two *s* two *d*. *Educ:* City and Guilds (Engineering) Coll. Whitworth Exhibition, 1921; BSc Eng. London, 1st Cl. Hons, 1923; Associate of City and Guilds Institute, 1923; DIC 1924; Hon. FRAeS (FRAeS 1944); Air Ministry; Royal Aircraft Establishment, 1924, Junior Technical Officer, 1925; Testing Establishment, Technical Officer, 1926; Senior Technical Officer, 1937; Testing Establishment, Chief Technical Officer, 1937; Headquarters, Asst Director, 1938; Ministry of Aircraft Production Headquarters, Deputy Director, Research and Develt of Aircraft, 1940; Director of Technical Development, Ministry of Aircraft Production, 1941–45; Director-General of Technical Development, 1945–46; Controller of Research and Special Developments, British European Airways Corporation (on resignation from Civil Service), 1946–51; Technical Director Blackburn and General Aircraft Ltd, E Yorks, 1952–61; Joint Managing Director of the Blackburn Aircraft Company, 1960–61; Director, Hawker Siddeley Aviation, 1961–62. Member: Air Registration Bd, 1968; ARC, 1969–72. Fellow Inst. Aeronautical Sciences of Amer., 1953; FCGI 1954. Pres. Royal Aeronautical Society, 1955–56, Hon. Fellow 1962. President: Helicopter Assoc. of GB, 1959–60; Whitworth Soc., 1974–75. Hon. Fellow, Canadian Aeronautics and Space Inst. (formerly Canadian Aerospace Inst.), 1965. *Address:* 22 Westfields Road, Mirfield, West Yorks WF14 9PW.

ROWE, Owen John Tressider, MA; retired; *b* 30 July 1922; *e s* of late Harold Ridges Rowe and Emma E. Rowe (*née* Matthews), Lymington, Hampshire; *m* 1946, Marcelle Ljufliny Hyde-Johnson (*d* 1986); one *s* one *d*. *Educ:* King Edward VI School, Southampton; Exeter College, Oxford (Scholar, MA); 1st Cl. Hons in Classical Hon. Mods, 1942. Served War of 1939–45, Lieut in Roy. Hampshire Regt, 1942–45. 1st Cl. Hons in Lit Hum, Dec. 1947; Assistant Master: Royal Grammar School, Lancaster, 1948–50; Charterhouse, 1950–60 (Head of Classical Dept); Officer Comdg Charterhouse CCF, 1954–60; Headmaster: Giggleswick School, 1961–70; Epsom College, 1970–82; Head of Classics, St John's Sch., Leatherhead, 1982–87. Governor: St John's Sch., Leatherhead, 1988–; Rosebery Sch., 1971–; Downside Sch., Purley, 1971– (Chm., 1987–), and others. *Recreations:* Rotary, gardening. *Address:* 8 Pine Hill, Epsom KT18 7BG. *Club:* Rotary (Epsom).

See also A. H. R. Rowe.

ROWE, Rear-Adm. Patrick Barton, CBE 1990; LVO 1975; Military Deputy, Defence Export Services, since 1990; *b* 14 April 1939; *e s* of Captain G. B. Rowe, DSC, RN and Doreen Rowe (*née* Robarts), Liphook, Hants; *m* 1964, Alexandra, *e d* of Alexander Mellor, OBE; one *s* one *d*. *Educ:* Wellington College; RNC Dartmouth. MRIN. Served Far East Fleet, 1960–65; specialised in Navigation, 1966; navigation appts, 1966–70; Comd, HMS Soberton, 1970–71; Army Staff Coll., 1972; Navigation Officer, HM Yacht Britannia, 1973–75; Comd, HMS Antelope, 1977–79; Naval Staff appts, 1979–82; Comd, HMS Keren, 1983; Comd, HMS Liverpool, 1983–85; RN Presentation Team, 1985–86; Commodore, Clyde, 1986–88; RCDS 1989. Younger Brother, Trinity House. FBIM; MIPM. *Recreations:* sailing, ski-ing. *Address:* c/o Lloyds Bank, Bishop's Waltham, Southampton SO3 1GS. *Clubs:* Army and Navy; Royal Yacht Squadron.

ROWE, Prof. Peter Noël, DSc (Eng); FEng, FIChemE; Ramsay Memorial Professor of Chemical Engineering, and Head of Department, University College London, 1965–85, now Professor Emeritus; *b* 25 Dec. 1919; *e s* of Charles Henry Rowe and Kate Winifred (*née* Storry); *m* 1952, Pauline Garmirian; two *s*. *Educ:* Preston Grammar Sch.; Manchester Coll. of Technology; Imperial Coll., London. Princ. Scientific Officer, AERE, Harwell, 1958–65. Crabtree Orator, 1980. Vis. Prof., Univ. Libre de Bruxelles, 1988. Non-exec. Dir, Bentham Fine Chemicals, 1985–; Consultant, SERC, 1990–. Pres., IChemE, 1981–82; Hon. Sec., Fellowship of Engrg, 1982–85. FCGI 1983. Hon. DSc Brussels, 1978. *Publications:* scientific articles in Trans IChemE, Chem. Eng. Science, etc. *Address:* Pamber Green, Upper Basildon, Reading, Berks RG8 8PG. *T:* Upper Basildon (0491) 671382.

ROWE, Peter Whitmill, MA; Schoolteacher at Kent College, Canterbury, 1983–90, retired; *b* 12 Feb. 1928; British; *s* of Gerald Whitmill Rowe, chartered accountant, one-time General Manager of Morris Commercials Co. Ltd; *m* 1952, Bridget Ann Moyle; two *s* one *d*. *Educ:* Bishop's Stortford College; St John's College, Cambridge. BA 1950; MA (Hons) 1956. VI Form History Master, Brentwood School, Essex, 1951–54; Senior History Master, Repton School, Derbys, 1954–57; Headmaster: Bishop's Stortford Coll., Herts, 1957–70; Cranbrook Sch., Kent, 1970–81; teacher, Williston-Northampton Sch., Mass., USA, 1981–83. JP Bishop's Stortford, 1968–70, Cranbrook, 1971–81. *Recreations:* literature, music, cricket, golf.

ROWE, Richard Brian; District Judge (formerly Registrar) of the High Court (Family Division), since 1979; *b* 28 April 1933; *s* of Charles Albert Rowe and Mabel Florence Rowe; *m* 1959, Shirley Ann Symons; two *d*. *Educ:* Greenford County Grammar Sch.; King's Coll., London Univ. (LLB). National Service, RAF, 1952–54. High Court (Probate, Divorce and Admiralty Div.), 1954–66; Land Commn, 1966–69; Lord Chancellor's Office, 1969–75; Sec., High Court (Family Div.), 1975–79. *Publications:* (ed) Rayden on Divorce, 10th edn, 1967; (ed) Tristram and Coote's Probate Practice, 25th edn, 1978, to 27th edn, 1989. *Recreations:* most sports. *Address:* High Court (Family Division), Somerset House, Strand, WC2R 1LP.

ROWE, Robert Stewart, CBE 1969; Director, Leeds City Art Gallery and Temple Newsam House, 1958–83 (and also of Lotherton Hall, 1968–83); *b* 31 Dec. 1920; *s* of late James Stewart Rowe and late Mrs A. G. Gillespie; *m* 1953, Barbara Elizabeth Hamilton Baynes; one *s* two *d*. *Educ:* privately; Downing Coll., Cambridge; Richmond Sch. of Art. Asst Keeper of Art, Birmingham Museum and Art Gallery, 1950–56; Dep. Dir, Manchester City Art Galls, 1956–58. Pres., Museums Assoc., 1973–74; Member: Arts Council of GB, 1981–86; Fine Arts Adv. Cttee, British Council, 1972–84; Chm., Bar Convent Museum Trust, York, 1986–91; Trustee, Henry Moore Sculpture Trust, 1983–. Liveryman, Worshipful Co. of Goldsmiths. Hon. LittD Leeds, 1983. *Publications:* Adam Silver, 1965; articles in Burlington Magazine, Museums Jl, etc. *Recreations:* gardening, reading. *Address:* Grove Lodge, Shadwell, Leeds LS17 8LB. *T:* Leeds (0532) 656365.

ROWE, Dr Roy Ernest, CBE 1977; FEng 1979; consultant; Director General, British Cement Association, 1977–87; *b* 26 Jan. 1929; *s* of Ernest Walter Rowe and Louisa Rowe; *m* 1954, Lillian Anderson; one *d*. *Educ:* Taunton's Sch., Southampton; Pembroke Coll., Cambridge (MA, ScD). FICE, FIStructE, FIHE. Cement and Concrete Association, later British Cement Association: Research Engineer, 1952–57; Head, Design Research Dept, 1958–65; Dir, R&D, 1966–77. President: IStructE, 1983–84; Comité Euro-Internat. du Béton, 1987–. Hon. Mem., Amer. Concrete Inst., 1978; For. Associate, Nat. Acad. of Engineering, USA, 1980. Hon. DEng Leeds, 1984. *Publications:* Concrete Bridge Design, 1962, 3rd impr. 1972; numerous papers in technical and professional jls. *Recreations:* fell walking, listening to music (and mutilating it on the piano). *Address:* 15 Hollesley Road, Alderton, Woodbridge, Suffolk IP12 3BX. *T:* Shottisham (0394) 411096.

ROWE-HAM, Sir David (Kenneth), GBE 1986; JP; chartered accountant, since 1962; Lord Mayor of London, 1986–87; Consultant to Touche Ross & Co., since 1984; Director of public and private companies; *b* 19 Dec. 1935; *o s* of late Kenneth Henry and of Muriel Phyllis Rowe-Ham; *m* Sandra Celia (*née* Nicholls), *widow* of Ian Glover; three *s*. *Educ:* Dragon School; Charterhouse. FCA; Mem., Soc. of Investment Analysts; FCIS. Commnd 3rd King's Own Hussars. Mem., Stock Exchange, 1964–84; Sen. Partner, Smith Keen Cutler, 1972–82. Chairman: Asset Trust plc, 1982–89; Jersey General Investment Trust Ltd, 1988–89. Dir, The Nineteen Twenty Eight Investment Trust, 1984–86; Regional Dir (London), Lloyds Bank, 1985–91; Director: W. Canning plc, 1981–86; Savoy Theatre Ltd, 1986–; Mem. Adv. Panel, Guinness Mahon Fund Managers Ltd, 1986– (Chm., 1987); Chm., Olayan Europe Ltd, 1989–. Alderman, City of London, Ward of Bridge and Bridge Without, 1976–; Sheriff, City of London, 1984–85; HM Lieut, City of London, 1987–; Admiral of the Port of London, 1986–87. Court Member: City Univ., 1981–86 (Chancellor, 1986–87); Worshipful Co. of Chartered Accountants in England and Wales (Master, 1985–86); Worshipful Co. of Wheelwrights; Hon. Mem., Worshipful Co. of Launderers; Mem. Ct, HAC; Member: Guild of Freemen; Prince's Youth Business Trust Council, 1986–; Gov., Royal Shakespeare Co.; Trustee, Friends of D'Oyly Carte. President: Black Country Mus. Develt Trust; St Bartholomew's College Council. Chm., Birmingham Municipal Bank, 1970–72; Mem., Birmingham CC, 1965–72. Chm., Political Council, Junior Carlton Club, 1977; Dep. Chm., Political Cttee, Carlton Club, 1977–79. Member: Lord's Taverners; Royal Soc. of St George. Governor, Christ's Hospital. JP City of London, 1976 (Chief Magistrate, 1986–87). Hon. DLitt City Univ., 1986. KJStJ 1986. Commandeur de l'Ordre Mérite, France, 1984; Commander, Order of the Lion, Malaŵi, 1985; Order of the Aztec Eagle (Cl. II), Mexico, 1985; Order of King Abdul Aziz (Cl. 1), 1987; Grand Officer, Order of Wissam Alouite, Morocco, 1987; Order of Diego Losada, Caracas, Venezuela, 1987; Pedro Ernesto Medal, Rio de Janeiro, 1987. *Recreations:* theatre, shooting. *Clubs:* Carlton, City Livery, Guildhall.

ROWELL, Sir John (Joseph), Kt 1980; CBE 1974; BA; Chairman, Legal Aid Commission of Queensland, 1979–90; Senior Partner, Neil O'Sullivan & Rowell, Solicitors, Brisbane, 1968–88; *b* 15 Feb. 1916; *s* of Joseph Alfred Rowell and Mary Lilian Rowell (*née* Hooper), both born in England; *m* 1947, Mary Kathleen (*née* de Silva); three *s* two *d*. *Educ:* Brisbane Grammar School; Univ. of Queensland (BA). Served AIF, 1940–46; Captain 2/10 Fd Regt (Efficiency Medal, 1946). Admitted Solicitor, 1939; Notary Public, 1959. Pres., Queensland Law Soc. Inc., 1964–66 (Mem. Council, 1956–67); Treas., Law Council of Aust., 1961–63 (Mem. Exec., 1960–67); Mem. Bd, Faculty of Law, Univ. of Queensland, 1959–78; Chm., Legal Assistance Cttee of Queensland, 1966–79; Member: Law Reform Commn of Qld, 1967–89; Commonwealth Legal Aid Commn, 1980–85. Chairman: Concrete Constructions (Qld) Pty Ltd; Qld Bulk Handling Pty Ltd; Gas Corp. of Qld Ltd, 1974–90; Qld Bd, Capita Financial Gp (formerly City Mutual Life Assce Soc. Ltd), 1986–88 (Mem. Bd, 1971–88); Dir of Principal Bd, Boral Ltd and Boral Resources Ltd, 1974–87. Former Hon. Consul of Qld for Federal Repub. of Germany, 1963–86; Dean, Consular Corps of Qld, 1978–80. Officer's Cross, Federal Republic of Germany, 1st class, 1979; Comdr's Cross, Order of Merit, FRG, 1986. *Recreations:* golf, fishing, reading. *Address:* Edgecliffe, 48 Walcott Street, St Lucia, Brisbane, Qld 4067, Australia. *T:* 870–9070. *Clubs:* Union, Australian (Sydney); Brisbane, United Service, Tattersall's, Queensland Turf (Brisbane); Indooroopilly Golf, Southport Golf.

ROWELL, John Martin, DPhil; FRS 1989; Chief Technical Officer, Conductus Inc., since 1989; *b* 27 June 1935; *s* of Frank L. and P. E. Rowell; *m* 1959, Judith A. Harte; two *s* one *d*. *Educ:* Wadham Coll., Oxford (BSc, MA; DPhil 1961). Bell Telephone Labs, 1961–84; Bell Communications Research, 1984–89. Fellow, Amer. Physical Soc., 1974. Fritz London Meml Low Temperature Physics Prize, 1978. *Publications:* about 100 pubns in jls. *Address:* Conductus Inc., 969 W Maude Avenue, Sunnyvale, Calif 94086, USA. *T:* 408–737–6707.

ROWLAND, Rev. Prof. Christopher Charles; Dean Ireland's Professor of the Exegesis of Holy Scripture, and Fellow of Queen's College, University of Oxford, since 1991; *b* Doncaster, 21 May 1947; *s* of Eric Rowland and Frances Mary Lawson; *m* 1969, Catherine Rogers; three *s* one *d*. *Educ:* Doncaster Grammar Sch.; Christ's Coll., Cambridge; Ridley Hall, Cambridge; BA 1969, PhD 1975, Cantab. Ordained deacon, 1975, priest 1976. Lectr in Religious Studies, Univ. of Newcastle upon Tyne, 1974–79; Curate: St James', Benwell, 1975–78; All Saints', Gosforth, 1978–79; Asst Lectr in Divinity, 1983–85, Lectr in Divinity, 1985–91, Univ. of Cambridge; Fellow and Dean, Jesus Coll., Cambridge, 1979–91. *Address:* Queen's College, Oxford OX1 4AW.

ROWLAND, David; *see* Rowland, J. D.

ROWLAND, David Powys; Stipendiary Magistrate, Mid Glamorgan (formerly Merthyr Tydfil), 1961–89, retired; *b* 7 Aug. 1917; *s* of late Henry Rowland, CBE, Weston-super-Mare; *m* 1st, 1946, Joan (*d* 1958), *d* of late Group Capt. J. McCrae, MBE, Weston-super-Mare; one *s* one *d*; 2nd, 1961, Jenny (marr. diss. 1977), *d* of late Percival Lance, Swanage, and *widow* of Michael A. Forester-Bennett, Alverstoke; one *s* one *d* (and one step-*d*); 3rd, 1980, Diana, *d* of late W. H. Smith, Cannock, and *widow* of Lt-Col W. D. H. McCardie, S Staffs Regt (two step-*d*). *Educ:* Cheltenham Coll.; Oriel Coll., Oxford (BA). Lieut, Royal Welch Fusiliers, 1940–46. Called to Bar, Middle Temple, 1947. Deputy Chairman: Glamorgan QS, 1961–71; Breconshire QS, 1964–71. Mem. Nat. Adv. Council on Training of Magistrates, 1964–73. *Recreations:* fly-fishing, gardening, golf. *Address:* Trosglwyd, Dyffryn Crawnon, Llangynidr, Crickhowell, Powys NP8 1NU. *T:* Bwlch (0874) 730635.

ROWLAND, Herbert Grimley; *b* 10 Feb. 1905; *s* of Frank Rowland, MRCS, LRCP, and Josephine Mary (*née* Quirke); *m* 1938, Margaret Jane Elizabeth, *yr d* of Robert Crawford Higginson and Mary Higginson; one *d*. *Educ:* Nautical Coll., Pangbourne; Peterhouse, Cambridge. Called to Bar, 1928; admitted Solicitor, 1933; private practice, Solicitor, 1933–40; joined Office of Solicitor of Inland Revenue, 1940; Princ. Asst Solicitor of Inland Revenue, 1961–65; Acting Solicitor of Inland Revenue, 1961; Special Commissioner of Income Tax, 1965–70. Chm., S Middlesex Rent Tribunal, 1972–76. *Recreation:* golf. *Address:* 10 Hillcrest, Durlston Road, Swanage, Dorset BH19 2HS. *T:* Swanage (0929) 423256. *Clubs:* Bramley Golf (Surrey); Isle of Purbeck (Swanage).

ROWLAND, Air Marshal Sir James (Anthony), AC 1987; KBE 1977; DFC 1944; AFC 1953; BE; CEng, FRAeS, FIE(Aust); Governor of New South Wales, 1981–89; Chancellor, University of Sydney, since 1990; Chairman, Preston Group Pty, since 1991; Director: Angus & Coote Ltd, since 1989; Focus Books Ltd, since 1990; *b* 1 Nov. 1922; *s* of Louis Claude Rowland and Elsie Jean Rowland; *m* 1955, Faye Alison (*née* Doughton); one *d*. *Educ:* Cranbrook Sch., Sydney; St Paul's Coll., Univ. of Sydney (BE Aero). CEng, FRAeS 1969; FIE (Aust) 1978; FTS 1988. Served War, Pilot, RAAF and RAF Bomber Comd, 1942–45. Sydney Univ., 1940–41 and 1946–47; Empire Test Pilots' Sch., Farnborough, 1949; Chief Test Pilot, RAAF R&D Unit, 1951–54; Staff Coll., 1956; Staff and unit posts, incl. OC R&D, 1957–60; RAAF Mirage Mission, Paris, 1961–64; CO No 1 Aircraft Depot, 1966; Sen. Engr SO, Ops Comd, 1968–69; RCDS, 1971; Dir Gen., Aircraft Engrg, RAAF, 1972; Air Mem. for Technical Services, 1973; Chief of Air Staff, RAAF, 1975–79. Member: Admin. Appeals Tribunal, 1979–80; Police Board of NSW, 1989–. Chm., NSW Air Transport Council, 1989–. Consultant, OFEMA Australia, 1980.

Pres., Royal Humane Soc. of NSW, 1990–. Hon. DEng Sydney, 1983. KStJ 1981. *Publications:* contribs to professional jls. *Recreations:* surfing, reading, golf. *Address:* 21/171 Walker Street, North Sydney, NSW 2060, Australia. *Clubs:* Royal Air Force; Australian Union (Sydney); United Services (Brisbane); Royal Sydney Golf.

ROWLAND, (John) David; Chairman, Sedgwick Group plc, since 1989 (Group Chief Executive, 1988–89); *b* 10 Aug. 1933; *s* of Cyril Arthur Rowland and Eileen Mary Rowland; *m* 1957, Giulia Powell; one *s* one *d*. *Educ:* St Paul's School; Trinity College, Cambridge (MA Natural Sciences). Joined Matthews Wrightson and Co., 1956, Dir, 1965; Dir, Matthews Wrightson Holdings, 1972; Dep. Chm., 1978–81, Chm., 1981–87, Stewart Wrightson Holdings plc; Dep. Chm., Willis Faber plc, 1987–88. Chm., Westminster Insurance Agencies, 1981–88; Dir, Royal London Mutual Insurance Soc., 1985–86. Director: Project Fullemploy, 1973–88; Fullemploy Gp Ltd, 1989–90. Mem. Council, Lloyd's, 1987–90; Mem., President's Cttee, Business in the Community, 1986– (Mem., City of London section, 1983–86). Vice-Pres., British Insurance and Investment Brokers' Assoc. (formerly British Insurance Brokers' Assoc.), 1980–; Member of Council: Industrial Soc., 1983–88; Contemporary Applied Arts (formerly British Crafts Centre), 1985–. Governor, Coll. of Insurance, 1983–85; Chm., 1985–, Mem. Council, 1980–, Templeton Coll. (Oxford Centre for Management Studies). *Recreations:* golf, running slowly. *Address:* 6 Mountfort Crescent, N1 1JW. *T:* 071–609 2041. *Clubs:* MCC; Royal and Ancient Golf (St Andrews), Royal St George's (Sandwich), Royal Worlington and Newmarket Golf, Sunningdale Golf.

ROWLAND, His Honour Robert Todd, QC 1969; County Court Judge of Northern Ireland, 1974–90; President, Lands Tribunal for Northern Ireland, 1983–90; *b* 12 Jan. 1922; *yr s* of late Lt-Col Charles Rowland and Jean Rowland; *m* 1952, Kathleen, *er d* of late H. J. Busby, Lambourn, Berks; two *s*. *Educ:* Crossley and Porter Sch., Halifax, Yorks; Ballyclare High Sch.; Queen's Univ. of Belfast (LLB 1948). Called to Bar of N Ireland, 1949; Mem., Bar Council, 1967–72. Served 2nd Punjab Regt, IA, in India, Assam, Burma, Thailand, Malaya, 1942–46. Counsel to Attorney-Gen. for N Ireland, 1966–69; Sen. Crown Prosecutor for Co. Tyrone, 1969–72; Vice-Pres., VAT Tribunal for N Ireland, 1972–74. Served on County Court Rules Cttee, 1965–72; Chairman: War Pensions Appeal Tribunal, 1962–72; Commn of Inquiry into Housing Contracts, 1978; Member: Bd of Governors, Strathearn Sch., 1969–89; Legal Adv. Cttee, Gen. Synod of Church of Ireland, 1975–89. Chancellor, dioceses of Armagh, and Down and Dromore, 1978–89. *Recreations:* fly-fishing, golf. *Address:* Greystones, Holmewood Drive, Kirby Fields, Kirby Muxloe, Leics LE9 9EF.

ROWLANDS, David, CB 1991; Under Secretary, Department of Transport, since 1990; *b* 31 May 1947; *s* of George and Margaret Rowlands; *m* 1975, Louise Marjorie Brown; two *s*. *Educ:* St Mary's Coll., Crosby; St Edmund Hall, Oxford. Entered Civil Service, 1974; Private Sec. to Minister of State for Industry, 1978–80; Principal, Dept of Trade, then of Transport, 1980–84; Asst Sec., Dept of Transport, 1984–90. *Address:* Department of Transport, 2 Marsham Street, SW1P 3EB.

ROWLANDS, Edward; MP (Lab) Merthyr Tydfil and Rhymney, since 1983 (Merthyr Tydfil, April 1972–1983); *b* 23 Jan. 1940; *e s* of W. S. Rowlands; *m* 1968, Janice Williams, Kidwelly, Carmarthenshire; two *s* one *d*. *Educ:* Rhondda Grammar Sch.; Wirral Grammar Sch.; King's Coll., London. BA Hons History (London) 1962. Research Asst, History of Parliament Trust, 1963–65; Lectr in Modern History and Govt, Welsh Coll. of Adv. Technology, 1965–. MP (Lab) Cardiff North, 1966–70; Parliamentary Under-Secretary of State: Welsh Office, 1969–70, 1974–75; FCO, 1975–76; Minister of State, FCO, 1976–79; Opposition spokesman on energy, 1980–87; Mem., Select Cttee on Foreign Affairs, 1987–. Member: Governing Body and Exec. Cttee, Commonwealth Inst., 1980–; Academic Council, Wilton Park, 1983–. A Booker Prize Judge, 1984. *Publications:* various articles. *Recreations:* music, golf. *Address:* House of Commons, SW1A 0AA; 5 Park Crescent, Thomastown, Merthyr Tydfil, Mid Glamorgan. *T:* Merthyr Tydfil (0685) 4912.

ROWLANDS, Rev. Canon John Henry Lewis; Warden, St Michael and All Angels' Theological College, Llandaff, since 1988; Dean of the Faculty of Theology, University of Wales, since 1991; *b* 16 Nov. 1947; *s* of William Lewis and Elizabeth Mary Rowlands; *m* 1976, Catryn Meryl Parry Edwards; one *s* two *d*. *Educ:* Queen Elizabeth Grammar Sch., Carmarthen; St David's University Coll., Lampeter (BA); Magdalene Coll., Cambridge (MA); Durham Univ. (MLitt); Wescott House, Cambridge. Ordained deacon, 1972, priest, 1973 (St David's Cathedral); Curate, Rectorial Benefice of Aberystwyth, 1972–76; Chaplain, St David's University Coll., Lampeter, 1976–79; Youth Chaplain, dio. of St David's, 1976–79; Dir, Academic Studies, St Michael's Coll., Llandaff, 1979–84, Sub-Warden, 1984–88. Lectr, Faculty of Theology, University Coll., Cardiff, now Univ. of Wales Coll. of Cardiff, 1979–, Asst Dean, 1981–83; Diocesan Dir of Ordinands, Dio. Llandaff, 1985–88; Exmng Chaplain to Archbishop of Wales, 1987. Hon. Canon, Llandaff Cathedral, 1990–. Pres., Diwinyddiaeth (Soc. of Theol. Grads, Univ. of Wales), 1989. *Publications:* (ed) Essays on the Kingdom of God, 1986; Church, State and Society 1827–45, 1989. *Recreations:* beachcombing, racket games, auctioneering, antique markets. *Address:* The Old Registry, Cardiff Road, Llandaff, Cardiff CF5 2DQ. *T:* Cardiff (0222) 563116.

ROWLANDS, John Kendall, FSA; Keeper, Department of Prints and Drawings, British Museum, 1981–91; *b* 18 Sept. 1931; *s* of Arthur and Margaret Rowlands; *m* 1st, 1957, Else A. H. Bachmann (marr. diss. 1981); one *s* two *d*; 2nd, 1982, Lorna Jane Lowe; one *d*. *Educ:* Chester Cathedral Choir Sch.; King's Sch., Chester; Gonville and Caius Coll., Cambridge. MA Cantab 1959; MA Oxon; FSA 1976. Asst Keeper, Dept of Art, City Mus. and Art Gall., Birmingham, 1956–60; Editor, Clarendon Press, Oxford, 1960–65; Asst Keeper, 1965–74, Dep. Keeper, 1974–81, Dept of Prints and Drawings, British Museum. Fellow Commoner, Corpus Christi Coll., Cambridge, 1989. *Publications:* David Cox Centenary Exhibition Catalogue, 1959; Graphic Work of Albrecht Dürer, 1971; Bosch, 1975; Rubens: drawings and sketches . . ., 1977; Urs Graf, 1977; Hercules Segers, 1979; Bosch, the Garden of Earthly Delights, 1979; German Drawings from a Private Collection, 1984; Master Drawings of Watercolours in the British Museum: from Angelico to Henry Moore, 1984; The Paintings of Hans Holbein the Younger, 1985; The Age of Dürer and Holbein, 1988; contribs to specialist journals. *Recreation:* playing the piano and organ. *Address:* The Old Rectory, Silk Willoughby, Lincs NG34 8NY. *Club:* Beefsteak.

ROWLANDS, (John) Martin, CBE 1980; Secretary for Civil Service, Hong Kong Government, 1978–85; *b* 20 July 1925; *s* of late John Walter Rowlands and of Mary Ace Maitland (*née* Roberts); *m* 1956, Christiane Germaine Madeleine Lacheny; two *d*. *Educ:* Charterhouse; Selwyn Coll., Cambridge (MA). Military service, 1943–47 (Captain, 3rd Royal Indian Artillery Field Regt, HQ XV Indian Corps, HQ ALFSEA). HMOCS, Hong Kong Admin. Service, 1952–85: Dep. Dir of Urban Services, 1966–68; Principal Asst Colonial Sec., 1968–71; Dep. Sec. for Home Affairs, 1971–74; Dir of Immigration, 1974–78; Mem., Hong Kong Legislative Council, 1978–84. *Recreations:* travel, railways, bird-watching. *Address:* Flat 3, 15 Collingham Road, SW5 0NU. *Clubs:* Hong Kong, Royal Hong Kong Jockey.

ROWLANDS, Air Marshal Sir John (Samuel), GC 1943; KBE 1971 (OBE 1954); Consultant, Civil Aviation Administration, since 1981; *b* 23 Sept. 1915; *s* of late Samuel and Sarah Rowlands; *m* 1942, Constance Wight; two *d*. *Educ:* Hawarden School; University of Wales (BSc Hons). Joined RAFVR, 1939; permanent commission in RAF, 1945. British Defence Staff, Washington, 1961–63; Imperial Defence College, 1964; Royal Air Force College, Cranwell, 1965–68; First Director General of Training, RAF, 1968–70; AOC-in-C, RAF Maintenance comd, 1970–73; Asst Principal, Sheffield Polytechnic, 1974–80. *Recreations:* photography, tennis, motoring. *Club:* Royal Air Force.

ROWLANDS, Maldwyn Jones, OBE 1979; FLA, FRGS, FLS; Head of Library Services, British Museum (Natural History), 1965–81, retired; *b* 7 March 1918; *s* of Thomas and Elizabeth Rowlands; *m* 1941, Sybil Elizabeth Price; two *s* one *d*. *Educ:* Newtown Grammar Sch., Montgomeryshire; University Coll. London. Served in Army, 1940–46: commnd 1941 (Lieut), HQ 21 Army Gp (Staff Captain), 1944–46 (C-in-C's Cert. 1945). Asst Librarian, Science Museum Library, 1946–54; Deputy Librarian: British Museum (Natural History), 1954–63; Patent Office, 1963–65. *Recreations:* old books and bindings, Welsh history and folk-lore. *Address:* Llys Hafren, Caersws, Powys SY17 5JA.

ROWLANDS, Martin; *see* Rowlands, J. M.

ROWLANDS, Martyn Omar, FCSD, FPRI; Chairman, Martyn Rowlands Design Consultants Ltd, 1960–88; retired; *b* 27 July 1923; *s* of Edward and Mildred Rowlands; *m* 1st, 1951, Ann Patricia (*d* 1974); two *s* one *d*; 2nd, 1978 (marr. diss. 1986). *Educ:* Eltham Coll.; Central Sch. of Art and Design. FSIAD 1960; FPRI 1973. Served War, RAF, 1940–45: India and Burma. Central Sch. of Art and Design, 1946–49; Head of Indust. Design, Ekco Plastics, 1954–59; started own design consultancy, 1959. Past Pres., SIAD (now CSD). *Recreation:* photography. *Address:* Parndon Mill, Harlow, Essex CM20 2HP. *T:* Harlow (0279) 641090.

ROWLEY, Sir Charles (Robert), 7th Bt *cr* 1836; *b* 15 March 1926; *s* of Sir William Joshua Rowley, 6th Bt and Beatrice Gwendoline, *d* of Rev. Augustus George Kirby; *S* father, 1971; *m* 1952, Astrid, *d* of Sir Arthur Massey, CBE; one *s* one *d*. *Educ:* Wellington. *Heir:* *s* Richard Charles Rowley [*b* 14 Aug. 1959; *m* 1989, Alison, *d* of late Henry Bellingham, and of Mrs Ian Baillie]. *Address:* 21 Tedworth Square, SW3; Naseby Hall, Northamptonshire.

ROWLEY, Frederick Allan, CMG 1978; OBE 1959; MC 1945; Major (retd); HM Diplomatic Service, retired; *b* 27 July 1922; *m* 1951, Anne Crawley; one *s* three *d*. *Educ:* Haig Sch., Aldershot. Served War of 1939–45: Ranks, 8th Worcs Regt (TA), 1939–40; Emergency Commnd Officer, 5th Bn, 10th Baluch Regt (KGVO), Jacob's Rifles, Indian Army, Burma Campaign (MC), June 1941–Nov. 1948. At partition of India, granted regular commn (back-dated, 1942) in Worcestershire Regt, but retd (wounded), sub. Major. Joined HM Diplomatic Service, Nov. 1948: served (with brief periods in FO) in: Egypt; Ethiopia; Turkey; Burma; Singapore; Australia; Malaysia; FCO 1971–72; Under-Sec., N Ireland Office (on secondment), 1972–73; Counsellor, FCO, 1973–79. Joint Services Staff College (jssc), 1959. *Recreations:* cricket, golf. *Club:* MCC.

ROWLEY, Geoffrey William, CBE 1989; Town Clerk, City of London, 1982–91; *b* 9 Sept. 1926; *s* of George Frederick Rowley and Ellen Mary Rowley; *m* 1950, Violet Gertrude Templeman; one *s* one *d*. *Educ:* Owens School. FIPM 1974. Served War, Royal Marines, 1944–47. Corporation of the City of London, 1947–: Head, Personnel Sect., 1965–74; Dep. Town Clerk, 1974–82. DCL *hc* City, 1989. Order of White Rose, Finland, 1969; Order of Orange Nassau, Holland, 1982; Légion d'Honneur, France, 1985. OStJ 1987. *Recreations:* sport: badminton as a player, cricket and soccer as a spectator. *Address:* 3 Wensley Avenue, Woodford Green, Essex. *T:* 081–504 6270.

ROWLEY, John Charles, CMG 1977; Director, Crown Agents Board of Management, 1980–84, retired; *b* 29 Sept. 1919; *s* of John Ernest Rowley and Edith Muriel (*née* Aldridge); *m* 1st, 1945, Pamela Hilda Godfrey (marr. diss. 1971); two *d*; 2nd, 1972, Anne Patricia Dening; one *s*. *Educ:* Ilford; King's College, London (LLB 1948, Upper Second Cl. Hons). Inland Revenue, 1938–40. RAF, 1940–46, pilot, Flight-Lieut; Iceland, 1944 (despatches). Inland Revenue, 1946–64; Min. of Overseas Development, 1964–79, Head, Middle East Develt Div., Beirut, Lebanon and Amman, Jordan, 1971–79; Crown Agents Regional Controller for Middle East, 1979–80. *Recreations:* choral singing, sailing. *Address:* 43 Half Moon Lane, SE24 9JX.

ROWLEY, John Vincent d'Alessio; General Manager, Bracknell New Town Development Corporation, 1955–73; *b* 12 Sept. 1907; 2nd *s* of late Ven. Hugh Rowley, Archdeacon of Kingwilliamstown, S Africa; *m* 1st, 1936, Violet Maud (*d* 1969), *d* of S. H. Day, Grahamstown, S Africa; one *s*; 2nd, 1972, Kathleen Mary Hawkesworth (*née* Pullom). *Educ:* St Andrews Coll., Grahamstown; Trinity Coll., Oxford (Rhodes Schol.). BA 1929; Oxford Univ. Rugby XV, 1929. Entered Sudan Political Service, 1930; Asst District Comr and District Comr, 1930–49; seconded Sudan Defence Force, 1940–42; Dep. Gov., Kordofan Province, 1950–52; Asst Financial Sec., 1952–53; Governor, Darfur Province, 1953–55. Chm., South Hill Park Arts Centre Trust, 1979–. *Recreations:* music, gardening, golf. *Address:* The Spring, Stanford Dingley, near Bradfield, Berks RG7 6LX. *T:* Bradfield (0734) 744270. *Club:* United Oxford & Cambridge University.

ROWLEY, Sir Joshua Francis, 7th Bt, *cr* 1786; JP; Lord-Lieutenant of Suffolk, since 1978; *b* 31 Dec. 1920; *o s* of 6th Bt and Margery Frances Bacon (*d* 1977); *S* father, 1962; *m* 1959, Hon. Celia Ella Vere Monckton, 2nd *d* of 8th Viscount Galway; one *d*. *Educ:* Eton; Trinity College, Cambridge. Grenadier Guards, 1940–46. Deputy Secretary, National Trust, 1952–55. Chairman: W Suffolk CC, 1971–74; Suffolk CC, 1976–78; DL 1968, High Sheriff 1971, Vice Lord-Lieutenant, 1973–78, JP 1978, Suffolk. *Address:* Holbecks, Hadleigh, Ipswich, Suffolk IP7 5PF. *T:* Hadleigh (0473) 823211. *Clubs:* Boodle's, Pratt's, MCC.

ROWLEY, Peter, MC 1944; Chairman: Cheshire Homes European Regional Council, since 1990; Leonard Cheshire Foundation, 1982–90; *b* 12 July 1918; *s* of late Roland and Catherine Isabel Rowley; *m* 1940, Ethnea Louis Florence Mary Howard Kyan; four *d*. *Educ:* Wembley County Sch.; University Coll., Oxford (MA). Served War of 1939–45: Queen's Westminster Rifles, 1938–39; 14th Bn Sherwood Foresters, 1940–46; Adjt, Middle East, N Africa; Company Comdr, Italy; Bde Major 13 Bde, 1944–45; GSOII 8 Corps, 1945–46. Admitted Solicitor, Titmuss Sainer & Webb, 1950; Sen. Partner, 1981–83, retd. Member, Law Society Land Law Cttee, 1970–87. Liveryman, Distillers Co., 1975. *Address:* Underlea, 34 Radnor Cliff, Folkestone, Kent CT20 2JL. *T:* Folkestone (0303) 48689. *Club:* Royal Automobile.

ROWLEY-CONWY, family name of **Baron Langford.**

ROWLEY HILL, Sir George Alfred; *see* Hill.

ROWLING, Rt. Hon. Sir Wallace (Edward), KCMG 1983; PC 1974; President, New Zealand Institute of International Affairs, since 1990; *b* Motueka, 15 Nov. 1927; *s* of A. Rowling; *m* 1951, Glen Elna, *d* of Captain J. M. Reeves; two *s* one *d*. *Educ:* Nelson Coll. MA. Fulbright Schol., 1955–56. Formerly Asst Dir of Educn, NZ Army. MP (Lab) for Buller (later for Tasman), NZ, 1962–84; Minister of Finance, 1972–74; Prime Minister of NZ, 1974–75; Leader of Opposition, 1975–83. Ambassador to USA, 1985–88. Governor for New Zealand, IMF. Rep. NZ at annual meeting of ADB, Kuala Lumpur,1974. Pres., Asia Pacific Socialist Orgn, 1977–83. Col Comdt, NZ Army Educn Corps, 1977–82. Hon. LLD Canterbury, NZ, 1987. *Recreation:* golf. *Address:* 3 Alton Lane, Nelson, New Zealand.

ROWLINSON, Prof. John Shipley, BSc, MA, DPhil Oxon; FRS 1970; FRSC; FEng 1976; FIChemE; Dr Lee's Professor of Physical Chemistry, Oxford University, since 1974; Fellow of Exeter College, since 1974; *b* 12 May 1926; *er s* of late Frank Rowlinson and Winifred Jones; *m* 1952, Nancy Gaskell; one *s* one *d*. *Educ:* Rossall School (Scholar); Trinity College, Oxford (Millard Scholar). Research Associate, Univ. of Wisconsin, USA, 1950–51; ICI Research Fellow, Lecturer, and Senior Lecturer in Chemistry, University of Manchester, 1951–60; Prof. of Chemical Technology, London Univ. (Imperial Coll.), 1961–73. Mary Upson Prof. of Engrg, 1988, Andrew D. White Prof.-at-large, 1990–, Cornell Univ. Lectures: Liversidge, Chem. Soc., 1978; von Hofmann, Gesell. Deutscher Chem., 1980; Faraday, 1983, Lennard-Jones, 1985, RSC; Guggenheim, Reading Univ., 1986; T. W. Leland, Rice Univ., Houston, Texas, 1990. Pres., Faraday Div., Chem. Soc., 1979–81; Hon. Treas., Faraday Society, 1968–71; Vice-Pres., Royal Instn of GB, 1974–76; Member, Sale Borough Council, 1956–59. Hon. FCGI 1987. Meldola Medal, Roy. Inst. of Chemistry, 1954; Marlow Medal, Faraday Soc., 1957. *Publications:* Liquids and Liquid Mixtures, 1959, (jtly) 3rd edn, 1982; The Perfect Gas, 1963; Physics of Simple Liquids (joint editor), 1968; (trans. jtly) The Metric System, 1969; (jtly) Thermodynamics for Chemical Engineers, 1975; (jtly) Molecular Theory of Capillarity, 1982; (ed) J. D. van der Waals, On the Continuity of the Gaseous and Liquid States, 1988; papers in scientific journals. *Recreation:* mountaineering. *Address:* 12 Pullens Field, Headington, Oxford OX3 0BU. *T:* Oxford (0865) 67507; Physical Chemistry Laboratory, South Parks Road, Oxford OX1 3QZ. *T:* Oxford (0865) 275401. *Club:* Alpine.

ROWNTREE CLIFFORD, Rev. Paul; *see* Clifford.

ROWSE, Alfred Leslie, MA, DLitt; FBA; Emeritus Fellow of All Souls College, Oxford; *b* St Austell, Cornwall, 4 Dec. 1903. *Educ:* Elementary and Grammar Schools, St Austell; Christ Church Oxford (Douglas Jerrold Scholar in English Literature). Sen. Res. Associate, Huntington Library, Calif, 1962–69. Fellow of the Royal Society of Literature; President of the English Association, 1952; Raleigh Lecturer, British Academy, 1957; Trevelyan Lecturer, Cambridge, 1958; Beatty Memorial Lecturer, McGill University, 1963. Pres., Shakespeare Club, Stratford-upon-Avon, 1970–71. Benson Medal, RSL, 1982. *Publications:* Politics and the Younger Generation, 1931; Mr Keynes and the Labour Movement, 1936; Sir Richard Grenville of the Revenge, 1937; Tudor Cornwall, 1941; Poems of a Decade, 1931–41; A Cornish Childhood, 1942; The Spirit of English History, 1943; Poems Chiefly Cornish, 1944; The English Spirit: Essays in History and Literature, 1944, rev. edn 1966; West Country Stories, 1945; The Use of History, 1946; Poems of Deliverance, 1946; The End of an Epoch, 1947; The England of Elizabeth, 1950; The English Past, 1951 (rev. edn, as Times, Persons, Places, 1965); Translation and completion of Lucien Romier's History of France, 1953; The Expansion of Elizabethan England, 1955; The Early Churchills, 1956; The Later Churchills, 1958; Poems Partly American, 1958; The Elizabethans and America, 1959; St Austell: Church, Town, Parish, 1960; All Souls and Appeasement, 1961; Ralegh and the Throckmortons, 1962; William Shakespeare: A Biography, 1963; Christopher Marlowe: A Biography, 1964; A Cornishman at Oxford, 1965; Shakespeare's Southampton: Patron of Virginia, 1965; Bosworth Field and the Wars of the Roses, 1966; Poems of Cornwall and America, 1967; Cornish Stories, 1967; A Cornish Anthology, 1968; The Cornish in America, 1969; The Elizabethan Renaissance: the Life of the Society, 1971; The Elizabethan Renaissance: The Cultural Achievement, 1972; Strange Encounter (poems), 1972; The Tower of London in the History of the Nation, 1972; Westminster Abbey in the History of the Nation, 1972; Shakespeare's Sonnets: a modern edition, 1973, rev. edn with introduction and prose versions, 1984; Shakespeare the Man, 1973, rev. edn, 1987; Simon Forman: Sex and Society in Shakespeare's Age, 1974; Windsor Castle in the History of the Nation, 1974; (with John Betjeman) Victorian and Edwardian Cornwall, 1974; Oxford in the History of the Nation, 1975; Discoveries and Reviews, 1975; Jonathan Swift: Major Prophet, 1975; A Cornishman Abroad, 1976; Brown Buck: a Californian fantasy, 1976; Matthew Arnold: Poet and Prophet, 1976; Shakespeare the Elizabethan, 1977; Homosexuals in History: Ambivalence in society, literature and the arts, 1977; Heritage of Britain, 1977; Milton the Puritan: Portrait of a Mind, 1977; The Road to Oxford: poems, 1978; (ed) The Poems of Shakespeare's Dark Lady, 1978; The Byrons and Trevanions, 1978; The Annotated Shakespeare, 3 vols (introds to vols and plays), 1978; A Man of the Thirties, 1979; Portraits and Views, 1979; Story of Britain, 1979; (ed) A Man of Singular Virtue: Roper's Life of Sir Thomas More, 1980; Memories of Men and Women, 1980; Shakespeare's Globe, 1980; A Life: Collected Poems, 1981; Eminent Elizabethans, 1983; Shakespeare's Characters: a complete guide, 1984; Night at the Carn, and Other Stories, 1984; Prefaces to Shakespeare's Plays, 1984; Shakespeare's Self-Portrait: Passages chosen from his work, with notes, 1984; Glimpses of the Great, 1985; (ed) The Contemporary Shakespeare, 1985–87; Reflections on the Puritan Revolution, 1986; The Little Land of Cornwall, 1986; Stories from Trenarren, 1986; A Quartet of Cornish Cats, 1986; The Poet Auden, 1987; Court and Country: studies in Tudor social history, 1987; Froude the Historian, 1988; Quiller Couch: portrait of Q, 1988; Shakespeare the Man, 1988; (ed and introd.) Froude, Spanish Story of the Armada, 1988; A. L. Rowse's Cornwall, 1988; Friends and Contemporaries, 1989; Transatlantic: Later Poems, 1989; The Controversial Colensos: South Africa and New Zealand, 1989; Discovering Shakespeare, 1989; Selected Poems, 1990; Prompting the Age: Poems Early and Late, 1990. *Address:* Trenarren House, St Austell, Cornwall PL26 6BH. *Club:* Athenæum.

ROWSELL, Edmund Lionel P.; *see* Penning-Rowsell.

ROWSON, John Anthony; Senior Partner, Herbert Smith, Solicitors, since 1988; *b* 6 May 1930; *s* of Thomas Herbert Rowson and Hilda Elizabeth Rowson; *m* 1st, 1955, Elizabeth Mary (*née* Fiddes) (marr. diss. 1980); two *s* one *d*; 2nd, 1989, Molly Lesley (*née* Newman). *Educ:* Beckenham Grammar Sch.; College of Law. Admitted Solicitor, 1959. Partner, Herbert Smith, 1960. *Recreations:* tennis, ski-ing, music. *Address:* 7 Wilton Street, SW1X 7AF. *Clubs:* Athenæum, City of London, Hurlingham, Royal Thames Yacht.

ROXBEE COX, family name of **Baron Kings Norton.**

ROXBURGH, Iain Edge; Chief Executive and Town Clerk, Coventry City Council, since 1989; *b* 4 Nov. 1943; *s* of John and Irene Roxburgh; *m* 1965, Tessa Breddy; two *s*. *Educ:* William Hulme's Grammar Sch., Manchester; Imperial Coll., London (BSc Eng, MSc, DIC). ACGI; CEng; MICE. Civil Engineer and transport planner, 1965–80; Greater London Council: Dep. Head of Personnel Services, 1981–83; Dir of Admin, 1983–85; Dep. Sec., AMA, 1985–89. *Recreations:* photography, motor cycling, walking, ski-ing. *Address:* Council House, Earl Street, Coventry CV1 5RR. *T:* Coventry (0203) 831100; Earlsdon, Coventry.

ROXBURGH, Prof. Ian Walter; Professor of Mathematics and Astronomy, since 1987, Head of School of Mathematical Sciences, since 1984, Director, Astronomy Unit, since 1983, Queen Mary and Westfield (formerly Queen Mary) College, London; *b* 31 Aug. 1939; *s* of Walter McRonald Roxburgh and Kathleen Joyce (*née* Prescott); *m* 1960, Diana Patricia (*née* Dunn); two *s* one *d*. *Educ:* King Edward VII Grammar Sch., Sheffield; Univ. of Nottingham (BSc Mathematics 1st Cl. Hons); Univ. of Cambridge (PhD); Elected Res. Fellow, Churchill Coll., Cambridge, 1963; Asst Lectr, Mathematics, 1963–64, Lectr, 1964–66, KCL; Reader in Astronomy, Univ. of Sussex, 1966–67; Queen Mary College, London University: Prof. of Applied Maths, 1967–87; Hd, Dept of Applied Maths, 1978–84; Pro-Principal, 1987. Chm., Cttee of Heads of Univ. Depts of Maths and Stats, 1988–. Contested: (L) Walthamstow W, 1970; (SDP) Ilford N, 1983. *Publications:* articles in Monthly Notices RAS, Astrophys. Jl, Astronomy and Astrophysics, Jl Geophysical Res., Phil. Trans Royal Soc., Gen. Relativity and Gravitation, Jl Physics A., Foundations of Physics, Nature, Solar Physics, Brit. Jl for the Philosophy of Science. *Recreations:* politics, philosophy. *Address:* 37 Leicester Road, Wanstead, E11 2DW. *T:* 081–989 7117.

ROXBURGH, Rt. Rev. James William; Assistant Bishop, Diocese of Liverpool, since 1991; *b* 5 July 1921; *s* of James Thomas and Margaret Roxburgh; *m* 1949, Marjorie Winifred (*née* Hipkiss); one *s* one *d*. *Educ:* Whitgift School; St Catharine's Coll., Cambridge (MA); Wycliffe Hall, Oxford. Deacon 1944, priest 1945; Curate: Christ Church and Holy Trinity, Folkestone, 1944–47; Handsworth, Birmingham, 1947–50; Vicar: S Matthew, Bootle, 1950–56; Drypool, Hull, 1956–65; Barking, 1965–77; Archdeacon of Colchester, 1977–83; Bishop Suffragan, later Area Bishop of Barking, 1983–90. Canon of Chelmsford, 1972–77. Pro-Prolocutor, Convocation of Canterbury, 1977–83. Pres. Barking Rotary Club, 1976–77. Hon. Freeman, Barking and Dagenham, 1990. *Recreations:* travel, philately. *Address:* 53 Preston Road, Southport, Merseyside PR9 9EE. *T:* Southport (0704) 542927. *Club:* Commonwealth Trust.

ROXBURGH, Vice-Adm. Sir John (Charles Young), KCB 1972 (CB 1969); CBE 1967; DSO 1943; DSC 1942 (Bar, 1945); *b* 29 June 1919; *s* of Sir (Thomas) James (Young) Roxburgh, CIE; *m* 1942, Philippa, 3rd *d* of late Major C. M. Hewlett, MC; one *s* one *d*. *Educ:* RNC, Dartmouth. Naval Cadet, 1933; Midshipman, 1937; Sub-Lt 1939; Lt 1941; Lt-Comdr 1949; Comdr 1952; Capt. 1958; Rear-Adm. 1967; Vice-Adm. 1970. Served in various ships, 1937–39; joined Submarine Br., 1940; served in ops off Norway, in Bay of Biscay and Mediterranean, 1940–42; comd HM Submarines H43, United and Tapir, 1942–45 in ops in Mediterranean and off Norway; HMS Vanguard, 1948–50; comd HM Submarine Turpin, 1951–53; HMS Triumph, 1955; HMS Ark Royal, 1955–56; comd HMS Contest, 1956–58; Brit. Jt Services Mission, Wash., 1958–60; comd 3rd Submarine Sqdn and HMS Adamant, 1960–61; idc 1962; Dep. Dir of Defence Plans (Navy), MoD, 1963–65; comd HMS Eagle, 1965–67; Flag Officer: Sea Training, 1967–69; Plymouth, 1969; Submarines, and NATO Comdr Submarines, E Atlantic, 1969–72, retired 1972. Chm., Grovebell Group Ltd, 1972–75. Mem. Management Cttee, The Freedom Assoc., 1978–85. Pres., Royal Naval Benevolent Trust, 1978–84. Co. Councillor, Surrey, 1977–81. *Recreations:* golf, sailing, walking, music. *Address:* Oakdene, Wood Road, Hindhead, Surrey GU26 6PT. *T:* Hindhead (0428) 605600. *Clubs:* Army and Navy; Liphook Golf, Woking Golf.

ROXBURGHE, 10th Duke of, *cr* 1707; **Guy David Innes-Ker;** Baron Roxburghe 1600; Earl of Roxburghe, Baron Ker of Cessford and Cavertoun, 1616; Bt (NS) 1625; Viscount Broxmouth, Earl of Kelso, Marquis of Bowmont and Cessford, 1707; Earl Innes (UK), 1837; *b* 18 Nov. 1954; *s* of 9th Duke of Roxburghe, and Margaret Elisabeth (*d* 1983) (who *m* 1976, Jocelyn Olaf Hambro, *qv*), *d* of late Frederick Bradshaw McConnel; *S* father, 1974; *m* 1977, Lady Jane Meriel Grosvenor (marr. diss. 1990), *yr d* of 5th Duke of Westminster, TD; two *s* one *d*. *Educ:* Eton; RMA Sandhurst (Sword of Honour, June 1974); Magdalene Coll., Cambridge (BA (Land Economy) 1980; MA 1984). Commnd into Royal Horse Guards/1st Dragoons, 1974; RARO 1977. Mem., Fishmongers' Co.; Freeman of City of London, 1983. *Recreations:* shooting, fishing, golf, racing, ski-ing. *Heir:* *s* Marquis of Bowmont, *qv*. *Address:* Floors Castle, Kelso TD5 7RW. *T:* Kelso (0573) 24288. *Clubs:* Turf, White's.

ROY, Andrew Donald; economist; *b* 28 June 1920; *er s* of late Donald Whatley Roy, FRCS, FRCOG, and late Beatrice Anne Roy (*née* Barstow); *m* 1947, Katherine Juliet Grove-White; one *s* two *d*. *Educ:* Malvern Coll.; Sidney Sussex Coll., Cambridge. Maths Trip. Pt I 1939 and Econ. Trip. Pt II 1948, Class I hons. 1939–45: served Royal Artillery, in UK, India and Burma (8 Medium Regt; Adjt, 1942–44). Cambridge Univ.: Asst Lecturer, 1949–51; Lecturer, 1951–64; Jun. Proctor, 1956–57; Sidney Sussex Coll.: Fellow, 1951–64; Tutor, 1953–56; Sen. Tutor, 1956–62; Financial Bursar, 1959–61. HM Treasury: Economic Consultant, 1962; Sen. Economic Adviser, 1964; Under-Sec. (Economics), 1969–72; Under-Sec., DTI, 1972–74, MoD, 1974–76; Chief Economic Adviser, DHSS, 1976–80. Consultant, NIESR, 1981–83. Governor, Malvern Coll., 1960–. *Publications:* British Economic Statistics (with C. F. Carter), 1954; articles in economic and statistical jls. *Address:* 15 Rusholme Road, Putney, SW15 3JX. *T:* 081–789 3180. *Club:* United Oxford & Cambridge University.

ROY, Prof. Arthur Douglas, FRCS, FRCSE, FRCSGlas, FRCSI; FACS; Chief of Surgical Services, Ministry of Health, Sultanate of Oman, 1985–88, and Professor of Surgery, Sultan Qaboos University, 1986–88, retired; Professor Emeritus, Queen's University of Belfast, 1985; *b* 10 April 1925; *s* of Arthur Roy and Edith Mary (*née* Brown); *m* 1st, 1954, Monica Cecilia Mary Bowley; three *d*; 2nd, 1973, Patricia Irene McColl. *Educ:* Paisley Grammar Sch.; Univ. of Glasgow (MB, ChB, Commendation). RAMC, 1948–50; Surgical Registrar posts in Glasgow and Inverness, 1950–54; Sen. Surgical Registrar, Aylesbury and Oxford, 1954–57; Cons. Surgeon and Hon. Lectr, Western Infirmary, Glasgow, 1957–68; Foundn Prof. of Surgery, Univ. of Nairobi, 1968–72; Prof. of Surgery, QUB, 1973–85. Mem. Council, RCSE, 1979–85. *Publications:* Lecture Notes in Surgery: tropical supplement, 1975; various papers on gastro-enterology, endocrine surgery, tropical medicine, etc. *Recreations:* sailing, gliding, gardening. *Address:* Garden House, Old Feniton Village, near Honiton, Devon EX14 0BE. *T:* Honiton (0404) 850055. *Club:* Commonwealth Trust.

ROY, Ian; Assistant Under-Secretary of State, Home Office, 1963–72; *b* 2 Aug. 1912; *o s* of late John Roy and Annie Froude Marshall; *m* 1939, Betty Louise Blissett; one *s* two *d*. *Educ:* Manchester Grammar School; Peterhouse, Cambridge. Assistant Inspector of Taxes, 1935; Assistant Principal, Home Office, 1936; Private Secretary to Permanent Under-Secretary of State, 1938; to Parliamentary Under-Secretary of State, 1939–40; Asst Secretary, 1947. *Address:* Flat 47, Cholmeley Lodge, Cholmeley Park, Highgate, N6. *T:* 081–340 3143.

ROY, Sheila; Director of Nursing Management and Research, North West Thames Regional Health Authority, since 1988; *b* 27 Feb. 1948; *d* of Bertie and Dorothy Atkinson; *m* 1970, Robert Neil Roy. *Educ:* BA Open Univ.; RGN; DN (London); Cert Ed Leeds

Univ.; RNT. Milton Keynes Health Authority: Dir, Nursing Studies, 1983–86; Actg Chief Nursing Officer and Dir, Nursing Studies, Feb.–May 1986; Dist Nursing Advr and Dir, Nurse Educn, Hillingdon HA, 1986–88. Gov., Hatfield Poly. Special Commendation, Richard J. Puttock Award, BIM, 1986. *Recreations:* riding, tennis, sailing. *Address:* North West Thames Regional Health Authority, 40 Eastbourne Terrace, W2 3QR. *T:* 071–262 8011.

ROYCE, David Nowill; Director-General, Institute of Export, 1980–85; *b* 10 Sept. 1920; *s* of late Bernard Royce and Ida Christine (*née* Nowill); *m* 1942, Esther Sylvia Yule; two *s* one *d*. *Educ:* Reading School; Vienna University. Served HM Forces, 1940–46. Major, Intelligence Corps, 1946; Asst Principal, Foreign Office, German Section, 1948; Foreign Service, 1949; First Secretary: Athens, 1953; Saigon, 1955; Foreign Office, 1957; Head of Chancery, Caracas, 1960; Counsellor (Commercial), Bonn, 1963; Counsellor (Commercial) and Consul-Gen., Helsinki, 1967–68; Commercial Inspector, FCO, 1969–71; Dir for Co-ordination of Export Services, DTI, 1971–73; Under-Secretary: Overseas Finance and Planning Div., Dept of Trade, 1973–75; CRE 3 and Export Develt Divs, Dept of Trade, 1975–77; Export Develt Div., Dept of Trade, 1977–80. Hon. Fellow, Inst. of Export, 1985. *Publication:* Successful Exporting for Small Businesses, 1990. *Recreation:* gardening. *Address:* 5 Sprimont Place, SW3. *T:* 071–589 9148. *Club:* Hurlingham.

ROYCE, (Roger) John; QC 1987; a Recorder, since 1986; *b* 27 Aug. 1944; *s* of J. Roger Royce and Margaret A. Royce (*née* Sibbald); *m* 1979, Gillian Wendy Adderley; two *s* one *d*. *Educ:* The Leys Sch., Cambridge; Trinity Hall, Cambridge (BA). Qualified as Solicitor, 1969; called to the Bar, Gray's Inn, 1970. Cambridge Hockey Blue, 1965, 1966; Captain Somerset Hockey, 1976; Austrian qualified ski instructor. *Recreations:* cricket, ski-ing, golf, collecting corkscrews. *Address:* Guildhall Chambers, Broad Street, Bristol BS1 2HG. *T:* Bristol (0272) 273366. *Clubs:* Hawks (Cambridge); St Enodoc Golf.

ROYDEN, Sir Christopher (John), 5th Bt *cr* 1905; Associate Director, Gerrard Vivian Gray Ltd, since 1988; *b* 26 Feb. 1937; *s* of Sir John Ledward Royden, 4th Bt, and of Dolores Catherine, *d* of late Cecil J. G. Coward; *S* father, 1976; *m* 1961, Diana Bridget, *d* of Lt-Col J. H. Goodhart, MC; two *s* one *d*. *Educ:* Winchester Coll.; Christ Church, Oxford (MA). Duncan Fox & Co. Ltd, 1960–71; Spencer Thornton & Co., 1971–88: Partner, 1974–86; Dir, 1986–88. *Recreations:* fishing, shooting, gardening. *Heir:* *s* John Michael Joseph Royden [*b* 17 March 1965; *m* 1989, Lucilla, *d* of J. R. Stourton]. *Address:* Flat 2, 8 Nevern Square, SW5. *Club:* Boodle's.

ROYDS, Rev. John Caress, MA Cantab; *b* 1920; 3rd *s* of Rev. Edward Thomas Hubert Royds, BA. *Educ:* Monkton Combe School, Bath; Queens' College, Cambridge. II 1 hons History, 1947. Military service with British and Indian Armies, 1940–46. Assistant master, Bryanston School, Dorset, 1947–61, House-master, 1951–61; Headmaster: General Wingate School, Addis Ababa, 1961–65; Uppingham Sch., 1965–75. Deacon, 1974; Priest, 1975; Dir of Educn for Peterborough diocese, 1976–81; Vicar of St James's, Northampton, 1981–85; with CMS, Peshawar, Pakistan, 1985–86. *Address:* 16B Donaldson Road, Salisbury SP1 3AD.

ROYLE, family name of **Baron Fanshawe of Richmond.**

ROYLE, Timothy Lancelot Fanshawe, FCIM; FBIBA; Chairman: Control Risks Group, 1975–91; Berry Palmer & Lyle, 1984–91; *b* 24 April 1931; *s* of Sir Lancelot Carrington Royle, KBE, and Barbara Rachel Royle; *m* 1959, Margaret Jill Stedeford; two *s* one *d*. *Educ:* Harrow; Mons Mil. Acad. FInstM 1977. Commnd 15th/19th King's Royal Hussars, 1949, Inns of Court Regt, TA, 1951–63. Joined Hogg Robinson Gp, 1951; Man. Dir, 1980–81. Dir, Wellmarine Reinsurance Brokers, 1976–. Member: Church Assembly of C of E, 1960–70; Gen. Synod of C of E, 1985–; Church Comr, 1966–83. Chairman: Lindley Educn Trust, 1970–; Christian Weekly Newspapers, 1979–. *Recreations:* country pursuits, ski-ing. *Address:* National Westminster Bank, 11 Leadenhall Street, EC3. *Clubs:* Cavalry and Guards, MCC; St Moritz Tobogganing (St Moritz).
See also Baron Fanshawe of Richmond.

ROZARIO, Most Rev. Michael; *see* Dhaka, Archbishop of, (RC).

ROZHDESTVENSKY, Gennadi Nikolaevich; Founder, Artistic Director and Chief Conductor, State Symphony Orchestra of Ministry of Culture, USSR (New Symphony Orchestra), since 1983; Professor of Conducting, Moscow State Conservatoire, since 1965; *b* 4 May 1931; *m* Victoria Postnikova, concert pianist. Studied piano at Moscow Conservatoire; started conducting at 18. Conductor Bolshoi Theatre, 1956–60 (Assistant Conductor, 1951); Chief Conductor, USSR Radio and Television Symphony Orchestra, 1960–74; Principal Conductor, Bolshoi Theatre, 1965–70; Chief Conductor: Stockholm Philharmonic Orchestra, 1974–77; BBC Symphony Orchestra, 1978–81; Moscow Chamber Opera, 1974–83; Vienna Symphony Orchestra, 1981–83. Guest conductor, Europe, Israel, America, Far East, Australia. Lenin Prize, 1970; People's Artist, USSR, 1972; Order of Red Banner of Labour, 1981. *Recreation:* music. *Address:* c/o Victor Hochhauser, 4 Oak Hill Way, NW3. *Club:* Athenæum.

RUBBIA, Prof. Carlo; physicist; Director-General, European Organisation for Nuclear Research, since 1989; *b* 31 March 1934; *s* of Silvio and Bice Rubbia; *m* Marisa; one *s* one *d*. *Educ:* Scuola Normale Superiore, Pisa; Univ. of Pisa (Dr 1957). Research Fellow, Columbia Univ., 1958–59; Lectr, Univ. of Rome, 1960–61; CERN, 1960– (head of team investigating fundamental particles on proton-antiproton collider); scientist, Fermi Nat. Accelerator Lab., USA, 1969–73; Prof. of Physics, Harvard Univ., 1971–88. Member: Papal Acad. of Science, 1985–; Amer. Acad. of Arts and Sciences, 1985; Accademia dei XL; Accademia dei Lincei; European Acad. of Sciences; Ateneo Veneto; Foreign Member: Royal Soc.; Soviet Acad. of Scis, 1988. Hon. Doctorates: Boston, Chicago, Geneva, Genoa, Northwestern, Udine, Carnegie-Mellon, and La Plata Universities. Gold Medal, Italian Physical Soc., 1983; Lorenzo il Magnifico Prize for Sciences, 1983; Achille de Gasperi Prize for Sciences, 1984; Nobel Prize for Physics (jtly), 1984; Leslie Prize for exceptional achievements, 1985; Castiglioni di Sicilia Prize, 1985; Carlo Capodieci Gold Medal, 1985; Jesolo d'Oro, 1986. Knight Grand Cross, Italy; Officer, Legion of Honour, France, 1989. *Publications:* papers on nuclear physics: weak force quanta (W−, W+ and Z particles, intermediate vector bosons); proton-antiproton collision; sixth quark. *Address:* CERN, 1211 Geneva 23, Switzerland.

RUBENS, Bernice Ruth; writer and director of documentary films, since 1957; *b* 26 July 1928; *m* 1947, Rudi Nassauer; two *d*. *Educ:* University of Wales, Cardiff (BA, Hons English; Fellow 1982; DLitt 1991). Followed teaching profession, 1950–55. American Blue Ribbon award for documentary film, Stress, 1968. *Publications:* Set on Edge, 1960; Madame Sousatzka, 1962 (filmed, 1989); Mate in Three, 1965; The Elected Member, 1969 (Booker Prize, 1970); Sunday Best, 1971; Go Tell the Lemming, 1973; I Sent a Letter to my Love, 1975; The Ponsonby Post, 1977; A Five Year Sentence, 1978; Spring Sonata, 1979; Birds of Passage, 1981; Brothers, 1983; Mr Wakefield's Crusade, 1985; Our Father, 1987; Kingdom Come, 1990; A Solitary Grief, 1991. *Recreation:* plays piano and 'cello. *Address:* 16A Belsize Park Gardens, NW3 4LD. *T:* 071–586 5365.

RUBERY, Dr Eileen Doris; Senior Principal Medical Officer, and Head of Medical Division, Health Promotion, Department of Health, since 1991; *b* 16 May 1943; *d* of James and Doris McDonnell; *m* 1969, Philip Huson Rubery; one *d*. *Educ:* Westcliff High Sch. for Girls; Sheffield Univ. Med. Sch. (MB ChB Hons); Cambridge Univ. (PhD). FRCR; MRCPath. Royal Infirmary, Sheffield, 1966–67; MRC Res. Fellow, Dept of Biochem., Cambridge, 1967; Meres' Sen. Student, St John's Coll., Cambridge, 1971; Addenbrooke's Hospital, Cambridge: Registrar in Radiotherapy and Oncology, 1973; Sen. Registrar, 1976; Wellcome Sen. Clinical Res. Fellow; Hon. Consultant, 1978; Sen. Res. Fellow and Dir of Med. Studies, Girton Coll., 1981; SMO (Toxicology), DHSS, 1983; Department of Health: PMO, 1988; SPMO and Hd of Med. Div., Communicable Disease and Immunisation, 1988–91. *Publications:* (ed) Indications for Iodine Prophylaxis following a Nuclear Accident, 1990; (ed) Medicine: a degree course guide, 1974–83; papers in professional jls. *Recreations:* music, theatre, tapestry work, reading Mme de Sévigné on the Underground. *Address:* Department of Health, Wellington House, 133–135 Waterloo Road, SE1 8UG. *T:* 071–972 2000.

RUBIN, Kenneth Warnell; His Honour Judge Rubin; DL; a Circuit Judge since 1972; *b* 8 March 1920; *s* of late Albert Reginald Rubin and late Mary Eales Rubin; *m* 1948, Jeanne Marie Louise de Wilde (*d* 1991); one *s* two *d*. *Educ:* King's College Sch., Wimbledon; King's Coll., London (LLB). Served HM Forces, 1939–45. Called to Bar, Gray's Inn, 1948. DL Surrey, 1989. *Address:* Tyrrellswood, Shere Road, West Horsley, Surrey KT24 6ER. *T:* East Horsley (04865) 2848.

RUBINS, Jack, FIPA; Chairman and Chief Executive Officer, McCann-Erickson Group UK, since 1990; *b* 4 Aug. 1931; *m* 1962, Ruth Davids; three *s*. *Educ:* Northern Polytechnic (Architecture). Chm. and Chief Exec., DFS Dorland Advertising, 1976–87; Chm., SMS Communications Gp, 1988–90. Chm., Hist. of Advertising Trust. *Recreations:* philately, golf. *Address:* Danehurst, 34 Northwick Circle, Harrow, Middx HA3 0EE.

RUBINSTEIN, Hilary Harold; Chairman and Managing Director, A. P. Watt Ltd (Literary Agents), since 1983; *b* 24 April 1926; *s* of H. F. and Lina Rubinstein; *m* 1955, Helge Kitzinger; three *s* one *d*. *Educ:* Cheltenham Coll.; Merton Coll., Oxford (MA). Editorial Dir, Victor Gollancz Ltd, 1952–63; Special Features Editor, The Observer, 1963–64; Dep. Editor, The Observer Magazine, 1964–65. Partner, 1965–, later Director, A. P. Watt Ltd. Mem. Council, ICA, 1976–; Trustee, Open Coll. of the Arts, 1987–. Founder-editor, The Good Hotel Guide (published in USA as Europe's Wonderful Little Hotels and Inns), 1978–. *Publications:* The Complete Insomniac, 1974; Hotels and Inns, an Oxford anthology, 1984. *Recreations:* hotel-watching, reading in bed. *Address:* 61 Clarendon Road, W11 4JE. *T:* 071–727 9550. *Club:* Garrick.
See also M. B. Rubinstein.

RUBINSTEIN, Michael Bernard; Consultant, Rubinstein Callingham Polden & Gale (formerly Rubinstein Callingham), Solicitors, since 1986 (Senior Partner, 1976–86); *b* 6 Nov. 1920; *s* of late H. F. Rubinstein and Lina (*née* Lowy); *m* 1955, Joy Douthwaite; two *s* two *d*. *Educ:* St Paul's Sch. Admitted solicitor, 1948. Served War, RE (TA), 1939, and RA; Captain 1945. Sen. Partner, Rubinstein, Nash & Co., later Rubinstein Callingham, 1969–86. Mem., Lord Chancellor's Cttee on Defamation, 1971–74. Trustee, SPNM, 1967– (Chm., 1986–). *Publications:* (ed and contrib.) Wicked, Wicked Libels, 1972; Rembrandt and Angels (monograph), 1982; (with Rowland Parker) The Cart-Ruts on Malta and Gozo (monograph), 1984, repr. with The People of the Temples of Malta and Gozo (monograph with Rowland Parker) as Malta's Ancient Temples and Ruts, 1988; Music to my Ear, 1985; contrib. legal and other jls. *Recreations:* faxing loose-ball letters to Editors when inspired, experiencing right hemisphere mentation, ruminating, practising. *Address:* 2 Raymond Buildings, Gray's Inn, WC1R 5BZ. *T:* 071–242 8404. *Club:* Garrick.
See also H. H. Rubinstein.

RUBINSTEIN, Prof. Nicolai, FBA 1971; FRHistS; Professor of History, Westfield College, London University, 1965–78, now Emeritus; *b* 13 July 1911; *s* of Bernhard and Irene Rubinstein; *m* 1954, Ruth Kidder Olitsky. *Educ:* Univs of Berlin and Florence. LittD Florence. Lectr, UC Southampton, 1942–45; Lectr, 1945–62, Reader, 1962–65, Westfield Coll., Univ. of London. Corresp. Mem., Accad. Toscana La Colombaria, 1976; Hon. Fellow: Warburg Inst., 1985; Westfield Coll., 1986. Hon. Diploma di perfezionamento, Scuola Normale Superiore, Pisa, 1991. Serena Medal, British Acad., 1974; Premio Internazionale Galileo Galilei, 1985; Fiorino d'oro, Florence, 1990. Hon. Citizen, Florence, 1991. *Publications:* The Government of Florence under the Medici 1434–94, 1966; (ed) Florentine Studies: politics and society in Renaissance Florence, 1968; Gen. Editor, Letters of Lorenzo de'Medici and ed vol. 3, 1977, and vol. 4, 1981; articles in Jl of Warburg and Courtauld Insts, Italian Studies, Archivio Storico Italiano, Rinascimento, etc. *Address:* 16 Gardnor Mansions, Church Row, NW3 6UR. *T:* 071–435 6995.

RUBNER, Ben; General Secretary, Furniture, Timber and Allied Trades Union, 1976–86; *b* 30 Sept. 1921; *s* of Charles and Lily Rubner; *m* 1952, Amelia Sonia Bagnari; one *s* one *d*. *Educ:* Mansford Street Central Sch., Bethnal Green, E2. Apprentice cabinet maker, 1935; Mem. Cttee, Trade Union Br., 1937. Served war in armed forces, Royal Corps of Signals: N Africa, Italy, Sicily, 1941–46. Shop Steward, Sec., Chm. and Convenor, London Furniture Workers Shop Stewards Council, 1947–52; NUFTO: London Dist Cttee, 1954; Gen. Exec. Council, 1958; London Dist Organiser, 1959. Nat. Trade Organiser, 1963; Asst Gen. Sec., FTAT, 1973–76. British TUC: London Delegate, 1955–58; full-time Officer Deleg., 1974–77. Mem., Central Arbitration Cttee, ACAS, 1977. *Recreations:* music (opera, light and grand), chess, table tennis, swimming. *Address:* 6 Oak Avenue, Bricket Wood, St Albans, Herts AL2 3LG. *Club:* Cambridge and Bethnal Green Old Boys.

RUBYTHON, Eric Gerald, CBE 1978; Member of Aerospace Board, British Aerospace, 1977–83, retired (Deputy Chief Executive of Aircraft Group, 1977–82); *b* 11 Feb. 1921; *s* of Reginald Rubython and Bessie Rubython; *m* 1943, Joan Ellen Mills. Joined Hawker Aircraft Ltd, 1948; Co. Sec., 1953; Exec. Dir, 1959; Dir and Gen. Man., 1960; Divl Dir and Gen. Man., Hawker Blackburn Div., 1963; Hawker Siddeley Aviation: Commercial Dir, 1965; Dir and Gen. Manager, 1970; Chm. and Man. Dir, 1977. *Recreations:* golf, gardening. *Address:* 1230 San Julian Drive, Lake San Marcos, Calif 92069, USA.

RUCK, Peter Frederick C.; *see* Carter-Ruck.

RUCK KEENE, John Robert, CBE 1977 (MBE 1946); TD 1950; Secretary General, Royal Society of Chemistry, 1980–81; *b* 2 Jan. 1917; *s* of late Major Robert Francis Ruck Keene, OBE, and Dorothy Mary (*née* Chester); *m* 1951, Beryl M Manistre; two *s*. *Educ:* Eton; Trinity Coll., Cambridge (BA 1938, MA 1955). Commissioned TA, Oxford and Bucks LI, 1939; served UK and NW Europe, 1939–45 (Major 1944, MBE 1946). First appointment with Chemical Society, 1946; General Secretary, 1947–80, when the Royal Society of Chemistry was formed by unification under Royal Charter of The Chemical Society and The Royal Institute of Chemistry, 1 June 1980. Hon. FRSC, 1982. *Address:* Chenies Cottage, 8 Copperkins Grove, Amersham, Bucks HP6 5QD. *T:* Amersham (0494) 727123.

RUCKER, Jeffrey Hamilton; His Honour Judge Rucker; a Circuit Judge, since 1988; *b* 19 Dec. 1942; *s* of Charles Edward Sigismund Rucker and Nancy Winifred Hodgson; *m* 1965, Caroline Mary Salkeld; three *s. Educ*: St Aubyn's, Rottingdean; Charterhouse. Called to the Bar, Middle Temple, 1967; a Recorder, 1984; a Circuit Judge, assigned to SE Circuit, 1988. *Recreations*: sailing, ski-ing, music. *Address*: 36 Essex Street, WC2 3AS.

RUDD, (Anthony) Nigel (Russell); Chairman, Williams Holdings, since 1982; *b* 31 Dec. 1946; *m* 1969, Lesley Elizabeth (*née* Hodgkinson); two *s* one *d. Educ*: Bemrose Grammar Sch., Derby. FCA. Qualified Chartered Accountant 1968; Divl Finance Dir, London & Northern Group, 1970–73; trouble shooting rôle, London & Northern, in loss making subs. cos, 1973–75; Finance Dir, Bardolin, 1975–77; (jtly) purchased C. Price & Son (building co.), 1977; purchased London & Provincial Properties (Chm.), 1981; C. Price & Son purchased W. Williams & Sons (Holdings), now Williams Holdings, 1982; sold C. Price & Son and London & Provincial Properties, 1986; Non-Executive Chairman: Raine Industries, 1986; Pendragon PLC, 1989–; Non-Exec. Director: Gartmore Value Investment, 1989–; East Midlands Electricity PLC, 1990–. Mem., City & Industrial Liaison Council, 1988. *Recreations*: squash, golf, shooting, ski-ing, swimming, theatre. *Address*: c/o Williams Holdings, Pentagon House, Sir Frank Whittle Road, Derby DE2 4XA. *T*: Derby (0332) 364257.

RUDD, Norman Julian Peter Joseph; His Honour Judge Rudd; a Circuit Judge, since 1988; *b* 12 May 1943; *s* of Norman Arthur Rudd and Winifred Rudd; *m* 1968, Judith Margaret Pottinger; three *s. Educ*: Paston Sch., N Walsham, Norfolk; University Coll. London (LLB, LLM). Called to the Bar, Inner Temple, 1968; Asst Recorder, 1982–87, Head of Chambers, 1982–87; a Recorder, 1987. *Recreations*: farming, shooting. *Address*: The Courts of Justice, London Road, Southampton SO9 5AF.

RUDD-JONES, Derek, CBE 1981; PhD; Director, Glasshouse Crops Research Institute, Littlehampton, Sussex, 1971–86; *b* 13 April 1924; 2nd *s* of late Walter Henry Jones and late Doris Mary, *er d* of H. Rudd Dawes; *m* 1948, Joan, 2nd *d* of late Edward Newhouse, Hong Kong, and Malvern, Worcs; two *s* one *d. Educ*: Whitgift; Repton; Emmanuel Coll., Cambridge. BA, MA, PhD (Cantab); FIBiol; FIHort. Agricultural Research Council, postgrad. student, Botany Sch., Univ. of Cambridge, 1945–48; Plant Pathologist, E African Agric. and Forestry Research Org., Kenya, 1949–52; Nat. Research Council, Postdoctoral Fellow, Univ. of Saskatchewan, Saskatoon, Canada, 1952–53. ICI Ltd, Akers Research Laboratory, The Frythe, Welwyn, Herts, 1953–56; Jealott's Hill Research Station, Bracknell, Berks, 1956–59; Scientific Adviser to Sec., Agricl Research Council, 1959–71; Foundn Chm., 1968–72, Managing Editor, 1986–, British Crop Protection Council (Mem., 1968–86); Pres., Section K, BAAS, 1981–82; Mem., Scientific Cttee, RHS, 1985–; formerly Mem., Adv. Cttee on Pesticides and Other Toxic Chemicals. Vis. Fellow, Univ. of Southampton, 1975–86. Governor, W Sussex Inst. of Higher Educn, 1980–; Trustee, Thomas Phillips Price Trust, 1988–. *Publications*: papers in scientific journals. *Recreations*: gardening, riding, fly-fishing. *Address*: Bignor Park Cottage, near Pulborough, West Sussex RH20 1HQ. *Club*: Farmers'.

RUDDEN, Prof. Bernard (Anthony), LLD; Professor of Comparative Law, University of Oxford, since 1979; Fellow of Brasenose College, Oxford, since 1979; *b* 21 Aug. 1933; *s* of John and Kathleen Rudden; *m* 1957, Nancy Campbell Painter; three *s* one *d. Educ*: City of Norwich Sch.; St John's Coll., Cambridge. LLD Cantab; DCL Oxon; PhD Wales. Solicitor. Fellow and Tutor, Oriel Coll., Oxford, 1965–79. Hon. LLD McGill, 1991. *Publications*: Soviet Insurance Law, 1966; The New River, 1985; Basic Community Cases, 1987; co-author or editor of: The Law of Mortgages, 1967; Source-Book on French Law, 1973, 3rd edn 1991; Basic Community Laws, 1980, 2nd edn 1986; The Law of Property, 1982; contrib. periodical pubns. *Address*: Brasenose College, Oxford OX1 4AJ. *T*: Oxford (0865) 277865. *Club*: United Oxford & Cambridge University.

RUDDEN, James; Advisory Head Teacher on Secondary Reorganisation, ILEA, 1976–78, retired; President: National Association of Head Teachers, 1971; London Head Teachers Association, 1969; Metropolitan Catholic Teachers Association, 1964; *b* 11 Dec. 1911; *s* of Bernard and Mary Rudden; *m* 1937, Eileen Finlay; one *s* four *d. Educ*: Carlisle Grammar Sch.; St Mary's Coll., Twickenham. BSc (Special, Geo.) (London Univ.); Teacher's Cert. (London Univ.). Asst Teacher, Carlisle, 1933–47; served War, RAF Educn Officer, 1940–45. First Head: St Cuthbert's Sec. Mod. Sch., Cleator, 1948–52; St Thomas More Sec. Mod. Sch., Tottenham, 1952–59; Bishop Thomas Grant Comprehensive Sch., Streatham, 1959–75. External Examnr for BEd, Avery Hill Coll. Chairman: London Comprehensive Head Teachers Conf., 1974–75; Southwark Diocesan Schs Commn; Governing Body of Schs Council; Adv. Council for Supply and Trng of Teachers. KSG 1969. *Publications*: numerous articles on educnl topics in educational and national press. *Recreation*: indulgence in retirement pursuits. *Address*: 5 The Gorse, Rissington Road, Bourton-on-the-Water, Glos. GL54 2EJ. *T*: Cotswold (0451) 21052.

RUDDOCK, Joan Mary; MP (Lab) Lewisham, Deptford, since 1987; *b* 28 Dec. 1943; *d* of Ken and Eileen Anthony; *m* 1963, Prof. Keith Ruddock. *Educ*: Pontypool Grammar Sch. for Girls; Imperial Coll., Univ. of London (BSc; ARCS). Worked for Shelter, national campaign for the homeless, 1968–73; Dir, Oxford Housing Aid Centre, 1973–77; Special Programmes Officer with unemployed young people, MSC, 1977–79; Organiser, CAB, Reading, 1979–86. Chairperson, CND, 1981–85, a Vice Chairperson, 1985–86. Active in politics and pressure groups, and mem. of anti-racist concerns, throughout working life. Frank Cousins' Peace Award, TGWU, 1984. *Publications*: CND Scrapbook, 1987; co-author of pubns on housing; (contrib.): The CND Story, 1983; Voices for One World, 1988. *Recreations*: music, travel, gardening. *Address*: c/o House of Commons, SW1.

RUDÉ, Prof. George Frederick Elliot; Professor of History, Concordia University, Montreal, 1970–87, Emeritus Professor, 1988; *b* 8 Feb. 1910; *s* of Jens Essendrop Rude, Norway, and Amy Geraldine Elliot Rude, England; *m* 1940, Doreen, *d* of J. W. De la Hoyde, Dublin; no *c. Educ*: Shrewsbury Sch.; Trinity Coll., Cambridge. Dr of Letters (Adelaide), 1967. Taught at: Stowe Sch., Bucks, 1931–35; St Paul's Sch., London, 1936–49; Sir Walter St John's Sch., London, 1950–54; Holloway Sch., London, 1954–59; Univ. of Adelaide: Sen. Lectr in History, 1960–63; Prof. of History, 1964–67; Prof. of History, Flinders Univ., SA, 1968–70; Leverhulme Vis. Prof., Univ. of Tokyo, Sept.-Nov. 1967; Vis. Prof., Univ. of Stirling, 1968; Vis. Prof. Fellow, Univ. of Sussex, 1979–82; Pinckney Harrison Vis. Prof., Coll. of William and Mary, Williamsburg, USA, 1980–81. Dir, Norway Mission, UNWRA, 1945. Mem., Australian Research Grants Cttee, 1969. Alexander Prize, Roy. Hist. Soc., 1955. FRHistS 1957; Fellow, Australian Acad. of Humanities, 1963. Kt of Mark Twain, 1986. *Publications*: The Crowd in the French Revolution, 1959; Wilkes and Liberty, 1962; Revolutionary Europe 1783–1815, 1964; The Crowd in History, 1964; (ed) The Eighteenth Century 1715–1815, 1965; (ed) Robespierre, 1967; (with E. J. Hobsbawm) Captain Swing, 1969; Paris and London in the 18th Century, 1970; Hanoverian London 1714–1808, 1971; Debate on Europe 1815–1850, 1972; Europe in the Eighteenth Century, 1972; Robespierre, 1975; Protest and Punishment, 1978; Ideology and Popular Protest, 1980; Criminal and Victim: crime and society in early 19th century England, 1985; The French Revolution after 200 years,

1988; contribs to Eng. Hist. Review, Eng. Econ. Hist. Review, Revue Historique, Past and Present, etc. *Recreations*: swimming, reading, public speaking. *Address*: 24 Cadborough Cliff, Rye, Sussex TN31 7EB. *T*: Rye (0797) 223442.

RUDENSTINE, Dr Neil Leon; President, and Professor of English and American Literature and Language, Harvard University, since 1991; *b* 21 Jan. 1935; *s* of Harry Rudenstine and Mae Esperito Rudenstine; *m* 1960, Angelica Zander; one *s* two *d. Educ*: Princeton Univ. (BA 1956); Oxford Univ. (BA 1959; MA 1963); Harvard Univ. (PhD 1964). Instructor, English and American Lit. and Lang., Harvard Univ., 1964–66, Asst Prof. 1966–68; Princeton University: Associate Prof., English Dept, 1968–73; Dean of Students, 1968–72; Prof. of English, 1973–88; Dean of College, 1972–77; Provost, 1977–88; Exec. Vice-Pres., Andrew W. Mellon Foundn, 1988–91. *Publications*: Sidney's Poetic Development, 1967; (ed with George Rousseau) English Poetic Satire: Wyatt to Byron, 1972. *Address*: Office of the President, Massachusetts Hall, Harvard University, Cambridge, Mass 02138, USA. *T*: (617) 495–1502.

RUDGE, Alan Walter, OBE 1987; PhD; FEng 1984; Managing Director, Development and Procurement, since 1990, and Member Main Board, since 1989, British Telecom; *b* 17 Oct. 1937; *s* of Walter Thomas Rudge and Emma (*née* McFayden); *m* 1969, Jennifer Joan Minott; one *s* one *d. Educ*: Hugh Myddelton Sch.; London Polytechnic; Univ. of Birmingham (PhD ElecEng). FIEE, FIEEE. Res. Engr, Illinois Inst. of Technol. Res. Inst., 1968–71; Lectr, Electronic and Elec. Engrg Dept, Univ. of Birmingham, 1971–74; Engrg Adviser, Illinois Inst. of Technol. Res. Inst., 1974–79; Man. Dir, Era Technology Ltd, 1979–86; Dir, Research and Technology, 1987–89, Group Technology and Develt Dir, 1989–90, British Telecom. Non-Exec. Director and Member Board: British Maritime Technology Ltd, 1984–89; Ricardo Consulting Engrs PLC, 1985–89; BT&D Technologies Ltd, 1987–; Telecom Securicor Cellular Radio, 1989–90. Vis. Prof., Queen Mary and Westfield Coll. (formerly QMC), Univ. of London, 1985–. Pres., AIRTO, 1986. Dep. Chm., IEE, 1991 (Vice Chm., 1989–91); Mem., Electronics Divl Bd, 1980–89, Chm., 1984; Faraday Medal, 1991); Chm., Learned Soc. Bd, 1989–; Member: Systems and Electronics Bd, MoD Defence Scientific Adv. Council, 1981–87; CBI Res. and Technol. Cttee, 1980–86; ACOST, 1987–90. FRSA. Freeman, City of London. Hon. DEng Birmingham, 1991. *Publications*: The Handbook of Antenna Design, vol. 1 1982, vol. 2 1983; papers in sci. and tech. jls on antennas, microwaves and satellite communications. *Recreations*: dabbler in cycling, sailing, reading. *Address*: Greenacres, Chapel Lane, Westhumble, Dorking, Surrey RH5 6AL. *T*: Dorking (0306) 881597. *Club*: Athenæum.

RUDIN, Toni Richard Perrott; Secretary, Magistrates' Association, since 1986; *b* 13 Oct. 1934; *s* of Richard William Rudin and Sarah Rowena Mary Rudin (*née* Perrott); *m* 1958, Heather Jean (*née* Farley); one *s* three *d. Educ*: Bootham Sch.; Millfield Sch.; RMA Sandhurst; Army Staff Coll.; Coll. of Law, Guildford. Commissioned Royal Artillery, 1954; served BAOR, Cyprus, UK; MoD, 1967–69; Battery Comdr and 2 i/c 26th Field Regt, RA, BAOR, 1969–72; MoD, 1972–75; retired, 1975. Solicitor, 1978; private practice as solicitor, 1978–80; Press and Public Relations, Law Soc., 1980–86. *Recreations*: riding, gardening, house renovation. *Address*: Otterbank House, 60 Wedgwood Avenue, Blakelands, Milton Keynes MK14 5HX.

RUDKIN, (James) David; playwright; *b* 29 June 1936; *s* of David Jonathan Rudkin and Anne Alice Martin; *m* 1967, Alexandra Margaret Thompson; two *s* two *d. Educ*: King Edward's Sch., Birmingham; St Catherine's Coll., Oxford (MA). Screenplays: Testimony, 1987; December Bride, 1991. *Publications*: plays: Afore Night Come, 1963; (trans.) Moses and Aaron, 1965; The Grace of Todd (orig. opera libretto), 1969; Cries from Casement as his Bones are Brought to Dublin, 1974; Penda's Fen (film), 1975; Burglars (for children), 1976; Ashes, 1978; (trans.) Hippolytus, 1980; The Sons of Light, 1981; The Triumph of Death, 1981; (trans.) Peer Gynt, 1983; The Saxon Shore, 1986; (trans.) When We Dead Waken, 1989; (trans.) Rosmersholm, 1990; articles, reviews etc. for Encounter, Drama, Tempo. *Recreations*: piano, geology, anthropology, languages, swimming, bridge. *Address*: c/o Margaret Ramsay Ltd, 14a Goodwin's Court, WC2N 4LL. *T*: 071–240 0691.

RUDKIN, Walter Charles, CBE 1981; Director of Economic Intelligence, 1973–81, of Economic and Logistic Intelligence, 1982, Ministry of Defence; retired; *b* 22 Sept. 1922; *e s* of Walter and Bertha Rudkin; *m* 1950, Hilda Mary Hope; two *s. Educ*: Carre's Grammar Sch., Sleaford; UC Hull. BSc (Econ) London. Served with RAF, 1942–46. Lectr, Dept of Econs and Econ. History, Univ. of Witwatersrand, 1948–52. Entered Min. of Defence, 1954; various appts, incl. Hong Kong, 1956–59; Junior Directing Staff, Imperial Defence Coll., 1962–64; Cabinet Office, 1968–71. *Recreation*: fishing. *Address*: 9 Speen Place, Speen, Newbury, Berks RG13 1RX. *T*: Newbury (0635) 49244. *Club*: Commonwealth Trust.

RUDLAND, Margaret Florence; Headmistress, Godolphin and Latymer School, since 1986; *b* 15 June 1945; *d* of Ernest George and Florence Hilda Rudland. *Educ*: Sweyne School, Rayleigh; Bedford College, Univ. of London (BSc); Inst. of Education (PGCE). Asst Mathematics Mistress, Godolphin and Latymer Sch., 1967–70; VSO, Ilorin, Nigeria, 1970–71; Asst Maths Mistress, Clapham County Sch., 1971–72; Asst Maths Mistress and Head of Dept, St Paul's Girls' Sch., 1972–83; Deputy Headmistress, Norwich High Sch., GPDST, 1983–85. *Address*: The Godolphin and Latymer School, Iffley Road, Hammersmith, W6 0PG. *T*: 081–741 1936.

RUDLOFF, Hans-Jörg; Chairman and Chief Executive: Financière Credit Suisse First-Boston, since 1989; Credit Suisse First Boston Ltd, since 1989; *b* Cologne, 1940. *Educ*: Univs of Grenoble and Berne (Econs, Hons). Exec. Trainee, Credit Suisse, 1965–68; with Kidder, Peabody, International, 1969–79: Manager, Swiss operation; Man. Dir; Chm., 1978; Mem. Bd, Kidder, Peabody Inc., 1978; joined Financière Credit Suisse First-Boston, 1980; Dep. Chm. and Mem. Bd, 1981–88. Director: Credit Suisse, 1986–90; CS First Boston, Inc., 1990–. *Address*: Credit Suisse First Boston, 2A Great Titchfield Street, W1P 7AA.

RUDMAN, Michael Edward; theatre director and producer; *b* Tyler, Texas, 14 Feb. 1939; *s* of M. B. Rudman and Josephine Davis; *m* 1963, Veronica Anne Bennett (marr. diss. 1981); two *d; m* 1983, Felicity Kendal, *qv*; one *s. Educ*: St Mark's Sch., Texas; Oberlin Coll. (BA *cum laude* Govt); St Edmund Hall, Oxford (MA). Pres., OUDS, 1963–64. Asst Dir and Associate Producer, Nottingham Playhouse and Newcastle Playhouse, 1964–68; Asst Dir, RSC, 1968; Artistic Director: Traverse Theatre Club, 1970–73; Hampstead Theatre, 1973–78 (Theatre won Evening Standard Award for Special Achievement, 1978); Associate Dir, Nat. Theatre, 1979–88; Dir, Lyttelton Theatre (National), 1979–81; Dir, Chichester Festival Theatre, 1989–91. *Plays directed* include: *Nottingham Playhouse*: Changing Gear, Measure for Measure, A Man for All Seasons, 1965; Julius Caesar, She Stoops to Conquer, Who's Afraid of Virginia Woolf, Death of a Salesman, 1966; Long Day's Journey into Night, 1967; Lily in Little India, 1968; *RSC Theatregoround*: The Fox and the Fly, 1968; *Traverse Theatre*: Curtains (transf. Open Space, 1971), Straight Up (transf. Piccadilly, 1971), A Game called Arthur (transf. Theatre Upstairs, 1971), Stand for my Father, (with Mike Wearing) A Triple Bill of David Halliwell plays, 1970; The Looneys, Pantagleize, 1971; Carravagio Buddy, Tell Charlie Thanks for the Truss, The

Relapse, 1972; *Hampstead Theatre:* Ride across Lake Constance, A Nightingale in Bloomsbury Square, 1973; The Black and White Minstrels, The Show-off, The Connection, The Looneys, 1974; Alphabetical Order (transf. May Fair), 1975; Clouds, 1977; Cakewalk, Beyond a Joke, Gloo-Joo (transf. Criterion), 1978; *National Theatre:* For Services Rendered (televised, 1980), Death of a Salesman, 1979; Thee and Me, The Browning Version/Harlequinade, Measure for Measure, 1980; The Second Mrs Tanqueray, 1981; Brighton Beach Memoirs, The Magistrate, 1986; Six Characters in Search of an Author, Fathers and Sons, Ting Tang Mine, Waiting for Godot, 1987; *Chichester:* The Merry Wives of Windsor, Rumours, 1990; *West End:* Donkeys Years, Globe, 1976; Clouds, Duke of York's, 1978; Taking Steps, Lyric, 1980; Camelot, 1982; The Winslow Boy, 1983; The Dragon's Tail, Apollo, 1985; Exclusive, Strand, 1989; *New York:* The Changing Room, 1973; Hamlet, 1976; Death of a Salesman, 1984. Mem., Bd of Directors, Hampstead Theatre, 1979–. *Address:* c/o Peter Murphy Esq., Curtis Brown Group, 162–168 Regent Street, W1R 5TA. *T:* 071–437 9700. *Clubs:* Royal Automobile; Dyrham Park Country, Cumberland Lawn Tennis, Royal Mid-Surrey Golf.

RUDOE, Wulf, CB 1975; *b* 9 March 1916; *m* 1942, Ellen Trilling; one *s* one *d*. *Educ:* Central Foundation School; Peterhouse, Cambridge (Open Schol. and Research Schol.). Mathematics Tripos Pt III, 1938, Distinction. Royal Aircraft Establishment, 1939. Operational Research, RAF, 1939–45. Operational Research in Building Industry, Min. of Works, 1946–48, Principal Scientific Officer 1948; Board of Trade, Statistician 1948, Chief Statistician 1952; Dir of Statistics and Research, DHSS (formerly Min. of Health), 1966–76; Asst Sec., Price Commn, 1976–79; Adviser to Govt of Ghana, 1980–81. Fellow Inst. of Statisticians; Mem. Council, 1962–78, Hon. Treasurer, 1965–74, Vice-Pres., 1974–75 and 1976–77, Roy. Statistical Soc. *Recreations:* walking, travel, languages. *Address:* 72 North End Road, NW11 7SY. *T:* 081–455 2890.

RUE, Dame (Elsie) Rosemary, DBE 1989 (CBE 1977); Regional General Manager, 1984–88, and Regional Medical Officer, 1973–88, Oxford Regional Health Authority; *b* 14 June 1928; *d* of Harry and Daisy Laurence; divorced; two *s*. *Educ:* Sydenham High Sch.; Univ. of London; Oxford Univ. Med. School. MB, BS; FRCP; DCH; FRCPsych (Hon. FRCPsych 1990); PFCM, 1986–89; FRCGP. MA Oxford, 1988. Gen. Practitioner, 1952–58; Public Health Service, 1958–65; Hospital Service, 1965–73; SAMO, Oxford RHB, 1971. Pres., BMA, 1990–91; Past-Pres., Medical Women's Fedn. Hon. Fellow, Green Coll., Oxford, 1985. *Publications:* papers on gen. practice, women in medicine, ward design, community hosps, health services, individuals requiring security. *Address:* 2 Stanton St John, Oxford OX9 1ET.

RUFF, William Willis, CBE 1973; DL; Clerk of the Surrey County Council, 1952–74; *b* 22 Sept. 1914; *s* of late William Ruff, Whitby, Yorks; *m* 1939, Agnes, *d* of late Howard Nankivell; two *s*. *Educ:* Durham School. Served War of 1939–45: Royal Signals, North Africa and India, 1940–45; Capt., 1942; Maj., 1943. Asst Solicitor: Scarborough Corp., 1937; Heston and Isleworth Corp., 1938; Surrey County Council: Asst Solicitor, 1939; Senior Asst Solicitor, 1947; Asst Clerk, 1948; Deputy Clerk, 1951. Chm., Soc. of Clerks of Peace and of Clerks of County Councils, 1969–72. Mem., Parly Boundary Commn for England, 1974–83. DL Surrey, 1964. *Recreations:* music, watching cricket. *Address:* 3 Brympton Close, Ridgeway Road, Dorking, Surrey RH4 3AU. *T:* Dorking (0306) 882406.

RUFFLE, Mary, (Mrs Thomas Ruffle); *see* Dilnot, Mary.

RUGAMBWA, HE Cardinal Laurean; *see* Dar-es-Salaam, Archbishop of, (RC).

RUGBY, 3rd Baron, *cr* 1947, of Rugby, Co. Warwick; **Robert Charles Maffey;** farmer; *b* 4 May 1951; *s* of 2nd Baron Rugby and of Margaret Helen, *d* of late Harold Bindley; *S* father, 1990; *m* 1974, Anne Penelope, *yr d* of late David Hale; two *s*. *Educ:* Brickwall House Sch., Northiam. *Recreations:* shooting, golf, woodwork and metal work. *Heir: s* Hon. Timothy James Howard Maffey, *b* 23 July 1975. *Address:* Grove Farm, Frankton, Rugby CV23 9QG.

RUGGE-PRICE, Sir Charles Keith Napier; *see* Price.

RUGGLES-BRISE, Captain Guy Edward, TD, DL; *b* 15 June 1914; *s* of late Col Sir Edward Archibald Ruggles-Brise, 1st Bt, MC, TD, DL, JP, MP, and Agatha, *e d* of J. H. Gurney, DL, JP, Keswick Hall, Norfolk; *b* and *heir pres.* of Sir John Ruggles-Brise, Bt, *qv*; *m* 1940, Elizabeth (*d* 1988), *o d* of James Knox, Smithstone House, Kilwinning, Ayrshire; three *s*. *Educ:* Eton. Captain 104th (Essex Yeo.) Field Bde RHA (TA), No 7 Commando. Served War of 1939–45 (PoW). DL 1967, High Sheriff 1967, Essex. *Recreations:* field sports. *Address:* Housham Tye, Harlow, Essex. *T:* Bishops Stortford (0279) 731236; Ledgowan Lodge, Achnasheen, Ross-shire. *T:* Achnasheen (044588) 245. *Club:* City of London.

RUGGLES-BRISE, Col Sir John Archibald, 2nd Bt, *cr* 1935; CB 1958; OBE (mil.) 1945; TD; JP; Lord-Lieutenant of Essex, 1958–78; Pro-Chancellor, University of Essex, 1964–79; *b* 13 June 1908; *er s* of Colonel Sir Edward Archibald Ruggles-Brise, 1st Bt, MC, TD, DL, JP, MP, and Agatha (*d* 1937), *e d* of J. H. Gurney, DL, JP, of Keswick Hall, Norfolk; *S* father, 1942. *Educ:* Eton. Served AA Comd, 1939–45 (comd 1st 450 Mixed HAA Regt, and 2nd AA Demonstration and User Trials Regt); formed and comd 599 HAA Regt, 1947. Member of Lloyd's. Pres., CLA, 1957–59 (helped promote Game Fair); Church Comr, 1959–64; Chm., Council of the Baronetage, 1958–63. Patron, Essex Agricl Soc., 1970–78. DL 1945, JP 1946, Vice-Lieutenant, 1947, Co. Essex. Hon. Freeman of Chelmsford. Governor of Felsted and Chigwell Schools, 1950–75. DUniv Essex, 1980. KStJ. *Recreation:* shooting. *Heir: b* Capt. Guy Edward Ruggles-Brise, *qv*. *Address:* Spains Hall, Finchingfield, Essex CM7 4PF. *T:* Great Dunmow (0371) 810266. *Club:* Carlton.

RUHFUS, Dr Jürgen; Officer's Cross, Order of Merit, Federal Republic of Germany, 1983; Hon. KBE, 1978; Ambassador of the Federal Republic of Germany to the United States of America, since 1987; *b* 4 Aug. 1930; three *d*. *Educ:* Universities of Munich, Münster and Denver, USA. Joined Federal Foreign Office, Bonn, 1955; Consulate General: Geneva, 1956–57; Dakar, 1958–59; Embassy, Athens, 1960–63; Dep. Spokesman of Federal Foreign Office, 1964, Official Spokesman, 1966; Ambassador to Kenya, 1970–73; Asst Under-Secretary, Federal Foreign Office, 1973–76; Adviser on Foreign Policy and Defence Affairs to Federal Chancellor Helmut Schmidt, 1976–80; Ambassador to UK, 1980–83; Head of Political Directorate-General (dealing with Third World and other overseas countries), Federal Foreign Office, Dec. 1983–June 1984; State Sec., Federal Foreign Office, FRG, 1984–87. *Recreations:* golf, tennis, skiing, shooting. *Address:* 4645 Reservoir Road NW, Washington, DC 20007, USA.

RUHNAU, Heinz; Chairman, Deutsche Lufthansa, 1982–91; *b* Danzig, 5 March 1929; *m* Edith Loers; three *d*. Dip. in Business Administration, 1954; Head, personal office of Chm., IG-Metall, Frankfurt; Regional Dir, IG-Metall, Hamburg, 1956–65; Mem., Supervisory Bd, Hapag Lloyd; Head of Dept of Internal Affairs and Mem., Senate of Free Hanseatic City of Hamburg, 1965–73; Mem., Exec. Bd, COOP, 1973; State Sec., Ministry of Transport, 1974–82; Mem., Supervisory Bd, Vereinigte Tanklager und Transportmittel, Hamburg and Hapag Lloyd. Chm., Assoc. of European Airlines, 1988. Federal Grand Cross of Merit, 1980, with Star, 1989, FRG. *Address:* Deutsche Lufthansa, von Gablenz Strasse 2–6, D5000 Köln 21, Germany.

RUIZ SOLER, Antonio, (Antonio); Cross of the Order of Isabella the Catholic, 1951; Comdr Order of Civil Merit, 1964; Spanish dancer; Director, Ballet Nacional Español; *b* Seville, 4 November 1921. Studied at the Realito Dance Academy. First stage appearance at the age of eight; subsequently toured North and South America Southern and Western Europe, and Scandinavia. First stage appearance in Great Britain, Edinburgh Festival, 1950; London début, Cambridge Theatre, 1951. Golden Medal, Fine Arts, 1952. Formed Ballet Company, 1953; début in Generalife Theatre, Granada, presenting his Ballet in Europe, S and N America. Has also appeared in many festivals in Spain. Appearances with Ballet in London: Stoll, 1954; Palace, 1956; Coliseum, 1958; Royalty, 1960; Drury Lane, 1963; Coliseum, 1975. Gala perf. in Washington to President Kennedy, Ed Sullivan Show in New York, appearances Europe, 1963. Festivals of Spain, 1964–65; Madrid Season, 1965; N Amer. tour, 1965; Ed Sullivan Show, 1965. Appears on TV. Gold Medal, Swedish Acad. of Dancing, 1963; Medal of Min. of Information and Tourism, Madrid, 1963; Golden Medal, Spanish Inst., NY, 1979. *Address:* Coslada 7, Madrid, Spain.

RULE, Brian Francis; Director General of Information Technology Systems, Ministry of Defence, since 1985; *s* of Sydney John and Josephine Rule, Pen-y-ffordd, near Chester; *m* 1963, Kay M., *d* of late Dr and Mrs N. A. Dyce-Sharp. *Educ:* Daniel Owen Sch., Mold; Loughborough Univ. of Technology (MSc). Engineer, de Havilland Aircraft Co., 1955–59; Res. Assistant, Loughborough Univ., 1963–65; Lectr, Univ. of Glasgow, 1965–67; University of Aberdeen: Lectr, 1967–70; Sen. Lectr, 1970–72; Dir of Computing, 1972–78; Dir, Honeywell Information Systems Ltd, 1978–79; Dir of Scientific Services, NERC, 1979–85. *Publications:* various papers in scientific jls. *Recreations:* motoring, boats, antique clocks. *Address:* Ministry of Defence, Northumberland House, Northumberland Avenue, WC2N 5BP. *T:* 071–218 4828. *Club:* Commonwealth Trust.

RULE, David Charles; Dean of Postgraduate Dental Studies (Thames Regions), British Postgraduate Medical Federation, since 1990; *b* April 1937; *s* of Cyril George Leonard Rule and Ivy Rule; *m* 1972, Linda Marion Meyer; two *d*. *Educ:* Univ. of Birmingham (BDS). FDS RCS, MCCD RCS, DOrthRCS. Qualified Dental Surgeon, 1959; RADC 1960–63; Eastman Dental Hosp., 1964, Registrar, Lectr, Sen. Registrar, Consultant, 1975. President: British Paedontic Soc., 1988–89; British Soc. of Dentistry for the Handicapped, 1980; Internat. Assoc. of Dentistry for the Handicapped, 1990–92. *Recreation:* sailing. *Address:* 7 Malmains Way, Beckenham, Kent BR2 2SA. *T:* 081–650 1895. *Clubs:* MCC.

RULE, Margaret Helen, (Mrs A. W. Rule), CBE 1983; FSA; Research Director, Mary Rose Trust, since 1983; *b* 27 Sept. 1928; *d* of Ernest Victor and Mabel Martin; *m* 1949, Arthur Walter Rule; one *s*. *Educ:* Univ. of London. FSA 1967. Dir of Excavations, Chichester Civic Soc., 1961–79; Hon. Curator, Fishbourne Roman Palace and Museum, 1968–79; Archaeol Dir, Mary Rose Trust, 1979–82. Hon. Fellow, Portsmouth Polytechnic, 1982. Hon. DLitt Liverpool, 1984. Reginald Mitchell Medal, Stoke-on-Trent Assoc. of Engrs, 1983. *Publications:* Chichester Excavations 1, 1967; The Mary Rose, 1982; many papers in jls in Britain and USA. *Recreations:* anything in or on the water. *Address:* Mill House, Westbourne, West Sussex PO10 8TG.

RUMBELOW, Arthur Anthony; QC 1990; a Recorder, since 1988; *b* Salford, Lancs, 9 Sept. 1943; *er s* of Arthur and Theresa Rumbelow; *m* 1971, Shelagh Lewtas; three *d*. *Educ:* Salford Grammar Sch.; Queens' Coll., Cambridge (Squire Schol.; BA 1966). Called to the Bar, Middle Temple, 1967 (Harmsworth Exhibnr, Astbury Schol.); Chm., Medical Appeal Tribunal, 1988–. Mem., Rochdale MBC, 1982–84. *Recreations:* wine, theatre, Rugby, collecting. *Address:* 28 St John Street, Manchester M3 4DJ. *T:* 061–834 8418.

RUMBELOW, (Roger) Martin, CEng; Under Secretary, Management Services and Manpower Division, Department of Trade and Industry, since 1987; *b* 3 June 1937; *s* of Leonard Rumbelow and Phyllis (*née* Perkins); *m* 1965, Marjorie Elizabeth Glover. *Educ:* Cardiff High Sch.; Bristol Univ. (BSc); Cranfield Inst. of Technol. (MSc). CEng 1966. National Service, RAF Pilot, 1955–57. British Aircraft Corporation, 1958–74: Dep. Prodn Controller, 1967–73; Concorde Manufg Project Manager, 1973–74; DTI, 1974–: Principal, 1974–78; Asst Sec., 1978–86. *Recreations:* singing, opera, theatre, computing, amateur radio, electronics, tennis. *Address:* c/o Department of Trade and Industry, 1–19 Victoria Street, SW1H 0ET. *Club:* Royal Air Force.

RUMBLE, Captain John Bertram, RN (retired); Director General, Royal Over-Seas League, 1979–91; *b* 30 Oct. 1928; *s* of late Major and Mrs Rumble; *m* 1953, Jennifer; one *s* three *d*. *Educ:* Hordle House Sch.; Sherborne Sch. FBIM 1980, FIIM 1980. Special Entry Cadet into Royal Navy, 1946; ADC (Lieut) to Governor of Malta, 1952–53; specialised in Communications, 1954; HMS Maidstone, 1955–56; Staff, BRNC Dartmouth, 1956–57; Exchange Service with RCN, 1957–59; Signal Officer, HMS Ark Royal, 1959–61; Comdr 1962; RN sc 1963; CO HMS Torquay, 1964–65; Staff Communications Officer to C-in-C EASTLANT, 1966–67; Exec. Officer, HMS Hermes, 1967–69; Captain 1970; Staff Dir, Gen. Weapons, 1970–71; CO HMS Fearless, 1974–75; Asst Chief of Staff Communications (as Cdre), C-in-C SOUTH, 1976–77; MoD (Intelligence), 1977–79. Younger Brother, Trinity House, 1977; Member: Council, Mayfair, Piccadilly and St James's Assoc., 1979–91 (Chm., 1988–90); Jt Commonwealth Societies Council, 1980–91. *Recreations:* shooting, sailing, fishing, gold leaf gilding. *Address:* 109 Gaskarth Road, SW12 9NP. *T:* 081–675 0164. *Clubs:* Farmers', Royal Navy of 1765 and 1785; Keyhaven Yacht.

RUMBLE, Peter William, CB 1984; Chief Executive, Historic Buildings and Monuments Commission, 1983–89; Director-General, Union of European Historic Houses Associations, since 1991; *b* 28 April 1929; *s* of Arthur Victor Rumble and Dorothy Emily (*née* Sadler); *m* 1953, Joyce Audrey Stephenson; one *s* one *d*. *Educ:* Harwich County High Sch.; Oriel Coll., Oxford (MA). Entered Civil Service, 1952; HM Inspector of Taxes, 1952; Principal, Min. of Housing and Local Govt, 1963; Asst Sec., 1972, Under Sec., 1977, DoE. Member: Council, Architectural Heritage Fund, 1988–; Cttee, Southern Region, NT, 1990–; Redundant Churches Fund, 1991–. Trustee, Amer. Friends of English Heritage, 1988–. *Recreation:* music. *Address:* 11 Hillside Road, Cheam, Surrey SM2 6ET. *T:* 081–643 1752.

RUMBOLD, Sir Algernon; *see* Rumbold, Sir H. A. F.

RUMBOLD, Rt. Hon. Angela (Claire Rosemary), CBE 1981; PC 1991; MP (C) Mitcham and Morden (formerly Merton, Mitcham and Morden), since June 1982; Minister of State, Home Office, since 1990; *b* 11 Aug. 1932; *d* of late Harry Jones, FRS; *m* 1958, John Marix Rumbold; two *s* one *d*. *Educ:* Notting Hill and Ealing High Sch.; King's Coll., London. Founder Member, National Assoc. for the Welfare of Children in Hospital, and National Chairman, 1974–76. Councillor, Royal Borough of Kingston upon Thames, 1974–83; Chairman: Educn Cttee, Assoc. of Metropolitan Authorities, 1979–80; Council, Local Educn Authorities, 1979–80. Mem., Doctors and Dentists Review Body, 1979–81. Co-Chm., Women's Nat. Commn, 1986–90. Mem., Social Services Select Cttee, 1982–83; PPS to Financial Sec. to the Treasury, 1983, to Sec. of State for Transport, 1983–85; Parly

Under Sec. of State, DoE, 1985–86; Minister of State, DES, 1986–90. Freeman, City of London, 1988. *Recreations:* swimming, cinema, reading, ballet. *Address:* House of Commons, SW1A 0AA.

RUMBOLD, Sir Henry (John Sebastian), 11th Bt *cr* 1779; Partner, Dawson Cornwell, since 1991; *b* 24 Dec. 1947; *s* of Sir Horace Anthony Claude Rumbold, 10th Bt, KCMG, KCVO, CB, and Felicity Ann Rumbold (*née* Bailey); *S* father, 1983; *m* 1978, Frances Ann (*née* Hawkes, formerly wife of Julian Berry). *Educ:* Eton College; College of William and Mary, Virginia, USA (BA). Articled Stileman, Neate and Topping, 1975–77; admitted solicitor, 1977; asst solicitor, Stileman, Neate and Topping, 1977–79; Partner, 1979–81; joined Stephenson Harwood, 1981, Partner, 1982–91. *Recreations:* riding, shooting, reading. *Heir: cousin* Sir (Horace) Algernon (Fraser) Rumbold, *qv*. *Address:* 19 Hollywood Road, SW10 9HT. *T:* 071–352 9148; Hatch House, Tisbury, Wilts. *T:* Tisbury (0747) 870622.

RUMBOLD, Sir (Horace) Algernon (Fraser), KCMG 1960 (CMG 1953); CIE 1947; *b* 27 Feb. 1906; *s* of late Colonel William Edwin Rumbold, CMG; *m* 1946, Margaret Adél, *d* of late Arthur Joseph Hughes, OBE; two *d*. *Educ:* Wellington College; Christ Church, Oxford. Assistant Principal, India Office, 1929; Private Sec. to Parliamentary Under-Secretaries of State for India, 1930–33, and to Permanent Under-Secretary of State, 1933–34; Principal, 1934; Asst Sec., 1943; transferred to Commonwealth Relations Office, 1947; Deputy High Commissioner in the Union of South Africa, 1949–53; Asst Under Sec. of State, 1954–58; Dep. Under Sec. of State, 1958–66; retired, 1966. Chm. Cttee on Inter-Territorial Questions in Central Africa, 1963; Advr, Welsh Office, 1967. Dep. Chm., Air Transport Licensing Bd, 1971–72. Mem. Governing Body, SOAS, 1965–80, Hon. Fellow, 1981. Pres., Tibet Soc. of the UK, 1977–88. *Publication:* Watershed in India 1914–1922, 1979. *Address:* Shortwoods, West Clandon, Surrey GU4 7UB. *T:* Guildford (0483) 222757. *Club:* Travellers'.

RUMBOLD, Sir Jack (Seddon), Kt 1984; QC (Zanzibar) 1963; President of the Industrial Tribunals, England and Wales, 1979–84, retired; *b* 5 March 1920; *s* of William Alexander Rumbold and Jean Lindsay Rumbold (*née* Mackay), Christchurch, NZ; *m* 1st, 1949, Helen Suzanne, *d* of Col J. B. Davis, Wanganui, NZ; two *d*; 2nd, 1970, Veronica Ellie Hurt (*née* Whigham). *Educ:* St Andrew's Coll., NZ; Canterbury Univ., NZ (LLB 1940); Brasenose Coll., Oxford (Rhodes Schol.; BCL 1948). Served Royal Navy, Lieut RNZNVR, 1941–45 (despatches). Called to Bar, Inner Temple, 1948; Crown Counsel, Kenya, 1957, Sen. Crown Counsel, 1959; Attorney General, Zanzibar, 1963; Legal Adviser, Kenya Govt, 1964–66; Academic Director, British Campus of Stanford Univ., USA, 1966–72; Chairman of Industrial Tribunals (part-time), 1968; (full-time) 1972; Regional Chairman (London South), 1977. FRSA 1985. *Recreations:* books, music; formerly cricket (Oxford Blue). *Address:* Il Vallone Alto, Sarteano, Siena, Italy; c/o 20 Sallcott Road, SW11. *Clubs:* Garrick, MCC.

RUNACRES, Eric Arthur; *b* 22 Aug. 1916; *s* of Arthur Selwyn Runacres and Mildred May (*née* Dye); *m* 1950, Penelope Jane Elizabeth Luxmoore; one *s* one *d*. *Educ:* Dulwich College; Merton College, Oxford. 1st cl. hons Lit. Hum. 1939. Commissioned Royal Engineers, Oct. 1939; served UK, Malta, Middle East, India, 1939–46 (Major). J. & P. Coats Ltd, 1946–48. Entered HM Foreign Service, 1948; First Secretary, 1951–53. British Productivity Council, 1954–71 (Deputy Director, 1959–71, and Secretary, 1962–71); Vice-Chm., OECD, Cttee on National Productivity Centres, 1960–66; Exec. Director, Commonwealth Agricultural Bureaux, 1973–77; Consultant, Industrial Facts & Forecasting Ltd, 1978–81. *Recreations:* European thought and literature; gardening. *Address:* Gables, Radbones Hill, Over Norton, Oxon OX7 5RA. *T:* Chipping Norton (0608) 643264.

RUNCIE, family name of **Baron Runcie.**

RUNCIE, Baron *cr* 1991 (Life Peer), of Cuddesdon in the County of Oxfordshire; **Rt. Rev. and Rt. Hon. Robert Alexander Kennedy Runcie,** MC 1945; PC 1980; Royal Victorian Chain, 1991; Archbishop of Canterbury, 1980–91; Hon. Assistant Bishop of St Albans, since 1991; High Steward of the University of Cambridge, since 1991; *b* 2 Oct. 1921; *s* of Robert Dalziel Runcie and Anne Runcie; *m* 1957, Angela Rosalind, *d* of J. W. Cecil Turner; one *s* one *d*. *Educ:* Merchant Taylors', Crosby; Brasenose Coll., Oxford (Squire Minor Schol.), Hon. Fellow, 1979; Westcott House, Cambridge. BA (1st Cl. Hons, Lit. Hum.), MA Oxon, 1948; FKC 1981. Served Scots Guards, War of 1939–45 (MC). Deacon, 1950; Priest, 1951; Curate, All Saints, Gosforth, 1950–52; Chaplain, Westcott House, Cambridge, 1953–54; Vice-Principal, 1954–56; Fellow, Dean and Asst Tutor of Trinity Hall, Cambridge, 1956–60, Hon. Fellow 1975; Vicar of Cuddesdon and Principal of Cuddesdon Coll., 1960–69; Bishop of St Albans, 1970–80. Canon and Prebendary of Lincoln, 1969. Hon. Bencher, Gray's Inn, 1980. Chm., BBC and IBA Central Religious Adv. Cttee, 1973–79. Teape Lectr, St Stephen's Coll., Delhi, 1962; William Noble Lectr, Harvard, 1986. Select Preacher: Cambridge, 1957 and 1975, Oxford 1959 and 1973. Anglican Chm., Anglican-Orthodox Jt Doctrinal Commn, 1973–80. Freeman: St Albans, 1979; City of London, 1981; Canterbury, 1984. Hon. Fellow, Merton Coll., Oxford, 1991. Hon. DD: Oxon, 1980; Cantab, 1981; New Raday Coll., Budapest, 1987; S Carolina, 1987; St Andrews, 1989; Yale, 1989; Univ. of the South, Sewanee, 1981; Trinity Coll., Toronto, 1986; Hon. DLitt Keele, 1981; Hon. LittD Liverpool, 1983; Hon. DCL West Indies, 1984; Hon. degree Berkeley Divinity Sch., USA, 1986; Hon. DrLitt Rikkyo, Japan, 1987. Council on Christian Unity's Patron of Christian Unity Award, Yale Univ., 1986; Order of St Vladimir Class II, Russian Orthodox Church, 1975; Cross of Order of the Holy Sepulchre, Greek Orthodox Church, 1986. *Publications:* (ed) Cathedral and City: St Albans Ancient and Modern, 1978; Windows onto God, 1983; Seasons of the Spirit, 1983; One Light for One World, 1988; Authority in Crisis? an Anglican response, 1988; The Unity We Seek, 1989. *Recreations:* opera, reading history and novels, owning Berkshire pigs. *Address:* 26a Jennings Road, St Albans, Herts AL1 4PD. *Clubs:* Athenæum, MCC.

RUNCIMAN, family name of **Viscount Runciman of Doxford.**

RUNCIMAN OF DOXFORD, 3rd Viscount, *cr* 1937; **Walter Garrison Runciman (Garry),** CBE 1987; FBA 1975; Bt 1906; Baron Runciman, 1933, of Shoreston; Chairman: Walter Runciman plc, 1976–90; Andrew Weir and Co. Ltd, since 1991; Runciman Investments Ltd, since 1990; Fellow, Trinity College, Cambridge, since 1971; *b* 10 Nov. 1934; *o s* of 2nd Viscount Runciman of Doxford, OBE, AFC, AE and of Katherine Schuyler, *y d* of late William R. Garrison, New York; *S* father, 1989; *m* 1963, Ruth (OBE 1991), *o d* of late Joseph Hellmann and late Dr Ellen Hellmann, Johannesburg; one *s* two *d*. *Educ:* Eton (Oppidan Schol.); Trinity Coll., Cambridge (Schol.; Fellow, 1959–63, 1971–). National Service, 1953–55 (2/Lt, Grenadier Guards); Harkness Fellow, 1958–60; part-time Reader in Sociology, Univ. of Sussex, 1967–69; Vis. Prof., Harvard Univ., 1970; Vis. Fellow, Nuffield Coll., Oxford, 1979–87. Lectures: Radcliffe-Brown, British Acad., 1986; Spencer, Oxford Univ., 1986. Treas., Child Poverty Action Gp, 1972–; Member: SSRC, 1974–79; Securities and Investments Board, 1986– (a Dep. Chm., 1990–). Pres., Gen. Council of British Shipping, 1986–87 (Vice-Pres., 1985–86). Chm., Royal Commn on Criminal Justice, 1991–. Hon. Foreign Mem., Amer. Acad. of Arts and Sciences, 1986. *Publications:* Plato's Later Epistemology, 1962; Social Science and Political Theory, 1963, 2nd edn 1969; Relative Deprivation and Social Justice, 1966, 2nd edn 1972; Sociology in its Place, and other essays, 1970; A Critique of Max Weber's Philosophy of Social Science, 1972; A Treatise on Social Theory: vol. I, 1983, vol. II, 1989; Confessions of a Reluctant Theorist, 1989; articles in academic jls. *Heir: s* Hon. David Walter Runciman, *b* 1 March 1967. *Address:* 36 Carlton Hill, NW8 0JY. *Club:* Brooks's.

See also Hon. Sir Steven Runciman.

RUNCIMAN, Hon. Sir Steven, (Hon. Sir James Cochran Stevenson Runciman), CH 1984; Kt 1958; CLit 1987; FBA 1957; FSA 1964; MA; *b* 7 July 1903; 2nd *s* of 1st Viscount Runciman of Doxford, PC. *Educ:* Eton (King's Schol.); Trinity College, Cambridge (Schol.). Fellow of Trinity College, Cambridge, 1927–38 (Hon. Fellow 1965); Lecturer at the University of Cambridge, 1932–38; Press Attaché, British Legation, Sofia, 1940; British Embassy, Cairo, 1941; Professor of Byzantine Art and History in Univ. of Istanbul, 1942–45; Rep. Brit. Council in Greece, 1945–47. Lectures: Waynflete, Magdalen Coll., Oxford, 1953–54; Gifford, St Andrews, 1960–62; Birkbeck, Trinity Coll., Cambridge, 1966; Wiles, Queen's Univ., Belfast, 1968; Robb, Auckland, 1970; Regents', Los Angeles, California, 1971; Weir, Cincinnati, 1973. Alexander White Prof., Chicago, 1963. Mem. Advisory Council, Victoria and Albert Museum, 1957–71; Pres., British Inst. of Archæology at Ankara, 1960–75; Chairman: Anglo-Hellenic League, 1951–67; Nat. Trust for Greece, 1977–84; Councillor Emeritus, Nat. Trust for Scotland, 1985–; Trustee: British Museum, 1960–67; Scottish Nat. Museum of Antiquities, 1972–77; Hon. Vice-Pres., RHistS, 1967–; Vice-Pres., London Library, 1974; Chm., Friends of Scottish Ballet, 1984–88. For. Mem., American Philosophical Soc.; Corresp. Mem. Real Academia de Historia, Madrid. Hon. MRIA 1979. Hon. LittD Cambridge, 1955; Hon. LLD Glasgow, 1955; Hon. DLitt: Durham, 1956; St Andrews, 1969; Oxon, 1971; Birmingham, 1973; Hon. LitD London, 1966; Hon. DPhil Salonika, 1951; Hon. DD Wabash, USA, 1962; Hon. DHL Chicago, 1963; Hon. DHum Ball State Univ., 1973; Hon. DLitt New York Univ., 1984. Wolfson Literary Award, 1982. Knight Commander, Order of the Phœnix (Greece), 1961. *Publications:* The Emperor Romanus Lecapenus, 1929; The First Bulgarian Empire, 1930; Byzantine Civilization, 1933; The Medieval Manichee, 1947; A History of the Crusades, Vol. I, 1951 (illustrated edn, as The First Crusade, 1980), Vol. II, 1952, Vol. III, 1954; The Eastern Schism, 1955; The Sicilian Vespers, 1958; The White Rajahs, 1960; The Fall of Constantinople, 1453, 1965; The Great Church in Captivity, 1968; The Last Byzantine Renaissance, 1970; The Orthodox Churches and the Secular State, 1972; Byzantine Style and Civilisation, 1975; The Byzantine Theocracy, 1977; Mistra, 1980; A Traveller's Alphabet, 1991; contributions to various historical journals. *Address:* Elshieshields, Lockerbie, Dumfriesshire DG11 1LY. *Club:* Athenæum.

RUNCORN, Prof. (Stanley) Keith, FRS 1965; Sydney Chapman Professor of Physical Science, University of Alaska, since 1988; Senior Research Fellow, Imperial College of Science, Technology and Medicine, since 1989; *b* 19 November 1922; *s* of W. H. Runcorn, Southport, Lancs; unmarried. *Educ:* King George V Sch., Southport; Gonville and Caius Coll., Cambridge. ScD 1963. Radar Research and Devel. Establishment (Min. of Supply), 1943–46; Asst Lecturer, 1946–48, and Lecturer, 1948–49, in Physics, Univ. of Manchester; Asst Dir of Research in Geophysics, Cambridge Univ., 1950–55; Research Geophysicist, Univ. of California at Los Angeles, 1952 and 1953; Fellow of Gonville and Caius Coll., Cambridge, 1948–55; Prof. of Physics, Univ. of Durham (King's Coll.), 1956–63, Univ. of Newcastle upon Tyne, 1963–88 (Head, Dept of Physics, 1963–88). Visiting Scientist, Dominion Observatory, Ottawa, 1955; Vis. Prof. of Geophysics: Cal. Inst. of Tech., 1957; Univ. of Miami, 1966; Pa State Univ., 1967; Florida State Univ., 1968; UCLA, 1975; J. Ellerton Becker Senior Visiting Fellow, Australian Academy of Science, 1963; Res. Associate, Mus. of N Arizona, 1957–72; Rutherford Memorial Lectr (Kenya, Tanzania and Uganda), 1970; du Toit Meml Lectr (S Africa), 1971; Halley Lectr, Oxford Univ., 1972–73; Hitchcock Foundn Prof., Univ. of California, Berkeley, 1981; Vis. Scholar, Sydney Univ., 1991. Mem., NERC, 1965–69. Pres., Section A (Phys. and Maths), British Assoc., 1980–81. Mem., Royal Netherlands Acad. of Arts and Sciences, 1970; For. Mem., Indian Nat. Acad. of Science, 1980; Mem., Pontifical Acad. of Sciences, 1981; Mem., Royal Norwegian Soc. of Sci. and Letters, 1985; Corresp. Mem., Bavarian Acad. of Sci., 1990. Napier Shaw Prize, Royal Met. Soc., 1959; Charles Chree Medal and Prize, Inst. of Physics, 1969; Vetlesen Prize, 1971; John Adams Fleming Medal, Amer. Geophysical Union, 1983; Gold Medal, Royal Astronomical Soc., 1984; Wegener Medal, European Union of Geoscis, 1987. Hon. DSc: Utrecht, 1969; Ghent, 1971; Paris, 1979; Bergen, 1980. *Publications:* scientific papers. *Recreations:* usual. *Address:* Blackett Laboratory, Imperial College, SW7 2BZ. *Clubs:* Athenæum; Union (Newcastle upon Tyne).

RUNDLE, Christopher John Spencer, OBE 1983; HM Diplomatic Service; Research Counsellor, Research and Analysis Department, Foreign and Commonwealth Office, since 1991; *b* 17 Aug. 1938; *s* of Percy William and Ruth Rundle (*née* Spencer); *m* 1970, Qamar Said; one *d*. *Educ:* Cranbrook Sch.; St John's Coll., Cambridge (MA). Served HM Forces, 1957–59. Central Asian Res. Centre, 1962–63; joined Diplomatic Service, 1963; Tehran, 1967–68; Oriental Sec., Kabul, 1968–70; FCO, 1970–75; seconded to Cabinet Office, 1975–77; First Secretary: FCO, 1977–81; Tehran, 1981–84; FCO, 1985; Sen. Principal Res. Officer, Res. and Analysis Dept, FCO, 1988–91. Member Council: RSAA, 1989–; British Inst. of Persian Studies, 1990–. *Recreations:* sports, foreign films and literature. *Address:* c/o Foreign and Commonwealth Office, SW1A 2AH.

RUNDLE, John Louis, AM 1981; JP; Agent-General for South Australia, 1980–85; *b* 11 Jan. 1930; *s* of late J. A. Rundle; *m* Elizabeth Phillipa, *d* of John P. Little, Melbourne; one *s* one *d*. *Educ:* Rostrevor Coll. Formerly Senior Partner, J. C. Rundle & Co., and Rundle, Parsons & Partners; Former Chairman: J. C. Rundle Holdings Pty Ltd; Seacliff Investments Pty Ltd; Thevenard Hotel Pty Ltd; former Director: Commonwealth Accommodation & Catering Service Ltd; Mallen & Co. Ltd; Commercial & Domestic Finance Ltd. Former Member: Nat. Employers Ind. Council (Dep. Chm., 1979–80); Confed. of Aust. Industry (Mem. Bd, 1978–80); State Develt Council, SA; Ind. Relations Adv. Council, SA; Adv. Curriculum Bd, SA; Council, Royal AA of SA. Pres., Junior Chambers, Adelaide, 1957, SA, 1958, Australia, 1959; Vice-Pres., JCI, 1960, 1963, Exec. Vice-Pres., 1964, World Pres., 1965, Pres. Senate, 1966; Councillor, Adelaide Chamber of Commerce, 1956–57, 1961–72, Vice-Pres., 1968–70, Dep. Pres., 1970–72; Vice-Pres., Chamber of Commerce & Industry, SA, 1973–75, Dep. Pres., 1975–77, Pres. 1977–79 (Chm., Commerce Div., 1973, 1974; Chm., Ind. Matters Cttee); Exec. Mem., Aust. Chamber of Commerce, 1980. Councillor: Red Cross Soc., SA Div., 1957–63 (Chm., Junior Red Cross, 1961–62); Burnside City Council, 1962–64; President: Assoc. of Indep. Schools of SA, 1972–75; Nat. Council of Indep. Schools, 1975–77; Chm., Bd of Governors, Rostrevor Coll., 1967–77. Freeman, City of London, 1981. JP SA, 1956. KHS 1989. *Address:* Waggoners, Tower Road, Hindhead, Surrey GU26 6ST. *T:* Hindhead (042873) 5217. *Clubs:* East India; Stock Exchange (Pres., 1979–80), Naval Military and Air Force, Tattersall's (Adelaide); Clipper (USA).

RUPERT'S LAND, Archbishop and Metropolitan of, since 1988; **Most Rev. Walter Heath Jones;** *b* 25 Dec. 1928; *s* of Harry Heath Jones and Anne Grace Evelyn Jones (*née*

Stoddart); *m* 1951, L. Marilyn Jones (*née* Lunney); one *s* three *d*. *Educ:* Univ. of Manitoba (BA); St John's College (LTh); Nashotah House (STM). Received into Episcopal Church of USA, 1958; Rector, St Mary's Church, Mitchell, S Dak, 1958–62; Vice-Pres. of Chapter, 1962–67; Dean of Calvary Cathedral, Sioux Falls, S Dak, 1968–70; Bishop of South Dakota, Sioux Falls, 1970–83; Bishop of Rupert's Land, 1983. Hon. DD: St John's Coll., 1970; Nashotah House; Trinity Coll., 1990. Hon. Citizen of St Boniface, 1966; Bush Fellow, 1978. *Address:* 935 Nesbitt Bay, Winnipeg, Manitoba R3T 1W6, Canada. *T:* (204) 453–6248.

RUSBRIDGE, Brian John, CBE 1984; Senior Partner, The Belgrave Consultants, since 1987; Editor, The Municipal Year Book, since 1987; Secretary, Local Authorities' Conditions of Service Advisory Board (and all Local Authority National Negotiating Councils), 1973–87; *b* 10 Sept. 1922; *s* of late Arthur John and Leonora Rusbridge, Appleton, Berks; *m* 1951, Joyce, *d* of late Joseph Young Elliott, Darlington; two *s*. *Educ:* Willowfield Sch., Eastbourne; Univ. of Oxford Dept of Social and Admin. Studies (Dip. Social Admin.). Served War of 1939–45, Lieut RNVR. Personnel Manager, Imperial Chemical Industries (Teesside), 1949; British Railways Board: Dir of Industrial Relations, 1963; Divisional Manager, London, 1970. Companion, Inst. of Personnel Management; Mem., Chartered Inst. of Transport. *Recreations:* walking, gardening. *Address:* 19 Beauchamp Road, East Molesey, Surrey KT8 0PA. *T:* 081–979 4952.

RUSBY, Vice-Adm. Sir Cameron, KCB 1979; LVO 1965; Chief Executive, Scottish Society for the Prevention of Cruelty to Animals, 1983–91; *b* 20 Feb. 1926; *s* of late Captain Victor Evelyn Rusby, CBE, RN, and Mrs Irene Margaret Rusby; *m* 1948, Marion Elizabeth Bell; two *d*. *Educ:* RNC, Dartmouth. Midshipman 1943; specialised in communications, 1950; CO HMS Ulster, 1958–59; Exec. Officer, HM Yacht Britannia, 1962–65; Dep. Dir, Naval Signals, 1965–68; CO HMS Tartar, 1968–69; Dep. ACOS (Plans and Policy), staff of Allied C-in-C Southern Europe, 1969–72; Sen. Naval Off., WI, 1972–74; Rear-Adm. 1974; ACDS (Ops), 1974–77; Vice-Adm. 1977; Flag Officer Scotland and N Ireland, 1977–79; Dep. Supreme Allied Comdr, Atlantic, 1980–82. *Recreations:* sailing, skiing, equitation. *Address:* c/o Bank of Scotland, 70 High Street, Peebles EH45 8AQ. *Club:* New (Edinburgh).

RUSH, Most Rev. Francis Roberts; *see* Brisbane, Archbishop of, (RC).

RUSHBROOKE, Prof. G(eorge) Stanley, MA, PhD; FRS 1982; FRSE; Professor of Theoretical Physics, University of Newcastle upon Tyne, 1951–80; Head of Department of Theoretical Physics, 1965–80; Deputy Head, School of Physics, 1972–80; *b* 19 January 1915; *s* of George Henry Rushbrooke and Frances Isobel Rushbrooke (*née* Wright), Willenhall, Staffs; *m* 1949, Thelma Barbara Cox (*d* 1977). *Educ:* Wolverhampton Grammar School; St John's College, Cambridge. Schol. St John's Coll., Camb., 1933–37; Research Asst, Bristol Univ., 1938–39; Senior DSIR award and Carnegie Teaching Fellowship, 1939–44, UC Dundee, Univ. of St Andrews; Lectr in Mathematical Chemistry, The Univ., Leeds, 1944–48; Sen. Lectr in Theoretical Physics, Oxford, Univ. and Lecturer in Mathematics, University Coll., Oxford, 1948–51. Leverhulme Emeritus Fellow, 1981. Visiting Prof., Dept of Chemistry, Univ. of Oregon, USA, 1962–63; Vis. Prof. of Physics and Chemistry, Rice Univ., Houston, 1967. *Publications:* Introduction to Statistical Mechanics, 1949; research papers in scientific journals. *Recreations:* hillwalking, birdwatching. *Address:* 46 Belle Vue Avenue, Newcastle upon Tyne NE3 1AH.

RUSHDIE, (Ahmed) Salman, FRSL; writer; *b* 19 June 1947; *s* of Anis Ahmed Rushdie and Negin Rushdie (*née* Butt); *m* 1976, Clarissa Luard (marr. diss. 1987); one *s*; *m* 1988, Marianne Wiggins. *Educ:* Cathedral Sch., Bombay; Rugby Sch.; King's Coll., Cambridge (MA (Hons) History). Member: Camden Cttee for Community Relations, 1975–82; Internat. PEN, 1981–; ICA Council, 1985–; BFI Production Bd, 1986–. FRSL 1983. Arts Council Literature Bursary Award. *Films for TV:* The Painter and the Pest, 1985; The Riddle of Midnight, 1988. *Publications:* Grimus, 1975; Midnight's Children, 1981 (Booker McConnell Prize for Fiction; James Tait Black Meml Book Prize; E-SU Literary Award); Shame, 1983 (Prix du Meilleur Livre Etranger, 1984); The Jaguar Smile: a Nicaraguan journey, 1987; The Satanic Verses, 1988 (Whitbread Novel Award); Hauroun and the Sea of Stories, 1990; Imaginary Homelands (essays), 1991; contribs to many journals. *Recreations:* cinema, reading, chess. *Address:* c/o Aitken & Stone Ltd, 29 Fernshaw Road, SW10 0TG.

RUSHFORD, Antony Redfern, CMG 1963; consultant on constitutional, international and commonwealth law; *b* 9 Feb.; *m* 1975, June Jeffrey, *d* of late C. R. Morrish, DSC, KPM, and *widow* of Roy Eustace Wells; one step *s* one step *d*. *Educ:* Taunton Sch.; Trinity Coll., Cambridge (BA 1948; LLM (LLB 1948); MA 1951). FRSA. RAFVR, 1942 (active service, 1943–47, reserve, 1947–59); Sqdn Ldr, 1946. Solicitor, 1944–57 (distinction in Law Soc. final exams, 1942); Called to the Bar, Inner Temple, 1983. Asst Solicitor, E. W. Marshall Harvey & Dalton, 1948. Home Civil Service, Colonial Office, 1949–68; joined HM Diplomatic Service, 1968; CO, later FCO, retd as Dep. Legal Advr (Asst Under-Sec. of State), 1982. Crown Counsel, Uganda, 1954; Principal Legal Adviser, British Indian Ocean Territory, 1983; Attorney-Gen., Anguilla, and St Helena, 1983; Legal Adviser for Commonwealth Sec.-Gen. to Governor-Gen. of Grenada, Mem. Interim Govt, Attorney-Gen., and JP, Grenada, 1983; consultancies: FCO (special duties), 1982; Commonwealth Sec.-Gen., St Kitts and Nevis independence, 1982–83, St Lucia treaties, 1983–85; E Caribbean courts, 1983; maritime legislation for Jamaica, Internat. Maritime Orgn, 1983 and 1985; constitutional advr, Govt of St Kitts and Nevis, and Govt of St Lucia, 1982–. Has drafted many constitutions for UK dependencies and Commonwealth countries attaining independence; presented paper on constitutional develt to meeting of Law Officers from Smaller Commonwealth Jurisdictions, IoM, 1983. UK deleg. or advr at many constitutional confs and discussions; CO Rep., Inst. of Advanced Legal Studies; participant, Symposium on Federalism, Chicago, 1962; Advr, Commonwealth Law Ministers Conf., 1973. Lectr, Overseas Legal Officers Course, 1964; Special Examnr, London Univ., 1963, 1987; a dir of studies, RIPA (Overseas Services Unit), and also associate consultant on statute law, 1982–86. Mem. Editl Bd, Inst. of Internat. Law and Econ. Develt, Washington, 1977–82. Foundn Mem. Exec. Council, Royal Commonwealth Soc. for the Blind, 1969–81, 1983– (Hon. Legal Adviser, 1984–); Hon. Sec., Services Race Club, Hong Kong, 1946–47. Member: Glyndebourne Fest. Soc., 1950–; Inst. of Advanced Motoring, 1959–73; Commonwealth Lawyers Assoc., 1982–90; Commonwealth Assoc. of Legislative Counsel, 1984–; Commonwealth Magistrates and Judges Assoc., 1986–90; Anglo-Arab Assoc. and Saudi-British Soc., 1990–. Governor, Taunton Sch., 1948–. CStJ 1989 (Hon. Legal Counsellor, 1978–; Mem., Chapter-Gen., 1983–). *Address:* 63 Pont Street, Knightsbridge, SW1X 0BD. *T:* 071–589 6448; (chambers) 12 King's Bench Walk, Temple, EC4Y 7EL. *T:* 071–353 5692/6. *Club:* Commonwealth Trust.

RUSHTON, Ian Lawton, FIA, FCII, FSS; Vice Chairman, Royal Insurance Holdings plc, since 1991 (Group Chief Executive, 1989–91); *b* 8 Sept. 1931; *s* of Arthur John and Mabel Lilian Rushton; *m* 1st, 1956, Julia Frankland (decd); one *d*.; 2nd, 1986, Anita Spencer; one step *s* one step *d*. *Educ:* Rock Ferry High Sch., Birkenhead; King's Coll., London (BSc Mathematics). FIA 1959; FCII 1961. Served RAF, 1953–56 (Flt-Lieut). Royal Insurance, 1956–: Dep. Gen. Man. (UK), 1972; Exec. Vice Pres., Royal US, 1980; Gen. Man. Royal UK, 1983; Exec. Dir and Gp Gen. Man., Royal Insurance plc, 1986. Chairman: Fire Protection Assoc., 1983–87; Assoc. of British Insurers, 1991–; Vice Pres., Inst. of Actuaries, 1986–89. FRSA. *Recreations:* golf, gardening, theatre, music. *Address:* Royal Insurance Holdings plc, 1 Cornhill, EC3V 3QR.

RUSHTON, William George; actor, author, cartoonist and broadcaster; *b* 18 Aug. 1937; *s* of John and Veronica Rushton; *m* 1968, Arlene Dorgan; three *s*. *Educ:* Shrewsbury Sch. Founder/Editor, Private Eye, 1961. Stage début in The Bed-sitting Room, by Spike Milligan, Marlowe Theatre, Canterbury, 1961; Gulliver's Travels, Mermaid, 1971, 1979; Pass the Butler, by Eric Idle, Globe, 1982; Tales from a Long Room, Hammersmith, 1988; *films:* Nothing but the Best, 1963; Those Magnificent Men in their Flying Machines, 1964, and several others; *television* includes: That Was the Week that Was, 1962; Up Sunday, 1975–78; Celebrity Squares, 1979–80; numerous Jackanory progs; *radio* includes: I'm Sorry I Haven't a Clue, 1976–; much other broadcasting in UK and Australia. *Publications:* written and illustrated: William Rushton's Dirty Book, 1964; How to Play Football: the art of dirty play, 1968; The Day of the Grocer, 1971; The Geranium of Flüt, 1975; Superpig, 1976; Pigsticking: a joy for life, 1977; The Reluctant Euro, 1980; The Filth Amendment, 1981; W. G. Grace's Last Case, 1984; Willie Rushton's Great Moments of History, 1985; The Alternative Gardener: a compost of quips for the green-fingered, 1986; Marylebone Versus the Rest of the World, 1987; (ed) Spy Thatcher, 1987; illustrations for many others. *Recreations:* losing weight, gaining weight, parking. *Address:* Wallgrave Road, SW5. *Clubs:* Tatty Bogle's, Lord's Taverners, Surrey CCC.

RUSHWORTH, Dr (Frank) Derek; Headmaster, Holland Park School, London, 1971–85; *b* 15 Sept. 1920; *s* of late Frank and Elizabeth Rushworth, Huddersfield; *m* 1941, Hamidah Begum, *d* of late Justice S. Akhlaque Hussain, Lahore, and Edith (*née* Bayliss), Oxford; three *d*. *Educ:* Huddersfield Coll.; St Edmund Hall, Oxford (Schol.; BA 1942, MA 1946); Doctorate of Univ. of Paris (Lettres), 1947. Served 6th Rajputana Rifles, Indian Army, 1942–45 (Major); began teaching, 1947; Head of Modern Languages: Tottenham Grammar Sch., 1953; Holland Park Sch., 1958; Head of Shoreditch Sch., London, 1965. Chairman: Associated Examining Board, French Committee, 1964–74; Schools Council, 16+ Examination Feasibility Study (French), 1971–75; Pres., London Head Teachers' Assoc., 1985. Governor, Holland Park Sch., 1990–. *Publications:* Our French Neighbours, 1963, 2nd edn 1966; French text-books and language-laboratory books; articles in French Studies, Modern Languages, also educnl jls. *Recreation:* photography. *Address:* 25c Lambolle Road, NW3 4HS. *T:* 071–794 3691.

RUSK, Dean, KBE (Hon.) 1976; Professor of International Law, University of Georgia School of Law, Athens, Georgia, since 1971; *b* 9 February 1909; *s* of Robert Hugh Rusk and Frances Elizabeth Clotfelter; *m* 1937, Virginia Foisie; two *s* one *d*. *Educ:* Davidson College, North Carolina; St John's College, Oxford. Assoc. Prof. of Government and Dean of Faculty, Mills Coll., 1934–40; US Army, 1940–46; Special Asst to Secretary of War, 1946; US Dept of State, 1947–51; Asst Sec. of State for UN Affairs, 1949; Dep. Under Sec. of State, 1949–50; Asst Sec. of State for Far Eastern Affairs, 1950–51; Sec. of State, 1961–69; President, The Rockefeller Foundation, 1952–61, Distinguished Fellow, 1969–. Hon. Fellow, St John's Coll., Oxford, 1955. Hon. LLD: Mills Coll., Calif, 1948; Davidson Coll., 1950; Univ. of Calif, 1961; Emory Univ., Georgia, 1961; Princeton Univ., NJ, 1961; Louisiana State Univ. 1962; Amherst Coll., 1962; Columbia Univ., 1963; Harvard Univ., 1963; Rhode Island Univ., 1963; Valparaiso Univ., 1964; Williams Coll., 1964; Univ. of N Carolina, 1964; George Washington Univ., 1965; Oberlin Coll., 1965; Maryville Coll., 1965; Denver Univ., 1966; Erskine Coll., 1967. Hon. DCL Oxford, 1962; Hon. LHD: Westminster Coll., 1962; Hebrew Union Coll., 1963; Hardin-Simmons Univ., 1967. Cecil Peace Prize, 1933. Legion of Merit (Oak Leaf Cluster). *Address:* 1 Lafayette Square, 620 Hill Street, Athens, Ga 30606, USA.

RUSSELL; *see* Hamilton-Russell, family name of Viscount Boyne.

RUSSELL, family name of **Duke of Bedford, Earl Russell, Baron Ampthill, Baron de Clifford** and **Baron Russell of Liverpool.**

RUSSELL, 5th Earl *cr* 1861; **Conrad Sebastian Robert Russell,** FBA 1991; Viscount Amberley 1861; Professor of British History, King's College London, since 1990; *b* 15 April 1937; *s* of 3rd Earl Russell, OM, FRS and Patricia Helen, *d* of H. E. Spence; *S* half brother, 1987; *m* 1962, Elizabeth Franklyn Sanders; two *s*. *Educ:* Merton College, Oxford (BA 1958, MA 1962); MA Yale 1979. FRHistS 1971. Lectr in History, Bedford College, London, 1960–74, Reader, 1974–79; Prof. of History, Yale Univ., 1979–84; Astor Prof. of British History, UCL, 1984–90. Ford Lectr, Univ. of Oxford, 1987–88. Takes Liberal Democrat whip, H of L. *Publications:* The Crisis of Parliaments: English History 1509–1660, 1971; (ed) The Origins of the English Civil War, 1973; Parliaments and English Politics 1621–1629, 1979; The Causes of the English Civil War, 1990; Unrevolutionary England 1603–1642, 1990; The Fall of the British Monarchies 1637–1642, 1991; articles in jls. *Recreations:* swimming, uxoriousness, cricket. *Heir:* *s* Viscount Amberley, *qv*. *Address:* Department of History, King's College, Strand, WC2R 2LS.

RUSSELL OF LIVERPOOL, 3rd Baron *cr* 1919; **Simon Gordon Jared Russell;** *b* 30 Aug. 1952; *s* of Captain Hon. Langley Gordon Haslingden Russell, MC (*d* 1975) (*o s* of 2nd Baron), and of Kiloran Margaret, *d* of late Hon. Sir Arthur Jared Palmer Howard, KBE, CVO; *S* grandfather, 1981; *m* 1984, Dr Gilda Albano, *y d* of late Signor F. Albano and of Signora Maria Caputo-Albano; two *s* one *d*. *Educ:* Charterhouse; Trinity Coll., Cambridge; INSEAD, Fontainebleau, France. *Heir:* *s* Hon. Edward Charles Stanley Russell, *b* 2 Sept. 1985. *Address:* House of Lords, SW1.

RUSSELL, Alan Keith; writer, consultant and company director; formerly official of the European Communities; *b* 22 Oct. 1932; *s* of Keith Russell and late Gertrude Ann Russell; *m* 1959, Philippa Margaret Stoneham; two *s* one *d*. *Educ:* Ardingly Coll.; Oxford Univ. BA; MA Econ and Pol Sci; DPhil. Colonial Office, ODM, FCO, 1959–69, 1972–75; CS Coll., 1969–71; Dir, Inter University Council for Higher Educn Overseas, 1980–81; a sen. official, Commn of EC, 1976–79 and 1981–85; Fellow, Lincoln Coll., Oxford and Sen. Res. Associate, Queen Elizabeth House, 1986–88; Internat. Develt Officer, Internat. League of Socs for Persons with Mental Handicap, Mem., Institut Robert Schumann and Manager, Whitstable Improvement Trust, 1989–. *Publications:* ed, The Economic and Social History of Mauritius, 1962; Liberal Landslide: the General Election of 1906, 1973; contrib. Edwardian Radicalism, 1974; The Unclosed Eye (poems), 1987; articles on commodity trade, development, and Europe. *Recreations:* West African history, services for the mentally handicapped, travel, town planning.

RUSSELL, (Alastair) Muir; Under Secretary, Cabinet Office, since 1990; *b* 9 Jan. 1949; *s* of Thomas and Anne Russell; *m* 1983, Eileen Alison Mackay, *qv*. *Educ:* High Sch. of Glasgow; Univ. of Glasgow (BSc Nat. Phil.). Joined Scottish Office, 1970; seconded as Sec. to Scottish Development Agency, 1975–76; Asst Sec., 1981; Principal Private Sec. to Sec. of State for Scotland, 1981–83. *Recreations:* music, food, wine. *Address:* Cabinet Office, 70 Whitehall, SW1A 2AS. *Club:* Commonwealth Trust.

RUSSELL, Albert Muir Galloway, CBE 1989; QC (Scot.) 1965; Sheriff of Grampian, Highland and Islands (formerly Aberdeen, Kincardine and Banff) at Aberdeen and Stonehaven, 1971–91; *b* 26 Oct. 1925; *s* of Hon. Lord Russell; *m* 1954, Margaret Winifred, *o d* of T. McW Millar, FRCS(E), Edinburgh; two *s* two *d. Educ:* Edinburgh Academy; Wellington College; Brasenose College, Oxford. BA (Hons) Oxon, 1949; LLB (Edin.), 1951. Lieut, Scots Guards, 1944–47. Member of Faculty of Advocates, 1951–. *Recreation:* golf. *Address:* Easter Ord House, Skene, Aberdeenshire AB3 6SQ. *T:* Aberdeen (0224) 740228. *Club:* Royal Northern (Aberdeen).

RUSSELL, Alexander William; Commissioner, HM Customs and Excise, since 1985; *b* 16 Oct. 1938; *s* of William and Elizabeth W. B. Russell (*née* Russell); *m* 1962, Elspeth Rae (*née* Robertson). *Educ:* Royal High Sch., Edinburgh; Edinburgh Univ. (MA Hons); Manitoba Univ. (MA). Assistant Principal, Scottish Development Dept, 1961–64; Private Sec. to Parliamentary Under Secretary of State, Scottish Office, 1964–65; Principal, Regional Development Div. and Scottish Development Dept, 1965–72; Principal Private Sec. to Secretary of State for Scotland, 1972–73; Asst Secretary: Scottish Development Dept, 1973–76; Civil Service Dept, 1976–79; Under-Secretary: Management and Personnel Office (formerly CSD), 1979–82. Hd of Treasury MPO Financial Management Unit, 1982–85. *Address:* c/o HM Customs and Excise, Dorset House, Stamford Street, SE1 9PS.

RUSSELL, Anna; International Concert Comedienne; *b* 27 Dec. 1911; *d* of Col C. Russell-Brown, CB, DSO, RE, and Beatrice M. Tandy; single. *Educ:* St Felix School, Southwold; Royal College of Music, London. Folk singer, BBC, 1935–40; Canadian Broadcasting Corp. programmes, 1942–46; Radio interviewer, CBC, 1945–46; Debut, Town Hall, New York, as concert comedienne, 1948; Broadway show, Anna Russell and her Little Show, 1953; Towns of USA, Canada, Great Britain, Australia, New Zealand, the Orient and South Africa, 1948–60. Television, Radio Summer Theatre, USA; recordings, Columbia Masterworks. Resident in Australia, 1968–75. Mayfair Theatre, London, 1976. *Publications:* The Power of Being a Positive Stinker (NY); The Anna Russell Song Book; I'm Not Making This Up, You Know (autobiog.). *Recreation:* gardening. *Address:* 70 Anna Russell Way, Unionville, Ontario L3R 3X3, Canada. *Club:* Zouta International (USA, Toronto Branch, Internat. Mem.).

RUSSELL, Rt. Rev. Anthony John; *see* Dorchester, Area Bishop of.

RUSSELL, Sir Archibald (Edward), Kt 1972; CBE 1954; FRS 1970; FEng 1976; Joint Chairman, Concorde Executive Committee of Directors, 1965–69; Vice-Chairman, BAC-Sud Aviation Concorde Committee, 1969–70, retired; *b* 30 May 1904; *m*; one *s* one *d. Educ:* Fairfield Secondary Sch.; Bristol Univ. Joined Bristol Aeroplane Co. Ltd, 1926; Chief Technician, 1931; Technical Designer, 1938; Chief Engineer, 1944; Dir, 1951; Tech. Dir, 1960–66; Chm., British Aircraft Corporation, Filton Div., 1967–69 (Man. Dir, 1966–67). Wright Bros Memorial Lecture, Washington, 1949; 42nd Wilbur Wright Memorial Lecture, London, 1954; RAeS British Gold Medal, 1951; David Guggenheim Medal, 1971; Hon. DSc Bristol, 1951. FIAeS; Hon. FRAeS 1967. *Publications:* papers in R&M Series of Aeronautical Research Cttee and RAeS Journal. *Address:* Glendower House, Clifton Down, Bristol BS8 3BP. *T:* Bristol (0272) 739208.

RUSSELL, Rev. Arthur Colin, CMG 1957; ED; MA; *b* 1906; *e s* of late Arthur W. Russell, OBE, WS; *m* 1939, Elma (*d* 1967), *d* of late Douglas Strachan, Hon. RSA; three *d. Educ:* Harrow; Brasenose College, Oxford. Barrister-at-law, Inner Temple. Cadet, Gold Coast (now Ghana), 1929; Asst Dist Comr, 1930; Dist Comr, 1940; Judicial Adviser, 1947; Senior, 1951; Regional Officer, 1952; Permanent Sec., Min. of Education and Social Welfare, 1953; Governor's Secretary, 1954; Chief Regional Officer, Ashanti, 1955–57, retd. Trained for the Ministry, 1957–59; Ordained (Church of Scotland), 1959; Parish Minister, Aberlemno, 1959–76; retd. District Councillor, Angus District, 1977–84. *Publication:* Stained Glass Windows of Douglas Strachan, 1972. *Address:* Balgavies Lodge, by Forfar, Angus DD8 2TH. *T:* Letham (Angus) (030781) 571.

RUSSELL, Barbara Winifred, MA; Headmistress, Berkhamsted School for Girls, 1950–71; *b* 5 Jan. 1910; *er d* of Lionel Wilfred and Elizabeth Martin Russell. *Educ:* St Oran's School, Edinburgh; Edinburgh University; Oxford University, Dept of Education. History Mistress, Brighton and Hove High School, 1932–38; Senior History Mistress, Roedean School, 1938–49. *Recreations:* reading, gardening, travel. *Address:* 1 Beech Road, Thame, Oxon OX9 2AL. *T:* Thame (084421) 2738. *Club:* East India, Devonshire, Sports and Public Schools.

RUSSELL, Brian Fitzgerald, MD, FRCP; Consulting Physician, formerly Physician, Department of Dermatology, The London Hospital (1951–69); Consulting Physician, formerly Physician, St John's Hospital for Diseases of the Skin (1947–69); formerly Civilian Consultant in Dermatology to the Royal Navy (1955–69); past Dean, Institute of Dermatology; *b* 1 Sept. 1904; *s* of Dr John Hutchinson Russell and Helen Margaret (*née* Collingwood); *m* 1932, Phyllis Daisy Woodward; three *s* one *d. Educ:* Merchant Taylors' School. MD (London) 1929; FRCP 1951; DPH (Eng.) 1943. Medical First Asst, London Hosp., 1930–32; general medical practice, 1933–45; Dermatologist, Prince of Wales's Hosp., Tottenham, 1946–51; Asst Physician, Dept of Dermatology St Bartholomew's Hosp., 1946–51. President: St John's Hosp. Dermatological Soc., 1958–60; Dermatological Sect., RSM, 1968–69 (Hon. Mem., 1977); Corr. Mem.: American Dermatological Soc.; Danish Dermatological Soc. *Publications:* St John's Hospital for Diseases of the Skin, 1863–1963, 1963; (with Eric Wittkower) Emotional Factors in Skin Diseases, 1953; Section on Dermatology in Price's Medicine (ed by Bodley Scott), 1973. *Recreation:* rustication. *Address:* Arches, Hilltop Lane, Saffron Walden, Essex CB11 4AS.

RUSSELL, Cecil Anthony Francis; Director of Intelligence, Greater London Council, 1970–76; *b* 7 June 1921; *s* of late Comdr S. F. Russell, OBE, RN retd and late Mrs M. E. Russell (*née* Sneyd-Kynnersley); *m* 1950, Editha May (*née* Birch); no *c. Educ:* Winchester Coll.; University Coll., Oxford (1940–41, 1945–47). Civil Service, 1949–70: Road Research Lab., 1949–50; Air Min., 1950–62; Dep. Statistical Adviser, Home Office, 1962–67; Head of Census Div., General Register Office, 1967–70. FSS. *Recreation:* ocean sailing. *Address:* Pagan Hill, Whiteleaf, Princes Risborough, Bucks. *T:* Princes Risborough (08444) 3655. *Clubs:* Cruising Association; Ocean Cruising, Royal Lymington Yacht.

RUSSELL, Sir Charles Ian, 3rd Bt, *cr* 1916; Partner, Charles Russell & Co., 1947–83; retired; Captain, RHA (despatches); *b* 13 March 1918; *s* of Captain Sir Alec Charles Russell, 2nd Bt, and Monica (who *m* 2nd, 1942, Brig. John Victor Faviell, CBE, MC; she *d* 1978), *d* of Hon. Sir Charles Russell, 1st Bt; *S* father, 1938; *m* 1947, Rosemary, *er d* of late Sir John Prestige; one *s* one *d. Educ:* Beaumont College; University College, Oxford. Admitted Solicitor, 1947. *Recreation:* golf. *Heir: s* Charles Dominic Russell [*b* 28 May 1956; *m* 1986, Sarah Jane Murray Chandor, *o d* of Anthony Chandor, Haslemere, Surrey; one *s*]. *Address:* Hidden House, Sandwich, Kent; 39 Egerton Gardens, SW3. *Clubs:* Garrick, Army and Navy; Royal St George's.

RUSSELL, Christopher; *see* Russell, R. C. G.

RUSSELL, Rt. Rev. David Hamilton; *see* Grahamstown, Bishop of.

RUSSELL, Sir David Sturrock W.; *see* West-Russell.

RUSSELL, Rev. David Syme, CBE 1982; MA, DD, DLitt; President, Baptist Union of Great Britain and Ireland, 1983–84 (General Secretary, 1967–82); *b* 21 Nov. 1916; second *s* of Peter Russell and Janet Marshall Syme; *m* 1943, Marion Hamilton Campbell; one *s* one *d. Educ:* Scottish Baptist Coll., Glasgow; Trinity Coll., Glasgow; Glasgow Univ. (MA, BD, DLitt, Hon. DD); Regent's Park Coll., Oxford Univ. (MA, MLitt). Minister of Baptist Churches: Berwick, 1939–41; Oxford, 1943–45; Acton, 1945–53. Principal of Rawdon Coll., Leeds, and lectr in Old Testament languages and literature, 1953–64; Joint Principal of the Northern Baptist College, Manchester, 1964–67. Moderator, Free Church Federal Council, 1974–75. Pres., European Baptist Fedn, 1979–81. Mem., Central Cttee, WCC, 1968–83; Vice-Pres., BCC, 1981–84. Hon. DD McMaster, 1991. *Publications:* Between the Testaments, 1960; Two Refugees (Ezekiel and Second Isaiah), 1962; The Method and Message of Jewish Apocalyptic, 1964; The Jews from Alexander to Herod, 1976; Apocalyptic: Ancient and Modern, 1978; Daniel (The Daily Study Bible), 1981; In Journeyings Often, 1982; From Early Judaism to Early Church, 1986; The Old Testament Pseudepigrapha: patriarchs and prophets in early Judaism, 1987; Daniel: an active volcano, 1989; Poles Apart: the Gospel in creative tension; contrib. to Encyc. Britannica, 1963. *Recreation:* woodwork. *Address:* 40 Northumbria Drive, Henleaze, Bristol BS9 4HP. *T:* Bristol (0272) 621410.

RUSSELL, Prof. Donald Andrew Frank Moore, FBA 1971; Fellow, St John's College, Oxford, 1948–88, now Emeritus; Professor of Classical Literature, Oxford, 1985–88; *b* 13 Oct. 1920; *s* of Samuel Charles Russell (schoolmaster) and Laura Moore; *m* 1967, Joycelyne Gledhill Dickinson. *Educ:* King's College Sch., Wimbledon; Balliol Coll., Oxford (MA 1946); DLitt Oxon 1985. Served War: Army (R Signals and Intelligence Corps), 1941–45. Craven Scholar, 1946; Lectr, Christ Church, Oxford, 1947; St John's College, Oxford: Tutor, 1948–84; Dean, 1957–64; Tutor for Admissions, 1968–72; Reader in Class. Lit., Oxford Univ., 1978–85. Paddison Vis. Prof., Univ. of N Carolina at Chapel Hill, 1985; Vis. Prof. of Classics, Stanford Univ., 1989, 1991. Co-editor, Classical Quarterly, 1965–70. *Publications:* Commentary on Longinus, On the Sublime, 1964; Ancient Literary Criticism (with M. Winterbottom), 1972; Plutarch, 1972; (with N. G. Wilson) Menander Rhetor, 1981; Criticism in Antiquity, 1981; Greek Declamation, 1984; (ed) Antonine Literature, 1990; articles and reviews in classical periodicals. *Address:* 35 Belsyre Court, Oxford OX2 6HU. *T:* Oxford (0865) 56135.

RUSSELL, Rev. Prof. Edward Augustine; Principal, Union Theological College, Belfast, 1981–87; Professor of New Testament (originally at Presbyterian College, Belfast), 1961–87, Emeritus 1987; *b* 29 Nov. 1916; *s* of William Russell and Annie (*née* Sudway); *m* 1st, 1948, Emily Frances Stevenson (*d* 1978); two *s* one *d*; 2nd, 1979, Joan Evelyn Rufli (*née* Craig). *Educ:* Royal Belfast Academical Instn; London Univ. (BA, BD, MTh); Magee UC, 1942–43; Presbyterian Coll., Belfast, 1943–44, 1945–46; New Coll., Edinburgh, 1944–45. Research at Göttingen Univ. Ordained to Ministry of Presbyterian Church in Ireland, 1948; Minister: Donacloney, 1948–53; Mountpottinger Churches, 1953–61. External Examiner, Glasgow Univ., 1968, 1972–73; extra-mural Lectr, QUB, 1972–. Vis. Prof., Southwestern Univ., Memphis, 1980. Member of various clerical associations. Editor, Irish Biblical Studies, 1979–. Hon. DD Presbyterian Theol Faculty of Ireland, 1966. *Publications:* contribs to: Studia Evangelica VI, Berlin 1973; Ministry and the Church, 1977; Studia Biblica vol. II, Sheffield 1980; Studia Evangelica VII, Berlin 1982; Proc. Irish Biblical Assoc., *et al. Recreations:* music, golf, painting, languages, bird-watching. *Address:* 30 Glenshesk Road, Ballycastle, N Ireland BT54 6PH.

RUSSELL, Edward Walter, CMG 1960; MA Cantab, PhD Cantab; Professor of Soil Science, Reading University, 1964–70, now Professor Emeritus; *b* Wye, Kent, 27 Oct. 1904; *e s* of late Sir (Edward) John Russell, OBE, FRS; *m* 1933, Margaret, *y d* of late Sir Hugh Calthrop Webster; one *s* two *d. Educ:* Oundle; Gonville and Caius College, Cambridge. Soil Physicist, Rothamsted Experimental Station, Harpenden, 1930–48; Reader in Soil Science, Oxford Univ., 1948–55; Director, East African Agriculture and Forestry Research Organisation, 1955–64. Member: Scientific Council for Africa, 1956–63; Agricultural Research Council of Central Africa, 1959–64. FInstP; FIBiol; FIAgrE. Hon. Member: British Soc. of Soil Science (Pres., 1968–70); Internat. Soc. of Soil Science. For. Corr. Mem., French Acad. of Agriculture, 1969. Hon. Councillor, Consejo Superior de Investigations Cientificas, Madrid, 1970. Hon DSc Univ. of East Africa, 1970. *Publications:* 8th, 9th and 10th Editions of Soil Conditions and Plant Growth; contrib. on physics and chemistry of soils to agricultural and soil science journals. *Address:* 31 Brooklyn Drive, Emmer Green, Reading, Berks RG4 8SR. *T:* Reading (0734) 472934.

RUSSELL, Edwin John Cumming, FRBS 1978; sculptor; *b* 4 May 1939; *s* of Edwin Russell and Mary Elizabeth Russell; *m* 1964, Lorne McKean; two *d. Educ:* Brighton Coll. of Art and Crafts; Royal Academy Schs (CertRAS). *Works:* Crucifix, limewood, pulpit, St Paul's Cathedral, 1964; St Catherine, lead, Little Cloister, Westminster Abbey, 1966; St Michael, oak, Chapel of St Michael and St George, St Paul's Cath., 1970; Bishop Bubwith, W Front Wells Cath., 1980; sundials: Jubilee Dolphin Dial, bronze, Nat. Maritime Mus., Greenwich, 1978; 3m, Sultan Qaboos Univ., Oman, 1986; Botanical Armillery, Kew Gardens, 1987; 5m, bronze, Parliament Square, Dubai, 1988; Forecourt sculpture, Rank Xerox Internat. HQ, 1989; shopping centre sculpture: Mad Hatter's Tea Party play sculpture, granite, Warrington, 1984; Lion and Lamb, teak, Farnham, 1986; public works: Suffragette Meml, 1968; 1st Gov. of Bahamas, Sheraton Hotel, Nassau, 1968; Lewis Carroll commemorative sculpture, Alice and the White Rabbit, Guildford, 1984; Panda, marble, WWF Internat. HQ, 1988; private collections: Goodwood House; Sir Robert McAlpine & Sons Ltd; Rosehaugh Stanhope Developments; Arup Associates; Bovis; YRM International; Trafalgar House plc; Cementation International; John Laing Construction; John Mowlem & Co.; ARC; Worshipful Co. of Stationers; City of London Grammar Shool. Royal Academy Gold Medal for Sculpture, 1960. *Recreation:* philosophy. *Address:* Lethendry, Polecat Valley, Hindhead, Surrey GU26 6BE. *T:* Hindhead (042873) 5655.

RUSSELL, Eileen Alison, (Mrs A. Muir Russell); *see* Mackay, E. A.

RUSSELL, Sir Evelyn (Charles Sackville), Kt 1982; Chief Metropolitan Stipendiary Magistrate, 1978–82; *b* 2 Dec. 1912; *s* of late Henry Frederick Russell and late Kathleen Isabel, *d* of Richard Morphy; *m* 1939, Joan (*d* 1990), *er d* of Harold Edward Jocelyn Camps; one *d. Educ:* Douai School; Château de Mesnières, Seine Maritime, France. Hon. Artillery Co., 1938. Served War of 1939–45, Royal Artillery, in UK, N Africa, Italy and Greece. Called to the Bar, Gray's Inn, 1945 (Hon. Bencher 1980); Metropolitan Stipendiary Magistrate, 1961. KCHS 1980 (KHS 1964). *Address:* The Gate House, Coopersale, Epping, Essex CM16 7QT. *T:* Epping (0378) 72568.

RUSSELL, Francis Mark; Chairman, B. Elliott plc, 1975–87 (Chief Executive, 1972–83); *b* 26 July 1927; *s* of W. Sidney and Beatrice M. Russell; *m* 1950, Joan Patricia Ryan; two *s* three *d. Educ:* Ratcliffe Coll., Leicester; Clare Coll., Cambridge (MA). CBIM. Palestine Police, 1946–48; Director: S. Russell & Sons Ltd, 1959; B. Elliott & Co. Ltd, 1967; Chief Executive, 1969, Dir, 1969–88, Chm., 1975–87, Goldfields Industrial Corporation; Dep. Chm., B. Elliott & Co. Ltd, 1971; Dir, Johnson & Firth Brown plc, 1982–. *Recreations:*

golf, gardening. *Address:* Welders Wood, Welders Lane, Chalfont St Peter, Bucks SL9 8TT. *T:* Chalfont St Giles (02407) 4559. *Clubs:* Boodle's; Denham Golf.

RUSSELL, George, CBE 1985; Chairman, since 1989, and Group Chief Executive, since 1986, Marley Plc; Chairman, Independent Television Commission, since 1991; *b* 25 Oct. 1935; *s* of William H. Russell and Frances A. Russell; *m* 1959, Dorothy Brown; three *d*. *Educ:* Gateshead Grammar Sch.; Durham Univ. (BA Hons). ICI, 1958–67 (graduate trainee, Commercial Res. Officer, Sales Rep., and Product Sales Man.); Vice President and General Manager: Welland Chemical Co. of Canada Ltd, 1968; St Clair Chemical Co. Ltd, 1968; Man. Dir, Alcan UK Ltd, 1976; Asst Man. Dir, 1977–81, Man. Dir, 1981–82, Alcan Aluminium (UK) Ltd; Man. Dir and Chief Exec., British Alcan Aluminium, 1982–86; Dep. Chm., Channel Four TV, 1987–88; Chm., ITN, 1988; Chairman: Luxfer Holdings Ltd, 1976; Alcan UK Ltd, 1978; Director: Alcan Aluminiumwerke GmbH, Frankfurt, 1977–82; Northern Rock Bldg Soc., 1985–; Alcan Aluminium Ltd, 1987–. Visiting Professor, Univ. of Newcastle upon Tyne, 1978. Chm., IBA, 1989–90 (Mem., 1979–86); Member: Board, Northern Sinfonia Orchestra, 1977–80; Northern Industrial Development Board, 1977–80; Washington Development Corporation, 1978–80; Board, Civil Service Pay Research Unit, 1980–81; Megaw Inquiry into Civil Service Pay, 1981–; Widdicombe Cttee of Inquiry into Conduct of Local Authority Business, 1985. Trustee, Beamish Develt Trust, 1985–. Hon. DEng Univ of Newcastle upon Tyne, 1985. *Recreations:* tennis, badminton, bird watching. *Address:* Marley plc, London Road, Riverhead, Sevenoaks, Kent TN13 2DS.

RUSSELL, Sir George Michael, 7th Bt, *cr* 1812; *b* 30 Sept. 1908; *s* of Sir Arthur Edward Ian Montagu Russell, 6th Bt, MBE and late Aileen Kerr, *y d* of Admiral Mark Robert Pechell; *S* father, 1964; *m* 1936, Joy Frances Bedford, *d* of late W. Mitchell, Irwin, Western Australia; two *d*. *Educ:* Radley, Berkshire, England. *Heir: half-b* Arthur Mervyn Russell, *b* 7 Feb. 1923.

See also Baron Broughshane.

RUSSELL, Gerald Francis Morris, MD, FRCP, FRCPE, FRCPsych, DPM; Professor of Psychiatry, Institute of Psychiatry, University of London, and Physician, Bethlem Royal and Maudsley Hospital, since 1979; *b* Grammont, Belgium, 12 Jan. 1928; 2nd *s* of late Maj. Daniel George Russell, MC, and late Berthe Marie Russell (*née* De Boe); *m* 1950, Margaret Taylor, MB, ChB; three *s*. *Educ:* Collège St Jean Berchmans, Brussels; George Watson's Coll., Edinburgh (Dux); Univ. of Edinburgh (Mouat Schol. in Practice of Physic). MD (with commendation), 1957. RAMC Regimental Med. Off., Queen's Bays, 1951–53; Neurological Registrar, Northern Gen. Hosp., Edin., 1954–56; MRC Clinical Res. Fellow, 1956–58; Inst. of Psychiatry, Maudsley Hospital: 1st Asst, 1959–60; Senior Lectr, 1961–70; Dean, 1966–70; Bethlem Royal and Maudsley Hospital: Physician, 1961–70; Mem. Bd of Governors, 1966–70; Mem., Special Health Authority, 1979–; Prof. of Psychiatry, Royal Free Hosp. Sch. of Medicine, 1971–79. Chairman: Educn Cttee, Royal Medico-Psychological Assoc., 1970 (Mem. Council, 1966–71); Sect. on Eating Disorders, World Psychiatric Assoc., 1989–; Assoc. of Univ. Teachers of Psychiatry, 1991–; Sec. of Sect. of Psychiatry, Roy. Soc. Med., 1966–68; European Soc. for Clinical Investigation, 1968–72; Pres., Soc. for Psychosomatic Res., 1989–91. Corr. Fellow, Amer. Psychiatric Assoc., 1967–. Member Editorial Boards: British Jl of Psychiatry, 1966–71; Psychological Medicine, 1970–; Jl Neurology, Neurosurgery and Psychiatry, 1971–75; Medical Education, 1975–; Internat. Jl of Eating Disorders, 1981–. Mem., 1942 Club, 1978–. *Publications:* contrib. to Psychiatrie der Gegenwart, vol. 3, 1975; (ed jtly with L. Hersov and contrib.) Handbook of Psychiatry, vol. 4, The Neuroses and Personality Disorders, 1984; (contrib. and ed with G. I. Szmukler, P. D. Slade, P. Harris and D. Benton) Anorexia Nervosa and Bulimic Disorders: current perspectives, 1985; (contrib.) Oxford Textbook of Medicine (ed D. J. Weatherall, J. G. G. Leddingham and D. A. Warrell), 2nd edn, 1987; articles in med. jls on psychiatry, disorders of eating, education and neurology. *Recreations:* roses, language, photography. *Address:* The Institute of Psychiatry, De Crespigny Park, SE5 8AF.

RUSSELL, Graham R.; *see* Ross Russell.

RUSSELL, Ven. Harold Ian Lyle; Archdeacon of Coventry, since 1989; *b* 17 Oct. 1934; *s* of Percy Harold and Emma Rebecca Russell; *m* 1961, Barbara Lillian Dixon; two *s* one *d*. *Educ:* Epsom College; London Coll. of Divinity (BD, ALCD). Shell Petroleum Co., 1951–53; RAF, Jan. 1953; RAF Regt, Nov. 1953–1956; London Coll. of Divinity, 1956–60; ordained, 1960; Curate of Iver, Bucks, 1960–63; Curate-in-charge of St Luke's, Lodge Moor, Parish of Fulwood, Sheffield, 1963–67; Vicar: St John's, Chapeltown, Sheffield, 1967–75; St Jude's, Mapperley, Nottingham, 1975–89. *Recreations:* walking, photography, sport, gardening. *Address:* 9 Armorial Road, Coventry CV3 6GH. *T:* Coventry (0203) (home) 417750, (office) 674328. *Club:* Royal Air Force.

RUSSELL, Prof. Ian John, FRS 1989; Professor of Neurobiology, Sussex University, since 1987; *b* 19 June 1943; *s* of Philip William George Russell and Joan Lillian Russell; *m* 1968, Janice Marion Russell; one *s* one *d*. *Educ:* Chatham Technical Sch.; Queen Mary Coll., London (BSc Zoology); Univ. of British Columbia (NATO Student; MSc Zool.); Univ. of Cambridge (SRC Student; Trinity Hall Res. Student; PhD Zool.). Res. Fellowship, Magdalene Coll., Cambridge, 1969–71; SRC Res. Fellowship, Cambridge, 1969–73; Royal Soc. Exchange Fellowship, King Gustav V Res. Inst., Stockholm, 1970–71; University of Sussex: Lectr in Neurobiology, 1971–79; Reader in Neurobiology, 1979–80 and 1982–87; MRC Sen. Res. Fellow, 1980–82. *Publications:* on lateral line system and the cochlea, in learned jls. *Recreations:* hockey, windsurfing, reading, music, gardening, walking. *Address:* Martins, Cuilfail, Lewes, East Sussex BN7 2BE. *T:* Lewes (0273) 472351.

RUSSELL, James Francis Buchanan, QC (NI) 1968; **His Honour Judge Russell;** County Court Judge of Northern Ireland, since 1978; *b* 7 July 1924; *e s* of John Buchanan Russell and Margaret Bellingham Russell; *m* 1946, Irene McKee; two *s* one *d* (and one *d* decd). *Educ:* King's Sch., Worcester; St Andrews Univ.; Queen's Univ., Belfast (LLB). Served Royal Air Force, 1941–47. Called to Bar, NI, 1952; Crown Prosecutor: Co. Fermanagh, 1970; Co. Tyrone, 1974; Co. Londonderry, 1976. Bencher, Inn of Court, N Ireland, 1972–78 and 1988–, Treasurer, 1977. Member, Standing Advisory Commn on Human Rights, 1974–78; Chairman, Pensions Appeal Tribunal, N Ireland, 1970–. *Recreations:* golf, gardening. *Address:* 5 Grey Point, Helen's Bay, Co. Down, Northern Ireland. *T:* Helen's Bay (0247) 852249. *Clubs:* Royal Air Force; Royal Belfast Golf.

RUSSELL, Prof. James Knox, MD; ChB; FRCOG; Emeritus Professor of Obstetrics and Gynæcology, University of Newcastle upon Tyne, since 1982; Dean of Postgraduate Medicine, 1968–77; Consultant Obstetrician, Princess Mary Maternity Hospital, Newcastle upon Tyne, 1956–82, now Hon. Consultant; Consultant Gynæcologist, Royal Victoria Infirmary, Newcastle upon Tyne, 1956–82, now Hon. Consultant; *b* 5 Sept. 1919; *s* of James Russell, Aberdeen; *m* 1944, Cecilia V. Urquhart, MD, DCH, *o d* of Patrick Urquhart, MA; three *d*. *Educ:* Aberdeen Grammar School; University of Aberdeen. MB, ChB 1942, MD 1954, Aberdeen; MRCOG 1949; FRCOG 1958. Served War, 1943–46, as MO in RAF, UK and Western Europe. First Assistant to Prof. of Obstetrics and Gynæcology, Univ. of Durham, 1950; Senior Lecturer in Obstetrics and Gynæcology, Univ. of Durham, 1956; Prof., first at Durham, then at Newcastle upon Tyne, 1958–82. Hon. Obstetrician, MRC Unit on Reproduction and Growth; Examiner in Obstetrics and Gynæcology, Univs of London, Birmingham, Manchester, Belfast, Aberdeen, Liverpool, RCOG, CMB, Tripoli and Kuala Lumpur; Presiding Examiner, CMB, Newcastle upon Tyne; Consultant in human reproduction, WHO. Commonwealth Fund Fellow 1962. Visiting Professor: New York, 1974; South Africa, 1978; Kuala Lumpur, 1980, 1982; Oviedo, Spain, 1987; Graham Waite Meml Lectr, Amer. Coll. of Obstetricians and Gynaecologists, Dallas, 1982. *Publications:* Teenage Pregnancy: Medical, Social and Educational Aspects, 1982; various papers, editorials and articles on obstetrical and gynæcological subjects and medical education to learned journals, newspapers and magazines. *Recreations:* writing, gardening, curing and smoking bacon, eels, salmon, etc. *Address:* Newlands, Tranwell Woods, Morpeth, Northumberland NE61 6AG. *T:* Morpeth (0670) 515666. *Club:* Royal Over-Seas League.

RUSSELL, John, CBE 1975; Art critic, The New York Times, since 1974 (Chief Art Critic, 1982–90); *b* 1919; *o s* of Isaac James Russell and Harriet Elizabeth Atkins; *m* 1st, 1945, Alexandrine Apponyi (marr. diss., 1950); one *d*; 2nd, 1956, Vera Poliakoff (marr. diss., 1971); 3rd, 1975, Rosamond Bernier. *Educ:* St Paul's Sch.; Magdalen Coll., Oxford (MA). Hon. Attaché, Tate Gall., 1940–41; MOI, 1941–43; Naval Intell. Div., Admty, 1943–46. Regular contributor, The Sunday Times, 1945–, art critic, 1949–74. Mem. art panel, Arts Council, 1958–68. Organised Arts Council exhibns: Modigliani, 1964, Rouault, 1966 and Balthus, 1968 (all at Tate Gallery); Pop Art (with Suzi Gablik), 1969 (at the Hayward Gallery); organised Vuillard exhibn (Toronto, Chicago, San Francisco), 1971. Hon. Fellow, Royal Acad. of Arts, 1989. Frank Jewett Mather Award (College Art Assoc.), 1979; Mitchell Prize for Art Criticism, 1984. Grand Medal of Honour (Austria), 1972; Officier de l'Ordre des Arts et des Lettres, 1975; Order of Merit, Fed. Repub. of Germany, 1982; Chevalier, Légion d'Honneur, 1986. *Publications:* books include: Shakespeare's Country, 1942; British Portrait Painters, 1945; Switzerland, 1950; Logan Pearsall Smith, 1950; Erich Kleiber, 1956; Paris, 1960, new and enlarged edn, 1983; Seurat, 1965; Private View (with Bryan Robertson and Lord Snowdon), 1965; Max Ernst, 1967; Henry Moore, 1968; Ben Nicholson, 1969; Pop Art Redefined (with Suzi Gablik), 1969; The World of Matisse, 1970; Francis Bacon, 1971; Edouard Vuillard, 1971; The Meanings of Modern Art, 1981, new and enlarged edn 1990; Reading Russell, 1989. *Recreations:* reading, writing, Raimund (1790–1836). *Address:* 166 East 61st Street, New York, NY 10021, USA. *Clubs:* Century, Knickerbocker (New York).

See also N. T. Grimshaw.

RUSSELL, John Harry; Chairman and Chief Executive, Duport plc, 1981–86; *b* 21 Feb. 1926; *s* of Joseph Harry Russell and Nellie Annie Russell; *m* 1951, Iris Mary Cooke; one *s* one *d*. *Educ:* Halesowen Grammar Sch. FCA; FBIM. War Service, RN. Joseph Lucas Ltd, 1948–52; Vono Ltd (Duport Gp Co.), 1952–59; Standard Motors Ltd, 1959–61; rejoined Duport Gp, 1961: Man. Dir, Duport Foundries Ltd, 1964; Dir, Duport Parent Bd, 1966; Chm., Burman & Sons Ltd (formerly part of Duport), 1968–72; Chief Exec., Duport Engrg Div., 1972–73; Dep. Gp Man. Dir, 1973–75; Gp Man. Dir, 1975–80, Dep. Chm., 1976–81, Duport Ltd. Non-exec. Dir, Birmingham Local Bd, Barclays Bank Ltd, 1976–88. Chm., Black Country Museum Trust Ltd, 1988–. Liveryman, Worshipful Co. of Glaziers and Freeman and Citizen of London, 1976. *Recreations:* reading, music, antiques. *Address:* 442 Bromsgrove Road, Hunnington, Halesowen, West Midlands B62 0JL.

RUSSELL, John Lawson; Commissioner for Local Administration in Scotland, 1978–82; *b* 29 May 1917; *er s* of late George William Russell and Joan Tait Russell; *m* 1946, Rachel Essington Howgate; three *s*. *Educ:* Central School and Anderson Inst., Lerwick; Edinburgh Univ. (BL). Enrolled Solicitor. Served Royal Scots, Royal Artillery, Gordon Highlanders and 30 Commando, 1939–46 (despatches). Assistant Secretary, Assoc. of County Councils in Scotland, 1946–49; Depute County Clerk: West Lothian, 1950–57; Caithness, 1957–58; County Clerk: Caithness, 1958–67; Aberdeen, 1967–75; Chief Executive, Grampian Region, 1974–77. Member, Countryside Commission for Scotland, 1978–82. *Recreations:* sailing, hill-walking, camping, photography. *Address:* 2A Montgomery Court, 110 Hepburn Gardens, St Andrews, Fife KY16 9LT. *T:* St Andrews (0334) 75727.

RUSSELL, Ken; film director since 1958; *b* 3 July 1927; *m* Shirley Kingdom (marr. diss. 1978); five *c*; *m* 1984, Vivian Jolly; one *s* one *d*. Merchant Navy, 1945; RAF, 1946–49. Ny Norsk Ballet, 1950; Garrick Players, 1951; free-lance photographer, 1951–57; Film Director, BBC, 1958–66; free-lance film director, 1966; *Films for TV:* Elgar; Bartok; Debussy; Henri Rousseau; Isadora Duncan; Delius; Richard Strauss; Clouds of Glory; The Planets; Vaughan Williams; ABC of British Music (Emmy award); *films:* French Dressing, 1964; The Billion Dollar Brain, 1967; Women in Love, 1969; The Music Lovers, 1970; The Devils, 1971; The Boy Friend, 1971; Savage Messiah, 1972; Mahler, 1973; Tommy, 1974; Lisztomania, 1975; Valentino, 1977; Altered States, 1981; Crimes of Passion, 1985; Gothic, 1987; (jtly) Aria, 1987; Salome's Last Dance, 1988; Lair of the White Worm, 1989; The Rainbow, 1989; Whore, 1991; *opera:* The Rake's Progress, Florence, 1982; Madam Butterfly, Spoleto, 1983; La Bohème, Macerata, 1984; Faust, Vienna, 1985. Screen Writers Guild Award for TV films Elgar, Debussy, Isadora and Dante's Inferno. *Publication:* A British Picture (autobiog.), 1989. *Recreation:* music, fell walking.

RUSSELL, Mrs Leonard; *see* Powell, (E.) Dilys.

RUSSELL, Sir Mark; *see* Russell, Sir R. M.

RUSSELL, Martin Guthrie, CBE 1970; Children's Division, Home Office, later Department of Health and Social Security, 1964–74; *b* 7 May 1914; *s* of William James Russell and Bessie Gertrude Meades; *m* 1951, Moira May Eynon, *d* of Capt. Richard Threlfell; one *d*. *Educ:* Alleyn's School; Sidney Sussex Coll., Cambridge (MA). Asst Principal, Home Office, 1937; Asst Private Sec. to Lord Privy Seal, 1942; Principal, Home Office, 1942; seconded to Treasury, 1949–51 and 1952–54; Asst Sec. 1950; Estabt Officer, 1954, Dep. Chm., 1960–64, Prison Commn. In charge of Interdepartmental Social Work Gp, 1969–70. *Recreations:* gardening, enjoying retirement. *Address:* 23 Sutton Lane, Banstead, Surrey SM7 3QX. *T:* Burgh Heath (0737) 54397. *Club:* United Oxford & Cambridge University.

RUSSELL, Muir; *see* Russell, A. M.

RUSSELL, Hon. Sir Patrick; *see* Russell, Hon. Sir T. P.

RUSSELL, Prof. Peter Edward Lionel Russell, DLitt; FBA 1977; (surname formerly Wheeler); King Alfonso XIII Professor of Spanish Studies, Oxford, 1953–81; *b* 24 Oct. 1913; *er s* of Hugh Bernard Wheeler and late Rita Muriel (*née* Russell), Christchurch, NZ. *Educ:* Cheltenham College; Queen's College, Oxford (DLitt 1981; Hon. Fellow, 1990). Lecturer of St John's College, 1937–53 and Queen's College, 1938–45. Enlisted, 1940; commissioned (Intelligence Corps) Dec. 1940; Temp. Lt-Col, 1945; specially employed in Caribbean, W Africa and SE Asia, 1942–46. Fellow of Queen's College, 1946–53, and Univ. Lectr in Spanish Studies, 1946–53; Fellow of Exeter Coll., 1953–81, Emeritus Fellow, 1981; Taylorian Special Lectr, Oxford, 1983; Visiting Professor: Univ. of

Virginia, 1982; Univ. of Texas, 1983, 1987; Johns Hopkins Univ., 1986; Vanderbilt Univ., 1987. Member: Portuguese Academy of History, 1956; Real Academia de Buenas Letras, Barcelona, 1972; UGC Cttee on Latin-American Studies in British Univs, 1962–64. FRHistS. Premio Antonio de Nebrija, Univ. of Salamanca, 1989. Comdr, Order of Isabel the Catholic (Spain), 1989. *Publications:* As Fontes de Fernão Lopes, 1941 (Coimbra); The English Intervention in Spain and Portugal in the Time of Edward III and Richard II, 1955; Prince Henry the Navigator, 1960; (with D. M. Rogers) Hispanic Manuscripts and Books in the Bodleian and Oxford College Libraries, 1962; (ed) Spain: a Companion to Spanish Studies, 1973, Spanish edn, 1982; Temas de la Celestina y otros estudios (del Cid al Quijote), 1978; Prince Henry the Navigator: the rise and fall of a culture hero, 1984; Traducción y traductores en la Península Ibérica 1400–1550, 1985; Cervantes, 1985; La Celestina, 1991; articles and reviews in Modern Language Review, Medium Aevum, Bulletin of Hispanic Studies, etc. *Recreation:* travel. *Address:* 23 Belsyre Court, Woodstock Road, Oxford OX2 6HU. *T:* Oxford (0865) 56086. *Club:* United Oxford & Cambridge University.

RUSSELL, Most Rev. Philip Welsford Richmond; *b* 21 Oct. 1919; *s* of Leslie Richmond Russell and Clarice Louisa Russell (*née* Welsford); *m* 1945, Violet Eirene, *d* of Ven. Dr. O. J. Hogarth, sometime Archdeacon of the Cape; one *s* three *d*. *Educ:* Durban High Sch.; Rhodes Univ. College (Univ. of South Africa), BA 1948; LTh 1950. Served War of 1939–45; MBE 1943. Deacon, 1950; Priest, 1951; Curate, St Peter's, Maritzburg, 1950–54; Vicar: Greytown, 1954–57; Ladysmith, 1957–61; Kloof, 1961–66; Archdeacon of Pinetown, 1961–66; Bishop Suffragan of Capetown, 1966–70; Bishop of Port Elizabeth, 1970–74; Bishop of Natal, 1974–81; Archbishop of Cape Town and Metropolitan of Southern Africa, 1981–86. *Recreations:* caravanning, fishing. *Address:* 400 Currie Road, Durban, Natal, South Africa.

RUSSELL, Robert Christopher Hamlyn, CBE 1981; formerly Director, Hydraulics Research Station, Department of the Environment (formerly Ministry of Technology), 1965–81; *b* Singapore, 1921; *s* of late Philip Charles and Hilda Gertrude Russell; *m* 1950, Cynthia Mary Roberts; one *s* two *d*. *Educ:* Stowe; King's Coll., Cambridge. Asst Engineer: BTH Co., Rugby, 1944; Dunlop Rubber Co., 1946; Sen. Scientific Officer, later PSO, then SPSO, in Hydraulics Research Station, 1949–65. Visiting Prof., Univ. of Strathclyde, 1967. *Publications:* Waves and Tides, 1951; papers on civil engineering hydraulics. *Address:* 29 St Mary's Street, Wallingford, Oxfordshire. *T:* Wallingford (0491) 37323.

RUSSELL, Sir (Robert) Mark, KCMG 1985 (CMG 1977); HM Diplomatic Service, retired; Chairman, Commonwealth Institute, Scotland, since 1989; *b* 3 Sept. 1929; *s* of Sir Robert E. Russell, CSI, CIE; *m* 1954, Virginia Mary Rogers; two *s* two *d*. *Educ:* Trinity Coll., Glenalmond; Exeter Coll., Oxford (MA). Hon. Mods cl. 2, Lit. Hum. cl. 1. Royal Artillery, 1952–54; FO, 1954–56; 3rd, later 2nd Sec., HM Legation, Budapest, 1956–58; 2nd Sec., Berne, 1958–61; FO, 1961–65; 1st Sec., 1962; 1st Sec. and Head of Chancery, Kabul, 1965–67; 1st Sec., DSAO, 1967–69; Counsellor, 1969; Dep. Head of Personnel (Ops) Dept, FCO, 1969–70; Commercial Counsellor, Bucharest, 1970–73; Counsellor, Washington, 1974–78, and Head of Chancery, 1977–78; Asst Under Sec. of State, FCO and Dep. Chief Clerk and Chief Inspector, HM Diplomatic Service, 1978–82; Ambassador to Turkey, 1983–86; Dep. Under-Sec. of State (Chief Clerk), FCO, 1986–89. Chairman: Martin Currie European Investment Trust, 1990–; Margaret Blackwood Housing Assoc.; Scottish Trust for the Physically Disabled, 1990–. Mem. Bd, British Council, 1990–. *Recreations:* travel, music. *Address:* 20 Meadow Place, Edinburgh EH9 1JR. *Clubs:* Commonwealth Trust; New (Edinburgh).

RUSSELL, Prof. Roger Wolcott; Vice Chancellor, and Professor of Psychobiology, Flinders University of South Australia, 1972–79, now Emeritus Professor (engaged in research, 1979–89); Visiting Professor of Pharmacology, School of Medicine, University of California at Los Angeles, 1976–77 and since 1980; Research Psychobiologist, School of Biological Sciences, Research Neurobiologist and Fellow of the Center for the Neurobiology of Learning and Memory, University of California at Irvine, since 1990; *b* 30 Aug. 1914; *s* of Leonard Walker and Sadie Stanhope Russell, Worcester, Mass, USA; *m* 1945, Kathleen Sherman Fortescue; one *s* one *d*. *Educ:* Worcester (Mass, USA) Public Schools; Clark Univ. (Livermore Schol., Clark Fellow in Psychology); BA 1935, MA 1936; Peabody Coll., Vanderbilt Univ. (Payne Schol.); University of Virginia (Du Pont Research Fellow); PhD 1939; DSc Univ. of London, 1954. Instructor in Psychology: Univ. of Nebraska, 1939–41, Michigan State Coll., 1941; Research Psychologist, USAF Sch. of Aviation Medicine, 1941–42; Officer USAF, 1942–46; Asst Prof. in Psychol., Univ. of Pittsburgh, 1946–47; Assoc. Prof. of Psychol., Univ. of Pittsburgh and Res. Fellow in Neurophysiol., Western Psychiatric Inst., 1947–49; Fulbright Advanced Research Schol. and Director, Animal Research Lab., Institute of Psychiatry, Univ. of London, 1949–50; Prof. of Psychology and Head of Dept of Psychol., University Coll., London 1950–57 (on leave of absence, 1956–57); Dean of Advanced Studies, Indiana Univ., 1966–67 (Prof. and Chm. Dept of Psychology, 1959–66); Vice Chancellor, Academic Affairs, and Prof. of Psychology, Psycho-Biology and of Clinical Pharmacology and Therapeutics, Univ. of Calif., Irvine, 1967–72. Member: Australian Vice-Chancellors' Cttee, 1972–79; Bd of Dirs, Australian-American Educnl Foundn, 1972–79; Commonwealth Educnl R&D Cttee, 1974–79. Visiting Professor: Dept of Psychology, Univ. of Reading, 1977; Dept of Psychology, Univ. of Stockholm, 1977. Executive Sec. of the American Psychological Assoc., 1956–59, Board of Directors, 1963–65, Pres. Div. 1, 1968–69; Mem., USPHS Adv. Cttee in Psychopharmacology, 1957–63, 1967–70, 1981–85; Member: Nat. Research Coun. (USA), 1958–61, 1963–65, 1967–71; Army Sci. Adv. Panel (USA), 1958–66; Sec.-Gen. Internat. Union of Psychological Science, 1960–66 (Vice-Pres., 1966–69; Pres., 1969–72; Mem. Exec. Cttee, 1972–80); Aust.-Amer. Educn Foundn Vis. Prof., Dept of Psychol., Univ. of Sydney, 1965–66; Vis. Erskine Fellow, Univ. of Canterbury, NZ, 1966. Member, Scientific and Professional Socs in Europe, USA, Australia. FACE 1972; FASSA 1973. Hon. DSc: Newcastle, NSW, 1978; Flinders, 1979. Bronze Star Medal (USA), 1945. Army Commendation Medal (USA), 1946. *Publications:* (ed) Frontiers in Psychology, 1964; (ed) Frontiers in physiological Psychology, 1966; (ed) Matthew Flinders: The Ifs of History, 1979; (ed) Behavioral Measures of Neurotoxicity, 1990; research papers on neurochemical bases of behaviour, experimental psycho-pathology, physiological, child and social psychology, psychopharmacology. *Recreation:* writing. *Address:* Center for the Neurobiology of Learning and Memory, University of California, Irvine, Calif 92717, USA; One Cherry North, Irvine, Calif 92715. *T:* (714) 651–0107.

RUSSELL, (Ronald) Christopher (Gordon), FRCS; Consultant Surgeon: Middlesex Hospital, since 1975; King Edward VII Hospital, since 1985; *b* 15 May 1940; *s* of Rognvald Gordon Russell and Doris Isa Russell (*née* Troup); *m* 1965, Mary Ruth Pitcher; two *s* (and one *s* decd). *Educ:* Epsom College; Middlesex Hosp. Med. Sch. (MB BS, MS). Sen. Lectr in Surgery, St Mary's Hosp., 1973–75. Associate Editor, 1978, Co-Editor, 1986–91, British Jl of Surgery; Gen. Editor, Operative Surgery, 1986–. *Publications:* (ed) Recent Advances in Surgery, vols XI, XII, XIII, 1991; (ed jtly) Bailey & Love Textbook of Surgery, 1991–; numerous contribs to surgical and gastroenterological jls. *Recreation:* travel. *Address:* 149 Harley Street, W1N 2DE; Little Orchards, Layters Way, Gerrards Cross SL9 7QY. *T:* Gerrards Cross (0753) 882264. *Club:* Royal Society of Medicine.

RUSSELL, Rudolf Rosenfeld; a Recorder of the Crown Court, since 1980; *b* 5 Feb. 1925; *s* of Robert and Johanna Rosenfeld; *m* 1952, Eva Maria Jaray; one *s*. *Educ:* Bryanston Sch.; Worcester Coll., Oxford (MA). Service in RAF, 1943–46. Called to the Bar, Middle Temple, 1950. *Recreations:* walking, music, skiing. *Address:* Devereux Chambers, Devereux Court, Temple, WC2R 3JJ. *T:* 071–353 7534.

RUSSELL, Sir Spencer (Thomas), Kt 1988; FCA; FCIS; FNZIM; Governor, Reserve Bank of New Zealand, 1984–88, retired; *b* 5 Oct. 1923; *s* of Thomas Spencer Russell and Ann Jane Russell; *m* 1953, Ainsley Russell (*née* Coull); three *s*. *Educ:* Wanganui Collegiate School. Served War, NZ Division, 1942–45. Joined National Bank of New Zealand, 1946; International Manager, 1956; Asst Gen. Man., 1960; Chief London Man., 1973; Chief Exec. and Dir, 1976. *Publications:* numerous articles in professional jls. *Recreations:* golf, gardening. *Address:* 6 Challenger Street, St Heliers, Auckland 5, New Zealand. *Clubs:* Wellington, Wellesley (Wellington); Wellington Golf.

RUSSELL, Terence Francis; Sheriff of North Strathclyde at Kilmarnock, since 1983; *b* 12 April 1931; *s* of Robert Russell and Catherine Cusker Russell; *m* 1965, Mary Ann Kennedy; two *d*. *Educ:* Glasgow Univ. (BL). Qualified as Solicitor, 1955; practised in Glasgow, 1955–58 and 1963–81; Solicitor in High Court, Bombay, 1958–63. Sheriff of N Strathclyde, and of Grampian, Highland and Islands, 1981–83. *Recreations:* gardening, painting.

RUSSELL, Thomas, CMG 1980; CBE 1970 (OBE 1963); HM Overseas Civil Service, retired; Representative of the Cayman Islands in UK, since 1982; *b* 27 May 1920; *s* of late Thomas Russell, OBE, MC and Margaret Thomson Russell; *m* 1951, Andrée Irma Désfossés (*d* 1989); one *s*. *Educ:* Hawick High Sch.; St Andrews Univ.; Peterhouse, Cambridge. MA St Andrews; Dip. Anthrop. Cantab. War Service, Cameronians (Scottish Rifles), 1941; 5th Bn (Scottish), Parachute Regt, 1943: served in N Africa and Italy; POW, 1944; Captain 1945; OC Parachute Trng Company, 1946. Cambridge Univ., 1946–47. Colonial Admin. Service, 1948; District Comr, British Solomon Is Protectorate, 1948; Asst Sec., Western Pacific High Commn, Fiji, 1951; District Comr, British Solomon Is Protectorate, 1954–56; seconded Colonial Office, 1956–57; Admin. Officer Class A, 1956; Dep. Financial Sec., 1962; Financial Sec., 1965; Chief Sec. to W Pacific High Commn, 1970–74; Governor of the Cayman Islands, 1974–81. FRAI. *Recreations:* anthropology, archæology. *Address:* 6 Eldon Drive, Frensham Road, The Bourne, Farnham, Surrey GU10 3JE. *Clubs:* Commonwealth Trust, Caledonian.

RUSSELL, Rt. Hon. Sir (Thomas) Patrick, Kt 1980; PC 1987; **Rt. Hon. Lord Justice Russell;** a Lord Justice of Appeal, since 1987; *b* 30 July 1926; *s* of late Sidney Arthur Russell and Elsie Russell; *m* 1951, Doreen (Janie) Ireland; two *d*. *Educ:* Urmston Grammar Sch.; Manchester Univ. (LLB). Served in Intelligence Corps and RASC, 1945–48. Called to Bar, Middle Temple, 1949, Bencher, 1978; Prosecuting Counsel to the Post Office (Northern Circuit), 1961–70; Asst Recorder of Bolton, 1963–70; Recorder of Barrow-in-Furness, 1970–71; QC 1971; a Recorder of the Crown Court, 1972–80; Leader, 1978–80, Presiding Judge, 1983–87, Northern Circuit; a Judge of the High Court of Justice, QBD, 1980–86. Mem. Senate, Inns of Court and Bar, 1978–80. Mem., Lord Justice James Cttee on Distribution of Criminal Business, 1973–76. Pres., Manchester and Dist Medico-Legal Soc., 1978–79 (Patron, 1987); Vice-Pres., Lancs CCC, 1980. Hon. LLD Manchester, 1988. *Recreation:* cricket. *Address:* Royal Courts of Justice, WC2.

RUSSELL, William Martin, (Willy); author since 1971; *b* 23 Aug. 1947; *s* of William and Margery Russell; *m* 1969, Ann Seagroatt; one *s* two *d*. *Educ:* St Katharine's Coll. of Educn, Liverpool, 1970–73 (Cert. of Educn). Ladies' Hairdresser, 1963–69; Teacher, 1973–74; Fellow in Creative Writing, Manchester Polytechnic, 1977–78. Founder Mem., and Dir, Quintet Films; Hon. Dir, Liverpool Playhouse. *Theatre:* Blind Scouse (3 short plays), 1971–72; When the Reds (adaptation), 1972; John, Paul, George, Ringo and Bert (musical), 1974; Breezeblock Park, 1975; One for the Road, 1976; Stags and Hens, 1978; Educating Rita, 1979; Blood Brothers (musical), 1983; Our Day Out (musical), 1983; Shirley Valentine, 1986; *television plays:* King of the Castle, 1972; Death of a Young, Young Man, 1972; Break In (for schools), 1974; Our Day Out, 1976; Lies (for schools), 1977; Daughters of Albion, 1978; Boy with Transistor Radio (for schools), 1979; One Summer (series), 1980; *radio play:* I Read the News Today (for schools), 1976; *screenplays:* Band on the Run, 1979 (not released); Educating Rita, 1981; Shirley Valentine, 1988; Dancing Through the Dark, 1989. Hon. MA Open Univ., 1983; Hon. DLit Liverpool. *Publications:* Breezeblock Park, 1978; One for the Road, 1980, rev. edn 1985; Educating Rita, 1981; Our Day Out, 1984; Stags and Hens, 1985; Blood Brothers, 1985 (also pubd as short non-musical version for schools, 1984); Shirley Valentine, 1989; several other plays included in general collections of plays; songs and poetry. *Recreations:* playing the guitar, composing songs, gardening, cooking. *Address:* c/o Margaret Ramsay Ltd, 14A Goodwin's Court, St Martin's Lane, WC2N 4LL. *T:* 071–240 0691. *Club:* Woolton Village (Liverpool).

RUSSELL, William Robert; Vice-President, Australian British Trade Association, 1980–86 (Chairman, 1967–72 and 1975–77; Deputy Chairman, 1972–74 and 1977–80); *b* 6 Aug. 1913; *s* of William Andrew Russell and Mary Margaret Russell; *m* 1940, Muriel Faith Rolfe; one *s* one *d*. *Educ:* Wakefield Road Central, East Ham. Served War of 1939–45: Mine-Sweeping and Anti-Submarine vessels; Commissioned, 1942; appointed to command, 1943. Joined Shaw Savill & Albion Co. Ltd, 1929; Director, 1958–; Manager, 1959; Gen. Manager, 1961; Dep. Chm., 1966; Chm. and Man. Dir, 1968–73. Chm., London Bd, Bank of NZ, 1981–84 (Dir, 1968–84). Chairman: Council of European and Japanese Nat. Shipowners Assocs, 1969–71 and 1973–75; Aust. and NZ Adv. Cttee to BOTB, 1975–77 (Dep. Chm., 1977–79); NZ/UK Chamber of Commerce and Industry, 1979–84. Mem., Tandridge Dist Council, 1978–82. *Recreations:* gardening, golf, sailing. *Address:* Westland, Uvedale Road, Limpsfield, Oxted, Surrey. *T:* Oxted (0883) 3080. *Clubs:* Naval; Royal Lymington Yacht.

RUSSELL-DAVIS, John Darelan, FRICS; chartered surveyor, retired; *b* 23 Dec. 1912; *s* of Edward David Darelan Davis, FRCS, and Alice Mildred (*née* Russell); *m* 1st, 1938, Barbarina Elizabeth Graham Arnould (*d* 1985); one *s* one *d*; 2nd, 1986, Gaynor, *widow* of Lt-Col A. V. Brooke-Webb, RA. *Educ:* Stowe Sch.; Germany; Coll. of Estate Management, London. FRICS 1934. Served War, HAC, 1939; commnd RA, 1940; Captain 1942; mentioned in despatches, 1945. Partner, C. P. Whiteley & Son, Chartered Surveyors, 1938; Sen. Partner, Whiteley, Ferris & Puckridge, and Kemsley, Whiteley & Ferris, City of London, 1948–72. Mem., Lands Tribunal, 1972–77. Royal Instn of Chartered Surveyors: formerly Mem. Council (twice); Chm., City branch, 1959; Hon. Treasurer, Benevolent Fund. Mem., East Grinstead UDC, 1957–60 (Vice-Chm., 1960). Formerly: Mem. Council, Wycombe Abbey Sch.; Trustee, Cordwainer and Bread Street Foundn; Mem. Court, Turners Co. (Renter-Warden, 1975). *Recreations:* gardening, Somerset and Dorset countryside. *Address:* 171 Goose Hill, Bower Hinton, Martock, Somerset TA12 6LJ. *T:* Martock (0935) 822307. *Clubs:* Army and Navy; Somerset CCC.
See also D. R. Davis.

RUSSELL VICK, Arnold Oughtred; His Honour Judge Russell Vick; *see* Vick.

RUSSON, David; Director General, Boston Spa (formerly Science, Technology and Industry), British Library, since 1988; *b* 12 June 1944; *s* of Thomas Charles Russon and Violet Russon (*née* Jarvis); *m* 1967, Kathleen Mary Gregory; one *s* two *d*. *Educ:* Wellington Grammar Sch.; University College London (BSc); Univ. of York. Various appts, Office for Scientific and Technical Information, DES, 1969–74; British Library: R & D Dept, 1974–75; Lending Div., 1975–85; Dir, Document Supply Centre, 1985–88; Mem., British Liby Bd, 1988–. FRSA; FIInfSc. *Publications:* contribs to professional jls of library and inf. science. *Recreations:* village tennis and badminton. *Address:* March House, Tollerton, York YO6 2EQ. *T:* Tollerton (03473) 253.

RUSTON, Rt. Rev. John Harry Gerald; *see* St Helena, Bishop of.

RUTHERFORD, Prof. Andrew; Warden of Goldsmiths' College, since 1984, and Professor since 1988, University of London; *b* Helmsdale, Sutherland, 23 July 1929; *s* of Thomas Armstrong and Christian P. Rutherford (*née* Russell); *m* 1953, Nancy Milroy Browning, MA, *d* of Dr Arthur Browning and Dr Jean G. Browning (*née* Thomson); two *s* one *d*. *Educ:* Helmsdale Sch.; George Watson's Boys' Coll.; Univ. of Edinburgh; Merton Coll., Oxford. MA Edinburgh Univ., First Cl. Hons Eng. Lang. and Lit., James Elliott Prize, and Vans Dunlop Schol., 1951; Carnegie Schol., 1953; BLitt Oxford, 1959. Seaforth Hldrs, 1952–53, serving with Somaliland Scouts; 11th Bn Seaforth Hldrs (TA), 1953–58. Asst Lectr in English, Univ. of Edinburgh, 1955; Lectr, 1956–64; Vis. Assoc. Prof., Univ. of Rochester (NY), 1963; University of Aberdeen: Sen. Lectr, 1964; Second Prof. of English, 1965–68; Regius (Chalmers) Prof. of Eng. Lit., 1968–84; Mem. Court, 1978–84; Dean, Faculty of Arts and Soc. Scis, 1979–82; Sen. Vice-Principal, 1982–84. Lectures: Byron Foundn, Nottingham Univ., 1964; Chatterton, British Acad., 1965; Stevenson, Edinburgh Univ., 1967. Chairman: English Bd, CNAA, 1966–73; Literature Adv. Cttee, British Council, 1987–; Pres., Internat. Assoc. of Univ. Profs of English, 1977–80. Mem., BBC Gen. Adv. Council, 1979–84; Trustee, Learning from Experience Trust, 1986–. British Council lecture tours in Europe, India and S America. Liveryman, Goldsmiths' Co., Freeman, City of London, 1991. Hon. DLitt SUNY, 1990. *Publications:* Byron: A Critical Study, 1961; (ed) Kipling's Mind and Art, 1964; (ed) Byron: The Critical Heritage, 1970; (ed) 20th Century Interpretations of A Passage to India, 1970; (ed) Kipling, A Sahibs' War and other stories, 1971; (ed) Kipling, Friendly Brook and other stories, 1971; The Literature of War, 1979, 2nd edn 1989; (ed) Early Verse by Rudyard Kipling, 1986; (ed) Kipling, Plain Tales from the Hills, 1987; (ed) Kipling, Selected Stories, 1987; (ed) Kipling, War Stories and Poems, 1990; (ed) Byron: Augustan and Romantic, 1990; articles in learned journals. *Address:* Goldsmiths' College, University of London, New Cross, SE14 6NW. *Clubs:* Athenæum, Commonwealth Trust.

RUTHERFORD, Derek Thomas Jones, FCA; financial and management accounting consultant, since 1990; *b* 9 April 1930; *s* of late Sydney Watson Rutherford and Elsie Rutherford; *m* 1956, Kathleen Robinson; one *s* four *d*. *Educ:* Doncaster Grammar School. Practising accountant and auditor, 1955–59; Company Sec./Accountant, P. Platt & Sons, 1959–61; Retail Accountant, MacFisheries, 1961–63; Factory Management Accountant, then Company Systems Manager, T. Wall & Son (Ice Cream), 1963–70; Dir of Finance, Alfa-Laval Co., 1970–74; Group Financial Dir, Oxley Printing Group, 1974; HMSO: Chief Accountant, Publications Group, 1975–76; Dir, Management Accounting Project, 1976–77; Dir of Finance and Planning Div., 1977–83; Principal Estabt and Finance Officer, 1983–84; Comr for Admin and Finance, Forestry Commn, 1984–90. *Recreations:* reading, gardening, home computing. *Address:* 83 Caiyside, Swanston, Edinburgh EH10 7HR. *T:* 031–445 1171. *Club:* Commonwealth Trust.

RUTHERFORD, (Gordon) Malcolm; Assistant Editor, Financial Times, since 1977; *b* 21 Aug. 1939; *s* of late Gordon Brown Rutherford and Bertha Brown Rutherford; *m* 1st, 1965, Susan Tyler (marr. diss. 1969); one *d*; 2nd, 1970, Elizabeth Maitland Pelen; three *d*. *Educ:* Newcastle Royal Grammar Sch.; Balliol Coll., Oxford. Arts Editor 1962, Foreign Editor 1964, The Spectator; founded the Newsletter, Latin America, 1965; Financial Times: Diplomatic Correspondent, 1967–69; Chief German Correspondent, 1969–74; Defence Specialist, 1974–77; Chief political commentator, 1977–88; Chief theatre critic, 1990. Founding Mem., Media Law Group, 1983. *Publication:* Can We Save the Common Market?, 1981, 2nd edn 1983. *Recreations:* travel, tennis, bridge. *Address:* 89 Bedford Gardens, W8. *T:* 071–229 2063. *Club:* Travellers'.

RUTHERFORD, Herman Graham, CBE 1966; QPM 1957; DL; Chief Constable of Surrey, 1956–68; retired, 1968; *b* 3 April 1908; *m* 1940, Dorothy Weaver (*d* 1987); three *s* one *d*. *Educ:* Grammar School, Consett, County Durham. Metropolitan Police, 1929–45; Chief Constable: of Oxfordshire, 1945–54; of Lincolnshire, 1954–56. Barrister, Gray's Inn, 1941. Served Army, Allied Military Government, 1943–45, Lt-Colonel. DL Surrey, 1968. *Recreation:* sailing. *Address:* Hankley Farm, Elstead, Surrey. *T:* Elstead (0252) 702200.

RUTHERFORD, Malcolm; *see* Rutherford, G. M.

RUTHERFORD, Thomas, CBE 1982; Chairman, North Eastern Electricity Board, 1977–89, retired; *b* 4 June 1924; *s* of Thomas and Catherine Rutherford; *m* 1950, Joyce Foreman; one *s* one *d*. *Educ:* Tynemouth High Sch.; King's Coll., Durham Univ. BSc(Hons); CEng, FIEE. Engrg Trainee, subseq. Research Engr, A Reyrolle & Co. Ltd, Hebburn-on-Tyne, 1943–49; North Eastern Electricity Bd: various engrg and commercial appts, 1949–61; Personal Asst to Chm., 1961–63; Area Commercial Engr, then Area Engr, Tees Area, 1964–69; Dep. Commercial Man., 1969–70; Commercial Man., 1970–72; Chief Engr, 1972–73; Dep. Chm., 1973–75; Chm., SE Electricity Board, 1975–77. *Address:* 76 Beach Road, Tynemouth, Northumberland NE30 2QW. *T:* 091–257 1775.

RUTHNASWAMY, Elizabeth Kuanghu, (Mrs Vincent Ruthnaswamy); *see* Han Suyin.

RUTHVEN; *see* Hore-Ruthven, family name of Earl of Gowrie.

RUTHVEN OF CANBERRA, Viscount; Patrick Leo Brer Hore-Ruthven; Fund Manager, Brewin Dolphin & Co. Ltd; *b* 4 Feb. 1964; *s* and *heir* of 2nd Earl of Gowrie, *qv*; *m* 1990, Julie Goldsmith; one *s*. Lead Singer of the Pleasure Splinters. *Heir:* *s* Hon. Heathcote Patrick Cornelius Hore-Ruthven, *b* 28 May 1990. *Address:* Basement Flat, 3 St Michael's Road, SW9.

RUTLAND, 10th Duke of, *cr* 1703; **Charles John Robert Manners,** CBE 1962; Marquess of Granby, 1703; Earl of Rutland, 1525; Baron Manners of Haddon, 1679; Baron Roos of Belvoir, 1896; Captain Grenadier Guards; *b* 28 May 1919; *e s* of 9th Duke and Kathleen (*d* 1989), 3rd *d* of late F. J. Tennant; *S* father, 1940; *m* 1946, Anne Bairstow Cumming (marr. diss. 1956), *e d* of late Major Cumming Bell, Binham Lodge, Edgerton, Huddersfield; one *d*; *m* 1958, Frances Helen, *d* of Charles Sweeny and of Margaret, Duchess of Argyll; two *s* one *d* (and one *s* decd). *Educ:* Eton; Trinity Coll., Cambridge. Owns 18,000 acres; minerals in Leicestershire and Derbyshire; picture gallery at Belvoir Castle. Chairman: E Midlands Economic Planning Council, 1971–74; Leicestershire County Council, 1974–77. *Heir:* *s* Marquis of Granby, *qv*. *Address:* Belvoir Castle, Grantham; Haddon Hall, Derby.

See also Marquess of Anglesey, Earl of Wemyss.

RUTT, Rt. Rev. Cecil Richard, CBE 1973; MA; Bishop of Leicester, 1979–90; *b* 27 Aug. 1925; *s* of Cecil Rutt and Mary Hare Turner; *m* 1969, Joan Mary Ford. *Educ:* Huntingdon Grammar School; Kelham Theol. Coll.; Pembroke Coll., Cambridge. RNVR, 1943–46. Deacon, 1951; Priest, 1952. Asst Curate, St George's, Cambridge, 1951–54; Dio. of Korea, 1954; Parish Priest of Anjung, 1956–58; Warden of St Bede's House Univ. Centre, Seoul, 1959–64; Rector of St Michael's Seminary, Oryu Dong, Seoul, 1964–66; Archdeacon, West Kyonggi (Dio. Seoul), 1965–66; Asst Bishop of Taejon, 1966–68; Bishop of Taejon, 1968–74; Bishop Suffragan of St Germans, 1974–79; Hon. Canon, St Mary's Cathedral, Truro, 1974–79. Associate Gen. Sec., Korean Bible Soc., 1964–74; Episcopal Sec., Council of the Church of SE Asia, 1968–74; Commissary, , 1974–90; Pres., Roy. Asiatic Soc., Korea Br., 1974. Chm., Adv. Council on Relations of Bishops and Religious Communities, 1980–90; Mem., Anglican/Orthodox Jt Doctrinal Discussions, 1983–89. Interested in the Cornish language. Bard of the Gorsedd of Cornwall, Cornwhylen, 1976. Hon. Fellow, Northumbrian Univs' E Asia Centre, 1990. Hon. DLitt, Confucian Univ., Seoul, 1974. Tasan Cultural Award (for writings on Korea), 1964. ChStJ 1978. Order of Civil Merit, Peony Class (Korea), 1974. *Publications:* (ed) Songgonghoe Songga (Korean Anglican Hymnal), 1961; Korean Works and Days, 1964; P'ungnyu Han'guk (in Korean), 1965; (trans.) An Anthology of Korean Sijo, 1970; The Bamboo Grove, an introduction to Korean Sijo poetry, 1971; James Scarth Gale and his History of the Korean People, 1972; Virtuous Women, three masterpieces of traditional Korean fiction, 1974; A History of Handknitting, 1987; contribs on Korean classical poetry and history to Trans. Royal Asiatic Soc. (Korea Br.) and various Korean publications. *Address:* 3 Marlborough Court, Falmouth, Cornwall TR11 2QU. *T:* Falmouth (0326) 312276. *Club:* United Oxford & Cambridge University.

RUTTER, Prof. Arthur John; Emeritus Professor and Senior Research Fellow, Imperial College, University of London (Professor of Botany, 1967–79 and Head of Department of Botany and Plant Technology, 1971–79); *b* 22 Nov. 1917; *s* of late W. Arthur Rutter, CBE, FRIBA and Amy, *d* of William Dyche, BA, Cardiff; *m* 1944, Betsy Rosier Stone (*d* 1978); two *s* one *d*. *Educ:* Royal Grammar Sch., Guildford; Imperial Coll. of Science and Technology. ARCS, BSc, PhD, FIBiol. Mem., ARC team for selection of oil-seed crops and develt selective herbicides, 1940–45; Asst Lectr, Imperial Coll., 1945, Lectr 1946; Reader in Ecology, Univ. of London, 1956. Vis. Prof., Univ. of the Panjab, Pakistan, 1960–61. *Publications:* papers, mainly in Annals of Botany, Jl of Ecology, Jl of Applied Ecology on water relations of plants, forest hydrology and effects of atmospheric pollution on trees. *Recreations:* gardening, walking. *Address:* Fairseat, Bagshot Road, Knaphill, Woking, Surrey. *T:* Brookwood (04867) 3347.

RUTTER, Sir Frank (William Eden), KBE 1986 (CBE 1981); general medical practitioner; *b* 5 June 1918; *s* of Edgar and Nellie Rutter; *m* 1947, Mary Elizabeth Milton; six *d*. *Educ:* Welsh National Sch. of Medicine, Cardiff; Westminster Hosp. Med. Sch., London. MRCGP, MRCS, LRCP; DipObst. RAMC (Airborne Forces), 1942–46; OC 195 (Parachute) Field Ambulance, 1946. Chm., Health Cttee, Cardiff RDC, 1960–62; Member: Auckland Hosp. Bd, 1971–88 (Chm., 1974–88); Auckland Area Health Bd, 1988–89; Pres., Hosp. Bds Assoc., NZ, 1977–81 and 1983–85; Chairman, National Advisory Committee: Cancer Treatment Services, 1978–89; Organ Imaging Services, 1982–89; Life-Mem., NZ National Multiple Sclerosis Soc. Patron, South Island Airedale Terrier Club, 1989–. CStJ 1989. Silver Jubilee Medal, 1977. *Recreations:* breeding Airedale terriers and Irish terriers, watching development of thirteen grandchildren. *Address:* 10 Staffa Street, Parnell, Auckland, New Zealand. *T:* 09/773070; (professional) 28 Hoteo Avenue, Papatoetoe, New Zealand. *T:* 09/2786564. *Club:* Northern (Auckland).

See also J. C. Rutter.

RUTTER, John Cleverdon; His Honour Judge Rutter; a Senior Circuit Judge, since 1990 (a Circuit Judge, since 1972); *b* 18 Sept. 1919; 2nd *s* of late Edgar John Rutter; *m* 1951, Jill, *d* of Maxwell Duncan McIntosh; one *s* one *d*. *Educ:* Cardiff High Sch.; Univ. Coll., of SW of England, Exeter (Open Schol.); Keble Coll., Oxford. MA Oxon; LLB London. Royal Artillery, 1939–46; commnd 1941; served overseas. Called to the Bar, Lincoln's Inn, 1948; practised Wales and Chester Circuit, 1948–66, Stipendiary Magistrate for City of Cardiff, 1966–71. A Legal Member, Mental Health Review Tribunal for Wales Region, 1960–66. An Assistant Recorder of: Cardiff, 1962–66; Merthyr Tydfil, 1962–66; Swansea, 1965–66; Dep. Chm., Glamorgan QS, 1969–71. *Recreations:* golf, reading. *Address:* Law Courts, Cardiff. *T:* Cardiff (0222) 45931.

See also Sir F. W. E. Rutter.

RUTTER, John Milford; composer and conductor; *b* 24 Sept. 1945; *s* of Laurence Frederick and Joan Mary Rutter; *m* 1980, JoAnne Redden; two *s* and one step *d*. *Educ:* Highgate Sch.; Clare Coll., Cambridge (MA, MusB). Fellow and Director of Music, Clare Coll., Cambridge, 1975–79; Founder and Director, Cambridge Singers, 1981–. Hon. FGCM 1988; Hon. Fellow, Westminster Choir Coll., Princeton, 1980. *Publications:* compositions include choral pieces, anthems and carols, 1969–. *Address:* Old Laceys, St John's Street, Duxford, Cambridge CB2 4RA. *T:* Cambridge (0223) 832474, *Fax:* Cambridge (0223) 836723.

RUTTER, Prof. Michael Llewellyn, CBE 1985; MD; FRCP, FRCPsych; FRS 1987; Professor of Child Psychiatry, University of London Institute of Psychiatry, since 1973; *b* 15 Aug. 1933; *s* of Llewellyn Charles Rutter and Winifred Olive Rutter; *m* 1958, Marjorie Heys; one *s* two *d*. *Educ:* Moorestown Friends' Sch., USA; Wolverhampton Grammar Sch.; Bootham Sch., York; Birmingham Univ. Med. Sch. (MB ChB 1955, MD Hons 1963). MRCS 1955; LRCP 1955, MRCP 1958, FRCP 1972; FRCPsych 1971. Training in paediatrics, neurology and internal medicine, 1955–58; Maudsley Hosp., 1958–61; Nuffield Med. Travelling Fellow, Albert Einstein Coll. of Medicine, NY, 1961–62; Mem., Sci. Staff, MRC Social Psych. Res. Unit, 1962–65; Institute of Psychiatry: Sen. Lectr, then Reader, 1966–73; Prof., 1973–; Hon. Dir, MRC Child Psych. Unit, 1984–. Fellow, Center for Advanced Study in Behavioral Scis, Stanford, Calif, 1979–80. Lectures: Goulstonian, RCP, 1973; Salmon, NY Acad. of Medicine, 1979; Adolf Meyer, Amer. Psych. Assoc., 1985; Maudsley, RCPsych, 1986. Founding Mem., Acad. Europaea, 1988; Foreign Associate Member: Inst. of Medicine, Nat. Acad. of Scis, USA, 1988; US Nat. Acad. of Educn, 1990; Foreign Hon. Mem., Amer. Acad. of Arts and Scis, 1989. Hon. FBPsS 1978; Hon. Fellow, Amer. Acad. of Pediatrics, 1981. Hon. DSSc Univ. of Leiden, 1985; Hon. Dr Leuven, 1990; Hon. DSc: Birmingham, 1990; Chicago, 1991; Hon. MD Edinburgh, 1990. Numerous awards, UK and USA. *Publications:* Children of Sick Parents, 1966; (jtly) A Neuropsychiatric Study in Childhood, 1970; (ed jtly) Education, Health and Behaviour, 1970; (ed) Infantile Autism, 1971; Maternal Deprivation Reassessed, 1972, 2nd edn 1981; (ed jtly) The Child with Delayed Speech, 1972; Helping Troubled Children, 1975; (jtly) Cycles of Disadvantage, 1976; (ed jtly) Child Psychiatry, 1977, 2nd edn as Child and Adolescent Psychiatry, 1985; (ed jtly) Autism, 1978; Changing Youth in a Changing Society, 1979; (jtly) Fifteen Thousand Hours: secondary schools and their effects on children, 1979; (ed) Scientific Foundations of Developmental Psychiatry, 1981; A Measure of Our Values: goals and dilemmas in the upbringing of children, 1983; (jtly)

Lead Versus Health, 1983; (jtly) Juvenile Delinquency, 1983; (ed) Developmental Neuropsychiatry, 1983; (ed jtly) Stress, Coping and Development, 1983; (ed jtly) Depression and Young People, 1986; (jtly) Treatment of Autistic Children, 1987; (ed jtly) Language Development and Disorders, 1987; (jtly) Parenting Breakdown: the making and breaking of inter-generational links, 1988; (ed jtly) Assessment and Diagnosis in Child Psychopathology, 1988; (ed) Studies of Psychological Risk: the power of longitudinal data, 1988; (ed jtly) Straight and Devious Pathways from Childhood to Adulthood, 1990; (ed jtly) Biological Risk Factors for Psychosocial Disorders, 1991. *Recreations:* fell walking, tennis, wine tasting, theatre. *Address:* 190 Court Lane, Dulwich, SE21 7ED. *Club:* Royal Society of Medicine.

RUTTER, Air Vice-Marshal (Retd) Norman Colpoy Simpson, CB 1965; CBE 1945; idc; jssc; psa; Sen. Tech. Staff Officer, Bomber Command, 1961–65; *b* 1909; *s* of Rufus John Rutter; *m* 1936, Irene Sophia (*d* 1983), *d* of late Colonel A. M. Lloyd; one *s* one *d*. Air Cdre, 1957; Air Officer Commanding and Commandant of the Royal Air Force Technical College, Henlow, 1959–61. CEng, FIMechE; FRAeS. *Address:* 37 Meadow Road, Pinner, Mddx HA5 1EB.

RUTTER, Trevor John, CBE 1990 (OBE 1976); Assistant Director General, British Council, since 1990; *b* 26 Jan. 1934; *s* of late Alfred and Agnes Rutter; *m* 1959, Josephine Henson; one *s*. *Educ:* Monmouth Sch.; Brasenose Coll., Oxford (BA). National Service, Army, 1955–57. British Council, Indonesia, W Germany (Munich), London, 1959–66; First Secretary, Foreign Office, 1967; British Council, 1968–: Representative: Singapore, 1968–71; Thailand, 1971–75; various appointments, London, 1975–85, including: Head, Home Div., 1980; Asst Dir Gen., 1981–85; Rep. in W Germany, 1986–90. *Address:* c/o British Council, 10 Spring Gardens, SW1; West House, West Street, Wivenhoe, Essex CO7 9DE. *T:* Wivenhoe (020682) 2562.

RUTTLE, His Honour Henry Samuel; a Circuit Judge (formerly Judge of County Courts), 1959–81; *b* 10 Nov. 1906; *yr s* of late Michael Ruttle, Portlaw, Co. Waterford, Ireland; *m* 1st, 1943, Joyce Mayo Moriarty (*d* 1968), *yr d* of late J. O. M. Moriarty, Plymouth; one *s* two *d*; 2nd, 1978, Mary Kathleen Scott, *d* of late F. T. Scott, Wimbledon. *Educ:* Wesley College, Dublin and Trinity College, Dublin. BA (Moderatorship in Legal and Political Science) and LLB, 1929; LLD 1933; MA 1950. Called to the Bar, Gray's Inn, 1933; practised in Common Law: London and Western Circuit. Served War of 1939–45: RAFVR, 1940–45; Squadron Leader. Deputy Judge Advocate Judge Advocate General's Office. Resumed practice at Bar, 1945. Member of Church Assembly, 1948–55; Mem., General Council of the Bar, 1957–59; Deputy Chairman Agricultural Land Tribunal (SW Area), 1958–59. JP, Co. Surrey, 1961. Mem., County Court Rules Cttee, 1969–81 (Chm., 1978–81). Jt Editor, The County Court Practice, 1973–81. *Recreations:* Rugby football (Leinster Inter-Provincial, 1927; Captain London Irish RFC, 1935–36; Middlesex County); fly-fishing. *Address:* 1 Rutland Lodge, Clifton Road, Wimbledon Common, SW19 4QZ.

RYAN, Prof. Alan James, FBA 1986; Professor of Politics, Princeton University, since 1988; Fellow of New College, University of Oxford, since 1969; *b* 9 May 1940; *s* of James William Ryan and Ivy Ryan; *m* 1971, Kathleen Alyson Lane; one *d*. *Educ:* Christ's Hospital; Balliol Coll., Oxford. Lectr in Politics, Univ. of Keele, 1963–66, Univ. of Essex, 1966–69; Lectr in Politics, 1969–78, Reader, 1978–87, Univ. of Oxford. Visiting Professor in Politics: City University of New York, 1967–68; Univs of Texas, 1972, California, 1977, the Witwatersrand, 1978; Vis. Fellow, ANU, 1974, 1979; de Carle Lectr, Univ. of Otago, 1983. Official Mem., CNAA, 1975–80. Delegate, Oxford Univ. Press, 1983–87. *Publications:* The Philosophy of John Stuart Mill, 1970, 2nd edn 1987; The Philosophy of the Social Sciences, 1970; J. S. Mill, 1975; Property and Political Theory, 1984; (ed jtly) The Blackwell Encyclopaedia of Political Thought, 1987; Property, 1987; Bertrand Russell: a political life, 1988. *Recreations:* dinghy sailing, long train journeys. *Address:* 41 Robert Road, Princeton, New Jersey 08540, USA. *T:* (609) 924–3515. *Club:* United Oxford & Cambridge University.

RYAN, (Christopher) Nigel (John), CBE 1977; freelance writer; Chairman, TV-am News, since 1989 (Director, since 1985); *b* 12 Dec. 1929; *s* of late Brig. C. E. Ryan, MC, RA. *Educ:* Ampleforth Coll.; Queen's Coll., Oxford (MA). Joined Reuters, London, 1954; Foreign Corresp., 1957–60; joined Independent Television News, 1961, Editor, 1968–71, Editor and Chief Executive, 1971–77; Vice-Pres., NBC News, America, 1977–80; Dir of Progs, Thames Television, 1980–82. Silver Medal, Royal Television Soc., 1970; Desmond Davis Award, 1972. *Publications:* A Hitch or Two in Afghanistan, 1983; trans. novels from French by Georges Simenon and others. *Address:* 28 St Petersburgh Place, W2 4LD. *T:* 071–221 4170. *Club:* Beefsteak.

RYAN, Maj.-Gen. Denis Edgar, CB 1987; Director of Army Education, 1984–87; *b* 18 June 1928; *s* of Reginald Arthur Ryan and Amelia (*née* Smith); *m* 1955, Jean Mary Bentley; one *s* one *d*. *Educ:* Sir William Borlase School, Marlow; King's College, London (LLB). Commissioned RAEC, 1950; served BAOR, 1950–54; Instr, RMA Sandhurst, 1954–56; Adjt, Army Sch. of Educn, 1957–59; Staff Coll., 1960; served in Cyprus, Kenya and UK, 1961–67; CAES, HQ 4 Div., BAOR, 1968–70; Cabinet Office, 1970–72; TDA, Staff Coll., 1972–75; Col GS MoD, 1976–78; Chief Education Officer: HQ SE Dist, 1978–79; HQ BAOR, 1979–82; Comd, Education, UK, 1982–84. Col Comdt, RAEC, 1990–. *Recreations:* cricket, tennis, rugby, music, theatre. *Address:* c/o Royal Bank of Scotland, Kirkland House, Whitehall, SW1A 2EB. *Club:* Army and Navy.

RYAN, Sir Derek (Gerald), 4th Bt *cr* 1919, of Hintlesham, Suffolk; architect; *b* 25 March 1954; *s* of Sir Derek Gerald Ryan, 3rd Bt and of Penelope Anne Hawkings; *S* father, 1990; *m* (marr. diss.). *Educ:* Univ. of California at Berkeley (BAED 1977). Washington State Architect License #4296, 1984; NCARB Certificate #32,269, 1984. *Recreations:* skiing, guitar. *Heir:* *cousin* Desmond Maurice Ryan [*b* 16 Sept. 1918; *m* 1942, Margaret Catherine, *d* of A. H. Brereton; three *s*]. *Address:* 111 South Jackson Street, Seattle, WA 98104, USA. *T:* 206 223 5204.

RYAN, Gerard Charles, QC 1981; a Recorder of the Crown Court, since 1986; *b* 16 Dec. 1931; *er s* of Frederick Charles Ryan, Hove, and Louie Violet Ryan (*née* Ball); *m* 1960, Sheila Morag Clark Cameron, *qv*; two *s*. *Educ:* Clayesmore Sch.; Brighton Coll.; Pembroke Coll., Cambridge (Exhibnr; MA). Served RA, 1955–57 (Lieut). Called to the Bar, Middle Temple, 1955, Bencher, 1988; Harmsworth Scholar, 1956. Chm., Tribunal of Inquiry into Loscoe (Derbyshire) gas explosion, 1986–87. Chm., Soc. of Sussex Downsmen, 1977–80. *Publication:* (with A. O. B. Harris) Outline of the Law of Common Land, 1967. *Recreations:* gardening, natural history, walking. *Address:* 13 Westmoreland Place, SW1V 4AA; 2 Harcourt Buildings, Temple, EC4Y 9DB. *T:* 071–353 8415. *Club:* United Oxford & Cambridge University.

RYAN, John; Management consultant and lecturer; *b* 30 April 1940; *m* 1964, Eunice Ann Edmonds; two *s*. *Educ:* Lanark Grammar School; Glasgow University. Member, National Association of Labour Student Organisations, 1958–62; formerly Youth Organiser, Lanark City Labour Party; Member, Executive Committee, North Paddington Labour Party, 1964–66. Contested (Lab) Buckinghamshire South, 1964; MP (Lab) Uxbridge, 1966–70. Member, Fabian Society, 1961; Dir, Tribune Publications Ltd, 1969–. Mem., Inst. of Marketing; Associate Member: Market Res. Soc.; BIM. *Recreations:* golf, walking.

RYAN, Most Rev. Laurence; *see* Kildare and Leighlin, Bishop of (RC).

RYAN, Nigel; *see* Ryan, C. N. J.

RYAN, Sheila Morag Clark, (Mrs G. C. Ryan); *see* Cameron, S. M. C.

RYAN, Dr Thomas Anthony, (Tony); Chairman and Chief Executive, GPA Group, since 1975; *b* 2 Feb. 1936; *m*; three *s*. *Educ:* Christian Brothers Sch., Thurles, Co. Tipperary; North Western Univ., Chicago. Aer Lingus, 1956–75; Non-Executive Director: Bank of Ireland, 1988–; Trafalgar House, 1989–. Consul for Republic of Mexico to Ireland. Mem., Bd of Govs, Nat. Gall. of Ireland. Mem., Europe Round Table. Hon. Mem., Univ. of Limerick, 1986. Hon. LLD: Dublin, 1987; NUI, 1987. *Recreations:* farming, the arts. *Address:* Kilboy House, Dolla, Co. Tipperary, Ireland. *T:* 353.67.25350.

RYBCZYNSKI, Tadeusz Mieczyslaw, FCIB; Director, Sund and Wrigley & Co. Ltd; *b* 21 May 1923; *s* of Karol Rybczynski and Helena (*née* Sawicka); *m* 1951, Helena Perucka; one *d*. *Educ:* primary and secondary schs, Lwow, Poland; LSE, Univ. of London (BCom, MScEcon). FCIB (FIB 1966). Lloyds Bank, 1949–53; Lazard Brothers & Co. Ltd, 1954–88; Dir, Lazard Securities Ltd, 1969–86; Econ. Advr, Lazard Brothers & Co. Ltd, 1973–88; Dir, Euro-Canadian Internat. Investment Management Ltd, 1987–90. Vis. Professor: Univ. of Surrey, 1968–74; City Univ., 1974–. Chm., Soc. of Business Economists, 1962–75 (Fellow, 1988). Member: Monopolies and Mergers Commn, 1978–81; Council of Management and Exec. Cttee, NIESR, 1968– (also Governor); Exec. Cttee and Council, Inst. of Fiscal Studies, 1988–. Member: Council, REconS, 1969– (Treas., 1974; Vice-Pres., 1976–); Governing Body, Trade Policy Res. Centre, 1968–; Cttee, Foreign Affairs Club, 1968–85; Adv. Bd in Banking and Finance, Univ. of Aston Management Centre, 1973–82; Sci. Cttee, Centre for Monetary and Banking Studies, Univ. of Geneva, 1973–; Court, Brunel Univ., 1976–79; Council, British Assoc., 1990–. Hon. DSc City Univ., 1990. Harms Award, Inst. for Economic Research, Univ. of Kiel, 1983; Abramson Award, Nat. Assoc. of Business Economists, USA, 1980. *Publications:* (contrib.) Comparative Banking, ed H. W. Auburn, 1960 (3rd edn 1969); (contrib.) Long Range Planning, Paris and New York, 1967; (ed jtly and contrib.) The Economist in Business, 1967; (contrib.) Readings in International Economics, ed R. E. Caves and H. Johnson, 1968; (ed and contrib.) Value Added Tax-the UK position and the European experience, 1969; (contrib.) Money in Britain 1959–69, ed R. Croome and H. Johnson, 1970; (contrib.) Problems of Investment, ed Sir Robert Shone, 1971; (contrib.) Users of Economics, ed G. D. N. Worswick, 1972; (ed) A New Era in Competition, 1973; (ed and contrib.) The Economics of the Oil Crisis, 1976; (contrib.) Financial Management Handbook, 1977; (contrib.) The International Monetary System 1971–80, 1983; (contrib.) International Lending in a Fragile World Economy, 1983; articles in serious jls, and in academic and bank revs. *Recreations:* opera, ballet, history, international affairs, travel. *Address:* 2 Windyridge Close, Parkside Avenue, SW19 5HB. *T:* 081–946 7363. *Club:* Reform.

RYBURN, Rev. Hubert James, CMG 1959; MA (Oxon and NZ), BD (Union); *b* 19 April 1897; *s* of Very Rev. Robert Middelton Ryburn and Anna Jane Steadman; *m* 1st, 1931, Jocelyn Maud Dunlop (*d* 1980), *d* of Prof. F. W. Dunlop; two *s* two *d*; 2nd, 1981, Isabella Paterson May. *Educ:* Otago University; Oxford University; Union Theological Seminary, NY. Rhodes Scholar, 1921–24. Ordained a minister of the Presbyterian Church of New Zealand, 1926; Minister: Bay of Islands, 1926–29; St Andrews', Dunedin, 1929–41; Master of Knox College, Dunedin, 1941–63. Member: Council of Otago University, 1946–71, Pro-Chancellor, 1954–55, Chancellor, 1955–70; Senate of Univ. of NZ, 1948–61. Hon. LLD (Otago). *Publication:* Te Hemara, James Hamlin, 1980. *Recreation:* fishing. *Address:* 15 Cornwall Street, Dunedin, New Zealand. *T:* 42–032.

RYCROFT, Sir Richard Newton, 7th Bt, *cr* 1784; *b* 23 Jan. 1918; *yr s* of Sir Nelson Edward Oliver Rycroft, 6th Bt, and Ethel Sylvia (*d* 1952), *d* of late Robert Nurton, Odcombe, Yeovil; *S* father 1958; *m* 1947, Ann, *d* of late Hugh Bellingham-Smith, Alfriston, Sussex, and Mrs Harvey Robarts; two *d*. *Educ:* Winchester; Christ Church, Oxford (BA). Served War of 1939–45: Bedfordshire and Hertfordshire Regt, on special service work in Balkans (Major, despatches); Knight's Cross of Royal Order of Phœnix with Swords (Greece). *Heir:* *cousin* Richard John Rycroft, *b* 15 June 1946. *Address:* Winalls Wood House, Stuckton, Fordingbridge, Hampshire. *T:* Fordingbridge (0425) 2263.
See also Viscount FitzHarris.

RYDBECK, Olof; Comdr 1st Class, Order of the Star of the North, Sweden, 1973; Commissioner-General, United Nations Relief and Works Agency, 1979–85; *b* Djursholm, 15 April 1913; *s* of Oscar Rydbeck and Signe Olson; *m* 1940, Monica Schnell; one *s* one *d*. *Educ:* Univ. of Uppsala, Sweden (BA 1934, LLB 1939). Attaché, Min. for Foreign Affairs, 1939; Berlin, 1940; Ankara, 1941; Stockholm, 1942; Second Sec., 1943; Washington, 1945–50 (First Sec., 1946); Bonn, 1950; Head of Press Sect., Min. for For. Affairs, 1952; Dir Gen., Swedish Broadcasting Corp., 1955–70; Perm. Rep. to UN, 1970–76; Rep. of Sweden to Security Council, 1975–76; Special Rep. of Sec. Gen. on Western Sahara, 1976; Ambassador of Sweden to the UK, 1977–79. Chairman: Adv. Cttee on Outer Space Communications, UNESCO, 1966–70; Working Gp on Direct Broadcast Satellites, UN Cttee on Peaceful Uses of Outer Space, 1969–75; Cttee of Trustees, UN Trust Fund for S Africa, 1970–75; Prep. Cttee, World Food Conf., 1974; Second Cttee, 30th Gen. Assembly, 1975. Chairman: Assoc. of Royal Swedish Nat. Defence Coll., 1957–70; Internat. Broadcasting Inst., Rome, 1967–70; Hon. Pres., EBU, 1964– (Pres., 1961–64). Member: Central Cttee, Swedish Red Cross; Nat. Swedish Preparedness Commn for Psychol. Defence, 1954–70 (Vice Chm., 1962–70); Royal Swed. Acad. of Music, 1962–. Member Boards: Swed. Inst., 1953–55; Amer.-Swed. News Exchange, 1953–55; Swed. Tourist Traffic Assoc., 1953–55; Stockholm Philharmonic Soc., 1955–62; Swed. Central News Agency, 1967–70; Swed. Inst. of Internat. Affairs, 1967–. King's Medal, 12th size, Sweden, 1980; Medal of Serahims, Sweden, 1987; Commander 1st Class: Order of the White Rose (Finland); Order of the Falcon (Iceland); Comdr, Order of the Dannebrog (Denmark); Verdienstkreutz (FRG). *Recreations:* music, books. *Address:* 3 avenue Charles de Gaulle, 69260 Charbonnières-les-Bains, France.

RYDEN, Kenneth, MC and Bar 1945; DL; *b* 15 Feb. 1917; *s* of Walter and Elizabeth Ryden; *m* 1950, Catherine Kershaw (*née* Wilkinson); two *s*. *Educ:* Queen Elizabeth's Grammar School, Blackburn. FRICS. Served War of 1939–45 (MC and Bar, despatches 1945): RE, attached Royal Bombay Sappers and Miners, India, Assam and Burma, 1940–46, retd (Captain). Articled pupil and prof. trng, 1936–39; Min. of Works: Estate Surveyor, 1946–47; attached UK High Commns, India and Pakistan, 1947–50; Sen. Estate Surveyor, Scotland, 1950–59. Founder and Sen. Partner, Kenneth Ryden & Partners (Chartered Surveyors) Edinburgh, Glasgow and London, 1959–74, retd, Consultant 1974–80. Chm., Scottish Br. Chartered Auctioneers and Estate Agents' Institute, 1960–61; Member: Edinburgh Valuation Appeal Cttee, 1965–75, 1981– (Chm., 1987–90); Scottish Solicitors' Discipline Tribunal, 1985–. Mem. Bd, Housing Corp., 1972–76. Master, Co. of Merchants of City of Edinburgh, 1976–78; Liveryman, Chartered Surveyors' Co. DL

City of Edinburgh, 1978. FRCPE 1985. *Recreations:* fishing, golf, Scottish art. *Address:* 19 Belgrave Crescent, Edinburgh EH4 3AJ. *T:* 031–332 5893. *Club:* New (Edinburgh).

RYDER, family name of **Earl of Harrowby** and of **Baron Ryder of Eaton Hastings.**

RYDER OF EATON HASTINGS, Baron *cr* 1975 (Life Peer), of Eaton Hastings, Oxfordshire; **Sydney Thomas Franklin, (Don), Ryder,** Kt 1972; Industrial Adviser to the Government, since 1974; Chairman, National Enterprise Board, 1975–77; *b* 16 Sept. 1916; *s* of John Ryder; *m* 1950; one *s* one *d. Educ:* Ealing. Editor, Stock Exchange Gazette, 1950–60; Jt Man. Dir, 1960–61, Sole Man. Dir, 1961–63, Kelly Iliffe Holdings, and Associated Iliffe Press Ltd; Dir, Internat. Publishing Corp., 1963–70; Man. Dir, Reed Paper Gp, 1963–68; Chm. and Chief Executive, Reed International Ltd, 1968–75; Dir, MEPC Ltd, 1972–75. Member: British Gas Corp., 1973–78; Reserve Pension Bd, 1973–; Council and Bd of Fellows, BIM, 1970–; Court and Council, Cranfield Inst. of Technology, 1970–74; Council, UK S Africa Trade Assoc., 1974–; Nat. Materials Handling Centre (Pres., 1970–77); Council, Industrial Soc., 1971–; NEDC, 1976–77. Vice-Pres., RoSPA, 1973–. *Recreations:* sailing, chess. *Address:* House of Lords, SW1.

RYDER OF WARSAW, Baroness *cr* 1979 (Life Peer), of Warsaw in Poland and of Cavendish in the County of Suffolk; **(Sue Ryder);** CMG 1976; OBE 1957; Founder and Social Worker, Sue Ryder Foundation for the Sick and Disabled of all Age Groups; *b* 3 July 1923; *d* of late Charles and Elizabeth Ryder; *m* 1959, Geoffrey Leonard Cheshire (*see* Baron Cheshire); one *s* one *d. Educ:* Benenden Sch., Kent. Served War of 1939–45 with FANY and with Special Ops Executive. Co-Founder, Mission for the Relief of Suffering; Trustee, Cheshire Foundn. Hon. LLD: Liverpool, 1973; Exeter, 1980; London, 1981; Leeds, 1984; Cambridge, 1989; Hon. DLitt Reading, 1982; Hon. DCL Kent, 1986. Holds Officer's Cross of Order of Polonia Restituta, Poland, 1965; Medal of Yugoslav Flag with Gold Wreath and Diploma, 1971; Golden Order of Merit, Polish People's Republic, 1976; Order of Smile (Poland), 1980. *Publications:* Remembrance (annual leaflet of the Sue Ryder Foundation); And the Morrow is Theirs (autobiog.), 1975; Child of My Love (autobiog.), 1986. *Address:* Sue Ryder Home, Cavendish, Sudbury, Suffolk CO10 8AY.

RYDER, Edward Alexander; HM Chief Inspector of Nuclear Installations, Health and Safety Executive, since 1985; *b* 9 Nov. 1931; *s* of Alexander Harry and Gwendoline Gladys Ryder; *m* 1956, Janet; one *s* one *d. Educ:* Cheltenham Grammar School; Bristol University (BSc). CPhys; FInstP. Flying Officer, RAF, 1953–55; Engineer, GEC Applied Electronics Labs, 1955–57; Control Engineer, Hawker Siddeley Nuclear Power Co., 1957–61; Sen. Engineer, CEGB, 1961–71; Principal Inspector, then Superintending Inspector, HM Nuclear Installations Inspectorate, 1971–80; Head of Hazardous Installations Policy Branch, 1980–85, Head of Nuclear Installations Policy Branch, 1985, HSE. Sec., Adv. Cttee on Major Hazards, 1980–85. Chairman: HSC Working Gp on Ionising Radiations, 1987–; IAEA Nuclear Safety Standards Adv. Gp, 1988–. *Recreation:* golf—or is it nature study. *Address:* Health and Safety Executive, Baynards House, 1 Chepstow Place, Westbourne Grove, W2 4TF.

RYDER, Eric Charles, MA, LLB; Barrister; Professor of English Law in the University of London (University College) 1960–82, now Professor Emeritus; *b* 28 July 1915; *er s* of late Charles Henry Ryder, solicitor, Hanley, Staffs, and of Ellen Miller; *m* 1941, Nancy Winifred Roberts. *Educ:* Hanley High School; Gonville and Caius College, Cambridge (scholar). BA (Law Tripos Parts I and II, 1st Cl.), 1936; LLB (1st Cl.) 1937; MA 1940; Tapp Law Scholar, Gonville and Caius College, 1937; called to Bar, Gray's Inn, 1937; practice at Chancery Bar. Ministry of Food, 1941–44; Lecturer in Law, King's College, Newcastle upon Tyne, 1944; Dean of Faculty of Law, Univ. of Durham, 1947–60; Professor of Law, Univ. of Durham (King's College), 1953–60. Practised as conveyancing counsel, Newcastle upon Tyne, 1944–53. *Publications:* Hawkins and Ryder on the Construction of Wills, 1965; contrib. to legal periodicals. *Address:* 9 Arlington Court, Kenton Avenue, Gosforth, Newcastle upon Tyne NE3 4JR. *T:* 091–285 1172.

RYDER, Dr Peter; Deputy Chief Executive and Director of Operations, Meteorological Office, since 1990; *b* 10 March 1942; *s* of Percival Henry Sussex Ryder and Bridget (*née* McCormack); *m* 1965, Jacqueline Doris Sylvia Rigby; two *s* one *d. Educ:* Yorebridge Grammar Sch., Askrigg; Univ. of Leeds (BSc 1963; PhD 1966). Research Asst, Physics Dept, Univ. of Leeds, 1966–67; Meteorological Office, 1967–: Asst Dir, Cloud Physics Res, 1976–82; Asst Dir, Systems Develt, 1982–84; Dep. Dir, Observational Services, 1984–88; Dep. Dir, Forecasting Services, 1988–89; Dir of Services, 1989–90. Royal Meteorological Society: Mem. Council, 1980–83; Mem., Qly Jl Editing Cttee, 1981–84. William Gaskell Meml Medal, 1981; L. G. Groves Meml Prize for Meteorology, 1982. *Publications:* papers in learned jls on experimental atmospheric physics and meteorology. *Recreations:* gardening, walking, fishing, photography, philately. *Address:* c/o Meteorological Office, London Road, Bracknell, Berks RG12 2SZ.

RYDER, Peter Hugh Dudley, MBE 1944; Managing Director, Thomas Tilling Ltd, 1957–68; *b* 28 April 1913; *s* of Hon. Archibald Dudley Ryder and Eleanor Frederica Fisher-Rowe; *m* 1940, Sarah Susannah Bowes-Lyon; two *s* one *d. Educ:* Oundle School. Provincial Newspapers Ltd, Hull and Leeds, 1930–33; Illustrated Newspapers Ltd, 1933–39; seconded from TA to Political Intell. Dept of FO, 1939–45 (Hon. Lt-Col 1944); Jt Man. Dir, Contact Publications Ltd, 1945; Man. Dir, Daimler Hire Ltd, 1950; Commercial Dir, James A. Jobling & Co. Ltd, Sunderland, 1953; Chairman: James A. Jobling & Co. Ltd, 1957–62 and 1967–68; Heinemann Gp of Publishers Ltd, 1961–68; Director: District Bank Ltd, 1961–69; Cornhill Insce Co. Ltd, 1965–68. Mem. Council, BIM, 1966–69 (Mem. Bd of Fellows, 1968–69); Mem. Bd of Govs, Ashridge Management Coll., 1968. *Address:* Ardmore, 21 Riverbank Road, Ramsey, Isle of Man.

RYDER, Rt. Hon. Richard Andrew, OBE 1981; PC 1990; MP (C) Mid Norfolk, since 1983; Parliamentary Secretary to HM Treasury and Government Chief Whip, since 1990; *b* 4 Feb. 1949; *s* of Richard Stephen Ryder, JP, DL, and Margaret MacKenzie; *m* 1981, Caroline, MBE, *o d* of Sir David Stephens; one *d* (one *s* decd). *Educ:* Radley; Magdalene Coll., Cambridge. BA Hons History, 1971. Chm., Univ. Cons. Assoc. Political Secretary: to Leader of the Opposition, 1975–79; to Prime Minister, 1979–81. Partner, M. Ryder and Sons; journalist. Contested (C) Gateshead E, Feb. and Oct., 1974. Parliamentary Private Secretary: to Financial Sec. to the Treasury, 1984; to Sec. of State for Foreign and Commonwealth Affairs, 1984–86; an Asst Govt Whip, 1986–88; Parly Under-Sec. of State, MAFF, 1988–89; Econ. Sec. to HM Treasury, 1989–90; Paymaster General, 1990. Chm., Cons. Foreign and Commonwealth Council, 1984–89. *Address:* House of Commons, SW1A 0AA.

RYDER, Richard Hood Jack Dudley; campaigner; *b* 3 July 1940; *s* of late Major D. C. D. Ryder, JP and Vera Mary (*née* Cook); *m* 1974, Audrey Jane Smith; one *s* one *d. Educ:* Sherborne Sch.; Cambridge Univ. (MA); Edinburgh Univ. (DCP); Columbia Univ., NY (Fellow). AFBPsS; FZS. Sen. Clinical Psychologist, Warneford Hosp., Oxford, 1967–84; Principal Clin. Psychologist, St James Hosp., Portsmouth, 1983–84. Chm., Oxford Div. of Clin. Psych., 1981–83; Member: Oxford Regional Adolescent Service, 1971–84; DHSS Health Adv. Service, 1977–78. Royal Society for Prevention of Cruelty to Animals: Council Mem., 1972–; Chm., 1977–79; Chm. Political Cttee, 1979–80; Chm., Animal Experimentation Adv. Cttee, 1983–85; Chm., Public Relns and Campaign Cttee, 1990–; Vice Chm., 1990–; Mem., Gen. Election Coordinating Cttee on Animal Protection, 1978; Prog. Organiser, IFAW, 1984–88; UK Delegate, Eurogroup, 1980. Chm., Liberal Animal Welfare Gp, 1981–88; Member: Liberal Party Council, 1983–87; Liberal Party Policy Panels on defence, health, home affairs, Eur. affairs, foreign affairs, environment, 1981–88; contested (L): Buckingham, 1983; Teignbridge, 1987. Pres., Lib. Democrats Animal Protection Gp, 1989–. Chairman: Teignbridge NSPCC, 1984–87; Teignbridge Home Start, 1987–89. Broadcaster and writer on psychological, political and animal protection subjects. *Publications:* Speciesism, 1970; Victims of Science, 1975, 2nd edn 1984; (ed) Animal Rights—a Symposium, 1979; Animal Revolution: changing attitudes to speciesism, 1989. *Recreations:* history, opera, croquet. *Clubs:* National Liberal, Royal Over-Seas League.

RYDILL, Prof. Louis Joseph, OBE 1962; FEng 1982; RCNC; Consultant in Naval Ship Design, since 1986; Professor of Naval Architecture, University College London, 1981–85, now Emeritus Professor; *b* 16 Aug. 1922; *s* of Louis and Queenie Rydill; *m* 1949, Eva (*née* Newman); two *d. Educ:* HM Dockyard Sch., Devonport; RNEC Keyham; RNC Greenwich; Royal Corps of Naval Constructors. FRINA (Gold Medallist). Asst Constructor, 1946–52; Constructor, 1952–62, incl. Asst Prof. of Naval Architecture, RNC Greenwich, 1953–57; Chief Constructor, 1962–72, incl. Prof. of Naval Architecture, RNC Greenwich and UCL, 1967–72; Asst Dir Submarines, Constructive, 1972–74; Dep. Dir Submarines (Polaris), 1974–76; Dir of Ship Design and Engrg (formerly Warship Design), MoD, 1976–81. Hon. Res. Fellow, UCL, 1974; Vis. Prof., US Naval Acad., Annapolis, Md, 1985–86. Silver Jubilee Medal, 1977. *Recreations:* literature, theatre, jazz and other music. *Address:* The Lodge, Entry Hill Drive, Bath, Avon. *T:* Bath (0225) 427888.

RYKWERT, Prof. Joseph, MA (Cantab), DrRCA; Paul Philippe Cret Professor of Architecture, University of Pennsylvania, since 1988; *b* 5 April 1926; *s* of Szymon Rykwert and Elizabeth Melup; *m* 1st, 1960 (marr. diss. 1967); 2nd, 1972, Anne-Marie Sandersley; one *s* one *d. Educ:* Charterhouse; Bartlett Sch. of Architecture; Architectural Assoc. Lectr, Hochschule für Gestaltung, Ulm, 1958; Librarian and Tutor, Royal Coll. of Art, 1961–67; Prof. of Art, Univ. of Essex, 1967–80; Lectr on Arch., 1980–85, Reader, 1985–88, Univ. of Cambridge. Fellow, Inst. for Arch. and Urban Studies, NY, 1969–71; Sen. Fellow, Council of Humanities, Princeton Univ., 1971; Visiting Professor: Institut d'Urbanisme, Univ. of Paris, 1974–76; Princeton Univ., 1977; Andrew Mellon Vis. Prof., Cooper Union, NY, 1977; Slade Prof. of Fine Art, Cambridge Univ., 1979–80; Vis. Fellow, Darwin Coll., Cambridge, 1979–80; Sen. Fellow, Center for the Advanced Studies in the Visual Arts. Nat. Gall. of Art, Washington; Visiting Professor: Univ. of Louvain, 1981–84; Univ. of Pennsylvania, 1982–88; George Lurcy Vis. Prof., Columbia, 1986. Mem., Comité Internat. des Critiques d'Architecture. Mem. Commn, Venice Biennale, 1974–78. Consultant, Min. of Urban Develt and Ecology, Republic of Mexico, 1986–88. Alfred Jurzykowski Foundn Award, 1990. Chevalier des Arts et des Lettres, 1984. Co-editor: Lotus, 1974–; RES (Anthropology and Aesthetics), 1981–. *Publications:* The Golden House, 1947; (ed) The Ten Books of Architecture, by L. B. Alberti (annotated edn of Leoni trans. of 1756), 1955, new translation from Latin, as On the Art of Building in Ten Books, 1988; The Idea of a Town, 1963, 3rd edn 1988; Church Building, 1966; On Adam's House in Paradise, 1972, 2nd edn 1982; (ed) Parole nel Vuoto, by A. Loos, 1972; The First Moderns, 1980; The Necessity of Artifice, 1981; (with Anne Rykwert) The Brothers Adam, 1985; contrib. Arch. Rev., Burlington Mag., Lotus. *Recreations:* rare. *Address:* University of Pennsylvania, Meyerson Hall, Philadelphia, Pa 19104–6311, USA. *Club:* Savile.

RYLAND, Judge John, CIE 1946; RIN (retired); Judge for British Columbia, 1969; retired; *b* 31 March 1900; *s* of late W. J. Ryland, Surbiton; *m* 1938, Lucy Lenore, *d* of J. W. Bryden, Victoria, BC; two *s. Educ:* King's College School; HMS Conway. *Address:* Royston, BC V0R 2V0, Canada.

RYLAND, Timothy Richard Godfrey Fetherstonhaugh; His Honour Judge Ryland; a Circuit Judge, since 1988; *b* 13 June 1938; *s* of late Richard Desmond Fetherstonhaugh Ryland and Frances Katharine Vernon Ryland; *m* 1991, Jean Margaret Muirhead. *Educ:* St Andrew's Coll.; TCD. BA (Moderatorship), LLB. Called to Bar, Gray's Inn, 1961. Dep. Circuit Judge, 1978; a Recorder, 1983–88. *Recreations:* opera, wine. *Club:* Kildare Street and University (Dublin).

RYLANDS, George Humphrey Wolferstan, CH 1987; CBE 1961; MA; Fellow of King's College, Cambridge; Sometime Dean, Bursar, College Lecturer, and Director of Studies; University Lecturer in English Literature (retd); *b* 23 October 1902; *s* of Thomas Kirkland Rylands. *Educ:* Eton (King's Scholar); King's Coll., Cambridge (Scholar). Chm. of Directors and Trustees of the Arts Theatre, Cambridge, 1946–82; Governor of the Old Vic, 1945–78; Chm. of Apollo Soc., 1946–72. Member: Cheltenham Coll. Council, 1946–76; Council of RADA. Directed Hamlet with Sir John Gielgud, 1945; LP Recordings of the Shakespeare canon and the English Poets, for the British Council. Hon. LittD Cambridge, 1976; Hon. degree, Durham, 1988. *Publications:* Words and Poetry, 1928; Shakespeare the Poet (in a Companion to Shakespeare Studies), 1934; Poems, 1931; The Ages of Man, a Shakespeare Anthology, 1939; Shakespeare's Poetic Energy (British Academy Lecture, 1951); Quoth the Raven "Nevermore": an anthology, 1984; Croaked the Raven: one NO more, 1988; College Verse, 1989. *Address:* King's College, Cambridge CB2 1ST. *T:* Cambridge (0223) 350411. *Club:* Athenæum.

RYLE, Kenneth Sherriff, CBE 1964; MC 1945; Secretary to the Church Commissioners for England, 1969–75; *b* 13 April 1912; *s* of Herbert Ryle, CVO, OBE; *m* 1941, Jean Margaret Watt; one *s* one *d. Educ:* Cheltenham Coll. Chartered Accountant, 1936; Queen Anne's Bounty, 1936–48. Served in RA, 1940–45: India, Persia, Middle East, Sicily, Italy, Germany; Captain 1944. Church Commissioners, 1948– (Dep. Sec., 1964–69). *Recreation:* golf. *Address:* 47 Albyfield, Bickley, Kent. *T:* 081–467 6319. *Club:* Chislehurst Golf.

RYLE, Michael Thomas; Clerk of Committees, House of Commons, 1987–89, retired; *b* 30 July 1927; *s* of Peter Johnston Ryle and Rebecca Katie (*née* Boxall); *m* 1952, Bridget Moyes; one *s* two *d. Educ:* Newcastle upon Tyne Royal Grammar Sch.; Merton Coll., Oxford (1st Cl. Hons PPE, 1951; MA). Served RA, 1946–48 and TA, 1950–57. Entered Clerk's Dept, House of Commons, 1951; served in various offices; Clerk of Overseas Office, 1979–83; Principal Clerk, Table Office, 1983–84; Clerk of the Journals, 1985–87; attached Nova Scotia Legislature, 1976. Member: Study of Parlt Gp, 1964– (Founding Mem.; Chm., 1975–78; Pres., 1986–); Council, Hansard Soc., 1974–; Council, RIPA, 1982–88; Lambeth HMC, 1960–64. Governor, St Thomas' Hosp., 1964–74. Hon. Res. Fellow, Univ. of Exeter, 1990–. *Publications:* (ed with S. Walkland) The Commons in the Seventies, 1977, 2nd edn, as The Commons Today, 1981; (contrib.) The House of Commons in the Twentieth Century, 1979; (ed with P. G. Richards) The Commons Under Scrutiny, 1988; (with J. A. G. Griffith) Parliament, 1989; contrib. to books on parly practice and procedure; articles in Pol Qly, Parly Affairs, The Table, etc. *Recreations:* cricket, golf, bridge, watching birds, caravanning. *Address:* Jasmine Cottage, Winsford, Minehead, Somerset TA24 7JE. *T:* Winsford (064385) 317.

RYMAN, John; *b* 7 Nov. 1930. *Educ:* Leighton Park; Pembroke College, Oxford. Inns of Court Regt (TA), 1948–51. Called to the Bar, Middle Temple, 1957. Harmsworth Law Scholar. MP (Lab): Blyth, Oct. 1974–1983; Blyth Valley, 1983–87. Mem. Council, Assoc. of the Clergy, 1976–. *Recreation:* Horses.

RYMER-JONES, Brig. John Murray, CBE 1950 (OBE 1941); MC 1917, and Bar 1918; QPM 1959; retired as Assistant Commissioner Metropolitan Police (1950–59); Secretary, Drinking Fountain Association, 1959–76; Committee Member, Royal Humane Society, 1957–77; *b* 12 July 1897; *s* of late John and Lilian Rymer-Jones; *m* 1930, Gertrude Alice Wobey; one *s* two *d*. *Educ:* Felsted School; RMA, Woolwich. Commissioned RFA 1916; served European War: France and Flanders, 1916–18; Army of Rhine, 1919. Ireland, 1920–21 with KORR (Lancaster); Plebiscite, Upper Silesia, 1921; HQ British Army in Egypt, 1921–25; HQ Shanghai Defence Force, 1927–28; Company Commander and Instructor, RMA, Woolwich, 1929–33; retired as Captain, RA. Joined Metropolitan Police as Chief Inspector, 1934; Superintendent, 1935; Chief Constable, 1936; Inspector-General and Brigadier commanding Palestine Police, 1943–46. Commander Metropolitan Police, 1946–50. Area Comr, St John Ambulance, North Kent, 1963–66. Commander of St John of Jerusalem, 1952; Chevalier, Légion d'Honneur, 1950. Unpublished memoirs lodged with Imperial War Mus., 1987. *Recreations:* talking and music. *Address:* Lion House Lodge, High Halden, Kent. *T:* High Halden (023385) 538.

RYRIE, Sir William (Sinclair), KCB 1982 (CB 1979); Executive Vice-President and Chief Executive, International Finance Corporation at World Bank, since 1984; *b* 10 Nov. 1928; *s* of Rev. Dr Frank Ryrie and Mabel Moncrieff Ryrie (*née* Watt); *m* 1st, 1953, Dorrit Klein (marr. diss. 1969); two *s* one *d*; 2nd, 1969, Christine Gray Thomson; one *s*. *Educ:* Mount Hermon Sch., Darjeeling; Heriot's Sch., Edinburgh; Edinburgh Univ. MA 1st cl. hons History, 1951. Nat. Service, 1951–53: Lieut, Intell. Corps, Malaya, 1952–53 (despatches). Colonial Office, 1953; seconded to Uganda, 1956–58; Principal 1958; transf. to Treasury, 1963; Asst Sec., internat. monetary affairs, 1966–69; Principal Private Sec. to Chancellor of Exchequer, 1969–71; Under-Sec., Public Sector Gp, HM Treasury, 1971–75; Econ. Minister and Head of UK Treasury and Supply Delegn, Washington, and UK Exec. Dir, IMF and IBRD, 1975–79; 2nd Perm. Sec. (Domestic Economy Sector), HM Treasury, 1980–82; Permanent Sec., ODA, FCO, 1982–84. *Recreations:* photography, walking, music. *Address:* 4840 Van Ness Street NW, Washington, DC 20016, USA. *Club:* Reform.

S

SAATCHI, Charles; Director, Saatchi & Saatchi Co., since 1970; *b* 9 June 1943; *m* 1973, Doris Lockhart. *Educ:* Christ's Coll., Finchley. Associate Director, Collett Dickenson Pearce, 1966–68; Director, Cramer Saatchi, 1968–70. *Address:* 80 Charlotte Street, W1.

SAATCHI, Maurice; Chairman, Saatchi & Saatchi Co. plc, since 1984; *b* 21 June 1946; *s* of Daisy and Nathan Saatchi; *m* 1984, Josephine Hart; one *s* one step *s*. *Educ:* London School of Economics and Political Science (1st class BSc Econ). Co-Founder of Saatchi & Saatchi Co., 1970. *Address:* (office) 80 Charlotte Street, W1A 1AQ. *T:* 071–636 5060.
See also C. Saatchi.

SABATINI, Lawrence John; retired; Assistant Under Secretary of State, Ministry of Defence, 1972–79; *b* 5 Dec. 1919; *s* of Frederick Laurence Sabatini and Elsie May Sabatini (*née* Friggens); *m* 1947, Patricia Dyson; one *s* one *d*. *Educ:* Watford Grammar School. Joined HM Office of Works, 1938. Army service, 1940–46: commnd in RTR, 1943: service in NW Europe with 5 RTR. Asst Principal, Min. of Works, 1947; Asst Private Sec. to Minister of Works, 1948–49; Principal, 1949; Principal Private Sec. to Ministers of Defence, 1958–60; Asst Sec., MoD, 1960; Defence Counsellor, UK Delegn to NATO, on secondment to Diplomatic Service, 1963–67. *Recreations:* gardening, photography, music. *Address:* 44a Batchworth Lane, Northwood, Mddx HA6 3DT. *T:* Northwood (09274) 23249. *Club:* MCC.

SABBEN-CLARE, Ernest E., MA Oxon, BA London; Information Officer to University of Oxford, 1970–77; *b* 11 Aug. 1910; *s* of late Mr and Mrs J. W. Sabben-Clare; *m* 1938, Rosamond Dorothy Mary Scott; two *s* one *d*. *Educ:* Winchester Coll. (schol.); New College, Oxford (schol.). 1st cl. Mod. Hist., Oxford, 1932. Asst Master, Winchester Coll., 1932–34; Asst Dist Officer, Tanganyika, 1935–40; seconded Colonial Office, 1940–47; Lt, 10th Essex Bn Home Guard; Colonial Attaché, British Embassy, Washington, and Comr, Caribbean Commn, 1947–49; Nigerian Govt, 1950–55; Permanent Sec., Min. of Commerce, 1953–55; 1st cl. French, London Univ. (external), 1954; Asst Master, Marlborough Coll., 1955–60, Under-Master from 1957; Headmaster, Bishop Wordsworth's School, Salisbury, 1960–63; Headmaster, Leeds Grammar Sch., 1963–70. Chairman of Governors: Bramcote Sch., Scarborough, 1970–80; Badminton Sch., 1981–85. Editor, Wilts Archaeological and Natural History Magazine, 1956–62. *Publication:* (ed jtly) Health in Tropical Africa during the Colonial Period, 1980. *Recreations:* walking, gardening. *Address:* 4 Denham Close, Abbey Hill Road, Winchester SO23 7BL. *Club:* Athenæum.
See also J.P. Sabben-Clare.

SABBEN-CLARE, James Paley; Headmaster, Winchester College, since 1985; *b* 9 Sept. 1941; *s* of Ernest Sabben-Clare, *qv*; *m* 1969, Geraldine Mary Borton, LLB; one *s* one *d*. *Educ:* Winchester College (Scholar); New College, Oxford (Scholar; 1st Class Classical Hon. Mods and Greats, 1964; MA). Asst Master, Marlborough College, 1964–68; Vis. Fellow, All Souls College, Oxford, 1967–68; Winchester College, 1968–; Head of Classics Dept, 1969–79; Second Master, 1979–85. *Publications:* Caesar and Roman Politics, 1971, 2nd edn 1981; Fables from Aesop, 1976; The Culture of Athens, 1978, 2nd edn 1980; Winchester College, 1981, 2nd edn 1988; contribs to educnl and classical jls. *Recreations:* fives, Italian opera, mountains, furniture making. *Address:* Headmaster's House, Winchester College, Winchester, Hants SO23 9NA. *T:* Winchester (0962) 854328.

SABIN, Professor Albert (Bruce); retired; Consultant to World Health Organization, 1969–86; Senior Expert Consultant, Fogarty International Center, National Institutes of Health, Bethesda, Md, 1984–86; *b* 26 Aug. 1906; *s* of Jacob Sabin and Tillie Krugman; *m* 1935, Sylvia Tregillus (*d* 1966); two *d*; *m* 1967, Jane Blach Warner (marr. diss. 1971); *m* 1972, Heloisa Dunshee de Abranches. *Educ:* New York Univ. (MD). Ho. Phys., Bellevue Hosp., NY, 1932–33; Nat. Research Council Fellow, Lister Inst., London, 1934; Rockefeller Inst. for Med. Research, NY, 1935–39; Associate Prof. of Research Pediatrics, Univ. of Cincinnati, 1939–43; active duty, US Army, 1943–46 (Legion of Merit, 1945); Prof. of Research Pediatrics, Univ. of Cincinnati Coll. of Medicine and The Children's Hosp. Research Foundn, 1946–60, Distinguished Service Prof., 1960–71, Emeritus, 1971–; Distinguished Res. Prof. of Biomedicine, Med. Univ. of SC, Charleston, 1974–82. Pres., Weizmann Inst. of Science, Israel, 1970–72. Fogarty Scholar, NIH, 1973. Mem. Nat. Acad. of Sciences of the USA; Fellow, Amer. Acad. of Arts and Sciences; Mem. and Hon. Mem. of various Amer. and foreign societies; Foreign Mem., USSR Acad. of Med. Scis, 1986; Hon. Member: Royal Acad. of Med. of Belgium; British Paediatric Association. Holds hon. degrees; awards include: Feltrinelli Prize ($40,000) of Accad. Naz. dei Lincei, Rome, 1964; Lasker ($10,000) Prize for Clinical Medicine Research, 1965. Gold Medal, Royal Soc. of Health, 1969; National Medal of Science (USA), 1970; Statesman in Medicine Award (USA), 1973; US Medal of Freedom, 1986; US Medal of Liberty, 1986; Order of Friendship Among Peoples, Presidium of Supreme Soviet, 1986; Carlos Finlay Medal (Cuba), 1987. Hon. FRSH London. *Publications:* numerous papers on pneumococcus infection, poliomyelitis, encephalitis, virus diseases of nervous system, toxoplasmosis, sandfly fever, dengue, other topics relating to various infectious diseases and virus-cancer relationships. *Recreations:* reading, music, home. *Address:* Sutton Towers, Apt 1001, 3101 New Mexico Avenue NW, Washington, DC 20016–5902, USA. *Club:* Cosmos (Washington, DC).

SABIN, Howard Westcott; Legal Adviser to Associated Newspapers Group Ltd, 1972–84; Chairman, William Morris Rolling Mills Ltd (formerly William Morris & Son (Birmingham) Ltd), since 1985; *b* 19 Oct. 1916; *s* of late John Howard Sabin and Octavia Roads (*née* Scruby); *m* 1st, 1942, Joan Eunice Noble (marr. diss. 1959); two *s* one *d*; 2nd, 1959, Janet Eileen Baillie. *Educ:* Shrewsbury; St John's Coll., Cambridge; MA (Hons in History and Law). Lieut, RNVR, 1939–46 (despatches 1944). Called to the Bar, Middle Temple, 1946. Dep. Chm., Bedfordshire QS, 1968–72; Assistant Recorder, Portsmouth, 1966, Bournemouth, 1967. Counsel for Post Office (Midland Circuit), 1964. *Recreations:* golf, swimming, music. *Address:* 40 Wynnstay Gardens, W8 6UT. *T:* 071–937 9247. *Club:* Hadley Wood Golf.

SABIN, Paul Robert; Chief Executive, Kent County Council, since 1986; *b* 29 March 1943; *s* of Robert Reginald and Dorothy Maude Sabin; *m* 1965, Vivien Furnival; one *s* two *d*. *Educ:* Oldbury Grammar Sch. DMS Aston Univ.; IPFA 1966; FBIM (MBIM 1967). West Bromwich CBC, 1961–69; Redditch Develt Corp., 1969–81, Chief Finance Officer, 1975–81; City of Birmingham, 1981–86: City Treas., 1982–86; Dep. Chief Exec., 1984–86. FRSA 1988. *Recreations:* antique maps and books, music. *Address:* County Hall, Maidstone ME14 1XQ. *T:* Maidstone (0622) 694001.

SABINE, Neville Warde, CMG 1960; CBE 1957; *b* 6 April 1910; *s* of late John William Sabine; *m* 1954, Zoë Margherita Bargna; two *d*. *Educ:* Manchester Grammar School; Brasenose College, Oxford. BA Hons. (Oxon) 1934. Colonial Service (Colonial Audit Dept) 1934; served Gold Coast, Malaya, Uganda, Leeward Islands, and N Borneo. Served War of 1939–45: Gold Coast Regt, 1939–40; Singapore RA (V), 1940–42; British Military Administration, Malaya, 1945–46. Auditor-General, Ghana, 1954–64; Secretary, Central Bd of Finance of Church of England, 1964–75. Sec., Soc. of Sussex Downsmen, 1976–84. *Recreations:* bridge, walking. *Address:* 11 Windlesham Road, Brighton BN1 3AG. *T:* Brighton (0273) 732157.

SABINE, Peter Aubrey, DSc; FRSE, FRSA, FIMM; CEng, CGeol, FGS; Deputy Director (Chief Scientific Officer, Chief Geologist), British Geological Survey (formerly Institute of Geological Sciences), 1977–84; *b* 29 Dec. 1924; *s* of Bernard Robert and Edith Lucy Sabine; *m* 1946, Peggy Willis Lambert, MSc, FBCS, FRSA, FSS; one *s*. *Educ:* Brockley County Sch.; Chelsea Polytechnic; Royal Coll. of Science, London. BSc, ARCS (1st Cl. Geol.; Watts medal) 1945; PhD 1951, DSc 1970 (London). Apptd Geological Survey of Gt Britain as Geologist, 1945; Geological Museum, 1946–50; in charge Petrographical Dept, Geol Survey and Museum, 1950, Chief Petrographer, 1959; Asst Dir, S England and Wales, 1970; Chief Geochemist, 1977; Dep. Dir, 1977–84. Sec., Geol Soc. of London, 1959–66, Vice-Pres., 1966–67, 1982–84 (Lyell Fund, 1955); International Union of Geological Sciences: Mem. Commn on Systematics of Igneous Rocks, 1969–; Mem. Commn on Systematics in Petrology, 1980– (Chm., 1984–); Chief UK Deleg., 1980–84; Mem. Council, 1980–; Member Council: Geologists' Assoc., 1966–70; Mineralogical Soc., 1950–53; Instn of Mining and Metallurgy, 1976–80; Mineral Industry Res. Orgn, 1983–86; Member: DTI Chem. and Mineral Research Requirements Bd, 1973–82; Minerals, Metals Extraction and Reclamation Cttee, 1981–84; EEC Cttees on minerals and geochemistry; Cttee of Dirs of W European Geolog. Surveys, 1978–84; Chm., Sub-Cttee on geochem. and cosmochem. of British Nat. Cttee for Geology, 1977–86. Royal Institution: Visitor, 1979–82; Mem., Audit Cttee, 1987–90 (Chm., 1989–90). FMSA. *Publications:* Chemical Analysis of Igneous Rocks (with E. M. Guppy), 1956; (with D. S. Sutherland) Petrography of British Igneous Rocks, 1982; (jtly) Classification of Igneous Rocks, 1989; numerous scientific contribs in Mem. Geol. Surv., Qly Jl Geol. Soc., Mineral. Mag., Phil. Trans Roy. Soc., etc. *Recreations:* gardening, genealogy. *Address:* 19 Beaufort Road, Ealing, W5 3EB. *T:* 081–997 2360. *Clubs:* Athenæum; Geological Society's.

SACHS, Michael Alexander Geddes; His Honour Judge Sachs; a Circuit Judge, since 1984; *b* 8 April 1932; *s* of Dr Joseph Sachs, MB, ChB, DPH, and Mrs Ruby Mary Sachs (*née* Ross); *m* 1957, Patricia Mary (*née* Conroy); two *s* two *d*. *Educ:* Sedbergh; Manchester Univ. (LLB 1954). Admitted solicitor, 1957. Partner in Slater, Heelis & Co., Solicitors, Manchester, 1962–84. A Recorder, 1980–84. Pres., Manchester Law Soc., 1978–79; Chm., Greater Manchester Legal Services Cttee, 1977–81; Member: No 7 (NW) Area, Legal Aid Cttee, 1966–80 (Chm., 1975–76); Council, Law Soc., 1979–84 (Chm., Standing Cttee on Criminal Law, 1982–84); Court, Univ. of Manchester, 1977–84. KSS 1980. *Address:* c/o Circuit Administrator, Aldine House, New Bailey Street, Salford M3 5EU.

SACKS, The Chief Rabbi Dr Jonathan Henry; Chief Rabbi of the United Hebrew Congregations of the British Commonwealth of Nations, since 1991; *b* 8 March 1948; *s* of Louis David Sacks and Louisa (*née* Frumkin); *m* 1970, Elaine (*née* Taylor); one *s* two *d*. *Educ:* Gonville and Caius Coll., Cambridge (MA 1972); New Coll., Oxford; PhD London, 1981. Rabbinic Ordination: Jews' Coll., London, 1976; Yeshivat Etz Hayyim, London, 1976. Lectr in Moral Philosophy, Middlesex Polytechnic, 1971–73; Jews' College, London: Lectr in Jewish Philosophy, 1973–76; Lectr on the Talmud and in Phil., 1976–82; apptd (first) Sir Immanuel (now Lord) Jakobovits Prof. of Modern Jewish Thought, 1982–; Dir, Rabbinic Faculty, 1983–90; Principal, 1984–90; Rabbi, Golders Green Synagogue, 1978–82; Minister, Marble Arch Synagogue, 1983–90. Member (Univ. of London): Bd of Phil., 1985–90; Bd of Studies in Oriental Languages and Literature, 1985–90; Bd of Studies in Theology and Religious Studies, 1986–90. Member: Theol. and Religious Studies Bd, CNAA, 1984–87; Central Religious Adv. Cttee, BBC and IBA, 1987–90. Vis. Prof. of Philosophy, Univ. of Essex, 1989–90. BBC Reith Lectr, 1990. Editor, L'Eylah: A Journal of Judaism Today, 1984–. *Publications:* Torah Studies, 1986; (ed) Tradition and Transition: essays presented to Sir Immanuel Jakobovits, 1986; Traditional Alternatives, 1989; Tradition in an Untraditional Age, 1990; The Persistence of Faith, 1991; articles, booklets and book reviews. *Address:* Adler House, Tavistock Square, WC1H 9HN. *T:* 071–387 1066.

SACKVILLE, family name of **Earl De la Warr.**

SACKVILLE, 6th Baron, *cr* 1876; **Lionel Bertrand Sackville-West;** *b* 30 May 1913; *s* of late Hon. Bertrand George Sackville-West, *y b* of 4th Baron and Eva Adela Mabel Inigo (*d* 1936), *d* of late Maj.-Gen. Inigo Richmond Jones, CB, CVO; *S* cousin, 1965; *m* 1st, 1953, Jacobine Napier (*d* 1971), *widow* of Captain John Hichens, RA, and *d* of J. R. Menzies-Wilson; five *d*; 2nd, 1974, Arlie, Lady de Guingand (marr. diss. 1983); 3rd,

1983, Jean, *widow* of Sir Edward Imbert-Terry, 3rd Bt. *Educ:* Winchester; Magdalen Coll., Oxford. Formerly Capt. Coldstream Gds; served War, 1939–42 (POW). Member of Lloyd's, 1949. *Heir: b* Hugh Rosslyn Inigo Sackville-West, MC [*b* 1 Feb. 1919; *m* 1957, Bridget Eleanor, *d* of late Capt. Robert Lionel Brooke Cunliffe, CBE, RN; two *s* three *d*]. *Address:* Knole, Sevenoaks, Kent.

See also Sir M. E. S. Imbert-Terry, Bt.

SACKVILLE, Hon. Thomas Geoffrey, (Tom); MP (C) Bolton West, since 1983; a Lord Commissioner of the Treasury (Government Whip), since 1990; *b* 26 Oct. 1950; 2nd *s* of 10th Earl De La Warr (*d* 1988) and of Anne Rachel, *o d* of Geoffrey Devas, MC, Hunton Court, Maidstone; *m* 1979, Catherine Theresa, *d* of Brig. James Windsor Lewis; one *s* one *d*. *Educ:* St Aubyn's, Rottingdean, Sussex; Eton Coll.; Lincoln Coll., Oxford (BA). Deltec Banking Corp., New York, 1971–74; Grindlays Bank Ltd, London, 1974–77; Internat. Bullion and Metal Brokers (London) Ltd, 1978–83. PPS to Minister of State at the Treasury, 1985, to Minister for Social Security, 1987–88; an Asst Govt Whip, 1988–90. Sec., All-Party Cttee on Drug Misuse, 1984–. *Recreations:* music, fishing. *Address:* House of Commons, SW1A 0AA. *T:* 071–219 4050.

SACKVILLE-WEST, family name of **Baron Sackville.**

SACKWOOD, Dr Mark; Regional Medical Officer, Northern Regional Health Authority, 1973–86, retired; *b* London, 18 Jan. 1926; *s* of Philip and Frances Sackwood; *m* 1953, Anne Harper Wilson; one *s* two *d*. *Educ:* King's Coll., London; Westminster Hosp. Med. School. MB, BS, FFCM, LRCP, MRCS, DPH, DRCOG. Various hosp. appts, South of England, 1949–58; mil. service, Far East, 1951–53; subseq. admin. med. appts, Middlesbrough and Newcastle upon Tyne, incl. Dep. Sen. Admin. MO with Newcastle RHB, 1968–73. *Recreations:* walking, reading, music. *Address:* 11 The Chesters, Beaumont Park, Whitley Bay, Tyne and Wear. *T:* 091–252 7401.

SADEQUE, Shahwar; a Governor, BBC, since 1990; *b* 31 Aug. 1942; *d* of late Ali Imam and of Akhtar Imam; *m* 1962, Pharhad Sadeque; one *s* one *d*. *Educ:* Dhaka Univ., Bangladesh (BSc (Hons) Physics); Bedford Coll., London (MPhil Physics); Kingston Poly (MSc Inf. Technol.). Computer Programmer with Baric Services Ltd, 1969–73; Teacher, Nonsuch High Sch., Sutton, 1973–84; research in computer integrated manufacture incorporating vision systems and artificial intelligence, Kingston Poly, 1985–. Mem., Commn for Racial Equality, 1989–. *Publications:* papers: Education and Ethnic Minorities, 1988; Manufacturing—towards the 21st Century, 1988; A Knowledge-Based System for Sensor Interaction and Real-Time Component Control, 1988. *Recreations:* collecting thimbles and perfume bottles, cooking Indian-style, passion for keeping up-to-date with current affairs. *Address:* 59 Cheam Road, East Ewell, Epsom, Surrey KT17 3EG. *T:* 081–393 8485.

SADIE, Stanley (John), CBE 1982; writer on music; Music Critic for The Times, 1964–81, thereafter freelance; Editor: The Musical Times, 1967–87; The New Grove Dictionary of Music and Musicians, since 1970; Master Musicians series, since 1976; Musical Consultant, Man and Music, Granada TV, since 1984; *b* 30 Oct. 1930; *s* of David Sadie and Deborah (*née* Simons); *m* 1st, 1953, Adèle Bloom (*d* 1978); two *s* one *d*; 2nd, 1978, Julie Anne Vertrees; one *s* one *d*. *Educ:* St Paul's Sch.; Gonville and Caius Coll., Cambridge Univ. (MA, PhD, MusB). Prof., Trinity Coll. of Music, London, 1957–65. Pres., Royal Musical Assoc., 1989– (Vice-Pres., 1985–89); Member: Internat. Musicological Soc., 1955–; Critics' Circle, 1963–; American Musicological Soc., 1970–; Directorium, 1987–. Hon. RAM 1981; Hon. DLitt Leicester, 1981. FRSA 1982. Writer and broadcaster on musical subjects, *circa* 1955–; editor of many edns of 18th-century music, *circa* 1955–; Series Editor, Man and Music, 8 vols, 1989–. *Publications:* Handel, 1962; Mozart, 1966; Beethoven, 1967; Handel, 1968; (with Arthur Jacobs) Pan Book of Opera/The Opera Guide, 1964, new edns 1969, 1984; Handel Concertos, 1973; (ed) The New Grove Dictionary of Music and Musicians, 1980; Mozart (The New Grove Biographies), 1982; (ed) New Grove Dictionary of Musical Instruments, 1984; (with Alison Latham) The Cambridge Music Guide, 1985; Mozart Symphonies, 1986; (ed with H. Wiley Hitchcock) The New Grove Dictionary of American Music, 1986; (ed) The Grove Concise Dictionary of Music, 1988; (ed) History of Opera, 1989; (ed with H. M. Brown) Performance Practice, 1989; (ed with D. W. Krummel) Music Printing and Publishing, 1989; contrib.: The Musical Times, Gramophone, Opera, Music and Letters, Musical Quarterly, Proc. Roy. Musical Assoc. *Recreations:* watching cricket, drinking (mainly wine and coffee), bridge, reading. *Address:* 12 Lyndhurst Road, NW3 5NL. *T:* 071–435 2482.

SADLER, Joan; Principal, Cheltenham Ladies' College, 1979–87; *b* 1 July 1927; *d* of Thomas Harold Sadler and Florence May Sadler. *Educ:* Cambridgeshire High Sch.; Univ. of Bristol (BA Hons (History); DipEd). Downe House, Cold Ash, Newbury, Berks: Asst History teacher, 1950–56; Head of History Dept, 1956–58; Heriots Wood School, Stanmore, Mddx: Head of History Dept, 1958–68; Sen. Mistress, 1966–68; Headmistress, Howell's School, Denbigh, 1968–79. Chairman: Boarding Schools' Assoc., 1983–85; Independent Schools' Curriculum Cttee, 1986–; Trustee: Central Bureau for Educnl Visits and Exchanges; Common Entrance Examination for Girls' Schools. MInstD 1986. Hon. Freewoman: City of London; Drapers' Co., 1979. FRSA. *Recreations:* music, theatre, travel, reading. *Address:* Locke's Cottage, Caudle Green, Cheltenham, Glos GL53 9PR.

SADLER, John Stephen, CBE 1982; Chairman, WRC plc, since 1989; *b* 6 May 1930; *s* of late Bernard and Phyllis Sadler; *m* 1952, Ella (*née* McCleery); three *s*. *Educ:* Reading Sch.; Corpus Christi Coll., Oxford (MA). Board of Trade, 1952–54; Treasury, 1954–56; Board of Trade, 1956–60; British Trade Commissioner, Lagos, Nigeria, 1960–64; Board of Trade, 1964–66. John Lewis Partnership Ltd, 1966–89: Finance Dir, 1971–87; Dep. Chm., 1984–89. Chm., UK Bd, Australian Mutual Provident Society and London Life, 1991–; Dep. Chm., West End Central London Region Bd, Sun Alliance Insurance Gp, 1987–; Dir, Debenham Tewson & Chinnock Hldgs plc, 1987–. Dir, IMRO, 1987–; Chm., Authorised Conveyancing Practitioners Bd, 1991–; Mem., Monopolies and Mergers Commn, 1973–85. Trustee, British Telecommunications Staff Superannuation Scheme, 1983–. *Recreations:* golf, boating. *Address:* 7 The Chilterns, 63 Chiltern Street, W1M 1HS. *Clubs:* Oriental, Reading Golf.

SAFFMAN, Prof. Philip Geoffrey, FRS 1988; Professor of Applied Mathematics, California Institute of Technology, since 1964; *b* 19 March 1931; *s* of Sam Ralph Saffman and Sarah Rebecca Leviten; *m* 1954, Ruth Arion; one *s* two *d*. *Educ:* Roundhay Sch., Leeds; Trinity Coll., Cambridge (BA, MA, PhD). Prize Fellow, Trinity Coll., Cambridge, 1955–59; Asst Lectr, Applied Math., Cambridge, 1958–60; Reader in Applied Math., King's Coll. London, 1960–64. Fellow, Amer. Acad. of Arts and Scis, 1978. *Publications:* numerous papers in sci. jls. *Recreations:* hiking, camping. *Address:* 399 Ninita Parkway, Pasadena, Calif 91106, USA.

SAGAN, Françoise, pen-name of Françoise Quoirez; authoress; *b* France, 21 June 1935; *y c* of Paul Quoirez; *m* 1958, Guy Schoeller (marr. diss. 1960); *m* 1962, Robert James Westhoff; one *s*. *Educ:* convent and private school. Published first novel at age of 18. Has written some songs and collaborated in scheme for ballet Le Rendez-vous Manqué, produced Paris and London, 1958. *Publications:* (all trans. into Eng., usually French title): Bonjour Tristesse, 1954; Un Certain Sourire, 1956 (filmed, 1958); Dans un mois, dans un an, 1957 (Eng. trans. Those Without Shadows, 1958); Aimez-vous Brahms . . . . 1959 (Eng. trans. 1960); Château en Suède (play), 1960; Les Violons, parfois . . . (play), 1961; La Robe Mauve de Valentine (play), 1963; Bonheur, impair et passe (play), 1964; Toxique . . . (tr. 1965); La Chamade, 1965 (tr. 1966) (film, 1970); Le Cheval Evanoui (play), 1966; L'Echarde, 1966; Le Garde du cœur, 1968 (tr., The Heart-Keeper, 1968); Un peu de soleil dans l'eau froide, 1969 (tr., Sunlight and Cold Water, 1971); Un piano dans l'herbe (play), 1970; Des bleus à l'âme, 1972 (tr., Scars on the Soul, 1974); Zaphorie (play), 1973; Lost Profile, 1976; Silken Eyes (short stories), 1977; The Unmade Bed, 1978; Le Chien Couchant, 1980; La femme fardée, 1981 (tr., The Painted Lady, 1982); The Still Storm, 1984; Incidental Music (short stories), 1985; Avec mon meilleur souvenir (tr. With Fondest Regards), 1986; Un sang d'aquarelle, 1987; Dear Sarah Bernhardt, 1989; (with W. Denker) The Eiffel Tower, 1989. *Address:* c/o Editions Flammarion, 26 rue Racine, 75006 Paris, France.

SAGE, Lorna; journalist and critic; Senior Lecturer in English Literature, since 1975, Dean of the School of English and American Studies, since 1985, University of East Anglia; *b* 13 Jan. 1943; *d* of Eric and Valma Stockton; *m* 1st, 1959, Victor Sage; one *d*; 2nd, 1979, Rupert Hodson. *Educ:* Univ. of Durham (BA 1st Cl. Hons 1964); Univ. of Birmingham (MA 1966). Asst Lectr in English Literature, Univ. of East Anglia, 1965, Lectr 1968. Florence B. Tucker Vis. Prof., Wellesley Coll., Mass, USA, 1981. *Publications:* (ed) Peacock, Satirical Novels, 1976; Doris Lessing, 1983; reviews in Observer, TLS, etc. *Address:* School of English and American Studies, University of East Anglia, Norwich NR4 7TJ. *T:* Norwich (0603) 56161.

SAINER, Leonard; *b* 12 Oct. 1909; *s* of late Archer and Sarah Sainer. Life President (formerly Chairman), Sears plc; Consultant, Titmuss Sainer & Webb, Solicitors. *Address:* (business) 40 Duke Street, W1; (home) 8 Farm Street, W1X 7RE.

SAINSBURY, family name of **Barons Sainsbury** and **Sainsbury of Preston Candover.**

SAINSBURY, Baron, *cr* 1962, of Drury Lane (Life Peer); **Alan John Sainsbury;** Joint President of J. Sainsbury plc, since 1967 (Chairman, 1956–67); *b* 13 Aug. 1902; *er s* of John Benjamin and Mabel Miriam Sainsbury; *m* 1st, 1925, Doreen Davan Adams (marr. diss. 1939; she *d* 1985); three *s*; 2nd, 1944, Anne Elizabeth Lewy (*d* 1988); one *d*. *Educ:* Haileybury. Joined Grocery and Provision Firm of J. Sainsbury, Ltd (founded by his grandparents), 1921. Served on many war-time consultative committees of Ministry of Food; Member Williams' Committee on Milk Distribution, 1947–48; Member: Food Research Advisory Cttee, 1960–70 (Chm., 1965–70); NEDC Cttee for the Distributive Trades, 1964–68; Exec. Cttee, PEP, 1970–76; House of Lords Select Cttee on the European Communities, 1978–81; Chm., Cttee of Inquiry into Relationship of Pharmaceutical Industry with National Health Service, 1965–67. President: Multiple Shops' Fedn, 1963–65; The Grocers' Inst., 1963–66; Internat. Assoc. of Chain Stores, 1965–68; The Royal Inst. of Public Health and Hygiene, 1965–70; Pestalozzi Children's Village Trust, 1963–; Distributive Trades Educn and Trng Council, 1975–83; a Vice-President, Assoc. of Agriculture, 1965–73; Royal Society for the Encouragement of Arts, Manufactures and Commerce, 1962–66; Mem., Court of Univ. of Essex, 1966–76; Governor, City Literary Inst., 1967–69; Chairman of Trustees: Overseas Students Adv. Bureau; Uganda Asian Relief Trust, 1972–74; Vice-President: World Development Movement; Internat. Voluntary Service, 1977–81; Parly Gp for World Govt, 1982–. Liberal candidate, Sudbury Div. of Suffolk, Gen. Elections of 1929, 1931 and 1935. Joined Labour Party, 1945, SDP, 1981. Hon. Fellow, Inst. of Food Sci, and Technology. *Address:* J. Sainsbury plc, Stamford House, Stamford Street, SE1 9LL.

See also Baron Sainsbury of Preston Candover, Hon. T. A. D. Sainsbury.

SAINSBURY OF PRESTON CANDOVER, Baron *cr* 1989 (Life Peer), of Preston Candover in the county of Hampshire; **John Davan Sainsbury;** Kt 1980; Chairman, J Sainsbury plc, since 1969 (Vice-Chairman, 1967–69; Director, since 1958); *b* 2 Nov. 1927; *e s* of Baron Sainsbury, *qv*; *m* 1963, Anya Linden, *qv*; two *s* one *d*. *Educ:* Stowe School; Worcester College, Oxford (Hon. Fellow 1982). Dir, Royal Opera House Trust, 1974–84 and 1987–; Chairman: Friends of Covent Garden, 1969–81; Benesh Inst. of Choreology, 1986–87; Royal Opera House, Covent Garden, 1987–91; Governor, Royal Ballet Sch., 1965–76, and 1987–. Dir, The Economist, 1972–80; Jt Hon. Treas., European Movt, 1972–75; Member: Council, Retail Consortium, 1975–79; Nat. Cttee for Electoral Reform, 1976–85; President's Cttee, CBI, 1982–84. Vice Pres., Contemporary Arts Soc., 1984– (Hon. Sec., 1965–71; Vice Chm., 1971–74); Trustee: Nat. Gall., 1976–83; Westminster Abbey Trust, 1977–83; Tate Gall., 1982–83; Rhodes Trust, 1984–. Hon. Bencher, Inner Temple, 1985. FIGD 1973. Hon. DScEcon London, 1985. Albert Medal, RSA, 1989. *Address:* c/o Stamford House, Stamford Street, SE1 9LL. *T:* 071–921 6000. *Clubs:* Athenæum, Garrick.

See also Hon. T. A. D. Sainsbury.

SAINSBURY OF PRESTON CANDOVER, Lady; *see* Linden, Anya.

SAINSBURY, David John; Deputy Chairman, J. Sainsbury plc, since 1988; *b* 24 Oct. 1940; *s* of Sir Robert Sainsbury, *qv*; *m* 1973, Susan Carole Reid; three *d*. *Educ:* King's Coll., Cambridge (BA); Columbia Univ., NY (MBA). Joined J. Sainsbury, 1963; Finance Dir, 1973–90. Mem., Cttee of Review of the Post Office (Carter Cttee), 1975–77. Trustee, Social Democratic Party, 1982–; Mem. Governing Body, London Business Sch., 1985–. Vis. Fellow, Nuffield Coll., Oxford, 1987–. Hon. DSc Salford, 1989. *Publications:* Government and Industry: a new partnership, 1981; (with Christopher Smallwood) Wealth Creation and Jobs, 1987.

SAINSBURY, Edward Hardwicke; TD 1945; Consultant Partner, Dawson, Hart & Co., Uckfield, since 1983; District Notary Public, Uckfield, since 1965; *b* 17 Sept. 1912; *e s* of Henry Morgan Sainsbury, and *g s* of James C. Hardwicke, a pioneer of technical and other education in S Wales; *m* 1946, Ann, 2nd *d* of late Kenneth Ellis, Tunbridge Wells; one *s* one *d*. *Educ:* Cardiff High School; University of S Wales and Monmouth. Solicitor in private practice, 1935; commissioned (TA) 1936; Prosecuting Solicitor, Cardiff, 1938, Sen. Pros. Solicitor, 1939. Served War of 1939–45; Adjutant, 77th HAA Regt, 1940; comd 240 HAA Battery Gibraltar, 1944; demobilised Nov. 1945. Hong Kong: Asst Crown Solicitor, 1946; commissioner for revision of the laws of Hong Kong, 1947; magistrate, 1948; registrar, High Court, 1949; sen. magistrate, Kowloon, 1951; Barrister, Inner Temple, 1951; Land Officer and sen. crown counsel, Hong Kong, 1952; legal draftsman, Nigeria, 1953; Principal Legal Draftsman, Fed. of Nigeria, 1958. President, Commonwealth Parliamentary Assoc., Southern Cameroons, 1959–63. Judge, High Court of Lagos, 1960–63, and of Southern Cameroons, 1961–63; Speaker, House of Assembly, 1958–63, Chm., Public Service Commn, 1961–63, Southern Cameroons. *Publication:* (jointly) Revised Laws of Hong Kong, 1948. *Recreations:* squash (a memory), golf. *Address:* Little Gassons, Fairwarp, Uckfield, East Sussex TN22 3BG. *T:* Nutley (082571) 2100.

SAINSBURY, Sir Robert, Kt 1967 (for services to the arts); Joint President, J. Sainsbury plc; *b* 24 Oct. 1906; *s* of late John Benjamin Sainsbury and late Mable Miriam (*née* Van den Bergh); *m* 1937, Lisa Ingeborg (*née* Van den Bergh; second cousin); one *s* two *d* (and one *d* decd). *Educ:* Haileybury Coll.; Pembroke Coll., Cambridge (MA; Hon. Fellow, 1983). ACA, 1930, FCA, 1935. Joined J. Sainsbury Ltd, 1930; Dir, 1934; Jt Gen. Man., 1938; Dep. Chm., 1956; Chm. 1967; Jt Pres., 1969. Formerly Mem. Art Panel of Arts Council; Member: Mngt Cttee, Courtauld Inst. of Art, Univ. of London, 1979–82; Vis. Cttee to Primitive Art Dept, Metropolitan Mus of Art, New York, until 1986; Pres., British Assoc. of Friends of Museums, 1985–. Trustee, Tate Gall., 1959–73 (Vice-Chm. 1967, Chm., 1969). Founder, with wife, Sainsbury Centre for Visual Arts, UEA, 1978. Hon. Treasurer, Inst. of Med. Social Workers, 1948–71; Governor, St Thomas' Hospital, 1939–68. Hon. FRIBA 1986. Hon. Dr RCA, 1976; Hon. LittD East Anglia, 1977; Hon. LLD Liverpool, 1988.
See also D. J. Sainsbury.

SAINSBURY, Rt. Rev. Roger Frederick; *see* Barking, Area Bishop of.

SAINSBURY, Hon. Timothy Alan Davan; MP (C) Hove, since Nov. 1973; Minister of State (Minister for Trade), Department of Trade and Industry, since 1990; *b* 11 June 1932; *y s* of Baron Sainsbury, *qv*; *m* 1961, Susan Mary Mitchell; two *s* two *d*. *Educ:* Eton; Worcester Coll., Oxford (MA; Hon. Fellow 1982). Dir, J. Sainsbury, 1962–83. Chm., Council for the Unit for Retail Planning Information Ltd, 1974–79. PPS to Sec. of State for the Environment, 1979–83, to Sec. of State for Defence, 1983; a Govt Whip, 1983–87; Parly Under-Sec. of State for Defence Procurement, 1987–89; Parly Under-Sec. of State, FCO, 1989–90. Mem. Council, RSA, 1981–83. *Address:* House of Commons, SW1A 0AA.
See also Baron Sainsbury of Preston Candover.

SAINT, Dora Jessie, (*pen name* Miss Read); writer, since 1950; *b* 17 April 1913; *d* of Arthur Gunnis Shafe and Grace Lilian Shafe; *m* 1940, Douglas Edward John Saint; one *d*. *Educ:* Bromley County Sch.; Homerton Coll., Cambridge. Teaching in Middlesex, 1933–40; occasional teaching, 1946–63. *Publications:* Village School, 1955; Village Diary, 1957; Storm in the Village, 1958; Thrush Green, 1959; Fresh from the Country, 1960; Winter in Thrush Green, 1961; Miss Clare Remembers, 1962; Chronicles of Fairacre, 1963; Over the Gate, 1964; Market Square, 1965; Village Christmas, 1966; Fairacre Festival, 1968; News from Thrush Green, 1970; Tiggy, 1971; Emily Davis, 1971; Tyler's Row, 1972; The Christmas Mouse, 1973; Farther Afield, 1974; Battles at Thrush Green, 1975; No Holly for Miss Quinn, 1976; Village Affairs, 1977; Return to Thrush Green, 1978; The White Robin, 1979; Village Centenary, 1980; Gossip from Thrush Green, 1981; Affairs at Thrush Green, 1983; Summer at Fairacre, 1984; At Home in Thrush Green, 1985; The School at Thrush Green, 1987; The World of Thrush Green, 1988; Mrs Pringle, 1989; Friends at Thrush Green, 1990; *for children*: Hobby Horse Cottage, 1958; Hob and the Horse-Bat, 1965; The Red Bus Series, 1965; *non-fiction:* County Bunch (anthology), 1963; Miss Read's Country Cooking, 1969; *autobiography:* A Fortunate Grandchild, 1982; Time Remembered, 1986. *Recreations:* theatre-going, reading. *Address:* Strouds, Shefford Woodlands, Newbury, Berks RG16 7AJ. *T:* Great Shefford (048839) 249.

ST ALBANS, 14th Duke of, *cr* 1684; **Murray de Vere Beauclerk;** Earl of Burford, Baron of Heddington, 1676; Baron Vere of Hanworth, 1750. Hereditary Grand Falconer of England; Hereditary Registrar, Court of Chancery; Partner: Burfords, chartered accountants, since 1981; Burford & Co., since 1981; *b* 19 Jan. 1939; *s* of 13th Duke of St Albans, OBE and Nathalie Chatham, *d* of P. F. Walker (later Mrs Nathalie C. Eldrid, *d* 1985); *S* father, 1988; *m* 1st, 1963, Rosemary Frances Scoones (marr. diss. 1974); one *s* one *d*; 2nd, 1974, Cynthia Theresa Mary, *d* of late Lt-Col W. J. H. Howard, DSO and formerly wife of Sir Anthony Robin Maurice Hooper, 2nd Bt. *Educ:* Tonbridge. Chartered Accountant, 1962. Gov.-Gen., Royal Stuart Soc., 1989–. *Heir: s* Earl of Burford, *qv*. *Address:* 3 St George's Court, Gloucester Road, SW7 4QZ. *T:* 071–589 1771. *Club:* Hurlingham.

ST ALBANS, Bishop of, since 1980; **Rt. Rev. John Bernard Taylor;** Lord High Almoner to HM the Queen, since 1988; *b* 6 May 1929; *s* of George Ernest and Gwendoline Irene Taylor; *m* 1956, Linda Courtenay Barnes; one *s* two *d*. *Educ:* Watford Grammar Sch.; Christ's Coll., Cambridge; Jesus Coll., Cambridge. MA Cantab. Vicar of Henham and Elsenham, Essex, 1959–64; Vice-Principal, Oak Hill Theological Coll., 1964–72; Vicar of All Saints', Woodford Wells, 1972–75; Archdeacon of West Ham, 1975–80. Examining Chaplain to Bishop of Chelmsford, 1962–80. Chm., Gen. Synod's Cttee for Communications, 1986–. Member: Churches' Council for Covenanting, 1978–82; Liturgical Commn, 1981–86; Doctrine Commn, 1989–. Chairman Council: Haileybury Coll., 1980–; Wycliffe Hall, Oxford, 1985–. President: Hildenborough Evangelistic Trust, 1985–; Garden Tomb Assoc., Jerusalem, 1986–. Took his seat in House of Lords, 1985. *Publications:* A Christian's Guide to the Old Testament, 1966; Evangelism among Children and Young People, 1967; Tyndale Commentary on Ezekiel, 1969; Preaching through the Prophets, 1983. *Address:* Abbey Gate House, St Albans, Herts AL3 4HD. *T:* St Albans (0727) 53305.

ST ALBANS, Dean of; *see* Moore, Very Rev. P. C.

ST ALBANS, Archdeacon of; *see* Davies, Ven. P. B.

ST ALDWYN, 2nd Earl, *cr* 1915, of Coln St Aldwyns; **Michael John Hicks Beach,** GBE 1980 (KBE 1964); TD 1949; PC 1959; JP; Bt 1619; Viscount St Aldwyn, 1906; Viscount Quenington, 1915; Vice Lord-Lieutenant, Gloucestershire, 1981–87; *b* 9 Oct. 1912; *s* of Visc. Quenington, Roy. Glos. Hussars Yeo. (*d* 1916; *o s* of 1st Earl) and Marjorie (*d* 1916), *d* of late H. Dent Brocklehurst, Sudeley Castle, Gloucs; *S* grandfather, 1916 (his father having been killed in action a week previously); *m* 1948, Diana Mary Christian, DStJ (she *m* 1st, 1939, Major Richard Patrick Pilkington Smyly, MC; marriage annulled, 1942), *o d* of late Henry C. G. and Mrs Mills; two *s* (and one *s* decd). *Educ:* Eton; Christ Church, Oxford. Major Royal Glos Hussars Yeomanry, 1942. Parliamentary Secretary, Ministry of Agriculture and Fisheries, 1954–58; Captain of the Honorable Corps of Gentlemen-at-Arms and Govt Chief Whip, House of Lords, 1958–64 and 1970–74; Opposition Chief Whip, House of Lords, 1964–70 and 1974–78. DL 1950, JP 1952, Glos. GCStJ 1978; Chancellor, Order of St John, 1978–87 (Vice-Chancellor, 1969–78). *Heir: s* Viscount Quenington, *qv*. *Address:* Williamstrip Park, Cirencester, Gloucestershire GL7 5AT. *T:* Coln St Aldwyns (028575) 226; 13 Upper Belgrave Street, SW1X 8BA. *T:* 071–235 8464. *Clubs:* Carlton, Pratt's; Royal Yacht Squadron.
See also Sir Richard Keane, Bt.

ST ANDREWS, Earl of; George Philip Nicholas Windsor; *b* 26 June 1962; *s* of HRH the Duke of Kent and HRH the Duchess of Kent; *m* 1988, Sylvana Tomaselli; one *s*. *Educ:* Eton (King's Scholar); Downing College, Cambridge. Attached to FCO, 1987–88. *Heir: s* Lord Downpatrick, *qv*. *Address:* York House, St James's Palace, SW1.
See under Royal Family.

ST ANDREWS AND EDINBURGH, Archbishop of, (RC), since 1985; **Most Rev. Keith Michael Patrick O'Brien;** *b* Ballycastle, Co. Antrim, 17 March 1938; *s* of late Mark Joseph O'Brien and Alice Mary (*née* Moriarty). *Educ:* schools in Ballycastle, Dumbarton and Edinburgh; Edinburgh Univ. (BSc 1959, DipEd 1966); St Andrew's Coll., Drygrange; Moray House Coll. of Education, Edinburgh. Ordained Priest, 1965; pastoral appointments: Holy Cross, Edinburgh, 1965–66; St Bride's, Cowdenbeath, 1966–71 (while Chaplain and teacher of Maths and Science, St Columba's High Sch., Cowdenbeath and Dunfermline); St Patrick's, Kilsyth, 1972–75; St Mary's, Bathgate, 1975–78. Spiritual Director, St Andrew's Coll., Drygrange, 1978–80; Rector of St Mary's Coll., Blair, Aberdeen, 1980–85. *Address:* St Bennet's, 42 Greenhill Gardens, Edinburgh EH10 4BJ. *T:* 031–447 3337.

ST ANDREWS AND EDINBURGH, Bishop Auxiliary of, (RC); *see* Rafferty, Rt Rev. K. L.

ST ANDREWS, DUNKELD AND DUNBLANE, Bishop of, since 1969; **Rt. Rev. Michael Geoffrey Hare Duke;** *b* 28 Nov. 1925; *s* of late A. R. A. Hare Duke, Civil Engineer; *m* 1949, Grace Lydia Frances McKean Dodd; one *s* three *d*. *Educ:* Bradfield Coll.; Trinity Coll., Oxford. BA 1949, MA 1951. Sub-Lt, RNVR, 1944–46. Deacon, 1952; Priest, 1953; Curate, St John's Wood Church, 1952–56; Vicar, St Mark's, Bury, 1956–62; Pastoral Dir, Clin. Theol. Assoc., 1962–64; Vicar, St Paul's, Daybrook, and Pastoral Consultant to Clin. Theol. Assoc., 1964–69; OCF, E Midland Dist HQ, 1968–69. Chm., Scottish Assoc. for Mental Health, 1978–85. Mem. Editorial Bd, Contact Magazine, 1962–79. *Publications:* (jtly) The Caring Church, 1963; (jtly) First Aid in Counselling, 1968; Understanding the Adolescent, 1969; The Break of Glory, 1970; Freud, 1972; Good News, 1976; Stories, Signs and Sacraments in the Emerging Church, 1982; (ed) Praying for Peace, 1991; contributor to: Expository Times, Blackfriars, New Christian, Church Quarterly Review, Church Times, Contact. *Address:* Bishop's House, Fairmount Road, Perth PH2 7AP. *T:* Perth (0738) 21580.

ST ANDREWS, DUNKELD AND DUNBLANE, Dean of; *see* Watt, Very Rev. A. I.

ST ASAPH, Bishop of, since 1982; **Rt. Rev. Alwyn Rice Jones;** *b* 25 March 1934; *s* of John Griffith and Annie Jones, Capel Curig, Caernarvonshire; *m* 1968, Meriel Anne Thomas; one *d*. *Educ:* Llanrwst Grammar School, Denbighshire; St David's Coll., Lampeter (BA Hons Welsh 1955); Fitzwilliam House, Cambridge (BA 1957 Theology Tripos, MA 1961); St Michael's Coll., Llandaff. Deacon 1958, priest 1959, Bangor Cathedral; Asst Curate, Llanfairisgaer, 1958–62; Secretary for SCM in N Wales Colleges and SCM in schools, 1962–65; Director of Education, Diocese of Bangor, 1965–75; Chaplain, St Winifred's School, Llanfairfechan, 1965–67; Diocesan Warden of Ordinands, 1970–75; Vicar of Porthmadog, dio. Bangor, 1975–79; Exam. Chaplain to Archbishop of Wales, 1970–79; Hon. Canon, Bangor Cathedral, 1974–78, Preb. of Llanfair, 1978–79; Dean of Brecon Cathedral, 1979–82. Mem., IBA Panel of Religious Advisers and Welsh Cttee, IBA, 1972–76; Asst Tutor in Religious Education, UCNW, Bangor, 1973–76. *Recreations:* music and walking. *Address:* Esgobty, St Asaph, Clwyd LL17 0TW. *T:* St Asaph (0745) 583503.

ST ASAPH, Dean of; *see* Renowden, Very Rev. C. R.

ST AUBYN, family name of **Baron St Levan.**

ST AUBYN, Sir (John) Arscott M.; *see* Molesworth-St Aubyn.

ST AUBYN, Major Thomas Edward, DL, FRGS; Lieutenant, HM Body Guard of Honourable Corps of Gentlemen at Arms, since 1990 (Clerk of the Cheque and Adjutant, 1986–90); *b* 13 June 1923; *s* of Hon. Lionel Michael St Aubyn, MVO, and Lady Mary St Aubyn; *m* 1953, Henrietta Mary, *d* of Sir Henry Studholme, 1st Bt; three *d*. *Educ:* Eton. Served in King's Royal Rifle Corps, 1941–62; Italian Campaign, 1944–45; Adjt 1st KRRC, 1946–48; seconded to Sudan Defence Force in rank of Bimbashi, 1948–52; leader of Tibesti Mountain Expedn in Chad, 1957; Bde Adjt Green Jackets Bde, 1960–62. Mem., HM Body Guard, 1973–. High Sheriff of Hampshire, 1979–80; DL Hampshire, 1984. FRGS 1959. *Recreations:* shooting, fishing, ski-ing, stalking. *Address:* Dairy House Farm, Ashford Hill, Newbury, Berks RG15 8BL. *T:* Kingsclere (0635) 298493. *Club:* Army and Navy.

ST BONIFACE, Archbishop of, (RC), since 1974; **Most Rev. Antoine Hacault,** STD; *b* Bruxelles, Manitoba, 17 Jan. 1926. *Educ:* Sainte-Marie Elem. Sch., Bruxelles; St Boniface Coll. (BA 1947); St Boniface Major Seminary; Angelicum Univ., Rome (STD 1954). Priest, 1951; Prof. of Theology, St Boniface Major Seminary, 1954–64; Auxiliary Bishop of St Boniface and Titular Bishop of Media, 1964; also Rector, St Boniface College, 1967–69; Bishop Coadjutor of St Boniface, 1972. Member: Vatican Secretariat for Non-Believers, 1973–83; Vatican Secretariat for promoting Christian Unity, 1976–; Pastoral Team, Canadian Catholic Conf. of Bishops, 1971–75 and 1983–87; Admin. Bd, St Boniface Gen. Hosp., 1984–; Gen. Bd of Canadian Council of Churches, 1986–. President: Canadian Episcopal Commn for Ecumenism, 1974–; Inter-Church Cttee, 1982–85. *Address:* Archbishop's Residence, 151 avenue de la Cathédrale, St Boniface, Manitoba R2H 0H6, Canada.

ST CLAIR, family name of **Lord Sinclair.**

ST CLAIR, Malcolm Archibald James; *b* 16 Feb. 1927; *o s* of late Maj.-Gen. George James Paul St Clair, CB, CBE, DSO and late Charlotte Theresa Orme Little; *m* 1955, Mary-Jean Rosalie Alice, *o d* of Wing-Comdr Caryl Liddell Hargreaves, Broadwood House, Sunningdale; two *s* one *d*. *Educ:* Eton. Served with Royal Scots Greys, 1944–48. Formerly Hon. Sec. to Sir Winston Churchill. Contested (C) Bristol South-East, 1959; MP (C) Bristol South-East, 1961–63. Lt Col Comdg, Royal Gloucestershire Hussars (TA), 1967–69. High Sheriff Glos, 1972. *Address:* Long Newnton Priory, Tetbury, Glos. *Club:* White's.

ST CLAIR, William Linn, FRSL; Under Secretary, HM Treasury, since 1990; *b* 7 Dec. 1937; *s* of late Joseph and Susan St Clair, Falkirk; two *d*. *Educ:* Edinburgh Acad.; St John's Coll., Oxford. FRSL 1973. Admiralty and MoD, 1961–66; First Sec., FCO, 1966–69; transferred to HM Treasury, 1969. Visiting Fellow: All Souls Coll., Oxford, 1981–82; Huntington Library, Calif., 1985; Fellow, All Souls Coll., Oxford, Oct. 1992–. Internat. Pres., Byron Soc.; Mem. Exec. Cttee, English Centre of Internat. PEN; Chm., Writers in Prison Cttee. *Publications:* Lord Elgin and the Marbles, 1967, rev. edn 1983; That Greece Might Still Be Free, 1972 (Heinemann prize); Trelawny, 1978; Policy Evaluation: a guide for managers, 1988; The Godwins and the Shelleys, 1989 (Time Life prize and Macmillan silver pen); contrib. Financial Times and other jls. *Recreations:* old books, Scottish hills. *Address:* c/o HM Treasury, Parliament Street, SW1P 3AG. *Clubs:* Athenæum, PEN.

ST CLAIR-ERSKINE, family name of **Earl of Rosslyn.**

ST CLAIR-FORD, Sir James Anson, 7th Bt *cr* 1793, of Ember Court, Surrey; *b* 16 March 1952; *s* of Capt. Sir Aubrey St Clair-Ford, 6th Bt, DSO, RN and of Anne, *o d* of Harold Cecil Christopherson; *S* father, 1991; *m* 1st, 1977, Jennifer Margaret (marr. diss.

1984), *yr d* of Comodore Robin Grindle, RN; 2nd, 1987, Mary Anne, *er d* of His Honour Nathaniel Robert Blaker, QC. *Educ:* Wellington; Bristol Univ. *Heir: cousin* Colin Anson St Clair-Ford [*b* 19 April 1939; *m* 1964, Gillian Mary, *er d* of Rear Adm. Peter Skelton, *qv*; two *d*]. *Address:* 161 Sheen Lane, SW14 8NA.

ST CYRES, Viscount; John Stafford Northcote; *b* 15 Feb. 1957; *s* and *heir* of 4th Earl of Iddesleigh, *qv*; *m* 1983, Fiona Caroline Elizabeth, *d* of P. Wakefield, Barcelona, and Mrs M. Hattrell, Burnham, Bucks; one *s* one *d*. *Educ:* Downside Sch.; RAC Cirencester. *Heir: s* Hon. Thomas Stafford Northcote, *b* 5 Aug. 1985. *Address:* Hayne Barton, Newton St Cyres, Devon EX5 5AH.

ST DAVIDS, 3rd Viscount *cr* 1918; **Colwyn Jestyn John Philipps;** Baron Strange of Knokin, 1299; Baron Hungerford, 1426; Baron de Moleyns, 1445; Bt 1621; Baron St Davids, 1908; *b* 30 Jan. 1939; *s* of 2nd Viscount St Davids and Doreen Guinness (*d* 1956), *o d* of late Captain Arthur Jowett; *S* father, 1991; *m* 1965, Augusta Victoria Correa Larrain, *d* of late Don Estantislao Correa Ugarte; two *s*. *Educ:* Sevenoaks Sch.; King's Coll., London (Cert. Advanced Musical Studies, 1989). Nat. Service, 1958–60; commnd 2nd Lt Welsh Guards. Securities Agency Ltd, 1960–65; Mem., Stock Exchange, 1965; investment analyst, Maguire Kingsmill and Co., 1968; Partner, Kemp-Gee and Co., later Scrimgeour Kemp-Gee and Co., 1971; Dir, Citicorp Scrimgeour Vickers (Securities) Ltd, 1985–88; Dir, 1989–90, Consultant, 1991–, Greig Middleton & Co. Ltd. Mem., Baden-Powell Fellowship, 1985–. Liveryman, Musicians' Co., 1971–. *Recreations:* music, literature, natural sciences. *Heir: s* Hon. Rhodri Colwyn Philipps, *b* 16 Sept. 1966. *Address:* House of Lords, SW1A 0PW. *Club:* City of London.

ST DAVIDS, Bishop of, since 1991; **Rt. Rev. (John) Ivor Rees;** *b* 19 Feb. 1926; *o s* of David Morgan Rees and Cecilia Perrott Rees; *m* 1954, Beverley Richards; three *s*. *Educ:* Llanelli Gram. Sch.; University Coll. of Wales (BA 1950); Westcott House, Cambridge. Served RN, Coastal Forces and British Pacific Fleet, 1943–47. Deacon 1952, priest 1953, Dio. St David's; Curate: Fishguard, 1952–55; Llangathen, 1955–57; Priest-in-Charge, Uzmaston, 1957–59; Vicar: Slebech and Uzmaston, 1959–65; Llangollen, 1965–74; Rural Dean of Llangollen, 1970–74; Rector of Wrexham, 1974–76; Dean of Bangor, 1976–88; Vicar of Cathedral Parish of Bangor, 1979–88; Archdeacon of St Davids and Asst Bp, Dio. of St Davids, 1988–91. Canon of St Asaph, 1975–76; Chaplain, Order of St John for County of Clwyd, 1974–76, County of Gwynedd, 1976–88. SBStJ 1975, OStJ 1981. *Publications:* Monograph—The Parish of Llangollen and its Churches, 1971; Keeping 40 Days—Sermons for Lent, 1989. *Recreations:* music and good light reading. *Address:* Llys Esgob, Abergwili, Carmarthen, Dyfed SA31 2JG. *T:* Carmarthen (0267) 236597.

ST DAVIDS, Dean of; *see* Lewis, Very Rev. B.

ST DAVIDS, Archdeacon of; *no new appointment at time of going to press.*

ST EDMUNDSBURY, Provost of; *see* Furnell, Very Rev. R.

ST EDMUNDSBURY AND IPSWICH, Bishop of, since 1986; **Rt. Rev. John Dennis;** *b* 19 June 1931; *s* of late Hubert Ronald and Evelyn Dennis; *m* 1956, Dorothy Mary (*née* Hinnels); two *s*. *Educ:* Rutlish School, Merton; St Catharine's Coll., Cambridge (BA 1954; MA 1959); Cuddesdon Coll., Oxford (1954–56). RAF, 1950–51. Curate, St Bartholomew's, Armley, Leeds, 1956–60; Curate of Kettering, 1960–62; Vicar of the Isle of Dogs, 1962–71; Vicar of John Keble, Mill Hill, 1971–79; Area Dean of West Barnet, 1973–79; Prebendary of St Paul's Cathedral, 1977–79; Bishop Suffragan of Knaresborough, 1979–86; Diocesan Dir of Ordinands, Dio. Ripon, 1980–86. Episcopal Guardian of Anglican Focolarini, 1981–; Chaplain to Franciscan Third Order, 1988–. Co-Chairman: English ARC, 1988–; Anglican-Oriental Orthodox Dialogue, 1989–. *Recreations:* walking, gardening, wood working. *Address:* Bishop's House, 4 Park Road, Ipswich IP1 3ST. *T:* Ipswich (0473) 252829. *Club:* Royal Air Force.

ST GEORGE, Sir George (Bligh), 9th Bt *cr* 1766 (Ire.), of Athlone, Co. Westmeath; *b* 23 Sept. 1908; *s* of Sir Theophilus John St George, 6th Bt and Florence Emma Vanderplank; *S* brother, 1989; *m* 1935, Mary Somerville, *d* of John Francis Fearly Sutcliffe; two *s* three *d*. *Educ:* Christian Bros Coll., Kimberley; Natal Univ. (BA). Natal Provincial Administration, 1929–73, last appointment Asst Dir (Admin), Addington Hospital, Durban. *Recreations:* music, bowls. *Heir: s* John Avenel Bligh [*b* 18 March 1940; *m* 1st, 1962, Margaret Carter (marr. diss. 1979); two *d*; 2nd, 1981, Linda, *d* of Robert Perry; two *s*]. *Address:* Hatley Cottage, 28 Waterfall Gardens Village, Private Bag X01, Link Hills 3652, Natal, South Africa. *T:* (031) 7633299.

ST GERMANS, 10th Earl of, *cr* 1815; **Peregrine Nicholas Eliot;** Baron Eliot 1784; *b* 2 Jan. 1941; *o s* of 9th Earl of St Germans, and Helen Mary (*d* 1951), *d* of late Lieut-Col Charles Walter Villiers, CBE, DSO, and Lady Kathleen Villiers; *S* father, 1988; *m* 1964, Hon. Jacquetta Jean Frederika Lampson (marr. diss. 1989), *d* of 1st Baron Killearn and Jacqueline Aldine Lesley (*née* Castellani); three *s*. *Educ:* Eton. *Recreation:* mucking about. *Heir: s* Lord Eliot, *q.v.* *Address:* Port Eliot, St Germans, Cornwall. *Clubs:* Pratt's; Cornish Club 1768.

ST GERMANS, Bishop Suffragan of, since 1985; **Rt. Rev. John Richard Allan Llewellin;** *b* 30 Sept. 1938; *s* of John Clarence Llewellin and Margaret Gwenllian Llewellin; *m* 1965, Jennifer Sally (*née* House); one *s* two *d*. *Educ:* Clifton College, Bristol; Westcott House and Fitzwilliam Coll., Cambridge (MA). Solicitor, 1960. Ordained deacon, 1964; priest, 1965; Curate at Radlett, Herts, 1964–68; Curate at Johannesburg Cathedral, 1968–71; Vicar of Waltham Cross, 1971–79; Rector of Harpenden, 1979–85. *Recreations:* sailing; DIY. *Address:* 32 Falmouth Road, Truro TR1 2HX. *T:* Truro (0872) 73190.

ST HELENA, Bishop of, since 1991; **Rt. Rev. John Harry Gerald Ruston,** OGS; *b* 1 Oct. 1929; *s* of late Alfred Francis Gerald Ruston and of Constance Mary (*née* Symonds). *Educ:* Berkhamsted Sch.; Sidney Sussex Coll., Cambridge (BA 1952; MA 1956); Ely Theol Coll. Ordained deacon 1954, priest 1955; Asst Curate, St Andrew's, Leicester, 1954–57; Tutor, Cuddesdon Coll., Oxford, 1957–61; Asst Curate, All Saints, Cuddesdon, 1957–61; Asst Priest, St Francis, Sekhukhuniland, Transvaal, dio. of Pretoria, 1962–70; Principal, St Francis's Coll., Sekhukhuniland, 1967–70; Canon, Pretoria, 1968–76; Sub-Dean, Pretoria, 1970–76; Archdeacon of Bloemfontein, 1976–83; Warden, Community of St Michael and All Angels, and Chaplain, St Michael's Sch., Bloemfontein, 1976–83; consecrated Bishop, 1983; Bishop Suffragan, Pretoria, 1983–91. *Recreation:* music (composition and adaptation for 3-part singing). *Address:* Bishopsholme, PO Box 62, Island of St Helena, South Atlantic Ocean. *T:* 290 4471, *Fax:* 290 4330.

ST HELENS, 2nd Baron *cr* 1964; **Richard Francis Hughes-Young;** *b* 4 Nov. 1945; *s* of 1st Baron St Helens, MC, and Elizabeth Agnes (*d* 1956), *y d* of late Captain Richard Blakiston-Houston; *S* father, 1980; *m* 1983, Mrs Emma R. Talbot-Smith; one *s* one *d*. *Educ:* Nautical College, Pangbourne. *Heir: s* Henry Thomas Hughes-Young, *b* 7 March 1986. *Address:* Marchfield House, Binfield, Berks.

ST JOHN, family name of **Baron St John of Bletso,** and of **Viscount Bolingbroke.**

ST JOHN OF BLETSO, 21st Baron *cr* 1558; **Anthony Tudor St John;** Bt 1660; stockbroker with Smith New Court plc, London; solicitor; *b* 16 May 1957; *s* of 20th Baron St John of Bletso, TD, and of Katharine, *d* of late A. G. von Berg; *S* father, 1978. *Educ:* Diocesan College, Rondebosch, Cape; Univ. of Cape Town (BSocSc 1977, BA (Law) 1978); Univ. of S Africa (BProc 1982); London Univ. (LLM 1983). Cross-bencher in House of Lords, specific interests foreign affairs, energy, financial services. *Recreations:* golf, tennis, surfing and ski-ing; bridge. *Heir: cousin* Edmund Oliver St John, WS [*b* 13 Oct. 1927; *m* 1959, Elizabeth Frances, *o d* of Lt-Col H. R. Nicholl; one *s* two *d*]. *Address:* 12 Collingham Gardens, SW5. *T:* 071–370 0870. *Clubs:* Royal Cape Golf, Western Province Sports.

ST JOHN OF FAWSLEY, Baron *cr* 1987 (Life Peer), of Preston Capes in the County of Northamptonshire; **Norman Antony Francis St John-Stevas;** PC 1979; FRSL 1966; Master, Emmanuel College, Cambridge, since 1991; Chairman, Royal Fine Art Commission, since 1985; author, barrister and journalist; *b* London, 18 May 1929; *o s* of late Stephen S. Stevas, civil engineer and company director, and late Kitty St John O'Connor; unmarried. *Educ:* Ratcliffe; Fitzwilliam, Cambridge (Hon. Fellow 1991); Christ Church, Oxford; Yale. Scholar, Clothworkers Exhibnr, 1946, 1947; BA (Cambridge) (1st cl. hons in law), 1950, MA 1954; President, Cambridge Union, 1950; Whitlock Prize, 1950; MA 1952, BCL 1954 (Oxon); Sec. Oxford Union, 1952. Barrister, Middle Temple, 1952; Blackstone and Harmsworth schol., 1952; Blackstone Prize, 1953. Lecturer, Southampton University, 1952–53, King's Coll., London, 1953–56, tutored in jurisprudence, Christ Church, 1953–55, and Merton, 1955–57, Oxford. Founder member, Inst. of Higher European Studies, Bolzano, 1955; PhD (Lond.) 1957; Yorke Prize, Cambridge Univ., 1957; Fellow Yale Law School, 1957; Fulbright Award, 1957; Fund for the Republic Fellow, 1958; Dr of Sc. of Law (Yale), 1960; Lecture tours of USA, 1958–68. Regents' Prof., Univ. of California at Santa Barbara, 1969; Regents' Lectr, Univ. of Calif at La Jolla, 1984. Legal Adviser to Sir Alan Herbert's Cttee on book censorship, 1954–59; joined The Economist, 1959, to edit collected works of Walter Bagehot and became legal, ecclesiastical and political correspondent. Contested (C) Dagenham, 1951. MP (C) Chelmsford, 1964–87. Mem. Shadow Cabinet, 1974–79, and Opposition Spokesman on Educn, 1975–78, Science and the Arts, 1975–79; Shadow Leader of the House, 1978–79; Parly Under-Sec. of State, DES, 1972–73; Min. of State for the Arts, DES, 1973–74; Chancellor of the Duchy of Lancaster, Leader of the House of Commons and Minister for the Arts, 1979–81. Sec., Cons. Parly Home Affairs Cttee, 1969–72; Vice-Chm., Cons. Parly N Ireland Cttee, 1972–74; Mem. Executive, Cons. Parly 1922 Cttee, 1971–72 and 1974; Vice Chm., Cons. Group for Europe, 1972–75; Member: Cons. Nat. Adv. Cttee on Policy, 1971; Fulbright Commission, 1961; Parly Select Cttee: on Race Relations and Immigration, 1970–72; on Civil List, 1971–73; on Foreign Affairs, 1983–89; Deleg., Council of Europe and WEU, 1967–71; Head, British delegn to Helsinki Cultural Forum, Budapest, 1985. Chm., New Bearings for the Re-Establishment, 1970–. Hon. Sec., Fedn of Cons. Students, 1971–73, Hon. Vice-Pres. 1973. Chm., Booker McConnell Prize, 1985. Mem. Council: RADA, 1983–88; Nat. Soc. for Dance, 1983–; Nat. Youth Theatre, 1983– (Patron, 1984–); RCA, 1985–; Mem., Pontifical Council for Culture, 1987–; Patron, Medieval Players, 1984–89; Dir, N. M. Rothschild Trust, 1990–; Trustee: Royal Philharmonic Orch., 1985–88; Philharmonic Orch., 1988–; Royal Soc. of Painters in Watercolours, 1984; Decorative Arts Soc., 1984–. Editor The Dublin (Wiseman) Review, 1961. Vice Pres., Les Amis de Napoléon III, 1974; Mem., Académie du Second Empire, 1975. Hon. FRIBA 1990; Presidential Fellow, Aspern Inst., 1980; Hon. Fellow, St Edmund's College, Cambridge, 1985. Romanes Lectr, Oxford, 1987. DD (*hc*) Univ. of Susquehanna, Pa, 1983; DLitt (*hc*): Schiller Univ., 1985; Bristol Univ., 1988; Hon. LLD Leicester, 1991. Silver Jubilee Medal, 1977. SBStJ. Gran Ufficiale, Order of Merit (Italian Republic), 1989 (Commendatore, 1965). GCKLJ 1976 (KSLJ 1963). *Publications:* Obscenity and the Law, 1956; Walter Bagehot, 1959; Life, Death and the Law, 1961; The Right to Life, 1963; Law and Morals, 1964; The Literary Works of Walter Bagehot, vols I, II, 1966, The Historical Works, vols III, IV, 1968, The Political Works, vols V, VI, VII, and VIII, 1974, The Economic Works, vols IX, X and XI, 1978, Letters and Miscellany, vols XII, XIII, XIV and XV, 1986; The Agonising Choice, 1971; Pope John Paul II, his travels and mission, 1982; The Two Cities, 1984; contrib. to: Critical Quarterly, Modern Law Review, Criminal Law Review, Law and Contemporary Problems, Twentieth Century, Times Lit. Supp., Dublin Review. *Recreations:* reading, talking, listening (to music), travelling, walking, appearing on television, sleeping. *Address:* The Master's Lodge, Emmanuel College, Cambridge CB2 3AP; The Old Rectory, Preston Capes, Daventry, Northants. *Clubs:* White's, Garrick, Pratt's, Arts (Hon. Mem., 1980), Grillions, The Other.

ST JOHN, Oliver Beauchamp, CEng, FRAeS; Chief Scientist, Civil Aviation Authority, 1978–82; *b* 22 Jan. 1922; 2nd *s* of late Harold and Ella Margaret St John; *m* 1945, Eileen (*née* Morris); three *s*. *Educ:* Monkton Combe Sch.; Queens Coll., Cambridge (MA); London Univ. (External) (BSc). Metropolitan Vickers, Manchester, 1939; Royal Aircraft Estabt, Farnborough, from 1946, on automatic control of fixed-wing aircraft and helicopters; Supt, Blind Landing Experimental Unit, RAE, Bedford, 1966; Director of Technical Research & Development, CAA, 1969–78. Queen's Commendation for Valuable Services in the Air, 1956. *Publication:* A Gallimaufry of Goffering: a history of early ironing implements, 1982. *Recreations:* mountaineering, skiing, early music, instrument making. *Address:* The Old Stables, Manor Farm Barns, East Hagbourne OX11 9ND. *T:* Didcot (0235) 818437. *Club:* Alpine.

ST JOHN, Maj.-Gen. Roger Ellis Tudor, CB 1965; MC 1944; *b* Hexham on Tyne, 4 Oct. 1911; *s* of late Major B. T. St John, Craigveigh, Aboyne, Aberdeenshire; *m* 1943, Rosemary Jean Douglas Vickers, Englefield Green, Surrey; one *s* three *d*. *Educ:* Wellington College; RMC Sandhurst. Joined Fifth Fusiliers, 1931; served War of 1939–45 (despatches, MC), in Hong Kong, UK and NW Europe; Bde Major 11 Armoured Div., 1944–45; GSO 2 Instructor Camberley Staff Coll., 1945–46; AA and QMG 1st Division, Tripoli, 1948–50; comd 1st Bn Royal Northumberland Fusiliers, 1953–55 (despatches), Mau Mau Rebellion; AMS Mil. Secretary's Branch, War Office, 1955–57; Comdr 11 Inf. Bde Group, BAOR, 1957–60; Asst Comdt, Camberley Staff Coll., 1960–62; Comdr, British Army Staff, Military Member, British Defence Staffs, and Military Attaché, Washington, 1963–65; President, Regular Army Commissions Board, 1965–67; retired, 1967. Colonel, Royal Northumberland Fusiliers, 1965–68. Personnel Adminr, Urwick, Orr and Partners Ltd, Management Consultants, 1967–73. *Address:* Harelaw, Gorse Hill Road, Virginia Water, Surrey GU25 4AS.

ST JOHN PARKER, Michael, MA (Cantab); Headmaster, Abingdon School, Oxfordshire, since 1975; *b* 21 July 1941; *s* of Rev. Canon J. W. Parker; *m* 1965, Annette Monica Ugle; two *s* two *d*. *Educ:* Stamford Sch.; King's Coll., Cambridge. Asst Master: Sevenoaks Sch., 1962–63; King's Sch., Canterbury, 1963–69; Winchester Coll., 1969–75; Head of History Dept, Winchester Coll., 1970–75. Schoolmaster Student, Christ Church, Oxford, 1984. Member: Council, Hansard Soc., 1972–; Marsh Cttee on Politics and Industry, 1978–79. Chm., Midland Div., HMC, 1984. Governor: St Helen's Sch., 1975–83; Christ Church Cathedral Sch.; Cokethorpe Sch. (Chm., 1990); Josca's Sch. *Publications:* The British Revolution—Social and Economic History 1750–1970, 1972;

various pamphlets and articles. *Recreations:* old buildings, music, books. *Address:* Lacies Court, Abingdon, Oxfordshire. *T:* Abingdon (0235) 520163. *Clubs:* East India, Devonshire, Sports and Public Schools; Leander.

ST JOHN-STEVAS, family name of **Baron St John of Fawsley.**

ST JOHN WILSON, Colin Alexander; *see* Wilson.

ST JOHN'S (Newfoundland), Archbishop of, (RC), since 1979; **Most Rev. Alphonsus Liguori Penney;** *b* 17 Sept. 1924; *s* of Alphonsus Penney and Catherine Penney (*née* Mullaly). *Educ:* St Bonaventure's Coll., St John's, Newfoundland; University Seminary, Ottawa (LPh, LTh). Assistant Priest: St Joseph's Parish, St John's, 1950–56; St Patrick's Parish, St John's, 1956; Parish Priest: Marystown, Placentia Bay, Newfoundland, 1957; Basilica Parish, St John's, 1969. Prelate of Honour, 1971. Bishop of Grand Falls, Newfoundland, 1972. Hon. LLD, Memorial Univ. of Newfoundland, 1980. Confederation Medal, 1967. *Recreations:* walking, golf. *Address:* Basilica Residence, PO Box 37, St John's, Newfoundland A1C 5H5, Canada. *T:* 709–726–3660.

ST JOHNSTON, Colin David; Managing Director, PRO NED (Promotion of Non-Executive Directors), since 1989; *b* 6 Sept. 1934; *s* of Hal and Sheilagh St Johnston; *m* 1958, Valerie Paget; three *s* one *d*. *Educ:* Shrewsbury Sch.; Lincoln Coll., Oxford. Booker McConnell Ltd, 1958–70; Ocean Transport and Trading Ltd, 1970–88: Dir, 1974–88; Dep. Chief Exec., 1987–88; non-Executive Director, FMC plc, 1981–83. Mem. Council: Royal Commonwealth Society for the Blind, 1967–; Industrial Soc., 1981–; Trustee, Frances Mary Buss Foundn, 1981–; Governor, Camden Sch., 1974–. *Recreations:* music, Real and lawn tennis. *Address:* 30 Fitzroy Road, NW1 8TY. *T:* 071–722 5932. *Club:* MCC.

ST JOHNSTON, Sir Kerry, Kt 1988; Chairman, Wilrig AS, Norway; Managing Director, Diehl and St Johnston Ltd, since 1989; *b* 30 July 1931; *s* of George Eric St Johnston and Viola Rhona Moriarty; *m* 1st, 1960, Judith Ann Nichols; two *s* one *d*; 2nd, 1980, Charlotte Ann Taylor. *Educ:* Summer Fields, Oxford; Eton Coll.; Worcester Coll., Oxford (MA Jurisprudence). Joined Ocean Steamship Co. Ltd, 1955, Man. Dir 1963; Overseas Containers Ltd: Founder Dir, 1965; Commerical Dir, 1966; Jt Man. Dir, 1969; Dep. Chm., 1973; Pres. and Chief Exec. Officer, Private Investment Co. for Asia (PICA), SA, Singapore, 1977–82; Chm. and Chief Exec., P & O (formerly Overseas) Containers Ltd, 1982–89. Director: Royal Insurance, 1973–76; Lloyds Bank Internat. Ltd, 1983–85; P&OSNCo., 1986–89. Pres., Gen. Council of British Shipping, 1987–88. *Recreations:* trout fishing, gardening. *Address:* Flat 5, 53 Drayton Gardens, SW10 9RX. *T:* 071–373 3947. *Club:* Boodle's.

ST JOSEPH, Prof. John Kenneth Sinclair, CBE 1979 (OBE 1964); FBA 1978; Professor of Aerial Photographic Studies, University of Cambridge, and Fellow of Selwyn College, since 1939 (Senior Fellow, since 1989, Professorial Fellow, 1973–80), Professor Emeritus since 1980; *b* 1912; *s* of late John D. St Joseph and of Irma Robertson (*née* Marris); *m* 1945, Daphne Margaret, *d* of late H. March, Worcester; two *s* two *d*. *Educ:* Bromsgrove Sch.; Selwyn Coll., Cambridge (Scholar). BA 1934, PhD 1937, MA 1938, LittD 1976. Harkness Scholar, 1934; Goldsmiths' Company Senior Student, 1935–37; DSIR Sen. Research Award, 1936–37; Lectr in Natural Sciences, Selwyn Coll., and Dean, 1939–62; Tutor, 1945–62; Librarian, 1946–62; Vice Master, 1974–80; Univ. Demonstrator in Geology, 1937–45; Operational Research, Min. of Aircraft Production, 1942–45; Univ. Lectr in Geology, 1945–48; Leverhulme Research Fellow, 1948–49; Curator in Aerial Photography at Cambridge, 1948–62; Dir in Aerial Photography, 1962–80. Has undertaken aerial reconnaissance and photography, in aid of research, over the United Kingdom, Ireland, Denmark, the Netherlands and Northern France. Governor, Stratton Sch., Biggleswade, 1952–64; Hon. Corresp. Mem., German Archæological Inst., 1964–; Member: Council for British Archaeology, 1944–; Ancient Monuments Bd (England), 1969–84; Royal Commn on Historical Monuments (England), 1972–81; Council, British Acad., 1980–83; Vice-Pres., Soc. for Promotion of Roman Studies, 1975–; Hon. Vice-Pres., Royal Archaeological Inst., 1982–. Lectures: Chatwin Meml, Birmingham, 1969; David Murray, Glasgow Univ., 1973; Kroon, Amsterdam Univ., 1981. Cuthbert Peek Award, RGS, 1976; President's Award, Inst. of Incorporated Photographers, 1977. FGS 1937; FSAScot 1940; FSA 1944; Hon. ScD Trinity Coll., Dublin; Hon. LLD Dundee, 1971; Dr *hc* in Maths and Science, Amsterdam, 1982. *Publications:* The Pentameracea of the Oslo Region, 1939; chapters in The Roman Occupation of SW Scotland (ed S. N. Miller), 1945; Monastic Sites from the Air (with M. C. Knowles), 1952; Medieval England, an aerial survey (with M. W. Beresford), 1958, 2nd rev. edn, 1979; (ed) The Uses of Air Photography, 1966, 2nd rev. edn 1977; The Early Development of Irish Society (with E. R. Norman), 1970; Roman Britain from the Air (with S. S. Frere), 1983; chapters in Inchtuthil: the Roman legionary fortress (ed S. S. Frere), 1985; papers in learned jls on fossil Silurian Brachiopoda, and on aerial photography and archæology, especially of Roman Britain. *Recreations:* gardening, lumbering. *Address:* Selwyn College, Cambridge CB3 9DQ. *T:* Cambridge (0223) 335846; Histon Manor, Cambridge CB4 4JJ. *T:* Cambridge (0223) 232383.

SAINT LAURENT, Yves (Henri Donat Mathieu); Officier de la Légion d'Honneur, 1985; couturier; *b* 1 Aug. 1936; *s* of Charles Mathieu and Lucienne-Andrée (Wilbaux) Mathieu Saint Laurent. *Educ:* Lycée d'Oran. Collaborator, 1954, then successor of Christian Dior, 1957–60; Dir, Société Yves Saint Laurent, 1962–. *Exhibitions:* Metropolitan Mus. of Art, NY, 1983; Fine Arts Mus., Beijing, 1985; Musée des Arts de la Mode, Paris, 1986; House of Painters of the USSR, Moscow, 1986; Hermitage Mus., Leningrad, 1987; Art Gall. of NSW, Sydney, 1987; Sezon Mus. of Art, Tokyo, 1990. *Costume design: for opera,* Le Mariage de Figaro, 1964; *for ballet:* Cyrano de Bergerac, 1959; Adage et Variations, 1965; Notre Dame de Paris, 1965; Delicate Balance, 1967; Scheherazade, 1973; *for films:* The Pink Panther, 1962; Belle de Jour, 1967; La Chamade, 1968; La Sirène du Mississippi, 1969; L'affaire Stavisky, 1974; *stage sets and costumes:* Les Chants de Maldoror, 1962; Spectacle Zizi Jeanmaire, 1961, 1963, 1968; Revue Zizi Jeanmaire, 1970, 1972, 1977; L'Aigle à deux têtes, 1978. Neiman-Marcus Award for fashion, 1958; Oscar from Harper's Bazaar, 1966; Internat. Award, Council of Fashion Designers of America, 1982; Best Fashion Designer Oscar, 1985. *Publication:* La Vilaine Lulu, 1967. *Address:* (office) 5 avenue Marceau, 75116 Paris; (home) 55 rue de Babylone, 75007 Paris, France.

ST LEGER, family name of **Viscount Doneraile.**

ST LEVAN, 4th Baron *cr* 1887; **John Francis Arthur St Aubyn,** DSC 1942; DL; Bt 1866; landowner and company director; *b* 23 Feb. 1919; *s* of 3rd Baron St Levan, and of Hon. Clementina Gwendolen Catharine Nicolson, *o d* of 1st Baron Carnock; *S* father, 1978; *m* 1970, Susan Maria Marcia, *d* of late Maj.-Gen. Sir John Kennedy, GCMG, KCVO, KBE, CB. *Educ:* Eton Coll.; Trinity Coll., Cambridge (BA). Admitted a Solicitor, 1948. High Sheriff of Cornwall, 1974; DL Cornwall, 1977. President: Friends of Plymouth City Museums and Art Gallery, 1985–; London Cornish Assoc., 1987–; Penwith NT Assoc.,1987; Penzance YMCA, 1987; St Ives Soc. of Artists, 1979; Vice President: Royal Bath and West and Southern Counties Soc. (Pres., 1983); Royal Cornwall Agricl Assoc. (Pres., 1979). FRSA 1974. CStJ 1990. *Publication:* Illustrated History of St Michael's Mount, 1974. *Recreation:* sailing. *Heir:* *b* Hon. (Oliver) Piers St Aubyn, MC [*b* 12 July 1920; *m* 1948, Mary (*d* 1987), *e d* of late Bailey Southwell; two *s* one *d*]. *Address:* St Michael's Mount, Marazion, Cornwall. *Clubs:* Brooks's; Royal Yacht Squadron.

ST OSWALD, 5th Baron *cr* 1885; **Derek Edward Anthony Winn;** DL; *b* 9 July 1919; *s* of 3rd Baron St Oswald and Eve Carew (*d* 1976), *d* of Charles Greene; *S* brother, 1984; *m* 1954, Charlotte Denise Eileen, *d* of Wilfred Haig Loyd; one *s* one *d*. *Educ:* Stowe. Joined 60th Rifles, KRRC, as 2nd Lieut, 1938; Parachute Regt, 1942; served N Africa (wounded). Malayan Police, 1948–51. Film Producer, 1953–67. Farm owner, Nostell Priory. President: Royal British Legion (S and W Yorks), 1985–; Wakefield Parachute Regt, 1985–; Wakefield Hospice, 1985–; Wakefield Multiple Sclerosis Soc., 1985–. DL W Yorks, 1987. *Publication:* I Served Caesar, 1972. *Recreation:* shooting. *Heir:* *s* Hon. Charles Rowland Andrew Winn [*b* 22 July 1959; *m* 1985, Louise Alexandra, *yr d* of Stewart Scott; one *s*]. *Address:* Nostell Priory, Wakefield, Yorks. *T:* Wakefield (0924) 862394; The Old Rectory, Bainton, Driffield, East Yorks. *Clubs:* Lansdowne, Special Forces.

ST PAUL'S, Dean of; *see* Evans, Very Rev. T. E.

ST VINCENT, 7th Viscount (*cr* 1801); **Ronald George James Jervis;** *b* 3 May 1905; *o* surv. *s* of 6th Viscount and Marion Annie (*d* 1911), *d* of James Brown, JP, Orchard, Carluke, Scotland; *S* father, 1940; *m* 1945, Phillida, *o d* of Lt-Col R. H. Logan, Taunton; two *s* one *d*. *Educ:* Sherborne. JP Somerset, 1950–55. *Heir:* *s* Hon. Edward Robert James Jervis [*b* 12 May 1951; *m* 1977, Victoria Margaret, *o d* of Wilton J. Oldham, St Peter, Jersey; one *s* one *d*]. *Address:* Les Charrieres, St Ouen, Jersey, CI.

ST VINCENT FERRERI, Marquis of; *see* San Vincenzo Ferreri.

SAINTONGE, Rolland A. A. C. de; *see* Chaput de Saintonge.

SAINTY, Sir John Christopher, KCB 1986; Clerk of the Parliaments, 1983–90, retired; *b* 31 Dec. 1934; *s* of late Christopher Lawrence Sainty and Nancy Lee Sainty (*née* Miller); *m* 1965, (Elizabeth) Frances Sherlock; three *s*. *Educ:* Winchester Coll.; New Coll., Oxford (MA). FSA; FRHistS. Clerk, Parlt Office, House of Lords, 1959; seconded as Private Sec. to Leader of House and Chief Whip, House of Lords, 1963; Clerk of Journals, House of Lords, 1965; Res. Asst and Editor, Inst. of Historical Research, 1970; Reading Clerk, House of Lords, 1974. Mem., Royal Commn on Historical MSS, 1991–. *Publications:* Treasury Officials 1660–1870, 1972; Officials of the Secretaries of State 1660–1782, 1973; Officials of the Boards of Trade 1660–1870, 1974; Admiralty Officials 1660–1870, 1975; Home Office Officials, 1782–1870, 1975; Colonial Office Officials 1794–1870, 1976; (with D. Dewar) Divisions in the House of Lords: an analytical list 1685–1857, 1976; Officers of the Exchequer, 1983; A List of English Law Officers, King's Counsel and Holders of Patents of Precedence, 1987; articles in Eng. Hist. Rev., Bull. Inst. Hist. Research. *Address:* 22 Kelso Place, W8 5QG. *T:* 071–937 9460.

SALAM, Professor Abdus, Hon. KBE 1989; Sitara-i-Pakistan, 1959; Order of Nishan-i-Imtiaz, Pakistan, 1979; PhD; FRS 1959; Professor of Theoretical Physics at the Imperial College in the University of London, since 1957; Director, International Centre for Theoretical Physics, Trieste, since 1964; *b* 29 Jan. 1926. *Educ:* Govt Coll., Lahore, Pakistan (MA); St John's Coll., Camb. (BA, PhD). Fellow, St John's Coll., Cambridge, 1951–56 (Hon. Fellow, 1972); Professor of Mathematics, Government College, Lahore, 1951–54; Lecturer in Mathematics, University of Cambridge, 1954–56. Sci. Advr to Pres. of Pakistan, 1961–74. Has made contributions to the theory of elementary particles. Member: UN Adv. Cttee on Science and Technology, 1964–75 (Chm., 1971–72); South Commn, 1987–; Vice-Pres., IUPAP, 1972–78. Founding Mem. and Pres., Third World Acad. of Scis, 1983; (first elected) Pres., Third World Network of Scientific Orgns, 1988–; Fellow, Royal Swedish Acad. of Sciences, 1970; For. Mem., USSR Acad. of Scis, 1971. Hon. DSc, universities in: Punjab (Lahore), 1957; Edinburgh, 1971; Trieste and Islamabad, 1979; Lima, Cuzco, Caracas, Wroclow, Yarmouk and Istanbul, 1980; Amritsar, Aligarh, Banaras, Chittagong, Bristol and Maiduguri, 1981; Philippines, 1982; Khartoum and Madrid, 1983; New York (City Coll.) and Nairobi, 1984; Cuyo, La Plata and Göteborg, 1985; Sofia, Glasgow, Hefei and London (City Univ.), 1986; Punjab (Chandigarh), Benin, Exeter and Colombo, 1987; Gent, 1988; Hon. ScD Cambridge, 1985. Hopkins Prize, Cambridge Philosophical Soc., 1957; Adams Prize, Cambridge Univ., 1958; Maxwell Medal and Prize, IPPS, 1961; Hughes Medal, Royal Society, 1964; Atoms for Peace Award, 1968; Oppenheimer Prize and Medal, 1971; Guthrie Medal and Prize, IPPS, 1976; Matteuci Medal, Accad. Naz. di XL, Rome, 1978; John Torrence Tate Medal, Amer. Inst. of Physics, 1978; Royal Medal, Royal Society, 1978; (jtly) Nobel Prize for Physics, 1979; Einstein Medal, UNESCO, Paris, 1979; Josef Stefan Medal, Josef Stefan Inst., Ljubljana, 1980; Gold Medal for outstanding contrib. to physics, Czechoslovak Acad. of Scis, Prague, 1981; Peace Medal, Charles Univ., Prague, 1981; Lomonosov Gold Medal, USSR Acad. of Scis, 1983; Edinburgh Medal and Prize, 1988; Genoa Internat. Develt of People's Prize, 1988. *Publications:* (ed with E. P. Wigner) Aspects of Quantum Mechanics, 1972; Ideals and Realities: selected essays, 1984, 2nd edn 1987; Science and Education in Pakistan, 1987; (with Ergin Sezgin) Supergravity in Diverse Dimensions, Vols I and II, 1988; (ed) From a Life of Physics, 1989; papers on physics of elementary particles and on scientific and educnl policies for developing countries and Pakistan; *relevant publication:* Abdus Salam, by Dr Abdul Ghani, 1982. *Address:* Imperial College of Science, Technology and Medicine, Prince Consort Road, SW7; International Centre for Theoretical Physics, PO Box 586, 34100 Trieste, Italy.

SALAMAN, Myer Head, MD; Research Pathologist, Royal College of Surgeons, 1968–74; *b* 2 August 1902; *e s* of Redcliffe N. Salaman, MD, FRS and Nina Salaman; *m* 1926, Esther Polianowsky; one *s* three *d*. *Educ:* Clifton College; Bedales School; Trinity College, Cambridge; London Hospital Medical College. Natural Science Tripos Pts I and II, Cambridge, 1921–25; London Hosp.: Clinical training, 1927–30; House Appts, 1931–32; Research on Viruses, 1932–34, and Lister Inst. (Junior Beit Mem. Fellow) 1935–38; Cancer Research, St Bartholomew's Hosp., 1939; Asst Pathologist, Emergency Public Health Service, 1940–42; Cancer and Virus Research, Strangeways Lab., 1942–43; Temp. Major, RAMC, 1943–46. Engaged in Cancer Research at the London Hospital, 1946–48; Dir, Dept of Cancer Research, London Hosp. Med. Sch., 1948–67; engaged in Cancer Research at RCS, 1968–74. MA 1926, MD 1936 Cantab; MRCS, LRCP, 1930; Dipl. Bact. London, 1936. FRSocMed. *Publications:* papers on virus diseases, and on cancer, in Jour. Pathology and Bacteriology, Proc. Roy. Soc. (B), Brit. Jl Cancer, etc. *Recreations:* reading, writing. *Address:* 23 Bisham Gardens, Highgate, N6 6DJ. *T:* 081–340 1019. *Club:* Athenæum.

See also Prof. H. B. Barlow.

SALAS, Dame Margaret Laurence, (Dame Laurie), DBE 1988; QSO 1982; *b* 8 Feb. 1922; *d* of Sir James Lawrence Hay, OBE and late Davidina Mertel (née Gunn); *m* 1946, Dr John Reuben Salas, FRCSE, FRACS; two *s* four *d*. *Educ:* Christchurch; Univ. of New Zealand (BA). Teacher, audiometrist in Med. practice. National Council of Women of NZ: legislative and parly work; Nat. Sec., 1976–80; Nat. Vice-Pres., 1982–86; Vice-Convener, Internat. Council, Women's Cttee on Develt; Nat. Sec., Women's Internat. League for Peace and Freedom, 1985–90; Pres., UN Assoc. of NZ, 1988–; Member:

Public Adv. Cttee, Disarmament and Arms Control, 1987–; Nat. Cons. Cttee on Disarmament (Chair, 1979–90); Adv. Cttee, External Aid and Develt, 1986–88; Standing Cttee, NZ Inst. of Internat. Affairs, 1989–; Educn Cttee, Alcoholic Liquor Adv. Council, 1976–81; Nat. Review Cttee on Social Studies, Educn Dept; Cttee, SCF, 1970–76; Nat. Commn, UN Internat. Year of the Child, 1978–80; UN Internat. Year of Peace, Aotearoa Cttee, (Vice-Chair, 1986). Pres., Wellington Branch, NZ Fedn of Univ. Women, 1970–72; repr. NZ, overseas meetings. Silver Jubilee Medal, 1977; NZ Commemoration Medal, 1990. *Publication:* Disarmament, 1982. *Recreations:* choral and classical music, enjoying extended family. *Address:* 2 Raumati Terrace, Khandallah, Wellington 4, New Zealand. *T:* (04) 793 415.

See also Sir David Hay, Sir Hamish Hay.

SALEM, Daniel Laurent Manuel; Chairman, The Condé Nast Publications Ltd, London, since 1968; Chairman, Condé Nast International Inc., since 1971; Deputy Chairman, The Condé Nast Publications Inc., New York, since 1986 (Vice President, 1965–86); *b* 29 Jan. 1925; *s* of Raphael Salem and Adriana Gentili di Giuseppe; *m* 1950, Marie-Pierre Arachtingi. *Educ:* Harvard Univ., Cambridge, Mass (BA, MA). Served Free French Forces, 1943–45. Exec. Asst, Lazard Frères & Co., New York, 1946–50; exec. positions, The Condé Nast Publications Inc., New York, 1950–60; Vice Pres., Banque Paribas, Paris, 1961–65. Chairman: Mercury Selected Trust, 1974–; Mercury Offshore Selected Trust, 1979–; Philharmonia Trust Ltd, 1985–. Chevalier, Legion of Honour (France), 1987; Comnmendatore, Order of Merit (Italy), 1988. *Recreations:* music, bridge, chess, golf. *Address:* 3 Ennismore Gardens, SW7 1NL. *T:* 071–584 0466. *Clubs:* White's, Portland; Harvard (New York City).

SALFORD, Bishop of, (RC), since 1984; **Rt. Rev. Patrick Altham Kelly;** *b* 23 Nov. 1938; *s* of John Joseph Kelly and Mary Ann Kelly (née Altham). *Educ:* St Mary's Primary School, Morecambe; Preston Catholic Coll.; English College and Gregorian Univ., Rome (STL, PhL). Curate, Lancaster Cathedral, 1964–66; Lectr in Theology, 1966–79 and Rector, 1979–84, St Mary's Coll., Oscott. *Address:* Wardley Hall, Worsley, Manchester M28 5ND.

SALINGER, Jerome David; American author; *b* New York City, 1919; *m;* one *s* one *d.* *Educ:* Manhattan public schools; Military Academy, Paris. Served with 4th Infantry Division, US Army, 1942–46 (Staff Sergeant). Travelled in Europe, 1937–38. Started writing at age of 15; first story published, 1940. *Publications:* The Catcher in the Rye, 1951; For Esme-with Love and Squalor, 1953; Franny and Zooey, 1962; Raise High the Roof Beam, Carpenters and Seymour: an Introduction, 1963. *Address:* c/o Harold Ober Associates, 425 Madison Avenue, New York, NY 10017, USA.

SALINGER, Pierre (Emil George); politician, journalist; Chief Foreign Correspondent, since 1983, and Senior Editor, Europe, since 1988, ABC News, American Broadcasting Company; *b* San Francisco, 14 June 1925; *s* of Herbert and Jehanne Salinger; *m* 1st; one *s* one *d;* 2nd, 1957, Nancy Brook Joy (marr. diss., 1965); 3rd, 1965, Nicole Gillmann (marr. diss. 1988), Paris, France; one *s;* 4th, 1989, Nicole Beauvillain. *Educ:* Lowell High School, San Francisco; State Coll., San Francisco; Univ. of San Francisco. Served War, 1942–45, with US Navy. With San Francisco Chronicle, 1942–55; Guest Lectr, Mills Coll., Calif, 1950–55; Press Officer, Democratic Presidential Campaign (Calif), 1952; West Coast Editor, Contributing Editor, Collier's Magazine, 1955–56; Investigator, Senate Labor Rackets Cttee, 1957–59; Press Sec. to President Kennedy (when Senator), 1959–61, and to President of the United States, 1961–64; appointed to serve as a US Senator, 4 Aug. 1964–2 Jan. 1965; Roving Editor, L'Express, Paris, 1973–78; Correspondent, Paris, 1978–79, Paris Bureau Chief, 1979–87, ABC News. Vice Pres.: Continental Airlines, Continental Air Services, 1965–68. Trustee, Robert F. Kennedy Meml Foundn; Hon. Chm., Bd of Trustees, American Coll. in Paris. Mem., Legion of Honour, 1978; US Navy and Marine Corps Medal, 1946. *Publications:* articles on county jail conditions in California, 1953; A Tribute to John F. Kennedy, Encyclopedia Britannica, 1964; With Kennedy, 1966; A Tribute to Robert F. Kennedy, 1968; For the Eyes of the President Only, 1971; Je suis un Americain, 1975; La France et le Nouveau Monde, 1976; America Held Hostage—the secret negotiations, 1981; (with Leonard Gross) The Dossier, 1984; (with Robert Cameron) Above Paris, 1985; (with Leonard Gross) Mortal Games, 1988; (with Eric Laurent) La Guerre du Golfe: le dossier secret, 1990. *Address:* c/o ABC News, 8 Carburton Street, W1P 7DT.

SALISBURY, 6th Marquess of, *cr* 1789; **Robert Edward Peter Cecil;** DL; Baron Cecil, 1603; Viscount Cranborne, 1604; Earl of Salisbury, 1605; Captain Grenadier Guards; High Steward of Hertford since 1972; *b* 24 Oct. 1916; *s* of 5th Marquess of Salisbury, KG, PC, FRS, and Elizabeth Vere (*d* 1982), *e d* of late Lord Richard Cavendish, PC, CB, CMG; *S* father, 1972; *m* 1945, Marjorie Olein (Mollie), *d* of late Captain Hon. Valentine Wyndham-Quin, RN; four *s* one *d* (and one *s* decd). MP (C) Bournemouth West, 1950–54. Pres., Monday Club, 1974–81. DL Dorset, 1974. *Heir: s* Viscount Cranborne, *qv.* *Address:* Hatfield House, Hatfield, Herts.

See also Dowager Duchess of Devonshire.

SALISBURY, Bishop of, since 1982; **Rt. Rev. John Austin Baker;** *b* 11 Jan. 1928; *s* of George Austin Baker and Grace Edna Baker; *m* 1974, Gillian Mary Leach. *Educ:* Marlborough; Oriel Coll., Oxford (MA, MLitt). Asst Curate, All Saints', Cuddesdon, and Lectr in Old Testament, Cuddesdon Theol Coll., 1954–57; Priest 1955; Asst Curate, St Anselm's, Hatch End, and Asst Lectr in NT Greek, King's Coll., London, 1957–59; Official Fellow, Chaplain and Lectr in Divinity, Corpus Christi Coll., Oxford, 1959–73, Emeritus Fellow, 1977; Lectr in Theology, Brasenose and Lincoln Colls, Oxford, 1959–73; Hebrew Lectr, Exeter Coll., Oxford, 1969–73; Canon of Westminster, 1973–82; Treas., 1974–78; Sub-Dean and Lector Theologiae, 1978–82; Rector of St Margaret's, Westminster, and Speaker's Chaplain, 1978–82. Governor of Pusey House, Oxford, 1970–78; Exam. Chaplain to Bp of Oxford, 1960–78, to Bp of Southwark, 1973–78. Governor: Westminster Sch., 1974–81; Ripon Coll., Cuddesdon, 1974–80; Westminster City Sch., 1978–81; Dorset Inst. of Higher Educn, 1982–86; Bishop Wordsworth's Sch., 1982–; Sherborne Sch., 1982–; Salisbury & Wells Theological Coll., 1982–; Pres. of Council, Marlborough Coll., 1982–; Trustee, Harold Buxton Trust, 1973–79. Dorrance Vis. Prof., Trinity Coll., Hartford, Conn, USA, 1967; Vis. Prof., King's Coll., London, 1974–77; Hulsean Preacher, Univ. of Cambridge, 1979; Select Preacher, Univ. of Oxford, 1983. Chairman: Defence Theol Working Party, C of E Bd for Social Responsibility, 1980–82; C of E Doctrine Commn, 1985–87 (Mem. 1967–76, 1977–81, 1984–87); Member: Faith and Order Advisory Gp, C of E Bd for Mission and Unity, 1976–81; Council of Christians and Jews, 1979–; Cttee for Theological Education, 1982–85; Standing Cttee, WCC Faith and Order Commn, 1983–87. Chaplain, Playing Card Makers' Co., 1977. DD Lambeth, 1991. *Publications:* The Foolishness of God, 1970; Travels in Oudamovia, 1976; The Living Splendour of Westminster Abbey, 1977; The Whole Family of God, 1981; Evidence for the Resurrection, 1986; contrib. to: Man: Fallen and Free (ed Kemp), 1969; Thinking about the Eucharist (ed Ramsey), 1972; Church Membership and Intercommunion (ed Kent and Murray), 1973; What about the New Testament? (ed Hooker and Hickling), 1975; Man and Nature (ed Montefiore), 1975; Studia Biblica I, 1978; Religious Studies and Public Examinations (ed Hulmes and Watson), 1980; Believing in the Church, 1981; Hospice: the living Idea (ed Saunders, Summers and Teller), 1981; Darwin: a Commemoration (ed R. J. Berry), 1982; Unholy Warfare (ed D. Martin and P. Mullen), 1983; The Challenge of Northern Ireland, 1984; Lessons before Midnight (ed J. White), 1984; Feminine in the Church (ed M. Furlong), 1984; Dropping the Bomb (ed J. Gladwin), 1985; Theology and Racism, I (ed K. Leech), 1985; Peace Together (ed C. Barrett), 1986; Working for the Kingdom (ed J. Fuller), 1986; Faith and Renewal (ed T. F. Best), 1986; Women Priests? (ed A. Peberdy), 1988; For the Love of Animals (ed B. and M. Annett), 1989; Liberating Life (ed S. McFague *et al*), 1990; The Extended Circle (ed J. Wynne Tyson), 1990; Praying for Peace (ed M. Hare Duke), 1991; *translations:* W. Eichrodt, Theology of the Old Testament, vol. 1 1961, vol. 2 1967; T. Bovet, That They May Have Life, 1964; J. Daniélou, Theology of Jewish Christianity, 1964; H. von Campenhausen, Ecclesiastical Authority and Spiritual Power, 1969; H. von Campenhausen, The Formation of the Christian Bible, 1972; J. Daniélou, Gospel Message and Hellenistic Culture, 1973; (with David Smith) J. Daniélou, The Origins of Latin Christianity, 1977. *Recreations:* music, walking. *Address:* South Canonry, 71 The Close, Salisbury, Wilts SP1 2ER. *Club:* United Oxford & Cambridge University.

SALISBURY, Dean of; *see* Dickinson, Very Rev. H. G.

SALISBURY, Harrison Evans; *b* 14 Nov. 1908; *s* of Percy Pritchard Salisbury and Georgiana Evans Salisbury; *m* 1st, 1933, Mary Hollis (marr. diss.); two *s;* 2nd, 1964, Charlotte Young Rand. *Educ:* Univ. of Minnesota (AB). United Press, 1930: London Manager, 1943; Foreign Editor, 1945. New York Times: Moscow Corresp., 1949–54; National Editor, 1962; Asst Man. Editor, 1964–69; Associate Editor and Editor Opposite-Editorial Page, 1970–73. Pres., Amer. Acad. and Inst. of Arts and Letters, 1975–77; Mem., Amer. Acad. of Arts and Letters, 1986. Pres., Authors' League, 1980–85. Amer. Philosophical Soc. Pulitzer Prize, International Correspondence, 1955. Holds hon. doctorates. *Publications:* Russia on the Way, 1946; American in Russia, 1955; The Shook-up Generation, 1958; To Moscow-And Beyond, 1960; Moscow Journal, 1961; The Northern Palmyra Affair, 1962; A New Russia?, 1962; Russia, 1965; Orbit of China, 1967; Behind the Lines-Hanoi 1967; The Soviet Union-The 50 Years, 1967; The 900 Days, the Siege of Leningrad, 1969; The Coming War Between Russia and China, 1969; The Many Americas Shall Be One, 1971; The Eloquence of Protest: voices of the seventies, 1972; To Peking-and Beyond, 1973; The Gates of Hell, 1975; Black Night, White Snow: Russia's Revolutions 1905–1917, 1978; Russia in Revolution 1900–1930, 1978; The Unknown War, 1978; Without Fear or Favor: The New York Times and *its* times, 1980; A Journey for Our Times, 1983; China: 100 Years of Revolution, 1983; The Long March: the untold story, 1985; A Time of Change, 1988; The Great Black Dragon Fire: a Chinese inferno, 1989; Tiananmen Diary: thirteen days in June, 1989; Disturber of the Peace, 1989. *Address:* Box 70, Taconic, Conn, USA. *Clubs:* Century Association (New York); National Press (Washington, DC).

SALISBURY, John; *see* Caute, J. D.

SALISSE, John Joseph, CBE 1986; Chairman, Retail Consortium, since 1986; *b* 24 March 1926; *s* of Joseph and Anne Salisse; *m* 1949, Margaret Horsfield; one *d.* *Educ:* Portsmouth Grammar Sch. Marks and Spencer, 1944–85, Dir 1968–85. Chairman: CBI Distributive Trades Survey Cttee, 1983–86; St Enoch Management Centre Ltd, 1986–; Jt London Tourism Forum, 1986–; London Enterprise Agency, 1983–88; Director: London Tourist Bd, 1984– (Vice-Chm., 1989–); City Shops, 1986–88; Fullemploy, 1984–86; Allied Internat. Designers, 1986–87. Jt Treas., European Movement, 1982–86; Member: CBI Council, 1984–89; Cttee, Amer. European Community Assoc., 1983–90; Nat. Employers' Liaison Cttee, 1987–; Cttee on Commerce and Distribution, 1988–; Council for Charitable Support, 1986–89; Inst. of Dirs; Trustee, London Educn Business Partnership, 1986–; Dir, CECD, 1986– (Vice-Pres., 1989–). Hon. Vice Pres., Magic Circle, 1975– (Hon. Sec., 1965–86); Hon. Life Mem., Acad. of Magical Arts and Scis, America, 1979–. *Publications:* various contribs to Magic literature. *Recreations:* golf, theatre, ballet, opera, history of magic, collecting Victorian theatre programmes. *Address:* 12 Hampstead Way, NW11 7LS. *Clubs:* Savage, Magic Circle, Highgate Golf; Magic Castle (Los Angeles).

SALK, Jonas Edward, BS, MD; Founding Director, since 1975, and Distinguished Professor in International Health Sciences, since 1984, Salk Institute for Biological Studies (Director, 1963–75; Fellow, 1963–84); Adjunct Professor of Health Sciences in Departments of Psychiatry, Community Medicine, and Medicine, University of California at San Diego, since 1970; *b* New York, 28 Oct. 1914; *s* of Daniel B. Salk; *m* 1st, 1939, Donna Lindsay (marr. diss. 1968); three *s;* 2nd, 1970, Françoise Gilot. *Educ:* NY University College of Medicine; Coll. of New York City (BS). Fellow, NY Univ. Coll. of Medicine, 1935–40; Mount Sinai Hosp., NYC, 1940–42; Nat. Research Council Fellow, Sch. of Public Health, Univ. of Michigan, 1942–43, Research Fellow in Epidemiology, 1943–44, Research Assoc., 1944–46, Asst Professor, 1946–47; Assoc. Prof. of Bacteriology, 1947–49, and Director of Virus Research Laboratory, 1947–63, School of Medicine, Univ. of Pittsburgh; Research Prof., 1949–54. Consultant in epidemic diseases to: Sec. of War, 1944–47, Sec. of Army, 1947–54; Commonwealth Professor of Experimental Medicine, 1957–62 (Professor of Preventive Med., Sch. of Med., Univ. of Pittsburgh, USA, and Chairman of the Department, 1954–57). Vis. Prof.-at-Large, Pittsburgh, 1963. Specialist in polio research; developed antipoliomyelitis vaccine, 1955. Emeritus Member: Amer. Epidemiological Soc.; Amer. Soc. of Clinical Investigation; Assoc. of Amer. Physicians; Soc. for Exptl Biol. and Medicine; Sen Mem., Inst. of Medicine, Nat. Acad. of Scis; mem. of other socs. Fellow: Amer. Public Health Assoc.; AAAS; Amer. Acad. of Arts and Scis; Hon. Fellow: Amer. Acad. of Pediatrics; Royal Soc. of Health. US Medal of Freedom, 1977. *Publications:* Man Unfolding, 1972; The Survival of the Wisest, 1973; (with Jonathan Salk) World Population and Human Values: a new reality, 1981; Anatomy of Reality: merging of intuition and reason, 1983. *Address:* The Salk Institute, PO Box 85800, San Diego, Calif 92138, USA.

SALMON, family name of **Baron Salmon.**

SALMON, Baron *cr* 1972 (Life Peer), of Sandwich, Kent; **Cyril Barnet Salmon,** PC 1964; Kt 1957; a Lord of Appeal in Ordinary, 1972–80; *b* 28 Dec. 1903; *s* of late Montagu Salmon; *m* 1st, 1929, Rencie (*d* 1942), *d* of late Sidney Gorton Vanderfelt, OBE; one *s* one *d;* 2nd, 1946, Jean, Lady Morris (*d* 1989), *d* of late Lt-Col D. Maitland-Makgill-Crichton. *Educ:* Mill Hill; Pembroke College, Cambridge. BA 1925. Called to Bar, Middle Temple, 1925 (Bencher, 1953; Treasurer, 1972); QC 1945; Recorder of Gravesend, 1947–57; Judge of High Court of Justice, Queen's Bench Division, 1957–64; a Lord Justice of Appeal, 1964–72. Chairman: Royal Commission on the Working of the Tribunals of Inquiry (Evidence) Act, 1921, 1966; Royal Commission on Standards of Conduct in Public Life, 1974–76. Commissioned Royal Artillery, 1940. 8th Army HQ Staff, 1943–44. JP (Kent), 1949. Commissioner of Assize, Wales and Chester Circuit, 1955. Captain of the Royal St George's, Sandwich, 1972–73. Commissary of Cambridge Univ., 1979–. Governor of Mill Hill School. Hon. Fellow, Pembroke College, Cambridge. Hon. DCL Kent, 1978; Hon. LLD Cambridge, 1982. *Recreations:* golf, fishing. *Address:* Eldon House, 1 Dorset Street, W1H 3FB. *T:* 071–487 3461.

See also A. G. Robinson.

SALMON, Brian Lawson, CBE 1972; Chairman, J. Lyons & Co. Ltd, 1972–77 (Director, 1961–77, Joint Managing Director, 1967–69, Deputy Chairman, 1969–71); *b* 30 June 1917; *s* of Julius Salmon; *m* 1946, Annette Wilson Mackay; two *s* one *d*. *Educ:* Grenham Hse; Malvern Coll. Chm., Cttee on Sen. Nursing Staff Structure, 1963–66. Vice-Chm., Bd of Governors, Westminster Hosp. Gp, 1963–74; Chairman: Camden and Islington AHA, 1974–77; Supply Bd Working Gp, DHSS, 1977–78. *Recreations:* theatre, ballet, food and wine. *Address:* 34 Kingston House North, Princes Gate, SW7 1LN.

SALMON, Dame Nancy (Marion); *see* Snagge, Dame Nancy.

SALMON, Thomas David; Assistant to Speaker's Counsel, House of Commons, 1980–86; retired; *b* 1 Nov. 1916; *s* of late Rev. Thomas Salmon and Isabel Salmon (*née* Littleton), North Stoneham, Hants; *m* 1950, Morris Patricia Reyner Turner, Ilford, Essex; one *s* two *d*. *Educ:* Winchester Coll.; Christ Church, Oxford (MA). Served War of 1939–45: Captain 133 Field Regt RA (despatches). Temp. Asst Principal, Cabinet Office, 1946. Admitted Solicitor, 1949; entered Treasury Solicitor's Dept, 1951; transf. to Bd of Trade, 1966; Under-Sec. (Legal), Solicitors' Dept, Depts of Industry and Trade, 1973–80. *Recreations:* walking, study of history and languages, gardening. *Address:* Tenures, 23 Sole Farm Road, Great Bookham, Surrey KT23 3DW. *T:* Bookham (0372) 452837.

SALMON, Very Rev. Thomas Noel Desmond Cornwall; Dean of Christ Church, Dublin, 1967–88; *b* Dublin, 5 Feb. 1913; *s* of Francis Allen Cornwall Salmon, BDS, and Emma Sophia, *d* of Dr Hamilton Jolly, Clonroche, Co. Wexford; unmarried. *Educ:* privately; Trinity College, Dublin; BA 1935, MA, BD. Deacon 1937; Priest 1938. Curate Assistant: Bangor, Co. Down, 1937–40; St James' Belfast, 1940–42; Larne, Co. Antrim, 1942–44; Clerical Vicar, Christ Church Cathedral, 1944–45; Curate Assistant, Rathfarnham, Dublin, 1945–50; Incumbent: Tullow, Carrickmines, 1950–62; St Ann, Dublin, 1962–67. Asst Lectr in Divinity School, TCD, 1945–63; Examining Chaplain to Archbishop of Dublin, 1949–. *Recreations:* in younger days Rugby football (Monkstown FC Dublin) and swimming; now walking, gardening and reading. *Address:* 3 Glenageary Terrace, Lower Glenageary Road, Dun Laoghaire, Co. Dublin. *T:* 2800101.

SALMON, Col William Alexander, OBE 1956; Assistant Ecclesiastical Secretary to Lord Chancellor, 1964–77, and to Prime Minister, 1964–77, retired; *b* 16 Nov. 1910; *o s* of late Lt-Colonel W. H. B. Salmon, late IA; *m* 1939, Jean Barbara Macmillan (*d* 1982), *o d* of late J. V. Macmillan, DD, OBE (Bishop of Guildford, 1934–49); one *s* two *d*. *Educ:* Haileybury College; RMC, Sandhurst. Commissioned 2nd Lt HLI 1930; ADC to Governor of Sind, 1936–38. Served during War of 1939–45: France, 1939; Middle East, Italy, Greece, Bde Major, 1942; GSO2 HQ Aegean Force, 1943; CO, 2nd Bn Beds and Herts Regt, 1945–46. CO, 2nd Bn Royal Irish Fusiliers, 1946–47; GSO1 (Trng), HQ Scottish Command, 1947–49; Chief of Staff to Lt-Gen. Glubb Pasha, HQ Arab Legion, 1950–53; CO 1st Bn HLI, 1953–55; Col, GS (O and T Div.) SHAPE, 1957–59; AQMG (QAE2), The War Office, 1959–62; AAG (AG14), The War Office, 1962–63; retd 1963. Life Governor, Haileybury and Imperial Service Coll., 1965–. Hashemite Order of El Istiqlal (2nd Cl.), 1953. *Publication:* Churches and Royal Patronage, 1983. *Recreations:* shooting, fishing, gardening. *Address:* Balcombe Place, Balcombe, Haywards Heath, West Sussex RH17 6QJ. *Club:* Army and Navy.

SALMOND, Alexander Elliot Anderson; MP (SNP) Banff and Buchan, since 1987; Leader, Scottish National Party, since 1990; *b* 31 Dec. 1954; *s* of Robert F. F. Salmond and Mary S. Milne; *m* 1981, Moira F. McGlashan. *Educ:* Linlithgow Acad.; St Andrews Univ. (MA Hons). Govt Econ. Service, 1980; Asst Agricl and Fisheries Economist, DAFS, 1978–80; Energy Economist, Royal Bank of Scotland plc, 1980–87. Scottish National Party: Mem. Nat. Exec., 1981–; Vice-Chair (Publicity), 1985–87; Sen. Vice-Convener (Dep. Leader) (formerly Sen. Vice-Chair), 1987–90. SNP/Plaid Cymru parly spokesperson on energy, treasury and fishing, 1987–88, on economy, energy, environment and poll tax, 1988–. *Publications:* articles and conference papers on oil and gas economics; contribs to Scottish Government Yearbook, Fraser of Allander Economic Commentary, Petroleum Review, Opec Bulletin, etc. *Address:* House of Commons, SW1A 0AA; 17 Maiden Street, Peterhead, Aberdeenshire AB42 6EE.

SALOP, Archdeacon of; *see* Frost, Ven. G.

SALT, George, FRS 1956; ScD; Fellow of King's College, Cambridge, since 1933; Reader in Animal Ecology, University of Cambridge, 1965–71, now Emeritus; *b* Loughborough, 12 Dec. 1903; *s* of late Walter Salt and Mary Cecilia (*née* Hulme); *m* 1939, Joyce Laing, Newnham Coll. and Stockton-on-Tees; two *s*. *Educ:* Crescent Heights Collegiate Inst., Calgary; Univ. of Alberta (BSc); Harvard Univ. (SM, SD); Univ. of Cambridge (PhD, ScD). National Research Fellow, Harvard Univ., 1927–28; Entomologist, Imperial Inst. Entom, 1929–31; Royal Soc. Moseley Research Student, 1932–33; Univ. Lectr in Zoology, Cambridge, 1937–65; Fellow of King's Coll., Cambridge, 1933–, Dean, 1939–45, Tutor for Advanced Students, 1945–51. Visiting Prof. Univ. of California, Berkeley, 1966. On biological expedns in NW Canada and Rocky Mts, Cuba, Republic of Colombia, E Africa, Pakistan. *Publications:* The Cellular Defence Reactions of Insects, 1970; papers in scientific jls on insect parasitism and ecology. *Recreations:* mountaineering, gardening, calligraphy and palaeography. *Address:* King's College, Cambridge CB2 1ST; 21 Barton Road, Cambridge CB3 9LB. *T:* Cambridge (0223) 355450.

SALT, Rear-Adm. James Frederick Thomas George, CB 1991; Assistant Chief of Naval Staff (Gulf War), 1990–91; *b* 19 April 1940; *s* of Lieut Comdr George Salt (lost in 1939–45 War in command HMS Triad, 1940) and Lillian Bridget Lamb; *m* 1975, Penelope Mary Walker; four *s*. *Educ:* Wellington College; RNC Dartmouth (1958–59). Served Far East, Mediterranean, South Atlantic and home waters; commanded HM Sub. Finwhale, 1969–71; 2 i/c HM Sub. Resolution (Polaris), 1973–74; Comd HM Nuclear Sub. Dreadnought, 1978–79; Comd HMS Sheffield, 1982 (sank Falklands); Comd HMS Southampton, 1983; ACOS Ops C-in-C Fleet, 1984–85; Dir, Defence Intell., 1986–87; Sen. Naval Mem., Directing Staff, RCDS, 1988–90. Liveryman, Cordwainers' Co. *Recreations:* sailing, ski-ing, shooting. *Address:* c/o Ministry of Defence, Whitehall, SW1.

SALT, Sir Patrick (Macdonnell), 7th Bt *cr* 1869, of Saltaire, Yorkshire; Director, Cassidy Davis Members Agency Ltd, since 1983; *b* 25 Sept. 1932; *s* of Sir John Salt, 4th Bt and Stella Houlton Jackson (*d* 1974); *S* brother, 1991; *m* 1976, Ann Elizabeth Mary Kilham Roberts, *widow* of Denys Kilham Roberts, OBE. *Educ:* Summer Fields, Oxford; Stowe Sch. *Recreation:* fishing. *Heir: cousin* Daniel Alexander Salt [*b* 15 Aug. 1943; *m* 1968, Merchide, *d* of Dr Ahmad Emami; two *d*]. *Address:* Hillwatering Farmhouse, Langham, Bury St Edmunds, Suffolk IP31 3ED. *T:* Walsham-le-Willows (0359) 259367. *Club:* City University.

SALT, Sir (Thomas) Michael (John), 4th Bt, *cr* 1899; *b* 7 Nov. 1946; *s* of Lt-Col Sir Thomas Henry Salt, 3rd Bt, and Meriel Sophia Wilmot, *d* of late Capt. Berkeley C. W. Williams and Hon. Mrs Williams, Herringston, Dorchester; *S* father 1965; *m* 1971, Caroline, *er d* of Henry Hildyard; two *d*. *Educ:* Eton. *Heir: b* Anthony William David Salt [*b* 5 Feb. 1950; *m* 1978, Olivia Anne, *yr d* of Martin Morgan Hudson; two *s*]. *Recreations:* cricket, shooting. *Address:* Shillingstone House, Shillingstone, Dorset. *Club:* Boodle's.

SALTER, Harry Charles, CMG 1983; DFC 1945; *b* 29 July 1918; *er s* of late Harry Arnold Salter and Irene Beatrice Salter; *m* 1st, 1946, Anne Hooper (marr. diss. 1980); one *d*; 2nd, 1983, Mrs Janet Watford. *Educ:* St Albans Sch. Entered Ministry of Health, 1936. Served War, Royal Artillery, 1939–46 (despatches, DFC). Asst Sec., Min. of Health, 1963; Under-Sec., DHSS, 1971–73; Dir, Financing of Community Budget, EEC, 1973–82, retd. *Recreations:* golf, bridge, walking, cooking. *Address:* 5 Clos des Acacias, 1150 Brussels, Belgium. *T:* 770 36 71.

SALTER, Ian George; a Deputy Chairman, The Stock Exchange, since 1990; *b* Hobart, Tasmania, 7 March 1943; *s* of Desmond and Diane Salter. *Educ:* Hutchins Sch., Hobart, Tasmania. AASA. Member: Hobart Stock Exchange, 1965–69; Stock Exchange, London, 1970–; Principal, Strauss Turnbull, now Société Générale Strauss Turnbull, 1978–. Mem., Stock Exchange Council, 1980–. DTI Inspector, 1984–87. *Recreations:* opera, travel, gardening. *Address:* (office) Exchange House, Primrose Street, Broadgate, EC2A 2DD. *T:* 071–638 5699.

SALTHOUSE, Edward Charles, PhD; CEng, FIEE; Master of University College, Durham University, since 1979; *b* 27 Dec. 1935; *s* of Edward Salthouse, MBE, and Mrs Salthouse (*née* Boyd); *m* 1961, Denise Kathleen Margot Reid; two *s*. *Educ:* Campbell Coll., Belfast; Queen's University of Belfast (BSc, PhD). Lecturer in Electrical Engrg, Univ. of Bristol, 1962–67; University of Durham: Reader in Elec. Engrg Science, 1967–79; Chairman, Board of Studies in Engrg Science, 1976–79; Dean, Faculty of Science, 1982–85; First Chm., School of Applied Science and Engrg, 1985–87; Pro-Vice-Chancellor, 1985–88. *Publications:* papers on electrical insulation in Proc. IEE and other appropriate jls. *Recreations:* travel by train, photography. *Address:* The Master's House, The Castle, Durham DH1 3RL. *T:* Durham (091) 3743800; Shieldaig, Hume, Kelso.

SALTHOUSE, Leonard; Assistant Under Secretary of State, Ministry of Defence, 1977–87; *b* 15 April 1927; *s* of late Edward Keith Salthouse and Dorothy Annie (*née* Clark); *m* 1950, Kathleen May (*née* Spittle); one *s* one *d*. *Educ:* Queen Elizabeth Grammar Sch., Atherstone, Warwickshire; University Coll. London (BScEcon). Home Civil Service: Asst Principal, Min. of Fuel and Power, 1950–55; Principal, Air Min., then Min. of Defence, 1955–66; Asst Sec., 1966–77. *Recreations:* gardening, music. *Address:* Highfield, 115 Cross Oak Road, Berkhamsted, Herts HP4 3HZ. *T:* Berkhamsted (0442) 877809.

SALTON, Prof. Milton Robert James, FRS 1979; Professor and Chairman of Microbiology, New York University School of Medicine, since 1964; *b* 29 April 1921; *s* of Robert Alexander Salton and Stella Salton; *m* 1951, Joy Marriott; two *s*. *Educ:* Univ. of Sydney (BSc Agr. 1945); Univ. of Cambridge (PhD 1951, ScD 1967). Beit Meml Res. Fellow, Univ. of Cambridge, 1950–52; Merck Internat. Fellow, Univ. of California, Berkeley, 1952–53; Reader, Univ. of Manchester, 1956–61; Prof. of Microbiology, Univ. of NSW, Australia, 1962–64. Hon. Mem., British Soc. for Antimicrobial Chemotherapy, 1983. Docteur en Médecine, *Dhc*, Université de Liège, 1967. *Publications:* Microbial Cell Walls, 1960; The Bacterial Cell Wall, 1964; Immunochemistry of Enzymes and their Antibodies, 1978; β-Lactam Antibiotics, 1981; (ed jtly) Antibiotic Inhibition of Bacterial Cell Surface Assembly and Function, 1988. *Address:* Department of Microbiology, New York University School of Medicine, 550 First Avenue, New York, NY 10016, USA. *Club:* United Oxford & Cambridge University.

SALTOUN, Lady (20th in line) *cr* 1445, of Abernethy; **Flora Marjory Fraser;** Chief of Clan Fraser; *b* 18 Oct. 1930; *d* of 19th Lord Saltoun, MC, and Dorothy (*d* 1985), *e d* of Sir Charles Welby, 5th Bt; *S* father, 1979; *m* 1956, Captain Alexander Ramsay of Mar, Grenadier Guards retd, *o s* of late Adm. Hon. Sir Alexander Ramsay, GCVO, KCB, DSO, and The Lady Patricia Ramsay, CI, VA, CD; three *d*. *Heiress: d* Hon. Katharine Ingrid Mary Isabel Fraser [*b* 11 Oct. 1957; *m* 1980, Captain Mark Malise Nicolson, Irish Guards; one *s* two *d*]. *Address:* Cairnbulg Castle, Fraserburgh, Aberdeenshire AB43 5TN.

SALTZMAN, Charles Eskridge, OBE (Hon.) 1943; DSM 1945 (US); Legion of Merit (US) 1943; Partner, Goldman, Sachs & Co. (investment banking), 1956, Limited Partner since 1973; *b* 19 Sept. 1903; *s* of Maj.-Gen. Charles McKinley Saltzman and Mary Saltzman (*née* Eskridge); *m* 1st, 1931, Gertrude Lamont (marr. diss.); one *s*; 2nd, 1947, Cynthia Southall Myrick (marr. diss.); two *d* (one *s* decd); 3rd, 1978, Clotilde McCormick (*née* Knapp). *Educ:* Cornell Univ.; US Mil. Acad.; Magdalen College, Oxford University. BS (US Mil. Acad.); BA, MA (Rhodes Scholar) (Oxford Univ.). Served as 2nd Lt, Corps of Engrs, US Army, 1925–30; commissioned 1st Lieut, NY National Guard, 1930; Lieutenant-Colonel 1940; on active duty in US Army, 1940–46, serving overseas, 1942–46; Brigadier-General 1945; relieved from active duty, 1946; Maj.-Gen. AUS (Retd). With NY Telephone Co., 1930–35; with NY Stock Exchange, 1935–49 (Asst to Exec. Vice-Pres., later Sec. and Vice-Pres.). Asst Sec. of State, 1947–49; Partner Henry Sears & Co., 1949–56; Under-Sec. of State for Admin., 1954–55. Former Dir, Continental Can Co. and A. H. Robins Co., Inc. President: English-Speaking Union of the US, 1961–66 (now Hon. Director); Assoc. of Graduates, US Mil. Academy, 1974–78 (now Emeritus); Mem. Pilgrims of the United States; Hon. Mem., Soc. of the Cincinnati. Member, Director, or Trustee of many boards, societies and religious, philanthropic and educational institutions. Hon. Dr Mil. Sci. Mil. Coll. of S Carolina, 1984. Holds foreign decorations. *Address:* (home) 30 E 62nd Street, New York, NY 10021, USA. *T:* (212) 759–5655; (office) 85 Broad Street, New York, NY 10004. *T:* (212) 902–1000. *Clubs:* Century Association, Union, University (New York); Metropolitan (Washington).

SALUSBURY-TRELAWNY, Sir J. B.; *see* Trelawny.

SALVIDGE, Paul; Under Secretary, Telecommunications and Posts Division, Department of Trade and Industry, since 1989; *b* 22 Aug. 1946; *s* of Herbert Stephen and Winifred Alice Elisabeth Salvidge; *m* 1972, Heather Margaret (*née* Johnson); one *d*. *Educ:* Cardiff High School; Birmingham Univ. (LLB). Ministry of Power, 1967; Dept of Trade and Industry, 1972; Asst Secretary, 1982. *Address:* Department of Trade and Industry, 151 Buckingham Palace Road, SW1W 9SS.

SAMARAKOON, Hon. Neville Dunbar Mirahawatte; Chief Justice, Democratic Socialist Republic of Sri Lanka, 1977–84; *b* 22 Oct. 1919; *s* of Alfred Charles Warnabarana Wickremasinghe Samarakoon and Rajapaksa Wasala Mudiyanselage Chandrawati Mirahawatte Kumarihamy; *m* 1949, Mary Patricia Mulholland; one *s* two *d*. *Educ:* Trinity Coll., Kandy; University Coll., Colombo; Law Coll., Colombo. Enrolled as Advocate, 1945; Crown Counsel, Attorney-General's Dept, 1948–51; reverted to Private Bar, 1951; QC 1968. Member: Bar Council, 1964–77; Disciplinary Bd for Lawyers 1971–74, 1976, 1977. Chairman: Judicial Service Commn, 1978–; Council of Legal Educn. *Address:* 129 Wijerama Mawatha, Colombo 7, Sri Lanka. *T:* Colombo 595364.

SAMARANCH, Juan Antonio; President, International Olympic Committee, since 1980 (Member, since 1966); *b* 17 July 1920; *s* of Francisco Samaranch and Juana Torello; *m* 1955, Maria Teresa Salisachs Rowe; one *s* one *d*. *Educ:* Instituto Superior Estudios de Empresas, Barcelona; German College; Higher Inst. of Business Studies, Barcelona. Industrialist, Bank Consultant; Pres., Barcelona Diputacion, 1973–77; Ambassador to USSR and to People's Republic of Mongolia, 1977–80. Mem., Spanish Olympic Cttee, 1954 (Pres., 1967–70); Nat. Deleg. for Physical Educn and Sport. Holds numerous decorations. *Publications:* Deporte 2000, 1967; Olympic Message, 1980. *Recreation:* philately. *Address:* Junqueras 18, 08003 Barcelona, Spain. *T:* 318 28 88; International Olympic Committee, Château de Vidy, 1007 Lausanne, Switzerland. *T:* 253271.

SAMBROOK, Gordon Hartley, CBE 1986; Chairman, Iron Trades Employers' Insurance Association, and Iron Trades Insurance Co. Ltd (formerly Iron Trades Mutual Insurance Co.), since 1984; *b* 9 Jan. 1930; *m* 1956, Patricia Joan Mary Havard; one *s. Educ:* Sheffield Univ. (BA(Hons), DipEd). Graduate Apprentice, Utd Steel, 1954; United Steel Cos, 1954–68; British Steel Corporation: General Manager, Rotherham, 1972; Dir, Tinplate Gp, 1973–75; Man. Dir, Personnel, 1975–77; Man. Dir, Commercial, 1977–80; Dir, 1978–90; Chief Exec., 1980–89, Chm., 1980–90, BSC General Steels, later General Steels. Director: Allied Steel & Wire Ltd, 1981–87; United Merchant Bar PLC, 1985–; United Engineering Steels Ltd, 1986–; Tuscaloosa Steel Corp., 1985–91. Chm. of Council, Steel Construction Inst.

SAMBROOK, Prof. Joseph Frank, PhD; FRS 1985; Director, McDermott Center for Human Growth and Development, Southwestern Medical School, Dallas, since 1991; *b* 1 March 1939; *s* of Thomas and Ethel Gertrude (*née* Lightfoot); *m* 1st, 1960, Thelma McGrady (marr. diss. 1984); two *s* one *d*; 2nd, 1986, Mary-Jane Gething; one *d. Educ:* Liverpool Univ. (BSc 1962); Australian Nat. Univ. (PhD 1965). Res. Fellow, John Curtin Sch. of Med. Res., ANU, 1965–66; Postdoctoral Fellow, MRC Lab. of Molecular Biol., 1966–67; Jun. Fellow, Salk Inst. for Biol Studies, 1967–69; Sen. Staff Investigator, 1969–77; Asst Dir, 1977–85, Cold Spring Harbor Lab.; Prof. and Chm., Dept of Biochemistry, Southwestern Medical Center, Dallas, 1985–91. *Publications:* contribs to learned jls. *Recreation:* music. *Address:* 4320 Irvin Simmons Drive, Dallas, Texas 75229, USA. *T:* (214) 688–3723, *Fax:* (214) 688–7579.

SAMMAN, Peter Derrick, MD, FRCP; Physician to Dermatological Department, Westminster Hospital, 1951–79, and St John's Hospital for Diseases of the Skin, 1959–79; Consultant Dermatologist, Orpington and Sevenoaks Hospitals, 1951–77; Dean, Institute of Dermatology, 1965–70; *b* 20 March 1914; *y s* of Herbert Frederick Samman and Emily Elizabeth Savage; *m* 1953, Judith Mary Kelly; three *d. Educ:* King William's Coll., IOM; Emmanual Coll., Cambridge; King's Coll. Hosp., London. BA (Nat. Scis. Tripos), 1936; MB, BChir Cantab 1939; MRCP 1946; MA, MD Cantab 1948; FRCP 1963. House Surg., King's Coll. Hosp., 1939; Sqdn Ldr, RAFVR, 1940–45; House Phys. and Registrar, King's Coll. Hosp., 1946; Sen. Dermatological Registrar and Tutor in Dermatology, United Bristol Hosps, 1947–48; Sen. Registrar, St John's Hosp. for Diseases of the Skin, 1949–50. FRSocMed; Mem. Brit. Assoc. of Dermatology; Hon. Mem., Dermatological Soc. of S Africa. *Publications:* The Nails in Disease, 1965, 4th edn 1986; chapters in Textbook of Dermatology (ed Rook, Wilkinson and Ebling), 1968; (jtly) Tutorials in Postgraduate Medicine: Dermatology, 1977; A History of St John's Hospital for Diseases of the Skin 1963–1988, 1990; various articles in med. jls. *Recreation:* gardening. *Address:* 18 Sutherland Avenue, Orpington, Kent BR5 1QZ. *T:* Orpington (0689) 820839.

SAMPLES, Reginald McCartney, CMG 1971; DSO 1942; OBE 1963; HM Diplomatic Service, retired; *b* 11 Aug. 1918; *o s* of late William and Jessie Samples; *m* 1947, Elsie Roberts Hide; two *s* one step *d. Educ:* Rhyl Grammar Sch.; Liverpool Univ. (BCom). Served, 1940–46; RNVR (Air Branch); torpedo action with 825 Sqn against German ships Scharnhorst, Gneisenau and Prinz Eugen in English Channel (wounded, DSO); Lieut (A). Central Office of Information (Economic Editor, Overseas Newspapers), 1947–48. CRO (Brit. Inf. Services, India), 1948; Economic Information Officer, Bombay, 1948–52; Editor-in-Chief, BIS, New Delhi, 1952; Dep.-Dir, BIS, New Delhi, 1952–56; Dir, BIS, Pakistan (Karachi), 1956–59; Dir, BIS, Canada (Ottawa), 1959–65, OBE; Counsellor (Information) to Brit. High Comr, India, and Dir, BIS, India (New Delhi), 1965–68; Asst Under-Sec. of State, Commonwealth Office, 1968; Head of British Govt Office, and Sen. British Trade Comr, Toronto, 1969; Consul-Gen., Toronto, 1974–78. Asst Dir, Royal Ontario Museum, 1978–83. *Recreations:* tennis, watching ballet. *Address:* Apartment 1105, 44 Jackes Avenue, Toronto, Ontario M4T 1E5, Canada. *Clubs:* Naval; Queens (Toronto).

SAMPSON, Anthony (Terrell Seward); writer and journalist; *b* 3 Aug. 1926; *s* of Michael Sampson and Phyllis, *d* of Sir Albert Seward, FRS; *m* 1965, Sally, *d* of Dr P. G. Bentlif, Jersey, and of Mrs G. Denison-Smith, Islip, Oxon; one *s* one *d. Educ:* Westminster School; Christ Church, Oxford. Served with Royal Navy, 1944–47; Sub-Lieut, RNVR, 1946. Editor of Drum Magazine, Johannesburg, 1951–55; Editorial staff of The Observer, 1955–66; Associate Prof., Univ. of Vincennes, Paris, 1968–70; Chief American Corresp., The Observer, 1973–74. Contributing Editor, Newsweek, 1977–; Editorial Conslt, The Brandt Commn, 1978–79; Editor, The Sampson Letter, 1984–86. Presenter and narrator, The Midas Touch (BBC2), 1990. *Publications:* Drum, a Venture into the New Africa, 1956; The Treason Cage, 1958; Commonsense about Africa, 1960; (with S. Pienaar) South Africa: two views of Separate Development 1960; Anatomy of Britain, 1962; Anatomy of Britain Today, 1965; Macmillan: a study in ambiguity, 1967; The New Europeans, 1968; The New Anatomy of Britain, 1971; The Sovereign State: the secret history of ITT, 1973; The Seven Sisters, 1975 (Prix International de la Presse, Nice, 1976); The Arms Bazaar, 1977; The Money Lenders, 1981; The Changing Anatomy of Britain, 1982; Empires of the Sky, 1984; (with Sally Sampson) The Oxford Book of Ages, 1985; Black and Gold: tycoons, revolutionaries and apartheid, 1987; The Midas Touch, 1989. *Recreations:* vertical gardening, opera. *Address:* 27 Ladbroke Grove, W11. *T:* 071–727 4188, *Fax:* 071–221 5738; Quarry Garden, Wardour, Wilts. *T:* Tisbury (0747) 870407. *Clubs:* Beefsteak, Groucho, Academy.

SAMPSON, Colin, CBE 1988; QPM 1978; HM Chief Inspector of Constabulary for Scotland, since 1991; *b* 26 May 1929; *s* of James and Nellie Sampson; *m* 1953, Kathleen Stones; two *s. Educ:* Stanley Sch., Wakefield; Univ. of Leeds (Criminology). Joined Police Force, 1949; served mainly in the CID (incl. training of detectives), at Dewsbury, Skipton, Doncaster, Goole, Wakefield, Huddersfield, Rotherham, Barnsley; Comdt, Home Office Detective Trng Sch., Wakefield, 1971–72; Asst Chief Constable, West Yorks, 1973; Dep. Chief Constable, Notts, 1976; Chief Constable, W Yorks, 1983–89; HM Inspector of Constabulary, 1989–90 (for NE England, 1990). CBIM 1987. OStJ 1988. DUniv Bradford, 1988; Hon. LLD Leeds, 1990. *Recreations:* choral music, walking, gardening. *Address:* HM Inspectorate of Constabulary, St Andrew's House, Edinburgh EH1 3DE.

SAMSOVA, Galina; producer; a Principal Dancer, Birmingham Royal Ballet (formerly Sadler's Wells Royal Ballet), since 1980; Teacher with the company in the Royal Ballet and Royal Ballet School; Artistic Director, Scottish Ballet, since 1991; *b* Stalingrad, 1937; *d* of a Byelorussian; *m* 1st, Alexander Ursuliak; 2nd, André Prokovsky. *Educ:* the Ballet Sch., Kiev (pupil of N. Verekundova). Joined Kiev Ballet, 1956 and became a soloist; Canadian Ballet, 1961; created chief rôle in Cendrillon, Paris 1963 (Gold Medal for best danseuse of Paris Festival). Ballerina, Festival Ballet, 1964–73; headed the group of André Prokovsky, The New London Ballet, (disbanded in 1977, revived for 3 new productions, The Theatre Royal, York, 1979); has danced principal rôles in Sleeping Beauty, Nutcracker, Giselle, Swan Lake, Anna Karenina, and other classical ballets; danced in

Europe, Far East and USA. Produced: Sequence from Paquita, Sadler's Wells, 1980; (with Peter Wright) Swan Lake, Sadler's Wells, 1983, Covent Garden, 1991; Giselle, London City Ballet, 1986. *Address:* Scottish Ballet, 261 West Princes Street, Glasgow G4 9EE.

SAMUEL, family name of **Viscounts Bearsted** and **Samuel.**

SAMUEL, 3rd Viscount *cr* 1937, of Mount Carmel and of Toxteth, Liverpool; **David Herbert Samuel;** Sherman Professor of Physical Chemistry, Weizmann Institute of Science, Rehovot, Israel, since 1967; President, Shenkar College of Textile Technology and Fashion, since 1987; *b* 8 July 1922; *s* of 2nd Viscount Samuel, CMG, and Hadassah (*d* 1986), *d* of Judah Goor (Grasovsky); *S* father, 1978; *m* 1st, 1950, Esther Berelowitz (marr. diss. 1957); one *d*; 2nd, 1960, Rinna Dafni (*née* Grossman) (marr. diss. 1978); one *d*; 3rd, 1980, Veronika Engelhardt Grimm. *Educ:* Balliol Coll., Oxford (MA 1948); Hebrew Univ. (PhD 1953). Served War of 1939–45 (despatches); Captain RA, in India, Burma and Sumatra. Member of Isotope Dept, 1949–86, of Dept of Neurobiology, 1986–, Dir, Center for Neurosciences and Behavioural Research, 1978–87, Weizmann Inst. of Sci., Rehovot, Israel; Head, Chemistry Gp, Science Teaching Dept, 1967–83; Dean, Faculty of Chemistry, 1971–73; Chm., Bd of Studies in Chemistry, Feinberg Grad. Sch., 1968–74. Post-doctoral Fellow, Chem. Dept, UCL, 1956; Res. Fellow, Chem. Dept, Harvard Univ., 1957–58; Res. Fellow, Lab. of Chemical Biodynamics (Lawrence Radiation Lab.), Univ. of California, Berkeley, 1965–66; Visiting Professor: Sch. of Molecular Scis, Univ. of Warwick, 1967; MRC Neuroimmunology Unit, Zoology Dept, UCL, 1974–75; Pharmacol. Dept, Yale Sch. of Medicine, 1983–84; McLaughlin Prof., Sch. of Medicine, McMaster Univ., 1984. Member: Adv. Bd, Bat-Sheva de Rothschild Foundn for Advancement of Science in Israel, 1970–83; Bd, US-Israel Educnl (Fulbright) Foundn, 1969–74 (Chm., 1974–75); Bd, Israel Center for Scientific and Technol Information, 1970–74; Scientific Adv. Cttee and Bd of Trustees of Israel Center for Psychobiol., 1973–; Acad. Adv. Cttee, Everyman's (Open) Univ., 1976–83; Bd of Govs, Bezalel Acad. of Arts and Design, 1977–; Council, Israel Chemical Soc., 1977–83; Internat. Brain Res. Org. (IBRO), 1977–; Israel Exec. Cttee, America-Israel Cultural Foundn, 1978–89 (Chm., 1986–89); Bd of Governors, Tel Aviv Museum, 1980–; Cttee on Teaching of Chemistry, IUPAC, 1981–89; Anglo-Israel Assoc., 1985–; British Israel Arts Foundn, 1986–; Bd of Trustees, Menninger Foundn, USA, 1988–. Member, Editorial Board: Jl of Labelled Compounds & Radiopharmaceuticals, 1967–; Alzheimer Disease and Associated Disorders, 1985–; Brain Behaviour and Immunity, 1985–. *Publications:* more than 300 papers, reviews and parts of collective volumes on isotopes, physical chemistry, reaction mechanisms, neurochemistry, psychopharmacology, animal behavior, education and the history and teaching of science. *Heir:* *b* Hon. Dan Judah Samuel [*b* 25 March 1925; *m* 1st, 1957, Nonni (Esther) (marr. diss. 1977), *d* of late Max Gordon, Johannesburg; one *s* two *d*; 2nd, 1981, Heather, *d* of Angus and Elsa Cumming, Haywards Heath; one *s* one *d*]. *Address:* Weizmann Institute of Science, Rehovot, Israel. *T:* (office) 03–7521133; (home) 08–468123.

SAMUEL, Adrian Christopher Ian, CMG 1959; CVO 1963; *b* 20 Aug. 1915; *s* of late George Christopher Samuel and Alma Richards; *m* 1942, Sheila, *er d* of late J. C. Barrett, Killiney, Co. Dublin; three *s* one *d. Educ:* Rugby Sch.; St John's Coll., Oxford. Entered HM Consular Service, 1938; served at Beirut, Tunis and Trieste. Served War, 1940–44, in Royal Air Force. Returned to HM Foreign Service and served at HM Embassies in Ankara, Cairo and Damascus; First Secretary, 1947; Counsellor, 1956; Principal Private Secretary to the Secretary of State for Foreign Affairs, Oct. 1959–63; Minister at HM Embassy, Madrid, 1963–65; resigned 1965. Director: British Chemical Engrg Contractors Assoc., 1966–69; British Agrochemicals Assoc., 1972–78; Dir-Gen., Groupement Internat. des Assocs Nats de Fabricants de Pesticides (GIFAP), 1978–79. *Publication:* An Astonishing Fellow: a life of Sir Robert Wilson, KMT, MP, 1986. *Recreations:* golf, shooting and reading. *Address:* The Laundry House, Handcross, near Haywards Heath, West Sussex RH17 6HQ. *T:* Handcross (0444) 400717. *Club:* Garrick.

SAMUEL, Sir John (Michael Glen), 5th Bt, *cr* 1898; Director, Clean Air Transport Holdings Ltd, since 1988; *b* 25 Jan. 1944; *o s* of Sir John Oliver Cecil Samuel, 4th Bt, and of Charlotte Mary, *d* of late R. H. Hoyt, Calgary, Canada; *S* father, 1962; *m* 1st, 1966, Antoinette Sandra, *d* of late Captain Antony Hewitt, RE, 2nd SAS Regt, and of Mrs K. A. H. Casson, Frith Farm, Wolverton, Hants; two *s*; 2nd, 1982, Mrs Elizabeth Ann Molinari, *y d* of Major R. G. Curry, Bournemouth, Dorset. *Educ:* Radley; London Univ. Director: Enfield Automotive, 1967–70; Advanced Vehicle Systems Ltd, 1971–78; Chairman: Electric Auto Corp. (USA), 1978–83; Whisper Electric Car A/S, Denmark, 1984–88. *Recreations:* motor racing, water ski-ing. *Heir:* *s* Anthony John Fulton Samuel, *b* 13 Oct. 1972.

SAMUEL, Richard Christopher, CMG 1983; CVO 1983; HM Diplomatic Service; Ambassador to Latvia, since 1991; *b* Edinburgh, 8 Aug. 1933; *m* 1986, Frances Draper; one *d. Educ:* Durham Sch.; St John's Coll., Cambridge (BA). Royal Navy, 1952–54. FO, 1957–58; Warsaw, 1958–59; Rome, 1960–63; FO, 1963; Private Sec. to Parly Under-Sec. of State, 1965–68; Hong Kong, 1968–69; 1st Sec. and Head of Chancery: Singapore, 1969–71; Peking, 1971–73; Counsellor, Washington, 1973–76; Head of Far Eastern Dept, FCO, 1976–79; Counsellor (Commercial), Moscow, 1980–82; Minister and Dep. High Comr, New Delhi, 1982–85; Under-Sec. for Asia and the Oceans, ODA, FCO, 1986–88; on loan to Inter-Amer. Develt Bank, Washington, as Exec. Dir for Belgium, Denmark, Finland, Germany, Italy, Netherlands, Norway, Sweden and UK, 1988–91. *Address:* c/o Foreign and Commonwealth Office, SW1A 2AH.

SAMUELS; *see* Turner-Samuels.

SAMUELS, John Edward Anthony; QC 1981; a Recorder, since 1985; *b* 15 Aug. 1940; *s* of late Albert Edward Samuels, solicitor, Reigate, Surrey; *m* 1967, Maxine (*née* Robertson), JP; two *s. Educ:* Charterhouse; Perugia; Queens' Coll., Cambridge (MA). Commnd, Queen's Royal Regt (TA), 1959; Lieut, Queen's Royal Surrey Regt (TA), 1961–67. Chairman, Cambridge Univ. United Nations Assoc., 1962. Called to Bar, Lincoln's Inn, 1964 (Mansfield Schol., 1963; Bencher, 1990); South Eastern Circuit; Mem., Senate of the Inns of Court and the Bar, 1983–86; Mem., Council of Legal Educn, 1983–90. Co-opted Mem., ILEA Education Cttee, 1964–67; Jt Chm., ILEA Disciplinary Tribunals, 1977–87; Alternate Chm., Burnham Cttee, 1981–87. Member: Richmond, Twickenham and Roehampton HA, 1982–85; Kingston and Richmond Family Practitioner Cttee, 1982–86; Chm., Jt Regulations Cttee, Inns' Council and Bar Council, 1987–90. Trustee, Richmond Parish Lands Charity, 1986– (Chairman: Educn Cttee, 1987–89; Property Cttee, 1987–). *Publications:* Action Pack: counsel's guide to chambers' administration, 1986, 2nd edn 1988; contributor to Halsbury's Laws of England, 4th edn. *Recreations:* conservation, restoration, serendipity. *Address:* 22 Old Buildings, Lincoln's Inn, WC2A 3UJ. *T:* 071–831 0222.

SAMUELS, Prof. Michael Louis, FRSE; Professor of English Language, University of Glasgow, 1959–89; *b* 1920; *s* of late Harry Samuels, OBE, MA, barrister-at-law, and Céline Samuels (*née* Aronowitz), London; *m* 1950, Hilary, *d* of late Julius and Ruth Samuel, Glasgow; one *d. Educ:* St Paul's School; Balliol College, Oxford. Domus Exhibitioner in Classics, Balliol College, Oxford, 1938–40 and 1945–47; MA 1947 (First

Class Hons English Lang. and Lit.). Worked for Air Ministry (Maintenance Command), 1940–45. Research Fellow, University of Birmingham, 1947–48; Assistant in English Language, University of Edinburgh, 1948–49; Lecturer in English Language, Univ. of Edinburgh, 1949–59. Chm., Scottish Studentships Selection Cttee, 1975–88. FRSE 1989. *Publications*: Linguistic Evolution, 1972; (ed jtly) A Linguistic Atlas of Late Medieval English, 1987; (jtly) Middle English Dialectology, 1989; (with J. J. Smith) The English of Chaucer, 1989; contribs to: Approaches to English Historical Linguistics, 1969; So Meny people Longages and Tonges (presented to A. McIntosh), 1981; Middle English Studies (presented to N. Davis), 1983; Proc. 4th Internat. Conf. on English Historical Linguistics, 1985; Explanation and Linguistic Change, 1987; A Companion to Piers Plowman, 1988; articles and reviews in linguistic and literary jls. *Address*: 4 Queen's Gate, Dowanhill, Glasgow G12 9DN. *T*: 041–334 4999.

SAMUELSON, Sir (Bernard) Michael (Francis), 5th Bt *cr* 1884; *b* 17 Jan. 1917; *s* of Sir Francis Henry Bernard Samuelson, 4th Bt, and Margaret Kendall (*d* 1980), *d* of H. Kendall Barnes; *S* father, 1981; *m* 1952, Janet Amy, *yr d* of Lt-Comdr L. G. Elkington, RN retd, Chelsea; two *s* two *d*. *Educ*: Eton. Served War of 1939–45 with RA and Leicestershire Regt (despatches). *Heir*: *s* James Francis Samuelson, *b* 20 Dec. 1956. *Address*: Hollingwood, Stunts Green, Herstmonceux, East Sussex.

SAMUELSON, Prof. Paul A.; Institute Professor, Massachusetts Institute of Technology, 1966–85, now Emeritus; Long-Term Credit Bank of Japan Visiting Professor of Political Economy, Center for Japan—US Business and Economic Studies, New York University, since 1987; *b* Gary, Indiana, 15 May 1915; *m* 1938, Marion Crawford (*d* 1978); four *s* two *d*; *m* 1981, Risha Claypool. *Educ*: Univs of Chicago (BS) and Harvard (MA, PhD). SSRC Predoctoral Fellow, 1935–37; Soc. of Fellows, Harvard, 1937–40; Guggenheim Fellow, 1948–49; Ford Faculty Research Fellow, 1958–59; Hoyt Vis. Fellow, Calhoun Coll., Yale, 1962; Carnegie Foundn Reflective Year, 1965–66. MIT: Asst Prof. of Econs, 1940; Assoc. Prof. of Econs, 1944; Staff Mem., Radiation Lab., 1944–45; Prof. of Econs, 1947; Prof. of Internat. Economic Relations (part-time), Fletcher Sch. of Law and Diplomacy, 1945. Consultant: to Nat. Resources Planning Bd, 1941–43; to Rand Corp., 1948–75; to US Treasury, 1945–52, 1961–; to Johnson Task Force on Sustained Prosperity, 1964; to Council of Econ. Advisers, 1960–; to Federal Reserve Bd, 1965–; to Congressional Budget Office, 1974–. Economic Adviser to Senator, Candidate and President-elect John F. Kennedy, informal adviser to President Kennedy. Member: War Prodn Bd and Office of War Mobilization and Reconstruction, 1945; Bureau of the Budget, 1952; Adv. Bd of Nat Commn on Money and Credit, 1958–60; Research Adv. Panel to President's Nat. Goals Commn, 1959–60; Research Adv. Bd Cttee for Econ. Develt, 1960; Nat. Task Force on Econ. Educn, 1960–61; Sen. Advr, Brookings Panel on Econ. Activity. Contrib. Editor and Columnist, Newsweek, 1966–81. Vernon F. Taylor Vis. Dist. Prof., Trinity Univ., Texas, 1989. Lectures: Stamp Meml, London, 1961; Wicksell, Stockholm, 1962; Franklin, Detroit, 1962; Gerhard Colm Meml, NYC, 1971; Davidson, Univ. of New Hampshire, 1971; 12th John von Neumann, Univ. of Wisconsin, 1971; J. Willard Gibbs, Amer. Mathematical Soc., 1974; 1st Sulzbacher, Columbia Law Sch., 1974; John Diebold, Harvard Univ., 1976; Alice Bourneauf, Boston Coll., 1981; Horowitz, Jerusalem and Tel Aviv, 1984; Marschak Meml, UCLA, 1984; Olin, Univ. of Virginia Law Sch., 1989; Joseph W. Martin Commemorative, Stonehill Coll., 1990; Lionel Robbins Meml, Claremont Coll., 1991. Corresp. Fellow, British Acad., 1960; Fellow: Amer. Philosoph. Soc.; Econometric Soc. (Mem. Council; Vice-Pres. 1950; Pres. 1951); AAAS, 1985; Member: Amer. Acad. Arts and Sciences; Amer. Econ. Assoc. (Pres. 1961; Hon. Fellow, 1965); Phi Beta Kappa; Commn on Social Sciences (NSF), 1967–; Internat. Econ. Assoc. (Pres. 1965–68; Hon. Pres. 1968–); Nat. Acad. of Sciences, 1970–; Omicron Delta Epsilon, Bd of Trustees (Internat. Honor Soc. in Econ.). Hon. Fellow: LSE; Peruvian Sch. of Economics, 1980. Hon. LLD: Chicago, 1961; Oberlin, 1961; Boston Coll., 1964; Indiana, 1966; Michigan, 1967; Claremont Grad. Sch., 1970; New Hampshire, 1971; Keio, Tokyo, 1971; Harvard, 1972; Gustavas Adolphus Coll., 1974; Univ. of Southern Calif, 1975; Univ. of Rochester, 1976; Univ. of Pennsylvania, 1976; Emmanuel Coll., 1977; Widener, 1982; Hon. DLitt: Ripon Coll., 1962; Northern Michigan Univ., 1973; Valparaiso Univ., 1987; Columbia Univ., 1988; Hon DSc: E Anglia, 1966; Massachusetts, 1972; Rhode Is., 1972; Hon. LHD: Seton Hall, 1971; Williams Coll., 1971; Stonehill Coll., 1978; Dhc: Université Catholique de Louvain, Belgium, 1976; Catholic Univ. at Riva Aguero Inst., Lima, 1980; City Univ. of London, 1980; Universidad Nacional de Educación a Distancia, Madrid, 1989; DUniv, New Univ. of Lisbon, Portugal, 1985; Hon. DSc Tufts Univ., 1988. David A. Wells Prize, Harvard, 1941; John Bates Clark Medal, Amer. Econ. Assoc., 1947; Medal of Honor, Univ. of Evansville, 1970; Nobel Prize in Econ. Science, 1970; Albert Einstein Commemorative Award, 1971; Alumni Medal, Chicago Univ., 1983; Britannica Award, 1989; Medal and Hon. Mem., Club of Economics and Management, Valencia, Spain, 1990; Gold Scanno Prize in Economy, Naples, Italy, 1990. *Publications*: Foundations of Economic Analysis, 1947, enlarged edn, 1982; Economics, 1948, (with Paul A. Samuelson and William D. Nordhaus) 12th edn, 1985, 13th edn, 1989, (trans. 24 langs) 1948); (jtly) Linear Programming and Economic Analysis, 1958 (trans. French, Japanese); Readings in Economics, 1955; The Collected Scientific Papers of Paul A. Samuelson (ed J. E. Stiglitz), vols I and II, 1966, vol. III (ed R. C. Merton), 1972, vol. IV (ed H. Nagatani and K. Crowley), 1977, vol. V (ed K. Crowley), 1986; co-author, other books in field, papers in various jls, etc. *Recreation*: tennis. *Address*: Department of Economics, Massachusetts Institute of Technology E52–383, Cambridge, Mass 02139, USA. *T*: 617–253–3368. *Club*: Belmont Hill (Mass).

SAMUELSON, Sydney Wylie, CBE 1978; President, Samuelson Group PLC, since 1990 (Chairman, 1966–90); *b* 7 Dec. 1925; 2nd *s* of G. B. and Marjorie Samuelson; *m* 1949, Doris (*née* Magen); three *s*. *Educ*: Irene Avenue Council Sch., Lancing, Sussex. Served RAF, 1943–47. From age 14, career devoted to various aspects of British film industry: cinema projectionist, 1939–42; Asst Film Editor, 1943; Asst Film Cameraman, Cameraman and Dir of Documentary Films, 1947–59; founded company to service film, TV and, later, audio-visual prodn organisations, supplying cameras and other technical equipment, with purchase of first camera, 1954; continued filming as technician on locations throughout world until 1959, when activities concentrated on expanding his company. First British Film Comr, 1991–. Permanent Trustee, 1973– and Chm. Bd of Management, 1976–, BAFTA (Vice-Chm. Film, 1971–73, Chm. of Council, 1973–76); Chm., BAFTA—Shell UK Venture Cttee; Member: Exec. Cttee, Cinema and Television Veterans (Pres., 1980–81); Exec. Cttee, Cinema and TV Benevolent Fund (Trustee, 1982–89; Pres., 1983–86); Brit. Soc. of Cinematographers (Governor, 1969–79; 1st Vice-Pres., 1976–77; award for Outstanding Contribution to Film Industry, 1967); Associate Mem., Amer. Soc. of Cinematographers; Hon. Mem., ACTT, 1990. Hon. Technical Adviser, Royal Naval Film Corp.; Hon. Fellow, Brit. Kinematograph Sound and TV Soc., 1970; Hon. Mem., Guild of British Camera Technicians. Guild of Film Production Executives Award of Merit, 1986. Pres., UK Friends of Akim (Israel Assoc. for Mentally Handicapped); Vice Pres., Muscular Dystrophy Assoc. of GB; Founder Mem., Charity Projects. Michael Balcon Award, BAFTA, 1985; Patron, Young Persons Concert Foundn. *Recreations*: collecting recorded film music, vintage motoring, veteran jogging (finished 13,006th London Marathon 1982). *Address*: 31 West Heath Avenue, NW11 7QJ. *T*: 081–458 4982, *Fax*: 081–458 1957.

SAMUELSSON, Prof. Bengt Ingemar; Professor of Medical and Physiological Chemistry, since 1972, and Rector, since 1983, Karolinska Institutet, Stockholm; *b* Halmstad, Sweden, 21 May 1934; *s* of Anders and Stina Samuelsson; *m* 1958, Inga Karin Bergstein; one *s* two *d*. *Educ*: Karolinska Institutet (DMedSci 1960, MD 1961). Res. Fellow, Harvard Univ., 1961–62; Asst Prof. of Med. Chemistry, Karolinska Inst, 1961–66; Prof., Royal Vet. Coll., Stockholm, 1967–72; Chm., Dept of Chemistry, 1973–83, Dean of Med. Faculty, 1978–83, Karolinska Inst, Stockholm. Vis. Prof., Harvard, 1976; T. Y. Shen Vis. Prof. in Med. Chem., MIT, 1977; Walker-Ames Prof., Washington Univ., 1987. Lectures: MacArthur, Univ. of Edinburgh, 1975; Shirley Johnson Meml, Philadelphia, 1977; Sixth Annual Marrs McLean, Houston, 1978; Rockwood Meml, Univ. of Iowa, 1978; Smith Kline and French, Vanderbilt Univ. Sch. of Medicine, 1979; Harvey, NY, 1979; Smith Kline and French Res., Philadelphia, 1979; Fifth McNeil-Ortho Chem., Philadelphia, 1980; Lane Medical, Stanford Univ., 1981; Shell, Univ. of Calif, 1981; Romanes, Univ. of Edinburgh, 1981; Eighth Annual Sci. in Med., Univ. of Washington, 1981; Fedn of European Chem. Socs, Helsinki, 1981; Arthur C. Corcoran Meml, Cleveland, Ohio, 1981; Carl V. Moore Meml, Washington Univ., 1982; Kober, Assoc. of Amer. Physicians, 1982; first Bayer, Yale Univ., 1983; Lorenzini Foundn, Milan, 1983; Brown-Razor, Rice Univ., Houston, 1984; Solomon A. Berson Meml, Mount Sinai Sch. of Medicine, NY, 1984; Immunology Council Annual, Johns Hopkins Univ., 1984; Dist. Lectr in Med. Scis, Mayo Foundn, 1980. Member: Swedish Govt Res. Adv. Bd, 1985–88; Nobel Cttee for Physiol. or Med., 1984– (Chm., 1987–89); Nat. Commn on Health Policy, 1987–90. Member: Royal Swedish Acad. of Scis, 1981–; Mediterranean Acad., Catania, 1982–; Hon. Prof., Bethune Univ. of Med. Scis, China, 1986; Hon. Member: Amer. Soc. of Biological Chemists, 1976; Assoc. of American Physicians, 1982; Swedish Med. Assoc., 1982; Italian Pharmacological Soc., 1985; Acad. Nac. de Medicina de Buenos Aires, 1986; Internat. Soc. of Haematology, 1986; Spanish Soc. of Allergology and Clinical Immunology, 1989; Mem., French Acad. of Scis, 1989; For. Associate, US Nat. Acad. of Scis, 1984; For. Hon. Mem., Amer. Acad. of Arts and Scis, 1982–; Founding Mem., Academia Europaea, 1988; Foreign Mem., Royal Soc., 1990; Mem., Real Academia Nacional de Medicina, Spain, 1991. Hon. DSc: Chicago, 1978; Illinois, 1983; DUniv: Rio de Janeiro, 1986; Buenos Aires, 1986. Nobel Prize in Physiology or Medicine (jtly), 1982; numerous awards and prizes. *Publications*: papers on biochemistry of prostaglandins, thromboxanes and leukotrienes. *Address*: Department of Physiological Chemistry 2, Karolinska Institutet, Box 60400, S-104 01 Stockholm, Sweden. *T*: 8 7287601, *Fax*: 8 7360439.

SAMWORTH, David Chetwode, CBE 1985; DL; Chairman, Samworth Brothers Ltd (formerly Gorran Foods Ltd), since 1984 (Director since 1981); *b* 25 June 1935; *s* of Frank and Phyllis Samworth; *m* 1969, Rosemary Grace Cadell; one *s* three *d*. *Educ*: Uppingham Sch. Chm., Pork Farms Ltd, 1968–81; Director: Northern Foods Ltd, 1978–81; Imperial Gp, 1983–85; (non-exec.) Thorntons Ltd, 1988–. Chm., Meat and Livestock Commn, 1980–84. Member: Leicester No 3 HMC, 1970–74; Trent RHA, 1974–78, 1980–84. DL Leics, 1984. *Recreations*: tennis, hunting. *Address*: Markham House, Thorpe Satchville, Melton Mowbray, Leics. *T*: Melton Mowbray (0664) 840510.

SAN VINCENZO FERRERI, 8th Marquis of, **Alfio Testaferrata Ghâxaq** (Marquis Testaferrata); *b* 1911; *s* of Daniel Testaferrata Bonici Ghâxaq and Agnese (*d* 1941), *d* of Baroncino Nicola Galea di San Marciano; *S* father, 1945. *Educ*: Stonyhurst College, Blackburn; University Coll., Oxford. Member: Cttee of Privileges of Maltese Nobility, 1948–65; Royal Numismatic Society, 1962–85; Société suisse de Numismatique, 1962–85. Hereditary Knight of the Holy Roman Empire; Patrician of Rome, Messina, and Citta di Castello. *Address*: 29 Villegaignon Street, Mdina, Malta, GC. *T*: Rabat 674139. *Club*: Casino Maltese (Valletta).

SANCTUARY, Gerald Philip; Secretary, National Union of Journalists Provident Fund, since 1984; *b* 22 Nov. 1930; *s* of late John Cyril Tabor Sanctuary, MD and of Maisie Toppin Sanctuary (*née* Brooks); *m* 1956, Rosemary Patricia L'Estrange, Dublin; three *s* two *d*. *Educ*: Bryanston Sch.; Law Soc.'s Sch. of Law. National Service Pilot, 1953–55; Asst Solicitor, Kingston, 1955–56; Partner in Hasties, Solicitors, Lincoln's Inn Fields, 1957–62; Field Sec., Nat. Marriage Guidance Council, 1963–65, Nat. Secretary 1965–69; Exec. Dir, Sex Information and Educn Council of US, 1969–71; Sec., Professional and Public Relations, The Law Soc., 1971–78; Exec. Dir, Internat. Bar Assoc., 1978–79; Legal Adviser and Regional and Local Affairs Dir, Mencap, 1979–84. Hon. Treas., GAPAN, 1986–. Editor, Law Soc. series, It's Your Law, 1973–79. Regular broadcaster on radio. *Publications*: Marriage Under Stress, 1968; Divorce — and After, 1970, 2nd edn 1976; Before You See a Solicitor, 1973, 2nd edn 1983; After I'm Gone—what will happen to my Handicapped Child?, 1984, 2nd edn 1991; contrib., Moral Implications of Marriage Counselling, 1971; Vie Affective et Sexuelle, 1972; Loss Prevention Manual, 1978; The English Legal Heritage, 1979; booklets: Fishpool Street—St Albans, 1984; Tudor St Albans; St Albans and the Wars of the Roses, 1985; The Romans in St Albans, 1986; The Monastery at St Albans, 1987. *Recreations*: amateur drama, organising murder mystery weekends. *Address*: 6 Mercers Row, St Albans, Herts. *T*: St Albans (0727) 42666.

SANDARS, Christopher Thomas; Assistant Under Secretary, Defence Export Services (Administration), Ministry of Defence, since 1990; *b* 6 March 1942; *s* of late Vice-Adm. Sir Thomas Sandars, KBE, CB and Lady Sandars; *m* 1966, Elizabeth Anne Yielder; three *s* one *d*. *Educ*: Oundle Sch.; Corpus Christi Coll., Cambridge (Foundation Schol.). Joined MoD, 1964; Asst Private Sec. to Minister of State, 1967–69; Central Policy Review Staff, Cabinet Office, 1971–74; Private Sec. to Minister of State, 1975–77; Hd, General Finance Div. 1, 1977–80; Hd, Defence Secretariat 13, 1980–84; RCDS, 1985; Hd, Secretariat 9 (Air), 1986–90. *Recreations*: tennis, squash, painting, gardening, theatre. *Address*: c/o Ministry of Defence, Whitehall, SW1A 2HB. *T*: 071–218 6748. *Club*: Commonwealth Trust.

SANDARS, Nancy Katharine, FBA 1984; FSA; archaeologist; *b* 29 June 1914; *d* of Edward Carew Sandars and Gertrude Annie Sandars (*née* Phipps). *Educ*: at home; Wychwood School, Oxford; Inst. of Archaeology, Univ. of London (Diploma 1949); St Hugh's College, Oxford (BLitt 1957). Archaeological research and travel in Europe, 1949–69; British School at Athens, 1954–55; Elizabeth Wordsworth Studentship, St Hugh's College, Oxford, 1958–61; travelled in Middle East, 1957, 1958, 1962, 1966; conferences, lectures (Prague, Sofia, McGill Univ.); excavations in British Isles and Greece. *Publications*: Bronze Age Cultures in France, 1957; The Epic of Gilgamesh, an English version, 1960; Prehistoric Art in Europe, 1967, rev. edn 1985; Poems of Heaven and Hell from Ancient Mesopotamia, 1971; The Sea-Peoples: warriors of the ancient Mediterranean, 1978. *Recreations*: walking, translating, looking at pictures. *Address*: The Manor House, Little Tew, Oxford OX7 4JF. *Club*: University Women's.

SANDARS, Prof. Patrick George Henry; Professor of Experimental Physics, since 1978, and Head of Atomic and Laser Physics, since 1990, Oxford University; *b* 29 March 1935; *s* of late P. R. and A. C. Sandars; *m* 1959, P. B. Hall; two *s*. *Educ*: Wellington Coll.; Balliol Coll., Oxford (MA, DPhil). Weir Junior Research Fellow, University Coll., and ICI Research Fellow, Clarendon Laboratory, Oxford, 1960–63; Tutorial Fellow, Balliol Coll., and Univ. Lectr, Oxford Univ., 1964–72; Reader in Physics, Oxford Univ.,

1972–77. Junior Proctor, Oxford Univ., 1971–72. *Address:* 3 Hawkswell Gardens, Oxford. *T:* Oxford (0865) 58535.

SANDBANK, Charles Peter, FEng; Assistant to Director of Engineering, BBC, since 1991; *b* 14 Aug. 1931; *s* of Gustav and Clare Sandbank; *m* 1955, Audrey Celia; one *s* two *d. Educ:* Bromley Grammar Sch.; London Univ. (BSc, DIC). FEng 1983; FIEE, FInstP. Prodn Engr, 1953–55, Develt Engr, 1955–60, Brimar Valve Co.; Develt Section Head, STC Transistor Div., 1960–64; Head of Electron Devices Lab., 1964–68, Manager, Communication Systems Div., 1968–78, Standard Telecommunication Laboratories; Head of BBC Research Dept, 1978–84; Asst Dir of Engrg, 1984–85, Dep. Dir of Engrg, 1985–91, BBC. Mem. Council: IEE, 1978–81, 1989– (Chm., Electronics Divisional Bd, 1979–80); Royal TV Soc., 1983–86, 1989–; Chairman: EBU New Systems and Services Cttee, 1984–89; EBU High Definition TV Cttee, 1981–84; EUREKA High Definition Television Project Adv. Bd, 1988–; Jt Technical Cttee, EBU/Eur. Telecommunications Standards Inst., 1990–; Bureau mem., EBU Tech. Cttee, 1989–. Ext. Examr, London Univ., 1982–89. Chm., Internal Cttee of Inquiry into Legionnaires Disease Outbreak at Broadcasting House, London, 1988. Liveryman, Scientific Instrument Makers' Co., 1988–. Fellow, SMPTE, 1989; FBKSTS 1991; FRTS; FRSA. *Publications:* Optical Fibre Communication Systems, 1980; Digital Television, 1990; papers and patents (about 200) on semiconductor devices, integrated circuits, solid-state bulk effects, compound semiconductors, micro-waves, electron-phonon interactions, navigational aids, electro-optics and broadcasting technology. *Recreations:* boatbuilding, sailing, film-making, music, garden-watching. *Address:* Grailands, Beech Road, Reigate, Surrey RH2 9NA. *T:* (office) 071-580 4468.

SANDBERG, Sir Michael (Graham Ruddock), Kt 1986; CBE 1982 (OBE 1977); Chairman: The Hongkong and Shanghai Banking Corporation, 1977–86; The British Bank of the Middle East, 1980–86; *b* 31 May 1927; *s* of Gerald Arthur Clifford Sandberg and Ethel Marion Sandberg; *m* 1954, Carmel Mary Roseleen Donnelly; two *s* two *d. Educ:* St Edward's Sch., Oxford. 6th Lancers (Indian Army) and First King's Dragoon Guards, 1945. Joined The Hongkong and Shanghai Banking Corp., 1949. Mem. Exec. Council, Hong Kong, 1978–86. Steward, Royal Hong Kong Jockey Club, 1972–86, Chm., 1981–86; Treasurer, Univ. of Hong Kong, 1977–86. FCIB (FIB 1977; Vice Pres. 1984–87); FRSA 1983. Freeman, City of London; Liveryman, Co. of Clockmakers. Hon. LLD: Hong Kong, 1984; Pepperdine, 1986. *Recreations:* horse racing, bridge, cricket, horology. *Address:* 54A Hyde Park Gate, SW7 5EB; Domaine de la Haute Germaine, Ste Marguerite, Le Broc, Alpes Maritimes, France. *Clubs:* Cavalry and Guards, Carlton, Portland, MCC, Surrey CCC (Pres. 1988).

SANDELL, Terry, OBE 1991; Director, Soviet Union, British Council, and Cultural Counsellor, British Embassy, Moscow, since 1989; *b* 8 Sept. 1948; *s* of James William Sandell and Helen Elizabeth McCombie; *m* 1984, Kate Ling; two *s. Educ:* Watford Grammar Sch. for Boys; Univ. of Nottingham (BA Hons); Univ. of Edinburgh. VSO, Berber, N Sudan, 1970–72. Joined British Council, 1974: Asst Rep. Dir, Omdurman Centre, Sudan, 1974–78; Regional Officer, Soviet Union and Mongolia, London, 1978–81; 1st Sec. (Cultural), British Embassy, Moscow, 1981–83; Asst Rep., Vienna, 1983–86, Rep. 1986–89; Projects Manager, Soviet Union, London, 1989. Mem. Bd of Trustees, State Liby for Foreign Lit., Moscow. *Publication:* (with Sadig Rashid) Non-Formal Education and Development in the Sudan, 1980. *Recreations:* walking, literature, theatre, travel. *Address:* c/o Foreign and Commonwealth Office, King Charles Street, SW1A 2AH; c/o British Council, 10 Spring Gardens, SW1A 2BN.

SANDELSON, Neville Devonshire; Barrister-at-Law; public affairs and business consultant; Deputy Chairman, Westminster and Overseas Trade Services Ltd, since 1985; Co-Founder, 1988, President, since 1990, The Radical Society (Co-Chairman, 1988–90); Executive Director, Profundis Ltd, since 1989; *b* Leeds, 27 Nov. 1923; *s* of late David I. Sandelson, OBE, and Dora Sandelson, (*née* Lightman); *m* 1959, Nana Karlinski, Neuilly sur Seine, France; one *s* two *d. Educ:* Westminster School; Trinity College, Cambridge; MA. Called to Bar, Inner Temple, 1946; for some years director of local newspaper and book publishing cos and producer of TV documentary programmes until resuming practice at Bar, 1964. Dep. Circuit Judge and Asst Recorder, 1977–85. Mem. London County Council, 1952–58. Travelled extensively in USA, Middle East, Asia and Europe. Contested (Lab): Ashford (Kent) 1950, 1951 and 1955; Beckenham (by-election) 1957; Rushcliffe 1959; Heston & Isleworth 1966; SW Leicester (by-election) 1967; Chichester 1970; (SDP) Hayes and Harlington, 1983. MP (Lab 1971–81, SDP 1981–83) Hayes and Harlington, June 1971–83; Founder Mem., SDP, 1981, resigned 1987. Parly spokesman on NI, 1981–82, and on the arts, 1982–83; Vice-Chm., All-Party Productivity Gp; Sec., All-Party Theatre Gp; Jt Sec., British-Greek Parly Gp; Sec., British Gibraltar Parly Gp; Vice-Chm., Afghanistan Parly Support Cttee. Promoted, as a Private Mem's Bill, the Matrimonial Proceedings (Polygamous Marriages) Act, 1972. Member: Council, Nat. Cttee for Electoral Reform, 1977–88 (resigned); Nat. Council of European Movement, 1985–; Exec. Cttee, Wider Share Ownership Council, 1979–; founder Mem., Manifesto Gp, 1975–80 (Hon. Treas.). Mem. Ct, Brunel Univ., 1975–81. *Address:* Yorkshire House, 8 Maddox Street, W1R 9PN. *T:* 071–408 1152. *Club:* Reform.

SANDERS, Cyril Woods, CB 1959; Lord of the Manor of Kavenham-Stoke-Wereham and Wretton in Norfolk; *b* 21 Feb. 1912; *er s* of Cyril Sturgis Sanders and Dorothy (*née* Woods); *m* 1944, Kate Emily Boyes, *qv*; one *s* three *d. Educ:* St Paul's Sch.; Queen's Coll., Oxford. BA Oxon 1934, Lit. Hum. Joined General Post Office as Assistant Principal, 1934; transferred to Board of Trade, 1935; retired from Dept of Trade and Industry (formerly Bd of Trade) as Under-Secretary, 1972. *Recreations:* walking, sailing, painting. *Address:* 41 Smith Street, Chelsea, SW3 4EP. *T:* 071–352 8053; Giles Point, Winchelsea, Sussex. *T:* Rye (0797) 226431; Canower, Cashel, Connemara, Eire. *Club:* Ski Club of Gt Britain.

SANDERS, Donald Neil, CB 1983; Chief Executive, since 1987, Managing Director, since 1991, Commonwealth Bank of Australia; Chairman, Australian European Finance Corporation Ltd, since 1988; *b* Sydney, 21 June 1927; *s* of L. G. and R. M. Sanders; *m* 1952, Betty Elaine, *d* of W. B. Constance; four *s* one *d. Educ:* Wollongong High Sch.; Univ. of Sydney (BEc). Commonwealth Bank of Australia, 1943–60; Australian Treasury, 1956; Bank of England, 1960; Reserve Bank of Australia, 1960–87: Supt, Credit Policy Div., Banking Dept, 1964–66; Dep. Manager: Banking Dept, 1966–67; Res. Dept, 1967–70; Aust. Embassy, Washington DC, 1968; Chief Manager: Securities Markets Dept, 1970–72; Banking and Finance Dept, 1972–74; Adviser and Chief Manager, Banking and Finance Dept, 1974–75; Dep. Governor and Dep. Chm., 1975–87. Man. Dir, Commonwealth Banking Corp., 1987–91. *Address:* Commonwealth Bank of Australia, 48 Martin Place, Sydney, NSW 2000, Australia.

SANDERS, Prof. Ed Parish, FBA 1989; Arts and Sciences Professor of Religion, Duke University, since 1990; *b* 18 April 1937; *s* of Mildred Sanders (*née* Parish) and Eula Thomas Sanders; *m* 1963, Becky Jill Hall (marr. diss. 1978); one *d. Educ:* Texas Wesleyan College (BA); Southern Methodist Univ. (BD); Union Theological Seminary, NY (ThD). Asst Prof. of Religious Studies, McMaster Univ., 1966–70, Associate Prof., 1970–74, Prof., 1974–88; Dean Ireland's Prof. of Exegesis of Holy Scripture, Oxford Univ., 1984–89. Visiting Professor: Jewish Theol. Seminary, 1980; Chair of Judeo-Christian Studies, Tulane Univ., 1980; Walter G. Mason Dist. Vis. Prof., Coll. of William and Mary in Virginia, 1981; Vis. Fellow Commoner, Trinity Coll., Cambridge, 1982. Donnellan Lectr, TCD, 1982. *Publications:* The Tendencies of the Synoptic Tradition, 1969; Paul and Palestinian Judaism, 1977, 2nd edn 1981; (ed) Jewish and Christian Self-Definition, vol. I, The Shaping of Christianity in the Second and Third Centuries, 1980, vol. II, Aspects of Judaism in the Graeco-Roman Period, 1981, vol. III, Self-Definition in the Graeco-Roman World, 1982; Paul, The Law and the Jewish People, 1983; Jesus and Judaism, 1985, 3rd edn 1987; (ed) Jesus, The Gospels and the Church, 1987; (with Margaret Davies) Studying the Synoptic Gospels, 1989; Jewish Law from Jesus to the Mishnah, 1990; Paul: past master, 1991; articles in NT Studies, Jl of Biblical Literature, Harvard Theol. Review, Jewish Quarterly Review. *Address:* Department of Religion, Duke University, Durham, NC 27706, USA.

SANDERS, John Derek, FRCO; Organist and Master of the Choristers, Gloucester Cathedral, since 1967; *b* 26 Nov. 1933; *s* of Alderman J. T. Sanders, JP, CA and Mrs E. M. Sanders (*née* Trivett); *m* 1967, Janet Ann Dawson; one *s* one *d. Educ:* Felsted Sch., Essex; Royal Coll. of Music; Gonville and Caius Coll., Cambridge. ARCM 1952; FRCO 1955; MusB 1956; MA 1958. Dir of Music, King's Sch., Gloucester, and Asst Organist, Gloucester Cathedral, 1958–63; Organist and Master of the Choristers, Chester Cathedral, 1964–67. Dir of Music, Cheltenham Ladies' Coll., 1968–. Conductor: Gloucestershire Symphony Orchestra, 1967–; Gloucester Choral Soc., 1967–. Conductor of Three Choirs Festival, triennially, 1968–. Pres., Cathedral Organists' Assoc., 1990–; Mem. Council, RCO, 1979–. Liveryman, Co. of Musicians, 1987. Freeman, City of London, 1986. Hon. DMus Lambeth, 1990. *Publications:* Festival Te Deum, 1962; Soliloquy for Organ, 1977; Toccata for Organ, 1979; Te Deum Laudamus, 1985; Jubilate Deo, 1986; Two Prayers, 1988. *Recreations:* gastronomy, travelling. *Address:* 7 Miller's Green, Gloucester GL1 2BN. *T:* Gloucester (0452) 524764.

SANDERS, John Leslie Yorath; HM Diplomatic Service, retired; furniture conservator and restorer; *b* 5 May 1929; *s* of late Reginald Yorath Sanders and Gladys Elizabeth Sanders (*née* Blything); *m* 1953, Brigit Mary Lucine Altounyan; one *s* two *d. Educ:* Dulwich Coll. Prep. Sch.; Cranleigh School. Higher Dip. in Furniture Prodn and Design, London Coll. of Furniture, 1982. Nat. Service in HM Forces (RA), 1948–50; entered HM Foreign Service, 1950; FO, 1950–52; MECAS, Lebanon, 1953; Damascus, 1954–55; Bahrain, 1955–56; Vice-Consul, Basra, 1956–60; Oriental Sec., Rabat, 1960–63; FO, 1964–67; 1st Sec., Beirut, 1968–70; 1st Sec. and Head of Chancery, Mexico City, 1970–73; Counsellor, Khartoum, 1973–75; Counsellor, Beirut, 1975–76; Dir of Res., FCO, 1976–78; Ambassador to Panama, 1978–80. *Recreations:* sailing, music. *Address:* Town Yeat, High Nibthwaite, Ulverston, Cumbria LA12 8DF.

SANDERS, Sir John Reynolds M.; *see* Mayhew-Sanders, Sir J. R.

SANDERS, Kate Emily Tyrrell, (Mrs C. W. Sanders); *see* Boyes, K. E. T.

SANDERS, Nicholas John, PhD; Principal Finance Officer, Department of Education and Science, since 1989; *b* 14 Sept. 1946; *s* of Ivor and Mollie Sanders; *m* 1971, Alison Ruth Carter; one *s* one *d. Educ:* King Edward's Sch., Birmingham; Magdalene Coll., Cambridge (MA, PhD). Joined DES, 1971; Principal Private Sec. to Sec. of State, 1974–75; Private Sec. to Prime Minister, 1978–81; Under Sec., 1989. *Address:* Department of Education and Science, Sanctuary Buildings, Great Smith Street, SW1.

SANDERS, Peter Basil; Chief Executive, Commission for Racial Equality, since 1988 (Director, 1977–88); *b* 9 June 1938; *s* of Basil Alfred Horace Sanders and Ellen May Sanders (*née* Cockrell); *m* 1961, Janet Valerie (*née* Child) (marr. diss. 1984); two *s* one *d. Educ:* Queen Elizabeth's Grammar Sch., Barnet; Wadham Coll., Oxford (MA, DPhil). Administrative Officer, Basutoland, 1961–66; Research in Oxford for DPhil, 1966–70; Officer, Min. of Defence, 1971–73; Race Relations Bd: Principal Conciliation Officer, 1973–74; Dep. Chief Officer, 1974–77. *Publications:* Lithoko: Sotho Praise-Poems (ed jtly and trans. with an Introd. and Notes), 1974; Moshoeshoe, Chief of the Sotho, 1975; The Simple Annals: the history of an Essex and East End family, 1989. *Address:* 5 Bentfield End Causeway, Stansted Mountfitchet, Essex. *T:* Bishop's Stortford (0279) 815096.

SANDERS, Raymond Adrian; Social Security Commissioner, since 1986; *b* 13 May 1932; *s* of Leslie Harry Sanders and Beatrice Sanders; *m* 1st, 1961, Anna Margaret Burton (marr. diss.); one *s*; 2nd, 1985, Virginia Varnell Dunn; two *d. Educ:* Auckland Univ. (LLB); London School of Economics (LLB). Barrister and Solicitor, New Zealand, 1956–66; Partner in Jackson, Russell and Co., Barristers and Solicitors, Auckland, NZ, 1962–66; part-time Lectr 1960–66 and Examiner 1961–66, Auckland Univ.; Solicitor, Allen and Overy, London, 1967–71; practising barrister, 1971–73; DHSS, 1973–74, 1975–84; Law Officers' Dept, 1974–75. Legal Advr to Warnock Inquiry (Human Fertilisation and Embryology), 1982–84; Regional Chm., Social Security and Medical Appeal Tribunals, 1984–86. *Publications:* Credit Management (jtly) 1966; Building Contracts and Practice, 1967. *Recreations:* theatre, music, cycling, tennis. *Address:* Office of the Social Security Commissioners, Harp House, 83 Farringdon Street, EC4.

SANDERS, Sir Robert (Tait), KBE 1980; CMG 1974; HMOCS; Secretary to the Cabinet, Government of Fiji, 1970–79; Treaties Adviser, Government of Fiji, 1985–87; *b* 2 Feb. 1925; *s* of late A. S. W. Sanders and Charlotte McCulloch; *m* 1951, Barbara, *d* of G. Sutcliffe; two *s* (and one *s* decd). *Educ:* Canmore Public Sch., Dunfermline; Dunfermline High Sch.; Fettes Coll., Edinburgh; Cambridge Univ. (Major Open Classical Schol., Pembroke Coll., 1943; John Stewart of Rannoch Schol. in Latin and Greek, 1947; 1st cl. Hons, Pts I and II of Classical Tripos); London Sch. of Economics, 1949–50; SOAS, 1949–50. Served War, 1943–46: Lieut, 1st Bn the Royal Scots, India and Malaya. Sir Arthur Thomson Travelling Schol., 1948; Sir William Browne Medal for Latin Epigram, 1948; MA (Cantab) 1951. Joined HM Overseas Civil Service, Fiji, as Dist Officer, 1950; Sec. to Govt of Tonga, 1956–58; Sec., Coconut Commn of Enquiry, 1963; MLC, Fiji, 1963–64; Sec. for Natural Resources, 1965–67; Actg Sec. Fijian Affairs, and Actg Chm. Native Lands and Fisheries Commn, 1967; MEC, Fiji, 1967; Sec. to Chief Minister and to Council of Ministers, 1967; apptd Sec. to Cabinet, 1970, also Sec. for Foreign Affairs, 1970–74, Sec. for Home Affairs, 1972–74 and Sec. for Information, 1975–76. Fiji Independence Medal, 1970. *Publications:* Interlude in Fiji, 1963; Fiji Treaty List, 1987; articles in Corona, jl of HMOCS. *Recreations:* golf, music, hill-walking. *Address:* Greystones Lodge, Broich Terrace, Crieff. *Clubs:* Royal Scots (Edinburgh); Nausori Golf (Fiji).

SANDERS, Roger Benedict; His Honour Judge Sanders; a Circuit Judge, since 1987; a Recorder of the Crown Court, since 1986; *b* 1 Oct. 1940; *s* of late Maurice and of Lilian Sanders; *m* 1969, Susan, *er d* of Simon and Phyllis Brenner; two *s* (one *d* decd). *Educ:* Highgate School. Co-founder, Inner Temple Debating Soc., 1961, Chm. 1962. Called to the Bar, Inner Temple, 1965; South Eastern Circuit. Metropolitan Stipendiary Magistrate, 1980–87. A Chm., Inner London Juvenile Courts, 1980–87; Chm., Legal Cttee, Inner London Juvenile Panel, 1983–86; First Chm., No 1 (London S) Regional Duty Solicitor Cttee, 1984–85; Inner London Magistrates' Training Panel, 1983–87; Mem., Mental

Health Review Tribunal, 1990–. Chairman, Walker School Assoc. (Southgate), 1976, 1977; Schools' Debating Assoc. Judge, 1976–; Mem., Haringey Schools Liaison Group, 1979. *Recreations:* model railways, music, gardening. *Address:* c/o Circuit Office, New Cavendish House, 18 Maltravers Street, WC2R 3EU.

SANDERS, Ronald; international affairs and business consultant; Director, Swiss American National Bank, Antigua, since 1990; Adviser to President, Atlantic Tele Network, USA, since 1989; *b* Guyana, 26 Jan. 1948; *m* 1975, Susan Indrani (*née* Ramphal). *Educ:* Sacred Heart RC Sch., Guyana; Westminster Sch., London; Boston Univ., USA; Sussex Univ. Gen. Man., Guyana Broadcasting Service, 1973–76; Communication Cons. to Pres., Caribbean Develt Bank, Barbados, 1977; UNDP and CFTC Cons. to Govt of Antigua, 1977–81; Advr to For. Minister of Antigua and Barbuda, 1981–82; Dep. Perm. Rep. to UN, 1982–83; High Comr for Antigua and Barbuda in UK, 1984–87; Ambassador to UNESCO and EEC, 1983–87, to FRG, 1986–87. Vis. Fellow, Oxford Univ., 1988–89. Advr to Govt of Antigua and Barbuda, 1989–91. Mem., Bd of Dirs, Guyana Telephone and Telegraph Co., 1991–. Member: Inter-Govtl Council, Internat. Prog. for Develt of Communications, UNESCO, 1983–87; Exec. Bd, UNESCO, 1985–87; RIIA, 1987–; Internat. Inst. of Communications, 1984–. *Publications:* Broadcasting in Guyana, 1977; Antigua and Barbuda: transition, trial, triumph, 1984; (ed) Inseparable Humanity—an anthology of reflections of Shridath Ramphal, Commonwealth Secretary-General, 1988; several contribs to internat. jls on communication, Antarctica, also political commentaries. *Recreations:* reading, cinema. *Address:* 24 Chelmsford Square, NW10 3AR. *Clubs:* Royal Automobile, St James's.

SANDERS, William George, CB 1991; RCNC, CEng, FRINA; Head of Royal Corps of Naval Constructors, 1986–91; Director General, Submarines, Ministry of Defence (PE), 1985–91; *b* 22 Jan. 1936; *s* of George and Alice Irene Sanders; *m* 1956, Marina Charlotte Burford; two *s* one *d*. *Educ:* Public Secondary Sch., Plymouth; Devonport Dockyard Tech. Coll.; RN Coll., Greenwich. Asst Constructor, Ship Dept, Admiralty, 1961–68; FNCO Western Fleet, 1968–70; Constructor, Ship Dept, MoD (Navy), 1970–77; Principal Naval Overseer, Scotland, 1977–79; Marconi Space and Defence Systems, 1979–82; Project Manager, Type 23, 1982–83; DG Future Material Projects (Naval), MoD (PE), 1983–85. *Recreations:* golf, painting, gardening. *Address:* The Old Barn, London Road West, Bath, Avon. *T:* Bath (0225) 317006.

SANDERSON, family name of **Baron Sanderson of Bowden.**

SANDERSON OF AYOT, 2nd Baron *cr* 1960, title disclaimed by the heir, Dr Alan Lindsay Sanderson, 1971.

SANDERSON OF BOWDEN, Baron *cr* 1985 (Life Peer), of Melrose in the District of Ettrick and Lauderdale; **Charles Russell Sanderson,** Kt 1981; DL; Chairman, Scottish Conservative Party, since 1990; *b* 30 April 1933; *s* of Charles Plummer Sanderson and Martha Evelyn Gardiner; *m* 1958, Frances Elizabeth Macaulay; one *s* two *d* (and one *s* decd). *Educ:* St Mary's Sch., Melrose; Trinity Coll., Glenalmond; Scottish Coll. of Textiles, Galashiels; Bradford Coll. (now Bradford Univ.). Commnd Royal Signals, 1952; served: 51 (Highland) Inf. Div. Signal Regt TA, 1953–56, KOSB TA, 1956–58. Partner, Chas P. Sanderson, Wool and Yarn Merchants, Melrose, 1958–87; Chairman: Edinburgh Financial Trust (formerly Yorkshire & Lancashire Investment Trust), 1983–87; Shires Investment Trust, 1984–87; Dir, Clydesdale Bank, 1986–87. Minister of State, Scottish Office, 1987–90. Chairman, Roxburgh, Selkirk and Peebles Cons. and Unionist Assoc., 1970–73; Scottish Cons. Unionist Association: Chm. Central and Southern Area, 1974–75; Vice-Pres. 1975–77; Pres. 1977–79; Vice-Chm. Nat. Union of Cons Assocs, 1979–81 (Mem. Exec. Cttee, 1975–); Chm. Exec. Cttee, Nat. Union of Cons. Assocs, 1981–86; Member: Cons. Party Policy Cttee, 1979–86; Standing Adv. Cttee of Parly Candidates, 1979–86 (Vice-Chm. with responsibility for Europe, 1980–81). Deacon, Galashiels Manufrs Corp., 1976; Chm., Eildon Housing Assoc., 1978–82. Governor, St Mary's Sch., Melrose, 1977–87; Mem. Council, Trinity Coll., Glenalmond, 1982–. Comr, Gen. Assembly of Ch. of Scotland, 1972. DL Roxburgh, Ettrick and Lauderdale, 1990. *Recreations:* golf, amateur operatics (Past Pres., Producer and Mem. Melrose Amateur Operatic Soc.). *Address:* Becketts Field, Bowden, Melrose, Roxburgh TD6 0ST. *T:* St Boswell's (0835) 22736. *Clubs:* Caledonian; Hon. Co. of Edinburgh Golfers (Muirfield).

SANDERSON, Sir Bryan; *see* Sanderson, Sir F. P. B.

SANDERSON, Charles Denis; HM Diplomatic Service, retired; Domestic Bursar and Fellow of St Peter's College, Oxford, since 1985; *b* 18 Dec. 1934; *s* of Norman and Elsie Sanderson; *m* 1960, Mary Joyce Gillow; one *s* two *d*. *Educ:* Bishopshalt Sch., Hillingdon, Mddx; Pembroke Coll., Oxford (MA). National Service, 1953–55; Oxford, 1955–58; British Petroleum Co. Ltd, 1958–64; Second, later First Secretary, Commonwealth Relations Office, 1964–67; First Sec., Kingston, and concurrently, Haiti, 1967–70; Acting Consul, Port au Prince, 1969; First Sec., Head of Chancery and Consul, Panama, 1970–73; First Sec., FCO, 1973–75; Consul (Commercial), British Trade Development Office, New York, 1975–77; Dep. Consul General and Director Industrial Development, New York, 1977–79; Counsellor, Caracas, 1979–84; Hd, W Indian and Atlantic Dept, FCO, 1984–85. *Address:* Gilletts Farm, Asthall Leigh, Oxford OX8 5PX. *T:* Asthall Leigh (099387) 455. *Club:* Commonwealth Trust.

SANDERSON, Sir (Frank Philip) Bryan, 2nd Bt, *cr* 1920; Lt-Comdr RNVR; *b* 18 Feb. 1910; *s* of Sir Frank Bernard Sanderson, 1st Bt, and Amy Edith (*d* 1949), *d* of David Wing, Scarborough; *S* father 1965; *m* 1933, Annette Irene Caroline (*d* 1967), *d* of late Col Korab Laskowski, Warsaw, (*g d* of General Count de Castellaz); two *s* one *d*. *Educ:* Stowe; Pembroke College, Oxford. Served War of 1939–45 with Fleet Air Arm. A Member of Lloyd's. Dir, Humber Fertilisers (formerly Humber Fishing and Fish Manure Co.), Hull, retd 1988 (Chm., 1965–80). *Recreation:* shooting. *Heir: s* Frank Linton Sanderson [*b* 21 Nov. 1933; *m* 1961, Margaret Ann, *o d* of John C. Maxwell; two *s* three *d*]. *Address:* Lychgate Cottage, Scaynes Hill, Haywards Heath, West Sussex RH17 7NH.

SANDERSON, George Rutherford, CBE 1978; British Council Representative, Spain, and Cultural Attaché, British Embassy, Madrid, 1976–79; *b* 23 Nov. 1919; *er s* of late George Sanderson and Edith Mary Sanderson, Blyth, Northumberland; *m* 1947, Jean Cecilia, *d* of late James C. McDougall, Chesterfield, Derbyshire; two *s*. *Educ:* Blyth Grammar Sch.; Univ. of London (BA 1st Cl. Hons French and Italian). War Service, 1940–46: RA, Malta and Egypt (Major). British Council, 1949–79: Actg Dir, Anglo Argentine Cultural Inst., La Plata, Argentina, 1949; Dir, Tucuman, Argentina, 1950–52; Asst Rep., Santiago, Chile, 1952–58; Dep. Area Officer, Oxford, 1958–62; Reg. Dir, and Dir Anglo Argentine Cultural Assoc., Rosario, Argentina, 1962–66; Asst Rep., Buenos Aires, 1966–69; Reg. Dir, and Dir Anglo Brazilian Cultural Soc., São Paulo, Brazil, 1969–72; Dir, Drama and Music Dept, and Dep. Controller, Arts Div., 1973; Educnl Attaché, British Embassy, Washington, 1973–76; Administering Officer, The Kennedy Scholarships and Knox Fellowships, ACU, 1979–82. *Recreations:* art, reading. *Address:* Leafield House, Holton, Oxford OX9 1PZ. *T:* Wheatley (08677) 2526. *Club:* Athenæum.

SANDERSON, Air Vice-Marshal Keith Fred, CB 1986; Planning Consultant, Ericsson Ltd, since 1989; *b* 25 Nov. 1932; *s* of late Arnold and Emily Sanderson; *m* 1957, Margaret

Ward; two *d*. *Educ:* Hutton Grammar Sch., Lancs. RAF Navigator, 1950–74; Staff of CDS, 1974–75; Comd RAF Leconfield, 1976; RCDS, 1977; AOA RAF Germany, 1978–80; AOC Personnel Management Centre and Dir of Personnel (Air), 1980–83; AOA, HQ Strike Command, 1983–87. BDO Binder Hamlyn, 1987–89. *Recreations:* walking, golf. *Club:* Royal Air Force.

SANDERSON, Very Rev. Peter Oliver; Provost of St Paul's Cathedral, Dundee, since 1984; *b* 26 Jan. 1929; *s* of Harold and Doris Sanderson; *m* 1956, Doreen Gibson; one *s* one *d* (and one *s* decd). *Educ:* St Chad's College, Durham Univ. (BA, DipTh). Asst Curate, Houghton-le-Spring, Durham Diocese, 1954–59; Rector, Linstead and St Thomas Ye Vale, Jamaica, 1959–63; Chaplain, RAF, 1963–67; Vicar, Winksley-cum-Grantley and Aldfield-with-Studley, Ripon, 1967–74; Vicar, St Aidan, Leeds, 1974–84. *Recreations:* gardening, music, reading. *Address:* St Paul's Cathedral Rectory, 4 Richmond Terrace, Dundee DD2 1BQ. *T:* Dundee (0382) 68548.

SANDERSON, Very Rev. Roy; *see* Sanderson, Very Rev. W. R.

SANDERSON, Roy, OBE 1983; National Secretary, Electrical and Engineering Staff Association, EETPU, since 1987; *b* 15 Feb. 1931; *s* of George and Lillian Sanderson; *m* 1951, Jean (*née* Booth); two *s* (and one *s* decd). *Educ:* Carfield Sch., Sheffield. EETPU Convenor, Lucas Aerospace, Hemel Hempstead, 1952–67; Asst Educn Officer, EETPU, 1967–69; Nat. Officer, EETPU, 1969–87. Non-exec. Dir, UKAEA, 1987–. Member: Armed Forces Pay Review Body, 1987–; Economic and Social Cttee, European Community, 1990. *Recreations:* golf, snooker; supporter of Watford Football Club. *Address:* 162 Belswains Lane, Hemel Hempstead HP3 9XA. *T:* Hemel Hempstead (0442) 242033. *Club:* Shendish (Hemel Hempstead).

SANDERSON, Very Rev. (William) Roy; Parish Minister at Stenton and Whittingehame, 1963–73; Extra Chaplain to the Queen in Scotland, since 1977 (Chaplain, 1965–77); *b* 23 Sept. 1907; *er s* of late Arthur Watson Sanderson, Leith, and late Ethel Catherine Watson, Dundee; *m* 1941, Annie Muriel Easton, Glasgow; three *s* two *d*. *Educ:* Cargilfield Sch.; Fettes Coll.; Oriel Coll., Oxford; Edinburgh University. BA 1929, MA 1933, Oxon. Ordained, 1933. Asst Minister, St Giles' Cath., Edin., 1932–34; Minister: at St Andrew's, Lochgelly, 1935–39; at the Barony of Glasgow, 1939–63. Moderator: Glasgow Presbytery, 1958; Haddington and Dunbar Presbytery, 1972–74; Convener of Assembly Cttees: on Religious Instruction of Youth, 1950–55; on Deaconesses, 1956–61; Panel of Doctrine, 1960–65; on Gen. Administration, 1967–72. Convener of Business Cttee and Leader of General Assembly of the Church of Scotland, 1965–66, 1968–72. Moderator of Gen. Assembly of the Church of Scotland, May 1967–May 1968. Chm., BBC Scottish Religious Advisory Committee, 1961–71; Member Central Religious Advisory Cttee of BBC and ITA, 1961–71. Governor, Fettes Coll., Edinburgh, 1967–76. Hon. DD Glasgow, 1959. *Publication:* Responsibility (Moderatorial address), 1967. *Recreations:* cooking, reading. *Address:* 1a York Road, North Berwick, East Lothian EH39 4LS. *T:* North Berwick (0620) 2780.

SANDFORD, 2nd Baron, *cr* 1945, of Banbury; **Rev. John Cyril Edmondson,** DSC 1942; Conservative Peer in House of Lords, since 1959; *b* 22 Dec. 1920; *e s* of 1st Baron Sandford; *S* father, 1959; *m* 1947, Catharine Mary Hunt; two *s* two *d*. *Educ:* Eton Coll.; Royal Naval Coll., Dartmouth; Westcott House, Cambridge. Served War of 1939–45: Mediterranean Fleet, 1940–41; Home Fleet, 1942; Normandy Landings, 1944 (wounded); Mediterranean Fleet, HMS Saumarez, 1946 (wounded). Staff of RN Coll., Dartmouth, 1947–49; HMS Vengeance, 1950; HMS Cleopatra, 1951–52; Staff Commander-in-Chief Far East, 1953–55; Commander of Home Fleet Flagship, HMS Tyne, 1956; retired 1956. Ordained in Church of England, 1958; Parish of St Nicholas, Harpenden, 1958–63; Exec. Chaplain to Bishop of St Albans, 1965–68. Opposition Whip, House of Lords, 1966–70; Parly Sec., Min. of Housing and Local Govt, June–Oct. 1970; Parliamentary Under-Secretary of State: DoE, 1970–73; DES, 1973–74. Dir, Ecclesiastical Insce Office, 1977–89. Chairman: Cttee to review the condition and future of National Parks in England and Wales, 1971; Standing Conf. of London and SE Regl Planning Authorities, 1981–89. A Church Comr, 1982–89. Chairman: Hertfordshire Council of Social Service, 1969–70; Church Army, 1969–70; Community Task Force, 1975–82; Redundant Churches Cttee, 1982–89; Mem., Adv. Council on Penal Reform, 1968–70. President: Anglo-Swiss Soc., 1974–84; Council for Environmental Educn, 1974–84; Assoc. of District Councils, 1980–86; Offa's Dyke Assoc., 1980–84; Countrywide Holidays Assoc., 1982–86; Vice-Pres., YHA, 1979–90. Founder Trustee, WaterAid, 1981 (Council Mem., 1984; Vice-Pres., 1991). Founder, Sandford Award for Heritage Educn; inaugurated Heritage Educn Trust. Hon. Fellow, Inst. of Landscape Architects. *Heir: s* Hon. James John Mowbray Edmondson [*b* 1 July 1949; *m* 1st, 1973, Ellen Sarah, *d* of Jack Shapiro, Toronto; one *d*; 2nd, 1986, Linda, *d* of Mr and Mrs Wheeler, Nova Scotia; one *s*]. *Address:* 27 Ashley Gardens, Ambrosden Avenue, Westminster, SW1P 1QD. *T:* 071–834 5722. *Club:* Ski Club of Gt Britain.

SANDFORD, Arthur; DL; Chief Executive, Football League, since 1990; *b* 12 May 1941; *s* of Arthur and Lilian Sandford; *m* 1963, Kathleen Entwistle; two *d*. *Educ:* Queen Elizabeth's Grammar Sch., Blackburn; University Coll., London (LLB Hons (Upper 2nd Class)). Preston County Borough Council: Articled Clerk to Town Clerk, 1962–65; Asst Solicitor, 1965–66; Sen. Asst Solicitor, 1966–68; Asst Solicitor, Hants CC, 1969–70; Nottinghamshire County Council: Second Asst Clerk, 1970–72; First Asst Clerk, 1972–74; Dep. Dir of Admin, 1973–75; Dir of Admin, 1975–77; Dep. Clerk and County Sec., 1977–78; Clerk and Chief Exec., 1978–89. DL Notts, 1990. *Recreations:* half-marathon running, gardening. *Address:* Fairford House, 66 Loughborough Road, Bunny, Nottingham NG11 6QD. *T:* Nottingham (0602) 212440. *Club:* Royal Over-Seas League.

SANDFORD, Prof. Cedric Thomas; Professor of Political Economy, University of Bath, 1965–87, now Professor Emeritus; Director of Bath University Centre for Fiscal Studies, 1974–86; *b* 21 Nov. 1924; *s* of Thomas Sandford and Louisa (*née* Hodge); *m* 1945, Evelyn Belch (*d* 1982); one *s* one *d*; *m* 1984, Christina Privett; one *d*. *Educ:* Manchester Univ. (BAEcon 1948, MAEcon 1949); London Univ. (BA History (external) 1955). Undergraduate, Manchester Univ., 1942–43 and 1946–48; RAF, 1943–46 (Pilot). Graduate Research Schol., Univ. of Manchester, 1948–49; Lectr, Burnley Municipal Coll., 1949–60; Sen. Lectr, subseq. Head of General and Social Studies Dept, Bristol Coll. of Science and Technology, 1960–65; Head of Sch. of Humanities and Social Sciences, Univ. of Bath, 1965–68, 1971–74, 1977–79. Visiting Prof., Univ. of Delaware, USA, 1969; Visiting Fellow: ANU, 1981, 1985; Univ. of Melbourne, 1990. Mem., Meade Cttee on Reform of Direct Tax System, 1975–78; Consultant: Fiscal Div., OECD, 1976–79, 1985–87; Irish Commn on Taxation, 1982–85; World Bank, 1986; UN 1986; IMF 1989. *Publications:* Taxing Inheritance and Capital Gains (Hobart Paper 32, IEA), 1965, 2nd edn 1967; Economics of Public Finance, 1969, 3rd edn 1984; Realistic Tax Reform, 1971; Taxing Personal Wealth, 1971; (sen. editor and jt author) Case Studies in Economics (3 vols), 1971, 2nd edn 1977; National Economic Planning, 1972, 2nd edn 1976; Hidden Costs of Taxation, 1973; (jtly) An Accessions Tax, 1973; (jtly) An Annual Wealth Tax, 1975; Social Economics, 1977; (jtly) Grants or Loans?, 1980; (jtly) The Costs and Benefits of VAT, 1981; The Economic Framework, 1982; (jtly) Tax Policy-Making in the United

Kingdom, 1983; (jtly) The Irish Wealth Tax: a study in economics and politics, 1985; Taxing Wealth in New Zealand, 1987; (jtly) Administrative and Compliance Costs of Taxation, 1989; numerous articles in wide range of learned jls. *Recreations:* fishing, gardening, busking. *Address:* Old Coach House, Fersfield, Perrymead, Bath BA2 5AR. *T:* Bath (0225) 832683.

SANDFORD, Herbert Henry, OBE 1963; DFM 1942; Member for Chelsea, ILEA, 1986–90; Chief Whip, minority party, 1986–90; opposition spokesman: Staff Committee, 1986–90; General Purposes Committee, 1986–90; *b* 19 Nov. 1916; *s* of Herbert Charles Sandford and Grace Ellen (*née* Onley); *m* 1st, 1938, Irene Lucy (*née* Porter) (marr. diss. 1944); 2nd, 1948, Jessie Irene (*née* Gray). *Educ:* Minchendon Secondary Sch., Southgate. Served War, Pathfinder Sqdns, RAF, 1939–45. Elected to St Marylebone Metrop. Bor. Council, 1953; Chm., Works Cttee. City of Westminster: Councillor, Lords Ward, 1964–68; Alderman, 1968–78; Dep. Leader of Council, 1975–76; Chairman: Traffic Cttee, 1964–67; Highways and Traffic Cttee, 1967–68; Highways Cttee, 1971–72 (Vice-Chm., 1969–71); Highways and Works Cttee, 1972–75; special sub-cttee of Highways and Town Planning Cttees on redevelt of Piccadilly Circus, 1972–76; Member: Policy Cttee, 1972–74; Town Planning Cttee, 1971–76; Road Safety Cttee, 1972–74; Road Safety Adv. Cttee, 1974–76; Co-ord. Cttee, 1974–75; Housing Management Cttee, 1975–77; London Transport Passenger Cttee, 1974–76. Greater London Council: Mem. for St Marylebone, 1976–86; Dep. Chm., 1985–86; Chm., Central Area Planning Cttee, 1977–81; Member: Public Services Safety Cttee, 1977–81; Covent Garden Cttee, 1977–81; Thames Water Regional Land Drainage Cttee, 1978–82; Leading Opposition Mem., Technical Services Cttee, 1983–86; Dep. Spokesman, Finance Cttee, 1983–86. Opposition Spokesman, Staff and Gen. Cttee, 1982–86, Opposition Chief Whip, 1986–90, ILEA. Chm., Grove End Housing Assoc., Ltd, 1986– (Dir, 1976–). Chairman: St Marylebone Sea Cadet Corps, 1953; St Marylebone Boy Scouts Assoc., 1958–64. Treasurer, Wiltons Music Hall Trust, 1982–. Governor: St John's Hosp. for Skin Diseases, 1973–76; London Inst., 1986–90. *Recreations:* golf, bridge, Yoga. *Address:* 5 Elmfield House, Carlton Hill, NW8 9XB. *T:* 071–624 9694. *Clubs:* Royal Air Force, Pathfinder.

SANDFORD, Jeremy; writer, journalist, musician, performer; *s* of late Christopher Sandford, owner/director of the Golden Cockerel Press, and of Lettice Sandford, wood engraver, craft worker; *m* 1956, Nell Dunn; three *s*. *Educ:* Eton; Oxford. Dir, The Cyrenians; Exec., Gypsy Council; Sponsor: Shelter; The Simon Community. Editor, Romano Drom (gypsy newspaper). Screen Writers' Guild of Gt Britain Award, 1967, 1971; Prix Italia prize for TV drama, 1968; Critics Award for TV drama, 1971. *Publications:* Synthetic Fun, 1967; Cathy Come Home, 1967; Whelks and Chromium, 1968; Edna the Inebriate Woman, 1971; Down and Out in Britain, 1971; In Search of the Magic Mushrooms, 1972; Gypsies, 1973; Tomorrow's People, 1974; Prostitutes, 1975; Smiling David, 1975; Virgin of the Clearways, 1977. *Recreations:* painting, music, travel, mountain exploration, riding, wandering, windsurfing, wondering, festivals, getting to know British people. *Address:* c/o 7 Earls Court Square, SW5. *Club:* Chelsea Arts.

SANDFORD, Kenneth Leslie, CMG 1974; retired barrister; *b* 14 Aug. 1915; *s* of Albert Edgar Sandford and Barbara Ivy (*née* Hill); *m* 1946, Airini Ethel Scott Sergel; one *s* one *d* (and one *d* decd). *Educ:* King's Coll., Auckland, NZ; Auckland University Coll. LLB 1938. Served War: 34 Bn (NZ), rank of Captain, 1940–45. Barrister and Solicitor, 1939–72; Crown Solicitor (Hamilton), 1950–72; Chm., Accident Compensation Commn (NZ), 1972–80. *Publications:* Dead Reckoning, 1955; Dead Secret, 1957; Mark of the Lion, 1962. *Recreation:* cricket (Pres. NZ Cricket Council, 1971–73). *Address:* 1523 Kawakawa Bay, RD5 Papakura, New Zealand.

SANDFORD, Rear-Adm. Sefton Ronald, CB 1976; *b* 23 July 1925; *s* of Col H. R. Sandford and Mrs Faye Sandford (*née* Renouf); *m* 1st, 1950, Mary Ann Prins (*d* 1972); one *s*; 2nd, 1972, Jennifer Rachel Newell; two *d*. *Educ:* St Aubyns, Rottingdean, 1934–38; Royal Naval Coll., Dartmouth, 1939–42. Served War: went to sea, July 1942; commanded HMMTB 2017, Lieut, 1946–47; ADC to Comdr British Forces, Hong Kong (Lt-Gen. Sir Terence Airey), 1952–53; commanded HMS Teazer (rank Comdr), 1958; Staff of Imperial Defence Coll., 1963–65; comd HMS Protector, Captain, 1965–67; Naval Attaché, Moscow, 1968–70; comd HMS Devonshire, 1971–73; ADC to the Queen, 1974; Flag Officer, Gibraltar, 1974–76. A Younger Brother of Trinity House, 1968. *Recreations:* cricket, sailing, fishing. *Address:* Dolphins, Rue de St Jean, St Lawrence, Jersey, Channel Islands. *T:* Jersey (0534) 62200. *Clubs:* Marylebone Cricket (MCC); Royal Yacht Squadron (Cowes).

SANDFORD SMITH, Richard Henry, FCIS; Chairman, Eastern Gas Region (formerly Eastern Gas Board), 1970–73; *b* 29 March 1909; *s* of late Dr H. Sandford Smith; *m* 1936, Dorothy Hewitt, *y d* of late Rev. J. F. Hewitt; one *s*. *Educ:* Haileybury Coll. London Stock Exchange, 1926. Qualified as Chartered Secretary and awarded Sir Ernest Clarke Prize, 1932. Joined Gas Light & Coke Co., 1932; Sec., SE Gas Corp. Ltd, 1939–49; Sec., SE Gas Bd, 1949–56 (Dep. Chm., 1956–69). *Recreations:* theatre, golf, gardening. *Address:* 60 The Marlowes, St John's Wood Park, NW8 6NA. *Club:* Savile.

SANDHURST, 5th Baron, *cr* 1871; **(John Edward) Terence Mansfield,** DFC 1944; *b* 4 Sept. 1920; *er s* of 4th Baron Sandhurst, OBE, and Morley Victoria (*née* Upcher; *d* 1961); *S* father 1964; *m* 1947, Janet Mary, *er d* of late John Edward Lloyd, NY, USA; one *s* one *d*. *Educ:* Harrow. Served RAFVR, 1939–46: Bomber Command (as Navigator and Bombing Leader): 149 Sqdn, 1941; 419 (RCAF) Sqdn, 1942; 12 Sqdn, 1943–45. 1946–55: Metropolitan Special Constabulary 'C' Div., Sergeant, 1949–52; long service medal, 1955. Hon. ADC to Lieutenant-Governor of Jersey, 1969–74. *Recreation:* golf. *Heir:* *s* Hon. Guy Rhys John Mansfield [*b* 3 March 1949; *m* 1976, Philippa St Clair, *er d* of late Digby Verdon-Roe, Cannes; one *s* one *d*. *Educ:* Harrow; Oriel Coll., Oxford (MA). Called to Bar, Middle Temple, 1972]. *Address:* Jersey, CI. *Clubs:* Royal Air Force, MCC; United (Jersey).

See also Earl of Macclesfield.

SANDIFORD, Rt. Hon. (Lloyd) Erskine, PC 1989; JP; MP St Michael South, since 1971; Prime Minister and Minister of Finance and Economic Affairs, Barbados, since 1987; *b* 24 March 1937; *s* of Cyril and Eunice Sandiford; *m* 1963, Angelita P. Rickett; one *s* two *d*. *Educ:* Coleridge/Parry Sec.; Harrison Coll.; Univ. of WI, Jamaica (BA Hons English); Univ. of Manchester (MAEcon). Assistant Master: Modern High Sch., Barbados, 1956–57; Kingston Coll., Jamaica, 1960–61; Asst Master, 1963–64, Sen. Graduate Master, 1964–66, Harrison Coll., Barbados; part-time Tutor and Lectr, Univ. of the WI, Barbados, 1963–65; Asst Tutor, Barbados Community Coll., 1976–86. Democratic Labour Party, Barbados: Mem., 1964–; Asst Sec., 1966–67; Gen. Sec., 1967–68; (first) Vice-Pres., 1972–74; Pres., 1974–75; Vice-Pres., 1975–76; Founder, Acad. of Politics. Member: Senate, 1967–71; House of Assembly, 1971–; Personal Asst to the Prime Minister, 1966–67; Minister: of Educn, 1967–71; of Educn, Youth Affairs, Community Develt and Sport, 1971–75; of Health and Welfare, 1975–76; Dep. Leader of Opposition, 1978–86; Dep. Prime Minister and Minister of Educn and Culture, 1986–87. Order of the Liberator (Venezuela), 1987. *Address:* Prime Minister's Office, Government Headquarters, Bridgetown, Barbados, West Indies. *T:* 426–3179.

SANDILANDS, family name of **Baron Torphichen.**

SANDILANDS, Sir Francis (Edwin Prescott), Kt 1976; CBE 1967; Director, 1965–83 and Chairman, 1972–83, Commercial Union Assurance Co. Ltd; *b* 11 December 1913; *s* of late Lieut-Col Prescott Sandilands, DSO, RM, and late Gladys Baird Murton; *m* 1939, Susan Gillian Jackson; two *s*. *Educ:* Eton; Corpus Christi College, Cambridge (Hon. Fellow, 1975). MA 1938. Served War of 1939–45, Royal Scots Fusiliers and General Staff, UK and NW Europe (Lt-Col; despatches). Joined Ocean Accident and Guarantee Corporation Ltd, 1935, Manager, 1955; General Manager, then Chief General Manager, 1958–72, Vice-Chm., 1968–72, Commercial Union Assurance Co. Ltd; Chairman: Royal Trust Company of Canada, 1974–84; Dir, Kleinwort, Benson, Lonsdale Ltd, 1979–86. Trustee: British Museum, 1977–85; Royal Opera House, 1974–86 (Chm. Trustees, 1980–84; Dir, 1975–85); Mem., Royal Fine Art Commn, 1980–85. Chairman: London Salvage Corps, 1962–63; British Insurance Assoc., 1965–67; Pres., Insurance Inst. of London, 1969–70. Chm., Govt Cttee of Enquiry on Inflation and Company Accounts, 1974–75; Cttee on Invisible Exports, 1975–83; Member: BOTB, 1976–83; Adv. Cttee, Queen's Award to Industry, 1976–83. Treas., UCL, 1973–81 (Hon. Fellow, 1981). Commandeur de l'Ordre de la Couronne (Belgium), 1974. *Address:* 53 Cadogan Square, SW1X 0HY. *T:* 071–235 6384.

SANDISON, Alexander, (Alec), FCCA; Director, Cruse-Bereavement Care, since 1990; *b* 24 May 1943; *s* of late Alexander Sandison and Mary Roscoe; *m* 1st, 1968, Janet Firmager; 2nd, 1977, Merralyn Martin (*née* Hill); two *s*. *Educ:* Cambs High Sch.; Trinity Sch. of John Whitgift, Croydon. FCCA 1970. Commercial Union Assce Co., 1962–63; John Mowlem PLC, 1964–71 (Gp Financial Accountant, 1970–71); Chief Accountant: and Co. Sec., J. E. Freeman & Co., 1972–73; Wings Ltd, 1973–78; Divl Financial Dir, Doulton Glass Inds, 1978–80; Sec. for Finance and Corporate Controller, RICS, 1980–90; Chief Exec., Surveyors Holdings Ltd, 1985–89; Chm., Imaginor Systems Ltd, 1989–90. *Publications:* People to People: course notes, 1985; Watton-at-Stone Village Guide, 1989; contribs, incl. poetry, to learned jls. *Recreations:* reading, writing; avoiding involvement with and conversations about, sport. *Address:* Cruse-Bereavement Care, 126 Sheen Road, Richmond, Surrey TW9 1UR. *T:* 081–940 4818.

SANDLE, Prof. Michael Leonard, RA 1989 (ARA 1982); DFA; sculptor; Professor at the Akademie der Bildenden Künste, Karlsruhe, West Germany, since 1980; *b* 18 May 1936; *s* of Charles Edward Sandle and Dorothy Gwendoline Gladys (*née* Vernon); *m* 1971, Cynthia Dora Koppel (marriage annulled 1974); *m* 1988, Demelza Spargo. *Educ:* Douglas High Sch., IOM; Douglas Sch. of Art and Technol.; Slade Sch. of Fine Art (DFA 1959). Studied painting and printmaking, Slade Sch. of Fine Art, 1956–59; changed to sculpture, 1962; various teaching posts in Britain, 1961–70, including Lectr, Coventry Coll. of Art, 1964–68; resident in Canada, 1970–73; Vis. Prof., Univ. of Calgary, Alberta, 1970–71; Vis. Associate Prof., Univ. of Victoria, BC, 1972–73; Lectr in Sculpture, Fachhochschule für Gestaltung, Pforzheim, W Germany, 1973–77, Prof., 1977–80. Has participated in exhibns in GB and internationally, 1957–, including: V Biennale, Paris, 1966; Documenta IV, Kassel, W Germany, 1968 and Documenta VI, 1977. Work in public collections, including: Arts Council of GB, Tate Gall.; Australian Nat. Gall., Canberra; Met. Mus., NY; Sztüki Mus., Lodz; Nat. Gall., Warsaw; Wilhelm Lehmbruck Mus., Duisburg, W Germany. Nobutaka Shikanai Special Prize, Utsukushi-Ga-Hara Open-Air Mus., Japan, 1986. Tokyo. *Address:* Schloss Scheibenhardt, 7500 Karlsruhe, West Germany. *T:* Karlsruhe 868633.

SANDLER, Prof. Merton, MD; FRCP, FRCPath, FRCPsych, CBiol, FIBiol; Professor of Chemical Pathology, Royal Postgraduate Medical School, Institute of Obstetrics and Gynaecology, University of London, 1973–91, Professor Emeritus, since 1991; Consultant Chemical Pathologist, Queen Charlotte's Maternity Hospital, 1958–91; *b* 28 March 1926; *s* of late Frank Sandler and Edith (*née* Stein), Salford, Lancs; *m* 1961, Lorna Rosemary, *d* of late Ian Michael and of Sally Grenby, Colindale, London; two *s* two *d*. *Educ:* Manchester Grammar Sch.; Manchester Univ. (MB ChB 1949; MD 1962). FRCPath 1970 (MRCPath 1963); FRCP 1974 (MRCP 1955); FRCPsych 1986. Jun. Specialist in Pathology, RAMC (Captain), 1951–53. Research Fellow in Clin. Path., Brompton Hosp., 1953–54; Lectr in Chem. Path., Royal Free Hosp. Sch. of Med., 1955–58. Visiting Professor: Univ. of New Mexico, 1983; Chicago Med. Sch., 1984; Univ. of S Fla, 1988. Recognized Teacher in Chem. Path., 1960–; extensive examining experience for various Brit. and for. univs and Royal Colls; Mem. Standing Adv. Cttee, Bd of Studies in Path., Univ. of London, 1972–76 (also Mem. Chem. Path. Sub-Cttee, 1973–); Chm., Academic Bd, 1972–73, Bd of Management, 1975–, Inst. of Obst. and Gyn.; Governor: Brit. Postgrad. Med. Fedn, 1976–78; Queen Charlotte's Hosp. for Women, 1978–84; Council Mem. and Meetings Sec., Assoc. of Clin. Pathologists, 1959–70; Mem. Council, Collegium Internat. Neuro-Psycho-pharmacologicum, 1982–90. Various offices in: RSM, incl. Hon. Librarian, 1977–, and Pres. Section of Med. Exper. Med. and Therapeutics, 1979–80; Brit. Assoc. for Psychopharm., incl. Pres., 1980–82; British Assoc. for Postnatal Illness (Pres., 1980–); office in many other learned socs and grant-giving bodies, incl. Med. Adv. Councils of Migraine Trust, 1975–80 (Chm., Scientific Adv. Cttee, 1985–), Schizophrenia Assoc. of GB, 1975–78, Parkinson's Disease Soc., 1981–, Chm. of Trustees, Nat. Soc. for Res. into Mental Health, 1983–. Chm. and Sec., Biol Council Symposium on Drug Action, 1979; Sec., Mem. Bd of Management and Chm. Awards Subcttee, Biological Council, 1983–91; Member, Executive Committee: Marcé Soc., 1983–86; Med. Council on Alcoholism, 1987–90; Sec. and Mem. Council, Harveian Soc. of London, 1979–89 (Vice Pres., 1990; Pres., Nov. 1991–92); Mem. Council of Management and Patron, Helping Hand Orgn, 1981–87. Organiser or Brit. rep. on org. cttees of many nat. and internat. meetings incl. Internat. Chm., 6th Internat. Catecholamine Congress, 1987. For. Corresp. Mem., Amer. Coll. of Neuropsychopharm., 1975; Hon. Member: Indian Acad. of Neuroscis, 1982; Hungarian Pharmacological Soc., 1985. Jt Editor: British Jl of Pharmacology, 1974–80; Clinical Science, 1975–77; Jl of Neural Transmission, 1979–82; Jt Editor-in-Chief, Jl of Psychiatric Research, 1982–, and present or past Mem. Editorial Bds of 17 other sci. jls; eponymous lectures to various learned socs incl. 1st Cumings Meml, 1976, James E. Beall II Meml, 1980, Biol Council Lecture and Medal, 1984; provision of Nat. Monoamine Ref. Laboratory Service, 1976–91. Anna Monika Internat. Prize (jtly), for Res. on Biol Aspects of Depression, 1973; Gold Medal, Brit. Migraine Assoc., 1974; Senator Dr Franz Burda Internat. Prize for Res. on Parkinson's Disease, 1988; Arnold Friedman Distinguished Clinician Researcher Award, 1991. *Publications:* Mental Illness in Pregnancy and the Puerperium, 1978; The Psychopharmacology of Aggression, 1979; Enzyme Inhibitors as Drugs, 1980; Amniotic Fluid and its Clinical Significance, 1980; The Psychopharmacology of Alcohol, 1980; The Psychopathology of Anticonvulsants, 1981; Nervous Laughter, 1990; *jointly:* The Adrenal Cortex, 1961; The Thyroid Gland, 1967; Advances in Pharmacology, 1968; Monoamine Oxidases, 1972; Serotonin—New Vistas, 1974; Sexual Behaviour: Pharmacology and Biochemistry, 1975; Trace Amines and the Brain, 1976; Phenolsulphotransferase in Mental Health Research, 1981; Tetrahydroisoquinolines and β-Carbolines, 1982; Progress towards a Male Contraceptive, 1982; Neurobiology of the

Trace Amines, 1984; Psychopharmacology and Food, 1985; Neurotransmitter Interactions, 1986; Progress in Catecholamine Research, 1988; Design of Enzyme Inhibitors as Drugs, Vol. 1, 1989; Migraine: a spectrum of ideas, 1990; 5-Hydroxytryptamine in Psychiatry, 1991; numerous research pubns on aspects of biologically-active monoamine metabolism. *Recreations:* reading, listening to music, lying in the sun. *Address:* 27 St Peter's Road, Twickenham, Mddx TW1 1QY. *T:* 081–892 8433. *Club:* Athenæum.

SANDON, Viscount; Dudley Adrian Conroy Ryder; chartered surveyor; *b* 18 March 1951; *s* and *heir* of Earl of Harrowby, *qv*; *m* 1977, Sarah Nicola Hobhouse Payne, *d* of Captain Anthony Payne; three *s*. *Educ:* Eton; Univ. of Newcastle upon Tyne; Magdalene Coll., Cambridge (MA). ARICS. Exec. Dir, Compton Street Securities Ltd, 1988–. Governor, John Archer Sch., Wandsworth, 1986–88. *Recreations:* shooting, fell walking, music, study of fine art and architecture. *Heir: s* Hon. Dudley Anthony Hugo Coventry Ryder, *b* 5 Sept. 1981. *Address:* Sandon Estate Office, Sandon, Stafford ST18 0DA.

SANDS, Roger Blakemore; Clerk of the Overseas Office, House of Commons, since 1987; *b* 6 May 1942; *s* of late Thomas Blakemore Sands and Edith Malyon (Betty) Sands (*née* Waldram); *m* 1966, Jennifer Ann Cattell; two *d*. *Educ:* University Coll. Sch., Hampstead; Oriel Coll., Oxford (scholar; MA LitHum). A Clerk, House of Commons, 1965–; Sec. to Chm. of Ways and Means, 1975–77; Clerk to Select Cttee on European Legislation, 1977–81, to Scottish Affairs Cttee, 1981–84; Sec. to H of C Commn and Clerk to H of C (Services) Cttee, 1985–87. Sec., History of Parlt Trust, 1974–80; Vice Chm, Study of Parlt Group, 1991– (Sec., 1977–79); Sec., Council, RIPA, 1989–. *Publications:* (ed) Official Guide to the Houses of Parliament, 13th edn, 1977; articles and reviews in parly jls. *Recreations:* gardening, listening to music, occasional golf. *Address:* House of Commons, SW1A 0AA. *T:* 071–219 3314.

SANDWICH, 10th Earl of, *cr* 1660; Viscount Hinchingbrooke and Baron Montagu of St Neots, 1660 [disclaimed his Peerages for life, 24 July 1964]; *see under* Montagu, A. V. E. P.

SANDYS, 7th Baron, *cr* 1802; **Richard Michael Oliver Hill;** DL; Captain of the Yeomen of the Guard (Deputy Government Chief Whip, House of Lords), 1979–82; Landowner; *b* 21 July 1931; *o s* of late Lt-Col the Lord Sandys and Cynthia Mary (*d* 1990), *o d* of late Col F. R. T. T. Gascoigne, DSO; *S* father, 1961; *m* 1961, Patricia Simpson Hall, *d* of late Captain Lionel Hall, MC. *Educ:* Royal Naval College, Dartmouth. Lieutenant in The Royal Scots Greys, 1950–55. A Lord in Waiting, 1974; an Opposition Whip, H of L, 1974–79. FRGS. DL Worcestershire, 1968. *Heir: cousin* Marcus Tufton Hill [*b* 13 March 1931; *m* 1980, Margaret Cato St Aubrey, *d* of late Maj. Gerald Lloyd St Aubrey Davies, OBE]. *Address:* Ombersley Court, Droitwich, Worcestershire WR9 0HH. *T:* Worcester (0905) 620220. *Club:* Cavalry and Guards.

SANDYS, Julian George Winston; QC 1983; *b* 19 Sept. 1936; *s* of Baron Duncan-Sandys, CH, PC; *m* 1970, Elisabeth Jane, *o d* of late John Besley Martin, CBE; three *s* one *d*. *Educ:* Eton; Salem; Trinity Coll., Melbourne. 2nd Lt, 4th Hussars, 1955; Captain, QRIH (AER), 1964. Called to the Bar, Inner Temple, 1959. Member: Midland Circuit, 1960–76; Western Circuit, 1982–; Gray's Inn, 1970–. Contested (C) Ashfield, Notts, 1959. *Recreations:* flying, computers.

SANER, Robert Morton; *see* Morton-Saner.

SANGER, Frederick, OM 1986; CH 1981; CBE 1963; PhD; FRS 1954; on staff of Medical Research Council, 1951–83; *b* 13 Aug. 1918; *s* of Frederick Sanger, MD, and Cicely Sanger; *m* 1940, M. Joan Howe; two *s* one *d*. *Educ:* Bryanston; St John's College, Cambridge. BA 1939; PhD 1943. From 1940, research in Biochemistry at Cambridge University; Beit Memorial Fellowship for Medical Research, 1944–51; at MRC Lab. of Molecular Biol., Cambridge, 1961–83; Fellowship at King's College, Cambridge, 1954. (Hon. Fellow 1983). For. Hon. Mem., Amer. Acad. of Arts and Sciences, 1958; Hon. Mem. Amer. Society of Biological Chemists, 1961; Foreign Assoc., Nat. Acad. of Sciences, 1967. Hon. DSc: Leicester, 1968; Oxon, 1970; Strasbourg, 1970; Cambridge, 1983. Corday-Morgan Medal and Prize, Chem. Soc., 1951; Nobel Prize for Chemistry, 1958, (jointly) 1980; Alfred Benzon Prize, 1966; Royal Medal, Royal Soc., 1969; Sir Frederick Gowland Hopkins Meml Medal, 1971; Gairdner Foundation Annual Award, 1971, 1979; William Bate Hardy Prize, Cambridge Philosophical Soc., 1976; Hanbury Meml Medal, 1976; Copley Medal, Royal Soc., 1977; Horwitz Prize, Albert Lasker Award, 1979; Biochem. Analysis Prize, German Soc. Clin. Chem., 1980; Gold Medal, RSM, 1983. *Publications:* papers on Chemistry of Insulin and Nucleic Acid Structure in Biochemical and other journals. *Address:* Far Leys, Fen Lane, Swaffham Bulbeck, Cambridge CB5 0NJ.

SANGER, Dr Ruth Ann, (Mrs R. R. Race), FRS 1972; Director, Medical Research Council Blood Group Unit, 1973–83 (Member of Scientific Staff, 1946–83); *b* 6 June 1918; *yr d* of late Rev. Hubert Sanger and late Katharine M. R. Sanger (*née* Cameron), Urunga, NSW; *m* 1956, Robert Russell Race, CBE, FRS (*d* 1984); no *c*. *Educ:* Abbotsleigh, Sydney; Sydney and London Univs. BSc Sydney 1939, PhD London 1948. Scientific Staff of Red Cross Blood Transfusion Service, Sydney, 1940–46. Hon. Member: Sociedad de Hematologia del Instituto Mexicano del Seguro Social; Deutsche Gesellschaft für Bluttransfusion; Toronto Antibody Club; Norwegian Soc. of Immunohaematology; Internat. Soc. of Blood Transfusion. Hon. MD Helsinki, 1990. (Jtly with R. R. Race) Landsteiner Meml Award, USA, 1957, Philip Levine Award, USA, 1970, and Gairdner Foundn Award, Canada, 1972; Oliver Meml Award for Blood Transfusion, British Red Cross, 1973. *Publications:* (with R. R. Race) Blood Groups in Man, 1950, 6th edn, 1975; many papers in genetical and med. jls. *Address:* 22 Vicarage Road, East Sheen, SW14 8RU. *T:* 081–876 1508.

SANGSTER, John Laing; *b* 21 Nov. 1922; *s* of Albert James Laing Sangster and Ottilie Elizabeth Ritzdorff; *m* 1952, Mary Louise Fitz-Alan Stuart; two *s*. *Educ:* Emanuel Sch., London; Emmanuel Coll., Cambridge (MA). Joined Bank of England, 1949; Adviser, Foreign Exchange, 1965; Deputy Chief Cashier, 1975; Chief Adviser, 1979; Asst Dir, Foreign Exchange Div., 1980–82. Exco International: Dep. Chm., 1983–84; Chm., 1984–86; Chm., London Forfaiting Co. Ltd, 1984–86. *Recreations:* touring, walking, bird watching. *Clubs:* Overseas Bankers'; Thames Rowing; Leander (Henley on Thames).

SANGSTER, Robert Edmund; *b* 23 May 1936; *o c* of late Mr Vernon Sangster and of Mrs Sangster. *Educ:* Repton Coll. Dir, Newmarket Thoroughbred Breeders plc, 1985–. Chm., Vernons Orgn, 1980–88. Owner of: The Minstrel (won Derby, 1977); Alleged (won Prix de l'Arc de Triomphe, 1977, 1978); Detroit (won Prix de l'Arc de Triomphe, 1980); Beldale Ball (won Melbourne Cup, 1980); Our Paddy Boy (won Australian Jockey Club Cup, 1981); Golden Fleece (won Derby, 1982); Assert (won Irish Sweeps Derby, 1982); Lomond (won 2,000 Guineas, 1983); Caerleon (won French Derby, 1983); El Gran Señor (won 2,000 Guineas, Irish Sweeps Derby, 1984); Sadler's Wells (won Irish 2,000 Guineas, 1984); Gildoran (won Ascot Gold Cup, 1984, 1985, Goodwood Cup, 1984); Committed (won Prix de l'Abbaye de Longchamp, Champion European Sprinter, Royal Heroine Champion Grass Mare, USA, 1984); Marooned (won Sydney Cup, 1986). Leading winning race-horse owner, 1977, 1978, 1982, 1983 and 1984 seasons. *Recreation:* golf. *Address:* The Nunnery, Douglas, Isle of Man. *T:* Douglas (0624) 23351. *Club:* Jockey.

SANKEY, Guy Richard; QC 1991; *b* 2 April 1944; *s* of Graham and Joan Sankey; *m* 1969, Pauline Mace Lamotte; three *d*. *Educ:* Marlborough College; New College, Oxford (MA). Called to the Bar, Inner Temple, 1966; Assistant Recorder, 1987–; Junior Counsel to the Crown, Common Law, 1987–91. *Recreations:* golf, ski-ing, tennis. *Address:* Fallowfield, Cokes Lane, Chalfont St Giles, Bucks HP8 4TZ; 1 Temple Gardens, Temple, EC4Y 9BB. *Club:* Denham Golf.

SANKEY, John Anthony, CMG 1983; Secretary General, Society of London Art Dealers, since 1991; *b* 8 June 1930; *m* 1958, Gwendoline Putman; two *s* two *d*. *Educ:* Cardinal Vaughan Sch., Kensington; Peterhouse, Cambridge (Classical Tripos Parts 1 and 2, Class 1; MA). 1st (Singapore) Regt, RA (2nd Lieut), 1952. Colonial Office, 1953; UK Mission to United Nations, 1961; Foreign Office, 1964; Guyana, 1968; Singapore, 1971; NATO Defence Coll., Rome, 1973; Malta, 1973–75; The Hague, 1975–79 (Gov., British Sch. in the Netherlands, 1975–79); Special Counsellor for African Affairs, FCO, 1980–82; High Comr, Tanzania, 1982–85; UK Perm. Rep. to UN Office, Geneva, 1985–90. Leader, British Govt Delegn to Internat. Red Cross Conf., 1986; Chm., Intergovtl Gp for the Least Developed Countries, 1990. Chm., GATT Wkg Group on trade in domestically prohibited goods, 1989–91. Sir Evelyn Wrench Lectr, ESU, 1990. *Recreations:* nineteenth century sculpture, historical portraits, walking. *Address:* 108 Lancaster Gate, W2 3NW.

SANKEY, Vernon Louis; Chief Executive, Reckitt & Colman plc, since 1992; *b* 9 May 1949; *s* of late Edward Sankey and Marguerite Elizabeth Louise (*née* van Maurik); *m* 1976, Elizabeth Knights; three *s* one *d*. *Educ:* Harrow School; Oriel Coll., Oxford (MA Mod. Langs). Joined Reckitt & Colman, 1971: General Manager, Denmark, 1978–80; PA to Chm. and Chief Exec., 1980–81; Man. Dir, France, 1981–85; Man. Dir, Colman's of Norwich, 1985–89; Chm. and Chief Exec. Officer, Reckitt & Colman Inc., USA, 1989–92. *Recreations:* various, including golf, tennis, theatre-going. *Address:* c/o Reckitt & Colman plc, One Burlington Lane, Chiswick W4 2RW. *Club:* Leander (Henley).

SANSBURY, Rt. Rev. (Cyril) Kenneth, MA Cantab; Hon. DD (Trinity College, Wycliffe College, Toronto); retired; *b* 21 Jan. 1905; *s* of late Cyril J. Sansbury; *m* 1931, Ada Ethelreda Mary, *d* of late Captain P. B. Wamsley; one *s* two *d*. *Educ:* St Paul's School; Peterhouse, Cambridge; Westcott House, Cambridge. 2nd cl. Classical Tripos, 1926; 1st cl. Theological Tripos, Pt I 1927 and Pt II 1928. Curate of St Peter's, Dulwich Common, 1928–31 and Wimbledon, 1931–32; SPG Missionary, Numazu, Japan, 1932–34; Prof. at Central Theological Coll. and British Chaplain at St Andrew's, Tokyo, 1934–41; Chaplain to HM Embassy, Tokyo, 1938–41; Chaplain, RCAF, 1941–45; Warden, Lincoln Theological Coll., 1945–52; Canon and Prebendary of Asgarby in Lincoln Cathedral, 1948–53; Warden, St Augustine's College, Canterbury (Central College of the Anglican Communion), 1952–61; Hon. Canon, Canterbury Cathedral, 1953–61; Bishop of Singapore and Malaya, 1961–66; Asst Bishop, dio. London, 1966–73; Gen. Sec., British Council of Churches, 1966–73; Priest-in-Charge of St Mary in the Marsh, Norwich, 1973–83. *Publications:* Truth, Unity and Concord, 1967; Combating Racism, 1975. *Address:* 20 The Close, Norwich NR1 4DZ. *Club:* Royal Over-Seas League.

SANSOM, Andrew William, FCCA; Secretary, Chartered Association of Certified Accountants, since 1988; *b* 1 Jan. 1937; *s* of Reginald Henry Charles Sansom and Marjorie Frances (*née* Pearce); *m* 1970, Rosanne Louise Best; one *s*. *Educ:* Sidcot School; Univ. of Wales (BA). FCCA 1975 (ACCA 1970). Served Welch Regt, 2nd Lieut, 1957–59. Joined HMOCS, 1959; Overseas Audit Service: Tanganyika, 1960–63; Bechuanaland (later Botswana), 1963–70; London Merchant Securities Ltd, 1971–73; Assoc. of Certified Accountants: Admin Sec., 1974–76; Dep. Sec., 1976–88. *Publications:* articles on accountancy profession in nat. and professional press. *Recreations:* theatre, horticulture, swimming, Church of England matters. *Address:* 29 Lincoln's Inn Fields, WC2A 3EE. *T:* 071–242 6855; Spring Cottage, Sheep Street, Charlbury, Oxon OX7 3RR. *T:* Charlbury (0608) 810914.

SANTER, Rt. Rev. Mark; *see* Birmingham, Bishop of.

SAOUMA, Edouard; Director-General of the Food and Agriculture Organization of the United Nations, Rome, since 1976; agricultural engineer and international official; *b* Beirut, Lebanon, 6 Nov. 1926; *m* Inés Forero; one *s* two *d*. *Educ:* St Joseph's University Sch. of Engineering, Beirut; École Nat. Supérieure d'Agronomie, Montpellier, France. Director: Tel Amara Agric. Sch., 1952–53; Nat. Centre for Farm Mechanization, 1954–55; Sec. Gen., Nat. Fedn of Lebanese Agronomists, 1955; Dir-Gen., Nat. Inst. for Agric. Research, 1957–62; Mem. Gov. Bd, Nat. Grains Office, 1960–62; Minister of Agric., Fisheries and Forestry, 1970. Food and Agric. Organization of UN: Dep. Regional Rep. for Asia and Far East, 1962–65; Dir, Land and Water Develt Div., 1965–75; Dir-Gen., 1976. Hon. Prof. of Agronomy, Agricl Univ. of Beijing, China. Said Akl Prize, Lebanon; Chevalier du Mérite Agricole, France; Grand Cross: Order of the Cedar, Lebanon; Ordre National du Tchad; Ordre Nat. du Ghana; Ordre National de Haute Volta; Mérito Agrícola of Spain; Orden Nacional al Mérito, Colombia; Kt Comdr, Order of Merit, Greece; Order of Agricl Merit, Colombia; Gran Oficial, Orden de Vasco Nuñez de Balboa, Panamá; Orden al Mérito Agrícola, Peru; Order of Merit, Egypt; Order of Merit, Mauritania; Grand Officier: Ordre de la République, Tunisia; Ordre National, Madagascar. Dr (*hc*): Univ. of Bologna, Italy; Agric. Univ. La Molina, Peru; Univ. of Seoul, Republic of Korea; Univ. of Uruguay; Univ. of Jakarta, Indonesia; Univ. of Warsaw; Univ. of Los Baños, Philippines; Punjab Agricultural Univ.; Faisalabad Agricultural Univ., Pakistan; Gödöllö Univ., Hungary; Univ. Nacional Autonoma, Nicaragua; Univ. of Florence, Italy; Univ. of Gembloux, Belgium; Univ. of Prague, Czechoslovakia; Catholic Univ. of America. Accademico Corrispondente, Accademià Nazionale di Agricultura, Bologna, Italy. *Publications:* technical publications on agriculture. *Address:* Food and Agriculture Organization of the United Nations, Via delle Terme di Caracalla, Rome 00100, Italy. *T:* 57971.

SAPPER, Alan Louis Geoffrey; General Secretary, Association of Cinematograph, Television and Allied Technicians, 1969–91; *b* 18 March 1931; *y s* of late Max and Kate Sapper; *m* 1959, Helen Rubens; one *s* one *d*. *Educ:* Upper Latymer Sch.; Univ. of London. Botanist, Royal Botanic Gardens, Kew, 1948–58; Asst Gen. Sec., 1958–64, Dep. Gen. Sec., 1967–69, Assoc. of Cinematograph, Television and Allied Technicians; Gen. Sec., Writers' Guild of Great Britain, 1964–67. Mem. General Council, Trades Union Congress, 1970–84 (Chm., 1982). President: Confedn of Entertainment Unions, 1970–91; Internat. Fedn of Audio-Visual Workers, 1974–; Sec., Fedn of Film Unions, 1968–91; Treas., Fedn of Broadcasting Unions, 1968–91; Member: British Copyright Council, 1964–; British Screen Adv. Council, 1985–. Governor: BFI, 1974–; Nat. Film School, 1980–; Hammersmith Hosp., 1965–72; Ealing Coll. of Higher Educn, 1976–78. Chm., League for Democracy in Greece, 1970–. Founder and Chief Executive, Interconnect. *Publications:* articles, short stories; stage plays, On Licence, Kith and Kin; TV play, The Return, 1961. *Recreations:* taxonomic botany, hill walking, politics and human nature. *Address:* 19 Lavington Road, West Ealing, W13 9NN. *T:* 081–567 4900.

SARAJČIĆ, Ivo; elected Member, Council of the Republic, Croatia, since 1983; President, Board for Foreign Policy and International Relations, National Assembly of Croatia, 1978–82, retired; *b* 10 March 1915; *s* of Ivan and Elizabeth Sarajčić; *m* 1944, Marija Godlar; three *s*. *Educ:* Univ. of Philosophy, Zagreb. Participated in War of Liberation from (beginning) 1941 (Partizan Remembrance Medal); held various prominent political positions. Subsequently: Secretary, Presidium of Nat. Assembly of Croatia; Editor-in-Chief of Borba; Asst Minister of Educn; Dir of Information Office of Yugoslav Govt; MEC, Croatia; also Mem. Central Cttee of League of Communists of Croatia, Mem. Federal Assembly, Mem. Council for Foreign Affairs and Internat. Relations. Yugoslav Diplomatic Service, 1959; Ambassador to Austria, 1960–63; Asst Sec. of State for Foreign Affairs, 1963–66; Ambassador to London, 1966–70; Dir, Inst. for Developing Countries, Zagreb, 1970–78.

SAREI, Sir Alexis Holyweek, Kt 1987; CBE 1981; PhD; Papua New Guinea Permanent Representative to the United Nations, and Ambassador to the United States of America, 1983–86; *b* 25 March 1934; *s* of late Joseph Nambong and Joanna Mota; *m* 1972, Claire Dionne; three *s* three *d* (all adopted). *Educ:* PNG Primary to Tertiary, 1949–66; Rome Univ., 1968–71 (PhD Canon Law). RC Priest, 1966–72; Secretary to Chief Minister, PNG, 1972–73; District Comr, 1973–75; Advisor to Bougainville people, 1975–76; Premier of North Solomons Provincial Govt, 1976–80; High Comr in UK, 1980–83. PNG Independence Medal 1977; CBE for work in Provincial Govt, pioneering work in the system in PNG. Successor to his uncle, Gregory Moah, as Chief of Clan, Petisuun. *Publication:* The Practice of Marriage Among the Solos, Buka Island, 1974. *Recreations:* music, sketching, golf, swimming, sports. *Address:* c/o Ministry for Foreign Affairs, Central Government Offices, Kumul Avenue, Post Office, Wards Strip, Waigani, Papua New Guinea.

SARELL, Captain Richard Iwan Alexander, DSO 1939; RN retd; *b* 22 Feb. 1909; *s* of late Philip Charles Sarell; *m* 1961, Mrs Ann Morgan (*née* Keenlyside). *Educ:* Royal Naval Coll., Dartmouth. Entered RNC Dartmouth, 1922; Comdr 1943; Capt. 1948; specialised in Gunnery, 1934; DSO for action against enemy submarines while in command of HMS Broke, 1939; despatches, 1943. Naval Attaché, Moscow and Helsinki, 1949–51; student Imperial Defence Coll., 1952; Defence Research Policy Staff, 1954; retd 1957. *Recreation:* fishing. *Address:* 43 Rivermead Court, Ranelagh Gardens, SW6 3RX.

SARELL, Sir Roderick (Francis Gisbert), KCMG 1968 (CMG 1958); KCVO 1971; HM Diplomatic Service, retired; *b* 23 Jan. 1913; *y s* of late Philip Charles Sarell, HM Consular Service and of Ethel Ida Rebecca, *d* of late John Dewar Campbell; *m* 1946, Pamela Muriel, *d* of late Vivian Francis Crowther-Smith; three *s*. *Educ:* Ashdown House, Sussex; Radley; Magdalen College, Oxford. HM Consular Service, 1936; Vice-Consul, Persia, 1937; Italian East Africa, 1939; Iraq, 1940; 2nd Secretary, Addis Ababa, 1942; 1st Secretary, HM Foreign Service, 1946; Rome, Bucharest, 1946; Foreign Office, 1949; Acting Counsellor, 1952; Counsellor and Consul-General, Rangoon, 1953; Consul-General, Algiers, 1956–59; Head of Southern Dept, Foreign Office, 1959–61, General Dept, 1961–63; Ambassador: to Libya, 1964–69; to Turkey, 1969–73. Coronation medal, 1953. *Recreations:* swimming, building, walking. *Address:* The Litten, Hampstead Norreys, Newbury, Berks RG16 0TD. *T:* Hermitage (0635) 201274. *Clubs:* Oriental, Royal Over-Seas League; Leander.

SARGAN, Prof. John Denis, FBA 1981; Emeritus Professor, London School of Economics and Political Science, since 1984 (Tooke Professor of Economic Science and Statistics, 1982–84; Professor of Econometrics, 1964–84); *b* 23 Aug. 1924; *s* of H. and G. A. Sargan; *m* 1953, Phyllis Mary Millard; two *s* one *d*. *Educ:* Doncaster Grammar Sch.; St John's Coll., Cambridge. Asst. Lectr, Lectr and Reader, Leeds Univ., 1948–63; Reader, 1963–64, Hon. Fellow, 1991, LSE. Fellow, Amer. Acad. of Arts and Scis, 1987. *Address:* 49 Dukes Avenue, Theydon Bois, Essex.

SARGANT, Sir (Henry) Edmund, Kt 1969; President of the Law Society, 1968–69; Partner in Radcliffes and Co., 1930–71, and Senior Partner for twenty years; *b* 24 May 1906; *s* of Rt Hon. Sir Charles Henry Sargant, Lord Justice of Appeal, and Amelia Julia Sargant, RRC; *m* 1st, 1930, Mary Kathleen Lemmey (*d* 1979); one *s*; 2nd, 1981, Evelyn Noel (*née* Arnold-Wallinger). *Educ:* Rugby School; Trinity College, Cambridge (MA). 3rd Cl. Hons Solicitors' final examination; admitted 1930. Served War of 1939–45 in RAF, Provost and Security Branch; (W Africa; Middle East; Acting Wing Comdr). Member, Council, Law Society, 1951–75; Chm., Disciplinary Cttee of Architects Registration Council, 1964, 1965, 1966. Master, Worshipful Co. of Merchant Taylors, 1954. *Address:* 902 Keyes House, Dolphin Square, SW1V 3NB. *Club:* United Oxford & Cambridge University.

See also Rt Hon. Lord Justice Nourse.

SARGANT, Naomi Ellen; *see* McIntosh, N. E. S.

SARGEANT, Frank Charles Douglas, CMG 1972; HM Diplomatic Service, retired 1977; *b* 7 Nov. 1917; *s* of late John Sargeant and Anna Sargeant; *m* 1946, Joan Adene Bickerton; one *s* one *d*. *Educ:* Lincoln; St Catharine's Coll., Cambridge. MA Cantab, Natural Sciences. Cadbury Bros. Ltd, 1939. Served War: Army, 1939–46; Lt-Col, Royal Signals. Imperial Chemical Industries Ltd, 1947–48. HM Diplomatic Service: Curacao, 1948; The Hague, 1951; Kuwait, 1954; Foreign Office, 1957 (First Sec. 1958); First Sec., Head of Chancery and Consul, Mogadishu, 1959; First Sec. (Commercial) Stockholm, 1962–66; First Sec., Head of Chancery, Colombo, and Consul for the Maldive Islands, 1967; Counsellor, 1968; Gonsul-General, Lubumbashi, 1968–70; Dep. High Comr, Dacca, 1970–71; Sen. Officers' War Course, RN Coll., Greenwich, 1971–72; Consul Gen., Lyons, 1972–77 (Doyen of the Consular Corps). *Recreations:* shooting, fishing. *Address:* c/o Lloyds Bank, Jersey, Channel Islands.

SARGEANT, Rt. Rev. Frank Pilkington; *see* Stockport, Bishop Suffragan of.

SARGEAUNT, Henry Anthony, CB 1961; OBE 1949; Scientific Consultant, United Nations, New York, 1968–69; *b* 11 June 1907; *o s* of Lt-Col Henry Sargeaunt and Norah Ierne Carden; *m* 1939, Winifred Doris Parkinson; two *s* one *d*. *Educ:* Clifton Coll.; University Coll., Reading (London Univ.); Cambridge Univ. Rhodes Research Grant, 1939–42; served with HM Forces, 1944–46: France, 1944; Staff Capt. with 21 Army Group, 1944; Supt Operational Research Group (ORG) (W&E), Min. of Supply, 1946; Supt, Army ORG, 1947–50; Dep. Scientific Adviser, 1950–52, Scientific Adviser, to Army Council, 1952–55; Asst Scientific Adviser to Supreme Allied Commander in Europe, Sept. 1955–57; Dep. Science Adviser, NATO, 1958–59; re-apptd Scientific Adviser to Army Council, 1959; Dep. Chief Scientist (B), War Office, 1960–62; Chief Scientific Adviser, Home Office, 1962–67. *Recreations:* yachting, horse-racing, bird-watching. *Address:* 7 Bond Close, Sway, Lymington, Hants. *T:* Lymington (0590) 683112.

SARGENT, Dick; *see* Sargent, J. R.

SARGENT, John Richard, (Dick); *b* 22 March 1925; *s* of John Philip Sargent and Ruth (*née* Taunton) *m* 1st, 1949, Anne Elizabeth Haigh (marr. diss. 1980); one *s* two *d*; 2nd, 1980, Hester Mary Campbell. *Educ:* Dragon Sch., Oxford; Rugby Sch.; Christ Church, Oxford (MA). Fellow and Lectr in Econs, Worcester Coll., Oxford, 1951–62; Econ. Consultant, HM Treasury and DEA, 1963–65; Prof. of Econs, Univ. of Warwick, 1965–73 (Pro-Vice-Chancellor, 1971–72), Hon. Prof., 1974–81. Vis. Prof. of Econs, LSE, 1981–82; Gp Economic Adviser, Midland Bank Ltd, 1974–84; Houblon-Norman Res. Fellow, Bank of England, 1984–85. Member: Doctors and Dentists Rev. Body, 1972–75; Armed Forces Pay Rev. Body, 1972–86; Channel Tunnel Adv. Gp, 1974–75; SSRC, 1980–85; Pharmacists Review Panel, 1986–; Pres., Société Universitaire Européenne de Recherches Financières, 1985–88. Editor, Midland Bank Rev., 1974–84. *Publications:* British Transport Policy, 1958; (ed with R. C. O. Matthews) Contemporary Problems of Economic Policy, 1983; articles in various economic jls, and in vols of conf. papers etc. *Recreation:* work. *Address:* Trentham House, Fulbrook, Burford, Oxon OX18 4BL. *T:* Burford (099382) 3525. *Club:* Reform.

SARGENT, Prof. Roger William Herbert, FEng 1976; Courtaulds Professor of Chemical Engineering, since 1966, and Director of Interdisciplinary Research Centre in Process Systems Engineering, since 1989, Imperial College; *b* 14 Oct. 1926; *s* of Herbert Alfred Sargent and May Elizabeth (*née* Gill); *m* 1951, Shirley Jane Levesque (*née* Spooner); two *s*. *Educ:* Bedford Sch.; Imperial Coll., London. BSc, ACGI, PhD, DScEng, DIC; FIChemE, FIMA. Design Engineer, Société l'Air Liquide, Paris, 1951–58; Imperial College: Sen. Lectr, 1958–62; Prof. of Chem. Engrg, 1962–66; Dean, City and Guilds Coll., 1973–76; Head of Dept of Chem. Engrg and Chem. Technology, 1975–88. Member: Engrg and Technol. Adv. Cttee, British Council, 1976–89 (Chm., 1984–89); Technol. Subcttee, UGC, 1984–88. Pres., Instn of Chem. Engrs, 1973–74. FRSA 1988. Hon. FCGI 1977. Dhc Institut Nat. Polytechnique de Lorraine. *Publications:* contribs to: Trans Instn Chem. Engrs, Computers and Chemical Engrg, Jl of Optimization Theory and Applications, SIAM Jl of Optimization, Mathematical Programming, Internat. Jl of Control, etc. *Address:* Mulberry Cottage, 291A Sheen Road, Richmond, Surrey TW10 5AW. *T:* 081–876 9623.

SARGENT, Prof. Wallace Leslie William, FRS 1981; Ira S. Bowen Professor of Astronomy, California Institute of Technology, since 1981; *b* 15 Feb. 1935; *s* of Leslie William Sargent and Eleanor (*née* Dennis); *m* 1964, Anneila Isabel Cassells, PhD; two *d*. *Educ:* Scunthorpe Tech. High Sch. (first pupil to go to univ., 1953); Manchester Univ. (BSc Hons, MSc, PhD). Research Fellow in Astronomy, California Inst. of Tech., 1959–62; Sen. Research Fellow, Royal Greenwich Observatory, 1962–64; Asst Prof. of Physics, Univ. of California, San Diego, 1964–66; Asst Prof. of Astronomy, Calif Inst. Tech., 1966–68, Associate Prof., 1968–71, Professor, 1971–81; Executive Officer for Astronomy, 1975–81. George Darwin Lectr, RAS, 1987. Fellow, American Acad. of Arts and Sciences, 1977. Warner Prize, American Astronomical Soc., 1968; Dannie Heineman Prize, 1991. *Publications:* many papers in learned jls. *Recreations:* reading, gardening, oriental carpets, watching sports. *Address:* Astronomy Dept 105–24, California Institute of Technology, Pasadena, Calif 91125, USA. *T:* 818–356–4055; 400 South Berkeley Avenue, Pasadena, Calif 91107, USA. *T:* 818–795–6345. *Club:* Athenæum (Pasadena).

SARGESON, Prof. Alan McLeod, FRS 1983; Professor of Inorganic Chemistry, Australian National University, since 1978; *b* 13 Oct. 1930; *s* of late H. L. Sargeson; *m* 1959, Marietta, *d* of F. Anders; two *s* two *d*. *Educ:* Maitland Boys' High Sch.; Sydney Univ. (BSc, PhD, DipEd). FRACI; FAA. Lectr, Chem. Dept, Univ. of Adelaide, 1956–57; Res. Fellow, John Curtin Sch. of Med. Research, ANU, 1958, Fellow 1960; Sen. Fellow, then Professorial Fellow, 1969–78, Res. Sch. of Chemistry, ANU. DSc *hc* Sydney, 1990. *Address:* Research School of Chemistry, Australian National University, GPO Box 4, Canberra, ACT 2601, Australia.

SARGINSON, Edward William; retired from Civil Service, 1976; with Confederation of British Industry until 1982; *b* 22 May 1919; *s* of Frederick William and Edith Sarginson; *m* 1944, Olive Pescod; one *s* one *d*. *Educ:* Barrow-in-Furness Grammar School. Entered Civil Service, War Office, 1936; served Infantry, 1939–46; Principal, Min. of Supply, 1955; Asst Sec., Min. of Aviation, 1965; Asst Under Sec. of State, MoD(PE), 1972–76. *Recreations:* local community work, bowls. *Address:* 41 Kendall Avenue South, Sanderstead, Surrey CR2 0QR. *T:* 081–660 4476.

SARK, Seigneur of; *see* Beaumont, J. M.

SAROOP, Narindar, CBE 1982; Adviser, Banque Belge, since 1987; *b* 14 Aug. 1929; *e s* of Chaudhri Ram Saroop, Ismaila, Rohtak, India and late Shyam Devi; *m* 1st, 1952, Ravi Gill (marr. diss. 1967), *o* surv. *c* of the Sardar and Sardarni of Premgarh, India; two *d* (one *s* decd); 2nd 1969, Stephanie Denise, *yr d* of Alexander and Cynthia Amie Cronopulo, Zakynthos, Greece. *Educ:* Aitchison Coll. for Punjab Chiefs, Lahore; Indian Military Acad., Dehra Dun. Served as regular officer, 2nd Royal Lancers (Gardner's Horse) and Queen Victoria's Own The Poona Horse; retired, 1954. Management Trainee, Yule Catto, 1954; senior executive and Dir of subsidiaries of various multinationals, to 1976; Hon. Administrator, Oxfam Relief Project, 1964; Director: Devi Grays Insurance Ltd, 1981–84; Capital Plant International Ltd, 1982–86. Advr, Develt, Clarkson Puckle Gp, 1976–87. Mem., BBC Adv. Council on Asian Programmes, 1977–81. Pres., Indian Welfare Soc., 1983–. Member Council: Freedom Assoc., 1978–86; Internat. Social Services, 1981–91; Inst. of Directors, 1983–; Founder Mem., Tory Asians for Representation Gp, 1984–85; Mem. Adv. Council, Efficiency in Local Govt, 1984. Contested (C) Greenwich, 1979 (first Asian Tory Parliamentary candidate this century); Founder and 1st Chm., UK Anglo Asian Cons. Soc., 1976–79, 1985–86; Vice Chm., Cons. Party Internat. Office, 1990–91. Councillor, Kensington and Chelsea, 1974–82; initiated Borough Community Relations Cttee (Chm., 1975–77, 1980–82); Chm., Working Party on Employment, 1978; Founder and Chm., Durbar Club, 1981–. *Publications:* In Defence of Freedom (jtly), 1978; A Squire of Hindoostan, 1983. *Recreations:* keeping fools, boredom and socialism at bay. *Address:* 25 de Vere Gardens, W8. *Clubs:* Beefsteak, Buck's, Cavalry and Guards, Pratt's; Imperial Delhi Gymkhana; Royal Bombay Yacht, Royal Calcutta Golf.

SARRAUTE, Nathalie; writer; *b* Ivanowo, Russia, 18 July 1900; *d* of Ilya Tcherniak and Pauline Chatounowski; *m* 1925, Raymond Sarraute; three *d*. *Educ:* Sorbonne; Ecole de Droit de Paris; Oxford. *Publications:* Tropismes, 1939 (trans. Tropisms, 1964); Portrait d'un inconnu, 1948 (Portrait of a Man Unknown, 1959); Martereau, 1953 (trans. 1964); L'Ere du soupçon, 1956 (The Age of Suspicion, 1964); Le Planétarium, 1959 (The Planetarium, 1962); Les Fruits d'or, 1963 (The Golden Fruits, 1965) (Prix international de Littérature, 1964); Entre la vie et la mort, 1968 (Between Life and Death, 1969); Vous les entendez?, 1972 (Do You Hear Them?, 1973); "disent les imbéciles", 1976 ("fools say", 1977); L'usage de la parole, 1980 (The Use of Speech, 1983); Enfance, 1983 (Childhood, 1984); Tu ne t'aimes pas, 1989 (You Don't Love Yourself, 1990); *plays:* Le Silence, Le Mensonge, 1967 (Silence and The Lie, 1969); Isma, 1970 (Izzum, 1975); C'est beau, 1973 (It is Beautiful, 1978); Elle est là, 1978 (It is There, 1980); Collected Plays, 1981; Pour un oui ou pour un non, 1982; *essay:* Paul Valéry et l'enfant d'éléphant, 1986. *Address:* 12 avenue Pierre I de Serbie, 75116 Paris, France. *T:* 47.20.58.28.

SARUM, Archdeacon of; *see* Hopkinson, Ven. B. J.

SASKATCHEWAN, Bishop of, since 1985; **Rt. Rev. Thomas Oliver Morgan;** *b* 20 Jan. 1941; *s* of Charles Edwin Morgan and Amy Amelia (*née* Hoyes); *m* 1963, Lillian Marie (*née* Textor); two *s* one *d*. *Educ:* Univ. of Saskatchewan (BA 1962); King's College, London (BD 1965); Tyndale Hall, Bristol (GOE 1966). Curate, Church of the Saviour, Blackburn, Lancs, 1966–69; Rector: Porcupine Plain, Sask, Canada, 1969–73; Kinistino, 1973–77; Shellbrook, 1977–83; Archdeacon of Indian Missions, Saskatchewan, 1983–85. Hon. DD, Coll. of Emmanuel and St Chad, Saskatoon, 1986. *Address:* Bishopsthorpe, 427 21 Street West, Prince Albert, Sask S6V 4J5, Canada.

SASKATOON, Bishop of, since 1981; **Rt. Rev. Roland Arthur Wood;** *b* 1 Jan. 1933; *s* of Cyril Arthur Wood and Evelyn Mae Wood (*née* Cave); *m* 1959, Elizabeth Nora (*née* Deacon); one *s* two *d*. *Educ:* Bishop's Univ., Lennoxville, Quebec (BA 1956, LST 1958). Deacon, May 1958, priest, Dec. 1958; Asst Curate, St Matthew's, Winnipeg, 1958–60; Rector, Christ Church, Selkirk, 1960–64; Assistant Priest, St John's Cathedral, Saskatoon, 1964–67; Rector, Holy Trinity Church, Yorkton, 1967–71; Dean, St John's Cathedral, Saskatoon, 1971–81. Hon. DD, Coll. of Emmanuel and St Chad, Saskatoon, 1979. *Recreations:* model railroading, camping, painting, refurbishing old furniture. *Address:* 1104 Elliott Street, Saskatoon, Saskatchewan S7N 0V3, Canada. *T:* 306–653–0890.

SATCHELL, Edward William John, CEng, FIEE, RCNC; Director of Engineering (Ships), 1973–76; *b* 23 Sept. 1916; *s* of Horsey John Robert Satchell and Ethel Satchell (*née* Chandler); *m* 1941, Stella Grace Cook; one *d*. *Educ:* Esplanade House Sch., Southsea; Royal Dockyard Sch., Portsmouth; RNC, Greenwich. Electrical Apprentice, Portsmouth Dockyard, 1932; Probationary Asst Electrical Engr, 1936; Asst Electrical Engr, 1939; Electrical Engr, 1943; Suptg Electrical Engr, 1955. Served with British Naval Mission in USA, 1951–53. Warship Electrical Supt, Scotland, 1958–61; Dep. Admty Repair Manager, Malta, 1961–64; Dep. Elec. Engrg Manager, Devonport, 1964–66; Asst Dir of Electrical Engineering, 1966; Dep. Dir of Elec. Engrg, 1970; Head of RN Engrng Service, 1973–75; Dep. Head, RCNC (L), 1975–76; retired 1976. *Recreations:* reading, gardening, bird watching. *Address:* 6 Badminton Gardens, Bath BA1 2XS. *T:* Bath (0225) 426974.

SATOW, Rear-Adm. Derek Graham, CB 1977; *b* 13 June 1923; *y s* of late Graham F. H. Satow, OBE, and of Evelyn M. Satow (*née* Moore); *m* 1944, Patricia E. A. Penaliggon; two *d*. *Educ:* Oakley Hall Sch.; Haileybury Coll.; Royal Naval Engineering Coll. CEng, FIMechE, FIMarE. HMS Ceylon, 1945–46; RNC, Greenwich, 1946–48; HMS Duke of York, 1948–49; RAE Farnborough, 1949–51; HMS Newcastle, 1951–53 (despatches, 1953); Naval Ordnance and Weapons Dept, Admiralty, 1953–59; Dir of Engineering, RNEC, 1959–62; HMS Tiger, 1962–64; Asst and Dep. Dir of Marine Engineering, MoD, 1964–67; IDC, 1968; Captain, RNEC, 1969–71; Dir, Naval Officer Appointments (Eng), MoD, 1971–73; Chief Staff Officer, Technical, later Engineering, to C-in-C Fleet, 1974–76; Dep. Dir-Gen., Ships, MoD, 1976–79; Chief Naval Engr Officer, 1977–79. Comdr, 1955; Captain, 1964; Rear-Adm., 1973.

SATTERTHWAITE, Rt. Rev. John Richard; *see* Gibraltar in Europe, Bishop of.

SATTERTHWAITE, Lt-Col Richard George, LVO 1985; OBE 1961; Director and General Secretary, 1972–85, Vice President, 1986, National Playing Fields Association; *b* 8 April 1920; *s* of R. E. Satterthwaite and A. M. Elers; *m* 1949, Rosemary Ann, *d* of Gen. Sir Frank Messervy, KCSI, KBE, CB, DSO; three *s* (one *d* decd). *Educ:* Rugby Sch.; RMC Sandhurst. 2nd Lieut, 19th King George V's Own Lancers, 1939; served India, Burma, Malaya; transf. to 17th/21st Lancers, 1949; comd 17th/21st Lancers, 1959–61; retd 1962. Vice Pres. and Chm. Management Cttee, British Sports Trust, 1988–. *Recreations:* cricket, golf. *Address:* Meadow Cottage, East Harting, Petersfield, Hants GU31 5LX. *T:* Harting (0730) 825516.

SAUGMAN, Per Gotfred, Hon. OBE 1990; Knight of the Order of Dannebrog; Chairman, Blackwell Scientific Publications Ltd, Oxford, 1972–90 (Managing Director, 1954–87); *b* 26 June 1925; *s* of Emanuel A. G. Saugman and Esther (*née* Lehmann); *m* 1950, Patricia (*née* Fulford); two *s* one *d* (and one *s* decd). *Educ:* Gentofte Grammar Sch.; Commercial Coll., Copenhagen. Bookselling and publishing training in Denmark, Switzerland and England, 1941–49; Sales Manager, Blackwell Scientific Publications Ltd, 1952; Director, University Bookshops (Oxford) Ltd, 1963; Mem. Board, B. H. Blackwell Ltd, 1964; Chairman: William George's Sons Ltd, Bristol, 1965; Blackwell North America, Inc., 1975; Ejnar Munksgaard Publishers Ltd, Copenhagen, 1967; Kooyker Boekhandel Leiden, 1973. Member Council: International Publishers' Assoc., 1976–79; Publishers' Assoc. of GB and Ireland, 1977–82; President, Internat. Group of Scientific, Technical and Medical Publishers, 1977–79. Chairman, Oxford Round Table, 1953–55; Hon. Mem., British Ecological Soc., 1960–; Governor: Oxford Polytechnic, 1972–85; Dragon Sch., Oxford, 1975–; Headington Sch., Oxford, 1988. Fellow, St Cross Coll., Oxford, 1978; Hon. MA Oxford, 1978; Hon. Fellow, Green Coll., Oxford, 1981. Chevalier, Order of Icelandic Falcon, 1984. *Recreations:* reading, art—English watercolours, golf. *Address:* Sunningwood House, Lincombe Lane, Boars Hill, Oxford OX1 5DZ. *T:* Oxford (0865) 735503. *Clubs:* Athenæum, Royal Automobile; Frilford Golf (Oxford).

SAUL, Prof. Samuel Berrick, PhD; Vice Chancellor, University of York, since 1979; *b* 20 Oct. 1924; *s* of Ernest Saul and Maud Eaton; *m* 1953, Sheila Stenton; one *s* one *d*. *Educ:* West Bromwich Grammar Sch.; Birmingham Univ. (BCom 1949, PhD 1953). National Service, 1944–47 (Lieut Sherwood Foresters). Lectr in Econ. History, Liverpool Univ., 1951–63; Edinburgh University: Prof. of Econ. History, 1963–78; Dean, Faculty of Social Sciences, 1970–75; Vice Principal, 1975–77; Actg Principal, 1978. Rockefeller Fellow, Univ. of Calif (Berkeley), and Columbia Univ., 1959; Ford Fellow, Stanford Univ., 1969–70. Vis. Prof., Harvard Univ., 1973. Chairman: Central Council for Educn and Trng in Social Work, 1986–; Standing Conf. on Univ. Entrance, 1986–. Hon. LLD York, Toronto, 1981; Hon. Dr *hc* Edinburgh, 1986. *Publications:* Studies in British Overseas Trade 1870–1914, 1960; The Myth of the Great Depression, 1969; Technological Change: the US and Britain in the 19th Century, 1970; (with A. S. Milward) The Economic Development of Continental Europe 1780–1870, 1973; (with A. S. Milward) The Development of the Economies of Continental Europe 1850–1914, 1977. *Recreations:* fell walking, brass rubbing, music. *Address:* Vice Chancellor's House, Spring Lane, Heslington, York YO1 5DZ. *T:* York (0904) 413601.

SAULL, Rear-Adm. Keith Michael, CB 1982; FCIT; Chairman, New Zealand Ports Authority, 1984–88; *b* 24 Aug. 1927; *s* of Harold Vincent Saull and Margaret Saull; *m* 1952, Linfield Mabel (*née* Barnsdale); two *s* one *d*. *Educ:* Altrincham Grammar Sch.; HMS Conway. Royal Navy, 1945–50; transferred to Royal New Zealand Navy, 1951; commanded HMNZ Ships: Kaniere, Taranaki, Canterbury, 1956–71; Naval Attaché, Washington DC, 1972–75; RCDS 1976; Commodore, Auckland, 1978; Chief of Naval Staff, RNZN, 1980–83. Vice Patron, NZ Coastguard Fedn, 1987–. *Recreations:* golf, fishing, sailing.

SAULTER, Paul Reginald; management consultant, since 1986; Managing Director, Cornwall of Mine Ltd, since 1989; Administrator, St Paul's, Knightsbridge, since 1987; *b* 27 Aug. 1935; *s* of Alfred Walter Saulter and Mabel Elizabeth Oliver. *Educ:* Truro Sch.; University Coll., Oxford. MA. Admin. Asst, Nat. Council of Social Service, 1960–63; Sen. Asst and Principal, CEGB, 1963–65; Dep. Head, Overseas Div., BEAMA, 1965–69; Dir, Internat. Affairs, ABCC, 1969–73; Sec.-Gen., British Chamber of Commerce in France, 1973–81; Chief Executive: Manchester Chamber of Commerce and Industry, 1981–85; Assoc. of Exhibn Organisers, 1985–86. Exhibn Advr, London Chamber of Commerce, 1986–88. Secretary: For. Trade Working Gp, ORGALIME, 1967–69; Council of British Chambers of Commerce in Continental Europe, 1977–80; Mem., Export Promotion Cttee, CBI, 1983–86. Member: RHS; Trevithick Soc., 1986–. *Recreations:* walking, music, theatre, researching Cornish mining history. *Address:* 24 Pembridge Crescent, W11 3DS. *T:* 071–229 2616. *Club:* Commonwealth Trust.

SAUMAREZ, family name of **Baron de Saumarez.**

SAUNDERS, Albert Edward, CMG 1975; OBE 1970; HM Diplomatic Service, retired; Ambassador to the United Republic of Cameroon and the Republic of Equatorial Guinea, 1975–79; *b* 5 June 1919; *s* of late Albert Edward and Marie Marguerite Saunders; *m* 1945, Dorothea Charlotte Mary Whittle (*d* 1985); one *s* one *d*. *Educ:* yes. Westminster Bank Ltd, 1937. Royal Navy, 1942–45: last appt, Asst Chief Port Security Officer, Middle East. Apptd to British Embassy, Cairo, 1938 and 1945; Asst Information Officer, Tripoli, 1949; Asst Admin. Officer, Athens, 1951; Middle East Centre for Arabic Studies, 1952; Third Sec., Office of UK Trade Comr, Khartoum, 1953; Third Sec. (Information), Beirut, 1954; POMEF, Cyprus, 1956; FO, 1957; Second Sec. (Oriental), Baghdad, 1958; FO, 1959; Vice-Consul, Casablanca, 1963; Second Sec. (Oriental), Rabat, 1963; Consul, Jerusalem, 1964; First Sec., FO, 1967; Chancery, Baghdad, 1968; Head of Chancery and Consul, Rabat, 1969; Counsellor and Consul General in charge British Embassy, Dubai, 1972; Chargé d'Affaires, Abu Dhabi, 1972 and 1973; RN War Coll., Greenwich, 1974, sowc, 1975. *Recreation:* iconoclasm (20th Century). *Address:* 3 Deanhill Road, SW14 7DQ.

SAUNDERS, Andrew Downing; Chief Inspector of Ancient Monuments and Historic Buildings, English Heritage (formerly Department of the Environment), 1973–89; *b* 22 Sept. 1931; *s* of Lionel Edward Saunders; *m* 1st, 1961, Hilary Jean (*née* Aikman) (marr. diss. 1980); two *s* one *d*; 2nd, 1985, Gillian Ruth Hutchinson; one *d*. *Educ:* Magdalen Coll. Sch., Oxford; Magdalen Coll., Oxford (MA). FSA, FRHistS, FSAScot. Joined Ancient Monuments Inspectorate, 1954; Inspector of Ancient Monuments for England, 1964. Vice-President: Royal Archaeol Inst.; Cornwall Archaeol Soc.; Hendon and Dist Archaeol Soc.; Mem., Adv. Cttee on Historic Wrecks. MIFA. Editor, Fortress, The Castles and Fortifications Qly, 1989–. *Publications:* ed jtly and contrib., Ancient Monuments and their Interpretation, 1977; Fortress Britain, 1989; excavation reports on various Roman and Medieval sites and monuments, papers on castles and artillery fortification in various archæological and historical jls; guidebooks to ancient monuments. *Recreations:* opera, sailing, Staffordshire Bull Terriers. *Address:* 12 Ashburnham Grove, Greenwich, SE10 8UH. *T:* 081–691 7192. *Club:* Athenæum.

SAUNDERS, Basil; public relations consultant; Director, Charles Barker Traverse-Healy (formerly Traverse-Healy & Regester Ltd), 1984–90; *b* 12 Aug. 1925; *s* of late Comdr J. E. Saunders, RN and Marjorie Saunders; *m* 1957, Betty Smith; two *s* four *d*. *Educ:* Merchant Taylors'; Wadham Coll., Oxford (MA). FIPR. Sub-Lt, RNVR, 1944–46. Assistant d'Anglais, Collège de Tarascon, 1950–51; Writer, General Electric Co. (USA), 1952–53; PRO, BIM, 1954–57; Public Relations Exec., Pritchard, Wood and Partners, 1957–63; Head of Public Relations Services, Wellcome Foundn Ltd, 1963–78; Dir-Gen., Aslib, 1978–80; Public Relations Officer, Arts Council, 1981. Consultant, Traverse-Healy Ltd, 1981–84. *Publications:* Crackle of Thorns (verse), 1968; short stories in magazines and on radio; backpagers in Manchester Guardian; reviews, articles, etc. *Recreation:* throwing things away. *Address:* 18 Dartmouth Park Avenue, NW5 1JN. *T:* 071–485 4672. *Club:* Savile.

SAUNDERS, Christopher John, MA; Headmaster, Eastbourne College, since 1981; *b* 7 May 1940; *s* of R. H. Saunders and G. S. Saunders (*née* Harris); *m* 1973, Cynthia Elizabeth Stiles; one *s* one *d*. *Educ:* Lancing Coll.; Fitzwilliam Coll., Cambridge (MA); PGCE Wadham Coll., Oxford. Assistant Master, Bradfield College, 1964–80 (Housemaster, 1972–80). Mem. Council, FA. *Recreations:* music, theatre, gardening, soccer (Oxford Blue 1963), cricket (Oxford Blue 1964), people. *Address:* Headmaster's House, Eastbourne College, Eastbourne, East Sussex BN21 4JX. *Clubs:* MCC; Hawks (Cambridge).

SAUNDERS, Christopher Thomas, CMG 1953; Visiting Fellow, Sussex European Research Centre and Science Policy Research Unit, University of Sussex, since 1973; *b* 5 Nov. 1907; *s* of Thomas Beckenn Avening Saunders, clergyman, and Mary Theodora Slater; *m* 1947, Cornelia Jacomijntje Gielstra; one *s*. *Educ:* Craig School, Windermere; St Edward's School; Christ Church, Oxford. BA 1929; MA 1932; University of Liverpool: Social Survey of Merseyside, 1930–33; University of Manchester: Economic Research Dept, 1933–35; Joint Committee of Cotton Trade Organisations, Manchester, 1935–40; Cotton Control, 1940–44; Combined Production and Resources Board, Washington, 1944–45; Min. of Labour, 1945–47; Central Statistical Office, 1947–57; Dir, Nat. Inst. of Econ. and Social Research, 1957–64; Economist, UN Econ. Commn for Europe, 1965–72. *Publications:* Red Oxford (with M. P. Ashley), 1929; Social Survey of Merseyside (collaborated in), 1934; Seasonal Variations in Employment, 1936; From Free Trade to Integration?, 1975; Winners and Losers, 1977; Engineering in Britain, West Germany and France, 1978; (with D. Marsden) Pay Inequalities in the European Community, 1981; (ed) The Political Economy of New and Old Industrial Countries, 1981; (ed jtly) Europe's Industries, 1983; (ed) 10 volumes in East-West European Economic Interaction Workshop Papers, 1977–91; articles in Economic Jl, Jl of Royal Statistical Soc., The Manchester School. *Recreations:* walking and other forms of travel; painting. *Address:* 73 Wick Hall, Furze Hill, Hove BN3 1NG. *Club:* Reform.

SAUNDERS, Dame Cicely (Mary Strode), OM 1989; DBE 1980 (OBE 1967); FRCP, FRCS; Chairman, St Christopher's Hospice, since 1985 (Medical Director, 1967–85); *b* 22 June 1918; *d* of Gordon Saunders and Mary Christian Knight; *m* 1980, Prof. Marian Bohusz-Szyszko, *s* of Antoni Bohusz-Szyszko, Wilno, Poland. *Educ:* Roedean Sch.; St Anne's Coll., Oxford; St Thomas's Hosp. Med. Sch.; Nightingale Sch. of Nursing. SRN 1944; MB, BS, 1957; MA 1960 (BA (war degree) 1945). FRCP 1974 (MRCP 1968); FRCN 1981; FRCS 1986. Founded St Christopher's Hospice, 1967 (St Christopher's has been a Registered Charity since 1961 and was opened as a Hospice in 1967). Mem., MRC, 1976–79; Dep. Chm., Attendance Allowance Bd, 1979–85. Hon. Consultant, St Thomas' Hosp., 1985. AIMSW 1947. Hon. FRCPsych 1988; Hon. Fellow: Sheffield City Polytechnic, 1983; Newnham Coll., Cambridge, 1986. Hon. DSc: Yale, 1969; London, 1983; Glasgow, 1990; Dr of Medicine, Lambeth, 1977; Hon. MD Belfast, 1984; DUniv Open, 1978; Hon. LLD: Columbia, NY, 1979; Leicester, 1983; DHL Jewish Theological Seminary of America, 1982; DU Essex, 1983; Hon. DCL: Canterbury, 1984; Cambridge, 1986; Oxford, 1986; Hon. Dr Med. TCD, 1988. Gold Medal, Soc. of Apothecaries of London, 1979; Gold Medal, BMA, 1987; Templeton Foundation Prize, 1981. *Publications:* Care of the Dying, 1960, 2nd edn 1977; (ed) The Management of Terminal Disease, 1978, 2nd edn 1984; (ed jtly) Hospice: the living idea, 1981; Living with Dying, 1983, 2nd edn 1989; (ed) St Christopher's in Celebration, 1988; Beyond the Horizon, 1990; (ed) Hospice and Palliative Care, 1990; various papers on terminal care. *Recreation*: home. *Address*: St Christopher's Hospice, 51–59 Lawrie Park Road, Sydenham, SE26 6DZ. *T*: 081–778 9252.

SAUNDERS, Air Vice-Marshal David John, CBE 1986; FIMechE; Assistant Chief of Defence Staff (Logistics), since 1991; *b* 12 June 1943; *s* of John Saunders and Nina Saunders (*née* Mabberley); *m* 1966, Elizabeth Jane Cairns; one *s* one *d*. *Educ*: Commonweal Grammar Sch.; RAF College; Cranfield Inst. of Technology. BSc, MSc, CEng. Joined RAF 1961; management appts, 1966–85; Station Comdr, RAF Sealand, 1983; Command Mechanical Engineer, HQ RAF Germany, 1986; Dir of Engineering Policy (RAF), MoD, 1989–91. *Recreations*: hill walking, cross country ski-ing, team sports. *Address*: Ministry of Defence, Main Building, Whitehall, SW1A 2HB. *T*: 071–218 3634. *Club*: Royal Air Force.

SAUNDERS, David Martin St George; HM Diplomatic Service, retired; *b* 23 July 1930; *s* of late Hilary St George Saunders and Helen (*née* Foley); *m* 1960, Patricia, *d* of James Methold, CBE; one *s* one *d*. *Educ*: Marlborough Coll.; RMA Sandhurst; Staff Coll., Quetta, Pakistan. Commnd Welsh Guards, 1950; Staff Captain Egypt, 1954–56; Asst Adjt, RMA Sandhurst, 1956–58; Adjt 1st Bn Welsh Guards, 1958–60; GSO III War Office, 1960–62; sc 1962–63; Company Comdr 1st Bn Welsh Guards, 1964; GSO II British Defence Liaison Staff, Canberra, 1965–67; Guards Depot, Pirbright, 1967–68; joined Foreign Service, 1968; Consul (Economic), Johannesburg, 1970–73; First Secretary: FCO, 1973–74; Dakar, 1974–76; FCO, 1976–77; Pretoria, 1977–79; The Hague, 1979–83; Counsellor, FCO, 1983–90. *Recreations*: military history, tennis, skiing, shooting, cinema, wines of Burgundy. *Address*: 18 Garfield Road, SW11 5PN.

SAUNDERS, David William, CB 1989; Parliamentary Counsel, since 1980; *b* 4 Nov. 1936; *s* of William Ernest Saunders and Lilian Grace (*née* Ward); *m* 1963, Margaret Susan Rose Bartholomew. *Educ*: Hornchurch Grammar Sch.; Worcester Coll., Oxford (MA). Admitted solicitor, 1964. Joined Office of Parly Counsel, 1970; Dep. Parly Counsel, 1978–80; with Law Commn, 1972–74, 1986–87. *Recreations*: golf, bridge. *Address*: 104A Belgrave Road, SW1V 2BJ. *T*: 071–834 4403. *Club*: United Oxford & Cambridge University.

SAUNDERS, Prof. Derek William, CBE 1986; Professor of Polymer Physics and Engineering, Cranfield Institute of Technology, 1967–87, retired 1988, Emeritus Professor, since 1989; Director, Science and Engineering Research Council/Department of Industry Teaching Company Scheme, 1981–88; *b* 4 Dec. 1925; *s* of Alfred and Elizabeth Hannah Saunders; *m* 1949, Mahalah Harrison; three *s* two *d*. *Educ*: Morley Grammar Sch.; Imperial Coll., Univ. of London. PhD, ARCS, FInstP, FPRI, FIM, CEng, CPhys. Building Res. Stn, Garston, 1945–47; British Rubber Producers Res. Assoc., 1947–51; Royal Instn, 1951–54; British Rayon Res. Assoc., 1954–60; Cranfield Inst. of Technology: Sen. Lectr 1960, subseq. Reader; Head of Materials Dept, 1969–81; Pro-Vice-Chancellor, 1973–76. Chm. Council, Plastics Inst., 1973–75; Chm. Council, 1975–76, Pres., 1983–85, Plastics and Rubber Inst. Mem. Harpur Trust (Bedford Charity), 1968–88. Hon. DTech CNAA, 1990. *Publications*: chapters in several books on polymeric materials; sci. papers in various learned jls. *Address*: 98 Topcliffe Road, Thirsk, N Yorks YO7 1RY. *T*: Thirsk (0845) 523344.

SAUNDERS, Ernest Walter, MA; FInstM; Chairman, 1986–87, and Chief Executive, 1981–87, Guinness PLC (formerly Arthur Guinness & Sons plc); Chairman: Arthur Guinness Son & Co. (Great Britain), 1982–87; Guinness Brewing Worldwide, 1982–87; *b* 21 Oct. 1935; *m* 1963, Carole Ann Stephings; two *s* one *d*. *Educ*: Emmanuel Coll., Cambridge (MA). Man. Dir, Beecham Products Internat., and Dir, Beecham Products, 1966–73; Chm., European Div., Great Universal Stores, 1973–77; Pres., Nestlé Nutrition SA, and Mem. Worldwide Management Cttee, Nestlé SA, Vevey, Switzerland, 1977–81; Chm., Beechnut Corp., USA, 1977–81; Dir, Brewers' Soc., 1983. Dir, Queens Park Rangers Football & Athletic Club, 1983. *Recreations*: skiing, tennis, football.

SAUNDERS, James; playwright; *b* Islington, 8 Jan. 1925; *s* of Walter Percival Saunders and Dorcas Geraldine (*née* Warren); *m* 1951, Audrey Cross; *s* two *d*. *Educ*: Wembley County Sch.; Southampton Univ. *Plays*: Moonshine, 1955; Alas, Poor Fred, The Ark, 1959; Committal, Barnstable, Return to a City, 1960; A Slight Accident, 1961; Double Double, 1962; Next Time I'll Sing to You (Evening Standard Drama Award), The Pedagogue, Who Was Hilary Maconochie?, 1963; A Scent of Flowers, Neighbours, 1964; Triangle, Opus, 1965; A Man's Best Friend, The Borage Pigeon Affair, 1969; After Liverpool, 1970; Games, Savoury Meringue, 1971; Hans Kohlhaas, 1972; Bye Bye Blues, 1973; The Island, 1975; Bodies, 1977; Birdsong, 1979; Fall, 1981; Emperor Waltz, 1983; Scandella, 1985; Menocchio, 1985 (BBC Radio Play Award, 1986); *stage adaptations*: The Italian Girl, 1968; The Travails of Sancho Panza, 1969; A Journey to London, 1973; Player Piano, 1978; Random Moments in a May Garden, 1980; The Girl in Melanie Klein, 1980; *television*: Watch Me I'm a Bird, 1964; Bloomers, 1979 (series); television adaptations of works by D. H. Lawrence, Henry James, H. E. Bates and R. F. Delderfield; *screenplays*: Sailor's Return; The Captain's Doll. Arts Council of GB Drama Bursary, 1960; Writers' Guild TV Adaptation Award, 1966; Arts Council Major Bursary, 1984. *Address*: c/o Margaret Ramsay Ltd, 14a Goodwin's Court, St Martin's Lane, WC2.

SAUNDERS, Sir John (Anthony Holt), Kt 1972; CBE 1970; DSO 1945; MC 1944; formerly Chairman and Chief Manager, Hongkong and Shanghai Banking Corporation, 1962–72; *b* 29 July 1917; *m* 1942, Enid Mary Durant Cassidy; two *d*. *Educ*: Bromsgrove Sch. War Service, 1940–45; OCTU Sandhurst (Belt of Honour); N Africa, Sicily and Italy. Lived in Hong Kong 1950–72; MEC Hong Kong Govt, 1966–72. Chm. of Stewards, Royal Hong Kong Jockey Club, 1967–72. Hon. DSocSc (Hong Kong) 1969. Comdr, Order of Prince Henry the Navigator (Portugal), 1966.

SAUNDERS, John Henry Boulton; QC 1991; *b* 15 March 1949; *s* of Kathleen Mary Saunders and Henry G. B. Saunders; *m* 1975, Susan Mary Chick; one *s* two *d*. *Educ*: Uppingham School; Magdalen College, Oxford (BA). Called to the Bar, Gray's Inn, 1972; a Recorder, 1990. *Recreations*: music, sailing. *Address*: 4 Fountain Court, Steelhouse Lane, Birmingham B4 6DR. *T*: 021–236 3476.

SAUNDERS, Maj.-Gen. Kenneth, CB 1979; OBE 1970; Paymaster in Chief and Inspector of Army Pay Services, 1975–79, retired; *b* 1 Jan. 1920; *m* 1953, Ann Lawrence Addison; one *s*. *Educ*: Lancastrian Sch., Shrewsbury. Enlisted King's Shropshire LI, 1939; commnd Royal Welch Fus., 1940; served in France, Belgium, Holland and Germany (despatches 1945); various staff appts, NW Europe and Far East, 1945–52; transf. to RAPC, 1952; Staff Paymaster: WO 1962–63; HQ Div./Malaya, 1965–67; MoD, 1967–70; Chief Paymaster: MoD, 1970–71; 1 British Corps, 1971–72; Dep. Paymaster in Chief, 1972–75; Maj.-Gen. 1975; Col Comdt, RAPC, 1979–84. *Recreations*: fishing, travel. *Address*: 31 Prestonville Court, Dyke Road, Brighton BN1 3UG. *T*: Brighton (0273) 28866.

SAUNDERS, Kenneth Herbert; Chief Architect, Commission for the New Towns, 1976–82, retired; *b* 5 April 1915; *s* of William James Saunders and Anne Elizabeth Baker; *m* 1940, Kathleen Bettye Fortune (*d* 1981); one *s* one *d*. *Educ*: elementary sch., Worthing;

Sch. of Art, Worthing; Brighton Coll. of Art. ARIBA 1940. Served War: RA Iraq and Persia; OCTU Bengal Sappers and Miners, India and Burma; Major RE ALFSEA, SORE II, 1940 (mentioned in despatches). Articled pupil, 1933; Dept of Architecture, Bor. of Worthing, 1936; City Architect's Dept, Portsmouth, 1937–39, 1946–49; Crawley Develt Corporation: Architect, 1949; Sen. Architect, 1952; Asst Chief Architect, 1958; Commission for New Towns: Asst Chief Architect, 1962; Exec. Architect, 1965; Manager (Crawley), 1978–80. *Recreations*: architecture, buildings. *Address*: Longthorpe, 22 Goffs Park Road, Crawley, West Sussex RH11 8AY. *T*: Crawley (0293) 521334.

SAUNDERS, Michael Lawrence, CB 1990; Solicitor to HM Customs and Excise, since 1989; *b* 13 April 1944; *s* of Samuel Reuben Saunders and Doris Saunders; *m* 1970, Anna Stobo; one *s* one *d*. *Educ*: Clifton College; Birmingham University (LLB Hons); Jesus College, Cambridge (LLB Hons). Called to the Bar, Gray's Inn, 1971. Third Sec., Hague Conf. on Private Internat. Law (Permt Bureau), 1966–68; Second Sec., 1968–72; Senior Legal Assistant: DTI, 1972–73; Treasury Solicitor's Dept (Energy Branch), 1973–76; Law Officers' Dept, 1976–79; Asst Treasury Solicitor (Cabinet Office European Secretariat Asst Legal Adviser), 1979–83; Asst Legal Sec., 1983–86, Legal Sec., 1986–89, Law Officers' Dept. *Publications*: contribs to jls on internat. law. *Address*: c/o HM Customs and Excise, New King's Beam House, SE1 9PJ.

SAUNDERS, Sir Owen (Alfred), Kt 1965; MA, DSc; FRS 1958; FEng; Hon. FIMechE; FInstP; FInstF; FRAeS; Hon. FCGI; Life Member of ASME; Emeritus Professor of Mechanical Engineering, University of London, Imperial College (Professor, 1946; Head of Department, 1946–65; Pro-Rector, 1964–67, Acting Rector, 1966–67); Vice-Chancellor, University of London, 1967–69; *b* 24 September 1904; *s* of Alfred George Saunders and Margaret Ellen Jones; *m* 1st, 1935, Marion Isabel McKechney (*d* 1981); one *s* two *d*; 2nd, 1981, Mrs Daphne Holmes. *Educ*: Emanuel School; Birkbeck College, London; Trinity College, Cambridge (Senior Scholar). Scientific Officer, Dept of Scientific and Industrial Research, 1926; Lecturer in Applied Mathematical Physics, Imperial College, 1932; Clothworkers' Reader in Applied Thermodynamics, Univ. of London, 1937; on loan to Directorate of Turbine Engines, MAP, 1942–45. Dean, City and Guilds Coll., 1955–64. Past Pres., IMechE; Mem., ITA, 1964–69; President: British Flame Research Cttee; Section G, British Assoc., 1959. Founder Fellow, Fellowship of Engineering, 1976. Honorary Member: Yugoslav Acad., 1959–; Japan Soc. of Mechanical Engrs, 1960–; ASME, 1961–; For. Assoc., Nat. Acad. of Engrg, USA, 1979. Hon. Fellow, RHC, 1983 (Chm. Council, 1971–85). Hon. DSc Strathclyde, 1964. Melchett medallist, Inst. of Fuel, 1962; Max Jakob Award, ASME, 1966. Hon. Mem., Mark Twain Soc., 1976. *Publications*: The Calculation of Heat Transmission, 1932; An Introduction to Heat Transfer, 1950; various scientific and technical papers in Proceedings of Royal Society, Phil. Mag., Physical Society, Engineering, and the Institutions. *Recreation*: music. *Address*: Oakbank, Sea Lane, Middleton, Sussex. *T*: Middleton-on-Sea (0243) 582966. *Club*: Athenæum.

SAUNDERS, Sir Peter, Kt 1982; Chairman and Managing Director: Peter Saunders Ltd; Peter Saunders Group Ltd; Director: West End Theatre Managers Ltd; Duke of York's Theatre Ltd; Theatre Investment Fund Ltd; Theatre Investment Finance Ltd; *b* 23 Nov. 1911; *s* of Ernest and Aletta Saunders; *m* 1st, 1959, Ann Stewart (*d* 1976); no *c*; 2nd, 1979, Catherine Baylis (*née* Imperiali dei Principi di Francavilla) (Katie Boyle); no *c*. *Educ*: Oundle Sch.; Lausanne. Film cameraman, film director, journalist and press agent; served War of 1939–45 (Captain); started in theatrical production, 1947; has presented over 100 plays incl. The Mousetrap, which has run since 1952 (world's longest ever run, Dec. 1971); other West End productions include: Fly Away Peter; The Perfect Woman; Breach of Marriage; My Mother Said; The Hollow; Witness for the Prosecution; The Manor of Northstead; Spider's Web; The Water Gipsies; The Bride and the Bachelor; Subway in the Sky; Verdict; The Trial of Mary Dugan; The Unexpected Guest; A Day in the Life Of; And Suddenly it's Spring; Go Back For Murder; You Prove It; Fit To Print; Rule of Three; Alfie; The Reluctant Peer; Hostile Witness; Every Other Evening; Return Ticket; Arsenic and Old Lace; Justice Is A Woman; As You Like It; Oh Clarence!; On A Foggy Day; The Jockey Club Stakes; Move Over Mrs Markham; Lover; Cockie; Double Edge; A Murder is Announced; The Family Reunion; Cards On The Table; in 1971 acquired Volcano Productions Ltd., whose productions include No Sex Please, We're British; The Mating Game; Lloyd George Knew My Father; At The End Of The Day; Touch Of Spring; Betzi; operated repertory at Royal Artillery Theatre, Woolwich, 1951, and at Prince of Wales Theatre, Cardiff, 1956; in 1958, took over a long lease of the Ambassadors Theatre; bought the Duchess Theatre, 1961, and sold it in 1968; acquired a long lease of the St Martin's Theatre, 1968; bought the Vaudeville Theatre, 1969, and sold it in 1983; bought the Duke of York's Theatre, 1976 and sold it in 1979 to Capital Radio on condition that it remained a live theatre in perpetuity; has produced more than 1500 programmes for Radio Luxembourg; an original Dir, Yorkshire Television; Mem. consortium awarded London Gen. Radio Station by IBA, which became Capital Radio, 1973. Vice-President: Actors' Benevolent Fund, 1972–; Royal General Theatrical Fund Assoc., 1985–; Mem. Exec. Council, SWET, 1954– (Pres. 1961–62 and 1967–69, Vice Pres., 1988–); Mem. Council, Theatrical Managers' Assoc., 1958–64; Pres., Stage Golfing Soc., 1963; Pres., Stage Cricket Club, 1956–65. Life Mem., Dogs Home Battersea Assoc., 1988. Governor, Christ's Hosp. Silver Heart award, Variety Club of GB, 1955. *Publications*: The Mousetrap Man (autobiog.), 1972; Scales of Justice (play), 1978. *Recreations*: cricket, chess, bridge, photography, music of George Gershwin, telephoning, collecting wills. *Address*: Vaudeville Theatre Offices, 10 Maiden Lane, WC2E 7NA. *T*: 071–240 3177. *Clubs*: Garrick, MCC; Highgate Golf.

SAUNDERS, Peter Gordon; Editor, The Birmingham Post, 1986–90; *b* 1 July 1940; *s* of Gordon and Winifred Saunders; *m* 1964, Teresa Geraldine Metcalf; two *d*. *Educ*: Newport High Sch. for Boys, Gwent; London Sch. of Econs and Pol Science (BScEcon 1961). Reporter, Gloucestershire Echo, 1961–63; Sports Reporter, Sunderland Echo, 1963–64; Sub-Editor, Yorkshire Post, 1964; The Birmingham Post, 1964–69; Lectr in Journalism, Cardiff Coll. of Commerce, 1969–70; The Birmingham Post, 1971–90: successively Dep. Chief Sub-Editor, Chief Sub-Editor, Asst Editor, Exec. Editor, and Editor. *Recreations*: Rugby Union, reading, rhythm and blues. *Address*: Well Cottage, West Street, Kingham, Oxon OX7 6YG. *T*: Kingham (0608) 659010. *Club*: Birmingham Press (Birmingham).

SAUNDERS, Raymond; Secretary, British Museum (Natural History), 1976–87; *b* 24 July 1933; *s* of late Herbert Charles Saunders and Doris May (*née* Kirkham-Jones); *m* 1959, Shirley Marion (*née* Stringer); two *s*. *Educ*: Poole Grammar Sch. WO, 1950; Air Min., 1956; Min. of Land and Natural Resources, 1966; Land Commn, 1967; Treasury, 1968; CSD, 1969. *Recreations*: reading biographies, gardening, sport (now as spectator). *Address*: The Old World Tea Gardens, High Street, Godshill, Isle of Wight.

SAUNDERS, Richard, FRICS; Chairman, Baker Harris Saunders Group Plc, since 1986; *b* 4 July 1937; *s* of late Edward E. Saunders and of Betty Saunders; *m* 1st, 1961, Suzannah Rhodes-Cooke (marr. diss.); one *s*; 2nd, 1970, Alison Fiddes. *Educ*: St Edmund's Sch., Hindhead; Uppingham. FRICS 1965. National Service, commnd The Life Guards, 1958–60. Jun. Partner, Richard Ellis, Chartered Surveyors, 1966–69; formed Richard

Saunders & Partners, 1969; Baker Harris Saunders, 1977. Chm., City Br., RICS, 1979–80; Pres., Associated Owners of City Properties, 1985–87; Member: Council, British Property Fedn, 1974–90 (Hon. Treas., 1974–85); Bd, Gen. Practice Finance Corp., 1984–89. Chairman: Barbican Residential Cttee, 1979–81; Barbican Centre Cttee, 1983–86; Metropolitan Public Gardens Assoc., 1984–90; Governor: Bridewell Royal Hosp. and King Edward's Sch., Witley, 1976–; St Edmund's Sch., Hindhead, 1979– (Chm., 1979–87); (also Almoner), Christ's Hosp., 1980–; Royal Star and Garter Home, 1984–. Mem., Court of Common Council, Corp. of London, 1975–; Deputy for Ward of Candlewick, 1983–; Liveryman: Clothworkers Co., 1960– (Warden, 1989); Co. of Chartered Surveyors, 1979–; Church Warden, St Lawrence Jewry-by-Guildhall, 1984–; Sheriff, City of London, 1987–88. *Recreations:* instant gardening, music, golf, tennis. *Address:* 13 Caroline Place, W2 4AW. *T:* 071–796 4000; The Old Rectory, Bagendon, Cirencester, Glos GL7 7DU. *Clubs:* Cavalry and Guards, City Livery, MCC.

SAUNDERS, Prof. Wilfred Leonard, CBE 1982; FLA; Director, University of Sheffield Postgraduate School of Librarianship and Information Science, 1963–82, now Professor Emeritus; *b* 18 April 1920; *s* of Leonard and Annie Saunders; *m* 1946, Joan Mary Rider, *er d* of late Major W. E. Rider; two *s*. *Educ:* King Edward's Grammar Sch. for Boys, Camp Hill, Birmingham; Fitzwilliam House, Univ. of Cambridge (MA). FLA 1952. Served War: France, 1940; N Africa, 1942–43; Italy, 1943–46; Captain Royal Signals. Library Asst, Birmingham Reference Library, 1936–39; Dep. Lib., Inst. of Bankers, 1948–49; Lib., Univ. of Birmingham Inst. of Educn, 1949–56; Dep. Lib., Univ. of Sheffield, 1956–63; 12 months' secondment to UNESCO as Expert in Educnl Documentation, Uganda, 1962; Univ. of Sheffield: Prof. of Librarianship and Inf. Science, 1968; Dean, Faculty of Educnl Studies, 1974–77. Visiting Professor: Pittsburgh Univ. Grad. Sch. of Library and Inf. Sciences, 1968; UCLA, 1985; Commonwealth Vis. Fellow, Australia, 1969; (1st) Elsie O. and Philip Sang Internat. Lectr, Rosary Grad. Sch. of Library Science, USA, 1974. UK Rep., Internat. Fedn for Documentation/Training of Documentalists Cttee, 1966–70; Hon. Consultant, E Africa Sch. of Librarianship, Makerere Univ., 1967–73; overseas consultancy and adv. missions. Mem. Council, Library Assoc., 1979–83 (Pres. 1980); Member: Council, ASLIB, 1965–71, 1972–78; British Council, 1970– (Mem., Libraries Adv. Panel, 1970–87, Chm. 1975–81); Bd of Librarianship, CNAA, 1966–79; Library Adv. Council (England), 1970–73; Adv. Cttee, British Library Ref. Div., 1975–80; *ad hoc* Cttee on Educn and Trng (Gen. Inf. Prog.), UNESCO, 1978–85; Adv. Cttee, British Library R&D Dept, 1980–88; British Library Adv. Council, 1981–84; Adv. Council on Public Records, 1986–; Chairman: Jt Consultative Cttee of Library Assoc., Aslib, SCONUL, Soc. of Archivists and IInfSc, 1980–81; Library and Information Services Council (formerly Library Adv. Council for Eng.), 1981–84. Hon. FIInfSc 1977; Hon. FCP 1983. Hon. LittD Sheffield, 1989. *Publications:* (ed) The Provision and Use of Library and Documentation Services, 1966; (ed) Librarianship in Britain Today, 1967; (with H. Schur and Lisbeth J. Pargeter) Education and Training for Scientific and Technological Library and Information Work, 1968; (ed) University and Research Library Studies, 1968; (with W. J. Hutchins and Lisbeth J. Pargeter) The Language Barrier: a study in depth of the place of foreign language materials in the research activity of an academic community, 1971; (ed) British Librarianship Today, 1977; (with E. M. Broome) The Library and Information Services of the British Council, 1977; Guidelines for Curriculum Development in Information Studies, 1978; Professional Education for Library and Information Work in the Socialist Republic of Macedonia, 1982; Post-graduate Training for Information Specialists (Venezuela), 1984; An Evaluation of Education for Librarianship in New Zealand, 1987; Towards a Unified Professional Organization for Library and Information Science and Services, 1989; Dunkirk Diary of a Very Young Soldier (autobiog.), 1989; jl articles and res. reports. *Recreations:* gardening, walking, listening to music, book collecting. *Address:* 15 Princess Drive, Sawston, Cambridge CB2 4DL. *Club:* Commonwealth Trust.

SAUNDERS WATSON, Comdr (Leslie) Michael (Macdonald), RN (retired); DL; Chairman, British Library Board, since 1990; *b* 9 Oct. 1934; *s* of Captain L. S. Saunders, DSO, RN (retd), and Elizabeth Saunders (*née* Culme-Seymour); *m* 1958, Georgina Elizabeth Laetitia, *d* of Adm. Sir William Davis, GCB, DSO; two *s* one *d*. *Educ:* Eton; BRNC, Dartmouth. Joined Royal Navy, 1951; specialised in Communications (Jackson Everett Prize); Comdr 1969; retired, 1971, on succession to Rockingham Castle Estate. Pres., Historic Houses Assoc., 1982–88 (Dep. Pres., 1978–82; Chm., Tax and Parly Cttee, 1975–82); Chairman: Northamptonshire Assoc. Youth Clubs, 1977–91; Heritage Educn Year, 1977; Corby Community Adv. Gp, 1979–86; Ironstone Royalty Owners Assoc., 1979–91; Nat. Curriculum History Wkg Gp, 1988–90; Heritage Educn Trust, 1988–; Vice-Chm., Northamptonshire Small Industries Cttee, 1974–79; Member: British Heritage Cttee, 1978–; BTA, 1978–88; Northamptonshire Enterprise Agency, 1986–90; Country Landowners' Association: Member: Taxation Cttee, 1975–90; Exec. Cttee, 1977–82, 1987–; Legal and Land Use Cttee, 1982–87; Chm., Northamptonshire Branch, 1981–84. Director: Lamport Hall Preservation Trust, 1978–91; English Sinfonia, 1981–. Trustee: Royal Botanic Gdns, Kew, 1983– (Chm., Bldgs and Design Cttee, 1985–); Nat. Heritage Meml Fund, 1987–. Chm., Governors Lodge Park Comprehensive Sch., 1977–82; Trustee, Oakham Sch., 1975–77. FRSA 1986. High Sheriff, 1978–79, DL 1979–, Northamptonshire. Hon. DLitt Warwick, 1991. *Recreations:* sailing, music, gardening. *Address:* Rockingham Castle, Market Harborough, Leicestershire LE16 8TH. *T:* Rockingham (0536) 770240/770326. *Club:* Brooks's.

SAUVAGNARGUES, Jean Victor; Commander, Légion d'Honneur, Croix de Guerre avec palme (1939–45); Hon. GCMG 1976; Commander of the National Order of Merit; French Ambassador; former Foreign Minister; *b* Paris, 2 April 1915; *s* of Edmond Sauvagnargues and Alice Caplan; *m* 1948, Lise Marie L'Evesque; two *s* two *d*. *Educ:* Higher Normal Sch.; Dip., Political Science Sch.; Univ. (German) (Agrégé). Attaché, Embassy, Bucharest, 1941. Served War with Free French Forces, 1943 (Army, June 1944–May 1945). Cabinet of: the High Commn, Beirut, 1943; M Massigli, 1944; Gen. de Gaulle, 1945–46; Specialist on German questions, Quai d'Orsay, 1947–55; Cabinet of M Pinay, 1955. In negotiations about the Saar, Jan.-June 1956; Ambassador to Ethiopia, 1956–60; Director, African and Middle-Eastern Affairs, Min. of Foreign Affairs, 1960–62; Ambassador to: Tunisia, 1962–70; the Federal Republic of Germany, Bonn, 1970–74; Minister for Foreign Affairs, France, 1974–76; Ambassadeur de France, 1976; Ambassador to UK, 1977–81. *Address:* 14 avenue Pierre 1er de Serbie, 75116 Paris, France.

SAUVÉ, Rt. Hon. Jeanne, CC (Canada) 1984; CMM 1984; CD 1984; PC (Can.) 1972; Governor-General and Commander-in-Chief of Canada, 1984–89; Founder, and Honorary Chairman, Jeanne Sauvé Youth Foundation, since 1990; *b* 26 April 1922; *d* of Charles Albert Benoit and Anna Vaillant; *m* 1948, Hon. Maurice Sauvé; one *s*. *Educ:* Notre-Dame du Rosaire Convent, Ottawa; Ottawa Univ.; Paris Univ. Journalist; Founder, Youth Movements Fedn, 1947; Asst to Dir of Youth Section, UNESCO, Paris, 1951; Union des Artistes, Montreal: Mem., Admin. Council, 1961–72; Deleg. to Film and TV Writers Congress, Moscow, 1968; Vice-Pres., 1968–70; Sec. Gen., Fédération des Auteurs et des Artistes du Canada, 1966–72. MP (L) for Montreal Laval- les-Rapides (formerly Montreal-Ahuntsic), 1972–84; Minister of State for Science and Technol., 1972–74; Minister of the Environment, 1974–75; Minister of Communications, 1975–79; Advisor to Sec. of State for External Affairs for relations with the French-speaking world, 1978–79; Speaker of the House of Commons, 1980–84. Pres., Canadian Inst. of Public Affairs, 1964 (Vice-Pres., 1962–64); Founding Mem., Inst. of Political Res., 1972; Member: Centennial Commn, 1967; Admin. Council, YMCA, 1969–72. Hon. DSc New Brunswick, 1974; Hon. LLD: Calgary, 1982; McGill, 1984; Toronto, 1984; Queen's, 1984; Carleton, 1986; Laurentian, 1987; Royal Mil. Coll., Kingston, 1987; Manitoba, 1988; Moncton, 1988; Hon. DHL: Mount St Vincent, 1983; St-Lawrence in Canton, NY, 1987; Hon. DU: Ottawa, 1984; Laval, 1984; Montreal, 1985; Hon. Dr in Political Science, Chulalongkorn, Bangkok, 1987. Médaille des Universités de Paris, 1988. *Recreations:* cultivating flowers and plants, reading, tennis. *Address:* 3474 de la Montagne, Montréal, Qué H3G 2A6, Canada.

SAUZIER, Sir (André) Guy, Kt 1973; CBE 1959; ED; retired General Overseas Representative of Mauritius Chamber of Agriculture, 1959–79; Minister Plenipotentiary, Mauritius Mission to EEC, 1972–79; *b* 20 Oct. 1910; *s* of J. Adrien Sauzier, Mauritius; *m* 1936, Thérèse, *d* of Henri Mallac; six *s* two *d*. *Educ:* Royal Coll., Mauritius. Served War of 1939–45; late Major, Mauritius TF. A nominated Member of the Legislative Council, Mauritius, 1949–57; Member, Mauritius Political Delegn to the UK, 1955; Minister of Works and Communications, 1957–59. Represented Mauritius at the Coronation, 1953. *Address:* 15 Marloes Road, W8 6LQ.

SAVA, George, (George Alexis Milkomanovich Milkomane); Author and Consulting Surgeon; *b* 15 Oct. 1903; *s* of Col Ivan Alexandrovitch and Countess Maria Ignatiev; *nephew* of Prince Alexander Milkomanovich Milkomane; *m* 1939, Jannette Hollingdale; two *s* two *d*. *Educ:* Public Schools in Bulgaria and Russia. Entered Russian Imperial Naval Academy in 1913; after the Revolution studied in various medical schools, Univ. of Paris, Florence, Rome, Munich, Berlin and Bonn; domiciled in this country since 1932; further medical education at Manchester, Glasgow and Edinburgh; naturalised British subject in 1938; Research scholarships in medicine and surgery, University of Rome, Libero Docente (Professorship) of Univ. of Rome, 1954. Grand Chev. of the Crown of Bulgaria; Commendatore dell' Ordine al Merito Della Repubblica Italiana, 1961. *Publications: autobiog. medical:* The Healing Knife, 1937; Beauty from the Surgeon's Knife, 1938; A Surgeon's Destiny, 1939; Donkey's Serenade, 1940; Twice the Clock Round, 1941; A Ring at the Door, 1941; Surgeon's Symphony, 1944; They come by Appointment, 1946; The Knife Heals Again, 1948; The Way of a Surgeon, 1949; Strange Cases, 1950; A Doctor's Odyssey, 1951; Patients' Progress, 1952; A Surgeon Remembers, 1953; Surgeon Under Capricorn, 1954; The Lure of Surgery, 1955; A Surgeon at Large, 1957; Surgery and Crime, 1957; All this and Surgery too, 1958; Surgery Holds the Door, 1960; A Surgeon in Rome, 1961; A Surgeon in California, 1962; Appointments in Rome, 1963; A Surgeon in New Zealand, 1964; A Surgeon in Cyprus, 1965; A Surgeon in Australia, 1966; Sex, Surgery, People, 1967; The Gates of Heaven are Narrow, 1968; Bitter-Sweet Surgery, 1969; One Russian's Story, 1970; A Stranger in Harley Street, 1970; A Surgeon and his Knife, 1978; Living with your Psoriasis (essays), 1978; *political and historical books:* Rasputin Speaks, 1941; Valley of Forgotten People, 1942; The Chetniks, 1943; School for War, 1943; They Stayed in London, 1943; Russia Triumphant, 1944; A Tale of Ten Cities, 1944; War Without Guns, 1944; Caught by Revolution, 1952; *novels:* Land Fit for Heroes, 1945; Link of Two Hearts, 1945; Gissy, 1946; Call it Life, 1946; Boy in Samarkand, 1950; Flight from the Palace, 1953; Pursuit in the Desert, 1955; The Emperor Story, 1959; Punishment Deferred, 1966; Man Without Label, 1967; Alias Dr Holtzman, 1968; City of Cain, 1969; The Imperfect Surgeon, 1969; Nothing Sacred, 1970; Of Guilt Possessed, 1970; A Skeleton for My Mate, 1971; The Beloved Nemesis, 1971; On the Wings of Angels, 1972; The Sins of Andrea, 1972; Tell Your Grief Softly, 1972; Cocaine for Breakfast, 1973; Return from the Valley, 1973; Sheilah of Buckleigh Manor, 1974; Every Sweet Hath Its Sour, 1974; The Way of the Healing Knife, 1976; Mary Mary Quite Contrary, 1977; Crusader's Clinic, 1977; Pretty Polly, 1977; No Man is Perfect, 1978; A Stranger in his Skull, 1979; Secret Surgeon, 1979; Crimson Eclipse, 1980; Innocence on Trial, 1981; The Price of Prejudice, 1982; The Killer Microbes, 1982; Betrayal in Style, 1983; Double Identity, 1984; A Smile Through Tears, 1985; Bill of Indictment, 1986; Rose By Any Other Name, 1987; The Roses Bloom Again, 1988; also wrote numerous novels as George Borodin. *Recreations:* tennis, golf, riding, aviation. *Address:* c/o A. P. Watt Ltd, 20 John Street, WC1N 2DL.

SAVAGE, Albert Walter, CMG 1954; Director-General (retired), Colonial Civil Aviation Service; *b* 12 June 1898; *s* of William Albert Savage, Wheathampstead, Herts; *m* 1923, Lilian Marie Gertrude Storch; one *s* one *d*. *Educ:* Northern Polytechnic, Northampton Institute and Sheffield University. Apprentice, Grahame White Flying School, 1914–16. Served European War, 1914–18, RFC, 1916 to end of war. Aeronautical Inspection Directorate, Air Ministry, UK 1921–34, India, 1934–36; seconded to Egyptian Govt as Chief Technical Inspector, Civil Aviation Dept, Cairo, 1936–46; Colonial Civil Aviation Service, 1946–; Director of Civil Aviation, W Africa, 1946–49; Director-General of Civil Aviation, Malaya/Borneo territories, 1949–54; Civil Aviation Adviser, Government of Jordan, 1954–55; Director of Civil Aviation, Leeward and Windward Islands, 1956–60. Director of Civil Aviation, Sierra Leone, 1961–62. *Recreations:* golf, tennis and squash. *Address:* 71 Eridge Road, Eastbourne BN21 2TS. *T:* Eastbourne (0323) 37905.

SAVAGE, Sir Ernest (Walter), Kt 1979; FCA; company director, retired; *b* 24 Aug. 1912; *s* of Walter Edwin Savage and Constance Mary Sutton; *m* 1938, Dorothy Winifred Nicholls; one *s* one *d*. *Educ:* Brisbane Grammar School; Scots Coll., Warwick, Qld. In public practice as chartered accountant, 1940–76; retd as Sen. Partner of Coopers & Lybrand, Queensland. Chairman, Bank of Queensland, 1960–84; Director of several other public companies, retired. Institute of Chartered Accountants in Australia: Mem. Queensland State Council, 1951–74 (Chm. three years); Nat. Council, 1961–73; Aust. Pres., 1968–70; elected Life Member, 1978. Hon. Consul for Norway at Brisbane, 1950–76. Chairman: Queensland Govt Cttee of Review of Business Regulations, 1985–86; Public Sector Review Cttee, 1987. Member: Bd of Governors, Cromwell Univ. Coll., 1950–77 (Chm. 1958–67); Faculty of Commerce and Economics, Univ. of Queensland, 1960–67; Bd of Advanced Education, 1978–82 (Finance Cttee, 1974–83); Salvation Army Adv. Bd, 1981–. Trustee, Leukaemia Foundn, 1983–; Chm., Geriatric Medical Foundn, 1986–. Knight 1st class, Order of St Olav (Norway), 1966. *Recreation:* brick and concrete work. *Address:* 12 Mount Ommaney Drive, Jindalee, Brisbane, Queensland 4074, Australia. *T:* 07–376.1086. *Clubs:* Queensland, Brisbane (Brisbane).

SAVAGE, Thomas Hixon, CBE 1990; Chairman and President, ITT Canada, since 1970; *b* Belfast, 21 Nov. 1928; *s* of Thomas Hixon Savage and Martha Foy Turkington; *m* 1st, 1950, Annie Marie Gloria Ethel Gilmore (marr. diss. 1975); one *s* two *d*; 2nd, 1976, Evelyn Phyllis Chapman. *Educ:* Belfast High Sch.; Indian Army Officers' Trng Coll.; Univ. of Toronto Dept of Extension (Indust. Management). Chm., Abbey Life Insurance Co., Canada; formerly Chief Industrial Engineer: Union Carbide, Dunlop Canada; J. J. Gage Co.; Hallmark Greeting Cards; Electric Reduction Co. Mem., Policy Cttee, Business Council on Nat. Issues; Business Co-Chm., Canadian Labour Market & Productivity Center, 1990. Dir, Nat. Retinitis Pigmentosa Eye Res. Foundn, Canada; Chairman: Bd of

Govs, West Park Hosp., 1991; Adv. Bd, Canadian Inst. of Management, 1971 (Life Mem.); Adv. Bd, Boys' and Girls' Clubs of Canada; NI Partnership in Canada. *Recreation*: golf. *Address*: ITT Canada Ltd, PO Box 138, Toronto-Dominion Centre, Toronto, Ont M5K 1H1, Canada; 41 Abilene Drive, Islington, Ont M9A 2N1, Canada. *Clubs*: Ontario (Toronto); Lambton Golf and Country (Islington).

SAVAGE, Wendy Diane, FRCOG; Senior Lecturer in Obstetrics and Gynaecology, Royal London Hospital Medical College, since 1977; *b* 12 April 1935; *d* of William George Edwards and Anne (*née* Smith); *m* 1960, Miguel Babatunde Richard Savage (marr. diss. 1973); two *s* two *d*. *Educ*: Croydon High School for Girls; Girton Coll., Cambridge (BA); London Hosp. Med. Coll. (MB BCh); FRCOG 1985 (MRCOG 1971). Res. Fellow, Harvard Univ., 1963–64; MO, Nigeria, 1964–67; Registrar: Surgery and Obst. and Gynaec., Kenya, 1967–69; Obst. and Gynaec., Royal Free Hosp., 1969–71; venereology, abortion work, family planning, Islington 1971–73; Specialist in obst. and gynaec., family planning and venereology, Gisborne, NZ 1973–76; Lectr, London Hosp., 1976–77. Contract as Hon. Cons. suspended for alleged incompetence, April 1985 — reinstated by unanimous vote of DHA after exoneration by HM61/112 Enquiry, July 1986. Mem., GMC, 1989–. *Publications*: Hysterectomy, 1982; (with Fran Reader) Coping with Caesarean Section and other difficult births, 1983; A Savage Enquiry — who controls childbirth?, 1986; papers on abortion, sexually transmitted disease, ultrasound, sex in pregnancy, cervical cytology, medical education. *Recreations*: playing piano duets, reading. *Address*: 19 Vincent Terrace, N1. *T*: 071–837 7635.

SAVARESE, Signora Fernando; *see* Elvin, Violetta.

SAVERNAKE, Viscount; Thomas James Brudenell-Bruce; *b* 11 Feb. 1982; *s* and heir of Earl of Cardigan, *qv*.

SAVILE, family name of **Earl of Mexborough**.

SAVILE, 3rd Baron, *cr* 1888; **George Halifax Lumley-Savile**; DL; JP; *b* 24 Jan. 1919; *s* of 2nd Baron and Esme Grace Virginia (*d* 1958), *d* of J. Wolton; *S* father, 1931. *Educ*: Eton. Served in 1939–45 War in Duke of Wellington's Regiment, and attached Lincolnshire Regiment during the Burma Campaigns. DL W Yorks, 1954. Is Patron of two livings. Owns about 18,000 acres. JP Borough of Dewsbury, 1955. CStJ 1982. *Recreations*: music and shooting. *Heir*: *b* Hon. Henry Leoline Thornhill Lumley-Savile [*b* 2 Oct. 1923; *m* 1st, 1946, Presiley June (marr. diss. 1951), *o d* of Major G. H. E. Inchbald, Halebourne House, Chobham, Surrey; one *s*; 2nd, 1961, Caroline Jeffie (*d* 1970), *o d* of Peter Clive, California, USA, and Elizabeth Clive, 58 Queens' Gate, SW7; 3rd, 1972, Margaret, *widow* of Peter Bruce; three *s* (triplets). Served War of 1939–45, in Grenadier Guards, Italy (wounded)]. *Address*: Gryce Hall, Shelley, Huddersfield. *T*: Huddersfield (0484) 602774; Walshaw, Hebden Bridge, Yorks. *T*: Hebden Bridge (0422) 842275. *Clubs*: Brooks's, Sloane.

SAVILE, Sir James (Wilson Vincent), Kt 1990; OBE 1971; TV and radio personality; *b* 31 Oct. 1926. *Educ*: St Anne's, Leeds. Presenter: Independent Radio weekly show; Radio One Weekly Show, 1969–89; television: Jim'll Fix It, making dreams come true, No 1 in the ratings every year; Mind How You Go, road safety show; Top of the Pops. Man of many parts but best known as a voluntary helper at Leeds Infirmary, Broadmoor Hospital, and Stoke Mandeville where he raised twelve million pounds to rebuild the National Spinal Injuries Centre. Chm., Broadmoor SHA (Chm., Hosp. Adv. Cttee). Fellow of Cybernetics, Reading Univ., 1990. Hon. LLD Leeds, 1986. Hon. KCSG (Holy See), 1982; Bronze and Gold medals, SMO, St John of Jerusalem. *Publications*: As It Happens (autobiog.), 1975; Love is an Uphill Thing (autobiog.), 1975; God'll Fix It, 1978. *Recreations*: running, cycling, wrestling. *Address*: c/o General Infirmary, Leeds LS1 3EX. *T*: Leeds (0532) 432 799. *Club*: Athenæum.

SAVILL, David Malcolm, QC 1969; **His Honour Judge Savill**; a Senior Circuit Judge and Resident Judge, Leeds Combined Court Centre, since 1991 (a Circuit Judge, 1984–91); *b* 18 Sept. 1930; *s* of late Lionel and of Lisbeth Savill; *m* 1955, Mary Arnott (*née* Eadie), JP, *d* of late Lady Hinchcliffe and step *d* of late Hon. Sir (George) Raymond Hinchcliffe; one *s* two *d*. *Educ*: Marlborough Coll.; Clare Coll., Cambridge. 2nd Lieut Grenadier Guards, 1949–50. BA (Hons) Cambridge, 1953. Called to the Bar, Middle Temple, 1954 (Bencher, 1977); Mem., Senate of Inns of Court and the Bar, 1976, 1980–83. A Recorder, 1972–84; Chancellor: diocese of Bradford, 1976–; diocese of Ripon, 1987–; Leader, NE Circuit, 1980–83. Chm., Adv. Cttee on Conscientious Objectors, 1978–91. *Recreations*: cricket, golf, gardening. *Address*: The Crown Court, Oxford Place, Leeds 1. *Club*: MCC.

SAVILL, Colonel Kenneth Edward, CVO 1976; DSO 1945; DL; Member, HM Bodyguard of Hon. Corps of Gentlemen at Arms, 1955–76 (Lieutenant, 1973–76; Standard Bearer, 1972–73); *b* 8 August 1906; *o s* of Walter Savill, Chilton Manor, Alresford and May, *d* of Major Charles Marriott; *m* 1935, Jacqueline (*d* 1980), *o d* of Brig. John Salusbury Hughes, MC; two *d* (and one *d* decd). *Educ*: Winchester College; RMC Sandhurst. Commissioned, 12th Royal Lancers, 1926; 1st King's Dragoon Guards, 1936; The Queen's Bays, 1947. Served War of 1939–45, France, 1939–40; N Africa and Italy, 1943–45; Col 1950; retd 1953. High Sheriff of Hampshire, 1961; DL Hampshire, 1965. Col, 1st The Queen's Dragoon Guards, 1964–68. *Address*: Chilton Manor, Alresford, Hants SO24 9TX. *T*: Preston Candover (025687) 246. *Club*: Cavalry and Guards.

SAVILLE, Clive Howard; Under Secretary, Department of Education and Science, since 1987; *b* 7 July 1943; *s* of Rev. Frank Saville and Gracie (*née* Mackie); *m* 1967, Camille Kathleen, *yr d* of late Edmund St C. Burke and Camille (*née* Andrea). *Educ*: Bishop Gore Grammar Sch., Swansea; University Coll., Swansea (BA). Asst Principal, DES, 1965; Private Sec. to Minister for the Arts, 1968–70; Principal, DES, 1970; UGC, 1973–75; Cabinet Office, 1975; Principal Private Sec. to Lord Pres. of the Council and Leader of House of Commons, 1975–77; Asst Sec., DES, 1977. Vis. Associate, Center for Studies in Higher Educn, Univ. of California, Berkeley, 1987. *Address*: Department of Education and Science, Sanctuary Buildings, Great Smith Street, SW1.

SAVILLE, Prof. John; Emeritus Professor of Economic and Social History, University of Hull; *b* 2 April 1916; *o s* of Orestes Stamatopoulos, Volos, Greece, and Edith Vessey (name changed by deed poll to that of step-father, 1937); *m* 1943, Constance Betty Saunders; three *s* one *d*. *Educ*: Royal Liberty Sch.; London Sch. of Economics. 1st Cl. Hons BSc (Econ) 1937. Served War, RA, 1940–46; Chief Scientific Adviser's Div., Min. of Works, 1946–47; Univ. of Hull, 1947–82, Prof. of Economic and Social History, 1972–82. Leverhulme Emeritus Fellow, 1984–86. Mem., British Communist Party, 1934–56; Chm., Oral Hist. Soc., 1976–87; Vice-Chm., and then Chm., Soc. for Study of Labour Hist., 1974–82; Mem. Exec. Cttee and Founder-Mem., Council for Academic Freedom and Democracy, 1971–81; Chm. 1982–89; Chm., Economic and Social Hist. Cttee, SSRC, 1977–79. Trustee, Michael Lipman Trust, 1977–. Vice-Chm., Friends of the Brynmor Jones Library, Hull Univ., 1988–. *Publications*: Ernest Jones, Chartist, 1952; Rural Depopulation in England and Wales 1851–1951, 1957; 1848; The British State and the Chartist Movement, 1987; The Labour Movement in Britain: a commentary, 1988; numerous articles; Co-Editor: (with E. P. Thompson) Reasoner and New Reasoner, 1956–59; (with Asa Briggs) Essays in Labour History, 1960, 1971, 1977; (with Ralph

Miliband) Socialist Register (annual, 1964–90); (with Joyce M. Bellamy) Dictionary of Labour Biography, 1972–. *Recreations*: working for socialism, looking at churches. *Address*: 152 Westbourne Avenue, Hull HU5 3HZ. *T*: Hull (0482) 43425.

SAVILLE, Hon. Sir Mark (Oliver), Kt 1985; **Hon. Mr Justice Saville**; a Judge of the High Court of Justice, Queen's Bench Division, since 1985; *b* 20 March 1936; *s* of Kenneth Vivian Saville and Olivia Sarah Frances Gray; *m* 1961, Jill Gray; two *s*. *Educ*: St Paul's Primary Sch., Hastings; Rye Grammar Sch.; Brasenose Coll., Oxford (BA, BCL). Nat. Service, 2nd Lieut Royal Sussex Regt, 1954–56; Oxford Univ., 1956–60 (Vinerian Schol. 1960). Called to Bar, Middle Temple, 1962 (Bencher, 1983); QC 1975. *Recreations*: sailing, flying. *Address*: Royal Courts of Justice, Strand, WC2A 2LL.

SAVORY, Hubert Newman, MA, DPhil Oxon, FSA; Keeper of Archæology, National Museum of Wales, Cardiff, 1956–76; *b* 7 Aug. 1911; *s* of William Charles Newman Savory and Alice Amelia (*née* Minns); *m* 1949, Priscilla Valerie Thirkell; four *s* two *d*. *Educ*: Magdalen College Sch., Oxford; St Edmund Hall, Oxford Univ. BA Oxon 1934 (Lit. Hum. 1st Cl.); DPhil Oxon 1937; Randall MacIver Student in Iberian Archæology, 1936–38. Assistant, 1938, Asst Keeper, 1939, Dept of Archæology, National Museum of Wales. Chm., Royal Commn on Ancient Monuments (Wales), 1979–83 (Mem., 1970–83); Mem., Ancient Monuments Board for Wales, 1957–84; Pres., Cambrian Archæological Assoc., 1975–76; Chm., Glamorgan Gwent Archæological Trust, 1975–84. Conducted excavations of various Welsh megaliths, round barrows, hill-forts, etc. Served War of 1939–45, in Army, 1940–45. *Publications*: Spain and Portugal: The Prehistory of the Iberian Peninsula, 1968; Guide Catalogues of the Early Iron Age Collections, 1976, and the Bronze Age Collections, 1980, National Museum of Wales; (ed) Glamorgan County History, vol. II, 1984; contrib. to: Celtic Art in Ancient Europe, 1976; Hillforts, 1976; Settlement and Society in Wales, 1989; Proc. of Prehistoric Soc.; Archæologia Cambrensis, etc. *Recreations*: walking, gardening. *Address*: 31 Lady Mary Road, Cardiff. *T*: Cardiff (0222) 753106.

SAVOURS, Dale Norman C.; *see* Campbell-Savours.

SAWARD, Rev. Canon Michael John; Treasurer and Canon Residentiary of St Paul's Cathedral, since 1991; *b* 14 May 1932; *s* of Donald and Lily Saward; *m* 1956, Jackie, *d* of late Col John Atkinson, DSO, OBE, and Eileen Atkinson, MBE; one *s* three *d*. *Educ*: Eltham Coll.; Bristol Univ. (BA Theology). 2nd Lieut, RA, 1950–52, RWAFF (Nat. Service). Deacon 1956, priest 1957; curacies in Croydon, 1956–59, and Edgware, 1959–64; Sec., Liverpool Council of Churches, 1965–67; C of E Radio and Television Officer, 1967–72; Vicar: St Matthew, Fulham, 1972–78; Ealing, 1978–91; Prebendary of St Paul's Cathedral, 1985–91. Mem., General Synod, 1975– (Mem., House of Clergy Standing Cttee, 1981–86); a Church Comr, 1978– (Member: Redundant Churches Cttee, 1978–81; Houses Cttee, 1981–88; Bd of Govs, 1986–; Pastoral Cttee, 1988–); Chm., C of E Pensions Measure Revision Cttee, 1987–88; Member: Lambeth Conf., Preparatory Cttee, 1967–68; Archbishops' Council on Evangelism, 1975–78; C of E Evangelical Council, 1976–; Nat. Partners in Mission Wkg Party, 1979–81; Dioceses Commn, 1981–89. Sec., Gen. Synod Broadcasting Commn, 1970–73. Trustee, Church Urban Fund, 1989–90. Mem. Council, Trinity Theol Coll., 1974–78. Journalist, broadcaster, lectr, reviewer. Winston Churchill Travelling Fellowship, 1984. Words Editor, Hymns for Today's Church, 1974–82. Prizewinner: Southern TV Hymn for Britain competition, 1966; BBC-TV Songs of Praise new hymn competition, 1985. *Publications*: Leisure, 1963 (Norwegian edn 1971); Christian Youth Groups, 1965; Cracking the God-Code, 1974, 3rd edn 1989 (Chinese and Swedish edns 1976); And So To Bed?, 1975; God's Friends, 1978; All Change, 1983; Evangelicals on the Move, 1987. *Recreations*: reading (esp. military history), music, cricket, travel, food and drink, writing hymns. *Address*: 6 Amen Court, EC4M 7BU. *T*: 071–248 8572. *Club*: Athenæum.

SAWDY, Peter Bryan; Chairman, Costain Group, since 1990; Deputy Chairman, Hogg Group, since 1987; Director: Griffin International Ltd, since 1988; Yule Catto PLC, since 1990; *b* 17 Sept. 1931; *s* of Alfred Eustace Leon Sawdy and Beatrice Sawdy; *m* 1st, 1955, Anne Stonor (marr. diss. 1989); two *d*; 2nd, 1989, Judith Mary Bowen. *Educ*: Ampleforth Coll.; Regent St Polytechnic; LSE. Trainee, Brooke Bond Ltd, 1952; Chm., Brooke Bond Ceylon Ltd, 1962–65; Director: Brooke Bond Ltd, 1965–68; Brooke Bond Liebig Ltd, 1968–75; Brooke Bond Group: Man. Dir, 1975–77; Gp Chief Exec., 1977–81; Dep. Chm. and Gp Chief Exec., 1981–85. *Recreations*: golf, opera, collecting modern first editions. *Address*: Costain Group, 111 Westminster Bridge Road, SE1 7UE. *Clubs*: Naval and Military; Royal Ashdown Golf (Forest Row), Royal Mid-Surrey Golf (Richmond).

SAWERS, David Richard Hall; writer and consultant; *b* 23 April 1931; *s* of late Edward and Madeline Sawers; unmarried. *Educ*: Westminster Sch.; Christ Church, Oxford (MA). Research Asst to Prof. J. Jewkes, Oxford Univ., 1954–58; Journalist, The Economist, 1959–64; Vis. Fellow, Princeton Univ., 1964–65; Econ. Adviser, Min. of Aviation and of Technology, 1966–68; Sen. Econ. Adviser, Min. of Technology, Aviation Supply, and DTI, 1968–72; Under-Sec., Depts of Industry, Trade and Prices and Consumer Protection, 1972–76; Under-Sec., Depts of Environment and Transport, 1976–83; Principal Res. Fellow, Technical Change Centre, 1984–86. *Publications*: (with John Jewkes and Richard Stillerman) The Sources of Invention, 1958; (with Ronald Miller) The Technical Development of Modern Aviation, 1968; Competition in the Air, 1987; articles in daily press and journals. *Recreations*: listening to music, looking at pictures, gardening. *Address*: 10 Seaview Avenue, Angmering-on-Sea, Littlehampton BN16 1PP. *T*: Worthing (0903) 785571.

SAWKO, Prof. Felicjan, DSc; Professor of Civil Engineering and Head of Department at the Sultan Qaboos University, Oman, since 1986; *b* 17 May 1937; *s* of Czeslaw Sawko and Franciszka (*née* Nawrot); *m* 1960, Genowefa Stefania (*née* Bak); four *s* one *d*. *Educ*: Leeds Univ. (BSc Civil Engrg, 1958; MSc 1960; DSc 1973). Engr, Rendel Palmer & Tritton, London, 1959–62; Lectr, 1962–67, Reader, 1967, Leeds University; Prof. of Civil Engrg, Liverpool Univ., 1967–86. Henry Adams Award, IStructE, 1980. *Publications*: (ed) Developments in Prestressed Concrete, Vols 1 and 2, 1968; (with Cope and Tickell) Numerical Methods for Civil Engineers, 1981; some 70 papers on computer methods and structural masonry. *Recreations*: travel, bridge, numismatics. *Address*: 9 Harthill Road, Liverpool L18 6HU. *T*: 051–724 2726; PO Box 32483, Al-Khod, Oman.

SAWYER, Anthony Charles; Director Outfield, and Commissioner, HM Customs and Excise, since 1991; *b* 3 Aug. 1939; *s* of Charles Bertram and Elizabeth Sawyer; *m* 1962, Kathleen Josephine McGill; two *s* one *d*. *Educ*: Surrey; Munster, W Germany. Nat. Service, RA, 1960. Underwriter, Northern Assurance Group, 1962; Customs and Excise, 1964–: Collector, Edinburgh, 1984; Dep. Dir, Outfield, 1988. *Recreations*: all sports, theatre, music. *Address*: HM Customs and Excise, New King's Beam House, 22 Upper Ground, SE1 9PS. *T*: 071–865 5017. *Club*: National Liberal.

SAWYER, John Stanley, MA; FRS 1962; Director of Research, Meteorological Office, 1965–76; *b* 19 June 1916; *s* of late Arthur Stanley Sawyer and Emily Florence Sawyer (*née* Frost); *m* 1951, Betty Vera Beeching (*née* Tooke), *widow*; one *d*. *Educ*: Latymer Upper Sch., Hammersmith; Jesus Coll., Cambridge. Entered Meteorological Office, 1937.

Mem., NERC, 1975–81. Pres., Commn for Atmospheric Sciences, World Meteorological Organisation, 1968–73 (IMO Prize, 1973); Pres., Royal Meteorological Soc., 1963–65 (Hugh Robert Mill Medal 1956, Buchan Prize 1962, Symons Medal 1971). *Publications:* Ways of the Weather, 1958; scientific papers largely in Quart. Jl Roy. Met. Soc. *Address:* Ivy Corner, Corfe, Taunton, Somerset TA3 7AN. *T:* Blagdon Hill (082342) 612.

SAXON, David Stephen, PhD; Hon. Chairman of the Corporation, Massachusetts Institute of Technology, since 1990 (Chairman, 1983–90); *b* 8 Feb. 1920; *s* of Ivan Saxon and Rebecca Moss; *m* 1940, Shirley Goodman; six *d.* *Educ:* Massachusetts Institute of Technology (BS 1941; PhD 1944). Massachusetts Institute of Technology: Res. physicist, Radiation Lab., 1943–46; Philips Labs, 1946–47. Univ. of California at Los Angeles: Mem. of Faculty, 1947–75; Prof. of Physics, 1958–75; Chm. of Dept, 1963–66; Dean of Physical Sciences, 1966–68; Vice-Chancellor, 1968–75; Provost, Univ. of California, 1974–75, Pres., 1975–83. Guggenheim Fellow, 1956–57 and 1961–62; Fulbright grant, 1961–62. Vis. Prof., Univ. of Paris, Orsay, France, 1961–62; Vis. scientist, Centre d'Etudes Nucléaires, France, 1968–69; Vis. Research Fellow, Merton Coll., Oxford, 1981; consultant to research organisations, 1948–. Special research into theoretical physics: nuclear physics, quantum mechanics, electromagnetic theory and scattering theory. Dir, Eastman Kodak Co., 1983–90. Fellow: Amer. Phys. Soc.; Amer. Acad. of Arts and Scis; Member: Amer. Assoc. Physics Teachers; Amer. Inst. Physics; Amer. Assoc. for the Advancement of Science; Technical Adv. Council for Ford Motor Co., 1979–; Corp. of MIT, 1977–; Dir, Houghton Mifflin Co., 1984–90. Recipient of several honorary degrees. Member: Phi Beta Kappa; Sigma Pi Sigma; Sigma Xi. Royal Order of the Northern Star (Nordstjärnan), 1979. *Publications:* Elementary Quantum Mechanics, 1968; The Nuclear Independent Particle Model (with A. E. S. Green and T. Sawada), 1968; Discontinuities in Wave Guides (with Julian Schwinger), 1968; Physics for the Liberal Arts Student (with William B. Fretter), 1971. *Address:* University of California, Los Angeles, Department of Physics, Knudsen Hall Room 2130J, 405 Hilgard Avenue, Los Angeles, Calif 90024-1547, USA.

SAXTON, Robert Louis Alfred; Head of Composition, Guildhall School of Music and Drama, since 1990; *b* 8 Oct. 1953; *s* of Jean Augusta Saxton (*née* Infield) and Ian Sanders Saxton. *Educ:* Bryanston Sch.; St Catharine's Coll., Cambridge (MA); Worcester Coll., Oxford (BMus). FGSM 1987. Lectr, Bristol Univ., 1984–85; Fulbright Arts award, 1985; Vis. Fellow, Princeton Univ., 1986. Finalist, BBC Young Composers' Comp., 1973; First Prize, Gaudeamus Music Fest., Holland, 1975; early works at ISCM Fest., Bonn, 1977, Royan Fest., 1977; later works include: The Ring of Eternity, 1983 (recorded); Concerto for Orchestra, 1984 (recorded); The Circles of Light, 1985; The Sentinel of the Rainbow, 1984 (recorded); Night Dance, 1986–87 (recorded); I Will Awake the Dawn, 1987; In the Beginning, 1987; Elijah's Violin, 1988; Chacony, 1988; Music to celebrate the Resurrection of Christ, 1988 (recorded); Violin Concerto, Leeds Fest., 1990; Caritas (opera with libretto by Arnold Wesker), 1990–91; works commissioned by: Fires of London, London Sinfonietta, BBC, LSO, ECO, Aldeburgh Fest., Cheltenham Fest., Opera North. *Publications:* numerous compositions. *Recreations:* reading, theatre, cinema, watching cricket. *Address:* c/o Chester Music, 8–9 Frith Street, W1V 5TZ. *T:* 071–434 0066.

SAY, Rt. Rev. Richard David, KCVO 1988; DD (Lambeth) 1961; an Assistant Bishop, diocese of Canterbury, since 1988; *b* 4 Oct. 1914; *s* of Commander Richard Say, OBE, RNVR, and Kathleen Mary (*née* Wildy); *m* 1943, Irene Frances (OBE 1980, JP 1960), *e d* of Seaburne and Frances Rayner, Exeter; one *s* two *d* (and one *s* decd). *Educ:* University Coll. Sch.; Christ's College, Cambridge (MA); Ridley Hall, Cambridge. Ordained deacon, 1939; priest, 1940. Curate of Croydon Parish Church, 1939–43; Curate of St Martin-in-the-Fields, London, 1943–50; Asst Sec. Church of England Youth Council, 1942–44; Gen. Sec., 1944–47; Gen. Sec. British Council of Churches, 1947–55; Church of England delegate to World Council of Churches, 1948, 1954 and 1961. Select Preacher, University of Cambridge, 1954 and University of Oxford, 1963; Rector of Bishop's Hatfield, 1955–61; Hon. Canon of St Albans, 1957–61; Bishop of Rochester, 1961–88; High Almoner to HM the Queen, 1970–88. Domestic Chaplain to Marquess of Salisbury and Chaplain of Welfield Hospital, 1955–61; Hon. Chaplain of The Pilgrims, 1968–. Entered House of Lords, 1969. Chaplain and Sub-Prelate, Order of St John, 1961. Mem., Court of Ecclesiastical Causes Reserved, 1984–. Dep. Pro-Chancellor, 1977–83, Pro-Chancellor, 1983–, Kent Univ.; Governor, University Coll. Sch., 1980–88. A Vice-Pres., UNA of GB, 1986–; Pres., Friends of Kent Churches, 1988–. Chm., Age Concern, England, 1986–89 (Vice Pres., 1990–). Freeman of City of London, 1953; Hon. Freeman: of Tonbridge and Malling, 1987; of Rochester upon Medway, 1988. Hon. Member: Smeatonian Soc., 1977; Instn of Royal Engineers, 1987. Hon. DCL Kent, 1987. *Recreations:* walking, travel. *Address:* 23 Chequers Park, Wye, Ashford, Kent TN25 5BB. *T:* Wye (0233) 812720. *Club:* United Oxford & Cambridge University.

SAYCE, Roy Beavan, FRICS; MRAC; Director, RPS Group (formerly Rural Planning Services) PLC, Didcot, 1980–88; *b* 19 July 1920; *s* of Roger Sayce, BScAgric, NDA, and Lilian Irene Sayce; *m* 1949, Barbara Sarah (*née* Leverton) (marr. diss. 1990); two *s.* *Educ:* Culford, Royal Agricultural Coll. (MRAC; Silver Medal 1948). FRICS 1949; FAAV. Univ. of London, 1938–40. Served War, Intell., RAFVR, 1940–46. Agricultural Land Service: Asst Land Comr, Chelmsford, 1949–50; Sen. Asst Land Comr, Norwich, 1950–63; Divl Land Comr, Oxford, 1963–71; Reg. Surveyor, Land Service, Agric. Develt and Adv. Service, Bristol, 1971–76; Chief Surveyor, Land Service, Agric. Develt and Adv. Service, MAFF, 1977–80. Royal Instn of Chartered Surveyors: Mem., Gen. and Divl Councils, 1970–80; Divl Pres., Land Agency and Agriculture Div., 1973–74. Chm., Farm Buildings Information Centre, 1980–85. Governor, Royal Agric. Coll., Cirencester, 1975–88. FRSA 1975; Hon. Mem., CAAV, 1978. *Publications:* Farm Buildings, 1966; (contrib.) Walmsley's Rural Estate Management, 1969; contrib. professional jls. *Recreations:* golf, historical writing. *Address:* 13 Haywards Close, Wantage, Oxon OX12 7AT. *T:* Wantage (02357) 66704. *Clubs:* Farmers', Civil Service.

SAYE AND SELE, 21st Baron *cr* 1447 and 1603; **Nathaniel Thomas Allen Fiennes;** DL; *b* 22 September 1920; *s* of Ivo Murray Twisleton-Wykeham-Fiennes, 20th Baron Saye and Sele, OBE, MC, and Hersey Cecilia Hester, *d* of late Captain Sir Thomas Dacres Butler, KCVO; *S* father, 1968; *m* 1958, Mariette Helena, *d* of Maj.-Gen. Sir Guy Salisbury-Jones, GCVO, CMG, CBE, MC; three *s* one *d* (and one *s* decd). *Educ:* Eton; New College, Oxford. Served with Rifle Brigade, 1941–49 (despatches twice). Chartered Surveyor. Partner in firm of Laws and Fiennes. Regional Dir, S Midlands Region, Lloyds Bank, 1983–. Chm. of Trustees, Ernest Cook Trust, 1965– (Trustee, 1960–). DL Oxfordshire, 1979. Fellow, Winchester Coll., 1967–83. *Heir:* *s* Hon. Richard Ingel Fiennes, *b* 19 August 1959. *Address:* Broughton Castle, Banbury, Oxon OX15 5EB. *T:* Banbury (0295) 262624.

See also Very Rev. Hon. O. W. Fiennes.

SAYEED, Dr (Abul Fatah) Akram, OBE 1976; FRSM; General Medical Practitioner in Leicester, since 1963; President, Standing Conference of Asian Organizations in UK, since 1977; Chairman, Overseas Doctors' Association in UK, since 1991; *b* Bangladesh, 23 Nov. 1935; *s* of late Mokhles Ahmed, school teacher; registered British; *m* 1959, Hosneara Ali, *d* of M. S. Ali; two *s* one *d.* *Educ:* St Joseph's Sch., Khulna; Dacca Univ. MB, BS 1958. FRSM 1981; FODA 1985. Editor, Dacca Med. Coll. Jl and Magazines, 1957–58; Lit. Sec., Students Union. Went to USA, 1960; resident in Britain from 1961. Mem. Staff, Leicester Royal Infirmary, 1964–89; Member: Leics Local Medical Cttee, 1977–; Leics Family Practitioner Cttee, 1982–87; Leics Div., BMA, 1979–; Leics Med. Audit and Adv. Gp. Member: DHSS Working Party on Asian Health Gp, 1979; DHSS Adv. Council on Violence Against NHS Staff, 1986–; Home Office Statutory Adv. Council on Community and Race Relations, 1983–88; Health Care Planning Team, Leics HA, 1984–86; Policy Planning (formerly Unit Management) Team, Leics Central Unit, 1986–. Sec., Inst. of Transcultural Health Care, 1985–. Co-founder, Nat. Fedn of Pakistani Assocs in GB, 1963; Adviser, NCCI, 1965–68; Founder Member: Leicester Council for Community Relations, 1965; British-Bangladesh Soc.; Member: Community Relations Commn, 1968–77; E Midlands Adv. Cttee, CRE, 1978–; Stop Rickets Campaign (Chm., Leicester Campaign); Central Exec. Council, Bangladesh Med. Assoc. in UK; Hon. Med. Advr in UK, Min. of Health, Govt of Bangladesh; Chm., Standing Conf. of Asian Orgns in UK, 1973–77 (Vice-Chm., 1970–73; Pres., 1977–90); Hon. Sec., Inst. of Transcultural Health Care; Pres., Pakistan Assoc., Leics, 1965–71. Mem., BBC Asian Programme Adv. Cttee, 1972–77. Special interest in problems of Asians; initiated study of problems of second generation Asians (CRE report Between Two Cultures); Overseas Doctors' Association: Founder Chm., 1975, Sponsor Chm., 1975; Gen. Sec., 1975–77; Vice-Pres., 1979–84; Vice-Chm., 1984–90; Fellow, 1985; Mem. Editl Bd, ODA News Review, 1986–; Associate Mem., MJA. Attended First World Conf. on Muslim Educn, Mecca, 1977; has done much work with disaster funds, etc. *Publications:* (ed jtly) Asian Who's Who, 1975–76, 7th edn 1991–92; contribs on socio-med. aspects of Asians in Britain to various jls. *Recreations:* gardening, reading, stamp collecting. *Address:* Ramna, 2 Mickleton Drive, Leicester LE5 6GD. *T:* Leicester (0533) 416703. *Clubs:* Royal Over-Seas League; Rotary (Leicester).

SAYEED, Jonathan; MP (C) Bristol East, since 1983; *b* 20 March 1948; *m* 1980, Nicola Anne Parkes Power; two *s.* *Educ:* Woolverstone Hall; Britannia Royal Naval Coll., Dartmouth; Royal Naval Engrg Coll., Manadon. PPS to Paymaster General and Minister of State for NI, 1991–. Vice-Chm., Cons. Backbench Shipping and Shipbuilding Cttee, 1987–; Dep. Chm., All Party Maritime Group, 1987–; Member: Environment Select Cttee, 1987–; Defence Select Cttee, 1988–91. *Recreations:* golf, riding, classical music, architecture. *Address:* House of Commons, SW1A 0AA. *T:* 071–219 6389.

SAYER, Guy Mowbray, CBE 1978; JP; retired banker; *b* 18 June 1924; *yr s* of late Geoffrey Robley and Winifred Lily Sayer; *m* 1951, Marie Anne Sophie, *o d* of late Henri-Marie and Elisabeth Mertens; one *s* two *d.* *Educ:* Mill Mead Prep. Sch.; Shrewsbury School. FIB 1971. Royal Navy, 1942–46. Joined Hongkong & Shanghai Banking Corp., 1946; Gen. Man. 1969; Exec. Dir 1970; Dep. Chm. 1971; Chm., 1972–77 (now Mem., London Adv. Cttee, 1979–). Treas., Hong Kong Univ., 1972–77. Member: Exchange Fund Adv. Cttee, Hong Kong, 1971–77; London Adv. Cttee, British Bank of the Middle East, 1980–. MLC, 1973–74, MEC, 1974–77, Hong Kong. JP Hong Kong, 1971. Governor, Suttons Hosp. in Charterhouse. Hon. LLD Hong Kong, 1978. *Recreations:* golf, walking. *Address:* 5 Pembroke Gardens, W8. *T:* 071–602 4578. *Clubs:* Oriental, MCC; Royal Wimbledon Golf; West Sussex Golf; Hong Kong, Shek O Country (Hong Kong).

SAYER, John Raymond Keer, MA; FBIM; Secretary, GTC (England and Wales), since 1990; Research Associate, Department of Educational Studies, University of Oxford, since 1991; Visiting Fellow, University of London Institute of Education, since 1985; *b* 8 Aug. 1931; *s* of Arthur and Hilda Sayer; *m* 1955, Ilserose (*née* Heyd); one *s* one *d.* *Educ:* Maidstone Grammar Sch.; Brasenose Coll., Oxford (Open Scholar; MA). FBIM 1979. Taught languages, 1955–63; Dep. Head, Nailsea Sch., Somerset, 1963–67; Headmaster, Minehead Sch., Somerset, 1967–73; Principal, Banbury Sch., 1973–84; Dir, Educn Management Unit, 1987–90. Chairman: Reform of Assessment at Sixteen-Plus, 1972–75; PUBANSCO publishing gp, 1975–; Chm., External Relations Cttee, Headmasters' Assoc., 1974–77; Secondary Heads Association: Mem. Exec., 1978–86; Press and Publications Officer, 1978–79, 1982–84; Pres., 1979–80. Chm., Jt Council of Heads, 1981; Member: Exec., UCCA, 1975–84; Schools Panel, CBI, 1975–82; Heads Panel, TUC, 1975–80; National Adv. Council on Educn for Industry and Commerce, 1974–77; Adv. Cttee on Supply and Educn of Teachers, 1982–85. Trustee and Mem. Exec., Education 2000, 1983–89 (Hon. Sec., 1987–89); Mem. Exec., Schools Curriculum Award, 1986–91. *Publications:* (ed) The School as a Centre of Enquiry, 1975; (ed) Staffing our Secondary Schools, 1980; (ed) Teacher Training and Special Educational Needs, 1985; What Future for Secondary Schools?, 1985; Secondary schools for All?, 1987; (ed) Management and the Psychology of Schooling, 1988; Schools and External Relations, 1989; Managing Schools, 1989; Towards the General Teaching Council, 1989; frequent contribs on educnl topics to learned jls and symposia. *Recreation:* postal history. *Address:* 8 Northmoor Road, Oxford OX2 6UP. *T:* Oxford (0865) 56932.

SAYERS, Prof. Bruce McArthur, PhD, DScEng; FEng 1990; FIEE; Kobler Professor of the Management of Information Technology and Director of the Centre for Cognitive Systems, Imperial College of Science, Technology and Medicine, since 1990; Dean of City and Guilds College, 1984–88, and since 1991; *b* 6 Feb. 1928; *s* of John William McArthur Sayers and Mabel Florence Sayers (*née* Howe); *m* 1951, R Woolls Humphery. *Educ:* Melbourne Boys' High School; Univ. of Melbourne (MSc); Imperial College, Univ. of London (PhD, DIC, DScEng). Biophysicist, Baker Med. Research Inst. and Clinical Research Unit, Alfred Hosp., Melbourne, 1949–54; Imperial College, London: Research Asst, 1955–56; Philips Elec. Ltd Research Fellow, 1957; Lectr, 1958; Senior Lectr, 1963; Reader, 1965; Prof. of Electrical Engrg Applied to Medicine, 1968–84; Head of Dept of Electrical Engrg, 1979–84; Prof. of Computing Applied to Medicine and Head of Dept of Computing, 1984–89. Pres., Section of Measurement in Medicine, Royal Soc. of Medicine, 1971–72; Hon. Consultant, Royal Throat, Nose and Ear Hosp., 1974–; UK rep., Bio-engineering Working Group, EEC Cttee for Med. Res., 1976–80; Temp. Adviser, WHO, 1970–76, 1981–87; Member: WHO Adv. Cttee for Health Res., 1988– (Vice Chm., 1990–91); Engrg Adv. Cttee, Science Mus., 1987–. Consultant: Data Laboratories, 1968–80; Data Beta, 1981–; Advent Eurofund, 1981–89; Shinan Investment Services SA, Switzerland, 1984–87; Advent Capital Ltd, 1985–89; Neuroscience Ltd, 1985–90; Transatlantic Capital (Biosciences) Fund, 1985–; Director: Imperial Software Technology Ltd, 1984–90; Imperial Information Technology Ltd, 1986–90. Former Visiting Prof., Univs of Melbourne, Rio de Janeiro, McGill, Toronto. Travelling Lectr: Nuffield Foundn-Nat. Research Council, Canada, 1971; Inst. of Electron. and Radio Engrs, Australia, 1976. Member: (PC nominee), Academic Adv. Council, Buckingham Univ., 1988–; Internat. Academic Cttee on Energy Studies, Ecole Polytechnique Fédérale de Lausanne, 1989–. FCGI 1983. Hon. Fellow, British Cybernetics Soc., 1986. Hon. Foreign Mem., Medico-Chirurgical Soc. of Bologna, 1965; Hon. Member, Eta Kappa Nu (USA), 1980. Freeman of the City of London, 1986; Liveryman, Scientific Instrument Makers' Co., 1986. *Publications:* papers, mainly on biomedical signals and control systems, epidemiology, cardiology and audiology. *Recreations:* writing comic verse, pottering around France, music. *Address:* Centre for Cognitive Systems, Imperial College, SW7 2AZ. *T:* 071–225 8930; 40 Queen's Gate, SW7 5HR. *T:* 071–581 3690; Lots Cottage, Compton Abbas, Dorset. *Club:* Athenæum.

SAYERS, Prof. James, MSc, PhD Cantab; Professor of Electron Physics, University of Birmingham, 1946–72; *b* 2 Sept. 1912; *s* of late J. Sayers; *m* 1943, Diana Ailsa Joan Montgomery; two *s* one *d*. *Educ:* Ballymena Academy; University of Belfast; St John's College, Cambridge. Fellow of St John's College, Cambridge, 1941–46. Research for Admiralty in Univ. of Birmingham, 1939–43, on micro-wave radar; Member of British Group of Atomic Scientists transferred to work on the US Manhattan Project, 1943–45. Award by the Royal Commission on Awards to Inventors, 1949. British delegate to Internat. Scientific Radio Union, Zürich, 1950. Life Fellow, Franklin Inst. of State of Pennsylvania. John Price Wetherill Medallist, for discovery in Physical Science, 1958. *Publications:* papers in Proc. Royal Soc., Proc. Phys. Soc., and in the reports of various Internat. Scientific Conferences, on Upper Atmosphere Physics and the Physics of Ionized Gases. *Recreations:* gardening, photography. *Address:* Edgewood Gables, The Holloway, Alvechurch, Worcestershire. *T:* Redditch (0527) 64414.

SAYERS, (Matthew Herbert) Patrick, OBE 1945; MD; FRCPath; Major-General, Army Medical Services (retired); formerly Consulting Pathologist, Employment Medical Advisory Service, Department of Employment and Health and Safety Executive, 1967–75; Hon. Physician to HM The Queen, 1965–67; Director of Army Pathology and Consulting Pathologist to the Army, 1964–67; *b* 17 Jan. 1908; *s* of late Herbert John Ireland Sayers, Musician, and late Julia Alice Sayers (*née* Tabb); *m* 1935, Moira, *d* of Robert Dougall; two *s* one *d*. *Educ:* Whitgift School; St Thomas's Hospital, London. MRCS, LRCP 1932; MB, BS London 1933; MD London 1961; FCPath 1964. Commissioned Lieutenant RAMC, 1935; served India and Far East, 1936–46: Asst Dir of Pathology, HQ 14th Army, 1943–44; Dep. Dir of Pathology, Allied Land Forces, SE Asia, 1945. Asst Dir-Gen., War Office, 1948; OC The David Bruce Laboratories, 1949–52 and 1955–61; Asst Dir of Pathology, Middle East Land Forces, 1953–55; Editor, Journal RAMC, 1955–61; Dep. Dir of Pathology, Far East Land Forces, 1961–64. Mem., Johnson Socs of London and Lichfield. CStJ 1968. *Publications:* contribs (jtly) to scientific jls on scrub typhus, immunology and industrial medicine. *Recreations:* gardening, music, cricket, field sports. *Address:* High Trees, Walmer, Kent CT14 7LP. *T:* Deal (0304) 363526. *Clubs:* Army and Navy; MCC.

See also J. C. O. R. Hopkinson.

SAYERS, Michael Patrick; QC 1988; a Recorder of the Crown Court, since 1986; *b* 28 March 1940; *s* of Major Herbert James Michael Sayers, RA (killed on active service, 1943) and late Joan Sheilah de Courcy Holroyd (*née* Stephenson); *m* 1976, Mrs Moussie Brougham (*née* Hallstrom); one *s* one *d*, and one step *s*. *Educ:* Harrow School; Fitzwilliam College, Cambridge (Evelyn Rothschild Scholar; MA). Called to the Bar, Inner Temple, 1970; South Eastern Circuit; Junior, Central Criminal Court Bar Mess, 1975–78; Supplementary Prosecuting Counsel to the Crown, Central Criminal Court, 1977. *Recreations:* shooting, stalking, theatre, Sweden. *Address:* 2 Harcourt Buildings, Temple, EC4Y 9DB. *T:* 071–353 2112; 1 Pembroke Villas, W8 6PG. *T:* 071–937 6033. *Clubs:* Garrick, Pratt's; Queen's, Swinley Forest Golf.

SAYLES, Prof. George Osborne, LittD, DLitt, LLD; FBA 1962; MRIA; *b* 20 April 1901; *s* of Rev. L. P. Sayles and Margaret Brown, Glasgow; *m* 1936, Agnes, *d* of George Sutherland, Glasgow; one *d* (one *s* decd). *Educ:* Ilkeston Grammar Sch.; Glasgow Univ.; University Coll., London. Open Bursar, Ewing Gold Medallist, First Cl. Hons History, Glasgow Univ., 1923; Carnegie Res. Schol., University Coll., London, 1923–24. Asst. 1924, Lectr, 1925 and Sen. Lectr, 1934–45, in History, Glasgow Univ.; Leverhulme Res. Fellow, 1939; Professor of Modern History in the Queen's University, Belfast, 1945–53; Burnett-Fletcher Professor of History in the Univ. of Aberdeen, 1953–62; first Kenan Prof. of History, New York Univ., 1967; Vis. Prof., Louvain Univ., Belgium, 1951; Woodward Lectr, Yale Univ., USA, 1952; Fellow, Folger Library, Washington, 1960–61; Corr. Fellow, American Soc. for Legal History, 1971; Hon. Fellow, Medieval Acad. of America, 1980. Vis. Mem., Inst. for Advanced Study, Princeton, NJ, 1969. Hon. LittD Trinity Coll. Dublin, 1965; Hon. LLD Glasgow, 1979. James Barr Ames Medal, Fac. of Law, Harvard Univ., 1958. Hon. Mem., Selden Soc., London, 1985 (Vice-Pres., 1954–86). Chm. Advisory Cttee, Official War History of Northern Ireland, 1949; Member: Commission Internationale pour l'Histoire des Assemblées d'Etats; Advisory Historical Committee, Official Histories of War (Gt Brit.), 1950; Irish Manuscripts Commn, Dublin, 1949; Scottish Cttee on History of Scottish Parliament, 1937; Council of Stair Soc. (Scotland). Intelligence Officer (voluntary) to District Commissioner for Civil Defence SW Scotland, 1939–44; HG, Glasgow 12th Bn 1940. *Publications:* Author, Editor or Joint Editor of: The Early Statutes, 1934; Rotuli Parliamentorum Anglie Hactenus Inediti, 1935; Select Cases in Court of King's Bench: under Edward I (3 vols), 1936–39; Edward II (1 vol.), 1956; Edward III (2 vols), 1958, 1965; Richard II, Henry IV, Henry V (1 vol.), 1972; Select Cases in Procedure without Writ, 1943; Parliaments and Councils of Medieval Ireland, 1947; Medieval Foundations of England, 1948, 3rd edn 1964, American edn, 1950; Irish Parliament in the Middle Ages, 1952, 2nd edn 1964; The Irish Parliament in 1782, 1954; Fleta, vol. I, 1955, vol. II, 1972, vol. III, 1984; Parliaments and Great Councils in Medieval England, 1961; Governance of Medieval England, 1963; The Administration of Ireland, 1172–1377, 1964; Law and Legislation in Medieval England, 1966; The King's Parliament of England, 1974; Documents on the Affairs of Ireland before the King's Council, 1979; The English Parliament in the Middle Ages, 1981; Scripta Diversa, 1983; The Functions of the Medieval Parliament of England, 1988; articles and reviews in Eng. Hist. Review, Scot. Hist. Review, Law Quarterly Review, Proc. RIA, etc. *Recreations:* travel, motoring. *Address:* Warren Hill, Crowborough, East Sussex TN6 1RA. *T:* Crowborough (0892) 661439.

SAYNOR, John, JP; Secretary and Director-General, Commonwealth War Graves Commission, since 1989; *b* 28 Sept. 1930; *s* of Charles Herbert Saynor and Emily Saynor (*née* Mundie); *m* 1954, Jennifer Ann Nelson; two *s*. *Educ:* Doncaster Grammar Sch. Commnd RASC, 1949–51. Post Office, 1951–69; Dept for National Savings, 1969–74; Commonwealth War Graves Commn, 1974–. JP Berks, 1983. *Recreations:* gardening, golf, bridge. *Address:* 12 The Meadows, Flackwell Heath, High Wycombe, Bucks HP10 9LX. *T:* Bourne End (06285) 23459.

SCADDING, John Guyett, MD (London), FRCP; Emeritus Professor of Medicine in the University of London; Hon. Consulting Physician, Brompton and Hammersmith Hospitals; *b* 30 August 1907; *e s* of late John William Scadding and Jessima Alice Guyett; *m* 1940, Mabel Pennington; one *s* two *d*. *Educ:* Mercers' School; Middlesex Hospital Medical School, University of London. MRCS, LRCP, 1929; MB, BS (London), 1930. Resident appts, Middx Hosp., Connaught Hosp., Walthamstow, and Brompton Hosp., 1930–35; MRCP 1932; MD (London, Univ. gold medal), 1932; First Asst, Dept of Med., Brit. Postgrad. Med. Sch., 1935; FRCP 1941; RAMC 1940–45 (Lt-Col, O i/c Med. Div.); Phys., Hammersmith Hosp., Royal Postgrad. Med. Sch., 1946–72; Physician, Brompton Hosp., 1939–72; Inst. of Diseases of the Chest: Dean, 1946–60; Dir of Studies, 1950–62; Prof. of Medicine, 1962–72; Hon. Cons. in Diseases of the Chest to the Army, 1953–72 (Guthrie Medal, 1973). Visiting Professor: Univ. Oklahoma, 1963; Stanford Univ. and Univ. Colorado, 1965; McMaster Univ., 1973; Univ. Manitoba, 1974; Univ. Chicago, 1976; Dalhousie Univ., 1977. Mem. Central Health Services Council, and Standing Medical Advisory Cttee, 1954–66; Mem. Clinical Research Board, 1960–65. Royal College of Physicians: Bradshaw Lectr, 1949; Mitchell Lectr, 1960; Tudor Edwards Lectr, 1970; Lumleian Lectr, 1973; Councillor, 1949–52; Censor, 1968–70; Second Vice-Pres., 1971–72; Moxon Medal, 1975; Lettsomian Lectr, Med. Soc. of London, 1955. Editor, Thorax, 1946–59. President: British Tuberculosis Assoc., 1959–61; Section of Medicine, RSM, 1969–71; Thoracic Soc., 1971–72. Dr *hc* Reims, 1978. *Publications:* Sarcoidosis, 1967, 2nd edn 1985; contributions to textbooks and articles, mainly on respiratory diseases, in medical journals. *Recreations:* music, pottering about. *Address:* 18 Seagrave Road, Beaconsfield, Bucks HP9 1SU. *T:* Beaconsfield (0494) 676033. *Club:* Athenæum.

SCALES, Prof. John Tracey, OBE 1986; FRCS, LRCP; CIMechE; Hon. Director, Department of Research in Plastic Surgery, Regional Plastic and Oral Surgery Centre, Mount Vernon Hospital, since 1987; Professor of Biomedical Engineering, Institute of Orthopaedics, University of London, 1974–87, now Emeritus; *b* 2 July 1920; *s* of late W. L. Scales and E. M. Scales (*née* Tracey); *m* 1945, Cecilia May, *d* of late A. W. Sparrow; two *d*. *Educ:* Haberdashers' Aske's Sch., Hampstead; King's Coll., London; Charing Cross Hosp. Med. Sch. MRCS, LRCP 1944; Hon. FRCS 1969. CIMechE 1966. Captain RAMC, 1945–47. Casualty Officer and Resident Anaesthetist, Charing Cross Hosp., 1944; Royal National Orthopaedic Hosp., Stanmore: House Surgeon, 1944–45 and 1947–49; MO i/c Plastics Res. Unit, 1949–50; Hon. Registrar, 1950–52; Hon. Sen Registrar, 1952–57; Lectr i/c Plastics Res. Unit, Inst. of Orth., Stanmore, 1951–52; Sen. Lectr i/c Plastics Res. Unit (re-named Dept. of Biomechanics and Surg. Materials, 1956; re-named Dept of Biomed. Engrg, 1968), Inst. of Orth., Univ. of London, 1952–68; Consultant in Orthopaedic Prosthetics, 1958–68, in Biomedical Engrg, 1968–87, Royal Nat. Orthopaedic Hosp., Stanmore and London; Reader in Biomed. Engrg, Dept of Biomed. Engrg, Inst. of Orth., Univ. of London, 1968–74; Consultant in Biomed. Engrg, Mt Vernon Hosp., Northwood, 1972–85; Consultant, Royal Orthopaedic Hosp., Birmingham, 1978–87. Chairman: BSI Cttee on Orthopaedic Joint-replacements, 1981–; ISO Cttee on Bone and Joint Replacements; Member: IMechE Engrg in Medicine Gp, 1966– (Founder Mem.); Adv. Panel on Med. Engrg, National Fund for Res. into Crippling Diseases (Chm., 1981–85); British Orth. Res. Soc., 1962–; Biol Engrg Soc., 1960– (Founder Mem.); Eur. Soc. of Biomaterials, 1974– (Founder Mem.); Hon. Mem., Eur. Soc. of Biomechanics, 1976– (Former Pres., Founder Mem.). Ext. Examiner, Univ. of Surrey, 1969–84, and other univs. FRSocMed 1950; Companion Fellow, British Orth. Assoc., 1959. Thomas Henry Green Prize in Surgery, Charing Cross Hosp. Med. Sch., 1943; Robert Danis Prize, Internat. Soc. of Surgery, Brussels, 1969; James Berrie Prize, RCS, 1973; Clemson Univ. Award, USA, 1974; S. G. Brown Award, Royal Soc., 1974; A. A. Griffith Silver Medal, Materials Science Club, 1980; Jackson Burrows Medal, Royal Nat. Orthopaedic Hosp., Stanmore, 1985; Don Julius Groen Prize, IMechE, 1988. Kentucky Colonel, 1986. Member Editorial Board: Engineering in Medicine; Clinical Materials, 1986–; Wounds, 1989–. *Publications: chapters in:* Modern Trends in Surgical Materials, ed Gillis, 1958; Aspects of Medical Physics, ed Rotblat, 1966; Surgical Dressings and Wound Healing, ed Harkiss, 1971; (and ed jtly) Bed Sore Biomechanics, 1976; Surgical Dressings in the Hospital Environment, ed Turner and Brain; Treatment of Burns, ed Donati, Burke and Bertelli, 1976; Scientific Foundations of Orthopaedics and Traumatology, ed Owen, Goodfellow and Bullough, 1980; also jt author of chapters in med. books; contrib. Proc. RSM, Proc. IMechE, Proc. Physiol Soc., BMJ, Jl of Bone and Jt Surg., Lancet, Nature, and other med. and scientific jls; contrib. conf. and symposia reports. *Recreations:* walking dogs, Goss china. *Address:* 17 Brockley Avenue, Stanmore, Mddx HA7 4LX. *T:* 081–958 8773. *Club:* Army and Navy.

SCALES, Prunella, (Prunella Margaret Rumney West); actress; *d* of John Richardson Illingworth and Catherine Scales; *m* 1963, Timothy Lancaster West, *qv*; two *s*. *Educ:* Moira House, Eastbourne; Old Vic Theatre School, London; Herbert Berghof Studio, New York (with Uta Hagen). Repertory in Huddersfield, Salisbury, Oxford, Bristol Old Vic, etc; seasons at Stratford-on-Avon and Chichester Festival Theatre, 1967–68; plays on London Stage include: The Promise, 1967; Hay Fever, 1968; It's a Two-Foot-Six-Inches-Above-The-Ground-World, 1970; The Wolf, 1975; Breezeblock Park, 1978; Make and Break, 1980; An Evening with Queen Victoria, 1980; The Merchant of Venice, 1981; Quartermaine's Terms, 1981; Big in Brazil, 1984; When We Are Married, 1986; Single Spies (double bill), 1988; The School for Scandal, 1990; Long Day's Journey into Night, 1991; *television:* Fawlty Towers (series), 1975, 1978; Grand Duo, The Merry Wives of Windsor, 1982; Mapp and Lucia (series), 1985–86; Absurd Person Singular, 1985; The Index Has Gone Fishing, What the Butler Saw, 1987; After Henry (series), 1988, 1990; frequent broadcasts, readings, poetry recitals and fringe productions. Has directed plays at Bristol Old Vic, Arts Theatre, Cambridge, Billingham Forum, Almost Free Theatre, London, Nottingham Playhouse, Palace Theatre, Watford, Nat. Theatre of WA, Perth, and taught at several drama schools. *Recreation:* growing vegetables. *Address:* c/o Jeremy Conway, 18–21 Jermyn Street, SW1Y 6HP. *Club:* BBC.

SCALIA, Antonin; Associate Justice, United States Supreme Court, since 1986; *b* 11 March 1936; *s* of S. Eugene Scalia and Catherine Louise (*née* Panaro); *m* 1960, Maureen McCarthy; five *s* four *d*. *Educ:* Georgetown Univ. (AB 1957); Fribourg Univ., Switzerland; Harvard (LLB 1960; Sheldon Fellow, 1960–61). Admitted to Ohio Bar, 1962, to Virginia Bar, 1970. Associate, Jones, Day, Cockley & Reavis, Cleveland, 1961–67; Associate Prof., 1967–70, Prof., 1970–74, Univ. of Virginia Law Sch.; Gen. Counsel, Office of Telecommunications, Exec. Office of Pres., 1971–72; Chm., Admin. Conf. US, Washington, 1972–74; Asst Attorney Gen., US Office of Legal Counsel, Justice Dept, 1974–77; Prof., Law Sch., Chicago Univ., 1977–82; Judge, US Court Appeals (DC Circuit), 1982–86. American Bar Association: Mem. Council, 1974–77, Chm., 1981–82, Section Admin. Law; Chm., Conf. Section, 1982–83. Jt Editor, Regulation Magazine, 1979–82. *Address:* US Supreme Court, 1 First Street NE, Washington, DC 20543, USA.

SCANLAN, Dorothy, (Mrs Charles Denis Scanlan); *see* Quick, Dorothy.

SCANLON, family name of **Baron Scanlon.**

SCANLON, Baron *cr* 1979 (Life Peer), of Davyhulme in the County of Greater Manchester; **Hugh Parr Scanlon;** President, Amalgamated Union of Engineering Workers, 1968–78; Member, British Gas Corporation, 1976–82; *b* 26 Oct. 1913; *m* 1943, Nora; two *d*. *Educ:* Stretford Elem. Sch.; NCLC. Apprentice, Instrument Maker, Shop Steward-Convener, AEI, Trafford Park; Divisional Organiser, AEU, Manchester, 1947–63; Member: Exec. Council, AEU, London, 1963–67; TUC Gen. Council, 1968–78; TUC Econ. Cttee, 1968–78. Member: NEDC, 1971–; Metrication Bd, 1973–78; NEB, 1977–79; Govt Cttee of Inquiry into Teaching of Maths in Primary and Secondary Schs in England and Wales, 1978–; Chm., Engineering Industry Training Bd, 1975–82. Vice-Pres., Internat. Metalworkers' Fedn, 1969–78; Pres., European Metal Workers' Fedn, 1974–78. Hon. DCL Kent, 1988. *Recreations:* golf, swimming, gardening. *Address:* 23 Seven Stones Drive, Broadstairs, Kent. *Club:* Eltham Warren Golf.

SCANNELL, Vernon, FRSL; free-lance author, poet and broadcaster, since 1962; *b* 23 Jan. 1922. *Educ:* elementary schools; Leeds Univ. Served with Gordon Highlanders (51st

Highland Div.), ME and Normandy, 1940–45; Leeds Univ. (reading Eng. Lit.), 1946–47; various jobs incl. professional boxer, 1945–46, English Master at Hazelwood Prep. Sch., 1955–62. Southern Arts Assoc. Writing Fellowship, 1975–76; Vis. Poet, Shrewsbury Sch., 1978–79; Res. Poet, King's Sch. Canterbury, Michaelmas Term 1979. FRSL 1960. Granted a civil list pension, 1981, for services to literature. *Publications: novels*: The Fight, 1953; The Wound and the Scar, 1953; The Big Chance, 1960; The Face of the Enemy, 1961; The Shadowed Place, 1961; The Dividing Night, 1962; The Big Time, 1965; The Dangerous Ones, 1970; A Lonely Game (for younger readers), 1979; Ring of Truth, 1983; *poetry*: The Masks of Love, 1960 (Heinemann Award, 1960); A Sense of Danger, 1962; Walking Wounded: poems 1962–65, 1968; Epithets of War: poems 1965–69, 1969; Mastering the Craft (Poets Today Series), 1970; (with J. Silkin) Pergamon Poets, No 8, 1970; Selected Poems, 1971; The Winter Man: new poems, 1973; The Apple Raid and other poems, 1974 (Cholmondeley Poetry Prize, 1974); The Loving Game, 1975 (also in paperback); New and Collected Poems 1950–80, 1980; Winterlude and other poems, 1982; Funeral Games and other poems, 1987; Soldiering On: poems of military life, 1989; A Time for Fires, 1991; Travelling Light, 1991; *edited*: (with Ted Hughes and Patricia Beer) New Poems: a PEN anthology, 1962; Sporting Literature: an anthology, 1987; *criticism*: Not Without Glory: poets of World War II, 1976; How to Enjoy Poetry, 1982; How to Enjoy Novels, 1984; *autobiography*: The Tiger and the Rose, 1971; A Proper Gentleman, 1977; Argument of Kings, 1987. *Recreations*: listening to radio (mainly music), drink, boxing (as a spectator), films, reading, learning French, loathing Tories. *Address*: 51 North Street, Otley, W Yorks LS21 1AH. *T*: Otley (0943) 467176.

SCARASCIA-MUGNOZZA, Carlo; President: International Centre for Advanced Mediterranean Agronomic Studies, Paris, since 1983; Accademia Nazionale di Danza, Rome; *b* Rome, 19 Jan. 1920. Mem., Italian Chamber of Deputies for Lecce-Brindisi-Taranto, 1953; Vice-Pres., Christian Democrat Parly Gp, 1958–62; Leader, Italian Delegn to UNESCO, 1962; Secretary of State: for Educn, 1962–63; for Justice, June 1963–Dec. 1963; Mem., European Parliament, 1961, Chm., Political Cttee, 1971–72; a Vice-Pres., EEC, 1972–77; Mem., Council of State, Italy, 1977–. Mem., Accademia Agricoltura di Francia. *Address*: Via Timavo 32, 00195 Rome, Italy. *T*: 06–3588842; International Centre for Advanced Mediterranean Agronomic Studies, 11 rue Newton, 75116 Paris, France; Accademia Nazionale di Danza, Largo Arrigo VII 5, 00153 Rome.

SCARBROUGH, 12th Earl of, *cr* 1690; **Richard Aldred Lumley;** Viscount Lumley (Ire.), 1628; Baron Lumley, 1681; Viscount Lumley, 1690; Vice Lord-Lieutenant of South Yorkshire, since 1990; *b* 5 Dec. 1932; *o s* of 11th Earl of Scarbrough, KG, PC, GCSI, GCIE, GCVO, and Katharine Isobel, Dowager Countess of Scarbrough, DCVO (*d* 1979), *d* of late R. F. McEwen; *S* father, 1969; *m* 1970, Lady Elizabeth Ramsay, *d* of Earl of Dalhousie, *qv*; two *s* one *d*. *Educ*: Eton; Magdalen College, Oxford. 2nd Lt 11th Hussars, 1951–52; formerly Lt Queen's Own Yorkshire Dragoons. ADC to Governor and C-in-C, Cyprus, 1956. Hon. Col, 1st Bn The Yorkshire Volunteers, 1975–88. President: Northern Area, Royal British Legion, 1984–; York Georgian Soc., 1985–; Northern Assoc. of Building Socs (formerly Yorkshire and North Western Assoc. of Building Socs), 1985–. Mem. Council, Univ. of Sheffield, 1974–79. Hon. RIBA, Yorks Region. DL S Yorks, 1974. *Heir: s* Viscount Lumley, *qv*. *Address*: Sandbeck Park, Maltby, Rotherham, S Yorks S66 8PF. *T*: Doncaster (0302) 742210. *Clubs*: White's; Pratt's; Jockey (Newmarket).

See also Lady Grimthorpe.

SCARFE, Gerald; artist; *b* 1 June 1936; *m* Jane Asher, *qv*; two *s* one *d*. *Educ*: scattered (due to chronic asthma as a child). Punch, 1960; Private Eye, 1961; Daily Mail, 1966; Sunday Times, 1967; cover artist to illustrator, Time Magazine, 1967; animation and film directing for BBC, 1969–. Has taken part in exhibitions: Grosvenor Gall., 1969 and 1970; Pavillon d'Humour, Montreal, 1967 and 1971; Expo '70, Osaka, 1970. One-man exhibitions of sculptures and lithographs: Waddell Gall., New York, 1968 and 1970; Grosvenor Gall., 1969; Vincent Price Gall., Chicago, 1969; National Portrait Gall., 1971; retrospective exhibn, Royal Festival Hall, 1983; Langton Gall., 1986; Chris Beetles Gall., 1989. Animated film for BBC, Long Drawn Out Trip, 1973 (prizewinner, Zagreb); Dir, Scarfe by Scarfe, BBC (BAFTA Award, 1987); Designer and Dir, animated sequences in film, The Wall, 1982; designer: Who's A Lucky Boy?, Royal Exchange, Manchester, 1984; Orpheus in the Underworld, ENO, 1985; Born Again, Chichester, 1990. *Publications*: Gerald Scarfe's People, 1966; Indecent Exposure (ltd edn), 1973; Expletive Deleted: the life and times of Richard Nixon (ltd edn), 1974; Gerald Scarfe, 1982; Father Kissmass and Mother Claws, 1985; Scarfe by Scarfe (autobiog), 1986 (televised, 1987); Scarfe's Seven Deadly Sins, 1988; Scarfe's Line of Attack, 1988; Scarfeland: a lost world of fabulous beasts and monsters, 1989. *Recreations*: drawing, painting and sculpting. *Address*: c/o Fraser & Dunlop Scripts Ltd, Fifth Floor, The Chambers, Chelsea Harbour, Lots Road, SW10.

SCARFE, Jane; see Asher, J.

SCARGILL, Arthur; President, National Union of Mineworkers, since 1981; *b* 11 Jan. 1938; *o c* of Harold and Alice Scargill; *m* 1961, Anne, *d* of Elliott Harper; one *d*. *Educ*: Worsbrough Dale School; White Cross Secondary School; Leeds Univ. Miner, Woolley Colliery, 1953; Mem., NUM branch cttee, 1960; Woolley branch deleg. to Yorks NUM Council, 1964; Mem., Nat. Exec., 1972, Pres., 1973, Yorks NUM. Mem., TUC Gen. Council, 1986–88. Member: Young Communists' League, 1955–62; Co-op Party, 1963; Labour Party, 1966; CND. *Address*: National Union of Mineworkers, Holly Street, Sheffield S1 2GT.

SCARLETT, family name of **Baron Abinger.**

SCARLETT, His Honour James Harvey Anglin; a Circuit Judge, 1974–89; *b* 27 Jan. 1924; *s* of Lt-Col James Alexander Scarlett, DSO, RA, and Muriel Scarlett, *d* of Walter Blease; unmarried. *Educ*: Shrewsbury Sch.; Christ Church, Oxford (MA). Barrister-at-law. Served War, Royal Artillery (Lieut) 1943–47. Called to the Bar, Inner Temple, 1950. A Recorder of the Crown Court, 1972–74. Malayan Civil Service, 1955–58. *Recreation*: fell walking. *Address*: Chilmington Green, Great Chart, near Ashford, Kent TN23 3DP. *Clubs*: Athenæum; Athenæum (Liverpool); Border County (Carlisle).

SCARLETT, Hon. John Leopold Campbell, CBE 1973; Deputy to Health Service Commissioner, 1973–76; *b* 18 Dec. 1916; 2nd *s* of 7th Baron Abinger and Marjorie, 2nd *d* of John McPhillamy, Bathurst, NSW; *m* 1947, Bridget Valerie, *d* of late H. B. Crook; two *s* one *d*. *Educ*: Eton; Magdalene Coll., Cambridge (MA). Served War of 1939–45, France, Madagascar, Burma (despatches); 2nd Lieut 1940; Major 1944, RA. House Governor, London Hosp., 1962–72. *Address*: Bramblewood, Castle Walk, Wadhurst, Sussex TN5 6DB. *T*: Wadhurst (089288) 2642. *Club*: Royal Automobile.

SCARMAN, family name of **Baron Scarman.**

SCARMAN, Baron *cr* 1977 (Life Peer), of Quatt in the county of Salop; **Leslie George Scarman,** PC 1973; Kt 1961; OBE 1944; a Lord of Appeal in Ordinary, 1977–86; *b* 29 July 1911; *s* of late George Charles and Ida Irene Scarman; *m* 1947, Ruth Clement Wright; one *s*. *Educ*: Radley College; Brasenose College, Oxford. Classical Scholar,

Radley, 1925; Open Classical Scholar, Brasenose Coll., 1930; Hon. Mods 1st cl., 1932; Lit. Hum. 1st cl., 1934; Harmsworth Law Scholar, Middle Temple, 1936, Barrister, 1936; QC 1957. A Judge of the High Court of Justice, Probate, Divorce, and Admiralty Div., later Family Div., 1961–73; a Lord Justice of Appeal, 1973–77. Chairman: Law Commn, 1965–73; Council of Legal Educn, 1973–76; President: Constitutional Reform Centre, 1984–; Citizen Action Compensation Campaign, 1988–. Chm., Univ. of London Court, 1970–86 (Dep. Chm., 1966–70); Chancellor, Univ. of Warwick, 1977–89. Vice-Chm., Statute Law Cttee, 1967–72. Pres., Senate of Inns of Court and Bar, 1976–79. Mem. Arts Council, 1968–70, 1972–73; Vice-Chm., ENO, 1976–81. Pres., RIPA, 1981–89. Hon. Fellow: Brasenose College, Oxford, 1966; Imperial Coll., Univ. of London, 1975; UCL, 1985; LSE, 1985; Leeds, 1987; Brunel, 1988. Hon. LLD: Exeter, 1965; Glasgow, 1969; London, 1971; Keele, 1972; Freiburg, 1973; Warwick, 1974; Bristol, 1976; Manchester, 1977; Kent, 1981; Wales, 1985; QUB, 1990; Dundee, 1990; Hon. DCL: City, 1980; Oxon, 1982. RAFVR, 1940–45; Chm., Malcolm Clubs, RAF. Order of Battle Merit (Russia), 1945. *Publications*: Pattern of Law Reform, 1967; English Law—The New Dimension, 1975. *Recreations*: gardening, walking. *Address*: House of Lords, SW1A 0PW. *Club*: Royal Air Force.

SCARSDALE, 3rd Viscount *cr* 1911; **Francis John Nathaniel Curzon;** Bt (Scotland) 1636, (England) 1641; Baron Scarsdale 1761; late Captain, Scots Guards; *b* 28 July 1924; *o s* of late Hon. Francis Nathaniel Curzon, 3rd *s* of 4th Baron Scarsdale, and late Winifred Phyllis (*née* Combe); *S* cousin, 1977; *m* 1st, 1948, Solange (marr. diss. 1967, she *d* 1974), *yr d* of late Oscar Hanse, Mont-sur-Marchienne, Belgium; two *s* one *d*; 2nd, 1968, Helene Gladys Frances, *o d* of late Maj. William Ferguson Thomson, Kinellar, Aberdeenshire; two *s*. *Educ*: Eton. *Recreations*: shooting, piping, photography. *Heir: s* Hon. Peter Ghislain Nathaniel Curzon [*b* 6 March 1949; *m* 1983, Mrs Karen Osborne; one *d*]. *Address*: Kedleston Hall, Derby. *T*: Derby (0332) 840386. *Club*: County (Derby).

SCATCHARD, Vice-Adm. John Percival, CB 1963; DSC 1941; first Bar, 1944; second Bar, 1945; *b* 5 Sept. 1910; *s* of Dr James P. Scatchard, MB, BS, Tadcaster, Yorks; *m* 1943, Edith Margaret Niven; one *d*. *Educ*: Aysgarth School, Yorkshire; RNC Dartmouth. Joined RN, 1924; served War of 1939–45, in HMS Kashmir-Garth and Termagent; Captain (D) Portsmouth, 1951–52; Captain 5th Destroyer Squadron, 1957–58; Director Naval Equipment, Admiralty, 1959–60; Commandant, Joint Services Staff College, Latimer, Bucks, 1960–62; Flag Officer, Second-in-Command, Far East Fleet, 1962–64; retd list, 1964. *Recreation*: gardening. *Address*: Reachfar, Warsash, near Southampton, Hants SO3 9FZ.

SCHAFFTER, Ernest Merill James; Secretary, Royal Aeronautical Society, 1973–82 (Deputy Secretary, 1970–73); Director, Engineering Sciences Data Unit Ltd, 1975–82; *b* 1922; *er s* of late Dr Charles Merill Schaffter and of Bertha Grace Brownrigg, of the CMS in Isfahan, Iran; *m* 1951, Barbara Joy, *o c* of Alfred Bennett Wallis and Hilda Frances Hammond; three *d*. *Educ*: Trent Coll., Nottinghamshire; King's Coll., Cambridge. BA 1950, MA 1955. Served War: RAF, as Pilot with Coastal and Transport Command, Flt Lt, 1941–46. De Havilland Aircraft Co., Hatfield, as Aerodynamicist and Engr, 1950–54; Marshall's Flying Sch., Cambridge, as Engr, 1954–60; Marshall of Cambridge (Eng) Ltd, as Personal Asst to Chief Designer and later as Design Office Manager, 1960–70. Freeman, GAPAN, 1978. FRAeS, AFAIAA, AFCASI, FBIM. *Address*: 43 Speldhurst Road, W4 1BX. *T*: 081–995 0708. *Clubs*: Royal Air Force, Les Ambassadeurs.

SCHALLY, Dr Andrew Victor; Chief of Endocrine, Polypeptide and Cancer Institute, since 1962 and Senior Medical Investigator, since 1973, Veterans Administration Medical Center, New Orleans; Professor of Medicine, since 1967, and Head, Section of Experimental Medicine, since 1978, Tulane University School of Medicine, New Orleans (Associate Professor, 1962–67); *b* Wilno, Poland, 30 Nov. 1926; US Citizen (formerly Canadian Citizen); *s* of Casimir and Maria Schally; *m* 1st, 1956, Margaret White (marr. diss.); one *s* one *d*; 2nd, 1976, Ana Maria Comaru. *Educ*: Bridge of Allan, Scotland (Higher Learning Cert.); London (studied chemistry); McGill Univ., Montreal, Canada (BSc Biochem., 1955; PhD Biochem., 1957). Res. Assistant: Dept of Biochem., Nat. Inst. for Med. Res., MRC, Mill Hill, 1949–52; Endocrine Unit, Allan Meml Inst. for Psych., McGill Univ., Montreal, 1952–57; Baylor University Coll. of Medicine, Texas Med. Center: Res. Associate, Dept of Physiol., 1957–60; Asst Prof. of Physiol., Dept of Physiol., and Asst Prof. of Biochem., Dept of Biochem., 1960–62. Member: Endocrine Soc., USA; AAAS; Soc. of Biol Chemists; Amer. Physiol Soc.; Soc. for Experimental Biol. and Med.; Internat. Soc. for Res. in Biol. of Reprodn; Internat. Brain Res. Org.; Nat. Acad. of Medicine, Mexico; Nat. Acad. of Medicine, Brazil; Nat. Acad. of Medicine, Venezuela; Nat. Acad. of Scis (US); Hungarian Acad. of Scis. Hon. Member: Internat. Family Planning Res. Assoc., Inc.; Chilean Endocrine Soc.; Mexican Soc. of Nutrition and Endocrinol.; Acad. of Med. Sciences of Cataluna and Baleares; Endocrine Soc. of Madrid; Polish Soc. of Internal Med.; Endocrine Soc. of Ecuador; Endocrine Soc. of Peru. Dr *hc* State Univ. of Rio de Janeiro, 1977; Rosario, Argentina, 1979; Univ. Peruana Cayetano Heredia, Lima, 1979; Univ. Nat. de San Marcos, Lima, 1979; MD *hc*: Tulane, 1978; Cadiz, 1979; Univ. Villareal-Lima, 1979; Copernicus Med. Acad., Cracow, 1979; Chile, 1979; Buenos Aires, 1980; Salamanca, 1981; Complutense Univ., Madrid, 1984; Pécs Univ., 1986; Hon. DSc McGill, 1979. Nobel Prize in Physiology or Medicine, 1977. Veterans Administration: William S. Middleton Award, 1970; Exceptional Service Award and Medal, 1978. Van Meter Prize, Amer. Thyroid Assoc., 1969; Ayerst-Squibb Award, US Endocrine Soc., 1970; Charles Mickle Award, Faculty of Med., Univ. of Toronto, 1974; Gairdner Foundn Internat. Award, Toronto, 1974; Edward T. Tyler Award, 1975; Borden Award, Assoc. of Amer. Med. Colls, 1975; Albert Lasker Basic Med. Res. Award, 1975; Spanish Pharmaceutical Soc., 1977; Laude Award, 1978; Heath Meml Award from M. D. Anderson Tumour Inst., 1989. Member Editorial Board: Proc. of Society for Experimental Biology and Medicine, 1973–; Life Sciences, 1980–; Peptides, 1980–; The Prostate, 1985–; Internat. Jl of Fertility, 1987–. *Publications*: (compiled and ed with William Locke) The Hypothalamus and Pituitary in Health and Disease, 1972; over 1700 other pubns (papers, revs, books, abstracts). *Address*: Quadrant F, 7th Floor Veterans Administration Medical Center, 1601 Perdido Street, New Orleans, La 70146, USA. *T*: (504) 589–5230.

SCHAPERA, Prof. Isaac, MA (Cape Town) 1925; PhD (London) 1929; DSc (London) 1939; FBA 1958; FRSSAf 1934; Emeritus Professor, University of London (London School of Economics), 1969; *b* Garies, South Africa, 23 June 1905; 3rd *s* of late Herman and Rose Schapera. *Educ*: S African Coll. Sch., Cape Town; Universities of Cape Town and London. Prof. of Social Anthropology, Univ. of Cape Town, 1935–50; Prof. of Anthropology, Univ. of London (LSE), 1950–69, now Emeritus; Hon. Fellow, 1974. Many anthropological field expeditions to Bechuanaland Protectorate, 1929–50. Chairman Association of Social Anthropologists of the British Commonwealth, 1954–57; President, Royal Anthropological Inst., 1961–63. Hon. DLitt: Cape Town, 1975; Botswana, 1985; Hon. LLD Witwatersrand, 1979. *Publications*: The Khoisan Peoples of South Africa, 1930; A Handbook of Tswana Law and Custom, 1938; Married Life in an African Tribe, 1940; Native Land Tenure in the Bechuanaland Protectorate, 1943; Migrant Labour and Tribal Life, 1948; The Ethnic Composition of Tswana Tribes, 1952; The Tswana, 1953;

Government and Politics in Tribal Societies, 1956; Praise Poems of Tswana Chiefs, 1965; Tribal Innovators, 1970; Rainmaking Rites of Tswana Tribes, 1971; Kinship Terminology in Jane Austen's Novels, 1977; Editor: Western Civilization and the Natives of South Africa, 1934; The Bantu-speaking Tribes of South Africa, 1937; David Livingstone's Journals and Letters, 1841–56 (6 vols), 1959–63; David Livingstone: South African Papers 1849–1853, 1974; contrib. to many learned journals. *Address*: 457 White House, Albany Street, NW1 3UP.

SCHAPIRO, Isabel Margaret; *see* Madariaga, I. M. de.

SCHAPIRO, Meyer; University Professor, Columbia University, 1965–73, now Emeritus Professor; *b* Shavly, Lithuania, 23 Sept. 1904; *s* of Nathan Menahem Schapiro and Fege Edelman; *m* 1928, Dr Lillian Milgram; one *s* one *d*. *Educ*: Boys' High Sch., Brooklyn; Columbia University. PhD Columbia, 1929. Columbia University: Lectr, Dept of Art History and Archæology, 1928; Asst Prof., 1936; Assoc. Prof., 1948; Prof., 1952; University Prof., 1965. Visiting Lecturer: Institute of Fine Arts, NY University, 1931–36; New School for Social Research, NY, 1938–50; Vis. Prof.: Univ. of London, 1947, 1957; Univ. of Jerusalem, 1961; Messenger Lectr, Cornell Univ., 1960; Patten Lectr, Indiana Univ., 1961; Charles Eliot Norton Prof., Harvard Univ., 1966–67; Slade Prof. of Fine Art, Oxford Univ., 1968; Vis. Lectr, Collège de France, 1974. Guggenheim Fellow, 1939, 1943; Fellow: Amer. Acad. of Arts and Sciences, 1952; Inst. for Advanced Study in Behavioral Sciences, Palo Alto, 1962–63; Amer. Philosophical Soc., 1969; Mediaeval Acad., 1970; Amer. Inst. of Arts and Letters, 1976; Corresponding FBA, 1990. Hon. degrees: Columbia Univ.; Harvard Univ.; Yale Univ.; Jewish Theological Seminary, NY; New Sch. for Social Research; Univ. of Hartford. Bd of Editors: Jl of History of Ideas; Semiotica; Dissent. Award for Distinction, Amer. Council of Learned Socs, 1960; Mitchell Prize, 1979; Aby M. Warburg Prize, Hamburg, 1985. *Publications*: The Romanesque Sculpture of Moissac, 1931; Van Gogh, 1950; Cézanne, 1952; The Parma Ildefonsus, 1964; Words and Pictures, 1973; Selected Papers, vol. I, Romanesque Art, 1976, vol. II, Modern Art, 1978; vol. III, Late Antique, Early Christian and Medieval Art, 1980; Style, Artiste et Société, 1983; articles in collective books and in Art Bulletin, Gazette des Beaux-Arts, Jl Warburg and Courtauld Insts, Jl History of Ideas, Jl Architectural Historians, Kritische Berichte, Amer. Jl Sociology, Partisan Review, Encounter, etc. *Address*: 279 West 4th Street, New York, NY 10014, USA.

SCHAUFUSS, Peter; ballet dancer, producer, choreographer; Director of Ballet, Deutsche Oper, Berlin, since 1990; *b* 26 April 1950; *s* of Frank Schaufuss and Mona Vangsaae, former solo dancers with Royal Danish Ballet. *Educ*: Royal Danish Ballet School. Apprentice, Royal Danish Ballet, 1965; soloist, Nat. Ballet of Canada, 1967–68; Royal Danish Ballet, 1969–70; Principal, London Festival Ballet, 1970–74; NY City Ballet, 1974–77; Principal, National Ballet of Canada, 1977–83; Artistic Dir, London Fest. Ballet, later English Nat. Ballet, 1984–90. Guest appearances in Austria, Canada, Denmark, France, Germany, Greece, Israel, Italy, Japan, Norway, S America, Turkey, UK, USA, USSR; Presenter, Dancer, BBC, 1984; numerous TV appearances. Roles created for him in: Phantom of the Opera; Orpheus; Verdi Variations; The Steadfast Tin Soldier; Rhapsodie Espagnole. Produced Bournonville ballets: La Sylphide (London Fest. Ballet, Stuttgart Ballet, Roland Petit's Ballet de Marseille, Deutsche Oper Berlin, Teatro Comunale, Florence, Vienna State Opera); Napoli (Nat. Ballet of Canada, Teatro San Carlo, English Nat. Ballet); Folktale (Deutsche Oper Berlin); Dances from Napoli (London Fest. Ballet); Bournonville (Aterballetto); The Nutcracker (London Fest. Ballet). Solo award, 2nd Internat. Ballet Competition, Moscow, 1973; Star of the Year, Munich Abendzeitung, 1978; Evening Standard and SWET ballet award, 1979; Manchester Evening News theatre award, 1986. Knight of the Dannebrog (Denmark), 1988. *Recreation*: boxing. *Address*: c/o Papoutsis Representation Ltd, 18 Sundial Avenue, SE25 4BX.

SCHAWLOW, Prof. Arthur Leonard, PhD; J. G. Jackson—C. J. Wood Professor of Physics, Stanford University, since 1961; *b* Mt Vernon, New York, 5 May 1921; *s* of Arthur Schawlow and Helen Schawlow (*née* Mason); *m* 1951, Aurelia Keith Townes; one *s* two *d*. *Educ*: Univ. of Toronto, Canada. BA 1941, MA 1942, PhD 1949. Postdoctoral Fellow and Research Associate, Columbia Univ., 1949–51; Research Physicist, Bell Telephone Laboratories, 1951–61; Visiting Assoc. Prof., Columbia Univ., 1960. Hon. MRIA 1991. Hon. DSc: Ghent, 1968; Bradford, 1970; Alabama, 1984; TCD, 1986; Hon. LLD, Toronto, 1970; Hon. DTech Lund, 1988. Ballantine Medal, Franklin Inst., 1962; Liebmann Prize, Inst. of Electrical and Electronic Engrs, 1963; Thomas Young Medal and Prize (GB), 1963; California Scientist of the Year, 1973; Ives Medal, Optical Soc. of America, 1975; Marconi Internat. Fellowship, 1977; (jtly) Nobel Prize in Physics, 1981; Arthur L. Schawlow Medal, Laser Inst. of America, 1982. *Publications*: (with C. H. Townes) Microwave Spectroscopy, 1955; many contribs to learned journals. *Recreation*: jazz music. *Address*: Department of Physics, Stanford University, Stanford, California 94305–4060, USA. *T*: (415) 723–4356.

SCHEEL, Walter; Grand Cross First Class of Order of Merit of Federal Republic of Germany; President of the Federal Republic of Germany, 1974–79; *b* 8 July 1919; *m* 1969, Dr Mildred Wirtz (*d* 1985); one *s* two *d*, and one *s* of previous *m*; *m* 1988, Barbara Wiese. *Educ*: Reform Gymnasium, Solingen. Served in German Air Force, War of 1939–45. Mem. of Bundestag, 1953–74; Federal Minister for Economic Co-operation, 1961–Oct. 1966, Vice-President of Bundestag, 1967–69; Vice-Chancellor and Foreign Minister, 1969–74. Mem., Landtag North Rhine Westphalia, 1950–54; Mem. European Parlt, 1958–61 (Vice-Chm., Liberal Gp; Chm., Cttee on Co-operation with Developing Countries). Free Democratic Party: Mem., 1946; Mem. Exec. Cttee for North Rhine/ Westphalia, 1953–74; Mem. Federal Exec., 1956–74; Chm., 1968–74; Hon. Pres., 1979. Holds numerous hon. degrees and foreign decorations. *Publications*: Konturen einer neuen Welt, 1965; Formeln deutscher Politik, 1968; Warum Mitbestimmung und wie—eine Diskussion, 1970; Reden und Interviews, 1969–79; Vom Recht des anderen, 1977; Die Zukunft der Freiheit, 1979; Wen schmerzt noch Deutschlands Teilung?, 1986. *Address*: Lindenallee 23, 5000 Köln 51, Germany.

SCHEMBRI, His Honour Carmelo; Chief Justice of Malta and President of the Constitutional Court, Court of Appeal and Court of Criminal Appeal, 1981–87; *b* 2 Sept. 1922; *s* of Joseph Schembri and Lucia (*née* Tabone Adami); *m* 1949, Helen (*née* Holland); six *s* five *d*. *Educ*: The Lyceum, Malta; Royal Univ. of Malta (LLD 1946). Called to the Bar, 1947; elected Mem., Malta Legislative Assembly (Nationalist Party), 1950; Dep. Speaker and Chm., Cttees until dissolution of Assembly, 1951; returned to Parliament in General Election, 1951 and re-elected Dep. Speaker and Chm. Cttees; Minister of Educn, 1952–53; Asst Crown Counsel and Officer i/c Inland Revenue Dept, Gozo, 1954–62; Magistrate: for Gozo, 1962–68; Malta, 1968–78; Judge of Superior Courts, 1978–81. Coronation Medal 1953. *Recreations*: football, woodwork, collecting match boxes. *Address*: 2 Holland Court, Bisazza Street, Sliema, Malta.

SCHERER, Prof. Jacques, DèsL; Professor, University of Paris-III, 1979–83, now Emeritus; *b* 24 Feb. 1912; *s* of Maurice Scherer and Madeleine Franck; *m* 1965, Colette Bié. *Educ*: Ecole Normale Supérieure; Sorbonne Univ., Paris (Agrégé des Lettres, Docteur

ès Lettres). Prof. of French Literature, Univ. of Nancy, 1946–54; Prof. of French Literature and Theatre, Sorbonne Univ., 1954–73; Marshal Foch Prof. of French Literature and Fellow of All Souls Coll., Univ. of Oxford, 1973–79. *Publications*: L'expression littéraire dans l'œuvre de Mallarmé, 1947; La dramaturgie classique en France, 1950; La dramaturgie de Beaumarchais, 1954; Le 'Livre' de Mallarmé, 1957 (new edn 1977); Structures de Tartuffe, 1966; Sur le Dom Juan de Molière, 1967; Le cardinal et l'orang-outang, essai sur Diderot, 1972; Théâtre du XVIIe siècle, 1975, vol. II (ed jtly), 1987; Grammaire de Mallarmé, 1977; Racine et/ou la cérémonie, 1982; Le théâtre de Corneille, 1984; Dramaturgies d'Œdipe, 1987. *Address*: 11 rue de la Colonie, 75013 Paris, France.

SCHERER, Paul Joseph; Managing Director and Chief Executive, Transworld Publishers Ltd, since 1982; President, Publishers Association, since 1991; *b* 28 Dec. 1933; *s* of François Joseph Scherer and Florence (*née* Haywood); *m* 1959, Mary Fieldus; one *s* three *d*. *Educ*: Stonyhurst Coll. National Service, commnd BUFFS (Royal E Kent Regt), 1952–54. Bailey Bros & Swinfen, 1954–56; Jun. Editor, G. Bell & Sons, 1956–58; Sales Man., Penguin Books, 1958–63; Gp Sales Dir, Paul Hamlyn, 1963–68; William Collins Sons & Co.: Man. Dir, Internat. Div., 1968–77; Pres., Collins & World USA, 1974–75; Man. Dir, Mills & Boon, 1977–82. Member Board: Book Develt Council, 1971–74; Book Marketing Council, 1977–84 (Chm., 1982–84); Mem. Council, Publishers Assoc., 1982–84 and 1989–. Founding Chm., Unicorn Sch., Kew, 1970–73. *Recreation*: laughing at my own jokes. *Address*: Flat 6, 62 Queen's Gate, SW7 5JP. *T*: 071–581 9831. *Clubs*: Savile, Arts, Hurlingham.

SCHERMERS, Prof. Dr Henry Gerhard; Knight of Netherlands Lion, 1974; Professor of Law, University of Leiden, since 1978; *b* 27 Sept. 1928; *s* of Petrus Schermers and Amelia M. Gooszen; *m* 1957, Hotsche A. C. Tans; one *s* two *d*. *Educ*: Leiden State Univ. (LLM 1953; LLD 1957). Ministry of Foreign Affairs: Internat. Orgns Dept, 1953–56; Asst Legal Advr, 1956–63; University of Amsterdam: Lectr in Internat. Law, 1963–65; Prof.of Law, 1965–78. Visiting Professor: Ann Arbor, Michigan, 1968; Louisiana, 1981; QMC, 1988. Mem., Eur. Commn of Human Rights, 1981–. Corresp. Fellow, British Acad., 1990; Mem., Inst. de Droit Internat., 1989. Chief Editor, Common Market Law Review, 1978–. Officer, Crown of Belgium, 1962. *Publications*: International Institutional Law, 1972, 2nd edn 1980; Judicial Protection in the European Communities, 1976, 5th edn 1991; numerous articles in Common Market Law Review and professional jls. *Recreations*: hiking, ski-ing, carpentry. *Address*: Herengracht 15, NL 2312 LA Leiden, Netherlands. *T*: 31–71–124294.

SCHIEMANN, Hon. Sir Konrad Hermann Theodor, Kt 1986; **Hon. Mr Justice Schiemann;** a Justice of the High Court, Queen's Bench Division, since 1986; *b* 15 Sept. 1937; *s* of Helmuth and Beate Schiemann; *m* 1965, Elisabeth Hanna Eleonore Holroyd-Reece; one *d*. *Educ*: King Edward's Sch., Birmingham; Pembroke Coll., Cambridge (Schol.; MA, LLB). Served Lancs Fusiliers, 1956–58 (commnd, 1957). Called to Bar, Inner Temple, 1962 (Bencher, 1985); Junior Counsel to the Crown, Common Law, 1978–80; QC 1980; a Recorder of the Crown Court, 1985–86. Chairman of panel conducting Examinations in Public of: North-East Hants and Mid Hants Structure Plans, 1979; Merseyside Structure Plan, 1980; Oxfordshire Structure Plan, 1984. Mem., Parole Bd, 1990– (Vice-Chm., 1991–). Trustee, St John's, Smith Square, 1990–. *Recreations*: music, reading. *Address*: c/o Royal Courts of Justice, Strand, WC2A 2LL.

SCHIFF, András; concert pianist; *b* 21 Dec. 1953; *s* of Odon Schiff and Klara Schiff (*née* Csengeri). *Educ*: Franz Liszt Academy of Music, Budapest; with Prof. Paul Kadosa and Ferenc Rados; private study with George Malcolm. Artistic Dir, September Chamber Music Fest., Mondsee, Austria, 1989–. Prizewinner, Tchaikovsky competition, Moscow, 1974 and Leeds comp., 1975; Liszt Prize, 1977. Regular orch. engagements include: NY Philharmonic, Chicago Symphony, Vienna Phil., Concertgebouw, Orch. de Paris, London Phil., London Symph., Royal Phil., Israel Phil., Philadelphia, Washington Nat. Symph.; major festival performances include: Salzburg, Edinburgh, Aldeburgh, Tanglewood. Recordings include: extensive Bach repertoire; all Mozart Piano Sonatas; all Mozart Piano Concertos; Lieder records with Peter Schreier. Grammy Award (for recording of Bach English Suites), 1990. *Recreations*: literature, languages, soccer. *Address*: c/o Harrison Operations Ltd, 9a Penzance Place, W11.

SCHILD, Geoffrey Christopher, PhD; FIBiol; Director, National Institute for Biological Standards and Control, since 1985; *b* 28 Nov. 1935; *s* of Christopher and Georgina Schild; *m* 1961, Tora Madland; two *s* one *d*. *Educ*: High Storrs Sch., Sheffield; Univ. of Reading (BSc Hons); Univ. of Sheffield (PhD). Res. Fellow 1961–63, Lectr in Virology 1963–67, Univ. of Sheffield; National Institute for Medical Research: Mem., Scientific Staff of MRC, 1967–75; Dir, World Influenza Centre, 1970–75; Hd, Div. of Virology, Nat. Inst. for Biol Standards, 1975–85; Dir, MRC Directed Prog. of AIDS Res., 1987–. Freeman, City of London. *Publications*: Influenza, the Virus and the Disease, 1975, 2nd edn 1985; some 300 original res. papers on virology in learned jls. *Recreations*: hill walking, music, ornithology. *Address*: National Institute for Biological Standards and Control, Blanche Lane, South Mimms, Potters Bar, Hertfordshire EN6 3QG. *T*: Potters Bar (0707) 54753.

SCHILLER, Prof. Dr Karl; Member of Deutscher Bundestag, 1965–72; Professor of Political Economy, University of Hamburg, and Director of Institute for Foreign Trade and Overseas Economy, 1947–72; Member, Ford European Advisory Council, since 1976; *b* 24 April 1911; *s* of Carl and Maria Schiller; *m*; one *s* three *d*. *Educ*: Univs of Kiel, Frankfurt, Berlin, Heidelberg. Research Asst, Institut für Weltwirtschaft, Kiel, 1935–39; Lectr, Univ. of Kiel, 1945–46; Rector, Univ. of Hamburg, 1956–58. Senator for Economic Affairs and Transportation, Hamburg, 1948–53; Mem., Bürgerschaft Hamburg, 1949–57; Senator for Economics, West Berlin, 1961–65; Federal Minister of Economics, 1966–71, of Economics and Finance, 1971–72. Pres., EDESA, 1973–79. Hon. Senator, Univ. of Hamburg, 1983. Alexander Ruestow Plaque, Ruestow Soc., 1976; Ludwig Erhard Prize, Ludwig Erhard Foundn, Bonn, 1978; Burgermeister Stolten Medal, Senate of Hamburg, 1986; Bernhard Harms Medal, Inst. of World Economics, Kiel, 1989. *Publications*: Sozialismus und Wettbewerb, 1955; Neuere Entwicklungen in der Theorie der Wirtschaftspolitik, 1958; Zur Wachstumsproblematik der Entwicklungsländer, 1960; Der Ökonom und die Gesellschaft, 1964; Reden zur Wirtschaft und Finanzpolitik (10 vols), 1966–72; Betrachtungen zur Geld- und Konjunkturpolitik, 1984, etc. *Address*: 2000 Hamburg 60, Leinpfad 71, Germany.

SCHILLING, Prof. Richard Selwyn Francis, CBE 1975; MD (London); DSc (London); FRCP; FFPHM; FFOM; DPH; Professor of Occupational Health, London School of Hygiene and Tropical Medicine, University of London, 1960–76, now Emeritus, Hon. Fellow 1979; Director and Consultant, Possum Controls Ltd, Langley, Slough, since 1986; Director, TUC Centenary Institute of Occupational Health, 1968–76; *b* 9 Jan. 1911; *s* of late George Schilling and of Florence Louise Schilling, Kessingland, Suffolk; *m* 1937, Heather Maude Elinor Norman; one *s* two *d*. *Educ*: Epsom College; St Thomas' Hospital. Obstetric house physician, St Thomas' Hosp., 1935; house physician, Addenbrooke's Hosp., Cambridge, 1936; Asst Industrial MO, ICI (metals) Ltd, Birmingham, 1937; Medical Inspector of Factories, 1939–42. Served War of 1939–45, Captain RAMC, France and Belgium, 1939–40. Sec. Industrial Health Research Board of

Med. Research Council, 1942–46; Nuffield Fellow in Industrial Health, 1946–47; Reader in Occupational Health, Univ. of Manchester, 1947–56; WHO Consultant, 1956–69. Lectures: Milroy, RCP, 1956; Mackenzie, BMA, 1956; Cantor, RSA, 1963; C.-E. A. Winslow, Yale Univ., 1963; Ernestine Henry, RCP, 1970. Former Vice-Pres., Perm. Commn, Internat. Assoc. Occupational Health. Former President: Assoc. of Industrial Medical Officers; British Occupational Hygiene Soc.; Occup. Med. Sect. of Roy. Soc. Med. Member: Committee of Inquiry into Trawler Safety, 1968; Royal Commn on Civil Liability and Compensation for Personal Injury, 1973–78. Hon. Mem., Amer. Occupational Med. Assoc., 1986. Hon. FRSM 1976; Hon. DIH, Soc. of Apothecaries; Hon. FFOM, RCPI. *Publications:* (ed) Modern Trends in Occupational Health, 1960; (ed) Occupational Health Practice, 1973, 2nd edn 1980; original papers on Byssinosis (respiratory disease of textile workers) and other subjects in occupational health in BMJ, Lancet, Brit. Jl of Industrial Medicine, and foreign journals. *Recreation:* fishing. *Address:* 11c Prior Bolton Street, N1 2NX. *T:* 071–359 1627.

SCHLESINGER, Arthur (Meier), Jr; writer; educator; Schweitzer Professor of the Humanities, City University of New York since 1966; *b* Columbus, Ohio, 15 Oct. 1917; *s* of late Arthur Meier and of Elizabeth Bancroft Schlesinger; *m* 1st, 1940, Marian Cannon (marr. diss. 1970); two *s* two *d*; 2nd, 1971, Alexandra Emmet; one *s*. *Educ:* Phillips Exeter Acad. AB (Harvard), 1938; Henry Fellow, Peterhouse, Cambridge, 1938–39. Soc. of Fellows, Harvard, 1939–42; US Office of War Information, 1942–43; US Office of Strategic Services, 1943–45; US Army, 1945. Mem. Adlai Stevenson Campaign Staff, 1952, 1956. Professor of History, Harvard University, 1954–61 (Associate, 1946–54); Special Assistant to President Kennedy, 1961–63. Film Reviewer: Show, 1962–65; Vogue (US), 1966–70; Saturday Review, 1977–80; Amer. Heritage, 1981. Member of Jury, Cannes Film Festival, 1964. Holds 21 honorary doctorates, incl. DLitt Oxford, 1987. Mem. of numerous Socs and Instns; Pres., Amer. Inst. of Arts and Letters, 1981–84; Chancellor, Amer. Acad., 1985–88. Pulitzer Prize: History, 1946; Biography, 1966; Nat. Book Award for Biog., 1966 (for A Thousand Days: John F. Kennedy in the White House), 1979 (for Robert Kennedy and His Times); Amer. Inst. of Arts and Letters, Gold Medal for History, 1967. Commander, Order of Orange-Nassau (Netherlands), 1987. *Publications:* Orestes A. Brownson: a Pilgrim's Progress, 1939; The Age of Jackson, 1945; The Vital Center, 1949, (in UK) The Politics of Freedom, 1950; The General and the President (with R. H. Rovere), 1951; (co-editor) Harvard Guide to American History, 1954; The Age of Roosevelt: I: The Crisis of the Old Order, 1957; II: The Coming of the New Deal, 1958; III: The Politics of Upheaval, 1960; Kennedy or Nixon, 1960; The Politics of Hope, 1963; (ed with Morton White) Paths of American Thought, 1963; A Thousand Days: John F. Kennedy in the White House, 1965; The Bitter Heritage: Vietnam and American Democracy 1941–1966, 1967; The Crisis of Confidence: ideas, power & violence in America, 1969; (ed with F. L. Israel) History of American Presidential Elections, 1971; The Imperial Presidency, 1973; (ed) History of US Political Parties, 1973; Robert Kennedy and His Times, 1978; The Cycles of American History, 1986; The Disuniting of America, 1991; articles to magazines and newspapers. *Recreations:* theatre, movies, tennis. *Address:* (office) 33 W 42nd Street, New York, NY 10036, USA. *T:* 212–642–2060; 171 E 64th Street, New York, NY 10021, USA. *Clubs:* Century (New York), Federal City (Washington).

SCHLESINGER, John Richard, CBE 1970; film director; *b* 16 Feb. 1926; *s* of late Bernard Schlesinger, OBE, MD, FRCP and Winifred Henrietta (*née* Regensburg). *Educ:* Uppingham; Balliol Coll., Oxford (BA; Hon. Fellow 1981). Associate Dir, Nat. Theatre, 1973–88. Mem., Theatre Dirs' Guild of GB, 1983–. Directed: *films:* for Monitor and Tonight (BBC TV), 1958–60; Terminus, for British Transport Films, 1960 (Golden Lion Award, Venice Film Fest., 1961); A Kind of Loving, 1961 (Golden Bear Award, Berlin Film Festival, 1962); Billy Liar, 1962–63; Darling, 1964–65 (NY Critics Award); Far from the Madding Crowd, 1966–67; Midnight Cowboy, 1968–69 (Soc. of TV and Film Acad. Award for Best Dir; Dir's Guild of America Award; American Oscar); Sunday, Bloody Sunday, 1971 (Soc. of TV and Film Acad. Award for Best Dir; David di Donatello Award); contrib. Visions of Eight, 1973; Day of the Locust, 1975; Marathon Man, 1976; Yanks, 1978 (New Evening Standard Award, 1980); Honky Tonk Freeway, 1980; The Falcon and the Snowman, 1984; The Believers, 1987; Madame Sousatzka, 1988 (screenplay with Ruth Prawer Jhabvala); Pacific Heights, 1991; *television:* Separate Tables, 1982; An Englishman Abroad, 1983 (BAFTA Award, Broadcasting Press Guild Award, Barcelona Film Fest. Award and Nat. Bd of Review Award, 1984); A Question of Attribution, 1991; *plays:* No, Why, for RSC, 1964; Timon of Athens, and Days in the Trees, for RSC, 1964–66; I and Albert, Piccadilly, 1972; Heartbreak House, 1975, Julius Caesar, 1977, and True West, 1981, for Nat. Theatre; *opera:* Les Contes d'Hoffmann, 1980 (SWET Award, 1981), and Der Rosenkavalier, 1984, for Covent Garden; Un Ballo in Maschera, for Salzburg Fest., 1989. David di Donatello Special Award, 1980; Shakespeare Prize, FVS Foundn of Hamburg, 1981. *Recreations:* gardening, travel, music, antiques. *Address:* c/o DHAL, Paramount House, 162 Wardour Street, W1.

SCHMIDHUBER, Peter M.; Member, Commission of the European Communities, since 1987; lawyer; *b* 15 Dec. 1931; *s* of Jakob Schmidhuber and Anna (*née* Mandlmayr); *m* 1960, Elisabeth Schweigart; one *d*. *Educ:* Univ. of Munich (MA Econs 1955). Qualified as lawyer, 1960. Member: Bundestag, 1965–69 and 1972–78; Bundesrat, Bavarian Parliament, 1978–87 (Bavarian Minister of State for Federal Affairs). Mem., CSU. *Address:* Commision of the European Communities, rue de la Loi 200, 1049 Bruxelles, Belgium.

SCHMIDT, Benno Charles, Jr; President, Yale University, since 1986; *b* 20 March 1942; *s* of Benno Charles Schmidt and Martha Chastain; *m* 1980, Helen Cutting Whitney; one *s* two *d*. *Educ:* Yale Univ. (BA 1963; LLB 1966). Mem., DC Bar, 1968; Law Clerk to Chief Justice Earl Warren, 1966–67; Special Asst Atty Gen., Office of Legal Counsel, US Dept of Justice, Washington, 1967–69; Harlan Fiske Stone Prof. of Constitutional Law, Columbia Univ., 1969–86, Dean of Law School, 1984–86; Professor of Law, Yale Univ., 1986–. Hon. Bencher, Gray's Inn, 1988. Hon. degrees: LLD Princeton, 1986; DLitt Johns Hopkins, 1987; LLD Harvard, 1987. Hon. AM, 1989. *Publications:* Freedom of the Press Versus Public Access, 1974; (with A. M. Bickel) The Judiciary and Responsible Government 1910–1921, 1985. *Address:* Yale University, Office of the President, New Haven, Conn 06520, USA. *T:* (203) 432–2550.

SCHMIDT, Helmut H. W.; Chancellor, Federal Republic of Germany, 1974–82; Member of Bundestag, Federal Republic of Germany, 1953–62, and 1965–86; Publisher, Die Zeit, since 1983; *b* 23 Dec. 1918; *s* of Gustav L. and Ludovica Schmidt; *m* 1942, Hannelore Glaser; one *d*. *Educ:* Univ. of Hamburg. Diplom-Volkswirt, 1948. Manager of Transport Administration, State of Hamburg, 1949–53; Social Democratic Party: Member, 1946–; Chm., Party Gp, 1967–69; Vice-Chm. of Party, 1968–84; Senator (Minister) for Domestic Affairs in Hamburg, 1961–65; Minister of Defence, 1969–72; Minister of Finance and Economics, 1972; Minister of Finance, 1972–74. Hon LLD: Newberry Coll., S Carolina, 1973; Johns Hopkins Univ., 1976; Cambridge, 1983; Hon. DCL Oxford, 1979; Hon. Doctorate: Harvard, 1979; Sorbonne, 1981.; Georgetown, 1986. Athinai Prize for Man and Mankind, Onassis Foundn, Greece, 1986. *Publications:* Defence or Retaliation, 1962; Beiträge, 1967; Balance of Power, 1971; Auf dem Fundament des Godesberger Programms, 1973; Bundestagsreden, 1975; Kontinuität und Konzentration, 1975; Als Christ in der politischen Entscheidung, 1976; (with Willy Brandt) Deutschland 1976—Zwei Sozialdemokraten im Gespräch, 1976; Der Kurs heisst Frieden, 1979; Freiheit verantworten, 1980; Pflicht zur Menschlichkeit, 1981; A Grand Strategy for the West, 1985; Menschen und Mächte, 1987 (trans. as Men and Powers, 1990); Die Deutschen und ihre Nachbarn, 1990. *Recreations:* sailing, chess, playing the organ. *Address:* c/o Deutscher Bundestag, Görresstrasse 15, Bundeshaus, 5300 Bonn 1, Germany.

SCHNEIDER, Rt. Hon. Sir Lancelot Raymond A.; *see* Adams-Schneider.

SCHNEIDER, Dr William George, OC 1977; FRS 1962; FRSC 1951; Research Consultant, National Research Council of Canada, Ottawa, since 1980 (President, 1967–80); *b* Wolseley, Saskatchewan, 1 June 1915; *s* of Michael Schneider and Phillipina Schneider (*née* Kraushaar); *m* 1940, Jean Frances Purves; two *d*. *Educ:* University of Saskatchewan; McGill University; Harvard University. BSc 1937, MSc 1939, University of Saskatchewan; PhD (in physical chem.), 1941, McGill Univ. Research physicist at Woods Hole Oceanographic Inst., Woods Hole, Mass, USA, 1943–46 (US Navy Certificate of Merit, 1946). Joined Nat. Research Council, Division of Pure Chemistry, Ottawa, 1946; Vice-President (Scientific), 1965–67. Pres., Internat. Union of Pure and Applied Chemistry, 1983–85. Chemical Inst. of Canada Medal, 1961, Montreal Medal, 1973; Henry Marshall Tory Medal, RSC, 1969. Hon. DSc: York, 1966; Memorial, 1968; Saskatchewan, 1969; Moncton, 1969; McMaster, 1969; Laval, 1969; New Brunswick, 1970; Montreal, 1970; McGill, 1970; Acadia, 1976; Regina, 1976; Ottawa, 1978; Hon. LLD: Alberta, 1968; Laurentian, 1968. *Publications:* (with J. A. Pople and H. J. Bernstein) High Resolution Nuclear Magnetic Resonance, 1959; scientific papers in chemistry and physics research jls. *Recreations:* tennis, ski-ing. *Address:* #2–65 Whitemarl Drive, Ottawa, Ontario K1L 8J9, Canada. *T:* (613) 748–9742.

SCHNEIDERHAN, Frau Wolfgang; *see* Seefried, Irmgard.

SCHNITTKE, Alfred; Soviet composer; *b* Engels, Saratov Region, 24 Nov. 1934; *s* of Harry Schnittke and Maria Vogel; *m* 1st, 1956, Galina Koltsina (marr. diss. 1958); 2nd, 1961, Irina Katayeva; one *s*. *Educ:* Moscow Conservatory. Teacher of instrumentation, polyphony and composition, Moscow Conservatory, 1961–71. Member: USSR Composers' Union, Film Makers' Union; W Berlin Acad. of Fine Arts; Royal Swedish Music Acad.; Corresp. Mem., Bavarian Acad. of Fine Arts; Hon. Mem., Hamburg Acad. of Fine Arts. State Prize, RSFSR, 1986. Compositions include: 5 symphonies, 4 violin concertos, 5 concerti grossi, 2 concertos for viola and orchestra, 2 concertos for 'cello and orchestra; Peer Gynt (ballet); choral music, chamber music, film and theatre music. *Publications:* musicological articles. *Address:* ul. Dmitrija Uljanowa d. 4, korp. 2, kw. 155, 117 333 Moscow, USSR. *T:* 137 48 17; Magdalenenstrasse 62, 2000 Hamburg 13, Germany. *T:* 44 63 91.

SCHNYDER, Félix; Ambassador of Switzerland to the United States, 1966–75; *b* 5 March 1910; Swiss; *s* of Maximilian Schnyder and Louise (*née* Steiner); *m* 1941, Sigrid Bucher; one *d*. *Educ:* University of Berne. Barrister, 1938; activities in private enterprise, 1938–40; joined Federal Political Dept, 1940; assigned to Swiss Legation in Moscow, 1947–49; Counsellor of Legation, Head of Swiss Delegation in Berlin, 1949–54; First Counsellor, Swiss Legation in Washington, 1954–57; Swiss Minister in Israel, 1957; Permanent Observer for Switzerland at UN in New York, 1958–61; Swiss Delegate to Technical Assistance Cttee; Swiss Delegate to Exec. Board of UNICEF (Chm. 1960); UN High Comr for Refugees, 1961–65. President: Swiss Nat. Cttee for UNESCO, 1976–80; Swiss Foreign Policy Assoc., 1976–84. *Address:* Via Navegna 25, 6648 Minusio-Locarno, Switzerland.

SCHOFIELD, Alfred, FCBSI; Director, Leeds Permanent Building Society, 1970–86; *b* 18 Feb. 1913; *s* of James Henry and Alice Schofield; *m* 1939, Kathleen Risingham; one *d*. *Educ:* Queen Elizabeth's Grammar Sch., Wakefield. Apptd General Manager, Leeds Permanent Bldg Soc., 1967; retd, 1973; Pres., 1975–78. Director: Homeowners Friendly Soc., 1983–; Springfield Trustees Ltd, 1987–. *Recreation:* orchid growing. *Address:* The Cottage, Rudding, Harrogate, N Yorks HG3 1DQ. *T:* Harrogate (0423) 872037.

SCHOFIELD, Prof. Andrew Noel, MA, PhD (Cantab); FEng 1986; FICE; Professor of Engineering, Cambridge University, since 1974; Fellow of Churchill College, Cambridge, 1963–66 and since 1974; *b* 1 Nov. 1930; *s* of late Rev. John Noel Schofield and of Winifred Jane Mary (*née* Eyles); *m* 1961, Margaret Eileen Green; two *s* two *d*. *Educ:* Mill Hill Sch.; Christ's Coll., Cambridge. John Winbolt Prize, 1954. Asst Engr, in Malawi, with Scott Wilson Kirkpatrick and Partners, 1951. Cambridge Univ.: Demonstrator, 1955, Lectr, 1959, Dept of Engrg. Research Fellow, California Inst. of Technology, 1963–64. Univ. of Manchester Inst. of Science and Technology: Prof. of Civil Engrg, 1968; Head of Dept of Civil and Structural Engrg, 1973. Chairman: Andrew N. Schofield & Associates Ltd, 1984–; Centrifuge Instrumentation and Equipment (formerly Cambridge Equipment) Ltd, 1987–. Rankine Lecture, ICE British Geotechnical Soc., 1980. Chm., Tech. Cttee on Centrifuge Testing, Int. Soc. for Soil Mech. and Foundn Engrg, 1982–85. US Army Award, Civilian Service 1979. *Publications:* (with C. P. Wroth) Critical State Soil Mechanics, 1968; (ed with W. H. Craig and R. G. James and contrib.) Centrifuges in Soil Mechanics, 1988; (ed with J. R. Gronow and R. K. Jain and contrib.) Land Disposal of Hazardous Waste, 1988; papers on soil mechanics and civil engrg. *Address:* 9 Little St Mary's Lane, Cambridge CB2 1RR. *T:* Cambridge (0223) 314536.

SCHOFIELD, Bertram, CBE 1959; MA, PhD, LittD; Keeper of Manuscripts and Egerton Librarian, British Museum, 1956–61; *b* 13 June 1896; *m* 1928, Edith (*d* 1981), *d* of Arthur William and Edith Emily Thomas; one *s* two *d*. *Educ:* University Sch., Southport; University of Liverpool (Charles Beard and University Fellow); Sorbonne, Ecole des Chartes and Ecole des Hautes Etudes, Paris; Emmanuel College, Cambridge (Open Research Student). Served European War, with Roy. Wilts Yeomanry, 1917–19. Asst Keeper, Dept of MSS, British Museum, 1922; Deputy-Keeper, 1947; Keeper, 1956. Seconded to Min. of Economic Warfare, 1940–42, and for special duties with Inter-Services Intelligence and Combined Ops, HQ, 1942–44. Member: Bd of Studies in Palæography, University of London; Committee of Inst. of Historical Research, 1951–61; Council of Royal Historical Society, 1956–59; Canterbury and York Society; Vice-Pres. British Records Assoc., 1956–61; Governor: North London Collegiate School and Camden High Sch. for Girls, 1955–64. *Publications:* Muchelney Memoranda (Somerset Record Soc.), 1927; (with A. J. Collins) Legal and Manorial Formularies, 1933; The Knyvett Letters, 1949; contrib. to Musical Quarterly, Music Review, Music and Letters. British Museum Quarterly, Studies presented to Sir Hilary Jenkinson, 1957; Musik in Geschichte und Gegenwart, etc. *Recreations:* gardening and music. *Address:* 4 Farm Close, Kidlington, Oxford OX5 2BE. *T:* Kidlington (08675) 4110.

SCHOFIELD, Grace Florence; Regional Nursing Officer to the South West Thames Regional Health Authority, 1974–82, retired; *b* 24 Feb. 1925; *d* of Percy and Matilda

Schofield. *Educ:* Mayfield Sch., Putney; University College Hosp. (SRN, SCM); Univ. of London (Dip. in Nursing); Royal College of Nursing (Dip. in Nursing Admin. (Hosp.)). Asst Matron, Guy's Hosp., 1960–61; Dep. Matron, Hammersmith Hosp., 1962–66; Matron, Mount Vernon Hosp. Northwood, and Harefield Hosp., Harefield, 1966–69; Chief Nursing Officer, University Coll. Hosp., 1969–73. *Address:* 42 Briarwood Road, Stoneleigh, Epsom, Surrey KT17 2LY.

SCHOFIELD, Dr Roger Snowden, FRHistS; FBA 1988; FSS; Director, Cambridge Group for the History of Population and Social Structure, Economic and Social Research Council, since 1974; Hon. Reader in Historical Demography, University of Cambridge, since 1991; Fellow of Clare College, Cambridge, since 1969; *b* 26 Aug. 1937; *s* of Ronald Snowden Schofield and Muriel Grace Braime; *m* 1961, Elizabeth Mary Cunliffe; one *d*. *Educ:* Leighton Park Sch., Reading; Clare Coll., Cambridge (BA (History); PhD 1963). FRHistS 1970; FSS 1987. Member: Computing Cttee, SSRC, 1970–75; Stats Cttee, SSRC, 1974–78; Software Provision Cttee, UK Computer Bd, 1977–79. Mem., Population Investigation Cttee, 1976– (Treas., 1987–); British Society for Population Studies: Mem., Council, 1979–87; Treas., 1981–85; Pres., 1985–87. *Publications:* (with E. A. Wrigley) The Population History of England 1541–1871: a reconstruction, 1981, repr. with introd. essay, 1989; (ed with John Walter) Famine, Disease, and the Social Order in Early Modern Society, 1989; contrib. to Population Studies, Jl of Interdisciplinary Hist., Jl of Family Hist. *Address:* Clare College, Cambridge CB2 1TL. *T:* Cambridge (0223) 333267.

SCHOLAR, Michael Charles, CB 1991; Deputy Secretary, HM Treasury, since 1987; *b* 3 Jan. 1942; *s* of Richard Herbert Scholar and Mary Blodwen Scholar; *m* 1964, Angela Mary (*née* Sweet); three *s* (one *d* decd). *Educ:* St Olave's Grammar School, Bermondsey; St John's College, Cambridge (PhD, MA); Univ. of California at Berkeley. ARCO. Loeb Fellow, Harvard Univ., 1967; Asst Lectr, Leicester Univ., 1968; Fellow, St John's College, Cambridge, 1969; HM Treasury, 1969; Private Sec. to Chief Sec., 1974–76; Barclays Bank International, 1979–81; Private Sec. to Prime Minister, 1981–83; Under Secretary, HM Treasury, 1983–87; Central Unit, 1985; Fiscal Policy Gp, 1986–87. *Publications:* contribs to philosophical jls. *Recreations:* music, walking. *Address:* HM Treasury, Parliament Street, SW1. *T:* 071–270 4389.

SCHOLEFIELD, Charles Edward, QC 1959; *b* 15 July 1902; *e s* of Edward Scholefield, Castleford, Yorks; *m* 1966, Catherine Heléne (formerly Childs), *o d* of Reginald and Marguerite Blyth; one step *s*; one step *d*. *Educ:* St Peter's School, York. Admitted a Solicitor, 1925; Barrister, Middle Temple, 1934; North Eastern Circuit. Served in Royal Army Pay Corps, 1940–45; Captain, 1943–45. Chm., Council of Professions supplementary to Medicine, 1966–73. Master of the Bench of the Middle Temple, 1966. *Publications:* (ed) 11th and 12th edns, Lumley's Public Health. *Recreations:* watching cricket and Rugby football; Sherlock Holmes Society of London; Society of Yorkshiremen in London (Past Chairman). *Address:* 4 Gray's Inn Square, WC1; Flat 12, Parkside Nursing Home, Park Road, Banstead, Surrey SM7 3BY. *T:* Burgh Heath (0737) 361334.

SCHOLES, Alwyn Denton; Senior Puisne Judge, Hong Kong, 1970–71 (Acting Chief Justice, 1970); *b* 16 Dec. 1910; *s* of Denton Scholes and Mrs Scholes (*née* Birch); *m* 1939, Juliet Angela Ierne Pyne; one *s* four *d*. *Educ:* Cheltenham College; Selwyn College, Cambridge. Legal Tripos Parts I and II, Cantab, 1932, 1933; MA 1933. Called to the Bar, 1934; practised at the Bar in London and on Midland Circuit, 1934–38; apptd District Magistrate, Gold Coast, 1938; Acting Crown Counsel and Solicitor General, Gold Coast, 1941; apptd Magistrate, Hong Kong, 1948; First Magistrate: Kowloon, 1949; Hong Kong, 1949. Appointed District Judge, Hong Kong, 1953, Puisne Judge, Hong Kong, 1958. Comr, Supreme Ct of State of Brunei, 1964–67, 1968–71. Pres. or Mem., Hong Kong Full Ct of Appeal, on occasions, 1949–71. Member: Sidmouth Parochial Church Council, 1972–82; Ottery Deanery Synod, 1973–82. Governor, St Nicholas Sch., Sidmouth, 1984–89. *Recreations:* walking, gardening. *Address:* West Hayes, Convent Road, Sidmouth, Devon EX10 8RL. *Club:* Commonwealth Trust.

SCHOLES, Gordon Glen Denton; MHR for Corio (Victoria), Australia, since 1967; *b* 7 June 1931; *s* of Glen Scholes and Mary Scholes; *m* 1957, Della Kathleen Robinson; two *d*. *Educ:* various schs. Loco-engine driver, Victorian Railways, 1949–67. Councillor, Geelong City, 1965–67; Pres., Geelong Trades Hall Council, 1965–66. House of Representatives: Chm. cttees, 1973–75; Speaker, 1975–76; Shadow Minister for Defence, 1977–83; Minister for Defence, 1983–84; Minister for Territories, 1984–87. Amateur Boxing Champion (Heavyweight), Vic, 1949. *Recreations:* golf, reading. *Address:* 20 Stephen Street, Newtown, Vic 3220, Australia.

SCHOLES, Hubert, CB 1977; a Commissioner of Customs and Excise, 1978–81; *b* 22 March 1921; *s* of late Hubert Scholes and Lucy (*née* Carter); *m* 1949, Patricia Caldwell; one *s*. *Educ:* Shrewsbury Sch.; Balliol Coll., Oxford. Served RA, 1940–45. Asst Principal, Min. of Fuel and Power, 1946; Principal, 1950; Ministry of Housing and Local Govt, 1956–57; Principal Private Sec. to Minister of Power, 1959–62; Asst Sec., 1962; Under-Sec., Min. of Power, subseq. Min. of Technol., DTI and Dept of Industry, 1968–78. Specialist Advr to H of C Employment Cttee, 1981–82. *Address:* 5A Lancaster Avenue, Farnham, Surrey GU9 8JY. *T:* Farnham (0252) 723992.

SCHOLES, Mary Elizabeth, (Mrs A. I. M. Haggart), OBE 1983; SRN; Chief Area Nursing Officer, Tayside Health Board, 1973–83; *b* 8 April 1924; *d* of late John Neville Carpenter Scholes and Margaret Elizabeth (*née* Hines); *m* 1983, Most Rev. Alastair Iain Macdonald Haggart, *qv*. *Educ:* Wyggeston Grammar Sch. for Girls, Leicester; Leicester Royal Infirmary and Children's Hosp. (SRN 1946); Guy's Hosp., London (CMB Pt I Cert. 1947); Royal Coll. of Nursing, London (Nursing Admin (Hosp.) Cert. 1962). Leicester Royal Infirmary and Children's Hospital: Staff Nurse, 1947–48; Night Sister, 1948–50; Ward Sister, 1950–56; Night Supt, 1956–58; Asst Matron, 1958–61; Asst Matron, Memorial/Brook Gen. Hosp., London, 1962–64; Matron, Dundee Royal Infirm. and Matron Designate, Ninewells Hosp., Dundee, 1964–68; Chief Nursing Officer, Bd of Management for Dundee Gen. Hosps and Bd of Man. for Ninewells and Associated Hosps, 1968–73. Pres., Scottish Assoc. of Nurse Administrators, 1973–77. Member: Scottish Bd, Royal Coll. of Nursing, 1965–70; Gen. Nursing Council for Scotland, 1966–70, 1979–; Standing Nursing and Midwifery Cttee, Scotland, 1971–74 (Vice-Chm., 1973–74); UK Central Council for Nursing, Midwifery and Health Visiting, 1980–84; Management Cttee, State Hosp., Carstairs, 1983; Scottish Hosp. Endowments Res. Trust, 1986–; Chm., Scottish National Bd for Nursing, Midwifery and Health Visiting, 1980–84. *Recreations:* travel, music. *Address:* 19 Eglinton Crescent, Edinburgh EH12 5BY. *Club:* Commonwealth Trust.

SCHOLES, Rodney James; QC 1987; a Recorder, since 1986; *b* 26 Sept. 1945; *s* of late Henry Scholes and of Margaret Bower; *m* 1977, Katherin Elizabeth (*née* Keogh); three *s*. *Educ:* Wade Deacon Grammar Sch., Widnes; St Catherine's Coll., Oxford (scholar) (BA; BCL). Lincoln's Inn: Hardwicke Schol., 1964; Mansfield Schol., 1967; called to the Bar, 1968. Mem., Northern Circuit, 1968–. *Recreations:* watching Rugby League football, dog walking. *Address:* 25 Byrom Street, Manchester M3 4PF. *T:* 061–834 5238; 5 Essex Court, Temple, EC4Y 9AH. *T:* 071–353 4363.

SCHOLEY, Sir David (Gerald), Kt 1987; CBE 1976; Chairman, S. G. Warburg Group plc (formerly Mercury International Group), since 1984; a Director, Bank of England, since 1981; *b* 28 June 1935; *s* of Dudley and Lois Scholey; *m* 1960, Alexandra Beatrix, *d* of Hon. George and Fiorenza Drew, Canada; one *s* one *d*. *Educ:* Wellington Coll., Berks; Christ Church, Oxford. Nat Service, RAC, 9th Queen's Royal Lancers, 1953–55. Thompson Graham & Co. (Lloyd's brokers), 1956–58; Dale & Co. (Insce brokers), Canada, 1958–59; Guinness Mahon & Co. Ltd, 1959–64; joined S. G. Warburg & Co. Ltd, 1964, Dir 1967, Dep. Chm., 1977, Jt Chm., 1980–87; Director: Mercury Securities plc, 1969 (Chm., 1984–86); Orion Insurance Co. Ltd, 1963–87; Stewart Wrightson Holdings Ltd, 1972–81; Union Discount Co. of London, Ltd, 1976–81; British Telecom plc, 1985–. Mem., Export Guarantees Adv. Council, 1970–75, (Dep. Chm. 1974–75); Chm., Construction Exports Adv. Bd, 1975–78; Mem., Cttee on Finance for Industry, NEDO, 1980–87. Trustee, Glyndebourne Arts Trust, 1989–. Hon. Treasurer, IISS, 1984–91. Governor: Wellington Coll., 1977–89; NIESR, 1984–. *Address:* (office) 1 Finsbury Avenue, EC2M 2PA.

SCHOLEY, Sir Robert, Kt 1987; CBE 1982; FEng 1990; Chairman, British Steel plc (formerly British Steel Corporation), since 1986; *b* 8 Oct. 1921; *s* of Harold and Eveline Scholey; *m* 1946, Joan Methley; two *d*. *Educ:* King Edward VII Sch. and Sheffield Univ. Associateship in Mech Engrg. United Steel Companies, 1947–68; British Steel Corporation, 1968–: Dir and Chief Executive, 1973–86; Dep. Chm., 1976–86. Dir, Eurotunnel Bd, 1987–. Mem., NHS Policy Bd, 1989–. Pres., Eurofer, 1985–90. Chm., Internat. Iron and Steel Inst., 1989–90; Pres., Inst. of Metals, 1989–90. Hon. DEng Sheffield, 1987. *Recreations:* outdoor life, history. *Address:* British Steel plc, 9 Albert Embankment, SE1 7SN. *T:* 071–735 7654.

SCHOLTENS, Sir James (Henry), KCVO 1977 (CVO 1963); Director, Office of Government Ceremonial and Hospitality, Department of the Prime Minister and Cabinet, Canberra, 1973–80, retired; Extra Gentleman Usher to the Queen, since 1981; *b* 12 June 1920; *s* of late Theo F. J. Scholtens and late Grace M. E. (*née* Nolan); *m* 1945, Mary Maguire, Brisbane; one *s* five *d*. *Educ:* St Patrick's Marist Brothers' Coll., Sale, Vic. Served War, RAAF, 1943–45. Joined Aust. Public Service, 1935; PMG's Dept, Melbourne, 1935; Dept of Commerce, Melb., 1938; transf. to Dept of Commerce, Canberra, 1941; Dept of Prime Minister, Canberra: Accountant, 1949; Ceremonial Officer, 1954; Asst Sec., Ceremonial and Hospitality Br., 1967. Dir of visits to Australia by the Sovereign and Members of the Royal Family, Heads of State, Monarchs and Presidents, and by Heads of Govt and Ministers of State. *Address:* 74 Boldrewood Street, Turner, Canberra, ACT 2601, Australia. *T:* 48 6639. *Clubs:* Canberra, Southern Cross (Canberra); Royal Automobile of Australia (Sydney).

SCHOLZ, Prof. Dr Rupert; Professor of Public Law, Institut für Politik und öffentliches Recht, University of Munich, since 1981; *b* 23 May 1937; *s* of Ernst and Gisela Scholz (*née* Merdas); *m* 1971, Dr Helga Scholz-Hoppe. *Educ:* Abitur, Berlin; studied law and economics, Berlin and Heidelberg; Dr Jur., Univ. of Munich. Prof., Univ. of Munich, taught in Munich, Berlin, Regensburg, Augsburg; Public Law Chair, Berlin and Munich, 1978. Senator of Justice, Land Berlin, 1981; Acting Senator for Federal Affairs; Mem., Bundesrat, 1982; Mem., N Atlantic Assembly, 1982; Senator for Federal Affairs, Land Berlin, 1983; MHR, Berlin, and Senator for Justice and Federal Affairs, 1985; Federal Minister of Defence, FRG, 1988–89; Mem., German Bundestag, 1990. *Publications:* numerous papers in jurisp., German policy, foreign policy, economic policy. *Address:* Institut für Politik und öffentliches Recht, Universität München, Ludwigstrasse 28, 8000 München, Federal Republic of Germany.

SCHON, family name of **Baron Schon.**

SCHON, Baron *cr* 1976 (Life Peer), of Whitehaven, Cumbria; **Frank Schon,** Kt 1966; Chairman, National Research Development Corporation, 1969–79 (Member, 1967–79); *b* 18 May 1912; *o s* of Dr Frederick Schon and Henriette (*née* Nettel); *m* 1936, Gertrude Secher; two *d*. *Educ:* Rainer Gymnasium, Vienna II; University of Prague; University of Vienna (studied law externally). Co-founder: Marchon Products Ltd, 1939; Solway Chemicals Ltd, 1943; Chm. and Man. Dir of both until May 1967; Dir, Albright & Wilson Ltd, 1956–67; Non-exec. Dir, Blue Circle Industries PLC (formerly Associated Portland Cement Manufacturers Ltd), 1967–82. Mem. Council, King's College, Durham, 1959–63; Mem. Council, 1963–66, Mem. Court, 1963–78, Univ. of Newcastle upon Tyne. Chm. Cumberland Development Council, 1964–68; Member: Northern Economic Planning Council, 1965–68; Industrial Reorganisation Corp., 1966–71; Adv. Council of Technology, 1968–70; part-time Mem., Northern Gas Bd, 1963–66. Hon. Freeman of Whitehaven, 1961. Hon. DCL Durham, 1961. *Recreations:* golf, reading. *Address:* Flat 82, Prince Albert Court, 33 Prince Albert Road, NW8 7LU. *T:* 071–586 1461.

SCHOPPER, Prof. Herwig Franz; Professor of Physics, University of Hamburg, 1973–89, now Emeritus; *b* 28 Feb. 1928; *s* of Franz Schopper and Margarete Hartmann; *m* 1949, Dora Klara Ingeborg (*née* Stieler); one *s* one *d*. *Educ:* Univ. of Hamburg. Dip. Phys. 1949, Dr rer nat 1951. Asst Prof. and Univ. Lectr, Univ. of Erlangen, 1954–57; Prof., Univ. of Mainz, 1957–60; Prof., Univ. of Karlsruhe and Dir of Inst. for Nuclear Physics, 1961–73; Chm., Scientific Council, Kerforschungszentrum, Karlsruhe, 1967–69; Chm., Deutsches Elektronen Synchrotron particle physics Lab., Hamburg, 1973–80; European Organisation for Nuclear Research (CERN): Res. Associate, 1966–67; Head, Dept of particle physics and Mem., Directorate for experimental prog., 1970–73; Chm., Intersecting Storage Ring Cttee, 1973–76; Mem., Sci. Policy Cttee, 1979–80; Dir-Gen., 1981–88. Chm., Assoc. of German Nat. Research Centres, 1978–80; Mem., Scientific Council, IN2P3, Paris. Pres., German Phys. Soc., 1992. Member: Akad. der Wissenschaften Leopoldina, Halle; Joachim Jungius Gesellschaft, Hamburg; Corresp. Mem., Bavarian Acad. of Scis, 1981; Sudetendeutsche Akad. der Wissenschaft, 1979. Dr *hc*: Univ. of Erlangen, 1982; Univ. of Moscow, 1989; Univ. of Geneva, 1989; Univ. of London, 1989. Physics Award, Göttinger Akad. der Wissenschaft, 1957; Carus Medal, Akad. Leopoldina, 1958; Ritter von Gerstner Medal, 1978; Sudetendeutscher Kulturpreis, 1984; Golden Plate Award, Amer. Acad. of Achievement, 1984; Gold Medal, Weizmann Inst., 1987. Grosses Bundesverdienstkreuz (FRG), 1989. *Publications:* Weak Interactions and Nuclear Beta Decay, 1966; Matter—Antimatter, 1989; papers on elementary particle physics, high energy accelerators, relation of science and society. *Recreations:* reading, music, gardening. *Address:* c/o CERN, CH 1211 Geneva 23, Switzerland. *T:* 767 5350.

SCHOUVALOFF, Alexander, MA; Curator, Theatre Museum, Victoria and Albert Museum, 1974–89; *b* 4 May 1934; *s* of Paul Schouvaloff (professional name Paul Sheriff) and Anna Schouvaloff (*née* Raevsky); *m* 1st, Gillian Baker; one *s*; 2nd, 1971, Daria Chorley (*née* de Mérindol). *Educ:* Harrow Sch.; Jesus Coll., Oxford (MA). Asst Director, Edinburgh Festival, 1965–67; Dir, North West Arts Assoc., 1967–74; Director: Rochdale Festival, 1971; Chester Festival, 1973. Sec. Gen., Société Internat. des Bibliothèques et des Musées des Arts du Spectacle, 1980–90. Trustee, London Archives of the Dance, 1976–. BBC Radio plays: Summer of the Bullshine Boys, 1981; No Saleable Value, 1982. Cross of Polonia Restituta, 1971. *Publications:* Place for the Arts, 1971; Summer of the Bullshine Boys, 1979; (with Victor Borovsky) Stravinsky on Stage, 1982; (with April FitzLyon) A

Month in the Country, 1983; Thyssen-Bornemisza Collection: catalogue of set and costume designs, 1987; (with Catherine Haill) The Theatre Museum, 1987; Theatre on Paper, 1990; Léon Bakst: The Theatre Art, 1991. *Recreation:* swimming. *Address:* 10 Avondale Park Gardens, W11 4PR. *T:* 071–727 7543. *Club:* Garrick.

SCHRAM, Prof. Stuart Reynolds; Professor of Politics (with reference to China) in the University of London, School of Oriental and African Studies, 1968–89, now Emeritus; *b* Excelsior, Minn, 27 Feb. 1924; *s* of Warren R. Schram and Nada Stedman Schram; *m* 1972, Marie-Annick Lancelot; one *s*. *Educ:* West High Sch., Minneapolis, Minn; Univ. of Minnesota (BA, 1944); Columbia Univ. (PhD 1954). Dir, Soviet and Chinese Section, Centre d'Etude des Relations Internationales, Fondation Nationale des Sciences Politiques, Paris, 1954–67; Head, Contemporary China Inst., SOAS, 1968–72. *Publications:* Protestantism and Politics in France, 1954; La théorie de la "révolution permanente" en Chine, 1963; The Political Thought of Mao Tse-Tung, 1963, rev. edn 1969; Le marxisme et l'Asie 1853–1964, 1965, rev. and enl. English edn 1969; Mao Tse-tung, 1966; (ed) Authority, Participation and Cultural Change in China, 1973; Mao Zedong: a preliminary re-assessment, 1983; Ideology and Policy in China since the Third Plenum, 1978–84, 1984; (ed) The Scope of State Power in China, 1985; (ed) Foundations and Limits of State Power in China, 1987; The Thought of Mao Tse-tung, 1989. *Recreations:* concert- and theatre-going, walking in the country, fishing. *Address:* John King Fairbank Center for East Asian Research, Harvard University, 1737 Cambridge Street, Cambridge, Mass 02138, USA; 4 Regal Lane, NW1.

SCHRAMEK, Sir Eric (Emil) von; *see* von Schramek.

SCHREIBER, family name of **Baron Marlesford.**

SCHREYER, Rt. Hon. Edward Richard, CC (Canada) 1979; CMM 1979; CD 1979; PC 1984; High Commissioner for Canada in Australia, 1984–88; *b* Beausejour, Man., 21 Dec. 1935; *s* of John and Elizabeth Schreyer, a pioneer family of the district; *m* 1960, Lily, *d* of Jacob Schulz, MP; two *s* two *d*. *Educ:* United Coll., Winnipeg; St John's Coll., Winnipeg, Univ. of Manitoba (BA, BEd, MA). While at university served as 2nd Lieut, COTC, Royal Canadian Armored Corps, 1954–56. Member, Legislative Assembly of Manitoba, 1958; re-elected, 1959 and 1962; MP: for Springfield, 1965, for Selkirk, 1968; chosen as Leader of New Democratic Party in Manitoba, 1969, and resigned seat in House of Commons; MLA for Rossmere and Premier of Manitoba, 1969–77; Minister of Hydro, 1970–77; Minister of Finance, 1972–74; re-elected MLA, 1977; Governor-Gen. and C-in-C of Canada, 1979–84. Prof. of Political Science and Internat. Relns, St John's Coll., Univ. of Manitoba, 1962–65. Member, Commonwealth Parly Assoc., Interparly Union, 1960–78. Hon. LLD: Manitoba, 1979; Ottawa 1980; ME Allison, 1983; McGill, 1984; Simon Fraser, 1984; Lakehead, 1985. Chancellor and Principal Companion of the Order of Canada, 1979; Chancellor and Commander of the Order of Military Merit, 1979. Gov.-Gen. Vanier Award as Outstanding Young Canadian, 1975. *Recreations:* curling, golf, canoeing. *Address:* 3069 Henderson Highway, RR3, Winnipeg, Man R3C 2E7, Canada. *Clubs:* Rideau (Ottawa); East St Paul Legion, East St Paul Curling.

SCHRIEFFER, Prof. John Robert, PhD; Professor of Physics, since 1980 and Chancellor's Professor, since 1984, University of California, Santa Barbara (Director, Institute for Theoretical Physics, 1984–89); *b* Oak Park, Ill, 31 May 1931; *s* of John Henry Schrieffer and Louise Anderson; *m* 1960, Anne Grete Thomsen; one *s* two *d*. *Educ:* MIT(BS); Univ. of Illinois (MS, PhD). Nat. Sci. Foundn Fellow, Univ. of Birmingham, and Niels Bohr Inst. for Theoretical Physics, Copenhagen, 1957–58; Asst Prof., Univ. of Chicago, 1957–59; Asst Prof., Univ. of Illinois, 1959–60, Associate Prof., 1960–62; Univ. of Pennsylvania: Mem. Faculty, 1962–79; Mary Amanda Wood Prof. of Physics, 1964–79. Guggenheim Fellow, Copenhagen, 1967. Member: Nat. Acad. Scis; Amer. Acad. of Arts and Scis; Amer. Philos. Soc.; Amer. Phys Soc.; Danish Royal Acad. Sci.; Acad. of Sci. of USSR, 1989. Hon. ScD: Technische Hochschule, Munich, 1968; Univ. of Geneva, 1968; Univ. of Pennsylvania, 1973; Illinois Univ., 1974; Univ. of Cincinnati, 1977; Hon. DSc Tel-Aviv Univ., 1987. Buckley Prize, Amer. Phys Soc., 1968; Comstock Prize, Nat. Acad. Scis, 1968; (jtly) Nobel Prize for Physics, 1972; John Ericsson Medal, Amer. Soc. of Swedish Engineers, 1976; Nat. Medal of Science, USA, 1985. *Publications:* Theory of Superconductivity, 1964; articles on solid state physics and chemistry. *Recreations:* painting, gardening, wood working. *Address:* Department of Physics, University of California, Santa Barbara, Calif 93106, USA.

SCHRODER, Ernest Melville, CMG 1970; retired 1980; *b* 23 Aug. 1901; *s* of Harold Schroder and Florence L. A. Schroder (*née* Stimson); *m* 1928, Winsome Dawson; two *s* one *d*. *Educ:* Newcastle (NSW) High Sch.; Newcastle Techn. College. Chief Chemist: Kandos Cement Co., Sydney, 1927–30; Australian Cement Ltd, Geelong, 1930–44; Man. Dir, Adelaide Cement Ltd, Adelaide, 1944–68, Chm., 1970–77; Dir, Quarry Industries Ltd, 1965–77. Pres., SA Chamber of Manufacturers, 1963–64, 1964–65; Vice-Pres., Assoc. Chamber of Manufrs of Aust., 1964–65; Pres., Cement and Concrete Assoc. of Aust., 1953–54, 1960–61; State Cttee Mem., CSIRO, 1954–71; Mem., CSIRO Adv. Council, 1955–61. FRACI; AIEAust. *Recreation:* gardening. *Address:* 23 Coreega Avenue, Springfield, SA 5062, Australia. *T:* Adelaide 796452.

SCHUBERT, Sir Sydney, Kt 1985; Chief Executive, Daikyo Group Australia, since 1988; Co-ordinator General and Permanent Head, 1982–88, Director General, 1987–88, Premier's Department, Government of Queensland, Australia; *b* 22 March 1928; *s* of Wilhelm F. Schubert and Mary A. Price; *m* 1961, Maureen Kistle; two *d*. *Educ:* Univ. of Queensland; Univ. of Durham. Queensland Government: Civil Engr, 1950; Dep. Chief Engr, Main Roads Dept, 1965–69; Chief Engr Dept., 1969–72; Dep. Co-ordinator General, 1972–76. Director: Jupiters Develt Ltd; Jupiters Management Ltd; Australian Provincial Newspapers Ltd; Coffey Internat. Ltd. Chancellor, Bond Univ., 1987–89. Mem., Gt Barrier Reef Marine Park Authy, 1978–88; Deputy Chairman: Brisbane Exposition and S Bank Redevelt Authy, 1984–88; Qld Cultural Centre Trust, 1986–88. Member: Bd of Management, Graduate Sch. of Management, Univ. of Queensland, 1985–88; Exec. Council, Australia Japan Assoc. Qld, 1988–90. Trustee, Australia Koala Foundn, 1988–. Eisenhower Fellow, Aust., 1972. FIE(Aust); FAIM; Hon. Fellow, Aust. Instn of Engrs. *Recreations:* golf, fishing. *Address:* 15 Apex Street, Clayfield, Brisbane, Qld 4011, Australia. *Clubs:* Queensland, Brisbane, Royal Queensland Golf.

SCHULTZ, Rt. Rev. Bruce Allan; *see* Grafton, NSW, Bishop of.

SCHULTZ, Prof. Theodore W., PhD; Charles L. Hutchinson Distinguished Service Professor of Economics, University of Chicago, since 1952; *b* 30 April 1902; *s* of Henry E. Schultz and Anna Elizabeth Weiss; *m* Esther Florence Werth; one *s* two *d*. *Educ:* South Dakota State Coll. (BS); Univ. of Wisconsin (MS, PhD). Iowa State College: Faculty of Economics, 1930–43; Head, Dept of Economics and Sociology, 1934–43; University of Chicago: Prof. of Economics, from 1943; Chairman, Dept of Economics, 1946–61. Hon. LLD: Grinnell Coll. 1949; Michigan State 1962; Illinois 1968; Wisconsin 1968; Catholic Univ. of Chile 1979; Dijon 1981; N Carolina State Univ. 1984. Francis A. Walker Medal, Amer. Econ. Assoc., 1972; Leonard Elmhirst Medal, Internat. Agricl Econ. Assoc., 1976; Nobel Prize for Economic Science, 1979. *Publications:* Redirecting Farm Policy, 1943; Agriculture in an Unstable Economy, 1945; The Economic Organization of Agriculture, 1953; The Economic Value of Education, 1963; Transforming Traditional Agriculture, 1964; Economic Growth and Agriculture, 1968; Investment in Human Capital: role of education and research, 1971; Human Resources: policy issues and research opportunities, 1972; (ed) Distortions of Agricultural Incentives, 1978; Investing in People: the economics of population quality, 1981; Restoring Economic Equilibrium: human capital in the modernizing economy, 1990. *Address:* 5620 South Kimbark Avenue, Chicago, Illinois 60637, USA. *T:* (312) 493–6083.

SCHUMANN, Maurice; Hon. GCMG 1972; Chevalier de la Légion d'Honneur; Compagnon de la Libération; Croix de Guerre (1939–45); Senator from the Department of the Nord, since 1974; Vice-President of the Senate, since 1977; Member, Académie Française, since 1974; writer and broadcaster; *b* Paris, 10 April 1911; *s* of Julien Schumann and Thérèse Michel; *m* 1944, Lucie Daniel; three *d*. *Educ:* Lycées of Janson-de-Sailly and Henry IV; Faculty of Letters, Univ. of Paris (Licencié ès Lettres). Attached to l'Agence Havas in London and later Paris, 1935–39; Chief Official Broadcaster, BBC French Service, 1940–44; Liaison Officer with Allied Expeditionary Forces at end of war; Mem. Provisional Consultative Assembly, Nov. 1944–July 1945; Deputy for Nord, 1945–67 and 1968–73; Mem. Constituent Assemblies, Oct. 1945–May 1946 and June-Nov. 1946. Chm., Popular Republican Movement (MRP); Deputy of this group, 1945–73 (Pres., 1945–49; Hon. Pres., 1949–); Dep. Minister for Foreign Affairs, 1951–54; Pres., For. Affairs Cttee of Nat. Assembly, 1959; Minister of State (Prime Minister's Office), April-May 1962; Minister of State, in charge of scientific res. and atomic and spacial questions, 1967–68; Minister of State for Social Affairs, 1968–69; Minister for Foreign Affairs, 1969–73. Has been Pres. of various organisations, incl. Internat. Movement for Atlantic Union, 1966–. Associate Prof., Faculté Catholique de Lille, 1975–. Pres., Assoc. des Ecrivains catholiques, 1980–. Hon. LLD: Cantab, 1972; St Andrews, 1974; Hon. Dr Oxon, 1972. *Publications:* Le Germanisme en marche, 1938; Mussolini, 1939; Les problèmes Ukrainiens et la paix européenne, 1939; Honneur et Patrie, 1945; Le vrai malaise des intellectuels de gauche, 1957; La Mort née de leur propre vie: essai sur Péguy, Simone Weil et Gandhi, 1974; Un Certain 18 Juin, 1980 (Prix Aujourd'hui); Qui a tué le duc d'Enghien?, 1984; Une grande Imprudence, 1986; *novels:* Le Rendezvous avec quelqu'un, 1962; Les Flots roulant au loin, 1973; La Communication, 1974; Angoisse et Certitude, 1978 (Grand Prix de Littérature Catholique); Le Concerto en Ut Majeur, 1982; La victoire et la nuit, 1989; chapters in: Mazarin, 1960; Talleyrand, 1962; Clemenceau, 1974; many articles etc (under pseudonym of André Sidobre) to L'Aube (Paris daily), Le Temps présent and La Vie catholique, etc. *Address:* 53 avenue du Maréchal-Lyautey, Paris 16e, France.

SCHUSTER, Sir (Felix) James (Moncrieff), 3rd Bt, *cr* 1906; OBE 1955; TD; Senior Partner, Sheppards and Chase, 1970–75, retired; *b* 8 January 1913; *o s* of Sir Victor Schuster, 2nd Bt, and Lucy, *d* of W. B. Skene, Pitlour-Halyards, Fife; *S* father, 1962; *m* 1937, Ragna, *er d* of late Direktor Sundø, Copenhagen; two *d*. *Educ:* Winchester. Served War of 1939–45, with The Rifle Brigade (Middle East and Combined Operations). Lt-Col comdg London Rifle Brigade. Rangers (RB), TA, 1952; Bt-Colonel, 1955. Hon. Col, 5th Bn Royal Green Jackets, 1970–75. *Heir:* none. *Address:* Piltdown Cottage, Piltdown, Uckfield, East Sussex TN22 3XB. *T:* Newick (082572) 2916. *Clubs:* Naval and Military, Lansdowne.

SCHUSTER, Sir James; *see* Schuster, Sir F. J. M.

SCHUSTER, Rt. Rev. James Leo; Assistant Bishop of George, since 1980; *b* 18 July 1912; *s* of Rev. Harold Vernon Schuster and Elsie Jane (*née* Roberton); *m* 1951, Ilse Henriette Emmy Gottschalk; three *s* two *d* (and one *s* decd). *Educ:* Lancing; Keble Coll., Oxford. Deacon, 1937; Priest, 1938; Asst Missioner, Clare Coll. Mission, Rotherhithe, 1937–38; Chaplain St Stephen's House, Oxford, 1938–40; CF (EC), 1940–46; wounded, 1942; despatches, 1943. Chaplain, St Stephen's House, Oxford, 1946–49; Principal St Bede's Coll., Umtata, 1949–56; Bishop of St John's, 1956–79; Archdeacon of Riversdale, 1980–86; Rector of Swellendam, 1980–87. *Address:* PO Box 285, 19 Aanhuizen Street, Swellendam 6740, South Africa.

SCHWARTZ, Melvin, PhD; Associate Director for High Energy and Nuclear Physics, Brookhaven National Laboratory, Upton, New York, since 1991; *b* 2 Nov. 1932; *s* of Harry Schwartz and Hannah Schwartz (*née* Shulman); *m* 1953, Marilyn Fenster; one *s* two *d*. *Educ:* Columbia College, NY (AB 1953); Columbia Univ., NY (PhD 1958). Associate Physicist, Brookhaven Nat. Lab., 1956–58; Asst Prof., Associate Prof. and Prof. of Physics, Columbia Univ., 1958–66; Prof. of Physics, 1966–83, Consulting Prof., 1983–, Stanford Univ. Mem., Nat. Acad. of Scis, 1975. Hughes Prize, 1964; (jtly) Nobel Prize in Physics, 1988. *Publication:* Principles of Electrodynamics, 1972. *Recreations:* ski-ing, photography, woodworking. *Address:* 61 So. Howells Pt Road, Bellport, New York, NY 11713, USA. *T:* (office) 516 282 7711.

SCHWARZ, Rudolf, CBE 1973; Conductor Laureate, Northern Sinfonia of England (formerly Northern Sinfonia Orchestra, Newcastle upon Tyne), 1982–85 (Principal Guest Conductor, 1973–82); *b* 29 April 1905; Austrian (British subject, 1952); *m* 1950, Greta Ohlson (*d* 1984); one *s* (and one step *d* and one step *s*). *Educ:* Vienna. Conductor, Opera House, Düsseldorf, 1923–27; Conductor, Opera House, Karlsruhe, 1927–33; Musical Director, Jewish Cultural Organisation, Berlin, 1936–41; Conductor, Bournemouth Municipal Orchestra, 1947–51; Conductor, City of Birmingham Symphony Orchestra, 1951–57; Chief Conductor of the BBC Symphony Orchestra, 1957–62; Principal Conductor, Northern Sinfonia Orchestra, Newcastle upon Tyne, 1964–73; Guest Conductor, Bergen Orchestra, Norway, 1964–71; Principal Guest Conductor, Bournemouth Symphony Orchestra, 1970–79. Hon. RAM; Hon. GSM; DMus (*hc*) Newcastle upon Tyne, 1972. *Address:* 24 Wildcroft Manor, SW15 3TS.

SCHWARZ-BART, André; French writer; *b* Metz, Lorraine, France, 23 May 1928; 2nd *s* of parents from Poland; *m* 1961, Simone Schwarz-Bart; two *c*. *Educ:* self-educated; Trades Sch., Sillac; Sorbonne. Joined French Resistance at 15. Has worked in factories as a fitter and in Les Halles, Paris, while writing; has travelled to Israel, Africa and to the West Indies. *Publications:* Le Dernier des Justes, 1959 (Prix Goncourt, 1959; Eng. trans., 1960); (with Simone Schwarz-Bart) Un plat de porc aux bananes vertes, 1967 (Jerusalem Prize, 1967); La Mulâtresse Solitude, 1972 (Eng. trans., A Woman Named Solitude, 1973). *Address:* c/o Editions du Seuil, 27 rue Jacob, 75261 Paris Cedex 06, France.

SCHWARZENBERGER, Prof. Georg; Professor of International Law in the University of London, 1962–75, now Emeritus; Dean, Faculty of Laws, University College, London, 1965–67 (Vice-Dean, 1949–55 and 1963–65); Director, London Institute of World Affairs since 1943; Barrister-at-Law, Gray's Inn, since 1955; *b* 20 May 1908; *o s* of Ludwig and Ferry Schwarzenberger; *m* 1931, Suse Schwarz; one *s*. *Educ:* Karls-Gymnasium, Heilbronn aN; Univs of Heidelberg, Frankfurt, Berlin, Tübingen, Paris and London. Dr Jur. (Tübingen) 1930; PhD (London) 1936. Sec. London Inst. of World Affairs (formerly New Commonwealth Inst.) 1934–43; Lectr in Internat. Law and Relations, University Coll., London, 1938–45; Sub-Dean and Tutor, Faculty of Laws, 1942–49; Reader in Internat. Law, 1945–62. Co-Editor (with G. W. Keeton) of: The Library of World

Affairs, 1946–; The Year Book of World Affairs, 1947–84; Current Legal Problems, 1948–72. Member, Permanent Finnish-Netherlands Conciliation Commission. Hon. LLD Dalhousie, 1979. *Publications:* The League of Nations and World Order, 1936; Power Politics: A Study of World Society (1st edn 1941, 3rd edn 1964); International Law and Totalitarian Lawlessness, 1943; International Law as Applied by International Court and Tribunals, 1945 (Vol. I, 3rd edn 1957, Vol. II, 1968, Vol. III, 1976, Vol. IV, 1986); A Manual of International Law, 1947 (6th edn (with E. D. Brown) 1976); The Fundamental Principles of International Law, Hague Academy of Internat. Law (Recueil, Vol. 87), 1955; The Legality of Nuclear Weapons, 1958; The Frontiers of International Law, 1962; The Inductive Approach to International Law, 1965; The Principles and Standards of International Economic Law, Hague Acad. of Internat. Law (Recueil, Vol. 117), 1966; Foreign Investments and International Law, 1969; International Law and Order, 1971; The Dynamics of International Law, 1976. *Recreations:* gardening, swimming. *Address:* 4 Bowers Way, Harpenden, Herts AL5 4EW. *T:* Harpenden (0582) 713497.

SCHWARZKOPF, Elisabeth; soprano; *b* 9 Dec. 1915; *o d* of Gymnasialdirektor Friedrich Schwarzkopf and Elisabeth (*née* Fröhlich); *m* Walter Legge (*d* 1979). *Educ:* High School for Music, Berlin; studied with Maria Ivogün-Raucheisen, Austrian concert singer. Sang at Vienna State Opera, Royal Opera House, Covent Garden, La Scala, Milan, 1948–64, Metropolitan Opera, NY, San Francisco Opera; Inauguration, Bayreuther Fest. after the war. Film, Der Rosenkavalier, 1961. Hon. Member: Royal Swedish Acad. for Arts and Sciences; Accad. S Cecilia, Roma; RAM; Corres. Mem., Bayerischer Akad. der Künste. MusD (*hc*) Cambridge, 1976; Hon. Dr Amer. Univ. Washington, DC, 1982. Lilli Lehmann Medal, Salzburg, 1950; first Premio Orfeo d'oro, Mantua; Lily Pons Medal, Paris; Hugo Wolf Verein Medal, Vienna, 1973. Grosse Verdienstkreuz, Germany, 1974; Order of Merit for Sci. and the Arts (Germany), 1983; 1st class Order of Dannebrog, Denmark. *Publication:* (ed) On and Off the Record: a memoire of Walter Legge, 1982. *Recreations:* music, theatre, gardening, ski-ing, mountain walking.

SCHWARZKOPF, Gen. H. Norman, Hon. KCB 1991; Commander, Allied Forces, Gulf War, Jan.–Feb. 1991; Commander in Chief, US Central Command, MacDill Air Force Base, Florida, 1988–91; *b* 22 Aug. 1934; *s* of Herbert Norman Schwarzkopf and Ruth (*née* Bowman); *m* 1968, Brenda Holsinger; one *s* two *d*. *Educ:* Bordentown Mil. Inst.; Valley Forge Mil. Acad. (football schol.); US Mil. Acad., West Point; Univ. of S Calif (MME 1964). Commnd 2nd Lieut. Inf. and airborne trng, Fort Benning, Ga; 101st Airborne Div., Fort Campbell, Ky; Teacher, Mil. Acad., West Point, 1964 and 1966–68; Task-Force Advr, S Vietnamese Airborne Div., 1965; Comdr, 1st Bn, 6th Inf., 198th Inf. Bde, American Div., 1969–73; Dep. Comdr, 172nd Inf. Bde, Fort Richardson, Alaska, 1974–76; Comdr, 1st Bde, 9th Inf. Div., Fort Lewis, Wash, 1976–78; Dep. Dir of Plans, US Pacific Comd, Camp Smith, Hawaii, 1978–80; Asst Div. Comdr, 8th Mechanized Inf. Div., W Germany, 1980–82; Dir, Military-Personnel Management, Office of Dep. Chief of Staff for Personnel Management, Office of Dep. Chief of Staff for Personnel, Washington, DC, 1982–83; Comdr, 24th Mechanized Inf. Div., Fort Stewart, Ga, 1983–85; Comdr, US Ground Forces and Dep. Comdr, Jt Task Force, Grenada op. Oct. 1983; Asst Dep. Chief of Staff, Army Ops, Washington DC, 1985–86; Comdr, I Corps, Fort Lewis, Wash, 1986–87; Dep. Chief for Ops and Plans, Washington, DC, 1987–88. DSM with oak leaf cluster; DFC; Silver Star with 2 oak leaf clusters; Bronze Star with 3 oak leaf clusters; Purple Heart with oak leaf cluster; Congressional Gold Medal, 1991. *Address:* c/o US Central Command, MacDill Air Force Base, Fla 33608, USA.

SCHWEITZER, Prof. Miguel; Minister for Foreign Affairs, Chile, 1983; *b* 22 July 1940; *s* of Miguel Schweitzer and Cora Walters; *m* 1964, Maria Luisa Fernándes; two *s* one *d*. *Educ:* The Grange School, Santiago (preparatory and secondary schooling); Law School, Univ. of Chile (law degree). Doctorate in Penal Law, Rome, 1964–65; Professor of Penal Law: Law Sch., Univ. of Chile, 1966; High Sch. of Carabineros (Police), 1968, 1970 and from 1974; Director, Dept of Penal Sciences, Univ. of Chile, 1974–76; Chile's Alternate Representative with the Chilean Delegn to UN, 1975, 1976, 1978; Ambassador on special missions, 1975–80; Chilean Delegate to OAS, 1976–78; Ambassador to the Court of St James's, 1980–83. *Publications:* El Error de Derecho en Materia Penal (Chile), 1964; Sull elemento soggettivo nel reato di bancarotta del l'imprenditore (Rome), 1965; Prospectus for a Course on the Special Part of Penal Law (USA), 1969. *Recreations:* music, reading, golf, tennis, Rugby. *Address:* Moneda 1040, Of. 703, Santiago, Chile. *Clubs:* Temple Golf; Prince of Wales Country (Santiago).

SCHWEITZER, Pierre-Paul; Grand Croix de la Légion d'Honneur; Croix de Guerre (1939–45); Médaille de la Résistance avec rosette; Inspecteur Général des Finances Honoraire, 1974; *b* 29 May 1912; *s* of Paul Schweitzer and Emma Munch; *m* 1941, Catherine Hatt; one *s* one *d*. *Educ:* Univs of Strasbourg and Paris; Ecole Libre des Sciences Politiques. Joined French Treasury as Inspecteur des Finances, 1936; Dep. Dir for Internat. Finance, French Treasury, Paris, 1946; Alternate Exec. Dir, IMF, Washington, 1947; Sec.-Gen. for European Economic Cooperation in the French Administration, Paris, 1948; Financial Counsellor, French Embassy, Washington, 1949; Director, Treasury, Paris, 1953; Dep. Governor of the Banque de France, Paris, 1960–63; Inspecteur Général des Finances, 1963; Man. Dir and Chm. Exec. Bd, IMF, 1963–73. Chairman: Bank of America International, Luxembourg, 1974–77; Cie Monégasque de Banque, Monaco, 1978–88; Director: Banque Pétrofigaz, Paris, 1974– (Chm., 1974–79); Robeco Gp, Rotterdam, 1974–82; Compagnie de Participations et d'Investissements Holding SA, Luxembourg, 1975–87 (Chm., 1975–84); Société Financière Internationale de Participations, Paris, 1976–87 (Chm., 1976–84); Adv. Dir, Bank of America, NY, 1974–77, and Unilever NV, Rotterdam, 1974–84. Hon. LLD: Yale, 1966; Harvard 1966; Leeds, 1968; New York, 1968; George Washington Univ., 1972; Wales, 1972; Williams, 1973. *Address:* 170 route de Mon Idée, 1253 Vandoeuvres, Switzerland. *T:* (022) 750.13.13.

SCHWINGER, Prof. Julian, AB, PhD; University Professor, University of California at Los Angeles, since 1980 (Professor of Physics, 1972–80); *b* 12 Feb. 1918; *s* of Benjamin Schwinger and Belle Schwinger (*née* Rosenfeld); *m* 1947, Clarice Carrol. *Educ:* Columbia University. Nat. Research Council Fellow, 1939–40; Research Associate, University of California at Berkeley, 1940–41; Instructor, later Assistant Professor, Purdue University, 1941–43; Member Staff: Radiation Laboratory, MIT, 1943–46; Metallurgy Laboratory, University of Chicago, 1943; Associate Professor of Physics, Harvard University, 1945–47, Prof., 1947–72, Higgins Prof. of Physics, 1966–72. Writer and presenter of series Understanding Space and Time, BBC (jt Univ. of Calif and Open Univ. prodn). Member, Board of Sponsors, Bulletin of the Atomic Scientists. Member: Nat. Acad. of Scis; Amer. Acad. of Arts and Scis; Amer. Assoc. for Advancement of Science; NY Acad. of Sciences; Bd of Sponsors, Amer. Fedn of Scientists; Civil Liberties Union. Guggenheim Fellow, 1970. Hon. DSc: Purdue, 1961; Harvard, 1962; Columbia, 1966; Brandeis, 1973; Gustavus Adolphus Coll., 1975; Hon. LLD City Univ. of NY, 1972; Hon. Dr Univ. of Paris, 1990. US Nat. Medal of Sci., 1964; Nobel Prize for Physics (with R. Feynman and S. Tomonaga), 1965; Humboldt Prize, 1981; many other awards and medals. *Publications:* Quantum Electrodynamics (editor), 1958; (with D. Saxon) Discontinuities in Wave Guides, 1968; Particles and Sources, 1969; Quantum Kinematics and Dynamics, 1970; Particles, Sources and Fields, vol. I, 1970, vol. II, 1973, vol. III, 1989. *Recreations:* tennis, swimming, ski-ing, driving, and being one of the world's worst pianists. *Address:* Department of Physics, University of California at Los Angeles, Calif 90024, USA; 10727 Stradella Court, Los Angeles, Calif 90077.

SCIAMA, Prof. Dennis William, PhD; FRS 1983; Extraordinary Fellow, Churchill College, Cambridge, since 1986; Professor of Astrophysics, International School of Advanced Studies, Trieste, since 1983; Consultant, International Centre for Theoretical Physics, Trieste, since 1983; *b* 18 Nov. 1926; *s* of Abraham and Nelly Sciama; *m* 1959, Lidia Dina; two *d*. *Educ:* Malvern Coll.; Trinity Coll., Cambridge (MA, PhD). Fellow, Trinity Coll., Cambridge, 1952–56; Mem., Inst. for Advanced Study, Princeton, 1954–55; Agassiz Fellow, Harvard Univ., 1955–56; Res. Associate, KCL, 1958–60; Lectr in Maths, 1961–70, and Fellow of Peterhouse, 1963–70, Cambridge Univ.; Sen. Res. Fellow, All Souls Coll., Oxford, 1970–85. Vis. Prof., Cornell Univ., 1960–61; Luce Prof., Mount Holyoke Coll., 1977–78; Prof. of Physics, Univ. of Texas at Austin, 1978–83. Foreign Member: Amer. Philosophical Soc., 1981; Amer. Acad. of Arts and Scis, 1982; Accademia Nazionale dei Lincei, 1984. Guthrie Medal, 1991. *Publications:* The Unity of the Universe, 1959; The Physical Foundations of General Relativity, 1969; Modern Cosmology, 1971, 2nd edn 1975; contribs to physics and astronomy jls. *Address:* 7 Park Town, Oxford. *T:* Oxford (0865) 59441.

SCLATER, Prof. John George, PhD; FRS 1982; Professor, Scripps Institution of Oceanography, University of California at San Diego, since 1991; *b* 17 June 1940; *s* of John George Sclater and Margaret Bennett Glen; *m* 1st, 1968, Fredrica Rose Felcyn; two *s*; 2nd, 1985, Paula Ann Edwards. *Educ:* Carlekemp Priory School; Stonyhurst College; Edinburgh Univ. (BSc); Cambridge Univ. (PhD 1966). Research Scientist, Scripps Instn of Oceanography, 1965; Massachusetts Institute of Technology: Associate Prof., 1972; Professor, 1977; Dir, Jt Prog. in Oceanography and Oceanographic Engrg with Woods Hole Oceanographic Instn, 1981; Prof., Dept of Geol Scis, and Associate Dir, Inst. for Geophysics, 1983–91, Shell Dist. Prof., 1983–88, Univ. of Texas at Austin. Fellow Geological Soc. of America; Fellow Amer. Geophysical Union; Mem., US Nat. Acad. of Scis, 1989. Rosenstiel Award in Oceanography, Rosenstiel Sch., Univ. of Miami, 1979; Bucher Medal, Amer. Geophysical Union, 1985. *Recreations:* running, swimming, golf. *Address:* Scripps Institution of Oceanography, La Jolla, Calif 92093–0215, USA.

SCLATER, John Richard; Chairman, Foreign and Colonial Investment Trust PLC, since 1985 (Director, since 1981); *b* 14 July 1940; *s* of Arthur William Sclater and Alice Sclater (*née* Collett); *m* 1st, 1967, Nicola Mary Gloria Cropper (marr. diss.); one *s* one *d*; 2nd, 1985, Grizel Elizabeth Catherine Dawson. *Educ:* Charterhouse; Gonville and Caius Coll., Cambridge (schol., 1st Cl. Hons History Tripos, BA, MA); Commonwealth Fellow, 1962–64; Yale Univ. (MA 1963); Harvard Univ. (MBA 1968). Glyn, Mills & Co., 1964–70; Dir, Williams, Glyn & Co., 1970–76; Man. Dir, Nordic Bank, 1976–85 (Chm., 1985); Dir, 1985–87, Jt Dep. Chm., 1987, Guinness Peat Gp PLC; Dir and Dep. Chm., 1985–87, Chm., 1987, Guinness Mahon & Co. Ltd; Chairman: F & C Enterprise Trust PLC, 1986–; Foreign & Colonial Ventures Ltd, 1989–; Chm., Berisford Internat. PLC, 1990– (Dir, 1986–); Vice-Chm., Hill Samuel, 1990–; Deputy Chairman: Yamaichi International (Europe) Ltd, 1985–; Union Discount Co. of London PLC, 1986– (Dir, 1981–); Director: James Cropper PLC, 1972–; Holker Estates Co. Ltd, 1974–; Equitable Life Assurance Soc., 1985–; Hypo Foreign & Colonial Management Hldgs, 1989–; Grosvenor Estate Hldgs, 1989–; Economic Insce Co. Ltd, 1989–; Wilrig AS, 1989–; Hafnia Hldgs (UK), 1989–; Fuel Tech (Europe), 1990–; Prolific Gp, 1990–; Member, London Bd of Halifax Building Soc., 1983–90. Mem., City Taxation Cttee, 1973–76. Chm., Assoc. of Consortium Banks, 1980–82. Mem., City Adv. Gp, CBI, 1988–. Trustee, Grosvenor Estate, 1973–; Mem. Council, Duchy of Lancaster, 1987–. Governor: Internat. Students House, 1976–; Brambletye Sch. Trust, 1976–. *Recreations:* country pursuits. *Address:* Sutton Hall, Barcombe, near Lewes, Sussex BN8 5EB. *T:* Barcombe (0273) 400450. *Clubs:* Brooks's, Pratt's; University Pitt (Cambridge).

SCLATER-BOOTH, family name of **Baron Basing.**

SCOBIE, Kenneth Charles, CA; Deputy Chairman and Chief Executive, Brent Walker Group PLC, since 1991; Chairman, Lovells Confectionery Ltd, since 1991; *b* 29 July 1938; *s* of Charles Scobie and Shena (*née* Melrose); *m* 1973, Adela Jane Hollebone; one *s* one *d*. *Educ:* Daniel Stewart's Coll., Edinburgh; Edinburgh Univ. CA 1961. Romanes-Munro, CA, 1956–61; BMC (Scotland) Ltd, 1961–63; Rolls-Royce Ltd, 1963–66; Robson Morrow & Co., 1966–70; Black & Decker, 1971–72; Vavasseur South Africa Ltd, 1972–76; H. C. Sleigh Ltd, 1979–83; Blackwood Hodge plc, 1984–90. Non-exec. Dir, Albrighton plc., 1990–. CBIM 1987. *Recreations:* sport, Bridge. *Address:* Path Hill House, Path Hill, Goring Heath, Oxon RG8 7RE. *T:* Reading (0734) 842417. *Clubs:* London Scottish Rugby; Huntercombe Golf.

SCOBLE, (Arthur William) John; Chairman, Economic Planning Board, South West Region (Bristol), 1965–71, retired; *er s* of Arthur Scoble; *m* 1935, Constance Aveline, *d* of Samuel Robbins; three *d*. Min. of Nat. Insce, 1945–50; jssc 1950; Min. of Works, 1951–59; UN, Buenos Aires, 1960–61; Min. of Works, 1962–64; Dept of Economic Affairs, 1965–70; Dept of the Environment, 1970–71, 1972–73. Chm., Agricl Housing Adv. Cttee, 1977–81. Dir, Bath Preservation Trust, 1973–74. Regional Advisor, Employment Fellowship, 1975–79. Clerk to Bathampton Council, 1980–86. *Address:* Cross Deep, Bathampton Lane, Bath BA2 6ST. *T:* Bath (0225) 460525.

SCOBLE, Christopher Lawrence; Assistant Under-Secretary of State, Establishment Department, Home Office, since 1991; *b* 21 Nov. 1943; *s* of Victor Arthur Oliphant Scoble and Mabel Crouch; *m* 1972, Rosemary Hunter; one *s* one *d*. *Educ:* Kent Coll., Canterbury; Corpus Christi Coll., Oxford. Asst Principal, Home Office, 1965; Private Sec. to Minister of State, Welsh Office, 1969–70; Principal, 1970; Sec. to Adv. Council on the Penal System, 1976–78; Asst Sec., 1978; Asst Under-Sec. of State, Broadcasting and Miscellaneous Dept, Home Office, 1988–91. Vice-Chm., Media Policy Cttee, Council of Europe, 1985–87. CS (Nuffield and Leverhulme) Travelling Fellowship, 1987–88. *Address:* Home Office, Grenadier House, 99–105 Horseferry Road, SW1P 2DD. *T:* 071–217 0174.

SCOFIELD, (David) Paul, CBE 1956; actor; *b* 21 Jan. 1922; *s* of Edward H. and M. Scofield; *m* 1943, Joy Parker (actress); one *s* one *d*. *Educ:* Varndean Sch. for Boys, Brighton. Theatre training, Croydon Repertory, 1939; London Mask Theatre School, 1940. Shakespeare with ENSA, 1940–41; Birmingham Repertory Theatre, 1942; CEMA Factory tours, 1942–43; Whitehall Theatre, 1943; Birmingham Repertory, 1943–44–45; Stratford-upon-Avon, 1946–47–48. Mem., Royal Shakespeare Directorate, 1966–68. Associate Dir, Nat. Theatre, 1970–71. London theatres: Arts, 1946; Phoenix, 1947; Adventure Story, and The Seagull, St James's, 1949; Ring Round the Moon, Globe, 1950; Much Ado About Nothing, Phœnix, 1952; The River Line, Edin. Fest., Lyric (Hammersmith), Strand, 1952; John Gielgud's Company, 1952–53: Richard II, The Way of the World, Venice Preserved, etc; A Question of Fact, Piccadilly, 1953–54; Time Remembered, Lyric, Hammersmith, New Theatre, 1954–55; Hamlet, Moscow, 1955; Paul Scofield-Peter Brook Season, Phœnix Theatre, 1956; Hamlet, The Power and the

Glory, Family Reunion; A Dead Secret, Piccadilly Theatre, 1957; Expresso Bongo, Saville Theatre, 1958; The Complaisant Lover, Globe Theatre, 1959; A Man For All Seasons, Globe Theatre, 1960, New York, 1961–62; Coriolanus and Love's Labour's Lost, at Shakespeare Festival Season, Stratford, Ont., 1961; King Lear: Stratford-on-Avon, Aldwych Theatre, 1962–63, Europe and US, 1964; Timon of Athens, Stratford-on-Avon, 1965; The Government Inspector, also Staircase, Aldwych, 1966; Macbeth, Stratford-on-Avon, 1967, Russia, Finland, 1967, Aldwych, 1968; The Hotel in Amsterdam, Royal Court, 1968; Uncle Vanya, Royal Court, 1970; Savages, Royal Court and Comedy, 1973; The Tempest, Wyndhams, 1975; Dimetos, Comedy, 1976; The Family, Royal Exchange, Manchester, and Haymarket, 1978; I am Not Rappaport, Apollo, 1986–87; Exclusive, Strand, 1989; *National Theatre:* The Captain of Kopenick, The Rules of the Game, 1971; Volpone, The Madras House, 1977; Amadeus, 1979; Othello, 1980; Don Quixote, A Midsummer Night's Dream, 1982. *Films:* The Train, 1964; A Man for All Seasons, 1966 (from the play); Bartleby, King Lear, 1971; Scorpio, 1973; A Delicate Balance, 1974; Nineteen Nineteen, 1985; When the Whales Came, 1989; Henry V, 1989; Hamlet, 1991; *TV films:* Anna Karenina, 1985; The Attic, 1988. Hon. LLD Glasgow, 1968; Hon. DLit Kent, 1973; Hon. DLitt Sussex, 1985. Shakespeare prize, Hamburg, 1972. *Relevant publication:* Paul Scofield, by J. C. Trewin, 1956. *Address:* The Gables, Balcombe, Sussex. *T:* Balcombe (0444) 378. *Club:* Athenæum.

SCOON, Sir Paul, GCMG 1979; GCVO 1985; OBE 1970; Governor General of Grenada, since 1978; *b* 4 July 1935; *m* 1970, Esmai Monica McNeilly (*née* Lumsden); two step *s* one step *d*. *Educ:* St John's Anglican Sch., Grenada; Grenada Boys' Secondary Sch.; Inst. of Education, Leeds; Toronto Univ. BA, MEd. Teacher, Grenada Boys' Secondary Sch., 1953–67. Chief Educn Officer, 1967–68, Permanent Sec., 1969, Secretary to the Cabinet, 1970–72, Grenada; Dep. Director, Commonwealth Foundn, 1973–78. Governor, Centre for Internat. Briefing, Farnham Castle, 1973–78; Vice-Pres., Civil Service Assoc., Grenada, 1968; Co-founder and former Pres., Assoc. of Masters and Mistresses, Grenada. *Recreations:* reading, tennis. *Address:* Governor General's House, St George's, Grenada. *T:* 2401.

SCOONES, Major-General Sir Reginald (Laurence), KBE 1955 (OBE 1941); CB 1951; DSO 1945; late Royal Armoured Corps; Director, The Brewers' Society, 1957–69; *b* 18 Dec. 1900; *s* of late Major Fitzmaurice Scoones, Royal Fusiliers; *m* 1933, Isabella Bowie, *d* of John Nisbet, Cumbrae Isles, Scotland; one *d*. *Educ:* Wellington College; RMC, Sandhurst. 2nd Lt R Fus., 1920; transferred Royal Tank Corps, 1923; attd Sudan Defence Force, 1926–34; Adj. 1 RTR, 1935; GSO3 Mobile Div., 1938; served War of 1939–45, Middle East and Burma; Brigade Major, Cavalry Brigade, Cairo, 1939; GSO2 Western Desert Corps, 1940; CO 42 RTR, 1941; GSO1 War Office, 1941; Brig. Dep. Dir Military Trng, 1942; Comdr, 254 Tank Brigade, Burma, 1943; Dep. Dir Military Trng, 1945; Asst Kaid, Sudan Defence Force, 1947–50; Maj.-Gen. 1950; Major-General Commanding British Troops Sudan and Commandant Sudan Defence Force, 1950–54. *Address:* Flat 51, 50 Sloane Street, SW1X 9SV.

SCOPES, Sir Leonard Arthur, KCVO 1961; CMG 1957; OBE 1946; *b* 19 March 1912; *s* of late Arthur Edward Scopes and Jessie Russell Hendry; *m* 1938, Brunhilde Slater Rolfe; two *s* two *d*. *Educ:* St Dunstan's College; Gonville and Caius College, Cambridge (MA). Joined HM Consular Service, 1933; Vice-Consul: Antwerp, 1933, Saigon, 1935; Canton, 1937; Acting Consul, Surabaya, 1941; Vice-Consul, Lourenço Marques, 1942; Consul, Skoplje and Ljubljana, 1945; Commercial Secretary, Bogota, 1947; Assistant in United Nations (Economic and Social) Department of Foreign Office, 1950; Counsellor, Djakarta, 1952; Foreign Service Inspector, 1954; HM Ambassador to Nepal, 1957–62; HM Ambassador to Paraguay, 1962–67; Mem., UN Jt Inspection Unit, Geneva, 1968–71. *Recreation:* retirement. *Address:* 2 Whaddon Hall Mews, Milton Keynes, Bucks MK17 0NA.

SCORER, Philip Segar; a Recorder of the Crown Court, since 1976; *b* 11 March 1916; *s* of late Eric W. Scorer and Maud Scorer (*née* Segar); *m* 1950, Monica Smith; one *s* three *d*. *Educ:* Repton. Admitted Solicitor, 1938; London County Council Legal Dept, 1938–40. Served War, Army (Royal Signals: War Office, SHAEF and BAS, Paris), 1940–46. Solicitors' Dept, New Scotland Yard, 1947–51; Partner in Burton & Co., Solicitors, Lincoln, 1952–; Clerk of the Peace, City of Lincoln, 1952–71; Under-Sheriff of Lincolnshire, 1954–; Pres., Under Sheriffs Assoc., 1978–. *Address:* Stonebow, Lincoln LN2 1DA. *T:* Lincoln (0522) 23215. *Club:* National Liberal.

SCORSESE, Martin; American film director; *b* 17 Nov. 1942; *s* of Charles Scorsese and Catherine (*née* Cappa); *m* 1st, 1965, Laraine Marie Brennan (marr. diss.); one *d*; 2nd, Julia Cameron (marr. diss.); one *d*; 3rd, 1979, Isabella Rosellini (marr. diss. 1983); 4th, 1985, Barbara DeFina. *Educ:* Univ. of New York (BS 1964; MA 1966). Faculty Asst, 1963–66, Lectr, 1968–70, Dept of Film, Univ. of New York; dir and writer of documentaries. *Films* include: Who's That Knocking At My Door? (also writer), 1968; Mean Streets (also co-writer), 1973; Alice Doesn't Live Here Any More, 1974; Taxi Driver, 1976; New York, New York, 1977; The Last Waltz (also actor), 1978; Raging Bull, 1980; After Hours, 1985 (Best Dir Award, Cannes Film Fest., 1986); The Color of Money, 1986; acted in 'Round Midnight, 1986; The Last Temptation of Christ, 1988; Goodfellas, 1990. *Address:* c/o CAA, 9830 Wilshire Boulevard, Los Angeles, Calif 90212, USA.

SCOTFORD, John Edward; Treasurer, Hampshire County Council, since 1983; *b* 15 Aug. 1939; *s* of Albert and Louisa Scotford; *m* 1962, Marjorie Clare Wells; one *s*. *Educ:* Reading Grammar Sch. IPFA. Reading County Borough Council, 1955–62; Coventry County Borough Council, 1962–65; Hampshire CC, 1965–; Dep. County Treasurer, 1977–83. *Address:* Hampshire County Council, The Castle, Winchester SO23 8UJ.

SCOTHORNE, Prof. Raymond John, BSc, MD Leeds; MD Chicago; FRSE; FRCSGlas; Regius Professor of Anatomy, University of Glasgow, 1972–90, now Emeritus; *b* 1920; *s* of late John and Lavinia Scothorne; *m* 1948, Audrey, *o d* of late Rev. Selwyn and Winifred Gillott; one *s* two *d*. *Educ:* Royal Grammar School, Newcastle upon Tyne; Universities of Leeds and Chicago, BSc (Hons) 1st cl. (Leeds), 1941; MD (Chicago), Rockefeller Student, 1941–43; MB (Hons) 1st cl. (Leeds), 1944; MD (with Distinction) (Leeds), 1951. Demonstrator and Lecturer in Anatomy, 1944–50, Univ. of Leeds; Sen. Lecturer in Anatomy, 1950–60, Univ. of Glasgow; Prof., Univ. of Newcastle upon Tyne, 1960–72. Hon. Sec., Anat. Soc. of Great Britain and Ireland, 1967–71, Pres., 1971–73; Fellow, British Assoc. of Clinical Anatomists (Pres., 1986–88); Mem., Med. Sub-Cttee, UGC, 1967–76. Hon. Mem., Assoc. des Anatomistes. Struthers Prize and Gold Medal in Anatomy, Univ. of Glasgow, 1957. Anatomical Editor, Companion to Medical Studies; Editor, Clinical Anatomy, 1987–. *Publications:* chapter on Peripheral Nervous System in Hamilton's Textbook of Anatomy, 2nd edn, 1975; chapters on Early Development, on Tissue and Organ Growth, on Skin and on the Nervous System in Companion to Medical Studies, 3rd edn, 1985; chapter on Development and Structure of Liver in Pathology of Liver, 1979, 2nd edn 1987; chapter on Respiratory System in Cunningham's Textbook, 12th edn, 1981; chapter on Development of Spinal Cord and Vertebral Column in Surgery of the Spine, 1991; papers on embryology, histology and tissue transplantation. *Address:* Southernknowe, Linlithgow, West Lothian. *T:* Linlithgow (0506) 842463.

SCOTT, family name of **Earl of Eldon.**

SCOTT; *see* Hepburne-Scott, family name of Lord Polwarth.

SCOTT; *see* Maxwell Scott and Maxwell-Scott.

SCOTT; *see* Montagu Douglas Scott, family name of Duke of Buccleuch.

SCOTT, Alan James, CVO 1986; CBE 1982; Governor, Cayman Islands, since 1987; *b* 14 Jan. 1934; *er s* of Rev. Harold James Scott and Mary Phyllis Barbara Scott; *m* 1st, 1958, Mary Elizabeth Ireland (*d* 1969); one *s* two *d*; 2nd, 1971, Joan Hall; one step *s* two step *d*. *Educ:* King's Sch., Ely; Selwyn Coll., Cambridge Univ. (BA Hons). Lieut, Suffolk Regt, Italy and Germany, 1952–54. HMOCS, 1958–87: Fiji: Dist Officer, 1958; Estabts Officer, 1960; Registry of Univ. of S Pacific, 1968; Controller, Organisation and Estabts, 1969; Hong Kong: Asst Financial Sec., 1971; Prin. Asst Financial Sec., 1972; Sec. for CS, 1973; MLC, 1976–85; Sec. for Housing, and Chm. Hong Kong Housing Authy, 1977; Sec. for Information, 1980; Sec. for Transport, 1982; Dep. Chief Sec., 1985–87. President: Fiji AAA, 1964–69; Hong Kong AAA, 1978–87. *Recreations:* bicycling, tennis, golf, sailing, dilatory travel. *Address:* Government House, Cayman Islands, BWI; Petraea, Claviers 83830, France. *Clubs:* Farmers'; Nautilus, Britannia Golf, Grand Cayman Yacht (Cayman).

SCOTT, Prof. Alastair Ian, FRS 1978; FRSE 1981; Davidson Professor of Chemistry and Biochemistry, Texas A & M University, since 1981; *b* 10 April 1928; *s* of William Scott and Nell Florence (*née* Newton); *m* 1950, Elizabeth Wilson (*née* Walters); one *s one d*. *Educ:* Glasgow Univ. (BSc, PhD, DSc). Postdoctoral Fellow, Ohio State Univ., 1952–53; Technical Officer, ICI (Nobel Div.), 1953–54; Postdoctoral Fellow, London and Glasgow Univs, 1954–57; Lectr, Glasgow Univ., 1957–62; Professor: Univ. of British Columbia, 1962–65; Univ. of Sussex, 1965–68; Yale Univ., 1968–77; Texas A&M Univ., 1977–80; Edinburgh Univ., 1980–83 (Forbes Prof., 1980–81). Lectures: Karl Folkers, Wisconsin Univ., 1964; Burger, Virginia Univ., 1975; Benjamin Rush, Pennsylvania Univ., 1975; 5 colls, Mass, 1977; Andrews, NSW Univ., 1979; Dreyfus, Indiana Univ., 1983. FAAAS 1988. Hon. Mem., Pharmaceutical Soc. of Japan, 1985. Hon. MA Yale, 1968; Hon. DSc Coimbra, 1990. Corday-Morgan Medallist, Chemical Soc., 1964; Ernest Guenther Medallist, Amer. Chem. Soc., 1976. *Publications:* Interpretation of Ultraviolet Spectra of Natural Products, 1964; (with T. K. Devon) Handbook of Naturally Occurring Compounds, 1972; numerous pubns in learned jls. *Recreations:* music, gardening. *Address:* Department of Chemistry, Texas A & M University, College Station, Texas 77843–3255, USA. *T:* 409–845 3243. *Club:* Athenæum.

SCOTT, Prof. Alexander Whiteford, CBE 1960; Professor of Chemical Engineering, University of Strathclyde, Glasgow, 1955–71; Hon. Engineering Consultant to Ministry of Agriculture, Fisheries and Food, 1946–62; *b* 28 January 1904; *s* of Alexander Scott, Glasgow; *m* 1933, Rowena Christianna (*d* 1970), *d* of John Craig, Glasgow; one *s*. *Educ:* Royal College of Science and Technology, Glasgow. BSc, PhD, ARCST, Glasgow. Pres., Instn of Engineers and Shipbuilders in Scotland, 1975–76 and 1976–77. FIMechE, FIChemE, Hon. FCIBS. Hon. LLD Strathclyde, 1980. *Address:* 9 Rowallan Road, Thornliebank, Glasgow G46 7EP. *T:* 041–638 2968.

SCOTT, Anthony Douglas, TD 1972; chartered accountant in public practice; *b* 6 Nov. 1933; *o s* of Douglas Ernest and Mary Gladys Scott; *m* 1962, Irene Robson; one *s* one *d*. *Educ:* Gateshead Central Technical Secondary Sch. Articled to Middleton & Middleton, also J. Stanley Armstrong, Chartered Accountants, Newcastle upon Tyne, 1952–57; National Service, WO Selection Bd, 1957–59; Accountant with Commercial Plastics Ltd, 1959; joined ICI Ltd (Agricl Div), 1961; seconded by ICI to Hargreaves Fertilisers Ltd, as Chief Accountant, 1966; ICI Ltd (Nobel Div.) as Asst Chief Acct, 1970; seconded by ICI to MoD as Dir-Gen. Internal Audit, 1972–74. Dir of Consumer Credit, Office of Fair Trading, 1974–80. Chief Exec. and Dir, CoSIRA, 1981–88. Chm., Teesside Soc. of Chartered Accts, 1969–70; Mem. Cttee, London Chartered Accountants, 1974–79. Chm., Jt Working Party on Students' Societies (ICAE&W), 1979–80. *Publications:* Accountants Digests on Consumer Credit Act 1974, 1980; Accountants Digest on Estate Agents Act 1979, 1982. *Recreations:* antiquary, walking, gardening; TA, 1959–91. *Address:* 33 Barlings Road, Harpenden, Herts. *T:* Harpenden (0582) 763067.

SCOTT, Sir Anthony (Percy), 3rd Bt *cr* 1913; Chairman and Managing Director, L. M. (Moneybrokers) Ltd, since 1986; *b* 1 May 1937; *s* of Sir Douglas Winchester Scott, 2nd Bt, and of Elizabeth Joyce, *d* of W. N. C. Grant; *S* father, 1984; *m* 1962, Caroline Theresa Anne, *er d* of Edward Bacon; two *s* one *d*. *Educ:* Harrow; Christ Church, Oxford. Barrister, Inner Temple, 1960. *Recreation:* racing. *Heir:* *s* Henry Douglas Edward Scott, *b* 26 March 1964. *Address:* 1 Groveside Court, Albion Wharf, Lombard Road, SW11 3RQ.

SCOTT, Brough; *see* Scott, J. B.

SCOTT, Dame Catherine Margaret Mary; *see* Scott, Dame M.

SCOTT, Sir (Charles) Peter, KBE 1978 (OBE 1948); CMG 1964; HM Diplomatic Service, retired; Member, Council of Anglo-Norse Society, since 1978; *b* 30 Dec. 1917; *er s* of late Rev. John Joseph Scott and late Dorothea Scott (*née* Senior); *m* 1954, Rachael, *yr d* of C. W. Lloyd Jones, CIE; one *s* two *d*. *Educ:* Weymouth Coll.; Pembroke Coll., Cambridge. Indian Civil Service: Probationer, 1939; appointed to Madras Presidency, 1940; Asst Private Sec. to Viceroy, 1946–47. Entered HM Diplomatic Service, 1947, Second Sec., Tokyo, 1948; First Sec., 1949; Foreign Office, 1950; Private Sec. to Gen. Lord Ismay at NATO, Paris, 1952; First Sec., Vienna, 1954; First Sec. at British Information Services, NY, 1956; Counsellor and Consul-General, Washington, 1959; Student at IDC, 1962; Head of UK Mission to European Office of the United Nations, Geneva, 1963; Minister at HM Embassy, Rome, 1966–69; Temp. Vis. Fellow at Centre for Contemporary European Studies, Univ. of Sussex, 1969–70; Asst Under-Sec. of State, FCO, 1970–75; Ambassador to Norway, 1975–77. Private Sec., 1978–79, Treasurer, 1979–81, to HRH Prince Michael of Kent. *Recreations:* walking, and such as offer. *Address:* Bisley Farmhouse, Irstead, near Norwich, Norfolk NR12 8XT. *T:* Horning (0692) 630413. *Clubs:* United Oxford & Cambridge University; Norfolk (Norwich).

SCOTT, Rt. Rev. Colin John Fraser; *see* Hulme, Bishop Suffragan of.

SCOTT, Prof. Dana Stewart, FBA 1976; Hillman University Professor of Computer Science and Mathematical Logic, Carnegie Mellon University, since 1981; *b* Berkeley, Calif, 11 Oct. 1932; *m* 1959, Irene Schreier; one *d*. *Educ:* Univ. of Calif, Berkeley (BA); Princeton Univ. (PhD). Instructor, Univ. of Chicago, 1958–60; Asst Prof., Univ. of Calif, Berkeley, 1960–63; Associate Prof. and Prof., Stanford Univ., 1963–69; Prof., Princeton, 1969–72; Prof. of Mathematical Logic, Oxford Univ., 1972–81. Visiting Prof., Amsterdam, 1968–69; Guggenheim Fellow, 1978–79. *Publications:* papers on logic and mathematics in technical jls. *Address:* School of Computer Science, Carnegie Mellon University, 5000 Forbes Avenue, Pittsburgh, Pa 15213-3890, USA.

SCOTT, Sir David; *see* Scott, Sir W. D. S.

SCOTT, David; *b* 6 Sept. 1916; *er s* of late Sir Basil Scott and late Gertrude, MBE, 2nd *d* of Henry Villiers Stuart of Dromana, MP; *m* 1951, Hester Mary, MA, *y d* of late Gilbert Ogilvy of Winton and Pencaitland; one *s* three *d*. *Educ:* Stowe; New College, Oxford

(MA). War Service 1939–45: Argyll and Sutherland Highlanders (SR), Reconnaissance Corps and Highland Light Infantry; T/Capt., 1941; Asst to Political Adviser for Khuzistan, Iran, 1944; Actg Vice Consul, Ahwaz, 1944–45. Clerk, House of Commons, 1946; Deputy Principal Clerk, 1962; Clerk of Standing Cttees, 1966–70; Clerk of Select Cttees, 1970–73; Clerk of Private Bills, an Examiner of Petitions for Private Bills and Taxing Officer, House of Commons, 1974–77; retired 1977. Mem., Cttee on Canons, General Synod, Scottish Episcopal Church, 1983–91. *Recreation:* fishing. *Address:* Glenaros, Aros, Isle of Mull PA72 6JP. *T:* Aros (0680) 300337; 6a Stafford House, Maida Avenue, W2 1TE. *T:* 071–723 8398. *Club:* New (Edinburgh).

SCOTT, Ven. David; Archdeacon of Stow, 1975–89; Chaplain to the Queen, since 1983; *b* 19 June 1924; *m*; two *c*. *Educ:* Trinity Hall, Cambridge (BA 1950, MA 1954); Cuddesdon Theological College. Deacon 1952, priest 1953, dio. Portsmouth; Curate of St Mark, Portsea, 1952–58; Asst Chaplain, Univ. of London, 1958–59; PC, Old Brumby, 1959–66; Vicar of Boston, Lincs, 1966–75; Rural Dean of Holland East, 1971–75; Surrogate, 1972–75; Vicar of Hackthorn with Cold Hanworth, 1975–89; Priest-in-Charge of North and South Carlton, 1978–89; Canon and Prebendary of Lincoln Cathedral, 1971–89. Mem. Gen. Synod, 1978–80, 1983–85, 1985–89. *Address:* 4 Honing Drive, Southwell, Notts NG25 0LB. *T:* Southwell (0636) 813900.

SCOTT, Sir David (Aubrey), GCMG 1979 (KCMG 1974; CMG 1966); HM Diplomatic Service, retired 1979; *b* 3 Aug. 1919; *s* of late Hugh Sumner Scott and of Barbara E. Scott, JP; *m* 1941, Vera Kathleen, *d* of late Major G. H. Ibbitson, MBE, RA; two *s* one *d*. *Educ:* Charterhouse; Birmingham University (Mining Engrg). Served War of 1939–45, Royal Artillery, 1939–47; Chief Radar Adviser, British Military Mission to Egyptian Army, 1945–47, Major. Appointed to CRO, 1948; Asst Private Secretary to Secretary of State, 1949; Cape Town/Pretoria, 1951–53; Cabinet Office, 1954–56; Malta Round Table Conf., 1955; Secretary-General, Malaya and Caribbean Constitutional Confs, 1956; Singapore, 1956–58; Monckton Commn, 1960; Dep. High Comr, Fedn of Rhodesia and Nyasaland, 1961–63; Imperial Defence College, 1964; Dep. High Comr, India, 1965–67; British High Comr in Uganda, and Ambassador (non-resident) to Rwanda, 1967–70; Asst Under-Sec. of State, FCO, 1970–72; British High Comr to New Zealand, and Governor, Pitcairn Is., 1973–75; HM Ambassador to Republic of S Africa, 1976–79. Chairman: Ellerman Lines plc, 1982–83; Nuclear Resources Ltd, 1984–88; Director: Barclays Bank International Ltd, 1979–85; Mitchell Cotts plc, 1980–86; Delta Metal Overseas Ltd, 1980–83; Bradbury Wilkinson plc, 1984–86; Consultant, Thomas De La Rue & Co. Ltd, 1986–88. Pres., Uganda Soc. for Disabled Children, 1984–; Vice-Pres., UK South Africa Trade Assoc., 1980–85. Mem., Manchester Olympic Bid Cttee, 1989–. Gov., Sadler's Wells Trust, 1984–89. Freeman, City of London, 1982; Liveryman, Shipwrights' Co., 1983. *Publication:* Ambassador in Black and White, 1981. *Recreations:* music, birdwatching. *Address:* Wayside, Moushill Lane, Milford, Surrey GU8 5BQ. *Club:* Royal Over-Seas League (Chm., 1981–86).

See also Sir J. B. Unwin.

SCOTT, David Gidley; Registrar of the High Court in Bankruptcy, since 1984; *b* 3 Jan. 1924; *s* of late Bernard Wardlaw Habershon Scott, FRIBA and of Florence May Scott; *m* 1948, Elinor Anne, *d* of late Major Alan Garthwaite, DSO, MC, and Mrs Garthwaite; two *s* two *d*. *Educ:* Sutton Valence School (scholarship); St John's College, Cambridge (exhibnr, MA, LLM). Army service, 1942–47, Royal Engineers; Assault RE European theatre, 1944–45 (wounded); Acting Major, Palestine. Called to the Bar, Lincoln's Inn, 1951; practised Chancery Bar, 1951–84. *Recreations:* sailing, choral singing. *Address:* Little Almshoe House, St Ippolyts, Hitchin, Herts SG4 7NP. *T:* Hitchin (0462) 434391. *Clubs:* Bar Yacht, Parkstone Yacht.

SCOTT, Donald; *see* Scott, W. D.

SCOTT, Prof. Douglas Frederick Schumacher; Professor of German in the University of Durham (late Durham Colleges), 1958–75, now Emeritus Professor; *b* Newcastle under Lyme, Staffs, 17 Sept. 1910; *o s* of Frederick Scott and Magdalena (*née* Gronbach); *m* 1942, Margaret (*d* 1972), *o d* of late Owen Gray Ellis, Beaumaris, Anglesey, and Helen (*née* Gibbs); two *d*. *Educ:* Queen Mary's Grammar School, Walsall, Staffs; Dillmann-Realgymnasium Stuttgart, Germany; University of Tübingen, Göttingen (Dr phil.); University College, London (MA). Part-time Assistant, German Dept, University Coll., London, 1935–37; Lecturer in charge German Dept, Huddersfield Technical Coll., 1937–38; Lecturer in German, King's Coll., Newcastle, 1938–46; released for service with Friends' Ambulance Unit, 1940–46; Lecturer in German, King's Coll., London, 1946–49; Reader and Head of Dept of German, The Durham Colls, 1949–58. *Publications:* Some English Correspondents of Goethe, 1949; W. v. Humboldt and the Idea of a University, 1960; Luke Howard: his correspondence with Goethe and his continental journey of 1816, 1976; articles and reviews on German lit. and Anglo-German literary relations in various English and German journals. *Recreations:* music, travel. *Address:* 6 Fieldhouse Terrace, Durham DH1 4NA. *T:* Durham (091) 3864518.

SCOTT, Douglas Keith, (Doug Scott); *b* Nottingham, 29 May 1941; *s* of George Douglas Scott and Edith Joyce Scott; *m* 1962, Janice Elaine Brook (marr. diss. 1988); one *s* two *d*. *Educ:* Cottesmore Secondary Modern Sch.; Mundella Grammar Sch., Nottingham; Loughborough Teachers' Trng Coll. (Teaching Certificate). Began climbing age of 12, British crag climbing, and most weekends thereafter; visited the Alps age of 17 and every year thereafter; first ascent, Tarso Teiroko, Tibest Mts, Sahara, 1965; first ascents, Cilo Dag Mts, SE Turkey, 1966; first ascent, S face Koh-i-Bandaka (6837 m), Hindu Kush, Afghanistan, 1967; first British ascent, Salathé Wall, El Capitain, Yosemite, 1971; 1972: Spring, Mem., European Mt Everest Expedn to SW face; Summer, first ascent, E Pillar of Mt Asgard, Baffin Island Expedn; Autumn, Mem., British Mt Everest Expedn to SW face; first ascent, Changabang (6864 m), 1974; first ascent, SE spur, Pic Lenin (7189 m), 1974; reached summit of Mt Everest, via SW face, with Dougal Haston, as Members, British Everest Expedn, 24th Sept. 1975 (first Britons on summit); first Alpine ascent of S face, Mt McKinley (6226 m), via new route, British Direct, with Dougal Haston, 1976; first ascent, East Face Direct, Mt Kenya, 1976; first ascent, Ogre (7330 m), Karakoram Mountains, 1977; first ascent, N Ridge route, Kangchenjunga (8593 m), without oxygen, 1979; first ascent, N Summit, Kussum Kangguru, 1979; first ascent, N Face, Nuptse, 1979; Alpine style, Kangchungtse (7640 m), 1980; first ascent Shivling E Pillar, 13-day Alpine Style push, 1981; Chamlang (7366 m) North Face to Central Summit, with Rheinhold Messner, 1981; first ascent, Pungpa Ri (7445 m), 1982; first ascent Shishapangma South Face (8046 m), 1982; first ascent, Lobsang Spire (Karakoram), and ascent Broad Peak (8047 m), 1983; Mt Baruntse (7143 m), first ascent, East Summit Mt Chamlang (7287 m), and traverse over unclimbed central summit Chamlang, Makalu SE Ridge, Alpine Style, to within 100 m of summit, 1984; first Alpine style ascent, Diran (7260 m), 1985; first ascent of rock climbs in S India, 1986; first ascent of rock climbs, Wadi Rum, Jordan, 1987; Mt Jitchu Drake (Bhutan) (6793 m), South face first ascent of peak, Alpine style, 1988; first ascent, Indian Arêt Latok III, 1990. Pres., Alpine Climbing Gp, 1976–82. A vegetarian, 1978–. *Publications:* Big Wall Climbing, 1974; (with Alex MacIntyre) Shishapangma, Tibet, 1984; contrib. to Alpine Jl, Amer. Alpine Jl and Mountain Magazine. *Recreations:* rock climbing, photography, organic gardening. *Address:* Chapel House, Low Cotehill, Carlisle CA4 0EL. *T:* Carlisle (0228) 562358. *Clubs:* Alpine; Alpine Climbing Group; Nottingham Climbers'.

SCOTT, Edward McM.; *see* McMillan-Scott.

SCOTT, Most Rev. Edward Walter, CC 1978; Archbishop, and Primate of All Canada, 1971–86; *b* Edmonton, Alberta; *s* of Tom Walter Scott and Kathleen Frances Ford; *m* 1942, Isabel Florence Brannan; one *s* three *d*. *Educ:* Univ. of British Columbia; Anglican Theological Coll. of BC. Vicar of St Peter's, Seal Cove, 1943–45; SCM Secretary, Univ. of Manitoba, 1945–59; Staff of St John's Coll., Winnipeg, 1947–48; Rector: St John the Baptist, Fort Garry, 1949–55; St Jude's, Winnipeg, 1955–60; Dir, Diocesan Council for Social Service, Diocese of Rupert's Land, and Priest Dir of Indian Work, 1960–64; Associate Sec., Council for Social Service, Anglican Church of Canada, 1964–66; Bishop of Kootenay, 1966–71. Moderator of Executive and Central Cttees, WCC, 1975–83; Pres., Canadian Council of Churches, 1985–. Mem. Commonwealth Eminent Persons Gp on South Africa, Dec. 1985–June 1986. DD Lambeth, 1986; Hon. DD: Anglican Theol Coll., BC, 1966; Trinity Coll., Toronto, 1971; Wycliffe Coll., Toronto, 1971; Huron Coll., Ont., 1973; United Theol Coll., Montreal, 1971; Renison Coll., Waterloo; Coll. of Emmanuel & St Chad, Saskatoon, 1979; Univ. of Victoria Coll., Toronto, 1986; Queen's Univ., Kingston, 1987; Hon. DCL St John's Coll., Winnipeg, 1971; Hon. STD: Dio. Theol Coll., Montreal, 1973; Thorneloe Coll., Ont., 1974; Hon. LLD York, 1987. Human Relations Award, Canadian CCJ, 1987. *Recreation:* carpentry. *Address:* 29 Hawthorn Avenue, Toronto, Ont M4W 2Z1, Canada.

SCOTT, Esme, (Lady Scott), CBE 1985; WS; Chair, Volunteer Development Scotland, since 1989; *b* 7 Jan. 1932; *d* of David Burnett, SSC and Jane Burnett (*née* Thornton); *m* 1st, 1956, Ian Macfarlane Walker, WS (*d* 1988); one *s*; 2nd, 1990, Sir Kenneth Scott, *qv*; one step *s* one step *d*. *Educ:* St George's School for Girls, Edinburgh; Univ. of Edinburgh (MA, LLB). NP; Mem., Law Soc. of Scotland; Vice-Pres., Inst. of Trading Standards Admin. Lectr in Legal Studies, Queen Margaret College, Edinburgh, 1977–83. Voluntary worker, Citizens' Advice Bureau, 1960–85; Chm., Scottish Assoc. of CABx, 1986–88. Comr, Equal Opportunities Commn, 1986–90. Chm., Scottish Consumer Council, 1980–85; Vice-Chm., Nat. Consumer Council, 1984–87; Member: Expert Cttee, Multiple Surveys and Valuations (Scotland), 1982–84; Working Party on Procedure for Judicial Review of Admin. Action, 1983–84; Cttee on Conveyancing, 1984; Scottish Cttee, Council on Tribunals, 1986–; Court, Edinburgh Univ., 1989–; Volunteer Centre UK Bd, 1989–; Social Security Adv. Cttee, 1990–; Direct Mail Services Standards Bd, 1990–; Privacy Adv. Cttee, Common Services Agency, 1990–. FRSA. *Recreation:* crosswords. *Address:* 13 Clinton Road, Edinburgh EH9 2AW. *T:* 031–447 5191; 25A Friary Court, St James's Palace, SW1A 1BJ. *T:* 071–839 6579. *Club:* New (Edinburgh).

SCOTT, Dr Graham Alexander; Consultant in Public Health Medicine, Borders Health Board, since 1990; *b* 26 Nov. 1927; *s* of Alexander Scott and Jessie Scott; *m* 1951, Helena Patricia Margaret Cavanagh; two *s* one *d*. *Educ:* Daniel Stewart's Coll., Edinburgh; Edinburgh Univ. (MB, ChB). FRCPE, FFCM, DPH. RAAMC, 1951–56 (Dep. Asst Dir, Army Health, 1st Commonwealth Div., Korea, 1953–54). Sen. Asst MO, Stirling CC, 1957–62, Dep. County MO, 1962–65; Scottish Home and Health Department: MO, 1965–68; SMO, 1968–74; PMO, 1974–75; Dep. CMO, 1975–89. QHP 1987–90. *Recreations:* gardening, walking. *Address:* Rosemains, Pathhead, Midlothian EH37 5UQ.

SCOTT, Hardiman; *see* Scott, P. H.

SCOTT, Sir Ian Dixon, KCMG 1962 (CMG 1959); KCVO 1965; CIE 1947; *b* Inverness, 6 March 1909; *s* of Thomas Henderson Scott, OBE, MICE, and Mary Agnes Dixon, Selkirk; *m* 1937, Hon. Anna Drusilla Lindsay, *d* of 1st Baron Lindsay of Birker, CBE, LLD; one *s* four *d*. *Educ:* Queen's Royal College, Trinidad; Balliol College, Oxford (MA); London School of Economics. Entered Indian Civil Service, 1932; Indian Political Service, 1935; Assistant Director of Intelligence, Peshawar, 1941; Principal, Islamia College, Peshawar, 1943; Deputy Private Secretary to the Viceroy of India, 1945–47. Dep. Dir of Personnel, John Lewis & Co. Ltd, 1948–50. Appointed to Foreign Service, 1950; First Secretary, Foreign Office, 1950–51; British Legation, Helsinki, 1952; British Embassy, Beirut, 1954; Counsellor, 1956; Chargé d'Affaires, 1956, 1957, 1958; idc 1959; Consul-General, then Ambassador to the Congo, 1960–61; Ambassador to Sudan, 1961–65, to Norway, 1965–68. Chm., Clarksons Holidays Ltd, 1972–73 (Dir, 1968–73). Chm., Suffolk AHA, 1973–77; Member: Council, Dr Barnardo's, 1970–84 (Chm., 1972–78; elected Vice-Pres., 1984–); Bd of Governors, Felixstowe Coll., 1971–84 (Chm., 1972–78); Chm., Indian Civil Service (retd) Assoc., 1977–. *Publication:* Tumbled House, 1969. *Recreation:* sailing. *Address:* Ash House, Alde Lane, Aldeburgh, Suffolk IP15 5DZ.

SCOTT, Prof. Ian Richard, PhD; Barber Professor of Law, since 1978, and Dean of the Faculty of Law, since 1985, University of Birmingham; *b* 8 Jan. 1940; *s* of Ernest and Edith Scott; *m* 1971, Ecce Cole; two *d*. *Educ:* Geelong Coll.; Queen's Coll., Univ. of Melbourne (LLB); King's Coll., Univ. of London (PhD). Barrister and Solicitor, Supreme Court of Victoria. Dir, Inst. of Judicial Admin, 1975–82. Exec. Dir, Victoria Law Foundn, 1982–84. Mem., Lord Chancellor's Civil Justice Review Body, 1985–88; Chm., N Yorks Magistrates' Courts Inquiry, 1989. Hon. Bencher, Gray's Inn, 1988. *Recreation:* law. *Address:* Faculty of Law, University of Birmingham, Birmingham B15 2TT. *T:* 021–414 6291.

SCOTT, Jack Hardiman; *see* Scott, (Peter) Hardiman.

SCOTT, Prof. James Alexander, CBE 1986; Regional Medical Officer, Trent Regional Health Authority, 1973–88, retired; Special Professor of Health Care Planning, Nottingham University, since 1974; Professor Associate in Health Service Planning, Department of Community Medicine, Sheffield University, since 1988; *b* 3 July 1931; *s* of Thomas Scott, MA Oxon and Margaret L. Scott; *m* 1957, Margaret Olive Slinger, BA, SRN; one *s* two *d*. *Educ:* Doncaster Grammar Sch.; Trinity Coll., Dublin Univ. BA 1953; MB, BCh, BAO 1955; MA, MD 1965; FFCM 1974; FRCP 1985. Pathologist, Sir Patrick Dun's Hosp., Dublin, 1957–59; Registrar in Clinical Pathology, United Sheffield Hosps, 1959–61; Trainee, later Asst and Principal Asst Sen. MO, Sheffield RHB, 1961–70; Sen. Lectr in Community Medicine, Nottingham Univ., 1967–71; Sen. Admin. MO, Sheffield RHB, 1971–73. Chm., English Regional MOs Gp, 1978–80; Pres., Hospital Cttee, EEC, 1980–86; Treas., Fac. of Community Medicine, RCP, 1984–86; Member: Health Services Res. Cttee, MRC, 1986–88; Nat. Cttee for Review of Blood Transfusion Service, 1986–87. Chm., Bd of Govs, Mid-Trent Coll. of Nursing and Midwifery, 1989–. Masur Fellow, Nuffield Provincial Hospitals Trust, 1983. QHP, 1980–83. Hon. LLD Sheffield, 1983. *Publications:* contrib. Lancet. *Recreation:* stamp collecting. *Address:* 5 Slayleigh Lane, Sheffield S10 3RE. *T:* Sheffield (0742) 302238; La Gardelle, 24260 Le Bugue, Dordogne, France.

SCOTT, James Alexander, OBE 1987; FCA; Partner, BDO Binder Hamlyn, Chartered Accountants, since 1969; *b* 30 April 1940; *s* of Douglas McPherson Scott and Mabel Mary (*née* Skepper); *m* 1965, Annette Goslett; three *s* two *d*. *Educ:* Uppingham Sch.; Magdalene Coll., Cambridge (Schol.; MA); London Business Sch. (MSc). Joined BDO Binder Hamlyn, 1961; Man. Partner, London Region, 1980–88; Nat. Man. Partner, 1988–89.

Mem., Agricl Wages Bd for England and Wales, 1971–86; Sec., Review Bd for Govt Contracts, 1969–; Mem., NHS Pharmacists Remuneration Review Panel, 1982. DTI Inspector, Atlantic Computers plc, 1990. *Recreations:* walking, golf, tennis, ski-ing. *Address:* Southbrook, Shrubbs Hill, Chobham, Surrey GU24 8ST. *T:* Chobham (Woking) (0276) 858431. *Clubs:* Berkshire Golf; St Enodoc Golf.

SCOTT, James Archibald, CB 1988; LVO 1961; Chief Executive, Scottish Development Agency, 1990–91; *b* 5 March 1932; *s* of late James Scott, MBE, and Agnes Bone Howie; *m* 1957, Elizabeth Agnes Joyce Buchan-Hepburn; three *s* one *d. Educ:* Dollar Acad.; Queen's Univ. of Ont.; Univ. of St Andrews (MA Hons). RAF aircrew, 1954–56. Asst Principal, CRO, 1956; served in New Delhi, 1958–62, and UK Mission to UN, New York, 1962–65; transf. to Scottish Office, 1965; Private Sec. to Sec. of State for Scotland, 1969–71; Asst Sec., Scottish Office, 1971; Under-Sec., Scottish Economic Planning Dept, later Industry Dept for Scotland, 1976–84; Sec., Scottish Educn Dept, 1984–87; Sec., Industry Dept for Scotland, 1987–90. *Recreations:* music, golf. *Address:* 38 Queen's Crescent, Edinburgh EH9 2BA. *T:* 031–667 8417. *Club:* Travellers'.

SCOTT, James Steel; Professor of Obstetrics and Gynæcology, 1961–89, and Dean of Faculty of Medicine, 1986–89, University of Leeds, now Professor Emeritus; *b* 18 April 1924; *s* of late Dr Angus M. Scott and late Margaret Scott; *m* 1958, Olive Sharpe; two *s. Educ:* Glasgow Academy; University of Glasgow. MB, ChB 1946, MD 1959; FRCSEd 1959; FRCOG 1962 (MRCOG 1953); FRCS (*ad eund*) 1986. Service in RAMC, 1947–49. Liverpool University: Obstetric Tutor, 1954; Lecturer, 1958; Senior Lecturer, 1960. *Publications:* contrib. to New Engl. Jl of Medicine, Lancet, BMJ, Jl of Obst. and Gynæc. of Brit. Empire, Amer. Jl of Obstetrics and Gynæcology, etc. *Recreations:* skiing, biography. *Address:* Byards Lodge, Boroughbridge Road, Knaresborough, N Yorks HG5 0LT.

SCOTT, Sir James (Walter), 2nd Bt, *cr* 1962; JP; Lord-Lieutenant of Hampshire, since 1982; Standard Bearer, HM Body Guard, Hon. Corps of Gentlemen-at-Arms, since 1990 (Member, since 1977); *b* 26 Oct. 1924; *e s* of Col Sir Jervoise Bolitho Scott, 1st Bt, and Kathleen Isabel, *yr d* of late Godfrey Walter, Malshanger, Basingstoke; *S* father 1965; *m* 1951, Anne Constantia, *e d* of late Lt-Col Clive Austin, Roundwood, Micheldever, Hants and the Lady Lilian Austin, *d* of late Brig. Lumley; three *s* one *d* (and one *d* decd). *Educ:* Eton. Lt-Col The Life Guards, formerly Grenadier Guards, retired 1969. Served War of 1939–45: NW Europe, 1944–45. Palestine, 1945–46; ADC to Viceroy and Gov.-Gen. of India, 1946–48; Malaya, 1948–49; Cyprus, 1958, 1960, 1964; Malaysia, 1966. Hon. Colonel: 2nd Bn Wessex Regt (Volunteers), 1985–90; Hants and IoW ACF, 1990–. Underwriting Member of Lloyd's. Master, Mercers' Co., 1976. Chm. Hants Branch, Country Landowners' Assoc., 1981–84. Councillor, Hants CC, 1973–83. DL 1978, High Sheriff 1981–82, JP 1982, Hants. KStJ 1983. *Heir: s* James Jervoise Scott [*b* 12 Oct. 1952; *m* 1982, Mrs Judy Lyndon-Skeggs, *d* of Brian Trafford; one *s* one *d* and two step *d*]. *Address:* Rotherfield Park, Alton, Hampshire GU34 3QL. *T:* Tisted (042058) 204. *Clubs:* Cavalry and Guards, Farmers', Institute of Directors.

SCOTT, Sir John; *see* Scott, Sir P. J.

SCOTT, (John) Brough; Editorial Director, Racing Post, since 1988; Chief Presenter, Channel 4 Racing, since 1985; sports journalist, The Independent on Sunday, since 1990; *b* 12 Dec. 1942; *s* of Mason Hogarth Scott and Irene Florence Scott, Broadway, Worcs; *m* 1973, Susan Eleanor MacInnes; two *s* two *d. Educ:* Radley College; Corpus Christi, Oxford (BA History). Amateur, then professional, Nat. Hunt jockey, 1962–71 (100 winners, incl. Imperial Cup and Mandarin Chase). ITV presenter, sports programmes and documentaries, 1971–; chief racing presenter, ITV, 1979–85; Evening Standard sports correspondent, 1972–74; sports journalist, Sunday Times, 1974–90. Vice-Pres., Jockeys' Assoc., 1969–71; Trustee: Injured Jockeys Fund; Professional Riders' Insurance Scheme; Racing Welfare. Lord Derby Award, 1978 (racing journalist of the year); Clive Graham Trophy, 1982; Sports Journalist of the Year, 1983; Sports Feature Writer of the Year, 1985, 1991. *Publications:* World of Flat Racing, 1983; On and Off the Rails, 1984. *Recreation:* making bonfires. *Address:* 120 Coombe Lane, Raynes Park, SW20 0BA. *T:* 081–879 3377.

SCOTT, Rev. Prof. John Fraser, AO 1990; Vice-Chancellor, La Trobe University, Melbourne, 1977–90; Assistant Curate, St George's, East Ivanhoe, since 1990; *b* 10 Oct. 1928; *s* of Douglas Fraser Scott and Cecilia Louise Scott; *m* 1956, Dorothea Elizabeth Paton Scott; one *s* three *d. Educ:* Bristol Grammar Sch.; Trinity Coll., Cambridge. MA, FIS. Research Asst, Univ. of Sheffield, 1950–53; Asst, Univ. of Aberdeen, 1953–55; Lectr in Biometry, Univ. of Oxford, 1955–65; University of Sussex: Reader in Statistics, 1965–67; Prof. of Applied Statistics, 1967–77; Pro-Vice-Chancellor, 1971–77. Adv. Prof., E China Normal Univ., 1988. Visiting Consultant in Statistics: Nigeria, 1961, 1965; Sweden, 1969; Kuwait, 1973, 1976; Iraq, 1973; Malaysia, 1976. Reader, Church of England, 1971–77; Examining Chaplain to Bp of Chichester, 1974–77; Diocesan Lay Reader, Anglican Dio. of Melbourne, 1977–90; ordained deacon, then priest, 1990. Chairman: Jt Cttee on Univ. Statistics, 1978–86; Cttee of Review of Student Finances, 1983; Aust. Univs Industrial Assoc., 1986–; AVCC, 1986–88 (Dep. Chm., 1986, Chm., Wkg Party on Attrition, 1981–86); Council for Chaplains in Tertiary Instns, 1990; Member: Grad. Careers Council of Aust., 1980–86; Council, 1986–, Exec. Cttee, 1986–88, ACU; ABC Victorian State Adv. Cttee, 1978–81; Pres., Victoria State Libraries Bd, 1990. Editor, Applied Statistics, 1971–76; Mem., Editl Bd, The Statistician, 1987–. DUniv La Trobe, 1990. *Publications:* The Comparability of Grade Standards in Mathematics, 1975; Report of Committee of Review of Student Finances, 1983; papers in JRSS, Lancet, BMJ, Chemistry and Industry, Statistician, etc. *Recreations:* wine, women and song; canals. *Address:* 1/18 Riversdale Road, Hawthorn, Victoria 3122, Australia. *T:* (03) 819 1862. *Club:* Melbourne.

SCOTT, John Gavin, FRCO; Organist and Director of Music, St Paul's Cathedral, since 1990; *b* 18 June 1956; *s* of Douglas Gavin Scott and Hetty Scott (*née* Murphy); *m* 1979, Carolyn Jane Lumsden; one *s* one *d. Educ:* Queen Elizabeth Grammar Sch., Wakefield; St John's Coll., Cambridge (MA, MusB). Asst Organist, Wakefield Cath., 1970–74; Organ Scholar, St John's Coll., Cambridge, 1974–78; Assistant Organist: Southwark Cath., 1978–85; St Paul's Cath., 1978–85; Sub-Organist, St Paul's Cath., 1985–90. Asst Conductor and Accompanist, Bach Choir, 1978–. Hon. RAM 1990. First Prizewinner: Manchester Internat. Organ Fest., 1978; Leipzig Internat. J. S. Bach Competition, 1984. *Recreations:* reading, travel, ecclesiastical architecture. *Address:* 5 Amen Court, EC4M 7BU. *T:* 071–248 6868.

SCOTT, John Hamilton; Vice Lord-Lieutenant for Shetland, since 1983; farming in Bressay and Noss; *b* 30 Nov. 1936; *s* of Dr Thomas Gilbert Scott and Elizabeth M. B. Scott; *m* 1965, Wendy Ronald; one *s* one *d. Educ:* Bryanston; Cambridge Univ.; Guy's Hosp., London. Shepherd, Scrabster, Caithness, 1961–64. Chm., Woolgrowers of Shetland Ltd, 1981–. Pres., Shetland NFU, 1976; Chm., Shetland Crofting, Farming and Wildlife Adv. Gp, 1984–; Mem., Nature Conservancy Council Cttee for Scotland, 1984–91; NE Regl Bd, Nature Conservancy Council for Scotland, 1991–92. *Recreations:* mountain climbing, Up-Helly-Aa, music. *Address:* Gardie House, Bressay, Shetland. *T:* Bressay (059582) 281. *Club:* Alpine.

SCOTT, John James; Managing Director, Dudmass Ltd, since 1983; Associate, Save & Prosper Group, since 1985; *b* 4 Sept. 1924; *s* of late Col John Creagh Scott, DSO, OBE and Mary Elizabeth Marjory (*née* Murray of Polmaise); *m* 1st, Katherine Mary (*née* Bruce); twin *d*; 2nd, Heather Marguerite (*née* Douglas Brown); 3rd, June Rose (*née* Mackie); twin *s. Educ:* Radley (Schol.); Corpus Christi Coll., Cambridge (Schol.); National Inst. for Medical Research, London. War Service, Captain, Argyll and Sutherland Highlanders, 1944–47. BA 1st cl. hons Nat. Sci. Tripos, Pts I and II, 1950, MA 1953, Cantab; PhD London 1954. Senior Lectr in Chem. Pathology, St Mary's Hosp., 1955–61; Mem. Editorial Bd, Biochem. Jl, 1956–61; Mem. Cttee of Biochem. Soc., 1961; Vis. Scientist, Nat. Insts of Health, Bethesda, Md, 1961. Entered Diplomatic Service, 1961; Office of Comr Gen. for SE Asia, Singapore, 1962; Office of Political Adviser to C-in-C, Singapore, 1963; FO, 1966; Counsellor, Rio de Janeiro and Brasilia, 1971; seconded to NI Office as Asst Sec., Stormont, 1974–76; Asst Under-Sec., FCO, 1978–80; Asst Managing Dir, later Commercial Dir, Industrial Engines (Sales) Ltd, Elbar Group, 1980. Francis Bacon Prize, Cambridge, 1950. *Publications:* papers in Biochem. Jl, Proc. Royal Soc. and other learned jls. *Recreations:* botany, photography, music. *Address:* The Cottage, South Rauceby, Sleaford, Lincs NG34 7QG. *T:* South Rauceby (05298) 254. *Clubs:* Carlton, Institute of Directors; Leander (Henley-on-Thames); Hawks (Cambridge); Ski Club of GB.

SCOTT, Sir Kenneth (Bertram Adam), KCVO 1990; CMG 1980; Deputy Private Secretary to the Queen, since 1990; *b* 23 Jan. 1931; *s* of late Adam Scott, OBE, and Lena Kaye; *m* 1st, 1966, Gabrielle Justine (*d* 1977), *d* of R. W. Smart, Christchurch, New Zealand; one *s* one *d*; 2nd, 1990, Esme Walker (*see* Esme Scott); one step *s. Educ:* George Watson's Coll., Edinburgh; Edinburgh Univ. MA Hons 1952. Foreign Office, 1954; Third Sec., Moscow 1956; Second Sec., (Commercial), Bonn, 1958; FO, 1961; First Sec., Washington, 1964; Head of Chancery and Consul, Vientiane, 1968; Counsellor and Head of Chancery, Moscow, 1971; Sen. Officers' War Course, RNC, Greenwich, 1973; Dep. Head, Personnel Ops Dept, FCO, 1973; Counsellor and Head of Chancery, Washington, 1975; Head of E European and Soviet Dept, FCO, 1977; Minister and Dep. UK Perm. Rep. to NATO, 1979–82; Ambassador to Yugoslavia, 1982–85; Asst Private Sec. to the Queen, 1985–90. *Address:* 25a Friary Court, St James's Palace, SW1A 1BJ. *T:* 071–839 6579. *Clubs:* Royal Automobile; New (Edinburgh).

SCOTT, Kenneth Farish, MC 1943 and Bar, 1944; FEng 1979, FICE; Senior Partner, 1977–84, Senior Consultant, 1984–87, Sir Alexander Gibb & Partners; *b* 21 Dec. 1918; *s* of Norman James Stewart and Ethel May Scott; *m* 1945, Elizabeth Mary Barrowcliff; one *s* one *d. Educ:* Stockton Grammar School; Constantine Tech. Coll. Served Royal Engineers, 1939–46. Joined Sir Alexander Gibb & Partners, 1946; Resident Engineer, Hydro-Electric Works, Scotland, 1946–52; Chief Rep., NZ, 1952–55, Scotland, 1955–59; Partner 1959, Senior Partner 1977; responsible for design and supervision of construction of major water resource develt projects, incl. Latiyan Dam, 1959–67, Lar Dam 1968–82, Greater Tehran Water Supply, 1959–82; major maritime works incl. modernisation Devonport Dockyard, 1970–80; internat. airports at Tripoli, 1966–70, Bahrain, 1970–72. Pres., Soc. des Ingénieurs et Scientifiques de France (British Section), 1975; Vice-Pres., ICE, 1985–87. Chm., Assoc. of Consulting Engineers, 1976. Hon. Mem., Instn of RE, 1982. *Publications:* papers to ICE and International Congress of Large Dams. *Recreations:* sailing, golf, wood working. *Address:* Forest House, Brookside Road, Brockenhurst, Hants SO42 7SS. *T:* Lymington (0590) 23531. *Clubs:* Special Forces, Royal Over-Seas League; RE Yacht, Island Sailing (Cowes), Royal Southampton Yacht.

SCOTT, Dame Margaret, (Dame Catherine Margaret Mary Denton), DBE 1981 (OBE 1977); Founding Director of the Australian Ballet School, since 1964; *b* 26 April 1922; *d* of John and Marjorie Douglas-Scott; *m* 1953, Prof. Derek Ashworth Denton, FAA, FRACP; two *s. Educ:* Parktown Convent, Johannesburg, S Africa. Sadler's Wells Ballet, London, 1940–43; Principal: Ballet Rambert, London and Australia, 1944–49; National Ballet, Australia, 1949–50; Ballet Rambert, and John Cranko Group, London, 1951–53; private ballet teaching, Australia, 1953–61; planned and prepared the founding of the Aust. Ballet Sch., 1962–64. Hon. Life Mem., Australian Ballet Foundn, 1988. Hon. LLD Melbourne, 1989. *Recreations:* music, theatre, garden. *Address:* 816 Orrong Road, Toorak, Melbourne, Vic 3142, Australia. *T:* (03) 827 2640. *Club:* Alexandra (Melbourne).

SCOTT, Maurice FitzGerald, FBA 1990; Official Fellow in Economics, Nuffield College, Oxford, since 1968; *b* 6 Dec. 1924; *s* of Colonel G. C. Scott, OBE and H. M. G. Scott; *m* 1953, Eleanor Warren (*née* Dawson) (*d* 1989); three *d. Educ:* Wadham Coll., Oxford (MA); Nuffield Coll., Oxford (BLitt). Served RE, 1943–46. OEEC, Paris, 1949–51; Paymaster-General's Office (Lord Cherwell), 1951–53; Cabinet Office, 1953–54; NIESR, London, 1954–57; Tutor in Economics and Student of Christ Church, Oxford, 1957–68; NEDO, London, 1962–63; OECD, Paris, 1967–68. *Publications:* A Study of U.K. Imports, 1963; (with I. M. D. Little and T. Scitovsky) Industry and Trade in Some Developing Countries, 1970; (with J. D. MacArthur and D. M. G. Newbery) Project Appraisal in Practice, 1976; (with R. A. Laslett) Can We get back to Full Employment?, 1978; (with W. M. Corden and I. M. D. Little) The Case against General Import Restrictions, 1980; A New View of Economic Growth, 1989. *Recreation:* walking. *Address:* 11 Blandford Avenue, Oxford OX2 8EA. *T:* Oxford (0865) 59115. *Club:* Political Economy (Oxford).

SCOTT, Sir Michael, KCVO 1979 (MVO 1961); CMG 1977; HM Diplomatic Service, retired; *b* 19 May 1923; *yr s* of late John Scott and Kathleen Scott; *m* 1st, 1944, Vivienne Sylvia Vincent-Barwood; three *s*; 2nd, 1971, Jennifer Slawikowski (*née* Cameron Smith), *widow* of Dr George J. M. Slawikowski. *Educ:* Dame Allan's School; Durham Univ. War Service: Durham Light Infantry, 1941; 1st Gurkha Rifles, 1943–47. Joined Colonial Office, 1949; CRO, 1957; First Secretary, Karachi, 1958–59; Deputy High Commissioner, Peshawar, 1959–62; Counsellor and Director, British Information Services in India, New Delhi, 1963–65; Head of E and Central Africa Dept, FCO, 1965–68; Dep. High Comr, British High Commn, Nicosia, 1968–72; RCDS, 1973; Ambassador to Nepal, 1974–77; High Comr in Malaŵi, 1977–79; High Comr in Bangladesh, 1980–81. Sec.-Gen., Royal Commonwealth Soc., 1983–88. Dir, Tiger Mountain Gp (Nepal and India), 1984–. Mem., King Mahendra Trust for Nature Conservation (Nepal), 1989–. Member: Governing Council, ODI, 1983–; Council, Internat. Agricl Trng Programme, 1988–. Trustee, Drive for Youth Programme, 1987–. *Address:* 87A Cornwall Gardens, SW7 4AY. *T:* 071–589 6794. *Clubs:* Oriental, Commonwealth Trust.

SCOTT, Maj.-Gen. Michael Frederick, JP; Farmer; *b* 25 Oct. 1911; *s* of Col F. W. Scott, Romsey, Hants; *m* 1961, Laila Wallis (*née* Tatchell). *Educ:* Harrow. Apprenticed as Mechanical Engr to John I. Thornycroft Co. Basingstoke, 1932–35; commnd Lieut, RAOC, 1935; transf. REME 1942. Served: India, 1938–44; Palestine, 1947–48; Germany, 1951–54; Cyprus, 1955–58. Inspector, REME, 1960–63; Commandant Technical Group, REME, 1963–65 (retd); Col Comdt, REME, 1968–73. CEng; FIMechE. JP Somerset, 1967. *Recreations:* sailing, shooting, country pursuits. *Address:* Parsonage Farm, South Barrow, Yeovil, Somerset BA22 7LF. *T:* North Cadbury (0963) 40417. *Club:* Royal Ocean Racing.

SCOTT, Michael John; broadcaster; *b* 8 Dec. 1932; *s* of Tony and Pam Scott; *m* 1956, Sylvia Hudson; one *d. Educ:* Latymer Upper Sch., Hammersmith; Clayesmore, Iwerne

Minster, Dorset. National Service, RAOC, 1951–53. Stagehand with Festival Ballet, and film extra, 1954; TV production trainee, Rank Organization, 1955; Granada TV: joined as floormanager, 1956; Programme Director, 1957; Producer/Performer, daily magazine programme, 1963–65; Presenter, Cinema, 1965–68; Executive Producer, local programmes, 1968–73; World in Action interviewer, and producer/performer of other programmes, 1974–75; Executive Producer and Reporter, Nuts and Bolts of the Economy, 1975–78; Dep. Programme Controller, 1978–79; Prog. Controller, 1979–87; returned to active broadcasting, Autumn 1987, via live daily programme The Time . . . The Place. Director: Channel 4 Television Co., 1984–87; Granada TV, 1978–87. *Recreations:* watching the box, jogging, a 1932 Lagonda, a garden. *Address:* Flat 1, 39 Gloucester Walk, W8. *T:* 071–937 3962.

SCOTT, Rt. Hon. Nicholas (Paul), PC 1989; MBE 1964; JP; MP (C) Chelsea, since Oct. 1974; Minister of State, Department of Social Security (formerly of Health and Social Security), since 1987; *b* 1933; *e s* of late Percival John Scott; *m* 1st, 1964, Elizabeth Robinson (marr. diss. 1976); one *s* two *d;* 2nd, 1979, Hon. Mrs Cecilia Anne Tapsell, *d* of 9th Baron Hawke; one *s* one *d. Educ:* Clapham College. Served Holborn Borough Coun., 1956–59 and 1962–65; contested (C) SW Islington, 1959 and 1964; MP (C) Paddington S, 1966–Feb. 1974; PPS to: Chancellor of the Exchequer, Rt Hon. Iain Macleod, 1970; Home Sec., Rt. Hon. Robert Carr, 1972–74; Parly Under-Sec. of State, Dept of Employment, 1974; Opposition spokesman on housing, 1974–75; Parly Under Sec. of State, 1981–86, Minister of State, 1986–87 Northern Ireland Office. Mem., 1922 Exec. Cttee, 1978–81; Dir, London Office, European Cons. Gp in European Parlt, 1974. Nat. Chm., Young Conservatives, 1963 (Vice-Pres., 1988–89); Chm., Conservative Parly Employment Cttee, 1979–81 (Vice-Chm., 1967–72). Chairman: Westminster Community Relations Council, 1967–72; Paddington Churches Housing Assoc., 1970–76; British Atlantic Gp Younger Politicians, 1970–73; Nat. Pres., Tory Reform Gp. Dep. Chm., British Caribbean Assoc.; Mem. Council, Community Service Volunteers; Governor, British Inst. of Human Rights; Dep. Chm., Youthaid, 1977–79. Mem., Cttee, MCC, 1972–75. Churchwarden, St Margaret's, Westminster, 1971–73. Man. Dir, E. Allom & Co., 1968–70; Chm., Creative Consultants Ltd, 1969–79; Director: A. S. Kerswill Ltd, 1970–81; Eastbourne Printers Ltd, 1970–81; Juniper Studios Ltd, 1970–81; Midhurst White Holdings Ltd, 1977–78; Bonusbond Hldgs Ltd, 1980–81; Bonusplan Ltd, 1977–81; Cleveland Offshore Fund Inc., 1970–81; Throgmorton Securities Ltd, 1970–74; Ede & Townsend, 1977–80; Learplan Ltd, 1978–81; Consultant: Campbell-Johnson Ltd, 1970–76; Roulston & Co. Inc., 1970–78; Lombard North Central Ltd, 1971–74; Clevebourne Investments Ltd, 1974–76; Claremont Textiles Ltd, 1974–76; Procter & Gamble Ltd, 1974–78; Hill & Knowlton (UK) Ltd, 1981; VSO, 1974–76; Council, Bank Staff Assocs, 1968–77. Freeman, City of London, 1979; Liveryman, GAPAN, 1988–. JP London, 1961. *Recreations:* cricket, tennis, golf, flying. *Address:* House of Commons, SW1A 0AA. *Clubs:* Pratt's, Buck's, MCC.

SCOTT, Sir Oliver (Christopher Anderson), 3rd Bt, of Yews, Westmorland, *cr* 1909; Radiobiologist, Richard Dimbleby Cancer Research Department, St Thomas' Hospital, 1982–88; Radiobiologist, 1954–66, Director, 1966–69, British Empire Cancer Campaign Research Unit in Radiobiology; *b* 6 November 1922; *s* of Sir Samuel H. Scott, 2nd Bt and Nancy Lilian (*née* Anderson); *S* father 1960; *m* 1951, Phoebe Ann Tolhurst; one *s* two *d. Educ:* Charterhouse; King's College, Cambridge. Clinical training at St Thomas' Hosp., 1943–46; MRCS, LRCP, 1946; MB, BCh, Cambridge, 1946; MD Cambridge, 1976; Surgeon-Lieutenant RNVR, 1947–49. Dir, Provincial Insurance Co., 1955–64. Hon. Consultant, Inst. of Cancer Res., Sutton, 1974–82. Pres., Section of Oncology, RSM, 1987–88. Mem. Council, Cancer Res. Campaign, 1978–. High Sheriff of Westmorland, 1966. *Publications:* contributions to scientific books and journals. *Recreations:* music, walking. *Heir: s* Christopher James Scott, [*b* 16 Jan. 1955; *m* 1988, Emma, *o d* of Michael Boxhall; one *s*]. *Address:* 31 Kensington Square, W8. *T:* 071–937 8556. *Club:* Brooks's.

SCOTT, Oliver Lester Schreiner; Emeritus Consultant: Skin Department, Charing Cross Hospital, since 1985; South West Metropolitan Regional Hospital Board, since 1985; *b* London, 16 June 1919; *s* of Ralph Lester Scott, FRCSE, and Ursula Hester Schreiner; *m* 1943, Katherine Ogle Branfoot (*d* 1987); two *d. Educ:* Diocesan College, Cape Town; Trinity College, Cambridge; St Thomas's Hospital, London. MRCS, LRCP 1942; MA, MB, BChir, (Cantab) 1943; MRCP (London) 1944. FRCP 1964. Med. Specialist, RAF Med. Branch, 1943–46. Consultant, Medical Insurance Agency, 1976–; former Hon. Consultant: Dispensaire Française; King Edward VII Hosp. for Officers, London. Pres., Dermatology Section, RSocMed, 1977–78; Hon. Treas., Royal Medical Foundn of Epsom Coll.; Hon. Mem., British Assoc. of Dermatologists, (Pres., 1982–83). Chevalier, l'Ordre National du Mérite, France. *Publications:* section on skin disorders in Clinical Genetics, ed A. Sorsby; medical articles in Lancet, British Journal of Dermatology, etc. *Recreations:* fishing, gardening. *Address:* South Lodge, 7 South Side, Wimbledon Common, SW19 4TL. *T:* 081–946 6662.

SCOTT, Paul Henderson, CMG 1974; writer; Rector, Dundee University, since 1989; HM Diplomatic Service, retired 1980; *b* 7 Nov. 1920; *s* of Alan Scott and Catherine Scott (*née* Henderson), Edinburgh; *m* 1953, Beatrice Celia Sharpe; one *s* one *d. Educ:* Royal High School, Edinburgh; Edinburgh University (MA, MLitt). HM Forces, 1941–47 (Major RA). Foreign Office, 1947–53; First Secretary, Warsaw, 1953–55; First Secretary, La Paz, 1955–59; Foreign Office, 1959–62; Counsellor, Havana, 1962–64; Canadian National Defence College, 1964–65; British Deputy Commissioner General for Montreal Exhibition, 1965–67; Counsellor and Consul-General, Vienna, 1968–71; Head of British Govt Office, 1971, Consul-Gen., 1974–75, Montreal; Research Associate, IISS, 1975–76; Asst Under Sec., FO (negotiator on behalf of EEC Presidency for negotiations with USSR, Poland and East Germany), 1977; Minister and Consul-General, Milan, 1977–80. Chairman: Adv. Council for the Arts in Scotland, 1981–; Steering Cttee for a Scottish Nat. Theatre, 1988–; Mem., Constitutional Steering Cttee, which drew up A Claim of Right for Scotland, published 1988; Dep. Chm., Saltire Soc., 1981–87; Member: Council, Nat. Trust for Scotland, 1981–87; Assoc. for Scottish Literary Studies, 1981–; Scots Language Soc., 1981–; Cockburn Assoc., 1982–85; Council, Edinburgh Internat. Fest., 1984–87. Mem., NEC, SNP, 1989–; Convener, Scottish Centre for Econ. and Social Res., 1990–. Grosse Goldene Ehrenzeichen, Austria, 1969. *Publications:* 1707: The Union of Scotland and England, 1979; (ed with A. C. Davis) The Age of MacDiarmid, 1980; Walter Scott and Scotland, 1981; (ed) Walter Scott's Letters of Malachi Malagrowther, 1981; (ed) Andrew Fletcher's United and Separate Parliaments, 1982; John Galt, 1985; In Bed with an Elephant, 1985; (ed with George Bruce) A Scottish Postbag, 1986; The Thinking Nation, 1989; Towards Independence, 1991; articles and book reviews esp. in Economist, Scotsman and other periodicals. *Recreations:* ski-ing, sailing. *Address:* 33 Drumsheugh Gardens, Edinburgh. *T:* 031–225 1038. *Clubs:* New, Scottish Arts (Edinburgh).

SCOTT, Sir Peter; *see* Scott, Sir C. P.

SCOTT, Peter Denys John, QC 1978; *b* 19 April 1935; *s* of John Ernest Dudley Scott and Joan G. Steinberg. *Educ:* Monroe High Sch., Rochester, NY, USA; Balliol Coll., Oxford (MA). Second Lieut, RHA, Lieut (TA), National Service, 1955. Called to the Bar, Middle Temple (Harmsworth Scholar), 1960, Bencher, 1984; Standing Counsel: to Dir, Gen. of Fair Trading, 1973–78; to Dept of Employment, 1974–78. Member: Home Sec's Cttee on Prison Disciplinary System, 1984; Interception of Communications Tribunal, 1986–; Lord Chancellor's Adv. Cttee on Legal Educn and Conduct, 1991–. Vice-Chm., Senate of the Inns of Court and the Bar, 1985–86; Chm., General Council of the Bar, 1987; Mem., Senate and Bar Council, 1981–87; Chm., London Common Law Bar Assoc., 1983–85. Chm., N Kensington Amenity Trust, 1981–85. *Recreations:* gardening, theatre. *Address:* 4 Eldon Road, W8. *T:* 071–937 3301.

SCOTT, (Peter) Hardiman, OBE 1989; Chief Assistant to Director General BBC, 1975–80; *b* King's Lynn, 2 April 1920; named Jack Hardiman Scott at birth; *s* of Thomas Hardiman Scott and Dorothy Constance Smith; *m* 1st, 1942, Sheilah Stewart Roberts (marr. diss.); two *s;* 2nd, Patricia Mary (Sue) Windle. *Educ:* Grammar Sch.; privately. Northampton Chronicle and Echo series, 1939; then various provincial newspapers; Associated Press, and finally Hants and Sussex News, when began freelance broadcasting, 1948. Joined BBC; Asst News Editor Midland Region, 1950; gen. reporting staff, London, 1954; various foreign assignments, incl. Suez war; BBC's first Polit. Corresp., 1960; subseq. first Polit. Editor until 1975. Member: Study Gp on Future of Broadcasting in Zimbabwe, 1980; Broadcasting Complaints Commn, 1981–89. Pres., Suffolk Poetry Soc., 1979–. *Publications:* Secret Sussex, 1949; (ed) How Shall I Vote?, 1976; Many a Summer, 1991; *poems:* Adam and Eve and Us, 1946; When the Words are Gone, 1972; Part of Silence, 1984; *novels:* Within the Centre, 1946; The Lonely River, 1950; Text for Murder, 1951; Operation 10, 1982; No Exit, 1984; Deadly Nature, 1985; (with Becky Allan) Bait of Lies, 1986; contribs to: TV and Elections, 1977; BBC Guide to Parliament, 1979; Politics and the Media, 1980. *Recreations:* poetry, paintings, listening to music, conservation, East Anglia. *Address:* 4 Butchers Lane, Boxford, via Colchester CO6 5DZ. *T:* Boxford (Suffolk) (0787) 210320.

SCOTT, Sir (Philip) John, KBE 1987; FRCP; FRACP; FRSNZ; Professor of Medicine, University of Auckland, since 1975; *b* 26 June 1931; *s* of Horace McD. Scott and Doris A. Scott (*née* Ruddock); *m* 1956, Elizabeth Jane MacMillan; one *s* three *d. Educ:* Univ. of Otago (BMedSci; MB, ChB); Univ. of Birmingham (MD). Qual. in medicine, Dunedin, 1955; hosp. and gen. practice experience, Auckland, 1956–58; postgrad. trng, RPMS, London, 1959–60; Queen Elizabeth Hosp. and Univ. of Birmingham, 1960–62; Med. Res. Fellowships, Auckland, 1962–68; Sen. Lectr, Univ. of Otago, based on Auckland Hosp., 1969–72; University of Auckland: Sen. Lectr, 1970–72; Associate Prof., 1973–75; Hd, Dept of Medicine, the Univ.'s Sch. of Medicine, 1979–87. Res. interests in lipoprotein metabolism, arterial disease, human nutrition, med. econs and educn, professional ethics. *Publications:* (first author/co-author) articles in sci./med. jls and in press, on aspects of coronary artery disease, atherosclerosis, lipoprotein metabolism, human nutrition, ethical issues. *Recreations:* music, pottery, gardening. *Address:* 64 Temple Street, Meadowbank, Auckland 5, New Zealand. *T:* (64)–(9)–521–5384.

SCOTT, Sheriff Richard John Dinwoodie; Sheriff of Lothian and Borders at Edinburgh, since 1986; *b* 28 May 1939; *s* of late Prof. Richard Scott and Mary Ellen Maclachlan; *m* 1969, Josephine Moretta Blake; two *d. Educ:* Edinburgh Academy; Univ. of Edinburgh (MA, LLB) (Vans Dunlop Schol. in Evidence and Pleading, 1963). Lektor in English, British Centre, Sweden, 1960–61; Tutor, Faculty of Law, Univ. of Edinburgh, 1964–72; admitted to Faculty of Advocates, 1965; Standing Jun. Counsel to Min. of Defence (Air) in Scotland, 1968–77. Sheriff of Grampian, Highland and Islands, at Aberdeen and Stonehaven, 1977–86. Hon. Lectr, Univ. of Aberdeen, 1980–86. *Publications:* various articles in legal jls. *Address:* Sheriff Court House, Lawnmarket, Edinburgh EH1 2NS.

SCOTT, Hon. Sir Richard (Rashleigh Folliott), Kt 1983; **Hon. Mr Justice Scott;** a Judge of the High Court of Justice, Chancery Division, since 1983; *b* 2 Oct. 1934; *s* of Lt-Col C. W. F. Scott, 2/9th Gurkha Rifles and Katharine Scott (*née* Rashleigh); *m* 1959, Rima Elisa, *d* of Salvador Ripoll and Blanca Korsi de Ripoll, Panama City; two *s* two *d. Educ:* Michaelhouse Coll., Natal; Univ. of Cape Town (BA); Trinity Coll., Cambridge (BA, LLB). Bigelow Fellow, Univ. of Chicago, 1958–59. Called to Bar, Inner Temple, 1959, Bencher, 1981. QC 1975; Attorney Gen., 1980–83, Vice-Chancellor, 1987–91, Duchy and County Palatine of Lancaster. Chm. of the Bar, 1982–83 (Vice-Chm., 1981–82). *Recreations:* hunting, tennis, bridge; formerly Rugby (Cambridge Blue, 1957). *Address:* Royal Courts of Justice, Strand, WC2. *Clubs:* Hawks (Cambridge); Vanderbilt Racquet.

SCOTT, Robert, CBE 1976; Director, Polytechnic, Wolverhampton, 1969–77, retired; *b* 7 July 1913; 2nd *s* of H. Scott, Westhoughton, Bolton; *m* 1940, Dorothy M. Howell, Westhoughton; one *s* one *d. Educ:* Hindley and Abram Grammar Sch., Lancs; Univ. of Liverpool; St John's Coll., Cambridge (Wrangler; MA). BSc 1st cl. hons 1934, DipEd 1937, Liverpool; BA Cantab, 1936; FIMA. Asst Master, Newton-le-Willows Grammar Sch., 1937–41; Army and WO Staff, 1941–46; Scientific Civil Service at RMCS Shrivenham, 1946–54; Vice-Principal, Bolton Techn. Coll., 1954–57; Principal, Wolverhampton and Staffs Coll. of Technology, 1958–69. *Recreations:* motoring, reading. *Address:* 25 Market Road, Battle, E Sussex TN33 0XA. *T:* Battle (04246) 4328.

SCOTT, Col Robert Edmond Gabriel, MBE 1959; MC 1953; Director General, Engineering Industries Association, 1981–82; *b* 3 Aug. 1920; *s* of Edmond James and Lilian Kate Scott; *m* 1942, Anna Maria Larkin; two *s. Educ:* Roan, Greenwich. Commissioned into Durham Light Inf., 1942; regimental service with this regt in Western Desert, Italy, Korea and Rhine Army, 1942–52; Staff duties, MoD and Eastern Comd, 1952–56; service with W African Frontier Force, 1956–60; comd inf. batt., Home Service, 1960–66; seconded to Diplomatic Service, as Defence Adviser, Lagos, 1966–70; Dep. Comd, W. Midland Dist, 1970–72; retired, 1972. Engineering Industries Association: Export Sec. and Dep. Dir, 1973–77; Dir, 1977–81. *Recreations:* rough shooting, country pursuits, philately. *Address:* Zaria, 22 Crail Close, Wokingham, Berks RG11 2PZ. *T:* Wokingham (0734) 776595.

SCOTT, Robin; *see* Scutt, R. H.

SCOTT, Ronald, OBE 1981; musician; *b* 28 Jan. 1927. *Educ:* Jews' Infant Sch., Aldgate, E1; Benthal Road Elementary Sch., N16; Central Foundation Sch., Cowper St, E1. Musician (Tenor Saxophone), 1943–. Opened Ronnie Scott's Club, 1959 (Director, with Pete King). *Publication:* (with Michael Hennessey) Some of My Best Friends are Blues, 1979; *relevant publication:* Let's Join Hands and Contact the Living (biography), by John Fordham, 1989. *Recreation:* motor sport. *Address:* 47 Frith Street, W1. *T:* 071–439 0747. *Club:* just his own.

SCOTT, Sir Terence Charles Stuart M.; *see* Morrison-Scott.

SCOTT, Prof. Thomas Frederick McNair, MA Cantab, MD Cantab, MRCS; FRCP; Associate Director of Ambulatory Pediatrics, 1983–85, retired, now Emeritus Professor of Paediatrics, Hahnemann University (Professor of Paediatrics, 1974, Co-ordinator of Ambulatory Care Teaching, 1974–75, and Co-Director of Ambulatory Paediatrics, 1975–83, Hahnemann Medical College and Hospital); Senior Physician, The Children's Hospital of Philadelphia, 1940–69, now Physician Emeritus; *b* 18 June 1901; *e s* of Robert

Frederick McNair Scott, MB, ChB (Edin.), and Alice Nystrom; *m* 1936, Mary Dwight Baker, PhD (Radcliffe), *o d* of late Clarence Dwight Baker, Wisconsin, USA; one *s* one *d*. *Educ:* Cheltenham College; Caius College, Cambridge (Scholar). Natural Science Tripos Pt I Class I, Part II (Physiology) Class II; Junior University Entrance Scholarship to St George's Hospital, 1924; Brackenbury Prize in Medicine, 1926; Qualified conjoint board, 1927; MRCP 1928; FRCP 1953; MD (Cantab) 1938; Casualty Officer, House Surgeon, House Physn, Resident Obst. Asst, Medical Registrar, at St George's Hospital, 1927–29; House Physician Queens Hospital for Children, 1930; Research Fellow of Medicine, Harvard University, Mass, USA, 1930–31; Instructor in Pædiatrics Johns Hopkins University, Baltimore, Md, USA, 1931–34; Assistant Resident Physician at Hospital of Rockefeller Institute for Medical Research, New York, USA, working on Virus diseases, 1934–36; Assistant Physician i/c of Children's Out-patients, Lecturer in Children's Diseases, at St George's Hospital, SW1, Assistant Physician at Queens Hospital for Children, E2, 1936–38; Prof. of Pediatrics, Temple Univ. Med. Sch., Philadelphia, 1938–40; Research Prof. of Pediatrics, Univ. of Pennsylvania, 1940–66, Prof. of Paediatrics, 1966–69, now Emeritus. Dist. Service Award, The Children's Hosp. of Philadelphia, 1977; Corp. medal, Hahnemann Med. Coll., 1978; Alumni Award, Children's Hosp. Alumni Orgn, 1989. Elected Faculty Mem., Medical Students' Honor Soc. (AOA), 1981. *Publications:* Papers on Cytology and Blood diseases, Lead poisoning in children, Virus diseases of the central nervous system, Herpes simplex infections, Common exanthemata, History of measles and herpes. *Address:* 2 Franklin Town Boulevard 1605, Philadelphia, Pennsylvania 19103, USA.

SCOTT, Thora; *see* Hird, T.

SCOTT, Sir Walter, 4th Bt, *cr* 1907; DL; *b* 29 July 1918; *s* of Sir Walter Scott, 3rd Bt, and Nancie Margot, *d* of S. H. March; *S* father, 1967; *m* 1945, Diana Mary, *d* of J. R. Owen; one *s* one *d*. *Educ:* Eton; Jesus College, Cambridge. Served 1st Royal Dragoons, 1939–46; Temp. Major, 1945. JP East Sussex, 1963; DL East Sussex, 1975. *Recreations:* field sports. *Heir: s* Walter John Scott [*b* 24 Feb. 1948; *m* 1st, 1969, Lowell Patria (marr. diss. 1971), *d* of late Pat Vaughan Goddard, Auckland, NZ; one *d*; 2nd, 1977, Mary Gavin, *d* of Alexander Fairly Anderson, of Gartocharn, Dunbartonshire; one *s* one *d*]. *Address:* Newhouse Farm, Chalvington, Hailsham, Sussex.

See also Duke of Hamilton and Brandon.

SCOTT, William Clifford Munro, MD; Consulting Psychiatrist, Montreal Children's Hospital, and Montreal General Hospital; *b* 11 March 1903; *o s* of late Rev. Robert Smyth Scott and late Katherine Munro Hopper; *m* 1934, Emmy Luise (marr. diss.), *er d* of late Hugo Böcking; two *s*; *m* 1970, Evelyn Freeman Fitch. *Educ:* Parkdale Collegiate, Toronto; University of Toronto. BSc (Med.), MD (Tor.), DPM (London), LMSSA. James H. Richardson Fellow, Department of Anat., 1922–24; Lectr in Anat. and Physiol., Margaret Eaton Sch. of Phys. Educ., Toronto, 1923–25; Post-Grad. Educ. in Psychiatry: Johns Hopkins Med. Sch., 1928–29; Boston Psychopathic Hosp., Harvard Univ. Med. Sch., 1929–30; Commonwealth Fund Fellow, Dept of Psychiatry, Harvard Univ., 1930–33; studied at Nat. Hosp., Queen Sq., London, 1931–32, and at Inst of Psycho-Analysis, London, 1931–33. Staff positions Maudsley Hosp., 1933–35, Cassel Hosp., 1935–38; private practice, 1938–. EMS Psychiatrist, Min. of Health, London, Sheffield and S Wales, 1939–46; Psychiatric Cons. to St Dunstan's, 1945. Mem. Cttee of Management, Inst. of Psychiatry (Univ. of London), 1951–53; Med. Dir London Clinic of Psycho-Analysis, 1947–53; Senior Psychotherapist, Bethlem Royal Hosp. and Maudsley Hosp., 1948–54; Teacher Inst. of Psychiatry (Univ. of London), 1948–54; Associate Professor in charge of Training in Psycho-Analysis, Department of Psychiatry, McGill University, Montreal, 1954–59; Post-Grad. Teacher (Psychiatry and Psycho-Analysis), 1945–. Chm. Psychotherapy and Social Psychiatry Section, Roy. Medico-Psychological Assoc., 1952–54; Pres. Brit. Psycho-Analytical Soc., 1953–54; Mem. Bd Dirs, Inst. of Psycho-Analysis, 1947–54 (Chm. 1954); Director of Canadian Inst. of Psycho-Analysis, 1965–67. FRCPsych; FBPsS; ex-Chm. Med. Sect. and Mem. Council, Brit. Psychological Soc.; ex-Mem. Cttee Sect. Psychiatry; Roy. Soc. Med.; Amer. Psychiatric Assoc.; Vice-Pres., Psychiatric Sect., BMA, 1952 and 1955; ex-Asst Ed. Internat. Jl Psycho-Analysis; ex-Asst Ed., Brit. Jl Med. Psychology. Mem., Montreal AAA. *Publications:* chiefly in Brit. Jl of Med. Psychol. and Internat. Jl of Psycho-Analysis. *Recreations:* people and books. *Address:* 488 Mount Pleasant, Westmount, Quebec H3Y 3H3, Canada.

SCOTT, Rear-Adm. Sir (William) David (Stewart), KBE 1977; CB 1974; *b* 5 April 1921; *y s* of Brig. H. St G. Scott, CB, DSO and Ida Christabel Trower Scott (*née* Hogg); *m* 1952, Pamela Dorothy Whitlock; one *s* two *d*. *Educ:* Tonbridge. Naval Cadet, 1938; comd HM Submarines: Umbra, 1944; Vulpine, Satyr, 1945; Andrew, 1953; Thermopylae, 1955; comd HM Ships: Gateshead, 1951; Surprise, 1960; Adamant, 1963; Fife, 1969; Chief of British Navy Staff, Washington, UK Rep. to SACLANT, and Naval Attaché to USA, 1971–73; Deputy Controller, Polaris, 1973–76; Chief Polaris Executive, 1976–80; Comdr 1956; Captain 1962; Rear-Adm. 1971. FInstD 1979. *Address:* c/o Lloyds Bank, 6 Pall Mall, SW1Y 5NH.

SCOTT, (William) Donald, CBE 1968; MA (Oxon); BSc (Yale); *b* 22 May 1903; *s* of late Reverend William Scott and Sara Jane (*née* Platt); *m* 1928, Muriel Barbara, *d* of late Louis F. Rothschild, NYC; two *s* one *d*. *Educ:* Taunton Sch., Taunton; Univ. College, Oxford (open scholar); Yale University, USA (Henry P. Davison Scholar). Hercules Powder Co., USA and Rotterdam, 1926–28; British Paint & Lacquer Co., Cowley, Oxford, 1928–35; ICI Ltd: Nobel Div., 1935–41; Dyestuffs Div., 1941–43; Southern Sales Region, Dep. Regional Manager, 1943–45; Regional Manager, 1945–51; Billingham Div., Jt Man. Dir, 1951–55; Main Board Director, 1954–65. Director, 1952–60, and Chairman, 1956–60, Scottish Agricultural Industries Ltd; Chm., Home Grown Cereals Authority, 1965–68; Director: Canadian Industries Ltd, 1957–62; Glaxo Group Ltd, 1965–68; Laporte Industries Ltd, 1965–68. Mem., Western Hemisphere Exports Council, 1961–64. FRSA 1968. *Recreations:* cricket, golf. *Address:* 42 Cumberland Terrace, Regent's Park, NW1 4HP.

SCOTT, Rev. W(illiam) G.; *see* Gardiner-Scott.

SCOTT, William Wootton, CB 1990; Under Secretary, Industry Department for Scotland, 1985–90; *b* 20 May 1930; *s* of Dr Archibald C. Scott and Barbara R. Scott; *m* 1958, Margaret Chandler, SRN; three *s* one *d*. *Educ:* Kilmarnock Academy; Dollar Academy; Glasgow Univ. (MA, 1st Cl. Hons History). National Service in Royal Artillery, 1952–54. Assistant Principal, 1954, Principal, 1958, Min. of Transport and Civil Aviation; Principal Private Sec. to Minister of Transport, 1965–66; Asst Sec., 1966; Regional Controller (Housing and Planning), Northern Regional Office of DoE, 1971–74; joined Scottish Development Dept, 1974, Under Sec., 1978. *Publications:* occasional historical notes. *Recreations:* historical research, music, gardening, reading. *Address:* Thornleigh, Kippford, Dalbeattie, DG5 4LJ. *T:* Kippford (055662) 641. *Clubs:* Commonwealth Trust; Scottish Arts (Edinburgh).

SCOTT-BARRETT, Lt-Gen. Sir David (William), KBE 1976 (MBE 1956); MC 1945; GOC Scotland and Governor of Edinburgh Castle, 1976–79; Chairman, Army Cadet Force Association, since 1982; *b* 16 Dec. 1922; 2nd *s* of late Brig. Rev. H. Scott-Barrett, CB, CBE; *m* 1948, Marie Elise (*d* 1985), *d* of late Norman Morris; three *s*. *Educ:* Westminster School. Commnd Scots Guards, 1942; served NW Europe, 3rd Armd Bn Scots Guards; GSO3 Gds Div., 1948; Co. Comdr 2nd Bn Malaya, 1951; GSO2, 1st Div., 1955; DS Camberley, 1961; Comdt Gds Depot, 1963; GSO1, 4th Div. BAOR, 1965; comd 6 Inf. Bde BAOR, 1967; idc 1970; GOC Eastern District, 1971–73; GOC Berlin, 1973–75. Col Comdt, Scottish Div., 1976–79; Hon. Col, 205 (Scottish) Gen. Hosp., RAMC, TAVR, 1981–88. *Address:* Hall House, Kersey, Ipswich, Suffolk IP7 6DZ. *T:* Hadleigh (0473) 822365. *Club:* Cavalry and Guards.

SCOTT-BOWDEN, Maj.-Gen. Logan, CBE 1972 (OBE 1964); DSO 1944; MC 1944 and Bar 1946; *b* 21 Feb. 1920; *s* of late Lt-Col Jonathan Scott-Bowden, OBE, TD, and Mary Scott-Bowden (*née* Logan); *m* 1950, Helen Jocelyn, *d* of late Major Sir Francis Caradoc Rose Price, 5th Bt, and late Marjorie Lady Price; three *s* three *d*. *Educ:* Malvern Coll.; RMA Woolwich. Commissioned Royal Engineers, 1939; served in War of 1939–45: Norway, 1940; Adjt, 53rd (Welsh) Div. RE, 1941; Liaison Duties in Canada and USA, 1942; Normandy Beach Reconnaissance Team (Major), 1943; OC 17 Fd Co RE, NW Europe, 1944; psc 1945; Singapore, Burma (Bde Maj. 98 Indian Inf. Bde), Palestine, Libya, 1946–51; Korea, 1953; jssc 1956; Arabia, 1958–60 (Lt-Col 1959); CRE 1st Div., BAOR, 1960; Head, UK Land Forces Planning Staff, 1963; Asst Dir, Def. Plans MoD (Col), 1964; Comd Trg Bde RE (Brig.), 1966; Nat. Defence Coll. (India), 1969; Comd Ulster Defence Regiment, 1970–71; Head of British Defence Liaison Staff, India, 1971–74, retd 1974. Col Comdt RE, 1975–80. *Recreations:* riding, ski-ing, travel.

SCOTT-ELLIOT, Aydua Helen, CVO 1970 (MVO 1958); FSA; retired 1970; *b* 1909; *d* of late Lewis Alexander Scott-Elliot and of Princess Eydua Odescalchi. *Educ:* St Paul's Girls' School and abroad. Temp. Asst Civilian Officer, Admty, 1941–46; Keeper of Prints and Drawings, Royal Library, Windsor Castle, 1946–69. *Publications:* articles in Burlington Magazine, Apollo, Papers of the Bibliographical Soc. of America, etc. *Address:* Shaldon, Mayfield, East Sussex. *Club:* University Women's.

SCOTT ELLIOT, Major-General James, CB 1954; CBE 1945 (OBE 1940); DSO 1943, Bar 1944; HM Lieutenant of the County of Dumfries, 1962–67; *b* 6 Nov. 1902; *s* of late Lt-Col W. Scott Elliot, DSO and Marie Theresa Scott Elliot (*née* Lyon); *m* 1st, 1932, Cecil Margaret Du Buisson; one *s* two *d*; 2nd, 1971, Mrs Fay Courtauld. *Educ:* Wellington College; Sandhurst. 2nd Lieut KOSB, 1923; Capt. Argyll and Sutherland Highlanders, 1936; psc 1937–38; Major, 1940; served in Egypt, China, India, Malta, Palestine. War of 1939–45: France, N Africa, Sicily, Italy; Temp. Lt-Col 1941; Temp. Brig. 1944; despatches, 1945; Germany, 1946–47; War Office, 1948–49; Maj.-Gen., 1954; GOC 51st (Highland) Division and Highland Dist, 1952–56; retd, 1956. Colonel King's Own Scottish Borderers, 1954–61. President: Dumfries and Galloway Natural History and Antiquarian Soc., 1962–65; Soc. of Antiquaries of Scotland, 1965–67; Brit. Soc. of Dowsers, 1966–75. *Publication:* Dowsing One Man's Way, 1977. *Address:* 14 King Street, Emsworth, Hants PO10 7AZ. *T:* Emsworth (0243) 372401. *Club:* Army and Navy.

SCOTT-ELLIS, family name of **Baron Howard de Walden.**

SCOTT-HOPKINS, Major Sir James (Sidney Rawdon), Kt 1981; Member (C) European Parliament, since 1973, elected Member for Hereford and Worcester, since 1979; *b* 29 Nov. 1921; *s* of late Col R. Scott-Hopkins, DSO, MC and late Mrs Scott-Hopkins; *m* 1946, Geraldine Elizabeth Mary Hargreaves, CBE; three *s* one *d*. *Educ:* Eton; Oxford. Army, 1939–50; farming, 1950–59. MP (C) North Cornwall, 1959–66, Derbyshire West, Nov. 1967–1979; Joint Parliamentary Secretary, Ministry of Agriculture, Fisheries and Food, 1962–64. European Parliament: Dep. Leader Cons. Gp and Spokesman on Agric., 1973–79; Vice-Pres., 1976–79; Chm., European Democratic Gp, 1979–82. *Recreations:* riding, shooting. *Address:* 602 Nelson House, Dolphin Square, SW1; Bicknor House, English Bicknor, Coleford, Glos GL16 7PF. *Club:* Carlton.

See also T. J. Smith.

SCOTT-JAMES, Anne Eleanor, (Lady Lancaster); author and journalist; *b* 5 April 1913; *d* of R. A. Scott-James and Violet Brooks; *m* 1st, 1944, Macdonald Hastings (*d* 1982); one *s* one *d*; 2nd, 1967, Sir Osbert Lancaster, CBE (*d* 1986). *Educ:* St Paul's Girls' Sch.; Somerville Coll., Oxford (Class. Schol.). Editorial staff of Vogue, 1934–41; Woman's Editor, Picture Post, 1941–45; Editor, Harper's Bazaar, 1945–51; Woman's Editor, Sunday Express, 1953–57; Woman's Adviser to Beaverbrook Newspapers, 1959–60; Columnist, Daily Mail, 1960–68; freelance journalist, broadcasting, TV, 1968–. Member: Council, RCA, 1948–51, 1954–56; Council, RHS, 1978–82. *Publications:* In the Mink, 1952; Down to Earth, 1971; Sissinghurst: The Making of a Garden, 1975; (with Osbert Lancaster) The Pleasure Garden, 1977; The Cottage Garden, 1981; (with Christopher Lloyd) Glyndebourne—the Gardens, 1983; The Language of the Garden: a personal anthology, 1984; (introd.) Our Village, by Mary Russell Mitford, 1987; The Best Plants for your Garden, 1988; (with Ray Desmond) The British Museum Book of Flowers, 1989; Gardening Letters to My Daughter, 1990. *Recreations:* reading, gardening, travelling looking at churches and flowers. *Address:* 78 Cheyne Court, Royal Hospital Road, SW3 5TT.

See also M. M. Hastings.

SCOTT-JOYNT, Rt. Rev. Michael Charles; *see* Stafford, Bishop Suffragan of.

SCOTT-MALDEN, (Charles) Peter, CB 1966; retired civil servant; *b* 29 June 1918; *e s* of late Gilbert Scott Scott-Malden and Phyllis Dorothy Scott-Malden (*née* Wilkinson); *m* 1941, Jean Honor Chamberlain Silver, *yr d* of late Lt-Col J. P. Silver, CBE, DSO, RAMC; two *s* two *d*. *Educ:* Winchester Coll. (Schol.); King's College, Cambridge (major Scholar). Entered Ministry of Transport, 1939. War of 1939–45; RAMC 1940–41; Glider Pilot Regiment, 1942–45. Min. of Transport (later DoE): Asst Sec., 1949; Under-Sec., 1959; Dep. Sec., 1968, retired, 1976. Member: Transport Tribunal, 1978–88; Management Cttee, Hanover Housing Assoc., 1978–; Nat. Exec. Cttee, Abbeyfield Soc., 1983–90. *Recreations:* music, golf. *Address:* 23 Burdon Lane, Cheam, Surrey SM2 7PP. *T:* 081–642 7086.

SCOTT-MALDEN, Air Vice-Marshal (Francis) David (Stephen), DSO 1942; DFC 1941; RAF (Retd); *b* 26 Dec. 1919; *s* of late Gilbert Scott Scott-Malden and Phyllis Dorothy Wilkinson; *m* 1955, Anne Elizabeth Watson; two *s* two *d*. *Educ:* Winchester Coll. (Scholar; Goddard Scholar, 1938); King's Coll., Cambridge (Scholar, Sir William Browne Medal for Greek Verse, 1939). Joined Cambridge University Air Squadron, Nov. 1938; called up into RAFVR as Pilot Officer, Oct 1939; flying on operations, 1940–42, as Pilot Officer, Flight Lt, Squadron Leader, and Wing Comdr (DFC and Bar, DSO, Norwegian War Cross; Commander, Order of Orange Nassau, 1945). Visited International Youth Assembly at Washington, DC, as rep. of English Universities, and toured USA as member of United Nations delegation, Sept.-Nov. 1942. RAF Selection Board (Dep. Pres.), 1946; on staff of RAF College, 1946–48; Central Fighter Establishment, 1948; RAF Staff Coll., Bracknell, 1951; psa; RAF Flying Coll., 1954–55; pfc; Jt Planning Staff, Min. of Defence, 1955–57; Group Capt. 1958; Imperial Defence College, 1957–59; idc. Dep. Dir Plans, Air Ministry, 1959–61; Air Cdre 1962; Air Vice-Marshal, 1965. Department of Transport, 1966–78. *Recreations:* shooting, fishing, sailing. *Address:*

Roughwood, 1 White House Gardens, Upgate, Poringland, Norwich, Norfolk NR14 7RU. *T:* Framingham Earl (05086) 4779.

SCOTT-MALDEN, Peter; *see* Scott-Malden, C. P.

SCOTT-MILLER, Commander Ronald, VRD 1942; RNVR (retired); *b* 1 Nov. 1904; *s* of late Colonel Walter Scott-Miller, DL; *m* 1932, Stella Louise Farquhar (*d* 1988), *d* of late Farquhar Deuchar, Shortridge Hall, Northumberland. *Educ:* Aldro School, Eastbourne; Uppingham. Joined London Division, RNVR, as Midshipman, 1924; War of 1939–45 (despatches): HMS Dunedin, Northern Patrol, 1939; HMS London, Atlantic, Russian Convoys, 1940–43; Combined Operations, Mediterranean, NW Europe, 1943–45. Commander, 1943; retired, 1946. MP (C) King's Lynn Division of Norfolk, 1951–59; Parliamentary Private Secretary: to Financial Secretary to Treasury, Dec. 1953–July 1954; to Minister of Transport, 1954–56; to Minister of Pensions and National Insurance, 1956–59. Trustee of Uppingham School, 1954–59. Freeman of the City of London, and Liveryman of Worshipful Company of Butchers, 1926. US Legion of Merit (Legionaire), 1943. *Recreations:* shooting, sailing. *Club:* Naval.

SCOTT-MONCRIEFF, William; Under-Secretary for Finance (Health), Department of Health and Social Security, 1977–82; *b* 22 Aug. 1922; *s* of Major R. Scott-Moncrieff and Mrs R. Scott-Moncrieff; *m* 1950, Dora Rosemary Knollys; two *d*. *Educ:* Trinity Coll., Glenalmond; Emmanuel Coll., Cambridge (BA Mech. Sciences). Served RE, 1941–65 (Lt-Col); DHSS (formerly Min. of Social Security), 1965–82. *Recreations:* golf, fishing. *Address:* Combe Cottage, Chiddingfold, Surrey. *T:* Wormley (0428) 682937.

SCOTT-SMITH, Catharine Mary, MA Cantab; Principal of Beechlawn Tutorial College, Oxford, 1966–71, retired; *b* 4 April 1912; *d* of Edward Montagu Scott-Smith and Catharine Lorance (*née* Garland). *Educ:* Wycombe Abbey School, Bucks; Girton College, Cambridge. Classics Mistress: St Katharine's School, Wantage, 1933–37; Godolphin School, Salisbury 1937–41; Classics Mistress and house-mistress, Headington School, Oxford, 1941–47, Second Mistress, 1946–47; Classics Mistress and house-mistress, Wycombe Abbey School, Bucks, 1947–55, Second Mistress, 1951–54; Headmistress of Westonbirt School, Tetbury, Gloucestershire, 1955–64. Member Council: Berkhamsted School for Girls; Berkhamsted School; Mem. Exec. Cttee, GBGSA, 1975–78. Pres., Wycombe Abbey School Seniors, 1974–79. *Address:* Graystones, Lower Waites Lane, Fairlight, Hastings, East Sussex. *T:* Hastings (0424) 813071. *Club:* University Women's.

SCOTT WHYTE, Stuart; *see* Whyte, J. S. S.

SCOTT WRIGHT, Prof. Margaret, PhD; Dean, 1979–84, and Professor, 1979–86, now Emeritus, Faculty of Nursing, University of Calgary; *b* 10 Sept. 1923; *d* of Ebenezer Wright and Margaret Greig Masson. *Educ:* Wallington County Grammar Sch.; Univ. of Edinburgh; St George's and Queen Charlotte's Hosps, London. MA Hons Hist., PhD and Dipl. Med. Services Admin, Edinburgh; SRN and SCM. Research Asst, Unilever Ltd, 1947–50; Student Nurse, St George's Hosp., 1950–53; Student Midwife, Queen Charlotte's Hosp. and E Sussex CC, 1954–55; Staff Nurse and Sister, St George's Hosp., London, 1955–57; Boots Research Fellow in Nursing, Dept of Social Medicine, Univ. of Edinburgh, 1957–61; Rockefeller Fellow, USA, 1961–62; Deputy Matron, St George's Hosp., 1962–64; Matron, Middlesex Hosp., 1965–68; Dir, Dept of Nursing Studies, Univ. of Edinburgh, 1968–71; Prof. of Nursing Studies, Univ. of Edinburgh, 1972–76; Dir and Prof. of Sch. of Nursing, Dalhousie Univ., Nova Scotia, 1976–79. Second Vice-Pres., Internat. Council of Nurses, 1973–77. Margaret Scott Wright Annual Lecture in Nursing Research established in Faculty of Nursing, Univ. of Alberta, 1984. Silver Jubilee Medal, 1977. *Publications:* Experimental Nurse Training at Glasgow Royal Infirmary, 1963; Student Nurses in Scotland, 1968. *Recreations:* walking, music, reading, travel. *Address:* 24 St Michael at Pleas, Norwich NR3 1EP. *Club:* University Women's.

SCOULLER, (John) Alan; independent consultant; Head of Industrial Relations, Midland Bank Group, 1975–88; Visiting Professor in Industrial Relations, Kingston Polytechnic, since 1988; Senior Visiting Fellow, City University Business School, since 1989; *b* 23 Sept. 1929; *e s* of late Charles James Scouller and Mary Helena Scouller; *m* 1954, Angela Geneste Ambrose; two *s* five *d*. *Educ:* John Fisher Sch., Purley. Army service, Queen's Own Royal W Kent Regt, 1948–58 (Captain). Joined Unilever as management trainee, 1958; Personnel Man., Wall's Ice Cream, 1959–62; Domestos, 1963–66; Holpak, 1966–68; Commercial Plastics and Holpak, 1968–69; left Unilever to join Commn on Industrial Relations, 1969; Dir of Industrial Relations until 1973, full-time Comr, 1973–74. Member: Employment Appeal Tribunal, 1976–; Educn Bd, RC Dio. of Westminster, 1990–. FIPM. *Recreations:* studying employment law, walking, listening to music, looking after grandchildren. *Address:* Shortlands, 32 Sollershott West, Letchworth, Herts. *T:* Letchworth (0462) 682781.

SCOURFIELD, Edward Grismond Beaumont D.; *see* Davies-Scourfield.

SCOWEN, Sir Eric (Frank), Kt 1973; MD, DSc; FRCP, FRCS, FRCPE, FRCPath, FRPharmS, FRCGP; Director, Medical Professorial Unit, 1955–75; Physician to St Bartholomew's Hospital, 1946–75; Professor of Medicine, University of London, 1961–75 (Reader in Medicine, 1938–61); *b* 22 April 1910; *s* of late Frank Edward Scowen and Eleanor Betsy (*née* Barnes) (*d* 1969). *Educ:* City of London School; St Bartholomew's Hospital Medical College. MD 1935, DSc 1962, MA 1988, London. FRCP 1941; FRCS 1960; FRCPE 1965; FRCPath 1965; FRPharmS 1984; FRCGP 1989. St Bartholomew's Hospital: House Physician, 1931, Second Assistant, 1933, to Medical Professorial Unit; Baly Research Fell. in Clin. Med., 1933; First Asst to Med. Professorial Unit, 1935; Asst Dir of Med. Prof. Unit, and Asst Phys, 1937; Rockefeller Research Fell. to Columbia Univ., New York, 1937. Chairman: Council, Imperial Cancer Research Fund, 1967–82 (Vice-Pres., 1982); Cttee on Safety of Drugs, 1969– (Mem., 1963); British Pharmacopœia Commission, 1963–69; Cttee on Safety of Medicines, 1970–80; Cttee on the Review of Medicines, 1975–78; Poisons Bd (Home Office), 1976–83. Chm. Council, Sch. of Pharmacy, Univ. of London, 1979–88 (Hon. Fellow, 1986). Hon. LLD Nottingham, 1979. *Publications:* various in medical and scientific journals. *Address:* Flat 77, 6/9 Charterhouse Square, EC1M 6EX. *T:* 071–251 3212. *Club:* Athenæum.

SCRASE-DICKINS, Mark Frederick Hakon, CMG 1991; HM Diplomatic Service, retired; *b* 31 May 1936; *s* of Alwyne Rory Macnamara Scrase-Dickins and Ingeborg Oscara Frederika Scrase-Dickins; *m* 1969, Martina Viviane Bayley; one *s* one *d* (and one *d* decd). *Educ:* Eton Coll.; RMA, Sandhurst. Commnd Rifle Bde (later Royal Green Jackets), 1956; Malaya, 1956–57 (despatches); ADC to GOC Ghana Army, 1958–59; ADC to Chief of Imperial Gen. Staff, 1959–60; SE Asia, 1962–65; Army Staff Coll., 1967; Hong Kong, 1968–70; transferred to FCO, 1973; Vientiane, 1975; Muscat, 1976; Counsellor: Jakarta, 1983; Riyadh, 1990. *Recreation:* field sports. *Address:* Coolhurst Grange, Horsham, West Sussex RH13 6LE. *T:* Horsham (0403) 52416. *Clubs:* Buck's, Special Forces.

SCREECH, Michael Andrew, FBA 1981; FRSL; Senior Research Fellow, All Souls College, Oxford, since 1984; *b* 2 May 1926; 3rd *s* of Richard John Screech, MM and Nellie Screech (*née* Maunder); *m* 1956, Anne (*née* Reeve); three *s*. *Educ:* Sutton High Sch., Plymouth; University Coll. London (BA (1st cl. Hons) 1950; Fellow, 1982); University of Montpellier, France. DLitt Birmingham, 1958, Oxon, 1990; DLit London, 1982. FRSL 1989. Other Rank, Intelligence Corps (Far East), 1944–48. Asst, UCL, 1950–51; Birmingham Univ.: Lectr, 1951–58; Sen. Lectr., 1959–61; UCL: Reader, 1961–66; Personal Chair of French, 1966–71; Fielden Prof. of French Language and Lit., London Univ., 1971–84. Visiting Professor: Univ. of Western Ontario, 1964–65; Univ. of New York, Albany, 1968–69; Johnson Prof., Inst. for Research in the Humanities, Madison, Wisconsin, 1978–79; Vis. Fellow, All Souls, Oxford, 1981; Edmund Campion Lectr, Regina, 1985; Wiley Vis. Prof., N Carolina, 1986; Professeur, Collège de France, 1989; Prof. Associé, Paris IV (Sorbonne), 1990. Member: Cttee, Warburg Inst., 1970–84; Comité d'Humanisme et Renaissance, 1971–; Comité de parrainage des Classiques de l'Humanisme, 1988–; Corresp. Mem., Société Historique de Genève, 1988. Chevalier dans l'Ordre National du Mérite, 1983; Hon. Citizen of the Ville de Tours, 1984. *Publications:* The Rabelaisian Marriage, 1958, rev. edn in French, 1991; L'Evangélisme de Rabelais, 1959, rev. edn in English, 1991; Tiers Livre de Pantagruel, 1964; Les épistres et évangiles de Lefèvre d'Etaples, 1964; (with John Jollife) Les Regrets et autres oeuvres poëtiques (Du Bellay), 1966; Marot évangélique, 1967; (with R. M. Calder) Gargantua, 1970; La Pantagrueline Prognostication, 1975; Rabelais, 1980, rev. edn in French, 1991; Ecstasy and the Praise of Folly, 1981, rev. edn in French, 1991; Montaigne and Melancholy, 1983, rev. edn in French, 1991; (with Anne Screech) Erasmus' Annotations on the New Testament: The Gospels, 1986, Acts, Romans, I and I Corinthians, 1990; (ed trans.) Montaigne, An Apology for Raymond Sebond, 1987; (with Stephen Rawles *et al.*) A New Rabelais Bibliography: editions before 1626, 1987; (ed trans.) The Essays of Montaigne, 1991; *edited reprints:* Le Nouveau Testament de Lefèvre d'Etaples, 1970; F. de Billon: Le Fort inexpugnable de l'Honneur du Sexe Femenin, 1970; Opuscules d'Amour par Héroët et autres divins poëtes, 1970; Amyot: Les œuvres morales et meslées de Plutarque, 1971; articles on Renaissance, Reformation, and the history of the classical and Christian tradition in: Bibliothèque d'Humanisme et Renaissance, Etudes rabelaisiennes, Jl of Warburg Inst., etc; contribs to several collective volumes. *Recreation:* walking. *Address:* 5 Swanston-field, Whitchurch-on-Thames RG8 7HP. *T:* Pangbourne (0734) 842513. *Club:* Athenæum.

SCRIMSHAW, Frank Herbert; *b* 25 Dec. 1917; *s* of late John Leonard Scrimshaw and Jessie Scrimshaw (*née* Sewell), Lincoln; *m* 1950, Joan Olive, *d* of Leslie Stephen Paskall, Felixstowe; one *s*. *Educ:* The City Sch., Lincoln; University Coll., Nottingham. BSc London. Joined Scientific Civil Service, 1939; various posts at RAE, Farnborough, and Blind Landing Experimental Unit, RAF Martlesham Heath, 1939–58; Dir of Scientific Research (Electronics), Min. of Aviation, 1959–61; RRE, Malvern: Head of Guided Weapons Group, 1961–65; Head of Mil. and Civil Systems Dept, 1965–67; Dir Gen., Electronics R&D, Min. of Technology, later MoD, 1967–72; Dep. Dir, RAE, Farnborough, 1972–78, retired. *Address:* 53 Feoffees Road, Somersham, near Huntingdon, Cambs PE17 3JQ. *T:* Ramsey (Cambs) (0487) 840143.

SCRIVEN, Wilton Maxwell, AO 1983; Member, Casino Supervisory Authority, since 1987; Director: Rib Loc International Ltd, since 1986; Merino Wool Harvesting Ltd, since 1987; *b* 10 Dec. 1924; *m* 1948, Marjorie Reta Shaw; two *s* two *d*. *Educ:* Univ. of Adelaide. BSc; FIEAust. Flying Officer RAAF; served with RAF Sqdn 622 Mildenhall, 1943–45. Engr, PMG's Dept, 1946–64; Regional Dir, Dept of Trade, 1965–66; Chm., Australian Industrial Research and Develt Grants Bd, 1967–68; Dir of Industrial Develt, S Australian Govt, 1969–76; Agent General for S Australia in London, 1977–80; Dir Gen., S Aust. Dept of Premier and Cabinet, 1980–83; Dir Gen., Dept of Lands, SA, 1983–84. *Recreations:* tennis, golf, flute. *Address:* 7 Knightsbridge Road, Leabrook, SA 5068, Australia. *Clubs:* Adelaide Rotary; Mount Osmond Golf.

SCRIVENER, Anthony Frank Bertram, QC 1975; a Recorder of the Crown Court, since 1976; *b* 31 July 1935; *s* of Frank Bertram Scrivener and Edna Scrivener; *m* 1964, Irén Becze; one *s* one *d*. *Educ:* Kent Coll., Canterbury; University Coll. London (LLB). Called to Bar, Gray's Inn, 1958 (Holt Scholar); Bencher, Lincoln's Inn, 1985. Lectr in Law, Ghana, 1959–61; practice as Junior, 1961–75. Chm., Gen. Council of Bar, 1991 (Vice-Chm., 1990). *Recreations:* tennis, chess, cricket, car racing, taking the dog for a walk. *Address:* Grenville Manor, Aston Road, Haddenham, Bucks HP17 8AF. *T:* Haddenham (0844) 291496; 8 New Square, Lincoln's Inn, WC2A 3QP.

SCRIVENER, Christiane, Chevalier de la Légion d'Honneur 1978; Member, Commission of the European Communities, since 1989; *b* 1 Sept. 1925; *m* 1944, Pierre Scrivener; one *s*. *Educ:* Lycée de Grenoble; Faculté de lettres et de droit de Paris. Dip. Psychol.; Dip. Harvard Business Sch. Directeur Général: l'Assoc. pour l'organisation des Stages en France, 1958–69; l'Assoc. pour l'organisation des missions de coopération technique, 1961–69; l'Agence pour la coopération technique industrielle et économique, 1969–76; Sec. d'Etat à la Consommation, 1976–78; Pres., la Commission chargée d'étudier les problèmes éthiques de la publicité, 1978; Sec. Gen. Adj. du parti républicain, 1978–79; Mem., Parlement européen (UDF), 1979–89; Mem., Conseil d'admin des Assurances Générales de France, 1986–89. Alumni Achievement Award (Harvard Business Sch.), 1976. Officier, Polonia Restituta, 1968; Médaille d'Or du Mérite Européen, 1990. *Publications:* L'Europe, une bataille pour l'avenir, 1984; (pour les enfants) L'histoire du Petit Troll, 1986. *Recreations:* ski-ing, tennis, classical music. *Address:* c/o Commission of the European Communities, Rue de la Loi 200, B–1049 Brussels, Belgium. *T:* 32–2–236.33.29.

SCRIVENER, Ronald Stratford, CMG 1965; HM Diplomatic Service, retired; *b* 29 Dec. 1919; *s* of Sir Patrick Scrivener, KCMG; *m* 1st, 1947, Elizabeth Drake-Brockman (marr. diss., 1952); 2nd, 1962, Mary Alice Olga Sofia Jane Hohler, *d* of late Squadron-Leader Robert Charlton Lane; two step-*s* two step-*d*. *Educ:* Westminster School; St Catharine's College, Cambridge. Served with Royal Air Force Volunteer Reserve, 1940–45. Appointed HM Diplomatic Service, Dec. 1945. Served in Berlin, Buenos Aires, Vienna, Caracas, Berne, Bangkok; Ambassador to: Panama, 1969–70; Czechoslovakia, 1971–74; Asst Under-Sec. of State, FCO, 1974–76. Mem. Council, Franco-British Soc., 1978–. Freeman of City of London, 1984; Liveryman, Scriveners' Co., 1984–. *Publications:* Economic Handbook to the Soviet Union, 1986; Market Survey of Spain, 1987. *Recreations:* travel, fishing. *Address:* 38 Lysia Street, SW6 6NG. *T:* 071–385 3013. *Clubs:* White's, Beefsteak.

SCRIVENOR, Sir Thomas (Vaisey), Kt 1960; CMG 1956; *b* 28 Aug. 1908; *e s* of late John Brooke Scrivenor, ISO, formerly Dir of Geological Survey, Malaya; *m* 1934, Mary Elizabeth Neatby; one *s* three *d*. *Educ:* King's School, Canterbury; Oriel College, Oxford (MA). Temp. Assistant Principal, Colonial Office, 1930–33; Assistant District Officer, Tanganyika, 1934–37; Assistant District Commissioner, Palestine, 1937–43; Assistant Lt-Governor, Malta, 1943–44; Principal, Colonial Office, 1944–46; Principal Asst Sec., Palestine, 1946–48; Civil Service Comr, Nigeria, 1948–53; Deputy High Commissioner for Basutoland, the Bechuanaland Protectorate, and Swaziland, 1953–60. Sec. to Exec. Council of Commonwealth Agric. Bureaux, 1961–73. *Address:* Vine Cottage, Minster Lovell, Oxon OX8 5RN. *T:* Witney (0993) 775620.

SCROGGIE, Alan Ure Reith, CBE 1973 (OBE 1961); QPM 1968; one of HM's Inspectors of Constabulary 1963–75; *b* 1912; *s* of late Col W. R. J. Scroggie, CIE, IMS,

Callander, Perthshire; *m* 1940, Shiela Catherine, *d* of late Finlay Mackenzie, Elgin, Morayshire; two *s*. *Educ:* Cargilfield Preparatory Sch.; Fettes Coll.; Edinburgh Univ. (BL). Joined Edinburgh City Police, 1930; Asst Chief Constable of Bucks, 1947–53; Chief Constable of Northumberland, 1953–63. OStJ 1955. *Recreations:* golf, fishing, gardening. *Address:* Fowler's Cottage, Abercrombie, by St Monans, Anstruther, Fife KY10 2DE. *Clubs:* Royal and Ancient (St Andrews); Golf House (Elie).

SCRUBY, Ven. Ronald Victor, MA; Archdeacon of Portsmouth, 1977–85, now Emeritus; *b* 23 Dec. 1919; 6th *s* of late Thomas Henry Scruby and late Florence Jane Scruby, Norwood Green, Southall, Middx; *m* 1955, Sylvia Tremayne Miles, *e d* of late Rear-Adm. Roderic B. T. Miles, Trotton, Sussex; two *s* one *d*. *Educ:* Southall Technical Coll.; Trinity Hall, Cambridge. Engineering Apprentice, London Transport, 1936–39. Royal Engineers, 1939–45; Capt. 1943. Trinity Hall, Cambridge, 1945–48; Cuddesdon Coll., Oxford, 1948–50. Asst Curate, Rogate, Sussex, 1950–53; Chaplain, King Edward VII Hosp., Midhurst, 1950–53; Chaplain, Saunders-Roe, Osborne, E Cowes, 1953–58; Vicar of Eastney, Portsmouth, 1958–65; Rural Dean of Portsmouth, 1960–65; Archdeacon of the Isle of Wight, 1965–77. *Address:* The Dower House, Rogate, Petersfield, Hants GU31 5EG. *T:* Rogate (073080) 325.

SCRUTON, Prof. Roger Vernon; Professor of Aesthetics, Birkbeck College, London, since 1985; *b* 27 Feb. 1944; *s* of John Scruton and Beryl C. Haynes; *m* 1973, Danielle Laffitte (marr. diss.). *Educ:* Jesus Coll., Cambridge (MA, PhD). Called to the Bar, Inner Temple, 1978. Res. Fellow, Peterhouse, 1969–71; Lectr in Philosophy, Birkbeck Coll., London, 1971–79, Reader, 1979–85. Founder and Dir, The Claridge Press, 1987–. Editor, Salisbury Review, 1982–. *Publications:* Art and Imagination, 1974, 2nd edn 1982; The Aesthetics of Architecture, 1979; The Meaning of Conservatism, 1980; From Descartes to Wittgenstein, 1981; Fortnight's Anger (novel), 1981; The Politics of Culture, 1981; Kant, 1982; A Dictionary of Political Thought, 1982; The Aesthetic Understanding, 1983; (with Baroness Cox) Peace Studies: A Critical Survey, 1984; Thinkers of the New Left, 1985; (jtly) Education and Indoctrination, 1985; Sexual Desire, 1986; A Land held Hostage, 1987; Untimely Tracts, 1987; The Philosopher on Dover Beach (essays), 1990; Francesca (novel), 1991; contribs to The Times, Guardian, etc. *Recreations:* music, architecture, literature. *Address:* Department of Philosophy, Birkbeck College, Malet Street, WC1E 7JG. *Club:* Athenæum.

SCRYMGEOUR, family name of **Earl of Dundee.**

SCRYMGEOUR, Lord; Henry David; *b* 20 June 1982; *s* and *heir* of 12th Earl of Dundee, *qv*.

SCUDAMORE, Peter Michael, MBE 1990; National Hunt jockey since 1979; Director, Chasing Promotions, since 1989; *b* 13 June 1958; *s* of Michael and Mary Scudamore; *m* 1980, Marilyn Linda Kington; two *s*. *Educ:* Belmont Abbey, Hereford. Champion Jockey, 1981–82 and annually since 1986; rode for British Jump Jockeys; winners in Australia, Belgium, Germany, New Zealand, Norway; John Player Amateur Flat Race, Galway; Leading Jockey, Ritz Club Charity Trophy, Cheltenham Festival, 1986; leading jockey, Cheltenham, 1986, 1987; set new record for number of winners ridden in career, 1989, for number in one season (221), 1989. *Publication:* (with Alan Lee) A Share of Success: the Scudamore Family, 1983. *Recreations:* cricket, music, watching sport. *Address:* Mucky Cottage, Grange Hill, Naunton, near Cheltenham, Glos GL54 3AY. *T:* Guiting Power (04515) 741.

SCULLARD, Geoffrey Layton, OBE 1971; HM Diplomatic Service, retired; Head of Accommodation and Services Department, Foreign and Commonwealth Office, 1978–80; *b* 5 July 1922; *s* of late William Harold Scullard and late Eleanor Mary Scullard (*née* Tomkin); *m* 1945, Catherine Margaret Pinington; three *d*. *Educ:* St Olave's Grammar Sch. Joined Foreign Office, 1939. Served War (RAF Signals), 1942–46. Diplomatic service at: Stockholm, Washington, Baghdad, Los Angeles, Moscow. *Recreations:* fishing, golf. *Address:* 2 Albury Heights, 8 Albury Road, Guildford, Surrey GU1 2BT. *T:* Guildford (0483) 39915. *Club:* Bramley Golf.

SCULLY, Prof. Crispian Michael, FDSRCPSG; FFDRCSI; Professor of Stomatology, University of Bristol, since 1982; *b* 24 May 1945; *s* of Patrick and Rosaleen Scully; *m* Zoitsa Boucoumani; one *d*. *Educ:* Univ. of London (BSc, BDS, PhD); Univ. of Glasgow; Univ. of Bristol (MD, MDS). MRCS; LRCP; LDS RCS; MRCPath. MRC Research Fellow, Guy's Hosp., 1975–78; Lectr, 1979–81, Sen. Lectr, 1981–82, Univ. of Glasgow. Consultant Adviser in Dental Research, DHSS, 1986–. Member: GDC, 1984–; Adv. Council for Misuse of Drugs, 1985–89; Chm., Central Examining Bd for Dental Hygienists, 1989–; Mem., Medicines Control Agency Cttee on Dental and Surgical Materials, 1990–. *Publications:* Medical Problems in Dentistry, 1982, 2nd edn 1987; (jtly) Multiple Choice Questions in Dentistry, 1985; Handbook for Hospital Dental Surgeons, 1985; (jtly) Slide Interpretation in Oral Disease, 1986; Dental Surgery Assistants' Handbook, 1988; Colour Atlas of Stomatology, 1988; Colour Aids to Oral Medicine, 1988; The Dental Patient, 1988; The Mouth and Perioral Tissues, 1989; Patient Care: a dental surgeon's guide, 1989; (jtly) Occupational Hazards in Dentistry, 1990; contribs to learned jls. *Recreation:* music. *Address:* University Department of Oral Medicine, Surgery, and Pathology, Bristol Dental Hospital and School, Lower Maudlin Street, Bristol BS1 2LY. *T:* Bristol (0272) 276201.

SCURR, Dr Cyril Frederick, CBE 1980; LVO 1952; FRCS, FFARCS; Hon. Consulting Anaesthetist, Westminster Hospital, since 1985 (Consultant Anaesthetist, 1949–85); Hon. Anaesthetist, Hospital of SS John and Elizabeth, since 1952; *b* 14 July 1920; *s* of Cyril Albert Scurr and Mabel Rose Scurr; *m* 1947, Isabel Jean Spiller; three *s* one *d*. *Educ:* King's Coll., London; Westminster Hosp. MB, BS. Served War of 1939–45: RAMC, 1942–47, Major, Specialist Anaesthetist. Faculty of Anaesthetists: Mem. Bd, 1961–77; Dean, 1970–73; Mem. Council, RCS, 1970–73; Pres., Assoc. of Anaesthetists of GB and Ireland, 1976–78; Mem. Health Services Bd, 1977–80; Chm., Scientific Programme, World Congress of Anaesthetists, London, 1968; Pres., 1978–79, Hon. Mem., 1988, Anaesthetics Section, RSocMed; Mem. Adv. Cttee on Distinction Awards, 1973–84; Vice-Chm., Jt Consultants Cttee, 1979–81; past Member: Cttee, Competence to Practise; Standing Med. Adv. Cttee, DHSS. Mem. d'Honneur, Société Française d'Anesthésie et de Réanimation, 1978; Academician, European Acad. of Anaesthesiology, 1978. Frederick Hewitt Lectr, RCS, 1971; Magill Centenary Oration, RCS, 1988. Dudley Buxton Prize, RCS, 1977; Gold Medal, Faculty of Anaesthetists, 1983; John Snow Medal, Assoc. of Anaesthetists of GB and Ireland, 1984. Fellow, RSocMed; Hon. FFARCSI 1977. *Publication:* Scientific Foundations of Anaesthesia, 1970, 4th edn 1990. *Recreations:* photography, gardening. *Address:* 16 Grange Avenue, Totteridge Common, N20 8AD. *T:* 081–445 7188.

SCUSE, Dennis George, MBE 1957; TD 1946; Managing Director, Dennis Scuse Ltd, PR Consultants in Radio and TV, 1976–87; *b* 19 May 1921; *yr s* of late Charles H. and Katherine Scuse; *m* 1948, Joyce Evelyn, *yr d* of late Frank and Frances Burt; one *s*. *Educ:* Park Sch., Ilford; Mercers' Sch., London. Joined Martins Bank, 1937. TA (RA), 1938; mobilised, Sept. 1939. Served War, commissioned 78th (HyAA) Regt, RA, 1940. Air Defence of Gt Britain, 1940–41; Command Entertainment Officer, Ceylon Army Comd, 1942; subseq. 65th (HyAA) Regt, in MELF and CMF, 1943–44; joined Army Broadcasting Service, CMF: commanded stations in Bari, Rome and Athens, 1945–46; demobilised, Sept. 1946. Joined Overseas Div. BBC and seconded to War Office for Forces Broadcasting Service in Benghasi and Canal Zone; Chief Programme Officer, 1947–48; Asst Dir, British Forces Network, Germany, 1949–50; Dir, 1950–57. Introduced "Two-Way Family Favourites", 1952–57; Sen. Planning Asst, BBC-TV, 1958–59; Chief Asst (Light Entertainment), BBC-TV, 1960; Chief Asst (TV), BBC New York Office, Sept. 1960; BBC Rep. in USA, July 1962; Gen. Manager, BBC-TV Enterprises, 1963–72, and BBC Radio Enterprises, 1968–72. Trident Management Ltd, 1972; Man. Dir, Trident Internat. TV Enterprises Ltd, 1972–76. Consultant, Hanson Trust, 1984–89. *Publications:* numerous articles on broadcasting, television programme exports, etc. *Recreations:* journalism, watching television. *Address:* 2 York House, Courtlands, Sheen Road, Richmond, Surrey. *T:* 081–948 4737. *Club:* Royal Greenjackets.

SCUTT, Robin Hugh, CBE 1976; Chairman, United Media Ltd, since 1983; Director of Production, NVC Arts, since 1991; Chairman, International Committee, Monte Carlo Television Festival, since 1989; *b* Sandgate, Kent, 24 Oct. 1920; *s* of late Rev. A. O. Scutt, MA and Freda M. Scutt (*née* Palmer); *m* 1st, 1943, Judy Watson (marr. diss. 1960); two *s*; 2nd, 1961, Patricia A. M. Smith. *Educ:* Fonthill; Bryanston; Jesus Coll., Cambridge (MA Mod. Lang.). Served Intell. Corps, 1941–42 (invalided out). BBC Eur. Service (French Section), 1942; BBC TV Outside Broadcasts Producer, 1955; BBC Paris Rep., 1958; Gen. Man., Trans Europe Television, 1962; rejoined BBC TV Outside Broadcasts, 1963; Asst Head of BBC TV Presentation (BBC1), 1966; Controller: BBC Radio 1 and 2, 1967–68; BBC 2, 1969–74; Development TV, 1974–77; Dep. Man. Dir, BBC TV, 1977–80. Dir, LWT, 1981–90. Chm., New Technologies Working Party, Broadcast Res. Unit, BFI, 1981–83. TV Exec. Producer for National Video Corp.: Tales of Hoffmann, Peter Grimes, La Bohème, Fanciulla del West, Manon Lescaut, Die Fledermaus, Der Rosenkavalier, Nutcracker and Don Carlo, Covent Gdn, 1981–85; Ernani, Il Trittico, I Lombardi, Andrea Chenier, Aida, Madame Butterfly and Nabucco, La Scala, 1982–86; Otello, Turandot, Madame Butterfly, Tosca, Il Trovatore and Attila, Verona, 1982–85; Don Quixote, and ABT at the Met, and at San Francisco, Amer. Ballet Theatre, 1983–85; Natasha (Natalia Makarova), and Carols for Christmas, 1985; Napoli and La Sylphide, Royal Theatre Copenhagen, 1986–88; Boris Godunov, and The Golden Age, Bolshoi Theatre, 1987; Cinderella, 1987, Diaghilev Tribute, 1990, Paris Opera Ballet; Le Corsaire, 1989, Swan Lake, 1990, Kirov Ballet, Leningrad. Mem., BAFTA. FRTS 1978 (Gold Medallist, 1980); FRSA 1984. Officier de la Légion d'Honneur, France, 1983. *Recreations:* music, theatre, gardening. *Address:* The Abbey Cottage, Cockfield, Suffolk. *Clubs:* Garrick, St James.

SEABORG, Glenn Theodore; University Professor of Chemistry, University of California, Berkeley, since 1971; *b* 19 April 1912; *s* of Herman Theodore and Selma Erickson Seaborg; *m* 1942, Helen Lucille Griggs; four *s* two *d*. *Educ:* Univ. of Calif, Los Angeles (BA); Univ. of Calif, Berkeley (PhD). University of California, Berkeley: Res. Associate (with Prof. Gilbert N. Lewis), Coll. of Chem., 1937–39; Instr, Dept of Chem., 1939–41, Asst Prof., 1941–45, Prof., 1945–71; Chancellor, 1958–61; Lawrence Berkeley Laboratory: Associate Dir, 1954–61, and 1972–; Dir, Nuclear Chem. Div., 1946–58, and 1972–75; Dir, Lawrence Hall of Science, 1982–; Head, Plutonium Chem. Metall. Lab., Univ. of Chicago, 1942–46; Chm., US Atomic Energy Commn, 1961–71. Member, US Delegns to: 3rd (Chm.) and 4th (Chm. and Pres.) UN Internat. Confs on Peaceful Uses of Atomic Energy, Geneva, 1964 and 1971; 5–15th annual Gen. Confs of Internat. Atomic Energy Agency, 1961–71; USSR, for signing of Memorandum on Cooperation in the Field of Utilization of Atomic Energy for Peaceful Purposes (Chm.), 1963; USSR, for signing of Limited Test Ban Treaty, 1963. Member: Nat. Council on Marine Resources and Engineering Development, 1966–71; Nat. Aeronautics and Space Council, 1961–71; Fed. Council for Science and Tech., 1961–71; Pres.'s Cttee on Manpower, 1964–69; Fed. Radiation Council, 1961–69; Nat. Sci. Bd, Nat. Sci. Foundn, 1960–61; Pres.'s Science Adv. Cttee, 1959–61; 1st Gen. Adv. Cttee, US Atomic Energy Commn, 1946–50; Commn on the Humanities, 1962–65; Scientific Adv. Bd, Robert A. Welch Foundn, 1957–; Bd of Dirs, Nat. Educnl TV and Radio Centre, 1958–64, 1967–70; Bd of Dirs, World Future Soc., 1969–; Nat. Programming Council for Public TV, 1970–72; Bd of Governors, Amer.-Swedish Hist. Foundn, 1972–; Steering Cttee, Chem. Educn Material Study (Chm.), 1959–74; Nat. Cttee on America's Goals and Resources, Nat. Planning Assoc., 1962–64; Electoral Coll. Hall of Fame for Great Americans, 1969–; California Inventors' Hall of Fame, 1983–; Council on Foreign Relations, 1965–; Bd of Trustees: Pacific Science Centre Foundn, 1962–; Science Service, 1965– (Pres., 1966–); Amer.-Scandinavian Foundn, 1968–; Educnl Broadcasting Corp., 1970–73; Amer. Assoc. for the Advancement of Science (Pres. 1972, Chm. 1973); Amer. Chem. Soc. (Pres., 1976); Chm. Bd, Swedish Council of America, 1978–. Mem. and Hon. Mem., Fellow and Hon. Fellow, numerous scientific and professional socs and instns, Argentina, German Dem. Republic., German Fed. Republic, Japan, Poland, Spain, Sweden, UK, USA, USSR; Foreign Mem., Royal Society, 1985; Hon. FRSC 1982. Holds 50 hon. doctorates from univs and colls. Named one of America's 10 Outstanding Young Men, 1947. Awards (1947–) include: Nobel Prize for Chemistry (jtly), 1951; Perkin Medal (Amer. Sect. Soc. Chem. Ind.), 1957; USAEC Enrico Fermi Award, 1959; Priestley Meml Award, 1960; Franklin Medal (Franklin Inst. of Philadelphia), 1963; Award in Pure Chem., 1947, Charles Lathrop Parsons Award, (Amer. Chem. Soc.), 1964; Chem. Pioneer Award, 1968, Gold Medal Award, (Am. Inst. of Chemists), 1973; Arches of Science Award (Pacific Science Centre, Seattle), 1968; John R. Kuebler Award, Alpha Chi Sigma, 1978; Priestley Medal, Amer. Chem. Soc., 1979; Henry DeWolf Smyth Award, Amer. Nuclear Soc., 1982; Actinide Award, 1984; Great Swedish Heritage Award, 1984. Officer, French Legion of Honour, 1973. Co-discoverer of: nuclear energy source isotopes Pu-239 and U-233; elements (1940–74): 94, plutonium; 95, americium; 96, curium; 97, berkelium; 98, californium; 99, einsteinium; 100, fermium; 101, mendelevium; 102, nobelium; element 106. *Publications:* (jtly) The Chemistry of the Actinide Elements, 1958, 2nd edn 1986; The Transuranium Elements (Silliman Lectures), 1958; (jtly) Elements of the Universe, 1958; Man-made Transuranium Elements, 1963; (jtly) Education and the Atom, 1964; (jtly) The Nuclear Properties of the Heavy Elements, 1964; (jtly) Oppenheimer, 1969; (jtly) Man and Atom, 1971; Nuclear Milestones, 1972; (ed) Transuranium Elements—Products of Modern Alchemy, 1978; Kennedy, Khrushchev and the Test Ban, 1981; (jtly) Nuclear Chemistry, 1982; Stemming the Tide: arms control Johnson years, 1987; contrib. numerous papers on nuclear chem. and nuclear physics, transuranium elements, high energy nuclear reactions and educn in Physical Rev., Jl Amer. Chm. Soc., Annual Rev. of Nuclear Science, etc. *Recreations:* golf, reading, hiking. *Address:* (business) Lawrence Berkeley Laboratory, University of California, Berkeley, Calif 94720, USA; (home) 1154 Glen Road, Lafayette, Calif 94549, USA. *Clubs:* Faculty (Univ. Calif, Berkeley); Commonwealth Club of California, Bohemian (San Francisco); Chemists (NY); Cosmos, University (Washington).

SEABORN, Most Rev. Robert Lowder; Chancellor, University of Trinity College, Toronto, since 1983; *b* 9 July 1911; *s* of Rev. Richard Seaborn and Muriel Kathleen Reid; *m* 1938, Mary Elizabeth Gilchrist; four *s* one *d*. *Educ:* Univ. of Toronto Schs; Trinity Coll., Univ. of Toronto (MA); Oxford Univ. Deacon, 1934; Priest, 1935; Asst Curate, St

Simon's, Toronto, 1934–36; Asst Curate, St James's Cathedral, Toronto, 1937–41; Rector, St Peter's, Cobourg, Ont., 1941–48; Chaplain, Canadian Army, 1942–45 (Padre Canadian Scottish Regt); Dean of Quebec and Rector of Parish of Quebec, 1948–57; Rector, St Mary's, Kerrisdale, Vancouver, BC, 1957–58; Asst Bishop of Newfoundland, 1958–65, Coadjutor, June-Dec. 1965; Bishop of Newfoundland, 1965–75, of Eastern Newfoundland and Labrador, 1975–80; Archbishop of Newfoundland and Metropolitan of Ecclesiastical Province of Canada, 1975–80; Bishop Ordinary (Anglican) to Canadian Forces, 1980–86. Croix de Guerre avec étoile de vermeil (French), 1945. DD, (*jure dignitatis*), Trinity Coll., 1948; DCL (*hc*), Bishop's Univ., 1962; Hon. LLD Meml Univ. of Newfoundland, 1972; Hon. DD Montreal Diocesan Theological Coll., 1980. *Publication:* Faith in our Time, 1963. *Recreations:* camping, golf. *Address:* 247 Lake Street, Cobourg, Ont K9A 1R6, Canada.

SEABROOK, Air Vice-Marshal Geoffrey Leonard, CB 1965; *b* 25 Aug. 1909; *s* of late Robert Leonard Seabrook; *m* 1949, Beryl Mary (*née* Hughes); one *s* one *d. Educ:* King's Sch., Canterbury. Commissioned in RAF (Accountant Branch), 1933; served in: Middle East, 1935–43; Bomber Command, 1943–45; Transport Command, 1945–47; Iraq, 1947–49; Signals Command, 1949–51; Air Ministry Organisation and Methods, 1951–53; Home Command Group Captain Organisation, 1953–56; Far East Air Force, 1957–59; idc 1960; Director of Personnel, Air Ministry, 1961–63; Air Officer Administration, HQ, RAF Tech. Trg Comd, 1963–66; retired June 1966. Air Cdre 1961; Air Vice-Marshal, 1964. Head of Secretarial Branch, Royal Air Force, 1963–66. FCA 1957 (Associate, 1932). *Recreations:* sailing, golf. *Address:* Long Pightle, Piltdown, Uckfield, E Sussex TN22 3XB. *T:* Newick (082572) 2322. *Clubs:* Royal Air Force; Piltdown Golf.

SEABROOK, Graeme; Managing Director, since 1988, and Chief Executive, since 1989, Kwik Save Group; *b* 1 May 1939; *s* of Norman and Amy Winifred Seabrook; *m* 1967, Lorraine Ellen Ludlow; one *s* one *d.* G. J. Coles & Co. (later Coles Myer), Australia, 1955; Chief Gen. Manager, G. J. Coles, 1982; acquisition of Myer, 1985; Man. Dir, Discount Stores Group, 1985; Jt Man. Dir, Coles Myer, 1987, resigned 1988; joined Dairy Farm International, Hong Kong and seconded to Kwik Save Group, 1988. *Recreations:* tennis, photography. *Address:* Kwik Save Group, Warren Drive, Prestatyn, Clwyd LL19 7HU. *T:* Prestatyn (0745) 887111, 882004.

SEABROOK, Robert John; QC 1983; a Recorder, since 1985; Leader, South Eastern Circuit, since 1989; *b* 6 Oct. 1941; *s* of Alan Thomas Pertwee Seabrook, MBE and late Mary Seabrook (*née* Parker); *m* 1965, Liv Karin Djupvik, Bergen, Norway; two *s* one *d. Educ:* St George's Coll., Salisbury, Southern Rhodesia; University Coll., London (LLB). Called to the Bar, Middle Temple, 1964, Bencher, 1990. The Recorder, SE Circuit Bar Mess, 1982–84. Member: Brighton Fest. Cttee, 1976–86; Court, Univ. of Sussex, 1988–. Liveryman, Curriers' Co., 1972. *Recreations:* travel, listening to music, wine. *Address:* (chambers) 1 Crown Office Row, Temple, EC4Y 7HH. *T:* 071–353 1801.

SEABROOKE, George Alfred; consultant in education and training; Director, The Polytechnic, Wolverhampton, 1977–85; *b* 8 Dec. 1923; *s* of late John Arthur Seabrooke and Elsie Seabrooke; *m* 1945, Evelyn Sargent; two *s. Educ:* Keighley Boys' Grammar Sch.; Bradford Technical Coll.; Stoke-on-Trent Tech. Coll.; King's Coll., London Univ. FBIM 1978. National Service, 1946–48. Post Office Engrg Dept, 1940–50; Estate Duty Office, Comrs of Inland Revenue, 1950–56; SW London Coll. of Commerce, 1956–60; Trent Polytechnic, Nottingham (and precursor Colls), 1960–73; Dep. Dir, NE London Polytechnic, 1974–77. *Publications:* Air Law, 1964; contrib. learned jls. *Recreations:* music, cricket, rugby. *Address:* 6 John Trundle Court, Barbican, EC2Y 8DJ.

SEABY, Wilfred Arthur; retired museum official; Director, Ulster Museum (previously Belfast Museum and Art Gallery), 1953–70; Numismatic Section, Department of Technology and Local History, 1970–73; *b* 16 Sept. 1910; *y s* of late Allen W. Seaby, sometime Prof. of Art, Univ. of Reading; *m* 1937, Nora, *d* of late A. E. Pecover, Reading; two *s* one *d. Educ:* Wycliffe College; Reading University, College of Art. Dip. Museums Assoc., 1939. Served War of 1939–45, Royal Air Force, 1940–46 (Flt-Lt). B. A. Seaby Ltd, 1927–30; Reading, Birmingham, and Taunton Museums, 1931–53. Volunteer Numismatist, Warwickshire Mus., 1974–. FSA 1948. Hon. MA QUB, 1971. *Publication:* Hiberno-Norse Coins in the Ulster Museum, 1984. *Recreation:* water colour painting. *Address:* 36 Ladbrook Road, Solihull, West Midlands.

SEAFIELD, 13th Earl of, *cr* 1701; **Ian Derek Francis Ogilvie-Grant;** Viscount Seafield, Baron Ogilvy of Cullen, 1698; Viscount Reidhaven, Baron Ogilvy of Deskford and Cullen, 1701; *b* 20 March 1939; *s* of Countess of Seafield (12th in line), and Derek Studley-Herbert (who assumed by deed poll, 1939, the additional surnames of Ogilvie-Grant; he *d* 1960); *S* mother, 1969; *m* 1st, 1960, Mary Dawn Mackenzie (marr. diss., 1971), *er d* of Henry Illingworth; two *s*; 2nd, 1971, Leila, *d* of Mahmoud Refaat, Cairo. *Educ:* Eton. *Recreations:* shooting, fishing, tennis. *Heir: s* Viscount Reidhaven, *qv. Address:* Old Cullen, Cullen, Banffshire AB5 2XW. *T:* Cullen (0542) 40221. *Club:* White's.

SEAGA, Rt. Hon. Edward Philip George, PC 1982; MP for Western Kingston, since 1962; Leader of the Jamaica Labour Party, since 1974; *b* 28 May 1930; *s* of late Philip Seaga and of Erna (*née* Maxwell); *m* 1965, Marie Elizabeth (*née* Constantine) (Miss Jamaica, 1964); two *s* one *d. Educ:* Wolmers Boys' Sch., Kingston, Jamaica; Harvard Univ., USA (BA Social Science, 1952). Did field research in connection with Inst. of Social and Econ. Res., University Coll. of the West Indies (now Univ. of the WI), Jamaica, on develt of the child, and revival spirit cults, by living in rural villages and urban slums; proposed estabt of Unesco Internat. Fund for Promotion of Culture, 1971, and is founding mem. of its Administrative Council. Nominated to Upper House (Legislative Council), 1959 (youngest mem. in its history); Asst Sec., Jamaica Labour Party, 1960–62, Sec., 1962; Minister of Develt and Social Welfare, 1962–67; Minister of Finance and Planning, 1967–72, and 1980–89; Leader of Opposition, 1974–80; Prime Minister, 1980–89. Director: Consulting Services Ltd, to 1979; Capital Finance Co. Ltd, to 1979. Hon. LLD Miami, 1981. Grand Collar, and Golden Mercury Internat. Award, Venezuela, 1981; Gold Key Award, Avenue of the Americas, NYC, 1981; Grand Cross, Order of Merit of Fed. Rep. of Germany, 1982. Religion Anglican. *Publications:* The Development of the Child; Revival Spirit Cults. *Recreations:* classical music, reading, shooting, hockey, football, cricket, tennis, swimming. *Address:* Vale Royal, Kingston, Jamaica. *Clubs:* Kingston Cricket, Jamaica Gun (Jamaica).

SEAGER, family name of **Baron Leighton of Saint Mellons.**

SEAGER, Major Ronald Frank, RA, retired; Executive Director, RSPCA, 1971–78 (Secretary, 1966–71); Advisory Director, International Society for Protection of Animals; *b* 27 May 1918; *s* of Frank Seager and Lilias K. (*née* Parr); *m* 1941, Josephine, *d* of Rev. R. M. Chadwick; one *s* one *d. Educ:* St Albans School. Royal Artillery (HAC), 1939; commnd, 1941; Italy, 1944–45; seconded Royal Pakistan Artillery, 1949–50; served Korean War, 1953–54; Perm. Pres. Courts Martial, Eastern Command, 1960–63. Joined RSPCA, 1963. *Recreations:* golf, gardening. *Address:* Merle Cottage, 3 The Tanyard, Shadrack Street, Beaminster, Dorset DT8 3BG. *T:* Beaminster (0308) 862806.

SEAGROATT, Conrad; QC 1983; barrister-at-law; a Recorder of the Crown Court, since 1980; *s* of late E. G. Seagroatt, Solicitor of the Supreme Court and Immigration Appeals Adjudicator, and of Gray's Inn, and of Barbara C. Seagroatt; *m* Cornelia Mary Anne Verdegaal; five *d. Educ:* Solihull Sch., Warwicks; Pembroke Coll., Oxford (MA Hons Modern History). Admitted Solicitor of the Supreme Court, 1967; called to the Bar, Gray's Inn, 1970; Member: Senate of the Inns of Court and the Bar, 1980–83; Criminal Injuries Compensation Bd, 1986–. *Recreations:* running, fairweather ski-ing, hockey. *Address:* 1 King's Bench Walk, Temple, EC4Y 7DB. *T:* 071–353 8436. *Club:* Western (Glasgow).

SEAL, Dr Barry Herbert; Member (Lab) Yorkshire West, European Parliament, since 1979; *b* 28 Oct. 1937; *s* of Herbert Seal and Rose Anne Seal; *m* 1963, Frances Catherine Wilkinson; one *s* one *d. Educ:* Heath Grammar Sch., Halifax; Univ. of Bradford (MSc, PhD); European Business Sch., Fontainebleau. CEng, MIChemE; FBIM. Served RAF, 1955–58. Trained as Chem. Engr, ICI Ltd, 1958–64; Div. Chem. Engr, Murex Ltd, 1964–68; Sen. Engr, BOC Internat., 1968–71; Principal Lectr in Systems, Huddersfield Polytechnic, 1971–79; consultant on microprocessors. Parly Candidate (Lab), Harrogate, 1974; Leader, Bradford Met. Dist Council Labour Gp, 1976–79. European Parliament: Leader, British Lab. Gp, 1988–89; Chm., Econ., Monetary and Industrial Policy Cttee, 1984–87. *Publications:* papers on computer and microprocessor applications. *Recreations:* running, reading, TV, flying. *Address:* (office) City Hall, Bradford, West Yorks BD1 1HY. *T:* Bradford (0274) 752091; (home) Brookfields Farm, Wyke, Bradford, West Yorks. *T:* Bradford (0274) 671888.

SEAL, Richard Godfrey, FRCO; FRSCM; Organist of Salisbury Cathedral, since 1968; *b* 4 Dec. 1935; *s* of William Godfrey Seal and Shelagh Seal (*née* Bagshaw); *m* 1975, Dr Sarah Helen Hamilton; two *s. Educ:* New Coll. Choir Sch., Oxford; Cranleigh Sch., Surrey; Christ's Coll., Cambridge (MA). FRCO 1958. Assistant Organist: Kingsway Hall, London, 1957–58; St Bartholomews the Great, London, 1960–61; Chichester Cathedral (and Dir of Music, Prebendal Sch.) Sussex, 1961–68. *Address:* 5 The Close, Salisbury, Wilts SP1 2EF. *T:* Salisbury (0722) 336828. *Club:* Crudgemens (Godalming).

SEALE, Douglas (Robert); producer, actor and director (stage); *b* 28 Oct. 1913; *s* of Robert Henry Seale and Margaret Seale (*née* Law). *Educ:* Rutlish. Studied for stage at Royal Academy of Dramatic Art and became an actor. First appeared as Starling in The Drums Begin, Embassy, 1934; subseq. in Repertory. Served in Army, 1940–46, commissioned in Royal Signals. Joined Shakespeare Memorial Theatre Company, Stratford-on-Avon season's 1946 and 1947. From 1948 produced at Birmingham Repertory Theatre, at The Bedford, Camden Town (under Donald Wolfit), and again at Birmingham where he became Director of Productions, 1950. Later Productions include: Figaro and Fidelio, Sadler's Wells; Shaw's Caesar and Cleopatra at Birmingham Rep. Theatre, 1956 (later presented at Théâtre Sarah Bernhardt, Paris, and Old Vic). Season 1957: The Tempest, at Univ. of BC, Vancouver; King John, Stratford-on-Avon; Richard III, Old Vic; Trilogy of Henry VI, Old Vic; Season 1958; The World of the Wonderful Dark, for first Vancouver Festival; King Lear, Old Vic; Much Ado about Nothing, Stratford-on-Avon. Old Vic productions as Associate Director, 1958: Julius Caesar; Macbeth; 1959: Molière's Tartuffe; Pinero's The Magistrate; Dryden-Davenant-Purcell version of Shakespeare's The Tempest; St Joan; She Stoops to Conquer, 1960, Landscape with Figures, by Cecil Beaton, Dublin Festival, 1960: King John, Festival Theatre, Stratford, Ontario, 1960; Director of tours in Russia and Poland for Old Vic Theatre Co., 1961: prod. The Importance of Being Earnest, New York, 1962; The Comedy of Errors, Henry V, Stratford, Connecticut, 1963; Regent's Prof., Univ. of Calif. at Santa Barbara, Jan.-June 1965; Artistic Director, Center Stage, Baltimore, Maryland, USA, 1965–67; directed and acted, Meadowbrook Theater, Rochester, Mich, 1968; co-producing Director, Goodman Theater, Chicago, 1969–72 (productions incl.: Soldiers, Marching Song, Heartbreak House (Jefferson award), The Tempest, Twelfth Night, own musical adaptation of Lady Audley's Secret); directed and acted in Lady Audley's Secret, Washington and New York, 1972; Giovani, in Pirandello's Henry IV, New York, 1973; directed: King Lear, Marin Shakespeare Festival, San Francisco; Doll's House and Look Back in Anger, Cleveland, Getting Married, New Haven, 1973; Sorin in The Seagull, Seattle; Artistic Dir, Philadelphia Drama Guild, 1974–80; The Last Few Days of Willie Callendar, Philadelphia, 1979; Summer, Philadelphia, 1980; directed at Shaw Festival, Ont.: Too True to be Good, 1974; Caesar and Cleopatra, 1975; Lady Audley's Secret, 1978; Director: The Winslow Boy, NY, 1980, and tour; The Dresser, Witness for the Prosecution, Miami, 1982; acted in: Frankenstein, NY, 1980; The Dresser, NY, 1981; Noises Off, 1983; acted in *films:* Amadeus, 1983; Heaven Help Us, 1984; Secret Passions, 1987; Ernest Saves Christmas, 1988; Triplicity, 1989; I'm No Angel, 1990; Mr Destiny, 1990; Rescue Down Under (voice), 1991; Aladin (voice), 1991; acted in, *TV:* Lucy Arnaz Show (series), 1985; Amazing Stories, 1985; Rags to Riches (series, 1987). Hon. DFA Washington Coll., Md, 1967. Mensa Annual Achievement Award, 1979. *Address:* Apt 14c, One University Place, New York, NY 10003, USA.

SEALE, Sir John Henry, 5th Bt, *cr* 1838; RIBA; *b* 3 March 1921; *s* of 4th Bt; *S* father, 1964; *m* 1953, Ray Josephine, *d* of Robert Gordon Charters, MC, Christchurch, New Zealand; one *s* one *d. Educ:* Eton; Christ Church, Oxford. Served War of 1939–45: Royal Artillery, North Africa and Italy; Captain, 1945. ARIBA 1951. *Heir: s* John Robert Charters Seale, *b* 17 Aug. 1954. *Address:* Slade, Kingsbridge, Devon TQ7 4BL. *T:* Kingsbridge (0548) 550226.

SEALES, Peter Clinton; Chairman, PSL Associates, since 1978; *s* of James Seales, Solicitor, and Angela Seales; *m* 1955, Bernadette Rogers; one *d.* Called to the Bar, King's Inns, 1953. Group Marketing Dir, Raleigh Industries Ltd, 1962–74; Dir, E Midlands Electricity Board, 1972–74; Man. Dir, Potterton International, and Chm. overseas subsidiaries in France, Belgium, Germany, Holland and Japan, 1974–76; International Marketing Dir, Ever Ready Holdings, 1977. Chief Executive: Sea Fish Industry Authority, 1982–83; Operation Raleigh, 1984–85; Consultant to Saatchi & Saatchi Compton, 1984; Group Marketing Dir, Wassen Internat. Ltd, 1986–; Hon. Council Mem., Operation Innervator, 1987–. *Recreations:* sailing, music. *Address:* 78 Northumberland Road, Leamington Spa, Warwickshire CV32 6HG. *T:* Leamington Spa (0926) 315624. *Clubs:* White Elephant, Wig and Pen, Institute of Directors; Leamington Real Tennis.

SEAMAN, Christopher; international conductor; Conductor-in-Residence, Baltimore Symphony Orchestra, since 1987; *b* 7 March 1942; *s* of late Albert Edward Seaman and Ethel Margery Seaman (*née* Chambers). *Educ:* Canterbury Cathedral Choir Sch.; The King's Sch., Canterbury; King's Coll., Cambridge. MA, double first cl. Hons in Music; ARCM, ARCO. Principal Timpanist, London Philharmonic Orch., 1964–68 (Mem., LPO Bd of Dirs, 1965–68); Asst Conductor, 1968–70, Principal Conductor, 1971–77, BBC Scottish Symphony Orchestra; Princ. Conductor and Artistic Dir, Northern Sinfonia Orch., 1974–79; Principal Guest Conductor, Utrecht Symphony Orch., 1979–83; Principal Conductor, BBC Robert Mayer concerts, 1978–87; now works widely as a guest conductor, and appears in America, Holland, France, Germany, Belgium, Italy, Norway, Spain, Portugal, Czechoslovakia, Israel, Hong Kong, Japan, Australia, New

Zealand and all parts of UK. FGSM 1972. *Recreations:* people, reading, walking, theology. *Address:* 25 Westfield Drive, Glasgow G52 2SG.

SEAMAN, Dick; *see* Seaman, R. J.

SEAMAN, Gilbert Frederick, AO 1981; CMG 1967; Chairman, State Bank of South Australia, 1963–83; Deputy Chairman, Electricity Trust of SA, 1970–84; Trustee, Savings Bank of SA, 1973–81; *b* 7 Sept. 1912; *s* of Eli S. Seaman, McLaren Vale, South Australia; *m* 1935, Avenal Essie Fong; one *s* one *d*. *Educ:* University of Adelaide. BEc, Associate of University of Adelaide, 1935, High School Teacher, Port Pirie and Unley, 1932–35; South Australian Public Service, 1936–41; Seconded to Commonwealth of Australia as Assistant Director of Manpower for SA, 1941–46; Economist, SA Treasury, 1946–60; Under Treasurer for SA, 1960–72. *Address:* 27 William Street, Hawthorn, SA 5062, Australia. *T:* 271–4271.

See also Sir K. D. Seaman.

SEAMAN, Sir Keith (Douglas), KCVO 1981; OBE 1976; Governor of South Australia, 1977–82; *b* 11 June 1920; *s* of late E. S. and E. M. Seaman; *m* 1946, Joan, *d* of F. Birbeck; one *s* one *d*. *Educ:* Unley High Sch.; Univ. of Adelaide (BA, LLB); Flinders Univ. (MA, DipHum). South Australian Public Service, 1937–54; RAAF Overseas HQ, London, 1941–45, Flt-Lieut. Entered Methodist Ministry, 1954: Renmark, 1954–58; Adelaide Central Methodist Mission, 1958–77 (Supt, 1971–77). Sec., Christian Television Assoc. of S Australia, 1959–73; Mem. Executive, World Assoc. of Christian Broadcasting, 1963–70; Director, 5KA, 5AU and 5RM Broadcasting Companies, 1960–77; Chm., 5KA, 5AU and 5RM, 1971–77. Mem., Australian Govt Social Welfare Commn, 1973–76. KStJ 1978. *Recreations:* reading, gardening. *Address:* Victor Harbor, SA 5211, Australia.

See also G. F. Seaman.

SEAMAN, Reginald Jaspar, (Dick Seaman); Director of Information, Department of Employment, 1978–80; *b* 19 March 1923; *o s* of Jaspar and Flora Seaman, Wandsworth; *m* 1950, Marian, *o d* of Henry and Ethel Sarah Moser. *Educ:* West Hill Elem. Sch., Wandsworth, SW18. Served War, 1940–46, RAF aircrew. Entered Civil Service as Post Office Messenger, 1937; Clerical Officer, HM Treasury, 1950; Asst Inf. Officer, Treasury, 1959–61; Inf. Officer, MAFF, 1961–64; Sen. Inf. Officer, DEA, 1964–67; Principal Inf. Officer, 1967–69; Chief Press Officer, DEP, 1969–72; Chief Inf. Officer, Northern Ireland Office, 1972–78. Silver Jubilee Medal, 1977. *Recreations:* orchids, horticulture (Chm., Caterham Horticultural Soc.). *Address:* 9 Ninehams Road, Caterham, Surrey.

SEAMMEN, Diana Jill; Director, VAT Control, and a Commissioner, HM Customs and Excise, since 1989; *b* 24 March 1948. *Educ:* Univ. of Sussex. HM Treasury, 1969–89. *Address:* The Boardroom, HM Customs and Excise, Wilberforce House, The Strand, Liverpool L2 7QA.

SEARBY, Philip James, CBE 1981; Secretary and Authority Finance Officer, UK Atomic Energy Authority, 1976–84; *b* 20 Sept. 1924; *s* of Leonard James and Lillian Mary Searby; *m* 1955, Mary Brent Dudley; two *s*. *Educ:* Bedford Sch.; Wadham Coll., Oxford (MA). Entered Civil Service, Min. of Nat. Insurance, 1949; Prime Minister's Statistical Branch, 1951; Private Sec. to Paymaster Gen. (Lord Cherwell), 1952; Principal, Atomic Energy Office, 1954. Joined UK Atomic Energy Authority, 1956; Dep. Gen. Sec., Harwell, 1959; Principal Economics and Programmes Officer, 1965; Authority Finance and Programmes Officer, 1971. St Albans Diocesan Reader, 1950. *Recreation:* gardening. *Address:* 35 Wordsworth Road, Harpenden, Herts AL5 4AG. *T:* Harpenden (05827) 60837. *Club:* United Oxford & Cambridge University.

SEARBY, Richard Henry; QC (Aust.) 1971; non-executive Deputy Chairman, News Corporation Ltd, since 1991 (Director, 1977–91; Chairman, 1981–91); non-executive Chairman: News Ltd, since 1991 (Director, 1977–91; Chairman, 1981–91); South China Morning Post, since 1991 (Director, 1986–91; Chairman, 1987–91); Deputy Chairman, Times Newspapers Holdings Ltd, 1981–91; Chairman, Equity Trustees Executors & Agency Co. Ltd, since 1980 (Director, since 1975); *b* 23 July 1931; *s* of late Henry and Mary Searby; *m* 1962, Caroline (*née* McAdam); three *s*. *Educ:* Geelong Grammar Sch., Corio, Vic; Corpus Christi Coll., Oxford Univ. (MA Hons). Called to Bar, Inner Temple, London, 1956; admitted Barrister and Solicitor, Victoria, Aust., 1956; called to Victorian Bar, 1957; Associate to late Rt Hon. Sir Owen Dixon, Chief Justice of Aust., 1956–59; commenced practice, Victorian Bar, 1959; Independent Lectr in Law relating to Executors and Trustees, Univ. of Melbourne, 1961–72. Director: CRA Ltd, 1979–; Shell Australia Ltd, 1979–; Ansett Transport Industries Ltd, 1979–; News Internat. plc, UK, 1982–91 (Chm., 1987–90). Reuter Trustee (Dir, Reuters Founders Share Co. Ltd), 1988–. Chm., Geelong Grammar Sch., 1983–89. *Recreations:* reading, music, tennis, fishing. *Address:* 126 Kooyong Road, Armadale, Vic 3143, Australia. *T:* (61)–(3)–205095. *Clubs:* Melbourne, Australian (Melbourne).

SEARLE, Rear-Adm. (retd) Malcolm Walter St Leger, CB 1955; CBE 1945; *b* Cape Colony, S Africa, 23 Dec. 1900; *e s* of late Sir Malcolm William Searle; *m* 1930, Betty Margaret Crampton; one *s* two *d*. *Educ:* accepted as Dominion cadet to enter RN, 1912; RN Colleges Osborne and Dartmouth, 1914–17. Served European War, 1914–19 (Grand Fleet and Baltic, 1917–1919); specialised in Gunnery, 1927; Comdr 1936 (Anti-aircraft Comdr); served War of 1939–45 (Fleet Gunnery Officer, Home Fleet, 1939–41; HMS Sheffield, Mediterranean and Arctic, 1941–43); Capt. 1943; CSO to Vice-Adm., E Fleet, 1943–44; COS to C-in-C East Indies Fleet, 1944–46; Dir of Plans (Q), Naval Staff, 1948–51; Commodore, RN Barracks, Portsmouth, 1951; Rear-Adm. 1952; Deputy Chief of Naval Personnel, 1953–55; retired, 1956. *Recreations:* formerly: small boat sailing, mountaineering, ski-ing. *Address:* Lindens, Kithurst Park, Storrington, Pulborough, West Sussex RH20 4JH.

SEARLE, Peter; Director-General, Mental Health Foundation, since 1990; *b* 5 Jan. 1941; *s* of Neville Searle and Edith Searle (*née* Hoyle); *m* 1964, (Margaret) Ann Parker; three *d* and one foster *d*. *Educ:* Manchester Grammar Sch.; Univ. of Bristol. Lewis's Ltd (retailers), 1961–67; Don Summers Evangelistic Assoc., 1968–70; Principal, St Brandon's Sch., Clevedon, 1971–78; Proprietor, Moxhull Hall, 1978–81; Exec. Dir, World Vision of Britain, 1981–89. Dep. Chm., Royal Commonwealth Soc. MInstD; MBIM. *Publications:* articles in professional jls. *Recreations:* sailing, talking, sleeping. *Address:* Mental Health Foundation, 8 Hallam Street, W1N 6DH. *T:* 071–580 0145. *Clubs:* Commonwealth Trust; Safari (Nairobi).

SEARLE, Ronald William Fordham, RDI 1988; AGI; artist; *b* Cambridge, 3 March 1920; *s* of late William James Searle and of Nellie Hunt; *m* 1st, Kaye Webb (marr. diss. 1967); one *s* one *d*; 2nd, 1967, Monica Koenig. *Educ:* Cambridge School of Art. Humorous work first published in Cambridge Daily News and Granta, 1935–39. Served with 287 Field Co. RE, 1939–46; captured by the Japanese at fall of Singapore, 1942; Prisoner of War in Siam and Malaya, 1942–45; Allied Force HQ Port Said Ops, 1956. Began contributing widely to nat. publications from 1946; creator of the schoolgirls of St Trinian's, 1941 (abandoned them in 1953); Cartoonist to Tribune, 1949–51; to Sunday Express, 1950–51; Special Feature artist, News Chronicle, 1951–53; Weekly Cartoonist, News Chronicle, 1954; Punch Theatre artist, 1949–62; Contributor, New Yorker. Designer of commemorative medals for: the French Mint, 1974–; British Art Medal Soc., 1983–. *Awards:* Art Dirs Club, Philadelphia, Medal, 1959; Nat. Cartoonists Soc. of America, Awards, 1959, 1960, 1966; Art Dirs Club, LA, Medal, 1959; Gold Medal, III Biennale Tolentino, 1965; Prix de la Critique Belge, 1968; Médaille de la ville d'Avignon, 1971; Prix d'Humour du Festival d'Avignon, 1971; Grand Prix de l'Humour noir "Grandville", 1971; Prix Internationale Charles Huard de dessin de presse, 1972. *One Man Exhibitions:* Batsford Gall., 1947; Leicester Galls, 1948, 1950, 1954, 1957; New York, 1959, 1963, 1969, 1976; Hannover, Tolentino (Italy), Stuttgart, Berlin, 1965; Bremerhaven, Basle, Linz, 1966; Galerie La Pochade, Paris, 1966, 1967, 1968, 1969, 1971; Galerie Gurlitt, Munich, 1967, 1968, 1969, 1970, 1971, 1973, 1976; Grosvenor Gall., London, Brussels, 1968; Frankfurt, 1969; Konstanz, Würzburg, 1970; Salzburg, 1971; Lausanne, Poncey, 1972; Paris, Vienna, 1973; Lausanne, 1974; Paris, 1975; Berlin, Hannover, Stuttgart, Mainz, Recklinghausen, New York, Stuttgart, Paris, 1976; Brussels, London, Paris, 1977; London, Vienna, Lausanne, Berlin, 1978; Graz, Tübingen, Salzburg, 1979; Bonn, Heidelberg, 1980; Rizzoli Gall., NY, Gal. Bartsch & Chariau, Munich, 1981; Cooper-Hewitt Museum, NY, 1984; Neue Galerie Wien, 1985, 1988; Imperial War Museum, BM, 1986; Fitzwilliam Museum, Cambridge, 1987; Mus. of Fine Arts, San Francisco, 1987–88. *Works in permanent collections:* V&A, BM, Imperial War Museum, Tate Gall.; Bibliothèque Nat., Paris; Kunsthalle, Bremen; Wilhelm-Busch Museum, Hanover; Stadtmuseum, Munich; Art Museum, Dallas, Texas; Staatlische Mus., Berlin-Dahlem; Cooper-Hewitt Museum, NY; Univ. of Texas, Austin; Mus. of Fine Arts, San Francisco. *Films based on the characters of St Trinian's:* The Belles of St Trinian's, 1954; Blue Murder at St Trinian's, 1957; The Pure Hell of St Trinian's, 1960; The Great St Trinian's Train Robbery, 1966; The Wildcats of St Trinian's, 1980. *Films designed:* John Gilpin, 1951; On the Twelfth Day, 1954 (Acad. Award Nomination); Energetically Yours (USA), 1957; Germany, 1960 (for Suddeutschen RTV); The King's Breakfast, 1962; Those Magnificent Men in their Flying Machines (Animation Sequence), 1965; Monte Carlo or Bust (Animation Sequence), 1969; Scrooge (Animation Sequence), 1970; Dick Deadeye, 1975. *Publications:* Forty Drawings, 1946; Le Nouveau Ballet Anglais, 1947; Hurrah for St Trinian's!, 1948; The Female Approach, 1949; Back to the Slaughterhouse, 1951; John Gilpin, 1952; Souls in Torment, 1953; Rake's Progress, 1955; Merry England, etc, 1956; A Christmas Carol, 1961; Which Way Did He Go, 1961; Searle in the Sixties, 1964; From Frozen North to Filthy Lucre, 1964; Pardong M'sieur, 1965; Searle's Cats, 1967; The Square Egg, 1968; Take one Toad, 1968; Baron Munchausen, 1960; Hello—where did all the people go?, 1969; Hommage à Toulouse-Lautrec, 1969; Secret Sketchbook, 1970; The Addict, 1971; More Cats, 1975; Drawings from Gilbert and Sullivan, 1975; The Zoodiac, 1977; Ronald Searle (Monograph), 1978; The King of Beasts, 1980; The Big Fat Cat Book, 1982; Illustrated Winespeak, 1983; Ronald Searle in Perspective (monograph), 1984; Ronald Searle's Golden Oldies 1941–61, 1985; To the Kwai—and Back, 1986; Something in the Cellar, 1986; Ah Yes, I Remember It Well . . ., 1987; Ronald Searle's Non-Sexist Dictionary, 1988; Slightly Foxed—but still desirable, 1989; *in collaboration:* (with D. B. Wyndham Lewis) The Terror of St Trinian's, 1952; (with Geoffrey Willans) Down with Skool, 1953; How to be Topp, 1954; Whizz for Atomms, 1956; The Compleet Molesworth, 1958; The Dog's Ear Book, 1958; Back in the Jug Agane, 1959; (with Kaye Webb) Paris Sketchbook, 1950 and 1957; Looking at London, 1953; The St Trinian's Story, 1959; Refugees 1960, 1960; (with Alex Atkinson) The Big City, 1958; USA for Beginners, 1959; Russia for Beginners, 1960; Escape from the Amazon!, 1964; (with A. Andrews & B. Richardson) Those Magnificent Men in their Flying Machines, 1965; (with Heinz Huber) Haven't We Met Before Somewhere?, 1966; (with Kildare Dobbs) The Great Fur Opera, 1970; (with Irwin Shaw) Paris! Paris!, 1977; Ronald Searle: a biography, by Russell Davies, 1990. *Address:* c/o Tessa Sayle, 11 Jubilee Place, SW3 3TE. *T:* 071–823 3883. *Club:* Garrick.

SEARS, Hon. Raymond Arthur William; Hon. Mr Justice Sears; Judge of the Supreme Court of Hong Kong, since 1986; Commissioner of the Supreme Court of Brunei Darussalam, since 1987; *b* 10 March 1933; *s* of William Arthur and Lillian Sears; *m* 1960 (marr. diss. 1981); one *s* one *d*. *Educ:* Epsom Coll.; Jesus Coll., Cambridge. BA 1956. Lieut RA (TA) Airborne, 1953. Called to Bar, Gray's Inn, 1957. QC 1975; Recorder of the Crown Court, 1977–86. *Recreations:* watching horse-racing; music. *Address:* Supreme Court, Hong Kong. *Clubs:* Royal Automobile; Hong Kong, Royal Hong Kong Jockey.

SEATON, Colin Robert; Secretary to the University Commissioners, since 1988; Chairman, Medical Appeal Tribunals, since 1989; Barrister-at-Law; *b* 21 Nov. 1928; 2nd *s* of late Arthur William Robert Seaton and Helen Amelia Seaton (*née* Stone); *m* 1952, Betty (*née* Gosling); two *s*. *Educ:* Wallington County Grammar Sch. for Boys; Worcester Coll., Oxford. BA 1953; MA 1956. Royal Air Force, 1947–49. Called to Bar, Inner Temple, 1956 (Profumo Prize, 1953, 1954); Schoolmaster for LCC, 1953–57; Solicitor's Dept, Ministries of Health and Housing and Local Govt, also Dept of the Environment, 1957–71; Sec. (Master) of Nat. Industrial Relations Court, 1971–74; Under Sec., Lord Chancellor's Dept, 1974–88; Circuit Administrator: Northern Circuit, 1974–82; SE Circuit, 1982–83; Head, Legislation Gp, 1983–88. Sec., Lord Chancellor's Law Reform Cttee, 1983–88. *Publication:* Aspects of the National Health Service Acts, 1966. *Recreations:* golf, reading. *Address:* Tree Tops, The Drive, Coulsdon, Surrey CR5 2BL. *T:* 081–668 5538. *Club:* Civil Service.

See also M. J. Seaton.

SEATON, Prof. Michael John, FRS 1967; Professor of Physics, Department of Physics and Astronomy, University College London, 1963–88, now Emeritus; Senior Fellow, Science and Engineering Research Council, 1984–88; *b* 16 Jan. 1923; *s* of late Arthur William Robert Seaton and Helen Amelia Seaton; *m* 1st, 1943, Olive May (*d* 1959), *d* of Charles Edward Singleton; one *s* one *d*; 2nd, 1960, Joy Clarice, *d* of Harry Albert Balchin; one *s*. *Educ:* Wallington Co. Sch., Surrey; University Coll., London (Fellow, 1972). BSc 1948, PhD 1951, London. Dept of Physics, UCL: Asst Lectr, 1950; Lectr, 1953; Reader, 1959; Prof., 1963. Chargé de Recherche, Institut d'Astrophysique, Paris, 1954–55; Univ. of Colorado, 1961; Fellow-Adjoint, Jt Inst. for Laboratory Astrophysics (Nat. Bureau of Standards and Univ. of Colorado), Boulder, Colo, 1964–. Hon. Mem., Amer. Astronomical Soc., 1983; For. Associate, Amer. Nat. Acad. of Scis, 1986. Pres., RAS, 1979–81, Gold Medal, 1983; Guthrie Medal and Prize, Inst. of Physics, 1984. Dr *hc* Observatoire de Paris, 1976; Hon. DSc QUB, 1982. *Publications:* papers on atomic physics and astrophysics in various jls. *Address:* 51 Hall Drive, Sydenham, SE26 6XL. *T:* 081–778 7121.

See also C. R. Seaton.

SEAWARD, Colin Hugh, CBE 1987; HM Diplomatic Service, retired; *b* 16 Sept. 1926; *s* of late Sydney W. Seaward and Molly W. Seaward; *m* 1st, 1949, Jean Bugler (decd); three *s* one *d*; 2nd, 1973, Judith Margaret Hinkley; two *d*. *Educ:* RNC, Dartmouth. Served Royal Navy, 1944–65. Joined HM Diplomatic Service, 1965; served: Accra, 1965; Bathurst (Banjul), 1966; FO, 1968; Rio de Janeiro, 1971; Prague, 1972; FCO, 1973; RNC, Greenwich (sowc), 1976; Counsellor (Econ. and Comm.), Islamabad, 1977–80; Consul-General, Rio de Janeiro, 1980–86, retd; re-employed in FCO, 1987–91. Hon. Sec., Anglo-Brazilian Soc., 1986–. Freeman, City of London, 1987. *Address:* Brasted House, Brasted, Westerham, Kent TN16 1JA.

SEBAG-MONTEFIORE, Harold Henry; Barrister-at-law; Deputy Circuit Judge, 1973–83; *b* 5 Dec. 1924; *e s* of late John Sebag-Montefiore and Violet, *o c* of late James Henry Solomon; *m* 1968, Harriet, *o d* of Benjamin Harrison Paley, New York; one step *d. Educ:* Stowe; Lower Canada Coll., Montreal; Pembroke Coll., Cambridge (MA). Served War of 1939–45, RAF. Called to Bar, Lincoln's Inn, 1951. Contested (C) North Paddington, Gen. Elec., 1959; Chm., Conservative Parly Candidates Assoc., 1960–64. Member: LCC, 1955–65; GLC, for Cities of London and Westminster, 1964–73, First Chm., GLC Arts and Recreation Cttee, 1968–73; Sports Council, 1972–74. Pres., Anglo-Jewish Assoc., 1966–71; Jt Pres., Barkingside Jewish Youth Centre, 1988–; Mem. Council, Anglo-Netherlands Soc., 1988–. Freeman, City of London, and Liveryman, Spectacle Makers' Co. Trustee: Nat. Theatre Foundn; Internat. Festival of Youth Orchestras; Whitechapel Art Gall.; Touro National Heritage, RI; Mem., Cttee of Honour: RAH Centenary; "Fanfare for Europe"; William and Mary Tercentenary; Centenary of Montefiore Hosp., NY. Rode winner of Bar Point-to-Point, 1957 and 1959. Chevalier, Légion d'Honneur, 1973. *Publications:* book reviews and articles on Polo under *nom-de-plume* of "Marco II". *Recreation:* collecting conductors' batons. *Address:* 4 Breams Buildings, Chancery Lane, EC4A 1AQ. *T:* 071–353 5835. *Clubs:* Carlton, Garrick, Hurlingham, Pegasus (Pres., 1979).

SEBASTIAN, Timothy; freelance writer and journalist; *b* 13 March 1952; *s* of Peter Sebastian and Pegitha Saunders; *m* 1977, Diane Buscombe; one *s* two *d. Educ:* Westminster School; New College, Oxford. BA (Hons) Mod. Lang. BBC Eastern Europe correspondent, 1979–82; BBC TV News: Europe correspondent, 1982–84; Moscow correspondent, 1984–85; Washington correspondent, 1986–89. TV journalist of the year, RTS, 1982; Richard Dimbleby Award, BAFTA, 1982. *Publications:* Nice Promises, 1985; I Spy in Russia, 1986; *novels:* The Spy in Question, 1988; Spy Shadow, 1989; Saviour's Gate, 1990.

SEBRIGHT, Sir Peter Giles Vivian, 15th Bt *cr* 1626, of Besford, Worcs; *b* 2 Aug. 1953; *s* of Sir Hugo Giles Edmund Sebright, 14th Bt and of Deirdre Ann, *d* of late Major Vivian Lionel Slingsby Bethell; *S* father, 1985; *m* 1st, 1977, Regina Maria (marr. diss.), *d* of Francis Steven Clarebrough, Melbourne; one *s*; 2nd, Madeleine; one *s. Heir: s* Rufus Hugo Giles Sebright, *b* 31 July 1978.

SECCOMBE, family name of **Baroness Seccombe.**

SECCOMBE, Baroness *cr* 1991 (Life Peer), of Kineton in the County of Warwickshire; **Joan Anna Dalziel Seccombe,** DBE 1984; JP; Vice-Chairman, with special responsibility for women, Conservative Party, since 1987; Chairman, National Union of Conservative and Unionist Associations, 1987–88 (Vice-Chairman, 1984–87; Member of Executive, since 1975); *b* 3 May 1930; *d* of Robert John Owen and Olive Barlow Owen; *m* 1950, Henry Lawrence Seccombe; two *s. Educ:* St Martin's Sch., Solihull. Member: Heart of England Tourist Bd, 1977–81 (Chm., Marketing Sub-Cttee, 1979–81); Women's Nat. Commn., 1984–90; Chairman: W Midlands Area Cons. Women's Cttee, 1975–78; Cons. Women's Nat. Cttee, 1981–84; Cons. Party Social Affairs Forum, 1985–87; Dep. Chm., W Midlands Area Cons. Council, 1979–81. Mem., W Midlands CC, 1979–81 (Chm., Trading Standards Cttee, 1979–81). Governor, Nuffield Hosps, 1988–. JP Solihull, 1968 (Chm., 1981–84). *Recreations:* golf, ski-ing. *Address:* Trethias, Norton Grange, Little Kineton, Warwicks CV35 0DP. *T:* Kineton (0926) 460562.
See also Hon. Sir J. A. D. Owen.

SECCOMBE, Hugh Digorie, CBE 1976; Chairman, Seccombe Marshall & Campion Ltd, 1962–77; *b* 3 June 1917; *s* of Lawrence Henry Seccombe, CBE and Norah (*née* Wood); *m* 1947, Eirene Rosemary Banister, *d* of Richard Whittow and Eirene, and *widow* of Lieut P. C. McC. Banister, DSC, RN; one *s* one *d. Educ:* Stowe; Sidney Sussex Coll., Cambridge (BA 1938, MA 1942). RNVR, 1939–50; retd, Lt-Comdr. Joined Seccombe Marshall & Campion, 1938; Dir, 1947. Chm., YWCA Central Club, 1971–86. Fellow, Inst. of Bankers, 1964. *Recreations:* gardening, fishing. *Address:* Sparkes Place, Wonersh, Guildford, Surrey GU5 0PH. *T:* Guildford (0483) 893296; Benmore Lodge, Isle of Mull, Argyllshire PA71 6HU. *T:* Aros (0680) 300351.

SECCOMBE, Sir (William) Vernon (Stephen), Kt 1988; JP; Chairman, Plymouth Health Authority, since 1990; former electrical contractor; *b* 14 Jan. 1928; *s* of Stephen Seccombe and Edith Violet (*née* Henbry-Smith); *m* 1950, Margaret Vera Profit; four *s. Educ:* Saltash Grammar Sch.; Plymouth and Devonport Tech. Coll. Mem., E Cornwall Water Bd, 1960–74 (Vice-Chm., 1963–66; Chm., 1966–69); Chairman: Cornwall and Isles of Scilly DHA, late AHA, 1981–82; S Western RHA, 1983–90; Dep. Comr, 1970–79, Comr, 1979–82, Western Area Traffic Comrs. Member: Saltash BC, 1953–74 (Chairman: Works Cttee, 1956–62; Finance and Estabs Cttee, 1963–74; Mayor, 1962–63); Caradon DC, 1973–79 (Vice-Chm., 1973–76; Chm., 1976–78). Governor, Saltash Comprehensive Sch., 1970–81 (Chm., 1974–78). JP Cornwall East South Bench, 1970. *Recreations:* industrial and local archaeology, genealogy, watching Association football, listening to military music. *Address:* Derriford Business Park, Plymouth PL6 5XP.

SECOMBE, Sir Harry (Donald), Kt 1981; CBE 1963; actor, comedian and singer; *b* 8 Sept. 1921; *m* 1948, Myra Joan Atherton, Swansea; two *s* two *d. Educ:* Dynevor School, Swansea. Served with Royal Artillery, 1939–46. Windmill Theatre, 1947–48; General Variety since 1948. Appearances include: at London Palladium, 1956, 1958, 1959, 1961, 1966; in Roy. Command Perfs, 1951, 1955, 1957, 1958, 1963, 1966, 1969, 1975, 1978, 1987; (musical) Pickwick, Saville, 1963; (musical) The Four Musketeers, Drury Lane, 1967; The Plumber's Progress, Prince of Wales, 1975. Radio: Goon Show, 1949–60, and special performance of Goon Show for 50th Anniversary of BBC, 1972. Television: BBC, ITV, CBS (New York), Yorkshire TV, 1950–; Presenter, Highway, Tyne Tees TV, 1983–. Films: Davy, for Ealing Films, 1957; Jetstorm, 1959; Bed-Sitting Room, 1968; Mr Bumble in Oliver!, 1968; Bjornsen in Song of Norway, 1969; Rhubarb, 1969; Doctor in Trouble, 1970; The Magnificent Seven Deadly Sins, 1971; Sunstruck, 1972. Has made recordings for HMV, 1953–54, Philips Records, 1955–80, Celebrity Records, 1980–; Telstar, and Word Records, 1987. FRSA 1971. Hon. DMus Wales, 1986. *Publications:* Twice Brightly, 1974; Goon for Lunch, 1975; Katy and the Nurgla, 1978; Welsh Fargo, 1981; Goon Abroad, 1982; The Harry Secombe Diet Book, 1983; Harry Secombe's Highway, 1984; The Highway Companion, 1987; Arias and Raspberries (autobiog.), 1989. *Recreations:* film photography, literature, travel, golf, cricket. *Address:* 46 St James's Place, SW1. *T:* 071–629 2768. *Clubs:* Savage, Royal Automobile, Lord's Taverners, Variety Club of Great Britain, St James's (Founder Mem.).

SECONDÉ, Sir Reginald (Louis), KCMG 1981 (CMG 1972); CVO 1968 (MVO 1957); HM Diplomatic Service, retired; Ambassador to Venezuela, 1979–82; *b* 28 July 1922; *s* of late Lt-Col Emile Charles Secondé and Doreen Secondé (*née* Sutherland); *m* 1951, Catherine Penelope, *d* of late Thomas Ralph Sneyd-Kynnersley, OBE, MC and late Alice Sneyd-Kynnersley; one *s* two *d. Educ:* Beaumont; King's Coll., Cambridge. Served, 1941–47, in Coldstream Guards: N Africa and Italy (despatches); Major. Entered Diplomatic Service, 1949; UK Delegn to the UN, New York, 1951–55; British Embassy: Lisbon, 1955–57; Cambodia, 1957–59; FO, 1959–62; British Embassy, Warsaw, 1962–64; First Secretary and later Political Counsellor, Rio de Janeiro, 1964–69; Head of S European Dept, FCO, 1969–72; Royal Coll. of Defence Studies, 1972–73; Ambassador to Chile, 1973–76, to Romania, 1977–79. Comdr, Order of the Southern Cross (Brazil), 1968. *Recreations:* gardening, shooting. *Address:* Wamil Hall, near Mildenhall, Suffolk IP28 7JZ. *T:* Mildenhall (0638) 714160. *Club:* Cavalry and Guards.

SECRETAN, Lance Hilary Kenyon; consultant, lecturer, journalist, author and entrepreneur, since 1981; President: The Thaler Corporation Inc., since 1980; Thaler Resources Ltd, since 1981; Chief Executive Officer, The Kenyon Corporation SA, since 1972; *b* 1 Aug. 1939; *s* of late Kenyon and of Marie-Therese Secretan; *m* 1961, Gloria Christina (marr. diss. 1990); two *d* (and one *d* decd). *Educ:* Los Cocos, Argentina; Italia Conti, London; St Peters, Bournemouth; Univ. of Waterloo, Canada; Univ. of Southern California (MA in International Relations, *cum laude*); LSE (PhD in International Relations). Toronto Stock Exchange, 1958–59; Office Overload Co. Ltd, 1959–67; Man. Dir, Manpower Ltd Gp of Cos, UK, Ireland, Middle East and Africa, 1967–81. Prof. of Entrepreneurship, York Univ., Toronto, 1983–85. FIEC 1969; FRSA 1981. *Publications:* How to be an Effective Secretary, 1972; Managerial Moxie, 1985; The State of Small Business in Ontario, 1986; The Masterclass, 1988; The Way of the Tiger, 1989. *Recreation:* life. *Address:* RR2, Alton, Ontario, L0N 1A0, Canada; 38 Chester Terrace, Regent's Park, NW1 4ND. *Clubs:* Mensa, White Elephant; University (Toronto).

SEDCOLE, Cecil Frazer, FCA; a Vice Chairman, Unilever PLC, 1982–85; *b* 15 March 1927; *s* of late William John Sedcole and Georgina Irene Kathleen Bluett (*née* Moffatt); *m* 1962, Jennifer Bennett Riggall; one *s* one *d. Educ:* Uppingham Sch., Rutland. FCA 1952; CBIM 1982. Joined Unilever Group of Cos, 1952: Dir, Birds Eye Foods, 1960–66; Vice-Chairman: Langnese-Iglo, Germany, 1966–67; Frozen Products Gp, Rotterdam, 1967–71; Dir, Unilever PLC and Unilever NV, 1974–85; Chm., UAC International, 1976–79; Mem., 1971–75, Chm., 1979–85, Overseas Cttee, Unilever; Dir, Tate & Lyle, 1982–90; Dep. Chm., Reed International, 1985–87. Mem., BOTB, 1982–86; Mem. Bd, Commonwealth Devlt Corp., 1984–88. Trustee, Leverhulme Trust, 1982–. Governor, Bedales Sch., 1983–90. *Recreation:* golf. *Address:* Beeches, Tyrrell's Wood, Leatherhead, Surrey KT22 8QH. *Club:* Royal Air Force.

SEDDON, Richard Harding, PhD; RWS 1976 (ARWS 1972); ARCA; artist and writer; *b* 1 May 1915; *s* of Cyril Harding Seddon; *m* 1946, Audrey Madeline Wareham. *Educ:* King Edward VII School; Roy. Coll. of Art; Univ. of Reading (PhD 1946). Demonstrator in Fine Art, Univ. of Reading, 1944; Extra-Mural Staff Tutor in Fine Art, Univ. of Birmingham, 1947; Director, Sheffield City Art Galleries, 1948–63; Curator, Ruskin Collection, 1948–63; Dir of Art History and Liberal Studies, Sch. of Design and Furniture, Buckinghamshire Coll. of Higher Educn, 1963–80. Hon. Advisory Panel, Hereford Art Galls, 1948; Arts Council Selection Bd (Art Students Exhib.), 1947; Pres. Ludlow Art Soc., 1947–67; Hon. Member: Sheffield Soc. of Artists; Oxford Folk Art Soc.; Sheffield Photographic Soc.; Mem., Oxford Bureau for Artists in War-time, 1940; Chm. Selection Cttee, Nottingham Artists Exhibition, 1953; Guest Speaker Educational Centres Association Annual Conference, 1951; West Riding Artists Exhibition Selection Committee, 1956; Northern Young Artists Exhibition Selection Committee, 1958; Member Sheffield Univ. Court; Sheffield Diocesan Advisory Cttee, 1948. Exhibitor at: RA; NEAC; RI; RBA; Internat. Artists; Architectural Assoc.; RIBA; National Gallery (War Artists) 1943; Leicester Galleries; Redfern Galleries. Official acquisitions: V. & A. Museum, 1939; Pilgrim Trust, 1942; Imperial War Museum (War Artists), 1943, 1956 (ten paintings); Graves Gall., Sheffield, 1943 and 1956; Atkinson Gall., Southport, 1953; Reading Art Gall., 1956; Leeds Education Cttee Collection, 1956. Extra Mural and Univ. Extension lectr on art to Univs of Oxford, Birmingham, London and Sheffield, 1948–; initiated Sheffield Conference on Nation's Art Treasures, 1958; FMA, 1951–74; Mem. Yorkshire Fed. Museums and Art Galls, 1948 (Committee 1952 and 1957, President, 1954–55, Vice-President, 1955–56); Secretary Yorks Museums Regional Fact Finding Committee, 1959; National Art Collections Fund Rep. for Yorks, 1954–63; Judge for Wakefield Art Galls Open Art Competition, 1984. Hon. Adviser to Co. of Cutlers in Hallamshire, 1950–64; Dep. Chm., Sheffield Design Council for Gold, Silver and Jewelry Trades, 1960; Mem. BBC '51 Soc., 1960; Mem. Govg Council, Design and Res. Centre, 1960; Mem. Art Adv. Cttee Yorks Area Scheme for Museums and Art Galleries, 1963; Art Critic: Birmingham Post, 1963–71; Yorkshire Post, 1974–; Jl Fedn of British Artists, 1975–83; Mem. Recognised Panel of London Univ. Extension Lectrs, 1964; Mem. Council and Hon. Treasurer, 1976, Trustee, 1983–86, RWS; Hon. Treas., Artists' League of GB, 1984–86. Hon. Mem., Mark Twain Soc., USA, 1976. War Service with RAOC Field Park, France, 1940 (King's Badge); facilities by War Office Order to make war drawings in Maginot Line, 1940. *Publications:* The Technical Methods of Paul Nash (Memorial Vol.), 1949; The Artist's Vision, 1949; The Academic Technique of Oil Painting, 1960; A Hand Uplifted (war memoirs), 1962; Art Collecting for Amateurs, 1964; (ed) Dictionary of Art Terms, 1981; The Artist's Studio Book, 1983; articles on fine art for Jl of Aesthetics (USA), Burlington Magazine, Apollo, The Studio, The Connoisseur, Arch. Review, The Artist, The Antique Collector and daily press; lectures on art in England and abroad; criticisms; book reviews; broadcasts. *Recreation:* gardening. *Address:* 6 Arlesey Close, Putney, SW15 2EX. *T:* 081–788 5899.

SEDGEMORE, Brian Charles John; MP (Lab) Hackney South and Shoreditch, since 1983; *b* 17 March 1937; *s* of Charles John Sedgemore, fisherman; *m* 1964 (marr. diss.); one *s. Educ:* Newtown Primary Sch.; Heles Sch.; Oxford Univ. (MA). Diploma in public and social administration. Called to Bar, Middle Temple, 1966. RAF, 1956–58; Oxford, 1958–62. Administrative Class, Civil Service, Min. of Housing and Local Govt, 1962–66 (Private Sec. to R. J. Mellish, MP, then junior Minister of Housing, 1964–66). Practising barrister, 1966–74. MP (Lab) Luton West, Feb. 1974–1979; PPS to Tony Benn, MP, 1977–78. Researcher, Granada TV, 1980–83. *Publications:* The How and Why of Socialism, 1977; Mr Secretary of State (fiction), 1979; The Secret Constitution, 1980; Power Failure (fiction), 1985; Big Bang 2000, 1986; contributor to Tribune, one time contributor to Britain's top satirical magazine. *Recreation:* sleeping on the grass. *Address:* 71 Riverside Walk, Hackney, E5; House of Commons, SW1.

SEDGMAN, Francis Arthur, AM 1980; Lawn Tennis Champion: Australia, 1949, 1950; USA, 1951, 1952; Wimbledon, 1952; Italy, 1952; Asia, 1952; Professional Tennis Player since 1953; *b* Victoria, Australia, 29 Oct. 1927; *m* 1952, Jean Margaret Spence; four *d. Educ:* Box Hill High School, Vic, Australia. First played in the Australian Davis Cup team, 1949; also played in winning Australian Davis Cup team, 1950, 1951, 1952. With John Bromwich, won Wimbledon doubles title, 1948; with Kenneth McGregor, won the Australian, French, Wimbledon and American doubles titles in the same year (1951), the only pair ever to do so; with Kenneth McGregor also won Australian, French and Wimbledon doubles titles, 1952; with Doris Hart, won French, Wimbledon and US mixed doubles titles, 1952. Last male player to win three titles at Wimbledon in one year, 1952. Director of many private companies including: Tennis Camps of Australia Pty Ltd; Reelco Industries Pty Ltd; Polytray Pty Ltd. Australian Hall of Fame, 1987. *Publication:* Winning Tennis, 1955. *Recreations:* golfing, racing. *Address:* 19 Bolton Avenue, Hampton, Victoria 3188, Australia. *T:* 598 6341. *Clubs:* All England Tennis and Croquet, Queen's; Melbourne Cricket (Melbourne); Kooyong Tennis; Grace Park Tennis; Victoria Amateur

Turf, Victoria Racing; Royal Melbourne Golf, Carbine (Melbourne); Mornington Racing.

SEDGWICK, Mrs A. R. M.; *see* Milkina, Nina.

SEDGWICK, Peter Norman; Head of International Finance Group (Under Secretary), HM Treasury, since 1990; *b* 4 Dec. 1943; *s* of Norman Victor Sedgwick and Lorna Clara (*née* Burton); *m* 1984, Catherine Jane, *d* of Mr and Mrs B. D. T. Saunders; two *s* two *d*. *Educ:* Westminster Cathedral Choir Sch.; Downside; Lincoln Coll., Oxford (MA PPE, BPhilEcon). HM Treasury: Economic Asst, 1969; Economic Adviser, 1971; Sen. Economic Adviser, 1977; Under Sec., 1984. Chm. 1979–84, Mem. Develt Cttee 1984–, London Symphony Chorus. *Recreation:* singing. *Address:* c/o HM Treasury, Parliament Street, SW1P 3AG.

SEDLEY, Stephen John; QC 1983; *b* 9 Oct. 1939; *s* of William and Rachel Sedley; *m* 1968, Ann Tate; one *s* two *d*. *Educ:* Mill Hill Sch.; Queens' Coll., Cambridge (BA Hons 1961). Freelance writer, interpreter, musician, translator, 1961–64; called to the Bar, Inner Temple, 1964, Bencher, 1989; a Pres., Nat. Reference Tribunals for the Coalmining Industry, 1983–88. Vis. Professorial Fellow, Warwick Univ., 1981; Vis. Fellow, Osgoode Hall Law Sch., Canada, 1987. A Dir, Public Law Project, 1989–. Mem., Internat. Commn on Mercenaries, Angola, 1976. Sec., Haldane Soc., 1964–69. *Publications:* (trans.) From Burgos Jail, by Marcos Ana and Vidal de Nicolas, 1964; (ed) Seeds of Love (anthology), 1967; (contrib.) Orwell: inside the myth, 1984; (contrib.) Civil Liberty, 1984; (contrib.) Police, the Constitution and the Community, 1986; (contrib.) Challenging Decisions, 1986; (contrib.) Public Interest Law, 1987; Whose Child? (report of inquiry into death of Tyra Henry), 1987; (contrib.) Civil Liberties in Conflict, 1988; (contrib.) Law in East and West, 1988; contrib. London Review of Books, Public Law, Modern Law Review, Jl of Law and Soc., Civil Justice Qly. *Recreations:* carpentry, music, cycling, walking, changing the world. *Address:* 3 Torriano Cottages, NW5 2TA. *T:* 071–485 3660.

SEDOV, Leonid I.; 6 Orders of Lenin, Hero of Socialist Labour, USSR; Professor, Moscow University, since 1937; Chief of Department of Hydrodynamics, since 1941; Member, USSR Academy of Sciences; *b* 14 Nov. 1907; *m* 1931, Galya Tolstova; one *s* one *d*. *Educ:* Moscow University. Chief Engineer, Associate Chief lab., N.E. Zhukovsky Aerohydrodynamic Inst., Moscow, 1930–47; Vice-President, International Astronautical Federation, 1962–80 (Pres., 1959–61); Internat. Astronautical Acad., 1980–. Hon. Member: American Academy of Arts and Sciences; Internat. Astronautical Acad.; Serbian Academy, Belgrade; Tech. Academy, Finland; For. Associate, Acad. of Sciences, Paris; Academia Leopoldina. Hon. doctorates from many foreign universities. Medal of Obert; State Prize; Chaplygin Prize; Lomonosov Prize; Lyapunov Medal; Guggenheim Award; Van Allen Award. Commandeur de la Légion d'Honneur (France). *Publications:* Theory of Plane Flow of Liquids, 1939; Plane Problems of Hydrodynamics and Aerodynamics, 1950, 1966, 1980; Similarity and Dimensional Methods in Mechanics, 1944, 1951, 1953, 1957, 1960, 1965, 1967, 1977; Introduction into the Mechanics of Continua, 1962; Mechanics of Continuous Media, 2 vols, 1970, 1973, 1976, 1983–84; Thoughts about Science and Scientists, 1980; (with A. G. Tsypkin) Fundamentals of Electromagnetical and Gravitational Macroscopic Theories, 1989; numerous articles. *Address:* Moscow University, Zone U, kv 84 Leninskie Gory, Moscow B-234, USSR.

SEEAR, family name of **Baroness Seear.**

SEEAR, Baroness *cr* 1971 (Life Peer), of Paddington; **Beatrice Nancy Seear,** PC 1985; formerly Reader in Personnel Management, University of London, The London School of Economics, retired 1978, Hon. Fellow, 1980; Deputy Leader, Social & Liberal Democrats, House of Lords, since 1988 (Liberal Leader, 1984–88); *b* 7 Aug. 1913; *d* of late Herbert Charles Seear and Beatrice Maud Catchpole. *Educ:* Croydon High Sch.; Newnham Coll., Cambridge (Hon. Fellow, 1983); London Sch. of Economics and Political Science. BA (Cambridge Hist. Tripos). Personnel Officer, C. & J. Clark Ltd, shoe manufacturers, 1936–46; seconded as Mem. (pt-time), staff of Production Efficiency Bd at Min. of Aircraft Production, 1943–45; Teacher at London School of Economics, 1946–78. Vis. Prof. of Personnel Management, City Univ., 1980–87. Member: Hansard Soc. Commn on Electoral Reform, 1975–76; Top Salaries Review Body, 1971–84. Council, Morley Coll. President: BSI, 1974–77; Women's Liberal Fedn, 1974; Fawcett Soc., 1970–85; Inst. of Personnel Management, 1977–79; Carers Nat. Assoc. Mem. Council, Industrial Soc., 1972–84. Hon. LLD: Leeds, 1979; Exeter, 1989; Hon. DLit Bath, 1982. *Publications:* (with P. Jephcott and J. H. Smith) Married Women Working, 1962; (with V. Roberts and J. Brock) A Career for Women in Industry?, 1964; Industrial Social Services, 1964; The Position of Women in Industry, 1967; The Re-Entry of Women into Employment, 1971. *Recreations:* travel, gardening. *Address:* 189b Kennington Road, SE11 6ST. *T:* 071–587 0205. *Club:* Commonwealth Trust.

SEEL, Derek, FDSRCS; Consultant in Orthodontics, Welsh Regional Health Authority, since 1969; Dental Postgraduate Dean, University of Bristol, since 1986; Dean, Faculty of Dental Surgery, Royal College of Surgeons, since 1990; *b* 2 April 1932; *s* of William Alfred and Olive Seel; *m* 1960, Gillian Henderson. *Educ:* Stockport Sch.; Manchester Univ. Inst. of Dental Surgery (BDS). MOrthRCS. General dental practice, 1956–62; orthodontic trainee, 1962–68; Lectr in Orthodontics, Bristol Univ., 1967–69; Univ. of Wales Coll. of Medicine, 1969–. *Recreations:* music, ski-ing. *Address:* 20 Blenheim Road, Bristol BS6 7JP. *T:* Bristol (0272) 736635.

SEELY, family name of **Baron Mottistone.**

SEELY, Sir Nigel (Edward), 5th Bt *cr* 1896; Dorland International; *b* 28 July 1923; *s* of Sir Victor Basil John Seely, 4th Bt and of Sybil Helen, *d* of late Sills Clifford Gibbons; *S* father, 1980; *m* 1949, Loraine, *d* of late W. W. Lindley-Travis; three *d*; *m* 1984, Trudi Pacter, *d* of Sydney Pacter. *Educ:* Stowe. *Heir: half-b* Victor Ronald Seely [*b* 1 Aug. 1941; *m* 1972, Annette Bruce, *d* of Lt-Col J. A. D. McEwen; one *s* one *d*]. *Address:* 3 Craven Hill Mews, W2 3DY. *Clubs:* Buck's; Royal Solent.

SEENEY, Leslie Elon Sidney, OBE 1978; Director General (formerly General Secretary), National Chamber of Trade, 1971–87; *b* 19 Jan. 1922; *s* of Sidney Leonard and Daisy Seeney, Forest Hill; *m* 1947, Marjory Doreen Greenwood, Spalding; one *s*. *Educ:* St Matthews, Camberwell. RAFVR, 1941–46 (Flt Lt, Pilot). Man. Dir, family manufrg business (clothing), 1946–63, with other interests in insce and advertising. Mem., West Lewisham Chamber of Commerce, 1951, subseq. Sec. and Chm.; Delegate to Nat. Chamber of Trade, 1960; joined NCT staff, 1966. Mem., Home Office Standing Cttee on Crime Prevention, 1971–87. Council Member: (founding) Retail Consortium, 1971–87; Assoc. for Prevention of Theft from Shops, 1976–87. Fellow, Soc. of Assoc. Executives, 1970. *Publications:* various articles. *Recreations:* reading, writing, travel, photography. *Address:* 16 Barn Close, Southcote, Reading, Berks RG3 3EE. *T:* Reading (0734) 575478.

SEENEY, Noel Conway; Commissioner of Stamp Duties, Queensland, 1975–86; *b* 7 April 1926; *s* of Percy Matthew Mark Seeney and Wilhelmina Augusta Zanow; *m* 1949, Valrae Muriel Uhlmann; two *d*. *Educ:* Teachers' Coll., Brisbane; Univ. of Queensland (BCom). Assoc. Accountancy, Assoc. Coll. of Preceptors, London. Teacher, 1944; Dep. Principal, Secondary Sch., 1960; Principal 1964; Official Sec., Office of Agent-General for Qld in London, 1969; Agent-General for Qld in London, 1973. *Recreations:* golf, tennis. *Address:* 20 Nawarra Street, Indooroopilly, Qld 4068, Australia. *Clubs:* United Service (Brisbane); Indooroopilly Golf.

SEETO, Sir (James Hip) Ling, Kt 1988; MBE 1975; Managing Director, Lingana Pty Ltd, Port Moresby, Papua New Guinea, since 1965; Director and part owner, Kwila Insurance Co., Port Moresby, since 1978; *b* 19 June 1933; *s* of Yeeying Seeto and Kamfoung Mack; *m* 1960, Anna Choiha Peng; two *s*. *Educ:* Rabaul Public Sch., PNG; Mowbray House Sch., Sydney, Australia; Trinity Grammar Sch., Sydney. Pings Co., Rabaul, PNG, 1954–58; Shell Co., Rabaul, 1958–62; Rabaul Metal Industries, Rabaul, 1962–64. Former Board Member: Nat. Investment and Develt Authy, PNG; PNG Develt Bank; Harbors Board; Water Resources Bd of PNG; Salvation Army Adv. Bd, PNG. A Youth Leader, Rabaul Methodist Ch., 1954–60. Silver Jubilee Medal, 1977; PNG Independence Medal, 1986. *Recreations:* golf, swimming, gardening, cooking. *Address:* PO Box 1756, Boroko, National Capital District, Papua New Guinea. *T:* (office) 254966, (home) 211873. *Clubs:* Cathay (Port Moresby) (Patron); Port Moresby Golf.

SEEYAVE, Sir René (Sow Choung), Kt 1985; CBE 1979; Group Chairman, Happy World Ltd, since 1986; (Group Managing Director, 1968–86); *b* 15 March 1935; *s* of late Antoine Seeyave, CBE and Lam Tung Ying; *m* 1961, Thérèse How Hong; one *s* four *d*. *Educ:* Royal College, Port Louis, Mauritius. Chm., Mauritius Farms Ltd, 1974–. Chm., Electricity Adv. Cttee, 1972–76. Vice Chairman: Mauritius Employers' Fedn, 1972; Mauritius Broadcasting Corp., 1980–81. Director: Mauritius Development Investment Trust Ltd, 1968–; Swan Insurance Co. Ltd, 1969–; Mauritius Marine Authority, 1980–. Vice-Chm. Council, Univ. of Mauritius, 1985–87. Hon. Pres., Heen Foh Soc. *Address:* Happy World Ltd, Old Council Street, Port Louis, Mauritius. *T:* 208 68 86. *Clubs:* Mauritius Gymkhana, Port Louis City.

SEFTON, family name of **Baron Sefton of Garston.**

SEFTON OF GARSTON, Baron *cr* 1978 (Life Peer), of Garston in the County of Merseyside; **William Henry Sefton;** Chairman, North West Economic Planning Council, since 1975; Vice-Chairman and Board Member, Warrington and Runcorn Development Corporation, 1981–85 (Chairman, 1974–81, Board Member, 1964–81, Runcorn Development Corporation); *b* 5 Aug. 1915; *s* of George and Emma Sefton; *m* 1940, Phyllis Kerr. *Educ:* Duncombe Road Sch., Liverpool. Joined Liverpool CC, 1953, Leader 1964; Chm. and Leader, Merseyside CC, 1974–77, Opposition Leader, 1977–79. Joined Runcorn Develt Corp., 1964, Dep. Chm. 1967. Member: New Towns Commn, 1978–85; SSRC, 1978. *Recreations:* gardening, woodwork. *Address:* House of Lords, SW1.

SEGAL, Prof. Erich; Adjunct Professor of Classics, Yale University, 1981–88; Hon. Research Fellow, Classics, University College London, since 1982; Supernumerary Fellow, Wolfson College, Oxford, since 1985; *b* 16 June 1937; *s* of Samuel M. Segal, PhD, DHL and Cynthia Shapiro Segal; *m* 1975, Karen James; two *d*. *Educ:* Harvard (Boylston Prize 1957, Bowdoin Prize 1959; AB 1958, AM 1959, PhD 1965). Teaching Fellow, Harvard, 1959–64; Lectr in Classics, Yale, 1964, Asst Prof., 1965–68, Associate Prof., 1968–73; Vis. Prof. in Classics: Munich, 1973; Princeton, 1974–75; Tel Aviv, 1976–77; Vis. Prof. in Comp. Lit., Dartmouth, 1976–78; Vis. Fellow, Wolfson Coll., Oxford, 1979–80, Mem. Common Room, 1984–. Member: Acad. of Literary Studies, USA, 1981; Nat. Adv. Council, 1970–72, Exec. Cttee, 1971–72, Peace Corps, USA (Presidential Commendation for Service to Peace Corps, 1971). Lectures: Amer. Philological Assoc., 1971; Amer. Comparative Lit. Assoc., 1971; German Classical Assoc., 1974; Boston Psychoanalytic Inst., 1974; Istituto Nazionale del Dramma Antico, Sicily, 1975; Brit. Classical Assoc., 1977; William Kelley Prentice Meml, Princeton, 1981. Author and narrator, The Ancient Games, 1972; radio and TV commentator, Olympic Games, 1972 and 1976. Screenplays include: The Beatles' Yellow Submarine, 1968; The Games, 1969; Love Story, 1970 (Golden Globe Award, 1970); Oliver's Story, 1978; Man, Woman and Child, 1983. (Jtly) Premio San Valentin di Terni, 1989. *Publications:* Roman Laughter: the comedy of Plautus, 1968, rev. edn 1987; (ed) Euripides: a collection of critical essays, 1968; (ed and trans.) Plautus: Three Comedies, 1969, rev. edn 1985; (ed) Oxford Readings in Greek Tragedy, 1983; (ed with Fergus Millar) Caesar Augustus, 1984; (ed) Plato's Dialogues, 1985; *novels:* Love Story, 1970; Fairy Tale (for children), 1973; Oliver's Story, 1977; Man, Woman and Child, 1980; The Class, 1985 (Prix Deauville, France, and Premio Bancarella Selezione, Italy, 1986); Doctors, 1988; Acts of Faith, 1990; articles and reviews in Amer. Jl of Philology, Classical World, Harvard Studies in Classical Philology, Greek, Roman and Byzantine Studies, TLS, New York Times Book Review, New Republic, The Independent, Washington Post. *Recreations:* swimming, athletics. *Address:* Wolfson College, Oxford OX2 6UD. *T:* Oxford (0865) 274100. *Clubs:* Athenæum; Harvard (New York and Boston); Yale (New York).

SEGAL, Prof. Graeme Bryce, DPhil; FRS 1982; Lowndean Professor of Astronomy and Geometry, and Fellow of St John's College, Cambridge University, since 1990; *b* 21 Dec. 1941; *s* of Reuben Segal and Iza Joan Harris; *m* 1962, Desley Rae Cheetham (marr. diss. 1972). *Educ:* Sydney Grammar School; Univ. of Sydney (BSc 1962); Univ. of Cambridge; Univ. of Oxford (MA, DPhil 1967). Oxford University: Junior Res. Fellow, Worcester Coll., 1964–66; Junior Lectr in Mathematics, 1965–66; Fellow, St Catherine's Coll., 1966–90; Reader in Maths, 1978–89; Prof. of Maths, 1989–90. Mem., Inst. for Advanced Study, Princeton, 1969–70. Editor, Topology, 1970–90. *Publications:* (with A. Pressley) Loop Groups, 1986; articles in learned jls. *Address:* 16 Champneys Walk, Cambridge CB3 9AW. *T:* Cambridge (0223) 64263.

SEGAL, Prof. Judah Benzion, MC 1942; FBA 1968; Professor of Semitic Languages in the University of London, School of Oriental and African Studies, 1961–79; now Emeritus; *b* 21 June 1912; *s* of Prof. Moses H. Segal and Hannah Leah Segal; *m* 1946, Leah (*née* Seidemann); two *d*. *Educ:* Magdalen College School, Oxford; St Catharine's College, Cambridge. Jarrett Schol., 1932; John Stewart of Rannoch Schol., in Hebrew, 1933; 1st Cl. Oriental Langs Tripos, 1935; Tyrwhitt Schol. and Mason Prizeman, 1936; BA (Cambridge), 1935; MA 1938. Colours, Cambridge Univ. Boxing Club, 1935, 1936. Mansel Research Exhibitioner, St John's Coll., Oxford, 1936–39; James Mew Schol., 1937; DPhil (Oxon.), 1939. Deputy Assistant Director, Public Security, Sudan Government, 1939–41; served War of 1939–45, GHQ, MEF, 1942–44, Captain; Education Officer, British Military Administration, Tripolitania, 1945–46. Head of Dept of Near and Middle East, Sch. of Oriental and African Studies, 1961–68 (Hon. Fellow 1983); Visiting Lectr, Ain Shams Univ., Cairo, 1979; Res. Fellow, Hebrew Univ., Jerusalem, 1980; Leverhulme Emeritus Fellowship, S India, 1981. Principal, Leo Baeck Coll., 1982–85, Pres., 1985–. Mem., Council of Christians and Jews; President: North Western Reform Synagogue; British Assoc. for Jewish Studies, 1980; Vice-Pres., Reform Synagogues of GB, 1985–. Freedom, City of Urfa, Turkey, 1973. *Publications:* The Diacritical Point and the Accents in Syriac, 1953; The Hebrew Passover, 1963; Edessa, 1970; Aramaic Texts From North Saqqara, 1983; articles in learned periodicals. *Recreations:* walking, meditation. *Address:* 17 Hillersdon Avenue, Edgware, Mddx HA8 7SG. *T:* 081–958 4993.

SEGAL, Michael John; District Judge (formerly Registrar), Principal Registry, Family Division, since 1985; *b* 20 Sept. 1937; *s* of Abraham Charles Segal and Iris Muriel (*née* Parsons); *m* 1963, Barbara Gina Fluxman; one *d.* *Educ:* Strode's Sch., Egham. Called to the Bar, Middle Temple, 1962. Practised at Bar, Midland and Oxford Circuit, 1962–84. Mem., Civil and Family Cttee, Judicial Studies Bd, 1990–. Editor, Family Div. section, Butterworth's Cost Service, 1987–; Jt Editor, Supreme Court Practice, 1991–. *Recreations:* reading, listening to music. *Address:* 28 Grange Road, N6 4AP. *T:* 081–348 0680. *Club:* Athenæum.

SEIFERT, Robin (also known as **Richard**); JP; FRIBA; Principal R. Seifert and Partners, Architects, since 1934; *b* 25 Nov. 1910; *s* of William Seifert; *m* 1939, Josephine Jeanette Harding; two *s* one *d.* *Educ:* Central Foundation Sch., City of London; University College, London (DipArch), Fellow, 1971. Commenced architectural practice, 1934. Corps of Royal Engineers, 1940–44; Indian Army, 1944–46; Hon. Lt-Col, 1946; Certif. for Meritorious Services Home Forces, 1943. Returned to private practice, 1948. Designed: ICI Laboratories, Dyestuffs Div., Blackley, Manchester; The Times Newspapers building, Printing House Square; Centre Point, St Giles Circus; Drapers Gardens, Nat. West. Bank Tower, City; The Royal Garden Hotel, Kensington; Tolworth Towers, Surbiton; Guiness Mahon Bank, Gracechurch Street; HQ of ICT, Putney; Kellogg House, Baker Street; Dunlop House, King Street, St James's; BSC Res. Labs, Middlesbrough; Britannia Hotel; Park Tower Hotel; London Heathrow Hotel; Sobell Sports Centre; ATV Centre, Birmingham; Central Television Complex, Nottingham; International Press Centre; Metropolitan Police HQ, Putney; Wembley Conference Centre; Princess Grace Hospital, Marylebone Road; Princess Grace Hospital, Windsor; Princess Margaret Hospital, Windsor; Churchill Hospital, Harrow; BUPA Hospital, Bushey; The Pirate Castle, Camden; British Rail HQ Offices, Euston Station. RIBA Architectural Exhibition (depicting 50 years of practice), Heinz Gall., 1984. Member: MoT Road Safety Council, 1969 (now disbanded); Home Office Cttee of Management, Housing Assoc. for Discharged Offenders; (part-time) British Waterways Bd, 1971–74; Council, RIBA, 1971–74. FRSA 1976. Liveryman, Glaziers' Co. City of London. JP Barnet, 1969. *Recreations:* chess, violin. *Address:* Eleventrees, Milespit Hill, Mill Hill, NW7. *T:* 081–959 3397. *Clubs:* Army and Navy, City Livery, Arts.

SEIGNORET, Sir Clarence (Henry Augustus), GCB 1985; OBE 1966; President of the Commonwealth of Dominica, since 1983; *b* 25 Feb. 1919; *s* of Clarence Augustus Seignoret and Violet Elizabeth (*née* Riviere); *m* 1950; two *s.* *Educ:* Dominica Grammar Sch.; Balliol Coll., Oxford. Civil Servant, 1936–77: Permanent Sec., 1956–67; Sec. to Cabinet, Hd of Civil Service, 1967–77; Administrator's Dep., Governor's Dep., Actg Pres. on six occasions, 1966–83. Exec. Sec., Dominica Assoc. of Industry and Commerce, 1980–83. Mem., Girl Guide Council of Dominica. Patron: Dominica Red Cross Soc.; Dominica Legion, Commonwealth Ex-Service League; Dominica Br., Duke of Edinburgh's Award Scheme; Community Hostels Inc.; Adventurer's Club (Envmt); Nat. Develt Foundn of Dominica; Dominica Special Olympics; Dominica Conservation Assoc. Collar of Order of the Liberator (Simon Bolivar), Venezuela, 1987. *Recreations:* agriculture, horticulture. *Address:* 24 Cork Street, Roseau, Commonwealth of Dominica, West Indies. *T:* (office) 82054; (home) 82108. *Clubs:* Rotary of Dominica (Patron), Lions Club of Dominica (Hon. Mem.).

SEIGNORET, Eustace Edward; High Commissioner for Trinidad and Tobago in Georgetown, Guyana, 1982–84; *b* 16 Feb. 1925; *m*; two *s* one *d.* *Educ:* Howard Univ., Washington; Univ. of Wales, Bangor. BSc. Agricultural Officer, Dept of Agriculture, Trinidad and Tobago, 1953–58; West Indies Fedn Public Service, 1958–62; Asst Sec., Trinidad and Tobago Public Service, 1962; First Sec., 1962–65, Counsellor, 1965–68, Trinidad and Tobago Perm. Mission to UN; Dep. High Comr in London, 1969–71; Perm. Rep. to UN, 1971–75; High Comr in London, 1977–82. *Address:* c/o Ministry of External Affairs, Port of Spain, Trinidad and Tobago.

SEIPP, Walter, Dr jur; Chairman, Supervisory Board, Commerzbank AG, since 1991; *b* 13 Dec. 1925; *m* 1954, Marianne Zimmermann; two *s.* *Educ:* matriculated 1943; Univ. of Frankfurt (Law studies); final legal examination and doctorate in Law, 1950–53. Military Service, 1943–45. Deutsche Bank AG, 1951–74: Exec. Vice Pres., 1970–74; Vice Chm., UBS-DB Corp., New York, 1972–74; Westdeutsche Landesbank Girozentrale, 1974–81: Mem. Bd, 1974–81, and Dep. Chm. of the Bd, 1977–81; Chm., Bd of Man. Dirs, Commerzbank AG, 1981–91; Member, Supervisory Board: Bayer AG, 1981–; VIAG AG, 1981–; Linde AG, 1983–; Allianz Versicherungs-AG, 1985–; Hochtief AG, 1986–; MAN AG, 1986–; Thyssen AG, 1986–; Deutsche Shell AG, 1989–; Non-Exec. Dir, GKN plc, 1989–. Pres., Internat. Monetary Conf., 1987–88. *Publications:* multiple. *Address:* Neue Mainzer Strasse 32–36, D–6000 Frankfurt/Main, Germany. *T:* 069/ 1362–2220.

SEITZ, Raymond George Hardenbergh; Ambassador of the United States of America to the Court of St James's, since 1991; *b* Hawaii, 8 Dec. 1940; *s* of Maj.-Gen. John Francis Regis Seitz and Helen Johnson Hardenbergh; two *s* one *d*; *m* 1985, Caroline Richardson. *Educ:* Yale University (BA History 1963). Joined Foreign Service, Dept of State, 1966; served Montreal, Nairobi, Bukavu, Zaire, 1966–72; Staff Officer, later Director, Secretariat Staff, Washington, Special Asst to Dir Gen., Foreign Service, 1972–75; Political Officer, London, 1975–79; Dep. Exec. Sec., Washington, 1979–81; Senior Dep. Asst Sec., Public Affairs, Washington, 1981–82; Exec. Asst to Secretary George P. Shultz, Washington, 1982–84; Minister and Dep. Chief of Mission, US Embassy, London, 1984–89; Asst Sec. for European and Canadian Affairs, State Dept, Washington, 1989–91. Kt Comdr's Cross (Germany), 1991. *Address:* American Embassy, 24 Grosvenor Square, W1A 1AE.

SEKERS, David Nicholas Oliver, OBE 1986; FMA; Regional Director of National Trust, Southern Region, since 1989; *b* 29 Sept. 1943; *s* of Sir Nicholas Sekers, MBE and Lady Sekers; *m* 1965, Simone, *er d* of Moran Caplat, *qv*; one *d.* *Educ:* Eton: Worcester College, Oxford (BA). West Cumberland Silk Mills, 1965–73, Dir, 1968–73; Dir, Gladstone Pottery Museum (Museum of the Year 1976), 1973–78; Museum Dir, Quarry Bank Mill (Museum of the Year 1984), 1978–89. Mem., Crafts Council, 1984–86; Chm., Assoc. of Independent Museums, 1987–89. *Publications:* Role of Museum Trustees, 1987; articles for museum jls. *Recreations:* fishing, fell-walking. *Address:* c/o National Trust, Polesden Lacey, Dorking, Surrey RH5 6BD. *T:* Bookham (0372) 453401. *Club:* Garrick.

SEKYI, Henry Van Hien; Permanent Representative of Ghana to the United Nations, 1979–80; *b* 15 Jan. 1928; *s* of W. E. G. Sekyi, MA London, BL, and Lily Anna Sekyi (*née* Cleland); *m* 1958, Maria Joyce Sekyi (*née* Tachie-Menson); one *s* one *d.* *Educ:* Adisadel Coll., Cape Coast; Univ. of Ghana; King's Coll., Cambridge; LSE. BA London 1953; BA Cantab 1955. Third Sec., Second Sec., and First Sec., in succession, Ghana Embassy, Washington, DC, USA, 1958–61; First Sec., later Counsellor, Ghana Embassy, Rome, 1961–62; Director, Min. Foreign Affairs, 1962–65, in charge of Divisions of: Eastern Europe and China; Middle East and Asia; UN Affairs; Personnel and Administration; Acting Principal Sec., Min. of Foreign Affairs, 1965–66; Ghana High Comr to Australia, 1966–70; Ghana Ambassador to Italy, 1970–72; High Comr in UK, 1972–75; Supervising Dir, Political Dept, Min. of Foreign Affairs, Ghana, 1975–76, Senior Principal Secretary 1976–79. *Recreations:* classics, music, Africana and gymnastics. *Address:* c/o Ministry of Foreign Affairs, Accra, Ghana.

SELBORNE, 4th Earl of, *cr* 1882; **John Roundell Palmer,** KBE 1987; FRS 1991; DL; Baron Selborne, 1872; Viscount Wolmer, 1882; Chairman, Joint Nature Conservation Committee, since 1991; *b* 24 March 1940; *er s* of William Matthew, Viscount Wolmer (killed on active service, 1942), and of Priscilla (who *m* 1948, Hon. Peter Legh, now 4th Baron Newton, *qv*), *d* of late Captain John Egerton-Warburton; *S* grandfather, 1971; *m* 1969, Joanna Van Antwerp, *yr d* of Evan Maitland James, *qv*; three *s* one *d.* *Educ:* Eton; Christ Church, Oxford (MA). Chm., AFRC, 1983–90 (Mem., 1975; Vice-Chm., 1980–83); Vice-Chm., Apple and Pear Develt Council, 1969–73; Mem., Hops Mkting Bd, 1972–82 (Chm., 1978–82); Pres., British Crop Protection Council, 1977–80; Chm., SE Regl Panel, MAFF, 1979–83. Dir, Agricl Mortgage Corp., 1990–. Pres., South of England Agric. Soc., 1984; Pres., RASE, 1988. Treas., Bridewell Royal Hosp. (King Edward's Sch., Witley), 1972–83; Mem., Hampshire County Council, 1967–74. FIBiol 1984; FRAgS 1986. Master, Mercers' Co., 1989–90. JP Hants 1971–78; DL Hants 1982. Hon. LLD Bristol, 1989; Hon. DSc Cranfield, 1991. *Heir:* *s* Viscount Wolmer, *qv.* *Address:* Temple Manor, Selborne, Alton, Hants GU34 3LR. *T:* Bordon (0420) 473646. *Club:* Brooks's.

SELBY, 4th Viscount, *cr* 1905; **Michael Guy John Gully;** *b* 15 Aug. 1942; *s* of 3rd Viscount and of Veronica, *er d* of late J. George and of Mrs Briscoe-George; *S* father, 1959; *m* 1965, Mary Theresa, *d* of late Capt. Thomas Powell, London, SW7; one *s* one *d.* *Heir:* *s* Hon. Edward Thomas William Gully, *b* 21 Sept. 1967.

SELBY, Bishop Suffragan of, since 1991; **Rt. Rev. Humphrey Vincent Taylor;** *b* 5 March 1938; *s* of late Maurice Humphrey Taylor and of Mary Patricia Stuart Taylor (*née* Wood), now Pearson; *m* 1965, Anne Katharine Dart; two *d.* *Educ:* Harrow School; Pembroke College, Cambridge (MA); London University (MA). Nat. Service Officer, RAF, 1956–58; Cambridge 1958–61; College of the Resurrection, Mirfield, 1961–63; Curate in London, 1963–66; Rector of Lilongwe, Malaŵi, 1967–71; Chaplain, Bishop Grosseteste Coll., Lincoln, 1971–74; Sec. for Chaplaincies in Higher Education, Gen. Synod Bd of Education, 1974–80; Mission Programmes Sec., USPG, 1980–84; Sec., USPG, 1984–91. Hon. Canon of Bristol Cathedral, 1986–91; Provincial Canon of Southern Africa, 1989–. Moderator, Conf. for World Mission, BCC, 1987–. *Recreations:* music, gardening. *Address:* 8 Bankside Close, Upper Poppleton, York YO2 6LH. *T:* York (0904) 795342.

SELBY, Sir Kenneth, Kt 1970; FCMA, FCCA, CBIM, FIQ; President, Bath & Portland Group plc, 1983–86; *b* 16 Feb. 1914; *s* of Thomas William Selby; *m* 1937, Elma Gertrude, *d* of Johnstone Sleator; two *s.* *Educ:* High School for Boys, Worthing. Bath & Portland Group Ltd: Managing Director, 1963–81; Chm., 1969–82. Governor, Wells Cathedral Sch., 1976–; Mem., Ct and Council, 1975–, Chm. Council, 1975–84, Pro Chancellor, 1975–, Bath Univ. Chm., Air Travel Reserve Fund Agency, 1975–86. Hon. LLD Bath, 1985. *Address:* 21 Clan House, Sydney Road, Bath, Avon BA2 6NS. *T:* Bath (0225) 465445. *Club:* Reform.

SELBY, Rt. Rev. Peter Stephen Maurice; *see* Kingston-upon-Thames, Bishop of.

SELBY, Ralph Walford, CMG 1961; HM Diplomatic Service, retired; *b* 20 March 1915; *e s* of late Sir Walford Selby, KCMG, CB, CVO; *m* 1947, Julianna Snell; three *d.* *Educ:* Eton; Christ Church, Oxford. Entered HM Diplomatic Service, Sept. 1938; served in Foreign Office until Oct. 1939. Enlisted in Army and served with Grenadier Guards, March 1940–Feb. 1945, when returned to Foreign Office; seconded to Treasury for service in India as First Secretary in Office of High Commissioner for UK, Sept. 1947; transferred to The Hague, 1950; returned to FO, 1953–56; transf. to Tokyo as Counsellor, 1956, to Copenhagen in 1958, to Djakarta in 1961, to Warsaw in 1964; Chargé d'Affaires in 1952, 1958, 1959, 1960, 1961, 1962, 1964, 1965, 1969, 1970; Consul-Gen., Boston, 1966–69; Minister, British Embassy, Rome, 1969–72; Ambassador to Norway, 1972–75. *Recreations:* beagling, sail cruising, hill walking. *Address:* Mengeham House, Mengham Lane, Hayling Island, Hants PO11 9JX. *Clubs:* MCC; Royal Yacht Squadron (Cowes).

SELBY, Rear-Adm. William Halford, CB 1955; DSC 1942; *b* 29 April 1902; *s* of E. H. Selby; *m* 1926, Hilary Elizabeth Salter (*d* 1960); two *d*; *m* 1961, Mrs R. Milne. *Educ:* Royal Naval Colleges, Osborne and Dartmouth. Entered Royal Navy, 1916; Midshipman, HMS Royal Oak, Black Sea and Dardanelles, 1920; Sub.-Lt HMS Vendetta and HMY Victoria and Albert, 1924. Destroyers, Medit and China Station between 1927 and 1936; Naval Staff Coll., 1939; War of 1939–45: in comd HMS Wren, Mashona (despatches), Onslaught (despatches). Capt. 1943; Chief of Staff, Londonderry, 1944–45; Capt. 'D' Third Flotilla in comd HMS Saumarez, 1946–47; Dep. Dir Ops Div., Admty, 1948–50; Capt-in-Charge, Simonstown, 1950–52; Rear-Adm. 1953; Head of British Naval Mission to Greece, 1953–55; retired, 1956. *Address:* The Old Cottage, Chittoe, Chippenham, Wilts SN15 2EN.

SELBY WRIGHT, Very Rev. Ronald (William Vernon); *see* Wright.

SELDON, Arthur, CBE 1983; economist and writer; a Founder President, Institute of Economic Affairs, 1990–91; Economic Consultant, since 1981; Founder Editor, Economic Affairs; *b* 29 May 1916; *m* Audrey Marjorie, *d* of Wilfred Willett and Eileen Willett (*née* Stenhouse) three *s.* *Educ:* Dempsey St Elementary Sch., Stepney; Raine's Foundation Sch. (State Scholar); LSE. BCom 1937 (1st cl. hons). Army service in Africa and Italy, 1942–45. Editor, Store, 1946–49; economist in industry, 1949–1959; Editorial Dir, 1959–81, Adv. Dir, 1981–88, Inst. of Economic Affairs; Chm., Liberal Party Cttee on the Aged, 1948–49; Mem., BMA Cttee on Health Financing, 1968–70; Adviser, Australian Cabinet Cttee on Welfare, 1968; Vice-Pres., Mont Pélerin Soc., 1980–86; Founder Trustee, Social Affairs Unit, 1980. Member of advisory board: Jl of Post-Misesian Economics (Washington), 1983–; Inst für Bildungs- und Forschungspolitik (Cologne), 1983–; Libertariansk Allianse (Oslo), 1983–; Ludwig von Mises Institut (Brussels), 1983–. *Publications:* (with Lord Harris of High Cross) Advertising in a Free Society, 1959; Pensions for Prosperity, 1960; Everyman's Dictionary of Economics (with F. G. Pennance), 1965, 2nd edn 1976; After the NHS, 1968; The Great Pensions Swindle, 1970; Charge, 1977; (with Lord Harris of High Cross) Over-ruled on Welfare 1963–78, 1979; Corrigible Capitalism, Incorrigible Socialism, 1980; Wither the Welfare State, 1981; Socialism Explained, 1983 (US edn as Socialism: the grand delusion, 1986); (ed) The New Right Enlightenment, 1985; The Riddle of the Voucher, 1986; (with Lord Harris of High Cross) Welfare Without the State, 1987; Capitalism, 1990; (contrib.) Democracy and Public Choice: essays in honour of Gordon Tullock, ed C. K. Rowley, 1987. *Recreations:* work, cricket, opera, parties for non-conformists. *Address:* The Thatched Cottage, Godden Green, Sevenoaks, Kent. *T:* Sevenoaks (0732) 61499.

SELF, Hugh Michael, QC 1973; a Recorder of the Crown Court, since 1975; *b* 19 March 1921; *s* of Sir (Albert) Henry Self, KCB, KCMG, KBE; *m* 1950, Penelope Ann, *d* of late John Drinkwater, poet and dramatist and Daisy (*née* Kennedy), violinist; two *d.* *Educ:* Lancing Coll.; Worcester Coll., Oxford (BA). Royal Navy, 1942–46, Lieut RNVR 1946. Called to Bar, Lincoln's Inn, 1951, Bencher, 1980. *Recreations:* golf, walking in England,

literature. *Address:* 59 Maresfield Gardens, Hampstead, NW3 5TE. *T:* 071–435 8311. *Club:* Savile.
See also Prof. P. J. O. Self.

SELF, Prof. Peter John Otter; Emeritus Professor of Public Administration, University of London; Visiting Fellow, Australian National University, since 1984; *b* 7 June 1919; *s* of Sir (Albert) Henry Self, KCB, KCMG, KBE; *m* 1st, 1950, Diana Mary Pitt (marr. diss.); 2nd, 1959, Elaine Rosenbloom Adams (marr. diss.); two *s*; 3rd, 1981, Sandra Guerita Gough (*née* Moiseiwitsch). *Educ:* Lancing Coll.; Balliol Coll., Oxford (MA). Editorial staff of The Economist, 1944–62; Extra-mural Lectr, London Univ., 1944–49; Lectr in Public Administration, LSE, 1948–61; Reader in Political Science, LSE, 1961–63; Prof. of Public Admin, Univ. of London, 1963–82; Sen. Res. Fellow, ANU, 1982–84. Dir of Studies (Administration), Civil Service Dept, 1969–70. Chm., Australian Govt Inquiry into Local Govt Finance, 1984–85. Mem. Exec. and Coun., 1954, Vice-Chm. Exec., 1955, Chm. Exec., 1961–69, Chm. Council, 1979–82, Town and Country Planning Assoc.; Mem., SE Regional Economic Planning Coun., 1966–79. Hon. Mem., RTPI. *Publications:* Regionalism, 1949; Cities in Flood: The Problems of Urban Growth, 1957; (with H. Storing) The State and the Farmer, 1962; Administrative Theories and Politics, 1972; Econocrats and the Policy Process, 1976; Planning the Urban Region, 1982; Political Theories of Modern Government, 1985; numerous articles on administration, politics and planning. *Recreations:* walking, golf, story-telling. *Address:* 7 Hobbs Street, O'Connor, ACT 2601, Australia. *T:* Canberra 477383. *Club:* Reform.
See also H. M. Self.

SELIGMAN, Henry, OBE 1958; PhD; President, EXEC AG, Basle, 1975–85; Scientific Consultant (part-time) to International Atomic Energy Agency, Vienna, since 1969; Scientific Adviser to various industries, since 1970; *b* Frankfurt am Main, 25 Feb. 1909; *s* of Milton Seligman and Marie (*née* Gans); *m* 1941, Lesley Bradley; two *s*. *Educ:* Liebigschule Frankfurt; Sorbonne; Universities of Lausanne and of Zürich. Staff, DSIR, Cavendish Lab., Cambridge, 1942–43. Joined British-Canadian Research Project at Montreal, 1943, Chalk River, Ontario, 1944–; Staff, Brit. Atomic Energy Project, 1946; Head of Isotope Div., Atomic Energy Research Establishment, Harwell, UK, 1947–58; Dep. Dir Gen., Dept of Research and Isotopes, Internat. Atomic Energy Agency, Vienna, 1958–69. Austrian Decoration for Science and Art, 1979; Austrian Commander's Cross, 2nd class, 1986. Editor-in-Chief: Scientific Jl; Internat. Jl of Applied Radiation and Isotopes, 1973–. *Publications:* papers on: physical constants necessary for reactor development; waste disposal; production and uses of radioisotopes; contrib. scientific journals. *Address:* Scherpegasse 8/6/3, A–1190 Vienna, Austria. *T:* Vienna 323225.

SELIGMAN, Madron; *see* Seligman, R. M.

SELIGMAN, Sir Peter (Wendel), Kt 1978; CBE 1969; BA; FIMechE; *b* 16 Jan. 1913; *s* of late Dr Richard Joseph Simon Seligman and of Hilda Mary Seligman; *m* 1937, Elizabeth Lavinia Mary Wheatley; two *s* four *d*. *Educ:* King's Coll. Sch., Wimbledon; Harrow Sch.; Kantonschule, Zürich; Caius Coll., Cambridge. Joined APV Co. Ltd, as Asst to Man. Dir, 1936; appointed Dir, 1939; Man. Dir, 1947; Dep. Chm., 1961; Chm., APV Holdings Ltd, 1966–77. Director: St Regis International Ltd, 1973–83 (Vice-Chm., 1981–83); EIBIS International Ltd, 1980–90; Bell Bryant Pty Ltd, 1976–80; St Regis ACI Pty Ltd, 1980–84. Mem., Engineering Industries Council, 1975–77. Chm., Nat. Ski Fedn of GB, 1977–81. *Recreations:* yachting, carpentry. *Address:* King's Lea, King's Saltern Road, Lymington, Hants SO41 9QF. *T:* Lymington (0590) 676569. *Clubs:* South Africa; Royal Lymington Yacht; Hawks (Cambridge); Ski of Great Britain (Invitation Life Mem.); Kandahar Ski (Chm., 1972–77; Hon. Mem.).
See also R. M. Seligman.

SELIGMAN, (Richard) Madron; Member (C) Sussex West, European Parliament, since 1979; *b* 10 Nov. 1918; 4th *s* of late Dr Richard Seligman, FCGI, FIM, and Hilda Mary (*née* MacDowell); *m* 1947, Nancy-Joan, *d* of Julian Marks; three *s* one *d*. *Educ:* Rokeby Sch., Wimbledon; Harrow Sch.; Balliol Coll., Oxford (BA (Hons) PPE; MA). Oxford Univ. ski team, 1938–39; President, Oxford Union, 1940. Served war, 6th Armoured Divisional Signals, N Africa and Italy, 1941–46, Major 1945. Chm., Incinerator Company, Eaton Socon, 1960–88. Vice Pres., European Energy Foundn, 1982–. *Recreations:* tennis, ski-ing, gardening, piano, sailing. *Address:* Micklepage House, Nuthurst, near Horsham, Sussex RH13 6RG. *T:* Horsham (0403) 891533 or 891259. *Clubs:* Royal Thames Yacht, Royal Institute of International Affairs, MCC.
See also Sir Peter Seligman.

SELKIRK, 10th Earl of, *cr* 1646; **George Nigel Douglas-Hamilton,** KT 1976; GCMG 1959; GBE 1963 (OBE 1941); AFC; AE; PC 1955; QC(Scot.), 1959; late Gp Capt. Auxiliary Air Force; Scottish Representative Peer, 1945–63; *b* Merly, Wimborne, Dorset, 4 Jan. 1906; 2nd *s* of 13th Duke of Hamilton and Brandon; *S* to earldom of father under terms of special remainder, 1940; *m* 1949, Audrey Durell, *o d* of late Maurice Drummond-Sale-Barker and of Mrs H. S. Brooks. *Educ:* Eton; Balliol College, Oxford, (MA); Edinburgh University, (LLB); Univs of Bonn, Vienna and Paris (Sorbonne). Admitted to Faculty of Advocates, 1935; Commanded 603 Squadron AAF, 1934–38; Captain, 44th Co., Boys' Brigade, 1932–38; Member of Edinburgh Town Council, 1935–40; Commisssioner of General Board of Control (Scotland), 1936–39; Commissioner for Special Areas in Scotland, 1937–39. Served War of 1939–45 (OBE, despatches twice). A Lord-in-Waiting to the Queen, 1952–53 (to King George VI, 1951–52); Paymaster-General, Nov. 1953–Dec. 1955; Chancellor of the Duchy of Lancaster, Dec. 1955–Jan. 1957; First Lord of the Admiralty, 1957–Oct. 1959; UK Commissioner for Singapore and Comr Gen. for SE Asia, 1959–63; also UK Council Representative to SEATO, 1960–63; Chm., Cons. Commonwealth Council, 1965–72. Freeman of Hamilton, 1938. President: National Ski Fedn of Great Britain, 1964–68; Anglo-Swiss Society, 1965–74; Building Societies Assoc., 1965–82; Royal Soc. for Asian Affairs, 1966–76; Assoc. of Independent Unionist Peers, 1967–79. Chm., Victoria League, 1971–77. Hon. Chief, Saulteaux Indians, 1967. Hon. Citizen of the City of Winnipeg and of the Town of Selkirk in Manitoba. *Address:* Rose Lawn Coppice, Wimborne, Dorset. *T:* Wimborne (0202) 883160; 60 Eaton Place, SW1. *T:* 071–235 6926. *Clubs:* Athenæum, Caledonian; New (Edinburgh).

SELLARS, John Ernest, CEng; FIMA, FRSA; MRAeS; Chief Executive, Business and Technician Education Council, since 1983; *b* 5 Feb. 1936; *s* of Ernest Buttle Sellars and Edna Grace Sellars; *m* 1958, Dorothy Beatrice (*née* Morrison); three *d*. *Educ:* Wintringham Grammar Sch., Grimsby; Manchester Univ. (BSc, MSc). Research Engineer, English Electric (GW) Ltd, 1958–61; Lectr, Royal College of Advanced Technology (now Univ. of Salford), 1961–67; Head of Mathematics, Lanchester College of Technology, Coventry, 1967–71; Head of Computer Science, Lanchester Polytechnic, Coventry/Rugby, 1971–74; Chief Officer, Business Educn Council, 1974–83. Member: Bd, Nat. Adv. Body for Public Sector Higher Educn, 1982–88; BBC School Broadcasting Council for UK, 1982–87; City Technology Colls Trust, 1989–; Engrg and Technol. Adv. Cttee, British Council, 1990–. MInstD. Hon. FCP 1989. *Publications:* papers on mathematics, computer science and business educn. *Recreation:* walking. *Address:* Business and Technician Education Council, Central House, Upper Woburn Place, WC1H 0HH. *T:* 071–413 8400. *Club:* Reform.

SELLERS, Basil Alfred; Chairman and Chief Executive, Gestetner Holdings, since 1987; *b* 19 June 1935; *s* of William Alfred Sellers and Irene Ethel Sellers (*née* Freemantle); *m* 2nd, 1980, Gillian Clare Heinrich; two *s* one *d* from previous marr. *Educ:* King's College, Adelaide, SA. Clerk, State Bank of SA, 1952; Clerk, Cutten & Harvey, Adelaide, 1954–69 (Investment Advr, 1969); owner, Devon Homes, SA, 1970; bought Ralph Symonds Ltd, 1975 (Man. Dir); Managing Director: National Textiles, 1983; Linter Group, 1985; AFP Group, 1986. *Recreations:* cricket, art, music. *Address:* 22 Chester Street, Belgravia, SW1X 7BL. *T:* 071–245 9694. *Clubs:* Cricketers'; University (Australia).

SELLERS, Geoffrey Bernard; CB 1991; Parliamentary Counsel, since 1987; *b* 5 June 1947; *s* of Bernard Whittaker Sellers and late Elsie (*née* Coop); *m* 1971, Susan Margaret Faulconbridge; two *s* two *d*. *Educ:* Manchester Grammar Sch. (Scholar); Magdalen Coll., Oxford (Mackinnon Scholar; BCL 1st Cl. Hons; MA). Called to the Bar, Gray's Inn, 1971 (Macaskie Scholar). Legal Assistant: Law Commn, 1971; Commn on Industrial Relations, 1971–74; joined Office of Parly Counsel, 1974; with Law Commn, 1982–85. *Address:* 36 Whitehall, SW1A 2AY. *Club:* Royal Automobile.

SELLERS, His Honour Norman William Malin, VRD; DL; a Circuit Judge, 1974–90; *b* 29 Aug. 1919; *e s* of late Rt Hon. Sir Frederic Sellers, MC, and Grace (*née* Malin); *m* 1946, Angela Laurie, *er d* of Sidney Jukes, Barnet; four *d*. *Educ:* Merchant Taylors' Sch., Crosby; Silcoates Sch., Wakefield; Hertford Coll., Oxford (MA). Officer, RNVR, 1940–65 (despatches, HMS Nelson, 1942); Lt Cdr 1953, comd HMS Mersey. Called to Bar, Gray's Inn, 1947; Northern Circuit; Asst Recorder of Blackpool, 1962–71; Recorder of Crown Court, 1972–74. Contested (L) Crosby Div. of Lancs, 1964. DL Lancs, 1986. *Recreation:* sailing. *Address:* Hillside, Lower Road, Longridge, Preston PR3 2YN. *T:* Longridge (0772) 703222. *Clubs:* Bar Yacht, Ribble Cruising.

SELLERS, Philip Edward; Chairman, CSL Group Ltd, since 1989; *b* 20 March 1937; *s* of George Edward and Helen Sellers; *m* 1962, Brenda Anne Bell; two *s*. *Educ:* Ernest Bailey Grammar School, Matlock; CIPFA. Local Govt, 1953–72; Controller of Audit, British Gas Corp., 1972–76; Finance Dir, North Thames Gas, 1976–80; Dir of Finance and Planning, British Rail Board, 1980–84; Board Mem. for Corporate Finance and Planning, Post Office, 1984–89. Trustee, Post Office Pension Funds, 1985–; Director: Postel Investment Management Ltd, 1986–; THFC Ltd, 1987–; (non-exec.) Etam Gp, 1991–; Chm., CFM Ltd, 1989–. UK rep., IFAC Public Sector Cttee, 1987–90; Philip Sellers Communications and Consultancy, 1989–. Mem., NCC Impact Adv. Bd, 1989–. Pres., CIPFA, 1985–86; Chm., Nationalised Industries Finance Panel, 1986–89. *Recreations:* tennis, ski-ing. *Address:* Yarrimba, 31 Howards Thicket, Gerrards Cross, Bucks SL9 7NT. *T:* Gerrards Cross (0753) 884669.

SELLERS, Robert Firth, ScD; FRSE; MRCVS; consultant on foreign animal diseases; *b* 9 June 1924; *s* of Frederick Sellers and Janet Walkinshaw Shiels; *m* 1951, Margaret Peterkin; one *s* one *d*. *Educ:* Christ's Hospital; Gonville and Caius Coll., Cambridge (MA, ScD); Royal (Dick) School of Veterinary Studies, Edinburgh (PhD, BSc). FIBiol. Served War, Royal Artillery, 1943–46. Research Institute (Animal Virus Diseases), Pirbright, 1953–58; Wellcome Research Laboratories, Beckenham, 1958–62; Instituto Venezolano de Investigaciones Cientificas, Venezuela, 1962–64; Animal Virus Research Institute, Pirbright, 1964–84, Dep. Dir, 1964–79, Dir, 1979–84; Consultant, Foreign Animal Disease Unit, Agriculture, Canada, 1985–88. J. T. Edwards Meml Medal, 1976. *Publications:* papers on animal viruses in scientific jls. *Recreation:* archaeology. *Address:* 4 Pewley Way, Guildford, Surrey GU1 3PY.

SELLIER, Robert Hugh, FICE; Chief Executive, Y. J. Lovell, since 1991; *b* 15 Nov. 1933; *s* of Major Philip Joseph Sellier and Lorna Geraldine Sellier (*née* Luxton); *m* 1st, 1963, Cynthia Ann Dwelly (*d* 1985); one *d*; 2nd, 1987, Gillian Dalley (*née* Clark). *Educ:* St Joseph's Coll., Oxford; King's Coll., Durham Univ. (BScCivEng). FIHT. Man. Dir, New Ideal Homes, 1972–74; Dep. Man. Dir, Cementation International, 1974–79; Man. Dir, Cementation Construction, 1979–83; Chm., Cementation Gp of Companies, 1983–86; Gp Man. Dir, George Wimpey, 1986–91. *Recreations:* ski-ing, squash, clay pigeon shooting. *Address:* Heatherlands, Glenmore Road, Crowborough, East Sussex TN6 1TN. *T:* Crowborough (0892) 663413.

SELLORS, Patrick John Holmes, LVO 1990; FRCS; Surgeon-Oculist to the Queen, since 1980; Ophthalmic Surgeon, King Edward VIIth Hospital for Officers, since 1975; Ophthalmic Surgeon, Croydon Eye Unit, since 1970; *b* 11 Feb. 1934; *s* of Sir Thomas Holmes Sellors, DM, MCh, FRCP, FRCS; *m* 1961, Gillian Gratton Swallow; two *s* one *d*. *Educ:* Rugby Sch.; Oriel Coll., Oxford; Middlesex Hosp. Med. School. MA Oxon; BM, BCh Oxon 1958; FRCS 1965. Registrar, Moorfields Eye Hosp., 1962–65; recognised teacher in Ophthalmology, St George's Hosp., 1966; Ophthalmic Surgeon, St George's Hosp., 1965–82 (Hon., 1983); Surgeon-Oculist to HM Household, 1974–80; Hon. Consultant Ophthalmic Surgeon, St Luke's Hosp. for the Clergy, 1983–. Sec. to Ophthalmic Soc. of UK, 1970–72; Examr for Diploma of Ophthalmology, 1974–77; Member, Council: Faculty of Ophthalmologists, 1977–88; Med. Defence Union, 1977–; Gen. Optical Council, 1978–; Coll. of Ophthalmologists, 1988–. Dep. Master, Oxford Congress, 1991. *Publications:* (jtly) Outline in Ophthalmology, 1985; articles in BMJ and Trans OSUK. *Recreations:* gardening, golf. *Address:* 149 Harley Street, W1N 2DE. *T:* 071–935 4444.

SELLS, Sir David (Perronet), Kt 1980; *b* 23 June 1918; *s* of late Edward Perronet Sells; *m* 1948, Beryl Cecilia, *er d* of late C. E. W. Charrington, MC; three *s*. *Educ:* Sandroyd Sch.; Repton Sch.; Christ Church, Oxford. Commissioned, Coldstream Guards, 1941; active service, N Africa and Italy. Called to Bar, Inner Temple, 1947. Chairman: Cambridgeshire Conservative and Unionist Assoc., 1962–67; Conservative Council for Europ. Constit. of Cambs, 1978–85; Mem. Executive Cttee, Nat. Union of Conservative and Unionist Assocs, 1965–81; Chairman, Conservative Central Council and Conservative Party Conf., 1977–78. *Recreations:* fishing, painting, shooting. *Address:* Garden House, Church Street, Guilden Morden, Royston, Herts SG8 0JD. *T:* Steeple Morden (0763) 853237. *Club:* Savile.

SELLY, Susan, (Mrs Clifford Selly); *see* Strange, S.

SELSDON, 3rd Baron, *cr* 1932, of Croydon; **Malcolm McEacharn Mitchell-Thomson;** Bt 1900; banker; *b* 27 Oct. 1937; *s* of 2nd Baron Selsdon (3rd Bt, *cr* 1900), DSC; *S* father, 1963; *m* 1965, Patricia Anne, *d* of Donald Smith; one *s*. *Educ:* Winchester College. Sub-Lieut, RNVR. Deleg. to Council of Europe and WEU, 1972–78. C. T. Bowring Gp, 1972–76; Midland Bank Group, 1976–90: EEC Advr, 1979–85; Public Finance Advr, 1985–90. Dir of various companies. Chm., Committee for Middle East Trade (COMET), 1979–86; Member: BOTB, 1983–86; E European Trade Council, 1985–87. Chm., Greater London and SE Regional Council for Sport and Recreation, 1977–83. *Recreations:* rackets, squash, tennis, lawn tennis, ski-ing, sailing. *Heir:* *s* Hon. Callum Malcolm McEacharn Mitchell-Thomson, *b* 7 Nov. 1969. *Address:* c/o House of Lords, SW1A 0PW. *Club:* MCC.

SELVON, Samuel Dickson; author since 1954; *b* Trinidad, West Indies, 20 May 1923; *m* 1st, 1947, Draupadi Persaud; one *d*; 2nd, 1963, Althea Nesta Daroux; two *s* one *d*. *Educ:* Naparima College, Trinidad. Wireless Operator, 1940–45; Journalist, 1946–50; Civil Servant, 1950–53. Fellow, John Simon Guggenheim Memorial Foundn (USA), 1954 and 1968; Travelling Schol., Soc. of Authors (London), 1958; Trinidad Govt Schol., 1962. Hon. DLitt: Univ. of West Indies, 1985; Warwick, 1989. Humming Bird Medal (Trinidad), 1969. *Publications:* A Brighter Sun, 1952; An Island is a World, 1954; The Lonely Londoners, 1956; Ways of Sunlight, 1957; Turn Again Tiger, 1959; I Hear Thunder, 1963; The Housing Lark, 1965; The Plains of Caroni, 1970; Those Who Eat the Cascadura, 1972; Moses Ascending, 1975; Moses Migrating, 1983; Foreday Morning, 1989; Eldorado West One, 1989; contribs to London Magazine, New Statesman and Nation, Sunday Times, also Evergreen Review (USA). *Recreations:* tennis, swimming, gardening, cooking.

SELWOOD, Maj.-Gen. David Henry Deering; Director of Army Legal Services, Ministry of Defence, since 1990; a Recorder of the Crown Court, since 1985; *b* 27 June 1934; *s* of Comdr George Deering Selwood, RN, and Enid Marguerite Selwood (*née* Rowlinson); *m* 1973, Barbara Dorothea (*née* Hütter); three *s* one *d*. *Educ:* Kelly Coll., Tavistock; University College of the South-West; Law Society's School of Law. Articled to G. C. Aldhouse, Esq., Plymouth, 1952–57; admitted Solicitor 1957; National Service, RASC 2/Lieut, 1957–59; private practice, Plymouth, 1959–61; TA 4 Devons, Lieut, 1959–61; commnd Army Legal Services Staff List, 1961; service on legal staffs, MoD, Headquarters: BAOR, MELF, FARELF, UKLF, Land Forces Cyprus, 1961–85; Brig., Legal, HQ BAOR, 1986–90; Asst Recorder, SE Circuit, 1980. Hon. Advocate, US Court of Military Appeals, 1972–. *Publication:* (jtly) Criminal Law and Psychiatry, 1987. *Address:* Directorate of Army Legal Services, Empress State Building, Lillie Road, SW6 1TR. *Club:* Lansdowne.

SELWYN, John Sidney Augustus, OBE 1962 (MBE 1939); HM Diplomatic Service, retired; *b* 17 Oct. 1908; *s* of Rev. A. L. H. Selwyn; *m* 1932, Cicely Georgina Armour (marr. diss.); one *s* one *d* (and one *d* decd); *m* 1952, Janette Bruce Mullin (*d* 1968); one *s*; *m* 1971, Sonja Fischer; one *d*. *Educ:* St Lawrence College, Ramsgate; Royal Military Coll., Sandhurst. Entered the Indian Police, 1928. Served in NWF Campaigns, 1930, 1937 and 1941. Major, 12th Frontier Force Regt, active service in Burma, 1942–46, Allied Control Commission, Germany, 1946–48. Entered Diplomatic Service, 1948. Served in Bucharest, Lisbon, London, Lima, Santos, Beirut; Consul-General: Berlin, 1963; Strasbourg, 1964–68; Vice-Consul, Calais, 1969–73. *Recreation:* walking. *Address:* Erlaufstrasse 35/2/6, A-2344 Maria Enzersdorf-Südstadt, Austria. *Club:* Civil Service.

SEMEGA-JANNEH, Bocar Ousman, MBE 1954; High Commissioner for The Gambia in London and Ambassador to Western Germany, Belgium, Sweden, Switzerland, France and Austria, 1971–80, to The Holy See, 1979–80; *b* 21 July 1910; *s* of late Ousman Semega-Janneh, merchant and late Koumba Tunkara, The Gambia; *m* 1936, and other Muslim marriages; several *c*. *Educ:* Mohammedan Primary Sch.; Methodist Boys' High School. Air Raid Warden, Bathurst, 1939–45. Gambia Surveys Dept: Surveys Asst 1931; Surveyor 1937; Sen. Surveyor 1948; Dir 1953; retd 1966. Gambian High Comr, Senegal, 1967; Ambassador to Mauritania, Mali, Guinea and Liberia, and High Comr, Sierra Leone, 1969; rep. Gambia at Gen. Assembly of UN, 1968–; rep. at meetings of Ministers of Foreign Affairs and Heads of State and Govt of members of Organisation of African Unity, 1968–. Rep. Gambia, triennial Survey Officers' Conf., Cambridge, 1955–65. Boy Scout, 1925; District Scout-master, 1938–42; Chief Comr of Scouts, The Gambia, 1947–66 (Silver Acorn 1954); Dep. Chief Scout, 1980–. Bathurst City Council: Councillor, 1951; Dep. Chm., 1957; Chm., 1960; first Mayor 1965; resigned 1967. Vice-Pres. 1955–56, Pres. 1957–67, Gambia Football Assoc.; formerly: Mem. Kombo Rural Authority; Governor, Gambia High Sch.; Actg Mem. Gambia Oilseeds Marketing Bd; Mem. Bathurst Colony Team and Town Planning Bd; Mem. Consultative Cttee for foundation of Constitution; Mem., Mohammedan Sch. Man. Cttee. Pres., Gambia Tennis Assoc., 1980–. Grand Officer, Order of Merit: Senegal, 1971; Mauritania, 1971; Officer of Republic of The Gambia. *Recreations:* football, cricket, golf, lawn tennis (singles champion, Gambia, 1932–50). *Address:* 15 Hagan Street, Banjul, Republic of The Gambia.

SEMKEN, John Douglas, CB 1980; MC 1944; Legal Adviser to the Home Office, 1977–83; *b* 9 Jan. 1921; *s* of Wm R. Semken and Mrs B. R. Semken (*née* Craymer); *m* 1952, Edna Margaret, *yr d* of T. R. Poole; three *s*. *Educ:* St Albans Sch.; Pembroke Coll., Oxford (MA, BCL). Solicitor's articled clerk, 1938–39. Commnd in Sherwood Rangers Yeo., 1940; 1st Lieut 1941, Captain 1942, Major 1944; 8th Armd Bde, N Africa, 1942–43; Normandy beaches to Germany, 1944. Called to Bar, Lincoln's Inn, 1949; practised at Chancery Bar, 1949–54; joined Legal Adviser's Br., Home Office, 1954; Mem., Criminal Law Revision Cttee, 1980–83. Silver Star Medal (USA), 1944. *Address:* 2 The Ridgeway, Mill Hill, NW7 1RS. *T:* 081–346 3092. *Club:* Lawrenny Yacht.

SEMMENCE, Dr Adrian Murdoch, CB 1986; Civil Service Medical Adviser, 1979–86, retired; Consultant, Cabinet Office (Office of the Minister for the Civil Service), since 1986; *b* 5 April 1926; *e s* of late Adrian George Semmence, MA, and Henrietta Scorgie Semmence (*née* Murdoch), MA; *m* 1949, Joan, *o d* of Hugh and Bobbie Wood; four *s* one *d*. *Educ:* Robert Gordon's Coll.; Univ. of Aberdeen (MB, ChB 1953; MD 1957); Univ. of London (MSc 1972); DObstRCOG, FRCGP, DIH, FFOM, FRSM. Served War, FAA 1943–44, RN 1944–47, HM Ships Sharpshooter, Ekins, Liverpool, and Anson in Mediterranean and Channel (able seaman). General Practitioner, E Yorks, Berks and Oxon, 1954–76; Upjohn Fellow, Univ. of Edinburgh, 1967; Nuffield Travelling Fellow, 1969–70; Unit of Clinical Epidemiology, Univ. of Oxford, 1970–76; Principal MO, CSD, 1976–79. FRSM (Pres. Sect. of Occupational Med., 1985–86). *Address:* Stone Cottage, Steventon, Abingdon OX13 6RZ. *T:* Abingdon (0235) 831527. *Club:* Royal Society of Medicine.

SEMPER, Very Rev. Colin (Douglas); Canon of Westminster, since 1987; *b* 5 Feb. 1938; *s* of William Frederick and Dorothy Anne Semper; *m* 1962, Janet Louise Greaves; two *s*. *Educ:* Lincoln School; Keble College, Oxford (BA); Westcott House, Cambridge. Curate of Holy Trinity with St Mary, Guildford, 1963–66; Recruitment and Selection Sec., ACCM, 1966–69; Head of Religious Programmes, BBC Radio, and Deputy Head of Religious Broadcasting, BBC, 1969–82; Provost of Coventry Cathedral, 1982–87. *Recreations:* travel, reading modern novels, canals. *Address:* 8 Little Cloister, Westminster Abbey, SW1P 3PL.

SEMPILL, family name of **Lady Sempill** (*née* Forbes-Sempill).

SEMPILL, Lady (20th in line, of the Lordship *cr* 1489); **Ann Moira Sempill** (*née* Forbes-Sempill); *b* 19 March 1920; *d* of 19th Lord Sempill, AFC; *S* father, 1965; *m* 1st, 1941, Captain Eric Holt (marr. diss., 1945); one *d*; 2nd, 1948, Lt-Col Stuart Whitemore Chant (*d* 1991), OBE, MC (who assumed by decree of Lyon Court, 1966, the additional surname of Sempill); two *s*. *Educ:* Austrian, German and English Convents. Served War, 1939–42 (Petty Officer, WRNS). Mem. Cttee, Anglo Austrian Soc., 1966–. *Heir: s* The Master of Sempill, *qv*. *Address:* East Lodge, Druminnor, Rhynie, Aberdeenshire AB5 4LT; 15 Onslow Court, Drayton Gardens, SW10.

SEMPILL, Master of; Hon. James William Stuart Whitemore Sempill; Account Director, Bates Wells (Pty) Ltd, Advertising Agency, since 1986; Marketing Manager, South African Breweries, since 1983; *b* 25 Feb 1949; *s* and *heir* of Lady Sempill, *qv*, and Lt-Col Stuart Whitemore Chant-Sempill (*d* 1991); *m* 1977, Josephine Ann Edith, *e d* of J. Norman Rees, Johannesburg; one *s* one *d*. *Educ:* The Oratory School; St Clare's Hall, Oxford (BA Hons History, 1971); Hertford Coll., Oxford. Gallaher Ltd, 1972–80; PA to Managing Director, Sentinel Engineering Pty Ltd, Johannesburg, 1980–81; Manager, TWS Public Relations Company, Johannesburg, 1981–83; investment manager, Alan Clarke and Partners, 1982–83. *Address:* 50 Fort Street, Birnam, Johannesburg, 2193, South Africa. *Clubs:* Vincent's, Carlton (Oxford); Wanderers' (Johannesburg).

SEMPLE, Prof. Andrew Best, CBE 1966; VRD 1953; QHP 1962; Professor of Community and Environmental Health (formerly of Public Health), University of Liverpool, 1953–77, now Professor Emeritus; *b* 3 May 1912; *m* 1941, Jean (*née* Sweet); one *d*. *Educ:* Allan Glen's School, Glasgow; Glasgow Univ. MB, ChB 1934, MD 1947, DPH 1936, Glasgow. FFCM 1972. Various hospital appointments, 1934–38; Asst MOH and Deputy Medical Superintendent, Infectious Diseases Hosp., Portsmouth, 1938–39; Asst MOH and Asst School Medical Officer, Blackburn, 1939–47 (interrupted by War Service); Senior Asst MOH, Manchester, 1947–48; Deputy MOH, City and Port of Liverpool, 1948–53, MOH and Principal Sch. Med. Officer, 1953–74; Area MO (teaching), Liverpool AHA, 1974–77. Served War of 1939–46; Surgeon Commander, RNVR; Naval MOH, Western Approaches, Malta and Central Mediterranean. Chm. Council and Hon. Treasurer, RSH, 1963. *Publications:* various regarding infectious disease, port health, hygiene, etc. *Address:* Kelvin, 433 Woolton Road, Gateacre, Liverpool L25 4SY. *T:* 051–428 2081.

SEMPLE, Andrew Greenlees; Vice-Chairman, Anglian Water plc, since 1990; *b* 16 Jan. 1934; *s* of late William Hugh Semple and Madeline, *d* of late E. H. Wood, Malvern, Worcs; *m* 1961, Janet Elizabeth, *d* of late H. R. G. Whates and of Mrs Whates, Ludlow, Salop; one *s* one *d*. *Educ:* Winchester Coll.; St John's Coll., Cambridge (MA). Entered Min. of Transport and Civil Aviation, 1957; Private Sec. to Permanent Sec., 1960–62; Principal, 1962; Asst Sec., 1970; Private Sec. to successive Secs of State for the Environment, 1972–74; Under Sec., DoE, 1976; Principal Finance Officer, PSA, DoE, 1980–83; Sec., Water Authorities Assoc., 1983–87; Man. Dir, Anglian Water Authority, 1987–89; Gp Man. Dir, Anglian Water plc, 1989–90. Member: Bd, Eureau, 1983–; Admin. Council, European Inst. for Water, 1987–. Chm., Huntingdonshire Enterprise Agency, 1990–. CompIWEM 1984; Hon. Mem., AWO, 1988. *Recreations:* walking, reading, gardening, watching cricket. *Address:* 83 Burbage Road, SE24 9HB. *T:* 071–274 6550; 3 Church Lane, Covington, Cambs PE18 0RT. *T:* Huntingdon (0480) 860497.

SEMPLE, John Laughlin; Permanent Secretary, Department of Finance and Personnel for Northern Ireland, since 1988; *b* 10 Aug. 1940; *s* of late James E. Semple and of Violet E. G. Semple; *m* 1970, Maureen Anne Kerr; two *s* one *d*. *Educ:* Campbell Coll., Belfast; Corpus Christi Coll., Cambridge (MA). BScEcon London. Joined Home CS as Asst Principal, Min. of Aviation, 1961; transf. to NI CS, 1962; Asst Principal, Mins of Health and Local Govt, Finance, and Health and Social Services, 1962–65; Dep. Principal, Min. of Health and Social Services, 1965; Principal: Min. of Finance, 1968; Min. of Community Relations, 1970–72; Asst Sec. (Planning), Min. of Develt, 1972; Asst Sec. (Housing), DoE, 1977–79; Under Sec. (Housing), DoE for N Ireland, 1979–83; Under Sec., Dept of Finance and Personnel for NI, 1983–88. *Recreations:* golf, tennis, gardening.

SEMPLE, Prof. Stephen John Greenhill, MD, FRCP; Professor of Medicine, University College and Middlesex School of Medicine, University College London, since 1987; *b* 4 Aug. 1926; *s* of late John Edward Stewart and Janet Semple; *m* 1961, Penelope Ann, *y d* of Sir Geoffrey Aldington, *qv*; three *s*. *Educ:* Westminster; London Univ. MB, BS, 1950, MD 1952, FRCP 1968. Research Asst, St Thomas' Hosp. Med. Sch., 1952; Jun. Med. Specialist, RAMC, Malaya, 1953–55; Instr, Med. Sch., Univ. of Pennsylvania, USA, 1957–59; St Thomas' Hosp. Medical Sch.: Lectr, 1959; Sen. Lectr, 1961; Reader, 1965; Prof. in Medicine, 1969; Prof. of Medicine, The Middlesex Hosp. Medical Sch., 1970–87, also at UCL, 1985–87. *Publications:* Disorders of Respiration, 1972; articles in: Lancet, Jl Physiol. (London), Jl Applied Physiol. *Recreations:* tennis, music. *Address:* White Lodge, 3 Claremont Park Road, Esher, Surrey KT10 9LT. *T:* Esher (0372) 465057. *Club:* Queen's.

SEMPLE, William David Crowe, CBE 1991; Director of Education, Lothian Region, since 1974; *b* 11 June 1933; *s* of late George Crowe and Helen Davidson Semple (*née* Paterson); *m* 1958, Margaret Bain Donald; one *s* one *d*. *Educ:* Glasgow Univ.; Jordanhill Coll. of Educn; London Univ. BSc Hons, DipEd. FBIM. Educn Officer, Northern Rhodesia, 1958–64; Zambia: Dep. Chief Educn Officer, 1964–66; Chief Educn Officer, 1966–67; Actg Dir of Techn. Educn, 1967–68; Edinburgh: Asst Dir of Educn, 1968–72; Depute Dir of Educn, 1972–74. Gen. Sec., Assoc. of Dirs of Educn, Scotland, 1985–; Member: Sec. of State (Scot.) Wkg Party on Educnl Catering, 1971–73; Council for Tertiary Educn in Scotland, 1979–83; STV Educn Adv. Cttee, 1979–85; UK Nat. Cttee for UNESCO, 1981–85; UGC, 1983–89; Sec. of State (Scot.) Cttee reviewing examinations in 5th and 6th years, 1990–. *Publications:* contrib. various journals. *Recreations:* gardening, reading, gastronomy. *Address:* 15 Essex Park, Edinburgh EH4 6LH. *T:* 031–339 6157.

SEN, Prof. Amartya Kumar, FBA 1977; Lamont University Professor, Harvard University, since 1988 (Professor of Economics and Philosophy, 1987); *b* 3 Nov. 1933; *s* of late Dr Ashutosh Sen, Dacca, and of Amita Sen, Santiniketan, India; *m* 1st, 1960, Nabaneeta Dev (marr. diss. 1975); two *d*; 2nd, 1978, Eva Colorni (*d* 1985); one *s* one *d*; *m* 1991, Emma Rothschild, *qv*. *Educ:* Calcutta Univ.; Cambridge Univ. MA, PhD. Prof. of Economics, Jadavpur Univ., Calcutta, 1956–58; Trinity Coll., Cambridge: Prize Fellow, 1957–61; Staff Fellow, 1961–63; Professor of Economics: Delhi Univ., 1963–71 (Chm., Dept of Economics, 1966–68, Hon. Prof., 1971–); LSE, 1971–77; Oxford Univ., 1977–80; Fellow, Nuffield College, Oxford, 1977–80; Drummond Prof. of Political Economy, and Fellow, All Souls Coll., Oxford, 1980–88. Hon. Dir, Agricultural Economics Research Centre, Delhi, 1966–68 and 1969–71. Res. Advr, World Inst. for Develt Econ. Res., Helsinki, Finland, 1985–. Vis. Professor: MIT, 1960–61; Univ. of Calif at Berkeley, 1964–65; Harvard Univ., 1968–69; Andrew D. White Professor-at-large, Cornell Univ., 1978–84. Chm., UN Expert Gp Meeting on Role of Advanced Skill and Technology, New York, 1967. President: Develt Studies Assoc., 1980–82; Econometric Soc., 1984 (Fellow 1968–, Vice-Pres. 1982–83); Internat. Economic Assoc., 1986–89; Indian Econ. Assoc., 1989; Vice-Pres., Royal Economic Soc., 1988– (Mem. Council, 1977–87); Trustee, Inst. for Advanced Study, Princeton, 1987–. Foreign Hon. Mem., Amer. Acad. of Arts and Sciences, 1981; Hon. Mem., Amer. Econ. Assoc., 1981. Hon. Fellow: Inst. of Social Studies, The Hague, 1982; LSE, 1984; IDS, Sussex Univ., 1984. Hon. DLitt: Saskatchewan, 1980; Visva-Bharati Univ., 1983; Georgetown, 1989; Jadavpur, 1990; Kalyani, 1990; Williams Coll., 1991; Hon. DSc Bath, 1984; DU Essex, 1984; Dr *hc*: Caen, 1987; Bologna, 1988; Univ. Catholique de Louvain, 1989; Athens Univ. of Econs and Business, 1991; Hon. LLD Tulane, 1990. Agnelli Internat. Prize, 1990; Alan Shawn Feinstein World Hunger Award, 1990. *Publications:* Choice of Techniques: an aspect of planned economic development, 1960 (3rd edn, 1968); Growth

Economics, 1970; Collective Choice and Social Welfare, 1971; On Economic Inequality, 1973; Employment, Technology and Development, 1975; Poverty and Famines: an essay on entitlement and deprivation, 1981; (ed with Bernard Williams) Utilitarianism and Beyond, 1982; Choice, Welfare and Measurement, 1982; Resources, Values and Development, 1984; Commodities and Capabilities, 1985; On Ethics and Economics, 1987; The Standard of Living, 1987; (with Jean Drèze) Hunger and Public Action, 1989; Inequality and Freedom, 1991; (ed with Jean Drèze) The Political Economy of Hunger, 3 vols, 1990–91; articles in various jls in economics, philosophy, political science, decision theory, demography and law. *Address:* Harvard University, Cambridge, Mass 02138, USA. *T:* (617)–495–1871.

SEN, Shri Binay Ranjan, Padmavibhusan 1970; CIE 1944; ICS; Director-General of the United Nations Food and Agriculture Organisation, Rome, 1956–67; *b* 1 Jan. 1898; *s* of Dr K. M. Sen; *m* 1931, Chiroprova Chatterjee. *Educ:* Calcutta and Oxford Universities. Secretary to Govt of Bengal, Political and Appointment Departments, and Press Officer, 1931–34; District Magistrate, Midnapore, 1937–40; Revenue Secretary to Government of Bengal, 1940–43; Director of Civil Evacuation, Bengal, 1942–43; Relief Commissioner, 1942–43; Director-General of Food, Government of India, 1943–46; Sec. to Food Dept, Govt of India, 1946; Minister of the Embassy of India, at Washington, 1947–50; Indian Ambassador to: Italy and Yugoslavia, 1950–51; US and Mexico, 1951–52; Italy and Yugoslavia, 1952–55; Japan, 1955–56. Member Indian Delegation to General Assembly of United Nations, 1947; India's Rep. to United Nations Security Council, 1947; Agriculture Sec. to Govt of India, 1948; Head of Jt Mission of FAO and ECAFE (Economic Commn for Asia and the Far East) to study agricultural rehabilitation in China and SE Asian countries; Head of Ind. Deleg. to: ECOSOC (Economic and Social Council of the UN), 1949 and 1953; Annual Conf. of FAO, 1949, and FAO Coun., 1950, 1951, 1953. Hon. Mem., Internat. Mark Twain Soc., 1976. Hon. Fellow, St Catherine's Coll., Oxford. Award, NFU of US, 1960. Several hon. degrees and decorations, incl. Kt Comdr Piani Ordinis, and Kt Grand Cross Ordinis Sancti Silvetri Papae. *Address:* 14/2 Palm Avenue, Calcutta 19, India.

SEN, Emma; *see* Rothschild, Emma.

SEN, Prof. Satyendra Nath, MA, PhD (Econ) London; Chairman, Board of Governors, Indian Institute of Technology, Kharagpur, since 1981; President, Calcutta Local Board and Member, Central Board of Directors, State Bank of India, since 1979; Vice-Chancellor, 1968–76, Professor of Economics, 1958–76, Calcutta University; *b* April 1909. Visited UK and other parts of Europe, 1949–51; Vis. Prof., Princeton and Stanford Univs (sponsored Ford Foundn), 1962–63; subseq. Dean, Faculties of Arts and Commerce, and Head of Dept of Econs, Calcutta University. Mem. Bd of Trustees: Indian Museum, Calcutta; Victoria Memorial, Calcutta; Mahajati Sadan, Calcutta; Mem. Research Programmes Cttee, Planning Commn, Govt of India (Chm. East Regional Cttee); Mem. Pay Commn, Govt of W Bengal, 1967–69; Discussion Leader, Section on Medium and Longterm Credit, Internat. Conf. on Agricultural Credit, Lahore (FAO and ECAFE), 1956; Mem. Industrial Tribunal adjudicating dispute between United Bank of India Ltd and its employees, 1954–55. Mem., Nat. Co-operative Union, Delhi; Vice-Pres., State Co-operative Union, W Bengal. Mem. Adv. Cttee of Vice-Chancellors, New Delhi, and Chm., Cttee on salary scales of univ. and coll. teachers, 1974, Univ. Grants Commn; Mem. Exec. Cttee, Assoc. of Commonwealth Univs, 1974; Pres., Assoc. of Indian Univs, 1976; Mem., Central Adv. Commn on Educn, Govt of India, 1976. Pres., Asiatic Soc., Calcutta, 1983– (Hon. Fellow, 1982). *Publications:* Central Banking in Undeveloped Money Markets, 1952; The City of Calcutta: a socio-economic survey, 1954–55 to 1957–58, 1960; The Co-operative Movement in West Bengal, 1966; (with T. Piplai) Industrial Relations in Jute Industry in West Bengal, 1968. *Address:* 18c Lake View Road, Calcutta, West Bengal, 700029, India.

SENDAK, Maurice Bernard; writer and illustrator of children's books; theatrical designer; Artistic Director, The Night Kitchen, national children's theater; *b* 10 June 1928; *yr s* of Philip Sendak and Sarah (*née* Schindler). *Educ:* Lafayette High School, Brooklyn; Art Students' League, NY. Worked part-time at All American Comics; window display work with Timely Service, 1946–48, F. A. O. Schwartz, 1948–50; illustrated over 50 books by other writers, 1951–. Retrospective one-man exhibitions: Sch. of Visual Arts, NY, 1964; Ashmolean, Oxford, 1975; Amer. Cultural Center, Paris, 1978. *Stage designs:* The Magic Flute, Houston, 1980; The Cunning Little Vixen, NY, 1981; The Love of Three Oranges, Glyndebourne, 1982; Where the Wild Things Are, NT, 1984; L'enfant et les sortilèges, L'Heure espagnole, Glyndebourne, 1987. Hon. RDI 1986. *Publications:* Kenny's Window, 1956; Very Far Away, 1957; The Sign on Rosie's Door, 1960; Nutshell Library set, 1962; Where the Wild Things Are, 1963 (Amer. Liby Assoc. Caldecott Medal, 1964; opera, by Oliver Knussen, Glyndebourne, 1984); Higglety Pigglety Pop!, 1967; Hector Protector, 1967; In the Night Kitchen, 1971; (with Charlotte Zolotow) Rabbit and the Lovely Present, 1971; Pictures, 1972; Maxfield Parrish Poster Book, 1974; (with Matthelo Margolis) Some Swell Pup, 1976; Charlotte and the White Horse, 1977; (ed) Disney Poster Book, 1977; Seven Little Monsters, 1977; (with Doris Orgel) Sarah's Room, 1977; Very Far Away, 1978; Outside Over There, 1981; (with Frank Corsaro) The Love for Three Oranges, 1984; (with Ralph Manheim) Nutcracker, 1984; Dear Mili, 1988; Caldecott and Company (essays), 1989. *Address:* c/o HarperCollins, 10 East 53rd Street, New York, NY 10022, USA.

SENDALL, Bernard Charles, CBE 1952; Deputy Director-General, Independent Broadcasting Authority (formerly Independent Television Authority), 1955–77; *b* 30 April 1913; *s* of late William Sendall, Malvern, Worcestershire; *m* 1963, Barbara Mary, *d* of late Ambrose Coviello, DCM, FRAM. *Educ:* Magdalen College, Oxford; Harvard University. Entered Civil Service in the Admiralty, 1935; Principal Private Secretary to Minister of Information 1941–45; Controller (Home), Central Office of Information, 1946–49; Controller, Festival of Britain Office, 1949–51; Assistant Secretary, Admiralty, 1951–55. *Publication:* Independent Television in Britain, vol. I, 1982, vol. II, 1983. *Address:* 144 Montagu Mansions, York Street, W1H 1LA.

SENIOR, (Alan) Gordon, CBE 1981; CEng, FICE, FIStructE; FRICS; Managing Partner, Gordon Senior Associates, Engineering and Management Consultants, since 1980; Chairman, Masta Corporation Ltd, since 1987; *b* 1 Jan. 1928; *s* of late Oscar Senior and Helen Senior (*née* Cooper); *m* 1st, 1955, Sheila Lockyer (marr. diss. 1961); 2nd, 1968, Lawmary Mitchell (marr. diss. 1978); one *s*. *Educ:* Normanton Grammar School; Leeds Univ. (BSc 1948, MSc 1949). J. B. Edwards (Whyteleafe) Ltd, 1949–51; Oscar Faber & Partners, Consulting Engineers, 1951–54; W. S. Atkins & Partners, Consulting Engineers, 1954–80: Technical Dir, 1967; Man. Dir of Atkins Research and Development, 1972; Director, W. S. Atkins & Partners, 1976. Chairman: Surface Engineering and Inspection Ltd, 1983–86; Aptech Ltd, 1988–89; Director: Ansen Offshore Consultants Ltd and McMillan Sloan & Partners, 1981–84; Armstrong Technology Services Ltd, 1986. Member, Navy Dept Advisory Cttee on Structural Steels, 1967–71. Science and Engineering Research Council: Mem., Engineering Bd, 1974–78; Chm., Transport and Civil Engineering Cttee, 1974–78; Chm., Marine Technology Management Cttee, 1980–83. Department of Trade and Industry: Mem., Ship and Marine Technology Requirements Bd, and Chm., Marine Technology Cttee, 1976–81; Mem., Maritime Technology Cttee, 1981–86; Chm., Adv. Cttee on Resources from the Sea, 1983–86. Member: Programme Cttee, Offshore Energy Technology Bd, 1978–85; Offshore Safety and Tech. Bd, 1985–. Chm., Greenwich Forum, 1991–; Vice-Pres. and Chm. of Council, Soc. for Underwater Technology, 1979–81. *Publications:* (co-author) Brittle Fracture of Steel Structures, 1970; papers on welding, fatigue, brittle fracture, design of steel structures and future developments offshore and in the oceans. *Recreations:* food and wine, travel, ski-ing. *Address:* Deanlands, Guildford Road, Normandy, Surrey GU3 2AR. *T:* Worplesdon (0483) 235496. *Club:* Athenæum.

SENIOR, Sir Edward (Walters), Kt 1970; CMG 1955; Chairman, Ransome Hoffman Pollard Ltd, 1953–72; Chairman, George Senior & Sons Ltd, since 1930 (Managing Director, 1929); *b* 29 March 1902; *s* of Albert Senior; *m* 1928, Stephanie Vera Heald (*d* 1990); one *s* one *d*. *Educ:* Repton School; Sheffield University. Vice-Consul for Sweden, in Sheffield, 1930; RA, TA, Major, 1938; General Director of Alloy and Special Steels, Iron and Steel Control, 1941; Director, Steel Division of Raw Materials Mission, Washington, DC, 1942; Controller of Ball and Roller Bearings, 1944; British Iron and Steel Federation: Commercial Dir, 1949–61; Dir, 1961–62; Dir-Gen., 1962–66; retd, Dec. 1966; Exec. Chm., Derbyshire Stone Ltd, 1967–68; Dep. Chm., Tarmac Derby Ltd, 1968–71. Master of Cutlers' Company of Hallamshire in County of York, 1947; Vice-President of the Sheffield Chamber of Commerce, 1948; Chairman of Steel Re-Armament Panel, 1951. FBIM, 1971. JP Sheffield, 1937–50. *Recreations:* normal country activities. *Address:* Hollies, Church Close, Brenchley, Tonbridge, Kent TN12 7AA. *T:* Brenchley (089272) 2359. *Clubs:* Naval and Military; Sheffield (Sheffield).

SENIOR, Gordon; *see* Senior, A. G.

SENIOR, Olive Edith, JP, MPhil, SRN; Regional Nursing Officer, Trent Regional Health Authority, 1973–86; Fellow, Nottingham University, 1988; *b* 26 April 1934; *d* of Harold and Doris Senior, Mansfield, Notts. *Educ:* Harlow Wood Orthopaedic Hosp., 1949–52; St George's Hosp., Hyde Park Corner, 1952–56; City Hosp., Nottingham (Pt I, CMB 1956); Nottingham Univ. (HV Cert. 1957, MPhil 1978). Health Visitor, Notts CC, 1958–60; St George's Hosp., London (Ward Sister), 1960–63; S Africa, June-Dec. 1963; Forest Gate Hosp., London (SCM), 1964; St Mary's Hosp., Portsmouth (Asst Matron/Night Supt), 1964–66; NE Metropolitan Regional Hosp. Bd (Management Services), 1966–71; Chief Nursing Officer, Nottingham and Dist. Hosp. Management Cttee, 1971–73. Secretary of State Fellow, 1973. JP Nottingham Guildhall, 1973. *Publications:* An Analysis of Nurse Staffing Levels in Hospitals in the Trent Region (1977 Data), 1978; Dependency and Establishments, 1979; contrib. to Nursing Times (Determining Nursing Establishments). *Address:* 94 Oak Tree Lane, Mansfield, Notts NG18 3HL. *Club:* Nottingham Univ. (Nottingham).

SENOUSSI, Badreddine; Officer, Order of Ouissame Alaouite, Morocco; Ambassador of the Kingdom of Morocco to the Court of St James's, 1977–80; *b* 30 March 1933; *m* 1958; three *s*. *Educ:* Univ. of Bordeaux, France (Lic. (MA) en Droit); Univ. Mohamed V Rabat, Morocco (Lic. ès Lettres). Counsellor, High Cherifian Tribunal, 1956; in charge of: State Min. of Public Functions, Mar. 1957; Nat. Defense Min., Mar.-Sept. 1958; Gen. Sec., Tobacco Management, Oct. 1958–Feb. 1963; Chief, Royal Cabinet, 1963–64; Under-Sec. of State for Commerce, Industry, Mines and Merchant Navy, Dec. 1964–June 1965; Under-Sec. of State for Admin. Affairs, June 1965–Feb. 1966; Post and Telecommunications Minister, Feb. 1966–Mar. 1970; Benslimane Dep., Mem. Representative Chamber, Aug. 1970; Youth, Sports and Social Affairs Minister, Mar. 1970–Aug. 1971; Ambassador of Kingdom of Morocco: in Washington, Sept 1971–Dec. 1974; in Teheran, Mar. 1974–Sept. 1976. Holds many foreign honours. *Address:* c/o Ministry of Foreign Affairs, Rabat, Morocco. *Clubs:* Les Ambassadeurs, Mark's.

SENSI, His Eminence Cardinal (Giuseppe M.); *b* 27 May 1907. Ordained, 1929; Sec. of Apostolic Nunciature in Roumania, 1934–38; Secretary and Auditor of Apostolic Nunciature in Switzerland, 1938–46; Councillor of Apostolic Nunciature in Belgium, 1946–47; Chargé d'Affaires of the Holy See in Prague, 1948–49; Councillor in the Secretariat of State of His Holiness, 1949–53; Permanent Observer of the Holy See at UNESCO in Paris, 1953–55; apptd Nuncio Apostolic to Costa Rica, May 1955, and consecrated Titular Archbishop of Sardi, July 1955; Apostolic Delegate to Jerusalem, 1957; Apostolic Nuncio to Ireland, 1962–67; Apostolic Nuncio to Portugal, 1967–76; Cardinal, 1976. Membre de la Commission Pontificale pour l'Etat de la cité du Vatican. Chevalier, Grand Cross SMO Malta, 1959; Grand Cross, Santi Maurizio e Lazzaro, 1975; Grand Cross, Ordre Militaire du Christ (Portugal), 1976; Grand Cross, Ordre Equestre du St Sepolcre de Gerusalemme, 1978. Hon. Mem., Accademia Cosentina, 1976. *Address:* Piazza S Calisto 16, 00153 Rome, Italy. *T:* 06–6987265/6987388/5897827.

SEPÚLVEDA, Bernardo, Hon. GCMG 1985; Ambassador of Mexico to the Court of St James's, since 1989; *b* 14 Dec. 1941; *s* of Bernardo Sepúlveda and Margarita Amor; *m* 1970, Ana Yturbe; three *s*. *Educ:* Univ. of Mexico (Law Degree *magna cum laude*, 1964); Univ. of Cambridge (LLB; Hon. Fellow, Queen's Coll., 1990). Prof. of Internat. Law, El Colegio de México, 1967–81; Dep. Dir Gen. for Legal Affairs to Secretary of the Presidency, 1968–70; Asst Sec. for Internat. Affairs, Min. of the Treasury, 1976–80; Principal Advisor on Internat. Affairs to the Minister of Planning and Budget, 1981; Ambassador to USA, 1982; Minister of Foreign Relations, Mexico, 1982–88. Dr *hc*: Univ. of San Diego, Calif, 1982; Univ. of Leningrad, 1987. Príncipe de Asturias Prize, Spain, 1984; Simón Bolívar Prize, UNESCO, 1985. Grand Cross, Order of: Civil Merit (Spain), 1979; Isabel the Catholic (Spain), 1983; Southern Cross (Brazil), 1983; Boyacá (Colombia), 1984; Merit (FRG), 1984; Liberator San Martín (Argentina), 1984; Vasco Núñez de Balboa (Panama), 1984; Manuel Amador Geurrero (Panama), 1985; Christ (Portugal), 1985; Crown (Belgium), 1985; Quetzal (Guatemala), 1986; Prince Henry the Navigator (Portugal), 1986; Sun (Peru), 1987; Rio Branco (Brazil), 1988; Grand Officier, Nat. Order of Legion of Honour (France), 1985; also orders and decorations from Korea, Venezuela, Poland, Yugoslavia, Greece, Japan, Egypt and Jamaica. *Publications:* The United Nations: dilemma at 25, 1970; Foreign Investment in Mexico, 1973; Transnational Corporations in Mexico, 1974; articles on internat. law in prof. jls. *Recreations:* reading, music. *Address:* 48 Belgrave Square, SW1X 8QY. *T:* 071–235 6515. *Clubs:* Brooks's, Travellers'.

SERAFÍN, David; *see* Michael, I. D. L.

SERBY, John Edward, CB 1958; CBE 1951; FRAeS; Consultant; *b* 15 March 1902; *m* 1933, Clarice Lilian (*née* Hawes); one *d*. *Educ:* Haberdashers' Aske's School; Emmanuel College, Cambridge (BA). Junior Scientific Officer, Admiralty, 1927–30; Scientific Officer, RAE, 1930–38; Headquarters, MAP, 1938–50; Deputy Director, Royal Aircraft Establishment, Farnborough, 1950–54; Dir-Gen. of Guided Weapons, Min. of Aviation, 1954–61. Dep. Controller Guided Weapons, Ministry of Aviation, 1961–63. *Recreation:* gardening. *Address:* Overwey, Bishopsmead, Farnham, Surrey. *T:* Farnham (0252) 713526.

SERGEANT, Sir Patrick (John Rushton), Kt 1984; City Editor, Daily Mail, 1960–84; Founder, 1969, and Chairman, since 1985, Euromoney Publications (Managing Director, 1969–85); *b* 17 March 1924; *s* of George and Rene Sergeant; *m* 1952, Gillian Anne Wilks, Cape Town; two *d*. *Educ:* Beaumont Coll. Served as Lieut, RNVR, 1945. Asst City Editor, News Chronicle, 1948; Dep. City Editor, Daily Mail, 1953. Director: Associated Newspapers Group, 1971–83; Daily Mail General Trust, 1983–. Domus Fellow, St Catherine's Coll., Oxford, 1988. Freeman, City of London, 1987. Wincott Award, Financial Journalist of the Year, 1979. *Publications:* Another Road to Samarkand, 1955; Money Matters, 1967; Inflation Fighters Handbook, 1976. *Recreations:* skiing, tennis, swimming, talking. *Address:* One The Grove, Highgate Village, N6 6JU. *T:* 081–340 1245. *Clubs:* Royal Automobile, Annabel's; All England Lawn Tennis and Croquet.

SERIES, Sir Emile; *see* Seriès, Sir J. M. E.

SERIES, Prof. George William, FRS 1971; Hon. Research Fellow, Clarendon Laboratory, Oxford, since 1983; Professor of Physics, University of Reading, 1968, Emeritus 1982; *b* 22 Feb. 1920; *s* of William Series and Alice (*née* Crosthwaite); *m* 1948, Annette (*née* Pepper); three *s* one *d*. *Educ:* Reading Sch.; St John's Coll., Oxford. MA 1946, DPhil 1950, DSc 1969, Oxford. Served with Friends' Ambulance Unit, 1942–46. Open Schol., Oxford, 1938; 1st cl. hons Physics, Oxford, 1947; Nuffield Research Fellow, 1950. University Demonstrator, Oxford, 1951; St Edmund Hall, Oxford: Lectr, 1953; Fellow, 1954; Emeritus Fellow, 1969. William Evans Vis. Prof., Univ. of Otago, 1972; Raman Vis. Prof., Indian Acad. of Sci., 1982–83. Hon. Fellow, Indian Acad. of Science, 1984. Hon. Editor, Jl of Physics B (Atomic and Molecular Physics), 1975–79; Editor, Europ. Jl Physics, 1980–85. William F. Meggers Award, Optical Soc. Amer., 1982. *Publications:* Spectrum of Atomic Hydrogen, 1957; Laser Spectroscopy and other topics, 1985; Spectrum of Atomic Hydrogen: advances, 1988. *Recreation:* family. *Address:* Clarendon Laboratory, Oxford OX1 3PU. *T:* Oxford (0865) 272200.

SERIES, Sir (Joseph Michel) Emile, Kt 1978; CBE 1974; FCIS, FAIA, FSCA, FREconS, FInstD, FRSA; Chairman and General Manager, Flacq United Estates Ltd and WEAL Group (West East Ltd), since 1968; *b* 29 Sept. 1918; *s* of late Emile Seriès and Julie (*née* Langlois); *m* 1942, Rose-Aimée Jullienne; two *s* two *d*. *Educ:* Royal Coll., Mauritius; London Univ. MCom Delhi Commercial Univ., 1967. FBIM; FCCS 1958. Accounts Dept, General Electric Supply Co. of Mauritius Ltd, 1936–52 (final position, Chief Acct); Chief Acct and Econ. Adviser, Union Flacq Sugar Estate Ltd and Flacq United Estates Ltd, 1952–61; Manager, Union Flacq Sugar Estate Ltd, 1961–68. Chairman: Rogers & Co. Ltd; Alcohol & Molasses Co. Ltd; Compagnie Mauricienne de Commerce Ltd. Director: Maur. Commercial Bank Ltd; Anglo-Maur. Assurance Society Ltd, and other cos in Mauritius. Past President: Maur. Chamber of Agriculture; Maur. Sugar Industry Research Inst. Member: Maur. Sugar Producers' Assoc.; Maur. Sugar Syndicate; Amer. Management Assoc., New York; National Assoc. of Accts, New York. Chevalier de l'Ordre National du Mérite (France), 1978; Chevalier de la Légion d'Honneur, 1988. *Recreations:* sailing, shooting, photography, classical music, horse racing. *Address:* Flacq United Estates Ltd, Union Flacq, Mauritius. *T:* 532–583 and 535535. *Clubs:* Dodo, Mauritius Turf, Le Morne Anglers', Grand'Baie Yacht (Mauritius).

SERJEANT, Graham Roger, CMG 1981; MD; FRCP; Director, Medical Research Council Laboratories, Jamaica, since 1974; *b* 26 Oct. 1938; *s* of Ewart Egbert and Violet Elizabeth Serjeant; *m* 1965, Beryl Elizabeth, *d* of late Ivor Edward King, CB, CBE. *Educ:* Sibford Sch., Banbury; Bootham Sch., York; Clare Coll., Cambridge (BA 1960, MA 1965); London Hosp. Med. Sch.; Makerere Coll., Kampala. MB BChir 1963, MD 1971, Cantab; MRCP 1966, FRCP 1977. House Physician: London Hosp., 1963–64; Royal United Hosp., Bath, 1965–66; RPMS, 1966; Med. Registrar, University Hosp. of WI, 1966–67; Wellcome Res. Fellow, Dept of Medicine, Univ. of WI, 1967–71; Medical Research Council: Mem., Scientific Staff, Abnormal Haemoglobin Unit, Cambridge, 1971–72; Epidemiology Res. Unit, Jamaica, 1972–74. Hon. Prof. Faculty of Medicine, Univ. of WI, 1981. *Publications:* The Clinical Features of Sickle Cell Disease, 1974; Sickle Cell Disease, 1985; numerous papers on the nat. hist. of sickle cell disease, in med. jls. *Recreation:* squash. *Address:* Medical Research Council Laboratories, University of the West Indies, Mona, Kingston 7, Jamaica, WI. *T:* (809) 927–2471, (809) 927–2984. *Club:* Liguanea (Kingston).

SERJEANT, Robert Bertram, FBA 1986; Sir Thomas Adams's Professor of Arabic, 1970–82, and Director, Middle East Centre, 1965–82, University of Cambridge; *b* 23 March 1915; *er s* of R. T. R. and A. B. Serjeant; *m* Marion Keith Serjeant (*née* Robertson), MB, ChB; one *s* one *d*. *Educ:* Edinburgh; Trinity Coll., Cambridge. Vans Dunlop Schol. 1935; Visit to Syria, 1935; MA 1st Cl. Hons Semitic Langs, Edinburgh Univ., 1936; PhD Cambridge 1939; Tweedie Fellow Edinburgh, 1939; Studentship, SOAS, for research in S Arabia, 1940; Governor's Commn in Aden Prot. G Guards, 1940–41. Attached Mission 106. Lectr, SOAS, 1941; Seconded to BBC Eastern Service, 1942; Editor, Arabic Listener, 1943–45; Min. of Inf., Editor Arabic pubns, 1944. Colonial Research Fell., in Hadramawt, 1947–48; Reader in Arabic, 1948; Research in S Arabia and Persian Gulf, 1953–54; in N Nigeria, Minister of Education's mission to examine instruction in Arabic, 1956; Sec. of State for Colonies' mission to examine Muslim Education in E Africa, 1957; Inter-University Council's Advisory Delegation on University of N Nigeria, 1961; Research in Trucial States, Yemen, Aden, 1963–64 and 1966; Professor of Arabic, 1955–64, Middle East Department, SOAS, University of London; Lectr in Islamic History, ME Centre, Univ. of Cambridge, 1964–66, Reader in Arabic Studies, 1966–70. Member: ME Comd Expedition to Socotra, 1967; Cambridge expedn to San'ā' and N Yemen, 1972. Member: Royal Soc. for Asian Affairs; Royal Asiatic Soc.; Mem., Arab Acad., Cairo, 1976. Hon. DLitt Edinburgh, 1985. Lawrence of Arabia Meml Medal, RCAS, 1974; Sir Richard Burton Meml Medal, RAS, 1981. Co-editor, Arabian Studies, 1973–; Mem. Editl Bd, Cambridge History of Arabic Literature, 1983–. *Publications:* Cat. Arabic, Persian & Hindustani MSS in New College, Edinburgh, 1942; Materials for a History of Islamic Textiles, 1942–51; Prose and Poetry from Hadramawt, I, 1950; Saiyids of Hadramawt, 1957; Portuguese off the South Arabian Coast, 1961; The South Arabian Hunt, 1976; (ed) The Islamic City, 1980; Studies in Arabic History and Civilisation, 1981; (ed with R. Lewcock) San'ā': an Arabian Islamic city, 1983; articles in BSOAS, RAS, Le Muséon, Rivista d. Studi Orientali, Islamic Culture, etc. *Address:* Summerhill Cottage, Denhead, near St Andrews, Fife KY16 8PA.

SERJEANT, William Ronald, FRHistS; County Archivist, Suffolk, 1974–82, retired; Vice-President, Society of Archivists, since 1988 (President, 1982–88); Hon. Archivist to the Lords de Saumarez and Tollemache; *b* 5 March 1921; *s* of Frederick William and Louisa (*née* Wood); *m* 1961, Ruth Kneale (*née* Bridson); one *s*. *Educ:* Univ. of Manchester (BA Hons History); Univ. of Liverpool (Dip. Archive Admin. and Study of Records). Archivist/Librarian: Univ. of Sheffield, Sheffield City Library, Liverpool Record Office, 1952–56; Librarian/Archivist, Manx Nat. Library and Archives, Dep. Dir, Manx Mus. and Nat. Trust, 1957–62; County Archivist, Notts, 1962–70; Jt County Bor. and County Archivist, Ipswich and E Suffolk, 1970–74. Member: Lord Chancellor's Adv. Council on Public Records, 1982–88; Suffolk Heraldry Soc., 1982–; Mem. Exec. Cttee, Suffolk Local History Council, 1970–; Council Member: Suffolk Inst. of Archeology and History, 1970–; Suffolk Records Soc., 1970–; British Records Soc., 1974–; Ipswich Building Preservation Trust, 1988–; Chm., Publications Cttee, British Assoc. for Local History, 1988–; Trustee, Leiston Long Shop Museum, 1983–. Editor: Jl of the Manx Museum, 1957–62; The Suffolk Review, 1970–82; The Blazon (Suffolk Heraldry Soc.), 1984–88. *Publications:* The History of Tuxford Grammar School, 1969; (ed) Index to the Probate Records of the Court of the Archdeacon of Suffolk 1444–1700, 1979–80; (ed) Index to the Probate Records of the Court of the Archdeacon of Sudbury 1354–1700, 1984; articles in county and other local history periodicals. *Recreations:* walking, participation in local historical and heraldic studies and activities, theatre and cinema going; any gaps filled by reading novels. *Address:* 51 Derwent Road, Ipswich, Suffolk IP3 0QR. *T:* Ipswich (0473) 728997.

SERMON, Thomas Richard, FCIS; Chief Executive, Shandwick International, since 1990; *b* 25 Feb. 1947; *s* of Eric Thomas Sermon and Marjorie Hilda (*née* Parsons); *m* 1970, Rosemary Diane, *yr d* of Thomas Smith; one *s* one *d*. *Educ:* Nottingham High Sch. FCIS 1972. Crest Hotels, 1969–74; Good Relations Gp, 1974–79; Shandwick Consultants: Man. Dir, 1979–83; Dep. Chm., 1983–87; Chm., 1987–90; Man. Dir, Shandwick Consulting Gp, 1987–88; Chief Exec., Shandwick Europe, 1988–90. Vice-Pres., RADAR, 1987–. *Address:* Friars Well, Aynho, Banbury, Oxon OX17 3BG. *T:* Croughton (0869) 810284. *Clubs:* City of London, City Livery.

SEROTA, family name of **Baroness Serota.**

SEROTA, Baroness, *cr* 1967 (Life Peer), of Hampstead in Greater London; **Beatrice Serota,** JP; Principal Deputy Chairman of Committees, and Chairman, European Communities Select Committee, since 1986, a Deputy Speaker, since 1985, House of Lords; *b* 15 Oct. 1919; *m* 1942, Stanley Serota, BSc (Eng), FICE; one *s* one *d*. *Educ:* John Howard School; London School of Economics (BSc (Econ); Hon. Fellow, 1976). Member: Hampstead Borough Council, 1945–49; LCC for Brixton, 1954–65 (Chm., Children's Cttee, 1958–65); GLC for Lambeth, 1964–67 (Chief Whip). Baroness in Waiting, 1968–69; Minister of State (Health), Dept of Health and Social Security, 1969–70. Founder Chm., Commn for Local Admin, 1974–82; Member: Adv. Council in Child Care, and Central Training Council in Child Care, 1958–68; Adv. Council on Treatment of Offenders, 1960–64; Longford Cttee on "Crime—A Challenge to us all", 1964; Royal Commn on Penal System, 1964–66; Latey Cttee on Age of Majority, 1965–67; Adv. Council on Penal System, 1966–68, 1974–79 (Chm., 1976–79); Seebohm Cttee on Organization of Local Authority Personal Social Services, 1966–68; Community Relations Commn, 1970–76; BBC Complaints Commn, 1975–77; Governor, BBC, 1977–82. Pres., Volunteer Centre. JP Inner London (West Central Division). Peerage conferred for services to children. Hon. DLitt Loughborough, 1983. *Recreations:* needlepoint, gardening, collecting shells. *Address:* The Coach House, 15 Lyndhurst Terrace, NW3 5QA.
See also N. A. Serota.

SEROTA, Daniel; QC 1989; *b* 27 Sept. 1945; *s* of Louis and N'eema Serota; *m* 1970; two *d*. *Educ:* Carmel Coll.; Jesus Coll., Oxford (BA). Called to the Bar, Lincoln's Inn, 1969. *Address:* 2 Crown Office Row, Temple, EC4Y 7HJ. *T:* 071–583 2681.

SEROTA, Nicholas Andrew; Director of the Tate Gallery, since 1988; *b* 27 April 1946; *s* of Stanley Serota and Beatrice Serota (*see* Baroness Serota); *m* 1973, Angela Mary Beveridge; two *d*. *Educ:* Haberdashers' Aske's Sch., Hampstead and Elstree; Christ's Coll., Cambridge (BA); Courtauld Inst. of Art, London (MA). Regional Art Officer and Exhibn Organiser, Arts Council of GB, 1970–73; Dir, Museum of Modern Art, Oxford, 1973–76; Dir, Whitechapel Art Gallery, 1976–88. Mem., Fine Arts Adv. Cttee, British Council, 1976–; Trustee: Public Art Develt Trust, 1983–87; Architecture Foundn, 1991–. Hon. Fellow, QMC 1988. Hon. DLitt City, 1990; Hon. Dr Arts City of London Polytechnic, 1990. *Recreation:* hanging pictures. *Address:* Tate Gallery, Millbank, SW1P 4RG. *T:* 071–821 1313.

SERPELL, Sir David Radford, KCB 1968 (CB 1962); CMG 1952; OBE 1944; FCIT; Member, British Railways Board, 1974–82; *b* 10 Nov. 1911; 2nd *s* of Charles Robert and Elsie Leila Serpell, Plymouth; *m* 1st, Ann Dooley (marr. diss.); three *s*; 2nd, Doris Farr. *Educ:* Plymouth Coll.; Exeter Coll., Oxford; Univ. of Toulouse (DèsL); Syracuse University, USA; Fletcher School of Law and Diplomacy, USA. (Fell.) Imp. Economic Cttee, 1937–39; Min. of Food, 1939–42; Min. of Fuel and Power, 1942–45; Under-Sec., HM Treasury, 1954–60; Dep. Sec., MoT, 1960–63; Second Sec., BoT, 1963–66; Second Permanent Sec., 1966–68; Second Sec., Treasury, 1968; Permanent Secretary: MoT, 1968–70; DoE, 1970–72. Private Sec. to Parly Sec., Ministry of Food, 1941–42; Principal Private Sec. to Minister of Fuel and Power, 1942–45. Chairman: Nature Conservancy Council, 1973–77; Ordnance Survey Review Cttee, 1978–79; Cttee on the Review of Railway Finances, 1982; Member: NERC, 1973–76; Council, National Trust, 1973–77. *Recreations:* walking, golf. *Address:* 25 Crossparks, Dartmouth, Devon TQ6 9HP. *T:* Dartmouth (0803) 832073. *Club:* United Oxford & Cambridge University.

SERVAN-SCHREIBER, Jean-Jacques; engineer, author, politician; *b* Paris, 13 Feb. 1924; *s* of late Emile Servan-Schreiber, journalist, and Denise Bresard; *m*; four *s*. *Educ:* Ecole Polytechnique, Paris. Served as US-trained fighter pilot, Free French Air Force, World War II. Diplomatic Editor of Le Monde, 1948–53; Founder and Editor of weekly news-magazine, L'Express, 1953–73. Deputy for Lorraine, French National Assembly, 1970–78; Minister of Reforms, June 1974. Pres., Region of Lorraine, 1975–78. Pres., Radical Party, 1971–79; Chm., World Center for Computer Literacy, Paris, 1981–85. Chm., Internat. Cttee, Carnegie-Mellon Univ., Pittsburgh, USA, 1986–. Holds military cross for valour, with bar. *Publications:* Lieutenant en Algérie, 1957 (Lieutenant in Algeria); Le Défi américain, 1967 (The American Challenge); Le Manifeste Radical, 1970 (The Radical Alternative); Le Défi mondial, 1980 (The World Challenge); The Chosen and the Choice, 1988. *Address:* Carnegie-Mellon University, Pittsburgh, Pa 15213, USA.

SERVICE, Alastair Stanley Douglas; writer, publisher and campaigner; Non-Executive Director, Wessex Regional Health Authority, since 1990; *b* 8 May 1933; *s* of late Douglas William Service and Evelyn Caroline (*née* Sharp); *m* 1959, Louisa Anne (*née* Hemming), *qv* (marr. diss. 1984); one *s* one *d*. *Educ:* Westminster Sch.; Queen's Coll., Oxford. Midshipman, RNR, 1952–54. Director: McKinlay, Watson and Co. Ltd, Brazil, USA and London, 1959–64 (export finance); Seeley, Service and Co. Ltd (publishers), 1965–79; Municipal Journal Ltd, 1970–78. Hon. Parly Officer: Abortion Law Reform Assoc., organising passage of Abortion Act, 1964–67; Divorce Law Reform Union, organising passage of Divorce Reform Act, 1967–69; Chm., Birth Control Campaign, organising passage of NHS (Family Planning) Amendment Act, 1972, and NHS Reorganisation Act, 1973 (made vasectomy and contraception available free from NHS); involved in other parly campaigns, incl.: Town and Country Amenities Act, 1974; Children's Act, 1975; Public Lending Right for Authors; One-Parent Families. Chm., 1975–80, Gen. Sec., 1980–89, FPA; Sec. of State appointee, 1976–87, Vice-Chm., 1979–87, Health Educn Council; Dep. Chm. (Sec. of State appointee), Health Educn Authy, 1987–89. Member: Nat. Cttee, Population Concern, 1973– (Chm., 1975–79); Nat. Cttee, Victorian Soc., 1976– (Chm., Publications Cttee, 1982–89); Hon. Sec., Action for River Kennet, 1990–. *Publications:* A Birth Control Plan for Britain (with Dr John Dunwoody and Dr Tom

Stuttaford), 1972; The Benefits of Birth Control—Aberdeen's Experience, 1973; Edwardian Architecture and its Origins, 1975; Edwardian Architecture, 1977; The Architects of London from 1066 to Present Day, 1979; London 1900, 1979; (with Jean Bradbery) Megaliths of Europe, 1979; Lost Worlds, 1981; Edwardian Interiors, 1982; series editor, The Buildings of Britain, 1981–84, and author, Anglo-Saxon and Norman Buildings vol., 1982; Victorian and Edwardian Hampstead, 1989; articles in Arch. Rev., Guardian, etc. *Recreations:* looking at buildings (old, new and megalithic), opera, cycling et al. *Address:* Swan House, Avebury, Wilts SN8 1RA. *Club:* Garrick.

SERVICE, Louisa Anne, JP; Joint Chairman: The Hemming Group of Companies, since 1976; Hemming Publishing Ltd, since 1987; *d* of late Henry Harold Hemming, OBE, MC, and of Alice Louisa Weaver, OBE; *m* 1959, Alastair Stanley Douglas Service, *qv* (marr. diss. 1984); one *s* one *d. Educ:* private and state schs, Canada, USA and Britain; Ecole des Sciences Politiques, Paris; St Hilda's Coll., Oxford (BA and MA, PPE). Export Dir, Ladybird Appliances Ltd, 1957–59; Municipal Journal Ltd and associated cos: Financial Dir, 1966; Dep. Chm., 1974; Chm., Merchant Printers Ltd, 1975–80; Dir, Brintex Ltd, 1965–; Dir, Glass's Guides Services Ltd, 1971, Dep. Chm. 1976–81, Chm., 1982–. Member: Dept of Trade Consumer Credit Act Appeals Panel, 1981–; Cttee of Magistrates, 1985–88; FIMBRA Appeals Panel, 1988–. JP Inner London Juvenile Courts, 1969; Chm., Hackney Juvenile Court, 1975–82, Westminster Juvenile Ct, 1982–88, Hammersmith and Fulham Juvenile Court, 1988–; JP Inner London (5) PSD, 1980–; Chairman: Exec. Cttee, Inner London Juvenile Courts, 1977–79; Inner London Juvenile Liaison Cttee, 1986–88 (Mem., 1980–86); Member: working party on re-org. of London Juvenile Courts, 1975; Inner London Family Panel, 1991–; Vice-Chm., Paddington Probation Hostel, 1976–86. Corres. mem., SDP Policy Gp on Citizens' Rights, 1982–89. Chm. Council, Mayer-Lismann Opera Workshop, 1976–91; Hon. Sec., Women's India Assoc. of UK, 1967–74. Dir, Arts Club Ltd, 1981–84; Mem. Management Council, Friends of Covent Garden, 1982–; Chm., Youth & Music, 1990– (Dir, 1988–90); Mem., E-SU Music Cttee, 1984–91. *Publications:* articles on a variety of subjects. *Recreations:* travel, and attractive and witty people including my family. *Address:* c/o Hemming Publishing Ltd, 32 Vauxhall Bridge Road, SW1V 2SS. *T:* 071–973 6404. *Club:* Arts.
See also J. H. Hemming.

SESHADRI, Prof. Conjeevaram Srirangachari, PhD; FRS 1988; Dean, School of Mathematics, SPIC Science Foundation, since 1989; *b* 29 Feb. 1932; *s* of C. Srirangachari and Chudamani; *m* 1962, Sundari; two *s. Educ:* Loyola College, Madras (BA Hons Maths Madras Univ. 1953); PhD Bombay Univ. 1958. Tata Institute of Fundamental Research: Student, 1953; Reader, 1961; Professor, 1963; Senior Professor, 1975–84; Sen. Prof., Inst. of Math. Scis, India, 1984–89. *Publications:* Fibres Vectorials sur les courtes algébriques, Asterisque, 96, 1982; Introduction to the Theory of Standard Monomials, 1985. *Recreation:* south Indian classical music. *Address:* School of Mathematics, SPIC Science Foundation, East Coast Chambers, IV Floor, 92 G. N. Chetty Road, T Nagar, Madras 600 017, India. *T:* 445232, 444251; (home) 4914534.

SESSFORD, Rt. Rev. George Minshull; *see* Moray, Ross and Caithness, Bishop of.

SESSIONS, John, (John Marshall); actor, writer; *b* 11 Jan. 1953; *s* of John Marshall and Esmé Richardson. *Educ:* Univ. of Wales (MA). Plays and one-man shows, 1982–85; *television:* Spitting Image, 1986; Porterhouse Blue, 1987; New Year Show, 1988; A Day in Summer, 1988; Whose Line is it, Anyway?, 1988; On the Spot, 1989; Single Voices, 1990; Tall Tales, 1991; Travelling Tales, 1991; *theatre:* The Life of Napoleon, Albery, 1987; The Common Pursuit, Phoenix, 1988; The American Napoleon, Phoenix, 1989. *Recreation:* dinner parties. *Address:* c/o Markham & Froggatt, 4 Windmill Street, W1P 1HF. *T:* 071–636 4412. *Club:* Groucho.

SETCHELL, Marcus Edward, FRCSE, FRCS, FRCOG; Surgeon-Gynaecologist to the Queen, since 1990; Head of Department of Obstetrics and Gynaecology, St Bartholomew's Hospital, since 1986; *b* 4 Oct. 1943; *s* of Eric Hedley Setchell and Barbara Mary Whitworth; *m* 1973, Dr Sarah French; two *s* two *d. Educ:* Felsted Sch.; Gonville and Caius Coll., Cambridge; St Bartholomew's Hosp. MA, MB BChir. Consultant Obstetrician and Gynaecologist, Bart's and Homerton Hosps, 1975–; Hon. Consultant Gynaecologist: King Edward Hosp. for Officers, 1982–; St Luke's Hosp. for Clergy, 1983–. Convener, Scientific Meetings, RCOG, 1989–; Mem., Council, RSocMed, 1990–. *Publications:* Multiple Choice Questions in Obstetrics and Gynaecology (with R. J. Lilford), 1985; Ten Teachers in Obstetrics and Gynaecology, 1990; (with E. E. Philipp) Scientific Foundations of Obstetrics and Gynaecology, 1991. *Recreations:* tennis, ski-ing, gardening, walking. *Address:* 137 Harley Street, W1N 1DJ. *T:* 071–935 6122. *Clubs:* Royal Society of Medicine, St Albans Medical; David Lloyd Tennis.

SETON, Lady, (Alice Ida), CBE 1949; Group Officer, WRAF, retired; *d* of late P. C. Hodge, Port Elizabeth, South Africa; *m* 1923, Capt. Sir John Hastings Seton, 10th Bt (from whom she obtained a divorce, 1950); one *s* (*see* Sir Robert Seton, 11th Bt) (one *d* decd). Joined WAAF as Assistant Section Officer, 1939. *Address:* Collin House, 108 Ridgway, Wimbledon, SW19 4RD.

SETON, Sir Iain (Bruce), 13th Bt *cr* 1663 (NS), of Abercorn; *b* 27 Aug. 1942; *s* of Sir (Christopher) Bruce Seton, 12th Bt and of Joyce Vivien, *d* of late O. G. Barnard; *S* father, 1988; *m* 1963, Margaret Ann, *d* of Walter Charles Faulkner; one *s* one *d. Educ:* Colchester and Chadacre. Farming until 1972; mining, 1972–. *Heir: s* Laurence Bruce Seton, *b* 1 July 1968. *Address:* Bellavista, PO Box 253, Bridgetown, WA 6255, Australia. *T:* 097–611349.

SETON, Lady, (Julia), OBE 1989; VMH; (Julia Clements, professionally); author, speaker, international floral art judge; flower arrangement judge for RHS and National Association of Flower Arrangement Societies; *d* of late Frank Clements; *m* 1962, Sir Alexander Hay Seton, 10th Bt, of Abercorn (*d* 1963); no *c. Educ:* Isle of Wight; Zwicker College, Belgium. Organised and conducted first Judges' School in England at Royal Horticultural Society Halls; has since conducted many other courses for judges all over Britain. VMH, RHS, 1974. *Publications:* Fun with Flowers; Fun without Flowers; 101 Ideas for Flower Arrangement; Party Pieces; The Julia Clements Colour Book of Flower Arrangements; Flower Arrangements in Stately Homes; Julia Clements' Gift Book of Flower Arranging; Flowers in Praise; The Art of Arranging a Flower, etc. *Address:* 122 Swan Court, SW3. *T:* 071–352 9039. *Clubs:* Women's Press, Anglo-Belge.

SETON, Sir Robert (James), 11th Bt, *cr* 1683; *b* 20 April 1926; *s* of Captain Sir John Hastings Seton, 10th Bt and Alice (*see* Lady Seton), *d* of Percy Hodge, Cape Civil Service; *S* father 1956; unmarried. *Educ:* HMS Worcester (Thames Nautical Training College). Midshipman RNVR (invalided), 1943–44. Banker, with Hong Kong and Shanghai Banking Corpn, 1946–61 (retd). *Heir: kinsman* James Christall Seton [*b* 21 Jan. 1913; *m* 1939, Evelyn, *d* of Ray Hafer]. *Address:* 4B Morella Road, Balham, SW12 8UH.

SETSHOGO, Boithoko Moonwa; Managing Director, Merchandising Associates Pty Ltd; Chairman: Via Afrika Pty Ltd; Wellcome Superstores Pty Ltd; *b* Serowe, 16 June 1941; *m* 1971, Jennifer Tlalane; two *d. Educ:* Moeng Coll.; Univ. of Botswana, Lesotho and Swaziland (BA). District Officer, Kanye, 1969–70; First Sec., High Commn, London, 1970–72; Clerk to the Cabinet, 1972–73; Under-Sec., Min. of Commerce and Industry, 1973–75; High Comr of Botswana in London, 1975–78; Dir of Inf. and Broadcasting, 1978–80. Director: Aeriel Services (Botswana) Pty; Maungo Consultancy Services Pty; Tswana Travel & Tours Pty. Mem., Central Cttee, Botswana Democratic Party, 1984–. *Address:* (office) PO Box 73, Gaborone, Botswana.

SEVER, (Eric) John; *b* 1 April 1943; *s* of Eric and Clara Sever. *Educ:* Sparkhill Commercial School. Travel Executive with tour operator, 1970–77. MP (Lab) Birmingham, Ladywood, Aug. 1977–1983; PPS to the Solicitor General, 1978–79. Contested (Lab) Meriden, 1983. *Recreations:* theatre, cinema, reading.

SEVERIN, Prof. Dorothy Virginia Sherman, PhD; FSA; Gilmour Professor of Spanish, since 1982, and Pro-Vice-Chancellor, since 1989, University of Liverpool; *b* 24 March 1942; *d* of Wilbur B. and Virginia L. Sherman; marr. diss.; one *d. Educ:* Harvard Univ. AB 1963; AM 1964; PhD 1967. FSA 1989. Teaching Fellow and Tutor, Harvard Univ., 1964–66; Vis. Lectr, Univ. of W Indies, 1967–68; Asst Prof., Vassar Coll., 1968; Lectr, Westfield Coll., London Univ., 1969–82. Vis. Associate Prof., Harvard Univ., 1982; Visiting Professor: Columbia Univ., 1985; Yale Univ., 1985. Editor, Bulletin of Hispanic Studies, 1982–. *Publications:* (ed) de Rojas, La Celestina, 1969, 15th edn 1988; Memory in La Celestina, 1970; (ed) Diego de San Pedro, La pasión trobada, 1973; (ed) La Lengua de Erasmo romançada por muy elegante estilo, 1975; The Cancionero de Martínez de Burgos, 1976; (ed with K. Whinnom) Diego de San Pedro, Poesía (Obras completas III), 1979; (ed with Angus MacKay) Cosas sacadas de la Historia del rey Juan el Segundo, 1982; (ed) Celestina, trans. James Mabbe (Eng./Spanish text), 1987; (ed) Celestina (Spanish edn), 1987; Tragicomedy and Novelistic Discourse in Celestina, 1989; Cancionero de Oñate-Castañeda, 1990; contribs to learned jls incl. Hispanic Rev., Romance Philology, Medium Aevum, MLR and THES. *Address:* Department of Hispanic Studies, The University, PO Box 147, Liverpool L69 3BX. *T:* 051–794 2773.

SEVERIN, (Giles) Timothy; author, traveller and historian; *b* 25 Sept. 1940; *s* of Maurice Watkins and Inge Severin; *m* 1966, Dorothy Virginia Sherman (marr. diss. 1979); one *d. Educ:* Tonbridge School; Keble Coll., Oxford. MA, BLitt. Commonwealth Fellow, USA, 1964–66. Expeditions: led motorcycle team along Marco Polo route, 1961; R Mississippi by canoe and launch, 1965; Brendan Voyage from W Ireland to N America, 1977; Sindbad Voyage from Oman to China, 1980–81; Jason Voyage from Iolkos to Colchis, 1984; Ulysses Voyage from Troy to Ithaca, 1985; first Crusade route by horse to Jerusalem, 1987–88; travels by horse in Mongolia, 1990. Founders Medal, RGS; Livingstone Medal, RSGS; Sykes Medal, RSAA. *Publications:* Tracking Marco Polo, 1964; Explorers of the Mississippi, 1967; The Golden Antilles, 1970; The African Adventure, 1973; Vanishing Primitive Man, 1973; The Oriental Adventure, 1976; The Brendan Voyage, 1978; The Sindbad Voyage, 1982; The Jason Voyage, 1985; The Ulysses Voyage, 1987; Crusader, 1989; In Search of Genghis Khan, 1991. *Address:* Courtmacsherry, Co. Cork, Eire. *T:* Bandon 46127. *Club:* United Oxford & Cambridge University.

SEVERN, David; *see* Unwin, David Storr.

SEVERN, Prof. Roy Thomas, FEng 1981; FICE; Professor of Civil Engineering, Bristol University, since 1968; *b* 6 Sept. 1929; *s* of Ernest Severn and Muriel Woollatt; *m* 1957, Hilary Irene Saxton; two *d. Educ:* Deacons School, Peterborough; Imperial College (DSc). Lectr, Imperial College, 1949–54; Royal Engineers (Survey), 1954–56; Bristol University: Lectr, 1956–65; Reader, 1965–68. Pres., ICE, 1991. *Publications:* (ed) Engineering Structures: developments in the twentieth century, 1983; contribs to Procs of ICE, Jl Earthquake Eng. and Structural Dynamics. *Recreations:* sailing, gardening, cricket. *Address:* 49 Gloucester Road, Rudgeway, Bristol BS12 2SF. *T:* Thornbury (0454) 412027.

SEVERNE, Air Vice-Marshal Sir John (de Milt), KCVO 1988 (LVO 1961); OBE 1968; AFC 1955; DL; Extra Equerry to the Queen, since 1984; *b* 15 Aug. 1925; *s* of late Dr A. de M. Severne, Wateringbury, Kent; *m* 1951, Katharine Veronica, *d* of late Captain V. E. Kemball, RN (Retd); three *d. Educ:* Marlborough. Joined RAF, 1944; Flying Instr, Cranwell, 1948; Staff Instr and PA to Comdt CFS, 1950–53; Flt Comdr No 98 Sqdn, Germany, 1954–55; Sqdn Comdr No 26 Sqdn, Germany, 1956–57; Air Min., 1958; Equerry to Duke of Edinburgh, 1958–61; psa 1962; Chief Instr No 226 Operational Conversion Unit (Lightning), 1963–65; jssc 1965; Jt HQ, ME Comd, Aden, and Air Adviser to the South Arabian Govt, 1966–67; DS, JSSC, 1968; Gp Captain Organisation, HQ Strike Comd, 1968–70; Stn Comdr, RAF Kinloss, 1971–72; RCDS 1973; Comdt, Central Flying School, RAF, 1974–76; Air Cdre Flying Training, HQ RAF Support Comd, 1976–78; Comdr, Southern Maritime Air Region, Central Sub-Area Eastern Atlantic Command, and Plymouth Sub-Area Channel Command, 1978–80, retd; recalled as Captain of the Queen's Flight, 1982–89. ADC to The Queen, 1972–73. Hon. Air Cdre, No 3 (Co. of Devon) Maritime HQ Unit, RAuxAF, 1990–. President: SW Area, RAFA, 1981–; Queen's Flight Assoc., 1990–. Won Kings Cup Air Race, British Air Racing Champion, 1960. Pres., RAF Equitation Assoc., 1976–79 (Chm. 1973); Chm., Combined Services Equitation Assoc., 1977–79 (Vice-Chm., 1976). DL Somerset, 1991. *Address:* c/o National Westminster Bank, 9 York Buildings, Cornhill, Bridgwater, Som TA6 3BA. *Club:* Royal Air Force.

SEWARD, Guy William, QC 1982; FRVA; *b* 10 June 1916; *s* of late William Guy Seward and Maud Peacock; *m* 1946, Peggy Dearman. *Educ:* Stationers' Sch. Called to the Bar, Inner Temple, 1956. FRVA 1948. Chairman: Medical Service Cttee, 1977–81; Examination in Public, Devon Structure Plan, 1980; E Herts Health Authority, 1982–90; Member: Mid-Herts HMC, 1966–70; Napsbury HMC, 1970–74 (Chm., 1972–74); Bd of Governors, UCH, 1970–74; Herts AHA, 1974–82 (Vice Chm., 1980–82); Herts FPC, 1974–82; Council, Rating and Valuation Assoc., 1983. Freeman, City of London, 1949. *Publications:* (jtly) Enforcement of Planning Control, 1956; (jtly) Local Government Act, 1958; Howard Roberts Law of Town and Country Planning, 1963; (jtly) Rent Act, 1965; (jtly) Land Commission Act, 1967; (jtly) Leasehold Reform, 1967. *Recreations:* travel, gardening. *Address:* Stocking Lane Cottage, Ayot St Lawrence, Welwyn, Herts AL6 9BW. *Club:* Garrick.

SEWARD, William Richard, RCNC; General Manager, HM Dockyard, Portsmouth, 1975–79, retired; *b* 7 Feb. 1922; *s* of William and Gertrude Seward, Portsmouth; *m* 1946, Mary Deas Ritchie; one *d. Educ:* Portsmouth Dockyard Techn. Coll.; RNC Greenwich; Royal Corps of Naval Constructors. Asst Constructor, HM Dockyard, Rosyth, 1945–47; Constructor, Naval Construction Dept, Admty, 1947–58; Admty Constructor Overseer, Birkenhead, 1958–63; Chief Constructor, MoD (N), 1963–70; Prodn Man., HM Dockyard, Chatham, 1970–73, Gen. Manager, 1973–75. *Recreations:* reading, music, caravanning, walking. *Club:* Civil Service.

SEWELL, Sir (John) Allan, Kt 1977; ISO 1968; company director; *b* 23 July 1915; *s* of George Allan Sewell and Francis Doris Sewell; *m* 1st, 1939, Thelma Edith Buchholz (*d* 1965); one *s* one *d*; 2nd, 1978, Yoko Fukano, *d* of I. Fukano, Kyoto, Japan. *Educ:* Brisbane Grammar Sch. Dir of Local Govt, 1948–60; Under Treasurer of Qld, 1960–70; Auditor-General of Qld, 1970–78; Chm., State Govt Insurance Office, Qld, 1979–81. *Recreation:* game fishing. *Address:* 63 Ryans Road, St Lucia, Brisbane, Qld 4067, Australia. *Clubs:*

Queensland (Brisbane); Cairns Game Fishing (Cairns); Moreton Bay Game Fishing (Brisbane).

SEWELL, Thomas Robert McKie; HM Diplomatic Service, retired; international grains consultant; *b* 18 Aug. 1921; *s* of late O. B. Fane Sewell and late Frances M. Sewell (*née* Sharp); *m* 1955, Jennifer Mary Sandeman; one *d* (and one *d* decd). *Educ:* Eastbourne Coll.; Trinity Coll., Oxford (Schol., Heath Harrison Prize, MA); Lausanne and Stockholm Univs (Schol.). HM Forces, 1940–45 (despatches); Major. Entered Foreign Service, 1949; Second Sec., Moscow, 1950–52; FO, 1952–55; First Sec., 1954; Madrid, 1955–59; Lima, 1959–61; Chargé d'Affaires, 1960; FO, 1961–63; Counsellor and Head of Chancery, Moscow, 1964–66; Diplomatic Service Rep. at IDC, 1966; Head of Associated States, West Indies and Swaziland Depts, Commonwealth Office, 1967–68; Head of N American and Caribbean Dept, FCO, 1968–70; Asst Sec., MAFF, 1970–81; UK Rep. to Internat. Wheat Council, 1972–81. Chm., World Grain Conf., Brussels, 1990. Contested (C) Greater Manchester Central, Europ. Parly elecn, 1984. Vis. Fellow, Hubert H. Humphrey Inst. of Public Affairs and Dept of Agricl and Applied Econs, Univ. of Minnesota, 1985. *Publication:* (with John de Courcy Ling) Famine and Surplus, 1985. *Recreations:* ski-ing, inland waterways cruising. *Address:* c/o Barclays Bank, 16 Whitehall, SW1. *Clubs:* Farmers', Airborne.

SEWELL, Maj.-Gen. Timothy Patrick T.; *see* Toyne Sewell.

SEXTON, Maj.-Gen. (Francis) Michael, CB 1980; OBE 1966; retired; Director of Military Survey and Chief of Geographic Section of General Staff, Ministry of Defence, 1977–80; *b* 15 July 1923; *s* of Timothy and Catherine Sexton; *m* 1947, Naomi, *d* of Bertram Alonzo and Dorothy May Middleton; one *s* one *d*. *Educ:* Wanstead County High Sch.; Birmingham Univ. Commnd Kirkee India into RE, 1943; Royal Bombay Sappers and Miners and 5th/16th Punjab Regt, India, Assam and Burma, 1943–46; RE units, UK, Egypt and Cyprus, 1946–53; Dept of Mines and Surveys, Canada, 1953–56; Asst Dir, MoD, 1964–65; Dep. Dir, Ordnance Survey, 1966–70; Chief Geographic Officer, SHAPE, Belgium, 1970–73; Brig. (Survey), 1973–77. Bursar and Fellow, St Peter's Coll., Oxford, 1980–85. Mem., Panel of Indep. Inspectors, 1980–. MA Oxon, 1980. *Clubs:* MCC; Geographical.

SEYCHELLES, Bishop of; *see* Indian Ocean, Archbishop of.

SEYMOUR, family name of **Marquess of Hertford** and **Duke of Somerset.**

SEYMOUR, Lord; Sebastian Edward Seymour; *b* 3 Feb. 1982; *s* and *heir* of 19th Duke of Somerset, *qv*.

SEYMOUR, Dr Francis, FFPHM; Director of Clinical and Scientific Services (formerly Regional Medical Officer), North West Thames Regional Health Authority, 1982–89; *b* 29 June 1928; *s* of Francis Reginald and Drusilla Seymour; *m* 1953, Ivy Esther; two *d*. *Educ:* Wallasey Grammar School; Liverpool University. MB ChB 1951; DPH 1955; MFCM 1972. Dep. MOH, N Bucks, 1955–58; MOH, Mid Bucks Districts, 1958–62; Div. MO, Runcorn and Mid Cheshire, 1962–70; Dep. County MO, Herts, 1970–74; Area MO, Herts AHA, 1974–82. Non-Exec. Mem., SW Herts DHA. FRSA 1984. *Recreations:* walking, sailing, theatre. *Address:* The Fennings, Back Ends, Chipping Campden, Glos GL55 6AU. *T:* Evesham (0386) 840483.

SEYMOUR, Lynn, CBE 1976; Ballerina; Artistic Director, Ballet of the Bavarian State Opera, Munich, 1979–80; *b* Wainwright, Alberta, 8 March 1939; *d* of E. V. Springbett; *m* 1st, 1963, Colin Jones, photo-journalist (marr. diss.); 2nd, 1974, Philip Pace; three *s*; 3rd, 1983, Vanya Hackel. *Educ:* Vancouver; Sadler's Wells Ballet School. Joined Sadler's Wells Ballet Company, 1957; Deutsche Oper, Berlin, 1966. *Roles created:* Adolescent, in The Burrow, Royal Opera House, 1958; Bride, in Le Baiser de la Fée, 1960; Girl, in The Invitation, 1960; Young Girl, in Les Deux Pigeons, 1961; Principal, in Symphony, 1963; Principal, in Images of Love, 1964; Juliet, in Romeo and Juliet, 1964; Albertine, BBC TV, 1966; Concerto, 1966; Anastasia, 1966; Flowers, 1972; Side Show, 1972; A Month in the Country, 1976; Five Brahms Waltzes in the manner of Isadora Duncan, 1976; mother, in Fourth Symphony, 1977; Mary Vetsera, in Mayerling, 1978; Take Five, 1978. *Other appearances include:* Danses Concertantes; Solitaire; La Fête Etrange; Sleeping Beauty; Swan Lake; Giselle (title-role); Cinderella; Das Lied von der Erde; The Four Seasons; Voluntaries; Manon, Sleeping Beauty, Dances at a Gathering, The Concert, Pillar of Fire, Romeo and Juliet (Tudor, Nureyev and Cranko), Las Hermañas, Moor's Pavane, Auriole, Apollon, Le Corsaire, Flower Festival, La Sylphide (Sylph and Madge), A Simple Man, Onegin. *Choreography for:* Rashomon, for Royal Ballet Touring Co., 1976; The Court of Love, for SWRB, 1977; Intimate Letters, 1978 and Mac and Polly, for Commonwealth Dance Gala, 1979; Boreas, and Tattoo, for Bavarian State Opera Ballet, 1980; Wolfi, for Ballet Rambert, 1987; Bastet, for SWRB, 1988. A Time to Dance (film), 1986. *Publication:* Lynn: leaps and boundaries (autobiog.), 1984. *Address:* c/o Artistes in Action, 16 Balderton Street, W1Y 1TF.

SEYMOUR, Commander Sir Michael Culme-, 5th Bt, *cr* 1809; Royal Navy (retired); *b* 26 April 1909; *o s* of Vice-Admiral Sir M. Culme-Seymour, 4th Bt, and Florence Agnes Louisa (*d* 1956), *y d* of late A. L. Nugent; *S* father, 1925; *m* 1948, Lady (Mary) Faith Nesbitt (*d* 1983), *er d* of 9th Earl of Sandwich; one step-*d* (adopted) (two *s* decd). Succeeded Rev. Wentworth Watson to the Rockingham Castle estates, 1925, and transferred them to his nephew, Cmdr L. M. M. Saunders Watson, RN, 1967; is a farmer and a landowner. ADC to Governor-General of Canada, 1933–35; served War of 1939–45 (despatches); served Imperial Defence College, 1946–47; retired from RN 1947. JP Northants, 1949; Mem. Northants CC 1948–55; DL Northants, 1958–71; High Sheriff of Northants, 1966. Bledisloe Gold Medal for Landowners, 1972. *Heir to baronetcy: cousin* Michael Patrick Culme-Seymour [*b* 28 April 1962; *m* 1986, Karin Fleig; two *s*]. *Address:* Wytherston, Powerstock, Bridport, Dorset DT6 3TQ. *T:* Powerstock (030885) 211. *Club:* Brooks's.

SEYMOUR, Richard William; QC 1991; *b* 4 May 1950; *e s* of Albert Percy and Vera Maud Seymour; *m* 1971, Clare Veronica, BSS, MSc, *d* of Stanley Victor Peskett, *qv*; one *s* one *d*. *Educ:* Brentwood Sch.; Royal Belfast Academical Instn; Christ's Coll., Cambridge (schol.; BA 1971; MA 1975). Holker Jun. Exhibn, 1970, Holker Sen. Schol., 1972, Gray's Inn; called to the Bar, Gray's Inn, 1972. *Publications:* (ed jtly) Kemp and Kemp, The Quantum of Damages, 4th edn 1975; legal chapters in: Willis and Willis, Practice and Procedure for the Quantity Surveyor, 8th edn 1980; Willis and George, The Architect in Practice, 6th edn 1981. *Recreations:* archaeology, walking, foreign travel. *Address:* 4 Raymond Buildings, Gray's Inn, WC1R 5BP. *T:* 071–405 7211.

SEYS-LLEWELLYN, His Honour John Desmond; a Circuit Judge (formerly a County Court Judge), 1971–85; *b* 3 May 1912; *s* of Charles Ernest Llewellyn, FAI and Hannah Margretta Llewellyn, of Cardiff; *m* 1st, 1939, Elaine (*d* 1984), *d* of H. Leonard Porcher, solicitor, and Mrs Hilda Porcher, JP, of Pontypridd; three *s*; 2nd, 1986, Mrs Joan Banfield James, *d* of R. H. Cumming, JP, of Plymouth. *Educ:* Cardiff High School; Jesus College, Oxford; Exhibitioner, MA. Joined Inner Temple, 1936. War Service, RTR, 1940–46 (Captain). Called to the Bar, Inner Temple, in absentia OAS, 1945; Profumo Prizeman, 1947; practised on Wales and Chester Circuit, 1947–71; Local Insurance Appeal Tribunal, 1958–71; Dep. Chm., Cheshire QS, 1968–71; joined Gray's Inn, *ad eundem*, same day as youngest son, 1967. Contested Chester Constituency (L), 1955 and 1956. *Recreations:* languages, travel, archaeology, art galleries, music, swimming, English Setter. *Address:* Little Chetwyn, Green Pastures, Gresford, Clwyd LL12 8RT. *T:* Gresford (0978) 852419. *Club:* Athenæum (Liverpool).

SHACKLE, Prof. Christopher, PhD; FBA 1990; Professor of Modern Languages of South Asia, University of London, since 1985; *b* 4 March 1942; *s* of late Francis Mark Shackle and Diana Margaret Shackle (*née* Harrington, subseq. Thomas); *m* 1st, 1964, Emma Margaret Richmond (marr. diss.); one *s* two *d*; 2nd, 1988, Shahrukh Husain; one *s* one *d*. *Educ:* Haileybury and ISC; Merton College, Oxford (BA 1963); St Antony's College, Oxford (DipSocAnthrop 1965; BLitt 1966); PhD London, 1972. School of Oriental and African Studies, University of London: Fellow in Indian Studies, 1966; Lectr in Urdu and Panjabi, 1969; Reader in Modern Languages of South Asia, 1979. *Publications:* Teach Yourself Punjabi, 1972; (with D. J. Matthews) An Anthology of Classical Urdu Love Lyrics, 1972; The Siraiki Language of Central Pakistan, 1976; Catalogue of the Panjabi and Sindhi Manuscripts in the India Office Library, 1977; A Guru Nanak Glossary, 1981; An Introduction to the Sacred Language of the Sikhs, 1983; The Sikhs, 1984; (with D. J. Matthews and S. Husain) Urdu Literature, 1985; (with R. Snell) Hindi and Urdu Since 1800, 1990; numerous articles. *Address:* Department of Indology/South Asia, School of Oriental and African Studies. Thornaugh Street, Russell Square, WC1H 0XG. *T:* 071–637 2388.

SHACKLE, Prof. George Lennox Sharman, FBA 1967; Brunner Professor of Economic Science in the University of Liverpool, 1951–69, now Professor Emeritus; *b* 14 July 1903; *s* of Robert Walker Shackle, MA (Cambridge) and of Fanny Shackle (*née* Sharman); *m* 1st, 1939, Gertrude Courtney Susan Rowe (*d* 1978); two *s* one *d* (and one *d* decd); 2nd, 1979, Catherine Squarey Gibb (*née* Weldsmith). *Educ:* The Perse School, Cambridge; The London School of Economics; New College, Oxford. BA (London) 1931; Leverhulme Research Schol., 1934; PhD (Econ) (London), 1937; DPhil (Oxford), 1940. Oxford University Institute of Statistics, 1937; University of St Andrews, 1939; Admiralty and Cabinet Office; Sir Winston Churchill's Statistical Branch, 1939; Economic Section of Cabinet Secretariat, 1945; Reader in Economic Theory, Univ. of Leeds, 1950. F. de Vries Lecturer, Amsterdam, 1957; Visiting Professor: Columbia University, 1957–58; of Economics and Philosophy, Univ. of Pittsburgh, 1967; Keynes Lectr, British Acad., 1976. Mem. Council, Royal Economic Society, 1955–69; Pres., Section F, BAAS, 1966. Fellow of Econometric Society, 1960; Distinguished Fellow, Amer. Hist. of Econs Soc., 1985. Hon. DSc NUU, 1974; Hon. DSocSc Birmingham, 1978; Hon. DLitt Strathclyde, 1988. *Publications:* Expectations, Investment, and Income, 1938, 2nd edn 1968; Expectation in Economics, 1949, 2nd edn 1952; Mathematics at the Fireside, 1952 (French edn 1967); Uncertainty in Economics and Other Reflections, 1955; Time in Economics, 1957; Economics for Pleasure, 1959, 2nd edn 1968 (also foreign editions); Decision, Order and Time in Human Affairs, 1961, 2nd edn 1969 (also foreign editions); A Scheme of Economic Theory, 1965 (also Portuguese edn); The Nature of Economic Thought, 1966 (also Spanish edn); The Years of High Theory, 1967 (Italian edn 1985); Expectation, Enterprise and Profit, 1970 (Spanish edn 1976); Epistemics and Economics, 1973 (Spanish edn 1976); An Economic Querist, 1973 (Spanish edn 1976); Keynesian Kaleidics, 1974; Imagination and the Nature of Choice, 1979; (ed and contrib.) Uncertainty and Business Decisions, 1954, 2nd edn, 1957; The Theory of General Static Equilibrium, 1957; A New Prospect of Economics, 1958; On the Nature of Business Success, 1968; Business, Time and Thought (essays), 1988; articles in Chambers's Encyclopædia, 1950, 1967, Internat. Encyclopedia of the Social Sciences, 1968, and in other books; seventy or more main articles in learned jls. *Address:* Rudloe, Alde House Drive, Aldeburgh, Suffolk IP15 5EE. *T:* Aldeburgh (072885) 2227 and 2003.

SHACKLETON, family name of **Baron Shackleton.**

SHACKLETON, Baron *cr* 1958 (Life Peer), of Burley; **Edward Arthur Alexander Shackleton,** KG 1974; OBE 1945; FRS 1989; PC 1966; an Adviser to RTZ Corporation, since 1982 (Director, 1973–82; Deputy Chairman 1975–82); Chairman: RTZ Development Enterprises, 1973–83; Anglesey Aluminium Ltd, 1981–86; *b* 15 July 1911; *s* of late Sir Ernest Shackleton, CVO, OBE; *m* 1938, Betty Homan; one *d* (and one *s* decd). *Educ:* Radley College; Magdalen College, Oxford (MA; Hon. Fellow, 1986). Surveyor, Oxford University Expedition to Sarawak, 1932; first ascent of Mt Mulu; Organiser and Surveyor, Oxford University Expedition to Ellesmereland, 1934–35; Lecture tours in Europe and America; BBC talks producer, MOI. Served War of 1939–45, 1940–45; RAF Station Intelligence Officer, St Eval; Anti-U-Boat Planner and Intelligence Officer, Coastal Command; Naval and Military Intelligence, Air Ministry; Wing Cdr (despatches twice, OBE). Contested (Lab) Epsom, General Election, and Bournemouth by-election, 1945; MP (Lab), Preston (by-election), 1946–50, Preston South, 1950–55. Parliamentary Private Secretary to Minister of Supply, 1949–50; Parliamentary Private Sec. to Foreign Sec., March-Oct. 1951 (to Lord President of the Council, 1950–51); Minister of Defence for the RAF, 1964–67; Mission to S Arabia, 1967; Minister Without Portfolio and Deputy Leader, House of Lords, 1967–68; Lord Privy Seal, Jan.-April, 1968; Paymaster-General, April-Oct. 1968; Leader of the House of Lords, April 1968–70; Lord Privy Seal, Oct. 1968–1970; Minister in charge, Civil Service Dept, Nov. 1968–70; Opposition Leader, House of Lords, 1970–74. Chm., H of L Select Cttee on Sci. and Technol., 1988–. Sen. Executive and Director, J. Lewis Partnership, 1955–64; Dir, Personnel and Admin, RTZ Corp. Ltd, 1974–82. Chairman: Adv. Council on Oil Pollution, 1962–64; Political Honours Scrutiny Committee, 1976–; East European Trade Council, 1977–86 (Hon. Pres., 1986–); Mem., BOTB, 1975–78. Member, Council: Industrial Soc., 1963–83; RIIA, 1980–86; President: British Assoc. of Industrial Editors, 1960–64; ASLIB, 1963–65; Royal Geographical Society, 1971–74 (formerly Vice-Pres.); Parly and Scientific Cttee, 1976–80 (formerly Vice-Pres.); British Standards Inst., 1977–80. Chm., Arctic Club, 1960, 1979. Pro-Chancellor, Southampton Univ. Vice-Pres., YHA. Governor: London Chest Hosps, 1947–51; Imperial Coll. of Science, 1950–53. Mem. Council, SSAFA, 1951–55. Freedom of Stanley, Falkland Is, 1988. Hon. Elder Brother, Trinity Hse, 1980; Hon. Fellow, St Hugh's Coll., Oxford; Hon. Mem., RICS. CBIM. Hon. LLD Univ. of Newfoundland, 1970; Hon. DSc: Warwick, 1978; Southampton, 1986. Cuthbert Peek Award, 1933, Special Gold Medal, 1990, RGS; Ludwig Medallist (Munich Geog. Soc.), 1938. Hon. AC 1990. *Publications:* Arctic Journeys; Nansen, the Explorer; (part-author) Borneo Jungle; Economic Survey of Falkland Is, 1976, updated 1982; Review of UK Anti-Terrorist Legislation, 1978; articles, broadcasts, etc. on geographical and political subjects and personnel and general administration. *Address:* 11 Grosvenor Crescent, SW1X 7EE.

SHACKLETON, Keith Hope; artist and naturalist; President, Society of Wildlife Artists, 1978–83; Chairman, Artists League of Great Britain; *b* 16 Jan. 1923; *s* of W. S. Shackleton; *m* 1951, Jacqueline Tate; two *s* one *d*. *Educ:* Oundle. Served RAF, 1941–46. Civil Pilot and Dir, Shackleton Aviation Ltd, 1948–63; natural history programmes for television, 1964–68; joined naturalist team aboard MS Lindblad Explorer, 1969. Pres., Royal Soc. of

Marine Artists, 1973–78. Member: RGS; Zool Soc. of London; NZ Antarctic Soc. Hon. LLD Birmingham, 1983. *Publications:* Tidelines, 1951; Wake, 1953; Wild Animals in Britain, 1959; Ship in the Wilderness, 1986; Wildlife and Wilderness, 1986; illustrations for books. *Recreations:* small Boat Sailing, exploration field work. *Address:* Woodley Wood Farm, Woodleigh, Devon TQ7 4DR. *Club:* Itchenor Sailing.

SHACKLETON, Prof. Nicholas John, PhD; FRS 1985; Director, Sub-Department of Quaternary Research, University of Cambridge, since 1988; Fellow of Clare Hall, since 1980; *b* 23 June 1937; *s* of Prof. Robert Millner Shackleton, *qv*; *m* 1986, Vivien Law. *Educ:* Cranbrook Sch.; Clare Coll., Cambridge (BA, PhD); ScD Cantab 1984. Cambridge University: Senior Asst in Research, 1965–72, Asst Dir of Res., 1972–87, Reader, 1987–91, Prof., 1991–, sub-dept of Quaternary Res.; Research Fellow, Clare Hall, 1974–80, Official Fellow, 1980–. Sen. Vis. Res. Fellow, Lamont Doherty Geol Observatory of Columbia Univ., 1974–75. Founding Mem., Academia Europaea, 1988. Carus Medal, Deutsche Akad. der Naturforscher Leopoldina, 1985; Sheppard Medal, SEPM, 1985; Lyell Medal, Geol Soc. of London, 1987; Huntsman Award, 1991. *Publications:* numerous articles on marine geology, geological history of climate, etc; articles in New Grove Dictionary of Music and Musicians. *Recreations:* clarinet playing, researching history of clarinet, Thai food. *Address:* 12 Tenison Avenue, Cambridge CB1 2DY. *T:* Cambridge (0223) 311938.

SHACKLETON, Prof. Robert Millner, BSc, PhD; FRS 1971; FGS; Hon. Senior Research Fellow, Open University, since 1977; Professor of Geology, University of Leeds, 1962–75, now Emeritus; Director, Research Institute of African Geology, University of Leeds, 1966–75; *b* 30 Dec. 1909; *m* 1st, 1934, Gwen Isabel Harland; one *s* two *d*; 2nd, 1949, Judith Wyndham Jeffreys (marr. diss. 1978); one *s* one *d*; 3rd, 1984, Peigi Wallace. *Educ:* Sidcot School; University of Liverpool. BSc (Hons) 1931, PhD 1934, Liverpool; Beit Fellow, Imperial College, 1932–34; Chief Geologist to Whitehall Explorations Ltd in Fiji, 1935–36; on teaching staff, Imperial College, 1936–40 and 1945–48; Geologist, Mining and Geological Dept, Kenya, 1940–45; Herdman Professor of Geology, University of Liverpool, 1948–62. Royal Society Leverhulme Vis. Prof., Haile Sellassie I Univ., 1970–71; Trevelyan Coll. Fellow, Durham Univ., 1984–85. Vice-Pres., Geolog. Soc. of London, 1966. Murchison Medal, 1970. *Publications:* Mining and Geological Dept of Kenya Reports 10, 11, 12; papers in geological journals, etc. *Address:* The Croft Barn, Church Street, East Hendred, Oxon OX12 8LA. *T:* Abingdon (0235) 834802.
See also N. J. Shackleton.

SHACKLETON BAILEY, D. R.; *see* Bailey.

SHACKLOCK, Constance, OBE 1971; LRAM 1940; FRAM 1953; International Opera and Concert Singer; Professor, Royal Academy of Music, 1968–84; *b* 16 April 1913; *e d* of Randolph and Hilda Shacklock, Nottingham; *m* 1947, Eric Mitchell (*d* 1965). *Educ:* Huntingdon Street Secondary School, Nottingham; RAM. Principal mezzo-soprano, Covent Garden, 1946–56. Outstanding rôles: Carmen, Amneris (Aida), Octavian (Der Rosenkavalier), Brangaene (Tristan und Isolde). Guest artist: Wagner Society, Holland, 1949; Berlin State Opera, 1951; Edinburgh Festival, 1954; Berlin Festival, 1956; Teatro Colon, Buenos Aires, 1956; Bolshoi Theatre, Moscow, 1957; Kirov Theatre, Leningrad, 1957; Elizabethan Theatre Trust, Sydney, 1958; Liège Opera, 1960; London production of The Sound of Music, 1961–66. President: English Singers and Speakers, 1978–79; Royal Acad. of Music, 1979–80; Royal Borough of Kingston Arts Fest., 1988–. *Recreations:* gardening, reading, tapestry. *Address:* East Dorincourt, Kingston Vale, SW15 3RN.

SHAFER, Prof. Byron Edwin; Andrew W. Mellon Professor of American Government, Oxford, since 1985; Professorial Fellow, Nuffield College, Oxford, since 1985; *b* 8 Jan. 1947; *s* of Byron Henry Shafer and Doris Marguerite (*née* Von Bergen); *m* 1981, Wanda K. Green; one *s*. *Educ:* Yale Univ. (BA Magna Cum Laude, Deptl Hons in Pol. Sci. with Excep. Dist. 1968); Univ. of California at Berkeley (PhD Pol. Sci. 1979). Resident Scholar, Russell Sage Foundn, USA, 1977–84; Associate Prof. of Pol. Sci., Florida State Univ., 1984–85. Hon. MA Oxford, 1985. E. E. Schattschneider Prize, 1980, Franklin L. Burdette Prize, 1990, Amer. Pol. Sci. Assoc. *Publications:* Presidential Politics: readings on nominations and elections, 1980; Quiet Revolution: the struggle for the Democratic Party and the shaping of post-reform politics, 1983; Bifurcated Politics: evolution and reform in the National Party Convention, 1988; Is America Different?: a new look at American exceptionalism, 1991; The End of Realignment?: interpreting American electoral eras, 1991; articles in learned jls. *Recreations:* furniture restoration, gardening, travel. *Address:* Nuffield College, Oxford OX1 1NF. *T:* Oxford (0865) 278509; 55 Stapleton Road, Headington, Oxford OX3 7LX. *T:* Oxford (0865) 64705.

SHAFFER, Anna; *see* Wintour, A.

SHAFFER, Peter Levin, CBE 1987; FRSL; playwright; *b* 15 May 1926; *s* of Jack Shaffer and Reka Shaffer (*née* Fredman). *Educ:* St Paul's School, London; Trinity College, Cambridge. Literary Critic, Truth, 1956–57; Music Critic, Time and Tide, 1961–62. Hamburg Shakespeare Prize, 1989. *Stage Plays:* Five Finger Exercise, prod. Comedy, London, 1958–60, and Music Box Theatre, NY, 1960–61 (Evening Standard Drama Award, 1958; NY Drama Critics Circle Award (best foreign play), 1959–60); (double bill) The Private Ear (filmed 1966) and The Public Eye, produced, Globe, London, 1962, Morosco Theater, New York 1963 (filmed 1972); The Merry Roosters Panto (with Joan Littlewood and Theatre Workshop) prod. Wyndham's Theatre, Christmas, 1963; The Royal Hunt of the Sun, Nat. Theatre, Chichester Festival, 1964, The Old Vic, and Queen's Theatres, 1964–67, NY, 1965–66 (filmed 1969); Black Comedy, Nat. Theatre, Chichester Fest., 1965, The Old Vic and Queen's Theatres, 1965–67; as double bill with White Lies, NY, 1967, Shaw, 1976; The White Liars, Lyric, 1968; The Battle of Shrivings, Lyric, 1970; Equus, Nat. Theatre, 1973–74, Plymouth Theatre, NY, 1976, Albery Theatre, 1976–77 (NY Drama Critics' and Antoinette Perry Awards) (filmed 1977); Amadeus, Nat. Theatre, 1979 (Evening Standard Drama Award, Plays and Players Award, London Theatre Critics Award), Broadhurst Theatre, NY, 1980 (Antoinette Perry Award, Drama Desk Award), Her Majesty's, 1981 (filmed 1984, Acad. Award, Golden Globe Award, Los Angeles Film Critics Assoc. Award, 1985); Yonadab, Nat. Theatre, 1985; Lettice and Lovage, Globe, 1987, Barrymore Theatre, NY, 1990 (Evening Standard Drama Award for Best Comedy, 1988). Plays produced on television and sound include: The Salt Land (ITV), 1955; Balance of Terror (BBC TV), 1957; Whom Do I Have the Honour of Addressing? (radio), 1989, etc. *Recreations:* music, architecture. *Address:* c/o McNaughton-Lowe Representation, 200 Fulham Road, SW10. *Club:* Garrick.

SHAFTESBURY, 10th Earl of, *cr* 1672; **Anthony Ashley-Cooper;** Bt 1622; Baron Ashley 1661; Baron Cooper of Paulet, 1672; *b* 22 May 1938; *o s* of Major Lord Ashley (*d* 1947; *e s* of 9th Earl of Shaftesbury, KP, PC, GCVO, CBE) and of Françoise Soulier; *S* grandfather, 1961; *m* 1st, 1966, Bianca Maria (marr. diss. 1976), *o d* of late Gino de Paolis; 2nd, 1976, Christina Eva, *o d* of Ambassador Nils Montan; two *s*. *Educ:* Eton; Christchurch, Oxford. Chm., London Philharmonic Orchestra Council, 1966–80. Hon. Pres., Shaftesbury Soc., 1961. Hon. Citizen, South Carolina, USA, 1967. Patron of seven livings. *Recreations:* mountains, music, ecology. *Heir: s* Lord Ashley, *qv*. *Address:* St Giles, Wimborne, Dorset BH21 5NH. *T:* Cranborne (07254) 312. *Clubs:* Pratt's, Turf.

SHAGARI, Alhaji Shehu Usman Aliyu; President of Nigeria and Commander-in-Chief of the Armed Forces, 1979–83; *b* April 1925; *s* of Magaji Aliyu; *m* 1946; three *s* three *d*. *Educ:* Middle Sch., Sokoto; Barewa Coll., Kaduna; Teacher Trg Coll., Zaria. Teacher of science, Sokoto Middle Sch., 1945–50; Headmaster, Argungu Sen. Primary Sch., 1951–52; Sen. Visiting Teacher, Sokoto Prov., 1953–58. Entered politics as Mem. Federal Parl., 1954–58; Parly Sec. to Prime Minister, 1958–59; Federal Minister: Economic Develt, 1959–60; Establishments, 1960–62; Internal Affairs, 1962–65; Works, 1965–66; Sec., Sokoto Prov. Educl Develt Fund, 1966–68; State Comr for Educn, Sokoto Province, 1968–70; Fed. Comr for Econ. Develt and Reconstruction, 1970–71; for Finance, 1971–75. Mem., Constituent Assembly, Oct. 1977–; Mem., Nat. Party of Nigeria. *Publications:* (poetry) Wakar Nijeriya, 1948; Dun Fodia, 1978; (collected speeches) My Vision of Nigeria, 1981. *Recreations:* Hausa poetry, reading, farming, indoor games.

SHAKER, Mohamed Ibrahim, PhD; Order of the Arab Republic of Egypt (Second Grade), 1976; Order of Merit (Egypt) (First Grade), 1983; Ambassador of the Arab Republic of Egypt to the Court of St James's, since 1988; *b* 16 Oct. 1933; *s* of Mahmoud Shaker and Zeinab Wasef; *m* 1960, Mona El Kony; one *s* one *d*. *Educ:* Cairo Univ. (Lic. en Droit); Inst. of Internat. Studies, Geneva (PhD). Representative of Dir-Gen. of IAEA to UN, New York, 1982–83; Amb. and Dep. Perm. Rep. of Egypt to UN, New York, 1984–86; Amb. to Austria, 1986–88; Hd of Dept of W Europe, Min. of For. Affairs, Cairo, 1988. President: Third Review Conf. of the Parties to the Treaty on Non-Proliferation of Nuclear Weapons, Geneva, 1985; UN Conf. for the Promotion of Internat. Co-operation in the Peaceful Uses of Nuclear Energy, Geneva, 1987; Mem., Core Gp of Prog. for Promotion of Non-Proliferation of Nuclear Weapons, 1987–. *Publications:* The Nuclear Non-Proliferation Treaty: origin and implementation 1959–1979, 1980; several articles. *Recreation:* tennis. *Address:* Egyptian Embassy, 75 South Audley Street, W1. *Clubs:* Queen's (Hon. Member); Guizera Sporting (Cairo).

SHAKERLEY, Sir Geoffrey (Adam), 6th Bt *cr* 1838; Director, Photographic Records Ltd, since 1970; *b* 9 Dec. 1932; *s* of Sir Cyril Holland Shakerley, 5th Bt, and Elizabeth Averil (MBE 1955; *d* 1990), *d* of late Edward Gwynne Eardley-Wilmot; *S* father, 1970; *m* 1st, 1962, Virginia Elizabeth (*d* 1968), *d* of W. E. Maskell; two *s*; 2nd, 1972, Lady Elizabeth Georgiana, *d* of late Viscount Anson and Princess Georg of Denmark; one *d*. *Educ:* Harrow; Trinity College, Oxford. *Publications:* Henry Moore Sculptures in Landscape, 1978; The English Dog at Home, 1986. *Heir: s* Nicholas Simon Adam Shakerley, *b* 20 Dec. 1963. *Address:* 57 Artesian Road, W2 5DB.

SHAKESPEARE, John William Richmond, CMG 1985; LVO 1968; HM Diplomatic Service, retired; *b* 11 June 1930; *s* of late Dr W. G. Shakespeare; *m* 1955, Lalage Ann, *d* of late S. P. B. Mais; three *s* one *d*. *Educ:* Winchester; Trinity Coll., Oxford (Scholar, MA). 2nd Lieut Irish Guards, 1949–50. Lectr in English, Ecole Normale Supérieure, Paris, 1953–54; on editorial staff, Times Educational Supplement, 1955–56 and Times, 1956–59; entered Diplomatic Service, 1959; Private Sec. to Ambassador in Paris, 1959–61; FO, 1961–63; 1st Sec., Phnom-Penh, 1963–64; 1st Sec., Office of Polit. Adviser to C-in-C Far East, Singapore, 1964–66; Dir of British Information Service in Brazil, 1966–69; FCO, 1969–73; Counsellor and Consul-Gen., Buenos Aires, 1973–75; Chargé d'Affaires, Buenos Aires, 1976–77; Head of Mexico and Caribbean Dept, FCO, 1977–79; Counsellor, Lisbon, 1979–83; Ambassador to Peru, 1983–87, to Kingdom of Morocco, 1987–90. Officer, Order of Southern Cross (Brazil), 1968. *Recreations:* tennis, sailing, bicycling, gardening, music (light), poetry. *Address:* 10 South End Row, Kensington, W8. *Club:* Garrick.
See also N. W. R. Shakespeare.

SHAKESPEARE, Nicholas William Richmond; author and journalist; *b* 3 March 1957; *s* of J. W. R. Shakespeare, *qv*. *Educ:* Dragon Sch., Oxford; Winchester Coll.; Magdalene Coll., Cambridge (MA English). BBC TV, 1980–84; Dep. Arts and Literary Editor, The Times, 1985–87; Literary Editor: London Daily News, 1987–88; Daily Telegraph, 1988–91; Sunday Telegraph, 1989–91; film critic, Illustrated London News, 1989. Work for TV includes: The Evelyn Waugh Trilogy; Cover to Cover; Mario Vargas Llosa (Omnibus); Iquitos; For the Sake of the Children. *Publications:* The Men who would be King, 1984; Londoners, 1986; The Vision of Elena Silves, 1989 (Somerset Maugham Prize, 1990). *Recreations:* travelling, drawing. *Address:* 5 Bassett Road, W10 6LA. *Clubs:* Beefsteak, Groucho.

SHAKESPEARE, Sir William (Geoffrey), 2nd Bt *cr* 1942; Medical Adviser to Buckinghamshire Adoption Panel, since 1987; General Practitioner, Aylesbury, 1968–87; Clinical Assistant, Mental Subnormality, Manor House Hospital, Aylesbury, since 1972; *b* 12 Oct. 1927; *s* of Rt Hon. Sir Geoffrey Hithersay Shakespeare, 1st Bt, and Aimée Constance (*d* 1950), *d* of Walter Loveridge; *S* father, 1980; *m* 1964, Susan Mary, *d* of A. D. Raffel, Colombo, Ceylon; two *s*. *Educ:* Radley; Clare Coll., Cambridge (BA Hons Nat. Scis, MA 1957); St George's Hospital. MB BChir Camb. 1958; DCH Eng. 1961. Boston Children's Hosp., USA, 1963–64; Paediatric Registrar, Stoke Mandeville Hosp., 1964–66. Mem., Snowdon Working Party, Integration of Handicapped, 1974–76. Vice-President: Physically Handicapped & Able-Bodied (PHAB), 1977–; Assoc. for Res. into Restricted Growth (ARRG), 1982–. Member BMA. *Heir: s* Thomas William Shakespeare, *b* 11 May 1966. *Address:* Manor Cottage, Stoke Mandeville, Bucks HP22 5XA. *Clubs:* MCC; Leander.

SHAMS-UD DOHA, Aminur Rahman; Minister for Foreign Affairs, Government of the People's Republic of Bangladesh, 1982–84; Publisher and Editor-in-Chief: Dialogue Publications Ltd, Dhaka; Dialogue, international English weekly, since 1988; *b* 1929; *m*; two *s*; *m* 1981, Wajiha Moukaddem. *Educ:* Calcutta and Dacca Univs (BSc Hons; BA). Commnd 2nd Lieut, Pakistan Artillery, 1952; Sch. of Artillery and Guided Missiles, Ft Sill, Okla, USA, 1957–58; Gen. Staff Coll., Quetta, 1962; GS Inf. Bde HQ, 1963; RMCS, Shrivenham, 1964–65; Sen. Instr, Gunnery, 1965; GS GHQ, 1965–66, retired. Editor and Publisher, Inter-Wing, Rawalpindi, 1968–71; Gen. Sec., Awami League, Rawalpindi, 1969–71, and Mem. Working Cttee; Ambassador of Bangladesh to: Yugoslavia and Roumania, 1972–74; Iran and Turkey, 1974–77; High Comr for Bangladesh in UK, 1977–82; Minister for Information, Bangladesh, March-June 1982. Member and Leader of Bangladesh delegns to numerous internat., Islamic and Commonwealth meetings. Associate Mem., Inst. of Strategic Studies, London. C-in-C's Commendation, 1964; several military awards and decorations. Order of the Lance and Flag, Cl. 1 (Yugoslavia); Order of Diplomatic Service, Gwanha Medal (S Korea). *Publications:* Arab-Israeli War, 1967; The Emergence of South Asia's First Nation State; Aryans on the Indus (MS); In the Shadow of the Eagle and the Bear (MS). *Recreations:* sport (selected for London Olympics, 1948), writing, gardening. *Address:* Farm View, Indira Road, Tejgaon, Dhaka 15, Bangladesh; Dialogue Publications Ltd, 19 Kazi Nazrul Islam Avenue, Dhaka 15. *Clubs:* English-Speaking Union; Golf (Dhaka).

SHAND, Major Bruce Middleton Hope, MC 1940, and Bar 1942; Vice Lord-Lieutenant, East Sussex, since 1974; *b* 22 Jan. 1917; *s* of late P. Morton Shand; *m* 1946, Rosalind Maud, *d* of 3rd Baron Ashcombe; one *s* two *d*. *Educ:* Rugby; RMC, Sandhurst. 2nd Lieut 12th Royal Lancers, 1937; Major 1942; wounded and PoW 1942; retd 1947.

Exon, Queen's Body Guard of the Yeomen of the Guard, 1971, Ensign, 1978–85, Adjutant and Clerk of the Cheque, 1985–87. Joint or Acting Master, Southdown Fox Hounds, 1956–75. DL Sussex, 1962. *Publication:* Previous Engagements, 1991. *Recreations:* hunting, gardening. *Address:* The Laines, Plumpton, near Lewes, East Sussex BN7 3AJ. *T:* Plumpton (0273) 890248. *Club:* Cavalry and Guards.

See also E. R. M. Howe.

SHAND, Rt. Rev. David Hubert Warner; Assistant Bishop and Bishop in Geelong, Diocese of Melbourne, Archbishop's Provincial Assistant, 1985–88; *b* 6 April 1921; *s* of late Rev. Canon Rupert Warner Shand and Madeleine Ethel Warner Shand; *m* 1946, Muriel Jean Horwood Bennett; one *s* three *d*. *Educ:* The Southport Sch., Queensland; St Francis' Theological Coll., Brisbane (ThL, 2nd Cl. Hons); Univ. of Queensland (BA, 2nd Cl. Hons). Served War, AIF, 1941–45: Lieut, 1942. St Francis' Coll., Brisbane, 1946–48. Deacon, 1948; Priest, 1949; Asst Curate, Lutwyche. Served in Parishes: Moorooka, Inglewood, Nambour, Ipswich; Org. Sec., Home Mission Fund, 1960–63; Rural Dean of Ipswich, 1963–66; Dio. of Brisbane: Chaplain CMF, 1950–57; Vicar, Christ Church, South Yarra, 1966–69; St Andrew's, Brighton, 1969–73; Rural Dean of St Kilda, 1972–73; Dio. of Melbourne: consecrated Bishop, St Paul's Cathedral, Melbourne, Nov. 1973; Bishop of St Arnaud, 1973–76 (when diocese amalgamated with that of Bendigo); Vicar of St Stephen's, Mt Waverley, 1976–78; Bishop of the Southern Region, 1978–85. Chm., Gen. Bd of Religious Educn, 1974–84. *Recreation:* carpentry. *Address:* 40 Volitans Avenue, Mount Eliza, Vic 3930, Australia.

SHAND, John Alexander Ogilvie; His Honour Judge Shand; a Circuit Judge, since 1988; *b* 6 Nov. 1942; *s* of late Alexander Shand and Marguerite Marie Shand; *m* 1965, Patricia Margaret (*née* Toynbee) (marr. diss.); two *s* one *d*; *m* 1990, Valerie Jean (*née* Bond). *Educ:* Nottingham High Sch.; Queens' Coll., Cambridge (MA, LLB; Chancellor's Medal for Law 1965). Called to the Bar, Middle Temple, 1965 (Harmsworth Scholarship); practised on Midland and Oxford Circuit (Birmingham), 1965–71 and 1973–81 (Dep. Circuit Judge, 1979); a Recorder, 1981–88. Chm. of Industrial Tribunals (Birmingham Reg.), 1981–88. Fellow and Tutor, Queens' Coll., Cambridge, 1971–73. Chancellor: Dio. Southwell, 1981–; Dio. Lichfield, 1989–. *Publications:* (with P. G. Stein) Legal Values in Western Society, 1974; contrib. various articles in Cambridge Law Jl. *Address:* c/o Courts Administrator's Office, Kemley House, 2 Victoria Road, Stafford ST16 2AE.

SHANKAR, Pandit Ravi; Presidential Padma Vibhushan Award, 1980; musician and composer; MP (Member of Rajya Sabha) since 1986; *b* 7 April 1920; *m* 1989, Sukanya Rajan; one *s* two *d*. Studied with brother Uday Shankar in Paris, 1930, with Ustad Allaudin Khan in Maihar, 1938–. Music Dir, All-India Radio, 1949–56; music and choreography for ASIAD 82 (Asian Games, New Delhi, 1982). Fellow, Sangeet Natak Akademi, 1977 (President's Award, 1962); Member, Nat. Acad. for Recording Arts and Sciences, 1966. Recordings with Yehudi Menuhin, Jean-Pierre Rampal, Philip Glass, and others. Has received hon. doctorates in letters and arts from California, 1968; Colgate, NY, 1972; Rabindra Bharati, Calcutta; Benares Hindu Univ. Deshikottam Award, 1982. *Compositions:* Indian ragas; music for ballet, and films incl. Gandhi, 1983; Concertos for sitar and orch., No 1, 1971, No 2, 1981; Ghanashyam—A Broken Branch, 1989. *Publication:* My Music My Life, 1968. *Recreations:* films, people, music, theatre. *Address:* c/o Mayur Arts, 3 Coxcomb Walk, Bewbush, Crawley, W Sussex RH11 8BA; Ravi Shankar Institute of Performing Arts, New Delhi.

SHANKS, Duncan Faichney, RSA 1990 (ARSA 1972); RGI 1982; RSW 1987; artist; *b* 30 Aug. 1937; *s* of Duncan Faichney Shanks and Elizabeth Clark; *m* 1966, Una Brown Gordon. *Educ:* Glasgow School of Art; DA (Post Diploma) 1960. Travelling scholarship to Italy, 1961; part-time teacher, Glasgow Sch. of Art, 1963–79; full-time artist, 1979–. *Recreations:* classical and contemporary music.

SHANKS, Ernest Pattison, CBE 1975; QC (Singapore) 1958; Deputy Bailiff of Guernsey, 1973–76; *b* 11 Jan. 1911; *e s* of late Hugh P. Shanks and Mary E. Shanks; *m* 1st, 1937, Audrey E. Moore; one *s*; 2nd, 1947, Betty Katherine Battersby (*d* 1991); two *s* one *d*. *Educ:* Mill Hill Sch.; Downing Coll., Cambridge (MA); Inner Temple; Staff Coll., Camberley. Called to the Bar, Inner Temple, 1936; N Eastern Circuit. SRO, Mddx Regt, 1939–44: Princess Louise's Kensington Regt, France (despatches); Sicily, Italy, 1944; Staff Coll., Camberley, 1944–46; Sen. Legal Officer, Schleswig-Holstein, Milit. Govt, Germany, 1946; Lt-Col RARO, 1946. Colonial Legal Service: Dist Judge, Trengganu, Malaya, 1946; Singapore: Dist Judge and First Magistrate, 1947; Crown Counsel and Solicitor-Gen.; Attorney-Gen. and Minister of Legal Affairs, 1957–59. HM Comptroller, Guernsey, 1960; HM Procureur, 1969. *Address:* Le Petit Mas, Clos des Fosses, St Martin's, Guernsey. *T:* Guernsey (0481) 38300. *Clubs:* Old Millhillians (Pres., 1979–80), Commonwealth Trust; Royal Channel Islands Yacht, Royal Guernsey Golf.

SHANKS, Ian Alexander, PhD; FRS 1984; Chief Scientist, THORN EMI plc, since 1986; *b* 22 June 1948; *s* of Alexander and Isabella Affleck (*née* Beaton); *m* 1971, Janice Smillie Coulter; one *d*. *Educ:* Dumbarton Acad.; Glasgow Univ. (BSc); Glasgow Coll. of Technology (PhD); CEng, MIEE 1983, FIEE 1990. Projects Manager, Scottish Colorfoto Labs, 1970–72; Research Student, Portsmouth Polytechnic, 1972–73 (liquid crystal displays); RSRE, Malvern, 1973–82 (displays and L-B films); Unilever Research, 1982, Principal Scientist, 1984–86 (electronic biosensors). Vis. Prof. of Electrical and Electronic Engrg, Univ. of Glasgow, 1985–. Chm., Inter-Agency Cttee for Marine Sci. and Technol., 1991–; Member: Opto-electronics Cttee, Rank Prize Funds, 1985–; Science Consultative Gp, BBC, 1989–91; ABRC, 1990–. A Vice-Pres., Royal Soc., 1989– (Mem. Council, 1989–). Paterson Medal and Prize, Inst. of Physics, 1984; Best Paper Award, Soc. for Inf. Display, 1983. *Publications:* numerous sci. and tech. papers; numerous patents. *Recreations:* music, horology. *Address:* Flintwood Cottage, Channer Drive, Penn, Bucks HP10 8HT.

SHANNON, 9th Earl of, *cr* 1756; **Richard Bentinck Boyle;** Viscount Boyle, Baron of Castle-Martyr, 1756; Baron Carleton (GB), 1786; late Captain Irish Guards; Director of companies; Chairman: Strategy Europe Ltd, since 1988; Access Parliamentary Public Affairs, since 1989; Community (formerly Birmingham) Team Television, since 1989; *b* 23 Oct. 1924; *o s* of 8th Earl of Shannon; *S* father, 1963; *m* 1st, 1947, Catherine Irene Helen (marr. diss. 1955), *d* of the Marquis Demetrio Imperiali di Francavilla; 2nd, 1957, Susan Margaret (marr. diss. 1979), *d* of late J. P. R. Hogg; one *s* two *d*. *Educ:* Eton College. A Dep. Speaker and Dep. Chm. of Cttees, House of Lords, 1968–78. Dir, Cttee of Dirs of Res. Assocs, 1969–85; Sec. and Treas., Fedn of Eur. Indust. Co-operative Res. Orgns, 1971–86; President: Architectural Metalwork Assoc., 1966–74; Kent Br., BIM, 1970–87; Vice-President: Aslib, 1974; British Hydromechanics Res. Assoc., 1975–87; Foundn for Sci. and Tech. (Chm., 1977–83); IWA. Hon. Pres., Foundn for the Educn of the Underachieving and Dyslexic. FRSA, FBIM, MBHI. *Heir: s* Viscount Boyle, *qv*. *Address:* Pimm's Cottage, Man's Hill, Burghfield Common, Berks RG7 3BD. *Club:* White's.

SHANNON, David William Francis, PhD; Chief Scientist (Agriculture and Horticulture), Ministry of Agriculture, Fisheries and Food, since 1986; *b* 16 Aug. 1941; *s* of late William Francis Shannon and Elizabeth (*née* Gibson); *m* 1967, Rosamond (*née* Bond); one *s* one *d*. *Educ:* Wallace High Sch., Lisburn, NI; Queen's Univ., Belfast (BAgr, PhD); DMS Napier Coll., Edinburgh, 1976. Poultry Res. Centre, ARC, Edinburgh, 1967; study leave; Dept of Animal Science, Univ. of Alberta, Edmonton, 1973–74; Hd of Nutrition Sect., Poultry Res. Centre, AFRC, 1977, Dir, 1978. Mem., AFRC, 1986–; Pres., UK Br., World's Poultry Science Assoc., 1986–90. *Publications:* contribs to learned jls on poultry science and animal nutrition. *Recreations:* golf, bridge. *Address:* Ministry of Agriculture, Fisheries and Food, Nobel House, 17 Smith Square, SW1P 3HX. *T:* 071–238 5526. *Club:* Commonwealth Trust.

SHAPCOTT, Sidney Edward, CEng, FIEE, FInstP; Director-General, Airborne Weapons and Electronic Systems, Ministry of Defence, 1976–80; *b* 20 June 1920; *s* of late Percy Thomas and Beatrice Shapcott; *m* 1943, Betty Jean Richens; two *s* one *d*. *Educ:* Hele's School, Exeter; King's College, London. BSc. Joined Air Defence Experimental Establishment, 1941; various appointments in Min. of Supply and Min. of Aviation, 1941–62; DCSO, 1963; Dir of Projects, ESRO, 1963–65; Min. of Defence, Navy Dept, 1965–75; CSO, 1968; Dep. Dir, Admiralty Surface Weapons Establishment, 1968–72; Dir, Underwater Weapon Projects, Admiralty Underwater Weapons Establishment, Portland, 1972–75. Defence Engrng Consultant, 1981–85. *Address:* 23 Upper Churston Rise, Seaton, Devon EX12 2HD. *T:* Seaton (0297) 21545.

SHAPER, Prof. (Andrew) Gerald, FRCP; FRCPath; FFPHM; Professor of Clinical Epidemiology, Royal Free Hospital School of Medicine, London, since 1975; Hon. Consultant in Public Health (formerly Community) Medicine, Hampstead Health Authority, since 1975; *b* 9 Aug. 1927; *s* of Jack and Molly Shaper; *m* 1952, Lorna June Clarke; one *s*. *Educ:* Univ. of Cape Town (MB ChB); DTM&H with Milne Medal (Liverpool). Ho. Phys./Surg., Harare, 1952; SHO, Trop. Diseases Unit, Sefton Gen. Hosp., Liverpool, and Res. Asst, Liverpool Sch. of Trop. Med., 1953–54; Registrar: Clatterbridge Gen. Hosp., 1954–55; Hammersmith Hosp. and Post Grad. Med. Sch., 1955–56; Lectr, Sen. Lectr, Reader in Medicine and Prof. of Cardiovascular Disease, Makerere Univ. Med. Sch., Kampala, 1957–69; Mem. Sci. Staff, MRC Social Medicine Unit, LSHTM, 1970–75; Hon. Cons. Phys. (Cardiology), UCH, 1975–87. RCP Milroy Lectr, 1972. Chm., Jt Wkg Party of RCP and Brit. Cardiac Soc. on Prevention of Coronary Heart Disease, 1976; Member: DHSS Cttee on Med. Aspects of Water Quality, 1978–84; DHSS Cttee on Med. Aspects of Food Policy, 1979–83; Chairman: MRC Health Services Res. Panel, 1981–86; Heads of Academic Depts of Public Health (formerly Community) Medicine, 1987–90; Member: WHO Expert Adv. Panel on Cardiovascular Disease, 1975–; DHSS Central Health Monitoring Unit Steering Gp, 1989–. Alwyn Smith Prize Medal, FPHM, 1991. *Publications:* (ed) Medicine in a Tropical Environment, 1972; (ed) Cardiovascular Disease in the Tropics, 1974; Coronary Heart Disease: risks and reasons, 1988. *Recreations:* walking, second-hand/antiquarian books, theatre. *Address:* 8 Wentworth Hall, The Ridgeway, Mill Hill, NW7 1RJ. *T:* 081–959 8742.

SHAPIRO, Erin Patria Margaret; Founder of first Shelter for Battered Wives and their children, 1971; therapeutic consultant and fund-raiser, Women's Aid Ltd; *b* 19 Feb. 1939; *d* of Cyril Edward Antony Carney and Ruth Patricia Balfour-Last; *m* 1st, 1961, John Leo Pizzey (marr. diss. 1979); one *s* one *d*; 2nd, 1980, Jeffrey Scott Shapiro. *Educ:* St Antony's; Leweston Manor, Sherborne, Dorset. Somewhat chequered career as pioneering attracts frequent clashes with the law; appearances at such places as Acton Magistrates Court and the House of Lords could be considered milestones in the fulfilment of a career dedicated to defending women and children. Member: Soc. of Authors; AFI; Smithsonian Instn. Diploma of Honour, Internat. order of volunteers for peace, 1981; Distinguished Leadership Award, World Congress of Victimology, 1987. *Publications:* (as Erin Pizzey) Scream Quietly or the Neighbours Will Hear, 1974 (paperback), 2nd edn 1978; Infernal Child (autobiog.), 1978; The Slut's Cookbook, 1981; (with Jeff Shapiro) Prone to Violence, 1982; Erin Pizzey Collects, 1983; *novels:* The Watershed, 1983; In the Shadow of the Castle, 1984; The Pleasure Palace, 1986; First Lady, 1987; The Consul General's Daughter, 1988; The Snow Leopard of Shanghai, 1989; Other Lovers, 1991; Pets, 1991; poems and short stories. *Recreations:* wine, books, travel. *Address:* c/o Christopher Little, 49 Queen Victoria Street, EC4N 4SA.

SHAPIRO, Dr Harold Tafler; President of Princeton University, since 1988; *b* Montreal, 1936; *m* Vivian; four *d*. *Educ:* McGill Univ. (Lieut Governor's Medal; BA 1956); Graduate Sch., Princeton (PhD Econ 1964). University of Michigan: Asst Prof. of Economics, 1964; Associate Prof., 1967; Prof., 1970–88; Vice-Pres. for Acad. Affairs and Chm., Cttee on Budget Admin, 1977; President, 1980–88; Prof. of Economics and Public Affairs, Princeton, 1988–. Director: Dow Chemical Co.; Amer. Council of Educn; Nat. Bureau of Economic Research; Member: Conference Board Inc.; Bretton Woods Cttee; Govt-Univ.-Industry Res. Round-table; Inst. of Medicine, Nat. Acad. of Scis; Pres., Council of Advrs, 1990–. Mem., Amer. Philosophical Soc.; Fellow, Amer. Acad. of Arts and Scis. Trustee: Alfred P. Sloan Foundn; Univs Res. Assoc. *Address:* Princeton University, Princeton, NJ 08544, USA.

SHAPLAND, Maj.-Gen. Peter Charles, CB 1977; MBE 1960; MA; Senior Planning Inspector, Department of the Environment, since 1980; *b* 14 July 1923; *s* of late F. C. Shapland, Merton Park, Surrey; *m* 1954, Joyce Barbara Shapland (*née* Peradon); two *s*. *Educ:* Rutlish Sch., Merton Park; St Catharine's Coll., Cambridge. Served War: commissioned Royal Engineers, 1944; QVO Madras Sappers and Miners, Indian Army, 1944–47. Served United Kingdom, Middle East (Canal Zone) and Cyprus, 1948–63. Attended Staff Coll., 1952; jssc, 1960. Lt-Col, 1965; comd in Aden, 1965–67; Brig., Dec. 1968; comd 30 Engineer Bde. Attended Royal Coll. of Defence Studies, 1971. Dep. Comdr and Chief of Staff, HQ SE Dist, 1972–74; Maj.-Gen. 1974; Dir, Volunteers Territorials and Cadets, MoD (Army), 1974–78, retired. Hon. Col, 73 Engineer Regt, TA, 1979–89; Col Comdt, RE, 1981–86. Chm., Combined Cadet Forces Assoc., 1982–; Pres., Instn of Royal Engrs, 1982–87. Mem., Worshipful Co. of Painter-Stainers, 1983–. *Publications:* contribs to Royal Engineers' Jl. *Recreations:* sailing, swimming, golf. *Address:* c/o Royal Bank of Scotland, Holts Branch, Kirkland House, Whitehall, SW1A 2EB. *Clubs:* Royal Ocean Racing, Lansdowne; Royal Engineer Yacht (Chatham).

SHAPLAND, Sir William (Arthur), Kt 1982; Trustee, Bernard Sunley Charitable Foundation; *b* 20 Oct. 1912; *s* of late Arthur Frederick Shapland and of Alice Maud (*née* Jackson); *m* 1943, Madeline Annie (*née* Amiss); two *d*. *Educ:* Tollington Sch., Muswell Hill. Incorporated Accountant, 1936; Chartered Accountant, 1946. Allan Charlesworth & Co, Chartered Accountants, London, Cambridge and Rangoon, 1929–55; Blackwood Hodge, 1955–83 (Chm., 1965–83). Waynflete Fellow, Magdalen Coll., Oxford, 1981–; Hon. Fellow, St Catherine's College, Oxford, 1982. Hon. FRCS 1978. Past Master, Paviors' Co. KStJ 1987 (OStJ 1981). Hon. DSc Buckingham, 1983; Hon. DLitt Leicester, 1985. *Recreations:* golf, gardening, travel. *Address:* 44 Beech Drive, N2 9NY. *T:* 081–883 5073.

SHARKEY, Colum John, CMG 1984; MBE 1973; HM Diplomatic Service; Personnel Management Department, Foreign and Commonwealth Office, since 1991; *b* 9 June 1931; *s* of late Andrew Sharkey and late Sarah Josephine Sharkey (*née* Whelan); *m* 1962, Olivia Anne (*née* Brassil); two *s* one *d*. Commonwealth Relations Office, 1954; served in New Delhi, 1955, Calcutta, 1956–58; Second Secretary: Dacca, 1959–61; Melbourne, 1962–66; Montevideo, 1967–68 (joined HM Diplomatic Service, 1968); First Sec. and Consul, Asuncion, 1969; First Sec., Montevideo, 1971; seconded to Dept of Trade,

1972–74; Consul, Vancouver, 1974–78; Consul-Gen., Bilbao, 1978–81; Ambassador to Honduras, 1981–84 and non-resident Ambassador to El Salvador, 1982–84; Head of British Interests Section, Buenos Aires, 1984–87; Ambassador to Bolivia, 1987–89, to Uruguay, 1989–91, retd, then re-engaged. *Recreations:* reading, tennis, golf. *Address:* c/o Foreign and Commonwealth Office, King Charles Street, SW1A 2AH.

SHARLAND, Edward John; HM Diplomatic Service; High Commissioner, Port Moresby, Papua New Guinea, 1989–91; *b* 25 Dec. 1937; *s* of William Rex Sharland and late Phyllis Eileen Sharland (*née* Pitts); *m* 1970, Susan Mary Rodway Millard; four *d*. *Educ:* Monmouth Sch.; Jesus Coll., Oxford. BA Hons History; MA. FO, 1961–62; Bangkok, 1962–67; Far Eastern Dept, FCO, 1967–69; Dep. Perm. Rep. to UNIDO and Dep. Resident Rep. to IAEA, Vienna, 1969–72; Bangkok, 1972–75; Montevideo, 1976–79; Cultural Relations Dept, FCO, 1979–82; Consul-Gen., Perth, 1982–87; Consul-Gen., Cleveland, 1987–89. *Recreations:* tennis, bridge, stamp collecting. *Address:* c/o Foreign and Commonwealth Office, SW1A 2AH. *Club:* Royal Bangkok Sports.

SHARMA, Dr Shanker Dayal; Vice-President of India, 1987–August 1992; *b* 19 Aug. 1918. *Educ:* Lucknow Univ.; Cambridge Univ.; Lincoln's Inn. MA, LLM, PhD. Lawyer, 1942–; Mem., All India Congress Cttee, 1950–; Pres., Bhopal State Congress Cttee, 1950–52; Chief Minister, Bhopal, 1952–56; Minister, Madhya Pradesh Govt, 1956–67; Gen. Sec., Indian Nat. Congress, 1968–72; Pres., All India Congress Cttee, 1972–74; Mem., Lokh Sabha, 1971–77; Minister of Communications, 1974–77; former Governor, Andhra Pradesh, 1985, Punjab, 1985–86; suspended from Congress Party (I), 1986. Editor in Chief, Light and Learning, Ilm-au-Noor; Editor, Lucknow Law Jl. Hon. DPA London; Hon. LLD Vikram and Bhopal Univs. *Publication:* Congress Approach to International Affairs. *Address:* Vice-President's House, New Delhi 110011, India.

SHARMA, Usha Kumari, (Mrs V. K. Sharma); *see* Prashar, U. K.

SHARMA, Vishnu Datt; President, Ealing Community Relations Council, since 1987 (Senior Supervisor, 1981–87); Member, Executive Committee, National Council for Civil Liberties, since 1982 (Race Relations Officer, 1979–80); *b* 19 Oct. 1921; *s* of late Pandit Girdhari Lal Kaushik and Shrimati Ganga Devi; *m* 1960, Krishna Sharma; one *d*. *Educ:* High Sch. in India. Came to UK from India, 1957; worked in factories until 1967; apptd Mem. Nat. Cttee for Commonwealth Immigrants (by the Prime Minister, Rt Hon. Harold Wilson); twice elected Gen. Sec. of Indian Workers' Assoc., Southall, 1961–63 and 1965–67, and once Pres., 1977–79; Nat. Organiser, Campaign Against Racial Discrimination (later Vice-Chm.); Chm., Jt Council for the Welfare of Immigrants (Gen. Sec., Exec. Sec. and again Gen. Sec., 1967–77); Vice-Chm., Steering Cttee, Anti-Nazi League. Member: Adv. Cttee BBC, Asian Magazine; Editl Bd, Sher-e-Punjab, 1987–; Chief Editor, Charcha (Punjabi journal). Has attended five internat. confs on migrant workers and race relns. *Recreations:* cinema, watching television, sight-seeing, etc. *Address:* 43 Lady Margaret Road, Southall, Mddx UB1 2PJ. *T:* 081–843 0518.

SHARMAN, Peter William, CBE 1984; Director since 1974 and Chief General Manager, 1975–84, Norwich Union Insurance Group; *b* 1 June 1924; *s* of William Charles Sharman and Olive Mabel (*née* Burl); *m* 1946, Eileen Barbara Crix; one *s* two *d*. *Educ:* Northgate Grammar Sch., Ipswich; Edinburgh Univ. MA 1950; FIA 1956. War service as Pilot, RAF. Joined Norwich Union Insce Gp, 1950; Gen. Man. and Actuary, 1969. Chairman: Life Offices' Assoc., 1977–78; British Insurance Assoc., 1982–83. *Recreations:* tennis, badminton, golf. *Address:* 28B Eaton Road, Norwich NR4 6PZ. *T:* Norwich (0603) 51230.

SHARP, family name of **Baron Sharp of Grimsdyke.**

SHARP OF GRIMSDYKE, Baron *cr* 1989 (Life Peer), of Stanmore in the London Borough of Harrow; **Eric Sharp;** Kt 1984; CBE 1980; Chairman, 1980–90, and Chief Executive, 1981–90, Cable and Wireless PLC; *b* 17 Aug. 1916; *s* of Isaac and Martha Sharp; *m* 1950, Marion (*née* Freeman); one *s* one *d* (and one *d* decd). *Educ:* London School of Economics (BScEcon Hons; Hon. Fellow, 1986). CBIM. Served Army, 1940–46, Staff Captain SOIII Southern Comd, 1944. Principal, Min. of Power, 1948; UK Delegate, Coal and Petroleum Cttees of OEEC, 1948–50; Vice-Chm., Electricity Cttee, OEEC, 1951–54; Sec. to Herbert Cttee of Inquiry into Electricity Supply Industry, 1955–56; British Nylon Spinners Ltd, 1957–64; Director, ICI Fibres Ltd, 1964–68; Mem. Board, Monsanto Europe, 1969; Resident USA, Mem. Management Bd, 1970–72; Dep. Chm., 1973–74, Chm., 1975–81, Monsanto Ltd; Chairman: Polyamide Intermediates Ltd, 1975–81; (non-exec.) Stanhope Properties, 1987–; non exec. Director: Morgan Grenfell Group, 1987–90; Carlton Communications, 1990–. Chm., Chemical Industry Safety and Health Council, 1977–79; President: Chemical Industries Assoc., 1979–80; Sino-British Trade Council, 1985–90; part-time Mem., London Electricity Bd, 1969–78; Member: EDC for Chemical Industry, 1980–82; Central Electricity Generating Board, 1980–86. Freeman, City of London, 1982. Officer, Order of Merit (Cameroon). *Recreations:* family, food, music, conversation. *Address:* c/o House of Lords, SW1A 0PW. *Club:* Athenæum.

SHARP, Sir Adrian, 4th Bt *cr* 1922, of Warden Court, Maidstone, Kent; *b* 17 Sept. 1951; *s* of Sir Edward Herbert Sharp, 3rd Bt and of Beryl Kathleen, *d* of Leonard Simmons-Green; *S* father, 1986; *m* 1976, Hazel Patricia Bothwell (marr. diss.), *o d* of James Trevor Wallace. *Heir: b* Owen Sharp [*b* 17 Sept. 1956; *m* 1980, Caroline, *d* of late Jerrard Collings Van Benge; two *s*].

SHARP, His Honour Alastair George, MBE 1945; QC 1961; DL; a Circuit Judge (formerly Judge of County Courts), 1962–84; Liaison Judge, Durham County Magistrates Courts, 1972–84; *b* 25 May 1911; *s* of late Alexander Sharp, Advocate in Aberdeen, and of late Mrs Isabella Sharp, OBE; *m* 1940, Daphne Sybil, *d* of late Maj. Harold Smithers, RGA, and late Mrs Connor; one *s* two *d*. *Educ:* Aberdeen Grammar School; Fettes; Clare College, Cambridge (Archdeacon Johnson Exhibitioner in Classics). BA 1933, 1st Class Hons Classical Tripos Part II, Aegrotat Part I. Boxed Cambridge Univ., 1931–32; Cambridge Union Debating Team in America, 1933. On staff of Bonar Law College, Ashridge, 1934–35; Barrister, Middle Temple, 1935; Harmsworth Law Scholar; North Eastern Circuit, 1936. Dep. Chm. of Agricultural Land Tribunal, Northern Area, 1958–62; Asst Recorder of Huddersfield, 1958–60; Recorder of Rotherham, 1960–62; Dep. Chm., N Riding Yorks QS, 1959–65; Dep. Chm., 1965–70, Chm., 1970–71, Durham QS. Chm., Washington New Town Licensed Premises Cttee, 1966–78; Jt Pres., Council of Circuit Judges, 1979. Commissioned, The Gordon Highlanders, Feb. 1939; served War of 1939–45: Staff Coll., 1943; 2nd Bn The London Scottish, 1943; Gen. Staff, War Office, 1944–45, Temp. Major. Governor, Sherburn Hosp. Charity, 1972–81. Mem. Board, Faculty of Law, Durham Univ., 1976–84. DL Co. Durham, 1973. *Recreations:* golf, gardening, music, hill walking, fishing. *Address:* High Point, Western Hill, Durham DH1 4RG; The Old Kennels, Tomintoul, Banffshire. *Clubs:* Durham County; Brancepeth Castle Golf.

See also Baron Mackie of Benshie, Sir R. L. Sharp.

SHARP, Sir Angus; *see* Sharp, Sir W. H. A.

SHARP, Derek Joseph; British Council Representative, Italy, 1981–85, retired; *b* 12 June 1925; *s* of Joseph Frank Sharp and Sylvia May (*née* Allen); *m* 1957, Hilda Francesca Cernigoj; two *s*. *Educ:* Preston Grammar School; Queen's Coll., Oxford; MA, DipEd. Lectr, British Inst., Milan, 1956–58; British Council, 1958; served Indonesia, Bristol, Bangkok, Addis Ababa, Pretoria and London, 1958–77; Controller, Africa and Middle East Div., 1977–81. Mem., British Cttee for Preservation of Venice (Venice in Peril Fund), 1989–. *Address:* 3 Hartley Close, Bickley, Kent BR1 2TP; Cristallo Residence, Lungomare Trieste, 154, 33054 Lignano Sabbiadoro (UD), Italy.

SHARP, Sir George, Kt 1976; OBE 1969; JP; DL; Managing Trustee, Municipal Mutual Insurance Co. Ltd, since 1979; Chairman, Glenrothes Development Corporation, 1978–86 (Vice-Chairman, 1973–78); *b* 8 April 1919; *s* of Angus Sharp and Mary S. McNee; *m* 1948, Elsie May Rodger, *o d* of David Porter Rodger and Williamina S. Young; one *s*. *Educ:* Thornton Public Sch.; Buckhaven High Sch. Engine driver, 1962; PRO, 1962–69. Fife County Council: Mem., 1945–75; Chm., Water and Drainage Cttee, 1955–61; Chm., Finance Cttee, 1961–72; Convener, 1972–75; Convener, Fife Regional Council, 1974–78. President: Assoc. of County Councils, 1972–74; Convention of Scottish Local Authorities, 1975–78. Chairman: Kirkcaldy Dist Council, 1958–75; Fife and Kinross Water Bd, 1967–75; Forth River Purification Bd, 1955–67 and 1975–78; Scottish River Purification Adv. Cttee, 1967–75; Scottish Tourist Consultative Council, 1979–83. Vice-Chm., Forth Road Bridge Cttee, 1972–78. Member: Scottish Water Adv. Cttee, 1962–69; Cttee of Enquiry into Salmon and Trout Fishing, 1963; Potato Marketing Bd, 1965–71; Scottish Valuation Adv. Cttee, 1972; Cttee of Enquiry into Local Govt Finance, 1974–76; Scottish Develt Agency, 1975–80; Royal Commn on Legal Services in Scotland, 1978–80; Econ. and Soc. Cttee, EEC, 1982–86. Director: Grampian Television, 1975–89; National Girobank Scotland, 1985–90. JP Fife, 1975; DL Fife, 1978. *Recreation:* golf. *Address:* Strathlea, 56 Station Road, Thornton, Fife KY1 4AY. *T:* Glenrothes (0592) 774347.

SHARP, Lt-Col Granville Maynard, MA (Cantab); *b* 5 Jan. 1906; *s* of Walter Sharp, Cleckheaton, Yorks; *m* 1935, Margaret, *d* of Dr J. H. Vincent, Wembley Hill; two *d*. *Educ:* Cleckheaton Grammar School; Ashville College, Harrogate; St John's College, Cambridge, MA (Hons) (Economics). Lecturer in Economics at West Riding Technical Institutes, 1929–34; Chairman, Spenborough Housing and Town Planning Committee, 1935–39; Hon. Secretary, Spen Valley Divisional Labour Party, 1936–39; Battery Capt. 68 Anti-Tank Regt RA, 1939–42; Staff Capt. and DAQMG Belfast Area, 1942–43; Senior British Staff Officer, Economics Section, Allied Control Commission, Italy, 1943–44; Chief Economics and Supply Officer, Military Govt, Austria, 1944–45. MP (Lab) for Spen Valley Div. of West Riding of Yorks, 1945–50; PPS Min. of Civil Aviation, 1946; Chairman, Select Cttee of Estimates Sub-Cttee, 1946–48; Parliamentary Private Sec. to Minister of Works, 1947–50. Keymer Parish Councillor, 1969–83 (Vice-Chm., 1976–80); CC E Sussex, 1970–74; CC W Sussex, 1973–85 (Chm., Rts of Way Cttee, 1974–83); Member: Cuckfield RDC, 1971–74; Mid-Sussex DC, 1973–76. *Recreations:* swimming, singing, scything, Sussex Downs; attempting to preserve the local rural environment by every practical means, from collecting litter and clearing Rights of Way to chivvying authority (Queen Mother's Tidy Britain Award Certificate, 1989). *Address:* 31 Wilmington Close, Hassocks, West Sussex. *T:* Hassocks (07918) 2294.

SHARP, Dr John; Headmaster of Rossall School, 1973–87; *b* 18 Dec. 1927; *o s* of late Alfred and May Sharp, North Ives, Oxenhope, Keighley; *m* 1950, Jean Prosser; one *s* two *d*. *Educ:* Boys' Grammar Sch., Keighley; Brasenose Coll., Oxford. MA, MSc, DPhil Oxon. RAF Educn Br., 1950–52; research at Oxford, 1952–54; Asst Master, Marlborough Coll., 1954–62; Senior Chemistry Master, 1956–62; Senior Science Master, 1959–62; Headmaster, Christ Coll., Brecon, 1962–72. Co-opted Mem., Oxford and Cambridge Schools Examn Bd, 1966–74; Selected Mem., Breconshire Educn Cttee, 1966–72; Co-opted Mem., Lancs Educn Cttee, 1974–81; Divisional Chm., HMC, SW 1971 and NW 1977–78; Chm., HMC Acad. Policy Sub-Cttee, 1982–85. Chm., Independent Schs' Jt Council Accreditation and Consultancy Service, 1987–; Gov., City Technology Coll., Kingshurst, Solihull, 1989–. *Publications:* contrib. Anal. Chim. Acta. *Recreations:* fishing, photography, roses and shrubs. *Address:* Wood End Cottage, St Michael's, Tenbury Wells, Worcs WR15 8TG. *Club:* East India.

SHARP, J(ohn) M(ichael) Cartwright; Secretary of Law Commission, 1968–78; *b* 11 Aug. 1918; *s* of W. H. Cartwright Sharp, KC, and Dorothy (*née* Shelton). *Educ:* Rossall Sch.; Lincoln Coll., Oxford. Royal Artillery, 1940–46. Called to Bar, Middle Temple, 1947. Lord Chancellor's Office, 1951–65; Legal Sec. to Law Officers, 1965; Asst Solicitor, Law Commn, 1966. *Recreations:* travel, reading. *Address:* 15 Bolton Gardens, SW5 0AL. *T:* 071–370 1896. *Clubs:* Reform, Beefsteak.

SHARP, Sir Kenneth (Johnston), Kt 1984; TD 1960; Partner, Baker, Tilly & Co. (formerly Howard, Tilly), Chartered Accountants, 1983–89; Chairman, T. M. Hunter Ltd, 1983–88; several directorships; *b* 29 Dec. 1926; *s* of Johnston Sharp and late Ann Sharp (*née* Routledge); *m* 1955, Barbara Maud Keating; one *s*. *Educ:* Shrewsbury Sch.; St John's Coll., Cambridge (MA). ACA 1955, FCA 1960. Partner, Armstrong, Watson & Co., Chartered Accountants, 1955–75; Head, Govt Accountancy Service and Accountancy Advr to DoI, 1975–83. Indian Army, 1945–48; TA, 251st (Westmorland and Cumberland Yeo.) Field Regt RA, 1948–62; 2nd-in-Comd, 1959–62. Inst. of Chartered Accountants: Mem. Council, 1966–83; Vice-Pres., 1972–73; Dep. Pres., 1973–74; Pres., 1974–75. Master, Co. of Chartered Accountants in England and Wales, 1979–80. Mem., Governing Body, Shrewsbury Sch., 1976–. JP Carlisle, 1957–73. *Publications:* The Family Business and the Companies Act 1967, 1967; articles in professional accountancy press. *Recreations:* messing about in boats, DIY, gardening. *Address:* Tavern Rocks, 25 Lower Castle Road, St Mawes, Cornwall TR2 5DR. *Club:* United Oxford & Cambridge University.

SHARP, Leslie, QPM 1986; Chief Constable of Strathclyde Police, since 1991; *b* 14 May 1936; *s* of George James Sharp and Lily Mabel (*née* Moys); *m* 1st, 1956, Maureen (*née* Tyson) (decd); two *d*; 2nd, 1985, Audrey (*née* Sidwell); two *d*. *Educ:* University Coll. London (LLB). MRC, 1952–54; Nat. Service, Mddx Regt, 1954–56; Metropolitan Police, 1956–80; Asst Chief Constable, 1980–83, Dep. Chief Constable, 1983–88, W Midlands Police; Chief Constable, Cumbria Constab., 1988–91. FBIM 1986. *Recreations:* angling, cricket umpire, watercolour painting, gardening. *Address:* Police Headquarters, 173 Pitt Street, Glasgow G2 4JS.

SHARP, Michael Cartwright; *see* Sharp, J. M. C.

SHARP, Sir Milton Reginald, 3rd Bt, *cr* 1920; Capt. REME, TA; *b* 21 Nov. 1909; *s* of Sir Milton Sharp, 2nd Bt, and Gertrude (*d* 1940), *d* of John Earl, of London; *S* father, 1941; *m* 1951, Marie-Louise de Vignon, Paris. *Educ:* Shrewsbury; Trinity Hall, Cambridge.

SHARP, Hon. Mitchell William, OC 1983; PC (Can.) 1963; Policy Associate, Strategicon Inc., Ottawa, since 1988; *b* 11 May 1911; *s* of Thomas Sharp and Elizabeth (*née* Little); *m* 1938, Daisy Boyd (decd); one *s*; *m* 1976, Jeannette Dugal. *Educ:* University of Manitoba; London School of Economics. Statistician, Sanford Evans Statistical Service, 1926–36; Economist, James Richardson & Sons Ltd, 1937–42; Officer, Canadian Dept of

Finance, Ottawa, 1942–51; Director Economic Policy Division, 1947–51; Associate Deputy Minister, Canadian Dept Trade and Commerce, 1951–57; Dep. Minister, 1957–58; Minister, 1963–65; elected to Canadian House of Commons, 1963; Minister of Finance, 1965–68; Sec. of State for External Affairs, 1968–74; Pres., Privy Council, 1974–76; Govt Leader in House of Commons, 1974–76; resigned from Parliament, 1978. Comr, Northern Pipeline Agency, 1978–88. Vice-Pres., Brazilian Traction, Light & Power Co., Toronto, 1958–62. Hon. LLD: Univ. of Manitoba, 1965; Univ. of Western Ontario, 1977; Hon. DrSocSci Ottawa, 1970. *Recreations:* music, walking, skating. *Address:* 33 Monkland Avenue, Ottawa, Ontario K1S 1Y8, Canada. *T:* (613) 238–8668.

SHARP, Sir Richard (Lyall), KCVO 1982; CB 1977; Ceremonial Officer, Management and Personnel Office (formerly Civil Service Department), 1977–82; *b* 27 March 1915; *s* of late Alexander Sharp, Advocate, Aberdeen, and late Mrs Isabella Sharp, OBE; *m* 1950, Jean Helen, *er d* of late Sir James Crombie, KCB, KBE, CMG; two *s* two *d* (and one *d* decd). *Educ:* Fettes Coll.; Aberdeen Univ.; Clare Coll., Cambridge. MA with 1st Class Hons Classics, Aberdeen 1937; BA with 1st Class in Classical Tripos pt II, Cambridge 1939. Served Royal Northumberland Fusiliers, 1939–46 (POW, Singapore and Siam, 1942–45). Principal, HM Treasury, 1946; Private Sec. to Chancellor of Exchequer, 1948–50 and to Minister of State for Economic Affairs, 1950; UK Treasury and Supply Delegn, Washington, 1952–56; Asst Sec., 1954; IDC, 1961; Under-Secretary: Nat. Bd for Prices and Incomes, 1966–68; HM Treasury, 1968–77. *Recreations:* playing the viola, viticulture, gardening. *Address:* Home Farm House, Briston, Melton Constable, Norfolk NR24 2HN. *T:* Melton Constable (0263) 860445.

See also Baron Mackie of Benshie, A. G. Sharp.

SHARP, Robert Charles, CMG 1971; Director of Public Works, Tasmania, 1949–71; *b* 20 Sept. 1907; *s* of Robert George Sharp and Gertrude Coral (*née* Bellette); *m* 1st, 1935, Margaret Fairbrass Andrewartha (*d* 1975); one *d*; 2nd, 1978, Marie, widow of Alan C. Wharton, St Albans, Herts. *Educ:* Univ. of Tasmania. BE 1929. Bridge Engr, Public Works, 1935. Enlisted RAE (Major): comd 2/4 Aust. Field Sqdn RAE, 1942; 1 Aust. Port Mtce Co. RAE, 1943; HQ Docks Ops Gp, 1944. Chief Engr, Public Works, 1946; State Co-ordinator of Works, 1949–71. *Address:* The Coach House, Wickwood Court, Sandpit Lane, St Albans, Herts AL1 4BP; 594 Sandy Bay Road, Hobart, Tasmania 7005, Australia. *Club:* Athenæum.

SHARP, Thomas, (Tom), CBE 1987; retired; General Manager, Names' Interests, Lloyd's of London, 1987–91; *b* 19 June 1931; *s* of late William Douglas Sharp and Margaret Sharp (*née* Tout); *m* 1962, Margaret Lucy Hailstone; two *d*. *Educ:* Brown Sch., Toronto; Abbotsholme Sch., Derbs; Jesus Coll., Oxford. BoT and DTI (with short interval HM Treasury), 1954–73; Counsellor (Commercial), British Embassy, Washington, 1973–76; Dept of Trade, 1976–79; Dept of Industry, 1979–83; DTI, 1983–87. Member (Lib Dem): Surrey CC, 1989–; Guildford BC, 1991–. *Address:* 96 London Road, Guildford, Surrey GU1 1TH. *T:* Guildford (0483) 572669.

SHARP, Sir (William Harold) Angus, KBE 1974; QPM 1969; *b* Auckland, 1915. *Educ:* Cathedral Grammar School, Christchurch. Graduated Imperial Defence College, 1966. Joined New Zealand Police Force, 1937; Commissioner of Police, 1970; retd NZ Police, 1975; Commissioner, Police and Prisons Dept, Western Samoa, 1977–78. *Address:* Rural Delivery 4, Rotorua, New Zealand.

SHARP, William Johnstone, CB 1983; Controller and Chief Executive, Her Majesty's Stationery Office and Queen's Printer of Acts of Parliament, 1981–86; *b* 30 May 1926; *s* of Frederick Matthew and Gladys Evelyn Sharp; *m* 1952, Joan Alice Clark, MBE, *d* of Arnold and Violet Clark. *Educ:* Queen Elizabeth Grammar Sch., Hexham; Emmanuel Coll., Cambridge (MA). Army Service, Reconnaissance Corps, Durham LI and Staff, 1944–48. Entered Min. of Transport, 1949; Private Sec. to Perm. Sec., 1951–53; Principal, Min. of Civil Aviation, 1953; Asst Sec., Min. of Transport, 1962; Under-Sec., DoE, 1970; Controller of Supplies, PSA, 1976–80. FRSA 1984. Hon. Life Member: Nat. State Printing Assoc. (USA), 1987; Internat. Govt Printers Assoc., 1988. *Recreation:* the Turf. *Address:* 43 Friars Quay, Norwich NR3 1ES. *T:* Norwich (0603) 624258.

SHARPE, Brian Sidney; Consultant, financial and marketing presentation, since 1985; *b* 12 Feb. 1927; *s* of S. H. Sharpe and Norah Sharpe; *m* 1967, Susan Lillywhite; two *s*. *Educ:* Haberdashers' Aske's Sch., Hampstead; Guildhall Sch. of Music and Drama. Royal Fusiliers (att. Forces Broadcasting Service), 1945–48; BBC: Announcer, Midland Region, 1955; Television Presentation, 1956; Producer, African Service, External Services, 1957; Senior Producer: Overseas Talks and Features, 1965; The Financial World Tonight, Radio 4, 1974; Money Programme, Sept-Dec. 1979; on secondment as Exec. Dir, City Communications Centre, 1976–79; Director: Charles Barker Lyons, 1980–85; Charles Barker City, 1983–85. Town Councillor (Soc & Lib Dem), Godalming, 1986–; Bor. Councillor (Soc & Lib Dem), Waverley, 1987–. *Publications:* How Money Works (with A. Wilson), 1975; several articles on corporate and other forms of communication. *Recreations:* offshore fishing, music. *Address:* 26 Hallam Road, Godalming, Surrey GU7 3HW. *T:* Godalming (04868) 21551.

SHARPE, David Thomas, OBE 1986; FRCS; Consultant Plastic Surgeon, St Luke's Hospital, Bradford, Bradford Royal Infirmary, Royal Halifax Infirmary and Huddersfield Royal Infirmary, since 1985; Visiting Consultant Plastic Surgeon, Yorkshire Clinic, Bradford, BUPA Hospital, Elland, West Yorkshire, Cromwell Hospital, London, since 1985; Director, Plastic Surgery and Burns Research Unit, University of Bradford, since 1986; Chairman and Managing Director, Plastech Research and Design Ltd, since 1984; *b* 14 Jan. 1946; *s* of Albert Edward Sharpe and Grace Emily Sharpe; *m* 1971, Patricia Lilian Meredith; one *s* two *d*. *Educ:* Grammar School for Boys, Gravesend; Downing Coll., Cambridge (MA); Clin. Med. Sch., Oxford (MB BChir); FRCS 1975. Ho. Surg., Radcliffe Inf., Oxford, 1970–71; Senior House Officer: Plastic Surgery, Churchill Hosp., Oxford, 1971–72; Accident Service, Radcliffe Inf., 1972; Pathology, Radcliffe Inf., 1972–73; Gen. Surgery, Royal United Hosp., Bath, 1973–75; Plastic Surgery, Welsh Plastic Surgery Unit, Chepstow, 1976; Registrar, Plastic Surgery: Chepstow, 1976–78; Canniesburn Hosp., Glasgow, 1978–80; Sen. Registrar, Plastic Surgery, Leeds and Bradford, 1980–84. Inventor and designer of med. equipment and surgical instruments and devices; exhibitor, Design Council, London, 1987. British Design Award, 1988; Prince of Wales Award for Innovation and Production, 1988. *Publications:* chapters, leading articles and papers on plastic surgery topics, major burn disaster management, tissue expansion and breast reconstruction. *Recreations:* painting, shooting, riding. *Address:* Hazelbrae, Calverley, Leeds LS28 5QQ. *T:* Leeds (0532) 570027.

SHARPE, Hon. Sir John (Henry), Kt 1977; CBE 1972; JP; MP for Warwick West, Bermuda, since 1963; *b* 8 Nov. 1921; *s* of Harry Sharpe; *m* 1948, Eileen Margaret, *d* of George Morrow, BC, Canada; one *s* one *d*. *Educ:* Warwick Acad., Warwick, Bermuda; Mount Allison Commercial Coll., Sackville, New Brunswick. Served War of 1939–45: Pilot Officer, with Bomber Comd, NW Europe, RCAF, attached RAF. Chm., Purvis Ltd (Importers), Bermuda. MHA for Warwick, Bermuda, 1963–; Minister of Finance, 1968–75; Dep. Leader of Govt, 1971–75; Premier of Bermuda, 1975–77, resigned; Minister: of Transport, May-Dec. 1980; of Marine and Air Services, 1980–82; of Home Affairs, 1982–88; of Legislative and Delegated Affairs, 1988–90, and of Labour; of Labour and Home Affairs, and of Delegated and Legislative Affairs, 1990–. Formerly Member several Parliamentary Select Cttees, and of Bd of Educn, Bermuda; also Dep. Chm., Central Planning Authority and Defence Bd. Delegate to Constitutional Conf., London, 1966. Mem., War Veterans Assoc., Bermuda; Warden, Anglican Church. *Address:* Uplands, Harbour Road, Warwick West, Bermuda.

SHARPE, John Herbert S.; *see* Subak-Sharpe.

SHARPE, Sir Reginald (Taaffe), Kt 1947; QC; *b* 20 November 1898; *o s* of late Herbert Sharpe, Lindfield, Sussex; *m* 1st, 1922, Phyllis Maude (marr. diss. 1929), *d* of late Major Edward Whinney, Haywards Heath, Sussex; one *d* (and one *d* decd); 2nd, 1930, Eileen Kate (*d* 1946), *d* of Thomas Howarth Usherwood, Christ's Hospital, Sussex; 3rd, 1947, Vivien Travers (*d* 1971), *d* of late Rev. Herbert Seddon Rowley, Wretham, Norfolk; 4th, 1976, Mary Millicent, *d* of late Maj.-Gen. Patrick Barclay Sangster, CB, CMG, DSO, Roehampton. *Educ:* Westminster School. Served European War: enlisted in Army, 1916; 2nd Lieut Grenadier Guards (SR), Jan. 1917; Lt, 1918; served with 2nd Bn in France (wounded). Called to Bar at Gray's Inn, Easter, 1920. Went South-Eastern Circuit and Sussex Sessions. Judge of High Court, Rangoon, 1937–48; Director of Supply, Burma (at Calcutta), 1942–44; Trustee of Rangoon University Endowment Fund, 1946–48; KC Feb. 1949; HM Comr of Assize: Western and Northern Circuits, 1949; Midland and Western Circuits, 1950; South-Eastern Circuit, 1952; North-Eastern Circuit, 1954; Birmingham October Assize, 1954; Midland Circuit, 1960. Special Comr for Divorce Causes, 1948–67. Chm., Nat. Health Service Tribunal for England and Wales, 1948–71. Deputy Chairman QS: E Sussex, 1949–69; W Kent, 1949–62; Kent, 1962–69; Mddx, 1963–65 (Asst Chm. 1951–63); Mddx area of Greater London, 1965–71; Asst Chm., W Sussex QS, 1950–70; Dep. Chm., Hailsham Petty Sessional Div., 1950–57 and 1959–70 (Chm., 1957–58). Mem. Standing Jt Cttee for E Sussex, 1958–65, for W Sussex, 1953–65. Mem., Nat. Arbitration Tribunal, 1951, and of Industrial Disputes Tribunal, 1951; Chairman, 1951–54, of Joint Council, and Independent Chairman, 1955–57, of Conciliation Board set up by Assoc. of Health and Pleasure Resorts and the Musicians' Union; Sole Commissioner to hold British Honduras Inquiry at Belize, March 1954; Chm., Departmental Cttee on Summary Trial of Minor Offences in Magistrates' Courts, 1954–55. Mem., Governing Body, Westminster Sch., 1955–83. JP East Sussex. *Address:* The Old Post Office, Rushlake Green, Sussex TN21 9QL. *T:* Rushlake Green (0435) 830253.

SHARPE, Thomas Ridley; novelist; *b* 30 March 1928; *s* of Rev. George Coverdale Sharpe and Grace Egerton Sharpe; *m* 1969, Nancy Anne Looper; three *d*. *Educ:* Lancing College; Pembroke Coll., Cambridge (MA). National service, Royal Marines, 1946–48. Social worker 1952, teacher 1952–56, photographer 1956–61, in S Africa; Lecturer in History, Cambridge Coll. of Arts and Technology, 1963–71; full time novelist, 1971–. *Publications:* Riotous Assembly, 1971; Indecent Exposure, 1973; Porterhouse Blue, 1974 (televised, 1987); Blott on the Landscape, 1975 (televised, 1985); Wilt, 1976 (filmed, 1989); The Great Pursuit, 1977; The Throwback, 1978; The Wilt Alternative, 1979; Ancestral Vices, 1980; Vintage Stuff, 1982; Wilt on High, 1984. *Recreations:* gardening, photography. *Address:* 38 Tunwells Lane, Great Shelford, Cambridge CB2 5LJ.

SHARPE, William, OBE 1967; HM Diplomatic Service, retired; Overseas Relations Adviser, Potato Marketing Board, 1979–89; *b* 9 Dec. 1923; *s* of late William Joseph Sharpe and of Phoebe Irene (*née* Standen); *m* 1959, Marie-Antoinette Rodesch; one *s*. *Educ:* High Sch., Chichester; London Univ. BA (Hons), MA, BSc Econ (Hons). Served RAF, 1943–47. Joined Foreign (subseq. Diplomatic) Service, 1947; Foreign Office 1947–52; Cologne and Bonn, 1952–54; Leopoldville, 1954–57; UK Mission to UN, New York, 1957–61; Foreign Office, 1961–66; Milan, 1966–70; FCO, 1971–72; Kuwait, 1972–75; Consul-Gen., Berlin, 1975–78. *Recreations:* reading, music, walking. *Address:* 15 Regis Avenue, Aldwick Bay, Bognor Regis, Sussex PO21 4HQ.

SHARPE, William Forsyth; President, William F. Sharpe Associates, since 1986; Timken Professor of Finance, Stanford University, 1970–89, now Professor Emeritus; *b* 16 June 1934; *s* of Russell Thornley Sharpe and Evelyn Jillson Maloy; *m* 1st, 1954, Roberta Ruth Brandon; one *s* one *d*; 2nd, 1986, Kathryn Peck. *Educ:* UCLA (AB 1955; MA 1956; PhD 1961). Economist, Rand Corp., 1957–61; University of Washington: Asst Prof. of Economics, 1961–63; Associate Prof., 1963–67; Prof., 1967–68; Prof., Univ. of California, Irvine, 1968–70. Graham and Dodd Award, 1972, 1973, 1986, 1988; Nicholas Molodovsky Award, 1989; (jtly) Nobel Prize in Economics, 1990. *Publications:* Economics of Computers, 1969; Portfolio Theory and Capital Markets, 1970; Investments, 1978, 4th edn 1989; Fundamentals of Investments, 1989. *Recreations:* sailing, opera, music. *Address:* (office) 95 First Street, Suite 215, Los Altos, Calif 94022, USA. *T:* (415) 941–3990.

SHARPE, William James, CBE 1967 (OBE 1950); Director of Communications, Foreign and Commonwealth Office (formerly Foreign Office), 1965–69, retired; *b* 3 Jan. 1908; *s* of James Sharpe; *m* 1940, Doreen Winifred Cockell; three *s*. *Educ:* Aldershot Grammar School. 1927–39: Merchant Navy; Marconi International; Marine Communications Company. Commissioned Royal Corps of Signals, 1940; Served in France and South East Asia; Lt-Col 1945. Diplomatic Wireless Service, 1947; Deputy Director of Communications, 1959. *Address:* The Mount, Tingewick, Buckingham MK18 4QN. *T:* Finmere (0280) 848291.

SHARPLES, family name of **Baroness Sharples.**

SHARPLES, Baroness *cr* 1973 (Life Peer); **Pamela Sharples;** Director, TVS, 1981–90 and since 1991; *b* 11 Feb. 1923; *o d* of late Lt-Comdr K. W. Newall and of Violet (who *m* 2nd, Lord Claud Hamilton, GCVO, CMG, DSO); *m* 1st, 1946, Major R. C. Sharples, MC, Welsh Guards (later Sir Richard Sharples, KCMG, OBE, MC, assassinated 1973); two *s* two *d*; 2nd, 1977, Patrick D. de Laszlo (*d* 1980); 3rd, 1983, Robert Douglas Swan. *Educ:* Southover Manor, Lewes; Florence. WAAF, 1941–46. Mem., Review Body on Armed Forces Pay, 1979–81. *Recreations:* sailing, fishing, tennis, golf. *Address:* 60 Westminster Gardens, SW1P 4JG. *T:* 071–821 1875; Nunswell, Higher Coombe, Shaftesbury, Dorset SP7 9LR. *T:* Shaftesbury (0747) 52971.

SHARPLES, Florence Elizabeth; Executive Director, Young Women's Christian Association of Great Britain, since 1987 (National General Secretary, 1978–87); *b* 27 May 1931; *d* of late Flying Officer Albert Sharples, RAFVR, and Kathleen (*née* Evans). *Educ:* Alice Ottley Sch., Worcester; Homerton Coll., Cambridge (Teachers' Cert.); King's Coll., London (Cert. Prof. in Religious Knowledge). Head of Religious Education: Bruton Sch. for Girls, Somerset, 1953–57; Loughton High Sch., Essex, 1957–60; Housemistress, Headington Sch., Oxford, 1960–66; Headmistress, Ancaster House, Bexhill, Sussex, 1966–78. Former Mem., New Philharmonia Chorus. *Recreation:* the theatre.

SHARPLEY, Ven. Roger Ernest Dion; Archdeacon of Hackney and Vicar of Guild Church of St Andrew, Holborn, since 1981; *b* 19 Dec. 1928; *s* of Frederick Charles and Doris Irene Sharpley; unmarried. *Educ:* Dulwich College; Christ Church, Oxford (MA); St Stephen's House, Oxford. Deacon, 1954; Priest, 1955; Curate of St Columba,

Southwick, 1954–60; Vicar of All Saints', Middlesbrough, 1960–81; Curate-in-charge, St Hilda with St Peter, Middlesbrough, 1964–72; RD of Middlesbrough, 1970–81; Canon and Prebendary of York Minster, 1974–81; Priest-in-charge, St Aidan, Middlesbrough, 1979–81. *Recreations:* hill and country walking. *Address:* St Andrew's Vicarage, 5 St Andrew Street, EC4A 3AB. *T:* 071–353 3544.

SHATTOCK, David John, QPM 1985; Chief Constable, Avon and Somerset Constabulary, since 1989; *b* 25 Jan. 1936; *s* of Herbert John Shattock and Lucy Margaret Shattock; *m* 1973, Freda Thums; three *s*. *Educ:* Sir Richard Huish's Sch., Taunton. Joined as Constable, final post Asst Chief Constable, Somerset and Bath, later Avon and Somerset Constabulary, 1956–82; Deputy Chief Constable: Wilts Constab., 1983–85; Dyfed-Powys Police, 1985–86; Chief Constable, Dyfed-Powys Police, 1986–89. OStJ 1989. *Recreations:* racket sports, particularly badminton, antique restoration, keeping fit, horse riding. *Address:* PO Box 188, Bristol BS99 7BH. *T:* Bristol (0272) 277777. *Club:* Bristol Shakespeare (Bristol).

SHATTOCK, Sir Gordon, Kt 1985; Vice-Chairman, Veterinary Drug Co. PLC, since 1990 (Director, since 1982); Divisional Bursar, Western Division, Woodard Schools, since 1988; *b* 12 May 1928; *s* of Frederick Thomas and Rose May Irene Shattock; *m* 1952, Jeanne Mary Watkins (*d* 1984); one *s* one *d*; *m* 1988, Mrs Wendy Sale. *Educ:* Hele's Sch., Exeter; Royal Veterinary Coll., London. MRCVS. Senior Partner, St David's Vet. Hosp., Exeter, 1954–84. Mem., Exeter HA, 1987–. Fellow of Woodard Corp., 1973–88; Executive Member: Animal Health Trust, 1978–; GBA, 1986–89; Mem. of Council, Guide Dogs for the Blind, 1985–; Chairman: Grenville Coll., 1982–88; Exeter Cathedral Music Foundn Trust, 1987–. FRSocMed 1987. Hon. Mem., BVA, 1989. Farriers' Company: Liveryman, 1978–; Mem. Ct of Assistants, 1986–; Upper Warden, 1991. *Publications:* contrib. to Jl Small Animal Practice; papers to British Veterinary Assoc. *Recreation:* gardening. *Address:* Glasshayes, Higher Shapter Street, Topsham, Exeter EX3 0AW.

SHATTOCK, John Swithun Harvey, CMG 1952; OBE 1946; HM Diplomatic Service, 1947–67; *b* 21 Nov. 1907; *s* of late Rev. E. A. Shattock, Kingston St Mary, Nr Taunton; unmarried. *Educ:* Westminster School; Christ Church, Oxford. Entered ICS, 1931; served in Bengal, 1931–36; Under Sec., Govt of India (Defence Dept), 1936–39; joined Indian Political Service, 1939; served in Kathiawar, Baroda, and Kashmir Residencies, 1939–44; Dep. Sec. to Crown Representative (Political Dept), New Delhi, 1944–46; Chief Minister, Chamba State, 1946–47; apptd HM Diplomatic Service, 1947; served in UK High Commission, New Delhi, 1947–49; Head of Far Eastern Dept, Foreign Office, London, 1950–51; Head of China and Korea Dept, FO 1951; FO Rep. at Imperial Defence Coll., London, 1952; Head of China and Korea Dept, FO, 1953; Counsellor, British Embassy, Belgrade, Dec. 1953–Nov. 1955; Political Representative, Middle East Forces, Cyprus, Jan. 1956–Nov. 1958. Deputy to UK Permanent Representative on North Atlantic Council, Paris, 1959–61; Minister, UK Delegation to Disarmament Conference, Geneva, 1961–63; FO, 1963–67. *Address:* St Mary's Cottage, Kingston St Mary, near Taunton, Somerset; Grindlay's Bank, 13 St James's Square, SW1. *Club:* Travellers'.

SHAUGHNESSY, family name of **Baron Shaughnessy.**

SHAUGHNESSY, 3rd Baron, *cr* 1916, of Montreal; **William Graham Shaughnessy,** CD 1955; Director: Arbor Capital Inc., Toronto, since 1972; Corona Corporation, Toronto, since 1987; *b* 28 March 1922; *s* of 2nd Baron and Marion (*d* 1936), *d* of late R. K. Graham, Montreal; *S* father, 1938; *m* 1944, Mary Whitley, *o d* of late John Whitley, Copthorne House, Letchworth; one *s* two *d* (and one *s* decd). *Educ:* Bishop's Coll. Sch. and Bishop's Univ., Lennoxville, Canada; BA 1941; MSc Columbia Univ., NY, 1947. Dir, Canada-UK Chamber of Commerce, 1981–; Trustee, The Last Post Fund Inc., Canada. Major (retd), Canadian Grenadier Guards; served NW Europe in World War II (despatches). *Heir:* *s* Hon. Michael James Shaughnessy, *b* 12 Nov. 1946. *Address:* 27 Melton Court, Old Brompton Road, SW7 3JQ. *Clubs:* Cavalry and Guards; University (Montreal).

SHAVE, Kenneth George, CEng, FIMechE; Member, London Transport Executive, 1967–73, retired; *b* 25 June 1908; *s* of George Shave and Frances Larkin; *m* 1935, Doris May Stone; one *s* one *d*. *Educ:* St Paul's School. Apprenticed London General Omnibus Company, 1925; Rolling Stock Engineer, East Surrey Traction Company, 1930; London Transport: Asst Divisional Engineer, 1935; Divisional Engineer, 1948; Rolling Stock Engineer, 1956; Chief Mechanical Engineer, 1965. CStJ 1971 (OStJ 1963). *Recreations:* golf, bridge, gardening. *Address:* 5 St Katherine's Road, Henley on Thames, Oxon RG9 1PJ. *T:* Henley (0491) 57 3379.

SHAW; *see* Byam Shaw.

SHAW, family name of **Baron Craigmyle.**

SHAW, Maj.-Gen. Anthony John, CB 1988; CBE 1985; Director General, Army Medical Services, 1988–90, retired; *b* 13 July 1930; *s* of late Lt Col W. A. Shaw, MC and Mrs E. Shaw (*née* Malley); *m* 1961, Gillian Shaw (*née* Best); one *s* one *d*. *Educ:* Epsom College; Clare College, Cambridge (MA; MB BChir); Westminster Hosp. MRCS; LRCP 1954; D(Obst)RCOG 1956; DTM&H 1961; FFCM 1983; FRCP 1989. Casualty Officer, Westminster Hosp.; House Surgeon and Obst. House Officer, Kingston Hosp., 1955–56; Commissioned Lieut RAMC, 1956; Staff College, 1963; served in UK, Malta, Berlin, BAOR, MoD, Malaya, Nepal, Penang, Cameron Highlands; CO Field Ambulance, 1969–70; Chief Instructor, RAMC Training Centre, 1970–72; Nat. Defence Coll., 1973; ADGMS, MoD, 1973–76; CO Cambridge Mil. Hosp., 1977–79; Comdr Med. 2 Armd Div., BAOR, 1979–81; Comdr Med. SE Dist., 1981; Dir of Med. Supply, MoD, 1981–83; DDGAMS, 1983–84; Dir, Army Community and Occupational Medicine, 1983–87; Comdr Medical Servs, UKLF, 1984–87. QHP 1983–90. Member: BMA; Board of Faculty of Community Medicine, 1983–87. FRSocMed. CStJ 1989. *Recreations:* sailing, skiing, gardening, music, military history. *Club:* Lansdowne.

SHAW, Sir Barry; *see* Shaw, Sir C. B.

SHAW, Prof. Bernard Leslie, FRS 1978; Professor of Chemistry, University of Leeds, since 1971; *b* Springhead, Yorks, 28 March 1930; *s* of Thomas Shaw and Vera Shaw (*née* Dale); *m* 1951, Mary Elizabeth Neild; two *s* (and one *s* decd). *Educ:* Hulme Grammar Sch., Oldham; Univ. of Manchester (BSc, PhD). Sen. DSIR Fellow, Torry Research Station, Aberdeen, 1953–55; Scientific Officer, CDEE, Porton, 1955–56; Technical Officer, ICI Ltd, Akers Research Labs, Welwyn, 1956–61; Lectr, Reader, and Prof., Univ. of Leeds, 1962–. Visiting Professor: Univ. of Western Ontario, 1969; Carnegie Mellon Univ., 1969; ANU, 1983; Univ. of Auckland, 1986; Liversidge Lectr, RSC, 1987–88. Member: Royal Soc. Cttees; Royal Chem. Soc. Cttees; SERC (formerly SRC) Chem. Cttee, 1975–78, 1981–84 (and Inorganic Panel, 1977–78, Co-operative Grants Panel, 1982–84); Tilden Lectr and Prizewinner, 1975; Chem. Soc. Medal and Prize for Transition Metal Chem., 1975. *Publications:* Transition Metal Hydrides, 1967; (with N. Tucker) Organotransition Metal Chemistry, and Related Aspects of Homogeneous Catalysis, 1973; numerous original papers and reviews in chem. jls. *Recreations:* squash, tennis, pottery, music, walking, gardening. *Address:* School of Chemistry, The University of Leeds, Leeds LS2 9JT. *T:* Leeds (0532) 336401.

SHAW, Sir Brian (Piers), Kt 1986; Chairman, ANZ Grindlays Bank plc, since 1987; Director, Enterprise Oil plc, since 1986; Chairman, River Committee, Port of London Authority, since 1991 (Member of the Authority, since 1987); Treasurer, Automobile Association, since 1990 (Committee Member, since 1988); *b* 21 March 1933; *s* of late Percy Augustus Shaw and late Olive Shaw (*née* Hart); *m* 1962, Penelope Reece; three *s*. *Educ:* Wrekin Coll.; Corpus Christi Coll., Cambridge (MA). National Service (2nd Lieut, Cheshire Regt), 1951–53. Called to Bar, Gray's Inn, 1957. Joined Pacific Steam Navigation Co., Liverpool, 1957; Company Secretary, 1960; Company Sec., Royal Mail Lines, London, 1961; Dir, Royal Mail Lines, 1968; Furness Withy & Co.: Manager, 1969; Dir, 1973; Man. Dir, 1977–87; Chm., 1979–90; Chm., Shaw Savill & Albion Co., 1973; Director: Overseas Containers Ltd, 1972–80; Nat. Bank of NZ, 1973–77 (London Board, 1977–80; Chm., London Adv. Cttee, 1980–84); New Zealand Line, 1974–79; Grindlays Bank, 1977–85; Orient Overseas (Holdings), 1980–91; ANZ Holdings (UK), 1985–87; Walter Runciman, 1988–90. Mem., Gen. Cttee, Lloyd's Register of Shipping, 1974–; Chairman: Internat Chamber of Shipping, 1987–; Council of European and Japanese Nat. Shipowners' Assocs (CENSA), 1979–84; Pres., Gen. Council of British Shipping, 1985–86. Pres., New Zealand Soc., 1979–80. Second Warden, Shipwrights' Co., 1991–92; Elder Brother, Trinity House, 1989–. *Recreations:* golf, music, theatre. *Address:* 42 Norland Square, W11 4PZ. *T:* 071–221 4066. *Clubs:* Brooks's, MCC; Denham Golf.

SHAW, Sir (Charles) Barry, Kt 1980; CB 1974; QC 1964; DL; Director of Public Prosecutions for Northern Ireland, 1972–89; *b* 12 April 1923; *s* of late Ernest Hunter Shaw and Sarah Gertrude Shaw, Mayfield, Balmoral, Belfast; *m* 1964, Jane (*née* Phillips). *Educ:* Inchmarlo House, Belfast; Pannal Ash Coll., Harrogate; The Queen's Univ. of Belfast (LLB). Served War: commissioned RA, 97 A/Tk Regt RA, 15th (Scottish) Div., 1942–46. Called to Bar of Northern Ireland, 1948, Bencher 1968; called to Bar, Middle Temple, 1970, Hon. Bencher, 1986. DL Co. Down, 1990. *Address:* c/o Royal Courts of Justice, Belfast, Northern Ireland BT1 3NX.

SHAW, Prof. C(harles) Thurstan, CBE 1972; FBA 1991; Professor of Archaeology, University of Ibadan, 1963–74; *b* 27 June 1914; 2nd *s* of late Rev. John Herbert Shaw and Grace Irene (*née* Woollatt); *m* Gilian Ione Maud, *e d* of late Edward John Penberthy Magor and Gilian Sarah (*née* Westmacott); two *s* three *d*. *Educ:* Blundell's Sch.; Sidney Sussex Coll., Cambridge; Univ. of London Inst. of Education. 1st cl. hons Arch. and Anthrop. Tripos 1936, MA, PhD Cantab; DipEd London. FRAI 1938; FSA 1947. Curator, Anthropology Museum, Achimota Coll., Gold Coast, 1937–45; Cambs Educn Cttee, 1945–51; Cambridge Inst. of Educn, 1951–63; Dir of Studies, Archaeol. and Anthrop., Magdalene Coll., Cambridge, 1976–79. Vis. Fellow, Clare Hall, Cambridge, 1973; Vis. Prof., Northwestern Univ., USA, 1969; Vis. Res. Prof., Ahmadu Bello Univ., 1975–78; Visiting Lecturer: Harvard, 1975; Yale, 1979; Calgary, 1980; Hans Wolff Meml Lectr, Indiana Univ., 1984. Founder and Editor: W African Archaeological Newsletter, 1964–70; W African Jl of Archaeology, 1971–75. Mem. Perm. Council, Internat. Union of Pre- and Proto-historic Sciences, 1965–74; Vice-Pres., Panafrican Congress on Prehistory and Study of Quaternary, 1966–77; Dir, and Mem. Exec. Cttee, World Archaeol Congress, 1986–89. Founder, and Chm., Icknield Way Assoc., 1984–89, Pres., 1989–; Pres., Prehistoric Soc., 1986–90. Mem. Council, Univ. of Ibadan, 1969–71. Hon. DSc: Univ. of Nigeria, 1982; Ibadan, 1989. Amaury Talbot Prize, Royal Anthrop. Inst., 1970 and 1978; Gold Medal, Soc. of Antiquaries, 1990. Onuna-Ekwulu Ora of Igbo-Ukwu, 1972; Onyofuonka of Igboland, 1989; Onuna Ekwulu Nri, 1989. *Publications:* Excavation at Dawu, 1961; Archaeology and Nigeria, 1964; (with J. Vanderburg) Bibliography of Nigerian Archaeology, 1969; (ed) Nigerian Prehistory and Archaeology, 1969; Igbo-Ukwu: an account of archaeological discoveries in eastern Nigeria, 2 vols, 1970; Discovering Nigeria's Past, 1975; Why 'Darkest' Africa?, 1975; Unearthing Igbo-Ukwu, 1977; Ancient People and Places: Nigeria, 1978; (with S. G. H. Daniels) Excavations at Iwo Eleru, Ondo State, Nigeria, 1988; (with K. D. Aiyedun) Prehistoric Settlement and Subsistence in the Kaduna Valley, Nigeria, 1989; numerous articles on African archaeology and prehistory in jls. *Recreations:* walking, music. *Address:* Silver Ley, 37 Hawthorne Road, Stapleford, Cambridge CB2 5DU. *T:* Cambridge (0223) 842283. *Clubs:* Athenæum; Explorers' (New York).

SHAW, Prof. Charles Timothy, CEng; Professor of Mining, since 1980, and Dean, since 1991, Royal School of Mines (Head of Department of Mineral Resources Engineering, 1980–85); *b* 4 Oct. 1934; *s* of Charles John and Constance Olive Shaw (*née* Scotton); *m* 1962, Tuulike Raili Linari-Linholm; one *s* two *d*. *Educ:* Univ. of Witwatersrand (BSc(Mining) 1956); McGill Univ. (MSc(Applied) (Mineral Exploration) 1959). Mine Manager's, Mine Overseer's and Mine Surveyor's Certs of SA; Chartered Engineer. Johannesburg Consolidated Investment Co. Ltd (JCI): numerous positions at various levels, 1960–67; Head of Computer Div., 1967–70; Manager, 1970–72 (as such an appointed dir of 14 cos incl. Consolidated Murchison Ltd and Alternate Dir of 9 cos); Consulting Engr, Consolidated Murchison Ltd, Randfontein Estates Gold Mining Co. (Wits.) Ltd and Shangani Mining Corp. (Zimbabwe), 1972–74; Consulting Engr and Alternate Dir, Rustenburg Platinum Mines Ltd, 1974–76; Chief Consulting Engr and Alternate Dir, Johannesburg Consolidated Investment Co. Ltd, also Man. Dir, Western Areas Gold Mining Co. Ltd, 1976–77; Associate Prof., Virginia Polytechnic Inst. and State Univ., 1977–80. Rep. for JCI on Technical Adv. Cttee of SA Chamber of Mines, 1974–77; Alternate Mem. for Gold Producers Cttee, 1976–77. Member Council: InstnMM, 1981–88; IMinE, 1989– (Pres., S Counties Br., 1988–89). *Publications:* (with J. R. Lucas) The Coal Industry: Industry Guides for Accountants, Auditors and Financial Executives, 1980; papers both in technical literature and in house at Johannesburg Consolidated Investment Co. Ltd. *Recreations:* golf, mining history. *Address:* Department of Mineral Resources Engineering, Royal School of Mines, SW7 2BP. *T:* 071–589 5111.

SHAW, Colin Don; writer and lecturer; Director, Broadcasting Standards Council, since 1988; *b* 2 Nov. 1928; *s* of late Rupert M. Shaw and Enid F. Shaw (*née* Smith); *m* 1955, Elizabeth Ann, *d* of late Paul Bowker; one *s* two *d*. *Educ:* Liverpool Coll.; St Peter's Hall, Oxford (MA). Called to the Bar, Inner Temple, 1960. Nat. Service, RAF, 1947–49. Joined BBC as Radio Drama Producer, North Region, 1953; Asst, BBC Secretariat, 1957–59; Asst Head of Programme Contracts Dept, 1959–60; Sen. Asst, BBC Secretariat, 1960–63; special duties in connection with recruitment for BBC2, 1963; Asst Head of Programmes, BBC North Region, 1963–66; various posts in TV Programme Planning, ending as Head of Group, 1966–69; Secretary to the BBC, 1969–72, Chief Secretary, 1972–76; Dir of Television, IBA, 1977–83; Dir, Programme Planning Secretariat, ITCA, 1983–87. Vis. Fellow, Europ. Inst. for the Media, Manchester, 1985–; Vis. Lectr, Annenberg Sch. of Communications, Univ. of Pa, 1988. Member: Arts Council of GB, 1978–80 (Chairman: Arts Council Research Adv. Gp, 1978–80; Housing the Arts Cttee, 1979–80; Touring Cttee, 1980); Home Office Working Party on Fear of Crime, 1990. Trustee, Internat. Inst. of Communications, 1983–89; Governor, E-SU of the Commonwealth, 1976–83; Chm., Bd of Governors, Hampden House Sch., 1972–77. FRTS 1987; FRSA 1978. *Publications:* several radio plays and a stage-play for children. *Recreations:* going to the theatre, reading.

Address: Lesters, Little Ickford, Aylesbury, Bucks HP18 9HS. *T:* Ickford (08447) 339225.*Club:* Reform.

SHAW, David; Director, Independent Television Association (formerly General Secretary, Independent Television Companies Association), since 1981; *b* 19 Oct. 1936; *s* of Thomas Young Boyd Shaw and Elizabeth Shaw; *m* 1961, Margaret Esmé Bagnall; one *s* one *d*. *Educ:* Univ. of Birmingham (BA (Hons) Geography); Univ. of Sussex (Adv. Dip. Educnl Technology). Education Officer in Royal Air Force, final rank Sqdn Ldr, 1960–76; Training Adviser to North Western Provincial Councils, 1976–78; Gen. Sec., British Amateur Athletic Bd, 1978–81. Represented Great Britain in Athletics (3000 metres steeplechase), 1958; British Universities Cross-Country Champion, 1959. *Recreations:* reading, hill-climbing, sketching. *Address:* (business) Independent Television Association, 56 Mortimer Street, W1N 8AN. *Club:* Royal Air Force.

SHAW, Prof. David Aitken, CBE 1989; FRCP, FRCPE; Professor of Clinical Neurology, University of Newcastle upon Tyne, 1976–89, now Emeritus; *b* 11 April 1924; *s* of John James McIntosh Shaw and Mina Draper; *m* 1960, Jill Parry; one *s* two *d*. *Educ:* Edinburgh Academy; Edinburgh Univ. MB ChB (Edin) 1951; FRCPE 1968; FRCP (Lond.) 1976. Served as Lieut RNVR, 1943–46. Hospital appts, Edinburgh Royal Infirmary, 1951–57; Lectr, Inst. of Neurology, Univ. of London, 1957–64; Mayo Foundation Fellow, 1962–63; University of Newcastle upon Tyne: Sen. Lectr, 1964–76; Public Orator, 1976–79; Dean of Medicine, 1981–89. Mem., GMC, 1979–. Hon. FCST. *Publications:* (with N. E. F. Cartlidge) Head Injury, 1981; chapters in books and scientific articles in medical jls. *Recreations:* golf and fishing. *Address:* The Coach House, 82 Moor Road North, Newcastle upon Tyne NE3 1AB. *T:* Newcastle upon Tyne (091) 2852029. *Club:* Athenæum.

SHAW, David Lawrence; MP (C) Dover, since 1987; chartered accountant; Founder and Managing Director, Sabrelance Ltd; *b* 14 Nov. 1950; *m* 1986, Dr Lesley Brown; one *s*. *Educ:* King's Sch., Wimbledon; City of London Polytechnic. FCA 1974. Coopers & Lybrand, 1971–79; County Bank, 1979–83. Director: Invicta Sound PLC; The Adscene Group PLC; Palladian Estates PLC. Mem., Royal Borough of Kingston upon Thames Council, 1974–78. Contested (C) Leigh, 1979. Chm., Bow Gp, 1983–84 (Founder, Transatlantic Conf., 1982); Jt Chm., All Party Cttee on Dolphins, 1989–; Mem., Social Security Cttee, 1991–; Vice Chm., Cons. Backbench Smaller Businesses Cttee; Sec., Cons. Backbench Finance Cttee. Vice-Chm., Kingston and Malden Cons. Assoc., 1979–86. *Address:* House of Commons, SW1A 0AA.

SHAW, Maj.-Gen. Dennis, CB 1991; CBE 1983 (OBE 1978); FIMechE; Director General Electrical and Mechanical Engineering (Army), 1988–91; *b* 11 May 1936; *s* of Nathan Shaw and Frances Ellen (*née* Cookson); *m* 1955, Barbara Tate; two *d*. *Educ:* Humberstone Foundn Sch.; Scunthorpe Grammar Sch.; Royal Military Coll. of Science. BScEng 1st Cl. Hons, London. Commd into REME, 1956; served in Cyprus, 1957–58, and with 3 Commando Bde, Far East, 1963–66; sc Shrivenham and Camberley, 1967–68; Staff of High Commn, Ottawa, 1969–70; comd 1 Corps Troops Workshop, W Germany, 1971–72; Dep. Asst Adjt Gen., MoD, 1972–74; NDC Latimer, 1974–75; comd Commando Logistic Regt, RM, 1975–78; Instr, Ghana Armed Forces Staff Coll., Accra, 1978–80; ACOS in Comd HQ, 1981–83; served Logistic Executive (Army), 1983; RCDS 1984; ACOS, HQ UKLF, 1985–87. Col Comdt, REME, 1991–. Director: Brown Shaw Assocs Ltd; Promotit Ltd; Fairway Europe Ltd; Mike Bennett Travel Ltd. Liveryman, Turners' Co., 1990. Freeman, City of London, 1990. *Recreations:* golf, motoring. *Address:* c/o Royal Bank of Scotland, Laurie House, Victoria Road, Farnborough, Hants GU14 7NR. *Club:* Army and Navy.

SHAW, Dr Dennis Frederick, CBE 1974; Fellow of Keble College, since 1957, Professorial Fellow, 1978; Keeper of Scientific Books, Bodleian Library, Oxford, 1975–91; *b* 20 April 1924; 2nd *s* of Albert Shaw and Lily (*née* Hill), Teddington; *m* 1949, Joan Irene, *er d* of Sidney and Maud Chandler; one *s* three *d*. *Educ:* Harrow County Sch.; Christ Church, Oxford. BA 1945, MA 1950, DPhil 1950. FInstP 1971, CPhys; FZS. Jun. Sci. Officer, MAP, 1944–46; Res. Officer in Physics, Clarendon Lab., Oxford, 1950–57, Sen. Res. Officer 1957–64; Univ. Lectr in Physics, Oxford, 1964–75. Vis. Prof. of Physics and Brown Foundn Fellow, Univ. of the South, Tennessee, 1974. Pres., Internat. Assoc. of Technol Univ. Libraries, 1986–90 (Sec., 1983–85); Chm., Cttee for Sci. and Technol. Libys, IFLA, 1987– (Mem., 1985–87). Mem., Oxford City Council, 1963–67; Chm., Oxford City Civil Emergency Cttee, 1966–67; Member: Home Office Sci. Adv. Council, 1966–78; Home Defence Sci. Adv. Cttee, 1978–; Hebdomadal Council, 1980–89; Chairman: Oxford Univ. Delegacy for Educnl Studies, 1969–73; Home Office Police Equipment Cttee, 1969–70; Home Office Police Sci. Develt Cttee, 1971–74. Member: Amer. Phys. Soc., 1957; NY Acad. of Scis, 1981. Almoner, Christ's Hosp., 1980–. *Publications:* An Introduction to Electronics, 1962, 2nd edn 1970; A Review of Oxford University Science Libraries, 1977, 2nd edn 1981; (ed) Information Sources in Physics, 1985; papers in sci. jls. *Recreations:* riding, gardening, enjoying music. *Address:* Keble College, Oxford OX1 3PG. *T:* Oxford (0865) 272727. *Club:* United Oxford & Cambridge University.

SHAW, Rev. Douglas William David; Professor of Divinity, 1979–91, and Principal, St Mary's College, since 1986, University of St Andrews; *b* 25 June 1928; *s* of William David Shaw and Nansie Smart. *Educ:* Edinburgh Acad.; Loretto; Ashbury Coll., Ottawa; Univs of Cambridge and Edinburgh. MA (Cantab), BD (Edin.), LLB (Edin.). WS. Practised law as Partner of Davidson and Syme, WS, Edinburgh, 1953–57. Ordained Minister of Church of Scotland, 1960; Asst Minister, St George's West Church, Edinburgh, 1960–63; Official Observer of World Alliance of Reformed Churches at Second Vatican Council, Rome, 1962. University of Edinburgh: Dean, Faculty of Divinity, and Principal, New College, 1974–78; Lectr in Divinity, 1963–79; Dean, Faculty of Divinity, Univ. of St Andrews, 1983–86. Croall Lectr, New Coll., Edinburgh, 1983. *Publications:* Who is God? 1968, 2nd edn 1970; The Dissuaders, 1978; trans. from German: F. Heyer: The Catholic Church from 1648 to 1870, 1969; (ed) In Divers Manners—a St Mary's Miscellany, 1990; various articles in theological jls. *Recreations:* squash (Scottish Amateur Champion, 1950–51–52), golf. *Address:* St Mary's College, St Andrews, Fife. *T:* St Andrews (0334) 76161. *Clubs:* New (Edinburgh); Royal and Ancient (St Andrews); Luffness New; Edinburgh Sports.

SHAW, Very Rev. Duncan, JP; PhD; Minister of the parish of Craigentinny, Edinburgh, since 1959; *b* 27 Jan. 1925; *s* of Neil Shaw (Mac Gille Sheathanaich), master carpenter, and Mary Thompson Borthwick; *m* 1st, 1955, Ilse (*d* 1989), *d* of Robert Peiter and Luise Else Mattig, Dusseldorf; one *s* two *d*; 2nd, 1991, Prof. Anna-Libera Irma Domitilla, DrPhil, *d* of Prof. Luigi Dallapiccola and Dr Laura Coen Luggatto, Florence. *Educ:* Univ. of Edinburgh (PhD). Served REME, TA(WR), 1943–47 (Warrant Officer, cl. I 1946). Minister of parish of St Margaret, Edinburgh, 1951–59. Scottish Rep. of Aktion Zühnezeichen, Berlin, 1966–71; Chm. of Bd, St Andrew Press, 1967–74; Editorial Dir, Edina Press, Edinburgh, 1974–; Chm., IMS Trust and Instant Muscle (Scotland) plc, 1988–. Dir. Centre for Theological Exploration Inc. USA, 1989–. Trustee: Nat. Museum of Antiquities of Scotland, 1974–85; Edinburgh Old Town Charitable Trust, 1989–; Founder and Chm. of Council, Scottish Soc. for Reformation History, 1980–. University of Edinburgh: Sec. of Gen. Council, 1965–; Sen. Hume Brown Prizeman for Scottish History, 1965; Visiting Fellow, Inst. for Advanced Studies in the Humanities, 1975; part-time Lectr in Theological German, Faculty of Divinity, 1975–81; Sec., Gen. Council Trust, 1982–90; Dr *hc* 1990. Guest Prof., Lancaster Theolog. Seminary and Vis. Lectr, Princeton Theolog. Seminary, USA, 1967; Hastie Lectr in Divinity, Univ. of Glasgow, 1968–71; Visiting Lecturer: Univ. of Munich, 1980; Univ. of Heidelberg, 1983; McGill Univ., Montreal, 1984; Univ. of Mainz, 1991. Member of Advisory Commitee: Christian Peace Conf., Prague, 1960–68; Conf. of European Churches, 1970–86 (acted as Gen. Sec., 1971). Hon. Mem., United Church of Berlin Brandenburg, 1969; Mem. of Cons. Cttee, Selly Oak Colls, Birmingham, 1976–87; Moderator, Presbytery of Edinburgh, 1978; Moderator, Gen. Assembly of Church of Scotland, 1987–88. Freeman, City of London, 1990; Liveryman, Scriveners' Co., 1990. JP 1974. KStJ 1983; Chancellor of Scotland, Order of St John, 1986–. ThDr *hc*, Comenius Faculty of Theology, Charles Univ., Prague, 1969. Patriarchal Cross of Romanian Orthodox Church, 1978; Bundesverdienstkreuz, 1st cl., 1980; Com. al Merito Melitense (SMO Malta), 1987; Order of St Sergius, second class, Russian Orthodox Church, 1987. *Publications:* The General Assemblies of the Church of Scotland 1560–1600: their Origins and Development, 1964; (contrib. and ed) Reformation and Revolution: Essays presented to Principal Emeritus Hugh Watt, 1967; Inauguration of Ministers in Scotland 1560–1600, 1968; (contrib. and ed) John Knox: A Quartercentenary Reappraisal, 1975; Knox and Mary, Queen of Scots; (contrib. foreword and supervised translation) Zwingli's Thought: New Perspectives (by G. W. Locher), 1981; (contrib. and ed with I. B. Cowan) The Renaissance and Reformation in Scotland: Essays in Honour of Gordon Donaldson, 1983; contribs to learned jls, particularly to Records of Scottish Church History Soc. *Address:* 4 Sydney Terrace, Edinburgh EH7 6SL. *T:* 031–669 1089; 12 Castelnau Gardens, Arundel Terrace, SW13 9DU. *T:* 081–746 3087.

SHAW, Dr Gavin Brown, CBE 1981; FRCP, FRCPE, FRCPGlas; Consultant Physician, Southern General Hospital, Glasgow, 1956–84, Hon. Consultant, since 1984; *b* 24 May 1919; *s* of Gavin Shaw and Christian Douglas Cormack; *m* 1943, Margaret Mabon Henderson (*d* 1990); two *d* (one *s* decd). *Educ:* Glasgow Academy; Glasgow Univ., 1936–42 (BSc, MB ChB). President, Students' Representative Council, 1940–41. House Phys. to Sir J. W. McNee, 1942; Temporary Surg.-Lieut, RNVR, 1942–45; Asst Phys., Southern Gen. Hosp., Glasgow, 1948–56. Actg post-Grad. Dean., Glasgow Univ., 1983–84. Royal College of Physicians and Surgeons of Glasgow: Hon. Sec., 1957–65; Visitor, 1977–78; Pres., 1978–80. Mem., West Regional Hosp. Bd, 1971–74; Chairman: Greater Glasgow Med. Adv. Cttee, 1973–76; Jt Cttee for Higher Med. Trng, 1979–83; Specialty Adviser in Medicine, W of Scotland Post-Graduate Cttee, 1971–83. Mem., GMC, 1982–89. Hon. FACP 1979; Hon. FRCPI 1979; Hon. FRCPsych 1980; Hon. FRCGP 1980. *Publications:* (ed jtly) Cardiac Resuscitation and Pacing, 1964; occasional contributor to BMJ, Brit. Heart Jl, Lancet, Practitioner, Amer. Heart Jl, Scottish Med. Jl. *Recreations:* walking, gardening, bird watching and one-time sailor, listening to music, reading. *Address:* 4 Horseshoe Road, Bearsden, Glasgow G61 2ST. *T:* 041–942 4553. *Club:* Royal Scottish Automobile.

SHAW, Rev. Canon Geoffrey Norman; Hon. Canon Emeritus of Christ Church Cathedral, Oxford, since 1989 (Hon. Canon, 1985–89); *b* 15 April 1926; *s* of Samuel Norman Shaw and Maud Shaw; *m* 1948, Cynthia Brown; one *s* two *d*. *Educ:* Holgate Grammar Sch., Barnsley; Jesus Coll., Oxford (MA); Wycliffe Hall, Oxford. Asst Curate, St Mary, Rushden, 1951–54; Vicar of St Paul, Woking, 1954–62; Rector of St Leonards-on-Sea, Sussex, 1962–68; Asst Master, Ecclesfield Grammar Sch., Sheffield, 1968–69; Head of Religious Educn and Classics, Silverdale Sch., Sheffield, 1969–72; Vice-Principal, Oak Hill Theol Coll., Southgate, 1972–79; Principal, Wycliffe Hall, Oxford, 1979–89. *Recreations:* bird watching, walking, golf, music. *Address:* Kingham, The Green, Thorpe Market, Norfolk NR11 8TL. *T:* Southrepps (0263) 833580.

SHAW, Geoffrey Peter; QC 1991; *b* 19 April 1944; *s* of late James Adamson Shaw and Hilda Gargett Shaw (*née* Edwards); *m* 1985, Susan Cochrane. *Educ:* Worksop College, Notts; Worcester College, Oxford (BA, BCL). Teaching Fellow, Univ. of Chicago Law Sch., 1966; Arden Scholar of Gray's Inn, 1967; called to the Bar, Gray's Inn, 1968. *Recreations:* walking, travel, gardening. *Address:* 1 Brick Court, Temple, EC4Y 9BY. *T:* 071–353 8845.

SHAW, Sir (George) Neville B.; *see* Bowman-Shaw.

SHAW, Sir Giles; *see* Shaw, Sir J. G. D.

SHAW, James John Sutherland, CB 1970; Chairman, Civil Service Appeal Board, 1973–77 (Deputy Chairman, 1972–73); *b* 5 Jan. 1912; *s* of Robert Shaw and Christina Macallum Sutherland; *m* 1947, Rosamond Chisholm Sharman. *Educ:* Ardrossan Academy, Ayrshire; Glasgow and London Universities. Glasgow University: MA 1st Class Hons History, 1932, PhD 1935; Lecturer in History, 1936–40. Served War with RAF, 1940–45, Navigator, AC2 to Sqdn Leader (despatches). Senior Lecturer in History, Glasgow Univ., 1945–46; HM Treasury, 1946–68: Principal, Asst Sec., Under-Sec.; Under-Sec., 1968–69, Dep. Sec., 1969–72, CSD. OECD Consltnt on Greek CS, 1973; Chm., Internat. Commn on Reform, Sudan CS, 1973–74; consultant to Commn on Structure and Functions, Ghana CS, 1974, to States of Jersey on Jersey CS, 1975. *Recreations:* talking, walking and gardening. *Address:* North Field, Neaves Lane, Stradbroke, Eye, Suffolk IP21 5JP. *T:* Stradbroke (0379) 384535.

SHAW, Prof. John Calman, CBE 1989; CA; Director (non-executive), since 1990, and Deputy Governor (non-executive), since 1991, Bank of Scotland; *b* 10 July 1932; *m* 1960, Shirley Botterill; three *d*. *Educ:* Strathallan Sch.; Edinburgh Univ. BL; FCMA, MBCS, JDipMA. Qualified Chartered Accountant, 1955. National Service, RAF, 1955–57. Partner in Graham, Smart & Annan (later Deloitte, Haskins & Sells), 1960, Sen. Edinburgh Partner, 1980–87; Exec. Dir, Scottish Financial Enterprise, 1986–90. Johnstone Smith Prof. of Accountancy (pt-time appt), 1977–82, Vis. Prof., 1986–, Glasgow Univ. Chm., Scottish American Investment Trust, 1991– (Dir, 1986–); Dir, Scottish Mortgage and Trust PLC, 1982–. Mem., Scottish Industrial Develt Adv. Bd, 1987–; Bd Mem., Scottish Enterprise, 1990–; Financial Reporting Council, 1990–; Mem., UFC, 1991–. Pres., Inst. of Chartered Accountants of Scotland, 1983–84 (Vice-Pres., 1981–83). Dep. Chm., Edinburgh Fest. Soc., 1991–. Commander of The Priory of Scotland of Most Venerable Order of St John, 1970; CStJ. *Publications:* (ed) Bogie on Group Accounts (3rd edn), 1973; The Audit Report, 1980; (jtly) Information Disclosure and the Multinational Corporation, 1984; numerous articles in Accountant's Magazine and Accounting and Business Research and Accountancy, etc. *Recreations:* opera, theatre, walking. *Address:* 10 Belgrave Crescent, Edinburgh EH4 3AH. *T:* 031–332 5697. *Clubs:* Caledonian; New (Edinburgh); Western (Glasgow).

SHAW, John Campbell; Managing Director, East Kilbride Development Corporation, since 1990; *b* 2 Aug. 1949; *s* of late John C. B. Shaw and of May B. Shaw; *m* 1974, Sheila Kerr Thomson; two *d*. *Educ:* Grosvenor High Sch., Belfast; QUB (BSc Hons in Urban Geography); Heriot-Watt Univ. (MSc in Town & Country Planning). Lanarkshire CC, 1973–75; Motherwell DC, 1975–78; East Kilbride Development Corporation, 1978–:

Head of Planning, 1982; Tech. Dir, 1986; Dir, Lanarkshire Develt Agency, 1991. *Recreation:* sport. *Address:* East Kilbride Development Corporation, Atholl House, East Kilbride G74 1LU. *T:* East Kilbride (03552) 41111, *Fax:* East Kilbride (03552) 43999; 7 Maidens, Stewartfield, East Kilbride G74 4RS. *T:* East Kilbride (03552) 65145.

SHAW, John Frederick; Under Secretary, Department of Health (formerly of Health and Social Security), since 1987; *b* 7 Dec. 1936; *s of* James Herbert and Barbara Shaw; *m* 1964, Ann Rodden; two *s* one *d*. *Educ:* Loretto Sch., Musselburgh; Worcester Coll., Oxford (MA). National Service, 2/Lieut KOYLI, 1955–57. Church Comrs, 1960–62; Industrial Christian Fellowship, 1962–63; HQ Staff, VSO, 1963–73; Principal (Direct Entry), DHSS, 1973, Asst Sec. 1978. Chm., REACH, 1988–. *Recreations:* church activities, singing, gardening. *Address:* Department of Health, Richmond House, 79 Whitehall, SW1A 2NS. *T:* 071–210 5639.

SHAW, Sir (John) Giles (Dunkerley), Kt 1987; MP (C) Pudsey since Feb. 1974; *b* 16 Nov. 1931; *y s* of Hugh D. Shaw; *m* 1962, Dione Patricia Crosthwaite Ellison; one *s* two *d*. *Educ:* Sedbergh Sch.; St. John's Coll., Cambridge (MA). President of the Union, Cambridge, 1954. Joined Rowntree & Co. Ltd, 1955. Served on Flaxton RDC, 1957–64. Marketing Dir, Confectionery Div., Rowntree Mackintosh Ltd, 1970–74. Contested (C) Kingston upon Hull West, 1966. Parliamentary Under-Secretary of State: NI Office, 1979–81; DoE, 1981–83; Dept of Energy, 1983–84; Minister of State: Home Office, 1984–86; DTI, 1986–87. Mem., House of Commons Select Cttee on Nationalised Industries, 1976–79; Vice-Chm., Cons. Prices and Consumer Affairs Cttee, 1976–78; Joint-Sec., All Party Wool Textile Group, 1978–79; Treasurer, 1922 Cttee, 1988–; Mem., Speaker's Panel of Chairmen, 1988–. *Recreations:* ornithology, fishing. *Address:* 20 Parkside, Horsforth, Leeds; House of Commons, SW1.

SHAW, John Michael, MC 1940; QC 1967; Barrister-at-Law; Regional Chairman of Industrial Tribunals, 1972–84; *b* 14 Nov. 1914; *yr s* of late M. J. Shaw (killed in action, 1916); *m* 1940, Margaret L. *yr d* of Robert T. D. Stoneham, CBE; two *s* two *d*. *Educ:* Rugby; Worcester Coll., Oxford. Called to the Bar, Gray's Inn, 1937. Served War of 1939–45 (Major): commissioned Royal Fusiliers, 1940. *Recreation:* gardening. *Address:* South Knighton House, South Knighton, near Newton Abbot, Devon TQ12 6NP.

SHAW, Sir John Michael Robert B.; *see* Best-Shaw.

SHAW, Dr Mark Robert; Keeper of Natural History, National Museums of Scotland (formerly Royal Scottish Museum), since 1983; *b* 11 May 1945; *s of* William Shaw and Mabel Courtenay Shaw (*née* Bower); *m* 1970, Francesca Dennis Wilkinson; two *d*. *Educ:* Dartington Hall Sch.; Oriel Coll., Oxford (BA 1968; MA, DPhil 1972). Res. Assistant, Manchester Univ., 1973–76; Univ. Res. Fellow, Reading Univ., 1977–80; Asst Keeper, Dept of Natural History, Royal Scottish Museum, 1980–83. *Publications:* contribs to chemical jls and (mainly on parasitic wasps) entomological jls. *Recreations:* field entomology, family life, gardening. *Address:* 48 St Alban's Road, Edinburgh EH9 2LU. *T:* 031–667 0577. *Club:* University of Edinburgh Staff (Edinburgh).

SHAW, Group Captain Mary Michal, RRC 1981; Director and Matron-in-Chief, Princess Mary's Royal Air Force Nursing Service, and Deputy Director, Defence Nursing Services (Operations and Plans), 1985–88; *b* 7 April 1933; *d* of Ven. Archdeacon Thorndike Shaw and Violet Rosario Shaw. *Educ:* Wokingham Grammar School for Girls. SRN 1955, Royal Berkshire Hosp., Reading; SCM 1957, Central Middlesex Hosp., London and Battle Hosp., Reading; PMRAFNS, 1963–88; QHNS, 1985–88. OStJ 1974. *Recreations:* gardening, home crafts. *Address:* 5 William Barnaby Yard, College Street, Bury St Edmunds, Suffolk IP33 1PQ. *T:* Bury St Edmunds (0284) 705836. *Club:* Royal Air Force.

SHAW, Max S.; *see* Stuart-Shaw.

SHAW, Michael Hewitt, CMG 1990; HM Diplomatic Service; Counsellor, Foreign and Commonwealth Office, since 1986; *b* 5 Jan. 1935; *s of* late Donald Shaw and of Marion (*née* Hewitt); *m* 1963, Elizabeth Rance; three *d* (and one *d* decd). *Educ:* Sedbergh; Clare College, Cambridge (MA). HM Forces, 1953. HMOCS Tanganyika, 1959–62; joined Diplomatic Service, 1963; served The Hague, FCO and Vientiane, 1964–68; First Sec., FCO, 1968–72, Valletta, 1972–76, FCO, 1976–82, Brussels, 1982–84; Counsellor, Brussels, 1984–86. *Recreations:* cricket, theatre, walking. *Address:* c/o Foreign and Commonwealth Office, SW1A 2AH. *Clubs:* Army and Navy, MCC.

SHAW, Sir Michael (Norman), Kt 1982; JP; DL; MP (C) Scarborough, since 1974 (Scarborough and Whitby, 1966–74); *b* 9 Oct. 1920; *e s* of late Norman Shaw; *m* 1951, Joan Mary Louise, *o d* of Sir Alfred L. Mowat, 2nd Bt; three *s*. *Educ:* Sedbergh. Chartered Accountant. MP (L and C) Brighouse and Spenborough, March 1960–Oct. 1964; PPS: to Minister of Labour, 1962–63; to Sec. of State, Dept of Trade and Industry, 1970–72; to Chancellor of the Duchy of Lancaster, 1973. Mem., UK Delegn to European Parlt, 1974–79. FCA. JP Dewsbury, 1953; DL W Yorks, 1977. *Address:* Duxbury Hall, Liversedge, W Yorkshire WF15 7NR. *T:* Heckmondwike (0924) 402270. *Club:* Carlton.

SHAW, Neil McGowan; Chairman and Chief Executive, Tate & Lyle PLC, London, since 1986 (Group Managing Director, 1980–86); Chairman: Tate & Lyle Hldgs, since 1981; Tate & Lyle Industries, since 1981; Tunnel Refineries, since 1982 (Director, since 1981); Vice-Chairman: Redpath Industries, since 1981 (Director, since 1972); A. E. Staley Manufacturing Co., since 1988; *b* 31 May 1929; *s of* late Harold LeRoy Shaw and Fabiola Marie Shaw; *m* 1952, Audrey Robinson (marr. diss.); two *s* three *d*; *m* 1985, Elizabeth Fern Mudge-Massey. *Educ:* Knowlton High Sch.; Lower Canada Coll., Canada. Trust Officer, Crown Trust Co., Montreal, 1947–54; Merchandising Manager, Canada & Dominion Sugar Co. (later Redpath Industries Ltd), Montreal, 1954–66; Vice Pres., Canada & Dominion Sugar Co., Toronto, 1967–72; Pres., Redpath Industries Ltd., 1972–80; Director: Mid Industries & Explorations, 1973–; Texaco Canada Inc., 1974–; Americare Corp., 1980–; G. R. Amylum nv, 1982–; Alcantara, 1983–; Canadian Imperial Bank of Commerce (Toronto), 1986–; Smiths Industries, 1986–90; Scottish & Newcastle Breweries, 1986–; United Biscuits (Hldgs), 1988–. Director, World Sugar Res. Orgn, 1982–; Gov., World Food and Agro Forum, 1988–. Chm., Business in the Community, 1991–. Member, Advisory Council: YES, 1986–; London Enterprise Agency, 1986–. Governor: Montreal Gen. Hosp.; Reddy Meml Hosp. *Recreations:* sailing, skiing, golfing. *Address:* Titness Park, Mill Lane, Sunninghill, Ascot SL5 7RU. *Clubs:* Brooks's; Island Sailing (Cowes); Toronto (Toronto).

SHAW, Sir Neville B.; *see* Bowman-Shaw.

SHAW, Captain Peter Jack, CBE 1990; RN (retd); General Secretary, British Group Inter-Parliamentary Union, 1979–90; *b* Geelong, Australia, 27 Oct. 1924; *s of* late Jack and Betty Shaw; *m* 1951, Pauline, *e d* of Sir Frank Madge, 2nd Bt, and Lady (Doris) Madge, East Grinstead; one *s* one *d*. *Educ:* Watford Grammar School; RNC Dartmouth; RN Staff Coll. Greenwich; NATO Defence Coll., Paris. FIL 1957. War service in HM Ships Kenya, Resolution, Quadrant, Kelvin, incl. Malta and Russian Convoys and Normandy invasion; comd HM Ships Venus, Carron, Vigilant, 1958–61; Staff, C-in-C

Portsmouth and MoD, 1961–65; SHAPE, Paris and Mons, 1966–68; Comdr, RN Coll. Greenwich, 1968–70; Defence and Naval Attaché, The Hague, 1971–73; Captain of Port and Queen's Harbourmaster, Plymouth, 1973–76; Captain of Port, Chatham, 1976–79. MBIM. *Recreations:* international relations, foreign languages, domestic pursuits. *Address:* Woodside, Rogate, Petersfield, Hants GU31 5DJ. *T:* Rogate (0730) 821 344.

SHAW, Sir Robert, 7th Bt *cr* 1821; Design Engineer, T. Lamb, McManus & Associates Ltd, Calgary, Alberta; *b* Nairobi, Kenya, 31 Jan. 1925; *s of* Sir Robert de Vere Shaw, 6th Bt, MC, and Joan (*d* 1967), *d* of Thomas Cross; *S* father, 1969; *m* 1954, Jocelyn, *d* of late Andrew McGuffie, Swaziland; two *d*. *Educ:* Harrow; Univs of Oklahoma and Missouri, USA. RN, 1943–47 (Lieut RN retd). BS Civil Eng. Oklahoma, 1962; MS Civil Eng. Missouri, 1964; Professional Engineer, Alberta; Mem. Engineering Inst. of Canada. *Recreation:* sailing. *Heir: n* Charles de Vere Shaw [*b* 1 March 1957; *m* 1985, Sonia, *e d* of Thomas Geoffrey Eden; one *s* one *d*]. *Address:* 234 40th Avenue SW, Calgary, Alberta T2S 0X3, Canada. *Club:* Alberta United Services Inst. (Calgary, Alberta).

SHAW, Dr Robert Macdonald, CB 1968; Deputy Chief Medical Officer, Department of Health and Social Security (formerly Ministry of Health), 1965–77; *b* 16 Sept. 1912; *s of* late Peter Macdonald and late Ellen Shaw; *m* 1941, Grace Helen Stringfellow; two *s* one *d*. *Educ:* Mill Hill School; Victoria Univ. of Manchester. Miscellaneous hospital appointments, etc, 1936–39. Emergency Commission, RAMC, 1939–45. Asst County MOH, Essex, 1945–48; Department of Health and Social Security (formerly Ministry of Health), 1948–77. QHP 1971–74. *Address:* The Lodge, Tor Bryan, Ingatestone, Essex CM4 9HN.

SHAW, Sir Roy, Kt 1979; writer and theatre critic; Secretary General of the Arts Council of Great Britain, 1975–83; *b* 8 July 1918; *s of* Frederick and Elsie Shaw; *m* 1946, Gwenyth Baron; five *s* two *d*. *Educ:* Firth Park Grammar School, Sheffield; Manchester Univ. BA(Hons). Newspaper printing department 'copy-holder', 1937; newspaper publicity, 1938; Library Asst, Sheffield City Library, 1939; Cataloguer, Manchester Univ. Library, 1945; Organizing Tutor, WEA, 1946; Adult Educn Lectr, Leeds Univ., 1947; Warden, Leeds Univ. Adult Educn Centre, Bradford, 1959; Professor and Dir of Adult Educn, Keele Univ., 1962. Vis. Prof., Centre for Arts, City Univ., London, 1977–83. Vice-Pres., Coleg Harlech, 1983. Hon. DLitt: City, 1978; Southampton, 1984; DUniv Open, 1981. *Publications:* The Arts and the people, 1987; contrib. chapters to: Trends in English Adult Education, 1959; The Committed Church, 1966; Your Sunday Paper, 1967; over 160 articles and book chapters on cultural policy, adult education and the mass media. *Recreations:* reading, theatre, opera, films, concerts and art galleries, swimming, watching the best of television—and sometimes, for clinical reasons, the worst. *Address:* 48 Farrer Road, N8 8LB. *T:* 081–348 1857. *Club:* Arts.

SHAW, Roy Edwin, OBE 1991; Council Member, London Borough of Camden, since 1964; *b* 21 July 1925; *s of* Edwin Victor and Edith Lily Shaw. Hampstead Borough Council, 1956–62; St Pancras Borough, 1962–65; Camden Borough Council: Chm., Planning Cttee, 1967–68; Chm., Finance Cttee, 1971–74; Chief Whip and Dep. Leader, 1965–73; Leader, 1975–82; Dep. Leader, 1990–. Vice-Chm., AMA, 1979–83; Dep. Chm. and Leader of Labour Party, London Boroughs Assoc. Part-time Mem., London Electricity Bd, 1977–83; Member: Transport Users Consultative Cttee for London, 1974–80; Adv. Cttee on Local Govt Audit, 1979–82; Audit Commn, 1983–91; Consult. Council on Local Govt Finances, 1978–84. *Recreations:* listening to music; entertaining attractive women. *Address:* Town Hall, Euston Road, NW1 2RU. *T:* 071–278 4444.

SHAW, Sir Run Run, Kt 1977; CBE 1974; Founder and Chairman, Shaw Organisation, since 1963; Founder and Chairman, Shaw Foundation, since 1973; *b* 14 Oct. 1907; *m* 1932, Lily Wong Mee Chun (decd); two *s* two *d*. Left China for Singapore and began making films and operating cinemas, 1927; left Singapore for Hong Kong and built Shaw Movietown, making and distributing films, 1959. Pres., Hong Kong Red Cross Soc., 1972–. Chairman: Hong Kong Arts Festival, 1974–88; Bd of Governors, Hong Kong Arts Centre, 1978–88; Television Broadcasts Ltd, 1980–. Chinese University of Hong Kong: Mem. Council, 1977–; Chm., Bd of Trustees, United Coll., 1983–; Founder, Shaw Coll., 1986. Hon. LLD Hong Kong Univ., 1980; Hon. Dr Soc. Scis: Chinese Univ. of Hong Kong, 1981; Univ. of E Asia, Macau, 1985; Hon. DLitt: Sussex, 1987; Hong Kong Baptist Coll., 1990; Hon. DHL State Univ. of NY at Stony Brook, 1989. Queen's Badge, Red Cross, 1982. Comdr, Order of the Crown of Belgium, 1989. *Recreations:* shadow-boxing, golf. *Address:* Shaw House, Lot 220 Clearwater Bay Road, Kowloon, Hong Kong. *T:* 7198371.

SHAW, Sydney Herbert, CMG 1963; OBE 1958; *b* 6 Nov. 1903; 2nd *s of* John Beaumont and Gertrude Shaw; *m* 1930, Mary Louise, *e d* of Ernest Lewin Chapman; one *s* one *d*. *Educ:* King's College School; Royal School of Mines, London University. BSc Hons 1st cl. Mining Engineering, 1925 and Mining Geology, 1926; MSc (Birm.) 1937; PhD (Lond.) 1949. Geophys. prospecting N and S Rhodesia, 1926–28; Imperial Geophys. Experimental Survey, Aust., 1928–30; geophys. prospecting, Cyprus, 1930. Demonstrator, Geolog. Dept, Roy. Sch. of Mines, 1931; Lectr in Geology, Birmingham Univ., 1932–37; Govt Geologist, Palestine, 1937–48 (seconded as Dep. Controller Heavy Industries, Palestine, 1942–45); Colonial (later Overseas) Geological Surveys, London, 1949, Deputy Director, 1950, Dir, 1959–65; Head, Overseas Div., Inst. of Geological Sciences, 1965–68. Geological Adviser, Colonial Office (subseq. Dept of Tech. Co-op., then Min. of Overseas Develt), 1959–68. Retd. 1968. FIMM (Pres., 1968–69); FGS. *Publications:* scientific papers in various jls. *Recreation:* gardening. *Address:* Bisham Edge, Stoney Ware, Marlow, Bucks SL7 1RN. *T:* Marlow (06284) 484951.

SHAW, Thurstan; *see* Shaw, C. T.

SHAW, Prof. William V., MD; Professor of Biochemistry, University of Leicester, since 1974; *b* Philadelphia, Pennsylvania, 13 May 1933. *Educ:* Williams Coll., Williamstown, Mass (BA Chemistry 1955); Columbia Univ., New York (MD 1959). Diplomate: Amer. Bd of Med. Examrs, 1960; Amer. Bd of Internal Med., 1968 (Examiner, 1970). Appts, Presbyterian Hosp., New York, Nat. Heart Inst., Bethesda, Maryland, and Columbia Univ., New York, until 1966; Asst Prof. of Medicine, Columbia Univ., New York, 1966–68; University of Miami School of Medicine, Miami, Florida: Associate Prof. of Medicine and Biochemistry, 1968–73; Chief, Infectious Diseases, 1971–74; Prof. of Medicine, 1973–74. Vis. Scientist, MRC Lab. of Molecular Biology, Cambridge, Eng., 1972–74. Member: MRC Cell Biology and Disorders Bd, 1976–80 (Bd Chm. and Mem. Council, 1978–80); Science Council, Celltech Ltd, 1980–89 (Chm., 1983–89); Lister Inst. Sci. Adv. Council, 1981–85; AFRC, 1990–. Member: Amer. Soc. for Clinical Investigation, 1971; Infectious Disease Soc. of Amer., 1969; Amer. Soc. of Biol Chemists; Biochem. Soc. (UK); Amer. Soc. for Microbiology; Soc. for Gen. Microbiology (UK). *Publications:* contribs to professional works and jls in microbial biochem. and molecular biology. *Address:* Department of Biochemistry, University of Leicester, University Road, Leicester LE1 7RH. *T:* Leicester (0533) 523470.

SHAW-STEWART, Sir Houston (Mark), 11th Bt *cr* 1667; MC 1950; TD; Vice Lord-Lieutenant, Strathclyde Region (Eastwood, Renfrew and Inverclyde Districts), since 1980;

b 24 April 1931; *s* of Sir Guy Shaw-Stewart, 9th Bt, MC, and Diana (*d* 1931), *d* of late George Bulteel; *S* brother, 1980; *m* 1982, Lucinda Victoria, *yr d* of Alexander Fletcher, Old Vicarage, Wighill, near Tadcaster; one *s*. *Educ:* Eton. Joined Coldstream Guards, 1949; served as 2/Lt Royal Ulster Rifles, Korea, 1950 (MC); joined Ayrshire Yeomanry, 1952; retired, 1969; Hon. Col A (Ayrshire Yeomanry) Sqdn, Queen's Own Yeomanry RAC, TA, 1984–87. Member of the Royal Company of Archers, Queen's Body Guard for Scotland. Joint Master, Lanark and Renfrewshire Foxhounds, 1974–79. DL Renfrewshire, 1970. *Recreations:* hunting, shooting and racing. *Heir: s* Ludovic Houston Shaw Stewart *b* 12 Nov. 1986. *Address:* Ardgowan, Inverkip, Renfrewshire PA16 0DW. *T:* Wemyss Bay (0475) 521226. *Clubs:* White's, Turf, Pratt's.

SHAWCROSS, family name of **Baron Shawcross.**

SHAWCROSS, Baron, *cr* 1959 (Life Peer), of Friston; **Hartley William Shawcross,** PC 1946; GBE 1974; Kt 1945; QC 1939; Special Adviser, Morgan Guaranty Trust of New York, since 1965 (Chairman, International Advisory Council, 1967–74); Director, Hawker Siddeley Group, 1968–82, now Consultant; Director, The Observer, since 1981; *b* 4 Feb. 1902; *s* of John Shawcross, MA, and Hilda Shawcross; *m* 1st, 1924, Rosita Alberta Shyvers (*d* 1943); 2nd, 1944, Joan Winifred Mather (*d* 1974); two *s* one *d*. *Educ:* Dulwich Coll.; abroad. Certificate of Honour for 1st place in Bar Final; called to Bar, Gray's Inn, 1925 (Bencher, 1939); practised on Northern Circuit. Sen. Law Lectr, Liverpool Univ., 1927–34. Chm., Enemy Aliens Tribunal, 1939–40; left practice at Bar for War Service, 1940; Chief Prosecutor for UK before Internat. Military Tribunal at Nuremberg. Asst Chm. of E Sussex QS, 1941; Recorder of Salford, 1941–45; Dep. Regional Comr, South-Eastern Region, 1941; Regional Comr, North-Western Region, 1942–45; Recorder of Kingston-upon-Thames, 1946–61; retired from practice at Bar, 1958. MP (Lab) St Helens, 1945–58; Attorney-General, 1945–51; Pres., BoT, April-Oct. 1951. A Principal Deleg. for UK to Assemblies of UN, 1945–49; a UK Mem., Permanent Court of Arbitration at The Hague, 1950–67. Independent Chm., Kent District Coal Mining Board, 1940–45; Chairman: Catering Wages Commn, 1943–45; Bar Council, 1952–57; Royal Commn on the Press, 1961–62; MRC, 1961–65; Internat. Law Section of British Inst. of Internat. and Comparative Law; Justice (British Br. of Internat. Commn of Jurists), 1956–72; Panel on Take-overs and Mergers, 1969–80; Press Council, 1974–78; ICC Commn on Unethical Practices, 1976. President: Rainer Foundn (formerly London Police Court Mission), 1951–71; British Hotels and Restaurants Assoc., 1959–71. Member: Home Secretary's Adv. Council on Treatment of Offenders, 1944–45; Council, Internat. Law Assoc., 1958–74; Exec. Cttee, Internat. Commn of Jurists, 1959. Hon. Member: Bar Council; Amer. and New York Bar Assoc.; Fellow, Amer. Bar Foundn. Director: Shell Transport and Trading Co., 1961–72; EMI Ltd, 1965–81; Rank-Hovis-McDougall Ltd, 1965–79; Caffyns Motors Ltd, 1965–; Morgan et Cie International SA, 1966–77; Morgan et Cie SA, 1967–; Times Newspapers Ltd, 1967–74; Upjohn & Co Ltd, 1967–76 (Chm.); Birmingham Small Arms Co. Ltd, 1968–73 (Chm., 1971–73); European Enterprises Development Co. SA, 1970–78 (Chm., 1973–78); Chairman: Dominion Lincoln Assurance Co. Ltd, 1969–76; Thames Television Ltd, 1969–74; London and Continental Bankers, 1974–80 (now Consultant); Chm. Bd of Governors, Dulwich Coll.; Member: Court, London Univ., 1958–74; Council and Exec. Cttee, Sussex Univ., 1959– (Pro-Chancellor, 1960–65; Chancellor, 1965–85); Council, Eastbourne Coll., 1965–70. Hon. FRCS 1981; Hon. FRCOG 1978. Hon. Degrees from Universities of Bristol, Columbia, Hull, Lehigh, Liverpool, London, Loughborough, Massachusetts (Ann Arbor), Michigan, Sussex. JP Sussex, 1941–68. Chm., Soc. of Sussex Downsmen, 1962–75. Knight Grand Cross, Imperial Iranian Order of Homayoon, 1st Cl., 1974. *Recreations:* sailing, riding. *Address:* Friston Place, Sussex BN20 0AH; I-1 Albany, W1V 9RP; The Anchorage, St Mawes, Cornwall. *Clubs:* White's, Buck's, Pratt's, Garrick; Travellers' (Paris); Royal Cornwall Yacht (Falmouth); Royal Yacht Squadron (Cowes); New York Yacht (US).

SHAWE-TAYLOR, Desmond (Christopher), CBE 1965; music critic and journalist; *b* 29 May 1907; *s* of Frank Shawe-Taylor and Agnes Ussher. *Educ:* Shrewsbury Sch.; Oriel Coll., Oxford. Literary and occasional musical criticism, New Statesman, etc until 1939. Served War of 1939–45 with the Royal Artillery. Music Critic, New Statesman, 1945–58; Guest Music Critic, New Yorker, 1973–74; Chief Music Critic, The Sunday Times, 1958–83, thereafter frequent contributor on music and gramophone records. *Publications:* Covent Garden, 1948; (with Edward Sackville-West, later Lord Sackville), The Record Guide (with supplements and revisions, 1951–56). *Recreations:* travel, croquet, gramophone. *Address:* Long Crichel House, Wimborne, Dorset BH21 5JU. *T:* Tarrant Hinton (025889) 250; 15 Furlong Road, N7 8LS. *T:* 071–607 4854. *Club:* Brooks's.

SHEA, Michael Sinclair MacAuslan, CVO 1987 (LVO 1985); PhD; Director of Public Affairs, Hanson PLC, since 1987; *b* 10 May 1938; *s* of late James Michael Shea and of Mary Dalrymple Davidson MacAuslan, North Berwick; *m* 1968, Mona Grec Stensen, Oslo; two *d*. *Educ:* Gordonstoun Sch.; Edinburgh Univ. (MA, PhD Econs). FO, 1963; Inst. of African Studies, Accra, Ghana, 1963; FO, 1964; Third, later Second Sec., CRO, 1965; Second, later First Sec. (Econ.), Bonn, 1966; seconded to Cabinet Office, 1969; FO, 1971; Head of Chancery, Bucharest, 1973; Dep. Dir Gen., Brit. Inf. Services, New York, 1976; Press Sec. to the Queen, 1978–87. Gov., Gordonstoun Sch., 1988–. *Publications:* Britain's Offshore Islands, 1981; Maritime England, 1981; Tomorrow's Men, 1982; Influence: how to make the system work for you, 1988; Leadership Rules, 1990; (as Michael Sinclair): Sonntag, 1971; Folio Forty-One, 1972; The Dollar Covenant, 1974; A Long Time Sleeping, 1976; The Master Players, 1978; (with David Frost): The Mid-Atlantic Companion, 1986; The Rich Tide, 1986. *Recreations:* writing, sailing. *Address:* c/o Hanson PLC, 1 Grosvenor Place, SW1X 7JH. *Club:* Garrick.

SHEARER, Rt. Hon. Hugh Lawson, PC 1969; MP South-east Clarendon, since 1967; Deputy Prime Minister of Jamaica, and Minister of Foreign Affairs and Foreign Trade, 1980–89; President, Bustamante Industrial Trade Union, since 1977; *b* 18 May 1923. *Educ:* St Simons Coll., Jamaica. Journalist on weekly newspaper, Jamaica Worker, 1941–44, subseq. Editor. Apptd Asst Gen. Sec., Bustamante Industrial TU, 1947, Island Supervisor, 1953–67, Vice-Pres., 1960–79 (on leave of absence, 1967–72). Mem. Kingston and St Andrew Corp. Council, 1947; MHR for West Kingston, 1955–59; MLC, later Senator, 1962–67; Leader of Govt Business in Senate, 1962–67; Prime Minister of Jamaica, 1967–72; Minister of Defence and of External Affairs, 1967–72; Leader of the Opposition, 1972–74; Leader, Jamaica Labour Party, 1967–74. Hon. Dr of Laws, Howard Univ., Washington, DC, 1968. *Address:* House of Representatives, Kingston, Jamaica.

SHEARER, Rt. Hon. Ian Hamilton; *see* Avonside, Rt Hon. Lord.

SHEARER, Janet Sutherland; *see* Avonside, Lady.

SHEARER, Very Rev. John; Dean of Belfast, since 1985; *b* 30 Dec. 1926; *s* of William and Isabelle Shearer; *m* 1956, Morag Williamson; one *s* one *d*. *Educ:* Trinity College, Dublin. BA (Respondent) 1948; MA, BD 1953. Ordained, 1950; Rector of Ballynahinch, Co. Down, 1958; Rector of Seagoe, Co. Armagh, 1964. *Publication:* Stewardship Step by Step, 1961. *Recreation:* bee-keeping. *Address:* The Deanery, 5 Deramore Drive, Belfast BT9 5JQ. *T:* Belfast (0232) 660980.

SHEARER, Magnus MacDonald; JP; Lord Lieutenant of Shetland since 1982; Managing Director, J. & M. Shearer Ltd (Est. 1919), 1960–85; *b* 27 Feb. 1924; *s* of late Lt-Col Magnus Shearer, OBE, TD, JP, and Flora MacDonald Stephen; *m* 1949, Martha Nicolson Henderson, *d* of late Captain John Henderson, DSM, and late Martha Nicolson; one *s*. *Educ:* Anderson Educational Institute, Shetland; George Watson's Coll., Edinburgh. Served RN in Atlantic, Mediterranean and Far East, 1942–46. 2nd Lieut, RA (TA), 1949; Captain, TARO, 1959. Hon. Consul: for Sweden in Shetland and Orkney, 1958–; for Federal Republic of Germany in Shetland, 1972–87. Mem., Lerwick Harbour Trust, 1960–75 (Chm., 1967–72); Hon. Sec., RNLI Lerwick Branch, 1968–; Mem. Lerwick Town Council, 1963–69; JP 1969, DL 1973, Shetland. Knight 1st Class, Royal Order of Vasa (Sweden), 1969; Officer 1st Class, Order of Merit (Federal Republic of Germany), 1983; Officer 1st Class, Order of Polar Star (Sweden), 1983. *Recreations:* reading, bird watching and ships. *Address:* Birka, Cruester, Bressay, Shetland ZE2 9EL. *T:* Bressay (059582) 363.

SHEARER, Moira, (Mrs L. Kennedy); writer; *b* Dunfermline, Fife, 17 Jan. 1926; *d* of Harold King; *m* 1950, Ludovic Kennedy, *qv*; one *s* three *d*. *Educ:* Dunfermline High School; Ndola, N Rhodesia; Bearsden, Scotland. Professional training: Mayfair Sch.; Legat Sch. Début with International Ballet, 1941; joined Sadler's Wells Ballet, 1942, during following ten years danced all major classic roles and full repertoire of revivals and new ballets; first ballerina rôle in Sleeping Beauty, Royal Opera House, Covent Gdn, 1946; created rôle of Cinderella, 1948; Carmen, with Roland Petit, Théâtre Marigny, 1950; George Balanchine's Ballet Imperial, Covent Garden, 1950; Titania in Old Vic production of A Midsummer Night's Dream (Edin. Festival, 1954, and tour of US and Canada); American tours with Sadler's Wells Ballet, 1949, 1950–51. Toured as Sally Bowles in I am a Camera, 1955; joined Bristol Old Vic, 1955; played in Man of Distinction, Edin. Fest., 1957; played Madame Ranevskaya in The Cherry Orchard, Royal Lyceum, Edin., 1977; Judith Bliss in Hay Fever, Royal Lyceum, 1978; Elizabeth Lowry, in A Simple Man (Gillian Lynne's ballet for L. S. Lowry's centenary), BBC TV, 1987. Recorded: Thomas Hardy's Tess of the D'Urbervilles, 1977; Muriel Spark's The Ballad of Peckham Rye, BBC Radio 4, 1982; Dame Ninette de Valois' short stories, Acad. of Sound and Vision, 1990. Member: Scottish Arts Council, 1971–73; BBC Gen. Adv. Council, 1970–77; Dir, Border TV, 1977–82. Toured US, lecturing on history of ballet, March-April 1973; regular lecturing in England and Wales. Lectured and gave recitals on three world cruises, Queen Elizabeth II. Poetry and prose recitals, Edinburgh Festivals, 1974 and 1975. *Films:* Ballerina in The Red Shoes (première, 1948); Tales of Hoffmann, 1950; Story of Three Loves, 1952; The Man Who Loved Redheads, 1954; Peeping Tom, 1960; Black Tights, 1961. *Publication:* Balletmaster: a dancer's view of George Balanchine, 1986 (USA 1987).

SHEARER, Thomas Hamilton, CB 1974; Director, Sheltered Property Rental Ltd, since 1989; *b* 7 Nov. 1923; *o s* of late Thomas Appleby Shearer, OBE; *m* 1945, Sybil Mary Robinson, Stratford-on-Avon; one *s* one *d*. *Educ:* Haberdashers' Aske's, Hatcham; Emmanuel Coll., Cambridge (open exhibition in English). Served RAF, 1942–45 (despatches). Entered Air Ministry, as Asst Principal, 1948; Principal, 1951; Sec. to Grigg Cttee on Recruitment to Armed Forces, 1958; Asst Sec., 1959; transf. Min. of Public Building and Works, 1963; student, IDC, 1965; Under-Sec., 1967; Dir of Establishments, MPBW, 1967–70, DoE, 1970; Dir of Personnel Management, DoE, 1970–72; Dep. Chief Exec. II, PSA, DoE, 1972–73; Deputy Secretary, 1973–81. Chairman: Maplin Develt Authority, 1974–77; British Channel Tunnel Company, 1975–77; Location of Offices Bureau, 1980. A Controller, Royal Opera House Develt Land Trust, 1981–86. *Recreations:* opera, claret. *Address:* 9 Denny Crescent, SE11 4UY. *T:* 071–587 0921.

SHEARLOCK, Very Rev. David John; Dean and Rector of St Mary's Cathedral, Truro, since 1982; *b* 1 July 1932; *s* of Arthur John Shearlock and Honora Frances Hawkins; *m* 1959, Jean Margaret Marr; one *s* one *d*. *Educ:* Univ. of Birmingham (BA); Westcott House, Cambridge. Assistant Curate: Guisborough, Yorks, 1957–60; Christchurch Priory, Hants, 1960–64; Vicar: Kingsclere, 1964–71; Romsey Abbey, 1971–82; Diocesan Director of Ordinands (Winchester), 1977–82; Hon. Canon of Winchester, 1978–82. *Publication:* The Practice of Preaching, 1990. *Recreations:* model railways, music, walking the Cornish coastal footpath. *Address:* The Deanery, Lemon Street, Truro, Cornwall TR1 2PE. *T:* Truro (0872) 72661.

SHEARMAN, Rt. Rev. Donald Norman, OBE 1978; Assistant Bishop, Diocese of Brisbane, 1989–91; *b* 6 Feb. 1926; *s* of late S. F. Shearman, Sydney; *m* 1952, Stuart Fay, *d* of late Chap. F. H. Bashford; three *s* three *d*. *Educ:* Fort St and Orange High Schools; St John's Theological College, Morpeth, NSW. Served War of 1939–45: air crew, 1944–46. Theological College, 1948–50. Deacon, 1950; Priest, 1951. Curate: of Dubbo, 1950–52; of Forbes, and Warden of St John's Hostel, 1953–56; Rector of Coonabarabran, 1957–59; Director of Promotion and Adult Christian Education 1959–62; Canon, All Saints Cathedral, Bathurst, 1962; Archdeacon of Mildura and Rector of St. Margaret's, 1963; Bishop of Rockhampton, 1963–71; Chairman, Australian Board of Missions, Sydney, 1971–73; Bishop of Grafton, 1973–85. Chaplain, Order of St John of Jerusalem, Qld, 1989–. *Address:* 123 Turner Street, Scarborough, Qld 4020, Australia.

SHEARMAN, Prof. John Kinder Gowran, PhD; FBA 1976; Professor of Fine Arts, since 1987, and Chairman, since 1990, Department of Fine Arts, Harvard University; *b* 24 June 1931; *s* of Brig. C. E. G. Shearman; *m* 1957, Jane Dalrymple Smith; one *s* three *d*; *m* 1983, Deirdre Roskill. *Educ:* St Edmund's, Hindhead; Felsted; Courtauld Inst., London Univ.; BA, PhD 1957. Lectr, Courtauld Inst., 1957–67; Research Fellow, Inst. for Advanced Study, Princeton, 1964; Reader, Courtauld Inst., 1967–74, Prof. of the History of Art, 1974–79 (Dep. Dir, 1974–78); Prof., Dept of Art and Archaeology, Princeton Univ., 1979–87 (Chm., 1979–85). Mem., Accademia del Disegno, Florence, 1979. Serena Medal, British Acad., 1979. *Publications:* Andrea del Sarto, 1965; Mannerism, 1967, 8th edn 1990; Raphael's Cartoons, 1972; Catalogue of the Early Italian Paintings in the Collection of HM the Queen, 1983; Funzione e Illusione, 1983; contribs to British, French, German, American jls. *Recreations:* sailing, music. *Address:* 3 Clement Circle, Cambridge, Mass 02138, USA. *Club:* Bembridge Sailing.

SHEBBEARE, Thomas Andrew, (Tom); Director, The Prince's Trust and The Royal Jubilee Trusts, since 1988; *b* 25 Jan. 1952; *s* of Robert Austin Shebbeare and Frances Dare Graham; *m* 1976, Cynthia Jane Cottrell; one *s* one *d*. *Educ:* Malvern Coll.; Univ. of Exeter (BA Politics). World University Service (UK), 1973–75; Gen. Sec., British Youth Council, 1975–80; Administrator, Council of Europe, 1980–85; Exec. Dir, European Youth Foundn, 1985–88. *Recreations:* family, cooking, food and drink. *Address:* (office) 8 Bedford Row, WC1R 4BA. *T:* 071–430 0524.

SHEEHAN, Albert Vincent; Sheriff of Tayside, Central and Fife, since 1983; *b* 23 Aug. 1936; *s* of Richard Greig Sheehan and May Moffat; *m* 1965, Edna Georgina Scott Hastings; two *d*. *Educ:* Bo'ness Acad.; Edinburgh Univ. (MA 1957; LLB 1959). Admitted as Solicitor, 1959. 2nd Lieut, 1st Bn The Royal Scots (The Royal Regt), 1960; Captain, Directorate of Army Legal Services, 1961. Depute Procurator Fiscal, Hamilton, 1961–71; Sen. Depute Procurator Fiscal, Glasgow, 1971–74; Depute Crown Agent for Scotland,

1974–79; Asst Solicitor, Scottish Law Commn, 1979–81; Sheriff of Lothian and Borders, 1981–83. Leverhulme Fellow, 1971. *Publications:* Criminal Procedure in Scotland and France, 1975; Criminal Procedure, 1990. *Recreations:* naval history, travel, legal history, curling. *Address:* Sheriff's Chambers, Sheriff Court House, Falkirk.

SHEEHY, Sir Patrick, Kt 1991; Chairman, B. A. T Industries, since 1982 (Vice-Chairman, 1981–82); *b* 2 Sept. 1930; *s* of Sir John Francis Sheehy, CSI and Jean Newton Simpson; *m* 1964, Jill Patricia Tindall; one *s* one *d*. *Educ:* Australia; Ampleforth Coll., Yorks. Served Irish Guards, 1948–50; rank on leaving 2nd Lieut. Joined British-American Tobacco Co., 1950, first appt in Nigeria; Ghana, 1951; Reg. Sales Manager, Nigeria, 1953; Ethiopian Tobacco Monopoly, 1954; Marketing Dir, Jamaica, 1957; General Manager: Barbados, 1961; Holland, 1967; Dir, 1970–82, Chm., 1976–82, British-American Tobacco Co.; Dir, 1976–, Mem., Chm's Policy Cttee, 1976–, Dep. Chm., 1976–81, B.A.T Industries; Chairman: B. A. T Financial Services, 1985–90; BATUS Holdings Inc., 1986–; S London Business Initiative, 1986–; Director: BATUS Inc., 1979–82; Eagle Star Hldgs, 1984–87; BP, 1984–; The Spectator (1828) Ltd, 1988–. Member: Trade Policy Res. Centre, 1984–89; Action Cttee for Europe, 1985–; Council of Internat. Advrs, Swiss Bank Corp., 1985–; President's Cttee, CBI, 1986–; European Round Table, 1986–. *Recreations:* golf, reading. *Address:* B. A. T Industries plc, Windsor House, 50 Victoria Street, SWIH 0NL. *T:* 071–222–7979.

SHEEHY, Terence Joseph; Editor, Catholic Herald, 1983–88; *b* 12 May 1918; 2nd *s* of Michael Sheehy and Mary (*née* O'Sullivan); *m* 1955, Margaret Patricia Barry, *y d* of Dr T. St John Barry; one *s* three *d*. *Educ:* by Jesuits in London and Dublin. Editorial staff, Irish Catholic, Dublin, 1942–46; publisher and Editor, Irish Cinema Quarterly, Editor, Irish Hotelier, and Editor, Irish Licensing World, 1946–50; Gen. Manager and Dir, Ron Harris (Ireland), film distributors, 1950–52; Bord Fáilte Éireann (Irish Tourist Board): Asst Gen. Manager, N America, 1952–56; Gen. Manager (Britain), and Dir of Publicity, 1956–82; Editor, Irish Observer, 1982. Allied Irish Banks' Irish Post Community Award, 1977. Knight Cross, Order of Polonia Restituta (Poland), 1989. *Publications:* Ireland in Colour, 1975; Ireland, 1978; Ireland and Her People, 1980; Journey through Ireland, 1986; An Irish Moment, 1989. *Recreations:* reading, writing, conversation. *Address:* Ballinona, 7 Tower Road, Tadworth, Surrey KT20 5QY. *T:* Tadworth (0737) 4241. *Club:* Garrick.

SHEEN, Hon. Sir Barry (Cross), Kt 1978; **Hon. Mr Justice Sheen;** a Judge of the High Court of Justice, Queen's Bench Division, since 1978; *b* 31 Aug. 1918; 2nd *s* of late Ronald Sheen, FCA, St John's Wood; *m* 1st, 1946, Diane (*d* 1986), *d* of late C. L. Donne, MD; three *s*; 2nd, 1988, Helen Ursula, *widow* of Philip Spink. Educ: Haileybury College, Hill School (USA); Trinity Hall, Cambridge (MA). Served in RNVR, 1939–46; Commanding Officer, HMS Kilkenzie, 1943–45. Called to Bar, Middle Temple, 1947, Master of the Bench, 1971, Reader, 1990; Member Bar Council, 1959–63; QC 1966. Junior Counsel to Admiralty, 1961–66; a Recorder of the Crown Court, 1972–78. On Panel of Wreck Comrs (Eng.) under Merchant Shipping Acts, 1966–78; Mem., Panel of Lloyd's Arbitrators in Salvage Cases, 1966–78, Appeal Arbitrator, 1977–78. Presided over Inquiry into Zeebrugge ferry disaster, 1987; Vice-Pres., British Maritime Law Assoc., 1979–. Life Governor, Haileybury (Pres., Haileybury Soc., 1982); Hon. Mem., Assoc. of Average Adjusters, 1979– (Chm., 1986). Liveryman, Shipwrights' Co. *Recreations:* golf, travel, DIY. *Address:* Royal Courts of Justice, WC2. *T:* 071–731 7275. *Clubs:* Hurlingham; Royal Wimbledon Golf.

SHEERIN, John Declan; His Honour Judge Sheerin; a Circuit Judge, since 1982; *b* 29 Nov. 1932; *s* of late John Patrick Sheerin and Agnes Mary Sheerin; *m* 1958, Helen Suzanne (*née* LeRoux); two *s* two *d*. *Educ:* Wimbledon Coll.; London Sch. of Econs and Polit Science (LLB 1954). Served RAF, 1958–60 (Flying Officer). Admitted solicitor, 1957; Partner, Greene & Greene, 1962–82; a Recorder of the Crown Court, 1979–82. Councillor (Ind.), W Suffolk CC, 1964–76 (Chm., Library and Museums Cttee). *Recreation:* golf. *Address:* c/o Crown Court, Ipswich. *Club:* Flempton Golf.

SHEERMAN, Barry John; MP (Lab and Co-op) Huddersfield, since 1983 (Huddersfield East, 1979–83); *b* 17 Aug. 1940; *s* of Albert William Sheerman and Florence Sheerman (*née* Pike); *m* 1965 Pamela Elizabeth (*née* Brenchley); one *s* three *d*. *Educ:* Hampton Grammar Sch.; Kingston Technical Coll.; LSE. BSc (Economics) Hons; MSc Hons. Chemical worker, laboratory assistant, technical sales trainee, etc., 1958–61; Lectr, Univ. Coll. of Swansea, 1966–79. An opposition front bench spokesman on: employment, dealing with training, small business and tourism, 1983–88; home affairs, dealing with police, prisons, crime prevention, drugs, civil defence and fire service, and deputy to Rt. Hon. Roy Hattersley, MP, 1988–. Chairman: Parly Adv. Council on Transport Safety, 1981–83; Labour Campaign for Criminal Justice, 1989–; Mem., Public Accounts Cttee, 1981–. Chm., Internat. Cttee for Andean Aid, 1989–. FRSA; FRGS 1989. *Publications:* various. *Address:* House of Commons, SW1A 0AA.

SHEFFIELD, 8th Baron; *see under* Stanley of Alderley, 8th Baron.

SHEFFIELD, Bishop of, since 1980; **Rt. Rev. David Ramsay Lunn;** *b* 1930. *Educ:* King's College, Cambridge (BA 1953, MA 1957); Cuddesdon College, Oxford. Deacon 1955, priest 1956, Newcastle upon Tyne; Curate of Sugley, 1955–59; N Gosforth, 1959–63; Chaplain, Lincoln Theological College, 1963–66; Sub-Warden, 1966–70; Vicar of St George, Cullercoats, 1970–75, Rector, 1975–80; Rural Dean of Tynemouth, 1975–80. *Address:* Bishopscroft, Snaithing Lane, Sheffield, S Yorks S10 3LG.

SHEFFIELD, Provost of; *see* Gladwin, Very Rev. J. W.

SHEFFIELD, Archdeacon of; *see* Lowe, Ven. S. R.

SHEFFIELD, John Julian Lionel George; Chairman: Portals Holdings PLC, since 1979 (Director, since 1969); Norcros plc, since 1989 (Director, since 1974); *b* 28 Aug. 1938; *s* of John Vincent Sheffield, *qv*; *m* 1961, Carolyn Alexander Abel Smith; three *s* one *d*. *Educ:* Eton Coll.; Christ's Coll., Cambridge. Joined Portals Ltd, 1962. Director: Guardian Royal Exchange, 1981– (Dep. Chm., 1988–); Tex Hldgs, 1985–; North Foreland Lodge, 1987–; Newbury Racecourse, 1988–. Mem., Economic and Commercial Cttee, EEF, 1974–90. Mem. Council, St John's Sch., Leatherhead, 1966–. Trustee, Winchester Cathedral Trust, 1984–. *Recreations:* outdoor sports, collecting. *Address:* Laverstoke Mill House, Whitchurch, Hants RG28 7NR. *T:* Basingstoke (0256) 892360. *Clubs:* White's, MCC.

SHEFFIELD, John Vincent, CBE 1984; Chairman, Norcros Ltd, 1956–81; *b* 11 Nov. 1913; *y s* of Sir Berkeley Sheffield, 6th Bt; *m* 1st, 1936, Anne (*d* 1969), *d* of Sir Lionel Faudel-Phillips, 3rd Bt; one *s* three *d*; 2nd, 1971, Mrs France Crosthwaite, *d* of Brig.-Gen. Goland Clarke, CMG, DSO. *Educ:* Eton; Magdalene College, Cambridge (MA). Private Secretary to Minister of Works, 1943–44; Chairman: Portals Ltd, 1968–78; Atlantic Assets Trust Ltd, 1972–83. Chm., BEC, 1980–83; Vice-Chm., BTEC, 1983. High Sheriff of Lincolnshire, 1944–45. *Address:* New Barn House, Laverstoke, Whitchurch, Hants RG28 7PF. *T:* Whitchurch (Hants) (0256) 893187. *Club:* White's.
See also J. J. L. G. Sheffield.

SHEFFIELD, Sir Reginald (Adrian Berkeley), 8th Bt *cr* 1755; DL; Chairman: Aylesford Holdings Ltd, since 1979; Alpwood Holdings plc, 1984–88; Director, Normanby Estate Co. Ltd, and other companies; Member of Lloyd's, since 1977; *b* 9 May 1946; *s* of Edmund Charles Reginald Sheffield, JP, DL (*d* 1977) and of Nancie Miriel Denise, *d* of Edward Roland Soames; *S* uncle, 1977; *m* 1st, 1969, Annabel Lucy Veronica (marr. diss.), *d* of late T. A. Jones; two *d*; 2nd, 1977, Victoria Penelope, *d* of late R. C. Walker, DFC; one *s* two *d*. *Educ:* Eton. Member of Stock Exchange, 1973–75. Vice-Chm., S Humberside Business Advice Centre Ltd, 1984–. Pres., S Humberside CPRE, 1985–; Member: Cttee, Lincs and S Humberside Br., CLA, 1987–; Taxation Cttee, CLA, 1989–; Central Transport Consultative Cttee (NE Reg.), 1988–. Mem. (C) for Ermine Ward, Humberside County Council, 1985–. Pres., Scunthorpe United Football Club, 1982–. Pres., Scunthorpe and Dist, Victim Support Scheme, 1989–. DL Humberside, 1985. *Heir:* *s* Robert Charles Berkeley Sheffield, *b* 1 Sept. 1984. *Address:* Estate Office, Normanby, Scunthorpe, S Humberside DN15 9HS. *T:* Scunthorpe (0724) 720618. *Club:* White's.

SHEFTON, Prof. Brian Benjamin, FBA 1985; FSA 1980; Professor of Greek Art and Archaeology, University of Newcastle upon Tyne, 1979–84, now Emeritus; *b* 11 Aug. 1919; *yr s* of late Prof. I. Scheftelowitz (Cologne, Germany, until 1933 and Oxford) and Frieda (*née* Kohn); *m* 1960, Jutta Ebel of Alingsås, Sweden; one *d*. *Educ:* Apostelngymnasium, Cologne; St Lawrence Coll., Ramsgate; Magdalen Coll. Sch., Oxford; Oriel Coll., Oxford (Open Scholar, 1938; Hon. Mods Greek and Latin Lit. 1940; Lit Hum 1947, Class I). War service, HM Forces (change of name), 1940–45. Sch. Student, British Sch. at Athens, 1947; Derby Scholar, Oxford, 1948; Bishop Fraser Scholar, Oriel Coll., Oxford, 1949, in Aegean to 1950; excavated at Old Smyrna; Lectr in Classics, University Coll., Exeter, 1950–55; Lectr in Greek Archaeology and Ancient History, 1955, Sen. Lectr, 1960, Reader, 1974–79, King's Coll., Univ. of Durham (later Univ. of Newcastle upon Tyne). Established and directed Univ.'s Greek Museum, 1956–84, Hon. Advr, 1985–; Trustee, Oriental Mus., Durham Univ., 1989–. Vis. Res. Fellow, Merton Coll., Oxford, 1969; British Acad. Vis. Scholar to Albania, 1973; Munro Lectr, Edinburgh Univ., 1974; British Acad. European Exchange Fellow, Marburg Univ., 1975; German Academic Exchange Fellow, Marburg and Cologne, 1976; Leverhulme Res. Fellow, 1977; Webster Meml Lectr, Stanford Univ., 1981; Vis. Prof. of Classical Archaeology, Vienna Univ. (winter), 1981–82; British Council Vis. Scholar to Soviet Union, 1982, to Spain, 1985; Jackson Knight Meml Lectr, Exeter Univ., 1983; Leverhulme Emeritus Fellow, 1984–86; Balsdon Sen. Fellow, British Sch. at Rome, 1985; Vis. Scholar, J. Paul Getty Museum, 1987. Mem., German Archaeological Inst., 1961; Foreign Mem., Inst. of Etruscan and Italic Studies, Rome, 1990. Hon. Dr.phil Cologne, 1989. Aylwin Cotton Award, 1977. *Publications:* History of Greek Vase Painting (with P. Arias and M. Hirmer), 1962; Die rhodischen Bronzekannen, 1979; chapters in: Perachora II, 1962; Phoenizier im Westen, 1982; The Eye of Greece, 1982; Das Kleinaspergle, 1988; articles in British and foreign periodicals. *Recreations:* music, travel. *Address:* 24 Holly Avenue, Newcastle upon Tyne NE2 2PY. *T:* 091–281 4184.

SHEGOG, Rev. Eric Marshall; Director of Communications, Church of England, since 1990; *b* 23 July 1937; *s* of George Marshall Shegog and Helen (*née* Whitefoot); *m* 1961, Anne Thomas; two *s* one *d*. *Educ:* Leigh Grammar School; College of St Mark and St John; Whitelands College; Lichfield Theol College; City Univ. (MA). CertEd London; DipTh London. Asst Master, Holy Trinity Primary Sch., Wimbledon, 1960–64; Asst Curate, All Saints, Benhilton, 1965–68; Asst Youth Adviser, Dio. of Southwark, 1968–70; Vicar, St Michael and All Angels, Abbey Wood, 1970–75; Town Centre Chaplain, Sunderland, 1976–83; Head of Religious Broadcasting, IBA, 1984–90. Chairman: BBC Adv. Cttee for NE, 1980–83; Age Concern, Sunderland, 1980–83; Dir, World Assoc. for Christian Communication, 1990– (Vice-Chm., Eur. Region, 1990–). *Publications:* (jtly) Religious Television: controversies and conclusions, 1990; (jtly) Religious Broadcasting in the 90s, 1991. *Recreations:* gardening, opera, jogging. *Address:* 3 The Pleasance, Harpenden, Herts AL5 3NA. *T:* Harpenden (0582) 460406.

SHEHADIE, Sir Nicholas (Michael), AC 1990; Kt 1976; OBE 1971; Managing Director, Nicholas Shehadie Pty Ltd, since 1959; *b* 15 Nov. 1926; *s* of Michael and Hannah Shehadie; *m* 1957, Dr Marie Roslyn Bashir, AO; one *s* two *d*. *Educ:* Sydney. Elected Alderman, City of Sydney, Dec. 1962; Dep. Lord Mayor, Sept. 1969–73; Lord Mayor of Sydney, Sept. 1973–75. Chm., Special Broadcasting Services. Rugby Union career: Captained NSW and Australia; played 30 Internationals and 6 overseas tours; Mem., Barbarians'. Chm., Sydney Cricket Ground, 1990–. *Recreations:* Rugby, surfing, horse racing, bowls. *Address:* 118 Old Canterbury Road, Lewisham, Sydney, NSW 2090, Australia. *Clubs:* Randwick Rugby, Tattersall's (Sydney).

SHEIL, Hon. Sir John (Joseph), Kt 1989; **Hon. Mr Justice Sheil;** a Judge of the High Court of Northern Ireland, since 1989; *b* 19 June 1938; *y s* of late Hon. Mr Justice (Charles Leo) Sheil and Elizabeth Josephine Sheil (*née* Cassidy); *m* 1979, Brenda Margaret Hale Patterson, *o d* of late Rev. Forde Patterson and Elizabeth Patterson (*née* Irwin); one *s*. *Educ:* Clongowes Wood Coll.; Queen's Univ. Belfast (LLB); Trinity Coll., Dublin (MA). Called to Bar: NI, 1964 (Bencher 1988), QC 1975; Gray's Inn, 1974; Ireland, 1976. Chairman: Mental Health Rev. Tribunal, 1985–87; Fair Employment Appeals Bd, 1986–89; Mem., Standing Adv. Commn on Human Rights, 1981–83. Senator, QUB, 1987–. *Recreations:* golf, travel. *Address:* Royal Courts of Justice, Belfast BT1 3JY.

SHELBOURNE, Sir Philip, Kt 1984; Chairman, Henry Ansbacher Holdings, 1988–91; Deputy Chairman, Panel on Take-overs and Mergers, 1987–91; *b* 15 June 1924; *s* of late Leslie John Shelbourne. *Educ:* Radley Coll.; Corpus Christi Coll., Oxford (MA); Harvard Law School. Called to Bar, Inner Temple, Hon. Bencher 1984. Barrister specialising in taxation, 1951–62; Partner, N. M. Rothschild & Sons, 1962–70; Chief Exec., Drayton Corp., 1971–72; Chm., Drayton Gp and Drayton Corp., 1973–74; Chm. and Chief Exec., Samuel Montagu & Co., 1974–80; Chm. and Chief Exec., BNOC, 1980–82; Chm., Britoil, 1982–88. Mem., SIB, 1987–88. *Recreation:* music. *Address:* Myles Place, 68 The Close, Salisbury, Wilts SP1 2EN. *Club:* Brooks's.

SHELBURNE, Earl of; Charles Maurice Petty-Fitzmaurice, DL; *b* 21 Feb. 1941; *s* and *heir* of 8th Marquess of Lansdowne, *qv*; *m* 1st, 1965, Lady Frances Eliot, *o d* of 9th Earl of St Germans; two *s* two *d*; 2nd, 1987, Fiona Merritt, *d* of Lady Davies and Donald Merritt. *Educ:* Eton. Page of Honour to The Queen, 1956–57. Served with Kenya Regt, 1960–61; with Wiltshire Yeomanry (TA), amalgamated with Royal Yeomanry Regt, 1963–73. Pres., Wiltshire Playing Fields Assoc., 1965–74; Wiltshire County Councillor, 1970–85; Mem., South West Economic Planning Council, 1972–77; Chairman: Working Committee Population & Settlement Pattern (SWEPC), 1972–77; North Wiltshire DC, 1973–76; Mem., Calne and Chippenham RDC, 1964–73. Mem., Historic Bldgs and Monuments Commn, 1983–89; Pres., HHA, 1988– (Dep. Pres., 1986–88). President: Wiltshire Assocs Boys Clubs and Youth Clubs, 1976–; North-West Wiltshire District Scout Council, 1977–88; N Wilts Cons. Assoc., 1986–. Contested (C) Coventry North East, 1979. DL Wilts, 1990. *Heir:* *s* Viscount Calne and Calstone, *qv*. *Address:* Bowood House, Calne, Wiltshire SN11 0LZ. *T:* Calne (0249) 813343. *Clubs:* Turf, White's.

SHELDON, Bernard, CB 1981; *b* 14 June 1924; *s* of Gerald Walter Sheldon and Doris Sheldon (*née* Hopkins); *m* 1951, Dorothy Kirkland; one *s* two *d*. *Educ:* Hurstpierpoint

Coll. (Scholar). War service, N Atlantic and Pacific, 1943–46 (Lieut RNVR). Called to the Bar, Middle Temple, 1949. Joined Colonial Legal Service, 1951; Federal Counsel and Dep. Public Prosecutor, Fedn of Malaya, 1951–59; Legal Adviser: Pahang, 1953; Kedah and Perlis, 1955–59; War Office, 1959–67; MoD, 1967–87, retired 1987. Badlishah Decoration for Loyalty, Kedah, 1958. *Recreation:* chess. *Address:* c/o Lloyds Bank, 64 High Street, Epsom, Surrey KT19 8AT. *Club:* Carlton.

SHELDON, Hon. Sir Gervase; *see* Sheldon, Hon. Sir J. G. K.

SHELDON, Harold; District Councillor; *b* 22 June 1918; *s* of Charles Edwin Sheldon and Lily Sheldon (*née* Taylor); *m* 1941, Bessie Sheldon (*née* Barratt); two *s* one *d*. HM Forces, 1939–45 (Sgt; wounded D Day landings). Local Government: elected Batley Borough Council, 1953; Mayor of Batley, 1962–63; W Yorkshire County Council, 1973–86 (Chm., 1976–77); re-elected 1977, 1981; elected Kirklees MDC, 1987. Chairman: Batley Sports Develt Council, 1965–; Kirklees Dist Sports Council, 1974–; Mem., Yorks and Humberside Council for Sport and Recreation, 1977–86 and 1991–; President: Batley Boys' Club (Founder Mem.), 1975–; Batley CAB, 1987–; Batley Sports for the Disabled Assoc., 1987–. *Address:* 5 Norfolk Avenue, Carlton Grange, Batley, West Yorkshire. *T:* Batley (0924) 473619.

SHELDON, John Denby; General Secretary, Civil Service Union, since 1982; *b* 31 Jan. 1941; *s* of Frank and Doreen Sheldon; *m* 1976; two *s*. *Educ:* Wingate County Primary and West Leeds High School. Oxford Univ. Diploma in Social Studies. Post Office Engineer, 1957–68; student, Ruskin Coll., 1968–70; full time Trade Union Official, Instn of Professional Civil Servants, 1970–72; National Officer, Civil Service Union, 1972–78; Deputy Gen. Sec., 1978–82. *Recreations:* cricket; Rugby League as spectator; family; representing the working man. *Address:* 2 Wincroft Road, Reading, Berks RG4 7HH. *T:* Reading (0734) 477810.

SHELDON, Sir (John) Gervase (Kensington), Kt 1978; a Judge of the High Court, Family Division, 1978–88; *b* 4 Oct. 1913; *s* of John Henry Sheldon, MD, DPH, and Eleanor Gladys Sheldon, MB, BS; *m* 1st, 1940, Patricia Mary Mardon; one *s*; 2nd, 1960, Janet Marguerite Seager; two *s* one *d*. *Educ:* Winchester Coll.; Trinity Coll., Cambridge (MA; 1st Cl. Hons Law). Barrister-at-Law, called Lincoln's Inn, 1939 (Cert. of Honour, Cholmeley Schol.), Bencher, 1978. Served RA (TA), 1939–45 (despatches twice): Egypt, N Africa, Italy; Major, RA, 1943. A Circuit Judge (formerly a County Court Judge), 1968–78; Presiding Judge, Western Circuit, 1980–84. *Recreation:* family and home. *Address:* Hopton, Churt, Surrey GU10 2LD. *T:* Frensham (025125) 2035. *Clubs:* United Oxford & Cambridge University, MCC.

SHELDON, Mark Hebberton; Senior Partner, 1988–91, Joint Senior Partner, since 1991, Linklaters & Paines, Solicitors; Vice-President of the Law Society, 1991–July 1992; *b* 6 Feb. 1931; *s* of late George Hebberton Sheldon and Marie Sheldon (*née* Hazlitt); *m* 1971, Catherine Ashworth; one *s* one *d*. *Educ:* Wycliffe Coll.; Corpus Christi Coll., Oxford (BA Jurisprudence (Hons), MA). National Service, 1949–50, TA, 1950–54, Royal Signals (Lieut). Linklaters & Paines: articled clerk, 1953–56; Asst Solicitor, 1957–59; Partner, 1959–; Resident Partner, New York, 1972–74. Mem. Council 1978–, Treas. 1981–86, Law Soc.; Mem. Court 1975–, Master 1987–88, City of London Solicitors' Co.; Pres., City of London Law Soc., 1987–88. Nominated Mem., Council of Corp. of Lloyd's, 1989–90; Mem., Financial Reporting Council, 1990–. Chm., Corpus Assoc., 1983–89. *Recreations:* music, English water-colours, wine, swimming. *Address:* 5 St Albans Grove, W8 5PN. *T:* 071–937 3120. *Clubs:* Travellers', City of London.

SHELDON, Rt. Hon. Robert (Edward), PC 1977; MP (Lab) Ashton-under-Lyne, since 1964; *b* 13 Sept. 1923; *m* 1st, 1945, Eileen Shamash (*d* 1969); one *s* one *d*; 2nd 1971, Mary Shield. *Educ:* Elementary and Grammar Schools; Engineering Apprenticeship; Technical Colleges in Stockport, Burnley and Salford; WhSch 1944. Engineering diplomas; external graduate, London University. Contested Withington, Manchester, 1959; Chm., Labour Parly Economic Affairs and Finance Group, 1967–68; Opposition Front Bench Spokesman on Civil Service and Machinery of Govt, also on Treasury matters, 1970–74; Minister of State, CSD, March-Oct. 1974; Minister of State, HM Treasury, Oct. 1974–June 1975; Financial Sec. to the Treasury, 1975–79; Opposition front bench spokesman on Treasury matters, 1981–83; Chm., Public Accounts Cttee, 1983– (Mem., 1965–70, 1975–79); Member: Public Expenditure Cttee (Chm. Gen. Sub-Cttee), 1972–74; Select Cttee on Treasury and Civil Service, 1979–81 (Chm., Sub-Cttee); Fulton Cttee on the Civil Service, 1966–68. Chm., NW Gp of Labour MPs, 1970–74. Dir, Manchester Chamber of Commerce, 1964–74, 1979–. *Recreations:* various crafts. *Address:* 27 Darley Avenue, Manchester M20 8ZD; 2 Ryder Street, SW1.

SHELFORD, Cornelius William, DL; retired; *b* 6 July 1908; *s* of William Heard Shelford and Maud Ethel Shelford, Horncastle, Sharpthorne, Sussex, and Singapore; *m* 1934, Helen Beatrice Hilda Schuster; one *s* two *d*. *Educ:* private tutor and Trinity College, Cambridge. Chartered Accountant, 1934; Partner, Rowley Pemberton & Co., 1940 (retd 1960); Chm., Mills & Allen Ltd, 1964 (retd 1969); Chm., London County Freehold & Leasehold Properties Ltd, 1964 (retd 1970). East Sussex CC, 1952 (CA, 1957; Chm., 1964–67; Chm., Finance Cttee, 1970–74); High Sheriff of Sussex, 1954; DL Sussex, 1968–. Governor and Mem. Management Cttee, Chailey Heritage Craft Schs and Hosp., for 30 years (Jt Founder, League of Friends); Pestalozzi Children's Village Trust: Mem. Council, 1974–; Vice-Chm., 1975–83; Chm., 1983–85. *Recreations:* travelling, walking, gardening. *Address:* Heasmans, Chailey Green, near Lewes, E Sussex BN8 4DA. *T:* Newick (082572) 2530. *Club:* Carlton.

SHELLARD, Maj.-Gen. Michael Francis Linton, CBE 1989; Commander Artillery, 1st British Corps, since 1990; *b* 19 Aug. 1937; *s* of Norman Shellard and Stella (*née* Linton); *m* 1960, Jean Mary Yates; one *s* one *d*. *Educ:* Queen's Coll., Taunton; RMA, Sandhurst. Commnd, RA, 1957; Staff Coll., Camberley, 1969; NDC, Latimer, 1974; GSO1 MO4, MoD, 1975–76; CO 22 AD Regt, 1977–79; Col, 1983; Brig., 1985; Comd 1st Artillery Bde and Dortmund Garrison, 1985–88. Gov., Queen's Coll., Taunton, 1989–. *Recreations:* golf, bird watching, gardening. *Address:* c/o Midland Bank, High Street, Amesbury, Wilts SP4 7DN.

SHELLEY, Alan John; Senior Partner, Knight, Frank & Rutley, since 1983; *b* 7 Aug. 1931; *s* of Stanley and Ivy Shelley; *m* 1958, Josephine (*née* Flood); one *s* one *d*. *Educ:* People's College, Nottingham. FRICS. Senior Partner, Knight, Frank & Rutley (Nigeria), 1965. General Commissioner of Income Tax, 1984–. Chm., W Africa Cttee, 1985–. Mem. Ct of Governors, Royal Shakespeare Theatre, 1990–. *Recreations:* theatre, squash. *Address:* 54 Bathurst Mews, W2 2SB. *T:* 071–262 1991; Thatch Farm, Glaston, Rutland, Leics LE15 9BX. *T:* Uppingham (0572) 282396. *Clubs:* Oriental, MCC.

SHELLEY, Charles William Evans; Charity Commissioner, 1968–74; *b* 15 Aug. 1912; *s* of George Shelley and Frances Mary Anne Shelley (*née* Dain); *m* 1939, Patricia May Dolby; three *d* (and one *d* decd). *Educ:* Alleyn's Sch., Dulwich; Fitzwilliam House, Cambridge. Called to Bar, Inner Temple, 1937; practised at the Bar, to 1940. Served in Army: first in RAPC and later in Dept of Judge Advocate-General, rank Major, 1940–47. Joined Charity Commn as Legal Asst, 1947; Sen. Legal Asst, 1958; Dep. Comr, 1964. *Recreations:* English literature, listening to music, mountaineering. *Address:* Pen y Bryn, Llansilin, Oswestry, Shropshire SY10 7QG. *T:* Llansilin (069170) 273.

SHELLEY, Howard Gordon; concert pianist and conductor; Associate Conductor, London Mozart Players, since 1990; *b* 9 March 1950; *s* of Frederick Gordon Shelley and Katharine Anne Taylor; *m* 1975, Hilary Mary Pauline Macnamara; one *s*, and one step *s*. *Educ:* Highgate Sch.; Royal College of Music (ARCM Hons 1966; Foundn Schol. 1967–71); Boise Schol. 1971–72; ARCO 1967. Studied with Vera Yelverton, Harold Craxton, Kendall Taylor, Lamar Crowson and Ilona Kabos. Recital début, Wigmore Hall, 1971; televised Henry Wood Prom début, 1972; conducting début, London Symphony Orch., Barbican, 1985. Internat. solo career extending over five continents; performed world's first complete exposition of solo piano works of Rachmaninov, Wigmore Hall, 1983. Discography includes: Rachmaninov solo works (7 vols), Rachmaninov two-piano works, Rachmaninov Complete Piano Concertos, Mozart Piano Concertos (conductor/soloist), Chopin, Schumann recitals, Schubert recital on fortepiano, piano concertos of Vaughan Williams, Howard Ferguson and Peter Dickinson. 2 piano partnership with Hilary Macnamara, 1976–. Chappell Gold Medal and Peter Morrison Prize, 1968, Dannreuther Concerto Prize, 1971, RCM; Silver Medal, Co. of Musicians, 1971. *Address:* c/o Intermusica, 16 Duncan Terrace, N1 8BZ. *T:* 071–278 5455.

SHELLEY, James Edward, CBE 1991; Secretary to Church Commissioners, since 1985; *b* 1932; *s* of Vice-Adm. Richard Shelley and Eve Cecil; *m* 1956, Judy Grubb; two *s* two *d*. *Educ:* Eton; University College, Oxford (MA). Joined Church Commissioners' staff, 1954; Under Secretary General, 1976–81; Assets Secretary, 1981–85. Dir, Save & Prosper, 1987–. *Recreations:* country pursuits. *Address:* Church Commissioners, 1 Millbank, SW1P 3JZ. *T:* 071–222 7010; Mays Farm House, Ramsdell, Basingstoke, Hants RG26 5RE. *T:* Basingstoke (0256) 850770. *Club:* Naval and Military.

SHELLEY, Sir John (Richard), 11th Bt *cr* 1611; (professionally Dr J. R. Shelley); general medical practitioner; Partner, Drs Shelley, Newth and Doddington (formerly Durstan-Smith, Shelley and Newth), Health Centre, South Molton, Devon, since 1974; *b* 18 Jan. 1943; *s* of John Shelley (*d* 1974), and of Dorothy, *d* of Arthur Irvine Ingram; *S* grandfather, 1976; *m* 1965, Clare, *d* of Claud Bicknell, *qv*; two *d*. *Educ:* King's Sch., Bruton; Trinity Coll., Cambridge (BA 1964, MA 1967); St Mary's Hosp., London Univ. MB, BChir 1967; DObstRCOG 1969; MRCGP 1978. Partner in Drs Harris, Barkworth, Savile, Shelley and Gurney, Eastbourne, Sx, 1969–74. Member: Exeter Diocesan Synod for South Molton Deanery, 1976–79; BMA; CLA; NFU. *Heir:* *b* Thomas Henry Shelley [*b* 3 Feb. 1945; *m* 1970, Katherine Mary Holton; three *d*]. *Address:* Molford House, 27 South Street, South Molton, Devon EX36 4AA. *T:* South Molton (07695) 3101.

SHELLEY, Ursula, MD, FRCP; retired 1971; Physician to Royal Free Hospital's Children's Department, 1940–71 (Assistant Physician, 1935–40), to Princess Louise (Kensington) Hospital for Children, 1944–71 (Assistant Physician, 1937–44), and to Queen Elizabeth Hospital for Children, 1946–71; *b* 11 Apr. 1906; *d* of Frederick Farey Shelley, FIC, and Rachel Hicks Shelley, MB, BS. *Educ:* St Paul's Girls' School; Royal Free Hospital School of Medicine. MB, BS Lond., Univ. Gold Medal, 1930; MD Lond., 1932; FRCP 1948. Examiner: Coll. of Physicians, 1960–70; Univ. of London, 1965–70. Vice-Pres., Nat. Assoc. of Family Life and Child Care (formerly Nat. Assoc. of Nursery Matrons), 1968– (Pres., 1960–65); Member: Medical Women's Fedn, 1936–; British Pædiatric Assoc., 1946–85. Liveryman, Worshipful Soc. of Apothecaries; Freeman of City of London, 1950. *Publications:* numerous articles in medical journals. *Recreations:* gardening, lion dogs. *Address:* 15 Hyde Park Gate, SW7 5DG. *T:* 071–584 7941; Threeways, 2 Mincing Lane, Chobham GU24 8RX.

SHELTON, Shirley Megan, (Mrs W. T. Shelton); Editor, Home & Freezer Digest, 1988–90; *b* 8 March 1934; *d* of Lt-Col T. F. Goodwin; *m* 1960, William Timothy Shelton; one *s* two *d*. *Educ:* various schs. Home Editor 1970–75, Assistant Editor, 1975–78, Editor, 1978–82, Woman and Home magazine. *Address:* 59 Croftdown Road, NW5 1EL. *T:* 071–485 4936.

SHELTON, Sir William (Jeremy Masefield), Kt 1989; MA Oxon; MP (C) Streatham, since 1974 (Clapham, 1970–74); *b* 30 Oct. 1929; *s* of late Lt-Col R. C. M. Shelton, MBE, St Saviour's, Guernsey, and Mrs R. E. P. Shelton (*née* Coode), London Place, Oxford; *m* 1960, Anne Patricia, *o d* of John Arthur Warder, CBE; one *s* one *d*. *Educ:* Radley Coll.; Tabor Academy, Marion, Mass; Worcester Coll., Oxford; Univ. of Texas, Austin, Texas. Colman, Prentis & Varley Ltd, 1952–55; Corpa, Caracas, Venezuela, 1955–60; Managing Director: CPV (Colombiana) Ltd, Bogota, Colombia, 1960–64; CPV (International) Ltd, 1967–74 (Dir, 1964); Grosvenor Advertising Ltd, 1969–74 (Dir, 1964); Chairman: Fletcher, Shelton, Delaney & Reynolds Ltd, 1974–81; GGK London Ltd, 1984–86. Member for Wandsworth, GLC, 1967–70; Chief Whip, on ILEA, 1968–70. PPS to Minister of Posts and Telecommunications, 1972–74; PPS to Rt Hon. Margaret Thatcher, MP, 1975; Parly Under-Sec. of State, DES, 1981–83. Mem., Council of Europe and WEU, 1987–. *Recreations:* golf, reading, painting. *Address:* 27 Ponsonby Terrace, SW1P 4PZ. *T:* 071–821 8204; The Manor House, Long Crendon, Bucks HP18 9AN. *T:* Long Crendon (0844) 208748. *Club:* Carlton.

SHENFIELD, Dame Barbara (Estelle), DBE 1986; Chairman, Women's Royal Voluntary Service, 1981–88 (Vice Chairman, 1976–81); *d* of George and Jane Farrow, Bearwood, Staffs; *m* 1st, Flt-Lt Gwilym Ivor Lewis, RAF (killed in action); one *s*; 2nd, Arthur A. Shenfield (*d* 1990); one *s*. *Educ:* Langley High Sch., Worcs; Univ. of Birmingham (Hons Social and Political Science). Lectr in Soc. Studies, Univ. of Birmingham, 1945–56; Lectr, Dept of Econs and Soc. Studies, Bedford Coll., London Univ., 1959–65; Academic Dir, UC at Buckingham, 1972–73. Visiting Professor: Michigan State Univ., 1960; Temple Univ., Philadelphia, 1974; Distinguished Vis. Prof., Rockford Coll., Ill, 1969–71, 1974. Consultant, US Dept of Labor, 1964; Dir, PEP Study of Co. Bds' Soc. Responsibilities, 1965–68. Member: UK Govt Cttee on Local Taxation, 1965–66; UK Govt Cttee on Abuse of Welfare Services, 1971–73; Govt Review Team on Social Security, 1984–85. Chairman: Nat Exec., Nat. Old People's Welfare Council (now Age Concern), 1971–73; Friends of the Imperial War Mus., 1991–. Trustee, Social Affairs Unit, 1990–. DUniv Buckingham, 1987. *Publications:* Social Policies for Old Age, 1957; The Social Responsibilities of Company Boards, 1971; The Organisation of a Voluntary Service, 1972; Myths of Social Policy, 1975; monographs and articles on gerontological and other social subjects. *Recreations:* gardening, music, viticulture. *Address:* 1 Albert Court, Kensington Gore, SW7 2BE. *T:* 071–581 0363.

SHENTON, Clive; QC (Scot.) 1990; barrister; *b* 7 Oct. 1946; *s* of John Shenton and Mary Louise Gutridge. *Educ:* Durban High Sch.; RMA, Sandhurst; Univ. of Edinburgh (LLB). Served: Black Watch, 1966–70; Parachute Regt (T&AVR), 1971–77 (Captain 1973, Major 1975). Called to the Scots Bar, 1975; called to the Bar, Middle Temple, 1990. Standing Jun. Counsel to MoD (Army Dept) in Scotland, 1983–90; Temp. Sheriff, 1988–90. Treasurer, Advocates' Criminal Law Gp, 1984–88. Contested (C) Dunfermline E, 1983, 1987. *Recreation:* cricket. *Address:* 8 Moray Place, Edinburgh EH3 6DS. *T:* 031–225 1118; 36 Essex Street, WC2R 3AD. *T:* 071–413 0353. *Clubs:* Army and Navy, MCC; New (Edinburgh).

SHEPARD, Giles Richard Carless; Managing Director, Savoy Hotel plc, since 1979; *b* 1 April 1937; *er s* of Richard S. H. Shepard, MC, TD; *m* 1966, Peter Carolyn Fern Keighley; one *s* one *d.* *Educ:* Heatherdown, Ascot; Eton (King's Scholar); Harvard Business School (PMD 1967). Commissioned Coldstream Guards, 1955–60. Director: Charrington & Co., 1960–64; H. P. Bulmer & Co., 1964–70; Managing Director: Findlater Mackie, Todd, 1967–70; Westminster & Country Properties, 1970–76; Director: Dorchester Hotel, 1972–76; Savoy Hotel, 1976–79. Dir, Kleinwort Develt Fund. Member: Council, Royal Sch. of Needlework; Exec. Cttee, Cystic Fibrosis Res. Trust. Chm., City and Guilds of London Art Sch. Mem., Court of Assistants, Fishmongers' Co. (Prime Warden, 1987–88); High Sheriff of Greater London, 1986–87. Governor, Gresham's School, Holt, 1980–. *Recreations:* gardening, shooting, embroidery. *Address:* 1 Savoy Hill, WC2R 0BP. *T:* 071–836 1533. *Clubs:* White's, Pratt's.

SHEPHARD, George Clifford, CBE 1979; retired as NCB Board Member for Industrial Relations, 1969–80; Member, Paul Finet Foundation, since 1974; *b* 2 Aug. 1915; British; *m* 1942, Mollie Dorothy Mansfield; one *s* (one *d* decd). *Educ:* Chesterfield Grammar School. Bolsover Colliery Co. Ltd, Head Office, 1933–40. Served in Army, N Africa, various Comd HQs, 1940–45, commnd 1942. Official, National Union of Mineworkers, 1945–69. Director, 1969–80: Coal Products Div., NCB; Associated Heat Services Ltd; Compower Ltd; British Investment; former Dir, Inst. of Occupational Medicine. Member: CBI Cttees; ECSC. Jt Hon. Sec., Coal Industry Social Welfare Organisation; Chm., Mineworkers' Pension Scheme. Editor, various bulletins and tracts. FCIS, ACMA, CBIM. *Recreations:* golf, music. *Address:* c/o Queensgate Hotel, 398–402 North Promenade, Blackpool FY1 2LB.

SHEPHARD, Gillian Patricia; MP (C) South West Norfolk, since 1987; Minister of State, Treasury, since 1990; *b* 22 Jan. 1940; *d* of Reginald and Bertha Watts; *m* 1975, Thomas Shephard; two step *s.* *Educ:* North Walsham High Sch. for Girls; St Hilda's Coll., Oxford (MA Mod. Langs; Hon. Fellow, 1991). Educn Officer and Schools Inspector, 1963–75; Lectr, Cambridge Univ. Extra-Mural Bd, 1965–. Councillor, Norfolk CC, 1977–89 (Chm. of Social Services Cttee, 1978–83, of Educn Cttee, 1983–85); Chairman: W Norfolk and Wisbech HA, 1981–85; Norwich HA, 1985–87; Co-Chm., Women's Nat. Commn, 1990–. PPS to Economic Sec. to the Treasury, 1988–89; Parly Under Sec. of State, DSS, 1989–90. *Recreations:* music, gardening, France. *Address:* House of Commons, SW1A 0AA. *T:* (constituency office) Downham Market (0366) 385072. *Club:* Commonwealth Trust.

SHEPHARD, Air Cdre Harold Montague, CBE 1974 (OBE 1959); Provost Marshal (RAF) and Director of Security, 1971–74, retired; *b* 15 Aug. 1918; *s* of late Rev. Leonard B. Shephard; *m* 1939, Margaret Isobel (*née* Girdlestone); one *s* one *d.* *Educ:* St John's, Leatherhead. Metropolitan Police (CID), 1937–41. Served War, RAF, 1941; commissioned for Provost duties, 1943. Seconded Public Safety Br., CCG, 1945; Wing Comdr, SIB, BAFO, 1947–50; OC, RAF Police Sch., 1951–52; DAPM, Hong Kong; PMI, Air Ministry; Command Provost Marshal, Cyprus; OC, 4 RAF Police District; PM4, Air Ministry; Comdt, RAF Police Depot, Debden, 1963–64; CPM, FEAF, 1964–67; Comdt, Police Depot, 1967–69; Comd Provost and Security Officer, RAF Germany, 1969–71; Air Cdre, 1971. MBIM. *Recreations:* watching all sports, reading. *Address:* 6 Bennetts Mews, Tenterden, Kent. *Club:* Royal Air Force.

SHEPHEARD, Major-General Joseph Kenneth, CB 1962; DSO 1943, and Bar, 1945; OBE 1949; *b* 15 Nov. 1908; *s* of late J. D. Shepheard, Poole and Bournemouth; *m* 1939, Maureen, *d* of late Capt. R. McG. Bowen-Colthurst, Oak Grove, County Cork; three *d.* *Educ:* Monmouth School; RMA Woolwich; Christ's Coll., Cambridge (BA Hons). Commissioned RE, 1928; served in India with King George V's Own Bengal Sappers and Miners, 1933–38; served in France with BEF as Adjt 4 Div. RE, 1939–40; Staff College, Camberley, 1940; Bde Major 161 (Essex) Inf. Bde in UK, Sierra Leone and Western Desert, 1940–41; Bde Major 18 Indian Inf. Bde in Iraq, 1941; GSO1 4 Indian Div. in N Africa and Italy, 1942–44; Comd 6 Assault Regt RE, Normandy to Baltic, 1944–46; JSSC, Latimer, Bucks, 1947; GSO1, FarELF, 1948–49; Staff Officer to Dir of Operations, Malaya, 1950; Comd 27 Fd Enrg Regt and CRE 6 Armd Div., 1951–53; Defence Research Policy Staff, 1953–56; Imperial Defence Coll., 1957; CCRE 1 (Br.) Corps in Germany, 1958–60; Chief of Staff, Northern Comd, 1960–62; Chief Engineer, Northern Army Group and BAOR, 1962–64. Col Comdt, RE, 1967–72. Gen. Sec., The Officers' Assoc., 1966–74. *Address:* Comfrey Cottage, Fields Farm Lane, Layer-de-la-Haye, Colchester, Essex.

SHEPHEARD, Sir Peter (Faulkner), Kt 1980; CBE 1972; PPRIBA, MRTPI, PPILA; architect, town planner and landscape architect in private practice since 1948 (Shepheard, Epstein & Hunter); Professor of Architecture and Environmental Design, Graduate School of Fine Arts, University of Pennsylvania, since 1971; *b* 11 Nov. 1913; *s* of Thomas Faulkner Shepheard, FRIBA, Liverpool; *m* 1943, Mary Bailey; one *s* one *d.* *Educ:* Birkenhead Sch.; Liverpool Sch. of Architecture. BArch. (1st Cl. Hons) Liverpool, 1936; Univ. Grad. Scholar in Civic Design, 1936–37. Asst to Derek Bridgwater, 1937–40; Min. of Supply, Royal Ordnance Factories, 1940–43; Min. of Town and Country Planning: technical officer, first on Greater London Plan (Sir Patrick Abercrombie's staff), later on research and master plan for Stevenage New Town, 1943–47. Dep. Chief Architect and Planner, Stevenage Develt Corp., 1947–48. Vis. Prof., Landscape Architecture, 1959 and 1962–71, and Dean of Fine Arts, 1971–79, Univ. of Pennsylvania. Member: Nat. Parks Commn, 1966–68; Countryside Commn, 1968–71; Royal Fine Art Commn, 1968–71; Environmental Bd, 1977–. Artistic Advr, Commonwealth War Graves Commn, 1977–. Works include: housing and schools for GLC and other authorities; Landscape of part of Festival of Britain South Bank Exhibition, London, 1951; Master plan and buildings for University of Lancaster; work for the Universities of Keele, Liverpool, Oxford, and Ghana, and for Winchester College; gardens in England and USA. President: RIBA, 1969–71; Architectural Association, 1954–55; Inst. of Landscape Architects, 1965–66. RIBA Distinction in Town Planning, 1956. Hon. FRAIC; Hon. FAIA. *Publications:* Modern Gardens, 1953; Gardens, 1969; various articles, lectures and broadcasts on architecture and landscape; drawings and illustrations of architecture and other things; illustr. A Book of Ducks, and Woodland Birds (King Penguins). *Recreations:* music and poetry; drawing, gardening and the study of natural history. *Address:* 21 Well Road, NW3 1LH. *T:* 071–435 3019. *Clubs:* Athenæum, Savile.

SHEPHERD, family name of **Baron Shepherd.**

SHEPHERD, 2nd Baron, *cr* 1946, of Spalding; **Malcolm Newton Shepherd,** PC 1965; Chairman, Chequepoint International, since 1989; *b* 27 Sept. 1918; *s* of 1st Baron Shepherd, PC, and Ada Newton (*d* 1975); *S* father, 1954; *m* 1941, Allison Wilson Redmond; two *s.* *Educ:* Lower Sch. of John Lyon; Friends' Sch., Saffron Walden. War of 1939–45: commissioned RASC, 1941; served in Desert, N Africa, Sicily, Italy. Deputy Opposition Chief Whip, House of Lords, 1960. Member Parly Labour Party Exec., 1964; Deputy Speaker, House of Lords, subseq. Opposition Chief Whip, 1964; Captain of the Hon. Corps of Gentlemen-at-Arms and Government Chief Whip, House of Lords, 1964–67; Minister of State, FCO, 1967–70; Deputy Leader of the House of Lords, 1968–70; Opposition Dep. Leader, House of Lords, 1970–74; Lord Privy Seal and Leader, House of Lords, 1974–76, resigned. Dep. Chm., Sterling Gp of Cos, 1976–86. First Chm., CS Pay Res. Unit Bd, 1978–81; Chairman: MRC, 1978–82; Packaging Council, 1978–82; Nat. Bus Co., 1979–84; President: Centre Européen de l'Enterprise Publique, 1985–; Inst. of Road Transport Engrs, 1987–. *Recreation:* golf. *Heir:* *s* Hon. Graeme George Shepherd, *b* 6 January 1949. *Address:* 29 Kennington Palace Court, Sancroft Street, SE11. *T:* 071–582 6772.

SHEPHERD, Alan Arthur, CBE 1984; PhD; FEng 1986; FIEE; FInstP; Director, Ferranti plc, since 1981; *b* 6 Sept. 1927; *s* of Arthur and Hannah Shepherd; *m* 1953, Edith Hudson; two *d.* *Educ:* Univ. of Manchester (BSc, MSc, PhD). Lectr, Physics Dept, Univ. of Keele, 1950–54; Ferranti Ltd: Chief Engineer, Electronic Components Div., 1954–67; Gen. Manager, Instrument Dept, 1967–70; Gen. Manager, Electronic Components Div., 1970–78; Man. Dir, Ferranti Electronics, 1978–87; Dep. Man. Dir, Ops, Ferranti, then Ferranti Internat. Signal plc, 1987–89; Chm., Ferranti California Group of Cos, 1978–87. Hon. Fellow, UMIST, 1988. J. J. Thomson Medal, IEE, 1985. *Publication:* The Physics of Semiconductors, 1957. *Recreations:* golf, swimming, photography. *Address:* 6 Southern Crescent, Bramhall, Cheshire SK7 3AH. *T:* 061–439 2824. *Club:* St James's (Manchester).

SHEPHERD, Archie; HM Diplomatic Service, retired; Counsellor and Head of Migration and Visa Department, Foreign and Commonwealth Office, 1977–80; *b* 2 Nov. 1922; *s* of William Shepherd and Edith (*née* Browning); *m* 1959, Dorothy Annette Walker; one *s.* *Educ:* Torquay Grammar Sch. Prison Commission, 1939; served War, RAF, 1942–46. Foreign Office, 1949; Asst Political Agent and Vice Consul, Muscat, 1951–53; FO, 1954–55; Second Sec., UK Delegn to United Nations, Geneva, 1956–57; HM Consul: Warsaw, 1958–60; Rabat, 1960–62; FO, 1963–67; Consul, Cape Town, 1968–72; First Sec. (Commercial), Beirut, 1973–75. *Recreations:* tennis, gardening. *Address:* 9 Oaks Way, Kenley, Surrey CR2 5DT. *T:* 081–660 1299. *Clubs:* Civil Service, Commonwealth Trust.

SHEPHERD, Rear-Adm. Charles William Haimes, CB 1972; CBE 1968 (OBE 1958); *b* 10 Dec. 1917; *s* of William Henry Haimes Shepherd and Florence (*née* Hayter); *m* 1940, Myra Betty Joan Major (*d* 1988); one *s.* *Educ:* Public Central Sch., Plymouth; HMS Fisgard and RNC Greenwich. Entered RN as Artificer Apprentice, 1933; specialised Engrg Officer, 1940; served War of 1939–45 in HMS: Repulse; Hero; Royal Sovereign; Gambia (RNZN); Staff of C-in-C Pacific (Sydney); R&D, Guided Weapons, 1946–49 and 1954–58 incl. Flotilla Eng Officer 3rd Trng Flotilla (HMS Crispin), 1949–51; Sen. Officers War Course, 1961–62; Tech. Dir, UK Polaris Weapon System, 1962–68; Dir Project Teams (Submarines), and Dep. Asst Controller (Polaris), MoD (Navy), 1968–71; Dep. Controller (Polaris), MoD, 1971–73. Sub-Lt 1940; Lieut 1941; Lt-Comdr 1949; Comdr 1952; Captain 1960; Rear-Adm. 1970; retired 1974. Past Pres., Plymouth Albion RFC. *Address:* 5 Underhill Road, Stoke, Plymouth PL3 4BP. *T:* Plymouth (0752) 556888. *Clubs:* Royal Western Yacht; Royal Plymouth Corinthian Yacht.

SHEPHERD, Colin; MP (C) Hereford, since Oct. 1974; *b* 13 Jan. 1938; *s* of late T. C. R. Shepherd, MBE; *m* 1966, Louise, *d* of late Lt-Col E. A. M. Cleveland, MC. *Educ:* Oundle; Caius Coll., Cambridge; McGill Univ., Montreal. RCN, 1959–63. Dir, Haigh Engineering Co. Ltd, 1963–. PPS to Sec. of State for Wales, 1987–90. Jt Sec., Cons. Parly Agr. Fish. and Food Cttee, 1975–79, Vice-Chm., 1979–87; Mem., Select Cttee on H of C Services, 1979–; Sec., Cons. Parly Hort. Sub-Cttee, 1976–87; Chairman: Library Sub-Cttee, 1983–91; Catering Sub-Cttee, 1991–. Council Mem., RCVS, 1983–; Governor, Commonwealth Inst., 1989–. Fellow, Industry and Parlt Trust, 1985. *Address:* House of Commons, SW1A 0AA; Manor House, Ganarew, near Monmouth, Gwent. *T:* Symonds Yat (0600) 890220. *Club:* Naval.

SHEPHERD, David; *see* Shepherd, R. D.

SHEPHERD, Eric William, CB 1967; *b* London, 17 May 1913; *s* of late Charles Thomas Shepherd; *m* 1938, Marie Noele Carpenter; two *d.* *Educ:* Hackney Downs School; The Polytechnic, Regent Street. BSc 1st Class Hons (Maths and Physics) London 1932. Entered Post Office as Executive Officer, 1932. Served War of 1939–45, with Royal Engineers (Postal Section), 1940–46. Principal, Post Office, 1948; Treasury, 1949–52; Asst Accountant General, Post Office, 1952; Dep. Comptroller and Accountant General, 1953; Assistant Secretary, 1956; Director of Finance and Accounts, 1960; Senior Director, 1967–73. *Recreations:* music, especially choral singing, golf. *Address:* 2 Arkley View, Arkley, Barnet, Herts EN5 3JP. *T:* 081–449 9316.

SHEPHERD, Geoffrey Thomas, CBE 1979; FIMechE, FIEE; engineering consultant, since 1982; *b* 1922; *s* of Thomas Henry and Louise Shepherd; *m* Irene Wilkes; one *d.* *Educ:* King Edward's Sch., Birmingham; Coll. of Technology, Birmingham. BSc (Hons). GEC Ltd; British Electricity Authority (several positions in management of power stations); Nuclear Ops Engr, CEGB, 1958–61; Regional Dir (Western Div.), 1962–65; Dir of Engrg, South of Scotland Electricity Bd, 1965–69; Dep. Chm., LEB, 1969–72; Chm., Midlands Electricity Bd, 1972–82; part-time Mem., CEGB, 1977–82. Pres., IEE, 1986–87. Hon. DSc Aston, 1986. *Recreations:* fair weather sailing, railways. *Address:* Tree Tops, Pensham Hill, Pershore, Worcs WR10 3HA. *T:* Pershore (0386) 553076.

SHEPHERD, George Anthony, CMG 1986; HM Diplomatic Service; Counsellor, Foreign and Commonwealth Office, since 1986; *b* 8 Sept. 1931; *m* 1961, Sarah Eirlys Adamson; one *s* two *d.* *Educ:* Blundell's School; RMA Sandhurst. Served 4th Royal Tank Regt, in Egypt and BAOR, 1951–57; Trucial Oman Scouts, 1957–59; 2nd RTR, 1959–60; Durham Univ., 1960–61; Federal Regular Army, Aden, 1961–64; 2nd RTR, 1965; Asst Defence Adviser, British High Commission, Lagos, 1967–69; retd as Major RTR, 1969. 1st Secretary, FCO, Bahrain, Dubai and Islamabad, 1969–82; Counsellor, British High Commn, New Delhi, 1982–86. Life Member, Fauna Preservation Soc., 1964. *Publications:* Arabian Adventure, 1961; Flight of the Unicorns, 1964. *Recreations:* walking, bird watching, poetry. *Address:* c/o Foreign and Commonwealth Office, SW1. *Club:* Army and Navy.

SHEPHERD, James Rodney; Under-Secretary, Department of Trade and Industry (formerly Department of Industry), 1980–89, retired; *b* 27 Nov. 1935; *s* of Richard James Shepherd and Winifred Mary Shepherd. *Educ:* Blundell's; Magdalen Coll., Oxford (PPE; Diploma in Statistics). National Inst. of Economic and Social Res., 1960–64; Consultant to OECD, 1964; HM Treasury, 1965–80 (Under-Sec., 1975–80). *Publications:* articles in technical jls.

SHEPHERD, John Alan, CMG 1989; HM Diplomatic Service; Minister, Bonn, since 1991; *b* 27 April 1943; *s* of William (Mathieson) Shepherd and (Elsie) Rae Shepherd; *m* 1969, Jessica Mary Nichols; one *d.* *Educ:* Charterhouse; Selwyn Coll., Cambridge (MA); Stanford Univ., Calif (MA). Merchant Navy, 1961; HM Diplomatic Service, 1965–: CO, 1965–66; MECAS, Lebanon, 1966–68; 3rd Sec., Amman, 1968–70; 2nd Sec., Rome, 1970–73; 1st Secretary: FCO, 1973–76; The Hague, 1977–80; First Sec., 1980–82, Counsellor and Hd of Chancery, 1982–84, Office of UK Rep. to EEC, Brussels; Head of European Community Dept (External), FCO, 1985–87; Ambassador to Bahrain, 1988–91. *Recreations:* hills, birds, tennis, squash. *Club:* United Oxford & Cambridge University.

SHEPHERD, John Dodson, CBE 1979; Regional Administrator, Yorkshire Regional Health Authority, 1977–82, retired; *b* 24 Dec. 1920; *s* of Norman and Elizabeth Ellen Shepherd; *m* 1948, Marjorie Nettleton; one *s* two *d*. *Educ:* Barrow Grammar School. RAF, 1940–46: N Africa, Italy, Middle East, 1943–46. Asst Sec., Oxford RHB, 1956–58; Dep. Sec., Newcastle upon Tyne HMC, 1958–62; Sec., East Cumberland HMC, 1962–67; Sec., Liverpool RHB, 1967–73; Reg. Administrator, Mersey RHA, 1973–77. Pres., Inst. of Health Service Administrators, 1974–75 (Mem. Council, 1969–78). Trustee, Leonard Cheshire Foundn, 1989–. *Recreations:* golf, music, caravanning. *Address:* 14 Leconfield Garth, Follifoot, Harrogate HG3 1NF. *T:* Harrogate (0423) 870520. *Clubs:* Harrogate Golf, Harrogate Rotary (Pres., 1990–91).

SHEPHERD, Sir Peter (Malcolm), Kt 1976; CBE 1967; DL; FCIOB; CBIM; Director: Shepherd Building Group Ltd (Chairman, 1958–86); Shepherd Construction Ltd, since 1940 (Chairman, 1958–88); *b* 18 Oct. 1916; *s* of Alderman Frederick Welton Shepherd and Mrs Martha Eleanor Shepherd; *m* 1940, Patricia Mary Welton; four *s*. *Educ:* Nunthorpe and Rossall Schs. Chairman: Wool, Jute and Flax ITB, 1964–74; Jt Cttee, Textile ITBs, 1966–74; Construction ITB, 1973–76; Mem. Council, CBI, 1976–89. Chartered Inst. of Building: Pres., 1964–65; Member: Nat. Council, 1956–87; Professional Practice Bd, 1963– (Chm. 1963–75; Vice-Chm., 1975–88); Mem., Bd of Bldg Educn, 1957–75 (Chm. 1965–68). British Inst. of Management: Mem., Nat. Council, 1965–71; Mem., Bd of Fellows, 1969–73; Founder Chm., Yorks and N Lincs Adv. Bd, 1969–71. Mem., President's Consult. Cttee, Building Employers Confedn (formerly Nat. Fedn of Building Trades Employers), 1956–89; Mem. Council, Fedn of Civil Eng Contractors, 1952–60; Founder Mem., TEC, 1973–79. Chm., York and N Yorks Scanner Trust, 1979–. Member: Co. of Merchant Adventurers of City of York (Governor, 1984–85); York Rotary Club. Mem. Court, York Univ., 1976–; Governor, St Peter's Sch., York, 1970–. DL N Yorks, 1981. FCIOB (Hon. Fellow, 1987); Hon. Fellow, Leeds Polytechnic, 1987. Hon. DSc Heriot-Watt, 1979; DUniv York, 1981. *Recreation:* sailing. *Address:* Galtres House, Rawcliffe Lane, York YO3 6NP. *T:* York (0904) 624250. *Club:* Yorkshire (York).

SHEPHERD, Richard Charles Scrimgeour; MP (C) Aldridge-Brownhills, since 1979; *b* 6 Dec. 1942; *s* of late Alfred Reginald Shepherd and of Davida Sophia Wallace. *Educ:* LSE; Johns Hopkins Univ. (Sch. of Advanced Internat. Studies). Director: Shepherd Foods (London) Ltd, 1970–; Partridges of Sloane Street Ltd, 1972–. Mem., SE Econ. Planning Council, 1970–74. Underwriting Mem. of Lloyds, 1974–. Mem., Treasury and Civil Service Select Cttee, 1979–83; Secretary: Cons. Parly Industry Cttee, 1980–81; Cons. Parly European Cttee, 1980–81. *Recreations:* book collecting; searching for the Home Service on the wireless. *Address:* House of Commons, SW1A 0AA. *Clubs:* Carlton, Beefsteak, Chelsea Arts.

SHEPHERD, (Richard) David, OBE 1980; artist; *b* 25 April 1931; *s* of Raymond Oxley Shepherd and Margaret Joyce Shepherd (*née* Williamson); *m* 1957, Avril Shirley Gaywood; four *d*. *Educ:* Stowe. Art trng under Robin Goodwin, 1950–53; started career as aviation artist (Founder Mem., Soc. of Aviation Artists). Exhibited, RA, 1956; began painting African wild life, 1960. First London one-man show, 1962; painted 15 ft reredos of Christ for army garrison church, Bordon, 1964; 2nd London exhibn, 1965; Johannesburg exhibns, 1966 and 1969; exhibn, Tryon Gall., London, 1978. Painted: HE Dr Kaunda, President of Zambia, 1967; HM the Queen Mother for King's Regt, 1969; HE Sheikh Zaid of Abu Dhabi, 1970; 3rd London exhibn, 1971. Auctioned 5 wildlife paintings in USA and raised sufficient to purchase Bell Jet Ranger helicopter to combat game poaching in Zambia, 1971; painted Tiger Fire, for Operation Tiger, 1973; presented with 1896 steam locomotive by Pres. of Zambia (its return to Britain subject of BBC TV documentary, Last Train to Mulobezi); purchased 2 main line steam locomotives from BR, 1967 (92203 Black Prince, 75209 The Green Knight); Founder Chm., E Somerset Railway. BBC made 50-minute colour life documentary, The Man Who Loves Giants, 1970; series, In Search of Wildlife, in which he is shown tracking down and painting endangered species, Thames TV, 1988. Established The David Shepherd Conservation Foundn, 1986. Mem. of Honour, World Wildlife Fund, 1979. FRGS 1989; FRSA 1986. Hon. DFA, Pratt Inst., New York, for services to wildlife conservation, 1971; Hon. DSc Hatfield Polytechnic, 1990. Order of the Golden Ark, Netherlands, for services to wildlife conservation (Zambia, Operation Tiger, etc), 1973. *Publications:* Artist in Africa, 1967; (autobiog.) The Man who Loves Giants, 1975; Paintings of Africa and India, 1978; A Brush with Steam, 1983; David Shepherd: the man and his paintings, 1985. *Recreations:* driving steam engines, raising money for wildlife. *Address:* Winkworth Farm, Hascombe, Godalming, Surrey GU8 4JW. *T:* Hascombe (048632) 220.

SHEPHERD, Rt. Rev. Ronald Francis; *see* British Columbia, Bishop of.

SHEPHERD, William Stanley; *b* 1918; *s* of W. D. Shepherd; *m* 1942, Betty, *d* of late T. F. Howard, MP for Islington South, 1931–35; two *s*. Served in Army, War of 1939–45. A managing director of businesses which he has established; MP (C) for Cheadle Division of Cheshire, 1950–66 (Bucklow Division of Cheshire, 1945–50); Member of the Select Committee on Estimates; Joint Hon. Sec. Conservative Parliamentary Committee in Trade and Industry, 1945–51. Joined SDP, 1982. Hon. Mem., Valuers Institution. FREconS. *Address:* (office) 77 George Street, W1. *T:* 071–935 0753; (home) 33 Queens Grove, St John's Wood, NW8. *T:* 071–722 7526. *Club:* Savile.

SHEPHERDSON, Prof. John Cedric, ScD; FBA 1990; FIMA; H. O. Wills Professor of Mathematics, Bristol University, 1977–91, now Emeritus; *b* 7 June 1926; *s* of Arnold Shepherdson and Elsie (*née* Aspinall); *m* 1957, Margaret Smith; one *s* two *d*. *Educ:* Manchester Grammar Sch.; Trinity Coll., Cambridge (BA, MA, ScD). Asst Experimental Officer, Aerodynamics and Maths Div., NPL, 1946; Bristol University: Asst Lectr in Maths, 1946–49; Lectr, 1949–55; Reader, 1955–63; Prof. of Pure Maths, 1964–77. Mem., Inst. for Advanced Study, Princeton, 1953–54; Vis. Associate Prof., 1958–59, Vis. Prof., 1966–67, Univ. of Calif at Berkeley; Vis. Prof., Monash Univ., 1971, 1986; Vis. Scientist, IBM Res. Labs, Yorktown Heights, NY, 1973, 1975, 1979; Guest, Technische Hochschule, Zürich, 1988. *Publications:* papers in mathematical, logical and computer sci. jls. *Recreations:* walking, ski-ing, board-sailing, occasional climbing. *Address:* Oakhurst, North Road, Leigh Woods, Bristol BS8 3PN. *T:* Bristol (0272) 735410. *Clubs:* Fell & Rock Climbing (Lake District); Bristol Corinthian Yacht.

SHEPPARD, Sir Allen (John George), Kt 1990; Chief Executive, since 1986 and Chairman, since 1987, Grand Metropolitan plc; *b* 25 Dec. 1932; *s* of John Baggott Sheppard and Lily Marjorie Sheppard (*née* Palmer); *m* 1st, 1959, Peggy Damaris (*née* Jones) (marr. diss. 1980); 2nd, 1980, Mary (*née* Stewart). *Educ:* Ilford County School; London School of Economics (BSc Econ). FCMA, FCIS, ATII. Ford of Britain and Ford of Europe, 1958–68; Rootes/Chrysler, 1968–71; British Leyland, 1971–75; Grand Metropolitan, 1975–, Gp Man. Dir, 1982–86; Non. Exec. Dir, later Chm., UBM Group, 1981–85; Chm., Mallinson-Denny Group, 1985–87. Dep. Chm., Meyer Internat., 1991– (Non-exec. Dir, 1989–). Part time Mem., BR Board, 1985–90. Member: Nat. Trng Task Force, 1989–; NEDC; Deputy Chairman: Business in the Community, 1989–; Internat. Business Leaders Forum, 1990–; Chm., Bd of Trustees, Prince's Youth Business Trust, 1990–. Chm., Adv. Bd, British American Chamber of Commerce, 1991–. Governor, LSE, 1989–. CBIM; FRSA. *Publications:* Your Business Matters, 1958; articles in professional jls. *Recreations:* gardens, reading, red setter dogs. *Address:* (office) 20 St James's Square, SW1Y 4RR.

SHEPPARD, Rt. Rev. David Stuart; *see* Liverpool, Bishop of.

SHEPPARD, Francis Henry Wollaston; General Editor, Survey of London, 1954–82, retired; *b* 10 Sept. 1921; *s* of late Leslie Alfred Sheppard; *m* 1st, 1949, Pamela Gordon Davies (*d* 1954); one *s* one *d*; 2nd, 1957, Elizabeth Fleur Lees; one *d*. *Educ:* Bradfield; King's Coll., Cambridge (MA); PhD London. FRHistS. Asst Archivist, West Sussex CC, Chichester, 1947–48; Asst Keeper, London Museum, 1948–53. Mayor of Henley on Thames, 1970–71; Pres., Henley Symphony Orchestra, 1973–76. Visiting Fellow, Leicester Univ., 1977–78; Alice Davis Hitchcock Medallion of Soc. of Architectural Historians of Gt Britain, 1964. *Publications:* Local Government in St Marylebone 1688–1835, 1958; London 1808–1870: The Infernal Wen, 1971; Brakspear's Brewery, Henley on Thames, 1779–1979, 1979; The Treasury of London's Past, 1991; (ed) Survey of London, Vols XXVI-XLI, 1956–83. *Recreation:* music. *Address:* 10 Albion Place, West Street, Henley on Thames, Oxon RG9 2DT. *T:* Henley on Thames (0491) 574658.

SHEPPARD, Maurice Raymond, RWS; painter; President, Royal Society of Painters in Water-Colours, 1984–87; *b* 25 Feb. 1947; *s* of late Wilfred Ernest Sheppard and of Florence Hilda (*née* Morris). *Educ:* Loughborough; Kingston upon Thames (Dip AD Hons 1970); Royal College of Art (MA 1973). ARWS 1974, RWS 1977, Vice-Pres., 1978–83, Trustee, 1987–. One man exhibitions: New Grafton Gallery, 1979; Christopher Wood Gall., 1989; inaugural exhibn of L'Institut Europ. de l'Aquarelle, Brussels, 1986; works in: Royal Library, Windsor; BM; Contemporary Art Soc. for Wales; V&A; Nat. Museum of Wales; Beecroft Museum and Art Gallery, Southend. British Instn Award, 1971; David Murray Landscape Award, 1972; Geoffrey Crawshay Meml Travelling Schol., Univ. of Wales, 1973. *Publications:* articles and essays in jls and catalogues; *relevant publication:* Maurice Sheppard, RWS, by Felicity Owen (Old Watercolour Society Club, vol. 59, 1984). *Recreations:* cycling, a small garden, the pursuit of quiet. *Address:* Mole Bridge Cottage, 14 Apsley Street, Rusthall Common, Tunbridge Wells, Kent TN4 8NU. *T:* Tunbridge Wells (0892) 513405.

SHEPPARD, Tan Sri Dato Mervyn Cecil ffranck, PSM (Malaysia) 1969; DPMS 1982; DSNS 1988; DJPD (Malaysia), 1967; JMN (Malaysia), 1963; CMG 1957; MBE 1946; ED 1947; Vice-President and Editor, Malaysian Branch, Royal Asiatic Society; *b* 1905; *s* of late Canon J. W. ff. Sheppard; *m* 1940, Rosemary, *d* of late Major Edward Oakeley; one *d*. *Educ:* Marlborough; Magdalene Coll., Cambridge (MA). Cadet, Federated Malay States, 1928; Private Sec. to Chief Sec., 1929. Interned by Japanese, 1942–45; Major, FMS Volunteer Force, retd 1946. Director of Public Relations, 1946; District Officer, Klang, 1947–50; British Adviser, Negri Sembilan, 1952; Head of the Emergency Food Denial Organisation, Federation of Malaya, 1956. First Keeper of Public Records, 1957–62, and Director of Museums, 1958–63, Federation of Malaya. Vice Pres. and Hon. Editor, Malaysian Br., RAS, 1971–; Co-Founder and Vice-Pres., Heritage of Malaysia Trust, 1983–. Hon. Curator, Nat. Museum, Kuala Lumpur. Hon. DLitt Univ. Sains Malaysia, 1984. Biennial Award, Tun Abdul Razak Foundn, 1983. *Publications:* Taman Indera, Royal Pleasure Ground, 1972; Living Crafts of Malaysia, 1978; Memoirs of an Unorthodox Civil Servant, 1979; Tunku: a pictorial biography, part 1, 1903–1957, 1984, part 2, 1957–1987, 1987. *Address:* Apartment 7C, Crescent Court, Brickfields, 50470 Kuala Lumpur, Malaysia. *Clubs:* United Oxford & Cambridge University; Royal Selangor (Kuala Lumpur).

SHEPPARD, Prof. Norman, FRS 1967; Professor of Chemical Sciences, University of East Anglia, Norwich, 1964–86, now Emeritus; *b* 16 May 1921; *s* of Walter Sheppard and Anne Clarges Sheppard (*née* Finding); *m* 1949, Kathleen Margery McLean; two *s* one *d* (and one *s* decd). *Educ:* Hymers Coll., Hull; St Catharine's Coll., Cambridge. BA Cantab 1st cl. hons 1943; PhD and MA Cantab 1947. Vis. Asst Prof., Pennsylvania State Univ., 1947–48; Ramsay Memorial Fellow, 1948–49; Senior 1851 Exhibn, 1949–51; Fellow of Trinity Coll., Cambridge and Asst Dir of Research in Spectroscopy, Cambridge Univ., 1957–64. *Publications:* scientific papers on spectroscopy in Proc. Roy. Soc., Trans. Faraday Soc., Jl Chem. Soc., Spectrochimica Acta, etc. *Recreations:* architecture, classical music, walking. *Address:* 5 Hornor Close, Norwich NR2 2LY. *T:* Norwich (0603) 53052.

SHEPPERD, Sir Alfred (Joseph), Kt 1989; Chairman and Chief Executive: Wellcome plc, 1986–90; The Wellcome Foundation Ltd, 1977–90; Chairman, Burroughs Wellcome Co., 1986–90; *b* 19 June 1925; *s* of Alfred Charles Shepperd and Mary Ann Williams; *m* 1950, Gabrielle Marie Yvette Bouloux; two *d*. *Educ:* Archbishop Tenison's Sch.; University Coll., London (BSc Econ; Fellow, 1986). Rank Organisation, 1949; Selincourt & Sons Ltd, 1963; Chamberlain Group, 1965; Managing Director, Keyser Ullmann Industries Ltd, 1967; Dir, Keyser Ullmann Ltd, 1967; Financial Dir, Laporte Industries Ltd, 1971, Wellcome Foundation Ltd, 1972; Director: Anglia Maltings (Holdings) Ltd, 1972–; Mercury Asset Management Holdings Ltd, 1987–; Mercury Asset Management Group plc, 1987–; Isoscelles plc; Dep. Chm., Zoo Ops Ltd, 1988–91. Mem., ACOST, 1989–. Member: Adv. Bd, British-Amer. Chamber of Commerce, 1988–; Governing Body, Internat. Chamber of Commerce UK, 1988–. Mem., Adv. Panel, Common Law Inst. of Intellectual Property, 1986–; Governor: NIESR, 1981–; Royal Agricl Soc. of England, 1977–90. Commendatore della Repubblica, Italy, 1983; Encomienda al Merito de Sanidad, Spain, 1988; Comdr, Order of Leopold II, Belgium, 1989. *Address:* Court Mead, 6 Guildown Avenue, Guildford, Surrey GU2 5HB. *Club:* Oriental.

SHEPPERSON, Prof. George Albert, CBE 1989; William Robertson Professor of Commonwealth and American History, University of Edinburgh, 1963–86, now Emeritus; *b* 7 Jan. 1922; *s* of late Albert Edward Shepperson and Bertha Agnes (*née* Jennings); *m* 1952, Joyce Irene (*née* Cooper); one *d*. *Educ:* King's Sch., Peterborough; St John's Coll., Cambridge (Schol.; 1st Class Hons: English Tripos, Pt I, 1942; Historical Tripos, Pt II, 1947); 1st Cl. CertEd (Cantab), 1948. Served War, commnd Northamptonshire Regt, seconded to KAR, 1942–46. Edinburgh University: Lectr in Imperial and American History, 1948, Sen. Lectr, 1960, Reader, 1961; Dean of Faculty of Arts, 1974–77. Visiting Professor: Roosevelt and Chicago Univs, 1959; Makerere Coll., Uganda, 1962; Dalhousie Univ., 1968–69; Rhode Is Coll., 1984; Vis. Scholar, W. E. B. DuBois Inst. for Afro-American Res., Harvard Univ., 1986–87; Lectures: Herskovits Meml, Northwestern Univ., 1966 and 1972; Livingstone Centenary, RGS, 1973; Soc. of the Cincinnati, State of Virginia, 1976; Sarah Tryphena Phillips, in Amer. Lit. and Hist., British Acad., 1979; Rhodes Commem., Rhodes Univ., 1981. Chairman: British Assoc. for American Studies, 1971–74; Mungo Park Bicentenary Cttee, 1971; David Livingstone Documentation Project, 1973–89; Commonwealth Inst., Scotland, 1973–89; Mem., Marshall Aid Commemoration Commn, 1976–88. FEIS 1990. DUniv: York, 1987; Edinburgh, 1991. Jt Editor, Oxford Studies in African Affairs, 1969–85. *Publications:* Independent African: John Chilembwe, 1958, 5th edn 1987; David Livingstone and the Rovuma, 1964; many articles and chapters in learned jls, collaborative vols and encycs.

Recreations: theatre; collecting African and Afro-American documents. *Address:* 15 Farleigh Fields, Orton Wistow, Peterborough PE2 0YB.

SHER, Antony; actor, writer; *b* 14 June 1949; *s* of Emmanuel and Margery Sher. *Educ:* Sea Point Boys' Junior and High Schools, Cape Town; Webber-Douglas Acad. of Dramatic Art, London, 1969–71. Repertory seasons at Liverpool Everyman, Nottingham Playhouse and Royal Lyceum, Edinburgh; John, Paul, George, Ringo and Bert; Teeth and Smiles; Goose-Pimples; Torch Song Trilogy, Albery, 1985; True West, NT; The Trial, The Resistable Rise of Arturo Ui, NT, 1991; Royal Shakespeare Co.: Associate Artist, 1982–; Richard III, Merchant of Venice, Twelfth Night, King Lear, The Revenger's Tragedy, Molière, Tartuffe, Hello and Goodbye, Maydays, Red Noses; Singer; *films:* Shadey, 1986; Mark Gertler; *television series:* The History Man, 1982; The Land of Dreams, 1990. Best Actor Awards: Drama Magazine, 1984; Laurence Olivier, 1985; London Standard, 1985. *Publications:* Year of the King, 1985; Middlepost (novel), 1988; Characters (paintings and drawings), 1989; Changing Step (TV filmscript), 1989; The Indoor Boy (novel), 1991. *Address:* c/o Hope and Lyne, 108 Leonard Street, EC2A 4RH. *T:* 071–739 6200.

SHER, Samuel Julius; QC 1981; a Recorder, since 1987; *b* 22 Oct. 1941; *s* of Philip and Isa Phyllis Sher; *m* 1965, Sandra Maris; one *s* two *d. Educ:* Athlone High Sch., Johannesburg; Univ. of the Witwatersrand (BComm, LLB); New Coll., Oxford (BCL). Called to the Bar, Inner Temple, 1968, Bencher, 1988. *Recreation:* tennis. *Address:* 12 Constable Close, NW11 6TY. *T:* 081–455 2753.
See also V. H. Sher.

SHER, Victor Herman, (Harold), CA (SA); Chief Executive, Amalgamated Metal Corporation Plc, since 1992 (Group Managing Director, 1988–92); *b* 13 Jan. 1947; *s* of Philip Sher and Isa Phyllis Sher; *m* 1979, Molly Sher; one *s* three *d. Educ:* King Edward VII Sch., Johannesburg; Univ. of the Witwatersrand, Johannesburg (BComm). Chartered Accountant, Fuller, Jenks Beechcroft, 1972–73; Amalgamated Metal Corporation: Taxation Manager, 1973; Finance Manager, 1977; Dir of Corporate Finance, 1978; Dir of Corporate Treasury, 1981; Finance Dir, 1983; Finance and Trading Dir, 1986. Chm. of Trustees, Amalgamated Metal Corp. Pension Scheme, 1983– (Trustee, 1978). *Recreation:* tennis. *Address:* 42 Southway, Hampstead Garden Suburb, NW11 6SA. *T:* 081–455 6160.
See also S. J. Sher.

SHERBORNE, Area Bishop of; Rt. Rev. John Dudley Galtrey Kirkham; appointed Bishop Suffragan of Sherborne, 1976; Canon and Prebendary of Salisbury Cathedral, since 1977; *b* 20 Sept. 1935; *s* of late Rev. Canon Charles Dudley Kirkham and Doreen Betty Galtrey; *m* 1986, Mrs Hester Gregory. *Educ:* Lancing Coll.; Trinity Coll., Cambridge (BA 1959, MA 1963). Commnd, Royal Hampshire Regt and seconded to 23 (K) Bn, King's African Rifles, 1954–56. Trinity Coll., Cambridge, 1956–59; Westcott House, 1960–62; Curate, St Mary-Le-Tower, Ipswich, 1962–65; Chaplain to Bishop of Norwich, 1965–69; Priest in Charge, Rockland St Mary w. Hellington, 1967–69; Chaplain to Bishop of New Guinea, 1969; Asst Priest, St Martin in the Fields and St Margaret's, Westminster, 1970–72; Domestic Chaplain to Archbishop of Canterbury, 1972–76; Canterbury Diocesan Director of Ordinands, 1972–76. Archbishop of Canterbury's Advr to HMC, 1990–. Commissary to Bp of Polynesia and Archbp of PNG. Serving Brother Chaplain of the Order of St John of Jerusalem; Chaplain to the Guild of the Nineteen Lubricators. Croix d'Argent de Saint-Rombaut, 1973. *Recreations:* skiing, walking, wood-work, reading. *Address:* Little Bailie, Sturminster Marshall, Wimborne, Dorset BH21 4AD. *Clubs:* Army and Navy, Ski of Great Britain, Kandahar.

SHERBORNE, Archdeacon of; *see* Wheatley, Ven. P. C.

SHERBOURNE, Stephen Ashley, CBE 1988; Senior Corporate Communications Consultant, Lowe Bell Communications, since 1988; *b* 15 Oct. 1945; *s* of late Jack and of Blanche Sherbourne. *Educ:* Burnage Grammar Sch., Manchester; St Edmund Hall, Oxford (BA PPE). Hill Samuel, 1968–70; Conservative Research Dept, 1970–75: Head of Economic Section, 1973–74; Asst Dir, 1974–75; Head of Rt Hon. Edward Heath's Office, 1975–76; Gallaher, 1978–82; Special Adviser to Rt Hon. Patrick Jenkin, (then) Sec. of State for Industry, 1982–83; Political Sec. to the Prime Minister, 1983–88. *Recreations:* cinema, tennis, music. *Club:* Reform.

SHERBROOKE, Archbishop of, (RC), since 1968; **Most Rev. Jean-Marie Fortier;** *b* 1 July 1920. *Educ:* Laval University, Quebec. Bishop Auxiliary, La Pocatière, PQ, 1961–65; Bishop of Gaspé, PQ, 1965–68. Elected Pres., Canadian Catholic Conference, 1973–75. Prés. de l'Assemblée des Evêques du Québec, 1984–89. *Publication:* contrib. to Dictionnaire d'Histoire et de Géographie. *Address:* 130 rue de la Cathédrale, Sherbrooke, PQ J1H 4M1, Canada. *T:* 569–6070.

SHERFIELD, 1st Baron, *cr* 1964; **Roger Mellor Makins,** GCB 1960 (KCB 1953); GCMG 1955 (KCMG 1949; CMG 1944); FRS 1986; DL; Chancellor of Reading University, since 1970; *b* 3 Feb. 1904; *e s* of late Brigadier-General Sir Ernest Makins, KBE, CB, DSO; *m* 1934, Alice (*d* 1985), *e d* of late Hon. Dwight F. Davis; two *s* four *d. Educ:* Winchester; Christ Church, Oxford. First Class Honours in History, 1925; Fellow of All Souls College, 1925–39 and 1957–; called to Bar, Inner Temple, 1927; Foreign Office, 1928; served Washington, 1931–34, Oslo, 1934; Foreign Office, 1934; Assistant Adviser on League of Nations Affairs, 1937; Sec. Intergovernmental Cttee on Refugees from Germany, 1938–39; Adviser on League of Nations Affairs, 1939; Acting First Secretary, 1939; Acting Counsellor, 1940; Adviser to British Delegation, International Labour Conference, New York, 1941; served on Staff of Resident Minister in West Africa, 1942; Counsellor, 1942; Asst to Resident Minister at Allied Force Headquarters, Mediterranean, 1943–44; Minister at British Embassy, Washington, 1945–47; UK rep. on United Nations Interim Commission for Food and Agriculture, 1945; Asst Under-Sec. of State, FO, 1947–48, Dep. Under-Sec. of State, 1948–52; British Ambassador to the United States, 1953–56; Joint Permanent Secretary of the Treasury, 1956–59; Chm., UKAEA, 1960–64. Chairman: Hill, Samuel Group, 1966–70; Finance for Industry Ltd, 1973–74; Finance Corp. for Industry Ltd, 1973–74; Industrial & Commercial Finance Corp., 1964–74; Estate Duties Investment Trust, 1966–73; Ship Mortgage Finance Co., 1966–74; Technical Develt Capital, 1966–74; A. C. Cossor, 1968–82; Raytheon Europe Internat. Co., 1970–82; Wells Fargo Ltd, 1972–84, and other companies; Director: Times Publishing Co., 1964–67; Badger Ltd, 1981–83. Pres., BSI, 1970–73. Pres., Parly and Scientific Cttee, 1969–73; Chm., H of L Select Cttee on Science and Technology, 1984–87. Vice-Chm., The Ditchley Foundn, 1965–74 (Chm., 1962–65); Pres., Centre for Internat. Briefing, 1972–85; Mem., Foundn for Science and Technology, 1990–. Chm., Governing Body and Fellow of Imperial Coll. of Science and Technology, 1962–74. Fellow, Winchester College, 1962–79 (Warden, 1974–79). Chairman: Marshall Aid Commemoration Commn, 1965–73; Lindemann Trust Fellowship Cttee, 1973–83; Mem. of Council, Royal Albert Hall, 1959–87; Trustee, The Times Trust, 1968–73. DL Hants, 1978. Attlee Foundn Lectr, 1986. Hon. Student, Christ Church, Oxford, 1973; Hon. FICE 1964; Hon. DCL Oxford; Hon. DLitt Reading; Hon. LLD: Sheffield; London; Hon. DL North Carolina; and other American universities and colleges. Benjamin Franklin Medal, RSA, 1982. *Publications:* (ed) Economic and Social Consequences of Nuclear Energy, 1972; lectures and articles on science policy. *Recreations:* shooting, gardening. *Heir: s* Hon. Christopher James Makins [*b* 23 July 1942; *m* 1976, Wendy Cortesi]. *Address:* 81 Onslow Square, SW7; Ham Farm House, Ramsdell, near Basingstoke, Hants. *Clubs:* Boodle's, Pratt's, MCC.
See also Baron Milford, Viscount Norwich.

SHERGOLD, Harold Taplin, CMG 1963; OBE 1958 (MBE 1945); served in Foreign and Commonwealth Office (formerly Foreign Office), 1954–80; *b* 5 Dec. 1915; *s* of late Ernest Henry Shergold; *m* 1949, Bevis Anael, *d* of late William Bernard Reid; no *c. Educ:* Peter Symonds' School, Winchester; St Edmund Hall, Oxford; Corpus Christi Coll., Cambridge. Asst Master, Cheltenham Grammar Sch., 1937–40. Joined Hampshire Regt, 1940; transferred to Intelligence Corps, 1941; served in Middle East and Italy, 1941–46 (despatches). Joined Foreign Office, 1947; served in Germany, 1947–54. Chm., 1983–90, Pres., 1990–, Richmond, Twickenham & Dist Br., Guide Dogs for the Blind Assoc. *Address:* 1 Ancaster Court, Queens Road, Richmond, Surrey TW10 6JJ. *T:* 081–948 2048.

SHERIDAN, Cecil Majella, CMG 1961; company director, since 1984; *b* 9 Dec. 1911; *s* of late J. P. Sheridan, Liverpool, and Mrs Sheridan (*née* Myerscough), Preston, Lancs; *m* 1949, Monica, *d* of H. F. Ereaut, MBE, Jersey, CI; two *s* one *d. Educ:* Ampleforth College, York. Admitted Solicitor, England, 1934; called to Bar, Inner Temple, 1952. Practised as solicitor in Liverpool (Messrs Yates, Sheridan & Co.), 1934–40. Served in RAFVR, General Duties Pilot, 1940–46; resigned with hon. rank of Squadron Leader. Joined Colonial Legal Service, 1946; Crown Counsel and Dep. Public Prosecutor, Malayan Union, 1946–48; Legal Adviser, Malay States of Pahang, Kelantan, Trengganu and Selangor and Settlement of Penang, 1948–55; Legal Draftsman, Fedn of Malaya, 1955–57; Solicitor-General, Fedn of Malaya, 1957–59; Attorney-General, Fedn of Malaya, 1959–63; Attorney-General, Malaysia, retd. Mem. (Fedn of Malaya) Inter-Governmental Cttees for Borneo Territories and Singapore, 1962–63. Chm. Traffic Comrs, E Midland Traffic Area, 1965–81, Dep. Chm., 1981–82. Pres., British Assoc. of Malaysia, 1964–65. Chm., Malaysia Housing Soc., 1964–65. Associate Mem., Commonwealth Parly Assoc. (UK Branch). Hon. PMN (Malaysia), 1963. *Address:* 18 Private Road, Sherwood, Nottingham NG5 4DB. *Clubs:* East India, Devonshire, Sports and Public Schools; Nottinghamshire.

SHERIDAN, Christopher Julian; Deputy Chairman, since 1988, and Chief Executive, since 1984, Samuel Montagu & Co.; *b* 18 Feb. 1943; *s* of late Mark Sheridan and of Olive Maud Sheridan (*née* Hobbs); *m* 1972, Diane Virginia (*née* Wadey); one *d. Educ:* Berkhamsted School. Joined Samuel Montagu & Co., 1962; Dir, 1974; Managing Dir, 1981. *Recreations:* theatre, tennis, ski-ing. *Address:* 5 Onslow Square, SW7 3NJ. *T:* 071–589 6092. *Club:* Buck's.

SHERIDAN, Prof. Lionel Astor, PhD, LLD; Professor of Law, University College, Cardiff, 1971–88 (Acting Principal, 1980 and 1987); retired; *b* 21 July 1927; *s* of Stanley Frederick and Anne Agnes Sheridan; *m* 1948, Margaret Helen (*née* Béghin); one *s* (one *d* decd). *Educ:* Whitgift Sch., Croydon; University College London (LLB 1947; LLD 1969); Queen's Univ., Belfast (PhD 1953). Called to the Bar, Lincoln's Inn, 1948. Part-time Lectr, Univ. of Nottingham, 1949; Lectr, QUB, 1949–56; Prof. of Law, Univ. of Singapore (formerly Univ. of Malaya in Singapore), 1956–63; Prof. of Comparative Law, QUB, 1963–71. Hon. LLD Univ. of Singapore, 1963. *Publications:* Fraud in Equity, 1957; Constitutional Protection, 1963; Rights in Security, 1974; *jointly:* The Cy-près Doctrine, 1959; Constitution of Malaysia, 1961, 4th edn 1987; Malaya, Singapore, The Borneo Territories, 1961; Equity, 1969, 3rd edn 1987; Survey of the Land Law of Northern Ireland, 1971; The Modern Law of Charities, 1971, 3rd edn 1983; The Law of Trusts, 10th edn 1974, 11th edn 1983; The Comparative Law of Trusts in the Commonwealth and the Irish Republic, 1976; Digest of the English Law of Trusts, 1979; papers in jls. *Recreations:* reading, walking, theatre-going. *Address:* Cherry Trees, Broadway Green, St Nicholas, South Glam CF5 6SR. *T:* Peterston-super-Ely (0446) 760403. *Club:* Athenæum.

SHERIDAN, Peter, QC 1977; *b* 29 May 1927; *s* of Hugo and Marie Sheridan. *Educ:* eight schools; Lincoln Coll., Oxford Univ. BA Hons, 1950. Called to the Bar, Middle Temple, 1955, Bencher, 1988. *Recreations:* motor cars, archery. *Address:* 2 Crown Office Row, Temple, EC4Y 7HJ; 17 Brompton Square, SW3. *T:* 071–584 7250; Pile Oak Lodge, Donhead St Andrew, Wilts. *T:* Donhead (074788) 484.

SHERIDAN, Roderick Gerald, OBE 1978; MVO 1968; HM Diplomatic Service, retired; Consul-General, Barcelona and Andorra, 1977–80; Hon. Vice-Consul, Menorca, since 1983; *b* 24 Jan. 1921; *s* of late Sir Joseph Sheridan; *m* 1942, Lois Mary (*née* Greene); one *s* one *d. Educ:* Downside Sch.; Pembroke Coll., Cambridge. Served War, Coldstream Guards, N Africa and Italy, 1940–46. HM Overseas Colonial Service: Zanzibar and Cyprus, 1946–60; retd as District Comr, Nicosia; HM Diplomatic Service, 1960–: First Sec., Cyprus, 1960–63; Foreign Office, 1964–66; First Sec., Brasilia, 1966–69; FO, 1969–70; Head of Chancery, Oslo, 1970–73; Consul, Algeciras, 1973–77. *Recreations:* tennis, golf, skiing.

SHERLOCK, Dr Alexander, CBE 1989; medical practitioner; *b* 14 Feb. 1922; *s* of Thomas Sherlock, MM, and Evelyn M. Sherlock (*née* Alexander); *m* 1st, 1945, Clarice C. Scarff; one *s* two *d*; 2nd, 1976, Eileen Hall; one step *d. Educ:* Magdalen College Sch., Oxford; Stowmarket Grammar Sch.; London Hospital. MB BS (Hons) 1945. Ho. Phys., Ho. Surg., London Hosp.; RAF, 1946–48; Medical Practitioner, Felixstowe, and Consultant/Adviser to many organisations in matters of occupational health, safety and welfare. Called to the Bar, Gray's Inn, 1961. Member: Felixstowe UDC, 1960–74; E Suffolk CC, 1966–74; Suffolk CC, 1974–79 (Chairman, Fire and Public Protection Cttee, 1977–79). MEP (C) SW Essex, 1979–89; former Mem. of Envmt Cttee (Eur. Democratic (C) Leader) and Develt Cttee; spokesman on Envmt, Health and Consumer Protection, 1979–89. Vice-President: Inst. of Trading Officers, 1981–; Assoc. of Envmtl Health Officers, 1981–; Soc. of Dist Councils, 1981–. FRSA. OStJ 1974. *Recreation:* gardening. *Address:* 58 Orwell Road, Felixstowe IP11 7PS. *T:* Felixstowe (0394) 284503. *Club:* Royal Air Force.

SHERLOCK, Prof. David Christopher, FCSD; Director of Development, Royal College of Art, since 1991; *b* 6 Nov. 1943; *s* of Frank Ernest Sherlock and Emily Edna (*née* Johnson); *m* 1st, 1970, Jean Earl; 2nd, 1976, Cynthia Mary (*née* Hood); one *s* one *d. Educ:* Rutlish Sch., Merton, Newcastle upon Tyne; College of Art and Industrial Design, Univ. of Nottingham (BA, MPhil). Nottingham Coll. of Art, 1966–70; Trent Polytechnic, 1970–74; Dep. Dir, Nat. College of Art and Design, Dublin, 1975–80; Principal, Winchester Sch. of Art, 1980–87; Exec. Chm., Hampshire Consortium for Art, Design and Architecture, 1985–87; Head of Central Saint Martin's Coll. of Art and Design and Asst Rector, London Inst., 1988–91. FRSA. *Recreations:* sailing, mountain biking, opera, advising developing countries on design, cooking, good wine. *Address:* Royal College of Art, Kensington Gore, SW7 2EU. *T:* 071–584 5020; Woodside, Park Road, Winchester, Hampshire. *T:* Winchester (0962) 854661. *Club:* Royal Southern Yacht (Hamble).

SHERLOCK, (Edward) Barry (Orton), CBE 1991; Chairman, Life Assurance and Unit Trust Regulatory Organisation, since 1986; *b* 10 Feb. 1932; *s* of Victor Edward and Irene

Octavia Sherlock; *m* 1955, Lucy Trerice Willey; two *d*. *Educ:* Merchant Taylors' School; Pembroke College, Cambridge (MA 1st cl. Hons Maths). FIA. Joined Equitable Life Assurance Society, 1956; qualified actuary, 1958; Asst Actuary, 1962; Asst Gen. Manager, 1968; Gen. Manager and Actuary, 1972–91; Dir, 1972–. Institute of Actuaries: Hon. Sec., 1978–80; Vice-Pres., 1981–84. Chairman: Life Offices' Assoc., 1985; Life Insurance Council, Assoc. of British Insurers, 1985–86. Liveryman, Co. of Actuaries. *Recreations:* music, gardening. *Address:* 63 Sunnyfield, Mill Hill, NW7 4RE. *T:* 081–959 5193. *Club:* Actuaries'.

SHERLOCK, Sir Philip (Manderson), KBE 1967 (CBE 1953); Vice President, Caribbean Resources Development Foundation Inc., since 1983; *b* Jamaica, 25 Feb. 1902; *s* of Rev. Terence Sherlock, Methodist Minister, and Adina Sherlock; *m* 1942, Grace Marjorye Verity; two *s* one *d*. *Educ:* Calabar High Sch., Jamaica. Headmaster, Wolmer's Boys' Sch., Jamaica, 1933–38; Sec., Inst. of Jamaica, 1939–44; Educn Officer, Jamaica Welfare, 1944–47; Dir, Extra-Mural Dept, University Coll. of West Indies, 1947–60, also Vice-Principal, University Coll. of W Indies, 1952–62; Pro-Vice-Chancellor, Univ. of West Indies, 1962, Vice-Chancellor, 1963–69; Sec.-Gen., Assoc. of Caribbean Univs & Res. Insts, 1969–79; Sec., Assoc. of Caribbean Univs Foundn, 1979–83. Hon. LLD: Leeds, 1959; Carleton, 1967; St Andrews, 1968; Hon. DCL New Brunswick, 1966; Hon. DLitt: Acadia, 1966; Miami, 1971; Univ. of WI, 1972; Florida, 1975. Order of Andres Bello with collar (Venezuela), 1978. *Publications:* Anansi the Spider Man, 1956; (with John Parry) Short History of the West Indies, 1956, 4th edn 1987; Caribbean Citizen, 1957; West Indian Story, 1960; Three Finger Jack, 1961; Jamaica, A Junior History, 1966; West Indian Folk Tales, 1966; West Indies, 1966; Land and People of the West Indies, 1967; Belize, a Junior History, 1969; The Iguana's Tail, 1969; West Indian Nations, 1973; Ears and Tails and Common Sense, 1974; Shout for Freedom, 1976; Norman Manley, a biography, 1980; Keeping Company with Jamaica, 1984; educational books and articles. *Recreations:* reading, writing, cooking. *Address:* Caribbean Resources Development Foundation Inc., PO Box 248074, Coral Gables, Florida 33124, USA. *Club:* National Liberal.

SHERLOCK, Prof. Dame Sheila (Patricia Violet), DBE 1978; MD; FRCP; FRCPEd; Professor of Medicine, University of London, at the Royal Free Hospital School of Medicine, since 1959; *b* 31 March 1918; *d* of late Samuel Philip Sherlock and Violet Mary Catherine Beckett; *m* 1951, David Geraint James, *qv*; two *d*. *Educ:* Folkestone County Sch.; Edinburgh Univ. Ettles Scholar, 1941; Beit Memorial Research Fellow, 1942–47; Rockefeller Fellow, Yale University, USA, 1948. Physician and Lecturer in Medicine, Postgraduate Medical School of London, 1948–59. RCP Lectures: Bradshaw, 1961; Rolleston, 1968; Lumleian, 1978; Harveian, 1985. RCP: Councillor, 1964–68; Censor, 1970–72; Senior Censor and Vice-Pres., 1976–77. Mem. Senate, Univ. of London, 1976–81. Hon. Member: Gastro-enterological Societies of America, 1963, Australasia, 1965, Mexico, 1968, Czechoslovakia, 1968, Yugoslavia, 1981, Sweden, 1983; Assoc. of Amer. Physicians, 1973; Assoc. of Alimentary Surgeons, 1973. Hon. FACP; Hon. FRCPC; Hon. FRACP 1984; Hon. FRCPI; Hon. FRCPS 1986; Hon. FRCS 1989. Hon. DSc: City Univ. of NY, 1977; Yale Univ., USA, 1983; Edinburgh, 1985; London, 1989; Hon. MD: Lisbon, 1981; Oslo, 1981; Leuven, 1984; Barcelona, 1991; Mainz, 1991; Hon. LLD Aberdeen, 1982. William Cullen Prize, 1962 (shared); Jimenez-Diaz Prize, 1980; Thannhauser Prize, 1980; Fothergill Gold Medal, Med. Soc. of London, 1983; Gold Medal, BMA, 1985. *Publications:* Diseases of the Liver and Biliary System, 1955, 8th edn 1989; papers on liver structure and function in various medical journals, since 1943. *Recreations:* cricket, travel. *Address:* 41 York Terrace East, NW1 4PT. *T:* 071–486 4560, 071–431 4589.

SHERMAN, Sir Alfred, Kt 1983; journalist; public affairs advisor in private practice; co-founder, Centre for Policy Studies, 1974 (Director of Studies until 1984); *b* 10 Nov. 1919; *m* 1958, Zahava (*née* Levin); one *s*. Served in International Brigade, Spanish Civil War, 1937–38; war of 1939–45 in field security and occupied enemy territory administration. Mem., economic adv. staff of Israeli Govt, in 1950s; leader writer, Jewish Chronicle; various appts with Daily Telegraph, 1965–86, as leader writer 1977–86. Vis. Fellow, LSE, 1983–85. Broadcaster. Councillor, RBK&C, 1971–78. Mem., West End Synagogue. *Publications:* Local Government Reorganisation and Industry, 1970; Councils, Councillors and Public Relations, 1973; Local Government Reorganization and the Salary Bill, 1974; (with D. Mallam) Waste in Wandsworth, 1976; Crisis Calls for a Minister for Denationalization, 1980; The Scott Report, 1981; (introd.) The Grenada Documents, ed Brian Crozier, 1987; (contrib.) Revisionism, 1961; Communism and Arab Nationalism: a reappraisal; Capitalism and Liberty; Our Complacent Satirists; Political Violence in Britain; contribs to newspapers and periodicals. *Address:* 14 Malvern Court, Onslow Square, SW7 3HU. *T:* 071–581 4075. *Cables:* SHERMANIA LONDON SW7. *Clubs:* Reform, Hurlingham.

SHERMAN, Sir Louis, (Sir Lou Sherman), Kt 1975; OBE 1967; JP; Chairman, Housing Corporation, 1977–80; Deputy Chairman, Harlow Development Corporation. Initiated Lea Valley Regional Park Authority. JP Inner London Area. *Recreations:* politics, reading, talking. *Club:* Reform.

SHERRARD, Michael David, QC 1968; a Recorder of the Crown Court, since 1974; *b* 23 June 1928; *er s* of late Morris and Ethel Sherrard; *m* 1952, Shirley (C. B. Piper, writer), *d* of late Maurice and Lucy Bagrit; two *s*. *Educ:* King's Coll., London. LLB 1949. Called to Bar, Middle Temple, 1949 (Bencher 1977); Mem., Inner Temple, 1980; Mem. Senate, 1977–80. Mem., SE Circuit, 1950. Mem., Winn Cttee on Personal Injury Litigation, 1966; Mem. Council and Exec. Cttee, Justice, British Section, Internat. Commn of Jurists, 1974–; Dept of Trade Inspector, London Capital Group, 1975–77; Chm., Normansfield Hosp. Inquiry, 1977–78; Comr for trial of local govt election petitions (under Representation of the People Act 1949), 1978–80. Mem., Bar Assoc. of NYC, 1986–. FRSA 1991. *Recreations:* oil painting, oriental art, listening to opera. *Address:* 2 Crown Office Row, Temple, EC4Y 7HJ. *T:* 071–583 2681; 26 Eton Avenue, Hampstead, NW3 3HL. *T:* 071–431 0713.

SHERRIN, Ned, (Edward George Sherrin); film, theatre and television producer, presenter, director and writer; *b* Low Ham, Som, 18 Feb. 1931; *s* of late T. A. Sherrin and D. F. Sherrin (*née* Drewett). *Educ:* Sexey's Sch., Bruton; Exeter Coll., Oxford; Gray's Inn. Producer: ATV, Birmingham, 1955–57; BBC TV, 1957–66 (prod. and dir. That Was The Week That Was). Produced films: The Virgin Soldiers (with Leslie Gilliat) 1968; Every Home Should Have One, 1969; (with Terry Glinwood) Up Pompeii, 1971; Up the Chastity Belt, 1971; Girl Stroke Boy, 1971; Rentadick, 1971; Up the Front, 1972; The National Health, 1972; TV plays (with Caryl Brahms) include: Little Beggars; Benbow was his Name; Take a Sapphire; The Great Inimitable Mr Dickens; Feydeau Farces; plays (with Caryl Brahms): No Bed for Bacon; Cindy-Ella or I Gotta Shoe, 1962–63; The Spoils, 1968; Nicholas Nickleby, 1969; Sing a Rude Song, 1970; Fish out of Water, 1971; Liberty Ranch, 1972; Nickleby and Me, 1975; Beecham, 1980; The Mitford Girls, 1981; Oh, Kay! (new book with Tony Geiss), 1984; directed: Come Spy with Me, Whitehall, 1967; (and appeared in) Side by Side by Sondheim, Mermaid, 1976, NY 1977; Only in America (with D. Yakir), Roundhouse, 1980; Noël, Goodspeed, USA, 1981; Mr & Mrs Nobody, Garrick, 1986; Jeffrey Bernard is Unwell, Apollo, 1989; Same Old Moon, Nuffield, Southampton, 1990; Bookends, Apollo, 1990; directed and co-adapted: The Ratepayers' Iolanthe, QEH, 1984 (Olivier Award); The Metropolitan Mikado, QEH, 1985; Small Expectations, QEH, 1986; dir, The Sloane Ranger Revue, Duchess, 1985; scripted (with A. Beaton) Ziegfeld, London Palladium, 1988. TV appearances include: Song by Song, BBC and Yorkshire TV series; Quiz of the Week, BBC; The Rather Reassuring Programme, BBC; We Interrupt this Week, PBS, NY; Friday Night Saturday Morning, BBC-2; Countdown, Channel 4; radio appearances: Midweek (host), Medium Dry Sherrin, Extra Dry Sherrin, And So to Ned; Loose Ends; Counterpoint. Governor, BFI, 1980–84. Guild of TV Producers and Directors' Awards; Ivor Novello Award, 1966. *Publications:* (with Caryl Brahms) Cindy-Ella or I Gotta Shoe, 1962; Rappell 1910, 1964; Benbow was his Name, 1967; Ooh la! la! (short stories), 1973; After You Mr Feydeau, 1975; A Small Thing—Like an Earthquake (memoirs), 1983; (with Caryl Brahms) Song by Song, 1984; Cutting Edge, 1984; (with Neil Shand) 1956 and all that, 1984; (with Caryl Brahms) Too Dirty for the Windmill, 1986; Loose Neds, 1990; many songs. *Address:* c/o Margaret Ramsay Ltd, 14a Goodwin's Court, WC2. *T:* 071–240 0691.

SHERRINGTON, Prof. David, PhD; CPhys, FInstP; Wykeham Professor of Physics, University of Oxford, since 1989; Fellow, New College, Oxford, since 1989; *b* 29 Oct. 1941; *s* of James Arthur Sherrington and Elfreda (*née* Cameron); *m* 1966, Margaret Gee-Clough; one *s* one *d*. *Educ:* St Mary's Coll.; Univ. of Manchester (BSc 1st Cl. Hons Physics, 1962; PhD Theoretical Physics, 1966). FInstP 1974; CPhys. Asst Lectr in Theoretical Physics, 1964–67, Lectr, 1967–69, Univ. of Manchester; Asst Res. Physicist, UCSD, 1967–69; Imperial College, University of London: Lectr in Theor. Solid State Phys, 1969–74; Reader in Theor. Solid State Phys, 1974–83; Prof. of Phys, 1983–89; Cadre Supérieur, Inst Laue Langevin, Grenoble, France, 1977–79. Fellow, Amer. Physical Soc., 1985. Editor, Advances in Physics; Hon. Editor, Jl of Physics A: Mathematical and General. *Publications:* (ed jtly) Phase Transitions in Soft Condensed Matter, 1990; papers in learned jls. *Recreations:* wine tasting, travel, theatre, occasional scuba diving, ski-ing. *Address:* 6 North Way, Pinner, Mddx HA5 3NY. *T:* 081–866 2605.

SHERRY, Prof. Norman, FRSL 1985; writer; Mitchell Distinguished Professor of Literature, Trinity University, San Antonio, Texas, 1983–91; *b* 6 July 1935; *m* 1960, Sylvia Brunt. *Educ:* Univ. of Durham (BA Eng Lit); Univ. of Singapore (PhD). Lectr, Univ. of Singapore, 1961–66; Lectr and Sen. Lectr, Univ. of Liverpool, 1966–70; Prof. of English, Univ. of Lancaster, 1970–82. Fellow, Humanities Research Center, N Carolina, 1982; Guggenheim Fellow, 1989–90. *Publications:* Conrad's Eastern World, 1966; The Novels of Jane Austen, 1966; Charlotte and Emily Bronte, 1969; Conrad's Western World, 1971; Conrad and his World, 1972; (ed) Conrad: the Critical Heritage, 1973; (ed) An Outpost of Progress and Heart of Darkness, 1973; (ed) Lord Jim, 1974; (ed) Nostromo, 1974; (ed) The Secret Agent, 1974; (ed) The Nigger of Narcissus, Typhoon, Falk and Other Stories, 1975; (ed) Joseph Conrad: a commemoration, 1976; The Life of Graham Greene, vol. I, 1904–1939, 1989 (Edgar Allan Poe Award, Britannica Book of the Year, 1990); contribs to Review of English Studies, Notes & Queries, Modern Language Review, TLS, Observer, The Daily Telegraph, The Guardian, The Independent. *Recreations:* reading, writing, jogging, talking. *Address:* 5 St Pancras Green, Kingston, near Lewes, Sussex BN7 3LH. *Club:* Savile.

SHERRY, Mrs Vincent; *see* Robinson, Kathleen M.

SHERSBY, (Julian) Michael; MP (C) Uxbridge, since Dec. 1972; *b* Ickenham, 17 Feb. 1933; *s* of William Henry and Elinor Shersby; *m* 1958, Barbara Joan, *d* of John Henry Barrow; one *s* one *d*. *Educ:* John Lyon Sch., Harrow-on-the-Hill. Mem., Paddington Borough Council, 1959–64; Mem., Westminster City Council, 1964–71; Deputy Lord Mayor of Westminster, 1967–68. Chm., Uxbridge Div. Young Conservatives, 1951–52; Conservative and Unionist Party Organisation, 1952–58; Sec., Assoc. of Specialised Film Producers, 1958–62; Dir, British Industrial Film Assoc., 1962–66; Dir, 1966–77, Dir-Gen., 1977–88, Sugar Bureau (formerly British Sugar Bureau); Sec., UK Sugar Industry Assoc., 1978–88, Parly Advr, 1988–; Treas., World Sugar Res. Orgn, 1982–. PPS to Minister of Aerospace and Shipping, DTI, 1974; Member: Speaker's Panel of Chairmen, 1983–; Public Accounts Cttee, 1983–. Parly Advr to Police Fedn, 1989–; promoted Private Member's Bills: Town and Country Amenities Act, 1974; Parks Regulation (Amendment) Act, 1974; Stock Exchange (Completion of Bargains) Act, 1976; Gaming (Amendment) Act, 1980; Copyright Act (1956) Amendment Act, 1982; British Nationality (Falkland Islands) Act, 1983. Jt Sec., 1977–80, Vice-Pres., 1980–83, Parly and Scientific Cttee. Mem. Exec. Cttee, UK Br., CPA, 1988–. Pres., London Green Belt Council, 1989–. Mem. Court, Brunel Univ., 1975–; Pres., Abbeyfield Uxbridge Soc., 1975–. Trustee, Harefield Heart Transplant Trust, 1989–. *Recreations:* theatre, gardening, travel. *Address:* House of Commons, SW1A 0AA. *T:* 071–219 5023; Bay Lodge, 36 Harefield Road, Uxbridge, Middx. *T:* Uxbridge (0895) 39465. *Clubs:* Carlton; Conservative (Uxbridge).

SHERSTON-BAKER, Sir Robert (George Humphrey), 7th Bt *cr* 1796, of Dunstable House, Richmond, Surrey; *b* 3 April 1951; *o s* of Sir Humphrey Sherston-Baker, 6th Bt and of Margaret Alice, *o d* of Henry William Binns; *S* father, 1990. *Heir: kinsman* Maj. Peter Sherston-Baker, MC [*b* 7 Aug. 1918; *m* 1947, Elizabeth, *yr d* of late W. H. Barham; three *d*]. *Address:* Deal House, Stour Street, Canterbury, Kent CT1 2NZ.

SHERVAL, Rear-Adm. David Robert, CB 1989; CEng; FIMechE; FIMarE; Chief Surveyor and Deputy General Manager, The Salvage Association, since 1990; *b* 4 July 1933; *s* of William Robert Sherval and Florence Margaret Sherval (*née* Luke); *m* 1961, Patricia Ann Phillips; one *s* one *d*. *Educ:* Portsmouth Southern Grammar School. Artificer Apprentice, 1950; BRNC Dartmouth, 1951; Training: at sea, HM Ships Devonshire, Forth and Glasgow, 1951–52 and 1955; RNEC, 1952–53, 1956; served: HM Ships Eagle, Tiger, Hampshire, HM Dockyard Gibraltar and HMY Britannia, 1957–68; BRNC, 1968–70; HMS Juno, 1970–72; NDC, 1972–73; Naval Plans, MoD, 1973–75; Staff of FO Sea Training, 1975–76; Naval Op. Requirements, MoD, 1976–77; NATO Defence Coll., Rome, 1979; ACOS (Intell.) to SACLANT, 1979–82; Fleet Marine Engineer Officer, 1982–84; Dir, Naval Logistic Planning, 1984–85; CSO (Engrg) to C-in-C Fleet, 1985–87; Dir Gen. Ship Refitting, 1987–89. *Recreation:* music.

SHERWIN-WHITE, Adrian Nicholas, MA; FBA 1956; Reader in Ancient History, University of Oxford, 1966–79; Fellow and Tutor of St John's College, Oxford, 1936–79, Fellow Emeritus 1979; Keeper of the Groves, 1970; *b* 1911; *s* of H. N. Sherwin-White, Solicitors' Dept of LCC. *Educ:* Merchant Taylors' School; St John's College, Oxford (Derby Scholar, 1935; Arnold Historical Essay Prize, 1935; MA, 1937). War Service in RN and Admiralty, 1942–45. Conington Prize, 1947. Sarum Lecturer, Oxford Univ., 1960–61; Gray Lecturer, Cambridge Univ., 1965–66; Special Lectr, Open Univ., 1973–81. Pres., Soc. for Promotion of Roman Studies, 1974–77. Corresp. Fellow, Bayerische Akademie der Wissenschaften, 1977. *Publications:* Roman Citizenship, 1939, enlarged edn 1973; Ancient Rome (Then and There Series), 1959; Roman Society and Roman Law in the New Testament, 1963; Historical Commentary on the Letters of Pliny the Younger, 1966; Racial Prejudice in Imperial Rome, 1967; Roman Foreign Policy in the East 167BC-AD1, 1983; (contrib.) Cambridge Ancient History, 1985; ed Geographical Handbook Series, Admiralty; contrib. Jl Roman Studies. *Recreations:* watching horses and growing hardy plants. *Address:* St John's College, Oxford. *T:* Frilford Heath (0865) 390496.

SHERWOOD, Bishop Suffragan of, since 1989; **Rt. Rev. Alan Wyndham Morgan;** *b* 22 June 1940; *s* of A. W. Morgan; *m* 1965, Margaret Patricia, *d* of W. O. Williams; one *s* one *d*. *Educ:* Boys' Grammar School, Gowerton; St David's Coll., Lampeter (BA 1962); St Michael's Coll., Llandaff. Deacon 1964, priest 1965; Assistant Curate: Llangyfelach with Morriston, 1964–69; Cockett, 1969–72; St Mark with St Barnabas, Coventry, 1972–73; Team Vicar, St Barnabas, Coventry East, 1973–77; Bishop's Officer for Social Responsibility, Diocese of Coventry, 1978–83; Archdeacon of Coventry, 1983–89. Mem., Gen. Synod, 1980–89. President: Nottingham Help the Homeless Assoc. Ltd, 1989; Notts Assoc. of Voluntary Orgns, 1991; Vice-Pres., NCVO, 1989– (Chm., 1986–89); Chairman: Dio. of Southwell Ministry Gp, 1990; Additional Needs and Equal Opportunities Gp; Dir, Greater Nottingham TEC, 1991. *Address:* Sherwood House, High Oakham Road, Mansfield, Notts NG18 5AJ.

SHERWOOD, James Blair; Founder and President, Sea Containers Group, Bermuda and London, since 1965; Chairman, Orient-Express Hotels, since 1987; *b* 8 Aug. 1933; *s* of William Earl Sherwood and Florence Balph Sherwood; *m* 1977, Shirley Angela Masser Cross; two step *s*. *Educ:* Yale Univ. (BA Economics 1955). Lieut US Naval Reserve, Far East service, afloat and ashore, 1955–58. Manager, French Ports, later Asst General Freight Traffic Manager, United States Lines Co., Le Havre and NY, 1959–62; Gen. Manager, Container Transport Internat. Inc., NY and Paris, 1963–64. In partnership with Mark Birley, established Harry's Bar Club in London, 1979. Restored, and brought into regular service, the Venice Simplon-Orient-Express, 1982. *Publication:* James Sherwood's Discriminating Guide to London, 1975, 2nd edn 1977. *Recreations:* sailing, tennis, skiing. *Address:* Hinton Manor, Hinton Waldrist, Oxon. *T:* Oxford (0865) 820260. *Clubs:* Hurlingham, Pilgrims.

SHERWOOD, (Peter) Louis (Michael); Chairman: HTV Group, since 1991; Airedale Holdings, since 1990; *b* 27 Oct. 1941; *s* of Peter Louis Sherwood and Mervyn Sherwood (*née* de Toll); *m* 1970, Nicole Dina; one *s* two *d*. *Educ:* New Coll., Oxford (BA 1963; MA 1966); Stanford Univ. (MBA 1965). Morgan Grenfell & Co., Corporate Finance Officer, 1965–68; Asst to Chm., Fine Fare (Supermarkets), 1968–69; Man. Dir, Melias (Fine Fare subsid.), 1969–72; Dir, Anglo-Continental Investment & Finance Co., 1972–79; Sen. Vice-Pres. for Development, Grand Union Co., USA, 1979–85; Pres., Great Atlantic & Pacific Tea Co., USA, 1985–88; Chm. and Chief Exec., Gateway Foodmarkets, 1988–89. *Recreations:* mountain walking, collecting fine wine. *Address:* 10 College Road, Clifton, Bristol BS8 3HZ. *Club:* Lansdowne.

SHERWOOD, (Robert) Antony (Frank), CMG 1981; Assistant Director-General, British Council, 1977–81, retired; *b* 29 May 1923; *s* of Frank Henry Sherwood and Mollie Sherwood (*née* Moore); *m* 1953, Margaret Elizabeth Simpson; two *s* two *d*. *Educ:* Christ's Hospital; St John's Coll., Oxford (BA 1949, MA 1953). War service, RAF, 1942–46. Apptd to British Council, 1949; served in Turkey, Nigeria (twice), Syria, Uganda, Somalia and at HQ. Help the Aged: Vice-Chm., Internat. Cttee, 1982–88, Chm., 1988–; Trustee, 1988–; Mem. Council and Exec. Cttee, HelpAge Internat., 1983–; Hon. PRO, Surrey Voluntary Service Council, 1982–88. Mem. Management Cttee and Chm. Finance Cttee, Guildford Inst. of Univ. of Surrey, 1988–. *Publication:* (ed) Directory of Statutory and Voluntary Health, Social and Welfare Services in Surrey, 1987. *Recreations:* travel, genealogy and family history, reading. *Address:* 18 Rivermount Gardens, Guildford, Surrey GU2 5DN. *T:* Guildford (0483) 38277.

SHERWOOD, Prof. Thomas, FRCP, FRCR; Professor of Radiology, since 1978, and Clinical Dean, since 1984, University of Cambridge; Fellow of Girton College, Cambridge, since 1982; *b* 25 Sept. 1934; *m* 1961, Margaret Gooch; two *s* one *d*. *Educ:* Frensham Heights Sch.; Guy's Hospital, London. MA; DCH. Consultant Radiologist, Hammersmith Hospital and St Peter's Hospitals, 1969–77. *Publications:* Uroradiology, 1980; Roads to Radiology, 1983; Blow the Wind Southerly, 1988; papers in medical and radiological jls, 1964–. *Recreations:* music, reading and writing. *Address:* Department of Radiology, Addenbrooke's Hospital, Hills Road, Cambridge CB2 2QQ. *T:* Cambridge (0223) 336891.

SHESTOPAL, Dawn Angela, (Mrs N. J. Shestopal); *see* Freedman, D. A.

SHETH, Pranlal; Director, Reed Executive plc, since 1990; Member, Independent Television Commission, since 1991; Hon. Legal Advisor, National Association of Victim Support Schemes, since 1988; *b* 20 Dec. 1924; *s* of Purashotam Virji Sheth and Sakarben Sheth; *m* 1951, Indumati Sheth; one *s* one *d*. Called to the Bar, Lincoln's Inn, 1962. Journalist, Kenya, 1943–52; Chm., Nyanza Farmers' Cooperative Soc., 1954–60; Mem., Central Agriculture Bd, Kenya, 1963–66; Chm., Asian Hosp. Authority, 1964–66; Mem., Economic Planning and Develt Council, Kenya, 1964–66. Group Sec., 1971, Legal Advr and Dir, 1985–88, Abbey Life Gp of Cos; Legal Dir, Hartford Europe Gp of Cos, 1977–86; Director: Abbey Life Assurance Co. Ltd, 1977–89; Ambassador Life Assce Co. Ltd, 1980–88; Abbey Life Assurance (Ireland), 1981–85; Gp Sec., ITT cos in UK, 1983–86. Dir, Round House Arts Centre, 1986–; Member: BBC Consultative Gp on Industry and Business Affairs, 1986–89; BBC Asian Progs Adv. Cttee, 1986–89; IBA, 1990. Founder, and Chief Editor, Gujarat Samachar Weekly, 1972–73; Mem., N Metropolitan Conciliation Cttee, Race Relations Bd, 1973–77; a Dep. Chm., CRE, 1977–80; Vice Pres., UKIAS, 1986–. Trustee: Project Fullemploy (Charitable Trust), 1977–89; Runnymede Trust, 1987–; Urban Trust, 1987–; Windsor Fellowship, 1988–; Womankind Worldwide Trust, 1989–; Vice-Patron, UK Assoc., Internat. Year of the Child, 1978–80; Patron, Internat. Centre for Child Studies. Dir, Shelter, 1987–91; Hon. Legal Advr and Mem. Exec. Cttee, Nat. Assoc. of Victim Support Schemes, 1988–. Fellow, Inst. of Directors, 1977; FBIM 1980. Mem., Bd of Dirs, Polytech. of N London, 1979–. Mem. Editorial Adv. Panel, Equal Opportunities Review, 1984. *Address:* (home) 70 Howberry Road, Edgware, Mddx. *T:* 081–952 2413; (business) 14 Theobalds Road, WC1X 8PF. *T:* 071–831 6969. *Clubs:* Royal Over-Seas League, Commonwealth Trust.

SHEUMACK, Rt. Rev. Colin Davies; *see* Gippsland, Bishop of.

SHEVARDNADZE, Eduard Amvrosiyevich; Minister of Foreign Affairs, USSR, 1985–90; Founder, Movement for Democratic Reform, 1991; *b* Georgia, 25 Jan. 1928. *Educ:* Pedagogical Institute, Kutaisi. Mem., CPSU, 1948–91; Sec., Komsomol Cttee in Kutaisi, 1952–56, of Georgia, 1956–61; 1st Sec., Regional Party Cttee, Mtsheta, 1961–63, Tbilisi, 1963–64; Minister of Internal Affairs, Georgia, 1964–72; 1st Sec., Republican Party Cttee, Georgia, 1972–85; Mem., Politburo, 1985–91. Order of Lenin (five times); Hero of Socialist Labour (twice); Order of Red Banner of Labour. *Publication:* The Future Belongs to Freedom, 1991.

SHEWRY, Prof. Peter Robert, CBiol, FIBiol; Head of Long Ashton Research Station (AFRC Institute of Arable Crops Research) and Professor of Agricultural Sciences, University of Bristol, since 1989; *b* 19 March 1948; *s* of Robert Thomas Shewry and Mary Helen Shewry; *m* 1969, Rosemary Willsdon; one *s* one *d*. *Educ:* Bristol Univ. (BSc, PhD, DSc). Postdoctoral Res. Fellow, Westfield Coll., Univ. of London, 1972; Rothamsted Experimental Station: Res. Scientist, 1974; Head of Biochem. Dept, 1986. *Publications:* Plant Protein Engineering (ed with Steven Gutteridge), 1991; numerous papers in sci. jls on plant genetics, biochem. and molecular biol. *Address:* AFRC Institute of Arable Crops Research, Long Ashton Research Station, Long Ashton, Bristol BS18 9AF. *T:* Bristol (0275) 392181.

SHIACH, Sheriff Gordon Iain Wilson; Sheriff of Lothian and Borders, at Edinburgh, since 1984; *b* 15 Oct. 1935; *o s* of late Dr John Crawford Shiach, FDS, QHDS, and of Florence Bygott Wilson; *m* 1962, Margaret Grant Smith; two *d*. *Educ:* Lathallan Sch.; Gordonstoun Sch.; Edinburgh Univ. (MA, LLB); Open Univ. (BA Hons). Admitted to Faculty of Advocates, 1960; practised as Advocate, 1960–72; Tutor, Dept of Evidence and Pleading, Univ. of Edinburgh, 1963–66; Clerk to Rules Council of Court of Session, 1963–72; Standing Jun. Counsel in Scotland to Post Office, 1969–72; Sheriff of: Fife and Kinross, later Tayside, Central and Fife, at Dunfermline, 1972–79; Lothian and Borders at Linlithgow, 1979–84; Hon. Sheriff at Elgin, 1986–. Member: Council, Sheriffs' Assoc., 1989–; Bd, Lothian Family Conciliation Service, 1989–; Standing Cttee on Criminal Procedure, 1989–; Parole Bd for Scotland, 1990–. *Recreations:* walking, swimming, music, art, theatre. *Address:* Sheriffs' Chambers, Sheriff Court House, Lawnmarket, Edinburgh EH1 2NS. *T:* 031–226 7181. *Club:* New (Edinburgh).

SHIELD, Leslie, TD; DL; a Recorder of the Crown Court, since 1980; *b* 8 May 1916; *s* of Tom Shield and Annie Maud Shield; *m* 1941, Doris Leather; one *s*. *Educ:* Cowley Sch., St Helens; Univ. of Liverpool (LLB 1936, LLM 1938). Qualified solicitor, 1939, admitted 1945. Served War, 1939–46: commnd 5th Bn Prince of Wales' Volunteers (S Lancs) Regt; demob., Major. Entered into gen. practice as solicitor, 1946. DL Merseyside, 1976. *Recreations:* gardening (particular interest, orchids), music. *Address:* 185 Higher Lane, Rainford, St Helens, Merseyside WA11 8NF. *T:* Rainford (074488) 2708.

SHIELDS, Elizabeth Lois; Chairman, Ryedale Housing Association, since 1990; *b* 27 Feb. 1928; *d* of Thomas Henry Teare and Dorothy Emma Elizabeth Roberts-Lawrence; *m* 1961, David Cathro Shields. *Educ:* Whyteleafe Girls' Grammar School; UCL (BA Hons Classics); Avery Hill College of Education (Cert Ed); MA York 1988. Asst Teacher, St Philomena's Sch., Carshalton, 1954–59; Head of Department: Jersey Coll. for Girls, 1959–61; Whyteleafe Girls' Grammar Sch., 1961–62; Trowbridge Girls' High Sch., 1962–64; St Swithun's, Winchester, 1964–65; Queen Ethelburga's, Harrogate, 1967–69; Malton Sch., N Yorks, 1976–86; Univ. of York (on secondment), 1985–86 (Medieval Studies). Mem., Ryedale DC, 1980– (Chm., 1989–90). Contested (L) Howden, 1979, Ryedale, 1983; MP (L) Ryedale, May 1986–87. Pres., Ryedale Area Motor Neurone Disease Assoc., 1990–. *Recreations:* gardening, music, theatre. *Address:* Firby Hall, Kirkham Abbey, Westow, York YO6 7LH. *T:* Whitwell-on-the-Hill (065381) 474. *Clubs:* National Liberal; Ryedale House.

SHIELDS, John Sinclair; *b* 4 Feb. 1903; *s* of Rev. W. H. Shields and Margaret Louisa (*née* Sinclair); *m* 1st, 1924, Norah Fane Smith; three *d*; 2nd, 1963, Mrs Noreen Moultrie, *widow* of Comdr John Moultrie. *Educ:* Charterhouse; Lincoln Coll., Oxford (MA). Headmaster: Wem Grammar School, 1934–47; Queen Mary's School, Basingstoke, 1947–56; Headmaster, Peter Symonds' School, Winchester, 1957–63; Vice-Pres. Classical Assoc., 1958; Mem., Broadcasting Cttee, 1960. *Recreations:* golf, gardening. *Address:* North End House, Hursley, Winchester, Hants SO21 2JR. *T:* Hursley (0962) 75271.

SHIELDS, (Leslie) Stuart, QC 1970; a Recorder of the Crown Court, since 1972; *b* 15 May 1919; *m* 1st, 1941, Maureen Margaret McKinstry (*d* 1989); two *s* two *d* (and one *s* decd); 2nd, 1990, Barbara Diana Lloyd. *Educ:* St Paul's School; Corpus Christi College, Oxford. Paid Local Serjeant, Oxford and Buckinghamshire Light Infantry, 1945–47. Called to the Bar, Middle Temple, 1948; Bencher, 1977. Member: Criminal Injuries Compensation Bd, 1981–; Independent Review Body for Coal Industry, 1985–. *Recreations:* music, travel. *Address:* Devereux Chambers, Devereux Court, Temple, WC2R 3JJ.

SHIELDS, Michael; *see* Shields, R. M. C.

SHIELDS, Sir Neil (Stanley), Kt 1964; MC 1946; management consultant and company director; Chairman, Commission for New Towns, since 1982 (Member, since 1981); Deputy Chairman, London Transport, since 1989; *b* 7 September 1919; *o s* of late Archie Shields and Mrs Hannah Shields; *m* 1970, Gloria Dawn Wilson. Member of Honourable Artillery Company 1939–. Served in Royal Artillery, 1939–46; commnd 1940; Major 1943. Chairman: Anglo Continental Investment & Finance Co., 1965–74; Standard Catalogue Co., 1976–84; Holcombe Hldgs, 1978–84; Trianco Redfyre, 1979–84; Director: Chesham Amalgamations & Investments, 1964–84; Continental Bankers Agents, 1965–74; Central and Sheerwood, 1969–84; Newton Chambers & Co., 1972–84; Paxall Engineering, 1976–79. London Transport (formerly London Regional Transport): Mem. Bd, 1986–; Chm., 1988–89; Chm., Property Bd, 1986–. Prospective candidate (C) North St Pancras 1947 and contested by-election 1949. Chairman: Camden Conservative Cttee, 1965–67; Hampstead Conservative Assoc., 1954–65 (Vice-Chm., 1951–54); Hon. Treas. 1965–67; National Union of Conservative and Unionist Assocs: Chm. of London Area, 1961–63 (Vice-Chm., 1959–61); Mem. of National Executive, 1955–59, 1961–67, 1968–69; Hampstead Borough Council: Mem. 1947–65; Deputy Leader, 1952–61; Chm. of Works Cttee, 1951–55; Chm. of Finance Cttee, 1955–59. Mem. Council, Aims of Industry, 1976–. Governor, Bedford Coll., London Univ., 1983–85. *Recreations:* reading, music, wining and dining. *Address:* 12 London House, Avenue Road, NW8 7PX. *Clubs:* Carlton, HAC.

SHIELDS, Sir Robert, Kt 1990; DL; MD, FRCS, FRCSE; Professor of Surgery, University of Liverpool, since 1969; Consultant Surgeon, Royal Liverpool Hospital and Broadgreen Hospital, since 1969; *b* 8 Nov. 1930; *o s* of late Robert Alexander Shields and Isobel Dougall Shields; *m* 1957, Grace Marianne Swinburn; one *s* two *d*. *Educ:* John Neilson Institution, Paisley; Univ. of Glasgow. MB, ChB 1953 (Asher-Asher Medal and MacLeod Medal); MD (Hons and Bellahouston Medal) 1965; FRCSE 1959; FRCS 1966. House appts, Western Infirmary, Glasgow, 1953–54; RAMC, Captain attached 1 Bn Argyll and Sutherland Highlanders, 1954–56; RAMC (TA), Major (Surg. Specialist) attached 7 Bn A & S H, 1956–61. Hall Fellow, Univ. of Glasgow, 1957–58; Mayo Foundn Fellow, 1959–60; Lectr in Surgery, Univ. of Glasgow, 1960–63; Sen. Lectr and Reader in Surgery, Welsh Nat. Sch. of Medicine, 1963–69; Dean, Faculty of Medicine, Univ. of Liverpool, 1982–85. General Medical Council: Mem., 1982–; Member: Educn Cttee, 1984–85, 1986–87, 1989–90; Exec. Cttee, 1985–86, 1989–90; Prof. Conduct Cttee, 1986–87; Royal College of Surgeons: Mem., Ct of Examrs, 1980–86; Mem. Bd, Hunterian Inst., 1986–; Non-Exec. Trustee, Royal Liverpool Univ. Hosp. Trust, 1991–; Member: Liverpool AHA (T) (Chm., Area/Univ. Liaison Cttee), 1974–78; Mersey RHA, 1982–85 (Vice-Chm., 1985; Regl Advr, 1986–); Liverpool Med. Instn (Vice-Pres., 1983–84; Pres., 1988–89); Council, RCSE, 1985–; MRC, 1987–91 (Member: Cell Bd, 1974–77; Strategy Cttee, 1987–91); Exec. Cttee, Council of Military Educn Cttees of Univs of UK, 1990–.

Member: Surgical Research Soc. (Hon. Sec. 1972–76 and Pres. 1983–85); British Soc. of Gastroenterology (Mem. Council, 1984–86; Pres., 1990–91); N of England Gastroent. Soc. (Pres., 1981–83); Internat. Surgical Gp; James IV Assoc. of Surgeons, 1986– (Dir, 1991–); Assoc. of Surgs of GB and Ire. (Mem. Council 1966–69; Pres., 1986–87); Chm., Med. Adv. Cttee, British Liver Foundn, 1991–; Vice-Chm., Brit. Jl of Surgery Soc., 1989–. Member: Panel of Assessors, Nat. Health and Med. Res. Council of Commonwealth and Australia, 1983–; List of Assessors for Cancer Grants, Anti-Cancer Council of Vic, Australia, 1986–. Marjorie Budd Prof., Univ. of Bristol, 1983; Wilson Wang Vis. Prof., Chinese Univ. of Hong Kong, 1990; Wellcome Prof., Coll. of Medicine of S Africa, 1991. Former Visiting Prof., Univs of Toronto, Virginia, Witwatersrand, Rochester (NY), Hong Kong, Calif, Yale, and Examiner in Surgery, Univs of Glasgow, Edinburgh, Dundee, Leicester, Sheffield, Cambridge, Lagos, Amman, Riyadh, Malta. Mem. Bd of Advrs in Surgery, London Univ., 1983–. Member: Editorial Board: Gut, 1969–76; Brit. Jl of Surgery, 1970–85; Internat. Editl Bd, Current Practice in Surgery, 1989–. DL Merseyside, 1991. Hon. FACS 1990; Hon. FCSSA, 1991. Hon. DSc Wales, 1990. Moynihan Medal, Assoc. of Surgs of GB and Ire., 1966. *Publications:* (ed jtly): Surgical Emergencies II, 1979; Textbook of Surgery, 1983; contribs to medical and surgical jls relating to surgery and gastroenterology. *Recreations:* sailing and walking. *Address:* 81 Meols Drive, West Kirby, Wirral L48 5DF. *T:* 051–632 3588. *Club:* Army and Navy.

SHIELDS, (Robert) Michael (Coverdale); Chief Executive, Trafford Park Development Corporation, since 1987; *b* 23 Jan. 1943; *s* of Thomas and Dorothy Shields; *m* 1965, Dorothy Jean Dennison; two *s* one *d. Educ:* Durham Johnston Grammar Tech. Sch.; Durham Univ. (BSc Hons); Newcastle Univ. (DipTP). MRTPI. Planning Departments: Newcastle upon Tyne, 1964–65; Durham CC, 1965–69; Nottingham, 1969–73; Dep. Dir of Planning, Leeds City Council, 1973–78; City Tech. Services Officer and Dep. Chief Exec., Salford City Council, 1978–83; Chief Exec., Trafford BC, 1983–87. *Recreations:* family, school and college Governor, books. *Address:* Trafford Park Development Corporation, Trafford Wharf Road, Wharfside, Trafford Park, Manchester M17 1EX. *T:* 061–848 8000. *Club:* St James's (Manchester).

SHIELDS, Stuart; *see* Shields, L. S.

SHIELL, James Wyllie, BSc, FICE; chartered civil engineer, retired; *b* 20 Aug. 1912; *yr s* of late George Douglas Shiell, farmer, Rennieston, Jedburgh and Janet Gladstone Wyllie; *m* 1941, Maureen Cameron Macpherson Hunter, *d* of late Thomas Hunter, Leeds; two *s. Educ:* Jedburgh Grammar and Kelso High Schools; Edinburgh Univ. Municipal Engrg posts in Edinburgh, Southampton, Sunderland and Leeds, 1934–39; Sen. Engr on Staff of J. D. & D. M. Watson, Consulting Engrs, Westminster, 1939–43 and 1945–47; Civil Engr on wartime service with Admty, 1943–45; Sen. Engr, Min. of Agriculture, 1947–49; Engrg Inspector, Dept of Health for Scotland, 1949–62; Dep. Chief Engr, Scottish Development Dept, 1962–68; Under Sec. and Chief Engr, Scottish Development Dept, 1968–75. Hon. FIWEM. *Recreations:* bowling, photography. *Address:* 25 Mortonhall Road, Edinburgh EH9 2HS. *T:* 031–667 8528.

SHIERLAW, Norman Craig; Senior Partner, N. C. Shierlaw & Associates (Stock and Sharebrokers), since 1968; *b* 17 Aug. 1921; *s* of Howard Alison Shierlaw and Margaret Bruce; *m* 1944, Patricia Yates; two *d. Educ:* Pulteney Grammar Sch., Adelaide; St Peter's Coll., Adelaide; Univ. of Adelaide (BE). Assoc. Mem. Australian Inst. Mining and Metallurgy; FSASM; Mining Manager's Certificate. War Service, AIF, 1941–45 (War Service medals). Mining Engr with North Broken Hill Ltd, 1949–58; Sharebroker's Clerk, 1959–60; Partner, F. W. Porter & Co. (Sharebrokers), 1960–68. Director: Australian Development Ltd, 1959–; Poseidon Ltd, 1968–77; North Flinders Mines Ltd, 1969–77; Nobelex NL, 1974–. FAIM 1971. *Recreations:* golf, tennis. *Address:* N. C. Shierlaw & Associates, 28 Grenfell Street, Adelaide, SA 5000, Australia. *T:* Adelaide 51–7468. *Clubs:* Royal Automobile (Sydney); Naval, Military and Air Force, Stock Exchange, Kooyonga Golf (Adelaide); West Australian (Perth).

SHIFFNER, Sir Henry David, 8th Bt, *cr* 1818; Company Director; *b* 2 Feb. 1930; *s* of Major Sir Henry Shiffner, 7th Bt, and Margaret Mary (*d* 1987), *er d* of late Sir Ernest Gowers, GCB, GBE; *S* father, 1941; *m* 1st, 1949, Dorothy Jackson (marr. diss. 1956); one *d* (and one *d* decd); 2nd, 1957, Beryl (marr. diss. 1970), *d* of George Milburn, Saltdean, Sussex; one *d*; 3rd, 1970, Joaquina Ramos Lopez. *Educ:* Rugby; Trinity Hall, Cambridge. *Heir: cousin* George Frederick Shiffner [*b* 3 August 1936; *m* 1961, Dorothea Helena Cynthia, *d* of late T. H. McLean; one *s* one *d*]. *Address:* PO Box 90, St Helier, Jersey, CI. *Club:* Royal Automobile.

SHILLINGFORD, Arden; *see* Shillingford, R. A. C.

SHILLINGFORD, Prof. John Parsons, CBE 1988; MD (Harvard and London), FRCP, FACP; FACC; Sir John McMichael Professor of Cardiovascular Medicine, Royal Postgraduate Medical School, London University, 1976–79, now Emeritus Professor (Director, Cardiovascular Research Unit, and Professor of Angiocardiology, 1966–76); Consultant Medical Director, British Heart Foundation, 1981–86; *b* 15 April 1914; *s* of Victor Shillingford and Ethel Eugenie Parsons; *m* 1947, Doris Margaret Franklin; two *s* one *d. Educ:* Bishops Stortford; Harvard Univ.; London Hosp. Med. Sch. Rockefeller Student, Harvard Med. Sch., 1939–42; House appts, Presbyterian Hosp., New York, and London Hosp., 1943–45; Med. First Asst, London Hosp., 1945–52; Sen. Lectr Royal Postgrad. Med. Sch., 1958–62. Pres., Sect. Experimental Med., Royal Soc. Med., 1968; Sec., Brit. Cardiac Soc., 1963–70; Chm. Org. Cttee, Sixth World Congress Cardiology, 1970; Lumleian Lectr, RCP, 1972. Member: Assoc. Physicians Gt Brit.; Med. Res. Soc.; Med. Soc. London; Royal Soc. Med.; Comité Recherche Médicale, EEC; various cttees, Brit. Heart Foundn. Hon. Mem.: Hellenic Cardiac Soc.; Cardiac Soc. of Yugoslavia; Polish Cardiac Soc.; Cardiological Soc. of India; French Cardiac Soc.; Corr. Mem., Australian Cardiac Soc.; Fellow, Amer. Coll. of Cardiology; Hon. FACP; Editor, Cardiovascular Research. Visiting Prof., Australian Heart Foundn, 1965; lectured extensively in Europe, USA, S America, Africa, Middle East. James Berry Prize, RCS. *Publications:* numerous scientific papers, mainly on heart disease and coronary thrombosis. *Recreation:* sailing. *Address:* Crohamhurst, Hesworth Lane, Fittleworth, W Sussex RH20 1EW. *T:* Fittleworth (079882) 290. *Club:* Hurlingham.

SHILLINGFORD, (Romeo) Arden (Coleridge), MBE 1977; Permanent Secretary, Ministry of Community Development and Social Affairs, Commonwealth of Dominica, since 1985; *b* 11 Feb. 1936; *s* of Stafford Shillingford and Ophelia Thomas, step *d* of Hosford Samuel O'Brien and *d* of Clarita (*née* Hunt), Roseau, Dominica; *m* 1st, Evelyn Blanche Hart; one *s* one *d*; 2nd, Maudline Joan Green; three *s. Educ:* Wesley High Sch., Roseau Boys' Sch., Dominica; grammar school; School of Law. Member, Hon. Soc. Inner Temple. Joined Dominican Civil Service, 1957, after brief period as solicitor's clerk; junior clerk, various Govt Depts, Dominica, 1957–59; Clerk of Court, then Chief Clerk, Magistrates' Office, 1960–61; joined staff, Eastern Caribbean Commn, London, on secondment from Dominican CS, 1965; served variously as Migrants' Welfare Officer, Students' Officer, Asst Trade Sec. and PA to Comr, 1968–71; Admin. Asst, Consular and Protocol Affairs, 1973–78 (actg Comr, several occasions, 1975–78); High Comr in UK, 1978–85 (concurrently non-resident Ambassador to France, Spain, Belgium, W Germany and EEC, Brussels, and Perm. Rep. to UNESCO). Past Member, numerous cttees and ad hoc bodies for West Indian Immigrant Welfare and Education; Dep. Chm., Bd of Governors, W Indian Students' Centre, 1970–75, Chm., 1976–79; Member, West India Cttee (Vice-Pres. 1979–). Liaison Officer, Victoria League for Commonwealth Friendship; Founder-Mem. and Vice-Chm., Jaycees (Dominica Jun. Chamber of Commerce). *Recreations:* cricket, collecting authentic folk music, swimming. *Address:* Ministry of Community Development and Social Affairs, Government Headquarters, Roseau, Commonwealth of Dominica, W Indies.

SHILLINGTON, Sir (Robert Edward) Graham, Kt 1972; CBE 1970 (OBE 1959; MBE 1951); DL; Chief Constable, Royal Ulster Constabulary, 1970–73; *b* 2 April 1911; *s* of Major D. Graham Shillington, DL, MP, and Mrs Louisa Shillington (*née* Collen); *m* 1935, Mary E. R. Bulloch (*d* 1977), Holywood, Co. Down; two *s* one *d. Educ:* Sedbergh Sch., Yorks; Clare Coll., Cambridge. Royal Ulster Constabulary: Officer Cadet, 1933; 3rd Class District Inspector, 1934; 2nd Class District Inspector, 1936; 1st Class District Inspector, 1944; County Inspector, 1953; Commissioner, Belfast, 1961; Deputy Inspector General (Deputy Chief Constable), 1969–70. Chm., Belfast Voluntary Welfare Soc., 1976–81. DL Co. Down, 1975. King's Coronation Medal, 1937; Queen's Coronation Medal, 1953; Police Long Service and Good Conduct Medal, 1955; RUC Service Medal, 1985. *Recreations:* golf, gardening. *Address:* Ardeevin, 184 Bangor Road, Holywood, Co. Down BT18 0BY. *T:* Holywood (02317) 3471. *Clubs:* Royal Over-Seas League; Royal Belfast Golf, Royal County Down Golf.

SHILLITO, Charles Henry; Under-Secretary, Ministry of Agriculture, Fisheries and Food, 1974–82; *b* 8 Jan. 1922; *s* of Charles Cawthorne and Florence Shillito; *m* 1947, Elizabeth Jean (*née* Bull); two *d. Educ:* Hugh Bell Sch., Middlesbrough. Clerk, Min. of Agriculture and Fisheries, 1938; War Service, Lieut RNVR, 1941–46; Principal, MAFF, 1957; Asst Sec. 1966; Section Head, Nat. Econ. Develt Office, 1966–69 (on secondment). Hon. ARCVS 1986; Hon. Mem., BVA, 1989. *Recreations:* gardening, nautical pursuits. *Address:* 62 Downs Road, Coulsdon, Surrey CR5 1AB. *T:* Downland (0737) 553392.

SHINDLER, George John, QC 1970; **His Honour Judge Shindler;** a Circuit Judge, since 1980; Senior Resident Judge, Inner London Crown Court, since 1987; *b* 27 Oct. 1922; *yr s* of late Dr Bruno and Mrs Alma Schindler; *m* 1955, Eva Muller; three *s. Educ:* Regent's Park Sch.; University Coll. Sch., Hampstead. Served in Royal Tank Regt, NW Europe, 1942–47. Called to Bar, Inner Temple, 1952; Bencher 1978. Standing Counsel to Inland Revenue at Central Criminal Court and all London sessions, 1965–70; a Recorder of the Crown Court, 1972–80. Legal Mem., Mental Health Review Tribunal, 1983–87; Mem., Inner London Probation Cttee, 1987–. Pres., Inner London Magistrates' Assoc., 1987–. *Recreations:* theatre, music, reading, watching soccer and cricket, travel. *Address:* Inner London Sessions House, Newington Causeway, SE1 6AZ. *T:* 071–407 7111. *Club:* MCC.

SHINGLES, Godfrey Stephen, (Geoff), CBE 1987; CEng, FIEE; FBCS; Chairman and Chief Executive, Digital Equipment Co. Ltd, since 1991 (Managing Director, 1983–91); Vice President, Digital Equipment Corporation, since 1981; *b* 9 April 1939; *s* of Sidney and Winifred Shingles; *m* 1963, Jaqueline Margaret Crouch (marr. diss.); two *s. Educ:* Paston Sch., N Walsham; Leeds Univ. (BSc). Joined Digital UK, 1965; UK Subsidiary Man., 1968; Man., N Europe, 1972; Man. Dir, UK Sales Subsidiary, and Dir, Scottish Manufacturing, 1974; European Marketing Vice Pres., 1976. Man. Dir, UK Country Gp, 1983. Vice Pres., Education 2000. FInstD. *Recreations:* sailing, squash, Rugby, ballet, ski-ing. *Address:* Worton Grange, Imperial Way, Reading, Berks RG2 0TE. *T:* Reading (0734) 868711.

SHINNIE, Prof. Peter Lewis; Professor of Archæology, in the University of Calgary, 1970–80, now Emeritus; *b* 1915; *s* of late Andrew James Shinnie, OBE; *m* 1st, 1940, Margaret Blanche Elizabeth Cloake; two *s* one *d*; 2nd, Ama Nantwi. *Educ:* Westminster Sch.; Christ Church, Oxford. Served War with RAF, 1939–45. Temp. Asst Keeper, Ashmolean Museum, 1945; Asst Commissioner for Archæology, Sudan Government, 1946; Commissioner for Archæology, Sudan Govt, 1948; Director of Antiquities, Uganda, 1956; Prof. of Archæology: Univ. of Ghana, 1958–66; Univ. of Khartoum, 1966–70. FSA. Hon. LLD Calgary, 1983. *Publications:* Excavation at Soba, 1955; Medieval Nubia, 1954; Ghazali: A Monastery in Northern Sudan, 1960; Meroe-Civilization of the Sudan, 1967; The African Iron Age, 1971; Debeira West, 1978; (with R. J. Bradley) The Capital of Kush, 1980; (ed with R. Haaland) African Iron Working: ancient and traditional, 1985; (with F. J. Kense) Archaeology in Gonja: excavations at Daboya, 1989; articles in Journal of Egyptian Archæology, Sudan Notes and Records, Kush. *Recreations:* reading, photography, travelling in Greece. *Address:* Department of Archæology, University of Calgary, Calgary, T2N 1N4 Canada. *T:* 403–220–5227. *Club:* Athenæum.

SHIRER, William Lawrence; broadcaster, journalist; author; *b* Chicago, 23 Feb. 1904; *s* of Seward Smith Shirer; *m* 1931, Theresa Stiberitz; two *d. Educ:* Coe College. DLitt (Hon.). Légion d'Honneur. *Publications:* Berlin Diary, 1941; End of a Berlin Diary, 1947; The Traitor, 1950; Mid-Century Journey, 1953; Stranger Come Home, 1954; The Challenge of Scandinavia, 1955; The Consul's Wife, 1956; The Rise and Fall of The Third Reich, 1960; The Rise and Fall of Adolf Hitler, 1961; The Sinking of the Bismarck, 1962; The Collapse of the Third Republic, 1970; 20th Century Journey: a memoir of a Life and the Times, vol. I, The Start 1904–1930, 1976, vol. II, The Nightmare Years 1930–1940, 1984, vol. III, A Native's Return 1945–1988, 1990; Gandhi, a Memoir, 1979. *Recreations:* walking, sailing. *Address:* Box 487, Lenox, Massachusetts 01240, USA. *Club:* Century (New York).

SHIRLEY, family name of **Earl Ferrers.**

SHIRLEY, David Andrew; a Special Commissioner of Income Tax, since 1988; *b* 23 Nov. 1926; *er s* of Rev. Canon F. J. Shirley, DD (Oxon), FSA, and Dorothy, *d* of John Howard, Aberfeldy; *m* 1st, 1955, Dorothy Evelyn Finn (*d* 1969); 2nd, 1973, Alysia Rosemary, *d* of Col Gerald Trimmer-Thompson, Cayton Park, Wargrave. *Educ:* Winchester Coll.; New Coll., Oxford (2nd Cl. Jurisprudence). 2nd Lieut Black Watch, 1946; ADC to Gov. of NW Frontier Province, 1947–48; Captain Black Watch (TA). Called to the Bar, Lincoln's Inn (Cholmeley Schol.), 1951; (*ad eundem*) Inner Temple, 1964; Bencher, Lincoln's Inn, 1978. Part-time Chm., VAT Tribunal, 1978–. *Recreations:* hunting, ski-ing, silviculture. *Address:* Litmore Shaw, Ibstone, High Wycombe, Bucks HP14 3XX. *T:* Turville Heath (049163) 204.

SHIRLEY, Philip Hammond; retired; *b* 4 Oct. 1912; *s* of Frank Shillito Shirley and Annie Lucy (*née* Hammond); *m* 1st, 1936, Marie Edna Walsh (*d* 1972); one *s* one *d*; 2nd, 1973, Norma Jones. *Educ:* Sydney Church of England Grammar School (Shore). Qualified in Australia as Chartered Accountant, 1934; with Peat Marwick Mitchell & Co., Chartered Accountants, London, 1937–49; with Unilever from 1951; Dep. Chief Accountant, 1951–52; Chief Accountant, 1952–58; Chm. Batchelors Foods Ltd 1958–61; Mem. BTC (Oct. 1961–Nov. 1962); Mem. BR Bd, 1962–67 (Vice-Chm. Bd, 1964–67); Dep. Chm., Cunard Steamship Co., 1968–71; Chief Commissioner of Public Transport,

NSW, 1972–75. *Recreation:* bowls. *Address:* 11, 25 Belmont Avenue, Wollstonecraft, NSW 2065, Australia.

SHIRLEY, Mrs Stephanie; *see* Shirley, Mrs V. S.

SHIRLEY, Mrs (Vera) Stephanie, (Steve), OBE 1980; CBIM, FBCS; Founder Director, FI Group PLC (formerly F International Group), since 1962; *b* 16 Sept. 1933; *d* of late Arnold Buchthal and Mrs Margaret Brook (formerly Buchthal, *née* Schick); name changed to Brook on naturalisation, 1951; *m* 1959, Derek George Millington Shirley; one *s*. *Educ:* Sir John Cass Coll., London. BSc (Spec.) London 1956. CBIM 1984; FBCS 1971. PO Res. Stn, Dollis Hill, 1951–59; CDL (subsid. of ICL), 1959–62; F International Group, later FI Group, and its associated cos, 1962–. Member: Computer, Systems and Electronics Requirements Bd, 1979–81; Electronics and Avionics Requirements Bd, 1981–83; Open Tech, MSC, 1983–86; Council, Industrial Soc., 1984–90; NCVQ, 1986–89. Pres., British Computer Soc., 1989–90. Consulting Editor on information processing, J. Wiley & Sons, 1978–87. Trustee, Help The Aged, 1987–90; Patron, Disablement Income Gp, 1989. Jun. Warden, Information Technologists' Co., 1990; Freeman, City of London, 1987. FRSA 1985. Hon. FCGI 1989. Hon. Fellow, Manchester Poly., 1989. Hon. DSc Buckingham, 1991; Hon. DTech Loughborough, 1991. Recognition of Industry Technology Achievement Award, 1985. *Publications:* articles in prof. jls, reviews, proc. of confs, and papers. *Recreation:* sleep. *Address:* c/o FI Group PLC, Campus 300, Maylands Avenue, Hemel Hempstead, Herts HP2 7EZ. *T:* Hemel Hempstead (0442) 233339, *Fax:* Hemel Hempstead (0442) 238400.

SHIRLEY-QUIRK, John Stanton, CBE 1975; bass-baritone singer; *b* 28 Aug. 1931; *s* of Joseph Stanley and Amelia Shirley-Quirk; *m* 1st, 1955, Patricia Hastie (*d* 1981); one *s* one *d*; 2nd, 1981, Sara V. Watkins; one *s* two *d*. *Educ:* Holt School, Liverpool; Liverpool University. Violin Scholarship, 1945; read Chemistry, Liverpool Univ., 1948–53; BSc (Hons), 1952; Dipl. in Educn 1953; became professional singer, 1961. Officer in Education Br., RAF, 1953–57. Asst Lectr in Chemistry, Acton Technical Coll., 1957–61; Lay-clerk in St Paul's Cathedral, 1961–62. First Appearance Glyndebourne Opera in Elegy for Young Lovers, 1961; subseq. 1962, 1963. Sang in first performance of Curlew River, 1964, The Burning Fiery Furnace, 1966, The Prodigal Son, 1968, Owen Wingrave, 1970, Death in Venice, 1973, Confessions of a Justified Sinner, 1976, The Ice Break, 1977. Has sung world wide. First American tour, 1966; Australian tour, 1967; first appearance Metropolitan Opera, NY, 1974. Has made numerous recordings: operas, songs, cantatas, etc. Mem. Court, Brunel Univ., 1977–. Hon. RAM 1972; Hon. DMus Liverpool, 1976; DUniv Brunel, 1981. Liverpool Univ. Chem. Soc. Medal, 1965; Sir Charles Santley Meml Gift, Worshipful Co. of Musicians, 1969. *Recreations:* trees, canals, clocks. *Address:* c/o Harrison/Parrott Ltd, 12 Penzance Place, W11 4PA.

SHIRRAS, Ven. Edward Scott; Archdeacon of Northolt, since 1985; *b* 23 April 1937; *s* of Edward Shirras and Alice Emma Shirras (*née* Morten); *m* 1962, Pamela Susan Mackenzie; two *s* two *d*. *Educ:* Sevenoaks School; St Andrews Univ. (BSc); Union Coll., Schenectady, NY, USA; Clifton Theolog. Coll., Bristol. Curate: Christ Church, Surbiton Hill, 1963–66; Jesmond Parish Church, Newcastle upon Tyne, 1966–68; Church Pastoral Aid Society: Youth Sec., 1968–71; Publications Sec., 1971–74; Asst Gen. Sec., 1974–75; Vicar of Christ Church, Roxeth, dio. London, 1975–85; Area Dean of Harrow, 1982–85. *Recreations:* transport photography (Scottish), Aberdeen FC. *Address:* 71 Gayton Road, Harrow, Middx HA1 2LY. *T:* 081–863 1530, *Fax:* 081–861 0684.

SHIVAS, Mark; Head of Drama, BBC Television, since 1988; *b* 24 April 1938; *s* of James Dallas Shivas and Winifred Alice Lighton (*née* Bristow). *Educ:* Whitgift School; Merton College, Oxford (MA Law). Asst Editor, Movie Magazine, 1962–64; freelance journalist; joined Granada TV, 1964, Director-Producer, 1965–68; Producer of Drama, 1969–88, Head of Drama series and serials, 1988, BBC TV; Creative Dir, Southern Pictures, 1979–81. Productions include: The Six Wives of Henry VIII (BAFTA awards, Prix Italia), The Evacuees (BAFTA and Emmy awards), Casanova, The Glittering Prizes, Rogue Male, Professional Foul (BAFTA award), Telford's Change, On Giant's Shoulders (Emmy award); for Channel 4: The Price, What if it's Raining?, The Storyteller (Emmy award); feature films include: Moonlighting, 1982; A Private Function, 1984; The Witches, 1988. *Publications:* articles in art jls. *Recreations:* Italy, gardens, swimming, cycling, moviegoing. *Address:* BBC TV, Wood Lane, W12. *T:* 081–743 8000.

SHOCK, Sir Maurice, Kt 1988; Rector, Lincoln College, Oxford, since 1987; *b* 15 April 1926; *o s* of Alfred and Ellen Shock; *m* 1947, Dorothy Donald; one *s* three *d*. *Educ:* King Edward's Sch., Birmingham; Balliol Coll., Oxford (MA); St Antony's Coll., Oxford. Served Intell. Corps, 1945–48. Lectr in Politics, Christ Church and Trinity Coll., Oxford, 1955–56; Fellow and Praelector in Politics, University Coll., Oxford, 1956–77, Hon. Fellow, 1986; Estates Bursar, 1959–74; Vice-Chancellor, Leicester Univ., 1977–87. Sen. Treasurer, Oxford Union Soc., 1954–72; Member: Franks Commn of Inquiry into the University of Oxford, 1964–66; Hebdomadal Council, Oxford Univ., 1969–75; Chairman: Univ. Authorities Panel, 1980–85; CVCP, 1985–87. Vis. Prof. of Govt, Pomona Coll., 1961–62, 1968–69. Mem., ESRC, 1981–85; a Governing Trustee, 1980–, Chm., 1988–, Nuffield Provincial Hosps Trust. Hon. LLD Leicester, 1987. *Publications:* The Liberal Tradition; articles on politics and recent history. *Recreations:* gardening, theatre. *Address:* Lincoln College, Oxford.

SHOENBERG, Prof. David, MBE 1944; FRS 1953; Professor of Physics, Cambridge University and Head of Low Temperature Physics Group, Cavendish Laboratory, 1973–78, now Emeritus; Life Fellow of Gonville and Caius College; *b* 4 Jan. 1911; *s* of Isaac and Esther Shoenberg; *m* 1940, Catherine Felicitée Fischmann; one *s* two *d*. *Educ:* Latymer Upper School, W6; Trinity College, Cambridge (Scholar). PhD 1935; Exhibition of 1851 Senior Student, 1936–39; Research in low temperature physics, 1932–, in charge of Royal Soc. Mond Laboratory, 1947–73; Univ. Lectr in Physics, 1944–52; Univ. Reader in Physics, 1952–73; UNESCO Adviser on Low Temperature Physics, NPL of India, 1953–54. Mellon Prof., Univ. of Pittsburgh, 1962; Gauss Prof., Univ. of Göttingen, 1964; Visiting Professor: Univ. of Maryland, 1968; Univ. of Toronto, 1974; Univ. of Waterloo, 1977; Lectures: Guthrie, 1961; Rutherford Meml, India and Sri Lanka, 1980; Krishnan Meml, New Delhi, 1988. Hon. Foreign Mem., Amer. Acad. of Arts and Sciences, 1982. Dr (*hc*) Univ. of Lausanne, 1973. Fritz London Award for Low Temperature Physics, 1964. *Publications:* Superconductivity, 1938, revised edn, 1952; Magnetism, 1949; Magnetic Oscillations in Metals, 1984; (ed jtly) Kapitza in Cambridge and Moscow, 1990; scientific papers on low temperature physics and magnetism. *Address:* 2 Long Road, Cambridge CB2 2PS; Cavendish Laboratory, Madingley Road, Cambridge CB3 0HE. *T:* Cambridge (0223) 337389.

SHOLL, Hon. Sir Reginald (Richard), Kt 1962; MA, BCL, Oxon; MA Melbourne; QC; retired Judge; former legal consultant and company director, Melbourne and Queensland; *b* 8 Oct. 1902; *e s* of late Reginald Frank and Alice Maud Sholl (*née* Mumby), Melbourne; *m* 1st, 1927, Hazel Ethel (*d* 1962), *yr d* of late Alfred L. and Fanny Bradshaw, Melbourne; two *s* two *d*; 2nd, 1964, Anna Campbell, *widow* of Alister Bruce McLean, Melbourne, and *e d* of late Campbell Colin and Edith Carpenter, Indiana, USA. *Educ:* Melbourne Church of England Grammar Sch.; Trinity Coll., Univ. of Melbourne; New Coll., Oxford. 1st Cl. Final Hons and exhibn, Sch. of Classical Philology, and Wyselaskie Schol. in Classical and Comparative Philology and Logic, Melbourne Univ., 1922; Rhodes Schol., Victoria, 1924; 1st Cl. Final Hons, School of Jurisprudence, Oxford, 1926, Bar Finals, London, 1926 and BCL, Oxford, 1927; Official Law Fellow, Brasenose Coll., Oxford, 1927. Called to Bar, Middle Temple, 1927; journalist, London, 1927; Tutor in Classics, Melbourne Univ., 1928–29; Lectr in law, 1928–38; Barrister, Melbourne, 1929–49; admitted to Bars of NSW and Tasmania, 1935. Served Aust. Army, 1940–44; Capt. retd. Chm. various Commonwealth Bds of Inquiry into Army contracts, 1941–42; KC Vic. and Tas., 1947, NSW 1948; Justice of the Supreme Court of Victoria, 1950–66; Australian Consul-Gen. in New York, 1966–69; Chm., Western Australian Parly Salaries Tribunal, 1971–77. Consultant: to Russell, Kennedy & Cook, solicitors, Melbourne, 1969–79; to Bell, Bell and Fradgley, solicitors, Qld, 1979–82; Dir, Nat. Trustees Executors and Agency Co. of Australasia Ltd, 1969–79, Vice-Chm., 1976–79, Consultant, 1979–85; Chm., Sperry Rand Corp. (Australia), 1969–74, and Mem. Internat. Adv. Bd, Sperry Rand Corp. (USA), 1971–74. Pres. ESU (Vic. Br.) 1961–66; Fed. Chm., ESU in Aust., 1961–63, 1969–73; Trustee, Northcote Trust Fund, 1978–; Member: Aust. Bd of Trustees, Northcote Children's Emigration Fund for Aust., 1950–78; Bd, US Educnl Foundn in Aust., 1961–64; Archbishop-in-Council, Dio. Melbourne, 1958–66, 1969–79; Advocate of Diocese of Melbourne, 1969–79; Mem. Councils: Trinity Coll., Melbourne, 1939–66; C of E Grammar Sch., Melbourne, 1960–66; Peninsula Sch., Mt Eliza, 1960–63; Toorak Coll., 1969–71; C of E Girls' Grammar Sch., Melbourne, 1969–75; Aust. Adv. Council of Elders, 1983–; Hon. Life Mem., Nat. Gall. of Vic., 1975 (Trustee, 1950–63, Dep. Chm. 1958). Pres. Somers Area, Boy Scouts Assoc. (Vic. Br.), 1955–64, 1972–76; Member: State Exec. Boy Scouts Assoc., 1958–66, (Vice-Pres., 1964–66); Nat. Council Australian Boy Scouts Assoc., 1959–69, 1975–; Cttee, Overseas Service Bureau (Australia), 1970–71; Foundn Dir, Winston Churchill Memorial Trust in Australia, 1965–66, Dep. Nat. Chm., 1969–75, Dep. Nat. Pres., 1975–81; Chm., Nat. Fellowship Cttee, 1965–66, 1969–75; Mem., Victoria Cttee, Duke of Edinburgh's Award in Australia, 1964–66; Chairman, Vict. Supreme Court Rules Cttee, 1960–66; Chm., Royal Commn, Western Australia Inquiry into the airline system, 1974–75. Stawell Orator, 1970; Fellow, Trinity Coll., Melbourne, 1981. *Publications:* contrib. to legal periodicals. *Recreations:* golf, bowls, sailing, gardening; formerly football (Melbourne Univ. blue) and lacrosse (Oxford half-blue). *Address:* 6/7 Britannia Avenue, Broadbeach, Qld 4218, Australia. *Clubs:* Melbourne, Australian (Melbourne); Queensland (Brisbane); Melbourne Cricket (1918–), Surfers Paradise Bridge (Qld).

SHONE, Rev. John Terence; Team Vicar, Cullercoats Team, Marden St Hilda, Diocese of Newcastle, since 1989; *b* 15 May 1935; *s* of late Arthur Shone and of E. B. Shone; *m* 1st, 1958, Ursula Ruth Buss (marr. diss.); three *s*; 2nd, 1987, Annette Simmons, *d* of William Caterer and late Ada Caterer. *Educ:* St Dunstan's College; Selwyn Coll., Cambridge (BA 1958, MA 1962); Lincoln Theological Coll. Deacon 1960, priest 1961, London; Curate, St Pancras Parish Church, 1960–62; Chaplain, St Andrew's Cathedral, Aberdeen, 1962–65; Chaplain to Anglican Students, Aberdeen, 1962–68; Lectr, Aberdeen Coll. of Education, 1965–68; Exam. Chaplain to Bishop of Aberdeen, 1966–68; Vicar, St Andrew and St Luke, Grimsby, 1968–69; Rector, St Saviour, Bridge of Allan, 1969–86; Chaplain, Stirling Univ., 1969–80; Priest i/c, St John's, Alloa, 1977–85, and St James', Dollar, 1981–86; Canon, St Ninian's Cathedral, Perth, 1980–82; Dean, United Dio. of St Andrews, Dunkeld and Dunblane, 1982–89; Diocesan R & D Officer, 1986–89. *Address:* St Hilda's Vicarage, Preston Gate, Marden, North Shields NE29 9QB. *T:* 091–257 6595.

SHONE, Sir Robert Minshull, Kt 1955; CBE 1949; *b* 27 May 1906; *s* of Robert Harold Shone. *Educ:* Sedbergh School; Liverpool University (MEng); Chicago Univ. (MA Economics). Commonwealth Fellow, USA, 1932–34; Lecturer, London School of Economics, 1935–36; British Iron and Steel Federation, 1936–39 and 1946–53, Director 1950–53; Iron and Steel Control, 1940–45, Gen. Dir, 1943–45; Executive Member, Iron and Steel Board, 1953–62; Joint Chairman, UK and ECSC Steel Committee, 1954–62; Dir-Gen., Nat. Economic Develt Council, 1962–66; Research Fellow, Nuffield Coll., Oxford, 1966–67; Special Prof., Nottingham Univ., 1971–73; Vis. Prof., City Univ., 1967–83. Director: M & G Gp, 1966–84; Rank Orgn, 1968–78; A. P. V. Holdings Ltd, 1969–75. Hon. Fellow, LSE. Pres., Soc. of Business Economists, 1963–68. *Publications:* Problems of Investment, 1971; Price and Investment Relationships, 1975; contributions to: Some Modern Business Problems, 1937; The Industrial Future of Great Britain, 1948; Large Scale Organisation, 1950; Models for Decision, 1965; Britain and the Common Market, 1967; Financial Management Handbook, 1978; articles in journals. *Recreation:* golf. *Address:* 7 Windmill Hill, Hampstead, NW3. *T:* 071–435 1930.

SHOOTER, Prof. Eric Manvers, FRS 1988; Professor of Neurobiology, Stanford University, since 1975; *b* 18 April 1924; *s* of Fred and Pattie Shooter; *m* 1949, Elaine Staley Arnold; one *d*. *Educ:* Gonville and Caius Coll., Cambridge (BA 1945; MA 1950; PhD 1950; ScD 1986); DSc London 1964. Senior Scientist, Brewing Industry Research Foundn, 1950–53; Lectr in Biochem., University Coll. London, 1953–63; Stanford University: Associate Prof. of Genetics, 1963–68; Prof. of Genetics and Prof. of Biochem., 1968–75; Prof. and Chm. of Neurobiol., 1975–87. Macy Faculty Scholar, Univ. of Geneva, 1974–75. Foreign Assoc., Inst. of Medicine, Nat. Acad. of Scis, USA, 1989–. Wakeman Award, 1988. *Publications:* (associate editor) Annual Review of Neuroscience, vols 6–13, 1983–90; numerous papers in sci jls. *Address:* Department of Neurobiology, Stanford University School of Medicine, Stanford, Calif 94305–5401, USA. *T:* 415 723 6638.

SHOOTER, Prof. Reginald Arthur, CBE 1980; Emeritus Professor of Medical Microbiology, London University, since 1981; *b* 1916; *s* of Rev. A. E. Shooter, TD and M. K. Shooter; *m* 1946, Jean Wallace, MB, ChB; one *s* three *d*. *Educ:* Mill Hill Sch.; Caius Coll., Cambridge; St Bartholomew's Hosp. BA 1937; MB, BChir 1940; MRCS, LRCP 1940; MA 1941; MD 1945; MRCP 1961; FRCP 1968; FRCS 1977; FRCPath 1963 (Vice-Pres., 1971–74). After various Hosp. appts became Surgeon Lieut, RNVR. Appointments at St Bartholomew's Hospital from 1946; Rockefeller Travelling Fellow in Medicine, 1950–51; Reader in Bacteriology, 1953–61, Prof. of Medical Microbiology, 1961–81, Univ. of London; Bacteriologist to St Bartholomew's Hosp., 1961–81 and Dean, Medical Coll., 1972–81. Member: City and E London AHA (T), 1974–81; Gloucester HA, 1981–85; Chm., Regional Computing Policy Steering Gp, SW RHA, 1983–85. Mem., Public Health Lab. Service Bd, 1970–82; Chm., Dangerous Pathogens Adv. Gp, 1975–81. Mem., Scientific Adv. Council, Stress Foundn, 1981–90. Governor: St Bartholomew's Hosp., 1972–74; Queen Mary Coll., 1972–81; Trustee: Mitchell City of London Trust, 1958–82; Jenner Trust, 1989–. Mem. Court, City Univ., 1972–81. Pybus Medal, N of England Surg. Soc., 1979. Asst Editor, British Jl of Exp. Pathology, 1953–58; Hon. Editor, RSocMed, 1960–65. *Publications:* books, and articles in medical journals. *Recreations:* archaeology, gardening, fishing. *Address:* Eastlea, Back Edge Lane, The Edge, Stroud, Glos GL6 6PE. *T:* Painswick (0452) 812408.

SHOPPEE, Prof. Charles William, FRS 1956; FAA 1958; Emeritus Professor of Chemistry, University of Sydney; *b* London, 24 Feb. 1904; *er s* of J. W. and Elizabeth Shoppee, Totteridge; *m* 1929, Eileen Alice West; one *d*. *Educ:* Stationers' Company's Sch.;

Univs of London and Leeds. PhD, DSc (London); MA, DPhil (Basle). Sen. Student of Royal Commn for Exhibition of 1851, 1926–28; Asst Lecturer and Lecturer in Organic Chemistry, Univ. of Leeds, 1929–39; Rockefeller Research Fellow, Univ. of Basle, 1939–45; Reader in Chemistry, Univ. of London, at Royal Cancer Hosp., 1945–48; Prof. of Chemistry, Univ. of Wales, at University Coll., Swansea, 1948–56; Prof. of Organic Chemistry, Univ. of Sydney, 1956–70; Foundation Welch Prof. of Chemistry, Texas Tech. Univ., 1970–75. Visiting Professor of Chemistry: Duke Univ., N Carolina, USA, 1963; Univ. of Georgia, USA, 1966; Univ. of Mississippi, USA, 1968; Hon. Professorial Fellow in Chem., Macquarie Univ., 1976–79; Hon. Vis. Prof. of Organic Chem., La Trobe Univ., 1980–. *Publications:* scientific papers in Jl Chem. Soc., Helvetica Chimica Acta and Aust. Jl Chem. *Recreations:* bowls, music, bridge. *Address:* Unit 1, 75 Normanby Road, Kew, Vic 3101, Australia. *T:* 817–2644. *Club:* Royal Automobile of Victoria.

SHORE, David Teignmouth, OBE 1982; FEng 1979; Director (Technical), APV PLC, 1984–88; *b* 15 Nov. 1928; *e s* of Geoffrey and Cecilia Mary Shore; *m* 1950, Pamela Goodge; one *s* two *d*. *Educ:* Tiffin Boys' Sch., Kingston; Imperial Coll., London (MSc(Eng)). FIMechE 1967; FIChemE 1970; FIFST 1970; FCGI 1979. Engrg apprenticeship, 1944–47; Thermal Engr, Foster Wheeler Ltd, 1953–54; APV Co. Ltd: Research Engr, 1950–52; Process Develt Engr, 1954–65; Research Dir, 1965–77; Man. Dir, 1977–82; Chm., 1982–84; Divisional Dir, APV Holdings PLC, 1982–84. Chm., British Food Manufg Industries Res. Assoc., 1984–87; Chm. Engrg Bd, 1985–89 and Mem. Council, 1985–89, SERC; Member: Bd of Advisers in Chemical Engrg, Univ. of London, 1983–; Bd of Food Studies, Univ. of Reading, 1984–; Jt Delegacy for Food Res. Inst., Reading, 1985–; Council, Univ. of Reading, 1987–. *Publications:* technical articles on rheology, heat transfer and food process engrg in learned jls. *Recreations:* walking, astronomy, wine-making. *Address:* Hembury, Garratts Lane, Banstead, Surrey. *T:* Burgh Heath (0737) 53721. *Club:* National Liberal.

SHORE, Dr Elizabeth Catherine, CB 1980; Dean of Postgraduate Medicine, North West Thames Region, since 1985; *b* 1927; *d* of Edward Murray Wrong and Rosalind Grace Smith; *m* 1948, Rt Hon. Peter David Shore, *qv*; one *s* two *d* (and one *s* decd). *Educ:* Newnham Coll., Cambridge; St Bartholomew's Hospital. MRCP, FRCP; MRCS, FFCM, DRCOG. Joined Medical Civil Service, 1962; Dep. Chief Medical Officer, DHSS, 1977–85. Mem., GMC, 1989– (Mem., Standards Cttee, 1989–). Trustee, Child Accident Prevention Trust, 1985– (Chm., Council and Professional Cttee, 1985–90). *Recreations:* reading, cookery, swimming in rough seas. *Address:* 33 Millman Street, WC1N 3EJ.

SHORE, Jack; Head of Chester School of Art, 1960–81; President, Royal Cambrian Academy of Art, 1977–83; *b* 17 July 1922; *s* of Frank and Maggie Shore; *m* 1970, Olive Brenda Williams; one *s* one *d*. *Educ:* Accrington and Manchester Schools of Art. Lectr, Blackpool School of Art, 1945–60. RCamA 1962 (ARCamA 1961). Jubilee Medal, 1977. *Recreations:* gardening, enjoyment of music. *Address:* 11 St George's Crescent, Queens Park, Chester CH4 7AR. *T:* Chester (0244) 675017.

SHORE, Rt. Hon. Peter (David), PC 1967; MP (Lab) Bethnal Green and Stepney, since 1983 (Stepney, 1964–74; Stepney and Poplar, 1974–83); *b* 20 May 1924; *m* 1948, Elizabeth Catherine Wrong (*see* E. C. Shore); one *s* two *d* (and one *s* decd). *Educ:* Quarry Bank High Sch., Liverpool; King's Coll., Cambridge. Political economist. Joined Labour Party, 1948; Head of Research Dept, Labour Party, 1959–64. Member of Fabian Society. Contested (Lab) St Ives, Cornwall, 1950, Halifax, 1959. PPS to the Prime Minister, 1965–66; Jt Parly Sec.: Min. of Technology, 1966–67; Dept of Economic Affairs, 1967; Sec. of State for Economic Affairs, 1967–69; Minister without Portfolio, 1969–70; Dep. Leader of House of Commons, 1969–70; Opposition Spokesman on Europe, 1971–74; Sec. of State for Trade, 1974–76; Sec. of State for the Environment, 1976–79; Opposition Spokesman on Foreign Affairs, 1979–80, on Treasury and Economic Affairs, 1980–83; Opposition Spokesman on Trade and Industry, 1983–84; Shadow Leader of the House of Commons, 1984–87. Mem., Select Cttee on Foreign Affairs, 1987–. *Publication:* Entitled to Know, 1966. *Recreation:* swimming. *Address:* House of Commons, SW1; 23 Dryburgh Road, SW15.

SHORROCK, John Michael; QC 1988; a Recorder of the Crown Court, since 1982; *b* 25 May 1943; *s* of late James Godby Shorrock; *m* 1971, Marianne (*née* Mills); two *d*. *Educ:* Clifton College, Bristol; Pembroke College, Cambridge. MA. Called to the Bar, Inner Temple, 1966; practising on Northern Circuit, 1966–: Junior, 1968; Sec., Exec. Cttee, 1981–85. *Recreations:* walking, gardening, opera, theatre, cinema. *Address:* 2 Old Bank Street, Manchester. *T:* 061–832 3791; 5 Essex Court, Temple, EC4.

SHORT, family name of **Baron Glenamara.**

SHORT, Bernard David; Chief Inspector, Further Education, HM Inspectorate of Schools, since 1986; *b* 9 June 1935; *s* of late Bernard Charles and of Ethel Florence Short; *m* 1960, Susan Yvonne Taylor; two *s* one *d*. *Educ:* St Edmund Hall, Oxford (MA). Served The Royal Scots, 1953–56 (commnd 1954). Taught at Ingiliz Erkek Lisesi, Istanbul, Turkey, 1960–63; Lectr, Univ. of Kyushu, Japan, 1963–65; Asst Lectr, Garretts Green Technical Coll., Birmingham, 1966–67; Lectr, Bournville Coll. of Further Educn, Birmingham, 1967–71; Sen. Lectr, Henley Coll. of Further Educn, Coventry, 1971–73; Head, Dept of Gen. Studies, Bournville Coll., Birmingham, 1973–76; HM Inspectorate of Schools, 1976–: Inspector, 1976; Staff Inspector, 1984. *Publications:* A Guide to Stress in English, 1967; Humour, 1970. *Recreations:* music, gardening, boats.

SHORT, Clare; MP (Lab) Birmingham Ladywood, since 1983; *b* 15 Feb. 1946; *d* of Frank and Joan Short; *m* 1981, Alexander Ward Lyon, *qv*. *Educ:* Keele Univ.; Leeds Univ. (BA Hons Political Sci.). Home Office, 1970–75; Dir, All Faiths for One Race, Birmingham, 1976–78; Dir, Youth Aid and the Unemployment Unit, 1979–83. Chm., All Party Parly Gp on Race Relations, 1985–86; Mem., Home Affairs Select Cttee, 1983–85; front bench spokesperson on employment, 1985–88, on social security, 1989–91. Mem., Labour Party NEC, 1988–. *Publications:* Talking Blues: a study of young West Indians' views of policing, 1978; Handbook of Immigration Law, 1978; Dear Clare . . . this is what women think about Page 3, 1991. *Recreations:* family and friends, swimming, and dog. *Address:* House of Commons, SW1. *T:* 071–219 3000.

SHORT, Prof. David Somerset, MD, FRCP, FRCPE; Clinical Professor in Medicine, University of Aberdeen, since 1983; Hon. Consultant Physician, Aberdeen Royal Infirmary, since 1983 (Consultant Physician, 1960–83); *b* 6 Aug. 1918; *s* of Latimer James Short, MD, DPH, Bristol, and Mabel Annie Wood, SRN, Nottingham; *m* 1948, Joan Anne McLay, BSc, MB, ChB, Cardiff; one *s* four *d*. *Educ:* Bristol Grammar Sch.; Cambridge Univ.; Bristol Royal Hospitals. MD 1948; PhD 1957; FRCP 1964; FRCPE 1966. Served with RAMC, 1944–47; Registrar, Southmead Hosp., Bristol, 1947–49; Sen. Registrar, National Heart Hosp. and London Hosp., 1950–54; Lecturer in Medicine, Middlesex Hosp., 1955–59. Physician to the Queen in Scotland, 1977–83. *Publications:* Medicine as a Vocation, 1978, 2nd edn 1987; contribs to medical journals, mainly on cardiovascular and pulmonary diseases. *Recreations:* walking, music. *Address:* 48 Victoria Street, Aberdeen, Scotland AB9 2PL. *T:* Aberdeen (0224) 645853.

SHORT, Rt. Rev. Hedley Vicars Roycraft; retired 1985; *b* 24 Jan. 1914; *s* of Hedley Vicars Short and Martha Hallam Parke; *m* 1953, Elizabeth Frances Louise Shirley; one *s* four *d*. *Educ:* Trinity College, Univ. of Toronto (BA, LTh, BD). Deacon, 1943, priest, 1944, Assistant Curate St Michael and All Angels, Toronto; Junior Chaplain, Coventry Cathedral, England, 1946–47; Lecturer, Trinity Coll., Toronto, 1947–51; Dean of Residence, 1949–51; Rector, Cochrane, Ont, 1951–56; Rector, St Barnabas, St Catharines, Ont, 1956–63; Canon, Christ's Church Cathedral, Hamilton, Ont, 1962; Dean of Saskatchewan, 1963–70; Archdeacon of Prince Albert, 1966–70; Bishop of Saskatchewan, 1970–85. Member of General Synod, 1955–83; Examining Chaplain successively to Bishops of Moosonee, Niagara and Saskatchewan. Mem., Northern Develt Adv. Council, Province of Saskatchewan, 1987–88. Pres. Council, Coll. of Emmanuel and St Chad, Saskatoon, 1974–80; Chm., Natonum Community Coll., Prince Albert, 1974–76; Chancellor, 1975–80, Hon. Fellow, 1980, Univ. of Emmanuel Coll. Hon. DD: Trinity Coll., Toronto, 1964; Emmanuel Coll., Saskatoon, 1983. *Publication:* (contrib.) Eucharistic Dimensions, 1977. *Recreations:* music, sketching, reading. *Address:* 355 19th Street W, Prince Albert, Saskatchewan S6V 4C8, Canada.

SHORT, Rev. John, MA (Edinburgh); PhD (Edinburgh); Hon. DD (St Andrews); Minister of St George's United Church, Toronto, Canada, 1951–64; *b* Berwickshire, 27 March 1896; *m* 1st; one *s* one *d*; 2nd, 1939, Anneliese, 2nd *d* of Dr C. J. F. Bechler, Danzig; two *s*. *Educ:* Edinburgh University. Trained for a business career but attracted by religious convictions to the Christian ministry; began to study for same just before the war of 1914–18, joined army and served for 3 years and 6 months; commenced studies at Edinburgh; graduated MA. First class honours in Philosophy; awarded John Edward Baxter Scholarship in Philosophy for 3 years; received University Diploma in Education and Medal; trained for Teacher's Certificate; awarded Doctorate in Philosophy for a thesis on the Philosophic Character of English XIVth Century Mysticism; medallist in class of Moral Philosophy, and in Metaphysics; Prizeman in Psychology; trained in Scottish Congregational College for Ministry under Principal T. Hywel Hughes, DLitt, DD; called to Bathgate E. U. Congregational Church, 1924; Minister of Lyndhurst Road Congregational Church, Hampstead, 1930–37. Minister of Richmond Hill Congregational Church, Bournemouth, 1937–51; Chairman of the Congregational Union of England and Wales, 1949–50. Mason: 3° Home Lodge Amity, Poole, Dorset, 18° Downend Chapter Rose Croix, Gloucester, 1953; affiliated Ashlar Lodge, 247 GRC, Toronto, 1952; 32° Moore Sovereign Consistory, Hamilton, Ont, 1964; 33° Supreme Council A&ASR, Dominion of Canada (Hon. Inspector Gen.), 1967. DD (hc): St Andrews Univ., 1950; McMaster Univ., Hamilton, Ontario, 1964. *Publications:* Can I Find Faith?, 1937; All Things are Yours (book of sermons), 1939; The Interpreter's Bible Exposition of I Corinthians; Triumphant Believing, 1952. *Recreations:* gardening, reading, and travel. *Address:* 162 Coldstream Avenue, Toronto, Ont M5N 1X9, Canada. *T:* 489–8614.

SHORT, Rt. Rev. Kenneth Herbert, AO 1988; Dean of Sydney (St Andrew's Cathedral), since 1989; *b* 6 July 1927; *s* of Cecil Charles Short and Joyce Ellen Begbie; *m* 1950, Gloria Noelle Funnell; one *s* two *d*. *Educ:* Moore Theological Coll. (ThL and Moore Coll. Dipl.). Commissioned AIF, 1946; with BCOF, 1946–48; theological training, 1949–52; ordained Anglican Ministry, 1952; Minister in Charge, Provisional Parish of Pittwater, 1952–54; with CMS in Tanzania, E Africa, 1955–64; Chaplain, Tabora 1955, Mwanza 1955–59; first Principal, Msalato Bible School, 1961–64; Gen. Secretary, CMS NSW Branch, 1964–71, including Sec. for S America. Canon of St Andrew's Cathedral, Sydney, 1970–75; Exam. Chaplain to Archbishop of Sydney, 1971–82; Rector of St Michael's, Vaucluse, 1971–75; Archdeacon of Wollongong and Camden, 1975–79; Chaplain General (CE), Australian Army, 1979–81; Bishop in Wollongong, Dio. of Sydney, 1975–82; Anglican Bishop to Aust. Defence Force (Army, Navy and Air Force), 1979–89; Bishop of Parramatta, Dio. of Sydney, 1982–89. ChStJ 1989. *Publications:* Guidance, 1969; (contrib.) Evangelism and Preaching in Secular Australia, 1989. *Recreations:* rock fishing, reading, walking, wood turning. *Address:* 46 Church Street, Lilyfield, NSW 2040, Australia. *T:* (02) 8103257. *Club:* Union (Sydney) (Hon. Mem.).

SHORT, Sir Noel (Edward Vivian), Kt 1977; MBE 1951; MC 1945; Speaker's Secretary, House of Commons, 1970–82; *b* 19 Jan. 1916; *s* of late Vivian A. Short, CIE, Indian Police, and late Annie W. Short; *m* 1st, 1949, Diana Hester Morison (*d* 1951); one *s*; 2nd, 1957, Karin Margarete Anders; one *s* one *d*. *Educ:* Radley College; RMA Sandhurst. Commissioned Indian Army, 1936; joined 6th Gurkha Rifles, 1937. Active service: NW Frontier of India, 1937, 1940–41; Assam and Burma, 1942, 1944–45; New Guinea, 1943–44; Malaysia, 1950–51, 1952–53, 1956–57. Staff College, 1946–47; jssc, 1953; Comdr, 63 Gurkha Bde, Malaysia, 1960–61; Comdr, 51 Infty Bde, Tidworth, 1962–63. Principal, Home Office, 1964–70. Col, 6th Queen Elizabeth's Own Gurkha Rifles, 1978–83.

SHORT, Peter, BA; IPFA; Deputy Chief Executive and Director of Finance, Greater Manchester Buses Ltd, since 1989; *b* 21 June 1945; *s* of Christopher John Grewcock Short and Isabella Short; *m* 1967, Eileen Short (*née* Makin); one *s* one *d*. *Educ:* South Shields Grammar Sch.; Univ. of Exeter (2nd Cl. Hons, Div. 1, Modern Economic History). IPFA (1st place Final, 1970). Local Govt Accountant with Manchester City Council, 1967–73; Leeds City Council, 1973–78; Dir of Finance, South Tyneside MDC, 1978–83; City Treas., Manchester CC, 1983–89. *Recreations:* reading, walking, caravanning, avoiding household maintenance, planning to walk the Pennine Way. *Address:* 2 Netherwood Road, Northenden, Manchester M22 4BQ.

SHORT, Mrs Renee; *m*; two *d*. *Educ:* Nottingham County Grammar Sch.; Manchester Univ. Freelance journalist. Member: Herts County Council, 1952–67; Watford RDC, 1952–64; West Herts Group Hosp. Management Cttee; former Chm. Shrodell's Hosp., Watford. Governor: Watford Coll. of Technology; Watford Grammar Sch. Contested (Lab) St Albans, 1955, Watford, 1959. MP (Lab) Wolverhampton NE, 1964–87; TGWU sponsored Member of Parliament. Member: Delegation to Council of Europe, 1964–68; Estimates Cttee, 1964–69; Expenditure Cttee, 1970–79 (Chm., Social Services and Employment Sub-Cttee); Chairman: Select Cttee for Social Services, 1979–87; Parly and Scientific Cttee, 1982–85 (Vice-Pres., 1986–); Associate Mem., Parly IT Cttee, 1987–. Vice-Chm., Parly East-West Trade Gp, 1968–87; Chairman: British-GDR Parly Gp, 1972–87; British-Soviet Parly Gp 1984–87 (Sec., 1972–84); Pres., British-Romanian Friendship Assoc. Mem., Nat. Exec. Cttee of Labour Party, 1970–81, 1983–88. Member: MRC, 1988–; Research in Patients Cttee, RCP, 1988–; IVF Cttee, BMA, 1988–; AIDS Study Gp, Inst. of Medical Ethics, 1989–. National President: Nursery Schools Assoc., 1970–80; Campaign for Nursery Educn, 1970–83; Pres., Action for the Newborn, 1988–; Vice-President: Women's Nat. Cancer Control Campaign; Health Visitors' Assoc. Mem., Roundhouse Theatre Council; Chm., Theatres' Advisory Council, 1974–80. Hon. Fellow, Wolverhampton Polytechnic, 1987; Hon. FRCPsych 1988; Hon. MRCP 1989. *Publication:* The Care of Long Term Prisoners, 1979. *Address:* 70 Westminster Gardens, Marsham Street, SW1P 4JG. *T:* 071–828 6110.

SHORT, Prof. Roger Valentine, FRCOG; FRS 1974; FRSE; FRCVS; FAA; Professor of Reproductive Biology, Monash University, Australia, since 1982; *b* 31 July 1930; *s* of F. A. and M. C. Short, Weybridge; *m* 1st, 1958, Dr Mary Bowen Wilson (marr. diss.

1981); one *s* three *d*; 2nd, 1982, Dr Marilyn Bernice Renfree; two *d*. *Educ*: Sherborne Sch.; Univs of Bristol (BVSc, MRCVS), Wisconsin (MSc) and Cambridge (PhD, ScD). FRSE 1974; FRCVS 1976; FAA 1984; FRCOG 1991. Mem., ARC Unit of Reproductive Physiology and Biochemistry, Cambridge, 1956–72; Fellow, Magdalene Coll., Cambridge, 1962–72; Lectr, then Reader, Dept of Veterinary Clinical Studies, Cambridge, 1961–72; Dir, MRC Unit of Reproductive Biology, Edinburgh, 1972–82. Hon. Prof., Univ. of Edinburgh, 1976–82. Chm., Bd of Dirs, Family Health Internat., NC, USA, 1984–90. Hon. DSc Guelph, 1988. *Publications*: (ed, with C. R. Austin) Reproduction in Mammals, vols 1–8, 1972–80, 2nd edn vols 1–5, 1982–86; (ed, with D. T. Baird) Contraceptives of the Future, 1976; contrib. Jl Endocrinology, Jl Reproduction and Fertility, Jl Zoology, Lancet, Nature. *Recreations*: gardening, wildlife, history of biology. *Address*: Department of Physiology, Monash University, Melbourne, Victoria 3168, Australia.

SHORTIS, Maj.-Gen. Colin Terry, CB 1988; CBE 1980 (OBE 1977; MBE 1974); General Officer Commanding North West District, 1986–89; *b* 18 Jan. 1934; *s* of late Tom Richardson Shortis and Marna Evelyn Shortis (*née* Kenworthy); *m* 1957, Sylvia Mary, *o d* of H. C. A. Jenkinson; two *s* two *d*. *Educ*: Bedford School. Enlisted Army 1951; 2nd Lieut Royal Fusiliers, 1953; transf. to Dorset Regt, 1955; served Hong Kong, Korea, Suez Canal Zone, Sudan, BAOR, Aden, Singapore and British Guiana, 1953–63; Instructor, Sch. of Infantry, 1964–65; Staff Coll., 1966; Co. Comdr, 1st Devonshire and Dorset, 1967–73; served Malta, NI, Belize, Cyprus, BAOR, CO 1974–77; Directing Staff, Staff Coll., 1977; Comdr, 8 Infantry Brigade, 1978–80; RCDS 1981; Comdr, British Mil. Adv. and Training Team, Zimbabwe, 1982–83; Dir of Infantry, 1983–86. Col Comdt, The Prince of Wales Div., 1983–88; Col, Devonshire and Dorset Regt, 1984–90. *Recreation*: sailing. *Address*: c/o Barclays Bank, 137 Brompton Road, SW3 1QF. *Club*: Army and Navy.

SHOTTER, Very Rev. Edward Frank; Dean of Rochester, since 1989; *b* 29 June 1933; *s* of late Frank Edward Shotter and Minnetta Shotter (*née* Gaskill); *m* 1978, Jane Edgcumbe; two *s* one *d*. *Educ*: Humberstone Foundation School, Clee; Durham Univ. School of Architecture; St David's Coll., Lampeter, Univ. of Wales (BA 1958); St Stephen's House, Oxford. Deacon 1960, priest 1961; Curate of St Peter, Plymouth, 1960–62; Intercollegiate Sec., SCM, London, 1962–66; Director of Studies, London Medical Group, 1966–89; Director, Inst. of Medical Ethics, 1974–89 (Amulree Fellow, 1991); Chaplain to Univ. of London, 1969–89; Prebendary of St Paul's Cathedral, 1977–89. Member: Archbishop of Canterbury's Counsellors on Foreign Relations, 1971–82; BCC East/West Relations Adv. Cttee, 1971–81; Liberal Party Foreign Affairs Panel (Chm. East Europe Sub-Cttee), 1974–81; St Christopher's Hospice Educn Cttee, 1982–89; Wking Party on ethics of med. involvement in torture, 1989–; C of E rep. on Churches Council of Health and Healing, 1975–76. Chm., Governing Body, King's School, Rochester, 1989. Founder, Jl of Medical Ethics, 1975. FRSocMed 1976. Patriarchal Cross, Romanian Orthodox Church, 1975. *Publications*: (ed) Matters of Life and Death, 1970; (with K. M. Boyd and B. Callaghan, SJ) Life Before Birth, 1986. *Recreations*: hill walking, restoring country houses and their gardens. *Address*: The Deanery, Rochester, Kent ME1 1TG. *T*: Medway (0634) 844023. *Club*: Reform.

SHOTTON, Prof. Edward; Professor of Pharmaceutics, University of London, 1956–77, now Emeritus; *b* 15 July 1910; *s* of Ernest Richard and Maud Shotton; *m* 1943, Mary Constance Louise Marchant; one *d*. *Educ*: Smethwick (Junior) Technical School; Birkbeck College, University of London. Pharmaceutical Chemist (PhC), 1933; BSc (London), 1939; PhD (London), 1955; Hon. ACT (Birmingham), 1961. FRIC 1949. Pharmaceutical research and development work at Burroughs, Wellcome & Co., Dartford, 1939–48. Sen. Lecturer in Pharmaceutics, Univ. of London, 1948–56. Chairman, British Pharmaceutical Conference, 1966. *Publications*: (with K. Ridgway) Physical Pharmaceutics, 1974; research papers, mainly in Jl of Pharmacy and Pharmacology. *Recreations*: gardening, cricket, fly-fishing. *Address*: 2 Raglan House, Kilfillan Gardens, Berkhamsted, Herts HP4 3LU. *T*: Berkhamsted (0442) 866402. *Club*: Athenæum.

SHOTTON, Dr Keith Crawford, FIEE, FInstP; Head of Information Technology Division, Department of Trade and Industry, since 1990; *b* 11 Sept. 1943; *s* of William Crawford Shotton and Mary Margaret Shotton (*née* Smith); *m* 1969, Maria Elizabeth Gonszor; two *d*. *Educ*: Newcastle upon Tyne Royal Grammar Sch.; Trinity Coll., Cambridge (Schol.; MA, PhD). CEng, CPhys. Post-doctoral Fellow (laser physics and spectroscopy), NRCC, 1969–71; National Physical Laboratory: mem. team measuring speed of light, 1971–77; Head, Ultrasonics Metrology Unit, 1977–80; Head, Marketing and Inf. Services, 1980–84; DCSO, Supt, Div. of Radiation Sci. and Acoustics, 1984–87; Dir, Radio Technology, Radio Communications Div., DTI, 1987–90. *Publications*: numerous papers in sci. jls, principally in spectroscopy, laser physics, ultrasonics and instrumentation. *Recreations*: fell walking, sailing, motor cars, food. *Address*: Department of Trade and Industry, 151 Buckingham Palace Road, SW1W 9SS. *T*: 071–215 1239.

SHOVELTON, Prof. David Scott, FDSRCS; Professor of Conservative Dentistry, University of Birmingham, 1964–89, Professor Emeritus, since 1990; Honorary Consultant in Conservative Dentistry, Central Birmingham Health Authority, since 1989; *b* 12 Sept. 1925; *s* of Leslie Shovelton, LDSRCS, and Marion de Winton (*née* Scott); *m* 1949, Pearl Holland; two *s*. *Educ*: The Downs Sch., Colwall; King's Sch., Worcester; Univ. of Birmingham (BSc, LDS, BDS). House Surg., Birmingham Dental Hosp., 1951; gen. dental practice, Evesham, Worcs, 1951; Dental Officer, RAF, 1951–53; Birmingham University: Lectr in Operative Dental Surg., 1953–60; Sen. Lectr, 1960–64; Dir, 1974–78, Dep. Dir, 1982–84, Dental Sch.; Consultant Dental Surgeon, Utd Birmingham Hosps, subseq. Central Birmingham HA, 1960–89. Vis. Asst Prof. of Clin. Dentistry, Univ. of Alabama, 1959–60. Hon. Cons. Dental Surg., Birmingham Reg. Hosp. Bd, 1962–74. Pres., British Soc. for Restorative Dentistry, 1970–71 (Vice-Pres., 1968–70 and 1971–72). Consultant, Commn on Dental Practice, Fédn Dentaire Internat., 1972–79; Consultant Adviser in Restorative Dentistry, DHSS, 1983–89. Member: Gen. Dental Council, 1974–89; Birmingham Area Health Authority (Teaching), 1973–79; Cttee of Management, Sch. for Dental Therapists, 1977–80; Jt Cttee for Higher Trng in Dentistry, 1979–84 (Chm., Specialist Adv. Cttee in Restorative Dentistry, 1979–84); Standing Dental Adv. Cttee, 1982–88; Bd, Faculty of Dental Surgery, RCS, 1983–91; Jt Dental Cttee of MRC, Health Depts and SERC, 1984–87; Cttee of Enquiry into unnecessary dental treatment, 1984–85. Ext. Examnr in dental subjects, univs and colls, 1968–. *Publications*: Inlays, Crowns and Bridges (jtly), 1963, 4th edn 1985; articles in med. and dental jls, 1957–. *Recreations*: music, learning about wine, gardening, caravanning. *Address*: 86 Broad Oaks Road, Solihull, West Midlands B91 1HZ. *T*: 021–705 3026. *Club*: Royal Air Force.

SHOVELTON, (Walter) Patrick, CB 1976; CMG 1972; FCIT; Chairman, Birmingham European Airways (formerly Birmingham Executive Airways), since 1988; Vice-Chairman, Maersk Co., since 1987 (Director, 1985); Director, Maersk Air Ltd, since 1988; *b* 18 Aug. 1919; *s* of late S. T. Shovelton, CBE, and May Catherine (*née* Kelly), cousin of Patrick and Willie Pearse; *m* 1st, 1942, Marjorie Lucy Joan Manners (marr. diss. 1967); one *d*; 2nd, Helena Richards, 3rd *d* of D. G. Richards, *qv*. *Educ*: Charterhouse; Keble Coll., Oxford (scholar of both). Rep. Oxford Univ. at Eton Fives. Served in RA and RHA, 1940–46; DAAG, War Office, 1945–46. Entered Administrative Civil Service as Asst Principal, Min. of War Transport, 1946; Principal 1947; Admin. Staff College, 1951; Private Sec. to Secretary of State for Co-ordination of Transport, Fuel and Power, 1951–53; Asst Sec., Road Transport, 1957; transferred to Min. of Aviation, 1959; IDC, 1962; Under Secretary, 1966; transferred to Min. of Technology, 1966, and to DTI, 1970; Mem., UK Negotiating Team for entry into EEC, 1970–72; Deputy Secretary: DTI, 1972–74; Dept of Prices and Consumer Protection, 1974–76; Dept of Trade, 1976–78; Dir-Gen., Gen. Council of British Shipping, 1978–85; Dir, British Airports Authy, 1982–85. Led UK Negotiating Team for Bermuda 2, 1977. William and Mary Tercentenary Trust: Chairman: Maritime Cttee, 1985–89; Finance and Sponsorship Cttee, 1988–89. Council, CIT, 1982–85; Advr, Inquiries into EEC Maritime Transport Policy H of L, 1985–86, into Merchant Shipping, H of C, 1986–88. Brancker Lectr (civil aviation), 1979; Grout Lectr (shipping), 1985. Officer, Order of Orange-Nassau (Netherlands), 1989. *Recreations*: competitive golf, reading, opera, gardening. *Address*: 63 London Road, Tunbridge Wells, Kent TN1 1DT. *T*: Tunbridge Wells (0892) 27885. *Clubs*: Brooks's; Hampstead Golf (Capt. 1975), Royal Ashdown Forest (Capt. 1988, Centenary Year), Rye Golf, Seniors' Golf, Jesters.

SHRAPNEL, Norman; Parliamentary Correspondent of the Guardian, 1958–75; *b* 5 Oct. 1912; *yr s* of Arthur Edward Scrope Shrapnel and Rosa Brosy; *m* 1940, Mary Lilian Myfanwy Edwards; two *s*. *Educ*: King's School, Grantham. Various weekly, evening and morning newspapers from 1930; Manchester Guardian (later the Guardian) from 1947, as reporter, theatre critic and reviewer; contributor to various journals. Political Writer of the Year Award (the Political Companion), 1969. *Publications*: A View of the Thames, 1977; The Performers: politics as theatre, 1978; The Seventies, 1980. *Recreations*: walking, music. *Address*: 27A Shooters Hill Road, Blackheath, SE3. *T*: 081–858 7123.

SHREEVE, Ven. David Herbert; Archdeacon of Bradford, since 1984; *b* 18 Jan. 1934; *s* of Hubert Ernest and Ivy Eleanor Shreeve; *m* 1957, Barbara (*née* Fogden); one *s* one *d*. *Educ*: Southfield School, Oxford; St Peter's Coll., Oxford (MA); Ridley Hall, Cambridge. Asst Curate, St Andrew's Church, Plymouth, 1959–64; Vicar: St Anne's, Bermondsey, 1964–71; St Luke's, Eccleshill, 1971–84; RD of Calverley, 1978–84. Mem., Gen. Synod and Proctor in Convocation, 1977–90. Hon. Canon of Bradford Cathedral, 1983–84. *Recreations*: walking, camping, jogging, photography. *Address*: Rowan House, 11 The Rowans, Baildon, Shipley, W Yorks BD17 5DB. *T*: Bradford (0274) 583735.

SHREWSBURY, Bishop Suffragan of, since 1987; **Rt. Rev. John Dudley Davies;** *b* 12 Aug. 1927; *s* of Charles Edward Steedman Davies and Minnie Paton Davies; *m* 1956, Shirley Dorothy Gough; one *s* two *d*. *Educ*: Trinity Coll., Cambridge (BA 1951, MA 1963); Lincoln Theol Coll. Deacon 1953, priest 1954, dio. Ripon; Curate: Halton, Leeds, 1953–56; Yeoville, Johannesburg, 1959; Priest-in-Charge, Evander, dio. Johannesburg, 1957–61; Rector and Dir of Missions, Empangeni, dio. Zululand and Swaziland, 1961–63; Anglican Chaplain, Univ. of Witwatersrand and Johannesburg Coll. of Educn, 1963–70; Chm., Div. of Christian Educn, S African Council of Churches, 1964–70; Mem. Exec., Univ. Christian Movement of Southern Africa, 1966–67; Sec. for Chaplaincies of Higher Educn, C of E Bd of Educn, 1970–74; Vicar of Keele and Chaplain, Univ. of Keele, 1974–76; Principal, Coll. of Ascension, Selly Oak, 1976–81; Preb. of Sandiacre, Lichfield Cathedral, 1976–87; Diocesan Missioner, St Asaph, 1982–87; Canon Res. and Hellins Lectr, St Asaph, 1982–85; Vicar/Rector, Llanrhaeadr-ym-Mochnant, Llanarmon-Mynydd-Mawr, Pennant, Hirnant and Llangynog, 1985–87. *Publications*: Free to Be, 1970; Beginning Now, 1971; Good News in Galatians, 1975; Creed and Conflict, 1979; The Faith Abroad, 1983; (with John J. Vincent) Mark at Work, 1986; contribs to jls. *Address*: Athlone House, 68 London Road, Shrewsbury SY2 6PG. *T*: Shrewsbury (0743) 235867.

SHREWSBURY, Bishop of, (RC), since 1980; **Rt. Rev. Joseph Gray,** DCL; *b* 20 Oct. 1919; *s* of Terence Gray and Mary Gray (*née* Alwill). *Educ*: Patrick's Coll., Cavan, Eire; St Mary's Seminary, Oscott, Birmingham; Dunboyne House, St Patrick's Coll., Maynooth, Eire; Pontifical Univ. of St Thomas Aquinas, Rome. Priest, 1943; Asst Priest, Sacred Heart, Aston, Birmingham, 1943–48; Dunboyne House, 1948–50 (Licentiate in Canon Law, 1950); Sec. to Archbp of Birmingham, 1950–55. Diocesan Chancellor, Birmingham, 1951–69; Pontifical Univ., 1959–60 (Doctorate in Canon Law, 1960); Vicar-Gen., Birmingham, 1960–69; Parish Priest, St Michael's, Birmingham, 1955–69. Papal Chamberlain, 1960; Domestic Prelate, 1966. Episcopal Ordination, Cathedral of Christ the King, Liverpool, Feb. 1969; Titular Bishop of Mercia and Auxiliary Bishop of Liverpool, 1969–80. Pres., Liturgy Commn of Bishops' Conf. of England and Wales, 1976–84; Chm., Commn for Religious Life, 1984–. *Recreations*: music, reading, travel. *Address*: Bishop's House, Eleanor Road, Birkenhead L43 7QW. *T*: 051–653 3600.

SHREWSBURY AND WATERFORD, 22nd Earl of, *cr* 1442 and 1446; **Charles Henry John Benedict Crofton Chetwynd Chetwynd-Talbot;** Baron Talbot, 1733; 7th Earl Talbot, Viscount Ingestre, 1784; Premier Earl on the Rolls of England and Ireland, Hereditary Great Seneschal or Lord High Steward of Ireland; director and consultant; Joint Deputy Chairman, Britannia Building Society, since 1989 (Deputy Chairman, 1987–89; Director, since 1984); *b* 18 Dec. 1952; *s* of 21st Earl of Shrewsbury and Waterford, and of Nadine, *yr d* of late Brig.-Gen. C. R. Crofton, CBE; *S* father, 1980; *m* 1974, Deborah, *o d* of Noel Hutchinson; two *s* one *d*. *Educ*: Harrow. Dir, Richmount Enterprise Zone Managers, 1988–. Executive Committee: Staffs Assoc. of Boys Clubs, 1981–; Staffs Br., Game Conservancy Trust, 1988–. Pres., Staffordshire Soc., 1989–; Vice-Pres., Midland & West Assoc. of Building Socs, 1984–. Patron: St Giles Hospice, Lichfield, 1988–; Staffs Br., BRCS, 1989–. Hon. President: Shropshire Bldg Preservation Trust, 1984–; Lord Roberts Wkshops and SSAFA (Wolverhampton Br.), 1987–; Staffs Small Bore Rifle Assoc., 1988–; Hon. Vice-Pres., Rugeley Rugby FC. Hon. Pres., Shropshire Hospice, 1983–88. Patron of 11 livings. *Recreations*: hunting, racing, shooting. *Heir*: *s* Viscount Ingestre, *qv*. *Address*: Wanfield Hall, Kingstone, Uttoxeter, Staffs ST14 8QT. *Club*: Flyfishers'.

SHRIMPLIN, John Steven; Deputy Director General and Director, Space Technology, British National Space Centre, since 1991; *b* 9 May 1934; *s* of late John Reginald Shrimplin and of Kathleen Mary (*née* Stevens); *m* 1957, Hazel Baughen; two *s*. *Educ*: Royal Grammar Sch., Colchester; King's Coll., London (BSc Maths). Joined RAE, Farnborough, 1956; Defence Operational Analysis Estabt, 1966; JSSC, 1970; Weapons Dept, RAE, 1971; Defence R&D Staff, British Embassy, Washington, 1972; Asst Dir, Future Systems, Air Systems Controllerate, MoD PE, 1974; Asst Chief Scientist, RAF, 1978; Head of Weapons Dept, RAE, 1983; Dep. Hd, British Defence Staff, and Minister/Counsellor, Defence Equipment, British Embassy, Washington, DC, 1985–88; Dir, Defence Science (Studies), MoD, 1988–91. *Recreations*: travel, camping, walking. *Address*: c/o National Westminster Bank, 2 Alexandra Road, Farnborough, Hants GU14 6BZ.

SHRIMSLEY, Bernard; journalist; Associate Editor, Daily Express, since 1986; *b* 13 Jan. 1931; *er s* of John and Alice Shrimsley, London; *m* 1952, Norma Jessie Alexandra, *d* of Albert and Maude Porter, Southport; one *d*. *Educ*: Kilburn Grammar School,

Northampton. Press Association, 1947; Southport Guardian, 1948; RAF, 1949–51; Daily Mirror, 1953; Sunday Express, 1958; Northern Editor, Daily Mirror, 1963; Editor, Daily Post, Liverpool, 1968; Editor, The Sun, 1972–75; Editor, News of the World, and Dir, News Group Newspapers Ltd, 1975–80; Editor-designate (subseq. Editor), The Mail on Sunday, and Dir (subseq. Vice-Chm.), The Mail on Sunday Ltd, 1980–82; Asst Editor, Daily Express, 1983–86. Mem., Press Council, 1989–90 (Jt Vice-Chm., 1990); Mem., Defence, Press and Broadcasting Cttee, 1989–. Mem. judging panel, British Press Awards, 1988–. *Publications:* The Candidates, 1968; Lion Rampant, 1984. *Address:* Daily Express, Ludgate House, 245 Blackfriars Road, SE1 9UX. *T:* 071–928 8000. *Club:* Garrick.

SHRIVER, (Robert) Sargent; Lawyer, Of Counsel, Fried, Frank, Harris, Shriver & Jacobson, since 1971; Chairman, Special Olympics International, since 1990 (President, 1984–90); *b* Westminster, Md, 9 Nov. 1915; *s* of Robert Sargent and Hilda Shriver; *m* 1953, Eunice Mary Kennedy; four *s* one *d*. *Educ:* parochial schools, Baltimore; Canterbury School, New Milford, Conn.; Yale College; Yale University. BA (*cum laude*) 1938; LLB 1941; LLD 1964. Apprentice Seaman, USNR, 1940; Ensign, 1941. Served War of 1941–45: Atlantic and Pacific Ocean Areas aboard battleships and submarines; Lt-Comdr, USNR. Admitted to: New York Bar, 1941; Illinois Bar, (retd) 1959; US Supreme Court, 1966; District of Columbia Bar, 1971. With legal firm of Winthrop, Stimson, Putnam & Roberts, NYC, 1940–41; Asst Editor, Newsweek, 1945–46; associated with Joseph P. Kennedy Enterprises, 1946–48; Asst Gen. Man., Merchandise Mart, 1948–61; President: Chicago Bd of Educn, 1955–60; Catholic Interracial Council of Chicago, 1954–59; Dir, Peace Corps, Washington, 1961–66; Dir, Office of Economic Opportunity and Special Asst to Pres. Johnson, 1964–68; US Ambassador to France, 1968–70. Vice-Presidential candidate (Democrat), Nov. 1972. Democrat; Roman Catholic. *Address:* 1350 New York Avenue NW, Washington, DC 20005, USA.

SHRUBSOLE, Alison Cheveley, CBE 1982; Principal, Homerton College, Cambridge, 1971–85; Fellow of Hughes Hall, Cambridge, 1974; *b* 7 April 1925; *d* of Rev. Stanley and Mrs Margaret Shrubsole. *Educ:* Milton Mount Coll.; Royal Holloway Coll.; Inst. of Education. BA Hons London; MA Cantab; Postgraduate Cert. in Educn. FCP. Teaching in schools in South London, 1946–50; Lectr and Sen. Lectr, Stockwell Coll., 1950–57; Principal: Machakos Training Coll., Kenya, 1957–62; Philippa Fawcett Coll., London SW16, 1963–71. DUniv. Open, 1985. *Publications:* articles in TES, THES, Dialogue, Learning for Teaching. *Recreations:* music, architecture, travel, mountaineering, gardening, cooking. *Address:* 4 Chancellor House, Mount Ephraim, Tunbridge Wells, Kent TN4 8BT; Cortijo Abulagar, Rubite, Granada, Spain.

SHTEREV, Kiril; Order of Georgi Dimitrov; Order of Narodna Republica Bulgaria, 2nd Degree; Ambassador of the People's Republic of Bulgaria to the Court of St James's, 1980–86; *b* 17 Feb. 1918; *s* of Shteriu Georgiev Gotchev and Dobra Shtereva; *m* 1945, Anna Shtereva; one *d* (and one *d* decd). *Educ:* Univ. of Sofia (degree in Economics). Joined Min. of Foreign Affairs, Sofia, 1947; Secretary: Bulgarian Embassy, Prague, 1950–54; Min. of Foreign Affairs, Sofia, 1954–56; Counsellor, Bulgarian Delegn to UN, 1956–59; Counsellor and Chargé d'Affaires, Bulgarian Embassy, Washington, 1959–63; Counsellor and Head of Dept, Min. of For. Affairs, Sofia, 1963–67; Ambassador to Ottawa, 1967–71; Head of State Protocol, Sofia, 1971–73; Ambassador to Teheran, 1973–79; Ambassador, Min. of For. Affairs, Sofia, 1979–80. Foreign Orders awarded by Govts of Czechoslovakia, Egypt, Ethiopia and Afghanistan. *Recreations:* reading, collection of postage stamps. *Address:* c/o Ministry of Foreign Affairs, Sofia, Bulgaria.

SHUCKBURGH, Sir (Charles Arthur) Evelyn, GCMG 1967 (KCMG 1959; CMG 1949); CB 1954; HM Diplomatic Service, retired; Chairman, Executive Committee, British Red Cross Society, 1970–80; Chairman, Council, 1976–80 (Vice-Chairman, 1980–81); Member, Standing Commission, International Red Cross, 1974–81 (Chairman, 1977–81); *b* 26 May 1909; *e s* of late Sir John Shuckburgh, KCMG, CB; *m* 1937, Nancy Brett, 2nd *d* of 3rd Viscount Esher, GBE; two *s* one *d*. *Educ:* Winchester; King's College, Cambridge. Entered Diplomatic Service, 1933; served at HM Embassy, Cairo, 1937–39; seconded for service on staff of UK High Comr in Ottawa, 1940; transferred to Buenos Aires, 1942; Chargé d'Affaires there in 1944; First Secretary at HM Embassy, Prague, 1945–47. Head of South American Department, FO, 1947–48; Western Dept, 1949–50; Western Organizations Dept, 1950–51; Principal Private Secretary to Secretary of State for Foreign Affairs, 1951–54; Assistant Under-Secretary, Foreign Office, 1954–56; Senior Civilian Instructor, IDC, 1956–58; Asst Sec.-Gen. (Polit.) of NATO, Paris, 1958–60; Dep. Under-Sec., FO, 1960–62; Perm. Brit. Rep. to N Atlantic Council, in Paris, 1962–66; Ambassador to Italy, 1966–69. Dir, Commercial Union Assurance, 1971–80. Chm., N Home Counties Regional Cttee, National Trust, 1975–79. *Publications:* Descent to Suez (Diaries, 1951–1956), 1986; (ed and trans.) The Memoirs of Madame Roland, 1989. *Address:* High Wood House, Watlington, Oxon OX9 5HG. *T:* Watlington (049161) 2433.

SHUCKBURGH, Sir Evelyn; *see* Shuckburgh, Sir C. A. E.

SHUCKBURGH, Sir Rupert (Charles Gerald), 13th Bt *cr* 1660, of Shuckburgh, Warwickshire; *b* 12 Feb. 1949; *s* of Sir Charles Gerald Stewkley Shuckburgh, 12th Bt, TD and Nancy Diana Mary, OBE (*d* 1984), *o d* of late Captain Rupert Lubbock, RN; *S* father, 1988; *m* 1st, 1976, Judith (marr. diss. 1987), *d* of W. G. Mackaness; two *s*; 2nd, 1987, Margaret Ida, *d* of late W. Evans. *Heir: s* James Rupert Charles Shuckburgh, *b* 4 Jan. 1978. *Address:* Shuckburgh Hall, Daventry, Northants NN11 6DT. *Club:* Farmers'.

SHUFFREY, Ralph Frederick Dendy, CB 1983; CVO 1981; Deputy Under-Secretary of State and Principal Establishment Officer, Home Office, 1980–84; *b* 9 Dec. 1925; *s* of late Frederick Arthur Shuffrey, MC and Mary Shuffrey (*née* Dendy) *m* 1953, Sheila, *d* of late Brig. John Lingham, CB, DSO, MC, and Juliet Judd; one *s* one *d*. *Educ:* Shrewsbury; Balliol Coll., Oxford. Served Army, 1944–47 (Captain). Entered Home Office, 1951; Private Sec. to Parly Under-Sec. of State, 1956–57; Private Sec. to Home Sec., 1965–66; Asst Sec., 1966–72; Asst Under-Sec. of State, 1972–80. Chairman: The Cranstoun Projects Ltd, 1988–; Fire Service Res. and Trng Trust, 1989–. Hon. Sec., Soc. for Individual Freedom, 1985–89. *Address:* 21 Claremont Road, Claygate, Surrey KT10 0PL. *T:* Esher (0372) 465123. *Club:* Reform.

SHULMAN, Drusilla Norman; *see* Beyfus, Drusilla N.

SHULMAN, Milton; writer, journalist, critic; *b* Toronto; *s* of late Samuel Shulman, merchant, and of Ethel Shulman; *m* 1956, Drusilla Beyfus, *qv*; one *s* two *d*. *Educ:* Univ. of Toronto (BA); Osgoode Hall, Toronto. Barrister, Toronto, 1937–40. Armoured Corps and Intelligence, Canadian Army, 1940–46 (despatches, Normandy, 1945); Major. Film critic, Evening Standard and Sunday Express, 1948–58; book critic, Sunday Express, 1957–58; theatre critic, Evening Standard, 1953–; TV critic, Evening Standard, 1964–73; columnist, social and political affairs, Daily Express, 1973–75; film critic, Vogue Magazine, 1975–87. Executive producer and producer, Granada TV, 1958–62; Asst Controller of Programmes, Rediffusion TV, 1962–64. Mem., Adv. Council, British Theatre Museum, 1981–83. Regular panel mem., Stop the Week, BBC Radio 4. IPC Award, Critic of the Year, 1966. *Publications:* Defeat in the West, 1948; How To Be a Celebrity, 1950; The Ravenous Eye, 1973; The Least Worst Television in the World, 1973; *children's books:* Preep, 1964; Preep in Paris, 1967; Preep and The Queen, 1970; *novel:* Kill Three, 1967; *novel and film story:* (with Herbert Kretzmer) Every Home Should Have One, 1970. *Recreations:* modern art, history, tennis. *Address:* 51 Eaton Square, SW1. *T:* 071–235 7162. *Clubs:* Garrick, Hurlingham.

See also Earl of Mulgrave.

SHULTZ, George Pratt; Secretary of State, United States of America, 1982–89; Distinguished Fellow, Hoover Institution, since 1989; *b* New York City, 13 Dec. 1920; *s* of Birl E. Shultz and Margaret Pratt; *m* 1946, Helena Maria O'Brien; two *s* three *d*. *Educ:* Princeton Univ., 1942 (BA Econ); Massachusetts Inst. of Technology, 1949 (PhD Industrial Econ). Served War, US Marine Corps, Pacific, 1942; Major, 1945. Faculty, MIT, 1949–57; Sen. staff economist, President's Council of Economic Advisers, 1955–56 (on leave, MIT); Univ. of Chicago, Graduate Sch. of Business: Prof. of Industrial Relations, 1957–62; Dean, 1962–69; Prof. of Management and Public Policy, Stanford Univ., Graduate Sch. of Business, 1974. Secretary of Labor, 1969–July 1, 1970; Dir, Office of Management and Budget, 1970–72; Secretary of the Treasury, 1972–74; Exec. Vice-Pres., Bechtel Corp., 1974–75, Pres. 1975–79; Vice-Chm., Bechtel Group, 1980; Pres., Bechtel Group Inc., San Francisco, 1981–82. Chm., President's Economic Policy Adv. Bd, 1981–82. Director: General Motors Corp., 1981–82, 1989–; Boeing Corp., 1989–; Dillon, Read & Co. Inc. Hon. Dr of Laws: Notre Dame Univ., 1969; Loyola Univ., 1972; Pennsylvania, 1973; Rochester, 1973; Princeton, 1973; Carnegie-Mellon Univ., 1975. *Publications:* Pressures on Wage Decisions, 1950; The Dynamics of a Labor Market (with C. A. Myers), 1951; Management Organization and the Computer (with T. A. Whisler), 1960; Strategies for the Displaced Worker (with Arnold R. Weber), 1966; Guidelines, Informal Controls, and the Market Place (with Rober Z. Aliber), 1966; Workers and Wages in the Urban Labor Market (with Albert Rees), 1970; Economic Policy Beyond the Headlines (with Kenneth W. Dam), 1978. *Recreations:* golf, tennis. *Address:* Hoover Institution, Stanford University, Stanford, Calif 94305–6010, USA.

SHURMAN, Laurence Paul Lyons; Banking Ombudsman, since 1989; *b* 25 Nov. 1930; *s* of Joseph and Sarah Shurman; *m* 1963, Mary Seamans (*née* McMullan); two *s* one *d*. *Educ:* Newcastle upon Tyne Royal Grammar Sch.; Magdalen Coll., Oxford (MA). Solicitor. Articles, John H. Sinton & Co., Newcastle, 1954–57; Assistant Solicitor: Haswell Croft, Newcastle, 1957–58; Hall Brydon, London, 1958–60; Kaufman & Siegal, London, 1960–61; Partner: Shurman & Bindman, Solicitors, London, 1961–64; Shurman & Co., London, 1964–67; Kingsley Napley, London, 1967–89 (Managing Partner, 1975–89). Legal Mem., Mental Health Review Tribunal, 1976–; Mem. Council, Justice, 1973–. Lectures: Gilbart, 1990; Ernest Sykes Meml, 1991. Pres., City of Westminster Law Soc., 1980–81; Governor: Channing Sch., 1985– (Vice-Chm., 1988–); Newcastle upon Tyne Royal Grammar Sch., 1991–. *Publications:* The Practical Skills of the Solicitor, 1981, 2nd edn 1985; contributor on Mental Health Tribunals in Vol. 26 of Atkin's Encyc. of Court Forms, 2nd edn 1985. *Recreations:* reading, fell walking, swimming, jogging, law reform. *Address:* Office of the Banking Ombudsman, Citadel House, 5/11 Fetter Lane, EC4A 1BR. *T:* 071–583 1395. *Club:* Leander (Henley).

SHUTE, Prof. Charles Cameron Donald, MD; Professor of Histology, Cambridge University, 1969–84, now Emeritus; Life Fellow of Christ's College, Cambridge, 1957; *b* 23 May 1917; *s* of late Cameron Deane Shute; *m* 1st, 1947, Patricia Cameron (*d* 1952), *d* of F. H. Doran; 2nd, 1954, Lydia May (Wendy) (*née* Harwood) (marr diss. 1980); one *s* three *d*; 3rd, 1980, Rosemary Gay Robins. *Educ:* Eton; King's Coll., Cambridge; Middlesex Hosp., London. MA, MB, BChir Cambridge, 1945; MD Cambridge 1958. Resident posts at Middlesex Hosp., 1945–47; RAMC (otologist), 1947–49; Demonstrator and Lectr in Anatomy, London Hosp. Med. Coll., 1951; Univ. Demonstrator and Lectr, Cambridge, 1952–69; Univ. Reader in Neuroanatomy, Cambridge, 1969. *Publications:* The McCollough Effect, 1979; (with R. G. Robins) The Rhind Mathematical Papyrus, 1987; papers in biological and Egyptological jls. *Recreation:* Egyptology. *Address:* 400 Princeton Way NE, Atlanta, Ga 30307, USA. *T:* 404/633 9452.

SHUTE, John Lawson, CMG 1970; OBE 1959; Member: Council of Egg Marketing Authorities of Australia, 1970–79; Egg Marketing Board of New South Wales, 1970–79; Director, Arthur Yates & Co. Pty Ltd, 1970–80; *b* Mudgee, NSW, 31 Jan. 1901; *s* of J. Shute, Mudgee; *m* 1937, Constance W. M., *d* of J. Douglas; two *s*. *Educ:* Parramatta High Sch. Asst Sec., Primary Producers' Union, NSW, 1923–33; Gen.-Sec., 1933–42; Sec., Federated Co-operative Bacon Factories, 1927–42; Member: NSW Dairy Products Bd, 1934–46; Commonwealth Air Beef Panel, 1962; Dir, Commonwealth Dairy Produce Equalisation Cttee, 1941–46; 1st Sec. Aust. Dairy Farmers' Fedn, 1942; Mem. Exec. and Asst Sec., Empire Producers' Conf., 1938; Mem. Special Dairy Industry Cttee apptd by Commonwealth Govt, 1942; Dep. Controller, Meat Supplies, NSW, 1942–46. Chairman: Aust. Meat Bd, 1946–70; Aust. Cttee of Animal Production, 1947–70; Aust. Cattle and Beef Research Cttee, 1960–66; Belmont-Brian Pastures Res. Cttee, 1962–76; Aust. Meat Research Cttee, 1966–70; Aust. Frozen Cargo Shippers' Cttee, 1967–70; Member: Export Development Council, 1958–66; Overseas Trade Publicity Cttee, 1955–70; Australia Japan Business Co-operation Cttee, 1962–70; Industry Co-operative Programme, FAO, 1973–78 (Chm., Working Gp on Integrated Meat Develt, 1975–78); NSW Rural Reconstruction Bd, 1942–71. Life Mem., Rural Youth Orgn of NSW, 1961. Life Mem., Australia-Britain Soc., 1979; Hon. Life Mem., Australian Veterinary Assoc., 1970–. Mem., Worshipful Co. of Butchers, 1950. Freedom, City of London, 1951. *Recreations:* Rugby Union (former Internat. rep.), cricket. *Address:* 5/2 Woonona Avenue, Wahroonga, NSW 2076, Australia. *Clubs:* Commercial Travellers' (NSW); Eastwood Rugby Union (NSW).

SHUTLER, (Ronald) Rex (Barry), FRICS; FAAV; Chief Executive, Valuation Office Agency (formerly Chief Valuer, Valuation Office (Inland Revenue)), since 1988; *b* 27 June 1933; *s* of Ronald Edgar Coggin Shutler and Helena Emily Shutler (*née* Lawes); *m* 1958, Patricia Elizabeth Longman; two *s*. *Educ:* Hardye's, Dorchester. Articled pupil and assistant, chartered surveyors, Dorchester, 1952–59; joined Valuation Office, 1959; District Valuer, Hereford and Worcester, 1970; Superintending Valuer, Wales, 1976; Dep. Chief Valuer, 1984–88. *Recreations:* golf, country pursuits, gardening. *Address:* Valuation Office Agency, New Court, Carey Street, WC2A 2JE. *T:* 071–324 1155. *Clubs:* Hereford Golf, Boxmoor Golf.

SHUTTLE, Penelope (Diane); writer and poet; *b* 12 May 1947; *d* of Jack Frederick Shuttle and Joan Shepherdess Lipscombe; *m* Peter Redgrove, *qv*; one *d*. *Educ:* Staines Grammar Sch.; Matthew Arnold County Secondary Sch., Mddx. Radio plays: The Girl who Lost her Glove, 1975 (Jt 3rd Prize Winner, Radio Times Drama Bursaries Comp., 1974); The Dauntless Girl, 1978. Poetry recorded for Poetry Room, Harvard Univ. Arts Council Awards, 1969, 1972 and 1985; Greenwood Poetry Prize, 1972; E. C. Gregory Award for Poetry, 1974. *Publications: novels:* An Excusable Vengeance, 1967; All the Usual Hours of Sleeping, 1969; Wailing Monkey Embracing a Tree, 1974; Rainsplitter in the Zodiac Garden, 1976; Mirror of the Giant, 1979; *poetry:* Nostalgia Neurosis, 1968; Midwinter Mandala, 1973; Photographs of Persephone, 1973; Autumn Piano, 1973; Songbook of the Snow, 1973; Webs on Fire, 1977; The Orchard Upstairs, 1981; The Child-Stealer, 1983; The Lion from Rio, 1986; Adventures with my Horse, 1988; *with*

Peter Redgrove: The Hermaphrodite Album (poems), 1973; The Terrors of Dr Treviles (novel), 1974; The Wise Wound (psychology), 1978, rev. edn 1986. *Recreations:* listening to music, Hatha Yoga, walking, a little philately. *Address:* c/o David Higham Associates Ltd, 5–8 Lower John Street, Golden Square, W1R 4HA.

SHUTTLEWORTH, 5th Baron *cr* 1902, of Gawthorpe; **Charles Geoffrey Nicholas Kay-Shuttleworth;** Bt 1850; DL; Partner, Burton, Barnes & Vigers, Chartered Surveyors, since 1977; Chairman, Rural Development Commission, since 1990; *b* 2 Aug. 1948; *s* of 4th Baron Shuttleworth, MC, and of Anne Elizabeth, *er d* of late Col Geoffrey Phillips, CBE, DSO; *S* father, 1975; *m* 1975, Mrs Ann Mary Barclay, *d* of James Whatman, MC; three *s*. *Educ:* Eton. Dir and Dep. Chm., National & Provincial Bldg Soc., 1983–; Dir, Burnley Bldg Soc., 1978–82 (Vice-Chm., 1982). Chairman: Lancs Small Industries Cttee, COSIRA, 1978–83; Lancs Youth Clubs Assoc., 1980–86, Pres., 1986–; Member: Skelmersdale Develt Corp., 1982–85; NW Regional Cttee, National Trust, 1980–89 (Vice Chm., 1983–89); President: Royal Lancashire Agricl Soc., 1985–86; Assoc. of Lancastrians in London, 1986–87; Governor, Giggleswick Sch., 1981– (Chm., 1984–). FRICS. DL Lancs, 1986. *Heir: s* Hon. Thomas Edward Kay-Shuttleworth, *b* 29 Sept. 1976. *Address:* 14 Sloane Avenue, SW3 3JE; Leck Hall, Carnforth, Lancs. *Clubs:* Brooks's, MCC.

SIBBALD, Maj.-Gen. Peter Frank Aubrey, CB 1982; OBE 1972; consultant in defence industries; *b* 24 March 1928; *s* of Major Francis Victor Sibbald, MBE, MM, BEM, and Mrs Alice Emma Hawking, The Hoe, Plymouth; *m* 1957, Margaret Maureen Entwistle (*d* 1991); one *s* one *d*. *Educ:* ISC, Haileybury. Commnd, 1948; served with 1 KOYLI, 1948–53; Malayan Emergency, 1948–51 (mentioned in despatches); Korea, 1953–54; Kenya Emergency, 1954–55; Instr, Sch. of Inf., 1955–57; psc 1961; Aden, 1965–66; Bde Maj., 151 Inf. Bde, 1962–64; jssc 1964; GSO2 HQ FARELF, 1966–68; CO 2 LI, 1968–71; Col GS HQ BAOR, 1972; Comdr 51 Inf. Bde, 1972–74; Div. Brig., Light Div., 1975–77; GOC NW District, 1977–80; Dir of Infantry, 1980–83. Dep. Col, Light Infantry (Yorks), 1977–80; Col Comdt, The Light Div., 1980–83. *Recreations:* game shooting, fishing, squash, swimming. *Club:* Army and Navy.

SIBERRY, John William Morgan; Under-Secretary, Welsh Office, 1964–73, retired; Secretary to Local Government Staff Commission for Wales, and NHS Staff Commission for Wales, 1973–75; *b* 26 Feb. 1913; *s* of late John William and Martha (*née* Morgan) Siberry; *m* 1949, Florence Jane Davies; one *s* one *d*. *Educ:* Porth County School, Rhondda; Univ. Coll. Cardiff. Entered Civil Service as Asst Principal, Unemployment Assistance Board (later Nat. Assistance Board), 1935; Principal, 1941; Asst Sec., 1947; transferred to Min. of Housing and Local Govt as Under-Sec., 1963; Welsh Secretary, Welsh Office and Office for Wales of the Ministry of Housing and Local Government, 1963–64. Chm., Working Party on Fourth Television Service in Wales, 1975. *Recreation:* golf. *Address:* Northgates, Pwllmelin Road, Llandaff, Cardiff CF5 2NG. *T:* Cardiff (0222) 564666. *Club:* Cardiff and County.

See also W. R. Siberry.

SIBERRY, William Richard; QC 1989; *b* 11 Dec. 1950; *s* of John William Morgan Siberry, *qv*; *m* 1976, Julia Christine Lancaster. *Educ:* King's Coll., Taunton; Pembroke Coll., Cambridge (MA, LLB). Fellow, Pembroke Coll., Cambridge, 1973–75. Called to the Bar, Middle Temple, 1974. *Recreations:* music, gardening, walking, photography, North West Highlands of Scotland. *Address:* 4 Essex Court, Temple, EC4Y 9AJ. *T:* 071–583 9191.

SIBLEY, Antoinette, CBE 1973; Prima Ballerina, The Royal Ballet, Covent Garden; Vice-President, Royal Academy of Dancing, since 1989; *b* 27 Feb. 1939; *d* of Edward G. Sibley and Winifred M. Sibley (*née* Smith); *m* 1964, M. G. Somes, CBE (marr. diss. 1973); *m* 1974, Panton Corbett; one *s* one *d*. *Educ:* Arts Educational Sch. and Royal Ballet Sch. 1st performance on stage as Student with Royal Ballet at Covent Garden, a swan, Jan. 1956; joined company, July 1956; has appeared with the company or as guest artist in many countries around the world. Leading role in: Swan Lake, Sleeping Beauty, Giselle, Coppelia, Cinderella, The Nutcracker, La Fille Mal Gardée, Romeo and Juliet, Harlequin in April, Les Rendezvous, Jabez and the Devil (created the role of Mary), La Fête Etrange, The Rakes Progress, Hamlet, Ballet Imperial, Two Pigeons, La Bayadère, Symphonic Variations, Scènes de Ballet, Lilac Garden, Daphnis and Chloe, Pas de Quatre (Dolin's), Konservatoriett, A Month in the Country, The Dream (created Titania), Laurentia, Good Humoured Ladies, Aristocrat in Mam'zelle Angot, Façade, Song of the Earth, Monotones (created role), Jazz Calendar (created Friday's Child), Enigma Variations (created Dorabella), Thais (created pas de deux), Anastasia (created Kshessinska), Afternoon of a Faun, Triad (created the Girl), Pavanne, Manon (created title role), Soupirs (created pas de deux), L'invitation au voyage (created), Impromptu (created pas de deux), Varii Capricci (created La Capricciosa), Fleeting Figures. *Film:* The Turning Point, 1978. *Relevant publications:* Sibley and Dowell, by Nicholas Dromgoole and Leslie Spatt, 1976; Antoinette Sibley, 1981, photographs with text by Mary Clarke; Reflections of a Ballerina, by Barbara Newman, 1986. *Recreations:* doing nothing; opera and books. *Address:* Royal Opera House, WC2.

SICH, Sir Rupert (Leigh), Kt 1968; CB 1953; Registrar of Restrictive Trading Agreements, 1956–73; *b* 3 Aug. 1908; *s* of late A. E. Sich, Caterham, Surrey; *m* 1933, Elizabeth Mary, *d* of late R. W. Hutchison, Gerrards Cross; one *s* two *d*. *Educ:* Radley College; Merton College, Oxford. Called to Bar, Inner Temple, 1930. Board of Trade Solicitor's Dept, 1932–48; Treasury Solicitor's Dept, 1948–56. *Recreations:* J. S. Bach; gardening. *Address:* Norfolk House, The Mall, Chiswick, W4. *T:* 081–994 2133. *Clubs:* United Oxford & Cambridge University, MCC.

SIDDALL, Sir Norman, Kt 1983; CBE 1975; DL; FEng; mining consultant; Member of the National Coal Board, 1971–83, Deputy Chairman 1973–82, Chairman 1982–83; *b* 4 May 1918; *s* of late Frederick and Mabel Siddall; *m* 1943, Pauline, *d* of late John Alexander and Edith Arthur; two *s* one *d*. *Educ:* King Edward VII School, Sheffield; Sheffield Univ. (BEng). National Coal Board: Production Manager, No 5 Area, East Midlands Div., 1951–56; General Manager, No 5 Area, East Midlands Div., 1956–57; General Manager, No 1 Area, East Midlands Div., 1957–66; Chief Mining Engineer, 1966–67; Dir Gen. of Production, 1967–71. Mem., Midland Cos Institn of Engrs (Silver Medal, 1951; Past Pres.). Chartered Engineer; FIMinE; CBIM. DL Notts, 1987. Hon. DSc Nottingham, 1982. National Association of Colliery Managers: Silver Medal, 1955; Bronze Medal, 1960; Coal Science Lecture Medal, 1972; CGLI Insignia Award in Technology (*hc*), 1978; Instn Medal, IME, 1982; Krupinski Medal, 1982. *Publications:* articles in professional journals. *Address:* Brentwood, High Oakham Road, Mansfield, Notts NG18 5AJ.

SIDDELEY, family name of **Baron Kenilworth.**

SIDDELEY, Randle; *see* Kenilworth, 4th Baron.

SIDDIQI, Prof. Obaid, Padma Bhushan 1984; FRS 1984; FIASc 1968; FNA 1977; Professor of Molecular Biology, Tata Institute of Fundamental Research, Bombay, since 1972; *b* 7 Jan. 1932; *s* of M. A. Qadeer Siddiqi and Umme Kulsum; *m* 1955, Asiya Siddiqi; two *s* two *d*. *Educ:* Univ. of Aligarh (MSc); Univ. of Glasgow (PhD). Lecturer, Aligarh Univ., 1954–57; Indian Agricl Res. Inst., 1957–58; Dept of Genetics, Glasgow Univ., 1958–61; Cold Spring Harbor Lab., NY, 1961; Univ. of Pennsylvania, 1961–62; joined Tata Inst. of Fundamental Research as Fellow, 1962. Vis. Associate, Yale Univ., 1966; Vis. Prof., MIT, 1970–71; CIT Gosney Fellow, 1971–72; Sherman Fairchild Distinguished Scholar, 1981–82; Fellow, Third World Acad. of Sciences, Trieste, 1986. Hon. DSc Aligarh, 1984. *Publications:* (co-ed) Development and Neurobiology of Drosophila, 1981; several papers in learned jls on genetics and neurobiology. *Recreations:* music, tennis, photography. *Address:* Molecular Biology Unit, Tata Institute of Fundamental Research, Homi Bhabha Road, Bombay 400 005, India. *T:* (office) 495–2311/320, (residence) 495–2140. *Club:* Bombay Gymkhana.

SIDDIQUI, Prof. Salimuzzaman, MBE 1946; Tamgha-i-Pakistan 1958; Sitara-i-Imtiaz (Pakistan) 1962; Hilal-e-Imtiaz, 1980; FRS 1961; DPhil. Nat.; Professor/Director, H. E. J. Research Institute of Chemistry, University of Karachi, since 1966; *b* 19 Oct. 1897. *Educ:* Lucknow; MAO College, Aligarh, UP; University College, London; Univ. of Frankfurt-on-Main. Returned to India, 1928; planned and directed Research Inst. at Ayurvedic and Unani Tibbi Coll., Delhi, 1928–40; joined Council of Scientific and Industrial Research (India): Asst Dir, later Dir, Chemical Laboratories, 1940–51; Director and Chairman of Pakistan Council of Scientific and Industrial Research, 1951–66. Chairman, Nat. Science Council, 1962–66; Pres., Pakistan Acad. of Sciences, 1967; Founding Fellow, Islamic Acad. of Scis, Saudi Arabia; Fellow: Pakistan Acad. of Med. Scis, 1987; Islamic Acad. of Scis, Jordan, 1988; Foreign Fellow, Indian Nat. Sci. Acad., 1989. A chemist, working on the chemistry of natural products; has led the promotion of scientific and industrial research in Pakistan; has rep. Pakistan at internat. scientific confs, etc. Elected Mem., Vatican Acad. of Sciences, and apptd Pontifical Academician, 1964. Hon. DMed Frankfurt-on-Main, 1958; Hon. DSc: Karachi, 1967; Leeds, 1967. Gold Medal, Russian Acad., 1958; President's Pride of Performance Medal (Pakistan), 1966; Prize of Islamic Medicine Orgn, Kuwait Foundn for Advancement of Scis, 1981; special prize, Council of Third World Acad. of Scis, for contribs to chemistry of Rauwolfia alkaloids, 1986. *Publications:* author of over 200 research papers. *Address:* Chair Professor, H. E. J. Research Institute of Chemistry, University of Karachi, Karachi, Pakistan. *T:* 472780.

SIDDONS, Arthur Harold Makins, MChir Cantab; FRCS; FRCP; Hon. Consulting Surgeon, St George's Hospital; *b* 17 Jan. 1911; *s* of late A. W. Siddons, Housemaster, Harrow School; *m* 1st, 1939, Joan Richardson Anderson (*née* McConnell) (*d* 1949); one *s* one *d*; 2nd, 1956, Eleanor Mary Oliver (*née* Hunter) (*d* 1970); 3rd, 1971, Margaret Christine Beardmore (*née* Smith). *Educ:* Harrow; Jesus College, Cambridge; St George's Hospital. MB, BCh Cantab 1935. Surgeon, St George's Hospital, 1941; Consultant General and Thoracic Surgeon, St George's Hosp. and others, 1948–76. Served RAF Medical Branch, 1942–46. Member of Court of Examiners, Royal College of Surgeons of England, 1958–63. *Publications:* Cardiac Pacemakers, 1967; sections on lung surgery in various textbooks. *Recreations:* travel, gardens, birds. *Address:* Robin Hey, Tilford Road, Farnham, Surrey GU9 8HX. *T:* Farnham (0252) 715667.

SIDEBOTTOM, Edward John; a Chief Inspector, Department of Education and Science, 1973–80 (Divisional Inspector, 1969–73); *b* 1918; *s* of late Ernest Sidebottom, Wylam, Northumberland; *m* 1949, Brenda Millicent, *d* of late Alec H. Sadler, Wandsworth. *Educ:* Queen Elizabeth Grammar School, Hexham; Hatfield College, Durham (BSc). Entered Iraq Government education service, 1939; lecturer, Leavesden Green Emergency Training College, 1946; County Youth Organiser for Hampshire, 1947; HM Inspector of Schools, 1949–80. Sec. to Albemarle Cttee on the Youth Service in England and Wales, 1958–59; seconded as first Principal, Nat. Coll. for the Training of Youth Leaders, 1960–64. Chm., Jt Working Gp on Training for Staff Working with Mentally Handicapped People, 1981–83. *Address:* 3 Queen's Court, Marlborough Road, West Cliff, Bournemouth, Dorset BH4 8DB.

SIDELL, Ron Daniel; architect; Sidell Gibson Partnership (private practice), since 1970; *b* 20 April 1941; *s* of Daniel Sidell and Dorothy Eady; *m* Sally Hodgson; one *d*. *Educ:* Canterbury Coll. of Architecture; York Univ. Winner: Grand Buildings Trafalgar Square Internat. Competition, 1986; City of Winchester Central Redevelt Proposal Comp., 1989. *Recreations:* just about most things. *Address:* Fitzroy Yard, Fitzroy Road, Primrose Hill, NW1 8TF. *T:* 071–722 5009.

SIDEY, Air Marshal Sir Ernest (Shaw), KBE 1972; CB 1965; MD, ChB, FFCM, DPH; Director-General, Chest, Heart and Stroke Association, 1974–85; *b* 2 Jan. 1913; *s* of Thomas Sidey, Alyth, Perthshire; *m* 1946, Doreen Florence, *y d* of late Cecil Ronald Lurring, Dalkey, Ireland; one *d* (and one *d* decd). *Educ:* Morgan Acad., Dundee; St Andrews Univ. Commissioned in RAF, 1937. Served in Burma Campaign during War of 1939–45. Recent appts include: Chief, Med. Adv. Staff, Allied Air Forces Central Europe, 1957–59; PMO: Flying Trg Comd, 1961–63; Middle East Comd, 1963–65; Transport Command, 1965–66; DDGMS, RAF, 1966–68. PMO, Strike Command, 1968–70; Dir-Gen., RAF Med. Services, 1971–74; QHS 1966–74. Governor, Royal Star and Garter Home, 1974–86. *Recreations:* racing, golf, bridge. *Address:* Callums, Tugwood Common, Cookham Dean, Berks SL6 9TU. *T:* Marlow (0628) 483006. *Club:* Royal Air Force.

SIDEY, Thomas Kay Stuart, CMG 1968; Executive Chairman, Wickliffe Press Ltd, since 1983 (Managing Director, 1961–83); Barrister and Solicitor, NZ, since 1932; *b* 8 Oct. 1908; *s* of Sir Thomas Kay Sidey; *m* 1933, Beryl, *d* of Harvey Richardson Thomas, Wellington, NZ; one *s* one *d*. *Educ:* Otago Boys' High School; Univ. of Otago (LLM; Hon LLD, 1978). Served War of 1939–45 (despatches): 2nd NZEF; 4 years, Middle East and Italy, rank of Major. Dunedin City Council, 1947–50, 1953–65, 1968–83; Dep. Mayor, 1956–59, 1968–77; Mayor, 1959–65. Mem., Univ. of Otago Council, 1947–83, Pro-Chancellor, 1959–70, Chancellor, 1970–76. Past President: Dunedin Chamber of Commerce; Automobile Assoc., Otago; Trusteebank Otago; NZ Library Assoc.; Otago Old People's Welfare Council; Otago Boys' High Sch. Old Boys' Soc. *Recreations:* fishing, boating, ski-ing. *Address:* 16 Tolcarne Avenue, Dunedin, New Zealand. *T:* 4775–694. *Club:* Dunedin (Dunedin, NZ).

SIDMOUTH, 7th Viscount *cr* 1805; **John Tonge Anthony Pellew Addington;** *b* 3 Oct. 1914; *s* of 6th Viscount Sidmouth and of Gladys Mary Dever (*d* 1983), *d* of late Thomas Francis Hughes; *S* father, 1976; *m* 1940, Barbara Mary (*d* 1989), *d* of Bernard Rochford, OBE; one *s* five *d* (and one *s* decd). *Educ:* Downside School (Scholar); Brasenose Coll., Oxford (Scholar). Colonial Service, E Africa, 1938–54. Mem. Council and Chm. Glasshouse Cttee, Nat. Farmers Union, 1962–69; Member: Agricultural Research Council, 1964–74; Central Council for Agricultural Cooperation, 1970–73. Mem., Select Cttee on European Communities, 1984–87. Pres., Nat. Council on Inland Transport, 1978–84. Trustee, John Innes Foundation, 1974–89. Chm. of Governing Body, Glasshouse Crops Research Inst., 1981–84. Knight of Malta, 1962. *Recreation:* gardening. *Heir: s* Hon. Jeremy Francis Addington [*b* 29 July 1947; *m* 1st, 1970, Grete Henningsen; one *s* one *d*; 2nd, 1986, Una Coogan; one *s* one *d*]. *Address:* 12 Brock Street, Bath, Avon BA1 2LN. *T:* Bath (0225) 301946.

SIDNEY, family name of **Viscount De L'Isle.**

SIDWELL, Martindale, FRAM; FRCO; Organist and Choirmaster, Hampstead Parish Church, since 1945; Organist and Director of Music, St Clement Danes (Central Church of the RAF), since 1957; Conductor: Martindale Sidwell Choir, since 1956; St Clement Danes Chorale and Martindale Sidwell Sinfonia, since 1983; St Clement's Orchestra, since 1984; *b* 23 Feb. 1916; *s* of John William Sidwell, Little Packington, Warwicks, and Mary Martindale, Liverpool; *m* 1944, Barbara Anne (*née* Hill) (pianist, harpsichordist and Prof. of Piano and Harpsichord, Royal Coll. of Music, under the name Barbara Hill); two *s*. *Educ:* Wells Cathedral Sch., Somerset; Royal Academy of Music. Sub-Organist, Wells Cathedral, 1932. Served War of 1939–45, Royal Engineers. Organist, Holy Trinity Church, Leamington Spa, and Director of Music, Warwick School, 1943, also at same time Conductor of Royal Leamington Spa Bach Choir; Conductor, Hampstead Choral Soc., 1946–81; Founder 1967, and Director and Conductor, 1967–81, London Bach Orch. Prof., RSCM, 1958–66; Prof. of Organ, RAM, 1963–84. Mem. Council, RCO, 1966–. Harriet Cohen International Bach Medal, 1967. Frequent broadcasts as Conductor and as Organ Recitalist, 1944–. *Address:* 1 Frognal Gardens, Hampstead, NW3. *T:* 071–435 9210. *Clubs:* Savage, Wig and Pen.

SIE, Sir Banja T.; *see* Tejan-Sie.

SIEFF, family name of **Baron Sieff of Brimpton** and of Sieff barony (extinct).

SIEFF OF BRIMPTON, Baron *cr* 1980 (Life Peer), of Brimpton in the Royal County of Berkshire; **Marcus Joseph Sieff;** Kt 1971; OBE 1944; Chairman, First International Bank of Israel Financial Trust Ltd, since 1983; Non-Executive Chairman, The Independent, since 1986; *b* 2 July 1913; *yr s* of late Baron Sieff; *m* 1st, 1937, Rosalie Fromson (marr. diss., 1947); one *s*; 2nd, 1951, Elsa Florence Gosen (marr. diss., 1953); 3rd, 1956, Brenda Mary Beith (marr. diss., 1962); one *d*; 4th, 1963, Mrs Pauline Lily Moretzki (*née* Spatz); one *d*. *Educ:* Manchester Grammar School; St Paul's; Corpus Christi College, Cambridge (MA), Hon. Fellow, 1975. Served War 1939–45, Royal Artillery. Joined Marks and Spencer Ltd, 1935; Dir, 1954; Asst Man. Dir, 1963; Vice-Chm., 1965; Jt Man. Dir, 1967–83; Dep. Chm., 1971; Chm., 1972–84; Pres., 1984–85; Hon. Pres., 1985–. Non-exec. director: Wickes PLC, 1986–; Sock Shop Internat. plc, 1987–89. Mem., BNEC, 1965–71 (Chm., Export Cttee for Israel, 1965–68). Hon. Pres., Joint Israel Appeal, 1984–. Vice Pres., Policy Studies Institute (formerly PEP) Exec., 1975–; Pres., Anglo-Israel Chamber of Commerce, 1975–. Trustee, Nat. Portrait Gallery, 1986–. Hon. FRCS 1984. Hon. LLD: St Andrews, 1983; Leicester, 1988; Hon. Dr Babson Coll., Mass, 1984; Hon. DLitt Reading; DUniv Stirling, 1986. Hambro Award, Businessman of the Year, 1977; Aims National Free Enterprise Award, 1978; B'nai B'rith Internat. gold medallion for humanitarianism, 1982; Retailer of the Year Award, National Retail Merchants' Assoc., USA, 1982; BIM Gold Medal, 1983. *Publications:* Don't Ask the Price (autobiog.), 1987; Marcus Sieff on Management, 1990. *Address:* Michael House, Baker Street, W1A 1DN.
See also Hon. D. D. Sieff.

SIEFF, Hon. David Daniel; Director, Marks and Spencer plc, since 1972; *b* 22 March 1939; *s* of Baron Sieff of Brimpton, *qv*, and late Rosalie Cottage; *m* 1962, Jennifer Walton; two *s*. *Educ:* Repton. Joined Marks & Spencer, 1957; Alternate Director, 1968; Full Director, 1972. Chairman, North Metropolitan Conciliation Cttee of Race Relations Board, 1969–71; Vice-Chm., Inst. of Race Relations, 1971–72; part-time Member, National Freight Corp., 1972–78; Member: Policy Studies Inst. (formerly PEP), 1976–84; Bd, Business in the Community; Council, Industrial Soc.; Council, Manchester Business Sch. Governor: Weizmann Inst. of Science, Rehovot, Israel, 1978– (Chm. Exec. Cttee, UK Foundn, 1984–); Shenkar Coll. of Textile Technology (Israel), 1980–; Hon. Pres., British ORT, 1983–. Trustee, Glyndebourne Arts Trust, 1971–. Pres., Racehorse Owners Assoc., 1975–78; Member: Jockey Club, 1977–; Bd, Newbury Racecourse; Horserace Totalisator Bd, 1991–. *Address:* Michael House, 47 Baker Street, W1A 1DN. *T:* 071–935 4422. *Club:* White's.

SIEGBAHN, Prof. Kai Manne Börje; Professor of Physics, University of Uppsala, since 1954; *b* 20 April 1918; *s* of Manne Siegbahn and Karin Siegbahn (*née* Högbom); *m* 1944, Anna-Brita (*née* Rhedin); three *s*. *Educ:* Univ. of Uppsala (BSc 1939; Licentiate of Philosophy 1942); Univ. of Stockholm (Dr of Philosophy 1944). Research Associate, Nobel Inst. of Physics, 1942–51; Prof. of Physics, Royal Inst. of Technology, Stockholm, 1951–54. Member: Roy. Swedish Acad. of Sci.; Roy. Swedish Acad. of Engrg Scis; Roy. Soc. of Sci.; Roy. Acad. of Arts and Sci. of Uppsala; Roy. Physiographical Soc. of Lund; Societas Scientiarum Fennica; Norwegian Acad. of Sci.; Roy. Norwegian Soc. of Scis and Letters; Nat. Acad. of Sciences; Pontifical Acad. of Sci.; European Acad. of Arts, Scis and Humanities; Acad. Europaea. Hon. Mem. Amer. Acad. of Arts and Scis; Membre de Comité des Poids et Mesures, Paris; Pres., IUPAP, 1981–84. Dr of Science, *hc*: Durham, 1972; Basel, 1980; Liège, 1980; Upsala Coll., East Orange, NJ, 1982; Sussex, 1983. Lindblom Prize, 1945; Björkén Prize, 1955, 1977; Celsius Medal, 1962; Sixten Heyman Award, 1971; Harrison Howe Award, 1973; Maurice F. Hasler Award, 1975; Charles Frederick Chandler Medal, 1976; Torbern Bergman Medal, 1979; (jtly) Nobel Prize for Physics, 1981; Pittsburgh Award of Spectroscopy, 1982; Röntgen Medal, 1985; Fiuggi Award, 1986; Humboldt Award, 1986; Premio Castiglione Di Sicilia, 1990. *Publications:* Beta- and Gamma-Ray Spectroscopy, 1955; Alpha-, Beta- and Gamma-Ray Spectroscopy, 1965; ESCA—Atomic, Molecular and Solid State Structure Studied by Means of Electron Spectroscopy, 1967; ESCA Applied to Free Molecules, 1969; around 400 scientific papers. *Recreations:* tennis, skiing and music. *Address:* Institute of Physics, University of Uppsala, Box 530, S-751 21 Uppsala, Sweden. *T:* 018/146963.

SIEGERT, Air Vice-Marshal Cyril Laurence, CB 1979; CBE 1975; MVO 1954; DFC 1944; AFC 1954; *b* 14 March 1923; *s* of Lawrence Siegert and Julia Ann Siegert; *m* 1948, Shirley Berenice Dick; two *s* two *d*. *Educ:* Fairlie High School; St Kevin's Coll., Oamaru; Victoria Univ. of Wellington. Joined RNZAF, 1942; served in UK with Nos 299 and 190 Sqdns; on loan to BOAC, 1945–47; Berlin airlift, 1949; NZ, 1952–54; NZ Defence Staff, Washington, 1954–56; RAF Staff Coll., 1957; NZ, 1958–62; Comdt, RNZAF's Command and Staff Sch., 1962; RAF Coll. of Air Warfare, 1963; Singapore, 1963–65; CO, No 3 Battlefield Support Sqdn and RNZAF Transport Wing, 1965–69; AOC RNZAF Ops Group, 1969–70; IDC 1970; RNZAF Air Staff, 1971; Chief of Staff, ANZUK Joint Force HQ, Singapore, 1971–73; Dep. Chief of Defence Staff (Policy), 1973–76; Chief of Air Staff, RNZAF, 1976–79. Gen. Manager, Marine Air Systems, 1980–84; Mem., Air Services Licensing Authority, 1980–87. *Recreations:* fishing, tramping, gardening. *Address:* 46 Wyndrum Avenue, Lower Hutt, New Zealand. *Clubs:* United Services (Wellington); Wellington Racing.

SIEPMANN, Mary Aline, (Mary Wesley); writer; *b* 24 June 1912; *d* of Col Harold Mynors Farmar, CMG, DSO and Violet Hyacinth (*née* Dalby); *m* 1st, 1937, 2nd Baron Swinfen (marr. diss. 1945); two *s*; 2nd, 1952, Eric Siepmann (*d* 1970); one *s*. *Educ:* at home (governesses); LSE. *Publications:* Speaking Terms (for children), 1968; The Sixth Seal (for children), 1968; Haphazard House (for children), 1983; Jumping the Queue, 1983; The Camomile Lawn, 1984; Harnessing Peacocks, 1985; The Vacillations of Poppy Carew, 1986; Not That Sort of Girl, 1987; Second Fiddle, 1988; A Sensible Life, 1990; The Tillotson Legacy, 1992. *Recreation:* reading. *Address:* c/o Transworld Publishers, 61–63 Uxbridge Road, W5 5SA.

SIEVE, James Ezekiel Balfour, PhD, FCA; *b* 31 July 1922; *s* of Isaac and Rachel Sieve; *m* 1953, Yvonne Manley; two *s*. *Educ:* London Sch. of Economics. BSc Econ, PhD. With Urwick Orr & Partners, 1950–54; Aquascutum & Associated Cos Ltd, 1954–68, Finance Dir, 1957–68; Metal Box Ltd, 1968, Finance Dir, 1970–80; Hacker Young, Chartered Accountants, 1981–83. Governor, Home Farm Trust (residential care of mentally handicapped), 1974–83; Member: Tax Reform Cttee, 1975–83; Nat. Freight Consortium, 1982–83 (Nat. Freight Corp., later Nat. Freight Co., 1977–82). *Publication:* Income Redistribution and the Welfare State (with Adrian Webb), 1971. *Recreation:* relaxing with family. *Address:* 56 Hampstead Lane, NW3 7JP.

SIGMON, Robert Leland; lawyer; *b* Roanoke, Va, 3 April 1929; *s* of Ottis Leland Sigmon and Aubrey Virginia (*née* Bishop); *m* 1963, Marianne Rita Gellner. *Educ:* Univ. of Virginia; Sorbonne; London Sch. of Economics. BA, DrJur. Member of the Bar: US Supreme Court; Court of Appeals, Second and District of Columbia Circuits; Virginia; District of Columbia. Chairman, Exec. Cttee, Pilgrims Soc. of Gt Britain, 1977–; Founder Mem., Associates of the Victoria and Albert Museum, 1976 (Dir, 1976–87); Mem., Council of Management, British Inst. of Internat. and Comparative Law, 1982–. Trustee: American Sch. in London, 1977–91; Magna Carta Trust, 1984–; Vice-Chm., Mid-Atlantic Club of London, 1977–; Vice-Pres., European-Atlantic Gp, 1978–; Member: Exec. Cttee, Amer. Soc. in London, 1969– (Chm. 1974); Amer. Soc. of Internat. Law; Selden Soc.; Guild of St Bride's Church, Fleet Street; Ends of the Earth; Gov., E-SU, 1984–90. Chevalier du Tastevin. *Publications:* contribs to legal periodicals. *Recreations:* collecting antiquarian books, oenology. *Address:* 2 Plowden Buildings, Middle Temple, EC4Y 9AS. *T:* 071–583 4851. *Club:* Reform.

SIGURDSSON, Niels P.; Minister of Foreign Affairs, Iceland, since 1990; *b* Reykjavik, 10 Feb. 1926; *s* of Sigurdur B. Sigurdsson and Karitas Einarsdóttir; *m* 1953, Olafia Rafnsdóttir; two *s* one *d*. *Educ:* Univ. of Iceland (Law). Joined Diplomatic Service 1952; First Sec., Paris Embassy, 1956–60; Dep. Permanent Rep. to NATO and OECD, 1957–60; Dir, Internat. Policy Div., Min. of Foreign Affairs, Reykjavik, 1961–67; Delegate to UN Gen. Assembly, 1965; Ambassador and Permanent Rep. of Iceland to N Atlantic Council, 1967–71. Ambassador: to Belgium and EEC, 1968–71; to UK, 1971–76; to Fed. Republic of Germany, 1976–78; Ministry of Foreign Affairs, Reykjavik, 1979–84; Ambassador to Norway, 1985–89. *Recreations:* swimming, riding. *Address:* Sólheimar 15, 104 Reykjavík, Iceland.

SIKORA, Prof. Karol, FRCP, FRCR; Professor of Clinical Oncology, Royal Postgraduate Medical School, Hammersmith Hospital, since 1986; *b* 17 June 1948; *s* of Witold Karol Sikora and Thomasina Sikora; *m* 1974, Alison Mary Rice; one *s* two *d*. *Educ:* Dulwich Coll.; Corpus Christi Coll., Cambridge (MA, MB, BChir, PhD); Middlesex Hospital. Middlesex Hosp., 1972; Hammersmith Hosp., 1973; MRC Clinical Fellow, Lab. for Molecular Biol., Cambridge, 1974–77; Clinical Fellow, Stanford Univ., 1978–79; Dir, Ludwig Inst. for Cancer Research, Cambridge, 1980–86. *Publications:* Monoclonal Antibodies, 1984; Interferon, 1985; Cancer: a student guide, 1988; Treatment of Cancer, 1990; Fight Cancer, 1990; Genes and Cancer, 1990. *Recreations:* boating, travelling. *Address:* Department of Clinical Oncology, Hammersmith Hospital, W12 0HS. *T:* 081–740 3060. *Clubs:* Athenæum, Polish Hearth.

SIKRI, Sarv Mittra; *b* 26 April 1908; *s* of late Dr Nihal Chand; *m* 1937, Mrs Leila Sikri; one *s*. *Educ:* Trinity Hall, Cambridge (BA). Barrister-at-Law (Lincoln's Inn). Started practice in Lahore High Court, 1930; Asst Advocate Gen., Punjab, 1949; Advocate Gen., Punjab, 1951–64; Judge, Supreme Ct of India, 1964–71; Chief Justice of India, 1971–73. Chm., Railway Accidents Enquiry Cttee, 1978–80; Chm., Jammu and Kashmir Enquiry Cttee, 1979–80. Alternate rep., UN Cttee on Codification and Develt of Internat. Law, 1947; Legal Adviser to Min. of Irrigation and Power, Govt of India, 1949; Mem. Internat. Law Assoc. Cttee on Internat. Rivers, 1955; Mem., Indian Law Commn, 1955–58. Delegate to: Law of the Sea Conf., Geneva, 1958; World Peace Through Law Conf., Tokyo, 1961, Athens, 1963; Accra Assembly, Accra, 1962. Pres., Indian Br. of Internat. Law Assoc., 1971–73; Member: Indian Commn of Jurists; Univ. Grants Commn, 1979–82; Chm., Sir Ganga Ram Hosp. Trust; Hon. Mem., Acad. of Political Sci., NY; Vice-Pres., Delhi Public School Soc. *Recreations:* golf, tennis, bridge. *Address:* 3 Nizam-ud-din East, New Delhi 110013, India. *T:* 692327. *Clubs:* Delhi Golf, Delhi Gymkhana (both in New Delhi).

SILBER, Stephen Robert; QC 1987; a Recorder, since 1987; *b* 26 March 1944; *s* of late J. J. Silber and of Marguerite Silber; *m* 1982, Lucinda, *d* of Lt-Col David St John Edwards, retd; one *s* one *d*. *Educ:* William Ellis Sch.; University Coll. London; Trinity Coll., Cambridge. Called to Bar, Gray's Inn, 1968. *Recreations:* walking, watching sport, theatre. *Address:* 3 Gray's Inn Place, WC1R 5EA. *T:* 071–831 8441.

SILBERSTON, Prof. (Zangwill) Aubrey, CBE 1987; Professor of Economics, University of London, at Imperial College of Science and Technology, 1978–87, now Emeritus, and Head of Department of Social and Economic Studies, 1981–87; Senior Research Fellow, Management School, Imperial College, since 1987; *b* 26 Jan. 1922; *s* of Louis and Polly Silberston; *m* 1st, 1945, Dorothy Marion Nicholls (marr. diss.); one *s* (one *d* decd); 2nd, 1985, Michèle Ledić. *Educ:* Hackney Downs Sch., London; Jesus Coll., Cambridge. MA (Cantab); MA (Oxon). Courtaulds Ltd, 1946–50; Kenward Res. Fellow in Industrial Admin, St Catharine's Coll., Cambridge, 1950–53; University Lectr in Economics, Cambridge, 1953–71; Fellow, 1958–71, Dir of Studies in Econs, 1965–71, St John's Coll., Cambridge; Chm., Faculty Bd of Econs and Politics, Cambridge, 1966–70; Official Fellow in Econs, 1971–78, and Dean, 1972–78, Nuffield Coll., Oxford. Rockefeller Fellow, Univ. of Calif, Berkeley, 1959–60; Visiting Professor: Queensland Univ., 1977; Univ. of the South, Sewanee, 1984. Member: Monopolies Commn, 1965–68; Board of British Steel Corp., 1967–76; Departmental Cttee on Patent System, 1967–70; Econs Cttee, SSRC, 1969–73; Royal Commn on the Press, 1974–77; Restrictive Practices Ct, 1986–; Royal Commn on Environmental Pollution, 1986–. Economic Adviser, CBI, 1972–74. Sec.-Gen., Royal Economic Soc., 1979–; Chm., Assoc. of Learned Societies in the Social Sciences, 1985–87; President: Section F, British Assoc., 1987; Confedn of European Economic Assocs, 1988–90 (Vice-Pres., 1990–). *Publications:* Education and Training for Industrial Management, 1955; (with G. Maxcy) The Motor Industry, 1959; (jtly)Economies of Large-scale Production in British Industry, 1965; (jtly) The Patent System, 1967; (with C. T. Taylor) The Economic Impact of the Patent System, 1973; (ed) Industrial Management: East and West, 1973; (with A. Cockerill) The Steel Industry, 1974; (jtly) Microeconomic Efficiency and Macroeconomic Performance, 1983; The Multi-Fibre Arrangement and the UK Economy, 1984; (jtly) British Manufacturing Investment Overseas, 1985; The Economic Importance of Patents, 1987; (ed) Technology and Economic Progress, 1989; Patent Policy: is the pharmaceutical industry a special case?, 1989; The Future of the Multi-Fibre Arrangement, 1989; articles in Econ. Jl, Bulletin of Oxford Inst. of Statistics, Oxford Economic Papers, Jl of Royal Statistical

Society. *Recreations:* music, ballet. *Address:* 53 Prince's Gate, SW7 2PG. *T:* 071–589 5111. *Club:* Travellers'.

SILK, Ven. David; *see* Silk, Ven. R. D.

SILK, Dennis Raoul Whitehall, JP; MA; Warden of Radley College, 1968–91; *b* 8 Oct. 1931; 2nd *s* of late Rev. Dr Claude Whitehall Silk and Mrs Louise Silk; *m* 1963, Diana Merilyn, 2nd *d* of W. F. Milton, Pitminster, Somerset; two *s* two *d. Educ:* Christ's Hosp.; Sidney Sussex Coll., Cambridge (Exhibr). MA (History) Cantab. Asst Master, Marlborough Coll., 1955–68 (Housemaster, 1957–68). JP Abingdon, 1972. *Publications:* Cricket for Schools, 1964; Attacking Cricket, 1965. *Recreations:* antiquarian, literary, sporting (Blues in cricket (Capt. Cambridge Univ. CC, 1955) and Rugby football). *Address:* Sturts Barn, Huntham Lane, Stoke St Gregory, Taunton, Somerset TA3 6EG. *T:* North Curry (0823) 490348. *Clubs:* East India, Devonshire, Sports and Public Schools; Hawks (Cambridge).

SILK, Ven. (Robert) David; Archdeacon of Leicester, since 1980; *b* 23 Aug. 1936; *s* of Robert Reeve Silk and Winifred Patience Silk; *m* 1957, Joyce Irene Bracey; one *s* one *d. Educ:* Gillingham Grammar School; Univ. of Exeter (BA Hons Theology 1958); St Stephen's House, Oxford. Deacon 1959, priest 1960, Rochester; Curate: St Barnabas, Gillingham, 1959–63; Holy Redeemer, Lamorbey, 1963–69; Priest-in-Charge of the Good Shepherd, Blackfen, 1967–69; Rector of Swanscombe, 1969–75; Rector of Beckenham, St George, 1975–80; Team Rector, Holy Spirit, Leicester, 1982–88. Proctor in Convocation, 1970–; Prolocutor of Lower House of Convocation of Canterbury, 1980–; Member of Liturgical Commission, 1976–91; Chm., Leicester Council of Faiths, 1986–; Moderator, Cttee for Relations with Peoples of Other Faiths, 1990–. *Publications:* Prayers for Use at the Alternative Services, 1980; Compline—an Alternative Order, 1980; In Penitence and Faith, 1988. *Recreations:* Richard III Society, Leicester FC, squash. *Address:* 13 Stoneygate Avenue, Stoneygate, Leicester. *T:* Leicester (0533) 704441. *Club:* Athenæum.

SILK, Robert K.; *see* Kilroy-Silk.

SILKE, Hon. William James; Hon. Mr Justice Silke; Justice of Appeal, Supreme Court of Hong Kong, since 1981; Vice-President, Court of Appeal, since 1987; *b* 21 Sept. 1929; *s* of William Joseph Silke and Gertrude (*née* Delany). *Educ:* Dominican Convent, Wicklow; Xavier Sch., Donnybrook; King's Inns, Dublin. Called to Irish Bar (South Eastern Circuit, Leinster Bar), 1955; Magistrate, North Borneo/Malaysia, 1959; Registrar, High Court in Borneo (Sabah-Sarawak), 1965; Puisne Judge, 1966; retired under compensation scheme during Malaysianisation, 1969; Hong Kong: Magistrate, 1969; President, Tenancy Tribunal, 1971; Acting Asst Registrar, High Court, 1972; President, Lands Tribunal, 1974; Judge, District Court, 1975; Judicial Commissioner, State of Brunei, 1978–91; Judge of the High Court, 1979. *Recreations:* horse racing/breeding, music, travel. *Address:* Supreme Court, Hong Kong. *T:* 8254606. *Clubs:* Stephen's Green (Dublin); Royal Sabah Turf (Sabah, Malaysia); Hong Kong, Royal Hong Kong Jockey (Hong Kong).

SILKIN, 2nd Baron, *cr* 1950, of Dulwich [disclaimed his peerage for life, 1972]; *see under* Silkin, Arthur.

SILKIN, Arthur; Lecturer in Public Administration, Civil Service College, Sunningdale, 1971–76, on secondment from Department of Employment; retired 1976; *b* 20 Oct. 1916; *e s* of 1st Baron Silkin, PC, CH; *S* father, 1972, as 2nd Baron Silkin, but disclaimed his peerage for life; *m* 1969, Audrey Bennett. *Educ:* Dulwich College; Peterhouse, Cambridge. BA 1938; Diploma in Govt Administration, 1959; Dip. in Hist. of Art, London Univ., 1990. Served 1940–45, Royal Air Force (A and SD Branch), Pilot Officer, 1941, subsequently Flying Officer. Entered Ministry of Labour and National Service, 1939; formerly 2nd Secretary, British Embassy, Paris. First Secretary: High Commissioner's Office, Calcutta, 1960–61; British Embassy, Dakar, May 1962–Mar. 1964; British Embassy, Kinshasa, 1964–66. *Publications:* contrib. to Public Administration, Political Qly. *Address:* Cuzco, 33 Woodnook Road, SW16. *T:* 081–677 8733.

SILKIN, Jon, FRSL 1986; poet; *b* 2 Dec. 1930; *s* of Dora Rubenstein and Joseph Silkin, solicitor (retd); three *s* one *d* (one *s* decd); *m* Lorna Tracy (American writer and co-editor of Stand). *Educ:* Wycliffe Coll.; Dulwich Coll.; Univ. of Leeds. BA Hons Eng. Lit. 1962. Journalist, 1947; Nat. Service, teaching in Educn Corps, Army; subseq. six years as manual labourer, London and two years teaching English to foreign students. Founded magazine Stand, 1952. Several poetry-reading tours, USA; Vis. Lectr, Denison Univ., Ohio; taught at Writers' Workshop, Univ. of Iowa, 1968–69; Visiting writer: for Australian Council for the Arts, 1974; College of Idaho, Caldwell, 1978; Mishkenot Sha'ananim, Jerusalem, 1980; Bingham Vis. Poet, Univ. of Louisville, 1981; Elliston Poet-in-Residence, Univ. of Cincinnati, 1983; Distinguished Writer in Residence, The Amer. Univ., 1989; Residency, Dumfries and Galloway Arts, 1990. C. Day Lewis Fellowship, 1976–77. Vis. Speaker, World Congress of Poets: Korea, 1979; Madrid, 1982; Corfu, 1985; Florence, 1986. *Publications:* The Peaceable Kingdom, 1954, reprint 1976; The Two Freedoms, 1958; The Re-ordering of the Stones, 1961; Nature with Man, 1965 (Geoffrey Faber Meml Prize, 1966); (with Murphy and Tarn) Penguin Modern Poets 7, 1965; Poems New and Selected, 1966; Killhope Wheel, 1971; Amana Grass, 1971; Out of Battle: the poetry of the Great War, 1972; (ed) Poetry of the Committed Individual, 1973; The Principle of Water, 1974; The Little Time-keeper, 1976; (ed) Penguin Book of First World War Poetry, 1979; (ed with Peter Redgrove) New Poetry, 1979; The Psalms with Their Spoils, 1980; Selected Poems, 1980, rev. and enl. edn 1988; (ed jtly) Stand One, 1984; Gurney (verse play), 1985; (ed) Wilfred Owen: the Collected Poems, 1985; The Ship's Pasture (poems), 1986; (with Jon Glover) The Penguin Book of First World War Prose, 1989. *Recreation:* travelling. *Address:* 19 Haldane Terrace, Newcastle upon Tyne NE2 3AN. *T:* 091–281 2614.

SILLARS, James; MP (SNP) Glasgow Govan, since Nov. 1988; management consultant; *b* Ayr, 4 Oct. 1937; *s* of Matthew Sillars; *m* 1st, 1957; one *s* one *d*; 2nd, 1981, Mrs Margo MacDonald, *qv. Educ:* Newton Park Sch., Ayr; Ayr Academy. Former official, Fire Brigades Union; Past Member Ayr Town Council and Ayr County Council Educn Cttee; Mem., T&GWU. Head of Organization and Social Services Dept, Scottish TUC, 1968–70. Full-time Labour Party agent, 1964 and 1966 elections. Contested (SNP) Linlithgow, 1987. MP (Lab) South Ayrshire, March 1970–1976, (SLP) 1976–79. Among the founders of the Scottish Labour Party, Jan. 1976. Man. Dir, Scoted Ltd, 1980–83. Especially interested in education, social services, industrial relations, development policies. *Publications:* Scotland—the Case for Optimism, 1986; Labour Party pamphlets on Scottish Nationalism; Tribune Gp pamphlet on Democracy within the Labour Party. *Recreations:* reading, camping, tennis, swimming. *Address:* House of Commons, SW1A 0AA.

SILLARS, Margo; *see* MacDonald, M.

SILLERY, William Moore; Headmaster, Belfast Royal Academy, since 1980; *b* 14 March 1941; *s* of William and Adeline Sillery; *m* 1963, Elizabeth Margaret Dunwoody; two *d. Educ:* Methodist Coll., Belfast; St Catharine's Coll., Cambridge. Head of Modern Languages, Belfast Royal Academy, 1968, Vice-Principal 1974, Deputy Headmaster 1976. Educnl Advr, Ulster Television. Chm., Ministerial Working Party on Modern Langs in NI Curriculum; Mem., NI Cttee, UGC. *Recreations:* golf, bridge. *Address:* Ardmore, 15 Saintfield Road, Belfast BT8 4AE. *T:* Belfast (0232) 645260. *Clubs:* East India; Belvoir Park (Belfast).

SILLITOE, Alan; writer since 1948; *b* 4 March 1928; *s* of Christopher Archibald Sillitoe and Sylvina (*née* Burton); *m* 1959, Ruth Fainlight; one *s* one *d. Educ:* various elementary schools in Nottingham. Raleigh Bicycle Factory, 1942; air traffic control asst, 1945–46; wireless operator, RAF, 1946–49. Lived in France and Spain, 1952–58. FRGS; Hon. Fellow, Manchester Polytechnic, 1977. Hon. DLitt Nottingham Polytechnic, 1990. *Publications: novels:* Saturday Night and Sunday Morning, 1958 (Authors' Club Award for best first novel of 1958; filmed, 1960, play, 1964); The General, 1960 (filmed 1967 as Counterpoint); Key to the Door, 1961; The Death of William Posters, 1965; A Tree on Fire, 1967; A Start in Life, 1970; Travels in Nihilon, 1971; Raw Material, 1972; The Flame of Life, 1974; The Widower's Son, 1976; The Storyteller, 1979; Her Victory, 1982; The Lost Flying Boat, 1983; Down from the Hill, 1984; Life Goes On, 1985; Out of the Whirlpool, 1987; The Open Door, 1989; Last Loves, 1990; Leonard's War, 1991; *stories:* The Loneliness of the Long Distance Runner, 1959 (Hawthornden Prize; filmed, 1962); The Ragman's Daughter, 1963 (filmed, 1972); Guzman, Go Home, 1968; Men, Women and Children, 1973; The Second Chance, 1981; The Far Side of the Street, 1988; *poetry:* The Rats and Other Poems, 1960; A Falling Out of Love, 1964; Love in the Environs of Voronezh, 1968; Storm and Other Poems, 1974; Snow on the North Side of Lucifer, 1979; Sun before Departure, 1984; Tides and Stone Walls, 1986; *for children:* The City Adventures of Marmalade Jim, 1967; Big John and the Stars, 1977; The Incredible Fencing Fleas, 1978; Marmalade Jim at the Farm, 1980; Marmalade Jim and the Fox, 1985; *travel:* Road to Volgograd, 1964; (with Fay Godwin) The Saxon Shore Way, 1983; (with David Sillitoe) Nottinghamshire, 1987; *plays:* (with Ruth Fainlight) All Citizens are Soldiers, 1969; Three Plays, 1978; *essays:* Mountains and Caverns, 1975; *miscellaneous:* Every Day of the Week, 1987. *Recreations:* travel, shortwave wireless telegraphy listening. *Club:* Savage.

SILLITOE, Leslie Richard, OBE 1977; JP; General Secretary, Ceramic and Allied Trades Union, 1975–80, now Life Member; *b* 30 Aug. 1915; *s* of Leonard Richard Sillitoe and Ellen (*née* Sutton); *m* 1939, Lucy (*née* Goulding); two *d. Educ:* St George's and St Giles' Sch., Newcastle, Staffs; Stoke-on-Trent School of Art; WEA, N Staffs Technical Coll. Modeller and mouldmaker on leaving school. Served War, Royal Artillery, sen. non-commnd officer, 1939–46. Ceramic and Allied Trades Union: General President, 1961–63; Organiser, 1963; Asst Gen. Sec., 1967. Dep. Chm., Ceramics, Glass and Mineral Products Industry Trng Bd, 1977–82; Chm., Nat. Jt Council for Ceramic Industry, 1975–81. Chm., N Staffs Manpower Services Cttee, 1975–83; Life Mem., N Staffs Trades Council (Pres., 1963–81); Member: N Staffs Tourist Assoc.; N Staffs Medical Inst.; Staffordshire Soc.; Pottery & Glass Benevolent Inst. (Vice-Pres., 1980–); N Staffs Community Health Council, 1975–85; Staffordshire War Pensions Cttee, 1980–; Council, Univ. of Keele, 1976–85, 1989– (Mem. Court, 1989–); BBC Local Radio Council, 1978–81; Wetley Moor Jt Cttee, 1989–; Mem. Bd of Management, and Custodian Trustee, N Staffs Trustee Savings Bank; Vice-President: N Staffs District WEA, 1976–86; Muscular Dystrophy N Staffs Gp, 1978–; Pres., Staffordshire Lads and Dads Assoc., 1981–82, Vice-Pres. 1982–; Sec. and Treas., Ceramic Ind. Welfare Soc., 1971–81. Mem., Staffs Develt Assoc., 1977–81. Mem., Magistrates' Assoc.; Gideons Internat. Mem., Stoke-on-Trent District Council, 1953–83, 1986– (Vice-Chm., Museums Cttee); Lord Mayor, Stoke-on-Trent, 1981–82, Dep. Lord Mayor 1982–83. Governor: St Peters High Sch., Penkhull, 1975–; Cauldon Coll. of Further Educn, Stoke-on-Trent, 1976–; Thistley Hough High Sch., Penkhull, 1982–86. Mem., W Midland TAVRA, 1979–83; Chairman: Friends of the Staffordshire Regt (N Staffs), 1982–; N Staffs Normandy Veterans' Assoc., 1986–. Gov., Stoke Harpfield Primary Sch., 1982–. Pres., Longton Rotary Club, 1987–88. Former Member: Boy Scouts; St John's Ambulance Brigade. Territorial Efficient Service Medal, 1944. JP Stoke-on-Trent 1963–. *Publication:* foreword to The History of the Potters Union, 1977. *Recreations:* walking, photography, swimming, history. *Address:* 19 Sillitoe Place, Penkhull, Stoke-on-Trent ST4 5DQ. *T:* Stoke-on-Trent (0782) 47866.

SILLS, Beverly, (Mrs P. B. Greenough); Director, New York City Opera, since 1979; former leading soprano, New York City Opera and Metropolitan Opera; *b* 25 May 1929; *d* of late Morris Silverman and of Sonia Bahn; *m* 1956, Peter B. Greenough; one *s* one *d. Educ:* Professional Children's Sch., NYC; privately. Vocal studies with Estelle Liebling, piano with Paulo Gallico. Operatic debut, Philadelphia Civic Opera, 1947; San Francisco Opera, 1953; New York City Opera, 1955; Vienna State Opera, 1967; Teatro Colon, Buenos Aires, 1968; La Scala, Milan, 1969; Teatro San Carlo, Naples, 1970; Royal Opera, Covent Garden, London, 1970; Deutsche Oper, W Berlin, 1971; NY Metropolitan Opera, 1975, etc. Repeated appearances as soloist with major US symphony orchestras; English orchestral debut with London Symphony Orch., London, 1971; Paris debut, orchestral concert, Salle Pleyel, 1971. Repertoire includes title roles of Norma, Manon, Lucia di Lammermoor, Maria Stuarda, Daughter of Regiment, Anna Bolena, Traviata, Lucrezia Borgia, Thais, Louise, Cleopatra in Giulio Cesare, Elizabeth in Roberto Devereux, Tales of Hoffmann, Elvira in Puritani, Rosina in Barber of Seville, Norina in Don Pasquale, Pamira in Siege of Corinth; created title role, La Loca, San Diego Opera, 1979. Subject of BBC-TV's Profile in Music (Nat. Acad. of TV Arts and Sciences Emmy Award, 1975); other TV includes: Sills and Burnett at the Met, 1976; Hostess/Commentator for Young People's Concerts, NY Philharmonic, 1977; Moderator/Hostess, Lifestyles with Beverly Sills, 1976, 1977 (Emmy 1978). Hon. DMus: Temple Univ., 1972; New York Univ., 1973; New England Conservatory, 1973; Harvard Univ., 1974. Woman of the Year, Hasty Pudding Club, Harvard, 1974; Handel Medallion, NYC; US Presidential Medal of Freedom. *Publications:* Bubbles: a self-portrait, 1976; (autobiog. with Lawrence Linderman) Beverly. *Recreations:* fishing, bridge. *Address:* c/o Edgar Vincent-Patrick Farrell Associates, 157 West 57 Street, New York City, NY 10019, USA. *Tel:* 212–541–7666, *Fax:* 212–541–7767.

SILSOE, 2nd Baron *cr* 1963; **David Malcolm Trustram Eve,** Bt 1943; QC 1972; Barrister, Inner Temple, since 1955; *b* 2 May 1930; *er* twin *s* of 1st Baron Silsoe, GBE, MC, TD, QC, and Marguerite (*d* 1945), *d* of late Sir Augustus Meredith Nanton, Winnipeg; *S* father, 1976; *m* 1963, Bridget Min, *d* of Sir Rupert Hart-Davis, *qv*; one *s* one *d. Educ:* Winchester; Christ Church, Oxford (MA); Columbia Univ., New York. 2nd Lt, Royal Welch Fusiliers, 1949–50; Lieut, Queen Victoria's Rifles (TA), 1950–53. Bar Auditor, Inner Temple, 1965–70; Bencher, 1970. *Recreation:* ski-ing. *Heir:* *s* Hon. Simon Rupert Trustram Eve, *b* 17 April 1966. *Address:* Neals Farm, Wyfold, Reading, Berks RG4 9JB. *Club:* Ski of Great Britain.

SILVER, Clinton Vita; Deputy Chairman, since 1991, and Managing Director, since 1990, Marks & Spencer; *b* 26 Sept. 1929; *s* of Sidney (Mick) Silver and Mina Silver (*née* Gabriel); *m* 1973, Patricia Ann (Jill) Vernon; one *s* one *d. Educ:* Upton Park Sch.; Southampton Univ. (BSc Econ). Nat. Service, 1950–52. Joined Marks & Spencer, 1952; Alternate Dir, 1974; Dir, 1978. Member: NEDC (Garment and Textile Sector Gp);

British Irish Industry Circle; Dir, Food Marketing Inst., Washington; Gov., World Economic Forum; Vice-Pres., British Overseas Trade Gp for Israel; Exec., British/Israel Chamber of Commerce. Member: Develt Bd, NACF; Bd, Youth and Music; Appeal Bd, Ashmolean Museum; Exec., Royal Acad. of Dancing. Vice-Chm., Bd of Caldicott Sch.; Chm., Israel/Diaspora Trust. *Recreations*: gardening, music, art. *Address*: Marks & Spencer, Michael House, 57 Baker Street, W1M 1AG. *T*: 071–268 6537.

SILVER, Prof. Ian Adair; Professor of Comparative Pathology since 1970, and Head of Department of Pathology and Microbiology (formerly Department of Pathology), since 1982, University of Bristol; Adjunct Professor of Neurology, University of Pennsylvania, since 1977; *b* 28 Dec. 1927; *s* of Captain George James Silver and Nora Adair Silver; *m* 1950, Dr Marian Scrase, *d* of Dr F. J. Scrase; two *s* two *d*. *Educ*: Rugby School; Corpus Christi Coll., Cambridge (BA, MA); Royal Veterinary Coll. MRCVS, FRCVS 1990. University of Cambridge: Univ. Demonstrator, Zoology, 1952–57; Univ. Lectr, Anatomy, 1957–70; Official Fellow and Coll. Lectr, Churchill Coll., 1965–70; Sen. Tutor for Advanced Students, Churchill Coll., 1966–70; Dean, Faculty of Medicine, Bristol Univ., 1987–90. Vis. Fellow, Weitzmann Inst., Rehovot, 1963; Vis. Prof., Louisiana Tech. Univ., 1973; Royal Soc. Vis. Prof., Fed. Univ. of Rio de Janeiro, 1977. Mem., SERC Biol. Scis Cttee, 1975–80; President: Internat. Soc. for O_2 Transport to Tissue, 1976 and 1986; RCVS, 1985–86 and 1987 (Sen. Vice-Pres., 1986–87 and 1987–88). RAgS Silver Medal, 1952; Sir Frederick Hobday Meml Medal, British Equine Vet. Assoc., 1982; Dalrymple-Champneys Medal, BVA, 1984. *Publications*: Editor of scientific books, 1971–; numerous articles in scientific jls. *Recreations*: farming, exploring, fishing, DIY. *Address*: Department of Pathology and Microbiology, School of Medical Sciences, University of Bristol, Bristol BS8 1TD. *T*: Bristol (0272) 303446.

SILVER, Prof. Peter Hele S.; *see* Spencer-Silver.

SILVER, Prof. Robert Simpson, CBE 1967; FRSE; FIMechE; FInstP; James Watt Professor of Mechanical Engineering, University of Glasgow, 1967–79; *b* Montrose, Angus, 13 March 1913; *s* of Alexander Clark Silver and Isabella Simpson; *m* 1937, Jean McIntyre Bruce, *er d* of Alexander and Elizabeth Bruce (*née* Livingstone); two *s*. *Educ*: Montrose Academy; University of Glasgow. MA, 1932; BSc (1st Class Hons Nat. Phil) 1934; PhD 1938; DSc 1945. Research Physicist, ICI (Explosives), 1936–39; Head of Research, G. & J. Weir Ltd, 1939–46; Asst Director, Gas Research Board, 1947–48; Director of Research, Federated Founderies Ltd, 1948–54; Chief Designer, John Brown Land Boilers Ltd, 1954–56; Chief of Development and Research, G. & J. Weir Ltd, 1956–62 (Director 1958–); Prof. of Mech. Engrng, Heriot-Watt Coll. (now Univ.), 1962–66. FInstP 1942; MIMechE 1953; FRSE 1963. Hon. DSc Strathclyde, 1984. Foreign Associate, Nat. Acad. of Engineering, USA, 1979. Unesco Prize for Science, 1968. *Publications*: An Introduction to Thermodynamics, 1971; The Bruce, Robert I King of Scots (play), 1986; papers on physics and engineering, with special emphasis on thermodynamics, desalination, combustion, phase-change, and heat transfer; also on philosophy of science and education; a few poems. *Recreations*: fishing, music, theatre, Scottish history and affairs. *Address*: 5 Panmure Street, Montrose, Angus DD10 8EZ. *T*: Montrose (0674) 77793.

SILVERLEAF, Alexander, CB 1980; FEng; FRINA; FICE; FCIT; Co-ordinator, International Transport Group (INTRA), since 1981; *b* 29 Oct. 1920; *m* 1950, Helen Marion Scott; two *d*. *Educ*: Kilburn Grammar Sch., London; Glasgow Univ. (BSc 1941). Wm Denny and Bros Ltd, Shipbuilders, Dumbarton, 1937–51: Student apprentice, 1937–41; Head, Design Office, 1947–51; National Physical Laboratory, 1951–71: Superintendent, Ship Div., 1962–67; Dep. Dir, 1966–71; Dir, Transport and Road Res. Lab., 1971–80. Chm., UK Council for Computing Develt, 1981–86. Hon. FIHT. *Publications*: papers in Trans. Royal Instn Naval Architects and other technical jls. *Address*: 64 Fairfax Road, Teddington, Mddx. *T*: 081–977 6261. *Club*: Athenæum.

SILVERMAN, Prof. Hugh Richard, ARIBA; Professor of Architecture and Head of Welsh School of Architecture, since 1986; *b* 23 Sept. 1940; *m* 1963, Kay Sønderskov-Madsen; two *d*. *Educ*: Edinburgh Univ. (MSc Soc. Sci). Lectr, then Sen. Lectr, Univ. of Bristol, 1971–82. Partner, Alec French Partnership, Architects, Bristol, 1984–86. Built project, 1 Bridewell St, Bristol, 1985 (RIBA Regl Award). Member: Bldg Sub-Cttee, SERC, 1983–85; Architecture Bd, CNAA, 1981–84; Board, Cardiff Bay Develt Corp., 1990–. FRSA 1989. *Address*: 15 Clifton Vale, Bristol BS8 4PT. *T*: Bristol (0272) 292676. *Club*: Commonwealth Trust.

SILVERMAN, Julius; Barrister-at-law; *b* Leeds, 8 Dec. 1905; *s* of Nathan Silverman; *m* 1959, Eva Price. *Educ*: Central High School, Leeds (Matriculated). Entered Gray's Inn as student in 1928; called to Bar, 1931; joined Midland Circuit, 1933, practised in Birmingham. Birmingham City Councillor, 1934–45. Contested Moseley Division, 1935. MP (Lab) Birmingham, Erdington, 1945–55 and 1974–83, Birmingham, Aston, 1955–74. Apptd Chm., by Birmingham City Council, of Handsworth Inquiry (into disturbances in Handsworth), 1985 (report published by Council, 1986). Chm., India League, 1971–. Freeman, City of Birmingham, 1982. Hon. Fellow, City of Birmingham Polytechnic, 1987. Padma Bhushan (India), 1990. *Publication*: (contrib.) Centenary History of the Indian National Congress, 1986. *Address*: c/o 132A Croxted Road, SE21 8NR.

SILVERWOOD-COPE, Maclachlan Alan Carl, CBE 1959; FCA 1960; ATII 1978; Chartered Accountant; HM Diplomatic Service, retired; *b* 15 Dec. 1915; *s* of late Alan Lachlan Silverwood-Cope and late Elizabeth Masters; *m* 1st, 1940, Hilkka (*née* Halme) (marr. diss. 1970); one *s* one *d*; 2nd, 1971, Jane (*née* Monier-Williams); one *s* one *d*. *Educ*: Malvern College. ACA 1939. HM Forces, 1939–45 (Major, RA). Foreign (later Diplomatic) Service, 1939–71: served as 3rd Sec., Stockholm, 1945–50; 1st Sec., Washington, 1951 and 1956–57; Tokyo, 1952–55; Copenhagen, 1960–64; Counsellor, Buenos Aires, 1966–68; FCO, 1968–71. Finance appts with Aspro-Nicholas Ltd, 1971–78. Home Front Medal (Finland), 1940; Freedom Cross (Norway), 1945. *Recreations*: tennis, bridge, music. *Address*: Brock Hill, Winkfield Row, Berks RG12 6LS. *T*: Winkfield Row (0344) 882746. *Club*: Middlesex County Cricket.

SILVESTER, Frederick John; Managing Director, Advocacy Partnership Ltd; *b* 20 Sept. 1933; *s* of William Thomas Silvester and Kathleen Gertrude (*née* Jones); *m* 1971, Victoria Ann, *d* of James Harold and Mary Lloyd Davies; two *d*. *Educ*: Sir George Monoux Grammar Sch.; Sidney Sussex Coll., Cambridge. Called to the Bar, Gray's Inn, 1957. Teacher, Wolstanton Grammar School, 1955–57; Political Education Officer, Conservative Political Centre, 1957–60. Member, Walthamstow Borough Council, 1961–64; Chairman, Walthamstow West Conservative Association, 1961–64. Contested (C) Manchester, Withington, 1987. MP (C): Walthamstow West, Sept. 1967–70; Manchester, Withington, Feb. 1974–1987. An Opposition Whip, 1974–76; PPS to Sec. of State for Employment, 1979–81, to Sec. of State for NI, 1981–83. Member: Public Accounts Cttee, 1983–87; Procedure Cttee, 1983–87; Exec., 1922 Cttee, 1985–87; Vice-Chm., Cons. Employment Cttee, 1976–79. Sen. Associate Dir, J. Walter Thompson, 1970–88. *Address*: 27 King Edward Walk, SE1 7PR.

SIM, John Mackay, MBE (mil.) 1945; Deputy Chairman, Inchcape & Co. Ltd, 1975–82 (Deputy Chairman/Managing Director, 1965–75); *b* 4 Oct. 1917; *s* of William Aberdeen Mackay Sim and Zoe Sim; *m* 1st, Dora Cecilia Plumridge Levita (*d* 1951); two *d*; 2nd, Mrs Muriel Harvard (Peggie) Norman. *Educ*: Glenalmond; Pembroke Coll., Cambridge (MA). Lieut RA, 1940, Captain 1942; served NW Europe (despatches). Smith Mackenzie & Co. Ltd (East Africa), 1946–62, Chm. 1960–62; Dir, subseq. Man. Dir, Inchcape & Co. Ltd, 1962. *Recreation*: gardening. *Address*: 6 Bryanston Mews West, W1H 7FR. *T*: 071–262 7673.

SIMCOX, Richard Alfred, CBE 1975 (MBE 1956); Hon. Member of the British Council; *b* 29 March 1915; *s* of Alfred William and Alice Simcox; *m* 1951, Patricia Elisabeth Gutteridge; one *s* two *d*. *Educ*: Gonville and Caius Coll., Cambridge. BA Class. Tripos. Served with N Staffs Regt, 1939–43; British Council from 1943: Rep. in Jordan, 1957–60; in Libya, 1960; in Jordan (again), 1960; Cultural Attaché, British Embassy, Cairo, 1968–71; British Council Representative, Iran, 1971–75. Governor, Gabbitas-Thring Educnl Trust. *Recreations*: gardening, philately. *Address*: Little Brockhurst, Lye Green Road, Chesham, Bucks HP5 3NH. *T*: Chesham (0494) 783797.

SIMEON, Sir John Edmund Barrington, 7th Bt, *cr* 1815; Civil Servant in Department of Social Welfare, Provincial Government, British Columbia, retired 1975; lately in Real Estate business; *b* 1 March 1911; *s* of Sir John Walter Barrington Simeon, 6th Bt, and Adelaide Emily (*d* 1934), *e d* of late Col Hon. E. A. Holmes-à-Court; *S* father 1957; *m* 1937, Anne Robina Mary Dean; one *s* two *d*. *Educ*: Eton; Christ Church, Oxford. Motor business, 1931–39. Served with RAF, 1939–43; invalided, rank of Flight Lt, 1943. Civil Servant, Ministry of Agriculture, 1943–51. Took up residence in Vancouver, Canada, 1951. *Recreations*: sailing, painting. *Heir*: *s* Richard Edmund Barrington Simeon, PhD Yale; Professor of Political Science, Queen's Univ., Kingston, Ont [*b* 2 March 1943; *m* 1966, Agnes Joan (marr. diss.), *d* of George Frederick Weld; one *s* one *d*]. *Address*: c/o Jerome & Co., Solicitors, 98 High Street, Newport, Isle of Wight PO30 1BD; 987 Wavertree Road, N Vancouver, BC V7R 1S6, Canada.

SIMEON, John Power Barrington, OBE 1978; HM Diplomatic Service, retired; *b* 15 Nov. 1929; *o s* of late Cornwall Barrington Simeon and Ellaline Margery Mary (*née* Le Poer Power, Clonmel, Co. Tipperary); *m* 1970, Carina Renate Elisabeth Schüller; one *s*. *Educ*: Beaumont Coll.; RMA, Sandhurst. Commnd 2nd Lieut Royal Corps of Signals, 1949; Lieut 1951; resigned, 1952. Ferrous and non-ferrous metal broker, London and Europe, 1953–57; Rank Organisation: served in Germany, Thailand, Singapore, India, ME, N Africa, Hong Kong and London, 1957–65; entered HM Diplomatic Service, 1965; First Sec. (Commercial): Colombo, 1967; Bonn, 1968–70; First Sec., and sometime Actg High Comr, Port of Spain, 1970–73; FCO, 1973–75; Dep. High Comr and Head of Post, Ibadan, Nigeria, 1975–79. Counsellor, 1978; HM Consul-General: Berlin, 1979–81; Hamburg, 1981–84. *Recreations*: travel, photography, reading, music. *Address*: 4 Cliff Road, Dovercourt, Harwich, Essex CO12 3PP. *T*: Harwich (0255) 552820.

SIMEONE, Reginald Nicola, CBE 1985; Adviser to the Chairman, Nuclear Electric plc, since 1990; *b* 12 July 1927; *s* of late Nicola Francisco Simeone, FCIS, and Phyllis Simeone (*née* Iles); *m* 1954, Josephine Frances, *d* of late Robert Hope and of Marjorie Hope; two *s*. *Educ*: Raynes Park Grammar Sch.; St John's Coll., Cambridge (Schol.; MA). Instr Lieut, Royal Navy, 1947–50; Admiralty: Asst Principal, 1950–55; Principal, 1955–59; UKAEA: Finance Br., 1959–61; Economics and Programmes Br., 1961–65; Chief Personnel Officer, AWRE, 1965–69; Principal Estabts Officer, 1970–76; Authority Personnel Officer, 1976–84; Comptroller of Finance and Administration, 1984–86; Bd Mem., 1987–88; Advr to the Chm., 1988–90. Chm., Atomic Energy Constabulary Police Cttee, 1986–90; Exec. Vice Pres., European Atomic Energy Soc., 1987–90. *Recreation*: travel. *Club*: United Oxford & Cambridge University.

SIMEONS, Charles Fitzmaurice Creighton, DL; MA; Consultant: Environmental Control, Market and Behavioural Studies, Health and Safety at Work, Electronic Information Technology, Communications with Government, technical programmes for conferences; Director, Action Learning Trust, 1978–82; *b* 22 Sept. 1921; *s* of Charles Albert Simeons and Vera Hildegarde Simeons; *m* 1945, Rosemary (*née* Tabrum) (*d* 1991); one *s* one *d*. *Educ*: Oundle; Queens' Coll., Cambridge. Royal Artillery with 8th Indian Div., 1942–45. Man. Dir, supplier to photographic industry, 1957–70. MP (C) Luton, 1970–Feb. 1974. Chm., Luton Cons. Assoc., 1960–63. Pres., Luton, Dunstable and District Chamber of Commerce, 1967–68; District Gov., Rotary International, 1967–68; Chm. of cttees raising funds for disabled and cancer research and for National Children's Homes; Member: Nat. Appeals Cttee, Cancer Res. Campaign, 1977–78; Children in Danger Campaign, 1985–. Chm., Adv. Cttee, Rotary Internat. Bd on Environmental Research and Resources, 1973–74; Vice Pres., Nat. Industrial Material Recovery Assoc., 1972–77; Member: Internat. Cttee, Water Pollution Control Federation, Washington, DC, 1974–77; Customer Consultative Cttee, Anglian Water, 1984–89, Thames Water, 1986–89; Anglian Customer Services Cttee, Water Srvices, 1990–; Council, Smaller Business Assoc., 1974–76; ABCC Small Firms Panel; Chm., Central Govt Cttee, Union of Independent Cos. Hon. Mem., Inst. of Water Pollution Control. Liveryman: Worshipful Co. of Feltmakers (Master, 1987–88); Guild of Freemen of City of London; Mem., Guild of Water Conservators, 1991. FIIM; FRSA. Hon. FIWEM. Pres., Old Oundelian Club, 1976–77; Hon. Sec., 8th Indian Clover Club, 1984–. JP Luton, 1959–74; DL Beds, 1987. *Publications*: Energy Research in Western Europe, 1976; Coal: its role in tomorrow's technology, 1978; Water as a Source of Energy, 1980; A Review of Chemical Response Data Bases in Europe and the United States, 1985; Studies on Incidents Involving Chemicals on Board Ship, in Port, and at Sea in Europe and the United States, 1985; Data Bases capable of response to Chemical Incidents Worldwide, 1986. *Recreations*: watching football, cricket, gardening. *Address*: 21 Ludlow Avenue, Luton, Beds. *T*: Luton (0582) 30965. *Club*: City Livery.

SIMHA, Maj.-Gen. Bharat Kesher; Tri Sakti Patta, 1st Class; Gorkha Dakchhina Bahu, 1st Class; Nepal Kirtimaya Shreepad, 3rd Class; Ambassador of Nepal to the Court of St James's, since 1988; concurrently accredited to Finland, Iceland, Sweden, Norway and Denmark; *b* 15 Aug. 1934; *s* of Lt-Gen. Dharma Bahadur Simha and Chaitanya Rajya Laxmi Simha; *m* 1955, Teeka Rajya Laxmi Simha; three *s*. *Educ*: Durbar High Sch., Kathmandu; Col Brown's Cambridge Sch., Dehradun; Indian Mil. Acad., Dehradun (grad. 1954). Commnd into Royal Nepalese Army, 1952; appts as Adjt, Co. Comdr, ADC to C-in-C, 1954–55; various courses in England, 1956; attached BAOR, 1956; Instr, Sch. of Inf., 1957–59; GSO 3 Directorate of Mil. Ops and Staff Duties, also ADC to C-in-C, 1960; Mem., Nepal–China Jt Boundary Commn, 1960–63; sc Camberley, 1964 (grad.); Resident Mil. Attaché, UK, with accreditation to France, W Germany, Belgium, Netherlands, Sweden, 1964–67; Dir of Mil. Intelligence, 1967–68; Para Overall Comdr, 1968–70; Dir of Res. and Planning, 1970; Asst Dir of Mil. Ops and Staff Duties, 1971; Dir of Mil. Trng, 1972–73; Officiating Dir of Mil. Ops and Staff Duties, 1974; Master-Gen. of Ordnance, 1975; Comdr, No 4 Bde, 1975–77; Dir, Mil. Ops, Staff Duties, Res. and Planning, 1978–80; Adjt-Gen., 1980; QMG, 1982–83; CGS, 1983–85 (retired); ADC Gen. to King of Nepal, 1986. Mem. Exec. Cttee, Pashupati Area Develt Trust, 1987–. Army Long Service Medal. Comdr OM (France), 1966; OM (Jugoslavia), 1974;

Grand Cross: Order of the Lion of Finland, 1989; Order of the Dannebrog (Denmark), 1989. *Recreations:* hunting, jogging, squash, tennis, trekking. *Address:* Royal Nepalese Embassy, 12a Kensington Palace Gardens, W8 4QU. *T:* (office) 071–229 6231/1594; (direct line) 071–229 4536; (permanent) Dharma Ashram, CHHA 3/150 Kaldhara, Kathmandu 3, Nepal. *T:* 412270. *Clubs:* Travellers', Royal Automobile; Tribhuwan Army Officers (Kathmandu).

SIMINOVITCH, Dr Louis, CC 1989 (OC 1980); PhD, FRS 1980; FRSC 1965; Director, Samuel Lunenfeld Research Institute of Mount Sinai Hospital (formerly Mount Sinai Hospital Research Institute), University of Toronto, since 1983; *b* Montreal, PQ, 1 May 1920; *s* of Nathan Siminovitch and Goldie Watchman; *m* 1944, Elinore, *d* of late Harry Faierman; three *d. Educ:* McGill Univ. (BSc 1941, PhD 1944; Arts and Sci. schol. 1939, Sir William McDonald schol. 1940, Anne Molson prize in Chem. 1941). With NRC at Ottawa and Chalk River, Ont., 1944–47; NRC Studentship and Fellowship, 1942–44; with Centre Nat. de la Recherche Scientifique, Paris, 1949–53; Nat. Cancer Inst. Canadian Fellowships, 1953–55; Connaught Med. Res. Labs, Univ. of Toronto, 1953–56. Head of Div. of Biolog. Research, Ontario Cancer Inst., Toronto, 1963–69; Chm., Dept of Med. Cell Biology, Univ. of Toronto, 1969–72; Chm., Dept of Med. Genetics, 1972–79, Univ. Prof., 1976–85, Toronto Univ. Founding Mem. and Pres., Editorial Bd, Science Forum, 1966–79; Pres., Canadian Cell Biology Soc., 1967. Member: Bd of Dirs, Nat. Cancer Inst. of Canada, 1975–85 (Pres., 1982–84); Nat. Bd of Dirs, Canadian Cancer Soc., 1981–84; Bd, Ontario Cancer Treatment and Res. Foundn, 1979–; Scientific Adv. Cttee, Connaught Res. Inst., 1980–84; Alfred P. Sloan, Jr, Selection Cttee, General Motors Cancer Res. Foundn, 1980–81, 1983–84; Health Res. and Develt Council of Ont, 1983–86. Ed., Jl of Molecular and Cellular Biology, 1980–90; Member Editorial Board: Jl Cancer Surveys (London), 1980–89; Somatic Cell and Molecular Genetics, 1984–. Hon. degrees: Meml Univ., Newfoundland, 1978; McMaster Univ., 1978; Univ. of Montreal, 1990; McGill Univ., Montreal, 1990; Univ. of Western Ont, London, 1990. Flavelle Gold Medal, RSC, 1978; Univ. of Toronto Alumni Assoc. Award, 1978; Izaak Walton Killam Meml Prize, 1981; Gairdner Foundn Wightman Award, 1981; Medal of Achievement Award, Institut de Recherches Cliniques de Montreal, 1985; Environmental Mutagen Society Award, Baltimore, Maryland, 1986; R. P. Taylor Award, Canadian Cancer Soc., Nat. Cancer Inst., 1986; Distinguished Service Award, Canadian Soc. for Clinical Investigation, 1990. Silver Jubilee Medal, 1977. Has specialised in the study of bacterial and somatic cell genetics. *Publications:* many contribs to scientific and learned journals. *Address:* Samuel Lunenfeld Research Institute of Mount Sinai Hospital, 600 University Avenue, Toronto, Ont M5G 1X5, Canada; 106 Wembley Road, Toronto, Ont., Canada.

SIMKINS, Charles Anthony Goodall, CB 1968; CBE 1963; *b* 2 March 1912; *s* of Charles Wyckens Simkins; *m* 1938, Sylvia, *d* of Thomas Hartley, Silchester, Hants; two *s* one *d. Educ:* Marlborough; New Coll., Oxford (1st Class Hons Mod. Hist.). Barrister, Lincoln's Inn, 1936; served 1939–45 as Captain, Rifle Bde (POW); attached War Office (later MoD), 1945–71. *Publication:* (with Sir Harry Hinsley) British Intelligence in the Second World War: vol. IV, security and counter-intelligence, 1990. *Address:* The Cottage, 94 Broad Street, near Guildford, Surrey. *T:* Guildford (0483) 572456. *Clubs:* Naval and Military, MCC.

SIMMONDS, Rt. Hon. Dr Kennedy Alphonse, PC 1984; Prime Minister, Federation of St Christopher (St Kitts) and Nevis, since 1983; *b* 12 April 1936; *s* of Bronte Clarke and Arthur Simmonds; *m* 1976, Mary Camella (*née* Matthew); three *s* two *d. Educ:* St Kitts and Nevis Grammar School; Leeward Islands Scholar, 1954; Univ. of West Indies (studies in Medicine), 1955–62. Senior Bench Chemist, Sugar Assoc. Res. Lab., St Kitts, 1955; Internship, Kingston Public Hosp., 1963; medical practice, St Kitts, Anguilla and Nevis, 1964–66; postgrad. studies, Princess Margaret Hosp., Bahamas, 1966; Resident in Anaesthesiology, Pittsburgh, 1968–69; medical practice, St Kitts, 1969–80; Premier of St Christopher (St Kitts) and Nevis, 1980–83. Foundn Mem., People's Action Movement Opposition Party, 1965, Pres., People's Action Movement, 1976. Fellow, Amer. Coll. of Anaesthesiology, 1970. *Recreations:* tennis, cricket, football, video taping. *Address:* PO Box 186, Government Headquarters, Basseterre, St Kitts, West Indies. *T:* 809–465 2103.

SIMMONDS, Prof. Kenneth Royston; Professor of International Law in the University of London, at Queen Mary and Westfield College (formerly Queen Mary College), since 1976; Gresham Professor of Law, City of London, since 1986; *b* 11 Nov. 1927; *s* of Frederick John Simmonds and Maude (*née* Coxhill) *m* 1958, Gloria Mary (*née* Tatchell); one *s* one *d. Educ:* Watford Grammar Sch.; Exeter Coll., Oxford. BA, MA, DPhil (Oxon). Amelia Jackson Sen. Fellow, Exeter Coll., Oxford, 1951–53; Lectr, UCW, 1953–58; Lectr, Univ. of Liverpool, 1958–61; Sen. Lectr, QUB, 1961–63; Prof. of Law, Univ. of Kent, 1970–72; British Institute of International and Comparative Law: Asst Dir, 1963–65; Dir, 1965–76; Hon. Dir, 1976–82; Dean, Faculty of Law, QMC, 1980–84. Gen. Editor, International and Comparative Law Qly, 1966–86; Editor, Common Market Law Review, 1967–; Gen. Editor, Encyclopedia of European Community Law, 1972–; Member Editorial Committee: British Year Book of International Law, 1967–; The International Lawyer, 1986–. Visiting Professor: McGill Univ., 1963; Univ. of Wyoming, 1969; Free Univ. of Brussels, 1972 and 1973; Univ. of Amsterdam, annually, 1979–; Univ. of Kentucky, 1985; Univ. of Texas at Austin, 1986–87; The Hague Acad. of Internat. Law, 1989. Mem., Legal Adv. Cttee, British Council, 1966–86; Chm., UK Nat. Cttee of Comparative Law, 1973–76; Pres., Internat. Assoc. of Legal Science, 1975–76; Mem. Bd, Eur. Maritime Law Assoc., 1991–. Consultant, EEC, 1983–84. Chevalier, l'Ordre de Mérite, 1973; Comdr's Cross of Order of Merit, Federal Republic of Germany, 1983. *Publications:* Resources of the Ocean Bed, 1970; New Directions in the Law of the Sea, 1972–; (ed) Legal Problems of an Enlarged European Community, 1972; (ed) Sweet and Maxwell's European Community Treaties, 1972, 4th edn 1980; Cases on the Law of the Sea, 1976–84, Second series, 1990–; (ed, with C. M. Schmitthoff) International Economic and Trade Law, 1976; Legal Problems of Multinational Corporations, 1978; (ed, with R. M. Goode) Commercial Operations in Europe, 1978; Multinational Corporations Law, 1979–; The UN Convention on the Law of the Sea, 1982; New Directions in the Law of the Sea, 1983–; (ed with B. H. W. Hill) Commercial Arbitration in Asia and the Pacific, 1987; (ed with B. H. W. Hill) GATT Law and Practice, 1987–; The European Community, the Soviet Union and Eastern Europe, 1991; numerous articles in Internat. and Comparative Law Qly, Common Market Law Rev., Europarecht. *Recreations:* travel (espec. in the Americas), classical music, cats. *Address:* The Oast Barn, Bell's Forstal, Throwley, near Faversham, Kent ME13 0JS.

SIMMONDS, Kenneth Willison, CMG 1956; FRSA; *b* Carmacoup, Douglas, Lanarkshire, 13 May 1912; *s* of late William Henry Simmonds, Civil Servant, and late Ida, *d* of John Willison, Acharn, Killin, Perthshire; *m* 1st, 1939, Ruth Constance Sargant (marr. diss. 1974); two *s*; 2nd, 1974, Mrs Catherine Clare Lewis, *y d* of late Col F. J. Brakenridge, CMG, Chew Magna. *Educ:* Bedford Sch.; Humberstone Sch.; St Catharine's Coll., Cambridge (MA). District Officer, Colonial Administrative Service, Kenya, 1935–48; Deputy Financial Secretary, Uganda, 1948–51; Financial Secretary, Nyasaland Protectorate, 1951–57; Chief Secretary, Aden, 1957–63. Exhibited paintings: Southern Arts Open Field; Royal Acad.; Royal West of England Acad.; Bladon, Andover; Westward Open; Royal Bath and West; group and collective exhbns. *Address:* 1 Fons George Road, Taunton, Somerset TA1 3JU. *T:* Taunton (0823) 333128.

SIMMONDS, Posy; freelance illustrator/cartoonist, since 1969; *b* 9 Aug. 1945; *d* of Reginald A. C. Simmonds and Betty Cahusac; *m* 1974, Richard Hollis. *Educ:* Queen Anne's Sch., Caversham; L'Ecole des Beaux Arts, Paris; Central Sch. of Art and Design, London (BA Art and Design). Cartoonist: The Guardian, 1977–87, 1988–90; The Spectator, 1988–90. Exhibitions: The Cartoon Gall. (formerly the Workshop), 1974, 1976, 1979, 1981, 1982, 1984; Mus. of Modern Art, Oxford, 1981; Manor House Mus. & Art Gall., Ilkley, 1985. TV documentary, Tresoddit for Easter, 1991. Cartoonist of the Year: Granada TV/What The Papers Say, 1980; British Press Awards, 1981. *Publications:* Bear Book, 1969; Mrs Weber's Diary, 1979; True Love, 1981; Pick of Posy, 1982; (illustrator) Daisy Ashford, The Young Visiters, 1984; Very Posy, 1985; Fred, 1987; Pure Posy, 1987; Lulu and the Flying Babies, 1988; The Chocolate Wedding, 1990; (illustrator) Hilaire Belloc, Matilda, who told such Dreadful Lies, 1991. *Address:* c/o Peters, Fraser & Dunlop, 5th Floor, The Chambers, Chelsea Harbour, Lots Road, SW10 0XF. *T:* 071–376 7676.

See also R. J. Simmonds.

SIMMONDS, Richard James; Member (C) Wight and Hampshire East, European Parliament, since 1984 (Midlands West, 1979–84); consultant surveyor and industrialist; farmer of free range poultry and breeder of Jersey cattle; *b* 2 Aug. 1944; *s* of Reginald A. C. Simmonds and Betty Cahusac; *m* 1967, Mary (*née* Stewart); one *s* two *d. Educ:* Trinity Coll., Glenalmond. Councillor, Berkshire CC (Chm. of Environment, Property, Transport, and Development Cttees), 1973–79. National Vice-Chm. of Young Conservatives, 1973–75; Founding Vice-Chm. of Young European Democrats, 1974; Personal Asst to Rt Hon. Edward Heath, 1973–75; PPS to Sir James Scott-Hopkins, Leader of European Democratic Gp, European Parlt, 1979–82; Cons. spokesman on youth and educn, European Parlt, 1982–84, on budget control, 1984–87; Whip, 1987–89. Member: Extnl Econ. Rels Cttee, 1990–; Cttee on Envmt, Public Health and Consumer Protection, 1991–. Fellow of Parly & Industry Trust. Founding Pres., Mounted Games Assoc. of GB, 1984–. Liveryman, Gunmakers' Co., 1989. Chm. of Governors, Berkshire Coll. of Agriculture, 1979–. *Publications:* The Common Agricultural Policy—a sad misnomer, 1979; An A to Z of Myths and Misunderstandings of the European Community, 1981; European Parliamentary report on farm animal welfare, 1985, 1987, 1990. *Recreation:* resisting bureaucracy. *Address:* Woodlands Farm, Cookham Dean, Berkshire SL6 9PJ. *Clubs:* Carlton, United & Cecil, Ancient Britons, Tamworth.

See also Posy Simmonds.

SIMMONS, Alan Gerald; His Honour Judge Simmons; a Circuit Judge, since 1990; *b* 7 Sept. 1936; *s* of late Maurice Simmons and Sophie Simmons (*née* Lasserson); *m* 1961, Mia Rosenstein; one *s* one *d. Educ:* Bedford Modern Sch.; Quintin Sch. RAF, 1956–58. Director: Aslon Labs; Record Productions (Surrey); Ashcourt. Called to the Bar, Gray's Inn, 1968; SE Circuit; Assistant Recorder, 1985; Recorder, 1989. Member: Board of Deputies of British Jews, 1982–88; Council, United Synagogue, 1979–. *Recreations:* music, reading, fencing.

SIMMONS, Fr Eric, CR; Superior of the Community of the Resurrection, Mirfield, Yorkshire, 1974–87; *b* 1930. *Educ:* Univ. of Leeds. BA (Phil) 1951. Coll. of the Resurrection, Mirfield, 1951; deacon, 1953, priest, 1954; Curate of St Luke, Chesterton, 1953–57; Chaplain, University Coll. of N Staffordshire, 1957–61; licensed to officiate: Dio. Wakefield, 1963–65 and 1967–; Dio. Ripon, 1965–67; Warden and Prior of Hostel of the Resurrection, Leeds, 1966–67; subseq. Novice Guardian, looking after young Community members; the Community is an Anglican foundation engaged in evangelism and teaching work, based in Yorkshire but with work in Southern Africa. *Address:* The Royal Foundation of St Katharine, 2 Butcher Row, E14 8DS. *T:* 071–790 3540.

SIMMONS, Guy Lintorn, MVO 1961; HM Diplomatic Service, retired; *b* 27 Feb. 1925; *s* of late Captain Geoffrey Larpent Simmons, RN and Frances Gladys Simmons (*née* Wright); *m* 1951, Sheila Jacob; three *d. Educ:* Bradfield Coll.; Oriel Coll., Oxford. RAF, 1943–46; CRO, 1949; 2nd Sec., British High Commn: Lahore, 1950; Dacca, 1952; CRO, 1954–58 and 1964–66; 1st Sec.: Bombay, 1958; New Delhi, 1961; Commercial Counsellor: New Delhi, 1966–68; Cairo, 1968–71; Head of Trade Policy Dept, FCO, 1971–73; Diplomatic Service Inspectorate, 1973–76; Commercial Counsellor, Copenhagen, 1976–79; Consul-General: Karachi, 1979–82; Montreal, 1982–84; FCO, 1984–90. *Recreations:* the arts, travel, country pursuits. *Address:* c/o Bank of Scotland, EC2P 2EH. *Clubs:* Oriental; Sind (Karachi).

SIMMONS, Jack; Professor of History, University of Leicester, 1947–75, now Professor Emeritus; Pro-Vice-Chancellor, 1960–63; Public Orator, 1965–68; *b* 30 Aug. 1915; *o c* of Seymour Francis Simmons and Katharine Lillias, *d* of Thomas Finch, MB, Babbacombe, Devon. *Educ:* Westminster Sch.; Christ Church, Oxford. Beit Lectr in the History of the British Empire, Oxford Univ., 1943–47. FSA. Mem., Adv. Council, Science Museum, 1969–84; Chm., Nat. Railway Museum Cttee, York, 1981–84; Leicestershire Archæological and Historical Society: Hon. Editor, 1948–61; Pres. 1966–77. Chm., Leicester Local Broadcasting Council, 1967–70. Jt Editor, The Journal of Transport History, 1953–73. Editor: A Visual History of Modern Britain; Classical County Histories. *Publications:* African Discovery: An Anthology of Exploration (edited with Margery Perham), 1942; Southey, 1945; Edition of Southey's Letters from England, 1951; Journeys in England: an Anthology, 1951; Parish and Empire, 1952; Livingstone and Africa, 1955; New University, 1958; The Railways of Britain, 1961, 3rd edn, 1986; Transport, 1962; Britain and the World, 1965; St Pancras Station, 1968; Transport Museums, 1970; A Devon Anthology, 1971; (ed) Memoirs of a Station Master, 1973; Leicester Past and Present (2 vols), 1974; (ed) Rail 150: The Stockton and Darlington Railway and What Followed, 1975; The Railway in England and Wales 1830–1914, 1978; A Selective Guide to England, 1979; Dandy Cart to Diesel: the National Railway Museum, 1981; (ed) F. R. Conder, The Men who Built Railways, 1983; The Railway in Town and Country 1830–1914, 1986; The Victorian Railway, 1991; Railways: an anthology, 1991. *Address:* Flat 6, 36 Victoria Park Road, Leicester LE2 1XB. *Club:* United Oxford & Cambridge University.

SIMMONS, Jean; film actress; *b* London, 31 Jan. 1929; *m* 1950, Stewart Granger, *qv* (marr. diss. 1960); one *d*; *m* 1960, Richard Brooks; one *d. Educ:* Orange Hill Sch.; Aida Foster School of Dancing. First film appearance in Give Us the Moon, 1942; minor parts in Cæsar and Cleopatra, The Way to the Stars, etc., 1942–44; since then has appeared in numerous British films, including: Great Expectations, Black Narcissus, Hungry Hill, Uncle Silas, Hamlet (Best Actress Award, Venice Film Festival, 1950), So Long at the Fair, The Blue Lagoon, Trio, Adam and Evalyn, Clouded Yellow; The Grass is Greener, 1960; Life at the Top, 1965; Say Hello to Yesterday, 1971; began American film career, 1950; American films include: Androcles and the Lion, Young Bess, The Actress, Desirée, Footsteps in the Fog, Guys and Dolls, This Could be the Night, Spartacus, Elmer Gantry, All the Way Home; Divorce, American Style, 1967; The Happy Ending, 1970; The Thorn Birds, 1982 (Emmy award, 1983); television includes: Down at the Hydro, 1982.

Musical: A Little Night Music, Adelphi, 1975. Outstanding Film Achievement Award, Italy, 1989. Comdr, Order of Arts and Letters (France), 1990. *Address:* c/o A. Morgan Maree, Jr & Assoc., Inc., 6363 Wilshire Boulevard, Los Angeles, California 90048, USA.

SIMMONS, John Barry Eves, OBE 1987; VMH 1987; Curator, Royal Botanic Gardens, Kew, since 1972; *b* 30 May 1937; *s* of Alfred John and Gladys Enid Simmons; *m* 1958, Valerie Lilian Dugan; two *s* one *d*. *Educ:* Harrow County Grammar Sch.; Herts Coll. of Agric. and Hort.; Regent Street Polytechnic; Sch. of Horticulture, Kew. MHort, FIHort; FIBiol, CBiol. Royal Botanic Gardens, Kew: Supervisor, Tropical Propagation Unit, 1961–64; Asst Curator, Temperate Section, 1964–68; Deputy Curator, 1968–72. Vice-Chm., Nat. Council for Conservation of Plants and Gardens, 1991– (Mem. Council, 1985–); Member: RHS Award and Judging Cttees, 1969–; Longwood Gardens (Pennsylvania) Visiting Cttee, 1984–91. Pres., Inst. of Horticulture, 1987–88. Gov., Writtle Agricl Coll., 1990–. *Publications:* The Life of Plants, 1974, 2nd edn 1990; (series editor) Kew Gardening Guides, 1987–; (gen. editor) Kew Gardens Book of Indoor Plants, 1988; ed and contrib. to learned jls. *Recreations:* photography, walking, gardening (own garden!).

SIMMONS, Air Marshal Sir Michael (George), KCB 1989 (CB 1988); AFC 1976; Deputy Controller Aircraft, Ministry of Defence, since 1989; *b* 8 May 1937; *s* of George and Thelma Simmons; *m* 1964, Jean Aliwell; two *d*. *Educ:* Shrewsbury Sch.; RAF Coll., Cranwell. Commissioned 1958; No 6 Squadron, Cyprus, 1959–61; ADC to AOC-in-C FTC, 1961–64; No 39 Sqdn, Malta, 1964–66; No 13 Sqdn, Malta, 1966–67; No 51 Sqdn, Wyton, 1967–69; RN Staff Coll., 1970; MoD, 1971–72; OC No XV Sqdn, Germany, 1973–76; MoD, 1976–79; OC RAF Cottesmore, 1980–82; MoD, 1982–84; SASO, HQ Strike Comd, 1984–85; AOC No 1 Gp, RAF, 1985–87; ACAS, 1987–89. ADC to the Queen, 1980–81. *Recreations:* walking, gardening, golf. *Address:* c/o Royal Bank of Scotland, Kirkland House, Whitehall, SW1A 2EB. *Club:* Royal Air Force.

SIMMONS, Prof. Robert Malcolm; Professor and Head of Department of Biophysics, King's College London, since 1983; *b* 23 Jan. 1938; *s* of Stanley Laurence Simmons and Marjorie Amys; *m* 1967, Mary Ann (Anna) Ross; one *s* one *d*. *Educ:* King's College London (BSc Physics 1960); PhD London 1965; University College London (MSc Physiol. 1967). Department of Physiology, University College London: Sharpey Scholar, 1967–70; Lectr, 1970–79; MRC Res. Fellow, 1979–81; King's College London: MRC Cell Biophysics Unit, 1981–83; Associate Dir, 1983–91; Head of Div. of Biomolecular Scis, 1988–91; Hon. Dir, Muscle and Cell Motility Unit, 1991–. *Publications:* contribs on physiol. and biophys to learned jls. *Recreations:* music, fishing.

SIMMONS, Stanley Clifford, FRCS, FRCOG; Consultant Obstetrician and Gynaecologist, Windsor, since 1965; *b* 28 July 1927; *s* of Lewis Alfred and Ann Simmons; *m* 1956, Ann Wine; one *s* three *d*. *Educ:* Hurstpierpoint Coll.; St Mary's Hosp., London Univ. (MB BS 1951). FRCS 1957, FRCOG 1971. National Service, Royal West African Frontier Force, 1953–55. Resident MO, Queen Charlotte's Hosp. and Chelsea Hosp. for Women, 1955–56; Registrar, St Mary's Hosp. Paddington, 1957–59; Sen. Registrar, St Thomas' Hosp., 1960–64. Member: GMC, 1975–84; Council, RCOG, 1971–72, 1973–78, 1982– (Vice-Pres., 1986; Sen. Vice-Pres., 1987; Pres., 1990); Council, RCS (co-opted), 1984–86; President: Hosp. Consultants and Specialists Assoc., 1972; Windsor Med. Soc., 1983; Section of Obst. and Gyn., RSocMed, 1985. *Publications:* (jtly) General Surgery in Gynaecological Practice, 1974; contribs to med. jls. *Recreations:* flying, sailing, golf, skiing, painting. *Address:* Coach House, Kennel Avenue, Ascot, Berks. *T:* Ascot (0344) 23184. *Clubs:* Royal Society of Medicine; Wentworth; Ocean Cruising.

SIMMS, Most Rev. George Otto, DD; MRIA 1957; *b* 4 July 1910; 3rd *s* of John F. A. Simms, Crown Solicitor, County Tyrone, and Mrs Simms, Combermore, Lifford, County Donegal; *m* 1941, Mercy Felicia, *o d* of Brian James Gwynn, Temple Hill, Terenure, Dublin; three *s* two *d*. *Educ:* St Edmund's School, Hindhead; Cheltenham College; Trinity College, Dublin; Scholar, 1930; Moderator in Classics, and History and Political Science, 1932; Berkeley Medallist; Vice-Chancellor's Latin Medallist; Theological Exhibnr; Hon. Fellow, 1978. MA 1935; BD 1936; PhD 1950; DD (*jure dignitatis*, Dublin), 1952; DD (*hc* Huron), 1963; Hon. DCL Kent, 1978. Deacon, 1935; Priest, 1936; Curate-asst, St Bartholomew's Church, Dublin, 1935–38; Chaplain Lincoln Theol. Coll., 1938–39; Dean of Residence, Trinity Coll., Dublin, 1939–52; Asst Lectr to Archbishop King's Prof. of Divinity, Dublin Univ., 1939–52; Chaplain-Secretary, Church of Ireland Training Coll., 1943–52; Hon. Clerical Vicar, Christ Church Cathedral, Dublin, 1937–52; Dean of Cork, 1952; Bishop of Cork, Cloyne, and Ross, 1952–56; Archbishop of Dublin and Primate of Ireland, 1956–69; also Bishop of Glendalough and Bishop of Kildare; Archbishop of Armagh and Primate of All Ireland, 1969–80. Member Governing Body, University College, Cork, 1953–57; President: The Leprosy Mission, 1964–; APCK, 1983–. Hon. Life Mem., Royal Dublin Soc., 1984. Hon. DLitt New Univ. of Ulster, 1981. *Publications:* joint-editor (with E. H. Alton and P. Meyer), The Book of Kells (fac. edn), Berne, 1951; For Better, for Worse, 1945; The Book of Kells: a short description, 1950; The Bible in Perspective, 1953; contributor, The Book of Durrow (fac. edn), 1960; Memoir of Michael Lloyd Ferrar, 1962; Christ within Me, 1975; (contrib.) Irish Life, by Sharon Gmelch, 1979; Irish Illuminated Manuscripts, 1980; In My Understanding, 1982; Tullow's Story, 1983; (contrib.) Ireland: a cultural encyclopaedia, ed B. de Breffny, 1983; (with R. G. F. Jenkins) Pioneers and Partners, 1985; (contrib.) Treasures of the Library of Trinity College Dublin, 1986; Angels and Saints, 1988; Exploring the Book of Kells, 1988; Brendan the Navigator, 1989; (contrib.) Faith in Place, by Adrian Hewson, 1990; articles in Hermathena, Theology, and Dublin Magazine, JTS; contrib. to New Divinity, Booklore, Search, Newman Review. *Address:* 62 Cypress Grove Road, Dublin 6W. *T:* Dublin 905594.

SIMON, family name of **Viscount Simon,** of **Baron Simon of Glaisdale** and of **Baron Simon of Wythenshawe.**

SIMON, 2nd Viscount, *cr* 1940, of Stackpole Elidor; **John Gilbert Simon,** CMG 1947; *b* 2 Sept. 1902; *o s* of 1st Viscount Simon, PC, GCSI, GCVO, and of Ethel Mary (*d* 1902), *d* of Gilbert Venables; *S* father, 1954; *m* 1930, Christie, *d* of William Stanley Hunt; one *s* one *d*. *Educ:* Winchester; Balliol College, Oxford (Scholar). With Ministry of War Transport, 1940–47. Man. Dir, 1947–58, Dep. Chm., 1951–58, Peninsular and Oriental Steam Navigation Co. Chm., PLA, 1958–71; Mem., Nat. Ports Council, 1967–71. President: Chamber of Shipping of UK, 1957–58; Inst. of Marine Engineers, 1960–61; RINA, 1961–71; British Hydromechanics Res. Assoc., 1968–80. Officer Order of Orange Nassau, Netherlands. *Heir:* *s* Hon. Jan David Simon [*b* 20 July 1940; *m* 1969, Mary Elizabeth Burns, Sydney; one *d*]. *Address:* 2 Church Cottages, Abbotskerswell, Newton Abbot, Devon TQ12 5NY. *T:* Newton Abbot (0626) 65573.

SIMON OF GLAISDALE, Baron *cr* 1971 (Life Peer), of Glaisdale, Yorks; **Jocelyn Edward Salis Simon,** PC 1961; Kt 1959; DL; a Lord of Appeal in Ordinary, 1971–77; *b* 15 Jan. 1911; *s* of Frank Cecil and Claire Evelyn Simon, 51 Belsize Pk, NW3; *m* 1st, 1934, Gwendolen Helen (*d* 1937), *d* of E. J. Evans; 2nd, 1948, Fay Elizabeth Leicester, JP, *d* of Brig. H. G. A. Pearson; three *s*. *Educ:* Gresham's School, Holt; Trinity Hall, Cambridge (Exhibitioner). Called to Bar, Middle Temple, 1934 (Blackstone Prizeman). Served War of 1939–45; commissioned RTR, 1939; comd Spec. Service Sqn, RAC, Madagascar, 1942; Burma Campaign, 1944; Lieut-Col. 1945. Resumed practice at Bar, 1946; QC 1951. MP (C) Middlesbrough West, 1951–62; Mem. of the Royal Commission on the Law relating to Mental Illness and Mental Deficiency, 1954–57. Jt Parly Under-Sec. of State, Home Office, 1957–58; Financial Sec. to the Treasury, 1958–59; Solicitor-General, 1959–62. President, Probate, Divorce and Admiralty Div. of the High Court of Justice, 1962–71. Hon. Elder Brother, Trinity House, 1975. Hon. Fellow, Trinity Hall, Cambridge, 1963. DL NR (now North) Yorks, 1973. *Publications:* Change is Our Ally, 1954 (part); Rule of Law, 1955 (part); The Church and the Law of Nullity, 1955 (part); articles in learned jls. *Address:* Midge Hall, Glaisdale Head, Whitby, North Yorks.

See also Hon. P. C. H. Simon.

SIMON OF WYTHENSHAWE, 2nd Baron, *cr* 1947, of Didsbury; **Roger Simon;** *b* 16 Oct. 1913; *S* father, 1960 (but does not use the title and wishes to be known as Roger Simon); *m* 1951 (Anthea) Daphne May; one *s* one *d*. *Educ:* Gresham's School; Gonville and Caius College, Cambridge. *Heir:* *s* Hon. Matthew Simon, *b* 10 April 1955. *Address:* Oakhill, Chester Avenue, Richmond, Surrey.

See also B. Simon.

SIMON, Prof. Brian; Emeritus Professor of Education, University of Leicester; *b* 26 March 1915; *yr s* of 1st Baron Simon of Wythenshawe and Shena D. Potter; *m* 1941, Joan Home Peel; two *s*. *Educ:* Gresham's Sch., Holt; Schloss Schule, Salem; Trinity Coll., Cambridge; Inst. of Educn, Univ. of London. MA. Pres., Nat. Union of Students, 1939–40; Royal Corps of Signals, GHQ Liaison Regt (Phantom), 1940–45; teaching Manchester and Salford schs, 1945–50; Univ. of Leicester: Lectr in Educn, 1950–64; Reader, 1964–66; Professor, 1966–80; Dir, Sch. of Educn, 1968–70, 1974–77. Chairman: History of Educn Soc., 1976–79; Internat. Standing Conf. for Hist. of Educn, 1979–82; Pres., British Educn Res. Assoc., 1977–78. Editor, Forum (for discussion of new trends in educn), 1958–90; Jt Editor, Students Library of Education, 1966–77. Dr *hc* Cath. Univ. of Leuven, 1980. DUniv Open Univ., 1981. *Publications:* A Student's View of the Universities, 1943; Intelligence Testing and the Comprehensive School, 1953; The Common Secondary School, 1955; (ed) New Trends in English Education, 1957; (ed) Psychology in the Soviet Union, 1957; Studies in the History of Education 1780–1870, 1960; (ed, with Joan Simon) Educational Psychology in the USSR, 1963; (ed) The Challenge of Marxism, 1963; (ed) Non-streaming in the Junior School, 1964; Education and the Labour Movement 1870–1920, 1965; (ed) Education in Leicestershire 1540–1940, 1968; (with D. Rubinstein) The Evolution of the Comprehensive School 1926–66, 1969 (revised edn 1973); (with Caroline Benn) Half-Way There: Report on the British Comprehensive School Reform, 1970 (revised edn 1972); Intelligence, Psychology and Education, 1971 (revised edn 1978); (ed) The Radical Tradition in Education in Britain, 1972; The Politics of Educational Reform 1920–1940, 1974; (ed with Ian Bradley) The Victorian Public School, 1975; (with Maurice Galton) Inside the Primary Classroom, 1980; Progress and Performance in the Primary Classroom, 1980; (ed with William Taylor) Education in the Eighties, the central issues, 1981; (ed with John Willcocks) Research and Practice in the Primary Classroom, 1981; Does Education Matter?, 1985; (ed with Detlef Müller and Fritz Ringer) The Rise of the Modern Educational System, 1987; Bending the Rules: the Baker "reform" of education, 1988; (ed) The Search for Enlightenment: the working class and adult education in the twentieth century, 1989; Education and the Social Order 1940–1990, 1990. *Address:* 11 Pendene Road, Leicester LE2 3DQ. *T:* Leicester (0533) 705176.

SIMON, Claude (Henri Eugène); French writer and vine grower; *b* Madagascar, 10 Oct. 1913; *s* of Antoine Simon and Suzanne (*née* Denamiel); *m* 1978, Réa Karavas. *Educ:* Collège Stanislas, Paris. Jury Mem., Prix Médicis, 1968–70. Nobel Prize for Literature, 1985. *Publications:* Le tricheur, 1945; La corde raide, 1947; Gulliver, 1952; Le sacre du printemps, 1954; Le vent, 1957; L'herbe, 1958 (trans. The Grass, 1961); La route des Flandres (Prix de l'Express), 1960 (trans. The Flanders Road, 1962); Le palace, 1962 (trans. 1964); Histoire (Prix Médicis), 1967 (trans. 1969); La bataille de Pharsale, 1969 (trans. The Battle of Pharsalus, 1971); Orion aveugle, 1970; Les corps conducteurs, 1971 (trans. Conducting Bodies, 1975); Triptyque, 1973 (trans. 1977); Leçon de choses, 1975; Les Géorgiques, 1981 (trans. 1985); L'Acacia, 1989; articles in journals. *Address:* c/o Editions de Minuit, 7 rue Bernard-Palissy, 75006 Paris, France.

SIMON, David Alec Gwyn, CBE 1991; Managing Director, since 1986, Deputy Chairman and Chief Operating Officer, since 1990, British Petroleum Co. plc; *b* 24 July 1939; *s* of Roger Albert Damas Jules Simon and Barbara (*née* Hudd); *m* 1964, Hanne (*née* Mohn) (marr. diss. 1987); two *s*. *Educ:* Christ's Hospital; Gonville and Caius College, Cambridge (MA Hons); MBA INSEAD. Joined BP 1961; Marketing Co-ordinator, European Region, 1975–80; Dir, BP Oil UK and Chm., National Benzole Co., 1980–82; Man. Dir, BP Oil International, 1982–85; Chairman: BP Finance Internat., 1986–90; BP Oil, 1989–90; Chm., Supervisory Bd, Deutsche BP; Director: BP France, 1982–; BP Nutrition, 1985–89; BP Holland, 1985–89; non-exec. Dir, Grand Metropolitan plc, 1989–. Member: International Council and UK Adv. Bd, INSEAD, 1985–; Council, Foundn for Management Educn, 1986–. Mem., Sports Council, 1988–. Liveryman: Worshipful Co. of Carmen, 1982–; Tallow Chandlers' Co., 1986–. *Recreations:* golf, books, music. *Address:* c/o The British Petroleum Co. plc, Britannic House, 1 Finsbury Circus, EC1Y 7BA. *T:* 071–496 4000. *Clubs:* Groucho; Hampstead Cricket, Highgate Golf, Hunstanton Golf.

SIMON, Prof. Herbert A(lexander), PhD; Richard King Mellon University Professor of Computer Science and Psychology, Carnegie-Mellon University, since 1967; *b* 15 June 1916; *s* of Arthur Simon and Edna Merkel Simon; *m* 1937, Dorothea Pye; one *s* two *d*. *Educ:* University of Chicago (BA, PhD). Staff member, Internat. City Managers' Assoc., 1936–39; Study Director, Bureau of Public Admin., Univ. of California (Berkeley), 1939–42; Asst Prof. to Professor, Illinois Inst. of Technology, 1942–49 (Head, Dept of Pol. and Social Sci., 1946–49); Professor of Administration, Carnegie-Mellon Univ., 1949–67 (Associate Dean, Graduate Sch. of Industrial Admin., 1957–73). Mem., Nat. Acad. of Scis, 1967 (Mem. Council, 1978–81, 1983–86). Hon. degrees: DSc: Case Inst. of Technol., 1963; Yale, 1963; Marquette, 1981; Columbia, 1983; Gustavus Adolphus, 1985; Duquesne, 1988; Illinois Inst. of Technol., 1988; Michigan Inst. of Technol., 1988; Carnegie Mellon, 1990; LLD: Chicago, 1964; McGill, 1970; Michigan, 1978; Pittsburgh, 1979; Univ. Paul-Valéry, 1984; Harvard, 1990; FilDr, Lund, 1968; DrEconSci, Erasmus (Rotterdam), 1973; DrPolitSci, Padua, 1988. Hon. Professor: Tianjin Univ., 1980; Beijing Univ., 1986; Hon. Res. Fellow, Inst. of Psych., Chinese Acad. of Sciences, 1985. Nobel Prize in Economics, 1978; Dist. Sci. Contrib. Award, Amer. Psych. Assoc., 1969; Turing Award, Assoc. for Computing Machinery, 1975; James Madison Award, Amer. Political Science Assoc., 1984; National Medal of Science, 1986; John Von Neumann Theory Prize, Operations Res. Soc. of Amer. and Inst. of Management Sci., 1988; Gold Medal Award in Psychol Sci., Amer. Psychol. Foundn, 1988. *Publications:* Administrative Behavior, 1947, 3rd edn 1976; Models of Man, 1957; (with J. G. March) Organizations, 1958; The New Science of Management Decision, 1960, rev. edn 1977; The Sciences of the Artificial, 1969, 2nd edn 1981; (with A. Newell) Human Problem Solving, 1972;

Models of Discovery, 1977; (with Y. Ijiri) Skew Distributions and the Sizes of Business Firms, 1977; Models of Thought, vol. 1, 1979, vol. 2, 1989; Models of Bounded Rationality (2 vols), 1982; Reason in Human Affairs, 1983; (with K. A. Ericsson) Protocol Analysis, 1984; (with P. Langley *et al*) Scientific Discovery, 1987; Models of my Life, 1991; other books, and articles in sci. jls. *Recreations:* walking, piano, painting. *Address:* Department of Psychology, Carnegie-Mellon University, Pittsburgh, Pa 15213, USA. *T:* 412–268–2787. *Clubs:* University (Pittsburgh); Cosmos (Washington).

SIMON, Neil; playwright; *b* NYC, 4 July 1927; *s* of Irving and Mamie Simon; *m* 1st, 1953, Joan Baim (decd); two *d*; 2nd, 1973, Marsha Mason; 3rd, 1987, Diane Lander (marr. diss.); 4th, 1990. *Educ:* De Witt Clinton High Sch.; entered Army Air Force Reserve training programme as an engineering student at New York University; discharged with rank of corporal, 1946. Went to New York Offices of Warner Brothers Pictures to work in mail room. Hon. LHD Hofstra Univ., 1981. *Screenplays include:* After The Fox (produced 1966); Barefoot in the Park, 1967; The Odd Couple, 1968; The Out-of-Towners, 1970; The Star-Spangled Girl, 1971; Plaza Suite, 1971; Last of the Red Hot Lovers, 1972; The Heartbreak Kid, 1973; The Prisoner of 2nd Avenue, 1975; The Sunshine Boys, 1975; Murder by Death, 1976; The Goodbye Girl, 1977; The Cheap Detective, 1978; California Suite, 1978; Chapter Two, 1979; Seems Like Old Times, 1980; Only When I Laugh, 1981; I Ought To Be In Pictures, 1982; Max Dugan Returns, 1983; adapt. The Lonely Guy, 1984; The Slugger's Wife, 1984; Brighton Beach Memoirs, 1986; Biloxi Blues, 1988; other films based on his stage plays: Come Blow Your Horn, 1963; Sweet Charity, 1969; The Star-Spangled Girl, 1971. *Plays produced:* Come Blow Your Horn, 1961 (publ. 1961); (jtly) Little Me, 1962 (publ. 1979), rev. version 1982, West End 1984; Barefoot in the Park, 1963 (publ. 1964); The Odd Couple, 1965 (publ. 1966); (jtly) Sweet Charity, 1966 (publ. 1966); The Star-Spangled Girl, 1966 (publ. 1967); Plaza Suite, 1968 (publ. 1969); (jtly) Promises, Promises, 1968 (publ. 1969); Last of the Red Hot Lovers, 1969 (publ. 1970), Criterion, 1979; The Gingerbread Lady, 1970 (publ. 1971); The Prisoner of Second Avenue, 1971 (publ. 1972); The Sunshine Boys, 1972 (publ. 1973); The Good Doctor, 1973 (publ. 1974); God's Favorite, 1974 (publ. 1975); California Suite, 1976 (publ. 1977); Chapter Two, 1977 (publ. 1978); (jtly) They're Playing Our Song, 1979 (publ. 1980); I Ought To Be In Pictures, 1980 (publ. 1981); Fools, 1981 (publ. 1982); Brighton Beach Memoirs, 1983 (publ. 1984), NT, 1986, West End, 1987; Biloxi Blues, 1985 (Tony Award for Best Play, 1985); The Odd Couple (female version), 1985; Broadway Bound, 1986 (publ. 1987); Rumors, 1988; Lost in Yonkers, 1991 (Pulitzer Prize, Tony Award for Best Play, 1991). *Address:* c/o A. DaSilva, 502 Park Avenue, New York, NY 10022, USA.

SIMON, Hon. Peregrine Charles Hugo, FLS; QC 1991; *b* 20 June 1950; *s* of Lord Simon of Glaisdale, *qv*, and Fay Elizabeth Leicester, *d* of Brig. Guy Pearson; *m* 1980, Francesca Fortescue Hitchins, *d* of Major Tom Fortescue Hitchins; two *s* two *d*. *Educ:* Westminster School; Trinity Hall, Cambridge (MA). Called to the Bar, Middle Temple, 1973. *Address:* Brick Court Chambers, 15/19 Devereux Court, WC2R 3JJ. *T:* 071–583 0777.

SIMON, Roger; *see* Simon of Wythenshawe barony.

SIMON, Prof. Ulrich Ernst, DD; Professor of Christian Literature, 1972–80, Dean, 1978–80, King's College, London; *b* 21 Sept. 1913; *s* of James and Anna Simon; *m* 1949, Joan Edith Raynor Westlake; two *s* one *d*. *Educ:* Grunewald Gymnasium, Berlin; King's Coll., London. BD, MTh, DD, FKC. Ordained in Church of England, 1938; Univ. Lectr, 1945; Reader, 1960. *Publications:* Theology of Crisis, 1948; Theology of Salvation, 1953; Heaven in the Christian Tradition, 1958; The Ascent to Heaven, 1961; The End is not Yet, 1964; Theology Observed, 1966; A Theology of Auschwitz, 1967 (paperback 1978); The Trial of Man, 1973; Story and Faith, 1975; Sitting in Judgment, 1978; Atonement, 1987; Pity and Terror, 1989. *Recreations:* gardening, chamber music, walking. *Address:* 22 Collingwood Avenue, N10 3ED. *T:* 081–883 4852.

SIMON, William Edward; Chairman, William E. Simon & Sons, Inc., Morristown, NJ; Co-Chairman, WSPG International Inc.; *b* 27 Nov. 1927; *s* of Charles Simon and Eleanor Kearns; *m* 1950, Carol Girard; two *s* five *d*. *Educ:* Newark Academy, NJ; Lafayette Coll. (BA). Joined Union Securities, NYC 1952, Asst Vice-Pres. and Manager of firm's Municipal Trading Dept, 1955–57; Vice Pres., Weeden & Co., 1957–64; Sen. Partner and Mem. Exec. Cttee, Salomon Brothers, NYC, 1964–72. Dep. Sec., US Treasury Dept, and Administrator, Federal Energy Office, 1973–74; Secretary of the Treasury, May 1974–Jan. 1977. Sen. Cons., Booz Allen & Hamilton Inc., 1977–79; Sen. Advr, Blyth Eastman Dillon & Co. Inc., 1977–80; Dep. Chm., Olayan Investments Co. Estabt, 1980; Chairman: Crescent Diversified Ltd, 1980; Wesray Corp., 1981–86, now Emeritus; Wesray Capital Corp., 1984–86, now Emeritus. Director: Castleton Inc.; Pompano Park Realty, Inc.; Sequoia Inst. Mem., President's Cttee on the Arts and Humanities; Director: Atlantic Council of US; Boys Harbor Catholic Big Brothers; Citizens Against Govt Waste; Citizens Network for Foreign Affairs; Covenant House; Gerald R. Ford Foundn; Internat. Foundn for Educn and Self-Help; Kissinger Assoc.; Nat. Football Hall of Fame; Space Studies Inst.; World Cup 1994 Organizing Cttee; Mem. Exec. Bd, US Olympic Cttee (former Pres.); Chm., Bd of Trustees, US Olympic Foundn. Trustee: Lafayette Coll.; Univ. of Rochester; Boston Univ.; Hudson Inst.; Hillsdale Coll. Hon. Dr of Laws: Lafayette Coll., 1973; Pepperdine Univ., 1975; Manhattanville Coll., 1978; Washington, Boston, 1980; Washington Coll., Rider Coll., Seton Hall, Fairleigh Dickenson, 1984; Rutgers, Rochester, 1985; Hon. DCL Jacksonville Univ., 1976; Hon. PhD Tel Aviv, 1976; Hon. Scriptural Degree, Israel Torah Res. Inst., 1976; Hon. DSc New England Coll., 1977; Dr of Econs Hanyang Univ., Seoul, Korea; Dr of Humanics Springfield, 1986. Numerous honours and awards. *Publications:* A Time for Truth, 1978; A Time for Action, 1980. *Address:* William E. Simon & Sons Inc., 310 South Street, PO Box 1913, Morristown, NJ 07960–1913, USA; Nomis Hill, Sand Spring Road, New Vernon, NJ 07976, USA. *Clubs:* River, Links, Brook, Bond, Municipal Bond, Explorers, Pilgrims of US, New York Yacht, New York Athletic (New York, NY); Maidstone (East Hampton, NY); Alfalfa (Washington, DC); Balboa Bay, Commonwealth (Calif); Morris County Golf (Convent Station, NJ); Rolling Rock (Pa); Country (Colo); Waialae Country, Oaho Country, Maui Country (Hawaii); Gulf Stream Golf (Fla); Lyford Cay (Bahamas).

SIMONDS-GOODING, Anthony James Joseph; *b* 10 Sept. 1937; *s* of Major and Mrs Hamilton Simonds-Gooding; *m* 1st, 1961, Fiona (*née* Menzies) (marr. diss. 1982); four *s* two *d*; 2nd, 1982, Marjorie Anne, *d* of late William and Wendy Pennock; one step *s*. *Educ:* Ampleforth Coll.; BRNC, Dartmouth. Served RN, 1953–59; Unilever, 1960–73; Marketing Dir, subseq. Man. Dir (UK), finally Gp Man. Dir, Whitbread & Co. plc, 1973–85; Saatchi plc, 1985–87 (Chm. and Chief Exec. of all communication and advertising cos worldwide); Chief Exec., British Satellite Broadcasting, 1987–90. Dir, Cancer Relief Macmillan Fund Appeal, 1991. *Recreations:* family, opera, tennis, travel, reading, ski-ing. *Address:* 60 Hurlingham Road, Fulham, SW6 3RQ. *Clubs:* Hurlingham, Queen's.

SIMONET, Henri François; Commander, Order of Leopold, 1974; Member, Belgian Parliament, since 1966; *b* Brussels, 10 May 1931; *m* 1960, Marie-Louise Angenent; one *s* one *d*. *Educ:* Univ. Libre de Bruxelles (DenD, DèsSc); Columbia Univ., USA. Assistant, Univ. Libre de Bruxelles, 1956–58, now Prof.; Financial Adv., Inst. Nat. d'Etudes pour le Développement du Bas-Congo, 1958–59; Legal Adv., Commn of Brussels Stock Exchange, 1956–60; Dep. Dir, Office of Econ. Programming, 1961; Director of Cabinet: of Min. of Econ. Affairs and Power, 1961–65; of Dep. Prime Minister responsible for co-ordination of Econ. Policy, 1965; Minister of Econ. Affairs, 1972; Vice-Pres., Commn of the European Communities, 1973–77; Foreign Minister, Belgium, 1977–80; Sec. of State, Brussels Regional Economy, 1977–79. Mayor of Anderlecht, 1966–84. Commander, Légion d'Honneur (France), 1985. *Publications:* various books and articles on economics, financial and political topics. *Address:* 34 avenue Franklin Roosevelt, 1050 Brussels, Belgium.

SIMONET, Sir (Louis Marcel) Pierre, Kt 1985; CBE 1980 (OBE 1972); Director and Proprietor, Pharmacie Simonet, since 1955 (founded by father, 1926); *b* 6 March 1934; *s* of Marcel Simonet and Marguerite Simonet. *Educ:* Collège du St Esprit up to Higher School Certificate. Town Council of Curepipe: Mem., 1960; Vice-Chm., 1962; Chm., 1964; 1st Mem. for Curepipe, Legislative Assembly, 1976; Pres., Mauritian Social Democratic Party, 1981. Judge Assessor, Permt Arbitration Tribunal, 1984. Dir, Central Electricity Bd, 1972. Chm., Central Housing Authority, 1986–88. Mem., Ex-servicemen's Assoc., 1977; Pres., Widows and Orphans Pension Fund, 1978; Vice-Chm., Lions Club of Curepipe, 1985; Vice-Chm., Centre Culturel d'Expressions Française (Founder Mem., 1960). Pres., Soc. of St Vincent de Paul. Testimonial, Royal Humane Soc. for life saving, 1962; Chevalier de l'Ordre National du Mérite (France), 1980. *Adddress:* Queen Mary Avenue, Floreal, Mauritius. *T:* (office) 6/3532, (residence) 86/5240. *Club:* Mauritius Racing.

SIMONS, (Alfred) Murray, CMG 1983; HM Diplomatic Service, retired; Head of UK Delegation to Negotiations on Mutual Reduction of Armed Forces and Armaments and Associated Measures in Central Europe, at Vienna, 1982–85, with personal rank of Ambassador; *b* 9 Aug. 1927; *s* of late Louis Simons and of Fay Simons; *m* 1975, Patricia Jill, *d* of late David and May Barclay, Westbury on Trym, Bristol; two *s*. *Educ:* City of London Sch.; Magdalen Coll., Oxford (MA). FO, 1951; 3rd Sec., Moscow, 1952–55; FO, 1955–56; Columbia Univ., 1956; 2nd Sec., Bogota, 1957; 1st Sec., Office of Comr-Gen. for SE Asia, Singapore, 1958–61; FO, 1961–64; 1st Sec., British High Commn, New Delhi, 1964–68; FCO, 1968–71; Counsellor, 1969; British Embassy, Washington, 1971–75; Head of SE Asia Dept, FCO, 1975–79; Consul General, Montreal, 1980–82. Mem., International Institute of Strategic Studies. Freeman, City of London, 1990. *Recreations:* tennis, theatre. *Address:* 128 Longland Drive, Totteridge, N20 8HL. *T:* 081–445 0896.

SIMONS, Prof. John Philip, PhD, ScD; FRS 1989; CChem, FRSC; Professor of Physical Chemistry, University of Nottingham, since 1981; *b* 20 April 1934; *s* of Mark Isaac Simons and Rose (*née* Pepper); *m* 1956, Althea Mary (*née* Screaton) (*d* 1989); three *s*. *Educ:* Haberdashers' Aske's Hampstead Sch.; Sidney Sussex Coll., Cambridge (BA; PhD 1958; ScD 1975). CChem, FRSC 1975. Chemistry Department, University of Birmingham: ICI Fellow, 1959; Lectr, 1961; Reader in Photochemistry, 1977; Prof. of Photochem., 1979. Royal Society of Chemistry: Vice Pres., and Hon. Sec., Faraday Div., 1981–; Tilden Lectr, 1983. Member: Chemistry Cttee, 1983–85, Laser Facility Cttee, 1983–87, SERC; Comité de Direction, CNRS Lab. de Photophysique Moleculaire, Orsay, 1985–90; specially promoted scientific programme panel, NATO, 1985–88. Member Editorial Boards: Jl of Photochemistry, 1972–; Molecular Physics, 1980–; Chemical Physics Letters, 1982–; Jl Chem. Soc. Faraday Trans, 1990–. *Publications:* Photochemistry and Spectroscopy, 1970; research papers in learned jls of molecular/chemical physics, *eg* Jl Chem. Soc. Faraday Trans, Molecular Physics, and Chem. Phys. Lett. *Recreations:* writing and reading verse. *Address:* Chemistry Department, The University, Nottingham NG7 2RD. *T:* Nottingham (0602) 484848.

SIMPLE, Peter; *see* Wharton, Michael B.

SIMPSON, Alan, MA, DPhil Oxon, LHD, LLD; President and Professor of History, Vassar College, Poughkeepsie, NY, 1964–77; *b* Gateshead, Durham, England, 23 July 1912; *s* of George Hardwick Simpson and Isabella Simpson (*née* Graham); *m* 1938, Mary McQueen McEldowney, Chicago Heights, Ill; one *s* two *d*. *Educ:* Worcester Coll., Oxford (BA); Merton Coll., Oxford (MA, DPhil); Harvard Univ. (Commonwealth Fellow). Served War of 1939–45, RA, Major. Sen. Lectr in Modern British History and American History, Univ. of St Andrews, and Lectr in Constitutional Law, Law Sch., University Coll., Dundee, 1938–46; Asst Prof. of History, Univ. of Chicago, 1946–54; Associate Prof., 1954–59; Thomas E. Donnelley Prof. of History and Dean of the College, Univ. of Chicago, 1959–64. Member Board of Trustees: Colonial Williamsburg; Salve Regina Coll., Newport; Old Dartmouth Hist. Soc.; Mem., Amer. Antiquarian Soc.; Former Member: Council of the Inst. of Early Amer. History and Culture, Williamsburg, Va, 1957–60; Midwest Conf. of British Historians (Co-Founder, 1954; Sec., 1954–61); Commn on Academic Affairs and Bd of Dirs, Amer. Council on Educn; Commn on Liberal Learning, Assoc. of Amer. Colls; Hudson River Valley Commn. *Publications:* (Co-Editor) The People Shall Judge: Readings in the Formation of American Policy, 1949; Puritanism in Old and New England, 1955; The Wealth of the Gentry, 1540–1660: East Anglian Studies, 1961; (co-ed with Mary Simpson): Diary of King Philip's War by Benjamin Church, 1975; (with Mary Simpson) I Too Am Here: selections from the letters of Jane Welsh Carlyle, 1977; (with Mary Simpson) Jean Webster, Storyteller, 1984; The Mysteries of the "Frenchman's Map" of Williamsburg, Virginia, 1984. *Address:* Yellow Gate Farm, Little Compton, RI 02837, USA. *Club:* Century (New York).

SIMPSON, Alan; author and scriptwriter since 1951 (in collaboration with Ray Galton, *qv*); *b* 27 Nov. 1929; *s* of Francis and Lilian Simpson; *m* 1958, Kathleen Phillips (*d* 1978). *Educ:* Mitcham Grammar Sch. *Television:* Hancock's Half Hour, 1954–61 (adaptation and trans., Fleksnes, Scandinavian TV, film and stage); Comedy Playhouse, 1962–63; Steptoe and Son, 1962–74 (US TV Version, Sanford and Son, Dutch TV, Stiefbeen And Zoon, Scandinavian TV, Albert Och Herbert); Galton-Simpson Comedy, 1969; Clochemerle, 1971; Casanova '74, 1974; Dawson's Weekly, 1975; The Galton and Simpson Playhouse, 1976–77; *films:* The Rebel, 1960; The Bargee, 1963; The Wrong Arm of the Law, 1963; The Spy with a Cold Nose, 1966; Loot, 1969; Steptoe and Son, 1971; Steptoe and Son Ride Again, 1973; Den Siste Fleksnes (Scandinavia), 1974; Skraphandlarne (Scandinavia), 1975; *theatre:* Way Out in Piccadilly, 1966; The Wind in the Sassafras Trees, 1968; Albert och Herbert (Sweden), 1981; Fleksnes (Norway), 1983; Mordet pa Skölgatan 15 (Sweden), 1984. Awards: Scriptwriters of the Year, 1959 (Guild of TV Producers and Directors); Best TV Comedy Series (Steptoe and Son, 1962, 1963, 1964, 1965 (Screenwriters Guild)); John Logie Baird Award (for outstanding contribution to Television), 1964; Best Comedy Series (Stiefbeen And Zoon, Dutch TV), 1966; Best Comedy Screenplay (Steptoe and Son, Screenwriters Guild), 1972. *Publications:* (jointly with Ray Galton, *qv*): Hancock, 1961; Steptoe and Son, 1963; The Reunion and Other Plays, 1966; Hancock Scripts, 1974; The Best of Hancock, 1986. *Recreations:* Hampton FC (Pres.), gourmet travelling, guest speaking. *Address:* c/o Tessa Le Bars Management, 18 Queen Anne Street, W1M 9LB. *T:* 071–636 3191.

SIMPSON, Alan; His Honour Judge Simpson; a Circuit Judge, since 1985; *b* 17 April 1937; *s* of William Henry Simpson and Gladys Simpson; *m* 1965, Maureen O'Shea; one *s* one *d*. *Educ:* Leeds Grammar Sch.; Corpus Christi Coll., Oxford (MA). Called to the Bar, Inner Temple, 1962; a Recorder, 1975–85. Prosecuting Counsel to DHSS, North Eastern Circuit, 1977–85. *Recreations:* music, books, sport (especially cricket and boxing). *Address:* c/o Sheffield Crown Court, Castle Street, Sheffield S1 1QN. *T:* Sheffield (0742) 737511.

SIMPSON, Sir Alfred (Henry), Kt 1985; Chief Justice of Kenya, 1982–85; *b* 29 Oct. 1914; *s* of John Robertson Simpson, Dundee; *m* 1941, Hilda Corson Rodgers; one *d*. *Educ:* Grove Academy; St Andrews University; Edinburgh University. MA St Andrews, 1935; LLB Edinburgh, 1938 and Solicitor. Served in RASC, 1940–46, Middle East and Italy; Military Mission to the Italian Army and Allied Commission, Austria. Legal Officer, BMA, Cyrenaica, 1946–48. Member of the Faculty of Advocates, 1952. Crown Counsel, Singapore, 1948–56; Legal Draftsman, Gold Coast, 1956; Solicitor-General, Ghana, 1957, then Puisne Judge, Supreme Court, 1957–61; Puisne Judge, Combined Judiciary of Sarawak, North Borneo and Brunei, 1962; Senior Puisne Judge, Fedn of Malaysia High Court in Borneo, 1964; Reader, Faculty of Law, ANU, Canberra, 1965; Barrister-at-Law, NSW, 1967; Puisne Judge, High Court of Kenya, 1967–82. *Publication:* (with others) The Laws of Singapore, revised edn, 1955. *Recreation:* golf. *Address:* 23 Downes Place, Hughes, ACT 2605, Australia. *Clubs:* Commonwealth Trust; Royal Canberra Golf.

SIMPSON, Alfred Moxon, AC 1978; CMG 1959; Chairman, SA Telecasters Ltd, since 1964 (Director since 1962); *b* 17 Nov. 1910; *s* of late A. A. Simpson, CMG, CBE; *m* 1938, Elizabeth Robson Cleland; one *s*. *Educ:* St Peter's College; University of Adelaide, (BSc). Associate (Commerce) of Univ. of Adelaide, 1940. Chm., Simpson Holdings Ltd, 1939–83. Pres. Adelaide Chamber of Commerce, 1950–52; Sen. Vice-Pres. Associated Chambers of Commerce of Aust., 1953–55; Pres. SA Chamber of Manufrs, 1956–58; Pres. Associated Chambers of Manufrs of Aust., 1957–58. Director: Bank of Adelaide, 1952–79; Elder Smith Goldsbrough Mort Ltd, 1954–81; Adelaide Steamship Co. Ltd, 1960–83; QBE Insurance Group Ltd, 1975–83 (Local Dir, 1935). Mem. Hulme Cttee on Rates of Depreciation, 1956; Report on employment security of overseas officers in Papua-New Guinea, 1972, adopted by govt, 1973. Mem. Council, Flinders Univ., 1965–76. *Recreations:* carpentry, lawnmowing. *Address:* 31 Heatherbank Terrace, Stonyfell, SA 5066, Australia. *T:* 31 12 85. *Clubs:* Adelaide, Mt Lofty Ski (Adelaide).

SIMPSON, Prof. (Alfred William) Brian, DCL; FBA 1983; JP; Charles F. and Edith J. Clyne Professor of Law, University of Michigan, since 1987; Professor of Law, University of Kent, 1973–85, now Emeritus; *b* 17 Aug. 1931; *s* of Rev. Canon Bernard W. Simpson and Mary E. Simpson; *m* 1st, 1954, Kathleen Anne Seston (marr. diss. 1968); one *s* one *d*; 2nd, 1969, Caroline Elizabeth Ann Brown; one *s* two *d*. *Educ:* Oakham Sch., Rutland; The Queen's Coll., Oxford (MA 1958, DCL 1976). Nat. Service with RWAFF, 1950–51. Junior Research Fellow, St Edmund Hall, Oxford, 1954–55; Fellow and Tutor, Lincoln Coll., Oxford, 1955–73; Dean: Faculty of Law, Univ. of Ghana, 1968–69; Faculty of Social Sciences, Univ. of Kent, 1975–78; Prof. of Law, Univ. of Chicago, 1984–86. Visiting Professor: Dalhousie Univ., 1964; Univ. of Chicago, 1979, 1980, 1982, 1984; Univ. of Michigan, 1985; Hon. Dep. District Attorney, Denver City, 1982. Member, Deptl Cttee on Obscenity and Film Censorship, 1977–79. JP Canterbury and St Augustine's, 1968–. *Publications:* Introduction to the History of the Land Law, 1961, new edn as A History of the Land Law, 1986; (ed) Oxford Essays in Jurisprudence, 2nd Series, 1973; A History of the Common Law of Contract, 1975; Pornography and Politics, 1983; Cannibalism and the Common Law, 1984; (ed) A Biographical Dictionary of the Common Law, 1984; Legal Theory and Legal History: essays on the common law, 1987; Invitation to Law, 1988; articles in legal jls. *Recreations:* sailing, flying. *Address:* University of Michigan Law School, Hutchins Hall, Ann Arbor, Michigan 48109–1215, USA. *T:* 313–763–0413; 36 High Street, Wingham, Canterbury, Kent CT3 1AB. *T:* Canterbury (0227) 720979.

SIMPSON, Anthony Maurice Herbert, TD 1973; Member (C) Northamptonshire, European Parliament, since 1979; *b* 28 Oct. 1935; *y s* of late Lt-Col Maurice Rowton Simpson, OBE, TD, DL and Mrs Renée Claire Simpson; *m* 1961, Penelope Gillian, *d* of late Howard Dixon Spackman; one *s* two *d*. *Educ:* Rugby; Magdalene College, Cambridge. BA 1959, LLM (LLB 1961), MA 1963. Leics and Derbys (PAO) Yeomanry, 1956–59; TA 1956–74, Major 1968. Called to Bar, Inner Temple, 1961; practised Midland and Oxford Circuit, 1961–75; Mem., Legal Service of European Commn, Brussels, 1975–79; Quaestor of the European Parlt, 1979–87, and 1989–; EDG spokesman on develt and co-operation, 1987–89. Contested (C) West Leicester, Feb. and Oct. 1974. Common Market Law Editor, Current Law, 1965–72. *Recreations:* walking, travelling. *Address:* Bassets, Great Glen, Leicestershire LE8 0GQ. *T:* Great Glen (053759) 2386; Avenue Michel-Ange 57, 1040 Brussels, Belgium. *T:* (02) 736–4219.

SIMPSON, Athol John Dundas, OBE 1976; Director of North American Operations, Crown Agents for Oversea Governments and Administrations, since 1985; *b* 4 May 1932; *s* of John Simpson and Helen Murray Simpson (*née* Cubie); *m* 1956, Ricki Ellen Carter; one *s* two *d*. *Educ:* Reigate Grammar Sch. Joined Crown Agents, 1950; served, Royal Air Force, 1951–53; Crown Agents' Representative in E Africa, 1965–69; seconded as Managing Director, Millbank Technical Services (Iran) Ltd, 1973–77; returned to Bd appt as Dir of Marketing and Development with Crown Agents, Nov. 1977; Dir, Crown Agents, 1978–85. *Recreations:* Rugby football, golf, reading. *Address:* 44F Whistlers Avenue, Morgans Walk, SW11. *T:* 071–223 3976. *Clubs:* Travellers'; International (Washington, DC).

SIMPSON, Prof. Brian; *see* Simpson, Prof. A. W. B.

SIMPSON, Brian; Member (Lab) Cheshire East, European Parliament, since 1989; *b* Leigh, Lancs, 6 Feb. 1953; *s* of John Hartley Simpson and Freda Simpson; *m* 1975, Linda Jane Gwynn; one *s* two *d*. *Educ:* Golborne Comprehensive Sch., Wigan; W Midlands Coll. of Educn, Walsall (Cert Ed). Teacher, City of Liverpool, 1974–89. Councillor: Merseyside CC, 1981–85; Warrington Bor. Council, 1987–91. *Recreations:* Rugby League, cricket, most sports, steam railways. *Address:* Gilbert Wakefield House, 67 Bewsey Street, Warrington WA2 7JQ. *T:* Warrington (0925) 54074. *Clubs:* Golborne Sports and Social (Wigan); Penketh Sports and Social (Warrington).

SIMPSON, Air Vice-Marshal Charles Ednam; Director (Scotland), Royal Air Force Benevolent Fund, since 1989; *b* 24 Sept. 1929; *s* of Charles and Margaret Simpson; *m* 1955, Margaret Riddell; two *s* one *d*. *Educ:* Stirling and Falkirk High Schools; Univ. of Glasgow (MB ChB); University of London (MSc). FFOM 1986; MFCM. British Defence Staff, Washington DC, 1975; Dep. Dir, Aviation Medicine, RAF, 1978; CO, RAF Hosp., Wegberg, 1981; CO, Princess Alexandra Hosp., Wroughton, 1982; Dir of Health and Research, RAF, 1984; Asst Surgeon General (Envtl Medicine and Res.), 1985; PMO HQ RAF Strike Comd, 1986–89; QHS 1985–89. *Recreations:* golf, birdwatching. *Address:* Am Bruach, Fore Road, Kippen, Stirling FK8 3DT. *T:* Kippen (078687) 281. *Club:* Royal Air Force.

SIMPSON, Commander Cortlandt James Woore, CBE 1956; DSC 1945; retired 1961; *b* 2 Sept. 1911; *s* of late Rear-Admiral C. H. Simpson, CBE, and, Edith Octavia (*née* Busby); *m* 1st, Lettice Mary Johnstone; 2nd, Ann Margaret Cubitt (*née* Tooth); 3rd, Joan Mary Watson; one *d*; 4th, Vanessa Ann Stainton (*née* Heald). *Educ:* St Ronans, Worthing; RN College, Dartmouth; London Univ. (BSc Engineering, Hons). Joined RN (Dartmouth), 1925; Lieut, 1934. Served War of 1939–45 in Home and Mediterranean Fleets; Commander, 1948. Summer expeditions to Greenland, 1950, 1951; Leader of British North Greenland Expedition, 1952–54. Polar Medal, 1954; Royal Geographical Society, Founder's Medal, 1955. *Publication:* North Ice, 1957. *Recreations:* mountaineering, sailing, walking. *Address:* Lower Lambie, Luxborough, Watchet, Somerset. *Club:* Alpine.

SIMPSON, David Rae Fisher; Economist, Standard Life Assurance Co., since 1988; *b* 29 Nov. 1936; *s* of late David Ebenezer Simpson and of Roberta Muriel Wilson; *m* 1980, Barbara Dianne Goalen, *d* of N. and Mrs G. Inglis, Edinburgh; one *s* (and one step *s* one step *d*). *Educ:* Skerry's Coll.; Edinburgh and Harvard Univs. MA 1st cl. hons Econs Edinburgh; PhD Econs Harvard. Instr in Econs, Harvard Univ., 1963–64; Assoc. Statistician, UN Hdqtrs, NY, 1964–65; Res. Officer, Econ. Res. Inst., Dublin, 1965–67; Lectr in Polit. Economy, UCL, 1967–69; Sen. Lectr in Econs, Univ. of Stirling, 1969–74; University of Strathclyde: Prof. and Dir, Fraser of Allander Inst., 1975–80, Res. Prof., 1980–85; Prof., Dept of Economics, 1985–88. Contested (SNP) Berwick and E Lothian Division, 1970 and Feb. 1974. *Publications:* Problems of Input-Output Tables and Analysis, 1966; General Equilibrium Analysis, 1975; The Political Economy of Growth, 1983; The Challenge of New Technology, 1987; articles in Econometrica, Rev. Econs and Statistics, Scientific American. *Recreations:* swimming, reading. *Address:* 11 Kingsburgh Road, Edinburgh EH12 6DZ.

SIMPSON, David Richard Salisbury, OBE 1989; Founder and Director, International Agency on Tobacco and Health, since 1991; *b* 1 Oct. 1945; *s* of Richard Salisbury Simpson and Joan Margaret Simpson (*née* Braund). *Educ:* Merchiston Castle School, Edinburgh. ACA 1969; FCA 1979 (but resigned from Institute, 1981). Teacher at Cadet College, Hasan Abdal, West Pakistan, 1963–64 (VSO). Peat, Marwick, Mitchell & Co., Chartered Accountants, 1964–72; Scottish Director, Shelter, Campaign for the Homeless, 1972–74; Director: Amnesty International (British Section), 1974–79; ASH, 1979–90. Sundry journalism, broadcasting and public lectures. Consultant, Internat. Union Against Cancer Special Project on Smoking and Cancer (responsibility for Indian Sub-Continent), 1980–. Trustee, The Consort of Musicke. Hon. MFPHM 1991. *Publications:* contribs to national newspapers and magazines. *Recreations:* friends, reading, music, hill-walking, Orkney. *Address:* c/o ASH, 5–11 Mortimer Street, W1N 7RH. *T:* 071–637 9843.

SIMPSON, Lt-Col (Retd) David Sackville Bruce, CBE 1990; Chief Executive, Civil Service Catering Organisation, 1981–89, retired; *b* 18 March 1930; *s* of Henry and Violet Simpson; *m* 1956, Margaret Elizabeth Goslin; two *s* three *d*. *Educ:* Brockley Grammar Sch.; Westminster Technical Coll. FHCIMA. Regular Officer, Army Catering Corps (retd in rank of Lt-Col), 1950–75; Principal Education Catering Organiser, Inner London Education Authority, 1975–81. *Recreations:* golf, squash. *Address:* 65 Gally Hill Road, Church Crookham, Hants. *T:* Fleet (0252) 613754.

SIMPSON, Dennis Charles; business consultant and lecturer; Managing Director, Axtel (UK) Ltd, 1986–88; *b* 24 Oct. 1931; *s* of late Arthur and Helen Simpson; *m* 1st, 1964, Margery Bruce Anderson (marr. diss.); three *s* one *d*; 2nd, 1983, Susan Gaynor Conway-Williams. *Educ:* Manchester Univ. (BA). FInstPS. 2nd Lieut Royal Signals, 1952–54; commercial appts, Philips Electrical Industries, 1956–63; Group Purchasing Manager, STC Ltd, 1963–66; Gp Purchasing Controller, Rank Organisation, 1966–69; Gen. Man., Cam Gears (S Wales) Ltd, 1969–72; Industrial Dir for Wales, Dept of Industry, 1972–75; Industrial Dir for Wales, Welsh Office, 1975–76; Business Agent, Welsh Develt Agency, 1983–85. Chairman: Spencer Harris Ltd, 1976–81; Grainger Hydraulics Ltd, 1976–81; Wellfield Engineering, 1976–81; Director: Beechwood Holdings, 1976–81; Gower Technology Ltd, 1983–87; Video Interactive Systems Ltd, 1983–87; Gower Alarms Ltd, 1985–87; Video Interactive Teaching Aids Ltd, 1985–87. *Recreations:* golf, bridge, reading war histories.

SIMPSON, Edward Hugh, CB 1976; FSS 1947; Deputy Secretary, Department of Education and Science, 1973–82, retired; *b* 10 Dec. 1922; *o s* of Hugh and Mary Simpson, of Brookfield, Ballymena, Co. Antrim; *m* 1947, Gladys Rebecca, *er d* of Sam and Elizabeth Gibson, Ernevale, Kesh, Co. Fermanagh; one *s* one *d*. *Educ:* Coleraine Academical Institution; Queen's Univ., Belfast (BSc (1st cl. Hons Mathematics), 1942); Mathematical Statistics res., Christ's Coll., Cambridge (Scholar), 1945–47. Foreign Office, Bletchley Park, 1942–45; Min. of Education, 1947–50 and 1952–56; HM Treasury, 1950–52; Commonwealth Fund Fellow, USA, 1956–57; Private Sec. to Lord President of Council and Lord Privy Seal, 1957–60; Dep. Dir, Commonwealth Educn Liaison Unit, 1960–62; Sec., Commonwealth Educn Conf., New Delhi, 1962; Asst Sec., DES, 1962–68; Under-Sec., Civil Service Dept, 1968–71, DES, 1971–73. Sen. Hon. Res. Fellow, Birmingham Univ., 1983–. Chairman: Nat. Assessment Panel, Schools Curriculum Award, 1983–; Educn Grants Adv. Service, 1987–; Governor and Chairman: Professional Cttee, Bishop Grosseteste Coll., Lincoln, 1984–; Acad. Affairs Cttee, Regent's Coll., London, 1986–; Trustee, Educn 2000, 1987–. Consultant: Educn Management Information Exchange, 1986–; Dixons plc, 1987–. *Publications:* articles in statistical and educn journals. *Address:* 40 Frays Avenue, West Drayton, Mddx UB7 7AG. *T:* West Drayton (0895) 443417. *Club:* Athenæum.

SIMPSON, Esther Eleanor, MD, FRCP, FFCM, DPH, DCH; former Senior Principal Medical Officer, Department of Education and Science, and Department of Health and Social Security, retired 1979; *b* 28 May 1919. *Educ:* Kendal High Sch.; London Univ. Medical Officer, London County Council, then to Province of Natal Centre, Inst. of Child Health; joined Medical Br., Min. of Education, 1961. *Recreations:* music, reading, walking. *Address:* 19 Belsize Lane, NW3 5AG. *T:* 071–794 5623.

SIMPSON, Ffreebairn Liddon, CMG 1967; General Manager, Central Water Authority, Mauritius, 1976–78; *b* 11 July 1916; *s* of late James Liddon Simpson and Dorothy (*née* Blyth); *m* 1947, Dorina Laura Magda, MBE (*née* Ilieva) (*d* 1991); one *s*. *Educ:* Westminster School; Trinity College, Cambridge. HM Diplomatic/Foreign Service, 1939–48; HM Treasury, 1948–50; Administrative Officer, Gold Coast, 1950–55; Dep. Colonial Sec., Mauritius, 1955; Perm. Secretary: Min. of Works and Internal Communications, 1961; Premier's Office, 1966; Sec. to the Cabinet, Mauritius, 1967–76. *Recreations:* reading, philately. *Club:* United Oxford & Cambridge University.

SIMPSON, George, FCCA; FIMI; Managing Director, Rover Group PLC, since 1989; Director, British Aerospace, since 1990; *b* 2 July 1942; *s* of William Simpson and Elizabeth Simpson; *m* 1964, Eva Chalmers; one *s* one *d*. *Educ:* Morgan Acad., Dundee; Dundee Inst. of Technology. ACIS. Sen. Accountant, Gas Industry, Scotland, 1962–69; Central Audit Man., BLMC, 1969–73; Financial Controller, Leyland Truck and Bus Div., 1973–76; Dir of Accounting, Leyland Cars, 1976–78; Finance and Systems Dir, Leyland Trucks, 1978–80; Managing Director: Coventry Climax Ltd, 1980–83; Freight Rover Ltd, 1983–86 ; Chief Exec. Officer, Leyland DAF, 1986–88. Mem., Exec. Cttee, and Council,

SMMT, 1986–. *Recreations:* golf, squash and Rugby (now spectating). *Address:* Rover Group PLC, Fletchamstead Highway, Coventry CV4 9DB. *T:* Coventry (0203) 675511. *Clubs:* Royal Birkdale Golf; Leamington and County golf; Kenilworth RFC; Warwick Boat (Squash).

SIMPSON, Gordon Russell, DSO 1944 and Bar 1945; LVO 1979; TD; DL; stockbroker; Partner, Bell, Cowan & Co. (now Bell, Lawrie, White & Co. Ltd), 1938–82; *b* 2 Jan. 1917; *s* of A. Russell Simpson, WS; *m* 1943, Marion Elizabeth King (*d* 1976); two *s*. *Educ:* Rugby School. Served with 2nd Lothians and Border Horse, 1939–46 (comd 1944–46). Chm., Edinburgh Stock Exchange, 1961–63; Chm., Scottish Stock Exchange, 1965–66; Pres., Council of Associated Stock Exchanges, 1971–73; Dep. Chm., Stock Exchange, 1973–78. Chm., General Accident Fire & Life Assurance Corporation Ltd, 1979–87 (Dir, 1967–87). Brigadier, Queen's Body Guard for Scotland (Royal Company of Archers). Mem. Court, Stirling Univ., 1980–88; Comr, Queen Victoria Sch., 1982–. DL Stirling and Falkirk Dists (Central Region), 1981. *Recreations:* music, ski-ing, archery. *Address:* c/o Bell, Lawrie, White & Co. Ltd, Erskine House, 7 Drumsheugh Gardens, Edinburgh EH3 7QH. *Club:* New (Edinburgh).

SIMPSON, Ian; artist and writer; Consultant, The Open College of the Arts, since 1988; *b* 12 Nov. 1933; *s* of Herbert William and Elsie Simpson; *m* 1st, 1958, Joan (*née* Charlton) (marr. diss. 1982); two *s* one *d*; 2nd, 1982, Birgitta Willcocks (*née* Brädde). *Educ:* Bede Grammar Sch., Sunderland; Sunderland Coll. of Art; Royal Coll. of Art. ARCA 1958. Freelance artist and illustrator, 1958–63; Hornsey Coll. of Art: Lectr, 1963–66; Head, Dept of Visual Research, 1966–69; Head, Dept of Co-ordinated Studies, 1969–72; Principal, 1972–86, Head, 1986–88, St Martin's Sch. of Art; Asst Rector, London Inst., 1986–88. Exhibited various exhibns, Britain, USA, etc; one-man exhibn, Cambridge, 1975, Durham, 1977, Blandford, 1985. Mem. Council, CNAA, 1974–80 (Chm., Fine Art Bd, 1976–81). Pres., Nat. Soc. for Art Educn, 1976. Consultant, Leisure Study Group Ltd, 1986–87. FSAE 1976; FRSA 1983. *Publications:* Eyeline, 1968; Drawing: seeing and observation, 1973; Picture Making, 1973; Guide to Painting and Composition, 1979; Painters Progress, 1983; Encyclopedia of Drawing Techniques, 1987; The Challenge of Landscape Painting, 1990. *Television Programmes:* Eyeline (10 programmes), 1968, 1969; Picture Making (10 programmes), 1973, 1976; Reading the Signs (5 programmes), 1977–78. *Recreations:* reading, music. *Address:* Motts Farm House, Chilton Street, Clare, Sudbury, Suffolk CO10 8QS.

SIMPSON, Ian Christopher; Sheriff of South Strathclyde, Dumfries and Galloway at Airdrie, since 1991 (Floating Sheriff, 1988–91); *b* 5 July 1949; *s* of David F. Simpson and J. O. S. Simpson (M. S. Dickie); *m* 1973, Anne Strang; two *s*. *Educ:* Glenalmond; Edinburgh Univ. (LLB). Admitted Faculty of Advocates, 1974. *Recreations:* golf, dog-walking. *Address:* 30 Cluny Drive, Edinburgh EH10 6DP. *T:* 031–447 3363. *Clubs:* Royal and Ancient (St Andrews); Dunbar Golf.

SIMPSON, Sir James (Joseph Trevor), KBE 1965 (CBE 1957); (forename James added by deed poll, 1965); Chairman, James Simpson & Co. Ltd; retired as Chairman, Uganda Development Corporation, Ltd (1952–64); *b* 9 Jan. 1908; reverted to British nationality, 1988, after Uganda citizenship, 1962–88; 2nd *s* of late Lieut-Colonel Herbert Simpson, OBE, MC, and of Mrs Henrietta Augusta Simpson; *m* 1940, Enid Florence (*née* Danzelman) (*d* 1979). *Educ:* Ardingly College, Sussex. Branch Manager, Vacuum Oil Co., Nakuru, Nairobi, Dar es Salaam, Mombasa, Kampala, 1932–46; General Manager, The Uganda Company Ltd, 1947–52; President, Uganda Chamber of Commerce, 1941, 1946–50. Member: Uganda Executive Council, 1952–55; Uganda Legislative Council, 1950–58 (Chm. Representative Members Organization 1951–58); E African Legislative Assembly, 1957–60, 1962–63; E African Railways and Harbours, Transport Advisory Council, 1948–61; E African Industrial Council, 1947–61; Uganda Electricity Bd, 1955–60; East African Airways Corporation, 1958–73; Minister of Economic Affairs, Uganda, 1962–63. *Recreation:* bridge. *Address:* PO Box 48816, Nairobi, Kenya. *Club:* Muthaiga (Kenya).

SIMPSON, John Andrew; Co-editor, Oxford English Dictionary, since 1986; *b* 13 Oct. 1953; *s* of Robert Morris Simpson and Joan Margaret (*née* Sersale); *m* 1976, Hilary Croxford; two *d*. *Educ:* Dean Close Sch., Cheltenham; Univ. of York (BA Hons English Literature); Univ. of Reading (MA Medieval Studies). Editorial Asst, Supplement to OED, 1976–79; Editor, Concise Oxford Dictionary of Proverbs, 1979–81; Sen. Editor, Supplement to OED, 1981–84; Editor (New Words), OED, 1984–86. Editl Consultant, Australian National Dictionary, 1986–88. Vis. Asst Prof., Dept of English, Univ. of Waterloo, Ont, Canada, 1985. *Publications:* (ed) Concise Oxford Dictionary of Proverbs, 1982; (contrib.) Oxford English, 1986; (contrib.) Words, 1989; (ed with E. S. C. Weiner) Oxford English Dictionary, 2nd edn 1989; (contrib.) Wörterbücher: ein internationales Handbuch zur Lexikographie, 1990; articles in Medium Aevum, English Today, and other lexicographical and linguistic periodicals. *Recreations:* cricket, computing. Address: 36 Kennett Road, Headington, Oxford OX3 7BJ. *T:* Oxford (0865) 68053.

SIMPSON, Very Rev. John Arthur; Dean of Canterbury, since 1986; *b* 7 June 1933; *s* of Arthur Simpson and Mary Esther Simpson; *m* 1968, Ruth Marian (*née* Dibbens); one *s* two *d*. *Educ:* Cathays High School, Cardiff; Keble Coll., Oxford (BA, 2nd cl. Mod. History 1956, MA 1960); Clifton Theological Coll. Deacon 1958, priest 1959; Curate: Leyton, 1958–59; Christ Church, Orpington, 1959–62; Tutor, Oak Hill Coll., Southgate N14, 1962–72; Vicar of Ridge, Herts, 1972–79; Director of Ordinands and Post-Ordination Training, Diocese of St Albans, 1975–81; Hon. Canon of St Albans Cathedral, 1977–79; Residentiary Canon, St Albans, and Priest-in-charge of Ridge, 1979–81; Archdeacon of Canterbury and Canon Res. of Canterbury Cathedral, 1981–86. Director: Ecclesiastical Insurance Group (formerly Ecclesiastical Insurance Office), 1983–; Merlin Internat. Green Investment Trust, 1989–. Chm. Govs, King's Sch., Canterbury, 1986–. *Recreations:* travel, theatre, opera. *Address:* The Deanery, Canterbury, Kent CT1 2EP. *T:* Canterbury (0227) 765983. *Club:* Athenæum.

SIMPSON, John (Cody Fidler-), CBE 1991; Foreign Affairs Editor, BBC-TV, since 1988; *b* 9 Aug. 1944; *s* of Roy Simpson Fidler-Simpson and Joyce Leila Vivienne Cody; *m* 1965, Diane Jean Petteys (separated), El Cajon, California; two *d*; lives with Tira Shubart. *Educ:* St Paul's School; Magdalene Coll., Cambridge (MA). Reporter, BBC Radio News, 1970; BBC correspondent, Dublin, 1972; Common Market correspondent (based in Brussels), 1975; Southern Africa correspondent (based in Johannesburg), 1977; Diplomatic correspondent, BBC Television News, 1978; BBC Political Editor, 1980; Presenter and Correspondent, BBC-TV News, 1981; Diplomatic Editor, BBC-TV, 1982–88. Contributing Editor, The Spectator, 1991. *Publications:* (ed jtly) The Best of Granta, 1966; The Disappeared: voices from a secret war, 1985; Behind Iranian Lines, 1988; Despatches from the Barricades, 1990; From the House of War: Baghdad and the Gulf, 1991; *novels:* Moscow Requiem, 1981; A Fine And Private Place, 1983. *Recreations:* collecting obscure books, travelling to obscure places, and returning to Suffolk. *Address:* BBC Television Centre, Wood Lane, W12. *T:* 081–743 8000. *Clubs:* Athenæum, Chelsea Arts.

SIMPSON, John Ernest Peter, FRCS; Regional Medical Officer, Mersey Regional Health Authority, since 1988; *b* 30 Jan. 1942; *s* of John and Alice Bewick Simpson; *m* 1964, Valerie Joan Lamb (marr. diss. 1987); one *s* one *d*. *Educ:* Jesus Coll., Oxford (MA, BM BCh); St Thomas's Hosp. Med. Sch. (Schol.). MFPHM. Surgical training, St Thomas' and Northwich Park Hosps, 1966–78; Lectr, Community Medicine, St Thomas' Hosp., 1974–75; Tutor, King's Fund Coll., 1975–78; Management, Planning Policy and Internat. Divs, DHSS, 1978–88. *Publications:* Going Home (from hospital) (ed jtly), 1981; articles on day case surgery and organisation of surgical and other clinical services. *Recreations:* golf, music. *Address:* 8 Talbot Court, Village Road, Oxton, Merseyside L43 5SR. *T:* 051–652 0005. *Clubs:* Hurlingham, Royal Society of Medicine.

SIMPSON, John Ferguson, FRCS; Consulting Surgeon to Ear, Nose and Throat Department, St Mary's Hospital, retired; formerly Civil Consultant, Ministry of Aviation; *b* 10 Oct. 1902; *s* of late Col P. J. Simpson, DSO, FRCVS, Maidenhead; *m* 1947, Winifred Beatrice Rood; one *s* one *d*. *Educ:* Reading Sch.; St Mary's Hosp. FRCS 1929; MRCS, LRCP 1926. Formerly: Lectr in Diseases of the Ear, Nose and Throat, Univ. of London; Specialist in Otorhino-laryngology, RAF; Hon. Surg. Royal Nat. Throat, Nose and Ear Hosp. FRSocMed (ex-President Section of Otology); Hon. Life Mem., Section of Laryngology); Hon. Life Mem., British Assoc. of Otolaryngologists. Liveryman, Farriers' Co. Sir W. Dalby Meml Prize in Otology (jtly), RSM, 1948. *Publications:* A Synopsis of Otorhinolaryngology (jointly), 1957; chapters: Operative Surgery, 1957; ENT Diseases, 1965. *Recreations:* entomology; formerly Rugby football. *Address:* Waverley Cottage, Upton Grey, Basingstoke, Hants RG25 2RA. *T:* Basingstoke (0256) 862433.

SIMPSON, John Liddle, CMG 1958; TD 1950; QC 1980; *b* 9 Oct. 1912; *s* of late James Simpson; *m* 1st, 1939, Nellie Lavender Mussett (*d* 1944); 2nd, 1959, Ursula Vaughan Washington (*nee* Rigby). *Educ:* George Watson's Coll.; Edinburgh Univ. (MA, DLitt). Barrister, Middle Temple, 1937. Served War of 1939–45; GSO1, 1945. Principal, Control Office for Germany and Austria, 1946; Senior legal assistant, FO (German Section), 1948; transferred to Foreign (now Diplomatic) Service and promoted Counsellor, 1954; Legal Counsellor, FO, 1954–59 and 1961–68; Legal Adviser, United Kingdom Mission to the United Nations, New York, 1959–61; Dep. Legal Adviser, 1968–71, Second Legal Adviser (Dep. Under-Sec. of State), 1971–72, FCO; returned to practice at the Bar, 1973; elected alternate Pres. of Arbitral Tribunals, Internat. Telecommunications Satellite Org., 1974 and 1976. Mem., Dubai/Sharjah Boundary Court of Arbitration, 1978–81; Chm., UNESCO Appeals Bd, 1980–85. Freeman, City of London, 1976. *Publications:* Germany and the North Atlantic Community: A Legal Survey (with M. E. Bathurst), 1956; International Arbitration; Law and Practice (with Hazel Fox), 1959; articles and notes in legal journals. *Address:* 137a Ashley Gardens, Thirleby Road, SW1P 1HN. *T:* 071–834 4814; 5 Paper Buildings, Temple, EC4Y 7HB. *T:* 071–353 8494.

SIMPSON, Keith Taylor; His Honour Judge Keith Simpson; a Circuit Judge, since 1990; *b* 8 May 1934; *m* 1961, Dorothy Preece; two *s* one *d*. *Educ:* privately; Jesus Coll., Oxford (MA). Called to the Bar, Middle Temple, 1958; joined SE Circuit; general Common Law practice. *Recreations:* walking, gardening, tennis, fishing, reading, opera. *Address:* c/o South Eastern Circuit Office, New Cavendish House, 18 Maltravers Street, WC2R 3EU.

SIMPSON, Kenneth John, CMG 1961; HM Diplomatic Service, retired; *b* 5 Feb. 1914; *s* of Bernard and Ann Simpson, Millhouses, Sheffield; *m* 1939, Harriet (Shan) Hughes; three *s*. *Educ:* Downing College, Cambridge. Entered HM Foreign (now Diplomatic) Service, 1937; lastly Consul-Gen., Hanoi and Stuttgart, Inspector, Diplomatic Service and Counsellor, FCO. *Address:* 76 Wood Ride, Petts Wood, Kent BR5 1PY. *T:* Orpington (0689) 824710.

SIMPSON, Malcolm Carter; Director of Finance, Leeds City Council, 1978–82, retired; *b* 15 June 1929; *s* of Arthur and Rhoda Simpson; *m* 1st, 1952, Doreen Patricia Wooler; two *d*; 2nd, 1980, Andrea Gillian Blythe. *Educ:* Stanningley Council Sch. DPA; CIPFA. Employed by Leeds CC for whole of working life, 1943–82: Asst Dir of Finance, 1968; Dep. Dir of Finance, 1973. Board Member: Yorks Water Authority, 1983–88; S Yorks Residuary Body, 1985–89. *Recreations:* golf, bridge. *Address:* Swiss Cottage, 44 Millbeck Green, Collingham Bridge, Leeds LS22 5AJ. *T:* Collingham Bridge (0937) 573917.

SIMPSON, Rear-Adm. Michael Frank, CB 1985; CEng, FIMechE; FRAeS; Managing Director, Field Airmotive Ltd (formerly Field Aircraft Services (Croydon) Ltd), since 1988 (Director and General Manager, 1985–88); Chairman, Somet Ltd, since 1988; *b* 27 Sept. 1928; *s* of Robert Michael Simpson and Florence Mabel Simpson; *m* 1973, Sandra MacDonald (*née* Clift); two *s* one *d*. *Educ:* King Edward VI Sch., Bath; RN Engrg Coll., Manadon. CEng, FIMechE 1983; FRAeS 1983. Joined RN, 1944; qual. as Air Engr Officer, 1956; served in FAA Sqdns, cruisers and carriers; served with US Navy on exchange, 1964–66; Air Engr Officer, HMS Ark Royal, 1970–72; MoD appts, 1972–78; Supt, RN Aircraft Yard, Fleetlands, 1978–80; Cdre, RN Barracks, Portsmouth, 1981–83; Dir Gen. Aircraft (Naval), 1983–85. Chairman: RN/RM Children's Home Management Cttee, 1980–83; RN Athletics Assoc., 1981–83. Mem. Court, Cranfield Inst. of Technology, 1983–86. *Publications:* articles on helicopter engrg in Jl of Naval Engrg; symposium paper on helicopter design, 1975. *Recreations:* sailing, ski-ing, shooting, making things, military history, swimming. *Address:* Keppel, Blackhills, Esher, Surrey KT10 9JW. *Clubs:* Army and Navy; Royal Naval Sailing Association (Captain, Portsmouth Br., 1981–83); Royal Navy Ski.

SIMPSON, Morag; *see* Macdonald, M.

SIMPSON, Oliver, CB 1977; MA, PhD, FInstP; Chief Scientist, Deputy Under-Secretary of State, Home Office, 1974–83; *b* 28 Oct. 1924; *y s* of late Sir George C. Simpson, KCB, FRS, and Dorothy (*née* Stephen); *m* 1946, Joan, *d* of late Walter and Maud Morgan; one *s* (and one *s* decd). *Educ:* Highgate Sch.; Trinity Coll., Cambridge. War Service: Admiralty Research Laboratory, Teddington, on submarine detection, 1944–46. Research Scholar, 1946–49, Fellow of Trinity Coll., Cambridge, 1949–53; Asst Prof. of Physics, Univ. of Michigan, USA, 1949–52; Imperial Chemical Industries Fellow in Dept. of Theoretical Chemistry, Cambridge, 1952–53; joined Services Electronics Research Laboratory, Admty, 1953, Head of Solid State Physics, 1956–63; Supt, Basic Physics Div., Nat. Physical Laboratory, 1964–66; Dep. Dir, Nat. Physical Laboratory, 1966–69; Under-Sec., Cabinet Office, 1969–74. *Publications:* articles in scientific jls on infra-red detectors, semiconductors, fluorescence and standards of measurement. *Address:* 4 Highbury Road, Wimbledon, SW19. *T:* 081–946 3871. *Club:* Athenæum.

SIMPSON, Peter Robert; His Honour Judge P. R. Simpson; a Circuit Judge, since 1989; *b* 9 Feb. 1936; *o s* of late Surg. Capt. (D) Donald Lee Simpson, RN and of Margaret Olive (*née* Lathan). *Educ:* St John's Coll., Southsea, Hants. Admitted Solicitor, 1960; called to the Bar, Inner Temple, 1970, *ad eundem* Lincoln's Inn, 1972. Practised on S Eastern Circuit, then at Chancery Bar, mainly in property and conveyancing matters; a Recorder, 1987–89. *Recreations:* playing chess, reading legal and political biographies, listening to music, dining out. *Address:* 12 New Square, Lincoln's Inn, WC2A 3SW; Erskine House, 1 Old Fold Close, Hadley Green, Barnet, Herts.

SIMPSON, Ven. Rennie, LVO 1974; MA Lambeth 1970; Archdeacon of Macclesfield, 1978–85, Emeritus since 1986; Rector of Gawsworth, 1978–85; Chaplain to the Queen, 1982–90; *b* 13 Jan. 1920; *o s* of late Doctor Taylor Simpson and late May Simpson, Rishton; *m* 1949, Margaret, *er d* of late Herbert Hardy and Olive Hardy, South Kirkby; one *s* one *d*. *Educ:* Blackburn Tech. Coll.; Kelham Theol College. Curate of S Elmsall, Yorks, 1945–49; Succentor of Blackburn Cath., 1949–52; Sacrist and Minor Canon of St Paul's Cath., 1952–58, Hon. Minor Canon, 1958–, Jun. Cardinal, 1954–55, Sen. Cardinal, 1955–58; Vicar of John Keble Church, Mill Hill, 1958–63; Precentor, 1963–74, Acting Sacrist, 1973–74, Westminster Abbey; Canon Residentiary, 1974–78, Vice-Dean, 1975–78, Chester Cathedral. Chaplain, RNVR, 1953–55; Dep. Chaplain, Gt Ormond St Hosp., 1954–58; Asst Chaplain, 1956–64, Officiating Chaplain, 1964–, Sub-Prelate, 1973–, Order of St John of Jerusalem; Deputy Priest to the Queen, 1956–67; Priest-in-Ordinary to the Queen, 1967–74. Life Governor, Imperial Cancer Research Fund, 1963. Liveryman of Waxchandlers' Co. and Freeman of City of London, 1955; Hon. Chaplain, Worshipful Soc. of Apothecaries of London, 1984–85. Jt Hon. Treas., Corp. Sons of the Clergy, 1967–74; Governor: King's School, Chester, 1974–78; King's Sch., Macclesfield, 1979–85. *Recreations:* football, cricket, theatre. *Address:* 18 Roseberry Green, North Stainley, Ripon, N Yorks HG4 3HZ.

SIMPSON, Rt. Hon. Dr Robert, PC (N Ireland) 1970; *b* 3 July 1923; *er s* of Samuel and Agnes Simpson, Craigbilly, Ballymena; *m* 1954, Dorothy Isobel, 2nd *d* of Dr Robert Strawbridge, MA, DD, and Anne Strawbridge; two *s* one *d*. *Educ:* Ballymena Academy; Queen's University, Belfast. MB, BCh, BAO, 1946; Founder Mem., RCGP; LRCPI (Occupational Medicine), 1980. House Surgeon, Belfast City Hosp., 1947; Resident Anaesthetist, Royal Infirmary, Leicester, 1948; GP, Ballymena, Co. Antrim, 1949–; Medical Correspondent: Belfast Telegraph, Irish Times (Dublin), Evening News (Edinburgh) and Leicester Mercury; Medical Representative, NI, Europ Assistance; Medical Officer, Flexibox Ltd, Ballymena, Northern Dairies Ltd. Founder Chm., Ballymena Round Table, 1951. NI Deleg. to CPA Conf. in NZ and Australia, 1965. Minister of Community Relations, N Ireland, 1969–71; MP (U) Mid-Antrim, Parlt of N Ireland, 1953–72. Vice-Pres., Co. Antrim Agricl Assoc., 1960–; Vice-Pres., Ballymena Musical Fest. Assoc. *Publications:* contribs to newspapers and magazines on medical, country and travel subjects. *Recreations:* gardening, trees and the countryside. *Address:* Random Cottage, Craigbilly, Ballymena, Co. Antrim BT42 4HL. *T:* Ballymena (0266) 653105. *Club:* Royal Over-Seas League.

SIMPSON, Robert Watson, (Robin); Under Secretary, and Head, Business Task Force Division I, Department of Trade and Industry, since 1990; *b* 14 June 1940; *s* of Robert Watson Simpson and Susan Gourlay Thomson Simpson (*née* Rolland). *Educ:* Perth Academy; University of St Andrews (BSc Hons). Board of Trade (Patent Office), 1962; Dept of Trade (Aviation), 1973; Dept of Industry (Indust. Develt Unit), 1976; Dept of Trade (Shipping), 1979; DTI (Management Services and Manpower), 1982; NE Regl Dir, DTI, 1986. *Recreations:* history, commemorative pottery, bridge. *Club:* Reform.

SIMPSON, Robert Wilfred Levick, DMus; composer; BBC Music Producer, 1951–80; *b* Leamington, Warwickshire, 2 March 1921; *s* of Robert Warren Simpson (British) and Helena Hendrika Govaars (Dutch); *m* 1946, Bessie Fraser (*d* 1981); *m* 1982, Angela Musgrave. *Educ:* Westminster City Sch.; studied with Herbert Howells. DMus (Dunelm) 1952. Holder of: Carl Nielsen Gold Medal (Denmark), 1956; Medal of Honor of Bruckner Soc. of America, 1962. Mem., British Astronomical Assoc.; FRAS. *Compositions:* Symphonies: No 1, 1951 (recorded); No 2, 1956 (recorded); No 3, 1962 (recorded); No 4, 1972 (recorded); No 5, 1972; Nos 6 and 7, 1977 (recorded); No 8, 1981; No 9, 1986 (recorded); No 10, 1988 (recorded); No 11, 1990; Concertos: Piano, 1967; Flute, 1989; String Quartets: No 1, 1952 (recorded); No 2, 1953 (recorded); No 3, 1954 (recorded); No 4, 1973 (recorded); No 5, 1974 (recorded); No 6, 1975 (recorded); No 7, 1977 (recorded); No 8, 1979 (recorded); No 9, 1982 (recorded); No 10 (For Peace), 1983 (recorded); No 11, 1984 (recorded); No 12, 1987 (recorded); No 13, 1989; No 14, 1990; Piano Sonata, 1946; Variations and Finale on a Theme of Haydn, for piano, 1948; Variations and Finale on a Theme of Beethoven for piano, 1990; Allegro Deciso, for string orchestra (from String Quartet No 3); Canzona for Brass, 1958 (recorded); Variations and Fugue for recorder and string quartet, 1959; Incidental Music to Ibsen's The Pretenders, 1965; Trio for clarinet, cello and piano, 1967; Quintet for clarinet, and strings, 1968 (recorded); Energy, Symphonic Study for brass band (test piece for 1971 World Championship) (recorded); Incidental Music to Milton's Samson Agonistes, 1974; *Media morte in vita sumus* (Motet for choir, brass, and timpani), 1975; Quartet for horn, violin, cello and piano, 1976; Volcano, for brass band, 1979 (test piece for Nat. Championship, 1979) (recorded); Sonata for two pianos, 1980; Quintet for double basses, clarinet and bass clarinet, 1981 (also for string trio, clarinet and bass clarinet); The Four Temperaments, for brass band, 1982 (recorded); Variations on a theme of Carl Nielsen, for orchestra, 1983; Trio for horn, violin and piano, 1984; Sonata for violin and piano, 1984; Eppur si muove, for organ, 1985; Introduction and Allegro on a bass by Max Reger, for brass band, 1986 (recorded); Tempi, for a cappella choir, 1987; String Quintet, 1987 (recorded); String Trio (Prelude and Fugue), 1987; Quintet for Brass, 1989; Vortex, for brass band, 1989 (recorded); Variations and Fugue on a theme of Bach, for string orch., 1991. *Publications:* Carl Nielsen, Symphonist, 1952, rev. edn 1977; The Essence of Bruckner, 1966; The Proms and Natural Justice, 1981; numerous articles in various jls and three BBC booklets (Bruckner and the Symphony, Sibelius and Nielsen, and The Beethoven Symphonies); contrib. to: Encycl. Brit.; Musik in Geschichte und Gegenwart; (ed) The Symphony (Pelican), 1966. *Recreation:* astronomy. *Address:* Síocháin, Killelton, near Camp, Tralee, Co. Kerry, Eire. *T:* Tralee 30213.

SIMPSON, Robin; *see* Simpson, Robert W.

SIMPSON, Robin Muschamp Garry; QC 1971; *b* 19 June 1927; *s* of Ronald Maitland Simpson, actor and Lila Maravan Simpson (*née* Muschamp); *m* 1st, 1956, Avril Carolyn Harrisson; one *s* one *d*; 2nd, 1968, Mary Faith Laughton-Scott; one *s* one *d*. *Educ:* Charterhouse; Peterhouse, Cambridge (MA). Called to Bar, Middle Temple, 1951, Bencher, 1979; SE Circuit; former Mem., Surrey and S London Sessions; a Recorder of the Crown Court, 1976–86. Mem., CCC Bar Mess. Appeal Steward, British Boxing Bd of Control. *Recreations:* real tennis, sailing. *Address:* 9 Drayton Gardens, SW10. *T:* 071–373 3284. *Clubs:* Garrick, MCC.

SIMPSON, William George; University Librarian, University of London, since 1990; *b* 27 June 1945; *s* of William Anion Simpson and Sarah Jane Simpson; *m* 1968, Margaret Lilian Pollard; two *d*. *Educ:* Liverpool Inst.; Univ. of Liverpool (BA 1st class Hons). ALA. Gilroy Scholar in Semitic Languages, Univ. of Aberdeen, 1968; Asst Librarian, Univ. of Durham, 1969–73; Asst Librarian, Sub-Librarian and Senior Sub-Librarian, John Rylands Univ. Library of Manchester, 1973–85; Univ. Librarian, Univ. of Surrey, 1985–90. Chm., Guildford Inst., 1987–90; Mem., Humanities and Social Scis Adv. Cttee, British Library, 1991–. FRSA. *Publications:* Libraries, Languages and the Interpretation of the Past, 1988; articles in learned jls. *Recreations:* astronomy, genealogy, languages, travel. *Address:* Cranhurst, Station Road, Farncombe, Godalming, Surrey GU7 3NF; University of London Library, Senate House, Malet Street, WC1E 7HU. *T:* 071–636 8000.

SIMPSON, Sir William (James), Kt 1984; Chairman, Health and Safety Commission, 1974–83; *b* Falkirk, 20 May 1920; *s* of William Simpson and Margaret Nimmo; *m* 1942, Catherine McEwan Nicol; one *s*. *Educ:* Victoria Sch. and Falkirk Techn. Sch., Falkirk. Served War of 1939–45, Argyll and Sutherland Highlanders (Sgt). Apprenticed to moulding trade, 1935; returned to foundry, 1946. Mem. Nat. Exec. Council, Amalgamated Union of Foundry Workers, 1955–67; Gen. Sec., AUEW (Foundry Section), 1967–75. Chm. of Labour Party, 1972–73; Member: Race Relations Board; Ct of Inquiry into Flixborough explosion, 1974; Chm., Adv. Cttee on Asbestos, 1976–79. *Publication:* Labour: The Unions and the Party, 1973.

SIMPSON-JONES, Peter Trevor, CBE 1971; Président d'Honneur, Société Française des Industries Lucas, since 1980 (Président-Directeur Général, 1957–80); *b* 20 March 1914; *s* of Frederick Henry Jones and Constance Agnès Simpson; *m* 1948, Marie-Lucy Sylvain; one *s* one *d*. *Educ:* Royal Navy School. British Chamber of Commerce, France: Vice-Pres., 1967–68 and 1970–72; Pres., 1968–70. Chevalier de la Légion d'Honneur, 1948, Officier 1973. *Recreation:* yachting. *Address:* 11 rue Max Blondat, 92 Boulogne-sur-Seine, France. *T:* 4825–01–20. *Clubs:* Special Forces; Polo (Paris).

SIMPSON-ORLEBAR, Sir Michael Keith Orlebar, KCMG 1991 (CMG 1982); HM Diplomatic Service; Ambassador to Mexico, 1989–Feb. 1992; *b* 5 Feb. 1932; *s* of Aubrey Orlebar Simpson, Royal Artillery and Laura Violet, *d* of Captain Frederick Keith-Jones; *m* 1964, Rosita Duarte Triana; two *s* one *d*. *Educ:* Eton; Christ Church, Oxford (MA). 2nd Lieut, KRRC, 1950–51. Joined Foreign Service, 1954; 3rd Sec., Tehran, 1955–57; FO, 1957–62; Private Sec. to Parly Under-Sec. of State, 1960–62; 1st Sec. (Commercial) and Consul, Bogotá, 1962–65; seconded to Urwick, Orr and Partners Ltd, 1966; FO, 1966–68; 1st Sec., Paris, 1969–72; Counsellor (Commercial), Tehran, 1972–76; Head of UN Dept, FCO, 1977–80; Minister, HM Embassy, Rome, 1980–83; Head of British Interests Section, Tehran, 1983–85; Ambassador to Portugal, 1986–89. *Recreations:* gardening, fishing. *Address:* 17a Barkston Gardens, SW5 0ER. *Club:* Travellers'.

SIMS, Prof. Andrew Charles Petter, FRCPsych; Professor of Psychiatry, University of Leeds, since 1979; President, Royal College of Psychiatrists, since 1990; *b* 5 Nov. 1938; *s* of Dr Charles Henry Sims and Dr Norah Winifred Kennan Sims (*née* Petter); *m* 1964, Ruth Marie Harvey; two *s* two *d*. *Educ:* Monkton Combe Sch.; Emmanuel Coll., Cambridge; Westminster Hosp. MA, MD; DObstRCOG. House Surgeon, Westminster Hosp., 1963–64; Registrar in Psychiatry, Manchester Royal Infirmary, 1966–69; Consultant Psychiatrist, All Saints Hosp., Birmingham, 1971–76; Sen. Lectr, Univ. of Birmingham, 1976–79; Head of Dept of Psychiatry, Univ. of Leeds, 1980–83, 1986–89. Dean, RCPsych, 1987–90 (Sub-Dean, 1984–87). *Publications:* Neurosis in Society, 1983; (with Sir William Trethowan) Psychiatry (Concise Medical Textbooks), 5th edn, 1983; (with W. I. Hume) Lecture Notes in Behavioural Sciences, 1984; Symptoms in the Mind: introduction to descriptive psychopathology, 1988; (with R. P. Snaith) Anxiety in Practice, 1988. *Recreations:* gardening, music, theatre, walking. *Address:* Gledholt, Oakwood Grove, Leeds LS8 2PA. *T:* Leeds (0532) 433144. *Clubs:* Christian Medical Fellowship, Royal Society of Medicine. *Club:* Athenæum.

SIMS, Prof. Geoffrey Donald, OBE 1971; FEng 1980; Vice-Chancellor, University of Sheffield, 1974–90; *b* 13 Dec. 1926; *s* of Albert Edward Hope Sims and Jessie Elizabeth Sims; *m* 1949, Pamela Audrey Richings; one *s* two *d*. *Educ:* Wembley County Grammar School; Imperial College of Science and Technology, London. Research physicist, GEC, 1948–54; Sen. Scientific Officer, UKAEA, 1954–56; Lecturer/Senior Lecturer, University College, London, 1956–63; University of Southampton: Prof. and Head of Dept of Electronics, 1963–74; Dean, Faculty of Engrg, 1967–70; Senior Dep. Vice-Chancellor, 1970–72. Member: Council, British Association for the Advancement of Science, 1965–69 (Chm., Sheffield Area Council, 1974–); EDC for Electronics Industry, 1966–75; Adv. Cttee for Scientific and Technical Information, 1969–74; CNAA Electrical Engineering Bd, 1970–73; Planning Cttee for British Library, 1971–73 (Chm., British Library R&D Adv. Cttee, 1975–81); Adv. Council, Science Museum, 1972–84; British Nat. Cttee for Physics, 1972–78; Royal Soc. Cttee on Sci. Information, 1972–81; Electronics Res. Council, 1973–74; Annan Cttee on Future of Broadcasting, 1974–77; Naval Educn Adv. Cttee, 1974–79; Trent RHA, 1975–84; British Council Engrg and Tech. Adv. Cttee, 1976–84 (Chm.); Interim Action Cttee on British Film Industry, 1977–81; EEC Adv. Cttee on Scientific and Technical Trng, 1977–81; Univs Council for Adult and Continuing Educn, 1978–84 (Chm., 1980–84); CNAA, 1979–83; Liaison Cttee on Highly Qualified Technol Manpower, 1979–82; Council, Nat. Inst. of Adult Educn, 1980–84; SRC, later SERC Engrg Bd, 1980–84; Inter Univ. and Polytechnic Council, 1981– (IUC and Exec. Cttee, 1974–81; Vice-Chm., IUPC, 1985–); Cttee for Internat. Co-operation in Higher Educn, 1981– (Vice-Chm., 1985–); EEC Adv. Cttee on Programme Management, 1981–84; BBC Engrg Adv. Cttee, 1981–90 (Chm.); Council, Fellowship of Engrg, 1986–88; Museums and Galleries Commn, 1983–88; Hong Kong City Polytechnic Sub-cttee, 1984–86, Hong Kong Univ. of Sci. and Technol. Sub-cttee, 1987–91, UPGC, Hong Kong; Mem. of Council and Hon. Dep. Treas., ACU, 1984–90; Chm., Council for Commonwealth Educn, 1991. UK rep. on Perm. Cttee of Conf. of European Rectors, 1981–84; *ad personem* rep. on Perm. Cttee and Bureau of Conf. of European Rectors, 1984–; rep. on Liaison Cttee, Rectors' Confs of EEC Mem. States, 1985– (Pres., 1987–). Chairman of Governors: Southampton College of Technology, 1967–69; Southampton Sch. of Navigation, 1972–74; Sheffield High Sch., 1978–85; Fellow, Midland Chapter, Woodard Schools, 1977–; Custos, Worksop Coll., 1984–. Trustee, Church Burgesses Trust, Sheffield, 1984–, Capital, 1988–89. FIEE 1963; FCGI 1980. Hon. Fellow, Sheffield City Polytechnic, 1990. Hon. DSc Southampton, 1979; Hon. ScD Allegheny Coll., Penn, USA, 1989; Hon. DSc (Eng) QUB, 1990; Hon. LLD: Dundee, 1987; Sheffield, 1991. Symons Medal, ACU, 1991. Founder Mem., 1966, Reviews Editor, 1969–, Chm., 1987, Jl of Materials Science Bd. *Publications:* Microwave Tubes and Semiconductor Devices (with I. M. Stephenson), 1963; Variational Techniques in Electromagnetism (trans.), 1965; numerous papers on microwaves, electronics and education in learned jls. *Recreations:* golf, travel, music. *Address:* North Leigh, 53 Sandygate Park Road, Sheffield S10 5TX. *Club:* Athenæum.

SIMS, Monica Louie, OBE 1971; MA, LRAM, LGSM; Director of Production, Children's Film and Television Foundation, since 1985; *d* of late Albert Charles Sims and Eva Elizabeth Preen, both of Gloucester. *Educ:* Girls' High School, Gloucester; St Hugh's College, Oxford. Tutor in Literature and Drama, Dept of Adult Educn, Hull Univ., 1947–50; Educn Tutor, Nat. Fedn of Women's Institutes, 1950–53; BBC Sound Talks Producer, 1953–55; BBC Television Producer, 1955–64; Editor of Woman's Hour, BBC, 1964–67; Head of Children's Programmes, BBC TV, 1967–78; Controller, BBC Radio 4, 1978–83; Dir of Programmes, BBC Radio, 1983–84. Vice-Pres., British Bd of Film Classification, 1985–; Chm., Careers Adv. Bd, Univ. of Bristol, 1991–. *Address:* 97 Gloucester Terrace, W2 3HB.

SIMS, Roger Edward, JP; MP (C) Chislehurst since Feb. 1974; *b* 27 Jan. 1930; *s* of late Herbert William Sims and Annie Amy Savidge; *m* 1957, Angela Mathews; two *s* one *d*. *Educ:* City Boys' Grammar Sch., Leicester; St Olave's Grammar Sch., London. MCInstM. National Service, 1948–50. Coutts & Co., 1950–51; Campbell Booker Carter Ltd,

1953–62; Dodwell & Co. Ltd, 1962–90; Dir, Inchcape International Ltd, 1981–90. Contested (C) Shoreditch and Finsbury, 1966 and 1970; PPS to Home Sec., 1979–83. Mem., GMC, 1989–. Mem., Central Exec. Cttee, NSPCC, 1980–. Mem. Chislehurst and Sidcup UDC, 1956–62; JP Bromley, 1960–72 (Dep. Chm. 1970–72); Chm., Juvenile Panel, 1971–72. *Recreations:* swimming; music, especially singing (Mem. Royal Choral Soc. from 1950). *Address:* House of Commons, SW1A 0AA. *Clubs:* Bromley Conservative (Bromley); Chislehurst British Legion.

SIMS-WILLIAMS, Dr Nicholas John, FBA 1988; Reader in Iranian Studies, School of Oriental and African Studies, University of London, since 1989; *b* 11 April 1949; *s* of Rev. M. V. S. Sims-Williams; *m* 1972, Ursula Mary Judith, *d* of late Prof. Hugh Seton-Watson, CBE, FBA; two *d. Educ:* Trinity Hall, Cambridge (BA, MA; PhD 1978). Res. Fellow, Gonville and Caius Coll., Cambridge, 1975–76; Lectr in Iranian Langs, SOAS, Univ. of London, 1976–89. Corresp. Mem., Austrian Acad. of Scis, 1990. *Publications:* The Christian Sogdian manuscript C2, 1985 (Prix Ghirshman, Inst. de France, 1988); Sogdian and other Iranian Inscriptions of the Upper Indus, vol. I, 1989; (with James Hamilton) Documents turco-sogdiens du IXe–Xe Siède de Touen-houang, 1990; contrib. on Iranian and Central Asian langs and culture to learned jls. *Recreation:* music. *Address:* 38 Parolles Road, N19 3RD. *T:* 071–272 5641.

SIMSON, Michael Ronald Fraser, OBE 1966; Secretary of the National Corporation for the Care of Old People, 1948–73; *b* 9 Oct. 1913; *er s* of Ronald Stuart Fraser Simson and Ethel Alice Henderson; *m* 1939, Elizabeth Joan Wilkinson; one *s. Educ:* Winchester Coll.; Christ Church, Oxford. OUAFC 1936 and 1937. Asst Master, West Downs Sch., 1938–40; RNVR, 1941–46; Asst Sec., Nat. Fedn of Housing Socs, 1946–48. Member: Min. of Labour Cttee on Employment of Older Men and Women, 1953–55; Cttee on Local Authority and Allied Personal Social Services (Seebohm Cttee), 1966–68; Supplementary Benefits Commn, 1967–76; Adv. Cttee on Rent Rebates and Rent Allowances, 1973–75, resigned 1975; Personal Social Services Council, 1973–78. *Recreations:* gardening, interested in all forms of sport. *Address:* Summerhill, Kingsdon, Somerton, Somerset TA11 7JU. *T:* Ilchester (0935) 840858.

SINATRA, Francis Albert, (Frank); singer, actor, film producer, publisher; *b* Hoboken, New Jersey, USA, 12 Dec. 1915; *s* of late Natalie and Martin Sinatra; *m* 1st, 1939, Nancy Barbato (marr. diss.); one *s* two *d*; 2nd 1951, Ava Gardner (marr. diss.); 3rd, 1966, Mia Farrow (marr. diss.); 4th, 1976, Barbara Marx. *Educ:* Demarest High School, New Jersey. Started in radio, 1936; then became band singer with orchestras. First appearance in films, 1943. *Films include:* From Here to Eternity (Oscar for best supporting actor, 1953), Anchors Aweigh, On the Town, The Tender Trap, High Society, Guys and Dolls, The Man with the Golden Arm, Johnny Concho, The Joker is Wild, Kings Go Forth, Some Came Running, A Hole in the Head, Ocean's 11, The Devil at Four O'Clock, Sergeants Three, Manchurian Candidate, Come Blow Your Horn, Four for Texas, Robin and the Seven Hoods, None But the Brave, Marriage on the Rocks, Von Ryan's Express, Assault on a Queen, The Naked Runner, Tony Rome, The Detective, Lady in Cement, Dirty Dingus Magee, The First Deadly Sin, Cannonball Run II. Owner music publishing companies, etc. Jean Hersholt Humanitarian Award, 1971. *Publications:* composed numerous popular songs. *Address:* Sinatra Enterprises, Goldwyn Studios, 1041 N Formosa, Los Angeles, Calif 90046, USA.

SINCLAIR, family name of **Earl of Caithness, Viscount Thurso,** and **Baron Sinclair of Cleeve.**

SINCLAIR, 17th Lord, *cr* 1449 (Scotland); **Charles Murray Kennedy St Clair,** CVO 1990 (LVO 1953); Major, late Coldstream Guards; Extra Equerry to Queen Elizabeth the Queen Mother since 1953; Lord-Lieutenant, Dumfries and Galloway Region (District of Stewartry), 1982–89 (Vice-Lord-Lieutenant, 1977–82); Member Queen's Body Guard for Scotland (Royal Company of Archers); *b* 21 June 1914; *o s* of 16th Lord Sinclair, MVO, and Violet (*d* 1953), *d* of Col J. Murray Kennedy, MVO; *S* father, 1957; *m* 1968, Anne Lettice, *yr d* of Sir Richard Cotterell, 5th Bt, CBE; one *s* two *d. Educ:* Eton; Magdalene Coll., Cambridge. Served War of 1939–45, Palestine, 1939 (wounded, despatches). Retired as Major Coldstream Guards, 1947. Portcullis Pursuivant of Arms, 1949–57; York Herald, 1957–68, retired. A Representative Peer for Scotland, 1959–63. DL Kirkcudbrightshire, 1969. *Heir: s* Master of Sinclair, *qv. Address:* Knocknalling, St John's Town of Dalry, Castle Douglas, Kirkcudbrightshire, Scotland DG7 3ST. *T:* Dalry (06443) 221. *Club:* New (Edinburgh).

SINCLAIR, Master of; Hon. Matthew Murray Kennedy St Clair; *b* 9 Dec. 1968; *s* and *heir* of 17th Lord Sinclair, *qv*.

SINCLAIR OF CLEEVE, 3rd Baron *cr* 1957, of Cleeve, Somerset; **John Lawrence Robert Sinclair;** Teaching Support Staff Governor at an Inner London comprehensive school, since 1985; *b* 6 Jan. 1953; *s* of 2nd Baron Sinclair of Cleeve, OBE, and of Patricia, *d* of late Major Lawrence Hellyer; *S* father, 1985. *Educ:* Winchester College; Manchester Univ. *Recreations:* motor cycling, mime, music.

SINCLAIR, Alexander Riddell; HM Diplomatic Service, retired; *b* 28 Aug. 1917; *s* of Henry W. Sinclair and Mary Turner; *m* 1948, Alice Evelyn Nottingham; three *d. Educ:* Greenock High School. DipCAM. Inland Revenue, 1935–37; Admty, 1938–47 (Comdr RNVR, 1945–46); 2nd Sec., HM Embassy, Moscow, 1947–48; Vice-Consul: Detroit, 1949; Mosul, 1950; FO, 1952; 1st Secretary, HM Embassy: Saigon, 1953–56; Amman, 1957–58; FO, 1959; 1st Sec. (Cultural), Budapest, 1962; FO, 1964; 1st Secretary (Information): Beirut, 1967–70; Rome, 1970–71; Consul-Gen., Genoa, 1972–76; FCO Library, 1977–85. Silver Jubilee Medal, 1977. *Publications:* literary articles in learned jls. *Recreations:* reading, book browsing, walking. *Address:* 2 Ruthven Place, St Andrews, Fife KY16 8SJ. *Club:* Civil Service.

SINCLAIR, Andrew Annandale; author; Managing Director: Lorrimer Publishing, since 1967; Timon Films, since 1967; *b* 21 Jan. 1935; *m* 1960, Marianne, *d* of Mr and Mrs Arsène Alexandre; *m* 1972, Miranda, *o d* of Mr and Hon. Mrs George Seymour; two *s*; *m* 1984, Sonia Lady Melchett, *d* of Dr and Mrs Roland Graham. *Educ:* Eton Coll.; Trinity Coll., Cambridge (BA, PhD); Harvard. Ensign, Coldstream Guards, 1953–55. Harkness Fellow of the Commonwealth Fund, 1959–61; Dir of Historical Studies, Churchill Coll., Cambridge, 1961–63; Fellow of American Council of Learned Societies, 1963–64; Lectr in American History, University Coll., London, 1965–67. Dir/Writer Mem., ACTT. FRSL 1973; Fellow Soc. of American Historians, 1974. Somerset Maugham Literary Prize, 1966. *Film:* (dir) Under Milk Wood, 1971. *Publications:* The Breaking of Bumbo, 1958; My Friend Judas, 1959; The Project, 1960; Prohibition, 1962; The Hallelujah Bum, 1963; The Available Man: Warren E. Harding, 1964; The Better Half, 1964; The Raker, 1965; Concise History of the United States, 1966; Albion Triptych: Gog, 1967, Magog, 1972, King Ludd, 1988; The Greek Anthology, 1967; Adventures in the Skin Trade, 1968; The Last of the Best, 1969; Guevara, 1970; Dylan Thomas: poet of his people, 1975; The Surrey Cat, 1976; The Savage, 1977; Jack: the biography of Jack London, 1977; A Patriot for Hire, 1978; John Ford, 1979; The Facts in the Case of E. A. Poe, 1979; Corsair, 1981; The Other Victoria, 1981; Sir Walter Raleigh and the Age of Discovery, 1984; Beau Bumbo, 1985; The Red and the Blue, 1986; Spiegel, 1987; War Like a Wasp, 1989; (ed) The War Decade, an anthology of the 1940s, 1989; The Need to Give, 1990; The Far Corners of the Earth, 1991. *Recreations:* old cities, old movies. *Address:* 16 Tite Street, SW3 4HZ.

SINCLAIR, Charles James Francis; Managing Director and Group Chief Executive, Daily Mail and General Trust PLC, since 1988; *b* 4 April 1948; *s* of Sir George (Evelyn) Sinclair, *qv*; *m* 1974, Nicola Bayliss; two *s. Educ:* Winchester Coll.; Magdalen Coll., Oxford (BA). ACA 1974. VSO, Zambia, 1966–67. Dearden Farrow, CA, 1970; joined Associated Newspapers Holdings, 1975; Asst Man. Dir and Mem. Main Bd, 1986; Man. Dir, 1988 (Associated Newspapers Holdings became the wholly-owned operating subsid. of Daily Mail and General Trust, 1988); Director: Whittle Communications, Tennessee, 1985–; Euromoney Publications, 1985–; Schroders plc, 1990–. Chm. of Trustees, Minack Theatre Trust, Porthcurno, Cornwall, 1985–. *Recreations:* opera, fishing, ski-ing. *Address:* Northcliffe House, 2 Derry Street, Kensington, W8 5TT. *Clubs:* Athenæum; Vincent's (Oxford).

SINCLAIR, Sir Clive (Marles), Kt 1983; Chairman, Sinclair Research Ltd, since 1979; *b* 30 July 1940; *s* of George William Carter Sinclair and Thora Edith Ella (*née* Marles); *m* 1962, Ann (*née* Trevor Briscoe) (marr. diss. 1985); two *s* one *d. Educ:* Boxgrove Prep. Sch., Guildford; Highgate; Reading; St George's Coll., Weybridge. Editor, Bernards Publishers Ltd, 1958–61; Chairman: Sinclair Radionics Ltd, 1962–79; Sinclair Browne Ltd, 1981–85; Cambridge Computer Ltd, 1986–90; Director: Shaye Communications Ltd; Anamartic Ltd. Vis. Fellow, Robinson Coll., Cambridge, 1982–; Vis. Prof., Dept of Elec. Engrg, Imperial Coll. of Science and Technol., London, 1984– (Hon. Fellow, 1984). Chm., British Mensa, 1980–. Hon. Fellow UMIST, 1984. Hon. DSc: Bath, 1983; Warwick, 1983; Heriot-Watt, 1983. Mullard Award, Royal Soc., 1984. *Publications:* Practical Transistor Receivers, 1959; British Semiconductor Survey, 1963. *Recreations:* music, poetry, mathematics, science. *Address:* 18 Shepherd House, 5 Shepherd Street, W1Y 7LD. *T:* 071–408 0199.

SINCLAIR of Freswick, Maj.-Gen. David Boyd A.; *see* Alexander-Sinclair.

SINCLAIR, Prof. David Cecil; Emeritus Professor, University of Western Australia; *b* 28 Aug. 1915; *s* of Norman James Sinclair and Annie Smart Sinclair; *m* 1945, Grace Elizabeth Simondson, Melbourne, Vic.; one *s* one *d. Educ:* Merchiston Castle Sch.; St Andrews University. MB, ChB (Commendation) St Andrews, 1937; MD (Hons and Rutherford Gold Medal) St Andrews, 1947; MA Oxon, 1948; DSc Western Australia, 1965. Served in RAMC, 1940–46: AMF, 1943–45; Head of Physiology Sect., Aust. Chem. Warfare Research and Experimental Stn, 1943–44; Dep. Chief Supt, Aust. Field Experimental Stn, 1944–45. Sen. Res. Off., Dept of Human Anatomy, Oxford, 1946–49; Univ. Demonstrator in Anatomy, Oxford, 1949–56; Lectr in Anatomy, Pembroke Coll., Oxford, 1950–56; Lectr in Anatomy, Ruskin Sch. of Fine Art, 1950–56; first Prof. of Anatomy, Univ. of W Australia, 1957–64, Dean of Med. Sch., 1964; Regius Prof. of Anatomy, Univ. of Aberdeen, 1965–75; Dir of Postgrad. Med. Educn, Queen Elizabeth II Med. Centre, WA, 1975–80. FRCSE 1966. Life Governor, Aust. Postgrad. Fedn in Medicine, 1983. *Publications:* Medical Students and Medical Sciences, 1955; An Introduction to Functional Anatomy, 1957 (5th edn 1975); A Student's Guide to Anatomy, 1961; Cutaneous Sensation, 1967, Japanese edn 1969; Human Growth after Birth, 1969 (5th edn 1989); Muscles and Fascia (section in Cunningham's Anatomy), 11th edn, 1972, 12th edn, 1981; Basic Medical Education, 1972; The Nerves of the Skin (section in Physiology and Pathophysiology of the Skin, ed Jarrett), 1973; Growth, section in Textbook of Human Anatomy (ed Hamilton), 1976; Mechanisms of Cutaneous Sensation, 1981; Not a Proper Doctor (autobiog.), 1989; Outside the Dissecting Room, 1989; papers on chemical warfare, neurological anatomy, experimental psychology, and medical education; Editor, Jl of Anatomy, 1970–73. *Recreations:* reading, writing, photography, chess problems. *Address:* Flat 3, Netherby, Netherby Road, Cults, Aberdeen.

SINCLAIR, Ernest Keith, CMG 1966; OBE 1946; DFC 1943; journalist-consultant; Commissioner, Australian Heritage Commission, 1976–81; Associate Commissioner, Industries Assistance Commission, 1974–81; *b* 13 November 1914; 2nd *s* of Ernest and Florence Sinclair, Victoria, Australia; *m* 1949, Jill, *d* of John and Muriel Nelder, Pangbourne; one *s. Educ:* Melbourne High School, Australia. Literary staff, The Age, 1932–38. Served War of 1939–45, RAF, 1940–45 (despatches, 1944). Associate Editor, The Age, Melbourne, 1946–59, Editor, 1959–66. Consultant to Dept of Prime Minister and Cabinet, 1967–74 and 1977–81 (to Prime Minister of Australia, 1967–72). Dep. Chm., Australian Tourist Commn, 1969–75 (Mem. 1966). Director: Australian Assoc. Press, 1959–66 (Chm., 1965–66); Gen. Television Corp. (Melbourne), 1959–66; Australian Paper Manufacturers Ltd, 1966–85; Member: Australian Council, Internat. Press Inst., 1959–66; Schools Bd for the Humanities, Victoria Inst. of Colleges, 1969–72 (Chm.); Library Council of Victoria, 1966–78; Council, Royal Historical Soc. of Victoria, 1981–86 (Hon. Editor, Jl, 1982–86); Observer, Nat. Capital Planning Cttee, 1967–72; Dep. Chm., Library Council, and Trustee, Nat. Museum and Sci. Museum of Victoria, 1976–78. *Publication:* The Spreading Tree: a history of APM and AMCOR 1844–1989, 1991. *Recreations:* historical writing, gardening, reading. *Address:* 138 Toorak Road West, South Yarra, Victoria 3141, Australia. *T:* 867–1405. *Club:* Melbourne (Melbourne).

SINCLAIR, Rear-Adm. Erroll Norman, CB 1963; DSC 1944; retired; *b* 6 Mar. 1909; *s* of late Col John Norman Sinclair, RHA; *m* 1940, Frances Elinor Knox-Gore; two *s. Educ:* RNC Dartmouth. Served HMS Cumberland, 1934–35; HMS Cairo, 1936–38; HMS Gallant, 1938–40 (Dunkirk); in comd HMS Fortune, 1940, HMS Antelope, 1941–43, N African Landings; in comd HMS Eskimo, 10th Destroyer Flotilla, 1943–45 (DSC); First Lieut, RN Barracks, Chatham, 1946, Comdr 1946; Exec. Officer, RN Air Station, Eglinton, 1947; Staff Officer Ops to C-in-C, S Atlantic Station, Simonstown, and UK Liaison Officer to S Af. Naval Forces, until 1951. In comd HMS St Kitts, 5th Destroyer Sqdn, Home Fleet, 1951–53; Capt. 1952; Pres. Second Admiralty Interview Board, 1953–54; Naval Attaché at Ankara, Teheran and Tel Aviv, 1955; Capt. (D) 4th Destroyer Sqdn, HMS Agincourt, 1957–59; in comd HMS Sea Eagle and Sen. Naval Officer N Ireland, and Naval Director, Joint A/S School, Londonderry, 1959–61; Flag Officer, Gibraltar, and Admiral Superintendent, HM Dockyard, Gibraltar, also NATO Commander of Gibraltar sub areas, 1962–64; retd list, 1964; Naval Regional Officer (North), 1964–68. *Club:* Rye Golf.

SINCLAIR, Maj.-Gen. George Brian, CB 1983; CBE 1975; FIHE; Engineer-in-Chief (Army), 1980–83; *b* 21 July 1928; *s* of Thomas S. Sinclair and Blanche Sinclair; *m* 1953, Edna Margaret Richardson; two *s* one *d. Educ:* Christ's College, Finchley; RMA Sandhurst. Commissioned, Royal Engineers, 1948; served UK, BAOR, Korea, and Christmas Island, 1948–66; Directing Staff, Staff College, Camberley, 1967–69; CRE, Near East, 1970–71; Col GS, HQ 1st British Corps, 1972–74; Nat. Defence Coll., India, 1975; Commandant Royal School of Military Engineering, 1976–77; BGS, Military Operations, MoD, 1978–80. Col Comdt, RE, 1983–91; Hon. Col, Engineer and Transport Staff Corps, 1988–. Vice Pres., Register of Engrs for Disaster Relief, 1985–; Trustee, Imperial War Mus., 1990–. Chm., Friends of Rochester Cathedral, 1988–. Governor, King's Sch.,

Rochester, 1984–. *Recreations:* hill walking, running, bird watching and discussion. *Address:* 6 Prospect Row, Brompton, Gillingham, Kent ME7 5AL. *T:* Medway (0634) 842364. *Club:* Army and Navy.

SINCLAIR, Sir George (Evelyn), Kt 1960; CMG 1956; OBE 1950; *b* Cornwall, 6 November 1912; 2nd *s* of late F. Sinclair, Chynance, St Buryan, Cornwall; *m* 1st, 1941, Katharine Jane Burdekin (*d* 1971); one *s* three *d*; 2nd, 1972, Mary Violet, *widow* of George Lester Sawday, Saxmundham, Suffolk. *Educ:* Abingdon School; Pembroke College, Oxford (MA; Hon. Fellow, 1986). Entered Colonial Administrative Service, 1936; appointed to Gold Coast Administration; Asst District Comr, 1937. Military service, 1940–43. District Commissioner, Gold Coast, 1943; seconded to Colonial Office, 1943–45; Sec. to Commn on Higher Education in West Africa, 1943–45; returned to Gold Coast, 1945; Senior Assistant Colonial Secretary, 1947; Principal Assistant Secretary, 1950; Regional Officer, Trans-Volta Togoland Region, 1952; Deputy Governor, Cyprus, 1955–60; retired, 1961. MP (C) Dorking, Surrey, Oct. 1964–1979. Member, Parly Select Committees on: Procedure, 1965–66; Race Relations, 1969–70; Overseas Aid, 1969–70; Race Relations and Immigration, 1970–74; Members Interests, 1975; Abortion Act (Amendment) Bill; Joint Secretary: Cons. Parly Commonwealth Affairs Cttee, 1966–68; Cons. Parly Educn Cttee, 1974–79, Vice-Chm., 1974; Member: Intermediate Technology Develt Gp (Vice-Pres., 1966–79; Dir, 1979–82); Nat. Exec. Cttee, UNA (UK Branch), 1968–70; Council, Overseas Services Resettlement Bureau; Council of PDSA, 1964–70; Council, Christian Aid, 1973–78; Steering Cttee, UN/FPA World Conf. of Parliamentarians on population and develt, 1978–79; Vice-Chm., Family Planning Assoc., 1979–81; Consultant: UN Fund for Population Affairs, 1979–82; IPPF, 1979–83; special advr to Global Cttee on Population and Develt, 1982–88. Trustee: Runnymede Trust, 1969–75; Human Rights Trust, 1971–74; Physically Handicapped and Able Bodied (Foundn Trustee), 1973–81; Wyndham Place Trust. Mem., Wimbledon Borough Council, 1962–65. Member, Board of Governors: Abingdon Sch., 1970–87 (Chm., 1971–79); Felixstowe Coll., 1980–87; Campion Sch., Athens, 1983–; Chm., Assoc. of Governing Bodies of Independent Schools, 1979–84 (Mem., 1973–); Member: Direct Grant Jt Cttee, 1974–80; Indep. Schools Jt Council, 1979–84 (Chm. 1980–83, Dep. Chm., 1984); Council, Oxford Soc., 1982–. Chm. Planning Office, 1988 Internat. Conf. of Spiritual and Parly Leaders on Human Survival, 1986–88. *Recreations:* golf, fishing. *Address:* Carlton Rookery, Saxmundham, Suffolk IP17 2NN; South Minack, Porthcurno, Cornwall. *Clubs:* Athenæum, Commonwealth Trust; Aldeburgh Golf.
See also C. J. F. Sinclair.

SINCLAIR, Hon. Ian David, OC 1979; QC (Can.) 1961; Member, Senate of Canada, 1983–88; *b* Winnipeg, 27 Dec. 1913; *s* of late John David Sinclair and late Lillian Sinclair; *m* 1942, Ruth Beatrice, *d* of Robert Parsons Drennan, Winnipeg; two *s* two *d*. *Educ:* public schs, Winnipeg; Univ. of Manitoba (BA Econs 1937); Manitoba Law School (LLB 1941). Barrister, Guy Chappell & Co., Winnipeg, 1937–41; Lectr in Torts, Univ. of Manitoba, 1942–43; joined Canadian Pacific Law Dept as Asst Solicitor, Winnipeg, 1942; Solicitor, Montreal, 1946; Asst to General Counsel, 1951; General Solicitor, 1953; Vice-Pres. and Gen. Counsel, 1960; Vice-Pres., Law, 1960; Canadian Pacific Railway Co.: Vice-Pres., Dir and Mem. Exec. Cttee, 1961; Pres., 1966; Chief Exec. Officer, 1969; Chm. and Chief Exec. Officer: Canadian Pacific Ltd, 1972–81; Canadian Pacific Enterprises Ltd, 1972–82 (Chm., 1982–84); Director: Canadian Investment Fund, Ltd, 1972–89; Canadian Marconi Co., 1967–; Union Carbide Canada Ltd, 1968–; Public Dir, Investment Dealers Assoc. of Canada, 1984–88; Mem., Internat. Adv. Cttee, Chase Manhattan Bank, N America, 1973–87; Trustee, Alliance Global Fund, 1987–. Hon. LLD Manitoba, 1967; Hon. DBA Laval, 1981; Hon. DCL Acadia, 1982. Mem., Canadian Business Hall of Fame. *Address:* Suite 1100, University Place, 123 Front Street West, Toronto, Ont M5J 2M2, Canada. *T:* (416) 860–0144. *Clubs:* Toronto (Toronto); Rideau (Ottawa).

SINCLAIR, Rt. Hon. Ian (McCahon), PC 1977; MHR for New England, NSW, since 1963; Leader, National Party of Australia, 1984–89 (Deputy Leader, 1971–84); *b* 10 June 1929; *s* of George McCahon Sinclair and Gertrude Hazel Sinclair; *m* 1st, 1956, Margaret Tarrant (*d* 1967); one *s* two *d*; 2nd, 1970, Rosemary Fenton; one *s*. *Educ:* Knox Grammar Sch., Wahroonga, NSW; Sydney Univ. BA, LLB. Grazier. Mem. Legislative Council, NSW, 1961–63; Minister for: Social Services, 1965–68; Trade and Industry (Minister Assisting Minister), 1966–71; Shipping and Transport, 1968–71; Primary Industry, 1971–72; Leader of House for Opposition, 1972–75; Country Party spokesman for Defence, Foreign Affairs, Law and Agriculture, 1973; Opposition spokesman on primary industry, 1974–75; Leader of House, 1975–79; Minister for: Agriculture and N Territory, Nov.-Dec. 1975; Primary Industry, 1975–79; Special Trade Representations, 1980; Communications, 1980–82; Defence, 1982–83; Leader of the House for the Opposition, 1983–89; Shadow Minister: Defence, 1983–87; Trade and Resources, 1987–89. Member Committee: House of Reps Standing Orders, 1974–79, 1980–82, 1983–84; Privileges, 1980–82; Legal and Constitutional Affairs, 1990–; Jt Foreign Affairs, Defence and Trade, 1990–; Nat. Crime Authority, 1990–; Mem., Jt Standing Cttee on Migration Regulations, 1990–. *Address:* Parliament House, Canberra, ACT 2600, Australia. *T:* (06) 2774064. *Clubs:* Australian, American, Union (Sydney); Tamworth; Killara Golf.

SINCLAIR, Sir Ian (McTaggart), KCMG 1977 (CMG 1972); QC 1979; Barrister-at-Law; Visiting Professor of International Law, King's College, London, since 1989; *b* 14 Jan. 1926; *s* of late John Sinclair, company director; *m* 1954, Barbara Elizabeth (*née* Lenton); two *s* one *d*. *Educ:* Merchiston Castle Sch. (Scholar); King's Coll., Cambridge; BA 1948, LLB 1949 (1st cl. hons). Served Intelligence Corps, 1944–47. Called to the Bar, Middle Temple, 1952; Bencher, 1980. Asst Legal Adviser, Foreign Office, 1950–56; Legal Adviser, HM Embassy, Bonn, 1957–60; Asst Legal Adviser, FO, 1960–64; Legal Adviser, UK Mission to the UN, New York, and HM Embassy, Washington, 1964–67; Foreign and Commonwealth Office: Legal Counsellor, 1967–71; Dep. Legal Advr, 1971–72; Second Legal Advr, 1973–75; Legal Advr, 1976–84. Has been Legal Adviser to UK delegn at numerous internat. confs, incl. Geneva Conf. on Korea and Indo-China, 1954, and Brussels negotiations for UK entry into the EEC, 1961–63; Dep. Chm., UK delegn to Law of Treaties Conf., Vienna, 1968–69; Legal Adviser to UK delegn on negotiations for UK entry into EEC, 1970–72; Member: Bureau of European Cttee on Legal Co-operation, Council of Europe, 1979–81; Panel of Conciliators, Annex to Vienna Convention on Law of Treaties, 1981–; Internat. Law Commn, 1981–86; Panel of Arbitrators, Internat. Centre for Settlement of Investment Disputes, 1988–; Panel of Legal Experts under INTELSAT Convention, 1990–. Mem., Committee of Management: British Inst. of Internat. and Comparative Law, 1976–; Inst. of Advanced Legal Studies, 1980–84. Associate Mem., Inst de Droit Internat., 1983, elected Mem., 1987; Hon. Mem., Amer. Soc. of Internat. Law, 1987. *Publications:* Vienna Convention on the Law of Treaties, 1973, 2nd edn 1984; International Law Commission, 1987; articles in British Yearbook of International Law, International and Comparative Law Qly and other legal jls. *Recreations:* golf, fishing, watching sea-birds. *Address:* Lassington, Chithurst, Petersfield, Hants GU31 5EU. *T:* Midhurst (0730) 815370; 10B South Park Road, Wimbledon, SW19 8ST. *T:* 081–543 1843; (chambers) 2 Hare Court, Temple, EC4. *T:* 071–583 1770. *Club:* Athenæum.

SINCLAIR, Isabel Lillias, (Mrs J. G. MacDonald), QC (Scotland) 1964; Sheriff of Lothian and Borders (formerly Roxburgh, Berwick, and Selkirk), 1968–79, now Honorary Sheriff; Honorary Sheriff of Bute; *d* of William Sinclair, Glasgow, and Isabella (*née* Thomson), Glasgow; *m* 1938, J. Gordon MacDonald (decd), BL, Solicitor, Glasgow. *Educ:* Shawlands Academy; Glasgow Univ. MA 1932; BL 1946. Worked as a newspaper-woman from 1932. Admitted to Faculty of Advocates, Edinburgh, 1949. Sheriff-Substitute of Lanarkshire at Airdrie, 1966–68. *Address:* 30 Ravelston Garden, Edinburgh EH4 3LE. *T:* 031–337 9797. *Club:* Royal Scottish Automobile (Glasgow).

SINCLAIR, Prof. John McHardy; Professor of Modern English Language, University of Birmingham, since 1965; *b* 14 June 1933; *s* of late George Ferguson Sinclair and of Isabella (*née* Palmer); *m* 1956, Margaret Myfanwy Lloyd; two *s* one *d*. *Educ:* George Heriot's Sch., Edinburgh; Edinburgh Univ. (MA). Served Royal Air Force (Flt-Lt), 1955–58. Lectr, Edinburgh Univ., 1959–65. Adjunct Prof., Shanghai Jiao Tong Univ., 1986–. *Publications:* A Course in Spoken English—Grammar, 1972; (with R. M. Coulthard) Towards an Analysis of Discourse, 1975, 2nd edn 1978; (with D. C. Brazil) Teacher Talk, 1982; Corpus, Concordance, Collocation, 1991; Editor in Chief, Cobuild: Collin's Cobuild English Language Dictionary, 1987; Collins Cobuild English Grammar, 1990. *Recreation:* printing. *Address:* School of English, The University, Edgbaston, Birmingham B15 2TT. *T:* 021–414 5688.

SINCLAIR, Prof. Sir Keith, Kt 1985; CBE 1983; Professor of History, University of Auckland, 1963–87, now Emeritus; *b* 5 Dec. 1922; *s* of Ernest Duncan and Florence Sinclair; *m* 1st, 1947, Mary Edith Land; four *s*; 2nd, 1976, Raewyn Mary Dalziel. *Educ:* Mount Albert Grammar Sch.; Auckland University Coll.; MA, PhD (NZ); LittD (Auckland); Univ. of London. War service, NZ Army, 1941–43; RNZNVR, in UK, 1944–45; Lectr in History, 1947, Senior Lectr, 1952, Associate Prof., 1960, Auckland University Coll. Carnegie Commonwealth Fellow, Inst. of Commonwealth Studies, London, 1954–55; Carnegie Travelling Grant, USA, 1955; Vis. Fellow, Inst. of Advanced Studies, ANU, 1967, 1978, 1983; Smuts Vis. Fellow, Cambridge, 1968–69. Labour candidate, Eden electorate, 1969 (elected for 3 weeks, defeated on postal ballot). Chm., NZ Authors' Fund Cttee, 1973–85; Trustee, NZ Nat. Library, 1981–90; Mem., NZ 1990 Commn (planning sesquicentenary), 1987–90. *Publications:* Maori Land League, 1950; Songs for a Summer, 1952; Strangers or Beasts, 1954; Imperial Federation, 1955; Origins of the Maori Wars, 1957; A History of New Zealand, 1959, rev. edn 1980; (ed) The Maori King, by J. E. Gorst, 1959; (with W. F. Mandle) The Bank of New South Wales in New Zealand, 1961; (ed) Distance Looks Our Way, 1961; A Time to Embrace, 1963; (ed with R. M. Chapman) Studies of a Small Democracy, 1963; William Pember Reeves, 1965; The Firewheel Tree, 1973; Walter Nash, 1977; The Reefs of Fire, 1977; (with Wendy Harrex) Looking Back: a photographic history of New Zealand, 1978; History of the University of Auckland, 1983; (with Judith Bassett and Marcia Stenson) The Story of New Zealand, 1985; A Destiny Apart: New Zealand's search for national identity, 1986; (ed) Tasman Relations: New Zealand and Australia 1788–1988, 1987; (ed) Oxford Illustrated History of New Zealand, 1990; Kinds of Peace: Maori people after the Wars 1870–85, 1991; articles in learned jls. *Recreations:* fishing, gardening. *Address:* 13 Mariposa Crescent, Birkenhead, Auckland 10, New Zealand. *T:* 480–5057.

SINCLAIR, Air Vice-Marshal Sir Laurence (Frank), GC 1941; KCB 1957 (CB 1946); CBE 1943; DSO 1940 (and Bar, 1943); *b* 1908; *m* 1941, Valerie (*d* 1990), *d* of Lt-Col Joseph Dalton White; one *s* one *d*. *Educ:* Imperial Service Coll.; RAF Coll. Cranwell. Comd No 110 Sqdn in 1940; Comd RAF Watton, 1941; Comd Tactical Light Bomber Force in North Africa and Italy, 1943–44; ADC to King George VI, 1943–44; subsequently Sen. Air Staff Officer, Balkan Air Force; Imperial Defence Coll., 1947; commanded No 2 Light Bomber Group (Germany), 1948–49; Assistant Commandant RAF Staff College, 1949–50; Commandant, Royal Air Force College Cranwell, 1950–52; Commandant, School of Land/Air Warfare, 1952–53; Asst Chief of the Air Staff (Operations), 1953–55; Comdr British Forces, Arabian Peninsula, 1955–57; Commandant Joint Services Staff College, 1958–60, retired from RAF. Controller of Ground Services, Min. of Aviation, 1960–61; Controller, Nat. Air Traffic Control Services, Min. of Aviation, and MoD, 1962–66. Legion of Merit (American), 1943; Legion of Honour, 1944; Partisan Star (Yugoslavia). *Address:* Haines Land, Great Brickhill, Milton Keynes MK17 9AQ.

SINCLAIR, Rt. Rev. Maurice Walter; *see* Northern Argentina, Bishop of.

SINCLAIR, Michael; *see* Shea, M. S. MacA.

SINCLAIR, Sir Patrick (Robert Richard), 10th Bt *cr* 1704 (NS), of Dunbeath, Caithness-shire; barrister; *b* 21 May 1936; *s* of Alexander Robert Sinclair (Robin) (*d* 1972) (*b* of 8th Bt) and Vera Mabel (*d* 1981), *d* of late Walter Stephings Baxendale; *S* cousin, 1990; *m* 1974, Susan Catherine Beresford Davies, *e d* of Geoffrey Clive Davies, OBE; one *s* one *d*. *Educ:* Winchester; Oriel Coll., Oxford. Nat. Service, RNVR, 1954–56 (Actg Sub-Lieut). Called to the Bar, Lincoln's Inn, 1961; in practice at Chancery Bar. *Recreations:* sailing, tennis. *Heir:* *s* William Robert Francis Sinclair, *b* 27 March 1979. *Address:* 5 New Square, Lincoln's Inn, WC2A 3RJ. *T:* 071–404 0404. *Club:* Pin Mill Sailing (Suffolk).

SINCLAIR, Rear-Adm. Peter Ross, AO 1986; Governor of New South Wales, since 1990; farmer, Flagship Poll Hereford Stud; *b* 16 Nov. 1934; *s* of G. P. Sinclair; *m* 1957, Shirley, *d* of J. A. McLellan; one *s* two *d*. *Educ:* North Sydney Boys' High Sch.; Royal Aust. Naval Coll.; Royal Coll. of Defence Studies. jssc. Joined RAN 1948; served HM Australian ships Australia, Tobruk, Vengeance, Arunta, Swan, Sydney, Vendetta, Vampire, Penguin, HMS Jutland; CO HMAS Duchess, 1970–72; CO HMAS Hobart, 1974–77; Dir, Naval Plans, 1979–80; Dir-Gen., Mil. Staff Branch, Strategic and Internat. Policy Div., Defence Dept, 1980–82; Chief of Staff, 1983–84; First Comdt, Aust. Defence Force Acad., 1984–86; Flag Officer Comdg Aust. Fleet, 1986–90 and Dep. Chief of Naval Staff, 1989. *Recreations:* painting, sketching, whittling, reading, cricket, golf, tennis. *Address:* Government House, Sydney, NSW 2000, Australia.

SINCLAIR, Sir Ronald Ormiston, KBE 1963; Kt 1956; President, Court of Appeal: for the Bahamas and for Bermuda, 1965–70; for British Honduras, 1968–70; Chairman, Industrial Tribunals (England and Wales), 1966–69; *b* 2 May 1903; *yr s* of Rev. W. A. Sinclair, Auckland, NZ; *m* 1935, Ellen Isabel Entrican; two *s*. *Educ:* New Plymouth Boys' High School, NZ; Auckland University College, NZ; Balliol College, Oxford. Barrister and Solicitor of Supreme Court of New Zealand, 1924; LLM (NZ) (Hons) 1925; Administrative Service, Nigeria, 1931; Magistrate, Nigeria, 1936; Resident Magistrate, Northern Rhodesia, 1938; Barrister-at-Law, Middle Temple, 1939; Puisne Judge, Tanganyika, 1946; Chief Justice, Nyasaland, 1953–55; Vice-President, East African Court of Appeal, 1956–57, Pres., 1962–64; Chief Justice of Kenya, 1957–62. *Address:* 158 Victoria Avenue, Remuera, Auckland, New Zealand.

SINCLAIR-LOCKHART, Sir Simon (John Edward Francis), 15th Bt *cr* 1636 (NS); *b* 22 July 1941; *s* of Sir Muir Edward Sinclair-Lockhart, 14th Bt, and of Olga Ann, *d* of late Claude Victor White-Parsons, Hawkes Bay, NZ; *S* father, 1985; *m* 1973, Felicity Edith, *d* of late I. L. C. Stewart, NZ; twin *s* one *d*. *Heir:* *er* twin *s* Robert Muir Sinclair-Lockhart, *b* 12 Sept. 1973. *Address:* 54 Duart Road, Havelock North, Hawke's Bay, New Zealand.

SINCLAIR-STEVENSON, Christopher Terence; publisher; Managing Director, Sinclair-Stevenson Ltd, since 1989; *b* 27 June 1939; *s* of George and Gloria Sinclair-Stevenson; *m* 1965, Deborah Susan (*née* Walker-Smith). *Educ:* Eton Coll.; St John's Coll., Cambridge (MA). Joined Hamish Hamilton Ltd, 1961, Dir, 1970, Man. Dir, 1974–89. *Publications:* The Gordon Highlanders, 1968; Inglorious Rebellion, 1971; The Life of a Regiment, 1974; Blood Royal, 1979; That Sweet Enemy, 1987. *Recreations:* music, travel, food, the written word. *Address:* 3 South Terrace, SW7 2TB. *T:* 071–584 8087.

SINDALL, Adrian John; HM Diplomatic Service; Middle East Marketing Director, Defence Export Services Organisation, Ministry of Defence, since 1988, on secondment; *b* 5 Oct. 1937; *s* of Stephen Sindall and Clare Mallet; *m* 1st, 1958; one *s* one *d*; 2nd, 1978, Jill Margaret Cowley. *Educ:* Battersea Grammar Sch. FO, 1956–58; ME Centre for Arab Studies, 1958–60; Third Sec. (Commercial), Baghdad, 1960–62; Second Sec., British Embassy, Rabat, 1962–67; First Secretary: FCO, 1967–70; Beirut, 1970–72; First Sec. and Head of Chancery, British Embassy, Lima, 1972–76; FCO, 1976–79; Counsellor, Head of Chancery and Consul-Gen., Amman, 1979–82; Hd of S America Dept, FCO, 1982–85; Consul-Gen., Sydney, 1985–88. *Address:* c/o Foreign and Commonwealth Office, SW1A 2AH.

SINDELL, Marion Harwood; Chief Executive, Equal Opportunities Commission, 1979–85; *b* 23 June 1925; *d* of Arthur Barrett Sindell and Ethel Maude Sindell. *Educ:* Lincoln Girls' High Sch.; St Hilda's Coll., Oxford (MA). Solicitor. Deputy Town Clerk: Workington, 1959–64; Nuneaton, 1964–66; Town Clerk, Goole, 1966–74; Chief Exec., Boothferry Bor. Council, 1974–79. *Address:* The Granary, Skelton, Penrith, Cumbria.

SINDEN, Donald Alfred, CBE 1979; actor; *b* 9 Oct. 1923; *s* of Alfred Edward Sinden and Mabel Agnes (*née* Fuller), Sussex; *m* 1948, Diana, *d* of Daniel and Muriel Mahony; two *s*. First appearance on stage, 1942, in Charles F. Smith's Co., Mobile Entertainments Southern Area; Leicester Repertory Co., 1945; Memorial Theatre Co., Stratford upon Avon, 1946 and 1947; Old Vic and Bristol Old Vic, 1948; The Heiress, Haymarket, 1949–50; Bristol Old Vic, 1950; Red Letter Day, Garrick, 1951. Under contract to Rank Organisation, 1952–60, appearing in 23 films including The Cruel Sea, Doctor in the House, etc. Returned to theatre, appearing in Odd Man In, St Martin's, 1957; Peter Pan, Scala, 1960; Guilty Party, St Martin's, 1961; Royal Shakespeare Co., playing Richard Plantagenet in Henry VI (The Wars of the Roses), Price in Eh!, etc, 1963 and 1964; British Council tour of S America in Dear Liar and Happy Days, 1965; There's a Girl in my Soup, Globe, 1966; Lord Foppington in The Relapse, RSC, Aldwych, 1967; Not Now Darling, Strand, 1968; RSC, Stratford, 1969 and Aldwych, 1970 playing Malvolio; Henry VIII; Sir Harcourt Courtly in London Assurance, revived at New Theatre, 1972, tour of the USA, 1974 (Drama Desk Award); In Praise of Love, Duchess, 1973; Stockmann in An Enemy of the People, Chichester, 1975; Habeas Corpus, USA, 1975; Benedick in Much Ado About Nothing, King Lear, RSC, Stratford, 1976, Aldwych, 1977 (Variety Club of GB Stage Actor of 1976; Evening Standard Drama Award, Best Actor, 1977); Shut Your Eyes and Think of England, Apollo, 1977; Othello, RSC, Stratford, 1979, Aldwych, 1980; Present Laughter, Vaudeville, 1981; Uncle Vanya, Haymarket, 1982; The School for Scandal, Haymarket and Duke of York's (Eur. tour, 1984), and Ariadne auf Naxos, Coliseum, 1983; Two Into One, Shaftesbury, 1984; The Scarlet Pimpernel, Chichester transf. to Her Majesty's, 1985; Major Barbara, Chichester, 1988; Over My Dead Body, Savoy, 1989; Oscar Wilde, Playhouse, 1990; Out of Order, Shaftesbury, 1990; dir, The Importance of Being Earnest, Royalty, 1987; *television series include:* Our Man from St Marks; Two's Company; Discovering English Churches; Never the Twain; has appeared in many films. Assoc. Artist, RSC, 1967–. Member: Council, British Actors Equity Assoc., 1966–77 (Trustee, 1988–); Council, RSA, 1972; Adv. Council, V&A Museum, 1973–80; Arts Council Drama Panel, 1973–77; Leicestershire Educn Arts Cttee, 1974–; BBC Archives Adv. Cttee, 1975–78; London Acad. of Music and Dramatic Art Council, 1976–; Kent and E Sussex Reg. Cttee, National Trust, 1978–82; Arts Council of GB, 1982–86; Chairman: British Theatre Museum Assoc., 1971–77; Theatre Museum Adv. Council, 1973–80; President: Fedn of Playgoers Socs, 1968–; Royal Theatrical Fund, 1983–; Vice-Pres., London Appreciation Soc., 1960–. FRSA 1966. *Publications:* A Touch of the Memoirs (autobiog.), 1982; Laughter in the Second Act (autobiog.), 1985; (ed) The Everyman Book of Theatrical Anecdotes, 1987; The English Country Church, 1988. *Recreations:* theatrical history, architecture, ecclesiology, genealogy, serendipity, London. *Address:* 60 Temple Fortune Lane, NW11 7UE; Rats Castle, Isle of Oxney, Kent. *Clubs:* Garrick (Trustee, 1980–), Beefsteak, MCC.

SINGER, Alfred Ernst; Chairman, London Trust PLC; Director, Ansbacher PLC; *b* 15 Nov. 1924; *s* of late Dr Robert Singer and Mrs Charlotte Singer; *m* 1st, 1951, Gwendoline Doris Barnett (*d* 1985); one *s* one *d*; 2nd, 1988, Christine Annette McCarron (*née* Evans). *Educ:* Halesowen Grammar Sch. Served War of 1939–45: Army, 1943–47. Subseq. professional and exec. posts with: Callingham, Brown & Co, Bunzl Pulp & Paper Ltd, David Brown Tractors Ltd; Rank Xerox Ltd, 1963–70 (Dir, 1967); Tesco Stores (Holdings) Ltd, 1970–73 (Dep. Managing Dir); Man. Dir (Giro), PO Corp., 1973–76; Chairman: PO Staff Superannuation Fund, 1977–79; Cannon Assurance Ltd, 1980–86. Chairman: Long Range Planning Soc., 1970–73; Council, Assoc. of Certified Accountants, 1972–81 (Vice-Pres., 1979–80); Member: Cttee for Industrial Technologies, DTI, 1972–76; National Economic Develt Council: Chm., Electronic Computers Sector Working Party; Member: Electronics EDC; Food and Drink Manufacturing Industry EDC, 1976–77; Governor, Centre for Environmental Studies, 1979–85 (Chm., 1981–85). *Address:* 7 Bacon's Lane, Highgate Village, N6 6BL. *T:* 081–340 0189; York Cottage, Lower Chedworth, Cheltenham, Glos GL54 5AN. *T:* Fossebridge (0285) 720523. *Clubs:* Athenæum, MCC.

SINGER, Aubrey Edward, CBE 1984; Chairman and Managing Director, White City Films, since 1984; *b* 21 Jan. 1927; *s* of Louis Henry Singer and late Elizabeth (*née* Walton); *m* 1949, Cynthia Hilda Adams; one *s* two *d* (and one *d* decd). *Educ:* Giggleswick; Bradford Grammar School. Joined film industry, 1944; directed various films teaching armed forces to shoot; worked extensively in Africa, 1946–48; worked on children's films in Austria, 1948–49; joined BBC TV Outside Broadcasts, 1949; TV Producer Scotland, 1951; BBC New York Office, 1953; returned to London as Producer, 1956; produced many scientific programmes; Asst Head of Outside Broadcasts, 1959; Head of Science and Features, 1961; Head of Features Gp, BBC TV, 1967; Controller, BBC 2, 1974–78; Man. Dir, BBC Radio, 1978–82; Dep. Dir-Gen., and Man. Dir, Television, BBC, 1982–84. Chm., Soc. of Film and Television Arts, 1971–73. President: TV and Radio Industries Club, 1984–85; Nat. Mus. of Photography, Film and TV, 1984–. FRTS 1978 (a Vice-Pres., 1982–88); FRAS; FRSA. Hon. DLitt Bradford, 1984. *Recreations:* walking, talking, archery. *Address:* 79 Sutton Court Road, Chiswick, W4 3EQ. *T:* 081–994 6795. *Club:* Savile.

SINGER, Harold Samuel; His Honour Judge Singer; a Circuit Judge, since 1984; *b* 17 July 1935; *s* of Ellis and Minnie Singer; *m* 1966, Adèle Berenice Emanuel; one *s* two *d*. *Educ:* Salford Grammar School; Fitzwilliam House, Cambridge. BA Cantab. Called to the Bar, Gray's Inn, 1957; a Recorder, 1981–84. *Recreations:* music, painting, books, photography, golf.

SINGER, Harry Bruce, TD 1955; DL; FCA; Senior Partner, Singer & Partners, Chartered Accountants, 1968–87; *b* 21 June 1921; *er s* of Geoffrey and Agnes Singer; *m* 1945, Betty Alison Brittan; one *s*. *Educ:* Cathedral Sch., Hereford. FCA 1960 (Mem., 1953). Served War: commnd 99th (London Welsh) HAA Regt, RA, 1941; served in UK and NW Europe; Instr, Sch. of AA Artillery, 1945; joined 281 (Glam Yeomanry) Field Regt, RA (TA), 1947; in comd, 1959–62. Pres., S Wales Soc. of Chartered Accountants, 1970–71; Inst. of Chartered Accountants in England and Wales: Mem. Council, 1973–85; Vice-Pres., 1979–80; Dep. Pres., 1980–81; Pres., 1981–82. Hon. Treasurer, SSAFA, 1990–. Liveryman, Worshipful Co. of Chartered Accountants, 1978; Freeman, City of London, 1978. Vice Chm. Wales, TA&VRA, 1984–87. DL Mid Glamorgan, 1985. *Recreations:* golf, foreign travel, Rugby football (originally as player). *Address:* 8 Windsor House, Castle Court, Cardiff CF1 1DG. *Clubs:* Army and Navy; Cardiff and County, Cardiff Golf (Cardiff).

SINGER, (Jan) Peter; QC 1987; a Recorder, since 1987; *b* 10 Sept. 1944; *s* of Dr Hanus Kurt Singer and Anita Singer; *m* 1970, Julia Mary Caney; one *s* one *d*. *Educ:* King Edward's School, Birmingham; Selwyn College, Cambridge. Called to the Bar, Inner Temple, 1967. Chm., Family Law Bar Assoc., 1990– (Sec., 1980–83, Treasurer, 1983–90); Member: Matrimonial Causes Rule Cttee, 1981–85; Senate of Inns of Court and Bar, 1983–86; Law Soc. Legal Aid Cttee, 1984–89; Gen. Council of the Bar, 1990–. *Publication:* (ed jtly) Rayden on Divorce, 14th edn, 1983. *Recreations:* gardening, walking, travel. *Address:* 1 Mitre Court Buildings, Temple, EC4Y 7BS. *T:* 071–353 0434, *Fax:* 071–353 3988.

SINGER, Norbert, CBE 1990; PhD, FRSC; Director, Thames Polytechnic, since 1978; *b* 3 May 1931; *s* of late Salomon Singer and late Mina Korn; *m* Brenda Margaret Walter, *e d* of Richard and Gladys Walter, Tunbridge Wells, Kent. *Educ:* Highbury County School; Queen Mary Coll., London. BSc, PhD, CChem, FRSC. Research Chemist and Project Leader, Morgan Crucible Co. Ltd, 1954–57; Lecturer, Senior Lectr, Principal Lectr and Dep. Head of Department, Dept of Chemistry, Northern Polytechnic, 1958–70; Head of Dept of Life Sciences 1971–74, Professor of Life Sciences 1972–74, Polytechnic of Central London; Asst Director, then Dep. Director, Polytechnic of North London, 1974–78. Council for National Academic Awards: Mem., 1982–88; Chm., Reviews Co-ordination Sub-Cttee, 1984–87; Vice Chm., Cttee for Academic and Institutional Policy, 1985–87; Mem., Accreditation Cttee, 1987–89; Chm., Cttee for CATs, 1990–. Mem., MSC Nat. Steering Gp, TVEI, 1984–88 (Mem., Quality and Standards Gp, 1987–89). *Publications:* research papers in electrochemistry, theoretical chemistry and surface chemistry in scientific jls. *Recreation:* squash. *Address:* Croft Lodge, Bayhall Road, Tunbridge Wells, Kent TN2 4TP. *T:* Tunbridge Wells (0892) 23821.

SINGER, Peter; see Singer, J. P.

SINGH, Kanwar N.; see Natwar-Singh.

SINGH, Khushwant; Padma Bhushan, 1974; Member of Parliament, India, since 1980; Barrister-at-Law; *b* Feb. 1915; *m* Kaval (*née* Malik); one *s* one *d*. *Educ:* Univ. of London (LLB); called to Bar. Practising Lawyer, High Court, Lahore, 1939–47; Min. of External Affairs, of India; PRO Ottawa and London, 1947–51; UNESCO, 1954–56. Visiting Lectr: Oxford (Spalding Trust); USA: Rochester, Princeton, Hawaii, Swarthmore; led Indian Delegn to Writers' Conf., Manila, Philippines, 1965; Guest Speaker at Montreal 'Expo 67'. Has written for many nat. dailies and foreign jls: New York Times; Observer and New Statesman (London); Harper's (USA); Evergreen Review (USA); London Magazine. Editor, The Illustrated Weekly of India, Bombay, 1969–78; Chief Editor, New Delhi, 1979–80; increased circulation of Illustrated Weekly of India from 80,000 to 410,000 in 9 yrs; Editor-in-chief, The Hindustan Times and Contour, New Delhi, 1980–83. *Broadcasting and Television:* All India Radio, BBC, CBC; LP recordings. Awards include: from Punjab Govt: 5,000 rupees and Robe of Honour, for contrib. to Sikh literature; Mohan Singh Award: 1,500 rupees for trans. of Sikh hymns, etc. *Publications: Sikh History and Religion:* The Sikhs, 1953; A History of the Sikhs: vol. i, 1469–1839, 1964; vol. ii, 1839–1964, 1967; Ranjit Singh, Maharajah of the Punjab, 1780–1839, 1963; Fall of the Kingdom of the Punjab; Sikhs Today; (ed) Sunset of the Sikh Empire, by Dr Sita Ram Kohli (posthumous); Hymns of Nanak The Guru. *Fiction:* The Mark of Vishnu and other stories, 1951; Train to Pakistan, 1956; I Shall Not Hear the Nightingales, 1961; *stories:* The Voice of God and other stories; Black Jasmine and other stories; A Bride for the Sahib and other stories. (*Co-author*) Sacred Writing of the Sikhs; (with Arun Joshi) Shri Ram: a biog., 1969; (with Satindra Singh) Ghadr Rebellion; (with Suneet Veer Singh) Homage to Guru Gobind Singh; *miscellaneous:* Love and Friendship (editor of anthology); Khushwant Singh's India—collection of articles (ed Rahul Singh); Shri Ram—a biography; Delhi—a Profile, 1982; The Sikhs, 1984; (with Kuldip Nayar) Punjab Tragedy, 1984; *translations:* Umrao Jan Ada, Courtesan of Lucknow, by Mohammed Ruswa (with M. A. Husaini); The Skeleton (by Amrita Pritam); Land of the Five Rivers; I Take This Woman, by Rajinder Singh Bedi; Iqbal's Dialogue with Allah (Shikwah and Jawab-e-Shikwah); We Indians. *Recreation:* bird watching. *Address:* 49E Sujan Singh Park, New Delhi 110003, India. *T:* 690159. *Clubs:* Authors'; Imperial Gymkhana (New Delhi); Bombay Gymkhana (Bombay 1).

SINGH, Mota; QC 1978; **His Honour Judge Mota Singh;** a Circuit Judge, since 1982; *b* 26 July 1930; *s* of Dalip Singh and Harnam Kaur; *m* 1950, Swaran Kaur; two *s* two *d*. *Educ:* Duke of Gloucester Sch., Nairobi, Kenya; Hon. Soc. of Lincoln's Inn. Called to the Bar, 1956. Left school, 1947; Solicitor's Clerk, Nairobi, 1948–54; Lincoln's Inn, London, 1954–56; Advocate, High Court of Kenya, 1957–65; Alderman, City of Nairobi, 1958–63; Vice-Chm., Kenya Justice; Sec., Law Soc. of Kenya, 1963–64. A Deputy Circuit Judge, 1976–82; a Recorder of the Crown Court, 1979–82. Member: London Rent Assessment Panel, 1965–67; Race Relations Bd, 1968–77. Hon. LLD Guru Nanak Dev Univ., Amritsar, 1981. *Recreations:* reading; formerly cricket (represented Kenya). *Address:* Cedarwood, 3 Somerset Road, Wimbledon SW19 5JU. *T:* 081–947 2271.

SINGH, Preetam; QC 1976; *b* 1 Oct. 1914; *s* of Waryam Singh and late Balwant Kaur; *m* 1934, Rattan Kaur (*née* Bura); three *s* one *d*. *Educ:* A. V. High Sch., Mombasa, Kenya; King's Coll., London. Called to the Bar, Gray's Inn, 1951; Mem. Bar Council and Senate of Inns of Court. Dep. Official Receiver, Kenya, 1960–64; Barrister, N Eastern Circuit, 1964–77; Advocate: Supreme Court, Kenya; High Court (Punjab and Haryana), India. Member: Commn for Racial Equality, 1977–78; BBC Adv. Cttee on Asian programmes, 1979–. Contested (L) Hallam (Sheffield), 1970. Hon. LLD Punjab, 1977. *Recreations:* hunting, politics, religion, Indian classical music. *Club:* Liberal.

SINGH, Sardar Swaran; President, Indian Council of World Affairs; *b* 19 Aug. 1907. *Educ:* Government College, Lahore; Lahore Law College. MSc (Physics) 1930; LLB 1932. Elected to Punjab Legislative Assembly, 1946; Punjab State Government: Minister for Development, Food and Civil Supplies, 1946–47; Member, Partition Committee, 1947; Minister: of Home, General Administration, Revenue, Irrigation and Electricity, 1947–49; of Capital Projects and Electricity, 1952; for Works, Housing and Supply, 1952–57, Govt of India; Member, Upper House of Indian Legislature, 1952–57; Member, Lower House of Indian Legislature, 1957; Minister: for Steel, Mines and Fuel, 1957–62;

for Railways, 1962–63; for Food and Agriculture, 1963–64; for Industry and Supply, 1964; for External Affairs, 1964–66; Foreign Minister, 1970–74, Minister of Defence, 1966–70 and 1974–75. Has led many Indian delegations to the United Nations, its agencies, foreign countries and international conferences. *Address:* c/o Indian National Congress, 5 Dr Rajendra Prasad Road, New Delhi, India.

SINGH, Vishwanath Pratap; Prime Minister of India, 1989–90; *b* 25 June 1931; *s* of Raja Bahadur Ram Gopal Singh; *m* 1955, Sita Kumari; two *s*. *Educ:* Poona Univ.; Allahabad Univ. (Vice-Pres., Students Union; LLB); Udip Pratap College, Varanasi (Pres., Students Union). Participated in Bhoodan Movement, 1957, and donated farm, Pasna, Allahabad; Mem. Exec., Allahabad Univ., 1969–71; founded Gopal Vidyalaya, Intermediate Coll., Koraon, Allahabad. Uttar Pradesh appointments: MLA, 1969–71 and 1981–83; Whip, Congress Legislature Party, 1970–71; MLC, 1980–81; Chief Minister, 1980–82; Pres., UP Congress Cttee, 1984. Mem., Lok Sabha, 1971–77, 1980, 1988–89 and 1989–; Mem., Rajya Sabha, 1983–88; Union Dep. Minister (Commerce), 1974–76; Union Minister of State (Commerce), 1976–77; Union Minister (Commerce), 1983 (also i/c Dept of Supply); Union Finance Minister, 1984–87; Defence Minister, Jan.–April 1987. Founded Jan Morcha, 1987; Pres., Janata Dal, 1988; Convenor, Nat. Front, 1988. *Address:* c/o Office of the Prime Minister, South Block, New Delhi 110011, India.

SINGH, Giani Zail; President of India, 1982–87; *b* Faridkot, 5 May 1916; *s* of Kishan Singh and Ind Kaur; *m* Pardan Kaur; one *s* three *d*. Founded Faridkot State Congress, 1946; formed govt in Faridkot State, 1948; Pres., State Praja Mandal, 1946–48; Government of Patiala and E Punjab States Union: Revenue Minister, 1948–49; Minister for Public Works and Agric., 1951–52; Pres., Provincial Congress Cttee, 1955–56; Member: Rajya Sabha, 1956–62; Punjab Assembly, 1962; Minister of State, and Pres. Punjab Provincial Congress Cttee, 1966–72; Chief Minister of Punjab, 1972–77; Minister of Home Affairs, 1980–82. *Address:* 4 Circular Road, Chanakyaduri, New Delhi 110023, India.

SINGHANIA, Sir Padampat, Kt 1943; President of the JK Organisation, India; *b* 1905; *s* of late Lala Kamlapat Singhania; *m* Srimati Anusiya Devi; four *s* one *d*. *Educ:* Home. A pioneer of Cotton, Rayon, Nylon, Jute, Woollen Textiles, Sugar, Aluminium, Steel and Engineering, Plastic, Strawboard, Paper, Chemicals, Oil Industries, Shipping, Cement, Tyres and Tubes, Dry Cell Batteries, Banking; Patron, large number of social, educational, political, and literary institutions. Founder of the Merchants' Chamber of UP: ex-Pres. of Federation of Indian Chambers of Commerce and Industry; ex-Pres., Employers' Assoc. of Northern India; Member 1st Indian Parliament, 1947–52, and many government and semi-govt bodies; formerly Chairman, Board of Governors, IIT Kanpur. Dr of Letters, Kanpur Univ., 1968. *Recreations:* riding, music, buildings, and studies. *Address:* Kamla Tower, Kanpur 208001, India. *TA:* Laljuggi, Kanpur. *T:* 69854, 51147 and 62988. *Telex* KP215.

SINGHVI, Dr Laxmi Mall; High Commissioner for India in the United Kingdom, since 1991; Senior Advocate, Supreme Court of India, since 1967 (Advocate, 1951–67); *b* 9 Nov. 1931; *s* of D. M. Singhvi and Akal Kaur Singhvi; *m* 1957, Kamla Singhvi; one *s* one *d*. *Educ:* Allahabad Univ. (BA); Rajasthan Univ. (LLB); Harvard Univ. Law Sch. (LLM); Cornell Univ. Law Sch. (SJD). MP, Independent, Lok Sabha, 1962–67; Senior Standing Counsel, State of UP, Union of India, 1967–71; Advocate-Gen., 1972–77. Dep. Leader, Indian Parly Delegn to CPA, 1964, Leader Parly Delegn, 1966; Chm. and Founder, Inst. of Constitutional and Parly Studies, 1964–. Chairman: Indian Fedn of Unesco Assocs, 1974–; World Colloquim on Legal Aid, 1975; State Bar Council, 1975–77; Indian Nat. Cttee for Abolition of Death Penalty, 1977–; Nat. Sch. of Drama, 1978–82; Supreme Court Law Reforms Cttee, 1981–82; Asian Conf. on Approaches to Human Rights, 1985; Govt of India Cttee on Revitalisation of Rural Local Self-Govt, 1986–87; Govt of India Task Force on Child Labour; Govt of India Cttee on Brain Death and Organ Transplantation; Founder Chm., 1972, Hon. Patron, 1983, Commonwealth Legal Educn Assoc.; Founder-Pres., Indian Centre for Human Rights Educn and Research; Pres., World Congress on Human Rights, 1990; Member: UN Human Rights Sub-Commn, Geneva, 1978–82 (Vice-Chm.); Nat. Commn for Unesco; Govt of India Expert Cttee on Legal Aid, 1971–73; Commn on Inf. and Broadcasting, 1964–68; Internat. Forum on Freedoms and Rights of Man, Paris, 1985–. President: Supreme Court Bar Assoc., 1977, 1978, 1980, 1982; Supreme Court Bar Trust, 1981–; Nat. Legal Aid Assoc., 1970–; Indian Centre for Independence of Judges and Lawyers, 1979–; UN Special Rapporteur on Independence of Judges and Lawyers, 1979–; Hon. Mem. and Adv. Panelist, Comparative Const. Law Project and Bicentennial of Amer. Constitution, Amer. Council of Learned Socs, 1986–88. President: World Culture; The Temple of Understanding (India); Life Trustee and Pres., India Internat. Centre; Pres. Emeritus, Authors Guild of India (Pres., 1986–90). Hon. Tagore Law Prof., 1975–. Hon. Bencher, Middle Temple, 1987. Hon. LLD: Banaras Hindu Univ. 1984; Jabalpur, 1983. Hon. Nyayavacaspati, Gurukul, 1968. Award, G. D. Birle Trust. Author, Jain Declaration on Nature. *Publications:* Horizons of Freedom, 1969; (ed) Law and Poverty, 1970; Indian Federalism, 1974; Legal Aid, 1985; Law Day, 1985; Independence of Justice, 1985; Freedom on Trial, 1991; The Evening Sun (poems), 1991; A Third International Covenant for the Prevention of Ecocide, 1991. *Recreations:* theatre, poetry, chess, gardening, classical Indian dance appreciation, archaeology. *Address:* Indian High Commission, India House, Aldwych WC2B 4NA.

SINGLETON, Barry Neill; QC 1989; *b* 12 April 1946; *s* of late Clifford and Moyna Singleton; *m* 1971, Anne Mary Potter; one *s* two *d*. *Educ:* Downside Sch.; Gonville and Caius Coll., Cambridge (MA). Called to the Bar, Gray's Inn, 1968. *Address:* 1 King's Bench Walk, Temple, EC4Y 7DB. *T:* 071–583 6266, *Fax:* 071–583 2068.

SINGLETON, Sir Edward (Henry Sibbald), Kt 1975; arbitrator and solicitor; Member of Council, The Law Society, 1961–80 (Vice-President of the Society, 1973, President, 1974); *b* 7 April 1921; *s* of W. P. Singleton, Colwall, and Florence, *d* of Sir Francis Sibbald Scott, 5th Bt; *m* 1943, Margaret Vere Hutton; three *s* one *d*. *Educ:* Shrewsbury; BNC, Oxford. MA 1946. Served War, as Pilot, Fleet Air Arm, 1941–45. Solicitor, 1949; Partner in Macfarlanes, 1954, consultant 1977–86; FCIArb 1982; Companion, Instn of Civil Engrs, 1982. Chm. and Dir of various public and private cos; Dir, Abbey Nat. Bldg Soc., 1977–89. Member: Council for the Securities Industry, 1978–83; Council of Management, The White Ensign Assoc. Ltd, 1984; Trustee: Fleet Air Arm Museum; Temple Bar Trust; Westminster Hospital, 1978–84. *Recreation:* relaxing. *Address:* Flat 7, 62 Queen's Gate, SW7 5JP. *T:* 071–581 3616.

SINGLETON, Norman, CB 1966; retired civil servant; *b* 21 March 1913; *s* of Charles and Alice Singleton, Bolton, Lancs; *m* 1936, Cicely Margaret Lucas, Claverdon, Warwick; one *s* two *d*. *Educ:* Bolton School; Emmanuel College, Cambridge. Min. of Labour, 1935; Under-Secretary: Civil Service Pay Research Unit, 1956–60; Min. of Labour (now Dept of Employment), 1960–69; Sec., 1969–72, Dep. Chm., 1973–74, Commn on Industrial Relns; Dep. Chm., Central Arbitration Cttee, 1976–85; Arbitrator and Mediator, ACAS, 1976–87. *Publication:* Industrial Relations Procedures, 1976. *Address:* 34 Willoughby Road, Hampstead, NW3 1RU. *T:* 071–435 1504.
See also E. A. Woods.

SINGLETON, Roger; Senior Director, Barnardo's, since 1984; *b* 6 Nov. 1942; *s* of late Malcolm and Ethel Singleton, Nether Edge, Sheffield; *m* 1966, Ann Hasler; two *d*. *Educ:* City Grammar Sch., Sheffield; Durham Univ. (MA); Bath Univ. (MSc); London Univ. (DipSocStud); Leeds (Cert. Ed.). Appts in care and educn of deprived and delinquent young people, 1961–71; professional adviser to Children's Regional Planning Cttee, 1971–74; Dep. Dir, Dr Barnardo's, 1974–84. Chm., Nat. Council of Voluntary Child Care Organisations, 1990; Member: Central Council for Educn and Training in Social Work, 1984–86; Council, Nat. Children's Bureau, 1982–84; Council, Nat. Youth Bureau, 1986–91. Company Dir. FBIM. *Publications:* contribs to professional jls. *Recreations:* home and garden. *Address:* Littleacres, Blackmore End, near Braintree, Essex CM7 4DT. *T:* Great Dunmow (0371) 850918; Barnardo's, Tanners Lane, Barkingside, Ilford, Essex IG6 1QG. *T:* 081–550 8822. *Club:* Reform.

SINGLETON, Valerie; television journalist and broadcaster; with BBC since 1962; presenter, Radio 4 PM, since 1981; *b* 9 April 1937; *d* of Wing Comdr Denis G. Singleton, OBE and Eileen Singleton, LRAM. *Educ:* Arts Educational Sch. (3 times Drama Cup); RADA (schol.). Bromley Rep.; commercial voice-overs; TV advertising magazines; joined BBC as announcer, 1962; presenter: Blue Peter, 1962–71; Blue Peter Special Assignments, covering capital cities, islands, famous houses, 1972–75, and Rivers Niagra and Yukon, 1980; Val Meets the VIPs, 1972–75; Nationwide, 1972–78; Tonight, and Tonight in Town, 1978–79; Echoes of Holocaust, documentary, BBC 2, Midweek, Radio 4, 1980; The Money Programme, BBC 2, 1980–88; numerous other radio and TV progs; corporate videos, business confs. Work for British Wildlife Appeal and Dr Barnardo's. *Recreations:* sailing, ski-ing, water ski-ing, photography, exploring London, travelling anywhere, riding, pottering in museums and antique shops. *Address:* c/o Arlington Enterprises, 1-3 Charlotte Street, W1. *Clubs:* Hurlingham; Hayling Island Sailing.

SINGLETON, William Brian, CBE 1974; FRCVS; retired; Director, Animal Health Trust, 1977–88; *b* 23 Feb. 1923; *s* of William Max Singleton and Blanche May Singleton; *m* 1947, Hilda Stott; two *s* one *d* (and one *s* decd). *Educ:* Queen Elizabeth Grammar Sch., Darlington; Royal (Dick) Sch. of Vet. Medicine, Edinburgh. Vis. Prof. Surgery, Ontario Vet. Coll., Guelph, Canada, 1973–74; Hon. Vet. Advr to Jockey Club, 1977–88. Member: Govt Cttee of Inquiry into Future Role of Veterinary Profession in GB (Chm., Sir Michael Swann), 1971–75; UGC Wkg Pty on Vet. Educn into the 21st Century (Chm., Sir Ralph Riley, FRS), 1987–89. President: British Small Animal Vet. Assoc., 1960–61; RCVS, 1969–70; World Small Animal Vet. Assoc., 1975–77. Hon. Diplomate, Amer. Coll. of Vet. Surgeons, 1973. Dalrymple-Champneys Award, 1987. *Publications:* (ed jtly) Canine Medicine and Therapeutics, 1979; chapter in International Encyclopaedia of Veterinary Medicine, 1966; chapters in Animal Nursing Part II, 1966; numerous papers in veterinary and comparative pathology jls. *Recreations:* gardening, sailing, bird watching, horse riding. *Address:* Vine Cottage, Morston Road, Blakeney, Holt, Norfolk NR25 7BE. *T:* Cley (0263) 740246. *Club:* Farmers'.

SINHA, 3rd Baron *cr* 1919, of Raipur; **Sudhindro Prosanno Sinha;** Chairman and Managing Director, MacNeill and Barry Ltd, Calcutta; *b* 29 Oct. 1920; *s* of Aroon Kumar, 2nd Baron Sinha (*s* of Satyendra Prasanna, 1st Baron Sinha, the first Indian to be created a peer) and Nirupama, *yr d* of Rai Bahadur Lalit Mohan Chatterjee; *S* father, 1967; *m* 1945, Madhabi, *d* of late Monoranjan Chatterjee, Calcutta; one *s* two *d* (and one *s* decd). *Educ:* Bryanston School, Blandford. *Heir:* *s* Hon. Susanta Prasanna Sinha [*b* 1953; *m* 1972, Patricia Orchard; one *d* (and one *s* one *d* decd]. *Address:* 7 Lord Sinha Road, Calcutta, India.

SINKER, Rev. Canon Michael Roy; Canon Emeritus of Lincoln Cathedral, 1969; *b* 28 Sept. 1908; 3rd *s* of late Rev. Francis Sinker, sometime Vicar of Ilkley; *m* 1939, Edith Watt Applegate; one *s* two *d*. *Educ:* Haileybury; Clare College, Cambridge (MA); Cuddesdon College, Oxford. Curate of Dalston, Cumberland, 1932–34; Chaplain to South African Church Railway Mission, 1935–38; Curate of Bishop's Hatfield 1938–39; Vicar of Dalton-in-Furness, 1939–46; Vicar of Saffron Walden, 1946–63; Hon. Canon of Chelmsford Cathedral, 1955–63; Rural Dean of Saffron Walden, 1948–63; Archdeacon of Stow, 1963–67; Rector of St Matthew, Ipswich, 1967–77. *Address:* 8 White Horse Way, Westbury, Wilts BA13 3AH.

SINNAMON, Sir Hercules Vincent, Kt 1985; OBE 1980; *b* 13 Nov. 1899; *s* of James Sinnamon and Janie Sinnamon (*née* Jackson). *Educ:* Taringa State School; Stott's Business College, Brisbane. FCISA; FIBA; AASA. Joined National Mutual Life Association, 1914; Manager, Townsville, Sub Accountant, and other executive positions; retired as Executive Officer, 1965. Retirement is happily spent furthering community projects and breeding beef and dairy cattle. *Publication:* The Gentleman Farmer's Paradise, 1980. *Recreations:* outdoors, riding, surfing. *Address:* Glen Ross, 619 Rocks and Sinnamon Roads, Sinnamon Park, Qld 4073, Australia. *T:* 07/3761540. *Club:* National Mutual Life 25 Years' and Retired Officers' (Brisbane).

SINNATT, Maj.-Gen. Martin Henry, CB 1984; Senior Executive and Secretary, Kennel Club, since 1984; *b* 28 Jan. 1928; *s* of Dr O. S. Sinnatt and Mrs M. H. Sinnatt (*née* Randall); *m* 1957, Susan Rosemary Clarke; four *d*. *Educ:* Hitchin Grammar School; Hertford College, Oxford (1 Year Army Short Course); RMA Sandhurst. Commissioned RTR, 1948; served Germany, Korea, UK, Hong Kong, 1948–58; psc 1959; Aden, 1959–62; Germany and UK, 1962–64; MA to C-in-C AFNE, Norway, 1964–66; jssc 1967; Germany and UK, 1967–69; CO 4 RTR, BAOR, 1969–71; Nat. Defence Coll., 1971–72; Comdr RAC, 1 (BR) Corps, BAOR, 1972–74; Dir Operational Requirements MoD, 1974–77; rcds 1978; Dir, Combat Development (Army), 1979–81; Chief of Staff to Live Oak, SHAPE, 1982–84; completed service, 1984. *Recreations:* medieval history, gardening and swimming; also, when time and finances permit, skiing and golf. *Address:* Meadowside Farmhouse, Tulls Lane, Standford, Bordon, Hants. *Clubs:* Army and Navy, Kennel; Liphook Golf.

SIRS, William, JP; General Secretary, Iron and Steel Trades Confederation, 1975–85, retired; *b* 6 Jan. 1920; *s* of Frederick Sirs and Margaret (*née* Powell); *m* 1941, Joan (*née* Clark); one *s* one *d*. *Educ:* Middleton St Johns, Hartlepool; WEA. Steel Industry, 1937–63; Iron and Steel Trades Confedn: Organiser, 1963; Divisional Officer, Manchester, 1970; Asst Gen. Sec., 1973. Member: Iron and Steel Industry Trng Bd, 1973; TUC Gen. Council, 1975–85; Trade Union Steel Industry Cons. Cttee, 1973– (Chm., 1975–) and Jt Accident Prevention Adv. Cttee, 1973; Employment Appeal Tribunal, 1976–; Jt Sec., Jt Industrial Council for Slag Industry, 1973; Exec. Mem., Paul Finet Foundn, European Coal and Steel Community, 1974; Hon. Sec. (British Section), Internat. Metalworkers Fedn, 1975. Mem., Management Cttee, BSC (Industry) Ltd, 1975–. Pres., Northern Home Counties Productivity Assoc., 1985–; Mem. RIIA, 1973. Mem. Council, Winston Churchill Meml Trust, 1985–90. JP Hartlepool, Co. Durham, Knutsford, Cheshire, Herts, 1963. Freeman, City of London, 1984. *Publication:* Hard Labour (autobiog.), 1985. *Recreations:* sailing, squash, swimming, running. *Address:* Hatfield, Hertfordshire.

SISSON, Charles Hubert; writer; *b* 22 April 1914; *s* of late Richard Percy Sisson and Ellen Minnie Sisson (*née* Worlock); *m* 1937, Nora Gilbertson; two *d*. *Educ:* University of Bristol, and in France and Germany. Entered Ministry of Labour as Assistant Principal, 1936; HM Forces, in the ranks, mainly in India, 1942–45; Simon Senior Research Fellow, 1956–57; Dir of Establishments, Min. of Labour, 1962–68; Dir of Occupational Safety and Health, Dept of Employment, 1972. FRSL 1975. Hon. DLitt Bristol, 1980. Jt Editor, PN Review, 1976–84. *Publications:* An Asiatic Romance, 1953; The Spirit of British Administration, 1959; Christopher Homm, 1965; Art and Action, 1965; Essays, 1967; English Poetry 1900–1950, 1971, rev. edn 1981; The Case of Walter Bagehot, 1972; (ed) The English Sermon, Vol. II 1650–1750, 1976; David Hume, 1976; (ed) Selected Poems of Jonathan Swift, 1977; The Avoidance of Literature, 1978; (ed) Autobiographical and Other Papers of Philip Mairet, 1981; Anglican Essays, 1983; (ed) Selected Poems of Christina Rossetti, 1984; On the Look-out (autobiog.), 1989; In Two Minds, 1990; (ed) Jeremy Taylor: selected writings, 1990; *poetry:* The London Zoo, 1961; Numbers, 1965; The Discarnation, 1967; Metamorphoses, 1968; In the Trojan Ditch, 1974; The Corridor, 1975; Anchises, 1976; Exactions, 1980; Selected Poems, 1981; Collected Poems, 1984; God Bless Karl Marx!, 1987; Antidotes, 1991; *translations:* Versions and Perversions of Heine, 1955; Catullus, 1966; The Poetic Art: a translation of the Ars Poetica of Horace, 1975; The Poem on Nature, 1976; Some Tales of La Fontaine, 1979; The Divine Comedy, 1980; The Song of Roland, 1983; Les Regrets of Joachim du Bellay, 1983; The Aeneid of Virgil, 1986; Britannicus, Phaedra, Athaliah, of Racine, 1987. *Address:* Moorfield Cottage, The Hill, Langport, Somerset TA10 9PU. *T:* Langport (0458) 250845.

SISSON, Rosemary Anne; writer since 1929; *b* 13 Oct. 1923; *d* of Prof. C. J. Sisson, MA, DèsL and Vera Kathleen (*née* Ginn). *Educ:* Cheltenham Ladies' Coll.; University Coll., London (BA Hons English); Newnham Coll., Cambridge (MLit). Served War, Royal Observer Corps, 1943–45. Instr in English, Univ. of Wisconsin, 1949; Lecturer in English: UCL, 1950–53; Univ. of Birmingham, 1953–54; Dramatic Critic, Stratford-upon-Avon Herald, 1954–57; after prodn of first play, The Queen and the Welshman, became full-time writer, 1957. Co-Chm., Writers Guild of GB, 1979 and 1980; Member: Dramatists' Club; BAFTA. Laurel Award, for service to writers, 1985; Prince Michael of Kent Award, for services to SSAFA, 1987. *Plays:* The Queen and the Welshman, 1957; Fear Came to Supper, 1958; The Splendid Outcasts, 1959; The Royal Captivity, 1960; Bitter Sanctuary, 1963; Ghost on Tiptoe (with Robert Morley), 1974; The Dark Horse, 1978. Contributed to *TV series:* Catherine of Aragon, in The Six Wives of Henry VIII; The Marriage Game, in Elizabeth R; Upstairs, Downstairs; A Town Like Alice; The Young Indiana Jones Chronicles; *TV scripts:* Irish RM; Seal Morning; The Manions of America; The Bretts (creator of series). *Film scripts* include: Ride a Wild Pony; Escape from the Dark; Candleshoe; Watcher in the Woods; The Black Cauldron (full-length animation film) (all for Walt Disney); The Wind in the Willows (animation film), 1983 (also TV series, 1984). *Other scripts:* Heart of a Nation (Son-et-Lumière), Horse Guards Parade, 1983; Dawn to Dusk, Royal Tournament, 1984; Joy to the World, Royal Albert Hall, 1988, 1989. *Publications:* children's books: The Adventures of Ambrose, 1951; The Young Shakespeare, 1959; The Young Jane Austen, 1962; The Young Shaftesbury, 1964; novels: The Exciseman, 1972; The Killer of Horseman's Flats, 1973; The Stratford Story, 1975; Escape from the Dark, 1976; The Queen and the Welshman, 1979; The Manions of America, 1982; Bury Love Deep, 1985; Beneath the Visiting Moon, 1986; The Bretts, 1987. *Recreations:* travel, walking, riding, writing poetry. *Address:* 167 New King's Road, Parson's Green, SW6.

SISSON, Sir Roy, Kt 1980; CEng; Hon. FRAeS; Chairman, Smiths Industries Ltd, 1976–85; *b* 17 June 1914; *s* of Bernard Sisson and Violet (*née* Hagg); *m* 1943, Constance Mary Cutchey; two *s* two *d*. *Educ:* Regent Street Polytechnic. De Havilland Aircraft Co. Ltd, 1933–37; Flight Engineer and Station Engineer, BOAC, 1944–47; BOAC rep. at de Havilland Aircraft Co., 1948; Smiths Industries: joined, 1955; Divl Dir, 1964; Chief Exec., Aviation Div., 1966; Managing Dir, 1973; Chm., 1976 (Chief Exec., 1976–81). Pres., SBAC, 1973–74. Councillor, Wheathampstead Parish Council, 1987–91. FBIM. Hon. FRAeS 1985. *Recreations:* sailing, tennis. *Address:* Gustard Wood House, Gustard Wood, near Wheathampstead, Herts AL4 8RP. *Clubs:* Royal Air Force; Royal Dart Yacht.

SISSONS, Prof. John Gerald Patrick, MD; FRCP; Professor of Medicine, University of Cambridge, and Fellow of Darwin College, since 1988; *b* 28 June 1945; *s* of Gerald William Sissons and Georgina Margaret Cockin; *m* 1971, Jennifer Ann Scovell (marr. diss. 1987); two *d*. *Educ:* Felstead Sch.; St Mary's Hosp. Med. Sch. MB London, MD. Hosp. appts, St Mary's, St George's and Hammersmith Hosps, 1968–71; Registrar and Lectr, Dept of Medicine, RPMS, 1972–77; NIH Research Fellow and Asst Mem., Res. Inst. of Scripps Clinic, California, 1977–80; Wellcome Sen. Lectr, Depts of Medicine and Virology, RPMS, 1980–86; Prof. of Infectious Diseases, RPMS, 1987. *Publications:* papers on immunology and pathogenesis of virus infections. *Address:* Department of Medicine, Addenbrookes Hospital, Hills Road, Cambridge CB2 2QQ. *T:* Cambridge (0223) 336849.

SISSONS, Peter George; presenter, BBC TV 6 o'clock news, and Chairman, BBC TV Question Time, since 1989; *b* 17 July 1942; *s* of George Robert Percival Sissons and Elsie Emma Evans; *m* 1965, Sylvia Bennett; two *s* one *d*. *Educ:* Liverpool Inst. High Sch. for Boys; University College Oxford (MA PPE). Independent Television News: graduate trainee, 1964; general reporter, 1967; industrial corresp., 1970; indust. editor, 1972–78; presenter, News at One, 1978–82; presenter, Channel Four News, 1982–89. Broadcasting Press Guild Award, 1984; RTS Judges' Award, 1988. *Recreations:* relaxing, supporting Liverpool FC. *Address:* BBC Television Centre, Wood Lane, W12 7RJ. *T:* 081–743 8000.

SISSONS, (Thomas) Michael (Beswick); Chairman and Managing Director, The Peters Fraser and Dunlop Group Ltd, since 1988; *b* 13 Oct. 1934; *s* of Captain T. E. B. Sissons (killed in action, 1940) and Marjorie (*née* Shepherd) *m* 1st, 1960, Nicola Ann Fowler; one *s* one *d*; 2nd, 1974, Ilze Kadegis; two *d*. *Educ:* Winchester Coll.; Exeter Coll., Oxford (BA 1958, MA 1964). National Service, 2nd Lieut 13/18 Royal Hussars, 1953–55. Lectr in History, Tulane Univ., New Orleans, USA, 1958–59; freelance writer and journalist, 1958–59; joined A.D. Peters, Literary Agent, 1959; Dir, 1965, Chm. and Man. Dir, 1973–88, A. D. Peters & Co. Ltd. Pres., Assoc. of Authors' Agents, 1978–81; Dir, London Broadcasting Co., 1973–75; Mem. Council, Consumers Assoc., 1974–77. *Publication:* (ed with Philip French) Age of Austerity, 1963, repr. 1986. *Recreations:* riding, gardening, cricket, music. *Address:* The White House, Broadleaze Farm, Westcot Lane, Sparsholt, Wantage, Oxon OX12 9PZ. *T:* Childrey (023559) 215, *Fax:* Childrey (023559) 561. *Clubs:* Garrick, Groucho, MCC (Mem. Cttee, 1984–87; Chm., Arts and Liby Sub-Cttee, 1985–).

SITWELL, Rev. Francis Gerard, OSB, MA; *b* 22 Dec. 1906; *s* of late Major Francis Sitwell and Margaret Elizabeth, *d* of late Matthew Culley, Coupland Castle, Northumberland. *Educ:* Ampleforth; St Benet's Hall, Oxford. Received Benedictine Habit, 1924; Professed, 1925; Priest, 1933; Assistant Master at Ampleforth, 1933–39; Assistant Procurator at Ampleforth, 1939–47; Subprior of Ampleforth, 1946–47; Master of St Benet's Hall, Oxford, 1947–64; Priest of Our Lady and St Wilfrid, Warwick Bridge, Carlisle, 1966–69. *Publications:* Walter Hilton, Scale of Perfection (trans. and ed); St Odo of Cluny; Medieval Spirituality; articles in Ampleforth Journal, Downside Review, Clergy Review, Month, etc. *Address:* Ampleforth Abbey, York YO6 4EN.

SITWELL, Peter Sacheverell W.; *see* Wilmot-Sitwell.

SITWELL, Sir (Sacheverell) Reresby, 7th Bt *cr* 1808, of Renishaw; DL; *b* 15 April 1927; *s* of Sir Sacheverell Sitwell, 6th Bt, CH and Georgia Louise (*d* 1980), *d* of Arthur Doble; *S* father, 1988; *m* 1952, Penelope, *yr d* of late Col Hon. Donald Alexander Forbes, DSO, MVO; one *d*. *Educ:* Eton College; King's Coll., Cambridge (schol.). Served Grenadier Guards, 1945–48, mainly as Lieut, 2nd Bn, BAOR. Advertising and PR executive, 1948–63; operated vending machines and wholesale wine business, 1963–73. Took over Renishaw and family estates from late uncle, Sir Osbert, 1965. High Sheriff of Derbyshire, 1983; DL Derbyshire 1984. Freedom of City of London, 1984. *Publications:* (with John Julius Norwich and A. Costa) Mount Athos, 1964; Hortus Sitwellianus (epilogue), 1984. *Recreations:* art and architecture, music, travel, photography, racing. *Heir: b* Francis Trajan Sacheverell Sitwell [*b* 17 Sept. 1935; *m* 1966, Susanna Carolyn, *d* of Sir Ronald Hibbert Cross, 1st Bt, KCMG, KCVO, PC; two *s* one *d*]. *Address:* Renishaw Hall, near Sheffield S31 9WB; 4 Southwick Place, W2 2TN. *T:* 071–262 3939. *Clubs:* White's, Brooks's, Pratt's, Society of Dilettanti; Pitt (Cambridge).

SIVEWRIGHT, Col Robert Charles Townsend, CB 1983; MC 1945; DL; Joint Principal (with Molly Sivewright) of the Talland School of Equitation, since 1959; *b* 7 Sept. 1923; *s* of late Captain R. H. V. Sivewright, DSC, RN and Sylvia Townsend (*née* Cobbold); *m* 1951, (Pamela) Molly Ryder-Richardson, FIH, FBHS (as Molly Sivewright, author of Thinking Riding); three *d*. *Educ:* Repton; Royal Agricultural Coll., Cirencester. Served Regular Army, 11th Hussars (PAO), 1943–52; TA, Royal Glos Hussars, 1959–67 (CO, 1964–67); Chm., Western Wessex TA&VRA, 1970–83; Vice-Chm., Council of TA&VRAs, 1979–83. DL 1965, High Sheriff 1977, Glos. *Recreation:* National Hunt racing. *Address:* Talland House, Clarks Hay, South Cerney, Cirencester, Glos GL7 6HU. *T:* Cirencester (0285) 860830.

SIZER, Prof. John, CBE 1989; DLitt; Professor of Financial Management, Loughborough University of Technology, since 1970; Director, Loughborough University Business School, since 1991; *b* 14 Sept. 1938; *s* of Mary and John Robert Sizer; *m* 1965, Valerie Davies; three *s*. *Educ:* Grimsby Coll. of Technology; Univ. of Nottingham (BA); DLitt Loughborough, 1989. FCMA. Teaching Fellow, later Lectr, Univ. of Edinburgh, 1965; Sen. Lectr, London Graduate Sch. of Business Studies, 1968; Loughborough University of Technology: Founding Head of Dept of Management Studies, 1971–84; Dean of Sch. of Human and Environmental Studies, 1973–76; Sen. Pro Vice-Chancellor, 1980–82. Chm., Directing Group, OECD/CERI Programme on Institutional Management in Higher Educn, 1980–84; Mem., UGC, 1984–89 (Chm., Business and Management Studies Sub-Cttee, 1984–89); Advr on Business and Management Studies, 1989–, Mem., NI Cttee, 1989–, UFC. Member: Council, CIMA, 1981–88 (Chairman: Internat. Cttee, 1982–86; Finance Cttee, 1986–88); Nat. Forum for Management Educn and Develt, 1989– (Chm., Finance and Resourcing Cttee, 1989–; Mem., Exec. Cttee, 1989–). FBIM; FRSA. *Publications:* An Insight into Management Accounting, 1969, 1979, 1989; Case Studies in Management Accounting, 1974; Perspectives in Management Accounting, 1981; (ed jtly) Resources and Higher Education, 1983; (jtly) A Casebook of British Management Accounting, vol. 1, 1984, vol. 2, 1985; Institutional Responses to Financial Reductions in the University Sector, 1987; numerous articles in accounting, higher educn and management jls. *Recreations:* table tennis, walking. *Address:* Loughborough University Business School, Loughborough, Leics LE11 3TU. *T:* Loughborough (0509) 263171.

SKAN, Peter Henry O.; *see* Ogle-Skan.

SKEAT, Theodore Cressy, BA; Keeper of Manuscripts and Egerton Librarian, British Museum, 1961–72; *b* 15 Feb. 1907; *s* of Walter William Skeat, MA; *m* 1942, Olive Martin; one *s*. *Educ:* Whitgift School, Croydon; Christ's College, Cambridge. Student at British School of Archaeology, Athens, 1929–31; Asst Keeper, Dept of Manuscripts, British Museum, 1931; Deputy Keeper, 1948. FBA, 1963–80. *Publications:* (with H. I. Bell) Fragments of an Unknown Gospel, 1935; (with H. J. M. Milne) Scribes and Correctors of the Codex Sinaiticus, 1938; The Reigns of the Ptolemies, 1954; Papyri from Panopolis, 1964; Catalogue of Greek Papyri in the British Museum, vol. VII, 1974; (with C. H. Roberts) The Birth of the Codex, 1983; articles in papyrological journals. *Address:* 63 Ashbourne Road, W5 3DH. *T:* 081–998 1246.

SKEATES, Basil George; Director, Ashdown Gallery, since 1985; Under Secretary, Department of the Environment, 1980–85; *b* 19 May 1929; *s* of George William Skeates and Florence Rachel Skeates; *m* 1957, Irene Margaret (*née* Hughes); four *s*. *Educ:* Hampton Grammar Sch. RIBA 1955. Mil. Service with RE, W Africa, 1947–49. Architect with LCC schs and special works, 1949–61; Principal Architect: NE Metrop. Reg. Hosp. Bd, 1961–64; MPBW, 1964–71; Superintending Architect, CSD, 1971–73; Asst Dir, Architectural Services, PSA, 1973–75; Dir of Works, PO Services, 1975–80; Dir of Def. Services II, DoE, 1980–85. *Publications:* articles in prof. and technical jls. *Recreation:* designing and making things.

SKEET, Muriel Harvey; Health Services adviser and consultant, World Health Organisation Headquarters and other international agencies and organisations, since 1978; *b* 12 July 1926; *y d* of late Col F. W. C. Harvey-Skeet, Suffolk. *Educ:* privately; Endsleigh House; Middlesex Hosp. SRN, MRSH; FRCN. Gen. Nursing Trg at Middx Hosp., 1946–49; also London Sch. of Hygiene and Tropical Med.; Ward Sister and Admin. Sister, Middx Hosp., 1949–60; Field Work Organiser, Opl Res. Unit, Nuffield Provincial Hosps Trust, 1961–64; Res. Org., Dan Mason Nursing Res. Cttee of Nat. Florence Nightingale Memorial Cttee of Gt Britain and N Ire., 1965–70; Chief Nursing Officer and Nursing Advr, BRCS, and St John of Jerusalem and BRCS Jt Cttee, 1970–78. WHO Res. Consultant, SE Asia, 1970; European Deleg. and First Chm. of Bd of Commonwealth Nurses' Fed., 1971. Leverhulme Fellowship, 1974–75. Member: Hosp. and Med. Services Cttee, 1970; Ex-Services War Disabled Help Cttee, 1970; British Commonwealth Nurses War Memorial Fund Cttee and Council, 1970; Council of Management of Nat. Florence Nightingale Memorial Cttee, 1970; Council of Queen's Inst. of District Nursing, 1970; Royal Coll. of Nursing and Nat. Council of Nurses; RSM, 1980. Fellow RCN, 1977. *Publications:* Waiting in Outpatient Departments (Nuffield Provincial Hospitals Trust), 1965; Marriage and Nursing (Dan Mason NRC), 1968; Home from Hospital (Dan Mason NRC), 1970; Home Nursing, 1975; Manual: Disaster Relief Work, 1977; Back to Our Basic Skills, 1977; Health needs Help, 1977; (jtly) Health Auxiliaries in the Health Team, 1978; Self Care for the People of Developing Countries, 1979; Discharge Procedures, 1980; Notes on Nursing 1860 and 1980, 1980; Emergency Procedures and First Aid for Nurses, 1981; The Third Age, 1982; Providing Continuing Care for Elderly People, 1983; First Aid for Developing Countries, 1983; Protecting the Health of the Elderly, 1983; Know Your Own Body, 1987; Add Life to Years, 1989; Tropical Health: concise notes, 1989; Better Opportunities for Disabled People, 1989; various articles in professional jls. *Recreations:* music, opera, painting, reading. *Address:* c/o Coutts & Co., 16 Cavendish Square, W1A 1EE. *Clubs:* New Cavendish, Royal Over-Seas League.

SKEET, Sir Trevor (Herbert Harry), Kt 1986; MP (C) Bedfordshire North, since 1983 (Bedford, 1970–83); Barrister, Writer and Consultant; *b* 28 Jan. 1918; British; *m* 1st, 1958, Elizabeth Margaret Gilling (*d* 1973); two *s*; 2nd, 1985, Mrs Valerie Anita Edwina Benson. *Educ:* King's College, Auckland; University of New Zealand, Auckland (LLB). Served War of 1939–45, with NZ Engineers (sergeant); 2nd Lieut, NZ Anti-Aircraft (Heavy); Sub-Lieutenant, NZ Roy. Naval Volunteer Reserve; demobilised, 1945. Formerly Barrister and Solicitor of Supreme Court of New Zealand; Barrister, Inner Temple, 1947. Has considerable experience in public speaking. Contested (C): Stoke Newington and Hackney, North, Gen. Election, 1951; Llanelly Div. of Carmarthenshire, Gen. Election, 1955; MP (C) Willesden East, 1959–64. Formerly associated with Commonwealth and Empire Industries Assoc.; Mem. Council, Royal Commonwealth Soc., 1952–55, and 1956–69. Vice-Chairman: Cons. Party Power Cttee, 1959–64; Energy Cttee, 1974–77; Chairman: Oil Sub-Cttee, 1959–64; Cons. Party Trade Cttee, 1971–74; Cons. Party Middle East Cttee (Foreign and Commonwealth Affairs), 1973–78; Secretary: All-Party Cttee on Airships, 1971–78; All-Party Gp on Minerals, 1971– (Co-Chm., 1979–); Vice-Pres., Steering Cttee, Parly and Scientific Cttee, 1988–91 (Mem., 1982–; Sec., 1983–85; Chm., 1985–88); Vice-Chm., British-Japanese and British-Brazilian Gps; Sec., British-Nigerian Gp. Mem., Econ. Cttee, Machine Tool Trades Association for several years; Member Technical Legislation Cttee, CBI. *Publications:* contrib. to numerous journals including New Commonwealth and Mining World, on oil, atomic energy, metals, commodities, finance, and Imperial and Commonwealth development. *Address:* (home) The Gables, Milton Ernest, Bedfordshire MK44 1RS. *T:* Oakley (02302) 2307. *Clubs:* Army and Navy, Commonwealth Trust.

SKEFFINGTON, family name of **Viscount Massereene and Ferrard.**

SKEFFINGTON-LODGE, Thomas Cecil; *b* 15 Jan. 1905; *s* of late Thomas Robert Lodge and late Winifred Marian Skeffington; unmarried. *Educ:* privately; Giggleswick and Westminster Schools. For some years engaged in Advertising and Publicity both in London and the North of England; later did Public Relations and administrative work in the Coal Trade as Northern Area Organiser for the Coal Utilisation Council, in which he served Cttees of Coal Trade in North-East, North-West and Yorkshire; on the outbreak of war, became a Mines Dept official; then volunteered for the Navy; from early 1941 a Naval Officer. Mem., Parly Delegn, Nüremberg Trials. Lecture tour in USA under auspices of Anglo-American Parly Gp, 1949. MP (Lab) Bedford, 1945–50; contested (Lab) York, 1951, Mid-Bedfordshire, 1955; Grantham, 1959; Brighton (Pavilion), March 1969; Personal Asst to Chm., Colonial Development Corp., 1950–52. Mem. of post-war Parly Delegns to Eire, Belgium, Luxembourg and USA; formerly Mem., Parly Ecclesiastical Cttee, and served on Parochial Church Council, St Margaret's, Westminster. Past-Pres. and Chm., Pudsey Divisional Labour Party; Pres., Brighton and Hove Fabian Soc.; Member: Labour Party many years; Socialist Christian Movement (Vice-Pres.); IPU; Exec. Cttee, Brighton and Hove Br. UNA; German-British Christian Fellowship (past Chm.); Union of Shop, Distributive and Allied Workers; Conservation Soc.; CPRE (Chm., Brighton Dist Cttee, Sussex Branch); RSPB; Georgian Group; Friends of the Lake District; Amnesty Internat.; British-Soviet Friendship Soc.; Anglo-German Assoc.; Anglo-Belgian Assoc.; former Chm., Socialist Christian League and Parly Socialist Christian Group. *Recreations:* travel, gardening, politics and associating Christianity with them, in the hope of erecting fairer national and international living conditions for mankind. *Address:* 5 Powis Grove, Brighton, East Sussex BN1 3HF. *T:* Brighton (0273) 25472. *Club:* Savile.

SKEGGS, Sir Clifford (George), Kt 1987; JP; FNZIM; Chairman and Chief Executive, Skeggs Group; Director of various public and private companies; Mayor, Dunedin City, 1978–89; *b* 19 March 1931; *s* of George Henry Skeggs and Beatrice Hannah (*née* Heathcote); *m* 1952, Marie Eleanor Ledgerwood; three *s*. *Educ:* Southland Technical Coll., New Zealand. Mem., 1968–80, Chm., 1973–77, Otago Harbour Bd. City Councillor, Dunedin, 1972–77. Mem. Council, Univ. of Otago, 1981–89. FNZIM 1985; Mem., Inst. of Dirs, 1984. JP Dunedin, 1978. OStJ 1987. *Publications:* contrib. fishing and general business publications. *Recreations:* yachting, golf, flying, power boating, squash, keen follower of Rugby. *Address:* Skeggs House, Box 5657, Dunedin, New Zealand; Skeggs Group, Dunedin, New Zealand. *Club:* Dunedin (Dunedin).

SKEHEL, John James, PhD; FRS 1984; Director: National Institute for Medical Research, since 1987; World Influenza Centre, since 1975; *b* 27 Feb. 1941; *s* of Joseph and Ann Josephine Skehel; *m* 1962, Anita Varley; two *s*. *Educ:* St Mary's Coll., Blackburn; University College of Wales, Aberystwyth (BSc); UMIST (PhD). Post-doctoral Fellow, Marischal Coll., Aberdeen, 1965–68; Fellow, Helen Hay Whitney Foundn, 1968–71; Nat. Inst. for Med. Res.: Mem., Scientific Staff, 1971–; Head of Div. of Virology, 1984–87. Leeuwenhoek Lecture, Royal Soc., 1990. Hon. Prof., Liverpool Polytechnic Sch. of Nat. Sci., 1990. Hon. DSc CNAA, 1990. Wilhelm Feldberg prize, 1986; Robert Koch prize, 1987; Prix Louis Jeantet de Médecine, 1988. *Publications:* scientific articles in various jls. *Address:* 49 Homewood Road, St Albans, Herts. *T:* St Albans (0727) 860603.

SKELMERSDALE, 7th Baron *cr* 1828; **Roger Bootle-Wilbraham;** Parliamentary Under-Secretary of State, Northern Ireland Office, 1989–90; *b* 2 April 1945; *o s* of 6th Baron Skelmersdale, DSO, MC, and Ann (*d* 1974), *d* of late Percy Cuthbert Quilter; *S* father, 1973; *m* 1972, Christine Joan, *o d* of Roy Morgan; one *s* one *d*. *Educ:* Eton; Lord Wandsworth Coll., Basingstoke; Somerset Farm Institute; Hadlow Coll. VSO (Zambia), 1969–71; Proprietor, Broadleigh Gardens, 1972; Man. Dir, Broadleigh Nurseries Ltd, 1973–81; Vice-Chm., Co En Co, 1979–81. A Lord in Waiting (Govt Whip), 1981–86; Parly Under-Sec. of State, DoE, 1986–87; Parly Under-Sec. of State, DHSS, 1987–88, Dept of Social Security, 1988–89. President: Somerset Trust for Nature Conservation, 1980–; British Naturalists Trust, 1980–. *Recreations:* gardening, reading, bridge playing. *Heir:* *s* Hon. Andrew Bootle-Wilbraham, *b* 9 Aug. 1977. *Address:* c/o House of Lords, SW1A 0PW.

SKELTON, Rt. Rev. Kenneth John Fraser, CBE 1972; an Assistant Bishop, Dioceses of Sheffield and Derby; *b* 16 May 1918; *s* of Henry Edmund and Kate Elizabeth Skelton; *m* 1945, Phyllis Barbara, *y d* of James Emerton; two *s* one *d*. *Educ:* Dulwich Coll.; Corpus Christi Coll., Cambridge; Wells Theological Coll. 1st Cl. Class. Tripos, Pt 1, 1939; 1st Cl. Theol. Tripos, Pt 1, 1940; BA 1940, MA 1944. Deacon, 1941; Priest, 1942; Curate: Normanton-by-Derby, 1941–43; Bakewell, 1943–45; Bolsover, 1945–46; Tutor, Wells Theol Coll., and Priest-Vicar, Wells Cathedral, 1946–50; Vicar of Howe Bridge, Atherton, 1950–55; Rector, Walton-on-the-Hill, Liverpool, 1955–62; Exam. Chap. to Bp of Liverpool, 1957–62; Bishop of Matabeleland, 1962–70; Asst Bishop, Dio. Durham, Rural Dean of Wearmouth and Rector of Bishopwearmouth, 1970–75; Bishop of Lichfield, 1975–84. Select Preacher, Cambridge Univ., 1971, 1973. *Publication:* Bishop in Smith's Rhodesia, 1985. *Recreation:* music. *Address:* 65 Crescent Road, Sheffield S7 1HN. *T:* Sheffield (0742) 551260.

SKELTON, Rear-Adm. Peter, CB 1956; *b* 27 Dec. 1901; *s* of Peter John and Selina Frances Skelton; *m* 1928, Janice Brown Clark; two *d*. *Educ:* RN Colleges, Osborne and Dartmouth; Trinity Hall, Cambridge. Cadet, 1915; Midshipman, HMS Valiant, 1918; Commander, 1936; Capt. 1944; Rear-Adm., 1953. Served War of 1939–45, as Staff Officer in HMS Aurora, later at Admiralty in Torpedo Division; Commander and Actg Capt. in HMS Royal Sovereign, 1942; Director of Trade Div., Admiralty, 1944; Supt of Torpedo Experimental Establishment, 1946; Sen. Naval Officer, Persian Gulf, 1949; Captain of Dockyard, Portsmouth, 1951; Admiral Superintendent, Rosyth, 1953–56; retired. Bucks CC, 1958. *Recreations:* golf, tennis, shooting. *Address:* Craigie Barns, Kippen, Stirlingshire.

SKELTON, Robert William, OBE 1989; Keeper, Indian Department, Victoria and Albert Museum, 1978–88; *b* 11 June 1929; *s* of John William Skelton and Victoria (*née* Wright); *m* 1954, Frances Aird; three *s*. *Educ:* Tiffin Boys' Sch., Kingston-upon-Thames. Joined Indian Section of Victoria and Albert Museum, 1950; Asst Keeper, 1960; Dep. Keeper, 1972; Nuffield Travelling Fellow in India, 1962. Mem. Council: Royal Asiatic Soc., 1970–73, 1975–78, 1988–; Soc. for S Asian Studies, 1984–; Trustee, Asia House Trust (London), 1977–. *Publications:* Indian Miniatures from the XVth to XIXth Centuries, 1961; Rajasthani Temple Hangings of the Krishna Cult, 1973; (jtly) Islamic Painting and Arts of the Book, 1976; (jtly) Indian Painting, 1978; (jtly) Arts of Bengal, 1979; (jtly) The Indian Heritage, 1982; (jtly) Islamic Art in the Keir Collection, 1988; various contribs to art periodicals and conf. proc., 1956–. *Recreations:* chamber music, walking. *Address:* 10 Spencer Road, South Croydon CR2 7EH. *T:* 081–688 7187.

SKELTON, Prof. Robin, FRSL; author; Professor of English, since 1966, and Chairman of Department of Creative Writing, 1973–76, University of Victoria, British Columbia; *b* 12 Oct. 1925; *o s* of Cyril Frederick William and Eliza Skelton; *m* 1957, Sylvia Mary Jarrett; one *s* two *d*. *Educ:* Pocklington Grammar Sch., 1936–43; Christ's Coll., Cambridge, 1943–44; Univ. of Leeds, 1947–51. BA 1950, MA 1951. Served RAF, 1944–47. Asst Lectr in English, Univ. of Manchester, 1951; Lectr, 1954. Managing Dir, The Lotus Press, 1950–52; Examiner for NUJMB, 1954–58; Chm. of Examrs in English, 'O' Level, 1958–60; Co-founder and Chm., Peterloo Gp, Manchester, 1957–60; Founding Mem. and Hon. Sec., Manchester Inst. of Contemporary Arts, 1960–63; Centenary Lectr at Univ. of Massachusetts, 1962–63; Gen. Editor, OUP edn of Works of J. M. Synge, 1962–68; Associate Prof. of English, Univ. of Victoria, BC, 1963–66. Visiting Prof., Univ. of Michigan, Ann Arbor, 1967; Dir, Creative Writing Programme, Univ. of Victoria, 1967–73; Founder and co-Editor, Malahat Review, 1967–71, Editor 1972–83. Mem. Bd of Dirs, Art Gall. of Greater Victoria, BC, 1968–69, 1970–73; Dir, Pharos Press, 1972–; Editor, Sono Nis Press, 1976–83. FRSL 1966. Chm., Writers' Union of Canada, 1982 (first Vice-Chm., 1981). *Publications: poetry* Patmos and Other Poems, 1955; Third Day Lucky, 1958; Two Ballads of the Muse, 1960; Begging the Dialect, 1960; The Dark Window, 1962; A Valedictory Poem, 1963; An Irish Gathering, 1964; A Ballad of Billy Barker, 1965; Inscriptions, 1967; Because of This, 1968; The Hold of Our Hands, 1968; Selected Poems, 1947–67, 1968; An Irish Album, 1969; Georges Zuk, Selected Verse, 1969; Answers, 1969; The Hunting Dark, 1971; Two Hundred Poems from the Greek Anthology, 1971; A Different Mountain, 1971; A Private Speech, 1971; Remembering Synge, 1971; Three for Herself, 1972; Musebook, 1972; Country Songs, 1973; Timelight, 1974; Georges Zuk: The Underwear of the Unicorn, 1975; Callsigns, 1976; Because of Love, 1977; Landmarks, 1979; Collected Shorter Poems 1947–1977, 1981; Limits, 1981; De Nihilo, 1982; Zuk, 1982; Wordsong, 1983; Distances, 1985; The Collected Longer Poems 1947–1977, 1985; Openings, 1988; *prose:* John Ruskin: The Final Years, 1955; The Poetic Pattern, 1956; Cavalier Poets, 1960; Poetry (in Teach Yourself series), 1963; The Writings of J. M. Synge, 1971; J. M. Synge and His World, 1971; The Practice of Poetry, 1971; J. M. Synge (Irish Writers series), 1972; The Poet's Calling, 1975; Poetic Truth, 1978; Spellcraft, 1978; They Call It The Cariboo, 1980; Talismanic Magic, 1985; The Memoirs of a Literary Blockhead (autobiog.), 1988; Portrait of My Father, 1989; (with Jean Kozocari) A Gathering of Ghosts, 1989; Celtic Contraries, 1990; *fiction:* The Man who sang in his Sleep, 1984; The Parrot who Could, 1987; Telling the Tale, 1987; The Fires of the Kindred, 1987; Hanky Panky, 1990; *drama:* The Paper Cage, 1982; *edited texts:* J. M. Synge: Translations, 1961; J. M. Synge, Four Plays and the Aran Islands, 1962; J. M. Synge, Collected Poems, 1962; Edward Thomas, Selected Poems, 1962; Selected Poems of Byron, 1965; David Gascoyne, Collected Poems, 1965; J. M. Synge, Riders to the Sea, 1969; David Gascoyne, Collected Verse Translations (with Alan Clodd), 1970; J. M. Synge, Translations of Petrarch, 1971; Jack B. Yeats, Collected Plays, 1971; (also trans.) George Faludy: selected poems, 1985; (also trans.) George Faludy: corpses brats and cricket music, 1987; The Selected Writings of Jack B. Yeats, 1991; *anthologies:* Leeds University Poetry, 1949, 1950; Viewpoint, 1962; Six Irish Poets, 1962; Poetry of the Thirties, 1964; Five Poets of the Pacific Northwest, 1964; Poetry of the Forties, 1968; The Cavalier Poets, 1970; Six Poets of British Columbia, 1980; *symposia:* The World of W. B. Yeats (with Ann Saddlemyer), 1965; Irish Renaissance (with David R. Clark), 1965; Herbert Read: a memorial symposium, 1970; Earth, Air, Fire and Water (with Margaret Blackwood), 1990. *Recreations:* book collecting, art collecting, making collages, stone carving, philately. *Address:* 1255 Victoria Avenue, Victoria, BC V8S 4P3, Canada. *T:* (604) 592–7032.

SKEMP, Prof. Joseph Bright, MA Cantab, PhD Edinburgh; Emeritus Professor of Greek, in the University of Durham; *b* 10 May 1910; *s* of late Thomas William Widlake Skemp, solicitor and local government officer, and Caroline (*née* Southall); *m* 1941, Ruby James (*d* 1987); no *c*. *Educ:* Wolverhampton Grammar School; Gonville and Caius College, Cambridge. Unofficial Drosier Fellow, Gonville and Caius College, Cambridge, 1936–47; Warden of Refugee Club and Asst Sec. to Refugee Cttee, Cambridge, 1940–46; Sec., Soc. for the Protection of Science and Learning, 1944–46; Lecturer in Greek and Latin, Univ. of Manchester, 1946–49; Reader in Greek, Univ. of Durham (Newcastle Div.), 1949–50; Prof. of Greek, Univ. of Durham, 1950–73; Vis. Prof., Univ. of Alexandria, 1977. Editor, Durham University Journal, 1953–57; Joint Editor, Phronesis, 1955–64. *Publications:* The Theory of Motion in Plato's Later Dialogues, 1942 (enlarged 1967); Plato's Statesman, 1952, repr. with postscript, 1987; The Greeks and the Gospel, 1964; Plato (supplementary vol. periodical Greece and Rome), 1976. *Recreations:* walking, history of railways. *Address:* Flat 6, 7 Clarence Road North, Weston-super-Mare BS23 4AT. *T:* Weston-super-Mare (0934) 641200.

SKEMP, Terence Rowland Frazer, CB 1973; QC 1984; Barrister-at-Law; *b* 14 Feb. 1915; *s* of Frank Whittingham Skemp and Dorothy Frazer; *m* 1939, Dorothy Norman Pringle; one *s* two *d*. *Educ:* Charterhouse; Christ Church, Oxford. Called to Bar, Gray's Inn, 1938. Served War, Army, 1939–46. Entered Parliamentary Counsel Office, 1946; Parliamentary Counsel, 1964; Second Parly Counsel, 1973–80; Counsel to the Speaker, 1980–85. *Address:* 997 Finchley Road, NW11 7HB.

SKEMPTON, Prof. Alec Westley, DSc London 1949; FRS 1961; FEng; FICE; Professor of Civil Engineering in the University of London (Imperial College), 1957–81, now Emeritus; Senior Research Fellow, Imperial College, since 1981; *b* 4 June 1914; *o c* of late A. W. Skempton, Northampton, and Beatrice Edridge Payne; *m* 1940, Mary, *d* of E. R. Wood, Brighouse, Yorks; two *d*. *Educ:* Northampton Grammar School; Imperial College, University of London (Goldsmiths' Bursar). Building Research Station, 1936–46; University Reader in Soil Mechanics, Imperial College, 1946–54; Professor of Soil

Mechanics, Imperial College, 1955–57. Vice-Pres., 1974–76 (Member Council, 1949–54), Institute Civil Engineers; Pres., Internat. Soc. Soil Mechanics and Foundn Eng, 1957–61; Chm. Jt Cttee on Soils, Min. of Supply and Road Research Bd, 1954–59; Mem., Cathedrals Advisory Cttee, 1964–70; Mem., NERC, 1973–76; President: Newcomen Soc., 1977–79; Smeatonian Soc., 1981. Hitchcock Foundn Prof., Univ. of Calif, Berkeley, 1978; Lectures: Copenhagen, Paris, Harvard, Univ. of Illinois, Oslo, Stockholm, Madrid, Florence, Sydney, Quebec, Mexico City, Tokyo, Berkeley; Special Lectr, Architectural Assoc., 1948–57; Vis. Lectr Cambridge Univ. School of Architecture, 1962–66; Consultant to Binnie & Partners, John Mowlem & Co., etc. For. Associate, Nat. Acad. of Engineering, USA, 1976. Hon. MRIA, 1990. Hon. DSc: Durham, 1968; Aston, 1980; Chalmers, 1982. Ewing Medal, 1968; Lyell Medal, 1972; Dickinson Medal, 1974; Karl Terzaghi Award, 1981; IStructE Gold Medal, 1981. Silver Jubilee Medal, 1977. *Publications:* Early Printed Reports in the Institution of Civil Engineers, 1977; (with C. Hadfield) William Jessop, Engineer, 1979; John Smeaton, FRS, 1981; Selected Papers on Soil Mechanics, 1984; British Civil Engineering Literature (1640–1840), 1987; numerous contribs on soil mechanics, engineering geology and history of construction. *Address:* Imperial College, SW7. *T:* 071–589 5111; 16 The Boltons, SW10. *T:* 071–370 3457. *Clubs:* Athenæum, Hurlingham.

SKERMAN, Ronald Sidney, CBE 1974; Deputy Chairman, Prudential Corporation plc, 1985–87 (Director, 1980–87; Group Chief Actuary, 1979); *b* 1 June 1914; *s* of S. H. Skerman; *m* 1939, Gladys Mary Fosdike; no *c*. *Educ:* Hertford Grammar School. BA Open Univ., 1989. FIA. Actuarial Trainee with Prudential Assurance Co., 1932; Chief Actuary, 1968–79. Pres., Inst. Actuaries, 1970–72; Chm., Life Offices Assoc., 1973–74; Chm., British Insurers European Cttee, 1972–82; Mem., Royal Commn on Civil Liability, 1973–78. Gold Medal, Inst. of Actuaries, 1980. *Publications:* contrib. Jl Inst. Actuaries. *Recreations:* walking, travel, music. *Address:* 1 Rookes, Little Walden Road, Saffron Walden, Essex CB10 2EP. *T:* Saffron Walden (0799) 513158.

SKEWIS, (William) Iain, PhD; consultant; *b* 1 May 1936; *s* of John Jamieson and Margaret Middlemass Skewis; *m* 1963, Jessie Frame Weir; two *s* one *d*. *Educ:* Hamilton Academy; Univ. of Glasgow (BSc, PhD). MCIT 1970; FTS 1987. British Rail, 1961–63; Transport Holding Co., 1963–66; Highlands and Islands Development Bd, 1966–72; Yorkshire and Humberside Development Assoc., 1973–77; Chief Exec., Develt Bd for Rural Wales, 1977–90. Chm., Regl Studies Assoc., 1990–. *Recreation:* soccer. *Address:* Rock House, The Square, Montgomery, Powys SY15 6RA. *T:* Montgomery (068681) 276.

SKIDELSKY, family name of **Baron Skidelsky.**

SKIDELSKY, Baron *cr* 1991 (Life Peer), of Tilton in the County of East Sussex; **Robert Jacob Alexander Skidelsky,** DPhil; FRHistS, FRSL; Professor of International Studies, Warwick University, since 1978; *b* 25 April 1939; *s* of late Boris Skidelsky and Galia Sapelkin; *m* 1970, Augusta Mary Clarissa Hope; two *s* one *d*. *Educ:* Brighton Coll.; Jesus Coll., Oxford (BA and MA Mod. Hist.; DPhil). FRHistS 1973; FRSL 1978. Res. Fellow: Nuffield Coll., Oxford, 1965–68; British Acad., 1968–70; Associate Prof. of History, Sch. of Advanced Internat. Studies, Johns Hopkins Univ., Washington, DC, 1970–76; Head, Dept of History, Philosophy and Eur. Studies, Polytechnic of N London, 1976–78. Dir, Social Market Foundn, 1989–; Mem., Policy Cttee, SDP, 1988–90. Chm., Charleston Trust, 1987–. Mem., Adv. Council on Public Records, 1988–. *Publications:* Politicians and the Slump, 1967; English Progressive Schools, 1969; Oswald Mosley, 1975, 2nd edn 1980; (ed) The End of the Keynesian Era, 1977; (ed, with Michael Holroyd) William Gerhardie's God's Fifth Column, 1981; John Maynard Keynes, vol. 1 1883–1920, Hopes Betrayed, 1983; (ed) Thatcherism, 1988. *Recreations:* opera, ballet, cinema, tennis, table tennis. *Address:* Tilton House, Firle, East Sussex BN8 6LL. *T:* Ripe (032183) 570. *Club:* United Oxford & Cambridge University.

SKILBECK, Diana Margaret; Headmistress, The Queen's School, Chester, since 1989; *b* 14 Nov. 1942; *d* of late William Allen Skilbeck and Elsie Almond Skilbeck. *Educ:* Wirral County Grammar School for Girls, Cheshire; Furzedown Coll., London (Teacher's Cert.); BA Hons London (External). Assistant Teacher: Mendell Primary Sch., 1964–67; Gayton Primary Sch., 1967–69; Wirral County Grammar Sch., 1969–74; Head of Geography, Wirral County Grammar Sch., 1974–78; Dep. Headmistress, West Kirby Grammar Sch., 1978–83; Headmistress, Sheffield High School, GPDST, 1983–89. *Recreations:* inland waterways, walking, singing, squash, skating, reading, industrial archaeology. *Address:* The Queen's School, City Walls Road, Chester CH1 2NN.

SKILBECK, Prof. Malcolm; Deputy Director, Division of Manpower, Social Affairs and Education, Organisation for Economic Co-operation and Development, Paris, since 1991; *b* 22 Sept. 1932; *s* of Charles Harrison Skilbeck and Elsie Muriel Nash Skilbeck; *m* Helen Connell. *Educ:* Univ. of Sydney (BA); Acad. DipEd London, PhD London; MA Illinois. Secondary school teacher and adult educn teacher, 1958–63; Lectr. Univ. of Bristol, 1963–71; Prof., New Univ. of Ulster, 1971–75; Dir, Australian Curriculum Develt Centre, 1975–81; Dir of Studies, Schs Council for Curriculum and Exams for England and Wales, 1981–83; Prof. of Education, Univ. of London, 1981–85; Prof. and Vice-Chancellor, Deakin Univ., Australia, 1986–91. Consultancies for Unesco, British Council, OECD, etc, intermittently, 1967–; active in voluntary organizations concerned with educn for internat. understanding, eg, Chm., World Educn Fellowship, 1981–85. *Publications:* John Dewey, 1970; (jtly) Classroom and Culture, 1976; (jtly) Inservice Education and Training, 1977; A Core Curriculum for the Common School 1982; (ed) Evaluating the Curriculum in the Eighties, 1984; School Based Curriculum Development, 1984; Readings in School-Based Curriculum Development, 1984; numerous contribs to jls, project reports, etc. *Recreations:* gardening, travelling, walking, reading. *Address:* OECD, 2 rue André-Pascal, 75116 Paris, France.

SKILLINGTON, William Patrick Denny, CB 1964; a Deputy Secretary, Department of the Environment (formerly Ministry of Public Building and Works), 1966–73; Housing Commissioner, for Clay Cross UDC, 1973–74; *b* 13 Feb. 1913; *s* of late S. J. Skillington, Leicester; *m* 1941, Dorin Kahn, Sydney, Australia; two *d*. *Educ:* Malvern College; Exeter College, Oxford. BA 1935, MA 1939, Oxford. Articled to Clerk of Leicestershire CC, 1936–39. Commissioned in R Welch Fusiliers (SR), 1933; served War of 1939–45 (despatches); regimental officer in France and Belgium, and on staff in Sicily, Italy and Greece; AA and QMG; Lt-Col. Entered Min. of Works as Principal, 1946; Asst Sec., 1952; Under-Sec. (Dir of Establishments), Min. of Public Building and Works, 1956–64; Asst Under-Sec. of State, Home Office, 1964–66. *Address:* 95a S Mark's Road, Henley-on-Thames, Oxon. *T:* Henley (0491) 573756. *Clubs:* United Oxford & Cambridge University; Phyllis Court (Henley).

SKINGSLEY, Air Chief Marshal Sir Anthony (Gerald), KCB 1986 (CB 1983); Deputy Commander-in-Chief, Allied Forces Central Europe, since 1989; *b* 19 Oct. 1933; *s* of Edward Roberts Skingsley; *m* 1957, Lilwen; two *s* one *d*. *Educ:* St Bartholomew's, Newbury; Cambridge Univ. (BA, MA). Commissioned RAFVR 1954, RAF 1955; several flying appointments, then Flt Comdr 13 Sqdn, 1961–62; OC Ops Sqdn, RAF Akrotiri, 1962–63; RAF Staff Coll., Bracknell, 1964; OC 45 Sqdn, RAF Tengah, Singapore, 1965–67; jssc Latimer, 1968; RAF Project Officer for Tornado in MoD, 1968–71; OC 214 Sqdn, RAF Marham, 1972–74; Station Comdr, RAF Laarbruch, Germany, 1974–76; Hon. ADC to the Queen, 1976–78; Asst Chief of Staff, Offensive Ops, HQ 2nd ATAF, 1977; RCDS 1978; Director of Air Staff Plans, MoD, 1978–80; Asst Chief of Staff, Plans and Policy, SHAPE, 1980–83; Comdt, RAF Staff Coll., Bracknell, 1983–84; ACAS, 1985–86; Air Mem. for Personnel, 1986–87; C-in-C RAF Germany, and Comdr, Second ATAF, 1987–89. Mem., Allgemeine Rheinlaendische Industrie Gesellschaft, 1975. *Recreations:* travel, off-shore sailing, music, walking, golf. *Address:* c/o National Westminster Bank, 43 Swan Street, West Malling, Kent ME19 6LE. *Clubs:* Royal Air Force, Royal Thames Yacht.

SKINNER, Prof. Andrew Forrester, MA, BSc, PhD (St Andrews); MA (Columbia); FEIS; Professor of Education, Ontario College of Education, University of Toronto, 1954–70, now Emeritus Professor; *b* 21 May 1902; *s* of Alexander H. and Jessie F. Skinner, Kingskettle, Scotland; *m* 1932, Elizabeth Balmer Lockhart (*d* 1983), Manchester. *Educ:* Bell-Baxter School, Cupar, Fife; University of St Andrews. MA, BSc, 1st Cl. Hons Maths and Phys Sci., 1925; Carnegie Research Fellow in Chemistry, PhD, 1928; Commonwealth Fund Fellow, Columbia, New York, 1929–31 (Educ. MA); Teacher in various schools, 1931–37; Asst Dir of Education, Co. of Aberdeen, 1937–39; Principal Lecturer in Methods, Dundee Trg Coll., 1939–41; Prof. of Education, Univ. of St Andrews, and Principal, Dundee Trg Coll., 1941–54. Vis. Prof. Ontario Coll. of Educ., Univ. of Toronto, 1950 and 1954; Visiting Professor: E Tennessee State Coll., 1951; State Univ. of Iowa, 1951–52; Univ. of British Columbia, 1962; Univ. of Victoria, 1964; Queen's Univ., Kingston, 1971. Former Member: Scottish Council for Research in Education; Scottish Universities Entrance Bd; School Broadcasting Council for Scotland; Mem., Bd of Directors, Comparative Educn Soc. of USA; Mem. Exec., Comparative and Internat. Educn Soc. of Canada, Vice-Pres., 1968–69, Pres., 1969–70, now Hon. Mem. *Publications:* (Booklet) Scottish Education in Schools, 1942; (Booklet) Introductory Course on Education in Scotland, 1944; Citizenship in the Training of Teachers, 1948; Teachers' Heritage: an introduction to the study of education, 1979; articles in Jl of Amer. Chem. Soc.; Trans Chem. Soc.; Scottish Educnl Jl; The Year Book of Education; Educnl Forum: Educational Record of Quebec; The American People's Encyclopedia; Canadian and International Education; Canadian Education and Research Digest. *Recreations:* golf, gardening and walking. *Address:* 296 Ferry Road, Edinburgh EH5 3NP. *T:* 031–552 4907.

SKINNER, Angus M. C.: Chief Social Work Adviser, Scottish Home and Health Department, since 1991; *b* 4 Jan. 1950; *s* of Dr Theodore Skinner, OBE and Morag Mackinnon Skinner; *m* 1977, Kate; one *s* two *d*. *Educ:* Univ. of Edinburgh (BSc 1971); London Univ. (CQSW 1973); Strathclyde Univ. (MBA 1988). Social Worker, Cheshire and Kent, 1971–75; Senior Social Worker, Area and Divl Manager, Lothian, 1975–87; Depute Dir, Borders, 1987–91. *Recreations:* music, painting, poetry. *Address:* Scottish Office, Edinburgh EH1 3DE. *T:* 031–244 5414; 37 Hadfast Road, Cousland, Midlothian EH22 2NZ. *T:* 031–663 6151.

SKINNER, Dennis Edward; MP (Lab) Bolsover since 1970; Miner at Glapwell Colliery; *b* 11 Feb. 1932; good working-class mining stock; *m* 1960; one *s* two *d*. *Educ:* Tupton Hall Grammar Sch.; Ruskin Coll., Oxford. Miner, 1949–70. Mem., Nat. Exec. Cttee of Labour Party, 1978–; Vice-Chm., Labour Party, 1987–88, Chm., 1988–89; Pres., Derbyshire Miners (NUM), 1966–70; Pres., NE Derbs Constituency Labour Party, 1968–71; Derbyshire CC, 1964–70; Clay Cross UDC, 1960–70. *Recreations:* tennis, cycling, walking. *Address:* House of Commons, SW1; 86 Thanet Street, Clay Cross, Chesterfield, Derbyshire. *T:* Chesterfield (0246) 863429. *Clubs:* Miners' Welfares in Derbyshire; Bestwood Working Men's.

SKINNER, James John; QC; Social Security Commissioner, since 1986; *b* 24 July 1923; *o s* of late William Skinner, Solicitor, Clonmel, Ireland; *m* 1950, Regina Brigitte Reiss; three *s* two *d*. *Educ:* Clongowes Wood Coll.; Trinity Coll., Dublin; King's Inns, Dublin. Called to Irish Bar, 1946; joined Leinster Circuit; called to English Bar, Gray's Inn, 1950; called to Bar of Northern Rhodesia, 1951; QC (Northern Rhodesia) 1964; MP (UNIP) Lusaka East, 1964–68; Minister of Justice, 1964–65; Attorney-General, 1965–69 (in addition, Minister of Legal Affairs, 1967–68); Chief Justice of Zambia, March-Sept. 1969; Chief Justice of Malaŵi, 1970–85. Grand Comdr, Order of Menelik II of Ethiopia, 1965. *Recreation:* reading. *Address:* Office of the Social Security Commissioners, 83 Farringdon Street, EC4A 4DH. *T:* 071–353 5145. *Club:* Commonwealth Trust.

SKINNER, Joyce Eva, CBE 1975; retired; *b* 5 Sept. 1920; *d* of Matthew and Ruth Eva Skinner. *Educ:* Christ's Hosp.; Girls' High Sch., Lincoln; Somerville Coll., Oxford. BA 1941, MA 1945. Bridlington Girls' High Sch., 1942–45; Perse Girls' Sch., 1946–50; Keswick Sch., 1950–52; Homerton Coll., Cambridge, 1952–64; Vis. Prof., Queen's Coll., NY, 1955–56; Principal, Bishop Grosseteste Coll., Lincoln, 1964–74; Dir, Cambridge Inst. of Educn, 1974–80; Academic Sec., Universities' Council for Educn of Teachers, 1979–84. Fellow: Hughes Hall, Cambridge, 1974–85; Worcester Coll. of Higher Educn, 1985. Hon. FCP 1971. Hon. DEd CNAA, 1989. *Recreations:* walking, reading, conversation. *Address:* 26 Rasen Lane, Lincoln. *T:* Lincoln (0522) 529483.

SKINNER, Sir Keith; *see* Skinner, Sir T. K. H.

SKINNER, Martyn; *b* 1906; *s* of late Sir Sydney Skinner; *m* 1938, Pauline Giles (marr. diss. 1987); three *s* one *d* (and one *s* one *d* decd). *Educ:* two well-known Public Schools; Magdalen College, Oxford (no degree taken). Hawthornden prize, 1943; Heinemann Award, 1947; Runner-up, Barley Championship, Brewers' Exhibition, 1949. *Publications:* Sir Elfadore and Mabyna, 1935; Letters to Malaya I and II, 1941; III and IV, 1943; V, 1947; Two Colloquies, 1949; The Return of Arthur, 1966; Old Rectory (Prologue), 1970; Old Rectory (The Session), 1973; Old Rectory (Epilogue), 1977; (with R. C. Hutchinson) Two Men of Letters, 1979; Alms for Oblivion, 1983; Old Rectory (complete edn), 1984. *Address:* Fitzhead, Taunton, Somerset. *T:* Milverton (0823) 400337.

SKINNER, Maj.-Gen. Michael Timothy, CB 1986; Lay Canon, Chapter Clerk and Comptroller of Rochester Cathedral, since 1988; *b* 5 Aug. 1931; *s* of Wilfred Skinner, MBE, FCIS and Ethel Skinner (*née* Jones); *m* 1959, Anne Kathleen Perry; three *s*. *Educ:* Merchant Taylors' School; RMA Sandhurst; psc, ptsc. Commissioned Royal Regt of Artillery, 1953; Malaya, 1955–58 (despatches); Parachute Brigade, UK, and Commando Brigade, Malta, 1958–62; RMCS and Staff Coll.; staff (weapon locating), RRE, 1967–68; GSO2 (future equipment), HQ Dir RA, 1971–72; CO 4th Regt RA, 1972–75, Germany and UK (despatches); MGO Secretariat, 1975–78; GS Op. Requirements and Dir, Heavy Weapons Projects, MoD, 1978–84; Vice Master-General of the Ordnance, 1984–86; Dir Gen. Weapons (Army), 1986–88. Hon. Col, 4th Regt RA, 1985–91. Chm., Kent SSAFA, 1990–. Chm., Bd of Govs, Fort Pitt Grammar Sch., 1990–. FBIM. Hon. MA Kent, 1991. *Recreations:* travel, opera, roses, campaign medals. *Address:* c/o Lloyds Bank, 18 Week Street, Maidstone, Kent ME14 1RW.

SKINNER, Prof. Quentin Robert Duthie, FBA 1981; Professor of Political Science, University of Cambridge, since 1978; Fellow of Christ's College, Cambridge, since 1962; *b* 26 Nov. 1940; 2nd *s* of late Alexander Skinner, CBE, and Winifred Skinner, MA; *m*

2nd, 1979, Susan Deborah Thorpe James, MA, PhD; one *s* one *d*. *Educ:* Bedford Sch.; Gonville and Caius Coll., Cambridge (BA 1962, MA 1965). Lecturer in History, Univ. of Cambridge, 1967–78. Visiting Fellow: Research Sch. of Social Science, ANU, 1970; Humanities Res. Centre, ANU, 1989; Institute for Advanced Study, Princeton: Mem., School of Historical Studies, 1974–75; longer-term Mem., School of Social Science, 1976–79; Gauss Seminars, Princeton Univ., 1980; Directeur d'Etudes Associé, Ecole des Hautes Etudes, 1987; Professeur Associé, Université Paris X, 1991. Carlyle Vis. Lectr, Univ. of Oxford, 1980–81; Lectures: Messenger, Cornell Univ., 1983; Tanner, Harvard Univ., 1984; James Ford, Univ. of Oxford, 1985; Raleigh, British Acad., 1986; Hart, Oxford Univ., 1988; Prothero, RHistS, 1989; Dawes Hicks, British Acad., 1990. Mem., Council, British Acad., 1987–90. Foreign Hon. Mem., Amer. Acad. of Arts and Sciences, 1986. Fellow, Academia Europaea, 1989. *Publications:* (ed jtly and contrib.) Philosophy, Politics and Society, Series 4, 1972; The Foundations of Modern Political Thought, Vol. 1, The Renaissance, 1978; Vol. 2, The Age of Reformation, 1978 (Wolfson Prize, 1979); Machiavelli, 1981; (ed jtly and contrib.) Philosophy in History, 1984; (ed and contrib.) The Return of Grand Theory in the Human Sciences, 1985; (ed jtly and contrib.) The Cambridge History of Renaissance Philosophy, 1988; Meaning and Context: Quentin Skinner and his critics, ed J. H. Tully, 1988; (ed and introd) Machiavelli: The Prince, 1988; (ed jtly and contrib.) Machiavelli and Republicanism, 1990. *Address:* c/o Christ's College, Cambridge CB2 3BU. *T:* Cambridge (0223) 334974.

SKINNER, Sir Thomas (Edward), KBE 1976; JP; Chairman, New Zealand Shipping Line, 1973–82; *b* 18 April 1909; *s* of Thomas Edward Skinner and Alice Skinner; *m* 1942, Mary Ethel Yardley; two *s* one *d*. *Educ:* Bayfield District Sch. Pres., NZ Fedn of Labour, 1963–79. Chairman: The Shipping Corp. of New Zealand Ltd, 1973–82; Container Terminals Ltd, 1975–82. Chm., St John Ambulance Trust Bd, Auckland, 1973–; KStJ 1970. JP New Zealand, 1943. *Recreations:* racing, boating, fishing. *Address:* 5 Dudley Road, Mission Bay, Auckland 5, New Zealand. *T:* 587–571. *Clubs:* Avondale Jockey (New Zealand); Auckland Branch, International Lions.

SKINNER, Sir (Thomas) Keith (Hewitt), 4th Bt *cr* 1912; Director, Reed International, 1980–90; Chairman and Chief Executive, Reed Publishing and Reed Regional Publishing, 1982–90, and other companies; *b* 6 Dec. 1927; *s* of Sir (Thomas) Gordon Skinner, 3rd Bt, and Mollie Barbara (*d* 1965), *d* of Herbert William Girling; *S* father, 1972; *m* 1959, Jill, *d* of Cedric Ivor Tuckett; two *s*. *Educ:* Charterhouse. Managing Director, Thomas Skinner & Co. (Publishers) Ltd, 1952–60; also Director, Iliffe & Co. Ltd, 1958–65; Director, Iliffe-NTP Ltd; Chairman: Industrial Trade Fairs Holdings Ltd, 1977–; Business Press Internat., 1970–84. *Recreations:* publishing, shooting, fishing, gardening, golf. *Heir:* *s* Thomas James Hewitt Skinner, *b* 11 Sept. 1962. *Address:* Wood Farm, Reydon, near Southwold, Suffolk. *Clubs:* Royal Automobile; Aldeburgh Golf.

SKINNER, Thomas Monier, CMG 1958; MBE; MA Oxon; *b* 2 Feb. 1913; *s* of Lt-Col and Mrs T. B. Skinner; *m* 1st, 1935, Margaret Adeline (*née* Pope) (*d* 1969); two *s*; 2nd, 1981, Elizabeth Jane Hardie, *d* of late Mr and Mrs P. L. Hardie. *Educ:* Cheltenham Coll.; Lincoln Coll., Oxford. Asst District Officer (Cadet), Tanganyika, 1935; Asst District Officer, 1937; District Officer, 1947; Senior Asst Secretary, East Africa High Commission, 1952; Director of Establishments (Kenya), 1955–62, retired 1962. Member, Civil Service Commission, East Caribbean Territories, 1962–63; Chairman, Nyasaland Local Civil Service Commission, 1963; Salaries Commissioner, Basutoland, The Bechuanaland Protectorate and Swaziland, 1964. Reports on Localisation of Civil Service, Gilbert and Ellice Islands Colony and of British National Service, New Hebrides, 1968. Chairman: Bear Securities, 1962–73; Exeter Trust, 1973–79; Edinburgh Bond and Mortgage Corp, 1988–; Dir, Business Mortgages Trust, 1979–87. *Recreation:* fishing. *Address:* Innerpeffray Lodge, by Crieff, Perthshire PH7 3QW. *Club:* Army and Navy.

SKIPPER, David John; Director, Westminster Centre In Service Teacher Training, Independent Schools Joint Council, since 1991; *b* 14 April 1931; *s* of Herbert G. and Edna Skipper; *m* 1955, Brenda Ann Williams; three *s* one *d*. *Educ:* Watford Grammar Sch.; Brasenose Coll., Oxford (2nd Cl. Hons Nat. Science (Chemistry)). Royal Air Force (Short Service Commn) (Education), 1954–57; Assistant Master: Radley Coll., 1957–63; Rugby Sch., 1963–69; Headmaster: Ellesmere Coll., Shropshire, 1969–81; Merchant Taylors' Sch., Northwood, 1982–91. Chairman: ISJC Special Educnl Needs, 1983–91; Soc. of Schoolmasters, 1985–. *Recreations:* golf, hill-walking, drawing, music. *Address:* Dolton's Farm, Newport Road, Woburn MK17 9HX. *T:* Woburn (0525) 290093. *Club:* East India, Devonshire, Sports and Public Schools.

SKIPWITH, Sir Patrick Alexander d'Estoteville, 12th Bt, *cr* 1622; *b* 1 Sept. 1938; *o s* of Grey d'Estoteville Townsend Skipwith (killed in action, 1942), Flying Officer, RAFVR, and Sofka, *d* of late Prince Peter Dolgorouky; *S* grandfather, 1950; *m* 1st, 1964, Gillian Patricia (marr. diss. 1970), *d* of late Charles F. Harwood; one *s* one *d*; 2nd, 1972, Ashkhain (separated 1986), *d* of Bedros Atikian, Calgary, Alta. *Educ:* Harrow; Dublin (MA); London (DIC, PhD). With Ocean Mining Inc., in Tasmania, 1966–67, Malaysia, 1967–69, W Africa, 1969–70; with Min. of Petroleum and Mineral Resources, Saudi Arabia, 1970–71 and 1972–73. Editor, Bureau de Recherches Géologiques et Minières, Jiddah, 1973–86; Man. Dir, Immel Publishing Ltd, 1988–89; Consultant Editor/Translator, GeoEdit, 1986–. *Heir:* *s* Alexander Sebastian Grey d'Estoteville Skipwith, *b* 9 April 1969. *Address:* 1 rue Jean Hupeau, 45000 Orléans, France. *Club:* Chelsea Arts.

SKITT, Baden Henry, BEM 1969; QPM 1990; Chief Constable of Hertfordshire, since 1990; *b* 5 Dec. 1941; *s* of Frederick Albert Skitt and Laura Kathleen (*née* Oakley). *Educ:* Rugeley Grammar Sch., Staffs; St Paul's Coll., Cheltenham (Dip of PE; CertEd). Schoolmaster, Sir Wilfrid Martineau Sch., Birmingham, 1963–67; Constable to Supt, Birmingham City, later W Midlands, Police, 1967–82; Chief Supt, 1982–84, Comdr, 1984–86, Metropolitan Police; Dep. Chief Constable, Northants, 1986–90. Visiting Lecturer: RIPA; The King's Fund. Dir, Educnl Broadcasting Services Trust. *Publications:* (jtly) In Service Training: a new approach, 1974; (jtly) Education 2000, 1984; contrib. to learned jls. *Recreations:* the history and travelling of inland waterways, Rugby football, music. *Address:* Police Headquarters, Stanborough Road, Welwyn Garden City, Herts AL8 6XF. *T:* Welwyn Garden City (0707) 322183, *Fax:* (0707) 336512. *Club:* Chief Constables'.

SKONE JAMES, Edmund Purcell; barrister; *b* 14 June 1927; *s* of Francis Edmund Skone James and Kate Eve Skone James; *m* 1952, Jean Norah Knight; one *s* one *d*. *Educ:* Westminster Sch.; New Coll., Oxford (MA). Served RASC, 2nd Lieut, 1946–48. Called to the Bar, Middle Temple, 1951; Bencher, Middle Temple, 1977. Mem., Whitford Cttee to Consider the Law on Copyright and Designs, 1973 (Report 1977). *Publication:* Copinger and Skone James on Copyright, 9th edn 1958–13th edn 1991. *Recreations:* gardening, walking, reading fiction. *Address:* 5 New Square, Lincoln's Inn, WC2A 3RJ. *T:* 071–404 0404.

SKYNNER, (Augustus Charles) Robin, FRCPsych; consultant psychiatrist in private practice; writer; *b* 16 Aug. 1922; *e s* of Reginald C. A. Skynner and Mary F. Skynner (*née* Johns); *m* 1st, 1948, Geraldine Annella (*née* Foley) (marr. diss. 1959); 2nd, 1959, Prudence Mary (*née* Fawcett) (*d* 1987); one *s* one *d*. *Educ:* St Austell County Sch.; Blundell's Sch. MB BS London; DPM; FRCPsych 1978. War service, 1940–46, RAF, as pilot, Flight-Lieut. Med. training at University Coll. and Hosp., London, 1947–52 (Trotter Medal in Clinical Surgery); postgrad. at Inst. Psych. and Maudsley Hosp.; consultant psychiatric posts, 1959–, incl. Physician-in-Charge, Dept of Psych., Queen Elizabeth Hosp. for Children, 1965–70; Sen. Tutor in Psychotherapy, Inst. of Psych. and Hon. Consultant, Maudsley Hosp., 1971–82. Founder Mem., RCPsych, 1971; Jt Founder: Inst. of Group Analysis, 1969; Inst. of Family Therapy, 1977 (Chm., 1977–79); Mem. Council, Tavistock Inst. of Med. Psychology, 1988–. *Publications:* One Flesh, Separate Persons, 1976; (with John Cleese) Families and How to Survive Them, 1983; Explorations with Families, 1987; Institutes and How to Survive Them, 1989. *Recreation:* wind-surfing. *Address:* 88 Montagu Mansions, W1H 1LF. *T:* 071–935 3103. *Club:* Royal Society of Medicine.

SKYRME, Sir (William) Thomas (Charles), KCVO 1974; CB 1966; CBE 1953; TD 1949; JP, DL; Chairman, Broadcasting Complaints Commission, 1985–87 (Member, 1981–87); Secretary of Commissions, 1948–77; Vice-President, Magistrates' Association of England and Wales, since 1981 (Member of Council, since 1974; Deputy Chairman, 1977–79; Chairman, 1979–81); *b* 20 March 1913; *s* of Charles G. Skyrme, Hereford, and of Katherine (*née* Smith), Maryland, USA; *m* 1st, 1938, Hon. Barbara Suzanne Lyle (marr. diss. 1953), *yr d* of 1st Baron Lyle of Westbourne; one *s* two *d*; 2nd, 1957, Mary, *d* of Dr R. C. Leaning. *Educ:* Rugby School; New College, Oxford (MA); Universities of Dresden and Paris. Called to the Bar, Inner Temple, 1935, Bencher 1988. Practised in London and on Western Circuit. Served War of 1939–45 in Royal Artillery in Middle East, North Africa and Italy (wounded twice). Lt-Col. Secretary to the Lord Chancellor, 1944. Governor and Member of Committee of Management of Queen Mary's Hosp., London, 1938–48. Mem., Magistrates' Courts Rule Cttee, 1950–66; Chm., Interdepartmental Working Party on Legal Proceedings against Justices and Clerks, 1960; Mem., Interdepartmental Cttee on Magistrates Courts in London, 1961; Life Vice-Pres., Commonwealth Magistrates' and Judges' Assoc. (formerly Commonwealth Magistrates' Assoc.), 1979 (Pres., 1970–79); Chm., Commonwealth Magistrates' Confs, London, 1970, Bermuda, 1972, Nairobi, 1973, Kuala Lumpur, 1975, Tonga, 1976, Jamaica, 1977, Oxford, 1979; Vice-Chm., Adv. Cttee on Training of Magistrates, 1974–80. Hon. Life Mem., Justices' Clerks' Soc., 1979–. A General Comr of Income Tax, 1977–88; Mem., Top Salaries Review Body, 1981–90; Chm., Judicial Salaries Cttee, 1983–90. Freeman of City of London, 1970; HM Lieut for City of London, 1977–. DL Glos 1983. FRGS. JP (Oxfordshire), 1948, (London), 1952, (Gloucestershire), 1976. *Publications:* The Changing Image of the Magistracy, 1979; History of the Justices of the Peace, 1989; contribs to legal jls. *Recreations:* travel; rifle shooting (captained Oxford University, 1934). *Address:* Elm Barns, Blockley, Gloucestershire; Casa Larissa, Klosters, Switzerland. *Clubs:* Army and Navy; Hurlingham.

See also Sir J. G. Waterlow, Bt.

SLABBERT, Dr Frederik Van Zyl; *b* 2 March 1940; *s* of Petrus Johannes and Barbara Zacharia Slabbert; *m* 1965, Marié Jordaan (marr. diss. 1983); one *s* one *d*. *Educ:* Univ. of Stellenbosch. BA, BA (Hons), MA 1964, DPhil 1967. Lectr in Sociology, Stellenbosch Univ., 1964–68; Senior Lecturer: Rhodes Univ., 1969; Stellenbosch Univ., 1970–71; Cape Town Univ., 1972–73; Prof. of Sociology, Univ. of the Witwatersrand, 1973–74. MP (Progressive Federal Party) Claremont, 1974–86; Leader, Official Opposition, S African Parlt, 1979–86. Founder and Dir, Inst. for a Democratic Alternative for South Africa, 1987. *Publications:* South African Society: its central perspectives, 1972; (jtly) South Africa's Options: strategies for sharing power, 1979; The Last White Parliament (autobiog.), 1986; contributions to: Change in Contemporary South Africa, 1975; Explorations in Social Theory, 1976; various SPROCAS (Study Project of a Christian in an Apartheid Society) publications. *Recreations:* jogging, swimming, squash, chess. *Address:* 33 Albion Road, Rondebosch, 7700, South Africa. *T:* Cape Town 6899468.

SLACK, Dr Charles Roger, FRS 1989; FRSNZ 1983; Senior Scientist, Crop Research Division, Department of Scientific and Industrial Research, New Zealand, since 1989; *b* 22 April 1937; *s* of Albert Oram Slack and Eva (*née* Simister); *m* 1963, Pamela Mary Shaw; one *s* one *d*. *Educ:* Audenshaw Grammar Sch., Lancs; Sch. of Agriculture, Univ. of Nottingham (BSc; PhD 1962). Biochemist, David North Plant Res. Centre, CSR Co. Ltd, Brisbane, Australia, 1962–70; Leader, Biochemistry Group, 1970–84, Leader, Crop Physiology Group and Dep. Dir, Plant Physiol. Div., 1984–89, DSIR, NZ. Charles F. Kettering Award for Photosynthesis Res., Amer. Soc. of Plant Physiologists, 1980; Rank Prize for Nutrition, 1981. *Publications:* scientific pubns, mainly on aspects of photosynthesis and plant lipid synthesis. *Recreations:* hiking, trout fishing, gardening. *Address:* Crop Research Division, Department of Scientific and Industrial Research, Private Bag, Palmerston North, New Zealand. *T:* Palmerston North 68019, ext. 7064.

SLACK, His Honour George Granville; a Circuit Judge (formerly a County Court Judge), 1966–81; *b* 11 July 1906; *s* of George Edwin and Amy Beatrice Slack; *m* 1st, 1935, Ella Kathleen (*d* 1957), *d* of Henry Alexander Eason; one *d*; 2nd, 1958, Vera Gertrude, *d* of Reginald Ackland Spencer; one *s* one *d*. *Educ:* Accrington Grammar School; London University. BA (Hons History) 1926; LLB 1929; LLM 1932. Called to Bar, Gray's Inn, 1929. Served RAFVR, 1943–46. Judge of Croydon County Court, 1969–75, of Willesden County Court, 1976–81. Contested (L): Twickenham, 1945; Dewsbury, 1950; Chairman: London Liberal Party, 1947–48, 1950–53; Liberal Party Organisation, 1956–57. Sec., Acton Baptist Church, 1954–77. Chm., West Gp Housing Soc. Ltd (West Haven), 1961–. *Publications:* Slack on War Damage, 1941; Liabilities (War Time Adjustment) Act, 1941; Liability for National Service, 1942. *Address:* 10 Baronsmede, Ealing, W5 4LT. *T:* 081–567 8164. *Club:* National Liberal.

SLACK, John Kenneth Edward, TD 1964; **His Honour Judge John Slack;** a Circuit Judge, since 1977; *b* 23 Dec. 1930; *o s* of late Ernest Edward Slack, formerly Chief Clerk Westminster County Court, and late Beatrice Mary Slack (*née* Shorten), Broadstairs; *m* 1959, Patricia Helen, MA Cantab, *o d* of late William Keith Metcalfe, Southport; two *s*. *Educ:* University College Sch., Hampstead; St John's Coll., Cambridge (MA). Captain, RAEC, 1950. Admitted Solicitor, 1957; Partner, Freeborough Slack & Co., 1958–76; Mem. No 1 (later No 14) Legal Aid Area, 1966–69; Deputy Registrar, County Courts, 1969–72; a Recorder of the Crown Court, 1972–77; Pres., Wireless Telegraphy Appeals Tribunal, 1974–77. Captain Club Cricket Conf., 1962–66; Captain Bucks County Cricket Club, 1967–69 (Minor County Champions 1969); Active Vice-Pres., Club Cricket Conf., 1969–77, Pres., 1978. Chm. Council, University Coll. Sch., 1980–87 (Mem., 1974–90). *Recreations:* cricket (Cambridge Blue 1954), golf. *Address:* c/o Crown Court, Aylesbury, Bucks HP20 1XF. *Clubs:* Hawks (Cambridge); Beaconsfield Golf.

SLACK, Dr Paul Alexander, FBA 1990; FRHistS; Reader in Modern History, University of Oxford, since 1990; Fellow and Tutor, Exeter College, Oxford, since 1973; *b* 23 Jan. 1943; *s* of Isaac Slack and Helen (*née* Firth); *m* 1965, Diana Gillian Manby; two *d*. *Educ:* Bradford Grammar Sch.; St John's Coll., Oxford (Casberd Exhibnr and Schol.; 1st cl. Hons Mod. Hist. 1964; MA; DPhil 1972). FRHistS 1972. A. M. P. Read Schol., Oxford Univ., and Harmsworth Sen. Schol., Merton Coll., Oxford, 1965–66; Jun. Res. Fellow, Balliol Coll., Oxford, 1966–69; Lectr in Hist., York Univ., 1969–72; Sub-Rector, 1983, Sen. Tutor, 1984–86, Exeter Coll., Oxford; Jun. Proctor, 1986–87, Mem., Hebdomadal

Council, 1987–, Oxford Univ. Vis. Prof., Univ. of S Carolina, 1980; Vis. Res. Associate, Rikkyo Univ., Tokyo, 1988. Mem., Internat. Commn for Hist. of Towns, 1976–. Pres., Soc. for Social Hist. of Medicine, 1991; Mem. Council, RHistS, 1984–87. Editor, Past and Present, 1985–. *Publications:* (ed with Peter Clark) Crisis and Order in English Towns 1500–1700, 1972; (ed) Poverty in Early Stuart Salisbury, 1975; (with P. Clark) English Towns in Transition 1500–1700, 1976 (Japanese edn 1989); (ed) Rebellion, Popular Protest and the Social Order in Early Modern England, 1984; The Impact of Plague in Tudor and Stuart England, 1985; Poverty and Policy in Tudor and Stuart England, 1988; The English Poor Law 1531–1782, 1990; contribs to learned jls. *Recreations:* opera, fell-walking. *Address:* Exeter College, Oxford OX1 3DP. *T:* Oxford (0865) 279600.

SLACK, Timothy Willatt, MA; Principal, St Catharine's Foundation at Cumberland Lodge, since 1985; *b* 18 April 1928; *yr s* of late Cecil Moorhouse Slack, MC, and Dora Willatt, Beverley, Yorks; *m* 1957, Katharine, 2nd *d* of late Walter Norman Hughes, MA, and of Jean Sorsbie, Chepstow, Mon.; one *s* three *d*. *Educ:* Winchester Coll.; New Coll., Oxford. Hons. PPE, 1951. Asst, Lycée de Rennes, France, 1951; Asst master, the Salem School, Baden, Germany, 1952; Assistant master, Repton School, 1953–59; Headmaster of Kambawsa College, Taunggyi, Shan State, Burma, 1959–62; Headmaster, Bedales Sch., 1962–74. Chairman, Society of Headmasters of Independent Schools, 1968–70. Dep. Dir, 1975–77, Dir, 1977–83, Wiston House FCO Conf. Centre (incorp. Wilton Park Confs), Steyning; Headmaster, Hellenic Coll. of London, 1983–84. Kurt Hahn Meml Lectr, 1982. Chm. Governors, The Royal Sch., Windsor Great Park. Contested (L): Petersfield, Feb. and Oct. 1974; Enfield, Southgate, Dec. 1984; (L/Alliance) Fareham, 1987. *Address:* Hamlet House, Hambledon, Portsmouth PO7 6RY; Cumberland Lodge, The Great Park, Windsor, Berks SL4 2HP.

See also Sir W. W. Slack.

SLACK, Sir William (Willatt), KCVO 1990; MA, MCh, BM, FRCS; Consultant Surgeon, Middlesex Hospital, 1962–91, now Emeritus Surgeon; Senior Lecturer in Surgery, 1962–91, and Dean, 1983–87, Middlesex Hospital Medical School; Dean, Faculty of Clinical Sciences, University College and Middlesex School of Medicine, University College London, 1987–91; also Surgeon: Hospital of St John and St Elizabeth, 1970–88; King Edward VII Hospital for Officers, 1975–91; *b* 22 Feb. 1925; *s* of late Cecil Moorhouse Slack, MC, and Dora Slack (*née* Willatt); *m* 1951, Joan, 4th *d* of late Lt-Col Talbot H. Wheelwright, OBE; two *s* two *d*. *Educ:* Winchester Coll.; New Coll., Oxford; Middlesex Hosp. Med. Sch. Ho. Surg., Surgical Registrar and Sen. Surgical Registrar, Mddx Hosp., 1950–59; Jun. Registrar, St Bartholomew's Hosp., 1953; Fulbright Scholar, R. & E. Hosp., Univ. of Illinois, Chicago, 1959. Surgeon to the Queen, 1975–83; Serjeant Surgeon to the Queen, 1983–90. Hon. Fellow, UCL, 1987. Master, Barbers' Co., 1991–Aug. 1992. *Publications:* various surgical articles in med. jls and textbooks. *Recreations:* skiing, gardening; Oxford blue for Association football, 1946. *Address:* 22 Platts Lane, NW3 7NS. *T:* 071–435 5887; Hillside Cottage, Tower Hill, Stawell, near Bridgwater, Somerset. *T:* Bridgwater (0278) 722719.

See also T. W. Slack.

SLADE, Adrian Carnegie, CBE 1988; Director, Longslade (Media Training) Ltd, since 1991; *b* 25 May 1936; *y s* of late George Penkivil Slade, KC and Mary Albinia Alice Slade; *m* 1960, Susan Elizabeth Forsyth; one *s* one *d*. *Educ:* Eton Coll.; Trinity Coll., Cambridge (BA Law). Pres., Cambridge Footlights, 1959. Served 9th Lancers, 1955–60 (AER, Cl. 1, 1957–60). Writer, J. Walter Thompson, 1959–64; S. H. Benson, 1964–71, Dir, 1970–71; Co-Founder and Managing Director: Slade Monico Bluff Ltd, 1971–75; Slade Bluff & Bigg Ltd, 1975–86; Slade Hamilton Fenech Ltd, 1986–90 (Chm., 1990–91). Dir, Orange Tree Th., Richmond, 1986–. Mem. (L) Richmond, GLC, 1981–86 (Leader, L/SDP Alliance Gp, 1982–86). Contested: (L) Putney, 1966, Feb. and Oct. 1974; (L/SDP Alliance) Wimbledon, 1987. Advertising and Pubns Advr to Liberal Party, gen. elections: 1966, 1970, Feb. and Oct. 1974, 1979; Pres. 1982–85, Chm. 1985–87, London Liberal Party; Pres., Liberal Party, 1987–88; Jt Pres., 1988, Vice-Pres., 1988–89, SLD; London Pres., Liberal Democrats, 1991–. Acting Advr for Public Affairs at Lambeth Palace, 1991. *Recreations:* music, theatre, films, piano playing, photography. *Address:* 28 St Leonard's Road, SW14 7LX. *T:* 081–876 8712.

See also Rt Hon. Sir C. J. Slade, J. P. Slade.

SLADE, (Sir) Benjamin Julian Alfred, (7th Bt *cr* 1831, but does not use the title); Chairman, Shirlstar Container Transport Ltd, since 1973, and director of subsidiary companies; *b* 22 May 1946; *s* of Sir Michael Slade, 6th Bt and Angela (*d* 1959), *d* of Captain Orlando Chichester; *S* father, 1962; *m* 1977, Pauline Carol (marr. diss. 1991), *er d* of Major Claude Myburgh. *Educ:* Millfield Sch. Chm., Pyman Bell (Holding) Ltd. Mem., Worshipful Co. of Ironmongers. Freeman, City of London, 1979. *Recreations:* hunting, shooting, racing, polo, bridge. *Heir:* none. *Address:* 164 Ashley Gardens, Emery Hill Street, SW1. *T:* 071–828 2809; Maunsel, North Newton, Bridgwater, Somerset. *T:* Bridgwater (0278) 663413, (Estate Office) Bridgwater (0278) 662387; *Telex:* (office) 917760; Shirlstar House, 37 St John's Road, Uxbridge, Mddx. *T:* Uxbridge (0895) 72929; *Telex:* 885639. *Clubs:* Turf, Buck's; Old Somerset Dining (Taunton).

SLADE, Brian John, FInstPS; Director General of Defence Contracts, Ministry of Defence, 1986–91; *b* 28 April 1931; *s* of Albert Edward Victor Slade and late Florence Elizabeth (*née* Eveleigh); *m* 1955, Grace, *d* of late W. McK. Murray and Mary Murray, Ayr; one *s* one *d*. *Educ:* Portsmouth Northern Grammar School; London University. Joined Min. of Supply, 1951; Private Sec. to Permanent Sec., Min. of Aviation, 1962–64; Head of Industrial Personnel Branch, Min. of Technology, 1968–73; Principal Dir of Contracts, Air, MoD, 1982–86. Mem. Synod, Methodist Church, London SW, 1981–90. *Recreations:* cricket, downs walking. *Address:* Doonbank, 16 Greenway, Great Bookham, Surrey KT23 3PA. *T:* Bookham (0372) 454359.

SLADE, Rt. Hon. Sir Christopher John, Kt 1975; PC 1982; a Lord Justice of Appeal, 1982–91; *b* 2 June 1927; *e s* of late George Penkivil Slade, KC, and Mary Albinia Alice Slade; *m* 1958, Jane Gwenllian Armstrong Buckley; one *e s* three *d*. *Educ:* Eton (Scholar); New Coll., Oxford (Scholar). Eldon Law Scholar, 1950. Called to Bar, Inner Temple, 1951; in practice at Chancery Bar, 1951–75; QC 1965; Bencher, Lincoln's Inn, 1973. Attorney General, Duchy of Lancaster and Attorney and Serjeant Within the County Palatine of Lancaster, 1972–75; a Judge of the High Ct, Chancery Division, 1975–82; a Judge of Restrictive Practices Ct, 1980–82, Pres., 1981–82. Member: Gen. Council of the Bar, 1958–62, 1965–69; Senate of Four Inns of Court, 1966–69; Lord Chancellor's Legal Educn Cttee, 1969–71. Master, Ironmongers' Co., 1973. *Address:* 12 Harley Gardens, SW10 9SW. *Club:* Garrick.

See also A. C. Slade, J. P. Slade.

SLADE, Julian Penkivil; author and composer since 1951; *b* 28 May 1930; *s* of G. P. Slade, KC. *Educ:* Eton College; Trinity College, Cambridge (BA). Went to Bristol Old Vic Theatre School, 1951; wrote incidental music for Bristol Old Vic production of Two Gentlemen of Verona, 1952; joined Bristol Old Vic Co. as musical director, 1952. Wrote and composed Christmas in King St (with Dorothy Reynolds and James Cairncross) Bristol, 1952; composed music for Sheridan's The Duenna, Bristol, 1953; transferred to Westminster Theatre, London, 1954; wrote and composed The Merry Gentleman (with Dorothy Reynolds), Bristol, 1953; composed incidental music for The Merchant of Venice (1953 Stratford season). Wrote musical version of The Comedy of Errors for TV, 1954, and for Arts Theatre, London, 1956; wrote (with Dorothy Reynolds) Salad Days, Bristol, 1954, Vaudeville, London, 1954, Duke of York's, 1976; Free as Air, Savoy, London, 1957; Hooray for Daisy!, Bristol, 1959, Lyric, Hammersmith, 1960; Follow that Girl, Vaudeville, London, 1960; Wildest Dreams, 1960; Vanity Fair (with Alan Pryce-Jones and Robin Miller), Queen's Theatre, London, 1962; Nutmeg and Ginger, Cheltenham, 1963, revived Orange Tree Theatre, Richmond, 1991; Sixty Thousand Nights (with George Rowell), Bristol, 1966; The Pursuit of Love, Bristol, 1967; composed music for songs in: As You Like It, Bristol, 1970; A Midsummer Night's Dream and Much Ado About Nothing, Regent's Park, 1970; adapted A. A. Milne's Winnie The Pooh, Phoenix Theatre, 1970, 1975; (music and lyrics) Trelawny, Bristol, then London West End, 1972; Out of Bounds (book, music and lyrics, based on Pinero's The Schoolmistress), 1973. Composed incidental music for Nancy Mitford's Love in a Cold Climate, Thames TV, 1980; adapted Salad Days for Yorkshire TV, 1983; (with Veronica Flint-Shipman and Kit Harvey) musical adaptation of J. M. Barrie's Dear Brutus, 1985; (with Gyles Brandreth) Now We Are Sixty (musical play based on works of A. A. Milne), Arts Theatre, Cambridge, 1986; (with Elizabeth Seal) concert performances of own songs, Easy to Sing, 1986–87. Played and sang for solo record album of own songs, Looking for a Piano, 1981; played for vocal album, Salad Days, 1982. Gold Badge of Merit, British Acad. of Songwriters, Composers and Authors, 1987. *Publications:* Nibble the Squirrel (children's book), 1946; music of: The Duenna, 1954; Salad Days, 1954; Free as Air, 1957; Follow That Girl, 1967; Trelawny, 1974; The Merry Gentleman, 1985. *Recreations:* drawing, going to theatres and cinemas, listening to music. *Address:* 86 Beaufort Street (Ground Floor/Basement), SW3 6BU. *T:* 071–376 4480.

See also A. C. Slade, Rt Hon. Sir C. J. Slade.

SLADE, Leslie William, JP; Agent General for Western Australia in London, 1978–82; *b* 17 July 1915; *s* of Leonard Barrington Slade and Gwendoline (*née* Fraser); *m* 1942, Marion Joan, *d* of V. J. Devitt, Perth, WA; one *d* decd. *Educ:* Scotch Coll., Melbourne, Australia. Accountant, Myer Emporium Ltd, Melbourne, 1933–39; served RAN (Lieut-Comdr), 1939–46; Proprietor of import/export business, Perth, WA, 1947–61; Export Consultant, W Australian Govt, Perth, 1962–68; Official Rep., Govt of W Australia for Far East, Tokyo, 1968–78. Freedom of City of London, 1978. JP WA, 1978. *Recreations:* golf, cricket, fishing, sailing. *Address:* Unit 8, Kyamala, 19 Broome Street, Mosman Park, WA 6012, Australia. *Clubs:* Weld, West Australian Cricket Association, Royal Perth Yacht, Nedlands Golf (Perth); Tokyo (Tokyo).

SLADE, Patrick Buxton M.; *see* Mitford-Slade.

SLADEN, Teresa; Secretary of the Victorian Society, since 1987; *b* 16 Sept. 1939; *d* of Robert John Fawcett and Anne (*née* Fairlie Clarke); *m* 1961, David Sladen; one *s* two *d*. *Educ:* Birkbeck Coll., London Univ. (BA Hons Hist. of Art/Italian); Courtauld Inst. (MA Medieval Art and Architecture, 1978). Royal Commn on Historical Monuments, 1978–79; part-time lectr and freelance researcher, 1980–82; Architectural Advr, Victorian Soc., 1983–87. *Publication:* contrib. jl of Garden History. *Recreations:* drawing, looking at 19th century stained glass, reading 19th century novels. *Address:* The Victorian Society, 1 Priory Gardens, W4 1TT. *T:* 081–994 0815.

SLANE, Viscount; Alexander Burton Conyngham; *b* 30 Jan. 1975; *s* and *heir* of Earl of Mount Charles, *qv*.

SLANEY, Prof. Sir Geoffrey, KBE 1984; FRCS; Barling Professor, Head of Department of Surgery, Queen Elizabeth Hospital, Birmingham University, 1971–86, now Emeritus; Hon. Consultant Surgeon: United Birmingham Hospitals and Regional Hospital Board, since 1959; Royal Prince Alfred Hospital, Sydney, since 1981; President, Royal College of Surgeons of England, 1982–86; Hon. Consulting Surgeon Emeritus, City of London and Hackney Health Authority, since 1983; *b* 19 Sept. 1922; *er s* of Richard and Gladys Lois Slaney; *m* 1956, Josephine Mary Davy; one *s* two *d*. *Educ:* Brewood Grammar Sch.; Univs of Birmingham, London and Illinois, USA. MB, ChB (Birmingham) 1947, FRCS 1953, MS (Ill) 1956, ChM (Birmingham) 1961; Hon. FRCSI 1983; Hon. FRACS 1983; Hon. FCSSL 1984; Hon. FACS 1985; Hon. FCSSA 1986; Hon. FRCSCan 1986; Hon. FCAnaes (Hon. FFARCS 1987). Ho. Surg. and Surgical Registrar, Gen. Hosp. Birmingham, 1947–48. Captain RAMC, 1948–50. Surgical Registrar, Coventry, London and Hackney Hosps, 1950–53; Surgical Registrar, Lectr in Surgery and Surgical Research Fellow, Queen Elizabeth Hosp., Birmingham, 1953–59; Hunterian Prof., RCS, 1961–62; Prof. of Surgery, Univ. of Birmingham, 1966–87. Member: London Adv. Group to Sec. of State, DHSS, 1980–81; Ministerial Adv. Gp on Med. Manpower, 1985–86; Res. Liaison Gp, DHSS, 1979–85; Midlands Med. Appeals Tribunal, 1964–. Former External Examr in Surgery to Univs of: Newcastle upon Tyne, London, Cambridge, Oxford, Liverpool, Nat. Univ. of Ireland, Lagos, Zimbabwe, and Licentiate Cttee, Hong Kong; Advisor in Surgery, Univs of Bristol and London. Lectures: Richardson Meml, Massachusetts Gen. Hosp., Boston, USA, 1975; Pybus Meml, Newcastle, 1978; Simpson Smith Meml, London, 1979; Legg Meml, KCH, London, 1982; Chesledon, St Thomas' Hosp., London, 1983; Miles Meml, London, 1983; Berrill Meml, Coventry, 1984; Sandblom, Lund, Sweden, 1984; Sir John Frazer Meml, Edinburgh, 1984; Tung Wah Inaugural, Tung Wah Hosp., Hong Kong, 1986; Sir Ernest Finch Meml, Sheffield, 1986; Hunterian Oration, RCS, 1987; Budd Meml, Bristol, 1987; Annual Guest Lecture, Chicago Surgical Soc., 1987; Barney Brooks Meml, Vanderbilt Univ., Tennessee, 1987; Rutherford-Morison, Newcastle, 1987; Walter C. Mackenzie, Edmonton, 1988; Francis C. Moore, Boston, 1988; Joseph C. Finneran, Indianapolis, 1988; Annual Oration, Osler Club, 1988; Qvist Meml, Royal Free Hosp., 1988; Duke Sesquicentennial, NC, 1988; Telford Meml, Manchester, 1989; (first) Bryan Brooke, Ileostomy Assoc., 1990. Visiting Professor: Durban, Cape Town, Witwatersrand, 1970; Sir Logan Campbell and RACS, NZ, 1977; Univ. of Calif and Cedars-Sinai Hosp., LA, 1978; Pearce Gould, Middlesex Hosp., 1980; McIlrath Guest, Sydney, 1981; G. B. Ong, Univ. of Hong Kong, 1983 (Ong Inaugural Lecture); Foundn Culpepper Prof., Univ. of California, 1984; Madras Med. Coll., and Univ. of Istanbul, 1986; Univ. of Alberta, Edmonton, 1988; Harvard, 1988; Uniformed Services Univ., Bethesda, 1988; Duke Univ., 1988; Wernicke-Marks-Elk, Univ. of Zimbabwe, 1989. Mem. Council, RCS, 1975–87; Member: Moynihan Chirurgical Club (Pres., 1986–87); James IV Assoc. of Surgeons (Pres., 1985–86); Internat. Surgical Gp (Pres., 1985–86); Surgical Research Soc.; Internat. Soc. of Cardio-Vascular Surgeons; Vascular Surgical Soc., GB (Pres., 1974–75); Chm., Assoc. of Profs of Surgery of GB and Ireland, 1979–82. Mem. Council, Univ. of Zimbabwe, 1973–82. Fellow: RSM; Assoc. of Surgeons GB and Ire. (Mem. Council, 1966–76, Treasurer, 1970–76); Assoc. Clinical Anatomists; Amer. Surgical Assoc.; Hon. FCS Sri Lanka, 1984. Hon. Life Member: Los Angeles Surgical Soc.; Chicago Surgical Soc.; Warren H. Cole Surgical Soc.; William H. Scott Surgical Soc.; Hon. Member: Grey Turner Surgical Club; Assoc. of Surgeons of India. Hon. Freeman, Barbers' Co. Jacksonian Prize and Medal, RCS, 1959; Pybus Meml Medal, NE Surgical Soc., 1978; Miles Medal, Royal Marsden Hosp., 1983; Vanderbilt Univ. Medal, 1987; Brooke Medal, Ileostomy Assoc. of GB and Ireland, 1990. *Publications:*

Metabolic Derangements in Gastrointestinal Surgery (with B. N. Brooke), 1967 (USA); numerous contribs to med. and surg. jls. *Recreations:* fishing and family. *Address:* 23 Aston Bury, Edgbaston, Birmingham B15 3QB. *T:* 021–454 0261.

SLATCHER, William Kenneth, CMG 1983; CVO 1975; HM Diplomatic Service, retired; High Commissioner in Guyana and non-resident Ambassador to Suriname, 1982–85; *b* 12 April 1926; *s* of John William and Ada Slatcher; *m* 1948, Erica Marjorie Konigs; one *s* one *d*. *Educ:* St John's Coll., Oxford. Royal Artillery, 1950–57; HM Diplomatic Service, 1958: Peking, 1959–60; Tokyo, 1961–63; Paris, 1965–68; New Delhi, 1968–71; Tokyo, 1974–77; Consul-Gen., Osaka, 1977–80; Head of Consular Dept, FCO, 1980–82. *Recreations:* travelling, oriental art and history, reading. *Address:* Le Bellevue, 6 Avenue Laurenti, 06500 Menton, France. *Club:* Commonwealth Trust.

SLATER, Bill; *see* Slater, W. J.

SLATER, Dr David Homfray; Chief Inspector, HM Inspectorate of Pollution, since 1991; *b* 16 Oct. 1940; *m* 1964, Edith Mildred Price; four *d*. *Educ:* University College of Wales Aberystwyth (BSc, PhD). CChem, FRIC, CEng, FInstE. Research Associate, Ohio State Univ., 1966–69; Sen. Res. Fellow, Dept of Chemistry, Univ. of Southampton, 1969–70; Lectr in Combustion, Dept of Chem. Engineering and Chem. Technology, Imperial College London, 1970–75; Cremer and Warner: Sen. Scientist, 1975; Partner, 1979–81; Founding Dir, Technica, 1981–91. *Publications:* numerous contribs to sci. jls and conference procs. *Recreations:* music, photography, fishing. *Address:* HM Inspectorate of Pollution, Romney House, 43 Marsham Street, SW1P 3PY.

SLATER, Duncan, CMG 1982; HM Diplomatic Service; Assistant Under Secretary of State, Foreign and Commonwealth Office, since 1986; *b* 15 July 1934; *m* 1972, Candida Coralie Anne Wheatley; one *s* two *d*. Joined FO, 1958; Asst Polit. Agent, Abu Dhabi, 1962–66; First Secretary: Islamabad, 1966; New Delhi, 1966–68; Head of Chancery, Aden, 1968–69; FO, 1969; Special Asst to Sir William Luce, 1970–71; First Sec., UK Representation to EEC, Brussels, 1973–75; UK Resident Rep. to IAEA and UK Perm. Rep. to UNIDO, Vienna, 1975–78; on staff of Government House, Salisbury, Dec. 1979–April 1980; Counsellor and Head of Chancery, Lagos, 1978–81; Ambassador to Oman, 1981–86. *Recreations:* walking, sailing, skiing, studying Islamic art. *Address:* c/o Foreign and Commonwealth Office, SW1.

SLATER, Prof. Edward Charles, ScD; FRS 1975; Professor of Physiological Chemistry, University of Amsterdam, The Netherlands, 1955–85; Hon. Professor, University of Southampton, since 1985; *b* 16 Jan. 1917; *s* of Edward Brunton Slater and Violet Podmore; *m* 1940, Marion Winifred Hutley; one *d*. *Educ:* Melbourne Univ. (BSc, MSc); Cambridge Univ. (PhD, ScD). Biochemist, Australian Inst. of Anatomy, Canberra, Aust., 1939–46; Research Fellow, Molteno Inst., Univ. of Cambridge, UK, 1946–55. Pres., Internat. Union of Biochem., 1988–91. Member: Royal Netherlands Acad. of Science and Letters, 1964; Hollandsche Maatschappij van Wetenschappen, 1970; Hon. Member: Amer. Soc. of Biological Chemists, 1971; Japanese Biochemical Soc., 1973; The Biochemical Soc., 1987; Nederlandse Vereniging voor Biochemie, 1989; For. Mem., Royal Swedish Acad. of Sciences, 1975; Hon. For. Mem., Académie Royal de Méd., Belgium, 1982; Corresponding Member: Acad. Nacional de Ciencas Exactas, Fisicasy Naturales, Argentina, 1973; Australian Acad. of Science, 1985. Kt, Order of the Netherlands Lion, 1984. *Publications:* Biochimica et Biophysica Acta: story of a biochemical journal, 1986; about 450 contribs to learned jls. *Recreations:* yachting, skiing. *Address:* 9 Oaklands, Lymington, Hants SO41 9TH. *T:* (home) Lymington (0590) 679455, (work) Southampton (0703) 554347.

SLATER, Gordon Charles Henry, CMG 1964; CBE 1956; Director, Branch Office in London of International Labour Office, 1964–70; Under-Secretary, Ministry of Labour, in the Overseas Department, 1960–64, retired; *b* 14 Dec. 1903; *s* of Matthew and Florence Slater; *m* 1928, Doris Primrose Hammond; one *s* one *d*. Entered Ministry of Labour, 1928, as Third Class Officer; Assistant Secretary, Organisation and Establishments, 1945, Disabled Persons Branch, 1949; Secretary of National Advisory Council on Employment of Disabled Persons, 1949–56; Sec. of Piercy Committee on Rehabilitation of Disabled, 1953–56; Under-Sec., Ministry of Labour, 1958. Member Governing Body, ILO, 1961–64; UK Govt delegate, IL Conf., 1961–64. Mem. Berkshire CC, 1970–81, Vice-Chm., 1977–79. *Address:* White House, Altwood Road, Maidenhead, Berks. *T:* Maidenhead (0628) 27463.

SLATER, Gordon James Augustus; HM Diplomatic Service, retired; Secretary to Government, and Adviser to Foreign Affairs Department, Tuvalu, 1985–86; *b* 8 July 1922; *s* of William Augustus Slater and Edith Garden; *m* 1st, 1952, Beryl Ruth Oliver (marr. diss. 1968); one *s* one *d*; 2nd, 1976, Gina Michelle Lambert (marr. diss. 1988); one *d*. *Educ:* Sydney, Australia. Foreign and Commonwealth Office (formerly Commonwealth Relations Office), 1958–82; High Comr, Honiara, Solomon Is, 1978–82. *Recreations:* sailing, diving, golf. *Address:* 5 Ordak Avenue, Gymea, NSW 2227, Australia.

SLATER, James Derrick, FCA; Chairman, Salar Properties Ltd, since 1983; *b* 13 March 1929; *o s* of Hubert and Jessica Slater; *m* 1965, Helen Wyndham Goodwyn; two *s* two *d*. *Educ:* Preston Manor County Sch. Accountant and then Gen. Man. to a gp of metal finishing cos, 1953–55; Sec., Park Royal Vehicles Ltd, 1955–58; Dep. Sales Dir, Leyland Motor Corp. Ltd, 1963; Chm., Slater Walker Securities Ltd, 1964–75; Dir, BLMC, 1969–75. FCA 1963 (ACA 1953). *Publications:* Return to Go, 1977; *for children:* Goldenrod, 1978; A. Mazing Monsters, 1979; Grasshopper and the Unwise Owl, 1979; The Boy Who Saved Earth, 1979. *Recreations:* chess, bridge, salmon fishing, table tennis. *Address:* Combe Court, Combe Lane, Chiddingfold, Surrey.

SLATER, John Christopher Nash; QC 1987; a Recorder, since 1990; *b* 14 June 1946; *er s* of Lt-Col Leonard Slater, *qv*; *m* 1971, Jane Schapiro; two *s* one *d*. *Educ:* Sedbergh School; University College, Oxford (MA). Called to the Bar, Middle Temple, 1969 (Harmsworth Scholar). Assistant Recorder, 1987–90. *Publications:* Concise College Texts: Cases and Statutes, Criminal Law, 1972, 2nd edn (jtly) 1981. *Recreations:* golf, acting, travel. *Address:* 7 Woodside Avenue, Highgate, N6 4SP. *T:* 081–883 3903. *Clubs:* Hampstead Golf; Hampstead Cricket.

SLATER, Adm. Sir John Cunningham Kirkwood, (Sir Jock), KCB 1988; LVO 1971; Commander-in-Chief, Fleet, Allied Commander-in-Chief, Channel, and Eastern Atlantic, since 1991; *b* 27 March 1938; *s* of late Dr James K. Slater, OBE, MD, FRCPE and M. C. B. Slater (*née* Bramwell); *m* 1972, Ann Frances, *d* of late Mr and Mrs W. P. Scott of Orkney; two *s*. *Educ:* Edinburgh Academy; Sedbergh. BRNC Dartmouth, 1956–58; served HM Ships Troubridge, Yaxham, HM Yacht Britannia, Cassandra, 1959–64; Comd HMS Soberton, 1965; specialised in navigation, HMS Dryad, 1965–66; HM Ships Victorious and Scarborough (Dartmouth Training Sqdn), 1966–68; Equerry to HM the Queen, 1968–71; Comdr 1971; Comd, HMS Jupiter, 1972–73; Directorate of Naval Ops, MoD, 1973–75; Captain 1976; Comd, HMS Kent, 1976–77; RCDS 1978; Asst Dir of Naval Warfare, MoD, 1979–81; Comd, HMS Illustrious, 1982–83; Captain, Sch. of Maritime Ops and Comd, HMS Dryad, 1983–85; Rear Adm. 1985; ACDS (Policy and Nuclear), 1985–87; Vice-Adm., 1987; Flag Officer, Scotland and NI, and NATO Comdr Northern sub area Eastern Atlantic, Comdr Nore sub area Channel and Naval Base Comdr, Rosyth, 1987–89; Chief of Fleet Support (Mem., Admiralty Bd), 1989–91; Adm. 1991. Mem., Bd of Management, BNSC, 1986–87. Mem., Nat. Youth Orchestra of GB, 1955. Younger Brother, Trinity Hse, 1978. Freeman: City of London, 1989; Shipwrights' Co., 1990. *Recreations:* outdoor. *Address:* c/o Royal Bank of Scotland, 142/144 Princes Street, Edinburgh EH2 4EQ. *Club:* Army and Navy.
See also P. J. B. Slater.

SLATER, John Fell, CMG 1972; Assistant Secretary, HM Treasury, 1968–83; *b* 3 July 1924; *s* of J. Alan Slater, FRIBA, and Freide R. Slater (*née* Flight); *m* 1951, Susan Baron; two *s* two *d* (and one *d* decd). *Educ:* Abinger Hill Preparatory Sch.; Leighton Park Sch.; New Coll., Oxford (BA). *Recreations:* fly-fishing, photography. *Address:* 20 Upham Park Road, W4 1PG. *T:* 071–994 6205.

SLATER, Kenneth Frederick, FEng 1985; FIEE; engineering consultant; *b* 31 July 1925; *s* of Charles Frederick and Emily Gertrude Slater; *m* 1965, Marjorie Gladys Beadsworth, Northampton. *Educ:* Hull Grammar Sch.; Manchester Univ. BSc Tech (Hons). Admiralty Signal Estab. Extension, 1943–46; RRE, 1949–63; UK Mem., NATO Air Defence Planning Team, 1964; Supt, Radar Div., RRE, 1965–68; Asst Dir of Electronics R&D, Min. of Technology, 1968–70, Dir, 1970–71; Head of various groups, RRE, 1971–76; Dep. Dir, RSRE, 1976–78; Dir, Admiralty Surface Weapons Estab., 1978–84; Dir of Engrg, Marconi Underwater Systems Ltd, 1984–88. *Publications:* specialist contribs on Radar to Encyclopaedia Britannica and Encyclopaedic Dictionary of Physics; technical articles. *Recreations:* photography, music. *Address:* Valinor, Blackheath Way, West Malvern WR14 4DR. *T:* Malvern (0684) 567641.

SLATER, Leonard, CBE 1976; JP; DL; *b* 23 July 1908; *s* of S. M. Slater, Oldham, and Heysham, Lancs; *m* 1943, Olga Patricia George (*d* 1983); two *s*. *Educ:* Hulme Grammar School, Oldham; St Catharine's College, Cambridge (MA). British Guiana Exped. 1929; Research at Cambridge, 1930–32; MA 1932. Lecturer in Geography, Univ. of Rangoon, 1932–37; Geography Master, Repton School, 1937. Served War, 1940–45; RE (Survey) in UK, India and SE Asia; Lieut-Col, 1944 and Hon. Lieut-Col, 1946. Univ. of Durham: Geography Dept, Lectr, 1939; Reader, 1948; Pro-Vice-Chancellor, 1969–73; Master, University Coll., Durham, 1953–73. Mem. Peterlee Develt Corp., 1956–63; Chairman: Durham Hosp. Management Cttee, 1961–73; Durham AHA, 1973–77; Mem., Newcastle Regional Hosp. Bd, 1965–69 and 1971–74. JP 1961, DL 1978, Durham. *Publications:* articles in geographical periodicals. *Recreation:* travel. *Address:* 8 Farnley Ridge, Durham DH1 4HB. *T:* Durham (091) 3863319.
See also J. C. N. Slater.

SLATER, Prof. Peter James Bramwell, FRSE; Kennedy Professor of Natural History, University of St Andrews, since 1984; *b* 26 Dec. 1942; *s* of Dr James Kirkwood Slater, OBE and Margaret Claire Byrom Slater (*née* Bramwell); *m* 1968, Elisabeth Priscilla Vernon Smith; two *s*. *Educ:* Edinburgh Academy; Glenalmond; Univ. of Edinburgh (BSc 1964; PhD 1968; DSc 1983). FIBiol 1986; FRSE 1991. Shaw Macfie Lang Fellow, 1964–66, Demonstrator in Zoology, 1966–68, Univ. of Edinburgh; Lectr in Biology, Univ. of Sussex, 1968–84. Hon. Sec., Assoc. for Study of Animal Behaviour, 1973–78, Hon. Pres., 1986–89. European Editor, Animal Behaviour, 1979–82; Editor: Advances in the Study of Behavior, 1989– (Associate Editor, 1982–88); Science Progress, 1983–89. *Publications:* Sex Hormones and Behaviour, 1978; (ed with T. R. Halliday) Animal Behaviour, 1983; An Introduction to Ethology, 1985; (ed) Collins Encyclopaedia of Animal Behaviour, 1986; numerous articles in learned jls. *Recreations:* ornithology, writing, listening to music. *Address:* Department of Biology and Preclinical Medicine, University of St Andrews, Fife KY16 9TS. *T:* St Andrews (0334) 76161.
See also Sir J. C. K. Slater.

SLATER, Richard Mercer Keene, CMG 1962; *b* 27 May 1915; *s* of late Samuel Henry Slater, CMG, CIE; *m* 1939, Barbara Janet Murdoch; four *s*. *Educ:* Eton; Magdalene Coll., Cambridge. Indian Civil Service (Punjab Commission), 1939–47; joined HM Diplomatic Service, 1947; served in Karachi (on secondment to Commonwealth Relations Office), Lima, Moscow, Rangoon and Foreign Office; Ambassador to Cuba, 1966–70; High Comr in Uganda and Ambassador to Rwanda, 1970–72; Asst Under-Sec. of State, FCO, 1973. Adviser to Commercial Union Assurance Co., 1973–81. Chm., Hampshire Br., CPRE, 1974–85. *Address:* Vicary's, Odiham, Hants RG25 1LE.

SLATER, William Bell, CBE 1982; VRD 1959; FCIT; Chairman, The Mersey Docks & Harbour Co., since 1987; Managing Director, The Cunard Steam-Ship Co. plc, 1974–85 (Director, 1971–85 and 1986–88); Director, Trafalgar House plc, 1975–88; *b* 7 Jan. 1925; *s* of William Bell and Mamie Slater; *m* 1950, Jean Mary Kiernan; two *s*. *Educ:* Lancaster Royal Grammar Sch. FCIT 1970. National Service, RM, 1943–47 (Captain, 3rd Commando Bde); RM Reserve, 1949–63 (Lt-Col and CO Merseyside Unit). Trainee, Thos & Jno Brocklebank Ltd, 1947, Dir 1966–85, also Chm.; Ops Dir, 1968, Dep. Man. Dir, 1969, Man. Dir, 1971–72, Chm. 1972–85, Cunard Brocklebank Ltd. Director: Atlantic Container Line Ltd, 1968–85 (Chm., 1977–78 and 1982–83); Associated Container Transportation (Australia) Ltd, 1974–85 (Chm., 1982–85); Associated Container Transportation Ltd, 1974–85 (Chm., 1982–85); The Mersey Docks & Harbour Co., 1980– (Dep. Chm., 1985–87). External Dir, British Internat. Freight Assoc., 1989–. Vice-Pres., CIT, 1984–87; Pres., Inst. of Freight Forwarders Ltd, 1987–88. Gen. Comr of Income Tax, 1987–. Hon. Col, RM Reserve, Merseyside, 1986–91. Order of El Istiqlal (2nd Cl.), Jordan, 1972. *Recreations:* Rugby and cricket (formerly Senior Club player). *Address:* Gayton Court, 419 Woodham Lane, Woodham, Weybridge, Surrey KT15 3PP. *T:* Byfleet (09323) 49389. *Club:* Naval.

SLATER, William John, (Bill Slater), OBE 1982; President, British Amateur Gymnastics Association, since 1989; Director of National Services, Sports Council, 1984–89; *b* 29 April 1927; *s* of John Rothwell Slater and Ethel May Slater; *m* 1952, Marion Warr; two *s* two *d*. *Educ:* Clitheroe Royal Grammar Sch.; Carnegie Coll. of Physical Educn (Dip. in Phys. Educn); Univ. of Birmingham (BSc). FPEA 1984. Dep. Dir, Crystal Palace Nat. Sports Centre, 1963–64; Dir of Phys. Educn, Univ. of Liverpool, 1964–70 (Warden, McNair Hall, 1966–69); Dir of Phys. Educn, Univ. of Birmingham, 1970–83. Member: Central Adv. Council for Educn (Newsom Cttee), 1961–63; Cttee of Enquiry into Association Football (Chester Cttee), 1966–68; Sports Council, 1974–83 (Chm., Nat. Resources Cttee, 1982–83); Nat. Olympic Cttee, 1990–. Chairman: Cttee of Advrs, Sports Aid Foundn, 1978–; Management Cttee, Lilleshall Nat. Sports Centre, 1979–83; West Midlands Council for Sport and Recreation, 1979–83. Wolverhampton Wanderers Football Club, 1951–62; rep. England in Association Football, 1951–60; Olympic Games, Helsinki, 1952; World Cup (Assoc. Football), Sweden, 1958. Hon. MSc Birmingham, 1990. Footballer of the Year, 1960. *Recreations:* games and sports of all kinds. *Address:* 10 Inglis Road, Ealing, W5 3RN. *T:* 081–992 7349.

SLATTERY, Dr David Antony Douglas, MBE (mil.) 1958; Chief Medical Officer, Rolls-Royce plc, since 1973; Dean, Faculty of Occupational Medicine, Royal College of Physicians, 1988–91 (Vice-Dean, 1986–88); *b* 28 Jan. 1930; *s* of Rear-Adm. Sir Matthew Slattery, KBE, CB and Mica Mary Slattery (*née* Swain); *m* 1st, 1954, Mary Winifred

Miller; two *s* two *d*; 2nd, 1974, Claire Louise McGuinness; one *s*. *Educ:* Ampleforth Coll.; St Thomas' Hosp., London. MB BS; FFOM RCPI 1977; FFOM RCP 1981; FRCP 1986. Capt., RAMC, 1954–58. MO, E Midlands Gas Bd, 1959–69; Manager, Health and Safety, BSC, Rotherham, 1969–73. Special Lectr, Dept of Community Health, Nottingham Univ., 1978–. Consultant Advr in occupational medicine, RAF, 1987–. Member: Standing Med. Adv. Cttee, DHSS, 1988–; Adv. Bd, CS Occupational Health Service, 1988–. Industrial Health Advr, Derbys Br., BRCS, 1976–. *Publications:* papers on occupational medicine and the employment of the disabled. *Recreations:* history, shooting, fishing, people. *Address:* The Croft, 83 Aston Lane, Shardlow, Derby DE7 2GX. *T:* Derby (0332) 792738. *Club:* Royal Society of Medicine.

SLATYER, Prof. Ralph Owen, AO 1982; FRS 1975; Chief Scientist, Department of the Prime Minister and Cabinet, Australia, since 1989; *b* 16 April 1929; *s* of Thomas Henry and Jean Slatyer; *m* 1953, June Helen Wade; one *s* two *d*. *Educ:* Univ. of Western Australia. BSc (Agric.), MSc, DSc. CSIRO Res. Scientist, subseq. Chief Res. Scientist, 1951–67; Prof., Inst. of Advanced Studies, 1967–89, Dir, Res. Sch. of Biol Scis, 1984–89, ANU. Aust. Amb. to UNESCO, 1978–81. Member: Australian Res. Grants Cttee, 1969–72; Nat. Capital Planning Cttee, 1973–76; Aust. Nat. Commn for UNESCO, 1975–78 (Chm., 1976–78); Policy Adv. Council and Bd of Management, Aust. Centre for Internat. Agricl Research, 1981–85; President: Ecol Soc. of Austr., 1969–71; UNESCO Man and the Biosphere Programme, 1977–81; UNESCO World Heritage Cttee, 1981–83; ICSU Sci. Cttee on Problems of the Environment, 1982–85; ANZAAS, 1983; Chairman: Aust. Biol. Resources Study, 1981–84; Australian Science and Technology Council, 1982–87. FAA 1967. Hon. DSc: Univ. of WA, 1983; Duke Univ., 1986. Edgeworth David Medal, 1960; Austr. Medal of Agric. Sci., 1968. For. Associate, US Nat. Acad. of Sciences, 1976; Hon. For. Mem., Amer. Acad. of Arts and Scis, 1981. *Publications:* (with I. C. McIlroy) Practical Microclimatology, 1961 (Russian edn 1964); Plant-Water Relationships, 1967 (Russian edn 1970); (ed with R. A. Perry) Arid Lands of Australia, 1969; (ed jtly) Photosynthesis and Photorespiration, 1971; (ed) Plant Response to Climatic Factors, 1974; papers in learned jls. *Recreations:* ski-ing, bushwalking. *Address:* Unit 15, 28 Black Street, Yarralumla, ACT 2600, Australia. *T:* (06) 285.1728.

SLAUGHTER, Audrey Cecelia, (Mrs C. V. Wintour); writer and freelance journalist; *b* 17 Jan. 1930; *d* of Frederick George Smith and Ethel Louise Smith; *m* 1st, 1950, W. A. Slaughter (marr. diss.); one *s* one *d*; 2nd, 1979, Charles Vere Wintour, *qv*. *Educ:* Chislehurst High Sch., Stand Grammar Sch., Manchester. Editor, Honey magazine, 1960; founded Petticoat magazine, 1964; columnist, Evening News, 1968; joined National Magazine Co., to edit Vanity Fair, 1969; founded and funded own magazine, Over 21, 1970; after sale to Morgan Grampian, 1972, remained as Dir and Editor until 1979; Associate Editor, Sunday Times, 1979; with husband founded Sunday Express colour magazine, 1981; Founder Editor, Working Woman magazine, 1984–86; Lifestyle Editor, The Independent, 1986–87. *Publications:* Every Man Should Have One (with Margaret Goodman), 1969; Getting Through . . ., 1981; Working Woman's Handbook, 1986; Your Brilliant Career, 1987; Private View (novel), 1990; Blooming (novel), 1992. *Recreations:* classical music, theatre, painting, gardening, entertaining. *Address:* 60 East Hatch, Tisbury, Wilts SP3 6PH. *T:* Tisbury (0747) 870880.

SLAUGHTER, Frank Gill, MC; MD, FACS; novelist (self-employed); physician and surgeon (retd); *b* Washington, USA, 25 Feb. 1908; *s* of Stephen Lucius Slaughter and Sallie Nicholson Gill; *m* 1933, Jane Mundy; two *s*. *Educ:* Duke Univ. (AB); Johns Hopkins (MD). Served War, 1942–46 (MC): Major to Lt-Col, US Army Med. Corps. Intern, asst resident, and resident surgeon, Jefferson Hosp., Roanoke, Va, 1930–34; practice, specializing in surgery, Jacksonville, Fla, 1934–42; retired, 1946; Lectr, W. Colston Leigh, Inc., NY City, 1947–49. Res. Diplomate, Amer. Bd of Surgery. Mem., Sons of Amer. Revolution. Presbyterian (Elder). Hon. DHL Jacksonville Univ., 1978. *Publications:* That None Should Die, 1941; Spencer Brade, MD, 1942; Air Surgeon, 1943; Battle Surgeon, 1944; A Touch of Glory, 1945; In a Dark Garden, 1946; The New Science of Surgery, 1946; The Golden Isle, 1947; Sangaree, 1948; Medicine for Moderns, 1948; Divine Mistress, 1949; The Stubborn Heart, 1950; Immortal Magyar, 1950; Fort Everglades, 1951; The Road to Bithynia, 1951; East Side General, 1952; The Galileians, 1953; Storm Haven, 1953; The Song of Ruth, 1954; Apalachee Gold, 1954; The Healer, 1955; Flight from Natchez, 1955; The Scarlet Cord, 1956; The Warrior, 1956; Sword and Scalpel, 1957; The Mapmaker, 1957; Daybreak, 1958; The Thorn of Arimathea, 1958; The Crown and the Cross, 1959; Lorena, 1959; The Land and the Promise, 1960; Pilgrims in Paradise, 1960; Epidemic, 1961; The Curse of Jezebel, 1961; David: Warrior and King, 1962; Tomorrow's Miracle, 1962; Devil's Harvest, 1963; Upon This Rock, 1963; A Savage Place, 1964; The Purple Quest, 1965; Constantine: The Miracle of the Flaming Cross, 1965; Surgeon, USA, 1966; God's Warrior, 1967; Doctor's Wives, 1967; The Sins of Herod, 1968; Surgeon's Choice, 1969; Countdown, 1970; Code Five, 1971; Convention, MD, 1972; Life blood, 1974; Stonewall Brigade, 1975; Plague Ship, 1977; Devil's Gamble, 1978; The Passionate Rebel, 1979; Gospel Fever, 1980; Doctor's Daughters, 1981; Doctors At Risk, 1983; No Greater Love, 1985; Transplant, 1987. *Recreations:* boating, hiking, reading. *Address:* 5051 Yacht Club Road, Jacksonville, Fla 32210, USA. *T:* 904–389–7677. *Club:* Timuquana Country (Jacksonville, Fla).

SLAUGHTER, Giles David, MA; Headmaster, University College School, since 1983; *b* 11 July 1937; *s* of Gerald Slaughter and Enid Lillian Slaughter (*née* Crane); *m* 1965, Gillian Rothwell Shepherd; three *d*. *Educ:* Royal Masonic School; King's College, Cambridge. MA. Pierrepont School, Frensham, 1961–65; Campbell College, Belfast, 1965–68; Stockport Grammar School, 1968–70; Housemaster, Ormiston House, Campbell Coll., 1970–73; Headmaster, Solihull School, 1973–82. Governor: Godolphin and Latymer Sch., 1988–; Cobham Hall, 1989–; Aldwickbury Sch., 1974–. JP Solihull, 1977–82. FRSA 1985. *Recreations:* gardening, cricket, golf, theatre. *Address:* 5 Redington Road, Hampstead, NW3 7QX. *Club:* East India, Devonshire, Sports and Public Schools.

SLEDGE, Ven. Richard Kitson; Archdeacon of Huntingdon, since 1978; Rector of Hemingford Abbots, 1978–89; *b* 13 April 1930; *s* of Sydney Kitson and Mary Sylvia Sledge; *m* 1958, Patricia Henley (*née* Sear); one *s* two *d* (and one *s* decd). *Educ:* Epsom College; Peterhouse, Cambridge (MA). Curate of Emmanuel, Plymouth, 1954–57; Curate-in-charge of St Stephen's, Exeter, 1957–63; Rector of Dronfield, 1963–78. *Address:* The Rectory, Hemingford Abbots, Huntingdon, Cambs PE18 9AN. *T:* St Ives (0480) 69856.

SLEEMAN, His Honour (Stuart) Colin; a Circuit Judge, 1976–86; *s* of Stuart Bertram Sleeman and Phyllis Grace (*née* Pitt); *m* 1944, Margaret Emily, *d* of late William Joseph Farmer; two *s* one *d*. *Educ:* Clifton Coll.; Merton Coll., Oxford (BA 1936, MA 1963). Called to the Bar, Gray's Inn, 1938; Bencher, 1974. World War II: Admin. Officer, Prize Dept, Min. of Economic Warfare, 1939–40; Lt-Col 16th-5th Lancers; Staff Captain: RAC Wing, Combined Trng Centre, 1941; 6th Armoured Div., 1942; Adjt, RAC Range, Minehead, 1942–44; Asst Judge Advocate Gen., HQ Allied Land Forces, SE Asia, 1945. London Corresp., Scottish Law Rev., 1949–54; a Recorder, 1975–76. *Publications:* The Trial of Gozawa Sadaichi and Nine Others, 1948; (with S. C. Silkin) The 'Double Tenth' Trial, 1950. *Recreations:* travel, genealogy. *Address:* West Walls, Cotmandene, Dorking, Surrey RH4 2BL. *T:* Dorking (0306) 883616.

SLEEP, Wayne; dancer, actor, choreographer; *b* Plymouth, 17 July 1948. *Educ:* Hartlepool; Royal Ballet Sch. (Leverhulme Scholar). Graduated into Royal Ballet, 1966; Soloist, 1970; Principal, 1973; roles in: Giselle; Dancers at a Gathering; The Nutcracker; Romeo and Juliet; The Grand Tour; Elite Syncopations; Swan Lake; The Four Seasons; Les Patineurs; Petroushka (title role); Cinderella; The Dream; Pineapple Poll; Mam'zelle Angot; 4th Symphony; La Fille mal gardée; A Month in the Country; A Good Night's Sleep (gala); chor., with Robert North, David & Goliath; also roles in operas, A Midsummer Night's Dream and Aida; roles created for him by Sir Frederick Ashton, Dame Ninette de Valois, Sir Kenneth MacMillan, Rudolf Nureyev, John Neumeier, Joe Layton and many others. *Theatre:* Ariel in The Tempest, New Shakespeare Co.; title role in Pinocchio, Birmingham Rep.; genie in Aladdin, Palladium; soldier in The Soldier's Tale, QEH, 1980 and 1981; Truffaldino in The Servant of Two Masters; chor. and played lead in The Point, Mermaid; Mr Mistoffelees in Cats, New London, 1981; co-starred in Song and Dance, Palace, 1982, Shaftesbury, 1990 (video, 1984); Cabaret, Strand, 1986. Formed own company, DASH, 1980: Chichester Fest., 1980, national tour and Sadler's Wells, 1982, Apollo Victoria and national tour, Christmas season, Dominion, 1983; danced in and jtly choreographed Bits and Pieces, Dominion, 1989. *Films:* The Virgin Soldiers; The First Great Train Robbery; The Tales of Beatrix Potter, 1971. Chor. films and television, inc. Adam's Rib, and appeared in many television progs inc. Dizzy Feet and series, The Hot Shoe Show, 1983, 1984; Tony Lumpkin in She Stoops to Conquer, radio. Show Business Personality of the Year, 1983. *Publication:* Variations on Wayne Sleep, 1983. *Recreation:* entertaining. *Address:* c/o London Management, 235 Regent Street, W1. *Clubs:* YMCA, Zanzibar.

SLEIGHT, Prof. Peter, MD (Cantab), DM (Oxon), FRCP; FACC; Field-Marshal Alexander Professor of Cardiovascular Medicine in the University of Oxford, and Fellow of Exeter College, Oxford, since 1973; *b* 27 June 1929; *s* of William and Mary Sleight, Boston Spa, Yorks; *m* 1953, Gillian France; two *s*. *Educ:* Leeds Grammar Sch.; Gonville and Caius Coll., Cambridge; St Bartholomew's Hosp., London. Ho. Phys. and Ho. Surg., Med. and Surg. Professorial Units, Bart's, 1953; Sen. Registrar, St George's Hosp., London, 1959–64; Bissinger Fellow, Cardiovascular Research Unit, Univ. of California, San Francisco, 1961–63; MRC Scientific Officer, Depts of Physiology and Medicine, Univ. of Oxford, 1964–66; Consultant Physician, Radcliffe Infirmary, Oxford, 1966–73; Visiting Prof., Univ. of Sydney (Warren McDonald Sen. Overseas Fellow of Aust. Heart Foundn), 1972–73; Hon. Prof. of Medicine, Federal Univ. of Pernambuco, 1975. Civil Consultant in Medicine, RAF, 1985–. Member Council: Internat. Soc. of Hypertension, 1978–86; European Soc. of Cardiology, 1983–88. Chm., ASH, 1982–. Mem. Editorial Bd, British Heart Jl, 1976–; Editor, Jl of Cardiovascular Res., 1983–. Young Investigators Award, Amer. Coll. of Cardiology, 1963; Evian Prize, 1988. *Films:* Control of Circulation; History of Hypertension (Medal, BMA Scientific Film Competition, 1981). *Publications:* Modern Trends in Cardiology, 1976; (ed) Arterial Baroreceptors and Hypertension, 1981; Hypertension, 1982; (ed) Scientific Foundations of Cardiology, 1983; contribs on nervous control of the circulation, hypertension and treatment of myocardial infarction in: Circulation Research; Jl Physiol; Lancet (Chm., Internat. Studies of Infarct Survival). *Recreations:* sailing, golf, travel. *Address:* Wayside, 32 Crown Road, Wheatley, Oxon. *Club:* Royal Air Force.

SLEIGHT, Sir Richard, 4th Bt *cr* 1920, of Weelsby Hall, Clee; *b* 27 May 1946; *s* of Sir John Frederick Sleight, 3rd Bt and of Jacqueline Margaret, *o d* of late Maj. H. R. Carter, Brisbane, Queensland; *S* father, 1990; *m* 1978, Marie-Thérèse, *o d* of O. M. Stepan, Bromley, Kent; two *s*. *Heir:* *s* James Alexander Sleight, *b* 5 Jan. 1981. *Address:* c/o National Westminster Bank, Hill Street, Richmond, Surrey TW9 1SY.

SLEMON, Air Marshal Charles Roy, CB 1946; CBE 1943; retired from RCAF, 1964; *b* Winnipeg, Manitoba, Canada, 7 November 1904; *s* of Samuel Slemon and Mary Bonser; *m* 1935, Marion Pamela Slemon, Bowmanville, Ont; one *s* two *d*. *Educ:* University of Manitoba (BSc). Lieut COTC (Army), Canada, 1923; Cadet Royal Canadian Air Force, 1923; Royal Air Force Staff College Course, England, 1938; Senior Air Staff Officer at Western Air Command Headquarters, Canada, 1939–41; commanded Western Air Command, Canada, for 5 months in 1941; Director of Operations at RCAF HQ Ottawa, 1941–42; Senior Air Staff Officer, No. 6 (RCAF) Bomber Group, England, 1942–44; Air Vice-Marshal, 1945; Deputy AOC-in-C, RCAF Overseas, March 1945; Commanded Canadian Air Forces preparing for the Pacific, 1945; Air Council Member for Supply and Organization, 1946; Air Council Member for Operations and Training, 1947–48; AOC Trg Comd, RCAF, 1949–53; Chief of the Air Staff, Canada, 1953–57; Dep. C-in-C, N American Defence Comd (Canada-USA), 1957–64, retd. Exec. Vice-Pres., US Air Force Acad. Foundn Inc., 1964–81. Hon. LLD (Univ. of Manitoba), 1953; Hon. DMSc (RMC), Kingston, Ont, 1965. USA Legion of Merit, 1946; French Legion of Honour and Croix de Guerre with Palm, 1947. *Recreations:* golf, swimming. *Address:* 8 Thayer Road, Broadmoor Heights, Colorado Springs, Colorado 80906, USA.

SLEVIN, Brian Francis Patrick, CMG 1975; OBE 1973; QPM 1968; CPM 1965; *b* 13 Aug. 1926; *s* of late Thomas and Helen Slevin; *m* 1972, Constance Gay (*d* 1991), *e d* of late Major Ronald Moody and of Amy Moody; one *s*. *Educ:* Blackrock Coll., Ireland. Palestine Police, 1946–48; Royal Hong Kong Police, 1949–79; Directing Staff, Overseas Police Courses, Metropolitan Police Coll., Hendon, London, 1955–57; Director, Special Branch, 1966–69; Sen. Asst Comr of Police, Comdg Kowloon Dist, 1969–70; Dir, Criminal Investigation Dept, 1971; Dep. Comr of Police, 1971, Comr of Police, 1974–79, Hong Kong; retired 1979. *Recreations:* walking, golf, reading, painting. *Address:* Lantau Lodge, 152 Coonanbarra Road, Wahroonga, Sydney, NSW 2076, Australia. *T:* (02) 4896671. *Clubs:* East India, Royal Automobile; Hong Kong, Royal Hong Kong Golf, Royal Hong Kong Jockey (Hong Kong).

SLIGO, 10th Marquess of, *cr* 1800; **Denis Edward Browne;** Baron Mount Eagle, 1760; Viscount Westport, 1768; Earl of Altamont, 1771; Earl of Clanricarde, 1543 and 1800 (special remainder); Baron Monteagle (UK), 1806; *b* 13 Dec. 1908; *er s* of late Lt-Col Lord Alfred Eden Browne, DSO (5th *s* of 5th Marquess) and late Cicely, *d* of Edward Wormald, 15 Berkeley Square, W; *S* uncle, 1952; *m* 1930, José Gauche; one *s*. *Educ:* Eton. *Heir:* *s* Earl of Altamont, *qv*. *Address:* c/o Messrs Trower, Still and Keeling, 5 New Square, Lincoln's Inn, WC2.

See also Baron Brabourne.

SLIM, family name of **Viscount Slim.**

SLIM, 2nd Viscount *cr* 1960, of Yarralumla and Bishopston; **John Douglas Slim,** OBE 1973; DL; Chairman, 1976–91, and non-executive Deputy Chairman, since 1991, Peek plc (formerly Peek Holdings); Director, Trailfinders Ltd, since 1984, and a number of other companies; *b* 20 July 1927; *s* of Field Marshal the 1st Viscount Slim, KG, GCB, GCMG, GCVO, GBE, DSO, MC, and of Aileen, *d* of Rev. J. A. Robertson, MA, Edinburgh; *S* father, 1970; *m* 1958, Elisabeth, *d* of Arthur Rawdon Spinney, CBE; two *s* one *d*. *Educ:* Prince of Wales Royal Indian Military College, Dehra Dun. Indian Army, 6 Gurkha Rifles, 1945–48; Argyll and Sutherland Highlanders, 1948; SAS, 1952; Staff.

Coll., Camberley, 1961; Brigade Major, HQ Highland Infantry Bde (TA), 1962–64; JSSC 1964; Lt-Col 1967; Comdr, 22 Special Air Service Regt, 1967–70; GSO1 (Special Forces) HQ UK Land Forces, 1970–72; retired 1972. President, Burma Star Association, 1971–. Vice-Pres., Britain-Australia Soc., 1988– (Chm., 1978–84); Vice-Chm., Arab-British Chamber of Commerce and Industry, 1977–. FRGS 1983. DL Greater London, 1988. *Heir:* *s* Hon. Mark William Rawdon Slim, *b* 13 Feb. 1960. *Address:* c/o Lloyds Bank, 7 Pall Mall, SW1Y 5NA. *Clubs:* White's, Special Forces.

SLIMMINGS, Sir William Kenneth MacLeod, Kt 1966; CBE 1960; *b* 15 Dec. 1912; *s* of George and Robina Slimmings; *m* 1943, Lilian Ellen Willis; one *s* one *d*. *Educ:* Dunfermline High School. Chartered Accountant: Partner in Thomson McLintock & Co., Chartered Accountants, London, etc, 1946–78. Member: Committee of Inquiry on the Cost of Housebuilding, 1947–53; Committee on Tax-paid Stocks, 1952–53; Committee on Cheque Endorsement, 1955–56; Performing Right Tribunal, 1963–77; Crown Agents Tribunal, 1978–82; Chairman: Board of Trade Advisory Committee, 1957–66; Review Bd for Govt Contracts, 1971–81; Accounting Standards Cttee, 1976–78. Member: Council, Inst. Chartered Accountants of Scotland, 1962–66 (Pres., 1969–70); Scottish Tourist Bd, 1969–76; Review Body on Doctors' and Dentists' Pay, 1976–83. Independent Chm., Cement Makers' Fedn, 1977–80. Hon. DLitt, Heriot-Watt, 1970. *Recreation:* gardening. *Address:* 62 The Avenue, Worcester Park, Surrey KT4 7HH. *T:* 081–337 2579. *Club:* Caledonian.

SLINGER, William, CBE 1991; *b* 27 Oct. 1917; *yr s* of late William Slinger and Maud Slinger, Newcastle, Co. Down; *m* 1944, Muriel, *o d* of late R. J. Johnston, Belfast; three *d*. *Educ:* Methodist Coll., Belfast; Queen's Univ., Belfast (BComSc). Entered Northern Ireland Civil Service, 1937; Private Secretary: to Minister of Labour, 1942–43 and 1945–46; to Minister of Public Security, 1944; Sec. to Nat. Arbitration Tribunal (NI), 1946–48; Principal, Min. of Labour and Nat. Insurance, Industrial Relations Div., 1954–60; Asst Sec. and Head of Industrial Relations Div., 1961–69; Sec., Dept of Community Relations, 1969–75; Dep. Sec., Dept of Educn for NI, 1975–77. CBIM. *Recreations:* gardening, walking. *Address:* Cairnfield, Circular Road, Belfast BT4 2GD. *T:* Belfast (0232) 768240. *Clubs:* East India, Devonshire, Sports and Public Schools; Ulster Reform (Belfast); Civil Service (N Ireland).

SLIPMAN, Sue; Director, National Council for One Parent Families, since 1985; *b* 3 Aug. 1949; *d* of Marks Slipman and Doris Barham; one *s*. *Educ:* Stockwell Manor Comprehensive School; Univ. of Wales (BA Hons 1st Class English; Post Graduate Cert Ed); Univs of Leeds and London. Sec. and Nat. Pres., Nat. Union of Students, 1975–78; Mem., Adv. Council for Adult and Continuing Educn, 1978–79; Area Officer, Nat. Union of Public Employees, 1979–85. Contested (SDP/Alliance) Hayes and Harlington, 1987. Mem. Exec., NCCL, 1974–75; Vice-Chair, British Youth Council, 1977–78; Chair, Women for Social Democracy, 1983–86; Mem. Exec. and Chair of Training, 300 Group, 1985–86; Mem. Exec., London Voluntary Service Council, 1986–; Dir, London East TEC, 1990–. *Publications:* Chapter in The Re-Birth of Britain, 1983; Helping Ourselves to Power: a handbook for women on the skills of public life, 1986. *Address:* c/o National Council for One Parent Families, 255 Kentish Town Road, NW5 2LX. *T:* 071–267 1361.

SLIVE, Prof. Seymour; Gleason Professor of Fine Arts at Harvard University, 1973–91, Emeritus since 1991; Director, Fogg Art Museum, 1975–82, sometime Elizabeth and John Moors Cabot Director of Harvard Art Museums; *b* Chicago, 15 Sept. 1920; *s* of Daniel Slive and Sonia (*née* Rapoport); *m* 1946, Zoya Gregorovna Sandomirsky; one *s* two *d*. *Educ:* Univ. of Chicago. BA 1943; PhD 1952. Served US Navy, Lieut, CO Small Craft, 1943–46. Instructor in Art History, Oberlin Coll., 1950–51; Asst Prof. and Chm. of Art Dept, Pomona Coll., 1952–54; Asst Prof. 1954–57, Assoc. Prof. 1957–61, Prof., 1961–73, Chm. of Dept 1968–71, Fine Arts, Harvard Univ.; Exchange Prof., Univ. of Leningrad, 1961. Ryerson Lectr, Yale, 1962. Slade Prof. of Fine Art, Univ. of Oxford, 1972–73. Trustee, Solomon R. Guggenheim Foundn, 1978–. FAAAS 1964. For. Mem., Netherlands Soc. of Sciences, 1971. Hon. MA Harvard, 1958; Hon. MA Oxford, 1972. Officer, Order of Orange Nassau, 1962. *Publications:* Rembrandt and His Critics: 1630–1730, 1953; Drawings of Rembrandt, 1965; (with J. Rosenberg and E. H. ter Kuile) Dutch Art and Architecture: 1600–1800, 1965, 2nd edn, 1978; Frans Hals, 3 vols, 1970–74; Jacob van Ruisdael, 1981; Frans Hals, 1989; contribs to learned jls. *Address:* 1 Walker Street Place, Cambridge, Mass 02138, USA.

SLOAN, Sir Andrew (Kirkpatrick), Kt 1991; QPM 1983; Chief Constable of Strathclyde, 1985–91; *b* 27 Feb. 1931; *s* of Andrew Kirkpatrick Sloan and Amelia Sarah (*née* Vernon), Kirkcudbright; *m* 1953, Agnes Sofie Storvik, Trondheim, Norway; three *d*. *Educ:* Kirkcudbright Acad.; Dumfries Acad.; Open Univ. (BA). Joined RN as boy seaman, 1947; served at home and abroad in cruisers and submarines, and worked in industry in Norway, 1947–55; joined W Riding Constab., 1955; apptd to CID, 1963; Det. Sgt, Barnsley, 1964; Det. Insp., Reg. Crime Squad, Leeds, 1966; Det. Chief Insp., Goole and Pontefract, 1969; Det. Supt, Reg. Crime Squad, Wakefield, 1970; Chief Supt, Toller Lane Div., Bradford, 1975; Asst Chief Constable, Operations, Lincolnshire Police, 1976–79; National Co-ordinator, Regional Crime Squads of England and Wales, 1979–81; Dep. Chief Constable, Lincs, 1981–83; Chief Constable, Beds, 1983–85. Pres., ACPO (Scotland), 1987–88. FSAScot 1987. *Recreations:* reading, travel, walking, conversation. *Address:* c/o Police HQ, 173 Pitt Street, Glasgow G2 4JS.

SLOAN, Norman Alexander; QC (Scot.) 1953; Legal Adviser, British Shipbuilders, 1978–81; *b* 27 Jan. 1914; *s* of George Scott Sloan and Margaret Hutcheson Smith; *m* 1st, 1944, Peggy Perry (*d* 1982); two *s* one *d*; 2nd, 1983, Norma Olsen (*d* 1985); 3rd, 1988, Beryl Maureen Hogg, Dublin. *Educ:* Glasgow Academy; Glasgow University (BL). Solicitor, 1935; Admitted to Faculty of Advocates, 1939; Served in RNVR 1940–46. Lecturer in Industrial Law, Edinburgh University, 1946–51; Standing Counsel to Department of Health for Scotland, 1946–51; Advocate-Depute, 1951–53. Director: The Shipbuilding Employers' Federation, 1955–68; Shipbuilders and Repairers Nat. Assoc., 1968–72; Swan Hunter Group Ltd, 1973–77; Swan Hunter Shipbuilders Ltd, 1973–78. *Recreations:* golf, gardening. *Address:* Fortuna 7, Villamartin, Torrevieja, Alicante, Spain.

SLOANE, Peter James, PhD; Jaffrey Professor of Political Economy, University of Aberdeen, since 1984; *b* 6 Aug. 1942; *s* of John Joseph Sloane and Elizabeth (*née* Clarke); *m* 1969, Avril Mary Urquhart; one *s*. *Educ:* Cheadle Hulme Sch.; Univ. of Sheffield (BAEcon Hons 1964); Univ. of Strathclyde (PhD 1966). Asst Lectr in Pol. Econ., Univ. of Aberdeen, 1966–67, Lectr in Pol. Econ., 1967–69; Lectr in Indust. Econs, Univ. of Nottingham, 1969–75; Economic Adviser, Unit for Manpower Studies, Dept of Employment (on secondment), 1973–74; Prof. of Econs and Management, Paisley Coll., 1975–84. Vis. Prof. (Commonwealth Fellow), Faculty of Business, McMaster Univ., Canada, 1978. Member: ESRC (formerly SSRC), 1979–85; Council, Scottish Economic Soc., 1983–. Sec., REconS Conf. of Heads of Univ. Depts of Econs, 1990–. *Publications:* (with B. Chiplin) Sex Discrimination in the Labour Market, 1976; (ed) Women and Low Pay, 1980; (with H. C. Jain) Equal Employment Issues, 1981; (with B. Chiplin) Tackling Discrimination, 1982; (with D. Carline *et al*) Labour Economics, 1985; monographs on changing patterns of working hours, discrimination and on sport in the market; articles in learned jls, incl. Econ. Jl, Economica, Econs Letters, Applied Econs, Bull. Econ. Res., Jl of Econ. Studies, Jl of Econ. Surveys, Scottish Jl of Pol. Econ., British Jl of Indust. Relations, Indust. Relations Jl, Internat. Labour Rev., Internat. Jl of Social Econs, Managerial and Decision Econs, Internat. Jl of Manpower, Leisure Studies and Jl of Management Studies. *Recreation:* sport. *Address:* Hillcrest, 45 Friarsfield Road, Cults, Aberdeen AB1 9LB. *T:* Aberdeen (0224) 869412. *Clubs:* Commonwealth Trust; Aboyne Golf.

SLOGGETT, Jolyon Edward, CEng, FIMarE, FRINA, FICS; Secretary, Institute of Marine Engineers, since 1986; *b* 30 May 1933; *s* of Edward Cornelius Sloggett and Lena May (*née* Norton); *m* 1970, Patricia Marjorie Iverson Ward; two *d*. *Educ:* John Lyon Sch.; Univ. of Glasgow (BSc). CDipAF. William Denny & Brothers Ltd, Leven Shipyard, Dumbarton, 1951–57 and 1959–60. Served, Royal Navy, TA Sub Lieut (E), RNVR, 1957–58; Houlder Brothers & Co. Ltd, 1960–78, Director, 1972–78; Man. Dir, Offshore, British Shipbuilders Corp., 1978–81; Dir, Vickers Shipbuilding Group, 1979–80; Chm., Vickers Offshore (Projects & Development) Ltd, 1979–81; Consultant to Marine and Offshore Industries, 1981–86. Liveryman, Shipwrights' Co. *Publication:* Shipping Finance, 1984. *Recreations:* sailing, gardening, woodwork. *Address:* Annington House, Steyning, West Sussex BN44 3WA. *T:* Steyning (0903) 812259.

SLOMAN, Sir Albert (Edward), Kt 1987; CBE 1980; DPhil; Vice-Chancellor of University of Essex, 1962–1987; *b* Launceston, Cornwall, 14 Feb. 1921; *y s* of Albert Sloman; *m* 1948, Marie Bernadette, *d* of Leo Bergeron, Cognac, France; three *d*. *Educ:* Launceston Coll., Cornwall; Wadham Coll., Oxford (Pope Exhibitioner, 1939; Hon. Fellow, 1982). BA Mediæval and Mod. Langs, 1941; MA (Oxon and Dublin); DPhil (Oxon). Served War of 1939–45 (despatches): night-fighter pilot with 219 and 68 squadrons; Flight-Lieut. Lecturer in Spanish, Univ. of California, Berkeley, USA, 1946–47; Reader in Spanish, in charge of Spanish studies, Univ. of Dublin, 1947–53; Fellow TCD, 1950–53; Gilmour Professor of Spanish, University of Liverpool, 1953–62; Dean, Faculty of Arts, 1961–62. Editor of Bulletin of Hispanic Studies, 1953–62. Reith Lecturer, 1963. Chairman: Dept of Education, subseq. British Acad., Studentship Cttee, 1965–87; Cttee of Vice-Chancellors and Principals of UK Univs, 1981–83 (Vice-Chm., 1979–81); Overseas Research Students Fees Support Scheme, 1980–87; Univs' Council for Adult and Continuing Educn, 1984–86; Inter-Univ. and Polytechnic Council, 1985–88; Cttee for Internat. Co-operation in Higher Educn, 1985–88; Selection Cttee of Commonwealth Scholarship Commn, 1986–; Internat. Bd, United World Colls, 1988– (Mem., 1985–); Member: Council of Europe Cttee for Higher Educn and Research, 1963–72; Inter-univ. Council for Higher Educn Overseas, 1964–81; Conf. of European Rectors and Vice-Chancellors, 1965–85 (Pres., 1969–74); Admin. Bd, Internat. Assoc. of Univs, 1965–75 (Vice-Pres., 1970–75); Economic and Social Cttee, EEC, 1973–82; Council, ACU, 1981–87 (Vice-Chm., 1985–87); Commonwealth Scholarship Commn, 1984–; Bd, British Council, 1985–88. Chm. Bd of Governors, Centre for Inf. on Lang. Teaching and Res., 1979–87; Member: Bd of Governors, Guyana Univ., 1966–; Cttee of Management, British Inst. in Paris, 1982–; Dir, Isys Ltd, 1987–. Hon. Doctorate: Nice, 1974; Essex, 1988; Liverpool, 1989. *Publications:* The Sources of Calderón's El Principe constante, 1950; The Dramatic Craftsmanship of Calderón, 1958; A University in the Making, 1964; articles and reviews in Modern Language Review, Bulletin of Hispanic Studies, Hispanic Review, Romance Philology and other journals. *Recreation:* travel. *Address:* 19 Inglis Road, Colchester CO3 3HU. *Club:* Savile.

SLOMAN, Mrs (Margaret) Barbara; Under Secretary, Management and Personnel Office (formerly Civil Service Department), 1975–84, retired; *b* 29 June 1925; *d* of Charles and Margaret Pilkington-Rogers; *m* 1950, Peter Sloman, *qv*; one *s* one *d*. *Educ:* Cheltenham Ladies' Coll.; Girton Coll., Cambridge. BA Hons Classics. FBIM. Asst Principal, Treasury, 1947, Principal 1954–65; Asst Sec., DES, 1965–69; Asst Sec., Civil Service Dept, 1970–75. *Address:* 11 Lowther Road, SW13 9NX. *T:* 081–748 2196.

SLOMAN, Peter; Education Officer, Association of Metropolitan Authorities, 1974–79; *b* Oct. 1919; *s* of H. N. P. and Mary Sloman (*née* Trinder); *m* 1950, Barbara (*see* M. B. Sloman); one *s* one *d*. *Educ:* Winchester Coll.; New Coll., Oxford (BA, MA 1945). War Service (RA), 1939–46. Home Civil Service, 1946–74: Under-Secretary, 1968; Min. (later Dept) of Education; Treasury; Ministries of Defence, Land and Natural Resources, Housing and Local Govt; IDC 1960. Principal Admin. Officer: Newham, 1980–83; Surrey CC, 1985; Principal Administrator, ACC, 1983–88; retired. *Address:* 11 Lowther Road, SW13 9NX. *T:* 081–748 2196.

SLOSS; *see* Butler-Sloss.

SLOT, Peter Maurice Joseph; His Honour Judge Slot; a Circuit Judge, since 1980; *b* 3 Dec. 1932; *s* of Joseph and Marie Slot; *m* 1962, Mary Eiluned Lewis; two *s* three *d*. *Educ:* Bradfield Coll.; St John's Coll., Oxford (MA). Called to Bar, Inner Temple, 1957. A Recorder of the Crown Court, 1974–80. *Recreations:* golf, madrigals, argument. *Address:* The Red House, Betchworth, Surrey RH3 7DR. *T:* Betchworth (073784) 2010. *Club:* Walton Heath Golf.

SLYNN, Hon. Sir Gordon, Kt 1976; a Judge of the Court of Justice of the European Communities at Luxembourg, since 1988 (an Advocate-General, 1981–88); *b* 17 Feb. 1930; *er s* of John and Edith Slynn; *m* 1962, Odile Marie Henriette Boutin. *Educ:* Sandbach Sch.; Goldsmiths' Coll.; Trinity Coll., Cambridge (Sen. Schol.; MA, LLB; Sub-Lector, 1956–61). Commnd RAF, 1951–54. Called to Bar, Gray's Inn, 1956, Bencher, 1970, Vice-Treas., 1987, Treas., 1988. Jun. Counsel, Min. of Labour, 1967–68; Jun. Counsel to the Treasury (Common Law), 1968–74; QC 1974; Leading Counsel to the Treasury, 1974–76. Recorder of Hereford, 1971; a Recorder, and Hon. Recorder of Hereford, 1972–76; a Judge of the High Ct of Justice, QBD, 1976–81. Pres., Employment Appeal Tribunal, 1978–81. Lecturer in Air Law, LSE, 1958–61; Visiting Professor in Law: Univ. of Durham, 1981–88; Cornell, 1983; KCL, 1985–; Univ. of Technol., Sydney, 1990–; Irvine Lectr, Cornell, 1984; Leon Ladner Lectr, Univ. of BC, 1987. Chief Steward of Hereford, 1978– (Dep. Chief Steward, 1977–78). Chm., Exec. Council, Internat. Law Assoc., 1988– (Vice-Chm., 1986–88); Hon. Vice-Pres., Union Internat. des Avocats, 1976– (Vice-Pres., 1973–76). Fellow, Internat. Soc. of Barristers, USA. Hon. Member: Canadian Bar Assoc.; Georgia Trial Lawyers' Assoc.; Florida Defense Lawyers' Assoc.; Soc. of Public Teachers of Law, 1986. Governor: Internat. Students' Trust, 1979–85 (Fellow, 1986–); Sadler's Wells Theatre; Chm., Develt Bd, Acad. of Ancient Music; Trustee, America-European Community Assoc. Trust, 1989–. Mem. Ct, Broderers' Co. Hon. Fellow: UC at Buckingham, 1982; St Andrews Coll., Univ. of Sydney, 1991. Hon. LLD: Birmingham, 1983; Buckingham, 1983; Exeter, 1985; Univ. of Technol., Sydney, 1991; Hon. DCL Durham, 1989. Hon. Decanus Legis, Mercer Univ., Ga, USA, 1986. Chevalier du Tastevin; Chevalier, Confrérie de St Cunibert; Commandeur d'Honneur, Commanderie du Bon Temps du Médoc et des Graves. *Publications:* (contrib.) Halsbury's Laws of England, 4th edn; (contrib.) Atkin's Court Forms, 3rd edn; lectures published in legal jls. *Address:* Court of Justice of the European Communities, Kirchberg, L-2925 Luxembourg. *Clubs:* Athenæum, Beefsteak, Garrick.

SMAILES, George Mason; retired barrister; *b* 23 Jan. 1916; *s* of late Thomas and Kate Smailes; *m* 1939, Evelyn Mabel Jones; one *s* two *d*. *Educ:* The Leys Sch., Cambridge; Leeds Univ. (LLB); Metropolitan Police College. Solicitor's articled clerk, 1933–37; Station Inspector, Metropolitan Police, 1937–47; served RAF, 1944–45. Called to Bar, Gray's Inn, 1946; practised on North-Eastern Circuit, 1947–67; acted as Deputy County Court Judge and Deputy and Asst Recorder of various boroughs, 1961–68. Part-time legal member of tribunals: Mental Health Review, 1960–67; National Insurance, Local, 1962–65; Medical Appeal (Industrial Injuries), 1965–67; Industrial, 1966–67; Regional Chm. of Industrial Tribunals, Leeds, 1967–82. Associate, Wellington Dist Law Soc. (NZ). *Recreations:* listening to music, gardening. *Clubs:* Leeds (Leeds); Masterton (Masterton).

SMALE, John Arthur, CBE 1953; AFC 1919; Technical consultant, Marconi's Wireless Telegraph Co. Ltd, 1957–62, retd; *b* 16 Feb. 1895; *s* of Charles Blackwell and Ann Smale; *m* 1920, Hilda Marguerita Watts; one *d* (one *s* killed on active service, RAF, 1941). *Educ:* Wycliffe Coll., Stonehouse; Bristol Univ. (BSc). Apprentice British Thompson Houston, Rugby, 1914; served European War, 1914–18, in RNAS; RAF, 1918–19. Engineer, Marconi's Wireless Telegraph Co. Ltd, 1919–29; Cable & Wireless Ltd, 1929–57, retired (Asst Engineer-in-Chief, 1935–48; Engineer-in-Chief, 1948–57). Chairman Cyprus Inland Telecommunications Authority, 1955–60, retired. FIEE 1941; Chairman, Radio Section of IEE, 1953; FIEEE 1958. *Recreations:* sport, music. *Address:* Cotswold, 21 Ilex Way, Goring-By-Sea, W Sussex BN12 4UZ.

SMALL, (Charles) John; development consultant, since 1985; economist; *b* Chengdu, Sichuan, China, 19 Dec. 1919; *s* of Rev. and Mrs Walter Small; *m* 1946, Jean McNeel; four *d*. *Educ:* Ontario Agricultural Coll. (BSA); Univ. of Toronto (BA). LLD *hc* Univ. of Guelph, 1975. Royal Canadian Navy service, 1941–46, in N Atlantic, Mediterranean, Normandy and Australia. Mem., Dept of Trade and Commerce, 1949–55; serving in The Hague as Commercial Sec. (Agriculture), 1950–55; Dept of External Affairs, 1955–84; Chinese studies at Univ. of Toronto, 1956–57; seconded to Dept of Trade and Commerce, and apptd Canadian Govt Trade Comr, Hong Kong, 1958–61; Ottawa, 1961–63; Counsellor, Canadian High Commn, Karachi, 1963–65; Perm. Rep. of Canada to OECD, Paris, concurrently Canadian observer, Council of Europe, Strasbourg, 1965–69; Amb. to Pakistan, 1969–72, concurrently Amb. to Afghanistan; Amb. to People's Repub. of China, 1972–76, concurrently to Socialist Repub. of Viet-Nam, 1975–76; Dep. Sec.-Gen. of the Commonwealth, 1978–83; High Comr to Malaysia and concurrently to Brunei, 1983–84. Administrator, Code of Conduct concerning employment practices of Canadian cos operating in South Africa, 1986–90. Chm., Presbyterian World Service and Develt Cttee, 1989–91. Patron, Ex Terra Foundn, 1987– (Canada/China Dinosaur Project). Member: CIIA; Agricl Inst. of Canada; Royal Commonwealth Society, Ottawa. *Recreations:* tennis, golf, swimming.

SMALL, David Purvis, CMG 1988; MBE 1966; HM Diplomatic Service, retired; High Commissioner to Guyana and non-resident Ambassador to Suriname, 1987–90; *b* 17 Oct. 1930; *s* of Joseph Small and Ann (*née* Purvis); *m* 1957, Patricia Kennedy; three *s*. *Educ:* Our Lady's High Sch., Motherwell. National Service, RAF Transport Comd, 1949–51. Metropolitan Vickers, 1951–53; Clerical Officer, Admiralty, Bath, 1953–55; Exec. Officer, HM Dockyard, Rosyth, 1955–58 and Singapore, 1958–60; Admiralty, London, 1960–61; CRO, 1961; Chief Clerk, Madras, 1962–64; Second Sec., Ibadan, 1964–68; Second, later First Sec. and Head of Chancery, Quito, 1968–73; FCO, 1973–76; Head of Chancery, Dacca, 1976–80; First Sec. (Commercial), Stockholm, 1980–82; Counsellor (Economic and Commercial), Copenhagen, 1982–87. *Recreations:* golf, soccer. *Address:* Ashbank, Strachur, Argyll PA27 8BX. *T:* Strachur (036986) 282. *Club:* Cowal Golf.

SMALL, John; *see* Small, C. J.

SMALL, Prof. John Rankin, CBE 1991; Professor and Head of Department of Accountancy and Finance, Heriot-Watt University, since 1967, and Deputy Principal, since 1990; *b* 28 Feb. 1933; *s* of David and Annie Small; *m* 1957, Catherine Wood; one *s* two *d*. *Educ:* Harris Academy, Dundee; Dundee Sch. of Econs. BScEcon London; FCCA, FCMA, JDipMA. Dunlop Rubber Co., 1956–60; Lectr, Univ. of Edinburgh, 1960–64; Sen. Lectr, Univ. of Glasgow, 1964–67; Dean of Faculty of Econ. and Social Studies, Heriot-Watt Univ., 1972–74; Vice-Principal, Heriot-Watt Univ., 1974–78, 1987–. Director: Edinburgh Instruments Ltd, 1976–; Orkney Water Test Centre, Ltd, 1987–. Chm., Nat. Appeal Panel for Entry to Pharmaceutical Lists (Scotland), 1987–. Trustee, Nat. Library of Scotland, 1991–. Pres., Assoc. of Certified Accountants, 1982 (Mem. Council, 1971–); Member: Educn Cttee, Internat. Fedn of Accountants, 1978–85 (Chm., 1978–82); Commn for Local Authority Accounts in Scotland, 1982– (Chm., 1983–); Chm., Inst. of Offshore Engrg, 1988–90. *Publications:* (jtly) Introduction to Managerial Economics, 1966; (contrib.) Business and Accounting in Europe, 1973; articles in accounting and financial jls on accounting and financial management. *Recreation:* golf. *Address:* 39 Caiystane Terrace, Edinburgh EH10 6ST. *T:* 031–445 2638. *Club:* New (Edinburgh).

SMALL, Dr Ramsay George; Chief Administrative Medical Officer, Tayside Health Board, 1986–89; *b* 5 Feb. 1930; *s* of Robert Small and Ann Ramsay; *m* 1951, Aileen Masterton; four *s*. *Educ:* Harris Academy, Dundee; Univ. of St Andrews (MB ChB); FFCM; FRCPE; DPH. Asst Medical Officer of Health, Ayr CC, 1958–61; Sen. Asst/PMO, City of Dundee, 1961–74; Community Medicine Specialist, Tayside Health Bd, 1974–86. Convener, Scottish Affairs Cttee, Faculty of Community Medicine, 1983–86. Pres., Baptist Union of Scotland, 1972–73. *Recreations:* music, bird watching, mediaeval ecclesiastical buildings. *Address:* 46 Monifieth Road, Broughty Ferry, Dundee DD5 2RX. *T:* Dundee (0382) 78408.

SMALL, Very Rev. Robert Leonard, CBE 1975 (OBE 1958); DD; Minister of St Cuthbert's Parish Church, Edinburgh, 1956–75; Chaplain to the Queen in Scotland, 1967–75, Extra Chaplain since 1975; *b* N Berwick, 12 May 1905; *s* of Rev. Robert Small, MA, and Marion C. McEwen; *m* 1931, Jane Hay McGregor; three *s* one *d*. *Educ:* N Berwick High Sch.; Edinburgh Univ.; New Coll., Edinburgh. MA 1st cl. hons Classics; Sen. Cunningham Fellowship; studied in Rome, Berlin and Zurich; DD 1957. Ordained, 1931, to St John's, Bathgate; W High Church, Kilmarnock, 1935–44; Cramond Church, Edinburgh 1944–56. Convener: C of S Cttee on Huts and Canteens for HM Forces, 1946–58; Cttee on Temperance and Morals, 1958–63; Social and Moral Welfare Bd, 1963–64; Stewardship and Budget Ctee, 1964–69; Mem., Scottish Adv. Cttee on Treatment of Offenders; Regional Chaplain (Scotland), Air Trng Corps; Hon. Vice-Pres., Boys' Brigade; awarded Silver Wolf by Chief Scout, 1990. Warrack Lectr on Preaching, 1959. Guest Preacher: Knox Church, Dunedin, 1950; Fifth Ave., Presbyterian Church, NY, 1960; St Stephen's Presbyterian Church, Sydney, 1962, 1971, 1976, 1981, 1987; Scots Church, Melbourne, 1971, 1976, 1979; St Columba's C of S, London, 1983–84; St Andrew's, Canberra, 1985. Moderator of the General Assembly of the Church of Scotland, 1966–67; First Chm., Scottish Parole Bd, 1967–73; Chm., Parkinson's Disease Soc., Edinburgh; Chm., Age Concern, Scotland, 1980–83 (Hon. Pres., 1989). TV Series, What I Believe, 1970. *Publications:* With Ardour and Accuracy (Warrack Lectures), 1959; No Uncertain Sound (Scholar as Preacher Series), 1964; No Other Name, 1966; contribs to The Expository Times. *Recreations:* boating, walking; formerly Association football (Edinburgh Univ. Blue, captained team, 1927–28; played as amateur for St Bernard's FC, 1928–29; capped *v* England (Amateur), 1929; Chaplain, Co-optimist RFC). *Address:* 5 Craighill Gardens, Edinburgh EH10 5PY. *T:* 031–447 4243. *Club:* Royal Over-Seas League.

SMALLBONE, Graham; Headmaster, Oakham School, since 1985; *b* 5 April 1934; *s* of Dr E. G. Smallbone and Jane Mann; *m* 1959, Dorothea Ruth Löw; two *s* two *d*. *Educ:* Uppingham School (music scholar); Worcester College, Oxford (Hadow Scholar; MA; Pres., Oxford Univ. Music Club, 1957). ARCO, ARCM. 2nd Lieut, RA, 1952–54. Asst Master, Oundle Sch., 1958–61; Director of Music: Dean Close Sch., 1961–66; Marlborough Coll., 1967–71; Precentor and Director of Music, Eton, 1971–85. Pres., Music Masters' Assoc., 1975; Warden, Music in Educn Section, ISM, 1977; Pres., International Cello Centre, 1985. Conductor: Cheltenham Chamber Orch., 1963–66; N Wilts Orch., 1966–71; Windsor and Eton Choral Soc., 1971–85. Chm., Peterborough Cathedral Fabric Adv. Cttee, 1990–. FRSA. *Recreations:* music, golf, photography. *Address:* Deanscroft, Oakham School, Station Road, Oakham, Rutland LE15 6QY. *T:* Oakham (0572) 722179. *Club:* East India.

SMALLEY, Very Rev. Stephen Stewart; Dean of Chester since 1987; *b* 11 May 1931; *s* of Arthur Thomas Smalley and May Elizabeth Selina Smalley; *m* 1974, Susan Jane Paterson; one *s* one *d*. *Educ:* Jesus Coll., Cambridge (MA, PhD); Eden Theological Seminary, USA (BD). Assistant Curate, St Paul's, Portman Square, London, 1958–60; Chaplain of Peterhouse, Cambridge, 1960–63; Lectr and Sen. Lectr in Religious Studies, Univ. of Ibadan, Nigeria, 1963–69; Lectr in New Testament, Univ. of Manchester, 1970–77, Sen. Lectr, 1977 (also Warden of St Anselm Hall, 1972–77); Canon Residentiary and Precentor of Coventry Cathedral, 1977–86, Vice-Provost, 1986. Mem., C of E Doctrine Commn, 1981–86. Mem., Studiorum Novi Testamenti Soc., 1965–. Manson Meml Lectr, Univ. of Manchester, 1986. *Publications:* Building for Worship, 1967; Heaven and Hell (Ibadan), 1968; The Spirit's Power (Achimota), 1972; ed, Christ and Spirit in the New Testament, 1973; John: Evangelist and Interpreter, 1978, USA 1984; 1, 2, 3 John, 1984; numerous articles in learned jls, incl. New Testament Studies, Novum Testamentum, Jl of Biblical Lit. *Recreations:* literature, music, drama, travel. *Address:* The Deanery, 7 Abbey Street, Chester CH1 2JF. *T:* Chester (0244) 351380; Hadrians, Bourton-on-the-Hill, Moreton-in-Marsh, Gloucestershire. *T:* Blockley (0386) 700564. *Club:* City (Chester).

SMALLMAN, Barry Granger, CMG 1976; CVO 1972; HM Diplomatic Service, retired; Founder, Granger Consultancies, 1984; *b* 22 Feb. 1924; *s* of late C. Stanley Smallman, CBE, ARCM, and Ruby Marian Granger; *m* 1952, Sheila Knight; two *s* one *d*. *Educ:* St Paul's School; Trinity College, Cambridge (Major Scholar, MA). Served War of 1939–45, Intelligence Corps, Australia 1944–46. Joined Colonial Office, 1947; Assistant Private Secretary to Secretary of State, 1951–52; Principal, 1953; attached to United Kingdom Delegation to United Nations, New York, 1956–57, 1958, 1961, 1962; seconded to Government of Western Nigeria, Senior Assistant Secretary, Governor's Office, Ibadan, 1959–60; transferred to CRO, 1961; British Deputy High Comr in Sierra Leone, 1963–64; British Dep. High Comr in NZ, 1964–67; Imp. Defence Coll., 1968; FCO, 1969–71; Counsellor and Consul-Gen., British Embassy, Bangkok, 1971–74; British High Comr to Bangladesh, 1975–78; Resident Diplomatic Service Chm., Civil Service Selection Bd, 1978–81; High Comr to Jamaica and non-resident Ambassador to Haiti, 1982–84. Mem. Governing Council: SPCK, 1984–; Leprosy Mission, 1985–; St Lawrence Coll., Ramsgate, 1984–; Benenden Sch., 1985–92 (Chm., 1986–92). *Recreations:* tennis, golf, making and listening to music, light verse, bird watching. *Address:* Beacon Shaw, Benenden, Kent TN17 4BU. *T:* Cranbrook (0580) 240625.

SMALLMAN, Prof. Raymond Edward, FRS 1986; FEng 1991; Feeney Professor of Metallurgy and Materials Science, since 1969, and Pro-Vice-Chancellor and Vice-Principal, since 1987, University of Birmingham; *b* 4 Aug. 1929; *s* of David Smallman and Edith French; *m* 1952, Joan Doreen Faulkner; one *s* one *d*. *Educ:* Rugeley Grammar Sch.; Univ. of Birmingham (BSc, PhD, DSc). CEng, FIM. AERE Harwell, 1953–58; University of Birmingham: Lectr in Dept of Physical Metallurgy, 1958, Sen Lectr, 1963; Prof. of Phys. Metall., 1964; Head of Dept of Phys. Metall. and Sci. of Materials, 1969–81, of Metallurgy and Materials, 1981–88; Dean of Faculty of Sci. and Eng., 1984–85, of Faculty of Eng., 1985–87. Visiting Professor: Pennsylvania, 1961; Stanford, 1962; NSW, 1974; UCLA Berkeley, 1978; Cape Town, 1982; Van Horn Dist. Lectr, Case Western Reserve Univ., 1978. IUC Consultant, Hong Kong, 1979. Member: Inter-Services Cttee, MoD, 1965; Metals and Materials Cttee, SRC, 1968–71; Materials Adv. Cttee, MoD, 1971; Cttee, Engrg Profs Conf., 1985; SERC Materials Commn, 1988–. Pres., Birmingham Metallurgical Assoc., 1972–73; Vice-Pres., Metals Soc., 1980–84 (Chm., Metals Sci Cttee, 1974–84); Member: Council, Inst. of Metals; Lunar Soc., 1991. Advr, ACU, 1985–. Hon. DSc: Wales, 1990; Novi Sad, Yugoslavia, 1990. Sir George Beilby Gold Medal, Inst. of Metals and Chem. Soc., 1969; Rosenhain Medal, Inst. Metals, 1972; Elegant Work Prize, Metals Soc., 1979; Platinum Medal, Inst. of Metals, 1989. *Publications:* Modern Physical Metallurgy, 1962, 4th edn 1985; (jtly) Modern Metallography, 1966; (jtly) Structure of Metal and Alloys, 1969; (jtly) Defect Analysis in Electron Microscopy, 1975; sci. papers on relationship of microstructure of materials to their properties in learned jls. *Recreations:* writing, travel, friendly golf, bridge. *Address:* 59 Woodthorne Road South, Tettenhall, Wolverhampton WV6 8SN. *T:* Wolverhampton (0902) 752545. *Clubs:* Athenæum; South Staffordshire Golf.

SMALLPEICE, Sir Basil, KCVO 1961; chartered accountant and air/sea transport executive, retired; *b* Rio de Janeiro, Brazil, 18 Sept. 1906; *s* of Herbert Charles Smallpeice, bank manager, and Georgina Ruth (*née* Rust); *m* 1931, Kathleen Ivey Singleton Brame (*d* 1973), *d* of late Edwin Singleton Brame; *m* 1973, Rita Burns, *yr d* of late Major William Burns, MBE. *Educ:* Shrewsbury. BComm London. Articled to Bullimore & Co., Chartered Accts, 1925–30. Accountant of Hoover Ltd, 1930–37; Chief Accountant and later Sec. of Doulton & Co. Ltd, 1937–48; Dir of Costs and Statistics, British Transport Commission, 1948–50; BOAC: Financial Comptroller, 1950–56; Member of Board, 1953–63; Deputy Chief Executive, 1954–56; Man. Dir, 1956–63; Chm., Nat. Jt Council for Civil Air Transport, 1960–61; Man. Dir, BOAC-Cunard Ltd, from its inception in 1962 till end of 1963; Administrative Adviser in HM Household, 1964–80; Chairman: Cunard Steam-Ship Co. Ltd, 1965–71 (Dir, 1964; a Dep. Chm., 1965); Cunard Line Ltd, 1965–71; Cunard-Brocklebank, 1967–70; Cunard Cargo Shipping, 1970–71; ACT (Australia)/Australian Nat. Line Co-ordinating Bd, 1969–79; Associated Container Transportation (Australia), 1971–79; a Dep. Chm., Lonrho Ltd, April 1972–May 1973; Director: Martins Bank Ltd, 1966–69; London Local Bd, Barclays Bank, 1969–74. Member Council: Inst. of Chartered Accountants, 1948–57; Inst. of Transport, 1958–61; Brit. Inst. of Management, 1959–64 and 1965–75 (Chm., 1970–72; a Vice-Pres., 1972–); Pres., Inst. of Freight Forwarders, 1977–78. Mem., Cttee for Exports to the US, 1964–66. Chairman: The English Speaking Union of the Commonwealth, 1965–68; Leatherhead New Theatre (Thorndike) Trust, 1966–74; Air League, 1971–74. President: Friends of Cobham Cottage Hosp., 1987–; Friends of St George's Church, Esher, 1987–. Companion,

RAeS, 1960–75; Liveryman: Guild of Air Pilots and Air Navigators, 1960; Coachmakers and Coach Harness Makers, 1961. Key to the City of San Francisco, 1959. Order of the Cedar, Lebanon, 1955. Pioneers Award for contribs to develt of containerization, Containerization Inst., NY, 1981. *Publications:* various articles in the 1940s on the development of industrial and management accounting; Of Comets and Queens (autobiog.), 1981. *Recreations:* gardening, golf. *Address:* Bridge House, 45 Leigh Hill Road, Cobham, Surrey KT11 2HU. *T:* Cobham (0932) 65425. *Clubs:* Athenæum, Boodle's; Melbourne (Melbourne, Australia).

SMALLWOOD, Anne Hunter, CMG 1976; Commissioner, Board of Inland Revenue, 1973–81; *b* 20 June 1922; *d* of Martin Wilkinson McNicol and Elizabeth Straiton Harper; *m* 1972, Peter Basil Smallwood (*d* 1977). *Educ:* High Sch. for Girls, Glasgow; Glasgow Univ. Entered Inland Revenue, 1943; Min. of Land and Natural Resources, 1964–66; Min. of Housing and Local Govt, 1966; Under-Sec., Inland Revenue, 1971–73. *Address:* 83 Lyncombe Hill, Bath BA2 4PJ. *Club:* United Oxford & Cambridge University.
See also G. P. McNicol.

SMALLWOOD, Air Chief Marshal Sir Denis (Graham), GBE 1975 (CBE 1961; MBE 1951); KCB 1969 (CB 1966); DSO 1944; DFC 1942; idc; jssc; psc; aws; FRSA; FRAeS; Military Adviser to British Aerospace, 1977–83; *b* 13 Aug. 1918; *s* of Frederick William Smallwood, Moseley, Birmingham; *m* 1940, Frances Jeanne, *d* of Walter Needham; one *s* one *d*. *Educ:* King Edward VI School, Birmingham. Joined Royal Air Force, 1938; Asst Adjt and Flying Instructor No 605 (County of Warwick) Sqdn, RAuxAF, 1938–39; served War of 1939–45, Fighter Command, as a fighter pilot in Nos 247 and 87 Hurricane Sqns, 1940–42, and Spitfire Wing Leader, 1943–44. Asst. Sec., COS Cttee, 1946–49; Directing Staff, JSSC, 1950–52; OC RAF Biggin Hill, 1953–55; Directing Staff, IDC, 1956; Group Captain, 1957; commanded RAF Guided Missiles Station, Lincs, 1959–61; AOC and Commandant, RAF Coll. of Air Warfare, Manby, 1961–62; ACAS (Ops), 1962–65; AOC No 3 Gp, RAF Bomber Comd, 1965–67; SASO, Bomber Comd, 1967–68; Dep. C-in-C, Strike Comd, 1968–69; AOC-in-C, NEAF, Comdr, British Forces Near East, and Administrator, Sovereign Base Area, Cyprus, 1969–70; Vice-Chief of the Air Staff, 1970–74; C-in-C, RAF Strike Command, 1974–76, and C-in-C, UK Air Forces, 1975–76. ADC to the Queen, 1959–64. Life Vice-Pres., Air League, 1984 (Pres., 1981–84, Chm., 1978–81). Freeman, City of London, 1976; Liveryman, Guild of Air Pilots and Navigators, 1975. *Recreations:* shooting, gun dog training, walking, swimming, gardening. *Address:* The Flint House, Owlswick, Bucks. *Clubs:* Royal Air Force, Les Ambassadeurs.

SMALLWOOD, John Frank Monton, CBE 1991; a Church Commissioner, since 1966 (Member, Board of Governors, since 1966 and Member, General Purposes Committee, since 1968); *b* 12 April 1926; *s* of late Frank Theodore and Edith Smallwood; *m* 1952, Jean Margaret Lovell; one *s* two *d*. *Educ:* City of London Sch.; Peterhouse, Cambridge, 1948–51 (MA Classics). Served RAF, 1944–48 (Japanese translation and interrogation). Joined Bank of England, 1951; Private Sec. to Governors, 1959–62; Adviser, 1967; Auditor, 1969; Dep. Chief Accountant, 1974–79. Member: Church Assembly/General Synod, 1965– (Standing Cttee, 1971–); numerous *ad hoc* Cttees, etc, over years, incl. Wkg Party on State Aid for Churches in use, 1971–; Central Bd of Finance, 1965– (Dep. Vice-Chm. 1972–82); Pensions Bd, 1985–; Anglican Consultative Council, 1975–87 (Trinidad, 1976, Lambeth Conf., 1978, Canada, 1979, Newcastle, 1981, Singapore, 1987). A Trustee: City Parochial Foundn, 1969– (Vice-Chm., 1977–81; Chm., 1981–); Trust for London, 1986– (Chm.); Overseas Bishoprics Fund, 1977–; Lambeth Palace Library, 1978–. Member: Southwark Dio. Bd of Finance, 1962– (Chm. 1975–); Southwark Ordination Course Council, 1960–74 and 1980– (Vice-Chm., 1980–); Corp. of Church House Council, 1986–; Churches' Main Cttee, 1987–; BCC 1987–90. Lee Abbey Council, 1969–74; Lay Reader, 1983–. *Recreations:* church finances (incl. various financial pamphlets), family, music, cathedrals, old churches, historic houses, gardens. *Address:* Downsview, 32 Brockham Lane, Brockham, Betchworth, Surrey RH3 7EL. *T:* Betchworth (0737) 842032.

SMART, (Alexander Basil) Peter, CMG 1990; HM Diplomatic Service; Ambassador to Fiji, and High Commissioner (non-resident) to Republic of Nauru and to Tuvalu, 1989–Feb. 1992; *b* 19 Feb. 1932; *s* of late Henry Prescott Smart and Mary Gertrude Todd; *m* 1955, Joan Mary Cumming; three *s* (incl. twin *s*). *Educ:* Ryhope Grammar Sch., Co. Durham. Commnd RAEC, 1951; Supervising Officer, Educn, Gibraltar Comd, 1951–52; entered HM Foreign (later Diplomatic) Service, 1953; Vice Consul, Duala, 1955; Polit. Office, ME Forces, Cyprus, 1956; 2nd Sec. (Information), Seoul, 1959; News Dept, FO, 1964; Head of Chancery, Rangoon, 1968; FCO, 1971; Head of Communications Technical Services Dept, 1975; Counsellor, 1977–82, and Dep. High Comr, 1981–82, Canberra; Counsellor and Head of Chancery, Prague, 1983–86; High Comr, Seychelles, 1986–89. FRSA. *Recreations:* wild nature, the arts: looking and listening. *Address:* 715 Willoughby House, Barbican, EC2Y 8BN.

SMART, Andrew, CB 1981; defence consultant; Director, Royal Signals and Radar Establishment, Malvern, 1978–84; *b* 12 Feb. 1924; *s* of late Mr and Mrs William S. Smart; *m* 1949, Pamela Kathleen Stephens; two *s* two *d*. *Educ:* Denny; High Sch. of Stirling; Glasgow Univ. MA 1944. TRE Malvern, 1943; Science 2 Air Min., 1950–53; Guided Weapons Gp, RRE, Malvern, 1953–70 (Head, 1968–70); Dep. Dir (Scientific B), DOAE, 1970; RAE, Farnborough: Head of Weapons Res. Gp, 1972; Head of Weapons Dept, 1973; Dep. Dir (W), 1974–77. *Recreations:* gardening, caravanning. *Address:* Hill Orchard, Shelsley Drive, Colwall, Malvern, Worcs. *T:* Colwall (0684) 40664.

SMART, Prof. (Arthur David) Gerald, CBE 1991; FRTPI; Emeritus Professor of Urban Planning, University of London, since 1984; Professor of Urban Planning at University College London, 1975–84 and part-time, 1984–87 (Head of Bartlett School of Architecture and Planning, University College London, 1975–80); *b* 19 March 1925; *s* of Dr A. H. J. Smart and A. O. M. Smart (*née* Evans); *m* 1955, Anne Patience Smart (*née* Baxter); two *d*. *Educ:* Rugby Sch.; King's Coll., Cambridge; Regent St Polytechnic. MA, DipTP; ARICS, FRSA. Served in The Rifle Brigade, 1943–47 (Captain). Appts in local govt (planning), London, NE England, E Midlands, 1950–63; County Planning Officer, Hants CC, 1963–75; Member: Planning Adv. Gp, 1964–65, Cttee on Public Participation in Planning, 1968–69, Min. of Housing and Local Govt; Planning and Transportation Res. Adv. Council, DoE, 1975–79; Working Party on alternative uses of Historic Buildings, Historic Bldgs Council and BTA, 1979–81; Council, TCPA, 1983–89; Council, RSPB, 1985–90; Governing Body, GB/E Europe Centre, 1985–; Council, Solent Protection Soc., 1986–; House Builders' Fedn Commn on Inner Cities, 1986–87; occasional Chm., Structure Plans Exams in Public for DoE; Consultant, Countryside Commn, 1989–90. Chm., Milford-on-Sea Parish Council, 1989– (Councillor, 1987–). *Publications:* articles, conf. papers, in books, professional and other jls, booklets and reports. *Recreations:* sailing, ornithology, music, walking. *Address:* 10 Harewood Green, Keyhaven, Lymington, Hants SO41 0TZ. *T:* Lymington (0590) 645475. *Clubs:* Royal Lymington Yacht, Keyhaven Yacht (Lymington).

SMART, Edwin; *see* Smart, L. E.

SMART, Professor Sir George (Algernon), Kt 1978; MD, FRCP; Director, British Postgraduate Medical Federation, 1971–78, retired; *b* 16 Dec. 1913; *er s* of A. Smart, Alnwick, Northumb; *m* 1939, Monica Helen Carrick; two *s* one *d*. *Educ:* Uppingham; Durham Univ., BSc 1935, MB, BS 1937. MD 1939 (Durham); MRCP 1940, FRCP 1952. Commonwealth Fund Fellow, 1948–49. Lectr in Med., Univ. of Bristol, 1946–50; Reader in Medicine, Univ. of Durham, 1950–56; Prof. of Medicine, Univ. of Durham, 1956–68, Univ. of Newcastle upon Tyne, 1968–71 (Post-graduate Sub-Dean, 1962–68, Dean of Medicine, 1968–71). Censor, 1965–67, Senior Censor and Senior Vice-Pres., 1972–73, RCP. Chairman: Review Bd for Overseas Qualified Practitioners, GMC, 1979–82; Cttee of Management, and Med. and Survival Cttee, RNLI, 1979–83. Hon. Fellow, Coll. of Physicians and Surgeons, Pakistan, 1976. *Publications:* contrib. to Price's Textbook of Medicine, and Progress in Clinical Medicine (Daley and Miller); (ed) Metabolic Disturbances in Clinical Medicine, 1958; (co-author) Fundamentals of Clinical Endocrinology, 1969, 2nd edn 1974. *Recreation:* photography. *Address:* Taffrail, Crede Lane, Old Bosham, Chichester, Sussex PO18 8NX.

SMART, Gerald; *see* Smart, A. D. G.

SMART, Sir Jack, Kt 1982; CBE 1976; JP; DL; Chairman, Wakefield District Health Authority, 1982–88; *b* 25 April 1920; *s* of James and Emily Smart; *m* 1941, Ethel King; one *d*. *Educ:* Altofts Colliery Sch. Miner, 1934–59; Branch Sec., Glasshoughton Colliery, NUM, 1949–59; Mem., Castleford Municipal Borough Council, 1949–74; Mayor of Castleford, 1962–63; Mem., Wakefield Metropolitan Dist Council, 1973–, Leader, 1973–86. Chm., Assoc. of Metropolitan Authorities, 1977–78, 1980–84; Leader of the Opposition Group, AMA, 1978–80. Chm., Wakefield AHA, 1977–81; Mem., Layfield Cttee of Enquiry into Local Govt Finance, 1974–76. Pres., Yorkshire Soc. (1980), 1988–. Hon. Fellow, Bretton Coll., 1983. Hon. Freeman, City of Wakefield, 1985. JP Castleford, 1960; DL West Yorks, 1987. FRSA. *Recreations:* golf, music. *Address:* Churchside, Weetworth, Pontefract Road, Castleford, West Yorks WF10 4QA. *T:* Castleford (0977) 554880.

SMART, Jack; *see* Smart, R. J.

SMART, (Louis) Edwin, JD; Chairman and Chief Executive Officer, Trans World Corporation, 1978–87; Chairman of Executive Committee, Hilton International Co., since 1986 (Chairman of Board, 1978–86); *b* Columbus, Ohio, 17 Nov. 1923; *s* of Louis Edwin Smart and Esther Guthery; *m* 1st, 1944, Virginia Alice Knouff (marr. diss. 1958); one *s* one *d*; 2nd, 1964, Jeanie Alberta Milone; one *s*. *Educ:* Harvard Coll. (AB *magna cum laude* 1947); Harvard Law Sch. (JD *magna cum laude* 1949). Served to Lieut, USNR, 1943–46. Admitted to NY Bar, 1950; Associate, Hughes, Hubbard & Ewing, NYC, 1949–56; Partner, Hughes, Hubbard & Reed, NYC, 1957–64; Pres., Bendix Internat. and Dir, Bendix Corp. and foreign subsids, 1964–67; Trans World Airlines Inc.: Sen. Vice Pres., External Affairs, 1967–71, Corp. Affairs, 1971–75; Vice Chm. 1976; Chief Exec. Officer, 1977–78; Chm. of Bd, 1977–85; also Dir, Mem. Exec., and Mem. Finance Cttee. Chairman: Canteen Corp., 1973–; Spartan Food Systems Inc., 1979–; Director: Sonat Inc.; The Continental Corp.; NY Stock Exchange; Trustee, Cttee for Econ. Develt, 1977–. Member: Conf. Bd, 1977–; Amer. Bar Assoc.; NY County Lawyers Assoc.; Phi Beta Kappa; Sigma Alpha Epsilon. *Address:* 535 E 86th Street, New York, NY 10028, USA; Coakley Bay, Christiansted, St Croix 00820, Virgin Islands. *Clubs:* Economic of New York, Presidents, Marco Polo, Sky (NYC); St Croix Yacht.

SMART, Ninian; *see* Smart, R. N.

SMART, Peter; *see* Smart, A. B. P.

SMART, (Raymond) Jack, DL; formerly Managing Director, Bus and Truck Group, British Leyland, retired; *b* 1 Aug. 1917; *s* of Frank Smart and Emily Rose Smart; *m* 1942, Jessie Alice Tyrrell; one *s* one *d*. *Educ:* Redhill Technical Coll. (HNC). Apprentice Prodn Engr, Lanston Monotype Corp., 1933–38; Aeronautical Inspection Directorate, Air Min., 1939–40; Rotol Airscrews/Dowty Rotol, 1940–59: successively Chief Inspector, Prodn Controller, Works Manager; Man. Dir, British Light Steel Pressings (subsidiary of Rootes Motors Ltd), 1960–65; British Leyland (formerly BM Corp.): Man. Dir, Truck Div., 1966–72; Gp Manufg Dir, 1972–76; Gp Exec. Dir and Dep. Man. Dir, 1976–79; Man. Dir, Aveling Barford Holdings Ltd, 1979–80; non-exec. Dir, Marshall Sons & Co. Ltd, 1981–84. DL W Yorks, 1987. *Recreations:* Rugby Union, gardening. *Address:* 17 Whitecroft Park, Northfield Road, Nailsworth, Glos GL6 0NS. *T:* Nailsworth (045383) 5634.

SMART, Reginald Piers Alexander de B.; *see* de Bernière-Smart.

SMART, Prof. (Roderick) Ninian; J. F. Rowny Professor of Religious Studies, University of California, Santa Barbara, since 1988 (Professor, since 1976); Professor Emeritus, University of Lancaster, since 1989 (Professor of Religious Studies, 1967–82; Hon. Professor, 1982–89); *b* 6 May 1927; *s* of late Prof. W. M. Smart, FRSE, and Isabel (*née* Carswell); *m* 1954, Libushka Clementina Baruffaldi; one *s* two *d*. *Educ:* Glasgow Academy; The Queen's College, Oxford. Army service with Intelligence Corps, 1945–48, 2nd Lt, Captain, 1947; overseas service in Ceylon. Oxford: Mods (shortened), Class II, 1949; Lit. Hum. Class I, 1951; BPhil 1954. Asst Lecturer in Philosophy, Univ. Coll. of Wales, Aberystwyth, 1952–55, Lecturer, 1955; Vis. Lecturer in Philosophy, Yale Univ., 1955–56; Lecturer in History and Philosophy of Religion, Univ. of London, King's College, 1956–61; H. G. Wood Professor of Theology, University of Birmingham, 1961–66. Pro-Vice-Chancellor, Univ. of Lancaster, 1969–72. Lectures: Banaras Hindu Univ., Summer, 1960; Teape, Univ. Delhi, 1964; Gifford, Univ. of Edinburgh, 1979–80; Visiting Professor: Univ. Wisconsin, 1965; Princeton and Otago, 1971; Queensland, 1980 and 1985; Univ. of Cape Town, 1982; Harvard, 1983; Hong Kong, 1989. President: Inst. of Religion and Theology, 1980–85 (first Gen. Sec., 1973–77); British Assoc. History of Religions, 1981–85; Amer. Soc. for Study of Religion, 1984–87. Hon. LHD Loyola, 1968; Hon. DLitt: Glasgow, 1984; Kelaniya, Sri Lanka, 1991; DUniv Stirling, 1986. *Publications:* Reasons and Faiths, 1958; A Dialogue of Religions, 1960; Historical Selections in the Philosophy of Religion, 1962; Philosophers and Religious Truth, 1964; Doctrine and Argument in Indian Philosophy, 1964, 2nd edn 1991; The Teacher and Christian Belief, 1966; The Yogi and the Devotee, 1968; Secular Education and the Logic of Religion, 1968; The Religious Experience of Mankind, 1969, 4th edn 1991; Philosophy of Religion, 1970; The Concept of Worship, 1972; The Phenomenon of Religion, 1973; The Science of Religion and the Sociology of Knowledge, 1973; Mao, 1974; A Companion to the Long Search, 1977; The Phenomenon of Christianity, 1979; Beyond Ideology, 1982; (with R. Hecht) Sacred Texts of the World, 1982; Worldviews, 1983; (with Swami Purnananda) Prophet of a New Hindu Age, 1985; Concept and Empathy, 1986; Religion and the Western Mind, 1986; World Religions, 1989; (with S. Konstantine) A Christian Systematic Theology in World Context, 1991; contrib. to Mind, Philosophy, Philosophical Quarterly, Review of Metaphysics, Religion, Religious Studies. *Recreations:* cricket, tennis, poetry. *Address:* Department of Religious Studies, University of Lancaster, Bailrigg, Lancaster LA1 4YG; Department of Religious Studies, University of California at Santa Barbara, Calif 93106, USA. *Club:* Athenæum.

SMART, William Norman H.; *see* Hunter Smart.

SMEALL, James Leathley, MA, JP; Principal, Saint Luke's College, Exeter, 1945–72; *b* 16 June 1907; *s* of late William Francis Smeall, MB, BCh (Edin.), and late Ethel Mary Leathley; *m* 1936, Joan Rachel Harris (*d* 1984); one *d*. *Educ:* Sorbonne; Queens' College, Cambridge (Scholar). Class I English Tripos, Class II Division 1 Anthropological and Archæological Tripos; Assistant Master, Merchiston, 1929–30; Staff, Royal Naval College, Dartmouth, 1930–34; Housemaster, Bradfield College, 1934–36; Head of the English Department, Epsom College, 1936–39; Headmaster, Chesterfield Grammar School, 1939–45; Commissioned RAFVR, 1941–44. Mayor of Exeter, 1965–66; President: Exeter Civic Soc., 1980–87; Exeter and Dist Br., E-SU, 1983–88. Hon. LLD Exeter, 1988. *Publication:* English Satire, Parody and Burlesque, 1952. *Recreations:* gardening and travel. *Address:* Follett Orchard, Topsham, Exeter EX3 0JP. *T:* Topsham (0392) 873892.

SMEDLEY, (Frank) Brian, QC 1977; **His Honour Judge Smedley;** a Circuit Judge, since 1987; *b* 28 Nov. 1934. *Educ:* West Bridgford Grammar Sch.; London Univ. LLB Hons, 1957. Called to the Bar, Gray's Inn, 1960; Midland Circuit; a Recorder, 1972; Sen. Judge, Sovereign Base Areas, Cyprus, 1991– (Dep. Sen. Judge, 1989–91). Mem., Senate of the Inns of Court and the Bar, 1973–77. Freeman, City of London, 1990. *Recreations:* travel, music. *Address:* Central Criminal Court, Old Bailey, EC4. *Club:* Garrick.

SMEDLEY, George; *see* Smedley, R. R. G. B.

SMEDLEY, Sir Harold, KCMG 1978 (CMG 1965); MBE 1946; HM Diplomatic Service, retired; *b* 19 June 1920; *s* of late Dr R. D. Smedley, MA, MD, DPH, Worthing; *m* 1950, Beryl Mary Harley Brown, Wellington, New Zealand; two *s* two *d*. *Educ:* Aldenham School; Pembroke College, Cambridge. Served War of 1939–45, Royal Marines. Entered Dominions Office (later Commonwealth Relations Office), 1946; Private Secretary to Permanent Under-Secretary of State, 1947–48; British High Commissioner's Office: Wellington, NZ, 1948–50; Salisbury, Southern Rhodesia, 1951–53; Principal Private Sec. to Sec. of State for Commonwealth Relations, 1954–57; Counsellor, British High Comr's Office: Calcutta, 1957; New Delhi, 1958–60; British High Comr in Ghana, 1964–67; Ambassador to Laos, 1967–70; Asst Under-Sec. of State, FCO, 1970–72; Sec. Gen., Commn on Rhodesian opinion, 1971–72; High Comr in Sri Lanka, and Ambassador to Republic of Maldives, 1972–75; High Comr in NZ and concurrently Governor of Pitcairn Island, 1976–80; High Comr in Western Samoa (non-resident), 1977–80. Chm., London Bd, Bank of NZ, 1983–89. Vice Chm., Victoria League, 1981–90. Pres., Hakluyt Soc., 1987–. Mem., W Sussex CC, 1989–. *Address:* 11A Beehive Lane, Ferring, Sussex BN12 5NN. *Clubs:* United Oxford & Cambridge University, Commonwealth Trust.

SMEDLEY, (Roscoe Relph) George (Boleyne); Barrister; Counsellor, HM Diplomatic Service, retired; *b* 3 Sept. 1919; *o s* of late Charles Boleyne Smedley and Aimie Blaine Smedley (*née* Relph); *m* 1st, 1947, Muriel Hallaway Murray (*d* 1975), *o d* of late Arthur Stanley Murray; one *s*; 2nd, 1979, Margaret Gerrard Gourlay (*d* 1991), *o c* of late Augustus Thorburn Hallaway and *widow* of Dr John Stewart Gourlay. *Educ:* King's Sch., Ely; King's Coll., London (LLB). Called to Bar, Inner Temple. Artists Rifles TA; commnd S Lancs Regt, 1940; Indian Army, 1942–46 (Captain); Foreign Office, 1937 and 1946; Foreign Service (subseq. Diplomatic Service): Rangoon, 1947; Maymyo, 1950; Brussels, 1952; Baghdad, 1954; FO, 1958; Beirut, 1963; Kuwait, 1965; FCO, 1969; Consul-Gen., Lubumbashi, 1972–74; British Mil. Govt, Berlin, 1974–76; FCO 1976; Head of Nationality and Treaty Dept, 1977–79. Part-time appointments (since retirement): Legal Mem., Mental Health Review Tribunal; Chm., Rent Assessment Cttee; Adjudicator under Immigration Act 1971; Inspector, Planning Inspectorate, Depts of the Environment and Transport; Dep. Traffic Comr for N Eastern Traffic Area; Mem., No 2 Dip. Service Appeal Bd. Churchwarden. *Address:* Garden House, Whorlton, Barnard Castle, Co. Durham DL12 8XQ. *T:* Teesdale (0833) 27381. *Clubs:* Royal Automobile, Royal Over-Seas League.

SMEDLEY, Susan M.; *see* Marsden.

SMEE, Clive Harrod; Chief Economic Adviser to Department of Health, since 1988 (to Department of Health and Social Security, 1984–88 and to Department of Social Security, 1988–89); *b* 29 April 1942; *s* of Victor Woolley Smee and Leila Olive Smee (*née* Harrod); *m* 1975, Denise Eileen Sell; one *s* two *d*. *Educ:* Royal Grammar Sch., Guildford; LSE (BSc Econ); Indiana Univ. (MBA); Inst. of Commonwealth Studies, Oxford. British Council, Nigeria, 1966–68; Economic Advr, ODM, 1969–75; Sen. Economic Advr, DHSS, 1975–82; Nuffield and Leverhulme Travelling Fellow, USA and Canada, 1978–79; Advr, Central Policy Review Staff, 1982–83; Sen. Economic Advr, HM Treasury, 1983–84. Consultant: NZ Treasury, 1988; NZ Dept of Health, 1991. Chm., OECD Social Policy Working Party, 1987–. *Publications:* articles on economics in learned jls. *Recreations:* running, gardening; Anna, David and Elizabeth. *Address:* c/o Department of Health, Friars House, Blackfriars Road, SE1 8EU. *T:* 071–972 3080.

SMEE, John Charles O.; *see* Odling-Smee, J. C.

SMEETON, Vice-Adm. Sir Richard Michael, KCB 1964 (CB 1961); MBE 1942; FRAeS 1973; DL; *b* 24 Sept. 1912; *s* of Edward Leaf Smeeton and Charlotte Mildred Leighton; *m* 1940, Maria Elizabeth Hawkins; no *c*. *Educ:* RNC, Dartmouth. 800 Squadron i/c HMS Ark Royal, 1940–41; Assistant Naval Attaché (Air), Washington, DC, 1941–43; staff of Admiral Nimitz, USN 1943–44; Air Plans Officer, British Pacific Fleet, 1944–45; Captain (Air) Med., 1952–54; Imperial Defence College, 1955; Captain, HMS Albion, 1956–57; Director of Plans, Admiralty, 1958–59; Flag Officer Aircraft Carriers, 1960–62; NATO Deputy Supreme Allied Commander, Atlantic, 1962–64; Flag Officer, Naval Air Command, 1964–65. Rear-Admiral, 1959; Vice-Admiral, 1962. Retired Nov. 1965, at own request. Dir and Chief Exec., Soc. of British Aerospace Cos, 1966–79; Sec., Defence Industries Council, 1970–79. Mem. Council, Inst. of Dirs. DL Surrey 1976. *Address:* St Mary's Cottage, Shamley Green, Guildford, Surrey GU5 0SP. *T:* Guildford (0483) 893478. *Club:* Army and Navy.

SMETHAM, Andrew James, MA; Headmaster, The Purbeck School, Wareham, Dorset, since 1985; *b* 22 Feb. 1937; *s* of Arthur James Smetham and Eunice (*née* Jones); *m* 1964, Sandra Mary (*née* Owen); two *s*. *Educ:* Vaynor and Penderyn Grammar Sch., Cefn Coed, Breconshire; King's Coll., Univ. of London (BA (Hons German) 1959, DipEd 1964, MA (Educn) 1968). Assistant Master: Wandsworth Sch., 1960–66; Sedgehill Sch., 1966–70; Dep. Headmaster, Holloway Sch., 1970–74; Headmaster, Wandsworth Sch., 1974–84. *Recreations:* music, walking. *Address:* The Water Barn, East Burton, Wareham, Dorset BH20 6HE. *T:* Bindon Abbey (0929) 463727.

SMETHURST, John Michael; Director-General, British Library, London, since 1991; *b* 25 April 1934; *s* of Albert Smethurst and Nelly Smethurst (*née* Kitchin); *m* 1960, Mary Clayworth; one *s* one *d*. *Educ:* William Hulme's Grammar School, Manchester; Manchester Univ. (BA). ALA. Librarian: Bede Coll., Durham Univ., 1964–66; Inst. of Educn, Newcastle upon Tyne, 1966–69; Dep. Librarian, Univ. of Glasgow, 1969–72; Univ. Librarian, Univ. of Aberdeen, 1972–86; British Library: Dir-Gen., Humanities and Social Sciences, 1986–91; Mem. Bd, 1986–; Mem., Lending Div. Adv. Cttee, 1976–80; Mem., Adv. Council, 1982–86 (Chm., Bibliog. Services Adv. Cttee, 1983–86). Hon. Res. Fellow, UCL, 1987–. Trustee, Nat. Library of Scotland, 1976–86; Chm., Library and Inf. Services Cttee (Scotland), 1982–86; Chm., SCONUL, 1984–86, 1989–90 (Vice-Chm., 1983–84, 1988; Mem. Council, 1977–80, 1983–); British Council Libraries Adv. Cttee, 1983–. President: Scottish Liby Assoc., 1983; LIBER, 1989–. FRSA. *Publications:* papers and articles in professional jls. *Recreations:* music, art, travel, gardening. *Address:* Romney, 72 Grove Road, Tring, Herts HP23 5PB. *Club:* Athenæum.

SMETHURST, Richard Good, MA; Provost, Worcester College, Oxford, since 1991; *b* 17 Jan. 1941; *s* of Thomas Good Smethurst and Madeleine Nora Foulkes; *m* 1964, Dorothy Joan (*née* Mitchenall); two *s* two *d*. *Educ:* Liverpool Coll.; Worcester Coll., Oxford; Nuffield Coll., Oxford. Webb Medley Jun. Schol. 1962; BA 1st Cl. 1963; MA Oxon. Research Fellow: St Edmund Hall, Oxford, 1964–65; Inst. for Commonwealth Studies, Oxford, 1965–66 (Consultant, UN/FAO World Food Program); University of Oxford: Fellow and Tutor in Economics, St Edmund Hall, 1966–67; Fellow and Tutor in Economics, Worcester Coll., and Univ. Lectr in Economics, 1967–76; Dir, Dept for External Studies, and Professorial Fellow, Worcester Coll., 1976–89; Supernumerary Fellow, Worcester Coll., and Chm., Gen. Bd of Faculties, 1989–91. Economic Adviser, HM Treasury, 1969–71; Policy Adviser, Prime Minister's Policy Unit, 1975–76. Dir, IMRO, 1987–. Member: Adv. Council for Adult and Continuing Educn, DES, 1977–83; Monopolies and Mergers Commn, 1978–89 (Dep. Chm., 1986–89); UGC/NAB Continuing Educn Standing Cttee, 1984–88; Acad. Consultative Cttee, Open Univ., 1986–; Adv. Bd, Music at Oxford, 1988–. Trustee, Eur. Community Baroque Orch., 1986–. Mem. Council, Templeton Coll., Oxford (Oxford Management Centre), 1982–; Life Governor, Liverpool Coll., 1968. Foundn Hon. Fellow, Rewley House, Oxford, 1990; Hon. Fellow, St Edmund Hall, Oxford, 1991. *Publications:* Impact of Food Aid on Donor Countries (with G. R. Allen), 1967; contribs to New Thinking About Welfare, 1969; Economic System in the UK, 1977, 2nd edn 1979; New Directions in Adult and Continuing Education, 1979; Continuing Education in Universities and Polytechnics, 1982; contrib. Jl of Development Studies, Oxford Rev. of Educn, Studies in Adult Education. *Recreation:* good food. *Address:* The Provost's Lodgings, Worcester College, Oxford OX1 2HB. *T:* Oxford (0865) 278362.

SMETTEM, Colin William; Chairman, North Eastern Region, British Gas Corporation, 1973–76; *b* 1 June 1916; *s* of William Home Smettem and Agnes Grace; *m* 1945, Sylvia Elisabeth (*née* Alcock); two *s* two *d*. Solicitor (Hons) 1938. Asst Solicitor, Scarborough Corp., 1938. Served War, 1939–45: UK, India, Assam; GII at Tactical Trng Centre, India Command, 1944. Asst Town Clerk, Wallasey, 1948; Solicitor, North Western Gas Bd, 1950; Commercial Manager, North Western Gas Bd, 1961, and Mem. Bd, 1965–68; Dep. Chm., Eastern Gas Bd, 1968. *Address:* The Rookery, Tinwell, via Stamford, Lincs PE9 3UJ. *T:* Stamford (0780) 53168. *Club:* Naval and Military.

SMIETON, Dame Mary Guillan, DBE 1949; MA Oxon; Permanent Secretary, Ministry of Education, 1959–63, retired; *b* 5 Dec. 1902; *d* of John Guillan Smieton, late librarian and bursar Westminster Coll., Cambridge, and of Maria Judith Toop. *Educ:* Perse Sch., Cambridge; Wimbledon High Sch.; Bedford Coll., London (1 year) (Hon. Fellow, 1971); Lady Margaret Hall. Assistant Keeper, Public Record Office, 1925–28; Ministry of Labour and National Service, 1928–46; on loan to Home Office as General Secretary, Women's Voluntary Services, 1938–40, and to UN as Director of Personnel, 1946–48; Deputy Secretary, Ministry of Labour and National Service, 1955–59 (Under-Secretary, 1946–55). UK representative, Unesco Executive Board, 1962–68. Trustee, British Museum, 1963–73; Chm., Bedford Coll. Council, 1964–70. Member: Advisory Council on Public Records, 1965–73; Standing Commn on Museums and Galleries, 1970–73; Vice Pres., Museums Assoc., 1974–77. Hon. Fellow, Lady Margaret Hall, Oxford, 1959. *Address:* 14 St George's Road, St Margaret's on Thames, Middlesex TW1 1QR. *T:* 081–892 9279. *Club:* United Oxford & Cambridge University.

SMIJTH-WINDHAM, Brig. William Russell, CBE 1946; DSO 1942; *b* 21 Oct. 1907; *s* of late Arthur Russell Smijth-Windham; *m* 1934, Helen Teresa, *d* of late Brig. H. Clementi Smith, DSO; one *s* three *d*. *Educ:* Wellington College; Royal Military Academy, Woolwich. Commissioned Royal Corps of Signals, 1927; Mount Everest Expedition, 1933 and 1936; Mohmand Ops, 1935; Army Revolver VIII, 1937–39; British Pistol VIII, 1939. Served War of 1939–45, Greece and Crete, 1941; Western Desert and Tunisia, 1942–43; France and Germany, 1944–45 (despatches); British Mil. Mission to Greece during Greek Civil War, 1948–49; Chief Signal Officer, Eastern Command and UKLF, 1957–60, retd 1960; ADC to the Queen, 1957–60. FIEE. *Address:* Icentown House, Pitney, Langport, Somerset. *T:* Langport (0458) 250525.

SMILEY, Lt-Col Sir John (Philip), 4th Bt *cr* 1903, of Drumalis, Larne, Co. Antrim and Gallowhill, Paisley, Co. Renfrew; *b* 24 Feb. 1934; *s* of Sir Hugh Houston Smiley, 3rd Bt and of Nancy Elizabeth Louise Hardy (*née* Beaton); *S* father, 1990; *m* 1963, Davina Elizabeth, *d* of late Denis Charles Griffiths; two *s* one *d*. *Educ:* Eton Coll.; RMA Sandhurst. Commnd Grenadier Guards, 1954; ADC to Governor of Bermuda, 1961–62; Regimental Adjt, 1970–73; served in Cyprus, BAOR, Hong Kong; Lt-Col, 1981; retired 1986. Governor, Oundle Sch., 1987–. Mem., Ct of Assts, Worshipful Co. of Grocers, 1987–. *Recreations:* gardening, travel. *Heir:* *s* Christopher Hugh Charles Smiley, *b* 7 Feb. 1968. *Address:* Cornerway House, Chobham, Woking, Surrey GU24 8SW. *T:* Chobham (0276) 858992. *Club:* Army and Navy.

SMILEY, Prof. Timothy John, PhD; FBA 1984; Knightbridge Professor of Philosophy, University of Cambridge, since 1980; Fellow of Clare College, Cambridge, since 1955; *b* 13 Nov. 1930; *s* of Prof. M. T. Smiley and Mrs T. M. Smiley (*née* Browne); *m* 1955, Benita Mary Bentley; four *d*. *Educ:* Ardwyn Grammar Sch., Aberystwyth; Ampleforth Coll.; Fribourg Univ.; Clare Coll., Cambridge (BA 1952, Math. Tripos; MA, PhD 1956). Holt Scholarship, Gray's Inn, 1954; called to the Bar, 1956. Pilot Officer, RAFVR, 1954. Scientific Officer, Air Min., 1955–56; Clare Coll., Cambridge: Res. Fellow, 1955–59; Asst Tutor, 1959–65; Sen. Tutor, 1966–69; Asst Lectr in Phil., Cambridge Univ., 1957–62, Lectr, 1962–79. Vis. Professor: Cornell Univ., 1964; Univ. of Virginia, 1972; Yale Univ., 1975; Univ. of Notre Dame, 1986; Yale Univ., 1990. *Publications:* (with D. J. Shoesmith) Multiple-conclusion Logic, 1978; articles in phil and math. jls. *Recreation:* orienteering. *Address:* Clare College, Cambridge. *T:* Cambridge (0223) 247106.

SMILLIE, William John Jones; Head of the Refreshment Department, House of Commons, since 1980; *b* 18 Feb. 1940; *s* of late John Smillie and Emily Mary Caroline (*née* Jones). *Educ:* Lauriston Sch., Falkirk; Territorial Sch., Stirling; Stirling High Sch. Scottish hotel family background; trained in all hotel depts in Scotland and Paris, with extensive kitchen work; progressed to management with Edward R. Barnett & Co. Ltd, industrial caterers (now taken over by Grand Metropolitan Gp), resp. for 50 outlets throughout Scotland, England and Wales (Asst Gen. Man., 1964–67); joined House of Commons Catering Dept as Personnel Manager, 1967; Personnel Manager and Asst to Catering Manager, 1970; Gen. Man., Refreshment Dept, 1971. Member: British Inst. of Cleaning Science, 1976–; Hine Soc., 1979–; FHCIMA 1979; Fellow, Cookery and Food

Assoc., 1967; Founder Mem., Wine Guild of UK, 1984–; Mem., Restaurateurs Assoc. of GB, 1983–; Hon. Member: Assoc. Culinaire Française, 1972; Conseil Culinaire Française de Grande Bretagne, en Reconnaissance des Services Rendus à l'Art Culinaire, 1987. Vice Pres., British Epilepsy Assoc., 1981; Mem., League Against Cruel Sports, 1983. *Publications:* articles for catering trade papers. *Recreations:* theatre, ballet, music, piano, motoring, boating, disc-jockey, travel, gourmandise, intervals at the opera, rock music. *Address:* House of Commons, SW1. *Clubs:* Mortons; Preston Cross Country; Jaguar Drivers (Luton).

SMIRNOVSKY, Mikhail Nikolaevich; Soviet Ambassador to the Court of St James's, 1966–73; non-resident Ambassador to Malta, 1967–73; *b* 7 Aug. 1921; *m* Liudmila A.; one *s* two *d*. *Educ:* Moscow Aviation Institute. Mem. Soviet Foreign Service, 1948; Assistant, 1955, Deputy Head of American Div., Ministry for Foreign Affairs, 1957–58; Counsellor, 1958, Minister-Counsellor, Soviet Embassy in Washington, 1960–62; Head of US Div. and Mem. Collegium, Ministry for Foreign Affairs, 1962–66. Member: Central Auditing Commn of CPSU, 1966–76; Soviet Delegations to several International Conferences. *Address:* Ministry of Foreign Affairs, 32–34 Smolenskaya Sennaya Ploshchad, Moscow, USSR.

SMITH; *see* Abel Smith and Abel-Smith.

SMITH; *see* Boys Smith and Boys-Smith.

SMITH; *see* Delacourt-Smith.

SMITH; *see* Gordon-Smith.

SMITH; *see* Hamilton-Smith, family name of Baron Colwyn.

SMITH; *see* Hugh Smith.

SMITH; *see* Llewellyn Smith and Llewellyn-Smith.

SMITH; *see* Macdonald-Smith.

SMITH; *see* Mackenzie Smith and McKenzie Smith.

SMITH; *see* Nowell-Smith.

SMITH; *see* Spencer Smith and Spencer-Smith.

SMITH; *see* Stewart-Smith.

SMITH; *see* Stuart-Smith.

SMITH; *see* Walker-Smith.

SMITH; *see* Wenban-Smith.

SMITH, family name of **Viscount Hambleden, Barons Bicester, Kirkhill** and **Smith.**

SMITH, Baron *cr* 1978 (Life Peer), of Marlow in the County of Buckinghamshire; **Rodney Smith,** KBE 1975; MS, FRCS; Hon. Consulting Surgeon: St George's Hospital London, 1978; Royal Prince Alfred Hospital, Sydney, NSW; Wimbledon Hospital; Examiner in Surgery, University of London; External Examiner in Surgery, Universities of Cambridge, Birmingham and Hong Kong; former Advisor in Surgery to Department of Health and Social Security; Hon. Consultant in Surgery to the Army, 1972, Emeritus Consultant, 1980; *b* 10 May 1914; *o s* of Dr Edwin Smith and Edith Catherine (*née* Dyer); *m* 1st, 1938, Mary Rodwell (marr. diss. 1971); three *s* one *d*; 2nd, 1971, Susan Fry. *Educ:* Westminster Sch.; London Univ. (St Thomas's Hospital). MB, BS London, MRCS, LRCP 1937; FRCS 1939; MS London 1941. Surgical Registrar, Middlesex Hospital, 1939–41; Surgeon RAMC, 1941–45; appointed Surgeon, St George's Hospital 1946. Royal College of Surgeons: Hunterian Professor, 1947 and 1952; Arris and Gale Lecturer, 1959; Jacksonian Prizewinner, 1951; Penrose May Tutor in Surgery, 1957–63; Dean, Inst. of Basic Medical Sciences, 1966–71; Mem., Ct of Examiners, 1963–69, Chm. Feb.-July 1969; Mem. Council, 1965–78; Pres., 1973–77; Mem. Ct of Patrons; Hunterian Orator, 1975. President: Brit. Assoc. Surg. Oncologists; Harveian Soc., 1965; Pancreatic Soc., GB and Ire., 1976; Roy. Soc. Med., 1978–80; London Med. Orchestra. Chairman: ASCAB; Conf. of Med. Roy. Coll. UK, 1976–78; Armed Forces Med. Adv. Bd, 1980–84. Member: Council, Brit. Empire Cancer Campaign; Exec., Internat. Fedn Surg. Colls. Trustee, Wolfson Foundn; Governor, Motability. Vis. Lectr to S Africa Assoc. of Surgeons, 1957; McIlrath Guest Prof. in Surgery, Royal Prince Alfred Hosp., Sydney, NSW, 1966; Vis. Prof., Surg. Unit, Univ. of Illinois, Chicago, 1978; Visiting Professor of Surgery: Jackson Univ., Miss, 1979; Johns Hopkins Hosp., Baltimore, 1979; Flint Univ., Mich, 1979. Lectures: First Datuk Abdul Majid Ismail Oration and Gold Medal, Malaysian Assoc. of Surgeons, 1972; Robert Whitmarsh Oration, Providence, 1972; Cheselden, St Thomas's Hosp., 1975; Philip Mitchiner, 1976; Balfour, Toronto, 1976; Colles, RCSI, 1976; Faltin (and Medal), Helsinki, 1976; Bradshaw, RCP, 1977; Sir Robert Bradlaw, Faculty of Dental Surgery, RCS, 1978; Sir Ernest Finch Meml, Sheffield, 1978; Telford Meml, Manchester, 1978; Annual Oration Med. Soc. of London, 1978; Sir William MacEwen Meml, Glasgow, 1978; Eisenberg, Boston, 1978; Judd, Minneapolis, 1979; first Samuel Jason Mixter, New England Surgical Soc., 1985. Hon. Member: Soc. of Grad. Surgeons of LA County Hosp., 1965; Finnish Surgical Soc., 1976; Surgical Res. Soc., 1976; Surgical Soc. of Phoenix, Arizona; Soc. Surg. Alimentary Tract; Hellenic Surg. Soc.; Kentucky Surg. Soc., 1979; Internat. Biliary Assoc., 1977. Hon. Fellow: Amer. Assoc. Surg.; Assoc. Clin. Anat.; Surgical Res. Soc., 1977; Assoc. of Surgeons of France, 1979; Philadelphia Acad. of Surg., 1979; Acad. de Chirurgie de Paris, 1981; Hon. FRACS 1957; Hon. FRCSEd 1975; Hon. FACS 1975; Hon. FRCSCan 1976; Hon. FRCSI 1976; Hon. FRCS S Africa 1976; Hon. FDS; Hon. FRSocMed 1981; Hon. FRCSGlas 1982. Hon. DSc: Exeter, 1974; Leeds, 1976; Hon. MD Zürich Univ., 1979. Biennial Prize, Internat. Soc. of Surgery, 1975; Gimbernat Surg. Prize, Surg. Soc. of Barcelona, 1980; Gold Medal, BMA, 1982. Hon. Freeman, Worshipful Co. of Barbers. *Publications:* Acute Intestinal Obstruction, 1947; Surgery of Pancreatic Neoplasms, 1951; Progress in Clinical Surgery, 1953, 1961, 1969; (ed with C. G. Rob) Operative Surgery (8 Vols) 1956–57 (14 Vols) 1968–69; Surgery of the Gallbladder and Bile Ducts, 1965; Clinical Surgery (Vols 1–14), 1965–67; papers in learned journals on pancreatic surgery, general abdominal surgery, intestinal obstruction. *Recreations:* music, painting, cricket, golf, bridge. *Address:* 135 Harley Street, W1. *T:* 071–935 1714. *Club:* MCC.

SMITH, Alan; Executive Secretary, The Newcomen Society, since 1988; *b* 19 Jan. 1930; *s* of John Smith and Alice (*née* Williams); *m* 1958, Adele Marguerite (*née* Buckle) (marr. diss. 1986); two *s* two *d*. *Educ:* Rossall; St Catherine's Soc., Oxford. BSc Leeds 1957. MIMinE 1958. NCB, 1957–64; Principal Sci. Officer, Min. of Power, 1964; Sci. Counsellor, HM Embassy, Paris, 1965–70; Cabinet Secretariat, 1970–71; DTI, 1971–73; Dept of Industry, 1973–74; Sci. and Technol. Counsellor, HM Embassy, Washington, 1975–77; Head of Sci. and Technol. Div., OECD, 1977–80; DTI Research Gp, 1980–84. De Laune Lectr, Apothecaries' Soc., 1980. *Publications:* learned articles on steam engines. *Recreation:* engineering history. *Address:* The Newcomen Society, The Science Museum, SW7 2DD.

SMITH, Sir Alan, Kt 1982; CBE 1976; DFC 1941, and Bar 1942; DL; President, Dawson International plc, since 1982; *b* 14 March 1917; *s* of Alfred and Lilian Smith; *m* 1st, 1943, Margaret Stewart Todd (*d* 1971); three *s* two *d*; 2nd, 1977, Alice Elizabeth Moncur. *Educ:* Bede College, Sunderland. Self employed, 1931–36; Unilever Ltd, 1937–39; RAF, 1939–45; Man. Dir, Todd & Duncan Ltd, 1946–60; Chm. and Chief Exec., Dawson International, 1960–82. DL Kinross, 1967. *Recreations:* sailing, swimming. *Address:* Ardgairney House, Cleish, by Kinross, Scotland. *T:* Cleish Hills (05775) 265. *Club:* Lansdowne.

SMITH, Alan Christopher; Chief Executive, Test and County Cricket Board, since 1987; *b* 25 Oct. 1936; *s* of Herbert Sidney and Elsie Smith; *m* 1963, Anne Elizabeth Boddy; one *s* one *d*. *Educ:* King Edward's Sch., Birmingham; Brasenose Coll., Oxford (BA). Played cricket: Oxford Univ. CC, 1958–60 (Captain, 1959 and 1960); Warwicks CCC, 1958–74 (Captain, 1968–74); rep. England in six Test Matches, Australia and NZ, 1962–63. Gen. Sec., Warwicks CCC, 1976–86; England overseas cricket tours: Asst Manager, Australia, 1974–75; Manager: West Indies, 1981; Fiji, NZ and Pakistan, 1984. Mem., England Cricket Selection Cttee, 1969–73, 1982–86. Director: Royds Advertising and Marketing, 1971–86; Aston Villa Football Club plc, 1972–78. *Recreations:* both football codes, golf, bridge, motoring. *Address:* (office) TCCB, Lord's Ground, NW8 8QZ. *T:* 071–286 4405; The Bridge House, Oversley Green, Alcester, Warwicks B49 6LE. *T:* Alcester (0789) 762847. *Clubs:* MCC, I Zingari; Vincent's (Oxford).

SMITH, Alan Frederick; Group Managing Director, Anglian Water PLC, since 1990; *b* 21 July 1944; *s* of Frederick Herbert Smith and Winifred Alice Bella (*née* Farthing); *m* 1966, Judith Mary Forshaw (marr. diss. 1991); one *s* one *d*. *Educ:* Gosfield Sch., Essex. CIPFA. Trainee, Colchester BC, 1961–66; Ipswich County Borough Council: Sen. Accountant, 1966–72; Asst Treas., 1972–74; Principal Accountant, Anglian Water Authy, 1974–75; Asst Dir of Finance, Southern Water Authy, 1975–80; Dir of Finance, Anglian Water Authy, 1980–89; Dep. Man. Dir and Dir of Finance, Anglian Water PLC, 1989–90. *Recreations:* walking, photography. *Address:* Anglian House, Ambury Road, Huntingdon, Cambs PE18 6NZ.

SMITH, Alan Guy E.; *see* Elliot-Smith.

SMITH, Alan Oliver, QPM 1986; Chief Constable of Derbyshire, 1985–90; *b* 9 Sept. 1929; *s* of Thomas Allen and Lily Oliver; *m* 1950, Jane (*née* Elliott); one *d*. *Educ:* elementary schools, Birmingham; Guiseley and Bradford Tech. Coll.; courses at Police Staff Coll., 1964, 1973, 1979. Constable to Supt, Bradford City Police, 1952–74; Supt and Chief Supt, W Yorks Metropolitan Police, 1974–79; Comdt, Bishopgarth Detective Training Sch., 1977–79; Asst Chief Constable, W Yorks, 1979–83; Dep. Chief Constable, Derbyshire Constabulary, 1983–84 (Acting Chief Constable, June 1984–Dec. 1985). Vice-President: Derbys Assoc. of Boys' Clubs, 1988–; Winksworth Br. Royal British Legion, 1988–; Derby and Dist Br. RSPCA, 1988–; Chm., Ashbourne and Dovedale Br., Children's Soc., 1991–. Formerly Mem., NE Consultative Cttee, Commn for Racial Equality; Mem., Professional Adv. Cttee, NSPCC, 1980–91; Mem., St John Council for Derbyshire, 1986– (formerly Hon. County Dir, St John Ambulance, S and W Yorks). OStJ 1988. *Recreations:* landscape artist (various exhibns; works in permt collections, Calderdale Authy, Leeds City Council, Bradford Univ.). *Address:* c/o Constabulary HQ, Butterley Hall, Ripley, Derbyshire DE5 3RS.

SMITH, Alastair Macleod M.; *see* Macleod-Smith.

SMITH, Sir Alex; *see* Smith, Sir Alexander M.

SMITH, Alexander; Member (Lab) Scotland South, European Parliament, since 1989; *b* Kilwinning, 2 Dec. 1943. *Educ:* Irvine Royal Acad. Former gardener. Chm., 1983–87, Trade Union Liaison Officer, 1986–88, Cunninghame S CLP; former Chm., Irvine and District Trades Council. Member: TGWU (Mem., Regl, Public Service and Political Cttees); Scottish CND. *Address:* Damside, Ayr KA8 8ER.

SMITH, Prof. Alexander Crampton, (Alex. Crampton Smith); Nuffield Professor of Anaesthetics, Oxford University, and Fellow of Pembroke College, Oxford, 1965–79; now Emeritus Professor; *b* 15 June 1917; *s* of William and Mary Elizabeth Crampton Smith; *m* 1953, Marjorie (*née* Mason); three *s*; two *d* by a former marriage. *Educ:* Inverness Royal Acad.; Edinburgh University. Edinburgh Univ., 1935–41. Served War of 1939–45 (Croix de Guerre, despatches), RNVR, 1942–46. Consultant Anaesthetist, United Oxford Hospitals, 1951; Clinical Lectr in Anaesthetics, Oxford Univ., 1961. FFARCS 1953; MA Oxon 1961. Civilian Consultant Anaesthetist to Royal Navy, 1968. Mem. Bd, Faculty of Anaesthetists, 1965–80. Mem. Trustees, Nuffield Medical Benefaction, 1973. *Publications:* Clinical Practice and Physiology of Artificial Respiration (with J. M. K. Spalding), 1963; contribs to anaesthetic, medical and physiological jls. *Recreations:* sailing, fishing. *Address:* 10 Horwood Close, Headington, Oxford OX3 7RF. *T:* Oxford (0865) 69593.

SMITH, Sir Alexander Mair, (Sir Alex), Kt 1975; Director of various companies; *b* 15 Oct. 1922; *s* of late John S. and Anne M. Smith; *m* 1st, 1944, Muriel (*née* Harris) (*d* 1950); one *d*; 2nd, 1956, Doris Neil (*née* Patrick) (*d* 1980); one *d* (and one *d* decd); 3rd, 1984, Jennifer Lewis (*née* Pearce); two step *s*. *Educ:* Univ. of Aberdeen. MA (Maths and Nat. Phil.), PhD, FInstP. Physicist, UKAEA, 1952–56; Head of Advanced Research, Rolls Royce Ltd, 1956–67; Dir and Chief Scientist, Rolls Royce & Associates Ltd, 1967–69; Dir, Manchester Polytechnic, 1969–81. Chairman: Cttee of Dirs of Polytechnics, 1974–76; Schools Council, 1975–78; Member: UGC, 1974–76; BBC Gen. Adv. Council, 1978–81; Council, RSA, 1979–84; Vice-Pres., CGLI, 1981–; Patron, Educnl Inst. of Design, Craft and Technology, 1977–83. *Publications:* papers in learned jls. *Recreation:* golf. *Address:* 33 Parkway, Wilmslow, Cheshire. *T:* Wilmslow (0625) 522011. *Club:* Athenæum.

SMITH, Alistair; *see* Smith, E. A.

SMITH, Alwyn; *see* Smith, Ernest A.

SMITH, Andreas W.; *see* Whittam Smith.

SMITH, Andrew Charles; QC 1990; *b* 31 Dec. 1947; *s* of Charles George Smith and Winifrid Smith; *m* 1986, Indu Nathoo; one *s* two *d*. *Educ:* Wyggeston Grammar Sch. for Boys, Leicester; Wadham Coll., Oxford (BA). Called to Bar, Middle Temple, 1974. *Address:* Fountain Court, Temple, EC4. *T:* 071–583 3335.

SMITH, Andrew David; MP (Lab) Oxford East, since 1987; *b* 1 Feb. 1951; *m*; one step *s*. *Educ:* Reading Grammar Sch.; St John's Coll., Oxford. Joined Labour Party, 1973. Mem., Oxford City Council, 1976–87 (Chairman: Recreation Cttee, 1980–83; Planning Cttee, 1984–87). Opposition spokesman on higher and continuing educn, 1988–. Contested (Lab) Oxford E, 1983. Chm., Bd, Oxford Polytechnic, 1987–. *Address:* 4 Flaxfield Road, Blackbird Leys, Oxford OX4 5QD; House of Commons, SW1A 0AA. *Club:* Headington Labour (Oxford).

SMITH, Maj.-Gen. Anthony Arthur D.; *see* Denison-Smith.

SMITH, Anthony David, CBE 1987; President, Magdalen College, Oxford, since 1988; *b* 14 March 1938; *s* of Henry and Esther Smith. *Educ:* Brasenose Coll., Oxford (BA). BBC TV Current Affairs Producer, 1960–71; Fellow, St Antony's Coll., Oxford, 1971–76; Director, BFI, 1979–88 (Fellow 1988). Bd Mem., Channel Four Television Co., 1980–84. Chm., Writers and Scholars Educnl Trust, 1989– (Mem., 1982–); Member: Arts Council, 1990–; Acton Soc. Trust, 1978–; Trustee, Cambodia Trust, 1990–. *Publications:* The Shadow in the Cave: the broadcaster, the audience and the state, 1973, 2nd edn 1976; British Broadcasting, 1974; The British Press since the War, 1976; Subsidies and the Press in Europe, 1977; The Politics of Information, 1978; Television and Political Life, 1979; The Newspaper: an international history, 1979; Newspapers and Democracy, 1980; Goodbye Gutenberg—the newspaper revolution of the 1980's, 1980; The Geopolitics of Information, 1980; The Age of the Behemoths, 1991. *Address:* Magdalen College, Oxford OX1 4AU; Albany, Piccadilly, W1V 9RP. *T:* 071–734 5494. *Club:* United Oxford & Cambridge University.

SMITH, Prof. (Anthony) David, DPhil; Professor and Head of the Department of Pharmacology, University of Oxford, since 1984; Hon. Director, MRC Anatomical Neuropharmacology Unit, Oxford, since 1985; Fellow, Lady Margaret Hall, Oxford, since 1984; *b* 16 Sept. 1938; *s* of Rev. William Beddard Smith and Evelyn Smith; *m* 1st, 1962, Wendy Diana Lee (marr. diss. 1974); one *s* one *d*; 2nd, 1975, Dr Ingegerd Östman; one *s*. *Educ:* Kingswood Sch., Bath; Christ Church, Oxford (Bostock Exhibnr; BA 1963, MA 1966, DPhil 1966). Royal Soc. Stothert Res. Fellow, Oxford, 1966–70; Res. Lectr, Christ Church, Oxford, 1966–71; Wellcome Res. Fellow, Oxford, 1970–71; Univ. Lectr in Pharmacology and Student of Christ Church, 1971–84. Member: Gen. Bd of the Faculties, Oxford, 1980–84; Neurosciences Bd, MRC, 1983–88; Physiol Soc.; Pharmacol Soc. Dir of Pubns, IBRO, 1977–; Editor: Methods in the Neurosciences (IBRO Handbook Series), 1981–; Neuroscience, 1976–; Mem., editorial bds of various scientific jls. (Seventh) Gaddum Meml Prize, British Pharmacol Soc., 1979. *Publications:* (ed) Handbook of Physiology, Section 7 Vol. 6, 1974; (ed) Commentaries in the Neurosciences, 1980; articles on neuropharmacology in jls. *Recreations:* music, travel. *Address:* University Department of Pharmacology, Mansfield Road, Oxford OX1 3QT. *T:* Oxford (0865) 275162.

SMITH, Anthony (John Francis); writer, broadcaster; *b* 30 March 1926; 2nd *s* of late Hubert Smith (formerly Chief Agent, National Trust) and of Diana Watkin; *m* 1st, 1956, Barbara Dorothy Newman (marr. diss. 1983); one *s* two *d*; 2nd, 1984, Margaret Ann Holloway; one *s*. *Educ:* Dragon School, Oxford; Blundell's School, Devon; Balliol College, Oxford. MA Oxon., 1951. Served with RAF, 1944–48. Oxford University, 1948–51. Manchester Guardian, 1953 and 1956–57; Drum, Africa, 1954–55; Science Correspondent, Daily Telegraph, 1957–63. Founded British Balloon and Airship Club, 1965 (Pres., 1970–). Scientific Fellow of Zoological Society. Glaxo Award for Science Writers, 1977; Cherry Kearton Medal and Award, RGS, 1978. TV series include: Balloon Safari, Balloons over the Alps, Great Zoos of the World, Great Parks of the World, Wilderness; radio series include: A Sideways Look, 1977–89; High Street Africa Revisited, 1983–84. *Publications:* Blind White Fish in Persia, 1953, repr. 1990; Sea Never Dry, 1958; High Street Africa, 1961; Throw Out Two Hands, 1963; The Body, 1968, new edn 1985; The Seasons, 1970; The Dangerous Sort, 1970; Mato Grosso, 1971; Beside the Seaside, 1972; Good Beach Guide, 1973; The Human Pedigree, 1975; Animals on View, 1977; Wilderness, 1978; A Persian Quarter Century, 1979; A Sideways Look, 1983; The Mind, 1984; Smith & Son, 1984; Which Animal Are You?, 1988; The Great Rift, 1988; Explorers of the Amazon, 1990. *Recreations:* travel, lighter-than-air flying. *Address:* 10 Aldbourne Road, W12 0LN. *T:* 081–743 6935; St Aidan's, Bamburgh, Northumberland. *T:* Bamburgh (06684) 253.

SMITH, Ven. (Anthony Michael) Percival; Archdeacon of Maidstone, 1979–89; *b* 5 Sept. 1924; *s* of Kenneth and Audrey Smith; *m* 1950, Mildred Elizabeth; two *d*. *Educ:* Shrewsbury; Gonville and Caius Coll., Cambridge (MA); Westcott House Theological Coll. Served Army, Rifle Brigade, 1942–46. Cambridge, 1946–48; Westcott House, 1948–50. Deacon 1950, priest 1951; Curate, Holy Trinity, Leamington, 1950–53; Domestic Chaplain to Archbishop of Canterbury, 1953–57; Vicar of All Saints, Upper Norwood, 1957–66; Vicar of Yeovil, 1966–72; Prebendary of Wells Cathedral, 1968–72; RD of Murston, 1968–72; Vicar of St Mildred's, Addiscombe, Croydon, 1972–80; Hon. Canon of Canterbury Cathedral, 1980–; Diocesan Dir of Ordinands, 1980–89. *Recreations:* reading, walking. *Address:* The Garden House, Horseshoe Lane, Beckley, East Sussex TN31 6RZ. *T:* Beckley (079726) 514.

SMITH, Anthony Patrick; Chief Executive, English National Board for Nursing, Midwifery and Health Visiting, since 1990; *b* 7 Aug. 1939; *s* of Edward Smith and Gladys Smith (*née* Green); *m* 1965, Barbara Marie Johnson; one *d*. *Educ:* Latymer Sch.; Open Univ. (BA Hons); Polytechnic of Central London (MA). RGN, RMN, RNT. Asst Dir, Nurse Education, St Bartholomew's Hosp., 1969–75; Dir, Nurse Education, Southampton, 1975–81. *Recreations:* countryside, breeding labradors, Staffordshire portrait figures. *Address:* English National Board for Nursing, Midwifery and Health Visiting, Victory House, 170 Tottenham Court Road, W1P 0HA. *T:* 071–388 3131.

SMITH, Anthony Thomas; QC 1977; a Recorder of the Crown Court, since 1977; *b* 21 June 1935; *s* of Sydney Ernest Smith and Winston Victoria Smith; *m* 1959, Letitia Ann Wheldon Griffith; one *s* two *d*. *Educ:* Northampton, Stafford, and Hinckley Grammar Schs; King's Coll., Cambridge (Exhibnr; MA). Called to the Bar, Inner Temple, 1958, Bencher, 1985. Flying Officer, RAF, 1958–60. Founder and Chm., Birmingham Free Representation Scheme. *Recreations:* music, reading, the countryside. *Address:* Berkeley House, 119 Hagley Road, Edgbaston, Birmingham B16 8LB. *T:* 021–456 3796.

SMITH, Arnold Cantwell, OC 1985; CH 1975; *b* 18 Jan. 1915; *m* 1st, 1938, Evelyn Hardwick Stewart (*d* 1987); two *s* one *d*; 2nd, 1989, Frances McFarland Lee. *Educ:* Upper Canada Coll., Toronto; Lycée Champoléon, Grenoble; Univ. of Toronto; Christ Church, Oxford (Rhodes Scholar for Ont), BA Toronto, 1935; BA (Juris) Oxon 1937 (MA 1968); BCL 1938. Editor, The Baltic Times, Tallinn, Estonia, and Assoc. Prof. of Polit. Econ., Univ. of Tartu, Estonia, 1939–40; Attaché, British Legation, Tallinn, 1940; Attaché, British Embassy, Cairo, 1940–43; part-time Lectr in Polit. Sci. and Econs, Egyptian State Univ., Cairo, 1940–42; transf. to Canadian Diplomatic Service, 1943; Sec., Canadian Legation, Kuibyshev, USSR, 1943; Sec., Canadian Embassy, Moscow, 1943–45; Dept of External Affairs, Ottawa, 1946–47; Assoc. Dir, Nat. Def. Coll. of Canada, Kingston, Ont, 1947–49; Mem. Canadian Delegns to various UN Confs, 1947–51; Alternate Perm. Deleg. of Canada to UN Security Coun. and Atomic Energy Commn, 1949–50; Counsellor, Canadian Embassy, Brussels, and Head of Canadian Delegn to Inter-Allied Reparations Agency, 1950–53; Special Asst to Sec. of State for External Affairs, 1953–55; Internat. Truce Comr in Indochina, 1955–56; Canadian Minister to UK, 1956–58; Canadian Ambassador to UAR, 1958–61; Canadian Ambassador to USSR, 1961–63; Asst Under-Sec. of State for External Affairs, Ottawa, 1963–65; Secretary-General of the Commonwealth, 1965–75; Lester B. Pearson Prof. of Internat. Affairs, Carleton Univ., Ottawa, 1975–81; Montague Burton Lectr in Internat. Relations, Leeds Univ., 1982, 75th Anniv. Lectr, Univ. of Alberta, 1983. Chairman: North-South Inst.; Hudson Inst. of Canada; Internat. Peace Acad., NY; Hon. Pres., Canadian Mediterranean Inst., 1981–; Trustee: Hudson Inst., Croton, NJ, 1976–81; Cambridge Univ. Commonwealth Trust, 1982–; Governor, Newsconcern Internat. Foundn; Mem. Univ. College Cttee, Univ. of Toronto, 1982–; Life Vice-Pres., Royal Commonwealth Soc. Hon. Fellow, Lady Eaton Coll., Trent Univ. R. B. Bennett Commonwealth Prize, RSA, 1975. Hon. LLD: Ricker Coll., 1964; Queen's Univ., Kingston, Ont, 1966; Univ. of New Brunswick, 1968; Univ. of BC, 1969; Univ. of Toronto, 1969; Leeds Univ., 1975; Trent Univ., 1979; Hon. DCL: Michigan, 1966; Oxon, 1975; Bishop's Univ., 1978. Zimbabwe Independence Medal, 1980. *Publications:* Stitches in Time—the Commonwealth in World Politics, 1981; The We-They Frontier: from international relations to world politics, 1983; (with Arthur Lall) Multilateral Negotiation and Mediation—Instruments and Methods, 1985; Tisserands de l'Histoire, 1987; reports; articles in learned jls. *Recreations:* fishing, reading, travelling, farming in France. *Address:* 260 Metcalfe Street, Apt 4–B, Ottawa, Ont K2P 1R6, Canada. *T:* (613) 235.3073; 120 Rosedale Valley Road, Apt 609, Toronto, Ont M4W 1P8; (summer) Aux Anjeaux, Gavaudun, 47150 Monflanquin, France. *T:* (53) 40.94.14. *Clubs:* Athenæum; Rideau, National Press (Ottawa); University, Arts and Letters (Toronto).

SMITH, Arnold Terence, MBE 1963; HM Diplomatic Service, retired; *b* 7 Oct. 1922; *s* of Thomas Smith and Minnie Louisa (*née* Mole); *m* 1st, 1944, Mary James (*d* 1983), Preston, Yorks; one *s* one *d*; 2nd, 1985, Brenda Day (*née* Edwards), Edmonton; one step *s*. *Educ:* Christ Church, Dover; Coll. of Technol., Dover. Enlisted HM Forces, Army, 1939; served War, 1939–45; released, 1947. Joined CRO, 1948; Attaché, Karachi, 1952–56; Second Sec., Madras, 1956–60; CRO, 1960–61; First Sec., Kuala Lumpur, 1961–65; Consul, Oslo, 1965–69; FCO, 1969–73; Head of Chancery, Mbabane, 1973–77; Head of Admin, Nairobi, 1977–78; Counsellor and Consul-Gen., Lagos, Nigeria, 1978–80. *Recreations:* hiking, gardening, golf, swimming. *Address:* Flowers Cottage, Streetly End, West Wickham, Cambridgeshire CB1 6RP. *T:* Cambridge (0223) 891247.

SMITH, Ven. Arthur Cyril, VRD 1955; MA; Archdeacon of Lincoln, 1960–76, now Archdeacon Emeritus; Rector of Algarkirk, 1960–76, now Canon Emeritus; *b* 26 Jan. 1909; *s* of late Arthur Smith and of Margaret Ryde, Manchester; *m* 1940, Patricia Marion Greenwood, *d* of late Lt-Col Ranolf Nelson Greenwood, MC, and Beatrice Marion, *d* of late Rev. Llewellyn L. Montford Bebb, DD; two *s* two *d*. *Educ:* St John's College, Winnipeg, Canada; Sheffield University; Westcott House, Cambridge. Curate of: Keighley, 1934–36; Bishop's Hatfield, 1936–40. Chaplain RNVR, 1940; HMS Hawkins, 1940–41; 13th Destroyer Flotilla Gibraltar, 1941–43; HMS Eaglet, 1943–44; Senior Chaplain, Liverpool 1945–46. Rector, South Ormsby Group of Parishes, 1946–60; Rural Dean, Hill North, 1955; Canon and Prebendary of Centum Solidorum, 1960. Member: Standing Cttee, House of Clergy, Church Assembly, 1966–70; General Synod, 1970–76; Inspections Cttee, Adv. Council for Churches Ministry, 1967. Church Comr, 1968. Dir, Ecclesiastical Insurance Office Ltd. *Publications:* The South Ormsby Experiment, 1960; Deaneries: Dead or Alive, 1963; Team and Group Ministry, 1965; contributor: to Mission and Communication, 1963; to Theology; to The Caring Church, 1964. *Address:* 2 Cavendish Court, 14 Blackwater Road, Eastbourne BN21 4JD. *T:* Eastbourne (0323) 36204. *Club:* Army and Navy.

SMITH, Barry Edward, PhD; Head of AFRC Institute of Plant Science Research, Nitrogen Fixation Laboratory, since 1987; *b* 15 Nov. 1939; *s* of late Ernest Smith and Agnes Mary Smith (*née* DeFraine); *m* 1963, Pamela Heather Pullen; one *s* one *d*. *Educ:* Dr Challoner's Grammar Sch., Amersham; Royal Melbourne Tech. Coll., Australia; Hatfield Tech. Coll.; Univ. of Exeter (BSc); Univ. of East Anglia (PhD). Lab. technician, ICIANZ, 1956–59; ICI, 1959–60; res. appts, Univ. of Washington, Seattle, 1966–68, Univ. of Oxford, 1968–69; ARC, subseq. AFRC, Unit of Nitrogen Fixation, 1969–; Asst Dir, 1986–87. Vis. Prof., Univ. of Essex, 1988–; Hon. Professorial Fellow, Univ. of Sussex, 1989–. *Publications:* numerous articles in sci. jls and chapters in books on excited state chem. and on nitrogen fixation. *Address:* AFRC Institute of Plant Science Research, Nitrogen Fixation Laboratory, University of Sussex, Brighton BN1 9RQ. *T:* Brighton (0273) 678252.

SMITH, Basil Gerald P.; *see* Parsons-Smith.

SMITH, Basil Gerrard, TD 1950; *b* 29 January 1911; *m* 1938, Marjorie Elizabeth Artz; one *s* two *d*. *Educ:* Epsom College, Surrey; Merton College, Oxford (MA). Solicitor (England), 1938. War Service, 1939–46; Hon. Lt-Col. District Judge, Pahang, 1946; joined Colonial Legal Service, 1946; District Judge: Selangor, 1947; Perak, 1948; President, Sessions Court: Ipoh, 1949; Georgetown, Penang, 1950; Barrister (Gray's Inn), 1950; Federal Counsel and Deputy Public Prosecutor, 1953; Asst Legal Draftsman, 1954; Actg Legal Draftsman, 1955; Judge, Supreme Court, Federation of Malaya, 1956–60; Attorney-General, Southern Cameroons, 1960–61; Legal Adviser to the UK Commissioner, Malta, 1962–64; Legal Asst, Solicitor's Dept, Post Office, 1964, Senior Legal Assistant, 1967–69; Treasury Solicitor's Office, 1969–77; Adjudicator, Immigration Act, 1977–81. Law Reviser, Kiribati and Tuvalu, 1970, 1976, 1980 and 1981. *Address:* 7 Langley Grove, New Malden, Surrey KT3 3AL. *T:* 081–949 4366.
See also S. A. Goldstein.

SMITH, Beverley; *see* Smith, Jenkyn B.

SMITH, Brian; *see* Smith, Eric B.

SMITH, Dr Brian; *see* Smith, Dr N. B.

SMITH, Brian, OBE 1975; HM Diplomatic Service; High Commissioner to Trinidad and Tobago, since 1991; *b* 15 Sept. 1935; *s* of Charles Francis Smith and Grace Amelia (*née* Pope); *m* 1955, Joan Patricia Rivers; one *s* two *d*. *Educ:* Hull Grammar School. Foreign Office, 1952; HM Forces, 1954–57; Bahrain, 1957; Doha, 1959; Vice-Consul, Luxembourg, 1960, Casablanca, 1962; Tehran, 1964; Berne, 1967; FCO, 1969; Kampala, 1973; Tehran, 1975; FCO, 1977; New York, 1979; Counsellor (Commercial), Bonn, 1982; Overseas Inspector, FCO, 1986; High Comr, Botswana, 1989. *Recreations:* riding, photography, music, handicrafts. *Address:* c/o Foreign and Commonwealth Office, SW1A 2AH.

SMITH, Brian, IPFA; County Treasurer, Staffordshire County Council, since 1983; *b* 16 May 1947; *s* of Albert Frederick and Gladys Smith; *m* 1972, Susan Jane Lund; two *s*. *Educ:* Bristol Univ. (BA Hons). Graduate trainee accountant, Derbyshire CC, 1968; Accountancy Asst, Berkshire CC, 1972; Group Technical Officer, South Yorkshire CC, 1974; Asst County Treasurer, Dorset CC, 1976; Sen. Asst County Treasurer, Avon CC, 1979; Dep. County Treasurer, Staffordshire CC, 1981. Hon. Sec., Soc. of County Treasurers, 1990–. *Publications:* various articles in local govt finance jls. *Recreations:* music, gardening, travel. *T:* (office) Stafford (0785) 223121, ext. 6300; (home) Stafford (0785) 660085.

SMITH, Ven. Brian Arthur; Archdeacon of Craven, since 1987; *b* 15 Aug. 1943; *s* of Arthur and Doris Marion Smith; *m* 1970, Elizabeth Berring (*née* Hutchinson); two *d*. *Educ:* George Heriot's School, Edinburgh; Edinburgh Univ. (MA Mental Philosophy 1966); Fitzwilliam Coll., Cambridge (BA Theology 1968, MA 1972); Westcott House, Cambridge; Jesus Coll., Cambridge (MLitt 1973). Curate of Cuddesdon, 1972–79; Tutor in Doctrine, Cuddesdon Coll., Oxford, 1972–75; Dir of Studies, Ripon Coll., Cuddesdon, 1975–78, Senior Tutor 1978–79. Diocese of Wakefield: Priest-in-charge of Cragg Vale, 1979–85; Dir of In-Service Training, 1979–81; Dir of Ministerial Trng, 1981–87; Warden of Readers, 1981–87; Sec. of Dio. Board of Ministry, 1979–87; Hon. Canon of Wakefield, 1981–87; Proctor in Convocation, 1985–87. Vice-Chairman, Northern Ordination Course, 1985–. A Director, Scottish Jl of Theology, 1977–81. *Recreations:* browsing in junk shops, walking, reading, music, short-wave radio listening. *Address:* Brooklands, Bridge End, Long Preston, Skipton BD23 4RA. *T:* Long Preston (0729) 840334. *Club:* National Liberal.

SMITH, Ven. Brian John; Archdeacon of Wilts, since 1980; Team Vicar, Redhorn team, Salisbury, since 1990; *b* 21 Sept. 1933; *s* of Stanley and Doris Jessie Smith; *m* 1965, Jean Margaret, *d* of Frank and Beryl Hanning; one *s* two *d*. *Educ:* St Marylebone Grammar School; Mill Hill School; St John's Coll., Durham; Salisbury Theological Coll. Army, 1952–55; professional photographer, 1956–62. Ordained, 1965; Curate of All Saints', Whitstable, 1965–69; Vicar of Woodford, Wilsford and Durnford, and Religious Drama Adviser to Diocese of Salisbury, 1969–76; Vicar of Mere, West Knoyle and Maiden Bradley, 1976–80; RD of Heytesbury, 1977–80; Vicar of Bishop's Cannings, All Cannings and Etchilhampton, 1980–83; Non-residentiary Canon, Salisbury Cath., 1980–. Member: Gen. Synod of C of E, 1985–90; Council of RADIUS (Religious Drama Soc. of GB), 1971–76; various cttees, Diocese of Salisbury, 1969–; Chm., Diocesan Christian Stewardship Cttee, 1983–. Author of a number of plays. *Publication:* contrib. to Religious Drama. *Recreations:* drama, photography, canals. *Address:* The Vicarage, 57 The Street, Chirton, Devizes, Wilts SN10 3QS. *T:* Devizes (0380) 840271.

SMITH, Brian Percival, CEng, FIProdE; CBIM; independent business consultant; *b* 3 Oct. 1919; *s* of Percival Smith and Hilda Judge; *m* 1942, Phoebe (Tina) Ginno; one *s*. *Educ:* Erith, Woolwich; London Univ. (BSc). Apprentice, 1936–41, Manager, 1941–46, Royal Ordnance Factories; Gen. Manager, Cumbrian Tool Co., 1946–49; PA Management Consultants: Consultant, 1949–59; Dir, R&D, 1959–66; Man. Dir, 1966–72; Chm. of Bd, 1972–76. Mem., CAA, 1981–84. Mem., Adv. Bd, LEK Partnership, 1987–. Mem., Design Council, 1975–80; Vice-Pres., Royal Soc. of Arts, 1976–80. Prof. of Design Management, RCA, 1977–81. Member Council: BIM, 1972–74; Instn of Prod. Engrs, 1972– (Pres., 1973–74). *Publications:* Leadership in Management, 1968; Bureaucracy in Management, 1969; Management Style, 1973; Going into Europe, Why and How, 1975; The Morality and Management of Design, 1977. *Recreations:* painting, writing, listening to music. *Address:* 4 Cliff Road, Eastbourne, East Sussex BN20 7RU. *T:* Eastbourne (0323) 31870.

SMITH, Brian Stanley, FSA, FRHistS; Secretary, Royal Commission on Historical Manuscripts, since 1982; *b* 15 May 1932; *s* of late Ernest Stanley Smith and Dorothy (*née* Palmer); *m* 1963, Alison Margaret Hemming; two *d*. *Educ:* Bloxham; Keble College, Oxford (Holroyd Scholar). MA 1957. FSA 1972, FRHistS 1980. Assistant Archivist, Worcestershire, 1956–58, Essex, 1958–60, Gloucestershire, 1961–68; County Archivist, Gloucestershire, 1968–79; Asst Sec., Royal Commn on Historical Manuscripts, 1980–81. Part-time Editor, Victoria County History of Gloucestershire, 1968–70; Editor, 1971–79, Pres., 1986–87, Bristol and Gloucestershire Archaeological Soc. Chm., Soc. of Archivists, 1979–80. Mem., Cttee of Management, Inst. of Historical Res., London Univ., 1982–87. Lay Mem., Gloucester Diocesan Synod, 1972–76. FRSA 1991. *Publications:* History of Malvern, 1964, 2nd edn 1978; (with Elizabeth Ralph) History of Bristol and Gloucestershire, 1972, 2nd edn 1982; The Cotswolds, 1976; History of Bloxham School, 1978; articles in learned jls on local history and archives. *Recreations:* mountaineering, gardening. *Address:* Midwoods, Shire Lane, Cholesbury, Tring, Herts HP23 6NA.

SMITH, Maj.-Gen. Sir Brian W.; *see* Wyldbore-Smith.

SMITH, Brian William, AO 1988; PhD, FIEAust; Vice-Chancellor and Professor, University of Western Sydney, since 1989; *b* 24 June 1938; *s* of William Lyle Smith and Grace Ellen Smith; *m* 1961, Josephine Peden; two *d* (one *s* decd). *Educ:* Univ. of Melbourne (BEng); Univ. of Cambridge (PhD). Australian Paper Manufacturers Ltd, 1964–70; Consolidated Electronic Industries Ltd, 1971–73; Head, School of Electrical Engineering, 1973–77, Dean, Faculty of Engineering, 1977–79, Dir, 1979–89, Royal Melbourne Inst. of Technology. FAIM. *Recreations:* golf, model railway. *Address:* 11 Greenvale Place, Castle Hill, NSW 2154, Australia. *T:* (02) 634 6423. *Clubs:* Castle Hill Country; Greenacres Golf, Melbourne Cricket.

SMITH, Bryan Crossley, CBE 1982; CEng, FIGasE; Member for Marketing, British Gas Corporation, 1977–82; Chairman: C.S.E. (Wendover) Ltd, Business Consultants, since 1985; Sports & Fitness Assessment Ltd, since 1985; Turbine Power Ltd (formerly Power Generation), since 1988; *b* 28 Feb. 1925; *s* of Frank Riley Smith and Fanny Smith; *m* 1948, Patricia Mabbott; one *s* one *d*. *Educ:* Hipperholme Grammar Sch.; Bradford Technical Coll. CEng, FIGasE 1944. Articled pupil to John Corrigan, 1941; Operating Engr, Humphreys & Glasgow, 1944; Works Engr, Middlesbrough Corp. Gas Dept, 1948; N Eastern Gas Board: Asst Works Manager, Huddersfield, 1952; Engr and Man., Dewsbury, 1956; Group Sales Man., Wakefield, 1961; Conversion Man., 1966; Dep. Commercial Man., 1968; Chief Service Man., Gas Council, 1970; Service Dir, British Gas Corp., 1973. Senior Vice-Pres., IGasE, 1980–81. Chm., Wendover Soc., 1985–. *Recreations:* golf, gardening. *Address:* Heron Path House, Wendover, Aylesbury, Bucks HP22 6NN. *T:* Wendover (0296) 622742.

SMITH, Campbell (Sherston); retired; *b* 24 April 1906; *s* of Herbert Smith and Carlotta Amelia Smith (*née* Newbury); *m* 1st, 1936, Leonora Florence Beeney (marr. diss., 1948); one *s*; 2nd, 1948, Gwenllian Elizabeth Anne Williams (marr. diss., 1963); one *s*; 3rd, 1964, Barbara Irene Winstone. *Educ:* City of London School. General Departmental Manager, Keith Prowse & Co. Ltd, 1932, Director and General Manager, 1936. Squadron Leader, RAF, 1939–45 (Defence Medal). Assistant Managing Director, Keith Prowse & Co. Ltd, 1945, Managing Director, 1951–54; Managing Director: Mechanical Copyright Protection Soc., 1945–57; Campbell Williams Ltd, 1960–75; Director: Performing Right Society, 1951–54; MEEC Productions Ltd, 1953–62; Proprietor, Mayfair Hotel, Worthing, 1964–75. Chm., Execs Assoc. of GB, 1939–40. Administrator of the Arts Theatre Club, 1954–62: *principal productions:* Saint Joan, 1954; The Immoralist, 1954; South, 1955; Waiting for Godot, 1955; Waltz of the Toreadors, 1956; The Bald Prima Donna, 1956; No Laughing Matter, 1957; The Balcony, 1957; The Iceman Cometh, 1958; The Imperial Nightingale, 1958; Madame de . . . . ., 1959; Traveller without Luggage, 1959; Ulysses in Nighttown, 1959; A Moon for the Misbegotten, 1959; The Caretaker, 1959; The Naked Island, 1960; Three, 1961; Stop It Whoever You Are, 1961; The Knacker's Yard, 1962; Everything in the Garden, 1962. *Recreation:* theatre. *Address:* 32 Wordsworth Road, Worthing, West Sussex BN11 3NJ. *Clubs:* Garrick, Arts Theatre.

SMITH, Catharine Mary S.; *see* Scott-Smith.

SMITH, Sheriff Charles; Sheriff of Tayside, Central and Fife at Cupar and Dundee, since 1991; *b* 15 Aug. 1930; *s* of late Charles Smith and Mary Allan Hunter or Smith; *m* 1959, Janet Elizabeth Hurst; one *s* one *d*. *Educ:* Kinnoull Primary Sch.; Perth Academy; St Andrews University. MA, LLB. Solicitor 1956. Practised as principal in Perth, 1961–82; Temporary Sheriff, 1977–82; Sheriff (floating appointment): of Glasgow and Strathkelvin, 1982–86; of Tayside, Central and Fife at Perth, 1986–91. Hon. Tutor, Dept of Law, Dundee Univ., 1982–. Member Council: Law Soc. of Scotland, 1977–82 (Convener, various cttees); Sheriffs' Assoc., 1987–90. Mem., Perth Town Council, 1966–68. *Recreations:* tennis, golf, croquet. *Address:* c/o Sheriff Court, County Buildings, St Catherine Street, Cupar, Fife KY15 4LX. *Club:* Kinnoull Lawn Tennis (Kinnoull).

SMITH, Sir Charles B.; *see* Bracewell-Smith.

SMITH, Charles Russell, CBE 1984; Chairman, Allied Textile Companies PLC, 1983–91 (Chief Executive, 1963–86); Director, Lloyds Bank plc, since 1985 (Regional Chairman, Yorkshire and Humberside, 1984–91; Regional Director, 1973–91); *b* 19 Aug. 1925; *m* 1951, Jean Rita Thomas; one *s* three *d*. *Educ:* Rastrick Grammar Sch., Brighouse, W Yorks. Served War, RNVR, 1943–46 (commnd). Armitage and Norton, Chartered Accountants, Huddersfield, 1941–50; Dir, subseq. Man. Dir, R. Beanland and Co. Ltd, 1950–63. Director: Yorkshire Bank PLC, 1978–84; Lloyds Bank UK Management Ltd, 1984–85; Lloyds & Scottish PLC, 1985–86; Lloyds Abbey Life PLC (formerly Abbey Life Gp), 1988–; Lloyds Merchant Bank (Hldgs) Ltd, 1989–; Heywood Williams Gp, 1990–. Pres., British Textile Confedn, 1982 and 1983; Chm., Wakefield Diocesan Bd of Finance, 1974–90; Mem., Yorks and Humberside Regional Develt Bd, 1975–79. *Recreations:* gardening, walking. *Address:* Tabara, 12 Wheatcroft Avenue, Scarborough, North Yorks YO11 3BN. *T:* Scarborough (0723) 376266.

SMITH, Prof. (Christopher) Colin; Professor of Spanish, University of Cambridge, 1975–90; *b* 17 Sept. 1927; *s* of Alfred Edward Smith and Dorothy May Berry; *m* 1954, Ruth Margaret Barnes; three *d* (one *s* decd). *Educ:* Varndean Grammar Sch., Brighton; St Catharine's Coll., Cambridge (MA, PhD; LittD). BA 1st cl. hons 1950. Dept of Spanish, Univ. of Leeds: Asst Lectr 1953; Lectr 1956; Sen. Lectr 1964; Sub-Dean of Arts, etc, 1963–67; Cambridge Univ.: Univ. Lectr in Spanish, 1968; Fellow, St Catharine's Coll., 1968–, Professorial Fellow, 1975–90, Tutor 1970; Chm. Faculty of Mod. and Med. Langs, 1973. Hon. Vice-Consul of Spain, Cambridge, 1983–. Comendador de número de la Orden de Isabel la Católica (Spain), 1988. General Editor, Modern Language Review, 1976–81 (Hispanic Editor, 1974–81). *Publications:* Spanish Ballads, 1964; (ed) Poema de mio Cid, 1972 (Spanish edn 1976); Collins' Spanish-English, English-Spanish Dictionary, 1971 (Spanish edn 1972), 3rd edn 1992; Estudios cidianos, 1977; (with A. L. F. Rivet) Place-names of Roman Britain, 1979; The Making of the Poema de mio Cid, 1983 (Spanish edn 1985); Christians and Moors in Spain, vol. I, 1988, vol. II, 1989; contrib. Bull. Hispanic Studies, Mod. Lang. Rev., Bull. Hispanique, etc. *Recreations:* theatre, opera, natural history (especially entomology), archaeology. *Address:* 56 Girton Road, Cambridge CB3 0LL. *T:* Cambridge (0223) 276214.

SMITH, Rev. Christopher Hughes; General Secretary, Methodist Division of Education and Youth, since 1988; President of the Methodist Conference, 1985–86; *b* 30 Nov. 1929; *s* of Rev. Bernard Hughes Smith and Dorothy Lucy Smith; *m* 1956, Margaret Jean Smith; three *s* and one foster *s*. *Educ:* Bolton School; Emmanuel College and Wesley House, Cambridge. MA Cantab. Intercollegiate Sec., SCM, 1955–58; ordained at Methodist Conf., Newcastle upon Tyne, 1958; Leicester South Methodist Circuit, 1958–65; Birmingham South-West Methodist Circuit, 1965–74; Chm., Birmingham Methodist Dist, 1974–87; Lancaster Methodist Circuit, 1987–88. Hon. MA Birmingham, 1985. *Publications:* contribs to Birmingham Post, Methodist Recorder, Epworth Review. *Recreations:* gardening, music, books, walking. *Address:* 3 Hazlehyrst, 7 Colney Hatch Lane, Muswell Hill, N10 1PN. *T:* 081–883 1304.

SMITH, Christopher Robert, PhD; MP (Lab) Islington South and Finsbury, since 1983; *b* 24 July 1951; *s* of Colin Smith and Gladys (*née* Luscombe). *Educ:* Cassiobury Primary Sch., Watford; George Watson's Coll., Edinburgh; Pembroke Coll., Cambridge Univ. (BA 1st cl. hons 1972, PhD 1979); Harvard Univ., Mass (Kennedy Scholar, 1975–76). Develt Sec., Shaftesbury Soc. Housing Assoc., 1977–80; Develt Co-ordinator, Soc. for Co-operative Dwellings, 1980–83. Councillor, London Bor. of Islington, 1978–83 (Chief Whip, 1978–79; Chm., Housing Cttee, 1981–83). Opposition spokesman on treasury and economic affairs, 1987–. Chairman: Tribune Gp of MPs, 1988–89 (Sec., 1985–88); Labour Campaign for Criminal Justice, 1985–88; Bd, Tribune Newspaper, 1990–; Mem. Exec., Fabian Soc., 1990–. Pres., Cambridge Union, 1972; Vice-Chm., Young Fabian Gp, 1974–75; Chm., Charing Cross Br., ASTMS, 1980–83; Member: Exec., NCCL, 1986–88; Bd, Shelter, 1986–. Governor, Sadler's Wells Theatre, 1987–. *Recreations:* mountaineering, literature, theatre, music. *Address:* House of Commons, SW1A 0AA. *T:* 071–219 5119.

SMITH, Sir Christopher Sydney Winwood, 5th Bt, *cr* 1809; *b* 20 Sept. 1906; *s* of Sir William Sydney Winwood Smith, 4th Bt, and Caroline, *o d* of James Harris, County Cork; *S* father 1953; *m* 1932, Phyllis Berenice, *y d* of late Thomas Robert O'Grady, Grafton, New South Wales, and County Waterford, Ireland; six *s* three *d* (and one *s* decd). *Heir:* *s* Robert Sydney Winwood Smith [*b* 1939; *m* 1971, Roslyn Nellie, *e d* of late James Keith McKensie; one *s* one *d*]. *Address:* Junction Road, via Grafton, New South Wales 2460, Australia.

SMITH, Claude C.; *see* Croxton-Smith.

SMITH, Clifford Bertram Bruce H.; *see* Heathcote-Smith.

SMITH, Colin; *see* Smith, Christopher C.

SMITH, Colin; Secretary-General, International Association Against Painful Experiments on Animals, since 1969; *b* 4 July 1941; *s* of Henry E. Smith and A. E. Smith. *Educ:* Upton House Sch., London. Asst Sec., National Anti-Vivisection Soc., 1962–71, Gen. Sec., 1971–81, Internat. Exec. Dir, 1981–86; Dir, American Fund for Alternatives to Animal Res., 1977–. Mem., Hon. Nederlandse Laureat van de Arbeid, 1981. Editor, Animals' Defender and Anti-Vivisection News, 1967–72, 1982–86. *Publications:* Progress without Pain, 1973; Animal Experiments: steps towards reform, 1975; Moral and Social Aspects of Vivisection, 1981; International Charter for Health and Humane Research, 1989; numerous contribs to med. and scientific jls on the anti-vivisection case. *Recreations:* music, theatre, travel. *Address:* 29 College Place, St Albans, Herts AL3 4PU.

SMITH, Colin Milner; QC 1985; **His Honour Judge Milner Smith;** a Circuit Judge, since 1991; *b* 2 Nov. 1936; *s* of Alan Milner Smith and late Vera Ivy Smith; *m* 1979, Moira Soraya, *d* of Reginald Braybrooke; one *s* one *d*. *Educ:* Tonbridge; Brasenose College, Oxford (MA); Univ. of Chicago (JD). Called to the Bar, Gray's Inn, 1962; a Recorder, 1987–91. *Publication:* (jtly) The Law of Betting, Gaming and Lotteries, 1987. *Recreations:* cricket, skiing, reading. *Address:* 3 Gray's Inn Place, Gray's Inn, WC1R 5DU. *T:* 071–831 8441. *Club:* MCC.

SMITH, Colin Roderick, CVO 1984; QPM 1987; HM Inspector of Constabulary, since 1991; *s* of Humphrey and Marie Smith; *m* 1961, Patricia Joan Coppin. *Educ:* Dorking County and Bexhill Grammar Schools; Univ. of Birmingham (BSocSc, Hons Social Admin.); rcds 1981. Royal Army Service Corps (Lieut), 18 Co. (Amph), 1959–62; East Sussex Constabulary, later Sussex Police, from Constable to Chief Supt, 1962–77; Asst Chief Constable, Thames Valley Police, 1977–82; Dep. Asst Comr, Metropolitan Police, 1982–85 (incl. founder, Royalty and Diplomatic Protection Dept); Chief Constable, Thames Valley Police, 1985–91. *Recreation:* horse riding. *Address:* Office of Her Majesty's Inspector of Constabulary, 10th Floor, Sheaf House, The Pennine Centre, Hawley Street, Sheffield S1 3GA. *T:* Sheffield (0742) 701054. *Club:* Naval and Military.

SMITH, Colin S.; *see* Stansfield Smith.

SMITH, Sir Cyril, Kt 1988; MBE 1966; DL; MP Rochdale, since Oct. 1972 (L 1972–88, Lib Dem since 1988); Liberal Chief Whip, 1975–76; Managing Director, Smith Springs (Rochdale) Ltd, 1963–87; *b* 28 June 1928; unmarried. *Educ:* Rochdale Grammar Sch. for Boys. Civil Service, 1944–45; Wages Clerk, 1945–48; Liberal Party Agent, Stockport, 1948–50; Labour Party Agent, Ashton-under-Lyne, 1950–53, Heywood and Royton 1953–55; rejoined Liberal Party, 1967. Newsagent (own account), 1955–58; Production Controller, Spring Manufacturing, 1958–63; founded Smith Springs (Rochdale) Ltd, 1963. Director: Ratcliffe Springs, 1987–90; Robert Riley Springs; Safe Buy UK. Councillor, 1952–66, Alderman, 1966–74, Mayor, 1966–67, Co. Borough of Rochdale (Chm., Education Cttee, 1966–72); Councillor, Rochdale Metropolitan DC, 1973–75. A Dep. Pro-Chancellor, Lancaster Univ., 1978–86. DL Greater Manchester, 1991. OStJ 1976. *Publications:* Big Cyril (autobiog.), 1977; Industrial Participation, 1977. *Recreations:* music (listener), reading, charitable work, local government. *Address:* 14 Emma Street, Rochdale, Lancs OL12 6QW. *T:* Rochdale (0706) 48840.

SMITH, Cyril Robert, OBE 1945; consultant and lecturer; *b* 28 Dec. 1907; *s* of late Robert Smith and Rose Smith (*née* Sommerville); *m* 1933, Margaret Jane Kathleen Gwladys Hughes; two *s*. *Educ:* Whitgift; Queen Mary's Coll., Univ. of London. Served in Army, Europe, N Africa, 1939–45 (despatches, OBE; Col). Entered PO as Asst Traffic Supt Telephones, 1927; Asst Inspector, Telephone Traffic PO Headquarters, 1930; Asst Surveyor, Postal Services, 1935; Asst Principal, PO Headquarters, 1936; Asst Postal Controller, 1941; Instructor, PO Management Training Centre, 1954; Postal Controller, 1955; Asst Sec. i/c of Central Organisation and Methods Br., PO Headquarters, 1958; Director, Computer Development, 1965–67; Dir, National Data Processing, GPO, 1967–68. UN Advisor to Greek Govt on computers in public service, 1971–74. FBCS; FBIM. *Publications:* various papers on computer matters in Computer Jl, etc. *Address:* 64 Copse Avenue, West Wickham, Kent. *T:* 081–777 1100.

SMITH, Cyril Stanley, CBE 1985; MSc, PhD; Managing Director, ReStrat, since 1985; Secretary to Economic and Social Research Council (formerly Social Science Research Council), 1975–85; *b* 21 July 1925; *s* of Walter and Beatrice May Smith; *m* 1968, Eileen Cameron; two *d* (by first marr.). *Educ:* Plaistow Municipal Secondary Sch.; London Sch. of Economics. HM Forces, Dorset Regt, 1943–47. Univ. of Birmingham, 1950–51; Univ. of Sheffield, 1951–52; Dulwich Coll. Mission, 1952–56; Nat. Coal Board, 1956–61; Univ. of Manchester, 1961–71; Civil Service Coll., 1971–75. Visiting Prof., Univ. of Virginia, 1965; Academic Visitor, Nuffield Coll., Oxford, 1980–81, 1985–86; Senior Res. Fellow, Wissenschaftszentrum Berlin für Sozialforschung, 1987. British Nat. Expert, European Poverty Prog., 1977–82. Mem., Sec. of State's Cttee on Inequalities in Health, DHSS, 1977–80. Chm., British Sociological Assoc., 1972–74; Pres., Sociol. Sect., British Assoc., 1979. *Publications:* Adolescence, 1968; (sen. author) The Wincroft Youth Project, 1972; (ed jtly) Society and Leisure in Britain, 1973; numerous articles on youth, leisure and developments in social science. *Address:* Cornwall House, Cornwall Gardens, SW7 4AE.

SMITH, Dan; *see* Smith, T. D.

SMITH, Prof. David; *see* Smith, Prof. A. D.

SMITH, Prof. David; *see* Smith, Prof. N. J. D.

SMITH, David, PhD; FInstPet; consultant; formerly Chairman and Managing Director, Esso Chemical Ltd; *b* 18 July 1927; *s* of Walter and Annie Smith; *m* 1951, Nancy Elizabeth (*née* Hawley); two *s* three *d*. *Educ:* Burton Grammar School; Univ. of Sheffield. BSc, PhD. Lectr in Fuel Technology and Chemical Engineering, Univ. of Sheffield, 1951–55; Esso Research Ltd, 1955–65; Dir, Products Research Div., Esso Research and Engineering, USA, 1966–68; Marketing Dir and Man. Dir, Esso Chemical Ltd, 1968–71; Vice-Pres., Essochem Europe Inc., Brussels, 1971–73; Vice-Pres., Exxon Chemical Inc., USA, 1973–78. *Recreation:* golf. *Address:* Meadowlands, Stockbridge Road, Winchester, Hants SO22 5JH. *T:* Winchester (0962) 864880. *Clubs:* MCC; Royal Winchester Golf.

SMITH, Prof. David, FRS 1988; CPhys, FInstP; Professor of Chemical Physics, University of Birmingham, since 1964; *b* 26 Nov. 1935; *s* of J. and F. L. Smith. *Educ:* Keele Univ. (BA 1959); DSc 1975, PhD 1962, Birmingham Univ. FInstP 1973. Res. Fellow, Birmingham Univ., 1962. Hon. DSc Keele, 1990. *Publications:* numerous res. pubns and review articles in physics, chemistry and astrophysics, for learned jls incl. British Inst. of Physics jls and Amer. Inst. of Physics jls. *Recreations:* classical music, sport. *Address:* 8 Coln Close, Northfield, Birmingham B31 1HN. *T:* 021–476 3338.

SMITH, David Arthur, QC 1982; **His Honour Judge David Smith;** a Circuit Judge, since 1986; *b* 7 May 1938; *s* of late Arthur Heber Smith and Marjorie Edith Pounds Smith; *m* 1967, Clementine Smith (*née* Urquhart); two *s*. *Educ:* Lancing College; Merton Coll., Oxford (MA Hons Jurisprudence). Called to Bar, Middle Temple, 1962; Official Principal of Archdeaconry of Hackney, 1973–; a Recorder, 1978–86. Mem., Parole Bd, 1989–. Wine Treasurer, Western Circuit, 1980–86. *Publications:* John Evelyn's Manuscript on Bees from Elysium Britannicum, 1966; Bibliography of British Bee Books, 1979. *Recreations:* bees (Sec. of Internat. Bee Research Assoc., 1963–), books, canals, Rossini. *Address:* Bristol Crown Court, Guildhall, Bristol.

SMITH, David Arthur George, JP; Headmaster of Bradford Grammar School, since 1974; *b* 17 Dec. 1934; *o s* of Stanley George and Winifred Smith, Bath, Somerset; *m* 1957, Jennifer, *e d* of John and Rhoda Anning, Launceston, Cornwall; one *s* two *d*. *Educ:* City of Bath Boys' Sch.; Balliol Coll., Oxford. MA, Dip. Ed (Oxon). Assistant Master, Manchester Grammar Sch., 1957–62; Head of History, Rossall School, 1963–70; Headmaster, The King's School, Peterborough, 1970–74. Chm., HMC, 1988. JP West Yorks, 1975. FRSA 1985. *Publications:* (with John Thorn and Roger Lockyer) A History of England, 1961; Left and Right in Twentieth Century Europe, 1970; Russia of the Tsars, 1971. *Recreations:* writing, walking. *Address:* Bradford Grammar School, Bradford, West Yorks. *T:* Bradford (0274) 545461. *Club:* Bradford Athenæum (Bradford).

SMITH, David Buchanan, FSAScot; Sheriff of North Strathclyde at Kilmarnock, since 1975; *b* 31 Oct. 1936; *s* of William Adam Smith and Irene Mary Calderwood Hogarth; *m* 1961, Hazel Mary Sinclair; one *s* one *d* (and one *s* decd). *Educ:* Paisley Grammar Sch.; Glasgow Univ. (MA); Edinburgh Univ. (LLB). Advocate, 1961; Standing Junior Counsel to Scottish Educn Dept, 1968–75. Tutor, Faculty of Law, Univ. of Edinburgh, 1964–72. Treas., Sheriffs' Assoc., 1979–89 (archivist, 1989–); Trustee, The Scottish Curling Museum Trust, 1980–. *Publications:* Curling: an illustrated history, 1981; The Roaring Game: memories of Scottish curling, 1985; George Washington Wilson in Ayrshire, 1991; contrib. The Laws of Scotland: Stair Memorial Encyclopedia, vol. 6; articles in Scots Law Times, Juridical Rev. and newspapers. *Recreations:* history of the law and institutions of Scotland, curling, collecting curliana, music, architecture. *Address:* 72 South Beach, Troon, Ayrshire KA10 6EG. *T:* Troon (0292) 312130; Sheriff's Chambers, Sheriff Court House, Kilmarnock. *T:* Kilmarnock (0563) 20211.

SMITH, David C.; *see* Calvert-Smith.

SMITH, Sir David (Cecil), Kt 1986; FRS 1975; FRSE; Principal and Vice-Chancellor, University of Edinburgh, since 1987; *b* 21 May 1930; *s* of William John Smith and Elva Emily Smith; *m* 1965, Lesley Margaret Mollison Mutch; two *s* one *d*. *Educ:* Colston's Sch., Bristol; St Paul's Sch., London; Queen's Coll., Oxford (Browne Schol., MA, DPhil). Christopher Welch Res. Schol., Oxford, 1951–54; Swedish Inst. Schol., Uppsala Univ., 1951–52; Browne Res. Fellow, Queen's Coll., Oxford, 1956–59; Harkness Fellow, Univ. Calif, Berkeley, 1959–60; Oxford University: Univ. Lectr, Dept Agric., 1960–74; Mem., Linacre Coll., 1962–64, Hon. Fellow, 1988; Royal Soc. Res. Fellow, 1964–71, Tutorial Fellow and Tutor for Admissions, 1971–74, Hon. Fellow, 1987, Wadham Coll.; Melville Wills Prof. of Botany, 1974–80, and Dir of Biological Studies, 1977–79, Bristol Univ.; Sibthorpian Prof. of Rural Economy, and Fellow of St John's Coll., Oxford Univ., 1980–87. Vis. Prof., UCLA, 1968. Chairman: NERC Aquatic Life Scis Cttee, 1978–81; Subject Area Rev. Cttee in Biol. Sci., London Univ., 1982–86; Member: NERC Terrestrial Life Scis Cttee, 1975–78; AFRC (formerly ARC), 1982–88 (Mem. Plants and Soils Cttee, 1976–86 (Chm., 1983–86)); Consultative Bd, JCO for Res. in Agric. and Food, 1981–83; SERC Science Board, 1983–85 (Chm., SERC Biol Scis Cttee, 1981–83); Co-ordinating Cttee on Marine Sci. and Technology, 1987–91; ABRC, 1989–90. President: British Lichen Soc., 1972–74; British Mycological Soc., 1980; Soc. for Experimental Biol., 1983–85 (Vice-Pres., 1981–83); Internat. Soc. Endocytobiology, 1981–89; Royal Society: a Vice-Pres., 1978–80, 1983–87; Biological Sec., 1983–87. Bidder Lecture, Soc. for Experimental Biology, 1985; Sir Joseph Banks Lectures, Australian bicentennial, 1988; L. F. Power Meml Lecture, James Cook Univ., 1988. Editor and Trustee, New Phytologist, 1965–. FRSE 1988. Hon. DSc: Liverpool, 1986; Exeter, 1986; Hull, 1987; Aberdeen, 1990; Hon. LLD Pennsylvania, 1990; Queen's Univ., Ontario, 1991. Linnean Medal, Linnean Soc., 1989. Commendatore dell'Ordine al Merito della Repubblica Italiana, 1991. *Publications:* (with A. Douglas) The Biology of Symbiosis, 1987; various articles on symbiosis, in New Phytol., Proc. Royal Soc., Biol. Rev., etc. *Address:* Old College, University of Edinburgh, South Bridge, Edinburgh EH8 9YL. *Clubs:* Farmers'; New (Edinburgh).

SMITH, David Douglas R.; *see* Rae Smith, D. D.

SMITH, David Dury H.; *see* Hindley-Smith.

SMITH, David Grahame G.; *see* Grahame-Smith.

SMITH, Air Marshal Sir David H.; *see* Harcourt-Smith.

SMITH, David Henry; Economics Editor, The Sunday Times, since 1989; *b* 3 April 1954; *s* of Charles Henry Smith and Elizabeth Mary Smith (*née* Williams), Walsall; *m* 1980, Jane Howells, Tenby; two *s* one *d*. *Educ:* West Bromwich Grammar Sch.; UC Cardiff (BSc Econ 1st cl. hons); Worcester Coll., Oxford; Birkbeck Coll., London (MSc Econ). Economic report writer, Lloyds Bank, 1976–77; economist, Henley Centre for Forecasting, 1977–79; economics and business writer, Now! magazine, 1979–81; Asst Editor, Financial Weekly, 1981–84; Economics Corresp., The Times, 1984–89. Univ. of Wales Tassie Medallion, 1975. *Publications:* The Rise and Fall of Monetarism, 1987; Mrs Thatcher's Economics, 1988; North and South, 1989. *Recreations:* squash, tennis, occasional cricket, music. *Address:* 9 Beechhill Road, Eltham, SE9 1HJ. *T:* 081–859 1350. *Club:* St James' Squash.

SMITH, Sir David (Iser), KCVO 1990 (CVO 1977); AO 1986; BA; Official Secretary to the Governor-General of Australia, 1973–90; Secretary of the Order of Australia, 1975–90; *b* 9 Aug. 1933; *s* of late W. M. Smith; *m* 1955, June F., *d* of M. A. W. Forestier; three *s*. *Educ:* Scotch Coll., Melbourne; Melbourne Univ.; Australian National Univ., Canberra (BA). Commnd CMF, Melb. Univ. Regt, 1956. Entered Aust. Public Service, 1954; Dept of Customs and Excise, Melb., 1954–57; Trng Officer, Dept of the Interior, Canberra, 1957–58; Private Sec. to Minister for the Interior and Minister for Works, 1958–63; Exec. Asst to Sec., Dept of the Interior, 1963–66; Exec. Officer (Govt), Dept of the Interior, 1966–69; Sen. Adviser, Govt Br., Prime Minister's Dept, 1969–71; Sec., Federal Exec. Council, 1971–73; Asst Sec., Govt Br., Dept of the Prime Minister and Cabinet, 1972–73. Attached to The Queen's Household, Buckingham Palace, June-July 1975. Dist Comr, Capital Hill Dist, Scout Assoc. of Australia, 1971–74. CStJ 1974. *Recreations:* music, reading. *Address:* 15 Adamson Crescent, Wanniassa, ACT 2903, Australia. *T:* 2312324. *Club:* Commonwealth (Canberra).

SMITH, Rt. Rev. David James; *see* Maidstone, Bishop Suffragan of.

SMITH, David John Leslie, PhD; CEng, FRAeS; Assistant Under-Secretary of State (Civilian Management) (Specialists), Ministry of Defence, since 1988; *b* 8 Oct. 1938; *s* of Gertrude Mary and late Arthur George Smith; *m* 1962, Wendy Lavinia (*née* Smith); two *d*. *Educ:* Cinderford Tech. Coll.; N Glos Tech. Coll.; Coll. of Aeronautics (MSc); Univ. of London; rcds. Mech. Engrg Apprentice, Rotol Ltd, 1954–59; Nat. Gas Turbine Estabt, Min. of Aviation, 1961, Head of Turbomachinery Dept, 1973; RCDS 1979; Ministry of Defence (PE): Dir, Aircraft Mech. and Elect. Equipment, Controllerate of Aircraft, 1980–81; Head of Aero. Dept, RAE, 1981–84; Dep. Dir (Marine Technology), 1984–85, Dep. Dir (Planning), 1986–87, ARE; Hd, Defence Res. Study Team, MoD, 1988. *Publications:* contribs to learned jls on gas turbine technology and fluid mechanics. *Recreation:* garden, including exhibiting flowers. *Address:* Ministry of Defence, Pinesgate East, Lower Bristol Road, Bath BA1 5AB.

SMITH, Very Rev. David MacIntyre Bell Armour; Minister at Logie Kirk, Stirling, 1965–89; Moderator of the General Assembly of the Church of Scotland, 1985–86; *b* 5 April 1923; *s* of Frederick Smith and Matilda Shearer; *m* 1960, Mary Kulvear Cumming; three *s*. *Educ:* Monkton Combe School; Peebles High School; St Andrews Univ. (MA 1947, BD 1950; Cook and Macfarlan Scholar). Served as Pilot, RAF, 1942–45. Warrender Church, Edinburgh, 1951–60; Old Partick Parish, Glasgow, 1960–65. Member: Stirlingshire Education Cttee, 1969–79; Central Region Educn Cttee, 1986–; Chm., Church of Scotland Bd of Education, 1979–83. DUniv Stirling, 1983. *Recreations:* gardening, philately. *Address:* 28 Millar Place, Stirling FK8 1XD. *T:* Stirling (0786) 75085.

SMITH, Delia; cookery writer and broadcaster; *m* Michael Wynn Jones. Several BBC TV series; cookery writer, Evening Standard, later the Standard, 1972–85; columnist, Radio Times. Is a Roman Catholic. *Publications:* How to Cheat at Cooking, 1973; Country Fare, 1973; Recipes from Country Inns and Restaurants, 1973; Family Fare, book 1, 1973, book 2, 1974; Evening Standard Cook Book, 1974; Country recipes from "Look East", 1975; More Country Recipes from "Look East", 1976; Frugal Food, 1976; Book of Cakes, 1977; Recipes from "Look East", 1977; Food for our Times, 1978; Cookery Course, part 1, 1978, part 2, 1979, part 3, 1981, The Complete Cookery Course, 1982; A Feast for Lent, 1983; A Feast for Advent, 1983; One is Fun, 1985; (ed) Food Aid Cookery Book, 1986; A Journey into God, 1988; Delia Smith's Christmas, 1990. *Address:* c/o BBC Books, Woodlands, 80 Wood Lane, W12 0TT.

SMITH, Denis M.; *see* Mack Smith.

SMITH, Derek B.; *see* Bryce-Smith.

SMITH, Derek Cyril; Under-Secretary, Export Credits Guarantee Department, 1974–87, retired; *b* 29 Jan. 1927; *s* of Albert Cyril and Edith Mary Elizabeth Smith; *m* 1st, 1949, Ursula Kulich (marr. diss. 1967); two *d*; 2nd, 1967, Nina Munday; one *s*. *Educ:* Pinner Grammar Sch.; St Catherine's Soc., Oxford. BA Mod. History 1951. Asst Principal, Min. of Materials, 1952–55; BoT, 1955–57: Asst Private Sec., Minister of State; Private Sec., Parly Sec.; Principal, ECGD, 1958–67; Asst Sec., BoT and DTI, 1967–72: Sec. to Lord Cromer's Survey of Capital Projects Contracting Overseas; Asst Sec., ECGD, 1972–74. *Recreations:* walking, reading, model-building.

SMITH, Derek Edward H.; *see* Hill-Smith.

SMITH, Derek Frank; Consultant, World Bank, 1986–87; *b* 11 Feb. 1929; *s* of late Frank H. and Rose V. Smith; *m* 1954, Anne Carpenter; one *s* one *d*. *Educ:* Chatham House Sch., Ramsgate. Served RAF, 1947–49. Colonial Office, 1949–66: Sec., Develt and Welfare Org. in WI, 1956–58; transf. to Min. of Overseas Develt, 1966; Financial Adviser, British Develt Div. in the Caribbean, 1966–68; Principal, India Sect., ODA, 1968–72; Asst Sec., 1972; Head of Southern African Develt Div., 1972–75; Establishment Officer, 1976–78, Head of UN Dept B, 1978–79, ODA; Alternate Exec. Dir of the World Bank, and Counsellor (Overseas Develt), Washington, 1979–84. Consultant, ODA, 1985. *Address:* 3 The Close, Montreal Park, Sevenoaks, Kent TN13 2HE. *T:* Sevenoaks (0732) 452534.

SMITH, Maj.-Gen. Desmond; *see* Smith, Maj.-Gen. J. D. B.

SMITH, Desmond; *see* Smith, S. D.

SMITH, Donald Charles; a Master of the Supreme Court of Judicature (Chancery Division), 1969–73; *b* 23 Jan. 1910; *o s* of Charles Frederic Smith and Cecilia Anastasia Smith (*née* Toomey); *m* 1941, Joan Rowsell, twin *d* of Richard Norman Rowsell Blaker, MC. *Educ:* Stonyhurst College. Articled, Peacock & Goddard, Gray's Inn, 1927–31; admitted Solicitor, 1932; Solicitor with Thorold, Brodie & Bonham-Carter, Westminster, 1931–34; Legal Staff of Public Trustee Office, 1934–39; joined Chancery Registrars' Office, 1939; Chancery Registrar, 1952; Chief Registrar, 1963; first Chancery Registrar to be appointed a Master. Pres., Stonyhurst Assoc., 1969. Served in RNVR, Fleet Air Arm, 1943–46; Lieut, 1944–46. *Publications:* (Revising Editor) Atkin's Encyclopaedia of Court Forms, 1st edn, (Advisory Editor) 2nd edn; contribs to Law Jl. *Recreations:* cricket, walking, theatre, philately. *Address:* Reading Hall, Denham, Eye, Suffolk IP21 5DR. *T:* Eye (0379) 870500. *Club:* MCC.

SMITH, Ven. Donald John; Archdeacon of Sudbury, 1984–91, Emeritus, since 1991; Hon. Canon of St Edmundsbury and Ipswich, 1973–92, Emeritus, since 1991; *b* 10 April 1926; *m* 1948, Violet Olive Goss; two *s* (one *d* decd). *Educ:* Clifton Theological Coll. Asst Curate: Edgware, 1953–56; St Margaret's, Ipswich, 1956–58; Vicar of St Mary, Hornsey Rise, Islington, 1958–62; Rector of Whitton, Ipswich, 1962–75; Rector of Redgrave cum Botesdale with The Rickinghalls, 1975–79; Archdeacon of Suffolk, 1975–84. HCF 1964. *Publications:* A Confirmation Course, 1974; (ed) Tourism and the Use of Church Buildings, 1983; Covenanting for Disunity, 1981; Thank you Lord for Alison, 1987; Straightforward and Simple: a guide for churchwardens, 1989. *Recreations:* driving, foreign travel, chess, collecting Meerschaum and antiques, drama, reading, photography, gardening, caravanning, good food, dining out, pastoral reorganisation, redundant churches. *Address:* St Peter's Cottage, Stretton-on-Fosse, Moreton-in-Marsh, Glos GL56 9SE.

SMITH, Donald MacKeen; Agent General of Nova Scotia, in London, 1980–91; *b* 26 Nov. 1923; *s* of Leonard Vernard and Lena Smith (*née* MacKeen); *m* 1949, Helen Elizabeth (*d* 1987), *d* of late Lt-Col David Guildford; three *d*. *Educ:* Halifax Public Schs; King's College Sch.; Dalhousie Univ., Nova Scotia. Served Canadian Armored Corps, 1942–45; 18th Armored Car Regt, 1944–45. J. E. Morse and Co. Ltd, Halifax: salesman, 1946; Vice-Pres., Director, 1951; Pres., 1956–. Pres., Tea Council of Canada, 1975–78; Vice-Pres. and Dir, Tea and Coffee Assoc. of Canada, 1960–78. Member, Executive Council of Nova Scotia, 1960–69; MLA Nova Scotia (Halifax Citadel), 1960–70; Minister of Mines, Minister in Charge of Liquor Control Act, 1960–69. Mem., Rotary Club. *Recreations:* swimming, sailing, fishing, walking. *Address:* PO Box 442, Station M, Halifax, Nova Scotia B3J 2P8, Canada. *Clubs:* Royal Automobile; Saraguay; Halifax; Royal Nova Scotia Yacht Squadron.

SMITH, Douglas; *see* Smith, I. D.

SMITH, Douglas Boucher, CB 1982; Chairman, Advisory, Conciliation and Arbitration Service, since 1987; *b* 9 June 1932; *m* 1956, Mary Barbara Tarran. *Educ:* Leeds Modern Sch.; Leeds Univ. Entered Ministry of Labour, 1953; successively: Private Sec. to Minister of Labour, 1967–68; to First Sec. of State and Sec. of State for Employment and Productivity, 1968–70; to Sec. of State for Employment, 1970–71; Chief Conciliation Officer, 1971–74, Under Secretary: Dept of Employment, 1974–77; Cabinet Office, 1977–79; Dep. Sec., Dept of Employment, 1979–87. *Address:* 17 Dundas Close, Bracknell, Berkshire RG12 4BX. *T:* Bracknell (0344) 54573. *Club:* Athenæum.

SMITH, Ven. Douglas Leslie B.; *see* Bartles-Smith.

SMITH, Drew; *see* Smith, F. D.

SMITH, Sir Dudley (Gordon), Kt 1983; DL; MP (C) Warwick and Leamington, since 1968 (Brentford and Chiswick, 1959–66); *b* 14 Nov. 1926; *o s* of late Hugh William and Florence Elizabeth Smith, Cambridge; 1st marr. diss.; one *s* two *d*; *m* 2nd, 1976, Catherine Amos, *o d* of late Mr and Mrs Thomas Amos, Liverpool. *Educ:* Chichester High Sch., Sussex. Worked for various provincial and national newspapers, as journalist and senior executive, 1943–66; Asst News Editor, Sunday Express, 1953–59. Vice-Chm. Southgate Conservative Assoc., 1958–59; CC Middlesex, 1958–65. Chief Whip of Majority Group, 1961–63. A Divl Dir, Beecham Group, 1966–70; Management Consultant. Contested (C) Camberwell-Peckham, General Election, 1955. PPS to Sec. for Tech. Co-operation, 1963–64; an Opposition Whip, 1964–66; an Opposition Spokesman on Employment and Productivity, 1969–70; Parliamentary Under-Secretary of State: Dept of Employment, 1970–74; (Army) MoD, 1974. Vice Chm., Parly Select Cttee on Race Relations and Immigration, 1974–79. UK delegate to Council of Europe and WEU, 1979– (Sec.-Gen., European Democratic Group, 1983–; Chm., WEU Defence Cttee, 1989–). Promoted Town and Country Planning (Amendment) Act, 1977, as a private member. Governor, Mill Hill Sch., 1958–89; Chm., United & Cecil Club, 1975–80. Freeman, City of London; Liveryman, Horners' Co. DL Warwickshire, 1988. *Publications:* Harold Wilson: A Critical Biography, 1964; etc. *Recreations:* books, travel, music, wild life and wilderness preservation. *Address:* Church Farm, Weston-under-Wetherley, near Leamington Spa, Warwicks. *T:* Marton (0926) 632 352.

SMITH, Dugal N.; *see* Nisbet-Smith.

SMITH, Dr (Edward) Alistair, CBE 1982; Director—North America, University of Aberdeen International Office, since 1989; *b* 16 Jan. 1939; *s* of Archibald Smith and Jean Milne Johnston. *Educ:* Aberdeen Grammar Sch.; Univ. of Aberdeen (MA, PhD); Univ. of Uppsala, Sweden. Lectr, Univ. of Aberdeen, 1963–88. Dir, Univ. of Aberdeen Develt Trust, 1982–90; Mem., Grampian Health Bd, 1983–91. Pres., Scottish Conservative and Unionist Assoc., 1979–81; Dep. Chm., Scottish Conservative Party, 1981–85. Member: Exec., Aberdeen and NE Council on Disability; Exec., Grampian ASH; Scottish Cttee, 1989–91, NE Scotland Regl Bd, 1991–, NCC; SCOTVEC, 1989–. *Publications:* (with R. E. H. Mellor) Europe: a geographical survey of the Continent, 1979; articles on Scandinavia, Europe and Scotland. *Recreations:* travel, photography, music. *Address:* 68A Beaconsfield Place, Aberdeen AB2 4AJ. *T:* Aberdeen (0224) 642932.

SMITH, Eileen S.; *see* Stamers-Smith.

SMITH, Emma; Author; *b* 1923; *m* 1951, Richard Stewart-Jones (*d* 1957); one *s* one *d*. *Publications:* Maidens' Trip, 1948 (awarded John Llewellyn Rhys Memorial Prize, 1948); The Far Cry, 1949 (awarded James Tait Black Memorial Prize, 1949); Emily, 1959; Out of Hand, 1963; Emily's Voyage, 1966; No Way of Telling, 1972; The Opportunity of a Lifetime, 1978. *Address:* c/o Curtis Brown, 162–168 Regent Street, W1R 5TB.

SMITH, (Eric) Brian, PhD, DSc; FRSC; Master, St Catherine's College, Oxford, since 1988 (Vice-Master, 1984–85); *b* 10 Oct. 1933; *s* of Eric Smith and Dilys Olwen (*née* Hughes); *m* 1st, 1957, Margaret Barr (marr. diss. 1978); two *s* one *d*; 2nd, 1983, Regina Arvidson Ball; two step *d*. *Educ:* Alun Grammar Sch., Mold; Wirral Grammar Sch.; Univ. of Liverpool (BSc; PhD 1957); MA Oxon 1960, DSc Oxon 1988. FRSC 1981. Res. Associate, Univ. of Calif, Berkeley, 1957–59; ICI Fellow, Oxford Univ., 1959–60; Fellow, St Catherine's Coll., and Lectr in Physical Chemistry, Univ. of Oxford, 1960–88. Vis. Prof., Univ. of Calif, Riverside, 1967; Vis. Lectr, Stanford Univ., 1983, 1984 and 1985; Priestley Lectr, RSC, 1986. Chm., Thermodynamics and Statistical Mechanics Section, RSC, 1979–83; Member: Southern Regional Council for Further Educn, 1965–76; Gen. Bd of Faculties, Oxford Univ., 1980– (Chm., 1985–87); Hebdomadal Council, Oxford Univ., 1985–. Pott's Medal, Univ. of Liverpool, 1969. *Publications:* (jtly) Virial Coefficients of Pure Gases and Mixtures, 1969, 2nd edn 1980; Basic Chemical Thermodynamics, 1973, 4th edn 1990; (jtly) Intermolecular Forces: origin and determination, 1981; (jtly) Forces between Molecules, 1986; papers in scientific jls. *Recreation:* mountaineering. *Address:* St Catherine's College, Oxford OX1 3UJ. *T:* Oxford (0865) 249541. *Clubs:* Alpine; Gorphwysfa.

SMITH, Eric John R.; *see* Radley-Smith.

SMITH, Eric Norman, CMG 1976; HM Diplomatic Service, retired; British High Commissioner in The Gambia, 1979–81; *b* 28 Jan. 1922; *s* of late Arthur Sidney David Smith; *m* 1955, Mary Gillian Horrocks. *Educ:* Colfe's Sch., London. Served War, Royal Corps of Signals, 1941–46. Foreign Office, 1947–53; HM Embassy, Cairo, 1953–55; UK Delegn to the UN, New York, 1955–57; FO, 1957–60; HM Embassy, Tehran, 1960–64; FO, 1964–68; British Information Services, New York, 1968–71; FCO, 1971–75; Singapore, 1975–79. *Recreations:* music, photography. *Address:* Kilsby, Llanwrtyd Wells, Powys LD5 4TL.

SMITH, Prof. (Ernest) Alwyn, CBE 1986; PhD; Professor of Epidemiology and Social Oncology, University of Manchester, 1979–90; *b* 9 Nov. 1925; *s* of Ernest Smith and Constance Barbara Smith; *m* 1950, Doreen Preston; one *s* one *d*. *Educ:* Queen Mary's Sch., Walsall; Birmingham Univ. MB, PhD; FRCP 1970; FRCGP 1973; FFCM 1974. Served War, RM, 1943–46. Res. Fellow in Social Medicine, Birmingham Univ., 1952–55; WHO Vis. Lectr, Univ. of Malaya, 1956–58; Lectr, Univ. of St. Andrews, 1959–61; Sen. Lectr. Univ. of Edinburgh, 1961–66; First Dir, Social Paediatric Res. Gp, Glasgow, 1966–67; Prof. of Community Medicine, Univ. of Manchester, 1967–79. Pres., FCM, 1981–86. *Publications:* Genetics in Medicine, 1966; The Science of Social Medicine, 1968; (ed) Cancer Control, 1979; (ed) Recent Advances in Community Medicine, 1982; papers on epidemiological subjects in Lancet, British Jl of Epidemiol., etc. *Recreations:* music, bird watching, sailing. *Address:* Plum Tree Cottage, Arnside, Cumbria, via Carnforth LA5 0AH. *T:* Carnforth (0524) 761976.

SMITH, E(rnest) Lester, DSc; FRS 1957; formerly Consultant, Glaxo Laboratories, Greenford; *b* 7 August 1904; *s* of Lester and Rose Smith; *m* 1931, Winifred R. Fitch; no *c*. *Educ:* Wood Green County School; Chelsea Polytechnic. Joined Glaxo Laboratories, 1926, as first post after graduation. Various posts in development, Fine Chemical Production (Head), then Biochemical Research. Shared responsibility for production of penicillin during War of 1939–45; isolation of vitamin B_{12} accomplished, 1948. *Publications:* Vitamin B_{12} (in series of Biochemical Monographs), 1960, 3rd edn 1965; Intelligence Came First, 1975, 2nd edn 1990; Our Last Adventure, 1982; Inner Adventures, 1988; numerous research papers in various scientific journals, 1927–. *Recreations:* horticulture, classical music. *Address:* Tinkers, Kingshall Green, Bradfield St George, Suffolk IP30 0BA.

SMITH, Sir Ewart; *see* Smith, Sir Frank Ewart.

SMITH, Maj.-Gen. Sir (Francis) Brian W.; *see* Wyldbore-Smith.

SMITH, Sir Francis Graham-, Kt 1986; FRS 1970; Langworthy Professor of Physics, Manchester University, 1987–90, now Emeritus (Professor of Radio Astronomy, 1964–74 and 1981–87); Director, Nuffield Radio Astronomy Laboratories, 1981–88; Astronomer Royal, 1982–90; *b* 25 April 1923; *s* of Claud Henry and Cicely Winifred Smith; *m* 1945, Dorothy Elizabeth (*née* Palmer); three *s* one *d*. *Educ:* Epsom Coll.; Rossall Sch.; Downing Coll., Cambridge. Nat. Sci. Tripos, Downing Coll., 1941–43 and 1946–47; PhD Cantab 1952. Telecommunications Research Estab., Malvern, 1943–46; Cavendish Lab., 1947–64; 1851 Exhibr 1951–52; Warren Research Fellow of Royal Soc., 1959–64; Fellow of Downing Coll., 1953–64, Hon. Fellow 1970; Dir-Designate, 1974–75, Dir, 1976–81, Royal Greenwich Observatory. Vis. Prof. of Astronomy, Univ. of Sussex, 1975. Sec., Royal Astronomical Soc., 1964–71, Pres., 1975–77. Mem. Council and Physical Sec., 1988–, Vice-Pres., 1990–, Royal Soc.; Hon. DSc: QUB, 1986; Keele, 1987; Birmingham, 1989; TCD, 1990; Nottingham, 1990. Royal Medal, Royal Soc., 1987; Glazebrook Medal, Inst. of Physics, 1991. *Publications:* Radio Astronomy, 1960; (with J. H. Thomson)

Optics, 1971; Pulsars, 1977; (with Sir Bernard Lovell) Pathways to the Universe, 1988; (with A. G. Lyne) Pulsar Astronomy, 1990; papers in Monthly Notices of RAS, Nature and other scientific jls. *Recreations:* sailing, walking. *Address:* Nuffield Radio Astronomy Laboratories, Jodrell Bank, Macclesfield, Cheshire SK11 9DL; Old School House, Henbury, Macclesfield, Cheshire SK11 9PH.

SMITH, Rev. Francis Taylor; Minister of St Paul's Parish Church, Dunfermline, since 1964; *b* 22 Jan. 1933; *s* of James William Smith and Jeannie Moir Catto Cockburn; *m* 1957, Jean Millar Wallace; three *s* one *d*. *Educ:* Aberdeen Grammar Sch.; Aberdeen Univ. (MA); Christ's Coll., Aberdeen (Licence to Preach). Student Assistant: Queen's Cross Church, Aberdeen, 1954–56; North Church, Aberdeen, 1956–57; Sen. Asst, Govan Old Church, Glasgow, 1957–58; Parish Minister, Aberlour, Banffshire, 1958–64. Chaplain: Dunfermline and West Fife Hosp., 1964–; Dunfermline Maternity Hosp., 1988–; Moderator of Presbytery, 1973–74. Councillor, Banff CC, 1964; Chairman, West Fife Local Health Council, 1975–84; Vice-Pres., Assoc. of Scottish Local Health Councils, 1978–79, Pres., 1980, 1981; Crown Lay Nominee, General Medical Council, 1979–89. Chm., Fife Marriage Counselling Service, 1984–85. Governor, Aberlour Orphanage, 1964. *Recreations:* work, music, fishing, shooting, reading. *Address:* St Paul's Manse, 6 Park Avenue, Dunfermline, Fife KY12 7HX. *T:* Dunfermline (0383) 721124.

SMITH, Sir (Frank) Ewart, Kt 1946; MA; FRS 1957; FEng; Hon. FIMechE; FIChemE; a past Deputy Chairman, Imperial Chemical Industries, Ltd; *b* 31 May 1897; *s* of late Richard Sidney Smith; *m* 1924, Kathleen Winifred (*d* 1978), *d* of late H. Rudd Dawes; one *d* (one *s* decd). *Educ:* Christ's Hospital; Sidney Sussex College, Cambridge (Scholar, 1st Class Mech. Science Tripos, John Winbolt Prizeman). War service, 1916–19, RA; ICI Ltd, Billingham Works in various engineering and managerial posts, 1923–42; chief engineer, 1932–42; Chief Engineer and Supt of Armament Design, Ministry of Supply, 1942–45; Formerly Member: Advisory Council on Scientific Policy; Scientific Advisory Council of Ministry of Works and Ministry of Fuel and Power; British Productivity Council, Cttee on Scientific Manpower; Chairman, National Health Service Advisory Council for Management Efficiency (England and Wales), etc. Hon. Fellow Sidney Sussex College; Hon. Member, City and Guilds of London Institute; Hon. FIMS; Hon. Associate, Univ. of Aston. James Clayton Prize, IMechE. American Medal of Freedom with Palm, 1946. *Publications:* various technical papers. *Recreation:* gardening. *Address:* Parkhill Cottage, Sandy Lane, Watersfield, Pulborough, W Sussex RH20 1NF. *T:* Bury (0798) 831354.

SMITH, Prof. Frank Thomas, FRS 1984; Goldsmid Professor of Applied Mathematics in the University of London, at University College London, since 1984; *b* 24 Feb. 1948; *s* of Leslie Maxwell Smith and Catherine Matilda Smith; *m* 1972, Valerie Sheila (*née* Hearn); three *d*. *Educ:* Bournemouth Grammar Sch.; Jesus Coll., Oxford (BA; DPhil); University College London. Research Fellow in Theoretical Aerodynamics Unit, Southampton, 1972–73; Lectr in Maths Dept, Imperial Coll., London, 1973–78; Vis. Scientist, Applied Mathematics Dept, Univ. of Western Ontario, Canada, 1978–79; Reader in Maths Dept, 1979–83, Prof. in Maths, 1983–84, Imperial Coll., London. *Publications:* on applied mathematics, fluid mechanics, computing and natural sciences, in jls. *Recreations:* the family, reading, music, sport. *Address:* Mathematics Department, University College, Gower Street, WC1E 6BT. *T:* 071–387 7050.

SMITH, Frank William G.; *see* Glaves-Smith.

SMITH, (Fraser) Drew; Publishing Director, Alfresco Leisure Publications, since 1990; *b* 30 March 1950; *s* of Frank and Beatrice Smith; *m* 1988, Susan Maloney; one *s* one *d*. *Educ:* Westminster School. Worked on Student magazine, 1967; IPC magazines, 1969–72; Westminster Press Newspapers, 1972–81. Editor, Good Food Guide, 1982–88; launched: Good Food Directory, 1985; Budget Good Food Guide, 1986–88; Head of Media Develt, Dir's Office, Consumers' Assoc., 1988–90. Columnist, Guardian, 1982–. Chm., Guild of Food Writers, 1990. Restaurant Writer of the Year, 1981, 1988. *Publication:* Modern Cooking, 1990. *Recreations:* walking, music, cooking, people. *Address:* Alfresco, 35 Tadema Road, SW10; Kins Cottage, Foxley Manor, Foxley, Wilts SN16 0JJ.

SMITH, Prof. Frederick Viggers; Professor of Psychology, University of Durham, 1950–77, now Emeritus; *b* Hamilton, New South Wales, 24 Jan. 1912; *s* of Frederick Thomas Smith and Agnes (*née* Viggers); unmarried. *Educ:* Newcastle (NSW) High School; Sydney and London Universities. BA 1938, MA 1941, Lithgow Schol., Sydney; PhD London 1948. FBPsS, 1950 (Pres., British Psychological Society, 1959–60). Research Office, Dept of Educ., NSW, 1936; Lecturer in Psychology, The Teachers' Coll., Sydney, 1938; Lectr, Birkbeck Coll., Univ. of London, 1946; Lectr, Univ. of Aberdeen, 1948. Visiting Prof., Cornell Univ., USA, 1957, Christchurch and Wellington Univs, NZ, 1960. Consultant, Council of Europe Sub-Cttee on Crime Problems, 1973; Unesco Consultant, Univ. of Riyadh, 1973. Hon. Research Associate, Univ. of Newcastle, NSW, 1980. *Publications:* The Child's Point of View (Sydney), 1946 (under pseudonym Victor Southward); Explanation of Human Behaviour (London), 1951, 1960; Attachment of the Young: Imprinting and Other Developments, 1969; Purpose in Animal Behaviour, 1971; papers to psychological and philosophical jls. *Recreations:* mountain walking, swimming, photography, music, golf. *Address:* 58 Harbourside Haven, Shoal Bay, Port Stephens, NSW 2315, Australia.

SMITH, Sir Geoffrey J.; *see* Johnson Smith.

SMITH, Geoffrey M.; *see* Maitland Smith.

SMITH, Prof. George, MBE 1945; FRSE 1979; Chief of Surgery, Veterans' Administration Hospital, Fayetteville, North Carolina, since 1982; Consultant Professor of Surgery, Duke University Medical Centre, since 1984; Regius Professor of Surgery, University of Aberdeen, 1962–82, now Emeritus; *b* 4 June 1919; *s* of late John Shand Smith and Lilimina Myles Mathers Smith; *m* 1951, Vivienne Marie Tuck, BA, Wooster, Ohio, USA, *d* of Rev. Robert Sidney Tuck, DD; two *s* one *d*. *Educ:* Grove Academy; Queen's College, Univ. of St Andrews. MB, ChB (St Andrews) 1942; MD (Hons) 1957, ChM (Hons) 1959; DSc (Glasgow) 1964; FRFP&S (Glasgow) 1949; FRCS (Edinburgh) 1949; FACS 1958; FACCP 1963; FInstBiol 1963. Commonwealth Fund Fellow, 1949–51 (Johns Hopkins, Columbia and Western Reserve Medical Schools). Formerly Reader in Cardiovascular Surgery, Univ. of Glasgow; Dean of Medicine, Aberdeen Univ., 1974–76, Dir, Inst. of Environmental and Offshore Med., 1975–78. Chm., NE Region Med. Postgrad. Cttee; Civil Consultant in surgery to RN; Governor: Robert Gordon's Colleges; Amer. Coll. of Chest Physicians. Mason: Scottish Rite, 32°; York Rite; Knight Templar; Sudan Shrine. *Publications:* (ed jtly) Resuscitation and Cardiac Pacing, 1965; The Biology of Affluence, 1972; The Staphylococci, 1981; (ed) Proceedings, 6th International Congress on Hyperbaric Medicine, 1979; sections in books and some 300 papers, mainly on cardio-vascular, respiratory, bacteriological and educnl topics. *Recreations:* sailing, gardening, golf. *Address:* 110 Ann Street, Beaufort, N Carolina 28516, USA. *T:* 919 728 7274. *Clubs:* Naval; RNVR (Glasgow); Fort Bragg Officers (Fayetteville).

SMITH, George; formerly Director-General of Ordnance Factories (Finance), 1972–76; *b* 13 Dec. 1914; *s* of George Smith and Catherine Annie Smith (*née* Ashby); *m* 1939, Alice May Smith; two *s*. *Educ:* Alderman Newton's Sch., Leicester. FCCA. Various posts in industry, 1929–40; joined Min. of Supply, 1940, various posts in Royal Ordnance factories, 1940–52; Asst Dir of Ordnance Factories (Accounts), 1952; Civil Asst, ROF Woolwich, 1958; Dir of Ordnance Factories (Accounts), 1962. *Recreations:* gardening, walking, bowls. *Address:* 14 Blenheim Gardens, Sanderstead, Surrey. *T:* 081–657 5826.

SMITH, (George) Neil, CMG 1987; HM Diplomatic Service; Ambassador to Finland, since 1989; *b* 12 July 1936; *s* of George Smith and Ena (*née* Hill); *m* 1956, Elvi Vappu Hämäläinen; one *s* one *d*. *Educ:* King Edward VII Sch., Sheffield. Joined HM Foreign (subseq. Diplomatic) Service, 1953; served RAF, 1954–56; Foreign Office, 1957; Rangoon, 1958–61; 2nd Sec., Berne, 1961–65; Diplomatic Service Administration, 1965–66; 1st Sec., CO, 1966–68; British Mil. Govt, Berlin, 1969–73; FCO, 1973–77; Counsellor (Commercial), Helsinki, 1977–80; Consul-Gen., Zürich and Principality of Liechtenstein, 1980–85; Head of Trade Relations and Export Dept, FCO, 1985–87; RCDS, 1988. *Recreations:* music, golf. *Address:* c/o Foreign and Commonwealth Office, SW1. *Club:* Travellers'.

SMITH, Prof. Gerald Stanton; Professor of Russian, University of Oxford, and Fellow of New College, since 1986; *b* 17 April 1938; *s* of Thomas Arthur Smith and Ruth Annie Stanton; *m* 1st, 1961, Frances Wetherill (marr. diss. 1981); one *s* one *d*; 2nd, 1982, Barbara Heldt; one step *s* one step *d*. *Educ:* Stretford Grammar Sch.; Sch. of Slavonic and E European Studies, Univ. of London (BA 1964; PhD 1977). Lectr in Russian, Univ. of Nottingham, 1964–71, Univ. of Birmingham, 1971–79; Univ. Research Fellow, Univ. of Liverpool, 1980–82. Visiting Professor: Indiana Univ., 1984; Univ. of California, Berkeley, 1984; Private Scholar, Social Scis and Humanities Res. Council, Canada, 1985; John Simon Guggenheim Meml Fellow, 1986. *Publications:* (ed) Alexander Galich, Songs and Poems, 1983; Songs to Seven Strings, 1984; Russian Inside and Out, 1989; (ed) D. S. Mirsky, Uncollected Writings on Russian Literature, 1989; papers in learned jls. *Recreation:* jazz music. *Address:* Taylor Institution, The University, Oxford OX1 3NA. *T:* Oxford (0865) 270476.

SMITH, Gerard Thomas C.; *see* Corley Smith.

SMITH, Sir Gilbert; *see* Smith, Sir T. G.

SMITH, Godfrey; writer; *b* 12 May 1926; *s* of Reginald Montague Smith and Ada May Smith (*née* Damen); *m* 1951, Mary, *d* of Jakub Schoenfeld, formerly of Vienna; three *d*. *Educ:* Surbiton County Sch.; Eggar's Grammar Sch.; Worcester Coll., Oxford (MA; Pres. of Oxford Union Soc. 1950). RAF, 1944–47. Joined Sunday Times as PA to Lord Kemsley, 1951; News Editor, 1956; Asst Editor, 1959; Editor, Magazine, 1965–72, Associate Editor, 1972–91; Editor, Weekly Review, 1972–79; columnist, 1979–; Director, 1968–81. Regent's Lectr, Univ. of California, 1970. *Publications: novels:* The Flaw in the Crystal, 1954; The Friends, 1957; The Business of Loving, 1961 (Book Society Choice); The Network, 1965; Caviare, 1976; *non-fiction:* The English Companion, 1984; The English Season, 1987; The English Reader, 1988; *anthologies:* The Best of Nat Gubbins, 1978; A World of Love, 1982; Beyond the Tingle Quotient, 1982; How it Was in the War, 1989; Take the Ball and Run, 1991. *Recreation:* chums. *Address:* Village Farmhouse, Charlton, Malmesbury, Wilts SN16 9DL. *T:* Malmesbury (0666) 822479; 10 Kensington Park Mews, W11 2EY. *T:* 071–727 4155. *Clubs:* Garrick, Savile, MCC; Leander.

SMITH, Gordon E.; *see* Etherington-Smith.

SMITH, Gordon Edward C.; *see* Connell-Smith.

SMITH, Prof. Hamilton Othanel, FRSE; Professor of Molecular Biology and Genetics, Johns Hopkins University School of Medicine, Maryland, USA, since 1981; *b* 23 Aug. 1931; *s* of Bunnie Othanel Smith and Tommie Harkey Smith; *m* 1957, Elizabeth Anne Bolton; four *s* one *d*. *Educ:* Univ. of Illinois; Univ. of California (AB); Johns Hopkins Univ. Sch. of Medicine (MD). FRSE 1991. Research Associate, Dept of Human Genetics, Univ. of Michigan, 1964–67; Asst Prof. of Microbiology, 1967–69, Associate Prof. of Microbiology, 1969–73, Prof. of Microbiology, 1973–81, Johns Hopkins Univ. Sch. of Medicine. During sabbatical leave in Zürich, worked in collaboration with Prof. Dr M. L. Birnstiel, Inst. für Molekularbiologie II der Univ. Zürich, July 1975–June 1976. Nobel Prize in Medicine (jtly), 1978. *Publications:* A restriction enzyme from *Hemophilus influenzae:* I. Purification and general properties (with K. W. Wilcox), in Jl Mol. Biol. *51*, 379, 1970; A restriction enzyme from *Hemophilus influenzae:* II. Base sequence of the recognition site (with T. J. Kelly), in Jl Mol. Biol. *51*, 393, 1970. *Recreations:* piano, classical music. *Address:* Department of Molecular Biology and Genetics, Johns Hopkins University School of Medicine, 725 N Wolfe Street, Baltimore, Maryland 21205, USA. *T:* (301) 955–3650.

SMITH, Prof. Harry, PhD, DSc; FRCPath; FRS 1979; FIBiol; Professor and Head, Department of Microbiology, University of Birmingham, 1965–88, now Emeritus Professor; *b* 7 Aug. 1921; *s* of Harry and Annie Smith; *m* 1947, Janet Mary Holmes; one *s* one *d*. *Educ:* Northampton Grammar Sch.; University Coll. (of London) at Nottingham. BPharm, BScChem (1st Cl. Hons), PhD, DSc London. Analyst, Boots Pure Drug Co., Nottingham, 1942–45; Asst Lectr, then Lectr, Dept of Chemistry, UCL at Nottingham, 1945–47; Microbiological Research Establishment, Porton: Sen. Scientific Officer, 1947; Principal Sci. Officer, 1951; Sen. Prin. Sci. Officer (Research Merit), 1956; Dep. Chief Sci. Officer (Res. Merit), 1964. Visiting Professor: Dept of Bacteriology, Univ. of Calif, Berkeley, USA, 1964, UCLA, 1972; (summer) Dept of Microbiol., Univ. of Washington, Seattle, USA, 1977, Univ. of Michigan, Ann Arbor, 1981, TCD, 1991. Society for General Microbiology: Mem. Council, 1960–64; Meetings Sec., 1964–68; Treas., 1968–75; Pres., 1975–78; Hon. Mem., 1986; Treas., Fedn of Europ. Microbiol Socs, 1975–82; Pres. and Chm., Organising Cttee, 14th (1986) Internat. Congress of Microbiology, Manchester. Member: Adv. Cttee on Dangerous Pathogens, 1985–88; PHLS Bd, 1985–89; Council, Royal Soc., 1989–; Assessor, AFRC, 1990–. Lectures: Amer. Soc. for Microbiol., 1984; Australian Soc. for Microbiol., 1985; Fred Griffith, Soc. for Gen. Microbiol., 1989; Leeuvenhoek, Royal Soc., 1991. Hon. MRCP 1986. *Publications:* over 250 papers in jls and books, mainly on mechanisms of microbial (bacterial, viral and fungal) pathogenicity. *Recreation:* interest in farming. *Address:* The Medical School, University of Birmingham, Birmingham B15 2TT. *T:* 021–472 1311 (ext. 4514). *Club:* Athenæum.

SMITH, Harvey; *see* Smith, R. H.

SMITH, Hedworth Cunningham, CBE 1972; Chairman: Medical Appeal Tribunals, England and Scotland, 1973–84; Pensions Appeal Tribunals, England, 1973–85; Judge of the Supreme Court of the Bahama Islands, 1965–72, retired; *b* 12 May 1912; *s* of James Smith and Elizabeth (*née* Brown); unmarried. *Educ:* George Watson's Coll., Edinburgh; Edinburgh University. MA 1933; LLB 1936. Solicitor, Scotland, 1937–40; Barrister-at-Law, Gray's Inn, London, 1950. Served War of 1939–45: commnd 1940; Staff Officer, GHQ India Command, 1943–46 (Major). District Magistrate, 1946, Senior District Magistrate, 1950, Gold Coast; Judge of Supreme Court of Ghana, 1957; retd from Ghana Govt service, 1961; Legal Adviser, Unilever Ltd Gp of Cos in Ghana, 1962–64. *Recreation:*

golf. *Address:* The Old (Police) House, Main Street, Aberlady, E Lothian. *T:* Aberlady (08757) 420. *Clubs:* East India, Devonshire, Sports and Public Schools; Kilspindie Golf.

SMITH, Helen Sylvester, MA; Headmistress, Perse School for Girls, Cambridge, since 1989; *b* 7 Jan. 1942; *d* of late S. J. Smith and of K. R. Smith. *Educ:* King Edward VI High Sch. for Girls, Birmingham; St Hilda's College, Oxford (BA 1963, MA 1967 Maths); Hughes Hall, Cambridge (PGCE 1964). Cheltenham Ladies' College, 1964–69; International School of Brussels, 1969–71; Perse Sch. for Girls, 1971– (Dep. Head, 1979–82, 1988–89). FRSA. *Recreations:* music, gardening. *Address:* 6A Cavendish Avenue, Cambridge CB1 4US. *T:* Cambridge (0223) 249200.

SMITH, Prof. Henry Sidney, FBA 1985; Edwards Professor of Egyptology, 1970–86, Head of Department of Egyptology, 1970–88, University College London, now Professor Emeritus; *b* 14 June 1928; *s* of Prof. Sidney Smith, FBA, and of Mary, *d* of H. W. Parker; *m* 1961, Hazel Flory Leeper (*d* 1991). *Educ:* Merchant Taylors' Sch., Northwood; Christ's Coll., Cambridge (MA); DLit London, 1987. Lectr in Egyptology, Univ. of Cambridge, 1954–63; Budge Fellow in Egyptology, Christ's Coll., Cambridge, 1955–63; Reader in Egyptian Archaeology, University Coll. London, 1963–70. Field Dir for Egypt Exploration Soc. in Nubia, 1961, 1964–65, and at Saqqara and Memphis, Egypt, 1970–88. *Publications:* Preliminary Reports of the Egypt Exploration Society's Nubian Survey, 1962; A Visit to Ancient Egypt, 1974; The Fortress of Buhen: the inscriptions, 1976; The Fortress of Buhen: the archaeological report, 1979; (with W. J. Tait) Saqqara Demotic Papyri I, 1983; (with D. G. Jeffreys) The Anubieion at Saqqara, Vol. I, 1988; articles in Kush, Jl of Egyptian Arch., Orientalia, Rev. d'Egyptologie, Bull. Inst. Français d'Arch. Or., Z für Äg. Sprache und Altertümskunde, etc. *Address:* Ailwyn House, Upwood, Huntingdon, Cambs PE17 1QE.

SMITH, Sir Howard (Frank Trayton), GCMG 1981 (KCMG 1976; CMG 1966); HM Diplomatic Service, retired; *b* 15 Oct. 1919; *m* 1st, 1943, Winifred Mary Cropper (*d* 1982); one *d*; 2nd, 1983, Mary Penney. *Educ:* Sidney Sussex Coll., Cambridge. Employed in FO, 1939; apptd Foreign Service, 1946. Served Oslo; transf. Washington, 2nd Sec. (Inf.) 1950; 1st Sec., Dec. 1950; 1st Sec. and Consul, Caracas, 1953; FO, 1956; Counsellor: Moscow, 1961–63; Foreign Office, 1964–68; Ambassador to Czechoslovakia, 1968–71; UK Rep. in NI, 1971–72; Dep. Sec., Cabinet Office, on secondment, 1972–75; Ambassador in Moscow, 1976–78. *Club:* Travellers'.
See also R. M. J. Lyne.

SMITH, Iain-Mór L.; *see* Lindsay-Smith.

SMITH, Ian Douglas, GCLM 1979; ID 1970; MP (Cons. Alliance, formerly Republican Front), Zimbabwe, since 1980; *b* 8 April 1919; *m* Janet Watt; two *s* one *d*. *Educ:* Selukwe Sch.; Chaplin Sch., Gwelo, S Rhodesia (now Zimbabwe); Rhodes Univ., Grahamstown, S Africa. Served War of 1939–45 in 237 (Rhodesia) Sqdn and 130 Sqdn, RAF. Farmer. Member: Southern Rhodesia Legislative Assembly, 1948–53; Parliament of Fedn of Rhodesia & Nyasaland, 1953–61; former Chief Whip (United Federal Party), 1958; resigned from United Federal Party, 1961; Foundn Mem. and Vice-Pres., Republican Front (formerly Rhodesian Front), 1962, President, 1964–87; Dep. Prime Minister and Minister of the Treasury, S Rhodesia, 1962–64; Prime Minister of Rhodesia, 1964–79; delivered Rhodesia's Unilateral Declaration of Independence, Nov. 1965; Minister Without Portfolio in Bishop Muzorewa's Govt, 1979; Mem., Transitional Exec. Council to prepare for transfer of power in Rhodesia, 1978–79. *Address:* Gwenoro Farm, Shurugwi, Zimbabwe; Box 8198, Causeway, Harare, Zimbabwe; (office) House of Assembly, Harare, Zimbabwe. *Clubs:* Harare, Harare Sports (Zimbabwe).

SMITH, Ivor Otterbein, CMG 1963; OBE 1952; retired as Chairman of Public Service and Police Service Commissions and Member of Judicial Service Commission, British Guiana (1961–66); *b* Georgetown, British Guiana, 13 Dec. 1907; *s* of late Bryce Otterbein Smith and Florette Maud Smith (*née* Chapman); *m* 1936, Leila Muriel Fowler; one *s* two *d*. *Educ:* Queen's Coll., British Guiana; Pitman's Commercial Coll., London. Joined Brit. Guiana CS, as Clerical Asst, Treas., 1925; Sec. Commissioners of Currency, 1933; Asst Dist. Comr, 1941; Private Sec. to Gov., 1943; Dist Comr, 1945; Comr, Cayman Is, 1946–52; Dep. Comr of Local Govt, Brit. Guiana, 1953; Governor's Sec., and Clerk Exec. Coun., 1956; Dep. Chief Sec., 1960; Acted as Chief Sec. on several occasions and was Officer Administering the Govt, Sept.-Oct. 1960. Served with S Caribbean Force, 1941–43; Major, Staff Officer, Brit. Guiana Garrison. Hon. Col, British Guiana Volunteer Force, 1962–66. Chm., Nat. Sports Coun, 1962–66. *Recreations:* tennis; interested in sports of all kinds; rep. Brit. Guiana at Association and Rugby football, cricket, hockey. *Address:* Suite No 606, 460 Westview Street, Coquitlam, BC V3K 6C9, Canada.

SMITH, Prof. Ivor Ramsay, FEng 1988; Pro-Vice-Chancellor, since 1987, and Professor of Electrical Power Engineering, since 1974, Loughborough University of Technology; *b* 8 Oct. 1929; *s* of Howard Smith and Elsie Emily Smith; *m* 1962, Pamela Mary Voake; three *s*. *Educ:* Univ. of Bristol (BSc, PhD, DSc), CEng, FIEE 1974. Design and Develt Engr, GEC, Birmingham, 1956–59; Lectr, Sen. Lectr, Reader, Univ. of Birmingham, 1959–74; Loughborough Univ. of Technology: Hd, Dept of Electronic and Electrical Engrg, 1980–90; Dean of Engrg, 1983–86. Director: Loughborough Consultants Ltd, 1980–; E Midlands Regl Technology Network, 1989–. *Publications:* about 150 technical papers and articles on range of power engrg topics, incl. the efficient computation of power supply systems and the prodn and processing of large pulses of energy. *Recreations:* gardening, walking, reading. *Address:* Department of Electronic and Electrical Engineering, Loughborough University of Technology, Loughborough, Leics LE11 3TU. *T:* Loughborough (0509) 222801.

SMITH, Jack, ARCA 1952; artist; *b* 18 June 1928; *s* of John Edward and Laura Smith; *m* 1956, Susan Craigie Halkett. *Educ:* Sheffield College of Art; St Martin's School of Art; Royal College of Art. Exhibitions: Whitechapel Art Gallery, 1959, 1971; Beaux Arts Gallery, 1952–58; Matthiesen Gallery, 1960, 1963; Catherine Viviano Gallery, New York, 1958, 1961; Pittsburgh International, 1955, 1957, 1964; Grosvenor Gallery, 1965; Marlborough Gallery, 1968; Konsthallen, Gothenburg, Sweden, 1968; Hull Univ., 1969; Bear Lane Gallery, Oxford, 1970; Whitechapel Gall., 1970; Redfern Gall., 1973 and 1976; Serpentine Gall., 1978; Fischer Fine Art, London, 1981, 1983; British Painting, Museo Municipal, Madrid, 1983; Flowers East Gall., London, 1990, 1991. Designer, sets and costumes: Carmen Arcadiae Mechanicae Perpetuum, Ballet Rambert, 1986; Pursuit, Royal Ballet, 1987. Guggenheim Award (Nat.), 1960. Work in permanent collections: Tate Gallery; Arts Council of Great Britain; Contemporary Art Society; British Council. *Address:* 29 Seafield Road, Hove, Sussex BN3 2TP. *T:* Brighton (0273) 738312.

SMITH, Jack Stanley, CMG 1970; Professor, and Chairman, Graduate School of Business Administration, University of Melbourne, 1973–77, retired; *b* 13 July 1916; *s* of C. P. T. Smith, Avoca, Victoria; *m* 1940, Nancy, *d* of J. C. Beckley, Melbourne; one *s* two *d*. *Educ:* Ballarat Grammar Sch.; Melbourne Univ. Construction Engineer, Australasian Petroleum Co., 1938–41. Served in Australian Imperial Forces, 1942–45, Lieut. Project Engineer, Melbourne & Metropolitan Bd of Works, 1946–48. P.A. Management Consultants, UK and Australia, 1949–72, Managing Dir, 1964–72. Hon. LLD Melbourne, 1987. *Recreations:* golf, tennis. *Address:* 15 Glyndebourne Avenue, Toorak, Victoria 3142, Australia. *T:* 822 4581. *Clubs:* Melbourne (Melbourne); Lawn Tennis Association of Victoria, Metropolitan Golf (Vic.).

SMITH, James Aikman, TD; Sheriff of Lothian and Borders (formerly the Lothians and Peebles) at Edinburgh, 1968–76; Hon. Sheriff, 1976; *b* 13 June 1914; *s* of Rev. W. J. Smith, DD; *m* 1947, Ann, *d* of Norman A. Millar, FRICS, Glasgow; three *d*. *Educ:* Glasgow Academy; The Queen's Coll., Oxford; Edinburgh Univ. BA (Oxford) 1936; LLB (Edinburgh) 1939; Mem. of Faculty of Advocates, 1939. Served War of 1939–45 (despatches): Royal Artillery, 1939–46; Lt-Col 1944. Sheriff-Substitute: of Renfrew and Argyll, 1948–52; of Roxburgh, Berwick and Selkirk, 1952–57; of Aberdeen, Kincardine and Banff, 1957–68. Pres., Sheriffs-Substitute Assoc., 1969; Pres., Sheriffs' Assoc., 1971–72. Member Departmental Cttee on Probation Service, 1959–62. Chm., Edinburgh and E of Scotland Br., English-Speaking Union, 1971. Bronze Star (US), 1945. *Publications:* occasional articles in legal journals. *Address:* 16 Murrayfield Avenue, Edinburgh EH12 6AX. *Club:* New (Edinburgh).

SMITH, Hon. Sir James (Alfred), Kt 1979; CBE 1964; TD; President of Court of Appeal for Belize, 1984–89; Member of the Court of Appeal for Turks and Caicos Islands, 1981–89; *b* Llandyssul, Cardiganshire, 11 May 1913; *s* of late Charles Silas and Elizabeth Smith (*née* Williams), Timberdine, Lampeter, Cardiganshire. *Educ:* Christ Coll., Brecon. Solicitor of the Supreme Court, 1937; called to the Bar, Lincoln's Inn, 1949. Served War of 1939–45: various Army Staff appointments; on staff of Supreme Allied Commander, South-East Asia, with rank of Major, 1944–45. Appointed to Colonial Legal Service, as Resident Magistrate, Nigeria, 1946; Chief Magistrate, 1951; Chief Registrar of the Supreme Court, Nigeria, 1953; Puisne Judge, Nigeria, 1955; Judge, High Court, Northern Nigeria, 1955; Senior Puisne Judge, High Court, N Nigeria, 1960–65; Puisne Judge, Supreme Court, Bahamas, 1965–75, Sen. Justice, 1975–78, Chief Justice, 1978–80; Justice of Appeal: for Bermuda, 1980–84; for Bahamas, 1981–83; for Belize, 1981–84. Pres., Commn of Inquiry into transshipment of drugs through Bahamas to USA, 1983–84. *Address:* PO Box CB 11508, Cable Beach, Nassau, Bahamas. *Clubs:* Naval and Military; Lyford Cay (Nassau).

SMITH, James Andrew Buchan, CBE 1959; DSc; FRSE 1952; retired as Director of the Hannah Dairy Research Institute, Ayr, Scotland, 1951–70 (Acting Director, 1948–51); *b* 26 May 1906; *yr s* of late Dr James Fleming Smith, JP, MB, CM, Whithorn, Wigtownshire; *m* 1933, Elizabeth Marion, *d* of James Kerr, Wallasey, Cheshire; four *d*. *Educ:* Leamington College, Warwicks; Univ. of Birmingham. PhD (Birmingham) 1929; DSc (London) 1940. Graduate Research Asst: at UCL, 1929–30; at Imperial College, London, 1930–32; Lectr in Biochemistry, Univ. of Liverpool, 1932–36; Biochemist, Hannah Dairy Research Inst., 1936–46; Lectr in Biochemistry, Univ. of Glasgow, 1946–47. President: Society of Dairy Technology, 1951–52; Nutrition Society, 1968–71; Treasurer, Internat. Union of Nutritional Sciences, 1969–75. Hon. LLD Glasgow, 1972. *Publications:* scientific papers in Biochemical Jl, Jl of Dairy Research, Proc. Nutrition Soc., etc. *Recreation:* gardening. *Address:* Flaxton House, 1 St Leonard's Road, Ayr KA7 2PR. *T:* Ayr (0292) 264865. *Club:* Farmers'.

SMITH, James Archibald Bruce, CBE 1981; British Council Representative, Indonesia, 1978–83; *b* 12 Sept. 1929; *s* of James Thom Smith and Anna Tyrie; *m* 1957, Anne Elizabeth Whittle; three *d*. *Educ:* Forfar Acad.; Edinburgh Univ. (MA 1952); Sch. of Econs, Dundee (BScEcon 1953); Jesus Coll., Cambridge. RAF, 1953–55. HMOCS, Dist Officer, Kenya, 1956–62; British Council, 1962–83: Asst, Edinburgh, 1962–65; Asst Rep., Tanzania, 1965–66; Reg. Dir, Kumasi, Ghana, 1966–69; Rep., Sierra Leone, 1969–72; seconded to ODM, 1973–75; Dir, Personnel Dept, 1975–77; Controller, Personnel and Staff Recruitment Div., 1977–78. *Recreations:* Angusiana, reading, walking, collecting. *Address:* Calluna, West Hemming Street, Letham, Angus. *T:* Forfar (0307) 81212.

SMITH, James Cadzow, CBE 1989; DRC; FEng 1988; FIMechE, FIEE, FIMarE; FRSE 1981; Chairman and Chief Executive, Eastern Electricity plc, since 1990; *b* 28 Nov. 1927; *s* of James Smith and Margaret Ann Cadzow; *m* 1954, Moira Barrie Hogg; one *s* one *d*. *Educ:* Bellvue Secondary Sch.; Heriot-Watt Coll.; Strathclyde Univ. Engineer Officer, Mercantile Marine, 1948–53; engineering and managerial appts in fossil and nuclear power generation with SSEB and CEGB, 1953–73; Director of Engineering, N Ireland Electricity Service, 1973–74; Deputy Chairman and Chief Executive, 1975–77; Chairman: E Midlands Electricity Bd, 1977–82; Eastern Electricity Bd, 1982–90. Vis. Prof., Strathclyde Univ. Pres., IEE, 1989–90. Freeman, 1984; Liveryman, 1984, Mem. Ct of Assistants, 1991–, Engineers' Co. Hon. LLD Strathclyde, 1988. *Recreations:* music, drama, mountaineering. *Address:* c/o Eastern Electricity plc, Wherstead Park, PO Box 40, Wherstead, Ipswich IP9 2AQ. *T:* Ipswich (0473) 688688.

SMITH, Maj.-Gen. (James) Desmond (Blaise), CBE 1944; DSO 1944; CD 1948; Chairman: Blaise Investments Ltd; Desmond Smith Investments Ltd; Dashabel Properties and Interiors Ltd; Member, Commonwealth War Graves Commission, since 1986; *b* 7 Oct. 1911; *s* of William George Smith, Ottawa, Canada; *m* 1st, 1937, Miriam Irene Blackburn (*d* 1969); two *s*; 2nd, 1979, Mrs Belle Shenkman, Ottawa. *Educ:* Ottawa University, Canada; Royal Military College, Canada. Joined Canadian Army, Royal Canadian Dragoons, 1933; National Defence HQ, Ottawa, as Assistant Field Officer in Bde Waiting to Governor-General of Canada, 1939. Served War of 1939–45, in England, Italy and N W Europe holding following commands and appts: CO Royal Canadian Dragoons; Comdr: 4th Cdn Armoured Bde; 5th Cdn Armoured Bde; 1st Cdn Inf. Bde: 5th Cdn Armoured Div.; 1st Cdn Inf. Div.; Chief of Staff, 1st Cdn Corps. Comdt Canadian Army Staff Coll., 1946; Imp. Defence Coll., 1947; Sec. Chiefs of Staff Cttee, 1948–50; Military Sec. Cdn Cabinet Defence Cttee, 1948–50; QMG, Canadian Army, 1951; Chairman, Canadian Joint Staff, London, 1951–54; Commandant, National Defence College of Canada, 1954–58; Adjutant-General of the Canadian Army, 1958–62. Colonel, HM Regt of Canadian Guards, 1961–66. Director, numerous cos; Chm. and Chief Exec. Officer, Pillar Engineering Ltd, 1966–82 (Queen's Award for Export Achievement, 1979); Dir, RTZ Pillar, 1973–82. Vice Pres., Engrg Assoc. of GB, 1974–77; Chairman: Nat. Export Cttee, EIA, 1977–81; Nat. Engrg Marketing Award Cttee, 1978–81; Sec. Gen., Canada Meml Foundn, 1988–90. Freedom, City of London, 1954. Croix de Guerre, 1944, Chevalier, Legion of Honour, 1944 (France); Comdr Military Order of Italy, 1944; Officer Legion of Merit (USA), 1944; Order of Valour (Greece), 1945. KStJ 1961 (CStJ 1952); KLJ 1985. *Recreations:* shooting, tennis, ski-ing, painting. *Address:* 50 Albert Court, SW7 2BH. *Clubs:* Mark's, Annabel's, Harry's Bar.

SMITH, James Ian, CB 1974; Member, Panel of Chairmen, Civil Service Selection Board, since 1984; *b* 22 April 1924; *s* of late James Smith, Ballater, Aberdeenshire, and of Agnes Michie; *m* 1947, Pearl Myra Fraser; one *s*. *Educ:* Alderman Newton's Sch., Leicester; St Andrews Univ. Served War of 1939–45: India and Burma; RA (attached Indian Mountain Artillery), Lieut, 1943–46. Entered Dept of Agriculture for Scotland, 1949; Private Sec. to Parly Under-Sec. of State, Scottish Office, 1953; Dept of Agriculture for Scotland: Principal, 1953; Asst Sec., 1959; Asst Sec., Scottish Development Dept, 1965–67; Under-

Sec., Dept of Agriculture and Fisheries for Scotland, 1967–72; Sec., Dept of Agriculture and Fisheries for Scotland, 1972–84. Mem., ARC, 1967–72, 1983–84; Mem., Potato Marketing Bd, 1985–87. Mem., St Andrews Links Trust, 1985–90 (Chm., 1989–90). *Recreation:* golf. *Address:* 7 Hillpark Loan, Edinburgh EH4 7ST. *T:* 031–336 4652. *Club:* Commonwealth Trust.

SMITH, Janet (B.) A.; *see* Adam Smith.

SMITH, Janet Hilary, (Mrs R. E. A. Mathieson); QC 1986; a Recorder, since 1988; *b* 29 Nov. 1940; *d* of Alexander Roe and Margaret Holt; *m* 1st, 1959, Edward Stuart Smith; two *s* one *d*; 2nd, 1984, Robin Edward Alexander Mathieson. *Educ:* Bolton School. Called to the Bar, Lincoln's Inn, 1972. Mem., Criminal Injuries Compensation Bd, 1988–. *Recreations:* gardening, music. *Address:* (chambers) 5 Essex Court, Temple, EC4Y 9AH; 25 Byrom Street, Manchester. *T:* 061–834 5238.

SMITH, Prof. (Jenkyn) Beverley, FRHistS; Sir John Williams Professor of Welsh History, University College of Wales, Aberystwyth, since 1986; Commissioner since 1984, Chairman since 1991, Royal Commission on Ancient and Historical Monuments for Wales; *b* 27 Sept. 1931; *s* of Cecil Nelson Smith and Hannah Jane (*née* Jenkins); *m* 1970, Llinos Olwen Wyn Vaughan; two *s*. *Educ:* Gowerton Grammar Sch.; UCW, Aberystwyth (BA, MA). FRHistS 1967. National Service, 1954–56. Researcher, Bd of Celtic Studies, Univ. of Wales, 1956–58; Asst Keeper, Dept of MSS and Records, Nat. Library of Wales, 1958–60; Lectr 1960–67, Sen. Lectr 1967–78, Reader 1978–86, Dept of Welsh History, UCW. Sir John Rhys Vis. Fellow, Univ. of Oxford, 1978–79. Member: Court and Council, Nat. Library of Wales, 1974–84; Bd of Celtic Studies, Univ. of Wales, 1965–91 (Sec., History and Law Cttee, 1979–85, Chm 1985–91). Jt Editor, Bulletin of Bd of Celtic Studies, 1972–91. *Publications:* Llywelyn ap Gruffudd, Tywysog Cymru, 1986; (ed) Medieval Welsh Society, Selected Essayss by T. Jones Pierce, 1972; (ed with G. H. Jenkins) Politics and Society in Wales 1840–1922, 1988; articles in English Hist. Review, Welsh Hist. Review, Bulletin Bd of Celtic Studies and other jls. *Recreations:* walking, Welsh terriers. *Address:* Department of Welsh History, University College of Wales, Aberystwyth, Dyfed SY23 3DY.

SMITH, Jeremy Fox Eric; DL; Chairman, Smith St Aubyn (Holdings) plc, 1973–86, retired; *b* 17 Nov. 1928; *s* of late Captain E. C. E. Smith, MC, and B. H. Smith (*née* Williams); *m* 1953, Julia Mary Rona, *d* of Sir Walter Burrell, 8th Bt, CBE, TD; two *s* two *d*. *Educ:* Eton; New College, Oxford. Chairman, Transparent Paper Ltd, 1965–76. Chairman, London Discount Market Assoc., 1978–80. DL 1988, High Sheriff, 1992–93, West Sussex. *Recreations:* hunting, shooting, stalking, skiing. *Address:* The Old Rectory, Slaugham, Haywards Heath, W Sussex RH17 6AG. *T:* Handcross (0444) 400341. *Clubs:* Beefsteak, Cavalry and Guards; Leander (Henley on Thames).

See also Duchess of Grafton, Sir J. L. E. Smith, Earl of Verulam.

SMITH, Jeremy James Russell; Chief Executive, London Borough of Camden, since 1990; *b* 12 June 1947; *s* of Horace James Smith and Joan Alistair Russell. *Educ:* Peterhouse, Cambridge (BA Law 1968). Called to the Bar, Lincoln's Inn, 1969; Barrister, 1971–78; Sen. Legal Adviser, Brent Community Law Centre, 1978–83; Legal Services Liaison Officer, GLC, 1983–86; Clerk and Legal Advr, ILEA, 1986–89; Dir of Law and Admin, London Borough of Camden, 1989–90. *Recreations:* history, current affairs, music, rambling. *Address:* London Borough of Camden, Town Hall, Euston Road, NW1 2RU. *T:* 071–860 5686.

SMITH, Jock; *see* Smith, John M. M.

SMITH, Dr John, OBE 1945; TD 1950; Deputy Chief Medical Officer, Scottish Home and Health Department, 1963–75, retired; *b* 13 July 1913; *e s* of late John Smith, DL, JP, Glasgow and Symington, and Agnes Smith; *m* 1942, Elizabeth Fleming (*d* 1981), twin *d* of late A. F. Wylie, Giffnock; three *s* one *d* (and one *s* decd). *Educ:* High Sch., Glasgow; Sedbergh Sch.; Christ's Coll., Cambridge; Glasgow Univ. BA 1935; MA 1943; MB, BChir Cantab 1938; MB, ChB Glasgow 1938; MRCPG 1965; FRCPG 1967; FRCPE 1969; FFPHM (FFCM 1972). TA (RA from 1935, RAMC from 1940); War Service, 1939–46; ADMS Second Army, DDMS (Ops and Plans) 21 Army Group (despatches); OC 155 (Lowland) Fd Amb., 1950–53; ADMS 52 (Lowland) Div., 1953–56; Hon. Col 52 Div. Medical Service, 1961–67. House appts Glasgow Victoria and Western Infirmaries; joined Dept of Health for Scotland, 1947; Medical Supt, Glasgow Victoria Hosps, 1955–58; rejoined Dept of Health for Scotland, 1958; specialised in hospital planning. QHP 1971–74. Officier, Ordre de Leopold I (Belgium), 1947. *Publications:* articles on medical administration and hospital services in various medical jls. *Recreations:* rifle shooting (shot in Scottish and TA representative teams); hill walking, gardening. *Address:* Murrayfield, Biggar, Lanarkshire ML12 6HA. *T:* Biggar (0899) 20036. *Clubs:* Naval and Military; New (Edinburgh).

See also Sir R. C. Smith.

SMITH, Rt. Hon. John, PC 1978; QC (Scot.) 1983; MP (Lab) Monklands East, since 1983 (Lanarkshire North, 1970–83); *b* 13 Sept. 1938; *s* of late Archibald Leitch Smith and of Sarah Cameron Smith; *m* 1967, Elizabeth Margaret Bennett; three *d*. *Educ:* Dunoon Grammar Sch.; Glasgow Univ. (MA, LLB). Advocate, Scottish Bar, 1967–. Contested East Fife, 1961 by-election and 1964. PPS to Sec. of State for Scotland, Feb.-Oct. 1974; Parly Under-Sec. of State, 1974–75, Minister of State, 1975–76, Dept of Energy; Minister of State, Privy Council Office, 1976–78; Sec. of State for Trade, 1978–79; principal Opposition Spokesman on Trade, Prices and Consumer Protection, 1979–82, on Energy, 1982–83, on Employment, 1983–84, on Trade and Industry, 1984–87, on Treasury and Economic Affairs, 1987–. Nat. Pres., Industrial Common Ownership Movement, 1988–. Vice-Chm., GB-USSR Assoc., 1985–. Gov., Ditchley Foundn, 1987–. Winner, Observer Mace, Nat. Debating Tournament, 1962. *Recreations:* opera, hill-walking. *Address:* 21 Cluny Drive, Edinburgh EH10 6DW. *T:* 031–447 3667.

SMITH, John Alfred, QPM 1986; Deputy Commisssioner of the Metropolitan Police, since 1991; *b* 21 Sept. 1938; *s* of Ruth Alice and Alfred Joseph Smith; *m* 1960, Joan Maria Smith; one *s* one *d*. *Educ:* St Olave's and St Saviour's Grammar School. Irish Guards, 1959–62. Metropolitan Police, 1962; Head, Scotland Yard drugs squad, 1979; Commander 'P' (Bromley–Lewisham) Dist., 1980; Dep. Chief Constable, Surrey Constabulary, 1981; Metropolitan Police: Dep. Asst Comr, 1984; Inspectorate and Force Reorganisation Team, 1985; Asst Comr, 1987–90; Management Support Dept, 1987–89; Specialist Ops Dept, 1989–90; Inspector of Constabulary for SE England, 1990–91. *Recreations:* gardening, sport spectating, horse riding. *Address:* New Scotland Yard, SW1. *T:* 071–230 3737. *Club:* Crystal Palace Football.

SMITH, Prof. John Cyril, CBE 1983; QC 1979; FBA 1973; Professor of Law in the University of Nottingham 1958–87, now Emeritus, and Head of Department of Law 1956–74, and 1977–86; *b* 15 Jan. 1922; 2nd *s* of Bernard and Madeline Smith; *m* 1957, Shirley Ann Walters; two *s* one *d*. *Educ:* St Mary's Grammar Sch., Darlington; Downing Coll., Cambridge (Hon. Fellow, 1977). Served Royal Artillery, 1942–47 (Captain). BA 1949, LLB 1950, MA 1954, LLD 1975 Cantab. Called to Bar, Lincoln's Inn, 1950; Hon. Bencher, 1977; Hon. Mem., Midland and Oxford Circuit Bar Mess. Nottingham University: Assistant Lecturer in Law, 1950–52; Lecturer, 1952–56; Reader, 1956–57; Pro-Vice-Chancellor, 1973–77; Hon. Pres. of Convocation, 1978–87. Arthur Goodhart Vis. Prof. in Legal Science, Cambridge, 1989–90. Commonwealth Fund Fellow, Harvard Law Sch., 1952–53. Member: Criminal Law Revision Cttee, 1977– (co-opted, 1960–66 (theft reference) and 1970–77); Policy Adv. Cttee, 1975–85. Pres., Soc. of Public Teachers of Law, 1979–80. Hon. LLD: Sheffield, 1984; Nottingham, 1989. *Publications:* (with J. A. C. Thomas) A Casebook on Contract, 1957, 8th edn 1987; (with Brian Hogan) Criminal Law, 1965, 6th edn 1988; Law of Theft, 1968, 6th edn 1989; Criminal Law, Cases and Materials, 1975, 4th edn 1990; (with I. H. Dennis and E. J. Griew) Codification of the Criminal Law, 1985; Justification and Excuse in the Criminal Law (Hamlyn Lectures), 1989; Contract, 1989. *Recreations:* walking, gardening. *Address:* 445 Derby Road, Lenton, Nottingham NG7 2EB. *T:* Nottingham (0602) 782323.

SMITH, John Derek, MA, PhD; FRS 1976; Member of Scientific Staff, Medical Research Council, Laboratory of Molecular Biology, Cambridge, 1962–88; *b* 8 Dec. 1924; *s* of Richard Ernest Smith and Winifred Strickland Smith (*née* Davis); *m* 1955, Ruth Irwin Aney (marr. diss. 1968). *Educ:* King James' Grammar Sch., Knaresborough; Clare Coll., Cambridge. Mem., Scientific Staff, Agricl Research Council Virus Research Unit, Cambridge, 1945–59; Research Fellow, Clare Coll., 1949–52; with Institut Pasteur, Paris, 1952–53; Rockefeller Foundn Fellow, Univ. of California, Berkeley, 1955–57; California Institute of Technology: Sen. Research Fellow, 1959–62; Sherman Fairchild Scholar, 1974–75. *Publications:* numerous papers in scientific jls on biochemistry and molecular biology. *Recreation:* travel. *Address:* 12 Stansgate Avenue, Cambridge CB2 2QZ. *T:* Cambridge (0223) 247841.

SMITH, Air Vice-Marshal John Edward, CB 1979; CBE 1972; AFC 1967; Air Officer Administration, Headquarters Strike Command, 1977–81; retired; *b* 8 June 1924; *m* 1944, Roseanne Margurite (*née* Eriksson); four *s* two *d* (and one *s* decd). *Educ:* Tonbridge Sch. Served in Far East, ME, USA and Germany as well as UK Stations since joining the Service in Nov. 1941. *Recreations:* sailing, travel. *Address:* 1 Butlers Grove, Great Linford, Bucks MK14 5DT. *Club:* Royal Air Force.

SMITH, Rear-Adm. John Edward D.; *see* Dyer-Smith.

SMITH, (John) Edward (McKenzie) L.; *see* Lucie-Smith.

SMITH, John Frederick; Lord Mayor of Cardiff, 1990–91; *b* 28 Sept. 1934; *s* of Charles Frederick Smith and Teresa Smith (*née* O'Brian); *m* 1962, Irene Rice (*d* 1982); one *s*. *Educ:* St Cuthbert's Jun. Sch.; St Illtyd's Grammar Sch.; Gwent Inst. of Higher Educn, 1981–82 (Dip. Trade Union Studies); University Coll., Cardiff, 1982–85 (BScEcon). Engrg apprenticeship, Edward Curran Engrg, 1951–56; Merchant Navy Engr, Blue Funnel and Andrew Weir, 1956–62; Steel Industry, GKN S Wales, 1964–81; Housing Officer, Adamsdown Housing Assoc. Ltd, 1985–. Member: Cardiff CC, 1972– (Chairman: Housing and Public Works Cttee, 1973–75; Land Cttee, 1987–90; Dep. Lord Mayor, 1988–89). S Glamorgan CC, 1973–81. AMIH 1990. JP Cardiff, 1977–87. *Recreations:* music, spectator of Cardiff RFC and Wales RU, Shakespeare, cooking. *Address:* 128 Corporation Road, Grangetown, Cardiff CF1 7AX. *T:* Cardiff (0222) 345176.

SMITH, John Herbert, CBE 1977; FCA, IPFA, CIGasE; Deputy Chairman and Chief Executive, British Gas Corporation, 1976–83; *b* 30 April 1918; *s* of Thomas Arthur Smith and Pattie Lord; *m* 1945, Phyllis Mary Baxter; two *s* three *d*. *Educ:* Salt High Sch., Shipley, Yorks. Articled Clerk, Bradford and Otley, 1934–39. Served War: RAMC, 1940–46. Dep. Clerk and Chief Financial Officer, Littleborough, Lancs, 1946–49; West Midlands Gas Bd, 1949–61 (various posts, finishing as Asst Chief Accountant); Chief Accountant, Southern Gas Bd, 1961–65; Director of Finance and Administration, East Midlands Gas Bd, 1965–68; Mem. (full-time), East Midlands Gas Bd, 1968 (Dep. Chm., 1968–72); Mem. for Finance, Gas Council, June-Dec. 1972; Mem. for Finance, British Gas Corp., 1973–76. Chm., Nationalised Industries Finance Panel, 1978–83. Chairman: Moracrest Investments, 1977–85; United Property Unit Trust (formerly Industrial and Commercial Property Unit Trust), 1986–89 (Mem., Management Cttee, 1983–89); Member, Management Committee: Pension Funds Property Unit Trust, 1975–89 (Dep. Chm., 1984–89); Lazard American Exempt Fund, 1976–; British American Property Unit Trust, 1982–. Member: Council, Inst. of Chartered Accountants, 1977–81; Trilateral Commn, 1976–85. FRSA 1985. *Recreations:* music, piano playing, walking. *Address:* 81 Albany, Manor Road, East Cliff, Bournemouth, Dorset BH1 3EJ. *T:* Bournemouth (0202) 298157. *Club:* Royal Automobile.

SMITH, John Hilary, CBE 1970 (OBE 1964); Procurator, since 1990, and Fellow, since 1991, University College, Oxford; *b* 20 March 1928; 2nd *s* of late P. R. Smith, OBE and Edith Prince; *m* 1964, Mary Sylvester Head; two *s* one *d*. *Educ:* Cardinal Vaughan Sch., London; University Coll. London (Fellow, 1987); University Coll., Oxford. BA Hons London 1948; MA Oxon 1991. Mil. service, 1948–50, commnd Queen's Own Royal W Kent Regt. Cadet, Northern Nigerian Administration, 1951; Supervisor, Admin. Service Trng, 1960; Dep. Sec. to Premier, 1963; Dir Staff, Develt Centre, 1964; Perm. Sec., Min. of Finance, Benue Plateau State, 1968; Vis. Lectr, Duke Univ., 1970; Financial Sec., British Solomon Is, 1970; Governor of Gilbert and Ellice Islands, 1973–76, of Gilbert Islands, 1976–78; Sec., Imperial Coll., and Clerk to the Govs, 1979–89. Dir, Fleming Ventures, 1985–. Mem. Council, Scout Assoc., 1980– (Chm., Cttee of Council, 1984–88); Pres., Pacific Is Soc. of UK and Ireland, 1981–85. Governor: St Mary's Coll., Strawberry Hill, 1980–88; Cardinal Vaughan School, 1982–88; Heythrop Coll., 1986–; Mem. Bd of Management, LSHTM, 1989–. *Publications:* How to Write Letters that get Results, 1965; Colonial Cadet in Nigeria, 1968; articles in S Atlantic Quarterly, Administration, Jl of Overseas Administration, Nigeria. *Recreations:* walking, writing, music. *Address:* Pound House, Dulverton, Som TA22 9HP. *Club:* Commonwealth Trust.

SMITH, Sir John Kenneth N.; *see* Newson-Smith.

SMITH, Sir John (Lindsay Eric), Kt 1988; CBE 1975; *b* 3 April 1923; *s* of Captain E. C. E. Smith, MC, LLD; *m* 1952, Christian, *d* of late Col U. E. C. Carnegy of Lour, DSO, MC; two *s* two *d* (and one *d* decd). *Educ:* Eton (Fellow, 1974–89); New Coll., Oxford (MA; Hon. Fellow, 1979). Served Fleet Air Arm 1942–46 (Lieut RNVR). MP (C) Cities of London and Westminster, Nov. 1965–1970; Mem., Public Accounts Cttee, 1968–69. National Trust: Mem., Historic Bldgs Cttee, 1952–61; Mem. Exec. Cttee, 1961–85; Mem. Council, 1961–; Dep. Chm., 1980–85. Member: Standing Commission on Museums and Galleries, 1958–66; Inland Waterways Redevelopment Cttee, 1959–62; Historic Buildings Council, 1971–78; Redundant Churches Fund, 1972–74; Nat. Heritage Memorial Fund, 1980–82. Director: Coutts & Co., 1950–; Financial Times Ltd, 1959–68; Rolls Royce Ltd, 1955–75; Dep. Governor, Royal Exchange Assurance, 1961–66. Founder, Manifold and Landmark Charitable Trusts. High Steward of Maidenhead, 1966–75. Freeman of Windsor and Maidenhead, 1975. FSA; Hon. FRIBA 1973; Hon. FRIAS 1983. JP Berks, 1964; DL 1978, Lord-Lieut, 1975–78, Berks. Hon. LLD Exeter, 1989. *Address:* Shottesbrooke Park, Maidenhead, Berks; 1 Smith Square, SW1. *Clubs:* Pratt's, Beefsteak, Brooks's; Tristan da Cunha Golf.

See also Duchess of Grafton, J. F. E. Smith.

SMITH, John M.; see Maynard Smith, J.

SMITH, John Mitchell Melvin, (Jock), WS; Partner, Masson & Glennie, Solicitors, Peterhead, since 1957; b 5 July 1930; s of John Mitchell Smith and Barbara Edda Smith or Glennie; m 1958, Elisabeth Marion Slight; two s one d. Educ: Fettes College; Edinburgh Univ. (BL). Pres., Law Soc. of Scotland, 1987–88. Recreations: golf, theatre. Address: 28 Blackhouse Terrace, Peterhead, Aberdeenshire. T: Peterhead (0779) 72450. Clubs: Royal Northern (Aberdeen); Club of Deir, Peterhead Burns.

SMITH, John P.; see Smith, J. W. P.

SMITH, John Roger B.; see Bickford Smith.

SMITH, John William Patrick, (John P. Smith); MP (Lab) Vale of Glamorgan, since May 1989; b 17 March 1951; s of John Henry Smith and Margaret Mary (née Collins); m 1971, Kathleen Mulvaney; two s one d. Educ: Penarth County Sch.; Gwent Coll. of Higher Educn (Dip. in Indust. Relations and Trade Union Studies); UCW Cardiff (BSc (Econ) Hons). Building worker, 1966–68; RAF, 1967–71; joiner, 1971–76; mature student, 1976–83; University Tutor, 1983–85; Sen. Lectr in Business Studies, 1985–89. Mem., Select Cttee on Welsh Affairs, 1990–. Recreations: reading, boating, camping. Address: House of Commons, SW1. T: 071–219 4487; Barry, S Glam. T: Barry (0446) 700482. Club: Sea View Labour (Barry).

SMITH, Sir John (Wilson), Kt 1990; CBE 1982; JP; DL; Chairman, British International Sports Committee, since 1988; b 6 Nov. 1920; m 1946, Doris Mabel Parfitt; one s. Educ: Oulton High School, Liverpool. Director: Tetley Walker Ltd, 1966–77; First Castle Electronics plc, 1978–. Member: Football Trust, 1980–; Football Assoc., 1981–86; Dir, Football League, 1981–86 (Mem., Restructuring Cttee, 1982); Chairman: Liverpool FC, 1973–90; Duke of Edinburgh's Merseyside Industrial Award Council, 1977–; Cttee of Inquiry into Lawn Tennis (report, 1980); Anfield Foundn, 1984–; Sports Council, 1985–89 (Mem. 1980–89); Dep. Chm., Merseyside Develt Corp., 1985–89. JP Liverpool, 1971; DL Merseyside, 1983. Recreation: golf. Address: Pine Close, Mill Lane, Gayton, Wirral, Merseyside. T: 051–342 5362. Club: Reform.

SMITH, Jonathan A.; see Ashley-Smith.

SMITH, Jonathan Simon Christopher R.; see Riley-Smith.

SMITH, Prof. Joseph Victor, FRS 1978; Louis Block Professor of Physical Sciences, since 1977, and Director, Consortium for Advanced Radiation Sources, since 1989, University of Chicago (Professor of Mineralogy and Crystallography, 1960–76); b 30 July 1928; s of Henry Victor Smith and Edith (née Robinson); m 1951, Brenda Florence Wallis; two d. Educ: Cambridge Univ. (MA, PhD). Fellow, Carnegie Instn of Washington, 1951–54; Demonstrator in Mineralogy and Petrology, Cambridge Univ., 1954–56; Asst then Associate Prof., Pennsylvania State Univ., 1956–60. Editor, Power Diffraction File, 1959–69. Visiting Prof., California Inst. of Technology, 1965; Consultant: Union Carbide Corp., 1956–85; UOP, 1985–. Member, US Nat. Acad. of Scis, 1986. Murchison Medal, 1980; Roebling Medal, 1982. Publications: Feldspar Minerals, Vols 1 and 2, 1975, 2nd edn 1987; Geometrical and Structural Crystallography, 1982; numerous articles on crystallography, inorganic chemistry, mineralogy, petrology and planetology. Recreations: music, art. Address: Department of the Geophysical Sciences, University of Chicago, 5734 S Ellis Avenue, Chicago, Ill 60637, USA. T: 312–702 8110. Club: Quadrangle (Chicago).

SMITH, Sir Joseph William Grenville, Kt 1991; MD; FRCP; FRCPath; FFPHM; FIBiol; Director, Public Health Laboratory Service, since 1985; b 14 Nov. 1930; s of Douglas Ralph and Hannah Letitia Margaret Smith; m 1954, Nira Jean (née Davies); one s. Educ: Cathays High School, Cardiff; Welsh Nat. Sch. of Medicine (MD 1966); Dip. Bact., London Univ.; FRCPath 1975; FFPHM (FFCM 1976); FRCP 1987. FIBiol 1978. Sen. Lectr, Dept of Bacteriology and Immunology, LSHTM, 1960–65; Consultant Clinical Bacteriologist, Radcliffe Infirmary, Oxford, 1965–69; Gen. Practitioner, Islington, 1970–71; Consultant Epidemiologist, Dep. Dir, Epidemiological Res. Lab., PHLS, 1971–76; Dir, Nat. Inst. for Biological Standards and Control, 1976–85. Consultant on immunisation to British Army, 1985–. Member: Cttee on Safety of Medicines, 1978–86 (Chm., Biol Sub-Cttee, 1981–86); Jt Cttee on Vaccination and Immunisation, 1976–; British Pharmacopoea Commn, 1976–85; MRC, 1989–; Council, RCPath, 1988–90; Chairman: Cttee on Vaccination and Immunization Procedures, MRC, 1976–; Simian Virus Cttee, MRC, 1982–; Tropical Medicine Res. Bd, MRC, 1989–90. Publications: (with E. B. Adams and D. R. Laurence) Tetanus, 1969; papers on tetanus, immunization, and epidemiology of infections in scientific and med. jls. Recreation: the arts. Address: Public Health Laboratory Service Board, 61 Colindale Avenue, NW9 5DF. T: 081–200 1295. Club: Athenæum.

SMITH, Hon. Kenneth George, OJ 1973; Justice of Appeal, Bahamas, 1985–90, retired; b 25 July 1920; s of Franklin C. Smith; m 1942, Hyacinth Whitfield Connell; two d. Educ: Primary schs; Cornwall Coll., Jamaica; Inns of Court Sch. of Law, London. Barrister-at-Law, Lincoln's Inn. Asst Clerk of Courts, 1940–48; Dep. Clerk of Courts, 1948–53; Clerk of Courts, 1953–56; Crown Counsel, 1956–62; Asst Attorney-Gen., 1962–65; Supreme Court Judge, 1965–70; Judge of Appeal, Jamaica, 1970–73; Chief Justice of Jamaica, 1973–85. Recreations: swimming, gardening. Address: 5 Wagner Avenue, Kingston 8, Jamaica.

SMITH, Kenneth Graeme Stewart, CMG 1958; JP; retired as Civil Secretary, The Gambia, West Africa, 1962; b 26 July 1918; 3rd s of late Prof. H. A. Smith, DCL; unmarried. Educ: Bradfield; Magdalen College, Oxford. Cadet, Colonial Administrative Service, Tanganyika, 1940; appointments in Colonial Service, 1945–62. JP Dorset, 1967. Address: The Old House, Newland, Sherborne, Dorset DT9 3AQ. T: Sherborne (0935) 812754.

SMITH, Kingsley Ward; Chief Executive, Durham County Council, since 1988; Clerk to the Lieutenancy, since 1990; b 24 Oct. 1946; s of Peter and Doris Evelyn Smith; m 1968, Kathy Rutherford; two s. Educ: Blue Coat Secondary Sch., Walsall, Staffs; Dame Allan's Boys' Sch., Newcastle upon Tyne. IPFA 1970. Trainee Accountant, Gateshead CBC, 1964–67; Durham County Council: Accountant, subseq. Sen. Accountant, 1967–76; Chief Internal Auditor, 1976–79; Sen. Asst County Treasurer, 1979–81; Dep. County Treasurer, 1981–84; County Treasurer, 1984–88. Director: Durham TEC, 1990–; Durham Agency Against Crime, 1990–. Chm., E Durham Task Force, 1990–; Vice-Chm., Prince's Trust Cttee for Cleveland and Durham, 1990–; Advr, Northern Develt Co., 1986–. Recreations: golfing, fishing, caravanning, walking his labrador (Sam). Address: Pointer House, 19 Church Street, Castleside, Consett, Co. Durham DH8 9QW. T: Consett (0207) 581095.

SMITH, Laura; see Duncan, A. L. A.

SMITH, Lawrence Delpré; Senior Puisne Judge of the Supreme Court of Sarawak, North Borneo and Brunei, 1951–64, retired; b 29 October 1905; m; one s three d. Educ: Christ's Hospital; Hertford College, Oxford; Gray's Inn. Colonial Administrative Service, 1929;

Colonial Legal Service, 1934; Tanganyika, 1929; Palestine, 1946; Gambia, 1948. Address: 34 The Avenue, Muswell Hill, N10 2QL. T: 081–883 7198.

SMITH, Lawrence Joseph, OBE 1976; Assistant General Secretary, Transport and General Workers Union, 1985–88; two d. Served in HM Forces, 1941–47; joined London Transport, 1947; District Officer, TGWU, 1961, London District Secretary, 1965, National Officer, 1966, National Secretary, Passenger Services Group, 1971, Exec. Officer, 1979–85. Part-time Mem., London Transport Bd, 1983–. Mem., TUC Gen. Council, 1979–88. Recreations: gardening, football. Address: c/o Transport House, Smith Square, SW1P 3JB. T: 071–828 7788.

SMITH, Lawrence Roger Hines, FSA; Keeper of Japanese Antiquities, British Museum, since 1987; b 19 Feb. 1941; s of Frank Ernest Smith and Eva Lilian Smith (née Hines); m 1965, Louise Geraldine Gallini (marr. diss. 1986); one s five d. Educ: Collyer's Grammar Sch., Horsham; Queens' Coll., Cambridge (BA). British Museum: Asst Keeper, Dept of Manuscripts, 1962; Dept of Oriental Antiquities, 1965; Dep. Keeper, 1976; Keeper, 1977. British Acad. Exchange Fellow, Nihon Gakujutsu Shinkōkai, Kyoto, 1974–75. Academic adviser, Great Japan Exhibn, RA, 1981–82, and contrib. to catalogue. Uchiyama Prize, Ukiyoe Soc. of Japan, 1986. Publications: Netsuke: the miniature sculpture of Japan (with R. Barker), 1976; Flowers in Art from East and West (with P. Hulton), 1979; Japanese Prints: 300 years of albums and books (with J. Hillier), 1980; Japanese Decorative Arts 1600–1900 (with V. Harris), 1982; The Japanese Print since 1900, 1983; Contemporary Japanese Prints, 1985; (ed) Ukiyoe: images of unknown Japan, 1988; (ed) Japanese Art: masterpieces in the British Museum, 1990; articles and reviews in learned jls. Recreations: walking, sailing, bellringing, music, wine. Address: 45 Lyme Farm Road, Lee, SE12 8JQ. T: 081–852 4789.

SMITH, Leslie Charles, OBE 1968; Founder Director, Eastway Zinc Alloy Co. Ltd, 1965–82; b 6 March 1918; s of Edward A. Smith and Elizabeth Smith; m 1948, Nancy Smith; two s one d. Educ: Enfield Central School. Export Buyer, 1938–40; Lieut, RNVR, 1940–46. Founder Dir, Lesney Products, 1947, Jt Man. Dir 1947–73, Man. Dir 1973–80; Chief Exec. Officer, 1980–81, Vice-Chm., 1981–82. FInstM; FBIM 1976; FInstD 1979. Recreations: ski-ing, sailing, golf. Address: White Timbers, 9a Broad Walk, N21 3DA. T: 081–886 1656. Clubs: Naval; Royal Thames Yacht, Royal Motor Yacht, Parkstone Yacht, Poole Harbour Yacht; Parkstone Golf, Hadley Wood Golf.

SMITH, Sir Leslie (Edward George), Kt 1977; Director, The BOC Group plc (formerly The British Oxygen Co. Ltd), since 1966 (Chairman, 1972–85); b 15 April 1919; m 1st, 1943, Lorna Bell Pickworth; two d; 2nd, 1964, Cynthia Barbara Holmes; one s one d. Educ: Christ's Hospital, Horsham, Sussex. Served War, Army (Royal Artillery, Royal Fusiliers), 1940–46. Variety of activities, 1946–55. Joined British Oxygen as Accountant, 1956, Group Man. Dir, 1969–72, Group Chm. and Chief Exec., 1972–79, Chm., 1979–85. Dir, British Gas plc (formerly British Gas Corp.), 1982–90. Mem., Exec. Cttee, King Edward VII Hospital for Officers, 1978–88. FCA. Recreations: unremarkable. Address: Forston Farm, Dorchester, Dorset DT2 7AB.

SMITH, Llewellyn; Member (Lab) South East Wales, European Parliament, since 1984; b 16 April 1944; m; two s one d. Educ: Cardiff University. Formerly with Pilkington Glass, George Wimpey and Workers' Educational Assoc. Prospective Parly Candidate (Lab), Blaenau Gwent, 1990–. Mem., CND. Address: The Mount, Uplands, Tynewydd, Newbridge, Gwent.

SMITH, Lloyd Barnaby; HM Diplomatic Service; Counsellor, Foreign and Commonwealth Office, since 1990; b 21 July 1945; s of Arthur and Zena Smith; m 1st, 1972, Nicola Mary Whitehead (marr. diss.); 2nd, 1983, Elizabeth Mary Sumner; one s one d. Educ: Merchant Taylors' Sch., Moor Park; Brasenose Coll., Oxford (MA). Joined Diplomatic Service, 1968; Third, later Second Sec., Bangkok, 1970–74; First Secretary: FCO, 1974–77; Paris, 1977–78; also Head of Chancery, Dublin, 1978–81; Ecole Nat. d'Admin, Paris, 1981–82; First Sec., then Counsellor, UK Repn to EEC, Brussels, 1982–86; Counsellor, Bangkok, 1987–90. Recreation: sailing. Address: c/o Foreign and Commonwealth Office, SW1A 2AH. Clubs: United Oxford & Cambridge University; Upper Thames Yacht.

SMITH, Dame Maggie, (Dame Margaret Natalie Cross), DBE 1990 (CBE 1970); actress; Director, United British Artists, since 1982; b 28 Dec. 1934; d of Nathaniel Smith and Margaret Little (née Hutton); m 1st, 1967, Robert Stephens, qv (marr. diss. 1975); two s; 2nd, 1975, Beverley Cross, qv. Educ: Oxford High School for Girls. Studied at Oxford Playhouse School under Isabel van Beers. First appearance, June 1952, as Viola in OUDS Twelfth Night; 1st New York appearance, Ethel Barrymore Theatre, June 1956, as comedienne in New Faces. Played in Share My Lettuce, Lyric, Hammersmith, 1957; The Stepmother, St Martin's, 1958. Old Vic Co., 1959–60 season: The Double Dealer; As You Like It; Richard II; The Merry Wives of Windsor; What Every Woman Knows; Rhinoceros, Strand, 1960; Strip the Willow, Cambridge, 1960; The Rehearsal, Globe, 1961; The Private Ear and The Public Eye (Evening Standard Drama Award, best actress of 1962), Globe, 1962; Mary, Mary, Queen's, 1963 (Variety Club of Gt Britain, best actress of the year); The Country Wife, Chichester, 1969; Design for Living, LA, 1971; Private Lives, Queen's, 1972, Globe, 1973, NY, 1975 (Variety Club of GB Stage Actress Award, 1972); Peter Pan, Coliseum, 1973; Snap, Vaudeville, 1974; Night and Day, Phoenix, 1979; Virginia, Haymarket, 1981 (Standard Best Actress Award, 1982); The Way of the World, Chichester and Haymarket, 1984 (Standard Best Actress Award, 1985); Interpreters, Queen's, 1985; Lettice and Lovage, Globe, 1987, NY, 1990 (Tony Award, best leading actress, 1990); at National Theatre: The Recruiting Officer, 1963; Othello, The Master Builder, Hay Fever, 1964; Much Ado About Nothing, Miss Julie, 1965; A Bond Honoured, 1966; The Beaux' Stratagem, 1970 (also USA); Hedda Gabler, 1970 (Evening Standard Best Actress award); War Plays, 1985; Coming in to Land, 1986; at Festival Theatre, Stratford, Ontario: 1976: Antony and Cleopatra, The Way of the World, Measure for Measure, The Three Sisters; 1977: Midsummer Night's Dream, Richard III, The Guardsman, As You Like It, Hay Fever; 1978: As You Like It, Macbeth, Private Lives; 1980: Virginia; Much Ado About Nothing. Films: The VIP's, 1963; The Pumpkin Eater, 1964; Young Cassidy, 1965; Othello, 1966; The Honey Pot, 1967; Hot Millions, 1968 (Variety Club of GB Award); The Prime of Miss Jean Brodie, 1968 (Oscar; SFTA award); Oh! What a Lovely War, 1968; Love and Pain (and the Whole Damned Thing), 1973; Travels with my Aunt, 1973; Murder by Death, 1976; California Suite, 1977 (Oscar); Death on the Nile, 1978; Quartet, 1981; Clash of the Titans, 1981; Evil Under the Sun, 1982; The Missionary, 1982; A Private Function, 1984 (BAFTA award, Best Actress, 1985); The Loves of Lily, 1985; A Room with a View, 1986 (Variety Club of GB Award; BAFTA award, Best Actress, 1986); The Lonely Passion of Judith Hearn, 1989 (Evening Standard British Films Award, 1988, and Best Film Actress BAFTA Award, 1988); television: Talking Heads: Bed Among the Lentils, BBC, 1989 (RTS Award). Hon. DLitt: St Andrews, 1971; London, 1991. Shakespeare Prize, 1991. Recreation: reading. Address: c/o Write on Cue, 10 Garrick Street, WC2E 9BH. T: 071–379 4915.

SMITH, Malcolm Andrew F.; see Ferguson-Smith.

SMITH, Dame Margôt, DBE 1974; *b* 5 Sept. 1918; *d* of Leonard Graham Brown, MC, FRCS, and Margaret Jane Menzies; *m* 1947, Roy Smith, MC, TD (*d* 1983); two *s* one *d*. *Educ:* Westonbirt. Chm., Nat. Conservative Women's Adv. Cttee, 1969–72; Chm., Nat. Union of Conservative and Unionist Assocs, 1973–74. Mem., NSPCC Central Exec. Cttee, 1969–86. *Address:* Howden Lodge, Spennithorne, Leyburn, N Yorks DL8 5PR. *T:* Wensleydale (0969) 23621.

SMITH, His Honour Mark Barnet; a Circuit Judge, 1972–87; *b* 11 Feb. 1917; *s* of David Smith and Sophie Smith (*née* Abrahams); *m* 1943, Edith Winifred Harrison; two *d*. *Educ:* Freehold Council Sch., Oldham; Manchester Grammar Sch.; Sidney Sussex Coll., Cambridge. MA (Hons) (Natural Sci.). Asst Examr in HM Patent Office, 1939 (and promoted Examr in 1944, while on war service). Served War, RA (Staff Sergt), 1940–46. Returned to Patent Office, 1946. Called to Bar, Middle Temple, 1948. Left Patent Office, end of 1948; pupil at the Bar, 1949. Temp. Recorder of Folkestone, 1971; a Recorder of the Crown Court, Jan.-Apr. 1972. *Address:* Munstead Lodge, Munstead Heath Road, Godalming, Surrey GU8 4AR.

SMITH, Maurice George, OBE 1988; retired; Under-Secretary, Ministry of Overseas Development, 1968–76; *b* 4 Sept. 1915; *s* of Alfred Graham and Laura Maria Smith; *m* 1940, Eva Margaret Vanstone; two *s*. *Educ:* Sir Walter St John's School, Battersea. Examiner, Estate Duty Office, 1939. Flt Lieut RAF, 1942–46. Asst Principal, Min. of Civil Aviation, 1947; Principal, 1948; transferred to Colonial Office, 1950; seconded Commonwealth Office, 1954–55; Asst Secretary, Colonial Office, 1959; transferred to Dept of Technical Co-operation, 1961; Min. of Overseas Development, 1964; Under-Sec. and Principal Finance Officer, ODM, 1968. Chairman, Knights' Assoc. of Christian Youth Clubs, Lambeth, 1970– (Hon. Sec., 1950–70). *Recreations:* voluntary work in youth service, travel. *Address:* 52 Woodfield Avenue, SW16 1LG. *T:* 081–769 5356.

SMITH, Melvin Kenneth; actor, writer, director; *b* 3 Dec. 1952; *s* of Kenneth and Vera Smith; *m* 1988, Pamela Gay-Rees. *Educ:* Latymer Upper Sch., Hammersmith; New Coll., Oxford. Asst Dir, Royal Court Th., 1973; freelance Dir, Bristol Old Vic, 1973, Liverpool Everyman, 1974, Bush Th., 1975; Associate Director: Crucible Th., Sheffield, 1975–78; Young Vic, 1978–79; Actor/writer, TV series, Not The Nine O'Clock News, Alas Smith and Jones, 1979–81; Smith & Jones, 1982–87; appeared in Small Doses (series of short plays), 1989. Films: The Tall Guy, 1989 (Dir); Wilt, 1989. Director: Talkback Prodns, 1982–; Playback Training Films, 1987–; Smith Jones Brown and Cassie Commercials, Ltd, 1988–. *Publications:* Not the book, 1981; Not the Nine O'Clock News Diary, 1982; Alas Smith and Jones Coffee Table Book, 1987; Janet Lives with Mel and Griff, 1988. *Club:* Groucho.

SMITH, Most Rev. Michael; *see* Meath, Bishop of, (RC).

SMITH, Prof. Michael, FRS 1986; FRSC 1981; Professor, Department of Biochemistry, since 1970, and Director, Biotechnology Laboratory, since 1987, University of British Columbia; *b* 26 April 1932; *s* of Rowland Smith and Mary Agnes Smith; *m* 1960, Helen Wood Smith; two *s* one *d*. *Educ:* Arnold Sch., Blackpool, England; Manchester Univ. (BSc Chemistry, PhD). Post-doctoral fellowship, Brit. Columbia Res. Council, 1956–60; Res. Associate, Inst. for Enzyme Res., Univ. of Wisconsin, 1960–61; Hd, Chemistry Sect., Vancouver Lab., Fisheries Res. Bd of Canada, 1961–66; Associate Prof., Dept of Biochem., Univ. of Brit. Columbia, 1966–70. Career Investigator, MRC of Canada, 1966–. *Recreations:* ski-ing, hiking, sailing. *Address:* University of British Columbia, Biotechnology Laboratory, Room 237 Wesbrook Building, 6174 University Boulevard, Vancouver, BC V6T 1W5, Canada. *Club:* Faculty (Univ. of British Columbia).

SMITH, Michael Edward C.; *see* Carleton-Smith.

SMITH, Prof. Michael G.; Crosby Professor of Human Environment, Department of Anthropology, Yale University, 1978–86, now Emeritus; Senior Research Fellow, Research Institute for the Study of Man, New York, since 1986; *b* 18 Aug. 1921; *m* 1947, Mary F. Morrison; three *s*. *Educ:* University College London. BA 1948, PhD 1951; Fellow, 1985. Research Fellow, Inst. of Social and Economic Research, University Coll. of the West Indies, 1952–56, Sen. Research Fellow, there, 1956–58; Sen. Research Fellow, Nigerian Inst. of Social and Economic Research, Ibadan, 1958–60; Sen. Lectr (Sociology), Univ. Coll. of the WI, 1960–61; Prof. of Anthropology: Univ. of California, Los Angeles, 1961–69; University Coll. London, 1969–75. Special Advr to Prime Minister of Jamaica, 1975–78. Hon. LLD McGill, 1976; Hon. DLitt Univ. of W Indies, 1989. Order of Merit (Jamaica), 1973. *Publications:* The Economy of Hausa Communities of Zaria, 1955; Labour Supply in Rural Jamaica, 1956; (with G. J. Kruijer) A Sociological Manual for Caribbean Extension Workers, 1957; Government in Zazzau, 1800–1950, 1960; Kinship and Community in Carriacou, 1962; West Indian Family Structure, 1962; Dark Puritan, 1963; The Plural Society in the British West Indies, 1965; Stratification in Grenada, 1965; (ed, with Leo Kuper) Pluralism in Africa, 1969; Corporations and Society, 1974; The Affairs of Daura, 1978; Culture, Race and Class in the Commonwealth Caribbean, 1986; Poverty in Jamaica, 1989; Pluralism, Politics and Ideology in the Creole Caribbean, 1991.

SMITH, Michael Gerard A.; *see* Austin-Smith.

SMITH, Michael K.; *see* Kinchin Smith.

SMITH, Neil; *see* Smith, G. N.

SMITH, Prof. Neilson Voyne; Professor of Linguistics, University College London, since 1981 (Head of Department of Phonetics and Linguistics, 1983–90); *b* 21 June 1939; *s* of Voyne Smith and Lilian Freda Smith (*née* Rose); *m* 1966, Saraswati Keskar; two *s*. *Educ:* Trinity College, Cambridge (BA 1961, MA 1964); UCL (PhD 1964). Lectr in W African Languages, SOAS, 1964–70; Harkness Fellow, MIT and UCLA, 1966–68; Lectr in Linguistics and W African Languages, SOAS, 1970–72; Reader in Linguistics, UCL, 1972–81. Chm., Linguistics Assoc., 1980–86. *Publications:* An Outline Grammar of Nupe, 1967; The Acquisition of Phonology, 1973; (with Deirdre Wilson) Modern Linguistics, 1979; (ed) Mutual Knowledge, 1982; Speculative Linguistics, 1983; The Twitter Machine, 1989; articles in learned jls. *Recreations:* music, walking, travel, playing with children. *Address:* 32 Long Buftlers, Harpenden, Herts AL5 1JE; Department of Phonetics and Linguistics, University College London, Gower Street, WC1E 6BT. *T:* 071–380 7173.

SMITH, Dr (Norman) Brian, CBE 1980; Chairman, BAA plc, since 1991; Deputy Chairman, Lister & Co. plc, since 1990 (Director, since 1985); Director, Davy Corporation, since 1986; *b* 10 Sept. 1928; *s* of late Vincent and Louise Smith; *m* 1955, Phyllis Crossley; one *s* one *d* (and one *s* decd). *Educ:* Sir John Deane's Grammar Sch., Northwich; Manchester Univ. (PhD Phys. Chemistry, 1954). FTI 1981. Joined ICI Ltd, Terylene Council, 1954; Fibres Division: Textile Develt Dir, 1969; Dep. Chm., 1972; Chm., 1975–78; ICI Main Bd, 1978–85; Director: Fiber Industries Inc., 1972–83; Canadian Industries Ltd, 1981–85; Territorial Dir for the Americas, and Chm., ICI Americas Inc., 1981–85 (Dir, 1980–85); Non-Exec. Dir, Carrington Viyella Ltd, 1979–81. Dep. Chm., 1985–86, Chm., 1986–89, Metal Box plc, subseq. MB Group; Director: Cable & Wireless, 1988–; Yorkshire Chemicals, 1990–; Mercury Communications, 1990–; Beresford Internat., 1990–. Pres., British Textile Confedn, 1977–79; Chairman: Man-Made Fibres Producers Cttee, 1976–78; EDC for Wool Textile Industry, 1979–81; Priorities Bd for R & D in Agric. and Food, 1987–; Mem., BOTB, 1980–81, 1983–87 (Chm., N American Adv. Group, 1983–87). Mem., Oxford Dio. Bd of Finance, 1990–. CBIM 1985; FCIM. Freeman, City of London, 1986; Liveryman, Glovers' Co., 1986. Hon. DBA Buckingham, 1990. *Recreations:* sailing, tennis, gardening. *Club:* Brooks's.

SMITH, Norman Jack, MA, MPhil; FInstPet; Chairman, Mentor Engineering Consultants Ltd, since 1988; Managing Director, Smith Rea Energy Associates Ltd, since 1981; *b* 14 April 1936; *s* of late Maurice Leslie and Ellen Dorothy Smith; *m* 1967, Valerie Ann, *o d* of late A. E. Frost; one *s* one *d*. *Educ:* Grammar Sch., Henley-on-Thames; Oriel Coll., Oxford (MA); City Univ. (MPhil). Dexion Ltd, 1957; Vickers Ltd, 1960; Baring Brothers & Co. Ltd, 1969; seconded as Industrial Director, 1977, Dir-Gen., 1978–80, Offshore Supplies Office, Dept of Energy; Chm., British Underwater Engineering Ltd, 1980–83. Director: Smith Rea Energy Analysts, 1985–; Smith Rea Energy Aberdeen, 1990–; Gas Transmission, 1989–. Mem., Offshore Energy Technology Bd, 1978–80. Fellow: Soc. of Business Economists (Mem., 1958–); Inst. of Dirs. *Publications:* sundry articles in economic and similar jls. *Recreations:* walking, swimming, photography, history. *Address:* c/o Smith Rea Energy Associates Ltd, Hunstead House, Nickle, Chartham, Canterbury, Kent CT4 7PL. *T:* Canterbury (0227) 738822. *Club:* United Oxford & Cambridge University.

SMITH, Prof. (Norman John) David; Head of Department of Dental Radiology, King's College School of Medicine and Dentistry (formerly King's College Hospital Dental School), since 1972, and Professor of Dental Radiology, University of London, since 1978; *b* 2 Feb. 1931; *s* of late Norman S. Smith; *m* 1st, 1954, Regina Eileen Lugg (marr. diss.); one *s*; 2nd, 1983, Mary Christine Pocock; one *d*. *Educ:* King's Coll. Sch., Wimbledon; King's Coll., London; KCH Dental Sch. (BDS 1963; MPhil 1969); Royal Free Hosp. Sch. of Medicine (MSc 1966). Apprenticed to Pacific Steam Navigation Co., 1948–51; Officer Service, Royal Mail Lines, 1952–58 (Master Mariner, 1957); part-time posts at KCH Dental Sch., Guy's Hosp. Dental Sch. and in gen. dental practice, 1966–69; Sen. Lectr in Dental Surg., KCH Dental Sch., 1969–72; Reader in Dental Radiol., Univ. of London, 1973. Civil Consultant to RAF, 1990–. Member: Southwark Bor. Council, 1974–78; GLC for Norwood, 1977–86 (Leader of Opposition, ILEA, 1979–86); Thames Water Authority, 1977–83; SE Thames RHA, 1978–86; Council, Open Univ., 1978–81, 1982–91; Court, Univ. of London, 1982–87; Governor, Bethlem Royal and Maudsley Hosps, 1980–82; Mem., Bethlem Royal and Maudsley SHA, 1982–86. Vis. Prof. and lectr worldwide. Liveryman, Hon. Co. of Master Mariners. Sir Charlton Briscoe Res. Prize, KCH Med. Sch., 1969. *Publications:* Simple Navigation by the Sun, 1974; Dental Radiography, 1980; articles in dental jls. *Recreations:* sailing, nature photography. *Address:* c/o King's College School of Medicine and Dentistry, Caldecot Road, SE5 9RW. *T:* 071–274 6222, ext. 2503.

SMITH, Ven. Percival; *see* Smith, Ven. A. M. P.

SMITH, Peter, FSA; Secretary, Royal Commission on Ancient Monuments in Wales, since 1973; *b* 15 June 1926; *s* of late L. W. Smith, HMI, and Mrs H. Smith (*née* Halsted); *m* 1954, Joyce Evelyn, *d* of late J. W. Abbott and of Alice Abbott (*née* Lloyd); two *s* one *d*. *Educ:* Peter Symonds' Sch., Winchester; Oriel Coll. and Lincoln Coll. (Open Scholar), Oxford (BA, Hons Mod. Hist. 1947); Hammersmith Sch. of Building (Inter ARIBA 1950). Royal Commission on Ancient Monuments in Wales: Jun. Investigator, 1949; Sen. Investigator, 1954; Investigator in Charge of Nat. Monuments Record, 1963. President: Cambrian Archaeological Assoc., 1979; Vernacular Architecture Gp, 1983–86. G. T. Clark Prize, 1969; Alice Davis Hitchcock Medallion, Soc. of Architectural Historians of GB, 1978. *Publications:* Houses of the Welsh Countryside, 1975; contribs to Agrarian History of England; periodical literature on historic domestic architecture. *Recreations:* reading, drawing, learning Welsh. *Address:* Tŷ-coch, Lluest, Llanbadarn Fawr, Aberystwyth, Dyfed SY23 3AU. *T:* Aberystwyth (0970) 623556.

SMITH, Peter Alexander Charles, OBE 1981; Chairman: Securicor Group plc, since 1974; Security Services plc, since 1974; *b* 18 Aug. 1920; *s* of Alexander Alfred Smith and Gwendoline Mary (*née* Beer); *m* 1945, Marjorie May Humphrey (*d* 1988); one *s*. *Educ:* St Paul's Sch., London. Admitted solicitor, 1948. Served RA, 1941–46: Captain; Adjt, 17th Medium Regt. Partner, Hextall, Erskine & Co., 1953–79. Chairman: British Security Industry Assoc. Ltd, 1977–81; Metal Closures Gp plc, 1983–87 (Dir, 1972, Dep. Chm., 1981). Mem. Council, Royal Warrant Holders Assoc., 1976–, Vice-Pres., 1981–82, Pres., 1982–83. Vice-Pres., Forest Philharmonic Symphony Orch., 1991–. CBIM. FRSA. *Recreations:* golf, music, photography. *Address:* Sutton Park House, 15 Carshalton Road, Sutton, Surrey SM1 4LE. *Club:* British Racing Drivers (Hon. Life Mem.).

SMITH, Peter Bruce; Head Master, Bradfield College, since 1985; *b* 18 March 1944; *s* of Alexander D. Smith and Grace Smith; *m* 1968, Diana Margaret Morgan; two *d*. *Educ:* Magdalen College School, Oxford; Lincoln College, Oxford (Old Members Scholar; MA). Asst Master, Rugby Sch., 1967–85 (Head of Hist. Dept, 1973–77, Housemaster of School Field, 1977–85). Mem. Governing Body, Downe House Sch., 1985–89. Captain Oxfordshire County Cricket Club, 1971–77 (Minor Counties Champions, 1974). *Recreations:* antiquarian, sporting, literary. *Address:* Headmaster's House, Bradfield College, Bradfield, Reading RG7 6AR. *Club:* Vincent's (Oxford).

SMITH, Peter Claudius G.; *see* Gautier-Smith.

SMITH, Dr Peter Graham, CB 1988; Director General Guided Weapons and Electronics, Ministry of Defence (Procurement Executive), 1982–88; *b* 12 June 1929; *s* of James A. and Florence L. Smith; *m* 1952, Doreen Millicent (*née* Wyatt); two *d*. *Educ:* Wellington Grammar Sch., Shropshire; Birmingham Univ. (BSc, PhD). Radar Res. Estab., 1953–75: seconded to British Defence Staff, Washington, 1966–68; Supt, Airborne Defensive Radar Div., 1970–75; Dir Defence Science 8, MoD, 1975–78; Dir Surveillance and Instrument Projs, MoD (PE), 1978–82. *Recreations:* gardening, reading, modelling. *Address:* c/o Lloyd's Bank, High Street, Harpenden AL5 2TA.

SMITH, Peter J.; *see* Jefferson Smith.

SMITH, Peter John, IPFA; public sector consultant; Executive Director, Westgate Trust plc, since 1990; Non-executive Director, N American Property Unit Trust, since 1982; County Treasurer, Tyne and Wear County Council, 1980–86; *b* 31 Dec. 1936; *s* of Frank and Sarah Ann Smith; *m* 1959, Marie Louise Smith; one *s* one *d*. *Educ:* Rastrick Grammar Sch., Brighouse, W Yorkshire. Trainee Accountant, Huddersfield CBC, 1953–59; Accountancy Asst, Bradford CBC, 1959–61; Asst Chief Accountant, Chester CBC, 1961–63; Computer Manager, Keighley BC, 1963–66; Asst City Treasurer, Gloucester CBC, 1966–69; Dep. Borough Treasurer, Gateshead CBC, 1969–73; Asst County Treasurer, Tyne and Wear CC, 1973–74, Dep. County Treasurer, 1974–80. Gen. Manager, Tyne and Wear Residuary Body, 1985–88. Treasurer: NE Regional Airport Jt Cttee, 1980–86; Northumbria Police Authority, 1980–86; Northumbria Probation and After Care Cttee, 1980–86; Mem., Tyne and Wear Passenger Transport Exec. Bd,

1981–86. Dir, Northern Investors Co., 1983–86. *Recreations:* fell walking, jogging. *Address:* Wheatsheaf House, Station Road, Beamish, Co. Durham DH9 0QU. *T:* Durham (091) 3700481.

SMITH, Peter Vivian Henworth, CB 1989; Solicitor, HM Customs and Excise, 1986–89; Legal Adviser: Broadcasting Standards Council, since 1989; Building Societies Commission, since 1990; *b* 5 Dec. 1928; *s* of Vivian and Dorothea Smith; *m* 1955, Mary Marjorie, *d* of Frank John Willsher and Sybil Marjorie Willsher; five *d. Educ:* Clacton County High Sch.; Brasenose Coll., Oxford (MA, BCL). Called to the Bar, Lincoln's Inn, 1953. HM Overseas Civil Service: Resident Magistrate, Nyasaland, 1955–63; Registrar, High Court, Nyasaland, 1963–64; Sen. Resident Magistrate, Malaŵi, 1964–69; Puisne Judge, Malaŵi, 1969–70; HM Customs and Excise: Legal Asst, 1970–72; Sen. Legal Asst, 1972–76; Asst Solicitor, 1976–82; Prin. Asst Solicitor, 1982–85. *Recreations:* classical music, walking, bridge, computers. *Address:* Likabula, 14 St Albans Road, Clacton-on-Sea CO15 6BA. *T:* Clacton-on-Sea (0255) 422053.

SMITH, Philip; Deputy Director Warship Design (Electrical), Ministry of Defence (Navy), 1969–73, retired; *b* 19 May 1913; *m* 1940, Joan Mary Harker; one *s* one *d. Educ:* Bishop Wordsworth's Sch., Salisbury; Bristol Univ. BSc (First Cl. Hons). Graduate Trainee Apprentice, BTH Co., 1934–37; Outside Construction Engrg, BTH Co., 1937–38; Central Electricity Bd, 1938–39; Admty (Electrical Engrg Dept) (now MoD Navy), 1939–73; past service at Chatham Dockyard and Dockyard Dept, HQ; Electrical Engrg Design Divs; Head of Electrical Dept, Admty Engrg Laboratory, West Drayton. CEng, FIEE, FIMechE; RCNC. *Recreations:* horticulture, golf, oil painting. *Address:* Myrfield, Summer Lane, Combe Down, Bath BA2 7EU. *T:* Combe Down (0225) 833408. *Club:* Bath Golf.

SMITH, Philip George, CBE 1973; Director, Metal Market & Exchange Co. Ltd, since 1954 (Chairman, 1967–84); Adviser, Triland Metals Ltd, since 1984; *b* 10 Sept. 1911. *Educ:* St Lawrence Coll., Ramsgate; Royal School of Mines, London. ARSM, BSc (Eng). Director: Bassett Smith & Co. Ltd, 1946–75; Bardyke Chemicals Ltd, 1968–90; (non-exec.), Comfin (Commodity & Finance) Co. Ltd, 1978–82. Mem. Cttee, London Metal Exchange, 1949–64 (Chm. 1954–64). Adviser to Dept of Trade and Industry, 1958–86; part-time Mem., Sugar Bd, 1967–76. *Address:* 67B Camlet Way, Hadley Wood, Barnet EN4 0NL.

SMITH, Ralph E. K. T.; *see* Taylor-Smith.

SMITH, (Raymond) Gordon (Antony); *see* Etherington-Smith.

SMITH, Sir Raymond (Horace), KBE 1967 (CBE 1960); Chairman of Hawker Siddeley and other British companies in Venezuela; Consultant to Rolls-Royce Ltd; *b* 1917; *s* of Horace P. Smith and Mabelle (*née* Osborne-Couzens); *m* 1943, Dorothy, *d* of Robert Cheney Hart. *Educ:* Salesian College, London; Barcelona University. Served War of 1939–45, with British Security Co-ordination, NY, and with Intelligence Corps, in France, India, Burma, Malaya, Indonesia. Civil Attaché British Embassy, Caracas, 1941; Negotiator, sale of British owned railway cos to Venezuelan Govt and other S American govts, 1946–50; Rep., London Reinsurers in Venezuela, 1954–60; Consultant: Cammell Laird; Mirrlees; British Aerospace, 1952–82; Provincial Insurance Co. Ltd; Director: Daily Journal; Anglo-Venezuelan Cultural Inst., 1946–80; British Venezuelan Chamber of Commerce, 1956–86 (Hon. Pres., 1987); Pres. British Commonwealth Assoc. of Venezuela, 1955–57. Companion of Royal Aeronautical Society. Knight Grand Cross, St Lazarus of Jerusalem; Venezuelan Air Force Cross. *Recreations:* tennis, water ski-ing, winter sports (Cresta Run and ski-ing). *Address:* Quinta San Antonio, Calle El Samancito, Avenida El Saman, Caracas Country Club, Caracas 1062, Venezuela; Carlton Lodge, 37 Lowndes Street, SW1. *Clubs:* White's, Naval and Military; Caracas Country, Jockey (Caracas); St Moritz Tobogganing (Switzerland).

SMITH, Sir Reginald Verdon; *see* Verdon-Smith.

SMITH, Richard; *see* Smith, W. R.

SMITH, Richard H. S.; *see* Sandford Smith.

SMITH, Richard John; High Commissioner for Australia in the United Kingdom, since 1991; *b* 14 Dec. 1934; *s* of C. A. Smith and T. A. O'Halloran; *m* 1958, Janet Campbell; two *s* two *d. Educ:* Sydney High Sch.; Sydney Univ. (BA, LLB Hons I 1958). Teacher, London, 1958–59; Solicitor, NSW, 1959–61; Foreign Affairs Trainee, 1961; First Sec., Australian Embassy, Washington, 1967–70; Dep. Perm. Rep., Australian Mission to UN, Geneva, 1972–74; Asst Sec., Internat. Legal Branch, 1974–75; Ambassador to Israel, 1975–77; First Assistant Secretary: Legal & Treaties Div., 1977–81; Management & Foreign Service Div., 1981–83; Actg Dep. Sec., Dept of Foreign Affairs, 1983–85; Ambassador to Thailand, 1985–88; Dep. Sec., Dept of Foreign Affairs and Trade, Canberra, 1988–90. *Recreations:* walking, reading, travel. *Address:* Australian High Commission, Strand, WC2B 4LA. *T:* 071–438 8209.

SMITH, Richard Maybury H.; *see* Hastie-Smith.

SMITH, Dr Richard Michael, FRHistS; FBA 1991; Reader in the History of Medicine and Director of Wellcome Unit for the History of Medicine, University of Oxford, since 1990; Fellow, All Souls College, Oxford, since 1983; *b* 3 Jan. 1946; *s* of Louis Gordon Smith and Elsie Fanny (*née* Ward); *m* 1971, Margaret Anne McFadden. *Educ:* Earls Colne Grammar Sch.; University Coll. London (BA Hons); St Catharine's Coll., Cambridge (MA 1977; PhD 1974). Lectr in Population Studies, Plymouth Poly., 1973–74; Cambridge University: Asst Lectr in Histl Geography, 1974–76; Sen. Res. Officer, 1976–81, Asst Dir, 1981–83, Cambridge Gp for the Hist. of Population and Social Structure; Fellow, 1977–83, Tutor, 1979–83, Fitzwilliam Coll.; Univ. Lectr in Histl Demography, Oxford, 1983–89. Mem. Council, British Soc. for Population Studies, 1987–91. Ed., Social Hist. of Medicine, 1986–. *Publications:* (ed jtly) Bastardy and its Comparative History, 1980; (ed) Land, Kinship and Lifecycle, 1984; (ed jtly) The World We Have Gained: histories of population and social structure, 1986; (ed jtly) Life, Death and the Elderly: historical perspectives, 1991; contribs to Annales ESC, Jl of Family Hist., Trans RHistS, Ageing and Society, Law and Hist. Rev., Population and Develt Rev. *Recreations:* listening to music, walking in Norfolk. *Address:* All Souls College, Oxford OX1 4AL. *T:* Oxford (0865) 279313.

SMITH, Sir Richard P.; *see* Prince-Smith, Sir (William) Richard.

SMITH, Sir Richard Robert L.; *see* Law-Smith.

SMITH, Sir Richard R. V.; *see* Vassar-Smith.

SMITH, Prof. R(ichard) Selby, OBE 1981; MA (Oxon), MA (Harvard); Professor of Education and Head of Department of Education, University of Tasmania, 1973–79, now Professor Emeritus; *b* 1914; *s* of Selby Smith, Hall Place, Barming, Maidstone, Kent, and Annie Rachel Smith (*née* Rawlins); *m* 1940, Rachel Hebe Philippa Pease, Rounton, Northallerton, Yorks; two *s. Educ:* Rugby Sch.; Magdalen Coll., Oxford; Harvard Univ. Asst Master, Milton Acad., Milton, Mass, USA, 1938–39; House Tutor and Sixth Form Master, Sedbergh Sch., 1939–40; War of 1939–45: Royal Navy, 1940–46; final rank of Lt-Comdr, RNVR. Administrative Asst, Kent Education Cttee, 1946–48; Asst Education Officer, Kent, 1948–50; Dep. Chief Education Officer, Warwickshire, 1950–53; Principal, Scotch Coll., Melbourne, 1953–64; Foundation Prof. of Educn, Monash Univ., 1964, Dean of Faculty of Educn, 1965–71; Principal, Tasmanian Coll. of Advanced Education, 1971–73. Chairman: Victorian Univs and Schools Examinations Bd, 1967–71; State Planning and Finance Cttee, Australian Schools Commn, 1974–77, 1980–83; Vice-Pres., Australian Council for Educnl Research, 1976–79. Hon. LLD Monash, 1989. *Publications:* Towards an Australian Philosophy of Education, 1965; (ed jtly) Fundamental Issues in Australian Education, 1971; The Education Policy Process in Tasmania, 1980; Australian Independent Schools: yesterday, today and tomorrow, 1983. *Recreations:* fishing, gardening, sailing, riding and ornithology. *Address:* Apt 234, Derwent Waters Residential Club, Cadbury Road, Claremont, Tas 7011, Australia.

SMITH, Richard Sydney William; Editor, British Medical Journal, since 1991; *b* 11 March 1952; *s* of Sydney Smith and Hazel Smith (*née* Kirk); *m* 1977, Linda Jean Arnott; two *s* one *d. Educ:* Roan Grammar Sch., London; Edinburgh Univ. (BSc 1973; MB ChB 1976); Stanford Univ. (MSc in Management 1990). MFPHM. Hosp. jobs in Scotland and New Zealand, 1976–79; Asst Editor, 1979, Sen. Asst Editor, 1984, BMJ. BBC Breakfast Time doctor, 1983–87. *Publications:* Alcohol Problems, 1982; Prison Health Care, 1984; The Good Health Kit, 1987; Unemployment and Health, 1987; articles in learned jls. *Recreations:* jazz, cycling, running, wine, talking first and thinking second. *Address:* British Medical Journal, BMA House, Tavistock Square, WC1H 9JR.

SMITH, Robert Carr, CBE 1989; PhD; Director, Kingston Polytechnic, since 1982; *b* 19 Nov. 1935; *s* of Edward Albert Smith and Olive Winifred Smith; *m* 1960, Rosalie Mary (*née* Spencer); one *s* one *d. Educ:* Queen Elizabeth's School, Barnet; Southampton Univ. (BSc); London Univ. (PhD). Research Asst, Guy's Hosp. Med. Sch., 1957–61; Lectr, Senior Lectr, Reader, Prof. of Electronics, Southampton Univ., 1961–82. Seconded to DoE, 1973–74. Chairman: Engineering Profs' Conf., 1980–82; Polytechnics and Colls Employers' Forum, 1988–90; Vice-Chm., Cttee of Dirs of Polytechnics, 1988–89; Member: Design Council, 1983–88; Council for Industry and Higher Educn, 1985–; Council, Inst. for Manpower Studies, 1987–; PCFC, 1989–. *Publications:* research papers on radiation physics, laser physics, new technology. *Recreations:* visual arts, collecting. *Address:* Maybury Cottage, Raleigh Drive, Claygate, Surrey KT10 9DE. *T:* Esher (0372) 463352.

SMITH, Sir Robert (Courtney), Kt 1987; CBE 1980; FRSE; MA, CA; Chairman, Alliance and Second Alliance Trust, since 1984; *b* 10 Sept. 1927; 4th *s* of late John Smith, DL, JP, and Agnes Smith, Glasgow and Symington; *m* 1954, Moira Rose, *d* of late Wilfred H. Macdougall, CA, Glasgow; one *s* two *d* (and one *s* decd). *Educ:* Kelvinside Academy, Glasgow; Sedbergh Sch.; Trinity Coll., Cambridge. BA 1950, MA 1957. Served, Royal Marines, 1945–47, and RMFVR, 1951–57. Partner, Arthur Young McClelland Moores & Co., Chartered Accountants, 1957–78. Director: Standard Life Assurance, 1975– (Chm., 1982–88); Sidlaw Gp, 1977– (Chm., 1980–88); Wm Collins, 1978–89 (Vice-Chm., 1979–89); Volvo Trucks (GB), 1979–; Edinburgh Investment Trust, 1983–; British Alcan Aluminium, 1983–; Bank of Scotland, 1985–. Mem., Scottish Industrial Develt Adv. Bd, 1972–88 (Chm., 1981–88); Pres., Business Archives Council of Scotland; Chancellor's Assessor, Glasgow Univ., 1984–. Mem., Horserace Betting Levy Bd, 1977–82; Deacon Convener, Trades House of Glasgow, 1976–78. Mem. Council, Inst. of Chartered Accountants of Scotland, 1974–79. Trustee, Carnegie Trust for Univs of Scotland. FRSE 1988. Hon. LLD: Glasgow, 1978; Aberdeen, 1991. OStJ. *Recreations:* racing, gardening. *Address:* North Lodge, Dunkeld, Perthshire PH8 0AR. *T:* Dunkeld (03502) 574; (professional) 64 Reform Street, Dundee DD1 1TJ. *Clubs:* East India; Western (Glasgow); Hawks (Cambridge).
See also John Smith.

SMITH, (Robert) Harvey; show jumper, farmer; *b* 29 Dec. 1938; *m* 1st, Irene Shuttleworth (marr. diss. 1986); two *s*; 2nd, 1987, Susan Dye. First major win with Farmer's Boy. Leading Show Jumper of the Year; other major wins include: King George V Cup, Royal Internat. Horse Show, 1958; has won the John Player Trophy 7 times, King George V Gold Cup once, and the British Jumping Derby 4 times; Grand Prix and Prix des Nations wins in UK, Ireland, Europe and USA; took part in Olympic Games, 1968 and 1972; best-known mounts: Farmer's Boy, Mattie Brown, Olympic Star, O'Malley, Salvador, Harvester. BBC TV Commentator, Los Angeles Olympics, 1984. *Publications:* Show Jumping with Harvey Smith, 1979; Bedside Jumping, 1985.

SMITH, Prof. Robert Henry Tufrey; Vice-Chancellor, University of New England, Australia, since 1990; *b* 22 May 1935; *s* of late Robert Davidson Smith and Gladys Smith (*née* Tufrey); *m* 1959, Elisabeth Jones; one *s* one *d. Educ:* Farrer Memorial Agricultural High Sch., Tamworth, NSW; Univ. of New England, NSW (BA, 1st Cl. Hons Geography); Northwestern Univ. (MA); ANU (PhD). Lectr in Geography, Univ. of Melbourne, 1961–62; University of Wisconsin: Asst Prof. of Geography, 1962–64; Associate Prof., 1964–67; Prof., 1967–70; Chm., African Studies Programme, 1968–69 (on leave, 1964–66: Associate Res. Fellow, Nigerian Inst. for Social and Econ. Res., and Hon. Vis. Lectr in Geography, Univ. of Ibadan, 1964–65; Vis. Fellow, Dept of Geography, Univ. of Sydney, 1965–66); Prof. of Geography and Head of Dept, Queen's Univ., Kingston, Ontario, 1970–72; Prof. of Geography, Monash Univ., 1972–75 (Chm. of Dept, 1973–75; Associate Dean, Faculty of Arts, 1974–75); University of British Columbia: Prof. of Geography, 1975–85; Head of Dept, 1975–80; Associate Vice-Pres., Academic, 1979–83; Vice-Pres., Academic, 1983–85; Pres. *pro tem*, March–Nov. 1985; Vice-Chancellor, Univ. of WA, 1985–89; Chm., Nat. Bd of Employment, Educn and Trng, Aust., 1989–90. *Address:* University of New England, Armidale, NSW 2351, Australia. *T:* 67 73 2001, *Fax:* 67 71 1571.

SMITH, Sir Robert Hill, 3rd Bt *cr* 1945, of Crowmallie, Co. Aberdeen; *b* 15 April 1958; *s* of Sir (William) Gordon Smith, 2nd Bt, VRD, and of Diana (*née* Goodchild); *S* father, 1983. *Educ:* Merchant Taylors' School; Aberdeen Univ. *Heir: b* Charles Gordon Smith, *b* 21 April 1959. *Address:* 5 Elmfield Avenue, Aberdeen AB2 3NU.

SMITH, Rt. Rev. Robin Jonathan Norman; *see* Hertford, Bishop Suffragan of.

SMITH, Rodger Hayward; *see* Hayward Smith.

SMITH, Roger Bonham; Chairman and Chief Executive Officer, General Motors, 1981–90 (Member, Board of Directors, since 1974); *b* Columbus, Ohio, 12 July 1925. *Educ:* Detroit University Sch.; Univ. of Michigan (BBA, MBA). Served US Navy, 1944–46. General Motors: Sen. Clerk, subseq. Director, general accounting, Detroit Central Office, 1949–58; Dir, financial analysis sect., NY Central Office, 1960, later Asst Treas.; transf. to Detroit as Gen. Asst Comptroller, then Gen. Asst Treas., 1968; Treasurer, 1970; Vice-Pres. i/c Financial Staff, 1971, also Mem. Admin Cttee, 1971–90; Vice-Pres. and Gp Exec. i/c Nonautomotive and Defense Gp, 1972; Exec. Vice-Pres., Mem. Bd of Dirs and Mem. Finance Cttee, 1974, also Mem. Exec. Cttee, 1974–90; Vice-Chm. Finance

Cttee, 1975–80, Chm., 1981–90. Conceived GM Cancer Res. Awards, 1978 (Trustee); Member: Business Council, 1981–; Soc. of Automotive Engrs, 1978–. Hon. degrees from several univs. Hon. Dr DePauw, 1979; Hon. Dr Albion Coll., 1982. *Address:* General Motors Corporation, 31 Judson Street, Pontiac, Mich 48342-2230, USA; (home) Bloomfield Hills, Michigan 48013. *Clubs:* Economic, Detroit, Detroit Athletic (Detroit); Links (NY).

SMITH, Roger John; Chairman and Chief Executive, Trimoco plc, since 1987; *b* 20 April 1939; *s* of Horace W. Smith and Marjorie E. Pummery; *m* 1962, Margaret R. Campbell; one *s* two *d. Educ:* Bedford School. Nat. Service, Subaltern, RCT, 1958–60. Dir, Family Group business, incl. Lea Heating Merchants (later part of Tricentrol), 1960–70; Man. Dir, Commercial Div., 1971–75, Dir, Special Projects, 1976–78, Tricentrol International; Dir, Group Co-ordination, Tricentrol, 1978–81; Man. Dir, Commercial Div., 1981–83; Dep. Chm., Tricentrol plc, 1983–88. Director: Combined Technologies Corp. plc; Brengreen Hldgs plc, and other cos. Pres., Retail Motor Industry Fedn, 1991. Sloan Fellow, Stanford Univ., 1976. Liveryman, Coach and Harnessmakers' Co. *Recreations:* Methodist church activities, sailing, shooting, squash, tennis, reading; Chm. of Luton Town Football Club. *Address:* Gilvers, Markyate, Herts. *T:* Luton (0582) 840536. *Clubs:* City of London, Royal Thames Yacht.

SMITH, Sir Roland, Kt 1991; Chairman, British Aerospace, since 1987; a Director, Bank of England, since 1991; Professor of Marketing (part-time), University of Manchester Institute of Science and Technology, 1966–88, now Emeritus; *b* 1 Oct. 1928; *s* of late Joshua Smith and of Mrs Hannah Smith; *m* 1954, Joan (*née* Shaw); no *c. Educ:* Univs of Birmingham and Manchester. BA, MSc, PhD (Econ). Flying Officer, RAF, 1953. Asst Dir, Footwear Manufacturers' Fedn, 1955; Lectr in Econs, Univ. of Liverpool, 1960; Dir, Univ. of Liverpool Business Sch., 1963. Non-Exec. Chm., Senior Engineering Ltd, 1973–; Chairman: Temple Bar Investment Trust Ltd, 1980–; House of Fraser, 1981–86 (Dep. Chm., 1980–81); Readicut International, 1984– (Dep. Chm., 1982–84); Hepworth plc, 1986–; Phoenix Properties and Finance, 1986–87; Kingston Oil & Gas, 1987–; P & P plc, 1988–; Manchester United FC, 1991–; Dir-Consultant to a number of public companies. *Recreation:* walking.

SMITH, Roland Hedley; HM Diplomatic Service; Head of Non-Proliferation and Defence Department, Foreign and Commonwealth Office, since 1990; *b* 11 April 1943; *s* of Alan Hedley Smith and Elizabeth Louise Smith; *m* 1971, Katherine Jane Lawrence; two *d. Educ:* King Edward VII School, Sheffield; Keble College, Oxford (BA 1st cl. hons 1965, MA 1981). Third Sec., Foreign Office, 1967; Second Sec., Moscow, 1969; Second, later First Sec., UK Delegn to NATO, Brussels, 1971; First Sec., FCO, 1974; First Sec. and Cultural Attaché, Moscow, 1978; FCO, 1980; attached to Internat. Inst. for Strategic Studies, 1983; Political Advr and Hd of Chancery, British Mil. Govt, Berlin, 1984–88; Dep. Hd, Sci., Energy and Nuclear Dept, FCO, 1988–90. *Publication:* Soviet Policy Towards West Germany, 1985. *Recreation:* music, esp. choral singing. *Address:* c/o Foreign and Commonwealth Office, SW1A 2AH. *Club:* Commonwealth Trust.

SMITH, Ron, CBE 1973; Member, British Steel Corporation, 1967–77 (Managing Director (Personnel and Social Policy), 1967–72); formed British Steel Corporation (Industry) Ltd and was first Chairman, 1974–77; *b* 15 July 1915; *s* of Henry Sidney Smith and Bertha Clara (*née* Barnwell); *m* 1940, Daisy Hope (*d* 1974), *d* of Herbert Leggatt Nicholson; one *d. Educ:* Workers' Education Association. Post Office Messenger, 1929; Postman, 1934; Postal and Telegraph Officer, 1951; Treasurer, Union of Post Office Workers, 1953; Gen. Sec., Union of Post Office Workers, 1957–66. General Council, TUC, 1957–66; Civil Service National Whitley Council, 1957–66; Exec. Cttee, Postal, Telegraph and Telephone International, 1957–66; Vice-Chairman, Post Office Dept, Whitley Council, 1959–66. Member: Cttee on Grants to Students, 1958–60; Development Areas, Treasury Advisory Cttee, 1959–60; Cttee on Company Law, 1960–62; National Economic Development Council, 1962–66; Court of Enquiry into Ford Motor Co. Dispute, 1963; Cttee of Enquiry into Pay, etc, of London Transport Bus Staff, 1963–64; Organising Cttee for Nat. Steel Corp., 1966; (part-time) Associated British Ports Hldgs plc (formerly BTDB), 1978–86. President, Postal, Telegraph and Telephone Internat., 1966. Director, BOAC, 1964–70. *Recreations:* photography, golf. *Address:* 3 Beech Grove, Epsom, Surrey KT18 5UD. *Club:* Tyrrells Wood Golf.

SMITH, Ronald A. D.; *see* Dingwall-Smith.

SMITH, Ronald Good; Sheriff of North Strathclyde, since 1984; *b* 24 July 1933; *s* of Adam Smith and Selina Spence Smith; *m* 1962, Joan Robertson Beharrie; two *s. Educ:* Glasgow University (BL 1962). Private practice to 1984. *Recreations:* philately, photography, gardening, reading. *Address:* 369 Mearns Road, Newton Mearns, Glasgow G77 5LZ. *T:* 041–639 3904.

SMITH, Rosemary Ann, (Mrs G. F. Smith); Headmistress, Wimbledon High School, GPDST, 1982–Sept. 1992; *b* 10 Feb. 1932; *d* of late Harold Edward Wincott, CBE, editor of the Investors Chronicle, and of Joyce Mary Wincott; *m* 1954, Rev. Canon Graham Francis Smith; two *s* two *d. Educ:* Brighton and Hove High School, GPDST; Westfield College, Univ. of London (BA Hons); London Univ. Inst. of Education (post grad. Cert. in Education). Assistant Teacher: Central Foundation Girls' School, 1964–69; Rosa Bassett Girls' School, 1970–77; Furzedown Secondary School, 1977–80; Deputy Head, Rowan High School, 1980–82. *Recreations:* theatre, gardening, dressmaking, reading, walking. *Address:* 30 Gorringe Park Avenue, Mitcham, Surrey CR4 2DG. *T:* 081–685 0772.

SMITH, Air Marshal Sir Roy David A.; *see* Austen-Smith.

SMITH, Sidney William; retired; Regional Administrator, East Anglian Regional Health Authority, 1975–83; *b* 17 May 1920; *s* of late Sidney John and Harriet May Smith; *m* 1943, Doreen Kelly; one *s* one *d. Educ:* Wirral Grammar Sch., Cheshire. FHSM; ACIS. Served RAF, 1940–46. Asst Sec., Bury Infirmary, 1939–48; Dep. Group Sec.: Mansfield Hosp. Management Cttee, 1948–61; Wolverhampton Hosp. Management Cttee, 1961–63; Group Sec., Wakefield Hosp. Management Cttee, 1963–73; Area Administrator, Wakefield Area Health Authority, 1973–75. Member: Management Side, Ancillary Staff, Whitley Council, 1969–83 (Chm., 1982–83); Cttee, Assoc. of Chief Administrators of Health Authorities, 1974–84 (Chm., 1974–76); Health Services Panel, Inst. of Chartered Secretaries and Administrators, 1978–84, 1986– (Chm., 1978–83); Council, Soc. of Family Practitioner Cttees, 1989–90; Vice Chm., Cambs FPC, 1985–90; Chm., Pharmaceutical Services Panel, Cambs FHSA, 1991–. Dir, Sketchley Hosp. Services Ltd, 1983–84. Freeman, City of London, 1985; Liveryman, Chartered Secretaries' and Administrators' Co., 1985–. *Recreations:* gardening, Rugby Union football. *Address:* 77 Gough Way, Cambridge CB3 9LN. *T:* Cambridge (0223) 62307.

SMITH, Prof. (Stanley) Desmond, FRS 1976; FRSE 1972; Professor of Physics and Head of Department of Physics, Heriot-Watt University, Edinburgh, since 1970 (Dean of the Faculty of Science, 1981–84); *b* 3 March 1931; *s* of Henry George Stanley Smith and Sarah Emily Ruth Smith; *m* 1956, Gillian Anne Parish; one *s* one *d. Educ:* Cotham Grammar Sch., Bristol; Bristol Univ. (BSc, DSc); Reading Univ. (PhD). SSO, RAE, Farnborough, 1956–58; Research Asst, Dept of Meteorology, Imperial Coll., London, 1958–59; Lectr, then Reader, Univ. of Reading, 1960–70. Chm., Edinburgh Instruments Ltd, 1971–. Member: ACARD, 1985–87; Defence Scientific Adv. Council, 1985–; Astronomy Bd, Space & Radio Bd, Engrg Bd, SERC, 1985–88; ACOST, 1987–88. Mem. Council, Inst. of Physics, 1984–87. C. V. Boys Prizeman, Inst. of Physics, 1976; Educn in Partnership with Industry or Commerce Prize, DTI, 1982; Technical or Business Innovation in Electronics Prize, Electronics Weekly, 1986; James Scott Prize, RSE, 1987. *Publications:* Infra-red Physics, 1966; numerous papers on semi-conductor and laser physics, satellite meteorology, nonlinear optics and optical computing. *Recreations:* tennis, skiing, mountaineering, golf. *Address:* Tree Tops, 29D Gillespie Road, Colinton, Edinburgh EH13 0NW. *T:* 031–441 7225; (office) 031–449 5542, *Fax:* 031–451 3136.

SMITH, Stanley Frank, MA; CEng, FIMechE, FCIT; Vice-President (Technology), Urban Transport Development Company, Kingston, Ontario, 1985–86, retired; *b* 15 Dec. 1924; *s* of Frederick and Edith Maria Smith; *m* 1st, 1946, Margaret (*née* Garrett) (*d* 1984); two *s* three *d*; 2nd, 1987, Catherine Cooke Murphy. *Educ:* Purley Sch.; Hertford Coll., Oxford (MA). Served War, RAF Pilot, 1943–46. Oxford Univ., 1946–49. Rolls-Royce Ltd, 1949–65 (Chief Research Engineer, 1963); British Railways, 1965–71 (Dir of Engineering Research, 1965; Dir of Research, 1966); joined London Transport, 1971: Dir-Gen. of Research and Develt, 1971–72; Chief Mech. Engr, 1972–81, retired; Gen. Manager, Res. Develt, Urban Transport Development Co., 1981–85. *Recreations:* tennis, windsurfing, cycling, walking, ski-ing, sailing. *Address:* Rural Route 1, Bath, Ontario K0H 1G0, Canada. *T:* 613–352–7429.

SMITH, Prof. Stephen Kevin, MD; Professor of Obstetrics and Gynaecology, University of Cambridge Clinical School, Rosie Maternity Hospital, Cambridge, since 1988; Fellow, Fitzwilliam College, Cambridge, since 1991; *b* 8 March 1951; *s* of Albert and Drusilla Smith; *m* 1978, Catriona Maclean Hobkirk Smith; one *s* two *d. Educ:* Birkenhead Sch.; Westminster Med. Sch., Univ. of London (MB BS 1974; MD 1982); MRCOG 1979. Lecturer: Univ. of Edinburgh, 1979–82; Univ. of Sheffield, 1982–85; Cons. Gynaecologist, MRC Reproductive Biology Unit, Edinburgh, 1985–88. *Publications:* numerous contribs to sci. and med. pubns on the subject of Reproductive Medicine. *Recreations:* cricket, football, music, natural history, politics. *Address:* 24 Hertford Street, Cambridge CB4 3AG. *T:* Cambridge (0223) 467169.

SMITH, Stewart Ranson, CBE 1986; Chairman, Consortium for Madrid Capital City of Culture 1992, since 1990; *b* 16 Feb. 1931; *s* of John Smith and Elizabeth Smith; *m* 1960, Lee Tjam Mui, Singapore. *Educ:* Bedlington Grammar Sch., Northumberland; Nottingham Univ. (BA, MA); Yale Univ., USA (MA). British Council: Asst Rep., Singapore, 1957–59; Reg. Officer, Overseas A, 1959–61; Dir, Curitiba, Brazil, 1961–65; Asst Rep., Sri Lanka, 1965–69; Planning Officer, London, 1969–70; seconded Min. of Overseas Develt, 1970–73; Rep., Kenya, 1973–76; Controller, Overseas B, 1976–80; Rep., Spain, 1980–87; Controller, Higher Educn Div., 1987–89; Controller, Europe Div., 1989–90. Cross, Order of Isabella la Católica (Spain). *Recreations:* music, cricket. *Address:* Zurbano 7, 28010 Madrid, Spain; Flat 1, Cumberland House, Clifton Gardens, W9 1DX. *Club:* Athenæum.

SMITH, Stuart Brian, FMA; Director, Ironbridge Gorge Museum, since 1983; *b* 19 Aug. 1944; *s* of Jack Fearnly Smith and Edith Dorothy Turner; *m* 1969, Jacqueline Slater; two *s* one *d. Educ:* Rochdale Grammar Sch.; Univ. of Surrey (BSc); Univ. of Manchester (MSc). Curator of Technology, Sunderland Museum, 1968–72; Curator of Technology, 1972, Dep. Dir, 1977–83, Ironbridge Gorge Museum. Hon. Lectr, Univ. of Birmingham, 1981–. Asst Sec., Assoc. for Industrial Archaeology, 1975–; Sec., Internat. Cttee for Conservation of Industrial Heritage, 1986–. Mem., Royal Commn on Ancient and Historical Monuments in Wales, 1991–. Pres., Midlands Fedn of Museums and Galls, 1991– (Vice-Pres. 1989); Vice-Pres., Chatterly Whitfield Mining Mus., 1988–. Mem. Cttee, Icomos UK, 1987–. Mem., Editl Bd, Blackwell Encyclopaedia of Industrial Archaeology, 1991–. FRSA. Freedom of City of London, 1984. *Publications:* A View from the Ironbridge, 1979; articles in learned jls. *Recreations:* restoration, gardening, collecting. *Address:* Ironbridge Gorge Museum, Ironbridge, Telford, Shropshire TF8 7AW. *T:* Ironbridge (0952) 433522.

SMITH, T(homas) Dan; Founder, New Directions, projects to assist ex-offenders, 1978; *b* 11 May 1915; *m* 1939; one *s* two *d.* City Councillor, Newcastle upon Tyne, 1950–65 (Chairman, Finance Cttee); Member: Nat. Sports Council, 1965–69; Royal Commission on Local Government, 1966–69; Shakespeare Theatre Trust, 1968–. Chairman: Northern Economic Planning Council, 1965–70; Peterlee and Aycliffe Develt Corp., 1968–70. Researcher for Amber Films, 1982–85. Consultant on the develt of an internat. science and technology paper, Change, 1982–86. Lecturer, broadcaster on constitutional reform and other subjects, 1987–88. Chairman: Mill House Tenants Assoc., 1987–; Spital Tongues Community Assoc., 1987–. Hon. DCL Newcastle University, 1966. *Publications:* Essays in Local Government, 1965; contrib. to Which Way, 1970; Education, Science and Technology (paper to British Assoc. for Advancement of Science), 1970; An Autobiography, 1971. *Recreations:* painting, music, writing, sport. *Address:* 92 Millhouse, 5 Hunters Road, Spital Tongues, Newcastle upon Tyne NE2 4AQ.

SMITH, Sir (Thomas) Gilbert, 4th Bt, *cr* 1897; Area Manager; *b* 2 July 1937; *er s* of Sir Thomas Turner Smith, 3rd Bt, and Agnes, *o d* of Bernard Page, Wellington, New Zealand; *S* father, 1961; *m* 1962, Patricia Christine Cooper; two *s* one *d. Educ:* Huntley Sch.; Nelson Coll. *Recreation:* skiing. *Heir: s* Andrew Thomas Smith, *b* 17 Oct. 1965.

SMITH, Rt. Rev. Timothy D.; *see* Dudley-Smith.

SMITH, Timothy John; MP (C) Beaconsfield, since May 1982; *b* 5 Oct. 1947; *s* of late Captain Norman Wesley Smith, CBE and Nancy Phyllis Smith; *m* 1980, Jennifer Jane Scott-Hopkins, *d* of Sir James Scott-Hopkins, *qv*; two *s. Educ:* Harrow Sch.; St Peter's Coll., Oxford (MA). FCA. Articled with Gibson, Harris & Turnbull, 1969; Audit Sen., Peat, Marwick, Mitchell & Co., 1971; Company Sec., Coubro & Scrutton (Hldgs) Ltd, 1973. Sec., Parly and Law Cttee, ICA, 1979–82. Pres., Oxford Univ. Conservative Assoc., 1968; Chm., Coningsby Club, 1977–78. MP (C) Ashfield, April 1977–1979; PPS to Chief Sec. HM Treasury, 1983, to Sec. of State for Home Dept, 1983–85. Vice-Chm., Conservative Finance Cttee, 1987–; Mem., Public Accts Cttee, 1987–. Dir, Gartmore Value Investments PLC, 1991–. *Recreations:* theatre, gardening. *Address:* 27 Rosenau Crescent, SW11. *T:* 071–223 3378.

SMITH, Prof. Trevor Arthur, FRHistS; Vice-Chancellor, University of Ulster, since 1991; *b* 14 June 1937; *e s* of Arthur and Vera Smith, London E5; *m* 1st, 1960, Brenda Eustace (marr. diss. 1973); two *s*; 2nd, 1979, Julia Bullock; one *d. Educ:* LSE (BSc Econ 1958). Schoolteacher, LCC, 1958–59; temp. Asst Lectr, Exeter Univ., 1959–60; Research Officer, Acton Soc. Trust, 1960–62; Lectr in Politics, Hull Univ., 1962–67; Queen Mary College, later Queen Mary & Westfield College, London: Lectr and Sen. Lectr in Political Studies, 1967–83; Prof., Political Studies, 1983–91; Head of Dept, 1972–85; Dean of Social Studies, 1979–82; Pro-Principal, 1985–87; Sen. Pro-Principal, 1987–89; Sen. Vice-Prin., 1989–91; Mem., Senate, London Univ., 1987–. Vis. Associate Prof., California State Univ., LA, 1969. Director: Job Ownership Ltd, 1978–85; New Society Ltd, 1986–88;

Statesman & Nation Publishing Co. Ltd, 1988–90 (Chm. 1990); G. Duckworth & Co., 1990–. Mem., Tower Hamlets DHA, 1987–91. Pres., Political Studies Assoc. of UK, 1991– (Chm., 1988–89); Vice-Pres., Patients' Assoc., 1988–. Mem., Liberal Party Exec., 1958–59; contested (L) Lewisham W, 1959. Trustee: Joseph Rowntree Reform (formerly Social Service) Trust, 1975– (Chm., 1987–); Acton Soc. Trust, 1975–87; Employment Inst., 1987–. Governor: Sir John Cass and Redcoats Sch., 1979–84; Univ. of Haifa, 1985–; Bell Educnl Trust, 1988–. Mem., Willesden Area Synod, 1985–88. *Publications:* (with M. Argyle) Training Managers, 1962; (with A. M. Rees) Town Councillors, 1964; Town and County Hall, 1966; Anti-Politics, 1972; (ed with R. Benewick) Direct Action and Democratic Politics, 1972; The Politics of the Corporate Economy, 1979; British Politics in the Post-Keynesian Era, 1986. *Recreation:* water colour painting. *Address:* University of Ulster, University House, Coleraine, Co. Londonderry, N Ireland BT52 1SA. *T:* Coleraine (0265) 44141. *Club:* Reform.

SMITH, Vernon Olivier; Senior Partner, Smith & Smith (Barbados), Solicitors/Attorneys-at-Law, since 1989 (Partner, 1974–86); *b* 25 June 1930; *s* of Cecil Gladstone Smith and Lilian Angelique Smith; *m* (marr. diss.); one *s* one *d. Educ:* Univ. of West Indies; BA London; qual. Solicitor, 1974. Classics Master, Harrison Coll., Barbados, 1953–54; Sen. Classics Master, Excelsior Coll., Jamaica, 1954–57; LCC Educn Authy, 1957–62; Sen. English Master, Ikwere-Etche Grammar Sch., E Nigeria, 1963–65; Berks Co. Educn Authy, 1965–68; Sen. Classics Master, Combermere Sch., Barbados, 1968–72; High Comr for Barbados in UK, 1986–89. *Recreations:* tennis, cricket. *Address:* Veronda, Browne's Gap, Hastings, Christ Church, Barbados.

SMITH, Adm. Sir Victor (Alfred Trumper), AC 1975; KBE 1969 (CBE 1963); CB 1968; DSC 1941; Chairman, Australian Chiefs of Staff Committee, 1970–75; Military Adviser to SEATO, 1970–74; *b* 9 May 1913; *s* of George Smith; *m* 1944, Nanette Suzanne Harrison; three *s. Educ:* Royal Australian Naval College. Sub-Lieut, 1935; Lieut, 1936; Lieut-Commander, 1944; Commander, 1947; Captain, 1953; Rear-Admiral, 1963; Vice-Admiral, 1968; Chief of Naval Staff and First Naval Member, Austr. Commonwealth Naval Bd, 1968–70; Admiral, 1970. *Recreation:* walking. *Address:* Fishburn Street, Red Hill, ACT 2603, Australia. *T:* Canberra 2958942.

SMITH, Walter Purvis, CB 1982; OBE 1960 (MBE 1945); Director General, Ordnance Survey, 1977–85, retired; *b* 8 March 1920; *s* of John William Smith and Margaret Jane (*née* Purvis); *m* 1946, Bettie Cox; one *s* one *d. Educ:* Wellfield Grammar Sch., Co. Durham; St Edmund Hall, Oxford (MA). FRICS 1951. Commnd RE (Survey), 1940; served War, UK and Europe, 1940–46; CO 135 Survey Engr Regt (TA), 1957–60. Directorate of Colonial (later Overseas) Surveys: served in Ghana, Tanzania, Malaŵi, 1946–50; Gen. Man., Air Survey Co. of Rhodesia Ltd, 1950–54; Fairey Surveys Ltd, 1954–75 (Man. Dir, 1969–75); Adviser: Surveying and Mapping, UN, NY, 1975–77; Ordnance Survey Review Cttee, 1978–79. Mem., Field Mission, Argentine-Chile Frontier Case, 1965. 15th British Commonwealth Lectr, RAeS, 1968. Dir, Sys Scan (UK) Ltd, 1985–90. President: Photogrammetric Soc., 1972–73; European Council of Heads of National Mapping Agencies, 1982–84; Eur. Orgn for Photogrammetric Res., 1984–85; Guild of Surveyors, 1985–88; Chm., National Cttee for Photogrammetry and Remote Sensing, 1985–88; Dep. Chm., Govt Cttee of Enquiry into Handling of Geographical Information, 1985–87; Mem., Gen. Council, RICS, 1967–70 (Chm., Land Survey Cttee, 1963–64). Patron's Medal, RGS, 1985. *Publications:* papers and technical jls. *Recreations:* music, walking, woodworking. *Address:* 15 Forest Gardens, Lyndhurst, Hants SO43 7AF. *T:* Lyndhurst (0703) 282566. *Club:* Oriental.

SMITH, (Walter) Richard; Regional Chairman of Industrial Tribunals, since 1976; *b* 12 Oct. 1926; *s* of Walter Richard and Ivy Millicent Smith; *m* 1959, Jean Monica Law; one *s* one *d. Educ:* Bromsgrove Sch.; Birmingham Univ. (LLB). Called to the Bar, Gray's Inn, 1954. A Chairman of Industrial Tribunals, 1971. *Address:* The Old Bakery, Broadwell, Moreton-in-Marsh, Glos GL56 0TW. *T:* Cotswold (0451) 30130.

SMITH, Wilbur Addison; author; *b* 1933; *m*; two *s* one *d. Educ:* Michaelhouse, Natal; Rhodes Univ. (BCom). Business executive, 1954–58; factory owner, 1958–64; full-time author, 1964–. *Publications:* When the Lion Feeds, 1964; Dark of the Sun, 1965; Sound of Thunder, 1966; Shout at the Devil, 1968; Gold Mine, 1970; Diamond Hunters, 1971; The Sunbird, 1972; Eagle in the Sky, 1974; Eye of the Tiger, 1975; Cry Wolf, 1976; Sparrow Falls, 1977; Hungry as the Sea, 1978; Wild Justice, 1979; A Falcon Flies, 1980; Men of Men, 1981; The Angels Weep, 1982; The Leopard hunts in Darkness, 1984; The Burning Shore, 1985; Power of the Sword, 1986; Rage, 1987; A Time to Die, 1989; Golden Fox, 1990; Elephant Song, 1991. *Recreations:* fly fishing, big game angling. *Address:* c/o Charles Pick Consultancy, Flat 3, 3 Bryanston Place, W1H 7FN.

SMITH, William Austin N.; *see* Nimmo Smith.

SMITH, William Frederick Bottrill, CBE 1964; Accountant and Comptroller General of Inland Revenue, 1958–68; Principal, Uganda Resettlement Board, 1972–74; *b* 29 Oct. 1903; *s* of late Arthur and Harriet Frances Smith; *m* 1926, Edyth Kilbourne (*d* 1970). *Educ:* Newton's, Leicester. Entered the Inland Revenue Dept, Civil Service, 1934. President, Inland Revenue Staff Federation, 1945–47. Vice-Pres., CS Fedn Drama Socs. Church Warden, Holy Trinity Church, Las Palmas. *Address:* 11 Preston Avenue, Rustington-on-Sea, W Sussex; 17 Bridge Avenue Mansions, Bridge Avenue, Hammersmith, W6 9JB. *T:* 081–748 3194.

SMITH, William Jeffrey, CB 1976; Under-Secretary, Northern Ireland Office, 1972–76; *b* 14 Oct. 1916; 2nd *s* of Frederick Smith, Sheffield, and Ellen Hickinson, Ringinglow, Derbyshire; *m* 1942, Marie Hughes; one *s* one *d. Educ:* King Edward VII Sch., Sheffield; University Coll., Oxford (Schol.) (MA). Employed by Calico Printers' Assoc., Manchester, 1938–40 and in 1946. Served War, Army: enlisted Sept. 1939, embodied, 1940; RA and York and Lancaster Regt (Captain), 1940–46. Dominions Office (subseq. CRO), 1946; Principal, 1948; Office of UK High Commissioner in South Africa, 1953–56; Asst Sec., 1959; sundry internat. confs; Dept of Technical Co-operation, 1961–64; Min. of Overseas Development, 1964–70; Overseas Develt Admin., 1970–72; UK Rep. to UNESCO, 1969–72. Sec. to Widgery Tribunal on loss of life in Londonderry, 1972; Northern Ireland Office, 1972. *Recreations:* theatre, scrambling up mountains, walking. *Address:* Lime Tree Cottage, Norris Field, Chaddleworth, Newbury, Berks RG16 0DZ. *T:* Chaddleworth (04882) 610.

SMITH, William McGregor, OBE 1970; HM Inspector of Constabulary for Scotland, 1970–75, retired; *b* 14 April 1910; *s* of John Smith, Milngavie and Agnes Smith (*née* Haldane); *m* 1939, Alice Mary Ewen, Montrose; one *s* one *d. Educ:* Bearsden Academy and Glasgow University (MA 1930). Joined City of Glasgow Police, 1933; Deputy Commandant, Scottish Police College, 1951; Chief Constable of Aberdeen, 1963. *Recreations:* golf, bridge. *Address:* Sherwood, 2 Cherry Tree Park, Balerno, Midlothian. *Clubs:* Luffness New Golf, Baberton Golf.

SMITH, Sir William Reardon Reardon-, 3rd Bt, *cr* 1920; Major, RA (TA); *b* 12 March 1911; *e s* of Sir Willie Reardon-Smith, 2nd Bt, and Elizabeth Ann (*d* 1986), *d* of John and Mary Wakely; *S* father, 1950; *m* 1st, 1935, Nesta (marr. diss., 1954; she *d* 1959), *d* of late Frederick J. Phillips; three *s* one *d*; 2nd, 1954, Beryl, *d* of William H. Powell; one *s* three *d. Educ:* Blundell's Sch., Tiverton. Served War of 1939–45. *Heir: s* (William) Antony (John) Reardon-Smith [*b* 20 June 1937; *m* 1962, Susan, *d* of H. W. Gibson, Cardiff; three *s* one *d. Educ:* Wycliffe Coll., Glos]. *Address:* Rhode Farm, Romansleigh, South Molton, Devon EX36 4JW. *T:* Bishops Nympton (07697) 371. *Club:* Cardiff and County (Cardiff).

SMITH, Sir William Reginald Verdon; *see* Verdon-Smith.

SMITH-DODSWORTH, Sir John (Christopher), 8th Bt, *cr* 1784; *b* 4 March 1935; *s* of Sir Claude Smith-Dodsworth, 7th Bt, and Cyrilla Marie Louise von Sobbe, (*d* 1984), 3rd *d* of William Ernest Taylor, Linnet Lane, Liverpool; *S* father, 1940; *m* 1st, 1961, Margaret Anne (*née* Jones) (marr. diss. 1971); one *s* one *d*; 2nd, 1972, Margaret Theresa (*née* Grey), Auckland, NZ; one *s. Educ:* Ampleforth Coll., Yorks. Now resident in Coromandel, New Zealand. *Heir: s* David John Smith-Dodsworth, *b* 23 Oct. 1963.

SMITH-GORDON, Sir (Lionel) Eldred (Peter), 5th Bt *cr* 1838; engaged in book publishing, since 1960; *b* 7 May 1935; *s* of Sir Lionel Eldred Pottinger Smith-Gordon, 4th Bt, and Eileen Laura (*d* 1979), *d* of late Captain H. G. Adams-Connor, CVO; *S* father, 1976; *m* 1962, Sandra Rosamund Ann, *d* of late Wing Commander Walter Farley, DFC and of Mrs Dennis Poore; one *s* one *d. Educ:* Eton College; Trinity College, Oxford. Chm., Smith-Gordon and Co. Ltd; Director: Consolidated Holdings (Gresham) Ltd; Dietetic Consultants Ltd. *Heir: s* Lionel George Eldred Smith-Gordon [*b* 1 July 1964. *Educ:* Eton; KCL]. *Address:* 13 Shalcomb Street, SW10. *T:* 071–352 8506.

SMITH-MARRIOTT, Sir Hugh Cavendish, 11th Bt *cr* 1774, of Sydling St Nicholas, Dorset; Public Relations and Marketing Executive Director; Director, Scope Marketing Ltd, Bristol, since 1988; *b* 22 March 1925; *s* of Sir Ralph George Cavendish Smith-Marriott,10th Bt and Phyllis Elizabeth (*d* 1932), *d* of Richard Kemp; *S* father, 1987; *m* 1953, Pauline Anne (*d* 1985), *d* of F. F. Holt; one *d. Educ:* Bristol Cathedral School. Man. Dir, Drawing Office Co., 1956; Group Marketing Executive, Bryan Brothers Group, 1976. *Recreations:* hockey (county level), cricket, painting. *Heir: b* Peter Francis Smith-Marriott [*b* 14 Feb. 1927; *m* 1961, Jean Graham Martin, *d* of James Sorley Ritchie; five *s* (including twin *s*)]. *Address:* 26 Shipley Road, Westbury-on-Trym, Bristol BS9 3HS. *T:* Bristol (0272) 502915. *Clubs:* MCC; Gloucestershire County Cricket (Mem. Management Cttee), Bristol Savages, Bristol RF.

SMITHERMAN, Frank, MBE 1951; HM Diplomatic Service, retired; *b* 13 Oct. 1913; *s* of Lt-Col H. C. Smitherman and Mildred E. Holten; *m* 1937, Frances Ellen Rivers Calvert; one *s* one *d. Educ:* Sir Joseph Williamson's Mathematical Sch., Rochester. Indian Police, Burma, 1933; served in: Yenangyaung; Rangoon; Myitkyina; Sagaing; Thayetmyo; Thaton. Served War of 1939–45 (despatches, 1945), Burma Army Reserve of Officers; Maj. 1945. Joined Civil Affairs Service; Foreign Office, 1949; subseq. service in: Amoy; Cairo; Rome; Khartoum; Miami; Consul-General, Bordeaux, 1967–69; Counsellor, Moscow, 1969–70; Ambassador to Togo and Dahomey, 1970–73. *Recreations:* fishing, gardening. *Address:* Grange Cottage, Grange Road, New Buckenham, Norfolk. *T:* Attleborough (0953) 860452.

See also Sir T. F. V. Buxton, Bt.

SMITHERS, Prof. Sir David (Waldron), Kt 1969; MD, FRCP, FRCS, FRCR; Professor of Radiotherapy in the University of London, 1943–73, now Emeritus; Director of the Radiotherapy Department at the Royal Marsden Hospital, 1943–73; *b* 17 Jan. 1908; *s* of late Sir Waldron Smithers, MP; *m* 1933, Gwladys Margaret (Marjorie), *d* of Harry Reeve Angel, Officer (1st class) Order of White Rose of Finland; one *s* one *d. Educ:* Boxgrove School, Guildford; Charterhouse; Clare College, Cambridge; St Thomas's Hospital. MRCS, LRCP 1933; MB, BChir (Cantab) 1934; MD (Cantab) 1937; DMR (London) 1937; MRCP 1946; FRCP 1952; FFR 1953, now FRCR; FRCS 1963. Pres. British Inst. of Radiology, 1946–47; President, Faculty of Radiologists, 1959–61; Kt Comdr, Order of St John of Jerusalem, Kts of Malta, 1973. *Publications:* Dickens's Doctors, 1979; Castles in Kent, 1980; Jane Austen in Kent, 1981; Not a Moment to Lose: some reminiscences, 1989; This Idle Trade: on doctors who were writers, 1989; papers on cancer and radiotherapy. *Recreations:* growing roses, book collecting. *Address:* Ringfield, Knockholt, Kent TN14 7JE. *T:* Knockholt (0959) 32122.

See also Maj.-Gen. B. C. Webster.

SMITHERS, Professor Geoffrey Victor; Professor of English Language, University of Durham, 1960–74, now Emeritus; *b* 5 May 1909; *s* of William Henry and Agnes Madeline Smithers; *m* 1953, Jean Buglass Hay McDonald; three *s* one *d. Educ:* Durban High School; Natal University College; Hertford College, Oxford. Rhodes Schol. for Natal, 1930; 1st Cl. in Final Hon. School of English, Oxford, 1933. Asst Lecturer: King's Coll., London, 1936; University Coll., London, 1938; Lectr in English Language, 1940, Senior Lecturer in English Language, 1950, Reader in Medieval English, 1954, Univ. of Oxford, and professorial Fellow of Merton Coll., 1954. *Publications:* 2nd edn of C. Brown's Religious Lyrics of the Fourteenth Century, 1952; Kyng Alisaunder, Vol. I 1952, Vol. II 1957; (with J. A. W. Bennett and N. Davis) Early Middle English Verse and Prose, 1966 (rev. edn 1974); Havelok, 1987; contribs to vols in honour of M. Schlauch, G. N. Garmonsway, D. Meritt, A. McIntosh and N. Davis; papers in Med. Ӕv., English and Germanic Studies, Archivum Linguisticum, Rev. Eng. Studies, Durham Univ. Jl. *Recreation:* music. *Address:* 6 Manor Close, Shincliffe, Durham DH1 2NS. *T:* Durham (091) 3861094.

SMITHERS, Sir Peter (Henry Berry Otway), Kt 1970; VRD with clasp; DPhil Oxon; Lt-Comdr RNR, retired; *b* 9 Dec. 1913; *o s* of late Lt-Col H. O. Smithers, JP, Hants, and Ethel Berry; *m* 1943, Dojean, *d* of late T. M. Sayman, St Louis, Mo; two *d. Educ:* Hawtrey's; Harrow Sch.; Magdalen Coll., Oxford. Demyship in History, 1931; 1st cl. Hons Modern History, 1934. Called to Bar, Inner Temple, 1936; joined Lincoln's Inn, 1937. Commn, London Div. RNVR, 1939; British Staff, Paris, 1940; Naval Intelligence Div., Admiralty; Asst Naval Attaché, British Embassy, Washington; Actg Naval Attaché, Mexico, Central Amer. Republics and Panama. RD Councillor, Winchester, 1946–49. MP (C) Winchester Div. of Hampshire, 1950–64; PPS to Minister of State for Colonies, 1952–56 and to Sec. of State for Colonies, 1956–59; Deleg., Consultative Assembly of Council of Europe, 1952–56 and 1960; UK Deleg. to UN Gen. Assembly, 1960–62; Parly Under-Sec. of State, FO, 1962–64; Sec.-Gen., Council of Europe, 1964–69; Senior Research Fellow, UN Inst. for Trng and Research, 1969–72; General Rapporteur, European Conf. of Parliamentarians and Scientists, 1970–77. Chairman: British-Mexican Soc., 1952–55; Conservative Overseas Bureau, 1956–59; Vice-Chm., Conservative Parly Foreign Affairs Cttee, 1958–62; Vice-Pres., European Assembly of Local Authorities, 1959–62. Master, Turners' Co., 1955; Liveryman, Goldsmiths' Co. Dr of Law *hc* Zürich, 1969. Marzotto Prize, Marzotto Foundn, Italy, 1969; Alexander von Humboldt Gold Medal, 1969; Medal of Honour, Parly Assembly, Council of Europe, 1984; Gold Medal (for photography), RHS, 1981, 1983, 1990, 1991, Gold Medal and Grenfell Medal, 1985. One-man shows of photography: Oklahoma Art Center, 1984; Musée Cernuschi, Paris, Norton Museum, Palm Beach, Brooklyn Botanic Garden, and Bois des Moutiers, Dieppe, 1985; Minneapolis, Pasadena, Philadelphia, Oklahoma City and Atlanta, 1986; Oklahoma

City, St Louis and NY, 1987; Atlanta Botanic Garden, Nat. Acad. of Sci., Washington, 1989. Chevalier de la Légion d'Honneur; Orden Mexicana del Aguila Azteca. *Publication:* Life of Joseph Addison, 1954, 2nd edn, 1966. *Recreation:* gardening. *Address:* CH-6921 Vico Morcote, Switzerland. *Clubs:* Carlton; The Everglades.

SMITHERS, Hon. Sir Reginald (Allfree), Kt 1980; Judge of Federal Court of Australia, 1977–86 (Judge, Australian Industrial Court, 1965–77); Additional Judge, Supreme Court of ACT and Supreme Court of NT, since 1964; *b* Echuca, 3 Feb. 1903; *s* of F. Smithers, Hove, Brighton, England; *m* 1932, Dorothy, *d* of J. Smalley, Bendigo; two *s* one *d*. *Educ:* Melbourne Grammar School; Melbourne Univ. (LLB 1924). Admitted to Victorian Bar, 1929; QC 1951. Served War, RAAF, 1942–45 (Sqdn Ldr); Censorship Liaison Officer to Gen. MacArthur, 1944–45, New Guinea and Philippines. Judge of Supreme Court of Papua and NG, 1962–64; Dep. Pres., Administrative Appeals Tribunal, 1977–80. Chancellor, La Trobe Univ., 1972–80 (DUniv 1982); Pres., Australian Assoc. of Youth Clubs, 1967–. *Address:* 11 Florence Avenue, Kew, Victoria 3101, Australia.

SMITHIES, Frederick Albert; General Secretary, National Association of Schoolmasters and Union of Women Teachers, 1983–90; *b* 12 May 1929; *s* of Frederick Albert and Lilian Smithies; *m* 1960, Olga Margaret Yates. *Educ:* St Mary's Coll., Blackburn, Lancs; St Mary's Coll., Twickenham, Mddx. Schoolteacher: Accrington, Lancs, 1948–60; Northampton, 1960–76. NAS/UWT (before 1975, NAS): Nat. Executive Member, 1966–76; Chm. of Education Cttee, 1972–76; Vice-President, 1976; Asst Gen. Secretary, 1976–81; Dep. Gen. Secretary, 1981–82; Gen. Sec. Designate, 1982–83. Member: TUC Gen. Council, 1983–89; Exec. Bd, European Trade Union Cttee for Educn, 1985–; Exec. Bd, Internat. Fedn of Free Teachers' Unions, 1985– (Hon. Treas., 1990–). *Recreations:* reading, music, theatre, fell-walking. *Address:* High Street, Guilsborough, Northampton NN6 8PY.

SMITHIES, His Honour Kenneth Charles Lester; a Circuit Judge, 1975–90; *b* 15 Aug. 1927; *s* of late Harold King Smithies and Kathleen Margaret (*née* Walsh); *m* 1950, Joan Winifred (*née* Ellis) (*d* 1983); one *s* two *d*. *Educ:* City of London Sch. (Corporation Scholar); University College London (LLB). Volunteered 60th Rifles, 1945, later commnd in Royal Artillery, in India; demobilised, 1948. Called to Bar, Gray's Inn, 1955. *Recreations:* music, gardening. *Address:* St Aldhelm's House, High Littleton, near Bristol BS18 5HG.

SMITHSON, Rt. Rev. Alan; *see* Jarrow, Bishop Suffragan of.

SMITHSON, Peter Denham; architect in private practice since 1950; *b* 18 Sept. 1923; *s* of William Blenkiron Smithson and Elizabeth Smithson; *m* 1949, Alison Margaret (*née* Gill); one *s* two *d*. *Educ:* The Grammar School, Stockton-on-Tees; King's College, Univ. of Durham. Served War of 1939–45: Queen Victoria's Own Madras Sappers and Miners, India and Burma, 1942–45. Asst in Schools Div. LCC, 1949–50; subseq. in private practice with wife. Banister Fletcher Prof. of Architecture, UCL, 1976–77; Vis. Prof. of Architecture: Bath Univ., 1978–90; Univ. of Delft, 1982–83; Univ. of Munich, 1984–85; Univ. of Barcelona, 1985–86. *Buildings:* Hunstanton School, 1950–54; The Economist Building, St James's, 1959–64, Porch 1983; Robin Hood Gardens, Tower Hamlets, 1963–72; Garden Bldg, St Hilda's Coll., Oxford, 1968–70; Ramp at Ansty, Wilts, 1987; for Bath University: Second Arts Bldg, 1978–81; Amenity Bldg, 1979–80, 1984; Arts Barn, 1980–90; Architecture and Building Engrg, 1982–88; *furniture:* for Tecta, Germany (with A. Smithson), 1982–. *Publications:* (all with A. Smithson) Uppercase 3, 1960; The Heroic Period of Modern Architecture, 1965, rev. edn 1981; Urban Structuring Studies of Alison and Peter Smithson, 1967; Team 10 Primer, 1968; The Euston Arch, 1968; Ordinariness and Light, 1970; Without Rhetoric, 1973; Bath: Walks Within the Walls, 1980; The Shift, 1982; AS in DS, 1983; The 1930s, 1985; Upper Lawn, 1986; theoretical work on town structuring in ILAUD Year Book, Spazio e Società and other periodicals; *relevant publications:* synopsis of professional life in Arch. Assoc.'s Arena, Feb. 1966; selective bibliography in The Shift, 1982; A. + P. Smithson, 1991. *Address:* 24 Gilston Road, SW10 9SR. *T:* 071–373 7423.

SMOUT, Prof. Thomas Christopher, PhD; FBA 1988; FRSE 1975; Director, St John's House Institute for Advanced Historical Studies, University of St Andrews, since 1992; *b* 19 Dec. 1933; *s* of Sir Arthur and Lady (Hilda) Smout; *m* 1959, Anne-Marie Schøning; one *s* one *d*. *Educ:* The Leys Sch., Cambridge; Clare Coll., Cambridge (MA; PhD 1960). Dept of Economic History, Edinburgh University: Asst Lectr, 1959; Lectr, 1962; Reader, 1964; Prof. of Econ. History, 1970; Prof. of Scottish History, Univ. of St Andrews, 1980–91. Vis. Prof., Strathclyde Univ., 1991–. Member: Cttee for Scotland, Nature Conservancy Council, 1986–91; Bd, NCC (Scotland), 1991–; Royal Commn on Ancient and Historic Monuments of Scotland, 1987–; Bd of Trustees, Nat. Museums of Scotland, 1991–. *Publications:* Scottish Trade on the Eve of Union, 1963; A History of the Scottish People, 1969; (with I. Levitt) The State of the Scottish Working Class in 1843, 1979; A Century of the Scottish People, 1986; (with S. Wood) Scottish Voices, 1990. *Recreations:* birdwatching, butterflies, ferns. *Address:* Chesterhill, Shore Road, Anstruther, Fife KY10 3DZ. *T:* Anstruther (0333) 310330.

SMYTH, Desmond; *see* Smyth, J.D.

SMYTH, (James) Robert Staples; His Honour Judge Robert Smyth; a Circuit Judge, since 1986; *b* 11 July 1926; *s* of late Major Robert Smyth, Gaybrook, Co. Westmeath, and Mabel Anne Georgiana (*née* MacGeough-Bond) *m* 1971, Fenella Joan Mowat; one *s*. *Educ:* St Columba's, Dublin; Merton Coll., Oxford (BA 1948, MA). Served RAF, 1944–46. Called to Bar, Inner Temple, 1949. Resident Magistrate, Northern Rhodesia, 1951–55; a Dep. Circuit Judge, 1974; Stipendiary Magistrate, W Midlands, 1978–86; a Recorder, 1983–86. Dep. Chairman, Agricultural Land Tribunal, 1974. *Recreations:* shooting, fishing, English literature. *Address:* Leys, Shelsley Beauchamp, Worcs WR6 6RB.

SMYTH, John Jackson; QC 1979; barrister-at-law; Director of Zambesi Ministries, Zimbabwe, since 1986; *b* 27 June 1941; *e s* of Col Edward Hugh Jackson Smyth, FRCSEd, and late Ursula Helen Lucie (*née* Ross) *m* 1968, Josephine Anne, *er d* of late Walter Leggott and Miriam Moss Leggott, Manor Farm, Burtoft, Lincs; one *s* three *d*. *Educ:* Strathcona Sch., Calgary, Alberta; St Lawrence Coll.; Trinity Hall, Cambridge. MA, LLB (Cantab). Called to Bar, Inner Temple (Major Schol.), 1965. A Recorder, 1978–84. *Publications:* Discovering Christianity Today, 1985; Following Christ Today, 1987. *Recreations:* skiing, sailing, trout fishing, real tennis. *Address:* 2 Crown Office Row, Temple, EC4; PO Box HG 167, Highlands, Harare, Zimbabwe. *Club:* Army and Navy.

SMYTH, (Joseph) Desmond, FCA; Managing Director, Ulster Television, since 1983; *b* 20 April 1950; *s* of Andrew and Annie Elizabeth Smyth; *m* 1975, Irene Janette (*née* Dale); one *s* one *d*. *Educ:* Limavady Grammar School; Queen's University, Belfast. BSc (Jt Hons Pure Maths and Statistics). Accountancy articles, Coopers and Lybrand, 1971–75; Ulster Television: Chief Accountant, 1975–76; Financial Controller and Company Secretary, 1976–83. Pres., NI Chamber of Commerce and Industry, 1991–92. *Recreations:* fishing, gardening. *Address:* Ulster Television plc, Havelock House, Ormeau Road, Belfast BT7 1EB.

SMYTH, Margaret Jane, CBE 1959 (OBE 1955); retired; *b* 23 Sept. 1897; *d* of late Colonel John Smyth, IMS. Trained at Univ. Settlement, Bristol; Health Visitors Certificate. Roy. Sanitary Inst., 1918; Central Midwives Board, SCM, 1920; Maternity and Child Welfare Certificate, RSI, 1921; SRN, 1925, trained in Nightingale Trng School, St Thomas Hosp.; Dep. Matron, St Thomas Hosp., 1939–45, Supt, Nightingale Trng School and Matron, St Thomas Hospital, 1945–55; Chairman of the General Nursing Council for England and Wales, 1955–60; President Royal College of Nursing, 1960–62; Chairman, South West Metropolitan Area, Nurse Training Cttee, 1952–64; Mem., Kingston and Long Grove Hosp. Management Cttee, 1967–69. *Address:* 9 Stockbridge Gardens, Chichester, West Sussex.

SMYTH, Rev. Martin; *see* Smyth, Rev. W. M.

SMYTH, Reginald; cartoonist (as Reginald Smythe); contracted to Mirror Publications, since 1955; *b* 10 July 1917; *s* of Richard Oliver Smyth and Florence Pearce; *m* 1949, Vera Toyne. *Educ:* Galleys Field Sch., Hartlepool, Cleveland. Served Army, Royal Northumberland Fusiliers, 1936–45. Civil Service, 1945–55. Creator, Andy Capp daily comic strip, 1956–. Best Brit. Cartoon Strip Awards, 1961–65; Premio Cartoon Award, Lucca, 1969; Best Cartoonist Award, Genoa, 1973; Best Strip Cartoon, USA Cartoonist Assoc., 1974; Italian Strip Award, Derthona, 1978. *Publications:* annual World of Andy Capp book, 1957–; annual Andy Capp books (USA), 1968–. *Address:* 96 Caledonian Road, Hartlepool, Cleveland TS25 5LB.

SMYTH, Robert Staples; *see* Smyth, J. R. S.

SMYTH, Sir Thomas Weyland Bowyer-, 15th Bt *cr* 1661; *b* 25 June 1960; *s* of Captain Sir Philip Weyland Bowyer-Smyth, 14th Bt, RN, and of Veronica Mary, *d* of Captain C. W. Bower, DSC, RN; *S* father, 1978. *Heir: kinsman* John Jeremy Windham [*b* 22 Nov. 1948; *m* 1976, Rachel Mary Finney; one *s* two *d*].

SMYTH, Dr Sir Timothy (John), 2nd Bt *cr* 1956, of Teignmouth, Co. Devon; General Manager, The St George Hospital, Sydney, since 1988; *b* 16 April 1953; *s* of Julian Smyth (*d* 1974) and of Phyllis, *d* of John Francis Cannon; *S* grandfather, Brig. Rt Hon. Sir John Smyth, 1st Bt, VC, MC, 1983; *m* 1981, Bernadette Mary, *d* of Leo Askew; two *s* two *d*. *Educ:* Univ. of New South Wales. MB, BS 1977; LLB 1987; MBA (AGSM) 1985; FRACMA 1985. Resident Medical Officer, 1977–79; Medical Administrator, Prince Henry Hosp., Prince of Wales Hosp. Gp, Sydney, 1980–86; Chief Exec. Officer, Sydney Health Service, 1986–88. *Heir: s* Brendan Julian Smyth, *b* 4 Oct. 1981. *Address:* 21 King Street, Randwick, NSW 2031, Australia.

SMYTH, Rev. (William) Martin; MP (UU) Belfast South, since March 1982 (resigned seat Dec. 1985 in protest against Anglo-Irish Agreement; re-elected Jan. 1986); *b* 15 June 1931; *s* of James Smyth, JP, and Minnie Kane; *m* 1957, Kathleen Jean Johnston, BA; two *d* (and one *d* decd). *Educ:* Methodist Coll., Belfast; Magee University Coll., Londonderry; Trinity Coll., Dublin (BA 1953, BD 1961); Assembly's Coll., Belfast. Assistant Minister, Lowe Memorial, Finaghy, 1953–57; Raffrey Presbyterian Church, Crossgar, 1957–63; Alexandra Presbyterian Church, Belfast, 1963–82. Member, Northern Ireland Convention, 1975; Mem. (UU) Belfast S, NI Assembly, 1982–86 (Chm., Health and Social Services Cttee, 1983–84; Chm., Finance and Personnel Cttee, 1984–86). Chm. of Executive 1974–76, Vice-Pres. 1974–, Ulster Unionist Council. Member: Select Cttee for Social Services, 1983–90; Select Cttee on Health, 1990–. Vice-Chm., Parly Cttee for Soviet Jewry, 1983–. Governor, Belfast City Mission. Grand Master, Grand Orange Lodge of Ireland, 1972–; Grand Master of World Orange Council, 1974–82, Pres., 1985–88; Hon. Past Grand Master, Canada, and Hon. Deputy Grand Master, USA, NZ, NSW, of Orange Order. *Publications:* (ed) Faith for Today, 1961; pamphlets: Why Presbyterian?, 1963; Till Death Us Do Part, 1965; In Defence of Ulster, 1970; The Battle for Northern Ireland, 1972; A Federated People, 1988; occasional papers, and articles in Christian Irishman, Evangelical Quarterly, Biblical Theology. *Recreations:* reading, photography; former Rugby player (capped for Magee University College). *Address:* 117 Cregagh Road, Belfast BT6 0LA. *T:* Belfast (0232) 457009.

SMYTHE, Clifford Anthony, (Tony); Director, Medical Campaign against Nuclear Weapons, since 1989; *b* 2 Aug. 1938; *s* of Clifford John and Florence May Smythe; *m*; four *d*. *Educ:* University College School. Conscientious Objector, 1958; General Secretary, War Resisters' International, 1959–64, Treasurer, 1982–86; Council Member, Internat. Confederation for Disarmament and Peace, 1963–71; Gen. Sec., Nat. Council for Civil Liberties, 1966–72; Field Dir, American Civil Liberties Union, 1973; Dir, Mind (Nat. Assoc. for Mental Health), 1973–81. Board Member: Volunteer Centre, 1977–81; Retired Execs Clearing Hse (REACH), 1978–90; Member: Nat. Adv. Council on Employment of Disabled People, 1975–81; Nat. Develt Council for Mentally Handicapped People, 1981; (co-opted), Mddx Area Probation Cttee, 1984–90. Chairman: Campaign for Homeless Single People, 1982–84; National Peace Council, 1982–86; Nat. Assoc. of Voluntary Hostels, 1991–; Director: Assoc. of Community Health Councils for England and Wales, 1983–86; SHAC, 1986–88. *Publications:* Conscription: a World Survey, 1968; (with D. Madgwick) The Invasion of Privacy, 1974. *Address:* 136 Stapleton Hall Road, N4 4QB.

SMYTHE, Patricia Rosemary K.; *see* Koechlin-Smythe.

SMYTHE, Captain Quentin George Murray, VC 1942; Officer Instructor, Department of Defence, South Africa, 1970–81, retired; *b* 6 Aug. 1916; *s* of Edric Murray Smythe and *g s* of 1st Administrator of Natal (Hon. Charles Smythe, Methven Castle, Perthshire, Scotland); *m* 1945, Dale Griffiths (marr. diss. 1970), Capetown; three *s* one *d*; *m* 1970, Margaret Joan Shatwell (*d* 1980); *m* 1984, Patricia Stamper. *Educ:* Estcourt High Sch. Went through Abyssinian Campaign with Regt, Natal Carabineers; Sgt at Alem Hanza, Egypt (VC). *Recreations:* bowls, fishing, shooting. *Address:* 54 Seadoone Road, Amanzimtoti 4126, Natal, Republic of South Africa.

SMYTHE, Reginald; *see* Smyth, R.

SMYTHE, Tony; *see* Smythe, C. A.

SNAGGE, John Derrick Mordaunt, OBE 1944; *b* 1904; 2nd *s* of late Judge Sir Mordaunt Snagge; *m* 1st, 1936, Eileen Mary (*d* 1980), *e d* of late H. P. Joscelyne; 2nd, 1983, Joan Mary, *e d* of late William Wilson. *Educ:* Winchester College; Pembroke College, Oxford. Assistant Station Director BBC, Stoke-on-Trent, 1924; Announcer London (Savoy Hill), 1928; Assistant Outside Broadcast Department 1933; Commentator Oxford and Cambridge Boat Race, 1931–80; Assistant Director Outside Broadcasts, 1939; Presentation Director BBC, 1939–45; Head of Presentation (Home Service), 1945–57; Head of Presentation (Sound) BBC, 1957–63; Special Duties, BBC, 1963–65. Retired from BBC 1965. Chairman of the Lord's Taverners, 1956, 1960, 1961; President, 1952, 1964; Secretary, 1965–67; Trustee, 1970–76. *Publication:* (with Michael Barsley) Those Vintage Years of Radio, 1972. *Recreation:* fishing. *Address:* Delgaty, Village Road, Dorney, near Windsor, Berks SL4 6QJ. *T:* Burnham (0628) 661303. *Clubs:* MCC, Leander, Lord's Taverners, Sportsman's.

SNAGGE, Dame Nancy (Marion), DBE 1955 (OBE 1945); *b* 2 May 1906; *d* of late Henry Thomas Salmon; *m* 1962, Thomas Geoffrey Mordaunt Snagge, DSC (*d* 1984), *e s* of late His Hon. Sir Mordaunt Snagge. *Educ:* Notting Hill, High Sch. Joined the WAAF on its inception, March 1939; served as a commnd officer in the WAAF and WRAF from Sept. 1939. ADC to King George VI, 1950–52; ADC to the Queen, 1952–56; Director Women's Royal Air Force, 1950–56, retired as Air Commandant. *Address:* 5 Headbourne Worthy House, Winchester, Hants SO23 7JG. *T:* Winchester (0962) 882489.

SNAITH, George Robert, FRINA; Consultant, Computervision Ltd, since 1985; *b* 9 July 1930; *s* of late Robert and Clara Snaith; *m* 1953, Verna Patricia (*née* Codling); one *s* one *d*. *Educ:* University of Durham. BSc Applied Science (Naval Architecture), 1952. A. Kari & Co., Consulting Naval Architects, Newcastle, 1952–57; Northern Aluminium Co. Ltd, Banbury, 1957–59; Burness, Corlett & Partners, Consulting Naval Architects, Basingstoke, 1959–64; British Ship Research Association, 1964–77, Dir of Research, 1976–77; British Shipbuilders: Dir of Research, 1977–81; Technol. and Systems Adviser (formerly Production Systems Adviser), 1981–85. Vis. Prof., Dept of Naval Architecture and Shipbldg, Univ. of Newcastle upon Tyne, 1980–. Vice-Pres., NE Coast Instn of Engrs and Shipbuilders, 1979; Member: Council, RINA, 1977–; Ship and Marine Technol. Requirements Bd, Dept of Industry, 1978–81; Bd, National Maritime Inst., 1978–82. *Recreations:* ships and shipbuilding, technology, reading, literature and discussion. *Address:* 10 Fieldhouse Close, Hepscott, Morpeth, Northumberland NE61 6LU. *T:* Morpeth (0670) 515319. *Club:* Athenæum.

SNAPE, Peter Charles; MP (Lab) West Bromwich East since Feb. 1974; *b* 12 Feb. 1942; *s* of Thomas and Kathleen Snape; *m* 1963, Winifred Grimshaw (marr. diss. 1980); two *d*. *Educ:* St Joseph's RC Sch., Stockport; St Winifred's Sch., Stockport. Railway signalman, 1957–61; regular soldier, RE & RCT, 1961–67; goods guard, 1967–70; clerical officer BR, 1970–74. Mem., Council of Europe and WEU, May-Nov. 1975. An Asst Govt Whip, 1975–77; a Lord Comr, HM Treasury, 1977–79; opposition spokesman for Defence, 1979–82, for Home Affairs, 1982–83, for Transport, 1983–. Mem., Bredbury and Romiley UDC, 1971–74 (Chm., Finance Cttee). *Address:* D4 Kenilworth Court, Edgbaston, Birmingham B16 9NU.

SNAPE, Royden Eric; a Recorder of the Crown Court, since 1979; *b* 20 April 1922; *s* of John Robert and Gwladys Constance Snape; *m* 1949, Unity Frances Money; one *s* one *d*. *Educ:* Bromsgrove Sch. Served War, Royal Regt of Artillery (Field), 1940–46; Adjt, 80th Field Regt, 1945. Admitted Solicitor, 1949; a Deputy Circuit Judge, 1975. Chm., Med. Appeal Tribunal, 1985–. Governor, St John's Sch., Porthcawl, 1971–88 (Chm., 1971–72). *Recreations:* golf, Rugby Union football, cricket, swimming. *Address:* West Winds, Love Lane, Llanblethian, Cowbridge, South Glamorgan, Wales CF7 7JQ. *T:* Cowbridge (0446) 772362. *Clubs:* Royal Porthcawl Golf; Cardiff Athletic; Glamorgan CCC.

SNAPE, Thomas Peter, OBE 1988; General Secretary, Secondary Heads Association and Headmasters' Conference, 1983–88; *b* 4 June 1925; *s* of Charles Snape and Jane Elizabeth Middleton; *m* 1951, Anne Christina McColl; one *s* three *d*. *Educ:* Cockburn High Sch., Leeds; Exeter Coll., Oxford (MA). PCE London Univ. Asst Master, grammar and comprehensive schs, 1950–60; Headmaster: Settle High Sch., Yorks, 1960–64; King Edward VI Grammar Sch., Totnes, 1964–66; King Edward VI Comprehensive Sch., Totnes, 1966–83; Warden, Totnes Community Coll., 1971–83. Leverhulme Res. Fellow, USA, 1970. Chm., Leechwell Press, 1989–. Member: Consultative Cttee, Assessment of Performance Unit, 1975–84; Teacher Educn Accreditation Council, 1984–86. FRSA 1989. JP Devon, 1975, Inner London 1983. *Publications:* Ten Sites in Totnes, 1990; chapters in edited works; sections of Open University readers; contrib. learned jls. *Address:* 10 Chalcot Square, NW1 8YB. *Club:* East India.

SNEDDEN, David King, CA; Chief Executive and Managing Director, Trinity International Holdings plc, since 1982; Chairman, Liverpool Daily Post and Echo, since 1985; *b* 23 Feb. 1933; *s* of David King Snedden and Isabella (*née* Martin); *m* 1958; two *s* one *d*. *Educ:* Daniel Stewart's College, Edinburgh. CA 1956. Flying Officer, RAF, 1956–57. Investment Adviser, Guinness Mahon, 1958–59; Chief Accountant, Scotsman Publications Ltd, Thomson British Publications Ltd, Thomson Scottish Associates Ltd, 1959–64; Commercial Controller, The Scotsman Publications Ltd, 1964–66; Managing Director: Belfast Telegraph Newspapers Ltd, 1967–70 (Director, 1979–82); The Scotsman Publications Ltd, 1970–78 (Director, 1970–82). Thomson Regional Newspapers Ltd: Dir, 1974–82; Gp Asst Man. Dir, 1979–80; Jt Man. Dir, 1980–82. Director: Radio Forth Ltd, 1973–77; Scottish Council Research Inst. Ltd, 1975–77; The Press Association Ltd, 1984– (Vice-Chm., 1988; Chm., 1989–); Reuters Holdings PLC, 1988–. Pres., Scottish Daily Newspaper Soc., 1975–78; Member: Press Council, 1976–80; Council, Newspaper Soc., 1983–; Regional Council, CBI, NI, 1968–70. *Recreations:* golf, shooting, fishing. *Address:* Apartment 223, The Colonnades, Albert Dock Village, Liverpool L3 4AA. *Clubs:* Caledonian; Bruntsfield Links Golfing Society.

SNEDDON, Hutchison Burt, CBE 1983 (OBE 1968); JP; DL; former Scottish Divisional Director, Nationwide Anglia Building Society (formerly Nationwide Building Society); *b* 17 April 1929; *s* of Robert and Catherine Sneddon; *m* 1960, Elizabeth Jardine; one *s* two *d*. *Educ:* Wishaw High School. Chm., Cumbernauld Develt Corp., 1979–83; Regl Sales Manager (Special Projects), Scottish Gas, 1983–88; Dir, National Bldg Agency, 1973–82; Vice-Chm., Scottish National Housing and Town Planning Council, 1965–71; Member: Bd, Housing Corp., 1977–83; Consultative Cttee, Scottish Develt Agency, 1979–83; Scottish Adv. Commn on Housing Rents, 1973–74; Anderson Cttee on Commercial Rating, 1972–74; Western Regional Hosp. Bd, 1968–70; Scottish Tourist Bd, 1969–83; Chm., Burns Heritage Trail, 1971–83; Sen. Vice Pres., 1988–89, Pres., 1989–90, World Fedn of Burns Clubs (Jun. Vice Pres., 1987–88). Dep. Pres., Convention of Scottish Local Authorities, 1974–76; Chairman: Gas Higher Managers Assoc., Scotland, 1984–88; Gas Higher Managers Assoc., GB, 1987–88. Motherwell and Wishaw Burgh Council: Councillor, 1958–77; Bailie, 1960–64; Chm., Housing Cttee, 1960–71; Chm., Policy and Resources Cttee, 1974–77; Leader, 1960–77; Chm., Motherwell DC, 1974–77; Provost, Burgh of Motherwell and Wishaw, 1971–75. JP Motherwell District, 1974 (Mem. JP Adv. Cttee); DL Motherwell, Hamilton, Monklands, E Kilbride and Clydesdale Districts, 1989. Gold Medal of Schweinfurt, Bavaria, 1977 (Internat. Relations). *Recreations:* football (watching), philately. *Address:* 36 Shand Street, Wishaw, Lanarks.

SNEDDON, Prof. Ian Naismith, OBE 1969; MA Cantab, DSc Glasgow; FRS 1983; FRSE; FIMA; FRSA; Member of the Polish Academy of Sciences; Emeritus Professor of Mathematics, University of Glasgow, 1985; Visiting Professor of Mathematics, University of Strathclyde, since 1985; *b* 8 Dec. 1919; *o s* of Naismith Sneddon and Mary Ann Cameron; *m* 1943, Mary Campbell Macgregor; two *s* one *d*. *Educ:* Hyndland School, Glasgow; The University of Glasgow; Trinity College, Cambridge (Senior Scholar, 1941). Scientific Officer, Ministry of Supply, 1942–45; Research Worker, H. H. Wills Physical Lab., Univ. of Bristol, 1945–46; Lecturer in Natural Philosophy, Univ. of Glasgow, 1946–50; Professor of Mathematics in University Coll. of N Staffordshire, 1950–56 (Senior Tutor of the College, 1954–56); Simson Prof. of Mathematics, Univ. of Glasgow, 1956–85 (Dean of Faculty of Science, 1970–72, Senate Assessor on Univ. Court, 1973–77); Visiting Professor: Duke Univ., North Carolina, 1959 and 1960; Michigan State Univ., 1967; Univ. of California, Berkeley, 1979; La Trobe Univ., 1984; Georgia Inst of Technol., 1986; Adjunct Prof., North Carolina State Univ., 1965–72; Visiting Lecturer: Univ. of Palermo, 1953 and 1980; Serbian Acad. of Sciences, 1958; Univ. of Warsaw, 1959, 1973, 1975; Canadian Mathematical Congress, 1961; Polish Acad. of Sciences, 1962; US Midwest Mechanics Research Seminar, 1963 and 1981; Univ. of Zagreb, 1964; Univ. of Calgary, 1968; Indiana Univ., 1970–80; Kuwait Univ., 1972; CISM, Udine, 1972, 1974; Britton Lectr, McMaster Univ., 1979; Huber Lectr, Polish Acad. of Sciences, 1980. NSF Distinguished Vis. Scientist, State Univ., New York, 1969. Member: various govt scientific cttees, 1950–80; Adv. Council on Scientific Research and Tech. Development, Min. of Supply, 1953–56, Min. of Defence, 1965–68; Univs Science and Technology Bd (SRC), 1965–69; Adv. Council of Scottish Opera, 1972– (Vice-Chm., 1979–); Bd of Scottish Nat. Orch., 1976–83; Bd of Citizens Theatre, Glasgow, 1975– (Vice-Chm.); BBC Central Music Adv. Cttee, 1978–85; Chm., BBC Scottish Music Adv. Cttee, 1978–85; Mem. Council, Scottish Soc. of Composers, 1981–83; Vice-Pres., RSE, 1966–69 and 1979–82. Kelvin Medal, Univ. of Glasgow, 1948; Makdougall-Brisbane Prize, RSE, 1956–58; Soc. of Engrg Sci. Medal, 1979. Mem., Order of Long-Leaf Pine, USA, 1964; Hon. Fellow, Soc. of Engng Sci., USA, 1977; Foreign Mem., Acad. of Scis, Turin. Hon. DSc: Warsaw, 1973; Heriot-Watt, 1982; Hull, 1983. Comdr's Cross, Order of Polonia Restituta, 1969; Comdr, Order of Merit (Poland), 1979; Medal of Cultural Merit, Poland, 1983. *Publications:* (with N. F. Mott) Wave Mechanics and Its Applications, 1948; Fourier Transforms, 1951; Special Functions of Mathematical Physics and Chemistry, 1956; The Elements of Partial Differential Equations, 1956; Introduction to the Mathematics of Biology and Medicine (with J. G. Defares), 1960; Fourier Series, 1961; Zagadnienie Szczelin w Teorii Sprezystasci, 1962; Mixed Boundary Value Problems in Potential Theory, 1966; Crack Problems in the Mathematical Theory of Elasticity (with M. Lowengrub), 1969; An Introduction to the Use of Integral Transforms, 1972; Metoda Transformacji Calkowych w Mieszanych Zogadnieniach Brzegowych, 1974; The Linear Theory of Thermoelasticity, 1974; (ed) Encyclopedic Dictionary of Mathematics for Engineers, 1976; (with G. Eason, W. Nowacki and Z. Olesiak) Integral Transform Methods in Elasticity, 1977; (with E. L. Ince) The Solution of Ordinary Differential Equations, 1987; articles in Handbuch der Physik, 1956–58; scientific papers on quantum theory of nuclei, theory of elasticity, and boundary value problems in jls. *Recreations:* music, painting and photography. *Address:* 19 Crown Terrace, Glasgow G12 9ES. *T:* 041–339 4114. *Club:* Glasgow Art.

SNEDDON, Robert, CMG 1976; MBE 1945; HM Diplomatic Service, retired; *b* 8 June 1920; *m* 1945, Kathleen Margaret Smith; two *d*. *Educ:* Dalziel High Sch., Motherwell; Kettering Grammar Sch.; University Coll., Nottingham. HM Forces, 1940–46: 8th Army, ME and Italy, 1942–45; 30 Corps, Germany (Major), 1945–46. Joined Foreign (subseq. Diplomatic) Service, 1946; 3rd Sec., Warsaw, 1946; 2nd Sec., Stockholm, 1950; FO, 1954; 1st Sec., Oslo, 1956; 1st Sec., Berlin, 1961; FO, 1963; Counsellor, Bonn, 1969; FCO, 1971, retired 1977. *Recreations:* golf, music. *Address:* Windrose, Church Road, Horsell, Woking, Surrey GU21 4QS. *T:* Woking (0483) 765745. *Club:* Westhill Golf.

SNELGROVE, Rt. Rev. Donald George; *see* Hull, Bishop Suffragan of.

SNELL, Rt. Rev. George Boyd, DD, PhD; *b* Toronto, Ontario, 17 June 1907; *s* of John George Snell and Minnie Alice Boyd; *m* 1934, Esther Mary. *Educ:* Trinity College, Toronto. BA 1929, MA 1930, PhD 1937, DD 1948. Deacon, Toronto, 1931; Priest, Niagara (for Tor.), 1932; Curate of St Michael and All Angels, Tor., 1931–39; Rector, 1940–48; Private Chaplain to Bp of Tor., 1945–48; Rector of Pro-Cathedral, Calgary, and Dean of Calgary, 1948–51; Exam. Chaplain to Bp of Calgary, 1948–51; Rector of St Clem. Eglinton, Tor., 1951–56; Archdeacon of Toronto, 1953–56; Exam. Chaplain to Bp of Toronto, 1953–55. Consecrated Bp Suffragan of Toronto, 1956; elected Bp-Coadjutor of Toronto, 1959; Bishop of Toronto, 1966–72. Hon. DD: Wycliffe Coll., Toronto, 1959; Huron Coll., Ontario, 1968. *Address:* 1210 Glen Road, Mississauga, Ont. L5H 3K8, Canada. *Club:* National (Toronto).

SNELL, Dr George Davis; geneticist; *b* Bradford, Mass, 19 Dec. 1903; *s* of Cullen Bryant and Katharine Davis Snell; *m* 1937, Rhoda Carson; three *s*. *Educ:* Dartmouth Coll. (BS 1926); Harvard Univ. (MS 1928; ScD 1930). Instr in Zoology, Dartmouth Coll., 1929–30, Brown Univ., 1930–31; Res. Fellow, Texas Univ., 1931–33; Asst Prof., Washington Univ., St Louis, 1933–34; Jackson Laboratory: Res. Associate, 1935–56; Sen. Staff Scientist, 1957–68, now Emeritus. Guggenheim Fellow, Texas Univ., 1953–54. Mem., Allergy and Immunology Study Sect., NIH, 1958–62. Member: Amer. Acad. of Arts and Scis; Nat. Acad. of Scis; French Acad. of Scis (foreign associate); Amer. Philosophical Soc., 1982; Hon. Member: British Transplantation Soc.; British Soc. for Immunology, 1983. Hon. MD Charles Univ., Prague, 1967; Hon. DSc: Dartmouth, 1974; Gustavus Adolphus Coll., 1981; Bates Coll., 1981; Ohio State Univ., 1984; Hon. LLD: Univ. of Maine, 1981; Colby Coll., 1982. Bertner Foundn Award, 1962; Gregor Mendel Medal, Czechoslovak Acad. of Scis, 1967; Gairdner Foundn Award, 1976; Prize in Medicine, Wolf Foundn, 1978; (jt) Nobel Prize for Physiology or Medicine, 1980. *Publications:* (ed) The Biology of the Laboratory Mouse, 1941; (jtly) Histocompatibility, 1976; Search for a Rational Ethic, 1988; contribs to learned jls. *Address:* The Jackson Laboratory, Bar Harbor, Maine 04609, USA; 21 Atlantic Avenue, Bar Harbor, Maine 04609, USA.

SNELL, John Nicholas B.; *see* Blashford-Snell.

SNELL, Philip D.; Member (Lab), Tyne and Wear County Council, 1974–86, Chairman, General Services Committee, 1981–86; *b* 14 Oct. 1915; *s* of Alfred William Snell and Jane Herdman; *m* 1939, Selina Waite; two *d*. *Educ:* Causey Road Council Sch., Gateshead. Miner, Marley Hill Colliery, Gateshead, 1929–57; Industrial Relations Advr, NCB, 1957–61; Education and Welfare Officer: Durham CC, 1961–73; Gateshead MDC, 1973. Chm., Tyne and Wear CC, 1980–81. Trustee, Whickham Glebe Sports Club. *Recreation:* enjoying Northern Federation Brewery Beer. *Address:* School House, Marley Hill, Whickham, Gateshead, Tyne and Wear. *T:* 091–488 7006. *Club:* Sunniside Social (Gateshead).

SNELLGROVE, Anthony; *see* Snellgrove, J. A.

SNELLGROVE, David Llewellyn, LittD, PhD; FBA 1969; Professor of Tibetan in the University of London, 1974–82, now Emeritus Professor (Reader, 1960–74, Lecturer, 1950–60); Founder Director of Institute of Tibetan Studies, Tring, 1966–82; *b* Portsmouth, 29 June 1920; *s* of Lt-Comdr Clifford Snellgrove, RN, and Eleanor Maud Snellgrove. *Educ:* Christ's Hospital, Horsham; Southampton Univ.; Queens' Coll., Cambridge. Served War of 1939–45: commissioned in Infantry, 1942; Intell. Officer in India until 1946. Then started seriously on oriental studies at Cambridge, 1946, cont. Rome, 1949–50. BA Cantab 1949, MA Cantab 1953; PhD London 1954; LittD Cantab 1969. Made expedns to India and the Himalayas, 1953–54, 1956, 1960, 1964, 1967, 1974–75, 1978–80, 1982, continued with regular travel in Indonesia, 1987–; founded with Mr Hugh E. Richardson an Inst. of Tibetan Studies, 1966. Apptd Consultant to Vatican in new Secretariat for non-Christian Religions, 1967. Many professional visits abroad, mainly to W Europe and

USA. *Publications:* Buddhist Himalaya, 1957; The Hevajra Tantra, 1959; Himalayan Pilgrimage, 1961, 2nd edn 1981; Four Lamas of Dolpo, 1967; The Nine Ways of Bon, 1967, repr. 1980; (with H. E. Richardson) A Cultural History of Tibet, 1968, 2nd edn 1980; (with T. Skorupski) The Cultural Heritage of Ladakh, vol. I, 1977, vol. II, 1980; (ed) The Image of the Buddha, 1978; Indo-Tibetan Buddhism, 1987; articles in Arts Asiatiques (Paris), Bulletin of the Secretariat for non-Christian Religions (Rome), etc. *Address:* Via Matteo Gay 26/7, 10066 Torre Pellice, Italy.

SNELLGROVE, (John) Anthony; HM Diplomatic Service, retired; Secretary, British Brush Manufacturers' Association, 1977–89; *b* 29 Jan. 1922; *s* of late John Snellgrove and Anne Mary Priscilla (*née* Brown); *m* 1956, Rose Jeanne Marie Suzanne (*née* Paris); two *d*. *Educ:* Wimbledon Coll.; Stonyhurst Coll.; Peterhouse, Cambridge (1940–41 and 1945–48; BA and MA). Served War, Royal Navy, latterly as temp. actg Lieut, RNVR, 1941–45. Asst Principal, Colonial Office, 1948–49; joined Foreign Service, Oct. 1949; 2nd Sec., Prague, 1950–51; FO (Econ. Relations Dept), 1951–53; HM Vice-Consul, Tamsui (Formosa), 1953–56; 1st Sec., 1954; FO (SE Asia Dept and UN (E&S) Dept), 1956–59; 1st Sec., Bangkok, 1959–62; 1st Sec. and Consul, Mogadishu (Somali Republic), 1962–63; FO (Arabian and European Econ. Org. Depts), 1963–66; 1st Sec., Holy See, 1967–71; Counsellor, 1971; Dep. Sec.-Gen. (Economic), CENTO, 1971–73; Counsellor and Head of Chancery, Carácas, 1973–75, retired, 1976. *Recreations:* music, bridge. *Address:* 13 Chantry Hurst, Woodcote, Epsom, Surrey KT18 7BN.

SNELLING, Sir Arthur (Wendell), KCMG 1960 (CMG 1954); KCVO 1962; HM Diplomatic Service, retired; *b* 7 May 1914; *s* of Arthur and Ellen Snelling; *m* 1939, Frieda, *d* of late Lt-Col F. C. Barnes; one *s*. *Educ:* Ackworth Sch., Yorks; University Coll., London (BSc Econ.). Study Gp Sec., Royal Inst. of Internat. Affairs, 1934–36; Dominions Office, 1936; Private Sec. to Parl. Under-Sec., 1939; Joint Sec. to UK Delegn to Internat. Monetary Conference, Bretton Woods, USA, 1944; accompanied Lord Keynes on missions to USA and Canada, 1943 and 1944; Dep. High Comr for UK in New Zealand, 1947–50, in S Africa, 1953–55; Assistant Under-Secretary of State, Commonwealth Relations Office, 1956–59; British High Comr in Ghana, 1959–61; Dep. Under-Sec. of State, FCO (formerly CRO), 1961–69; Ambassador to South Africa, 1970–72. Dir, Gordon and Gotch Holdings Ltd, 1973–81. Fellow, UCL, 1970; Mem., College Council, UCL, 1976–86. Vice-Pres., UK-S Africa Trade Assoc., 1974–80; Mem., Ciskei Commn, 1978–80. *Address:* 19 Albany Park Road, Kingston-upon-Thames, Surrey KT2 5SW. *T:* 081–549 4160. *Club:* Reform.

SNELSON, Sir Edward Alec Abbott, KBE 1954 (OBE 1946); Justice, Supreme Restitution Court, Herford, German Federal Republic, 1962–81; Judge, Arbitral Tribunal for Agreement on German External Debts and Mixed Commission, Koblenz, 1969–77; *b* 31 Oct. 1904; *er s* of Thomas Edward and Alice Martha Snelson; *m* 1956, Prof. Jean Johnston Mackay, MA, 3rd *d* of Donald and Isabella Mackay; two *s*. *Educ:* St Olave's; Gonville and Caius Coll., Cambridge. Called to Bar, Gray's Inn, 1929; entered ICS 1929; served in Central Provinces, District and Sessions Judge, 1936; Registrar, High Court, 1941; Legal Secretary, 1946; Joint Secretary, Govt of India, 1947; retired, 1947; Official Draftsman, Govt of Pakistan, 1948; Sec. Min. of Law, 1951–61, also of Parliamentary Affairs, 1952–58. Mem. Exec. Cttee, Arts Council of Pakistan, 1953–61. *Publication:* Father Damien, 1938. *Recreations:* sailing, music, theatre. *Address:* The Forge House, Binstead, Alton, Hants GU34 4PB. *Clubs:* United Oxford & Cambridge University; Challoner.

SNODGRASS, Prof. Anthony McElrea, FSA; FBA 1979; Laurence Professor of Classical Archaeology, University of Cambridge, since 1976; Fellow of Clare College, Cambridge, since 1977; *b* 7 July 1934; *s* of William McElrea Snodgrass, MC (Major, RAMC), and Kathleen Mabel (*née* Owen); *m* 1st, 1959, Ann Elizabeth Vaughan (marr. diss.); three *d*; 2nd, 1983, Annemarie Künzl; one *s*. *Educ:* Marlborough Coll.; Worcester Coll., Oxford (BA 1959, MA, DPhil 1963). FSA 1978. Served with RAF in Iraq, 1953–55 (National Service). Student of the British School, Athens, 1959–60; University of Edinburgh: Lectr in Classical Archaeology, 1961; Reader, 1969; Prof., 1975. Sather Classical Prof., Univ. of California, Berkeley, 1984–85. Myres Meml Lectr, Oxford, 1981. Vice-Pres., British Academy, 1991–. Corresp. Mem., German Archaeol. Inst., 1977. *Publications:* Early Greek Armour and Weapons, 1964; Arms and Armour of the Greeks, 1967; The Dark Age of Greece, 1971; Archaic Greece, 1980; Narration and Allusion in Early Greek Art, 1982; An Archaeology of Greece, 1987; contrib. Jl of Hellenic Studies, Proc. of Prehistoric Soc., Gnomon, etc. *Recreations:* mountaineering, skiing. *Address:* Museum of Classical Archaeology, Sidgwick Avenue, Cambridge CB3 9DA. *T:* Cambridge (0223) 335155. *Club:* Alpine Ski.

See also J. M. O. Snodgrass.

SNODGRASS, John Michael Owen, CMG 1981; HM Diplomatic Service, retired; *b* 12 Aug. 1928; *e s* of Major W. M. Snodgrass, MC, RAMC; *m* 1957, Jennifer James; three *s*. *Educ:* Marlborough Coll.; Trinity Hall, Cambridge (MA, Maths and Moral Scis). Diplomatic Service: 3rd Sec., Rome, 1953–56; FO, 1956–60; 1st Sec., Beirut, 1960–63; S Africa, 1964–67; FCO, 1967–70; Consul-Gen., Jerusalem, 1970–74; Counsellor, South Africa, 1974–77; Hd of South Pacific Dept, FCO, 1977–80; Ambassador: to Zaire, 1980–83 (also to Burundi, Rwanda and Congo); to Bulgaria, 1983–86. CStJ 1975. *Recreations:* ski-ing, tennis, travel. *Address:* The Barn House, North Warnborough, Basingstoke, Hants RG25 1ET. *T:* Basingstoke (0256) 702816.

See also A. McE. Snodgrass.

SNOW, Adrian John, MA, MEd; Warden, The Oratory School Association, since 1989; *b* 20 March 1939; *e s* of Edward Percy John Snow and Marjory Ellen Nicholls; *m* 1963, Alessina Teresa Kilkelly; one *s* one *d*. *Educ:* Hurstpierpoint Coll.; Trinity Coll., Dublin (BA, MA, HDipEd); Reading Univ. (MEd). Asst Master, The New Beacon, Sevenoaks, 1958–59; RAF Pilot Officer, 1963; Assistant Master: King's Sch., Sherborne, 1964; High Sch., Dublin, 1964–65 (part-time); Brighton Coll., 1965–66; The Oratory School: Head of Econ. and Pol Studies, 1966–73; Head of Hist., 1967–73; Housemaster, 1967–73; acting Headmaster, Sept. 1972–Mar. 1973; Headmaster, 1973–88. Governor: Prior Park Coll., 1981–87 (Mem., Action Cttee, 1980–81); Moreton Hall Prep. Sch., 1984–; St Mary's Sch., Ascot, 1986–; St Edward's Sch. and Highlands Sch., Reading, 1987– (Chm., 1990–). Member: Berks Cttee, Prince's Trust, 1989– (Vice-Chm., 1990–91); RYA. *Recreations:* athletics (univ. colour), cricket, farming, hockey (Jun. Internat. trialist), Real Tennis, Rugby (Combined Univs), sailing. *Address:* c/o The Oratory School, Woodcote, near Reading RG8 0PJ. *T:* Checkendon (0491) 680207. *Club:* Leander (Henley).

SNOW, Antony Edmund, MIPA, FIPR; Chief Executive and Deputy Chairman: Hill and Knowlton Public Relations, since 1990; Hogg Group Plc, since 1988; Hogg Robinson & Gardner Mountain PLC, since 1988; *b* 5 Dec. 1932; 2nd *s* of Thomas Maitland Snow, *qv*; *m* 1961, Caroline Wilson; one *s* two *d*. *Educ:* Sherborne Sch.; New College, Oxford. National Service, commnd in 10th Royal Hussars, 1952–53; Royal Wiltshire Yeomanry, TA, 1953–63. W. S. Crawford, 1958; Charles Barker & Sons, 1961, Dep. Chairman, 1975. Vice-Pres., Market Planning, Steuben Glass, 1976; Dep. Dir, Corning Museum of Glass, 1978 (Trustee, 1983–); Dir, Rockwell Museum, 1979. Member: Cttee of Management, Courtauld Institute of Art, 1984–; Exec. Cttee, Nat. Art-Collections Fund, 1985–; Ancient Monuments Adv. Cttee, English Heritage, 1988–; Design Council, 1989–. Trustee, Monteverdi Choir, 1988–. *Recreations:* windsurfing, ski-ing, tennis, English watercolours. *Address:* 16 Rumbold Road, SW6. *Clubs:* Cavalry and Guards, City of London; The Pilgrims (New York).

See also Thomas Snow.

SNOW, Jonathan George, (Jon Snow); television journalist; Presenter, Channel Four News, since 1989; *b* 28 Sept. 1947; *s* of late Rt Rev. George Snow and Joan Snow; partner, Madeleine Colvin; two *d*. *Educ:* St Edward's School, Oxford; Liverpool Univ. (no degree; sent down following political disturbances, 1970). VSO, Uganda, 1967–68; Co-ordinator, New Horizon Youth Centre, Covent Garden, 1970–73 (Chm., 1986–); Journalist, Independent Radio News, LBC, 1973–76; Independent Television News: Reporter, 1976–83; Washington Correspondent, 1983–86; Diplomatic Editor, 1986–89. Mem., NUJ. Monte Carlo Golden Nymph Award, for Eritrea Air Attack reporting, 1979; TV Reporter of the Year, for Afghanistan, Iran and Iraq reporting, RTS, 1980; Valiant for Truth Award, for El Salvador reporting, 1982; Internat. Award, for El Salvador reporting, RTS, 1982; Home News Award, for Kegworth Air Crash reporting, RTS, 1989. *Publication:* Atlas of Today, 1987. *Address:* Channel Four News, ITN, 200 Gray's Inn Road, WC1X 8HB. *T:* 071–430 4237.

SNOW, Rear-Adm. Kenneth Arthur, CB 1987; Receiver-General and Chapter Clerk, Westminster Abbey, since 1987; *b* 14 April 1934; *s* of Arthur Chandos Pole Snow and Evelyn (*née* Joyce); *m* 1956, Pamela Elizabeth Terry (*née* Sorrell); one *s* two *d*. *Educ:* St Andrews College, Grahamstown; South African Nautical College. Joined RN, 1952; commanded HMS Kirkliston, 1962; qualified navigation specialist, 1963; commanded: HMS Llandaff, 1970; HMS Arethusa, 1979; HMS Hermes, 1983; Dep. Asst Chief of Staff (Ops), SACEUR, 1984–87, retired. *Recreations:* gardening, painting. *Address:* 2 The Cloister, Westminster Abbey, SW1P 3PA. *Club:* Army and Navy.

See also Rear-Adm. R. E. Snow.

SNOW, Peter John; television presenter, reporter and author; *b* Dublin, 20 April 1938; *s* of Brig. John F. Snow, CBE and Peggy Mary Pringle; *m* 1st, 1964, Alison Carter (marr. diss. 1975); one *s* one *d*; 2nd, 1976, Ann Macmillan; one *s* two *d*. *Educ:* Wellington College; Balliol College, Oxford (BA Hons Greats 1962). 2nd Lieut, Somerset Light Infantry, 1956–58, served Plymouth and Warminster. Independent Television News: newscaster amd reporter, 1962–66; diplomatic and defence corresp., 1966–79; events covered include: Cyprus, 1964; Vietnam, Laos, Malaysia, 1968–70; China, 1972; Mideast war, 1973; Nigerian civil war, 1969; Oman, 1975; Rhodesia, 1965–79; Britain and EEC, 1970–73; co-presenter, Gen. Elections, Feb. and Oct. 1974, 1979; BBC: presenter, Newsnight, 1979–; events covered or reported include: Zimbabwe independence, 1980; Falklands war, 1982; S Africa, 1986; co-presenter, Gen. Elections, 1983 and 1987, US elections. *Publications:* (jtly) Leila's Hijack War, 1970; Hussein: a biography, 1972. *Recreations:* sailing, ski-ing, model railways, photography. *Address:* c/o BBC TV Centre, Wood Lane, W12 7RJ. *T:* 081–576 7306.

SNOW, Philip Albert, OBE 1985 (MBE 1979); JP; MA; FRSA; FRAI; author; *b* 7 Aug. 1915; *s* of William Edward Snow, FRCO and Ada Sophia Robinson; *m* 1940, Anne Harris; one *d*. *Educ:* Newton's Sch., Leicester; Christ's Coll., Cambridge (MA Hons). FRAI 1952. Provincial Comr, Magistrate and Asst Colonial Sec., Fiji and Western Pacific, 1937–52; ADC to Governor and C-in-C, Fiji, 1939; Fiji Govt Liaison Officer, US and NZ Forces, 1942–44. Bursar, Rugby Sch., 1952–76. Mem., Jt Cttee, Governing Bodies of Schools' Assoc., 1958–64. President: Public Schs Bursars' Assoc., 1962–65; The Worthing Soc., 1983–; Vice-Pres., Fiji Soc., 1944–52. Founder, Fiji Cricket Assoc., 1946, Vice-Patron, 1952–; Captain, Fiji Cricket Team, NZ first-class tour, 1948; Liaison Officer/Manager, first Fiji Cricket Team in England, 1979. International Cricket Conference: Perm. Rep. of Fiji, 1965–90; Mem., first World Cup Cttee, 1971–75; Chm., Associate Member Countries, 1982–87; Perm. Rep. of Fiji, Internat. Cricket Council, 1990–. Literary Executor and Executor of Lord Snow. JP Warwicks, 1967–76, and W Sussex, 1976–. FRSA 1984. Foreign Specialist Award, USA Govt, 1964. *Publications:* Cricket in the Fiji Islands, 1949; Report on the Visit of Three Bursars to the United States of America in 1964, 1965; Best Stories of the South Seas, 1967; Bibliography of Fiji, Tonga and Rotuma, 1969; (with Stefanie Waine) The People from the Horizon: an illustrated history of the Europeans among the South Sea Islanders, 1979; Stranger and Brother: a portrait of C. P. Snow, 1982; contrib. TLS, Sunday Times, Daily Telegraph, The Times, Jls of RAI, RGS, Fiji Museum and Polynesian Soc., Jl de la Société des Océanistes, Amer. Anthropologist, Wisden's Almanack, Barclays World of Cricket, Dictionary of Nat. Biog; numerous reviews of, and introductions to, Pacific and general books. *Recreations:* taming robins; formerly cricket (Leics 2nd XI, Cambridge Crusaders, Googlies, MCC, Authors, Fiji first-class), chess (half-Blue), table-tennis (half-Blue and Cambs), deck-tennis, tennis. *Address:* Gables, Station Road, Angmering, West Sussex BN16 4HY. *T:* Rustington (0903) 773594. *Clubs:* MCC (Hon. Life Mem. for services to internat. cricket, 1970), Stragglers of Asia (Hon. Mem.); Mastermind; Hawks (Cambridge); De Flamingos (Hon. Mem.) (Holland).

SNOW, Surg. Rear-Adm. Ronald Edward, CB 1991; LVO 1972; OBE 1977; Surgeon Rear Admiral (Operational Medical Services), 1988–91; *b* 17 May 1933; *s* of Arthur Chandos Pole Snow (formerly Soppitt) and Evelyn Dorothea Snow (*née* Joyce); *m* 1959, Valerie Melian French; two *d*. *Educ:* St Andrew's Coll., Grahamstown, S Africa; Trinity Coll., Dublin (MA, MB, BCh, BAO); MFOM, DA, LMCC. HMS Victorious, 1966; HMS Dolphin, 1967; HMY Britannia, 1970; MoD, 1973 and 1977; Inst. of Naval Medicine, 1975 and 1984; Staff of Surg. Rear Adm. (Naval Hosps), 1980; Staff of C-in-C Fleet, 1982; Asst Surg. Gen. (Service Hosps), 1985; Surg. Rear Adm. (Support Med. Services), 1987. QHP 1984–91. OStJ 1986. *Recreations:* National Hunt racing, cruising. *Clubs:* Army and Navy; Royal Naval Sailing Association (Portsmouth).

See also Rear-Adm. K. A. Snow.

SNOW, Thomas; Director, Oxford University Careers Service (formerly Secretary, Oxford University Appointments Committee), since 1970; Fellow, New College, Oxford, since 1973; *b* 16 June 1929; *e s* of Thomas Maitland Snow, *qv*; *m* 1961, Elena Tidmarsh; two *s* one *d*. *Educ:* Winchester Coll. (Fellow, 1985); New Coll., Oxford. Joined Crittall Manufacturing Co. Ltd as Management Trainee, 1952; Dir 1966; Director: Crittall Hope Ltd, Darlington Simpson Rolling Mills, Minex Metals Ltd, 1968. Mem. Standing Cttee, Assoc. of Graduate Careers Adv. Services, 1973–77, 1985–89. Held various positions in local govt; Marriage Counsellor, 1964–70; Chm., Relate—Oxfordshire Marriage Guidance (formerly Oxford Marriage Guidance Council), 1974–90. JP 1964–69. *Address:* 157 Woodstock Road, Oxford OX2 7NA.

See also A. E. Snow.

SNOW, Thomas Maitland, CMG 1934; *b* 21 May 1890; *s* of Thomas Snow, Cleve, Exeter, and Edith Banbury; *m* 1st, 1927, Phyllis Annette Malcolmson; three *s*; 2nd, 1949, Sylvia, *d* of W. Delmar, Buda-Pest. *Educ:* Winchester; New Coll., Oxford. 1st Secretary, HM Diplomatic Service, 1923; Counsellor, 1930; Minister: to Cuba, 1935–37; to

Finland, 1937–40; to Colombia, 1941–44 (Ambassador, 1944–45); to Switzerland, 1946–49. Retired, 1950. *Recreation:* metaphysics. *Address:* Chemin des Vuarennes 35, 1820 Montreux, Switzerland.
See also A. E. Snow, Thomas Snow.

SNOWDEN, Rt. Rev. John Samuel Philip; Bishop of Cariboo, 1974–91. *Educ:* Anglican Theological Coll., Vancouver (LTh 1951); Univ. of British Columbia (BA 1956). Deacon 1951, priest 1952; Curate: Kaslo-Kokanee, 1951–53; Oak Bay, 1953–57; Nanaimo, 1957–60; Incumbent of St Timothy, Vancouver, 1960–64; Priest Pastoral, Christ Church Cathedral, Vancouver, 1964–66; Rector of St Timothy, Edmonton, 1966–71; Dean and Rector of St Paul's Cathedral, Kamloops, 1971–74. Domestic Chaplain to Bishop of Cariboo, 1971–73. *Address:* 1–440 Victoria Street, Kamloops, BC V2C 2A7, Canada.

SNOWDON, 1st Earl of, *cr* 1961; **Antony Charles Robert Armstrong-Jones,** GCVO 1969; RDI 1978; FCSD; Viscount Linley, 1961; Photographer, Telegraph Magazine, since 1990; Constable of Caernarfon Castle since 1963; *b* 7 March 1930; *s* of Ronald Owen Lloyd Armstrong-Jones, MBE, QC, DL (*d* 1966), and of Anne, *o d* of Lt-Col Leonard Messel, OBE (later Countess of Rosse); *m* 1st, 1960, HRH The Princess Margaret (marr. diss. 1978); one *s* one *d*; 2nd, 1978, Lucy Lindsay-Hogg, *d* of Donald Davies; one *d*. *Educ:* Eton; Jesus Coll., Cambridge (coxed winning Univ. crew, 1950). Joined Staff of Council of Industrial Design, 1961, continued on a consultative basis, 1962–87, also an Editorial Adviser of Design Magazine, 1961–87; an Artistic Adviser to the Sunday Times and Sunday Times Publications Ltd, 1962–90. Designed: Snowdon Aviary, London Zoo, 1965; Chairmobile, 1972. Mem. Council, National Fund for Research for Crippling Diseases; Patron, Circle of Guide Dog Owners; Chm., Working Party on Integrating the Disabled (Report 1976); Pres. for England, Cttee, International Year for Disabled People, 1981. Hon. Fellow: Institute of British Photographers; Royal Photographic Soc.; Manchester College of Art and Design; Hon. Member: North Wales Society of Architects; South Wales Institute of Architects; Royal Welsh Yacht Club; Patron: Welsh Nat. Rowing Club; Metropolitan Union of YMCAs; British Water Ski Federation. President: Contemp. Art Society for Wales; Civic Trust for Wales; Welsh Theatre Company; Mem. Council, English Stage Co., 1978–82. Senior Fellow, RCA, 1986. FRSA. Dr *hc* Bradford, 1989; Hon. LLD Bath, 1989. Silver Progress Medal, RPS, 1985. *Television films:* Don't Count the Candles, 1968 (2 Hollywood Emmy Awards; St George Prize, Venice; awards at Prague and Barcelona film festivals); Love of a Kind, 1969; Born to be Small, 1971 (Chicago Hugo Award); Happy being Happy, 1973; Mary Kingsley, 1975; Burke and Wills, 1975; Peter, Tina and Steve, 1977; Snowdon on Camera, BBC (presenter), 1981. *Exhibitions include:* Photocall, London, 1958; Assignments, Cologne, London, Brussels, USA, 1972, Japan, Canada, Denmark, Holland, 1975, Australia, 1976, France, 1977; Serendipity, Brighton, Bradford, 1989, Bath, 1990. *Publications:* London, 1958; Malta (in collaboration), 1958; Private View (in collaboration), 1965; A View of Venice, 1972; Assignments, 1972; Inchcape Review, 1977; (jtly) Pride of the Shires, 1979; Personal View, 1979; Sittings, 1983; Israel: a first view, 1986; (with Viscount Tonypandy) My Wales, 1986; Stills 1983–1987, 1987. *Heir: s* Viscount Linley, *qv*. *Address:* 22 Launceston Place, W8 5RL. *Clubs:* Buck's, United Oxford & Cambridge University; Leander (Henley-on-Thames); Hawks (Cambridge).
See also under Royal Family, and Earl of Rosse.

SNOWLING, (George) Christopher (Edward); Head of Quality Control and Professional Standards, Durnford Ford, Solicitors in London and the South-East, since 1989; *b* 12 Aug. 1934; *s* of George Edward Snowling and Winifred Beryl (*née* Cave); *m* 1961, Flora Skells; one *s* one *d*. *Educ:* The Mercers' Sch.; Fitzwilliam House, Cambridge (MA). Admitted Solicitor, 1961; various local govt posts, 1958–71; Law Society: Legal Aid Admin, 1971–78; Secretary: Educn and Trng, 1978–85, Professional Purposes, 1985–86; Dir, Legal Aid, 1986–89. Mem., Cuckfield UDC, 1971–74; Mem. (C) Mid Sussex District Council, 1973–: Chm., 1981–82, 1986–87, 1987–88; Chm., Policy and Finance Cttee, 1988–91; Leader majority gp, 1991–; Mem. Council, Assoc. of Dist Councils, 1990–. Member: Mid Downs CHC, 1988–; Crawley & Horsham Med. Ethics Cttee, 1990–. FBIM 1988. *Recreations:* local government, painting. *Address:* Eldon Lodge, Pondcroft Road, Lindfield, West Sussex RH16 2HQ. *T:* Lindfield (0444) 482172.

SNOWMAN, (Michael) Nicholas; General Director (Arts), South Bank Centre, London, since 1986; *b* 18 March 1944; *s* of Kenneth Snowman and Sallie Snowman (*née* Moghi-Levkine); *m* 1983, Margo Michelle Rouard; one *s*. *Educ:* Hall Sch. and Highgate Sch., London; Magdalene Coll., Cambridge (BA Hons Eng. Lit.). Asst to Hd of Music Staff, Glyndebourne Fest., 1967–69; Co-Founder and Gen. Man., London Sinfonietta, 1968–72; Administrator, Music Th. Ensemble, 1968–71; Artistic Dir, IRCAM, Centre d'Art et de Culture Georges Pompidou, 1972–86. Co-Founder and Artistic Advr, Ensemble InterContemporain, 1975–; Mem. Music Cttee, Venice Biennale, 1979–86; Artistic Dir, Projects in 1980 (Stravinsky), 1981 (Webern), 1983 (Boulez), Fest. d'Automne de Paris; Programme Consultant, Cité de la Musique, La Villette, Paris, 1991–. Officier de l'Ordre des Arts et des Lettres (France), 1990 (Chevalier, 1985); Order of Cultural Merit (Poland), 1990. *Publications:* (co-ed) The Best of Granta, 1967; (series ed.) The Contemporary Composers, 1982–; papers and articles on music, opera, cultural policy. *Recreations:* films, eating, spy novels. *Address:* South Bank Centre, Royal Festival Hall, SE1 8XX. *T:* 071–921 0600. *Club:* Garrick.

SNYDER, Prof. Allan Whitenack, FRS 1990; FAA; FTS; Professor of Optical Physics and Visual Sciences, and Head of Optical Sciences Centre, Australian National University, since 1987; *b* 23 Nov. 1940; *s* of Edward H. Snyder, philanthropist, and Zelda (*née* Cotton), Broadway actress and psychodramatherapist; *m* 1967, Margo F. Collett (marr. diss. 1975); *m* 1986, Mandy Thomas; one *s*. *Educ:* Central High Sch., Phil. (AB); Pennsylvania State Univ. (BS); MIT (SM); Harvard Univ. (MS); University Coll. London (PhD); DSc London. Greenland Ice Cap Communications Project, 1961; Gen. Telecom. and Elec. Res. Lab., 1963–67; Cons. to Brit. PO and Standard Telecom. Lab., 1968–70; Nat. Sci. Foundn Fellow, Yale Univ., 1970–71; Sen. Res. Fellow, Sen. Fellow, Professorial Fellow, ANU, 1971–79; John Simon Guggenheim Fellow, Yale Univ. Med. Sch., 1977–78; Hd, Dept of Applied Maths, Inst. for Advanced Studies, ANU, 1980–83; Royal Soc. Quest Res. Fellow, Cambridge Univ., 1987. Associate Editor, Jl of Optical Soc. of America, 1981–83. Fellow, Optical Soc. of Amer., 1980; Foundn Fellow, Nat. Vision Res. Inst. of Aust., 1983. Research Medal, Royal Soc. Vic., 1974; Edgeworth David Medal, Royal Soc. NSW, 1974; Thomas Rankin Lyle Medal, Aust. Acad. of Sci., 1985. *Publications:* Photoreceptor Optics, 1975; Optical Waveguide Theory, 1983; Optical Waveguide Sciences, 1983; articles on the visual system of animals and on the physics of light propagation in internat sci. jls. *Recreations:* art, culture, language and thought. *Address:* Optical Sciences Centre, Institute of Advanced Studies, Australian National University, Canberra, ACT 2601, Australia. *T:* (6) 2492626, *Fax* (6) 2495184.

SOAME, Sir Charles (John) Buckworth-Herne-, 12th Bt *cr* 1697; *b* 28 May 1932; *s* of Sir Charles Burnett Buckworth-Herne-Soame, 11th Bt, and Elsie May (*d* 1972), *d* of Walter Alfred Lloyd; *S* father, 1977; *m* 1958, Eileen Margaret Mary, *d* of Leonard Minton; one *s*. *Heir: s* Richard John Buckworth-Herne-Soame, *b* 17 Aug. 1970. *Address:* Sheen Cottage, Coalbrookdale, Telford, Salop.

SOAMES, Lady; Mary Soames, DBE 1980 (MBE (mil.) 1945); President, National Benevolent Fund for the Aged, since 1978; Chairman, Winston Churchill Memorial Trust Council, since 1991 (Member, since 1978); Chairman, Royal National Theatre Board, since 1989; Member, South Bank Centre Board, since 1989; *b* 15 Sept. 1922; *y d* of late Rt Hon. Sir Winston Churchill, KG, OM, CH, FRS, and late Baroness Spencer-Churchill, GBE; *m* 1947, Captain Christopher Soames, Coldstream Guards, later Baron Soames, PC, GCMG, GCVO, CH, CBE (*d* 1987); three *s* two *d*. *Educ:* privately. Served War: Red Cross and WVS, 1939–41; ATS, 1941–46, with mixed anti-aircraft batteries in UK and Europe (Jun. Comdr). Accompanied father on various journeys; campaigned with husband through six elections whilst he was Conservative MP for Bedford, 1950–66; accompanied husband to Paris where he was Ambassador, 1968–72, and to Brussels where he was first British Vice Pres. of Eur. Commn, 1973–76; accompanied husband when he was appointed last British Governor of Southern Rhodesia, Dec. 1979–April 1980. Chm., UK Assoc. for Internat. Year of the Child, 1979. Governor, Harrow Sch., 1980–. Hon. Fellow, Churchill Coll., Cambridge, 1983. JP E Sussex, 1960–74. Hon DLitt Sussex, 1989. *Publications:* Clementine Churchill by Her Daughter Mary Soames, 1979 (a Wolfson Prize for History, and Yorkshire Post Prize for Best First Work, 1979); A Churchill Family Album—A Personal Anthology Selected by Mary Soames, 1982; The Profligate Duke: George Spencer-Churchill 5th Duke of Marlborough and his Duchess, 1987; Winston Churchill: his Life as a Painter: a Memoir by his Daughter Mary Soames, 1990. *Recreations:* reading, sight-seeing, gardening. *Club:* Grillions.
See also Earl Peel, Hon. A. N. W. Soames.

SOAMES, Hon. (Arthur) Nicholas (Winston); MP (C) Crawley, since 1983; *b* 12 Feb. 1948; *s* of Baron Soames, PC, GCMG, GCVO, CH, CBE and of Lady Soames, *qv*; *m* 1981, Catherine Weatherall; one *s*. *Educ:* Eton. Served 11th Hussars (PAO), 1967–70 (2nd Lieut); Equerry to the Prince of Wales, 1970–72; Asst Dir, Sedgwick Group, 1976–82. PPS to Minister of State for Employment, 1984–85, to Sec. of State, DoE, 1987–89, to Sec. of State, DTI, 1989–90. *Recreation:* country pursuits. *Address:* House of Commons, SW1A 0AA. *T:* 071–219 3000. *Clubs:* White's, Turf.

SOANE, Leslie James, OBE 1985; CEng, MICE; FCIT, FBIM; FRSA; Member of Board and Director, Railway Heritage Trust, since 1985; *b* 15 Jan. 1926; *s* of Arthur Edward Soane and Florence May Herring; *m* 1950, Joan Edith Mayo; one *s* one *d*. *Educ:* Watford Central Sch.; London Univ. Civil Engineer posts: London Midland Region, 1948–55; Eastern Region, 1955–62; LMR, 1962–71; Chief Civil Engr, Western Region, 1971–75; Dep. Gen. Manager, WR, 1975–77; Gen. Manager, Scottish Region, 1977–83; Man. Dir (Reorganisation), BRB, 1983–85. Lt-Col, then Col, Engr and Transport Staff Corps, RE (TA), 1985–. *Recreations:* theatre, reading, golf. *Address:* St Michael's Croft, Woodcock Hill, Berkhamsted, Herts HP4 3PJ. *T:* Berkhamsted (0442) 875831.

SOARES, Dr Mário Alberto Nobre Lopes; President of Portugal, since 1986; *b* 7 Dec. 1924; *s* of João Lopes Soares and Elisa Nobre Soares; *m* 1949, Maria Barroso Soares; one *s* one *d*. *Educ:* Univ. of Lisbon; Faculty of Law, Sorbonne. LèsL, DenD. Leader, United Democratic Youth Movement and Mem., Central Cttee, 1946–48; Mem. Exec., Social Democratic Action, 1952–60; Democratic Opposition candidate, Lisbon, legis. elections, 1965, 1969; deported to São Tomé, March-Nov. 1968; Rep., Internat. League of Human Rights; imprisoned 12 times; exile, Paris, 1970–74; elected to Legis. Assembly as Mem. (Socialist Party) for Lisbon, 1974; Minister of Foreign Affairs, 1974–75; Minister without Portfolio, 1975; Deputy Constituent Assistant, 1975, Legis. Assembly, 1976; Mem., Council of State; Prime Minister of Portugal 3 times, 1976–85. Founder, Portuguese Socialist Party, 1973, Sec. Gen., 1973–86. Joseph Lemaire Prize, 1975; Internat. Prize of Human Rights, 1977; Robert Schuman Prize, 1987; numerous hon. degrees, decorations and orders. *Publications:* As ideias politico-sociais de Teófilo Braga, 1950; Escritos Politicos, 1969; Le Portugal Bâillonné, 1972; Destruir o Sistema, Construir uma Vida Nova, 1973; Caminho Difícil, do Salazarismo ao Caetanismo, 1973; Escritos do Exílio, 1975; (with Willy Brandt and Bruno Kreisky) Liberdade para Portugal, 1975; Portugal, quelle Révolution?, 1976; O Futuro será o Socialismo Democrático, 1979; Resposta Socialista para o Mundo em Crise, 1983; A Árvore e a Floresta, 1985; Intervenções: Vol. I, 1987; Vol. II, 1988; Vol. III, 1989; Vol. IV, 1990; Vol. V, 1991. *Recreations:* bibliophile; collector of contemporary Portuguese paintings. *Address:* Presidência da República Palácio de Belém, 1300 Lisboa, Portugal; Rua Dr João Soares, 2-3°, 1600 Lisboa, Portugal.

SOBELL, Sir Michael, Kt 1972; Chairman, GEC (Radio & Television) Ltd, since 1968; *b* 1 Nov. 1892; *s* of Lewis and Esther Sobell; *m* 1917, Anne Rakusen; two *d*. *Educ:* Central 7118London Foundation Sch. Freeman and Liveryman, Carmen Co. Hon. FRCPath, 1981; Hon. Fellow: Bar Ilan Univ.; Jews' Coll.; Hon. Dr Science and Technol., Technion Inst., Haifa, 1980; Hon. Dr Bar-Ilan Univ. *Recreations:* racing, charitable work. *Address:* Bakeham House, Englefield Green, Surrey TW20 9TX. *Clubs:* City Livery; Jockey (Newmarket).
See also Baron Weinstock.

SOBER, Phillip, FCA; European Regional Director, Horwath International, since 1990; *b* 1 April 1931; *s* of Abraham and Sandra Sober; *m* 1957, Vivien Louise Oppenheimer; three *d*. *Educ:* Haberdashers' Aske's. Qual. as Chartered Accountant, 1953; FCA 1963. Stoy Hayward, Chartered Accountants: Partner, 1958; Internat. Partner, 1975–90; Sen. Partner, 1985–90. Crown Estate Comr, 1983–. Mem. Council, UK Central Council for Nursing, Midwifery and Health Visiting, 1980–83. Trustee, Royal Opera House Trust, 1985–. *Publications:* articles in prof. press on various subjects but primarily on property co. accounting. *Recreations:* interested in all the arts, partic. music; golf main sporting activity. *Address:* 10 Longwood Drive, Roehampton, SW15 5DL. *T:* 081–789 0437. *Clubs:* Savile, Royal Automobile, Hurlingham, Roehampton.

SOBERS, Sir Garfield (St Auburn), (Sir Garry Sobers), Kt 1975; cricketer; *b* Bridgetown, Barbados, 28 July 1936; *m* 1969, Prudence Kirby; two *s* one *d*. *Educ:* Bay Street Sch., Barbados. First major match, 1953, for Barbados; played in 93 Test Matches for West Indies, 39 as Captain, 1953–74 (made world record Test Match score, Kingston, 1958); captained West Indies and Barbados teams, 1965–74; Captain of Nottinghamshire CCC, 1968–74. On retirement from Test cricket held the following world records in Test Matches: 365 not out; 26 centuries; 235 wickets; 110 catches. *Publications:* Cricket Advance, 1965; Cricket Crusader, 1966; King Cricket, 1967; (with J. S. Barker) Cricket in the Sun, 1967; Bonaventure and the Flashing Blade, 1967; (with Brian Scovell) Sobers: Twenty Years At The Top (autobiog.), 1988; *relevant publication:* Sir Gary: a biography by Trevor Bailey, 1976.

SOBHI, Mohamed Ibrahim; Order of Merit, 1st Class, Egypt, 1974; Director General, International Bureau of Universal Postal Union, Berne, 1975–84, retired; *b* Alexandria, 28 March 1925; *s* of Gen. Ibrahim Sobhi and Mrs Zenab Affifi; *m* 1950, Laila Ahmed Sobhi; two *s* one *d*. *Educ:* Cairo Univ. (BE 1949). Construction of roads and airports, Engr Corps, 1950; Technical Sec., Communications Commn, Permanent Council for Develt and National Prodn, Cairo, 1954; Fellow, Vanderbilt Univ., Nashville, Tenn (studying transport and communications services in USA), 1955–56; Tech. Dir, Office of Minister of Communications for Posts, Railways and Coordination between means of transp. and communications, Cairo, 1956–61; Dir-Gen., Sea Transp. Authority (remaining Mem. Tech. Cttees, Postal Org.), 1961–64; Under Sec. of State for Communications and Mem. Bd, Postal Org., Cairo, 1964–68; Chm. Bd, Postal Org., and Sec.-Gen., African Postal Union, Cairo, 1968–74. Universal Postal Union: attended Congress, Ottawa, 1957; attended Cons. Council for Postal Studies session, Brussels, 1958; Head of Egyptian Delegn, Tokyo and Lausanne Congresses, and sessions of CCPS (set up by Tokyo Congress), 1969–74; Dir, Exec. Bureau i/c Egyptian projects in Africa, incl. construction of Hôtel de l'Amitié, Bamako, Mali, and roads, Republic of Mali, 1963–74; as Director-General of UPU, acted as Sec.-Gen. of the Congress, Exec. Council, and Cons. Council for Postal Studies; acted as intermediary between UPU and Restricted Unions, UN and internat. orgns; visited member countries and attended many meetings and congresses, inc. those of Restricted Unions, in all continents. Chm., Communications Cttee, Nat. Dem. Party of Egypt, 1985; Mem., Nat. Council of Production and Econ. Affairs of Egypt, 1985. Heinrich von Stephan Medal (Germany), 1979; Order of Postal Merit (Gran Placa) (Spain), 1979. *Recreations:* croquet, philately, music. *Address:* 4 Sheik Zakaria El-Ansary Street, Heliopolis, Cairo, Egypt.

SODOR AND MAN, Bishop of, since 1989; **Rt. Rev. Noël Debroy Jones,** CB 1986; *b* 25 Dec. 1932; *s* of Brinley and Gwendoline Jones; *m* 1969, Joyce Barbara Leelavathy Arulanandam; one *s* one *d. Educ:* Haberdasher's West Monmouth, 1955–59; Vicar of Kano, N Nigeria, 1960–62; Chaplain, RN, 1962; GSM Brunei 1962, Borneo 1963; RM Commando Course prior to service in Aden with 42 Cdo, 1967; GSM S Arabia, 1967; Mid Service Clergy Course at St George's House, Windsor Castle, 1974; Staff Chaplain, MoD, 1974–77; Chaplain of the Fleet and Archdeacon for the Royal Navy, 1984–89. QHC 1983–89. *Recreations:* squash, swimming, music, family; formerly Rugby. *Address:* The Bishop's House, Quarterbridge Road, Douglas, Isle of Man. *Clubs:* Army and Navy; Sion College.

SOEHARTO, General, Hon. GCB 1974; President of Indonesia, since 1968; *b* 8 June 1921; *s* of Kertosudiro and Sukirah; *m* 1947, Siti Hartinah; three *s* three *d. Educ:* Elementary Sch., Puluhan Village; Junior High Sch., Wonogiri and Yogyakarta; Senior High Sch., Semarang. Military Basic Training Course and Non Commissioned Officers' Sch., 1940; Asst Police Chief, Yogyakarta (Japanese Police Unit Keibuho), 1941; Platoon Leader, Volunteer Corps, Wates, 1943; Co. Comdrs Sch., 1944; Mem., People's Security Army during Physical Revolution's counter insurgency ops against Indonesian Communist Party, 1945–50; crushed rebellion of Andi Aziz, Ujung Pandang, 1950; ops against Moslem rebels, Central Java, 1951–59; Comdg Gen., Liberation of W Irian (Western New Guinea), 1962; ops against Indonesian Communist Party, 1965; took measures to control the country, 1966; Acting President, 1967–68. Holds numerous decorations. *Address:* Office of the President, Jakarta, Indonesia.

SOFER, Mrs Anne Hallowell; Chief Education Officer, London Borough of Tower Hamlets, since 1989; *b* 19 April 1937; *d* of Geoffrey Crowther (later Baron Crowther) and Margaret Worth; *m* 1958, Jonathan Sofer; two *s* one *d. Educ:* St Paul's Sch.; Swarthmore Coll., USA; Somerville Coll., Oxford (MA); DipEd London. Secretary, National Assoc. of Governors and Managers, 1972–75; Additional Member, ILEA Education Cttee, 1974–77; Chairman, ILEA Schools Sub-Cttee, 1978–81; Mem. (SDP), GLC/ILEA for St Pancras N, Oct. 1981–86 (by-election) (Labour, 1977–81). Dir, Channel Four Television Co. Ltd, 1981–83; Columnist, The Times, 1983–87. Mem., SDP Nat. Cttee, 1982–. Contested Hampstead and Highgate (SDP) 1983, (SDP/Alliance) 1987. *Publication:* (with Tyrrell Burgess) The School Governors and Managers Handbook and Training Guide, 1978. *Address:* 46 Regent's Park Road, NW1 7SX. *T:* 071–722 8970.

SOLANKI, Ramniklal Chhaganlal; Editor: Garavi Gujarat, newsweekly, since 1968; Asian Trader, trade journal, with controlled circulation in English, Gujarati and Urdu, since 1985; GGII, since 1990; Correspondent, Janmabhoomi Group, Bombay, since 1968; *b* 12 July 1931; *s* of Chhaganlal Kalidas and Mrs Ichchhaben Solanki, Surat, Gujarat, India; *m* 1955, Mrs Parvatiben, *d* of Makanji Dullabhji Chavda, Nani Pethan, India; two *s* two *d. Educ:* Irish Presbyterian Mission Sch., Surat (Matriculation Gold Medal, 1949); MTB Coll., Gujarat Univ. (BA(Econ)); Sarvajanik Law Coll., Surat, Gujarat (LLB). Pres., Rander Student Union, 1950–54; Sec., Surat Dist Students' Assoc., 1954–55. Sub-Editor, Nutan Bharat and Lok Vani, Surat, 1954–56; freelance columnist for several newspapers, while serving State Govt in India, 1956–63; London correspondent, Gujarat Mitra Surat, 1964–68; European Correspondent, Janmabhoomi Gp of Newspapers, 1968–; Managing Director: Garavi Gujarat Publications Ltd and Garavi Gujarat Property Ltd; Asian Trade Publications Ltd. Author and columnist of thought of the week on Indian philosophy. Member: Guild of British Newspaper Editors, 1976–; Asian Adv. Cttee, BBC, 1976–80; Nat. Centre for Ind. Language Trng Steering Gp, 1976–; Exec. Cttee, Gujarati Arya Kshtriya Maha Sabha UK, 1979–84; Exec. Cttee, Gujarati Arya Assoc., 1974–84 (Vice-Pres., 1980–81, 1982–83); CPU, 1964–; Foreign Press Assoc., 1984–; Parly Press Gallery, House of Commons; Sec., Indian Journalists Assoc. of Europe, 1978–79. Best Reporter of the Year in Gujarati, 1970. *Publications:* contrib. many articles. *Recreations:* reading, writing. *Address:* 74 Harrowdene Road, N Wembley, Mddx HA0 2JF. *T:* 081–902 2879; (office): Garavi Gujarat House, 1/2 Silex Street, SE1 0DW. *T:* 071–928 1234; *Telex:* 8955335 Gujrat G; *Telefax:* 071–261 0055.

SOLDATOV, Aleksandr Alekseyevich; Rector, Moscow State Institute of International Relations, 1970; *b* 27 Aug. 1915; *m* Rufina B.; two *d. Educ:* Moscow Teachers' Training Inst. (grad. Hist. Sciences, 1939). Member Soviet Foreign Service, 1941; Senior Counsellor of Soviet Delegation to the UN and Representative on Trusteeship Council, 1948–53; Head of UN Div., 1953–54, of American Div., 1954–60, Soviet Foreign Ministry; Soviet Ambassador to the Court of St James's, 1960–66; Deputy Foreign Minister, 1966–68; Ambassador in Cuba, 1968–70; Ambassador to Lebanon, 1974–86. Member Soviet Delegation to Geneva Conferences: on Germany, 1959; on Laos, 1961. Mem., CPSU Central Auditing Commn, 1966–71.

SOLÉ-ROMEO, Dr Luis Alberto; Ambassador Extraordinary and Plenipotentiary of the Oriental Republic of Uruguay to the Court of St James's, since 1987; *b* 31 Aug. 1934; *m* 1st; three *d*; 2nd, 1984, Mrs Mónica de Assumpçao de Solé-Romeo. *Educ:* Univ. of Oriental Republic of Uruguay (Dr in Law and Soc. Scis). Attorney Counsellor of the Government Exchequer, 1973–84; Dir, Maritime and Fluvial Matters Office, Min. of Foreign Affairs, 1985–87; Legal Diplomatic Counsel, Min. of Foreign Affairs, 1985–. Pres., Nat. Assoc. of Broadcasters, 1971–75; Dir Gen., Internat. Assoc. of Broadcasting, 1974–87; Dir, Correo de los viernes (weekly), 1981–85; Co-Dir, El Día (daily newspaper), Montevideo, 1985–86. Mem., Exec. Cttee, World Press Freedom Cttee, Washington, DC, 1978–. Gold Medal, Ethics and Permanent Cttee, IAAB, for professional ethics and defence of freedom of expression 1975–77, 1977. *Publications:* Bases for an Educational Policy for Private Broadcasting in America, 1971, USA 1976; Uruguayan Laws and Regulations on Broadcasting, 2 vols, 1974; (with Gonzalo Aguirre Ramírez) Broadcasting Law: some basic concepts, 1974; Preventive Control of the Exchequer, 1976; Freedom, essential for a Cultural Broadcasting, 1977; The Sex of the Angels: sketches on freedom, 1978; articles and essays in newspapers and jls. *Recreations:* reading, travelling, music, gardening. *Address:* 1 Campden Hill, W8. *T:* 071–727 6557. *Clubs:* Athenæum, Travellers', Les Ambassadeurs; Six Continents; Golf del Uruguay (Montevideo, Uruguay).

SOLER, Antonio R.; *see* Ruiz Soler, A.

SOLESBURY, William Booth; Secretary, Economic and Social Research Council, since 1990; *b* 10 April 1940; *s* of William and Hannah Solesbury; *m* 1966, Felicity Andrew; one *s* two *d. Educ:* Hertford Grammar Sch.; Univ. of Cambridge (BA Hons Geography); Univ. of Liverpool (MCD Town Planning). London County Council, 1961–65; London Borough of Camden, 1965–66; City of Munich, 1966–67; Min. of Housing, 1967–72; NATO Res. Fellow, Univ. of California, Berkeley, 1973; Dept of Environment, 1974–89. Gwilym Gibbon Res. Fellow, Nuffield Coll., Oxford, 1989–90. *Publications:* Policy in Urban Planning, 1974; articles in Public Administration, Policy and Politics. *Recreations:* home life, films, reading, travel. *Address:* Economic and Social Research Council, Polaris House, North Star Avenue, Swindon, Wilts SN2 1UJ.

SOLESBY, Tessa Audrey Hilda, CMG 1986; HM Diplomatic Service; Leader, UK Delegation to Conference on Disarmament, Geneva (with personal rank of Ambassador), since 1987; *b* 1932; *d* of Charles Solesby and Hilda Solesby (*née* Willis). *Educ:* Clifton High School; St Hugh's College, Oxford. MA; Hon. Fellow, 1988. Min. of Labour and Nat. Service, 1954–55; joined Diplomatic Service, 1956; FO, 1956; Manila, 1957–59; Lisbon, 1959–62; FO, 1962–64; First Sec., UK Mission to UN, Geneva, 1964–68; FO, 1968–70; First Sec., UK Mission to UN, NY, 1970–72; FCO, 1972–75, Counsellor, 1975; on secondment to NATO Internat. Staff, Brussels, 1975–78; Counsellor, East Berlin, 1978–81; temp. Minister, UK Mission to UN, NY, 1981–82; Head of Central African Dept, FCO, 1982–86; Minister, Pretoria, 1986–87. *Recreations:* hill-walking, music. *Address:* c/o Foreign and Commonwealth Office, SW1A 2AH.

SOLEY, Clive Stafford; MP (Lab) Hammersmith, since 1983 (Hammersmith North, 1979–83); *b* 7 May 1939. *Educ:* Downshall Sec. Modern School; Newbattle Abbey Coll.; Strathclyde Univ. (BA Hons); Southampton Univ. (Dip. in Applied Social Studies). Various appointments; Probation Officer, 1970–75; Senior Probation Officer, 1975–79. Chm., Alcohol Educn Centre, 1977–83. Opposition front bench spokesman on N Ireland, 1981–84, on Home Affairs, 1984–87, on Housing, 1987–. *Address:* House of Commons, SW1.

SOLLEY, Stephen Malcolm; QC 1989; a Recorder, since 1989; *b* 5 Nov. 1946; *s* of Leslie Solley, sometime MP, and Jose Solley; *m* 1971, Helen Olivia Cox; four *s. Educ:* University College London (LLB 1968). Called to the Bar, Inner Temple, 1969. The Recorder, South Eastern Circuit, 1984–87. *Recreations:* jazz, opera, classic cars, wine, football, cooking. *Address:* Cloisters, Temple, EC4Y 7AA. *T:* 071–583 0303.

SOLOMON, His Honour (Alan) Peter; a Circuit Judge, 1973–86; *b* 6 July 1923; *s* of late Jacob Ovid Solomon, Manchester; *m* 1st, 1954; one *d*; 2nd, 1973; one *d*; 3rd, 1981, Susan Jennifer Hunter. *Educ:* Mill Hill Sch.; Lincoln College, Oxford; MA. Served War 1942–46, Fleet Air Arm, Petty Officer Airman. Called to Bar, Inner Temple, 1949; practised South-Eastern circuit. *Publications: poetry:* The Lunatic, Balance, in Keats Prize Poems, 1973. *Recreations:* the turf, travel, poetry, burgundy. *Club:* Garrick.

SOLOMON, Sir David (Arnold), Kt 1973; MBE 1944; *b* 13 Nov. 1907; *s* of Richard Solomon and Sarah Annie Solomon (*née* Simpson); *m* 1935, Marjorie Miles (*d* 1990); two *s* one *d. Educ:* Leys Sch., Cambridge; Liverpool Univ. Qualified a Solicitor, 1933; became Mem. Liverpool Stock Exchange, 1935. Served War of 1939–45, RAF (MBE). Practised as a Stockbroker until retirement, March 1969. Chairman: Liverpool RHB, 1968–73; Community Health Council, SE Cumbria, 1973–76. *Recreation:* music. *Address:* Tithe Barn, Cartmel, Grange over Sands, Cumbria LA11 6PP. *T:* Cartmel (05395) 36558.

SOLOMON, Sir Harry, Kt 1991; Chairman, Hillsdown Holdings, since 1987 (Joint Chairman, 1984–87); *b* 20 March 1937; *s* of Jacob and Belle Solomon; *m* 1962, Judith Diana Manuel; one *s* two *d. Educ:* St Albans School; Law Society School of Law. Qualified solicitor, 1960; in private practice, 1960–75; Managing Dir, Hillsdown Holdings, 1975–84. *Recreations:* jogging, tennis, theatre, collector of historical autographed letters. *Address:* Hillsdown House, 32 Hampstead High Street, NW3 1QD. *T:* 071–794 0677.

SOLOMON, Jonathan Hilali Moïse; Member, Court of Directors, since 1987, and Director, Corporate Business Development, since 1989, Cable and Wireless PLC; Director, International Digital Communications, Japan, since 1987; *b* 3 March 1939; *s* of Samuel and Moselle Solomon; *m* 1966, Hester McFarland; one *s. Educ:* Clifton College; King's College, Cambridge. BA Hons, MA. Research worker, Supervisor and Tutor, Cambridge and London Univs, 1960–63, 1965. Entered Home Civil Service, 1963; Asst Private Sec. to Pres. of Board of Trade, 1966–67; Principal, Companies Div., BoT, transferred to DTI, 1970; to Treasury, 1972; Asst Sec., Dept of Prices and Consumer Protection, 1974; returned to Dept of Industry, Electronics Divs, 1977–80; Under-Sec., Telecomns (formerly Posts and Telecomns) Div., DoI, 1980–84; Under Sec., Quality and Educn Div., DTI, 1984–85; Cable and Wireless: Dir of Special Projects, 1985–87; Dir, Corporate Strategy, 1987–89. Head UK Delegn, ITU Plenipotentiary Conf., Nairobi, 1982. Member Editorial Board: Telecommunications Policy, 1984–; Utilities Policy, 1990–. *Publications:* contribs to journals such as Platon, Contemporary Review, New Outlook, Frontier, Tablet, Telecommunications Policy. *Recreations:* sport, futurology, writing. *Address:* 12 Kidderpore Gardens, NW3 7SR. *T:* 071–794 6230. *Clubs:* English-Speaking Union, Royal Automobile.

SOLOMON, Dr Patrick Vincent Joseph, TC 1978; retired from Trinidad and Tobago Diplomatic Service, 1977; High Commissioner for Trinidad and Tobago in London, 1971–76, concurrently Ambassador for Trinidad and Tobago to Switzerland, France, Germany, Austria, Luxembourg, Denmark, Norway, Sweden, Italy, Netherlands and Finland; Chairman, Crown Life (Caribbean) Ltd, since 1977; *b* 12 April 1910; *s* of late Charles William Solomon and late Euphemia Alexia (*née* Payne); *m*; two *s*; *m* 1974, Mrs Leslie Richardson, *widow* of late William A. Richardson, Trinidad and Tobago. *Educ:* Tranquility Boys' Sch.; St Mary's Coll., Trinidad; Island Science Scholar, 1928; studied Medicine at Belfast and Edinburgh Univs, graduating in 1934. Practised medicine in Scotland, Ireland and Wales, to 1939; Leeward Island Medical Service, 1939–42; practised medicine in Trinidad, 1943–. Entered Politics, 1944. Elected: MLC, 1946–50 and 1956; MP (MHR) 1961; Minister of: Education, 1956–60; Home Affairs, 1960–64; External Affairs, 1964–66; Dep. Prime Minister, 1962–66; Dep. Political Leader of People's Nat. Movement, 1956–66; Permanent Rep. of Trinidad and Tobago to the United Nations, NY, 1966–71; Vice-Pres., UN General Assembly, 21st Session, 1966; Chm., UN Fourth Cttee, 23rd Session, 1968; Trinidad and Tobago Rep., Special Cttee on Apartheid, 1966–71, and Special Cttee of 24 on question of Decolonization; Mem. Preparatory Cttees concerning: celebration of Tenth Anniversary of Declaration on granting of Independence to Colonial Countries and Peoples (Resolution 1514, xv), 1968 and 1969; Commemoration of 25th Anniversary of United Nations. Pres. of Assembly, IMCO, 1976–77. Chm., Trinidad Assoc. in Aid of the Deaf. Kt Great Band, Most Humane order of African Redemption, Liberia, 1963; Gran Cordon del Libertador, Venezuela, 1963; Grand Croix de l'Ordre de Mérite, Luxembourg, 1977. Is a Roman Catholic. *Publication:* Solomon: an autobiography, 1981. *Recreations:* bridge, fishing. *Address:* 8 Woodlands Road, Valsayn Park, Trinidad and Tobago, West Indies.

SOLOMON, Peter; *see* Solomon, A. P.

SOLOMONIDES, Valerie Ann, (Mrs Constantine Solomonides); *see* Karn, V. A.

SOLOMONS, Hon. Sir Adrian; *see* Solomons, Hon. Sir L. A.

SOLOMONS, Anthony Nathan, FCA; Chairman: Singer & Friedlander Ltd, since 1976 (Chief Executive, 1973–90); Singer & Friedlander Group plc, since 1987; Director: Bullough Ltd, since 1983; Invesco MIM plc (formerly Britannia Arrow Holdings) since 1984 (Deputy Chairman, 1984–87); Director, Milton Keynes Development Corporation, since 1985; ACT plc, since 1990; *b* 26 Jan. 1930; *s* of Leslie Emanuel Solomons and Susie Schneiders; *m* 1957, Jean Golding; two *d*. Qual. as chartered accountant, 1953; FCA 1963. National Service, 1953–54: commnd Dorset Regt. Accountant, Kennedy & Fox Oldfield & Co., 1955; Asst Accountant, then Chief Accountant, Lobitos Oilfields Ltd, 1955–58; Singer & Friedlander 1958–: successively Exec. Dir, Man. Dir, and Jt Chief Exec. Member: Property Adv. Gp, DoE, 1976–; Educnl Assets Bd, 1988–. *Address:* 21 New Street, EC2M 4HR. *T:* 071–623 3000. *Club:* Carlton.

SOLOMONS, Prof. David; Professor of Accounting in the University of Pennsylvania (Wharton School), USA, 1959–83, now Professor Emeritus; Chairman of Accounting Department, 1969–75, designated Arthur Young Professor, 1974; *b* London, 11 Oct. 1912; *e s* of Louis Solomons and Hannah Solomons (*née* Isaacs); *m* 1945, Kate Miriam (*née* Goldschmidt); one *s* one *d*. *Educ:* Hackney Downs Sch., London, E8; London School of Economics. BCom (London) 1932; DSc (Econ.) (London), 1966. Chartered accountant, 1936; engaged in professional accountancy until Sept. 1939. Enlisted in ranks on outbreak of war; 2nd Lieut, RASC, 1941; Temp. Captain, 1942; Petrol Supply Officer, HQ 88 Area (Tobruk), 1942; prisoner-of-war in Italy and Germany, 1942–45. Lectr in Accounting, LSE, 1946; Reader in Accounting, Univ. of London, 1948–55; Prof. of Accounting, University of Bristol, 1955–59. Visiting Assoc. Prof., University of California, 1954; Prof. at Institut pour l'Etude des Méthodes de Direction de l'Entreprise (IMEDE), Lausanne, 1963–64; Visiting Professor: Nat. Univ. of Singapore, 1984; Graduate Inst. of Business Admin, Chulalongkorn Univ., Bangkok, 1985 and 1986; Univ. of Auckland, NZ, 1991; Vis. Erskine Fellow, Univ. of Canterbury, NZ, 1976; AAA Distinguished Internat. Lectr, 1984; Lee Kuan Yew Disting. Visitor, Nat. Univ. of Singapore, 1986. Mem., AICPA Study on Establishment of Accounting Principles, 1971–72; directed (UK) Adv. Bd of Accountancy Educn Long-range Enquiry into Educn and Trng for Accountancy Profession, 1972–74; Dir of Res., Amer. Accounting Assoc., 1968–70, Pres., 1977–78. Mem., Financial Accounting Standards Adv. Council, 1982–85. Hon. DHL Widener, 1986; Hon. DSc Buckingham, 1987. AICPA Award for Notable Contribution to Accounting Literature, 1969; Jl of Accountancy Literary Award, 1979; AAA Outstanding Accounting Educator Award, 1980; Walter Taplin Prize, Accounting and Business Research, 1984; Internat. Award, ICA, 1989. *Publications:* Divisional Performance: Measurement and Control, 1965; ed and contrib. to Studies in Cost Analysis, 1968; Prospectus for a Profession, 1974; Collected Papers on Accounting and Accounting Education (2 vols), 1984; Making Accounting Policy: the Quest for Credibility in Financial Reporting, 1986; Guidelines for Financial Reporting Standards, 1989. *Address:* 205 Elm Avenue, Swarthmore, Pa 19081, USA. *T:* 215–544–8193.

SOLOMONS, Hon. Sir (Louis) Adrian, Kt 1982; Member since 1969, and Deputy President and Chairman of Committees since 1988, Legislative Council of New South Wales; Consultant, Messrs Everingham, Solomons & Co., Solicitors, since 1986 (Senior Partner, 1975–86); *b* 9 June 1922; *s* of George Albert Solomons and Katie Isabel (*née* Rowland); *m* 1944 (whilst on War Service), Olwyn Ainslie Bishop; two *s*. *Educ:* New England University Coll.; Sydney Univ. (BA *in absentia* 1945, LLB 1949). Admitted solicitor, 1949. National Country Party of Australia (now National Party), NSW: Mem., Central Exec., 1964–67; Vice Chm., 1967–69; Chm., 1969–74; National Pres., 1974–80. Mem., Bd of Governors, Law Foundn of NSW, 1984–. *Recreation:* deep sea fishing. *Address:* Fairview, 17 Campbell Road, Calala, Tamworth, NSW 2340, Australia. *T:* (067) 65–9899. *Clubs:* National Liberal, Lansdowne; Tattersall's (Sydney); Tamworth (NSW).

SOLOW, Prof. Robert Merton; Professor of Economics, Massachusetts Institute of Technology, since 1949; *b* 23 Aug. 1924; *s* of Milton H. Solow and Hannah Solow (*née* Sarney); *m* 1945, Barbara Lewis; two *s* one *d*. *Educ:* New York City schools; Harvard College (BA 1947); Harvard University (MA 1949, PhD 1951). Served US forces, 1942–45 (Bronze Star, 1944). Joined MIT Faculty as Asst Prof. of Statistics, 1949, Inst. Prof. of Economics, 1974–. Senior Economist, Council of Economic Advisers, 1961–62. Eastman Prof. and Fellow of Balliol Coll., Oxford, 1968–69; Overseas Fellow, Churchill Coll., Cambridge, 1984, 1991. President: Econometric Soc., 1965; Amer. Econ. Assoc., 1976; Member: Amer. Acad. of Arts and Scis, 1963; Nat. Acad. of Sciences, USA, 1972; Accademia dei Lincei, 1984; Corr. Mem., British Acad., 1975; Mem., Amer. Philosophical Soc., 1974–. Hon. degrees: Chicago, 1967; Brown, 1972; Williams, 1974; Warwick, 1976; Paris I, 1975; Lehigh, 1977; Geneva, 1982; Wesleyan, 1982; Tulane, 1983; Yale, 1986; Bryant, 1987; Massachusetts at Boston, 1989; Colgate, 1990; Dartmouth, 1990; Helsinki, 1990. Nobel Prize for Economics, 1987. *Publications:* Linear Programming and Economic Analysis (with P. Samuelson and R. Dorfman), 1958; Capital Theory and the Rate of Return, 1964; The Sources of Unemployment in the US, 1964; Growth Theory: an exposition, 1970; The Labor Market as a Social Institution, 1990; articles in learned jls. *Recreation:* sailing. *Address:* 528 Lewis Wharf, Boston, Mass 02110, USA. *T:* (617) 227 4436.

SOLTI, Sir Georg, KBE 1971 (CBE (Hon.) 1968); Artistic Director, Salzburg Easter Festival, from March 1992; Music Director, Chicago Symphony Orchestra, 1969–91, Music Director Laureate, since 1991; Principal Conductor and Artistic Director, London Philharmonic Orchestra, 1979–83, then Conductor Emeritus; *b* Budapest, 21 Oct. 1912; adopted British nationality, 1972; *m* 1st, 1946, Hedwig Oeschli; 2nd, 1967, Anne Valerie Pitts; two *d*. *Educ:* High School of Music, Budapest. Studied with Kodály, Bartók, and Dohnányi. Conductor and pianist, State Opera, Budapest, 1930–39; first prize, as pianist, Concours Internationale, Geneva, 1942; Musical Director, Bavarian State Opera, 1946–52; Musical Director, Frankfurt Opera, and Permanent Conductor, Museums Concerts, Frankfurt, 1952–61; Musical Director: Covent Garden Opera Co., 1961–71; Orchestre de Paris, 1972–75. Guest Conductor: Berlin, Salzburg, Vienna, Munich, Paris, London (first conducted London Philharmonic Orchestra, 1947; Covent Garden début, 1959), Glyndebourne Festival, Edinburgh Festival, Bayreuth Festival, San Francisco, New York, Los Angeles, Chicago, etc. Has made numerous recordings (many of which have received international awards or prizes, incl. Grand Prix Mondiale du Disque (14 times), and 29 Grammy Awards (incl. special Trustees Grammy Award for recording of The Ring Cycle), Nat. Acad. of Recorded Arts and Scis). Hon. FRCM, 1980; Hon. Prof., Baden-Württemberg, 1985. Hon. Fellow, Jesus Coll., Oxford, 1990. Hon. DMus: Leeds, 1971; Oxon, 1972; Yale Univ., 1974; Harvard, 1979; Furman, 1983; Surrey, 1983; London, 1986; Hon. Dr DePaul, 1975. Médaille de Vermeil, Ville de Paris, 1985; Loyola-Mellon Humanities Award, 1987; Medal of Merit, City of Chicago, 1987; Gold Medal, Royal Philharmonic Soc., 1989. Kt Commander's Cross, OM (FRG), 1987; Order of the Flag (Hungarian People's Republic), 1987. *Address:* Chalet Haut Pré, Villars s. Ollon, CH-1884, Switzerland. *Club:* Athenæum.

SOLYMAR, Dr Laszlo; Donald Pollock Reader in Engineering Science, University of Oxford and Professorial Fellow of Hertford College, since 1986; *b* 1930; *s* of Pál and Aranka Solymar; *m* 1955, Marianne Klopfer; two *d*. *Educ:* Technical University, Budapest (Hungarian equivalents of BSc and PhD in Engineering). Lectr, Technical Univ., Budapest, 1952–53; Research Engineer, Res. Inst. for Telecommunications, Budapest, 1953–56; Res. Engineer, Standard Telecom Labs, Harlow, 1956–65; Fellow in Engineering, Brasenose Coll., Oxford, 1966–86; Lectr, Univ. of Oxford, 1971–86. Visiting Professor: Ecole Normale Supérieure, Paris, 1965–66; Tech. Univ. of Denmark, 1972–73; Univ. Osnabrück, 1987; Tech. Univ., Berlin, 1990. Consultant: Tech. Univ. of Denmark, 1973–76; Thomson-CSF, Orsay, 1984; British Telecom, 1986–88; GEC Wembley, 1986–88; Pilkington Technol. Centre, 1989–90. *Publications:* Lectures on the Electrical Properties of Materials (with D. Walsh), 1970, 4th edn 1988; Superconductive Tunnelling and Applications, 1972; (ed) A Review of the Principles of Electrical and Electronic Engineering, 1974; Lectures on Electromagnetic Theory, 1976, 2nd edn 1984; (with D. J. Cooke) Volume Holography and Volume Gratings, 1981; Lectures on Fourier Series, 1988; articles. *Recreations:* history, languages, chess, swimming, ski-ing. *Address:* Department of Engineering Science, University of Oxford OX1 3PJ. *T:* Oxford (0865) 273110.

SOLZHENITSYN, Alexander Isayevitch; author; Hon. Fellow, Hoover Institution on War, Revolution and Peace, 1975; *b* 11 Dec. 1918; *m*; three *s*. *Educ:* Univ. of Rostov (degree in maths and physics); Moscow Inst. of History, Philosophy and Literature (correspondence course). Joined Army, 1941; grad. from Artillery School, 1942; in comd artillery battery and served at front until 1945 (twice decorated); sentenced to eight years' imprisonment, 1945, released, 1953; exile in Siberia, 1953–56; officially rehabilitated, 1957; taught and wrote in Ryazan and Moscow; expelled from Soviet Union, 1974; Soviet citizenship restored, 1990. Member Union of Soviet writers, 1962, expelled 1969; Member Amer. Acad. of Arts and Sciences, 1969. Awarded Nobel Prize for Literature, 1970; Templeton Prize for Progress in Religion, 1983; Russian State Literature Prize, 1990. *Publications:* One Day in the Life of Ivan Denisovich, 1962, new edn 1991, filmed 1971; An Incident at Krechetovka Station, and Matryona's House (publ. US as We Never Make Mistakes, 1969), 1963; For the Good of the Cause, 1964; The First Circle, 1968; Cancer Ward, part 1, 1968, part 2, 1969 (Prix du Meilleur Livre Etranger, Paris); Stories and Prose Poems, 1970; August 1914, 1972; One Word of Truth: the Nobel speech on literature, 1972; The Gulag Archipelago: an experiment in literary investigation, vol. 1, 1973, vol. 2, 1974, vol. 3, 1976 (first Russian edn, 1989); The Oak and the Calf (autobiog.), 1975; Lenin in Zurich, 1975; Prussian Nights (poem), 1977; The Red Wheel: August 1914, 1983 (revd edn of 1972 publication); October 1916, 1985; *plays:* trilogy: The Love Girl and the Innocent, 1969, Victory Celebrations, Prisoners, 1983. *Address:* c/o Harper & Row Inc., 10 East 53rd Street, New York, NY 10022, USA.

SOMARE, Rt. Hon. Sir Michael Thomas, GCMG 1990; CH 1978; PC 1977; MP; Minister for Foreign Affairs, Papua New Guinea, since 1988; *b* 9 April 1936; *m* 1965, Veronica Somare; three *s* two *d*. *Educ:* Sogeri Secondary Sch.; Admin. Coll. Teaching, 1956–62; Asst Area Educn Officer, Madang, 1962–63; Broadcasts Officer, Dept of Information and Extension Services, Wewack, 1963–66; Journalism, 1966–68. Member for E Sepik Region (Nat. Parl.), PNG House of Assembly, 1968–; Parly Leader, Pangu Pati, 1968–; First Chief Minister, 1972–75; first Prime Minister, 1975–80, 1982–85; Leader of Opposition in House of Assembly, 1980–82. Dep. Chm., Exec. Council, 1972–73, Chm., 1973–75. Mem., Second Select Cttee on Constitutional Develt, 1968–72; Mem. Adv. Cttee, Australian Broadcasting Commission. *Address:* House of Assembly, Port Moresby, Papua New Guinea; (home) Karan, Murik Lakes, East Sepik, Papua New Guinea.

SOMERFIELD, Stafford William; editorial consultant, since 1970; *b* 9 Jan. 1911; *m* 1st, 1933, Gertrude Camfield (marr. diss. 1951); two *d*; 2nd, 1951, Elizabeth Montgomery (*d* 1977); 3rd, 1977, Ferelith Hamilton. *Educ:* Ashleigh Road School, Barnstaple. Exeter Express and Echo, Bristol Evening World, Daily Telegraph, 1934–39; News Chronicle, 1939, until outbreak of War. Rifleman, Queen's Westminsters, 1939–40; Major, Gloucestershire Regt. 1945. News of the World: Features Editor, Asst Editor, Northern Editor, Dep. Editor; Editor, 1960–70; Chm., Dog World, 1982. *Publications:* John George Haigh, 1950; Banner Headlines, 1979; The Boxer, 1985. *Recreation:* pedigree dogs. *Address:* Ivy Lodge, Ivychurch, Romney Marsh, Kent TN29 0AL. *T:* Brookland (06794) 240. *Club:* Kennel.

SOMERLEYTON, 3rd Baron *cr* 1916; **Savile William Francis Crossley;** Bt 1863; DL; farmer; a Lord in Waiting to the Queen, since 1978; *b* 17 Sept. 1928; *er s* of 2nd Baron Somerleyton, MC; *S* father, 1959; *m* 1963, Belinda Maris Loyd, *d* of late Vivian Loyd and of Mrs Gerald Critchley; one *s* four *d*. *Educ:* Eton Coll. Captain Coldstream Guards, 1948; retired, 1956. Royal Agricultural Coll., Cirencester, 1958–59; farming, 1959–. Dir, E Anglian Water Co., 1961–. DL Suffolk, 1964. *Heir:* *s* Hon. Hugh Francis Savile Crossley, *b* 27 Sept. 1971. *Address:* Somerleyton Hall, Lowestoft, Suffolk NR32 5QQ. *T:* Lowestoft (0502) 730308. *Club:* White's.

SOMERS, 8th Baron *cr* 1784; **John Patrick Somers Cocks;** Bt 1772; *b* 30 April 1907; *o s* of 7th Baron and Mary Benita (*d* 1950), *d* of late Major Luther M. Sabin, United States Army; *S* father, 1953; *m* 1st, 1935, Barbara Marianne (*d* 1959), *d* of Charles Henry Southall, Norwich; 2nd, 1961, Dora Helen, *d* of late John Mountfort. *Educ:* privately; Royal College of Music, London. 2nd Music Master, Westonbirt School, 1935–38; Director of Music, Epsom Coll., 1949–53; Prof. of Composition and Theory, RCM, 1967–77. BMus, ARCM. *Heir:* *cousin* Philip Sebastian Somers-Cocks, *b* 4 Jan. 1948. *Address:* 35 Links Road, Epsom, Surrey KT17 3PP.

SOMERS, Rt Hon. Sir Edward (Jonathan), Kt 1989; PC 1981; Judge of the Court of Appeal, New Zealand, 1981–90; *b* 9 Sept. 1928; *s* of Ewart Somers and Muriel Ann Crossley; *m* 1953, Mollie Louise Morison; one *s* two *d*. *Educ:* Christ's Coll., Christchurch; Canterbury University Coll., Christchurch, NZ (BA, LLB). Practised as barrister and solicitor, 1952–71; practised as barrister, 1971; QC (NZ) 1973; Judge of Supreme Court of New Zealand, 1974. *Recreation:* gardening. *Address:* Waverley, Kaiapoi, RD2, New Zealand. *T:* Kaiapoi 7094. *Club:* Christchurch (New Zealand).

SOMERS COCKS, Anna Gwenllian, FSA; Editor, The Art Newspaper, since 1990; *b* 18 April 1950; *d* of John Sebastian Somers Cocks, CVO, CBE and Marjorie Olive Weller; *m* 1st, 1971, Martin Walker (marr. diss.); 2nd, 1978, John Hardy (marr. diss.); one *s* one *d*. *Educ:* abroad; Convent of the Sacred Heart, Woldingham; St Anne's College, Oxford (MA); Courtauld Inst., Univ. of London (MA). Asst Keeper, Dept of Metal Work, 1973–85, Dept of Ceramics, 1985–87, Victoria and Albert Museum; Ed., Apollo Magazine, 1987–90. FRSA. *Publications:* The Victoria and Albert Museum: the making of the collection, 1980; (ed and jt author) Princely Magnificence: court jewels of the Renaissance, 1980; (with C. Truman) Renaissance Jewels, Gold Boxes and Objets de Vertu in the Thyssen Collection, 1985. *Recreations:* ski-ing, entertaining, travelling, walking. *Address:* c/o The Art Newspaper, 44–46 Fleet Street, EC4. *Club:* Arts.

SOMERSCALES, Thomas Lawrence, CBE 1970; General Secretary, Joint Committee of the Order of St John of Jerusalem and the British Red Cross Society, 1960–78; *b* 1 July 1913; *s* of Wilfred Somerscales; *m* 1941, Ann Teresa, *d* of Robert Victor Kearney; three *s* one *d. Educ:* Riley High Sch., Hull. FCA 1939. KStJ 1978. Finance Sec., Jt Cttee, OStJ and BRCS, 1953–60. Mem., Adv. Council, ITA, 1964–67. *Address:* The Dormer House, The Rookery, Alveston, Stratford-upon-Avon.

SOMERSET, family name of **Duke of Beaufort** and of **Baron Raglan.**

SOMERSET, 19th Duke of, *cr* 1547; **John Michael Edward Seymour,** FRICS; Baron Seymour 1547; Bt 1611; *b* 30 Dec. 1952; *s* of 18th Duke of Somerset and of Gwendoline Collette (Jane), 2nd *d* of Major J. C. C. Thomas; *S* father, 1984; *m* 1978, Judith-Rose, *d* of J. F. C. Hull, *qv*; one *s* two *d. Educ:* Eton. *Heir: s* Lord Seymour, *qv. Address:* Maiden Bradley, Warminster, Wilts; Berry Pomeroy, Totnes, Devon.

SOMERSET, David Henry Fitzroy, FCIB; Fellow and Financial Adviser, Peterhouse, Cambridge, since 1988; *b* 19 June 1930; *s* of late Brig. Hon. Nigel Somerset, CBE, DSO, MC and Phyllis Marion Offley (*née* Irwin); *m* 1955, Ruth Ivy, *d* of late W. R. Wildbur; one *s* one *d. Educ:* Wellington Coll.; Peterhouse, Cambridge (MA). Entered Bank of England, 1952; Personal Asst to Managing Director, International Monetary Fund, Washington DC, 1959–62; Private Secretary to Governor of Bank of England, 1962–63; Asst Chief Cashier, 1968–69; Asst Chief of Establishments, 1969–73; Dep. Chief Cashier, 1973–80; Chief of Banking Dept and Chief Cashier, 1980–88. Chairman: EBS Investments Ltd, 1977–; London Adv. Bd, Bank Julius Baer, 1991–; Director: Prolific Gp PLC, 1988–; Yamaichi Bank (UK) PLC, 1988–; Hafnia Hldgs (UK) Ltd, 1990–. Comr, English Heritage, 1988–91. Mem. Council, Friends of Peterhouse, 1982–; Chm., Old Wellingtonian Soc., 1988–; Gov., Wellington Coll., 1989–. *Recreations:* gardening, racing, shooting. *Address:* White Wickets, Boars Head, Crowborough, Sussex TN6 3HE. *T:* Crowborough (0892) 661111. *Club:* Royal Automobile.

SOMERSET, Sir Henry Beaufort, Kt 1966; CBE 1961; *b* 21 May 1906; *s* of Henry St John Somerset; *m* 1930, Patricia Agnes Strickland; two *d. Educ:* St Peter's Coll., Adelaide; Trinity Coll., University of Melbourne; MSc 1928. Director: Humes Ltd, 1957–82 (Chm., 1961–82); Goliath Cement Hldgs Ltd, 1947–82 (Chm., 1967–82); Associated Pulp & Paper Mills Ltd, 1937–81 (Man. Dir, 1948–70; Dep. Chm., 1970–81); Electrolytic Zinc Co. of Australasia Ltd, 1953–78; Perpetual Exors Trustees Ltd, 1971–81 (Chm., 1973–81); Tioxide Australia Pty Ltd, 1949–82 (Chm., 1953–76); Central Norseman Gold Corp. Ltd, 1977–82. Chancellor, University of Tasmania, 1964–72; Member: Council, Australasian Inst. of Mining and Metallurgy, 1956– (President, 1958 and 1966); Exec., CSIRO, 1965–74; Council, Nat. Museum of Victoria, 1968–77; Pres., Australian Mineral Foundn, 1972–83. FRACI; FTS. Hon. DSc Tasmania, 1973. *Address:* 193 Domain Road, South Yarra, Victoria 3141, Australia. *Clubs:* Melbourne, Australian (Melbourne).

SOMERSET FRY, Peter George Robin Plantagenet; author and journalist, since 1955; *b* 3 Jan. 1931; *s* of late Comdr Peter K. Ll. Fry, OBE, RN, and Ruth Emily (*née* Marriott), LRAM; *m* 1st, 1958, Daphne Diana Elizabeth Caroline Yorke (*d* 1961); 2nd, 1961, Hon. Mrs Leri Butler (marr. diss. 1973, she *d* 1985); 3rd, 1974, Pamela Fiona Ileene (author: Horses, 1981; A Soldier in Wellington's Army, 1987), *d* of late Col H. M. Whitcombe, MBE. *Educ:* Lancing; St Thomas's Hosp. Med. Sch., London; St Catherine's Coll., Oxford (Sec. Oxford Union, Hilary 1956). Mem. editorial staff: Atomics and Nuclear Energy, 1957–58; The Tatler and Bystander, 1958; public relations, 1960–64; Information Officer: Incorp. Assoc. of Architects and Surveyors, 1965–67; MPBW, 1967–70; Head of Inf. Services, COSIRA, 1970–74; Editor of Books, HM Stationery Office, 1975–80. Gen. Editor, Macmillan History in Pictures Series, 1977–. Vis. Scholar, 1980–84, Sen. Mem., 1984–, Wolfson Coll., Cambridge. Mem. Council, East Anglian Writers, 1977–82; Co-founder, Congress of Indep. Archaeologists, 1985; Founder and Hon. Secretary: Little Bardfield Village Community Trust, 1971–74; Daphne Somerset Fry Meml Trust for Kidney Disease Res., 1961–; Burgh Soc., 1978–80. FRSA 1966. *Publications:* Mysteries of History, 1957; The Cankered Rose, 1959; Rulers of Britain, 1967, 3rd edn 1973; They Made History, 1970, 2nd edn 1973; The World of Antiques, 1970, 4th edn 1972; Antique Furniture, 1971, 2nd edn 1972; Constantinople, 1970; The Wonderful Story of the Jews, 1970; Children's History of the World, 1972, 11th edn 1987; Answer Book of History, 1972, 2nd edn 1973; Zebra Book of Famous Men, 1972; Zebra Book of Famous Women, 1972; Collecting Inexpensive Antiques, 1973, 5th edn 1980; Zebra Book of Castles, 1974; Great Caesar, 1974; British Mediaeval Castles, 1974; 1000 Great Lives, 1975, 8th edn 1984; Questions, 1976; 2,000 Years of British Life, 1976; Chequers: the country home of Britain's Prime Ministers, 1977 (official history); 3,000 Questions and Answers, 1977, 12th edn 1984; Boudicca, 1978; David & Charles Book of Castles, 1980, 2nd edn 1990; Fountains Abbey (official souvenir guide), 1980; Beautiful Britain, 1981; (with Fiona Somerset Fry) History of Scotland, 1982; Revolt Against Rome, 1982; Great Cathedrals, 1982; (ed) Longman Pocket History Dictionary, 1983; Roman Britain: history and sites, 1984; Battle Abbey and the Battle of Hastings (official souvenir guide), 1984, 2nd edn 1990; 3,000 More Questions and Answers, 1984; Antiques, 1985; Rievaulx Abbey (official souvenir guide), 1986; Children's Illustrated Dictionary, 1987; (with Fiona Somerset Fry) History of Ireland, 1988, 2nd edn 1991; 1000 Great People Through the Ages, 1989; Kings & Queens of England & Scotland, 1990; The Tower of London, 1990. *Recreations:* studying 18th Century French furniture, Roman history, visiting British castles, promoting freedom of information. *Address:* Wood Cottage, Wattisfield, Bury St Edmunds, Suffolk IP22 1NE. *T:* Stanton (0359) 51324.

SOMERSET JONES, Eric, QC 1978; a Recorder of the Crown Court, since 1975; *b* 21 Nov. 1925; *s* of late Daniel and Florence Somerset Jones; *m* 1966, Brenda Marion, *yr d* of late Hedley Shimmin and Doris Shimmin (*née* Beacroft) two *d. Educ:* Birkenhead Institute; Lincoln College, Oxford. MA Oxon. RAF, 1944–47. Called to Bar, Middle Temple, 1952, Bencher, 1988; Mem., Northern Circuit; Member, Lord Chancellor's County Courts Rule Cttee, 1975–78. *Recreations:* family pursuits; travel; listening to music; photography. *Address:* (home) Southmead, Mill Lane, Willaston, Wirral, Cheshire L64 1RL. *T:* 051–327 5138; Cloisters, Temple, EC4Y 7AA. *T:* 071–353 0461; (chambers) Goldsmith Building, Temple, EC4Y 7BL. *T:* 071–353 7881. *Club:* Royal Chester Rowing (Chester).

SOMERTON, Viscount; James Shaun Christian Welbore Ellis Agar; *b* 7 Sept. 1982; *s* and *heir* of 6th Earl of Normanton, *qv*.

SOMERVILLE, Prof. Christopher Roland, PhD; FRS 1991; Professor of Botany and Genetics, Michigan State University, since 1982; *b* 11 Oct. 1947; *s* of Hubert Roland Somerville and Teresa Marie (*née* Bond); *m* 1976, Shauna Christine Phimester. *Educ:* Univ. of Alberta, Canada (PhD, BS). Asst Prof. of Genetics, Univ. of Alberta, Canada, 1980–82; Associate Prof. of Botany and Genetics, Michigan State Univ., Mich, 1982–86. *Publications:* numerous research articles on genetics, physiology and biochemistry of plants. *Recreation:* sailing. *Address:* 4596 Herron Road, Okemos, Mich 48864, USA. *T:* 517–337–7137.

SOMERVILLE, David, CB 1971; Under-Secretary, Department of Health and Social Security, 1968–77; *b* 27 Feb. 1917; *e s* of late Rev. David Somerville and Euphemia Somerville; *m* 1950, Patricia Amy Johnston; two *s* two *d. Educ:* George Watson's Coll.; Fettes Coll.; Edinburgh Univ.; Christ Church, Oxford. Served with Army, 1940–45; Major, Royal Artillery. Entered Civil Service as Asst Principal, Ministry of Health, 1946; Under-Secretary, Min. of Health, 1963–67. *Recreations:* golf, gardening, adult education. *Address:* 5 Glebe Road, Dorking, Surrey RH4 3DS. *T:* Dorking (0306) 885102. *Club:* Betchworth Park Golf.

SOMERVILLE, Jane, MD; FRCP; Consultant Physician: Royal Brompton & National Heart Hospital (formerly National Heart Hospital), since 1974; Cardiac Department, Grown-Up Congenital Heart Disease Clinic, St Bartholomew's Hospital, since 1988; *b* 24 Jan. 1933; *d* of Joseph Bertram Platnauer and Pearl Ashton; *m* 1957, Dr Walter Somerville, *qv*; three *s* one *d. Educ:* Queen's Coll., London; Guy's Hosp., London Univ. MB, BS (Treasurer's Gold Medal for Clin. Surg.) 1955; MD 1966. MRCS 1955; FRCP 1973 (LRCP 1955, MRCP 1957). FACC 1972. Med. Registrar, Guy's Hosp., 1956–58; Registrar, Nat. Heart Hosp., 1958–59; First Asst to Dr Paul Wood, 1959–63, Sen. Lectr 1964–74, Inst. of Cardiol.; Hon. Cons. Phys., Nat. Heart Hosp., 1967–74, Hosp. for Sick Children, Gt Ormond St, 1968–88. Lectr in Cardiovascular Disease, Turin Univ., 1973. Vis. Prof. and Guest Lectr, Europe, ME, USA, Mexico, S America, USSR, China; St Cyres Lectr, Imperial Coll., London, 1976; 6th Mahboubian Lectr, NY, 1981; World Congress Gold Medal Lectr, Bombay, 1982; Edgar Mannheimer, Hamburg, 1987; John Keith, Montreal, 1988; Tudor Edwards, RCP, 1991. Chm., Staff Cttee, 1988–89, Jt Adv. Cttee, 1989–90, Nat. Heart Hosp.; Chm., Cardiol. Cttee, Royal Brompton & Nat. Heart Hosp., 1990–. Sci. Sec., World Congress, Paed. Cardiol., 1980; Advr on congenital heart disease, Sec. of State's Hon. Med. Adv. Panel on driving and disorders of cardiovascular system, 1986–. Member: Assoc. Europ. Pæd. Cardiol.; British Cardiac Soc. (Mem., Paediatric Cardiol. Services Sub-cttee, 1987–); British Paed. Assoc.; RSocMed; Harveian Soc.; French Cardiac Soc.; 300 Gp; Sci. Council, Monaco Cardiothoracic Centre. Hon. Member: Argentine Pæd. Soc.; Chilean Cardiac Soc.; Argentine Soc. of Cardiol.; Brazilian Cardiac Soc.; Argentine Cardiac Soc. Founding Fellow, Europ. Soc. of Cardiol. Mem. Council, Stonham Housing Assoc. Governor: Queen's Coll., London; Nat. Heart and Chest Hosps, 1977–82, 1988–90. Woman of the Year, 1968. *Publications:* numerous contribs to med. lit. on heart disease in children, adolescents and adults, congenital heart disease and results of cardiac surgery; chapters in Paul Wood's Diseases of Heart and Circulation (3rd edn), Oxford Textbook of Medicine, and Perspectives in Pediatric Cardiology, Vols I and II. *Recreations:* collecting antiques, pictures, porcelain soldiers; chess, roof gardening, orchid culture. *Address:* 30 York House, Upper Montagu Street, W1H 1FR. *T:* 071–262 2144; 071–351 8200, *Fax:* 071–351 8201.

SOMERVILLE, John Arthur Fownes, CB 1977; CBE 1964; DL; an Under-Secretary, Government Communications Headquarters, 1969–78; *b* 5 Dec. 1917; *s* of late Admiral of the Fleet Sir James Fownes Somerville, GCB, GBE, DSO; *m* 1945, Julia Elizabeth Payne; one *s* two *d. Educ:* RNC Dartmouth. Midshipman 1936; Sub-Lieut 1938; Lieut 1940; Lieut-Comdr 1945; retd 1950. Govt Communications Headquarters, 1950–78. DL Somerset, 1985. *Recreation:* walking. *Address:* The Old Rectory, Dinder, Wells, Som BA5 3PL. *T:* Wells (0749) 74900. *Club:* Army and Navy.

SOMERVILLE, Brig. Sir (John) Nicholas, Kt 1985; CBE 1975; self employed consultant, personnel selection, since 1984; *b* 16 Jan. 1924; *s* of Brig. Desmond Henry Sykes Somerville and Moira Burke Somerville; *m* 1951, Jenifer Dorothea Nash; one *s* two *d. Educ:* Winchester College. Commissioned, The South Wales Borderers, 24th Regt, 1943; served: France and Germany, D-day—VE day, 1944–45 (despatches 1945); BAOR, War Office, FARELF, Aden, 1967–68 (despatches 1968); Directing Staff, JSSC, 1967–69; Comdt, Junior Div., Staff Coll., 1969–72; Dir of Army Recruiting, 1973–75; retired, 1978. Managing Director, Saladin Security Ltd, 1981–84; voluntary consultant responsible for designing Cons. Party Parly selection board procedure, 1980–. *Recreations:* sailing, gardening, house designing. *Address:* Deptford Cottage, Greywell, near Basingstoke, Hants RG25 1BS. *T:* Odiham (0256) 702796. *Club:* Lansdowne.

SOMERVILLE, Very Rev. Dr John Spenser, ONZ 1991; CMG 1978; MC 1945; Master, Knox College, Dunedin, 1963–78, retired; *b* 7 July 1910; *s* of James Cleland Hall Somerville and Grace Isabella (*née* Isherwood); *m* 1951, Janet Christina Macky (*d* 1988); four *s. Educ:* Univ. of Otago (MA 1934); Theol Hall, Knox Coll., Dunedin. Ordained Tapanui, 1938; Chaplain, 2 NZEF, 1942–45; Minister, St Andrews, Wellington, 1947–63. Moderator, Gen. Assembly of Presbyterian Church of NZ, 1960. Mem. Council, 1969–85, Chancellor, 1976–82, Univ. of Otago. Pres., Otago Early Settlers' Assoc., 1979–91. Hon. DD St Andrews, 1969; Hon. LLD Otago, 1979. *Publication:* Jack in the Pulpit (autobiog.), 1987. *Recreations:* cricket, bowls, reading, gardening. *Address:* 19 Constitution Street, Dunedin 9001, New Zealand. *T:* (03) 4779876. *Clubs:* Dunedin, University (Dunedin).

SOMERVILLE, Brig. Sir Nicholas; *see* Somerville, Sir J. N.

SOMERVILLE, Sir Quentin Charles Somerville A.; *see* Agnew-Somerville.

SOMERVILLE, Sir Robert, KCVO 1961 (CVO 1953); MA; FSA; FRHistS; Clerk of the Council of the Duchy of Lancaster, 1952–70; *b* 5 June 1906; *s* of late Robert Somerville, FRSE, Dunfermline; *m* 1st, 1932, Marie-Louise Cornelia Bergené (*d* 1976), Aachen; one *d*; 2nd, 1981, Mrs Jessie B. Warburton, Sydney. *Educ:* Fettes; St John's Coll., Cambridge (1st cl. Class. Tripos, 1929); Edinburgh Univ. DLitt. Entered Duchy of Lancaster Office, 1930; Ministry of Shipping, 1940–44; Chief Clerk, Duchy of Lancaster, 1945; Hon. Research Asst, History of Medicine, UCL, 1935–38; Chairman: Council, British Records Assoc., 1957–67 (Hon. Secretary, 1947–56); London Record Soc., 1964–84; Member: Advisory Council on Public Records, 1959–64; Royal Commn on Historical MSS, 1966–88. Hon. DLitt Lancaster, 1990. Alexander Medallist, Royal Historical Society, 1940. *Publications:* History of the Duchy of Lancaster, 2 vols, 1953, 1970; The Savoy, 1960; Handlist of Record Publications, 1951; Duchy of Lancaster Office-Holders from 1603, 1972; (joint editor) John of Gaunt's Register, 1937; contribs to historical journals, etc. *Address:* 3 Hunt's Close, Morden Road, SE3 0AH.

SOMERVILLE, Most Rev. Thomas David; Archbishop of New Westminster and Metropolitan of Ecclesiastical Province of British Columbia, 1975–80, retired; Anglican Chaplain, Vancouver School of Theology, 1981–84; *b* 11 Nov. 1915; *s* of Thomas Alexander Somerville and Martha Stephenson Scott; *m* 1985, Frances Best. *Educ:* King George High Sch., Vancouver; Univ. of British Columbia (BA 1937); Anglican Theological Coll. of BC (LTh 1939, BD 1951). Deacon, 1939; priest, 1940; Incumbent of: Princeton, 1940–44; Sardis with Rosedale, 1944–49; Curate of St James, Vancouver, 1949–52, Rector, 1952–60; Chapter Canon, Dio. of New Westminster, 1957; Dean of Residence, Anglican Theological Coll. of BC, 1960–65; Gen. Sec., Gen. Bd of Religious Education, Anglican Church of Canada, 1965–66; Director of Planning and Research, Anglican Church of Canada, 1966–69; Coadjutor Bishop of New Westminster, 1969–71;

Bishop of New Westminster, 1971. Hon. DD: Anglican Theol. Coll. of BC, 1969; Vancouver Sch. of Theology, 1981. *Recreations:* music, botany. *Address:* 3485 Capilano Road, North Vancouver, BC V7R 4H9, Canada.

SOMERVILLE, Walter, CBE 1979; MD, FRCP; Hon. Physician to Department of Cardiology, Middlesex Hospital, since 1979 (Physician, 1954–79); to Cardiac Surgical Unit, Harefield Hospital, 1952–78; Lecturer in Cardiology, Middlesex Hospital Medical School, 1954–79; Consultant in Cardiology: to Royal Hospital Chelsea, 1963–79; to the Army, 1963–79, Hon. Consultant, 1980–85, Emeritus Consultant, 1985; Hon. Civil Consultant in Cardiology: to Royal Air Force, since 1963; to Association of Naval Officers, since 1960; to King Edward VII Convalescent Home for Officers, Osborne, since 1970; *b* 2 Oct. 1913; *s* of late Patrick and Catherine Somerville, Dublin; *m* 1957, Jane Platnauer (*see* Jane Somerville); three *s* one *d. Educ:* Belvedere Coll., Dublin; University College, Dublin. House appts, Mater Hosp., Dublin, 1937; out-patients Assistant, Brompton Hosp. and Chelsea Chest Clinic, 1938–39. Served in War 1939–45; attached: Canadian Dept of Defense, 1942; US Army, 1943; Lt-Col RAMC 1944. Fellow in Med., Mass General Hosp., Boston, 1946; Registrar, British Postgraduate Med. School, Hammersmith, 1947; studied in Paris, Stockholm and Univ. of Michigan, 1948; Fellow in Medicine, Peter Bent Brigham Hosp. Boston and Harvard Med. Sch., 1949; Med. Registrar, Nat. Heart Hosp. and Inst. of Cardiology, 1951; Sen. Med. Registrar, Middlesex Hosp., 1951–54. Lectures: Carey Coombs, Bristol Univ., 1977; St Cyres, Nat. Heart Hosp., 1978; William Stokes, Irish Cardiac Soc., Belfast, 1983. Editor, British Heart Journal, 1973–80; Editorial Board: American Heart Journal, 1975–; Revista Portuguesa de cardiologia, 1982–. Pres., British Cardiac Soc., 1976–80; former Pres., British Acad. of Forensic Sciences; Mem., Assoc. of Physicians of Great Britain and Ireland and other socs; Corr. Member: Colombian Soc. of Cardiology; Chilean Soc. of Cardiology; Fellow, Amer. Coll. of Cardiology. Vis. Prof., Cleveland Clinic, Cleveland, Ohio, 1980. Purkyne Medal, Czechoslovakian Cardiac Soc., 1981. Officer, Legion of Merit, USA, 1945. *Publications:* (ed) Paul Wood's Diseases of the Heart and Circulation (3rd edn), 1968; various articles on cardiovascular subjects in British, continental European and American journals. *Address:* 149 Harley Street, W1N 1HG. *T:* 071–935 4444; 30 York House, Upper Montagu Street, W1H 1FR. *T:* 071–262 2144.

SOMES, Michael (George), CBE 1959; Principal Repetiteur, Royal Ballet, Covent Garden 1970–84; *b* 28 Sept. 1917; British; *m* 1956, Deirdre Annette Dixon (*d* 1959). *Educ:* Huish's Grammar Sch., Taunton, Somerset. Started dancing at Sadler's Wells, 1934; first important rôle in Horoscope, 1938; Leading Male Dancer, Royal Ballet, Covent Garden, 1951–68; Asst Director, 1963–70. *Recreation:* music.

SOMMARUGA, Cornelio; President, International Committee of the Red Cross, since 1987; *b* 29 Dec. 1932; *s* of Carlo Sommaruga and Anna-Maria Valagussa; *m* 1957, Ornella Marzorati; two *s* four *d. Educ:* Rome; Paris; Univ. of Zürich (LLD). Bank trainee, Zürich, 1957–59; joined Diplomatic Service, 1960: Attaché, Swiss Embassy, The Hague, 1961; Sec., Bonn, 1962–64; Rome, 1965–68; Dep. Hd of Delegn to EFTA, GATT and UNCTAD, Geneva, 1969–73; Asst Sec. Gen., EFTA, 1973–75; Minister plenipotentiary, Div. of Commerce, Fed. Dept of Public Economy, Berne, 1976; Amb., 1977; Delegate, Fed. Council for Trade Agreements, 1980–84; State Sec. for External Econ. Affairs, 1984–86. Hon. Dr: (Political Affairs) Fribourg, 1985; (Internat. Relns) Minho, Braga (Portugal), 1990. *Publications:* La posizione costituzionale del Capo dello Stato nelle Costituzioni francese ed italiana da dopoguerra, 1957; numerous articles in jls and periodicals. *Address:* International Committee of the Red Cross, 19 avenue de la Paix, CH–1202 Geneva, Switzerland. *T:* (022) 734 60 01.

SONDES, 5th Earl *cr* 1880; **Henry George Herbert Milles-Lade;** Baron Sondes, 1760; Viscount Throwley, 1880; *b* 1 May 1940; *o s* of 4th Earl Sondes, and Pamela (*d* 1967), *d* of Col H. McDougall; *S* father, 1970; *m* 1st, 1968, Primrose Creswell (marr. diss. 1969), *d* of late Lawrence Stopford Llewellyn Cotter; 2nd, 1976, Sissy Fürstin zu Salm-Reifferscheidt-Raitz (marr. diss. 1981); *m* 1981, Sharon McCluskey (marr. diss. 1984); *m* 1986, Phyllis Kane Schmertz. *Educ:* Eton; La Rosey. Vice Chm., Gillingham FC, 1985–. *Recreations:* shooting, skiing, the Turf. *Address:* Stringman's Farm, Faversham, Kent. *T:* (0227) 730336. *Club:* Brooks's.

SONDHEIM, Stephen Joshua; composer-lyricist; *b* 22 March 1930; *s* of Herbert Sondheim and Janet (*née* Fox). *Educ:* Williams Coll. (BA 1950). Lyrics: West Side Story, 1957; Gypsy, 1959; Do I Hear a Waltz?, 1965; (additional lyrics) Candide, 1973; music and lyrics: A Funny Thing Happened on the Way to the Forum, 1962; Anyone Can Whistle, 1964; Company, 1970; Follies, 1971; A Little Night Music, 1973 (filmed, 1976); The Frogs, 1974; Pacific Overtures, 1976; Sweeney Todd, 1979; Merrily We Roll Along, 1981; Sunday in the Park with George, 1984 (Pulitzer Prize, 1985); Into The Woods, 1987; Assassins, 1991; incidental music: Girls of Summer, 1956; Invitation to a March, 1961; Twigs, 1971; film scores: Stavisky, 1974; Reds, 1981; Dick Tracy, 1990; co-author, The Last of Sheila (film), 1973; songs for Evening Primrose (TV), 1966; anthologies: Side By Side By Sondheim, 1976; Marry Me A Little, 1981; You're Gonna Love Tomorrow, 1983. Vis. Prof. of Drama, and Fellow of St Catherine's Coll., Oxford, Jan.–June 1990. Mem. Council, Dramatists Guild, 1963 (Pres., 1973–81); Mem., AAIL, 1983. Hon. Doctorate, Williams Coll., 1971. Tony Awards and New York Drama Critics' Circle Award for Into the Woods, Sweeney Todd, A Little Night Music, Follies, and Company; London Evening Standard Best Musical Award for Into the Woods; New York Drama Critics' Circle Award for Pacific Overtures and Sunday in the Park with George; London Evening Standard Best Musical Award, 1987, and SWET Laurence Olivier Award, 1988, for Follies. *Publications:* (book and vocal score): West Side Story, 1958; Gypsy, 1960; A Funny Thing Happened on the Way to the Forum, 1963; Anyone Can Whistle, 1965; Do I Hear a Waltz?, 1966; Company, 1971; Follies, 1972; A Little Night Music, 1974; Pacific Overtures, 1977; Sweeney Todd, 1979; Sunday in the Park with George, 1986. *Address:* c/o Flora Roberts, 157 West 57th Street, New York, NY 10019, USA.

SONDHEIMER, Professor Ernst Helmut, MA, ScD; Professor Emeritus of Mathematics, University of London; *b* 8 Sept. 1923; *er s* of late Max and of Ida Sondheimer; *m* 1950, Janet Harrington Matthews, PhD; one *s* one *d. Educ:* University College School; Trinity Coll., Cambridge. Smith's Prize, 1947; Fellow of Trinity Coll., 1948–52; Research Fellow, H. H. Wills Physical Lab., University of Bristol, 1948–49; Research Associate, Massachusetts Inst. of Technology, 1949–50; London University: Lecturer in Mathematics, Imperial College of Science and Technology, 1951–54; Reader in Applied Mathematics, Queen Mary Coll., 1954–60; Prof. of Mathematics, Westfield Coll., 1960–82. Vis. Research Asst Prof. of Physics, Univ. of Illinois, USA, 1958–59; Vis. Prof. of Theoretical Physics, University of Cologne, 1967. FKC 1985; Fellow, Queen Mary and Westfield Coll., London, 1989. Editor, Alpine Journal, 1986–91. *Publications:* (with S. Doniach) Green's Functions for Solid State Physicists, 1974; (with A. Rogerson) Numbers and Infinity, 1981; papers on the electron theory of metals. *Recreations:* mountains, photography, books, growing alpines. *Address:* 51 Cholmeley Crescent, Highgate, N6 5EX. *T:* 081–340 6607. *Club:* Alpine.

SONDHI, Ranjit; Senior Lecturer, Westhill College, Birmingham, since 1985; Member, Radio Authority, since 1991; *b* 22 Oct. 1950; *s* of Prem Lal Sondhi and Kanta Sondhi; *m*

1979, Anita Kumari Bhalla; one *s* one *d. Educ:* Bedford Sch.; Univ. of Birmingham (BSc Hons Physics). Handsworth Action Centre, Birmingham, 1972–76; Dir, Asian Resource Centre, Birmingham, 1976–85. Freelance lectr and researcher, 1975–. Mem., IBA, 1987–90; Chairman: Jt Council of Welfare for Immigrants, West Midlands, 1987–90; Refugee Employment, Trng and Educn Forum, 1990–; Member: Digbeth Trust, 1986–90; Prince's Youth Business Trust, Birmingham, 1986–; Royal Jubilee and Prince's Trust, Birmingham, 1986–88; Admin. Council, Prince's Trust, 1986–88; Council for Educn and Trng in Youth and Community Work, 1987–; CRE, 1991–. Dir, Birmingham TEC, 1990–. FRSA 1988. *Publications:* (jtly) Race in the Provincial Press, 1977; Divided Families, 1987; contribs to: Ethnicity and Social Work, 1982; Community Work and Racism, 1982; Minorities: community and identity, 1983; Analysing Inter-cultural Communication, 1987. *Recreations:* Indian classical music, yoga, cooking, reading, travel, family activities. *Address:* 89 Hamstead Hall Avenue, Handsworth Wood, Birmingham B20 1JU. *T:* 021–357 1216.

SONTAG, Susan; writer; *b* 16 Jan. 1933; one *s. Educ:* Univ. of Chicago (BA 1952); Harvard Univ. (MA 1955). Mem., American Acad.-Inst. of Arts and Letters; Pres., PEN Amer. Center, 1987–89. Officier de l'Ordre des Arts et des Lettres, France. Films: Duet for Cannibals, 1969; Brother Carl, 1971; Promised Lands, 1974; Unguided Tour, 1983. *Publications:* The Benefactor, 1963; Against Interpretation, 1966; Death Kit, 1967; Styles of Radical Will, 1969; On Photography, 1977; Illness as Metaphor, 1978; I, Etcetera, 1978; Under the Sign of Saturn, 1980; Aids and its Metaphors, 1989. *Address:* c/o Farrar, Straus & Giroux, 19 Union Square West, New York, NY 10003, USA.

SOPER, family name of **Baron Soper.**

SOPER, Baron, *cr* 1965 (Life Peer); **Rev. Donald Oliver Soper,** MA Cantab; PhD (London); Methodist Minister; President of the Methodist Conference, 1953, Superintendent West London Mission, Kingsway Hall, 1936–78; *b* 31 Jan. 1903; *s* of late Ernest and Caroline Soper; *m* 1929, Marie Dean, *d* of late Arthur Dean, Norbury; four *d. Educ:* Aske's School, Hatcham; St Catharine's College, Cambridge (Hon. Fellow, 1966); Wesley House, Cambridge; London School of Economics, London University. Minister, South London Mission, 1926–29; Central London Mission, 1929–36. Chm., Shelter, 1974–78. President, League Against Cruel Sports. Hon. DD Cambridge, 1988. Peace Award, World Methodist Council, 1981. *Publications:* Christianity and its Critics; Popular Fallacies about the Christian Faith; Will Christianity Work?; Practical Christianity To-day; Questions and Answers in Ceylon; All His Grace (Methodist Lent Book for 1957); It is hard to work for God; The Advocacy of the Gospel; Tower Hill 12.30; Aflame with Faith; Christian Politics; Calling for Action, 1984. *Recreations:* music, golf. *Address:* 19 Thayer Street, W1M 5LJ.

SOPER, Rt. Rev. (Andrew) Laurence, OSB; STD; Abbot of Ealing, since 1991; *b* 17 Sept. 1943; *s* of Alan and Anne Soper. *Educ:* St Benedict's Sch., Ealing; Blackfriars, Oxford; Sant Anselmo, Rome (STD); Strawberry Hill (PGCE). Banking until 1964; entered Novitiate at Ealing, 1964; St Benedict's School: Teacher, 1973–83; Bursar, 1975–91; Prior, 1984–91; Asst Chaplain, Harrow Sch., 1981–91. Substitute Prison Chaplain, 1988–. FRSA. *Publications:* (ed with Rev. Peter Elliott) Thoughts of Jesus Christ, 1970; articles and thesis on T. H. Green and 19th century English theology. *Recreations:* pastoral activities, reading, hill walking. *Address:* Ealing Abbey, W5 2DY. *T:* 081–998 2158.

SOPWITH, Sir Charles (Ronald), Kt 1966; Second Counsel to Chairman of Committees, House of Lords, 1974–82; *b* 12 Nov. 1905; *s* of Alfred Sopwith, S Shields, Co. Durham; *m* 1946, Ivy Violet (*d* 1968), *d* of Frederick Leonard Yeates, Gidea Park, Essex. *Educ:* S Shields High School. Chartered Accountant, 1928; Solicitor, 1938. Assistant Director, Press Censorship, 1943–45; Assistant Solicitor, 1952–56, Principal Asst Solicitor, 1956–61, Solicitor, 1963–70, Board of Inland Revenue; Public Trustee, 1961–63; Deputy Sec., Cabinet Office, 1970–72. Hon. FRAM, 1984. *Recreations:* music, reading history. *Address:* 18 Moor Lane, Rickmansworth, Herts WD3 1LG. *Club:* Reform.

SORABJI, Prof. Richard Rustom Kharsedji, FBA 1989; Professor of Ancient Philosphy, King's College London, since 1981; Director, Institute of Classical Studies, London, since 1991; *b* 8 Nov. 1934; *s* of Richard Kaikushru Sorabji and late Mary Katherine (*née* Monkhouse); *m* 1958, Margaret Anne Catherine Taster; one *s* two *d. Educ:* Dragon Sch.; Charterhouse; Pembroke Coll., Oxford (BA Greats; MA; BPhil). CS Commn in Russian Lang. Joined Sage Sch. of Philosophy, Cornell Univ., 1962, Associate Prof., 1968; KCL, 1970–: Dir, King's Coll. Centre for Philosophical Studies, 1989–91; FKC 1990. Chm., Bd of Philosophical Studies, London Univ., 1979–82. Pres., Aristotelian Soc., 1985–86. Founder and organiser of internat. project for translating the Ancient Commentators on Aristotle, 1985–. *Publications:* Aristotle on Memory, 1973; (ed jtly) Articles on Aristotle, 4 vols, 1975–79; Necessity, Cause and Blame, 1980; Time, Creation and the Continuum, 1983; (ed) Philoponus and the Rejection of Aristotelian Science, 1987; (ed) The Ancient Commentators on Aristotle, first 5 of 40 vols, 1987–; Matter, Space and Motion, 1988 (Choice Award for Outstanding Academic Book, 1989–90); (ed) Aristotle Transformed, 1990. *Recreations:* medieval architecture. *Address:* Department of Philosophy, King's College, Strand, WC2R 2LS. *T:* 071–873 2231.

SOREF, Harold Benjamin; Chairman and Managing Director, Soref Brothers Ltd, 1955–88; *b* 18 Dec. 1916; *o s* of late Paul Soref and Zelma Soref (*née* Goodman), Hampstead. *Educ:* Hall Sch., Hampstead; St Paul's Sch.; Queen's Coll., Oxford. Served with Royal Scots and Intell. Corps, 1940–46. Editor, The Debater (Britain's first inter-public schs magazine), 1934–35; Co-Editor, Equator, 1945–46; Founder and Editor, The Jewish Monthly, 1947–51. Contested (C): Dudley, 1951; Rugby, 1955. MP (C) Lancashire, Ormskirk, 1970–Feb. 1974. Delegate, first all-British Africa Conf. held Bulawayo, 1938, to form Africa Defence Fedn; formerly Vice-Chm., Monday Club and Chm., Africa Cttee, Monday Club; Mem. Council, Anglo-Jewish Assoc.; Founder Mem., Conservative Commonwealth Council. *Publications:* (jtly) The War of 1939, 1940; (with Ian Greig) The Puppeteers, 1965; numerous articles in press and periodicals. *Recreations:* research, reading, writing. *Address:* 20 Meriden Court, Chelsea Manor Street, SW3 3TT. *T:* 071–352 0691.

SORENSEN, (Kenneth) Eric (Correll); Chief Executive, London Docklands Development Corporation, since 1991; *b* 15 Oct. 1942; *m* Susan; two *s* one *d. Educ:* Bedford Sch.; Keele Univ. (BA(Hons) Econs and History). Voluntary work, India; joined DoE, 1967; Private Sec. to Sec. of State for Envmt, 1977; Chm., NW Regl Bd and NW Regl Dir, Depts of the Envmt and Transport, 1980–81; Dir, Merseyside Task Force, DoE, 1981–84; Dir, Inner Cities Directorate, DoE, 1984–87; Head of Urban Policy Unit, Cabinet Office, 1987–88; Dir of Personnel Management and Trng, Depts of Envmt and Transport, 1988–90; Dep. Sec., Housing and Construction Comd, DoE, 1990–91. *Address:* London Docklands Development Corporation, Thames Quay, 191 Marsh Wall, E14 9TJ.

SORINJ, Dr L. T.; *see* Tončić-Sorinj.

SOROKOS, Lt-Gen. John A., Greek Gold Medal for Gallantry (3 times); Greek Military Cross (twice); Medal for Distinguished Services (3 times); Silver and Gold Cross (with swords) of Order of George I; Comdr, Order of George I and Order of Phoenix; Military Medal of Merit (1st Class); Ambassador of Greece to the United States of America, 1972–74; *b* 1917; *s* of A. and P. Sorokos; *m* 1954, Pia Madaros; one *s*. *Educ:* Mil. Acad. of Greece; Staff and Nat. Defence Colls, Greece; British Staff Coll., Camberley; US Mil. Schools. Company Comdr: in Second World War in Greece, 1940–41; in El Alamein Campaign, N Africa, 1942–43; Div. Staff Officer and Bn Comdr, 1947–49; served as Staff Officer: in Mil. Units in Army HQ and Armed Forces HQ, 1952–63; in NATO Allied Forces Southern Europe, 1957–59; Instructor, Nat. Defence Coll., Greece, 1963–64; Regt Comdr, 1965; Mil. Attaché to Greek Embassies in Washington and Ottawa, 1966–68; Div. Comdr, 1968–69; Dep. Comdr, Greek Armed Forces, 1969; Ambassador to UK, 1969–72. Officer, Legion of Merit (US). *Recreations:* horses, boating, fishing. *Address:* Mimnermou 2, Athens 106 74, Greece.

SORRELL, Alec Albert; Director of Statistics, Department of the Environment, 1981–83, retired; *b* 20 July 1925; *s* of Albert Edward Sorrell and Jessie (*née* Morris); *m* 1962, Eileen Joan Orchard; one *s*. *Educ:* George Gascoigne Sch., Walthamstow; SW Essex Technical College. BSc (Econ). Statistical Officer, MAP, 1945; Board of Trade: Asst Statistician, 1950; Statistician, 1954; Chief Statistician, 1966; Chief Statistician: Min. of Technology, 1969; Dept of Trade and Industry, 1970; Central Statistical Office, 1971; Asst Dir, Central Statistical Office, Cabinet Office, 1972–78; Principal Dir of Statistics, Depts of the Environment and Transport, 1978–81. *Publications:* various articles in trade, professional and learned jls. *Recreations:* walking, reading, music, gardening. *Address:* Ranelagh, Stewarts Road, Week St Mary, Holsworthy, Devon EX22 6XA. *T:* Week St Mary (028884) 436.

SORRELL, Martin Stuart; Group Chief Executive, WPP Group, since 1986; *b* 14 Feb. 1945; *s* of late Jack and of Sally Sorrell; *m* 1971, Sandra Carol Ann Finestone; three *s*. *Educ:* Haberdashers' Aske's School; Christ's College, Cambridge (MA); Harvard Graduate School of Business (MBA 1968). Consultant, Glendinning Associates, Conn, 1968–69; Vice-Pres., Mark McCormack Orgn, London, 1970–74; Dir, James Gulliver Associates, 1975–77; Gp Financial Dir, Saatchi & Saatchi, 1977–86. *Recreations:* ski-ing, cricket (annual fathers' match). *Address:* WPP Group, 27 Farm Street, W1X 6RD. *T:* 071–408 2204. *Clubs:* Reform; Harvard (NY).

SORRIE, George Strath; Medical Adviser and Director, Civil Service Occupational Health Service, since 1987; *b* 19 May 1933; *s* of Alexander James Sorrie and Florence Edith Sorrie (*née* Strath); *m* 1959, Gabrielle Ann Baird; three *d*. *Educ:* Woodside Sch., Aberdeen; Robert Gordon's Coll., Aberdeen; Univ. of Aberdeen (MB ChB); Univs of London and Dundee. FFOM, DPH, DIH. Medical Branch, RAF, 1958–61; Lectr in Epidemiology, London Sch. of Hygiene and Tropical Medicine, 1965–67; GP, Rhynie, Aberdeenshire, 1967–72. Health and Safety Exec., 1972, Dep. Dir of Med. Services, 1980–87. *Recreations:* book-keeping, practising patience. *Address:* Occupational Health Service, 18–20 Hill Street, Edinburgh EH2 3NB. *T:* 031–220 4177. *Club:* Athenæum.

SOUHAMI, Mark; Group Managing Director, Dixons Group, since 1986; *b* 25 Sept. 1935; *s* of John Souhami and Freda Souhami (*née* Harris); *m* 1964, Margaret Austin; two *d*. *Educ:* St Marylebone Grammar School. Lieut RA, 1954–56; early career in City and timber industry; joined Dixons 1970: Group Marketing Dir, 1970; Retail Man. Dir, 1973; Group Board, 1978. Trustee, Photographers' Gallery. Founder Mem., of Marketors' Co. *Recreations:* gardening, English watercolours. *Address:* Brewham House, Brewham, Somerset BA10 0JG. *Clubs:* Savile, Royal Automobile.

SOUHAMI, Prof. Robert Leon, MD; FRCP; Kathleen Ferrier Professor of Clinical Oncology, University College and Middlesex School of Medicine, since 1987; *b* 26 April 1938; *s* of John Souhami and Freda Harris; *m* 1966. *Educ:* St Marylebone Grammar Sch.; University Coll. Hosp. Med. Sch. (BSc, MB BS). Registrar, UCH, 1966–69; Hon. Lectr, St Mary's Hosp. Med. Sch., 1969–71; Sen. Registrar, UCH, 1971–73; Consultant Physician, Poole Gen. Hosp., 1973–75; Consultant Physician and Sen. Lectr, UCH, 1975–87; Hon. Consultant Physician, Whittington Hosp. and Royal Nat. Orthopaedic Hosp., 1976–. Chairman: Cancer Therapy Cttee, MRC, 1987–; Assoc. of Cancer Physicians, 1989–. Fellow, UCL, 1990. *Publications:* Tutorials in Differential Diagnosis, 1974, 3rd edn 1991; Cancer and its Management, 1986; Textbook of Medicine, 1990; articles on aspects of cancer medicine.
See also M. Souhami.

SOUKOP, Wilhelm Josef, RA 1969 (ARA 1963); RBA 1950; FRBS 1956; freelance sculptor; Master of Sculpture, Royal Academy Schools, 1969–82; *b* 5 Jan. 1907; *s* of Karl Soukop and Anna Soukop (*née* Vogel); *m* 1945, Simone (*née* Moser), Paris; one *s* one *d*. *Educ:* Vienna State School; apprenticed to an engraver; Academy of Fine Art, Vienna. Arrived in England, Dartington Hall, 1934; taught at Dartington Hall, Bryanston and Blundell's Schools, 1935–45; moved to London, 1945, and taught at Bromley Sch. of Art, 1945–46, Guildford Sch. of Art, 1945–47; sculpture teacher, Chelsea Sch. of Art, 1947–72. Examr for Scotland, 1959–62. Sculptures for new schools in Herts, Leics, Derbs, Staffs, LCC. Work for housing estates. Sculptures in museums: USA; Cordova Mus., Boston; Chantry Bequest; Tate Gallery; Cheltenham Mus. and Gall.; Collection of LCC Educn Cttee. Work in many private collections England, America, Canada, Europe. Archibald McIndoe Award, 1964. *Recreation:* gardening. *Address:* 26 Greville Road, NW6 5JA. *T:* 071–624 5987.

SOULBURY, 2nd Viscount *cr* 1954, of Soulbury; **James Herwald Ramsbotham;** Baron 1941; *b* 21 March 1915; *s* of 1st Viscount Soulbury, PC, GCMG, GCVO, OBE, MC, and Doris Violet (*d* 1954), *d* of late S. de Stein; *S* father, 1971; *m* 1949, Anthea Margaret (*d* 1950), *d* of late David Wilton. *Educ:* Eton; Magdalen College, Oxford. *Heir:* *b* Hon. Sir Peter Edward Ramsbotham, *qv*.

SOULSBY, family name of **Baron Soulsby of Swaffham Prior.**

SOULSBY OF SWAFFHAM PRIOR, Baron *cr* 1990 (Life Peer), of Swaffham Prior in the County of Cambridgeshire; **Ernest Jackson Lawson Soulsby;** Professor of Animal Pathology, University of Cambridge, since 1978; Fellow, Wolfson College, Cambridge, since 1978; *b* 23 June 1926; *s* of William George Lawson Soulsby and Agnes Soulsby; *m* 1962, Georgina Elizabeth Annette Williams; one *s* one *d*. *Educ:* Queen Elizabeth Grammar Sch., Penrith; Univ. of Edinburgh. MRCVS; DVSM; PhD; MA (Cantab). Veterinary Officer, City of Edinburgh, 1949–52; Lectr in Clinical Parasitology, Univ. of Bristol, 1952–54; Univ. Lectr in Animal Pathology, Univ. of Cambridge, 1954–63; Prof. of Parasitology, Univ. of Pennsylvania, 1964–78. Ian McMaster Fellow, CSIRO, 1958; Sen. Vis. Fellow, EEC, Poland, 1961; WHO Vis. Worker, USSR, 1962; UN Special Fund Expert, IAEA, Vienna and Zemun, Yugoslavia, 1964; Ford Foundn Visiting Prof., Univ. of Ibadan, 1964; Richard Merton Guest Prof., Justus Liebig Univ., 1974–75. Lectures: Hume Meml, Univ. Fedn Animal Welfare, 1985; Wooldridge Meml, BVA, 1986; Sir Frederick Hobday Meml, British Equine Vet. Assoc., 1986. Member: AFRC, 1984– (Chm., Animal Res. Grants Bd, 1986–); Vet. Adv. Cttee, Horserace Betting Levy Bd, 1984– (Chm., 1985–); EEC Adv. Cttee on Vet. Trng, 1981–86. Royal College of Veterinary Surgeons: Mem. Council, 1978–; Jun. Vice-Pres., 1983; Pres., 1984; Sen. Vice-Pres., 1985. President: World Assoc. Adv. Vet. Parasit., 1963–67 (Hon. Mem., 1985); Helminthol. Soc., Washington, 1970–71; Cambridge Soc. for Comp. Medicine, 1984–85; Vet. Res. Club, 1985–86. Council Mem., Amer. Soc. Parasitologists, 1974–78. Corresp. Mem., German Parasitology Soc.; Hon. Member: Mexican Parasitology Soc.; Argentinian Parasitological Soc.; Expert Advisor and Consultant, and Member, Scientific Groups: various internat. agencies and govts. Hon. AM 1972, Hon. DSc 1984, Univ. of Pennsylvania. R. N. Chaudhury Gold Medal, Calcutta Sch. of Tropical Med., Calcutta, 1976; Behring-Bilharz Prize, Cairo, 1977; Ludwig-Schunk Prize, Justus-Liebig Universität, Giessen, 1979; Diploma and Medal, XXI World Vet. Congress, Moscow, 1979. *Publications:* Textbook of Veterinary Clinical Parasitology, 1965; Biology of Parasites, 1966; Reaction of the Host to Parasitism, 1968; Helminths, Arthropods and Protozoa of Domesticated Animals, 6th edn 1968, 7th edn 1982; Immunity to Animal Parasites, 1972; Parasitic Zoonoses, 1974; Pathophysiology of Parasitic Infections, 1976; Epidemiology and Control of Nematodiasis in Cattle, 1981; Immunology, Immunopathology and Immunoprophylaxis of Parasitic Infections, Vols I, II, III & IV, 1986; articles in jls of parasitology, immunology and pathology. *Recreations:* travel, gardening, photography. *Address:* Old Barn House, Swaffham Prior, Cambridge CB5 0LD. *T:* Newmarket (0638) 741304. *Clubs:* Farmers', United Oxford & Cambridge University.

SOUROZH, Metropolitan of; *see* Anthony, Archbishop.

SOUTAR, Air Marshal Sir Charles (John Williamson), KBE 1978 (MBE 1958); Director-General, Medical Services (RAF), 1978–81; *b* 12 June 1920; *s* of Charles Alexander Soutar and Mary Helen (*née* Watson); *m* 1944, Joy Dorée Upton; *s* two *d*. *Educ:* Brentwood Sch.; London Hosp. MB, BS, LMSSA, FFCM, DPH, DIH. Commissioned RAF, 1946. Various appts, then PMO, Middle East Command, 1967–68; Dep. Dir, Med. Organisation, RAF, 1968–70; OC, PMRAF Hosp., Halton, 1970–73; Comdt, RAF Inst. of Aviation Medicine, 1973–75; PMO, Strike Command, 1975–78. QHS 1974–81. CStJ 1972. *Recreations:* sport, gardening, ornithology, music. *Address:* Oak Cottage, High Street, Aldeburgh, Suffolk IP15 5AU. *T:* Aldeburgh (0728) 452201. *Club:* Royal Air Force.

SOUTER, family name of **Baron Audley.**

SOUTH, Sir Arthur, Kt 1974; JP; Partner, Norwich Fur Company, since 1947; *b* 29 Oct. 1914; *s* of Arthur and Violet South, Norwich; *m* 1st, 1937, May Adamson (marr. diss. 1976); two *s*; 2nd, 1976, Mary June (*d* 1982), *widow* of Robert Edward Carter, JP, DL. *Educ:* City of Norwich Sch. RAF and MAP, 1941–46. Mem., Norwich, Lowestoft, Gt Yarmouth Hosp. Management Cttee, 1948–74 (Vice-Chm., 1954–66, Chm., 1966–74); Chairman: Norfolk Area Health Authority, 1974–78; E Anglian RHA, 1978–87; Mem., E Anglia Regional Hosp. Bd, 1969–74. Member: Assoc. of Educn Cttees, 1963–74; Assoc. of Municipal Corporations, 1965–74; E Anglia Econ. Planning Council, 1966–80; E Anglia Rent Assessment Panel, 1967–74; E Anglia Adv. Cttee to BBC, 1970–74; Univ. of E Anglia Council, 1964–80 (Life Mem., Court, 1964); Chairman: E Anglia Roads to Prosperity, 1987–; Norfolk Energy Forum, 1988–. Norwich: City Councillor, 1935–41 and 1946–61; Alderman, 1961–74; Sheriff, 1953–54; Lord Mayor, 1956–57, Dep. Lord Mayor, 1959–60; JP 1949; Dep. Leader, Norwich City Council, 1959–60; Chm., Labour Party Gp and Leader Norwich City Council, 1960–78. Norwich City Football Club: Vice-Pres., 1957–66; Dir, 1966–73; Chm., 1973–85; Member: FA Council, 1981–86; Football League: Mem., Management Cttee, 1981–85; Life Vice-Pres., 1985. Hon. DCL East Anglia, 1989. *Recreations:* football, bowls, cricket. *Address:* The Lowlands, Drayton, Norfolk NR8 6HA. *T:* Norwich (0603) 867355, ext. 207. *Clubs:* MCC; Mitre Bowls, Norfolk Cricket, Norwich City Football.

SOUTHALL, Kenneth Charles; Under-Secretary, Inland Revenue, 1975–82; *b* 3 Aug. 1922; *s* of Arthur and Margarette Jane Southall; *m* 1947, Audrey Kathleen Skeels; one *s*. *Educ:* Queen Elizabeth's Grammar Sch., Hartlebury, Worcs. Inland Revenue, 1939; RAF, 1942–46; Administrative Staff College, 1962. *Address:* The Green, Brill, Bucks HP18 9RU.

SOUTHAM, Gordon Ronald, BSc; AInstP; Headmaster, Ashville College, 1958–77; *b* 20 March 1918; *s* of late G. H. Southam, Brackley; *m* 1948, Joan, *d* of late W. Thompson; one *d*. *Educ:* Magdalen College School, Brackley; Westminster College, and King's College, London. BSc (Gen. Hons) 1938, BSc (Special Physics) 1st Class Hons 1939. Teacher's diploma, 1947, AInstP 1947. Served Royal Air Force, 1940–46: Bomber Comd, 1940–43; Staff Officer in HQ, ACSEA, 1943–46 (Sqdn Ldr). Senior Physics Master, Culford School, 1947–49; Lecturer, Royal Military Academy, Sandhurst, 1950–52; Head of Department of Science, Royal Military Academy, Sandhurst, 1953–57. *Recreations:* motoring, electronics; formerly Rugby football, athletics. *Address:* Culford, 20 Oak Tree Drive, Bedale, N Yorks DL8 1UL.

SOUTHAMPTON, 6th Baron *cr* 1780; **Charles James FitzRoy;** *b* 12 Aug. 1928; *o s* of Charles FitzRoy (5th Baron, disclaimed peerage for life, 1964) and Margaret (*d* 1931), *d* of Rev. Preb. Herbert Mackworth Drake; *S* father, 1989; *m* 1951, Pamela Anne, *d* of Edward Percy Henniker; one *s* one *d* (and one *s* decd). *Educ:* Stowe. Master: Easton Harriers, 1968–71; Blaikney Foxhounds, 1971–72. *Recreations:* shooting, fishing, golf. *Heir:* *s* Hon. Edward Charles FitzRoy [*b* 8 July 1955; *m* 1978, Rachel Caroline Vincent, 2nd *d* of Peter John Curnow Millett; one *s* three *d*]. *Address:* Stone Cross, Stone Lane, Chagford, Newton Abbot, Devon.

SOUTHAMPTON, Bishop Suffragan of, since 1989; **Rt. Rev. John Freeman Perry;** *b* 15 June 1935; *s* of Richard and Elsie Perry; *m* 1959, Gay Valerie Brown; three *s* two *d*. *Educ:* Mill Hill School; London College of Divinity (ALCD). LTh St John's Coll., Nottingham, 1974; MPhil CNAA, 1986. Assistant Curate: Christ Church, Woking, 1959–62; Christ Church, Chorleywood, 1962–63; Vicar, St Andrew's, Chorleywood, 1963–77; RD of Rickmansworth, 1972–77; Warden, Lee Abbey, Lynton, Devon, 1977–89; RD of Shirwell, 1980–84. Hon. Canon, Winchester Cathedral, 1989–. *Publication:* Christian Leadership, 1983. *Recreations:* a large family, jogging and walking, sport, travel, classical music. *Address:* Ham House, The Crescent, Romsey, Hants SO51 7NG. *T:* Romsey (0794) 516005.

SOUTHAN, Robert Joseph; His Honour Judge Southan; a Circuit Judge, since 1986; *b* 13 July 1928; *s* of late Thomas Southan and of Kathleen Southan; *m* 1960, Elizabeth Andreas Evatt, *qv*; one *d* (one *s* decd). *Educ:* Rugby; St Edmund Hall, Oxford (MA); University Coll., London (LLM). Called to the Bar, Inner Temple, 1953; called to the Bar of NSW, 1976; a Recorder, 1983–86. *Recreations:* theatre, opera, sailing, ski-ing, squash, tennis. *Address:* c/o Snaresbrook Crown Court, Hollybush Hill, E11 1QW. *T:* 081–989 6666. *Clubs:* Royal Corinthian Yacht, Bar Yacht; Cumberland Lawn Tennis.

SOUTHBOROUGH, 4th Baron *cr* 1917; **Francis Michael Hopwood;** *b* 3 May 1922; *s* of 3rd Baron Southborough and of Audrey, Baroness Southborough (Audrey Evelyn Dorothy, *d* of late Edgar George Money); *S* father, 1982; *m* 1945, Moyna Kemp (*d* 1987), *d* of Robert John Kemp Chattey; one *d*. *Educ:* Wellington College; Christ Church, Oxford. An Underwriting Member of Lloyd's, 1949–; Dep. Chairman, Glanvill,

Enthoven & Co. Ltd, 1977–80 (Director, 1954); Chairman, Robert Woodson Ltd, 1970–72 (Director, 1950). Served War of 1939–45 as Lieut, The Rifle Brigade. *Heir:* none. *Address:* 50A Eaton Square, SW1W 9BE. *Clubs:* Brooks's, City of London.

SOUTHBY, Sir John (Richard Bilbe), 3rd Bt *cr* 1937, of Burford, Co. Oxford; District Manager, East Midlands Electricity, Milton Keynes, since 1991; *b* 2 April 1948; *s* of Sir Archibald Richard Charles Southby, 2nd Bt, OBE and of Olive Marion, *d* of late Sir Thomas Bilbe-Robinson; *S* father, 1988; *m* 1971, Victoria Jane, *d* of John Wilfred Sturrock; two *s* one *d*. *Educ:* Peterhouse, Marandellas, Rhodesia; Loughborough Univ. of Technology (BSc Elec. Eng). CEng, MIEE. East Midlands Electricity Board: Graduate Trainee, 1971; Asst Engineer 1973, O & M Engineer 1976, Shepshed, Leics; Senior Asst Engineer 1979, O & M Engineer 1981, Boston, Lincs; District Engineer, Grantham, 1986. *Recreations:* ski-ing, gardening, tennis, squash, DIY. *Heir: s* Peter John Southby, *b* 20 Aug. 1973. *Address:* Lomagundi, High Street, Nash, Bucks MK17 0EP. *Club:* Rotary (Grantham).

SOUTHEND, Archdeacon of; *see* Bailey, Ven. J. S.

SOUTHERN, Michael William; Adviser to HE the Minister of Health, Kingdom of Saudi Arabia, 1978, now retired; Regional Administrator, South West Thames Regional Health Authority, 1973–77; *b* 22 June 1918; *s* of William Southern and Ida Frances Southern; *m* 1945, Nancy Russell Golsworthy; three *d*. *Educ:* Tiffin Boys' Sch., Kingston-upon-Thames; London Univ. (DPA); Open Univ. (BA Humanities). FHSM. Surrey CC Public Health Dept, 1934–39 and 1945–48; served with RAMC (NCO), 1939–45: Technician in No 1 Malaria Field Lab., 1940–41; POW Germany, 1941–44; Planning Officer and later Sec. of SW Metropolitan Regional Hosp. Bd, 1948–73. Chairman: Surrey Council, Royal British Legion, 1985–88; Richard Sharples Court, Sutton, 1988–. *Publications:* various articles in Hospital and Health Services Review, Health and Social Service Jl. *Recreations:* music, travel, philately. *Address:* 14 Poole Road, West Ewell, Epsom, Surrey KT19 9RY. *T:* 081–393 5096.

SOUTHERN, Sir Richard (William), Kt 1974; FBA 1960; FRSL 1973; President of St John's College, Oxford, 1969–81, Honorary Fellow, 1981; *b* 8 Feb. 1912; 2nd *s* of Matthew Henry Southern, Newcastle upon Tyne; *m* 1944, Sheila (*née* Cobley), *widow* of Sqdn Ldr C. Crichton-Miller; two *s*. *Educ:* Royal Grammar Sch., Newcastle upon Tyne; Balliol College, Oxford (Domus Exhibnr). 1st Class Hons Modern History, 1932. Junior Research Fellow, Exeter College, Oxford, 1933–37 (Hon. Fellow, 1991); studied in Paris, 1933–34 and Munich, 1935; Fellow and Tutor, Balliol Coll., Oxford, 1937–61 (Hon. Fellow 1966). Served Oxford and Bucks LI, 1940; 2nd Lt Durham LI 1941; 155th Regt RAC, 1942; Captain 1943; Major 1944; Political Intelligence Dept, Foreign Office, 1943–45. Junior Proctor, Oxford Univ., 1948–49; Birkbeck Lectr in Ecclesiastical History, Trinity College, Cambridge, 1959–60; Chichele Prof. of Modern History, Oxford, 1961–69; President: Royal Historical Soc., 1968–72; Selden Soc., 1973–76. Lectures: Raleigh, British Academy, 1962; David Murray, Glasgow Univ., 1963; Gifford, Glasgow Univ., 1970–72; G. M. Trevelyan, Cambridge Univ., 1980–81. Corresponding Fellow: Medieval Academy of America, 1965; Monumenta Germaniae Historica, 1982; For. Hon. Mem., Amer. Acad. of Arts and Scis, 1972. Hon. Fellow, Sidney Sussex Coll., Cambridge, 1971; Hon. DLitt: Glasgow, 1964; Durham, 1969; Cantab, 1971; Bristol, 1974; Newcastle, 1977; Warwick, 1978; St Anselm's Coll., 1981; Columbia, 1982; Univ. of the South, 1985; Hon. LLD Harvard, 1977. Balzan Prize, Fondazione Internazionale Balzan, Milan, 1987. *Publications:* The Making of the Middle Ages, 1953 (numerous foreign translations); (ed) Eadmer's Vita Anselmi, 1963; St Anselm and his Biographer, 1963; Western Views of Islam in the Middle Ages, 1962; (ed with F. S. Schmitt) Memorials of St Anselm, 1969; Medieval Humanism and other studies, 1970 (RSL award 1970); Western Society and the Church in the Middle Ages, 1970; Robert Grosseteste, 1986; St Anselm: a portrait in a landscape, 1990; articles in English Historical Review, Medieval and Renaissance Studies, etc. *Address:* 40 St John Street, Oxford OX1 2LH.

SOUTHERN, Sir Robert, Kt 1970; CBE 1953; General Secretary, Co-operative Union Ltd, 1948–72; *b* 17 March 1907; *s* of Job Southern and Margaret (*née* Tonge); *m* 1933, Lena Chapman; one *s* one *d*. *Educ:* Stand Grammar Sch.; Co-operative Coll.; Manchester University. Co-operative Wholesale Soc., Bank Dept, 1925–29; Co-operative Union Ltd, 1929. *Publication:* Handbook to the Industrial and Provident Societies' Act, 1938. *Recreations:* photography, gardening. *Address:* 22 Glebelands Road, Prestwich, Manchester M25 5NE. *T:* 061–773 2699.

SOUTHERTON, Thomas Henry, BSc (Eng); CEng, MIEE; Senior Director, Data Processing, Post Office, 1975–78, retired; *b* 1 July 1917; *s* of C. H. Southerton, Birmingham; *m* 1st, 1945, Marjorie Elizabeth Sheen (*d* 1979); one *s*; 2nd, 1981, Joyce Try. *Educ:* Bemrose Sch., Derby; Northampton Coll., London (BSc(Eng)). PO Apprentice, Derby, 1933–36; Engineering Workman, Derby and Nottingham, 1936–40; Inspector, Engineer-in-Chief's Office, 1940–45; Engineer, 1945–50; Sen. Exec. Engr, 1950–53; Factory Manager, PO Provinces, 1953–56; Dep. Controller, Factories Dept, 1956–64; Controller, Factories Dept, 1964–67; Dir, Telecommunications Management Services, 1967–73; Sen. Dir Telecommunications Personnel, 1973–75. Mem., Industrial Tribunals, 1978–86. *Recreations:* art, architecture, music.

SOUTHESK, 11th Earl of *cr* 1633; **Charles Alexander Carnegie,** KCVO 1926; Major late Scots Guards; Baron Carnegie, 1616; Baron Balinhard (UK), 1869; Bt of Nova Scotia, 1663; *b* 23 Sept. 1893; *e s* of 10th Earl of Southesk and Ethel (*d* 1947), *o c* of Sir Alexander Bannerman, 9th Bt of Elsick; *S* father, 1941; *m* 1st, 1923, HH Princess Maud (*d* 1945), 2nd *d* of HRH Princess Louise, Princess Royal and late Duke of Fife; one *s*; 2nd, 1952, Evelyn, *e d* of Lieut-Colonel A. P. Williams-Freeman, and *widow* of Major Ion E. F. Campbell, DCLI. *Educ:* Eton; Sandhurst. *Heir: s* Duke of Fife, *qv*. *Address:* Kinnaird Castle, Brechin, Angus DD9 6TZ. *T:* Bridge of Dun (067481) 209.

SOUTHEY, Sir Robert (John), Kt 1976; CMG 1970; Chairman, NZI Insurance Australia (formerly General Accident Insurance Company Australia) Ltd, since 1987; Federal President, Liberal Party of Australia, 1970–75; Chairman, Australian Ballet, 1980–90; *b* 20 March 1922; *s* of Allen Hope Southey and Ethel Thorpe McComas, MBE; *m* 1st, 1946, Valerie Janet Cotton (*d* 1977), *y d* of late Hon. Sir Francis Grenville Clarke, KBE, MLC; five *s*; 2nd, 1982, Marigold Merlyn Baillieu, *yr d* of late Sidney and Dame Merlyn Myer, DBE, and *widow* of Ross Shelmerdine, CMG, OBE. *Educ:* Geelong Grammar Sch.; Magdalen Coll., Oxford (MA). Coldstream Guards, 1941–46 (Captain 1944, served N Africa, Italy). BA, 1st cl. PPE Oxon, 1948. Wm Haughton & Co. Ltd: Dir 1953; Man. Dir, 1959–75; Chm. 1968–80; Director: ICL Australia Pty Ltd, 1961–72, 1977–90; BP Australia Holdings Ltd, 1962–91; Kinnears Ltd, 1975–84; National Westminster Finance Australia Ltd, 1983–85; Nat West Australia Bank Ltd, 1985–87; Kawasaki (Australia) Pty Ltd, 1986–; Chairman: McArthur Shipping (Vic.) Pty Ltd, 1974–81; Australian Adv. Council, General Accident Assurance Corp. PLC, 1978–89. Mem. Executive, Liberal Party, 1966–82; Victorian State Pres., Liberal Party, 1966–70; Chm. of Council, Geelong Grammar Sch., 1966–72; Pres., Geelong Grammar Foundn, 1975–88; Chm. Australian Adv. Cttee, Nuffield Foundn, 1970–81; Mem., Rhodes Scholarship Selection Cttee, Victoria, 1973–76. *Publication:* (with C. J. Puplick) Liberal Thinking, 1980. *Recreations:* fishing, golf, music. *Address:* 3 Denistoun Avenue, Mount Eliza, Victoria 3930, Australia. *T:* (03)7871701. *Clubs:* Cavalry and Guards, MCC; Melbourne, Australian (Melbourne); Union (Sydney); Vincent's (Oxford); Leander.

SOUTHGATE, Colin Grieve; Chief Executive, since 1987, and Chairman, since 1989, THORN EMI plc; Director, Bank of England, since 1991; *b* 24 July 1938; *s* of Cyril Alfred and Edith Isabelle Southgate; *m* 1962, Sally Patricia Mead; two *s* two *d*. *Educ:* City of London Sch. ICT, later ICL, 1960–70; formed Software Sciences, 1970; apptd Chief Exec., BOC Computer Services Div. on sale of Software Sciences to BOC, 1980; Chief Exec., THORN EMI Information Technology, 1983; Dir, 1984–, Man. Dir, 1985–, THORN EMI. Non-executive Director: Lucas, 1987–; Prudential Corp., 1989–; Powergen, 1990–. Dir, South Bank Bd, 1990–. Mem., Industry and Commerce Gp, Save the Children Fund, 1991–; Vice Patron, Home Farm Develt Trust, 1991– (Trustee, 1988–91). Gov., Wellington Coll., 1989–; Mem. Court of Govs, Henley, the Management Coll., 1991–. *Recreation:* gardening. *Address:* THORN EMI plc, 4 Tenterden Street, Hanover Square, W1A 2AY. *T:* 071–355 4848.

SOUTHGATE, Air Vice-Marshal Harry Charles, CB 1976; CBE 1973 (MBE 1950); Director General of Engineering and Supply Policy and Planning, Ministry of Defence (Air), 1973–76, retired; *b* 30 Oct. 1921; *s* of George Harry Southgate and Lily Maud (*née* Clarke); *m* 1945, Violet Louise Davies; one *s*. *Educ:* St Saviour's Sch., Walthamstow. Entered RAF, 1941; India, 1942–45; HQ 90 Gp, 1946–50; RAF Stafford, 1950–52; Air Min., 1952–53; transf. to Equipment Br., 1953; RAF Tangmere, 1953–55; Singapore, 1955–57; psc 1957; Air Min., 1958–60; jssc 1961; Dirg Staff, RAF Staff Coll., Bracknell, 1961–64; CO 35 MU RAF Heywood, 1965–66; SESO, RAF Germany, 1967–68; idc 1969; Dir Supply Management, MoD Air, 1970–73. *Recreations:* travel, golf, painting, bird-watching. *Address:* The Rushings, Winksley, near Ripon, North Yorkshire HG4 3NR. *T:* Kirkby Malzeard (0765658) 582. *Club:* Royal Air Force.

SOUTHGATE, Very Rev. John Eliot; Dean of York, since 1984; *b* 2 Sept. 1926; *m* 1958, Patricia Mary Plumb; two *s* one *d*. *Educ:* City of Norwich Sch.; Durham Univ. BA 1953, DipTh 1955. Ordained 1955; Vicar of Plumstead, 1962; Rector of Old Charlton, 1966; Dean of Greenwich, 1968; York Diocesan Sec. for Mission and Evangelism, 1972–81, and Vicar of Harome, 1972–77; Archdeacon of Cleveland, 1974–84. A Church Comr, 1987–. Chairman: Nat. Assoc. of Victim Support Schemes, 1988–; Assoc. of English Cathedrals, 1990–. DUniv York, 1989. *Recreations:* music, sailing, Egyptology. *Address:* The Deanery, York, N Yorks YO1 2JD. *T:* York (0904) 623608. *Club:* Commonwealth Trust.

SOUTHGATE, Malcolm John; Director, Channel Tunnel, British Railways Board, since 1986; *b* 11 Nov. 1933; *s* of Harold Edwin Southgate and Mary (*née* Kelleher); *m* 1959, Anne Margaret Yeoman; two *s*. *Educ:* Royal Grammar Sch., Colchester; Corpus Christi Coll., Cambridge (BA). British Railways: Divl Manager, S Eastern Div., 1972; Chief Operating Manager, 1975, Dep. Gen. Man., 1977, Southern Region; Dir of Ops, 1980, Dir of Policy Unit, 1983, BR Board; Gen. Man., LMR, 1983. *Recreations:* Rugby, education administration, transport affairs. *Address:* 4 Langdale Rise, Maidstone, Kent ME16 0EU. *T:* Maidstone (0622) 753792.

SOUTHWARD, Sir Leonard (Bingley), (Sir Len), Kt 1986; OBE 1978; Founder (with Lady Southward) of Southward Museum Trust Inc., Paraparaumu, New Zealand, 1972; *b* 20 Sept. 1905; *s* of Philip Edmund Southward and Elizabeth Sarah Southward; *m* 2nd, 1954, Vera Thelma Bellamore; two *s* of former marriage. *Educ:* Te Aro Sch., Wellington, NZ. Started motorcycle repair business, 1926; changed to car repairs, 1935; started prodn engrg and manufacture of steel tubing, 1939; Governing Dir, Southward Engrg Co. Ltd, 1957–. The Southward Museum, which was opened to the public in 1979, contains one of the largest and most varied privately owned collection of veteran and vintage cars in the Southern Hemisphere. *Recreations:* veteran and vintage cars, rallies, etc; formerly speed boat racing, Australasia (first man in region to travel at over 100 mph on water). *Address:* Main Road North, Paraparaumu, New Zealand. *T:* 84–627.

SOUTHWARD, Dr Nigel Ralph, LVO 1985; Apothecary to the Queen, Apothecary to the Household and to the Households of Princess Margaret Countess of Snowdon, Princess Alice Duchess of Gloucester and the Duke and Duchess of Gloucester, since 1975, and of Queen Elizabeth the Queen Mother, since 1986; *b* 8 Feb. 1941; *s* of Sir Ralph Southward, *qv*; *m* 1965, Annette, *d* of J. H. Hoffmann; one *s* two *d*. *Educ:* Rugby Sch.; Trinity Hall, Cambridge; Middlesex Hosp. Med. Sch. MA, MB, BChir, 1965; MRCP 1969. Ho. Surg., Mddx Hosp., 1965; Ho. Phys., Royal Berkshire Hosp., Reading, 1966; Ho. Phys., Central Mddx Hosp., 1966; Casualty MO, Mddx Hosp., 1967; Vis. MO, King Edward VII Hosp. for Officers, 1972–. *Recreations:* sailing, golf, ski-ing. *Address:* 9 Devonshire Place, W1N 1PB. *T:* 071–935 8425; 56 Primrose Gardens, NW3 4TP. *Club:* Royal Yacht Squadron.

SOUTHWARD, Sir Ralph, KCVO 1975; Apothecary to the Household of Queen Elizabeth the Queen Mother, 1966–86, to the Household of HRH the Duke of Gloucester, 1966–75, to HM Household, 1964–74, to HM the Queen, 1972–74; *b* 2 Jan. 1908; *s* of Henry Stalker Southward; *m* 1935, Evelyn, *d* of J. G. Tassell; four *s*. *Educ:* High School of Glasgow; Glasgow Univ. MB, ChB (Glasgow) 1930; MRCP 1939; FRCP 1970. Western Infirmary, and Royal Hospital for Sick Children, Glasgow; Postgraduate Medical School, Hammersmith, London. Served War of 1939–45: Medical Officer, 215 Field Ambulance, North Africa, 1940–41; Medical Specialist, Egypt, India and Ceylon, and Lieut-Colonel in charge Medical Division, 1942–43; Colonel Comdg Combined General Hospital, 1944–45. Hon. Freeman, Worshipful Soc. of Apothecaries of London, 1975. *Recreations:* trout and salmon fishing, golf, travel. *Address:* 9 Devonshire Place, W1N 1PB. *T:* 071–935 7969; Amerden Priory, Amerden Lane, Taplow, Maidenhead, Berks SL6 0EE. *T:* Maidenhead (0628) 23525.

See also N. R. Southward.

SOUTHWARK, Archbishop and Metropolitan of, (RC), since 1977; **Most Rev. Michael George Bowen;** *b* 23 April 1930; *s* of late Major C. L. J. Bowen and Lady Makins (who *m* 1945, Sir Paul Makins, Bt, *qv*). *Educ:* Downside; Trinity Coll., Cambridge; Gregorian Univ., Rome. Army, 1948–49, 2nd Lieut Irish Guards; Wine Trade, 1951–52; English Coll., Rome, 1952–59; ordained 1958; Curate at Earlsfield and at Walworth, South London, 1959–63; taught theology, Beda Coll., Rome, 1963–66; Chancellor of Diocese of Arundel and Brighton, 1966–70; Coadjutor Bishop with right of succession to See of Arundel and Brighton, 1970–71; Bishop of Arundel and Brighton, 1971–77. *Recreations:* golf, tennis. *Address:* Archbishop's House, St George's Road, Southwark, SE1 6HX. *T:* 071–928 2495/5592.

SOUTHWARK, Bishop of, since 1991; **Rt. Rev. Robert Kerr Williamson;** *b* 18 Dec. 1932; *s* of James and Elizabeth Williamson; *m* 1956, Anne Boyd Smith; three *s* two *d*. *Educ:* Elmgrove School, Belfast; Oak Hill College, London. London City Missionary, 1955–61; Oak Hill Coll., 1961–63; Asst Curate, Crowborough Parish Church, 1963–66; Vicar: St Paul, Hyson Green, Nottingham, 1966–71; St Ann w. Emmanuel, Nottingham, 1971–76; St Michael and All Angels, Bramcote, 1976–79; Archdeacon of Nottingham,

1978–84; Bishop of Bradford, 1984–91. *Recreations:* walking, bird watching, reading, music. *Address:* Bishop's House, 38 Tooting Bec Gardens, SW16 1QZ.

SOUTHWARK, Auxiliary Bishops in, (RC); *see* Henderson, Rt Rev. C. J.; Jukes, Rt Rev. J.; Tripp, Rt Rev. H. G.

SOUTHWARK, Provost of; *see* Edwards, Very Rev. D. L.

SOUTHWARK, Archdeacon of; *see* Bartles-Smith, Ven. D. L.

SOUTHWELL, family name of **Viscount Southwell.**

SOUTHWELL, 7th Viscount, *cr* 1776; **Pyers Anthony Joseph Southwell**; Bt 1662; Baron Southwell, 1717; International Management and Marketing Consultant; *b* 14 Sept. 1930; *s* of Hon. Francis Joseph Southwell (2nd *s* of 5th Viscount) and Agnes Mary Annette Southwell (*née* Clifford); *S* uncle, 1960; *m* 1955, Barbara Jacqueline Raynes; two *s*. *Educ:* Beaumont Coll., Old Windsor, Berks; Royal Military Academy, Sandhurst. Commissioned into 8th King's Royal Irish Hussars, 1951; resigned commission, 1955. *Recreation:* golf. *Heir:* *s* Hon. Richard Andrew Pyers Southwell, *b* 15 June 1956. *Address:* 4 Rosebery Avenue, Harpenden, Herts AL5 2QP. *T:* Harpenden (0582) 5831. *Clubs:* Army and Navy, MCC.

SOUTHWELL, Bishop of, since 1988; **Rt. Rev. Patrick Burnet Harris**; *b* 30 Sept. 1934; *s* of Edward James Burnet Harris and Astrid Kendall; *m* 1968, Valerie Margaret Pilbrow; two *s* one *d*. *Educ:* St Albans School; Keble Coll., Oxford (MA). Asst Curate, St Ebbe's, Oxford, 1960–63; Missionary with S American Missionary Soc., 1963–73; Archdeacon of Salta, Argentina, 1969–73; Diocesan Bishop of Northern Argentina, 1973–80; Rector of Kirkheaton and Asst Bishop, Dio. Wakefield, 1981–85; Sec., Partnership for World Mission, 1986–88; Asst Bishop, Dio. Oxford, 1986–88. *Recreations:* ornithology, S American Indian culture, music. *Address:* Bishop's Manor, Southwell, Notts NG25 0JR. *Club:* Commonwealth Trust.

SOUTHWELL, Provost of; *see* Leaning, Very Rev. D.

SOUTHWELL, Richard Charles; QC 1977; *s* of late Sir Philip Southwell, CBE, MC and Mary Burnett; *m* Belinda Mary, *d* of Col F. H. Pownall, MC; two *s* one *d*. *Address:* 1 Hare Court, Temple, EC4Y 7BE. *T:* 071–353 3171, *Fax:* 071–583 9127.

SOUTHWELL, Ven. Roy; Archdeacon of Northolt, 1970–80, Archdeacon Emeritus, since 1980; Warden of the Community of All Hallows, Ditchingham, Norfolk, 1983–89; *b* 3 Dec. 1914; *s* of William Thomas and Lilian Southwell; *m* 1948, Nancy Elizabeth Lindsay Sharp; two *d*. *Educ:* Sudbury Grammar Sch.; King's Coll., London (AKC 1942). Curate: St Michael's, Wigan, 1942–44; St John the Divine, Kennington, 1944–48; Vicar of Ixworth, 1948–51; Vicar of St John's, Bury St Edmunds, 1951–56; Rector of Bucklesham with Brightwell and Foxhall, 1956–59; Asst Director of Religious Education, Diocese of St Edmundsbury and Ipswich, 1956–58, Director, 1959–67. Hon. Canon of St Edmundsbury, 1959–68; Vicar of Hendon, 1968–71. *Recreations:* reading, singing and watching TV. *Address:* 397 Sprowston Road, Norwich NR3 4HY. *T:* Norwich (0603) 405977.

SOUTHWOOD, Captain Horace Gerald, CBE 1966; DSC 1941; Royal Navy; Managing Director, Silley, Cox & Co. Ltd, Falmouth Docks, 1974–78; Chairman, Falmouth Group, 1976–78; *b* 19 April 1912; *s* of late Horace George Southwood; *m* 1936, Ruby Edith Hayes; two *s* one *d*. *Educ:* HMS Fisgard, RN Coll., Greenwich. Joined RN, 1927; HMS Resolution, Medit. Stn, 1932–34; HMS Barham, 1934–35; RN Coll., Greenwich, 1935–36; HMS Royal Oak, Home Fleet, 1936–38; specialised in Submarines, 1938; HMS Lucia, 1938–39. HM Submarine, Regent, 1939–41, China and Medit. (despatches, DSC); HMS Medway, Medit., 1941–42; HM Submarine, Amphion (first of Class), 1943–45. HMS Dolphin, 1946–48; HMS Vengeance, 1948–49; Comdr, 1948; HMS Glory, 1949–51; HMS Forth, 1951–52; Admty, Whitehall, 1952–54; HM Dockyard, Portsmouth (Dep. Man.), 1954–58; jssc, 1958–59; Capt., 1958. Chief Engr, Singapore, 1959–62; Sen. Officers' War Course, 1962; Manager, Engrg Dept, HM Dockyard, Portsmouth, 1963–67; Gen. Manager, HM Dockyard, Devonport, 1967–72, retd. Management Consultant, Productivity and Management Services Ltd, 1972–74. CEng, FIMechE. *Recreations:* sailing, fishing, golf, caravanning. *Address:* Dolphin Cottage, Riverside, Newton Ferrers, Devon PL8 1AA. *T:* Plymouth (0752) 872401. *Clubs:* Royal Western Yacht (Plymouth); Yealm Yacht (Newton Ferrers).

SOUTHWOOD, Prof. Sir (Thomas) Richard (Edmund), Kt 1984; FRS 1977; Linacre Professor of Zoology, University of Oxford and Fellow of Merton College, Oxford, since 1979; Vice-Chancellor, University of Oxford, since 1989; Chairman, National Radiological Protection Board, since 1985 (Member, since 1980); *b* 20 June 1931; *s* of late Edmund W. Southwood and A. Mary, *d* of Archdeacon T. R. Regg, and *g s* of W. E. W. Southwood; *m* 1955, Alison Langley, *d* of late A. L. Harden, Harpenden, Herts; two *s*. *Educ:* Gravesend Grammar Sch.; Imperial Coll., London. BSc, ARCS 1952; PhD London 1955; DSc London 1963; MA Oxon 1979; DSc Oxon 1987. FIBiol 1968; Hon. FRCP 1991. ARC Research Schol., Rothamsted Experimental Station, 1952–55; Res. Asst and Lecturer, Zoology Dept, Imperial Coll., London, 1955–64; Vis. Prof., Dept. of Entomology, University of California, Berkeley, 1964–65; Reader in Insect Ecology, University of London, 1964–67; Prof. of Zoology and Applied Entomology, London Univ., Head of Dept of Zoology and Applied Entomol., and Dir of Field Station, Imperial Coll., 1967–79; Dean, Royal Coll. of Science, 1971–72; Chm., Division of Life Sciences, Imperial Coll., 1974–77. A. D. White Prof.-at-Large, Cornell Univ., 1985–91. Member: ARC Adv. Cttee on Plants and Soils, 1970–72; ARC Res. Grants Bd, 1972–78; JCO Arable and Forage Crops Bd, 1972–79; NERC Terrestrial Life Sciences (formerly Nature Conservancy) Grants Cttee, 1971–76 (Chm., 1972–76); Council, St George's House, Windsor, 1974–80; Adv. Bd Research Councils, 1977–80; Trop. Medicine Panel, Wellcome Trust, 1977–79; Chairman: Royal Commn on Envmtl Pollution, 1981–86 (Mem., 1974–86); Management Cttee, Royal Soc., Royal Swedish Acad. and Norwegian Acad. Surface Water Acidification Prog., 1984–90; Dept of Health and MAFF Working Party on Bovine Spongiform Encephalopathy, 1988–89; UGC Working Party on Biology in Univs, 1988–89. Vice-Pres., Royal Soc., 1982–84; President: British Ecological Soc., 1976–78 (Hon. Treas., 1960–64 and 1967–68; Hon. Mem., 1988); Royal Entomological Soc., 1983 (Vice-Pres., 1963–64); Hon. Vice-President: Inst. of Envmtl Health Offices, 1984–; Game Conservancy, 1986–. Governor, Glasshouse Crops Research Inst., 1969–81; Trustee: British Museum (Natural History), 1974–83 (Chm., 1980–83); East Malling Trust, 1984–; Rhodes Trust, 1986–; Lawes Trust, 1987–; Delegate, OUP, 1980–; Mem., Hebdomadal Council, 1981–. Plenary speaker, 15th Internat. Congress on Entomology, Washington, 1976; Lectures: Spencer, Univ. of British Columbia, 1978; Bawden, British Crop Protection Conf., 1979; Le Conte, Georgia, 1989; F. E. Williams, RCP, 1990. Mem., Academia Europaea, 1989; Foreign Member: Amer. Acad. of Arts and Sciences, 1981; Norwegian Acad. of Sci. and Letters, 1987; US Nat. Acad. of Science, 1988; Hon. Mem., Ecol Soc. of America, 1986. Hon. Fellow: Imperial Coll., 1984; Entomological Soc. of Amer., 1986. Hon. DSc: Griffith, 1983; McGill, 1988; Warwick, 1989; London, 1991; Fil. Doc. *hc* Lund, 1986; Hon. ScD E Anglia, 1987. Scientific Medal, Zool. Soc., London, 1969; Linnean Medal, Linnean Soc. of London, 1988. Cavaliere Ufficale, Order of Merit, Republic of Italy, 1991. *Publications:* (with D. Leston) Land and Water Bugs of the British Isles, 1959; Life of the Wayside and Woodland, 1963; Ecological Methods, 1966, 2nd edn 1978; (jtly) Insects on Plants, 1984; (ed with B. J. Juniper) Insects and the Plant Surface, 1986; (ed with R. R. Jones) Radiation and Health: the biological effects of low-level exposure to ionizing radiation, 1987; many papers in entomological and ecological jls. *Recreations:* natural history, reading, travel, conversation. *Address:* Merton College, Oxford. *Clubs:* Athenæum, United Oxford & Cambridge University.

See also W. F. W. Southwood.

SOUTHWOOD, William Frederick Walter, MD; MChir; FRCS; Consultant Surgeon, Bath Health District, 1966–90; *b* 8 June 1925; *s* of late Stuart W. Southwood, MC, and of Mildred M. Southwood, and *g s* of W. E. W. Southwood; *m* 1965, Margaret Carleton Holderness, *d* of late Sir Ernest Holderness, Bt, CBE, and Lady Holderness; two *s*. *Educ:* Charterhouse; Trinity Coll., Cambridge (MA 1951, MD 1964, MChir 1956); Guy's Hosp. FRCS 1954. Captain, RAMC, 1949–51. Surg. Registrar, West London Hosp. and St Mark's Hosp. for Diseases of the Rectum, 1954–60; Sen. Surg. Registrar, Royal Infirmary, Bristol, 1960–66. Hunterian Prof., RCS, 1961. Vis. Prof. of Surgery, Univ. of Cape Town, 1987. Chm., Professional and Linguistic Assessment Bd, 1984–87 (Mem., 1976–87; Vice-Chm., 1983–84). Member: Court of Assts, Worshipful Soc. of Apothecaries of London, 1975– (Chm., Exams Cttee, 1981–85; Jun. Warden, 1984–85; Sen. Warden, 1985–86; Master, 1986–87); Cttee, Non-Univ. Medical Licencing Bodies, 1979–90. Examr in Anatomy and Surgery to GNC, 1957–72. *Publications:* articles in surgical jls. *Recreations:* fishing, snooker. *Address:* Upton House, Bathwick Hill, Bath, Avon. *T:* Bath (0225) 65152. *Clubs:* East India; Bath and County (Bath).

SOUTHWORTH, Sir Frederick, Kt 1965; QC; Chief Justice, Malawi, 1964–70, retired 1970; *b* Blackburn, Lancashire, 9 May 1910; *s* of late Harper Southworth, Blackburn, Lancs; *m* 1942, Margaret, *d* of James Rice, Monaghan, Ireland; three *d*. *Educ:* Queen Elizabeth's Grammar Sch., Blackburn; Exeter Coll., Oxford. Called to the Bar, Gray's Inn, 1936. War of 1939–45; commissioned 1939; served with South Lancashire Regiment and Lancashire Fusiliers, and with Department of the Judge Advocate General in India, 1939–46; Hon. Colonel, Crown Counsel, Palestine, 1946–47; Crown Counsel, Tanganyika, 1947–51; Attorney-General, Bahamas, 1951–55; QC Bahamas, 1952; Acting Governor, July-Aug. 1952; Acting Chief Justice, July-Oct. 1954; Puisne Judge, Nyasaland, 1955–64; Acting Governor-General, Malawi, 1964 and 1965. *Publications:* Specimen Charges, in use in the courts of Tanzania, Zanzibar, Kenya and Uganda; The Southworth Commission Report: an inquiry into allegations made by the international press against the Nyasaland Police, 1960. *Address:* c/o Barclays Bank, Darwen Street, Blackburn, Lancs.

SOUTHWORTH, Jean May, QC 1973; a Recorder of the Crown Court, since 1972; *b* 20 April 1926; *o c* of late Edgar and Jane Southworth, Clitheroe. *Educ:* Queen Ethelburga's Sch., Harrogate; St Anne's Coll., Oxford (MA). Served in WRNS, 1944–45. Called to Bar, Gray's Inn, 1954; Bencher, 1980. Standing Counsel to Dept of Trade and Industry for Central Criminal Court and Inner London Sessions, 1969–73. Chm., Police Discipline Appeals Tribunal, 1990–. Fellow, Woodard Corporation (Northern Div.), 1974–90. *Recreations:* music, tapestry. *Address:* 21 Caroline Place, W2 4AN; Queen Elizabeth Building, Temple, EC4Y 9BS.

SOUYAVE, Sir (Louis) Georges, Kt 1971; District Judge, Hong Kong, 1980–89; *b* 29 May 1926; *m* 1953, Mona de Chermont; two *s* four *d*. *Educ:* St Louis Coll., Seychelles; Gray's Inn, London. Barrister-at-Law, Gray's Inn, 1949. In private practice, Seychelles, 1949–56; Asst Attorney-Gen., Seychelles, 1956–62; Supreme Court, Seychelles: Additional Judge, 1962–64; Puisne Judge, 1964–70; Chief Justice, 1970–76; New Hebrides: Resident Judge of the High Court (British jurisdiction) and British Judge of the Supreme Ct of the Condominium, 1976–80. *Recreations:* walking, swimming. *Address:* 1 Flinders Court, Mount Ommaney, Brisbane, Qld 4074, Australia.

SOUZA e SILVA, Celso de; Grand Cross, Order of Rio Branco; Brazilian Ambassador to the Court of St James's, 1986–90; *b* 28 Sept. 1924; *s* of Oswaldo and Silvia de Souza e Silva; *m* Maria Alice de Souza e Silva; two *s*. *Educ:* (Faculty of Law) Catholic Univ. of Rio de Janeiro, Rio-Branco Inst. (diplomacy course); (Diplomatic and Consular Law) Inst. de Hautes Etudes Internat., Geneva Univ. Entered Diplomatic Service, 1948; Sec. of Embassy, Geneva, Caracas, El Salvador, Paris; Representative Adjunct, UN, New York, 1966–73; Amb. in Moscow, 1974–79; Special Rep. for Disarmament, 1979–86. Special missions for promotion of inter-Amer. relns in Buenos Aires, Santiago, Bogotá, Washington. Chief of Cabinet for Minister of External Relns; Asst to Pres. of Republic in Pan-Amer. Operation; Chairman: Disarmament Cttee, Geneva, 1979; Disarmament Commn of UN in New York, 1983; First Commn (Political and on Security), Gen. Assembly (UN Org.), 1984; Pres., Disarmament Conf., Geneva, 1986. Political Editor, Jornal do Brasil, 1962–66. Comdr or Grand Officer, several S American and European Orders. *Address:* Ladeira Dos Guararapes 76, Cosme Velho, Rio de Janeiro, RJ 22241, Brazil.

SOUZAY, Gérard, (*né* Gérard Marcel Tisserand), Chevalier, Légion d'Honneur; Chevalier de l'Ordre des Arts et Lettres; French baritone; *b* 8 Dec. 1921. *Educ:* Paris Conservatoire Musique. World Première, Stravinsky's Canticum Sacrum, Venice Festival, 1956; Bach B Minor Mass at Salzburg Festival; Pelléas et Mélisande, Rome Opera, Opera Comique, 1962, Scala, Milan, 1973; Don Giovanni, Paris Opera, 1963; second tour of Australia and New Zealand, 1964. Also tours in US, South America, Japan, Africa, Europe. Annual Lieder recitals, Salzburg Festival. Has made recordings; Grand Prix du Disque, for Ravel Recital, etc. *Recreations:* tennis, painting. *Address:* 26 rue Freycinet, 75116 Paris, France.

SOWARD, Prof. Andrew Michael, FRS 1991; Professor of Fluid Dynamics, since 1986 and Head, Division of Applied Mathematics, since 1985, University of Newcastle upon Tyne; *b* 20 Oct. 1943; *s* of Arthur Layton Soward and Sybil Jessica Lilian Soward (*née* Greathurst); *m* Elaine Celia McCaully; one *s* one *d*. *Educ:* St Edward's Sch., Oxford; Queen's College, Cambridge (BA 1st cl. Hons Maths 1965; PhD 1969; ScD 1984). Lectr, 1971, Reader, 1981–86, Dept of Maths and Stats, Univ. of Newcastle upon Tyne. Visiting appointments: Courant Inst. of Mathematical Scis, NY, 1969–70; CIRES, Boulder, Colorado, 1970–71; IGPP, UCLA, 1977–78. *Publications:* contribs to learned jls. *Recreations:* rock-climbing, running. *Address:* Department of Mathematics and Statistics, The University, Newcastle upon Tyne, NE1 7RU; Elton, Elm Bank Road, Wylam, Northumberland NE41 8HT. *T:* Wylam (0661) 853678.

SOWDEN, John Percival; Chairman, Costain Group Ltd (formerly Richard Costain Ltd), 1972–80 (Director, 1967–82); Regional Director, Central London and City of London Regional Boards, Lloyds Bank, 1980–87; *b* 6 Jan. 1917; *s* of Percy Sowden and Gertrude Sowden (*née* Moss); *m* 1st, 1940, Ruth Dorothy Keane (marr. diss. 1969); one *s*; 2nd, 1969, Joyce Diana Timson. *Educ:* Silcoates Sch., Wakefield, Yorks; The Grammar Sch., Hebden Bridge, Yorks; City and Guilds Coll., Imperial Coll. of Science (BScEng, ACGI; FCGI 1973). FIStructE. Served War: commnd RE, with service in UK, ME and Italy, 1939–46 (despatches, 1943). Joined Richard Costain Ltd, 1948; Site Project Manager on various construction projects, incl. Festival of Britain, Apapa Wharf, Nigeria, and

Bridgetown Harbour, Barbados, 1948–60; Joint Managing Director: Richard Costain (Associates) Ltd, 1961–62; Costain-Blankevoort Internat. Dredging Co. Ltd, 1963–65; Richard Costain Ltd: Manager, Civil Engrg Div., 1965–69; Board Member, 1967; Chief Executive, Internat. Area, 1969–70; Group Chief Executive, 1970–75. Member, Governing Body, Imperial Coll. of Science and Technology, 1971–, Fellow, 1980. FRSA 1983. *Recreations:* reading, joinery. *Address:* Below Star Cottage, East Tytherley Road, Lockerley, Romsey, Hants SO5 0LW. *T:* Romsey (0794) 41172. *Club:* Royal Automobile.

SOWDEN, Terence Cubitt; QC 1989; HM's Solicitor General for Jersey, since 1986; *b* 30 July 1929; *s* of George Henry Sowden, RNR, Master Mariner and Margaret Duncan Cubitt; *m* 1955, Doreen Mary Lucas (*d* 1983); one *s* two *d*. *Educ:* Victoria Coll. Prep. Sch.; Victoria Coll.; Hendon Tech. Coll., London. Called to the Bar, Middle Temple, 1951; Advocate, Royal Court of Jersey, 1951; in private practice in Jersey, 1951–85; Deputy for St Helier, States of Jersey, 1960–63; Sen. Partner, Crill Cubitt Sowden & Tomes, Advocates and Solicitors, 1962–83. *Publication:* (with Paul Matthews) The Jersey Law of Trusts, 1988, 2nd edn 1990. *Recreations:* writing, walking the low tide. *Address:* Chant de la Mer, Travers Farm Lane, Noirmont, St Brelade, Jersey, CI JE3 8AJ. *T:* Jersey (0534) 69044.

SOWREY, Air Marshal Sir Frederick (Beresford), KCB 1978 (CB 1968); CBE 1965; AFC 1954; *b* 14 Sept. 1922; *s* of late Group Captain Frederick Sowrey, DSO, MC, AFC; *m* 1946, Anne Margaret, *d* of late Captain C. T. A. Bunbury, OBE, RN; one *s* one *d*. *Educ:* Charterhouse. Joined RAF 1940; flying training in Canada, 1941; Fighter-reconnaissance Squadron, European theatre, 1942–44; Flying Instructors Sch., 1944; Airborne Forces, 1945; No 615 (Co. of Surrey) Squadron, RAuxAF ('Winston Churchill's Own'), 1946–48; Fighter Gunnery Sch., 1949–50, comdg 615 Sqdn, 1951–54; RAF Staff Coll., Bracknell, 1954; Chiefs of Staff Secretariat, 1955–58; comdg No 46 Sqdn, 1958–60; Personal Staff Officer to CAS, 1960–62; comdg RAF Abingdon, 1962–64; IDC 1965; SASO, Middle East Comd (Aden), 1966–67; Dir Defence Policy, MoD, 1968–70; SASO, RAF Trng Comd, 1970–72; Comdt, Nat. Defence Coll., 1972–75; Dir-Gen. RAF Training, 1975–77; UK Representative, Permanent Military Deputies Group CENTO, 1977–79. Research Fellow, IISS, 1980–81. Chm., Sussex Indust. Archaeology Soc., 1981–; Mem., Bd of Conservators, Ashdown Forest, 1984–; Pres., Victory Services Assoc., 1989– (Chm., 1985–89); Chm., RAF Historical Soc., 1986–; Trustee: Guild of Aviation Artists, 1990–; Amberley Chalk Pits Museum, 1990–. *Publications:* contribs and book reviews for defence jls. *Recreations:* motoring sport (world class records 1956), veteran cars, mechanical devices of any kind and age. *Address:* c/o National Westminster Bank, 67 High Street, Staines, Middx. *Club:* Royal Air Force.

SOWRY, Dr (George Stephen) Clive, FRCP, FRCPEd; FFOM; Physician, Edgware General Hospital, 1953–82; *b* 26 Dec. 1917; *s* of Dr George H. Sowry and Mrs Stella Sowry; *m* 1943, Jeanne (*née* Adams); one *s* one *d*. *Educ:* Bilton Grange, near Rugby; Epsom Coll., Surrey; St Mary's Hosp. Med. Sch., London (MB, BS 1940; MD 1947). FRCP 1963 (MRCP 1946); FRCPEd 1986; FFOM 1987. Served War, RNVR, 1941–45 (Surg. Lieut). Med. appts, St Mary's Hosp., Brompton Hosp. and Hammersmith Hosp., until 1953; med. admin, Edgware Gen. Hosp., 1957–73. Royal College of Physicians: Pro Censor, 1975; Censor, 1976; Sen. Censor and Vice-Pres., 1978–79; Mem. Qualification Cttee, 1981–86, Examnr, 1981–86, Board Mem., 1987–, Faculty of Occupational Medicine. Med. Sec., MRCP (UK) Pt 2 Exam. Bd., 1983–87; Member: Jt Academic Cttee, Conjoint Bd, 1983–89 (Chm., 1985–87); Med. Adv. Cttee, HSE, 1983–87. Silver Jubilee Medal, 1977. *Publication:* (jtly) article on aetiology of essential hypertension in Clin. Science. *Recreations:* sailing, singing. *Address:* 53 Aldenham Avenue, Radlett, Herts WD7 8JA. *T:* Radlett (0923) 856046.

SOYINKA, Wole; Nigerian writer; Goldwin Smith Professor of Africana Studies and Theatre, Cornell University, since 1988; *s* of Ayo and Eniola Soyinka; *b* 13 July 1934; *m*; *c*. *Educ:* Univ. of Ibadan, Nigeria; Univ. of Leeds. Res. Fellow in Drama, Univ. of Ibadan, 1960–61; Lectr in English, Univ. of Ife, 1962–63; Sen. Lectr in English, Univ. of Lagos, 1965–67; political prisoner, 1967–69; Artistic Dir and Head of Dept of Theatre Arts, Univ. of Ibadan, 1969–72; Res. Prof. in Dramatic Literature, 1972, Prof. of Comparative Literature, 1976–85, Univ. of Ife. Fellow, Churchill Coll., Cambridge, 1973–74. Hon. DLitt: Leeds, 1973; Yale, 1981; Paul Valéry, 1984; Morehouse Coll., 1988. Nobel Prize for Literature, 1986; AGIP/Enrico Mattei Award for the Humanities, 1986. *Publications: plays:* The Lion and the Jewel, 1959; The Swamp Dwellers, 1959; A Dance of the Forests, 1960; The Trials of Brother Jero, 1961; The Strong Breed, 1962; The Road, 1964; Kongi's Harvest, 1965; Madmen and Specialists, 1971; Before the Blackout, 1971; Jero's Metamorphosis, 1973; Camwood on the Leaves, 1973; The Bacchae of Euripides, 1974; Death and the King's Horsemen, 1975; Opera Wonyosi, 1978; A Play of Giants, 1984; *novels:* The Interpreters, 1964; The Forest of a Thousand Daemons (trans.), Season of Anomy, 1973; *poetry:* Idanre and other poems, 1967; A Shuttle in the Crypt, 1972; (ed) Poems of Black Africa, 1975; Ogun Abibman, 1977; Mandela's Earth and other Poems, 1989; *non-fiction:* The Man Died (prison memoirs), 1972; Myth, Literature and the African World (lectures), 1972; Ake, the Years of Childhood (autobiog.), 1982; Art, Dialogue and Outrage (essays), 1988; Isara: a voyage around "Essay" (biog.), 1989. *Address:* PO Box 935, Abeokuta, Ogun State, Nigeria.

SOYSA, Sir Warusahennedige Abraham Bastian, Kt 1954; CBE 1953 (MBE 1950); JP; formerly Mayor of Kandy, Sri Lanka. *Address:* 32/36 Sangaraja Mawatha, Kandy, Sri Lanka.

SPACIE, Maj.-Gen. Keith, CB 1987; OBE 1974; Chairman: Sudbury Consultants Ltd, since 1989; LEaD Ltd, since 1989; *b* 21 June 1935; *s* of Frederick and Kathleen Spacie; *m* 1961, Valerie Rich; one *s*. Commnd Royal Lincolns, 1955; transf. Parachute Regt, 1959; Staff Coll., Camberley, 1966; DAA&QMG 16 Parachute Bde, 1968–70; Staff, RMA, Sandhurst, 1970–72; Comd, 3rd Bn Parachute Regt, 1973–75; SHAPE, 1976–78; Comdr 7 Field Force, 1979–81; RCDS, 1982; Mil. Comr and Comdr, British Forces Falkland Is, 1983–84; Dir of Army Training, 1984–87. *Recreations:* cross-country running, athletics, walking, battlefield touring, Victorian paintings. *Address:* c/o Lloyds Bank, Obelisk Way, Camberley, Surrey GU15 3SE. *Clubs:* Army and Navy; Thames Hare and Hounds.

SPACKMAN, Brig. John William Charles, PhD; Director: European Telecommunications Informatics Services, since 1991; ACT Logsys, since 1991; *b* 12 May 1932; *s* of Lt-Col Robert Thomas Spackman, MBE and Ann (*née* Rees); *m* 1955, Jeanette Vera; two *s* one *d*. *Educ:* Cyfarthfa Castle Grammar School, Merthyr Tydfil; Wellington Grammar School; RMCS. BSc 1st cl. Hons London (external) 1960, PhD 1964; MSc (Management Sci.) UMIST, 1968. Nat. Service, 1950–52; Regular Commission, RAOC, 1952; Regtl appts, 1952–72; Project Wavell, 1969–72; RARDE, 1972–75; Senior Mil. Officer, Chem. Defence and Microbiological Defence Estab., Porton Down, 1975–78; Branch Chief, Inf. Systems Div., SHAPE, 1978–80; Dir, Supply Computer Services, 1980–83; retired from Army, 1983 (Brig.); Under Sec., and Dir, Social Security Operational Strategy, DHSS, 1983–87; Dir, Computing and Information Services, BT, 1987–90. FBCS 1987 (MBCS 1970); CEng 1990; MBIM 1970; MInstD 1983. Asst to Court, Co. of Information Technologists, 1989 (Mem., 1987). Freeman, City of London, 1987. *Recreations:* gardening, tennis, hill walking, opera. *Address:* 4 The Green, Evenley, Brackley, Northants. *T:* Brackley (0280) 703317. *Club:* Naval and Military.

SPACKMAN, Michael John; Chief Economic Adviser, Department of Transport, since 1991; *b* 8 Oct. 1936; *s* of late Geoffrey Spackman and Audrey (*née* Morecombe); *m* 1965, Judith Ann Leathem; two *s* two *d*. *Educ:* Malvern Coll.; Clare Coll., Cambridge (MA); Queen Mary Coll., London (MScEcon). Served RA (2nd Lieut), 1955–57; Physicist, UKAEA, Capenhurst, 1960–69; Sen. Physicist/Engr, Nuclear Power Gp Ltd, 1969–71; PSO, then Economic Advr, Dept of Energy, 1971–77; Economic Advr, HM Treasury, 1977–79; Dir of Econs and Accountancy, CS Coll., 1979–80; Hd of Public Services Econs Div., HM Treasury, 1980–85; Under Sec., 1985; Head of Public Expenditure Econs Gp, HM Treasury, 1985–91. *Recreations:* walking, children. *Address:* 44 Gibson Square, Islington, N1 0RA. *T:* 071–359 1053.

SPAFFORD, Rev. Christopher Garnett Howsin; Provost and Vicar of Newcastle, 1976–89; *b* 10 Sept. 1924; *s* of late Rev. Canon Douglas Norman Spafford and Frances Alison Spafford; *m* 1953, Stephanie Peel; three *s*. *Educ:* Marlborough Coll.; St John's Coll., Oxford (MA 2nd Cl. Hons Modern History); Wells Theological Coll. Curate of Brighouse, 1950; Curate of Huddersfield Parish Church, 1953; Vicar of Hebden Bridge, 1955; Rector of Thornhill, Dewsbury, 1961; Vicar of St Chad's, Shrewsbury, 1969. *Recreations:* reading, gardening, walking. *Address:* Low Moor, Elm Close, Leominster, Herefordshire HR6 8JX. *T:* Leominster (0568) 614395.

SPAFFORD, George Christopher Howsin; Chancellor, Manchester Diocese, since 1976; a Recorder of the Crown Court, 1975–88; *b* 1 Sept. 1921; *s* of Christopher Howsin Spafford and Clara Margaret Spafford; *m* 1959, Iola Margaret, 3rd *d* of Bertrand Leslie Hallward, *qv*; one *s* one *d*. *Educ:* Rugby; Brasenose Coll., Oxford (MA, BCL Hons). Served RA, 1939–46 (Captain). Called to Bar, Middle Temple, 1948. Mem., Legal Adv. Commn of Gen. Synod, 1981–. Treasurer, Friends of the Manchester City Art Gall., 1986–; Former Treasurer: Parish and People; Red Rose Guild of Designer Craftsmen. RCA 1989 (ARCamA 1986). *Recreation:* painting pictures. *Address:* 57 Hawthorn Lane, Wilmslow, Cheshire SK9 5DQ.

SPAGHT, Monroe E., MA, PhD; retired Director, Royal Dutch/Shell companies; Director: Shell Oil Co., USA, 1953–80 (Chairman, 1965–70); Royal Dutch Petroleum Co., 1965–80; various Royal Dutch/Shell companies, 1965–80; *b* Eureka, California, 9 Dec. 1909; *s* of Fred E. and Alpha L. Spaght; *m* two *s* one *d*. *Educ:* Humboldt State Univ.; Stanford Univ.; University of Leipzig. AB 1929, MA 1930, PhD 1933, Stanford Univ. (Chemistry). Research scientist and technologist, Shell Oil Co., 1933–45; Vice-President, Shell Development Co., 1945–48, President, 1949–52; Exec. Vice-President, Shell Oil Co., 1953–60, President, 1961–65; Man. Dir, Royal Dutch/Shell Group, 1965–70; Director: Stanford Research Inst., 1953–70; Inst. of International Education, 1953– (Chm., 1971–74); American Petroleum Inst., 1953–; American Standard, 1972–82; Belden & Blake Cos, 1984–; Mem. Adv. Bd, The Boston Co., 1979–80 (Dir, 1971–79). Chm., Internat. Adv. Bd of Chemical Bank, 1977–80; Mem., Internat. Adv. Cttee, Wells Fargo Bank, 1977–84. Trustee, Stanford Univ., 1955–65. President, Economic Club of New York, 1964–65. Mem., Nat. Acad. of Engrg, USA, 1969. Hon. DSc: Rensselaer Polytechnic Inst., 1958; Drexel Inst. of Technology, 1962; Hon. LLD: Manchester, 1964; California State Colleges, 1965; Millikin Univ., Illinois, 1967; Wesleyan Univ., Middletown, Conn, 1968; Hon. DEng, Colorado Sch. of Mines, 1971. Order of Francisco de Miranda, Venezuela, 1968; Comdr, Order of Oranje–Nassau, Netherlands, 1970. *Publications:* The Bright Key, 1965; Minding My Own Business, 1971; Here's What I Said, 1977; The Multinational Corporation, its Manners, Methods and Myths, 1977; The Long Road from Eureka, 1986; contribs to scientific journals. *Address:* 2 Lyall Mews, Belgravia, SW1X 8DJ. *Clubs:* Athenæum; Sunningdale; Blind Brook Country (New York).

SPALDING, Prof. (Dudley) Brian, MA, ScD; FRS 1983; FEng 1989; FIMechE, FInstF; Professor of Heat Transfer, London University, 1958–88, now Emeritus, and Head, Computational Fluid Dynamics Unit, Imperial College of Science, Technology and Medicine, 1981–88; *b* New Malden, Surrey, 9 Jan. 1923; *s* of H. A. Spalding; *m* 1st, Eda Ilse-Lotte (*née* Goericke); two *s* two *d*; 2nd, Colleen (*née* King); two *s*. *Educ:* King's College Sch., Wimbledon; The Queen's Coll., Oxford; Pembroke Coll., Cambridge. BA (Oxon) 1944; MA (Cantab) 1948, PhD (Cantab) 1951. Bataafsche Petroleum Matschapij, 1944–45; Ministry of Supply, 1945–47; National Physical Laboratory, 1947–48; ICI Research Fellow at Cambridge Univ., 1948–50; Cambridge University Demonstrator in Engineering, 1950–54; Reader in Applied Heat, Imperial College of Science and Technology, 1954–58. Managing Director: Combustion, Heat and Mass Transfer Ltd, 1970–; Concentration, Heat and Momentum Ltd, 1975–; Chm., CHAM of N America Inc., 1977–. *Publications:* Some Fundamentals of Combustion, 1955; (with E. H. Cole) Engineering Thermodynamics, 1958; Convective Mass Transfer, 1963; (with S. V. Patankar) Heat and Mass Transfer in Boundary Layers, 1967, rev. edn 1970; (co-author) Heat and Mass Transfer in Recirculating Flows, 1969; (with B. E. Launder) Mathematical Models of Turbulence, 1972; GENMIX: a general computer program for two-dimensional parabolic phenomena, 1978; Combustion and Mass Transfer, 1979; (jtly) Heat Exchanger Design Handbook, 1982; Numerical Prediction of Flow, Heat Transfer, Turbulence and Combustion (selected works), 1983; numerous scientific papers. *Recreations:* squash, poetry. *Address:* CHAM Ltd, Bakery House, 40 High Street, Wimbledon, SW19 5AU.

SPALDING, Rear-Adm. Ian Jaffery L.; *see* Lees-Spalding.

SPALDING, John Oliver, CBE 1988; Chairman, National House-Building Council, since 1988 (Member, since 1985); *b* 4 Aug. 1924; *m* 1952, Mary Whitworth Hull; one *d* one *s*. *Educ:* William Hulme's Grammar School, Manchester; Jesus College, Cambridge (MA). Served War: Capt. RA, attached IA; served India, Burma, Singapore, Java. Admitted a Solicitor, 1952; service with Manchester Corporation and Hampshire CC, 1952–62; Halifax Building Society: Assistant Solicitor, 1962–64; Head Office Solicitor, 1964–74; General Manager, 1970; Director, 1975–88; Deputy Chief General Manager, 1981; Chief Exec., 1982–88. Member: BSA Legal Adv. Panel, 1965–80; Council of BSA, 1981–88; Chairman: Future Constitution and Powers of Bldg Socs Working Party (Spalding Cttee), 1981–83; Calderdale Small Business Advice Centre, 1983–88; Mem., Farrand Cttee investigating Conveyancing, 1984. Director: NMW Computers Plc, 1989–; Morton, Hodson Ltd, 1989–. *Recreations:* boats and bird-watching. *Address:* Water's Edge, Springe Lane, Swanley, Nantwich, Cheshire CW5 8NR; National House-Building Council, Chiltern Avenue, Amersham, Bucks HP6 5AP.

SPALDING, Julian, FMA; Director, Glasgow Museums and Art Galleries, since 1989; *b* 15 June 1947; *s* of Eric Peter Spalding and Margaret Grace Savager; *m* 1974, Frances (*née* Crabtree), author; one *s*. *Educ:* Chislehurst and Sidcup Grammar Sch. for Boys; Univ. of Nottingham (BA Hons Fine Art). Dip. Museums Assoc., 1973; FMA 1983. Art Assistant: Leicester Museum and Art Gall., 1970; Durham Light Infantry Mus. and Arts Centre, 1971; Sheffield City Art Galleries: Keeper, Mappin Art Gall., 1972–76; Dep. Dir, 1976–82; Dir of Arts, Sheffield City Council, 1982–85; Dir, Manchester City Art Galls, 1985–89; Acting Dir, Nat. Mus. of Labour History, 1987–88. Art Panel Mem., Arts

Council of GB, 1978–82 (Chm., Exhibns Sub-Cttee, 1981–82 and 1986–); Founder, Art Galleries Assoc., 1976, Mem. Cttee, 1976–, Chm., 1987–; Dir, Guild of St George (John Ruskin's Guild), 1983– (Companion, 1978); Member: Crafts Council, 1986– (Member: Projects and Orgn Cttee, 1985–87; Purchasing Cttee, 1986–; Exhibns Cttee, 1986–90); British Council, 1987– (Mem., Fine Arts Adv. Cttee, 1987–). BBC broadcaster (talks and reviews); Third Ear, BBC Radio Three, 1988. *Publications:* L. S. Lowry, 1979; Three Little Books on Painting, 1984; pamphlets and exhibition catalogues, including: Modern British Painting 1900–1960, 1975; Fragments against Ruin, 1981; Francis Davison, 1983; George Fullard Drawings, 1984; The Forgotten Fifties, 1984; Modern Art in Manchester, 1986; The Art of Watercolour, 1987; L. S. Lowry, 1987; Ken Currie, 1988; Funfair or Church?, RSA, 1989; Glasgow's Great British Art Exhibition, 1990; contrib. Burlington Magazine. *Recreations:* painting, cycling, gardening. *Address:* Art Gallery and Museum, Kelvingrove, Glasgow G3 8AG.

SPALVINS, Janis Gunars; Managing Director, Adelaide Steamship Co., since 1981; *b* 26 May 1936; *s* of Peter Spalvins and Hilda Blumentals; *m* 1961, Cecily Westall Rymill; two *s*. *Educ:* Concordia College, Adelaide; Univ. of Adelaide (BEc). FCIS 1961; FASA 1967. Camelec Group of Cos, 1955–73 (Group Sec./Dir, subsidiary cos); Adelaide Steamship Co.: Asst Gen. Manager, 1973; Gen. Manager, 1977; Chief Gen. Manager and Dir, 1979. Dir and Chief Exec., David Jones Ltd, 1980–. Mem., Business Council of Australia, 1986–. FAIM; MInstD Australia, 1981. *Recreations:* snow ski-ing, water ski-ing, tennis, sailing. *Address:* 2 Brookside Road, Springfield, SA 5062, Australia. *T:* (08) 79 2965. *Clubs:* Cruising Yacht Club of SA, Royal SA Yacht Squadron (Adelaide); Ski Club of Victoria (Mount Buller).

SPANIER, Suzy Peta, (Mrs D. G. Spanier); *see* Menkes, S. P.

SPANKIE, Hugh Oliver; HM Diplomatic Service, retired 1986; *b* 11 Dec. 1936; *s* of late Col Hugh Vernon Spankie and Elizabeth Ursula (*née* Hills); *m* 1963, Anne Bridget Colville (marr. diss. 1981); one *s* one *d*. *Educ:* Tonbridge Sch. RM Officer, 1955–66; HM Diplomatic Service, 1967–: Helsinki, 1968–71; FCO, 1971–74; Helsinki, 1974–77; FCO and CSD, 1977–81; Counsellor, Copenhagen, 1981–85. *Address:* c/o Barclays Bank plc, 29 Stone Street, Cranbrook, Kent TN17 3HH.

SPANN, Keith, CB 1980; CVO 1977; Secretary, Premier's Department, Queensland, 1978–82; retired; *b* 8 Nov. 1922; *s* of late G. F. A. Spann; *m* 1946, Marjorie, *d* of W. R. Golding, CMG, MBE; three *s*. *Educ:* State High School, Gympie. Joined Queensland Public Service, 1938; Dept of Auditor-Gen., 1948–61; Sec. to Cabinet, 1961–64; Asst Under Sec., Premier's Dept, 1964–70, Under Sec., 1970–78. *Recreations:* fishing, golf, woodworking, gemmology. *Address:* 2 Quaver Court, Bridgeman Downs, Queensland 4035, Australia.

SPANTON, (Harry) Merrik, OBE 1975; CEng; CBIM; Chairman, British Coal Enterprise Ltd (formerly NCB (Enterprise) Ltd), 1984–91; *b* 27 Nov. 1924; *s* of late Henry Broadley Spanton and Edith Jane Spanton; *m* 1945, Mary Margaret Hawkins; one *s*. *Educ:* Eastbourne Coll.; Royal Sch. of Mines (BSc (Min) (Eng) 1945; ARSM). CEng, FIMinE 1957 (Hon. FIMinE 1986); CBIM 1979. Colliery Manager, 1950; Agent, 1954; Gp Man., 1956; Dep. Prodn Man., 1958; Dep. Prodn Dir, 1960; Asst Gen. Man., 1962; Gen. Man., 1964; Area Dir, 1967–80; Mem., NCB, 1980–85. Chairman: J. H. Sankey & Son, 1982–83; Coal Industry (Patents) Ltd, 1982–85; Director: British Mining Consultants Ltd, 1980–87 (Chm., 1981–83); Overseas Coal Develts Ltd, 1980–83; Compower, 1981–85 (Chm., 1984–85); NCB (Coal Products) Ltd, 1981–83; Coal Processing Consultants, 1981–83; Staveley Chemicals Ltd, 1981–83; NCB (Ancillaries) Ltd, 1982–85; British Fuel Co., 1983–87; Berry Hill Investments Ltd, 1984–85; CIBT Insurance Services Ltd, 1984–85; CIBT Developments Ltd, 1984–85; Coal Industry Social Welfare Orgn, 1983–85. Member: W European Coal Producers Assoc., 1980–85; CBI Overseas Cttee, 1981–85. Vice-Pres., Coal Trade Benevolent Assoc., 1979– (Chm., 1978). *Publications:* articles in prof. jls. *Recreations:* travel, shooting. *Address:* 4 Roselands Gardens, Canterbury, Kent CT2 7LP. *T:* Canterbury (0227) 769356.

SPAREY, John Raymond, MA; Director (Association of Municipal Engineers), Institution of Civil Engineers, 1984–85; Secretary-General, International Federation of Municipal Engineers, 1979–85; *b* 28 July 1924; *s* of late Henry Sparey and Lilian May (*née* Coles); *m* 1950, Audrie Kathleen, *d* of late Col E. J. W. Porter, OBE, TD, Portsmouth; two *s* one *d*. *Educ:* City of Bath Sch.; King's Coll., London; Trinity Coll., Cambridge (BA 1950, MA 1954). Royal Naval Scientific Service, 1944–47; Asst Secretary, Assoc. of Certified Accountants, 1952–69; Royal Institution of Chartered Surveyors: Dep. Sec., 1969–70; Sec. for Educn and Membership, 1970–74; Sec., Planning and Development Div., 1976; Sec., Instn of Municipal Engrs, 1977–84. *Recreations:* gardening, sailing. *Address:* Seaview House, Circular Road, Seaview, Isle of Wight PO34 5ET. *T:* Isle of Wight (0983) 613482. *Clubs:* Reform; Seaview Yacht (Seaview, IoW).

SPARK, Mrs Muriel Sarah, OBE 1967; writer; *b* Edinburgh; *d* of Bernard Camberg and Sarah Elizabeth Maud (*née* Uezzell); *m* 1937 (marr. diss.); one *s*. *Educ:* James Gillespie's School for Girls, Edinburgh; Heriot Watt Coll., Edinburgh. FO, 1944; General Secretary, The Poetry Society, Editor, The Poetry Review, 1947–49. FRSL 1963. Hon. Mem., Amer. Acad. of Arts and Letters, 1978. Hon. DLitt: Strathclyde, 1971; Edinburgh, 1989. Officier de l'Ordre des Arts et des Lettres, France, 1988. *Publications: critical and biographical:* (ed jtly) Tribute to Wordsworth, 1950; (ed) Selected Poems of Emily Brontë, 1952; Child of Light: a Reassessment of Mary Shelley, 1951, rev. edn, Mary Shelley, 1988; (ed jtly) My Best Mary: the letters of Mary Shelley, 1953; John Masefield, 1953; (joint) Emily Brontë: her Life and Work, 1953; (ed) The Brontë Letters, 1954; (ed jointly) Letters of John Henry Newman, 1957; *poems:* The Fanfarlo and Other Verse, 1952; Collected Poems I, 1967; Going Up to Sotheby's and other poems, 1982; *fiction:* The Comforters, 1957; Robinson, 1958; The Go-Away Bird, 1958; Memento Mori, 1959 (adapted for stage, 1964); The Ballad of Peckham Rye, 1960 (Italia prize, for dramatic radio, 1962); The Bachelors, 1960; Voices at Play, 1961; The Prime of Miss Jean Brodie, 1961 (adapted for stage, 1966, filmed 1969, and BBC TV, 1978); Doctors of Philosophy (play), 1963; The Girls of Slender Means, 1963 (adapted for radio, 1964, and BBC TV, 1975); The Mandelbaum Gate, 1965 (James Tait Black Memorial Prize); Collected Stories I, 1967; The Public Image, 1968; The Very Fine Clock (for children), 1969; The Driver's Seat, 1970 (filmed 1974); Not to Disturb, 1971; The Hothouse by the East River, 1973; The Abbess of Crewe, 1974 (filmed 1977); The Takeover, 1976; Territorial Rights, 1979; Loitering with Intent, 1981; Bang-Bang You're Dead and other stories, 1982; The Only Problem, 1984; The Stories of Muriel Spark, 1987 (Scottish Book of Year Award); A Far Cry from Kensington, 1988; Symposium, 1990. *Recreations:* reading, travel. *Address:* c/o David Higham Associates Ltd, 5–8 Lower John Street, Golden Square, W1R 4HA.

SPARKES, Sir Robert Lyndley, Kt 1979; State President, National Party of Australia (formerly Country Party), Queensland, 1970–90; Managing Partner, Lyndley Pastoral Co., since 1974; *b* 30 May 1929; *s* of late Sir James Sparkes, Jandowae, Queensland; *m* 1953, June, *d* of M. Morgan; two *s*. *Educ:* Southport Sch., Queensland. Chairman: National Party (formerly Country Party) Lands Cttee, Queensland, 1966–; NPA Nominees Pty Ltd; Wambo Shire Council, 1967– (Mem., 1952–55 and 1964–). *Recreation:* reading. *Address:* Dundonald, PO Box 117, Jandowae, Queensland 4410, Australia. *T:* (074) 68 5196.

SPARKS, Arthur Charles, BSc (Econ); Under-Secretary, Ministry of Agriculture, Fisheries and Food, 1959–74; *b* 1914; *s* of late Charles Herbert and Kate Dorothy Sparks; *m* 1939, Betty Joan (*d* 1978), *d* of late Harry Oswald and Lilian Mary Simmons; three *d*. *Educ:* Selhurst Grammar Sch.; London School of Economics. Clerk, Ministry of Agriculture and Fisheries, 1931; Administrative Grade, 1936; National Fire Service, 1942–44; Principal Private Secretary to Minister of Agriculture and Fisheries, 1946–47; Asst Secretary, Ministry of Agriculture and Fisheries, 1947–49 and 1951–59; Asst Secretary, Treasury, 1949–51. Chm., Internat. Wheat Council, 1968–69. *Recreations:* reading, walking. *Address:* 2 Stratton Close, Merton Park, SW19 3JF. *T:* 081–542 4827.

SPARKS, Rev. Hedley Frederick Davis, DD Oxon, 1949; FBA 1959; ATCL 1927; Oriel Professor of the Interpretation of Holy Scripture, University of Oxford, 1952–76; *b* 14 Nov. 1908; *s* of late Rev. Frederick Sparks and late Blanche Barnes Sparks (formerly Jackson); *m* 1953, Margaret Joan, *d* of late C. H. Davy; two *s* one *d*. *Educ:* St Edmund's Sch., Canterbury; BNC, Oxford (Hon. Fellow, 1987); Ripon Hall, Oxford. Hon. DD: St Andrews, 1963; Birmingham, 1983. Hon. Fellow, Oriel Coll., Oxford, 1980. Jt Editor, Jl of Theol Studies, 1954–77. *Publications:* The Old Testament in the Christian Church, 1944; The Formation of the New Testament, 1952; A Synopsis of the Gospels, part I: The Synoptic Gospels with the Johannine Parallels, 1964, 2nd edn 1970; part II: The Gospel according to St John with the Synoptic Parallels, 1974, combined volume edn, 1977; *Editor:* The Apocryphal Old Testament, 1984; *Joint Editor:* Novum Testamentum Domini Nostri Iesu Christi Latine secundum editionem Sancti Hieronymi, Part ii, fasc. 5, 1937, fasc. 6, 1939, fasc. 7, 1941, Part iii, fasc. 2, 1949, fasc. 3, 1953; Biblia Sacra iuxta Vulgatam versionem, 1969, 3rd edn 1983; *Contributor:* The Bible in its Ancient and English Versions, 1940, 2nd edn 1954; Studies in the Gospels, 1955; The Cambridge History of the Bible, vol. 1, 1970, 2nd edn, 1975. *Recreations:* music and railways. *Address:* 14 Longport, Canterbury, Kent CT1 1PE. *T:* Canterbury (0227) 766265.

SPARKS, Ian Leslie; Director, The Children's Society, since 1986; *b* 26 May 1943; *s* of Ronald Leslie and Hilda Sparks; *m* 1967, Eunice Jean; one *d*. *Educ:* Whitefield Road Primary School, Liverpool; Holt High School, Liverpool; Brunel Univ. (MA); AIB. Bank clerk, 1959–68; social worker, Liverpool, 1971–75; Asst Divl Dir, Barnardo's, 1975–80; Social Work Dir, The Children's Soc., 1981–86. Chair: Social Policy Cttee, NCVCCO, 1990–; Christian Child Care Network, 1991–; Trustee, LinkAge, 1989–. *Recreations:* piano playing, gardening in miniature. *Address:* Edward Rudolf House, Margery Street, WC1X 0JL. *T:* 071–837 4299.

SPARKS, Prof. Robert Stephen John, FRS 1988; Chaning Wills Professor of Geology, Bristol University, since 1990 (Professor of Geology, since 1989); *b* 15 May 1949; *s* of Kenneth Grenfell Sparks and Ruth Joan Rugman; *m* 1971, Ann Elizabeth Talbot; two *s*. *Educ:* Imperial College London (BSc Hons 1971, PhD 1974). Postdoctoral fellowships, Lancaster Univ., 1974–76, Univ. of Rhode Island, 1976–78, studying physics of volcanic eruptions; Cambridge University: Demonstrator, 1978–82; Lectr in Geology, 1982–89; Fellow, Trinity Hall, 1981–89. Sherman Fairchild Dist. Scholar, Calif. Inst. of Technology, 1987; studies of volcanic eruptions: Heimaey, Iceland, 1973; Etna, 1975; Soufriere, WI, 1979; Mount St Helens, 1980. Wager Prize for Volcanology, Internat. Assoc. of Volcanology and Chemistry of Earth's Interior, 1983; Bigsby Medal, Geol Soc., 1985. *Publications:* numerous papers on physics of volcanic eruptions, geology of young volcanoes and origins of volcanism. *Recreations:* music, soccer, squash, travel, cooking. *Address:* 28 Stonewell Drive, Congresbury, Avon.

SPARROW, (Albert) Charles; QC 1966; DL; barrister; *b* Kasauli, India, 16 Sept. 1925; *e s* of Captain Charles Thomas Sparrow, sometime Essex Regt, and Antonia Sparrow; *m* 1949, Edith Rosalie Taylor (*d* 1985); two *s* one *d*. *Educ:* Royal Grammar Sch., Colchester. Served Civil Defence, 1939–43; joined Army, 1943; posted as cadet to India, commnd into Royal Signals and served in Far East, 1944–47; OC, GHQ Signals, Simla, 1947. Admitted to Gray's Inn, 1947 (Holker Senior Scholar, Atkin Scholar, Lee Prizeman and Richards Prizeman); called to Bar, 1950, Master of the Bench, 1976; LLB London Univ., 1951; admitted to Lincoln's Inn, 1967; in practice in Chancery and before Parliament, 1950–. Member: General Council of the Bar, 1969–73; Senate of the Four Inns of Court, 1970–73; Incorp. Council of Law Reporting, 1977–83. Hon. Legal Adviser to Council for British Archæology (concerned notably with legal protection of antiquities and reform of treasure trove; produced two draft Antiquities Bills), 1966–. Chairman: independent Panel of Inquiry for affairs of RSPCA, 1973–74; independent Cttee of Inquiry for Girl Guides Rally at Crystal Palace, 1985. FSA 1972; Pres., Essex Archaeological Soc., 1975–78. Chm., Stock Branch, British Legion, 1970–75. Mem., Court, Univ. of Essex, 1985–. Advr to assocs of customary freemen, 1972–; Hon. Counsellor to Freemen of England, 1978–; Freeman, City of London; Hon. Life Mem., Gild of Freemen of City of York. CStJ 1987 (OStJ 1982); Comr for Essex, St John Ambulance Bde, 1983–90; Comdr, St John Ambulance for Essex, 1989–. DL Essex, 1985. *Recreation:* Romano-British archæology. *Address:* 13 Old Square, Lincoln's Inn, WC2A 3UA. *T:* 071–242 6105; Croyde Lodge, Stock, Essex.

SPARROW, Bryan; HM Diplomatic Service; Consul-General, Lyon, since 1989; *b* 8 June 1933; *m* 1958, Fiona Mary Mylechreest; one *s* one *d*. *Educ:* Hemel Hempstead Grammar Sch.; Pembroke Coll., Oxford (BA Hons). Served Army, 1951–53. Belgrade, 1958–61; FO, 1961–64; Moscow, 1964–66; Tunis, 1967–68; Casablanca, 1968–70; FO, 1970–72; Kinshasa, 1972–76; Prague, 1976–78; Counsellor (Commercial), Belgrade, 1978–81; Ambassador, United Republic of Cameroon, 1981–84, and concurrently to Republic of Equatorial Guinea and Central African Republic, 1982–84; Canadian Nat. Defence Coll., 1984–85; Consul-Gen., Toronto, 1985–89. *Recreations:* fishing, gardening, travel. *Address:* c/o Foreign and Commonwealth Office, SW1.

SPARROW, Charles; *see* Sparrow, A. C.

SPARROW, Sir John, Kt 1984; FCA; Chairman: Universities Superannuation Scheme Ltd, since 1988; Horserace Betting Levy Board, since 1991; *b* 4 June 1933; *s* of Richard A. and Winifred R. Sparrow; *m* 1967, Cynthia Whitehouse. *Educ:* Stationers' Company's School; London School of Economics (BSc Econ). FCA 1957. With Rawlinson & Hunter, Chartered Accountants, 1954–59; Ford Motor Co. Ltd, 1960; AEI-Hotpoint Ltd, 1960–63; United Leasing Corporation, 1963–64; Morgan Grenfell Group (formerly Morgan Grenfell & Co.), 1964–88; Dir, Morgan Grenfell Gp (formerly Morgan Grenfell Hldgs), 1971–88; Chm., Morgan Grenfell Asset Management, 1985–88; Morgan Grenfell Laurie Hldgs, 1985–88. Director: Federated Chemicals, 1969–78 (Chm., 1974–78); Harris Lebus, 1973–79; United Gas Industries, 1974–82 (Dep. Chm., 1981–82); Coalite Group plc, 1974–82, 1984–89; Gas and Oil Acreage, 1975–78; Tioxide Gp, 1977–78; Mather & Platt, 1979–81; Peterborough Develt Corp., 1981–88; Short Brothers plc, 1984–89 (Dep. Chm., 1985–89); ASW Holdings Plc, 1987–; National & Provincial Building Soc., 1989– (Mem., London Adv. Bd, 1986–); Regalian Properties PLC, 1990–. Seconded as Head of Central Policy Review Staff, Cabinet Office, 1982–83. Chm., EDC for Process Plant Industry, 1984–85; Chm., National Stud, 1988–91. Vice-Chm.,

Governors, LSE, 1984– (Actg Chm., 1987–88). Hon. Fellow, Wolfson Coll., Cambridge, 1987. *Recreations:* cricket, crosswords, horse-racing. *Address:* 52 Grosvenor Gardens, SW1W 0AU. *T:* 071–730 4540. *Club:* MCC.

SPARROW, John Hanbury Angus, OBE 1946; Warden of All Souls College, Oxford, 1952–77; *b* New Oxley, near Wolverhampton, 13 Nov. 1906; *e s* of I. S. Sparrow and Margaret Macgregor; unmarried. *Educ:* Winchester (Scholar); New Coll., Oxford (Scholar). 1st Class, Hon. Mods, 1927; 1st Class, Lit Hum, 1929; Fellow of All Souls Coll., 1929 (re-elected 1937, 1946); Chancellor's Prize for Latin Verse, 1929; Eldon Scholar, 1929; called to Bar, Middle Temple, 1931; practised in Chancery Division, 1931–39; enlisted in Oxford and Bucks LI, 1939; Commnd Coldstream Guards, 1940; Military Asst to Lt-Gen. Sir H. C. B. Wemyss in War Office and on Military Mission in Washington, Feb.-Dec. 1941; rejoined regt in England, 1942; DAAG and AAG, War Office, 1942–45; resumed practice at Bar, 1946; ceased to practise on appointment as Warden of All Souls Coll., 1952; Hon. Bencher, Middle Temple, 1952; Fellow of Winchester Coll., 1951–81; Hon. Fellow, New Coll., 1956. Hon. DLitt, Univ. of Warwick, 1967. *Publications:* various; mostly reviews and essays in periodicals, some of which were collected in Independent Essays, 1963, and Controversial Essays, 1966; Half-lines and Repetitions in Virgil, 1931; Sense and Poetry: essays on the place of meaning in contemporary verse, 1934; Mark Pattison and the Idea of a University (Clark Lectures), 1967; After the Assassination, 1968; Visible Words (Sandars Lectures), 1969; (with A. Perosa) Renaissance Latin Verse: an anthology, 1979; Grave Epigrams and Other Verses, 1981; Words on the Air, 1981; (ed with John Gere) Geoffrey Madan's Notebooks, 1981; Leaves from a Victorian Diary, 1985. *Address:* Beechwood House, Iffley Turn, Oxford. *Clubs:* Garrick, Reform, Beefsteak.

SPAWFORTH, David Meredith, MA; Headmaster, Merchiston Castle School, Edinburgh, since April 1981; *b* 2 Jan. 1938; *s* of Lawrence and Gwen Spawforth, Wakefield, Yorks; *m* 1963, Yvonne Mary Gude; one *s* one *d. Educ:* Silcoates School; Hertford Coll., Oxford (Heath Harrison Travelling Schol.; MA ModLang). Assistant Master: Winchester Coll., 1961–64; Wellington Coll., 1964–80; Housemaster, Wellington Coll., 1968–80. British Petroleum Education Fellow, Keble Coll., Oxford, 1977. *Publications:* articles in Conference and Teaching about Europe. *Recreations:* gardening, France, history, theatre, walking. *Address:* Castle Gates, Merchiston Castle School, Colinton, Edinburgh EH13 0PU. *T:* 031–441 3468.

SPEAKMAN-PITT, William, VC 1951; *b* 21 Sept. 1927; *m* 1st, 1956, Rachel Snitch; one *s*; 2nd, Jill; one *d. Educ:* Wellington Road Senior Boys' Sch., Altrincham. Entered Army as Private. Served Korean War, 1950–53 (VC), King's Own Scottish Borderers. *Recreations:* swimming, and ski-ing.

SPEAR, Harold Cumming, CBE 1976; Member, Electricity Council, 1972–76; *b* 26 Oct. 1909; *yr s* of late Rev. Edwin A. and Elizabeth Spear; *m* 1935, Gwendolen (*née* Richards); one *s* one *d. Educ:* Kingswood Sch., Bath. Asst to Employment Manager, Gramophone Co. Ltd, 1928–33; Labour and Welfare Supervisor, Mitcham Works Ltd, 1933–35; Employment Supervisor, Hoover Ltd, 1935–38; Personnel Manager, Sperry Gyroscope Co. Ltd, 1938–40; appts with British Overseas Airways Corp., finally as Chief Personnel Officer, 1941–59; Dir of Personnel Management, Central Electricity Generating Bd, 1959–72; Mem., Central Arbitration Cttee, 1976–85. Pres., Inst. of Personnel Management, 1969–71; CIPM. *Recreation:* golf. *Address:* The Almonry, Newlands, Pershore, Worcs WR10 1BW. *Club:* Roehampton.

SPEAR, Prof. Walter Eric, PhD, DSc; FRS 1980, FRSE; Harris Professor of Physics, University of Dundee, 1968–90, now Emeritus Professor; *b* 20 Jan. 1921; *s* of David and Eva Spear; *m* 1952, Hilda Doris King; two *d. Educ:* Musterschule, Frankfurt/Main; Univ. of London (BSc 1947, PhD 1950, DSc 1967). Lecturer, 1953, Reader, 1967, in Physics, Univ. of Leicester; Vis. Professor, Purdue Univ., 1957–58. FRSE 1972; FInstP 1962. Max Born Prize and Medal, 1977; Europhysics Prize, 1977; Makdougal-Brisbane Medal, RSE, 1981; Rank Prize, 1988; Mott Award, 1989; Rumford Medal, Royal Soc., 1990. *Publications:* numerous research papers on electronic and transport properties in crystalline solids, liquids and amorphous semiconductors. *Recreations:* literature, music (particularly chamber music), languages. *Address:* Carnegie Laboratory of Physics, University of Dundee, Dundee DD1 4HN. *T:* Dundee (0382) 23181; 323 Blackness Road, Dundee DD2 1SH. *T:* Dundee (0382) 67649.

SPEARING, Prof. Anthony Colin; William R. Kenan Professor of English, University of Virginia, since 1989 (Professor of English, since 1987); *b* 31 Jan. 1936; *s* of Frederick Spearing and Gertrude Spearing (*née* Calnin); *m* 1961, Elizabeth; one *s* one *d. Educ:* Alleyn's Sch., Dulwich; Jesus Coll., Cambridge (BA 1957; MA 1960). University of Cambridge: W. M. Tapp Res. Fellow, Gonville and Caius Coll., 1959–60; Univ. Asst Lectr in English, 1960–64; Supernumerary Fellow, Gonville and Caius Coll., 1960; Official Fellow, Queens' Coll., 1960–87; Univ. Lectr in English, 1964–85; Dir of Studies in English, Queens' Coll., 1967–85; Reader in Medieval English Literature, 1985–87; Life Fellow, Queens' Coll., 1987. Vis. Prof. of English, Univ. of Virginia, 1979–80, 1984. *Publications:* Criticism and Medieval Poetry, 1964, 2nd edn 1972; The Gawain-Poet: a critical study, 1970; Chaucer: Troilus and Criseyde, 1976; Medieval Dream-Poetry, 1976; Medieval to Renaissance in English Poetry, 1985; Readings in Medieval Poetry, 1987; texts, articles in learned jls. *Address:* Department of English, Wilson Hall, University of Virginia, Charlottesville, Va 22903, USA.

SPEARING, George David; Technical Adviser, Institution of Highways and Transportation, 1984–86, retired; *b* 16 Dec. 1927; *s* of late George Thomas and Edith Lydia Anna Spearing; *m* 1951, Josephine Mary Newbould; two *s* one *d. Educ:* Rotherham Grammar Sch.; Sheffield Univ. BEng; MICE, FIHE. RAF, Airfield Construction Br., 1948. Asst Divl Surveyor, Somerset CC, 1951; Asst Civil Engr, W Riding of Yorks CC, 1953; Asst Engr, MoT, 1957; Supt. Engr, Midland Road Construction Unit, 1967; Asst Chief Engr, MoT, 1969; Regional Controller (Roads and Transportation), West Midlands, 1972; Dep. Chief Engr, DoE, 1973; Under Sec., DoE, 1974; Under Sec., Dept of Transport, and Dir Highways Planning and Management, 1974–78; Regional Dir, Eastern Reg., Depts of the Environment and Transport, and Chm., E Anglia Regional Bd, 1978–83. *Publications:* papers in Proc. Instn CE and Jl Instn HE. *Address:* 23 Colburn Avenue, Caterham, Surrey CR3 6HW. *T:* Caterham (0883) 347472.

SPEARING, Nigel John; MP (Lab) Newham South, since May 1974; *b* 8 Oct. 1930; *s* of late Austen and of May Spearing; *m* 1956, Wendy, *d* of Percy and Molly Newman, Newport, Mon; one *s* two *d. Educ:* Latymer Upper School, Hammersmith. Ranks and commission, Royal Signals, 1950–52; St Catharine's Coll., Cambridge, 1953–56. Tutor, Wandsworth School, 1956–68 (Sen. Geography Master, 1967–68); Director, Thameside Research and Development Group, Inst. of Community Studies, 1968–69; Housemaster, Elliott School, Putney, 1969–70. Chairman: Barons Court Labour Party, 1961–63; Hammersmith Local Govt Cttee of the Labour Party, 1966–68. Contested (Lab) Warwick and Leamington, 1964. MP (Lab) Acton, 1970–74; Secretary: Parly Lab. Party Educn Gp, 1971–74; Parly Inland Waterways Gp, 1970–74; Member Select Cttee: Overseas Develt, 1973–74, 1977–79; Members' Interests, 1974–75; Procedure, 1975–79; EEC Legislation, 1979– (Chm., 1983–); Foreign and Commonwealth Affairs, 1980–87; Chair, Parly Affairs Cttee, PLP, 1989–. Vice-Pres., River Thames Soc.; Pres., Socialist Envt and Resources Assoc., 1977–86; Chm., British Anti-Common Market Campaign, 1977–83. Co-opted Mem. GLC Cttees, 1966–73. Mem. Bd, Christian Aid, 1987–91. *Publication:* The Thames Barrier-Barrage Controversy (Inst. of Community Studies), 1969. *Recreations:* rowing, reading. *Address:* House of Commons, SW1. *T:* 071–219 3000.

SPEARMAN, Sir Alexander Young Richard Mainwaring, 5th Bt *cr* 1840; *b* 3 Feb. 1969; *s* of Sir Alexander Bowyer Spearman, 4th Bt, and Martha, *d* of John Green, Naauwpoort, S Africa; *S* father, 1977. *Heir: uncle* Dr Richard Ian Campbell Spearman, FLS, FZS, *b* 14 Aug. 1926. *Address:* 19 Cogill Road, Wynberg, Cape Town, 7800, S Africa.

SPEARMAN, Clement, CBE 1979; HM Diplomatic Service, retired; Ambassador and Consul-General to the Dominican Republic, 1975–79; *b* 10 Sept. 1919; *y s* of late Edward and Clara Spearman; *m* 1950, Olwen Regina Morgan; one *s* two *d. Educ:* Cardiff High School. RN (Air Arm), 1942–46. Entered Foreign (subseq. Diplomatic) Service, 1947; 3rd Sec., Brussels, 1948–49; 2nd Sec., FO, 1949–51; HM Consul, Skoplje, 1951–53; FO, 1953–56; 1st Sec., Buenos Aires, 1956–60; FO, 1960–62; Counsellor, CENTO, Ankara, 1962–65; Reykjavik, 1965–69; FCO, 1969–71; Manila, 1971–74; Toronto, 1974–75. *Recreations:* tennis, swimming. *Address:* 56 Riverview Gardens, SW13 9QZ. *T:* 081–748 9339. *Clubs:* Naval, Roehampton.

SPECTOR, Prof. Roy Geoffrey, MD, PhD; FRCP, FRCPath; Professor of Applied Pharmacology, Guy's Hospital Medical School, 1972–89, now Emeritus; Hon. Physician, Guy's Hospital, since 1967; *b* 27 Aug. 1931; *s* of Paul Spector and Esther Cohen; *m* 1960, Evie Joan Freeman (marr. diss. 1979); two *s* one *d. Educ:* Roundhay Sch., Leeds; Sch. of Medicine, Leeds Univ. (MB, ChB, MD); PhD Lond 1964, Dip. in Biochem. 1966. FRCP 1971; FRCPath 1976; FRSM. Lectr in Paediatric Res. Unit, Guy's Hosp., 1961–67; Guy's Hosp. Medical School, subseq. United Medical and Dental Schools of Guy's and St Thomas's Hosps: Reader in Pharmacology, 1968–71; Sub Dean for Admissions, 1975–89; Chm., Div. of Pharmacology, 1985–88. Vis. Prof. in Clin. Pharmacology, West China Med. Univ., Chengdu, 1986–87. Vice Chm., British Univs' Film Council, 1976–87. *Publications:* (jtly) The Nerve Cell, 1964, 2nd edn 1986; (jtly) Clinical Pharmacology in Dentistry, 1975, 5th edn 1989; (jtly) Mechanisms in Pharmacology and Therapeutics, 1976; (jtly) Aids to Pharmacology, 1980, 2nd edn 1986; (jtly) Textbook of Clinical Pharmacology, 1981, 2nd edn 1986; (jtly) Aids to Clinical Pharmacology and Therapeutics, 1984, 2nd edn 1989; (jtly) Common Drug Treatments in Psychiatry, 1984; Catechism in Clinical Pharmacology Therapeutics, 1986; (jtly) Drugs and Medicines, 1989; contribs to jls on pathology, gen. science, and applied pharmacology. *Recreations:* music, walking. *Address:* 60 Crescent Drive, Petts Wood, Orpington, Kent BR5 1BD. *T:* Orpington (0689) 875885.

SPEDDING, Prof. Colin Raymond William, CBE 1988; Professor of Agricultural Systems, 1975–90, and Pro-Vice-Chancellor, 1986–90, University of Reading; *b* 22 March 1925; *s* of Robert Kewley Spedding and Ilynn Spedding; *m* 1952, Betty Noreen George (*d* 1988); one *s* one *d* (and one *s* decd). *Educ:* London Univ. (External) (BSc 1951; MSc 1953; PhD 1955; DSc 1967). FIBiol 1967, CBiol 1984; FRASE 1984; FIHort 1986; FRAgS 1986. Ilford Ltd, 1940–43; RNVR, 1943–46; Allen & Hanbury, 1947; Grassland Research Institute: joined 1949; Head of Ecology Div., 1967–75; Asst Dir, 1969–72; Dep. Dir, 1972–75; Univ. of Reading: Visiting, then part-time Prof. of Agric. Systems, 1970–75; Head of Dept of Agric. and Horticl., 1975–83; Dean, Faculty of Agriculture and Food, 1983–86; Dir, Centre for Agricl Strategy, 1981–90. Mem., Programme Cttee, Internat. Livestock Centre for Africa, Addis Ababa, 1976–80, Vice Chm., 1980–83; Special Advr, H of C Select Cttee on Agric., 1980–83; Chairman: UK Register of Organic Food Standards Bd, 1987–; Farm Animal Welfare Council, 1988–; Apple and Pear Res. Council, 1989–. Dir, Lands Improvement Gp Ltd., 1986– (Dep. Chm., 1990). President: European Assoc. of Animal Production Study Commn for Sheep and Goat Production, 1970–76; British Soc. for Animal Production, 1979–80; Vice-Pres., Inst. of Biology, 1989–91 (Pres. elect, 1991; Chairman: Agricl Scis Div., 1980; Natural Resources Policy Gp, 1988–). Governor: Royal Agricl Coll., 1982–88; Inst. of Grassland and Envmtl Res. (formerly Inst. for Grassland and Animal Production), 1987–; Mem., Council of Management, PDSA, 1988–. Editor, Agricultural Systems, 1976–88. *Publications:* Sheep Production and Grazing Management, 1965, 2nd edn 1970; Grassland Ecology, 1971; (ed with E. C. Diekmahns) Grasses and Legumes in British Agriculture, 1972; The Biology of Agricultural Systems, 1975; An Introduction to Agricultural Systems, 1979, 2nd edn 1988; (ed) Vegetable Productivity, 1981; (with J. M. Walsingham and A. M. Hoxey) Biological Efficiency in Agriculture, 1981; (ed) Fream's Agriculture, 1983; numerous sci papers in learned jls. *Address:* Vine Cottage, Orchard Road, Hurst, Berks RG10 0SD. *Clubs:* Athenæum, Farmers'.

SPEDDING, David Rolland, CVO 1984; OBE 1980; HM Diplomatic Service; Counsellor, Foreign and Commonwealth Office, since 1987; *b* 7 March 1943; *s* of Lt Col Carlisle Montagu Rodney Spedding and Gwynfydd Joan Llewellyn; *m* 1970, Gillian Leslie Kinnear; two *s. Educ:* Sherborne School; Hertford College, Oxford (MA). Third Sec., FO, 1967; Middle East Centre for Arabic Studies, 1968; Second Sec., Beirut, 1970; Santiago, 1972; First Sec., FCO, 1974; Abu Dhabi, 1978; FCO, 1981–83; Counsellor, Amman, 1983–86. *Recreations:* golf, tennis, reading, walking. *Address:* c/o Foreign and Commonwealth Office, King Charles Street, SW1A 2AH. *Club:* Huntercombe Golf.

SPEED, (Herbert) Keith, RD 1967; MP (C) Ashford, since Oct. 1974; *b* 11 March 1934; *s* of late Herbert Victor Speed and of Dorothy Barbara (*née* Mumford); *m* 1961, Peggy Voss Clarke; two *s* one *d* (and one *s* decd). *Educ:* Greenhill Sch., Evesham; Bedford Modern Sch.; RNC, Dartmouth and Greenwich. Officer, RN, 1947–56; Lt-Comdr RNR, 1964–79. Sales Man., Amos (Electronics) Ltd, 1957–60; Marketing Man., Plysu Products Ltd, 1960–65; Officer, Conservative Res. Dept, 1965–68. MP (C) Meriden, March 1968–Feb. 1974; An Asst Govt Whip, 1970–71; a Lord Comr of HM Treasury, 1971–72; Parly Under-Sec. of State, DoE, 1972–74; Opposition spokesman on local govt, 1976–77, on home affairs, 1977–79; Parly Under Sec. of State for Defence for RN, 1979–81; Mem., Parly Select Cttee on Defence, 1983–87; UK Rep. to Parly Assembly of Council of Europe and WEU, 1987–. Parly Consultant, Professional Assoc. of Teachers, 1982–. Chm., Westminster Communications Ltd, 1982–; Dir, Folkestone and District Water Co., 1986–. *Publications:* Blue Print for Britain, 1965; Sea Change, 1982; contribs to various political and defence jls. *Recreations:* classical music, reading. *Address:* House of Commons, SW1A 0AA. *Club:* Garrick.

SPEED, Sir Robert (William Arney), Kt 1954; CB 1946; QC 1963; Counsel to the Speaker, 1960–80; *b* 1905; *s* of late Sir Edwin Arney Speed; *m* 1929, Phyllis, *d* of Rev. P. Armitage; one *s* one *d. Educ:* Rugby; Trinity College, Cambridge. Called to Bar, Inner Temple, 1928; Bencher, 1961; Principal Assistant Solicitor, Office of HM Procurator-General and Treasury Solicitor, 1945–48; Solicitor to the Board of Trade, 1948–60. *Address:* Upper Culham, Wargrave, Berks RG10 8NR. *T:* Henley-on-Thames (0491) 574271. *Club:* United Oxford & Cambridge University.

SPEELMAN, Sir Cornelis Jacob, 8th Bt *cr* 1686; BA; *b* 17 March 1917; *s* of Sir Cornelis Jacob Speelman, 7th Bt and Maria Catharina Helena, Castendijk; *S* father, 1949; *m* 1972, Julia Mona Le Besque (*d* 1978); *m* 1986, Irene Agnes van Leeuwen; two step *c.* Education Dept, Royal Dutch Army, 1947–49; with The Shell Company (Marketing Service Dept), 1950. Student, Univ. of Western Australia, 1952; formerly Master of Modern Languages at Clifton Coll., Geelong Grammar Sch.; Exeter Tutorial Coll. *Address:* Lake's Edge Villas No 3, Wembley, Perth, WA, Australia.

SPEIGHT, Hon. Sir Graham (Davies), Kt 1983; Judge of the High Court of New Zealand, since 1966; *b* 21 July 1921; *s* of Henry Baxter and Anna May Speight; *m* 1947, Elisabeth Muriel Booth; one *s* one *d. Educ:* Auckland Grammar Sch.; Univ. of Auckland (LLB). Qualified barrister and solicitor, 1942; served 2nd NZ Expeditionary Force, Middle East and Italy, 1943–46: Lieut Royal NZ Artillery, 1943–46; Aide-de-Camp, General B. C. Freyberg, VC (later 1st Baron Freyberg), 1944–45; practising barrister, 1946–66. Justice of Appeal, Fiji, 1980–87; Chief Justice, Cook Is, 1982–87. Chairman: Eden Park Bd; Rothman Foundn. Chancellor, Univ. of Auckland, 1973–79; Hon. LLD Auckland, 1983. *Publication:* (jt ed) Adams: Criminal Law in New Zealand, 1986. *Recreations:* golf, yachting. *Address:* 5/163 Victoria Avenue, Remvera, Auckland 5, New Zealand. *T:* 544 464. *Clubs:* Auckland Golf, Royal New Zealand Yacht Squadron (Auckland) (Cdre 1961–63).

SPEIGHT, Johnny; writer; *b* 2 June 1920; *s* of John and Johanna Speight; *m* 1956, Constance Beatrice Barrett; two *s* one *d. Educ:* St Helen's RC School. Has written for: Arthur Haynes Show; Morecambe and Wise Show; Peter Sellers; Till Death Us Do Part (Screenwriters Guild Award, 1966, 1967, 1968); The Lady is a Tramp (Pye TV Award, 1982); In Sickness and in Health; with Ray Galton: Tea Ladies, 1979; Spooner's Patch, 1979. *Plays:* Compartment (Screenwriters Guild Award, 1962); Playmates; Salesman; Knackers Yard; If There Weren't any Blacks You Would Have to Invent Them (Prague Festival Award, 1969). Evening Standard Drama Award for Best Comedy. *Publications:* It Stands to Reason, 1974; The Thoughts of Chairman Alf, 1974; various scripts. *Recreation:* golf. *Address:* Fouracres, Heronsgate, Chorleywood, Herts. *T:* Chorleywood (09278) 2463. *Clubs:* 21; White Elephant; Stage Golf, Variety Golf, Pinner Hill Golf.

SPEIR, Sir Rupert (Malise), Kt 1964; *b* 10 Sept. 1910; *y s* of late Guy Thomas Speir and late Mary Lucy Fletcher, of Saltoun. *Educ:* Eton Coll.; Pembroke Coll., Cambridge (BA). Admitted Solicitor, 1936. Special Mem., Hops Marketing Board, 1958. Served in Army throughout War of 1939–45; commissioned in Intelligence Corps, Sept. 1939; retired with rank of Lt-Col, 1945. Contested (C) Linlithgow, 1945, Leek, 1950; MP (C) Hexham Div. of Northumberland, 1951–66, retired. Sponsor of: Litter Act, 1958; Noise Abatement Act, 1960; Local Government (Financial Provisions) Act, 1963; Parliamentary Private Secretary: to Minister of State for Foreign Affairs and to Parly Sec., CRO, 1956–59; to Parly and Fin. Sec., Admty and to Civil Lord of Admty, 1952–56. Hon. Fellow, Inst. of Public Cleansing; Vice-Pres., Keep Britain Tidy Group. *Recreations:* golf, shooting. *Address:* Birtley Hall, Hexham, Northumberland NE48 3HL. *T:* Bellingham (0434) 30275.

SPEIRS, Graham Hamilton; *b* 9 Jan. 1927; *s* of Graham Mushet Speirs and Jane (*née* McChesney) *m* 1954, Myra Reid (*née* Mills); one *s* one *d. Educ:* High Sch. of Glasgow Glasgow Univ. (MA 1950, LLB 1952). Anderson, Young and Dickson, Writers, Glasgow, 1950–52; Legal Asst, Dunbarton CC, 1952–54; Sen. Legal Asst, Stirling CC, 1954–59; Depute Sec., then Sec., Assoc. of County Councils in Scotland, 1959–75; Sec., Convention of Scottish Local Authorities, 1975–86, retd. Sec. Gen., Council of European Municipalities (British Section), 1980–84. Member: Scottish Legal Aid Bd, 1986–; Bd, Bield Housing Assoc., 1986–. *Recreation:* golf. *Address:* 3 Dirleton Avenue, North Berwick EH39 4AX. *T:* North Berwick (0620) 2801. *Clubs:* Club de la Fondation Universitaire (Brussels); North Berwick Golf (North Berwick).

SPEIRS, William James McLaren; HM Diplomatic Service, retired; Adviser, Sultanate of Oman; *b* 22 Nov. 1924; *s* of Alec McLaren Speirs and Olivia (*née* Petersen) *m* 1952, Jane Downing; two *s* one *d* (and one *d* decd). *Educ:* Clifton Coll.; Jesus Coll., Cambridge. Served Royal Signals, 1943–47; ADC to Governor of Singapore, 1946–47. HM Diplomatic Service, 1948–79: Rangoon, 1950; Jakarta, 1953; Berlin, 1957; Munich, 1963; Tel Aviv, 1970; Counsellor, FCO, 1979. Gp Security Adviser, Gallaher Ltd, 1979–85. *Recreations:* walking, collecting topographical books. *Address:* 24 Kingswood Firs, Grayshott, Hindhead, Surrey GU26 6ET. *Clubs:* Army and Navy, Special Forces.

SPELLER, Antony; MP (C) North Devon, since 1979; *b* 12 June 1929; *s* of late John and Ethel Speller; *m* 1st, Margaret Lloyd-Jones (marr. diss.); two *s* one *d*; 2nd, 1960, Maureen R. McLellan; one *s* one *d. Educ:* Univ. of London (BScEcon); Univ. of Exeter (BA Social Studies); FHCIMA. Nat. Service, Subaltern, Devonshire Regt, 1951; Major, Devonshire Regt TA, 1965. Nigerian Produce Marketing Boards, 1952–54; Dir, Atlas Ltd, Nigeria, 1955–61. Chairman: Exeter Photo-Copying, 1963–; EuroSpeedy Printing Centres UK, 1988–; Copyshops of SW England, 1989–. Councillor, Exeter CC, 1963–74 (Chairman: Public Works Cttee, 1965–69; Education Cttee, 1971–72). Mem., Select Cttee on Energy, 1982–88; Chairman: All-Party Alternative Energy Gp, 1984–; W Africa Cttee, 1987–; Treasurer: Anglo Nepal Gp, 1988–90; Anglo Korea Gp, 1989–90. Chm., W Country Cons. MPs, 1983–87. *Address:* House of Commons, SW1A 0AA. *T:* 071–219 4589, *Fax:* Barnstaple (0271) 22931. *Clubs:* Carlton; North Devon Yacht (Instow); Lagos Motor Boat (Nigeria).

SPELLER, Maj.-Gen. Norman Henry, CB 1976; Government Relations Adviser, ICL, 1976–86, retired; *b* 5 March 1921; *s* of late Col Norman Speller and Emily Florence Speller (*née* Lambert); *m* 1950, Barbara Eleanor (*née* Earle); two *s. Educ:* Wallingford Grammar School. Commnd RA, 1940; War Service N Africa; transf. to RAOC, 1945; psc 1952; DAA&QMG 39 Inf. Bde, 1953–55; Dirg Staff, Staff Coll., 1955–58; OC 20 Ordnance Field Park, 1958–60; Admin. Staff Coll., 1961; AA&QMG N Ireland, 1961–63; D/SPO COD Donnington, 1964–65; Col AQ 54 (EA) Div./District, 1965–66; AAG AG9, MoD, 1967; DDOS 1 British Corps, 1968–69; idc 1970; Dir of Systems Coordination, MoD, 1971–73; Dir of Ordnance Services, MoD, 1973–76, retired. Col Comdt, RAOC, 1978–83. Chm. Management Cttee, The Royal Homes for Officers' Widows and Daughters (SSAFA), 1987–. *Recreations:* sailing, golf. *Address:* 1 Steeple Close, SW6 3LE. *Club:* Roehampton.

SPENCE, Prof. Alastair Andrew, MD; FCAnaes, FRCSE, FRCPG; Professor of Anaesthetics, University of Edinburgh, since 1984; *b* 18 Sept. 1936; *s* of James Glendinning Spence and Margaret Macdonald; *m* 1963, Maureen Isobel Aitchison; two *s. Educ:* Ayr Acad.; Glasgow Univ. Western Infirmary, Glasgow, 1961–65; MRC Res. Fellow, Univ. of Glasgow Dept of Surgery, 1965–66; Steinberg Res. Fellow and Clinical Asst to Prof. of Anaesthesia, Univ. of Leeds, 1966–69; Sen. Lectr and Head of Dept of Anaesthesia, later Reader and Prof., Western Infirmary, Glasgow, 1969–84. Hon. Consultant Anaesthetist, Lothian Health Bd, 1984–. Pres., Coll. of Anaesthetists, 1991– (Vice-Pres., 1988–91). Editor, British Jl of Anaesthesia, 1973–83 (Chm. Bd, 1983–). *Publications:* books, chapters and papers on anaesthesia and respiratory care. *Recreations:* golf, gardening. *Address:* Harewood, Kilmacolm, Renfrewshire PA13 4HX. *T:* Kilmacolm (050587) 2962; 3/9 Dun-Ard Garden, Oswald Road, Edinburgh EH9 2HZ. *T:* 031–667 0231. *Club:* Caledonian.

SPENCE, Most Rev. Francis John; *see* Kingston (Ontario), Archbishop of.

SPENCE, Captain (Frederick) Michael (Alexander) T.; *see* Torrens-Spence.

SPENCE, Gabriel John; Under Secretary, Department of Education and Science, retired; *b* 5 April 1924; *s* of G. S. and D. A. Spence, Hope, Flints; *m* 1950, Averil Kingston (*née* Beresford); one *s* decd. *Educ:* Arnold House; King's Sch., Chester (King's Schol., Head of School); Wadham Coll., Oxon (Schol.). MA 1949; Stanhope Prize and Proxime, Gibbs Schol., Oxon, 1947; Haldane Essay Prize, Inst. Public Admin, 1959. Civil Service from 1949 (Min. of Works, Science Office, Min. of Housing and Local Govt, DES); Jt Sec., Adv. Council on Scientific Policy, 1959–62; Asst Sec., DES, 1964–73; Sec., Council for Scientific Policy, 1964–67; Under Sec., DES, 1973–81; Dep. Sec., UGC, 1978–81. Admin. Staff Coll., Henley, 1957. Trustee, The Oates Meml and Gilbert White Library and Museum, 1982–. *Recreations:* natural history, photography, golf. *Address:* Old Heath, Hillbrow Road, Liss, Hants. *T:* Liss (0730) 893235.

SPENCE, Malcolm Hugh; QC 1979; a Recorder, since 1985; barrister-at-law, since 1958; *b* 23 March 1934; *s* of late Dr Allan William and Martha Lena Spence; *m* 1967, Jennifer Jane, *d* of Lt-Gen. Sir George Cole, KCB, CBE; one *s* one *d. Educ:* Summer Fields, Oxford; Stowe Sch.; Gonville and Caius Coll., Cambridge (MA, LLM). Gray's Inn: James Mould Schol., Holker Sen. Exhibnr, Lee Prizeman; called to the Bar, 1958; Bencher, 1988. Worcester Regt, First Lieut, 1954. Marshal to Mr Justice McNair, 1957; Pupil to Mr Nigel Bridge (now Lord Bridge of Harwich), 1958; entered chambers of Mr John Widgery, QC, 1958; practises mainly in Town and Country Planning and Compensation for Compulsory Purchase. Assistant Recorder, 1982–85. Chairman of Panel, Examination-in-Public of Hartlepool and Cleveland Structure Plans, 1979–. *Publication:* (jtly) Rating Law and Valuation, 1961. *Recreations:* trout fishing, forestry and golf (Captain: Cambridge University Stymies, 1957; Old Stoic Golfing Soc., 1972; Semi-finalist, Scandinavian Amateur Championship, 1964). *Address:* 23 Ennerdale Road, Kew, Surrey TW9 3PE. *T:* 081–940 9884; Scamadale, Arisaig, Inverness-shire. *T:* Arisaig (06875) 698; 8 New Square, Lincoln's Inn, WC2. *T:* 071–242 4986. *Club:* Hawks (Cambridge).

SPENCE, Prof. Robert, FEng 1990; Professor of Information Engineering, Imperial College of Science, Technology and Medicine, since 1984; *b* 11 July 1933; *s* of Robert Whitehair Spence and Minnie Grace Spence (*née* Wood); *m* 1960, Kathleen Potts; one *s* one *d. Educ:* Hymers Coll., Hull; Hull Coll. of Technology (BScEng Hons London External 1954); Imperial College, London (DIC 1955; PhDEng 1959; DScEng 1983). FIEE, FIEEE, FCGI. Hull Corp. Telephones, 1950–51; General Dynamics/Electronics, Rochester, NY, 1959–62; Department of Electrical Engineering, Imperial College: Lectr, 1962–68; Reader, 1968–84; Prof., 1984–. Chm. and Founding Dir, Interactive Solutions Ltd, 1985–90. FRSA. Chevalier de l'Ordre des Palmes Académiques (France), 1985. *Publications:* Linear Active Networks, 1970; Tellegen's Theorem and Electrical Networks, 1970 (trans. Russian and Chinese); Resistive Circuit Theory, 1974; Modern Network Theory, 1978; Sensitivity and Optimization, 1980; Circuit Analysis by Computer, 1986; Tolerance Design of Electronic Circuits, 1988 (trans. Japanese); numerous papers in learned jls. *Recreations:* steel band (bass player), concrete aspects of gardening. *Address:* 1 Regent's Close, Whyteleafe, Surrey CR3 0AH. *T:* 081–668 3649.

SPENCE, Stanley Brian; His Honour Judge Spence; a Circuit Judge, since 1991; *b* 3 May 1937; *s* of George Henry Spence and Sarah Spence (*née* Hoad); *m* 1961, Victoria Rosaleen Tapper; one *s* one *d. Educ:* Portsmouth Grammar Sch.; Britannia Royal Naval College, Dartmouth. Commissioned Supply and Secretariat Specialisation, RN, 1958; served: HMS Eagle; Staff of FO2 i/c, FEF; Portsmouth; 3rd Frigate Sqdn; HMS St Vincent; legal training, 1966–68; called to the Bar, Middle Temple, 1968; served: HMS Terror, Singapore; Staff of Commander FEF; 8th Frigate Sqdn; Legal Advr to C-in-C Naval Home Command and Flag Officer Spithead, 1974–75; retired from RN, 1975; DJA and AJAG, Office of Judge Advocate General of the Forces (Army and RAF), 1975–90; Recorder of the Crown Court, 1987–91. *Recreations:* maintaining a cottage in France, drinking wine, general DIY, enforced gardening, English history to 1485. *Address:* The Crown Court, Reading, Berks.

SPENCER, family name of **Viscount Churchill** and of **Earl Spencer.**

SPENCER, 8th Earl *cr* 1765; **Edward John Spencer,** LVO 1954; DL; Baron and Viscount Spencer, 1761; Viscount Althorp, 1765; Viscount Althorp (UK), 1905; President, Northamptonshire Association of Boys' Clubs; Deputy President, National Association of Boys' Clubs, since 1980 (Chairman, 1962–80); *b* 24 Jan. 1924; *o s* of 7th Earl Spencer, TD, and Lady Cynthia Elinor Beatrix Hamilton, DCVO, OBE (*d* 1972), *d* of 3rd Duke of Abercorn; *S* father, 1975; *m* 1st, 1954, Hon. Frances Ruth Burke Roche (marr. diss. 1969), *yr d* of 4th Baron Fermoy; one *s* three *d* (and one *s* decd); 2nd, 1976, Raine (*see* Countess Spencer). *Educ:* Eton; RMC Sandhurst and RAC, Cirencester. ADC to Gov. of South Australia, 1947–50; Equerry to the Queen, 1952–54 (to King George VI, 1950–52). Formerly Capt RS Greys. Hon. Col The Northamptonshire Regt (Territorials), T&AVR, 1967–71; a Dep. Hon. Col, The Royal Anglian Regt, 1971–79. Chairman: SGBI, 1962–; The Nene Foundn, 1978–. Trustee: King George's Jubilee Trust; Queen's Silver Jubilee Appeal; Mem. UK Council European Architectural Heritage Year, 1975. CC Northants, 1952–81; High Sheriff of Northants, 1959; DL Northants, 1961; JP Norfolk, 1970. *Publications:* photographs for The Spencers on Spas, by Countess Spencer, 1983; Japan and the East (book of photographs), 1986. *Heir: s* Viscount Althorp, *qv. Address:* Althorp, Northampton NN7 4HG. *T:* (estate office) Northampton (0604) 770006. *Clubs:* Turf, Brooks's, MCC, Royal Over-Seas League.

See also under Royal Family, and Sir R. Fellowes.

SPENCER, Countess; Raine Spencer; *b* 9 Sept. 1929; *d* of late Alexander George McCorquodale and of Dame Barbara Cartland, *qv*; *m* 1st, 1948, Earl of Dartmouth (marr. diss. 1976), *qv*; three *s* one *d*; 2nd, 1976, Earl Spencer, *qv*. Westminster City Councillor, 1954–65 (served on various cttees); Member: for Lewisham West, LCC, 1958–65 (served on Town Planning, Parks, Staff Appeals Cttees); for Richmond upon Thames, GLC, 1967–73; GLC Gen. Purposes Cttee, 1971–73; Chm., GLC Historic Buildings Bd, 1968–71; Mem., Environmental Planning Cttee, 1967–71; Chm., Covent Garden Develt Cttee, 1971–72; Chm., Govt working party on Human Habitat in connection with UN Conf. on Environment, Stockholm (June 1972), 1971–72 (report: How Do You Want to Live?); Chm., UK Exec., European Architectural Heritage Year, 1975. British Tourist Authority: Member: Infrastructure Cttee, 1972–86; Board, 1982–; Chairman: Spas Cttee, 1982–83; Accommodation Cttee (formerly Hotels and Restaurants Cttee), 1983–; Develt Cttee, 1986–; Commended Hotels Panel, 1986–90; Member: English Tourist Bd, 1971–75; Adv. Council, V&A Museum, 1980–83; Cttee of Honour, Business Sponsorship of the Arts, 1980–; Chairman: Cttee, Britain Welcomes Japan, 1990–; Come to Britain Awards, 1990–. Formerly LCC Voluntary Care Cttee Worker, Wandsworth and Vauxhall. Hon. Dr Laws, Dartmouth Coll., USA. *Publications:* What Is Our Heritage?, 1975; The Spencers on Spas (with photographs by Earl Spencer), 1983; Japan and the East (with photographs by Earl Spencer), 1986. *Address:* Althorp, Northampton NN7 4HG. *T:* (estate office) Northampton (0604) 770042, *Fax:* (secretary) Northampton (0604) 770147.

SPENCER, Alan Douglas, CBIM; Director: Owen Owen plc, 1980–86; Johnson Wax (UK) Ltd, 1981–90; Member, East Midlands Electricity Board, 1976–86; *b* 22 Aug. 1920; *s* of Thomas Spencer and late Laura Spencer; *m* 1944, Dorothy Joan Harper; two *d.* *Educ:* Prince Henry's Grammar Sch., Evesham. FBIM 1975. Commnd Gloucester Regt, 1940; served War with Green Howards, 1940–45; Instr, Sch. of Infantry, 1945–47. Joined Boots Co., 1938; rejoined 1947; Dir, 1963–81, Man. Dir, 1975, Vice-Chm., 1978–80, Boots Co. Ltd; Man. Dir, 1977–79, Chm., 1977–80, Boots The Chemist Ltd. Pres., British Retailers' Assoc., 1983–84 (British Multiple Retailers Assoc., 1981–83). Governor, Trent Coll., 1979–90. *Recreation:* shooting. *Address:* Oakwood, Grange Road, Edwalton, Nottingham. *T:* Nottingham (0602) 231722. *Club:* Naval and Military.
See also Sir G. M. Brown.

SPENCER, Comdt Anne Christine; Director, Women's Royal Naval Service, since 1991; ADC to HM Queen, since 1991; *b* 15 Dec. 1938; *d* of late Ernest Spencer and Dora Harrie (*née* Hauxwell). *Educ:* Newlands High Sch.; Yorks Coll. of Housecraft (HCIMA 1959). Direct Entry Officer, WRNS, 1962; commnd 1963; HMS Victory, 1963–64; HMS Dauntless, 1964–66; HMS Terror, Singapore, 1966–68; HMS St Vincent, 1968–69; HMS Nelson, 1969–70; Officer i/c WRNS, HMS Excellent, 1970–73; HMS Pembroke, 1973–74; Mess Manager, RNC, Greenwich, 1974–76; Defence Intelligence Staff, MoD, 1976–78; RNSC, 1978; Directorate of Naval Service Conditions, MoD, 1978–79; Terminology Co-ordinator, NATO HQ Brussels, 1979–81; WRNS Officers Appointer, MoD, 1981–83; Dep. Dir, WRNS, MoD, 1984–86; Naval Dir, NAAFI Bd of Management, 1986–88; Chief Staff Officer (Admin) to Flag Officer, Plymouth, 1988–91. *Recreations:* theatre, art, food, friends, Yorkshire. *Address:* c/o The Naval Secretary, Ministry of Defence, Old Admiralty Building, Spring Gardens, SW1A 2BE. *T:* 071–218 2975.

SPENCER, Prof. Anthony James Merrill, FRS 1987; Professor of Theoretical Mechanics, University of Nottingham, since 1965; *b* 23 Aug. 1929; *s* of James Lawrence Spencer and Gladys Spencer; *m* 1955, Margaret Bosker; three *s.* *Educ:* Queen Mary's Grammar Sch., Walsall; Queens' Coll., Cambridge (MA, PhD, ScD). Research Associate, Brown Univ., USA, 1955–57; Senior Scientific Officer, UKAEA, 1957–60; Lectr, Reader, Prof., Univ. of Nottingham, 1960–. Visiting Professor: Brown Univ., 1966 and 1971; Lehigh Univ., 1978; Univ. of Queensland, 1982. *Publications:* Deformations of Fibre-reinforced Materials, 1972; (jtly) Engineering Mathematics, Vols I and II, 1977; Continuum Mechanics, 1980; Continuum Theory of the Mechanics of Fibre-reinforced composites, 1984; numerous articles in math. and eng. jls. *Address:* 43 Stanton Lane, Stanton-on-the-Wolds, Keyworth, Nottingham NG12 5BE. *T:* Plumtree (06077) 3134; Department of Theoretical Mechanics, The University, Nottingham NG7 2RD. *T:* Nottingham (0602) 484848.

SPENCER, Cyril; Director, Richmond Metal Group, since 1988; *b* 31 Aug. 1924; *s* of Isaac and Lily Spencer; *m* 1971, Wendy Lois Sutton; two *s* one *d* and two step *s* one step *d.* *Educ:* Christ Coll., Finchley; London Univ. (BSc). Joined Evans (Outsizes) Ltd, 1946: Managing Director, 1956; Chairman, 1969; Take Over of Evans by Burton Group Ltd, 1971; Head of Womenswear, 1972; Group Man. Dir and Chief Exec., 1976; Chairman, Burton Menswear, 1977; Exec. Chm., Burton Group Ltd, 1979–81; Chm., Waring and Gillow, 1985–88. *Recreations:* tennis, swimming, golf. *Address:* Eliot House, The Bishops Avenue, N2 0BA.

SPENCER, Cyril Charles, CMG 1951; First Deputy Executive Director, International Coffee Organisation, London, 1964–68; *b* 1 Feb. 1912; *s* of late Albert Edward Spencer, CBE, and Elsie Maud Spencer; *m* 1st, 1938; one *d*; 2nd, 1949, Catherine Dewar Robertson. *Educ:* Royal Grammar Sch., Worcester; St John's Coll., Cambridge (BA 1934). Uganda: Asst Treas., 1935; Asst District Officer, 1937; Asst Financial Sec., 1946; Economic Sec., E Africa High Commission, 1948; Financial Sec., 1948; Acting Chief Sec. at various dates; Acting Governor, July 1951; Chairman: Uganda Lint Marketing Bd; Uganda Coffee Marketing Board; Member: Uganda Electricity Board; Uganda Development Corp.; Comr on Special Duty, Uganda, 1953–61; Sec.-Gen., Inter-African Coffee Organisation, Paris, 1961–64. *Recreations:* golf, fishing. *Address:* Flat No 2, Norton Garth, Sidmouth, Devon EX10 8NY. *Club:* MCC.

SPENCER, Derek Harold, QC 1980; a Recorder of the Crown Court, since 1979; *b* 31 March 1936; *s* of Thomas Harold Spencer and Gladys Spencer (*née* Heslop); *m* 1st, 1960, Joan (*née* Nutter) (marr. diss.); two *s* one *d*; 2nd, 1988, Caroline Alexandra, *yr d* of Dr Franziskus Pärn, Hamburg; one *s.* *Educ:* Clitheroe Royal Grammar Sch.; Keble Coll., Oxford (MA, BCL). 2nd/Lieut King's Own Royal Regt, 1954–56; served in Nigeria. Part-time Law Tutor, Keble Coll., Oxford, 1960–64; called to the Bar, Gray's Inn, 1961 (Holt Scholar; Arden Scholar; Bencher, 1991); in practice SE Circuit. Councillor, London Borough of Camden, 1978–83; Dep. Leader, Conservative Party, London Borough of Camden, 1979–81. Contested (C) Leicester South, 1987; Prospective Parly Cand. (C), Brighton Pavilion, 1991–. MP (C) Leicester South, 1983–87. PPS to: Home Office Ministers, 1986; the Attorney General, 1986–87. Joint Sec. Cons. Parly Legal Affairs Cttee, 1985–87. Vice-Chm., St Pancras North Cons. Assoc., 1977–78; Treas., City of London and Westminster Cons. Assoc., 1990–. *Recreations:* reading, swimming, walking. *Address:* 179 Ashley Gardens, Emery Hill Street, SW1. *T:* 071–828 2517; 5 King's Bench Walk, Temple, EC4. *T:* 071–353 4713. *Club:* Norfolk (Norwich).

SPENCER, Prof. Herbert, MD London, PhD; FRCP, FRCS, FRCPath; Professor of Morbid Anatomy, St Thomas's Hospital Medical School, 1965–80, now Emeritus Professor; *b* 8 Feb. 1915; *s* of Hubert and Edith Maude Spencer; *m* 1940, Eileen Mabel Morgan; one *s* three *d.* *Educ:* Highgate Sch.; St Mary's Hosp. Med. Sch. Served War of 1939–45: Specialist Pathologist, RAMC, 1942–47. Reader in Pathology, St Thomas's Hosp. Med. Sch., 1954–65. Visiting Associate Prof. of Pathology, Yale Univ. Sch. of Med., 1961. Erasmus Wilson Lectr, RCS. Mem., Histopathology Unit, RCS/ICRF. Examiner: RCS, 1958–70; Univ. of London, 1974–77; Univ. of Liverpool, 1972–76; RCP, 1973–. *Publications:* Pathology of the Lung, 1962, 4th edn 1985; Tropical Pathology, 1973; contribs to numerous British and foreign med. jls and books. *Recreation:* woodwork. *Address:* Uplands Cottage, Barnet Road, Arkley, Barnet, Herts EN5 3ET. *T:* 081–449 7030.

SPENCER, Herbert, RDI 1965; DrRCA; Professor of Graphic Arts, Royal College of Art, 1978–85; *b* 22 June 1924; *m* 1954, Marianne Möls, Dordrecht; one *d.* DrRCA 1970; FSIA 1947. Sen. Res. Fellow, RCA, 1966–78, Hon. Fellow, 1985. Internat. Pres., Alliance Graphique Internat., 1971–74; Mem., PO Stamp Adv. Cttee, 1968–; External advr to Design Cttee, British Telecom, 1981–83. Dir, Lund Humphries Publishers Ltd, 1970–88. Consultant: W. H. Smith Ltd (formerly W. H. Smith & Son Ltd), 1973–; Tate Gall., 1981–89; British Rail, 1984–86. Master, Faculty of Royal Designers for Industry, 1979–81; Vice-Pres., RSA, 1979–81. Governor, Bath Acad. of Art, Corsham, 1982–83. One-man exhibitions of paintings: Bleddfa Trust, 1986; Gallery 202, London, 1988–89 and 1990; exhibition of photographs: Zelda Cheatle Gall., London, 1991; photographs in perm. collection of V & A Museum. Editor: Typographica, 1949–67; Penrose Annual, 1964–73. *Publications:* Design in Business Printing, 1952; London's Canal, 1961, 2nd edn 1976; Traces of Man, 1967; The Visible Word, 1968, 2nd edn 1969; Pioneers of Modern Typography, 1969, 2nd edn 1982, German edn 1970, Dutch edn 1983; (with Colin Forbes) New Alphabets A-Z, 1973, French edn 1974; (with Mafalda Spencer) The Book of Numbers, 1975; The Liberated Page, 1987. *Address:* 75 Deodar Road, Putney, SW15 2NU. *T:* 081–874 6352. *Club:* Chelsea Arts.

SPENCER, Air Vice-Marshal Ian James, CB 1963; DFC 1941 (Bar 1943); *b* 6 June 1916; *s* of late Percival James Spencer; *m* 1940, Kathleen Jeune Follis, *d* of late Canon Charles Follis; two *s.* Commissioned 1937. War of 1939–45: bomber sqdns of No 2 Gp (despatches). RAF Staff College, 1948; Air Attaché, Berne, 1950–53; CO, Univ. of London Air Sqdn, 1954–56; Director of Plans Second Allied TAF, 1956–59; commanded RAF Benson, 1959–61; AOA, Transport Command, 1961–64; Dir of Personnel, MoD, 1964–65; AOA, Far East Air Force, 1965–67; retired 1968. Member: CPRE; Franco-British Soc.; Anglo-Swiss Soc.; BIM. Croix de Guerre, 1944; Légion d'Honneur 1945. Interests: internat. affairs, the countryside.

SPENCER, Isobel; *see* Johnstone, I. T.

SPENCER, James; QC 1991; *b* 27 May 1947; *s* of James Henry Spencer and Irene Dulcie (*née* Wilson); *m* 1968, Patricia Johnson; two *s* one *d.* *Educ:* The King's Sch., Pontefract; Univ. of Newcastle upon Tyne (LLB). Admitted solicitor, 1971; called to the Bar, Gray's Inn, 1975. *Recreations:* watching Rugby League, playing golf. *Address:* 11 King's Bench Walk, Temple, EC4Y 7EQ. *T:* 071–353 3337.

SPENCER, Mrs Joanna Miriam, CB 1971; CBE 1961; CompIGasE; *b* 26 July 1910; *d* of late Rev. R. S. Franks; *m* 1954, Frank Woolley Sim Spencer (*d* 1975). *Educ:* Redland High School for Girls, Bristol; Girton College, Cambridge (MA). Asst, Lancs County Library, 1934–35; Asst Librarian: Hull Univ. Coll., 1936–37; Regent Street Polytechnic, 1938; Librarian, Selly Oak Colls, 1938–42. Temp. Civil Servant, Min. of Aircraft Production, 1942–45. Principal, Min. of Supply, 1946; Assistant Secretary, Min. of Supply, 1949–55, Board of Trade, 1955–56, Min. of Power, 1957–64; Under-Secretary: Min. of Power, 1964–69; Min. of Technology, 1969–70; DTI, 1970–72. *Address:* 4 Rostrevor Road, SW19 7AP. *T:* 081–946 4969.

SPENCER, John Loraine, TD; Headmaster, Berkhamsted School, 1972–83; Assistant Director, GAP Activity Projects Ltd, since 1985; *b* 19 Jan. 1923; *s* of late Arthur Loraine Spencer, OBE, and Emily Maude Spencer, OBE, Woodford Green; *m* 1954, Brenda Elizabeth (*née* Loft); two *s* one *d.* *Educ:* Bancroft's Sch.; Gonville and Caius Coll., Cambridge (MA). 1st cl. hons Class. Tripos Pts I and II. War Service in Essex Regt, 1942–45 (Captain, despatches). Asst Master, Housemaster and Sixth Form Classics Master, Haileybury Coll., 1947–61; Headmaster, Lancaster Royal Grammar Sch., 1961–72. Mem. Chairman's Panel, Civil Service Selection Bds, 1985–. Pres., Soc. of Schoolmasters, 1985–. Mem. Council, Lancaster Univ., 1968–72. *Address:* Crofts Close, 7 Aston Road, Haddenham, Bucks HP17 8AF. *T:* Haddenham (0844) 291235. *Club:* Commonwealth Trust.

SPENCER, Sir Kelvin (Tallent), Kt 1959; CBE 1950; MC 1918; Chief Scientist, Ministry of Power, 1954–59, retired; awaiting ecological recycling; *b* 7 July 1898; *s* of Charles Tallent and Edith Ælfrida Spencer; *m* 1927, Phœbe Mary Wills (*d* 1989); one *s.* *Educ:* University College School, Hampstead; City and Guilds Engineering Coll., London Univ. Founder Mem., Scientific and Medical Network. FCGI 1959. Formerly MICE, FRAeS. Hon. LLD Exeter, 1981. *Address:* Wootans, Branscombe, Seaton, Devon EX12 3DN. *T:* Branscombe (029780) 242; Honey Ditches House, Seaton Down Road, Seaton, Devon EX12 2JD.

SPENCER, Michael Gerald; QC 1989; a Recorder, since 1987; *b* 1 Dec. 1947; *s* of Dr Seymour J. G. Spencer and Margaret (*née* Behn); *m* 1969, Catherine Helen (*née* Dickinson); three *s.* *Educ:* Ampleforth Coll.; Hertford Coll., Oxford (MA Hons). Called to the Bar, Inner Temple, 1970. Mem., Oxford Circuit, 1971, Midland and Oxford Circuit, 1972–. Dir, Marina Developments Group, 1989–. Member: Hertford Coll. Boat Club Soc.; Ampleforth Soc. *Publication:* (contrib.) Medical Negligence, 1990. *Recreations:* Rugby football (coaching and referee), sailing, reading, classical music (16th century polyphony). *Address:* 1 Paper Buildings, Temple, EC4Y 7EP. *T:* 071–583 7355. *Clubs:* Pegasus, Bar Yacht, Royal Thames Yacht; Chiltern Rugby Football, Bucks Society of Rugby Football Referees.

SPENCER, Oscar Alan, CMG 1957; economic consultant; Economic Adviser to Government of Seychelles, 1976–83; *b* Eastleigh, Hants, 12 Dec. 1913; *m* 1952, Diana Mary, *d* of late Edmund Walker, Henley-on-Thames; two *s* one *d.* *Educ:* Mayfield Coll., Sussex; London Sch. of Economics. BCom (Hons) 1936. Premchand Prize in Banking and Currency, 1936; John Coleman Postgraduate Scholar in Business Administration, 1936–37. Served War of 1939–45, Lt-Col (despatches twice). HM Colonial Service, 1945–60: Economic Adviser and Development Comr, British Guiana, 1945; also Comr, Interior, 1949; Economic Sec., Malaya, 1950; Member, 1951, Minister, 1955, for Economic Affairs, Economic Adviser, and Head of Economic Secretariat, Fedn of Malaya, 1956–60; UN Technical Assistance Service, 1960–76: Econ. Adviser to Govt of Sudan, 1960–64; Sen. Regl Advr on Public Finance and Hd of Fiscal Section, UN Econ. Commn for Africa, 1964–66; Financial Advr to Govt of Ethiopia, 1966–76; Dep. Chm., Seychelles Nat. Investment Corp., 1979–81. Chm., Central Electricity Board, Malaya, 1952–55, 1956–60; British Guiana Delegate, Caribbean Commn, 1948; Malayan Adviser to Sec. of State. Commonwealth Finance Ministers' Conf., 1951; Leader of Malayan Reps, Internat. Rubber Study Gp, London, 1952, Copenhagen, 1953; Malayan Deleg., Internat. Tin Conf., Geneva, 1953; Adviser to Malayan Delegation, London Constitutional and Financial Confs, 1956 and 1957. Comdr, Order of St Agatha, San Marino, 1944; Knight of the Order of Defenders of the Realm (PMN), Malaya, 1958. *Publications:* The Finances of British Guiana, 1920–45, 1946; The Development Plan of British Guiana, 1947. *Recreations:* swimming, history, fine wines (Confrérie de Tastevin de Bourgogne). *Address:* Gatehurst, Pett, near Hastings, East Sussex. *T:* Hastings (0424) 812197. *Club:* East India, Devonshire, Sports and Public Schools.

SPENCER, Rosemary Jane, CMG 1991; HM Diplomatic Service; Assistant Under-Secretary of State, Foreign and Commonwealth Office, since 1989; *b* 1 April 1941; *d* of Air Vice-Marshal Geoffrey Roger Cole Spencer, CB, CBE, and Juliet Mary Spencer (*née* Warwick). *Educ:* Upper Chine Sch., Shanklin, IoW; St Hilda's Coll., Oxford (BA Hons Modern Langs). Joined Foreign Office, 1962; FO, 1962–65; Third Secretary, Nairobi, 1965–67; Second Sec., FCO, 1967–70; Second Sec., UK Delegn to EEC, and Private Sec. to Hon. Sir Con O'Neill, Official Leader of UK negotiating team, 1970–71; First Sec., Office of UK Permanent Representative to EEC, Brussels, 1972–73; First Sec. (Economic), Lagos, 1974–77; First Sec., Asst Head of Rhodesia Dept, FCO, 1977–80; RCDS 1980; Counsellor (Agric. and Economic Affairs), Paris, 1980–84; Counsellor (External Relations), Office of UK Perm. Rep. to EEC, 1984–87; Hd of European Community Dept (External),

FCO, 1987–89. Chm., Governing Bd, Upper Chine Sch., 1989– (Mem., 1984–). *Recreations:* country walking, travel, domestic arts. *Address:* c/o Foreign and Commonwealth Office, SW1A 2AH. *Clubs:* United Oxford & Cambridge University, Commonwealth Trust.

SPENCER, Sarah Ann; Research Fellow, Institute of Public Policy Research, since 1990; *b* 11 Dec. 1952; *d* of late Dr I. O. B. Spencer and of Dr Elspeth Wilkinson; *m* 1978, Brian Hackland; two *s*. *Educ:* Nottingham Univ. (BA Hons); University Coll. London (MPhil). Researcher, Law Faculty, UCL, 1977–79; Res. Officer, Cobden Trust (Civil Liberties Charity), 1979–84, Dir 1984–85. Trustee: Cobden Trust, 1985–89; Prisoners' Legal Services Foundn, 1985–89. Editor, Rights Jl, 1979–84. *Publications:* Called to Account: police accountability in England and Wales, 1985; (jtly) The New Prevention of Terrorism Act, 1985; The Role of Police Authorities during the Miners' Strike, 1985; (jtly) A British Bill of Rights, 1990. *Address:* 30–32 Southampton Street, WC2E 7HE.

SPENCER, Shaun Michael; QC 1988; a Recorder, since 1985; *b* 4 Feb. 1944; *s* of Edward Michael Spencer, Leeds and Barbara Spencer (*née* Williams); *m* 1971, Nicola, *e d* of F. G. Greenwood, Tockwith, York; two *s* two *d*. *Educ:* Middleton Boys' Sch., Leeds; Cockburn High Sch., Leeds; King's Coll., Newcastle (Univ. of Durham). LLB 1st cl. Hons 1965. Asst Lectr and Lectr in Law, Univ. of Sheffield, 1965–68; called to the Bar, Lincoln's Inn, 1968. *Recreations:* beagling, cookery, books. *Address:* 34A Rutland Drive, Harrogate, N Yorks HG1 2NX.

SPENCER, Thomas Newnham Bayley, (Tom Spencer); Member (C) Surrey West, European Parliament, since 1989; *b* 10 April 1948; *s* of Thomas Henry Newnham Spencer and Anne Hester (*née* Readett-Bayley); *m* 1979, Elizabeth Nan Maltby, *er d* of late Captain Ronald Edgar Bath and of Doreen Lester (*née* Bush); two *d* and one step *d*. *Educ:* Nautical Coll., Pangbourne; Southampton Univ. (BSc Social Sciences). Peat, Marwick, Mitchell & Co., 1972–75; Asst to Dir, Britain-in-Europe Campaign, 1975; J. Walter Thompson & Co., 1975–79. Associate Dean, Templeton Coll., Oxford, 1984–89; Exec. Dir, Eur. Centre for Public Affairs, Oxford, 1987–89. Mem. (C) Derbyshire, European Parlt, 1979–84, contested same seat, 1984; European Democratic Group: Dep. Chief Whip, 1989–; spokesman on: Social Affairs and Employment, 1979–81; External Econ. Relations, 1982–84; Member: External Trade Cttee; Agric. Cttee. Chm., European Union Cons. and Christian-Democratic Students, 1971–73. Mem., Global Legislation for a Balanced Environment. *Recreations:* gardening, swimming, opera. *Address:* Thornfalcon House, Northchapel, West Sussex GU28 9HP. *Clubs:* Carlton, Brass Monkey.

SPENCER-CHURCHILL, family name of **Duke of Marlborough.**

SPENCER CHURCHILL, John George; *see* Churchill, J. G. S.

SPENCER-NAIRN, Sir Robert (Arnold), 3rd Bt *cr* 1933; *b* 11 Oct. 1933; *s* of Sir Douglas Spencer-Nairn, 2nd Bt, TD, and Elizabeth Livingston (*d* 1985), *d* of late Arnold J. Henderson; *S* father, 1970; *m* 1963, Joanna Elizabeth, *d* of late Lt-Comdr G. S. Salt, RN; two *s* one *d*. *Educ:* Eton College; Trinity Hall, Cambridge (MA). *Heir: s* James Robert Spencer-Nairn, *b* 7 Dec. 1966. *Address:* Barham, Cupar, Fife KY15 5RG. *Clubs:* New (Edinburgh); Royal and Ancient Golf (St Andrews).

SPENCER PATERSON, Arthur; *see* Paterson, A. S.

SPENCER-SILVER, Prof. Peter Hele; S. A. Courtauld Professor of Anatomy in the University of London, at the Middlesex Hospital Medical School, 1974–82, now Emeritus; *b* 29 Oct. 1922; 2nd *s* of late Lt-Col J. H. Spencer Silver; *m* 1948, Patricia Anne, *e d* of late Col J. A. F. Cuffe, CMG, DSO, Wyke Mark, Winchester; two *s* one *d*. *Educ:* Harrow School; Middlesex Hosp. Med. School, Univ. of London. MRCS, LRCP; MB, BS London 1945; PhD London 1952. Res., Middlesex Hosp., 1945–46. RAF, 1946–48. Demonstrator in Anatomy, Middlesex Hosp. Med. Sch., 1948–57; Mem. 2nd Internat. Team in Embryology, Hübrecht Laboratory, Utrecht, Netherlands Govt Fellowship, 1956; Reader in Anatomy, Univ. of London, 1957; US Nat. Inst. of Health Post-doctoral Travelling Fellowship, 1961; Carnegie Inst. of Washington, Dept of Embryology, Baltimore, 1961–62; Prof. of Embryology, Mddx Hosp. Medical Sch., 1964–74, Sub-Dean, 1976–81. WHO Vis. Prof., 1976, 1979, 1981; Chm., Dept of Anatomy, King Saud Univ. (Abha Br.), Saudi Arabia, 1984–86. FRSM. *Publications:* An Introduction to Human Anatomy, 1981; contribs to Jl Embryology and Experimental Morphology, Jl Physiol., Jl Anat., Lancet, etc. *Recreation:* music. *Address:* c/o Barclays Bank, Jewry Street, Winchester, Hants SO23 8RG.

SPENCER SMITH, Prof. David, PhD; Hope Professor of Zoology/Entomology, University of Oxford, and Fellow of Jesus College, Oxford, since 1980; *b* 10 April 1934; *s* of Rev. Harry Chadwick Smith and Mary Edith (*née* Lupton); *m* 1st, 1964, Una Scully; one *d*; 2nd, 1974, Sylvia Hyder. *Educ:* Kingswood Sch.; Cambridge Univ. (BA, MA, PhD). Research Fellow: Rockefeller Univ., NY, 1958–61; St Catharine's Coll., Cambridge, 1961–63 (Res. Fellow); Asst Prof., Univ. of Virginia, 1963–66; Associate Prof. of Medicine and Biology, Univ. of Miami, Fla, 1966–70; Prof. of Medicine, Pharmacology and Biology, Univ. of Miami, 1970–80. Trustee, BM (Natural Hist.), 1984–88. Editor, Tissue & Cell, 1969–. *Publications:* Insect Cells: their structure and function, 1968; Muscle: a monograph, 1972; contrib. Standard Catalog of World Coins, annually, 1983–; papers and chapters in books and jls. *Recreations:* the ceramics and coinage of China; the coinage of the Indian subcontinent; cricket. *Address:* Jesus College, Oxford.

SPENCER-SMITH, Sir John Hamilton-, 7th Bt, *cr* 1804; quarantine kennel owner; *b* 18 March 1947; *s* of Sir Thomas Cospatric Hamilton-Spencer-Smith, 6th Bt, and Lucy Ashton, *o d* of late Thomas Ashton Ingram, Hopes, Norton-sub-Hamdon, Somerset; *S* father, 1959; *m* 1980, Christine (separated), *d* of late John Theodore Charles Osborne, Durrington, Worthing, Sussex; one *d*. *Educ:* Milton Abbey; Lackham College of Agriculture, Wilts. *Recreation:* watching polo. *Heir: cousin* Peter Compton Hamilton-Spencer-Smith [*b* 12 Nov. 1912; *m* 1950, Philippa Mary, *yr d* of late Captain Richard Ford; two *s*]. *Address:* Hazel House Quarantine Kennels, Elsted Marsh, Midhurst, West Sussex GU29 0JT. *T:* Midhurst (0730) 813616.

SPENCER WILLS; *see* Wills.

SPENDER, Sir Stephen (Harold), Kt 1983; CBE 1962; CLit 1977; FRSL; poet and critic; Professor of English, University College, London University, 1970–77, now Emeritus; *b* 28 Feb. 1909; *s* of Edward Harold Spender and Violet Hilda Schuster; *m* 1st, 1936, Agnes Marie (Inez), *o d* of late William Henry Pearn; 2nd, 1941, Natasha Litvin; one *s* one *d*. *Educ:* University College Sch.; University College, Oxford (Hon. Fellow, 1973). Co-editor Horizon Magazine, 1939–41; Counsellor, Section of Letters, Unesco, 1947; Co-Editor, Encounter, 1953–67. Fireman in NFS, 1941–44. Hon. Mem. Phi Beta Kappa (Harvard Univ.); Elliston Chair of Poetry, Univ. of Cincinnati, 1953; Beckman Prof., Univ. of California, 1959; Visiting Lecturer, Northwestern Univ., Illinois, 1963; Consultant in Poetry in English, Library of Congress, Washington, 1965; Clark Lectures (Cambridge), 1966; Mellon Lectures, Washington, DC, 1968; Northcliffe Lectures (London Univ.), 1969. Pres., English Centre, PEN Internat., 1975; Vice-Pres., RSL, 1987–. Fellow, Inst. of Advanced Studies, Wesleyan Univ., 1967. Visiting Professor: Univ. of Connecticut, 1969; Vanderbilt Univ., 1979; Emory Univ. Hon. Mem. Amer. Acad. of Arts and Letters and Nat. Inst. of Arts and Letters, 1969. Queen's Gold Medal for Poetry for 1971. Hon. DLitt: Montpellier Univ.; Cornell Coll.; Loyola Univ.; Macerata Univ. *Publications:* 20 Poems; Poems, the Destructive Element, 1934; Vienna, 1934; The Burning Cactus, 1936; Forward from Liberalism, 1937; Trial of a Judge (verse play), 1937; Poems for Spain, 1939; The Still Centre, 1939; Ruins and Visions, 1941; Life and the Poet, 1942; Citizens in War and After, 1945; Poems of Dedication, 1946; European Witness, 1946; The Edge of Being, 1949; essay, in The God that Failed, 1949; World Within World (autobiog.), 1951; Learning Laughter (travels in Israel), 1952; The Creative Element, 1953; Collected Poems, 1954; The Making of a Poem, 1955; Engaged in Writing (stories), 1958; Schiller's Mary Stuart (trans.), 1958 (staged at Old Vic, 1961); The Struggle of the Modern, 1963; Selected Poems, 1965; The Year of the Young Rebels, 1969; The Generous Days (poems), 1971; (ed) A Choice of Shelley's Verse, 1971; (ed) D. H. Lawrence: novelist, poet, prophet, 1973; Love-Hate Relations, 1974; T. S. Eliot, 1975; (ed) W. H. Auden: a tribute, 1975; The Thirties and After, 1978; (with David Hockney) China Diary, 1982; Oedipus Trilogy (trans.), 1983 (staged, Oxford Playhouse, 1983); Journals 1939–1983, 1985; Collected Poems 1930–1985, 1985; The Temple (novel), 1988. *Address:* 15 Loudoun Road, NW8. *Clubs:* Savile, Beefsteak.

See also J. B. Humphries.

SPENDLOVE, Peter Roy, CVO 1981; HM Diplomatic Service, retired; consultant in development and public administration; Chairman, Norfolk Ambulance Service NHS Trust, since 1990; *b* 11 Nov. 1925; *s* of H. A. Spendlove and Florence (*née* Jackson) *m* 1952, Wendy Margaret Valentine; two *s* three *d*. *Educ:* Chichester High Sch.; London Sch. of Economics; Edinburgh and Cambridge Univs. BScEcon Hons 1951. Called to Bar, Middle Temple, 1964. Served HM Forces, 1943–47: commnd, Indian Army/Royal Indian Artillery. LSE, 1948–51; Internat. Law Scholar at The Hague, 1951; Univ. of Cambridge, 1951–52. Apptd District Officer, Kenya, 1952; retired after serving in Provincial Admin and Central Govt, 1964. First Secretary, FCO, 1964; served in E Malaysia, Washington, Manila, FO, Jamaica; Counsellor, Economic, Commercial and Aid, Jakarta, 1977–80; Deputy High Comr, Sri Lanka, 1981–82; Dep. Chief Administrator, Broads Authority (E Anglia), 1983–86. *Recreation:* riding. *Address:* 120 Newmarket Road, Norwich NR4 6SA.

SPENS, family name of **Baron Spens.**

SPENS, 3rd Baron *cr* 1959, of Blairsanquhar, Co. Fife; **Patrick Michael Rex Spens,** FCA; Director: London & Midland Industries; Arlington Securities; *b* 22 July 1942; *s* of 2nd Baron Spens and of Joan Elizabeth, *d* of late Reginald Goodall; *S* father, 1984; *m* 1966, Barbara Janet Lindsay, *d* of Rear-Adm. Ralph Lindsay Fisher, CB, DSO, OBE, DSC; one *s* one *d*. *Educ:* Rugby; Corpus Christi Coll., Cambridge (MA). FCA 1967. Director of Morgan Grenfell & Co. Ltd, 1972–82; Man. Dir, Henry Ansbacher & Co. Ltd, 1983–87. *Heir: s* Hon. Patrick Nathaniel George Spens, *b* 14 Oct 1968. *Address:* Gould, Frittenden, Kent. *Clubs:* Carlton, City of London.

SPENS, Colin Hope, CB 1962; FICE, FIWEM; *b* 22 May 1906; *er s* of late Archibald Hope Spens, Lathallan, Fifeshire and Hilda Constance Hooper; *m* 1941, Josephine, *d* of late Septimus Simond; two *s* one *d*. *Educ:* Lancing Coll.; Imperial College of Science and Technology. Consulting engineering experience, 1928–39. Served War of 1939–45 with Royal Signals, 1939–41; PA to Director of Works in Ministry of Works, 1941–44; Engineering Inspectorate of Min. of Health, 1944–51, Min. of Housing and Local Govt, 1951–60; Chief Engineer, Min. of Housing and Local Govt, 1960–67. Senior Consultant, Rofe, Kennard and Lapworth, 1967–76; Dep. Chm., Sutton District Water Co., 1971–83. Pres., IWES, 1974–75. Hon. FInstPHE. *Address:* 10 Ashbourne Court, Burlington Place, Eastbourne BN21 4AX. *T:* Eastbourne (0323) 638742.

SPENS, John Alexander, RD 1970; WS; Partner, Maclay, Murray & Spens, Solicitors, Glasgow and Edinburgh, since 1960; *b* 7 June 1933; *s* of Thomas Patrick Spens and Nancy F. Spens (*née* Anderson); *m* 1961, Finella Jane, *d* of Donald Duff Gilroy; two *s* one *d* (and one *s* decd). *Educ:* Cargilfield; Rugby School; Corpus Christi College, Cambridge (BA); Glasgow Univ. (LLB). WS 1977. Director: Scottish Amicable Life Assurance Soc., 1963– (Chairman, 1978–81); Standard Property Investment PLC, 1977–87. Carrick Pursuivant, 1974–85; Albany Herald, 1985–. *Recreations:* sailing, countryside and opera. *Address:* The Old Manse, Gartocharn, Dunbartonshire G83 8RX. *T:* Gartocharn (038983) 329. *Clubs:* Naval; Western (Glasgow).

SPENSLEY, Philip Calvert, DPhil; CChem, FRSC; Editor, Tropical Science, since 1984; Director, Tropical Products Institute, Overseas Development Administration, Foreign and Commonwealth Office, 1966–81; *b* 7 May 1920; *s* of late Kent and Mary Spensley, Ealing; *m* 1957, Sheila Ross Fraser, *d* of late Alexander and Annie Fraser, Forres, Scotland; one *s* three *d*. *Educ:* St Paul's Sch., London; Keble Coll., Oxford (MA, BSc). Technical Officer, Royal Ordnance Factories, Ministry of Supply, 1940–45; Research Chemist, Nat. Inst. for Medical Research, MRC, 1950–54; Scientific Secretary, Colonial Products Council, Colonial Office, 1954–58; Asst Director, Tropical Products Inst., DSIR, 1958–61, Dep. Director, 1961–66, Director, 1966. Freelance consultant in post-harvest sci. and technol. and orgn of R&D, 1981–84. Mem., Panel of Chairmen, Sci. Div., Civil Service Commn, 1982–86; Mem. Council, Royal Institution, 1985–88 (Chm., Cttee of Visitors, 1959). Member: FAO/WHO/Unicef Protein Adv. Gp, 1968–71; Cttee on Needs of Developing Countries, Internat. Union of Food Science and Technology, 1970–78; Food Science and Technol. Bd, MAFF/ARC/Dept of Agric. and Fisheries for Scotland Jt Consultative Organisation, 1973–79; UK Rep., CENTO Council for Scientific Educn and Research, 1970–78. Member: Internat. Cttee, RSC, 1982–87; British Nat. Cttee for Chemistry, Royal Soc., 1986–89. Hon. Treas., Keble Assoc., 1987–. Received MRC/NRDC Inventors Awards, 1963 and 1971. Freeman, City of London, 1951. *Publications:* Tropical Products Institute Crop and Product Digests, vol. 1, 1971; various research and review papers, particularly in the fields of chemotherapeutic substances, plant sources of drugs, aflatoxin (name coined 1962), food losses, and work of Tropical Products Inst.; patents on extraction of hecogenin from sisal. *Recreations:* house and garden design, DIY, travel. *Address:* Hardy House, 96 Laurel Way, Totteridge, N20 8HU. *T:* 081–445 7895. *Clubs:* Athenæum, Royal Automobile; Island Cruising (Salcombe).

SPERRY, Rt. Rev. John Reginald, CD 1987; Bishop of The Arctic, 1974–90; National President, Canadian Bible Society, since 1990; *b* 2 May 1924; *s* of William Reginald Sperry and Elsie Agnes (*née* Priest); *m* 1952, Elizabeth Maclaren; one *s* one *d* (and one *d* decd). *Educ:* St Augustine's Coll., Canterbury; King's Coll., Halifax (STh). Deacon, 1950; priest, 1951; St Andrew's Mission, Coppermine, NWT, 1950–69; Canon of All Saints' Cathedral, Aklavik, 1957–59; Archdeacon of Coppermine, 1959–69; Rector of St John's, Fort Smith, NWT, 1969–73; Rector of Holy Trinity, Yellowknife, NWT, 1974. Hon. DD: Coll. of Emmanuel, St Chad, 1974; Wycliffe Coll., Toronto, 1979. *Publications:* translations into Copper Eskimo: Canadian Book of Common Prayer (1962), 1969; Four Gospels and Acts of the Apostles, 1972. *Address:* 1 Dakota Court, Yellowknife, Northwest Territories, X1A 2A4, Canada. *T:* 403–873–6163.

SPERRY, Prof. Roger Wolcott, PhD; Hixon Professor of Psychobiology, 1954–84, Trustee Professor Emeritus, since 1984, California Institute of Technology; *b* 20 Aug. 1913; *s* of Francis Bushnell Sperry and Florence Kraemer Sperry; *m* 1949, Norma Gay Deupree; one *s* one *d*. *Educ:* Oberlin Coll. (Amos C. Miller Schol.; AB English 1935; MA Psych. 1937); Univ. of Chicago (PhD Zoology 1941). Nat. Research Council Fellow, Harvard Univ., 1941–42; Biology Research Fellow, Harvard Univ. at Yerkes Labs of Primate Biology, 1942–46; Asst Prof., Dept of Anatomy, Univ. of Chicago, 1946–52; Section Chief, Neurolog. Diseases and Blindness, NIH, 1952–53; Assoc. Prof. of Psychology, Univ. of Chicago, 1952–53. For. Mem. of Royal Soc., 1976–; Fellow: Amer. Psycholog. Assoc. (Distinguished Scientific Contribn Award, 1971); Amer. Assoc. for Advancement of Sci.; Member: Nat. Acad. of Scis, 1960–; Pontifical Acad. of Scis, 1978–; Amer. Philosophical Soc., 1974– (Karl Lashley Award, 1976); Amer. Acad. of Arts and Scis, 1963–; (Hon.) Amer. Neurolog. Assoc., 1974–; Internat. Neuropsychology Soc.; Amer. Assoc. for Anatomists; Soc. for Developmental Biology; Amer. Physiological Soc.; Psychonomic Soc.; Soc. for Neuroscience (Ralph Gerard Award, 1979); Internat. Brain Res. Org.; Internat. Soc. of Developmental Biologists; Soc. of Sigma XI; Amer. Assoc. of Univ. Profs; For. Mem., USSR Acad. of Sciences, 1988. Hon. Dr of Science: Cambridge, 1972; Chicago, 1976; Kenyon Coll., 1979; Rockefeller, 1980; Oberlin Coll., 1982; Howard Crosby Warren Medal, Soc. of Exper. Psychologists, 1969; Calif. Scientist of the Year Award, Calif. Mus. of Sci. and Industry, 1972; (jtly) William Thomson Wakeman Res. Award, Nat. Paraplegia Foundn, 1972; Passano Award in Med. Sci., 1973; Claude Bernard Science Journalism Award, 1975; (jtly) Wolf Prize in Medicine, 1979; Internat. Visual Literacy Assoc. Special Award, 1979; Albert Lasker Med. Res. Award, 1979; Golden Plate Award of Amer. Acad. of Achievement, 1980; (jtly) Nobel Prize in Physiology or Medicine, 1981; Realia Award, Inst. for Advanced Philosophic Res., 1985; Nat. Medal of Science, USA, 1989. *Publications:* Science and Moral Priority, 1982; many contribs to scientific jls, chapters in books, and scattered theoretical, philosophical and humanistic articles. *Recreations:* paleontology, camping, ceramics and sculpture. *Address:* 3625 Lombardy Road, Pasadena, California 91107, USA. *T:* (818) 793–0117. *Club:* Athenæum of Pasadena (Calif.).

SPERRYN, Simon George; Chief Executive, Manchester Chamber of Commerce and Industry, since 1986; *b* 7 April 1946; *s* of George Roland Neville Sperryn and Wendy Sperryn (*née* King). *Educ:* Rydal School; Pembroke College, Cambridge (MA); Cranfield School of Management (MBA). Birmingham Chamber of Commerce and Industry, 1967–77; Chief Exec., Northants Chamber of Commerce and Industry, 1979–85. Regional Sec., NW Region Chambers of Commerce Council, 1986–; Member: Exec. Cttee, British Chambers of Commerce Executives, 1984–; Nat. Council, ABCC, 1986–; Exec. Cttee, Manchester Business Venture, 1986–; Director: Manchester TEC, 1990–; Manchester Phoenix Initiative, 1988–; Chm., Manchester Camerata, 1989–. Governor, Salford Coll. of Technol., 1988–. FBIM. *Recreations:* singing, reading, walking. *Address:* Manchester Chamber of Commerce and Industry, 56 Oxford Street, Manchester M60 7HJ. *T:* 061–236 3210; Lilac Cottage, Wincle, Macclesfield, Cheshire SK11 0QE. *T:* Wincle (0260) 620. *Club:* St James's (Manchester).

SPICER, Clive Colquhoun; Honorary Research Fellow, Exeter University, 1979–88; Director, Medical Research Council Computer Unit, 1967–79; *b* 5 Nov. 1917; *s* of John Bishop Spicer and Marion Isobel Spicer; *m* 1st, 1941, Faith Haughton James, MB (marr. diss. 1979); one *s* two *d*; 2nd, 1979, Anne Nolan. *Educ:* Charterhouse Sch.; Guy's Hospital. Operational research on war casualties, 1941–46; Hon. Sqdn Leader, RAF; Staff, Imperial Cancer Research Fund, 1946–49; Dept of Biometry, University Coll., London, 1946–47; Public Health Laboratory Service, 1949–59; WHO Fellow, Univ. of Wisconsin, 1952–53; Vis. Scientist, US Nat. Insts of Health, 1959–60; Statistician, Imperial Cancer Research Fund, 1960–62; Chief Medical Statistician, General Register Office, 1962–66. Main interest has been in application of mathematical methods to medical problems. *Publications:* papers in scientific journals on epidemiology and medical statistics. *Recreations:* sailing, reading. *Address:* Churchtown, Michaelstow, St Tudy, Bodmin PL30 3PD.

SPICER, Sir James (Wilton), Kt 1988; MP (C) Dorset West since Feb. 1974; a Vice Chairman, Conservative Party Organisation, and Chairman of the International Office, since 1985; company director; *b* 4 Oct. 1925; *s* of James and Florence Clara Spicer; *m* 1954, Winifred Douglas Shanks; two *d*. *Educ:* Latymer. Regular army, 1943–57, retd (Major); commnd Royal Fusiliers, 1944; Para. Regt, 1951–57. Nat. Chm., CPC, 1968–71. Mem., Select Cttee on Agriculture, 1984–85. Mem. (C) European Parlt, 1975–84 (elected Mem. for Wessex, 1979–84); Chief Whip, European Democratic Gp, 1975–79; Chairman: Cons. Group for Europe, 1975–78 (Dir, 1972–74); Conservatives Abroad, 1986–. *Recreations:* swimming, tennis. *Address:* Whatley, Beaminster, Dorset. *T:* Beaminster (0308) 862337. *Club:* Naval and Military.

SPICER, Michael; *see* Spicer, W. M. H.

SPICER, (Sir) Peter James, 4th Bt *cr* 1906 (but does not use the title); retired; *b* 20 May 1921; *s* of Captain Sir Stewart Dykes Spicer, 3rd Bt, RN, and Margaret Grace (*née* Gillespie) (*d* 1967); *S* father, 1968; *m* 1949, Margaret, *e d* of Sir Steuart Wilson (*d* 1966), and Ann Mary Grace, afterwards Lady Boult (*d* 1989); one *s* three *d* (and one *d* decd). *Educ:* Winchester Coll. (Schol.); Trinity Coll., Cambridge (Exhibr); Christ Church, Oxford (MA). Served War of 1939–45 (despatches, 1944); Royal Sussex Regt, then RN (Temp. Lieut, RNVR). Trinity Coll., Cambridge, 1939–40; Christ Church, Oxford, 1945–47. Member of publishing staff, Oxford University Press, 1947–81. Co-opted Member, Educn Cttee of Oxfordshire CC, 1959–74 (Chairman, Libraries Sub-Cttee, 1961–74). Congregational Rep., British Council of Churches, 1963–72; Chm., Educational Publishers' Council, 1976–78. Trustee, Mansfield Coll., Oxford, 1988–. *Recreations:* theology, gardening, walking, sailing, music, large family gatherings. *Heir:* *s* Dr Nicholas Adrian Albert Spicer, *b* 28 Oct. 1953. *Address:* Salt Mill House, Fishbourne, Chichester PO19 3JN. *T:* Chichester (0243) 782825.

SPICER, (William) Michael (Hardy); MP (C) South Worcestershire since Feb. 1974; *b* 22 Jan. 1943; *s* of late Brig. L. H. Spicer; *m* 1967, Patricia Ann Hunter; one *s* two *d*. *Educ:* Wellington Coll.; Emmanuel Coll., Cambridge (MA Econs). Asst to Editor, The Statist, 1964–66; Conservative Research Dept, 1966–68; Dir, Conservative Systems Research Centre, 1968–70; Man. Dir, Economic Models Ltd, 1970–80. PPS, Dept of Trade, 1979–81; Parly Under Sec. of State, 1984–87, and Minister for Aviation, 1985–87, Dept of Transport; Parly Under Sec. of State (Minister for Coal and Power), Dept of Energy, 1987–90; Minister of State (Minister for Housing and Planning), DoE, 1990. A Vice-Chm., 1981–83, Dep. Chm., 1983–84, Conservative Party. *Publications:* Final Act (political novel), 1981; Prime Minister Spy (novel), 1986; Cotswold Manners (novel), 1989; Cotswold Murders (novel), 1990; contrib. Jl Royal Inst. Public Admin. *Recreations:* painting, tennis, writing, travelling. *Address:* House of Commons, SW1A 0AA. *T:* 071–219 3000.

SPICKERNELL, Rear-Adm. Derek Garland, CB 1974; CEng, FIMechE, FIProdE, CBIM, FIMarE; Chairman: Ritec (UK) Ltd, since 1987; Jeniva Landfill PLC, since 1987; Director General, British Standards Institution, 1981–86 (Technical Director, 1976–81); *b* 1 June 1921; *s* of late Comdr Sidney Garland Spickernell, RN, and Florence Elizabeth (*née* March); *m* 1946, Ursula Rosemary Sheila Money; one *s* one *d* (and one *s* decd). *Educ:* RNEC, Keyham. Served War, HM Ships Abdiel, Wayland, and Engr Officer HM Submarine Statesman, 1943–45. Engr Officer HM Submarines Telemachus, Tudor and Alcide, 1945–50; Submarine Trials Officer, 1950–51; Engrg Dept, HM Dockyard, Portsmouth, 1951–53; SEO: Portsmouth Frigate Sqdn, 1954–55; 2nd Submarine Sqdn, 1956–57; Supt, ULE, Bournemouth, 1958–59; Dep. Captain Supt, AUWE, Portland, 1959–62; Dep. Manager, Engrg Dept, HM Dockyard, Portsmouth, 1962–64; in command, HMS Fisgard, 1965–66; Dep. Dir, Naval Ship Production, 1967–70; Dep. Chief Exec., Defence Quality Assurance Bd, 1970–71; Dir-Gen., Quality Assurance, MoD (PE), 1972–75. Dir, James Martin Associates PLC, 1986–90; Bd Mem., Southern Water, 1987–89. Chm., Nat. Council for Quality and Reliability, 1973–75; A Vice-Pres., Inst. of Quality Assurance, 1974– (Hon. FIQA); Vice-Pres., Internat. Orgn for Standardisation, 1985–87; Bd Mem. for Internat. Affairs, BSI, 1986–87; Dir, Turkish Standards Inst., 1987–90; Member: Internat. Acad. of Quality Assurance, 1977–; Design Council, 1984–87; Council, Cranfield Inst. of Technol. FRSA. *Publications:* papers on Quality Assurance. *Recreation:* golf. *Clubs:* English-Speaking Union, Institute of Directors; Royal Fowey Yacht.

SPIEGL, Fritz; musician, writer, broadcaster; *b* 27 Jan. 1926; *s* of Rudolf Spiegl and Josefine Geiringer; *m* 1st, 1952, Bridget Fry; three *d*; 2nd, 1976, Ingrid Frances Romnes. *Educ:* Magdalen College Sch.; Royal Academy of Music (ARAM, FRAM 1986). Designer/typographer, Colman Prentis & Varley, 1941–46; Principal Flautist, Royal Liverpool Philharmonic, 1948–63; occasional spare flautist: RPO; CBSO; Hallé; BBC NSO; Founder/Conductor, Liverpool Music Group, Liverpool Wind Ensemble, 1949–; Director, The Spieglers, 1975–. Columnist: Liverpool Daily Post, 1970–; Classical Music, 1979–81; contributor to: Daily Telegraph; Guardian; Independent; broadcaster in various capacities. *Publications:* various edns of music; What the Papers Didn't Mean to Say, 1964; Lern Yerself Scouse, 1965; ABZ of Scouse, 1967; The Growth of a City, 1967; Liverpool Ballads, 1967; The Liverpool Manchester Railway, 1970; Slavers and Privateers, 1970; A Small Book of Grave Humour, 1971; Dead Funny, 1982; Keep Taking the Tabloids, 1983; Music Through the Looking-Glass, 1984; The Joy of Words, 1986; Fritz Spiegl's In-words & Out-words, 1987; Mediaspeak/Mediawrite, 1989; contrib. Grove's Dictionary of Music. *Recreations:* printing, cooking, inventing and several deadly sins. *Address:* 4 Windermere Terrace, Liverpool L8 3SB. *T:* 051–727 2727.

SPIELBERG, Steven; American film director and producer; *b* 18 Dec. 1947; *s* of Arnold Spielberg and Leah (*née* Posner); *m* 1985, Amy Irving; one *s*. *Educ:* Calif State Coll. TV Director, Universal Pictures, 1968. Founder, Amblin Entertainment. Fellow, BAFTA, 1986. *Films include: directed:* Sugarland Express, 1974; Jaws, 1975; Close Encounters of the Third Kind, 1977; 1941, 1979; Raiders of the Lost Ark, 1981; (also produced) E.T., 1982; (also produced) Twilight Zone—the movie, 1983; Indiana Jones and the Temple of Doom, 1984; The Color Purple, 1985; Empire of the Sun, 1988; Indiana Jones and the Last Crusade, 1989; *produced:* I Wanna Hold Your Hand, 1978; (also co-wrote) Poltergeist, 1982; Gremlins, 1984; Goonies, 1985; Young Sherlock Holmes, 1985; Back to the Future, 1986; Who Framed Roger Rabbit, 1988; Always, 1990. *Publication:* (jtly) Close Encounters of the Third Kind. *Address:* Amblin Entertainment, 100 Universal City Plaza, Universal City, Calif 91608, USA.

SPIERS, Donald Maurice, CB 1987; TD 1966; Controller Aircraft, and Head of Profession Defence Science and Engineering, Ministry of Defence, since 1989; *b* 27 Jan. 1934; *s* of Harold Herbert Spiers and Emma (*née* Foster); *m* 1958, Sylvia Mary Lowman; two *s*. *Educ:* Raynes Park County Grammar Sch.; Trinity Coll., Cambridge (MA). CEng, FRAeS. Commnd RE, 1952–54. de Havilland Engine Co., Hatfield, 1957–60; joined Air Min. as SSO, 1960; operational res. on deterrence, 1960–63; trials and analysis, Aden and Radfan, 1964; Kestrel evaluation trial, 1965; Scientific Adviser to FEAF, Singapore, 1967–70; Asst Chief Scientist (RAF), MoD, 1972–77; Asst Dir, Mil. Aircraft Projs, MoD (PE), 1978; Dir of Aircraft Post Design Services, MoD (PE), 1979–81; Dir Gen. Aircraft 1, MoD (PE), 1981–84; Dep. Controller Aircraft, MoD (PE), 1984–86; Controller of R&D Estabts, later of Estabts, Res. and Nuclear Programmes, and Hd of Profession Defence Engrg Service, MoD, 1986–89. Gold Medal, RAeS, 1989. *Recreations:* flying aeroplanes, mending cars. *Address:* Ministry of Defence, Whitehall, SW1. *Club:* Royal Air Force.

SPIERS, Prof. Frederick William, CBE 1962; Professor of Medical Physics, University of Leeds, 1950–72, now Emeritus; *b* 29 July 1907; *er s* of Charles Edward and Annie Spiers; *m* 1936, Kathleen M. Brown; one *d*. *Educ:* Prince Henry's Grammar Sch., Evesham; University of Birmingham. 1st Class Hons Physics, 1929; PhD 1932; DSc 1952. Anglo-German Exchange Scholar, Univ. of Munich, 1930. Demonstrator in Physics, University of Leeds, 1931; Senior Physicist, General Infirmary, Leeds, 1935; Vis. Lecturer, Washington Univ., St Louis, USA, 1950; Chief Regional Scientific Advr for Civil Defence, NE Region, 1952–77; Hon. Director: MRC Environmental Radiation Unit, 1959–72; MRC Regional Radiological Protection Service, Leeds, 1963–70; Consultant to the Dir, NRPB, 1972–87; Pt-time Dir, Bone Dosimetry Res., Univ. of Leeds, 1972–78. President, British Inst. of Radiology, 1955–56; Chairman: Hospital Physicists Assoc., 1944–45; British Cttee on Radiation Units and Measurements, 1967–77; Home Defence Scientific Adv. Standing Conference, 1972–77; Hon. Mem., Royal Coll. of Radiologists; Member: MRC Protection Cttee; Radio-active Substances Adv. Cttee, 1960–70; Internat. Commn on Radiation Units and Measurements, 1969–73; Statutory Adv. Cttee to National Radiological Protection Bd; Adv. Council on Calibration and Measurement, 1973–77. Silvanus Thompson Meml Lectr, British Inst. Radiology, 1973; Douglas Lea Meml Lectr, Inst. of Physical Sciences in Medicine, 1987. Vis. Scientist, Argonne Nat. Laboratory, Univ. of Chicago, 1979. Röntgen Prize, 1950; Barclay Medal, 1970; Silver Jubilee Medal, 1977. FInstP 1970. *Publications:* Radioisotopes in the Human Body, 1968; articles on radiation physics and radiobiology in scientific journals; contribs in: British Practice in Radiotherapy, 1955; Radiation Dosimetry, 1956, 1969; Encyclopedia of Medical Radiology, 1968; Manual on Radiation Haematology, 1971. *Recreations:* photography, music, gardening. *Address:* Lanesfield House, Old Lane, Bramhope, near Leeds LS16 9AZ. *T:* Leeds (0532) 842680.

SPIERS, Ven. Graeme Hendry Gordon; Archdeacon of Liverpool, 1979–91, Archdeacon Emeritus, since 1991; *b* 15 Jan. 1925; *s* of Gordon and Mary Spiers; *m* 1958, Ann Chadwick; two *s*. *Educ:* Mercers Sch.; London College of Divinity. Westminster Bank, 1941–49; served RNVR, 1943–47. Deacon 1952, Priest 1953; Curate of Addiscombe, 1952–56; Succentor of Bradford Cathedral, 1956–58; Vicar of Speke, 1958–66; Vicar of Aigburth, 1966–80 and Rural Dean of Childwall, 1975–79. Hon. Canon, Liverpool Cathedral, 1977. *Recreation:* gardening. *Address:* 19 Barkfield Lane, Formby, Merseyside L37 1LY. *T:* Formby (07048) 72902.

SPIERS, Air Cdre Reginald James, OBE 1972; FRAeS; Marketing Executive, GEC (formerly Marconi) Avionics, 1984–91; *b* 8 Nov. 1928; *s* of Alfred James Oscar and Rose Emma Alice Spiers; *m* 1956, Cynthia Jeanette Williams; two *d*. *Educ:* Haberdashers' Aske's Sch.; RAF Coll., Cranwell. FRAeS 1975. Commissioned 1949; 247 and 64 Fighter Sqdns,

1950–54; Graduate, Empire Test Pilots' Sch., 1955; Fighter Test Sqdn, A&AEE, 1955–58; CO 4 Fighter Sqdn, 1958–61; PSO to C-in-C RAF Germany, 1961–63; RAF Staff Coll., 1964; FCO, 1965–67; CO RAF Masirah, 1967–68; Chief Test Flying Instructor, ETPS, 1968–71; Air Warfare Course, 1972; Air Secretary's Dept, MoD, 1972–73; MA to Governor of Gibraltar, 1973–75; CO Experimental Flying Dept, RAE Farnborough, 1975–78; Director, Defence Operational Requirements Staff, MoD, 1978–79; Comdt, A&AEE, Boscombe Down, 1979–83, retd. *Recreations:* shooting, aviation. *Address:* Barnside, Chalkcroft Lane, Penton Mewsey, near Andover, Hants SP11 0RQ. *T:* Weyhill (0264) 772376. *Club:* Royal Air Force.

SPIERS, Ronald Ian; Under-Secretary-General, Department of Political and General Assembly Affairs and Secretariat Services, United Nations, since 1989; *b* 9 July 1925; *s* of Tomas H. and Blanca De P. Spiers; *m* 1949, Patience Baker; one *s* three *d. Educ:* Dartmouth Coll., New Hampshire (BA); Princeton Univ. (Master in Public Affairs, PhD). Mem., US Delegn to UN, 1956–60; US Department of State: Dir, Office of Disarmament and Arms Control, 1960–62; Dir, Office of NATO Affairs, 1962–66; Political Counsellor, London, 1966–69; Asst Sec. of State, Politico-Military Affairs, 1969–73; Ambassador to the Bahamas, 1973–74; Minister, London, 1974–77; Ambassador to Turkey, 1977–80; Dir, Bureau of Intelligence and Research, Dept of State, 1980–81; Ambassador to Pakistan, 1981–83; Under Sec. of State for Management, 1983–89. *Recreations:* swimming, music, theatre-going, gardening. *Address:* United Nations, Room S-3862, New York, NY 10017, USA.

SPIKINGS, Barry Peter; President and Chief Operating Officer: Nelson Holdings International, since 1986; Nelson Entertainment Inc., since 1986; Joint Chairman, Nelson Vending Technology Ltd, since 1986; *b* Boston, Lincs, 23 Nov. 1939; *m* 1st, 1962, Judith Anne Spikings; one *s* one *d*; 2nd, 1978, Dorothy Spikings; two step *d. Educ:* Boston Grammar School. Joint Managing Director: British Lion Films Ltd, 1973–75; EMI Films Ltd, 1975–78; Director, EMI Films Inc., 1975–78; Chm. and Chief Exec. Officer, EMI Film and Theatre Corp., 1978–80; Chm., Elstree Studios, 1978–82; Chm. and Chief Exec., Thorn EMI Films Worldwide, 1980–82. Oscar award as Producer of Best Picture of the Year, for The Deer Hunter, Acad. of Motion Picture Arts and Sciences, 1979. *Recreation:* making films. *Address:* Nelson Entertainment Inc., 335 North Maple Drive, Suite 350, Beverly Hills, Calif 90210, USA. *Club:* Mark's.

SPILLER, John Anthony Walsh, MBE 1979; County Liaison Officer, Devonshire, PHAB Organisation UK, since 1990; *b* 29 Dec. 1942; *s* of C. H. Spiller and Sarah (*née* Walsh), Moycullen, Co. Galway, Eire; *m* 1972, Angela, *d* of Surtees Gleghorn; one *s* one *d. Educ:* County Secondary Sch., Bideford; North Devon College. Member Executive, Nat. League of Young Liberals, 1960–61; Organiser, Torrington Constituency Liberal Assoc., 1962–64; Divl Liberal Agent, Cornwall (Northern) Parly Constituency, 1965–71; Northern Regional Organiser (Election Agent, Rochdale By-Elec. 1972 and Berwick-upon-Tweed By-Elec. 1973), 1972–74; Nat. Agent, Liberal Central Assoc., 1974–76; Mem., Liberal Party Gen. Elec. Campaign Cttee, and Press Officer, Gen. Elections Feb. and Oct. 1974; Western Area Agent, 1977–80; Advisor, African Peoples Union, Independence Elections, Zimbabwe, 1980; By-Elec. and Marginal Seats Agent, Liberal Party Org. Headquarters, 1981–82; Sec. Gen., Liberal Party, 1983–85. *Recreation:* growing old roses. *Address:* 5 Royston Road, Bideford, Devonshire.

SPIRO, Sidney, MC 1945; Consultant, Hambros Bank Ltd, since 1985; Chairman, Landor Associates (Europe) Ltd, since 1985; *b* 27 July 1914; *m* 1949, Diana Susskind; two *d.* Law degree. RA in Middle East, Italy, 1939–45. Joined Anglo American Corp., 1953, Exec. Dir 1961–77; International Banking Consultant, 1977–; Man. Dir, 1969–71, and Chm., 1971–76, Charter Consolidated; Dir, Hambros plc, 1977–84. Dir, De Beers Consolidated Mines Ltd, 1970–. Founder Mem., Nat. Bd, Scripps Clinic and Res. Foundn. FRSA. *Recreations:* shooting, golf, tennis, music. *Address:* 9 Cedar House, Marloes Road, W8. *Clubs:* White's; Swinley Forest Golf.

SPITZ, Kathleen Emily, (Mrs Heinz Spitz); *see* Gales, Kathleen Emily.

SPITZ, Prof. Lewis, PhD; FRCS, FRCSE; Nuffield Professor of Paediatric Surgery, Institute of Child Health, London, since 1979; Hon. Consultant Surgeon, Hospital for Sick Children, Great Ormond Street, and Queen Elizabeth Hospital for Children, London, since 1979; *b* 25 Aug. 1939; *s* of Woolf and Selma Spitz; *m* 1972, Louise Ruth Dyzenhaus; one *s* one *d. Educ:* Univ. of Pretoria (MB, ChB); Univ. of the Witwatersrand (PhD). FRCS (*ad eundem*) 1980; FRCSE 1969; Hon. FAAP 1987. Smith and Nephew Fellow, Liverpool and London, 1971; Paediatric Surgeon, Johannesburg, 1971–74; Consultant Paediatric Surgeon, Sheffield Children's Hosp., 1974–79. Hon. Consultant in Paediatric Surgery to the Army, 1983–. Member: British Assoc. of Paediatric Surgeons; Assoc. of Surgeons of GB and Ireland; British Paediatric Assoc. (Mem. Acad. Bd, 1991–); British Soc. of Gastroenterology; Specialist Adv. Cttee in Paediatric Surgery, 1991–; MRSocMed. Exec. Editor, Progress in Paediatric Surgery, 1982; Member, Editorial Board: Jl of Paediatric Surgery, 1980–; Archives of Diseases in Childhood, 1984–89; Turkish Jl of Paediatric Surgery, 1987–; Associate Editor, Pediatric Surgery International, 1986–. *Publications:* A Colour Atlas of Paediatric Surgical Diagnosis, 1981; A Colour Atlas of Surgery for Undescended Testes, 1984; (ed jtly and contrib.) Paediatric Surgery, 4th edn 1988 (Rob and Smith Operative Surgery series); chapters in books on paediatrics and surgery; articles on oesophageal atresia, oesophageal replacement, gastro-oesophageal reflux, neonatal surgical conditions, and paediatric oncology. *Recreation:* tennis. *Address:* Institute of Child Health, 30 Guilford Street, WC1N 1EH. *T:* 071-242 9789.

SPITZER, Prof. Lyman, (Jr), BA; PhD; Professor of Astronomy, 1947–82 (Charles A. Young Professor, 1952–82), Princeton University; Chairman of Astrophysical Sciences Department, and Director of Observatory, Princeton University, 1947–79; Chairman, Research Board, 1967–72; *b* 26 June 1914; *s* of Lyman Spitzer and Blanche B. (*née* Brumback); *m* 1940, Doreen D. Canaday; one *s* three *d. Educ:* Phillips Academy, Andover; Yale Univ. (BA); Cambridge Univ., England; Princeton Univ. (PhD). Instructor in Physics and Astronomy, Yale Univ., 1939–42; Scientist, Special Studies Group, Columbia Univ. Div. of War Research, 1942–44; Dir, Sonar Analysis Group, Columbia Univ. Div. of War Research, 1944–46; Assoc. Prof. of Astrophysics, Yale Univ., 1946–47. Dir Project Matterhorn, Princeton Univ., 1953–61; Chm. Exec. Cttee, Plasma Physics Lab., Princeton Univ., 1961–66; Principal Investigator, Princeton telescope on Copernicus satellite; Chm., Space Telescope Inst. Council, 1981–90. Member: Nat. Acad. of Sciences; American Academy of Arts and Sciences; American Philosophical Society; Internat. Acad. of Astronautics; Corr. Member, Société Royale des Sciences, Liège; Foreign Mem., Royal Soc., 1990; Foreign Associate, Royal Astronomical Soc.; Pres., American Astronomical Soc., 1959–61. Hon. Dr of Science: Yale Univ., 1958; Case Inst. of Technology, 1961; Harvard, 1975; Princeton, 1984; Hon. Dr of Laws, Toledo Univ., 1963. Rittenhouse Medal, Franklin Inst., 1957; NASA Medal, 1972; Bruce Medal, Astron. Soc. of the Pacific, 1973; Draper Medal, Nat. Acad. of Scis, 1974; Maxwell Prize, Amer. Physical Soc., 1975; Schwarzschild Medal, Deutsche Astron. Ges., 1975; Dist. Public Service Medal, NASA, 1976; Gold Medal, RAS, 1978; Nat. Medal of Science, 1980; Janssen Medal, Soc. Astron. de France, 1980; Franklin Medal, Franklin Inst., 1980; Crafoord Prize, Royal Swedish Acad. Sci., 1985; Madison Medal, Princeton Univ., 1989; Franklin Medal, Amer. Philosophical Soc., 1991. *Publications:* (ed) Physics of Sound in the Sea, 1946; Physics of Fully Ionized Gases, 1956 (2nd edn 1962); Diffuse Matter in Space, 1968; Physical Processes in the Interstellar Medium, 1978; Searching between the Stars, 1982; Dynamical Evolution of Globular Clusters, 1987; papers in Astrophysical Jl, Monthly Notices of Royal Astronomical Soc., Physical Review, Physics of Fluids, on interstellar matter, stellar dynamics, plasma physics, space astronomy, etc. *Recreations:* ski-ing, mountain climbing. *Address:* 659 Lake Drive, Princeton, NJ 08540, USA. *T:* 609–924 3007. *Clubs:* Alpine; American Alpine.

SPOCK, Dr Benjamin McLane; Professor of Child Development, Western Reserve University, USA, 1955–67, now lecturing, writing and working for peace; *b* New Haven, Connecticut, 2 May 1903; *s* of Benjamin Ives Spock and Mildred Louise (*née* Stoughton); *m* 1st, 1927, Jane Davenport Cheney (marr. diss. 1975); two *s*; 2nd, 1976, Mary Morgan; one step *d. Educ:* Yale Univ. (BA); Yale Medical Sch.; Coll. Physicians and Surgeons, Columbia Univ. (MD). In practice (Pediatrics) from 1933; Cornell Med. Coll.; NY Hospital; NYC Health Dept. Served, 1944–46 in US Navy. Subseq. on Staff of: Rochester (Minn) Child Health Inst., Mayo Clinic, University of Minnesota; Prof. of Child Development, University of Pittsburgh, 1951–55. *Publications:* The Pocket Book of Baby and Child Care (also published as The Common Sense Book of Baby and Child Care), 1946, 6th edn as Dr Spock's Baby and Child Care, 1992; (with John Reinhart and Wayne Miller) A Baby's First Year, 1955; (with Miriam E. Lowenberg) Feeding Your Baby and Child, 1955; Dr Spock Talks with Mothers, 1961; Problems of Parents, 1962; (with Marion Lerrigo) Caring for Your Disabled Child, 1964; (with Mitchell Zimmerman) Dr Spock on Vietnam, 1968; Decent and Indecent: our personal and political behaviour, 1970; A Young Person's Guide to Life and Love, 1971; Raising Children in a Difficult Time, 1974 (UK as Bringing Up Children in a Difficult Time, 1974). *Relevant publications:* The Trial of Doctor Spock, by Jessica Mitford, 1969; Dr Spock: biography of a conservative radical, by Lynn Z. Bloom, 1972. *Address:* PO Box 1890, St Thomas, USVI 00803–1890, USA.

SPOKES, Ann; *see* Spokes Symonds, A. H.

SPOKES, John Arthur Clayton, QC 1973; a Recorder of the Crown Court, since 1972; *b* 6 Feb. 1931; 2nd *s* of late Peter Spencer Spokes and Lilla Jane Spokes (*née* Clayton), Oxford; *m* 1961, Jean, *yr d* of late Dr Robert McLean, Carluke, and Jean Symington McLean (*née* Barr); one *s* one *d. Educ:* Westminster Sch.; Brasenose Coll., Oxford. BA 1954; MA 1959. Nat. Service, Royal Artillery, 1949–51 (commnd 1950). Called to Bar, Gray's Inn, 1955, Bencher, 1985. Chm., Data Protection Tribunal, 1985–. Chancellor, Dio. of Winchester, 1985–. *Recreations:* gardening, walking. *Address:* 3 Pump Court, Temple, EC4Y 7AJ. *T:* 071–353 0711. *Club:* Leander (Henley-on-Thames).

See also A. H. Spokes Symonds.

SPOKES SYMONDS, Ann (Hazel); Vice President, Age Concern England, since 1987 (Chairman, 1983–86); *b* 10 Nov. 1925; *d* of Peter Spencer Spokes and Lilla Jane Spokes (*née* Clayton); *m* 1980, (John) Richard (Charters) Symonds, *qv. Educ:* Wychwood Sch., Oxford; Masters Sch., Dobbs Ferry, NY, USA; St Anne's Coll., Oxford (BA 1947; MA). Organising Secretary: Oxford Council of Social Service, 1959–74; Age Concern Oxford, 1958–80. Dir, ATV, 1978–81; Mem. W Midlands Bd, Central Indep. Television plc, 1981–. Mem., Thames Valley Police Authy, 1973–85; Chm., No 5 Police Dist. Authy Cttee, 1982–85; Vice-Chm., Personal Social Services Council, 1978–80; Chm., Social Services Cttee, ACC, 1978–82; Mem. Bd, Anchor Housing Assoc., 1976–83, 1985–; Member: Prince of Wales' Adv. Gp on Disability, 1983–90; Oftel Adv. Cttee for Disabled and Elderly People, 1985–91; Hearing Aid Council, 1986–89; Trustee, CERT, 1986–89. Member: Oxford City Council, 1957– (Lord Mayor, 1976–77); Oxfordshire CC, 1974–85 (Chm., 1981–83). Contested (C) NE Leicester, 1959, Brigg, 1966 and 1970. *Publications:* Celebrating Age: an anthology, 1987; Heavens Across the Sea, 1990. *Recreations:* lawn tennis, photography, enjoying cats. *Address:* 43 Davenant Road, Oxford OX2 8BU. *T:* Oxford (0865) 515661. *Club:* Royal Over-Seas League.

See also J. A. C. Spokes.

SPOONER, Edward Tenney Casswell, CMG 1966; MD, MA, MRCS, LRCP; FRCP; *b* 22 May 1904; *s* of William Casswell Spooner, MB, and Edith Maud Spooner, Blandford, Dorset; *m* 1948, Colin Mary Stewart. *Educ:* Epsom Coll.; Clare Coll., Cambridge; St Bartholomew's Hospital. Foundation Scholar of Clare Coll., 1923; House Physician, St Bartholomew's Hospital, 1927–28; Commonwealth Fellow, Harvard Medical Sch., 1929–31; Fellow of Clare Coll., 1929–47; Tutor of Clare Coll., 1939–47; University Demonstrator and Lecturer, Dept of Pathology, University of Cambridge, 1931–46; Professor of Bacteriology and Immunology, London School of Hygiene and Tropical Medicine, 1947–60, Dean, 1960–70. Temporary Major, RAMC, in No 1 Medical Research Section, 1942–43; Director, Emergency Public Health Laboratory, Cambridge, 1943–44; Editor, Journal of Hygiene, 1949–55; Member Medical Research Council, 1953–57; Member Council Epsom Coll., 1955–65; Chm., Public Health Lab. Service Bd, 1963–72. *Publications:* papers on tetanus, certain virus diseases and wound infection. *Address:* Ellergarth, Dalditch Lane, Knowle, Budleigh Salterton, Devon EX9 7AH.

SPOONER, Prof. Frank Clyffurde, MA, PhD, LittD; Professor of Economic History, University of Durham, 1966–85, now Emeritus; *b* 5 March 1924; *s* of Harry Gordon Morrison Spooner. *Educ:* Bromley Grammar Sch.; Christ's Coll., Cambridge. Hist. Tripos, 1st cl., Pt I 1947 and Pt II 1948; MA 1949; PhD 1953; LittD 1985. War Service, Sub-Lt (S) RNVR, 1943–46; Bachelor Research Scholar, 1948; Chargé de Recherches, CNRS, Paris, 1949–50; Allen Scholar, 1951; Fellow, Christ's Coll., Cambridge, 1951–57; Commonwealth Fund Fellow, 1955–57 at Chicago, Columbia, New York, and Harvard Univs; Ecole Pratique des Hautes Etudes, VI Section, Sorbonne, 1957–61; Lectr, Univ. of Oxford, 1958–59; Vis. Lectr in Econs, Harvard Univ., 1961–62; Irving Fisher Research Prof. of Econs, Yale Univ., 1962–63; Univ. of Durham: Lectr, 1963; Reader, 1964; Resident Tutor-in-charge, Lumley Castle, 1965–70; Dir, Inst. of European Studies, 1969–76; Leverhulme Fellow, 1976–78; Leverhulme Emeritus Fellow, 1985–86. FRHistS 1970; FSA 1983. Prix Limantour de l'Académie des Sciences Morales et Politiques, 1957; West European Award, British Academy, 1979; Ernst Meyer Award, 1983. *Publications:* L'économie mondiale et les frappes monétaires en France, 1493–1680, 1956, revised edn The International Economy and Monetary Movements in France, 1493–1725, 1972; Risks at Sea: Amsterdam insurance and maritime Europe 1766–1780, 1983; contribs to joint works and to jls. *Recreations:* music, photography, walking. *Club:* United Oxford & Cambridge University.

SPOONER, Sir James (Douglas), Kt 1981; Chairman, Morgan Crucible, since 1983 (Director, since 1978); Director, John Swire & Sons, since 1970; *b* 11 July 1932; *s* of late Vice-Adm. E. J. Spooner, DSO, and Megan Spooner (*née* Megan Foster, the singer); *m* 1958, Jane Alyson, *d* of late Sir Gerald Glover; two *s* one *d. Educ:* Eton Coll. (Fellow, 1990); Christ Church, Oxford. Chartered Accountant 1962; Partner, Dixon Wilson & Co., Chartered Accountants, 1963–72; Chm., Vantona Viyella, subseq. Coats Viyella, 1969–89. Chm., NAAFI, 1973–86 (Dir, 1968–86); Director: Abingworth, 1973–; J.

Sainsbury, 1981–; Barclays Bank, 1983–; Hogg Robinson Gp, 1971–85 (Dep. Chm., 1971–85); Royal Opera House, Covent Garden, 1987–. Chm. Council, King's College London, 1986–. *Recreations:* music, history, shooting. *Address:* Swire House, 59 Buckingham Gate, SW1E 6AJ. *Clubs:* White's, Beefsteak.

SPORBORG, Christopher Henry; Vice-Chairman, Hambros plc, since 1986; *b* 17 April 1939; *s* of H. N. Sporborg and Mary (*née* Rowlands); *m* 1961, Lucinda Jane (*née* Hanbury); two *s* two *d. Educ:* Rugby School; Emmanuel College, Cambridge (BA Hons). Nat. Service, Coldstream Guards, 1957–59 (Lieut). Hambros Bank, 1962–: Dir, 1970; Dep. Chm., 1983; Chm., Hambro Countrywide, 1986–, and Hambro overseas cos. Director: TNT; BMSS. Mem., Jockey Club and Dir, Jockey Club Estates; Treasurer, British Field Sport Soc. Trustee: Home Farm Trust; Sir Jules Thorn Charitable Trust; Fitzwilliam Family Trusts. *Recreations:* hunting (Joint Master, Puckeridge and Thurlow Foxhounds), racing (owner and permit holder), bridge. *Address:* Walkers Farm House, Farnham, Bishop's Stortford, Herts. *T:* Bishop's Stortford (0279) 74444. *Club:* Boodle's.

SPOTSWOOD, Marshal of the Royal Air Force Sir Denis (Frank), GCB 1971 (KCB 1966; CB 1961); CBE 1946; DSO 1943; DFC 1942; Director, Smiths Industries International Aerospace and Defence Companies, since 1982 (Chairman, 1980–82); *b* 26 Sept. 1916; *s* of late F. H. Spotswood and M. C. Spotswood; *m* 1942, Ann (*née* Child); one *s.* Commissioned in RAF, 1936; UK Service in Squadrons, 1937–41; No 209 Squadron, 1939–41. Served War of 1939–45 (despatches twice, DSO). Chief Instructor, Operation Training Unit, 1941–42; Officer Commanding No 500 (County of Kent) Squadron, RAuxAF, 1942–43; Director of Plans, HQ Supreme Allied Commander, South-East Asia, 1944–46; Directing Staff, RAF Staff Coll., 1946–48; Officer Commanding RAF (Fighter) Stations, Horsham St Faith and Coltishall, 1948–50; Directing Staff, Imperial Defence Coll., 1950–52; Exchange Duties, HQUSAF in USA, 1952–54; Officer Commanding RAF (Fighter) Station, Linton-on-Ouse, 1954–56; Deputy Director of Plans, Air Ministry, 1956–58; AOC and Commandant, RAF Coll., Cranwell, 1958–61; Assistant Chief of Staff (Air Defence), SHAPE, 1961–63; AOC No 3 Group, RAF Bomber Command, 1964–65; C-in-C RAF Germany, 1965–68; Commander, 2nd Allied Tactical Air Force, 1966–68; AOC-in-C, RAF Strike Command, 1968–71; Comdr, UK Air Defence Region, 1968–71; Chief of the Air Staff, 1971–74. Group Captain, 1954; Air Commodore, 1958; Air Vice-Marshal, 1961; Air Marshal, 1965; Air Chief Marshal, 1968; Marshal of the RAF, 1974. ADC to the Queen, 1957–61, Air ADC to the Queen, 1970–74. Vice-Chm. and Dir, Rolls Royce Ltd, 1974–80; Chm., Turbo Union Ltd, 1975–80; Director: RR/Turbomeca Ltd; Dowty Gp, 1980–87. Pres., SBAC, 1978–79. Chm. of Governors, Royal Star and Garter Home, 1981–85 (Gov., 1974–80); Vice-Patron, RAF Museum (Chm. of Trustees, 1974–80). FRAeS 1975. Officer of the Legion of Merit (USA). *Recreations:* golf, sailing, shooting, bridge. *Address:* Coombe Cottage, Hambleden, Henley-on-Thames, Oxon RG9 6SD. *Clubs:* Royal Air Force; Phyllis Court (Henley); Huntercombe Golf.

SPOTTISWOOD, Air Vice-Marshal James Donald, CB 1988; CVO 1977; AFC 1971; Managing Director, Airwork Ltd, Bournemouth International Airport, since 1989; *b* 27 May 1934; *s* of James Thomas Spottiswood and Caroline Margaret Spottiswood; *m* 1957, Margaret Maxwell (*née* Harrison); two *s* one *d. Educ:* West Hartlepool Grammar School; Boston Univ., USA (MA). Enlisted RAF, 1951, commissioned, 1952; 617 Sqn, 1962–64; Royal Naval Staff Coll., 1965; PSO to C-in-C Middle East, 1966–67; Commanded 53 Sqn, 1968–70; JSSC, 1970; Commanded: RAF Thorney Island, 1972–75; RAF Benson, 1975–76; Dep. Captain, the Queen's Flight, 1975–76; RCDS, 1978; Secretary to IMS, HQ NATO, 1980–83; DG of Trng, RAF, 1983–85; Air Officer Trng, RAF Support Comd, 1985–89, retired. FBIM 1983. *Recreations:* gliding, sailing, golf. *Address:* Royal Bank of Scotland, High Street, Oxford. *Club:* Royal Air Force.

SPRACKLING, Maj.-Gen. Ian Oliver John, OBE 1977; Special Adviser, Andersen Consulting, since 1989; *b* 3 Oct. 1936; *m* 1959, Ann Vonda (*née* Coote); two *s. Educ:* Bristol Grammar School; RMCS (BSc Eng); psc, RCDS. RMA Sandhurst, 1955; 2nd Lieut, Royal Corps of Signals, 1957; RMCS, 1958–61; served Far East, UK, BAOR, 1961–75; Staff Officer, Sultan of Oman's Armed Forces, 1975–77; CO, Electronic Warfare Regt, BAOR, 1977–79; Col, Cabinet Office, 1979–81; Comdr, Catterick Garrison, 1982–84; RCDS 1984; Director: Mil. Assistance Overseas, 1985–86; Management and Support of Intelligence, MoD, 1986–89, retired. *Recreations:* bridge, socialising, keep fit, watching Rugby. *Address:* 2 Arundel Street, WC2. *Clubs:* Army and Navy; Clifton (Bristol).

SPRAGGS, Rear-Adm. Trevor Owen Keith, CB 1983; CEng, FIEE; Chief of Staff to Commander-in-Chief, Naval Home Command, 1981–83; *b* 17 June 1926; *s* of Cecil James Spraggs and Gladys Maude (*née* Morey); *m* 1st, 1955, Mary Patricia Light (*d* 1983); two *s*; 2nd, 1986, Gwynedd Kate (*née* Adams) *widow* of Reginald A. W. Green, CEng, MIMechE. *Educ:* Portsmouth Grammar Sch.; St John's Coll., Southsea; Imperial College of Science and Technology, London (BScEng, ACGI). Joined Royal Navy, 1945; courses: HM Ships: King Alfred, Leander, Harrier, 1945–47; Admiralty Compass Obs., Slough, 1948; BRNC, Dartmouth, 1948–50; HM Ships: Dryad, Vanguard, Vernon, Collingwood, Ariel, Falcon, 1950–61; AEI, Manchester, 1962; RNEC, 1962–66; HMS Collingwood, 1966–69 and 1972–75; RNEC, 1969–72, and, as Dean, 1979–80; Dean, RNC, Greenwich, 1975–77; Dir of Naval Trng Support, Dir of Naval Educn and Trng Support, 1977–79; Chief Naval Instr Officer, 1981–83. ADC to the Queen, 1979. Member: Nautical Studies Bd of CNAA, 1975–80; Maritime Studies Adv. Cttee of Plymouth Polytech., 1979–80; Cttee of Management, Royal Hosp. Sch., Holbrook, 1981–83; Governor: Fareham Technical Coll., 1972–75; RN Sch. for Officers' Daughters, Haslemere, 1975–77. Pres., Combined Services and RN Amateur Athletic Assocs, 1981–83. *Recreations:* golf, sailing, rifle shooting, gardening. *Address:* 46 Sinah Lane, Hayling Island, Hants PO11 0HH. *Clubs:* Royal Naval Sailing Association; Hayling Golf; Hayling Island Sailing.

SPRAGUE, David Keith, MVO 1972; HM Diplomatic Service; High Commissioner, Sierra Leone, since 1991; *b* 20 Feb. 1935; *m* 1958, Audrey Mellon; two *s* one *d. Educ:* King Edward's Grammar Sch., Camp Hill, Birmingham. Foreign Office, 1953; Nat. Service, 1953–55; FO, 1955, served Addis Ababa, Paris, Belgrade, Budapest, Kuala Lumpur, Abidjan, Sofia, and FCO; Dep. High Comr, Madras, 1986–89; Ambassador to Mongolia, 1989–91. *Recreation:* golf. *Address:* c/o Foreign and Commonwealth Office, SW1A 2AH.

SPRATT, Sir Greville (Douglas), GBE 1987; TD 1962, Bar 1968; DL; JP; Underwriting Member of Lloyd's, since 1950; Lord Mayor of London, 1987–88; *b* 1 May 1927; *e s* of Hugh Douglas Spratt and Sheelah Ivy (*née* Stace); *m* 1954, Sheila Farrow Wade; three *d. Educ:* Leighton Park; Charterhouse. Served Coldstream Guards, 1945–46; commnd Oxfordshire and Bucks LI, 1946; seconded to Arab Legion; served Palestine, Trans Jordan and Egypt, 1946–48; GSO III (Ops and Intell.), 1948. Lloyd's, 1948–61; Joined J. & N. Wade Gp of Electrical Distributors, 1961; Dir, 1969–76 and Man. Dir, 1972–76. Chm., City and West End Regl Adv. Bd, National Westminster Bank, 1991–; Director: Williams Lea Gp; Forest Mere Ltd; Charterhouse Enterprises Ltd. Lieut of the City of London, 1972; Life Mem., Guild of Freemen, 1977 (Mem. Court, 1982–90); Liveryman, Ironmongers' Co., 1977– (Mem. Ct, 1982–); Alderman, Castle Baynard Ward, 1978–; JP 1978; Sheriff of the City of London, 1984–85; DL Greater London, 1986. Joined HAC Infantry Bn as private, 1950; re-commnd 1950; CO, 1962–65; Regtl Col, 1966–70; Mem., Ct of Assts, HAC, 1960–70 and 1978–; ADC to the Queen, 1973–78; Mem., City TA&VRA, 1960– (Vice Chm., 1973–77, Chm., 1977–82); Chm., TA&VRA for Greater London, 1991– (Mem., Exec. and Finance Cttee, 1977–); Hon. Colonel: City and NE sector, London ACF, 1983–; 8th Bn, The Queen's Fusiliers (City of London), 1988–. Chm., Action Res. for the Crippled Child, 1989– (Mem. Council, 1982–; Mem. Haslemere Cttee, 1971–82); President: Royal British Legion, Haslemere (St James Vice Pres., 1991–); London Fedn of Old Comrades Assocs, 1983–; Vice Pres., Not Forgotten Assoc., 1990–; Dep. Pres., London, British Red Cross, 1983–91; Mem. Council, Reserve Forces Assoc., 1981–84. Mem., City of London, Police Cttee, 1989–; Mem., Planning and Communications Cttee, 1990–. Chm., Anglo Jordanian Soc., 1990–; Member: Cttee, Guildhall Sch. of Music and Drama, 1978–80 and 1989– (Hon. Mem., GSMD 1988); Court, City Univ., 1981– (Chancellor, 1987–88); Governing Bodies of Girls' Schs Assoc., 1982–90; Governor: St Ives Sch., 1976– (Vice Chm., 1977–86; Chm., 1986–90); King Edward's Sch., Witley, 1978– (Vice-Pres., 1989–); Christ's Hosp., 1978–; Bridewell Royal Hosp., 1978–; City of London Sch. for Girls, 1981–82; Malvern Girls' Coll., 1982–90; St Paul's Cathedral Choir Sch., 1985–; Charterhouse, 1985– (Chm. Governing Body, 1989–); Life Governor, Corp. of the Sons of the Clergy, 1985–; Patron: Internat. Centre for Child Studies, 1985–; Surrey Charity Gp, 1989–. Mem., Surrey Scout Council, 1990–. Blackdown Cttee, Nat. Trust, 1977–87. Trustee: Chichester Theatre; Endowment of St Paul's Cathedral; Childrens' Research Internat. Carthusian Trust; Castle Baynard Educnl Trust; Special Trustee, St Bartholomew's Hosp. FRSA. Hon. DLitt City Univ., 1988. KStJ 1987 (OStJ 1985). Chevalier de la Légion d'Honneur, 1961; Commandeur de l'Ordre National du Mérite, 1984; Commander, Order of the Lion, Malaŵi, 1985; Mem., Nat. Order of Aztec Eagle, Mexico, 1985; Order of St Olav, Norway, 1988; Order of Merit, Senegal, 1988. *Recreations:* tennis, music, military history, forestry. *Address:* Grayswood Place, Haslemere, Surrey GU27 2ET. *T:* Haslemere (0428) 4367. *Clubs:* City Livery, Guildhall, United Wards; Cowdray Park Golf and Polo.

SPRECKLEY, Sir (John) Nicholas (Teague), KCVO 1989; CMG 1983; HM Diplomatic Service; British High Commissioner in Kuala Lumpur, since 1986; *b* 6 Dec. 1934; *s* of late Air Marshal Sir Herbert Spreckley, KBE, CB, and Winifred Emery Teague; *m* 1958, Margaret Paula Jane, *er d* of late Prof. W. McC. Stewart; one *s* one *d. Educ:* Winchester Coll.; Magdalene Coll., Cambridge (BA). Tokyo, 1957–62; American Dept, FO, 1962–64; Asst Private Sec. to Lord Carrington and Mr Padley, 1964; Defence Dept, FO, 1964–66; Head of Chancery, Dakar, 1966–70; Paris, 1970–75; Head of Referendum Unit, FCO, 1975; Counsellor and Head of Chancery, Tokyo, 1976–78; Fellow, Center for Internat. Affairs, Harvard Univ., 1978–79; Head of European Community Dept (Internal), FCO, 1979–83; Ambassador to Republic of Korea, 1983–86. *Address:* c/o Foreign and Commonwealth Office, SW1A 2AL. *Club:* Army and Navy.

SPREULL, Professor James (Spreull Andrew); William Dick Professor of Veterinary Surgery, at the University of Edinburgh, 1959–78, now Emeritus; *b* 2 May 1908; *s* of late Lt-Col Andrew Spreull, DSO, TD, MRCVS, and Effie Andrew Spreull; *m* 1951, Kirsten Brummerstedt-Hansen; three *s. Educ:* Dundee High Sch.; Edinburgh Univ. (PhD); Royal Dick Veterinary Coll. (MRCVS). Royal Dick Veterinary College: Demonstrator of Anatomy, 1930–34, Lecturer in Applied Anatomy, 1931–34. Engaged in general practice in Dundee, 1934–59. FRSE 1965. *Publications:* various contributions to Veterinary Journals. *Recreations:* agriculture, fishing, badminton, antiques. *Address:* 2 Marlee Road, Broughty Ferry, Dundee DD5 3HA. *T:* Dundee (0382) 75916.

SPRIDDELL, Peter Henry; Director, Marks & Spencer, since 1970; *b* 18 Aug. 1928; *s* of Thomas Henry Spriddell and Eva Florence Spriddell; *m* 1952, Joyce Patricia (*née* Haycock); two *s* one *d. Educ:* Plymouth Coll.; Exeter Coll., Oxford (MA); Harvard Business Sch. Joined Marks & Spencer Ltd, 1951: Alternate Dir Store Ops, 1970, full Dir, 1972; Dir of Personnel, 1972–75; Dir Estates, Bldg, Store Ops, Physical Distribution, 1975–. Dir, NFC, 1978–82; non-exec. Mem., British Rail Property Bd, 1986–. Member Council: Templeton Coll; Oxford (formerly Oxford Centre for Management Studies), 1978–; Town and Country Planning Assoc.; Vice-Pres., Devon Historic Bldgs Trust, 1978–. FRSA. Freeman, City of London; Liveryman, Worshipful Co. of Paviors, 1984. *Recreations:* music, golf. *Address:* 37 Main Avenue, Moor Park Estate, Northwood, Mddx. *T:* Northwood (09274) 29654. *Club:* Moor Park Golf.

SPRIGGE, Prof. Timothy Lauro Squire, PhD; Professor Emeritus and Endowment Fellow, University of Edinburgh, since 1989; *b* 14 Jan. 1932; *s* of Cecil and Katriona Sprigge; *m* 1959, Giglia Gordon; one *s* twin *d. Educ:* Gonville and Caius Coll., Cambridge (MA, PhD). Lecturer in Philosophy, University Coll. London, 1961–63; Lectr in Philosophy, 1963–70, Reader in Philosophy, 1970–79, Univ. of Sussex; Prof. of Logic and Metaphysics, Univ. of Edinburgh, 1979–89. Visiting Associate Professor, Univ. of Cincinnati, 1968–69. Member: Aristotelian Soc., 1960–; Mind Assoc., 1955–; Assoc. for the Advancement of Amer. Philosophy, 1978–; Scots Philosophical Club, 1979–. *Publications:* ed, Correspondence of Jeremy Bentham, vols 1 and 2, 1968; Facts, Words and Beliefs, 1970; Santayana: an examination of his philosophy, 1974; The Vindication of Absolute Idealism, 1983; Theories of Existence, 1985; The Rational Foundation of Ethics, 1988; contribs to various vols of philosophical essays and to periodicals, incl. Mind, Philosophy, Inquiry, Nous. *Recreation:* backgammon. *Address:* David Hume Tower, University of Edinburgh, George Square, Edinburgh EH8 9JX. *T:* 031–667 1011.

SPRIGGS, Leslie, JP; *b* 22 April 1910; British; *m* 1931, Elfrida Mary Brindle Parkinson. *Educ:* Council Sch.; Trade Union Adult Schools. TU Scholarship to Belgium, 1951. Merchant Service, then Railwayman until 1958. Formerly: President, NW (NUR) District Council, Political Section, 1954; Vice-President, Industrial Section, 1955. Served as Auditor to Lancs and Cheshire Region of the Labour Party. Formerly Lecturer, National Council of Labour Colleges on Industrial Law, Economics, Foreign Affairs, Local Government, Trade Union History. MP (Lab) St Helens, June 1958–1983; Member Parliamentary Groups: Employment, Environment, Health, Industry, Transport, and Trade, incl. aviation, shipping, textiles, clothing and footwear. JP N Fylde, 1955. *Recreations:* Rugby League, athletics, water polo, soccer, bowls, gardening. *Address:* 38 Knowle Avenue, Cleveleys, Lancs FY5 3PP. *T:* Cleveleys (0253) 852746.

SPRING, Frank Stuart, FRS 1952; DSc (Manchester), PhD (Liverpool), FRSC; Director, Laporte Industries Ltd, London, W1, 1959–71; *b* 5 Sept. 1907; 3rd *s* of John Spring and Isabella Spring, Crosby, Liverpool; *m* 1932, Mary, 2nd *d* of Rev. John Mackintosh, MA, Heswall; one *s* one *d. Educ:* Waterloo Grammar Sch.; University of Liverpool. United Alkali Research Scholar, University of Liverpool, 1928–29; University Fellow, Liverpool, 1929–30. Assistant Lecturer, Lecturer and Senior Lecturer in Chemistry, University of Manchester, 1930–46; Freeland Professor of Chemistry, The Royal College of Science and Technology, Glasgow, 1946–59. Chemical Society, Tilden Lecturer, 1950. Hon. DSc: Salford, 1967; Strathclyde, 1981. *Publications:* papers (mostly jtly) in chemical journals. *Address:* Flat 26, 1 Hyde Park Square, W2 2JZ. *T:* 071–262 8174.

SPRING, Richard, (Dick Spring); Member of the Dáil (TD) (Lab), North Kerry, since 1981; Leader of the Irish Labour Party, since 1982; *b* 29 Aug. 1950; *s* of Daniel and Anne Spring; *m* 1977, Kristi Lee Hutcheson; two *s* one *d*. *Educ:* Mt St Joseph Coll., Roscrea; Trinity Coll., Dublin (BA 1972). Called to the Bar, King's Inns, Dublin, 1975; in practice on Munster Circuit, 1977–81. Minister of State, Dept of Justice, 1981–82; Minister for the Environment, 1982–83; Dep. Prime Minister, 1982–87, and Minister for Energy, 1983–87. *Recreations:* swimming, reading. *Address:* Dunroamin, Cloonanorig, Tralee, Co. Kerry, Ireland. *T:* Tralee 25337, Dublin 717763.

SPRING RICE, family name of **Baron Monteagle of Brandon.**

SPRINGER, Sir Hugh (Worrell), GCMG 1984 (KCMG 1971); GCVO 1985; KA 1984; CBE 1961 (OBE 1954); Governor-General, Barbados, 1984–90; Barrister-at-Law; *b* 1913; 2nd *s* of late Charles W. Springer, Barbados, and late Florence Springer; *m* 1942, Dorothy Drinan, 3rd *d* of late Lionel Gittens, Barbados, and Cora Gittens; three *s* one *d*. *Educ:* Harrison Coll., Barbados; Hertford Coll., Oxford (Hon. Fellow 1974). BA 1936, MA 1944. Called to Bar, Inner Temple, 1938. Practice at the Bar, Barbados, 1938–47; MCP, 1940–47, MEC 1944–47, Barbados; Gen.-Sec., Barbados Lab. Party, 1940–47; Organiser and first Gen.-Sec., Workers' Union, 1940–47; Mem., West Indies Cttee of the Asquith Commn on Higher Educn, 1944; Mem., Provisional Council, University Coll. of the West Indies, 1947; first Registrar, Univ. Coll. of WI, 1947–63; John Simon Guggenheim Fellow and Fellow of Harvard Center for Internat. Affairs, 1961–62; first Dir, Univ. of WI Inst. of Educn, 1963–66; Commonwealth Asst Sec.-Gen., 1966–70; Sec.-Gen., ACU, 1970–80. Past Mem., Public Service and other Commns and Cttees in Barbados, Jamaica and W Indies; Sen. Vis. Fellow of All Souls Coll., Oxford, 1962–63 (Hon. Fellow 1988); Actg Governor of Barbados, 1964; Mem., Bermuda Civil Disorder Commn, 1968. Chm., Commonwealth Caribbean Med. Res. Council (formerly Brit. Caribbean Med. Research Cttee), 1965–84; Vice-Pres., British Caribbean Assoc., 1974–80; Trustee, Bernard Van Leer Foundn, 1967–78; Barbados Trustee, Commonwealth Foundn, 1967–80, and Chm., 1974–77; Member, Court of Governors: LSE, 1970–80; Exeter Univ., 1970–80; Hull Univ., 1970–80; London Sch. of Hygiene and Tropical Medicine, 1974–77; Inst. of Commonwealth Studies, 1974–80. Trustee, Harlow Campus, Meml Univ. of Newfoundland, 1975–79. Jt Sec., UK Commonwealth Scholarships Commn, 1970–80; Exec. Sec., Marshall Scholarships Commn, 1970–80; Sec., Kennedy Memorial Trust, 1970–80; Chm., Commonwealth Human Ecology Council, 1971–84 (Hon. Pres., 1984–); Member: Council, USPG, 1972–79; Adv. Cttee, Sci. Policy Foundn, 1977–; Bd of Dirs, United World Colleges, 1978–90; Bd of Trustees, Sir Ernest Cassel Educational Trust, 1978–81; Pres., Educn Section, British Assoc., 1974–75; Mem., President's Cttee, Campaign for Oxford, 1988–; Chm., Jt Commonwealth Socs Council, 1978–80. Hon. Prof. of Educn, Mauritius, 1981. Hon. DSc Soc Laval, 1958; Hon. LLD: Victoria, BC, 1972; Univ. of WI, 1973; City, 1978; Manchester, 1979; York, Ontario, 1980; Zimbabwe, 1981; Bristol, 1982; Birmingham, 1983; Hon. DLitt: Warwick, 1974; Ulster, 1974; Heriot-Watt, 1976; Hong Kong, 1977; St Andrews, 1977; Hon. DCL: New Brunswick, 1980; Oxon, 1980; East Anglia, 1980. KStJ 1985. *Publications:* Reflections on the Failure of the First West Indian Federation, 1962 (USA); articles and lectures on West Indian and Commonwealth Educn and Development, in: The Round Table, Commonwealth, RSA Jl, Caribbean Quarterly, Internat. Organisation, Jl of Negro History, etc. *Recreations:* walking, talking. *Address:* Gibbes, St Peter, Barbados. *T:* (809) 422 2591. *Clubs:* Athenæum, Commonwealth Trust.

SPRINGER, Tobias; a Metropolitan Stipendiary Magistrate, 1963–82; Barrister-at-law; *b* 3 April 1907; *o c* of late Samuel Springer, MBE; *m* 1937, Stella Rauchwerger. *Educ:* Mill Hill Sch.; Caius Coll., Cambridge. Law Tripos 1928; called to Bar, Gray's Inn, 1929. Practised London and SE Circuit. Served War of 1939–45: 60th Rifles, 1940–45; Lt-Col GSO1, GHQ, H Forces, 1944. Returned to practise at Bar, 1945. Actg Dep. Chm., Co. London Sessions, periods 1962, 1963; sometime Dep. Circuit Judge. Life Governor: Mill Hill School; Metropolitan Hosp. Freedom, City of London, 1982. *Recreations:* travel, golf, reading. *Address:* 82 Cholmley Gardens, Fortune Green Road, NW6 1UN. *T:* 071–435 0817. *Clubs:* Hurlingham, Old Mill Hillians; Porters Park Golf.

SPRINGETT, Jack Allan, CBE 1978; MA (Cantab); Education Officer, Association of Metropolitan Authorities, 1980–82; *b* 1 Feb. 1916; *s* of Arthur John and Agnes Springett; *m* 1950, Patricia Winifred Singleton; three *s* one *d*. *Educ:* Windsor Grammar Sch.; Fitzwilliam House, Cambridge. Asst Master, Christ's Hospital, Horsham, 1938–47. Served War, Royal Signals and Gen. Staff, 1940–46. Administrative Asst, North Riding, 1947–52; Asst Educn Officer, Birmingham, 1952–62; Dep. Educn Officer, Essex, 1962–73; County Educn Officer, Essex, 1973–80. *Address:* 3 Roxwell Road, Chelmsford, Essex CM1 2LY. *T:* Chelmsford (0245) 258669.

SPRINGFORD, John Frederick Charles, CBE 1980 (OBE 1970); retired British Council Officer; *b* 6 June 1919; *s* of Frederick Charles Springford and Bertha Agnes Springford (*née* Trenery); *m* 1945, Phyllis Wharton; one *s* two *d*. *Educ:* Latymer Upper Sch.; Christ's College, Cambridge (MA). Served War 1940–46, RAC; seconded Indian Armoured Corps, 1942; Asst Political Agent II in Mekran, 1945. British Council Service, Baghdad and Mosul, Iraq, 1947–51, Isfahan, Iran, 1951–52; British Council Representative: Tanzania, 1952–57; Sudan, 1957–62; Dir, Overseas Students Dept, 1962–66; Representative: Jordan, 1966–69; Iraq, 1969–74; Canada, 1974–79, and Counsellor, Cultural Affairs, British High Commission, Ottawa. Mem. Council, British Sch. of Archaeology in Iraq, 1980–86. Hon. Sec., Sussex Heritage Trust, 1980–83; Chm., Sussex Eastern Sub-Area, RSCM, 1981–85, Chm., Sussex Area, 1985–. *Recreations:* archaeology, church music. *Address:* Precinct, Crowhurst, Battle, East Sussex TN33 9AA. *T:* Crowhurst (042483) 200.

SPROAT, Iain Mac Donald; Chairman: Milner and Co. Ltd; Cricketers' Who's Who Ltd; Director: D'Arcy Masius Benton and Bowles Ltd; College of Petroleum Studies, Oxford; *b* Dollar, Clackmannanshire, 8 Nov. 1938; *s* of late William Bigham Sproat and Lydia Bain Sproat (*née* MacDonald); *m* 1979, Judith Mary Kernot (*née* King); one step *s*. *Educ:* St Mary's Sch., Melrose; Winchester Coll.; Univ. of Aix-en-Provence; Magdalen Coll., Oxford. Served RGJ (4th Bn), 1972–76. Contested (C) Roxburgh and Berwickshire, 1983; Prospective Parly Candidate (C) Harwich, 1990–. MP (C) Aberdeen South, 1970–83. PPS to Sec. of State for Scotland, 1973–74; Parly Under-Sec. of State, Dept of Trade (Minister: of Aviation and Shipping; of Tourism; responsible for: Govt Statistics; Retail Trade; Distributive Trades; Video, Cinema and Film Industry), 1981–83; Special Advr to Prime Minister, Gen. Election, 1987. Leader, Cons. Gp, Scottish Select Cttee, 1979–81; Chm., Scottish Cons. Cttee, 1979–81; Chm., Soviet and E European Gp, Cons. Foreign Affairs Cttee, 1975–81. Member: British Parly Delegn to oversee S Vietnamese Elections, 1973; British Parly Delegn to Soviet Union, 1974; Leader, British Parly Delegn to Austria, 1980. Lecturer: on guerilla warfare, RCDS, 1973; on Kurdish guerilla warfare in Iran/Iraq, RUSI, 1975. Trustee: African Med. and Res. Foundn; Scottish Self-Governing Schools Trust. Cricket Writer of the Year, Wombwell Cricket Lovers' Soc., 1983. *Publications:* (ed) Cricketers' Who's Who, annually 1980–; Wodehouse at War, 1981; Edward Heath, a pictorial biography; with Adam Sykes: The Wit of Sir Winston; The Wit of Westminster; The Wit of the Wig; The Harold Wilson Bunkside Book; The Cabinet Bedside Book; (contrib.) The British Prime Ministers. *Recreations:* collecting books, cricket. *Address:* c/o Coutts and Co., 2 Lower Sloane Streett, SW1. *Clubs:* Cavalry and Guards, United Oxford & Cambridge University.

SPROT, Lt-Col Aidan Mark, MC 1944; JP; Lord-Lieutenant of Tweeddale, since 1980; landed proprietor and farmer (Haystoun Estate); *b* 17 June 1919; *s* of Major Mark Sprot of Riddell. *Educ:* Stowe. Commissioned Royal Scots Greys, 1940; served: Middle East, 1941–43; Italy, 1943–44; NW Europe, 1944–45, and after the war in Germany, Libya, Egypt, Jordan and UK; Adjt 1945–46; CO, 1959–62, retired. Councillor, Peeblesshire CC, 1963–75; JP 1966, DL 1966–80, Peeblesshire. Member, Royal Company of Archers (Queen's Body Guard for Scotland), 1950–; Pres., Lowlands of Scotland, TAVRA, 1986–89. County Dir, 1966–74, Patron, 1983–, Tweeddale Br., British Red Cross Soc.; County Comr, 1968–73, Chm., 1975–80, Pres., 1980–, Tweeddale Scout Assoc. *Recreations:* country pursuits, motor cycle touring. *Address:* Crookston, Peebles EH45 9JQ. *T:* Kirkton Manor (07214) 209. *Club:* New (Edinburgh).

SPRY, Brig. Sir Charles Chambers Fowell, Kt 1964; CBE 1956; DSO 1943; retired as Director-General, Australian Security Intelligence Organization, 1950–70; *b* 26 June 1910; *s* of A. F. Spry, Brisbane; *m* 1939, Kathleen Edith Hull, *d* of Rev. Godfrey Smith; one *s* two *d*. *Educ:* Brisbane Grammar School. Graduated Royal Military College, Duntroon. Served War of 1939–45 as Col, Australian Imperial Force in SW Pacific (DSO) and Middle East. Director of Military Intelligence, 1946. Hon. ADC to Gov. Gen., 1946. *Recreation:* golf. *Address:* 2 Mandeville Crescent, Toorak, Victoria 3142, Australia. *Clubs:* Melbourne; Royal Melbourne Golf.

SPRY, Christopher John; Regional General Manager, South West Thames Regional Health Authority, since 1989; *b* 29 Aug. 1946; *s* of late Reginald Charles Spry and Kathleen Edith Spry (*née* Hobart); *m* 1st, Jean Banks (marr. diss. 1989); two *s*; 2nd, 1989, Judith Christina (*née* Ryder). *Educ:* Sir Roger Manwood's Sch., Sandwich; Exeter Univ. (BA 1967). AHSM. Dep. Hosp. Sec., Lewisham Hosp., 1970; Hosp. Sec., Nottingham Gen. Hosp., 1973; Asst. Dist Administrator, S Nottingham, 1975, Dist Administrator, 1978; Dist Administrator, 1981, Dist Gen. Manager, 1984, Newcastle HA. Member: ACARD Working Gp on UK Med. Equipment Industry, 1986; Working Party on Alternative Delivery and Funding of Health Services, 1988. *Publications:* (contrib.) The Future of Acute Services: doctors as managers, 1990; articles in health care management jls. *Recreations:* swimming, books, enjoying townscapes. *Address:* 36 King's Road, Wimbledon, SW19 8QW.

SPRY, Sir John (Farley), Kt 1975; Chief Justice, St Helena and its Dependencies, since 1983; *b* 11 March 1910; *s* of Joseph Farley Spry and Fanny Seagrave Treloar Spry; *m* 1st (marr. diss. 1940); one *s* one *d*; 2nd, Stella Marie (*née* Fichat). *Educ:* Perse School and Peterhouse, Cambridge (MA). Solicitor, 1935; Asst Registrar of Titles and Conveyancer, Uganda, 1936–44; Chief Inspector of Land Registration, Palestine, 1944; Asst Director of Land Registration, Palestine, 1944–48; Registrar-General, Tanganyika 1948–50, Kenya 1950–52; Tanganyika: Registrar-Gen., 1952–56; Legal Draftsman, 1956–60; Principal Sec., Public Service Commn, 1960–61; Puisne Judge, 1961–64; Justice of Appeal, Court of Appeal for Eastern Africa, 1964–70; Vice-President, 1970–75; Chm., Pensions Appeal Tribunals, 1975–76; Chief Justice of Gibraltar, 1976–80, Justice of Appeal, 1980–83, Pres., Court of Appeal, 1983–91; Chief Justice, British Indian Ocean Territory, 1981–87. Comr for Revision of Laws of Gibraltar, 1981–85. *Publications:* Sea Shells of Dar es Salaam, Part I, 1961 (3rd edn 1968), Part II, 1964; Civil Procedure in East Africa, 1969; Civil Law of Defamation in East Africa, 1976. *Recreation:* conchology. *Address:* 15 De Vere Gardens, W8 5AN.

SPURGEON, Maj.-Gen. Peter Lester, CB 1980; Chief Executive, Royal Agricultural Benevolent Institution, 1982–91; *b* 27 Aug. 1927; *s* of Harold Sidney Spurgeon and Emily Anne (*née* Bolton); *m* 1959, Susan Ann (*née* Aylward); one *s* one *d*. *Educ:* Merchant Taylors' Sch., Northwood. Commnd, 1946; 1949–66: HMS Glory; Depot, RM Deal; 40 Commando RM; ADC to Maj.-Gen. Plymouth Gp RM; DS Officers' Sch., RM; RAF Staff Coll., Bracknell; Staff of Comdt Gen. RM; 40 Commando RM; Jt Warfare Estab.; GS02 HQ: ME Comd, Aden, 1967; Army Strategic Comd, 1968–69; Second-in-Comd, 41 Commando RM, 1969–71; DS National Defence Coll., Latimer, 1971–73; CO RM Poole, 1973–75; Dir of Drafting and Records, RM, 1975–76; Comdr, Training Gp, RM, 1977–79 and Training and Reserve Forces, RM, 1979–80; retd 1980. Col Comdt, RM, 1987–90. Pres., RM Assoc., 1986–90. *Recreations:* golf, dinghy sailing. *Address:* c/o Lloyds Bank, 1 High Street, Oxford OX1 4AA. *Club:* Army and Navy.

SPURLING, (Susan) Hilary; writer and critic; *b* 25 Dec. 1940; *d* of Gilbert Alexander Forrest and Emily Maureen Forrest; *m* 1961, John Spurling; two *s* one *d*. *Educ:* Somerville Coll., Oxford (BA). Theatre Critic of the Spectator, 1964–70, Literary Editor, 1966–70. *Publications:* Ivy When Young: the early life of I. Compton-Burnett 1884–1919, 1974; Handbook to Anthony Powell's Music of Time, 1977; Secrets of a Woman's Heart: the later life of I. Compton-Burnett 1920–1969, 1984 (Duff Cooper Meml Prize, 1984; Heinemann Literary Award (jtly), 1985); Elinor Fettiplace's Receipt Book, 1986; Paul Scott, A Life, 1990. *Recreations:* reading, ratting, country walks. *Address:* c/o David Higham Associates, 5–8 Lower John Street, Golden Square, W1R 4HA.

SPURR, Margaret Anne; Headmistress, Bolton School, Girls' Division, since 1979; Consultant, Scholaservices, since 1990; *b* 7 Oct. 1933; *m* 1953, John Spurr; one *s* one *d*. *Educ:* Abbeydale Girls' Grammar Sch., Sheffield; Univ. of Keele. BA (Hons); PGCE. Tutor: Eng. Lit., Univ. of Glasgow, 1971; Eng. Lit. Dept, Adult Educn, Univ. of Keele, 1972–73; Dep. Hd, Fair Oak School, Rugeley, 1973–79. Sen. Examiner, Univ. of London, 1971–80. Pres., 1985–86, Chm., Public Relns Cttee, 1986–, GSA; Chm., Nat. ISIS Cttee, 1987–90; Member: Adv. Cttee, American Studies Resources Centre, Polytechnic of Central London, 1977–90; Scholarship Selection Cttee, ESU, 1983–; CBI Schools Panel, 1985–89. Fellow, Woodard Schs. Governor: Denstone Coll., 1989–; Huyton Coll., 1989–; St Dominic's Sch., Stone, 1989–. *Publications:* (ed) A Curriculum for Capability, 1986; (ed) Girls First, 1987. *Recreations:* gardening, theatre, poetry. *Address:* Hulme Lodge, Ladybridge Lane, Bolton BL1 5DE. *T:* Bolton (0204) 493594; The Old Vicarage, Croxden, Uttoxeter, Staffs ST14 5JQ. *T:* Hollington (088926) 424. *Clubs:* University Women's, Royal Over-Seas League.

SPY, James; Sheriff of North Strathclyde at Paisley, since 1988; *b* 1 Dec. 1952; *s* of James Spy and Jean Learmond; *m* 1980, Jennifer Margaret Malcolm; three *d*. *Educ:* Hermitage Acad., Helensburgh; Glasgow Univ. (LLB Hons). Admitted Solicitor, 1976; passed Advocate, 1979. *Recreations:* music, clocks, model ships, model trains. *Address:* St Ann's, 171 Nithsdale Road, Glasgow G41 5QS. *T:* 041–423 5317.

SQUAIR, George Alexander; Chairman and Chief Executive, SEEBOARD plc (formerly South Eastern Electricity Board), since 1983; *b* 26 July 1929; *s* of Alexander Squair and Elizabeth (*née* Macdonald); *m* 1953, Joy Honeybone; two *s* one *d*. *Educ:* Woolwich Polytechnic; Oxford Technical Coll.; Southampton Univ. CEng, FIEE 1986; CBIM 1984. Gen. distribution engrg posts, 1950–68; Southern Electricity Board: 1st Asst Dist Engr, 1968–69; Dist Engr, Swindon, 1969–70; Area Engr, Newbury, 1970–73; Dist

Manager, Oxford, 1973–74; Area Manager, Newbury, 1974–78; Mem., Exec. Bd, 1976–78; Dep. Chm., 1978–83. *Recreations:* reading, golf. *Address:* SEEBOARD plc, Grand Avenue, Hove BN3 2LS. *T:* Brighton (0273) 724522.

SQUIBB, George Drewry, LVO 1982; QC 1956; Norfolk Herald Extraordinary since 1959; Earl Marshal's Lieutenant, Assessor and Surrogate in the Court of Chivalry, since 1976; *b* 1 Dec. 1906; *o s* of Reginald Augustus Hodder Squibb, Chester; *m* 1st, 1936, Bessie (*d* 1954), *d* of George Whittaker, Burley, Hants; one *d*; 2nd, 1955, Evelyn May, *d* of Frederick Richard Higgins, of Overleigh Manor, Chester. *Educ:* King's School, Chester; Queen's College, Oxford (BCL, MA). Barrister-at-Law, Inner Temple, 1930; Bencher, 1951; Reader, 1975; Treasurer, 1976. Army Officers' Emergency Reserve, 1938. Deputy Chairman Dorset Quarter Sessions, 1950–53, Chairman, 1953–71; Junior Counsel to the Crown in Peerage and Baronetcy Cases, 1954–56; Hon. Historical Adviser in Peerage Cases to the Attorney-General, 1965–; Pres., Transport Tribunal, 1962–81; Chief Commons Commissioner, 1971–85. Member: Cttee on Rating of Charities, 1958–59; Adv. Council on Public Records, 1964–81; Council, Selden Soc., 1961–90 (Vice-Pres., 1969–72). FSA 1946; FSG 1973; FRHistS 1978. Master, Scriveners' Co., 1979–80. JP Dorset, 1943. *Publications:* The Law of Arms in England, 1953; Wiltshire Visitation Pedigrees, 1623, 1955; Reports of Heraldic Cases in the Court of Chivalry, 1956; The High Court of Chivalry, 1959; Visitation Pedigrees and the Genealogist, 1964, 2nd edn 1978; Founders' Kin, 1972; Doctors' Commons, 1977; Visitation of Dorset 1677, 1977; Precedence in England and Wales, 1981; Munimenta Heraldica, 1985; Visitation of Nottinghamshire 1662–64, 1986; Dugdale's Nottinghamshire and Derbyshire Visitation Papers, 1987; Visitation of Derbyshire 1662–64, 1989; Visitation of Hampshire and the Isle of Wight 1686, 1991; papers in legal and antiquarian journals. *Recreation:* genealogical and heraldic research. *Address:* The Old House, Cerne Abbas, Dorset DT2 7JQ. *T:* Cerne Abbas (0300) 341272. *Clubs:* Athenæum, United Oxford & Cambridge University.

SQUIRE, (Clifford) William, CMG 1978; LVO 1972; HM Diplomatic Service, retired; Development Director, University of Cambridge, since 1988; *b* 7 Oct. 1928; *s* of Clifford John Squire and Eleanor Eliza Harpley; *m* 1st, 1959, Marie José Carlier (*d* 1973); one *s* two *d* (and one *s* decd); 2nd, 1976, Sara Laetitia Hutchison; one *s* one *d*. *Educ:* Royal Masonic Sch., Bushey; St John's Coll., Oxford; Coll. of Europe, Bruges. PhD London 1979. British Army, 1947–49. Nigerian Admin. Service, 1953–59; FO, 1959–60; British Legation, Bucharest, 1961–63; FO, 1963–65; UK Mission to UN, New York, 1965–69; Head of Chancery, Bangkok, 1969–72; Head of SE Asian Dept, FCO, 1972–75; Extramural Fellow, Sch. of Oriental and African Studies, London Univ., 1975–76; Counsellor, later Head of Chancery, Washington, 1976–79; Ambassador to Senegal, 1979–82, concurrently to Cape Verde Is, Guinea (Bissau), Guinea (Conakry), Mali and Mauritania; Asst Under-Sec. of State, FCO, 1982–84; Ambassador to Israel, 1984–88. *Address:* Wolfson College, Cambridge. *Clubs:* Travellers'; Cosmos (Washington, DC).

SQUIRE, Peter John; Headmaster, Bedford Modern School, since 1977; *b* 15 Feb. 1937; *s* of Leslie Ernest Squire and Doris Eileen Squire; *m* 1965, Susan Elizabeth (*née* Edwards); one *s* one *d*. *Educ:* King Edward's Sch., Birmingham; Jesus Coll., Oxford (BA 1960, MA 1964); Pembroke Coll. and Dept of Educn, Cambridge (Cert. in Educn 1961). Asst Master, Monkton Combe Sch., Bath, 1961–65; Haberdashers' Aske's Sch., Elstree, 1965–77: Sen. Boarding Housemaster, 1968–77; Sen. History Master, 1970–77. *Recreations:* tennis, gardening, antique collecting. *Address:* Bedford Modern School, Manton Lane, Bedford MK41 7NT. *T:* Bedford (0234) 64331.

SQUIRE, Raglan, FRIBA, MSIA; Consultant, Raglan Squire & Partners, Architects, Engineers and Town Planners, since 1981 (Senior Partner, 1948–81); *b* 30 Jan. 1912; *e s* of late Sir John Squire, Kt; *m* 1st, 1938, Rachel, (*d* 1968), *d* of James Atkey, Oxshott, Surrey; two *s*; 2nd, 1968, Bridget Lawless. *Educ:* Blundell's; St John's Coll., Cambridge. Private practice in London, 1935–. War service with Royal Engineers, 1942–45. Founded firm of Raglan Squire & Partners, 1948. Principal projects: housing, educational and industrial work, 1935–41; pre-fabricated bldgs and industrial design, 1945–48; Eaton Sq. Conversion Scheme, 1945–56; Rangoon Univ. Engineering Coll., 1953–56; Associated Architect, Transport Pavilion, Festival of Britain Exhib., 1951; Town Planning Scheme for Mosul, Iraq, 1955; Bagdad airport report, 1955; factories at Weybridge, Huddersfield, etc; office buildings London, Eastbourne, Bournemouth, etc; gen. practice at home and over-seas incl. major hotels at Teheran, Tunis, Nicosia, Malta and Singapore, Gibraltar, Caribbean and Middle East, 1955–81, retired from active practice. Sec. RIBA Reconstruction Cttee, 1941–42; Council of Architectural Assoc., 1951–52; Guest Editor Architects' Journal, 1947. *Publications:* Portrait of an Architect (autobiog.), 1985; articles in technical press on organisation of Building Industry, Architectural Education, etc. *Recreations:* gardening, chess, ocean racing and designing small yachts. *Address:* 1 Chester Row, SW1. *T:* 071–730 7225. *Clubs:* Royal Thames Yacht, Royal Ocean Racing; Royal Southern Yacht.

SQUIRE, Robin Clifford; MP (C) Hornchurch, since 1979; *b* 12 July 1944; *s* of late Sidney John Squire and Mabel Alice Squire (*née* Gilmore); *m* 1981 Susan Margaret Fey, *d* of Arthur Frederick Branch and Mahala Branch (*née* Parker); one step *s* one step *d*. *Educ:* Tiffin School, Kingston-upon-Thames. FCA. Qualified as Chartered Accountant, 1966; joined Lombard Banking Ltd (subsequently Lombard North Central Ltd) as Accountant, 1968, becoming Dep. Chief Accountant, 1972–79. Councillor, London Borough of Sutton, 1968–82; Chm., Finance Cttee, 1972–76; Leader of Council, 1976–79. Chm., Greater London Young Conservatives, 1973; Vice-Chm., Nat. Young Conservatives, 1974–75. Personal Asst to Rt Hon. Robert Carr, Gen. Election, Feb. 1974; contested (C) Havering, Hornchurch, Oct. 1974. PPS to Minister of State for Transport, 1983–85, to Rt Hon. Chris Patten, Chm. of Cons. Party, 1991–. Mem., Commons Select Cttee on Environment, 1979–83 and 1987–91, on European Legislation, 1985–88; Sec., Cons. Parly European Affairs Cttee, 1979–80; Vice-Chm., Cons. Parly Trade Cttee, 1980–83; Chm., Cons. Parly Environment Cttee, 1990–91 (Jt Vice-Chm., 1985–89); Originator of Local Govt (Access to Information) Act, 1985. Chm., Cons. Action for Electoral Reform, 1983–86 (Vice-Chm., 1982–83); Dep. Chm., Anglo-Asian Cons. Soc., 1982–83. Mem. Bd, Shelter, 1982–; Dir, Link Assured Homes series of cos, 1988–. *Publication:* (jtly) Set the Party Free, 1969. *Recreations:* films, bridge, modern music. *Address:* House of Commons, SW1A 0AA. *T:* 071–219 4526.

SQUIRE, Warwick Nevison, CBE 1982; FRAeS; aviation and defence consultant; *b* 19 July 1921; *s* of late Alfred Squire and Elizabeth Timms; *m* 1947, Adelheid Elli Behrendt; one *d*. *Educ:* Cheltenham Higher Technical Sch. Apprenticeship, H. H. Martyn, Cheltenham, 1936–40; Aircraft Components Ltd (now Dowty Gp), 1940–42; HM Forces and German Control Commn, 1942–46; Dowty Group Plc: Gen. Management, 1946–75; Group Dir and Man. Dir, 1975–83 and Chm., 1983–84, Aerospace and Defence Div. FRAeS 1980; FRSA 1982. *Recreations:* gardening, golf, cricket. *Address:* Highlands, Daisy Bank Road, Leckhampton Hill, Cheltenham, Glos GL53 9QQ. *T:* Cheltenham (0242) 521038.

SQUIRE, William; *see* Squire, C. W.

SRISKANDAN, Kanagaretnam, CEng, FICE, FIStructE, FIHT; Divisional Director, Mott, MacDonald Group (formerly Mott, Hay and Anderson), Consulting Engineers, since 1988; *b* 12 Aug. 1930; *s* of Kanagaretnam Kathiravelu and Kanmanyammal Kumaraswamy; *m* 1956, Dorothy (*née* Harley); two *s* one *d*. *Educ:* Royal College, Colombo; Univ. of Ceylon. BSc Hons London 1952. Junior Asst Engineer, PWD, Ceylon, 1953; Asst Engr, Sir William Halcrow and Partners, Cons. Engrs, London, 1956; Section Engr, Tarmac Civil Engineering Ltd, 1958; Asst Engr, West Riding of Yorkshire CC, 1959, left as Principal Engr; Dept of Transport: Superintending Engr, Midland Road Construction Unit, 1968; Asst Chief Engr, 1971; Deputy Chief Highway Engr, 1976; Chief Highway Engr, 1980–87. *Publications:* papers on various engrg topics. *Recreations:* squash, golf. *Address:* Mott, MacDonald Group, St Anne House, 20–26 Wellesley Road, Croydon CR9 2UL.

SRIVASTAVA, Chandrika Prasad, Padma Bhushan 1972; Secretary-General, International Maritime Organization (formerly IMCO), 1974–89; Chancellor, World Maritime University, since 1983; *b* 8 July 1920; *s* of B. B. Srivastava; *m* 1947, Nirmala Salve; two *d*. *Educ:* Lucknow, India. 1st cl. BA 1940, 1st cl. BA Hons 1941, 1st cl. MA 1942, 1st cl. LLB 1944; gold medals for proficiency in Eng. Lit. and Polit. Science. Under-Sec., Min. of Commerce, India, 1948–49; City Magistrate, Lucknow, 1950; Addtl Dist. Magistrate, Meerut, 1951–52; Directorate-Gen. of Shipping, 1953; Dep. Dir-Gen. of Shipping, 1954–57; Dep. Sec., Min. of Transport, and Pvte Sec. to Minister of Transport and Communications, 1958; Sen. Dep. Dir-Gen. of Shipping, 1959–60; Man. Dir, Shipping Corp. of India, 1961–64; Jt Sec. to Prime Minister, 1964–66; Chm. and Man. Dir, Shipping Corp. of India, 1966–73; Director: Central Inland Water Transport Corp., 1967; Central Bd, Reserve Bank of India, 1972–73; Chm., Mogul Line Ltd, 1967–73. Vice-Pres., Sea Cadet Council, 1970–73. President: Indian Nat. Shipowners' Assoc., 1971–73; Inst. Mar. Technologists, India, 1972 (Hon. Mem., 1981); UN Conf. on Code of Conduct for Liner Confs, 1973–74; Internat. Maritime Lectrs' Assoc., 1980–; Chm., Cttee of Invisibles, 3rd UN Conf. on Trade and Develt, 1972; Member: Nat. Shipping Bd, 1959–73; Merchant Navy Trng Bd, 1959–73; Nat. Welfare Bd for Seafarers, 1966–73; Amer. Bureau of Shipping, 1969; Governing Body, Indian Inst. of Foreign Trade, 1970; State Bd of Tourism, 1970; Nat. Harbour Bd, 1970–73; Gen. Cttee, Bombay Chamber of Commerce and Ind., 1971; Governing Body Indian Inst. of Management, 1972–73; Adv. Bd, Seatrade Acad., 1978– (Chm. Awarding Body, Seatrade Annual Awards for Achievement, 1988); Europort Internat. Cttee of Honour, 1980–; Internat. Chamber of Commerce Internat. Maritime Bureau, 1981–; Bd of Dirs, ICC Centre for Maritime Co-operation, 1985–; Hon. Adv. Cttee, Internat. Congress on The Port—an Ecological Challenge, Hamburg, 1989–; Marine Soc., 1984. Vice Pres., Welsh Centre for Internat. Affairs, 1989–. FRSA 1981. Hon. Member: Master Mariners' Co., 1978; Royal Inst. of Navigation, 1984; Internat. Fedn of Shipmasters' Assocs, 1985; The Warsash Assoc., 1988; Internat. Maritime Pilots' Assoc., 1988; Hon. Fellow: Plymouth Polytech., 1979; Nautical Inst., 1985. Hon. LLD: Bhopal, 1984; Wales, 1987; Malta, 1988. Admiral Padilla Award, Colombia, 1978; Gran Amigo del Mar Award, Colombia, 1978; Gold Mercury Internat. Award Ad Personam, 1984; Award, Seatrade Acad., 1988. Commandeur du Mérite Maritime, France, 1982; Comdr, Order of St Olav, Norway, 1982; Grande Ufficiale dell'Ordine al Merito, Italy, 1983; Comdr, Order of Prince Henry the Navigator, Portugal, 1983; Gold Order of Distinguished Seafarers, Poland, 1983; Nautical Medal, 1st cl., Greece, 1983; Gran Cruz Distintivo Blanco, Orden Cruz Peruana al Mérito Naval, Peru, 1984; Gran Cruz, Orden de Manuel Amador Guerrero, Panama, 1985; Grande-Oficial, Ordem do Mérito Naval, Brazil, 1986; Commander's Cross, Order of Merit, Poland, 1986; Silver Medal of Honour, Malmö, Sweden, 1988; Kt Great Band, Order of Humane African Redemption, Liberia, 1989; Comdr's Cross of Order of Merit, FRG, 1989; Comdr Grand Cross, Royal Order of the Star of the North, Sweden, 1989. *Publications:* articles on shipping in newspapers and jls. *Recreation:* music. *Address:* c/o International Maritime Organization, 4 Albert Embankment, SE1 7SR. *Clubs:* Athenæum, Anglo-Belgian; Willingdon (Bombay).

STABB, His Honour Sir William (Walter), Kt 1981; QC 1968; FCIArb; retired; a Circuit Judge (formerly Official Referee, Supreme Court of Judicature), 1969–78; Senior Official Referee, 1978–85; *b* 6 Oct. 1913; 2nd *s* of late Sir Newton Stabb, OBE and late Lady E. M. Stabb; *m* 1940, Dorothy Margaret Leckie; four *d*. *Educ:* Rugby; University Coll., Oxford. Called to the Bar, 1936; Master of the Bench, Inner Temple, 1964, Treasurer, 1985. Served with RAF, 1940–46, attaining rank of Sqdn Ldr. Junior Counsel to Ministry of Labour, 1960; Prosecuting Counsel to BoT, 1962–68. Chm. 1961–69, Dep. Chm. 1969–71, Bedfordshire QS. *Recreations:* fishing, golf. *Address:* The Pale Farm, Chipperfield, Kings Langley, Herts WD4 9BH. *T:* Kings Langley (0923) 263124; 1 King's Bench Walk, Temple, EC4. *T:* 071–353 8436.

STABLE, (Rondle) Owen (Charles), QC 1963; **His Honour Judge Stable;** a Circuit Judge, since 1979; Senior Circuit Judge, Snaresbrook Crown Court, since 1982; *b* 28 Jan. 1923; *yr s* of late Rt Hon. Sir Wintringham Norton Stable, MC, and Lucie Haden (*née* Freeman); *m* 1949, Yvonne Brook, *y d* of late Maj. L. B. Holliday, OBE; two *d*. *Educ:* Winchester. Served with Rifle Bde, 1940–46 (Captain). Barrister, Middle Temple, 1948; Bencher, 1969. Dep. Chm., QS, Herts, 1963–71; a Recorder of the Crown Court, 1972–79. Board of Trade Inspector: Cadco Group of Cos, 1963–64; H. S. Whiteside & Co Ltd, 1965–67; International Learning Systems Corp. Ltd, 1969–71; Pergamon Press, 1969–73. Sec. National Reference Tribunal for the Coal Mining Industry, 1953–64; Chancellor of Diocese of Bangor, 1959–88; Member, Governing Body of the Church in Wales, 1960–88; Licensed Parochial Lay Reader, Diocese of St Albans, 1961–; Member: General Council of the Bar, 1962–66; Senate of 4 Inns of Court, 1971–74; Senate of the Inns of Court and the Bar, 1974–75. Chm., Horserace Betting Levy Appeal Tribunal, 1969–74. JP Hertfordshire, 1963–71. *Publication:* (with R. M. Stuttard) A Review of Coursing, 1971. *Recreations:* shooting, listening to music. *Address:* Snaresbrook Crown Court, Hollybush Hill, E11 1QW. *Club:* Boodle's.

See also P. L. W. Owen.

STABLER, Arthur Fletcher; District Councillor, Newcastle upon Tyne; Member, Supplementary Benefits Commission, 1976–79; *b* 1919; *s* of Edward and Maggie Stabler; *m* 1948, Margaret Stabler; two *s*. *Educ:* Cruddas Park Sch. Engineer apprenticeship, Vickers Armstrong, 1935–39. Served War, Royal Northumberland Fusiliers, 1939–46. With Vickers Armstrong, 1946–78. Newcastle upon Tyne: City Councillor, 1963–74; District Councillor, 1973–; Dep. Lord Mayor, 1982–83; Lord Mayor, 1983–84; Chairman: Housing Renewals, 1975–76; Arts and Recreation, 1976–77; Case Work Sub-Cttee, 1974–77; Tenancy Relations Sub-Cttee, 1975–77; Community Develt Sub-Cttee, 1975–76; Town Moor Sub-Cttee, 1976–77; Personnel Sub-Cttee, 1982–; Area Housing Cttee, 1984–85; Priority Area Sub-Cttee, 1984–85; Health Adv. Cttee, 1986–87; District HA Jt Consultative Cttee; Festival Cttee, 1987–88; Public Works Cttee, 1987–88; Vice-Chairman: Social Services Cttee, 1974–76; Housing Management Cttee, 1975–76; Tyneside Summer Exhibn Cttee, 1982–; Tyne and Wear Jt Fire and Civil Defence Cttee, 1986–89; Cityworks Cttee, 1989. Chm., Axwell Park Community Homes, 1978–79; Mem., numerous Tenants' Assocs. Chm., Newcastle upon Tyne Central Labour Party, 1965–78. Pres., No 6 Br., AUEW. Chm., Westerhope Golf Club Jt Sub-Cttee, 1976–77.

President: Newcastle upon Tyne and District Allotments and Garden Council, 1980–; Elswick Park Bowling Club, 1980–; Cttee, Tyne Wear Polish Solidarity Club, 1981–; Mem., Theatre Royal Trust, 1988–. Life Mem., High Pitt Social Club; Hon. Member: Casino Royal Club, 1980; St Joseph's Club, 1983; Royal British Legion Club, 1983. *Publication*: Gannin Along the Scotswood Road, 1976. *Recreations*: social work, local history. *Address*: 10 Whitebeam Place, Elswick, Newcastle upon Tyne NE4 7EJ. *T*: 091–273 2362. *Clubs*: Pineapple CIU, Polish White Eagle, Ryton Social, Tyneside Irish (Hon.), Maddison's (Hon.) (Newcastle upon Tyne).

STACEY, Air Vice-Marshal John Nichol, CBE 1971; DSO 1945; DFC 1942; *b* 14 Sept. 1920; *s* of Captain Herbert Chambers Stacey and Mrs May Stacey; *m* 1950, Veronica Satterly; two *d*. *Educ*: Whitgift Middle Sch., Croydon. Merchant Marine Apprentice, 1937–38; joined RAF, 1938; flying throughout War of 1939–45 (despatches thrice); comd No 160 Sqdn, 1944–45; Asst Air Attaché, Washington, 1947–48; psc 1949; on staff at Staff Coll., 1958–60; Chief of Air Staff, Royal Malayan Air Force, 1960–63 (JMN); comd RAF Laarbruch, Germany, 1963–66; AOC, Air Cadets, 1968–71; Dir, Orgn and Admin. Planning (RAF), MoD, 1971–74; AOA, Support Comd, 1974–75, retired. Dir, Stonham Housing Assoc., 1976–81; Member: Tunbridge Wells HA, 1981–91; RAFA Housing Assoc., 1982–86; Tunbridge Wells and Dist Housing Assoc., 1989–. President: Royal British Legion Gondhurst Br., 1991–; Headcorn Br., RAFA; Trustee: Housing Assoc. Charitable Trust, 1978–86; Tunbridge Wells Cancer Help Centre; Bedgebury Sch., 1983–. *Recreations*: sailing, golf. *Address*: Riseden Cottage, Riseden, Goudhurst, Cranbrook, Kent TN17 1HJ. *T*: Goudhurst (0580) 211239. *Clubs*: Royal Air Force; Dale Hill Golf.

STACEY, Prof. Margaret; Professor of Sociology, University of Warwick, 1974–89, Emeritus Professor, 1989; *b* 27 March 1922; *d* of Conrad Eugene Petrie and Grace Priscilla Boyce; *m* 1945, Frank Arthur Stacey (*d* 1977); three *s* two *d*. *Educ*: City of London Sch. for Girls; London Sch. of Econs (BScEcon, 1st Cl. Hons Sociology). Labour Officer, Royal Ordnance Factory, 1943–44; Tutor, Oxford Univ., 1944–51; University Coll. of Swansea: Res. Officer and Fellow, 1961–63; Lectr in Sociol., 1963–70; Sen. Lectr in Sociol., 1970–74; Dir, Medical Sociol. Res. Centre, 1972–74. Lucille Petry Loene Vis. Prof. Univ. of Calif., San Francisco, 1988. British Sociol Association: Mem. Exec. Cttee, 1965–70, 1975–79; Hon. Gen. Sec., 1968–70; Chairperson, 1977–79; Pres., 1981–83; Mem. Women's Caucus, 1974–. Pres., Section N, BAAS, 1990. Scientific Advr to DHSS: Temp. Advr to Reg. Dir, WHO EURO. Pres., Assoc. for Welfare of Children in Hosp. (Wales), 1974–; Member: Assoc. for Welfare of Children in Hosp., 1960–; Welsh Hosp. Bd, 1970–74; Davies Cttee on Hosp. Complaints Procedure, 1971–73; GMC, 1976–84; Sociol. Cttee, SSRC, 1969–71; Health and Health Policy Cttee, SSRC, 1976–77. FRSM. Hon. Fellow, UC of Swansea, 1987. *Publications*: Tradition and Change: a study of Banbury, 1960, paperback 1970; (ed) Comparability in Social Research, 1969; (ed and jt author) Hospitals, Children and their Families: a study of the welfare of children in hospital, 1970; Methods of Social Research, 1970; (jtly) Power, Persistence and Change: a second study of Banbury, 1975; (ed) The Sociology of the NHS, 1976; (ed jtly and contrib.) Beyond Separation: further studies of children in hospital, 1979; (jtly) Women, Power and Politics, 1981 (Fawcett Book Prize, 1982); (ed jtly) Concepts of Health, Illness and Disease: a comparative perspective, 1986; Sociology of Health and Healing: a textbook, 1988; contrib. to Feminist Rev., Sociol Rev., Sociol., Brit. Jl of Sociol., Social Science and Med., Jl of Med. Ethics, and Sociol. of Health and Illness. *Recreations*: walking, gardening. *Address*: 8 Lansdowne Circus, Leamington Spa, Warwicks CV32 4SW. *T*: Leamington Spa (0926) 312094.

STACEY, Prof. Maurice, CBE 1966; FRS 1950; Mason Professor of Chemistry, 1956–74, now Emeritus, and Head of Department, 1956–74, University of Birmingham; Dean of Faculty of Science, 1963–66; Hon. Senior Research Fellow, 1974–76; *b* 8 April 1907; *s* of J. H. Stacey, Bromstead, Newport, Shropshire; *m* 1937, Constance Mary, *d* of Wm Pugh, Birmingham; two *s* two *d*. *Educ*: Adam's School, Newport, Shropshire; Universities of Birmingham, London and Columbia (New York). BSc (Hons) Birmingham Univ., 1929; Demonstrator, Chemistry, Birmingham Univ., 1929–32; PhD 1932; Meldola Medal, 1933; Beit Memorial Fellow for Medical Research, School of Tropical Medicine, London Univ., 1933–37 (DSc 1939); Travelling Fellow, Columbia Univ., New York, 1937; Lecturer in Chemistry, Univ. of Birmingham, 1937–44, Reader in Biological Chemistry, 1944–46, Prof. of Chemistry, 1946–56. Tilden Lecturer of Chemical Society, 1946; P. F. Frankland Lectr, Roy. Inst. of Chemistry, 1955; Ivan Levinstein Lectr, 1956, Jubilee Meml Lectr, 1973, Soc. Chem. Industry; Vice-Pres. Chemical Society, 1950–53, 1955–58, 1960–63, 1968–71; Associate Editor, Advances in Carbohydrate Chem., 1950–; Editor, Advances in Fluorine Chem., 1960–73; Founder Editor, European Polymer Jl. Chief Scientific Adviser for Civil Defence, Midland Region, 1957–78; Vice-Pres., Home Office Sci. Council, 1974– (Mem., 1963–74); Governor, National Vegetable Research Institute, 1961–73; Former Member, Court of Governors: Univ. of Keele; Univ. of Warwick; Univ. of Loughborough; Gov., Adam's Sch., 1956–74; Mem. Council, Edgbaston High Sch. for Girls, 1963–84 (Vice-Pres. 1984–). Sugar Research Prize of National Academy of Science, New York, 1950; John Scott Medal and Award, 1969; Haworth Meml Medal, 1970. Captain, 2nd in Command Birmingham Home Guard, Chemical Warfare School, 1942–44. Defence Medal, 1945. Visiting Lecturer, Universities of Oslo, Stockholm, Uppsala and Lund, 1949, Helsinki, 1955. Has foreign Hon. doctorate and medals. Hon. DSc Keele, 1977. *Publications*: (with S. A. Barker) Polysaccharides of Micro-organisms, 1961, and Carbohydrates of Living Tissues; about 400 scientific contribs to Jl of Chem. Soc., Proc. Royal Soc., etc., on organic and biological chemistry subjects. *Recreations*: foreign travel, athletics (Life Mem. AAA), horticulture, science antiques. *Address*: 12 Bryony Road, Weoley Hill, Birmingham B29 4BU. *T*: 021–475 2065; The University, Birmingham. *T*: 021–472 1301. *Club*: Athenæum.

STACEY, Rear-Adm. Michael Lawrence, CB 1979; private consultant in marine pollution; Vice President, Advisory Committee on Protection of the Sea, since 1988; Director, Marine Emergency Operations, Marine Division, Department of Transport (formerly Department of Trade), 1979–87; *b* 6 July 1924; *s* of Maurice Stacey and Dorice Evelyn (*née* Bulling); *m* 1955, Penelope Leana (*née* Riddoch); two *s*. *Educ*: Epsom Coll. Entered RN as Cadet, 1942; Normandy landings, HMS Hawkins, 1944; served on HM Ships Rotherham, Cambrian, Shoreham, Hornet, Vernon, Euryalus, Bermuda, Vigilant, Comdr 1958; staff of RN Staff Coll.; in comd HMS Blackpool, 1960–62; JSSC; Captain 1966; Chief Staff Officer to Admiral Commanding Reserves, 1966–68; in comd HMS Andromeda and Captain (F) Sixth Frigate Sqdn, 1968–70; Dep. Dir of Naval Warfare, 1970–73; in comd HMS Tiger, 1973–75; Asst Chief of Naval Staff (Policy), 1975–76; Flag Officer, Gibraltar, 1976–78. ADC to the Queen, 1975. FNI; FBIM. Younger Brother, Trinity House, 1979. *Recreations*: fishing, yachting. *Address*: Little Hintock, 40 Lynch Road, Farnham, Surrey GU9 8BY. *T*: Farnham (0252) 713032. *Clubs*: Army and Navy, Royal Naval Sailing Association.

STACEY, Morna Dorothy, (Mrs W. D. Stacey); see Hooker, Prof. M. D.

STACEY, Rev. Nicolas David; social services consultant, since 1985; *b* 27 Nov. 1927; *s* of late David and of Gwen Stacey; *m* 1955, Hon. Anne Bridgeman, *er d* of 2nd Viscount Bridgeman, KBE, CB, DSO, MC; one *s* two *d*. *Educ*: RNC, Dartmouth; St Edmund Hall, Oxford (hons degree Mod. Hist.); Cuddesdon Theol Coll., Oxford. Midshipman, HMS Anson, 1945–46; Sub-Lt, 1946–48. Asst Curate, St Mark's, Portsea, 1953–58; Domestic Chap. to Bp of Birmingham, 1958–60; Rector of Woolwich, 1960–68; Dean of London Borough of Greenwich, 1965–68; Dep. Dir of Oxfam, 1968–70; Director of Social Services: London Borough of Ealing, 1971–74; Kent County Council, 1974–85; Dir, AIDS Policy Unit, sponsored by Citizen Action, 1988–89. Chm., Youth Call, 1981–; Vice-Chm., TV South Charitable Trust, 1988–. Six Preacher, Canterbury Cathedral, 1984–89. Sporting career: internat. sprinter, 1948–52, incl. British Empire Games, 1949, and Olympic Games, 1952 (semi-finalist 200 metres and finalist 4 × 400 metres relay); Pres., OUAC, 1951; winner, Oxf. v Cambridge 220 yds, 1948–51; Captain, Combined Oxf. and Camb. Athletic Team, 1951. *Publication*: Who Cares (autobiog.), 1971. *Address*: The Old Vicarage, Selling, Faversham, Kent ME13 9RD. *T*: Canterbury (0227) 752833. *Clubs*: Beefsteak; Royal St George's Golf (Sandwich, Kent).

STACK, (Ann) Prunella, (Mrs Brian St Quentin Power), OBE 1980; President, The Women's League of Health and Beauty, since 1982 (Member of Council, since 1950); *b* 28 July 1914; *d* of Capt. Hugh Bagot Stack, 8th Ghurka Rifles, and Mary Meta Bagot Stack, Founder of The Women's League of Health and Beauty; *m* 1st, 1938, Lord David Douglas-Hamilton (*d* 1944); two *s*; 2nd, 1950, Alfred G. Albers, FRCS (*d* 1951), Cape Town, S Africa; 3rd, 1964, Brian St Quentin Power. *Educ*: The Abbey, Malvern Wells. Mem. of the National Fitness Council, 1937–39. Vice-Pres., Outward Bound Trust, 1980–. *Publications*: The Way to Health and Beauty, 1938; Movement is Life, 1973; Island Quest, 1979; Zest for Life, 1988; Style for Life, 1990. *Recreations*: poetry, music, travel. *Address*: 14 Gertrude Street, SW10 0JN.

STACK, Rt. Rev. Mgr George; Vicar General, Archdiocese of Westminster, since 1990; *b* 9 May 1946; *s* of Gerald Stack and Elizabeth (*née* McKenzie). *Educ*: St Aloysius Coll., Highgate; St Edmund's Coll., Ware; St Mary's Coll., Strawberry Hill. BEd (Hons). Ordained priest, 1972; Curate, St Joseph's, Hanwell 1972–75; Diocesan Catechetical Office, 1975–77; Curate, St Paul's, Wood Green, 1977–83; Parish Priest, Our Lady Help of Christians, Kentish Town, 1983–90. *Recreations*: gardening, calligraphy, media studies. *Address*: Archbishop's House, Westminster, SW1P 1QJ. *T*: 071–834 3144.

STACK, Air Chief Marshal Sir Neville; see Stack, Air Chief Marshal Sir T. N.

STACK, Neville; international editorial consultant; *b* 2 Sept. 1928; *m* 1953, Molly Rowe; one *s* one *d*. *Educ*: Arnold School. Reporter: Ashton-under-Lyne Reporter, 1948; Express & Star, 1950; Sheffield Telegraph, and Kemsley National Papers, 1955; Northern News Editor, IPC national papers, 1971; Sub-editor, Daily Express, 1973; Editor, Stockport Advertiser, 1974; Editor, Leicester Mercury, 1974–87; Dir, F. Hewitt and Co. (1927) Ltd (Mercury Publishers), 1982–88; Editorial Consultant, Straits Times, Singapore, 1988–89. Press Fellow, Wolfson Coll., Cambridge, 1987–88; Vis. Fellow, Graduate Centre for Journalism, City Univ., 1988. Hon. MA Leicester, 1988. *Publications*: The Empty Palace, 1976; Editing for the Nineties, 1988. *Recreations*: writing, sailing, riding, flying. *Address*: 34 Main Street, Belton-in-Rutland, Leicestershire LE15 9LB. *T*: Belton (057286) 645.

STACK, Prunella; see Stack, A. P.

STACK, Air Chief Marshal Sir (Thomas) Neville, KCB 1972 (CB 1969); CVO 1963; CBE 1965; AFC 1957; Extra Gentleman Usher to the Queen, since 1989 (Gentleman Usher, 1978–89); *b* 19 Oct. 1919; *s* of T. Neville Stack, AFC, pioneer airman, and Edythe Neville Stack; *m* 1955, Diana Virginia, *d* of late Oliver Stuart Todd, MBE; one *s* one *d*. *Educ*: St Edmund's College, Ware; RAF College, Cranwell. Served on flying boats, 1939–45 (mentioned in despatches); Coastal Command, 1945–52; Transport Support flying in Far East (Malaya Ops) and UK, 1954–59; Dep. Captain of The Queen's Flight, 1960–62; Transport Support in Far East (Borneo Ops), 1963–64; Comdt, RAF Coll., Cranwell, 1967–70; UK Perm. Mil. Deputy, CENTO, Ankara, 1970–72; AOC-in-C, RAF Trng Comd, 1973–75; Air Sec., 1976–78. Air ADC to the Queen, 1976–78. Dir-Gen., Asbestos Internat. Assoc., 1978–89. Mem. Council, CRC, 1978– (Mem. Exec. Cttee, 1978–88). Pres., Old Cranwellian Assoc., 1984–. Governor, Wellington Coll., 1978–90. Freeman, City of London; Liveryman, Guild of Air Pilots and Air Navigators. FRMetS, 1945–90; FBIM, 1970–88. *Recreations*: various outdoor sports; undergardening. *Address*: 4 Perrymead Street, Fulham, SW6 3SP. *Clubs*: Royal Air Force, Boodle's, Hurlingham.

STACPOOLE, John Wentworth; Deputy Secretary, Department of Health and Social Security, 1979–82; *b* 16 June 1926; *s* of late G. W. Stacpoole and of Mrs M. G. Butt; *m* 1954, Charmian, *d* of late J. P. Bishop and Mrs E. M. Bishop; one *s* one *d*. *Educ*: Sedbergh; Magdalen Coll., Oxford (Demy; MA). Army, 1944–47 (Lieut, Assam Regt). Colonial Office, 1951–68, Private Sec. to Sec. of State, 1964–65; transf. to Min. of Social Security, 1968; Under-Sec., DHSS, 1973. Mem., Maidstone HA, 1982–. Chm., Maidstone Hospice Appeal, 1987–. *Recreations*: reading, walking, sketching. *Address*: Fairseat Lodge, Fairseat, near Sevenoaks, Kent. *T*: Fairseat (0732) 822201.

STADLEN, Nicholas Felix; QC 1991; *b* 3 May 1950; *s* of Peter Stadlen and Hedi (*née* Simon); *m* 1972, Frances Edith Howarth, *d* of T. E. B. and Margaret Howarth; three *s*. *Educ*: St Paul's School (Scholar); Trinity Coll., Cambridge (Open Scholarship and McGill Exhibition; BA Hons Classics Part 1, History Part 2). Pres., Cambridge Union Soc., 1970. First in order of merit, Part 1 Bar Exams, 1975; called to the Bar, Inner Temple, 1976. Mem., Bar Council Public Affairs Cttee, 1987. First Sec., British-Irish Assoc., 1972–74. *Publications*: (with Michael Barnes) Gulbenkian Foundation Reports on National Music and Drama Education, 1974–75; (contrib.) Convention: an account of the 1976 US Democratic Party Presidential Nominating Convention, 1976. *Recreation*: listening to classical music. *Address*: Fountain Court, Temple, EC4Y 9DH. *T*: 071–583 3335.

STAFFORD, 15th Baron *cr* 1640; **Francis Melfort William Fitzherbert;** *b* 13 March 1954; *s* of 14th Baron Stafford and of Morag Nada, *yr d* of late Lt-Col Alastair Campbell; *S* father, 1986; *m* 1980, Katharine Mary Codrington; two *s* two *d*. *Educ*: Ampleforth College; Reading Univ.; RAC, Cirencester. Director (non-executive): Tarmac Industrial Products Div.; Mid Staffs Mental Health Foundn. Pres. and Patron various orgns in North Staffs. Governor, Harper Adams Agricl Coll. *Recreations*: shooting, cricket, golf. *Heir*: *s* Hon. Benjamin John Basil Fitzherbert, *b* 8 Nov. 1983. *Address*: Swynnerton Park, Stone, Staffordshire ST15 0QE. *T*: Swynnerton (078135) 228. *Clubs*: Farmers'; Lord's Taverners.

STAFFORD, Bishop Suffragan of, since 1987; **Rt. Rev. Michael Charles Scott-Joynt;** *b* 1943; *m* 1965, Louise White; two *s* one *d*. *Educ*: King's College, Cambridge (BA 1965, MA 1968); Cuddesdon Theological College. Deacon 1967, priest 1968; Curate, Cuddesdon, 1967–70; Tutor, Cuddesdon Coll., 1967–71; Chaplain 1971–72; Team Vicar, Newbury, 1972–75; Priest-in-charge: Caversfield, 1975–79; Bicester, 1975–79; Bucknell, 1976–79; Rector, Bicester Area Team Ministry, 1979–81; RD of Bicester and Islip, 1976–81; Canon Residentiary of St Albans, 1982–87; Dir of Ordinands and In-Service Training, Diocese of St Albans, 1982–87. *Address*: Ash Garth, Broughton Crescent, Barlaston, Stoke-on-Trent ST12 9DD.

STAFFORD, Archdeaconry of; see Lichfield.

STAFFORD, David Valentine; Secretary, Economic and Social Research Council, 1988–90; *b* 14 Feb. 1930; *s* of Augustus Everard and Emily Blanche Stafford; *m* 1953, Aileen Patricia Wood; one *s* one *d*. *Educ:* Rutlish School, Merton. Dept of Educn and Science, 1951–88; Sec., Open Univ. Planning Cttee, 1967–69. Acting Chm., ESRC, Feb.–Sept. 1988. *Recreations:* reading, gardening, theatre, music. *Address:* 3 Bloomfield Park, Bath, Avon BA2 2BY. *T:* Bath (0225) 312563.

STAFFORD, Frank Edmund, CMG 1951; CBE 1946 (OBE 1931); Malayan CS, retired 1951; *b* 24 Aug. 1895; *s* of late Frank Stafford and Marie Stafford; *m* 1943, Ida Wadham (marr. diss., 1950), *d* of late Conway Burton-Durham; one *s*; *m* 1953, Catherine Rolfe (*d* 1984); *m* 1985, Mrs Doreen Voll. *Educ:* Royal Gram. School, Guildford. Served World War I, 1914–19, India and Mesopotamia, Queen's Royal West Surrey Regt. Joined staff of Civil Commissioner, Iraq, 1919; appointed to High Commission, Iraq, 1921; Financial Secretary, 1924; Financial Adviser, British Embassy, Baghdad, 1931; Colonial Service, Nigeria, 1936 (Asst Treasurer, Principal Asst Sec., Actg Financial Sec.). War of 1939–45, commissioned in Army (Lt-Col) for service with Occupied Enemy Territory Administration, 1941; Financial Adviser, Ethiopian Govt, 1942; attached LHQ Australia, 1944; Col, Military Administration, British Borneo, 1945; demobilized, 1946 (Brig.); seconded to Foreign Office, 1946; Member UK Delegn Italian Peace Conference and Council of Foreign Ministers; Head UK Delegn Four Power Commission, 1947; Member UK Delegn to UN, 1948, 1949, 1950, 1952; Foreign Office Adviser (Minister) to Chief Administrator, Eritrea, 1951–53; Adviser to Ethiopian Govt, 1953–60. Chm. Council, Royal Soc. of St George, 1978. FRAS, FRGS. Order Star of Ethiopia, 1944; Grand Officer, Star of Honour, 1955. *Publications:* contributions to Encyc. Britannica and to Kipling Jl, and International Affairs. *Recreations:* horticulture, hagiology. *Address:* 3 Holbrook Park, Horsham, West Sussex RH12 5PW. *T:* Horsham (0403) 52497. *Club:* National Liberal.

STAFFORD, Godfrey Harry, CBE 1976; PhD; FRS 1979; FInstP; Master of St Cross College, Oxford, 1979–87; *b* 15 April 1920; *s* of Henry and Sarah Stafford; *m* 1950, Helen Goldthorp (*née* Clark); one *s* twin *d*. *Educ:* Rondebosch Boys High Sch., S Africa; Univ. of Cape Town; Gonville and Caius Coll., Cambridge. MSc Cape Town, 1941; Ebden Scholar, PhD Cantab 1950; MA Oxon 1971. South African Naval Forces, 1941–46. Harwell, 1949–51; Head of Biophysics Subdiv., CSIR, Pretoria, 1951–54; Cyclotron Gp, AERE, 1954–57; Rutherford Laboratory: Head of Proton Linear Accelerator Gp, 1957; Head of High Energy Physics Div., 1963; Dep. Dir, 1966; Dir, Rutherford Lab., Chilton, 1969–79; Dir Gen., 1979–81, Hon. Scientist, 1987–, Rutherford Appleton Laboratory; Fellow, St Cross Coll., Oxford, 1971–79 (Hon. Fellow, 1987). CERN appointments: UK deleg. to Council, 1973; Vice-Pres., Council, 1973; Scientific Policy Cttee, 1973, Vice-Chm., 1976, Chm., 1978. Vice-Pres. for meetings, Inst. of Physics, 1976; President: European Physical Soc., 1984–86 (Vice-Pres., 1982–84); Inst. of Physics, 1986–88. Governor: Oxford Centre for Post-Graduate Hebrew Studies, 1983–; Westminster Coll., 1987–91. Glazebrook Prize and Medal, Inst. of Physics, 1981. Hon. DSc Birmingham, 1980. *Publications:* papers and articles in learned jls on: biophysics, nuclear physics, high energy physics. *Recreations:* walking, foreign travel, music. *Address:* Ferry Cottage, North Hinksey Village, Oxford OX2 0NA. *T:* Oxford (0865) 247621.

STAFFORD, John, OBE 1977; HM Diplomatic Service, retired; *b* 15 June 1920; *s* of late Frank and Gertrude Stafford, Sheffield; *m* 1949, Mary Jocelyn Goodwin, *d* of late Capt. J. G. Budge, RN. *Educ:* High Storrs Grammar Sch. Exchequer and Audit Dept, 1939. RAF, W/O Pilot, 1940. Board of Trade, 1946; Assistant Trade Commissioner, Delhi, Karachi, Bulawayo, 1946–56; Trade Commissioner, Karachi, Lahore, Bombay, Madras, Lahore, 1956–65; Dep. High Comr, Lahore, 1965–69; Consul, Houston, Texas, 1969–71; First Sec. (Commercial), New Delhi, 1974–77; Consul Gen., Brisbane, 1978–80. *Recreations:* cricket, tennis, theatre, music. *Address:* Leacroft, 268 Brooklands Road, Weybridge, Surrey KT13 0QX. *Clubs:* East India, Devonshire, Sports and Public Schools; Royal Bombay Yacht; Punjab (Lahore).

STAFFORD-CLARK, Dr David, MD; FRCP; FRCPsych; DPM; Consultant Emeritus, Guy's Hospital and Joint Hospitals, Institute of Psychiatry, University of London; formerly Physician in Charge, Department of Psychological Medicine, and Director of The York Clinic, Guy's Hospital, 1954–73; Chairman, Psychiatric Division, Guy's Group, 1973–74; Consultant Physician, Bethlem Royal and Maudsley Hospitals and the Institute of Psychiatry, 1954–73; retired; *b* 17 March 1916; *s* of Francis and Cordelia Susan Stafford Clark; *m* 1941, Dorothy Stewart (*née* Oldfield); three *s* one *d*. *Educ:* Felsted; University of London. Guy's Hospital. MRCS, LRCP, 1939; MB, BS, 1939. Served War of 1939–45, RAFVR; trained as Medical Parachutist (despatches twice); demobilised 1945. Guy's Hosp., MRCP, Nuffield Med. Fellow, 1946; 3 years postgrad. trg appts, Inst. of Psychiatry, Maudsley Hosp.; MD London, 1947, DPM London, 1948; Registrar, Nat. Hosp., Queen Sq., 1948. Resident Massachusetts Gen. Hosp., Dept of Psychiatry, and Teaching Clinical Fellow, Harvard Med. School, 1949; First Asst, Professorial Unit, Maudsley Hosp., 1950; Mem. Assoc. for Research in Mental and Nervous Disorders, NY, 1950–53; Consultant Staff, Guy's Hosp., 1950; Lectureship, Psychology (Faculty of Letters), Reading Univ., 1950–54. Hon. Vis. Prof., Johns Hopkins Univ., USA, 1964; Gifford Lectr and Vis. Prof., St Andrews Univ., 1978. Member: Archbishop of Canterbury's Commn on Divine Healing; Council, Royal Medico-Psychological Assoc.; Council, Medico-Legal Soc.; Examr, RCP London and Cambridge MD; Editorial Bds, Guy's Hosp. Reports, and Mod. Med. of Gt Britain. Acted as adviser to various motion picture companies (Universal International etc) on medical aspects of their productions; has also acted as adviser and director on a large number of medical programmes on sound radio, and both BBC and Independent Television, including the "Lifeline" series of programmes for the BBC, and documentary programmes for ITV on the emotional and intellectual growth of normal children, and the life and work of Freud; Author of Brain and Behaviour Series in Adult Education Television Programmes on BBC Channel 2; Mind and Motive Series, 1966. FRCP, 1958; Mem., NY Acad. of Sciences; FRSA (Silver Medal), 1959; Hon. RCM, 1966; Foundn Fellow, RCPsych, 1972, Hon. Fellow, 1976; FRSM. Hon. Pres., Guy's Hosp. RUFC, 1972; Hon. Mem., Cambridge RUFC, 1972. Gate Prize for Poetry, 1933. *Publications: poetry:* Autumn Shadow, 1941; Sound in the Sky, 1944; *novel:* Soldier Without a Rifle, 1979; *medical:* Psychiatry Today (Pelican), 1951; Psychiatry for Students, 1964, 7th (rev.) edn, 1989; What Freud Really Said, 1965; Five Questions in Search of an Answer, 1970; chapters in: Emergencies in Medical Practice, 1st, 2nd and 3rd edns, 1948, 1950, 1952; Compendium of Emergencies, 1st and 2nd edns; Case Histories in Psychosomatic Medicine, 1952; Taylor's Medical Jurisprudence, 12th edn, 1965; Schizophrenia: Somatic Aspects, 1st edn, 1957; Frontiers in General Hospital Psychiatry, 1961; A Short Textbook of Medicine, 1963; The Pathology and Treatment of Sexual Deviation, 1964; Modern Trends in Psychological Medicine, 1970; Psychiatric Treatment, Concepts of, in Encyclopædia Britannica, 200th anniv. edn, 1973; contributions to various medical textbooks and to medical and scientific jls. *Recreations:* travel, reading, writing, making and watching films, theatre. *Club:* Royal Air Force.

See also M. Stafford-Clark.

STAFFORD-CLARK, Max; artistic director, English Stage Company at Royal Court Theatre, since 1981; *b* 17 March 1941; *s* of David Stafford-Clark, *qv*; *m* 1st, 1971, Carole Hayman; 2nd, 1981, Ann Pennington; one *d*. *Educ:* Felstead School; Riverdale Country Day School, NY; Trinity College, Dublin. Associate dir, Traverse, 1966, artistic dir, 1968–70; dir, Traverse Workshop Co., 1970–74; founder, Joint Stock Theatre Group, 1974; at Abbey Theatre, Dublin, Nottingham Rep. and NY Shakespeare Festival Public Theatre. Best Drama Director Award, British Theatre Assoc., 1981 (for Outskirts and Borderline); Obie Award, 1983 (for Top Girls, NY). *Publication:* Letters to George, 1989. *Recreation:* lobbying Arts Council. *Address:* Royal Court Theatre, Sloane Square, SW1W 8AS. *T:* 071–730 5174. *Club:* Groucho.

STAGG, Prof. Geoffrey Leonard, MBE 1945; Professor Emeritus, Department of Spanish and Portuguese, University of Toronto; *b* 10 May 1913; *s* of Henry Percy Stagg and Maude Emily Bradbury; *m* 1948, Amy Southwell, Wellesley Hills, Mass, USA; two *s* one *d*. *Educ:* King Edward's School, Birmingham (Scholar); Trinity Hall, Cambridge (Scholar). BA 1st cl. Hons Modern and Medieval Languages Tripos, 1934; MA 1946; Joseph Hodges Choate Mem. Fellow, Harvard Univ., 1934–36; AM (Harvard), 1935; Modern Languages Master, King Edward's School, Birmingham, 1938–40, 1946–47; served in Intelligence Corps, 1940–46; Lecturer in Spanish and Italian, Nottingham Univ., 1947–53, and Head of Dept of Spanish, 1954–56; Dept of Italian and Hispanic Studies, Toronto Univ.: Prof., 1956–78; Chm., 1956–66, 1969–78. Vice-Pres., Assoc. of Teachers of Spanish and Portuguese of GB and Ireland, 1948–; Pres., Canadian Assoc. of Hispanists, 1964–66, 1972–74; Vice-Pres., Asociación Internacional de Hispanistas, 1977–83. Fellow, New Coll., Univ. of Toronto, 1962–; Senior Fellow, Massey Coll., Univ. of Toronto, 1965–70; Canada Council Senior Fellowship, 1967–68. *Publications:* articles on Spanish literature in learned jls. *Address:* 30 Old Bridle Path, Toronto, Ont M4T 1A7, Canada.

STAHL, Professor Ernest Ludwig, DLitt Oxon; retired; Taylor Professor of the German Language and Literature and Fellow of The Queen's College, Oxford, 1959–69, Supernumerary Fellow, since 1969; Student Emeritus of Christ Church Oxford, since 1960 (Student, 1945–59); *b* Senekal, OFS, S Africa, 10 Dec. 1902; *s* of Philip and Theresa Stahl; *m* 1942, Kathleen Mary Hudson, MA Oxon, author. *Educ:* Univ. of Capetown (MA 1925); Heidelberg Univ.; Oxford Univ. (First Class Hons, 1927; DLitt 1980); Berne Univ. (PhD *magna cum laude* 1931). Assistant Lecturer in German, Birmingham, 1932–35; Lecturer in German, Oxford, 1935–45; Reader in German Literature, Oxford, 1945–59. Vis. Professor: Cornell, 1956; Princeton, 1958; Yale, 1964; Kansas, 1968; Calif (Davis), 1969–70. Gold Medal, Goethe Gesellschaft, 1966. *Publications:* Die religiöse und die philosophische Bildungsidee und die Entstehung des Bildungsromans, 1934; Hölderlin's Symbolism, 1944; The Dramas of Heinrich von Kleist, 1948 (revised edn, 1961); (trans. with Louis MacNeice) Goethe's Faust pts I and II (abridged), 1951; Schiller's Drama: Theory and Practice, 1954; Goethe's Iphigenie auf Tauris, 1962. Editions of Goethe's Werther, 1942 (new edn, 1972), Lessing's Emilia Galotti, 1946, Goethe's Torquato Tasso, 1962, and R. M. Rilke's Duino Elegies, 1965; revised edn, Oxford Book of German Verse, 1967; (with W. E. Yuill) Introduction to German Literature, vol. III, 1970; The Faust Translation in Time Was Away: the world of Louis MacNeice, 1975; articles in Modern Language Review, Germanic Review, German Life and Letters, Journal of English and Germanic Philology, Oxford German Studies, Yearbook of Comparative Criticism; contrib. to Festschrift for Ralph Farrell. *Address:* 43 Plantation Road, Oxford OX2 6JE. *T:* Oxford (0865) 515896.

STAINFORTH, Maj.-Gen. Charles Herbert, CB 1969; OBE 1955; Editor, Army Quarterly and Defence Journal, since 1974; *b* 12 Dec. 1914; *s* of Lt-Col Stainforth, CMG, 4th Cavalry, IA, and Georgina Helen, *d* of Maj.-Gen. H. Pipon, CB; *m* Elizabeth, *d* of late John Tait Easdale; one *s* one *d*. *Educ:* Wellington Coll.; RMC, Sandhurst. Commnd into 2nd Royal Lancers, IA; transferred British Army, 1947; Chief of Staff, Southern Comd, 1965–66; GOC Aldershot District and SE Dist, 1966–69; Head of UK Future Command Structure, MoD, 1969–72. Col Comdt, RCT, 1970–72. Chm. Combined Cadet Forces, 1970–72. Consultant to Nat. Tourist Bds, 1973–75. *Address:* Powderham House, Dippenhall, near Farnham, Surrey. *Clubs:* Army and Navy, MCC.

STAINTON, Sir (John) Ross, Kt 1981; CBE 1971; retired; *b* 27 May 1914; *s* of late George Stainton and Helen Ross; *m* 1939, Doreen Werner; three *d*. *Educ:* Glengorse, Eastbourne; Malvern Coll., Worcestershire. Joined Imperial Airways as Trainee, 1933; served in Italy, Egypt, Sudan. Served with RAF in England, West Indies and USA, 1940–46. Man. N America, BOAC, 1949–53; General Sales Man. BOAC, and other Head Office posts, 1954–68; Dep. Man. Dir, 1968–71; Man. Dir, 1971–72; Mem., BOAC Bd, 1968, Chm. and Chief Exec., 1972, until merged into British Airways, 1974; Mem., 1971–, Dep. Chm. and Chief Exec., 1977–79, Chairman, 1979–80, British Airways Bd. Vice Pres., Private Patients Plan, 1986– (Dir, 1979–86). Hon. Treasurer, Air League Council, 1986–91. FCIT (Pres., 1970–71); CRAeS 1978. *Clubs:* Royal Air Force; Royal and Ancient Golf (St Andrews); Sunningdale Golf.

STAINTON, Keith; *b* 8 Nov. 1921; *m* 1946, Vanessa Ann Heald (marr. diss.); three *s* three *d*; *m* 1980, Frances Easton. *Educ:* Kendal Sch.; Manchester Univ. (BA (Com.) Dist. in Economics). Insurance clerk, 1936–39. Served War of 1939–45: Lieut, RNVR, Submarines and with French Resistance, 1940–46. Manchester Univ., 1946–49; Leader Writer, Financial Times, 1949–52; Industrial Consultant, 1952–57; joined Burton, Son & Sanders, Ltd, 1957, Man. Dir 1961–69, Chm. 1962–69; Chm. Scotia Investments Ltd, 1969–72. MP (C) Sudbury and Woodbridge, Dec. 1963–1983; Mem., House of Commons Select Cttees on Expenditure and Science and Technology. Mem. Council of Europe and WEU, 1979–83. Légion d'Honneur, Croix de Guerre avec Palmes, Croix de l'Armée, 1943. *Address:* Little Bealings House, near Woodbridge, Suffolk. *T:* Ipswich (0473) 624205; 5 Chelsea Studios, 410 Fulham Road, SW6. *T:* 071–385 3672.

STAINTON, Sir Ross; *see* Stainton, Sir J. R.

STAIR, 13th Earl of, *cr* 1703; **John Aymer Dalrymple,** KCVO 1978 (CVO 1964); MBE 1941; Bt 1664 and (Scot.) 1698; Viscount Stair, Lord Glenluce and Stranraer, 1690; Viscount Dalrymple, Lord Newliston, 1703; Baron Oxenfoord (UK) 1841; Colonel (retired) Scots Guards; Lord-Lieutenant of Wigtown, 1961–81; Captain General of the Queen's Body Guard for Scotland, Royal Company of Archers, 1973–88; *b* 9 Oct. 1906; *e s* of 12th Earl of Stair, KT, DSO, and Violet Evelyn (*née* Harford) (*d* 1968); *S* father, 1961; *m* 1960, Davina, *d* of late Hon. Sir David Bowes-Lyon, KCVO; three *s*. *Educ:* Eton; Sandhurst. Bde Major, 3rd (London) Infantry Bde and Regimental Adjt Scots Guards, 1935–38; served Middle East, 1941; Bde Major, 16th Inf. Bde (despatches, MBE); Lieut-Colonel 1942; commanded 1st Scots Guards, 1942–43; AMS Headquarters AAI, 1944; Comd Trg Bn Scots Guards, 1945; Comd 2nd Scots Guards, 1946–49; Comd Scots Guards, Temp. Colonel, 1949–52; retired, 1953; retired as Hon. Colonel Scots Guards, 1953. *Heir: s* Viscount Dalrymple, *qv*. *Address:* Lochinch Castle, Stranraer, Wigtownshire. *Club:* Cavalry and Guards.

See also Lady Marion Philipps, Lady Jean Rankin.

STAKIS, Sir Reo (Argyros), Kt 1988; Founder, and Chairman, 1947–91, President, since 1986, Stakis plc; *b* 13 March 1913; *s* of Anastasis and Katerina Stakis; *m* 1946, Annitsa Petropoulos; two *s* four *d*. *Educ:* American Acad., Larnaca. Stakis plc includes hotels, restaurants, casinos, public houses and nursing homes. Hon. Comr for Cyprus at Glasgow,

1968–. Hon. LLD Strathclyde, 1986. *Recreations:* shooting, fishing. *Address:* (office) 58 West Regent Street, Glasgow G2 2QZ. *T:* 041–332 7773; 54 Aytoun Road, Glasgow; Grant House, Dunblane, Perthshire.

STALLARD, family name of **Baron Stallard.**

STALLARD, Baron *cr* 1983 (Life Peer), of St Pancras in the London Borough of Camden; **Albert William Stallard;** *b* 5 Nov. 1921; *m* 1944; one *s* one *d.* *Educ:* Low Waters Public School; Hamilton Academy, Scotland. Engineer, 1937–65; Technical Training Officer, 1965–70. Councillor, St Pancras, 1953–59, Alderman, 1962–65; Councillor, Camden, 1965–70, Alderman, 1971–78. MP (Lab) St Pancras N, 1970–83; PPS to: Minister of State, Agriculture, Fisheries and Food, 1974; Minister of State for Housing and Construction, 1974–76; an Asst Govt Whip, 1976–78; a Lord Comr, HM Treasury, 1978–79. Chairman: Camden Town Disablement Cttee (Mem., 1951–); Camden Assoc. for Mental Health. Mem., Inst. of Training Officers, 1971. AEU Order of Merit, 1968. *Address:* Flat 2, 2 Belmont Street, NW1.

STALLARD, Sir Peter (Hyla Gawne), KCMG 1961 (CMG 1960); CVO 1956; MBE 1945; Secretary to the Prime Minister of the Federation of Nigeria, 1958–61; *b* 6 March 1915; *y c* of Rev. L. B. Stallard and Eleanor, *e d* of Colonel J. M. Gawne; *m* 1941, Mary Elizabeth Kirke, CStJ; one *s* one *d.* *Educ:* Bromsgrove Sch.; Corpus Christi Coll., Oxford (MA). Cadet, Colonial Administrative Service, Northern Nigeria, 1937. Military Service, Nigeria, Gold Coast, Burma, 1939–45. Governor and Commander-in-Chief of British Honduras, 1961–66; Lt Governor of the Isle of Man, 1966–74. Pres., Devon and Cornwall Rent Assessment Panel, 1976–85. Pres., Somerset Assoc. of Boys Clubs, 1977–91; Chm., Dartmoor Steering Gp, 1978–89. KStJ 1961; Chapter-Gen., Order of St John, 1976–. *Recreation:* golf. *Address:* 18 Henley Road, Taunton, Somerset TA1 5BJ. *T:* Taunton (0823) 331505. *Club:* Athenæum.
See also R. D. Wilson.

STALLIBRASS, Geoffrey Ward, CB 1972; OBE 1952; FRAeS; Controller, National Air Traffic Services (Civil Aviation Authority/Ministry of Defence), 1969–74 (Joint Field Commander, 1966–69); *b* 17 Dec. 1911; *s* of Thomas and Ivy Stallibrass, Midhurst; *m* 1940, Alison, *e d* of late James and Rita Scott, Norwich; two *s* three *d.* *Educ:* Wellingborough Sch. Air Service Training, Hamble (Commercial Pilot/Instrument Rating Course), 1948. Dep. Director, Civil Aviation Ops, Ministry of Civil Aviation, 1946; attached to BOAC, 1949; Dep. Director of Control and Navigation (Development), 1950; Director of Aerodromes (Tech.), Ministry of Transport and Civil Aviation, 1953; Director of Flight Safety, Min. of Aviation, 1962. *Publications:* articles on conservation subjects. *Recreations:* walking, birdwatching, conservation work, music. *Address:* Turkey Island Corner, East Harting, Petersfield, Hants GU31 5LT. *T:* Harting (0730) 825220.

STALLWORTHY, Sir John (Arthur), Kt 1972; Nuffield Professor of Obstetrics and Gynæcology, University of Oxford, 1967–73, now Emeritus; Fellow Emeritus, Oriel College, Oxford, 1973, Hon. Fellow, 1974; *b* 26 July 1906; *s* of Arthur John Stallworthy; *m* 1934, Margaret Wright Howie (*d* 1980); one *s* twin *d.* *Educ:* Auckland Grammar Sch.; Universities of Auckland and Otago, NZ. Distinction and gold medal in surgery, gynæcology and obstetrics, 1930; travelling med. schol., 1931; obstetrical travelling schol., 1932; postgrad. experience in Melbourne, London and Vienna. MRCOG 1935; FRCS 1936; FRCOG 1951. Joseph Price Orator, US, 1950; McIlrath Guest Prof., Sydney, 1952; Sommer Mem. Lecturer, US, 1958; Hunterian Prof., RCS, 1963; Sims Black Prof. S Africa, 1964. Sometime Examiner in Obstetrics and Gynæcology for RCOG, RCS of S Africa, Universities of Oxford, Birmingham, Leeds, E Africa and Singapore. Hon. Cons., Royal Prince Alfred Hospital, Sydney, 1952; Assoc. Obstetrician, National Maternity Hospital, Dublin, 1959. Vice-Pres., RCOG, 1969; President: RSM, 1974–75, 1980–81 (Hon. Fellow, 1976; Chm. Appeal Cttee); Medical Protection Soc.; BMA, 1975 (Gold Medal, 1981; Chm. Working Party, The Medical Effects of Nuclear War, 1981–83). Hon. Fellow, Surgical, Obstetrical and Gynæcological Societies in US, Wales, Canada, S Africa, Spain and Turkey; Hon. FACS 1954; Hon. FCOG (SA) 1964; Hon. FACOG 1974; Hon. FRCSI 1976. Hon. DSc: Otago, 1975; Leeds, 1975. Victor Bonney Prize, RCS, 1970. Member, Honourable Order of Kentucky Colonels, 1968. *Publications:* (jointly) Problems of Fertility in General Practice, 1948; (jointly) Recent Advances in Obstetrics and Gynæcology, 1966–79; (jointly) Bonney's Gynaecological Surgery, 8th edn; (ed jtly) The Medical Effects of Nuclear War, 1983; (contrib.) Cancer of the Uterine Cervix, 1984; joint contrib. to British Obstetric Practice and British Gynæcological Practice, 1959, and 1963. *Recreations:* formerly Rugby football, tennis, swimming, driving fast cars; now gardening, writing, driving fast cars more slowly. *Address:* 8a College Green, Gloucester GL1 2LX. *T:* Gloucester (0452) 421243. *Club:* Athenæum.
See also J. H. Stallworthy.

STALLWORTHY, Jon Howie, FBA 1990; Reader in English Literature, and Fellow of Wolfson College, Oxford University, since 1986; *b* 18 Jan. 1935; *s* of Sir John (Arthur) Stallworthy, *qv*; *m* 1960, Gillian Meredith (*née* Waldock); two *s* one *d.* *Educ:* The Dragon Sch., Oxford; Rugby Sch.; Magdalen Coll., Oxford (MA, BLitt). Served RWAFF (pre-Oxford). At Oxford won Newdigate Prize, 1958 (runner-up, 1957). Joined Oxford Univ. Press, 1959, Dep. Head, Academic Div., 1975–77; John Wendell Anderson Prof. of English Lit., Cornell Univ., 1977–86. Gave Chatterton Lecture on an English Poet to British Academy, 1970; during a sabbatical year, 1971–72, was a Visiting Fellow at All Souls Coll., Oxford. FRSL, 1971. *Publications: poems:* (8 collections) The Astronomy of Love, 1961; Out of Bounds, 1963; Root and Branch, 1969; Positives, 1969; The Apple Barrel: selected poems, 1955–63, 1974; Hand in Hand, 1974; A Familiar Tree, 1978; The Anzac Sonata: new and selected poems, 1986; *criticism:* Between the Lines, W. B. Yeats's Poetry in the Making, 1963; Vision and Revision in Yeats's Last Poems, 1969; *biography:* Wilfred Owen, 1974 (winner of Duff Cooper Meml Prize, W. H. Smith Literary Award and E. M. Forster Award); *translations:* (with Peter France) Alexander Blok: The Twelve and other poems, 1970; (with Jerzy Peterkiewicz) poems for 2nd edn of Five Centuries of Polish Poetry, 1970; (with Peter France) Boris Pasternak: Selected Poems, 1983; *edited:* The Penguin Book of Love Poetry, 1973; Wilfred Owen: Complete Poems and Fragments, 1983; The Oxford Book of War Poetry, 1984; The Poems of Wilfred Owen, 1985; First Lines: poems written in youth, from Herbert to Heaney, 1987; Henry Reed: Collected Poems, 1991. *Address:* Wolfson College, Oxford; Long Farm, Elsfield Road, Old Marston, Oxford. *Club:* Vincent's (Oxford).

STAMENKOVIĆ, Dragi; Order of National Hero, Yugoslavia, 1952; Yugoslav Star with ribbon, 1981; Yugoslav Ambassador to the Court of St James's, 1981–85, retired; *b* 29 Feb. 1920; *s* of Todor Stamenković and Darinka Malešević; *m* 1945, Jelica Purić; two *s* one *d.* *Educ:* Belgrade Univ. Mem., Supreme HQ, Nat. Liberation Army for Serbia, 1941–45. Mem., Liberation Cttee for Belgrade Dist, 1945–48; Minister in Govt of Serbia, 1949–51; Pres., Fedn of Trade Unions of Serbia 1951–62; President: Exec. Council of Serbia, 1964–67; Working People of Serbia, 1967–71; Mem., Presidency of Yugoslavia, 1971–74; Ambassador to Brazil, 1974–78; Ambassador in Federal Secretariat for Foreign Affairs, 1978–81. Mem. Council, Fedn of Yugoslavia, 1985–. Deputy of Fed. Assembly in three convocations, and of Republican Assembly in four; Mem., Presidency of Fed. Conf., Socialist Alliance of Working People of Yugoslavia; sometime head or mem., Yugoslav delegns abroad. Holder of many Yugoslav and foreign decorations. *Publications:* From Travels through China, 1955; contribs to jls and newspapers on economic and political affairs of Yugoslavia, 1945–75. *Recreations:* tennis, football. *Address:* Užička 10, 11040 Beograd, Yugoslavia. *Club:* Hurlingham.

STAMER, Sir (Lovelace) Anthony, 5th Bt, *cr* 1809; MA; AMIMI; *b* 28 Feb. 1917; *s* of Sir Lovelace Stamer, 4th Bt, and Eva Mary (*d* 1974), *e d* of R. C. Otter; *S* father, 1941; *m* 1st, 1948, Stella Huguette (marr. diss., 1953), *d* of Paul Burnell Binnie, Brussels; one *s* one *d*; 2nd, 1955, Margaret Lucy (marr. diss., 1959), *d* of late Major Belben and Mrs Stewart, Marandellas, Zimbabwe; 3rd, 1960, Marjorie June (marr. diss. 1968), *d* of late T. C. Noakes, St James, Cape; 4th, 1983, Mrs Elizabeth Graham Smith, *widow* of G. P. H. Smith, Colyton, Devon. *Educ:* Harrow; Trinity Coll., Cambridge; Royal Agricultural Coll., Cirencester. BA 1947; MA 1963; AMIMI 1963. Served RAF 1939–41; Officer in ATA 1941–45. Executive Director: Bentley Drivers Club Ltd, 1969–73; Bugatti & Ferrari Owners Club, 1973–75; Hon. Treasurer, Ferrari Owners' Club, 1975–81. *Heir: s* Peter Tomlinson Stamer, Sqn Leader, RAF, retd [*b* 19 Nov. 1951; *m* 1979, Dinah Louise Berry (marr. diss. 1989); one *s* one *d*]. *Address:* White Farm Cottage, White Farm Lane, West Hill, Ottery St Mary, Devon EX11 1XF.

STAMERS-SMITH, Eileen, MA; Headmistress, Malvern Girls' College, 1984–85; *b* 17 April 1929; *d* of Charles and May Fairey; *m* 1970, Henry Arthur Stamers-Smith, CBE, MA (*d* 1982). *Educ:* Castleford Grammar Sch., Yorks; Lady Margaret Hall, Oxford (BA Hons English Lang. and Lit., Cl. II, 1951; MA; DipEd). Asst English Teacher: Abbeydale Girls' Grammar Sch., Sheffield, 1952–57; Cheltenham Ladies' Coll., 1957–67; Headmistress, Bermuda Girls' High Sch., 1967–71. Tutor/lecturer in garden history and English literature for Dept for Continuing Educn, Univ. of Oxford, Denman Coll., WI, WEA, English Sch. of Gardening, Inchbald Sch. of Design, V & A, etc., 1985–; Guest Lectr, Swan's Hellenic Art Treasures Tours, 1990–. Hon. Editor: Garden Hist. Soc. Newsletter, 1986–; Garden Hist. Soc. Jl, 1989. *Publications:* articles in Garden Hist. Soc. Jl and Newsletter, and in The Northern Gardener and HORTUS. *Recreations:* music, garden history, Venice, photography, calligraphy, writing poetry, sketching, fell walking. *Address:* 8 Mavor Close, Old Woodstock, Oxon OX7 1YL. *T:* Woodstock (0993) 811383.

STAMLER, Samuel Aaron, QC 1971; a Recorder of the Crown Court, 1974–89; *b* 3 Dec. 1925; *s* of late Herman Stamler and Bronia Stamler; *m* 1953, Honor, *d* of A. G. Brotman; two *s* one *d.* *Educ:* Berkhamsted; King's College, Cambridge. Called to Bar, Middle Temple, 1949, Bencher, 1979. *Recreations:* walking, grandchildren. *Address:* 1 Essex Court, Temple, EC4Y 9AR. *T:* 071–353 5362. *Club:* Athenæum.

STAMM, Temple Theodore, FRCS; Orthopædic Surgeon Emeritus, Guy's Hospital; *b* 22 Dec. 1905; *s* of Dr Louis Edward Stamm, Streatham, and Louisa Ethel (*née* Perry), Caterham, Surrey; *m* 1945, Pamela, *d* of Charles Russell, Chislehurst, Kent. *Educ:* Rose Hill Sch., Surrey; Haileybury Coll.; Guy's Hospital Medical School. MB, BS (London), 1930, MRCS, LRCP 1928, FRCS 1934. Fellow Royal Society of Medicine; Fellow British Orthopædic Assoc.; Member British Med. Assoc. Formerly: Orthopædic Surgeon, Bromley Hospital, 1941–66; Asst Orthopædic Surgeon and Orthopædic Registrar, Royal Nat. Orthopædic Hospital; Asst Orthopædic Surgeon, Orthopædic Registrar, Asst Anæsthetist and Demonstrator of Anatomy, Guy's Hospital. Major RAMC. *Publications:* Foot Troubles, 1957; Guide to Orthopædics, 1958; Surgery of the Foot, British Surgical Practice, Vol. 4; contributions to Blackburn and Lawrie's Textbook of Surgery, 1958; articles in: Lancet, Guy's Hospital Reports, Journal of Bone and Joint Surgery, Medical Press, etc. *Recreations:* farming, sailing, music. *Address:* Hambrook Lodge, West Ashling, Chichester, West Sussex PO18 8DQ.

STAMP, family name of **Baron Stamp.**

STAMP, 4th Baron *cr* 1938, of Shortlands; **Trevor Charles Bosworth Stamp,** MD; FRCP; Consultant Physician and Director, Department of Bone and Mineral Metabolism, Institute of Orthopaedics, Royal National Orthopaedic Hospital, since 1974; *b* 18 Sept. 1935; *s* of 3rd Baron Stamp, MD, FRCPath and of Frances Hammond, *d* of late Charles Henry Bosworth, Evanston, Illinois, USA; *S* father, 1987; *m* 1st, 1963, Anne Carolynn Churchill (marr. diss. 1971); two *d*; 2nd, 1975, Carol Anne, *d* of Robert Keith Russell; one *s* one *d.* *Educ:* The Leys School; Gonville and Caius Coll., Cambridge; Yale Univ.; St Mary's Hosp. Medical School. MSc (Yale) 1957; MD (Cantab) 1972; FRCP 1978. Qualified in medicine, 1960; Med. Registrar, Professorial Medical Unit, St Mary's Hosp., 1964–66; Hon. Senior Registrar 1968–73, and Hon. Sen. Lecturer 1972–73, Dept of Human Metabolism, University College Hosp. and Medical School; Hon. Consultant Physician and Sen. Lectr, Middlesex Hosp. and UCL School of Medicine, 1974–. Prix André Lichtwitz, France, 1973. *Publications:* numerous papers on disorders of mineral metabolism. *Recreations:* music, tennis, contract bridge. *Heir: s* Hon. Nicholas Charles Trevor Stamp, *b* 27 Feb. 1978. *Address:* Pennyroyal, Village Lane, Hedgerley, Bucks SL2 3UY. *T:* Farnham Common (0753) 642737.

STAMP, Gavin Mark, MA, PhD; architectural historian and writer; Lecturer, Mackintosh School of Architecture, Glasgow, since 1990; *b* 15 March 1948; *s* of Barry Hartnell Stamp and Norah Clara (*née* Rich); *m* 1982, Alexandra Frances Artley; two *d.* *Educ:* Dulwich Coll.; Gonville & Caius Coll., Cambridge (MA, PhD). Contributor to The Spectator, The Independent, Daily Telegraph, Private Eye, Architects' Jl, etc. Chm., Thirties Soc., 1983–; acting Sec., Alexander Thomson Soc., 1991–. *Publications:* The Architect's Calendar, 1973; Silent Cities, 1977; (text only) Temples of Power, 1979; (jtly) The Victorian Buildings of London 1837–1887, 1980; Robert Weir Schultz and his work for the Marquesses of Bute, 1981; The Great Perspectivists, 1982; The Changing Metropolis, 1984; The English House 1860–1914, 1986; (jtly) The Church in Crisis, 1986; The Telephone Boxes, 1989; articles in Arch. History, Arch. Design, Jl of RSA, etc. *Address:* 1 Moray Place, Glasgow G41 2AQ. *T:* 041–423 3747.

STAMP, Terence Henry; actor and director; *b* 22 July 1938; *s* of Thomas Stamp and Ethel Esther Perrott. *Educ:* Plaistow County Grammar School; Webber-Douglas Dramatic Acad. (Amehurst Webber Meml Schol., 1958). *Films include:* Billy Budd, 1962; The Collector, 1964; Far from the Madding Crowd, 1966; Blue, 1967; Spirits of the Dead, 1967; Theorem, 1968; Superman, 1977; Meetings with Remarkable Men, 1977; Superman 2, 1978; The Hit, 1984; Legal Eagles, 1985; Wall Street, 1987; Young Guns, 1988; The Sicilian, 1988; Alien Nation, 1989; Prince of Shadows, 1991; *stage:* Alfie, Morosco, NY, 1965; Dracula, Shaftesbury, 1978; Lady from the Sea, Roundhouse, 1979. *Publications:* autobiography: Stamp Album, 1987; Coming Attractions, 1988; Double Feature, 1989. *Address:* c/o Markham & Froggatt, 4 Windmill Street, W1. *Club:* New York Athletic (New York).

STAMPER, John Trevor, MA; FEng, Hon. FRAeS, CBIM; Corporate Technical Director, British Aerospace, 1977–85, retired; *b* 12 Oct. 1926; *s* of late Col Horace John Stamper and Clara Jane (*née* Collin); *m* 1950, Cynthia Joan Parsons; two *s* one *d.* *Educ:* Loughborough Grammar Sch.; Jesus Coll., Cambridge (MA 1951). FRAeS 1965 (Hon. FRAeS 1984); CEng 1966; FEng 1977; CBIM 1983. Blackburn Aircraft Ltd: Post-grad.

apprenticeship, 1947; Dep. Head of Aerodynamics, 1955; Head of Structures, 1956; Flight Test Manager, 1960; Chief Designer (Buccaneer), 1961; Dir and Chief Designer, 1963; Hawker Siddeley Aviation Ltd (following merger): Exec. Dir Design (Military), 1966; Exec. Dir and Dep. Chief Engr (Civil), 1968; Tech. Dir, 1968–77. Member: Council, RAeS, 1971–77, 1978–88 (Pres., 1981–82); Tech. Bd, SBAC, 1966–85 (Chm., 1972–74); Council, SBAC, 1981–84; Council, Aircraft Res. Assoc., 1966–85 (Chm., 1976–78); Aeronautical Res. Council, 1971–74; Air Warfare Adv. Bd, Defence Scientific Adv. Council, 1973–84; Noise Adv. Council, 1975–78; Comité Technique et Industriel, Assoc. Européenne des Constructeurs de Matériel Aerospatial, 1971–81 (Chm., 1974–81); Airworthiness Requirements Bd, CAA, 1976–78, 1987–88. Hon. DSc Loughborough, 1986. Hodgeson Prize, RAeS, 1975 and 1986; British Gold Medal for Aeronautics, RAeS, 1976. *Publications*: (contrib.) The Future of Aeronautics, 1970; Air Power in the Next Generation, 1979; papers in Jl RAeS. *Recreations*: sailing, photography. *Address*: 7 Sycamore Close, The Mount, Fetcham, Surrey KT22 9EX. *T*: Fetcham (0372) 370336.

STANAGE, Rt. Rev. Thomas Shaun; *see* Bloemfontein, Bishop of.

STANBRIDGE, Air Vice-Marshal Sir Brian (Gerald Tivy), KCVO 1979 (MVO 1958); CBE 1974; AFC 1952; Director-General, Air Transport Users' Committee, 1979–85; *b* 6 July 1924; *s* of late Gerald Edward and Violet Georgina Stanbridge; *m* 1st, 1949, Kathleen Diana Hayes (marr. diss. 1983); two *d*; 2nd, 1984, Jennifer Anne Jenkins. *Educ*: Thurlestone Coll., Dartmouth. Served War: RAFVR, 1942; commnd, 1944; No 31 Sqdn (SE Asia), 1944–46; No 47 Sqdn, 1947–49; 2FTS/CFS, 1950–52; British Services Mission to Burma, 1952–54; The Queen's Flight (personal pilot and flying instructor to Duke of Edinburgh), 1954–58; Naval Staff Coll., 1958; PSO to AOC-in-C Coastal Comd, 1958–59; W/Cdr, Flying, RAF St Mawgan, 1960–62; jssc, 1962; RAFDS, Army Staff Coll., Camberley, 1962–63; Gp Captain on staff of NATO Standing Gp, Washington, DC, 1963–66; RAF Dir, Jt Anti-Submarine Sch., Londonderry, and Sen. RAF Officer, NI, 1966–68; Gp Captain Ops, HQ Coastal Comd, 1968–70; IDC, 1970; Air Cdre, 1970; Sec., Chiefs of Staff Cttee, MoD, 1971–73; Dep. Comdt, RAF Staff Coll., Bracknell, 1973–75; ADC to the Queen, 1973–75; Air Vice-Marshal, 1975; Defence Services Sec. to the Queen, 1975–79; retired 1979. Vice Pres., RAF Gliding and Soaring Assoc. *Address*: 20 Durrant Way, Sway, Lymington, Hants SO41 6DQ. *Club*: Royal Air Force.

STANBRIDGE, Ven. Leslie Cyril; Archdeacon of York, 1972–88, Archdeacon Emeritus since 1988; *b* 19 May 1920. *Educ*: Bromley County Grammar Sch., Kent; St John's Coll., Durham Univ. (MA, DipTheol). Asst Curate of Erith Parish Church, Kent, 1949–51; Tutor and Chaplain, St John's Coll., Durham, 1951–55; Vicar of St Martin's, Hull, 1955–64; Examining Chaplain to the Archbishop of York, 1962–74; Rector of Cottingham, Yorks, 1964–72; Canon of York, 1968–; Succentor Canonicorum, 1988–; Rural Dean of Kingston-upon-Hull, 1970–72; Warden, York Diocesan Readers' Assoc., 1988–. *Recreations*: fell walking, cycling. *Address*: 1 Deangate, York YO1 2JB. *T*: York (0904) 621174.

STANBROOK, Clive St George Clement, OBE 1987; QC 1989; Partner, Stanbrook & Hooper, since 1980; *b* 10 April 1948; *s* of Ivor Robert Stanbrook, *qv*; *m* 1971, Julia Suzanne Stanbrook; one *s* three *d*. *Educ*: Dragon Sch.; Westminster; University Coll. London. Called to the Bar, Inner Temple, 1972; called to New York Bar, 1988. Founded Stanbrook & Hooper, 1980. *Publications*: Extradition: the law and practice, 1979; Dumping: manual of EEC rules, 1980; Dumping and Subsidies, 1985. *Recreations*: tennis, travel. *Address*: 42 Rue du Taciturne, Brussels 1040, Belgium.

STANBROOK, Ivor Robert; MP (C) Orpington, since 1970; Barrister-at-Law; *b* 13 Jan. 1924; *y* *s* of Arthur William and Lilian Stanbrook; *m* 1946, Joan (*née* Clement); two *s*. *Educ*: state schools and London and Oxford Universities. Served RAF, 1942–46. Colonial Administrative Service, Nigeria, 1950–60: Asst Sec., Council of Ministers, Lagos, 1956; Dist Officer, N Region, 1957–60. Called to the Bar, Inner Temple, 1960; practising barrister, 1960–. Founded Britain-Nigerian Assoc., 1961. *Publications*: Extradition—the Law and Practice, 1979; British Nationality—the New Law, 1981; A Year in Politics, 1988. *Recreations*: music, gardening. *Address*: 6 Sevenoaks Road, Orpington, Kent BR6 9JJ. *T*: Orpington (0689) 820347. *Club*: Carlton.
See also C. St G. C. Stanbrook.

STANBURY, Richard Vivian Macaulay; HM Diplomatic Service, retired; *b* 5 Feb. 1916; *s* of late Gilbert Vivian Stanbury and Doris Marguerite (*née* Smythe); *m* 1953, Geraldine Anne, *d* of late R. F. W. Grant and of Winifred Helen Grant; one *s* one *d*. *Educ*: Shrewsbury Sch. (exhibnr); Magdalene Coll., Cambridge (exhibnr, 1st cl. Hons in Classical Tripos). Sudan Political Service, 1937–50 (District Comr in 12 districts, and Magistrate); HM Foreign (subseq. Diplomatic) Service, 1951–71: 2nd Sec., Cairo, 1951; FO 1954; Bahrain, Persian Gulf, 1956; FO 1959; Counsellor, Buenos Aires, 1968. *Recreations*: tennis, golf, and watching cricket (played for Somerset); fighting a losing battle to avoid playing bridge. *Address*: Shepherds House, Peasmarsh, near Rye, East Sussex. *Clubs*: Naval & Military; Hawks (Cambridge); Rye Golf; Hurlingham (Buenos Aires).

STANBURY, Prof. Sydney William, MD, FRCP; Professor of Medicine, University of Manchester, 1965–84, now Emeritus; *b* 21 April 1919; *s* of F. A. W. Stanbury and A. B. Stanbury (*née* Rowe); *m* 1943, Helen, *d* of Harry and Patty Jackson; one *s* four *d*. *Educ*: Hulme Grammar Sch., Oldham; Manchester Univ. MB, ChB (1st Cl. Hons) 1942; MD (Gold Medal) 1948; MRCP 1947, FRCP 1958. Served RAMC, Burma and India, 1944–47. Beit Meml Res. Fellow, 1948–51; Rockefeller Travelling Fellow, 1951–52; Registrar, Lectr and Reader, Dept of Medicine, Manchester Royal Infirmary, 1947–65; Consultant Phys., United Manchester Hosps, 1959–. Member: Assoc. of Physicians; Medical Res. Soc.; Bone and Tooth Soc. Visiting Professor: John Howard Means, Massachusetts Gen. Hosp., Boston, 1958; Henry M. Winans, Univ. of Texas, Dallas, 1958; W. T. Connoll, Queen's Univ., Kingston, Ont, 1978; Weild Lectr, RCP and S, Glasgow, 1958; Lumleian Lectr, RCP, 1981; Vis. Lectr: Univ. of Washington, Mayo Clinic, etc. *Publications*: contrib. European and American med. books and jls on: renal function, electrolyte metabolism, metabolic bone disease and vitamin D metabolism. *Recreation*: gardening. *Address*: Halamana, Gillan, Manaccan, Helston, Cornwall TR12 6HL. *T*: Manaccan (032623) 586.

STANCLIFFE, Very Rev. David Staffurth; Provost of Portsmouth, since 1982; *b* 1 Oct. 1942; *s* of late Very Rev. Michael Staffurth Stancliffe; *m* 1965, Sarah Loveday Smith; one *s* two *d*. *Educ*: Westminster School; Trinity College, Oxford (MA); Cuddesdon Theological College. Assistant Curate, St Bartholomew's, Armley, Leeds, 1967–70; Chaplain to Clifton Coll., Bristol, 1970–77; Canon Residentiary of Portsmouth Cathedral, Diocesan Director of Ordinands and Lay Ministry Adviser, 1977–82. Member: Gen. Synod, 1985–; Liturgical Commn, 1986–; Cathedrals' Fabric Commn 1991–. *Recreations*: old music, Italy. *Address*: Provost's House, Pembroke Road, Portsmouth PO1 2NS. *T*: Portsmouth (0705) 824400.
See also M. J. Stancliffe.

STANCLIFFE, Martin John, RIBA; Director, Martin Stancliffe Architects, since 1987; Surveyor to the Fabric, St Paul's Cathedral, since 1990; *b* 28 Dec. 1944; *s* of Very Rev. Michael Staffurth Stancliffe and Barbara Elizabeth Tatlow; *m* 1979, Sara Judith Sanders; two *d*. *Educ*: Westminster Sch.; Magdalene Coll., Cambridge (MA, DipArch). Private architectural practice, 1975–; restoration of Beningbrough Hall, York, for NT, 1979; Architect to: Lichfield Cath., 1983–; Southwell Minster, 1989–; Christ Church Cath., Oxford, 1990–. Member: Exec. Cttee, Council for the Care of Churches, 1980–91; Cathedrals' Fabric Commn for England, 1991–. *Recreations*: the baroque oboe, old buildings, travel, esp. in Italy and Greece. *Address*: 29 Marygate, York YO3 7BH. *T*: York (0904) 644001.
See also Very Rev. D. S. Stancliffe.

STANDARD, Prof. Sir Kenneth (Livingstone), Kt 1982; CD 1976; MD, MPH; FFPHM; Professor, 1968, and Head of Department of Social and Preventive Medicine, 1966–89, University of the West Indies at Mona; Emeritus Professor, University of the West Indies, 1990; *b* 8 Dec. 1920; *m* 1955, Evelyn Francis; one *d*. *Educ*: UC of West Indies (MB BS); Univ. of Pittsburgh (MPH); Univ. of London (MD). FFPHM (FFCM 1972). Schoolmaster, Lynch's Secondary Sch., Barbados, 1940–48 (Headmaster, 1948); Med. House Officer, UCH of WI, 1956; MO, Nutrition Res., Jamaica, 1957–58; MOH, Barbados, 1958–61; MO, MRC Epidemiol. Res. Unit, Jamaica, 1961–66; Lectr, 1961–65, Sen. Lectr, 1965–68, Dept of Social and Preventive Medicine, Univ. of WI, Jamaica. Adjunct Prof. of Public Health, Grad. Sch. Public Health, Univ. of Pittsburgh, 1972–75; Stubenbord Vis. Prof., Cornell Univ. Med. Coll., USA, 1975–. Thomas Parran Lecture, Grad. Sch. of Public Health, Univ. of Pittsburgh, 1984. Member: WHO Adv. Cttee on Med. Res., 1969–72; WHO Expert Adv. Panel on Public Health Admin, 1969–. Foundn Pres., Caribbean Public Health Assoc., 1988–. Fellow, Caribbean Coll. of Family Physicians, 1988. Fellowship, 1980, Medal, 1981, Jacques Parisot Foundn, WHO; Abraham Horwitz Award, Pan American Health and Educn Foundn, 1988; Health for All Medal, WHO, 1988; Medical Alumni Pioneer Award, Univ. of WI, 1988. *Publications*: (ed jtly) Manual for Community Health Workers, 1974, rev. edn 1983; Epidemiology and Community Health in Warm Climate Countries, 1976; Alternatives in the Delivery of Health Services, 1976; Four Decades of Advances in Health in the Commonwealth Caribbean, 1979. *Recreations*: reading, poetry, gardening. *Address*: Department of Social and Preventive Medicine, University of the West Indies, Mona, Kingston 7, Jamaica. *T*: 809 92 72476. *Club*: Commonwealth Trust.

STANDING, John; *see* Leon, Sir J. R.

STANESBY, Rev. Canon Derek Malcolm, PhD; Canon of St George's Chapel, Windsor, since 1985; *b* 28 March 1931; *s* of Laurence J. C. Stanesby and late Elsie L. Stanesby (*née* Stean); *m* 1958, Christine A. Payne; three *s* one *d*. *Educ*: Orange Hill Central School, London; Northampton Polytechnic, London; Leeds Univ. (BA Hons); Manchester Univ. (MEd, PhD); College of the Resurrection, Mirfield. GPO Radio Research Station, Dollis Hill, 1947–51; RAF (Navigator), 1951–53. Ordained, 1958; Curate: Old Lakenham, Norwich, 1958–61; St Mary, Welling, Dio. Southwark, 1961–63; Vicar, St Mark, Bury, Dio. Manchester, 1963–67; Rector, St Chad, Ladybarn, Manchester, 1967–85. Mem., Archbishop's Commn on Christian Doctrine, 1986–91. *Publications*: Science, Reason and Religion, 1985; various articles. *Recreations*: hill walking, sailing, woodwork, idling. *Address*: 4 The Cloisters, Windsor Castle, Berks SL4 1NJ. *T*: Windsor (0753) 864142.

STANFIELD, Hon. Robert Lorne, PC (Canada) 1967; QC; Chairman, Institute for Research on Public Policy, 1981–86; *b* Truro, NS, 11 April 1914; *s* of late Frank Stanfield, sometime MLA and Lieutenant-Governor of NS, and Sarah (*née* Thomas); *m* 1st, 1940, N. Joyce (*d* 1954), *d* of C. W. Frazee, Vancouver; one *s* three *d*; 2nd, 1957, Mary Margaret (*d* 1977), *d* of late Hon. W. L. Hall, Judge of Supreme Court and formerly Attorney-Gen. of NS; 3rd, 1978, Anne Margaret Austin, *d* of Dr D. Nelson, Henderson, Toronto. *Educ*: Colchester County Academy, Truro; Ashbury Coll., Ottawa; Dalhousie Univ.; Harvard Law Sch. Southam Cup, Ashbury Coll.; BA Political Science and Economics 1936, Governor-General's Gold Medal, Dalhousie Univ.; LLB Harvard, 1939. War of 1939–45: attached Halifax Office of Wartime Prices and Trade Bd as Regional Rentals Officer, later as Enforcement Counsel. Admitted Bar of NS, 1940. Practised law, McInnes and Stanfield, Halifax, 1945–56; KC 1950. President, Nova Scotia Progressive Cons. Assoc., 1947–48; Leader, Nova Scotia Progressive Cons. Party, 1948–67; elected to Legislature of NS, 1949, Mem. for Colchester Co.; re-elected Mem., 1953, 1960, 1963, 1967; Premier and Minister of Education, NS, 1956; resigned as Premier of NS, 1967; MP (Progressive C): Colchester-Hants, NS, 1967–68; Halifax, NS, 1968–79; Leader, Progressive Cons. Party of Canada, and of Opposition in House of Commons, 1967–74. Ambassador at Large and special representative of Govt of Canada in Middle East, 1979–80. Dir, Canada Life. Chm., Commonwealth Foundn. Hon. LLD: University of New Brunswick, 1958; St Dunstan's Univ., PEI, 1964; McGill Univ., PQ, 1967; St Mary's Univ., NS, 1969; Dalhousie, 1982; Université Sainte-Anne, NS, Acadia Univ., NS, and Univ. of Toronto, 1987; Mount Allison Univ., 1990. Anglican. *Address*: 136 Acacia Avenue, Rockcliffe Park, Ottawa, Ontario K1M 0R1, Canada.

STANFORD, Peter James; Editor, The Catholic Herald, since 1988; *b* 23 Nov. 1961; *s* of Reginald James Hughes Stanford and Mary Catherine (*née* Fleming). *Educ*: St Anselm's Coll., Birkenhead; Merton Coll., Oxford (BA Hons 1983). Reporter, The Tablet, 1983–84; News Editor, The Catholic Herald, 1984–88. Restaurant Critic, Girl About Town, 1987–90. *Publications*: (ed) Hidden Hands: child workers around the world, 1988; (with Simon Lee) Believing Bishops, 1990; (ed) The Seven Deadly Sins, 1990; (with Kate Saunders) Catholics and Sex, 1992. *Recreations*: soap operas, vases, photography, credit cards. *Address*: Fife Cottage, Wellington Way, Bow, E3 4NE. *T*: 081–980 5980; Catholic Herald, Herald House, Lambs Passage, Bunhill Row, EC1Y 8TQ.

STANGER, David Harry, OBE 1987; FFB, FIQA, FBIM; Chairman, Harry Stanger Ltd, 1975–90 (Senior Partner, 1972–85; Managing Director, 1976–86); Director, Stanger Consultants Ltd, since 1990; *b* 14 Feb. 1939; *s* of Charles Harry Stanger, CBE and Florence Bessie Hepworth Stanger; *m* 1963, Jill Patricia (*née* Barnes); one *s* two *d*. *Educ*: Oundle Sch.; Millfield Sch. TEng 1971; FFB 1977; FIQA 1982; FBIM 1980; MSocIS 1982. Served Corps of RE, 1960–66; joined R. H. Harry Stanger, 1966; Partner, Al Hoty-Stanger Ltd, 1975. Internat. Exec. Officer, Materials Consultants (Internat.) Ltd, 1983–. Chm., Adv. Cttee, NAMAS, 1985–87. Sec. Gen., Union Internationale des Laboratoires Indépendants, 1983–. Member: Steering Cttee, NATLAS, 1981–87; Adv. Council for Calibration and Measurement, 1982–87; Council, EUROLAB, 1990–; Chairman: Standards, Quality and Measurement Adv. Cttee, 1988–; British Measurement and Testing Assoc., 1990–; Inst of Quality Assurance, 1990– (a Vice-Pres., 1986–); Adv. Bd, Brunel Centre for Manufacturing Metrology. Pingat Peringatan, Malaysia, 1966. *Recreation*: collecting vintage wines. *Address*: Summerfield House, Barnet Lane, Elstree, Herts WD6 3HQ. *T*: 081–953 0022. *Club*: Carlton.

STANHOPE, family name of **Earl of Harrington**.

STANIER, Brigadier Sir Alexander Beville Gibbons, 2nd Bt, *cr* 1917; DSO 1940 (and Bar, 1945); MC; DL, JP; CStJ; *b* 31 Jan. 1899; *s* of Sir Beville Stanier, 1st Bt, MP and Constance (*d* 1948), *d* of late Rev. B. Gibbons; *S* father, 1921; *m* 1927, Dorothy Gladys (*d* 1973), *e d* of late Brig.-Gen. Alfred Douglas Miller, CBE, DSO; one *s* one *d*. *Educ:* Eton; RMC, Sandhurst. Served European War in France, 1918 (MC); served War of 1939–45, in France 1940 and 1944 (despatches, DSO and Bar, American Silver Star, Comdr Order of Leopold of Belgium with palm, Belgian Croix de Guerre with palm). Adjutant 1st Bn Welsh Guards, 1923–26; Military Secretary, Gibraltar, 1927–30; commanded 2nd Battalion Welsh Guards, 1939–40; temp. Brigadier, 1940–45; Lieut-Colonel Commanding Welsh Guards, 1945–48. CC Salop, 1950–58. High Sheriff of Shropshire, 1951. County President of the St John Ambulance Bde, 1950–60. Comdr, Order of Legion of Honour (France), 1988. *Heir: s* Beville Douglas Stanier [*b* 20 April 1934; *m* 1963, Shelagh, *er d* of late Major and Mrs J. S. Sinnott, Tetbury, Glos; one *s* two *d*]. *Address:* Hill House, Shotover Park, Wheatley, Oxford OX9 1QN. *T:* Wheatley (08677) 2996; Park Cottage, Ludford, Ludlow SY8 1PP. *T:* Ludlow (0584) 2675.

STANIER, Field Marshal Sir John (Wilfred), GCB 1982 (KCB 1978); MBE 1961; DL; Constable, HM Tower of London, since 1990; Chairman, Control Risks (GS), since 1985; *b* 6 Oct. 1925; *s* of late Harold Allan Stanier and Penelope Rose Stanier (*née* Price); *m* 1955, Cicely Constance Lambert; four *d*. *Educ:* Marlborough Coll.; Merton Coll., Oxford. MBIM, FRGS. Commd in 7th Queen's Own Hussars, 1946; served in N Italy, Germany and Hong Kong; comd Royal Scots Greys, 1966–68; comd 20th Armd Bde, 1969–70; GOC 1st Div., 1973–75; Comdt, Staff Coll., Camberley, 1975–78; Vice Chief of the General Staff, 1978–80; C-in-C, UKLF, 1981–82; CGS, 1982–85. ADC General to the Queen, 1981–85. Col, The Royal Scots Dragoon Guards, 1979–84; Col Comdt, RAC, 1982–85. Chm., RUSI, 1986–89. Pres., Hampshire Br., British Red Cross Soc., 1986–; Mem. Council, WWF. Comr, Royal Hosp., Chelsea, 1986–. Mem. Council, Marlborough Coll., 1984–. DL Hampshire, 1987. *Recreations:* hunting, fishing, sailing, talking. *Address:* c/o Coutts & Co., Chandos Branch, 440 Strand, WC2R 0QS. *Club:* Cavalry and Guards.

STANIFORTH, John Arthur Reginald, CBE 1969; Director: Constructors John Brown, 1947–84 (Chief Executive and Deputy Chairman, 1958–84); John Brown & Co., Ltd, 1965–84; John Brown Engineering (Clydebank) Ltd, 1968–84 (Chm., 1970–77); St Wilfrid's Hospice (South Coast) Ltd, since 1981; *b* 19 Sept. 1912; *o s* of Captain Staniforth, MC, Anston House, Anston, Yorks; *m* 1936, Penelope Cecile, *y d* of Maj.-Gen. Sir Henry Freeland; one *d* (one *s* decd). *Educ:* Marlborough Coll. With John Brown Group, 1929–84. Mem., Export Guarantees Adv. Council, 1971–76, Dep. Chm., 1975–76. Founder Chm., British Chemical Engrg Contractors Assoc., 1965–68. Governor, Bryanston Sch., 1962–. *Recreations:* golf, fishing. *Address:* 11 The Holdens, Old Bosham, West Sussex PO18 8LN. *T:* Bosham (0243) 572401. *Clubs:* MCC; Goodwood Golf.

STANISZEWSKI, Stefan; Commander's Cross, Order of Polonia Restituta, and other orders; Ambassador of Poland to Libya, since 1990; *b* 11 Feb. 1931; *s* of Andrzej and Katarzyna Staniszewski; *m* 1953, Wanda Szuszkiewicz; one *d*. *Educ:* Warsaw Univ. (BA Philosophy); Jagiellonian Univ. (BA Pol. Sciences). Active in students' and social organizations, 1951–58; Head of Editorial Dept, ISKRY state publishing firm, 1958–60; entered foreign service, 1960; Minister's Cabinet, Min. of Foreign Affairs, 1960–63; successively 2nd Sec., 1st Sec. and Counsellor, Polish Embassy, Paris, 1963–69; Head of West European Dept and Mem. of Minister's Council, Min. of Foreign Affairs, 1969–72; Ambassador to Sweden, 1972–77; Head of Press, Cultural and Scientific Co-operation Dept, Min. of Foreign Affairs, 1977–81; Ambassador to UK, 1981–86, and to Ireland, 1984–86; Head of Press and Information Dept, 1986–90, and spokesman, 1988–90, Polish Min. of Foreign Affairs. Commander, Légion d'Honneur, 1972; Order of the Star of the North, Sweden, 1977; Commander, Order of the Aztec Eagle, Mexico, 1979. *Recreation:* swimming. *Address:* Embassy of the Republic of Poland, PO Box 519, 61 Shia Ben Ashour, Tripoli, Libya. *T:* 607619.

STANLEY, family name of **Earl of Derby** and **Baron Stanley of Alderley.**

STANLEY OF ALDERLEY, 8th Baron (UK) *cr* 1839; **Thomas Henry Oliver Stanley;** Bt 1660; Baron Sheffield (Ire), 1783; Baron Eddisbury, 1848; DL; Captain (retired), Coldstream Guards; Tenant Farmer of New College, Oxford, since 1954; *b* 28 Sept. 1927; *s* of Lt-Col The Hon. Oliver Hugh Stanley, DSO, JP (3rd *s* of 4th Baron) (*d* 1952), and Lady Kathleen Stanley (*d* 1977), *e d* of 5th Marquess of Bath; *S* cousin (known as Baron Sheffield), 1971; *m* 1955, Jane Barrett, *d* of Ernest George Hartley; three *s* one *d*. *Educ:* Wellington College, Berks. Coldstream Guards, 1945–52; Guards Parachute Battalion and Independent Company, 1947–50; Northamptonshire Institute of Agriculture, 1952–53. Mem., Cttee of Management, RNLI, 1981–; Chm., Fund Raising Cttee, RNLI, 1986–. Governor, St Edward's Sch., Oxford, 1979–. DL Gwynedd, 1985. *Recreations:* sailing, skiing, fishing. *Heir: e s* Hon. Richard Oliver Stanley, BSc [*b* 24 April 1956; *m* 1983, Carla, *er d* of Dr K. T. C. McKenzie, Solihull; two *d* (one *s* decd)]. *Address:* Trysglwyn Fawr, Amlwch, Anglesey. *T:* Amlwch (0407) 830364; Rectory Farm, Stanton St John, Oxford. *T:* Stanton St John (086735) 214. *Club:* Farmers'.

STANLEY, Prof. Eric Gerald, MA (Oxford and Yale); PhD (Birmingham); FBA 1985; Rawlinson and Bosworth Professor of Anglo-Saxon in the University of Oxford, and Fellow of Pembroke College, Oxford, 1977–91; Emeritus Professor and Supernumerary Fellow, since 1991; *b* 19 Oct. 1923; *m* 1959, Mary Bateman, MD, FRCP; one *d*. *Educ:* Queen Elizabeth's Grammar Sch., Blackburn; University Coll., Oxford. Lectr in Eng. Lang. and Lit., Birmingham Univ., 1951–62; Reader in Eng. Lang. and Lit., 1962–64, Prof. of English, 1964–75, Univ. of London at QMC; Prof. of English, Yale Univ., 1975–76. Member: Mediaeval Acad. of America, 1975–; Connecticut Acad. of Arts and Scis, 1976–. Sir Israel Gollancz Meml Lectr, British Acad., 1984. Co-Editor, Notes and Queries, 1963–. *Publications:* (ed) The Owl and the Nightingale, 1960, 2nd edn 1972; The Search for Anglo-Saxon Paganism, 1975; A Collection of Papers with Emphasis on Old English Literature, 1987; academic articles. *Recreation:* photography. *Address:* Pembroke College, Oxford OX1 1DW. *Club:* Athenæum.

STANLEY, Henry Sydney Herbert Cloete, CMG 1968; HM Diplomatic Service, retired; British High Commissioner to Trinidad and Tobago and (non-resident) to Grenada, 1977–80; *b* 5 March 1920; *er s* of late Sir Herbert Stanley, GCMG and Reniera (*née* Cloete), DBE; *m* 1941, Margaret, *d* of late Professor H. B. Dixon, CBE, FRS; three *s*. *Educ:* Eton; Balliol College, Oxford. Served with King's Royal Rifle Corps, 1940–46 (Capt.); N-W Europe, 1944–46, also HQ, CCG. Appointed to Commonwealth Relations Office, 1947. Served in Pakistan, 1950–52; Swaziland and South Africa, 1954–57; USA, 1959–61; Tanganyika, 1961–63; Kenya, 1963–65; Inspector, HM Diplomatic Service, 1966–68, Chief Inspector, 1968–70; High Comr, Ghana, 1970–75; Asst Under Sec. of State, FCO, 1975–77; High Comr for the New Hebrides (non-resident), 1976–77. *Address:* Silver How, 7 Harberton Mead, Oxford OX3 0DB.

STANLEY, John Mallalieu; Under Secretary (Legal), Department of Trade and Industry, since 1989; *b* 30 Sept. 1941; *s* of William and Rose Margaret Stanley; *m* 1968, Christine Mary Cunningham; two *s* one *d*. *Educ:* Welwyn Garden City Grammar Sch.; Clare College, Cambridge (MA). Solicitor. Church, Adams, Tatham & Co., 1965–68; Jaques & Co., 1968–75; Dept of Industry, later of Trade and Industry, 1975–. *Address:* Department of Trade and Industry, 10–18 Victoria Street, SW1H 0NN. *T:* 071–215 3470.

STANLEY, Rt. Hon. Sir John (Paul), Kt 1988; PC 1984; MP (C) Tonbridge and Malling since Feb. 1974; *b* 19 Jan. 1942; *s* of Mr and Mrs H. Stanley; *m* 1968, Susan Elizabeth Giles; two *s* one *d*. *Educ:* Repton Sch.; Lincoln Coll., Oxford (MA). Conservative Research Dept with responsibility for Housing, 1967–68; Research Associate, Internat. Inst. for Strategic Studies, 1968–69; Rio Tinto-Zinc Corp. Ltd, 1969–79. PPS to Rt Hon. Margaret Thatcher, 1976–79; Minister of State (Minister for Housing and Construction), DoE, 1979–83; Minister of State: for the Armed Forces, MoD, 1983–87; Northern Ireland Office, 1987–88. Mem., Parly Select Cttee on Nationalised Industries, 1974. Director: Conder Group plc, 1989–; Henderson Highland Trust plc, 1990–. Trustee, ActionAid, 1989–. *Publication:* (jtly) The International Trade in Arms, 1972. *Recreations:* music, photography, sailing. *Address:* House of Commons, SW1A 0AA.

STANLEY, Oliver Duncan; Chairman and Chief Executive, Rathbone Brothers (formerly Comprehensive Financial Services) PLC, since 1972; *b* 5 June 1925; *s* of Bernard Stanley and Mabel Best; *m* 1954, Ruth Brenner, JP, BA; one *s* three *d*. *Educ:* Christ Church, Oxford (MA); Harvard Univ., USA. Called to the Bar, Middle Temple, 1963. Served War, 8 Hussars, 1943–47. HM Inspector of Taxes, 1952–65; Dir, Gray Dawes Bank, 1966–72; founded Comprehensive Financial Services Gp of Cos, 1971. Chief Taxation Adviser, CLA, 1975–83 (Mem., Tax Cttee, 1983–). Mem., Soc. of Authors, 1967–. *Publications:* A Guide to Taxation, 1967; Taxology, 1971; Creation and Protection of Capital, 1974; Taxation of Farmers and Landowners, 1981, 4th edn 1991; Offshore Tax Planning, 1986; contrib. The Times and The Sunday Times, 1966–83; numerous articles in legal and agricultural periodicals. *Recreations:* music, tennis, French civilisation. *Address:* 5 The Park, NW11 7SR. *Club:* Travellers'.

STANLEY PRICE, His Honour Peter, QC 1956; a Circuit Judge (formerly a Judge of the Central Criminal Court), 1969–83; President, National Reference Tribunal for the Coal Mining Industry, 1979–83; Judge of the Chancery Court of York, 1967–83; *b* 27 Nov. 1911; *s* of late Herbert Stanley Price and late Gertrude Rangeley S. P. (*née* Wightman); *m* 1st, 1946, Harriett Ella Theresa (*d* 1948), *o d* of late Rev. R. E. Pownall; two *s*; 2nd, 1950, Margaret Jane, *o d* of late Samuel Milkins (she *m* 1937, William Hebditch, RAF; he *d* 1941); one *d* one step *s*. *Educ:* Cheltenham; Exeter College, Oxford (1st cl. Final Hons Sch. of Jurisprudence, 1933). Barrister, Inner Temple, 1936, Master of the Bench, 1963. Served War of 1939–45, Lieut (S) RNVR. Recorder of Pontefract, 1954, of York, 1955, of Kingston-upon-Hull, 1958, of Sheffield, 1965–69. Dep. Chm., N Riding QS, 1955–58, 1970–71, Chm., 1958–70; Judge of Appeal, Jersey and Guernsey, 1964–69; Solicitor-General, County Palatine of Durham, 1965–69. Pres., Nat. Reference Tribunal, Officials Conciliation Scheme, 1967–79. *Recreations:* birds and trees; gardening, shooting. *Address:* Church Hill, Great Ouseburn, York. *T:* Boroughbridge (0423) 330252. *Clubs:* Brooks's; Yorkshire (York).

STANNARD, Ven. Colin Percy, TD 1966; Archdeacon of Carlisle and Residentiary Canon of Carlisle Cathedral, since 1984; *b* 8 Feb. 1924; *s* of Percy and Grace Adelaide Stannard; *m* 1950, Joan Callow; one *s* two *d*. *Educ:* Woodbridge School; Selwyn Coll., Cambridge (BA 1947, MA 1949); Lincoln Theological Coll. Deacon 1949, priest 1950; Curate, St James Cathedral, Bury St Edmunds, 1949–52; Priest-in-charge, St Martin's, Grimsby, 1952–55; CF (TA), 1953–67; Vicar: St James's, Barrow-in-Furness, 1955–64; St John the Baptist's, Upperby, 1964–70; Rector of Gosforth, 1970–75; RD of Calder, 1970–75; Hon. Canon of Carlisle, 1975–84; Priest-in-charge of Natland, 1975–76, Vicar, 1976–84; RD of Kendal, 1975–84. *Recreations:* walking, bringing order out of chaos—especially in gardens. *Address:* 38 Longlands Road, Carlisle, Cumbria CA3 9AE. *T:* Carlisle (0228) 27622.

STANNARD, John Anthony; His Honour Judge Stannard; a Circuit Judge, since 1983; nominated to conduct Official Referee's business on Northern Circuit, since 1984; Circuit Commercial Judge, Northern Circuit, since 1990; *b* 30 Sept. 1931; *s* of late Anthony Stannard and Joan Stannard (*née* Joslin); *m* 1956, Madeline Betty (*née* Limb); two *d*. *Educ:* Quarry Bank High School, Liverpool (state scholar); Trinity College, Cambridge (Major Scholar, 1951; Sen. Scholar, 1953; Whittaker Scholar, 1955; 1st Cl. History Tripos; Prizeman; MA). Called to the Bar, Lincoln's Inn, 1956 (Chomley Scholar, 1953; Cassels Scholar, 1954). Practised on Northern Circuit, 1956–83; a Recorder, 1980–83. Captain RARO. *Recreations:* walking, reading. *Address:* Robinswood, Glenrose Road, Woolton, Liverpool L25 5JT. *T:* 051–428 1187; Queen Elizabeth II Law Courts, Derby Square, Liverpool L2 1XA. *Club:* Athenæum (Liverpool).

STANSBY, John; Chairman, UIE (UK) Ltd, since 1974 (UK parent company of UIE Scotland Ltd and part of Bouygues Group); Deputy Chairman, Energy Resources Ltd, since 1990; *b* 2 July 1930; *s* of late Dumon Stansby and Vera Margaret Main; *m* 1966, Anna Maria Kruschewsky; one *d* and one step *s* one step *d*. *Educ:* Oundle; Jesus Coll., Cambridge (Schol., MA). FInstPet, FCIT, FRSA, MInstM. Commissioned, Queen's Royal Regt, 1949; Service, 1949–50, Somaliland Scouts. Shell Mex & BP Ltd, 1955–62; AIC Ltd, 1962–66; Dir, Rank Leisure Services, Rank Organisation, 1966–70; Dir, P&O Energy, P&OSN Co., 1970–74; Chm., Dumon Stansby & Co. Ltd, 1974–; Dep. Chm., London Transport Exec., 1978–80; Chairman: SAUR (UK) Ltd, 1986–89; Cementation–SAUR Water Services Ltd, 1986–88; Bouygues (UK) Ltd, 1987–89; SAUR UK Development PLC, 1989–91; Director: Cambrian Environmental Services PLC, 1990–91; Stalwart Environmental Services PLC, 1989–91. European Bobsleigh Champion, 1952. *Address:* 19 Brook Green, W6 7BL. *T:* 071–603 0886. *Club:* Travellers'.

STANSFIELD, George Norman, CBE 1985 (OBE 1980); HM Diplomatic Service, retired; *b* 28 Feb. 1926; *s* of George Stansfield and Martha Alice (*née* Leadbetter); *m* 1947, Elizabeth Margaret Williams. *Educ:* Liscard High Sch. Served War, RAF, 1944–47. Ministries of Food and Supply, 1948–58; Private Sec. to Dir-Gen. of Armament Prodn, 1958–61; CRO, 1961; Second Secretary: Calcutta, 1962–66; Port of Spain, 1966–68; First Secretary: FCO, 1968–71; Singapore, 1971–74; Consul, Durban, 1974–78; FCO, 1978; Counsellor, and Head of Overseas Estate Dept, 1980–82; High Comr, Solomon Islands, 1982–86. Mem. Council, Pacific Islands Soc, 1986–. *Recreations:* sailing, cine-photography, wildlife. *Address:* Deryn's Wood, 80 Westfield Road, Woking, Surrey GU22 9QA. *Clubs:* Commonwealth Trust; Royal Southampton Yacht.

STANSFIELD, His Honour James Warden; a Circuit Judge (formerly County Court Judge), 1963–78, retired; *b* 7 April 1906; *s* of James Hampson Stansfield, Sunny Lea, Wilmslow, Cheshire; *m* 1937, Florence Evelyn, *d* of Arthur Harry Holdcroft, Congleton, Cheshire; two *s* one *d*. *Educ:* King's School, Macclesfield; Sidney Sussex College, University of Cambridge. Called to the Bar, Inner Temple, 1929; practised Northern Circuit. Contested (C) Platting Division of Manchester, 1935. Served War of 1939–45: Royal Air Force, Middle East, and Staff of Judge Advocate-General; formerly RAFVR (Squadron Leader). Chairman: Manchester Licensing Planning Cttee, 1955–63; Manchester Mental Health Review Tribunal, 1962; Warrington Licensed Premises Cttee, 1970. *Recreations:* golf, walking. *Address:* Oak Lea, Victoria Road, Wilmslow, Cheshire. *T:* Wilmslow (0625) 523915.

STANSFIELD SMITH, Prof. Colin, CBE 1988; County Architect, Hampshire County Council, since 1973; Professor of Architectural Design, Portsmouth Polytechnic, since

1990; *b* 1 Oct. 1932; *s* of Stansfield Smith and Mary (*née* Simpson); *m* 1961, Angela Jean Earnshaw; one *s* one *d*. *Educ:* William Hulme's Grammar Sch., Manchester; Cambridge Univ. Sch. of Architecture (MA, DipArch). ARIBA. Schools Div., LCC, 1958–60; Sen. Asst then Associate Partner, Emberton Frank & Tardrew, Architects, 1960–65; Partner, Emberton Tardrew & Partners, 1965–71; Dep. County Architect, Cheshire CC, 1971–73. RIBA Royal Gold Medal, 1991. *Publications:* Hampshire Architecture (1974–1984), 1985; articles in Architects' Jl and Architectural Review. *Recreations:* golf, painting. *Address:* 8 Christchurch Road, Winchester, Hants SO23 9SR. *T:* Winchester (0962) 851970. *Club:* Hockley Golf (Twyford, Hants).

STANSGATE, Viscountcy of (*cr* 1942, of Stansgate); title disclaimed by 2nd Viscount (*see* Benn, Rt Hon. Tony).

STANTON, David; Chief Economist (Grade 3), Department of Employment, since 1988; *b* 5 Nov. 1942; *s* of Frederick Charles Patrick Stanton and Ethel (*née* Cout); *m* 1967, Isobel Joan Blair; one *s* one *d*. *Educ:* Bishops Stortford Coll.; Worcester Coll., Oxford (BA PPE 1965); LSE (MSc(Econ) 1971). ODI/Nuffield Fellow, Govt of Uganda, 1965–67; Lectr, Brunel Univ., 1967–70; Economic Adviser: Min. of Transport, 1970; Min. of Housing, then DoE, 1971–74; HM Treasury, 1974–75; Senior Economic Adviser: seconded to Hong Kong Govt, 1975–77; also Head of Unit for Manpower Studies, Dept of Employment, 1977–81; Econs Br., Dept of Employment, 1981–83; also Dir, Employment Market Res. Unit, 1983–87. *Recreations:* people, dogs and other animals, singing. *Address:* Department of Employment, Caxton House, Tothill Street, SW1H 9NF; 5 Darell Road, Richmond, Surrey TW9 4LF. *T:* 081–392 2107.

STANTON, Rev. John Maurice, MA; Rector of Chesham Bois, 1973–83; *b* 29 Aug. 1918; *s* of Frederick William Stanton, MInstCE and Maude Lozel (*née* Cole); *m* 1947, Helen Winifred (*née* Bowden); one *s* two *d*. *Educ:* King's School, Rochester; University College, Oxford (Gunsley Exhibnr; 2nd Class Hons, Final Hon. Sch. of Nat. Science, 1947; MA 1947). Commissioned Royal Artillery, 1940, 92nd Field Regt, RA, 1940–43. ISLD, CMF, 1943–46. Assistant Master, Tonbridge School, 1947–59; Headmaster, Blundell's School, 1959–71; Curate, St Matthew's, Exeter, 1972. Ordained Deacon, 1952; Priest, 1953. Sec., Oxford Diocesan Bd of Patronage, 1984–90. *Recreations:* water colour painting, gardening. *Address:* 37A St Andrew's Road, Old Headington, Oxford OX3 9DL. *T:* Oxford (0865) 65206.

STANYER, Maj.-Gen. John Turner, CBE 1971 (OBE 1967); *b* 28 July 1920; *s* of late Charles T. Stanyer and late Mrs R. H. Stanyer; *m* 1942, Mary Patricia Pattie; three *s* four *d*. *Educ:* Latymer Upper Sch., Hammersmith. Served War, 2/Lieut The Middlesex Regt, 1941; Lieut to Captain, The Middlesex Regt, 1941–47: Iceland, France, Germany, Palestine. Captain, Royal Army Ordnance Corps, 1947; Student, Staff Coll., Camberley, 1951; AA&QMG, UN Force in Cyprus, 1966; Dir of Ordnance Services, BAOR, 1968–71; Commandant, Central Ordnance Depot, Bicester, 1971–73; Comdr, Base Orgn, RAOC, 1973–75, retired. Col Comdt, RAOC, 1977–82. Dir Gen., Supply Co-ordination, MoD, 1975–80. Mem., Oxford City Council, 1983–87. CBIM. *Recreation:* sailing. *Address:* Sandy House, Manor Close, Walberswick, Southwold, Suffolk IP18 6UQ. *T:* Southwold (0502) 724533.

STAPLE, Rev. David; General Secretary, Free Church Federal Council, since 1986; *b* 30 March 1930; *s* of William Hill Staple and Elsie Staple; *m* 1955, Margaret Lilian Berrington; one *s* three *d*. *Educ:* Watford Boys' Grammar Sch.; Christ's Coll., Cambridge (MA); Regent's Park Coll., Oxford; Wadham Coll., Oxford (MA); BD London (external). Baptist Minister: West Ham Central Mission, 1955–58; Llanishen, Cardiff, 1958–74; College Road, Harrow, 1974–86. Chm., Baptist Missionary Soc., 1981–82. *Recreations:* fell walking, music. *Address:* Free Church Federal Council, 27 Tavistock Square, WC1H 9HH. *T:* 071–387 8413.

STAPLES, Rev. Canon Edward Eric, CBE 1977 (OBE 1973); Chaplain to The Queen, 1973–80; Chaplain to the Anglican congregations in Helsinki and throughout Finland, in Moscow, Leningrad and elsewhere in the Soviet Union, and in Outer Mongolia, 1964–80; Hon. Chaplain, British Embassy: Helsinki, 1967–80, Moscow, 1968–80, Ulan Bator, 1970–81; Hon. Lecturer, English History, University of Helsinki, 1972–80; Hon. Canon of Gibraltar Cathedral, since 1974; *b* 15 Nov. 1910; *yr s* of Christopher Walter Staples and Esther Jane Staples; *m* 1962, Kate Ethel Thusberg (*née* Rönngren); two step *d*. *Educ:* Chichester Theol Coll. (earlier opportunities so misused that it is unwise to name the establishments concerned!). MA, PhD. Niger Company, 1932. Served with RNVR, 1939–46. Ordained 1948. Assistant of Court of Russia Company, 1977–89, Consul, 1978–88. Life Mem., Finnish-British Soc.; Mem., Anglo-Mongolian Soc. Medal of Univ. of Helsinki, 1980. Kt, Order of the Lion (Finland), 1976; Order of St Vladimir (3rd cl.) (Russian Orthodox Church), 1977. *Recreations:* climbing, cricket, fishing, gardening (no longer actively), historical research. *Address:* The Old School House, Sutton Benger, near Chippenham, Wilts SN15 4RX; 10 Woodlands Close, Hermanus, 7200, Republic of South Africa. *Clubs:* MCC; City (Cape Town); Helsinki Cricket (Founder Mem.); Moscow Cricket (Founder Mem.); Ulan Bator Golf (Hon. Life Mem.).

STAPLES, (Hubert Anthony) Justin, CMG 1981; HM Diplomatic Service, retired; Ambassador to Finland, 1986–89; *b* 14 Nov. 1929; *s* of late Francis Hammond Staples, formerly ICS, and Catherine Margaret Mary Pownall; *m* 1962, Susan Angela Collingwood Carter; one *s* one *d*. *Educ:* Downside; Oriel Coll., Oxford. Served in RAF 1952–54 (Pilot Officer). Entered Foreign (later Diplomatic) Service, 1954; 3rd Sec., Bangkok, 1955; Foreign Office, 1959; 1st Sec., Berlin (Dep. Political Adviser), 1962; Vientiane, 1965 (acted as Chargé d'Affaires in 1966 and 1967); transf. to FO and seconded to Cabinet Office, 1968; Counsellor, UK Delegn to NATO, Brussels, 1971; Counsellor and Consul-General, Bangkok, 1974 (acted as Chargé d'affaires, 1975 and 1977); Counsellor, Dublin, 1978–81; Ambassador to Thailand, 1981–86 and concurrently to Laos, 1985–86. *Recreations:* ski-ing, golf. *Address:* 48 Crescent Road, Kingston, Surrey KT2 7RF. *Clubs:* Travellers'; Roehampton; Royal Bangkok Sports (Bangkok).

STAPLES, Justin; *see* Staples, H. A. J.

STAPLES, Sir Thomas, 15th Bt *cr* 1628 (Ire.), of Lissan, Co. Tyrone; *b* 9 Feb. 1905; *s* of Thomas Staples (*d* 1963) (nephew of 10th Bt) and Mary Ussher (*d* 1966), *d* of Frederick Greer; *S* cousin, 1989; *m* 1952, Frances Ann Irvine (*d* 1981). *Heir: b* Gerald James Arland Staples [*b* 2 Dec. 1909; *m* 1951, Henrietta Owen, *d* of Arland Ussher; two *d*]. *Address:* 219, 3051 Shelbourne Street, Victoria, BC V8R 6T2, Canada.

STAPLETON, Sir Alfred; *see* Stapleton, Sir H. A.

STAPLETON, Air Vice-Marshal Deryck Cameron, CB 1960; CBE 1948; DFC; AFC; psa; *b* 1918; *s* of John Rouse Stapleton, OBE, Sarnia, Natal; *m* 1942, Ethleen Joan Clifford, *d* of late Sir Cuthbert William Whiteside. *Educ:* King Edward VI Sch., Totnes. Joined RAF, 1936; served Transjordan and Palestine (AFC), 1937–39; War of 1939–45 (DFC). Middle East, N Africa, Italy. Asst Sec. (Air), War Cabinet Offices, 1945–46; Secretary, Chiefs of Staff Cttee, Ministry of Defence, 1947–49; OC RAF, Odiham, 1949–51; subsequently, Plans, Fighter Comd HQ and Ops at AFCENT Fontainebleu; then OC, RAF, Oldenburg (Germany); Plans, Bomber Comd HQ, 1957–60; Air Ministry, 1960–62; Dir, Defence Plans, Min. of Defence, 1963–64; AOC No 1 Group, RAF Bomber Command, 1964–66; Comdt, RAF Staff Coll., Bracknell, 1966–68. BAC Area Manager, Libya, 1969–70; BAC Rep. CENTO Area, Tehran, later BAe Chief Exec. Iran, and Man. Dir, Irano-British Dynamics Co. Iran, 1970–79; Rep. BAe, Peking, China, and Chm., British Cos Assoc., Peking, 1979–83. Associate Fellow, British Interplanetary Soc., 1960. *Recreations:* most sports. *Address:* c/o National Westminster Bank, Haymarket, SW1.

STAPLETON, Guy; Chief Executive, Intervention Board Executive Agency (formerly Intervention Board for Agricultural Produce), since 1986; *b* 10 Nov. 1935; *s* of William Algernon Swann Stapleton and Joan Denise Stapleton (*née* Wilson). *Educ:* Malvern Coll. Clerical Officer, Min. of Transport and Civil Aviation, 1954–58; Exec. Officer, 1958; transf. to Min. of Aviation, 1959; Civil Aviation Asst, British Embassy, Rome, 1960–63; Private Sec. to Controller of National Air Traffic Control Services, 1963–65; Asst Principal, MAFF, 1965; Private Sec. to Jt Parly Sec., 1967–68; Principal, 1968; Asst Sec., 1973; Dept of Prices and Consumer Protection, 1974–76; Under Sec., 1981; European Secretariat, Cabinet Office, 1982–85; Dir of Establishments, MAFF, 1985–86. *Publications:* A Walk of Verse, 1961; (compiled) Poet's England: 2, Gloucestershire, 1977, 2nd edn 1982; 4, Avon and Somerset, 1981; 7, Devon, 1986; 9, Hertfordshire, 1988; Vale of Moreton Churches, 1989; (ed) Memories of Moreton, 1989. *Recreations:* history of North Cotswolds, genealogy, topographical verse. *Address:* c/o Fountain House, 2 Queen's Walk, Reading RG1 7QW. *T:* Reading (0734) 583626. *Clubs:* Civil Service, Commonwealth Trust.

STAPLETON, Sir (Henry) Alfred, 10th Bt *cr* 1679; *b* 2 May 1913; *s* of Brig. Francis Harry Stapleton, CMG (*d* 1956) and *g g s* of 7th Bt, and Maud Ellen (*d* 1958), *d* of late Major Alfred Edward Wrottesley; *S* kinsman, 1977; *m* 1961, Rosslyne Murray, *d* of late Captain H. S. Warren, RN. *Educ:* Marlborough; Christ Church, Oxford. Served War of 1939–45, Oxfordshire and Bucks Light Infantry. *Recreations:* cricket umpiring, gardening. *Heir:* none. *Address:* 7 Ridgeway, Horsecastles Lane, Sherborne, Dorset DT9 6BZ. *T:* Sherborne (0935) 812295. *Clubs:* Garrick, MCC.

STAPLETON, Very Rev. Henry Edward Champneys; Dean of Carlisle, since 1988; *b* 17 June 1932; *s* of Edward Parker Stapleton and Frances Mary Stapleton; *m* 1964, Mary Deborah Sapwell; two *d*. *Educ:* Lancing College; Pembroke Coll., Cambridge (BA 1954, MA 1958); Ely Theological Coll. Deacon 1956, priest 1957, York; Assistant Curate: St Olave with St Giles, 1956–59; Pocklington, 1959–61; Vicar of Seaton Ross with Everingham, Harswell and Bielby, 1961–67; RD of Weighton, 1966–67; Rector of Skelton, 1967–75; Vicar of Wroxham with Hoveton, 1975–81; Priest in Charge of Belaugh, 1976–81, with Hoveton St Peter, 1979–81; Canon Residentiary and Precentor of Rochester Cathedral, 1981–88; Warden of Readers, 1981–88. Member: Council for the Care of Churches, 1965–91; Redundant Churches Fund, 1976–. FSA 1974. Editor, Cathedral, 1976–82. *Publications:* Skelton Village, 1971; Heirs without Title, 1974; The Skilful Master Builder, 1975; The Model Working Parson, 1976; (ed and contrib.) Churchyards Handbook, 2nd edn 1976, 3rd edn 1988; articles in Churchscape and other ecclesiastical jls. *Recreations:* visiting churches, second-hand bookshops. *Address:* The Deanery, Carlisle, Cumbria CA3 8TZ. *T:* Carlisle (0228) 23335.

STAPLETON, Prof. Richard Christopher, PhD; Wolfson Professor of Finance, Lancaster University, since 1989; *b* 11 Oct. 1942; *s* of Leonard Stapleton and Rosamund Kathleen May Stapleton; *m* 1968, Linda Cairns; one *s* one *d*. *Educ:* Univ. of Sheffield (BAEcon, PhD Business Studies); Open Univ. (BA Maths). Lectr in Business Finance, Sheffield Univ., 1965–73; Asst Prof. of Finance, New York Univ., 1973–76; Sen. Res. Fellow, 1976–77, Nat. West. Bank Prof. of Business Finance, 1977–86, Manchester Business Sch., Univ. of Manchester; Fellow, Churchill Coll., Cambridge, 1986–89. Hon. MBA Manchester, 1980. *Publications:* The Theory of Corporate Finance, 1970; International Tax Systems and Financing Policy, 1978; Capital Markets and Corporate Financial Decisions, 1980; contrib. Econ. Jl, Jl of Finance, Jl of Financial Econs, Qly Jl of Econs. *Recreations:* running, golf, reading, travel. *Address:* Lancaster University, University House, Lancaster LA1 4YW.

STAPLETON-COTTON, family name of **Viscount Combermere.**

STAREWICZ, Artur, 2 Orders of Banner of Labour (1st cl.); Polonia Restituta; and other orders; Ambassador of Poland to the Court of St James's, 1971–78; *b* Warsaw, 20 March 1917; *m* 1947, Maria Rutkiewicz; two *s* two *d*. *Educ:* Warsaw Univ.; Institut Chimique de Rouen, 1938–39; Lvov Technical Univ., 1940–41; Grad. Engr, Soviet Electrochemical Inst., 1943. Chemical engr. Mem., revolutionary youth orgns incl. Communist Union of Polish Youth; arrested 1935 and 1936; Mem., Polish Workers Party (PPR), 1944–48; worked in PPR Voivoidship Cttees: Rzeszow; Cracow; Warsaw; First Sec., Wroclaw, 1947–48; Polish United Workers Party (PZPR): Mem., 1948–; Head of Propaganda, Central Cttee, 1948–53; Sec., Central Council of Trade Unions, 1954–56; Dep. Editor-in-Chief, daily newspaper Trybuna Ludu, 1956; Alternate Mem., Central Cttee, 1954–59, Mem., 1959–71; Head of Press Office, 1957–63; Sec., Central Cttee, 1963–71. Mem., Seym, 1957–72; Chairman: Polish Gp, Inter-Parly Union; Polish Cttee for Security and Cooperation in Europe, 1978–86; Editor, Polish Perspectives, 1979–86. *Recreation:* aquatic sport. *Address:* Swietojerska 16 m3, Warsaw, Poland.

STARK, Sir Andrew (Alexander Steel), KCMG 1975 (CMG 1964); CVO 1965; DL; HM Diplomatic Service, retired; Director, The Maersk Co., 1978–90 (Chairman, 1978–87); Adviser on European Affairs, Society of Motor Manufacturers and Traders, 1977–89; *b* 30 Dec. 1916; *yr s* of late Thomas Bow Stark and of late Barbara Black Stark (*née* Steel), Fauldhouse, West Lothian; *m* 1944, Helen Rosemary, *er d* of late Lt-Col J. Oxley Parker, TD, and Mary Monica (*née* Hills); two *s* (and one *s* decd). *Educ:* Bathgate Acad.; Edinburgh Univ. MA (Hons), Eng. Lit, Edinburgh, 1938. Served War of 1939–45, Green Howards and Staff appts. Major 1945. Entered Foreign Service, 1948, and served in Foreign Office until 1950; 1st Secretary, Vienna, 1951–53; Asst Private Sec. to Foreign Secretary, 1953–55; Head of Chancery: Belgrade, 1956–58; Rome, 1958–60; Counsellor: FO, 1960–64; Bonn, 1964–68; attached to Mission to UN with rank of Ambassador, Jan. 1968; British Mem., Seven Nation Cttee on Reorganisation of UN Secretariat; seconded to UN, NY, as Under-Secretary-General, Oct. 1968–1971; HM Ambassador to Denmark, 1971–76; Dep. Under-Sec. of State, FCO, 1976–78. Director: Scandinavian Bank Ltd, 1978–88; Carlsberg Brewery Ltd, 1980–87. Mem., CBI Europe Cttee, 1980–85. Chairman: Anglo-Danish Soc., 1983–; Anglo-Danish Trade Adv. Bd, 1983–. President: British Assoc. of Former UN Civil Servants, 1989–; Essex Physically Handicapped Assoc., 1979–; Chm., Rural Community Council of Essex, 1990–. University of Essex: Mem. Council, 1978– (Chm. Council, 1983–89); Pro-Chancellor, 1983–; DU 1990. DL Essex, 1981. Grosses Verdienstkreuz, German Federal Republic, 1965; Grand Cross, Order of the Dannebrog, Denmark, 1974. *Recreations:* ski-ing, tennis, shooting. *Address:* Fambridge Hall, White Notley, Witham, Essex CM8 1RN. *T:* Silver End (0376) 83117. *Clubs:* Travellers' (Chairman 1978–81), MCC.

STARK, Dame Freya (Madeline), DBE 1972 (CBE 1953); *b* 31 Jan. 1893; *d* of late Robert Stark, sculptor, Ford Park, Chagford, Devon; *m* 1947, Stewart Perowne, OBE (*d* 1989). *Educ:* privately in Italy; Bedford College, London University; School of Oriental Studies, London. Engaged on Govt service in Middle East and elsewhere, 1939–45. Awarded Back Grant, 1933, for travel in Luristan; Triennial Burton Memorial Medal from Royal Asiatic Society, 1934; Mungo Park Medal from Royal Scottish Geographical Society, 1936; Founder's Medal from Royal Geographical Society, 1942; Percy Sykes Memorial Medal from R Central Asian Soc., 1951. Sister of the Order of St John of Jerusalem, 1949, Sister Comdr, 1981. LLD Glasgow Univ., 1951; DLitt Durham, 1971. *Publications:* Bagdad Sketches, 1933, enlarged edition, 1937; The Valleys of the Assassins, 1934; The Southern Gates of Arabia, 1936; Seen in the Hadhramaut, 1938; A Winter in Arabia, 1940; Letters from Syria, 1942; East is West, 1945; Perseus in the Wind, 1948; Traveller's Prelude, 1950, reissued 1989; Beyond Euphrates, 1951, reissued 1989; The Coast of Incense, 1953; Ionia: a Quest, 1954; The Lycian Shore, 1956, reissued 1989; Alexander's Path, 1958; Riding to the Tigris, 1959; Dust in the Lion's Paw, 1961; The Journey's Echo, 1963; Rome on the Euphrates, 1966; The Zodiac Arch, 1968; Space, Time and Movement in Landscape, 1969; The Minaret of Djam, 1970; Turkey: a sketch of Turkish History, 1971; A Peak in Darien, 1976; Rivers of Time, 1982; Letters (vols 1–6 ed Lucy Moorehead; vols 7–8 ed Caroline Moorehead): vol. 1, The Furnace and the Cup, 1914–1930, 1974; vol. 2, The Open Road, 1930–1935, 1975; vol. 3, The Growth of Danger, 1935–1939, 1976; vol. 4, The Bridge of the Levant, 1940–1943, 1977; vol. 5, New Worlds for Old, 1943–1946, 1978; vol. 6, The Broken Road, 1947–1952, 1981; vol. 7, Some Talk of Alexander, 1952–59, 1982; vol. 8, Traveller's Epilogue, 1960–80, 1982; (ed Caroline Moorehead) Over the Rim of the World: selected letters, 1988. *Recreations:* travel, mountaineering and embroidery. *Address:* Via Canova, Asolo (Treviso), Italy; c/o John Murray, 50 Albemarle Street, W1.

STARK, George Robert, PhD; FRS 1990; Associate Director of Research, Imperial Cancer Research Fund, since 1989; *b* 4 July 1933; *s* of Jack and Florence Stark; *m* 1956, Mary Beck; one *s* one *d*. *Educ:* Columbia College, NY (BA 1955); Columbia Univ., NY (Chemistry; PhD 1959). Asst Prof., Rockefeller Univ., 1961; Stanford University: Asst Prof., 1963; Associate Prof., 1966; Prof. of Biochemistry, 1971; ICRF, 1983–. Member: Nat. Acad. of Scis, USA, 1987; European Molecular Biol. Orgn, 1985. *Publications:* contribs to scientific jls. *Recreations:* sports, stamps, books, records. *Address:* Imperial Cancer Research Fund, Lincoln's Inn Fields, WC2A 3PX. *T:* 071–269 3265.

STARKE, Hon. Sir John Erskine, Kt 1976; Judge of Supreme Court of Victoria, Australia, 1964–85; Trustee, Australian War Memorial, Canberra; *b* 1 Dec. 1913; *s* of Hon. Sir Hayden Starke, KCMG; *m* Elizabeth, *d* of late Colin Campbell. Admitted to Victorian Bar, 1939; QC 1955; Judge, 1946. *Address:* Mount Eliza, Vic 3930, Australia.

STARKER, Janos; concert cellist, recording artist; Distinguished Professor of Music, Indiana University, since 1958; *b* 5 July 1924; *s* of F. Sandor and M. Margit; *m* 1944, Eva Uranyi; one *d*; *m* 1960, Rae D. Busch; one *d*. *Educ:* Franz Liszt Academy of Music, Budapest; Zrinyi Gymnasium, Budapest. Solo cellist: Budapest Opera and Philh., 1945–46; Dallas Symphony, 1948–49; Metropolitan Opera, 1949–53; Chicago Symphony, 1953–58; concert tours on all continents in recitals and as soloist with orchestras; numerous recordings. Grand Prix du Disque, 1948; George Washington Award, 1972; Sanford Fellowship Award, Yale, 1974; Herzl Award, 1978; Ed Press Award, 1983; Kodály Commemorative Medallion, NY, 1983; Arturo Toscanini Award, Toscanini Foundn, 1986; Tracy Sonneborn Award, Indiana Univ., 1986. Mem., Amer. Fedn Musicians; Hon. RAM, 1981. Hon. DMus: Chicago Conservatory Coll., 1961; Cornell, 1978; East-West Univ., 1982; Williams Coll., 1983; Lawrence Univ., 1990. Invented the Starker Bridge. *Publications:* Cello Method: an organised method of string playing, 1963; Bach Suites, 1971; Concerto Cadenzas, 1976; Beethoven Sonatas, 1978; Beethoven Variations, 1979; Bach Sonatas, 1979; Schubert-Starker Sonatina, 1980; Dvorak Concerto, 1981; Bottermund-Starker Variations, 1982; Encores, 1985; many articles and essays. *Recreations:* writing, swimming, staying alive. *Address:* Indiana University Music Department, Bloomington, Ind 47401, USA.

STARKEY, Sir John (Philip), 3rd Bt *cr* 1935; DL; *b* 8 May 1938; *s* of Sir William Randle Starkey, 2nd Bt, and Irene Myrtle Starkey (*née* Francklin) (*d* 1965); *S* father, 1977; *m* 1966, Victoria Henrietta Fleetwood, *y d* of Lt-Col Christopher Fuller, TD; one *s* three *d*. *Educ:* Eton College; Christ Church, Oxford. Sloan Fellow, London Business School. A Church Commissioner and Mem. Commissioners' Assets Cttee, 1985–; Mem., Archbishop's Commn on Rural Areas, 1988–90. Chairman: Notts Br., CLA, 1977–80; E Midlands Regional Cttee, Nat. Trust, 1986–. UK Vice Pres., Confedn of European Agriculture, 1989–; Pres., Newark Chamber of Commerce, 1980–82. Notts: DL, 1981; High Sheriff, 1987–88; JP Newark, 1981–88. FRSA 1990. *Recreation:* cricket. *Heir: s* Henry John Starkey, *b* 13 Oct. 1973. *Address:* Norwood Park, Southwell, Notts NG25 0PF. *T:* Southwell (0636) 812762. *Clubs:* Boodle's, MCC.

STASSEN, Harold Edward; lawyer, politician, educator, United States; Partner in law firm Stassen, Kostos and Mason; Chairman, International Law Committee of Philadelphia Bar Association, 1973; *b* W St Paul, Minn, 13 April 1907; *s* of William Andrew Stassen and Elsie Emma Mueller; *m* 1929, Esther G. Glewwe, artist; one *s* one *d*. *Educ:* Univ. of Minnesota Coll. (BA 1927; LLB 1929); Law School. Has several hon. degrees. Admitted to Minnesota Bar, 1929; practised South St Paul; County Attorney, Dakota County, 1930–38; thrice elected Governor of Minnesota, 1939–43; resigned for service with Navy; Lt Comdr, USN; Comdr on staff of Admiral Halsey in South Pacific, 1943–44; Asst Chief of Staff, 1944; Capt., USN; released to inactive duty, 1945. One of US delegates to San Francisco Conference, drafting and signing UN Charter, 1945. Pres., Minnesota Young Republicans; Delegate to Republican Convention, 1936; Temporary Chairman and Keynoter of Republican National Convention and floor manager for Wendell Wilkie, 1940; twice elected National Chairman National Governors' Conference, and of Council of State Governments, 1940–41. President, University of Pennsylvania, 1948–53. President International Council of Religious Education, 1942, 1950; Vice-Pres. and a Founder, Nat. Council of Churches, 1951–52; President, Div. of Christian Educ. of Nat. Council of Churches, 1953–. Director Foreign Operations Admin., 1953–55; Special Assistant to the President for Disarmament, 1955–58; Dep. US Rep. on Disarmament Commn, UN, 1955–58. Chief Consultant to ME Tech. Univ., Ankara, 1958; Mem., Nat. Security Council, 1953–58. Delivered Godkind Lectures on Human Rights, Harvard Univ., 1946; candidate for Republican nomination for President of US, 1948. Chm., World Law Day, Geneva, 1968. Bronze Star, 1944; Legion of Merit, Six Battle Stars (Western Pacific campaign), 1945. Baptist. Mason. *Publications:* Where I Stand, 1947; Man was meant to be Free, 1951.

STATHAM, Sir Norman, KCMG 1977 (CMG 1967); CVO 1968; HM Diplomatic Service, retired; *b* Stretford, Lancs, 15 Aug. 1922; *s* of Frederick William and Maud Statham; *m* 1948, Hedwig Gerlich; one *s* one *d* (and one *s* decd). *Educ:* Seymour Park Council School, Stretford; Manchester Grammar School; Gonville and Caius College, Cambridge (MA). Intelligence Corps, 1943–47; Manchester Oil Refinery Ltd and Petrochemicals Ltd, 1948–50; Foreign Service, 1951: Foreign Office, 1951; Consul (Commercial), New York, 1954; First Secretary (Commercial), Bonn, 1958; Administrative Staff College, Henley, 1963; Foreign Office, 1964; Counsellor, Head of European Economic Integration Dept, 1965–68, 1970–71; Consul-General, São Paulo, 1968–70; Minister (Economic), Bonn, 1971; Asst Under Sec. of State, FCO, 1975; Dep. Under Sec. of State, FCO, 1975; Ambassador to Brazil, 1977–79. FCO Special Rep. for British-German Co-operation, 1984–86. Vice-Pres., British Chamber of Commerce in Germany, 1981–85; Pres., Council of British Chambers of Commerce in Continental Europe, 1982–84. *Recreations:* gardening, reading, birdwatching. *Address:* 11 Underhill Park Road, Reigate, Surrey RH2 9LU.

STATHATOS, Stephanos; Commander, Order of Phoenix; Officer, Order of George I; Greek Ambassador to the Court of St James's, 1986–89, and non-resident Ambassador to Iceland; *b* 1922; *s* of Gerassimo and Eugenia Stathatos; *m* 1947, Thalia Mouzina. *Educ:* Law School, Athens Univ.; post graduate studies: Ecole des Sciences Politiques, Paris; LSE. Entered Greek Diplomatic Service, 1953; served Cairo, NATO, Paris, Athens, Washington; Dep. Perm. Rep. to UN, NY, 1968–72; Dir, Middle East Political Affairs, Min. of Foreign Affairs, 1972–74; Ambassador, Perm. Rep. to EEC, 1974–79; Ambassador, Paris, 1979–82; non-resident Ambassador to Holy See, 1981–82; Dep. Political Dir, 1982–84, Political Dir, 1984–85, Min. of Foreign Affairs. Holds numerous foreign orders and decorations. *Address:* 24 Raviné Street, Athens 11521, Greece. *T:* 7222004. *Club:* Athenæum.

STAUGHTON, Rt. Hon. Sir Christopher (Stephen Thomas Jonathan Thayer), Kt 1981; PC 1988; **Rt. Hon. Lord Justice Staughton;** a Lord Justice of Appeal, since 1987; *b* 24 May 1933; *yr s* of late Simon Thomas Samuel Staughton of Melbourne, Australia and Edith Madeline Jones of Halifax, Canada; *m* 1960, Joanna Susan Elizabeth, *er d* of late George Frederick Arthur Burgess; two *d*. *Educ:* Eton Coll. (Scholar); Magdalene Coll., Cambridge (Scholar; Hon. Fellow 1988). 2nd Lieut, 11th Hussars PAO, 1952–53; Lieut, Derbyshire Yeomanry TA, 1954–56. George Long Prize for Roman Law, Cambridge, 1955; BA 1956; MA 1961. Called to Bar, Inner Temple, 1957, Bencher, 1978; QC 1970; a Recorder of the Crown Court, 1972–81; a Judge of the High Court of Justice, QBD, 1981–87. Mem., Senate of the Inns of Court and the Bar, 1974–81; Chm., Code of Conduct sub-cttee, 1979–80. Chm., St Peter's Eaton Square Church of England Sch., 1974–83. *Publications:* (Jt Editor) The Law of General Average (British Shipping Laws vol. 7), 1964, new edn, 1975; (jtly) Profits of Crime and their Recovery, 1984; articles on plain English in the law. *Recreations:* bridge, growing dahlias. *Address:* Royal Courts of Justice, Strand, WC2. *T:* 071–936 6000.

STAUNTON, Marie; Editor, Solicitors' Journal, since 1990; *b* 28 May 1952; *d* of Ann and Austin Staunton; *m* 1986, James Albert Provan; one *d*. *Educ:* Lancaster Univ.; College of Law (BA). Solicitor. Head of casework for Simon Community Hostels for Addicts, Alcoholics and Homeless Families (England, NI and Eire), 1970–72; Articled Clerk and Solicitor in private practice and Law Centres, 1976–83; Legal Officer, NCCL, 1983–87; Dir, British Section, Amnesty Internat., 1987–90. *Publications:* Data Protection: putting the record straight, 1987; contribs to NCCL works; chapters in books on allied subjects. *Recreations:* playing with daughter, dancing, walking, gardening. *Address:* (office) 21–27 Lambs Conduit Street, WC1N 3NJ. *T:* 071–242 2548.

STAVELEY, Sir John (Malfroy), KBE 1980 (OBE 1972); MC 1941; FRCP; FRACPath; Haematologist, Auckland Hospital Board, 1950–64; Director, Auckland Blood Transfusion Service, 1965–76; *b* 30 Aug. 1914; *s* of William Staveley and Annie May Staveley (*née* Malfroy); *m* 1940, Elvira Cliafe Wycherley; one *s* one *d*. *Educ:* Univ. of Dunedin (MB ChB); Univ. of Edinburgh. FRCP 1958; FRACPath 1965. House Surgeon, Auckland Hosp., 1939; war service with 2NZEF, Middle East, 1940–45; post graduate educn, UK, 1946–47; Pathologist, Auckland Hosp., 1948–50. Landsteiner Award, USA, for medical research, 1980. *Publications:* papers in medical and scientific jls (British, American and NZ). *Recreations:* mountaineering, fishing, music. *Address:* 11 Matanui Street, Northcote, Auckland 9, New Zealand.

STAVELEY, Martin Samuel, CMG 1966; CVO 1966; CBE 1962 (MBE 1955); *b* 3 Oct. 1921; fourth *s* of late Herbert Samuel Staveley and Edith Ellen Staveley (*née* Shepherd); *m* 1942, Edith Eileen Baker; one *s* two *d*. *Educ:* Stamford School; Trinity College, Oxford. Appointed Cadet, Colonial Administrative Service, Nigeria, 1942; Secretary, Development and Welfare Organisation in the West Indies, 1946–57; Secretary to Governor-General, Federation of the West Indies, 1958–62; Administrator, British Virgin Islands, 1962–67; HM Diplomatic Service, 1967–74; Home Civil Service, 1974–84. *Address:* Centre Flat, Monkton Farleigh Manor, Bradford-on-Avon, Wilts BA15 2QE.

STAVELEY, Maj.-Gen. Robert; Administrative Controller, Norton Rose, solicitors, 1983–91; *b* 3 June 1928; *s* of Brig. Robin Staveley, DSO, and Ilys (*née* Sutherland); *m* 1958, Airlie, *d* of Maj.-Gen. W. H. Lambert, CB, CBE; one *s* one *d*. *Educ:* Wellington. RMA, Sandhurst, 1947; commissioned RA, 1948; served BAOR, 1949–51; ADC to GOC Malta, 1951–53; Air OP pilot, Malaya, 1954–57 (despatches); ADC to GOC-in-C Northern Command, 1957–58; Indian Staff Coll., 1959; Staff Officer and Missile Battery Comdr, BAOR, 1960–65; Instructor, Staff Coll., 1966–68; commanded 47 Lt Regt RA, UK and Hong Kong, 1969–71; CRA 2nd Div., BAOR, 1973–74; RCDS 1975; Director of Operational Requirements, MoD, 1976–79; C of S, Logistic Exec. (Army), 1979–82. Col Comdt, RA, 1982–87. FBIM 1983. *Recreations:* good food, sailing, skiing, music. *Address:* c/o Lloyds Bank (Cox's & King's Branch), 7 Pall Mall, SW1Y 5NA. *Clubs:* Army and Navy, Royal Ocean Racing; Royal Artillery Yacht (Commodore, 1980–83; Admiral, 1991–).

STAVELEY, Admiral of the Fleet Sir William (Doveton Minet), GCB 1984 (KCB 1981); Chairman, Royal London Hospital and Associated Community Services NHS Trust, since 1991; First Sea Lord and Chief of Naval Staff, 1985–89; First and Principal Naval Aide-de-Camp to the Queen, 1985–89; *b* 10 Nov. 1928; *s* of late Adm. Cecil Minet Staveley, CB, CMG, and Margaret Adela (*née* Sturdee); *m* 1954, Bettina Kirstine Shuter; one *s* one *d*. *Educ:* West Downs, Winchester; RN Colls, Dartmouth and Greenwich. Entered Royal Navy as Cadet, 1942; Midshipman, HMS Ajax, Mediterranean, 1946–47; Sub-Lieut/Lieut, HM Ships Nigeria and Bermuda, S Atlantic, 1949–51; Flag Lieut to Adm. Sir George Creasy, C-in-C Home Fleet, HM Ships Indomitable and Vanguard, 1952–54; Staff, Britannia, RNC, Dartmouth, 1954–56; HM Yacht Britannia, 1957; First Lieut, HMS Cavalier, Far East, 1958–59; Lt-Comdr, 1958; RN Staff Coll., 1959; Staff, C-in-C Nore and Flag Officer Medway, 1959–61; Comdr 1961; Sen. Officer, 104th and 6th Minesweeping Sqdn, HMS Houghton, Far East, 1962–63; Comdr, Sea Trng, Staff of Flag Officer, Sea Trng, Portland, 1964–66; comd HMS Zulu, ME and Home Station, 1967; Captain 1967; Asst Dir, Naval Plans, Naval Staff, 1967–70; Command: HM Ships Intrepid, Far and ME, 1970–72; Albion, Home Station, 1972; RCDS, 1973; Dir of Naval Plans, Naval Staff, 1974–76; Flag Officer, Second Flotilla, 1976–77; Flag Officer, Carriers and Amphibious Ships, and NATO Commander, Carrier Striking Group Two, 1977–78; Chief of Staff to C-in-C Fleet, 1978–80; Vice-Chief of Naval Staff, 1980–82; C-in-C, Fleet, and Allied C-in-C, Channel and E Atlantic, 1982–85. Chairman: Combined Services

Equitation Assoc., 1980–82; Council, British Horse Soc., 1982; Member: London Adv. Cttee, English Heritage, 1990–; RHS; Royal Nat. Rose Soc. Trustee: Florence Nightingale Mus. Trust, 1988–; Chatham Historic Dockyard Trust, 1988–. Dir, British Sch. of Osteopathy, 1990–. Mem. Court, Univ. of Kent, 1988–. Governor, Sutton Valence Sch., 1990–. A Younger Brother of Trinity House, 1973. Freeman, City of London, 1987; Liveryman and Hon. Freeman, Shipwrights' Co., 1987. CBIM 1983. *Recreations:* country sports, gardening. *Address:* The Royal London Trust, The Royal London Hospital, Whitechapel, E1 1BB. *T:* 071–377 7010. *Clubs:* Boodle's; Royal Naval Sailing Association.

STAVERT, Rt. Rev. Alexander Bruce; *see* Quebec, Bishop of.

STEAD, Rev. Canon (George) Christopher, LittD; FBA 1980; Fellow, King's College, Cambridge, 1938–49 and 1971–85 (Professorial Fellow, 1971–80); Emeritus Fellow, Keble College, Oxford, since 1981; *b* 9 April 1913; *s* of Francis Bernard Stead, CBE, and Rachel Elizabeth, *d* of Rev. Canon G. C. Bell; *m* 1958, Doris Elizabeth Odom; two *s* one *d.* *Educ:* Marlborough Coll.; King's Coll., Cambridge (scholar). 1st cl. Classical Tripos Pt I, 1933; Pitt Scholar, 1934; 1st cl. Moral Science Tripos Pt II, 1935; BA 1935, MA 1938, LittD Cantab 1978; New Coll., Oxford (BA 1935); Cuddesdon Coll., Oxford, 1938. Ordained, 1938; Curate, St John's, Newcastle upon Tyne, 1939; Lectr in Divinity, King's Coll., Cambridge, 1938–49; Asst Master, Eton Coll., 1940–44; Fellow and Chaplain, Keble Coll., Oxford, 1949–71 (MA Oxon 1949); Ely Professor of Divinity, Cambridge, and Canon Residentiary of Ely Cathedral, 1971–80, Canon Emeritus, 1981. *Publications:* Divine Substance, 1977; Substance and Illusion in the Christian Fathers, 1985; Philosophie und Theologie I, 1990; contributor to: Faith and Logic, 1957; New Testament Apocrypha, 1965; The Philosophical Frontiers of Christian Theology, 1981; Platonismus und Christentum, 1983; A New Dictionary of Christian Theology, 1983; Dizionario di Patristica, 1983; about 20 major articles, mostly in Jl of Theol Studies, Vigiliae Christianae. *Recreations:* walking, sailing, music. *Address:* 13 Station Road, Haddenham, Ely, Cambs.

STEAD, Ian Mathieson, PhD; FSA; FBA 1991; Deputy Keeper, Department of Prehistoric and Romano-British Antiquities, British Museum, since 1977 (Assistant Keeper, 1974–77); *b* 9 Jan. 1936; *er s* of Sidney William Stead and Edith Johann (*née* Mathieson); *m* 1962, Sheelagh Mary Johnson; one *s* one *d.* *Educ:* Nunthorpe Grammar Sch., York; Fitzwilliam House, Cambridge Univ. (MA; PhD 1965). FSA 1966. Asst Inspector of Ancient Monuments, 1962, Inspector, 1964–74, Min. of Works. Chairman: Herts Archaeol Council, 1970–75; Humberside Jt Archaeol Cttee, 1974–81; Sec., Prehistoric Soc., 1974–76. Hon. Life Mem., Yorks Philosophical Soc., 1982; Corresp. Mem., Deutsches Archäologisches Institut, 1976. *Publications:* La Tène Cultures of Eastern Yorkshire, 1965; Winterton Roman Villa, 1976; Arras Culture, 1979; (with J.-L. Flouest) Iron Age Cemeteries in Champagne, 1979; Rudston Roman Villa, 1980; The Gauls, 1981; Celtic Art in Britain, 1985; Battersea Shield, 1985; (with J. B. Bourke and D. Brothwell) Lindow Man, the Body in the Bog, 1986; (with V. Rigby) Baldock, 1986; (with V. Rigby) Verulamium, the King Harry Lane Site, 1989; Iron Age Cemeteries in East Yorkshire, 1991; papers in learned jls. *Address:* Ratcliffe House, Ashwell, Herts SG7 5NP. *T:* Ashwell (046274) 2396.

STEAD, Ralph Edmund, FCA, FCMA; retired; Chairman, Eastern Region, British Gas Corporation, 1977–81; *b* 7 Jan. 1917; *s* of Albert Stead and Mabel Stead; *m* 1946, Evelyn Annie Ness; two *s* two *d.* *Educ:* Manchester Grammar Sch.; Ilford County High Sch. FCA 1949; FCMA 1952. Served War, RASC, 1940–46. Asst Divl Accountant, Cambridge Div., Eastern Gas Bd, 1949–50; N Eastern Gas Board: Asst Chief Accountant, 1950–53; Group Accountant, Bradford Gp, 1953–57; N Western Gas Board: Gp Accountant, Manchester Gp, 1957–61; Gen. Man., West Lancs Gp, 1961–65; Head of Management Services, 1966–71; Dir of Finance, 1971–73; Dep. Chm., Eastern Reg., British Gas Corp., 1973–77. Member: Financial Instns Gp, DoE, 1981–82; Management Cttee, Lazards Property Unit Trust, 1979–; Rent Assessment Panel for Scotland, 1983–87. *Recreations:* golf, gardening, reading. *Address:* 88 Craiglockhart Road, Edinburgh EH14 1SP.

STEAD, Robert, CBE 1965; retired as Controller, BBC North Region, 1958–69; *b* 10 Aug. 1909; *s* of Charles Fearnley Stead and Mary Ellen Taylor; *m* 1932, Constance Ann Sharpley (*d* 1989); two *s.* *Educ:* Morley Grammar Sch. In journalism, 1926–40; served in RN, 1940–45. Talks Producer, BBC North Region, 1946–48; Head of North Regional Programmes, 1948–53; BBC Australian Representative, 1953–57. *Recreations:* golf, gardening, theatre. *Address:* 20 Fulshaw Court, Wilmslow, Cheshire SK9 5JB. *T:* Wilmslow (0625) 525536.

STEADMAN, Dr John Hubert; Senior Principal Medical Officer, Head of Division of Toxicology and Environmental Health, Department of Health, since 1988; *b* 10 Aug. 1938; *s* of late Dr Harry Hubert Steadman and Janet Gilchrist Steadman (*née* MacDonald); *m* 1972, Dr Anthea Howell; one *s* one *d.* *Educ:* Wimbledon Coll.; Guy's Hosp. (MB, BS); University Coll. London (MSc). University College Hospital, London: Beit Meml Fellowship, 1968–72; Sen. Registrar, Dept of Haematology, 1972–78, with secondments to Ahmadu Bello Univ. Hosp., Nigeria, 1973, and Royal Perth Hosp., WA, 1974; Cons. Haematologist, King George Hosp., Ilford, 1978–81; MO 1981, SMO 1982, PMO 1984, DHSS. Expert Advr on food safety, WHO, 1988–. *Publications:* articles in learned jls on regulatory toxicology, haematology and biochemistry. *Recreations:* cooking, political philosophy. *Address:* Division of Toxicology and Environmental Health, Department of Health, Hannibal House, SE1 6TE. *T:* 071–972 2142.

See also J. M. M. Curtis-Raleigh.

STEADMAN, Ralph Idris; freelance cartoonist, illustrator and writer; *b* 15 May 1936; *s* of Lionel Raphael Steadman (English), and Gwendoline (Welsh); *m* 1st, 1959, Sheila Thwaite (marr. diss. 1971); two *s* two *d*; 2nd, 1972, Anna Deverson; one *d.* *Educ:* Abergele Grammar Sch.; London Coll. of Printing and Graphic Arts. Apprentice, de Havilland Aircraft Co., 1952; Cartoonist, Kemsley (Thomson) Newspapers, 1956–59; freelance for Punch, Private Eye, Telegraph, during 1960s; Political Cartoonist, New Statesman, 1978–80; retired to work on book about Leonardo da Vinci; as a positive political statement, refuses to draw another politician; 15 Save the Children originals auctioned in aid of Ethiopia Fund, 1990. Retrospective exhibitions: Nat. Theatre, 1977; Royal Festival Hall, 1984; Wilhelm Busch Mus., Hannover, 1988; October Gall. (sculptures and silk screen prints), 1990, Gulf war collages, 1991. Designed set of stamps of Halley's Comet, 1986; opera libretto and concept, The Plague and the Moonflower, Exeter Cathedral and Festival, 1989 (artist-in-residence), St Paul's Cathedral, 1989, Canterbury Cathedral and Festival, 1990. Designers and Art Directors Assoc. Gold Award (for outstanding contribution to illustration), 1977, and Silver Award (for outstanding editorial illustration), 1977; Black Humour Award, France, 1986; W. H. Smith Illustration Award for best illustrated book for last five years, 1987; BBC Design Award for postage stamps, 1987. *Publications:* Jelly Book, 1968; Still Life with Raspberry: collected drawings, 1969; The Little Red Computer, 1970; Dogs Bodies, 1971; Bumper to Bumper Book, 1973; Two Donkeys and the Bridge, 1974; Flowers for the Moon, 1974; The Watchdog and the Lazy Dog, 1974; America: drawings, 1975; America: collected drawings, 1977 (rev. edn, Scar Strangled Banger, 1987); Between the Eyes, 1984; Paranoids, 1986; *written and illustrated:* Sigmund Freud, 1979 (as The Penguin Sigmund Freud, 1982); A Leg in the Wind and other Canine Curses, 1982; I, Leonardo, 1983; That's My Dad, 1986 (Critici in Erba Prize, 1987); The Big I Am, 1988; No Room to Swing a Cat, 1989; Near the Bone, 1990; Tales of the Weirrd, 1990; designed and printed, Steam Press Broadsheets; *illustrated:* Frank Dickens, Fly Away Peter, 1961; Mischa Damjan: The Big Squirrel and the Little Rhinoceros, 1962; The False Flamingoes, 1963; The Little Prince and the Tiger Cat, 1964; Richard Ingrams, The Tale of Driver Grope, 1964; Love and Marriage, 1964; Daisy Ashford, Where Love Lies Deepest, 1964; Fiona Saint, The Yellow Flowers, 1965; Alice in Wonderland, 1967; Midnight, 1967; Mischa Damjan, Two Cats in America, 1968; Tariq Ali, The Thoughts of Chairman Harold, 1968; Dr Hunter S. Thompson: Fear and Loathing in Las Vegas, 1972; The Curse of Lono, 1984; Contemporary Poets set to Music series, 1972; Through the Looking Glass, 1972; Night Edge: poems, 1973; The Poor Mouth, 1973; John Letts Limericks, 1974; The Hunting of the Snark, 1975; Dmitri Sidjanski, Cherrywood Cannon, 1978; Bernard Stone: Emergency Mouse, 1978; Inspector Mouse, 1980; Quasimodo Mouse, 1984; Ted Hughes, The Threshold (limited edn), 1979; Adrian Mitchell, For Beauty Douglas, 1982; Flann O'Brien, More of Myles, 1982; Wolf Mankowitz, The Devil in Texas, 1984; Treasure Island, 1985; The Complete Alice and The Hunting of the Snark, 1986; Friendship (short stories), 1990 (in aid of John McCarthy). *Recreations:* gardening (planted vineyard), collecting, writing, sheep husbandry, fishing, guitar, trumpet. *Club:* Chelsea Arts.

STEAR, Air Marshal Sir Michael (James Douglas), KCB 1990; CBE 1982; QCVSA 1969; Air Officer Commanding No 18 Group, RAF, and Commander Maritime Air Eastern Atlantic and Channel, since 1989; *b* 11 Oct. 1938; *s* of late Melbourne Douglas Stear and Barbara Jane Stear (*née* Fletcher); *m* 1966, Elizabeth Jane, *d* of late Donald Edward Macrae, FRCS and of Janet Wallace Macpherson Simpson; two *s* one *d.* *Educ:* Monkton Combe Sch.; Emmanuel Coll., Cambridge (MA; CU Air Sqn (RAFVR), 1959–62). Nat. Service, 1957–59. Joined RAF, 1962; served on 1 Sqn, 1964–67, on 208 Sqn, Persian Gulf, 1967–69; exchange tour with USAF, 1969–71; Air Sec.'s Br., MoD, 1972–74; OC 17 Sqn, Germany, 1974–76; OC 56 Sqn, RAF Wattisham, 1976; PSO to CAS, MoD, 1976–79; OC RAF Gutersloh, 1980–82; Asst C of S (Ops), HQ 2 ATAF, 1982; Air Cdre Plans, HQ Strike Command, 1982–85; AOC No 11 Gp, 1985–87; ACDS (Nato/UK), 1987–89. Mem., RUSI, 1989–. Member: Council, Malcolm Clubs, 1988–; RFU Cttee, 1987–; Vice-Pres., RAF RU, 1986– (Chm., 1983–86). Mem. Council, Epsom Coll., 1990–. *Recreations:* Rugby football, gardening, fishing, shooting. *Address:* HQ No 18 Group, RAF Northwood, Middlesex HA6 3EP. *Club:* Royal Air Force (Vice-Pres., 1990–).

STEARN, Dr William Thomas; botanical consultant; retired as Senior Principal Scientific Officer, Department of Botany, British Museum (Natural History), 1976; Editor, Annales Musei Goulandris, since 1976; *b* 16 April 1911; *e s* of late Thomas Stearn, Cambridge; *m* 1940, Eldwyth Ruth Alford, *d* of late Roger R. Alford, Tavistock; one *s* two *d.* *Educ:* Cambridge High Sch. for Boys; part-time research at Botany Sch., Cambridge; apprentice antiquarian bookseller, Bowes & Bowes, Cambridge, 1929–32. Librarian, Royal Horticultural Soc., 1933–41, 1946–52. Served RAF, in Britain, India and Burma, 1941–46. Botanist, British Museum (Natural History), 1952–76. Hon. Sec., Internat. Cttee for Nomenclature of Cultivated Plants, 1950–53; former Council Member: Botanical Soc. of British Isles (Vice-Pres., 1973–77); British Soc. for History of Science (Vice-Pres., 1969–72); British Soc. for History of Medicine; Field Studies Council; Garden History Soc. (Founder Mem., 1965; Pres., 1977–82); Linnean Soc. (Vice-Pres., 1961–62; Pres., 1979–82; Hon. Botanical Curator, 1959–85); Ray Soc. (Vice-Pres., 1964–67, 1970–73, Pres., 1974–77); Richmond Scientific Soc. (Pres., 1969–71); Soc. for Bibliography of Natural History (Founder Mem., 1936, Hon. Mem., 1976); Systematics Assoc.; Mem., Old Cantabrigian Soc. (Pres., 1984–85). Masters Meml Lectr, 1964; Sandars Reader in Bibliography, Cambridge, 1965; Vis. Prof., Dept of Botany and Agricl Botany, 1977–83, Hon. Res. Fellow, 1983, Univ. of Reading; Wilkins Lectr, Royal Soc., 1985. Botanical collections made in Europe, Jamaica, USA, Australia. Royal Horticultural Society: Hon. Fellow, 1946; Vice-Pres., 1986–; Veitch Meml Medal, 1964; Victoria Medal of Honour, 1965. FLS 1934; FIBiol 1967 (MIBiol 1965); Hon. Member: Kungl. Vetenskaps-Societeten i Uppsala, 1967; Svenska Linnésällskapet, 1971; Botanical Soc. of Amer., 1982; For. Mem., Royal Swedish Acad. of Sci., 1983; Corr. Mem., Amer. Soc. of Plant Taxonomists, 1980. Freeman, Gardeners' Co., 1982. Hon. Fellow, Sidney Sussex Coll., Cambridge, 1968. DSc *hc* Leiden, 1960; Hon. ScD Cantab, 1967; FilDr *hc* Uppsala, 1972. Boerhaave Commem. Medal, Leiden, 1969; Linnaeus Medal, Royal Swedish Acad. of Sciences, 1972; Linnean Gold Medal, Linnean Soc., 1976; Hutchinson Medal, Chicago Horticultural Soc., 1985; Founders Medal, Soc. for the Hist. of Natural Hist., 1986. Comdr, Order of the Star of the North (Sweden), 1980. *Publications:* (with H. B. D. Woodcock) Lilies of the World, 1950; (with E. Blatter and W. S. Millard) Some Beautiful Indian Trees, 1955; Introduction to the *Species Plantarum* of Carl Linnaeus, 1957; Early Leyden Botany, 1961; Botanical Latin, 1966, 3rd edn 1983 (trans. Chinese, 1981); Three Prefaces on Linnaeus and Robert Brown, 1967; Humboldt, Bonpland, Kunth and Tropical American Botany, 1968; (with C. N. Goulimis and N. Goulandris) Wild Flowers of Greece, 1968; (with A. W. Smith) Gardener's Dictionary of Plant Names, 1972; (with W. Blunt) Captain Cook's Florilegium, 1973; (with M. Page) Culinary Herbs, 1974; (with W. Blunt) Australian Flower Paintings of Ferdinand Bauer, 1976; The Wondrous Transformation of Caterpillars: M. S. Merian (Biog.), 1978; (with H. Hara and L. H. J. Williams) Enumeration of Flowering Plants of Nepal, vol. 1, 1978; The Natural History Museum at South Kensington, 1981; (with E. Rücker) Merian in Surinam, 1982; Plant Portraits from the *Flora Danica*, 1983; (with E. Roberts and C. Opsomer) Livre des Simples Médicines, English trans. and commentaries, 1984; (with P. H. Davis) Peonies of Greece, 1984; (with M. Rix) Redouté's Fairest Flowers, 1987; (with C. Brickell and M. Grierson) An English Florilegium, 1987; (with A. T. Gage) A Bicentenary History of the Linnean Society of London, 1988; (with A. W. Roach) Hooker's Fairest Fruits, 1989; Flower Artists of Kew, 1990; numerous bibliographical, biographical, botanical and horticultural contribs to learned jls (listed in Biological Jl of Linnean Soc. vol. 8, 1976), RHS Dictionary of Gardening, Chambers's Encyclopaedia, Dictionary of Scientific Biography, Flora Europaea, European Garden Flora, Flora of Australia, etc. *Recreations:* gardening, talking. *Address:* 17 High Park Road, Kew Gardens, Richmond, Surrey TW9 4BL.

STEDMAN, family name of **Baroness Stedman.**

STEDMAN, Baroness *cr* 1974 (Life Peer), of Longthorpe, Peterborough; **Phyllis Stedman,** OBE 1965; *b* 14 July 1916; *o d* of Percy and Emmie Adams; *m* 1941, Henry William Stedman (*d* 1989), OBE 1981. *Educ:* County Grammar Sch., Peterborough. Branch Librarian, Peterborough City Council, 1934–41; Group Officer, National Fire Service, 1942–45. Baroness-in-Waiting (a Govt Whip), 1975–79; Parly Under-Sec. of State, DoE, 1979; Govt spokesman for Transport, the Environment, Educn and Trade, 1975–79; Opposition spokesman on the environment, local govt, new towns and transport, 1979–81; Leader of SDP in House of Lords, 1988–91 (Mem., 1981–, SDP Whip, 1982–86, SDP Chief Whip, 1986–88). County Councillor: Soke of Peterborough, 1946–65; Huntingdon and Peterborough, 1965–74; Cambridgeshire, 1974–76; Vice-Chm.,

Cambridgeshire County Council, 1974–76. Member: Board, Peterborough Development Corp., 1972–76; IBA, 1974–75; Board, Hereward Radio, 1979–85; Vice-Chm., Nat. PHAB, 1978–; Vice-President: Assoc. of District Councils, 1979–; Nat. Assoc. of Local Councils, 1982–; ACC, 1986–; Building Societies Assoc., 1985–90. Mem. Exec. Council, Fire Services Nat. Benevolent Fund, 1976–. *Address:* 1 Grovelands, Thorpe Road, Peterborough PE3 6AQ. *T:* Peterborough (0733) 61109.

STEEDMAN, Air Chief Marshal Sir Alasdair, (Alexander McKay Sinclair), GCB 1980 (KCB 1976; CB 1973); CBE 1965; DFC 1944; Controller, Royal Air Force Benevolent Fund, 1981–88; *b* 29 Jan. 1922; *s* of late James Steedman, Hampton-on-Thames, Mddx, and late Anna McKay Steedman (*née* Sinclair); *m* 1945, Dorothy Isobel (*d* 1983), *d* of late Col Walter Todd, Knockbrex, Kirkcudbright; one *s* two *d*. *Educ:* Hampton Grammar School. Entered RAF, Jan. 1941; reconnaissance ops, 1942–45; (241 and 2 Sqns) Air Ministry (DP2), 1945–48; comd 39 Sqdn, Khartoum, 1948–49; comd 8 Sqdn, Aden, 1949–50; CFS Course, 1951; Training Sqn Comdr 201 Advanced Flying Sch., 1951–53; Syndicate Leader Aircrew Selection Centre, Hornchurch, 1953–54; psa 1955; Chief Instructor, CFS (B), 1955–57; Comdr Royal Ceylon Air Force, Katanayake, 1957–59; jssc 1959; Dir Staff, Jt Services Staff Coll., 1960–62; Comdr RAF Lyneham, 1962–65; CAS, Royal Malaysian Air Force, 1965–67; Dir of Defence Plans (Air), 1967–68; Dir Defence Operations Staff, 1968–69; ACAS (Policy), MoD, 1969–71; SASO, HQ Strike Comd, 1971–72; Comdt, RAF Staff Coll., 1972–75; Air Member of Air Force Bd for Supply and Organisation, 1976–77; UK Mil. Rep. to NATO, 1977–80; RAF retd, 1981. Mem., Security Commn, 1982–. Vice-Pres., Nat. Adv. Centre for Careers for Women, 1988–; Member of Council: ISCO, 1986–; GBA, 1988–. Governor: Hampton Sch., 1976– (Chm. of Govs, 1988–); Gordon Sch., 1987– (Mem. Foundn Cttee, 1981–). Patron, Central Flying Sch. Assoc., 1984–; Vice Patron: RAF Small Arms Assoc., 1978–; Internat. Air Tattoo, 1988– (Chm., 1981–88); Pres., British Pistol Club, 1986–. Liveryman, GAPAN, 1985 (Chm., Guild Benevolent Fund, 1990–). FRAeS 1981; CBIM 1979. Johan Mangku Negara (Malaysia), 1967; Commander, Order of Polonia Restituta (Poland), 1990. *Recreations:* defence, golf, reading. *Address:* Rutherford, St Chloe Lane, Amberley, Stroud, Glos GL5 5AS. *Club:* Royal Air Force.

STEEDMAN, Martha, (Mrs R. R. Steedman); *see* Hamilton, M.

STEEDMAN, Robert Russell, RSA 1979 (ARSA 1973); RIBA; FRIAS; ALI; Partner, Morris and Steedman, Architects and Landscape Architects, Edinburgh, since 1959; *b* 3 Jan. 1929; *s* of late Robert Smith Steedman and Helen Hope Brazier; *m* 1st, 1956, Susan Elizabeth (marr. diss. 1974), *d* of Sir Robert Scott, GCMG, CBE; one *s* two *d*; 2nd, 1977, Martha Hamilton, *qv*. *Educ:* Loretto Sch.; School of Architecture, Edinburgh College of Art (DA); Univ. of Pennsylvania (MLA). RIBA 1955; ALI 1979. Lieut, RWAFF, 1947–48. Worked in office, Alfred Roth, Zürich, 1953. Architectural works include: Principal's House, Univ. of Stirling; Head Offices for Christian Salvesen, Edinburgh; Administration Building for Shell UK Exploration and Production; Moss Morran Fife; Restoration of Old Waterworks, Perth, to form Tourist Information Centre and Offices. Ten Civic Trust Awards, 1963–88; British Steel Award, 1971; Saltire Award, 1971; RIBA Award for Scotland, 1974 and 1989; European Architectural Heritage Medal, 1975; Assoc. for Preservation of Rural Scotland Award, 1977 and 1989. Chm., Central Scotland Woodlands Project, 1984–87; Member: Countryside Commn for Scotland, 1980–88; Adv. Panel on Management of Popular Mountain Areas in Scotland, 1989; Royal Fine Art Commn for Scotland, 1984–; Sec., Royal Scottish Acad., 1983–90 (Mem. Council 1981–, Dep. Pres. 1982–83); Mem. Bd, Friends of Royal Scottish Acad., 1984–; Governor, Edinburgh College of Art, 1974–88; Mem., Edinburgh Festival Soc., 1978–; past Mem. Council, RIAS and Soc. of Scottish Artists. Hon. Senior, St Leonards Sch., 1987–. *Recreations:* skiing, sketching. *Address:* 11B Belford Mews, Edinburgh; (office) 38 Young Street North Lane, Edinburgh EH2 4JD. *T:* 031–226 6563. *Clubs:* New (Edinburgh); Royal & Ancient Golf (St Andrews).

STEEDS, Prof. John Wickham, FRS 1988; FInstP; Research Professor in Physics and Head of Microstructural Group, since 1985 and Director, Interface Analysis Centre, since 1990, Bristol University; *b* 9 Feb. 1940; *s* of John Henry William Steeds and Ethel Amelia Tyler; *m* 1969, Diana Mary Kettlewell; two *d*. *Educ:* University College London (BSc 1961); PhD Cantab 1965. FInstP 1991. Research Fellow, Selwyn Coll., Cambridge, 1964–67; IBM Res. Fellow, 1966–67; Fellow, Selwyn Coll., Cambridge, 1967; Lectr in Physics, 1967–77, Reader, 1977–85, Bristol Univ. Visiting Professor: Univ. of Santiago, Chile, 1971; Univ. of California, Berkeley, 1981. Chm., Science Res. Foundn, Emersons Green, 1989–. *Publications:* Introduction to Anistropic Elasticity Theory of Dislocations, 1973; (with J. F. Mansfield) Electron Diffraction of Phases in Alloys, 1984; papers on electron diffraction, materials science and solid state physics. *Recreations:* tennis, cycling, overseas travel. *Address:* 21 Canynge Square, Clifton, Bristol BS8 3LA. *T:* Bristol (0272) 732183.

STEEGMULLER, Francis; writer; *b* New Haven, Conn, 3 July 1906; *s* of Joseph Francis Steegmuller and Bertha Tierney; *m* 1st, 1935, Beatrice Stein (decd); 2nd, 1963, Shirley Hazzard. *Educ:* Columbia University, New York. Member, Nat. Inst. of Arts and Letters, 1966. Gold Medal for Biography, 1982. Chevalier de la Légion d'Honneur, 1957; Chevalier de l'Ordre des Arts et des Lettres, 1984. *Publications:* O Rare Ben Jonson (under pseudonym Byron Steel), 1928; Flaubert and Madame Bovary, 1939, reprinted 1947, 1958, 1968; States of Grace, 1947; Maupassant, 1950, repr. 1973; Blue Harpsichord (under pseudonym David Keith), 1950, repr. 1977 (under name Steegmuller); The Two Lives of James Jackson Jarves, 1953; (trans. and ed) The Selected Letters of Gustave Flaubert, 1954; La Grande Mademoiselle, 1955; The Christening Party, 1961; Le Hibou et la Poussiquette, 1961; Apollinaire, 1963, repr. 1986; Papillot, Clignot et Dodo (with Norbert Guterman), 1965; (trans.) Gustave Flaubert, Intimate Notebook, 1967; Cocteau, 1970, repr. 1986 (Nat. Book Award 1971); Stories and True Stories, 1972; (trans. and ed) Flaubert in Egypt, 1972, repr. 1982; (ed) Your Isadora, 1975; (trans. and ed) The Letters of Gustave Flaubert, 1830–1857, 1980 (American Book Award 1981), 2nd vol. 1983; A Woman, a Man, and Two Kingdoms: the story of Madame d'Épinay and the Abbé Galiani, 1991; works published abroad include a translation of Madame Bovary, 1957, Silence at Salerno (novel), 1979, and many short stories and articles in The New Yorker. *Address:* 200 East 66th Street, New York, NY 10021, USA. *Clubs:* Century, University (New York); Circolo del Remo e della Vela "Italia" (Naples).

STEEL, (Anne) Heather, (Mrs D. K.-M. Beattie); Her Honour Judge Steel; a Circuit Judge, since 1986; *b* 3 July 1940; *d* of late His Honour Edward Steel and Mary Evelyn Griffith Steel; *m* 1967, David Kerr-Muir Beattie; one *s* one *d*. *Educ:* Howell's School, Denbigh; Liverpool University (LLB). Called to the Bar, Gray's Inn, 1963; practice on N Circuit; Prosecuting Counsel to DHSS on N Circuit, 1984–86; a Recorder, 1984–86. Mem. Council, Rossall Sch., 1990–. *Recreations:* theatre, gardening, art, antiques. *Address:* The Sessions House, 37 Lancaster Road, Preston PR1 2PD. *T:* Preston (0772) 23431.

STEEL, Byron; *see* Steegmuller, Francis.

STEEL, Brig. Charles Deane, CMG 1957; OBE 1941; *b* 29 May 1901; *s* of Dr Gerard Steel, JP, Leominster, Herefs; *m* 1932, Elizabeth Chenevix-Trench (*d* 1973); two *s*. *Educ:* Bedford; Royal Military Academy, Woolwich. Prize Cadetship, Woolwich, 1919. Armstrong Memorial Prize, 1921. Commissioned 2nd Lieut RE, 1921; served in India (Bengal Sappers and Miners), 1924–29; Staff College, Camberley, 1936–37; War of 1939–45; E Africa and Abyssinia, 1941; Western Desert, 1942; POW, 1942; Switzerland, 1943; Dep. Head, British Mil. Mission to Greece, 1945–49; Dep. Mil. Sec., 1949–52; retd Feb. 1952; Head of Conference and Supply Dept, Foreign Office, 1952–64; Head of Accommodation Department Diplomatic Service, 1965–67. *Recreations:* golf, and gardening. *Address:* Little Hill, Nettlebed, Oxfordshire RG9 5BD. *T:* Nettlebed (0491) 641287.

STEEL, Very Rev. David; Minister of St Michael's, Linlithgow, 1959–76, now Minister Emeritus; Moderator of the General Assembly of the Church of Scotland, 1974–75; *b* 5 Oct. 1910; *s* of John S. G. Steel and Jane Scott, Hamilton; *m* 1937, Sheila Martin, Aberdeen; three *s* two *d*. *Educ:* Peterhead Academy; Robert Gordon's Coll., Aberdeen; Aberdeen Univ. MA 1932, BD 1935. Minister of Church of Scotland: Denbeath, Fife, 1936–41; Bridgend, Dumbarton, 1941–46; Home Organisation Foreign Mission Secretary, 1946–49; Minister of Parish of East Africa and of St Andrew's, Nairobi, 1949–57; Associate Minister, St Cuthbert's, Edinburgh, 1957–59. Vis. Prof., Columbia Theol Seminary, Atlanta, 1979–85. Chm. of Governors, Callendar Park Coll. of Educn, 1974–79; Vice-Pres., Boys' Brigade, 1974–79. Hon. Vice-President: Nat. Bible Soc. of Scotland; W Lothian History and Amenity Soc.; Boys' Brigade. Hon. DD Aberdeen 1964; Hon. LLD Dundee, 1977. *Publications:* History of St Michael's, Linlithgow, 1961; Preaching Through the Year, 1980; contrib. theological and church jls. *Recreation:* trout fishing. *Address:* 39 Newbattle Terrace, Edinburgh EH10 4SF. *T:* 031–447 2180. *Clubs:* Scottish Liberal (Edinburgh); Aberdeen University Senior Common Room; Edinburgh Amateur Angling.

See also Rt Hon. Sir D. M. S. Steel.

STEEL, Sir David (Edward Charles), Kt 1977; DSO 1940; MC 1945; TD; Chairman, The Wellcome Trust, 1982–89; *b* 29 Nov. 1916; *s* of late Gerald Arthur Steel, CB; *m* 1956, Ann Wynne, *d* of Maj.-Gen. C. B. Price, CB, DSO, DCM, VD, CD; one *s* two *d*. *Educ:* Rugby School; University Coll., Oxford (BA; Hon. Fellow, 1981). Inns of Court Regt, 1938; Commissioned 9 QR Lancers, 1940; served 1940–45 France, Middle East, North Africa, Italy (DSO, MC, despatches thrice). Admitted a Solicitor, June 1948; Linklaters and Paines, 1948–50; Legal Dept of The British Petroleum Co. Ltd, 1950–56; Pres. BP (N Amer.) Ltd, 1959–61; Man. Dir, Kuwait Oil Co. Ltd, 1962–65; Man. Dir, 1965–75, a Dep. Chm., 1972–75 and Chm., 1975–81, BP. A Dir, Bank of England, 1978–85; Dir, Kleinwort Benson Gp (formerly Kleinwort, Benson, Lonsdale), 1985–. Pres., London Chamber of Commerce and Industry, 1982–85. Trustee, The Economist, 1979–; Chairman: Lenta Educn Trust, 1986–90; London Educn Business Partnership, 1986–89; Governors, Rugby Sch., 1984–88. Hon. Freeman, Tallow Chandlers' Co., 1980. Hon. DCL City Univ., 1983. Order of Taj III, Iran, 1974; Comdr, Order of Leopold, Belgium, 1980. *Recreations:* gardening, golf. *Clubs:* Cavalry and Guards, MCC, Hurlingham; Royal and Ancient (St Andrews).

STEEL, Rt. Hon. Sir David (Martin Scott), KBE 1990; PC 1977; DL; MP Tweeddale, Ettrick and Lauderdale, since 1983 (Roxburgh, Selkirk and Peebles, 1965–83) (L 1965–88, Lib Dem, since 1988); Co-Founder, Social and Liberal Democrats, 1988; journalist and broadcaster; *b* Scotland, 31 March 1938; *s* of Very Rev. Dr David Steel, *qv*; *m* 1962, Judith Mary, *d* of W. D. MacGregor, CBE, Dunblane; two *s* one *d* and one adopted *s*. *Educ:* Prince of Wales School, Nairobi, Kenya; George Watson's College and Edinburgh University. MA 1960; LLB 1962. Rector, Edinburgh Univ., 1982–85. President: Edinburgh University Liberals, 1959; Students' Representative Council, 1960. Asst Secretary, Scottish Liberal Party, 1962–64; Youngest Member of 1964–66 Parliament, of Privy Council, 1977; Liberal Chief Whip, 1970–75; Mem. Parly Delegn to UN Gen. Assembly, 1967; Sponsor, Private Member's Bill to reform law on abortion, 1966–67. Leader of Liberal Party, 1976–88. Vice-Pres., Liberal International, 1978–. Pres., Anti-Apartheid Movement of GB, 1966–69; Chm., Shelter, Scotland, 1969–73. Member: Acton Trust, 1970–; British Council of Churches, 1971–75; Council of Management, Centre for Studies in Social Policy, 1971–76; Adv. Council, European Discussion Centre, 1971–76; Chubb Fellow, Yale Univ., 1987. BBC television interviewer in Scotland, 1964–65; Presenter of STV weekly religious programme, 1966–67, and for Granada, 1969, and BBC, 1971–76. FRSA 1990. DL Roxburgh, Ettrick and Lauderdale, 1990. Awarded Freedom of Tweeddale, 1988, of Ettrick and Lauderdale, 1990. DUniv Stirling, 1991. *Publications:* Boost for the Borders, 1964; Out of Control, 1968; No Entry, 1969; The Liberal Way Forward, 1975; A New Political Agenda, 1976; Militant for the Reasonable Man, 1977; New Majority for a New Parliament, 1978; High Ground of Politics, 1979; A House Divided, 1980; (with Judy Steel) Border Country, 1985; (presenter) Partners in One Nation: a new vision of Britain 2000, 1985; (with Judy Steel) Mary Stuart's Scotland, 1987; Against Goliath: David Steel's story, 1989; contrib. to The Times, The Guardian, The Scotsman, other newspapers and political weeklies. *Recreations:* angling, vintage motoring. *Address:* House of Commons, SW1A 0AA; Cherry Dene, Ettrick Bridge, Selkirkshire.

STEEL, David William, QC 1981; *b* 7 May 1943; *s* of Sir Lincoln Steel and of Barbara (*née* Goldschmidt); *m* 1970, Charlotte Elizabeth Ramsay; two *s*. *Educ:* Eton Coll.; Keble Coll., Oxford (MA Hons Jurisprudence). Called to the Bar, Inner Temple, 1966, Bencher, 1991. With Coudert Bros (Attorneys), New York, 1967–68; commenced practice in England, 1969; Junior Counsel to the Treasury (Common Law) 1978–81; Junior Counsel to the Treasury (Admiralty), 1978–81. Wreck Commissioner for England and Wales, 1982–. Mem., panel of Lloyd's Salvage Arbitrators, 1982–. *Publications:* Editor: Temperley: Merchant Shipping Acts, 1976–; Forms and Precedents: British Shipping Laws, 1977–; Kennedy: Salvage, 1981–. *Recreations:* shooting, fishing. *Address:* Chinnor Hill Manor, Chinnor, Oxford. *T:* Kingston Blount (0844) 51469. *Clubs:* Turf, Beefsteak; Leander (Henley-on-Thames).

STEEL, Donald MacLennan Arklay; golf correspondent and golf course architect; *b* 23 Aug. 1937; *s* of William Arklay Steel and Catherine Fanny (*née* Jacob), internat. golfer; *m* 1988, Rachel Ellen. *Educ:* Fettes Coll; Christ's Coll., Cambridge (MA). Golf correspondent: Sunday Telegraph, 1961–90; Country Life, 1983–; golf course architect, 1965–: with C. K. Cotton, Pennink, Lawrie and Partners; with C. K. Cotton, Pennink, Steel & Co.; with Donald Steel & Co. Pres., British Assoc of Golf Course Architects, 1989–91 (Hon. Sec., 1971–83; Chm., 1983–86). *Publications:* (ed jtly) Shell World Encyclopaedia of Golf, 1975; (ed) Guinness Book of Golf Facts and Feats, 1980; Bedside Books of Golf, 1965, 1971; The Classic Links; (ed) 8 edns, The Golf Course Guide of the British Isles (Daily Telegraph). *Recreations:* cricket, wine. *Address:* 1 March Square, Chichester, West Sussex PO19 4AN. *T:* Chichester (0243) 528506. *Clubs:* MCC; Hawks (Cambridge); Royal and Ancient Golf.

STEEL, Major Sir (Fiennes) William Strang, 2nd Bt, *cr* 1938; DL; JP; Major (retired), 17/21st Lancers; Forestry Commissioner, 1958–73; *b* 24 July 1912; *e s* of Sir Samuel Steel,

1st Bt and of Hon. Vere Mabel (*d* 1964), *d* of 1st Baron Cornwallis; *S* father, 1961; *m* 1941, Joan (*d* 1982), *d* of late Brig.-Gen. Sir Brodie Haldane Henderson, KCMG, CB, Braughing, Ware; two *s* (one *d* decd). *Educ:* Eton; RMC, Sandhurst; joined 17/21st Lancers, 1933; Major, 1941; retired, 1947. Convener, Selkirk CC, 1967–75. DL Selkirkshire, 1955, JP 1965. *Heir: s* Major (Fiennes) Michael Strang Steel, DL, 17/21 Lancers [*b* 22 Feb. 1943; *m* 1977, Sarah Russell; two *s* one *d*]. *Address:* Philiphaugh, Selkirk. *T:* Selkirk (0750) 21216. *Club:* Cavalry and Guards.

STEEL, Henry, CMG 1976; OBE 1965; Leader, United Kingdom Delegation to UN Human Rights Commission, Geneva, since 1987; Principal Legal Adviser, Government of British Antarctic Territory, since 1989; consultant on international and commonwealth law; *b* 13 Jan. 1926; *yr s* of late Raphael Steel; *m* 1960, Jennifer Isobel Margaret, *d* of late Brig. M. M. Simpson, MBE; two *s* two *d*. *Educ:* Christ's Coll., Finchley; New Coll., Oxford. BA Oxon 1950. Military Service, RASC and Intell. Corps, 1944–47. Called to Bar, Lincoln's Inn, 1951; Legal Asst, Colonial Office, 1955; Senior Legal Asst, CO, 1960; Asst Legal Adviser, CRO, 1965; Legal Counsellor, FCO, 1967–73; Legal Adviser, UK Mission to UN, NY, 1973–76; Legal Counsellor, FCO, 1976–79; Asst Under-Sec. of State (on loan to Law Officers' Dept), 1979; Legal Adviser to Governor of Southern Rhodesia, 1979–80; Asst Legal Secretary (Under-Secretary), Law Officers' Dept, 1980–83, Legal Sec. (Dep. Sec.), 1983–86; Dir, Commonwealth Legal Adv. Service, British Inst. of Internat. and Comparative Law, 1986–87. *Address:* College Place, Chapel Lane, Bledington, Oxon OX7 6UZ.

STEEL, Sir James, Kt 1967; CBE 1964; Lord-Lieutenant of Tyne and Wear, 1974–84; Chairman, Furness Withy & Co. Ltd, 1975–79; *b* 19 May 1909; *s* of Alfred Steel and Katharine (*née* Meikle); *m* 1935, Margaret Jean MacLauchlan (*d* 1987); two *s* two *d*. *Educ:* Trent College. Mem., Commn on the Constitution, 1969–73. Trustee, Sir John Priestman Charity Trust. Chairman: British Productivity Council, 1966–67; Textile Council, 1968–72; Washington Develt Corp., 1964–77. Pres., TA for N of England, 1979–84; Vice-Pres., Wildfowl Trust. Liveryman, Worshipful Co. of Founders. JP Sunderland, 1964; Durham: DL 1969; Sheriff 1972–73. KStJ 1975. Hon. DCL Dunelm, 1978. *Publication:* Bird Quest, 1989. *Recreation:* ornithology. *Address:* Fawnlees Hall, Wolsingham, County Durham DL13 3LW. *T:* Weardale (0388) 527307.

STEEL, Patricia Ann, OBE 1990; Non-Executive Director, London Regional Transport, since 1984; *b* 30 Oct. 1941; *d* of Thomas Norman Steel and Winifred Steel. *Educ:* Hunmanby Hall, near Filey, Yorks; Exeter Univ. (BA). Parly Liaison, Chamber of Shipping of UK and British Shipping Fedn, 1968–71; Sec., Highway and Traffic Technicians Assoc., 1972–73; Sec., Instn of Highways and Transportation, 1973–90. Director: Docklands Light Railway, 1984– (Chm., 1988–89); Victoria Coach Station Ltd, 1988–. Mem., Occupational Pensions Bd, 1979–84. *Recreations:* music, travel, politics. *Address:* 7 The Strathmore, 27 Petersham Road, Richmond, Surrey.

STEEL, Robert, CBE 1979; Secretary-General, Royal Institution of Chartered Surveyors, 1968–85 (Fellow, 1961; Hon. Mem., 1985); *b* 7 April 1920; *e s* of late John Thomas Steel and Jane (*née* Gordon), Wooler, Northumberland; *m* 1943, Averal Frances, *d* of Arthur Pettitt; one *s* one *d*. *Educ:* Duke's Sch., Alnwick, Northumb.; Univ. of London (BSc 1945); Gray's Inn (Barrister, 1956). Surveyor, 1937–46; Asst Sec., Under Sec., Royal Instn of Surveyors, 1946–61; Dir of Town Development, Basingstoke, 1962–67. Sec.-Gen., Internat. Fedn of Surveyors, 1967–69, Vice-Pres., 1970–72, Hon. Mem., 1983; Sec., Commonwealth Assoc. of Surveying and Land Economy, 1969–90; Sec., Aubrey Barker Trust, 1970–91; Member: South East Economic Planning Council, 1974–76; Council, British Consultants Bureau, 1977–85. Chm., Geometers Liaison Cttee, EEC, 1972–86. Hon. Editor, Commonwealth Surveying and Land Economy, 1975–90. Founder Mem., 1977, Mem. Ct of Assts, 1977–, Master, 1988–89, Worshipful Co. of Chartered Surveyors. Organised national networks of beacons for Queen's Silver Jubilee celebrations, 1977, and for the Wedding of Prince Charles and Lady Diana Spencer, 1981. Raised: £71,210 for RICS Benev. Fund by sponsored walk of 1000 miles, John O'Groats to Land's End, 1979 (world record for largest sum raised by a single walker); £66,333 for RICS Benev. Fund and The Prince's Trust by walk of 1100 miles, Cape Wrath to Dover and London, 1985; £111,039 for Lord Mayor of London's Charity Appeal for Children, 1988, by walk of 1,200 miles from Strathy Point, Sutherland, to Portland Bill, Dorset, and London; £130,500 for National Trust Enterprise Neptune, 1990, by walk of 2,000 miles around the perimeter of England. Hon. Mem., Union Belge des Geomètres Experts, 1976; Hon. Fellow, Inst. of Surveyors, Malaysia, 1983. Hon. LLD Aberdeen, 1985. Distinguished Service Award, Surveyors Inst. of Sri Lanka, 1986. *Publications:* on Property Law; contrib. professional jls and internat. conferences. *Recreations:* mountain walking, travel, music. *Address:* 701 Hood House, Dolphin Square, SW1V 3NJ.

STEEL, Prof. Robert Walter, CBE 1983; BSc, MA Oxon; Principal, University College of Swansea, 1974–82; Vice-Chancellor, 1979–81, Emeritus Professor 1982, University of Wales; *b* 31 July 1915; *er s* of late Frederick Grabham and Winifred Barry Steel; *m* 1940, Eileen Margaret, *er d* of late Arthur Ernest and Evelyn Beatrice Page, Bournemouth; one *s* two *d*. *Educ:* Great Yarmouth Grammar Sch.; Cambridge and County High School for Boys; Jesus College, Oxford (Open Exhibitioner in Geography; Hon. Fellow 1982). RGS Essay Prize, 1936. Drapers' Co. Research Scholarship for Geography, 1937–39, for work in Sierra Leone; Departmental Lectr in Geography, Univ. of Oxford, 1939–47; Naval Intelligence Div., Admiralty, 1940–45; attached to Sociological Dept of W African Inst. of Arts, Industry and Social Science as geographer to Ashanti Social Survey, Gold Coast, 1945–46; University of Oxford: Univ. Lectr in Commonwealth Geography, 1947–56; Lectr in Geography, St Peter's Hall, 1951–56; Official Fellow and Tutor in Geography, Jesus Coll., 1954–56 (Supernumary Welsh Fellow, 1974–75 and 1979–80; Hon. Fellow 1982); Univ. of Liverpool: John Rankin Prof. of Geography, 1957–74; Dean, Faculty of Arts, 1965–68, Pro-Vice-Chancellor, 1971–73. Murchison Grant (RGS), 1948; Council RGS, 1949–53, 1968–71; Inst. of Brit. Geographers: Council, 1947–60; Actg Sec., 1948, Asst Sec., 1949–50; Hon. Editor of Publications, 1950–60; Vice-Pres., 1966–67, Pres. 1968, Hon. Mem. 1974; President: Section E (Geography), BAAS, 1966; African Studies Assoc. of the UK, 1970–71 (Vice-Pres., 1969–70); Geographical Assoc., 1973 (Hon. Mem. 1982); Glamorgan Trust for Nature Conservation, 1982–86. Dir, Commonwealth Geographical Bureau, 1972–81; Member: Inter-Univ. Council for Higher Educn Overseas, 1974–81; Welsh Adv. Cttee, British Council, 1978–90; Cttee for Internat. Co-operation in Higher Educn, British Council (Higher Educn Div.), 1981–85; Chairman: Universities Council for Adult Educn, 1976–80; Governors, Westhill Coll., Birmingham, 1981–; Bd, Wales Adv. Body for Local Authority Higher Educn, 1982–86; Swansea Festival of Music and the Arts, 1982–; Lower Swansea Valley Develt Gp, 1979–88; Swansea Civic Soc., 1988–; Commonwealth Human Ecology Council, 1988–90; Pres., Council for Church and Associated Colls, 1990– (Vice-Chm., 1988–90); Mem., ESRC, 1983–86 (Chm., Internat. Activities Cttee, 1985–86). Member Council: National Univ. of Lesotho, 1981–85; Univ. of Swaziland, 1987–. Vice-Pres., Royal African Soc., 1977–; Council, Nat. Inst. of Adult Educn, 1977–80. Vis. Prof., Univ. of Ghana, 1964; Canadian Commonwealth Vis. Fellow, Carleton Univ., 1970. Hon. Fellow, UC Swansea, 1991. Hon. DSc Salford, 1977; Hon. LLD: Wales, 1983; Liverpool, 1985; DUniv Open, 1987. *Publications:* ed (with A. F. Martin), and contrib. to The Oxford Region: a Scientific and Historical Survey, 1954; ed (with C. A. Fisher), and contrib. to Geographical Essays on British Tropical Lands, 1956; ed (with R. M. Prothero), and contrib. to Geographers and the Tropics: Liverpool Essays, 1964; ed (with R. Lawton), and contrib. to Liverpool Essays on Geography: a Jubilee Collection, 1967; (with Eileen M. Steel) Africa, 1974, 3rd edn 1982; ed, Human Ecology and Hong Kong: report for the Commonwealth Human Ecology Council, 1975; The Institute of British Geographers, the First Fifty Years, 1984; (contrib. and ed) British Geography 1918–45, 1987; articles, mainly on tropical Africa, in Geographical Jl and other geog. jls. *Recreations:* walking, gardening, music. *Address:* 12 Cambridge Road, Langland, Swansea SA3 4PE. *T:* Swansea (0792) 369087. *Club:* Commonwealth Trust.

STEEL, Rupert Oliver; *b* 30 April 1922; *s* of Joseph Steel and Beatrice Elizabeth Courage; *m* 1st, Marigold Katharine, *d* of Percy Lowe; two *s*; 2nd, Lucinda Evelyn Tennant, *d* of Arthur James; one *s* one *d*. *Educ:* Eton. Served War of 1939–45 (despatches), Pilot, RNVR, Fleet Air Arm, 1941–46. Courage & Co. Ltd, 1946–78; Imperial Group Ltd, 1975–78; Chm., Everards Brewery Ltd, 1978–84; Director: Lloyds Bank Ltd, 1977–79; Lloyds Bank UK Management, 1979–85; Umeco plc, 1979–; South Uist Estates Ltd, 1980–. High Sheriff, Berks, 1985–86. *Recreation:* country. *Address:* Winterbourne Holt, Newbury, Berks RG16 8AP. *T:* Chieveley (0635) 248220. *Club:* Brooks's.

STEEL, Major Sir William Strang; *see* Steel, Major Sir F. W. S.

STEELE, Prof. Alan John; Professor of French, University of Edinburgh, 1972–80, retired; *b* Bellshill, Lanark, 11 April 1916; *s* of John Steele, MA, BD, and Anne (*née* Lawson); *m* 1947, Claire Alice Louise Belet; one *d* (one *s* decd). *Educ:* Royal Grammar School, Newcastle upon Tyne; Blyth Secondary School, Northumberland; Universities of Edinburgh, Grenoble and Paris. MA 1st Cl. Hons in French Language and Literature, Vans Dunlop Schol., Univ. of Edinburgh, 1938. Served War of 1939–45, at sea with 4th Maritime AA Regt, RA, 1941–42; commissioned, 1942, with 64th LAA Regt RA in Algeria, Italy and Greece. Lecturer in French, University of Edinburgh, 1946, Prof. of French Literature, 1961–72. Chairman: Scottish Central Cttee for Modern Languages, 1972–81; Assoc. of Univ. Profs of French, 1974–75; Consultative Cttee, Institut Français d'Ecosse, 1981–88; Vice-Pres., Franco-Scottish Soc., 1961–. Mem., Church of Scotland Panel on Doctrine, 1978–86. Editor, Modern Language Review (French Section), 1971–79. Chevalier, Légion d'Honneur, 1973; Commandeur, Palmes Académiques, 1988. *Publications:* (with R. A. Leigh) Contemporary French Translation Passages, 1956; Three Centuries of French Verse, 1956, new edn, 1961; contrib. to Cahiers de l'Assoc. Internat. des Etudes françaises, Modern Language Review. *Recreation:* music. *Address:* 17 Polwarth Grove, Edinburgh EH11 1LY. *T:* 031–337 5092.

STEELE, Dr Bernard Robert; Development and Property Director (formerly Property Secretary), Methodist Homes for the Aged, since 1987; *b* 21 July 1929; *s* of Robert Walter and late Phyllis Mabel Steele; *m* 1953, Dorothy Anne Newman; one *s* two *d*. *Educ:* Oakham Sch.; Selwyn Coll., Cambridge (MA, PhD). Scientific Officer, Min. of Supply, 1953–55; Section Leader, UKAEA, Springfields, 1955–66; Building Research Station: Head, Materials Div., 1966–69; Asst Dir, 1969–72; Dep. Dir, Building Res. Estabt, 1972–75; Borough Housing Officer, Haringey, 1975–78; Dir, Science and Research Policy, DoE, 1978–82; Head, Housing Services, GLC, 1982–86. Vis. Prof., Bartlett Sch. of Architecture and Planning, UCL, 1987–89. Chm., Environment Cttee, SRC, later SERC, 1978–81. Pres., RILEM (Internat. Union of Testing and Res. Labs for Materials and Structures), 1974–75. Chm., Watford Churches Housing Assoc., 1975–78. *Publications:* contrib. numerous scientific publications on chemistry, materials science and building. *Recreations:* travelling, photography. *Address:* 1 Broom Grove, Watford WD1 3RY. *T:* Watford (0923) 241271.

STEELE, Frank Fenwick, OBE 1969; consultant; *b* 11 Feb. 1923; *s* of Frank Robert and Mary Fenwick Steele; *m*; one *s* one *d*. *Educ:* St Peter's Sch., York; Emmanuel Coll., Cambridge (MA). Army, 1943–47. HM Colonial Service, Uganda, 1948–50; joined HM Diplomatic Service, 1951; FO, 1951; Vice-Consul, Basra, 1951; Third, later Second Sec., Tripoli, 1953; Foreign Office, 1956; Second Sec., Beirut, 1958; FO, 1961; First Sec.: Amman, 1965; Nairobi, 1968; Counsellor and Dep. UK Rep., Belfast, 1971; FCO, 1973; resigned 1975. Joined Kleinwort, Benson as Adviser, 1975; Dir, and Hd of Export Finance Dept, Kleinwort Benson, 1985–87; Dir, cos in Cluff group, 1979–87; Chm., Network Television Ltd, 1981–87. Mem., Export Promotion Cttee, CBI, 1983–87. Dir, Arab British Chamber of Commerce, 1978–87; Member Council: Anglo-Jordanian Soc., 1980–; Royal Soc. for Asian Affairs, 1981–88 (Vice-Pres., 1985–88); Royal Asiatic Soc., 1986– (Pres., 1988–); Mem., F and GP Cttee, 1986–, Mem. Council, 1990–, RGS; Mem. Cttee, Mount Everest Foundn, 1990–. *Publications:* articles on Tibet. *Recreation:* travel. *Address:* 9 Ashley Gardens, SW1P 1QD. *T:* 071–834 7596. *Clubs:* Beefsteak, Shikar, Travellers'.

STEELE, John Ernest, FInstPS; consultant to shipbuilding and allied industries, since 1989; Director, Morganite Special Carbons Ltd, since 1990; Chairman, Executive Committee, Rigby Metal Components Ltd, since 1990; *b* 4 June 1935; *s* of William Steele and Amelia Steele (*née* Graham); *m* 1958, Lucy Wilkinson; one *s* three *d*. *Educ:* Rutherford College of Technology, Newcastle upon Tyne. MNECInst. Swan Hunter and Wigham Richardson Ltd: apprentice shipbuilder, 1951–56; Management Progression, 1956–68; Swan Hunter Shipbuilders Ltd: Local Dir, 1968–71; Purchasing Dir, 1971–74; Dep. Chm. and Dep. Chief Exec., 1974–78; Chief Exec., 1977–83; Chm. and Chief Exec., 1978–83; British Shipbuilders: Div. Man. Dir, Composite Yards, 1981–83; Chm., Cammell Laird Shipbuilders Ltd, 1981–84; part time Bd Mem., 1979–82; Exec. Bd Mem., Offshore, 1982–84; a Corp. Man. Dir, Offshore, 1982–84; Exec. Bd Mem., Procurement, 1984–85; Corporate Man. Dir, Procurement and Special Projects, 1985–89; Commercial Dir, 1986–89, Man. Dir, 1989–90, North East Shipbuilders Ltd. Chairman: V. O. Offshore Ltd, 1982–84; Scott Lithgow Ltd, 1983–84; Lyon Street Railway Ltd, 1977–84; Vosper Thorneycroft (UK) Ltd, 1984–86; Sunderland Forge Services, 1987–89. British Cttee Mem., Det Norske Veritas, 1981–. Director: Euroroute Construction Ltd, 1985–89; Sunderland Shipbuilders Ltd, 1988–89; Non-Exec. Dir, Gibraltar Shiprepair Ltd, 1987–90. Liveryman, Shipwrights' Co. *Recreations:* rugby football, golf, reading. *Address:* 7 Denebank, Monkseaton, Whitley Bay, NE25 9AE. *T:* 091–252 8373.

STEELE, Dr John Hyslop, FRS 1978; FRSE; President, Woods Hole Oceanographic Institution, Mass, since 1986 (Director, 1977–89); *b* 15 Nov. 1926; *s* of Adam Steele and Annie Hyslop Steele; *m* 1956, Margaret Evelyn Travis; one *s*. *Educ:* George Watson's Boys' Coll., Edinburgh (Higher Cert. of Educn); University Coll., London Univ. (BSc, DSc). FRSE 1968. Marine Lab., Aberdeen, Scotland: Marine Scientist, 1951–66; Sen. Principal Scientific Officer, 1966–73; Dep. Dir, 1973–77. Fellow, Amer. Acad. of Arts and Sciences, 1980; FAAAS 1985. Agassiz Medal, Nat. Acad. of Sciences, USA, 1973. *Publications:* Structure of Marine Ecosystems, 1974; over 80 pubns in oceanographic and ecological jls. *Recreation:* sailing. *Address:* Woods Hole Oceanographic Institution, Woods Hole, Mass 02543, USA. *T:* (508) 548–1400. *Club:* St Botolph (Boston).

STEELE, John Martin, OBE 1986 (MBE 1979); TD 1970; Under Secretary, Northern Ireland Office, since 1987; *b* 20 May 1938; *s* of John and Margaret Steele; *m* 1961, Molly Fulton (*d* 1988); one *s* two *d. Educ:* Belfast High Sch.; Queen's Univ., Belfast. Various posts, NI Civil Service, 1962–66; staff of NI Parlt, 1966–72; Dept of Community Relations, 1972–73; Second Clerk Asst, NI Assembly, 1973–74; Co-Sec., Gardiner Cttee on measures to deal with terrorism in NI, 1974; Second Clerk Asst, NI Constitutional Convention, 1975–76; DoE, NI, 1976–78; DHSS, NI, 1978–82; Dir, NI Court Service, 1982–87. Mem., TA, 1958–85; formerly Dep. Comd 23 Artillery Bde and CO 102 Air Defence Regt, RA(V); Hon. Col, 102 AD Regt, 1987–; Vice-Chm., RA Council of NI, 1986–. *Recreations:* gardening, cycling, reading, cooking. *T:* (office) Belfast (0232) 63255. *Club:* Army and Navy.

STEELE, John Roderic, CB 1979; transport consultant; Chairman, P & O European Transport Service, since 1989; *b* 22 Feb. 1929; *s* of late Harold Graham Steele and Doris Steele (*née* Hall); *m* 1956, Margaret Marie, *d* of late Joseph and Alice Stevens; two *s* two *d. Educ:* Queen Elizabeth Grammar Sch., Wakefield; Queen's Coll., Oxford (MA). Asst Principal, Min. Civil Aviation, 1951; Private Sec. to Parly Sec., MTCA, 1954; Principal, Road Trans. Div., 1957; Sea Transport, 1960; Shipping Policy, 1962; Asst Sec., Shipping Policy, BoT, 1964; Counsellor (Shipping), British Embassy, Washington, 1967; Asst Sec., Civil Aviation Div., DTI, 1971, Under-Sec., Space Div., 1973, Shipping Policy Div., 1974, Gen. Div., 1975, Dept of Trade; Dep. Sec., Dept of Trade, 1976–80, Dept of Industry, 1980–81; Dir-Gen. for Transport, EEC, 1981–86. Dir, P & O Containers Ltd, 1987–. Mem., Dover Harbour Bd, 1990–. *Recreations:* normal. *Address:* Brocas Oast, Hever, Edenbridge, Kent; Square Ambiorix 30, Bte 30, 1040 Bruxelles, Belgium. *Clubs:* United Oxford & Cambridge University; Philippics.

STEELE, Kenneth Walter Lawrence, CBE 1980 (OBE 1967); KPM 1936; Chief Constable, Avon and Somerset Constabulary, 1974–79; *b* 28 July 1914; *s* of Walter and Susan Steele, Godalming, Surrey; *m* 1987, Irene Koh, Malaysia. *Educ:* Wellington Sch., Wellington, Somerset. Served War: with Somerset LI and Royal Northumberland Fusiliers, 1942–45. Asst Chief Constable, Buckinghamshire, 1953–55; Chief Constable: Somerset, 1955–66; Somerset and Bath, 1966–74. *Recreation:* tennis. *Address:* Lloyds Bank Ltd, 31 Fore Street, Taunton, Somerset TA1 1HN.

STEELE, Maj.-Gen. Michael Chandos Merrett, MBE 1972; Chief of Joint Services Liaison Organization, Bonn, 1983–86; Regimental Comptroller, Royal Artillery, since 1989; *b* 1 Dec. 1931; *s* of late William Chandos Steele and Daisy Rhoda Steele (*née* Merrett); *m* 1961, Judith Ann Huxford; two *s* one *d. Educ:* Westminster School; RMA Sandhurst. Commissioned RA, 1952; Staff Coll., Camberley, 1962; BM RA, 53rd Welsh Div., 1965–67; BM, 8th Inf. Brigade, 1970–72; CO 22nd Light Air Defence Regt, RA, 1972–74; GSO1, HQ DRA, 1974–76; Comdr, 7th Artillery Brigade, 1976–78; Nat. Defence Coll., Canada, 1978–79; BGS, Defence Sales Organization, 1979–82. Col Comdt, RA, 1988–. Hon. Col 104 Air Defence Regt, RA(V)TA, 1987–. *Recreations:* lawn tennis, gardening. *Address:* Elders, Masons Bridge Road, Redhill, Surrey RH1 5LE. *T:* Redhill (0737) 763982.

STEELE, Sir (Philip John) Rupert, Kt 1980; Director, Trust Company of Australia Ltd (formerly Union Fidelity Trustee Co. of Australia), since 1984; *b* 3 Nov. 1920; *s* of late C. Steele; *m* 1946, Judith, *d* of Dr Clifford Sharp; one *s* two *d. Educ:* Melbourne C of E Grammar School. Served RAAF and 115 Sqdn (Lancaster), RAF; POW 1944. Director: Steele & Co. Ltd, 1949–59; Carlton Brewery Ltd, 1964–73; Carlton and United Breweries, 1973–84. Mem. Council, Royal Agr. Soc. of Victoria, 1961–74. Pres., Prahan Football Club, 1980–85; Mem. Cttee, Victoria Racing Club, 1958–85, Hon. Treasurer, 1971–73, Vice-Chm., 1973–77, Chm., 1977–82; Mem., Racecourses Licensing Board, 1975–81. *Recreation:* racing thoroughbred horses. *Address:* 2/64 Irving Road, Toorak, Victoria 3142, Australia.

STEELE, Richard Charles, FIBiol, FICFor; Director General, Nature Conservancy Council, 1980–88; *b* 26 May 1928; *s* of Richard Orson Steele and Helen Curtis Steele (*née* Robertson); *m* 1966, Anne Freda Nelson; two *s* one *d. Educ:* Univ. of Wales (BSc Forestry and Botany); Univ. of Oxford. National Service, 1946–48. Assistant Conservator of Forests, Colonial Forest Service (later HMOCS), Tanganyika (later Tanzania), 1951–63; Head: Woodland Management Section, Nature Conservancy, Monks Wood, 1963–73; Terrestrial Life Sciences Section, Natural Environment Research Council, London, 1973–78; Division of Scientific Services, NERC Inst. of Terrestrial Ecology, Cambridge, 1978–80. Past Pres., Inst. of Foresters of Gt Britain. *Publications:* Wildlife Conservation in Woodlands, 1972; ed, Monks Wood: a nature reserve record, 1974; numerous papers on nature conservation, ecology and forestry in professional and scientific jls. *Recreations:* hill-walking, gardening, collecting books on natural history and E African travel. *Address:* Treetops, 20 Deepdene Wood, Dorking, Surrey, RH5 4BQ. *T:* Dorking (0306) 883106. *Club:* Athenæum.

STEELE, Sir Rupert; see Steele, Sir P. J. R.

STEELE, Tommy, (Thomas Hicks), OBE 1979; actor; *b* Bermondsey, London, 17 Dec. 1936; *s* of late Thomas Walter Hicks and Elizabeth Ellen (*née* Bennett); *m* 1960, Ann Donoghue; one *d. Educ:* Bacon's Sch. for Boys, Bermondsey. First appearance on stage in variety, Empire Theatre, Sunderland, Nov. 1956; first London appearance, variety, Dominion Theatre, 1957; Buttons in Rodgers and Hammerstein's Cinderella, Coliseum, 1958; Tony Lumpkin in She Stoops to Conquer, Old Vic, 1960; Arthur Kipps in Half a Sixpence, Cambridge Theatre, London, 1963–64 and Broadhurst Theatre (first NY appearance), 1965; Truffaldino in The Servant of Two Masters, Queen's, 1969; Dick Whittington, London Palladium, 1969; Meet Me In London, Adelphi, 1971; Jack Point, in The Yeomen of the Guard, City of London Fest., 1978; London Palladium: The Tommy Steele Show, 1973; Hans Andersen, 1974 and 1977; one-man show, Prince of Wales, 1979; Singin' in the Rain (also dir.), 1983; *films:* Kill Me Tomorrow, 1956; The Tommy Steele Story; The Duke Wore Jeans; Tommy the Toreador; Touch It Light; It's All Happening; The Happiest Millionaire; Half a Sixpence; Finian's Rainbow; Where's Jack?; *television:* wrote and acted in Quincy's Quest, 1979. Composed and recorded, My Life, My Song, 1974; composed: A Portrait of Pablo, 1985; Rock Suite—an Elderly Person's Guide to Rock, 1987. *Publications:* Quincy, 1981; The Final Run, 1983. *Recreations:* squash, sculpture. *Address:* c/o Michael Anderson, ICM Ltd, 388 Oxford Street, W1N 9HE. *T:* 071–629 8080.

STEELE-BODGER, Prof. Alasdair, CBE 1980; FRCVS; Professor of Veterinary Clinical Studies, University of Cambridge, 1979–91; *b* 1 Jan. 1924; *s* of late Harry Steele-Bodger, MRCVS, and Mrs K. Steele-Bodger (*née* MacDonald); *m* 1948, Anne, 2nd *d* of late Captain A. W. J. Finlayson, RN, and Mrs Nancy Finlayson; three *d. Educ:* Shrewsbury Sch.; Caius Coll., Cambridge (BA 1945, MA); Royal 'Dick' Veterinary Coll., Edinburgh Univ. (BSc, MRCVS 1948). Hon. FRCVS 1975; Scientific FZS 1989. Gen. vet. practice, Lichfield, Staffs, 1948–77; consultant practice, Fordingbridge, Hants, 1977–79. Hon. Vet. Consultant to British Agricl Export Council, 1967–. Vis. Prof., Univ. of Toronto, 1973. Pres., British Small Animal Vet. Assoc., 1962; Member: Horserace Scientific Adv. Cttee (formerly Jockey Club's Horserace Anti-Doping Cttee), 1973–; UGC's Agricl and Vet. Sub-Cttee, 1973–81; Council: BVA, 1957–85 (Pres., 1966; Hon. Mem., 1985); RCVS, 1960–90 (Pres., 1972); Jt RCVS/BVA Cttee on Eur. Vet. Affairs, 1967–90; Eur. Liaison Gp for Agriculture, 1972–90; Cttee of Inquiry on Experiments on Animals, 1963–65; Council, Royal Agricl Soc. of England, 1967–; Animal Feedingstuffs Industry/BVA/ADAS HQ Liaison Cttee, 1967–85. UK Deleg. to Fedn of Veterinarians of EEC, 1967–90; EEC Official Vet. Expert, 1974–; Member: EEC Adv. Cttee on Vet. Trng, 1981–90; Home Office Panel of Assessors under Animals (Scientific Procedures) Act, 1986–. Vice-Pres., Inst. of Animal Technology, 1988–. Dir, Bantin & Kingman Ltd, 1980–. Hon. Vet. Consultant, Nat. Cattle Breeders' Assoc., 1979–. Mem. Bd of Advisers, Univ. of London, 1984–. Gov., Cambs Coll. of Agric. and Hortic., 1989–90. Gen. Comr to Bd of Inland Revenue, 1969–81. Chairman: Editorial Bd, Veterinary Times (formerly Veterinary Drug), 1978–88; Adv. Bd, British Veterinary Formulary, 1987–. Crookes' Prize, 1970; Dalrymple-Champneys Cup and Medal, 1972. Cambridge Triple Blue. *Publications:* Society of Practising Veterinary Surgeons Economics Report, 1961, and papers in vet. jls on clinical subjects and vet. econs. *Recreations:* swimming, fishing, travel. *Address:* The Old House, Catton Lane, Walton-on-Trent, Derbyshire DE12 8LL. *Clubs:* Farmers'; Hawks (Cambridge).
See also M. R. Steele-Bodger.

STEELE-BODGER, Michael Roland, CBE 1990; veterinary surgeon in private practice; *b* 4 Sept. 1925; *s* of late Henry William Steele-Bodger and Kathrine Macdonald; *m* 1955, Violet Mary St Clair Murray; two *s* one *d. Educ:* Rugby Sch.; Gonville and Caius Coll., Cambridge. MRCVS. Mem., Sports Council, 1976–82. England Rugby Selector, 1954–70; Pres., RFU, 1973–74; Mem., Internat. Rugby Football Bd, 1974–84; Chm., Four Home Rugby Unions' Tours Cttee, 1976–. Cambridge Univ. Rugby Blue, Captain 1946; England Rugby Internat., 1947–48. *Recreation:* interest in all sport. *Address:* Laxford Lodge, Bonehill, Tamworth, Staffs. *T:* Tamworth (0827) 251001. *Clubs:* East India, Devonshire, Sports and Public Schools; Hawks (Cambridge).
See also A. Steele-Bodger.

STEELE-PERKINS, Surgeon Vice-Admiral Sir Derek (Duncombe), KCB 1966 (CB 1963); KCVO 1964 (CVO 1954); FRCS; FRACS; *b* 19 June 1908; *s* of late Dr Duncombe Steele-Perkins, Honiton, Devon, and Sybil Mary Hill-Jones, Edinburgh; *m* 1937, Joan Boddan (*d* 1985), Birkdale, Lancashire; three *d. Educ:* Allhallows School, Rousdon; College of Surgeons (Edin.). Entered RN, 1932; RN Hosp., Haslar, 1932; HMS Mantis, China, 1934–36; HMS Ganges, Shotley, 1936–38; HMS Vindictive, 1938–39; RN Hospitals: Haslar, 1939–40; Chatham, 1940–44; Sydney, Australia, 1944–46; Malta, 1946–50; RY Gothic, 1951–52; Chatham, 1952–59; Senior Surgical Specialist, RN Hosp., Bighi, Malta, Oct. 1959–61; Medical Officer-in-Charge, Royal Naval Hospital, Haslar, 1961; Command MO to C-in-C, Portsmouth, 1962–63; Medical Director of the Navy, 1963–66. FRSocMed. Royal Commonwealth Tours, 1953–66. QHS 1961. CStJ. *Recreations:* sailing, fly-fishing, shooting. *Address:* c/o National Westminster Bank, Lymington, Hants. *Club:* Royal Lymington Yacht (Cdre 1969–72).

STEEN, Anthony David; MP (C) South Hams, since 1983 (Liverpool Wavertree, Feb. 1974–1983); barrister; youth leader; social worker; underwriter; *b* 22 July 1939; *s* of late Stephen Nicholas Steen; *m* 1965, Carolyn Padfield, educational psychologist; one *s* one *d. Educ:* Westminster Sch.; occasional student University Coll., London. Called to Bar, Gray's Inn, 1962; practising Barrister, 1962–74; Defence Counsel, MoD (Court Martials). Lectr in Law, Council of Legal Educn, 1964–68; Adv. Tutor, Sch. of Environment, Central London Poly, 1981–83. Founder and First Director: Task Force to help London's old and lonely, with Govt support, 1964; Govt Foundn YVFF, tackling urban deprivation, 1968–74; Consultant to Canadian Govt on student and employment matters, 1970–71. Mem., Select Cttee on Race Relations, 1975–79; Chairman: Cons. Cttee on Cities, Urban and New Town Affairs, 1979–83; Parly Urban and Inner City Cttee, 1987–; All Party Friends of Cycling, 1979–88; Parly PNG Gp; Vice-Chm., Health and Social Services, 1979–80; Sec., Parly Caribbean Gp, 1979–; Chm., Chm's Unit Marginal Seats, Cons. Central Office, 1982–84; Jt Nat. Chm., Impact 80's Campaign. Member: Exec. Council, NPFA; Board, Community Transport; Council of Reference, Internat. Christian Relief; Council Mem., Anglo-Jewish Assoc.; Chm., Outlandos Charitable Trust; Vice-Chm., Task Force Trust; Vice-President: Ecology Bldg Soc.; Internat. Centre for Child Studies; Bentley Operatic Soc. Patron, Liverpool's Open Circle for Detached Youth Work; Pres., Devon Youth Assoc. *Publications:* New Life for Old Cities, 1981; Tested Ideas for Political Success, 1983; Plums, 1988. *Recreations:* piano, hill climbing, swimming, cycling. *Address:* House of Commons, SW1; 46 Fore Street, Totnes, South Devon. *T:* Totnes (0803) 866069. *Clubs:* Royal Automobile; Churchill (Liverpool); Brixham; Totnes Conservative (South Hams).

STEER, Prof. John Richardson, FSA 1981; Emeritus Professor of the History of Art, University of London; art-historian and director; *b* 14 Oct. 1928; *s* of Walter Wallis Steer and Elsie Gertrude (*née* Colman). *Educ:* Clayesmore Sch., Dorset; Keble Coll., Oxford (MA); Courtauld Inst. of Art, Univ. of London (BA). Gen. Asst, City Art Gall., Birmingham, 1953–56; Asst Lectr, Dept of Fine Art, Univ. of Glasgow, 1956–59; Lectr in Hist. of European Art, Univ. of Bristol, 1959–67; Prof. of Fine Arts, Univ. of St Andrews, 1967–80; Prof. of Hist. of Art, Birkbeck Coll., Univ. of London, 1980–84. Chm., Adv. Cttee on Validation, Heriot-Watt Univ./Edinburgh Coll. of Art, 1978–91; Chm., Art Historians Assoc. of GB, 1980–83; Vice-Chm., Scottish Theatre Ballet, 1969–71; Mem., Cttee for Art and Design, CNAA, 1977–82 (Chm., Hist. of Art/Design and Complementary Studies Bd, 1977–79); Member: Theatre Museum Adv. Council, 1981–83; Theatre Museum Cttee, V&A Mus., 1984–; Exec., Genius of Venice Exhibn, RA, 1983–84. Trustee, V&A Mus., 1991–. Adjudicator, National Student Drama Festival, 1977. Theatrical prodns include: The Seagull, St Andrews, 1971; And When Love Speaks, Edinburgh, 1975; The Privacy of the Patients, Edinburgh Fringe, 1977, ICA, 1978; Waiting for Godot, St Andrews, 1978; Minna von Barnhelm, plc theatre co., Young Vic Studio, 1987. Hon. DLitt: St Andrews, 1990; Heriot-Watt, 1991. *Publications:* A Concise History of Venetian Painting, 1967; Mr Bacon's Titian (Selwyn Brinton Lecture, RSA), 1977; Alvise Vivarini, 1982; contribs to Burlington Magazine, Art History. *Recreation:* travel. *Address:* 1 Cheriton Square, SW17 8AE.

STEER, Kenneth Arthur, CBE 1978; MA, PhD, FSA, FSAScot; Secretary, Royal Commission on the Ancient and Historical Monuments of Scotland, 1957–78; *b* 12 Nov. 1913; *o s* of Harold Steer and Emily Florence Thompson; *m* 1st, 1941, Rona Mary Mitchell (*d* 1983); one *d*; 2nd, 1985, Eileen Alice Nelson. *Educ:* Wath Grammar School; Durham University. Research Fellowship, 1936–38. Joined staff of Royal Commission on Ancient and Historical Monuments of Scotland, 1938. Intelligence Officer in Army, 1941–45 (despatches twice). Monuments, Fine Arts and Archives Officer, North Rhine Region, 1945–46. Corresponding Member, German Archæological Inst.; Horsley Memorial Lectr, Durham University, 1963; Rhind Lectr, Edinburgh, 1968. Pres., Soc. of Antiquaries of Scotland, 1972–75. Arts Council Literary Award, 1978. *Publications:* Late Medieval Monumental Sculpture in the West Highlands (with J. W. M. Bannerman), 1976; numerous articles in archæological journals. *Address:* 2 Morningside Courtyard, Idsall Drive, Prestbury, Cheltenham, Glos GL52 3BU.

STEER, Rt. Rev. Stanley Charles; Bishop of Saskatoon, 1950–70; *s* of S. E. and E. G. Steer; *m* 1936, Marjorie Slater. *Educ:* Guildford Gram. Sch.; Univ. of Saskatchewan (BA); Oxford Univ. (MA). Hon. DD: Wycliffe Coll., Toronto, 1947, Emmanuel Coll., Saskatoon, 1952; St Chad's Coll., Regina, 1964. Missionary at Vanderhoof, BC, 1929; Chaplain, St Mark's Church, Alexandria, 1931; Chaplain, University Coll., Oxford, 1932–33; St John's Hall, Univ. of London: Tutor, 1933; Vice-Principal, 1936. Chaplain, The Mercers' Company, City of London, 1937; Principal, Emmanuel Coll., Saskatoon, 1941; Hon. Canon of St John's Cathedral, Saskatoon, and CF (R of O), 1943. *Recreation:* tennis. *Address:* 2383 Lincoln Road, Victoria, BC V8R 6A3, Canada. *T:* 592 9888.

STEER, Wilfred Reed; QC 1972; *b* 23 Aug. 1926; *s* of George William and Dorothy Steer; *m* 1953, Jill Park; one *s* one *d*, and two step *s*. *Educ:* Bede Collegiate Sch., Sunderland, Co. Durham; London Sch. of Economics. LLB (Lond.) 1949. Called to the Bar, Gray's Inn, 1950. *Address:* Park Court Chambers, 40 Park Cross Street, Leeds LS1 2QH. *T:* Leeds (0532) 433277.

STEER, William Reed Hornby, MA, LLM; Barrister-at-Law; Recorder of South Molton, 1936–51; Deputy Chairman, London County Council, 1948–49; Lt-Col in the Army (released July 1945); *b* 5 April 1899; *s* of late Rev. W. H. Hornby Steer, TD MA, JP; unmarried. *Educ:* Eton; Trinity College, Cambridge. Commissioned in Royal Field Artillery; served European War, France and Belgium; called to Bar, Inner Temple, 1922; joined Western Circuit; Standing Counsel: to Commons, Open Spaces, and Footpaths Preservation Society; to Council for Preservation of Rural England; to National Smoke Abatement Society and to Pure Rivers Society; an Examiner in Law to Chartered Institute of Secretaries; Legal Member of Town Planning Inst.; Fellow of Royal Soc. of Health; Associate of Royal Institution of Chartered Surveyors; a representative for Hampstead on London County Council, 1931–52; a representative of London County Council on International Union of Local Authorities; Master of Worshipful Company of Turners, 1949–50; a Governor of Haberdashers' Aske's Schools and of Royal Free Hospital; a Governor and an Almoner of Christ's Hospital, Dep. Chm. Council of Almoners, 1970–75; Chairman Children's Hospital, Hampstead; Vice-Chairman London Old Age Pensions Committee; Treasurer, London Soc.; Kt of Justice, Order of St John; Joint Hon. Secretary of League of Mercy; Gold Staff Officer at Coronation of King George VI; Inspector of Metropolitan Special Constabulary; Army Officers Emergency Reserve, 1938; Extra Regimentally Employed, Military Dept, Judge Advocate-General's Office, 1939; Deputy Judge Advocate-General, Malta, 1941–43; graded Assistant Adjutant-General, War Office, 1944; Staff Officer (I), Control Commission for Germany, 1945; Captain, 1939; Major, 1941; Lt-Col 1943; Member of Territorial Army and Air Force Association of the County of London. *Publications:* articles on the law relating to Highways; Assistant Editor of Glen's Public Health Act, 1936; Steer's Law of Smoke Nuisances, 1938, 2nd edn 1948; contributions to Lord Macmillan's Local Government Law and Administration. *Recreation:* sailing. *Address:* 71A Whitehall Court, SW1A 2EL. *T:* 071–930 3160. *Clubs:* United Oxford & Cambridge University, Carlton, Pratt's, MCC; Royal Corinthian Yacht (Burnham-on-Crouch).

STEERE, Sir Ernest H. L.; *see* Lee-Steere, Sir E. H.

STEFF-LANGSTON, Group Captain John Antony, MBE 1959; Executive Secretary, Royal Astronomical Society, since 1980; *b* 5 Nov. 1926; *s* of William Austen Paul Steff-Langston, organist and composer, and Ethel Maude (*née* Fletcher); *m* 1959, Joyce Marian Brown. *Educ:* Cathedral Choir Sch., Canterbury; King's Sch., Canterbury; Pembroke Coll., Cambridge. RAF Coll., 1945–46; 45 Sqn, Ceylon, 1948; 61 Gp, Kenley, 1949; 34 Sqn, 1950–51; 80 Sqn, Hong Kong, 1951–54; 540, 58 and 82 Sqns, Wyton and Singapore, 1955–57; HQ 3 Gp, 1957–59; 80 Sqn, Germany, 1959–62; Staff Coll., Andover, 1962–63; Air Sec.'s Dept, 1963–65; OC 114 Sqn, Benson, 1966–68; aws 1968; CO Northolt, 1969–71; Defence Advr to High Comrs to NZ and Fiji, 1971–74; sowc Greenwich, 1974–75; AMPs Dept, 1975–78; retd 1978. FBIM 1978. *Recreations:* ornithology, photography, travel, music, cricket. *Address:* 6 Beech Wood, Church Hill, Caterham, Surrey CR3 6SB. *T:* Caterham (0883) 344348. *Club:* Royal Air Force.

STEGGLE, Terence Harry, CMG 1990; HM Diplomatic Service, retired; Ambassador to Paraguay, 1989–91; *b* 4 March 1932; *s* of Henry Richard Steggle and Jane Steggle; *m* 1st, 1954, Odette Marie (*née* Audisio) (*d* 1988); two *d*; 2nd, 1989, Annemarie Klara Johanne (*née* Wohle). *Educ:* Chislehurst and Sidcup County Grammar School. Crown Agents, 1950–57; Lieut RA (TA), 1951–53; seconded to Govt of E Nigeria, 1957–58, 1960–62; FO 1963; served Laos, 1963, France, 1964, Zaire, 1970, Bolivia, 1978–82; Ambassador to Panama, 1983–86; Consul-Gen., São Paulo, 1986–87; Counsellor, FCO, 1987–89. *Recreations:* swimming, philately, bridge. *Address:* c/o Foreign and Commonwealth Office, SW1A 2AH. *Club:* Asuncion Rotary.

STEIN, Cyril; Chairman and Joint Managing Director, Ladbroke Group PLC; *b* 20 Feb. 1928; *s* of late Jack Stein and Rebecca Stein (*née* Selner); *m* 1949, Betty Young; two *s* one *d*. *Address:* Ladbroke Group, 10 Cavendish Place, W1M 9DJ.

STEIN, Prof. Peter Gonville, FBA 1974; JP; Regius Professor of Civil Law in the University of Cambridge, and Fellow of Queens' College, since 1968; *b* 29 May 1926; *o s* of late Walter Stein, MA, Solicitor, and Effie Drummond Stein (*née* Walker); *m* 1st, 1953, Janet Chamberlain; three *d*; 2nd, 1978, Anne M. Howard; one step *s*. *Educ:* Liverpool Coll.; Gonville and Caius Coll., Camb. (Classical Exhibitioner); University of Pavia. Served in RN, Sub-lieut (Sp) RNVR, 1944–47. Admitted a Solicitor, 1951; Italian Govt Scholar, 1951–52; Asst Lecturer in Law, Nottingham Univ., 1952–53; Lecturer in Jurisprudence, 1953–56, Prof. of Jurisprudence, 1956–68, Dean of Faculty of Law, 1961–64, Aberdeen Univ.; Chm., Faculty Bd of Law, Cambridge, 1973–76; Vice Pres., Queens' Coll., 1974–81 (Acting Pres., 1976 and 1980–81). Visiting Prof. of Law: Univ. of Virginia, 1965–66, 1978–79; Colorado, 1966; Witwatersrand, 1970; Louisiana State, 1974, 1977, 1983, 1985; Chicago, 1985, 1988, 1990; Padua, 1991; Lectures: R. M. Jones, QUB, 1978; Irvine, Cornell, 1979; Sherman, Boston, 1979; Tucker, Louisiana State, 1985; David Murray, Glasgow, 1987. Fellow, Winchester Coll., 1976–91. Member: Council, Max Planck Inst. for European Legal History, Frankfurt, 1966–88; Council, Internat. Assoc. of Legal History, 1970– (Vice-Pres, 1985–); Sec. of State for Scotland's Working Party on Hospital Endowments, 1966–69; Bd of Management, Royal Cornhill and Assoc. (Mental) Hospitals, Aberdeen, 1963–68 (Chm. 1967–68); UGC, 1971–75; US–UK Educnl Commn, 1985–91; Council, British Acad., 1988–90. Chm., Ely Diocesan Trust Cttee, 1987–. Pres., Soc. of Public Teachers of Law, 1980–81; Vice-Pres., Selden Soc., 1984–87. Foreign Fellow: Accad. di Scienze morali e politiche, Naples, 1982; Accademia Nazionale dei Lincei, Rome, 1987; Corres. Fellow, Accademia degli Intronati, Siena, 1988; Fellow, Academia Europaea, 1989. JP Cambridge, 1970 (Supplementary List, 1988). Hon. Dr jur Göttingen, 1980; Hon. Dott. Giur. Ferrara, 1990. *Publications:* Fault in the formation of Contract in Roman Law and Scots Law, 1958; editor, Buckland's Textbook of Roman Law, 3rd edn, 1963; Regulae Iuris: from juristic rules to legal maxims, 1966; Roman Law in Scotland in Ius Romanum Medii Aevi, 1968; Roman Law and English Jurisprudence (inaugural lect.), 1969; (with J. Shand) Legal Values in Western Society, 1974, Italian edn 1981; (ed jtly) Adam Smith's Lectures on Jurisprudence, 1978; Legal Evolution, 1980, Japanese edn 1987; (ed jtly) Studies in Justinian's Institutes, 1983; Legal Institutions: the development of dispute settlement, 1984, Italian edn 1987; The Character and Influence of the Roman Civil Law: historical essays, 1988; (with F. de Zulueta) The Teaching of Roman Law in England around 1200, 1990; (ed and contrib.) Notaries Public in England since the Reformation (English and Italian edns), 1991; articles in legal periodicals mainly on Roman Law and legal history. *Recreations:* hill walking, gardening. *Address:* Queens' College, Cambridge CB3 9ET. *T:* Cambridge (0223) 335511; Wimpole Cottage, Wimpole Road, Great Eversden, Cambridge CB3 7HR. *T:* Cambridge (0223) 262349.

STEINBERG, Gerald Neil, (Gerry); MP (Lab) City of Durham, since 1987; *b* 20 April 1945; *s* of Harry and Esther Steinberg; *m* 1969, Margaret Cruddace Thornton; one *s* one *d*. *Educ:* St Margaret's Primary Sch.; Whinney Hill Secondary Sch.; Durham Johnston Sch.; Sheffield Coll. of Education; Newcastle Polytechnic. Cert. of Educn for Backward Children. Teacher, Dukeshouse Wood Camp Sch., Hexham, 1966–69; Teacher, Elemore Hall, 1969–75, Dep. Head, 1975–79; Head Teacher, Whitworth House Special Sch., 1979–87. Mem., Durham City Council, 1975–87 (Sec., Labour Gp, 1981–87). Mem., Parly Select Cttee on Education, 1987–. *Recreations:* Sunderland AFC supporter; cricket, squash, loves all sport (Pres., Bearpark Cricket Club). *Address:* 20 Briardene, Durham. *T:* Durham (091) 3861082. *Clubs:* Sherburn Workman's, Sherburn Hill Workman's, Brandon Workman's.

STEINBERG, Professor Hannah; Professor of Psychopharmacology in the University of London at University College, since 1970; Head of Psychopharmacology Group, Department of Psychology, University College London, since 1979; *d* of late Michael Steinberg, doctor of law, and Marie (*née* Wein). *Educ:* Schwarzwaldschule, Vienna; Putney High School; Queen Anne's School, Caversham; Univ. of Reading (Cert. Comm.); Denton Secretarial Coll., London; University College London (BA 1st cl. Hons Psychology, PhD; Troughton Schol., 1948–50). FBPsS, CPsychol 1990; FZS. Pres., Univ. of London Union, 1947–48; Univ. of London Postgrad. Studentship, 1948–50. Sec. to Man. Dir, Omes Ltd, 1943–44. University College London: Asst Lectr in Pharmacology, 1954–55; Lectr, 1955–62; Reader in Psychopharmacology, 1962–70; Prof. of Psychopharmacology (first in W Europe), 1970–. Hon. consulting Clinical Psychologist, Dept of Psychological Medicine, Royal Free Hosp., 1970. Member MRC working parties on: Biochemistry and Pharmacology of Drug Dependence, 1968–73; Biological Aspects of Drug Dependence, 1971–75. Vice-President: Collegium Internationale Neuro-Psychopharmacologicum (CINP), 1968–74; Brit. Assoc. of Psychopharmacology, 1973–77 (Hon. Mem., 1987); Mem., Biological Council, 1977–80. Distinguished Affiliate of Amer. Psychol Assoc., Psychopharmacology Div., 1978; Member: British Pharmacol Soc.; Experimental Psychol. Soc.; Assoc. for Study of Animal Behaviour; Soc. for Study of Addiction; European Coll. of Neuropsychopharmacology; European Behavioural Pharmacol Soc., etc. Convener, Academic Women's Achievement Gp, 1979–. Special Trustee, Middx Hosp., 1988–. Past and present ed. of scientific jls. *Publications:* (trans. and ed jtly) Animals and Men, 1951; organiser of symposia and editor: Animal Behaviour and Drug Action (jt), 1963; Scientific Basis of Drug Dependence, 1968; Psychopharmacology, Sexual Disorders and Drug Abuse (jt), 1972, etc; articles and reviews on psychopharmacology and physical exercise and mental health. *Address:* University College London, Gower Street, WC1E 6BT. *T:* 071–387 7050.

STEINBERG, Saul Phillip; Founder, 1961, and Chairman and Chief Executive Officer, since 1961, Reliance Group Holdings Inc.; *b* 13 Aug. 1939; *m* 3rd, 1984, Gayfryd McNabb; one *d* and one step *s*; and three *s* one *d* by previous marriages. *Educ:* Wharton School of Univ. of Pennsylvania (BScEcon). Director: Zenith National Insurance Corp.; Symbol Technologies Inc.; Chairman: Exec. Cttee, Frank B. Hall & Co. Inc.; Bd, Telemundo Gp Inc. Dir, Long Island Jewish Medical Center. Mem., Bd of Overseers, Cornell Univ. Medical Coll.; Chm., Wharton Bd of Overseers; Trustee: Univ. of Pennsylvania; NY Public Library. *Address:* Park Avenue Plaza, 55 E 52 Street, New York, NY 10055, USA. *T:* (212) 909–1110. *Clubs:* Glen Oaks, The Board Room (NY).

STEINBERGER, Prof. Jack; Gallilean Professor of Physics, Scuola Normale Superiore, Pisa, since 1986; *b* 25 May 1921; *s* of Ludwig and Bertha Steinberger; *m* 1st, 1943, Joan Beauregard; two *s*; 2nd, 1962, Cynthia Eve Alff; one *s* one *d*. *Educ:* New Trier Township High Sch.; Armour Inst. of Technology; Univ. of Chicago (BS Chem 1942; PhD Phys 1948). Mem., Inst. of Advanced Study, Princeton, 1948–49; Asst, Univ. of California, Berkeley, 1949–50; Prof., Columbia Univ., 1950–68 (Higgins Prof., 1965–68); Physicist, CERN, Geneva, 1968–86. Member: Nat. Acad. of Sciences; Amer. Acad. of Arts and Sciences; Heidelberg Acad. of Science. (Jtly) President's Science Award, USA, 1988; (jtly) Nobel Prize for Physics, 1988. *Publications:* papers in learned jls on discoveries leading to better understanding of elementary particles. *Recreations:* flute; formerly mountaineering, tennis, yachting. *Address:* CERN, 1211 Geneva 23, Switzerland; 25 Ch. des Merles, CH 1213 Onex, Switzerland.

STEINER, Prof. George, MA, DPhil; Extraordinary Fellow, Churchill College, Cambridge, since 1969; Professor of English and Comparative Literature, University of Geneva, since 1974; *b* 23 April 1929; *s* of Dr F. G. and Mrs E. Steiner; *m* 1955, Zara Steiner (*née* Shakow); one *s* one *d*. *Educ:* Paris (BèsL); Univ. of Chicago (BA); Harvard (MA); Oxford (DPhil). Member, staff of the Economist, in London, 1952–56; Inst. for Advanced Study, Princeton, 1956–58; Gauss Lectr, Princeton Univ., 1959–60; Fellow of Churchill Coll., Cambridge, 1961–. Lectures: Massey, 1974; Leslie Stephen, Cambridge, 1986; W. P. Ker, 1986, Gifford, 1990, Univ. of Glasgow; Page-Barbour, Univ. of Virginia, 1987. Fulbright Professorship, 1958–69; O. Henry Short Story Award, 1958; Guggenheim Fellowship, 1971–72; Zabel Award of Nat. Inst. of Arts and Letters of the Us, 1970; Faulkner Stipend for Fiction, PEN, 1983. Pres., English Assoc., 1975; Corresp. Mem., (Federal) German Acad. of Literature, 1981; Hon. Mem., Amer. Acad. of Arts and Scis, 1989. FRSL 1964. Hon. DLitt: East Anglia, 1976; Louvain, 1980; Mount Holyoke Coll., USA, 1983; Bristol, 1989; Glasgow, 1990; Liège, 1990. Chevalier de la Légion d'Honneur, 1984. *Publications:* Tolstoy or Dostoevsky, 1958; The Death of Tragedy, 1960; Anno Domini, 1964; Language and Silence, 1967; Extraterritorial, 1971; In Bluebeard's Castle, 1971; The Sporting Scene: White Knights in Reykjavik, 1973; After Babel, 1975 (adapted for TV as The Tongues of Men, 1977); Heidegger, 1978; On Difficulty and Other Essays, 1978; The Portage to San Cristobal of A. H., 1981; Antigones, 1984; George Steiner: a reader, 1984; Real Presences: is there anything in what we say?, 1989. *Recreations:* music, chess, mountain walking. *Address:* 32 Barrow Road, Cambridge. *T:* Cambridge (0223) 61200. *Clubs:* Athenæum, Savile; Harvard (New York).

STEINER, Rear-Adm. Ottokar Harold Mojmir St John, CB 1967; Assistant Chief of Defence Staff, 1966–68, retired; *b* 8 July 1916; *e s* of late O. F. Steiner; *m* 1st, 1940, Evelyn Mary Young (marr. diss. 1975); one *s* one *d*; 2nd, 1975, Eleanor, *widow* of Sqdn Leader W. J. H. Powell, RAF. *Educ:* St Paul's School. Special entry cadet, RN, 1935. Served War of 1939–45 (despatches twice), HMS Ilex, Havelock, Frobisher, Superb. Naval Staff Course, 1947; Staff of C-in-C, Far East Fleet, 1948–50; Comdr 1950; jssc 1953; HMS Ceylon, 1953–54; NATO Defence Coll., 1955; HMS Daedalus, 1955–56; Capt. 1956; Admiralty, 1956–58; in comd HMS Saintes and Capt. (D) 3rd Destroyer Squdn, 1958–60;

Naval Adviser to UK High Commission, Canada, 1960–62; Senior Offrs War Course, 1962; in comd HMS Centaur, 1963–65; ADC to HM the Queen, 1965; Rear-Adm., 1966. Vice-Pres., Shipwrecked Fishermen and Mariners Royal Benevolent Soc. Freeman, City of London; Liveryman, Coachmakers and Coach Harness Makers. *Recreations:* sailing, golf. *Clubs:* Royal Cruising, Isle of Wight Motor Yacht (Adm.); Royal Naval Sailing Association; Union (Malta).

STEINER, Prof. Robert Emil, CBE 1979; Professor of Diagnostic Radiology, University of London, Royal Postgraduate Medical School, 1961–83, now Emeritus; *b* 1 Feb. 1918; *s* of Rudolf Steiner and Clary (*née* Nordlinger); *m* 1945, Gertrude Margaret Konirsch; two *d. Educ:* University of Vienna; University College, Dublin. Dep. Director, Dept of Radiology, Hammersmith Hosp.; Lecturer Diagnostic Radiology, Postgraduate Med. School of London, 1950, Sen. Lecturer, 1955, Director, 1955–. Vice-Chm., Nat. Radiological Protection Bd, 1972–83. Past Consultant Adviser in Radiology to DHSS; Past Civil Consultant in Radiology to Med. Dir-Gen., Navy. Warden of Fellowship, Faculty of Radiologists. Former Mem. Council, RCS; Past Pres., British Inst. Radiology; Pres., RCR, 1977–80. Hon. Fellow: Amer. Coll. of Radiology; Australian Coll. of Radiology; Faculty of Radiologists, RCSI. Hon. Member: Radiological Soc. of Finland; Radiological Soc. of N America; Amer. Roentgen Ray Soc.; Germany Roentgen Soc. Barclay Medal British Inst. of Radiology; Gold Medal, RCR, 1986. Former Editor, British Jl of Radiology. *Publications:* Clinical Disorders of the Pulmonary Circulation, 1960; Recent Advances of Radiology, vols 4–8, 1979–85; contrib. to British Journal of Radiology, Clinical Radiology, British Heart Jl, Lancet, BMJ, etc. *Address:* 12 Stonehill Road, East Sheen, SW14 8RW. *T:* 081–876 4038. *Club:* Hurlingham.

STEINFELD, Alan Geoffrey; QC 1987; *b* 13 July 1946; *s* of Henry Chaim Steinfeld and Deborah Steinfeld; *m* 1976, Josephine Nicole (*née* Gros); two *s. Educ:* City of London Sch.; Downing Coll., Cambridge (BA Hons, LLB). Arnold McNair Schol. in Internat. Law, 1967; Whewell Schol. in Internat. Law, 1968. Called to the Bar, Lincoln's Inn, 1968; commenced pupillage at the Bar, 1968, practice at the Bar, 1969. *Recreations:* tennis, skiing, opera. *Address:* (home) 29 Boundary Road, NW8 0JE. *T:* 071–624 8995; (chambers) 24 Old Buildings, Lincoln's Inn, WC2A 3UJ. *T:* 071–404 0946. *Clubs:* Royal Automobile; Cumberland Lawn Tennis.

STELL, Prof. Philip Michael, FRCS, FRCSE; Professor of Oto-rhino-laryngology, University of Liverpool, since 1979; *b* 14 Aug. 1934; *s* of Frank Law Stell and Ada Stell; *m* 1959, Shirley Kathleen Mills; four *s* one *d. Educ:* Archbishop Holgate's Grammar Sch., York; Edinburgh Univ. (MB, ChB 1958). ChM Liverpool, 1976. FRCS 1966; FRCSE 1962. Jun. hosp. appts, Edinburgh and Liverpool, 1958–63; Fellow, Washington Univ., St Louis, USA, 1964–65; Sen. Lectr, Univ. of Liverpool, 1965–78. Hunterian Prof., RCS, 1976. President: Otorhinolaryngological Res. Soc., 1983–86; Assoc. of Head and Neck Oncologists of GB, 1986–89; Liverpool Med. Inst., 1986–87 and 1987–88. Leegaard Lecture, Norwegian ENT Soc., 1989; Sect. of Laryngology, RSM, 1990–91. Mem., Deutsche Akademie der Naturforscher Leopoldina, 1990. Yearsley Gold Medal, 1980; Harrison Prize, RSM, 1982; Semon Medal, Univ. of London, 1986; George Davey Meml Prize, Univ. of London, 1987. *Publications:* approx. 20 books and 80 articles in learned jls on surgery for cancer of head and neck. *Recreations:* squash, rowing, gardening. *Address:* 7 Partridge Road, Blundellsands, Liverpool L23 6UH. *T:* 051–924 2725.

STEMBRIDGE, David Harry, QC 1990; a Recorder of the Crown Court, since 1977; *b* 23 Dec. 1932; *s* of Percy G. Stembridge and Emily W. Stembridge; *m* 1956, Therese C. Furer; three *s* one *d. Educ:* St Chad's Cathedral Choir Sch., Lichfield; Bromsgrove Sch.; Birmingham Univ. (LLB Hons). Called to the Bar, Gray's Inn, 1955; practising barrister, 1956–. *Recreations:* organ playing, sailing. *Club:* Bar Yacht.

STENHAM, Anthony William Paul, (Cob), FCA; Chairman, Arjo Wiggins Appleton plc (formerly Wiggins Teape Appleton), since 1990; *b* 28 Jan. 1932; *s* of Bernard Basil Stenham and Annie Josephine (*née* Naylor); *m* 1st, 1966, Hon. Sheila Marion Poole (marr. diss.); 2nd, 1983, Anne Martha Mary O'Rawe; two *d. Educ:* Eton Coll.; Trinity Coll., Cambridge. MA. Qualified Accountant FCA 1958. Mem., Inner Temple, 1955. Price Waterhouse, 1955–61; Philip Hill Higginson Erlanger, 1962–64; William Baird & Co., 1964–69: Finance Dir and Jt Man. Dir; Unilever, 1969–86: Financial Dir, 1970–86, Corporate Develt Dir, 1984–86, Unilever PLC and Unilever NV; Chm., Unilever United States Inc., 1978–79; a Man. Dir, Bankers Trust Co. of NY, 1986–90 (Non-Exec. Chm., Bankers Trust UK and Europe). Director: Equity Capital for Industry, 1976–81; Capital Radio, 1982–; Virgin Gp, 1986–89; Rank Organisation, 1987–; VSEL Consortium, 1987– (Dep. Chm.); Colonial Mutual Life Assurance Society Ltd, 1987–; Rothmans Internat., 1988–; Unigate, 1989–; STC, 1990–91; Arjomari Prioux; Pechelbronn, 1991–. Institute of Contemporary Arts: Chm. Council, 1977–87; Chm., Adv. Bd, 1987–89; Mem. Council, Architectural Assoc., 1982–84; Royal Coll. of Art: Mem. Court, 1978–; Mem. Council, 1978–81; Chm. Council and Pro-Provost, 1979–81; Hon. Fellow, 1980. Governor: Museum of London, 1986–; Theatres Trust, 1989–. FRSA. *Recreations:* cinema, opera, painting. *Address:* 4 The Grove, Highgate, N6 6JU. *T:* 081–340 2266; 071–839 7505. *Clubs:* Turf, White's.

STENHOUSE, John Godwyn, TD with bar; FCIB; Chairman, Stenhouse Holdings plc, 1978–80 (Director, 1947–84); retired; *b* 16 Nov. 1908; *s* of Alexander Rennie Stenhouse and Hughina Cowan Stenhouse; *m* 1st, 1936, Margaret Constance Thornton (*d* 1965); two *d*; 2nd, 1967, Jean Ann Bennie (*née* Finlayson); one step *s. Educ:* Warriston Sch., Moffat; Kelvinside Acad., Glasgow. With an insurance co., 1927; joined A. R. Stenhouse & Partners, Ltd, Insurance Brokers (later Stenhouse Holdings Ltd), 1931. *Recreations:* sailing, mechanical engineering. *Address:* 2 St Germains, Bearsden, Glasgow G61 2RS. *T:* 041–942 0151. *Club:* Royal Scottish Automobile (Glasgow).

STENHOUSE, Sir Nicol, Kt 1962; *b* 14 Feb. 1911; 2nd *s* of late John Stenhouse, Shanghai, China, and Tring, Hertfordshire; *m* 1951, Barbara Heath Wilson (*d* 1991); two *s* one *d. Educ:* Repton. Joined Andrew Yule & Co. Ltd, Calcutta, India, 1937; Managing Director, 1953–59; Chairman and Senior Managing Director, 1959–62; President: Bengal Chamber of Commerce and Industry, Calcutta, 1961–62; Associated Chambers of Commerce of India, Calcutta, 1961–62. *Recreation:* gardening. *Address:* 3 St Mary's Court, Sixpenny Handley, near Salisbury, Wilts SP5 5PH.

STENING, Sir George (Grafton Lees), Kt 1968; ED; Hon. Consultant Gynæcological Surgeon, Royal Prince Alfred Hosp., Sydney; Emeritus Consultant, St Luke's Hospital, Sydney; *b* 16 Feb. 1904; *s* of George Smith Stening and Muriel Grafton Lees; *m* 1935, Kathleen Mary Packer, DStJ; one *s* one *d. Educ:* Sydney High Sch.; Univ. of Sydney. MB, BS (Syd.) 1927 (Hons Cl. II); FRCS (Ed.) 1931; FRACS 1935; FRCOG 1947; FRACOG, 1980. Carnegie Trav. Fellow, 1948. Served War of 1939–45: Middle East, New Guinea, Australia; OC, 3rd Aust. Surgical Team, Libyan Desert, 1941; CO, 2/11 Aust. Gen. Hosp., 1941–44; CO, 113 Aust. Gen. Hosp., 1945. Hon. Col, RAAMC. GCStJ 1971; Chancellor, Order of St John, in Australia, 1961–82. Past Pres., Sen. Golfers' Soc. of Aust. *Publication:* A Text Book of Gynæcology (co-author), 1948. *Recreations:* golf, yachting. *Address:* 2/22 Wolseley Road, Point Piper, NSW 2027, Australia. *Clubs:* Royal Sydney Golf (Sydney); Australian Jockey.

STEPHEN, David; *see* Stephen, J. D.

STEPHEN, Derek Ronald James, CB 1975; Deputy Under-Secretary of State, Ministry of Defence, 1973–82; *b* 22 June 1922; *s* of late Ronald James Stephen; *m* 1948, Gwendolen Margaret, *d* of late William James Heasman, CBE; two *s* one *d* (and one *s* decd). *Educ:* Bec Sch.; Christ's Coll., Cambridge (1st cl. Hons Classics). Served War, 1941–45; 11th Hussars and HQ 7th Armoured Div., N Africa, Italy, NW Europe; Captain. Asst Principal, War Office, 1946; Asst Private Sec. to Sec. of State for War, 1949–50; Principal, 1951; Private Sec. to Sec. of Cabinet, 1958–60; Asst Sec., WO (later MoD), 1960; IDC 1966; HM Treasury, 1968; Civil Service Dept (on its formation), 1968; Under-Sec., 1969–71; Asst Under-Sec. of State, MoD, 1972–73; Dep. Under-Sec. of State (Navy), MoD, and Mem. Admiralty Bd, 1973–78; Dep. Under-Sec. of State (Army), MoD, and Mem., Army Bd, 1978–82; Asst Sec., Royal Hosp., Chelsea, 1982–88. Army Benevolent Fund: Member: Grants Cttee, 1984–; Finance Cttee, 1988–; Mem. Council, Royal Cambridge Home for Soldiers' Widows, 1987–. Trustee, Tank Museum, 1982–. Gov., Royal Sch., Hampstead, 1984–. *Recreations:* music, golf. *Club:* Naval and Military.

STEPHEN, Dr (George) Martin; Headmaster, Perse School for Boys, Cambridge, since 1987; *b* 18 July 1949; *s* of Sir Andrew Stephen, MB, ChB and Lady Stephen (*née* Frances Barker); *m* 1971, Jennifer Elaine Fisher; three *s. Educ:* Uppingham Sch., Univ. of Leeds (BA); Univ. of Sheffield (Dip Ed, Dist., PhD). Child supervisor, Leeds and Oxford Remand Homes, 1966–67; Teacher of English, Uppingham, 1971–72, Haileybury, 1972–83 (and Housemaster); Second Master, Sedbergh, 1983–87. Mem., ESRC. Associate Mem., Combination Room, GCCC. *Publications:* British Warship Designs since 1906, 1984; An Introductory Guide to English Literature, 1984; Studying Shakespeare, 1984; English Literature, 1986, 2nd edn, 1991; (ed) Never Such Innocence, 1988; Sea Battles in Close Up, 1988; The Fighting Admirals, 1990; contrib. York Notes series; articles and reviews for various jls. *Recreations:* writing, directing plays, pen and ink drawing, field and water sports, music. *Address:* 80 Glebe Road, Cambridge CB1 4SZ. *T:* Cambridge (0223) 247964. *Club:* East India (Hon. Mem.).

STEPHEN, Harbourne Mackay, CBE 1985; DSO 1941; DFC and bar 1940; AE 1943; Director, Daily Telegraph, since 1963 (non-executive, since 1986); *b* 18 April 1916; *s* of Thomas Milne Stephen, JP, and Kathleen Vincent Park; *m* 1947, Sybil Erica Palmer; two *d. Educ:* Shrewsbury. Staff of Allied Newspapers, London, 1931; Evening Standard, 1936–39. RAFVR, 1937; served RAF, 1939–45 (destroyed numerous enemy aircraft): 605 and 74 Sqdns, 1939–40; at MAP, 1941, then joined 130 Sqdn and comd 234 Sqdn; served Far East, 1942–45; Wing Comdr (Flying) Dum Dum; RAF Jessore, Bengal; comd 166 Fighter Wing; then to Fighter Ops, 224 Gp Arakan; Ops "A" Air Comd SEA, 1945. Was OC 602 City of Glasgow (F) Sqdn RAuxAF, 1950–52. Returned to Beaverbrook Newspapers, Oct. 1945; worked on Scottish Daily Express, Scottish Sunday Express, and Evening Citizen in Glasgow, 1945–55; General Manager, Sunday Express, 1958; General Manager, Sunday Graphic, 1960, and thereafter General Manager, Thomson Papers, London; Man. Dir, Daily Telegraph and Sunday Telegraph, 1963–86; retired, 1986. Dir, Internat. Newspaper Colour Assoc., Darmstadt, 1964–69. Council Mem., RSPB, 1972–73. *Recreations:* normal, occasionally. *Address:* Donnington Fields, Newbury, Berks RG16 9BA. *T:* Newbury (0635) 40105. *Clubs:* Naval and Military, Royal Air Force.

STEPHEN, Henrietta Hamilton, (Rita Stephen), MBE 1973; National Officer, GMB, since 1989; *b* 9 Dec. 1925; *d* of late James Pithie Stephen, engine driver, Montrose and late Mary Hamilton Morton, South Queensferry. *Educ:* Wolseley Street and King's Park Elem. Schs, Glasgow; Queen's Park Sen. Secondary, Glasgow; Glasgow Univ. (extra-mural); LSE (TUC Schol.). McGill Univ. and Canada/US Travel, 1958–59. Law office junior, 1941; Clerk, Labour Exchange (Mem. MLSA), 1941–42; Post Office Telephonist, 1942–60; Officer and delegate, Union of Post Office Workers, Glasgow Br., 1942–60; Member: UPW Parly Panel, 1957; Glasgow City Labour Party; Cathcart Ward Labour Party; Election Agent (Municipal), 1955–60; London and Home Counties Area Organiser, CAWU, 1960–65; Nat. Sec., CAWU, subseq. APEX, 1965–89. Negotiator in public and private sectors of industry, 1960–; Editor, The Clerk, 1965–71; Union Educn Officer, 1965–72; Delegate: TUC; Labour Party Annual Confs; Member: EDC for Food and Drink Manufacturing, 1976–; Food Standards Cttee, 1968–80; Industrial Soc. Council and Exec., 1968–; Mary Macarthur Educnl Trust, 1965–; Distributive Industry Trng Bd, 1968–73; Monopolies and Mergers Commn, 1973–83; British Wool Marketing Bd, 1973–; Duke of Edinburgh's Commonwealth Study Conf., UK Trust; LSE Court, 1976–. Mem., TUC Women's Adv. Cttee, 1983; Chair, Nat. Jt Cttee of Working Women's Organisations, 1983–84; Jt Sec., British Coal Nat. Jt Council (Clerical), 1988–. *Publications:* (jtly) Training Shop Stewards, 1968; (with Roy Moore) Statistics for Negotiators, 1973; contrib. Clerk, Industrial Soc. Jl, Target, etc. *Recreations:* food, walking, conversation, theatre, reading. *Address:* 3 Pond Road, SE3. *T:* 081–852 7797, 081–947 3131.

STEPHEN, (John) David; Member of Management Board, since 1985, and Director of Corporate Relations, since 1989, Commonwealth Development Corporation; *b* 3 April 1942; *s* of late John Stephen and of Anne Eileen Stephen; *m* 1968, Susan Dorothy (*née* Harris); three *s* one *d. Educ:* Denbigh Road Primary Sch., Luton; Luton Grammar Sch.; King's Coll., Cambridge (BA Mod. Langs, 1964); Univ. of San Marcos, Lima, Peru; Univ. of Essex (MA Govt, 1968). Educn Officer, CRC, 1969–70; with Runnymede Trust, 1970–75 (Dir, 1973–75); Latin American Regional Rep., Internat. Univ. Exchange Fund, 1975–77; Special Adviser to Sec. of State for Foreign and Commonwealth Affairs, 1977–79; Editor, International Affairs, 1979–83; Dir, UK Immigrants Advisory Service, 1983–84; Head of External Relations, Commonwealth Develt Corp., 1985–89. Member: Bd of Trustees, Action Aid, 1981–; Latin America and Caribbean Cttee, Christian Aid, 1980–84. Broadcaster in English, French and Spanish, BBC Ext. Services, 1980–. Contested (SDP-Liberal Alliance), N Luton, 1983, 1987. *Publications:* The San of the Kalahari, 1982; articles in New Society, The Times and other jls. *Recreations:* the family, music, the countryside. *Address:* 123 Sundon Road, Harlington, Bedfordshire LU5 6LW. *T:* Toddington (05255) 4799.

STEPHEN, John Low, ChM (Aberdeen), FRCSE, FRCS; Surgeon, St Mary's Hospital, W2, since 1958; Senior Surgeon, St Mary's Hospital, W9, 1948–77, retired; *b* 13 May 1912; 2nd *s* of late Dr J. H. Stephen, Aberdeen; *m* 1938, Mary Milne, MA, BSc; one *s* one *d. Educ:* Aberdeen Grammar School; Aberdeen and Edinburgh Universities. MA 1931, MB 1935, Aberd.; FRCSEd, 1937; ChM Aberd., 1945; FRCS (ad eundem), 1968. Various university and hospital appointments in Scotland and England. Associate Teacher in Surgery, St Mary's Hosp. Med. School, 1950–. FRSocMed. *Publications:* chapters in Operative Surgery (Smith and Rob); various articles on abdominal surgery in Brit. Jl of Surgery. *Recreations:* golf, motoring. *Address:* Luibeg, Groombridge, Tunbridge Wells TN3 9PR.

STEPHEN, His Honour Lessel Bruce; a Circuit Judge, 1972–89; *b* 15 Feb. 1920; *s* of L. P. Stephen, FRCS(E); *m* 1949, Brenda (*née* Tinkler). *Educ:* Marlborough; Sydney Sussex Coll., Cambridge (BA). Called to the Bar, Inner Temple, 1948; subsequently practised NE Circuit; Recorder, 1972. *Recreations:* golf, wine. *Address:* 2 Harcourt Buildings, Temple, EC4Y 9DB. *T:* 071–353 2548.

STEPHEN, Martin; *see* Stephen, G. M.

STEPHEN, Rt. Hon. Sir Ninian (Martin), AK 1982; GCMG 1982; GCVO 1982; KBE 1972; PC 1979; Australian Ambassador for the Environment, since 1989; *b* 15 June 1923; *o s* of late Frederick Stephen and Barbara Stephen (*née* Cruickshank); *m* 1949, Valery Mary, *d* of late A. Q. Sinclair and of Mrs G. M. Sinclair; five *d*. *Educ:* George Watson's Sch., Edinburgh; Edinburgh Acad.; St Paul's Sch., London; Chillon Coll., Switzerland; Scotch Coll., Melbourne; Melbourne Univ. (LLB). Served War, HM Forces (Australian Army), 1941–46. Admitted as Barrister and Solicitor, in State of Victoria, 1949; signed Roll of Victorian Bar, 1951; QC 1966. Appointed Judge of Supreme Court of Victoria, 1970; Justice of High Court of Australia, 1972–82; Gov.-Gen. of Australia, 1982–89. Hon. Bencher Gray's Inn, 1981. Chm. , Nat. Liby of Aust., 1989–. Hon. Liveryman, Clothworkers' Co., 1991. Hon. LLD: Sydney, 1984; Melbourne, 1985; Griffith, 1988. KStJ 1982. *Address:* Flat 12/1, 193 Domain Road, South Yarra, Vic 3141, Australia.

STEPHEN, Rita; *see* Stephen, H. H.

STEPHENS, Air Commandant Dame Anne, DBE 1961 (MBE 1946); Hon. ADC to the Queen, 1960–63; Director, Women's Royal Air Force, 1960–63; *b* 4 Nov. 1912; *d* of late General Sir Reginald Byng Stephens, KCB, CMG and late Lady Stephens. *Educ:* privately. Joined WAAF, 1939; served in UK, Belgium and Germany, 1939–45. Command WRAF Depot, Hawkinge, 1950–52; promoted Group Officer, 1951; Inspector WRAF, 1952–54; Deputy Director, 1954–57; Staff Officer, HQ 2nd TAF, 1957–59; promoted Air Commandant, 1960. *Address:* The Forge, Sibford Ferris, Banbury, Oxfordshire. *T:* Swalcliffe (029578) 452.

STEPHENS, Anthony William, CB 1989; CMG 1976; Deputy Under Secretary of State, Northern Ireland Office, 1985–90; *b* 9 Jan. 1930; *s* of late Donald Martyn Stephens and Norah Stephens (*née* Smith-Cleburne); *m* 1954, Mytyl Joy, *d* of late William Gay Burdett; four *d*. *Educ:* Bradfield Coll.; Bristol Univ. (LLB); Corpus Christi Coll., Cambridge. RM (commnd), 1948–50. Colonial Administrative Service, 1953; District Officer, Kenya, 1954–63; Home Civil Service, 1964; Principal, MoD, 1964–70; Asst Private Sec. to successive Secretaries of State for Defence, 1970–71; Asst Sec., 1971; Chief Officer, Sovereign Base Areas, Cyprus, 1974–76; Under Sec., NI Office, 1976–79; Asst Under Sec. of State, General Staff, 1979–83, Ordnance, 1983–84, MoD. *Recreations:* travel and the outdoor life, music, theatre. *Club:* Commonwealth Trust.

STEPHENS, Prof. Arthur Veryan, MA Cantab; CEng; FRAeS; Professor of Aeronautical Engineering, The Queen's University, Belfast, 1956–73, now Emeritus Professor; *b* 9 July 1908; *s* of Arthur John Stephens and Mildred, *d* of Robert Fowler Sturge; *m* 1st, 1938, Jane Dows, *d* of F. W. Lester; three *s* one *d*; 2nd, 1981, Marjorie Phyllis Irene Sprince (*d* 1986); 3rd, 1987, Sheila Joy Franglen. *Educ:* Clifton Coll.; St John's Coll., Cambridge (Mechanical Sciences Tripos, John Bernard Seely Prize). Scientific Officer, Royal Aircraft Establishment, 1930–34; Fellow of St John's College, Cambridge, 1934–39; Lawrence Hargrave Professor of Aeronautics, 1939–56, Dean of the Faculty of Engineering, 1947–56, University of Sydney, NSW. Edward Busk Meml Prize of RAeS, 1934; Member: Australian Flying Personnel Research Cttee, 1940–45; Australian Council for Aeronautics, 1941–46; Chairman: Aeronautical Research Consultative Cttee, 1947–54; Australian Aeronautical Research Cttee, 1954–56; Member, Australian Defence Research and Development Policy Cttee, 1953–56; Chairman, Australian Division of Royal Aeronautical Society, 1947–56. Dean of Faculty of Applied Science and Technology, 1961–64; Vice-President (Buildings), 1964–67. *Publications:* numerous papers on applied aerodynamics published by Aeronautical Research Council, Australian Dept of Supply and in Jl of RAeS. *Recreations:* golf, real tennis, antiquarian horology. *Address:* 2 St Mary's Gardens, Chichester, W Sussex PO19 1NW. *Club:* Athenæum.

STEPHENS, Cedric John; Chairman, Exford (Highcliffe) Ltd, since 1987; *b* 13 Feb. 1921; *s* of late Col J. E. Stephens, Truro, Cornwall. *Educ:* London University (BSc (Eng.) Hons); CEng, FRAeS, FIEE. Entered Scientific Civil Service, 1951; Dir, Space Activities, Min. of Aviation, 1961; Mem. Coun., European Launcher Development Organisation, Paris, 1962; Chm. Technical Cttee, European Coun. on Satellite Communications, 1964; Imperial Defence Coll., 1965; Director, Signals Research and Develt Estabt, Min. of Technology, 1966–67; Chief Scientific Adviser, Home Office, 1968; Dir-Gen. of Research and Chief Scientist, Home Office, 1969–73 (Mem., Defence Scientific Adv. Council, 1970–72). Called to Bar, Gray's Inn, 1971. Mem., Electronics Div. Bd, IEE, 1972. *Recreation:* viola playing. *Address:* 6 Newlyn Road, Welling, Kent DA16 3LH. *Club:* Athenæum.

STEPHENS, Christopher Wilson T.; *see* Stephens, Wilson T.

STEPHENS, Maj.-Gen. Keith Fielding, CB 1970; OBE 1957; Medical Officer, Department of Health and Social Security, 1970–85, retired; *b* Taplow, Bucks, 28 July 1910; *s* of late Edgar Percy and Mary Louise Stephens; *m* 1937, Margaret Ann, *d* of late Alexander MacGregor; two *s*. *Educ:* Eastbourne College; St Bartholomew's Hospital. MB, BS London 1934; FFARCS 1953; DA 1945. Commissioned into RAMC, 1937; served in India, 1937–43; France and Germany, 1944–46; Cyprus, 1954–56; Adviser in Anæsthetics to the Army, 1949–53 and 1957–66; Commandant and Director of Studies, Royal Army Medical College, 1966–68; DDMS, Southern Command, 1968–70, retired. FRSocMed (Pres., Sect. of Anæsthetics, 1970–71); Hon. Member, Assoc. of Anæsthetists of Gt Brit. and Ireland. Fellow, Med. Soc. of London. Hon. FFARCS (Ireland), 1970; QHS, 1964–70. Hon. Col, 221 (Surrey) Field Ambulance RAMC(V), 1972–76. Mitchiner Medal, 1962. CStJ 1967. *Publications:* numerous articles in medical journals. *Address:* 3 Carnegie Place, Parkside, Wimbledon, SW19. *T:* 081–946 0911. *Club:* Naval and Military.

STEPHENS, Prof. Kenneth Gilbert, CEng, FIEE; CPhys, FInstP; Professor of Electronic and Electrical Engineering, since 1978, and Dean of the Faculty of Engineering, since 1991, University of Surrey; *b* 3 May 1931; *s* of George Harry Stephens and Christiana Stephens; *m* 1980, Elizabeth Carolynn (*née* Jones); one *s* one *d*, and two step *s*. *Educ:* Bablake Sch., Coventry; Birmingham Univ. (BSc, PhD). Nuclear Reactor Res. Physicist, AEI Ltd, Aldermaston, 1955–62; Sen. Res. Engr, Pye Ltd, Cambridge, 1963–66; University of Surrey: Lectr 1966; Reader 1967; Head, Dept of Electronic and Electrical Engrg, 1983–91. *Publications:* (ed jtly) Low Energy Ion Beams (conf. procs), 1978, 1980; (ed jtly) Ion Implantation Technology (conf. procs), 1991; articles on ion beam effects on semiconductors in learned jls. *Recreations:* reading, music, gardening, watching sport, especially cricket. *Address:* 10 Brockway Close, Merrow, Guildford, Surrey GU1 2LW. *T:* Guildford (0483) 575087. *Clubs:* MCC; Blackheath Cricket (Chm.).

STEPHENS, Malcolm George, CB 1991; Chief Executive, Export Credits Guarantee Department, since 1987; *b* 14 July 1937; *s* of Frank Ernest Stephens and Janet (*née* McQueen); *m* 1975, Lynette Marie Caffery, Brisbane, Australia. *Educ:* St Michael's and All Angels; Shooter's Hill Grammar Sch.; St John's Coll., Oxford (Casberd Scholar; BA 1st Cl. Hons PPE). National Service, RAOC, 1956–58. CRO, 1953; British High Commission: Ghana, 1959–62; Kenya, 1963–65; Export Credits Guarantee Dept, 1965–82: Principal, 1970; seconded to Civil Service Coll., 1971–72; Asst Sec., 1973; Estab. Officer, 1977; Under Sec., 1978; Head of Proj. Gp B, 1978–79; Principal Finance Officer, 1979–82; Internat. Finance Dir, Barclays Bank Internat. Ltd, 1982; Dir, Barclays Export Services, 1983–87; Export Finance Dir, Barclays Bank PLC, 1985–87. Member: Overseas Projects Bd, 1985; BOTB, 1987; Pres., Internat. Union of Credit and Investment Insurers (Berne Union), 1989–. FCIB (FIB 1984); FIEx 1987; MICM 1990. *Recreations:* gardening, reading. *Address:* 111 Woolwich Road, Bexleyheath, Kent DA7 4LP. *T:* 081–303 6782. *Club:* Travellers'.

STEPHENS, Martin; *see* Stephens, S. M.

STEPHENS, Peter Norman Stuart; Director, News Group Newspapers, 1978–87, Editorial Director, 1981–87; *b* 19 Dec. 1927; *s* of J. G. Stephens; *m* 1950, Constance Mary Ratheram; two *s* one *d*. *Educ:* Mundella Grammar Sch., Nottingham. Newark Advertiser, 1945–48; Northern Echo, 1948–50; Daily Dispatch, 1950–55; Daily Mirror, Manchester, 1955–57; Asst Editor, Newcastle Journal, 1957–60; Asst Editor, Evening Chronicle, Newcastle, 1960–62, Editor 1962–66; Editor, Newcastle Journal, 1966–70; Asst Editor, The Sun, 1970–72, Dep. Editor 1972; Associate Editor, News of the World, 1973, Editor, 1974–75; Associate Editor, The Sun, 1975–81. *Recreation:* supporting Derby County Football Club. *Address:* The Friary, Newark on Trent, Notts.

STEPHENS, Major Robert, CVO 1964; ERD; Administrative Officer, Hillsborough Castle (formerly Government House), 1973–78; retired; *b* 1909; *s* of late John Samuel Stephens; *m* 1939, Kathleen, *d* of late R. I. Trelford, Helen's Bay, Belfast. *Educ:* Campbell Coll., Belfast. Ulster Bank, 1929–39. Served War of 1939–45: RA, Middle East, 1941–45. Commercial Manager, Newforge Ltd, 1946–55; Private Secretary to the Governor of Northern Ireland, 1955–73; Comptroller to: Lord Wakehurst, 1955–64; Lord Erskine of Rerrick, 1964–68; Lord Grey of Naunton, 1968–73. Hon. Sec., SSAFA (NI), 1979. OStJ 1980. *Recreation:* golf. *Address:* 13 Ballynahinch Street, Hillsborough, Co. Down, Northern Ireland. *T:* Hillsborough (0846) 682550.

STEPHENS, Robert; actor; *b* 14 July 1931; *s* of Rueben Stephens and Gladys (*née* Deverell); *m* Tarn Bassett; one *d*; *m* 1967, Maggie Smith, (*see* Dame Maggie Smith) (marr. diss. 1975); two *s*. *Educ:* Bradford Civic Theatre School. Started with Caryl Jenner Mobile Theatre Co.; Mem. English Stage Co., Royal Court, 1956. *Stage:* The Crucible, Don Juan, The Death of Satan, Cards of Identity, The Good Woman of Setzuan and The Country Wife (also at Adelphi, 1957); The Apollo de Bellac, Yes-and After, The Making of Moo, How Can We Save Father?, The Waters of Babylon, Royal Court, 1957; The Entertainer, Palace, 1957; Epitaph for George Dillon, Royal Court, Comedy, Golden (NY), 1958 and Henry Miller, 1959; Look After Lulu (also at New) and The Kitchen (also 1961), Royal Court, 1959; The Wrong Side of the Park, Cambridge, 1960; The Sponge Room, Squat Betty, Royal Court, 1962; Chichester and Edinburgh Festival, 1963; Design for Living (Los Angeles), 1971; Private Lives, Queen's, 1972; The Seagull, Chichester, 1973; Apropos The Falling Sleet (dir.), Open Space, 1973; Ghosts, The Seagull, Hamlet, Greenwich, 1974; Sherlock Holmes, NY and Canada, 1975; Murderer, Garrick, 1975; Zoo Story, 1975, Othello, 1976, Open Air, Regent's Park; Pygmalion, Los Angeles, 1979; Othello, Cape Town, SA, 1982; WCPC, Half Moon, 1982; Light Up the Sky, Old Vic, 1985; Henry IV, parts I and II, and Julius Caesar, RSC, 1991; *National Theatre Company:* Hamlet, St Joan, The Recruiting Officer, 1963; Andorra, Play, The Royal Hunt of the Sun (also Chichester Fest.), Hay Fever, 1964; Much Ado About Nothing, Armstrong's Last Goodnight, Trelawny of the Wells (also Chichester Fest.), 1965; A Bond Honoured, Black Comedy, 1966; The Dance of Death, The Three Sisters (at Los Angeles, 1968), As You Like It, Tartuffe, 1967; Most Unwarrantable Intrusion (also dir.), Home and Beauty, 1968; Macrune's Guevara (also co-dir), 1969; The Beaux' Stratagem (also Los Angeles), Hedda Gabler, 1970; The Cherry Orchard, Brand, The Double Dealer, Has "Washington" Legs?, 1978; A Midsummer Night's Dream, Inner Voices, Cinderella, 1983. *Films:* A Taste of Honey, 1961; The Small World of Sammy Lee, 1962; Cleopatra, 1963; The Prime of Miss Jean Brodie, 1967; The Private Life of Sherlock Holmes, 1969; Travels with my Aunt, 1972; The Asphyx, 1972; Luther, 1972; QBVII, 1973; Alexander the Great, 1980; Ill Fares The Land, 1982; High Seasons, 1986; Comrades, 1987; Empire of the Sun, 1987; The Fruit Machine, 1988; Henry V, 1989. *Television* includes: Vienna 1900 (6 part series), 1973; Tribute to J. B. Priestley, 1974; Kean, 1978; Voyage of Charles Darwin, 1978; Office Story, 1978; Friends in Space, 1979; Suez, 1979; The Executioner, 1980; Adelaide Bartlett (series), 1980; Winter's Tale, 1980; The Double Dealer, 1980; The Trial of Madame Famay, 1980; Holocaust (USA), 1980; Eden End, 1981; The Year of the French (RTE), 1981; Anyone for Denis?, 1982; Tales Out of School, 1982; Box of Delights, 1984; Puccini, 1984; By the Sword Divided (series), 1984; Hells Bells (series), 1985; War and Remembrance, (film series), 1986; Fortunes of War (series), 1986; Lizzie's Pictures (series), 1986; Shostokovich, 1987. *Radio* plays include: The Light Shines in the Darkness (BBC), 1985; Timon of Athens (BBC), 1989. Variety Club Award for stage actor, 1965. *Recreations:* cooking, gymnastics, swimming. *Address:* c/o Film Rights Ltd, 4 New Burlington Place, Regent Street, W1X 2AS. *T:* 071–437 7151.

STEPHENS, (Stephen) Martin; QC 1982; **His Honour Judge Stephens;** a Circuit Judge, since 1986; *b* 26 June 1939; *s* of late Abraham Stephens and of Freda Stephens, Swansea; *m* 1965, Patricia Alison, *d* of late Joseph and of Anne Morris, Mapperley, Nottingham; one *s* one *d* (and one *s* decd). *Educ:* Swansea Grammar Sch.; Wadham Coll., Oxford (MA). Called to the Bar, Middle Temple, 1963; Wales and Chester Circuit; a Recorder, 1979–86. *Recreations:* cricket, theatre. *Address:* c/o The Law Courts, Glebeland Place, Merthyr Tydfil, Mid Glam CF47 8BH.

STEPHENS, William Henry, CB 1961; DSc, MSc, CEng, FRAeS; FBIS; retired; Non-Executive Director, General Technology Systems Ltd, 1987–89 (Senior Executive Director, 1973–87); *b* Kilkenny, Ireland, 18 March 1913; *s* of William Henry Stephens, MBE, and Helena Read Stephens (*née* Cantley); *m* 1938, Elizabeth Margaret Brown, BSc; one *s* one *d*. *Educ:* Methodist College and Queen's University, Belfast. Air Ministry, Royal Aircraft Establishment (Aerodynamic Research), 1935–38; War Office, Woolwich (Rocket Research), 1938–39; Ministry of Aircraft Prod., London (Air Defence Research), 1939–44; Asst Scientific Attaché and Asst Director, UK Scientific Mission, British Commonwealth Scientific Office, Washington, USA, 1944–47; Min. of Supply, RAE, Head of Guided Weapons Dept and later Dep. Director, 1947–58; Dir-Gen. Ballistic Missiles, Ministry of Aviation, 1959–62; Technical Dir, European Space Launcher Develt Organisation, Paris, 1962–69; Minister, Defence R&D, British Embassy, Washington, 1969–72; Special Advr (Internat. Affairs), Controllerate of Res., MoD, 1972–73. Mem., Internat. Acad. of Astronautics; Fellow, British Interplanetary Soc. *Publications:* contrib. to Jl Royal Aeronautical Soc.; Proc. Brit. Assoc.; Proc. Internat. Congress of Aeronautical Sciences. *Recreations:* travel, music, art, theatre. *Address:* Rosebrook House, Oriel Hill, Camberley, Surrey. *Club:* Athenæum.

STEPHENS, Wilson (Treeve); Editor of The Field, 1950–77, Consultant 1987–90; *b* 2 June 1912; *s* of Rev. Arthur Treeve Stephens, Shepton Beauchamp, Somerset, and Margaret Wilson; *m* 1st, 1934, Nina, *d* of Arthur Frederick Curzon, Derby; two *d*; 2nd, 1960, Marygold Anne, *o d* of Major-General G. O. Crawford, *qv*; two *d*. *Educ:* Christ's

Hosp. Formerly on editorial staffs of several provincial newspapers, and of The Daily Express. Served War of 1939–45, Royal Artillery. *Publications:* The Guinness Guide to Field Sports, 1979; Gundog Sense and Sensibility, 1982; Pigeon Racing, 1983; A Year Observed, 1984; Rivers of Britain (series) 1985–; contribs to numerous publications. *Recreations:* fly-fishing, shooting. *Address:* c/o Blake, Friedmann, 37–41 Gower Street, WC1E 6HH.

STEPHENSON, Ashley; *see* Stephenson, R. A. S.

STEPHENSON, Donald, CBE 1957 (OBE 1943); Controller, Overseas and Foreign Relations, BBC, 1966–71; *b* 18 May 1909; *yr s* of late J. V. G. Stephenson; *m* 1st, 1940, Alison (*d* 1965), *yr d* of late Wynn ap H. Thomas, OBE, LLB; three *d* (one *s* decd); 2nd, 1982, Francesca, *yr d* of late Captain Charles Francis Ward, RHA. *Educ:* Denstone College (Scholar); Paris; Baghdad. Banking business, 1925–31; permanent commission, RAF, 1932; Flt Lt, 1936; served France and Middle East, 1935–37; language specialist (interpreter, French and Arabic); Special Duty List, 1938; Arabic Editor, BBC, 1939; Director, BBC, New Delhi, 1944–45; Director, Eastern Services, 1946–47; Asst Controller in Overseas Div., 1948; Controller, North Region, 1948–56; Controller, Overseas Services, BBC, 1956–58; Chief Executive, Anglia Television Ltd, 1959; Head of Overseas and Foreign Relations, BBC, Dec. 1960. A Governor of Manchester Univ., 1950–58. A delegate to 5th Commonwealth Broadcasting Conf., Canada, 1963, to 7th Conf., NZ, 1968, and 8th Conf., Jamaica, 1970. *Recreation:* family life. *Address:* 21 Boulthurst Way, Oxted, Surrey. *T:* Oxted (0883) 723151.

STEPHENSON, Prof. Gordon, CBE 1967; FRIBA, FRTPI, LFRAIA, LFRAPI, FLI, DistTP; Professor Emeritus of Architecture, University of Western Australia; *b* 6 June 1908; *s* of Francis E. and Eva E. Stephenson, Liverpool; *m* 1938, Flora Bartlett Crockett (decd), Boston, USA; three *d.* *Educ:* Liverpool Institute; University of Liverpool; University of Paris; Massachusetts Institute of Technology. Elmes Scholar, Univ. of Liverpool, 1925–30; Holt Scholar, 1928; First Cl. Hons in Architecture, 1930; Chadwick Scholar at Brit. Inst. in Paris and Univ. of Paris, 1930–32; BArch; MCP(MIT). Lecturer and Studio Instructor in Architecture, University of Liverpool, 1932–36; Commonwealth Fellow and Medallist, Massachusetts Inst. of Technology, 1936–38; Studio Master, Architectural Assoc., School of Architecture, 1939–40; Lever Professor of Civic Design, School of Architecture, University of Liverpool, 1948–53; Professor of Town and Regional Planning in the University of Toronto, Canada, 1955–60; Prof. of Architecture, Univ. of WA, 1960–72. Architectural and Planning practice: asst to Corbett, Harrison and McMurray, NY City, 1929; asst to Le Corbusier and Pierre Jeanneret, Paris, 1930–32; Div. Architect, with W. G. Holford, on Royal Ordnance Factory work, 1940–42; Research Officer, Sen. Research Officer, and Chief Planning Officer, Min. of Works and Planning, and Min. of Town and Country Planning, 1942–47; seconded to assist Sir Patrick Abercrombie on Greater London Plan, 1943–44; Cnslt Architect, Univ. of WA, 1960–69; in partnership with R. J. Ferguson, as architects and planners for Murdoch Univ., WA, 1972–76; in private practice, houses, militia camp, university bldgs, community centre, housing schemes, town and regional planning studies. Mem., Nat. Capital Planning Cttee, Canberra, 1967–73; Consultant, Perth Northwestern Suburbs Railway Project, 1989–90. Editor, Town Planning Review, 1949–54. Hon. MCIP 1960. Hon. LLD Univ. of WA, 1976; Hon. DArch Univ. of Melbourne, 1984; Hon. DSc Flinders Univ., 1987; DUniv Murdoch Univ., 1988. *Publications:* (with Flora Stephenson) Community Centres, 1941; (with F. R. S. Yorke) Planning for Reconstruction, 1944; (with J. A. Hepburn) Plan for the Metropolitan Region of Perth and Fremantle, 1955; a Redevelopment Study of Halifax, Nova Scotia, 1957; (with G. G. Muirhead) A Planning Study of Kingston, Ontario, 1959; The Design of Central Perth, 1975; Joondalup Regional Centre, 1977; Planning for the University of Western Australia: 1914–70, 1986; articles and papers in British, Australian, Canadian Technical Professional Jls. *Recreations:* architectural practice, drawing and travel. *Address:* Unit 55, 14 Albert Street, St Louis Estate, Claremont, WA 6010, Australia. *T:* (09) 385 2309.

STEPHENSON, Henry Shepherd, CEng, FIMinE; Chairman, Mining Qualifications Board, 1970–75; *b* 1 Oct. 1905; *m* 1934, Faith Estelle, 3rd *d* of Tom Edward Arnold, Bolton Old Hall, Bradford; two *d.* *Educ:* Whitehaven Grammar School; Armstrong College, Durham University (BSc). Articled apprentice Mining Engineer, Whitehaven Colliery Co., 1924–28; official posts, Whitehaven Colliery Co., 1928–35; HM Junior Inspector of Mines Northern Div., 1935–39; Mining Agent, Cumberland Coal Co., 1939–41; HM Junior Inspector of Mines and Quarries (Yorkshire), 1941–44; Senior Inspector (Scotland), 1944–47; Senior Dist Inspector (Durham), 1948–52; Senior Dist Inspector (West Midland), 1952–58; Divisional Inspector (East Midland), 1958–62; Deputy Chief Inspector, Jan. 1962; Chief Inspector, 1962–70. Hon. DSc Newcastle upon Tyne, 1971. *Address:* 4 St Margarets Court, Topsham, Devon EX3 0JL.

STEPHENSON, Sir Henry Upton, 3rd Bt *cr* 1936; TD; Director: Stephenson, Blake (Holdings) Ltd; Thos Turton and Sons Ltd; *b* 26 Nov. 1926; *s* of Lt-Col Sir Henry Francis Blake Stephenson, 2nd Bt, OBE, TD, and of Joan, *d* of Major John Herbert Upton (formerly Upton Cottrell-Dormer); *S* father, 1982; *m* 1962, Susan, *o d* of Major J. E. Clowes, Ashbourne, Derbyshire; four *d.* *Educ:* Eton. Formerly Major, QO Yorkshire Dragoons. High Sheriff of Derbyshire, 1975. *Heir: cousin* Timothy Hugh Stephenson [*b* 5 Jan. 1930; *m* 1959, Susan Lesley, *yr d* of late George Arthur Harris; two *s*]. *Address:* Tissington Cottage, Rowland, Bakewell, Derbyshire.

STEPHENSON, Prof. Hugh; writer and journalist; Professor of Journalism, City University, since 1986; *b* 18 July 1938; *s* of late Sir Hugh and Lady Stephenson; *m* 1st, 1962, Auriol Stevens (marr. diss. 1987); two *s* one *d*; 2nd, 1990, Diana Eden. *Educ:* Winchester Coll.; New Coll., Oxford (BA); Univ. of Calif, Berkeley. Pres., Oxford Union, 1962. HM Diplomatic Service, 1964–68; joined The Times, 1968; Editor, The Times Business News, 1972–81; Editor, The New Statesman, 1982–86. Mem., Cttee to Review Functioning of Financial Instns, 1977–80. Councillor, London Bor. of Wandsworth, 1971–78. FRSA 1987. *Publications:* The Coming Clash, 1972; Mrs Thatcher's First Year, 1980; Claret and Chips, 1982. *Address:* Graduate Centre for Journalism, City University, Northampton Square, EC1.

STEPHENSON, (James) Ian (Love), RA 1986 (ARA 1975); painter; *b* 11 Jan. 1934; *o s* of James Stephenson and May (*née* Emery); *m* 1959, Kate, *o d* of James Brown; one *s* one *d.* *Educ:* King Edward VII School of Art, King's Coll., Univ. of Durham, Newcastle upon Tyne (3 prizes; Hatton Schol.; BA Dunelm 1956, 1st Class Hons in Fine Art). Tutorial Student, 1956–57, Studio Demonstrator, 1957–58, King's Coll., Newcastle upon Tyne (pioneered 1st foundn course in UK dedicated to new creativity in art); Boise Schol. (Italy), Univ. of London, 1958–59; Vis. Lectr, Polytechnic Sch. of Art, London, 1959–62; Vis. Painter, Chelsea Sch. of Art, 1959–66; Dir, Foundn Studies, Dept of Fine Art, Univ. of Newcastle, 1966–70 (introd alternating approach between perceptual and conceptual studies to academic syllabus for first time); Dir, Postgrad. Painting, Chelsea Sch. of Art, 1970–89 (attained Master's Degree status, 1974, the only CNAA Fine Art MA course in UK approved in nationwide survey, 1977–78); Internat. Course Leader, Voss Summer Sch., 1979. Member: Visual Arts Panel, Northern Arts Assoc., Newcastle, 1967–70; Fine Art Panel, NCDAD, 1972–74; Perm. Cttee, New Contemp. Assoc., 1973–75 (revived annual nat. student exhibns); Fine Art Board, CNAA, 1974–75; Adv. Cttee, Nat. Exhibn of Children's Art, Manchester, 1975–; Working Party, RA Jubilee Exhbn, 1976–77; Selection Cttee, Arts Council Awards, 1977–78; Painting Faculty, Rome and Abbey Major Scholarships, 1978–82; Recommending Cttee, Chantrey Bequest, 1979–80; RA Steward, Artists' Gen. Benevolent Instn, 1979–80; Fine Art Advr, Canterbury Art Coll., 1974–79; 1st Specialist Advr, CNAA, 1980–83; Vice-Pres., Sunderland Arts Centre, 1982–86; Boise Scholarship Cttee, UCL, 1983; Chm., Cttee, David Murray Studentship Fund, 1990. Examiner: Birmingham Poly., 1972–73; Portsmouth Poly., 1973–76; London Univ., 1975–83 (Sen. Postgrad. Examiner); Leicester Poly., 1976–78; Ulster Poly., 1979–82; Canterbury Art Coll., 1981–83; Newcastle Poly., 1982–85; Kingston Poly., 1985–88; Edinburgh Art Coll., 1989–. Juror: Contemporary Art, Portsmouth, 1966; Fedn N Art Socs, Newcastle, 1966; Pernod Competition NAA, Newcastle, 1970; Yorkshire Artists' Exhibn, Leeds, 1971; Open Field SAA, Reading, 1972; N Young Contemps, Manchester, 1973; British Painting, London, 1974; Winsor & Newton Award, Birmingham, 1975; Second Chance Charity Exhibn, London, 1977; RA Summer Exhibn, London, 1980; JM 12 Exhibn, Liverpool, 1980. Hon. Member: CAS, 1980–81; Accademia Italia, 1980–; Mark Twain Soc., 1978–. *Exhibitions include:* British Painting in the Sixties, London, 1963; Mostra di Pittura Contemporanea, Amsterdam and Europe, 1964–65; 9o Biennio, Lugano, 1966; 5e Biennale and 18e Salon, Paris, 1967; Recent British Painting, London and world tour, 1967–75; Junge Generation Grossbritannien, Berlin, 1968; Retrospective, Newcastle, 1970; La Peinture Anglaise Aujourd'hui, Paris, 1973; Elf Englische Zeichner, Baden Baden and Bremen, 1973; Recente Britse Tekenkunst, Antwerp, 1973; 13a Bienal, São Paulo and Latin America, 1975; Arte Inglese Oggi, Milan, 1976; Retrospective, London and Bristol, 1977; Englische Kunst der Gegenwart, Bregenz, 1977; British Painting 1952–77, London, 1977; Color en la Pintura Britanica, Rio de Janeiro and Latin America, 1977–79; Abstract Paintings from UK, Washington, 1978; Retrospective, Birmingham and Cardiff, 1978; Royal Acad. of Arts, Edinburgh, 1979–80; Art Anglais d'Aujourd'hui, Geneva, 1980; British Art 1940–80, London, 1980; Colour in British Painting, Hong Kong and Far East, 1980–81; Contemporary British Drawings, Tel-Aviv and Near East, 1980–82; The Deck of Cards, Athens and Arabia, 1980–82; A Taste of British Art Today, Brussels, 1982; Arteder Muestra Internacional, Bilbao, 1982; La Couleur en la Peinture Britannique, Luxembourg and Bucharest, 1982–83; 7th, 8th and 9th Internat. Print Biennales, Bradford, 1982, 1984 and 1986; 15a Bienale, Ljubljana, 1983; Peintiadau Prydeinig 1946–72, Penarth, 1985; *illustrations include:* Cubism and After (BBC film), 1962; Contemporary British Art, 1965; Private View, 1965; Blow Up (film), 1966; Art of Our Time, 1967; Recent British Painting, 1968; Adventure in Art, 1969; In Vogue, 1975; Painting in Britain 1525–1975, 1976; British Painting, 1976; Contemporary Artists, 1977, 1983 and 1989; Contemporary British Artists, 1979; Tendenze e Testimonianze, 1983; *work in collections:* Arnolfini Trust, Arts Council, Birmingham and Bristol City Art Galls, British Council, BP Chemicals and Co., Bury Art Gall., Contemp. Art Soc., Creasey Lit. Museum, DoE, Economist Newspaper, Granada TV, Gulbenkian Foundn, Hatton Gall., Hunterian Museum, Kettle's Yard, Leeds City Art Gall., Leicestershire Educn Authority, Madison Art Center, Marzotto Roma, Nat. West. Bank, Northern Arts Assoc., Nuffield Foundn, Queen Elizabeth II Conf. Centre, Stuyvesant Foundn, Sunderland Art Gall., Tate Gall., Unilever Ltd, Union Bank of Switzerland, V&A Museum, Victoria Nat. Gall., Welsh Nat. Museum, Whitworth Art Gall. *Prizes include:* Junior Section, Moores Exhibn, Liverpool, 1957; European Selection, Premio Marzotto, Valdagno, 1964; First, Northern Painters' Exhibn, 1966. *Address:* c/o Royal Academy of Arts, Piccadilly, W1V 0DS.

STEPHENSON, Jim; His Honour Judge Stephenson; a Circuit Judge, since 1983; *b* 17 July 1932; *s* of late Alex and Norah Stephenson, Heworth, Co. Durham; *m* 1964, Jill Christine, *d* of Dr Lindeck, Fairwarp, Sussex; three *s.* *Educ:* Royal Grammar Sch. and Dame Allan's Sch., Newcastle; Exeter Coll., Oxford (Exhibnr, BA). Pres., Oxford Univ. Law Society, Michaelmas, 1955. Called to Bar, Gray's Inn, 1957. Mem., General Council of the Bar, 1961–64; Junior, NE Circuit, 1961; a Recorder of the Crown Court, 1974–83. Pres., NE Br., Magistrates' Assoc., 1988–. Additional Mem. of Bd, Faculty of Law, Newcastle upon Tyne, 1984–90. Gov., Newcastle Prep. Sch., 1985–. *Recreations:* reading, walking, history. *Address:* Crown Court, Quayside, Newcastle upon Tyne NE1 2LA.

STEPHENSON, Maj.-Gen. John Aubrey, CB 1982; OBE 1971; defence consultant; Managing Director, Weapon Systems Ltd, 1982–91; Director, ATX Ltd, since 1984; Deputy Master General of the Ordnance, 1980–81; *b* 15 May 1929; *s* of Reginald Jack Stephenson and Florence Stephenson; *m* 1953, Sheila Colbeck; two *s* one *d.* *Educ:* Dorchester Grammar School. Commnd RA, 1948; served Malaya (despatches, 1951), Libya, Canal Zone and Germany, 1949–58 (student pilot, 1953–54); student, RMCS, 1958–60; 39 Missile Regt, 1960–61; student, RMCS and Staff Coll., 1961–62; served UK and Germany, 1962–67; Staff, RMCS, 1967–69; CO 16 Light Air Defence Regt RA, 1969–71; Project Manager, 155mm Systems, Woolwich, 1971–73; student, RCDS, 1974; Comdr, 1st Artillery Bde, Germany, 1975–77; Sen. Mil. Officer, RARDE, 1977–78; Dir Gen. Weapons (Army), 1978–80. Col Comdt, RA, 1984–89; Hon. Regtl Col, 16 Air Defence Regt, RA, 1989–. Governor, Hardye's Sch., Dorchester, 1984–. MInstD; FBIM. *Recreations:* fishing, sailing, gardening, bridge, golf, military history. *Address:* Collingwood, 27 Trafalgar Way, Stockbridge, Hants SO20 6ET. *T:* Andover (0264) 810458. *Club:* Commonwealth Trust.

STEPHENSON, Rt. Hon. Sir John (Frederick Eustace), PC 1971; Kt 1962; a Lord Justice of Appeal, 1971–85; *b* 28 March 1910; 2nd *s* of late Sir Guy Stephenson, CB, and of late Gwendolen, *d* of Rt Hon. J. G. Talbot; *m* 1951, Frances Rose, *yr d* of late Lord Asquith of Bishopstone, PC; two *s* two *d.* *Educ:* Winchester College (Schol.); New Coll., Oxford (Schol.); Hon. Fellow, 1979. 1st Cl. Hon. Mods. 1930, 1st Cl. Litt Hum. 1932, BA 1932, MA 1956. Called to Bar, Inner Temple (Entrance Scholarship), 1934; Bencher, 1962. Sapper RE (TA), 1938; War Office, 1940; Intelligence Corps, Captain 1943, Major 1944 and Lieut-Col 1946; Middle East and NW Europe; Regional Intelligence Officer, Hamburg, 1946; Recorder of Bridgwater, 1954–59; Recorder of Winchester, 1959–62; Chancellor of the Diocese: of Peterborough, 1956–62; of Winchester, 1958–62; QC 1960; Dep. Chm., Dorset QS, 1962–71; Judge of Queen's Bench Div., High Court of Justice, 1962–71. *Publication:* A Royal Correspondence, 1938. *Address:* 26 Doneraile Street, SW6. *T:* 071–736 6782. *Clubs:* Hurlingham, MCC; Royal Wimbledon Golf.

STEPHENSON, Lt-Col John Robin, OBE 1976; Secretary: Marylebone Cricket Club, since 1987; International Cricket Council (formerly International Cricket Conference), since 1987; *b* 25 Feb. 1931; *s* of John Stewart Stephenson and Edith Gerda Greenwell Stephenson; *m* 1962, Karen Margrethe Koppang; one *s* two *d.* *Educ:* Christ's Hospital; RMA Sandhurst. Commissioned Royal Sussex Regt, 1951; served Egypt, Korea, Gibraltar, Libya, Germany, N Ireland; Instructor, Mons Officer Cadet Sch., 1958–60; Infantry Rep., Sch. of Signals, 1968–70; SOWC, 1972–73; Comdg Officer, 5 (V) Queen's Regt, 1973–75; Dep. Pres., Regular Commissions Bd, 1976; Staff Officer, Cs-in-C Cttee, 1977–79. Asst Sec. (Cricket), MCC, 1979–86; managed MCC tours, Bangladesh, 1979–80, E Africa, 1980–81, Canada, 1985. Governor: St Bede's Sch., Eastbourne, 1989–; Clayesmore Sch., Dorset, 1989–. Order of Orange-Nassau, 1972. *Recreations:* Rugby football (RMA (Capt.),

Richmond, Army, Sussex), cricket (RMA, MCC, IZ, FF, Army), squash, golf, boating, gardening. *Address:* Plum Tree Cottage, Barford St Martin, Salisbury, Wilts SP3 4BL. *T:* Salisbury (0722) 743443. *Clubs:* MCC, IZ.

STEPHENSON, Lynne, (Mrs Chaim Stephenson); *see* Banks, L. R.

STEPHENSON, Margaret Maud; *see* Tyzack, M. M.

STEPHENSON, Prof. Patrick Hay, MA, CEng, FIMechE; retired consultant Mechanical Engineer; *b* 31 March 1916; *e s* of late Stanley George Stephenson; *m* 1947, Pauline Coupland; two *s* one *d*. *Educ:* Wyggeston Sch., Leicester; Cambridge Univ. (MA). Apprenticeship and Research Engr, Brit. United Shoe Machinery Co., 1932–39. War Service as Ordnance Mechanical Engr and REME, India and Far East, 1939–45; held as POW by Japanese, 1942–45. Chief Mechanical Engr, Pye Ltd, 1949–67; Prof. of Mech. Engrg, Univ. of Strathclyde, 1967–79; Dir, Inst. of Advanced Machine Tool and Control Technology, Min. of Technology, 1967–70; Dir, Birniehill Inst. and Manufacturing Systems Group, DTI, 1970–72; Head of Research Requirements Branch 2, DoI, 1972–77. Research advisor to Institution of Mechanical Engineers; senior industrial advisor to the Design Council. Mem. Council, IMechE, 1960–68; Member: Bd, UKAC, 1964–73; Engrg Bd, SRC, 1973–. *Publications:* papers and articles in technical press. *Recreations:* music, vintage motoring. *Address:* Toft Lane, Great Wilbraham, Cambridge CB1 5JH. *T:* Cambridge (0223) 880405.

STEPHENSON, Paul; Senior Liaison Officer, Commission for Racial Equality, since 1980; *b* 6 May 1937; *s* of Olive Stephenson; *m* 1965, Joyce Annikie; one *s* one *d*. *Educ:* Westhill Coll. of Educn, Selly Oak, Birmingham. MIPR 1978. Youth Tutor, St Paul's, Bristol, 1962–68; Sen. Community Relations Officer, Coventry, 1968–72; National Youth Trng Officer, Community Relations Commn, 1972–77. Chm., Muhammad Ali Sports Develt Assoc., Brixton and Lambeth, 1974–; Member: British Sports Council, 1976–82; Press Council, 1984–90. *Recreations:* travel, cinema, reading, international politics. *Address:* 12 Downs Park East, Westbury Park, Bristol. *T:* Bristol (0272) 623638.

STEPHENSON, Philip Robert, CMG 1962; OBE 1951; *b* 29 May 1914; *s* of late Robert Barnard Stephenson and Lilian Stephenson (*née* Sharp); *m* 1947, Marianne Hurst Wraith; two *s*. *Educ:* Berkhamsted School; Imperial College, London; Downing College, Cambridge; Imperial College of Tropical Agriculture, Trinidad. Colonial Agricultural Service, Entomologist, Uganda, 1938. Military Service, 1940–43. East African Anti-Locust Directorate, 1943–47, Director, Desert Locust Survey, 1948–62, HM Overseas Service. Member, British Advisory Mission on Tropical Agriculture in Bolivia, Dept of Technical Co-operation, 1963–64. *Address:* c/o Lloyds Bank, Berkhamsted, Herts. *Club:* MCC.

STEPHENSON, (Robert) Ashley (Shute), LVO 1990 (MVO 1979); Bailiff of the Royal Parks, 1980–90; Consultant on horticulture, Trusthouse Forte, since 1990; *b* 1 Sept. 1927; *s* of late James Stephenson and Agnes Maud Stephenson; *m* 1955, Isabel Dunn; one *s* one *d*. *Educ:* Walbottle Secondary Sch. Diploma in Horticulture, RHS, Wisley, 1954; MIHort 1987. Apprenticeship, Newcastle upon Tyne Parks Dept, 1942; served RASC, Palestine and Cyprus, 1946; Landscape Gardener, Donald Ireland Ltd, 1949; Student, RHS's gardens, Wisley, 1952; Royal Parks, 1954–: Supt, Regent's Park, 1969; Supt, Central Royal Parks, 1972. Gardening Correspondent, The Times, 1982–87. Pres., British Pelargonium and Geranium Soc., 1983–; Member: Cttee, RHS, 1981–; London in Bloom Cttee, English Tourist Bd, 1980– (Vice-Chm., 1983); Chm., South East in Bloom, 1990–. Dir, Gardens for Pleasure, 1987–. Contributor to television and radio programmes; gardening correspondent to professional and amateur papers. *Publications:* The Garden Planner, 1981; contribs to nat. press. *Recreations:* sport, judging horticultural shows, natural history, walking, golf. *Address:* 17 Sandore Road, Seaford, E Sussex BN25 3PR. *Club:* Arts.

STEPHENSON, Stanley, CMG 1987; HM Diplomatic Service, retired; *b* 30 Sept. 1926; *s* of George Stephenson and Margaret Jane (*née* Nicholson); *m* 1957, Grace Claire Lyons (*d* 1987); one *s* one *d*. *Educ:* Bede Sch., Sunderland. Inland Revenue, 1942; Royal Navy, 1944–48; Foreign (later Diplomatic) Service, 1948–: Cairo, Jedda, Damascus, Curaçao, Ciudad Trujillo (now Santo Domingo), San José, Seoul, Santiago de Cuba, Bogotá (twice), Asunción, San Francisco, FCO; Diplomatic Service Inspector, 1978–80; Ambassador to Panama, 1981–83; Consul-Gen., Vancouver, 1983–86. *Recreations:* tennis, cricket, Rugby, theatre, gardening. *Address:* Marymount, Raggleswood, Chislehurst, Kent. *T:* 081–467 6066. *Clubs:* Civil Service; Crescent Lawn Tennis (Sidcup).

STEPHENSON, Air Vice-Marshal Tom Birkett, CB 1982; Assistant Chief of Defence Staff (Signals), 1980–82, retired; *b* 18 Aug. 1926; *s* of Richard and Isabel Stephenson; *m* 1951, Rosemary Patricia (*née* Kaye) (*d* 1984); one *s* three *d*. *Educ:* Workington Secondary Sch.; Manchester Univ.; Southampton Univ. (DipEl). Commissioned in RAF Engrg Branch, 1945; Staff Coll., 1962; Wing Comdr, Station and Staff appointments, until 1967; Command Electrical Engr, HQASC, 1967–69; Dep. Director Op. Requirements, 1969–72; AOEng, HQ NEAF, 1972–74; RCDS 1975; Director of Signals (Air), 1976–79. *Recreations:* sport, walking, reading. *Address:* c/o National Westminster Bank, 14 Coney Street, York Y01 1YH. *Club:* Royal Air Force.

STEPNEY, Area Bishop of; *no new appointment at time of going to press.*

STERLING, family name of **Baron Sterling of Plaistow.**

STERLING OF PLAISTOW, Baron *cr* 1991 (Life Peer), of Pall Mall in the City of Westminster; **Jeffrey Maurice Sterling,** Kt 1985; CBE 1977; Chairman, The Peninsular and Oriental Steam Navigation Company, since 1983; *b* 27 Dec. 1934; *s* of late Harry and of Alice Sterling; *m* 1985, Dorothy Ann Smith; one *d*. *Educ:* Reigate Grammar Sch.; Preston Manor County Sch.; Guildhall School of Music. Paul Schweder & Co. (Stock Exchange), 1955–57; G. Eberstadt & Co., 1957–62; Fin. Dir, General Guarantee Corp., 1962–64; Man. Dir, Gula Investments Ltd, 1964–69; Chm., Sterling Guarantee Trust plc, 1969–85, when it merged with P&O Steam Navigation Co. Mem., British Airways Bd, 1979–82. Special Advr to Sec. of State for Industry, later for Trade and Industry, 1982–90. Mem. Exec., 1966–, Chm. Organisation Cttee, 1969–73, World ORT Union; Chm., ORT Technical Services, 1974–; Vice-Pres., British ORT, 1978–; Pres., Gen. Council of British Shipping, 1990–91. Dep. Chm. and Hon. Treasurer, London Celebrations Cttee, Queen's Silver Jubilee, 1975–83. Chm., Young Vic Co., 1975–83; Chm., of the Governors, Royal Ballet Sch., 1983–; Gov., Royal Ballet, 1986–; Vice-Chm. and Chm. of the Exec., Motability, 1977–. Freeman, City of London. Hon. Captain, RNR, 1991. Elder Brother, Trinity House, 1991. *Recreations:* music, swimming, tennis. *Address:* The Peninsular & Oriental Steam Navigation Company, 79 Pall Mall, SW1Y 5EJ. *Clubs:* Garrick, Carlton, Hurlingham.

STERLING, Michael John Howard, CEng, FIEE; FInstMC; Vice-Chancellor and Principal, Brunel University, since 1990; *b* 9 Feb. 1946; *s* of Richard Howard Sterling and Joan Valeria Sterling (*née* Skinner); *m* 1969, Wendy Karla Anstead; two *s*. *Educ:* Hampton Grammar Sch., Middx; Univ. of Sheffield (BEng 1968; PhD 1971; DEng 1988). Student apprentice, AEI, 1964–68; research engineer, GEC-Eliott Process Automation, 1968–71; Sheffield University: Lectr in Control Engineering, 1971–78; Industrial Liaison Officer, 1976–80; Sen. Lectr in Control Engineering, 1978–80; Prof. of Engineering, Univ. of Durham, 1980–90 (Dir, Microprocessor Centre, 1980–85). Nat. Pres., InstMC, 1988. FRSA. *Publications:* Power Systems Control, 1978; contribs to: Large Scale Systems Engineering Applications, 1980; Computer Control of Industrial Processes, 1982; Real Time Computer Control, 1984; Comparative Models for Electrical Load Forecasting, 1985; papers in learned jls. *Recreations:* gardening, DIY, canoeing, model engineering. *Address:* Brunel University, Uxbridge, Middx UB8 3PH. *T:* Uxbridge (0895) 74000.

STERN, Isaac; violinist; *b* Kreminiecz, Russia, 21 July 1920; *s* of Solomon and Clara Stern; *m* 1948, Nora Kaye (*d* 1987); *m* 1951, Vera Lindenblit; three *c*. Studied San Francisco Conservatory, 1930–37. First public concert as guest artist San Francisco Symphony Orchestra, 1934; played with Los Angeles Philharmonic Orchestra and in concerts in Pacific Coast cities; New York début, 1937. Has since played in concerts throughout USA, in Europe, Israel, Australia, South America, Japan, China, India, The Philippines, Soviet Union and Iceland; has played with major American and European orchestras. Took part in Prades Festivals, 1950–52; Edinburgh and other major festivals in Europe and US. Film, Mao to Mozart: Isaac Stern in China (Best Full-length Documentary Acad. Award, 1981); (TV prodn) Carnegie Hall—The Grand Reopening, 1987 (Emmy Award). Chm., America-Israel Cultural Foundn, NY, 1964–; President, Carnegie Hall, NY, 1960–. Hon. Degrees from Univs of Columbia, Johns Hopkins, Dalhousie, Brown, and San Francisco Conservatory of Music. Over 100 recordings for which many Grammy Awards received. Albert Schweitzer Music Award, 1975; Kennedy Center Honors, 1984. Commandeur, Légion d'Honneur (France), 1989. *Address:* c/o ICM Artists Ltd, 40 West 57th Street, New York, NY 10019, USA.

STERN, Prof. Joseph Peter Maria, PhD, LittD; FBA 1990; Professor of German, University of London, and Head of Department, University College, 1972–86, now Professor Emeritus; Research Fellow, University College London, since 1990; *b* 25 Dec. 1920; *s* of Gustav Stern and Louisa (*née* Bondy); *m* 1944, Sheila Frances, *d* of late Joseph Patrick and Frances McMullan; two *s* two *d*. *Educ:* Czech schs in Prague and Vienna; Barry County Sch. for Boys, Glam; St John's Coll., Cambridge (MA 1947, PhD 1949, LittD 1975; Hon. Fellow, 1990). Wartime service in Czech Army and RAF (VR). Asst Lectr, Bedford Coll., London, 1950–52; Asst Lectr, then Lectr, Cambridge Univ., 1952–72; Fellow, St John's Coll., Cambridge, 1954–72 (Tutor, 1963–70, 1972); Chm. of Bd, Germanic Languages and Literature, Univ. of London, 1978–79; Hon. Dir, Inst. of Germanic Studies, Univ. of London, 1981–85. Prof.-at-Large, Cornell Univ., Ithaca, NY, 1976–82. Vis. Professor: City Coll. of New York, 1958; Univ. of Calif at Berkeley, 1964 and 1967; State Univ. of NY at Buffalo, 1969; Univ. of Va, Charlottesville, 1971; Univ. of Calif at Irvine, 1988; Merton Prof., Univ. of Göttingen, 1965; Bernhard Vis. Prof., Williams Coll., Williamstown, Mass, 1986–87; Hochschule für angewandte Kunst, Vienna, 1988–89. Fellow, Center for Humanities, Wesleyan Univ., 1972. Lewis Fry Meml Lectr, Univ. of Bristol, 1973; British Academy Master Mind Lectr, 1978. General Editor, Landmarks of World Literature, 1986–. Mem., Acad. of Sciences, Göttingen, 1988–. Goethe Medal, Goethe Inst., 1980; Alexander von Humboldt Research Prize, 1980. *Publications:* Ernst Jünger: a writer of our time, 1952; (trans.) R. W. Meyer, Leibnitz and the seventeenth-century revolution, 1952; (trans.) H.-E. Holthusen, R. M. Rilke: a study of his later poetry, 1952; G. C. Lichtenberg: a doctrine of scattered occasions, 1959; Re-Interpretations: seven studies in nineteenth-century German literature, 1964, repr. 1981; (ed) Arthur Schnitzler: Liebelei, Leutnant Gustl, and Die letzten Masken, 1966; Idylls and Realities: studies in nineteenth-century German literature, 1971; On Realism, 1973, rev. German version, 1982; Hitler: the Führer and the People, 1975 (3rd edn 1990, German version 1978, French trans. rev. by S. F. Stern, 1985, Czech version, 1987); Nietzsche (Fontana Modern Masters), 1978; A Study of Nietzsche, 1979, rev. German version, 1982; (with Michael Silk) Nietzsche on Tragedy, 1981 (J. G. Robertson Prize, 1988); (ed) The World of Franz Kafka, 1981; (ed) London German Studies II, 1984, III, 1986; (ed) Paths and Labyrinths: a Kafka symposium, 1985; The Heart of Europe: essays on literature and ideology, 1992; contribs (incl. 42 Poems from the Czech, trans. with S. F. Stern) and articles in English and foreign jls and newspapers. *Address:* 83 Barton Road, Cambridge CB3 9LL. *T:* Cambridge (0223) 353078.
See also M. B. McMullan.

STERN, Linda Joy; QC 1991; a Recorder of the Crown Court, since 1990; *b* 21 Dec. 1941; *d* of Mrs L. R. Saville; *m* 1st, 1961, Michael Brian Rose (decd); two *s*; 2nd, 1978, Nigel Maurice Stern. *Educ:* St Paul's Girls' Sch. Called to the Bar, Gray's Inn, 1971; Mem., S Eastern Circuit. *Recreations:* music, theatre, reading, travel. *Address:* 5 King's Bench Walk, Temple, EC4Y 7DN. *T:* 071–353 4713.

STERN, Michael Charles, FCA; MP (C) Bristol North West, since 1983; *b* 3 Aug. 1942; *s* of late Maurice Leonard Stern and of Rose Stern; *m* 1976, Jillian Denise Aldridge; one *d*. *Educ:* Christ's College Grammar School, Finchley. Mem. ICA 1964; FCA 1969. Partner, Percy Phillips & Co., Accountants, 1964–80; Partner, Halpern & Woolf, Chartered Accountants, 1980–. Chm., The Bow Group, 1977–78; coopted Mem., Educn Cttee, Borough of Ealing, 1980–83. Contested (C) Derby S, 1979. PPS to Minister of State, HM Treasury, 1986–87, to Paymaster General, 1987–89, to Minister for Corporate Affairs, DTI, 1991. Chief Finance Officer, 1990–91, Vice-Chm., 1991–, Cons. party. *Publications:* papers for The Bow Group. *Recreations:* fell walking, bridge, chess. *Address:* House of Commons, SW1. *Clubs:* United and Cecil, Millbank, London Mountaineering.

STERN, Prof. Nicholas Herbert; Sir John Hicks Professor of Economics, London School of Economics and Political Science, since 1986; Chairman, Suntory Toyota International Centre for Economics and Related Disciplines, since 1987; *b* 22 April 1946; *s* of Adalbert Stern and Marion Fatima Stern; *m* 1968, Susan Ruth (*née* Chesterton); two *s* one *d*. *Educ:* Peterhouse, Cambridge (BA Mathematics); Nuffield Coll., Oxford (DPhilEcon). Jun. Res. Fellow, The Queen's Coll., Oxford, 1969–70; Fellow/Tutor in Econs, St Catherine's Coll., and Univ. Lectr, Oxford, 1970–77; Prof. of Econs, Univ. of Warwick, 1978–85. Research Associate/Vis. Professor: MIT, 1972; Ecole Polytech., 1977; Indian Statistical Inst. (Overseas Vis. Fellow of British Acad., 1974–75, and Ford Foundn Vis. Prof., 1981–82); People's Univ. of China, Beijing, 1988. Fellow, Econometric Soc., 1978. Editor, Journal of Public Economics, 1980–. *Publications:* An Appraisal of Tea Production on Smallholdings in Kenya, 1972; (ed jtly) Theories of Economic Growth, 1973; (jtly) Crime, the Police and Criminal Statistics, 1979; (jtly) Palanpur: the economy of an Indian village, 1982; (jtly) The Theory of Taxation for Developing Countries, 1987; articles in Econ. Jl, Rev. of Econ. Studies, Jl of Public Econs, Jl of Develt Econs, and others. *Recreations:* reading novels, walking, watching sport, food. *Address:* London School of Economics, Houghton Street, WC2A 2AE. *T:* 071–405 7686.

STERN, Vivien Helen; Director, National Association for the Care and Resettlement of Offenders (NACRO), since 1977; *b* 25 Sept. 1941; *d* of Frederick Stern and Renate Mills. *Educ:* Kent Coll., Pembury, Kent; Bristol Univ. (BA, MLitt, CertEd). Lectr in Further Educn until 1970; Community Relations Commn, 1970–77. Member: Special

Programmes Bd, Manpower Services Commn, 1980–82; Youth Training Bd, 1982–88; Gen. Adv. Council, IBA, 1982–87; Cttee on the Prison Disciplinary System, 1984–85. Vis. Fellow, Nuffield Coll., Oxford, 1984–. Hon. LLD Bristol, 1990. *Publications:* Bricks of Shame, 1987; Imprisoned by Our Prisons, 1989; Deprived of their Liberty, a report for Caribbean Rights, 1990. *Address:* National Association for the Care and Resettlement of Offenders, 169 Clapham Road, SW9.

STERNBERG, Sir Sigmund, Kt 1976; JP; FSCA; Chairman: Martin Slowe Estates Ltd, since 1971; ISYS Ltd, since 1986; Lloyd's Underwriter, since 1969; *b* Budapest, 2 June 1921; *s* of Abraham and Elizabeth Sternberg; *m* 1970, Hazel (*née* Everett Jones); one *s* one *d*, and one *s* one *d* from a previous marriage. Served War of 1939–45, Civil Defence Corps. Former Ring-Dealing Mem., London Metal Exchange. Co-Chm., Arbitration Cttee, Bureau Internat. de la Récupération, 1966. Instituted Res. Gp for Labour Shadow Cabinet, 1973–74; Econ. and Industry Cttee, Fabian Soc., 1976 (Chm., Appeals Cttee, 1975–77); Dep. Chm., Labour Finance and Industry Gp. Chm., St Charles Gp, HMC, 1974; NW Metrop. RHB, 1974; Member: Camden and Islington AHA, 1974–77; Gen. Purposes Cttee, NAMH, 1972; Vice-President: Coll. of Speech Therapists; Association for all Speech Impaired Children; Chm., Inst. for Archaeo-Metallurgical Studies. Pres., VOCAL (Voluntary Organisation Communications and Language); Hon. Treasurer: Cruse Bereavement Care; Council of Christians and Jews; Chm., Internat. Council of Christians and Jews; Mem., Board of Deputies of British Jews; Governor, Hebrew Univ. of Jerusalem; Mem. Bd of Management, Spiro Inst; Trustee, Manor House Trust (Sternberg Centre for Judaism), 1984–; Convenor, Religious Press Gp. Life Mem., Magistrates' Assoc., 1965; Mem., Commonwealth Magistrates' and Judges' Assoc., 1985; Vice Pres., Reform Synagogues of GB, 1991. Speaker Chm., Rotary Club of London, 1980–83. Mem., Editl Bd, Christian/Jewish Relations, 1989. Mem., Court, Essex Univ. Liveryman, Co. of Horners; Freeman, City of London. JP Middlesex, 1965 (Middlesex Probation (Case) Cttee, 1973). FRSA 1979. Hon. FRSM 1981; Hon. FCST, 1989. Judge, Templeton Foundn, 1988. Paul Harris Fellow, Rotary Foundn of Rotary Internat., 1989; Hon. Mem., Rotary Club, Budapest, 1989. Order of the Orthodox Hospitallers, First Class with Star and Badge of Religion, 1986; OStJ 1988. Brotherhood Award, Nat. Conf. of Christians and Jews Inc., 1980; Silver Pontifical Medal, 1986; Benemerenti Medal (Vatican), 1988, in Silver, 1990; Order of Merit, Poland, 1989; Order of the Gold Star, Hungary, 1990; Medaglia d'Argento di Benemerenza, Sacred Mil. Constantinian Order of St George, 1991; Good Servant Medal, Canadian CCJ, 1991; Silver Jerusalem Mayoral Award, 1991. KCSG 1985. *Recreations:* golf, swimming. *Address:* The Sternberg Centre for Judaism, 80 East End Road, N3 2SY. *T:* 071–485 2538, *Fax:* 071–485 4512. *Clubs:* Reform, City Livery.

STERNE, Laurence Henry Gordon; *b* 2 July 1916; *o s* of late Henry Herbert Sterne and late Hilda Davey; *m* 1944, Katharine Clover; two *d*. *Educ:* Culford Sch.; Jesus Coll. (Open Exhibnr and Hon. Schol.), Oxford (MA). Joined Royal Aircraft Establishment, 1940; Chief Supt at Bedford, 1955. Dir, von Karman Inst., Rhode Saint Genèse, Belgium, 1958; Research Policy Staff, MoD, 1962; Dir, Royal Naval Aircraft and Helicopters, 1964; Dep. Dir, Nat. Engineering Lab., E Kilbride, 1968–77. Vis. Prof., Strathclyde Univ., 1971–76. *Publications:* reports and memoranda of Aeronautical Research Council; ed jtly, early vols of Progress in Aeronautical Sciences. *Recreation:* gardening. *Address:* 10 Trinity Street, Bungay, Suffolk NR35 1EH.

STEVAS; *see* St John-Stevas, family name of Baron St John of Fawsley.

STEVEN, Stewart; Editor, The Mail on Sunday, since 1982; *b* 30 Sept. 1938; *s* of Rudolph and Trude Steven; *m* 1965, Inka Sobieniewska; one *s*. *Educ:* Mayfield Coll., Sussex. Political Reporter, Central Press Features, 1961–63; Political Correspondent, Western Daily Press, 1963–64; Daily Express: Political Reporter, 1964–65; Diplomatic Correspondent, 1965–67; Foreign Editor, 1967–72; Daily Mail: Asst Editor, 1972–74; Associate Editor, 1974–82. Director: The Mail on Sunday; Mail Newspapers plc; Associated Newspapers Holdings Ltd, 1989–. *Publications:* Operation Splinter-Factor, 1974; The Spymasters of Israel, 1976; The Poles, 1982. *Recreations:* classical guitar, writing, ski-ing. *Address:* Northcliffe House, 2 Derry Street, Kensington, W8 5EE. *Clubs:* Groucho; Surrey County Cricket.

STEVENS, family name of **Baron Stevens of Ludgate**.

STEVENS OF LUDGATE, Baron *cr* 1987 (Life Peer), of Ludgate in the City of London; **David Robert Stevens;** Chairman: United Newspapers plc, since 1981 (Director, since 1974); Express Newspapers, since 1985; MIM Britannia Ltd (formerly Montagu Investment Management Ltd), since 1980 (Chief Executive, 1980–87); INVESCO MIM (formerly Britannia Arrow Holdings) plc, since 1989 (Deputy Chairman, 1987–89); *b* 26 May 1936; *s* of (Arthur) Edwin Stevens, *qv*; *m* 1st Patricia Rose (marr. diss. 1971); 2nd, 1977, Melissa Milicevich (*d* 1989); one *s* one *d*; 3rd, 1990, Meriza Giori. *Educ:* Stowe Sch.; Sidney Sussex Coll., Cambridge (MA Hons Econ). Management Trainee, Elliott Automation, 1959; Director: Hill Samuel Securities, 1959–68; Drayton Group, 1968–74. Chairman: Alexander Proudfoot Hldgs (formerly City & Foreign), 1976–; Drayton Far East, 1976–; English & International, 1976–79; Consolidated Venture (formerly Montagu Boston), 1979–; Drayton Consolidated, 1980–; Drayton Japan, 1980–88. Chm., EDC for Civil Engrg, 1984–86. *Recreation:* golf. *Address:* 11 Devonshire Square, EC2M 4YR. *Clubs:* White's; Sunningdale Golf.

STEVENS, Anthony John; Post Graduate Veterinary Dean for London and South East England, Royal College of Veterinary Surgeons/British Veterinary Association, since 1986; engaged in consultancy and literary work; *b* 29 July 1926; *s* of John Walker Stevens and Hilda Stevens; *m* 1954, Patricia Frances, *d* of Robert Gill, Ponteland; one *s* two *d*. *Educ:* Liverpool and Manchester Univs; Magdalene Coll., Cambridge. MA, BVSc, MRCVS, DipBact. Veterinary Investigation Officer, Cambridge, 1956–65; Animal Health Expert for UNO, 1959–63; Suptg Veterinary Investigation Officer, Leeds, 1965–68; Ministry of Agriculture, Fisheries and Food: Dep. Dir, Central Vet. Lab., 1968–71; Asst Chief Vet. Officer, 1971–73; Dep. Chief Vet. Officer, 1973–78; Dir, Vet. Labs, MAFF, 1979–86. External Examr, Dublin, Liverpool and Edinburgh Univs., 1964–70. Past Pres., Veterinary Research Club. Vice Pres., Zoological Soc., 1989–90 (Mem. Council, 1987–). FRSA. *Publications:* UN/FAO Manual of Diagnostic Techniques; regular contributor to Veterinary Record, etc. *Recreations:* industrial archaeology particularly canals, riding, and all forms of livestock. *Address:* Marigold Cottage, Great Halfpenny Farm, Guildford, Surrey GU4 8PY. *T:* Guildford (0483) 65375.

STEVENS, (Arthur) Edwin, CBE 1979; *b* 17 Oct. 1905; *s* of Arthur Edwin Stevens and Bessie Annie (*née* Dowden); *m* 1933, Kathleen Alberta James; three *s*. *Educ:* West Monmouth Sch.; University Coll., Cardiff (BSc Hons 1927; Hon. Fellow 1981); Jesus Coll., Oxford (MA Hons 1929). Founder, Amplivox Ltd: Chm. and Man. Dir, 1935–75; designed world's first wearable electronic hearing aid, 1935; collector of world's most comprehensive exhibn of aids to hearing covering 400 yrs. Hon. Fellow, Jesus Coll., Oxford, 1973; financed building of Stevens Close, Jesus Coll. Hall of Residence opened by the Queen, 1976; New Assembly Hall, Jesus Coll., 1988; inaugurated Princess Alice Hospice, Esher, 1979; founded RSM Edwin Stevens Lectures for Laity, 1970. Hon. FRSM 1981. Hon. LLD Wales, 1984. *Recreations:* golf, gardening. *Address:* Oak Lawn, 1 Copsem Way, Esher, Surrey KT10 9ER. *T:* Esher (0372) 466767.

See also Baron Stevens of Ludgate.

STEVENS, Clifford David; Director, Industry Department, Welsh Office, since 1987; *b* 11 June 1941; *s* of late Robert Stevens and of Ivy (*née* White); *m* 1964, Mary Olive (*née* Bradford); one *s* two *d*. *Educ:* Stationers' Company's Sch., London. FO, 1959–63; BoT, 1963–64; DEA, 1964–70 (Private Sec. to successive Ministers, 1967–70); CSD, 1970–76; Cabinet Office, 1976–78; CSD, 1978–81; Management and Personnel Office, 1981–86; Welsh Office, 1986–. *Recreations:* gardening, bowls. *Address:* c/o Welsh Office, Cathays Park, Cardiff CF1 3NQ. *T:* Cardiff (0222) 823325.

STEVENS, Prof. Denis William, CBE 1984; President and Artistic Director, Accademia Monteverdiana, since 1961; *b* 2 March 1922; *s* of William J. Stevens and Edith Driver; *m* 1st, 1949, Sheila Elizabeth Holloway; two *s* one *d*; 2nd, 1975, Leocadia Elzbieta Kwasny. *Educ:* Royal Grammar Sch., High Wycombe; Jesus College, Oxford. Served War of 1939–45, RAF Intelligence, India and Burma, 1942–46. Producer, BBC Music Div., 1949–54; Assoc. Founder and Conductor, Ambrosian Singers, 1952; Vis. Professor of Musicology, Cornell Univ., 1955, Columbia Univ., 1956; Secretary, Plainsong and Mediaeval Music Soc., 1958–63; Editor, Grove's Dictionary of Music and Musicians, 1959–63. Professor, Royal Acad. of Music, 1960. Vis. Prof. Univ. of California (Berkeley), 1962; Dist. Vis. Prof., Pennsylvania State Univ., 1962–63; Prof. of Musicology, Columbia Univ., 1964–76; Vis. Prof. Univ. of California (Santa Barbara), 1974–75; Brechemin Dist. Vis. Prof., Univ. of Washington, Seattle, 1976; Vis. Prof., Univ. of Michigan, Ann Arbor, 1977, San Diego State Univ., 1978. Lectures on music, especially British, in England, France, Germany, Italy, USA; concerts, conducting own and ancillary ensembles at internat. festivals in GB, Europe and USA; TV and radio programmes in Europe and N America; cons. for films. FSA; Member Worshipful Company of Musicians. Hon. RAM, 1960. Hon.D, Humane Letters, Fairfield Univ., Connecticut, 1967. *Publications:* The Mulliner Book, 1952; Thomas Tomkins, 1957, rev. edn 1966; A History of Song, 1960, rev. edn, 1971; Tudor Church Music, 1966; A Treasury of English Church Music (I), 1965; (ed) First and Second Penguin Book of English Madrigals, 1967, 1971; Early Tudor Organ Music (II), 1969; Music in Honour of St Thomas of Canterbury, 1970; Monteverdi: sacred, secular and occasional music, 1978; Musicology: a practical guide, 1980; The Letters of Monteverdi, 1980; Renaissance Dialogues, 1981; The Worcester Fragments, 1981; Musicology in Practice, Pt I 1987, Pt II 1991; many edns of early music, including Monteverdi Vespers and Orfeo; choral works by Gabrieli, Lassus, Machaut, Tallis, Tomkins; articles in English and foreign journals; also many stereo recordings ranging from plainsong to Beethoven. *Recreations:* travel, photography. *Address:* 1624 Garden Street, Apt 2, Santa Barbara, Calif 93101, USA. *Club:* Garrick.

STEVENS, Edwin; *see* Stevens, A. E.

STEVENS, Handley Michael Gambrell; Under Secretary, Finance, Department of Transport, since 1988; *b* 29 June 1941; *s* of Ernest Norman Stevens and Kathleen Emily Gambrell; *m* 1966, Anne Frances Ross; three *d*. *Educ:* The Leys Sch., Cambridge; Phillips Acad., Andover, Mass (E-SU schol.); King's Coll., Cambridge (BA). Translator, Chrysler Internat., 1963; joined Foreign Office, 1964; Third, later Second, Sec., Kuala Lumpur, 1966; Asst Private Sec. to the Lord Privy Seal, 1970; Principal: CSD, 1971; DTI, 1973; Asst Sec., Dept of Trade, 1976; Under Sec. (Internat. Aviation), Dept of Transport, 1983. *Recreations:* music, hill walking, travel. *Address:* Department of Transport, 2 Marsham Street, SW1P 3EB.

STEVENS, Jocelyn Edward Greville; Rector and Vice-Provost, Royal College of Art, 1984–July 1992 (Senior Fellow, 1990); Chairman, English Heritage, from April 1992; Deputy Chairman, Independent Television Commission, since 1991; *b* 14 Feb. 1932; *s* of Major C. G. B. Stewart-Stevens and late Mrs Greville Stevens; *m* 1956, Jane Armyne Sheffield (marr. diss. 1979); one *s* two *d* (and one *s* decd). *Educ:* Eton; Cambridge. Military service in Rifle Bde, 1950–52; Journalist, Hulton Press Ltd, 1955–56; Chairman and Managing Dir, Stevens Press Ltd, and Editor of Queen Magazine, 1957–68; Personal Asst to Chairman of Beaverbrook Newspapers, May-Dec. 1968; Director, 1971–81; Managing Director: Evening Standard Co. Ltd, 1969–72; Daily Express, 1972–74; Beaverbrook Newspapers, 1974–77; Express Newspapers, 1977–81 (Dep. Chm. and Man. Dir); Editor and Publisher, The Magazine, 1982–84; Dir, Centaur Communications, 1982–84. Chm., Silver Trust, 1990–; Trustee, Eureka! The Children's Mus.; Pres., Cheyne Walk Trust. Governor: Imperial Coll. of Science, Technology and Medicine, 1985–; Winchester Sch. of Art, 1986–89. FRSA 1984. Hon. FCSD 1990. Hon. DLitt Loughborough, 1989. *Address:* Testbourne, Longparish, near Andover, Hants SP11 6QT. *T:* Longparish (026472) 232. *Clubs:* Buck's, Beefsteak, White's.

STEVENS, John Christopher Courtenay; Member (C) Thames Valley, European Parliament, since 1989; *b* 23 May 1955; *s* of Sir John Melior Stevens, KCMG, DSO, OBE and of Anne Hely-Hutchinson. *Educ:* Winchester Coll.; Magdalen Coll., Oxford (BA Jurisprudence). Foreign exchange and Bond trader, Banque Indosuez, Paris, 1976–77; Bayerische Hypotheken und Wechselbank, Munich, 1977–78; Morgan Grenfell, London, 1979–89, Internat. Dir, 1986–89; Man. Dir, RIT Capital Partners Securities; Advr, St James's Place Capital plc. *Recreations:* riding, ski-ing. *Address:* 15 St James's Place, SW1. *T:* 071–493 8111. *Club:* Carlton.

STEVENS, Prof. John Edgar, CBE 1980; PhD; FBA 1975; President of Magdalene College, Cambridge, 1983–88, Fellow, 1950–88, now Emeritus; Professor of Medieval and Renaissance English, University of Cambridge, 1978–88, now Emeritus; *b* 8 Oct. 1921; *s* of William Charles James and Fanny Stevens; *m* 1946, Charlotte Ethel Mary (*née* Somner); two *s* two *d*. *Educ:* Christ's Hospital, Horsham; Magdalene College, Cambridge (Schol.; MA, PhD). Served Royal Navy; Temp. Lieut RNVR. Cambridge University: Bye-Fellow 1948, Research Fellow 1950, Fellow 1953 and Tutor 1958–74, Magdalene Coll.; Univ. Lectr in English, 1954–74; Reader in English and Musical History, 1974–78. Vis. Dist. Prof. of Medieval Studies, Univ. of California, Berkeley, 1989. Chm., Plainsong and Medieval Music Soc., 1988–. Hon. MusD Exeter, 1989. *Publications:* Medieval Carols (Musica Britannica vol. 4), 1952, 2nd edn 1958; Music and Poetry in the Early Tudor Court, 1961; Music at the Court of Henry VIII (Musica Britannica vol. 18), 1962, 2nd edn 1969; (with Richard Axton) Medieval French Plays, 1971; Medieval Romance, 1973; Early Tudor Songs & Carols (Musica Britannica vol. 36), 1975; Words and Music in the Middle Ages, 1986. *Recreations:* viol-playing, sailing, bricklaying. *Address:* 4 & 5 Bell's Court, Cambridge.

STEVENS, Hon. John Paul; Associate Justice, Supreme Court of the United States, since 1975; *b* 20 April 1920; *s* of Ernest James Stevens and Elizabeth Stevens (*née* Street); *m* 1st, 1942, Elizabeth Jane Sheeren; one *s* three *d*; 2nd, 1979, Maryan Mulholland Simon. *Educ:* Univ. of Chicago (AB 1941); Northwestern Univ. (JD 1947). Served War, USNR, 1942–45 (Bronze Star). Law Clerk to US Supreme Ct Justice Wiley Rutledge, 1947–48; Associate, Poppenhusen, Johnston, Thompson & Raymond, 1948–50; Associate Counsel, sub-cttee on Study Monopoly Power, Cttee on Judiciary, US House of Reps, 1951; Partner, Rothschild, Hart, Stevens & Barry, 1952–70; US Circuit Judge, 1970–75. Lectr, anti-trust law, Northwestern Univ. Sch. of Law, 1953; Univ. of Chicago Law Sch., 1954–55; Mem., Attorney-Gen.'s Nat. Cttee to study Anti-Trust Laws, 1953–55. Mem., Chicago Bar Assoc. (2nd Vice-Pres. 1970). Order of Coif, Phi Beta Kappa, Psi Upsilon, Phi Delta Phi. *Publications:* chap. in book, Mr Justice (ed Dunham and Kurland); contrib. to Antitrust Developments: a supp. to Report of Attorney-Gen.'s Nat. Cttee to Study the Anti-trust Laws, 1955–68; various articles etc, in Ill. Law Rev., Proc. confs, and reports. *Recreations:* flying, tennis, bridge, reading, travel. *Address:* Supreme Court of the United States, Washington, DC 20543, USA.

STEVENS, John Williams, CB 1988; Official Side Member, Civil Service Appeal Board, since 1989; *b* 27 Feb. 1929; *s* of John Williams and Kathleen Stevens; *m* 1949, Grace Stevens; one *s* one *d*. *Educ:* St Ives School. Min. of Supply, 1952; UK Defence Res. and Supply Staff, Australia, 1958–61; HM Treasury, 1966; Civil Service Dept, 1969–73; Price Commn, 1973–74; Head of Personnel, Stock Exchange, 1975–76; Principal Private Sec. to Lord Pres. of the Council and Leader of the House of Commons, 1977–79, to Chancellor of Duchy of Lancaster and Leader of the House, 1979–80; Principal Estabts and Finance Officer, Cabinet Office, 1980–89; Under Sec. 1984. *Recreations:* Cornwall, reading, theatre. *Address:* 14 Highbury Crescent, Portsmouth Road, Camberley, Surrey GU15 1JZ. *Club:* Athenæum.

STEVENS, Kenneth Henry, CBE 1983; DL; Chief Executive Commissioner, The Scout Association, 1970–87; *b* 8 Oct. 1922; *s* of late Horace J. Stevens, CBE, sometime Senior Principal Inspector of Taxes, and late Nora Stevens (*née* Kauntze); *m* 1947, Yvonne Grace Ruth (*née* Mitchell); one *s* one *d*. *Educ:* Brighton Coll.; Brighton Technical Coll. South Coast Civil Defence, 1941–44. Alliance Assurance Co., 1944–47; Asst Dir of Adult Leader Training, Internat. Scout Training Centre, Gilwell Park, Chingford, 1947–56; Organising Comr, World Scout Jamboree, Indaba and Rover Moot, Sutton Coldfield, 1956–58; Dep. Dir of Adult Leader Training, Internat. Scout Training Centre, 1958–61; Asst Chief Exec. Comr, The Scout Assoc., 1961–63; Dep. Chief Exec. Comr, 1963–70. DL Surrey, 1989. *Publication:* Ceremonies of The Scout Movement, 1958. *Recreations:* motoring, gardening. *Address:* Drovers, Crampshaw Lane, Ashtead, Surrey KT21 2UF. *T:* Ashtead (0372) 277841. *Club:* MCC.

STEVENS, Prof. Kenneth William Harry; Professor of Theoretical Physics, 1958–87, now Emeritus, and Senior Research Fellow, 1987–88, University of Nottingham; *b* 17 Sept. 1922; *s* of Harry and Rose Stevens; *m* 1949, Audrey A. Gawthrop; one *s* one *d*. *Educ:* Magdalen College School, Oxford; Jesus and Merton Colleges, Oxford. MA 1947, DPhil 1949. Pressed Steel Company Ltd Research Fellow, Oxford University, 1949–53; Research Fellow, Harvard University, 1953–54; Reader in Theoretical Physics, University of Nottingham, 1953–58. Leverhulme Emeritus Fellow, 1990. Mem., IUPAP Commn on Magnetism, 1984–87. (Jointly) Maxwell Medal and Prize, 1968. *Publications:* contrib. to learned journals. *Recreations:* music, tennis, walking. *Address:* The University, Nottingham.

STEVENS, Sir Laurence (Houghton), Kt 1983; CBE 1979; company director and business consultant; *b* 9 Jan. 1920; *s* of Laurence Stevens and Annie (*née* Houghton); *m* 1943, Beryl J. Dickson; one *s* two *d*. *Educ:* Auckland Boys' Grammar Sch.; Auckland Univ. (BCom). FCA NZ 1969; CMA 1966. Served War, Pacific (Tonga Defence Force) and ME (2NZEF). Joined Auckland Knitting Mills Ltd, 1946; Man. Dir, 1952; retd 1980. Chairman: Thorn EMI Gp of Cos, NZ, 1980–; Chambard Property Develt (formerly Les Mills Corporation) Ltd, 1985–; Fay Richwhite & Co. (formerly Capital Markets Ltd), 1986–; Ascent Corp. Ltd, 1986–88; Auckland Internat. Airport Ltd, 1988–; Director: Guardian Royal Exchange, 1983–; Wormald International NZ Ltd, 1983–90; Reserve Bank of New Zealand, 1978–86; Petroleum Corp. of New Zealand Ltd, 1984–88; R. W. Saunders Ltd, 1984–87; Petralgas Chemicals NZ Ltd, 1986–87; Wormald Pacific Ltd, 1987–90. Past President and Life Member: NZ Knitting Industries Fedn; Textile and Garment Fedn of NZ; Auckland Manufrs' Assoc.; Pres., NZ Manufrs' Fedn, 1970–71 and 1980–81; Chm., Auckland Agricl, Pastoral and Indust. Shows Bd, 1976–86; Mem., Melanesian Trust Bd, 1977–. *Recreation:* tennis (Pres., Auckland Lawn Tennis Assoc., 1983–84). *Address:* 1/1 Watene Crescent, Orakei, Auckland 5, New Zealand. *T:* Auckland 521 0476. *Club:* Northern (Auckland).

STEVENS, Lewis David, MBE 1982; MP (C) Nuneaton, since 1983; *b* 13 April 1936; *s* of Richard and Winnifred Stevens; *m* 1959, Margaret Eileen Gibson; two *s* one *d*. *Educ:* Oldbury Grammar Sch.; Liverpool Univ.; Lanchester Coll. RAF 1956–58. Various engrg cos, mainly in industrial engrg and production management positions, 1958–79; management and industrial engrg consultant (self-employed), 1979–. Mem., Nuneaton Borough Council, 1966–72. *Address:* 151 Sherbourne Avenue, Nuneaton, Warwicks CV10 9JN. *T:* Chapel End (0203) 396105.

STEVENS, Philip Theodore; Professor of Greek in the University of London (Bedford College), 1950–74, now Emeritus; *b* 11 Nov. 1906; *s* of late Rev. Herbert Stevens, Vicar of Milwich; *m* 1939, Evelyn Grace (*d* 1990), 2nd *d* of late G. L. Crickmay, FRIBA, Oatlands Park, Weybridge, Surrey; one *s*. *Educ:* Wolverhampton Grammar School; New Coll., Oxford (Scholar; 1st Cl. Hon. Mods, 1927; 2nd Cl. Lit. Hum., 1929); PhD Aberdeen, 1939. Asst Master, Liverpool Institute, 1929–30; Tutor at Univ. Corresp. Coll., Cambridge, 1930–32; Asst Lecturer in Greek, Univ. of Aberdeen, 1933–38; Lectr in Classics, Univ. of Cape Town, 1938–41. War Service, S African Mil. Intelligence, 1941–45. Lecturer in Latin and Greek, University of Liverpool, 1945–50. Trustee, Hellenic Soc., 1961–. *Publications:* Euripides, Andromache, 1971; Colloquial Expressions in Euripides, 1976; The Society for the Promotion of Hellenic Studies 1879–1979, 1979; contribs to English and foreign classical periodicals. *Recreation:* music. *Address:* The Old Prebendal House, Shipton-under-Wychwood, Oxon OX7 6BQ.

STEVENS, Richard William, RDI 1973; BSc; FCSD; FCIBS; Partner, Richard Stevens Design Associates, since 1987; *b* 1 Oct. 1924; *s* of William Edward Stevens and Caroline Alice (*née* Mills); *m* 1947, Anne Clara Hammond; one *s* one *d*. *Educ:* Dorking County Grammar Sch.; Regent St Polytechnic (BSc). FCSD (FSIAD 1960); FCIBS 1977. Designer, then Chief Designer, Atlas Lighting Ltd, 1954–63; Industrial Design Manager, Standard Telephones and Cables Ltd, 1963–69; Design Manager, Post Office Telecommunications (later British Telecom), 1969–83. Pres., SIAD, 1972–73; Treasurer, ICSID, 1975–77. Gold Medal, Milan Triennale, 1957; three Design Centre Awards, London. *Recreations:* gardening, music, photography, walking. *Address:* Hazel Cottage, Ewood Lane, Newdigate, Dorking, Surrey RH5 5AR.

STEVENS, Prof. Thomas Stevens, FRS 1963; FRSE 1964; Emeritus Professor of Chemistry, University of Sheffield; *b* 8 Oct. 1900; *o c* of John Stevens and Jane E. Stevens (*née* Irving); *m* 1949, Janet Wilson Forsyth; no *c*. *Educ:* Paisley Grammar School; Glasgow Academy; Universities of Glasgow and Oxford. DPhil 1925. Assistant in Chemistry, Univ. of Glasgow, 1921–23, Lecturer, 1925–47; Ramsay Memorial Fellow, Oxford, 1923–25; Sen. Lectr in Organic Chemistry, Univ. of Sheffield, 1947–49, Reader, 1949–63, Prof., 1963–66; Visiting Prof. of Chemistry, Univ. of Strathclyde, Oct. 1966–Sept. 1967. Hon. DSc Glasgow, 1985. *Publications:* (with W. E. Watts) Selected Molecular Rearrangements, 1973; contrib. to Elsevier-Rodd, Chemistry of Carbon Compounds, 1957–60. Papers in scientific jls. *Recreation:* unsophisticated bridge. *Address:* 313 Albert Drive, Glasgow G41 5RP. *T:* 041–423 6928

STEVENS, Timothy John; Keeper of Art, National Museum of Wales, since 1987; *b* 17 Jan. 1940; *s* of Seymour Stevens; *m* 1969, Caroline Sankey; twin *s*. *Educ:* King's Sch., Canterbury; Hertford Coll., Oxford (MA); Courtauld Inst., Univ. of London (Academic Diploma, History of Art). Walker Art Gallery: Asst Keeper of British Art, 1964–65; Keeper of Foreign Art, 1965–67; Dep. Dir, 1967–70; Dir, 1971–74; Dir, Merseyside CC Art Galls, 1974–86; Dep. Dir, Nat. Museums and Galleries on Merseyside, 1986–87. Hon. LittD Liverpool, 1985. Chevalier de l'Ordre des Arts et des Lettres (France), 1988. *Recreation:* gardening. *Address:* National Museum of Wales, Cathays Park, Cardiff CF1 3NP. *T:* Cardiff (0222) 397951.

STEVENS, Ven. Timothy John; Archdeacon of West Ham, since 1991; *b* 31 Dec. 1946; *s* of Ralph and Jean Ursula Stevens; *m* 1973, Wendi Kathleen; one *s* one *d*. *Educ:* Chigwell Sch.; Selwyn Coll., Cambridge (BA 1968; MA 1972); Ripon Hall, Oxford (DipTh). BOAC, 1968–72; FCO, 1972–73. Ordained priest, 1976; Curate, East Ham, 1976–79; Team Vicar, Upton Park, 1979–80; Team Rector, Canvey Island, 1980–88; Bp of Chelsmford's Urban Officer, 1988–91. Hon. Canon of Chelmsford, 1987–. *Recreations:* golf, cricket. *Address:* 86 Aldersbrook Road, E12 5DH. *T:* 081–989 8557.

STEVENS, William David; President, Exxon Company, USA, since 1988; *b* USA, 18 Sept. 1934; *s* of Walter Gerald and Amy Grace Stevens; *m* 1954, Barbara Ann Duncan; one *s* three *d*. *Educ:* Texas A&I Univ. (BScEng). Joined Humble Oil, 1958: various assignments, US Gulf Coast, 1958–73; Exxon Corporation: Executive Asst to President, 1974; various assignments, New York, 1974–77; Vice Pres., Gas, 1977–78; Man. Dir, Esso UK Ltd, London, and Vice Pres. Upstream, Esso Europe, Inc., 1978–85; Executive Vice President: Esso Europe, 1985–86; Exxon Co., USA, Houston, 1986–87. *Recreations:* golf, shooting, hiking. *Address:* Exxon Co., USA, Division of Exxon Corporation, 800 Bell Street, Houston, Texas 77252–2180, USA.

STEVENSON, Dr Alan Carruth; *b* 27 Jan. 1909; *s* of Allan Stevenson, CBE, and Christina Kennedy Lawson; *m* 1937, Annie Gordon Sheila Steven (*d* 1989); two *s* one *d*. *Educ:* Glasgow Academy; Glasgow University. BSc 1930, MB, ChB 1933, MD 1946, Glasgow; MRCP 1935; FRCP 1955. Appointments: Royal Infirmary, Glasgow; Highgate Hospital, London; London Hospital. Served RAMC 1939–45 (despatches); retired with hon. rank of Lieutenant-Colonel, 1946–48. Professor of Social and Preventive Medicine, The Queen's University, Belfast, 1948–58; Reader in Public Health, London University; Dir, MRC Population Genetics Unit, Oxford, and Lectr in Human Genetics, Oxford Univ., 1958–74. *Publications:* Build your own Enlarger, 1943; Recent Advances in Social Medicine, 1948; Genetic Counselling, 1971; articles on Tropical and Preventive Medicine and human genetics in appropriate scientific journals. *Recreation:* fishing. *Address:* 17 Little Dene Copse, Pennington, Lymington, Hants SO41 8EW. *T:* Lymington (0590) 76444.

STEVENSON, Christopher Terence S.; *see* Sinclair Stevenson.

STEVENSON, Sir David; *see* Stevenson, Sir H. D.

STEVENSON, Dennis; *see* Stevenson, H. D.

STEVENSON, Dr Derek Paul, CBE 1972; MRCS, LRCP; *b* 11 July 1911; *s* of late Frederick Stevenson and Maud Coucher; *m* 1941, Pamela Mary, *d* of late Col C. N. Jervelund, OBE; two *s* one *d*. *Educ:* Epsom College; Guy's Hospital. Lieut RAMC, 1935 (Montefiore Prize, Royal Army Med. Coll., 1935); Capt. RAMC 1936; Maj. 1942; Lt-Col 1943; service in China and Malaya. Asst Director-General Army Medical Service, War Office, 1942–46; Sec. Army Medical Advisory Bd 1943–46. War Office rep. on Central Med., War Cttee, 1943–46. British Medical Association: Asst Sec., 1946–48; Dep. Sec., 1948–58; Sec., 1958–76. Sec. Jt Consultants Cttee, 1958–76; Mem., Health Services Bd, and Scottish Cttee, 1977–80. Vice-Pres. British Medical Students Assoc.; Hon. Sec./Treas., British Commonwealth Med. Conf.; Delegate, Gen. Assembly World Medical Association: Sydney, 1968, Paris, 1969, Oslo, 1970, Ottawa, 1971, Amsterdam, 1972, Munich, 1973, Stockholm, 1974, Chm. Council, 1969, 1970–71 (Mem. Council, 1967–). Medical Sec. to Nat. Ophthalmic Treatment Board Assoc.; Mem. Council of London Hospital Service Plan; Mem. Cttee of Management: Medical Insurance Agency; Medical and Dental Retirement Adv. Service; Vice Pres., Private Patients Plan, 1984–. Adviser: Sterling Winthrop, Mediscope Jl; Mem. Adv. Bd, Allied Investments; Dir, Tavistock Computer Services; Gen. Comr, Inland Revenue. Hon. Sec. and Treas., British Commonwealth Medical Assoc., 1964; Sec. Gen., Permanent Cttee of Doctors, EEC, 1973–76; Member: Chichester HA; West Sussex Gen. Practitioners' Cttee; Hon. Sec., British Life Assurance Trust. Liaison Officer, MoD, 1964. Mem. Bd of Governors, Epsom College; Governor, Midhurst Grammar Sch.; Pres., Old Epsomian Club, 1974–75. Mem., Chichester Dio. Bd; Lay Chm., Rural Deanery. Mem., West Sussex CC, 1980–85. Fellow, Royal Commonwealth Soc., 1968; Fellow, BMA, 1976 (Gold Medal, 1976). Hon. LLD, Manchester, 1964. *Publications:* contrib. Irish Medical Jl; BMA Lecture delivered to Irish Medical Assoc.; contrib. Canadian Med. Assoc. Jl, and address at Centennial meeting, Montreal; NHS Reorganisation (in RSH Jl), address to RSH Congress 1973; regular contribs to Medical Interface. *Recreations:* golf, sailing, gardening. *Address:* 19 Marchwood Gate, Chichester, West Sussex PO19 4HA. *T:* Chichester (0243) 774237. *Clubs:* Athenæum, Commonwealth Trust.

STEVENSON, Prof. George Telford; Professor of Immunochemistry, Faculty of Medicine, University of Southampton, since 1974; *b* 18 April 1932; *s* of Ernest George Stevenson and Mary Josephine Madden; *m* 1963, Freda Kathryn Hartley; three *s*. *Educ:* North Sydney High Sch.; Univ. of Sydney (MB, BS; MD); Univ. of Oxford (DPhil). Resident MO, 1955–56, Resident Pathologist, 1957, Sydney Hosp.; Research Fellow, Dept of Medicine, Univ. of Sydney, 1958–61; Nuffield Dominions Demonstrator, Dept of Biochemistry, Univ. of Oxford, 1962–64; Sen. Research Fellow, Dept of Biochemistry, Univ. of Sydney, 1965–66; Scientific Staff, MRC Immunochemistry Unit, Univ. of Oxford, 1967–70; Dir, Tenovus Research Lab., Southampton Gen. Hosp., 1970–; Consultant Immunologist, Southampton Univ. Hosps, 1976–. Hammer Prize for Cancer Research (jtly) (Armand Hammer Foundn, LA), 1982. *Publications:* Immunological Investigation of Lymphoid Neoplasms (with J. L. Smith and T. J. Hamblin), 1983; research papers on immunology and cancer, considered mainly at molecular level. *Address:* 9 Meadowhead Road, Bassett, Southampton SO1 7AD. *T:* Southampton (0703) 769092.

STEVENSON, George William; Member (Lab) Staffordshire East, European Parliament, since 1984; *b* 30 Aug. 1938; *s* of Harold and Elsie May Stevenson; *m* 1958, Doreen June (decd); two *s* one *d*. *Educ:* Uttoxeter Road Primary School; Queensberry Road Secondary School, Stoke-on-Trent. Pottery caster, 1953–57; coal miner, 1957–64; transport driver, 1964–66; bus driver, 1966–84; shop steward, TGWU 5/24 Branch, 1968–84 (Mem., 1964–; Chm., 1975–81). Member: Stoke-on-Trent City Council, 1972–86; Staffs County Council, 1981–85. Pres., Eur. Parlt Delegn for Relations with S Asia, 1989– (Vice-Pres., 1984–89). Prospective Parly Cand. (Lab) Stoke-on-Trent S, 1990–. *Recreations:* reading, crown green bowling. *Address:* (home) 291 Weston Road, Meir, Stoke-on-Trent, Staffs;

(office) Euro-Constituency Office, Pioneer House, 76/80 Lonsdale Street, Stoke-on-Trent, Staffs ST4 4DP. *T:* Stoke-on-Trent (0782) 414232. *Club:* Meir Sports and Social.

STEVENSON, Henry Dennistoun, (Dennis Stevenson), CBE 1981; Chairman: SRU Group of companies, since 1972; Board of Trustees, Tate Gallery, since 1988; *b* 19 July 1945; *s* of Alexander James Stevenson and Sylvia Florence Stevenson (*née* Ingleby); *m* 1972, Charlotte Susan, *d* of Hon. Sir Peter Vanneck, *qv*; four *s*. *Educ:* Glenalmond; King's Coll., Cambridge (MA). Chm., Newton Aycliffe and Peterlee New Town Develt Corp., 1971–80; Dir, LDDC, 1981–88. Chairman: govt working party on role of voluntary movements and youth in the environment, 1971, '50 Million Volunteers' (HMSO); Indep. Advisory Cttee on Pop Festivals, 1972–76, 'Pop Festivals, Report and Code of Practice' (HMSO); Adviser on Agricultural Marketing to Minister of Agriculture, 1979–83. Mem. Admin. Council, Royal Jubilee Trusts, 1978–80. Chm., Intermediate Technology Develt Gp, 1983–90; Director: Nat. Building Agency, 1977–81; British Technology Gp, 1979–89; Tyne Tees Television, 1982–87; Pearson plc, 1986–; Manpower plc (formerly Blue Arrow), 1988–; Thames Television, 1991–. Chairman: NAYC, 1973–81; Docklands Sinfonietta, 1990–. *Recreation:* home. *Clubs:* Brooks's, MCC.

STEVENSON, Vice-Adm. Sir (Hugh) David, AC 1976; KBE 1977 (CBE 1970); Royal Australian Navy, retired; *b* 24 Aug. 1918; *s* of late Rt Rev. William Henry Webster Stevenson, Bishop of Grafton, NSW, and Mrs Katherine Saumarez Stevenson; *m* 1st, 1944, Myra Joyce Clarke (*d* 1978); one *s* one *d*; 2nd, 1979, Margaret Wheeler Wright. *Educ:* Southport Sch., Qld; RAN Coll. psc RN 1956; idc 1966. Commnd, 1938; served War: Mediterranean, East Indies, Pacific; minesweeping post, SW Pacific; specialised in navigation, 1944 (HM Navigation Sch.); Commands: HMAS Tobruk and 10th Destroyer Sqdn, 1959–60; HMNZS Royalist, 1960–61; HMAS Sydney, 1964; HMAS Melbourne, 1965–66; Dir of Plans, 1962–63; Naval Officer i/c W Australian area, 1967; Dep. Chief of Naval Staff, 1968–69; Comdr Aust. Fleet, 1970–71; Chief of: Naval Personnel, 1972–73; Naval Staff, 1973–76; retd 1976. Comdr 1952; Captain 1958; Cdre 1967; Rear-Adm. 1968; Vice-Adm. 1973–85. Chm. for Territories, Queen Elizabeth Jubilee Fund for Young Australians, 1977. *Publication:* (contrib.) The Use of Radar at Sea, 1952. *Recreations:* reading, opera, bridge. *Address:* 109 Jefferson Lane, Palm Beach, Qld 4221, Australia. *T* and *Fax:* 075–344103. *Clubs:* Commonwealth Trust; Canberra Yacht, Federal Golf (Canberra).

STEVENSON, Dr Jim; Chief Executive, Educational Broadcasting Services Trust, since 1988; *b* 9 May 1937; *s* of George Stevenson and Frances Mildred Groat; *m* 1963, Brenda Cooley; one *s* one *d*. *Educ:* Kirkham Grammar Sch.; Univ. of Liverpool (BSc, PhD). NATO Res. Fellow, Univ. of Trondheim, 1963–65; Lectr in Biochemistry, Univ. of Warwick, 1965–69; BBC Open Univ. Production Centre: Producer, 1969–75; Exec. Producer, 1975–76; Editor (Science), 1976–79; Head of Programmes, 1979–82; Dep. Sec., BBC, 1982–83; Head of Educnl Broadcasting Services and Educn Sec., BBC, 1983–89. *Publications:* contribs to sci. jls and communications jls. *Recreations:* television, reading, drawing. *Address:* 34 Vallance Road, N22 4UB. *T:* 081–889 6261. *Club:* Savile.

STEVENSON, John, CBE 1987; Deputy Licensing Authority: South East Traffic Area, since 1987; Metropolitan Traffic Area, since 1989; Eastern Traffic Area, since 1990; Western Traffic Area, since 1991; *b* 15 June 1927; *s* of John and Harriet Esther Stevenson; *m* 1956, Kathleen Petch; one *s* one *d*. *Educ:* Durham Univ. (LLB); MA Oxon 1982. Solicitor. Legal Asst, Borough of Hartlepool, 1951; Junior Solicitor, County Borough of Sunderland, 1952; Solicitor, Hertfordshire CC, 1953, Asst Clerk, 1964; Clerk of the Peace and County Solicitor, Gloucestershire CC, 1969; Chief Executive, Buckinghamshire CC, 1974; Sec., ACC, 1980–87. Hon. Fellow, Inst. Local Govt Studies, Birmingham Univ., 1981–; Vis. Fellow, Nuffield Coll., Oxford, 1982–90. Vice President, Inst. of Trading Standards Administration, 1988. *Address:* 2 Water's Edge, Port La Salle, Bouldnor, Yarmouth, Isle of Wight; 405 Keyes House, Dolphin Square, SW1. *T:* 071–834 2149.

STEVENSON, Joseph Aidan; Chief Executive Officer, since 1989, Vice Chairman, since 1991, Johnson Matthey plc; *b* 19 April 1931; *s* of Robert and Bridget Stevenson; *m* 1956, Marjorie Skinner; one *s* two *d*. *Educ:* Birmingham Univ. (BSc Hons Metallurgy). Instr Lieut, RN, 1955–58. Joined Johnson Matthey, 1958, as development metallurgist; held a number of sen. management, operating and div. dirships within the Johnson Matthey Gp; Gp Exec. Dir, 1982–. Chm. of Govs, Combe Bank Indep. Girls' Sch., Kent, 1985–. Mem. Council, Royal London Soc. for the Blind, 1990–. Liveryman: Goldsmiths' Co.; Clockmakers' Co. Distinguished Achievement Award, Inst. of Precious Metals, 1989. *Recreations:* golf, sailing. *Address:* Johnson Matthey, 2–4 Cockspur Street, Trafalgar Square, SW1Y 5BQ. *Club:* Knole Park Golf (Sevenoaks).

STEVENSON, Prof. Olive; Professor of Social Work Studies, University of Nottingham, since 1984 (Head, School of Social Studies, 1987–91); Fellow, St Anne's College, University of Oxford, since 1970; *b* 13 Dec. 1930; *d* of John and Evelyn Stevenson. *Educ:* Purley County Grammar Sch. for Girls; Lady Margaret Hall, Oxford (BA EngLitt, MA 1955); London Sch. of Economics (Dip. in Social Studies, Dip. in Child Care). Tavistock Clinic; Child Care Officer, Devon CC, 1954–58; Lecturer in Applied Social Studies: Univ. of Bristol, 1959–61; Univ. of Oxford, 1961–68; Social Work Adviser, Supplementary Benefits Commn, 1968–70; Reader in Applied Social Studies, Univ. of Oxford, 1970–76; Prof. of Social Policy and Social Work: Univ. of Keele, 1976–82; Univ. of Liverpool, 1983–84. Member: Royal Commn on Civil Liability, 1973–78; Social Security Adv. Cttee, 1982–; Registered Homes Tribunal, 1985–90; Chairman: Adv. Cttee, Rent Rebates and Rent Allowances, 1977–83; Age Concern England, 1980–83; Councils of Voluntary Service Nat. Assoc., 1985–88. *Publications:* Someone Else's Child, 1965, rev. edn 1977; Claimant or Client?, 1970; Social Service Teams: the practitioner's view, 1978; Child Abuse: interprofessional communication, 1979; Specialisation in Social Service Teams, 1981; (with Fuller) Policies, Programmes and Disadvantage, 1983; Age and Vulnerability, a guide to better care, 1988; (ed) Child Abuse: public policy and professional practice, 1989. *Recreations:* music, cookery, conversation. *Address:* School of Social Studies, University of Nottingham, Nottingham NG7 2RD.

STEVENSON, Robert Barron Kerr, CBE 1976; MA; FSA; Keeper, National Museum of Antiquities of Scotland, 1946–78, Trustee, 1975–78; *b* 16 July 1913; *s* of late Professor William B. Stevenson; *m* 1950, Elizabeth M. Begg; twin *s*. Member: Ancient Monuments Board for Scotland, 1961–79; Cttees of Inquiry: Field Monuments, 1966–68; Provincial Museums, 1972–73. Pres., Soc. of Antiquaries of Scotland, 1975–78. Mem., Deutsches Archäologisches Institut, 1953–. Fellow, UCL, 1977. FMA, 1953–78. Hon. FRNS 1979; Hon. DLitt Edinburgh, 1981. *Address:* 51/1 Mortonhall Road, Edinburgh EH9 2HN. *T:* 031–662 0826.

STEVENSON, Robert Bryce; General President, National Union of Footwear Leather and Allied Trades, 1980–90, retired; *b* 26 June 1926; *s* of Daniel Liddle Stevenson and Christina Stevenson; *m* 1947, Margaret Eugenia; two *d*. *Educ:* Caldercruix Advanced Sch., Airdrie, Lanarks. Full-time Officer NUFLAT, Street, Som. Branch, 1961–80. Member, 1980–: Internat. Textile, Garment and Leather Workers Fedn Exec. Council and Cttee (Brussels); Jt Cttee, Footwear Industry in Europe (Brussels); Footwear Econ. Develt Cttee, 1980–88; TUC Textile, Clothing and Footwear Industries Cttee; Council, Shoe and Allied Trades Res. Assoc.; Boot and Shoe Repairing Wages Council for GB; Bd of Management, Boot Trade Benevolent Soc.; Mem., Footwear Leather and Fur Skin Industry Trng Bd, 1980–82; Mem., TUC Gen. Council, 1984–. JP Wells and Glastonbury 1970 (on Supplementary List, Northants, 1981). *Recreations:* listening to and playing music, all sports. *Address:* 27 Wentworth Avenue, Wellingborough, NorthantsNN8 3PE. *T:* Wellingborough (0933) 676959.

STEVENSON, Robert Wilfrid, (Wilf); Director, British Film Institute, since 1988; *b* 19 April 1947; *s* of James Alexander Stevenson and Elizabeth Anne Stevenson (*née* Macrae); *m* 1st, 1972, Jennifer Grace Antonio (marr. diss. 1979); 2nd, 1991, Elizabeth Ann Minogue. *Educ:* Edinburgh Academy; University College, Oxford (BA Natural Sciences, Chemistry); Napier Polytechnic. ACCA. Research Officer, Edinburgh Univ. Students' Assoc., 1970–74; Sec., Napier Polytechnic, Edinburgh, 1974–87; Dep. Dir, BFI, 1987–88. *Recreations:* cinema, hill walking, bridge. *Address:* (office) 21 Stephen Street, W1P 1PL. *T:* 071–255 1444.

STEVENSON, Sir Simpson, Kt 1976; DL; *b* 18 Aug. 1921; *s* of T. H. Stevenson, Greenock; *m* 1945, Jean Holmes Henry, JP, Port Glasgow. *Educ:* Greenock High Sch. Member: Greenock Town Council, 1949–67 and 1971– (Provost of Greenock, 1962–65); Inverclyde DC, 1974– (Provost, 1984–88); Vice-Chm., Clyde Port Authority, 1966–69; Chm., Greater Glasgow Health Bd, 1973–83; Chm., Scottish Health Services Common Service Agency, 1973–77, 1983–87. Member: Western Regional Hosp. Bd (Scotland), 1959–; Scottish Hosp. Administrative Staffs Cttee, 1965–74 (Chm., 1972–74); Chm., W Regional Hosp. Bd (Scotland), Glasgow, 1967–74; Member: Scottish Hosp. Endowments Commn, 1969–70; Scottish Health Services Planning Council; Royal Commn on the NHS, 1976–79. Chm., Consortium of Local Authorities Special Programme (CLASP), 1974. DL Renfrewshire, 1990. Hon. LLD Glasgow, 1982. *Recreations:* football, reading, choral singing. *Address:* 64A Reservoir Road, Gourock, Renfrewshire PA19 1YQ.

STEVENSON, Wilf; *see* Stevenson, R. W.

STEVENSON, William Trevor, CBE 1985; DL; *b* 21 March 1921; *o s* of late William Houston Stevenson and Mabel Rose Stevenson (*née* Hunt); *m* Alison Wilson (*née* Roy). *Educ:* Edinburgh Acad. Apprentice mechanical engineer, 1937–41; engineer, 1941–45; entered family food manufacturing business, Cottage Rusks, 1945; Man. Dir, 1948–54; Chm., 1954–59; Chief Executive, Cottage Rusks Associates, (following merger with Joseph Rank Ltd), 1959–69; Reg. Dir, Ranks Hovis McDougall, 1969–74; Dir, various cos in food, engrg, medical, hotel and aviation industries, 1974–; Chairman: Gleneagles Hotels, 1981–83; Scottish Transport Gp, 1981–86; Hodgson Martin Ventures, 1982–88; Alexander Wilkie, 1977–90. Master, Co. of Merchants of City of Edinburgh, 1978–80. DL City of Edinburgh, 1984. *Recreations:* flying, sailing, curling. *Address:* 45 Pentland View, Edinburgh EH10 6PY. *T:* 031–445 1512. *Clubs:* Caledonian; New (Edinburgh).

STEWARD, Rear Adm. Cedric John, CB 1984; Director: Antric Park, since 1986; Fontainebleau (Orewa, Auckland), since 1987; Horse Stud Owner, Antric Park, Auckland; Chief of Naval Staff, New Zealand, 1983–86, retired; *b* 31 Jan. 1931; *s* of Ethelbert Harold Steward and Anne Isabelle Steward; *m* 1952, Marie Antoinette Gurr; three *s*. *Educ:* Northcote College, Auckland, NZ; RNC Dartmouth; RNC Greenwich. Served: HMS Devonshire, 1950; HMS Illustrious, 1950; HMS Glory, 1951 (Korean Campaign and UN Medals, 1951); HMAS Australia, HMAS Barcoo, 1952; HM NZ Ships Hawea, 1953, Kaniere, 1954 (Korea), Tamaki, 1955–58, Stawell, 1958–59; HMAS Creswell (RAN College), 1959–62; HM NZ Ships Rotoiti, 1962–63 (Antarctic support), Tamaki, 1963–64, Royalist, 1965–66 (Confrontation), Philomel, 1966, Inverell (in Command), 1966–67; JSSC Latimer, 1968; Dep. Head, NZ Defence Liaison Staff, Canberra, 1969–73; in Command, HMNZS Otago, 1973–74; in Command and Captain F11, HMNZS Canterbury, 1974–75; Defence HQ, 1976–77; RCDS, 1978; Dep. Chief of Naval Staff, NZ, 1979–81; Commodore, Auckland, 1981–83. *Recreations:* rugby, golf, tennis, equestrian events, fishing, boating, philately, farming. *Clubs:* Helensville Golf (Kaukapakapa), Auckland Racing (Ellerslie).

STEWARD, Prof. Frederick Campion, FRS 1957; Charles A. Alexander Professor of Biological Sciences and Director of Laboratory for Cell Physiology and Growth, Cornell University, Ithaca, NY, 1965–72, now Professor Emeritus (Professor of Botany, 1950–65); *b* 16 June 1904; *s* of Frederick Walter and Mary Daglish Steward; *m* 1929, Anne Temple Gordon, Richmond, Va, USA; one *s*. *Educ:* Heckmondwike Gram. Sch., Yorks; Leeds Univ. BSc 1924 (1st Class Hons); PhD 1926. DSc London 1937. Demonstrator in Botany, Leeds Univ., 1926; Rockefeller Fellow: Cornell Univ., 1927, Univ. of California, 1928; Asst Lecturer, Univ. of Leeds (Botany), 1929; Rockefeller Foundation Fellow, 1933–34; Reader in Botany, Univ. of London (Birkbeck Coll.), 1934; War Service with MAP (Dir of Aircraft Equipment), 1940–45; Prof. of Botany and Chm. of Dept, Univ. of Rochester, Rochester, NY, 1946–50. John Simon Guggenheim Fell., 1963–64; Sir C. V. Raman Vis. Prof., Madras Univ., 1974. Fellow American Academy of Arts and Sciences, 1956. Merit Award, Botanical Society of America, 1961. Hon. DSc: Delhi, 1974; William and Mary, 1982; Guelph, 1983. *Publications:* Plants at Work, 1964; Growth and Organisation in Plants, 1968; Plants, Chemicals and Growth, 1971; (ed) Treatise on Plant Physiology, 6 vols and 11 tomes, 1959–72, Vols 7–9, 1983–86; papers in scientific journals and proceedings of learned societies. *Recreations:* gardening, swimming. *Address:* 4947 Woodland Forrest Drive, Tuscaloosa, Ala 35405, USA.

STEWARD, Stanley Feargus, CBE 1947; CEng; FIProdE; Chairman: George Thurlow and Sons (Holdings) Ltd; ERA Technology Ltd, 1983–84; *b* 9 July 1904; *s* of late Arthur Robert and late Minnie Elizabeth Steward, Mundesley, Norfolk; *m* 1929, Phyllis Winifred, *d* of late J. Thurlow, Stowmarket, Suffolk; one *s* one *d*. *Educ:* The Paston Sch., North Walsham, Norfolk. Was apprenticed to East Anglian Engineering Co. (subseq. Bull Motors Ltd) and subseq. held positions of Chief Designer, Sales Manager and Managing Dir; Min. of Supply Electrical Adviser to Machine Tool Control, 1940; Director of Industrial Electrical Equipment, 1941–44; Dir Gen. of Machine Tools, 1944–45; Chm. Machine Tool Advisory Council, 1946–47; Chm. Gauge & Tool Advisory Council, 1946–47. Director: E. R. & F. Turner, Ltd, Ipswich, 1944–48. Chm., South Western Electricity Board, 1948–55; Man. Dir, Lancashire Dynamo Holdings Ltd, 1956–59 (Chm., 1957–58); Former Chm., Lancashire Dynamo and Crypto Ltd, Lancashire Dynamo Electronic Products Ltd and Lancashire Dynamo Group Sales; Chairman: William Steward (Holdings) Ltd and William Steward & Co. Ltd, 1970–80; Thurlow, Nunn & Sons Ltd, 1970–84; Dir, Bull Motors Ltd, 1981–85. Member: British Electricity Authority, 1952–53; Elect. Engineering EDC, 1962–71; Machine Tool EDC, 1971–80; Chm., British Electrical Development Assoc., 1954; President: Ipswich and District Electrical Assoc., 1964–67, 1972–78; Electrical Industries Club, 1966–67; Assoc. of Supervisory and Exec. Engineers, 1970–74; Electrical and Electronic Industries Benevolent Assoc., 1971–72; Instn of Engineers-in-Charge, 1982–84; Man. Dir, BEAMA, 1959–71; Pres., Exec. Cttee, Organisme de Liaison des Industries Metalliques Europeénes, 1963–67. Freeman of City of London; Master, Worshipful Company of Glaziers and

Painters of Glass, 1964. *Publications:* Electricity and Food Production, 1953; British Electrical Manufacture in the National Economy, 1961; Twenty Five Years of South Western Electricity, 1973; The Story of the Dynamicables, 1983; The Story of Electrex, 1984; regular 'Personal View' contribs to Electrical Review and other jls. *Recreations:* books, music, watching cricket. *Address:* 41 Fairacres, Roehampton Lane, SW15 5LX. *T:* 081–876 2457. *Clubs:* Athenæum, MCC.

STEWART, family name of **Earl of Galloway.**

STEWART; *see* Vane-Tempest-Stewart, family name of Marquess of Londonderry.

STEWART, Sir Alan, KBE 1981 (CBE 1972); Vice-Chancellor of Massey University, 1964–83; *b* 8 Dec. 1917; *s* of Kenneth and Vera Mary Stewart; *m* 1950, Joan Cecily Sisam; one *s* three *d*. *Educ:* Massey Agricultural College; University College, Oxford. Sen. Lectr, Massey Agric. Coll., 1950–54; Chief Consulting Officer, Milk Marketing Board, England and Wales, 1954–58; Principal, Massey Agric. Coll., 1959–63. Hon. DSc Massey, 1984. *Address:* PO Box 3, Whakatane, New Zealand. *T:* Whakatane 86–619.

STEWART, Sir Alan (d'Arcy), 13th Bt *cr* 1623; yachtbuilder; *b* 29 Nov. 1932; *s* of Sir Jocelyn Harry Stewart, 12th Bt, and Constance Mary (*d* 1940), *d* of D'Arcy Shillaber; *S* father, 1982; *m* 1952, Patricia, *d* of Lawrence Turner; two *s* two *d*. *Educ:* All Saints College, Bathurst, NSW. *Heir:* *s* Nicholas Courtney d'Arcy Stewart, BSc, HDipEd, *b* 4 Aug. 1953. *Address:* One Acre House, Ramelton, Co. Donegal. *T:* Ramelton 82.

STEWART, Alastair Lindsay; Sheriff of Tayside, Central and Fife at Dundee, since 1990; *b* 28 Nov. 1938; *s* of Alexander Lindsay Stewart and Anna Stewart; *m* 1st, 1968, Annabel Claire Stewart (marr. diss.), *yr d* of late Prof. W. McC. Stewart; two *s*; 2nd, 1991, Sheila Ann Mackinnon (*née* Flockhart), *o d* of David H. Flockhart. *Educ:* Edinburgh Academy; St Edmund Hall, Oxford (BA); Univ. of Edinburgh (LLB). Admitted to Faculty of Advocates, 1963; Tutor, Faculty of Law, Univ. of Edinburgh, 1963–73; Standing Junior Counsel to Registrar of Restrictive Trading Agreements, 1968–70; Advocate Depute, 1970–73; Sheriff of South Strathclyde, Dumfries and Galloway, at Airdrie, 1973–79, of Grampian, Highland and Islands, at Aberdeen and Stonehaven, 1979–90. Chairman: Grampian Family Conciliation Service, 1984–87 (Hon. Pres., 1987–90); Scottish Assoc. of Family Conciliation Services, 1986–89. Governor, Robert Gordon's Inst. of Technology, 1982–90 (Vice-Chm. of Governors, 1985–90). *Publications:* contrib. chapter in Sheriff Court Practice, by I. D. Macphail, 1988; The Scottish Criminal Courts in Action, 1990; various articles in legal jls. *Recreations:* reading, music, walking. *Address:* Sheriffs' Chambers, Sheriff Court House, PO Box 2, Dundee DD1 9AD. *T:* Dundee (0382) 29961.

STEWART, Allan; *see* Stewart, J. A.

STEWART, Andrew, CBE 1954; *b* 23 June 1907; *s* of James Stewart; *m* 1937, Agnes Isabella Burnet, *d* of James McKechnie, JP. *Educ:* Glasgow University (MA). Hon LLD Glasgow, 1970. Joined BBC at Glasgow, 1926; Glasgow Representative, 1931–35; Scottish Programme Director, 1935–48; Controller (N Ire.), 1948–52; Controller (Home Service), 1953–57; Controller, Scotland, 1957–68. Min. of Information, 1939–41. Director, Scottish Television, 1968–77. Chm., Scottish Music Archive, 1972–82; Chm., Films of Scotland Committee. Governor, National Film School, 1971–76. Hon. Pres., Scottish Radio Industries Club, 1972–89. *Recreations:* reading, the theatre, mountaineering. *Address:* 36 Sherbrooke Avenue, Glasgow G41 4EP.

STEWART, Andrew Struthers, (Andy); MP (C) Sherwood, since 1983; farmer; *b* 27 May 1937; *s* of late James Stewart and of Elizabeth Stewart; *m* 1961, Louise Melvin (*née* Skimming); one *s* one *d*. *Educ:* Strathaven Acad., Scotland; West of Scotland Agricl Coll. Farming Beesthorpe Manor Farm, 1961–. Mem., Caunton Parish Council, 1973–83; Conservative Mem., Notts CC, 1975–83; Cons. spokesman on leisure services, 1981–83. PPS to Minister of Agriculture, Fisheries and Food, 1987–89, to Sec. of State for Educn and Science, 1989–90, to Lord Pres. of Council and Leader of H of C, 1990–. Chairman: Strathaven Br., Young Conservatives, 1957 and 1958; Caunton, Maplebeck and Kersall Cons. Br., 1970–73 (Founder Mem.). Member: Newark Br., NFU, 1961– (Mem., County Exec. Cttee, 1966–); Newark and Notts Agricl Soc.; Adv. Mem., Nottingham University Coll. of Agriculture, 1977–82 (formerly Chm., Notts Coll. of Agriculture Brackenhurst); formerly Chm., Governing Bd, Rufford Comprehensive Sch. Youth Club Leader, 1965–76; Life Vice President: Southwell Rugby Club; Caunton Cricket Club; Trustee, Southwell Recreation Centre, 1979–83. *Address:* Beesthorpe Manor Farm, Caunton, Newark, Notts NG23 6AT. *T:* Caunton (063686)270. *Clubs:* Farmers'; Bentinck Conservative (Hucknall, Notts).

STEWART, Angus; QC (Scot.); *b* 14 Dec. 1946; *s* of Archibald Ian Balfour Stewart, CBE, BL, FSAScot and Ailsa Rosamund Mary Massey; *m* 1975, Jennifer Margaret Stewart; one *d*. *Educ:* Edinburgh Acad.; Balliol Coll., Oxford (BA); Edinburgh Univ. (LLB). Called to the Scottish Bar, 1975. *Address:* 8 Ann Street, Edinburgh EH4 1PJ. *T:* 031–332 4083.

STEWART, Rt. Hon. Sir (Bernard Harold) Ian (Halley), Kt 1991; PC 1989; RD 1972; FBA 1981; FRSE 1986; MP (C) Hertfordshire North, since 1983 (Hitchin, Feb. 1974–1983); *b* 10 Aug. 1935; *s* of Prof. H. C. Stewart, *qv*; *m* 1966, Deborah Charlotte, *d* of Hon. William Buchan and late Barbara Howard Ensor, JP; one *s* two *d*. *Educ:* Haileybury; Jesus Coll., Cambridge (MA; LittD 1978). 1st cl. hons Class. Tripos Cantab. Nat. Service, RNVR, 1954–56; subseq. Lt-Cmdr RNR. Seccombe, Marshall & Campion Ltd, bill brokers, 1959–60; joined Brown, Shipley & Co. Ltd, 1960, Asst Man. 1963, Man. 1966, Dir 1971–83; Director: Brown Shipley Holdings Ltd, 1980–83; Victory Insurance Co. Ltd, 1976–83; Seccombe Marshall & Campion Hldgs Ltd, 1989–; Diploma plc, 1990–; Standard Chartered plc, 1990–; Chm., Throgmorton Trust, 1990–. Opposition spokesman on Banking Bill, 1978–79; PPS to Chancellor of the Exchequer, 1979–83; Parly Under-Sec. of State for Defence Procurement, MoD, Jan.-Oct. 1983; Economic Sec. to HM Treasury, 1983–87; Minister of State: for the Armed Forces, MoD, 1987–88; NI Office, 1988–89. Jt Sec., Cons. Parly Finance Cttee, 1975–76, 1977–79; Mem. Public Expenditure Cttee, 1977–79. Mem. British Academy Cttee for Sylloge of Coins of British Isles, 1967–; Hon. Treas., Westminster Cttee for Protection of Children, 1960–70, Vice-Chm., 1975–. FSA (Mem. Council 1974–76); FSA Scot; Dir, British Numismatic Soc., 1965–75 (Sanford Saltus Gold Medal 1971); FRNS (Parkes Weber Prize). Vice-Pres., Hertfordshire Soc., 1974–; Mem. Council, British Museum Soc., 1975–76. Life Governor, 1977, Mem. Council, 1980–, Haileybury; Trustee, Sir Halley Stewart Trust, 1978–. Hon. Vice-Pres., Stewart Soc. 1989–. County Vice-Pres., St John Ambulance for Herts, 1978–; CStJ 1986. *Publications:* The Scottish Coinage, 1955 (2nd edn 1967); Scottish Mints, 1971; (ed with C. N. L. Brooke and others) Studies in Numismatic Method, 1983; (with C. E. Blunt and C. S. S. Lyon) Coinage in Tenth-Century England, 1989; many papers in Proc. Soc. Antiquaries of Scotland, Numismatic Chronicle, British Numismatic Jl, etc. *Recreations:* history; tennis (Captain CU Tennis Club, 1958–59; 1st string v Oxford, 1958 and 1959; winner Coupe de Bordeaux 1959; led 1st Oxford and Cambridge Tennis and Rackets team to USA, 1958; played squash for Herts); Homer. *Address:* House of Commons, SW1A 0AA. *Clubs:* MCC; Hawks, Pitt (Cambridge).

STEWART, Brian John; Group Chief Executive, Scottish and Newcastle plc (formerly Scottish & Newcastle Breweries), since 1991; *b* 9 April 1945; *m* 1971, Shona Duncan; two *s* one *d*. *Educ:* Edinburgh Univ. (MSc). Mem., Scottish Inst. of Chartered Accountants. Scottish and Newcastle Breweries: joined 1976; Finance Dir, 1988–91. *Recreations:* golf, ski-ing. *Address:* Abbey Brewery, Holyrood Road, Edinburgh EH8 8YS. *T:* 031–556 2591.

STEWART, Brian Thomas Webster, CMG 1969; Director of Operations (China), Racal Electronics, since 1982; *b* 27 April 1922; *s* of late Redvers Buller Stewart and Mabel Banks Sparks, Broich, Crieff; *m* 1946, Millicent Peggy Pollock (marr. diss. 1970); two *d*; *m* 1972, Sally Nugent; one *s* one *d*. *Educ:* Trinity Coll., Glenalmond; Worcester Coll., Oxford (MA). Commnd The Black Watch (RHR), 1942; served Europe and Far East (Capt.). Joined Malayan Civil Service, 1946; studying Chinese Macau, 1947; Asst Sec., Chinese Affairs, Singapore, 1949; Devonshire Course, Oxford, 1950; Asst Comr for Labour, Kuala Lumpur, 1951; Sec. for Chinese Affairs, Supt of Chinese Schs, Malacca and Penang, 1952–57; joined HM Diplomatic Service, 1957; served Rangoon, Peking, Shanghai, Manila, Kuala Lumpur, Hanoi; Asst Sec., Cabinet Office, 1968–72; Counsellor, Hong Kong, 1972–74; FCO, 1974–78. Special Rep., Rubber Growers Assoc., Malaysia, 1979–82. Hon. Lectr, Hong Kong Univ., 1986–. *Publication:* All Men's Wisdom (anthology of Chinese Proverbs), 1957. *Recreations:* climbing, sailing, ski-ing, chamber music, orientalia particularly chinoiserie. *Address:* c/o Royal Bank of Scotland, Crieff, Perthshire. *Clubs:* Athenæum, Special Forces; Hong Kong.

STEWART, Colin MacDonald, CB 1983; FIA, FSS; Directing Actuary, Government Actuary's Department, 1974–84; *b* 26 Dec. 1922; *s* of John Stewart and Lillias Cecilia MacDonald Fraser; *m* 1948, Gladys Edith Thwaites; three *d*. *Educ:* Queen's Park Secondary Sch., Glasgow. Clerical Officer, Rosyth Dockyard, 1939–42. Served War: Fleet Air Arm (Lieut (A) RNVR), 1942–46. Govt Actuary's Dept, London, 1946–84. Head of Actuarial Res., Godwins Ltd, 1985–88. FIA 1953. *Publications:* The Students' Society Log 1960–85, 1985; numerous articles on actuarial and demographic subjects in British and internat. jls. *Recreations:* genealogical research, foreign travel, grandchilding. *Address:* 8 The Chase, Coulsdon, Surrey CR5 2EG. *T:* 081–660 3966.

STEWART, Sir David (Brodribb), 2nd Bt *cr* 1960, TD 1948; Managing Director, Francis Price (Fabrics) Ltd, Manchester, 1960–81; retired; *b* 20 Dec. 1913; *s* of Sir Kenneth Dugald Stewart, 1st Bt, GBE, and Noel (*d* 1946), *y d* of Kenric Brodribb, Melbourne; *S* father, 1972; *m* 1963, Barbara Dykes, *widow* of Donald Ian Stewart and *d* of late Harry Dykes Lloyd. *Educ:* Marlborough College; Manchester College of Technology (BSc (Tech), Textile Technology). Joined Stewart Thomson & Co. Ltd, Textile Merchant Converters, 1935; continuously employed in this company, except for six years war service, until absorbed into the Haighton & Dewhurst Group, 1958; Francis Price (Fabrics) Ltd is a subsidiary of this Group. Commissioned 8th Bn Lancashire Fusiliers (TA), 1934; war service, 1939–45; joined Duke of Lancaster's Own Yeomanry (TA) on re-formation of TA, 1947; in comd, 1952–56; retd with rank of Bt Col. *Recreation:* gardening. *Heir:* *b* Robin Alastair Stewart [*b* 26 Sept. 1925; *m* 1953, Patricia Helen, *d* of late J. A. Merrett; one *s* three *d*]. *Address:* Delamere, Heyes Lane, Alderley Edge, Cheshire SK9 7JY. *T:* Alderley Edge (0625) 582312.

STEWART, Sir David James H.; *see* Henderson-Stewart.

STEWART, Rt. Hon. Donald James, PC 1977; *b* 17 Oct. 1920; *m* 1955, Christina Macaulay. *Educ:* Nicolson Institute, Stornoway. Provost of Stornoway, 1958–64 and 1968–70; Hon. Sheriff, 1960. MP (SNP) Western Isles, 1970–87; Leader, Parly SNP, 1974–87; Pres., SNP, 1982–87. *Recreations:* fishing, photography, gardening. *Address:* Hillcrest, 41 Goathill Road, Stornoway, Isle of Lewis. *T:* Stornoway (0851) 2672.

STEWART, Duncan Montgomery; Principal of Lady Margaret Hall, Oxford, since 1979; *b* 14 Feb. 1930; *s* of William Montgomery Stewart and Mary Pauline (*née* Checkley); *m* 1961, Valerie Mary Grace, *er d* of Major E. H. T. Boileau, Rampisham, Dorset; one *s* one *d*. *Educ:* Greymouth Technical High Sch.; Christ's Coll., NZ; Canterbury University Coll., NZ (MA 1st Cl. French 1951, 1st Cl. Latin 1952); Rhodes Scholar, 1953; Queen's Coll., Oxford (1st Cl. Hons Mod. Langs 1955). Lectr, Wadham Coll., Oxford, 1955, Fellow, 1956–79. Vice-Chm., Oxford Univ. Gen. Bd of Faculties, 1976–78; Oxford Chm., Oxford and Cambridge Schs Exam. Bd, 1986–. Mem., Hebdomadal Council, 1976–; Rhodes Trustee, 1986–. *Publications:* articles and revs on French Literature, esp. later medieval. *Recreations:* growing vegetables, opera, wine. *Address:* 6 Fyfield Road, Oxford.

STEWART, Sir Edward (Jackson), Kt 1980; Chairman, Stewarts Hotels Pty Ltd, since 1956; *b* 10 Dec. 1923; *s* of Charles Jackson Stewart and Jessie Stewart (*née* Dobbie); *m* 1956, Shirley Patricia Holmes; four *s*. *Educ:* St Joseph's College, Brisbane. Fellow Catering Inst. of Australia (FCIA); FAIM. Served with Australian Army, RAA, 1942–44. Chairman: Castlemaine Perkins Ltd, 1977–80 (Dir, 1970); Castlemaine Tooheys Ltd, 1980–85; Director: Birch Carroll & Coyle Ltd, 1967–; Roadshow (Qld) Pty Ltd, 1970–; Darwin Cinemas Pty Ltd, 1972–; G. R. E. (Australia) Ltd, 1980–; Besser (Qld) Ltd, 1981–87; Bank of Queensland Ltd, 1986–; QUF Industries Ltd, 1986–. President: Queensland Hotels Assoc., 1963–69; Aust. Hotels Assoc., 1966–69. Mem. Totalisator Administration Bd of Queensland, 1977–81. Chm., Queensland Inst. of Medical Research Trust, 1980–88. *Recreations:* reading, fishing and thoroughbred breeding. *Address:* Box 25, Post Office, S Brisbane, Qld 4101, Australia. *Clubs:* Australian (Sydney); Brisbane, Tattersall's (Past Pres.) (Brisbane); Queensland Turf, Victorian Racing.

STEWART, Ewen; Sheriff at Wick, Caithness, since 1962, at Dornoch, Sutherland and Tain, Ross and Cromarty, since 1977, and at Stornoway, Western Isles, since 1990; *b* 22 April 1926; *o s* of late Duncan Stewart and Kate Blunt, and *gs* of late Ewen Stewart, Kinlocheil; *m* 1959, Norma Porteous Hollands, *d* of late William Charteris Hollands, Earlston; one *d*. *Educ:* Edinburgh University. BSc (Agric.) 1945; MA (Econ.) 1950; LLB 1952. Asst Agricultural Economist, East of Scotland Coll. of Agriculture, 1946–49; practised at Scottish Bar, 1952–62; lectr on Agricultural Law, Univ. of Edinburgh, 1957–62; former standing junior counsel, Min. of Fuel and Power. Parly Cand. (Lab.) Banffshire, 1962. *Address:* 16 Bignold Court, George Street, Wick, Caithness KW1 4DL.

STEWART, Prof. Sir Frederick (Henry), Kt 1974; FRS 1964; PhD Cantab; FRSE; FGS; Regius Professor of Geology, 1956–82, now Emeritus, Dean of Science Faculty, 1966–68, and Member, University Court, 1969–70, Edinburgh University; *b* 16 Jan. 1916; *o s* of Frederick Robert Stewart and Hester Alexander, Aberdeen; *m* 1945, Mary Florence Elinor Rainbow (*see* Mary Stewart); no *c*. *Educ:* Fettes Coll.; Univ. of Aberdeen (BSc); Emmanuel Coll., Cambridge. Mineralogist in Research Dept of ICI Ltd (Billingham Div.), 1941–43; Lectr in Geology, Durham Colls in the Univ. of Durham, 1943–56. Vice-Pres., Geological Soc. of London, 1965–66; Member: Council for Scientific Policy, 1967–71; Adv. Council for Applied R&D, 1976–79; Chairman: NERC, 1971–73 (Mem., Geol. Geophysics Cttee, 1967–70); Adv. Bd for Res. Councils, 1973–79 (Mem., 1972–73); Mem. Council, Royal Soc., 1969–70; Trustee, BM (Nat. Hist.), 1983–87; Mem. Council, Scottish Marine Biol Assoc., 1983–89. Lyell Fund Award, 1951, J. B. Tyrrell Fund, 1952,

Geological Soc. of London; Mineralogical Soc. of America Award, 1952; Lyell Medal, Geological Soc. of London, 1970; Clough Medal, Edinburgh Geol. Soc., 1971; Sorby Medal, Yorks Geol. Soc., 1975. Hon. DSc: Aberdeen, 1975; Leicester, 1977; Heriot-Watt, 1978; Durham, 1983; Glasgow, 1988. *Publications:* The British Caledonides (ed with M. R. W. Johnson), 1963; Marine Evaporites, 1963; papers in Mineralogical Magazine, Jl of Geol. Soc. of London, etc., dealing with igneous and metamorphic petrology and salt deposits. *Recreation:* fishing. *Address:* 79 Morningside Park, Edinburgh EH10 5EZ. *T:* 031–447 2620; House of Letterawe, Lochawe, Argyll PA33 1AH. *T:* Dalmally (08382) 329. *Club:* New (Edinburgh).

STEWART, George Girdwood, CB 1979; MC 1945; TD 1954; Cairngorm Estate Adviser, Highlands and Islands Enterprise, since 1988; Forestry Consultant, National Trust for Scotland, since 1989; Associate Director, Oakwood Environmental, since 1990; *b* 12 Dec. 1919; *o s* of late Herbert A. Stewart, BSc, and of Janetta Dunlop Girdwood; *m* 1950, Shelagh Jean Morven Murray; one *s* one *d*. *Educ:* Kelvinside Academy, Glasgow; Glasgow Univ.; Edinburgh Univ. (BSc). Served RA, 1940–46 (MC, despatches); CO 278 (Lowland) Field Regt RA (TA), 1957–60. Dist Officer, Forestry Commn, 1949; Asst Conservator, 1961; Conservator, West Scotland, 1966; Comr for Forest and Estate Management, 1969–79; National Trust for Scotland: Rep., Branklyn Garden, Perth, 1980–84; Regional Rep., Central and Tayside, 1984–88. Member: BR Bd Envt Panel, 1980–88; Countryside Commn for Scotland, 1981–88; Chm., Scottish Wildlife Trust, 1981–87. Pres., Scottish Nat. Ski Council, 1988–. FRSA; FICFor; Hon. FLI. Pres., Scottish Ski Club, 1971–75; Vice-Pres., Nat. Ski Fedn of GB; Chm., Alpine Racing Cttee, 1975–78. *Recreations:* ski-ing, tennis, studying Scottish painting. *Address:* Stormont House, 11 Mansfield Road, Scone, Perth PH2 6SA. *T:* Scone (0738) 51815. *Club:* Ski Club of Great Britain.

STEWART, (George Robert) Gordon, OBE 1984; Secretary, 1976–83, Legal Adviser 1983–89, Institute of Chartered Accountants of Scotland; *b* 13 Oct. 1924; *s* of David Gordon Stewart and Mary Grant Thompson or Stewart; *m* 1952, Rachel Jean Morrison; two *s* one *d*. *Educ:* George Watson's Coll., Edinburgh; Edinburgh Univ. (MA 1947, LLB 1949). WS and Mem., Law Soc. of Scotland, 1949. Served War, 1943–46: Captain, Royal Signals; Burma and SEAC. In practice as WS, Melville & Lindesay, WS, Edinburgh, 1950–59; Asst Sec., subseq. Sec., and Dir, Ideal-Standard Ltd, Hull, 1959–75. *Recreation:* gardening. *Address:* 15 Hillpark Loan, Edinburgh EH4 7BH. *T:* 031–312 7079. *Club:* University Staff (Edinburgh).

STEWART, Prof. George Russell, PhD; Quain Professor of Botany, since 1985 and Head of Department of Biology, since 1987, University College London; Dean of Faculty of Science, University of London, since 1990; *b* 25 Feb. 1944; *s* of George and Isobella Stewart; *m* 1978, Janice Anne Grimes; three *d*. *Educ:* Pinner County Grammar Sch.; Univ. of Bristol (BSc 1965; PhD 1968). Lectr in Botany, Univ. of Manchester, 1968–81; Prof. of Botany and Head of Dept, Birkbeck Coll., Univ. of London, 1981–85. Vis. Lectr, Dept of Biology, Univ. of Lagos, Nigeria; Visiting Professor: Dept of Botany, Univ. of Queensland, Aust.; Dept of Biology, Univ. of Campinas, Brazil; Dept of Biology, Univ. of WA. Member: Plants and Envmt Cttee, AFRC, 1989–; Plants and Envmt Res. Bd, AFRC (Chm., 1989–); Agriculture Cttee, Long Ashton Res. Station, 1990–; Inter-Agency Cttee on Res. into Global Envmtl Change (Working Gp 2), 1990–; Inst. of Zoology Cttee, 1989–. *Publications:* (ed jtly) The Genetic Manipulation of Plants and its Application to Agriculture, 1984; numerous scientific papers on plant physiology and metabolism and chapters in books and conf. proc. *Recreations:* cycling, cooking. *Address:* Department of Biology, Darwin Building, University College London, Gower Street, WC1E 6BT. *T:* 071–387 7050.

STEWART, Prof. Gordon Thallon, MD; Mechan Professor of Public Health, University of Glasgow, 1972–84, now Emeritus Professor; Hon. Consultant in Epidemiology and Preventive Medicine, Glasgow Area Health Board; *b* 5 Feb. 1919; *s* of John Stewart and Mary L. Thallon; *m* 1946, Joan Kego; two *s* two *d*; *m* 1975, Neena Walker. *Educ:* Paisley Grammar Sch.; Univs of Glasgow and Liverpool. BSc 1939; MB, ChB 1942; DTM&H 1947; MD (High Commendation) 1949; FRCPath 1964; FFCM 1972; MRCPGlas 1972; FRCPGlas 1975. House Phys. and House Surg., 1942–43; Surg. Lieut RNVR, 1943–46; Res. Fellow (MRC), Univ. of Liverpool, 1946–48; Sen. Registrar and Tutor, Wright-Fleming Inst., St Mary's Hosp., London, 1948–52; Cons. Pathologist, SW Metrop. Regional Hosp. Bd, 1954–63; Res. Worker at MRC Labs Carshalton, 1955–63; Prof. of Epidem. and Path., Univ. of N Carolina, 1964–68; Watkins Prof. of Epidem., Tulane Univ. Med. Center, New Orleans, 1968–72. Vis. Prof., Dow Med. Coll., Karachi, 1952–53 and Cornell Univ. Med. Coll., 1970–71; Cons. to WHO, and to NYC Dept of Health; Vis. Lectr and Examr, various univs in UK and overseas. Sen. Fellow, Nat. Science Foundn, Washington, 1964; Delta omega, 1969. *Publications:* (ed) Trends in Epidemiology, 1972; (ed jtly) Penicillin Allergy, 1970; Penicillin Group of Drugs, 1965; papers on chemotherapy of infectious diseases, drug allergy and epidemiology in various med. and sci. jls. *Recreations:* gardening, drawing, music. *Address:* Glenavon, The Promenade, Clifton, Bristol BS8 3HT. *T:* Bristol (0272) 736532.

STEWART, Prof. Harold Charles, CBE 1975; FRCP; FRSE; DL; Head of Pharmacology Department, St Mary's Hospital Medical School, 1950–74; Professor of Pharmacology in the University of London 1965–74, now Emeritus Professor (Reader, 1949–64); Consultant in Pharmacology to: St Mary's Hospital, 1946; Ministry of Defence (Army), since 1961; *b* 23 Nov. 1906; *s* of Bernard Halley Stewart, MA, MD, FRSE, FKC, Pres. of Sir Halley Stewart Trust, and Mabel Florence Wyatt; *m* 1st, 1929, Dorothy Irene Lowen (*d* 1969); one *s* one *d*; 2nd, 1970, Audrey Patricia Nicolle. *Educ:* Mill Hill Sch.; University Coll. London; Jesus Coll., Cambridge; University Coll. Hospital. Cambridge Univ.: BA 1928, MA 1934; MB, BCh 1931, MD 1935. London Univ.: PhD 1941, MRCP 1949. Gen. practice, Barnet, Herts, 1932–36. Sub-Dean, St Mary's Hospital Med. Sch., 1950–52; Gresham Prof. in Physic, City Univ., 1968–70. Examr now or formerly, Univs of London, Cambridge, Birmingham, Bristol and Wales, RCS, Soc. of Apothecaries. Research work, mainly on fat absorption and transport in the human subject, and on problems of pain and analgesia. Cons. in Pharmacology to Army; Med. Adviser and Mem. Commonwealth Council, Brit. Commonwealth Ex-Services League; Pres., Sir Halley Stewart Trust for Research, 1986– (Chm., 1979–86); Mem. Asthma Research Council; Dir-Gen., St John Ambulance Assoc., 1976–78 (Dep Dir-Gen., 1973–76; Dist Surg. for London, SJAB, 1950–64); Mem. Chapter-Gen., Order of St John (KStJ); Mem. Council, Stewart Soc.; Chm., Buttle Trust for Children, 1979–; Vice-Chairman: Med. Council of Alcoholism, 1986–87 (now Patron); St Christopher's Hospice for terminal cases, 1963–87 (Vice Pres., 1987); Sen. Vice-Pres. and British Rep., Assoc. Internat. de Sauvetage et de Premiers Secours en Cas d'Accidents, 1974–. Hon. Vice Pres., Stewart Soc., 1988. Liveryman, Soc. of Apothecaries of London; Freeman, City of London: Mem. Physiolog., Brit. Pharmacolog., Nutrition and Genealog. Socs. FFA, RCS, 1969. FRSE 1974. RAMC, T, 1935; Mem. LDV, later Major and Med. Adviser, HG; comd and reformed Med. Unit, Univ. of London STC as Major RAMC, 1942–46. Defence Medal; Gen. Serv. Medal, 1939–46; Coronation Medal, 1953; Guthrie Meml Medal, 1974. DL Greater London, 1967–82. *Publications:* Drugs in Anæsthetic Practice (with F. G. Wood-Smith), 1962; (with W. H. Hughes) Concise Antibiotic Treatment, 2nd edn 1973; contribs to jls. *Recreations:* voluntary service; sport (lacrosse: Cambridge Half-Blue 1928; lawn tennis); genealogy and heraldry. *Address:* 41 The Glen, Green Lane, Northwood, Mddx HA6 2UR. *T:* Northwood (09274) 24893. *Club:* Athenæum.

See also Rt. Hon. Sir B. H. I. H. Stewart.

STEWART, Sir Houston Mark S.; *see* Shaw-Stewart.

STEWART, Sir Hugh Charlie Godfray, 6th Bt, *cr* 1803, of Athenree; Major; DL; High Sheriff, Co. Tyrone, 1955; *b* 13 April 1897; *s* of Colonel Sir George Powell Stewart, 5th Bt, and Florence Maria Georgina, *d* of Sir James Godfray; *S* father, 1945; *m* 1st, 1929 (marr. diss. 1942); one *s* one *d*; 2nd, 1948, Diana Margaret, *d* of late Capt. J. E. Hibbert, MC, DFC, and late Mrs R. B. Bannon, Jersey; one *s* one *d*. *Educ:* Bradfield Coll., Berkshire; RMC, Sandhurst. Served European War, Royal Inniskilling Fusiliers, 1916; Arras, 1917 (wounded); France, 1939–40. Foreign Service has included India, Iraq, China, Malaya, South Africa and Syria; retired. DL Co. Tyrone, 1971. *Heir:* *s* David John Christopher Stewart [*b* 19 June 1935; *m* 1959, Bridget Anne, *er d* of late Patrick W. Sim and of Mrs Leslie Parkhouse; three *d*]. *Address:* Cottesbrook, Sandy Pluck Lane, Bentham, near Cheltenham, Glos.

STEWART, Hugh Parker, FCA; Chairman, Programming Research Ltd, since 1990; *b* 23 May 1934; *s* of George and Barbara Stewart; *m* 1960, Marion Gordon Cairns; one *s* one *d*. *Educ:* Sullivan Upper Sch., Holywood, Co. Down; Queen's Univ., Belfast (LLB Hons). Audit Manager, Hill Vellacott & Bailey, Belfast, 1959–62; Financial Comptroller, STC(NI) Ltd, Monkstown, Co. Antrim, 1962–67; Admin Manager, AMF Beaird, Belfast, 1967–70; Gp Financial Controller, Brightside Engrg Holdings Ltd, Sheffield, 1970–71; SMM Ltd, Greenwich: Financial Dir., 1971–74; Overseas Dir, 1974–78; Man. Dir, SMM Foundries Ltd, Greenwich, 1978–79; Finance Dir, Westland plc, 1979–81; Finance Dir, Westland plc, and Exec. Dir, Westland Technologies Ltd, 1981–84; Man. Dir, Westland Technologies Ltd, 1984–85; Chief Exec., Westland Gp plc, 1985–88. Chm., Scheduling Technology Gp, 1989–90; Practice Chm., Aaron & Partners, Solicitors, 1989–91; Non-Executive Director: DSK Systems Ltd, 1989–91; Wooton Jeffreys Consultants Ltd, 1990–. Dir, SBAC, 1986–88. Member: Council, CBI, 1987–88; Management Bd, EEF, 1988. Governor, Sherborne Sch., 1982–. *Recreations:* golf, gardening. *Address:* Ferncroft House, Walton Elm, Marnhull, Dorset DT10 1QG. *T:* Marnhull (0258) 820406; Flat 3, 80 Cambridge Street, SW1V 4QQ. *T:* 071–931 0531. *Club:* Royal Automobile.

STEWART, Rt. Hon. Sir Ian; *see* Stewart, Rt Hon. Sir B. H. I. H.

STEWART, Prof. Ian George; Professor of Economics, University of Edinburgh, 1967–84; *b* 24 June 1923; *s* of David Tweedie Stewart, MA and Ada Doris Montgomery Haldane; *m* 1949, Mary Katharine Oddie; one *s* two *d*. *Educ:* Fettes Coll.; Univ. of St Andrews (MA 1st Class Hons); MA Cantab 1954. Pilot, RAF, 1942–46. Commonwealth Fund Fellow, 1948–50. Research Officer, Dept of Applied Economics, Univ. of Cambridge, 1950–57; University of Edinburgh: Lectr in Economics, 1957–58; Sen. Lectr, 1958–61; Reader, 1961–67; Curator of Patronage, 1979–84. Vis. Associate Prof., Univ. of Michigan, 1962; Vis. Prof., Univ. of S Carolina, 1975. Dir, Scottish Provident Instn, 1980–90, Dep. Chm., 1983–85. Mem., British Library Bd, 1980–87. Governor, Fettes Coll., 1976–89. *Publications:* National Income of Nigeria (with A. R. Prest), 1953; (ed) Economic Development and Structural Change, 1969; articles in jls and bank reviews. *Recreations:* golf, fishing, gardening. *Address:* 571 Lanark Road West, Edinburgh EH14 7BL. *Club:* New (Edinburgh).

STEWART, Jackie; *see* Stewart, John Young.

STEWART, James Cecil Campbell, CBE 1960; Consultant; Chairman: British Nuclear Forum, since 1974; Nuclear Power Company Pension Trustee Ltd, since 1979; *b* 1916; *s* of late James Stewart and Mary Campbell Stewart; *m* 1946, Pamela Rouselle, *d* of William King-Smith; one *d*. *Educ:* Armstrong College and King's College, Durham University (BSc Physics). Telecommunications Research Establishment, 1939–46; Atomic Energy Research Establishment, Harwell, 1946–49; Industrial Group, UKAEA, 1949–63; Dep. Chm., British Nuclear Design and Construction, 1969–75; Member: UKAEA, 1963–69; Central Electricity Generating Bd, 1965–69; Dep. Chm., Nuclear Power Co. Ltd, 1975–80; Dir, National Nuclear Corp. Ltd, 1980–82. *Recreation:* tending a garden. *Address:* Whitethorns, Higher Whitley, Cheshire WA4 4QJ. *T:* Norcott Brook (0925) 730377; 901 Keyes House, Dolphin Square, SW1V 3NB. *T:* 071–798 8395. *Club:* East India, Devonshire, Sports and Public Schools.

STEWART, Sir James (Douglas), Kt 1983; agricultural consultant; Principal, Lincoln University College of Agriculture, 1974–84, retired; *b* 11 Aug. 1925; *s* of Charles Edward Stewart and Edith May Stewart (*née* Caldwell); *m* 1953, Nancy Elizabeth Dunbar; one *s* three *d*. *Educ:* Lincoln UC (Dip. Valuation and Farm Management); Canterbury Univ. (MA); Reading Univ. (DPhil). Lectr in Farm Management, Lincoln Coll., NZ, 1951–59; Research Fellow, Reading Univ., 1959–61; Sen. Lectr, Lincoln Coll., 1962–64; Prof. of Farm Management, Lincoln Coll., 1964–74. Chairman: NZ Vice-Chancellors Cttee, 1981–82; NZ Wheat Bd, 1986–87 (Dep. Chm., 1984–86); NZ Nat. Educn Qualifications Authority, 1989–. Chm., Pyne Gould Guinness Internat. Ltd, 1987–; Director: Pyne Gould Corp., 1982–; Alpine Dairy Products Ltd, 1985–. Chairman: Canterbury Develt Corp., 1983–89 (Dir, 1983–); Christchurch Sch. of Medicine, 1987–88. Silver Jubilee Medal, 1977. *Publications:* contrib. Jl Agricl Econs, Jl Farm Econs, Econ. Record, etc. *Recreations:* swimming, part-time farming. *Address:* 5 Glenharrow Avenue, Avonhead, Christchurch, New Zealand.

STEWART, James Harvey; Chief Executive (formerly District General Manager), Barking, Havering and Brentwood Health Authority, since 1985; *b* 15 Aug. 1939; *s* of Harvey Stewart and Annie (*née* Gray); *m* 1965, Fiona Maria Maclay Reid; three *s* one *d*. *Educ:* Peterhead Acad.; Aberdeen Univ. (MA 1962); Manchester Univ. (DSA 1964). Pres., Jun. Common Room, Crombie Hall, Aberdeen Univ., 1961–62. Hosp. Sec., Princess Margaret Rose Orthopaedic Hosp., Edinburgh, 1965–67; Principal Admin. Asst, 1967–68, and Dep. Gp Sec. and sometime Acting Gp Sec., 1968–73, York A HMC; Area Administrator, 1973–82, and Dist Administrator, 1982–83, Northumberland AHA; Regional Administrator, East Anglian RHA, 1983–85. Hon. Treasurer, Assoc. of Chief Administrators of Health Authorities in England and Wales, 1982–85 (Mem. Council, 1975–82). *Recreations:* music, reading, walking, playing squash, watching Rugby. *Address:* Barking, Havering and Brentwood Health Authority, The Grange, Harold Wood Hospital, Gubbins Lane, Romford RM3 0BE; White Cottage, Hardwick, Cambridge CB3 7QU. *T:* Madingley (0954) 210961. *Clubs:* Rotary (Cambridge); Cambridge Rugby Union Football.

STEWART, James Lablache; *see* Granger, Stewart.

STEWART, James (Maitland), DFC with 2 oak leaf clusters (US); Air Medal with 3 oak leaf clusters; DSM (US); actor, stage and film; *b* Indiana, Pa, 20 May 1908; *s* of Alexander Maitland Stewart and Elizabeth Ruth (*née* Jackson); *m* 1949, Gloria McLean; two *s* twin *d*. *Educ:* Mercersburg Academy, Pa; Princeton University (BS Arch.). War Service,

1942–45: Lt-Col Air Corps; Europe, 1943–45 (Air Medal, DFC); Colonel, 1945. USAF Reserve; Brig.-Gen. 1959. Dir, Air Force Assoc. First New York appearance, Carry Nation, 1932; subseq. played in Goodbye Again, Spring in Autumn, All Good Americans, Yellow Jack, Divided by Three, Page Miss Glory, A Journey by Night. Entered films, 1935; *films include:* Murder Man, Next Time We Love, Seventh Heaven, You Can't Take It With You, Made for Each Other, Vivacious Lady, The Shopworn Angel, Mr Smith Goes to Washington, Destry Rides Again, No Time for Comedy, Philadelphia Story, The Shop around the Corner, Pot o' Gold, Ziegfeld Girl, Come Live with Me, It's a Wonderful Life, Magic Town, On Our Merry Way, You Gotta Stay Happy, Call Northside 777, Rope, The Stratton Story, Malaya, The Jackpot, Harvey, Winchester '73, Broken Arrow, No Highway in the Sky, Bend of the River, Carbine Williams, The Greatest Show on Earth, Thunder Bay, Naked Spur, The Glenn Miller Story, Rear Window, The Man from Laramie, The Far Country, Strategic Air Command, The Man Who Knew Too Much, Night Passage, Spirit of St Louis, Midnight Story, Vertigo, Bell, Book and Candle, Anatomy of a Murder, The FBI Story, The Mountain Road, The Man Who Shot Liberty Valance, Mr Hobbs Takes a Vacation, Take her, She's Mine, Cheyenne Autumn, Shenandoah, The Rare Breed, Firecreek, Bandalero, The Cheyenne Social Club, Fool's Parade, Dynamite Man from Glory Jail, The Shootist, Airport 77, The Big Sleep, Magic of Lassie. *Play:* Harvey (Broadway), 1970, (Prince of Wales), 1975. Holds many awards including: five Academy Award nominations; Oscar award as best actor of the year; Hon. Oscar Award; two NY Film Critics best actor awards; Venice Film Festival best actor award; France's Victoire Trophy for best actor; Screen Actors Guild award. Hon. degrees include: DLitt, Pennsylvania; MA, Princeton. *Address:* PO Box 90, Beverly Hills, Calif 90213, USA.

STEWART, (James) Moray, CB 1990; Second Permanent Under Secretary of State, Ministry of Defence, since 1990; *b* 21 June 1938; third *s* of James and Evelyn Stewart; *m* 1963, Dorothy May Batey, *o d* of Alan and Maud Batey; three *s*. *Educ:* Marlborough Coll.; Univ. of Keele (BA First Cl. Hons History and Econs). Sec., Univ. of Keele Union, 1960–61. Breakdown and Information Service Operator, AA, 1956–57; Asst Master, Northcliffe Sch., Bognor Regis, 1957–58; Asst Principal, Air Min., 1962–65; Private Sec. to 2nd Permanent Under Sec. of State (RAF), MoD, 1965–66; Principal, MoD, 1966–70; First Sec. (Defence), UK Delegn to NATO, 1970–73; Asst Sec., MoD, 1974–75; Private Sec. to successive Secs of State for NI, 1975–77; Dir, Naval Manpower Requirements, MoD, 1977; Dir, Defence Policy Staff, MoD, 1978–80; Asst Under Sec. of State, MoD, 1980–84; Asst Sec. Gen. for Defence Planning and Policy, NATO, 1984–86; Dep. Under Sec. of State, Personnel and Logistics, 1986–88, Defence Procurement, 1988–90, MoD. Comr, Royal Hosp. Chelsea, 1986–88; Trustee, Imperial War Museum, 1986–88; Mem. Council, RUSI, 1988–. *Recreations:* reading, listening to music, walking. *Address:* Ministry of Defence, Whitehall, SW1A 2HB. *Club:* Commonwealth Trust.

STEWART, James Robertson, CBE 1971 (OBE 1964); Principal, University of London, 1978–83; *b* 1917; *s* of James and Isabella Stewart; *m* 1941, Grace Margaret Kirsop; two *s* one *d*. *Educ:* Perth Acad.; Whitley and Monkseaton High Sch.; Armstrong Coll. (later King's Coll.), Newcastle, Univ. of Durham. BA Dunelm (1st cl. hons Mod. History) 1937; DThPT (1st cl.) 1938; research in Canada (Canada Co.), 1938–39; awarded Holland Rose Studentship, Cambridge, and William Black Noble Fellowship, Durham, 1939; admitted to Christ's Coll., Cambridge, 1939; MA Dunelm 1941. Served Army, 1939–46: Royal Artillery (BEF); Combined Ops HQ; Directorate of Combined Ops, India and SE Asia; Major (Actg Lt-Col); Certif. of Good Service. Dep. Clerk of Court, Univ. of London, 1946–49, Clerk of Court, 1950–82. Member, governing bodies: RPMS, 1983–89; Sch. of Pharmacy, London Univ., 1983– (Hon. Treas.); Wye Coll., 1983–; Inst. of Educn, 1983–; RVC, 1983– (Hon. Treas.); LSE, 1984–89; Brunel Univ., 1984–89; Inst. of Germanic Studies, 1984– (Chm.); Roedean Sch., 1984–; Sussex Univ., 1985–; Westfield Coll., London, 1985–89. Hon. Fellow: KCL, 1982; Sch. of Pharmacy, London Univ., 1982; Birkbeck Coll., London, 1982; LSE, 1982; UCL, 1982; Wye Coll., 1987; Queen Mary and Westfield Coll., London, 1989 (Westfield Coll., 1981). Hon. LLD: London, 1983; Western Ontario, 1984. Symons Medal, ACU, 1983. *Recreations:* golf, gardening, watching soccer and cricket. *Address:* 2 Hilltop, Dyke Road Avenue, Brighton, Sussex BN1 5LY. *T:* Brighton (0273) 551039. *Clubs:* Athenæum; Dyke Golf (Brighton).

STEWART, James Simeon Hamilton, QC 1982; barrister; a Recorder of the Crown Court, since 1982; *b* 2 May 1943; *s* of late Henry Hamilton Stewart, MD, FRCS and of Edna Mary Hamilton Stewart; *m* 1972, Helen Margaret Whiteley; two *d*. *Educ:* Cheltenham Coll.; Univ. of Leeds (LLB Hons). Called to the Bar, Inner Temple, 1966. *Recreations:* cricket, golf, gardening. *Address:* 40 Park Cross Street, Leeds LS1 2QH. *T:* Bradford 493043. *Clubs:* Bradford (Bradford); Leeds Taverners (Leeds).

STEWART, (John) Allan; MP (C) Eastwood, since 1983 (East Renfrewshire, 1979–83); *b* 1 June 1942; *s* of Edward MacPherson Stewart and Eadie Barrie Stewart; *m* 1973, Marjorie Sally (Susie); one *s* one *d*. *Educ:* Bell Baxter High Sch., Cupar; St Andrews Univ. (1st Cl. Hons MA 1964); Harvard Univ. (Rotary Internat. Foundn Fellow, 1964–65). Lectr in Polit. Economy, St Andrews Univ., 1965–70 (Warden, John Burnet Hall, 1968–70); Confederation of British Industry: Head of Regional Develt Dept, 1971–73; Dep. Dir (Econs), 1973–76; Scottish Sec., 1976–78; Scottish Dir, 1978–79. Conservative Parly Candidate, Dundee E, 1970; Councillor, London Bor. of Bromley, 1975–76. PPS to Minister of State for Energy, 1981; Parly Under Sec. of State, Scottish Office, 1981–86, 1990–. Mem., Select Cttee on Scottish Affairs, 1979–81. *Publications:* articles in academic and gen. pubns on econ. and polit. affairs. *Recreations:* bridge, hedgehogs. *Address:* Crofthead House, by Neilston, Renfrewshire G78 3NB. *T:* 041–881 2892.

STEWART, John Anthony Benedict, CMG 1979; OBE 1973; HM Diplomatic Service, retired; Chairman, Civil Service Selection Board, since 1987; consultant; *b* 24 May 1927; *e s* of late Edward Vincent Stewart and Emily Veronica (*née* Jones); *m* 1960, Geraldine Margaret, *o d* of late Captain G. C. Clifton; one *s* one *d* (and one *s* decd). *Educ:* St Illtyd's Coll.; Univ. of Wales; Cambridge Univ.; Imperial Coll. of Science and Technology; Cox Gold medal for Geology, 1950. RNVR Ordinary Seaman, later Midshipman, 1944–47. Colonial Geol. Survey Service, Somaliland Protectorate, 1952–56; Dist Officer, 1956–57; seconded to Anglo-Ethiopian Liaison Service, 1957–60 (Sen. Liaison Officer, 1960); transf. N Rhodesia as Dist Officer, 1960, Dist Comr, 1962–64; Resident Local Govt Officer, Barotseland, 1964–67. Entered HM Diplomatic Service, 1968; served FCO, Barbados, Uganda; RCDS, 1974; Ambassador to Democratic Republic of Vietnam, 1975–76; Head of Hong Kong Dept, FCO, 1976–78; Ambassador: to Laos, 1978–80; to Mozambique, 1980–84; High Comr to Sri Lanka, 1984–87. *Publications:* The Geology of the Mait Area, 1955; papers in geological jls. *Recreations:* shooting, fishing. *Clubs:* Flyfishers', Commonwealth Trust; Guildford County (Guildford).

STEWART, Rt. Rev. John Craig; Assistant Bishop, diocese of Melbourne, since 1984; *b* 10 Aug. 1940; *s* of J. J. Stewart; *m* 1967, Janine (*née* Schahinger); two *s*. *Educ:* Newington Coll., Sydney; Wesley Coll., Melbourne; Ridley Theol Coll., Melbourne. Ordained: deacon, 1965; priest, 1966; Curate, S Australia, 1965–68; Asst Priest, St John's, Crawley, 1968–70; Vicar: St Aidan's, Parkdale, 1970–74; St Luke's, Frankston, 1974–79; Gen. Sec., Church Missionary Soc., Victoria, 1979–84. *Recreations:* music, genealogy, reading. *Address:* St Paul's Cathedral Building, Flinders Lane, Melbourne, Vic 3000, Australia.

STEWART, John Hall; Sheriff of South Strathclyde Dumfries and Galloway at Airdrie, since 1985; *b* 15 March 1944; *s* of Cecil Francis Wilson Stewart and Mary Fyfe Hall or Stewart; *m* 1968, Marion MacCalman; one *s* two *d*. *Educ:* Airdrie Acad.; St Andrews Univ. (LLB). Advocate. Enrolled solicitor, 1970–77; Mem. Faculty of Advocates, 1978–. *Recreations:* golf, spectator sports, his children. *Address:* 3 Fife Crescent, Bothwell, Glasgow G71 8DG. *T:* Bothwell (0698) 853854. *Clubs:* Caledonian (Edinburgh); Uddingston Rugby.

STEWART, John Innes Mackintosh; Reader in English Literature, Oxford University, 1969–73; Student of Christ Church, Oxford, 1949–73, now Emeritus; *b* 30 Sept. 1906; *s* of late John Stewart, Director of Education in the City of Edinburgh, and Eliza Jane, *d* of James Clark, Golford, Nairn; *m* 1932, Margaret Hardwick (*d* 1979); three *s* two *d*. *Educ:* Edinburgh Academy; Oriel College, Oxford. Bishop Fraser's Scholar, 1930; 1st class Eng. Lang. and Lit. 1928; Matthew Arnold Memorial Prize, 1929; Lectr in English in Univ. of Leeds, 1930–35; Jury Professor of English in Univ. of Adelaide, 1935–45; Lectr in Queen's Univ., Belfast, 1946–48; Walker-Ames Prof., Univ. of Washington, 1961. Hon. FRSE 1990. Hon. DLitt: New Brunswick, 1962; Leicester, 1979; St Andrews, 1980. *Publications:* Montaigne's Essays: John Florio's Translation, 1931; Character and Motive in Shakespeare, 1949; Eight Modern Writers, 1963; Rudyard Kipling, 1966; Joseph Conrad, 1968; Thomas Hardy, 1971; Shakespeare's Lofty Scene (Shakespeare Lectr, British Acad.), 1971. Detective novels and broadcast scripts (under pseudonym of Michael Innes) Death at the President's Lodging, 1936; Hamlet Revenge!, 1937; Lament for a Maker, 1938; Stop Press, 1939; There Came Both Mist and Snow, 1940; The Secret Vanguard, 1940; Appleby on Ararat, 1941; The Daffodil Affair, 1942; The Weight of the Evidence, 1944; Appleby's End, 1945; From London Far, 1946; What Happened at Hazelwood, 1947; A Night of Errors, 1948; The Hawk and the Handsaw, 1948; The Journeying Boy, 1949; Operation Pax, 1951; A Private View, 1952; Christmas at Candleshoe, 1953; Appleby Talking, 1954; The Man From the Sea, 1955; Old Hall, New Hall, 1956; Appleby Talks Again, 1956; Appleby Plays Chicken, 1956; The Long Farewell, 1958; Hare Sitting Up, 1959; The New Sonia Wayward, 1960; Silence Observed, 1961; A Connoisseur's Case, 1962; Money from Holme, 1964; The Bloody Wood, 1966; A Change of Heir, 1966; Appleby at Allington, 1968; A Family Affair, 1969; Death at the Chase, 1970; An Awkward Lie, 1971; The Open House, 1972; Appleby's Answer, 1973; Appleby's Other Story, 1974; The Mysterious Commission, 1974; The Appleby File, 1975; The Gay Phoenix, 1976; Honeybath's Haven, 1977; The Ampersand Papers, 1978; Going It Alone, 1980; Lord Mullion's Secret, 1981; Sheiks and Adders, 1982; Appleby and Honeybath, 1983; Carson's Conspiracy, 1984; Appleby and the Ospreys, 1986; *novels* (as J. I. M. Stewart): Mark Lambert's Supper, 1954; The Guardians, 1955; A Use of Riches, 1957; The Man Who Wrote Detective Stories, 1959; The Man Who Won the Pools, 1961; The Last Tresilians, 1963; An Acre of Grass, 1965; The Aylwins, 1966; Vanderlyn's Kingdom, 1967; Cucumber Sandwiches, 1969; Avery's Mission, 1971; A Palace of Art, 1972; Mungo's Dream, 1973; quintet, A Staircase in Surrey, 1974–78 (The Gaudy, 1974; Young Pattullo, 1975; A Memorial Service, 1976; The Madonna of the Astrolabe, 1977; Full Term, 1978); Our England is a Garden and other stories, 1979; Andrew and Tobias, 1981; The Bridge at Arta and other stories, 1981; A Villa in France, 1982; My Aunt Christina and Other Stories, 1983; An Open Prison, 1984; The Naylors, 1985; Parlour 4 and other stories, 1986; *autobiography:* Myself and Michael Innes, 1987. *Recreation:* walking. *Address:* Lower Park House, Occupation Road, Lindley, Huddersfield HD3 3EE.

See also M. J. Stewart.

STEWART, Sir (John) Simon (Watson), 6th Bt *cr* 1920, of Balgownie; MD, MRCP, FRCR; Consultant in Clinical Oncology at St Mary's Hospital and The Royal Postgraduate Medical School, since 1989; *b* 5 July 1955; *s* of Sir John Keith Watson Stewart, 5th Bt and of Mary Elizabeth, *d* of John Francis Moxon; *S* father, 1990; *m* 1978, Dr Catherine Stewart, *d* of H. Gordon Bond; one *s* one *d*. *Educ:* Uppingham Sch.; Charing Cross Hosp. Med. Sch. BSc (1st cl. Hons) 1977; MB BS Lond. 1980; MRCP 1983; FRCR 1986; MD 1989. Mem., Cavalhead, 1978–. *Heir:* *s* John Hamish Watson Stewart, *b* 12 Dec. 1983. *Address:* 52 Grosvenor Road, Chiswick, W4 4EG. *T:* 081–995 2213. *Club:* Oriental.

STEWART, John Young, (Jackie Stewart), OBE 1972; racing driver, retired 1973; *b* 11 June 1939; *s* of late Robert Paul Stewart and of Jean Clark Young; *m* 1962, Helen McGregor; two *s*. *Educ:* Dumbarton Academy. First raced, 1961; competed in 4 meetings, 1961–62, driving for Barry Filer, Glasgow; drove for Ecurie Ecosse and Barry Filer, winning 14 out of 23 starts, 1963; 28 wins out of 53 starts, 1964; drove Formula 1 for BRM, 1965–67 and for Ken Tyrrell, 1968–73; has won Australian, New Zealand, Swedish, Mediterranean, Japanese and many other non-championship, major internat. Motor Races; set up new world record by winning his 26th World Championship Grand Prix (Zandvoort), July 1973, and 27th (Nurburgring), Aug. 1973; 3rd in World Championship, 1965; 2nd in 1968 and 1972; World Champion, 1969, 1971, 1973. BARC Gold Medal, 1971, 1973. Daily Express Sportsman of the Year, 1971, 1973; BBC Sports Personality of the Year, 1973; Scottish Sportsman of the Year, 1973; US Sportsman of the Year, 1973; Segrave Trophy, 1973. Hon. Dr Automotive Engrg, Lawrence Inst. of Technology, Mich, USA, 1986. *Film:* Weekend of a Champion, 1972. *Publications:* World Champion, 1970 (with Eric Dymock); Faster!, 1972 (with Peter Manso); On the Road, 1983; Jackie Stewart's Principles of Performance Driving, 1986. *Recreations:* golf, fishing, tennis, shooting (Mem. British Team for Clay Pigeon shooting; former Scottish, English, Irish, Welsh and British Champion; won Coupe des Nations, 1959 and 1960; reserve for two-man team, 1960 Olympics). *Address:* 24 route de Divonne, 1260 Nyon, Switzerland. *T:* Geneva 61.01.52, *Fax:* 62.10.96. *Clubs:* (Hon.) Royal Automobile, British Racing Drivers' (Vice-Pres.); (Hon.) Royal Scottish Automobile; (Pres.) Scottish Motor Racing (Duns); Royal and Ancient (St Andrews); Prestwick Golf; Geneva Golf.

STEWART, Kenneth Albert; Member (Lab) Merseyside West, European Parliament, since 1984; *b* Liverpool, 28 July 1925; *m* 1946, Margaret Robertson Vass; one *s* two *d*. *Educ:* local schs. Parachute Regt (Sgt). Former joiner. Former Member: Merseyside CC; Liverpool CC (Chm., Housing Cttee); former Chm. and Sec., Liverpool West Derby Labour Party. *Address:* 62 Ballantyne Road, Liverpool L13 9AL.

STEWART, Kenneth Hope, PhD; Director of Research, Meteorological Office, 1976–82; *b* 29 March 1922; *s* of Harry Sinclair Stewart and Nora Hassan Parry; *m* 1950, Hilary Guest; four *s* four *d*. *Educ:* Trinity Coll., Cambridge (MA, PhD). Entered Meteorol Office, 1949; Dep. Dir, Physical Res., 1974. *Publications:* Ferromagnetic Domains, 1951; contrib. physical and meteorol jls. *Address:* 19 Harston Road, Newton, Cambridge.

STEWART, Hon. Kevin James, AO 1989; Director, KJ Consulting Services, since 1989; Consultant, United Health Serv Pty Ltd, Sydney, since 1989; *b* 20 Sept. 1928; *m* 1952, Jean, *d* of late F. I. Keating; two *s* five *d*. *Educ:* Christian Brothers School, Lewisham, NSW; De La Salle College, NSW. Officer, NSW Govt Rlys, 1944–62 (Regional Pres., Aust. Transport Officers' Assoc. and Fedn, 1959–62). MLA for Canterbury, NSW,

1962–85; Exec., NSW Parly Labor Party and Spokesman on Health Matters, 1967; NSW State Exec., Aust. Labor Party, 1968; Minister, NSW: for Health, 1976–81; for Youth and Community Services, 1981–83; for Mineral Resources, 1983–84; for Local Govt, 1984–85. Mem., Labor Transport Cttee, 1965–76; Chm., Labor Health Cttee, 1968–76; Mem., Jt Cttee, Legislative Council upon Drugs. Agent General for NSW in UK, 1986–88. Life Mem., British-Australia Soc., 1988. Chm., Bd of Canterbury Hosp., 1955–76 (Dir, 1954). FRSA 1988. Freeman, City of London, 1987. Hon. Citizen of Tokyo, Japan, 1985. *Recreations:* supporter of community services, Rugby Football League, swimming, bowls. *Address:* 44 Chalmers Street, Belmore, NSW 2192, Australia. *T:* (02) 759 7777. *Clubs:* International Nippon-Australia, Canterbury Bankstown League (Patron) (Sydney).

STEWART, Mary (Florence Elinor), (Lady Stewart); *b* 17 Sept. 1916; *d* of Rev. Frederick A. Rainbow, Durham Diocese, and Mary Edith (*née* Matthews), NZ; *m* 1945, Sir Frederick Henry Stewart, *qv*; no *c*. *Educ:* Eden Hall, Penrith, Cumberland; Skellfield School, Ripon, Yorks; St Hild's Coll., Durham Univ. BA 1938; MA 1941. Asst Lectr in English, Durham Univ., 1941–45; Part-time Lectr in English, St Hild's Training Coll., Durham, and Durham Univ., 1948–56. FRSA 1968. Hon. Fellow, Newnham Coll., Cambridge, 1986. *Publications: novels:* Madam, Will You Talk?, 1954; Wildfire at Midnight, 1956; Thunder on the Right, 1957; Nine Coaches Waiting, 1958; My Brother Michael, 1959; The Ivy Tree, 1961; The Moonspinners, 1962; This Rough Magic, 1964; Airs Above the Ground, 1965; The Gabriel Hounds, 1967; The Wind Off The Small Isles, 1968; The Crystal Cave, 1970 (Frederick Niven Award); The Little Broomstick, 1971; The Hollow Hills, 1973; Ludo and the Star Horse, 1974 (Scottish Arts Council Award); Touch Not the Cat, 1976; The Last Enchantment, 1979; A Walk in Wolf Wood, 1980; The Wicked Day, 1983; Thornyhold, 1988; Frost on the Window and Other Poems, 1990; also articles, radio plays. *Recreations:* gardening, music, painting. *Address:* 79 Morningside Park, Edinburgh EH10 5EZ. *T:* 031–447 2620.

STEWART, Michael James; Reader in Political Economy, University College, London University, since 1969; *b* 6 Feb. 1933; *s* of John Innes Mackintosh Stewart, *qv*; *m* 1962, Frances Kaldor, *d* of Baron Kaldor, FBA; one *s* two *d* (and one *d* decd). *Educ:* Campbell Coll., Belfast; St Edward's Sch., Oxford; Magdalen Coll., Oxford. 1st cl. PPE (Oxon), 1955. Asst Res. Officer, Oxford Univ. Inst. of Statistics, 1955–56; Barnett Fellow, Cornell Univ., 1956–57; Econ. Asst, HM Treasury, 1957–60; Sec. to Council on Prices, Productivity and Incomes, 1960–61; Econ. Adviser, HM Treasury, 1961–62, Cabinet Office, 1964–67 (Senior Econ. Advr, 1967), Kenya Treasury, 1967–69; Special Adviser to Sec. of State for Trade, Apr.-Oct. 1974; Economic Adviser to Malta Labour Party, 1970–73; Special Econ. Advr to Foreign Sec., 1977–78. Guest Scholar, Brookings Instn, Washington, DC, 1978–79. Mem., Acad. Adv. Panel, Bank of England, 1977–83. Contested (Lab): Folkestone and Hythe, 1964; Croydon North-West, 1966. Asst Editor, Nat. Inst. Econ. Review, 1962–64. Consultant to various UN agencies, 1971–. *Publications:* Keynes and After, 1967; The Jekyll and Hyde Years: politics and economic policy since 1964, 1977; Controlling the Economic Future: policy dilemmas in a shrinking world, 1983; (with Peter Jay) Apocalypse 2000: economic breakdown and the suicide of democracy 1989–2000, 1987. *Recreations:* looking at paintings, eating in restaurants. *Address:* 79 South Hill Park, NW3 2SS. *T:* 071–435 3686. *Club:* United Oxford & Cambridge University.

STEWART, Sir Michael (Norman Francis), KCMG 1966 (CMG 1957); OBE 1948; HM Diplomatic Service, retired; Director, Sotheby's, since 1977; *b* 18 Jan. 1911; *s* of late Sir Francis Stewart, CIE, and of Lady Stewart; *m* 1951, Katharine Damaris Houssemayne du Boulay; one *s* two *d*. *Educ:* Shrewsbury; Trinity College, Cambridge. Assistant Keeper, Victoria and Albert Museum, 1935–39; Ministry of Information, 1939–41; Press Attaché: HM Embassy, Lisbon, 1941–44; HM Embassy, Rome, 1944–48; employed in Foreign Office, 1948–51; Counsellor: Office of Comr-Gen. for UK in SE Asia, 1951–54; HM Embassy, Ankara, 1954–59; HM Chargé d'Affaires, Peking, 1959–62; Senior Civilian Instructor, IDC, 1962–64; HM Minister, British Embassy, Washington, 1964–67; Ambassador to Greece, 1967–71. Dir, Ditchley Foundn, 1971–76. *Recreation:* country life. *Address:* Combe, near Newbury, Berks RG15 0EH. *Club:* Buck's.

STEWART, Moray; *see* Stewart, J. M.

STEWART, Dame Muriel (Acadia), DBE 1968; Headmistress, Northumberland LEA, 1940–70; *b* 22 Oct. 1905; *d* of late James Edmund Stewart. *Educ:* Gateshead Grammar Sch.; Durham Univ. BA Hons 1926; MA 1929. Teacher: Newcastle upon Tyne, 1927–29; Northumberland, 1929–70 (a headteacher of Secondary Schools, 1940–69); Headmistress, Shiremoor Middle School, 1969–70. Nat. Pres., Nat. Union of Teachers, 1964–65; Chm., Schools Council, 1969–72. Vice-Chm., Bullock Cttee, 1972–74. Hon. MEd, Newcastle Univ., 1965. *Recreation:* music. *Address:* 44 Caldwell Road, Gosforth, Newcastle upon Tyne NE3 2AX. *T:* 091–285 3400.

STEWART, Nicholas John Cameron; QC 1987; *b* 16 April 1947; *s* of John Cameron Stewart and Margaret Mary (*née* Botsford); *m* 1974, Pamela Jean Windham; one *s* two *d*. *Educ:* Bedford Modern Sch.; Worcester Coll., Oxford (BA). CDipAF. Called to the Bar, Inner Temple, 1971. Chm., Internat. Practice Cttee, Bar Council, 1991. *Recreations:* walking, climbing. *Address:* 15 Old Square, Lincoln's Inn, WC2A 3UH. *T:* 071–405 9471.

STEWART, Norman MacLeod; Senior Partner, Allan, Black & McCaskie; President, The Law Society of Scotland, May 1985–86; *b* 2 Dec. 1934; *s* of George and Elspeth Stewart; *m* 1959, Mary Slater Campbell; four *d*. *Educ:* Elgin Acad.; Univ. of Edinburgh (BL); SSC. Alex. Morison & Co., WS, Edinburgh, 1954–58; Allan, Black & McCaskie, Solicitors, Elgin, 1959–; Partner, 1961–. Law Society of Scotland: Mem. Council, 1976–87; Convener: Public Relations Cttee, 1979–81; Professional Practice Cttee, 1981–84; Vice-Pres., 1984–85. Hon. Mem., American Bar Assoc., 1985–. *Recreations:* walking, golf, music, Spanish culture. *Address:* Argyll Lodge, Lossiemouth, Moray IV31 6QT. *T:* Lossiemouth (034381) 3150. *Club:* New (Edinburgh).

STEWART, Lt-Col Robert Christie, CBE 1983; TD 1962; Lord Lieutenant of Kinross-shire, 1966–74; *b* 3 Aug. 1926; *m* 1953, Ann Grizel Cochrane; three *s* two *d*. *Educ:* Eton; University College, Oxford. Lt Scots Guards, 1945–49. Oxford Univ., 1949–51 (BA Agric.). TA, 7 Argyll and Sutherland Highlanders, 1948–66; Lt-Col Comdg 7 A & SH, 1963–66. Hon. Col, 1/51 Highland Volunteers, 1972–75. Chm. and Pres., Bd of Governors, E of Scotland Coll. of Agric., 1970–83. DL Kinross 1956, VL 1958; Chairman Kinross County Council, 1963–73. *Address:* Arndean, by Dollar, Kinross-shire. *T:* Dollar (0259) 42527. *Club:* Royal Perth Golfing Society.

STEWART, Dr Robert William, OC 1979; FRS 1970; FRSC 1967; Adjunct Professor, Department of Physics, University of Victoria, since 1989; Hon. Professor of Physics and Oceanography, University of British Columbia, since 1971; Hon. Professor of Science, University of Alberta, since 1985; *b* 21 Aug. 1923; *m* 1st, 1948, V. Brande (marr. diss. 1972); two *s* one *d*; 2nd, 1973, Anne-Marie Robert; one *s*. *Educ:* Queen's Univ., Ontario. BSc 1945, MSc 1947, Queen's; PhD Cantab 1952. Canadian Defence Research Bd, 1950–61; Prof. of Physics and Oceanography, Univ. of British Columbia, 1961–70; Dir, Marine Scis Br., Pacific Reg., Environment Canada, 1970–74; Dir-Gen., Ocean and Aquatic Scis, Pacific Reg., Fisheries and Marine Service, Dept of Fisheries and Oceans, Canada, 1974–79; Dep. Minister, Ministry of Univs, Science and Communications, BC, Canada, 1979–84; Pres., Alberta Res. Council, 1984–87; Dir, Centre for Earth and Ocean Res., Univ. of Victoria, 1987–89. Vis. Professor: Dalhousie Univ., 1960–61; Harvard Univ., 1964; Pennsylvania State Univ., 1964; Commonwealth Vis. Prof., Cambridge Univ., 1967–68. Vice-Chm., 1968–72, Chm., 1972–76, Jt Organizing Cttee, Global Atmospheric Res. Program; Pres., Internat. Assoc. of Physical Scis of Ocean, 1975–79; Mem., Cttee on Climatic Changes and the Ocean, 1980– (Chm., 1983–87). *Publications:* numerous, on turbulence, oceanography and meteorology. *Address:* Department of Physics, University of Victoria, PO Box 1700, Victoria, British Columbia V8W 2Y2, Canada.

STEWART, Sir Robertson (Huntly), Kt 1979; CBE 1970; CEng, FIProdE, FPRI, FNZIM, FInstD; Executive Chairman: PDL Holdings Ltd (manufacturers of electrical and plastic products), since 1982 (Chairman and Managing Director, 1957–82); PDL (Asia), since 1975; *b* 21 Sept. 1913; *s* of Robert McGregor Stewart and Ivy Emily (*née* Grigg); *m* 1st, 1937, Ada Gladys Gunter; two *s* one *d*; 2nd, 1970, Ellen Adrienne Cansdale; two *s*. *Educ:* Christchurch Boys' High Sch.; Christchurch Technical Inst. CEng, FIProdE 1967, FPRI 1960, FNZIM 1962, FInstD 1970. Introd plastics industry to NZ, 1936; commenced manuf. of electrical products in NZ, 1937; estabd PDL Gp of Cos, 1947. Led NZ Trade Missions, 1962, 1964, 1966, 1967, 1970 and 1972. Pres., NZ Manufrs Fedn, 1963–64. Hon. Malaysian Consul. *Recreations:* motor racing, tennis, fishing. *Address:* Park Penthouse, Heatherlea, 10 Ayr Street, Christchurch, New Zealand. *T:* Christchurch 488984. *Club:* Canterbury (Christchurch).

STEWART, Robin Milton, QC 1978; a Recorder of the Crown Court, since 1978; *b* 5 Aug. 1938; *s* of late Brig. Guy Milton Stewart and of Dr Elaine Oenone Stewart, MD, BS; *m* 1962, Lynda Grace Medhurst; three *s*. *Educ:* Winchester; New Coll., Oxford (MA). Called to the Bar, Middle Temple, 1963, Bencher, 1988; called to the Irish Bar, King's Inns, Dublin, 1975. Prosecuting Counsel to Inland Revenue, NE Circuit, 1976–78. Freeman, City of London, 1966; Liveryman, Co. of Glaziers, 1966. *Recreations:* pictures, gardening, Scottish family history. *Address:* 199 Strand, WC2R 1DJ. *T:* 071–379 9779; Little Chart, 46 Oak Hill Road, Sevenoaks, Kent TN13 1NS. *T:* Sevenoaks (0732) 453475. *Club:* Oriental.

STEWART, Sir Ronald (Compton), 2nd Bt, *cr* 1937; DL; Chairman, London Brick Co. Ltd, 1966–79; *b* 14 Aug. 1903; *s* of Sir (Percy) Malcolm Stewart, 1st Bt, OBE, and Cordelia (*d* 1906,) *d* of late Rt Hon. Sir Joseph Compton Rickett, DL, MP; *S* father, 1951; *m* 1936, Cynthia, OBE, JP (*d* 1987), *d* of Harold Farmiloe. *Educ:* Rugby; Jesus College, Cambridge. High Sheriff of Bedfordshire, 1954, DL 1974. *Heir:* none. *Address:* Maulden Grange, Maulden, Bedfordshire.

STEWART, Sir Simon; *see* Stewart, Sir J. S. W.

STEWART, Stanley Toft, CMG 1958; PJG Singapore, 1962; *b* 13 June 1910; *s* of Charles Campbell Stewart and Jeanette Matilda Doral; *m* 1935, Therese Zelie de Souza; seven *d*. *Educ:* St Xavier's Instn, Penang; Raffles Coll., Singapore. Straits Settlements CS, 1934–46; Overseas Civil Service, 1946–55; District Officer, Butterworth, Province Wellesley, 1947–52; Dep. Chm., Rural Board, Singapore, 1952–54; Chm., Rural Board, Singapore, 1954; Dep. Sec., Ministry of Local Government, Lands and Housing, Singapore, 1955, Actg Permanent Sec., 1955; Actg Chief Sec., Singapore, Oct. 1957–Jan. 1958; Permanent Secretary: Home Affairs, 1959–63; to Prime Minister, 1961–66; Singapore High Comr in Australia, 1966–69; Permanent Sec., Min. of Foreign Affairs, Singapore, 1969–72; Exec. Sec., Nat. Stadium Corp., 1973. *Recreations:* tennis, gardening. *Clubs:* Singapore Recreation, Club 200 (Singapore).

STEWART, Stephen Malcolm, CBE 1986; QC 1979; Chairman, Common Law Institute of Intellectual Property, since 1981; *b* 22 April 1914; *s* of Dr Siegmund and Helen Strauss; *m* 1946, Marie Josephine (*née* Bere); two *s*. *Educ:* Univ. of Vienna (LLD 1936); Ecole des Sciences Politiques, Paris (Diploma 1938); Univ. of London. Overseas Service, BBC, 1939; served Army, 1940–47; Captain, Liaison Officer, Free French Forces and Belgian Army, 1944–45; Major JAG's Branch, 21 Army Group, 1945; Chief Prosecuting Officer, War Crimes Trials, 1946–47; UN War Crimes Commn, 1947–48; called to the Bar, Inner Temple, 1948; practice at the Bar, 1948–61; Director General, IFPI, 1961–79. Mem., Gen. Council of the Bar, 1969–71; Vice-Chm., Bar Assoc. for Commerce, Finance and Industry, 1974–76, Chm., 1976–78; Member of Senate of the Inns of Court and Bar, 1976–81. Governor: Polytechnic of the South Bank, 1967–70; Sevenoaks School, 1968–83. Golden Cross of the Republic, Austria, 1983. *Publications:* The Clearinghouse System for Copyright Licences, 1966; 200 Years of English Copyright Law, 1976; International Copyright in the 1980s (Geiringer Meml Lecture, NY), 1980; International Copyright and Neighbouring Rights, 1983, 2nd edn 1989. *Recreations:* music, tennis. *Address:* Oakwood, Chittoe, Wilts SN15 2EW. *T:* Devizes (0380) 850066. *Club:* Reform.

STEWART, Mrs Suzanne Freda; *see* Norwood, S. F.

STEWART, Victor Colvin, FCA; Registrar General for Scotland, 1978–82; *b* 12 April 1921; *s* of Victor Stewart and Jean Cameron; *m* 1949, Aileen Laurie; one *s*. *Educ:* Selkirk High Sch.; Edinburgh Univ. (BCom). FCA 1954. Served War in RAF, Africa and ME, 1942–46. Joined Dept of Health for Scotland, 1938; Chief Exec. Officer, 1959; Principal, SHHD, 1963, Asst Sec. 1971; Dep. Registrar Gen. for Scotland, 1976. *Recreations:* golf, walking, bridge. *Address:* Tynet, Lodgehill Road, Nairn IV12 4QL. *T:* Nairn (0667) 52050. *Club:* Commonwealth Trust.

STEWART, Dr William, CB 1977; DSc; aerospace consultant, since 1983; *b* Hamilton, 29 Aug. 1921; *m* 1955, Helen Cairney; two *d*. *Educ:* St John's Grammar Sch.; Hamilton Acad.; Glasgow Univ. BSc Hons (engin.); DSc 1958. RAE, Farnborough, 1942–53; British Jt Services Mission, Washington, 1953–56; Dep. Head of Naval Air Dept, RAE, Bedford, 1956–63; Imperial Defence College, 1964; Asst Dir, Project Time and Cost Analysis, 1965–66; Dir, Anglo-French Combat Trainer Aircraft Projects, 1966–70; Dir-Gen., Multi-Role Combat Aircraft, 1970–73; Dep. Controller, Aircraft A, 1973–78, Aircraft, 1978–81, MoD (PE). Silver Medal, RAeS, 1981. *Address:* 25 Brickhill Drive, Bedford MK41 7QA.

STEWART, Prof. William Alexander Campbell, MA, PhD; DL; Vice-Chancellor, University of Keele, 1967–79; *b* Glasgow, 17 Dec. 1915; *s* of late Thomas Stewart, Glasgow, and Helen Fraser, Elgin, Morayshire; *m* 1947, Ella Elizabeth Burnett, of Edinburgh; one *s* one *d*. *Educ:* Colfe's Grammar Sch., London; University Coll., and Inst. of Education, Univ. of London. Exhibitioner, University Coll., London., 1934–37; BA 1937; MA 1941; PhD 1947; Diploma in Education, 1938; Fellow, UCL, 1975. Sen. English Master: (and Housemaster), Friends' School, Saffron Walden, Essex, 1938–43; Abbotsholme School, Derbyshire, 1943–44 (Member of Governing Body, 1960–80; Chm., Council, 1974–80); Asst Lectr and Lectr in Education, University Coll.,

Nottingham, 1944–47; Lectr in Education, Univ. of Wales (Cardiff), 1947–50; Prof. of Education, Univ. of Keele (formerly UC of N Staffs), 1950–67, Prof. Emeritus, 1979. Vis. Prof., McGill Univ., 1957, Univ. of Calif., Los Angeles 1959; Simon Vis. Prof., Univ. of Manchester, 1962–63; Prestige Fellow, NZ Univs, 1969; Hon. Vis. Professorial Fellow, Univ. of Sussex, 1979–84. Chairman: YMCA Educn Cttee, 1962–67; Nat. Adv. Council for Child Care, 1968–71; Univs Council for Adult Educn, 1969–73; Council, Roehampton Inst. of Higher Educn, 1979–88 (Fellow, 1988); Member: Inter-Univ. and Polytech. Council for Higher Education Overseas; Commonwealth Univ. Interchange Council, 1968–80; Council, Univ. of Sierra Leone, 1968–83; Adv. Council, Supply and Training of Teachers, 1974–78; US-UK Educnl Commn, 1977–81. Fellow, Internat. Inst. of Art and Letters. DL Stafford, 1973. Hon. DLitt: Ulster, 1973; Keele, 1981. *Publications:* Quakers and Education, 1953; (ed with J. Eros) Systematic Sociology of Karl Mannheim, 1957; (with K. Mannheim) An Introduction to the Sociology of Education, 1962; contrib. to The American College (ed Sanford), 1962; The Educational Innovators, Vol. 1, with W. P. McCann, 1967, Vol. 2, 1968; Progressives and Radicals in English Education 1750–1970, 1972; Higher Education in Postwar Britain, 1989. *Recreations:* talking and listening, theatre, music. *Address:* Flat 4, 74 Westgate, Chichester, West Sussex PO19 3HH. *T:* Chichester (0243) 785528. *Clubs:* Oriental; Federation House (Stoke on Trent).

STEWART, Prof. William Duncan Paterson, PhD, DSc; FRS 1977; FRSE; Chief Scientific Adviser, Cabinet Office, since 1990; *b* 7 June 1935; *s* of John Stewart and Margaret (*née* Paterson); *m* 1958, Catherine MacLeod; one *s*. *Educ:* Bowmore Junior Secondary Sch., Isle-of-Islay; Dunoon Grammar Sch.; Glasgow Univ. (BSc, PhD, DSc). FRSE 1973. Asst Lectr, Univ. of Nottingham, 1961–63; Lectr, Westfield Coll., Univ. of London, 1963–68; University of Dundee: Hd of Dept of Biol Scis, 1968–83; Boyd Baxter Prof. of Biology, 1968–88; Vice-Principal, 1985–87; Sec. and Dep. Chm., AFRC, 1988–90. Vis. Res. Worker, Univ. of Wisconsin, 1966 and 1968; Vis. Professor: Univ. of Kuwait, 1980; Univ. of Otago, 1984. Chairman: Royal Soc. Biological Educn Cttee, 1977–80; Aquatic Life Sciences Grants Cttee, NERC, 1973–78; Sci. Adv. Cttee, Freshwater Biol. Assoc., 1974–85; Royal Soc. Study Group on Nitrogen Cycle, 1979–84; Internat. Cttee on Microbial Ecology, 1983–86 (Sec., 1980–83); Royal Soc. Biotechnology and Educn Wkg Gp, 1980–81; Independent Adv. Gp on Gruinard Is., 1986–; Vice-Pres., 1973–75, Pres., 1975–77, British Phycological Soc.; President: Section K, BAAS, 1984; Council, Scottish Marine Biol. Assoc., 1985–87 (Mem., 1969–74, 1982–); Vice-Pres., Freshwater Biol. Assoc., 1984–. Trustee, Estuarine and Brackish-Water Sciences Assoc., 1978–88; Member: Council, RSE, 1976–79; Council, Marine Biol. Assoc., 1973–76, 1977–80, 1981–84; Plants and Soils Res. Grants Bd, ARC, 1978–84; Governing Body, Scottish Hort. Res. Inst., 1971–80; British Nat. Cttee for problems of environment, Royal Soc., 1979–85; UNESCO Panel on Microbiology, 1975–81; Council, NERC, 1979–85 (Chm., Marine Life Scis Preparatory Gp, 1982–85); Internat. Cell Res. Org., 1979–84; Governing Body, Scottish Crop Res. Inst., 1980–88; Governing Body, Macaulay Land Use Res. Inst., 1987–88; Royal Soc. Study Gp on Science Educn, 1981–82; Royal Soc. Study Gp on Pollution Control Priorities, 1987–; Council, Royal Soc., 1984–86; Royal Commn on Environmental Pollution, 1986–; Biol Sciences Sub-Cttee, UGC, 1988. Royal Soc. Assessor, AFRC, 1985–87. Lectures: Phycological Soc. of America Dist., 1977; Barton-Wright, Inst. Biol., 1977; Sir David Martin Royal Soc.-BAYS, 1979; Plenary, 2nd Internat. Symp. on Microbial Ecology, 1980; Holden, Nottingham Univ., 1983; Leeuwenhoek, Royal Soc., 1984; Plenary, 2nd Internat. Phycological Congress, Copenhagen, 1985; Diamond Jubilee, Hannah Res. Inst., 1989. Hon. DSc: Edinburgh, 1990; UEA, Glasgow, Nottingham, and Sheffield, 1991; DUniv Stirling, 1991. *Publications:* Nitrogen Fixation in Plants, 1966; (jtly) The Blue-Green Algae, 1973; Algal Physiology and Biochemistry, 1974; (ed) Nitrogen Fixation by Free-living Organisms, 1975; (ed jtly) Nitrogen Fixation, 1980; (ed jtly) The Nitrogen Cycle of the United Kingdom, 1984; papers in learned jls of repute. *Recreations:* watching soccer, playing the bagpipes (occasionally). *Address:* c/o Cabinet Office, 70 Whitehall, SW1A 2AS. *Club:* Athenæum.

STEWART, William Ian; *see* Allanbridge, Hon. Lord.

STEWART-CLARK, Sir John, (Sir Jack), 3rd Bt *cr* 1918; Member (C) Sussex East, European Parliament, since 1979; *b* 17 Sept. 1929; *e s* of Sir Stewart Stewart-Clark, 2nd Bt, and of Jane Pamela, *d* of late Major Arundell Clarke; *S* father, 1971; *m* 1958, Lydia Frederike, *d* of J. W. Loudon, Holland; one *s* four *d*. *Educ:* Eton; Balliol College, Oxford; Harvard Business School. Commissioned with HM Coldstream Guards, 1948–49. Oxford, 1949–52. With J. & P. Coats Ltd, 1952–69; Managing Director: J. & P. Coats, Pakistan, Ltd, 1961–67; J. A. Carp's Garenfabrieken, Holland, 1967–69; Philips Electrical Ltd, London, 1971–75; Pye of Cambridge Ltd, 1975–79. Director: Low and Bonar plc; A. T. Kearney Ltd; Pioneer Concrete plc; TSB Scotland, 1986–89. Pres. Supervisory Bd, Eur. Inst. for Security, 1984–86; Mem. Council, RUSI, 1979–83. Dir and Trustee, Eur. Centre for Work and Society, 1982–; Chm., Conf. of Regions of North Western Europe, 1986–. Treas., Eur. Democratic Group, 1979–. Member Royal Company of Archers, Queen's Body Guard for Scotland. Contested (U) North Aberdeen, Gen. Election, 1959. *Recreations:* golf, tennis, shooting, photography, vintage cars. *Heir: s* Alexander Dudley Stewart-Clark, *b* 21 Nov. 1960. *Address:* Puckstye House, Holtye Common, Cowden, Kent TN8 7EL. *T:* Cowden (0342) 850541. *Clubs:* White's; Royal Ashdown Golf.

STEWART COX, Maj.-Gen. Arthur George Ernest, DFC 1952; General Officer Commanding Wales, 1978–80; *b* 11 April 1925; *s* of Lt-Col Arthur Stewart Cox and Mrs Dorothea Stewart Cox, *d* of Maj.-Gen. Sir Edward May; *m* 1953, Mary Pamela, *d* of Hon. George Lyttelton; three *s* one *d*. *Educ:* Marlborough Coll.; Aberdeen Univ. Commissioned RA, 1944; parachutist, RA regts, 1945–50; army pilot, Far East and Korea, 1950–52; ADC to Comdt, RMA Sandhurst, 1954–56; Staff Coll., 1956; SO 99 Gurkha Inf. Bde, 1957–58; SO MoD, Malaya, 1963–65; CO 29 Commando Light Regt, RA, 1965–68; SO Sch. of Artillery, 1968–69; Comdr RA 4th Div., 1969–72; RCDS, 1973; Dep. Dir of Manning (Army), MoD, 1974–76. Col Comdt, RA, 1980–90; Hon. Colonel: 3rd Bn RWF, TAVR, 1980–85; 289 Commando Battery, RA, TAVR, 1983–91. *Recreations:* shooting, fishing, lepidoptery, gardening. *Address:* Long Mead, Brixton Deverill, Warminster, Wilts BA12 7EJ. *T:* Warminster (0985) 40872.

STEWART-JONES, Mrs Richard; *see* Smith, Emma.

STEWART-MOORE, Alexander Wyndham Hume; DL; Chairman, Gallaher Ltd, 1975–79 (Managing Director, 1966–75); Director, American Brands Inc., 1975–79; *b* 14 Feb. 1915; 2nd *s* of late James Stewart-Moore, DL, Ballydivity, Dervock, Co. Antrim, and of Katherine Marion (*née* Jackson); *m* 1948, Magdalene Clare, *y d* of Sir David Richard Llewellyn, 1st Bt, LLD, JP; three *s* one *d*. *Educ:* Shrewsbury. Joined Gallaher Ltd, Nov. 1934. Served War, Royal Artillery (Middle East and Italy), 1939–46. DL Co. Antrim. *Recreations:* farming, fishing, gardening. *Address:* Moyarget Farm, 98 Moyarget Road, Ballycastle, Co. Antrim, NI. *T:* Ballycastle (02657) 62287.

STEWART-RICHARDSON, Sir Simon (Alaisdair), 17th Bt *cr* 1630; *b* 9 June 1947; *er s* of Sir Ian Rorie Hay Stewart-Richardson, 16th Bt, and of Audrey Meryl (who *m* 1975, P. A. P. Robertson, *qv*), *e d* of late Claude Odlum; *S* father, 1969. *Educ:* Trinity College, Glenalmond. *Heir: b* Ninian Rorie Stewart-Richardson [*b* 20 Jan. 1949; *m* 1983, Joan Kristina, *d* of Howard Smee; one *s* one *d*]. *Address:* Lynedale, Longcross, near Chertsey, Surrey KT16 0DP. *T:* Ottershaw (0932) 872329.

STEWART-ROBERTS, Phyllida Katharine, JP; DL; Superintendent-in-Chief, St John Ambulance Brigade, since 1990; *b* 19 Aug. 1933; *d* of Lt-Col Walter Harold Bamfield, Royal Welch Fusiliers and Veronica Grissell; *m* 1955, Andrew Kerr Stewart-Roberts; one *s* one *d*. *Educ:* Tormead Sch.; RAM (Diploma). Love Walk Hostel for Disabled Workers: Mem., Management Cttee, 1972–; Chm., 1983–89. Trustee, Community Service Volunteers, 1984–; Management Cttee, Habinteg Housing Assoc., 1988–; St John Ambulance Brigade, Sussex, 1962–89 (County Pres., 1984–89); Order of St John of Jerusalem: Jt Cttee, BRCS, 1990–; Florence Nightingale Meml Cttee, 1990–; Vice-Pres., VAD Assoc., 1991–. JP Inner London, 1980; Inner London Juvenile Panel, 1981–. DL E Sussex, 1991. OStJ 1987. *Recreations:* needlework, the gentler country pursuits. *Address:* 48 Grove Lane, SE5 8ST.

STEWART-SMITH, Christopher Dudley; Chairman, Conder Group plc, since 1987; *b* 21 Jan. 1941; *s* of late Ean Stewart-Smith and Edmee von Wallerstain und Marnegg; *m* 1964, Olivia (marr. diss. 1989), *d* of Col John Barstow, DSO; one *s* two *d*. *Educ:* Winchester; King's Coll., Cambridge (MA Mod Langs); MIT (SM Management). Courtaulds, 1962–65; McKinsey & Co. Management Consultants, 1966–71; joined Sterling Guarantee Trust, 1971, Dir, 1973; served on main bd after merger with Town & City Properties and later with P&OSNCo., until 1986; Chairman: Earls Court and Olympia Exhibns Gp, 1974–85; Sutcliffe Catering Gp, 1975–85; Butlers Warehousing & Distribution, 1971–85; Sterling Guards, 1974–85, P & O Cruises, Swan Hellenic, and Princess Cruises, 1985–86; Southern Adv. Bd, Nat. Westminster Bank, 1988– (Dir, Outer Reg., 1984–88); Collett Dickenson Pearce Internat., 1990–91; Healthcall plc, 1991–. Director: Williamson Tea Holdings, 1986–; Life Sciences Internat., 1987–. Chm., London Chamber of Commerce and Industry, 1988–90 (Dep. Chm., 1986–88); Dep. Pres., ABCC, 1990–. Trustee: Conder Conserv. Trust, 1987–; Res. Fund for Complementary Med., 1988–; Member: Council, Centre for World Develt Educn, 1988–; Council of Management, Acad. of St Martin-in-the-Fields, 1990–; Cttee, Royal Tournament, 1976–85; Vice-Pres., Olympia Internat. Showjumping, 1977–85; Hon. Mem., Royal Smithfield Club, 1985–. Liveryman, Grocers' Co., 1972. FRSA. *Recreations:* design of gardens and buildings, tennis, shooting, ski-ing. *Address:* (office) 25/28 Old Burlington Street, W1X 1LB. *T:* 071–734 7701. *Clubs:* Buck's, Travellers'.

STEWART-SMITH, Rev. Canon David Cree, MA; *b* 22 May 1913; 3rd *s* of late Thomas Stewart Stewart-Smith, JP, Heathlands, Kinver, Staffs, and Mabel (*née* McDougall); *m* 1943, Kathleen Georgiana Maule Ffinch, *d* of Rev. K. M. Ffinch, Ifield, Kent. *Educ:* Marlborough; King's Coll., Cambridge; Cuddesdon Theol. College. BA 1939, MA 1943. Vicar-Choral and Sacrist, York Minster, 1944–49; Vicar of Shadwell, Leeds, 1949–52; Warden, Brasted Place Coll., 1952–63; Dean of St George's Cath., Jerusalem, and Administrator of St George's Coll., 1964–67; Commissary for Archbishop in Jerusalem, 1968–76; Archdeacon of Bromley and Hon. Canon of Rochester, 1968–69; Archdeacon of Rochester and Canon Residentiary of Rochester Cathedral, 1969–76; Hon. Canon of Rochester, 1976–78, Canon Emeritus, 1978–; Director of Ordinands, dio. Rochester, 1968–74; Mem., C of E Pensions Bd, 1970–84; a Church Commissioner, 1973–78; Home Sec., Jerusalem and Middle East Church Assoc., 1976–78; Fellow of Woodard Corp.: Northern Div., 1949–52; Southern Div., 1959–64. *Recreations:* architecture, music, travel. *Address:* 16 Capel Court, Prestbury, near Cheltenham GL52 3EL. *T:* Cheltenham (0242) 510972. *Club:* United Oxford & Cambridge University.

STEWART-SMITH, (Dudley) Geoffrey; *b* 28 Dec. 1933; *s* of Dudley Cautley Stewart-Smith; *m* 1956, Kay Mary; three *s*. *Educ:* Winchester; RMA Sandhurst. Regular Officer, The Black Watch, 1952–60. Dir, Foreign Affairs Res. Inst., 1976–86. Director: Foreign Affairs Circle; Freedom Communications Internat. News Agency; Editor, East-West Digest; Dir, Foreign Affairs Publishing Co.; Financial Times, 1968. MP (C) Derbyshire, Belper, 1970–Feb 1974. Liveryman, Grocers' Co., 1962. *Publications:* The Defeat of Communism, 1964; No Vision Here: Non-Military Warfare in Britain, 1966; (ed) Brandt and the Destruction of NATO, 1973; The Struggle for Freedom, 1980; contribs to various foreign, defence and communist affairs jls at home and overseas. *Recreations:* walking, swimming, shooting and stalking.

STEWART-WILSON, Lt-Col Blair Aubyn, CVO 1989 (LVO 1983); Deputy Master of the Household and Equerry to Her Majesty, since 1976; *b* 17 July 1929; *s* of late Aubyn Wilson and late Muriel Stewart Stevens; *m* 1962, Helen Mary Fox; three *d*. *Educ:* Eton; Sandhurst. Commnd Scots Guards, 1949; served with Regt in UK, Germany and Far East; Adjutant 2nd Bn, 1955–57; ADC to Viscount Cobham, Governor General and C-in-C, New Zealand, 1957–59; Equerry to late Duke of Gloucester, 1960–62; Regtl Adjutant, 1966–68; GSO1, Foreign Liaison Sect. (Army), MoD, 1970–73; Defence, Military and Air Attaché, British Embassy, Vienna, 1975–76. *Address:* c/o Royal Bank of Scotland, 84 Atholl Road, Pitlochry PH16 5BJ. *Clubs:* Pratt's, White's.

STEYN, Hon. Sir Johan, Kt 1985; **Hon. Mr Justice Steyn;** a Judge of the High Court, Queen's Bench Division, since 1985; *b* 15 Aug. 1932; *m* Susan Leonore (*née* Lewis); two *s* two *d* by previous *m*, and one step *s* one step *d*. *Educ:* Jan van Riebeeck Sch., Cape Town, S Africa; Univ. of Stellenbosch, S Africa (BA, LLB); University Coll., Oxford (MA). Cape Province Rhodes Scholar, 1955; commenced practice at S African Bar, 1958; Sen. Counsel of Supreme Court of SA, 1970; settled in UK; commenced practice at English Bar, 1973 (Bencher, Lincoln's Inn, 1985); QC 1979; a Presiding Judge, Northern Circuit, 1989–. Member: Supreme Court Rule Cttee, 1985–89; Deptl Adv. Cttee on Arbitration Law, 1986–89 (Chm., 1990–); Chm., Race Relations Cttee of the Bar, 1987–88. *Address:* c/o Royal Courts of Justice, WC2A 2LL. *Club:* Garrick.

STEYN, Hon. (Stephanus Jacobus) Marais, DMS 1981; South African Ambassador: to United Kingdom, 1980–84; to Transkei, 1984–87; retired 1987; *b* 25 Dec. 1914; *m* 1940, Susanne Moolman; two *s* two *d*. *Educ:* Univ. of Cape Town (BA); Univ. of the Witwatersrand (LLB). Journalist, various newspapers and on staff of State Information Office, 1938–42; Sec., United Party, Witwatersrand, 1942–48 (Asst Chief Sec., 1946–48); Opposition MP representing consecutively constituencies of Alberton, Vereeniging and Yeoville, specialising in labour and transport matters, 1948–73; National Party MP for Turffontein, 1974–80; Minister of: Indian Affairs and Tourism, 1975; Community Develt, 1976–80; Community Develt, Coloured Relations and Indian Affairs, 1980. *Recreations:* bowls, chess, grandchildren. *Address:* PO Box 6077, Uniedal, 7612, South Africa. *Club:* City and Civil Service (Cape Town).

STIBBARD, Peter Jack; Director of Statistics, Department of Employment, since 1989; *b* 15 May 1936; *s* of late Frederick Stibbard and Gladys Stibbard (*née* Daines); *m* 1964, Christine Fuller; two *d*. *Educ:* City of Norwich Grammar School; Hull Univ. (BSc Econ; MIS). Served RAF, 1954–56. Kodak Ltd, 1959–64; Thos Potterton Ltd, 1964–66; Greater London Council, 1966–68; Central Statistical Office, 1968–82 (Chief Statistician 1973); HM Treasury, 1982–85; Under Sec., Statistics Div. 2, DTI, 1985–89. *Publications:* articles in official and trade jls. *Address:* Department of Employment, Caxton House, Tothill Street, SW1H 9NF.

STIBBE, Philip Godfrey, MA; Head Master of Norwich School, 1975–84; *b* 20 July 1921; *m* 1956, Mary Joy, *d* of late Canon C. G. Thornton; two *s* one *d*. *Educ:* Mill Hill Sch.; Merton Coll., Oxford (MA). Served War of 1939–45; joined Royal Sussex Regt, 1941; seconded King's (Liverpool) Regt, 1942; 1st Wingate Expedn into Burma (wounded, despatches), 1943; POW, 1943–45. Asst Master, 1948–75, Housemaster, 1953–74, Bradfield Coll. JP Norwich, 1979–84. *Publication:* Return via Rangoon, 1947. *Recreations:* people, places, books. *Address:* 29A Bracondale, Norwich NR1 2AT. *T:* Norwich (0603) 630704.

STIBBON, Gen. Sir John (James), KCB 1988; OBE 1979; CEng, FICE; Master General of the Ordnance, 1987–91; *b* 5 Jan. 1935; *s* of Jack Stibbon and Elizabeth Matilda Stibbon (*née* Dixon); *m* 1957, Jean Fergusson Skeggs, *d* of John Robert Skeggs and Florence Skeggs (*née* Hayes); two *d*. *Educ:* Portsmouth Southern Grammar School; Royal Military Academy; Royal Military College of Science. BSc (Eng). CEng 1989; FICE 1989. Commissioned RE, 1954; CO 28 Amphibious Engineer Regt, 1975–77; Asst Military Secretary, 1977–79; Comd 20 Armoured Brigade, 1979–81; Comdt, RMCS, 1983–85; ACDS Operational Requirements (Land Systems), 1985–87. Colonel Commandant: RAPC, 1985–; RPC, 1986–; RE, 1987–. Hon DSc Cranfield Inst. of Technology, 1989. *Recreations:* Association football, athletics, painting, palaeontology. *Club:* Lansdowne.

STIBBS, Prof. Douglas Walter Noble, MSc Sydney, DPhil Oxon; FRSE; Napier Professor of Astronomy and Director of the University Observatory, 1959–89, and Senior Professor Senatus Academicus, 1987–89, University of St Andrews; Visiting Fellow, Mount Stromlo and Siding Spring Observatories, and Visiting Professor, Department of Mathematics, Australian National University, since 1990; *b* 17 Feb. 1919; 2nd *s* of Edward John Stibbs, Sydney, NSW; *m* 1949, Margaret Lilian Calvert, BSc, DipEd (Sydney), *er d* of Rev. John Calvert, Sydney, NSW; two *d*. *Educ:* Sydney High Sch.; Univ. of Sydney; New College, Oxford. Deas Thomson Scholar, Sch. of Physics, Univ. of Sydney, 1940; BSc (Sydney), 1st Class Hons, Univ. Medal in Physics, 1942; MSc (Sydney), 1943; DPhil (Oxon), 1954. Johnson Memorial Prize and Gold Medal for Advancement of Astronomy and Meteorology, Oxford Univ., 1956. Res. Asst, Commonwealth Solar Observatory, Canberra, ACT, 1940–42; Asst Lectr, Dept of Mathematics and Physics, New England University Coll., Armidale, NSW (now the Univ. of New England), 1942–45; Scientific Officer and Sen. Scientific Officer, Commonwealth Observatory, Canberra, ACT, 1945–51; Radcliffe Travelling Fellow in Astronomy, Radcliffe Observatory, Pretoria, S Africa, and Univ. Observatory, Oxford, 1951–54; PSO, UKAEA, 1955–59. Vis. Prof. of Astrophysics, Yale Univ. Observatory, 1966–67; British Council Vis. Prof., Univ. of Utrecht, 1968; Prof., Collège de France, 1975–76 (Médaille du Collège, 1976). Member: Internat. Astronomical Union, 1951– (Chm. Finance Cttee, 1964–67, 1973–76, 1976–79); Amer. Astronomical Soc., 1956–73; Adv. Cttee on Meteorology for Scotland, 1960–69, 1972–75, 1978–80; Board of Visitors, Royal Greenwich Observatory, 1963–65; Council RAS, 1964–67, 1970–73 (Vice-Pres., 1972–73), Editorial Board, 1970–73; Council, RSE, 1970–72; National Cttee for Astronomy, 1964–76; SRC Cttees for Royal Greenwich Observatory, 1966–70, and Royal Observatory, Edinburgh, 1966–76, Chm., 1970–76; SRC Astronomy, Space and Radio Bd, 1970–76; SRC, 1972–76; S African Astron. Obs. Adv. Cttee, 1972–76; Chairman: Astronomy Policy and Grants Cttee, 1972–74; Northern Hemisphere Observatory Planning Cttee, 1972–75; Astronomy II Cttee, 1974–75; Mem., Centre National de la Recherche Scientifique Cttee, Obs. de Haute Provence, 1973–82. Life Member: Sydney Univ. Union, 1942; New Coll. Soc., 1953; New England Univ. Union, NSW, 1957. Mem., Western Province Masters Athletics Assoc., Cape Town, 1983–. Marathon Medals: Paris, Caithness, Edinburgh (3hrs 59mins), Flying Fox (British Veterans Championships), Honolulu, 1983; London, Loch Rannoch, and Aberdeen (Veterans Trophy Winner), 1984; Stoke-on-Trent (Potteries), Athens, Honolulu, 1985; London, Edinburgh (Commonwealth Games Peoples Marathon), Stoke-on-Trent (Potteries), Berlin, Honolulu, 1986; Boston, 1987; Half-marathon Gold Medal, Australian Veterans Games, NSW, 1991. *Publications:* The Outer Layers of a Star (with Sir Richard Woolley), 1953; contrib. Theoretical Astrophysics and Astronomy in Monthly Notices of RAS and other jls. *Recreations:* music, ornithology, photography, golf, long-distance running. *Address:* Mount Stromlo Observatory, Australian National University, Canberra, ACT 2601, Australia. *T:* Canberra (06) 290–1773. *Club:* Royal and Ancient (St Andrews).

STIFF, Rt. Rev. Hugh Vernon; retired; *b* 15 Sept. 1916; unmarried. *Educ:* Univ. of Toronto (BA); Trinity Coll., Toronto (LTh). BD General Synod; Hon. DD, Trinity Coll., Toronto. Bishop of Keewatin, 1969–74; Rector of St James Cathedral and Dean of Toronto, 1974–86; Asst Bishop, Diocese of Toronto, 1977–86. *Address:* Apt #207, 83 Elm Avenue, Toronto, Ontario M4W IP1, Canada.

STIGLER, Prof. George Joseph, PhD; economist; Charles R. Walgreen Distinguished Service Professor Emeritus of American Institutions, University of Chicago, since 1981; *b* 17 Jan. 1911; *s* of Joseph Stigler and Elizabeth Stigler (*née* Hungler); *m* 1936, Margaret Mack (*d* 1970); three *s*. *Educ:* Seattle schools; Univ. of Washington (BBA); Northwestern Univ. (MBA); Univ. of Chicago (PhD 1938). Asst Prof., Iowa State Univ., 1936–38; Asst Prof., later Prof., Univ. of Minnesota, 1938–46 (war-time Mem., Stats Res. Group, Columbia Univ.); Professor: Brown Univ., 1946–47; Columbia Univ., 1947–58; Charles R. Walgreen Prof. of Amer. Instns, Graduate Sch. of Business, Univ. of Chicago, 1958, Dist. Service Prof., 1963; Founder, Center for Study of the Economy and the States, Univ. of Chicago, 1977. Member: Nat. Acad. of Sciences, 1975; Amer. Economic Assoc. (Pres., 1964); Guggenheim Fellow, 1955. Nobel Prize for Economic Science, 1982; Nat. Medal of Science, 1987. Editor, Jl of Political Economy, 1974–. *Publications:* Production and Distribution Theories, 1940; The Theory of Competitive Price, 1942; The Theory of Price, 1946 (numerous rev. edns); Trends in Employment in the Service Industries, 1956; The Intellectual and the Market Place, 1964, rev. edn 1984; Essays in the History of Economics, 1965; The Organization of Industry, 1968; The Citizen and the State, 1975; The Economist as Preacher, 1982; Memoirs of an Unregulated Economist (autobiog.), 1988; essays and articles for Nat. Bureau of Economic Research, Fortune, Jl of Political Economy (The Economics of Information, 1961), Jl of Business, Jl of Law and Economics, Bell Jl of Economics and Management Science, Antitrust Bulletin and other learned jls. *Recreations:* book collecting, golf, photography. *Address:* University of Chicago Graduate School of Business, 1101 East 58th Street, Chicago, Ill 60637, USA; 5825 Dorchester Avenue, Chicago, Ill 60637, USA.

STIGLITZ, Prof. Joseph Eugene, PhD; Professor of Economics, Stanford University, since 1988; *b* 9 Feb. 1943; *m* M. J. Hannaway; two *s* two *d*. *Educ:* Amherst Coll. (BA 1964); MIT (PhD 1966); Cambridge Univ. (MA 1970). Professor of Economics: Yale Univ. 1970–74; Stanford Univ., 1974–76; Drummond Prof. of Political Economy, Oxford Univ. and All Souls Coll., 1976–79; Prof. of Economics, Princeton Univ., 1979–88. Fellowships: Nat. Sci. Foundn, 1964–65; Fulbright, 1965–66; SSRC Faculty, 1969–70; Guggenheim, 1969–70; Oskar Morgenstern Distinguished Fellowship, Mathematica and Inst. for Advanced Study, Princeton, 1978–79. Consultant: Nat. Sci. Foundn, 1972–75; Ford Foundn Energy Policy Study, 1973; Dept of Labor (Pensions and Labor Turnover), 1974; Dept of Interior (Offshore Oil Leasing Programs), 1975; Federal Energy Admin (Intertemporal Biases in Market Allocation of Natural Resources), 1975–79; World Bank (Cost Benefit Analysis; Urban Rural Migration; Natural Resources), 1975–; Electric Power Res. Inst., 1976–; OECD; Office of Fair Trading; Treasury (Office of Tax Analysis), 1980; US AID (commodity price stabilization), 1977; Inter-American Development Bank; Bell Laboratories; Bell Communications Research; State of Alaska; Seneca Indian Nation. Internat. Prize, Academia Lincei, 1988; Union des Assurances de Paris Scientific Prize, 1989. Gen. Editor, Econometric Soc. Reprint Series; Associate Editor: Jl of Economic Theory, 1968–73; American Economic Rev., 1972–75; Jl of Economic Perspectives, 1988–; Co-editor, Jl of Public Economics, 1968–83; American Editor, Rev. of Economic Studies, 1968–76; Editorial Bd, World Bank Economic Review, The Geneva Papers, Revista de Econometrica, Assicurazioni. Vice-Pres., American Econ. Assoc., 1985. Fellow: Econometric Soc., 1972 (Sec./Treasurer, 1972–75); Amer. Acad. of Arts and Scis; Inst. for Policy Reform, 1990–; Sen. Fellow, Hoover Instn, 1988–. Hon. MA Yale, 1970; Hon. DHL Amherst, 1974. John Bates Clark Medal, Amer. Econ. Assoc. *Publications:* (ed) Collected Scientific Papers of P. A. Samuelson, 1965; (ed with H. Uzawa) Readings in Modern Theory of Economic Growth, 1969; (with A. B. Atkinson) Lectures in Public Finance, 1980; (with D. Newbery) The Economic Impact of Price Stabilization, 1980; Economics of the Public Sector, 1986; contribs on economics of growth, development, natural resources, information, uncertainty, imperfect competition, corporate finance and public finance in Amer. Econ. Rev., Qly Jl of Econs, Jl of Pol. Econ., Econometrica, Internat. Econ. Rev., Econ. Jl, Rev. of Econ. Studies, Jl of Public Econs, Jl of Econ. Theory, Oxford Econ. Papers. *Address:* Department of Economics, Stanford University, Stanford, Calif 94305–6072, USA.

STILGOE, Richard Henry Simpson; songwriter, lyricist, entertainer and broadcaster, since 1962; *b* 28 March 1943; *s* of John Henry Tweedie Stilgoe and Joan Lucy Strutt Stilgoe; *m* 1st, 1964, Elizabeth Caroline Gross; one *s* one *d*; 2nd, 1975, Annabel Margaret Hunt; two *s* one *d*. *Educ:* Liverpool Coll.; Monkton Combe Sch.; Clare Coll., Cambridge (choral exhibnr). One-man show worldwide, incl. Windsor Castle, 1982 and British Embassy, Washington, 1986; Two-man show with Peter Skellern, London, 1985–86; author and composer of Bodywork (children's musical), 1987. Word-processor for Andrew Lloyd Webber on Cats, Starlight Express and Phantom of the Opera. Founder and Dir, Orpheus Trust (music and the disabled), 1985–; Pres., Surrey Care Trust, 1986–. Monaco Radio Prize, 1984; NY Radio Fest. Gold Award, 1989. *Publication:* The Richard Stilgoe Letters, 1981. *Recreations:* sailing, cricket, architecture, building, demolition, children. *Address:* c/o The Orpheus Trust, North Park, Godstone, Surrey. *Club:* Lord's Taverners.

STIMSON, Robert Frederick; HM Diplomatic Service; Governor and Commander in Chief of St Helena and its Dependencies, 1987–91; *b* 16 May 1939; *s* of Frederick Henry and Gladys Alma Stimson (*née* Joel); *m* 1961, Margaret Faith Kerry; two *s* one *d*. *Educ:* Rendcomb Coll.; Queen Mary Coll., London (BSc First Cl. Hons; MSc (by thesis) mathematical physics). HM Diplomatic Service: FO, 1966–67; Saigon, 1967–68; Singapore, 1968–70; Cabinet Office, 1970–73; Mexico City, 1973–75; FCO, 1975–80; Counsellor, East Berlin, 1980–81; Head of Home Inspectorate, 1982–83; Counsellor and Hd of Chancery, Dublin, 1984–87. Order of Aztec Eagle, Mexico, 1975. *Publications:* contrib. Jl Physics and Chemistry of Solids. *Address:* c/o Foreign and Commonwealth Office, SW1A 2AH.

STINSON, His Honour David John; a Circuit Judge (formerly County Court Judge), 1969–86; President, Parents' Conciliation Trust, Suffolk, since 1987; *b* 22 Feb. 1921; *s* of late Henry John Edwin Stinson, MC, MA, LLB, Beckenham, Kent (sometime Chief Commoner of City of London, solicitor), and late Margaret Stinson (*née* Little); *m* 1950, Eleanor Judith (*née* Chance); two *s* two *d* (and one *s* decd). *Educ:* Eastbourne Coll.; Emmanuel Coll., Cambridge. MA 1946; Jesters Club, 1949 (Rugby Fives). Served War of 1939–45: Essex Yeomanry, Captain, RA, and Air OP, 1941–46 (despatches). Called to Bar, Middle Temple, 1947; Dep. Chm., Herts QS, 1965–71; Suffolk and Essex County Court Circuit, 1973–86. Chancellor, dio. of Carlisle, 1971–90. Chm., Ipswich Family Conciliation Service, 1982–89. *Recreations:* bird-watching, sailing. *Address:* Barrack Row, Waldringfield, Woodbridge, Suffolk IP12 4QX. *T:* Waldringfield (047336) 280. *Clubs:* Army and Navy; Waldringfield Sailing.

STIRLING, Sir Alexander (John Dickson), KBE 1981; CMG 1976; HM Diplomatic Service, retired; Chairman, Society for Protection of Animals in North Africa, since 1989; *b* 20 Oct. 1926; *e s* of late Brig. A. Dickson Stirling, DSO, MB, ChB, DPH, and Isobel Stirling, MA, DipEd, DipPsych, *d* of late Rev. J. C. Matthew (former senior Presidency Chaplain, Bombay); *m* 1955, Alison Mary, *y d* of Gp Capt. A. P. Campbell, CBE; two *s* two *d*. *Educ:* Edinburgh Academy; Lincoln Coll., Oxford (MA). RAFVR, 1945–48 (Egypt, 1945–47). Entered Foreign Office, 1951; Lebanon, 1952; British Embassy, Cairo, 1952–56 (Oriental Sec., 1955–56); FO, 1956–59; First Sec., British Embassy, Baghdad, 1959–62; First Sec. and Consul, Amman, 1962–64; First Sec., British Embassy, Santiago, 1965–67 (led UK Delegn to Fourth Antarctic Treaty Consultative Meeting, 1966); FO, 1967–69; British Political Agent, Bahrain, 1969–71, Ambassador, 1971–72; Counsellor, Beirut, 1972–75; RCDS 1976; Ambassador to Iraq, 1977–80, to the Tunisian Republic, 1981–84, to the Sudan, 1984–86.

See also C. J. M. Stirling.

STIRLING, Angus Duncan Æneas; Director-General, The National Trust, since 1983 (Deputy Director-General, 1979–83); Chairman, Royal Opera House, Covent Garden, since 1990 (Member of the Board, since 1979); 1979); *b* 10 Dec. 1933; *s* of late Duncan Alexander Stirling and of Lady Marjorie, *e d* of 8th Earl of Dunmore, VC, DSO, MVO; *m* 1959, Armyne Morar Helen Schofield, *e d* of W. G. B. Schofield; one *s* two *d*. *Educ:* Eton Coll.; Trinity Coll., Cambridge; London Univ. (Extra Mural) (Dip. History of Art). Christie, Manson and Woods Ltd, 1954–57; Lazard Bros and Co. Ltd, 1957–66; Asst Dir, Paul Mellon Foundn for British Art, 1966–69 (Jt Dir, 1969–70); Dep. Sec.-General, Arts Council of GB, 1971–79. Chm., Friends of Covent Garden, 1981–91; Dep. Chm., Royal Ballet Bd, 1988–91; a Gov., Royal Ballet, 1988–; Member: Crafts Council, 1980–85; Council of Management, Byam Shaw Sch. of Art, 1965–89; Management Cttee, Courtauld Inst. of Art, 1981–83 (Trustee, Home House (Courtald Collection), 1983–); Exec. Cttee, London Symphony Orchestra, 1979–89; Bd of Governors, Live Music Now, 1982–89; Bd of Trustees, The Theatres Trust, 1983–91; Bd of Trustees, Heritage of London Trust, 1983–. CBIM; FRSA. *Recreations:* music, travel, walking, landscape photography. *Clubs:* Garrick, Brooks's.

STIRLING, Prof. Charles James Matthew, FRS 1986; CChem, FRSC; Professor and Head of Department of Organic Chemistry, University of Sheffield, since 1991; *b* 8 Dec. 1930; *s* of Brig. Alexander Dickson Stirling, DSO, MB, ChB, DPH, RAMC, and Isobel Millicent Stirling, MA, DipPsych; *m* 1956, Eileen Gibson Powell, BA, MEd, *yr d* of William Leslie and Elsie May Powell; two *d* (and one *d* decd). *Educ:* Edinburgh Acad.; Univ. of St Andrews (Harkness Exhibn; BSc; Biochem. Medal 1951); Univ. of London (PhD, DSc). FRSC, CChem 1967. Civil Service Jun. Res. Fellowship, Porton, 1955, Sen.

Fellowship, 1956; ICI Fellowship, Univ. of Edinburgh, 1957; Lectr, QUB, 1959; Reader in Org. Chem., KCL, 1965; Prof. of Organic Chemistry, 1969–81, Dean of Faculty of Science, 1977–79, Hd of Dept of Chemistry, 1981–90, Univ. of Wales, Bangor. Vis. Prof., Hebrew Univ. of Jerusalem, 1981. Mem., Perkin Council, RSC, 1971 (Vice-Pres., 1985–88 and 1991, Pres., 1989–91); Pres., Section B (Chemistry), BAAS, 1990. Award for Organic Reaction Mechanisms, RSC, 1988. *Publications:* Radicals in Organic Chemistry, 1965; (ed) Organic Sulphur Chemistry, 1975; (ed) The Chemistry of the Sulphonium Group, 1981; (ed) The Chemistry of Sulphones and Sulphoxides, 1988; numerous res. papers mainly in Jls of RSC. *Recreations:* choral music, travel, furniture restoration. *Address:* Department of Chemistry, University of Sheffield, Sheffield S3 7HF. *T:* Sheffield (0742) 768555; 114 Westbourne Road, Sheffield S10 2QT.

See also Sir A. J. D. Stirling.

STIRLING of Garden, Col James, CBE 1987; TD; FRICS; Lord-Lieutenant of Stirling and Falkirk (Central Region), since 1983; *b* 8 Sept. 1930; *s* of Col Archibald Stirling of Garden, OBE; *m* 1958, Fiona Janetta Sophia Wood Parker; two *s* two *d. Educ:* Rugby; Trinity Coll., Cambridge. BA; Dip. Estate Management. Chartered Surveyor in private practice. Partner, K. Ryden and Partners, Chartered Surveyors, 1962–89, Consultant, 1989–; Director: Local Bd, Scotland and N Ireland, Woolwich Building Soc., 1973–; Scottish Widows and Life Insurance Fund, 1975–. Chm., Highland TAVR Assoc., 1982–87. DL 1970, Vice-Lieutenant 1979–83, Stirling. Hon. Col, 3/51st Highland Volunteers, TA, 1979–86. KStJ 1987. *Address:* Garden, Buchlyvie, Stirlingshire. *T:* Buchlyvie (036085) 212. *Club:* New (Edinburgh).

STIRLING, James Frazer, RA 1991 (ARA 1985); ARIBA 1950; Architect; *b* 1926; *s* of Joseph Stirling and Louisa Frazer; *m* 1966, Mary, *d* of Morton Shand and Sybil Sissons; one *s* two *d. Educ:* Quarry Bank High Sch., Liverpool; Liverpool Sch. of Art, 1942. Served War of 1939–45: Lieut, Black Watch and Paratroops (D-Day Landing). Sch. of Architecture, Liverpool Univ., 1945–50. With Assoc. of Town Planning and Regional Research, London, 1950–52; worked for Lyons, Israel and Ellis, London, 1953–56; entered a series of architectural competitions, and Mem. ICA Indep. Gp, 1952–56. Private practice, 1956– (Partners: James Gowan until 1963 and Michael Wilford, 1971–). Projects include: Flats at Ham Common, 1955–58; Churchill Coll. Comp., 1958; Selwyn Coll., Cambridge, 1959; Leicester Univ. Engrg Bldg, 1959–63 (USA Reynolds Award); Andrew Melville Hall, St Andrews Univ., 1964–68; Dorman Long Steel Co. HQ, 1965; Runcorn New Town Housing, 1968–; Olivetti Trng Sch., Surrey, 1969–; New State Art Gall., Stuttgart, 1977–83; Clore Gall., Tate, 1983–87. Visiting teacher at: Architectural Assoc., London, 1955; Regent Street Polytechnic, London, 1956–57; Cambridge Univ. Sch. of Architecture, 1958; Charles Davenport Visiting Prof., Yale Univ. Sch. of Architecture, USA, 1970; Master Class, Kunstakademie, Dusseldorf, 1977–. Redevelopment plan of West Mid-Town Manhatten, for New York City Planning Commn, USA, 1968–69; invited UK Architect, in internat. limited competitions for Govt/United Nations low cost housing for Peru, 1969, and Siemens AG Computer Centre Munich, 1970; buildings in Iran, Berlin and Stuttgart, 1977; Museum buildings for Univs of Harvard, Columbia and Rice, Houston, 1979. Hon. Mem., Akademie der Kunst, Berlin, 1969; Hon. FAIA, 1976; Hon. Dr RCA, 1979. Exhibitions: "James Stirling—Three Buildings", at Museum of Modern Art, NY, USA, 1969; (drawings) RIBA Heinz Gall., 1974 (associated pubn, James Stirling, 1974); "Foster, Rogers and Stirling", RA, 1987. BBC/Arts Council film, James Stirling's Architecture, 1973. Brunner Award, USA, 1976; Aalto Medal, Finland, 1978; Royal Gold Medal, RIBA, 1980; Pritzker Prize, 1981. *Relevant publication:* James Stirling: Buildings and Projects, 1985. *Address:* 8 Fitzroy Square, W1P 5AH.

STIRLING, Rear-Adm. Michael Grote; Agent-General for British Columbia in the United Kingdom and Europe, 1968–75; *b* 29 June 1915; *s* of late Hon. Grote Stirling and late Mabel Katherine (*née* Brigstocke), Kelowna, British Columbia; *m* 1942, Sheelagh Kathleen Russell; two *s* one *d. Educ:* Shawnigan Lake School, BC; RNC Greenwich. Cadet, RCN, 1933; HMS Frobisher for training till 1934, then as Midshipman and Sub-Lt in RN, returning Canada Jan. 1938; Ships of RCN until 1941; specialized in Signals at HM Signal School, Portsmouth, then Home Fleet; Deputy Director, Signal Div., Naval Service HQ, Ottawa, 1942–43; SSO to C-in-C, Canadian North-West Atlantic, 1943–44; Commanded destroyers, 1944–46; Director Naval Communications, rank of Commander, 1949–51; promoted Captain and staff of Supreme Allied Commander Atlantic, Norfolk, Va, 1953–55; Commanded HMCS Cornwallis, 1955–57; 2nd Cdn Escort Sqdn, 1957–58; Naval Member of Directing Staff, Nat. Defence College as Commodore, 1958–61; Senior Canadian Officer Afloat, 1961–62; Chief of Naval Personnel, 1962–64; Maritime Comdr, Pacific, 1964–66. Rear-Adm. 1962. Dir, Univ. of Victoria Foundation, 1967–68. *Recreations:* golf, ski-ing. *Address:* 302–1280 Newport Avenue, Victoria, BC V8S 5E7, Canada. *Club:* Victoria Golf (Victoria, BC).

STIRLING of Fairburn, Captain Roderick William Kenneth, TD 1965; JP; Lord Lieutenant of Ross and Cromarty and Skye and Lochalsh, since 1988; *b* 17 June 1932; *s* of late Major Sir John Stirling, KT, MBE and Lady Marjory Kythé, *d* of Sir Kenneth Mackenzie, 7th Bt of Gairloch; *m* 1963, Penelope Jane Wright; four *d. Educ:* Wellesley House; Harrow. National Service, Scots Guards, 1950–52; commissioned 1951; TA Seaforth Highlanders and Queen's Own Highlanders (Seaforth and Cameron), 1953–69. Member: Ross and Cromarty County Council, 1970–74 (Chm. of Highways, 1973–74); Ross and Cromarty District Council, 1984–. Mem., Red Deer Commn, 1964–89 (Vice-Chm., 1975–89); Director: Moray Firth Salmon Fishing Co., 1973–; Scottish Salmon and Whitefish Co., 1972– (Chm., 1980–). Mem., Scottish Council, NPFA, 1971– (Chm., Highland Cttee). JP Ross and Cromarty, 1975. *Recreations:* stalking, shooting, fishing, gardening, curling. *Address:* Arcan, Muir of Ord, Ross and Cromarty IV6 7UL. *T:* Urray (09973) 207. *Club:* New (Edinburgh).

STIRLING-HAMILTON, Sir Malcolm William Bruce, 14th Bt *cr* 1673 (NS), of Preston, Haddingtonshire; *b* 6 Aug. 1979; *s* of Sir Bruce Stirling-Hamilton, 13th Bt and of Stephanie (who *m* 1990, Anthony Tinsley), *d* of Dr William Campbell, LRCP, LRCS; *S* father, 1989. *Heir: cousin* Robert William Hamilton, *qv. Address:* Langrick Grange, Boston, Lincs PE22 7AH.

STIRRAT, Prof. Gordon Macmillan, MA, MD; FRCOG; Professor of Obstetrics and Gynaecology, since 1982, Dean of Faculty of Medicine, since 1990, University of Bristol; *b* 12 March 1940; *s* of Alexander and Caroline Mary Stirrat; *m* 1965, Janeen Mary (*née* Brown); three *d. Educ:* Hutcheson's Boys' Grammar Sch., Glasgow; Glasgow Univ. (MB, ChB). MA Oxon, MD London. FRCOG 1981. Jun. hosp. doctor appts, Glasgow and environs, and London, 1964–71; Lectr, St Mary's Hosp. Med. Sch., London, 1971–75; Clinical Reader, Univ. of Oxford, 1975–81. *Publications:* Obstetrics Pocket Consultant, 1981, 2nd edn 1986; (jtly) You and Your Baby—a Mother's Guide to Health, 1982; Aids to Reproductive Biology, 1982; Aids to Obstetrics and Gynaecology, 1983, 3rd edn 1991. *Recreations:* fly-fishing, walking, writing. *Address:* Malpas Lodge, 24 Henbury Road, Westbury-on-Trym, Bristol BS9 3HJ. *T:* Bristol (0272) 505310.

STOATE, Isabel Dorothy; HM Diplomatic Service, retired; Counsellor, Foreign and Commonwealth Office, 1980–82; *b* 31 May 1927; *d* of late William Maurice Stoate and Dorothy Evelyn Stoate (*née* French). *Educ:* Talbot Heath Sch., Bournemouth; St Andrews Univ. Athlone Press, London Univ., 1950–52; joined HM Diplomatic Service, 1952; served Cyprus, Vienna, Buenos Aires, Tokyo, Athens, Rio de Janeiro and FCO, 1952–80. *Recreations:* travel, tapestry. *Address:* 177 Gloucester Street, Cirencester, Glos.

STOBART, Patrick Desmond, CBE 1976 (MBE 1950); HM Diplomatic Service, retired; *b* 14 Feb. 1920; *s* of late Reginald and Eva Stobart; *m* 1951, Sheila (marr. diss. 1973), *d* of late A. W. Brown, Belfast; three *s* one *d. Educ:* Cathedral and Cleveland House Schools, Salisbury; St Edmund Hall, Oxford. Served Royal Artillery and Wilts Regiment, 1940–46. Tübingen University, 1946; Political Officer, Trucial Oman, 1947; Chancery, Bonn, 1951–53; FO, 1953–54; Consul, Benghazi, 1954–58; FO, 1958–60; Commercial Counsellor, British Embassy, Helsinki, 1960–64, Copenhagen, 1964–66; Consul-General, Gothenburg, 1966–68; seconded to Aero-Engine Div., Rolls-Royce Ltd, 1968–69; Gwilym Gibbon Research Fellow, Nuffield College, Oxford, 1969–70; Head of Export Promotion Dept, FCO, 1970–71; Consul-Gen., Zürich, 1971–75; seconded to Commercial Relations and Exports Div., DoT, 1976–79. Mem. of Secretariat, Internat. Primary Aluminium Inst., 1979–86. *Publication:* (also ed) The Centenary Book of the Hall and Héroult Processes for the Production of Aluminium, 1986. *Recreation:* history.

STOCK, Prof. Francis Edgar, CBE 1977 (OBE 1961); FRCS, FACS; Principal and Vice-Chancellor of the University of Natal, South Africa, 1970–77; now Emeritus Professor; *b* 5 July 1914; *o s* of late Edgar Stephen and Olive Blanche Stock; *m* 1939, Gwendoline Mary Thomas; two *s* one *d. Educ:* Colfe's Grammar Sch., Lewisham; King's Coll., London (Sambrooke schol.); King's Coll. Hosp., London (Jelf medal, Todd medal and prize in clin. med.; Hygiene and Psychological med. prizes); Univ. of Edinburgh. AKC, MB, BS (Lond.), FRCS, FACS, DTMH (Edin.). Ho. Surg., Cancer Research Registrar, Radium Registrar, King's Coll. Hosp., 1938–39; MO, Colonial Med. Service, Nigeria, 1940–45; Lectr and Asst to Prof. of Surg., Univ. of Liverpool, 1946–48; Prof. of Surgery, Univ. of Hong Kong, 1948–63; Cons. in Surg. to Hong Kong Govt, Brit. Mil. Hosps in Hong Kong, and Ruttonjee Sanatorium, 1948–63; Cons. Surg., RN, 1949–70; Dean, Fac. of Med., Univ. of Hong Kong, 1957–62; Med. Coun., Hong Kong, 1957–60; Pro-Vice-Chancellor, Univ. of Hong Kong, 1959–63; McIlrath Guest Prof., Royal Prince Alfred Hosp., Sydney, NSW, 1960 (Hon. Cons. Surg., 1960–); Prof. of Surg., Univ. of Liverpool, 1964–70; Cons. Surg., Liverpool Royal Infirmary and Liverpool Regional Hosp. Bd, 1964–70; Dean, Fac. of Med., Univ. of Liverpool, 1969–70. Visiting Prof. or Lectr: Univs of Alberta, Edinburgh, Qld, Singapore, W Australia, QUB, State Univ. of NY. Brit. Council Lectr: in Thailand, Burma, Fiji, Mauritius; Hunterian Prof., RCS London, 1948 and 1951. Member: BMA (Council 1964–69; Bd of Science and Educn, 1978–80); Bd of Governors, United Liverpool Hosps, 1967–70; Med. Adv. Council and Chm. Techn. Adv. Cttee on Surg., Liverpool Reg. Hosp. Bd, 1964–70; Gen. Med. Council, 1969–70; Med. Appeals Tribunals, Liverpool and N Wales, 1966–70; Council, Edgewood Coll. of Education, 1976–77; Univs Adv. Council, 1976–; Cttee of Univ. Principals, 1970–77 (Chm., 1976–77). Examr in Surgery: to Univs of Edinburgh, Glasgow, Liverpool, Hong Kong, Malaya, Singapore and NUI, at various times, 1949–70; to Soc. of Apothecaries, 1958–60; Mem. Ct of Examrs, RCS, 1965–69. Sen. Fellow, Assoc. of Surgeons of GB and Ire.; Sen. Mem. Pan Pacific Surg. Assoc. (past Mem. Coun. and Bd of Trustees). Mem., Board of Control, Nat. Inst. of Metallurgy, 1975–77. Liveryman, Soc. of Apothecaries. Hon. FACCP. *Publications:* Surgical Principles (with J. Moroney), 1968; chapters in: Surgery of Liver and Bile Ducts (ed Smith and Sherlock); Clinical Surgery (ed Rob and Smith); Scientific Foundations of Surgery (ed Wells and Kyle); Abdominal Operations (ed Maingot), and others; numerous articles in scientific jls. *Recreations:* swimming (Univ. of London colours, 1934, Kent Co. colours, 1935), sailing (Pres., Hong Kong Yacht Racing Assoc., 1961–63, Vice-Pres., Far East Yacht Racing Fedn, 1961–62), gardening, photography, music (Dep. Organist, Grouville Parish Church, Jersey, 1978–82). *Address:* 5 Links Court, Grouville, Jersey, CI JE3 9DD. *T:* Jersey (0534) 53269. *Clubs:* Royal Over-Seas League; Royal Hong Kong Yacht (Cdre, 1957–63).

STOCK, His Honour Raymond, QC 1964; DL; a Circuit Judge (formerly Judge of County Courts), 1971–88; *b* 1913; *s* of late A. E. and M. E. Stock; *m* 1969, E. Dorothy Thorpe, JP. *Educ:* West Monmouth School; Balliol College, Oxford. Barrister-at-law, Gray's Inn, 1936, Bencher, 1969. Royal Artillery, 1939–45. Recorder: Penzance, 1962–64; Exeter, 1964–66; Southampton, 1966–71; Dep. Chm., Dorset QS, 1964–71. DL Hants, 1991. *Address:* Brambridge House, Bishopstoke, Hants SO5 7HL. *Clubs:* Athenæum; Hampshire (Winchester).

STOCKDALE, Sir (Arthur) Noel, Kt 1986; DFM 1942; Life President, ASDA–MFI, 1986 (Chairman, 1969–86); *b* 25 Dec. 1920; *s* of Arthur and Florence Stockdale; *m* 1944, Betty Monica Shaw; two *s. Educ:* Woodhouse Grove School; Reading University. Joined Hindells Dairy Farmers, 1939; RAF, 1940–46; rejoined Hindells Dairy Farmers, 1946, subseq. Associated Dairies & Farm Stores (Leeds) Ltd, 1949, Associated Dairies Group PLC, 1977 and ASDA–MFI Group PLC, 1985; Chm., 1969–. Hon. LLD Leeds, 1986. *Recreations:* fishing, garden. *Address:* Granary Gap, Main Street, Linton, Wetherby, Yorks LS22 4HT. *T:* Wetherby (0937) 582970.

STOCKDALE, Eric; His Honour Judge Eric Stockdale; a Circuit Judge since 1972; *b* 8 Feb. 1929; *m* 1952, Joan (*née* Berry); two *s. Educ:* Collyers Sch., Horsham; London Sch. of Economics. LLB, BSc(Econ.), LLM, PhD (Lond.); MSc (Cranfield). 2nd Lieut, RA, 1947–49. Called to the Bar, Middle Temple, 1950; practised in London and on Midland Circuit until 1972; admitted to State Bar, Calif, 1983. Mem., Supreme Court Procedure Cttee, 1982–. Tech. Advr, Central Council of Probation Cttees, 1979–84; Vice-Pres., NACRO, 1980– (Mem. Council, 1970–80); President: British Soc. of Criminology, 1978–81; Soc. of English and Amer. Lawyers, 1986–89 (Chm., 1984–86). Member: Central Council for Educn and Trng in Social Work, 1984–89; Parole Board, 1985–89. Vis. Prof., Queen Mary and Westfield Coll., London Univ., 1989–. Governor, 1977–89, Vis. Fellow, 1985–, Hatfield Polytechnic. *Publications:* The Court and the Offender, 1967; A Study of Bedford Prison 1660–1877, 1977; Law and Order in Georgian Bedfordshire, 1982; The Probation Volunteer, 1985; (with Keith Devlin) Sentencing, 1987; (Cons. Ed.) Blackstone's Criminal Practice, 1991. *Address:* 20 Lyonsdown Road, New Barnet, Barnet EN5 1JE. *T:* 081–449 7181. *Club:* Athenæum.

STOCKDALE, Sir Noel; *see* Stockdale, Sir A. N.

STOCKDALE, Sir Thomas (Minshull), 2nd Bt *cr* 1960, of Hoddington, Co. Southampton; barrister; *b* 7 Jan. 1940; *s* of Sir Edmund Villiers Minshull Stockdale, 1st Bt and of Hon. Louise Fermor-Hesketh, *er d* of 1st Lord Hesketh; *S* father, 1989; *m* 1965, Jacqueline Ha-Van-Vuong; one *s* one *d. Educ:* Eton; Worcester Coll., Oxford (MA). Called to Bar, Inner Temple, 1966. *Recreations:* shooting, travel. *Heir: s* John Minshull Stockdale, *b* 13 Dec. 1967. *Address:* Conington Hall, Conington, Cambridge CB3 8LT; 73 Alderney Street, SW1. *Clubs:* Turf, MCC.

STOCKER, Prof. Bruce Arnold Dunbar, FRS 1966; MD; Professor of Medical Microbiology in Stanford University, 1966–87, now Emeritus Active; *b* 26 May 1917. *Educ:* King's College, London; Westminster Hosp. Med. Sch. MB, BS, 1940; MRCS, LRCP, 1940; MD 1947. Guinness Prof. of Microbiology, Univ. of London, and Dir of

Guinness-Lister Microbiological Research Unit, Lister Inst. of Preventive Med., until Dec. 1965. *Publications:* articles in scientific jls. *Address:* Department of Microbiology and Immunology, Stanford University School of Medicine, Stanford, Calif 94305–5402, USA. *T:* 415–723 2006.

STOCKER, Rt. Hon. Sir John (Dexter), Kt 1973; MC; TD; PC 1986; **Rt. Hon. Lord Justice Stocker;** a Lord Justice of Appeal, since 1986; *b* 7 Oct. 1918; *s* of late John Augustus Stocker and Emma Eyre Stocker (*née* Kettle), Hampstead; *m* 1956, Margaret Mary Hegarty (*d* 1987); no *c. Educ:* Westminster Sch.; London University. 2nd Lt, QO Royal West Kent Regt, 1939; France, 1940; Middle East, 1942–43; Italy, 1943–46; Maj. 1943; Lt-Col 1945. LLB London 1947. Called to Bar, Middle Temple, 1948, Master of the Bench, 1971. QC 1965; a Recorder, 1972–73; Judge of the High Court, Queen's Bench Div., 1973–86; Presiding Judge, SE Circuit, 1976–79. *Recreations:* golf, cricket. *Address:* Royal Courts of Justice, Strand, WC2A 2LL. *Clubs:* Naval and Military, Army and Navy, MCC; Royal Wimbledon Golf.

STOCKHAUSEN, Karlheinz; composer and conductor; *b* 22 Aug. 1928; *s* of late Simon and Gertrud Stockhausen; *m* 1st, 1951, Doris Andreae; one *s* three *d*; 2nd, 1967, Mary Bauermeister; one *s* one *d. Educ:* Hochschule für Musik, and Univ., Cologne, 1947–51; studied with: Messaien, 1952–53; Prof. Werner Meyer-Eppler, Bonn Univ., 1954–56. With Westdeutscher Rundfunk Electronic Music Studio, 1953–, Artistic Dir, 1963–. Lectr, Internat. Summer Sch. for New Music, Darmstadt, 1953–; Dir, Interpretation Group for live electronic music, 1964–; Founder, and Artistic Dir, Kölner Kurse für Neue Musik, 1963–68; Visiting Professor: Univ. of Pa, 1965; Univ. of Calif, 1966–67; Prof. of Composition, Cologne State Conservatory, 1971–77. Co-Editor, Die Reihe, 1954–59. First annual tour of 30 concerts and lectures, 1958, USA and Canada, since then throughout world. Has composed 214 individually performable works and made more than 100 records of his own works. Member or Foreign Member: Akad. der Künste, Hamburg, 1968; Kungl. Musikaliska Akad., Sweden, 1970; Akad. der Künste, Berlin, 1973; Amer. Acad. and Inst. of Arts and Letters, 1977; Acad. Filarmonica Romana, 1979; Acad. Européenne des Sciences, des Arts et des Lettres, 1980; Hon. RAM 1987. Awards and Prizes from France, Germany, Italy and USA; Prix Ars Electronica, Cluiz, Austria, 1990; Bundesverdienstkreuz 1st class, 1974. *Publications:* Texte, 6 vols, 1963–89; Stockhausen on Music, 1989; *compositions:* Chöre für Doris, Drei Lieder, Choral, 1950–51; Sonatine, Kreuzspiel, Formel, 1951; Schlagtrio, Spiel für Orchester, Etude, 1952; Punkte, 1952, rev. 1962, Klavierstücke I-XI, 1952–56; Kontra-Punkte, 1953; Elektronische Studien I and II, 1953–54; Zeitmasze, Gesang der Jünglinge, 1956; Gruppen, 1957; Zyklus, Refrain, 1959; Carré, Kontakte für elektronische Klänge, Kontakte für elektronische Klänge, Klavier und Schlagzeug, 1960; Originale (musical play with Kontakte), 1961; Plus Minus, 1963; Momente, 1962–64, completed, 1969; Mixtur (new arr. 1967), Mikrophonie I, 1964; Mikrophonie II, Stop (new arr. 1969), 1965; Telemusik, Solo, Adieu, 1966; Hymnen, Prozession, Ensemble, 1967; Kurzwellen, Stimmung, Aus den sieben Tagen, Spiral, Musik für ein Haus, 1968; Für Kommende Zeiten, 1968–70; Hymnen mit Orchester, Fresco, Dr K-Sextett, 1969; Pole, Expo, Mantra, 1970; Sternklang, Trans, 1971; Alphabet für Liège, Am Himmel wandre ich, (Indianerlieder), Ylem, 1972; Inori, 1973–74; Vortrag über Hu, Herbstmusik, Atmen gibt das Leben..., 1974; Musik im Bauch, Harlekin, Der Kleine Harlekin, 1975; Tierkreis, 1975–76; Sirius, 1975–77; Amour, 1976; Jubiläum, In Freundschaft, 1977; Licht, die sieben Tage der Woche (an operatic cycle for solo voices, solo instruments, solo dancers/choirs, orchestras, ballet and mimes/electronic and concrete music), 1977–: Donnerstag 1978–80 (Donnerstags-Gruss, or Michaels-Gruss, 1978; Unsichtbare Chöre, 1978–79; Michaels Jugend, 1979; Michaels Reise um die Erde, 1978; Michaels Heimkehr, 1980; Donnerstags-Abschied, 1980); Samstag, 1981–84 (Samstags-Gruss or Luzifers-Gruss, 1983; Luzifers Traum or Klavierstück XIII, 1981; Traum-Formel, 1981; Kathinkas Gesang als Luzifers Requiem, 1982–83; Luzifers Tanz, 1983; Luzifers Abschied, 1982); Montag, 1984–88 (Montags-Gruss, or Eva-Gruss, 1984/88; Evas Erstgeburt, 1987; Evas Zweitgeburt, 1984/87; Klavierstück XIV, 1984; Evas Zauber, 1986; Montags-Abschied, or Eva-Abschied, 1988); Dienstag, 1977/1990–91 (Jahreslauf, 1977–91; Invasion-Explosion mit Abschied, 1990–91). *Address:* Stockhausen-Verlag, 5067 Kürten, West Germany.

STOCKPORT, Bishop Suffragan of, since 1984; **Rt. Rev. Frank Pilkington Sargeant;** *b* 12 Sept. 1932; *s* of John Stanley and Grace Sargeant; *m* 1958, Sally Jeanette McDermott; three *s* two *d. Educ:* Boston Grammar School; Durham Univ., St John's Coll. and Cranmer Hall (BA, Dip Theol); Nottingham Univ. (Diploma in Adult Education). National Service Commission, RA (20th Field Regt), 1955–57. Assistant Curate: Gainsborough Parish Church, 1958–62; Grimsby Parish Church, and Priest-in-Charge of St Martin's, Grimsby, 1962–67; Vicar of North Hykeham and Rector of South Hykeham, 1967–73; Residentiary Canon, Bradford Cathedral, 1973–77; Archdeacon of Bradford, 1977–84. Mem., House of Bishops, Gen. Synod of C of E, 1990–. *Address:* 32 Park Gates Drive, Cheadle Hulme, Cheadle, Stockport, Cheshire SK8 7DF. *T:* 061–486 9715.

STOCKTON, 2nd Earl of, *cr* 1984; **Alexander Daniel Alan Macmillan;** Viscount Macmillan of Ovenden, 1984; President, Macmillan Ltd, since 1990; *b* Oswestry, Shropshire, 10 Oct. 1943; *s* of Viscount Macmillan of Ovenden, PC, MP (*d* 1984) and of Katharine Viscountess Macmillan of Ovenden, DBE; *S* grandfather, 1986; *m* 1970, Hélène Birgitte (marr. diss. 1991), *o d* of late Alan D. C. Hamilton, Mitford, Northumberland; one *s* two *d. Educ:* Eton; Université de Paris, Strathclyde Univ. MBIM 1981; FRSA 1987. Liveryman: Worshipful Co. of Merchant Taylors, 1972 (Mem., Ct of Assts, 1987–); Worshipful Co. of Stationers and Newspaper Makers, 1973. *Heir: s* Viscount Macmillan of Ovenden, *qv. Address:* 4 Little Essex Street, WC2R 3LF. *T:* 071–836 6633. *Clubs:* Beefsteak, Buck's, Garrick, Pratt's, White's.

STOCKWELL, Air Cdre Edmund Arthur, CB 1967; MA; Command Education Officer, Training Command, 1968–72 (Flying Training Command, 1964–68); retired 1972; *b* 15 Dec. 1911; *e s* of Arthur Davenport Stockwell, Dewsbury; *m* 1937, Pearl Arber; two *d* (one *s* decd); *m* 1955, Lillian Gertrude Moore (*d* 1965), OBE, MRCP; two *s*; *m* 1970, Mrs Kathleen (Betty) Clarke, Chesham. *Educ:* Wheelwright Grammar School; Balliol Coll., Oxford (BA 1934; MA 1939). Entered RAF Educational Service, Cranwell, 1935; RAF Educn in India, 1936; Punjab and NW Frontier, 1936–38; RAFVR (Admin and Special Duties), 1939; Lahore, Simla, Delhi, 1939–44; Group Educn Officer, No 6 (RCAF) Group, 1944; Air Min., 1944–48; OC, RAF Sch. of Educn, 1948–51; Comd Educn Officer, Coastal Comd, 1951–53; Comd Educn Officer, Far East Air Force, 1953–55; Principal Educn Officer, Halton, 1956–59; Comd Educn Officer, Maintenance Comd, 1959–62; Dep. Dir of Educational Services, Air Min., 1962–64. Group Captain, 1954; Air Commodore, 1964. FRAeS 1963. *Recreations:* golf, gardening. *Address:* 95 Newland, Sherborne, Dorset DT9 3AS. *T:* Sherborne (0935) 815689.

STOCKWIN, Prof. James Arthur Ainscow; Nissan Professor of Modern Japanese Studies, University of Oxford and Fellow, St Antony's College, Oxford, since 1982; *b* 28 Nov. 1935; *s* of Wilfred Arthur Stockwin and Edith Mary Stockwin; *m* 1960, Audrey Lucretia Hobson Stockwin (*née* Wood); one *s* two *d* (and one *s* decd). *Educ:* Exeter Coll., Oxford Univ. (MA); Australian Nat. Univ. (PhD). Australian National University: Lectr, Dept of Political Science, 1964–66; Sen. Lectr, 1966–72; Reader, 1972–81. *Publications:* The Japanese Socialist Party and Neutralism, 1968; (ed) Japan and Australia in the Seventies, 1972; Japan, Divided Politics in a Growth Economy, 1975, 2nd edn 1982; Why Japan Matters, 1983; (jtly, also ed) Dynamic and Immobilist Politics in Japan, 1988; articles, largely on Japanese politics and foreign policy, in Pacific Affairs, Aust. Outlook, Aust. Jl Politics and History, Japan Interpreter, East Asia, Asian and African Studies, Asian Survey, etc. *Recreations:* languages, exercise. *Address:* Nissan Institute of Japanese Studies, 1 Church Walk, Oxford OX2 6LY. *T:* Oxford (0865) 274570.

STOCKWOOD, Rt. Rev. (Arthur) Mervyn, DD; Hon. Assistant Bishop, Diocese of Bath and Wells; *b* 27 May 1913; *s* of late Arthur Stockwood, solicitor, and Beatrice Ethel Stockwood; unmarried. *Educ:* Kelly Coll., Tavistock; Christ's Coll., Cambridge (MA). Curate of St Matthew, Moorfields, Bristol, 1936–41; Blundell's Sch., Missioner, 1936–41; Vicar, St Matthew, Moorfields, Bristol, 1941–55; Hon. Canon of Bristol, 1952–55; Vicar of the University Church, Cambridge, 1955–59; Bishop of Southwark, 1959–80. Member: Bristol CC, 1946–55; Cambridge CC, 1956–59; House of Lords, 1963–80. Mem. Council, Bath Univ., 1980–. Freeman of City of London, 1976. DD Lambeth, 1959; Hon. DLitt Sussex, 1963; Hon. DD Bucharest, 1977. *Publications:* There is a Tide, 1946; Whom They Pierced, 1948; Christianity and Marxism, 1949; I Went to Moscow, 1955; The Faith To-day, 1959; Cambridge Sermons, 1959; Bishop's Journal, 1965; The Cross and the Sickle, 1978; From Strength to Strength, 1980; Chanctonbury Ring (autobiog.), 1982. *Address:* 15 Sydney Buildings, Bath, Avon BA2 6BZ. *T:* Bath (0225) 62788.

STODART, family name of **Baron Stodart of Leaston.**

STODART OF LEASTON, Baron *cr* 1981 (Life Peer), of Humbie in the District of East Lothian; **James Anthony Stodart;** PC 1974; *b* 6 June 1916; *yr s* of late Col Thomas Stodart, CIE, IMS, and of Mary Alice Coullie; *m* 1940, Hazel Jean Usher. *Educ:* Wellington. Farming at Kingston, North Berwick, 1934–58, and now at Leaston, Humbie, East Lothian. Hon. Pres., Edinburgh Univ. Agricultural Soc., 1952; Pres. East Lothian Boy Scouts' Assoc., 1960–63. Contested: (L) Berwick and East Lothian, 1950; (C) Midlothian and Peebles, 1951; Midlothian, 1955; MP (C) Edinburgh West, 1959–Oct. 1974; Jt Parly Under-Sec. of State, Scottish Office, Sept. 1963–Oct. 1964; An Opposition spokesman on Agriculture and on Scottish Affairs, 1966–69; Parly Sec., MAFF, 1970–72; Minister of State, MAFF, 1972–74; Vice-Chm., Conservative Agric. Cttee, House of Commons, 1962–63, 1964–65, 1966–70. Led Parly Delegns to Canada, 1974, 1983. Dir, FMC, 1980–82; Chm., Agricultural Credit Corp. Ltd, 1975–87. Chairman: Cttee of Inquiry into Local Govt in Scotland, 1980; Manpower Review of Vet. Profession in UK, 1984–85. *Publications:* (jt author) Land of Abundance, a study of Scottish Agriculture in the 20th Century, 1962; contrib. on farming topics to agricultural journals and newspapers. *Recreations:* music, playing golf and preserving a sense of humour. *Address:* Lorimers, North Berwick, East Lothian. *T:* North Berwick (0620) 2457; Leaston, Humbie, E Lothian. *T:* Humbie (0875) 233213. *Clubs:* Caledonian; New (Edinburgh); Hon. Company of Edinburgh Golfers.

STODDART, family name of **Baron Stoddart of Swindon.**

STODDART OF SWINDON, Baron *cr* 1983 (Life Peer), of Reading in the Royal County of Berkshire; **David Leonard Stoddart;** *b* 4 May 1926; *s* of Arthur Leonard Stoddart, coal miner, and Queenie Victoria Stoddart (*née* Price); *m* 1961, Jennifer Percival-Alwyn; two *s* (one *d* by previous marr.). *Educ:* elementary; St Clement Danes and Henley Grammar Schools. Youth in training, PO Telephones, 1942–44; business on own account, 1944–46; Railway Clerk, 1947–49; Hospital Clerk, 1949–51; Power Station Clerical Worker, 1951–70. Joined Labour Party, 1947; Member Reading County Borough Council, 1954–72; served at various times as Chairman of Housing, Transport and Finance Cttees; Leader of the Reading Labour Group of Councillors, 1962–70. Contested (Lab) Newbury, 1959 and 1964, Swindon, 1969, 1983. MP (Lab) Swindon, 1970–83; PPS to Minister for Housing and Construction, 1974–75; an Asst Govt Whip, 1975; a Lord Comr, HM Treasury, 1976–77; an opposition whip, and opposition spokesman on energy, House of Lords, 1983–88. *Recreations:* gardening, music. *Address:* Sintra, 37A Bath Road, Reading, Berks. *T:* Reading (0734) 576726.

STODDART, Anne Elizabeth; HM Diplomatic Service; Deputy Permanent Representative (Economic Affairs), UK Mission to the United Nations, Geneva, since 1991; *b* 29 March 1937; *d* of late James Stoddart and Ann Jack Stoddart (*née* Inglis). *Educ:* Kirby Grammar School, Middlesbrough; Somerville College, Oxford. MA. Entered Foreign Office, 1960; British Military Govt, Berlin, 1963–67; FCO, 1967–70; First Secretary (Economic), Ankara, 1970–73; Head of Chancery, Colombo, 1974–76; FCO, 1977–81; Dep. Permanent UK Rep. to Council of Europe, Strasbourg, 1981–87; seconded to External Eur. Policy Div., DTI, 1987–91. *Address:* c/o Foreign and Commonwealth Office, SW1A 2AH.

STODDART, Charles Norman, PhD; Sheriff of North Strathclyde at Paisley, since 1988; *b* 4 April 1948; *s* of Robert Stoddart and Margaret (*née* Allenby); *m* 1981, Anne Lees; one *d. Educ:* Edinburgh Univ. (LLB, PhD); McGill Univ. (LLM). Admitted Solicitor, 1972, practised, 1972–73, 1980–88; Lectr in Scots Law, Edinburgh Univ., 1973–80. *Publications:* The Law and Practice of Legal Aid in Scotland, 1979, 3rd edn 1990; (with C. H. W. Gane) A Casebook on Scottish Criminal Law, 1980, 2nd edn 1988; Bible John (crime documentary), 1980; (with C. H. W. Gane) Cases and Materials on Scottish Criminal Procedure, 1983; contribs to professional jls. *Recreations:* music, foreign travel, ski-ing and other sport. *Address:* Sheriff's Chambers, Sheriff Court House, St James Street, Paisley PA3 2HW. *T:* 041–887 5291.

STODDART, Prof. John Little, PhD, DSc; FIBiol; Director of Research, Institute of Grassland and Environmental Research, Agricultural and Food Research Council, since 1988; *b* 1 Oct. 1933; *s* of John Little Stoddart and Margaret Pickering Dye; *m* 1957, Wendy Dalton Leardie; one *d* (one *s* decd). *Educ:* South Shields High Sch. for Boys; University Coll., Durham (BSc Botany 1954); University of Wales, Aberystwyth (PhD 1961); Durham Univ. (DSc 1973). FIBiol 1984; ARPS 1985. Nat. Service, RA, UK, Hong Kong and Malaya, 1954–56. Fulbright-Hays Sen. Fellow, 1966–67; Res. Associate, Mich. State Univ./Atomic Energy Commn Plant Res. Lab., 1966–67; Welsh Plant Breeding Station: Dep. Dir, 1985–87; Dir, 1987–88; Head of Plants and Soils Div., 1985–88. Vis. Prof., Reading Univ., 1988–; Hon. Prof., Sch. of Agric. and Biol Scis, Univ. of Wales, 1988–. Mem. Council, NIAB, 1988–. Mem., Stapledon Meml Trust, 1988–. *Publications:* scientific articles, reviews and contribs to scientific books. *Recreations:* photography (pictorial), tennis, golf. *Address:* Institute of Grassland and Environmental Research, Plas Gogerddan, Aberystwyth, Dyfed SY23 3EB.

STODDART, John Maurice; Principal, Sheffield City Polytechnic, since 1983; Chairman, Committee of Directors of Polytechnics, since 1990 (Vice-Chairman, 1988–90); *b* 18 Sept. 1938; *s* of Gordon Stoddart and May (*née* Ledder). *Educ:* Wallasey Grammar Sch.; Univ. of Reading (BA Pol Econ.). FBIM 1977. Teacher, Wallasey GS, 1960–62; Lectr, Mid Cheshire Coll. of Further Educn, 1962–64; Lectr, Enfield Coll., 1964–70; Head,

Dept of Econs and Business Studies, Sheffield Polytechnic, 1970–72; Asst Dir, NE London Polytechnic, 1972–76; Dir, Hull Coll. of Higher Educn (now Humberside Poly.), 1976–83. Dir, Sheffield Science Park Co. Ltd, 1988–. Chm., CNAA Cttee for Business and Management, 1985–88 (Chm., Undergrad. Courses Bd, 1976–83); Mem., CNAA, 1982–88. Member: Sea Fisheries Trng Council, 1976–80; Architects Registration Council, UK, 1979–85; Council for Management Educn and Develt, 1988–. Mem., Bd of Management, Crucible Theatre, 1986–. Member: Court, Univ. of Hull, 1976–83; Council, Univ. of Sheffield, 1983–. Companion, British Business Graduates Soc., 1983; Hon. Fellow, Humberside Coll., 1983; FRSA 1977. *Publications:* articles on business and management educn. *Address:* 58 Riverdale Road, Sheffield S10 3FB. *T:* Sheffield (0742) 683636. *Clubs:* Reform; Leander (Henley-on-Thames).

STODDART, Sir Kenneth (Maxwell), KCVO 1989; AE 1942; JP; DL; Lord-Lieutenant, Metropolitan County of Merseyside, 1979–89; *b* 26 May 1914; *s* of late Wilfrid Bowring Stoddart and Mary Hyslop Stoddart (*née* Maxwell); *m* 1940, Jean Roberta Benson Young, DL; two *d. Educ:* Sedbergh; Clare Coll., Cambridge. Chairman: Cearns and Brown Ltd, 1973–84; United Mersey Supply Co. Ltd, 1978–81. Commissioned No 611 (West Lancashire) Sqdn, Auxiliary Air Force, 1936; served War, UK and Europe; comd W Lancashire Wing, Air Trng Corps, 1946–54; Vice-Chm. (Air) W Lancashire T&AFA, 1954–64. Chairman, Liverpool Child Welfare Assoc., 1965–81. DL Lancashire 1958 (transf. to Metropolitan County of Merseyside, 1974); JP Liverpool 1952; High Sheriff of Merseyside, 1974. Hon. Fellow, Liverpool Poly., 1989. Hon. LLD Liverpool, 1986. KStJ 1979. *Recreations:* gardening, walking. *Address:* The Spinney, Overdale Road, Willaston, South Wirral L64 1SY. *T:* 051–327 5183. *Clubs:* Athenæum (Liverpool); Liverpool Racquet.

STODDART, Michael Craig, FCA; Chairman: Electra Investment Trust, since 1986; Electra Kingsway, since 1990; *b* 27 March 1932; *s* of Frank Ogle Boyd Stoddart and Barbara Craig; *m* 1961, Susan Brigid (*née* O'Halloran); two *s* two *d. Educ:* Abberley Hall, Worcs; Marlborough Coll. Chartered Accountant 1955; joined Singer & Friedlander, 1955: resp. for opening provincial network; retired as Jt Chief Exec., 1973; Dep. Chm. and Chief Exec., Electra Investment Trust, 1974; pioneered into substantial unlisted investments, incl. developing venture capital arm. Non-exec. Chm., BPCC Ltd; non-executive Director: Globe Investment Trust, 1973–90; Next plc; Summit Gp plc; Bullough; Sphere Drake, and other cos in UK and USA. *Recreations:* country pursuits, shooting, tennis, golf, theatre. *Address:* Compton House, Kinver, Worcs DY7 5LY. *Club:* Boodle's.

STOGDON, Norman Francis; a Recorder of the Crown Court, 1972–83; *b* 14 June 1909; *s* of late F. R. Stogdon and late L. Stogdon (*née* Reynolds); *m* 1959, Yvonne (*née* Jaques). *Educ:* Harrow; Brasenose Coll., Oxford (BA, BCL). Called to Bar, Middle Temple, 1932. War Service, Army, 1939–45: served with Royal Fusiliers, King's African Rifles, 1941–45; Staff Officer; sc Middle East 1944. Part-time Chairman: Mental Health Tribunal, 1960–81; Industrial Tribunal, 1975–83. Contested (Lab): Gosport, 1951; Banbury and N Oxford, 1955. ACIArb 1984. *Publications:* contrib. 2nd, 3rd and 4th edns Halsbury's Laws of England. *Recreations:* golf, ski-ing. *Address:* The Cloisters, Temple, EC4Y 7AA. *T:* 071–353 2548. *Club:* Moor Park Golf.

STOICHEFF, Prof. Boris Peter, OC 1982; FRS 1975; FRSC 1965; Professor of Physics, 1964–89, now Emeritus, and University Professor, 1977–89, now Emeritus, University of Toronto; *b* 1 June 1924; *s* of Peter and Vasilka Stoicheff; *m* 1954, Lillian Joan Ambridge; one *s. Educ:* Univ. of Toronto, Faculty of Applied Science and Engineering (BASc), Dept of Physics (MA, PhD). McKee-Gilchrist Fellowship, Univ. of Toronto, 1950–51; National Research Council of Canada: Fellowship, Ottawa, 1952–53; Res. Officer in Div. of Pure Physics, 1953–64; Member, 1978–83. Exec. Dir, Ontario Laser and Lightware Res. Centre, 1988–. Visiting Scientist, Mass Inst. of Technology, 1963–64. Chm., Engrg Science, Univ. of Toronto, 1972–77. Izaak Walton Killam Meml Scholarship, 1977–79; Senior Fellow, Massey Coll., Univ. of Toronto, 1979. H. L. Welsh Lecture, Univ. of Toronto, 1984; Elizabeth Laird Meml Lecture, Univ. Western Ontario, 1985; UK/Canada Rutherford Lectr, 1989. Pres., Canadian Assoc. of Physicists, 1983–84; Council Mem., Assoc. of Professional Engrs of Ontario, 1985–. Fellow, Optical Soc. of America, 1965 (Pres. 1976); Fellow, Amer. Phys. Soc., 1969; Geoffrey Frew Fellow, Australian Acad. of Science, 1980. Hon. Fellow: Indian Acad. of Scis, 1971; Macedonian Acad. of Sci. and Arts, 1981; Foreign Hon. Fellow, Amer. Acad. of Arts and Scis, 1989. Hon. DSc: York, Canada, 1982; Skopje, Yugoslavia, 1982; Windsor, Canada, 1989. Gold Medal for Achievement in Physics of Canadian Assoc. of Physicists, 1974; William F. Meggers Award, Optical Soc. of America, 1981; Frederic Ives Medal, Optical Soc. of America, 1983; Henry Marshall Tory Medal, RSC, 1989. Centennial Medal of Canada, 1967. *Publications:* numerous scientific contribs to phys. and chem. jls. *Address:* Department of Physics, University of Toronto, Toronto, Ontario M5S 1A7, Canada. *T:* (416) 978–2948.

STOKE-UPON-TRENT, Archdeacon of; *see* Ede, Ven. D.

STOKER, Dr Dennis James, FRCP, FRCR; Consultant Radiologist, Royal National Orthopaedic Hospital, since 1972; Dean, Institute of Orthopaedics, since 1987; *b* 22 March 1928; *yr s* of Dr George Morris Stoker and Elsie Margaret Stoker (*née* Macqueen); *m* 1951, Anne Sylvia Nelson Forster; two *s* two *d. Educ:* Oundle Sch.; Guy's Hosp. Med. Sch. MB BS; DMRD. Guy's Hosp. appts, 1951–52; RAF Med. Branch, 1951–68; served Cyprus and Aden; Wing Cdr (retd). Consultant Physician, RAF, 1964–68; Registrar and Sen. Registrar, Diagnostic Radiology, St George's Hosp., London, 1968–72; Sen. Lectr and Dir Radiological Studies, Inst. of Orthopaedics, 1977–. Royal Society of Medicine: Fellow, 1958; Mem. Council, Section of Radiol., 1975–77; Vice-Pres., 1978–80; Royal College of Radiologists: Fellow, 1976; Examr, 1981–84 and 1985–88; George Simon Lectr, 1988; Dean and Vice-Pres., 1989–91; Fellow, British Orth. Assoc.; Mem., Internat. Skeletal Soc., 1974–. Editor, Skeletal Radiology, 1984–; Mem., Editl Bd, Clinical Radiology, 1974–84. *Publications:* Knee Arthrography, 1980; (jtly) Self Assessment in Orthopaedic Radiology, 1988; The Radiology of Skeletal Disorders, 1990; chapters in textbooks; papers on metabolic medicine, tropical disease and skeletal radiology. *Recreations:* philology, medical history, dinghy sailing in warm climates. *Address:* 4 Waterloo Terrace, Islington, N1 1TQ. *T:* 071–359 0615. *Club:* Royal Air Force.

STOKER, Sir Michael (George Parke), Kt 1980; CBE 1974; FRCP 1979; FRS 1968; FRSE 1960; President of Clare Hall, Cambridge, 1980–87 (Fellow, 1978); *b* 4 July 1918; *e s* of Dr S. P. Stoker, Maypole, Monmouth; *m* 1942, Veronica Mary English; three *s* two *d. Educ:* Oakham Sch.; Sidney Sussex Coll., Cambridge (Hon. Fellow 1981); St Thomas' Hosp., London. MRCS, LRCP 1942; MB, BChir 1943; MD 1947. RAMC, 1942–47; Demonstrator in Pathology, Cambridge Univ., 1947–48; Univ. Lecturer in Pathology, 1948–50; Huddersfield Lecturer in Special Pathology, 1950–58; Asst Tutor and Dir of Medical Studies, Clare Coll., 1949–58; Fellow of Clare College, 1948–58, Hon. Fellow, 1976; Prof. of Virology, Glasgow Univ., and Hon. Dir, MRC Experimental Virus Research Unit, 1959–68; Dir, Imperial Cancer Res. Fund Laboratories, 1968–79. WHO Travel Fellow, 1951; Rockefeller Foundn Travel Fellow, 1958; Vis. Prof., UCL, 1968–79. Royal Society: For. Sec., 1977–81; a Vice-Pres., 1977–81; Leeuwenhoek Lecture, 1971, Blackett Meml Lecture, 1980; Mendel Gold Medal, 1978. Dir, Celltech Ltd, 1980–86. Member: European Molecular Biology Organisation; Council for Scientific Policy, DES, 1970–73; Gen. Cttee, Internat. Council of Scientific Unions, 1977–81; Eur. Acad. of Arts, Scis and Humanities, 1980; Med. Res. Council, 1982–86; Chairman: UK Co-ordinating Cttee, Cancer Res., 1983–86; Scientific Cttee, Ludwig Inst. Cancer Res., 1985–. Foreign Hon. Member: Amer. Acad. of Arts and Scis, 1973; Czech Acad. of Scis, 1980. Chm. of Trustees, Strangeways Res. Lab., Cambridge, 1981–. Hon. DSc Glasgow, 1982. *Publications:* various articles on cell biology and virology. *Recreation:* painting. *Address:* 12 Willow Walk, Cambridge CB1 1LA. *Club:* United Oxford & Cambridge University.

STOKES, family name of **Baron Stokes.**

STOKES, Baron *cr* 1969 (Life Peer), of Leyland; **Donald Gresham Stokes,** Kt 1965; TD; DL; FEng, FIMechE; MSAE; FIMI; FCIT; FICE; Chairman: Jack Barclay Ltd, since 1980 (President, 1989–90); KBH Communications, since 1987; Chairman and Managing Director, 1968–75, Chief Executive, 1973–75, British Leyland Motor Corporation Ltd; President, BL Ltd, 1975–79; Consultant to Leyland Vehicles, 1979–81; *b* 22 March 1914; *o s* of Harry Potts Stokes; *m* 1939, Laura Elizabeth Courteney Lamb; one *s. Educ:* Blundell's School; Harris Institute of Technology, Preston. Started Student Apprenticeship, Leyland Motors Ltd, 1930. Served War of 1939–45: REME (Lt-Col). Re-joined Leyland as Exports Manager, 1946; General Sales and Service Manager, 1950; Director, 1954; Managing Director, and Deputy Chairman, Leyland Motor Corp., 1963, Chm. 1967; Chm. and Man. Dir, British Leyland Ltd, 1973. Director: National Westminster Bank, 1969–81; London Weekend Television Ltd, 1967–71; Opus Public Relations Ltd, 1979–84; Scottish & Universal Investments Ltd, 1980–; Dovercourt Motor Co. Ltd, 1982–90; Beherman Auto-Transport SA, 1983–89; GWR Gp, 1990–. Vice-President, Empresa Nacional de Autocamiones SA, Spain, 1959–73. Chairman: British Arabian Adv. Co. Ltd, 1977–85; Two Counties Radio Ltd, 1978–84, 1990– (Pres., 1984–90); British Arabian Technical Co-operation Ltd, 1981–85; Reliant Group, 1990; Dutton Forshaw Motor Gp, 1980–90. Vice-Pres., Engineering Employers Fedn, 1967–75; President: SMMT, 1961–62; Motor Industry Res. Assoc., 1965–66; Manchester Univ. Inst. of Science and Technology, 1972–76 (Vice-Pres., 1967–71); Vice-Pres., IMechE, 1971, Pres., 1972; Chm., EDC for Electronics Industry, 1966–67; Member: NW Economic Planning Council, 1965–70; IRC, 1966–71 (Dep. Chm. 1969); EDC for the Motor Manufacturing Industry, 1967–; Council, Public Transport Assoc.; Worshipful Co. of Carmen. Fellow, IRTE (Pres., 1983–84), Hon. FIRTE. DL Lancs 1968. Hon. Fellow, Keble Coll., Oxford, 1968. Hon. LLD Lancaster, 1967; Hon. DTech Loughborough, 1968; Hon. DSc: Southampton, 1969; Salford, 1971. Officier de l'Ordre de la Couronne (Belgium), 1964; Commandeur de l'ordre de Leopold II (Belgium), 1972. *Recreation:* sailing. *Address:* 2 Branksome Cliff, Westminster Road, Poole, Dorset BH1 3 6JW. *Clubs:* Beefsteak, Army and Navy; Royal Motor Yacht (Commodore, 1979–81).

STOKES, Dr Adrian Victor, OBE 1983; CChem; CEng; FBCS; FInstD; MRSC; MBIM; Principal Consultant, NHS Information Management Centre (formerly Centre for Information Technology), since 1989 (Consultant, on secondment, 1986–88); *b* 25 June 1945; *s* of Alfred Samuel and Edna Stokes; *m* (marr. diss.). *Educ:* Orange Hill Grammar School, Edgware; University College London. BSc 1966 (1st cl. Hons), PhD 1970; FBCS 1978; MBIM 1986; CEng 1990. Research Programmer, GEC-Computers Ltd, 1969–71; Research Asst, Inst. of Computer Science, 1971–73; Research Fellow, UCL, 1973–77; Sen. Research Fellow and Sen. Lectr, Hatfield Polytechnic, 1977–81; Dir of Computing, St Thomas' Hosp., 1981–88 (King's Fund Fellow, 1981–84). Member: Silver Jubilee Cttee on Improving Access for Disabled People, 1977–78; Cttee on Restrictions Against Disabled People, 1979–81; Social Security Adv. Cttee, 1980–; Dept of Transport Panel of Advisers on Disability, 1983–85; Disabled Persons' Transport Adv. Cttee, 1986–89; Chm., Disabled Drivers' Motor Club, 1972–82, Vice-Pres., 1982–; Chm., Exec. Cttee, RADAR, 1985–. Governor, Motability, 1978–; Trustee, PHAB, 1982–90. Freeman, City of London, 1988; Freeman, Co. of Information Technologists, 1988. *Publications:* An Introduction to Data Processing Networks, 1978; Viewdata: a public information utility, 1979, 2nd edn 1980; The Concise Encyclopaedia of Computer Terminology, 1981; Networks, 1981; (with C. Saiady) What to Read in Microcomputing, 1982; Concise Encyclopaedia of Information Technology, 1982, 3rd edn 1986, USA edn 1983; Integrated Office Systems, 1982; (with M. D. Bacon and J. M. Bacon) Computer Networks: fundamentals and practice, 1984; Overview of Data Communications, 1985; The A to Z of Business Computing, 1986; Communications Standards, 1986; OSI Standards and Acronyms, 1987, 3rd edn 1991; numerous papers and articles, mainly concerned with computer technology. *Recreations:* philately, science fiction, collecting Elvis Presley records, computer programming. *Address:* 97 Millway, Mill Hill, NW7 3JL. *T:* 081–959 6665; (mobile) 0860 549584, *Fax:* 081–906 4137.

STOKES, Dr Alistair Michael; Managing Director, Operations, Porton International, since 1990; *b* 22 July 1948; *s* of Alan Philip and Janet Ross Stokes; *m* 1970, Stephanie Mary Garland; two *d. Educ:* University College, Cardiff (BSc, PhD). With Pharmacia AB (Sweden), 1974–76; Monsanto Co., St Louis, USA, 1976–82; Glaxo Pharmaceuticals, 1982–85; Regional Gen. Manager, Yorkshire RHA, 1985–87; Dir, Glaxo Pharmaceuticals, 1987–90. *Publications:* Plasma Proteins, 1977; biochemical and scientific papers. *Recreations:* music, cricket, travel. *Address:* Porton International, 100 Piccadilly, W1V 9FN.

STOKES, David Mayhew Allen; QC 1989; a Recorder of the Crown Court, since 1985; *b* 12 Feb. 1944; *s* of Henry Pauntley Allen Stokes and Marjorie Joan Stokes; *m* 1970, Ruth Elizabeth, *d* of late Charles Tunstall Evans, CMG, Haywards Heath; one *s* one *d. Educ:* Radley College; Inst. de Touraine (Tours); Churchill College, Cambridge (MA History/Law). Admitted Student, Gray's Inn, 1964; Holt Scholar, 1966; called to the Bar, 1968. Mem., Gen. Council of the Bar, 1989–. Vis. Instructor/Team Leader, Nat. Inst. Trial Advocacy Workshop, Osgoode Hall Law Sch., York Univ., Toronto, 1986–. Trustee/Dir, London Suzuki Gp, 1988–. Chm., Cambridge Bar Mess, 1991–. *Recreations:* amateur dramatics, badminton, madrigals. *Address:* 5 Paper Buildings, Temple, EC4Y 7HB. *T:* 071–583 6117. *Club:* Norfolk (Norwich).

STOKES, Harry Michael; HM Diplomatic Service, retired; Counsellor, Foreign and Commonwealth Office, 1979–81; *b* 22 July 1926; *s* of late Wing Comdr Henry Alban Stokes, RAF, and Lilian Frances (*née* Ede); *m* 1951, Prudence Mary Watling; two *s* one *d. Educ:* Rossall Sch.; Worcester Coll., Oxford (BA, Dip. Slavonic Studies). Served RAF, 1944–47. Joined Foreign Service, 1951; attached Control Commission, Germany, 1952–55; Foreign Office, 1955; Singapore, 1958; FO, 1959; Washington, 1961; Copenhagen, 1963; FO 1965; New Delhi, 1976; FO, 1977. Chm., British Assoc. for Cemeteries in S Asia, 1985–. Dir, Indo-British Review, 1988–. *Recreations:* walking, racquet games, photography, music. *Club:* Commonwealth Trust.

STOKES, John Fisher, MA, MD, FRCP; Physician, University College Hospital, since 1947; *b* 19 Sept. 1912; *e s* of late Dr Kenneth Stokes and Mary (*née* Fisher); *m* 1940, Elizabeth Joan, *d* of Thomas Rooke and Elizabeth Frances (*née* Pearce); one *s* one *d. Educ:*

Haileybury (exhibitioner); Gonville and Caius Coll., Cambridge (exhibitioner); University Coll. Hosp. (Fellowes Silver Medal for clinical medicine). MB BChir (Cambridge) 1937; MRCP 1939; MD (Cambridge) 1947 (proxime accessit, Horton Smith prize); FRCP 1947; FRCPE 1975; Thruston Medal, Gonville and Caius Coll., 1948. Appointments on junior staff University Coll. Hosp. and Victoria Hosp. for Children, Tite St, 1937–42; RAMC 1942–46; served in Far East, 1943–46, Lt-Col (despatches). Examiner in Medicine, various Univs, 1949–70. Member of Council, Royal Soc. of Med., 1951–54, 1967–69. Vice-Pres., RCP, 1968–69; Harveian Orator, RCP, 1981. Trustee, Leeds Castle Foundn, 1984–. Amateur Squash Rackets Champion of Surrey, 1935, of East of England, 1936, Runner-up of British Isles, 1937; English International, 1938; Technical Adviser to Squash Rackets Assoc., 1948–52; Chm. Jesters Club, 1953–59. *Publications:* Examinations in Medicine (jtly), 1976; contrib. on liver disease and general medicine in medical journals. *Recreations:* music, tennis, painting. *Address:* Ossicles, Newnham Hill, near Henley-on-Thames, Oxon RG9 5TL. *Clubs:* Athenæum, Savile.

See also Prof. Sir W. D. M. Paton.

STOKES, Sir John (Heydon Romaine), Kt 1988; MP (C) Halesowen and Stourbridge, since 1974 (Oldbury and Halesowen, 1970–74); *b* 23 July 1917; *o* surv. *s* of late Victor Romaine Stokes, Hitchin; *m* 1st, 1939, Barbara Esmée (*d* 1988), *y d* of late R. E. Yorke, Wellingborough; one *s* two *d*; 2nd, 1989, Elsie Frances (*d* 1990), *widow* of John Plowman; 3rd, 1991, Ruth, *widow* of Sir Timothy Bligh, KBE, DSO, DSC. *Educ:* Temple Grove; Haileybury Coll.; Queen's Coll., Oxford. BA 1938; MA 1946. Hon. Agent and Treas., Oxford Univ. Conservative Assoc., 1937; Pres., Monarchist Soc., 1937; Pres., Mermaid Club, 1937. Asst Master, Prep. Sch., 1938–39. Served War, 1939–46: Dakar Expedn, 1940; wounded in N Africa, 1943; Mil. Asst to HM Minister Beirut and Damascus, 1944–46; Major, Royal Fusiliers. Personnel Officer, Imperial Chemical Industries, 1946–51; Personnel Manager, British Celanese, 1951–59; Dep. Personnel Manager, Courtaulds, 1957–59; Dir, Clive & Stokes, Personnel Consultants, 1959–80. Mem., Gen. Synod of C of E, 1985–90. Contested (C): Gloucester, 1964; Hitchin, 1966. Mem., Select Cttee on Parly Commn for Admin (Ombudsman), 1979–83. Leader, Parly delegations: to Portugal, 1980; to Falkland Islands, 1985; to Malta, 1988; to Trinidad and Tobago, 1991. Mem., Delegn to Council of Europe and WEU, 1983–. Pres., W Midlands Cons. Clubs, 1971–84. Mem. Exec. Cttee, Oxford Soc.; Chm., Gen. Purposes Cttee, Primrose League, 1971–85; Vice-Pres., Royal Stuart Soc. *Publications:* articles on political and personnel subjects. *Recreations:* gardening, travel, English history, church affairs. *Address:* Top Barn, Church End, Haddenham, Bucks HP17 8AE. *Clubs:* Carlton, Buck's.

STOLLERY, Prof. John Leslie, DScEng; FRAeS; FCGI; FAIAA; Professor of Aerodynamics since 1973, and Head, College of Aeronautics, 1976–86, Cranfield Institute of Technology; *b* 21 April 1930; *s* of George and Emma Stollery; *m* 1956, Jane Elizabeth, *d* of Walter and Mildred Reynolds; four *s*. *Educ:* East Barnet Grammar Sch.; Imperial Coll. of Science and Technol., London Univ. (BScEng 1951, MScEng 1953, DScEng 1973). DIC; CEng; FRAeS 1975; FCGI 1984; FAIAA 1988. Aerodynamics Dept, De Havilland Aircraft Co., 1952–56; Lectr, 1956, Reader, 1962, Aeronautics Dept, Imperial Coll., London; Dean, Faculty of Engrg, 1976–79, Pro Vice-Chancellor, 1982–85, Cranfield Inst. of Technol. Chairman: Aerospace Technology Bd, MoD, 1986–89; Aviation Cttee, DTI, 1986–; Mem., Airworthiness Requirements Bd, 1990–. Pres., RAeS, 1987–88. Visiting Professor: Cornell Aeronautical Labs, Buffalo, USA, 1964; Aeronaut. Res. Lab., Wright Patterson Air Force Base, 1971; Nat. Aeronaut. Lab., Bangalore, India, 1977; Peking Inst. of Aeronautics and Astronautics, 1979; Univ. of Queensland, 1983. *Publications:* (Chief Editor) Shock Tube Research, 1971; papers in Jl of Fluid Mechanics, and various other aeronautical jls. *Recreations:* playing tennis, watching football, travelling. *Address:* 28 The Embankment, Bedford. *T:* Bedford (0234) 355087.

STOLTENBERG, Gerhard, DrPhil; Minister of Defence, Federal Republic of Germany, since 1989; *b* 29 Sept. 1928; *m* 1958, Margot Rann; one *s* one *d*. *Educ:* Bad Oldesloe; Kiel Univ. (DrPhil 1954). Military service, 1944–45; local govt, 1945–46; Asst Lectr, 1954–60, Lectr, 1960–65, Kiel Univ. Mem., CDU, 1947–: Dep. Chm., 1955–71, Chm., 1971–82, Schleswig-Holstein CDU; Nat. Dep. Chm., 1969–. Nat. Chm., Young Union, 1955–61. Schleswig-Holstein Parliament: Mem., 1954–57, 1971–; Prime Minister, 1971–82. Bundestag: Mem., 1957–71 and 1982–; Minister of Scientific Research, 1965–69; Dep. Chm., CDU/CSU, Bundestag, 1969–71; Minister of Finance, 1982–89. *Publications:* The German Reichstag 1871–1873, 1954; Political Currents in Rural Schleswig-Holstein 1919–1933, 1960; State and Science, 1969; Schleswig-Holstein: present and future, 1978. *Address:* Postfach 1328, 5300 Bonn 1, Federal Republic of Germany.

STONE, Maj.-Gen. Anthony Charles Peter; Director General Policy and Special Projects, Ministry of Defence, since 1990; *b* 25 March 1939; *s* of Major (retd) Charles C. Stone and Kathleen M. Stone (*née* Grogan); *m* 1967, (Elizabeth) Mary, *d* of Rev. Canon Gideon Davies; two *s*. *Educ:* St Joseph's Coll.; RMA, Sandhurst; Staff Coll., Camberley. Commnd RA, 1960; served in light, field, medium, heavy, locating and air defence artillery in BAOR, FE and ME and in various general and weapons staff appts in MoD; commanded 5th Regt, RA, 1980–83; founded Special OP Troop, 1982; Col, Defence Progs Staff, MoD, 1983–84; Mil. Dir of Studies, RMCS, 1985–86; Dir of Operational Requirements (Land), MoD, 1986–89; Dir of Light Weapons Projects, MoD, 1989–90. *Recreations:* shooting (game), family, country pursuits. *Club:* Army and Navy.

STONE, Evan David Robert, QC 1979; a Recorder of the Crown Court, since 1979; *b* 26 Aug. 1928; *s* of Laurence George and Lillian Stone; *m* 1959, Gisela Bridget Mann; one *s*. *Educ:* Berkhamsted; Worcester Coll., Oxford (MA). National Service (commnd, Army), 1947–49; served Middle East and UK. Called to Bar, Inner Temple, 1954, Bencher, 1985; sometime HM Deputy Coroner: Inner West London; West Middlesex; City of London. Mem. Senate of Inns of Court and the Bar, 1985–86. Formerly Associate Editor, Medico-Legal Journal. Councillor, later Alderman, London Borough of Islington, 1969–74 (Dep. Leader, later Leader of Opposition). Chm., City and Hackney HA, 1984–. Mem., Criminal Injuries Compensation Bd, 1989–. Governor: Moorfields Eye Hosp., 1970–79; Highbury Grove Sch., 1971–86 (Chm. of Governors, 1978–83). *Publications:* Forensic Medicine, 1987 (with Prof. H. Johnson); contrib. Social Welfare and the Citizen (paperback), 1957; contribs to Medico-Legal Jl and other professional jls. *Recreations:* reading, writing, sport, listening to music. *Address:* 60 Canonbury Park South, N1 2JG. *T:* 071–226 6820; The Mill House, Ridgewell, Halstead, Essex. *T:* Ridgewell (044085) 338; (chambers) 5 Raymond Buildings, Gray's Inn, WC1R 5BP. *T:* 071–831 0720. *Clubs:* Garrick, MCC; Norfolk (Norwich), Western (Glasgow).

STONE, Prof. (Francis) Gordon (Albert), CBE 1990; FRS 1976; Head of Department of Inorganic Chemistry, and Professor, Bristol University, 1963–90, now Professor Emeritus; Robert A. Welch Distinguished Professor of Chemistry, Baylor University, Texas, since 1990; *b* 19 May 1925; *s* of Sidney Charles and Florence Stone; *m* 1956, Judith M. Hislop, Sydney, Australia; three *s*. *Educ:* Exeter Sch.; Christ's Coll., Cambridge. BA 1948, MA and PhD 1952, ScD 1963, Cambridge. Fulbright Schol., Univ. of Southern Calif., 1952–54; Instructor and Asst Prof., Harvard Univ., 1954–62; Reader, Queen Mary Coll., London, 1962–63. Vis. Professor: Monash Univ., 1966; Princeton Univ., 1967; Univ. of Arizona, 1970; Carnegie-Mellon Univ., 1972; Texas A&M Univ., 1980; ANU, 1982; Guggenheim Fellow, 1961; Sen. Vis. Fellow, Australian Acad. of Sciences, 1966; A. R. Gordon Distinguished Lectr, Univ. of Toronto, 1977; Misha Strassberg Vis. Lectr, Univ. of WA, 1982. Lectures: Boomer, Univ. of Alberta, 1965; Firestone, Univ. of Wisconsin, 1970; Tilden, Chem. Soc., 1971; Ludwig Mond, RSC, 1982; Reilly, Univ. of Notre Dame, 1983; Waddington, Univ. of Durham, 1984; Sir Edward Frankland Prize, RSC, 1987; G. W. Watt, Univ. of Texas (Austin), 1988. Member: Council, Royal Soc. of Chemistry (formerly Chemical Soc.), 1968–70, 1981–83; Dalton Div. Council, 1971–74, 1981–85 (Vice-Pres. 1973 and 1984–85; Pres., 1981–83); Chemistry Cttee, SERC, 1982–85 (Mem., Chem. Cttee, SRC, 1971–74); Council, Royal Soc., 1986–88 (Vice-Pres., 1987–88). Organometallic Chemistry Medal, 1972, Transition Metal Chemistry Medal, 1979, RSC; Chugaev Medal, Inst. of Inorganic Chem., USSR Acad. of Sciences, 1978; Amer. Chem. Soc. Award in Inorg. Chem., 1985; Davy Medal, Royal Soc., 1989; Longstaff Medal, RSC, 1990. *Publications:* (Editor) Inorganic Polymers, 1962; Hydrogen Compounds of the Group IV Elements, 1962; (Editor) Advances in Organometallic Chemistry, vols 1–33, 1964–92; (ed) Comprehensive Organometallic Chemistry, 1984; numerous papers in Jl Chem. Soc., Jl Amer. Chem. Soc., etc. *Recreation:* world travel. *Address:* 60 Coombe Lane, Bristol BS9 2AY. *T:* Bristol (0272) 686107; 1605 South 4th Street, Apt 106, Waco, Tex 76706, USA. *T:* (817) 752–7208.

STONE, Frederick Alistair, CBE 1988; DL; solicitor; Clerk and Chief Executive, Surrey County Council, 1973–88; *b* 13 Sept. 1927; *s* of Cyril Jackson and Elsie May Stone; *m* 1963, Anne Teresa Connor; one *s* one *d*. *Educ:* William Hulme's Grammar Sch.; Dulwich Coll.; Brasenose Coll., Oxford (BCL, MA). Asst Solicitor: Norwich City Council, 1954–58; Hampshire CC, 1958–60; Sen. Solicitor, CC of Lincoln (Parts of Lindsey), 1960–63; Asst Clerk, Hampshire CC, 1963–65; Dep. Clerk, Cheshire CC, 1965–73. Chairman: RIPA, 1979–81; Assoc. of County Chief Executives, 1986–87. DL Surrey, 1988. *Recreations:* music, walking, gardening. *Address:* North Lodge, Brockham Green, Betchworth RH3 7JS. *T:* Betchworth (073784) 2178.

STONE, Gilbert Seymour, FCA; Chairman, Manganese Bronze Holdings plc, since 1987 (Director, since 1976); *b* 4 Feb. 1915; *s* of J. Stone; *m* 1941, Josephine Tolhurst; one *s*. *Educ:* Clifton College. War service as Air Crew with RAF, 1939–45 (Sqdn-Ldr); with Industrial & Commercial Finance Corp. Ltd, 1945–59, latterly Asst Gen. Manager; Dir, Gresham Trust Ltd, 1959–61; practised on own account, 1961–72 and 1974–85; Dir, Industrial Develt Unit, DTI, 1972–74. Director: Babcock Internat. Gp plc (formerly FKI Babcock plc); Smith New Court plc; Household Mortgage Corp. plc. *Recreations:* golf, travel. *Address:* 2 Priory Close, Sunningdale, Berks SL5 9SE. *Clubs:* Garrick; Sunningdale Golf.

STONE, Gordon; *see* Stone, F. G. A.

STONE, Sir (John) Richard (Nicholas), Kt 1978; CBE 1946; ScD; FBA 1956; P. D. Leake Professor of Finance and Accounting, University of Cambridge, 1955–80, retired; Fellow of King's College, Cambridge, since 1945; *b* 30 Aug. 1913; *o c* of late Sir Gilbert Stone; *m* 1936, Winifred Jenkins (marr. diss.); *m* 1941, Feodora Leontinoff (*d* 1956); one *d*; *m* 1960, Mrs Giovanna Croft-Murray, *d* of Count Aurelio Saffi. *Educ:* Westminster School (Hon. Fellow, 1989); Gonville and Caius College, Cambridge (Hon. Fellow, 1976). MA 1938; ScD 1957. With C. E. Heath and Co., Lloyd's Brokers, 1936–39; Ministry of Economic Warfare, 1939–40; Offices of the War Cabinet, Central Statistical Office, 1940–45; Dir Dept of Applied Economics, Cambridge, 1945–55. Mem., Internat. Statistical Inst. President: Econometric Soc., 1955; Royal Econ. Soc., 1978–80; Hon. Member: Soc. of Incorp. Accountants, 1954; Amer. Economic Assoc., 1976; For. Hon. Mem., Amer. Acad. of Arts and Sciences, 1968; For. Mem., Accad. dei Lincei, 1987. Hon. doctorates, Univs of Oslo and Brussels, 1965, Geneva, 1971, Warwick, 1975, Paris, 1977, Bristol, 1978. Lectures: Mattioli, 1986; Solari, 1987. Nobel Prize for Economics, 1984. *Publications:* National Income and Expenditure, 1st edn (with J. E. Meade), 1944, 10th edn (with G. Stone), 1977; The Role of Measurement in Economics, 1951; (with others) The Measurement of Consumers' Expenditure and Behaviour in the United Kingdom 1920–1938, vol. 1 1954, vol. 2 1966; Quantity and Price Indexes in National Accounts, 1956; Input-Output and National Accounts, 1961; Mathematics in the Social Sciences, and Other Essays, 1966; Mathematical Models of the Economy, and Other Essays, 1970; Demographic Accounting and Model Building, 1971; Aspects of Economic and Social Modelling, 1980; gen. editor and pt author series A Programme for Growth, 1962–74; numerous articles in learned journals, particularly on social accounting and econometrics, 1936–. *Recreation:* staying at home. *Address:* 13 Millington Road, Cambridge.

STONE, Prof. Lawrence, MA Oxon; Dodge Professor of History, 1963–90, and Director, Shelby Cullom Davis Center for Historical Studies, 1968–90, Princeton University; *b* 4 Dec. 1919; *s* of Lawrence Frederick Stone and Mabel Julia Annie Stone; *m* 1943, Jeanne Caecilia, *d* of Prof. Robert Fawtier, Membre de l'Institut, Paris; one *s* one *d*. *Educ:* Charterhouse School, 1933–38; Sorbonne, Paris, 1938; Christ Church, Oxford, 1938–40, 1945–46. Lieut RNVR 1940–45. Bryce Research Student, Oxford Univ., 1946–47; Lectr, University Coll. Oxford, 1947–50; Fellow, Wadham Coll., Oxford, 1950–63 (Hon. Fellow, 1983); Mem. Inst. for Advanced Study, Princeton, 1960–61; Chm., Dept of History, 1967–70. Mem., Amer. Philosophical Soc., 1970. Fellow, Amer. Acad. of Arts and Sciences, 1968; Corresp. FBA 1983. Hon. DHL: Chicago, 1979; Pennsylvania, 1986; Hon. DLitt Edinburgh, 1983. *Publications:* Sculpture in Britain: The Middle Ages, 1955; An Elizabethan: Sir Horatio Palavicino, 1956; The Crisis of the Aristocracy, 1558–1641, 1965; The Causes of the English Revolution, 1529–1642, 1972; Family and Fortune: Studies in Aristocratic Finance in the 16th and 17th Centuries, 1973; (ed) The University in Society, 1975; (ed) Schooling and Society, 1977; Family, Sex and Marriage in England 1500–1800, 1977; The Past and the Present, 1981; An Open Elite? England 1540–1880, 1984; The Past and the Present Revisited, 1987; Road to Divorce: England 1530–1987, 1990; numerous articles in History, Economic History Review, Past and Present, Archæological Jl, English Historical Review, Bulletin of the Inst. for Historical Research, Malone Soc., Comparative Studies in Society and History, History Today, etc. *Address:* 266 Moore Street, Princeton, NJ 08540, USA. *T:* 609 921.2717; 231A Woodstock Road, Oxford. *T:* Oxford (0865) 59174.

STONE, Marcus; Sheriff of Lothian and Borders, since 1984; Advocate; *b* 22 March 1921; *s* of Morris and Reva Stone; *m* 1956, Jacqueline Barnoin; three *s* two *d*. *Educ:* High Sch. of Glasgow; Univ. of Glasgow (MA 1940, LLB 1948). Served War of 1939–45, RASC: overseas service, West Africa, att. RWAFF. Admitted Solicitor, 1949; Post Grad. Dip., Psychology, Univ. of Glasgow, 1953; admitted Faculty of Advocates, 1965; apptd Hon. Sheriff Substitute, 1967, Sheriff, 1971–76, of Stirling, Dunbarton and Clackmannan, later N Strathclyde at Dumbarton; Sheriff of Glasgow and Strathkelvin, 1976–84. *Publications:* Proof of Fact in Criminal Trials, 1984; Cross-examination in Criminal Trials, 1988; Fact-finding for Magistrates, 1990; Criminal Advocacy and Evidence, 1992. *Recreations:* swimming, music. *Address:* Sheriff's Chambers, Sheriff Court House, Court Square, Linlithgow EH49 7EQ.

STONE, Prof. Norman; Professor of Modern History, and Fellow of Worcester College, University of Oxford, since 1984; *b* 8 March 1941; *s* of late Norman Stone and Mary

Stone (*née* Pettigrew); *m* 1st, 1966, Nicole Aubry (marr. diss. 1977); two *s*; 2nd, 1982, Christine Margaret Booker (*née* Verity); one *s*. *Educ*: Glasgow Acad.; Gonville and Caius Coll., Cambridge (MA). Research student in Austria and Hungary, 1962–65; University of Cambridge: Research Fellow, Gonville and Caius Coll., 1965–67; Univ. Lectr in Russian History, 1967–84; Fellow and Dir of Studies in History, Jesus Coll., 1971–79; Fellow of Trinity Coll., 1979–84. Vis. Lectr, Sydney Univ., 1978. *Publications*: The Eastern Front 1914–1917, 1975, 3rd edn 1978 (Wolfson Prize for History, 1976); Hitler, 1980; Europe Transformed 1878–1919 (Fontana History of Europe), 1983; (ed jtly) Czechoslovakia, 1989; (jtly) The Other Russia, 1990; The Russian Chronicles, 1990. *Recreations*: Eastern Europe, music, languages, journalism. *Address*: 18 Thorncliffe Road, Oxford. *T*: Oxford (0865) 311081. *Clubs*: Savile, Beefsteak, Garrick.

STONE, Maj.-Gen. Patrick Philip Dennant, CBE 1984 (OBE 1981; MBE 1975); Director General, Personal Services (Army), 1988–91; *b* 7 Feb. 1939; *s* of Philip Hartley Stone and Elsie Maude Stone (*née* Dennant); *m* 1967, Christine Iredale Trent; two *s* one *d*. *Educ*: Christ's Hospital; psc 1972. Nat. Service, 1959; commissioned East Anglian Regt, 1959; seconded 6 KAR, 1960–62 (Tanganyika); served British Guyana and Aden, 1962–65; ADC to Governor of W Australia, 1965–67; RAF Staff Coll., 1972; Comd 2nd Bn, Royal Anglian Regt, 1977–80 (UK and Berlin); Chief of Staff, 1st Armoured Div., 1981–84; Comdr, Berlin Inf. Bde, 1985–86; Dep. Mil. Sec. (B), 1987. Dep. Col, Royal Anglian Regt, 1986; Col Comdt, Mil. Provost Staff Corps, 1988–. *Recreations*: country interests, travel, conservation. *Address*: c/o Lloyds Bank, 90A Mill Road, Cambridge. *Club*: Army and Navy.

STONE, Sir Richard; *see* Stone, Sir J. R. N.

STONE, Richard Frederick, QC 1968; *b* 11 March 1928; *s* of Sir Leonard Stone, OBE, QC, and Madeleine Marie (*née* Scheffler); *m* 1st, 1957, Georgina Maxwell Morris (decd); two *d*; 2nd, 1964, Susan van Heel; two *d*. *Educ*: Lakefield College Sch., Canada; Rugby; Trinity Hall, Cambridge (MA). Lt, Worcs Regt, 1946–48. Called to Bar, Gray's Inn, 1952, Bencher, 1974; Mem., Bar Council, 1957–61; Member: Panel of Lloyd's Arbitrators in Salvage Cases; Panel of Wreck Comrs. *Recreation*: sailing. *Address*: 5 Raymond Buildings, Gray's Inn, WC1R 5BP. *T*: 071–242 2697; Orchard Gap, Wittering Road, Hayling Island, Hants PO11 9SP. *T*: Hayling Island (0705) 463645.

STONEFROST, Maurice Frank, CBE 1983; DL; Chairman, Municipal Mutual Insurance, since 1990; *b* 1 Sept. 1927; *s* of Arthur and Anne Stonefrost, Bristol; *m* 1953, Audrey Jean Fishlock; one *s* one *d*. *Educ*: Merrywood Grammar Sch., Bristol (DPA). IPFA. Nat. Service, RAF, 1948–51; local govt finance: Bristol County Borough, 1951–54; Slough Borough, 1954–56; Coventry County Borough, 1956–61; W Sussex CC, 1961–64; Sec., Inst. of Municipal Treasurers and Accountants, 1964–73; Comptroller of Financial Services, GLC, 1973–84; Dir Gen. and Clerk, GLC, 1984–85; Chief Exec., BR Pension Fund, 1986–90. President: Soc. of County Treasurers, 1982–83; CIPFA, 1984–85. Chm., Commn on Citizenship, 1989–90. DL Greater London, 1986. Hon. DSc City Univ., 1987. *Recreation*: gardening. *Address*: 611 Hood House, Dolphin Square, SW1V 3LX. *T*: 071–798 3247.

STONEHAM, Arthur Marshall, PhD; FRS 1989; Director of Research, AEA Industrial Technology, since 1990; Fellow, Wolfson College, Oxford, since 1989; *b* 18 May 1940; *s* of Garth Rivers Stoneham and Nancy Wooler Stoneham (*née* Leslie); *m* 1962, Doreen Montgomery; two *d*. *Educ*: Univ. of Bristol (BSc 1961; PhD 1964). CPhys, FInstP 1981. Harwell Laboratory, UKAEA, 1964–: Group Leader, 1974; Individual Merit promotions to Band level, 1974, and Sen. level, 1979; Hd of Materials Physics and Metallurgy Div., 1989–90; Hd of Technical Area, Core and Fuel Studies, UKAEA, 1988–90. Wolfson Industrial Fellow, Oxford Univ., 1985–89. Visiting Professor: Univ. of Illinois, 1969; Univ. of Connecticut, 1973; Univ. of Keele, 1988–; visiting scientist: Gen. Electric, Schenectady, 1969; Centre d'Etudes Nucléaires Grenoble, 1970; KFA Julich, 1973; IBM Yorktown Heights, 1982; PTB Braunschweig, 1985, etc. Dir, Inst. of Physics Publications; Editor, Jl of Physics C: Solid State Physics, 1983–88; mem. editl bds of other learned jls. *Publications*: Theory of Defects in Solids, 1975, new edn 1985 (Russian edn 1978); (with W. Hayes) Defects and Defect Processes in Non-Metallic Solids, 1985; (with M. G. Silk and J. A. G. Temple) Current Issues in Semiconductor Science, 1986; Current Issues in Condensed Matter Structure, 1987; Reliability of Non-Destructive Inspection, 1987; Ionic Solids at High Temperatures, 1989; research papers on defect properties of the solid state, quantum diffusion, and ordered structures in Jl Phys C: Solid State Phys, Phys Rev., Phys Rev. Lett., Procs of Royal Soc., etc. *Recreations*: music, esp. horn playing in orchestral and chamber music, musical scholarship, reading. *Address*: Riding Mill, Bridge End, Dorchester-on-Thames, Wallingford, Oxon OX10 7JP. *T*: Oxford (0865) 340066.

STONES, (Elsie) Margaret, AM 1988; MBE 1977; botanical artist; *b* 28 Aug. 1920; *d* of Frederick Stones and Agnes Kirkwood (*née* Fleming). *Educ*: Swinburne Technical Coll., Melbourne; Melbourne National Gall. Art Sch. Came to England, 1951; working independently as botanical artist, 1951–: at Royal Botanic Gardens, Kew; Nat. Hist. Museum; Royal Horticultural Soc., and at other botanical instns; Contrib. Artist to Curtis's Botanical Magazine, 1957–82. Drawings (water-colour): 20, Aust. plants, National Library, Canberra, 1962–63; 250, Tasmanian endemic plants, 1962–77; Basalt Plains flora, Melbourne Univ., 1975–76; Vis. Botanical Artist, Louisiana State Univ., 1977–86 (200 drawings of Louisiana flora, exhibited: Fitzwilliam, Cambridge, Royal Botanic Garden, Edinburgh, Ashmolean Mus., Oxford, 1991). Exhibitions: Colnaghi's, London, 1967–; Retrospective Exhibn, Melbourne Univ., 1976; Louisiana Drawings, Smithsonian, USA, 1980, Louisiana State Mus., 1985; Baskett & Day, 1984, 1989. Workshop, Cornell Univ., USA, 1990. Hon. DSc: Louisiana State Univ. Bâton Rouge, 1986; Melbourne Univ., 1989. Eloise Payne Luquer Medal, Garden Club of Amer., 1987; Gold Veitch Meml Medal, RHS, 1989. *Publications*: The Endemic Flora of Tasmania (text by W. M. Curtis), 6 Parts, 1967–78; Flora of Louisiana: water-colour drawings, 1991; illus. various books. *Recreations*: gardening, reading. *Address*: 1 Bushwood Road, Kew, Richmond, Surrey TW9 3BG. *T*: 081–940 6183.

STONES, Sir William (Frederick), Kt 1990; OBE 1980; Managing Director, China Light & Power Co., since 1984; Chairman, Hong Kong Nuclear Investment Co., since 1985; *b* 3 March 1923; *s* of Ralph William Stones and Ada Stones (*née* Armstrong); *m* 1st, 1946, Irene Mary Punter (marr. diss.); one *s* one *d*; 2nd, 1968, Margaret Joy Catton. *Educ*: Rutherford Coll., Newcastle upon Tyne. Chief Chemist, Michie & Davidson, 1948–51; Regional Res. Dir, CEGB NE Region, 1951–63; Supt, Ferrybridge Power Station, 1963–66; CEGB NE Region: Group Manager, 1966–68; Dir, Operational Planning, 1968–71; Dir, Generation, and Dep. Dir-Gen., 1971–75; Dir and Gen. Manager, China Light & Power Co., 1975–83. Dep. Chm., Guandong Nuclear Power Joint Venture Co., 1985–. Commander, Order of Leopold II (Belgium), 1986. *Recreations*: fishing, country life. *Address*: Pirnie House, Kelso, Roxburghshire TD5 8NS. T: St Boswells (0835) 23854. *Clubs*: New (Edinburgh); Hong Kong.

STONEY, Brigadier Ralph Francis Ewart, CBE 1952 (OBE, 1943); Director-General, The Royal Society for the Prevention of Accidents, 1959–68; *b* 28 June 1903; *o s* of late Col R. D. S. Stoney, The Downs, Delgany, Co. Wicklow and Mrs E. M. M. Stoney; *m* 1st, 1939, Kathleen Nina (*née* Kirkland) (*d* 1973); one *d*; 2nd, 1979, Bridget Mary St John Browne. *Educ*: Royal Naval Colleges, Osborne and Dartmouth; Royal Military Academy, Woolwich. Commissioned Royal Engineers, 1923; Staff College, Camberley, 1937–38. Served War of 1939–45 as GSO, 1939–43 (OBE) and as CRE, 82 Div., 1943–46, in Burma (despatches twice). CRE 5th Div. and 2nd Div., 1947–48; Col GS (Intelligence), War Office, 1949–51; Brig. GS (Intelligence), Middle East, 1952–54. Retired, 1954. *Recreations*: sailing; workshop practice. *Address*: Kinsale, Hook Heath Avenue, Woking, Surrey GU22 0HN.

STONHOUSE, Sir Philip (Allan), 18th Bt, *cr* 1628, and 14th Bt *cr* 1670; Assessor and Land Appraiser, Government of Alberta; *b* 24 Oct. 1916; *s* of Sir Arthur Allan Stonhouse, 17th Bt, and Beatrice C. Féron; *S* father, 1967; *m* 1946, Winnifred Emily Shield; two *s*. *Educ*: Western Canada Coll.; Queen's Univ., Kingston, Ontario. Gold Mining, 1936–40; General Construction, 1940–42; Ranching, 1942–54; Assessing, 1954–68. Is a Freemason. *Recreations*: water-fowl and upland game hunting, tennis, ski-ing. *Heir*: *s* Rev. Michael Philip Stonhouse, BA, LTh [*b* 4 Sept. 1948; *m* 1977, Colleen Coueill, Toronto; two *s*. *Educ*: Wycliffe Coll., Toronto]. *Address*: 521–12 Street SW, Medicine Hat, Alberta, Canada. *T*: 526–5832. *Club*: Medicine Hat Ski.

STONOR, family name of **Baron Camoys.**

STONOR, Air Marshal Sir Thomas (Henry), KCB 1989; Group Director and Controller, National Air Traffic Services, 1988–91; *b* 5 March 1936; *s* of Alphonsus and Ann Stonor; *m* 1964, Robin Antoinette, *er d* of late Wilfrid and Rita Budd; two *s* one *d*. *Educ*: St Cuthbert's High Sch., Newcastle upon Tyne; King's Coll., Univ. of Durham (BSc (Mech Eng) 1957). Commissioned, RAF, 1959; served No 3 Sqn, 2ATAF, 1961–64; CFS, 6 FTS and RAF Coll., Cranwell, 1964–67; No 231 Operational Conversion Unit, 1967–69; RAF Staff Coll., Bracknell, 1970; HQ, RAF Germany, 1971–73; OC 31 Sqn, 1974–76; Mil. Asst to VCDS, MoD, 1976–78; OC RAF Coltishall, 1978–80; RCDS, 1981; Inspector of Flight Safety, RAF, 1982–84; Dir of Control (Airspace Policy), NATS, 1985–86; Dep. Controller, NATS, 1986–88. *Recreations*: gardening, music. *Address*: c/o Barclays Bank, Haymarket Branch, Newcastle upon Tyne NE1 7BH. *Club*: Royal Air Force.

STOODLEY, Peter Ernest William; County Treasurer of Kent, 1972–80; *b* 27 July 1925; *s* of Ernest and Esther Stoodley; *m* 1970, June (*née* Bennett). *Educ*: Weymouth Grammar Sch.; Administrative Staff Coll.; Inst. of Public Finance Accountants. Accountant with County Council of: Dorset, 1947–56; Staffordshire, 1956–61; Kent, 1961–65; Asst Co. Treasurer of Kent, 1965–69; Dep. Co. Treasurer of Kent, 1969–72. *Recreations*: ornithology, cricket. *Address*: Cranby, Horseshoe Lane, Leeds, Maidstone, Kent ME17 1SR. *T*: Maidstone (0622) 861287.

STOPFORD, family name of **Earl of Courtown.**

STOPFORD, Viscount; James Richard Ian Montagu Stopford; *b* 30 March 1988; *s* and *heir* of Earl of Courtown, *qv*.

STOPFORD, Maj.-Gen. Stephen Robert Anthony, CB 1988; MBE 1971; Director, David Brown Vehicle Transmissions Ltd, since 1990; Director General Fighting Vehicles and Engineer Equipment, Ministry of Defence (Procurement Executive), 1985–89; *b* 1 April 1934; *s* of Comdr Robert Stopford, RN, and Elsie Stopford; *m* 1963, Vanessa (*née* Baron). *Educ*: Downside; Millfield. Graduate MIERE. Commissioned Royal Scots Greys, 1954; regimental service and various staff appts until 1977; Project Manager, MBT80, 1977–80; Military Attaché, Washington, 1983–85. *Recreations*: sailing, scuba diving, shooting. *Address*: 18 Thornton Avenue, SW2 4HG. *T*: 081–674 1416. *Club*: Cavalry and Guards.

STOPPARD, Miriam, MD, MRCP; writer and broadcaster; *b* 12 May 1937; *d* of Sydney and Jenny Stern; *m* 1972, Tom Stoppard, *qv*; two *s* and two step *s*. *Educ*: Newcastle upon Tyne Central High Sch. (State Scholar, 1955); Royal Free Hosp. Sch. of Medicine, Univ. of London (Prize for Experimental Physiol., 1958); King's Coll. Med. Sch. (Univ. of Durham), Newcastle upon Tyne (MB, BS Durham, 1961; MD Newcastle, 1966). MRCP 1964. Royal Victoria Infirmary, King's Coll. Hosp., Newcastle upon Tyne: House Surg., 1961; House Phys., 1962; Sen. House Officer in Medicine, 1962–63; Univ. of Bristol: Res. Fellow, Dept of Chem. Pathol., 1963–65 (MRC Scholar in Chem. Pathol.); Registrar in Dermatol., 1965–66 (MRC Scholar in Dermatol.); Sen. Registrar in Dermatol., 1966–68; Syntex Pharmaceuticals Ltd: Associate Med. Dir, 1968; Dep. Med. Dir, 1971; Med. Dir, 1974; Dep. Man. Dir, 1976; Man. Dir, 1977–81. TV series: Where There's Life (5 series), 1981–; Baby & Co. (2 series), 1984–; Woman to Woman, 1985–; Miriam Stoppard's Health and Beauty Show, 1988–; Dear Miriam, 1989. MRSocMed (Mem. Dermatol. Sect., Endocrinol. Sect.); Member: Heberden Soc.; Brit. Assoc. of Rheumatology and Rehabilitation. *Publications*: Miriam Stoppard's Book of Baby Care, 1977; (contrib.) My Medical School, 1978; Miriam Stoppard's Book of Health Care, 1979; The Face and Body Book, 1980; Everywoman's Lifeguide, 1982; Your Baby, 1982; Fifty Plus Lifeguide, 1982; Your Growing Child, 1983; Baby Care Book, 1983; Pregnancy and Birth Book, 1984; Baby and Child Medical Handbook, 1986; Everygirl's Lifeguide, 1987; Feeding Your Family, 1987; Miriam Stoppard's Health and Beauty Book, 1988; Every Woman's Medical Handbook, 1988; Lose 7 lb in 7 Days, 1990; Test Your Child, 1991; The Magic of Sex, 1991; over 40 pubns in med. jls. *Recreations*: my family, gardening. *Address*: Iver Grove, Iver, Bucks.

STOPPARD, Tom, CBE 1978; FRSL; playwright and novelist; *b* 3 July 1937; *yr s* of late Eugene Straussler and of Mrs Martha Stoppard; *m* 1st, 1965, Jose (marr. diss. 1972), *yr d* of John and Alice Ingle; two *s*; 2nd, 1972, Dr Miriam Moore-Robinson (*see* Miriam Stoppard); two *s*. *Educ*: abroad; Dolphin Sch., Notts; Pocklington, Yorks. Journalist: Western Daily Press, Bristol, 1954–58; Bristol Evening World, 1958–60; freelance, 1960–63. Mem., Royal Nat. Theatre Bd, 1989–. Hon. degrees: Bristol, 1976; Brunel, 1979; Leeds, 1980; Sussex, 1980; London, 1982; Kenyon Coll., 1984; York, 1984. Shakespeare Prize, 1979. *Plays*: Enter a Free Man, London, 1968 (TV play, A Walk on the Water, 1963); Rosencrantz and Guildenstern are Dead, Nat. Theatre, 1967, subseq. NY, etc (Tony Award, NY, 1968; NY Drama Critics Circle Award, 1968); The Real Inspector Hound, London, 1968; After Magritte, Ambiance Theatre, 1970; Dogg's Our Pet, Ambiance Theatre, 1972; Jumpers, National Theatre, 1972 (Evening Standard Award); Travesties, Aldwych, 1974 (Evening Standard Award; Tony Award, NY, 1976); Dirty Linen, Newfoundland, Ambiance Theatre, 1976; Every Good Boy Deserves Favour (music-theatre), 1977; Night and Day, Phoenix, 1978 (Evening Standard Award); Dogg's Hamlet and Cahoot's Macbeth, Collegiate, 1979; Undiscovered Country (adaptation), NT, 1979; On the Razzle, NT, 1981; The Real Thing, Strand, 1982 (Standard Award), subseq. NY (Tony Award, 1984); Rough Crossing (adaptation), NT, 1984; Dalliance (adaptation), NT, 1986; Hapgood, Aldwych, 1988; *radio*: The Dissolution of Dominic Boot, 1964; M is for Moon Among Other Things, 1964; If You're Glad I'll Be Frank, 1965; Albert's Bridge, 1967 (Prix Italia); Where Are They Now?, 1970; Artist Descending a Staircase, 1972; The Dog it was That Died, 1982 (Giles Cooper Award; televised 1988); In the Native State, 1991; *television*: A Separate Peace, 1966; Teeth, 1967;

Another Moon Called Earth, 1967; Neutral Ground, 1968; (with Clive Exton) Boundaries, 1975; (adapted) Three Men in a Boat, 1976; Professional Foul, 1977; Squaring the Circle, 1984; *screenplays*: (with T. Wiseman) The Romantic Englishwoman, 1975; Despair, 1978; The Human Factor, 1979; (with Terry Gilliam and Charles McKeown) Brazil, 1985; Empire of the Sun, 1987; Rosencrantz and Guildenstern are Dead, 1990 (also dir); The Russian House, 1991; Billy Bathgate, 1991. John Whiting Award, Arts Council, 1967; Evening Standard Award for Most Promising Playwright, 1968. *Publications*: (short stories) Introduction 2, 1964; (novel) Lord Malquist and Mr Moon, 1965; *plays*: Rosencrantz and Guildenstern are Dead, 1967; The Real Inspector Hound, 1968; Albert's Bridge, 1968; Enter a Free Man, 1968; After Magritte, 1971; Jumpers, 1972; Artists Descending a Staircase, and, Where Are They Now?, 1973; Travesties, 1975; Dirty Linen, and New-Found-Land, 1976; Every Good Boy Deserves Favour, 1978; Professional Foul, 1978; Night and Day, 1978; Undiscovered Country, 1980; Dogg's Hamlet, Cahoot's Macbeth, 1980; On the Razzle, 1982; The Real Thing, 1983; The Dog it was that Died, 1983; Squaring the Circle, 1984; Four plays for radio, 1984; Rough Crossing, 1985; Dalliance and Undiscovered Country, 1986; (trans.) Largo Desolato, by Vaclav Havel, 1987; Hapgood, 1988; In the Native State, 1991. *Address*: c/o Peters, Fraser & Dunlop, The Chambers, Chelsea Harbour, Lots Road, SW10 0XF.

STOPS; *see* Jackson-Stops.

STORAR, John Robert Allan Montague, CA; Chairman, Mitchell Cotts PLC, 1985–87 (Director, 1973–87; Deputy Chairman, 1978); *b* 6 Nov. 1925; *s* of James and Leonore Storar; *m* 1952, Catherine Swanson Henderson; two *s* one *d*. *Educ*: Dollar Academy. Dir 1960–74, Dep. Chief Exec. 1972–74, Drayton Corporation Ltd; Dir 1974–85, Dep. Chm. 1974–81, Man. Dir 1981–82, Samuel Montagu & Co. Ltd; Dir, Consolidated Gold Fields PLC, 1969–89. Chm., Assoc. of Investment Trust Cos, 1979–81. *Recreation*: fly fishing. *Address*: 3 Parkside Avenue, Wimbledon, SW19 5ES. *Club*: Caledonian.
See also L. E. T. Storar.

STORAR, Leonore Elizabeth Therese; retired; *b* 3 May 1920. Served HM Forces, 1942–46. Min. of Labour, 1941; Min. of Works, 1947; joined CRO, 1948; First Sec., Delhi and Calcutta, 1951–53; Salisbury, 1956–58; Colombo, 1960–62; Counsellor, 1963; Head of General and Migration Dept, CRO, 1962; Dep. Consul-Gen., NY, 1967; Consul-Gen., Boston, 1969; Head of Commonwealth Co-ordination Dept, FCO, 1971–75; Dir, Colombo Plan Bureau, Colombo, Sri Lanka, 1976–78. *Address*: Lavender Cottage, Dippenhall Street, Crondall, Farnham, Surrey GU10 5PF.
See also J. R. A. M. Storar.

STORER, David George; Under Secretary, Department of Social Security (formerly of Health and Social Security), 1984–89; *b* 27 June 1929; *s* of Herbert Edwards Storer; *m* 1960, Jean Mary Isobel Jenkin; one *s* two *d*. *Educ*: Monmouth School; St John's Coll., Cambridge (MA). Assistant Principal, Min. of Labour, 1952; Principal, 1957; Cabinet Office, 1963–66; Asst Secretary, Dept of Employment, 1966–73; Director, Training Opportunities Scheme, 1973–77; Dir of Corporate Services, MSC, 1977–84. *Recreations*: reading, walking. *Address*: Barclays Bank, 27 Regent Street, SW1.

STORER, James Donald, CEng, MRAeS; author and museum consultant; Keeper, Department of Science, Technology and Working Life, Royal Museum of Scotland, Edinburgh, 1985–88; *b* 11 Jan. 1928; *s* of James Arthur Storer and Elizabeth May Gartshore (*née* Pirie); *m* 1955, Shirley Anne (*née* Kent); one *s* one *d*. *Educ*: Hemsworth Grammar Sch., Yorks; Imperial Coll., London (BSc Hons, ACGI). Design Office, Vickers Armstrongs (Aircraft) Ltd, and British Aircraft Corporation, Weybridge, 1948–66; Dept of Technology, Royal Scottish Museum, 1966–85. MRAeS (AFRAeS 1958). *Publications*: Steel and Engineering, 1959; Behind the Scenes in an Aircraft Factory, 1965; It's Made Like This: Cars, 1967; The World We Are Making: Aviation, 1968; A Simple History of the Steam Engine, 1969; How to Run An Airport, 1971; How We Find Out About Flight, 1973; Flying Feats, 1977; Book of the Air, 1979; Great Inventions, 1980; (jtly) Encyclopedia of Transport, 1983; (jtly) East Fortune: Museum of Flight and history of the airfield, 1983; The Silver Burdett Encyclopedia of Transport: Air, 1984; Ship Models in the Royal Scottish Museum, 1986; The Conservation of Industrial Collections, 1989. *Recreations*: aircraft preservation, industrial archaeology, gardening. *Address*: Stonewharf, 2 Dale Road, Coalbrookdale, Telford, Shropshire TF8 7DT. *T*: Ironbridge (0952) 433534.

STORER, Prof. Roy; Professor of Prosthodontics since 1968 and Dean of Dentistry since 1977 (Clinical Sub-Dean, 1970–77) The Dental School, University of Newcastle upon Tyne; *b* 21 Feb. 1928; *s* of late Harry and Jessie Storer; *m* 1953, Kathleen Mary Frances Pitman; one *s* two *d*. *Educ*: Wallasey Grammar Sch.; Univ. of Liverpool. LDS (Liverpool) 1950; FDSRCS 1954; MSc (Liverpool) 1960; DRD RCS Ed, 1978. House Surg., 1950, and Registrar, 1952–54, United Liverpool Hosps; Lieut (later Captain) Royal Army Dental Corps, 1950–52; Lectr in Dental Prosthetics, Univ. of Liverpool, 1954–61; Visiting Associate Prof., Northwestern Univ., Chicago, 1961–62; Sen. Lectr in Dental Prosthetics, Univ. of Liverpool, 1962–67; Hon. Cons. Dental Surgeon: United Liverpool Hosps, 1962–67; United Newcastle Hosps (now Newcastle Health Authority), 1968–. Mem. Council and Sec., British Soc. for the Study of Prosthetic Dentistry, 1960–69 (Pres., 1968–69); Member: GDC, 1977–; Bd of Faculty, RCS, 1982–90 (Chm. Educn Cttee, 1986–91); Dental Sub-Cttee, UGC, 1982–89; EC Dental Cttee for trng of dental practitioners, 1986–; Med. Cttee, UFC, 1989–. Pres., Med. Rugby Football Club (Newcastle), 1968–82; Mem., Northern Sports Council, 1973–88; Chm., Div. of Dentistry, Newcastle Univ. Hosps, 1972–75. External Examiner in Dental Subjects: Univs of Belfast, Birmingham, Bristol, Dublin, Dundee, Leeds, London, Newcastle upon Tyne, and Royal Coll. of Surgeons of England. *Publications*: A Laboratory Course in Dental Materials for Dental Hygienists (with D. C. Smith), 1963; Immediate and Replacement Dentures (with J. N. Anderson), 3rd edn, 1981; papers on sci. and clin. subjects in dental and med. jls. *Recreations*: Rugby football, cricket, gardening. *Address*: The Dental School, Framlington Place, Newcastle upon Tyne NE2 4BW; 164 Eastern Way, Darras Hall, Ponteland, Newcastle upon Tyne NE20 9RH. *T*: Ponteland 23286. *Clubs*: Athenæum, MCC, East India.

STOREY, Christopher, MA, PhD; Headmaster, Culford School, Bury St Edmunds, 1951–71; *b* 23 July 1908; *s* of William Storey and Margaret T. B. Cowan, Newcastle upon Tyne; *m* 1937, Gertrude Appleby, Scarborough; four *s*. *Educ*: Rutherford Coll., Newcastle upon Tyne; King's Coll., Univ. of Durham (BA Hons French, cl. I); Univ. of Strasbourg (PhD). Modern Languages Master, Mundella Sch., Nottingham, 1931–34; French Master: Scarborough High Sch. for Boys, 1934–36; City of London Sch., 1936–42. Headmaster, Johnston Grammar Sch., Durham, 1942–51. Officier d'Académie, 1947. *Publications*: Etude critique de la Vie de St Alexis, 1934; Apprenons le mot juste!, 1939; (ed) La Vie de St Alexis, 1946, 2nd rev. edn, 1968; Sprechen und Schreiben (with C. E. Bond), 1950; A Guide to Alexis Studies, 1987; articles in Modern Language Review, French Studies, and Medium Aevum. *Address*: 13 The Paddox, Oxford OX2 7PN. *T*: Oxford (0865) 52328.

STOREY, David Malcolm; writer and dramatist; *b* 13 July 1933; *s* of Frank Richmond Storey and Lily (*née* Cartwright); *m* 1956, Barbara Rudd Hamilton; two *s* two *d*. *Educ*: Queen Elizabeth Grammar Sch., Wakefield, Yorks; Slade School of Fine Art, London; Fellow, UCL, 1974. *Plays*: The Restoration of Arnold Middleton, 1967 (Evening Standard Award); In Celebration, 1969 (Los Angeles Critics' Award); The Contractor, 1969 (Writer of the Year Award, Variety Club of GB, NY Critics' Award) (televised, 1989); Home, 1970 (Evening Standard Award, Critics' Award, NY); The Changing Room, 1971 (Critics' Award, NY); Cromwell, 1973; The Farm, 1973; Life Class, 1974; Mother's Day, 1976; Sisters, 1978; Early Days, 1980; The March on Russia, 1989. *Publications*: This Sporting Life, 1960 (Macmillan Fiction Award, US); Flight into Camden, 1960 (John Llewellyn Meml Prize, Somerset Maugham award); Radcliffe, 1963; Pasmore, 1972 (Geoffrey Faber Meml Prize, 1973); A Temporary Life, 1973; Edward, 1973; Saville, 1976 (Booker Prize, 1976); A Prodigal Child, 1982; Present Times, 1984. *Address*: c/o Jonathan Cape Ltd, Random Century House, 20 Vauxhall Bridge Road, SW1V 2SA.

STOREY, Graham; Emeritus Reader in English, and Emeritus Fellow of Trinity Hall, Cambridge University, since 1988; *b* 8 Nov. 1920; *o surv. s* of late Stanley Runton Storey, LDS RCS and Winifred Storey (*née* Graham). *Educ*: St Edward's Sch., Oxford; Trinity Hall, Cambridge (MA 1944). Served War, RA, 1941–45; Lieut 1942; mentioned in despatches. Called to the Bar, Middle Temple, 1950, but did not practise. Cambridge University: Fellow, 1949–88, Sen. Tutor, 1958–68, Vice-Master, 1970–74, Trinity Hall; Univ. Lectr in English, 1965–81; Reader, 1981–88; Chm., Faculty Bd of English, 1972–74. Vis. Fellow, All Souls Coll., Oxford, 1968. Leverhulme Emeritus Res. Fellowship, 1988. Warton Lectr, British Acad., 1984; Lecture tours for British Council overseas. Syndic, CUP, 1983. Vice-Pres., G. M. Hopkins Soc., 1971; Pres., Dickens Soc. of America, 1983–84. Governor: St Edward's, Oxford, 1959–69; Eastbourne Coll., 1965–69. Jt Gen. Editor, Letters of Dickens, Pilgrim edn, 1965–; General Editor: Cambridge Renaissance and Restoration Dramatists, 1975–89; Cambridge English Prose Texts, 1980–. *Publications*: Reuters' Century, 1951; Journals and Papers of G. M. Hopkins, 1959 (completed edn on death of Humphry House); (ed) A. P. Rossiter, Angel with Horns, 1961; (ed) Selected Verse and Prose of G. M. Hopkins, 1966; Letters of Charles Dickens, vol. I, 1965, vol. II, 1969, vol. III, 1974, vol. V, 1981, vol. VI, 1988 (ed jtly); A Preface to Hopkins, 1981; (ed with Howard Erskine-Hill) Revolutionary Prose of the English Civil War, 1983; Bleak House (critical study), 1987; contributions to: New Cambridge Bibliography, 1967; Writers and their Work, 1982; Dickens and Other Victorians, 1988; periodicals. *Recreations*: theatre, gardening, travel, tennis. *Address*: Trinity Hall, Cambridge. *T*: Cambridge (0223) 332500; Crown House, Caxton, Cambs. *T*: Caxton (0954) 719316.

STOREY, Maude, CBE 1987; President, Royal College of Nursing, 1986–90; *b* 24 March 1930; *d* of late Henry Storey and of Sarah Farrimond Storey. *Educ*: Wigan and District Mining and Techn. Coll.; St Mary's Hosp., Manchester; Lancaster Royal Infirmary; Paddington Gen. Hosp.; Royal Coll. of Nursing, Edinburgh; Queen Elizabeth Coll., London. SRN 1952; SCM 1953; RCI (Edin.) 1962; RNT 1965. Domiciliary Midwife, Wigan County Borough, 1953–56; Midwifery Sister, St Mary's Hosp., Manchester, 1956–57; Charge Nurse, Intensive Therapy, Mayo Clinic, USA, 1957–59; Theatre Sister, Clinical Instructor, 1959–63, subseq. Nurse Tutor, 1965–68, Royal Albert Edward Infirmary, Wigan; Lectr in Community Nursing, Manchester Univ., 1968–71; Asst, subseq. Principal Regional Nursing Officer, Liverpool Regional Hosp. Bd, 1971–73; Regional Nursing Officer, Mersey RHA, 1973–77; Registrar, GNC for England and Wales, 1977–81; Registrar and Chief Exec., UKCC, 1981–87. Member: Standing Nursing and Midwifery Adv. Cttee, 1977–90; West Berks HA, 1982–. Mem. Council, Reading Univ., 1988–. CStJ 1987. *Recreations*: travel, theatre, amateur dramatics. *Address*: 14 Conifer Drive, Long Lane, Tilehurst, Berks. *T*: Reading (0734) 412082.

STOREY, Hon. Sir Richard, 2nd Bt *cr* 1960; Chairman of Portsmouth and Sunderland Newspapers plc, since 1973 (Director, since 1962); *b* 23 Jan. 1937; *s* of Baron Buckton (Life Peer) and Elisabeth (*d* 1951), *d* of late Brig.-Gen. W. J. Woodcock, DSO; *S* to baronetcy of father, 1978; *m* 1961, Virginia Anne, 3rd *d* of Sir Kenelm Cayley, 10th Bt; one *s* two *d*. *Educ*: Winchester; Trinity Coll., Cambridge (BA, LLB). National service commission, RNVR, 1956. Called to the Bar, Inner Temple, 1962. Director: Reuters Hldgs PLC, 1986–; Press Association Ltd, 1986– (Vice Chm., 1989–); Fleming Enterprise Investment Trust PLC, 1989–. Member: Nat. Council and Exec., CLA, 1980–84, Yorks Exec., CLA (Chm., 1974–76); Employment Policy Cttee, CBI, 1984–88, CBI Regl Council, Yorks and Humberside, 1974–76; Press Council, 1980–86; Pres., Newspaper Soc., 1990– (Mem. Council, 1980–). Chm., Hillier Arboretum Management Cttee, 1989–. Mem. Council, INCA-FIEJ Res. Assoc., 1983–88. Contested (C): Don Valley, 1966; Huddersfield W, 1970. *Recreations*: sport and silviculture, farms and administers land in Yorkshire. *Heir*: *s* Kenelm Storey, *b* 4 Jan. 1963. *Address*: Settrington House, Malton, Yorks YO17 8NP. *T*: North Grimston (09446) 200; 7 Douro Place, W8 5PH. *T*: 071–937 8823.

STORIE-PUGH, Col Peter David, CBE 1981 (MBE 1945); MC 1940; TD 1945 and 3 clasps; DL; Lecturer, University of Cambridge, 1953–82; Fellow of Wolfson College, Cambridge, since 1967; *b* 1 Nov. 1919; *s* of late Prof. Leslie Pugh, CBE, FRCVS and Paula Storie; *m* 1st, 1946, Alison (marr. diss. 1971), *d* of late Sir Oliver Lyle, OBE; one *s* two *d*; 2nd, 1971, Leslie Helen, *d* of Earl Striegel; three *s* one *d*. *Educ*: Malvern; Queens' Coll., Cambridge (Hon. Foundn Scholar; MA, PhD); Royal Veterinary Coll., Univ. of London(FRCVS). CChem, FRSC. Served War of 1939–45, Queen's Own Royal W Kent Regt (escaped from Spangenberg and Colditz); comd 1st Bn, Cambs Regt, comd 1st Bn Suffolk and Cambs Regt; Col, Dep. Comdr, 161 Inf. Bde, ACF County Comdt. Wellcome Res. Fellow, Cambridge, 1950–52. Mem. Council, RCVS, 1956–84 (Chm. Parly Cttee, 1962–67; Pres., 1977–78); President: Cambridge Soc. for Study of Comparative Medicine, 1966–67; Internat. Pig Vet. Soc., 1967–69 (Life Pres., 1969); British Veterinary Assoc., 1968–69 and 1970–71 (Hon. Life Mem., 1984; Dalrymple-Champneys Cup and Medal, 1986); Mem. Exec. Cttee, Cambridgeshire Farmers Union, 1960–65; UK delegate, EEC Vet. Liaison Cttee, 1962–75 (Pres., 1973–75); UK Rep., Fedn of Veterinarians of EEC, 1975–83 (Pres. of Fedn, 1975–79); Chm., Eurovet, 1971–73; Mem. Jt RCVS/BVA Cttee on European Vet. Affairs, 1971–; Observer, European Liaison Gp for Agric., 1972–80; Jt Pres., 1st European Vet. Congress, Wiesbaden, 1972; Permanent Mem. EEC Adv. Vet. Cttee, 1976–82; Mem. Council, Secrétariat Européen des Professions Libérales, 1976–80; Mem. Permanent Cttee, World Vet. Assoc., 1964–75. Member: Parly and Sci. Cttee, 1962–67; Home Sec.'s Adv. Cttee (Cruelty to Animals Act, 1876), 1963–80; Nat. Agric. Centre Adv. Bd, 1966–69; Production Cttee, Meat and Livestock Commn, 1967–70; Min. of Agriculture's Farm Animal Adv. Cttee, 1970–73; Econ. and Social Cttee, EEC, 1982–90. Chm., Nat. Sheep Breeders' Assoc., 1964–68; Vice-Pres., Agric. Section, British Assoc., 1970–71. Corresp. Mem., Bund Deutscher Veterinäroffiziere, 1979–. Robert von Ostertag Medal, German Vet. Assoc., 1972. DL Cambs, 1963. *Publications*: (and ed jtly) Eurovet: an Anatomy of Veterinary Europe, 1972; Eurovet-2, 1975. *Address*: Duxford Grange, Duxford, Cambridge CB2 4QF. *T*: Fowlmere (076382) 403. *Club*: United Oxford & Cambridge University.

STORMONT, Viscount; Alexander David Mungo Murray; *b* 17 Oct. 1956; *s* and *heir* of 8th Earl of Mansfield and Mansfield, *qv*; *m* 1985, Sophia Mary Veronica, *o d* of Biden Ashbrooke, St John, Jersey; one *s* one *d*. *Educ*: Eton. *Heir*: *s* Master of Stormont, *qv*. *Address*: Scone Palace, Perthshire PH2 6BE.

STORMONT, Master of; Hon. William Philip David Mungo Murray; *b* 1 Nov. 1988; *s* and *heir* of Viscount Stormont, *qv*.

STORMONTH DARLING, Sir James Carlisle, (Sir Jamie Stormonth Darling), Kt 1983; CBE 1972; MC 1945; TD; WS; Director, 1971–83, Vice-President Emeritus, since 1986, The National Trust for Scotland (Secretary, as Chief Executive, 1949–71); *b* 18 July 1918; *s* of late Robert Stormonth Darling, Writer to the Signet, Rosebank, Kelso, Roxburghshire, and late Beryl Madeleine Sayer, Battle, Sussex; *m* 1948, Mary Finella, BEM 1945, DL, *d* of late Lt-Gen. Sir James Gammell, KCB, DSO, MC; one *s* two *d*. *Educ:* Winchester Coll.; Christ Church, Oxford; BA 1939, MA 1972; Edinburgh Univ.; LLB 1949. 2nd Lt KOSB (TA), 1938; War Service, 1939–46, in KOSB and 52nd (L) Reconnaissance Regt, RAC, of which Lt-Col comdg in 1945 (TD). Admitted Writer to the Signet, 1949. Member, Queen's Body Guard for Scotland (Royal Company of Archers), 1958–. Mem., Ancient Monuments Bd for Scotland, 1983–. Dir, Scottish Widows Fund and Life Assce Soc., 1981–89. Vice-President: Scotland's Gardens Scheme, 1983–; Scottish Conservation Projects Trust, 1989– (Pres., 1984–89); Trustee: Scottish Churches Architectural Heritage Trust, 1983–; Edinburgh Old Town Trust, 1990– (Chm., 1985–90); Edinburgh Old Town Charitable Trust, 1990– (Chm., 1985–90). Hon. FRIAS 1982. DUniv Stirling, 1983; Hon. LLD Aberdeen, 1984. *Address:* Chapelhill House, Dirleton, East Lothian. *T:* Dirleton (062085) 296. *Clubs:* New, Hon. Co. of Edinburgh Golfers (Edinburgh).

STORMONTH DARLING, Peter; Chairman, Mercury Asset Management Group plc (formerly Warburg Investment Management Ltd), since 1979; *b* 29 Sept. 1932; *s* of Patrick Stormonth Darling and Edith Mary Ormston Lamb; *m* 1st, 1958, Candis Hitzig; three *d*: 2nd, 1970, Maureen O'Leary. *Educ:* Winchester; New Coll., Oxford (MA). 2nd Lieut, Black Watch, 1950–53, served Korean War; RAFVR, 1953–56. Director: S. G. Warburg & Co. Ltd, 1967–85 (Vice-Chm., 1977–85); S. G. Warburg Group plc, 1974; Orion Insurance, 1987–; Europe Fund, 1990–. Mem., UN Pension Fund Investments Cttee. *Address:* 33 King William Street, EC4R 9AS.

See also R. A. Stormonth-Darling.

STORMONTH-DARLING, Robin Andrew; Chairman, Tranwood (formerly Tranwood Group) Plc, since 1987; *b* 1 Oct. 1926; *s* of Patrick Stormonth-Darling and Edith Mary Ormston Lamb; *m* 1st, 1956, Susan Marion Clifford-Turner (marr. diss. 1970); three *s* one *d*; 2nd, 1974, Harriet Heathcoat-Amory (*née* Nye) (marr. diss. 1978); 3rd, 1981, Carola Marion Brooke, *er d* of Sir Robert Erskine-Hill, 2nd Bt. *Educ:* Abberley Hall; Winchester Coll. Served Fleet Air Arm (Pilot), 1945; 9th Queen's Royal Lancers, 1946–54: ADC to GOC-in-C Scotland, 1950–52; Officer Cadet Instr, 1952–54. Alexanders Laing & Cruickshank (formerly Laing & Cruickshank), 1954–87, Chm., 1980–87; Director: Austin Motor Co., 1959; British Motor Corp., 1960–68; British Leyland, 1968–75. Director: London Scottish Bank (formerly London Scottish Finance Corp.), 1984–; Mercantile House Holdings, 1984–87 (non-exec. Dep. Chm., 1987); GPI Leisure Corp. (Australia). Stock Exchange: Mem., 1956–87; Mem. Council, 1978–86; Chairman: Quotations Cttee, 1981–85; Disciplinary Appeals Cttee, 1985–. Dep. Chm., Panel on Take-Overs and Mergers, 1985–87; Mem., Securities and Investments Bd, 1985–87. *Recreations:* shooting, ski-ing, flying, swimming. *Address:* Balvarran, Enochdhu, Blairgowrie, Perthshire PH10 7PA. *T:* Strathardle (025081) 248; 21 Paradise Walk, SW3. *T:* 071–352 4161. *Clubs:* White's, City of London, MCC, Hurlingham; Perth Hunt.

See also P. M. Stormonth Darling.

STORR, (Charles) Anthony, FRCP, FRCPsych; FRSL; writer and psychiatrist; Clinical Lecturer in Psychiatry, Faculty of Medicine, University of Oxford, 1974–84; Fellow, Green College, Oxford, 1979–84, now Emeritus; Hon. Consulting Psychiatrist, Oxford Health Authority, since 1986; *b* 18 May 1920; *y s* of Vernon Faithfull Storr, Subdean of Westminster and Katherine Cecilia Storr; *m* 1st, 1942, Catherine Cole; three *d*; 2nd, 1970, Catherine Barton (*née* Peters). *Educ:* Winchester Coll.; Christ's Coll., Cambridge; Westminster Hosp. Medical School. MB, BChir Cantab. FRSL 1990. Qual. in medicine, 1944; postgrad. trng in psychiatry, Maudsley Hosp., 1947–50; held various positions as psychiatrist in different hospitals; Consltnt Psychotherapist, Oxford AHA, 1974–84. Member: Parole Bd, 1976–77; Cttee on Obscenity and Film Censorship, 1977–79. *Publications:* The Integrity of the Personality, 1960; Sexual Deviation, 1964; Human Aggression, 1968; Human Destructiveness, 1972; The Dynamics of Creation, 1972; Jung, 1973; The Art of Psychotherapy, 1979; (ed) Jung: selected writings, 1983; Solitude, 1988; Freud, 1989; Churchill's Black Dog and Other Phenomena of the Human Mind, 1989; contrib. several books and jls. *Recreations:* music, broadcasting, journalism. *Address:* 45 Chalfont Road, Oxford OX2 6TJ. *T:* Oxford (0865) 53348. *Club:* Savile.

STOTT, Rt. Hon. Lord; George Gordon Stott, PC 1964; Senator of College of Justice in Scotland, 1967–84; *b* 22 Dec. 1909; *s* of Rev. Dr G. Gordon Stott; *m* 1947, Nancy, *d* of A. D. Braggins; one *s* one *d*. *Educ:* Cramond Sch.; Edinburgh Acad.; Edinburgh Univ. Advocate 1936; QC (Scotland) 1950; Advocate-Depute, 1947–51; Editor, Edinburgh Clarion, 1939–44; Member, Monopolies Commission, 1949–56; Sheriff of Roxburgh, Berwick and Selkirk, 1961–64; Lord Advocate, 1964–67. *Address:* 12 Midmar Gardens, Edinburgh. *T:* 031–447 4251.

STOTT, Sir Adrian (George Ellingham), 4th Bt *cr* 1920; management consultant, since 1989; *b* 7 Oct. 1948; *s* of Sir Philip Sidney Stott, 3rd Bt, and of Cicely Florence, *o d* of Bertram Ellingham; *S* father, 1979. *Educ:* Univ. of British Columbia (BSc (Maths) 1968, MSc (Town Planning) 1974); Univ. of Waterloo, Ont (MMaths (Computer Science) 1971). Dir of Planning for a rural region of BC, 1974; formed own consulting practice, 1977; property develt, gen. management and town planning consultant, 1977–85; Manager: BC Govt Real Estate Portfolio, 1980; Islands Trust (coastal conservation and property develt control agency), 1985; Man. Dir, direct sales marketing company, 1986–88. Member: Cdn Inst. of Planners (MCIP); Assoc. for Computing Machinery; MENSA. *Recreations:* music, inland waterways, computers, politics. *Heir:* *b* Vyvyan Philip Stott, *b* 5 Aug. 1952. *Address:* 1566 Admiral Tryon Boulevard, Parksville, BC V9P 1Y3, Canada. *T:* (604) 752–5774.

STOTT, (Charlotte) Mary, OBE 1975; journalist, retired; *b* 1907; *d* of Robert Guy Waddington and Amalie Waddington (*née* Bates); *m* 1937, Kenneth Stott (*d* 1967); one *d*. *Educ:* Wyggeston Grammar Sch., Leicester. Leicester Mail, 1925–31; Bolton Evening News, 1931–33; Co-operative Press, Manchester, editing women's and children's publications, 1933–45; News sub-editor, Manchester Evening News, 1945–50; Women's Editor, The Guardian, 1957–72. Last Pres., Women's Press Club, 1970; Chm., Fawcett Soc., 1980–82; Trustee, Nat. Assoc. of Widows. Hon. Fellow, Manchester Polytechnic, 1972. Hon. MA Open, 1991. *Publications:* Forgetting's No Excuse, 1973; Organization Woman, 1978; Ageing for Beginners, 1981; Before I Go . . ., 1985; Women Talking, 1987. *Recreations:* committees, music (especially choir singing), painting (water colours), gardening. *Address:* 4/11 Morden Road, Blackheath, SE3 0AA. *T:* 081–852 2901. *Club:* University Women's.

STOTT, Rt. Hon. George Gordon; *see* Stott, Rt Hon. Lord.

STOTT, Rev. John Robert Walmsley, MA Cantab; DD Lambeth; Director, London Institute for Contemporary Christianity, 1982–86, now President; Chaplain to the Queen, 1959–91, Extra Chaplain, since 1991; *b* 27 April 1921; *s* of late Sir Arnold W. Stott, KBE, physician, and late Emily Caroline Holland. *Educ:* Rugby Sch.; Trinity Coll., Cambridge; Ridley Hall, Cambridge. Curate of All Souls, Langham Place, 1945; Rector of All Souls, 1950–75 (with St Peter's, Vere Street, 1952), now Rector Emeritus. Hon. DD, Trinity Evangelical Divinity Sch., Deerfield, USA, 1971. *Publications:* Men with a Message, 1954; What Christ Thinks of the Church, 1958; Basic Christianity, 1958; Your Confirmation, 1958; Fundamentalism and Evangelism, 1959; The Preacher's Portrait, 1961; Confess Your Sins, 1964; The Epistles of John, 1964; Canticles and Selected Psalms, 1966; Men Made New, 1966; Our Guilty Silence, 1967; The Message of Galatians, 1968; One People, 1969; Christ the Controversialist, 1970; Understanding the Bible, 1972; Guard the Gospel, 1973; Balanced Christianity, 1975; Christian Mission in the Modern World, 1975; Baptism and Fullness, 1975; The Lausanne Covenant, 1975; Christian Counter-Culture, 1978; Focus on Christ, 1979, rev. edn as Life in Christ, 1991; God's New Society, 1979; I Believe in Preaching, 1982; The Bible Book for Today, 1982; Issues Facing Christians Today, 1984; The Authentic Jesus, 1985; The Cross of Christ, 1986; Essentials, 1988; The Message of Acts, 1990; The Message of I and II Thessalonians, 1991. *Recreations:* bird watching, photography. *Address:* 13 Bridford Mews, Devonshire Street, W1N 1LQ.

STOTT, Mary; *see* Stott, C. M.

STOTT, Prof. Peter Frank, CBE 1978; MA, FEng, FICE, FIHT, FIEAust, FCIT; Nash Professor of Civil Engineering, King's College, London University, 1983–89, now Professor Emeritus; *b* 8 Aug. 1927; *s* of late Clarence Stott and of Mabel Sutcliffe; *m* 1953, Vera Watkins; two *s*. *Educ:* Bradford Grammar Sch.; Clare Coll., Cambridge. Partner, G. Maunsell & Partners, Consulting Engineers, 1955–63; Deputy Chief Engineer (Roads) and later Chief Engineer, London County Council, 1963–65; Dir of Highways and Transportation, GLC, 1964–67; Traffic Comr and Dir of Transportation, GLC, 1967–69; Controller of Planning and Transportation, GLC, 1969–73; Dir-Gen., Nat. Water Council, 1973–83. Sec.-Gen., Internat. Water Supply Assoc., 1980–83. President: Reinforced Concrete Assoc., 1964; Concrete Soc., 1967; Instn of Highway Engineers, 1971–72; ICE, 1989–90 (Vice-Pres., 1987–89). Chm., Quality Scheme for Ready Mixed Concrete Ltd, 1984–; Dir, Mid Kent Hldgs, 1991–. *Recreations:* fine arts, pottery. *Address:* 7 Frank Dixon Way, SE21 7BB. *T:* 081–693 5121. *Club:* Athenæum.

STOTT, Richard Keith; Editor, Daily Mirror, since 1991; *b* 17 Aug. 1943; *s* of late Fred B. Stott and of Bertha Stott; *m* 1970, Penny, *yr d* of Air Vice-Marshal Sir Colin Scragg, KBE, CB, AFC; one *s* two *d*. *Educ:* Clifton College, Bristol. Bucks Herald, 1963–65; Ferrari Press Agency, 1965–68; Daily Mirror: Reporter, 1968–79; Features Editor, 1979–81; Asst Editor, 1981; Editor: Sunday People, 1984; Daily Mirror, 1985–89; The People, 1990–91. Dir, People Publishing Co., 1990–. Reporter of the Year, British Press Awards, 1977. *Recreations:* theatre, reading. *Address:* Daily Mirror, Holborn Circus, EC1P 1DQ.

STOTT, Roger, CBE 1979; MP (Lab) Wigan, since 1983 (Westhoughton, May 1973–1983); *b* 7 Aug. 1943; *s* of Richard and Edith Stott; *m* 1st, 1969, Irene Mills (marr. diss. 1982); two *s*; 2nd, 1985, Gillian Pye, Wigan; one *s*. *Educ:* Rochdale Tech. Coll. Served in Merchant Navy, 1959–64. Post Office Telephone Engineer, 1964–73. PPS to Sec. of State for Industry, 1975–76; PPS to the Prime Minister, 1976–79, to Leader of the Opposition, 1979; opposition spokesman on transport, 1980–83, 1984–86, on trade and industry, with special responsibility for IT, 1983–89, on NI, 1989–. Mem., Select Cttee on Agriculture, 1980–. Pres., Bass Wingates Band, 1980–. *Recreations:* cricket, gardening, Rugby League. *Address:* House of Commons, SW1A 0AA; 26 Spelding Drive, Standish Lower Ground, Wigan WN6 8LW.

STOUGHTON-HARRIS, Anthony Geoffrey, CBE 1989; FCA; Deputy Chairman, Nationwide Anglia Building Society; *b* 5 June 1932; *s* of Geoffrey Stoughton-Harris and Kathleen Mary (*née* Baker Brown); *m* 1959, Elizabeth Thackery (*née* White); one *s* two *d*. *Educ:* Sherborne Sch., Dorset. FCA 1956. Partner, Norton Keen & Co., chartered accountants, 1958–74; Dir, Maidenhead & Berkshire Building Soc., subseq. re-named South of England, London & South of England, Anglia, then Nationwide Anglia Building Soc., 1967–; Man. Dir, London & South of England Building Soc., 1975; Chief Gen. Manager, Anglia Building Soc., 1983–87. Chm., Electronic Funds Transfer Ltd, 1984–89; Director: Southern Electric, 1981–; EftPos UK Ltd, 1988–89; Guardian Royal Exchange, 1990–. Gen. Comr, Inland Revenue, 1982–. Part-time Treasurer, W Herts Main Drainage Authority, 1964–70. Chairman: Metropolitan Assoc. of Building Socs, 1979–80; BSA, 1987–89; Northants TEC, 1990–. FRSA; FCBSI. *Recreations:* sport, gardening, DIY. *Address:* Old Farm House, Blackmile Lane, Grendon, Northants NN7 1JR. *T:* Wellingborough (0933) 664235.

STOURTON, family name of **Baron Mowbray, Segrave and Stourton.**

STOURTON, Hon. John Joseph, TD; *b* 5 March 1899; *yr s* of 24th Lord Mowbray; *m* 1st, 1923, Kathleen Alice (marr. diss. 1933; she *d* 1986), *d* of late Robert Louis George Gunther, of 8 Princes Gardens and Park Wood, Englefield Green, Surrey; two *s* two *d*; 2nd, 1934, Gladys Leila (marr. diss. 1947), *d* of late Col Sir W. J. Waldron. *Educ:* Downside School. MP (C) South Salford, 1931–45. Sec., Cons. Foreign Affairs Cttee, 1944–45. Served N Russian Relief Force at Archangel, 1919; and in European War, 1939–43; late Lt 10th Royal Hussars; Major The Royal Norfolk Regiment. *Address:* 3 Rosebery Avenue, Hampden Park, Eastbourne, East Sussex.

See also Earl of Gainsborough, H. L. C. Greig.

STOUT, Prof. David Ker; Head of Economics, Unilever, since 1982; Visiting Professor of Economics, Leicester University, since 1982 (Professor of Economics, 1980–81); *b* Bangor, N Wales, 27 Jan. 1932; *s* of late Prof. Alan Ker Stout, FAHA, FASSA and of Evelyn Roberts; *m* 1956, Margaret Sugden; two *s* two *d*. *Educ:* Sydney High Sch.; Sydney Univ., NSW (BA 1st Cl. English Lit, Econs, and University Medal in Econs, 1953); NSW Rhodes Scholar 1954; Magdalen Coll., Oxford; George Webb Medley Jun. Scholar 1955, Sen. Scholar 1956; PPE 1st Cl. 1956; Nuffield Coll., Oxford (Studentship 1956); Magdalen Prize Fellow by Examination, 1958–59. Fellow and Lectr in Econs, University Coll., Oxford, 1959–76; Economic Dir, NEDO, 1971–72 and 1976–80. Adviser on tax structure to Syrian Govt, 1965, and New Hebrides Condominium, 1966; Sen. Econ. Adviser to Monopolies Commn, 1969; Consultant on VAT, Nat. Bureau of Econ. Res., NY, 1970; Adviser to Australian Govt on Prices Justification, 1973, and on Wage Indexation, 1975–76. Member: Management Cttee, NIESR, 1974–; EEC Expert Gp on Community Planning, 1976–78, and on Adjustment Policy, 1979–80; ESRC, 1989– (Mem., Econ. Affairs Cttee, 1980–86; Chm., Industry, Economics and Envmt Cttee); Bd of Trustees, Strategic Planning Inst., Cambridge, Mass, 1983–87. *Publications:* papers on taxation policy, VAT, investment, incomes policy, trade performance, indust. policy, de-industrialisation, and European planning. *Recreations:* music, chess, bivalves. *Address:* Unilever, PO Box 68, EC4P 4BQ. *T:* 071–822 6557.

STOUT, Samuel Coredon; HM Diplomatic Service, retired; *b* 17 Feb. 1913; *m* 1st, Mary Finn (*d* 1965); two *s* one *d*; 2nd, 1966, Jill Emery. Ministry of National Insurance, 1937–40; Admiralty, 1940–46; Board of Trade, 1946–65 (Trade Commissioner, Singapore, Bombay and Melbourne); Counsellor (Commercial), Canberra, 1966–68; Dep. High Comr and Minister (Commercial), Karachi, 1968–70; Consul-Gen., St Louis, USA, 1970–72. *Address:* 7 Horncastle Road, Woodhall Spa, Lincs LN10 6UY.

STOUT, William Ferguson, CB 1964; Security Adviser to Government of Northern Ireland, 1971–72, retired; *b* Holywood, Co. Down, 22 Feb. 1907; *s* of late Robert and Amelia Stout; *m* 1938, Muriel Kilner; one *s* one *d*. *Educ:* Sullivan Upper Sch., Holywood; Queen's Univ., Belfast. Ministry of Home Affairs: Principal, 1943; Asst Sec., 1954; Senior Asst Sec., 1959; Permanent Sec., 1961–64; Permanent Secretary: Min. of Health and Local Govt, 1964; Min. of Development, 1965–71. *Recreation:* golf.

STOUTE, Michael Ronald; race horse trainer, since 1972; *b* 22 Oct. 1945; *m* 1969, Joan Patricia Baker; one *s* one *d*. *Educ:* Harrison College, Barbados. Leading flat racing trainer, 1981 and 1986; trained: Derby winners, Shergar, 1981, Shahrastani, 1986; Irish Derby winners, Shergar, 1981, Shareef Dancer, 1983, Shahrastani, 1986; 1000 Guineas winner, Musical Bliss, 1989; Irish 1000 Guineas winner, Sonic Lady, 1986; 2000 Guineas Winners, Shadeed, 1985, Doyoun, 1988; Irish 2000 Guineas winner, Shaadi, 1989; Oaks winners, Fair Salinia, 1978, Unite, 1987; Irish Oaks winners, Fair Salinia, 1978, Colorspin, 1986, Unite, 1987, Methodist, 1988. *Recreations:* cricket, ski-ing. *Address:* Freemason Lodge, Bury Road, Newmarket, Suffolk CB8 7BT. *T:* Newmarket (0638) 663801.

STOW, Archdeacon of; *see* Wells, Ven. R. J.

STOW, Sir Christopher P.; *see* Philipson-Stow.

STOW, Sir John Montague, GCMG 1966 (KCMG 1959; CMG 1950); KCVO 1966; Governor-General of Barbados, 1966–67; retired, 1967; *b* 3 Oct. 1911; *s* of late Sir Alexander Stow, KCIE; *m* 1939, Beatrice Tryhorne; two *s*. *Educ:* Harrow School; Pembroke College, Cambridge. Administrative Officer, Nigeria, 1934; Secretariat, Gambia, 1938; Chief Sec., Windward Islands, 1944; Administrator, St Lucia, BWI, 1947; Dir of Establishments, Kenya, 1952–55; Chief Sec., Jamaica, 1955–59; Governor and C-in-C Barbados, 1959–66. With Stewart, Wrightson Ltd, 1967–77; Dir, Buckmaster Management Co. Ltd, 1981–. Chm., Commonwealth Soc. for Deaf, 1983–85. KStJ 1959. *Recreations:* cricket, tennis. *Address:* 26a Tregunter Road, SW10. *T:* 071–370 1921. *Clubs:* Caledonian, MCC.

STOW, (Julian) Randolph; writer; *b* Geraldton, W Australia, 28 Nov. 1935; *s* of Cedric Ernest Stow, barrister and Mary Stow (*née* Sewell). *Educ:* Guildford Grammar Sch., W Australia; Univ. of Western Australia. Lecturer in English Literature: Univ. of Leeds, 1962; Univ. of Western Australia, 1963–64; Harkness Fellow, United States, 1964–66; Lectr in English and Commonwealth Lit., Univ. of Leeds, 1968–69. Miles Franklin Award, 1958; Britannica Australia Award, 1966; Patrick White Award, 1979. *Publications: poems:* Outrider, 1962; A Counterfeit Silence, 1969; *novels:* To The Islands, 1958, rev. edn 1981; Tourmaline, 1963; The Merry-go-round in the Sea, 1965; Visitants, 1979; The Girl Green as Elderflower, 1980; The Suburbs of Hell, 1984; *music theatre* (with Peter Maxwell Davies): Eight Songs for a Mad King, 1969; Miss Donnithorne's Maggot, 1974; *for children:* Midnite, 1967. *Address:* c/o Richard Scott Simon Ltd, 43 Doughty Street, WC1N 2LF.

STOW, Ralph Conyers, CBE 1981; FCIS, FCBSI; President and Chairman, Cheltenham & Gloucester Building Society, 1982–87 (Managing Director, 1973–82); *b* 19 Dec. 1916; *s* of Albert Conyers Stow and Mabel Louise Bourlet; *m* 1943, Eleanor Joyce Appleby; one *s* one *d*. *Educ:* Woodhouse Sch., Finchley. FCIS 1959; FBS 1952. Supt of Branches, Temperance Permanent Bldg Soc., 1950, Asst Manager 1958; Gen. Man. and Sec., Cheltenham & Gloucester Bldg Soc., 1962, Dir 1967. Pres., Bldg Socs Inst., 1971–72; Chm., Midland Assoc. of Bldg Socs, 1973–74; Chm., Bldg Socs Assoc., 1977–79. Mem., Glos AHA, 1973–81; Chm., Cheltenham DHA, 1981–88. Mem. Council, Cheltenham Coll.; Governor, Bournside Sch., Cheltenham. *Recreations:* photography, oil painting. *Club:* Rotary (Cheltenham).

STOW, Randolph; *see* Stow, J. R.

STOW, Timothy Montague Fenwick; QC 1989; a Recorder, since 1989; *b* 31 Jan. 1943; *s* of Geoffrey Montague Fenwick Stow and Joan Fortescue Stow (*née* Flannery); *m* 1965, Alisoun Mary Francis Homberger; one *s* one *d*. *Educ:* Eton Coll. Called to the Bar, Gray's Inn, 1965; became a tenant in common law chambers of David Croom-Johnson, QC (later Lord Justice Croom-Johnson), 1966. *Recreations:* swimming, squash, tennis, foreign travel, music, looking after their country property. *Address:* 12 King's Bench Walk, Temple, EC4Y 7EL. *T:* 071–583 0811.

STOWE, Sir Kenneth (Ronald), GCB 1986 (KCB 1980; CB 1977); CVO 1979; Chairman, Institute of Cancer Research, since 1987; *b* 17 July 1927; *er s* of Arthur and Emily Stowe; *m* 1949, Joan Frances Cullen; two *s* one *d*. *Educ:* County High Sch., Dagenham; Exeter Coll., Oxford (MA; Hon. Fellow, 1989). Asst Principal, Nat. Assistance Board, 1951; Principal, 1956; seconded UN Secretariat, New York, 1958; Asst Sec., 1964; Asst Under-Sec. of State, DHSS, 1970–73; Under Sec., Cabinet Office, 1973–75, Dep. Sec., 1976; Principal Private Sec. to the Prime Minister, 1975–79; Permanent Under Sec. of State, NI Office, 1979–81; Perm. Sec., DHSS, 1981–87. Dep. Chm., English Estates Corp., 1990–. Mem., President's Commn to review Public Service of Zimbabwe, 1987–89. Life Trustee, Carnegie UK Trust, 1988–. *Recreations:* opera, theatre, hill walking. *Club:* Athenæum.

STOWELL, Dr Michael James, FRS 1984; Research Director, Alcan International Ltd, since 1990 (Principal Consulting Scientist, 1989–90); *b* 10 July 1935; *s* of Albert James Stowell and Kathleen Maude (*née* Poole); *m* 1962, Rosemary Allen (marr. diss. 1990); one *s* one *d*. *Educ:* St Julian's High Sch., Newport; Bristol Univ. (BSc 1957, PhD 1961). Res. Scientist and Gp Leader, Tube Investments Research Labs, 1960–78; Research Manager, Materials Dept, TI Research, 1978–88. Post-doctoral Res. Fellow, Ohio State Univ., 1962–63; Res. Fellow, Univ. of Minnesota, 1970. L. B. Pfeil Medal, Metals Soc., 1976; Sir Robert Hadfield Medal, Metals Soc., 1981. *Publications:* papers on electron microscopy, epitaxy, nucleation theory, superplasticity and physical metallurgy, in various jls. *Recreation:* music. *Address:* Alcan International Ltd, Banbury Laboratories, Banbury, Oxon OX16 7SP. *T:* Banbury (0295) 274419.

STOY, Prof. Philip Joseph; Professor of Dentistry, Queen's University of Belfast, 1948–73, now Professor Emeritus; *b* 19 Jan. 1906; *m* 1945, Isabella Mary Beatrice Crispin; two *s*. *Educ:* Wolverhampton School. Queen's Scholar, Birmingham Univ., 1929; LDS, RCS, 1931; BDS (Hons), Birmingham 1932; FDS, RCS, 1947; Fellow of the Faculty of Dentistry, RCSI, 1963 (FFDRCSI). Lectr in Dental Mechanics, Univ. of Bristol, 1934; Lectr in Dental Surgery, Univ. of Bristol, 1940. Hon. MD QUB, 1987. *Publications:* articles in British Dental Journal, Dental Record. *Recreations:* reading, painting, dental history, chess. *Address:* Westward Ho!, 57 Imperial Road, Exmouth, Devon EX8 1DQ. *T:* Exmouth (0395) 265113.

STOYLE, Roger John B.; *see* Blin-Stoyle.

STRABOLGI, 11th Baron of England, *cr* 1318; **David Montague de Burgh Kenworthy;** a Deputy Speaker and Deputy Chairman of Committees, House of Lords, since 1986; *b* 1 Nov. 1914; *e s* of 10th Baron Strabolgi and Doris Whitley (*d* 1988), *o c* of late Sir Frederick Whitley-Thomson, MP; *S* father, 1953; *m* 1961, Doreen Margaret, *e d* of late Alexander Morgan, Ashton-under-Lyne, and Emma Morgan (*née* Mellor). *Educ:* Gresham's School; Chelsea Sch. of Art; Paris. Served with HM Forces, BEF, 1939–40; MEF, 1940–45, as Lt-Col RAOC. Mem. Parly Delegations to USSR, 1954, SHAPE, 1955, and France, 1981, 1983 and 1985; PPS to Minister of State, Home Office, 1968–69; PPS to Leader of the House of Lords and Lord Privy Seal, 1969–70; Asst Opposition Whip, and spokesman on the Arts, House of Lords, 1970–74; Captain of the Yeomen of the Guard (Dep. Govt Chief Whip), and Govt spokesman on Energy and Agriculture, 1974–79; Opposition spokesman on arts and libraries, 1979–85. Member: Jt Cttee on Consolidation Bills, 1986–; Select Cttee for Privileges, 1987–; Procedure Cttee, 1987–90. A Vice-Pres., Franco-British Soc.; Member: Franco-British Parly Relations Cttee; British Sect., Franco-British Council, 1981; Council, Alliance Française in GB. Dir, Bolton Building Soc., 1958–74, 1979–87 (Dep. Chm., 1983, Chm., 1986–87). Hon. Life Mem., RPO, 1977. FIPR 1990. Freeman, City of London, 1960. Officier de la Légion d'Honneur, 1981. *Recreations:* books, music, travel. *Heir-pres:* *nephew* Andrew David Whitley Kenworthy, *b* 11 Feb. 1967. *Address:* House of Lords, SW1A 0PW. *Club:* Reform.

See also Sir Harold Hood, Bt.

STRACEY, Sir John (Simon), 9th Bt *cr* 1818; *b* 30 Nov. 1938; *s* of Captain Algernon Augustus Henry Stracey (2nd *s* of 6th Bt) (*d* 1940) and Olive Beryl (*d* 1972), *d* of late Major Charles Robert Eustace Radclyffe; *S* cousin, 1971; *m* 1968, Martha Maria, *d* of late Johann Egger; two *d*. *Heir:* *cousin* Henry Mounteney Stracey [*b* 24 April 1920; *m* 1st, 1943, Susanna, *d* of Adair Tracey; one *d*; 2nd, 1950, Lysbeth, *o d* of Charles Ashford, NZ; one *s* one *d*; 3rd, 1961, Jeltje, *y d* of Scholte de Boer]. *Address:* 32 Park Road, Southborough, near Tunbridge Wells, Kent TN4 0NX. *T:* Tunbridge Wells (0892) 20771.

STRACHAN, Alan Lockhart Thomson; theatre director; *b* 3 Sept. 1946; *s* of Roualeyn Robert Scott Strachan and Ellen Strachan (*née* Graham); *m* 1977, Jennifer Piercey-Thompson. *Educ:* Morgan Acad., Dundee; St Andrews Univ. (MA); Merton Coll., Oxford (B.Litt). Associate Dir, Mermaid Theatre, 1970–75; Artistic Director: Greenwich Th., 1978–88; Theatre of Comedy, 1991–. *Productions include: Mermaid:* The Watched Pot, 1970; John Bull's Other Island, The Old Boys, 1971; (co-deviser) Cowardy Custard, 1972; Misalliance, 1973; Children, (co-deviser and dir) Cole, 1974; *Greenwich:* An Audience Called Edouard, 1978; The Play's the Thing, I Sent a Letter to my Love, 1979; Private Lives (transf. Duchess), Time and the Conways, 1980; Present Laughter (transf. Vaudeville), The Golden Age, The Doctor's Dilemma, 1981; Design for Living (transf. Globe), The Paranormalist, French Without Tears, 1982; The Dining Room, An Inspector Calls, A Streetcar Named Desire, 1983 (transf. Mermaid, 1984); The Glass Menagerie, Biography, 1985; One of Us, Relatively Speaking, For King and Country, 1986; The Viewing, The Perfect Party, 1987; How the Other Half Loves (transf. Duke of York's), 1988; *freelance:* Family and a Fortune, Apollo, 1975; (deviser and dir) Shakespeare's People, world tours, 1975–78; Confusions, Apollo, 1976; (also jt author) Yahoo, Queen's, 1976; Just Between Ourselves, Queen's, 1977; The Immortal Haydon, Mermaid, 1977 (transf. Greenwich, 1978); Bedroom Farce, Amsterdam, 1978; Noël and Gertie, King's Head, 1983, Comedy, 1989; (replacement cast) Woman in Mind, Vaudeville, 1987; The Deep Blue Sea, Haymarket, 1988; Re: Joyce!, Fortune, 1988 (transf. Vaudeville, 1989; USA, 1990), Vaudeville, 1991; (replacement cast) Henceforward . . ., Vaudeville, 1989; June Moon, Scarborough, 1989; Toekomstmuziek, Amsterdam, 1989; Alphabetical Order, Scarborough, 1990; (replacement cast) Man of the Moment, Globe, 1990; Other People's Money, Lyric, 1990; Taking Steps, NY, 1991. *Publications:* contribs to periodicals. *Recreations:* music, tennis, travelling. *Address:* 11 Garlies Road, SE23 2RU. *T:* 081–699 3360.

STRACHAN, Alexander William Bruce, OBE 1971; HM Diplomatic Service, retired; *b* 2 July 1917; *s* of William Fyfe and Winifred Orchar Strachan; *m* 1940, Rebecca Prince MacFarlane; one *s* one *d*. *Educ:* Daniel Stewart's Coll., Edinburgh; Allen Glen's High Sch., Glasgow. Served Army, 1939–46 (dispatches). GPO, 1935; Asst Postal Controller, 1949–64; Postal Adviser to Iraq Govt, 1964–66; First Sec., FCO, 1967–68; Jordan, 1968–72; Addis Ababa, 1972–73; Consul General, Lahore, 1973–74; Counsellor (Economic and Commercial) and Consul General, Islamabad, 1975–77. Order of Istiqlal, Hashemite Kingdom of Jordan, 1971. *Address:* 24 St Margarets, London Road, Guildford, Surrey GU1 1TJ.

STRACHAN, Major Benjamin Leckie, CMG 1978; HM Diplomatic Service, retired; Principal, Mill of Strachan Language Institute, since 1984; Special Adviser (Middle East), Foreign and Commonwealth Office, 1990–91; *b* 4 Jan. 1924; *e s* of late Dr C. G. Strachan, MC FRCPE and Annie Primrose (*née* Leckie); *m* 1958, Lize Lund; three *s* and one step *s* one step *d*. *Educ:* Rossall Sch. (Scholar); RMCS. Royal Dragoons, 1944; France and Germany Campaign, 1944–45 (despatches); 4th QO Hussars, Malayan Campaign, 1948–51; Middle East Centre for Arab Studies, 1952–53; GSO2, HQ British Troops Egypt, 1954–55; Technical Staff Course, RMCS, 1956–58; 10th Royal Hussars, 1959–61; GSO2, WO, 1961; retd from Army and joined Foreign (subseq. Diplomatic) Service, 1961; 1st Sec., FO, 1961–62; Information Adviser to Governor of Aden, 1962–63; FO, 1964–66; Commercial Sec., Kuwait, 1966–69; Counsellor, Amman, 1969–71; Trade Comr, Toronto, 1971–74; Consul General, Vancouver, 1974–76; Ambassador to Yemen Arab Republic, 1977–78, and to Republic of Jibuti (non-resident), 1978, to the Lebanon, 1978–81, to Algeria, 1981–84. *Recreations:* golf, tennis, writing, fishing. *Address:* Mill of Strachan, Strachan, Kincardineshire. *T:* Feughside (033045) 663. *Club:* Lansdowne.

STRACHAN, Douglas Frederick; Chairman: Somerset Family Health Services Authority, since 1989; Dartington Foods (UK) Ltd, since 1990; *b* 26 July 1933; *s* of Hon. Lord Strachan and Lady (Irene Louise) Strachan (*née* Warren); *m* 1st, 1956, Mary Scott Hardie (*d* 1976); four *s* one *d*; 2nd, 1980, Jane, *widow* of Lt-Col I. D. Corden-Lloyd, OBE, MC; three step *s*. *Educ:* Rugby Sch.; Corpus Christi Coll., Oxford (MA). Brewer, Arthur Guinness Son & Co. (Dublin) Ltd, 1956–67; Man. Dir, Cantrell & Cochrane Gp Ltd, Dublin, 1967–72; Dir, Showerings, Vine Products & Whiteways Ltd, 1972–77; Man. Dir, Allied Breweries Ltd, 1977–85; Dir, Allied-Lyons Plc, 1976–85; Dir (Chief Executive) PRO NED, 1985–89. Dir, Cheltenham & Gloucester BS, 1991–; Mem., South Western RHA, 1990–. *Recreations:* gardening, music, shooting. *Address:* Hewletts Mill, Galhampton, Yeovil, Somerset BA22 7BG. *T:* North Cadbury (0963) 40308.

STRACHAN, Douglas Mark Arthur; QC 1987; a Recorder, since 1990; *b* 25 Sept. 1946; *s* of William Arthur Watkin Strachan and Joyce Olive Strachan. *Educ:* Orange Hill Grammar Sch., Edgware, Middx; St Catherine's Coll., Oxford (Open Exhibnr in Eng. Lit.; BCL, MA); Nancy Univ. (French Govt Schol.). Called to the Bar, Inner Temple, 1969 (Major Schol. 1969–71); Asst Recorder, 1987–90. *Publications:* contributor to

Modern Law Rev. *Recreations:* France, antiques, food. *Address:* 38 Bedford Gardens, W8 7EH. *T:* 071–727 4729.

STRACHAN, Graham Robert, CBE 1977; DL; FEng, FIMechE, FIMarE; Director, Scott Lithgow Ltd, since 1984; *b* 1 Nov. 1931; *o c* of late George Strachan and of Lily Elizabeth (*née* Ayres); *m* 1960, Catherine Nicol Liston, *o d* of late John and of Eileen Vivian; two *s. Educ:* Trinity Coll., Glenalmond; Trinity Coll., Cambridge (MA, 3rd Cl. Hons Mech. Scis Tripos). Apprentice Engineer: Alexander Stephen and Sons Ltd, 1950–52; John Brown & Co. (Clydebank) Ltd, 1952–55. National Service, RNVR, Temp. Sub-Lieut (E), 1955–57. John Brown & Co. (Clydebank) Ltd: Design Engr, 1957; Develt Engr, 1959; Engrg Dir, 1963; John Brown Engineering Ltd: Dir and Gen. Manager, 1966, Man. Dir, 1968, Gp Man. Dir, 1975, Dep. Chm., 1983–84; Director: British Smelter Constructions Ltd, 1968–73; CJB Offshore Ltd, 1975–80; John Brown & Co. (Overseas), 1976–84; Chairman: JBE Offshore Ltd, 1976–81 (Dep. Chm., 1974); JBE Gas Turbines, 1976–84; Stephens of Linthouse Ltd, 1982–84. Member: CBI Oil Steering Gp, 1975–79; Exec. Cttee, Scottish Engrg Employers' Assoc., 1966–82; Vice Pres., Scottish Council (Develt and Industry), 1983–; Mem. Council, Inst. of Engineers and Shipbuilders in Scotland, 1985–88. Dir, Glasgow Chamber of Commerce, 1978–. Mem. Court, Univ. of Strathclyde, 1979–83. DL Dumbarton, 1979. *Recreations:* skiing, golf, early jazz. *Address:* The Mill House, Strathblane, Glasgow G63 9EP. *T:* Blanefield (0360) 70220. *Clubs:* Caledonian, Royal Over-Seas League; Buchananan Castle Golf (Drymen).

STRACHAN, Michael Francis, CBE 1980 (MBE 1945); FRSE 1979; Chairman, Ben Line Steamers Ltd and Ben Line Containers Ltd, 1970–82; Director, Bank of Scotland, 1972–90; *b* 23 Oct. 1919; *s* of Francis William Strachan and Violet Blackwell (*née* Palmer); *m* 1948, Iris Hemingway; two *s* two *d. Educ:* Rugby Sch. (Scholar); Corpus Christi Coll., Cambridge (Exhibnr, MA). Served in Army, 1939–46; demobilised 1946 (Lt-Col). Joined Wm Thomson & Co., Edinburgh, Managers of Ben Line, 1946; Partner, 1950–64; Jt Man. Dir, Ben Line Steamers Ltd, 1964. Chm., Associated Container Transportation Ltd, 1971–75. Trustee: Nat. Galleries of Scotland, 1972–74; Nat. Library of Scotland, 1974– (Chm., 1974–90); Carnegie Trust for Univs of Scotland, 1976–; Hakluyt Soc., 1984–. Member of Queen's Body Guard for Scotland. *Publications:* The Life and Adventures of Thomas Coryate, 1962; (ed jtly) The East India Company Journals of Captain William Keeling and Master Thomas Bonner, 1615–1617, 1971; Sir Thomas Roe (1581–1644) A Life, 1989; (contrib.) Oxford Book of Military Anecdotes, 1987; The Ben Line 1825–1982; articles in Blackwood's, Hakluyt Society's Hakluyt Handbook, History Today, Jl Soc. for Nautical Research. *Recreations:* country pursuits, silviculture. *Address:* 33 St Mary's Street, Edinburgh EH1 1TN. *Clubs:* Naval and Military; New (Edinburgh).

STRACHAN, Mrs Valerie Patricia Marie, CB 1991; a Deputy Chairman, Board of Customs and Excise, since 1987; *b* 10 Jan. 1940; *d* of John Jonas Nicholls and Louise Nicholls; *m* 1965, John Strachan; one *s* one *d. Educ:* Newland High Sch., Hull; Manchester Univ. (BA). Joined Customs and Excise, 1961; Dept of Economic Affairs, 1964; Home Office, 1966; Principal, Customs and Excise, 1966; Treasury, 1972; Asst Secretary, Customs and Excise, 1974, Comr, 1980; Head, Joint Management Unit, HM Treasury/Cabinet Office, 1985–87. Vice-Chm., RIPA, 1991– (Mem. Council, 1988–). CBIM. *Address:* c/o Customs and Excise, New King's Beam House, 22 Upper Ground, SE1 9PJ.

STRACHAN, Walter, CBE 1967; CEng, FRAeS; Consulting Engineer since 1971; *b* 14 Oct. 1910; *s* of William John Strachan, Rothes, Morayshire, and Eva Hitchins, Bristol; *m* 1937, Elizabeth Dora Bradshaw, Aldershot; two *s. Educ:* Newfoundland Road Sch., Bristol; Merchant Venturers Technical Coll., Bristol. Bristol Aeroplane Co.: Apprentice, 1925; Aircraft Ground Engr, 1932; RAE, Farnborough, 1934; Inspector: Bristol Aeroplane Co., 1937. BAC Service Engr, RAF Martlesham Heath, 1938; BAC: Asst Service Manager, 1940; Asst Works Manager, 1942; Manager, Banwell, building Beaufort and Tempest aircraft, 1943; Gen.-Manager, Banwell and Weston Factories, manufrg Aluminium Houses, 1945; Gen. Manager, Banwell and Weston Factories, building helicopters and aircraft components, 1951; Managing Dir, Bristol Aerojet, Banwell, Rocket Motor Develt and Prod., 1958. *Recreations:* golf, music, ornithology. *Address:* 18 Clarence Road East, Weston-super-Mare, Somerset BS23 4BW. *T:* Weston-super-Mare (0934) 623878. *Clubs:* Naval and Military; Royal Automobile.

STRACHEY, family name of **Baron O'Hagan.**

STRACHEY, Charles, (6th Bt *cr* 1801, but does not use the title); *b* 20 June 1934; *s* of Rt Hon. Evelyn John St Loe Strachey (*d* 1963) and Celia (*d* 1980), 3rd *d* of late Rev. Arthur Hume Simpson; *S* to baronetcy of cousin, 2nd Baron Strachie, 1973; *m* 1973, Janet Megan, *d* of Alexander Miller; one *d. Heir: kinsman* Henry Leofric Benvenuto Strachey, *b* 17 April 1947. *Address:* 31 Northchurch Terrace, N1 4EB. *T:* 071–249 1055.

STRADBROKE, 6th Earl of, *cr* 1821; **Robert Keith Rous;** Bt 1660; Baron Rous 1796; Viscount Dunwich 1821; *b* 25 March 1937; *s* of 5th Earl of Stradbroke and Pamela Catherine Mabell (*d* 1972), *d* of Captain Hon. Edward James Kay-Shuttleworth; *S* father, 1983; *m* 1960, Dawn Antoinette (marr. diss. 1976), *d* of Thomas Edward Beverley, Brisbane; two *s* five *d*; 2nd, 1977, Roseanna Mary Blanche, *d* of late Francis Reitman, MD; five *s* two *d. Educ:* Harrow. *Heir: s* Viscount Dunwich, *qv. Address:* Mount Fyans, RSD Darlington, Vic 3271, Australia. *T:* 055–901298, *Fax:* 055–901294. *Club:* Royal Automobile of Victoria.

See also Hon. W. E. Rous.

STRADLING, Donald George; Group Personnel Director, John Laing & Son Ltd, then John Laing plc, 1969–89; *b* 7 Sept. 1929; *s* of George Frederic and Olive Emily Stradling; *m* 1955, Mary Anne Hartridge; two *d. Educ:* Clifton Coll.; Magdalen Coll., Oxford (Open Exhibnr; MA). CIPM. School Master, St Albans Sch., 1954–55; Group Trng and Educn Officer, John Laing & Son Ltd, Building and Civil Engrg Contractors, 1955. Vis. Prof., Univ. of Salford, 1989–. Comr, Manpower Services Commn, 1980–82; Mem. Council, Inst. of Manpower Studies, 1975–81; Member: Employment Policy Cttee, CBI, 1978–84, 1986–; Council, CBI, 1982–86; FCEC Wages and Industrial Cttee, 1978–; Council, FCEC, 1985–; National Steering Gp, New Technical and Vocational Educn Initiative, 1983–88. Director: Building and Civil Engrg Benefits Scheme (Trustee, 1984–); Building and Civil Engrg Holidays Scheme Management, 1984–; Construction ITB, 1985–90. NHS Trng Authy, 1985–89. Vice-Pres., Inst. of Personnel Management, 1974–76. Vice-Chm. of Governors, St Albans High Sch., 1977–; Mem. Council, Tyndale House, 1977–. Liveryman, Glaziers' and Painters of Glass Co., 1983–. Hon. PhD Internat. Management Centre, Buckingham, 1987. *Publications:* contribs on music and musical instruments, et al. to New Bible Dictionary, 1962. *Recreations:* singing (St Albans Bach Choir), oboe (Abbey Gateway Orchestra), listening to music (espec. opera), walking. *Address:* Courts Edge, 12 The Warren, Harpenden, Herts AL5 2NH. *T:* Harpenden (0582) 712744. *Club:* Institute of Directors.

STRADLING, Rt. Rev. Leslie Edward, MA; *b* 11 Feb. 1908; *er s* of late Rev. W. H. Stradling; unmarried. *Educ:* King Edward VII Sch., Sheffield; The Queen's Coll., Oxford; Westcott House, Cambridge. Curate of St Paul's, Lorrimore Square, 1933–38; Vicar of St Luke's Camberwell, 1938–43; of St Anne's, Wandsworth, 1943–45; Bishop of Masasi, 1945–52; Bishop of South West Tanganyika, 1952–61; Bishop of Johannesburg, 1961–74. Hon. DCL Bishops' Univ., Lennoxville, Canada, 1968. *Publications:* A Bishop on Safari, 1960; The Acts through Modern Eyes, 1963; An Open Door, 1966; A Bishop at Prayer, 1971; Praying Now, 1976; Praying the Psalms, 1977. *Address:* Braehead House, Auburn Road, Kenilworth 7700, Republic of South Africa. *Club:* City and Civil Service (Cape Town).

STRAFFORD, 8th Earl of, *cr* 1847; **Thomas Edmund Byng;** Baron Strafford, 1835; Viscount Enfield, 1847; *b* 26 Sept. 1936; *s* of 7th Earl of Strafford, and Maria Magdalena Elizabeth, *d* of late Henry Cloete, CMG, Alphen, S Africa; *S* father, 1984; *m* 1963, Jennifer Mary (marr. diss. 1981), *er d* of late Rt Hon. W. M. May, FCA, PC, MP, and of Mrs May, Mertoun Hall, Holywood, Co. Down; two *s* two *d*; 2nd, 1981, Mrs Julia Mary Howard, (Judy), *d* of Sir Dennis Pilcher, *qv. Educ:* Eton; Clare Coll., Cambridge. Lieut, Royal Sussex Regt (National Service). *Recreation:* gardening. *Heir: s* Viscount Enfield, *qv. Address:* 11 St James Terrace, Winchester, Hants SO22 4PP. *T:* Winchester (0962) 53905.

STRAKER, Rear-Adm. Bryan John, CB 1980; OBE 1966; Appeal Director, West Sussex Macmillan (Cancer Relief) Service, since 1990; *b* 26 May 1929; *s* of late George and Marjorie Straker; *m* 1954, Elizabeth Rosemary, *d* of Maj.-Gen. C. W. Greenway, CB, CBE, and Mrs C. W. Greenway; two *d. Educ:* St Albans Sch. FBIM 1978. Cadet, RNC Dartmouth, 1946; Flag Lieut to Flag Officer, Malayan Area, 1952–53; qual. in communications, 1955; CO: HMS Malcolm, 1962–63; HMS Defender, 1966–67; Asst Dir, Naval Operational Requirements, MoD, 1968–70; CO HMS Fearless, 1970–72; Dir of Naval Plans, MoD, 1972–74; Comdr British Forces Caribbean Area and Island Comdr, Bermuda, 1974–76; Asst Chief of Naval Staff (Policy), 1976–78; Sen. Naval Mem., DS, RCDS, 1978–80; RN retd, 1981. Hd of Personnel Services, ICRF, 1981–89. Freeman, City of London. *Recreations:* tennis, cricket, gardening. *Address:* c/o National Westminster Bank, Petersfield, Hants. *Clubs:* Farmers', Forty, West India; Steep Lawn Tennis.

STRAKER, Major Ivan Charles; Chairman, Seagram Distillers plc, since 1984 (Chief Executive, 1983–90); *b* 17 June 1928; *s* of Arthur Coppin Straker and Cicely Longueville Straker; *m* 1st, 1954, Gillian Elizabeth Grant (marr. diss. 1971); two *s* one *d*; 2nd, 1976, Sally Jane Hastings (marr. diss. 1986); one *s. Educ:* Harrow; RMA, Sandhurst. Commissioned 11th Hussars (PAO), 1948; served Germany, N Ireland, Middle East and Mil. Intell. Staff, War Office; left HM Armed Forces, 1962. Man. Dir, D. Rintoul & Co., 1964; Man. Dir, The Glenlivet and Glen Grant Agencies, 1964–71; apptd Main Board, The Glenlivet and Glen Grant Distillers, 1967; Chief Exec., The Glenlivet Distillers Ltd, 1971. Dir, Lothians Racing Syndicate Ltd, 1986–. Council Mem., Scotch Whisky Assoc., 1978–90 (Chm., Public Affairs Cttee, 1986–90). *Recreations:* fishing, shooting, golf, racing. *Address:* 33 Cluny Drive, Edinburgh. *T:* 031–447 6621. *Clubs:* Cavalry and Guards, Boodle's.

STRAKER, Sir Michael (Ian Bowstead), Kt 1984; CBE 1973; JP; DL; farmer, since 1951; Chairman: Aycliffe and Peterlee Development Corporations, 1980–88; Northumbrian Water Authority, since 1982; *b* 10 March 1928; *s* of late Edward Charles Straker and Margaret Alice Bridget Straker. *Educ:* Eton. Served in Coldstream Guards, 1946–50. Dir, Newcastle and Gateshead Water Co., 1975–82 (Chm., 1979–82); Member, Board: Port of Tyne Authority, 1986–; British Shipbuilders, 1990–. Chairman: Newcastle upon Tyne AHA(T), 1973–81; Newcastle Univ. HMC, 1971; Mem. Newcastle Univ. Court and Council, 1972– (Chm. Council, 1983–). Mem. Council, RASE, 1970–86. Chm., Northern Area Conservative Assoc., 1969–72. High Sheriff of Northumberland, 1977; JP, 1962, DL 1988, Northumberland. Hon. DCL Newcastle, 1987. *Address:* High Warden, Hexham, Northumberland NE46 4SR. *T:* Hexham (0434) 602083. *Club:* Northern Counties (Newcastle upon Tyne).

STRAND, Prof. Kenneth T.; Professor, Department of Economics, Simon Fraser University, 1968–86, now Emeritus; *b* Yakima, Wash, 30 June 1931; Canadian citizen since 1974; *m* 1960, Elna K. Tomaske; no *c. Educ:* Washington State Coll. (BA); Univ. of Wisconsin (PhD, MS). Woodrow Wilson Fellow, 1955–56; Ford Foundn Fellow, 1957–58; Herfurth Award, Univ. of Wisconsin, 1961 (for PhD thesis). Asst Exec. Sec., Hanford Contractors Negotiation Cttee, Richland, Wash, 1953–55; Asst Prof., Washington State Univ., 1959–60; Asst Prof., Oberlin Coll., 1960–65 (on leave, 1963–65); Economist, Manpower and Social Affairs Div., OECD, Paris, 1964–66; Assoc. Prof., Dept of Econs, Simon Fraser Univ., 1966–68; Pres., Simon Fraser Univ., 1969–74 (Acting Pres., 1968–69). Member: Industrial Relations Research Assoc.; Internat. Industrial Relations Assoc.; Canadian Industrial Relations Assoc. (Pres., 1983). Hon. LLD Simon Fraser Univ., 1983. FRSA 1972. *Publications:* Jurisdictional Disputes in Construction: The Causes, The Joint Board and the NLRB, 1961; contribs to Review of Econs and Statistics, Amer. Econ. Review, Industrial Relations, Sociaal Mannblad Arbeid. *Recreations:* fishing, ski-ing. *Address:* 3475 Main Avenue, Belcarra, BC V3H 4R2, Canada.

STRANG, family name of **Baron Strang.**

STRANG, 2nd Baron *cr* 1954, of Stonesfield; **Colin Strang;** Professor of Philosophy, University of Newcastle upon Tyne, 1975–82; Dean of the Faculty of Arts, 1976–79; retired 1982; *b* 12 June 1922; *s* of 1st Baron Strang, GCB, GCMG, MBE, and Elsie Wynne (*d* 1974), *d* of late J. E. Jones; *S* father, 1978; *m* 1st, 1948, Patricia Marie, *d* of Meiert C. Avis, Johannesburg; 2nd, 1955, Barbara Mary Hope Carr (*d* 1982); one *d*; 3rd, 1984, Mary Shewell. *Educ:* Merchant Taylors' School; St John's Coll., Oxford (MA, BPhil). *Heir:* none. *Address:* The Manse, Heptonstall Slack, Hebden Bridge, W Yorks HX7 7EZ.

STRANG, Gavin Steel; MP (Lab) Edinburgh East since 1970; *b* 10 July 1943; *s* of James Steel Strang and Marie Strang (*née* Finkle); *m. Educ:* Univs of Edinburgh and Cambridge. BSc Hons Edinburgh, 1964; DipAgricSci Cambridge, 1965; PhD Edinburgh, 1968. Mem., Tayside Econ. Planning Consultative Group, 1966–68; Scientist with ARC, 1968–70. Opposition front bench spokesman on Scottish affairs, 1972–73, on energy, 1973–74; Parly Under-Sec. of State, Dept of Energy, March-Oct. 1974; Parly Sec., MAFF, 1974–79; Opposition front bench spokesman on agriculture, 1979–82, on employment, 1987–89. Chm., PLP Defence Group, 1984–87. *Publications:* articles in Animal Production. *Recreations:* golf, swimming, watching football. *Address:* House of Commons, SW1A 0AA. *T:* 071–219 5155. *Club:* Newcraighall Miners' Welfare (Edinburgh).

STRANG, William John, CBE 1973; PhD; FRS 1977; FEng 1977; FRAeS; Deputy Technical Director, British Aerospace, Aircraft Group, 1978–83, retired; *b* 29 June 1921; *s* of late John F. Strang and Violet Strang (*née* Terrell); *m* 1946, Margaret Nicholas Howells; three *s* one *d. Educ:* Torquay Grammar Sch.; King's Coll., London Univ. (BSc). Bristol Aeroplane Co., Ltd, Stress Office, 1939–46; King's Coll., London Univ., 1946–48; Aeronautical Research Lab., Melbourne, Aust., 1948–51; Bristol Aeroplane Co. Ltd: Dep. Head, Guided Weapons Dept, 1951–52; Head of Aerodynamics and Flight Research, 1952–55; Chief Designer, 1955–60; British Aircraft Corporation: Dir and Chief Engr, 1960–67, Technical Dir, 1967–71, Filton Div.; Technical Dir, 1971–77, Commercial

Aircraft Div. Chm., Airworthiness Requirements Bd, 1983–90 (Mem., 1979–90). *Address:* April Cottage, Castle Combe, Wilts SN14 7HH. *T:* Castle Combe (0249) 782220.

STRANG STEEL, Major Sir (Fiennes) William; *see* Steel, Major Sir F. W. S.

STRANGE, Baroness (16th in line), *cr* 1628; **Jean Cherry Drummond;** *b* 17 Dec. 1928; *e c* of 15th Baron Strange (*d* 1982) and Violet Margaret Florence (*d* 1975), *d* of Sir Robert William Buchanan-Jardine, 2nd Bt; *S* (after termination of abeyance) 1986; *m* 1952, Captain Humphrey ap Evans, MC, who assumed name of Drummond of Megginch by decree of Lord Lyon, 1965; three *s* three *d*. *Educ:* St Andrews Univ. (MA 1951); Cambridge Univ. Pres., War Widows' Assoc. of GB, 1990. *Publications:* Love from Belinda, 1960; Lalage in Love, 1962; Creatures Great and Small, 1968; Love is For Ever, 1988. *Heir: s* Hon. Adam Humphrey Drummond, Major Grenadier Guards [*b* 20 April 1953; *m* 1988, Mary Emma, *e d* of Hon. John and Lady Elizabeth Dewar; one *d*]. *Address:* Megginch Castle, Errol, Perthshire. *T:* Errol (08212) 222; Tresco, 160 Kennington Road, SE11. *T:* 071–735 3681.

STRANGE, Prof. Susan, (Mrs Clifford Selly); Professor of International Relations at European University Institute, Florence, since 1989; *b* 9 June 1923; *d* of Col Louis Strange and Marjorie Beath; *m* 1st, 1942, Dr Denis Merritt (marr. diss. 1955); one *s* one *d*; 2nd, 1955, Clifford Selly; three *s* one *d*. *Educ:* Royal Sch., Bath; Université de Caen; London Sch. of Econs (BScEcon). The Economist, 1944–46; The Observer, 1946–57 (Washington, UN, and Econ. Corresp.); Lectr in Internat. Relations, University Coll., London, 1949–64; Res. Fellow, RIIA, 1965–76; German Marshall Fund Fellow, 1976–78; Montague Burton Prof. of Internat. Relns, LSE, 1978–88. Vis. Prof., Univ. of Southern Calif, 1978. *Publications:* Sterling and British Policy, 1971; International Monetary Relations, 1976; (ed with R. Tooze) The International Politics of Surplus Capacity, 1981; (ed) Paths to International Political Economy, 1984; Casino Capitalism, 1986; States and Markets, 1988; (with J. Stopford) Rival States, Rival Firms, 1991. *Recreations:* cooking, gardening, tennis. *Address:* Weedon Hill House, Aylesbury, Bucks. *T:* Aylesbury (0296) 22236.

STRANGWAYS; *see* Fox-Strangways, family name of Earl of Ilchester.

STRANRAER-MULL, Very Rev. Gerald; Dean of Aberdeen and Orkney, since 1988; Rector of Ellon and Cruden Bay, since 1972; *b* 24 Nov. 1942; *s* of Gerald and Lena Stranraer-Mull; *m* 1967, Glynis Mary Kempe; one *s* one *d* (and one *s* decd). *Educ:* Woodhouse Grove School, Apperley Bridge; King's College, London (AKC 1969); Saint Augustine's College, Canterbury. Journalist, 1960–66. Curate: Hexham Abbey, 1970–72; Corbridge, 1972; Editor of Aberdeen and Buchan Churchman, 1976–84, 1991–; Director of Training for Ministry, Diocese of Aberdeen and Orkney, 1982–90; Canon of Saint Andrew's Cathedral, Aberdeen, 1981–. *Address:* The Rectory, Ellon, Aberdeenshire AB41 9NP. *T:* Ellon (0358) 20366.

STRATFORD, Neil Martin; Keeper of Medieval and Later Antiquities, British Museum, since 1975; *b* 26 April 1938; *s* of Dr Martin Gould Stratford and Dr Mavis Stratford (*née* Beddall); *m* 1966, Anita Jennifer Lewis; two *d*. *Educ:* Marlborough Coll.; Magdalene Coll., Cambridge (BA Hons English 1961, MA); Courtauld Inst., London Univ. (BA Hons History of Art 1966). 2nd Lieut Coldstream Guards, 1956–58; Trainee Kleinwort, Benson, Lonsdale Ltd, 1961–63; Lecturer, Westfield Coll., London Univ., 1969–75. British Academy/Leverhulme Sen. Res. Fellow, 1991. Liveryman, Haberdashers' Company 1959–. Hon. Mem., Académie de Dijon, 1975; For. Mem., Société Nationale des Antiquaires de France, 1985. FSA 1976. *Publications:* La Sculpture Oubliée de Vézelay, 1984; articles in French and English periodicals. *Recreations:* opera, food and wine, cricket and football. *Address:* 17 Church Row, NW3. *T:* 071–794 5688. *Clubs:* Beefsteak, Garrick, MCC, I Zingari; University Pitt, Hawks (Cambridge).

STRATHALLAN, Viscount; John Eric Drummond; *b* 7 July 1935; *e s* of 17th Earl of Perth, *qv*; *m* 1963, Margaret Ann (marr. diss.), *o d* of Robin Gordon; two *s*; *m* 1988, Mrs Marion Elliot. *Heir: s* Hon. James David Drummond, *b* 24 Oct. 1965. *Address:* Stobhall, by Perth.

STRATHALMOND, 3rd Baron *cr* 1955; **William Roberton Fraser,** CA; Managing Director, London Wall Members Agency Ltd, since 1986 (Director, since 1985); *b* 22 July 1947; *s* of 2nd Baron Strathalmond, CMG, OBE, TD, and of Letitia, *d* of late Walter Krementz, New Jersey, USA; *S* father, 1976; *m* 1973, Amanda Rose, *yr d* of Rev. Gordon Clifford Taylor; two *s* one *d*. *Educ:* Loretto. Dir, London Wall Hldgs plc, 1986–. *Heir: s* Hon. William Gordon Fraser, *b* 24 Sept. 1976. *Address:* Holt House, Elstead, near Godalming, Surrey GU8 6LF.

STRATHCARRON, 2nd Baron, *cr* 1936, of Banchor; **David William Anthony Blyth Macpherson;** Bt, *cr* 1933; Partner, Strathcarron & Co.; Director: Kirchhoff (London) Ltd; Seabourne Express Ltd; Forster and Hales Ltd; Kent International Airport Ltd (formerly Seabourne Aviation); *b* 23 Jan. 1924; *s* of 1st Baron and Jill (*d* 1956), *o d* of Sir George Rhodes, 1st Bt; *S* father, 1937; *m* 1st, 1947, Valerie Cole (marr. annulled on his petition, 1947); 2nd, 1948, Mrs Diana Hawtrey Curle (*d* 1973), *o d* of Comdr R. H. Deane; two *s*; 3rd 1974, Mrs Eve Samuel, *o d* of late J. C. Higgins, CIE. *Educ:* Eton; Jesus College, Cambridge. Served War of 1939–45, RAFVR, 1942–47. Motoring Correspondent of The Field, 1954–. Member, British Parly Delegn to Austria, 1964. Pres., Inst. of Freight Forwarders, 1974–75. Member Council: Inst. of Advanced Motorists, 1972–; Order of the Road, 1974–. President: Guild of Motoring Writers, 1971–; Guild of Experienced Motorists, 1980–86; National Breakdown Recovery Club, 1982–; Driving Instructors' Assoc., 1982–; Vehicle Builders' and Repairers' Assoc., 1983–; IRTE, 1990–. *Publication:* Motoring for Pleasure, 1963. *Recreations:* motor-racing, sailing, motorcycling, golf. *Heir: s* Hon. Ian David Patrick Macpherson, *b* 31 March 1949. *Address:* 22 Rutland Gate, SW7 1BB. *T:* 071–584 1240; Otterwood, Beaulieu, Hants. *T:* Beaulieu (0590) 612334. *Clubs:* Boodle's, Royal Air Force.

STRATHCLYDE, 2nd Baron *cr* 1955, of Barskimming; **Thomas Galloway Dunlop du Roy de Blicquy Galbraith;** Parliamentary Under-Secretary of State, Scottish Office, since 1990; *b* 22 Feb. 1960; *s* of Hon. Sir Thomas Galloway Dunlop Galbraith, KBE, MP (*d* 1982) (*e s* of 1st Baron) and of Simone Clothilde Fernande Marie Ghislaine, *e d* of late Jean du Roy de Blicquy; *S* grandfather, 1985. *Educ:* Wellington College; Univ. of East Anglia (BA 1982); Université d'Aix-en-Provence. Insurance Broker, Bain Dawes, subseq. Bain Clarkson Ltd, 1982–88. Contested (C) Merseyside East, European Parly Election, 1984. Spokesman for DTI, Treasury and Scotland; Govt Whip, 1988–89; Parly Under-Sec. of State, Dept of Employment, 1989–90, DoE, 1990. *Heir: b* Hon. Charles William du Roy de Blicquy Galbraith, *b* 20 May 1962. *Address:* Old Barskimming, Mauchline, Ayrshire. *T:* Mauchline (0290) 50334; 2 Cowley Street, SW1. *T:* 071–222 2966.

STRATHCONA AND MOUNT ROYAL, 4th Baron, *cr* 1900; **Donald Euan Palmer Howard;** *b* 26 Nov. 1923; *s* of 3rd Baron Strathcona and Mount Royal and Diana Evelyn (*d* 1985), twin *d* of 1st Baron Wakehurst; *S* father 1959; *m* 1st, 1954, Lady Jane Mary Waldegrave (marr. diss. 1977), 2nd *d* of Earl Waldegrave, *qv*; two *s* four *d*; 2nd, 1978, Patricia (*née* Thomas), *widow* of John Middleton. *Educ:* King's Mead, Seaford; Eton; Trinity Coll., Cambridge; McGill University, Montreal (1947–50). Served War of 1939–45: RN, 1942–47: Midshipman, RNVR, 1943; Lieutenant, 1945. With Urwick, Orr and Partners (Industrial Consultants), 1950–56. Lord in Waiting (Govt Whip), 1973–74; Parly Under-Sec. of State for Defence (RAF), MoD, 1974; Jt Dep. Leader of the Opposition, House of Lords, 1976–79; Minister of State, MoD, 1979–81. Dir, Computing Devices, Hastings, 1981–. Chairman, Bath Festival Society, 1966–70. Dep. Chm., SS Great Britain Project, 1970–73; Pres., Falkland Is Trust, 1982–. *Recreations:* gardening, sailing. *Heir: s* Hon. Donald Alexander Smith Howard, *b* 24 June 1961. *Address:* 5 Ridgway Gardens, Wimbledon, SW19. *T:* 081–947 8157; Kiloran, Isle of Colonsay, Scotland. *T:* Colonsay (09512) 301. *Clubs:* Brooks's, Pratt's; Royal Yacht Squadron.

STRATHEDEN, 6th Baron *cr* 1836, **AND CAMPBELL,** 6th Baron *cr* 1841; **Donald Campbell;** *b* 4 April 1934; *s* of 5th Baron Stratheden and Campbell and of Evelyn Mary Austen, *d* of late Col Herbert Austen Smith, CIE; *S* father, 1987; *m* 1957, Hilary Ann Holland, *d* of Lt-Col William D. Turner; one *s* three *d*. *Educ:* Eton. *Heir: s* Hon. David Anthony Campbell, *b* 13 Feb. 1963. *Address:* Yalara, M5 401, Cooroy, Queensland 4563, Australia.

STRATHERN, Prof. Andrew Jamieson, PhD; Andrew Mellon Professor of Anthropology, University of Pittsburgh, since 1987; Emeritus Professor of Anthropology, University of London; Hon. Research Fellow, Institute of Papua New Guinea Studies, Port Moresby, since 1977 (Director, 1981–86); *b* 19 Jan. 1939; *s* of Robert Strathern and Mary Strathern (*née* Sharp); *m* 1963, Ann Marilyn Evans (marr. diss. 1986); two *s* one *d*; *m* 1990, Gabriele Stürzenhofecker. *Educ:* Colchester Royal Grammar Sch.; Trinity Coll., Cambridge (BA, PhD). Research Fellow, Trinity Coll., Cambridge, 1965–68; Research Fellow, then Fellow, Australian National Univ., 1969–72; Professor, later Vis. Professor, Dept of Anthropology and Sociology, Univ. of Papua New Guinea, 1973–77; Prof. of Anthropology and Hd of Dept of Anthropology, UCL, 1976–83. Rivers Memorial Medal, RAI, 1976. 10th Independence Anniv. Medal (PNG), 1987. *Publications:* The Rope of Moka, 1971; One Father, One Blood, 1972; (with M. Strathern) Self-decoration in Mount Hagen, 1972; Melpa Amb Kenan, 1974; Myths and Legends from Mt Hagen, 1977; Beneath the Andaiya Tree, 1977; Ongka, 1979; (with Malcolm Kirk) Man as Art, 1981; Inequality in New Guinea Highlands Societies, 1982; Wiru Laa, 1983; A line of power, 1984; (ed jtly) Strauss, The Mi: culture of the Mount Hagen people, 1990; (with P. Birnbaum) Faces of Papua New Guinea, 1991; articles in Man, Oceania, Ethnology, Jl Polyn Soc., Amer. Anthropology, Amer. Ethnology, Mankind, Bijdragen, Jl de la Soc. des Océanistes, Oral History, Bikmaus. *Address:* Department of Anthropology, University of Pittsburgh, Pittsburgh, Penn 15260, USA. *T:* (office) 412–648–7519.

STRATHERN, Prof. (Ann) Marilyn, FBA 1987; Professor of Social Anthropology and Head of the Department, Manchester University, since 1985; *b* 6 March 1941; *d* of Eric Charles Evans and Joyce Florence Evans; *m* 1963, Andrew Jamieson Strathern, *qv* (marr. diss. 1986); twin *s* one *d*. *Educ:* Bromley High Sch (GPDST); Girton Coll., Cambridge (MA, PhD). Asst Curator, Mus. of Ethnology, Cambridge, 1966–68; Res. Fellow, ANU, 1970–72 and 1974–75; Bye-Fellow, Sen. Res. Fellow, then Official Fellow, Girton Coll., 1976–83; Fellow and Lectr, Trinity Coll., Cambridge, 1984–85. Sen. Res. Fellow, ANU, 1983–84; Vis. Prof., Univ. of California, Berkeley, 1984. Rivers Meml Medal, RAI, 1976. *Publications:* Self-Decoration in Mt Hagen (jtly), 1971; Women In Between, 1972; (co-ed) Nature, Culture and Gender, 1980; Kinship at the Core: an anthropology of Elmdon, Essex, 1981; (ed) Dealing With Inequality, 1987; The Gender of the Gift, 1988; Partial Connections, 1991. *Address:* 8 Darley Avenue, Didsbury, Manchester M20 8XF.

STRATHMORE AND KINGHORNE, 18th Earl of, *cr* 1677 (Scot.); Earl (UK) *cr* 1937; **Michael Fergus Bowes Lyon;** Lord Glamis, 1445; Earl of Kinghorne, Lord Lyon and Glamis, 1606; Viscount Lyon, Lord Glamis, Tannadyce, Sidlaw and Strathdichtie, 1677; Baron Bowes (UK), 1887; Captain, Scots Guards; a Lord in Waiting (Government Whip), since 1989; *b* 7 June 1957; *s* of 17th Earl of Strathmore and Kinghorne and of Mary Pamela, DL, *d* of Brig. Norman Duncan McCorquodale, MC; *S* father, 1987; *m* 1984, Isobel, *yr d* of Capt. A. E. Weatherall, Cowhill, Dumfries; two *s*. *Educ:* Univ. of Aberdeen (BLE 1979). Page of Honour to HM Queen Elizabeth The Queen Mother, 1971–73; commissioned, Scots Guards, 1980. *Heir: s* Lord Glamis, *qv*. *Address:* Glamis Castle, Forfar, Angus. *Clubs:* Turf, Buck's, Pratt's; Third Guards'; Perth (Perth).

STRATHNAVER, Lord; Alistair Charles St Clair Sutherland, DL; Master of Sutherland; with Sutherland Estates, since 1978; *b* 7 Jan. 1947; *e s* of Charles Noel Janson, DL, and the Countess of Sutherland, *qv*; *heir* to mother's titles; *m* 1st, 1968, Eileen Elizabeth, *o d* of Richard Wheeler Baker, Jr, Princeton, NJ; two *d*; 2nd, 1980, Gillian, *er d* of Robert Murray, Gourock, Renfrewshire; one *s* one *d*. *Educ:* Eton; Christ Church, Oxford. BA. Metropolitan Police, 1969–74; with IBM UK Ltd, 1975–78. DL Sutherland, 1991. *Heir: s* Hon. Alexander Charles Robert Sutherland, *b* 1 Oct. 1981. *Address:* Sutherland Estates Office, Golspie, Sutherland KW10 6RR. *T:* Golspie (04083) 3268.

STRATHSPEY, 5th Baron, *cr* 1884; **Donald Patrick Trevor Grant of Grant,** 17th Bt, of Nova Scotia, *cr* 1625; 32nd Chief of Grant; Lieutenant-Colonel retired; *b* 18 March 1912; *s* of 4th Baron and Alice Louisa (*d* 1945), *d* of T. M. Hardy-Johnston, MICE London, of Christchurch, NZ; *S* father, 1948; *m* 1st, 1938, Alice (marr. diss. 1951), *o c* of late Francis Bowe, Timaru, NZ; one *s* two *d*; 2nd, 1951, Olive, *d* of W. H. Grant, Norwich; one *s* one *d*. *Educ:* Stowe Sch.; South Eastern Agricultural Coll. War Dept Land Agent and Valuer, Portsmouth, 1944–48; Command Land Agent, HQ Scottish Command, 1948–60; Asst Chief Land Agent and Valuer, War Office, 1960–63; Command Land Agent, HQ Cyprus District, 1963–64; Asst Director of Lands, NW Europe, 1964–66; Asst Chief Land Agent, MoD HQ, 1966–72. Associate, Land Agents' Soc. Fellow, Royal Institution of Chartered Surveyors, retd 1972. Member: Standing Council of Scottish Chiefs; Highland Soc. of London; Pres., Clan Grant Socs of Australia, Canada, Nova Scotia, UK and USA. Hon. Mem., Los Angeles Saint Andrew's Soc.; Knight, Mark Twain Soc., Missouri; Patron: American Scottish Foundn; Soc. for Protection of Endangered Species. Defence Medal; Coronation medal. *Publication:* A History of Clan Grant, 1983. *Recreations:* yachting, gardening, carpentry. *Heir: s* Hon. James Patrick Grant of Grant, *b* 9 Sept. 1943. *Address:* Elms Cottage, Elms Ride, West Wittering, West Sussex. *Clubs:* Lancia Motor, House of Lords Motor, House of Lords Sailing, Civil Service Motoring Association (Pres.), West Wittering Sailing; West Wittering Horticultural and Produce Assoc.

STRATTON, Andrew, MSc, FInstP, CEng, FIEE, FInstNav, FIMA; consulting engineer; applied systems analyst; *b* 5 Sept. 1918; *m* 1949, Ruth Deutsch (*d* 1987); one *s* one *d*. *Educ:* Skinners' Company Sch., Tunbridge Wells; University Coll. of the South West, Exeter; Univ. of London (BSc 1st cl. Hons Physics). RAE Farnborough: Air Defence and Armament Depts, 1939–54; Supt, Instruments and Inertial Navigation Div., 1954–62; Head of Weapon Research and Assessment Group, 1962–66; Prof. and Head of Maths Dept, Coll. of Aeronautics, Cranfield, 1966–68; Dir, Defence Operational Analysis Estabt, 1968–76; Under Sec., MoD, on secondment as Consultant, 1977, Senior Consultant, 1978–81, ICI Ltd. Technical Dir, Terrafix Ltd, 1983–88. Pt-time Mem., CAA, 1980–83; Chm., Civil Aviation R&D Prog. Bd, 1981–84. Faraday Lecture, IEE, 1972–73. Former Chm. and Mem. of Cttees, Aeronautical and Electronics Research Councils; former Mem.,

Home Office Scientific Adv. Council. Pres., Inst. of Navigation, 1967–70; Chm. of Convocation, Univ. of Exeter, 1959–83. Hon. DSc Exeter, 1972. Hodgson Prize, RAeS, 1969; Bronze Medal, 1971 and 1975, Gold Medal, 1973, Royal Inst of Navigation. US Medal of Freedom with Bronze Palm, 1947. *Publications:* (ed) Energy and Feedstocks in the Chemical Industry, 1983; contrib. to Unless Peace Comes, 1968; to The Future of Aeronautics, 1970; papers on: aircraft instruments, navigation, air traffic, operational analysis in Jl IEE, Jl IMechE, Jl RAeS, Jl Inst. Navigation; energy, and chemical feedstock in Chem. and Ind., Omega, Process Econ. Internat. *Recreations:* painting, rambling. *Address:* Chartley, 39 Salisbury Road, Farnborough, Hants GU14 7AJ. *T:* Farnborough (0252)542514.

STRATTON, Ven. Basil; Archdeacon of Stafford and Canon Residentiary of Lichfield Cathedral, 1959–74, Archdeacon Emeritus, since 1974; Chaplain to the Queen, 1965–76; *b* 27 April 1906; *s* of Reverend Samuel Henry Stratton and Kate Mabel Stratton; *m* 1934, Euphemia Frances Stuart; one *s* three *d. Educ:* Lincoln School; Hatfield College, Durham University. BA 1929, MA 1932. Deacon 1930; Priest 1931; Curate, St Stephen's, Grimsby, 1930–32; SPG Missionary, India, 1932–34; Indian Ecclesiastical Establishment, 1935–47. Chaplain to the Forces on service in Iraq, India, Burma and Malaya, 1941–46 (despatches); officiated as Chaplain-General in India, 1946. Vicar of Figheldean with Milston, Wilts, 1948–53; Vicar of Market Drayton, Shropshire, 1953–59. *Address:* Woodlands Cottage, Mere, Wilts BA12 6BY. *T:* Mere (0747) 860235.

STRATTON, Julius Adams, ScD; President Emeritus, Massachusetts Institute of Technology; *b* Seattle, 18 May 1901; *s* of Julius A. Stratton and Laura (*née* Adams); *m* 1935, Catherine N. Coffman; three *d. Educ:* Univ. of Washington; Mass Inst. of Technology (SB, SM); Eidgenössische Technische Hochschule, Zurich (ScD). Expert Consultant, Sec. of War, 1942–46. MIT: Res. Assistant, Elect. Engrg, 1924–26; Asst Prof., Electrical Engrg, 1928–30; Asst Prof., Physics, 1930–35; Assoc. Prof., Physics, 1935–41; Prof., Physics, 1941–51; Mem. Staff, Radiation Lab., 1940–45; Dir, Res. Lab. of Electronics, 1944–49; Provost, 1949–56; Vice-Pres., 1951–56; Chancellor, 1956–59; Actg Pres., 1957–59; Pres., 1959–66; Pres. Emer., 1966–. Trustee, Ford Foundn, 1955–71 (Chm. of Board, 1966–71). Chm., Commn on Marine Science, Engrg and Resources, 1967–69; Member: National Adv. Cttee on Oceans and Atmosphere, 1971–73; National Science Bd, 1956–62 and 1964–67; Naval Res. Adv. Cttee, 1954–59 (Chm., 1956–57). Life Mem. Corp., MIT; Life Trustee, Boston Museum of Science. Hon. Life FIEEE; FAAAS; Fellow: Amer. Acad. of Arts and Scis; Amer. Phys. Soc.; Founding Mem., National Acad. of Engrg; Member: Council on For. Relations; Amer. Philos. Soc.; Nat. Acad. of Scis (Vice-Pres., 1961–65); Sigma Xi; Tau Beta Pi; Eminent Mem., Eta Kappa Nu. Hon. Fellow, Coll. of Science and Technology, Manchester, England, 1963; Hon. Mem. Senate, Technical Univ. of Berlin, 1966. Holds numerous hon. doctorates of Engrg, Humane Letters, Laws and Science incl. DSc: Leeds, 1967; Heriot-Watt, 1971; ScD Cantab 1972. Medal for Merit, 1946; Distinguished Public Service Award, US Navy, 1957; Medal of Honor, Inst. Radio Engrs, 1957; Faraday Medal, IEE (England), 1961; Boston Medal for Distinguished Achievement, 1966. Officer, Legion of Honour, France, 1961; Orden de Boyacá, Colombia, 1964; Kt Comdr, Order of Merit, Germany, 1966. *Publications:* Electromagnetic Theory, 1941; Science and the Educated Man, 1966; numerous papers in scientific and professional jls. *Address:* (home) 100 Memorial Drive, Cambridge, Mass 02142, USA; (office) Massachusetts Institute of Technology, Cambridge, Mass 02139. *Clubs:* Century Association (New York); St Botolph (Boston).

STRATTON, Mrs Roy Olin; *see* Dickens, Monica Enid.

STRATTON, Air Vice-Marshal William Hector, CB 1970; CBE 1963; DFC 1939 and Bar 1944; company director; Chief of the Air Staff, RNZAF, 1969–71, retired 1971; *b* 22 July 1916; *s* of V. J. Stratton; *m* 1954, Dorothy M., *d* of J. D. Whyte; one *s* two *d. Educ:* Hawera Tech. High School, and privately. RAF, 1937–44. Appointments include: in comd RNZAF, Ohakea; Air Member for Personnel; assistant chief of Air Staff; Head NZ Defence Staff, Canberra; Head NZ Defence Staff, London. *Address:* 41 Goldsworthy Road, Claremont, Perth, WA 6010, Australia.

STRAUB, Marianne, OBE 1985; RDI 1972; textile designer; *b* 23 Sept. 1909; *d* of Karl Straub and Cécile (*née* Kappeler). *Educ:* in Switzerland. Dip. Kunstgewerbeschule Zürich. Textile Designer: Rural Industries Bureau, 1934–37; Helios Ltd, Bolton, 1937–50; Warner & Sons Ltd, Braintree, 1950–69. Teaching posts: Central School of Art and Design, 1958–63; Hornsey College of Art, 1963–68; Royal College of Art, 1968–74. Now retired, but working freelance and teaching by invitation at various colleges. Hon. Fellow: RCA, 1981; Liverpool Polytechnic, 1991. *Publication:* Hand Weaving and Cloth Design, 1977. *Address:* 67 Highsett, Hills Road, Cambridge CB2 1NZ. *T:* Cambridge (0223) 61947.

STRAUSS, family name of **Baron Strauss.**

STRAUSS, Baron *cr* 1979 (Life Peer), of Vauxhall in the London Borough of Lambeth; **George Russell Strauss;** PC 1947; *b* 18 July 1901; *s* of Arthur Strauss, formerly MP (C) Camborne Div. of Cornwall and N Paddington; *m* 1st, 1932, Patricia O'Flynn (*d* 1987); two *s* one *d*; 2nd, 1987, Benita Armstrong. *Educ:* Rugby. MP (Lab) Lambeth North, 1929–31 and 1934–50, Lambeth, Vauxhall, 1950–79; PPS to Minister of Transport, 1929–31, to Lord Privy Seal, and later Minister of Aircraft Production, 1942–45; Parly Sec., Min. of Transport, 1945–47; Minister of Supply, 1947–51 (introd. Iron and Steel Nationalisation Bill, 1949). LCC Representative: N Lambeth, 1925–31; SE Southwark, 1932–46; LCC: Chm. Highways Cttee, 1934–37; Vice-Chm. Finance Cttee, 1934–37; Chm. Supplies Cttee, 1937–39; Mem. London and Home Counties Traffic Advisory Cttee, 1934–39. Introduced Theatres Bill for the abolition of stage censorship, 1968. Father of the House of Commons, 1974. *Recreations:* painting and chess. *Address:* 1 Palace Green, W8 4QA. *T:* 071–937 1630; House of Lords, SW1A 0PW.

STRAUSS, Claude L.; *see* Levi-Strauss.

STRAUSS, Hon. Jacobus Gideon Nel, QC (South Africa) 1944; Leader of the South African United Party, 1950–56; MP for Germiston District 1932–57; *b* Calvinia CP, 17 Dec. 1900; *s* of late H. J. Strauss; *m* 1928, Joy Carpenter; two *s* two *d* (and one *s* decd). *Educ:* Calvinia High Sch.; Univ. of Cape Town; Univ. of South Africa. Private Sec. to the Prime Minister (General J. C. Smuts), 1923–24; practice at Johannesburg Bar, 1926–53; Minister of Agriculture and Forestry in Smuts Cabinet, 1944; succeeded Field Marshal J. C. Smuts as Leader of the Opposition, 1950. *Recreations:* riding, mountaineering and golf. *Address:* PO Box 67398, Bryanston, Transvaal, 2021, South Africa. *Clubs:* Rand, Royal Johannesburg Golf (Johannesburg).

STRAUSS, Nicholas Albert; QC 1984; *b* 29 July 1942; *s* of late Walter Strauss and of Ilse Strauss (*née* Leon); *m* 1972, Christine M. MacColl; two *d. Educ:* Highgate School; Jesus College, Cambridge. BA 1964; LLB 1965. Called to the Bar, Middle Temple, 1965; Harmsworth Scholar, 1965. *Address:* 1 Essex Court, Temple, EC4Y 9AR. *T:* 071–353 5362.

STRAW, Alice Elizabeth, (Mrs J. W. Straw); *see* Perkins, A. E.

STRAW, Jack, (John Whitaker Straw); MP (Lab) Blackburn, since 1979; barrister; *b* 3 Aug. 1946; *s* of Walter Arthur Whitaker Straw and of Joan Sylvia Straw; *m* 1st, 1968, Anthea Lilian Weston (marr. diss. 1978); one *d* (decd); 2nd, 1978, Alice Elizabeth Perkins, *qv*; one *s* one *d. Educ:* Brentwood Sch., Essex; Univ. of Leeds. LLB 1967. Called to Bar, Inner Temple, 1972. Political Advr to Sec. of State for Social Services, 1974–76; Special Advr to Sec. of State for Environment, 1976–77; on staff of Granada TV (World in Action), 1977–79. Pres., Leeds Univ. Union, 1967–68; Pres., Nat. Union of Students, 1969–71; Mem., Islington Borough Council, 1971–78; Dep. Leader, Inner London Educn Authority, 1973–74; Mem., Labour Party's Nat. Exec. Sub-Cttee on Educn and Science, 1970–82; Chm., Jt Adv. Cttee on Polytechnic of N London, 1973–75. Vice-Pres., Assoc. of District Councils, 1984–. Contested (Lab) Tonbridge and Malling, Feb. 1974. Opposition spokesman on the Treasury, 1980–83, on the environment, 1983–87; Principal Opposition Spokesman on educn, 1987–; Mem., Shadow Cabinet, 1987–. Vis. Fellow, Nuffield Coll., Oxford, 1990–. Member, Council: Inst. for Fiscal Studies, 1983–; Lancaster Univ., 1988–; Gov., Blackburn Coll., 1990–. *Publications:* Granada Guildhall Lecture, 1969; University of Leeds Convocation Lecture, 1978; contrib. pamphlets, articles. *Recreations:* walking, cycling, cooking puddings, music. *Address:* House of Commons, SW1A 0AA; Union House, Freckleton Street, Blackburn BB2 2HL.

STRAWSON, Maj.-Gen. John Michael, CB 1975; OBE 1964; idc, jssc, psc; Senior Military Adviser, Westland Aircraft Ltd, 1978–85 (Head of Cairo Office, 1976–78); *b* 1 Jan. 1921; *s* of late Cyril Walter and Nellie Dora Strawson; *m* 1960, Baroness Wilfried von Schellersheim; two *d. Educ:* Christ's Coll., Finchley. Joined Army, 1940; commnd, 1942; served with 4th QO Hussars in Middle East, Italy, Germany, Malaya, 1942–50, 1953–54, 1956–58; Staff Coll., Camberley, 1950; Bde Major, 1951–53; Instructor, Staff Coll. and Master of Drag Hounds, 1958–60; GSO1 and Col GS in WO and MoD, 1961–62 and 1965–66; comd QR Irish Hussars, Malaysia and BAOR, 1963–65; comd 39 Inf. Bde, 1967–68; idc 1969; COS, Live Oak, SHAPE, 1970–72; COS, HQ UKLF, 1972–76. Col, Queen's Royal Irish Hussars, 1975–85. US Bronze Star, 1945. *Publications:* The Battle for North Africa, 1969; Hitler as Military Commander, 1971; The Battle for the Ardennes, 1972; The Battle for Berlin, 1974; (jtly) The Third World War, 1978; El Alamein, 1981; (jtly) The Third World War: the untold story, 1982; A History of the SAS Regiment, 1984; The Italian Campaign, 1987; Gentlemen in Khaki: the British Army 1890–1990, 1989; Beggars in Red: the British Army 1789–1889, 1991. *Recreations:* equitation, shooting, reading. *Address:* The Old Rectory, Boyton, Warminster, Wilts BA12 0SS. *Club:* Cavalry and Guards.

See also Sir P. F. Strawson.

STRAWSON, Sir Peter (Frederick), Kt 1977; FBA 1960; Fellow of Magdalen College, Oxford, 1968–87, Hon. Fellow, 1989; Waynflete Professor of Metaphysical Philosophy in the University of Oxford, 1968–87 (Reader, 1966–68); Fellow of University College, Oxford, 1948–68, Honorary Fellow since 1979; *b* 23 November 1919; *s* of late Cyril Walter and Nellie Dora Strawson; *m* 1945, Grace Hall Martin; two *s* two *d. Educ:* Christ's College, Finchley; St John's College, Oxford (scholar; Hon. Fellow, 1973). Served War of 1939–45, RA, REME, Capt. Asst Lecturer in Philosophy, University Coll. of N. Wales, 1946; John Locke Schol., Univ. of Oxford, 1946; Lecturer in Philosophy, 1947, Fellow and Praelector, 1948, University Coll., Oxford. Vis. Prof., Duke Univ., N Carolina, 1955–56; Fellow of Humanities Council and Vis. Associate Prof., Princeton Univ., 1960–61, Vis. Prof., 1972; Woodbridge Lectr, Columbia Univ., NY, 1983; Immanuel Kant Lectr, Munich, 1985; Vis. Prof., Collège de France, 1985. Mem., Academia Europaea, 1990; For. Hon. Mem., Amer. Acad. Arts and Scis, 1971. *Publications:* Introduction to Logical Theory, 1952; Individuals, 1959; The Bounds of Sense, 1966; (ed) Philosophical Logic, 1967; (ed) Studies in the Philosophy of Thought and Action, 1968; Logico-Linguistic Papers, 1971; Freedom and Resentment, 1974; Subject and Predicate in Logic and Grammar, 1974; Scepticism and Naturalism: some varieties, 1985; Analyse et Métaphysique, 1985; contrib. to Mind, Philosophy, Proc. Aristotelian Soc., Philosophical Review, etc. *Address:* 25 Farndon Road, Oxford. *T:* Oxford (0865) 515026. *Club:* Athenæum.

See also J. M. Strawson.

STREAMS, Peter John, CMG 1986; HM Diplomatic Service; Ambassador to Honduras, and concurrently to El Salvador, since 1989; *b* 8 March 1935; *s* of Horace Stanley Streams and Isabel Esther (*née Ellaway*); *m* 1956, Margareta Decker; two *s* one *d. Educ:* Wallington County Grammar Sch. BoT, 1953; Bombay, 1960, Calcutta, 1962, Oslo, 1966; FCO, 1970; Mexico, 1973; FCO, 1977, Counsellor, 1979; Consul-Gen., Karachi, 1982; Counsellor, Stockholm, 1985. *Recreations:* walking, golf. *Address:* c/o Foreign and Commonwealth Office, SW1.

STREATFEILD, Maj.-Gen. Timothy Stuart Champion, CB 1980; MBE 1960; Director, Royal Artillery, 1978–81; *b* 9 Sept. 1926; *s* of Henry Grey Champion and Edythe Streatfeild; *m* 1951, Annette Catherine, *d* of Sir John Clague, CMG, CIE, and Lady Clague; two *s* one *d. Educ:* Eton; Christ Church, Oxford. FBIM. Commnd into RA, 1946; Instructor, Staff Coll., Camberley, 1963–65; Chief Instructor, Sudan Armed Forces Staff Coll., 1965–67; Commander, 7th Parachute Regt, RHA, 1967–69; Col Adjt and QMG, 4 Div., 1969–70; Commander, RA 2 Div., 1971–72; RCDS, 1973; Brigadier Adjt and QMG, 1st Corps, 1974–75; COS, Logistic Exec., MoD, 1976–78. Col. Commandant: RA, 1980–; RHA, 1981–. *Recreations:* fishing, sporting, the countryside, music. *Address:* Toatley Farm, Chawleigh, Chulmleigh, N Devon. *T:* Lapford (03635) 363. *Clubs:* Army and Navy, MCC.

STREATFEILD-JAMES, Captain John Jocelyn, RN retired; *b* 14 April 1929; *s* of Comdr Rev. Eric Cardew Streatfeild-James, OBE, and Elizabeth Ann (*né Kirby*); *m* 1962, Sally Madeline (*née* Stewart); three *s* (one *d* decd). *Educ:* RNC, Dartmouth. Specialist in Undersea Warfare. FBIM; MNI 1982. Naval Cadet, 1943–47; Midshipman, 1947–49; Sub-Lt, 1949–51; Lieutenant: Minesweeping, Diving and Anti-Bandit Ops, Far East Stn, 1951; Officer and Rating Trng, Home Stn, 1952–53; specialised in Undersea Warfare, 1954–55; Ship and Staff Duties, Far East Stn, 1955–57; Exchange Service, RAN, 1957–59; Lieutenant-Commander: instructed Officers specialising in Undersea Warfare, 1960–61; Sea Duty, Staff Home Stn, 1962–63; Sen. Instr, Jt Anti-Submarine Sch., HMS Sea Eagle, 1964–65; Commander: Staff of C-in-C Western Fleet and C-in-C Eastern Atlantic Area, 1965–67; Jt Services Staff Coll., 1968; Staff of Comdr Allied Naval Forces, Southern Europe, Malta, 1968–71; HMS Dryad, 1971–73; Captain: Sen. Officers' War Course, RNC, Greenwich, 1974; Dir, OPCON Proj., 1974–77; HMS Howard (i/c), Head of British Defence Liaison Staff, Ottawa, and Defence Advr to British High Comr in Canada, 1978–80 (as Cdre); HMS Excellent (i/c), 1981–82; ADC to the Queen, 1982–83. *Recreations:* sailing, carpentry, painting. *Address:* South Lodge, Tower Road, Hindhead, Surrey. *T:* Hindhead (0428) 606064. *Club:* Naval.

STREATOR, Edward James; Chairman, International Advisory Committee, Ruder Finn International, since 1990; UK Representative, Carlyle Group, since 1989; *b* 12 Dec. 1930; *s* of Edward J. and Ella S. Streator; *m* 1957, Priscilla Craig Kenney; one *s* two *d. Educ:* Princeton Univ. (AB). US Naval Reserve, served to Lieut (jg), 1952–56; entered Foreign Service, 1956; Third Sec., US Embassy, Addis Ababa, 1958–60; Second Sec.,

Lome, 1960–62; Office of Intelligence and Research, Dept of State, 1962–64; Staff Asst to Sec. of State, 1964–66; First Sec., US Mission to NATO, 1966–69; Dep. Director, then Director, Office of NATO Affairs, Dept of State, 1969–75; Dep. US Permanent Representative to NATO, Brussels, 1975–77; Minister, US Embassy, London, 1977–84; US Ambassador to OECD, 1984–87. Dir, Playhouse Theatre Co., 1989–; Mem., South Bank Bd, 1990–. Member: Council, RUSI, 1988–; Exec. Cttee, IISS, 1988–; Bd, British Amer. Arts Assoc., 1989–. Pres., American Chamber of Commerce (UK), 1989–. Mem. Exec. Cttee, The Pilgrims, 1984–; Governor: Ditchley Foundn, 1984–; E–SU, 1989–. *Recreation:* swimming. *Address:* 32 Phillimore Gardens, W8 7QF. *T:* 071–937 4772. *Clubs:* White's, Brooks's, Beefsteak, Buck's, Garrick; Metropolitan (Washington); Mill Reef (Antigua).

STREDDER, James Cecil; Headmaster, Wellington School, Somerset, 1957–73; *b* 22 Sept. 1912; 4th *s* of late Rev. J. Clifton Stredder and late Mrs Stredder; *m* 1938, Catherine Jane, *er d* of late Rev. A. R. Price, RN (Retd), Paignton, Devon; one *d. Educ:* King Edward VI School, Stratford-on-Avon; Jesus College, Oxford. Senior Chemistry Master at: Victoria College, Alexandria, Egypt, 1935; St Lawrence Coll., Ramsgate, 1936; Fettes Coll., Edinburgh, 1940; Tonbridge School, 1942–57. BA (Hons) Natural Science (Chemistry) Oxon 1935, MA 1943. *Recreation:* walking. *Address:* 44 Bedford Street, Hitchin, Herts SG5 2JG.

STREEP, Meryl (Mary Louise); American actress; *b* 22 June 1949; *d* of Harry and Mary Streep; *m* 1978, Donald Gummer; one *s* two *d. Educ:* Vassar Coll. (BA 1971); Yale (MA 1975). *Stage appearances include:* New York Shakespeare Fest., 1976; Alice in Concert, NY Public Theater, 1981; *television appearances include:* The Deadliest Season (film), 1977; Holocaust, 1978; *films include:* The Deer Hunter, 1978; Manhattan, 1979; The Seduction of Joe Tynan, 1979; Kramer versus Kramer, 1979 (Academy Award, 1980); The French Lieutenant's Woman (BAFTA Award), 1981; Sophie's Choice (Academy Award), 1982; Still of the Night, 1982; Silkwood, 1983; Falling in Love, 1984; Plenty, 1985; Out of Africa, 1985; Heartburn, 1986; Ironweed, 1987; A Cry in the Dark, 1989; She-Devil, 1990; Postcards from the Edge, 1991; Defending your Life, 1991. Hon. DFA: Dartmouth Coll., 1981; Yale, 1983. *Address:* c/o International Creative Management, 40 West 57th Street, New York, NY 10019, USA.

STREET, Hon. Anthony Austin; manager and company director; *b* 8 Feb. 1926; *s* of late Brig. the Hon. G. A. Street, MC, MHR; *m* 1951, Valerie Erica, *d* of J. A. Rickard; three *s. Educ:* Melbourne C of E Grammar Sch. RAN, 1945–46. MP (L) Corangamite, Vic, 1966–84 (resigned); Mem., various Govt Mems Cttees, 1967–71; Mem., Fed. Exec. Council, 1971–; Asst Minister for Labour and Nat. Service, 1971–72; Mem., Opposition Exec., 1973–75 (Special Asst to Leader of Opposition and Shadow Minister for Labour and Immigration, March-Nov. 1975); Minister for Labour and Immigration, Caretaker Ministry after dissolution of Parliament, Nov. 1975; Minister for Employment and Industrial Relations and Minister Assisting Prime Minister in Public Service Matters, 1975–78; Minister for: Industrial Relations, 1978–80; Foreign Affairs, 1980–83. Chm., Fed. Rural Cttee, Liberal Party, 1970–74. *Recreations:* cricket, golf, tennis, flying. *Address:* 153 The Terrace, Ocean Grove, Vic 3226, Australia. *Clubs:* MCC; Royal Melbourne Golf, Barwon Heads Golf.

STREET, John Edmund Dudley, CMG 1966; retired; *b* 21 April 1918; *er s* of late Philip Edmund Wells Street and of Elinor Gladys Whittington-Ince; *m* 1st, 1940, Noreen Mary (*d* 1981), *o d* of Edward John Griffin Comerford and Mary Elizabeth Winstone; three *s* one *d*; 2nd, 1983, Mrs Patricia Curzon. *Educ:* Tonbridge School; Exeter College, Oxford. Served War of 1939–45, HM Forces, 1940–46. Entered Foreign Service, 1947; First Secretary: British Embassy, Oslo, 1950; British Embassy, Lisbon, 1952; Foreign Office, 1954; First Secretary and Head of Chancery, British Legation, Budapest, 1957–60; HM Ambassador to Malagasy Republic, 1961–62, also Consul-General for the Island of Réunion and the Comoro Islands, 1961–62; Asst Sec., MoD, 1967–76; Asst Under-Sec. of State, MoD, 1976–78. *Recreations:* reading, golf, bridge. *Address:* Cornerways, High Street, Old Woking, Surrey GU22 9JH. *T:* Guildford (0483) 764371.

STREET, Hon. Sir Laurence (Whistler), AC 1989; KCMG 1976; Lieutenant-Governor of New South Wales, 1974–89; Chief Justice of New South Wales, 1974–88; *b* Sydney, 3 July 1926; *s* of Hon. Sir Kenneth Street, KCMG; *m* 1st, 1952, Susan Gai, AM, *d* of E. A. S. Watt; two *s* two *d*; 2nd, Penelope Patricia, *d* of G. Ferguson. *Educ:* Cranbrook Sch.; Univ. of Sydney (LLB Hons). Ord. Seaman, RANR, 1943–44; Midshipman, RANVR, 1944–45; Sub-Lt 1945–47; Comdr, Sen. Officer RANR Legal Br., 1964–65. Admitted to NSW Bar, 1951; QC 1963; Judge, Supreme Court of NSW, 1965; Judge of Appeal, 1972–74; Chief Judge in Equity, 1972–74. Lectr in Procedure, Univ. of Sydney, 1962–63, Lectr in Bankruptcy, 1964–65; Member: Public Accountants Regn Bd, 1962–65; Companies Auditors Bd, 1962–65; Pres., Courts-Martial Appeal Tribunal, 1971–74. Mem., London Court of Internat. Arbitration, 1988– (Pres., Asia-Pacific Council, 1989–). Chairman: Television Oceania, 1990–; Tourtalk Internat. Pty, 1990–. Pres., Aust. Br., 1990–, World Pres., 1990–, Internat. Law Assoc.; Chm., Judiciary Appeals Bd, NSW Rugby League, 1989–. President: Cranbrook Sch. Council, 1966–74; Sydney Univ. Law Sch. Foundn, 1990–; St John Amb. Aust. (NSW), 1974–. Hon. Col, 1st/15th Royal NSW Lancers, 1986–. Fellow, UTS Sydney, 1990; Hon. FIArbA 1989. KStJ 1976. Hon. LLD: Sydney, 1984; Macquarie Univ., 1989. Grand Officer of Merit, SMO Malta, 1977. *Address:* State Office Block, Macquarie Street, Sydney, NSW 2000, Australia. *Clubs:* Union (Sydney); Royal Sydney Golf.

STREET, Prof. Robert, AO 1985; DSc; Vice-Chancellor, University of Western Australia, 1978–86, Hon. Research Fellow, since 1986; *b* 16 Dec. 1920; *s* of late J. Street, Allerton Bywater, Yorkshire, UK; *m* 1943, Joan Marjorie Bere; one *s* one *d. Educ:* Hanley High Sch.; King's Coll., London. BSc, MSc, PhD, DSc (London). MIEE, FInstP, FAIP, FAA. Scientific Officer, Dept of Supply, UK, 1942–45; Lectr, Dept of Physics, Univ. of Nottingham, 1945–54; Sen. Lectr, Dept of Physics, Univ. of Sheffield, 1954–60; Foundn Prof. of Physics, Monash Univ., Melbourne, Vic., 1960–74; Dir, Research Sch. of Physical Sciences, Aust. Nat. Univ., 1974–78. Former President: Aust. Inst. of Nuclear Science and Engrg; Aust. Inst. of Physics; Mem. and Chm., Aust. Research Grants Cttee, 1970–76; Chm., Nat. Standards Commn, 1967–78; Member: State Energy Adv. Council, WA, 1981–86; Australian Science and Technology Council, 1977–80; Council, Univ. of Technology, Lae, Papua New Guinea, 1982–84; Bd of Management, Royal Perth Hosp., 1978–85. Fellow, Aust. Acad. of Science, 1973 (Treas., 1976–77). Hon. DSc: Sheffield, 1986; Western Australia, 1988. *Publications:* research papers in scientific jls. *Recreation:* swimming. *Address:* Department of Physics, University of Western Australia, Nedlands, WA 6009, Australia. *Club:* Weld (Perth).

STREETEN, Frank; *see* Streeten, R. H.

STREETEN, Paul Patrick, DLitt; Director, World Development Institute, since 1984, Professor, since 1980, Boston University (Director, Center for Asian Development Studies, 1980–84); *b* 18 July 1917; *e s* of Wilhelm Hornig, Vienna; changed name to Streeten under Army Council Instruction, 1943; *m* 1951, Ann Hilary Palmer, *d* of Edgar Higgins, Woodstock, Vermont; two *d* (and one step *s*). *Educ:* Vienna; Aberdeen Univ.;

Balliol Coll., Oxford (Hon. Schol.); 1st cl. PPE, 1947; Student, Nuffield Coll., Oxford, 1947–48. DLitt Oxon, 1976. Mil. service in Commandos, 1941–43; wounded in Sicily, 1943. Fellow, Balliol Coll., Oxford, 1948–66 (Hon. Fellow, 1986); Associate, Oxford Univ. Inst. of Econs and Statistics, 1960–64; Dep. Dir-Gen., Econ. Planning Staff, Min. of Overseas Develt, 1964–66; Prof. of Econs, Fellow, Acting and Dep. Dir of Inst. of Develt Studies, Sussex Univ., 1966–68; Warden of Queen Elizabeth House, Dir, Inst. of Commonwealth Studies, Univ. of Oxford, and Fellow of Balliol Coll., 1968–78; Special Adviser, World Bank, 1976–79; Dir of Studies, Overseas Develt Council, 1979–80. Rockefeller Fellow, USA, 1950–51; Fellow, Johns Hopkins Univ., Baltimore, 1955–56; Fellow, Center for Advanced Studies, Wesleyan Univ., Conn.; Vis. Prof., Econ. Develt Inst. of World Bank, 1984–86. European Univ. Inst., Florence, 1991. Sec., Oxford Econ. Papers, until 1961, Mem. Edit. Bd, 1971–78; Editor, Bulletin of Oxford Univ. Inst. of Econs and Statistics, 1961–64; Member: UK Nat. Commn of Unesco, 1966; Provisional Council of Univ. of Mauritius, 1966–72; Commonwealth Develt Corp., 1967–72; Statutory Commn, Royal Univ. of Malta, 1972–; Royal Commn on Environmental Pollution, 1974–76. Mem., Internat. Adv. Panel, Canadian Univ. Service Overseas. Vice-Chm., Social Sciences Adv. Cttee, 1971; Member, Governing Body: Queen Elizabeth House, Oxford, 1966–68; Inst. of Develt Studies, Univ. of Sussex, 1968–80 (Vice-Chm.); Dominion Students' Hall Trust, London House; Mem. Council, Overseas Develt Institute, until 1979. Pres., UK Chapter, Soc. for Internat. Develt until 1976. Mem., Phi Beta Delta. Hon. Fellow, Inst. of Develt Studies, Sussex, 1980. Raffaele Mattioli Lectr, Milan, 1991. Hon. LLD Aberdeen, 1980. Development Prize, Justus Liebig Univ., Giessen. Chm. Editorial Bd, World Develt, 1972–. *Publications:* (ed) Value in Social Theory, 1958; Economic Integration, 1961, 2nd edn 1964; (contrib.) Economic Growth in Britain, 1966; The Teaching of Development Economics, 1967; (ed with M. Lipton) Crisis in Indian Planning, 1968; (contrib. to) Gunnar Myrdal, Asian Drama, 1968; (ed) Unfashionable Economics, 1970; (ed, with Hugh Corbet) Commonwealth Policy in a Global Context, 1971; Frontiers of Development Studies, 1972; (ed) Trade Strategies for Development, 1973; The Limits of Development Research, 1975; (with S. Lall) Foreign Investment, Transnationals and Developing Countries, 1977; Development Perspectives, 1981; First Things First, 1981; (ed with Richard Jolly) Recent Issues in World Development, 1981; (ed with H. Maier) Human Resources, Employment and Development, 1983; What Price Food?, 1987; (ed) Beyond Adjustment, 1988; Mobilizing Human Potential, 1989; contribs to learned journals. *Address:* World Development Institute, Boston University, 270 Bay State Road, Boston, Mass 02215, USA. *Club:* United Oxford & Cambridge University.

STREETEN, Reginald Hawkins, (Frank), CBE 1991; Head of Statute Law Revision, Law Commission, since 1978; *b* 19 March 1928; *s* of late Reginald Craufurd Streeten, BA, LLB and Olive Gladys Streeten (*née* Palmer); *m* 1962, Bodile Westergren, Lappland, Sweden; two *s. Educ:* Grey Coll., S Africa; Rhodes University Coll. (BA, LLB). Called to the Bar, S Rhodesia, 1959. Crown Counsel and Legal Draftsman, S Rhodesia and Fedn of Rhodesia and Nyasaland, 1952–63; Jun. Counsel for Fed. Govt at inquiry into aircraft accident involving late Dag Hammarskjöld, 1961; Parly Draftsman, Zambia, 1964–66; Mem. Legal Staff, 1967–, Sec., 1981–82, Law Commn. Legal Mem., Med. Council of S Rhodesia, 1959–63. *Address:* 32 Holme Chase, St George's Avenue, Weybridge, Surrey KT13 0BZ.

STREETER, His Honour John Stuart; DL; a Circuit Judge, 1972–86 (Deputy Chairman 1967–71, Chairman 1971, Kent Quarter Sessions); *b* 20 May 1920; *yr s* of late Wilfrid A. Streeter, osteopath, and late Mrs R. L. Streeter; *m* 1956, (Margaret) Nancy Richardson; one *s* two *d. Educ:* Sherborne. Served War of 1939–45 (despatches): Captain, Royal Scots Fusiliers, 1940–46. Called to Bar, Gray's Inn, Nov. 1947. Post Office Counsel SE Circuit, 1957; Treasury Counsel, London Sessions, 1959; Part-time Dep. Chm., Kent Quarter Sessions, 1963. Trustee and Chm., Sherborne House, Bermondsey, 1990–; Pres., Old Shirburnian Soc., 1990. DL Kent, 1986. *Recreation:* gardening. *Address:* Playstole, Sissinghurst, Cranbrook, Kent TN17 2JN. *T:* Cranbrook (0580) 712847.

STREETON, Sir Terence (George), KBE 1989 (MBE 1969); CMG 1981; HM Diplomatic Service, retired; Adviser, APS (Singapore) Pte Ltd, since 1990; Chairman, International Social Service of Great Britain, since 1990; *b* 12 Jan. 1930; *er s* of late Alfred Victor Streeton and Edith Streeton (*née* Deiton); *m* 1962, Molly Horsburgh; two *s* two *d. Educ:* Wellingborough Grammar School. Inland Revenue, 1946; Prison Commission, 1947; Government Communications Headquarters, 1952; Foreign Office (Diplomatic Wireless Service), 1953; Diplomatic Service, 1965–89: First Secretary, Bonn, 1966; FCO, 1970; First Secretary and Head of Chancery, Bombay, 1972; Counsellor and Head of Joint Admin Office, Brussels, 1975; Head of Finance Dept, FCO, 1979; Asst Under-Sec. of State and Prin. Finance Officer, FCO, 1982–83; High Comr to Bangladesh, 1983–89. *Recreations:* walking, golf. *Address:* The Langtons, Beech Avenue, Olney, Bucks MK46 5AE. *T:* Bedford (0234) 711761. *Club:* Oriental.

STRETTON, Eric Hugh Alexander, CB 1972; Deputy Chief Executive in Property Services Agency, Department of the Environment, 1972–76, Deputy Chairman, 1973–76; *b* 22 June 1916; *y s* of Major S. G. Stretton, Wigston, Leicester; *m* 1946, Sheila Woodroffe Anderson, MB, BS, *d* of Dr A. W. Anderson, Cardiff (formerly of Ogmore Vale); one *s* one *d. Educ:* Wyggeston Sch; Pembroke Coll., Oxford. BA 1939, MA 1942. Leics Regt and 2/4 PWO Gurkha Rifles (Major), 1939–46. Asst Sec., Birmingham Univ. Appointments Board, 1946. Entered Ministry of Works, 1947; Prin. Private Sec. to Minister of Works, 1952–54; Asst Sec., 1954; Under-Secretary: MPBW, 1962–70; DoE, 1970–72; Dep. Sec., 1972. Chm., Structure Plan Examns in Public, Salop, 1979, Lincs, 1980, Central and N Lancs, 1981. *Address:* Dacre Castle, Penrith, Cumbria CA11 0HL. *T:* Pooley Bridge (07684) 86375. *Club:* United Oxford & Cambridge University.

STRETTON, Peter John; His Honour Judge Stretton; a Circuit Judge, since 1986; *b* 14 June 1938; *s* of Frank and Ella Stretton; *m* 1973, Eleanor Anne Wait; two *s* one *d. Educ:* Bedford Modern Sch. Called to the Bar, Middle Temple, 1962; Head of Chambers, 1985. A Recorder, 1982–86. *Recreations:* squash, gardening. *Address:* 1 Fountain Court, Steelhouse Lane, Birmingham. *T:* 021–236 5721.

STRICK, Robert Charles Gordon; Clerk to the Drapers' Company, since 1980; *b* 23 March 1931; *m* 1960, Jennifer Mary Hathway; one *s* one *d. Educ:* Royal Grammar Sch., Guildford; Sidney Sussex Coll., Cambridge. MA. Served RA, 1949–51; TA, 1951–55. Spicers Ltd, 1954–55; joined HMOCS, 1955; Dist Officer, Fiji, 1955–59; Sec., Burns Commn into Natural Resources and Population Trends, 1959–60; Asst Sec., Suva, 1960–61; Sec. to Govt, Tonga, 1961–63; Develt Officer and Divl Comr, 1963–67, Sec. for Natural Resources, 1967–71, Fiji; retired 1971; Under Sec., ICA, 1971–72; Asst Sec.-Gen., RICS, 1972–80; Clerk, Chartered Surveyors' Co., 1977–80. Clerk to Governors, Howells Sch., Denbigh, 1980–; Gov., QMC, 1980–89, Mem. Council, QMW, 1989–. *Recreations:* the countryside, walking, cycling, gardening. *Address:* Highstead Corner, Lickfold, West Sussex GU28 9DX. *T:* Lodsworth (07985) 367.

STRICKLAND, Benjamin Vincent Michael, FCA; Group Managing Director, Operations (including Group Strategy), and Director, Schroders PLC, 1983–91; *b* 20 Sept.

1939; *s* of Maj.-Gen. Eugene Vincent Michael Strickland, CMG, DSO, OBE, MM, and of Barbara Mary Farquharson Meares Lamb, *d* of Major Benjamin Lamb, RFA; *m* 1965, Tessa Mary Edwina, *d* of Rear-Adm. John Grant, *qv*; one *s* one *d*. *Educ:* Mayfield; University Coll., Oxford, 1960–63 (MA PPE); Harvard Business Sch. (AMPDip 1978). FCA 1967. Lieutenant: 17/21 Lancers, BAOR, 1959–60; Inns of Court and City Yeomanry, 1963–67. Jun. Man., Price Waterhouse & Co., 1963–68; joined J. Henry Schroder Wagg & Co. in Corp. Finance, 1968: Dir, Schroder Wagg, 1974–; Chm., G. D. Peters Engineering, 1972–74; Dir, Property Hldgs Internat. (USA), 1974–75; Chm. and Chief Exec., Schroders Australia, 1978–82. Dir, Oakley Investments (subsidiary of Chelsea Land), 1991–. Financial Advr, Westminster Cathedral, 1991. FRSA. *Publications:* Bow Group pamphlet on Resources of the Sea (with Laurance Reed), 1965; (contrib.) Financial Services Handbook, 1986. *Recreations:* travel, military and general history, shooting, theatre. *Address:* 6 Queen's Elm Square, Chelsea, SW3 6ED. *T:* 071–351 0372. *Clubs:* Boodle's, Hurlingham.

STRICKLAND, Frank, OBE 1986; Director, 1975 (Executive Deputy Chairman, 1989–91); North of England Building Society, since 1989; *b* 4 Feb. 1928; *s* of Robert and Esther Strickland; *m* 1953, Marian Holt; one *d*. *Educ:* Harris Inst., Preston, Lancs. Asst Sec., Chorley and District Building Soc., 1952; Branch Manager, Hastings and Thanet Building Soc., 1955; Asst Sec., later Jt Sec., Corporation and Eligible Building Soc., 1965; Gen. Manager, Sunderland and Shields Building Soc., 1969, Dir, 1982; Chief Exec., 1975–89, Gen. Manager, 1986–89, North of England Building Soc. Chm., Building Socs Assoc., 1989–91 (Dep. Chm., 1987–89); Pres., European Fedn of Bldg Socs, 1989–91. *Recreations:* golf, cricket. *Address:* 383 Sunderland Road, South Shields, Tyne and Wear NE34 8DG. *T:* 091–456 1216. *Clubs:* Royal Over-Seas League, MCC; Sunderland, Sunderland Rotary.

STRICKLAND-CONSTABLE, Sir Robert (Frederick), 11th Bt *cr* 1641; *b* 22 Oct. 1903; 2nd *s* of Lt-Col Frederick Charles Strickland-Constable (*d* 1917) (*g g s* of 7th Bt) and Margaret Elizabeth (*d* 1961), *d* of late Rear-Adm. Hon. Thomas Alexander Pakenham; *S* brother, 1975; *m* 1936, Lettice, *y d* of late Major Frederick Strickland; two *s* two *d*. *Educ:* Magdalen Coll., Oxford (BA 1925, MA 1936, DPhil 1940). Served War of 1939–45, Lieut Comdr RNVR. Teaching Staff, Chem. Engineering Dept, Imperial Coll., Univ. of London, 1948–71, Readership 1963–71. Mem. Faraday Soc. *Publications:* Kinetics and Mechanism of Crystallization, 1968; approx. 50 contribs to scientific jls. *Recreations:* music, mountains, bird-watching. *Heir:* *s* Frederick Strickland-Constable [*b* 21 Oct. 1944; *m* 1982, Pauline Margaret Harding; one *s* one *d*].

STRINGER, Donald Arthur, OBE 1975; Deputy Chairman, Associated British Ports (formerly British Transport Docks Board), 1982–85 (Member, 1969–85; Deputy Managing Director, 1967–71 and 1978–82; Joint Managing Director, 1982–85); *b* 15 June 1922; *s* of late Harry William Stringer and Helen Stringer; *m* 1945, Hazel Handley; one *s* one *d*. *Educ:* Dorking High Sch.; Borden Grammar Sch. FCIT; CBIM. Joined Southern Railway Co., 1938; service with RAF, 1941–46; Docks Manager: Fleetwood, 1957–58; East Coast Scottish Ports, 1958–62; Chief Docks Man., Southampton, 1963–67, Port Director, 1970–77. Chairman: ABP (formerly BTDB) Bds: Southampton, 1972–85; Humber, 1978–85; Southampton Cargo Handling Co. Ltd, 1968–85; Nat. Assoc. of Port Employers, 1982–85 (Mem. Exec. Cttee, 1964–85); Mem., National Dock Labour Bd, 1976–85; Past Pres., Southampton Chamber of Commerce. Col, Engr and Transport Staff Corps, RE(TA). *Recreation:* gardening. *Address:* Hillcrest, Pinehurst Road, Bassett, Southampton SO1 7FZ. *T:* Southampton (0703) 768887. *Clubs:* Army and Navy; Royal Southampton Yacht.

STRINGER, Pamela Mary; Headmistress, Clifton High School for Girls, 1965–85; *b* 30 Aug. 1928; *e d* of late E. Allen Stringer. *Educ:* Worcester Grammar Sch. for Girls; St Hugh's Coll., Oxford. MA (Hons Lit Hum). Asst Classics Mistress, Sherborne Sch. for Girls, 1950–59; Head of Classics Dept, Pate's Grammar Sch. for Girls, Cheltenham, 1959–64 (Dep. Head, 1963–64). Member: Exec. Cttee, Assoc. of Headmistresses, 1975–; Exec. Cttee, Girls Schools Assoc., 1975– (Pres., 1978–79; Chm., Educn Cttee, 1981–84); Council, Secondary Heads Assoc., 1978–79 (Pres. Area 7, 1978–79). *Recreations:* travel in Tuscany and Umbria, reading, arctophily, cooking. *Address:* 36 Henleaze Gardens, Bristol BS9 4HJ.

STRONACH, David Brian, OBE 1975; FSA; Professor of Near Eastern Studies, University of California, Berkeley, since 1981; Curator of Near Eastern Archaeology, Lowie Museum of Anthropology, Berkeley, since 1982; *b* 10 June 1931; *s* of Ian David Stronach, MB, FRCSE, and Marjorie Jessie Duncan (*née* Minto); *m* 1966, Ruth Vaadia; two *d*. *Educ:* Gordonstoun; St John's Coll., Cambridge (MA). Pres., Cambridge Univ. Archaeological Field Club, 1954. British Inst. of Archaeology at Ankara: Scholar, 1955–56; Fellow, 1957–58; Fellow, British Sch. of Archaeology in Iraq, 1957–60; Brit. Acad. Archaeological Attaché in Iran, 1960–61; Dir, British Inst. of Persian Studies, 1961–80, Hon. Vice Pres., 1981–. Asst on excavations at: Istanbul, 1954; Tell Rifa'at, 1956; Beycesultan, 1956–57; Hacilar, 1957–59; Nimrud, 1957–60; Charsada, 1958. Dir, excavations at: Ras al'Amiya, 1960; Yarim Tepe, 1960–62; Pasargadae, 1961–63; Tepe Nush-i Jan, 1967–77; Nineveh, 1987–; Co-dir, excavs at Shahr-i Qumis, 1967–78. Mem., Internat. Cttee of Internat. Congresses of Iranian Art and Archaeology, 1968–80. Hagop Kevorkian Visiting Lectr in Iranian Art and Archaeology, Univ. of Pennsylvania, 1967; Rhind Lectr, Edin., 1973; Norton Lectr, Amer. Inst. of Archaeology, 1980; Columbia Lectr in Iranian Studies, Columbia Univ., 1986. Vis. Prof. of Archaeology, Hebrew Univ., Jerusalem, 1977; Vis. Prof. of Archaeology and Iranian Studies, Univ. of Arizona, Tucson, 1980–81. Mem., German Archaeological Inst., 1973 (Corr. Mem., 1966); Associate Mem., Royal Belgian Acad., 1988–. Ghirshman Prize, Académie des Inscriptions et Belles-Lettres, Paris, 1979; Sir Percy Sykes Meml Medal, Royal Soc. for Asian Affairs, 1980. Adv. Editor: Jl of Mithraic Studies, 1976–79; Iran, 1980–; Iranica Antiqua, 1984–; Bulletin of Asia Inst., 1986–; Amer. Jl of Archaeol., 1989. *Publications:* Pasargadae, a Report on the Excavations conducted by the British Institute of Persian Studies, 1978; archaeological articles in: Jl of Near Eastern Studies; Iran; Iraq; Anatolian Studies, etc. *Recreations:* fly fishing, mediaeval architecture, tribal carpets; repr. Cambridge in athletics, 1953. *Address:* Department of Near Eastern Studies, University of California, Berkeley, Calif 94720, USA. *Clubs:* Achilles; Hawks (Cambridge); Explorers' (New York).

STRONG, Air Cdre David Malcolm, CB 1964; AFC 1941; *b* 30 Sept. 1913; *s* of Theo Strong; *m* 1941, Daphne Irene Warren-Brown; two *s* one *d*. *Educ:* Cardiff High School. Pilot, under trng, 1936; Bomber Sqdn, 1937–41; POW, 1941–45. Station Commander, RAF Jurby, RAF Driffield, 1946–48; Staff Coll. (psa), 1949; Staff Officer, Rhodesian Air Trng Grp, 1949–51; Directing Staff, Staff Coll., 1952–55; Air Warfare Coll. (pfc), 1956; Station Comdr, RAF Coningsby, 1957–59; Dir of Personnel, Air Min., 1959–61; Senior Air Staff Officer, RAF Germany, 1962–63; Officer Commanding, RAF Halton, 1964–66. Retired, 1966. Chairman: RAF Rugby Union, 1954–56; RAF Golf Soc., 1964–66. *Recreation:* golf. *Address:* Old Coach House, Wendover, Bucks. *T:* Wendover (0296) 624724. *Clubs:* Royal Air Force; Ashridge Golf.

STRONG, Dr John Anderson, CBE 1978 (MBE (mil.) 1942); MD; FRCP; FRCPE; FRSE; President, Royal College of Physicians of Edinburgh, 1979–82; *b* 18 Feb. 1915; *s* of Charles James Strong and Mabel Emma Strong (*née* Anderson); *m* 1939, Anne Frances Moira Heaney; one *s* two *d*. *Educ:* Monkton Combe Sch., Bath; Trinity Coll., Dublin (MB 1937, MA, MD). Served RAMC, UK, India and Burma, 1939–46 (despatches, Burma, 1945); Hon. Lt-Col RAMC, 1946. Senior Lecturer, Dept of Medicine, Univ. of Edinburgh, 1949; Hon. Cons. Phys., Western General Hosp., Edinburgh, 1949; Hon. Physician, MRC Clinical and Population Cytogenetics Unit, 1959–80; Professor of Medicine, Univ. of Edinburgh, 1966–80, Professor Emeritus, 1981. Mem., Medicines Commn, 1976–83; Chm., Scottish Health Educn Co-ordinating Cttee, 1986–88. Hon. FACP 1980; Hon. FRCPI 1980; Hon. Fellow: Coll. of Physicians of Philadelphia, 1981; TCD, 1982; Coll. of Physicians of S Africa, 1982; Fellow *ad eundem*, RCGP, 1982; Mem., Acad. of Medicine, Singapore, 1982. *Publications:* chapter on Endocrinology in Principles and Practice of Medicine, ed L. S. P. Davidson, 1952, 12th edn 1977; articles in general medical and endocrinological jls. *Recreations:* fishing, golf, stalking, natural history. *Address:* 6 York Road, Edinburgh EH5 3EH. *T:* 031–552 2865. *Clubs:* New (Edinburgh); Hon. Company of Edinburgh Golfers (Muirfield).

STRONG, John Clifford, CBE 1980; HM Diplomatic Service, retired; Governor, Turks and Caicos Islands, 1978–82; *b* 14 Jan. 1922; *m* 1942, Janet Browning; three *d*. *Educ:* Beckenham Grammar Sch.; London Sch. of Economics and Political Science. LLB 1953. Served RN, 1942–46; HMOCS Tanzania, 1946–63; CRO, 1963; First Sec., Nairobi, 1964–68; FCO, 1968–73; Counsellor and Head of Chancery, Dar es Salaam, 1973–78. *Address:* Oakover, 24 Crescent Road, Beckenham BR3 2NE. *Club:* Royal Over-Seas League.

STRONG, Julia Trevelyan; *see* Oman, J. T.

STRONG, Maurice F., OC 1976; FRSC 1987; Chairman: Strovest Holdings Inc., since 1984; American Water Development Inc., Denver, Colorado, since 1986; President: World Federation of United Nations Associations, since 1987; Better World Society, since 1988; Chairman, World Economic Forum Council, since 1988; *b* 29 April 1929; *s* of Frederick Milton Strong and late Mary Fyfe Strong; *m* 1st, 1950 (marr. diss. 1980); two *s* two *d*; 2nd, 1981, Hanne Marstrand; one foster *d*. *Educ:* Public and High Sch., Oak Lake, Manitoba, Canada. Served in UN Secretariat, 1947; worked in industry and Pres. or Dir, various Canadian and internat. corporations, 1948–66; Dir-Gen., External Aid Office (later Canadian Internat. Develt Agency), Canadian Govt, 1966–71; Under-Sec.-Gen. with responsibility for envmtl affairs, and Sec.-Gen. of 1972 Conf. on the Human Environment, Stockholm, 1971–72; Exec. Dir, UN Envmtl Programme, 1972–75; Pres., Chm. of Bd and Chm. of Exec. Cttee, Petro-Canada, 1976–78; Chm. of Bd, AZL Resources Inc., USA, 1978–83; Under-Sec.-Gen., UN, and Exec. Co-ordinator, UN Office for Emergency Ops in Africa, NY, 1985–87. Dir, Massey Ferguson, Canada; Dir, Mem. Exec. Cttee and Vice Chm., Canadaa Develt Corp., Toronto. Chairman: Centre for Internat. Management Studies, Geneva, 1971–78; Internat. Energy Develt Corp., Geneva (also Special Advr); Canada Develt Investment Corp., Vancouver; Bd of Govs, Internat. Develt Res. Centre, 1977–78; Co-Chm., Interaction Policy Bd, Vienna; Vice-Chm. and Dir, Soc. Gén. pour l'Energie et les Ressources, Geneva, 1980–86; Member: Internat. Adv. Bd, Unisys Corp., USA; Bd, Bretton Woods Cttee, Washington; World Commn on Envmt and Develt; Alt. Gov., IBRD, ADB, Caribbean Develt Bank. Chairman: North South Energy Roundtable, Washington, DC; North South Energy Roundtable, Rome; Adv. Cttee, UN Univ., Tokyo, Japan. Dir, Lindisfarne Assoc.; Mem., Internat. Asia Soc., NY. Trustee: Rockefeller Foundn, 1971–78; Aspen Inst., 1971–; Internat. Foundn for Develt Alternatives. FRSA. Holds numerous hon. degrees from univs and colls in Canada, USA and UK. *Publications:* articles in various jls, including Foreign Affairs Magazine, Natural History Magazine. *Recreations:* swimming, skin-diving, farming, reading. *Address:* Suite 2950, 1099 18th Street, Denver, Colorado 80202, USA. *Clubs:* Yale (New York); Rideau (Ottawa); University (Vancouver); Petroleum (Denver).

STRONG, Sir Roy (Colin), Kt 1982; PhD, FSA; writer and historian, lecturer, critic, columnist, contributor to radio and television and organiser of exhibitions; Director, Oman Productions Ltd; *b* 23 Aug. 1935; *s* of G. E. C. Strong; *m* 1971, Julia Trevelyan Oman, *qv*. *Educ:* Edmonton Co. Grammar Sch.; Queen Mary Coll., London (Fellow, 1976); Warburg Inst., London. Asst Keeper, 1959, Director, Keeper and Secretary 1967–73, Nat. Portrait Gallery; Dir, Victoria and Albert Museum, 1974–87. Ferens Prof. of Fine Art, Univ. of Hull, 1972. Walls Lectures, Pierpont Morgan Library, 1974. Member: Fine Arts Adv. Cttee, British Council, 1974–87; Westminster Abbey Architectl Panel, 1975–89; Council, RCA, 1979–87; Arts Council of GB, 1983–87 (Chm., Arts Panel, 1983–87); Vice-Chm., South Bank Centre (formerly South Bank Bd), 1985–90. Trustee: Arundel Castle, 1974–86; Chevening, 1974–87; Sutton Place, 1982–84; Patron, Pallant House, Chichester, 1986– (Trustee, 1980–86). Hon. DLitt: Leeds, 1983; Keele, 1984. Sen. Fellow, RCA, 1983. Shakespeare Prize, FVS Foundn, Hamburg, 1980. *Publications:* Portraits of Queen Elizabeth I, 1963; (with J. A. van Dorsten) Leicester's Triumph, 1964; Holbein and Henry VIII, 1967; Tudor and Jacobean Portraits, 1969; The English Icon: Elizabethan and Jacobean Portraiture, 1969; (with Julia Trevelyan Oman) Elizabeth R, 1971; Van Dyck: Charles I on Horseback, 1972; (with Julia Trevelyan Oman) Mary Queen of Scots, 1972; (with Stephen Orgel) Inigo Jones: the theatre of the Stuart court, 1973; contrib. Burke's Guide to the Royal Family, 1973; Splendour at Court: Renaissance Spectacle and the Theatre of Power, 1973; (with Colin Ford) An Early Victorian Album: the Hill-Adamson collection, 1974; Nicholas Hilliard, 1975; (contrib.) Spirit of the Age, 1975; The Cult of Elizabeth: Elizabethan Portraiture and Pageantry, 1977; And When Did You Last See Your Father?, 1978; The Renaissance Garden in England, 1979; (contrib.) The Garden, 1979; Britannia Triumphans: Inigo Jones, Rubens and Whitehall Palace, 1980; (introd.) Holbein, 1980; (contrib.) Designing for the Dancer, 1981; (jtly) The English Miniature, 1981; (with Julia Trevelyan Oman) The English Year, 1982; (contrib.) Pelican Guide to English Literature vol. 3, 1982; (with J. Murrell) Artists of the Tudor Court, 1983; The English Renaissance Miniature, 1983; (contrib.) Glyndebourne: a celebration, 1984; Art & Power, 1984; Strong Points, 1985; Henry, Prince of Wales and England's Lost Renaissance, 1986; (contrib.) For Veronica Wedgwood These, 1986; Creating Small Gardens, 1986; Gloriana, Portraits of Queen Elizabeth I, 1987; A Small Garden Designer's Handbook, 1987; Cecil Beaton: the Royal portraits, 1988; Creating Small Formal Gardens, 1989; (contrib.) British Theatre Design, 1989; Lost Treasures of Britain, 1990; (contrib.) Sir Philip Sidney's Achievements, 1990; (contrib.) England and the Continental Renaissance, 1990. *Recreations:* gardening, cooking, keeping fit. *Address:* The Laskett, Much Birch, Herefords HR2 8HZ. *Clubs:* Garrick, Grillions.

STRONGE, Christopher James; Partner, Coopers & Lybrand Deloitte, since 1967; *b* 16 Aug. 1933; *s* of Reginald Herbert James Stronge and Doreen Marjorie Stronge; *m* 1964, Gabrielle; one *s* one *d*. *Educ:* Chigwell Sch.; Magdalene Coll., Cambridge (MA Math.). FCA. Deloitte Haskins & Sells: joined 1957; Partner 1967; Dep. Sen. Partner, 1985. Member: Accounting Standards Cttee, 1980–83; Internat. Accounting Standards Cttee, 1985–90; Treasurer, RIIA, 1981. *Recreations:* opera, golf, sailing. *Address:* (office) Coopers, Lybrand Deloitte, PO Box 207, 128 Queen Victoria Street, EC4P 4JX; 7 Woodhall Drive, SE21 7HJ. *T:* 081–693 6778. *Club:* Gresham.

STRONGE, Sir James Anselan Maxwell, 10th Bt *cr* 1803; *b* 17 July 1946; *s* of Maxwell Du Pré James Stronge (*d* 1973) (*g g s* of 2nd Bt) and Eileen Mary (*d* 1976), *d* of Rt Hon. Maurice Marcus McCausland, PC, Drenagh, Limavady, Co. Londonderry; *S* cousin, 1981. *Heir:* none. *Address:* Shannagh Camphill Community, Kilkeel, Co. Down; c/o Helen Allen-Morgan, Manor South, Bishopstone, Sussex BN25 2UD.

STROUD, Sir (Charles) Eric, Kt 1989; FRCP; Professor of Child Health, King's College School of Medicine and Dentistry (formerly King's College Hospital Medical School), and Director, Department of Child Health, 1968–88; Paediatric Consultant to RAF, since 1976; *b* 15 May 1924; *s* of Frank Edmund and Lavinia May Stroud; *m* 1950, June, *d* of Harold Neep; one *s* two *d*. *Educ:* Cardiff High Sch. for Boys; Welsh National Sch. of Medicine. BSc 1945, MB, BCh 1948 (Wales); MRCP 1955, DCH 1955, FRCP 1968 (London). Sqdn Ldr, RAF, 1950–52. Med. Qual., 1948; Paediatric Registrar, Welsh Nat. Sch. of Med.; Sen. Registrar, Great Ormond Street Children's Hosp., 1957–61; Paediatrician, Uganda Govt, 1958–60; Asst to Dir, Dept of Child Health, Guy's Hosp., 1961–62; Cons. Paediatrician, King's Coll. Hosp., 1962–68. Med. Advr, Eastern Hemisphere, Variety Clubs Internat., 1985–; Hon. Med. Dir, Children Nationwide Med. Res. Fund. FKC 1989. *Publications:* chapters in Textbook of Obstetrics, 1958; Childhealth in the Tropics, 1961; various articles in med. jls, mainly on sickle cell anaemia, nutrition and health of ethnic minorities. *Recreations:* bad golf, good fishing, cheap antiques, planning for retirement. *Address:* 84 Copse Hill, Wimbledon, SW20. *T:* 081–947 1336.

STROUD, Derek H.; *see* Hammond-Stroud.

STROUD, Dorothy Nancy, MBE 1968; Assistant Curator, Sir John Soane's Museum, 1945–84; *b* London, 11 Jan. 1910; *o c* of late Nancy and Alfred Stroud, London. *Educ:* Claremont, Eastbourne; Edgbaston High Sch. On staff of: Country Life, 1930–41; National Monuments Record, 1941–45. Vice-Pres., Garden History Soc., 1982–; Mem., Historic Buildings Council, 1974–82. FSA 1951; Hon. RIBA, 1975. *Publications:* Capability Brown, 1950, new edn 1975; The Thurloe Estate, 1959; The Architecture of Sir John Soane, 1961; Humphry Repton, 1962; Henry Holland, 1966; George Dance, 1971; The South Kensington Estate of Henry Smith's Charity, 1975; Sir John Soane, Architect, 1984. *Address:* 24 Onslow Square, SW7 3NS.

STROUD, Sir Eric; *see* Stroud, Sir C. E.

STROUD, Ven. Ernest Charles Frederick; Archdeacon of Colchester, since 1983; *b* 20 May 1931; *s* of Charles Henry and Irene Doris Stroud; *m* 1959, Jeanne Marguerite Evans; two *d*. *Educ:* Merrywood Grammar School; Merchant Venturers' Technical College; St Chad's Coll., Univ. of Durham. BA (Hons Theology), Diploma in Theology, Diploma in Rural Ministry and Mission. Esso Petroleum Co. Ltd, 1947–55. Deacon 1960, priest 1961, dio. Wakefield; Asst Curate, All Saints, S Kirkby, Yorks, 1960–63; Priest-in-Charge, St Ninian, Whitby, 1963–66; Minister of Conventional District, and first Vicar, All Saints, Chelmsford, 1966–75; Vicar of St Margaret of Antioch, Leigh on Sea, 1975–83; Asst RD of Southend, 1976–79; RD of Hadleigh, 1979–83; Hon. Canon of Chelmsford, 1982–. Member: General Synod, 1981–; C of E Pensions Bd; Vice-Chm., Finance and Investment Cttee. Chairman: Additional Curates Soc., 1988–; Church Union, 1989–. *Publication:* contrib. on ministry of healing to Christian. *Recreations:* travel, music, theatre. *Address:* 63 Powers Hall End, Witham, Essex CM8 1NH. *T:* Witham (0376) 513130, *Fax:* Witham (0376) 500789.

STROWGER, Gaston Jack, CBE 1976; Managing Director, Thorn Electrical Industries, 1970–79; Chairman: Hornby Hobbies PLC, since 1981; Wiltminster Ltd, since 1981; Director, Harland Simon; *b* 8 Feb. 1916; *s* of Alfred Henry Strowger, Lowestoft boat-owner, and Lily Ellen Tripp; *m* 1939, Katherine Ellen Gilbert; two *s* one *d*. *Educ:* Lowestoft Grammar School. Joined London Electrical Supply Co., 1934; HM Forces, 1939–43. Joined TEI, as an Accountant, 1943; Group Chief Accountant, 1952; joined Tricity Finance Corp. as Dir, 1959; Exec. Dir, TEI, 1961; full Dir 1966; Financial Dir 1967; Dep. Chm., Tricity Finance Corp., 1968; Chm., Thorn-Ericsson, 1974–81. FBIM 1971. *Recreations:* gardening, bowling. *Address:* The Penthouse, 46 Maplin Close, Eversley Park Road, Winchmore Hill, N21 1NB.

STROYAN, Ronald Angus Ropner, QC 1972; **His Honour Judge Stroyan;** a Circuit Judge, since 1975; *b* 27 Nov. 1924; *e s* of Ronald S. Stroyan of Boreland, Killin; *m* 1st, 1952, Elisabeth Anna Grant (marr. diss. 1965), *y d* of Col J. P. Grant of Rothiemurchus; one *s* two *d*; 2nd, 1967, Jill Annette Johnston, *d* of late Sir Douglas Marshall; one *s* (and two step *s* two step *d*). *Educ:* Harrow School; Trinity College, Cambridge; BA(Hons). Served 1943–45 with The Black Watch (NW Europe); attd Argyll and Sutherland Highlanders, Palestine, 1945–47 (despatches); Captain; later with Black Watch TA. Barrister-at-Law, 1950, Inner Temple. Dep. Chm., North Riding QS, 1962–70, Chm., 1970–71; a Recorder of the Crown Court, 1972–75. Mem. Gen. Council of the Bar, 1963–67, 1969–73 and 1975. *Recreations:* shooting, stalking, fishing. *Address:* Chapel Cottage, Whashton, near Richmond, Yorks; Boreland, Killin, Perthshire. *T:* Killin (05672) 252. *Clubs:* Caledonian; Yorkshire (York).

STRUDWICK, Air Cdre Arthur Sidney Ronald, CB 1976; DFC 1945; *b* 16 April 1921; *s* of Percival and Mary Strudwick; *m* 1941, Cissily (*d* 1983); two *s* one *d*. *Educ:* Guildford Tech. Coll.; RAF Colls. Joined RAF 1940; War Service as Fighter Pilot, 1941–43; POW Germany, 1944; Test Flying, Canada, 1948–50; CO No 98 Sqdn, 1951–53; Staff Coll., Camberley, 1954; Commanded Jt Services Trials Unit, Woomera, 1956–59; JSSC, 1959–60; MoD Planning Staff, 1960–62; Dir of Plans, Far East, 1962–64; Commanded RAF Leuchars, 1965–67; Air Cdre Plans, Strategic Comd, 1967–69; IDC 1969; Dir of Flying (R&D), MoD PE, 1970–73; AOC Central Tactics and Trials Orgn, 1973–76, retired 1976. Defence Liaison Officer, Singer Co., Link-Miles Div., 1976–86. *Recreations:* golf, gardening. *Club:* Royal Air Force.

STRUDWICK, John Philip, CBE 1970; CVO 1973; Assistant Secretary, Board of Inland Revenue, 1950–74, retired; *b* 30 May 1914; *s* of Philip Strudwick, FRICS and Marjorie Strudwick (*née* Clements); *m* 1942, Elizabeth Marion Stemson; two *s* three *d* (and one *d* decd). *Educ:* Eltham Coll.; St John's Coll., Cambridge. BA 1936, MA 1973. Asst Principal, Bd of Inland Revenue, 1937; Principal 1942. Sec., Millard Tucker Cttee on Taxation Treatment of Provisions for Retirement, 1951–53. KSG 1977. *Recreations:* music, gardening, voluntary social work (Chm. of Univ. of Sussex Catholic Chaplaincy Assoc., 1972–76 and Edenbridge Volunteer Bureau, 1978–82). *Address:* The Moat, Cowden, Edenbridge, Kent TN8 7DP. *T:* Cowden (0342) 850441.

STRUTT, family name of **Barons Belper** and **Rayleigh.**

STRUTT, Sir Nigel (Edward), Kt 1972; TD; DL; *b* 18 Jan. 1916; *yr s* of late Edward Jolliffe Strutt. *Educ:* Winchester; Wye Agricultural College (Fellow, 1970). Essex Yeomanry (Major), 1937–56. Member: Eastern Electricity Bd, 1964–76; Agricultural Advisory Council, 1963– (Chm. 1969–73; Chm., Adv. Council for Agriculture and Horticulture, 1973–80); NEDC for Agriculture, 1967–82. President: Country Landowners' Association, 1967–69; British Friesian Cattle Soc., 1974–75; Royal Agricultural Soc. of England, 1982–83. Master, Farmers' Co., 1976–77. DL Essex 1954; High Sheriff of Essex, 1966. Hon. FRASE, 1971. Hon. DSc Cranfield, 1979; DU Essex, 1981. Massey Ferguson Award, 1976. Von Thünen Gold Medal, Kiel Univ., 1974. *Recreations:* shooting, ski-ing. *Address:* Sparrows, Terling, Essex. *T:* Terling (024533) 213. *Clubs:* Brooks's, Farmers'.

STUART, family name of **Earl Castle Stewart, Earl of Moray** and **Viscount Stuart of Findhorn.**

STUART; *see* Crichton-Stuart, family name of Marquess of Bute.

STUART; *see* Mackenzie Stuart, family name of Baron Mackenzie-Stuart.

STUART, Viscount; Andrew Richard Charles Stuart; *b* 7 Oct. 1953; *s* and *heir* of 8th Earl Castle Stewart, *qv*; *m* 1973, Annie Le Poulain, St Malo, France; one *d*. *Educ:* Wynstones, Glos; Millfield, Som. *Recreations:* flying, sailing. *Address:* Combe Hayes Farm, Buckerell, near Honiton, Devon EX14 0ET.

STUART OF FINDHORN, 2nd Viscount *cr* 1959; **David Randolph Moray Stuart;** *b* 20 June 1924; *s* of 1st Viscount Stuart of Findhorn, PC, CH, MVO, MC, and Lady Rachel Cavendish, OBE (*d* 1977), 4th *d* of 9th Duke of Devonshire; *S* father, 1971; *m* 1st, 1945, Grizel Mary Wilfreda (*d* 1948), *d* of D. T. Fyfe and *widow* of Michael Gillilan; one *s*; 2nd, 1951, Marian Emelia (marr. diss. 1979), *d* of Gerald H. Wilson; one *s* three *d*; 3rd, 1979, Margaret Anne, *yr d* of Comdr Peter Du Cane, CBE, RN. *Educ:* Eton; Cirencester Agricultural College. FRICS. Page of Honour to HM George VI, 1937–39. Served KRRC LI, 1942–47. Later RWF Major, TA. DL Caernarvonshire (retired). *Heir:* *s* Hon. James Dominic Stuart [*b* 25 March 1948; *m* 1979, Yvonne Lucienne, *d* of Edgar Després, Ottawa]. *Address:* Findhorn, Forres, Moray.

STUART, Andrew Christopher, CMG 1979; CPM 1961; HM Diplomatic Service, retired; Consultant to Voluntary Service Overseas, since 1990; *b* 30 Nov. 1928; *s* of late Rt Rev. Cyril Edgar Stuart and Mary Summerhayes; *m* 1959, Patricia Kelly; two *s* one *d*. *Educ:* Bryanston; Clare Coll., Cambridge (MA). Royal Navy, 1947–49. Colonial Admin. Service, Uganda, 1953; retd from HMOCS as Judicial Adviser, 1965. Called to Bar, Middle Temple, 1965. Entered HM Diplomatic Service, 1965; 1st Sec. and Head of Chancery, Helsinki, 1968; Asst, S Asian Dept, FCO, 1971; Head of Hong Kong and Indian Ocean Dept, FCO, 1972–75; Counsellor, Jakarta, 1975–78; British Resident Comr, New Hebrides, 1978–80; Ambassador to Finland, 1980–83. Principal, United World Coll. of the Atlantic, 1983–90. Order of the Lion (Finland), 1990. *Recreations:* sailing, gliding. *Address:* 34 Queensgate Terrace, SW7. *T:* 071–589 7769. *Clubs:* United Oxford & Cambridge University, Alpine; Jesters; Royal Naval Sailing Association.

STUART, Antony James Cobham E.; *see* Edwards-Stuart.

STUART, (Charles) Murray; Chief Executive, Berisford International, since 1991; *b* 28 July 1933; *s* of Charles Maitland Stuart and Grace Forrester Stuart (*née* Kerr); *m* 1963, Netta Caroline; one *s* one *d*. *Educ:* Glasgow Acad.; Glasgow Univ. (MA, LLB). Scottish Chartered Accountant; CA. With P. & W. McLellan, Ford Motor Co., Sheffield Twist Drill & Steel Co., and Unicorn Industries, 1961–73; Finance Dir, Hepworths, 1973–74; Finance Dir and Dep. Man. Dir, ICL, 1974–81; Metal Box, subseq. MB Group: Finance Dir, Dir—Finance, Planning and Admin, 1981–86; Man. Dir, Dec. 1986–Dec. 1987; Gp Chief Exec., 1988–89; Chm., 1989–90; Finance Dir, Berisford International, 1990–91. Vice Chm., CMB Packaging SA, 1989–90; Non-exec. Director: Save & Prosper Insurance, 1989–91; Save & Prosper Securities, 1989–91; Scottish Power, 1990–; Hunter Saphir, 1991–. Dep. Chm., Audit Commn, 1991– (Mem., 1986–). Mem., W Surrey and NE Hants HA, 1990–. *Recreations:* sailing, tennis. *Address:* Longacre, Guildford Road, Chobham, Woking, Surrey GU24 8EA. *T:* Chobham (0276) 857144.

STUART, Charles Rowell, FRAeS, FCIT; Chairman, South Western Regional Health Authority, since 1990; *b* 20 May 1928; *s* of Charles Stuart and Agnes (*née* Spence); *m* 1951, Anne Grace Mingo; one *s* two *d*. *Educ:* St Olave's and St Saviour's Grammar Sch.; LSE (BSc Econ). FCIT 1964; FRAeS 1977. With British Rail, 1951–69; Marketing Dir and Mem. Bd, BEA, 1969–77; Hd of Commercial Develt and Exec. Bd Mem., British Airways, 1977–83; also Dir of travel cos, 1969–83; Chm. and Chief Exec., Brymon Airways, Plymouth City Airport, 1983–91. Director: SW Water plc, 1987–; Exeter and Devon Airport Ltd, 1991–. Governor: Polytechnic SW, 1986–; E Devon Coll., 1986–. Trustee, Bishop Simeon CR Trust. Voluntary driver, Exe Valley Market Bus, 1988–. FInstD 1985. *Publications:* articles in professional jls. *Recreations:* running, reading. *Address:* c/o South Western Regional Health Authority, King Square House, Bristol BS2 8EF. *T:* Bristol (0272) 423271. *Clubs:* Oriental, Farmers', Royal Automobile.

STUART, Duncan, CMG 1989; HM Diplomatic Service; Counsellor, Foreign and Commonwealth Office, since 1989; *b* 1 July 1934; *s* of late Ian Cameron Stuart and Patricia Forbes; *m* 1961, Leonore Luise Liederwald; one *s* one *d*. *Educ:* Rugby Sch.; Brasenose Coll., Oxford (MA). Served 1st Bn Oxfordshire and Bucks LI, 1955–57 (2nd Lieut). Joined Foreign, later Diplomatic, Service, 1959; Office of Political Advr, Berlin, 1960–61; FO, 1961–64; Helsinki, 1964–66; Head of Chancery, Dar-es-Salaam, 1966–69; FCO, 1969–70; Helsinki, 1970–74; FCO, 1974–80; Bonn, 1980–83; FCO, 1983–86; Washington, 1986–88. *Address:* c/o Foreign and Commonwealth Office, SW1A 2AH. *Clubs:* Boodle's, United Oxford & Cambridge University, MCC.

STUART, Francis; *b* Queensland, Australia, 1902; *s* of Henry and Elizabeth Stuart, Co. Antrim, Ireland; *m* 1st, 1920, Iseult Gonne; one *s* one *d*; 2nd, 1954, Gertrude Meiszner; 3rd, 1987, Finola Graham. *Educ:* Rugby. First book, poems, which received an American prize and also award of the Royal Irish Academy, published at age of 21; first novel published in 1931 at age of 29; contributor to various newspapers and periodicals. *Publications:* *novels:* Women and God, 1931; Pigeon Irish, 1932; The Coloured Dome, 1933; Try the Sky, 1933; Glory, 1934; The Pillar of Cloud, 1948; Redemption, 1949; The Flowering Cross, 1950; Good Friday's Daughter, 1951; The Chariot, 1953; The Pilgrimage, 1955; Victors and Vanquished, 1958; Angels of Providence, 1959; Black List, Section H, 1971; Memorial, 1973; A Hole in the Head, 1977; The High Consistory, 1980; Faillandia, 1985; The Abandoned Snail Shell, 1987; A Compendium of Lovers, 1990; *short stories:* Selected Stories, 1983; *poetry:* We Have Kept the Faith, 1923; Night Pilot, 1988; *autobiography:* Things to Live For, 1936. *Recreations:* horse-racing, golf. *Address:* 2 Highfield Park, Dublin 14, Ireland.

STUART, Rev. Canon Herbert James, CB 1983; Canon Emeritus of Lincoln Cathedral, since 1983 (Canon, 1980–83); *b* 16 Nov. 1926; *s* of Joseph and Jane Stuart; *m* 1955, Adrienne Le Fanu; two *s* one *d*. *Educ:* Mountjoy School, Dublin; Trinity Coll., Dublin (BA Hons, MA). Priest, 1950; served in Church of Ireland, 1950–55; Chaplain, RAF, 1955; Asst Chaplain-in-Chief, RAF, 1973; Chaplain-in-Chief and Archdeacon, RAF, 1980–83; QHC, 1978–83; Rector of Cherbury, 1983–87. *Recreations:* gardening, travel, books. *Address:* Abbots Walk, Lechlade Park, Lechlade, Glos GL7 3DB. *Club:* Royal Air Force.

STUART, Sir (James) Keith, Kt 1986; Chairman, Associated British Ports Holdings PLC, since 1983; *b* 4 March 1940; *s* of James and Marjorie Stuart; *m* 1966, Kathleen Anne

Pinder (*née* Woodman); three *s* one *d.* *Educ:* King George V School, Southport; Gonville and Caius College, Cambridge (MA). FCIT, CBIM, FRSA. District Manager, South Western Electricity Bd, 1970–72; British Transport Docks Board: Sec., 1972–75; Gen. Manager, 1976–77; Man. Dir, 1977–82; Dep. Chm., 1980–82; Chm., 1982–83. Dir, Internat. Assoc. of Ports and Harbors, 1983, Vice-Pres., 1985–87; Chm., Cttee on Internat. Port Develt, 1979–85; Pres., Inst. of Freight Forwarders, 1983–84. Director: Royal Ordnance Factories, 1983–85; BAA Plc, 1986–; SEEBOARD plc, 1990–. Chartered Inst. of Transport: Mem. Council, 1979–88; Vice-Pres., 1982–83; Pres., 1985–86. Liveryman, Clockmakers' Co., 1987. *Recreation:* music. *Address:* Associated British Ports Holdings PLC, 150 Holborn, EC1N 2LR. *T:* 071–430 1177. *Clubs:* Brooks's, United Oxford & Cambridge University (Trustee, 1989–).

STUART, Prof. John Trevor, FRS 1974; Professor of Theoretical Fluid Mechanics, Imperial College of Science, Technology and Medicine, University of London, since 1966; Dean, Royal College of Science, since 1990; *b* 28 Jan. 1929; *s* of Horace Stuart and Phyllis Emily Stuart (*née* Potter); *m* 1957, Christine Mary (*née* Tracy); two *s* one *d.* *Educ:* Gateway Sch., Leicester; Imperial Coll., London. BSc 1949, PhD 1951. Aerodynamics Div., Nat. Physical Lab., Teddington, 1951–66; Sen. Principal Scientific Officer (Special Merit), 1961; Hd, Maths Dept, Imperial Coll., London, 1974–79, 1983–86. Vis. Lectr, Dept of Maths, MIT, 1956–57; Vis. Prof. of Maths, MIT, 1965–66; Vis. Prof. of Theoretical Fluid Mechanics, Brown Univ., 1978–; Hon. Prof., Tianjin Univ., China, 1983–. Member: Council, Royal Soc., 1982–84; SERC, 1989– (Chm., Mathematics Cttee, 1985–88). 1st Stewartson Meml Lectr, Long Beach, Calif., 1985; 1st DiPrima Meml Lectr, Troy, NY, 1985; Ludwig Prandtl Meml Lectr, Dortmund, 1986. Hon. ScD: Brown Univ., 1986; East Anglia, 1987. Senior Whitehead Prize, London Mathematical Soc., 1984; Otto Laporte Award, Amer. Physical Soc., 1987. *Publications:* (contrib.) Laminar Boundary Layers, ed L. Rosenhead, 1963; articles in Proc. Royal Soc., Phil. Trans Royal Soc., Jl Fluid Mech., Proc. 10th Int. Cong. Appl. Mech., Jl Lub. Tech. (ASME). *Recreations:* theatre, music, gardening, reading, do-it-yourself, ornithology. *Address:* Mathematics Department, Imperial College, SW7 2AZ. *T:* 071–589 5111; 3 Steeple Close, Wimbledon, SW19 5AD. *T:* 081–946 7019.

STUART, Joseph B.; *see* Burnett-Stuart.

STUART, Sir Keith; *see* Stuart, Sir J. K.

STUART, Prof. Sir Kenneth (Lamonte), Kt 1977; MD, FRCP, FRCPE, FACP, DTM&H; Hon. Medical and Scientific Adviser, Barbados High Commission, since 1991; *b* 16 June 1920; *s* of Egbert and Louise Stuart; *m* 1958, Barbara Cecille Ashby; one *s* two *d.* *Educ:* Harrison Coll., Barbados; Queen's Univ., Belfast (MB, BCh, BAO 1948). Consultant Physician, University Coll. Hospital of the West Indies, 1954–76; University of the West Indies: Prof. of Medicine, 1966–76; Dean, Medical Faculty, 1969–71; Head, Dept of Medicine, 1972–76; Mem. Council, 1971–76; Medical Adviser, Commonwealth Secretariat, 1976–84. Rockefeller Foundation Fellow in Cardiology, Massachusetts Gen. Hosp., Boston, 1956–57; Wellcome Foundation Research Fellow, Harvard Univ., Boston, 1960–61; Gresham Prof. of Physic, 1988–. Consultant to WHO on Cardiovascular Disorders, 1969–. Chm., Commonwealth Caribbean MRC, 1989–. Chm., Court of Governors, LSHTM, 1982–; Mem., Court of Governors, Internat. Develt Res. Centre of Canada, 1985–. Hon. DSc QUB, 1986. *Publications:* articles on hepatic and cardiovascular disorders in medical journals. *Recreations:* tennis, music. *Address:* Barbados High Commission, 1 Great Russell Street, WC1B 3JY.

STUART, Marian Elizabeth; Under Secretary, Department of Health, since 1989; *b* 17 July 1944; *d* of William and Greta Stuart; one *s* one *d.* *Educ:* Eye Grammar School, Suffolk; Mount Grace Comprehensive School, Potters Bar; Leicester Univ. (MA). Joined DHSS, 1967. *Recreations:* reading, bridge, ski-ing. *Address:* Department of Health, Friars House, 157–168 Blackfriars Road, SE1 8EU.

STUART, Michael Francis Harvey; Treasury Adviser, UK Mission to the United Nations, 1974–82, retired; *b* 3 Oct. 1926; *s* of late Willoughby Stuart and Ethel Candy; *m* 1961, Ruth Tennyson-d'Eyncourt; one *s* one *d.* *Educ:* Harrow; Magdalen Coll., Oxford. Air Min., 1950–65; DEA, 1965–69; HM Treasury, 1969–74. Mem., UN Adv. Cttee on Administrative and Budgetary Questions, 1975–80. *Recreations:* music, tennis. *Address:* Bourne House, Chertsey Road, Chobham, Woking, Surrey GU24 8NB. *T:* Chobham (0276) 857954.

STUART, Murray; *see* Stuart, C. M.

STUART, Nicholas Willoughby, CB 1990; Deputy Secretary, Department of Education and Science, since 1987; *b* 2 Oct. 1942; *s* of Douglas Willoughby Stuart and Margaret Eileen Stuart; *m* 1st, 1963, Sarah Mustard (marr. diss. 1974); one *d* (one *s* decd); 2nd, 1975, Susan Jane Fletcher; one *s* one *d.* *Educ:* Harrow Sch.; Christ Church Coll., Oxford (MA). Asst Principal, DES, 1964–68; Private Sec. to Minister for the Arts, 1968–69; Principal, DES, 1969–73; Private Secretary to: Head of the Civil Service, 1973; Prime Minister, 1973–76; Asst Sec., DES, 1976–78; Advr, Cabinet of Pres. of EEC, 1978–80; Under Sec., DES, 1981–87. *Recreation:* collecting Tunbridgeware.

STUART, Sir Phillip (Luttrell), 9th Bt *cr* 1660; late F/O RCAF; President, Agassiz Industries Ltd; *b* 7 September 1937; *s* of late Luttrell Hamilton Stuart and late Irene Ethel Jackman; *S* uncle, Sir Houlton John Stuart, 8th Bt, 1959; *m* 1st, 1962, Marlene Rose Muth (marr. diss. 1968); two *d*; 2nd, 1969, Beverley Clare Pieri; one *s* one *d.* *Educ:* Vancouver. Enlisted RCAF, Nov. 1955; commnd FO (1957–62). *Heir:* *s* Geoffrey Phillip Stuart, *b* 5 July 1973.

[*But his name does not, at the time of going to press, appear on the official Roll of Baronets.*

STUART-COLE, James; DL; Chairman, Merseyside Region, Co-operative Retail Services Ltd, 1974; *b* 6 March 1916; *s* of Charles Albert Stuart-Cole and Gertrude Mary Stuart-Cole; *m* 1937, Margaret Evelyn Robb; one *s* two *d.* *Educ:* Birley Street Central Sch., Manchester. Engr, 1930–55; Political Organiser, Labour Party, 1955–60; Political Sec., Co-operative Soc., 1960–81. Mem. Bd, Merseyside Development Corp, 1981. Merseyside County Council: Mem., 1973–86; Leader, 1981–82; Chm., 1983–84. DL Merseyside, 1983. *Recreations:* sport, grandchildren. *Address:* 85 Kylemore Drive, Pensby, Wirral, Merseyside L61 6XZ. *T:* 051–342 6180.

STUART-FORBES, Sir Charles Edward; *see* Forbes.

STUART-HARRIS, Sir Charles (Herbert), Kt 1970; CBE 1961; MD; FRCP; Fogarty Scholar-in-Residence, National Institutes of Health, Bethesda, Maryland, USA, 1979–80; Postgraduate Dean of Medicine, University of Sheffield, 1972–77, Professor of Medicine, 1946–72, now Emeritus Professor; Physician, United Sheffield Hospitals, 1946–74; *b* 12 July 1909; *s* of late Dr and Mrs Herbert Harris, Birmingham; *m* 1937, Marjorie, *y d* of late Mr and Mrs F. Robinson, Dulwich; two *s* one *d.* *Educ:* King Edward's School, Birmingham; St Bartholomew's Hospital Medical School. MB, BS London 1931 (Gold Medal); MD 1933 (Gold Medal); FRCP 1944. House-Physician and Demonstrator in Pathology, St Bartholomew's Hosp.; First Asst, Dept of Medicine, Brit. Postgrad. Medical Sch., 1935; Sir Henry Royce Research Fellow. Univ. of London, 1935; Foulerton Research Fellow, Royal Society, 1938. War Service, 1939–46; Specialist Pathologist Comdg Mobile Bacteriological, Command and Field Laboratories; Colonel RAMC, 1945. Goulstonian Lectr, Royal College of Physicians, 1944; Visiting Prof. of Medicine, Albany Medical Coll., New York, 1953; Sir Arthur Sims Commonwealth Travelling Prof., 1962. Vis. Professor of Medicine: Vanderbilt Univ., Tennessee, 1961; Univ. of Southern California, Los Angeles, 1962; Croonian Lectr, Royal Coll. of Physicians, 1962; Henry Cohen Lectr, Hebrew Univ. of Jerusalem, 1966; Waring Prof., Univ. of Colorado and Stanford Univ., Calif., 1967; Harveian Orator, RCP, 1974. Member: MRC, 1957–61; Public Health Lab. Service Bd, 1954–66; UGC 1968–77 (Chm., Med. Sub-Cttee, 1973–77); UPGC, Hong Kong, 1978–84. Pres., Assoc. of Physicians of GB and Ireland, 1971. Hon. Member: Assoc. of Amer. Physicians; Infectious Diseases Soc. of Amer. Hon. DSc: Hull, 1973; Sheffield, 1978. *Publications:* (co-author) Chronic bronchitis emphysema and cor pulmonale, 1957; Influenza and other virus infections of the respiratory tract, 1965; (co-author) Virus and Rickettsial Diseases, 1967; (co-author) Influenza—the Viruses and the Disease, 1976, 2nd edn 1985; papers in med. and scientific jls on influenza, typhus and bronchitis. *Recreation:* music. *Address:* 28 Whitworth Road, Sheffield S10 3HD. *T:* Sheffield (0742) 301200.

STUART-MENTETH, Sir James; *see* Menteth.

STUART-MOORE, Michael, QC 1990; a Recorder of the Crown Court, since 1985; *b* 7 July 1944; *s* of (Kenneth) Basil Moore and Marjorie (Elizabeth) Moore; *m* 1973, Katherine Ann, *d* of William and Ruth Scott; one *s* one *d.* *Educ:* Cranleigh School. Called to the Bar, Middle Temple, 1966. *Recreations:* cine photography, travel to outlandish places, music, tennis. *Address:* 1 Hare Court, Temple, EC4Y 7BE. *T:* 071–353 5324.

STUART-PAUL, Air Marshal Sir Ronald (Ian), KBE 1990 (MBE 1967); Director General, Saudi Air Force Project, 1985–92; *b* 7 Nov. 1934; *s* of Dr J. G. Stuart-Paul and Mary (*née* McDonald); *m* 1963, Priscilla Frances (*née* Kay); one *s* one *d.* *Educ:* Dollar Acad.; RAF Coll., Cranwell. Served 14, 19, 56 and 92 Sqns and 11 and 12 Groups, 1957–73; Defence Attaché, Saudi Arabia, 1974–75; Stn Comdr, RAF Lossiemouth, 1976–78; RCDS, 1979; Dep. Comdr, NAEW Force, SHAPE, 1980–82; Dir of Ops Air Defence, RAF, 1982–83; AO Training, RAF Support Command, 1984–85. *Recreations:* golf, campanology, sailing, rug-making. *Address:* 27 Church Way, Little Stukeley, Huntingdon, Cambs PE17 5BQ. *T:* Huntingdon (0480) 457660. *Club:* Royal Air Force.

STUART-SHAW, Max, CBE 1963; Executive Director, Olympic Airways, 1969–71; *b* 20 Dec. 1912; *e s* of Herman and Anne Louise Stuart-Shaw; *m* 1967, Janna Job, *d* of C. W. Howard. *Educ:* Belmont School, Sussex; St Paul's, London. Imperial Airways/BOAC, 1931–46; Aer Lingus Irish Airlines; Traffic Manager, Commercial Manager, Asst Gen. Manager, 1947–57; Chief Exec. and Gen. Manager Central African Airways, Salisbury, Rhodesia, 1958–65; Man. Dir, BUA, 1966–67; Vice-Chairman, British United Airways, 1967–68. FCIT. *Recreation:* air transport. *Club:* Harare (Zimbabwe).

STUART-SMITH, James, CB 1986; QC 1988; Judge Advocate General, 1984–91 (Vice Judge Advocate General, 1979–84); a Recorder, 1985–91; *b* 13 Sept. 1919; *s* of James Stuart-Smith and Florence Emma (*née* Armfield); *m* 1957, Jean Marie Therese Young Groundsell, *d* of Hubert Young Groundsell, Newport, IoW; one *s* one *d.* *Educ:* Brighton Coll.; London Hospital. Medical student, 1938. Served War of 1939–45: commnd KRRC, 1940; served ME and Italy, and staff appointments in UK; demobilised 1947. Called to Bar, Middle Temple, 1948; practised in London, 1948–55; Legal Asst, JAG's Office, 1955; Dep. Judge Advocate, 1957; Asst Judge Advocate General, 1968; Dep. Judge Advocate, Middle East Comd (Aden), 1964–65; Dep. Judge Advocate General, British Forces Germany, 1976–79. Pres., Internat. Soc. for Military Law and the Law of War, 1985–91 (Vice-Pres., 1979–85). *Publications:* contribs to Internat. Soc. for Military Law and Law of War Rev. and Law Qly Rev., on history and practice of British military law. *Recreations:* composing letters, lawn tennis, mowing lawns. *Address:* The Firs, Copthorne, Sussex RH10 4HH. *T:* Copthorne (0342) 712395. *Club:* Royal Air Force.

STUART-SMITH, Rt. Hon. Sir Murray, Kt 1981; PC 1988; **Rt. Hon. Lord Justice Stuart-Smith;** a Lord Justice of Appeal, since 1988; *b* 18 Nov. 1927; *s* of Edward Stuart-Smith and Doris Mary Laughland; *m* 1953, Joan Elizabeth Mary Motion, BA, JP, DL (High Sheriff of Herts, 1983); three *s* three *d.* *Educ:* Radley; Corpus Christi Coll., Cambridge (Foundn Scholar; 1st Cl. Hons Law Tripos, Pts I and II; 1st Cl. Hons LLM; MA). 2nd Lieut, 5th Royal Inniskilling Dragoon Guards, 1947. Called to the Bar, Gray's Inn, 1952 (Atkin Scholar), Bencher 1977; QC 1970; a Recorder of the Crown Court, 1972–81; a Judge of the High Court of Justice, QBD, 1981–88; Presiding Judge, Western Circuit, 1983–87. Jt Inspector into Grays Bldg Soc., 1979. Mem., Criminal Injuries Compensation Bd, 1980–81. *Recreations:* playing 'cello, shooting, building, playing bridge. *Address:* Royal Courts of Justice, Strand, WC2.

STUART TAYLOR, Sir Nicholas (Richard), 4th Bt *cr* 1917; solicitor; *b* 14 Jan. 1952; *s* of Sir Richard Laurence Stuart Taylor, 3rd Bt, and of Iris Mary, *d* of Rev. Edwin John Gargery; *S* father, 1978; *m* 1984, Malvena Elizabeth Sullivan, BSc, MB, BS, FFARCS, *d* of late Daniel David Charles Sullivan and Kathleen Sullivan; one *d.* *Educ:* Bradfield. Admitted Solicitor, 1977. *Recreations:* ski-ing and other sports. *Heir:* none. *Address:* 3 Horseshoe Drive, Romsey, Hampshire. *Club:* Ski Club of Great Britain.

STUART-WHITE, Christopher Stuart; His Honour Judge Stuart-White; a Circuit Judge, since 1978; *b* 18 Dec. 1933; *s* of Reginald Stuart-White and Catherine Mary Wigmore Stuart-White (*née* Higginson); *m* 1957, Pamela (*née* Grant); one *s* two *d.* *Educ:* Winchester; Trinity Coll., Oxford (BA). Called to Bar, Inner Temple, 1957. Practising Barrister on the Midland and Oxford Circuit, 1958–78; a Recorder of the Crown Court, 1974–78. Chairman: Magisterial Cttee, Judicial Studies Bd, 1985–90; County Court Rule Cttee, 1988–90. *Recreation:* gardening.

STUBBLEFIELD, Sir (Cyril) James, Kt 1965; FRS 1944; FGS; FZS; DSc (London); ARCS; formerly Director, Geological Survey of Great Britain and Museum of Practical Geology, 1960–66; Director, Geological Survey in Northern Ireland, 1960–66; *b* Cambridge, 6 Sept. 1901; *s* of James and Jane Stubblefield; *m* 1932, Muriel Elizabeth, *d* of L. R. Yakchee; two *s.* *Educ:* The Perse Sch.; Chelsea Polytechnic; Royal College of Science, London (Royal Scholar); London Univ. Geology Scholar, 1921. Demonstrator in Geology, Imperial College of Science and Technology, 1923–28; Warden of pioneer Imperial Coll. Hostel, 1926–28. Apptd Geological Survey as Geologist, 1928; Chief Palæontologist, 1947–53; Asst Director, 1953–60. Mem., Anglo-French Commn of Surveillance, Channel Tunnel, 1964–67. Pres. Geological Soc. of London, 1958–60; Bigsby Medallist, 1941; Murchison Medallist, 1955. Sec. of Palæontographical Soc., 1934–48; Pres., 1966–71, Hon. Mem., 1974. Member Council Brit. Assoc. for Advancement of Science, 1946–52, 1958–63; Pres. Section C (Geology), Oxford, 1954. Pres. Cambrian Subcommn, Internat. Geol. Union's Commn on Stratigraphy, 1964–72. Pres. Internat. Congress Carboniferous Stratigraphy and Geology, 6th Session, Sheffield, 1967, and Editor, 4 vol. Compte rendu, 1968–72. Vice-Pres. International Paleontological Union, 1948–56. Corresp. Paleont. Soc. (USA), 1950–; Corresp. Mem. Geol. Soc. Stockholm, 1952–; Senckenbergische Naturforschende Gesellschaft, 1957–. Member:

Gov. Body (later Council), Chelsea Coll. of Science and Technology, 1958–82; Council, Royal Soc., 1960–62. Hon. Fellow: Pal. Soc. India, 1961–; Chelsea Coll., 1985; KCL, 1985–. Fellow Imperial Coll., 1962–; Hon. Member: Geologists' Assoc., 1973–; Liverpool Geol. Soc., 1960–; Petroleum Exploration Soc. GB, 1966–; For. Corr., Geol. Soc., France, 1963–, For. Vice-Pres., 1966. Hon. DSc Southampton, 1965. *Publications:* papers in journals, on Palæozoic fossils and rocks; also contributions to: Geological Survey Memoirs; Trilobita, Zoological Record, 1938–51, 1965–77. Joint Editor of the Handbook of the Geology of Great Britain, 1929; Reviser, Introduction to Palæontology (A. Morley Davies), 3rd edn, 1961. *Address:* 35 Kent Avenue, Ealing, W13 8BE. *T:* 081–997 5051.

STUBBS, Sir James (Wilfrid), KCVO 1979; TD 1946; Grand Secretary, United Grand Lodge of England, 1958–80; *b* 13 Aug. 1910; *s* of Rev. Wilfrid Thomas Stubbs and Muriel Elizabeth (*née* Pope); *m* Richenda Katherine Theodora Streatfeild; one *s* (and one *d* decd). *Educ:* Charterhouse (Junior and Senior Scholar); Brasenose Coll., Oxford (Scholar; MA). Assistant Master, St Paul's Sch., London, 1934–46. Served War, Royal Signals, 1941–46: Captain 1941, Major 1945, Lt-Col 1946 (2nd Lieut, SR, 1932, Lieut 1935). Asst Grand Sec., United Grand Lodge of England, 1948–54; Dep. Grand Sec., 1954–58. *Publications:* Grand Lodge 1717–1967, 1967; The Four Corners, 1983; Freemasonry in My Life, 1985. *Recreations:* family history, travel. *Address:* 5 Pensioners Court, The Charterhouse, EC1M 6AU. *T:* 071–253 1982. *Club:* Athenæum.

STUBBS, John F. A. H.; see Heath-Stubbs.

STUBBS, Prof. Michael Wesley, PhD; Professor of English Linguistics, University of Trier, Germany, since 1990; *b* 23 Dec. 1947; *s* of late Leonard Garforth Stubbs and of Isabella Wardop (*née* McGavin). *Educ:* Glasgow High Sch. for Boys; King's Coll., Cambridge (MA); Univ. of Edinburgh (PhD 1975). Res. Associate, Univ. of Birmingham, 1973–74; Lectr in Linguistics, Univ. of Nottingham, 1974–85; Prof. of English in Educn, Inst. of Educn, Univ. of London, 1985–90. Vis. Prof. of Linguistics, Univ. of Tübingen, Germany, 1985. *Publications:* Language, Schools and Classrooms, 1976, 2nd edn 1983; Language and Literacy, 1980; Discourse Analysis, 1983; Educational Linguistics, 1986; articles in Lang. and Educn, Applied Linguistics, Jl of Pragmatics. *Recreation:* walking. *Address:* FB2 Anglistik, University of Trier, 5500 Trier, Germany. *T:* 0651 201 2278.

STUBBS, Thomas, OBE 1980; HM Diplomatic Service, retired; *b* 12 July 1926; *s* of Thomas Stubbs and Lillian Marguerite (*née* Rumball, formerly Bell); *m* 1951, Dorothy Miller; one *s* one *d*. *Educ:* Heaton Tech. Sch., Newcastle upon Tyne. Served in Army, 1944–48. Joined Min. of Nat. Insce, later Min. of Pensions and Nat. Insce, 1948; transf. to CRO, 1960; New Delhi, 1962; CRO, 1964; Wellington, NZ, 1965; Vice-Consul, Düsseldorf, 1970; seconded to BOTB, 1974; First Sec. (Commercial) and Consul, Addis Ababa, 1977; Consul, Hannover, 1980; Dep. High Comr, Madras, 1983–86. Dep. Mayor, Spelthorne Borough Council, 1991–May 1992 (Mem., 1987–; Vice-Chm., Leisure and Amenities Cttee, 1987–89; Chm., Personnel Cttee, 1989–91). *Recreations:* reading, golf. *Address:* 17 Chester Close, Ashford Common, Middlesex TW15 1PH.

STUBBS, William Frederick, QC 1978; *b* 27 Nov. 1934; *s* of William John Stubbs and Winifred Hilda (*née* Johnson); *m* 1961, Anne Katharine (*d* 1966), *d* of late Prof. W. K. C. Guthrie, FBA; one *s* one *d*. *Educ:* The High Sch., Newcastle-under-Lyme, Staffs; Gonville and Caius Coll., Cambridge; Harvard Law Sch. Open Minor Scholar in Nat. Sci., Gonville and Caius Coll., 1951; Student, Gray's Inn, 1953; 1st Cl. Hons Law Tripos Pt I, and George Long Prize for Roman Law, Cambridge, 1954; Major Scholar, Gonville and Caius Coll., 1954; 1st Cl. Hons with Distinction Law Tripos Pt II, Cambridge, 1955; LLB 1st Cl. Hons with Dist., and Chancellor's Medal for English Law, Cambridge, 1956; Tapp Post-Grad. Law Scholar, Gonville and Caius Coll., 1956 (also awarded Schuldham Plate); Joseph Hodges Choate Meml Fellow, Harvard Coll., 1957; Bar Final Exam., 2nd Cl. Hons Div. 1, 1957; Holker Sen. Scholar and Macaskie Scholar, Gray's Inn, 1957; called to the Bar, Gray's Inn, 1957, Bencher, 1987. Has practised in Courts of Malaysia, Singapore and Hong Kong. *Recreations:* reading, walking, natural history. *Address:* Erskine Chambers, 30 Lincoln's Inn Fields, WC2A 3PF. *T:* 071–242 5532; 3 Atherton Drive, SW19 5LB. *T:* 081–947 3986. *Club:* MCC.

STUBBS, William Hamilton; Chief Executive, Polytechnics and Colleges Funding Council, since 1988; *b* 5 Nov. 1937; *s* of Joseph Stubbs and Mary Stubbs (*née* McNicol); *m* 1963, Marie Margaret Pierce; three *d*. *Educ:* Workington Grammar Sch.; St Aloysius Coll., Glasgow; Glasgow Univ. (BSc, PhD). Res. Associate, Univ. of Arizona, 1963–64; with Shell Oil Co., San Francisco, 1964–67; teaching, 1967–72; Asst Dir of Educn, Carlisle, 1972–74; Asst Dir of Educn, 1974–76, Second Dep. Dir of Educn, 1976–77, Cumbria; Second Dep. Educn Officer, 1977–79, Dir of Educn (Schools), 1979–82, Educn Officer and Chief Exec., 1982–88, ILEA. Trustee, Thames/LWT Telethon Trust, 1987–. CBIM; FRSA. *Address:* 122 Cromwell Tower, Barbican, EC2.

STÜCKLEN, Richard; Grosskreuz des Verdienstordens der Bundesrepublik Deutschland; Bayerischer Verdienstorden; Vice-President of the Bundestag, Federal Republic of Germany, since 1983 (President, 1979–83); *b* 20 Aug. 1916; *s* of Georg Stücklen and Mathilde (*née* Bach); *m* 1943, Ruth Stücklen (*née* Geissler); one *s* one *d*. *Educ:* primary sch.; technical sch.; engineering sch. Industrial Dept Manager and Manager in family business, 1945–49. Mem. of Bundestag, 1949–; Dep. Chm., CDU/Christian Social Union and Party Leader, Christian Social Union, 1953–57 and 1967–76; Federal Minister of Posts and Telegraphs, 1957–66; Vice-Pres. of Bundestag, 1976–79. *Publications:* Bundestagsreden und Zeitdokumente, 1979; and others. *Recreations:* skating, chess, soccer. *Address:* Bundeshaus, 5300 Bonn, Germany. *T:* Bonn 16 29 12. *Club:* Lions.

STUCLEY, Sir Hugh (George Coplestone Bampfylde), 6th Bt *cr* 1859; Lieut Royal Horse Guards, retired; *b* 8 Jan. 1945; *s* of Major Sir Dennis Frederic Bankes Stucley, 5th Bt, and of Hon. Sheila Bampfylde, *o d* of 4th Baron Poltimore; *S* father, 1983; *m* 1969, Angela Caroline, *e d* of Richard Charles Robertson Toller, MC, Theale, Berks; two *s* two *d*. *Educ:* Milton Abbey School; Royal Agricultural College, Cirencester. *Heir: s* George Dennis Bampfylde Stucley, *b* 26 Dec. 1970. *Address:* Affeton Castle, Worlington, Crediton, Devon EX17 4TU. *Club:* Sloane.

STUDD, Sir Edward (Fairfax), 4th Bt *cr* 1929; Chairman, Gray Dawes Travel, and director of other companies; *b* 3 May 1929; *s* of Sir Eric Studd, 2nd Bt, OBE, and Stephana (*d* 1976), *o d* of L. J. Langmead; *S* brother, 1977; *m* 1960, Prudence Janet, *o d* of Alastair Douglas Fyfe, OBE, Riding Mill, Northumberland; two *s* one *d*. *Educ:* Winchester College. Lieutenant Coldstream Guards, London and Malaya, 1947–49; Macneill & Barry Ltd, Calcutta, 1951–62; Inchcape & Co. Ltd, London, 1962–86 (Dir, 1974–86). Master, Merchant Taylor's Co., 1987–88. *Recreations:* walking, shooting, fishing. *Heir: s* Philip Alastair Fairfax Studd [*b* 27 Oct. 1961; *m* 1987, Georgina, *d* of Roger Neville; one *d*].

STUDD, Sir Peter Malden, GBE 1971; KCVO 1979; Kt 1969; DL; MA, DSc; *b* 15 Sept. 1916; *s* of late Brig. Malden Augustus Studd, DSO, MC and Netta Cramsie; *m* 1943, Angela Mary Hamilton (*née* Garnier); two *s*. *Educ:* Harrow; Clare Coll., Cambridge (MA). Captain of cricket, Harrow and Cambridge Univ. Served War of 1939–45, Royal Artillery, ME and European campaigns. De La Rue Co., 1939–81. Alderman, Cripplegate Ward, City of London, 1959–76; Sheriff, 1967–68; Lord Mayor of London, 1970–71;

Hon. DSc City Univ., 1971. Chm., King George's Jubilee Trust, 1972; Dep. Chm., Queen's Silver Jubilee Trust, 1976–80; Vice-Pres., Britain-Australia Bicentennial Cttee '88, 1985–; Pres., British Chiropractic Advancement Assoc., 1987–90; Vice-Pres., The Arts Educational Schools, 1984–; Trustee, Royal Jubilee Trusts, 1980–. Liveryman, Merchant Taylors' Co., 1959 (Asst, 1959–, Master, 1973–74); Hon. Liveryman, Worshipful Cos of Fruiterers and Plaisterers. DL Wilts, 1983. KStJ 1968. *Recreations:* gardening, fishing, shooting, 'lighting up the Thames'. *Address:* c/o Messrs C. Hoare & Co., 37 Fleet Street, EC4P 4DQ. *Clubs:* MCC, I Zingari; Hawks (Cambridge); Houghton (Stockbridge).

STUDHOLME, Sir Henry (William), 3rd Bt *cr* 1956, of Perridge, Co. Devon; Managing Director, Wood & Wood International Signs Ltd; *b* 31 Jan. 1958; *s* of Sir Paul Henry William Studholme, 2nd Bt and Virginia (*d* 1990), *yr d* of Sir (Herbert) Richmond Palmer, KCMG, CBE; *S* father, 1990; *m* 1988, Sarah Lucy Rosita (*née* Deans-Chrystall); one *d*. *Educ:* Eton; Trinity Hall, Cambridge (MA). ACA, ATII. *Recreations:* wine, agriculture. *Heir: b* James Paul Gilfred Studholme, *b* 10 Feb. 1960. *Address:* Perridge House, Longdown, Exeter, Devon EX6 7RU. *Club:* Brooks's.

STURDEE, Rear-Adm. Arthur Rodney Barry, CB 1971; DSC 1945; *b* 6 Dec. 1919; *s* of Comdr Barry V. Sturdee, RN, and Barbara (*née* Sturdee); *m* 1953, Marie-Claire Amstoutz, Mulhouse, France; one *s* one *d*. *Educ:* Canford Sch. Entered Royal Navy as Special Entry Cadet, 1937. Served War of 1939–45: Midshipman in HMS Exeter at Battle of the River Plate, 1939; Lieut, 1941; specialised in Navigation, 1944; minesweeping in Mediterranean, 1944–45 (DSC). Lt-Comdr, 1949; RN Staff Coll., 1950–51; Staff of Navigation Sch., 1951–52; Comdr, 1952; JSSC, 1953; BJSM, Washington, 1953–55; Fleet Navigating Officer, Medit., 1955–57; Exec. Officer, RNAS, Culdrose, 1958–59; Captain 1960; NATO Defence Coll., 1960–63; Queen's Harbour-Master, Singapore, 1963–65; Staff of Chief of Defence Staff, 1965–67; Chief of Staff to C-in-C, Portsmouth (as Cdre), 1967–69; Rear-Adm. 1969; Flag Officer, Gibraltar, 1969–72; retired 1972. ADC to the Queen, 1969. *Address:* 3 Tibberton Mews, Tibberton Road, Malvern, Worcestershire WR14 3AS. *T:* Malvern (0684) 575402.

STURDY, Henry William, OBE 1975 (MBE 1968); HM Diplomatic Service, retired; Deputy Consul General and Counsellor Commercial, Chicago, 1976–78; *b* 17 Feb. 1919; *s* of late Henry William Dawson Sturdy and Jemima Aixill; *m* 1945, Anne Jamieson Marr; one *s* one *d*. *Educ:* Woolwich Polytechnic (Mechanical Engineering). Served War in Middle East, 1939–45; Allied Control Commission, Germany, 1946. Executive Branch of Civil Service and Board of Trade, 1951; tour in Trade Commission Service, 1953; appointments: Pakistan, Bangladesh, Sri Lanka, Canada. First Secretary, Diplomatic Service, 1965; Counsellor, Korea, 1976. Defence Medal; 1939–45 Medal; General Service Medal, 1939, with Palestine Clasp, 1945. *Recreations:* squash, bridge, reading, argument, international cuisine. *Address:* 17 Clock Tower Court, Park Avenue, Bexhill-on-Sea, E Sussex TN39 3HP.

STURGE, Harold Francis Ralph; Metropolitan Magistrate, 1947–68; *b* 15 May 1902; *y s* of Ernest Harold Sturge; *m* 1936, Doreen, *e d* of Sir Percy Greenaway, 1st Bt; two *s* (and one *s* decd). *Educ:* Highgate Sch.; Oriel Coll., Oxford, MA (Lit. Hum.). Called to Bar, Inner Temple, 1925; Midland Circuit. War of 1939–45, served on staff of Judge Advocate-General. Mem., Departmental Cttee on the Probation Service, 1959–62; President, Old Cholmelian Society, 1962–63. *Publications:* The Road Haulage Wages Act, 1938; (with T. D. Corpe, OBE) Road Haulage Law and Compensation, 1947; (with C. A. Reston, LLB) The Main Rules of Evidence in Criminal Cases, 1972. *Recreation:* painting. *Address:* 10 Tilney Court, Catherine Road, Surbiton, Surrey KT6 4HA.

STURGE, Maj.-Gen. (Henry Arthur) John, CB 1978; Chairman, Logica Defence and Civil Government Ltd, since 1991; *b* 27 April 1925; *s* of Henry George Arthur Sturge and Lilian Beatrice Sturge; *m* 1953, Jean Ailsa Mountain; two *s* one *d*. *Educ:* Wilson's Sch., (formerly) Camberwell, London; Queen Mary Coll., London. Commissioned, Royal Signals, 1946; UK, 1946–50; Egypt, 1950–53; UK, incl. psc, 1953–59; Far East, 1959–62; jssc, 1962; BAOR, 1963–64; RMA, Sandhurst, 1965–66; BAOR, incl. Command, 1966–69; Min. of Defence, 1970–75; Chief Signal Officer, BAOR, 1975–77; ACDS (Signals), 1977–80. Col Comdt, Royal Corps of Signals, 1977–85. Colonel, Queen's Gurkha Signals, 1980–86. Gen. Manager, 1981–84, Dir, 1983–84, Marconi Space and Defence Systems; Man. Dir, 1984–85, Chm., 1985–86, Marconi Secure Radio Systems; Prin. Consultant, Logica Space and Defence Systems, 1986–90. Vice Chm., Governors, Wilson's Sch., 1979–. *Recreations:* sailing, (formerly) Rugby. *Address:* 18 High Street, Odiham, Hampshire RG25 1LG. *Club:* Army and Navy.

STURKEY, (Robert) Douglas; Official Secretary to the Governor-General of Australia, since 1990; Secretary of the Order of Australia, since 1990; *b* 7 Sept. 1935; *s* of late James Robert Sturkey and Jessie Grace (*née* Meares). *Educ:* Wesley Coll., S Perth; Univ. of WA (BA Hons). Mem., Australian Diplomatic Service, 1957–90: service abroad at Wellington, Lagos, Suva, Malta, Calcutta; Counsellor, later Dep. Perm. Rep., UN, New York, 1974–77; Ambassador to Saudi Arabia (also concurrently to countries of Arabian peninsula), 1979–84; Head, S Asia, Africa and ME Br., Dept of Foreign Affairs, Canberra, 1984–87; Principal Advr, Asia Div., Dept of Foreign Affairs and Trade, Canberra, 1987–90. *Recreations:* opera, music, theatre. *Address:* Government House, Canberra, ACT 2600, Australia. *T:* (06) 2833 533.

STURROCK, Philip James; Chairman and Managing Director, Cassell, since 1986; *b* 5 Oct. 1947; *s* of James Cars Sturrock and Joyce Sturrock (*née* Knowles); *m* 1972, Susan Haycock; one *s* two *d*. *Educ:* Queen Mary's School, Walsall; Trinity College, Oxford (MA); Manchester Business School (MBA). Managing Director: IBIS Informatin Services, 1972–80; Pitman Books, 1980–83; Group Man. Dir, Routledge & Kegan Paul, 1983–85. Governor, Pusey House, Oxford, 1975–. *Recreations:* reading, walking, music. *Address:* 52 Hill Street, St Albans, Herts. *T:* St Albans (0727) 58849. *Club:* United Oxford & Cambridge University.

STUTTAFORD, Dr (Irving) Thomas; medical practitioner; *b* 4 May 1931; 2nd *s* of late Dr W. J. E. Stuttaford, MC, Horning, Norfolk; *m* 1957, Pamela, *d* of late Col Richard Ropner, TD, DL, Tain; three *s*. *Educ:* Gresham's Sch.; Brasenose Coll., Oxford; West London Hosp. 2nd Lieut, 10th Royal Hussars (PWO), 1953–55; Lieut, Scottish Horse (TA), 1955–59. Qualif. MRCS, LRCP, 1959; junior hosp. appts, 1959 and 1960. Gen. Med. practice, 1960–70. Mem. Blofield and Flegg RDC, 1964–66; Mem., Norwich City Council, 1969–71. MP (C) Norwich S, 1970–Feb. 1974; Mem. Select Cttee Science and Technology, 1970–74. Contested (C) Isle of Ely, Oct. 1974, 1979. Physician, BUPA Medical Centre; Clinical Assistant to: The London Hosp.; Queen Mary's Hosp. for East End, 1974–79; Moorfields Eye Hosp., 1975–79. Member: Council, Research Defence Soc., 1970–79; Birth Control Campaign Cttee, 1970–79; British Cancer Council, 1970–79. Medical Adviser, Rank Organisation, 1980–85; Medical Corresp. to The Times, 1982–. *Recreation:* country life. *Address:* The Grange, Bressingham, Diss, Norfolk IP22 2AT. *T:* Bressingham (037988) 245. *Clubs:* Athenæum, Reform, Cavalry and Guards; Norfolk (Norwich).

See also W. R. Stuttaford.

STUTTAFORD, William Royden, CBE 1989 (OBE 1983); Chairman: Brown Shipley Investment Management, since 1990; Brown Shipley Stockbroking, since 1991; *b* 21 Nov. 1928; *s* of Dr William Joseph Edward Stuttaford and Mary Marjorie Dean Stuttaford; *m* 1st, 1958, Sarah Jane Legge; two *s* two *d*; 2nd, 1974, Susan d'Esterre Grahame (*née* Curteis). *Educ:* Gresham's Sch., Holt; Trinity Coll., Oxford (MA Nat. Scis). 2nd Lieut, 10th Royal Hussars (PWO), 1952–53. Mem. Stock Exchange, 1959–; Chairman: Framlington Unit Management, 1974–87; Framlington Gp, 1983–89; Senior Partner, Laurence, Prust & Co., 1983–86. Dir, Gen. Portfolio Gp, 1988–. Chm., Unit Trust Assoc., 1987–89. Chairman: Conservative Political Centre, 1978–81; Eastern Area Cons. Council, 1986–89; Jt Vice-Chm., Nat. Union of Cons. and Unionist Assocs, 1991–. *Address:* Moulshams Manor, Great Wigborough, Colchester, Essex CO5 7RL. *T:* Peldon (020635) 330. *Club:* Cavalry & Guards.

See also I. T. Stuttaford.

STYLE, Lt-Comdr Sir Godfrey (William), Kt 1973; CBE 1961; DSC 1941; RN; Governor, Queen Elizabeth's Foundation, since 1975; Director, Star Centre for Youth, Cheltenham, since 1967; also Member of a number of allied advisory bodies and panels; a Member of Lloyd's, since 1945; *b* 3 April 1915; *er s* of Brig.-Gen. R. C. Style (*y s* of Sir William Henry Marsham Style, 9th Bt), and Hélène Pauline, *d* of Herman Greverus Kleinwort; *m* 1st, 1942, Jill Elizabeth Caruth (marr. diss. 1951); one *s* two *d*; 2nd, 1951, Sigrid Elisabeth Julin (*née* Carlberg) (*d* 1985); one *s*; 3rd, 1986, Valerie Beauclerk (*née* Hulton-Sams), *widow* of W. D. McClure. *Educ:* Eton. Joined Royal Navy as a Regular Officer, 1933; served in Royal Yacht Victoria and Albert, 1938. Served War, Flag-Lieut to C-in-C, Home Fleet, 1939–41 (despatches, DSC, 1941; wounded, 1942, in Mediterranean); despatches, 1943; invalided from Royal Navy, due to war wounds and injuries, 1945. Dep. Underwriter at Lloyd's, 1945–55; Mem., National Advisory Council on Employment of Disabled People, 1944–74 (Chm., 1963–74). Mem. Council, Sir Oswald Stoll Foundn, 1975–84. *Recreations:* the field sports, horticulture, lapidary work. *Address:* 30 Carlyle Court, Chelsea Harbour, SW10 0UQ. T: 071–352 6512. *Club:* Naval and Military.

STYLE, Sir William Frederick, 13th Bt *cr* 1627, of Wateringbury, Kent; *b* 13 May 1945; *s* of Sir William Montague Style, 12th Bt, and of La Verne, *d* of late T. M. Comstock; *S* father, 1981; *m* 1st, 1968, Wendy Gay (marr. diss. 1971), *d* of Gene Wittenberger, Hartford, Wisconsin, USA; two *d*; 2nd, 1986, Linnea Lorna, *d* of Donn Erickson, Sussex, Wisconsin, USA; two *d*. *Heir: b* Frederick Montague Style [*b* 5 Nov. 1947; *m* 1971, Sharon (marr. diss. 1988), *d* of William H. Kurz; two *d*]. *Address:* 2430 N 3rd Lane, Oconomowoc, Wisconsin 53066, USA.

STYLES, (Frank) Showell, FRGS; author; *b* 14 March 1908; *s* of Frank Styles and Edith (*née* Showell); *m* 1954, Kathleen Jane Humphreys; one *s* two *d*. *Educ:* Bishop Vesey's Grammar Sch., Sutton Coldfield. Served Royal Navy, 1939; retd (Comdr), 1946. Professional author, 1946–76, retd. Led two private Arctic expedns, 1952–53; led private Himalayan expedn, 1954. FRGS 1954. *Publications:* 119 books: *travel*, incl. Mountains of the Midnight Sun, 1954; Blue Remembered Hills, 1965; *biography*, incl. Mr Nelson's Ladies, 1954; Mallory of Everest, 1967; *mountain guidebooks*, incl. The Mountains of North Wales, 1973; The Glyder Range, 1973; *instructional books*, incl. Modern Mountaineering, 1964; Introduction to Mountaineering, 1955; *naval historical fiction*, incl. Stella and the Fireships, 1985; The Lee Shore, 1986; Gun-brig Captain, 1987; HMS Cracker, 1988; Nelson's Midshipman, 1990; *children's fiction*, incl. Kami the Sherpa, 1957; The Shop in the Mountain, 1961; *detective fiction* (under *pen-name*, Glyn Carr), incl. Death under Snowdon, 1954; The Corpse in the Crevasse, 1957. *Recreations:* mountaineering, gardening, music. *Address:* Trwyn Cae Iago, Borth-y-Gest, Porthmadog, Gwynedd. *T:* Porthmadog (0766) 2849. *Club:* Midland Association of Mountaineers (Birmingham).

STYLES, Fredrick William, BEM 1943; Director, Royal Arsenal Co-operative Society, 1968–84 (Chairman, 1975–79); *b* 18 Dec. 1914; *s* of Henry Albert Styles and Mabel Louise (*née* Sherwood); *m* 1942, Mary Gwendoline Harrison; one *s* three *d*. *Educ:* LCC elementary sch.; London Univ. (Dipl. economics); NCLC (Dipls Local and Central Govt). Salesman, Co-op, 1929–39. RAFVR Air Sea Rescue Service, 1939–46. Royal Humane Soc. Silver Medal, 1939; BEM for gallantry, 1943. Trade union official, NUPE (London divisional officer), 1946–52; social worker, hospital, 1952–58; social worker, LCC and GLC, 1958–68. Mem. Exec., 1973, Vice-Chm., 1974–79, Chm., 1979–80, Bexley and Greenwich AHA. Mem. for Greenwich, GLC, 1974–81; Mem., Greenwich Borough Council, 1971–78; Mem., 1971–81, Vice-Chm., 1974–75, Chm., 1975–76, ILEA; Chm. Staff and General Cttee, ILEA, 1977–81; Chm., ILEA schools, 1983– (Vice Chm., 1976–83): Nansen (partially sighted), now incorporated into Hawthorn Cottage (physically handicapped), and Rose Cottage (educationally sub-normal). Chm., Co-operative Metropolitan Industrial Relations Cttee, 1979– (Exec. Mem., 1970; Vice-Chm., 1973); first Chm., Heronsgate Community Centre, Thamesmead, 1982–; Sen. Vice-Chm. 1986–, Chm., 1988–, Governors, Thames Polytechnic (Chm. Governors, Avery Hill Teachers Trng Coll. (incorporated in Thames Polytechnic, 1986), 1971–86); Governor: Woolwich Coll., 1971– (Vice-Chm., 1983–); Thameside Inst., 1971– (Vice Chm., 1983–87, Chm., 1987). *Recreations:* problems, people, pensioners, politics. *Address:* 49 Court Farm Road, Mottingham, SE9 4JN. *T:* 081–857 1508.

STYLES, Lt-Col George; *see* Styles, Lt-Col S. G.

STYLES, Showell; *see* Styles, F. S.

STYLES, Lt-Col (Stephen) George, GC 1972; retired; company director, since 1974; *b* 16 March 1928; *s* of Stephen Styles and Grace Lily Styles (*née* Preston) *m* 1952, Mary Rose Styles (*née* Woolgar); one *s* two *d*. *Educ:* Collyers Sch., Horsham; Royal Military Coll. of Science. Ammunition Technical Officer, commissioned RAOC, Nov. 1947; seconded to 1 Bn KOYLI, 1949–51 (despatches, 1952); RMCS, 1952–56; HQ Ammunition Organisation, 1956–58; OC 28 Commonwealth Bde, Ordnance Field Park, Malaya, 1958–61; 2i/c 16 Bn RAOC, Bicester, 1961–64; OC Eastern Command Ammunition Inspectorate, 1964–67; Sen. Ammo Tech. Officer, 3 BAPD, BAOR, 1967–68; OC 1(BR) Corps Vehicle Company, 1968–69; Sen. Ammo Tech. Officer, Northern Ireland, 1969–72; Chief Ammo Tech. Officer (EOD), HQ DOS (CILSA), 1972–74. Member: Royal Soc. of St George, NRA, NSRA. *Publications:* Bombs Have No Pity, 1975; contrib. Proc. ICE, Jl of Forensic Science Soc. *Recreation:* rifle and game shooting, cartridge collector. *Address:* c/o Barclays Bank, Abingdon.

SUAREZ, Juan L.; *see* Lechin-Suarez.

SUBAK-SHARPE, Prof. John Herbert, CBE 1991; FRSE 1970; Professor of Virology, University of Glasgow, since 1968; Hon. Director, Medical Research Council Virology Unit, since 1968; *b* 14 Feb. 1924; *s* of late Robert Subak and late Nelly (*née* Bruell), Vienna, Austria; *m* 1953, Barbara Naomi Morris; two *s* one *d*. *Educ:* Humanistic Gymnasium, Vienna; Univ. of Birmingham. BSc (Genetics) (1st Cl. Hons) 1952; PhD 1956. Refugee from Nazi oppression, 1939; farm pupil, 1939–44; HM Forces (Parachute Regt), 1944–47. Asst Lectr in Genetics, Glasgow Univ., 1954–56; Mem. scientific staff, ARC Animal Virus Research Inst., Pirbright, 1956–60; Nat. Foundn Fellow, California Inst. of Technology, 1961; Mem. Scientific staff of MRC, in Experimental Virus Research Unit, Glasgow, 1961–68. Visiting Professor: US Nat. Insts of Health, Bethesda, Md, 1967; US Univ. of Health Services, Bethesda, Md, 1985; Vis. Fellow, Clare Hall, Cambridge, 1986–87. Sec., Genetical Soc., 1966–72, Vice-Pres. 1972–75, Trustee 1971–. Member: European Molecular Biology Orgn, 1969– (Chm., Course and Workshops Cttee, 1976–78); Genetic Manipulation Adv. Gp, 1976–80; Biomed. Res. Cttee, SHHD Chief Scientist Orgn, 1979–84; British Nat. Cttee of Biophysics, 1970–76; Governing Body, W of Scotland Oncological Orgn, 1974–; Scientific Adv. Body, W German Cancer Res. Centre, 1977–82; Governing Body, Animal Virus Res. Inst., Pirbright, 1986–87; MRC Training Awards Panel, 1985–89 (Chm., 1986–89); Scientific Adv. Gp of Equine Virology Res. Foundn, 1987–; MRC Cell and Disorders Bd, 1988–. *Publications:* articles in scientific jls on genetic studies with viruses and cells. *Recreations:* travel, hill walking, bridge. *Address:* 17 Kingsborough Gardens, Glasgow G12 9NH. *T:* 041–334 1863. *Club:* Athenæum.

SUBBA ROW, Raman, CBE 1991; Managing Director, Management Public Relations Ltd, since 1969; Chairman, Test and County Cricket Board, 1985–90; *b* 29 Jan. 1932; *s* of Panguluri Venkata Subba Row and Doris Mildred Subba Row; *m* 1960, Anne Dorothy (*née* Harrison); two *s* one *d*. *Educ:* Whitgift Sch., Croydon; Trinity Hall, Cambridge (MA Hons). Associate Dir, W. S. Crawford Ltd, 1963–69. *Recreation:* golf. *Address:* Leeward, Manor Way, South Croydon, Surrey CR2 7BT. *T:* 081–688 3388. *Clubs:* Institute of Directors, MCC, Surrey County Cricket; Addington Golf.

SUBRAMANIAM, Chidambaram; Chairman, Rajaji International Institute of Public Affairs and Administration, since 1980; President, Madras Voluntary Health Services, since 1987; *b* 30 Jan. 1910; *s* of Chidambara Gounder and Valliammal; *m* 1945, Sakuntala; one *s* two *d*. *Educ:* Madras (BA, LLB). Set up legal practice, Coimbatore, 1936; took active part in freedom movt, imprisoned 1932, 1941 and again 1942; Pres., District Congress Committee, Coimbatore; Mem. Working Cttee of State Congress Cttee; Mem. Constituent Assembly; Minister of Finance, Educn and Law, Govt of Madras, 1952; MP 1962; Minister of Steel, 1962–63; Minister of Steel, Mines and Heavy Engrg, 1963–64; Minister of Food and Agric., 1964–66; Minister of Food and Agriculture, CD and Coopn, 1966–67; Chm. Cttee on Aeronautics Industry, 1967–69; Interim Pres., Indian Nat. Congress, July-Dec. 1969; Chm. Nat. Commn on Agric., 1970; Minister of Planning and Dep. Chm., Planning Commn, 1971; also i/c Dept of Science and Technology; Minister of Industrial Develt and Science and Technology, 1972 (also Agric., temp., 1974); Minister of Finance, 1974–77; Minister of Defence, 1979. Hon. Pres., Internat. Inst. of Public Enterprises, Ljubljana, 1985–87; Sen. Vice-Pres., Bharatiya Vidyabhavan, Bombay, 1985–. Hon. DLitt: Wattair; Sri Venkateswara; Madurai; Madras; Annamalai; Hon. LLD Andhra. *Publications:* Nan Sendra Sila Nadugal (Travelogues); War on Poverty; Ulagam Sutrinen (in Tamil); India of My Dreams (in English); Strategy Statement for Fighting Protein Hunger in Developing Countries; The New Strategy in Indian Agriculture. *Recreation:* yoga. *Address:* River View, Madras 85, India. *T:* 414298. *Clubs:* Cosmopolitan, Gymkhana (Madras); Cosmopolitan (Coimbatore).

SUCH, Frederick Rudolph Charles; a Recorder of the Crown Court, since 1979; *b* 19 June 1936; *s* of Frederick Sidney Such and Anne Marie Louise (*née* Martin); *m* 1961, Elizabeth, *d* of late Judge Norman and Mrs Harper, Cloughton, Yorkshire; one *s* one *d*. *Educ:* Mbeya Sch., Tanganyika Territory, E Africa (Tanzania); Taunton Sch.; Keble Coll., Oxford (MA). Called to the Bar, Gray's Inn, 1960; practised: London, 1960–69, then North Eastern Circuit, 1969–. *Recreations:* theatre, opera, hockey, squash, tennis. *Address:* The Rift Barns, Wylam, Northumberland NE41 8BL. *T:* Wylam (0661) 852763. *Club:* Northern Counties (Newcastle upon Tyne).

SUCHET, David; actor; associate artiste, Royal Shakespeare Co.; *b* 2 May 1946; *s* of Jack and Joan Suchet; *m* 1976, Sheila Ferris, actress; one *s* one *d*. *Educ:* Wellington Sch.; LAMDA (Best Drama Student, 1968). *Stage:* repertory theatres, incl. Chester, Birmingham, Exeter, Worthing, Coventry, 1969–73; for Royal Shakespeare Co.: Romeo and Juliet (Mercutio and Tybalt), As You Like It (Orlando), Once in a Lifetime (Glogauer), Measure for Measure (Angelo), The Tempest (Caliban), King Lear, King John, Merchant of Venice (Shylock), Troilus and Cressida (Achilles), Richard II (Bolingbroke), Every Good Boy Deserves Favour, 1983, Othello (Iago), 1986, Timon of Athens (title rôle), 1991; Separation, Comedy, 1988; *films include:* Falcon and the Snowman, 1983; Thirteen at Dinner, 1985; Song for Europe, 1985; Harry and the Hendersons, 1986; When the Whales came, 1990; serials and series for *television:* Oppenheimer, 1978; Reilly, 1981; Saigon, 1982; Freud, 1983; Blott on the Landscape, 1984; Oxbridge Blues, 1984; Playing Shakespeare, 1985; Great Writers, 1988; Agatha Christie's Hercule Poirot, 1989, 1991; numerous radio parts. Mem. Council, LAMDA, 1985–. Lectr, US Univs; Vis. Prof., Univ. of Nebraska, 1975. Numerous awards, incl. Best Actor, RTS, 1986. *Publications:* (contrib.) Players of Shakespeare, 2 vols, 1985 and 1988; essays on interpretation of roles. *Recreations:* clarinet, photography, reading, ornithology, theology. *Address:* c/o Aude Powell, Brunskill Management, Suite 8, 169 Queens Gate, SW7 5EH.

SUCKLING, Dr Charles Walter, CBE 1989; FRS 1978; FRSC; Chairman, Bradbury, Suckling and Partners Ltd, since 1982; *b* 24 July 1920; *s* of Edward Ernest and Barbara Suckling (*née* Thomson); *m* 1946, (Eleanor) Margaret Watterson; two *s* one *d*. *Educ:* Oldershaw Grammar Sch., Wallasey; Liverpool Univ. (BSc, PhD). ICI: joined Gen. Chemicals Div., 1942; R&D Director, Mond Div., 1967; Dep. Chairman, Mond Div., 1969; Chairman, Paints Div., 1972; Gen. Man., Res. and Technol., 1977–82; Dir, Albright and Wilson, 1982–89. Hon. Vis. Prof., Univ. of Stirling. Member: BBC Science Consultative Gp, 1980–85; Royal Commn on Environmental Pollution, 1982–91; Electricity Supply Res. Council, 1983–90; ABRC/NERC Gp into Geol Surveying, 1985–87; Cttee of Inquiry into Teaching of English Language, 1987–88; Nat. Curriculum English Working Gp, 1988–89; Nat. Curriculum Mod. For. Langs Wkg Gp, 1989–90; Council, RCA, 1981–90 (Treasurer, 1984–90); Chm., Roy. Soc. Study Gp on Pollution Control Priorities, 1988–; Nat. Adv. Gp on Eco-labelling, 1990–. Bicentennial Lecture, Washington Coll., Maryland, 1981; Robbins Lecture, Stirling Univ., 1990. Senior Fellow, RCA, 1986. Hon. DSc Liverpool, 1980; DUniv Stirling, 1985. Liverpool Univ. Chem. Soc. Medal, 1964; John Scott Medal, City of Philadelphia, 1973. *Publications:* (with A. Baines and F. R. Bradbury) Research in the Chemical Industry, 1969; (with C. J. Suckling and K. E. Suckling) Chemistry through Models, 1978; papers on anaesthetics, industrial research and strategy in journals. *Recreations:* music, gardening, languages, writing. *Address:* Willowhay, Shoppenhangers Road, Maidenhead, Berks SL6 2QA. *T:* Maidenhead (0628) 27502.

SUCKSDORFF, Mrs Åke; *see* Jonzen, Mrs Karin.

SUDBURY, Archdeacon of; *see* Garrard, Ven. Richard.

SUDDABY, Arthur, CBE 1980; PhD, MSc; CChem, FRSC; CEng, MIChemE; scientific consultant on the carriage of goods by sea, until 1990; Provost, City of London Polytechnic, 1970–81; *b* 26 Feb. 1919; *e s* of George Suddaby, Kingston-upon-Hull, Yorks; *m* 1944, Elizabeth Bullin Vyse (decd), *d* of Charles Vyse; two *s*. *Educ:* Riley High Sch., Kingston-upon-Hull; Hull Technical Coll.; Chelsea Polytechnic; Queen Mary Coll.

London. Chemist and Chemical Engr, in industry, 1937–47; Lectr in Physical Chemistry, and later Sen. Lectr in Chem. Engrg, West Ham Coll. of Technology, 1947–50; Sir John Cass Coll.: Sen. Lectr in Physics, 1950–61; Head of Dept of Physics, 1961–66; Principal, 1966–70. Chm., Cttee of Directors of Polytechnics, 1976–78; Member: Chem. Engrg Cttee, 1948–51; London and Home Counties Regional Adv. Council, 1971–; Bd of Examrs and Educn Cttee, Inst. of Chem. Engrs, 1948–51; CNAA: Chem. Engrg Bd, 1969–75; Nautical Studies Bd, 1972–75; Chm., Standing Conf. of Approved Coll. Res. Deg. Cttees, 1979–81; Court of the City University, 1967–81; Vis. Cttee, Cranfield Inst. of Technology, 1979–85; Chm., Assoc. of Navigation Schs, 1972. *Publications:* various original research papers in theoretical physics, in scientific jls; review articles. *Recreations:* fishing, occasional hunting. *Address:* Flat 3, 16 Elm Park Gardens, Chelsea, SW10. *T:* 071–352 9164; Castle Hill House, Godshill Wood, near Fordingbridge, Hants. *T:* Fordingbridge (0425) 652234. *Club:* Athenæum.

SUDDARDS, His Honour (Henry) Gaunt; a Circuit Judge (formerly Judge of County Courts), 1963–80; *b* 30 July 1910; *s* of Fred Suddards and Agnes Suddards (*née* Gaunt); unmarried. *Educ:* Cheltenham College; Trinity College, Cambridge (MA). Barrister, Inner Temple, 1932; joined NE Circuit, 1933. Served War of 1939–45, RAFVR, 1940–46. Recorder of Pontefract, 1960–61; Recorder of Middlesbrough, 1961–63; Dep. Chm., West Riding QS, 1961–71; Chairman, Agricultural Land Tribunal, Northern Area, 1961–63, Dep. Chairman 1960. *Recreations:* fishing, shooting, sailing. *Address:* Rockville, Frizinghall, Shipley, West Yorkshire BD18 3AA. *Club:* Bradford (Bradford).

SUDDARDS, Roger Whitley, CBE 1987; DL; Consultant, Hammond Suddards, since 1988; Chairman, Hammond Suddards Research Ltd, since 1989; *b* 5 June 1930; *s* of John Whitley Suddards, OBE and Jean Suddards (*née* Rollitt); *m* 1963, Elizabeth Anne Rayner; two *d.* *Educ:* Bradford Grammar Sch. Admitted solicitor, 1952; Partner, Last Suddards, 1952–88; Chm., Yorkshire BS, 1988–91. Vis. Lectr, Leeds Sch. of Town Planning, 1964–74; Planning Law Consultant: to UN, 1974–77; to Govt of Mauritius, 1981–82 and 1989. Former Chairman: Examinations Bd, ISVA; Adv. Cttee for Land Commn for Yorks and Humberside; Chm., Working Party on Future of Bradford Churches, 1978–79. Member: Law Society Bye-Laws Revision Cttee, 1984–87; Law Society Planning Law Cttee, 1964–81; Pres., Bradford Law Soc., 1969; Legal Mem., RTPI. Sec., Hand Knitting Assoc., 1958–75. Chm., Bradford Disaster Appeal Trust, 1985–89. Mem. Cttee, Nat. Mus. Photography, Film and TV, 1984–; Dir, Mus. Trng Inst.; Member: W Yorks Residuary Body, 1986–89; Civic Trust, 1988–. Pro-Chancellor, and Chm. of Council, Bradford Univ., 1987–. Mem. of Bd, 1969–86, Vice Chm. and Chm, 1985–88, Bradford Grammar Sch. Hon. FSVA. DL W Yorks, 1990. *Publications:* Town Planning Law of West Indies, 1974; History of Bradford Law Society, 1975; Listed Buildings, 1982, 3rd edn 1992; A Lawyer's Peregrination, 1984, 2nd edn 1987; Bradford Diaster Appeal, 1986; articles in Jl of Planning and Environmental Law (Mem. Editl Bd), and Law Society Gazette. *Recreations:* theatre, music, reading, travel. *Address:* Low House, High Eldwick, Bingley, West Yorks BD16 3AZ. *T:* Bradford (0274) 564832, 532233. *Clubs:* Arts; Bradford (Bradford).

SUDELEY, 7th Baron *cr* 1838; **Merlin Charles Sainthill Hanbury-Tracy,** FSA; *b* 17 June 1939; *o c* of late Captain Michael David Charles Hanbury-Tracy, Scots Guards, and Colline Ammabel (*d* 1985), *d* of late Lt-Col C. G. H. St Hill and *widow* of Lt-Col Frank King, DSO, OBE; *S* cousin, 1941; *m* 1980, Hon. Mrs Elizabeth Villiers (marr. diss. 1988), *d* of late Viscount Bury (*s* of 9th Earl of Albemarle). *Educ:* at Eton and in the ranks of the Scots Guards. Pres., Monday Club; Vice-Chancellor, Monarchist League; Vice-Pres., Western Goals. Patron: Assoc. of Bankrupts; Prayer Book Soc.; Anglican Assoc.; St Peter's, Petersham, Richmond, Surrey. *Publications:* (jtly) The Sudeleys—Lords of Toddington, 1987; contribs to Quarterly Review, Contemporary Review, Family History, Trans of Bristol and Gloucestershire Archaeol. Soc., Montgomeryshire Collections, Bull. of Manorial Soc., Die Waage (Zeitschrift der Chemie Grünenthal). *Recreations:* ancestor worship; cultivating his sensibility. *Heir: kinsman* Desmond Andrew John Hanbury-Tracy [*b* 30 Nov. 1928; *m* 1st, 1957, Jennifer Lynn (marr. diss. 1966), *d* of Dr R. C. Hodges; one *s*; 2nd, 1967, Lillian, *d* of Nathaniel Laurie; one *s*; 3rd, 1988, Mrs Margaret Cecilia White, *d* of late Alfred Henry Marmaduke Purse]. *Address:* c/o Royal Bank of Scotland, 21 Grosvenor Gardens, SW1. *Club:* Brooks's.

SUENENS, His Eminence Cardinal Leo Joseph, DTheol, DPhil; Cardinal since 1962; Archbishop of Malines-Brussels and Primate of Belgium, 1961–79; *b* Ixelles (Brussels), 16 July 1904. *Educ:* primary sch., Inst. of Marist Brothers, Brussels; secondary sch., St Mary's High Sch., Brussels; Gregorian Univ., Rome (BCL, DPhil, DrTheol). Priest, 1927; Teacher, St Mary's High Sch., Brussels, 1929; Prof. of Philosophy, Diocesan Seminary, Malines, 1930; Vice-Rector, Cath. Univ. of Louvain, 1940; Vicar-Gen., Archdio. of Malines, 1945; Auxiliary Bp to Archbp of Malines, 1945. Moderator of Second Vatican Council, 1962–65; Pres., Belgian Bishops' Conf.; Internat. Pastoral Delegate for Catholic Charismatic Renewal. Templeton Prize for Religion, 1976. *Publications:* Theology of the Apostolate of the Legion of Mary, 1951 (Cork); Edel Quinn, 1952 (Dublin); (ed) The Right View on Moral Rearmament, 1953 (London); (ed) The Gospel to Every Creature, 1955 (London); (ed) Mary the Mother of God, 1957 (New York); (ed) Love and Control, 1959 (London); (ed) Christian Life Day by Day, 1961 (London); (ed) The Nun in the World, 1962 (London); (ed) Co-responsibility in the Church, 1968 (New York), 1969 (London); (ed, with Archbp Ramsey) The Future of the Christian Church, 1971 (New York); A New Pentecost?, 1975 (New York); Open the Frontiers, 1980; Renewal and Powers of Darkness, 1982; Nature and Grace, 1986. *Address:* Boulevard de Smet de Mayer 570, 1020 Bruxelles, Belgium. *T:* 02/4791950.

SUENSON-TAYLOR, family name of **Baron Grantchester.**

SUFFIAN, Tun Mohamed, SSM 1975 (PSM 1967); SPCM 1978; SPMK 1989; DIMP 1969; JMN 1961; PJK 1963; Judge, Administrative Tribunal, World Bank, Washington DC, since 1985; Vice President, International Labour Organisation Administrative Tribunal, Geneva, since 1987 (Judge, 1986–87); *b* 12 Nov. 1917; *s* of late Haji Mohamed Hashim and Zaharah binti Ibrahim; *m* 1946, Dora Evelina Grange. *Educ:* Gonville and Caius Coll., Cambridge (BA Hons, LLB); SOAS; LSE. Called to the Bar, Middle Temple, 1941 (Hon. Bencher, 1984). All India Radio, New Delhi, 1942–45; BBC, London, 1945–46; Malayan Civil Service, 1948; Malayan Judicial and Legal Service, 1949–61; Solicitor General, 1959; High Court Judge, 1961; Federal Judge, 1968; Chief Justice of Malaya, 1973; Lord Pres., Federal Court, 1974–82. Advr, Standard Chartered Bank in Malaysia, 1982–90. Pro-Chancellor, Univ. of Malaya, 1963–86. President: Commonwealth Magistrates Assoc., 1979–85; Asean Law Assoc., 1982–84. Pres., Malaysian Br., Royal Asiatic Soc., 1978–. Fellow, Univ. Coll. at Buckingham, 1979. Hon. LLD: Singapore, 1975; Buckingham, 1983; Hon. DLitt Malaya, 1975; DUniv Murdoch, WA, 1988. Ramon Magsaysay Foundn Award for Government Service, 1975. SMB (Brunei), 1959. *Publications:* Malayan Constitution (official trans.), 1963; An Introduction to the Constitution of Malaysia, 1972, 2nd edn 1976; (ed jtly) The Constitution of Malaysia: its development 1957–1977, 1978; Introduction to the Legal System of Malaysia, 1987, 2nd edn 1989. *Recreations:* gardening, swimming, reading. *Address:* Suite 1B, Bangunan Dato Zainal, 23 Jalan Melaka, 50100 Kuala Lumpur, Malaysia. *T:* 03–292 0527, *Fax:* 03–298 7237. *Clubs:* Lake, Bankers' (Kuala Lumpur).

SUFFIELD, 11th Baron *cr* 1786; **Anthony Philip Harbord-Hamond,** Bt, *cr* 1745; MC 1950; Major, retired, 1961; *b* 19 June 1922; *o s* of 10th Baron and Nina Annette Mary Crawfuird (*d* 1955), *e d* of John Hutchison of Laurieston and Edingham, Stewartry of Kirkcudbright; *S* father 1951; *m* 1952, Elizabeth Eve, *er d* of late Judge Edgedale; three *s* one *d.* *Educ:* Eton. Commission, Coldstream Guards, 1942; served War of 1939–45, in North African and Italian campaigns, 1942–45; Malaya, 1948–50. One of HM Hon. Corps of Gentlemen-at-Arms, 1973– (Harbinger, 1990–). *Recreations:* normal. *Heir: s* Hon. Charles Anthony Assheton Harbord-Hamond [*b* 3 Dec. 1953; *m* 1983, Lucy (marr. diss.), *yr d* of Comdr A. S. Hutchinson. Commissioned Coldstream Guards, 1972, RARO 1979]. *Address:* Wood Norton Grange, Dereham, Norfolk NR20 5BD. *T:* Foulsham (036284) 235. *Clubs:* Army and Navy, Pratt's.

SUFFIELD, Sir (Henry John) Lester, Kt 1973; Head of Defence Sales, Ministry of Defence, 1969–76; *b* 28 April 1911; *m* 1940, Elizabeth Mary White (*d* 1985); one *s* one *d.* *Educ:* Camberwell Central, LCC. Served with RASC, 1939–45 (Major). LNER, 1926–35; Morris Motors, 1935–38 and 1945–52; Pres., British Motor Corp., Canada and USA, 1952–64; Dep. Man. Dir, British Motor Corp., Birmingham, 1964–68; Sales Dir, British Leyland Motor Corp., 1968–69. Freeman of City of London, 1978; Liveryman, Coachmakers and Coach Harness Makers Co. *Recreation:* golf. *Address:* 16 Glebe Court, Fleet, Hants. *T:* Fleet (0252) 616861. *Clubs:* Royal Automobile; Royal Wimbledon Golf.

SUFFOLK AND BERKSHIRE, 21st Earl of, *cr* 1603; **Michael John James George Robert Howard;** Viscount Andover and Baron Howard, 1622; Earl of Berkshire, 1626; *b* 27 March 1935; *s* of 20th Earl (killed by enemy action, 1941) and Mimi (*d* 1966), *yr d* of late A. G. Forde Pigott; *S* father 1941; *m* 1st, 1960, Mme Simone Paulmier (marr. diss. 1967), *d* of late Georges Litman, Paris; (one *d* decd); 2nd, 1973, Anita (marr. diss. 1980), *d* of R. R. Fuglesang, Haywards Heath, Sussex; one *s* one *d*; 3rd, 1983, Linda Viscountess Bridport; two *d.* Owns 5,000 acres. *Heir: s* Viscount Andover, *qv.* *Address:* Charlton Park, Malmesbury, Wilts.

SUFFOLK, Archdeacon of; *see* Robinson, Ven. N.

SUGAR, Alan Michael; Chairman, Amstrad plc, since 1968; *b* 24 March 1947; *s* of Nathan and Fay Sugar; *m* 1968, Ann Simons; two *s* one *d.* *Educ:* Brooke House School, London. Chm. of Amstrad since formation in 1968. Hon. DSc City, 1988. *Recreation:* tennis. *Address:* 169 King's Road, Brentwood, Essex CM14 4EF. *T:* Brentwood (0277) 228888.

SUGDEN, Sir Arthur, Kt 1978; Director: A. S. Marketing Enterprises Ltd, since 1987; A.S.G. Insurance Consultants Ltd, since 1988; Chief Executive Officer, Co-operative Wholesale Society Ltd, 1974–80; Chairman: Co-operative Bank Ltd, 1974–80; Co-operative Commercial Bank Ltd, 1974–80; *b* 12 Sept. 1918; *s* of late Arthur and Elizabeth Ann Sugden; *m* 1946, Agnes Grayston; two *s.* *Educ:* Thomas Street, Manchester. Certified Accountant, Chartered Secretary. FIB 1975. Served War of 1939–45, Royal Artillery; CPO 6th Super Heavy Battery; Adjt 12th Medium Regt; Staff Captain 16th Army Group. CWS Ltd: Accountancy Asst, 1946; Office Man., 1950; Factory Man., 1954; Group Man., Edible Oils and Fats Factories, 1964; Controller, Food Div., 1967; Dep. Chief Exec. Officer, 1971. Chairman, 1974–80: FC Finance Ltd; CWS (Longburn) Ltd; CWS (New Zealand) Holdings Ltd; CWS Marketing Ltd; CWS (India) Ltd; Ocean Beach Freezing Co. Ltd; Shaw's Smokers' Products Ltd; Former Director: Co-operative City Investments Ltd; Co-operative Pension Funds Unit Trust Managers' Ltd; Associated Co-operative Creameries Ltd; CWS Svineslagterier A/S Denmark; CWS (Overseas) Ltd; Tukuyu Tea Estates Ltd; Spillers French Holdings Ltd; J. W. French (Milling & Baking Holdings) Ltd; North Eastern Co-operative Soc. Ltd; Manchester Ship Canal Ltd, 1978–87; Manchester Chamber of Commerce. Former Vice-President: Inst. of Bankers; Inst. of Grocery Distribution Ltd. Member: Central Cttee, Internat. Co-operative Alliance; Management Bds, Euro-Coop and Inter-Coop (Pres., 1979–80). Pres., Co-operative Congress, 1978. CBIM; FIGD. *Recreations:* music, reading, walking. *Address:* 56 Old Wool Lane, Cheadle Hulme, Cheadle, Cheshire SK8 5JA.

SUGDEN, Maj.-Gen. Francis George, CB 1991; CBE 1989 (OBE 1980); Chief of Staff, HQ British Army of the Rhine, 1989–91; *b* IOM, 27 July 1938; *s* of Maj.-Gen. Sir Henry H. C. Sugden, KBE, CB, DSO and Joan Morgan Sugden (*née* Francis); *m* 1964, Elizabeth Blackburn Bradbury; two *s* one *d.* *Educ:* Wellington Coll. Commnd RE, 1958; service on Christmas Is, in England and Germany; sc 1970; GSO2 Defence Secretariat 6, MoD, 1971–72; OC 4 Field Sqn RE, BAOR, 1973–74; GSO2 RE HQ 1 (BR) Corps, 1974–77; GSO1 Staff of CDS, MoD, 1977–78; CO 22 Engr Regt, UK and Rhodesia, 1978–80; Col GS HQ 1 (BR) Corps, 1980–83; RCDS, 1984; Comdr Engr HQ 1 (BR) Corps and Comdr Hameln Garrison, 1985–86; GS Dir, MoD, 1986–89. Zimbabwe Independence Medal, 1980. *Recreations:* golf, gardening, ski-ing.

SUGDEN, John Goldthorp, MA; ARCM; Headmaster, Wellingborough School, 1965–73; *b* 22 July 1921; *s* of A. G. Sugden, Brighouse, Yorkshire; *m* 1954, Jane Machin; two *s.* *Educ:* Radley; Magdalene College, Cambridge. War Service, Royal Signals, 1941–46. Asst Master, Bilton Grange Prep. School, 1948–52; Asst Master, The King's School, Canterbury, 1952–59; Headmaster, Foster's School, Sherborne, 1959–64. *Publication:* Niccolo Paganini, 1980. *Recreations:* music, golf. *Address:* Woodlands, 2 Linksview Avenue, Parkstone, Poole, Dorset BH14 9QT. *T:* Parkstone (0202) 707497.

SUGG, Aldhelm St John, CMG 1963; retired as Provincial Commissioner, Southern Province of Northern Rhodesia, August 1963; *b* 21 Oct. 1909; *s* of H. G. St J. Sugg; *m* 1935, Jessie May Parker; one *s* one *d.* *Educ:* Colchester Royal Grammar School. Palestine Police, 1930–31; Northern Rhodesia Police, 1932–43; Colonial Administrative Service, in N Rhodesia, 1943–63. Retired to England, 1963. *Recreations:* sailing, field sports. *Address:* Bushbury, Blackboys, Uckfield, East Sussex TN22 5JE. *T:* Framfield (0825) 890282. *Club:* Commonwealth Trust.

SUHARTO, Gen.; *see* Soeharto.

SUHARTOYO, S.; Indonesian Ambassador to the Court of St James's and to the Republic of Ireland, 1986–89; *b* 2 Sept. 1926; *m* 1954, Umi Sudiyati; two *s* four *d.* *Educ:* Gajahmada Univ., Yogyakarta, Indonesia (Faculty of Technology, Engrg). Lectr, Faculty of Technology, Gajahmada Univ., 1954–58; Mem. Bd of Management, NV Molenvliet, Jakarta, 1958–61; Dir, Bd of Management, Mech. and Elec. Equipment Ind., 1961–65, Pres. Dir, Bd of Management, Mech./Elec. and Transport Equip. Ind., 1965–66, Dept of Basic Industry and Mining, Republic of Indonesia; Dir Gen., Metal and Mech. Ind., Dept of Industry, 1966–81; Hd of BKPM (Investment Coordinating Bd), Indonesia, 1981–85. Indonesian Star: Satya Lencana Pembangunan, 1962; 3rd Class, Mahaputra Utama, 1974; Comdr, Order of Leopold, Belgium, 1975. *Recreation:* golf. *Address:* c/o Ministry of Foreign Affairs, Jakarta, Indonesia. *Club:* Highgate Golf.

SUIRDALE, Viscount; John Michael James Hely-Hutchinson; company director since 1981; *b* 7 Aug. 1952; *s* and *heir* of 8th Earl of Donoughmore, *qv*; *m* 1976, Marie-Claire Carola Etienne van den Driessche; one *s* two *d*. *Educ:* Harrow. *Recreations:* shooting, ski-ing, fishing, etc. *Heir:* *s* Hon. Richard Gregory Hely-Hutchinson, *b* 3 July 1980. *Address:* 34 Perryn Road, Acton, W3 7NA.

SULLIVAN, David Douglas Hooper, QC 1975; author and historian; *b* 10 April 1926; *s* of Michael and Maude Sullivan; *m* 1st, 1951, Sheila, *d* of Henry and Georgina Bathurst; three *d*; 2nd, 1981, Ann Munro, *d* of Malcolm and Eva Betten. *Educ:* Haileybury (schol.); Christ Church, Oxford (schol.). MA 1949, BCL 1951. Served War, with RNVR (Sub-Lieut), 1944–46. Called to Bar, Inner Temple, 1951, Bencher, 1984. Mem., Central Policy Cttee, Mental Health Act Commn, 1983–86. Author of various plays and media programmes. *Recreations:* painting, medieval history. *Address:* Well Mount Cottage, Well Road, NW3 1LJ. *T:* 071–431 3433.

SULLIVAN, Sir Desmond (John), Kt 1985; Chief District Court Judge, New Zealand, 1979–85, retired; Member, Treaty of Waitangi Tribunal, since 1986; *b* 3 March 1920; *s* of Patrick James Sullivan and Annie Sullivan; *m* 1947, Phyllis Maude Mahon; two *s* four *d* (and one *s* decd). *Educ:* Timaru Marist; Timaru Boys' High Sch.; Canterbury Univ. (LLB). Served NZ Army and Navy, 1940–45. Barrister and solicitor: Westport, 1949–59; Palmerston North, 1960–66; Stipendiary Magistrate, Wellington, 1966–79. Member, Westport Bor. Council, 1955–59; Chairman: NZ Council for Recreation and Sport, 1973–76; Film Industry Board, 1962–85. *Publication:* (jtly) Violence in the Community, 1975. *Recreations:* golf, swimming, reading. *Address:* 208 Whites Line East, Lower Hutt, New Zealand. *T:* 695–440. *Club:* Wellington.

SULLIVAN, Prof. (Donovan) Michael; Professor of Oriental Art, 1966–85, Christensen Professor, 1975–85, Stanford University, California; Fellow, St Catherine's College, Oxford, 1979–90, now Emeritus Fellow; *b* 29 Oct. 1916; *s* of Alan Sullivan and Elisabeth Hees; *m* 1943, Khoan, *d* of Ngo Eng-lim, Kulangsu, Amoy, China; no *c*. *Educ:* Rugby School; Corpus Christi College, Cambridge (MA); Univ. of London (BA Hons); Harvard Univ. (PhD); LittD Cambridge, 1966; MA, DLitt Oxon, 1973. Chinese Govt Scholarship, Univ. of London, 1947–50; Rockefeller Foundn Travelling Fellowship in USA, 1950–51; Bollingen Foundn Research Fellowship, 1952–54; Curator of Art Museum and Lectr in the History of Art, Univ. of Malaya (now Univ. of Singapore), Singapore, 1954–60; Lectr in Asian Art, Sch. of Oriental and African Studies, Univ. of London, 1960–66. Vis. Prof. of Far Eastern Art, Univ. of Michigan (Spring Semester), 1964; Slade Prof. of Fine Art, Oxford Univ., 1973–74, Cambridge Univ., 1983–84; Guggenheim Foundn Fellowship, 1974; Vis. Fellow, St Antony's Coll., Oxford, 1976–77; Nat. Endowment for the Humanities Fellowship, 1976–77; Professorial Fellow, Corpus Christi Coll., Cambridge, 1983–84; Vis. Fellow, Humanities Centre, ANU, 1987. Fellow, Amer. Acad. of Arts and Sciences, 1977. *Publications:* Chinese Art in the Twentieth Century, 1959; An Introduction to Chinese Art, 1961; The Birth of Landscape Painting in China, 1962; Chinese Ceramics, Bronzes and Jades in the Collection of Sir Alan and Lady Barlow, 1963; Chinese and Japanese Art, 1965; A Short History of Chinese Art, 1967, 3rd edn as The Arts of China, 1973, rev. edns 1977, 1984, 1986; The Cave Temples of Maichishan, 1969; The Meeting of Eastern and Western Art, 1973, rev. and expanded edn 1989; Chinese Art: recent discoveries, 1973; The Three Perfections, 1975; Chinese Landscape Painting, vol. II, The Sui and T'ang Dynasties, 1979; Symbols of Eternity: the art of landscape painting in China, 1979; contrib. to learned journals, Encyclopedia Britannica, Chambers's Encyclopædia, etc. *Address:* St Catherine's College, Oxford OX1 3UJ. *Club:* Athenæum.

SULLIVAN, Edmund Wendell, FRCVS; Chief Veterinary Officer, Department of Agriculture for Northern Ireland, 1983–90; *b* 21 March 1925; *s* of Thomas Llewellyn Sullivan and Letitia Sullivan; *m* 1957, Elinor Wilson Melville; two *s* one *d*. *Educ:* Portadown College; Queen's University, Belfast; Royal (Dick) Veterinary College. FRCVS 1991. General Veterinary Practice, Appleby, Westmoreland, 1947; joined staff of State Veterinary Service, Dept. of Agriculture for N Ireland, 1948; Headquarters staff, 1966–90. *Recreations:* hill walking, wood craft, following rugby and cricket. *Address:* Kinfauns, 26 Dillon's Avenue, Newtownabbey, Co. Antrim BT37 0SX. *T:* Belfast (0232) 862323.

SULLIVAN, Jeremy Mirth; QC 1982; a Recorder, since 1989; *b* 17 Sept. 1945; *s* of Arthur Brian and Pamela Jean Sullivan; *m* 1970, Ursula Klara Marie Hildenbrock (separated); two *s*. *Educ:* Framlingham Coll.; King's Coll., London. LLB 1967, LLM 1968; LAMTPI 1970, LMRTPI 1976. 2nd Lieut, Suffolk & Cambs Regt (TA), 1963–65. Called to the Bar, Inner Temple, 1968; Lectr in Law, City of London Polytechnic, 1968–71; in practice, Planning and Local Govt Bar, Parly Bar, 1971–. Mem. Council, RTPI, 1984–87. Gov., Highgate Sch., 1991–. *Publications:* contribs to Jl of Planning Law. *Recreations:* walking, railways, canals, reading history. *Address:* 4–5 Gray's Inn Square, WC1R 5JA. *T:* 071–404 5252.

SULLIVAN, Prof. Michael; *see* Sullivan, D. M.

SULLIVAN, Michael Frederick, MBE 1981; HM Diplomatic Service; Head of Nationality, Treaty and Claims Department, Foreign and Commonwealth Office, since 1990; *b* 22 June 1940; *s* of late Frederick Franklin Sullivan and of Leonora Mary Sullivan; *m* 1967, Jennifer Enid Saunders. *Educ:* King's Sch., Canterbury; Jesus Coll., Oxford (BA). CRO 1962–66; Moscow, 1967; Ulan Bator, Mongolia, 1967–69; Sydney, 1970–74; FCO, 1975–77; First Sec., W Indian and Atlantic Dept, FCO, 1977–79; Consul (Industrial Develt), British Trade Develt Office, NY, 1979–81; Cultural Attaché, Moscow, 1981–85; Assistant Head: Personnel Services Dept, FCO, 1985–86; Energy, Sci. and Space Dept, FCO, 1986–88; Counsellor (Cultural Affairs), Moscow, 1988–89; Counsellor, Export Promotion Policy Unit, DTI, 1989–90. *Recreations:* piano playing, music and the arts, tennis, jogging, swimming. *Address:* c/o Foreign and Commonwealth Office, SW1A 2AH.

SULLIVAN, Richard Arthur, (9th Bt *cr* 1804, but does not use the title); Woodward-Clyde Consultants; *b* 9 Aug. 1931; *s* of Sir Richard Benjamin Magniac Sullivan, 8th Bt, and Muriel Mary Paget (*d* 1988), *d* of late Francis Charles Trayler Pineo; *S* father, 1977; *m* 1962, Elenor Mary, *e d* of late K. M. Thorpe; one *s* three *d*. *Educ:* Univ. of Cape Town (BSc); Massachusetts Inst. of Technology (SM). Chartered Engineer, UK; Professional Engineer, Ontario, Texas and Louisiana. *Publications:* technical papers to international conferences and geotechnical journals. *Recreation:* tennis. *Heir:* *s* Charles Merson Sullivan, *b* 15 Dec. 1962. *Address:* PO Box 1954, Tustin, Calif 92681, USA.

SULLIVAN, Tod; National Secretary, Association of Clerical, Technical and Supervisory Staffs, Transport and General Workers' Union, since 1974; *b* 3 Jan. 1934; *s* of Timothy William and Elizabeth Sullivan; *m* 1963, Patricia Norma Roughsedge; one *s* three *d*. *Educ:* Fanshawe Crescent Sch., Dagenham. Merchant Navy, 1950–52; RAF, 1952–55; Electrician, 1955–60; Children's Journalist, 1960–68; Industrial Relations Officer: ATV, 1968–71; CIR, 1971–72; Gen. Sec., Union of Kodak Workers, 1973–74 (until transfer of engagements to TGWU). *Recreations:* reading, music, golf. *Address:* 267 Luton Road, Harpenden, Herts. *T:* Harpenden (05827) 5034.

SULLY, Leonard Thomas George, CBE 1963; Covent Garden Market Authority, 1967–80; Member, Industrial Tribunals Panel, 1976–80; *b* 25 June 1909; British; *m* 1935, Phyllis Emily Phipps, Bristol; one *d*. *Educ:* elementary schs; Fairfield Grammar Sch., Bristol. Public Health Dept, Bristol Corp., 1927; Assistance Officer, Unemployment Assistance Board, Bristol District, 1934; subseq. served in Bath, Weston-super-Mare, etc.; Staff Officer, Air Ministry, London, 1943; Principal, and allocated to Air Ministry, 1949; Asst Sec., 1954, Dir of Contracts, 1960; Dir of Contracts (Air) MoD, 1964. *Recreation:* gardening. *Address:* Coppins, 20 Brackendale Close, Camberley, Surrey. *T:* Camberley (0276) 63604.

SULSTON, John Edward, PhD; FRS 1986; Staff Scientist, Laboratory of Molecular Biology, Cambridge, since 1969; *b* 27 March 1942; *s* of late Rev. Canon Arthur Edward Aubrey Sulston and of Josephine Muriel Frearson (*née* Blocksidge); *m* 1966, Daphne Edith Bate; one *s* one *d*. *Educ:* Merchant Taylors' School; Pembroke College, Cambridge (BA, PhD). Postdoctoral Fellow, Salk Inst., San Diego, 1966–69. *Publications:* articles on organic chemistry, molecular and developmental biology in sci. jls. *Recreations:* gardening, walking, avoiding people. *Address:* 39 Mingle Lane, Stapleford, Cambridge CB2 5BG. *T:* Cambridge (0223) 842248.

SULZBERGER, Arthur Ochs; Chairman, New York Times Co., since 1973; Publisher of The New York Times since 1963; *b* 5 Feb. 1926; *s* of late Arthur Hays Sulzberger; *m* 1st, 1948, Barbara Grant (marr. diss. 1956); one *s* one *d*; 2nd, 1956, Carol Fox Fuhrman; one *d* (and one adopted *d*). *Educ:* Browning School, New York City; Loomis School, Windsor, Conn; Columbia University, NYC. Reporter, Milwaukee Journal, 1953–54; Foreign Correspondent, New York Times, 1954–55; Asst to the Publisher, New York Times, 1956–57; Asst Treasurer, New York Times, 1957–63. Trustee: Metropolitan Mus. of Art; Columbia Univ. Hon. LLD: Dartmouth, 1964; Bard, 1967; Hon LHD: Montclair State Coll.; Tufts Univ., 1984. *Recreation:* fishing. *Address:* 229 West 43rd Street, New York, NY 10036, USA. *T:* 556–1771. *Clubs:* Overseas Press, Century Country, Explorers (New York); Metropolitan (Washington, DC).

SUMBERG, David Anthony Gerald; MP (C) Bury South, since 1983; *b* 2 June 1941; *s* of Joshua and Lorna Sumberg; *m* 1972, Carolyn Ann Rae Franks; one *s* one *d*. *Educ:* Tettenhall Coll., Staffs; Coll. of Law, London. Qualified as a Solicitor, 1964. Mem. (C) Manchester City Council, 1982–84. Contested (C) Manchester, Wythenshawe, 1979. PPS to: Solicitor-General, 1986–87; Attorney-General, 1987–90. Mem., Home Affairs Select Cttee, 1991–. *Recreation:* family. *Address:* 19 New Road, Radcliffe, Manchester. *T:* 061–723 3457.

SUMMERFIELD, Prof. Arthur, BSc Tech; BSc; CPsychol, FBPsS; Chairman, Learnit Ltd, since 1991; Professor of Psychology, University of London, 1961–88, now Emeritus, and Head of the Department of Psychology at Birkbeck College, 1961–88; *b* 31 March 1923; *s* of late Arthur and Dora Gertrude Summerfield; *m* 1st, 1946, Aline Whalley; one *s* one *d*; 2nd, 1974, Angela Barbara, MA Cantab, PhD London, CPsychol, FBPsS, *d* of late George Frederick and Estelle Steer. *Educ:* Manchester Grammar Sch.; Manchester Univ.; University Coll. London (1st cl. hons Psychology). Served War of 1939–45, Electrical Officer, RNVR, 1943–46: Naval Air Stations, 1943–46; Dept of Sen. Psychologist to the Admiralty, 1946. Asst Lectr in Psychology, University Coll. London, 1949–51, Lectr, 1951–61, Hon. Research Associate, 1961–70, Hon. Research Fellow, 1970–; first Dean, Fac. of Econs, Birkbeck Coll., 1971–72, Governor, 1982–86; Hon. Lectr in Psychology, Westminster Med. Sch., 1974–76. Member: Univ. of London Bd of Studies in Psychology, 1956–88 (Chm., 1967–70); Special Adv. Cttee on Ergonomics, 1968–88 (Chm., 1983–88); Acad. Adv. Bd in Medicine, 1974–88; Acad. Council Standing Sub-Cttee on Science and Engrg, 1974–77. Mem. Council, British Psychological Soc., 1953–65, 1967–75, 1977–84 (Hon. Gen. Sec., 1954–59; Pres., 1963–64; Vice-Pres., 1964–65; first Chm., Scientific Affairs Bd, 1974–75); Member: Cttee on Internat. Relations in Psychology, Amer. Psychological Assoc., 1977–79; Bd of Dirs, European Coordination Centre for Res. and Documentation in Social Scis (Vienna Centre), 1977–81; ICSU Study Gp on biol, med. and physical effects of large scale use of nuclear weapons, 1983–87; Pres., International Union of Psychological Science, 1976–80 (Mem., Exec. Cttee, 1963–84, Assembly, 1957–84; Vice-Pres., 1972–76); Pres., Section J (Psychology) BAAS, 1976–77; Pres., Internat. Soc. Sci. Council, 1977–81 (Mem. Prog. Cttee, 1973–83; Mem. Exec. Cttee, 1977–83); Chm., DES Working Party on Psychologists in Educn Services, 1965–68 (Summerfield report). Member: DSIR Human Sciences Res. Grants Cttee, 1962–65; SSRC, 1979–81; Psychology Cttee, SSRC, 1979–81. Vis. Prof., Univ. of California (at Dept of Psychobiology, Irvine Campus), 1968. Governor, Enfield Coll. of Technology, 1968–72. Dir, British Jl of Educnl Psychology Ltd, 1976–; Asst Editor, Brit. Jl Psychology (Statistical Section), 1950–54; Editor, British Journal of Psychology, 1964–67; Scientific Editor, British Med. Bulletin issues on Experimental Psychology, 1964, Cognitive Psychology, 1971, (with D. M. Warburton) Psychobiology, 1981. *Publications:* articles on perception, memory, statistical methods and psycho-pharmacology in scientific periodicals. *Address:* 14 Colonels Walk, The Ridgeway, Enfield EN2 8HN. *Club:* Athenæum.

SUMMERFIELD, Sir John (Crampton), Kt 1973; CBE 1966 (OBE 1961); Judge of the Grand Court and Chief Justice of the Cayman Islands, 1977–87, retired; *b* 20 Sept. 1920; *s* of late Arthur Fred Summerfield and late Lilian Winifred Summerfield (*née* Staas); *m* 1945, Patricia Sandra Musgrave; two *s* two *d*. *Educ:* Lucton Sch., Herefordshire. Called to Bar, Gray's Inn, 1949. Served War, 1939–46: East Africa, Abyssinia, Somaliland, Madagascar; Captain, Royal Signals. Crown Counsel, Tanganyika (now Tanzania), 1949; Legal Draftsman, 1953; Dep. Legal Sec., EA High Commission, 1958. Attorney-Gen., Bermuda, 1962; QC (Bermuda) 1963; MEC, 1962–68, and MLC, 1962–68 (Bermuda); Chief Justice of Bermuda, 1972–77; Judge of Supreme Court, Turks and Caicos Islands, 1977–82; Justice of Appeal for Bermuda, 1979–87; Pres., Ct of Appeal for Belize, 1982–84. *Publications:* Preparation of Revised Laws of Bermuda, 1963 and 1971 edns. *Recreations:* photography, chess, sailing. *Address:* 3 The Corniche, Sandgate, Folkestone, Kent CT20 3TA. *Club:* Commonwealth Trust.

SUMMERHAYES, Dr Colin Peter; Director, Institute of Oceanographic Sciences Deacon Laboratory, since 1988; *b* 7 March 1942; *s* of late Leonard Percy Summerhayes and of Jessica Adelaide (*née* Crump); *m* 1st, 1966 (marr. diss. 1977); one *s* one *d*; 2nd, 1981, Diana Ridley (*née* Perry); one step *s* one step *d*. *Educ:* Slough Grammar Sch.; UCL (BSc 1963); Keble Coll., Oxford; Victoria Univ., Wellington, NZ (MSc 1967; DSc 1986); Imperial Coll., London (DIC; PhD 1970). FRGS 1990. Scientific Officer, DSIR, NZ Oceanographic Inst., 1964–67; Res. Asst, Geol. Dept, Imperial Coll., London, 1967–70; Sen. Scientific Officer, CSIR, Marine Geosci. Unit, Univ. of Cape Town, 1970–72; Asst Scientist, Geol. and Geophys Dept, Woods Hole Oceanographic Instn, 1972–76; Research Associate/Project Leader: Geochem. Br., Exxon Prodn Res. Centre, Houston, 1976–82; Global Paleoreconstruction Sect., Stratigraphy Br., BP Res. Centre, 1982–85; Manager and Sen. Res. Associate, Stratigraphy Br., BP Res. Centre, 1985–88.

Vis. Prof., UCL, 1987–91. Vice-Pres., Houston Audubon Soc., 1980–82. Member: Geol Soc.; Geol Soc. Dining Club; Challenger Soc. for Marine Sci.; Soc. for Underwater Technology; RSPB. MBIM. *Publications:* (with N. J. Shackleton) North Atlantic Palaeoceanography, 1986; 90 papers in various geol, geochem., oceanographic jls, 3 on seabirds. *Recreations:* ornithology, jogging, reading, films and theatre. *Address:* Institute of Oceanographic Sciences Deacon Laboratory, Brook Road, Wormley, Godalming, Surrey GU8 5UB. *T:* Wormley (0428) 684141.

SUMMERHAYES, David Michael, CMG 1975; HM Diplomatic Service, retired; Disarmament Adviser, Foreign and Commonwealth Office, since 1983; *b* 29 Sept. 1922; *s* of Sir Christopher Summerhayes, KBE, CMG and late Anna (*née* Johnson); *m* 1959, June van der Hardt Aberson; two *s* one *d*. *Educ:* Marlborough; Emmanuel Coll., Cambridge. Served War of 1939–45 in Royal Artillery (Capt.) N Africa and Italy. 3rd Sec., FO, 1948; Baghdad, 1949; Brussels, 1950–53; 2nd Sec., FO, 1953–56; 1st Sec. (Commercial), The Hague, 1956–59; 1st Sec. and Consul, Reykjavik, 1959–61; FO, 1961–65; Consul-General and Counsellor, Buenos Aires, 1965–70; Head of Arms Control and Disarmament Dept, FCO, 1970–74; Minister, Pretoria/Cape Town, 1974–78; Ambassador and Leader, UK Delegn to Cttee on Disarmament, Geneva, 1979–82. Hon. Officer, Order of Orange Nassau. *Recreations:* tennis, golf, walking. *Address:* Ivy House, South Harting, Petersfield, Hants GU31 5QQ. *Club:* United Oxford & Cambridge University.

SUMMERHAYES, Gerald Victor, CMG 1979; OBE 1969; *b* 28 Jan. 1928; *s* of Victor Samuel and Florence A. V. Summerhayes. Administrative Service, Nigeria, 1952–81; Permanent Secretary: Local Govt, North Western State, 1975–76, Sokoto State, 1976–77; Cabinet Office (Political and Trng), 1977–79; Dir of Trng, Cabinet Office, Sokoto, 1979–81. *Address:* Bridge Cottage, Bridge Street, Sidbury, Devon EX10 0RU. *T:* Sidbury (03957) 311; PO Box 172, Sokoto, Nigeria.

SUMMERS, (Sir) Felix Roland Brattan, 2nd Bt *cr* 1952; does not use the title and his name is not on the Official Roll of Baronets.

SUMMERS, Henry Forbes, CB 1961; Under-Secretary, Department of the Environment (formerly Ministry of Housing and Local Government), 1955–71; *b* 18 August 1911; *s* of late Rev. H. H. Summers, Harrogate, Yorks; *m* 1937, Rosemary, *d* of late Robert L. Roberts, CBE; two *s* one *d*. *Educ:* Fettes Coll., Edinburgh; Trinity College, Oxford. *Publications:* Smoke After Flame, 1944; Hinterland, 1947; Tomorrow is my Love, 1978; The Burning Book, 1982. *Address:* Folly Fields, Tunbridge Wells, Kent TN2 5QU. *T:* Tunbridge Wells (0892) 27671.

See also N. Summers.

SUMMERS, Janet Margaret, (Mrs L. J. Summers); *see* Bately, J. M.

SUMMERS, Nicholas; Under Secretary, Department of Education and Science, since 1981; *b* 11 July 1939; *s* of Henry Forbes Summers, *qv*; *m* 1965, Marian Elizabeth Ottley; four *s*. *Educ:* Tonbridge Sch.; Corpus Christi Coll., Oxford. Min. of Educn, 1961–64; DES, 1964–74; Private Sec. to Minister for the Arts, 1965–66; Cabinet Office, 1974–76; DES, 1976–. *Recreations:* family, music. *Address:* c/o Department of Education and Science, Sanctuary Buildings, Great Smith Street, SW1.

SUMMERSCALE, David Michael, MA; Head Master of Westminster School, since 1986; *b* 22 April 1937; *s* of Noel Tynwald Summerscale and Beatrice (*née* Wilson); *m* 1975, Pauline, *d* of Prof. Michel Fleury, Président de l'Ecole des Hautes Etudes, Paris, Directeur des Antiquités Historiques de l'Ile-de-France; one *s* one *d*. *Educ:* Northaw; Sherborne Sch.; Trinity Hall, Cambridge. Lectr in English Literature and Tutor, St Stephen's Coll., Univ. of Delhi, 1959–63; Charterhouse, 1963–75 (Head of English, Housemaster); Master of Haileybury, 1976–86. Oxford and Cambridge Schs Examination Bd Awarder and Reviser in English. Vice-Chm., E-SU Scholarship Cttee, 1982–; Member: Managing Cttee of Cambridge Mission to Delhi, 1965; C. F. Andrews Centenary Appeal Cttee, 1970; HMC Academic Policy Sub-Cttee, 1982–86; Council, Charing Cross and Westminster Med. Sch., 1986–. Governor: The Hall Sch., Hampstead, 1986–; Arnold House Sch., St John's Wood, 1988–; Staff Advr, Governing Body, Westminster Abbey Choir Sch., 1989–; Nominated Mem., Sch. Cttee, Merchant Taylors' Co., 1988–; Consultant and Gov., Assam Valley Sch., India, 1989–. FRSA 1984. *Publications:* articles on English and Indian literature; dramatisations of novels and verse. *Recreations:* music, reading, mountaineering, games (squash (Mem. SRA), cricket, tennis, rackets (Mem. Tennis and Rackets Assoc.), golf. *Address:* 17 Dean's Yard, SW1P 3PB. *Clubs:* Athenæum, I Zingari, Free Foresters, Jesters; Club Alpin Suisse.

SUMMERSCALE, Peter Wayne; HM Diplomatic Service, retired; *b* 22 April 1935; *s* of Sir John Summerscale, KBE; *m* 1st, 1964, Valerie Turner (marr. diss. 1983); one *s* two *d*; 2nd, 1985, Cristina Fournier (marr. diss. 1986); 3rd, 1989, Elizabeth Carro. *Educ:* Rugby Sch.; New Coll., Oxford Univ. (Exhibnr; 1st Cl. Hons Modern History); Russian Res. Centre, Harvard Univ. FO, 1960–62; Polit. Residency, Bahrain, 1962–65; 1st Sec., Tokyo, 1965–68; FCO, 1968–69; Cabinet Office, 1969–71; 1st Sec. and Head of Chancery, Santiago, Chile, 1971–75; Head of CSCE Unit, FCO, 1976–77; Dep. Leader, UK Delegn, Belgrade Rev. Conf., 1977–78; Counsellor and Head of Chancery, Brussels, 1978–79; Vis. FCO Res. Fellow, RIIA, Chatham House, 1979–81; Head of Civilian Faculty, Nat. Defence Coll., 1981–82; Ambassador to Costa Rica, 1982–86, and concurrently (non-resident) to Nicaragua; Dep. Leader, UK Delegn to CSCE, 1986–88; Hd, CSCE Unit, FCO, 1989–90. *Publications:* (jtly) Soviet—East European Dilemmas, 1981; The East European Predicament, 1982; articles on E Europe and communism. *Recreations:* sailing, skiing, walking. *Address:* 5 Grove Terrace, NW5 1PH.

SUMMERSKILL, Dr the Hon. Shirley Catherine Wynne; Medical Practitioner; Medical Officer in Blood Transfusion Service, since 1983; *b* London, 9 Sept. 1931; *d* of late Dr E. J. Samuel and Baroness Summerskill, CH, PC. *Educ:* St Paul's Girls' Sch.; Somerville Coll., Oxford; St Thomas' Hospital. MA, BM, BCh., 1958. Treas., Oxford Univ. Labour Club, 1952. Resident House Surgeon, later House Physician, St Helier Hosp., Carshalton, 1959; Partner in Gen. Practice, 1960–68. Contested (Lab): Blackpool North by-election, 1962; Halifax, 1983. MP (Lab) Halifax, 1964–83; opposition spokesman on health, 1970–74; Parly Under-Sec. of State, Home Office, 1974–79; opposition spokesman on home affairs, 1979–83. Vice-Chm., PLP Health Gp, 1964–69, Chm., 1969–70; Mem., Labour Party NEC, 1981–83. UK delegate, UN Status of Women Commn, 1968 and 1969; Mem. British delegn, Council of Europe and WEU, 1968, 1969. *Publications:* A Surgical Affair (novel), 1963; Destined to Love (novel), 1986.

SUMMERSON, Hugo Hawksley Fitzthomas; MP (C) Walthamstow, since 1987; *b* 21 July 1950; *s* of late Thomas Hawksley Summerson, OBE and of Joan Florence Summerson; *m* 1989, Rosemary, *d* of late John Pitts, Exeter. *Educ:* Harrow School; Royal Agricultural College. FRICS; MRAC. Land Agent with Knight, Frank and Rutley, 1973–76; travel in S America, 1977; self-employment, 1978–83; Dir, Palatine Properties, 1983–. Contested (C) Barking, 1983. Select Cttee on Envmt, 1991–; Treas., British Latin-American Parly Gp, 1990. Chm., Greater London Area Adopted Parly Candidates Assoc., 1986; Vice-Pres., Greater London Area, Nat. Soc. of Cons. and Unionist Agents, 1989; Mem. Council, British Atlantic Gp of Young Politicians, 1989; Parly Advr to Drinking Fountain Assoc., 1989. Fellow-Elect, Industry and Parlt Trust, 1990. Sir Anthony Berry Meml Scholar, 1985. *Recreations:* fishing, music, cricket. *Address:* House of Commons, SW1A 0AA. *T:* 071–219 3000. *Club:* Royal Over-Seas League.

SUMMERSON, Sir John (Newenham), CH 1987; Kt 1958; CBE 1952; BA(Arch); FBA 1954; FSA; ARIBA; Curator of Sir John Soane's Museum, 1945–84; *b* 25 Nov. 1904; *o s* of late Samuel James Summerson of Darlington and Dorothea Worth Newenham; *m* 1938, Elizabeth Alison (*d* 1991), *d* of H. R. Hepworth, CBE, Leeds; three *s*. *Educ:* Harrow; University College, London. From 1926 worked in architects' offices, including those of late W. D. Caröe and Sir Giles Gilbert Scott, OM. Instructor in Sch. of Architecture, Edinburgh Coll. of Art, 1929–30. Asst Editor, Architect and Building News, 1934–41; Dep. Dir, National Buildings Record, 1941–45. Lectr in History of Architecture: Architectural Assoc., 1949–62; Birkbeck Coll., 1950–67; Slade Prof. of Fine Art, Oxford, 1958–59; Ferens Prof. of Fine Art, Hull, 1960–61 and 1970–71; Slade Prof. of Fine Art, Cambridge, 1966–67; Bampton Lectr, Columbia Univ., 1968; Page-Barbour Lectr, Virginia Univ., 1972; Banister Fletcher Prof., UCL, 1981. Member: Royal Fine Art Commn, 1947–54; Royal Commn on Historical Monuments (England), 1953–74; Historic Buildings Council, 1953–78; Arts Council Art Panel, 1953–56; Historical Manuscripts Commn, 1959–83; Listed Buildings Cttee Min. of Housing and Local Govt, 1944–66 (Chm., 1960–62); Adv. Council on Public Records, 1968–74; Council, Architectural Assoc., 1940–45; Trustee, National Portrait Gallery, 1966–73. Hon. Fellow, Trinity Hall, Cambridge, 1968; Fellow, UCL. Foreign Hon. Mem., Amer. Acad. of Arts and Sciences, 1967; Chairman, National Council for Diplomas in Art and Design, 1961–70. Hon. DLitt: Leicester, 1959; Oxford, 1963; Hull, 1971; Newcastle, 1973; Hon. DSc Edinburgh, 1968; Hon. Dr, RCA, 1975. Hon. RSA 1982. RIBA Silver Medal (Essay), 1937; RIBA Royal Gold Medal for Architecture, 1976. *Publications:* Architecture Here and Now (with C. Williams-Ellis), 1934; John Nash, Architect to George IV, 1935; The Bombed Buildings of Britain (with J. M. Richards), 1942 and 1945; Georgian London, 1946, rev. edn 1988; The Architectural Association (Centenary History), 1947; Ben Nicholson (Penguin Modern Painters), 1948; Heavenly Mansions (essays), 1949; Sir John Soane, 1952; Sir Christopher Wren, 1953; Architecture in Britain, 1530–1830 (Pelican History of Art), 1953, 8th edn 1991; New Description of Sir J. Soane's Museum, 1955; The Classical Language of Architecture, 1964, rev. edn 1980; The Book of John Thorpe (Walpole Soc., vol. 40), 1966; Inigo Jones, 1966; Victorian Architecture (four studies in evaluation), 1969; (ed) Concerning Architecture, 1969; The London Building World of the Eighteen-Sixties, 1974; (jt author) The History of the King's Works (ed H. M. Colvin), vol. 3, 1976, vol. 4, 1982; The Life and Work of John Nash, Architect, 1981; The Architecture of the Eighteenth Century, 1986; The Unromantic Castle (essays), 1990. *Address:* 1 Eton Villas, NW3 4SX. *T:* 01–722 6247. *Club:* Athenæum.

SUMMERTON, Dr Neil William; Under Secretary, Local Government Finance Policy, Department of the Environment, since 1988; *b* 5 April 1942; *s* of H. E. W. Summerton and Nancy Summerton; *m* 1965, Pauline Webb; two *s*. *Educ:* Wellington Grammar Sch., Shropshire; King's Coll., London (BA History 1963; PhD War Studies 1970). Min. of Transport, 1966–69; PA to Principal, 1969–71, Asst Sec. (Co-ordination), 1971–74, KCL; DoE, 1974–; Asst Sec., heading various housing Divs, 1978–85; Under Sec., Planning Land-Use Policy Directorate, 1985–87; Under Sec., Planning and Develt Control Directorate, 1987–88. Attended HM Treasury Centre for Admin. Studies, 1968–69; Civil Service Top Management Programme, 1985. Non-exec. Dir, Redland Bricks Ltd, 1988–; Director: Harvester Trust Ltd, 1989–; Christian Impact Ltd, 1989–; London Christian Housing plc, 1990–. Elder of a Christian congregation; other Christian activities; Member: Cttee of Management, Council on Christian Approaches to Defence and Disarmament, 1983– (Hon. Sec., 1984–91); Council, Evangelical Alliance, 1990–. *Publications:* A Noble Task: eldership and ministry in the local church, 1987; articles and essays on historical, theological and ethical matters.

SUMNER, Christopher John; His Honour Judge Sumner; a Circuit Judge, since 1987; *b* 28 Aug. 1939; *s* of His Honour W. D. M. Sumner, OBE, QC; *m* 1970, Carole Ashley Mann; one *s* two *d*. *Educ:* Charterhouse; Sidney Sussex Coll., Cambridge (MA). Called to the Bar, Inner Temple, 1961; Asst Recorder, 1983; Recorder, 1986. *Recreations:* reading, sport, theatre, listening to music. *Address:* 26 Stevenage Road, SW6 6ET. *T:* 071–736 5632. *Club:* Hurlingham.

SUMNER, Victor Emmanuel, MRSL 1983; Chairman, Public Service Commission, Sierra Leone, since 1989; *b* 17 April 1929; *s* of D. R. Sumner; *m* 1962, Gladys Victoria Small; two *s* one *d*. *Educ:* Fourah Bay Coll., Sierra Leone; Otterbein Coll., Ohio, USA; Laval Univ., Canada. BA, MA. School teacher, 1949–55; Sierra Leone Commonwealth and Foreign Service: Asst Sec., 1961; Sen. Asst Sec., 1965; Dep. Sec., 1968; Counsellor: Washington, 1969; Bonn, 1970; Permanent Secretary: Min. of For. Affairs, 1971; Min. of Health, 1974–76; Asst to Sec. to Pres., 1976–77; Permanent Sec., Min. of For. Affairs, 1977–80; High Comr in UK and Ambassador to Sweden, Denmark and Norway, 1980–87, to Spain, Portugal, Greece and Algeria, 1983–87. *Recreations:* fishing, walking, volleyball, football. *Address:* Public Service Commission, 5 Gloucester Street, Freetown, Sierra Leone.

SUMPTION, Anthony James Chadwick, DSC 1944; *b* 15 May 1919; *s* of late John Chadwick Sumption and late Winifred Fanny Sumption; *m* 1946, Hedy Hedigan (marr. diss. 1979); two *s* two *d*. *Educ:* Cheltenham Coll.; London Sch. of Economics. Served RNVR, 1939–46; HM Submarines, 1941–45: comd Varangian, 1944; Upright, 1945. Solicitor, 1946; called to the Bar, Lincoln's Inn, 1971; a Recorder of the Crown Court, 1980–84. Member (C): LCC, 1949–52; Westminster City Council, 1953–56. Contested (C): Hayes and Harlington, March 1953; Middlesbrough W, 1964. *Publications:* Taxation of Overseas Income and Gains, 1973, 4th edn 1982; Tax Planning, (with Philip Lawton) 6th edn 1973–8th edn 1979, (with Giles Clarke) 9th edn 1981–10th edn 1982; Capital Gains Tax, 1981. *Recreations:* painting, angling. *Address:* c/o Coutts & Co., 188 Fleet Street, EC4. *Club:* Garrick.

See also J. P. C. Sumption.

SUMPTION, Jonathan Philip Chadwick; QC 1986; *b* 9 Dec. 1948; *s* of Anthony James Chadwick Sumption, *qv*; *m* 1971, Teresa Mary (*née* Whelan); one *s* two *d*. *Educ:* Eton; Magdalen College, Oxford (MA). Fellow (in History) of Magdalen College, Oxford, 1971–75; called to the Bar, Inner Temple, 1975, Bencher, 1990. *Publications:* Pilgrimage: an image of medieval religion, 1975; The Albigensian Crusade, 1978; The Hundred Years' War, 1990. *Recreations:* music, history. *Address:* 34 Crooms Hill, Greenwich, SE10. *T:* 081–858 4444.

SUMRAY, Monty; CBE 1989; Chairman and Managing Director, FII Group, since 1965; *b* 12 Oct. 1918; *m* 1939, Catherine Beber; one *s* one *d*. *Educ:* Upton House, London. Royal Berkshire Regt, 1939–46; served in Burma (Captain). UK footwear manufacturing, 1934–; Dir, FII Group subsid. cos and other cos. Pres., British Footwear Manufacturers' Fedn, 1976–77, formerly: Member: Footwear Industry Study Steering Gp (Chm., Home Working Cttee); Footwear Economic Develt Cttee (4 years); Pres., London Footwear

Manufacturers' Assoc.; Chm., London Branch, British Boot & Shoe Instn. FCFI 1974; FInstD 1981. *Recreations:* tennis, reading, social and charitable work. *Address:* 11 Neville Drive, N2 0QS. *T:* 081–458 2788.

SUMSION, Herbert Whitton, CBE 1961; DMus Lambeth; FRCM, Hon. RAM, FRCO, FRSCM; Organist of Gloucester Cathedral, 1928–67; Director of Music, Ladies' College, Cheltenham, 1935–68; *b* Gloucester, 19 Jan. 1899; *m* 1927, Alice Hartley Garlichs, BA; three *s*. *Educ:* Durham Univ. (MusBac 1920). DMus Lambeth, 1947. Organist and Choirmaster at Christ Church, Lancaster Gate; Director of Music, Bishop's Stortford College; Asst Instructor in Music at Morley Coll., London; Teacher of Harmony and Counterpoint, Curtis Institute, Philadelphia, 1926–28; Conductor Three Choirs Fest., 1928, 1931, 1934, 1937, 1947, 1950, 1953, 1956, 1959, 1962, 1965. *Publications:* Introduction and Theme for Organ, 1935; Morning and Evening Service in G, 1935; Two pieces for Cello and Piano, 1939 (No 1 arranged for String Orchestra); Magnificat and Nunc Dimittis in G for Boys' Voices, 1953, for Men's Voices, 1953, for Boys' Voices in D, 1973; Cradle Song for Organ, 1953; Benedicite in B flat, 1955; Four Carol Preludes for Organ, 1956; Festival Benedicite in D, 1971; They That Go Down to the Sea in Ships (anthem), 1979; Transposition Exercises, 1980; Piano Technique, a Book of Exercises, 1980; There is a Green Hill Far Away (anthem), 1981; Two Anthems for Holy Communion, 1981; In Exile (By the Waters of Babylon) (anthem), 1981; A Unison Communion Service, 1991; (contrib.) Sing The Seasons, 1991; Cello Sonata, 1992. *Address:* Church End House, Frampton-on-Severn, Glos GL2 7EH. *T:* Gloucester (0452) 741074.

See also J. W. Sumsion.

SUMSION, John Walbridge, OBE 1991; Director, Library and Information Statistics Unit, Loughborough University, since 1991; *b* 16 Aug. 1928; *s* of Dr Herbert Sumsion, *qv*; *m* 1st, 1961, Annette Dorothea Wilson (marr. diss. 1979); two *s* two *d*; 2nd, 1979, Hazel Mary Jones (*née* English). *Educ:* St George's Choir Sch., Windsor Castle; St Thomas' Choir Sch., New York City; Rendcomb Coll., Cirencester; Clare Coll., Cambridge (BA (Hons) History); Yale Univ., USA (MA Economics); Cornell Univ., USA (Teaching Fellow). FBIM. Somervell Brothers (K Shoemakers) Ltd: Graduate trainee, 1954; Production Manager (Women's Shoes), 1959; Director, 1962–81; Registrar, Public Lending Right, 1981–91. Mem., Copyright Tribunal, 1990–. Hon. FLA 1990. *Publications:* Setting Up Public Lending Right, 1984; PLR in Practice, 1988. *Recreations:* music (flute, singing), tennis. *Address:* Library and Information Statistics Unit, Loughborough University, Leics LE11 3TU. *T:* Loughborough (0509) 223071. *Club:* United Oxford & Cambridge University.

SUNDARAVADIVELU, Neyyadupakkam Duraiswamy; Vice President, Madras State Board for Adult Education; Vice-Chancellor, University of Madras, 1969–75; *b* 15 Oct. 1912. *Educ:* Univ. of Madras (MA, Licentiate in Teaching). Asst Panchayat Officer (organising and directing village panchayats), 1935–40; Madras Educnl Subordinate Service, inspection of primary schs, 1940–42; Madras Educnl Service, inspection of secondary schs and gen. direction of primary schs, 1942–51; Dep. Dir of Public Instruction, 1951–56 and Comr for Public Examns, 1954–65, Tamil Nadu; Dir of Higher Educn, Tamil Nadu, 1965–66; Dir of Public Libraries, Tamil Nadu, 1954–65; Jt Educnl Adviser to Govt of India, Min. of Educn, New Delhi, 1966–68; Chief Educnl Adviser and Additional Sec. to Govt of Tamil Nadu, Educn Dept, 1968–69; Dir of Collegiate Educn, Tamil Nadu, 1968–69. Visited: UK, 1951, 1962, 1973; USSR, 1961, 1967, 1971, 1973; USA, 1964, 1970; France, 1951, 1968, 1970, 1971, 1973; Malaysia, 1966, 1975; Philippines, 1971, 1972; Ghana, 1971; Canada, 1970; Singapore, 1966, 1975; Hong Kong, 1970, 1975; German Dem. Republic, 1973; participated in various confs, meetings, etc. Past Member: Nat. Council of Educnl Research and Trng, New Delhi; Nat. Commn on UNESCO; Mem., Nat. Council for Rural Higher Educn; Pres., Madras Cttee of World Univ. Service (Vice-Pres., Indian Nat. Cttee); Mem., Nat. Bd of Adult Educn; Chm., Southern Languages Book Trust; Mem., Standing Cttee of Inter-Univ. Bd of India and Ceylon, New Delhi; Vice-Pres., Indian Adult Educn Assoc.; Mem., Central Cttee of Tamil Nadu Tuberculosis Assoc.; Chm., Kendriya Vidyalaya, Gill Nagar, Madras. Originator of schemes, Free Mid-day Meals, School Improvement, and Free Supply of Uniforms to School Children, recommended to all Asian countries for adoption (personally commended by Pres. of India, 1960). Hon. DLitt Madras, 1983. Padma Shri (presidential award), 1961. *Publications:* 45 books in Tamil, incl. 13 for children and Autobiography, part I, 1983; State awards for best travelogue, 1968, 1981. *Address:* 90C Shenoynagar, Madras 600030, India. *T:* Madras 612516.

SUNDERLAND, (Arthur) John; Commissioner-in-Chief, St John Ambulance Brigade, 1986–90; *b* 24 Feb. 1932; *s* of George Frederick Irvon Sunderland and Mary Katharine Sunderland; *m* 1958, Audrey Ann Thompson; three *s*. *Educ:* Marlborough Coll. Served Army, RE, 1953–55 (2nd Lieut). Director: James Upton Ltd, 1963–69; Surrey Fine Art Press Ltd, 1963–69; Sunderland Print Ltd, 1969–84; Randall Bros Ltd, 1970–84; Alday Green & Welburn, 1978–84; Foxplan Ltd, 1984–; Rapidflow Ltd, 1985–; SADC Ltd, 1986–. Dep. County Comr, 1976–78, County Comr, 1978–86, St John Ambulance Bde, W Midlands; KStJ 1986 (CStJ 1982; OStJ 1978). Chm., Ladypool Road Neighbourhood Centre, Balsall Heath, 1970–76. Governor, West House Sch., Birmingham, 1973–. *Recreations:* walking, sport generally. *Address:* Rowans, Grafton Flyford, Worcs WR7 4PJ. *T:* Himbleton (090569) 281.

SUNDERLAND, Prof. Eric, PhD; FIBiol; Principal, University College of North Wales, Bangor, since 1984; *b* 18 March 1930; *s* of Leonard Sunderland and Mary Agnes (*née* Davies); *m* 1957, Jean Patricia (*née* Watson); two *d*. *Educ:* Amman Valley Grammar Sch.; Univ. of Wales (BA, MA); Univ. of London (PhD). FIBiol 1975. Commnd Officer, RA, 1955–56. Res. Asst, UCL, 1953–54; Res. Scientist, NCB, 1957–58; Univ. of Durham: Lectr, 1958–66; Sen. Lectr, 1966–71; Prof. of Anthropology, 1971–84; Pro Vice-Chancellor, 1979–84; Vice-Chancellor, Univ. of Wales, 1989–91. Welsh Supernumerary Fellow, Jesus Coll., Oxford, 1987–88. Sec.-Gen., Internat. Union of Anthropol and Ethnol Sciences, 1978–; President, Royal Anthropol Inst., 1989–91 (Hon. Sec., 1978–85; Hon. Treasurer, 1985–89); Chm., Biosocial Soc., 1981–85. Member: Welsh Language Bd, 1988–; Ct of Govs, Nat. Mus. of Wales, 1991–; Chm., Welsh Language Educn Develt Cttee, 1987–. Hon. Mem., The Gorsedd, 1985. *Publications:* Elements of Human and Social Geography: some anthropological perspectives, 1973; (ed jtly) Genetic Variation in Britain, 1973; (ed jtly) The Operation of Intelligence: biological preconditions for the operation of intelligence, 1980; (ed jtly) Genetic and Population Studies in Wales, 1986; contrib. Annals of Human Biol., Human Heredity, Man, Human Biol., Nature, Amer. Jl of Phys. Anthropol., and Trans Royal Soc. *Recreations:* travel, gardening, book collecting, reading. *Address:* University College of North Wales, Bangor, Gwynedd LL57 2DG. *T:* Bangor (0248) 351151. *Club:* Athenæum.

SUNDERLAND, (Godfrey) Russell, CB 1991; Deputy Secretary, Aviation, Shipping and International, Department of Transport, since 1988; *b* 28 July 1936; *s* of Allan and Laura Sunderland; *m* 1965, Greta Jones; one *s* one *d*. *Educ:* Heath Grammar Sch., Halifax; The Queen's College, Oxford (MA). Ministry of Aviation: Asst Principal, 1962; Asst Private Sec. to Minister, 1964; Principal, 1965; HM Diplomatic Service: First Sec. (Civil Air), Beirut, and other Middle East posts, 1969; Principal, Board of Trade, 1971; Asst Sec., DTI, 1973; Under Sec., DTI, 1979; Dir of Shipping Policy and Emergency Planning, Dept of Transport, 1984. Chairman, Consultative Shipping Group, 1984–88. *Address:* Department of Transport, 2 Marsham Street, SW1P 3EB.

SUNDERLAND, John; *see* Sunderland, A. J.

SUNDERLAND, Russell; *see* Sunderland, G. R.

SUNDERLAND, Prof. Sir Sydney, Kt 1971; CMG 1961; FAA 1954; Professor of Experimental Neurology, 1961–75, now Emeritus Professor, and Dean of the Faculty of Medicine 1953–71, University of Melbourne; *b* Brisbane, Aust., 31 Dec. 1910; *s* of Harry and Anne Sunderland; *m* 1939, Nina Gwendoline Johnston, LLB; one *s*. *Educ:* University of Melbourne. BM, BS 1935, DSc 1945, DMed 1946, Melbourne. FRACP 1941; FRACS 1952. Sen. Lectr in Anatomy, Univ. of Melbourne, 1936–37; Demonstrator in Human Anatomy, Oxford, 1938–39; Prof. of Anatomy, Univ. of Melbourne, 1940–61. Visiting Specialist (Hon. Major) 115 Aust. Gen. Mil. Hosp., 1941–45. Mem. Zool Bd of Vict., 1944–65 (Chm. Scientific Cttee, 1958–62); Dep. Chm., Adv. Cttee to Mental Hygiene Dept, Vict., 1952–63; Mem. Nat. Health and MRC, 1953–69; Chm., Med. Research Adv. Cttee of Nat. Health and MRC, 1964–69. Visiting Prof. of Anatomy, Johns Hopkins Univ., 1953–54; Sec., Div. of Biol Sciences, Aust. Acad. Sci., 1955–58; Member: Nat. Radiation Adv. Cttee, 1957–64 (Chm. 1958–64); Defence Research and Development Policy Cttee, 1957–75; Med. Services Cttee, Dept of Defence, 1957–78; Council, AMA, Victorian Branch, 1960–68; Safety Review Cttee, Aust. Atomic Energy Commn, 1961–74 (Chm.); Aust. Univs Commn, 1962–76; Cttee of Management, Royal Melbourne Hosp., 1963–71; Protective Chemistry Research Adv. Cttee, Dept of Supply, 1964–73 (Chm.); Victorian Med. Adv. Cttee, 1962–71; Board of Walter and Eliza Hall Inst. of Med. Research, 1968–75. Governor, Ian Potter Foundn, 1964–. Trustee: National Museum, 1954–82; Van Cleef Foundn, 1971–. Fogarty Scholar in residence, Nat. Inst. of Health, Bethesda, USA, 1972–73. Foundn Fellow, Aust. Acad. of Science, 1954, and rep. on Pacific Science Council, 1957–69. Hon. MD: Tasmania, 1970; Queensland, 1975; Hon. LLD: Melbourne, 1975; Monash, 1977. *Publications:* Nerves and Nerve Injuries, 1968, 2nd edn 1978; Nerve Injuries and Their Repair: a critical appraisal, 1991; about 100 articles in scientific jls in Gt Britain, Europe, US and Australia. *Address:* 72 Kingstoun, 461 St Kilda Road, Melbourne, Victoria 3004, Australia. *T:* 2665858. *Club:* Melbourne.

SUPHAMONGKHON, Dr Konthi, Kt Grand Cordon of the White Elephant, Kt Grand Cordon, Order of the Crown of Thailand; Kt Grand Commander, Order of Chula Chom Klao; Hon. GCVO 1972; Member, National Legislative Assembly, 1977–79 and Adviser to the Prime Minister, 1978–79; *b* 3 Aug. 1916; *m* 1951, Dootsdi Atthakravi; two *s* one *d*. *Educ:* Univ. of Moral and Political Sciences, Bangkok (LLB); Univ. of Paris (Dr-en-Droit). Joined Min. of Foreign Affairs, 1940; Second Sec., Tokyo, 1942–44; Chief of Polit. Div., 1944–48; Dir-Gen., Western Affairs Dept, 1948–50; UN Affairs Dept, 1950–52; Minister to Australia, 1952–56, Ambassador, June 1956–59, and to New Zealand, Oct. 1956–59; Dir-Gen. of Internat. Organizations, 1959–63; Adviser on Foreign Affairs to the Prime Minister, 1962–64; Sec.-Gen., SEATO, 1964–65; Ambassador to Federal Republic of Germany, 1965–70, and to Finland, 1967–70; Ambassador to Court of St James's, 1970–76. Frequent Lecturer, 1944–; notably at Thammasat Univ., 1944–52, at National Defence Coll., 1960–62, and at Army War Coll., Bangkok, 1960–63. Mem., Internat. Law Assoc. Holds foreign decorations. *Publications:* Thailand and her relations with France, 1940 (in French); Thai Foreign Policy, 1984 (in Thai). *Recreations:* tennis, golf, swimming. *Address:* c/o Ministry of Foreign Affairs, Bangkok, Thailand. *Clubs:* Siam Society, Rotary of Bangkok, Royal Sport of Bangkok, Royal Turf (Bangkok).

SUPPERSTONE, Michael Alan; QC 1991; *b* 30 March 1950; *s* of Harold Bernard Supperstone and late Muriel Supperstone; *m* 1985, Dianne Jaffe; one *s* one *d*. *Educ:* St Paul's School; Lincoln College, Oxford (MA, BCL). Called to the Bar, Middle Temple, 1973; in practice, 1974. Vis. Scholar, Harvard Law Sch., 1979–80; Vis. Lectr, Nat. Univ. of Singapore, 1981, 1982. Treas., Administrative Law Bar Assoc., 1991– (Sec., 1986–91). *Publications:* Brownlie's Law of Public Order and National Security, 2nd edn, 1981; Immigration: the law and practice, 1983, 2nd edn 1988; (principal contributor) Administrative Law Title in Halsbury's Laws of England, 4th edn reissue, 1989; articles on public law. *Recreations:* playing tennis, watching Association Football. *Address:* 11 King's Bench Walk, Temple, EC4Y 7EQ. *T:* 071–583 0610. *Clubs:* Garrick, Royal Automobile, Roehampton.

SUPPLE, Prof. Barry Emanuel, FRHistS; FBA 1987; Professor of Economic History, University of Cambridge, since 1981; Master of St Catharine's College, Cambridge, since 1984; *b* 27 Oct. 1930; *s* of Solomon and Rose Supple; *m* 1958, Sonia (*née* Caller); two *s* one *d*. *Educ:* Hackney Downs Grammar Sch.; London Sch. of Econs and Polit. Science (BScEcon 1952); Christ's Coll., Cambridge (PhD 1955). FRHistS 1972. Asst Prof. of Business History, Grad. Sch. of Business Admin, Harvard Univ., 1955–60; Associate Prof. of Econ. Hist., McGill Univ., 1960–62; University of Sussex: Lectr, Reader, then Prof. of Econ. and Social Hist., 1962–78; Dean, Sch. of Social Sciences, 1965–68; Pro-Vice-Chancellor (Arts and Social Studies), 1968–72; Pro-Vice-Chancellor, 1978; University of Oxford: Reader in Recent Social and Econ. Hist., 1978–81; Professorial Fellow, Nuffield Coll., 1978–81; Professorial Fellow, 1981–83, Hon. Fellow, 1984, Christ's Coll., Cambridge. Hon. Fellow, Worcester Coll., 1986; Associate Fellow, Trumbull Coll., Yale, 1986. Chm., Consultative Cttee of Assessment of Performance Unit, DES, 1975–80; Member: Council, SSRC, 1972–77; Social Science Fellowship Cttee, Nuffield Foundn, 1974–. Co-editor, Econ. Hist. Rev., 1973–82. *Publications:* Commercial Crisis and Change in England, 1600–42, 1959; (ed) The Experience of Economic Growth, 1963; Boston Capitalists and Western Railroads, 1967; The Royal Exchange Assurance: a history of British insurance, 1720–1970, 1970; (ed) Essays in Business History, 1977; History of the British Coal Industry: vol. 4, 1914–46, The Political Economy of Decline, 1987; (ed) The State and Economic Knowledge: the American and British experience, 1990; articles and revs in learned jls. *Recreations:* tennis, photography. *Address:* The Master's Lodge, St Catharine's College, Cambridge CB2 1RL. *T:* Cambridge (0223) 338347. *Club:* United Oxford & Cambridge University.

SURR, Jeremy Bernard; Director Operations (South and East), Training Enterprise and Education Directorate, Department of Employment, since 1990; *b* 23 Jan. 1938; *s* of Thomas Bernard Surr, ISO, and Mabel Edith Moore; *m* 1965, Gillian Mary Lapage. *Educ:* Rutlish Sch., Wimbledon; Bury Grammar Sch., Lancs. National Service, RCS, 1956–58. Min. of Labour, 1959–65; computer systems analyst, 1965–70; Asst Private Sec. to Sec. of State for Employment, 1971–74; Principal, Employment Protection, Incomes Policy and Res. and Planning, 1974–78; on secondment to Australian Dept of Employment and Industrial Relations, 1978–80; joined MSC as Head of Sheltered Employment and Employment Rehabilitation Br., 1980; Head of Special Measures Br., 1982–85; Dir of Special Measures, 1985–86; Chief Exec., Employment and Enterprise Gp, 1986–87; Dir of Adult Programmes, 1987–89, Dir, Operations and Trng and Enterprise Councils Develt, 1989–90, Training Agency (formerly MSC, later Training Commn). *Recreations:*

golf, walking, gardening, DIY. *Address:* 48 Oak Hill Road, Nether Edge, Sheffield S7 1SH. *T:* Sheffield (0742) 557554. *Club:* Abbeydale Golf (Sheffield).

SURREY, Archdeacon of; *see* Went, Ven. J. S.

SURTEES, John, MBE 1961; controls companies in automotive research and development and property development; *b* 11 Feb. 1934; *s* of late John Norman and Dorothy Surtees; *m* 1st, 1962, Patricia Phyllis Burke (marr. diss. 1979); 2nd, 1987, Jane A. Sparrow; one *s* two *d.* *Educ:* Ashburton School, Croydon. 5 year engineering apprenticeship, Vincent Engrs, Stevenage, Herts. Motorcycle racing, 1952–60; British Champion, 1954, 1955; World 500 cc Motorcycle Champion, 1956; World 350 and 500 cc Motorcycle Champion, 1958, 1959, 1960. At end of 1960 he retd from motorcycling; motor racing, 1961–72; with Ferrari Co., won World Motor Racing title, 1964; 5th in World Championship, 1965 (following accident in Canada due to suspension failure); in 1966 left Ferrari in mid-season and joined Cooper, finishing 2nd in World Championship; in 1967 with Honda Motor Co. as first driver and develt engr (1967–68); 3rd in World Championship; with BRM as No 1 driver, 1969; designed and built own Formula 1 car, 1970. *Publications:* Motorcycle Racing and Preparation, 1958; John Surtees Book of Motorcycling, 1960; Speed, 1963; Six Days in August, 1968. *Recreations:* music, architecture; interested in most sports. *Address:* c/o John Surtees Ltd, Enterprise Way, Station Road, Edenbridge, Kent. *T:* Edenbridge (0732) 863773.

SUTCLIFF, Rosemary, OBE 1975 (for services to children's literature); FRSL 1982; writer of historical novels for adults and children; *b* 14 Dec. 1920; *d* of George Ernest Sutcliff and Elizabeth Sutcliff (*née* Lawton). *Educ:* privately. Carne Medal, 1959; The Other Award, 1978; Phoenix Award, 1985. *Publications:* Chronicles of Robin Hood, 1950; The Queen Elizabeth Story, 1950; The Armourer's House, 1951; Brother Dusty-feet, 1952; Simon, 1953; The Eagle of the Ninth, 1954; Outcast, 1955; Lady in Waiting, 1956; The Shield Ring, 1956; The Silver Branch, 1957; Warrior Scarlet, 1958; Rider of the White Horse, 1959; Lantern Bearers, 1959; Houses and History, 1960; Knights Fee, 1960; Rudyard Kipling, 1960; Beowulf, 1961; Dawn Wind, 1961; Sword at Sunset, 1963; The Hound of Ulster, 1963; The Mark of the Horse Lord, 1965; Heroes and History, 1965; The Chief's Daughter, 1967; The High Deeds of Finn McCool, 1967; A Circlet of Oak Leaves, 1968; The Flowers of Adonis, 1969; The Witches' Brat, 1970; Tristan and Iseult, 1971; The Capricorn Bracelet, 1973; The Changeling, 1974; Blood Feud, 1977; Sun Horse, Moon Horse, 1977; Shifting Sands, 1977; Song for a Dark Queen, 1978; The Light Beyond the Forest, 1979; Frontier Wolf, 1980; The Sword and the Circle: King Arthur and the Knights of the Round Table, 1981; Eagle's Egg, 1981; The Road to Camlann, 1981; Blue Remembered Hills (childhood memoir), 1982; Bonnie Dundee, 1983; Flame Coloured Taffeta, 1985; The Roundabout Horse, 1986; A Little Dog Like You, 1987; Blood and Sand, 1987; The Shining Company, 1990. *Recreations:* painting, needlework, dogs, travel. *Address:* Swallowshaw, Walberton, Arundel, West Sussex BN18 0PQ. *T:* Yapton (0243) 551316.

SUTCLIFFE, Allan; Group Managing Director, Finance, British Gas plc, since 1991; *b* 30 Jan. 1936; *s* of Bertie and May Sutcliffe; *m* 1983, Pauline, *d* of Mark and Lilian Abrahams; one *s* one *d* by a previous marr. *Educ:* Neath Grammar Sch.; University Coll. London (LLB); FCMA, CIGasE. Graduate trainee, BR, 1957–60; various positions in Finance in Western, Eastern and Southern Regions and at HQ, BR, 1960–70; Wales Gas Board: Chief Accountant, 1970; Dir of Finance, 1972; Deputy Chairman: British Gas W Midlands, 1980; British Gas N Thames, 1983; British Gas plc: Dir, 1986–; Man. Dir, Finance, 1987–89; Man. Dir, Gp Finance, 1989–91. *Recreations:* music, books, old buildings. *Address:* British Gas plc, 152 Grosvenor Road, SW1V 3JL. *T:* 071–821 1444. *Club:* Royal Automobile.

SUTCLIFFE, His Honour Edward Davis, QC 1959; a Circuit Judge and Additional Judge of the Central Criminal Court, 1969–84; *b* 25 Aug. 1917; 3rd *s* of late Richard Joseph and Anne Sutcliffe; *m* 1939, Elsie Eileen Brooks; two *d.* *Educ:* University College School, Hampstead; Wadham College, Oxford (MA). Served Royal Artillery, 1939–46 (despatches). Called to Bar, Inner Temple, 1946; Bencher, 1966. Recorder of Canterbury, 1968–69, and Hon. Recorder, 1974–84. Mem., Criminal Injuries Compensation Board, 1964–69; Legal Assessor, GMC and GDC, 1967–69; Chm., Statutory Cttee, Pharmaceutical Soc., 1986–90. Governor: Bedford Coll., London, 1968–76; St Michael's Sch., Otford, 1973–83. Hon. Freedom of Canterbury, 1983. Liveryman, Needlemakers' Co. *Address:* 39 Southwood Park, Southwood Lawn Road, Highgate, N6 5SG.
See also A. J. C. Britton.

SUTCLIFFE, Geoffrey Scott, OBE 1944; TD 1952; *b* 12 June 1912; *o s* of late John Walton Sutcliffe and late Alice Mary Sutcliffe (*née* Scott); *m* 1946, Mary Sylvia, *d* of late George Herbert Kay; two *s* one *d.* *Educ:* Repton. TA 2nd Lieut, 1939; Lt-Col, 1943; GSO1, AFHQ, N Africa and Italy; served France and Belgium, 1940; N Africa and Italy, 1943–45 (despatches, OBE). Ferodo Ltd, 1932: Works Dir, 1947; Home Sales Dir, 1952; Man. Dir, 1955; Chm., 1956–67; Turner & Newall Ltd: Dir, 1957–75; Jt Man. Dir, 1963–74; Dep. Chm., 1967–74. *Recreations:* gardening, reading. *Address:* Crosswinds, 25b Coopers Drive, Bridport, Dorset DT6 4JU. *Club:* Army and Navy.

SUTCLIFFE, John Harold Vick; DL; company director; Chairman: North Housing Association Ltd, since 1985; North Housing Ltd, since 1985; Teesside Development Corporation, since 1987; *b* 30 April 1931; *o s* of late Sir Harold Sutcliffe and Emily Theodora Cochrane; *m* 1959, Cecilia Mary, *e d* of Ralph Meredyth Turton; three *s* one *d.* *Educ:* Winchester Coll.; New Coll., Oxford (MA). 2nd Lieut RA, 1950–51. Called to Bar, Inner Temple, 1956; practised until 1960, Midland Circuit. Chm., Great Fosters (1931) Ltd, 1958–; Director: Allied Investors Trusts Ltd, 1958–69; Norton Junction Sand & Gravel Ltd, 1958–64; Tyne Tees Waste Disposal Ltd, 1964–71. Manager, Kildale Estate, 1965–. Mem., Housing Corp., 1982–88. Chm., North East Civic Trust (Northern Heritage), 1989– (Chm., Northern Heritage Trust, 1981–89; Vice-Chm., Civic Trust NE, 1977–89). Contested (C): Oldham West, 1959; Chorley, Lancs, 1964; Middlesbrough West, 1966. MP (C) Middlesbrough W, 1970–Feb. 1974. Contested (C) Teesside Thornaby, Oct. 1974. Chm., Bow Street Project, Guisborough, 1988–; Pres., N Yorks Youth Clubs (Chm., 1966–70); Mem., N Yorks Moors Nat. Park Cttee, 1982–88. DL Cleveland, 1983; High Sheriff, N Yorks, 1987–88. *Recreations:* woodland cultivation, gardening, travel, shooting. *Address:* Chapelgarth, Great Broughton, Middlesbrough, N Yorks TS9 7ET. *T:* Stokesley (0642) 712228.

SUTCLIFFE, Kenneth Edward; Headmaster, Latymer Upper School, Hammersmith, W6, 1958–71; *b* 24 March 1911; *s* of late Rev. James Sutcliffe; *m* 1937, Nora, *d* of late Charles Herbert Burcham; two *d.* *Educ:* Manchester Grammar School; King's College, Cambridge (Scholar). BA Modern and Medieval Languages Tripos 1932; MA 1936. Assistant Master, Stockport Grammar School, 1933–38; Assistant Master, Liverpool Institute High School, 1938–46; Headmaster, Cockburn High School, Leeds, 1946–57. Served with Royal Armoured Corps and Intelligence Corps, 1940–46, Captain (General Staff). Lay Reader, dios of Ripon, Guildford, Bath and Wells, 1953–81. *Publications:* German Translation and Composition, 1948; French Translation and Composition, 1951; Fahrt ins Blaue (a German course for schools), 1960. *Address:* Hatherlow, Springfield Drive, Wedmore, Somerset BS28 4BT. *T:* Wedmore (0934) 712049.

SUTER, Michael; Chief Executive, Shropshire County Council, since 1987; *b* 21 Jan. 1944; *s* of Robert and Rose Suter; *m* 1963, Sandra Harrison; two *s.* *Educ:* Liverpool Collegiate Sch.; Liverpool Univ. (LLB). Solicitor. Dep. Chief Exec., Notts CC, 1980–87. *Recreations:* music, gardening, watching old Hollywood films, visiting Spain. *Address:* Redcliffe House, Weston-under-Redcastle, Shrewsbury, Shropshire.

SUTHERLAND, family name of **Countess of Sutherland.**

SUTHERLAND, 6th Duke of, *cr* 1833; **John Sutherland Egerton,** TD; DL; Bt 1620; Baron Gower, 1703; Earl Gower, Viscount Trentham, 1746; Marquis of Stafford (county), 1786; Viscount Brackley and Earl of Ellesmere, 1846; *b* 10 May 1915; *o s* of 4th Earl of Ellesmere and Violet (*d* 1976), *e d* of 4th Earl of Durham; *S* father, 1944; *S* kinsman as Duke of Sutherland, 1963; *m* 1st, 1939, Lady Diana Percy (*d* 1978), *yr d* of 8th Duke of Northumberland; 2nd, 1979, Evelyn, *e d* of late Maj. Robert Moubray. Served War of 1939–45 (prisoner). DL Berwickshire, 1955. *Heir:* *c* Cyril Reginald Egerton [*b* 7 Sept. 1905; *m* 1st, 1934, Mary (*d* 1949), *d* of late Rt Hon. Sir Ronald Hugh Campbell, PC, GCMG; one *s* three *d*; 2nd, 1954, Mary (*d* 1982), *d* of late Sir Sydney Lea, Dunley Hall, Worcestershire]. *Address:* Mertoun, St Boswell's, Melrose, Roxburghshire; Lingay Cottage, Hall Farm, Newmarket. *Clubs:* White's, Turf; Jockey (Newmarket).
See also J. M. E. Askew, Lady M. Colville, Baron Home of the Hirsel, Viscount Rochdale.

SUTHERLAND, Countess of (24th in line) *cr* (*c*) 1235; **Elizabeth Millicent Sutherland;** Lady Strathnaver (*c*) 1235; Chief of Clan Sutherland; *b* 30 March 1921; *o c* of Lord Alastair St Clair Sutherland-Leveson-Gower, MC (*d* 1921; 2nd *s* of 4th Duke), and Baroness Osten Driesen (*d* 1931); *niece* of 5th Duke of Sutherland, KT, PC; *S* (to uncle's Earldom of Sutherland and Lordship of Strathnaver), 1963; *m* 1946, Charles Noel Janson, DL, late Welsh Guards; two *s* one *d* (and one *s* decd). *Educ:* Queen's College, Harley Street, W1, and abroad. Land Army, 1939–41; Laboratory Technician: Raigmore Hospital, Inverness, 1941–43; St Thomas' Hospital, SE1, 1943–45. Chm., Dunrobin Castle Ltd; Dir, The Northern Times Ltd. *Recreations:* reading, swimming. *Heir:* *e s* Lord Strathnaver, *qv.* *Address:* Dunrobin Castle, Sutherland; House of Tongue, by Lairg, Sutherland; 39 Edwardes Square, W8 6HJ. *T:* 071–603 0659.

SUTHERLAND, Hon. Lord; Ranald Iain Sutherland; a Senator of the College of Justice in Scotland, since 1985; *b* 23 Jan. 1932; *s* of J. W. and A. K. Sutherland, Edinburgh; *m* 1964, Janice Mary, *d* of W. S. Miller, Edinburgh; two *s.* *Educ:* Edinburgh Academy; Edinburgh University. MA 1951, LLB 1953. Admitted to Faculty of Advocates, 1956; QC (Scot.) 1969. Advocate Depute, 1962–64, 1971–77; Standing Junior Counsel to Min. of Defence (Army Dept), 1964–69. Mem., Criminal Injuries Compensation Bd, 1977–85. *Recreations:* sailing, shooting. *Address:* 38 Lauder Road, Edinburgh. *T:* 031–667 5280. *Clubs:* New (Edinburgh); Hon. Company of Edinburgh Golfers.

SUTHERLAND, Anthony (Frederic Arthur); Under-Secretary, Department of Employment, retired; *b* 19 Oct. 1916; *e s* of Bertram and Grace Sutherland; *m* 1940, Betty Josephine Glass; one *s* two *d.* *Educ:* Christ's Hosp.; Gonville and Caius Coll., Cambridge (Classical Schol.). 1st cl. hons Classics, 1938; MA 1944. HM Forces, 1940–45 (Major, Mddx Regt). Asst Prin., Min. of Labour, 1938; Prin., 1943; Prin. Private Sec. to Ministers of Labour, 1948–53; Counsellor (Labour), British Embassy, Rome, 1953–55; Asst Sec., 1955; Imp. Def. Coll., 1960; Under-Sec., 1967. Coronation Medal, 1953; Silver Jubilee Medal, 1977. *Recreations:* philately, bird watching. *Address:* 53 Wieland Road, Northwood, Mddx HA6 3QX. *T:* Northwood (09274) 22078. *Club:* Civil Service.

SUTHERLAND, Colin John MacLean; QC (Scot.) 1990; *b* 20 May 1954; *s* of Eric Alexander Cruickshank Sutherland and Mary Macaulay or Sutherland; *m* 1988, Jane Alexander Turnbull or Sutherland; one *s.* *Educ:* Hurst Grange Prep. Sch., Stirling; Edinburgh Acad.; Edinburgh Univ. (LLB Hons). Advocate, 1977; Advocate Depute, 1986–89. *Address:* 10 Eton Terrace, Edinburgh EH4 1QD. *T:* 031–332 6725. *Club:* Scottish Arts (Edinburgh).

SUTHERLAND, Ian, MA; Director of Education and Training to Health Education Council, 1971–85; *b* 7 July 1926; *m* 1951, Virginia Scovil Bliss (marr. diss. 1978); one *s* one *d.* *Educ:* Wyggeston Grammar School, Leicester; Sidney Sussex College, Cambridge. Assistant Professor of Classics, Univ. of New Brunswick, NB, Canada, 1949–50; Asst Master: Christ's Hospital, 1951–52; Harrow School, 1952–60; Head Master, St John's School, Leatherhead, 1960–70; Dir of Educn, Health Educn Council, 1970–71. Mem., Wandsworth HA, 1986–89. Governor, Reeds Sch., 1980–. *Publications:* From Pericles to Cleophon, 1954; (ed) Health Education: perspectives and choices, 1979; Health Education, Half a Policy: the rise and fall of the Health Education Council, 1987; Around the World by Train, 1991. *Recreations:* painting, cricket. *Address:* 57 Burntwood Grange Road, Wandsworth Common, SW18 3JY. *Clubs:* United Oxford & Cambridge University, MCC, Free Foresters'.

SUTHERLAND, Dr Ian Boyd; Senior Administrative Medical Officer, South Western Regional Hospital Board, 1970–73; Regional Medical Officer, South Western Regional Health Authority, 1973–80; *b* 19 Oct. 1926; *s* of William Sutherland and Grace Alexandra Campbell; *m* 1950, Charlotte Winifred Cordin; two *d.* *Educ:* Bradford Grammar Sch.; Edinburgh Univ. MB, ChB; FRCPE, FFCM, DPH. Medical Officer, RAF, 1950–52; Asst MOH, Counties of Roxburgh and Selkirk, 1953–55; Dep. MOH, County and Borough of Inverness, 1955–59; Dep. County MOH, Oxfordshire CC, 1959–60; Asst SMO, Leeds Regional Hosp. Bd, 1960–63; Dep. Sen. Admin. MO, SW Regl Hosp Bd, 1963–70; Community Medicine Specialist, Lothian Health Bd, 1980–86. Research Fellow, Dept of Clin. Surgery, Univ. of Edinburgh, 1986–88. *Recreations:* reading, art. *Address:* 8 Chesterfield Road, Eastbourne, E Sussex BN20 7NU.

SUTHERLAND, James, CBE 1974; Partner, McClure Naismith, Anderson & Gardiner (formerly McClure Naismith), Solicitors, Glasgow and Edinburgh, 1951–87; *b* 15 Feb. 1920; *s* of James Sutherland, JP and Agnes Walker; *m* 1st, 1948, Elizabeth Kelly Barr; two *s*; 2nd, 1984, Grace Williamson Dawson. *Educ:* Queens Park Secondary Sch., Glasgow; Glasgow Univ. MA 1940, LLB 1948; Hon. LLD 1985. Served Royal Signals, 1940–46. Examr in Scots Law, 1951–55 and Mercantile Law and Industrial Law, 1968–69, Glasgow Univ.; Chm., Glasgow South Nat. Insce Tribunal, 1964–66; Member: Bd of Management, Glasgow Maternity and Women's Hosps, 1964–74 (Chm. 1966–74); Council, Law Soc. of Scotland, 1959–77 (Vice-Pres. 1969–70; Pres. 1972–74); Council, Internat. Bar Assoc., 1972– (Chm., Gen. Practice Section, 1978–80; Sec.-Gen., 1980–84; Pres., 1984–86); GDC, 1975–89; Scottish Dental Estimates Bd, 1982–87; Vice-Chm., Glasgow Eastern Health Council, 1975–77; Deacon, Incorporation of Barbers, Glasgow, 1962–63; Sec., Local Dental Cttee, City of Glasgow, 1955–65; Dean, Royal Faculty of Procurators in Glasgow, 1977–80. Mem. Court, Univ. of Strathclyde, 1977–. *Recreation:* golf. *Address:* Greenacres, 20/1 Easter Belmont Road, Edinburgh EH12 6EX. *T:* 031–337 1888. *Clubs:* Western (Glasgow); Royal and Ancient.

SUTHERLAND, Prof. James Runcieman, FBA 1953; MA, BLitt; Emeritus Professor of Modern English Literature, University College, London (Lord Northcliffe Professor, 1951–67); *b* Aberdeen, 26 April 1900; *s* of Henry Edward Sutherland, Stockbroker; *m* 1st, 1931, Helen (*d* 1975) *d* of Will H. Dircks; 2nd, 1977, Eve Betts, *widow* of Ernest Betts. *Educ:* Aberdeen Grammar Sch.; Univ. of Aberdeen; Oxford Univ. BLitt Oxford, 1927. Lecturer in English, Univ. of Saskatchewan, 1921–23; Merton Coll., Oxford, 1923–25; Chancellor's English Essay Prize, Oxford, 1925; Lecturer in English, University College, Southampton, 1925; Lecturer in English, University of Glasgow, 1925–30; Senior Lecturer in English, University College, London, 1930–36; Professor of English Literature, Birkbeck College, London, 1936–44; Prof. of English Language and Literature, Queen Mary College, London, 1944–51. Warton lecturer on English Poetry to the British Academy, 1944; editor of The Review of English Studies, 1940–47. Visiting Professor: Harvard Univ., 1947; Indiana Univ., 1950–51; UCLA, 1967–68; Mellon Prof., Univ. of Pittsburgh, 1965; Berg Prof., NY Univ., 1969–70. Sir Walter Scott Lectures, Edinburgh University, 1952; Clark Lectures, Cambridge University, 1956; Alexander Lectures, Toronto University, 1956; Public Orator, University of London, 1957–62; W. P. Ker Memorial Lecture, Glasgow Univ., 1962; Clark Library Fellow, Univ. of California, Los Angeles, 1962–63. Hon. Mem. Modern Language Assoc. of America, 1960. Hon. LLD Aberdeen, 1955; Hon. DLitt Edinburgh, 1968; Hon. Doctor, Liège, 1974. *Publications:* Leucocholy (Poems), 1926; Jasper Weeple, 1930; The Medium of Poetry, 1934; Defoe, 1937; Background for Queen Anne, 1939; (ed) The Dunciad, 1943; English in the Universities, 1945; A Preface to Eighteenth Century Poetry, 1948; The English Critic, 1952; The Oxford Book of English Talk, 1953; On English Prose, 1957; English Satire, 1958; English Literature of the late Seventeenth Century, 1969; Daniel Defoe: a critical study, 1971; editions of plays by Nicholas Rowe, Thomas Dekker, John Dryden, William Shakespeare, and of Lucy Hutchinson's Memoirs of the Life of Colonel Hutchinson, 1973; (ed) The Oxford Book of Literary Anecdotes, 1975; The Restoration Newspaper and its Development, 1986; contributions to various literary journals. *Recreations:* fishing, second-hand book catalogues. *Address:* 16 Murray Court, 80 Banbury Road, Oxford OX2 6LQ. *T:* Oxford (0865) 510469.

SUTHERLAND, Dame Joan, AC 1975; DBE 1979 (CBE 1961); soprano; *b* 7 Nov. 1926; *d* of McDonald Sutherland, Sydney, NSW, and Muriel Alston Sutherland; *m* 1954, Richard Bonynge, *qv*; one *s*. *Educ:* St Catherine's, Waverley, Sydney. Début as Dido in Purcell's Dido and Aeneas, Sydney, 1947; subsequently concerts, oratorios and broadcasts throughout Australia. Came to London, 1951; joined Covent Garden, 1952, where she remained resident soprano for 7 years; won international fame with début as Lucia di Lammermoor, Covent Garden, 1959, and by early 1960s had sung throughout the Americas and Europe. Has specialised throughout her career in the popular and lesser-known bel canto operatic repertoire of 18th and 19th centuries, and has made many recordings. Hon. DMus Sydney, 1984. *Publication:* The Joan Sutherland Album (autobiog., with Richard Bonynge), 1986; *Relevant publications:* Joan Sutherland, by R. Braddon, 1962; Joan Sutherland, by E. Greenfield, 1972; La Stupenda, by B. Adams, 1980; Joan Sutherland, by Norma Major, 1987. *Recreations:* reading, gardening, needlepoint. *Address:* c/o Ingpen & Williams, 14 Kensington Court, W8 5DN.

SUTHERLAND, John Alexander Muir; Chief Executive, Celtic Films Ltd, since 1986; *b* 5 April 1933; *m* 1970, Mercedes Gonzalez; two *s*. *Educ:* India; Trinity Coll., Glenalmond; Hertford Coll., Oxford (MA). 2nd Lieut, HLI, 1952–53. Economist, Fed. Govt of Nigeria, 1957–58; film production, Spain and Portugal, 1958–62; Head of Presentation and Programme Planning, Border TV, 1963–66; Programme Co-Ordinator: ABC TV, 1966–68; Thames TV, 1968–72; Controller of Programme Sales, Thames TV, 1973–74; Man. Dir, 1975–82, Dep Chm., 1982–86, Thames TV Internat.; Dir of Programmes, Thames TV, 1982–86. *Address:* Celtic Films Ltd, 1–2 Bromley Place, W1. *T:* 071–637 7651.

SUTHERLAND, John Brewer; (3rd Bt *cr* 1921, but does not use the title); *b* 19 Oct. 1931; *s* of Sir (Benjamin) Ivan Sutherland, 2nd Bt, and Marjorie Constance Daniel (*d* 1980), *yr d* of Frederic William Brewer, OBE; *S* father, 1980; *m* 1st, 1958, Alice Muireall (*d* 1984), *d* of late W. Stamford Henderson, Kelso; three *s* one *d*; 2nd, 1988, Heather, *d* of late David A. Gray, Chester-le-Street. *Educ:* Sedbergh; St Catharine's Coll., Cambridge. *Heir:* *s* Peter William Sutherland, *b* 18 May 1963.

SUTHERLAND, John Menzies, FICE, FIStructE, FASCE; Secretary, Joint Board of Moderators, Institution of Civil Engineers, since 1985; *b* 19 June 1928; *s* of John Menzies and Margaret Rae Sutherland; *m* 1962, Margaret Mary (*née* Collins); one *s* one *d*. *Educ:* Royal Technical Coll., Glasgow. CEng; Eur. Ing. 1988. Indentured Civil Engineer, City Engineer, Glasgow, 1945–51; Engineer, Costains Group, 1952–56; Site Agent, Pakistan and Chief Engineer, Middle East, Gammon Group, 1956–61; Engineer Adsviser (Colombo Plan), new capital city, Islamabad, 1962–66; Associate Partner, Bullen & Partners, 1966–69; Chief Civil Engineer, overseas plant construction, Union International Co. (Vestey Gp Holding Co.), 1970–74; Board Dir and Dir Engineering Projects, Internat. Military Services Ltd, 1974–83 (2 years Malaysia); Gen. Manager, BTR-Swire Projects, Singapore, 1983–85. *Publication:* Naval Bases and Infrastructure, 1979. *Recreations:* music, collecting Victorian ceramics. *Address:* 13 Ravenshill, Chislehurst, Kent BR7 5PD. *T:* 081–467 0037. *Clubs;* Royal Over-Seas League; Chislehurst Golf.

SUTHERLAND, Sir Maurice, Kt 1976; Member, Cleveland County Council, since 1973 (Leader, 1973–77 and 1981–85; Leader of Opposition, 1977–81); *b* 12 July 1915; *s* of Thomas Daniel and Ada Sutherland; *m* 1st, 1941, Beatrice (*née* Skinner); one *s*; 2nd, 1960, Jane Ellen (*née* Bell); one step-*d*; 3rd, Ellen Margaret (*née* Guy). *Educ:* Stockton Secondary Sch. War service with Green Howards and RCS, N Africa and NW Europe. Solicitor, 1937–. Mem. Stockton Borough Council, 1957–67; Chm., Teesside Steering Cttee, 1966–67; Leader of Labour Party, Teesside County Borough Council, 1967–74; Mayor of Teesside, 1972–73. Chm., Northern Econ. Planning Council, 1977–79. *Recreations:* cricket, walking, chess, politics. *Address:* 8 Manor Close, Low Worsall, Yarm, Cleveland. *T:* Eaglescliffe (0642) 782799.

SUTHERLAND, Muir; *see* Sutherland, J. A. M.

SUTHERLAND, Prof. (Norman) Stuart, MA, DPhil; Professor of Experimental Psychology, University of Sussex, since 1965; *b* 26 March 1927; *s* of Norman McLeod Sutherland; *m* 1966, Jose Louise Fogden; two *d*. *Educ:* Magdalen Coll., Oxford. BA Hons Lit. Hum. 1949 and PPP 1953; John Locke Scholar 1953. Fellow; Magdalen Coll., 1954–58; Merton Coll., 1962–64; Oxford Univ. Lectr in Exper. Psychol., 1960–64. Vis. Prof., MIT, 1961–62, 1964–65. Dir, William Schlackman Ltd, 1968–81. *Publications:* Shape Discrimination by Animals, 1959; (ed jtly) Animal Discrimination Learning, 1969; (with N. J. Mackintosh) Mechanisms of Animal Discrimination Learning, 1971; Breakdown: a personal crisis and a medical dilemma, 1976, 2nd edn 1987; (ed) Tutorial Essays in Psychology, vol. 1, 1977, vol. 2, 1979; Discovering the Human Mind, 1982; Men Change Too, 1987; Macmillan Dictionary of Psychology, 1989; scientific papers mainly on perception and learning. *Address:* Centre for Research on Perception and Cognition, Sussex University, Brighton BN1 9QG. *T:* Brighton (0273) 678304.

SUTHERLAND, Peter Denis, SC; Chairman, Allied Irish Banks, since 1989; *b* 25 April 1946; *s* of W. G. Sutherland and Barbara Sutherland (*née* Neahon); *m* 1971, Maria Del Pilar Cabria Valcarcel; two *s* one *d*. *Educ:* Gonzaga Coll.; University Coll. Dublin (BCL). Called to Bar: King's Inns, 1968; Middle Temple, 1976; Attorney of New York Bar, 1981; Attorney and Counsellor of Supreme Court of USA, 1986. Tutor in Law, University Coll., Dublin, 1968–71; practising member of Irish Bar, 1968–81, and 1981–82; Senior Counsel 1980; Attorney General of Ireland, June 1981–Feb. 1982 and Dec. 1982–Dec. 1984; Mem. Council of State, 1981–82 and 1982–84; Comr for Competition and Comr for Social Affairs and Educn, EEC, 1985–86, for Competition and Relns with European Parliament, 1986–88. Director: GPA, 1989–; BP Oil Ltd; CRH plc; James Crean plc. Chm., Bd of Govs, Eur. Inst. of Public Admin, 1991–. Hon. LLD: St Louis, 1985; NUI, 1990. Gold Medal, Eur. Parlt, 1988. Grand Cross, King Leopold II (Belgium), 1989; Grand Cross of Civil Merit (Spain), 1989. *Publications:* Premier Janvier 1993 ce qui va changer en Europe, 1988; contribs to law jls. *Recreations:* sports generally, reading. *Address:* Allied Irish Banks, Bankcentre, Ballsbridge, Dublin 4, Eire. *Clubs:* Hibernian United Service, Fitzwilliam (Dublin); Lansdowne FC.

SUTHERLAND, Ranald Iain; *see* Sutherland, Hon. Lord.

SUTHERLAND, Prof. Stewart Ross; Vice-Chancellor, University of London, since 1990; *b* 25 Feb. 1941; *s* of late George A. C. Sutherland and of Ethel (*née* Masson); *m* 1964, Sheena Robertson; one *s* two *d*. *Educ:* Woodside Sch.; Robert Gordon's Coll.; Univ. of Aberdeen (MA); Corpus Christi Coll., Cambridge (Hon. Schol.; MA; Hon. Fellow, 1989). Asst Lectr in Philosophy, UCNW, 1965; Lectr in Philosophy, 1968, Sen. Lectr, 1972, Reader, 1976, Univ. of Stirling; King's College London: Prof. of Hist. and Philos. of Religion, 1977–85, Titular Prof., 1985–; Vice-Principal, 1981–85; Principal, 1985–90; FKC 1983. Vis. Fellow, ANU, 1974; Gillespie Vis. Prof., Wooster Ohio, 1975. Lectures: Hope, Stirling, 1979; Ferguson, Manchester, 1982; Wilde, Oxford, 1981–84; Boutwood, Cambridge, 1990. Chairman: British Acad. Postgrad. Studentships Cttee, 1987–; Royal Inst. of Philosophy, 1988–; Vice-Chm., CVCP, 1989–91. Member: C of E Bd of Educn, 1980–84; Arts Sub-Cttee, UGC, 1983–85; City Parochial Foundn, 1988–90. Pres., Soc. for the Study of Theology, 1985, 1986. Chm., Ethiopian Gemini Trust, 1987–. Editor, Religious Studies, 1984–90; Member, Editorial Board: Scottish Jl of Religious Studies, 1980–; Modern Theology, 1984–91. Associate Fellow, Warwick Univ., 1986–; Hon. Fellow, UCNW, 1990. Hon. LHD Wooster, Ohio, 1986; Hon. LLD Aberdeen, 1990. *Publications:* Atheism and the Rejection of God, 1977, 2nd edn 1980; (ed with B. L. Hebblethwaite) The Philosophical Frontiers of Christian Theology, 1983; God, Jesus and Belief, 1984; Faith and Ambiguity, 1984; (ed) The World's Religions, 1988; (ed with T. A. Roberts) Religion, Reason and the Self, 1989; articles in books and learned jls. *Recreations:* Tassie medallions, theatre, jazz. *Address:* Senate House, Malet Street, WC1E 7HU. *T:* 071–636 8000. *Clubs:* Athenæum, Ronnie Scott's.

SUTHERLAND, Prof. Stuart; *see* Sutherland, Prof. N. S.

SUTHERLAND, Veronica Evelyn, (Mrs A. J. Sutherland), CMG 1988; HM Diplomatic Service; Assistant Under-Secretary of State (Deputy Chief Clerk), Foreign and Commonwealth Office, since 1990; *b* 25 April 1939; *d* of late Lt-Col Maurice George Beckett, KOYLI, and of Constance Mary Cavenagh-Mainwaring; *m* 1981, Alex James Sutherland. *Educ:* Royal Sch., Bath; London Univ. (BA); Southampton Univ. (MA). Joined HM Diplomatic Service, 1965; Second, later First Sec., Copenhagen, 1967–70; FCO, 1970–75; First Sec., New Delhi, 1975–78; FCO, 1978–80; Counsellor, 1981; Perm. UK Deleg. to UNESCO, 1981–84; Counsellor, FCO, 1984–87; Ambassador to Côte d'Ivoire, 1987–90. *Address:* c/o Foreign and Commonwealth Office, SW1.

SUTHERLAND, Sir William (George MacKenzie), Kt 1988; QPM 1981; Chief Constable, Lothian and Borders Police, since 1983; *b* 12 Nov. 1933; *m* 1957, Jennie Abbott; two *d*. *Educ:* Inverness Technical High Sch. Cheshire Police, 1954–73; Surrey Police, 1973–75; Hertfordshire Police, 1975–79; Chief Constable of Bedfordshire, 1979–83. *Recreations:* squash, hill walking. *Address:* Police Headquarters, Fettes Avenue, Edinburgh EH4 1RB. *T:* 031–311 3131.

SUTHIWART-NARUEPUT, Dr Owart; Kt Grand Cordon: Order of Crown of Thailand, 1981; Order of White Elephant, 1985; Hon. CMG 1972; Lecturer, since 1987, Director, Language Institute, since 1990, Thammasat University; *b* 19 Sept. 1926; *s* of Luang Suthiwart-Narueput and Mrs Khae; *m* 1959, Angkana (*née* Sthapitanond); one *s* one *d*. *Educ:* Thammasat Univ., Thailand (BA Law); Fletcher Sch. of Law and Diplomacy, Tufts Univ., USA (MA, PhD); Nat. Defence Coll. Joined Min. of For. Affairs, 1945; Asst Sec. to Minister, 1958; SEATO Res. Officer, 1959; Protocol Dept, 1963; Econ. Dept, 1964; Counsellor, Thai Embassy, Canberra, 1965; Dir-Gen. of Inf. Dept, 1969; Ambassador to India, Nepal, Sri Lanka, and Minister to Afghanistan, 1972; Ambassador to Poland, E Germany and Bulgaria, 1976; Dir-Gen. of Political Dept, 1977; Under-Sec. of State (Permanent Sec.) for For. Affairs, 1979; Ambassador to France and Perm. Representative to UNESCO, 1980; Ambassador: to Switzerland and to Holy See, 1983; to UK, 1984–86, concurrently to Ireland, 1985–86. Chm. Adv. Gp, Thai Investors Assoc., 1990–. Mem. Exec. Cttee, Internat. Understanding Program, Inst. Asian Studies, Chulalongkorn Univ., 1988–. Commander: Order of Phoenix, Greece, 1963; Order of Orange-Nassau, Netherlands, 1963; Bintang Djasa (1st Cl.), Indonesia, 1970; Order of Merit, Poland, 1979; Grand Officier, L'Ordre Nat. du Mérite, France, 1983. *Publication:* The Evolution of Thailand's Foreign Relations since 1855: from extraterritoriality to equality, 1955. *Recreations:* reading, music. *Address:* 193 Lane 4 Navathanee, Sukha-Pibarn 2 Road, Kannayao, Bangkapi, Bangkok 10230, Thailand. *Clubs:* Old England Students' Assoc., Amer. Univs Alumni Assoc. (Bangkok).

SUTTIE, Sir (George) Philip Grant-, 8th Bt, *cr* 1702; *b* 20 Dec. 1938; *o s* of late Maj. George Donald Grant-Suttie and Marjorie Neville, *d* of Capt. C. E. Carter, RN, of Newfoundland; *S* cousin, 1947; *m* 1962, Elspeth Mary (marr. diss. 1969), *e d* of Maj.-Gen. R. E. Urquhart, CB, DSO; one *s*. *Educ:* Sussex Composite High School, NB, Canada; Macdonald College, McGill University, Montreal. *Recreations:* flying, fishing, farming, forestry. *Heir:* *s* James Edward Grant-Suttie, *b* 29 May 1965. *Address:* (seat) Balgone, North Berwick; The Granary, Sheriff Hall, North Berwick, East Lothian. *T:* North Berwick (0620) 2569, (office) 3750.

SUTTILL, Dr Margaret Joan, (Mrs G. A. Rink); *d* of Ernest Montrose and Caroline Hyde; *m* 1st, 1935, F. A. Suttill, DSO, LLB (*d* 1945); two *s*; 2nd, 1949, G. A. Rink, QC (*d* 1983). *Educ:* Royal Free Hospital Medical School. MB, BS 1935; MRCP 1972. Director, Medical Dept, and Chief Medical Advr, British Council, retired. *Recreations:* music (especially opera), reading, walking, bird watching, consumer problems. *Address:* 173 Oakwood Court, W14 8JE. *T:* 071–602 2143.

SUTTON, Alan John; Founder Chairman and Chief Executive, Anglolink Ltd, since 1985; *b* 16 March 1936; *s* of William Clifford Sutton and Emily Sutton (*née* Batten); *m* 1957, Glenis (*née* Henry); one *s* one *d*. *Educ:* Bristol Univ. BSc (Hons) Elec. Engrg; MIEE. Design, Production and Trials Evaluation of Guided Missiles, English Electric Aviation Ltd, 1957–63; Design, Production, Sales and General Management of Scientific Digital,

Analogue and Hybrid Computers, Solartron Electronic Group Ltd, 1963–69; International Sales Manager, Sales Director, of A. B. Electronic Components Ltd, 1969–73; Managing Director, A. B. Connectors, 1973–76; Industrial Dir, Welsh Office, 1976–79; Welsh Development Agency: Exec. Dir (Industry and Investment), 1979–83; Exec. Dir (Marketing), 1983–85; Sen. Vice-Pres., USA W Coast Div., WINvest, 1985–88. *Recreation:* golf. *Address:* 56 Heol-y-Delyn, Lisvane, Cardiff CF4 5SR. *T:* Cardiff (0222) 753194.

SUTTON, Barry Bridge; Headmaster, Taunton School, since 1987; *b* 21 Jan. 1937; *s* of Albert and Ethel Sutton; *m* 1961, Margaret Helen (*née* Palmer); one *s* two *d. Educ:* Eltham Coll.; Peterhouse, Cambridge (MA Hist. Tripos); Bristol Univ. (PGCE). Asst Master and Housemaster, Wycliffe College, 1961–75; Headmaster, Hereford Cathedral School, 1975–87. *Recreations:* hill-walking, scouting. *Address:* Taunton School, Taunton, Somerset TA2 6AD. *T:* Taunton (0823) 284596. *Club:* East India and Public Schools.

SUTTON, Colin Bertie John, QPM 1985; Director, Police Requirements Support Unit, Home Office, since 1988; *b* 6 Dec. 1938; *s* of Bertie Sidney Russell Sutton and Phyllis May; *m* 1960, Anne Margaret Davis. *Educ:* King Edward VI Grammar School, Stratford-upon-Avon; University College London (LLB 1970). Police Constable, 1957, Sergeant, 1964, Inspector, 1966, Warwicks County Police; Chief Inspector, 1970, Supt, 1972, Chief Supt, 1974, Warwicks and Coventry Constabulary; Chief Supt, W Midlands Police, 1974–77; Asst Chief Constable, Leics Constabulary, 1977; Metropolitan Police: Dep. Asst Comr, 1983–84; Asst Comr, 1984–88. Freeman, City of London, 1988; Liveryman, Fletchers' Co., 1989. SBStJ 1990. *Recreations:* golf, angling, squash, music, art, literature. *Address:* Horseferry House, Dean Ryle Street, SW1P 2AW. *T:* 071–217 8409.

SUTTON, Sir Frederick (Walter), Kt 1974; OBE 1971; Founder and Chairman of Directors of the Sutton Group of Companies; *b* 1 Feb. 1915; *s* of late William W. Sutton and Daisy Sutton; *m* 1934; three *s*; *m* 1977, Morna Patricia Smyth. *Educ:* Sydney Technical College. Motor Engineer, founder and Chief Executive of the Sutton group of Companies; Mem. Bd of Directors, and life Governor, Royal New South Wales Inst. for Deaf and Blind Children. *Recreations:* flying, going fishing, boating. *Address:* (office) 114 Bourke Street, Potts Point, Sydney, NSW 2011, Australia. *T:* Sydney 357–1777. *Clubs:* Royal Aero of NSW (Life Member); Royal Automobile of Australia; Royal Automobile of Victoria; American (Sydney).

SUTTON, Prof. John, DSc, PhD, ARCS; FRS 1966; FGS; Senior Research Fellow, Centre for Environmental Technology, since 1983, Professor of Geology, 1958–83, now Emeritus, Imperial College of Science and Technology, London; *b* 8 July 1919; *e s* of Gerald John Sutton; *m* 1st, 1949, Janet Vida Watson, FRS (*d* 1985); 2nd, 1985, Betty Middleton-Sandford. *Educ:* King's School, Worcester; Royal College of Science, London. Service with RAOC and REME, 1941–46. Imperial College: Research, 1946–48; Lecturer in Geology, 1948; Reader in Geology, 1956; Head of Geol. Dept, 1964–74; Dean, Royal Sch. of Mines, 1965–68, 1974–77; Pro-Rector, External Develt, 1979–80, Pro-Rector, 1980–83; Fellow, 1985. A Trustee, BM (Nat. Hist.), 1976–81. Mem., NERC, 1977–79. Mem. Council, Univ. of Zimbabwe, 1980–83. President, Geologists' Association, 1966–68. A Vice-Pres., Royal Society, 1975–77; Pres., Remote Sensing Soc., 1977–84. For. Mem., Royal Netherlands Acad., 1978; Hon. For. Fellow, Geol Soc. of Amer. Bigsby Medal, Geological Society of London, 1965 (jointly with Janet Watson); Murchison Medal, 1975. *Publications:* papers dealing with the Geology of the Scottish Highlands. *Recreation:* gardening. *Address:* Imperial College of Science, Technology and Medicine, SW7.

SUTTON, Air Marshal Sir John (Matthias Dobson), KCB 1986 (CB 1981); Lieutenant-Governor and Commander-in-Chief, Jersey, since 1990; *b* 9 July 1932; *s* of late Harry Rowston Sutton and Gertrude Sutton; *m* 1954 (marr. diss. 1968); one *s* one *d*; *m* 1969, Angela Faith Gray; two *s. Educ:* Queen Elizabeth's Grammar Sch., Alford, Lincs. Joined RAF, 1950; pilot trng, commnd, 1951; served on Fighter Sqdns, UK and Germany; Staff Coll., 1963; OC 249 Sqdn, 1964–66; Asst Sec., Chiefs of Staff Cttee, 1966–69; OC 14 Sqdn, 1970–71; Asst Chief of Staff (Policy and Plans), HQ 2 ATAF, 1971–73; Staff, Chief of Def. Staff, 1973–74; RCDS, 1975; Comdt Central Flying Sch., 1976–77; Asst Chief of Air Staff (Policy), 1977–79; Dep. Comdr, RAF Germany, 1980–82; ACDS (Commitments), 1982–84; ACDS (Overseas), 1985; C-in-C, RAF Support Comd, 1986–89. KStJ 1990. *Recreations:* golf, ski-ing. *Address:* Government House, Jersey, Channel Islands JY2 7GH; c/o Royal Bank of Scotland, Holt's Branch, Whitehall, SW1A 2EB. *Clubs:* Royal Air Force; Luffenham Heath Golf.

SUTTON, John Sydney; General Secretary, Secondary Heads Association, since 1988; *b* 9 June 1936; *s* of Sydney and Mabel Sutton; *m* 1961, Carmen Grandoso Martinez; three *s. Educ:* King Edward VI Sch., Southampton; Univ. of Keele (BA Hons, MA). Asst Teacher, Christopher Wren Sch., London, 1958–60; Asst Master, later Head of History, Bemrose Sch., Derby, 1960–68; Head, Social Studies Dept, Sir Wilfrid Martineau Sch., Birmingham, 1968–73; Headmaster: Corby Grammar Sch., 1973; Southwood Sch., Corby, 1973–82; Queen Elizabeth Sch., Corby, 1982–88. *Publications:* American Government, 1974; Understanding Politics in Modern Britain, 1977; (with L. Robbins and T. Brennan) People and Politics in Britain, 1985; (jtly) School Management in Practice, 1985. *Recreations:* wine appreciation, Geddington Volunteer Fire Brigade. *Address:* 24 Bright Trees Road, Geddington, Kettering, Northants NN14 1BS. *T:* Kettering (0536) 742559. *Clubs:* Commonwealth Trust; Rotary (Kettering Huxloe).

SUTTON, Rt. Rev. Keith Norman; *see* Lichfield, Bishop of.

SUTTON, Leslie Ernest, MA, DPhil Oxon; FRS 1950; Fellow and Lecturer in Chemistry, Magdalen College, Oxford, 1936–73, Fellow Emeritus, 1973; Reader in Physical Chemistry, 1962–73 (University Demonstrator and Lecturer in Chemistry, 1945–62); *b* 22 June 1906; *o c* of Edgar William Sutton; *m* 1st, 1932, Catharine Virginia Stock (*d* 1962), *er d* of Wallace Teall Stock, Maplewood, NY, USA; two *s* one *d*; 2nd, 1963, Rachel Ann Long (*d* 1987), *er d* of Lt-Col J. F. Batten, Swyncombe, Henley-on-Thames; two *s. Educ:* Watford Gram. Sch.; Lincoln Coll., Oxford (Scholar). 1st Class Hon. School Chemistry, 1928; research at Leipzig Univ., 1928–29, and at Oxford University; Fellow by Examination, Magdalen College, 1932–36; Rockefeller Fellow, California Inst. of Technology, 1933–34; Tilden Lectr, Chemical Soc., 1940; Visiting Prof., Heidelberg Univ., 1960, 1964, 1967. Vice-Pres., Magdalen College, 1947–48. Hon. Sec., Chemical Soc., 1951–57, Vice-Pres., 1957–60. Chairman: Lawes Agricl Trust Cttee, Rothamsted Experimental Stn, 1982–89 (Treas., 1978–82); Dielectrics Soc., 1975–86. Hon. DSc Salford, 1973. Meldola Medal, RIC, 1932; Harrison Prize, Chemical Soc., 1935. *Publications:* papers in scientific jls; (as scientific Editor) Tables of Interatomic Distances and Configuration in Molecules and Ions, 1958, 1964; Chemische Bindung und Molekülstruktur, 1961. *Address:* 62 Osler Road, Headington, Oxford OX3 9BN. *T:* Oxford (0865) 66456.

SUTTON, Rt. Rev. Peter (Eves), CBE 1990; Bishop of Nelson, New Zealand, 1965–90; Senior Anglican Bishop, 1979–90; Acting Primate, New Zealand, 1985–86; *b* Wellington, NZ, 7 June 1923; *m* 1956, Pamela Cherrington, *e d* of R. A. Dalley, Patin House, Kidderminster; one *s* one *d. Educ:* Wellesley Coll.; Nelson Coll.; University of New Zealand. BA 1945; MA 1947; LTh 1948. Deacon, 1947; Priest, 1948 (Wellington); Curate of Wanganui, New Zealand, 1947–50; St John the Evangelist, Bethnal Green, 1950–51; Bishops Hatfield, Diocese of St Albans (England), 1951–52; Vicar of St Cuthberts, Berhampore (NZ), 1952–58; Whangarei, Diocese of Auckland, New Zealand, 1958–64; Archdeacon of Waimate, 1962–64; Dean of Dunedin and Vicar of St Paul's Cathedral, Dunedin, 1964–65. Chm., Cawthron Inst., 1977–90, 1991–. Sub-Prelate, Order of St John, NZ, 1987–. ChStJ 1986. NZ Commemoration Medal, 1990. *Publication:* Freedom for Convictions, 1971. *Recreation:* golf (Canterbury Univ. Blue). *Address:* 3 Ngatiawa Street, Nelson, New Zealand. *Club:* Nelson (New Zealand).

SUTTON, Dr Peter Morgan; Director, Public Health Laboratory Service Centre for Applied Microbiology and Research, Porton Down, since 1979; *b* 21 June 1932; *s* of Sir Graham Sutton, CBE, FRS and late Lady Sutton (*née* Doris Morgan); *m* 1959, Helen Ersy Economides; two *s* two *d. Educ:* Bishop Wordsworth Sch., Salisbury; Wrekin Coll., Wellington; University Coll. (Fellow, 1985) and University Coll. Hosp. Med. Sch., London. House Surgeon and House Physician, UCH, 1956–57; Graham Scholar in Pathology, Univ. of London, 1958–59; on academic staff of UCH Med. Sch., 1960–65; Vis. Asst Prof. of Pathology, Univ. of Pittsburg, USA, 1966–67; Hon. Consultant Pathologist, UCH, 1967–79; Reader in Pathology, Univ. of London, 1971–79; Vice-Dean, UCH Med. Sch., 1973–78. Vis. Prof., Dept of Biochemical Pathology, UCL, 1983–. Sometime Examr in Pathology, Univ. of London and RCS. *Publications:* The Nature of Cancer, 1962; various papers on fibrinolytic enzymes and novel antiviral compounds. *Recreations:* English literature, history of science. *Address:* Manderley, 34 Bower Gardens, Salisbury, Wilts SP1 2RL. *T:* Salisbury (0722) 323902.

SUTTON, Philip John, RA 1989 (ARA 1977); *b* 20 Oct. 1928; *m* 1954; one *s* three *d. Educ:* Slade Sch. of Fine Art, UCL. Artist-in-residence, Fulham Pottery, 1987–. One-man exhibitions: Roland Browse and Delbanco (now Browse and Darby) Gallery, London, 1953–; Geffrye Museum, London, 1959; Leeds City Art Gallery, 1960; Newcastle-on-Tyne, 1962; Bradford, 1962; Edinburgh, 1962; Sydney, 1963, 1966, 1970, 1973; Perth, 1963; Battersea, 1963, 1972; Detroit, 1967; Bristol, 1970; Folkestone, 1970, 1974; Cape Town, 1976; Johannesburg, 1976; Falmouth Sch. of Art, 1977; Royal Acad. (Diploma Gall.), London, 1977; Annexe Gall., London, 1979; Holsworthy Gall., London, 1980; David Jones Gall., Sydney, 1980; Annexe Art Gall., 1980; Minden Gall., CI, 1981; Bonython Art Gall., Adelaide, 1981; Norwich, Bath and New York, 1983; Lichfield Fest., 1985; Beaux Arts Gall., Bath, 1985; Galerie Joël Salaün, Paris, 1988; exhibn of ceramics, Oditte Gilbert Gall., London, 1987. Designed: Post Office 'Greetings' stamps, 1989; London Transport poster 'Soho', 1989. *Recreations:* swimming, running. *Address:* 10 Soudan Road, Battersea, SW11 4HH. *T:* 071–622 2647.

SUTTON, Dr Richard, DSc (Med); FRCP, FACC; Consultant Cardiologist: Westminster Hospital, London, since 1976; to British Airways, since 1976; *b* 1 Sept. 1940; *s* of late Dick Brasnett Sutton and of Greta Mary (*née* Leadbeter); *m* 1964, Anna Gunilla (*née* Cassö); one *s. Educ:* Gresham's Sch.; King's Coll., London; King's Coll. Hosp. (MB, BS 1964); DSc (Med) London 1988. FRCP 1983 (MRCP 1967); FACC 1975; FESC 1990. Gen. medical trng followed graduation; career in cardiology began at St George's Hosp., London, 1967; Fellow in Cardiol., Univ. of NC, 1968–69; Registrar, Sen. Registrar, then Temp. Consultant, National Heart Hosp., London, 1970–76. Cons. Cardiologist, St Stephen's Hosp., 1976–89; Hon. Cons. Cardiologist: Italian Hosp., London, 1977–89; SW Thames RHA, 1979–; St Luke's Hosp., London, 1980–. Member: British Medical Assoc.; British Cardiac Soc.; British Pacing and Electrophysiology Group (Co-Founder, Pres. and Past Hon. Sec.). Governors' Award, Amer. Coll. of Cardiol., 1979 (Scientific Exhibit, Physiol Cardiac Pacing), and 1982 (1st Prize; Scientific Exhibit, 5 yrs of Physiol Cardiac Pacing). Editor in Chief, European Jl of Cardiac Pacing and Electrophysiology. *Publications:* Foundations of Cardiac Pacing, 1991; articles on many aspects of cardiology incl. cardiac pacing, coronary artery disease, left ventricular function, and assessment of pharm. agents, in Circulation, Amer. Jl of Cardiol., Amer. Heart Jl, Brit. Heart Jl, Pace, Lancet, BMJ, and Oxford Textbook of Medicine, 1967–. *Recreations:* opera, foreign travel, tennis. *Address:* 149 Harley Street, W1N 1HG. *T:* 071–935 4444.

SUTTON, Richard Lewis; Regional Director, Northern Region, Department of Industry, 1974–81; *b* 3 Feb. 1923; *s* of William Richard Sutton and Marina Susan Sutton (*née* Chudleigh); *m* 1944, Jean Muriel (*née* Turner). *Educ:* Ealing County Grammar Sch. Board of Trade, 1939. Served War: HM Forces (Lieut RA), 1942–47. Asst Trade Comr, Port of Spain, 1950–52; BoT, 1953–62; Trade Comr, Kuala Lumpur, 1962–66; Monopolies Commn, 1966; BoT, 1967–68; Dir, British Industrial Develt Office, New York, 1968–71; Regional Dir, West Midland Region, Dept of Trade and Industry, 1971–74. *Recreations:* music, walking, bridge. *Address:* Barton Toft, Dowlish Wake, Ilminster, Somerset TA19 0QG. *T:* Ilminster (0460) 57127.

SUTTON, Sir Richard (Lexington), 9th Bt *cr* 1772; farmer; *b* 27 April 1937; *s* of Sir Robert Lexington Sutton, 8th Bt, and of Gwynneth Gwladys, *o d* of Major Arnold Charles Gover, MC; *S* father, 1981; *m* 1959, Fiamma, *o d* of G. M. Ferrari, Rome; one *s* one *d. Educ:* Stowe. *Recreations:* ski-ing, sailing, swimming, tennis. *Heir: s* David Robert Sutton, *b* 26 Feb. 1960. *Address:* Moorhill, Langham, Gillingham, Dorset. *T:* Gillingham (07476) 2665.

SUTTON, Robert William, CB 1962; OBE 1946; retired as Superintendent and Chief Scientific Officer, Services Electronics Research Laboratories, Baldock, Herts, 1946–70; *b* 13 Nov. 1905; *s* of late William Sutton; *m* 1951, Elizabeth Mary, *d* of George Maurice Wright, CBE, Chelmsford; one *s* two *d. Educ:* Brighton College; Royal College of Science, London University. Formerly with Ferranti Ltd, and then with E. K. Cole Ltd until 1938. Admiralty, 1939–68. *Address:* 33 Hitchin Street, Baldock, Herts SG7 6AQ. *T:* Baldock (0462) 893373.

SUTTON, Shaun Alfred Graham, OBE 1979; television producer and writer; Head of Drama Group, BBC Television, 1969–81; Consultant Director, Prime Time Television, since 1987; *b* 14 Oct. 1919; *s* of Eric Graham Sutton and Beryl Astley-Marsden; *m* 1948, Barbara Leslie; one *s* three *d. Educ:* Latymer Upper Sch.; Embassy Sch. of Acting, London. Actor and Stage Manager, Q, Embassy, Aldwych, Adelphi, Arts, Criterion Theatres, 1938–40. Royal Navy, 1940–46, Lieut RNVR. Stage Dir, Embassy and provincial theatres, 1946–48; Producer, Embassy, Buxton, Croydon Theatres, 1948–50; toured S Africa as Producer, 1950; Producer, Embassy, Ipswich, Buxton, 1951–52; entered BBC TV Service, 1952; produced and wrote many children's TV plays and serials; directed many series incl. Z Cars, Softly Softly, Sherlock Holmes, Kipling, etc.; Head of BBC Drama Serials Dept, 1966–69; dramatised Rogue Herries and Judith Paris for BBC Radio, 1971; Producer: BBC TV Shakespeare series, 1982–84; Theatre Night series, BBC 2, including Season's Greetings, Make and Break, The Devil's Disciple, What the Butler Saw, Absent Friends, The Master Builder, Strife, The Miser, The Rivals, Journey's End, When We are Married, Once in a Lifetime, Benefactors, The Contractor, The Winslow Boy, Relatively Speaking, Merlin. Fellow, Royal TV Soc.; Mem., BAFTA. *Publications:* A Christmas Carol (stage adaptation), 1949; Queen's Champion (children's novel), 1961; The Largest Theatre in the World, 1982. *Recreations:* gardening, walking. *Address:* 15 Corringham

Court, Corringham Road, NW11 7BY. *T:* 081–455 5417; The Cottage, Brewery Road, Trunch, Norfolk. *Club:* Lord's Taverners.

SUTTON, Sir Stafford William Powell F.; *see* Foster-Sutton.

SUTTON, Thomas Francis; Chairman, AE-International Inc., since 1981; Director and Executive Vice-President, J. Walter Thompson Co., New York, 1965–85; Executive Vice-President, JWT Group Inc., New York, 1982–86; *b* 9 Feb. 1923; *m* 1st, 1950, Anne Fleming (marr. diss. 1974); one *s* two *d*; 2nd, 1982, Maki Watanabe. *Educ:* King's School, Worcester; St Peter's College, Oxford. Research Officer, British Market Research Bureau Ltd, 1949–51; Advertising Manager, Pasolds Ltd, 1951–52; Managing Director, J. Walter Thompson GmbH, Frankfurt, Germany, 1952–59; Dir, J. Walter Thompson Co. Ltd, 1960–73, Man. Dir, 1960–66; Dir, internat. operations, J. Walter Thompson, NY, 1966–72; Man. Dir, J. Walter Thompson Co. Japan, Tokyo, 1972–80; Exec. Vice-Pres./Dir, J. Walter Thompson Asia/Pacific, 1980–81. Chm., E-A Advertising, NY, 1982–86; Dir, Lansdowneuro, 1982–85 (Chm., 1984). Part-time Lecturer in advertising and marketing: Rutger's Univ., NJ, 1968–71; Columbia Univ., NY, 1971–73; Sophia Univ., Tokyo, 1974–81. Chm., Internat. Support Gp, YMCA Japan, 1981–82. FIPA; FIS; FSS. Internat. Advertising Man of the Year Award, 1970. *Recreations:* chess, riding, Pudding Club. *Address:* Rushway House, Willington, Shipston-on-Stour, Warwicks CV36 5AS. *Clubs:* Princeton of New York; Probus (Shipston-on-Stour); Walton Hall Country (Warwickshire).

SUVA, Archbishop of, (RC), since 1976; **Most Rev. Petero Mataca;** *b* 28 April 1933; *s* of Gaberiele Daunivucu and Akeneta Taina. *Educ:* Holy Name Seminary, Dunedin, NZ; Propaganda Fidei, Rome. Priest, Rome, 1959; Vicar-Gen. of Archdiocese of Suva, 1966; Rector of Pacific Regional Seminary, 1973; Auxiliary Bishop of Suva, 1974. Pres., Episcopal Conf. of South Pacific, 1981. *Address:* Archbishop's House, Box 393, Suva, Fiji. *T:* 301955.

SUYIN; *see* Han Suyin.

SUZMAN, Mrs Helen, Hon. DBE 1989; *b* 7 Nov. 1917; *d* of late Samuel Gavronsky; *m* Dr M. M. Suzman, FRCP; two *d*. *Educ:* Parktown Convent, Johannesburg; Univ. of Witwatersrand (BCom). Lectr in Economic History, Univ. of Witwatersrand, 1944–52. Elected MP for Houghton, RSA, 1953; United Party 1953–61; Progressive Party (later Progressive Reform Party and Progressive Federal Party), 1961–89. Hon. Fellow: St Hugh's Coll., Oxford, 1973; London Sch. of Economics, 1975. Hon. DCL Oxford, 1973; Hon. LLD: Harvard, Witwatersrand, 1976; Columbia, Smith Coll., 1977; Brandeis, 1981; Jewish Theological Seminary, NY, Cape Town, 1986; Ohio, Western Ontario, 1989; Rhodes, S Africa, Cambridge, Glasgow, Nottingham, Warwick, Ulster, 1990; Hon. DHL: Denison, 1982; New Sch. for Social Res., NY, Sacred Heart Univ., USA, 1984; DUniv. Brunel, 1991. UN Human Rights Award, 1978; Roger E. Joseph Award, Hebrew Union Coll., NY, 1986; Moses Mendelssohn Prize, Berlin Senate, 1988. *Recreations:* golf, swimming, fishing, bridge. *Address:* 49 Melville Road, Hyde Park, Sandton, Transvaal 2196, South Africa. *T:* 788–2833. *Clubs:* Lansdowne; River, Wanderers, Wanderers Golf, Houghton Golf, Glendower (Johannesburg).

SUZMAN, Janet; actress; *b* 9 Feb. 1939; *d* of Saul Suzman; *m* 1969, Trevor Nunn, *qv* (marr. diss. 1986); one *s*. *Educ:* Kingsmead Coll., Johannesburg; Univ. of the Witwatersrand (BA); London Acad. of Music and Dramatic Art. Vis Prof of Drama Studies, Westfield Coll., London, 1983–84. Mem., LAMDA Council, 1978–. Rôles played for *Royal Shakespeare Co.* incl.: Joan La Pucelle in The Wars of the Roses, 1963–64; Lulu in The Birthday Party, Rosaline, Portia, 1965; Ophelia, 1965–66; Katharina, Celia, and Berinthia in The Relapse, 1967; Beatrice, Rosalind, 1968–69; Cleopatra and Lavinia, 1972–73; Clytemnestra and Helen of Troy in The Greeks, 1980; *other rôles* incl.: Kate Hardcastle, and Carmen in The Balcony, Oxford Playhouse, 1966; Hester in Hello and Goodbye, King's Head Theatre, 1973; Masha in Three Sisters, Cambridge, 1976; Good Woman of Setzuan, Newcastle, 1976, Royal Court, 1977; Hedda Gabler, Duke of York's, 1977; Boo-hoo, Open Space, 1978; The Duchess of Malfi, Birmingham, 1979; Cowardice, Ambassadors, 1983; Boesman and Lena, Hampstead, 1984; Vassa, Greenwich, 1985; Andromache, Old Vic, 1988; Hippolytus, Almeida, 1991. Director: Othello, MK Theatre, Johannesburg, 1987; Another Time, Wyndham's, 1989; A Dream of People, The Pit, 1990. *Films:* A Day in the Death of Joe Egg, 1970; Nicholas and Alexandra, 1971; The Priest of Love, 1980; The Draughtsman's Contract, 1981; E la Nave Va, 1983; A Dry White Season, 1990; Nuns on the Run, 1990; *television:* plays for BBC and ITV incl.: St Joan, 1968; Three Sisters, 1969; Macbeth, 1970; Hedda Gabler, 1972; Twelfth Night, 1973; Antony and Cleopatra, 1974; Miss Nightingale, 1974; Clayhanger, serial, 1975–76; Mountbatten—The Last Viceroy, 1986; The Singing Detective, 1986, The Miser, 1987; dir., Othello, 1988; Cripples, 1989; The Amazon, 1989; master class on Shakespearean comedy, BBC, 1990. Acad. Award Nomination, Best Actress, 1971; Evening Standard Drama Awards, Best Actress, 1973, 1976; Plays and Players Award, Best Actress, 1976. Hon. MA Open, 1984; Hon. DLitt Warwick, 1990. *Address:* William Morris (UK) Ltd, 31/32 Soho Square, W1V 5DG. *T:* 071–434 2191.

SVENSON, Dame Beryl; *see* Grey, Dame Beryl.

SVOBODA, Prof. Josef, RDI 1989; Chief Scenographer, National Theatre, Prague, since 1948; Professor at Academy of Applied Arts, since 1968; *b* Čáslav, 10 May 1920; *m* 1948, Libuše Svobodová; one *d*. *Educ:* Gymnasium; special sch. for interior architecture; Academy of Applied Arts (architecture). EXPO 58, Brussels: success with Laterna Magica; EXPO 67, Montreal: polyvision, polydiaekran. He co-operates with many theatres all over the world (Metropolitan Opera, New York; Covent Garden; Geneva; Bayreuth; Frankfurt, etc); Chief of Laterna Magica, experimental scene of National Theatre, Prague, 1973–. Hon. RA 1969. Hon. DFA: Denison, Ohio, 1978; Western Michigan, 1984. Internat. Theatre Award, ATA, 1976; Internat. Prize for scenery and costumes, Teatro de l'Europa, 1984. Laureate of State Prize, 1954; Merited Artist of CSSR, 1966; National Artist of CSSR, 1968; Chevalier, Ordre des Arts et des Lettres (France), 1976. *Publications:* relevant monographs: Josef Svoboda (by Theatre Inst.) 1967 (Prague); Josef Svoboda (by Denis Bablet) 1970 (France); The Scenography of J. Svoboda (by Jarka Burian) 1971, 1974 (USA); Teatr Josefa Svobody (by V. Berjozkin) 1973 (USSR). *Recreations:* theatre, photography, creative arts, music, literature. *Address:* Filmařská 535/17, 15200 Prague 5, Czechoslovakia.

SWAFFIELD, Sir James (Chesebrough), Kt 1976; CBE 1971; RD 1967; DL; Chairman, British Rail Property Board, 1984–91; solicitor, retired; *b* 16 Feb. 1924; *s* of Frederick and Kate Elizabeth Swaffield, Cheltenham; *m* 1950, Elizabeth Margaret Ellen, 2nd *d* of A. V. and K. E. Maunder, Belfast; two *s* two *d*. *Educ:* Cheltenham Grammar Sch.; Haberdashers' Aske's Hampstead Sch.; London Univ. (LLB); MA Oxon 1974. RNVR, 1942–46. Articled Town Clerk, Lincoln, 1946–49; Asst Solicitor: Norwich Corp., 1949–52; Cheltenham Corp., 1952–53; Southend-on-Sea Corp., 1953–56; Dep. Town Clerk, subseq. Town Clerk and Clerk of Peace, Blackpool, 1956–62; Sec., Assoc. of Municipal Corpns, 1962–72; Dir-Gen. and Clerk to GLC, Clerk to ILEA and Clerk of Lieutenancy for Greater London, 1973–84. Chairman: St Paul's Cathedral Ct of Advrs; Outward Bound Trust; Vice-President: Age Concern, Greater London; RSNC; Trustee, Civic Trust. Chm., Governors, Dulwich Coll. FRSA. Hon. Fellow, Inst. Local Govt Studies, Birmingham Univ. DL Greater London, 1978. OStJ. Dist. Service Award (Internat. City Management Assoc.), 1984. *Address:* 10 Kelsey Way, Beckenham, Kent BR3 3LL. *Clubs:* Reform, Naval.

SWAIN, Henry Thornhill, CBE 1971; RIBA; County Architect, Nottinghamshire County Council, 1964–88, retired; *b* 14 Feb. 1924; *s* of Thornhill Madge Swain and Bessie Marion Swain; *m*; three *d*. *Educ:* Bryanston Sch.; Architectural Assoc. (Hons Dipl.). Served with RN, 1943–46. Herts County Architect's Dept, 1949; worked in primary school group; Notts CC, 1955; Group Leader i/c initial develt of CLASP construction; Dep. County Architect, 1958. *Publications:* many articles in architectural jls. *Recreation:* sailing. *Address:* 50 Loughborough Road, West Bridgford, Nottingham. *T:* Nottingham (0602) 818059.

SWAINE, Edward Thomas William, CMG 1968; MBE 1952; Director, Exhibitions Division, Central Office of Information, 1961–71, retired; *b* 17 July 1907; *s* of Edward James Swaine; *m* 1942, Ruby Louise (*née* Ticehurst) (*d* 1974). Entered Govt Service, Min. of Information, 1940; Festival of Britain, 1948–52; Dir of Exhibns, British Pavilion, Montreal World Exhibn, 1967; UK Dep. Comr-Gen. and Dir of Exhbns, Japan World Exhibn, 1970. *Recreation:* photography. *Address:* 6/12 Northwood Hall, Highgate, N6 5PN. *T:* 081–340 4392.

SWAINSON, Eric, CBE 1981; Vice-Chairman, Fairey Group, since 1987; Director, AMEC, since 1987; *b* 5 Dec. 1926; *m* 1953, Betty Heywood; two *d*. *Educ:* Sheffield Univ. (BMet 1st cl. Hons; W. H. A. Robertson medal, 1959). Joined Imperial Chemical Industries Metals Div. (now IMI), 1946; Technical Officer, Res. Dept, 1946–53; Manager, Titanium Melting Plant, 1953–56; Asst Manager, Technical Dept, 1956–59; Gen. Manager and Man. Dir, Lightning Fasteners, 1961–69; Dir, IMI, 1969–86; Asst Man. Dir, 1972–74; Man. Dir, 1974–86; Dep. Chm., Pegler-Hattersley plc, 1986. Director: Birmingham Broadcasting, 1973–; Midlands Radio Hldgs, 1988–; Lloyds Bank plc, 1986–; Lloyds Merchant Bank Hldgs, 1989–; Chm., Birmingham and West Midlands Reg. Bd, Lloyds Bank, 1985–91 (Reg. Dir, 1979–91). Chm., W Midlands Industrial Develt Bd, 1985–90; Member: Review Bd for Govt Contracts, 1978–; NEDC Cttee on Finance for Industry, 1978–86; Council, CBI, 1975–86; W Midlands Reg. Council, CBI, 1973–83 (Chm. 1976–78); Industrial Develt Adv. Bd, 1982–88. Pro-Chancellor, Aston Univ., 1981–86. FRSA 1985. Hon. DSc Aston, 1986. *Address:* Paddox Hollow, Norton Lindsey, Warwick CV35 8JA.

SWALLOW, Comdt (Daphne) Patricia, CBE 1986; *b* 25 Sept. 1932; *d* of Captain Ralph Geoffrey Swallow, RN retd and Daphne Lucy Regina Swallow (*née* Parry). *Educ:* St George's Sch., Ascot; Portsmouth Polytechnic (Hon. Fellow, 1983). Joined WRNS as Signal Wren, 1950; qualified as WRNS Communications Officer, 1955; served in HMS Drake and Malta, 1956–58; Oslo, Portsmouth, HMS Mercury, Northwood and Gibraltar, 1958–67; HMS Pembroke and HMS Heron, 1968–71; passed Naval Staff Course, 1972; HMS Dauntless, 1973–74; Staff of C-in-C Naval Home Comd and MoD, 1974–76; National Defence College Latimer Course, 1976–77; Staff of Naval Secretary, 1977; Command Personnel Officer to C-in-C Naval Home Comd, 1977–79; Dep. Dir, WRNS, 1979–81; Staff Officer Training Co-ordination and Comd WRNS Officer to C-in-C Naval Home Comd, 1981–82; Dir, WRNS, 1982–86; Hon. ADC to the Queen, 1982–86. Asst Sec., Benevolent Dept, Officers' Assoc., 1987–89; Case Sec., DGAA, 1989–90. Member: Nat. Exec. Cttee, Forces Help Soc. and Lord Roberts Workshops, 1986–; Council and Exec. Cttee, Shipwrecked Fishermen and Mariners Royal Benevolent Soc., 1991–. FBIM 1986. *Recreations:* tennis, dressmaking and needlework, reading, theatre, opera, music. *Address:* c/o Lloyds Bank plc, 15 The Village, Blackheath, SE3 9LH. *Club:* Naval.

SWALLOW, John Crossley, PhD; FRS 1968; physical oceanographer, Institute of Oceanographic Sciences (formerly National Institute of Oceanography), 1954–83; *b* 11 Oct. 1923; *s* of Alfred Swallow and Elizabeth (*née* Crossley); *m* 1958, Mary Morgan (*née* McKenzie); one step *d*. *Educ:* Holme Valley Gram. Sch.; St John's Coll., Cambridge. Admty Signal Estabt, 1943–47; research in marine geophysics, at Cambridge and in HMS Challenger, 1948–54; work on ocean circulation, in RRS Discovery II, and in RRS Discovery, and other vessels, 1954–83. Rossby Fellow, Woods Hole Oceanographic Inst., 1973–74. Murchison Grant of RGS, 1965. Foreign Hon. Mem., Amer. Acad. of Arts and Sciences, 1975. Holds American awards in oceanography. Commem. medal of Prince Albert I of Monaco, Inst Océanographique, Paris, 1982. *Publications:* papers on physical oceanography. *Address:* Heath Cottage, Station Road, Drakewalls, Gunnislake, Cornwall. *T:* Tavistock (0822) 832100.

SWALLOW, Comdt Patricia; *see* Swallow, Comdt D. P.

SWALLOW, Sydney; Senior Director, Procurement, Post Office, 1977–81; Chief Procurement Officer, British Telecommunications, 1981–83; *b* 29 June 1919; *s* of William and Charlotte Lucy Swallow; *m* 1950, Monica Williams; one *s*. *Educ:* Woking County Sch.; St Catharine's Coll., Cambridge (MA). Mines Dept, Board of Trade, 1940–42. Served War: Royal Engineers (Survey), 1942–46. Nat. Coal Bd, 1946–59; Central Electricity Generating Bd, 1959–65; Associated Electrical Industries Ltd, 1965–68; General Electric Co. Ltd, 1968; Dir of Supplies, GLC, 1968–77. Chm., Educn Cttee, Inst. of Purchasing and Supply, 1967–77; Visiting Prof., Univ. of Bradford Management Centre, 1972–75; Vis. Fellow, ASC, 1976–80. FInstPS. *Publications:* various articles on purchasing and supply in professional jls. *Recreations:* gardening, cricket. *Address:* 101 Muswell Hill Road, N10. *T:* 081–444 8775.

SWALLOW, Sir William, Kt 1967; FIMechE; *b* 2 Jan. 1905; *s* of William Turner Swallow, Gomersal, Yorks; *m* 1929, Kathleen Lucy Smith; no *c*. *Educ:* Batley and Huddersfield Technical Colleges. Draughtsman, Karrier Motors Ltd, 1923; senior draughtsman, chief body designer, Short Bros, 1926; Gilford Motors Ltd, 1930; development engineer, Pressed Steel Co., 1932; chief production engineer, Short Bros, 1943; development engineer, General Motors Overseas Operations, New York, 1947; i/c manufacturing staff, General Motors Ltd, 1948; gen. man., A. C. Sphinx Spark Plug Div. of Gen. Motors Ltd, 1950; Managing Director, General Motors Ltd, 1953, Chairman, 1958; Chm., Vauxhall Motors Ltd, Luton, Beds, 1961–66 (Man. Dir, 1961–65). Mem., Advisory Council on Technology, 1968–70; Chairman: NPL Adv. Bd, 1969–; Shipbuilding and Shiprepairing Council, 1967–71; EDC for Hotel and Catering Industry, 1966–72; Shipbuilding Industry Bd, 1966–71. Governor, Ashridge Coll., 1965–72. ARAeS; MSAE. President: SMMT, 1964–65 (Dep. Pres. 1966–67); Inst. Road Tspt Engrs, 1966–68. *Address:* Alderton Lodge, Ashridge Park, Berkhamsted, Herts HP4 1NA. *T:* Little Gaddesden (0442) 842284.

SWAMINATHAN, Dr Monkombu Sambasivan, FRS 1973; President, International Union for the Conservation of Nature and Natural Resources, since 1988; *b* 7 Aug. 1925; *m* Mina Swaminathan; three *d*. *Educ:* Univs of Kerala, Madras and Cambridge. BSc Kerala, 1944; BSc (Agric.) Madras, 1947; Assoc. IARI 1949; PhD Cantab, 1952.

Responsible for developing Nat. Demonstration Project, 1964, and for evolving Seed Village concept; actively involved in develt of High Yielding Varieties, Dryland Farming and Multiple Cropping Programmes. Vice-Pres., Internat. Congress of Genetics, The Hague, 1963; Gen. Pres., Indian Science Congress, 1976; Mem. (Agriculture), Planning Commn, 1980–82 (formerly Dir-Gen., Indian Council of Agricultural Research); Dir-Gen., Internat. Rice Res. Inst., Manila, 1982–88. First Zakir Hussain Meml Lectr, 1970; UGC Nat. Lectr, 1971; lectures at many internat. scientific symposia. Foreign Associate, US Nat. Acad. of Scis; For. Mem., All Union Acad. of Agricl Scis, USSR; Hon. Mem., Swedish Seed Assoc.; Hon. Fellow, Indian Nat. Acad. of Sciences. FNA; Fellow, Italian Nat. Sci. Acad. Shanti Swarup Bhatnagar Award for contribs in Biological Scis, 1961; Mendel Centenary Award, Czechoslovak Acad. of Scis, 1965; Birbal Sahni Award, Indian Bot. Soc., 1965; Ramon Magsaysay Award for Community Leadership, 1971; Silver Jubilee Award, 1973, Meghnath Saha Medal, 1981, Indian Nat. Science Acad.; R. B. Bennett Commonwealth Prize, RSA, 1984; Albert Einstein World Science Award, 1986; World Food Prize, 1987; Tyler Prize for Envmtl Achievement, 1991. Padma Shri, 1967; Padma Bhushan, 1972; Padma Vibhushan, 1989. Hon. DSc from thirty-three universities. *Publications:* numerous scientific papers. *Address:* 11 Rathna Nagar, Teynampet, Madras 600018, India.

SWAN, Conrad Marshall John Fisher, CVO 1986 (LVO 1978); PhD; York Herald of Arms, since 1968; Registrar, College of Arms, since 1982; Genealogist: of Order of the Bath, since 1972; of Grand Priory, OStJ, since 1976; First Hon. Genealogist, Order of St Michael and St George, since 1989; *b* 13 May 1924; *yr s* of late Dr Henry Peter Swan, Major RAMC and RCAMC, of BC, Canada and Colchester, Essex, and of Edna Hanson Magdalen (*née* Green), Cross of Honour Pro Ecclesia et Pontifice *m* 1957, Lady Hilda Susan Mary Northcote, Dame of Honour and Devotion, SMO Malta, 1979, and of Justice of SMO of Constantine St George, 1975, *yr d* of 3rd Earl of Iddesleigh; one *s* four *d*. *Educ:* St George's Coll., Weybridge; Sch. of Oriental and African Studies, Univ. of London; Univ. of Western Ontario; Peterhouse, Cambridge. BA 1949, MA 1951, Univ. of W Ont; PhD 1955, Cambridge. Served Europe and India (Capt. Madras Regt, IA), 1942–47. Assumption Univ. of Windsor, Ont.: Lectr in History, 1955–57; Asst Prof. of Hist., 1957–60; Univ. Beadle, 1957–60. Rouge Dragon Pursuivant of Arms, 1962–68. On Earl Marshal's staff for State Funeral of Sir Winston Churchill, 1965 and Investiture of HRH Prince of Wales, 1969. In attendance: upon HM The Queen at Installation of HRH Prince of Wales as Great Master of Order of the Bath, 1975; during Silver Jubilee Thanksgiving Service, 1977; on Australasian Tour, 1977; at Commonwealth Heads of Govt Conf., 1987; Gentleman Usher-in-Waiting to HH the Pope, GB visit, 1982. Woodward Lectr, Yale, 1964; Centennial Lectr, St Thomas More Coll., Univ. of Saskatchewan, 1967; Inaugural Sir William Scott Meml Lectr, Ulster-Scot Hist. Foundn, 1968; 60th Anniv. Lectr, St Joseph's Coll., Univ. of Alberta, 1987; first Herald to execute duties across Atlantic (Bermuda, 1969) and in S Hemisphere (Brisbane, Qld, 1977) (both in tabard) and in Canada in attendance upon the Sovereign (Vancouver, 1987), to visit Australia, 1970, S America, 1972, Thailand, Japan, 1973, NZ, 1976. World lecture tours, 1970, 1973, 1976. Adviser to PM of Canada on establishment of Nat. Flag of Canada and Order of Canada, 1964–67; at invitation of Sec. of State of Canada participated in nat. forum on heraldry in Canada, 1987. Co-founder (with Lady Hilda Swan), Heraldic Garden, Boxford, Suffolk, 1983. Hon. Citizen, State of Texas; Freemanships in USA; Freeman: St George's, Bermuda, 1969; City of London, 1974. Fellow, 1976, Hon. Vice-Pres. and a Founder, Heraldry Soc. of Canada; Fellow, Geneal. Soc. of Victoria (Australia), 1970; FSA 1971; FZS 1986. Liveryman and Freeman, 1974, and Mem., Ct of Assts, 1983, Gunmakers' Co. KStJ 1976. Kt of Honour and Devotion, SMO of Malta, 1979 (Kt of Grace and Devotion, 1964) (Genealogist Br. Assoc., 1974–); Cross of Comdr of Order of Merit, SMO of Malta, 1983. *Publications:* Heraldry: Ulster and North American Connections, 1972; Canada: Symbols of Sovereignty, 1977; many articles in learned jls on heraldic, sigillographic and related subjects. *Recreations:* hunting, driving (horse drawn vehicles), rearing ornamental pheasants and waterfowl, marine biology. *Address:* College of Arms, Queen Victoria Street, EC4V 4BT. *T:* 071–248 1850; Boxford House, Suffolk CO6 5JT. *T:* Boxford (Suffolk) (0787) 210208.

SWAN, Maj.-Gen. Dennis Charles Tarrant, CB 1953; CBE 1948; *b* 2 Sept. 1900; *s* of late Lt-Col C. T. Swan, IA; *m* 1930, Patricia Ethel Mary Thorne (*d* 1960); one *s* one *d*. *Educ:* Wellington Coll., Berks; Royal Military Academy, Woolwich. Commissioned as 2nd Lt RE, 1919; served War of 1939–45 (despatches twice): with BEF France, Feb.-May 1940; CRE 1 Burma Div., 1941; Comdt No 6 Mech. Eqpt Group, IE, 1944; Chief Engineer, 15 Ind. Corps, 1945; District Chief Engineer, BAOR, 1946, Chief Engineer, 1948; Director of Fortification and Works, War Office, 1952–55, retired. Captain 1930; Adjutant, 36 (Mx) AA Bn, 1935; Major, 1938; Lt-Col, 1945; Colonel 1947; Brig. 1948; Maj.-Gen., 1952. Pres., Instn of Royal Engineers, 1961–65. *Address:* Lordington Park, Chichester, West Sussex. *T:* Emsworth (0243) 378229; c/o Hindon House, 30 Havant Road, Emsworth, Hampshire PO10 7JE. *T:* Emsworth (0243) 372528.

SWAN, Dermot Joseph, MVO 1972; HM Diplomatic Service, retired; HM Consul-General, Marseilles, 1971–77; *b* 24 Oct. 1917; *s* of Dr William Swan and Anne Cosgrave; *m* 1947, Jeanne Labat; one *d*. *Educ:* St George's, Weybridge; University Coll., London Univ. BA (Hons) French and German. Served War, HM Forces, 1939–46. HM Foreign (later Diplomatic) Service: Vice-Consul, Marseilles, 1947; Saigon, 1949; Foreign Office, 1951; Brazzaville, 1951; Budapest, 1953; FO 1955; First Sec., 1958; Head of Chancery, Phnom Penh, 1959, and Budapest, 1961; UK Mission, New York, 1963; FO (later FCO), 1967; Counsellor, Special Asst to Sec.-Gen. of CENTO, Ankara, 1969. *Recreations:* ice-skating, skiing, swimming. *Address:* Résidence du Golf, 66120 Font Romeu, France. *Club:* Roehampton.

SWAN, Hon. Sir John (William David), KBE 1990; JP; MP (United Bermuda Party) Paget East, since 1972; Premier of Bermuda, since 1982; *b* 3 July 1935; *s* of late John N. Swan and of Margaret E. Swan; *m* 1965, Jacqueline A. D. Roberts; one *s* two *d*. *Educ:* West Virginia Wesleyan Coll. (BA). Mem., Lloyd's of London. Salesman, Real Estate, Rego Ltd, 1960–62; Founder, Chairman and Chief Exec., John W. Swan Ltd, 1962–. Minister for: Marine and Air Services; Labour and Immigration, 1977–78; Home Affairs, 1978–82; formerly: Parly Sec. for Finance; Chairman: Bermuda Hosps Bd; Dept of Civil Aviation; Young Presidents' Organization, 1974–86. Member: Chief Execs Orgn; World Business Council, 1986. Hon. Freeman of London, 1985. Hon. LLD: Univ. of Tampa, Fla, 1985; W Virginia Wesleyan Coll., 1987; Atlantic Union Coll., Mass, 1991. Internat. Medal of Excellence (1st recipient), Poor Richard Club of Philadelphia, 1987. *Recreations:* sailing, tennis. *Address:* 11 Grape Bay Drive, Paget PG 06, Bermuda. *T:* 809–236–1303. *Clubs:* Hamilton Rotary, Royal Bermuda Yacht (Bermuda); Bohemian (San Francisco).

SWANN, Benjamin Colin Lewis; Controller, Finance, British Council, 1975–79, retired; *b* 9 May 1922; *s* of Henry Basil Swann and Olivia Ophelia Lewis; *m* 1946, Phyllis Julia Sybil Lewis; three *s* one *d*. *Educ:* Bridgend County School. CA. RAFVR, 1941; Transatlantic Ferry, 1942; Flt Lieut, Transport Command, 1944; Flt Supervisor, BOAC, 1946. Apprentice Chartered Accountant, 1950; Audit Asst, George A. Touche & Co., 1953; Treasury Acct, Malaya, 1954; Financial Adviser, Petaling Jaya, 1956; Partner, Milligan Swann & Co., Chartered Accountants, Exeter, 1957; British Council, 1960; Regional Acct, SE Asia, 1961; Dep. Dir Audit, 1965; Asst Representative, Delhi, 1970; Director, Budget, 1972; Dep. Controller, Finance, 1972. *Recreations:* cuisine, lepidoptery. *Address:* Les Malardeaux, St Sernin de Duras 47120, France.

SWANN, Donald Ibrahim, MA; composer and performer, free-lance since 1948; *b* 30 Sept. 1923; *s* of late Dr Herbert William Swann, Richmond, Surrey and Naguimé Sultan; *m* 1955, Janet Mary (*née* Oxborrow) (marr. diss. 1983), Ipswich, Suffolk; two *d*. *Educ:* Westminster School; Christ Church, Oxford. Hons Degree Mod. Lang. (Russian and Mod. Greek). Contributed music to London revues, including Airs on a Shoestring, 1953–54, as joint leader writer with Michael Flanders; Wild Thyme, musical play, with Philip Guard, 1955; in At the Drop of a Hat, 1957, appeared for first time (with Michael Flanders) as singer and accompanist of own songs (this show ran over 2 yrs in London, was part of Edinburgh Festival, 1959; Broadway, 1959–60; American and Canadian tour, 1960–61; tour of Great Britain and Ireland, 1962–63); At the Drop of Another Hat (with Michael Flanders), Haymarket, 1963–64, Globe, 1965; Aust. and NZ tour, 1964; US Tour, 1966–67. Arranged concerts of own settings: Set by Swann, An Evening in Crete; Soundings by Swann; Between the Bars: an autobiography in music; A Crack in Time, a concert in search of peace. Musician in Residence, Quaker Study Center, Pendle Hill, USA, Jan.-June 1983; has worked in song-writing and performing partnerships with Jeremy Taylor, Sydney Carter, Frank Topping, John Amis; solo entertainments in theatres and concert halls (Stand Clear for Wonders, with peace exploration songs); with Digby Fairweather and jazz group, Swann in Jazz, 1987; Swann's Way, synoptic concert series, Brighton Fest., 1988. Founded Albert House Press for special publications, 1974. *Compositions and publications include:* Lucy and the Hunter, musical play with Sydney Carter; satirical music to Third Programme series by Henry Reed, ghosting for Hilda Tablet. London Sketches with Sebastian Shaw, 1958; Festival Matins, 1962; Perelandra, music drama with David Marsh based on the novel of C. S. Lewis, 1961–62; Settings of John Betjeman Poems, 1964; Sing Round the Year (Book of New Carols for Children), 1965; The Road Goes Ever On, book of songs with J. R. R. Tolkien, 1968, rev. edn 1978; The Space Between the Bars: a book of reflections, 1968; Requiem for the Living, to words of C. Day Lewis, 1969; The Rope of Love: around the earth in song, 1973; Swann's Way Out: a posthumous adventure, 1974; (with Albert Friedlander) The Five Scrolls, 1975; Omnibus Flanders and Swann Songbook, 1977; Round the Piano with Donald Swann, 1979; (with Alec Davison) The Yeast Factory, music drama, 1979; South African Song Cycle, 1982; Alphabetaphon: 26 essays A-Z (illus. by Natasha Etheridge and Robert Poulter), 1987, also trilogy of cassettes, 80 Songs A to Z in personal performance; (with Alison Smith) Art, Music and the Numinous (lectures), 1990; Beyond War: can the Arts mediate?, 1991; Swann's Way, an autobiography (as told to Lyn Smith), 1991; *songs and operas* with Arthur Scholey: The Song of Caedmon, 1971; Singalive, 1978; Wacky and his Fuddlejig (children's musical play), 1978; Candle Tree, 1980; Baboushka (a Christmas cantata), 1980; The Visitors (based on Tolstoy), 1984; Brendan A-hoy!, 1985; (with Evelyn Kirkhart and Mary Morgan) Mamahuhu (musical play), 1986; (with Richard Crane) Envy (musical play), 1986; Victorian Song Cycle, 1987; William Blake and John Clare Song Cycle, 1989. *Recreation:* travelling in Greece. *Address:* 13 Albert Bridge Road, SW11 4PX. *T:* 071–622 4281.

SWANN, Frederick Ralph Holland, CBE 1974 (OBE (mil.) 1944); Life Vice President, Royal National Lifeboat Institution (Chairman, 1972–75); *b* 4 Oct. 1904; *s* of F. Holland Swann, JP, Steeple, Dorset; *m* 1940, Philippa Jocelyn Braithwaite (*d* 1968); no *c*. *Educ:* Eton; Trinity Coll., Cambridge (MA). Mem. London Stock Exchange, 1932–64. Joined RNVSR, 1937; served in HMS Northern Gift, 1939–40 (despatches); comd HMS Sapphire, 1940–41; Senior Fighter Direction Officer, HMS Formidable, 1941–43; Comdr RNVR 1944, QO status, 1945; Exec. Officer, HMS Biter, 1944 and HMS Hunter, 1944–45 (in comd, 1945). Mem. Cttee of Management, RNLI, 1953, Dep. Chm. 1964–72. A Vice-Pres., Royal Humane Soc., 1973; Hon. Life Mem., Norwegian Soc. for Sea Rescue, 1975. A Comr of Income Tax, City of London, 1964–76. *Recreations:* fishing, gardening. *Address:* Stratford Mill, Stratford-sub-Castle, Salisbury, Wilts SP1 3LJ. *T:* Salisbury (0722) 336563. *Clubs:* United Oxford & Cambridge University, Royal Cruising (Cdre 1966–72), Cruising Association (Hon. Mem.); Royal Corinthian Yacht.

SWANN, Julian Dana Nimmo H.; *see* Hartland-Swann.

SWANN, Sir Michael (Christopher), 4th Bt *cr* 1906, of Prince's Gardens, Royal Borough of Kensington; TD 1979; Director: GVG Financial Services Ltd, since 1988; Reyker Securities Ltd, since 1990; *b* 23 Sept. 1941; *s* of Sir Anthony Swann, 3rd Bt, CMG, OBE and of Jean Margaret, *d* of late John Herbert Niblock-Stuart; *S* father, 1991; *m* 1st, 1965, Hon. Lydia Hewitt (marr. diss. 1985), *e d* of 8th Viscount Lifford; two *s* one *d*; 2nd, 1988, Marilyn Ann Morse (*née* Tobitt). *Educ:* Eton Coll. APMI 1978. Lt KRRC (The Royal Green Jackets), 1960–63; T&AVR 4th Bn The Royal Green Jackets, 1964–79 (Brevet Lt-Col 1979). Director: Wright Deen (Life and Estate Duty), 1964–74; Richards Longstaff (Holdings) Ltd, 1974–86; Richards Longstaff Ltd, 1974–88. Governor, Gabbitas Truman and Thring, 1987–. General Comr of Income Tax, 1988–. *Recreations:* cricket, golf, skiing, gardening, growing orchids, racing. *Heir:* *s* Jonathan Christopher Swann, *b* 17 Nov. 1966. *Address:* 100 Hurlingham Road, SW6 3NR. *T:* 071–731 5601. *Clubs:* Hurlingham, IZ, MCC; Rye Golf.

SWANSEA, 4th Baron *cr* 1893; **John Hussey Hamilton Vivian,** Bt 1882; DL; *b* 1 Jan. 1925; *s* of 3rd Baron and Hon. Winifred Hamilton (*d* 1944), 4th *d* of 1st Baron Holm Patrick; *S* father, 1934; *m* 1st, 1956, Miriam Antoinette (marr. diss. 1973; she *d* 1975), 2nd *d* of A. W. F. Caccia-Birch, MC, of Guernsey Lodge, Marton, NZ; one *s* two *d*; 2nd, 1982, Mrs Lucy Temple-Richards (*née* Gough). *Educ:* Eton; Trinity Coll., Cambridge. DL Powys (formerly Brecknock), 1962. OStJ 1980. *Recreations:* shooting, fishing, rifle shooting. *Heir:* *s* Hon. Richard Anthony Hussey Vivian, *b* 24 Jan. 1957. *Address:* 16 Cheyne Gardens, SW3 5QT. *T:* 071–352 7455; Chapel House Cottage, Alltmawr, Builth Wells, Powys LD2 3LX. *T:* Erwood (0982) 560662. *Club:* Carlton.

SWANSEA and BRECON, Bishop of; since 1988; **Rt. Rev. Dewi Morris Bridges;** *b* 18 Nov. 1933; *s* of Harold Davies Bridges and Elsie Margaret Bridges; *m* 1959, Rhiannon Williams; one *s* one *d*. *Educ:* St David's University College, Lampeter (BA 1954, 1st cl. Hons History); Corpus Christi Coll., Cambridge (BA 1956 II 1, Pt 2 Theol. Tripos, MA 1960); Westcott House, Cambridge. Assistant Curate: Rhymney, Gwent, 1957–60; Chepstow, 1960–63; Vicar of St James', Tredegar, 1963–65; Lecturer and Senior Lectr, Summerfield Coll. of Education, Kidderminster, 1965–69; Vicar of Kempsey, Worcester, 1969–79; RD of Upton-upon-Severn, 1974–79; Rector of Tenby, Pembs, 1979–88; RD of Narberth, 1980–82; Archdeacon of St Davids, 1982–88. *Recreations:* walking, gardening, photography. *Address:* Ely Tower, Brecon, Powys, LD3 9DE. *T:* Brecon (0874) 2008.

SWANSON, Prof. Sydney Alan Vasey, FEng 1987; Professor of Biomechanics, Imperial College, University of London, since 1974; *b* 31 Oct. 1931; *s* of Charles Henry William Swanson and Hannah Elizabeth Swanson (*née* Vasey); *m* 1956, Mary Howarth; one *s* one *d*. *Educ:* Scarborough Boys' High Sch.; Imperial Coll., London. DSc (Eng), PhD, DIC,

FCGI, FIMechE. Engineering Laboratories, Bristol Aircraft Ltd, 1955–58; Imperial College, London: Lectr, Mechanical Engineering, 1958–69; Reader in Biomechanics, 1969–74; Dean, City and Guilds Coll., 1976–79; Head of Mechanical Engineering Dept, 1978–83; Pro Rector, 1983–86. FRSA. *Publications:* Engineering Dynamics, 1963; Engineering in Medicine (with B. M. Sayers and B. Watson), 1975; (with M. A. R. Freeman) The Scientific Basis of Joint Replacement, 1977; papers on bone, cartilage and joints in learned jls. *Recreations:* photography, fell-walking. *Address:* Mechanical Engineering Department, Imperial College, SW7 2BX. *T:* 071–589 5111. *Club:* Lyke Wake (Northallerton).

SWANTON, Ernest William, OBE 1965; author; Cricket and Rugby football Correspondent to the Daily Telegraph, retired 1975; BBC Commentator, 1934–75; *b* 11 Feb. 1907; *s* of late William Swanton; *m* 1958, Ann, *d* of late R. H. de Montmorency and *widow* of G. H. Carbutt. *Educ:* Cranleigh. Evening Standard, 1927–39. Played Cricket for Middlesex, 1937–38. Served 1939–46; captured at Singapore, 1942; POW Siam, 1942–45; Actg Maj. Bedfordshire Yeomanry (RA). Joined Daily Telegraph staff, 1946. Covered 20 Test tours to Australia, W Indies, S Africa, New Zealand and India; managed own XI to West Indies, 1956 and 1961 and to Malaya and Far East, 1964. Pres., The Cricketer, 1988– (Editorial Director, 1967–88). Hon. Life Vice-Pres., MCC, 1989 (Mem. Cttee, 1975–84). Mem. Cttee, Kent CCC, 1971–91 (Pres., 1981); President: Cricket Soc., 1976–83; Forty Club, 1983–86. *Publications:* (with H. S. Altham) A History of Cricket, 1938, 4th edn 1962; Denis Compton, A Cricket Sketch, 1948; Elusive Victory, 1951; Cricket and The Clock, 1952; Best Cricket Stories, 1953; West Indian Adventure, 1954; Victory in Australia, 1954/5, 1955; Report from South Africa, 1957; West Indies Revisited, 1960; The Ashes in Suspense, 1963; Cricket from all Angles, 1968; Sort of a Cricket Person (memoirs), 1972; Swanton in Australia, 1975; Follow On (memoirs), 1977; As I Said at the Time: a lifetime of cricket, 1983; Gubby Allen: Man of Cricket, 1985; (with C. H. Taylor) Kent Cricket: a photographic history 1744–1984, 1985; Back Page Cricket, 1987; The Essential E. W. Swanton (anthol.), 1990; General Editor, The World of Cricket, 1966, revised as Barclays World of Cricket, 1980, 3rd edn 1986. *Recreations:* cricket, golf. *Address:* Delf House, Sandwich, Kent CT13 9HB. *Clubs:* Naval and Military, MCC; Vincent's (Oxford); Royal St George's Golf.

SWANWICK, Sir Graham Russell, Kt 1966; MBE 1944; Judge of the High Court of Justice (Queen's Bench Division), 1966–80; Presiding Judge, Midland and Oxford Circuit, 1975–78; *b* 24 August 1906; *s* of Eric Drayton Swanwick and Margery Eleanor (*née* Norton), Whittington House, Chesterfield; *m* 1st, 1933, Helen Barbara Reid (marr. diss., 1945; she *d* 1970); two *s*; 2nd, 1952, Audrey Celia Parkinson (*d* 1987). *Educ:* Winchester Coll.; University Coll., Oxford (BA). Called to Bar, Inner Temple, 1930, Master of the Bench, 1962; QC 1956; Leader Midland Circuit, 1961–65. Wing Comdr RAFVR, 1940–45 (MBE, despatches). Recorder: City of Lincoln, 1957–59; City of Leicester, 1959–66; Judge of Appeal, Channel Islands, 1964–66; Derbyshire QS: Chm., 1963–66; Dep. Chm., 1966–71. *Recreation:* country pursuits. *Address:* Burnett's Ashurst, Steyning, West Sussex BN44 3AY. *T:* Partridge Green (0403) 710241. *Club:* Royal Air Force.

SWARBRICK, Prof. James, PhD, DSc; FRSC, CChem; Professor of Pharmaceutics and Chairman, Division of Pharmaceutics, University of North Carolina, since 1981; *b* 8 May 1934; *s* of George Winston Swarbrick and Edith M. C. Cooper; *m* 1960, Pamela Margaret Oliver. *Educ:* Sloane Grammar Sch.; Chelsea Coll., Univ. of London (BPharm Hons 1960; PhD 1964; DSc 1972). MPS 1961; FRIC 1970; FPS 1978. Asst Lectr, 1962, Lectr, 1964, Chelsea Coll.; Vis. Asst Prof., Purdue Univ., 1964; Associate Prof., 1966, Prof. and Chm. of Dept of Pharmaceutics, 1969, Asst Dean, 1970, Univ. of Conn; Dir of Product Develt, Sterling-Winthrop Res. Inst., NY, 1972; first Prof. of Pharmaceutics, Univ. of Sydney, 1975–76; Dean, Sch. of Pharmacy, Univ. of London, 1976–78; Prof. of Pharmacy and Chm., Res. Council, Univ. of S California, Los Angeles, 1978–81. Vis. Scientist, Astra Labs, Sweden, 1971; Vis. Prof., Shanghai Med. Univ., 1991–June 1992. Indust. Cons., 1965–72, 1975–; Cons., Aust. Dept. of Health, 1975–76; Mem., Cttee on Specifications, National Formulary, 1970–75; Chm., Jt US Pharmacopoeia-Nat. Formulary Panel on Disintegration and Dissolution Testing, 1971–75. Member: Cttee on Grad. Programs, Amer. Assoc. of Colls of Pharmacy, 1969–71; Practice Trng Cttee, Pharm. Soc. of NSW, 1975–76; Academic Bd, Univ. of Sydney, 1975–76; Collegiate Council, 1976–78; Educn Cttee, Pharmaceutical Soc. of GB, 1976–78; Working Party on Pre-Registration Training, 1977–78. Pharmaceutical Manufacturers Assoc. Foundation: Mem., Basic Pharmacology Adv. Cttee, 1982–; Chm., Pharmaceutics Adv. Cttee, 1986–; Mem., Scientific Adv. Cttee, 1986–. FAAAS 1966; Fellow: Acad. of Pharm. Sciences, 1973; Amer. Assoc. of Pharmaceutical Scientists, 1987. Kenan Res. Study Award, 1988. Mem. Editorial Board: Jl of Biopharmaceutics and Pharmacokinetics, 1973–79; Drug Development Communications, 1974–82; Pharmaceutical Technology, 1978–; Biopharmaceutics and Drug Disposition, 1979–; series Editor, Current Concepts in the Pharmaceutical Sciences, Drugs and the Pharmaceutical Sciences. *Publications:* (with A. N. Martin and A. Cammarata) Physical Pharmacy, 2nd edn 1969, 3rd edn 1983; (ed jtly) Encyclopedia of Pharmaceutical Technology; contributed: American Pharmacy, 6th edn 1966 and 7th edn 1974; Remington's Pharmaceutical Sciences, 14th edn 1970 to 18th edn 1990; contrib. Current Concepts in the Pharmaceutical Sciences: Biopharmaceutics, 1970; res. contribs to internat. sci. jls. *Recreation:* woodworking, listening to music, golf. *Address:* School of Pharmacy, University of North Carolina at Chapel Hill, CB #7360, Chapel Hill, NC 27599–7360, USA. *T:* (919) 962–0092.

SWARTZ, Rt. Rev. George Alfred; Bishop of Kimberley and Kuruman, 1983–91; *b* 8 Sept. 1928; *s* of Philip and Julia Swartz; *m* 1957, Sylvia Agatha (*née* George); one *s* one *d*. *Educ:* Umbilo Road High Sch., Durban; Univ. of the Witwatersrand, Johannesburg; Coll. of the Resurrection, Mirfield, Yorks; St Augustine's Coll., Canterbury. BA, Primary Lower Teacher's Cert., Central Coll. Dip. (Canterbury). Asst Teacher, Sydenham Primary Sch., 1951–52; Deacon, 1954; Priest, 1955; Asst Curate, St Paul's Church, Cape Town, 1955–56; Priest in Charge, Parochial Dist of St Helena Bay, Cape, 1957–60; St Augustine's Coll., Canterbury, 1960–61; Dir, Cape Town Dio. Mission to Muslims, 1962–63; Dir, Mission to Muslims and Rector St Philip's Church, Cape Town, 1963–70; Regional Dean of Woodstock Deanery, 1966–70; Priest in Charge, Church of the Resurrection, Bonteheuwel, Cape, 1971–72; a Bishop Suffragan of Cape Town, 1972–83; Canon of St George's Cathedral, Cape Town, 1969–72. Dean of the Province, Church of the Province of Southern Africa, 1986–89. *Recreations:* cinema, music (traditional jazz; instruments played are guitar and saxophone). *Address:* 11 Tanglin, Thomas Road, Kenilworth, Cape Town, 7700, Republic of South Africa. *T:* (021) 79–79079.

SWARTZ, Col Hon. Sir Reginald (William Colin), KBE 1972 (MBE (mil.) 1948); ED; FAIM, FBIM; retired parliamentarian and company director (director of nine companies, 1973–83); *b* 14 April 1911; *s* of late J. Swartz, Toowoomba, Qld; *m* 1936, Hilda, *d* of late G. C. Robinson; two *s* one *d*. *Educ:* Toowoomba and Brisbane Grammar Schs. Commonwealth Military Forces, 1928–40, Lieut, 1934. Served War of 1939–45: Captain 2–26 Bn, 8 Div., AIF, 1940; Malaya (PoW): Singapore, Malaya, Thailand (Burma-Thailand Rly); CMF, in Darling Downs Regt, Lt-Col, AQMG, CMF, N Comd, Col (RL), 1961. Hon. Col Australian Army Aviation Corps, 1969–75. MHR (L) Darling Downs, Qld, 1949–72; Parly Under-Sec. for Commerce and Agric., 1952–56; Parly Sec. for Trade, 1956–61; Minister: (of State) for Repatriation, Dec. 1961–Dec. 1964; for Health, 1964–66; for Social Services, 1965; for Civil Aviation, 1966–69; for Nat. Develt, 1969–72; Leader, House of Representatives, Canberra, 1971–72. Leader of many delegns overseas incl. Aust. Delegn to India, 1967, and Trade Mission to SE Asia, 1958; Parly Delegn to S and SE Asia, 1966. Patron and/or Vice-Pres. or Mem. of numerous public organizations. Life Chm. of Trustees, Australian Army Aviation Corps. Past Chm., Inst. of Dirs (Queensland). Member, RSL. JP Queensland, 1947–81. *Recreation:* bowls. *Address:* 39/110 King Street, Doncaster East, Victoria 3109, Australia. *Clubs:* United Service (Brisbane); Royal Automobile Club of Victoria; Australian (Melbourne); Twin Towns Services (Tweed Head); Darling Downs Aero; Probus (Doncaster) (Foundation Pres.); Templestowe Bowling (Melbourne).

SWARUP, Prof. Govind, PhD; FRS 1991; Professor of Eminence, since 1990, and Director, Giant Mehrewave Radio Telescope Project, since 1986, Tata Institute of Fundamental Research, Bombay; *b* 29 March 1929; *m* Bina Jain; one *s* one *d*. *Educ:* Allahabad Univ. (BSc 1948; MSc 1950); Stanford Univ., USA (PhD 1961). Sec., Radio Res. Cttee, CSIR, Nat. Physical Lab., New Delhi, 1950–53; Colombo-Plan Fellowship, CSIRO, Sydney, 1953–55; Res. Associate, Harvard Univ., 1956–57; Grad. Student, Stanford Univ., USA, 1957–60, Asst Prof. 1961–63; Tata Institute of Fundamental Research, Bombay: Reader, 1963–65; Associate Prof., 1965–70; Prof., 1970–79; Sen. Prof., 1979–90. Visiting Professor: Univ. of Md, USA, 1980; Univ. of Groningen, Netherlands, 1980–81; Univ. of Leiden, Netherlands, 1981. Chm., URSI, 1986–88; Mem., Exec. Cttee, Inter Union Commn for Frequency Allocation. Fellow: Indian Nat. Sci. Acad.; Indian Acad. Scis; Nat. Acad. Scis, India; Indian Geophysical Union. Associate, RAS; Member: Astronomical Soc. India (Pres., 1975–77); IAU; Indian Physics Assoc.; Indian Physical Soc. Member Editorial Board: Indian Jl Radio and Space Physics; Nat. Acad. of Science, India. Numerous awards, incl. Tskolovosky medal, Fedn of Cosmonautics, USSR. *Publications:* (ed jtly) Quasars, 1986; (ed jtly) History of Oriental Astronomy, 1987. *Address:* National Centre for Radio Astrophysics, Tata Institute of Fundamental Research, Poona University Campus, Post Bag 3, Ganeshkhind, Pune 411007, India. *T:* (office) 336111; (home) 336100.

SWASH, Stanley Victor, MC 1917 and Bar 1918; *b* 29 February 1896; British; *s* of A. W. Swash, JP and Sylvia Swash; *m* 1924; *m* 1955, Jane Henderson. *Educ:* Llandovery College; St John's College, Oxford; Lincoln's Inn. Served European War, 1915–19, RFA. MA (Mathematics); short period in Ministry of Pensions; served Royal Navy as Lieut Inst., 1921–24; worked in Woolworth Company, 1924–55; Director, 1939, Chairman, 1951–55; retired 1955. Called to Bar, Lincoln's Inn, 1938. OC 57 County of London Home Guard Battalion, Lieut-Colonel, 1940–45. Chairman, Horticultural Marketing Advisory Council, 1958; Member Milk Marketing Board, 1957–63; Chm. BOAC/MEA Cttee of Enquiry, 1963–64. *Recreations:* swimming, bridge. *Address:* Park Avenue, St Andrews, Malta. *Club:* United Oxford & Cambridge University.

SWAYNE, Sir Ronald (Oliver Carless), Kt 1979; MC 1945; Director: National Freight Co., 1973–85 (Consortium since 1982); Banque Nationale de Paris Ltd, since 1981; Member, Monopolies and Mergers Commission, 1982–86; *b* 11 May 1918; *s* of Col O. R. Swayne, DSO, and Brenda (*née* Butler); *m* 1941, Charmian (*d* 1984), *d* of Major W. E. P. Cairnes, Bollingham, Herefordshire; one *s* one *d*. *Educ:* Bromsgrove Sch., Worcester; University Coll., Oxford, 1936–39 and 1945–46 (MA). Served with Herefordshire Regt, 1939–40, No 1 Commando, 1940–45 (MC). Joined Ocean Steam Ship Co., 1946; became partner of Alfred Holt & Co. and Man. Dir of Ocean Steam Ship Co., 1955. Dir, 1965, Dep. Chm., 1969, Chm., 1973–82, Man. Dir, 1978–82, Overseas Containers Ltd. Vice-Chm., British Shipping Fedn, 1967; President: Cttee des Assocs d'Armateurs of EEC, 1974–75; Gen. Council of British Shipping, 1978–79; Inst. of Freight Forwarders, 1980. Industrial Adviser, Churchill Coll., Cambridge, 1974–82; Member: Design Council, 1975–78; Careers Res. Adv. Council, 1975–82; New Philharmonia Trust, 1968–82; Dir, ENO, 1980–86; Vice-Pres., British Maritime League, 1982–84. *Recreations:* fishing, shooting, music. *Address:* Puddle House, Chicksgrove, Tisbury, Salisbury SP3 6NA. *T:* Teffont (072276) 454; 32 Edith Road, W14. *T:* 071–602 4103. *Clubs:* Flyfishers'; Houghton (Stockbridge).

SWAYTHLING, 4th Baron, *cr* 1907; **David Charles Samuel Montagu;** Bt *cr* 1984; Chairman, Rothmans International PLC, since 1988; *b* 6 Aug. 1928; *e s* of 3rd Baron Swaythling, OBE, and Mary Violet, *e d* of Major Levy, DSO; *S* father, 1990; *m* 1951, Christiane Françoise (Ninette), *d* of Edgar Dreyfus, Paris; one *s* one *d* (and one *d* decd). *Educ:* Trinity Coll., Cambridge. Exec. Dir, 1954, Chm., 1970–73, Samuel Montagu & Co. Ltd; Chm. and Chief Exec., Orion Bank, 1974–79; Chm., Ailsa Investment Trust plc, 1981–88; Director: J. Rothschild Holdings PLC, 1983–89; The Daily Telegraph PLC, 1985–. *Recreations:* shooting, racing, theatre. *Heir: s* Hon. Charles Edgar Samuel Montagu, *b* 20 Feb. 1954. *Address:* 14 Craven Hill Mews, Devonshire Terrace, W2 3DY. *T:* 071–724 7860; (office) 15 Hill Street, W1X 7FB. *T:* 071–491 4366. *Clubs:* White's, Portland, Pratt's; Knickerbocker (New York).

SWAYTHLING, Jean Marcia, (The Dowager Lady Swaythling), CBE 1943; Chief Controller and Director, Auxilliary Territorial Service, 1941–43 (as Mrs Jean Knox); *b* 14 Aug. 1908; *m* Squadron Leader G. R. M. Knox; one *d*; *m* 1945, 3rd Baron Swaythling, OBE (*d* 1990). *Address:* Terwick Hill House, Rogate, Petersfield, Hants GU31 5EH. *T:* Rogate (0730) 821279.

SWEANEY, William Douglas, CMG 1965; retired 1972, as Establishment Officer, Overseas Development Administration, Foreign and Commonwealth Office; *b* 12 Nov. 1912; *s* of late Lt-Comdr William Sweaney, MBE, RN, and late Elizabeth Bridson; *m* 1939, Dorothy Beatrice Parsons; one *s*. *Educ:* Gillingham County Sch.; London Sch. of Economics. BSc(Econ). Clerical Officer, Inland Revenue (Special Comrs of Income Tax), 1929; Officer of Customs and Excise, 1932; seconded to Colonial Office, 1943 (promoted Surveyor of Customs and Excise *in absentia*); transferred to Colonial Office, 1948; Principal, 1948; Private Sec. to Minister of State for Colonial Affairs, 1953; Asst Sec., 1955; Dept of Technical Co-operation, 1961; ODM, later ODA, FCO, 1964–72; Establishment Officer, 1965. Panel of Chairmen, Agricl Dwelling House Adv. Cttees, 1977–86. *Recreations:* travel, ornithology. *Address:* 1 Beech Hurst Close, Haywards Heath, West Sussex RH16 4AE. *T:* Haywards Heath (0444) 450341.

SWEENEY, Thomas Kevin; Senior Medical Officer, Department of Health and Social Security, 1983–88, retired; *b* 10 Aug. 1923; *s* of John Francis and Mildred Sweeney; *m* 1950, Eveleen Moira Ryan; two *s* two *d*. *Educ:* O'Connell Sch., Dublin; University Coll., Dublin (MB, BCh, BAO NUI; DTM&H London; TDD Wales). FFPHM (FFCM 1983). Principal Med. Officer, Colonial Medical Service, 1950–65, retd; Asst Sen. Med. Officer, Welsh Hosp. Bd, 1965–68; Department of Health and Social Security: Med. Officer, 1968–72; Sen. Med. Officer, 1972–79; SPMO, 1979–83. QHP 1984–87. *Publication:* contrib. BMJ. *Recreations:* gardening, golf, cathedrals. *Address:* Tresanton, Wych Hill Way, Woking, Surrey GU22 0AE. *T:* Woking (0483) 760404.

SWEET, Prof. Peter Alan, MA, PhD; FRAS; Regius Professor of Astronomy in the University of Glasgow, 1959–82; retired; *b* 15 May 1921; *s* of David Frank Sweet; *m* 1947, Myrtle Vera Parnell; two *s*. *Educ:* Kingsbury County Grammar School, London; Sidney Sussex College, Cambridge. Open Maj. Schol. in Maths, Sidney Sussex Coll., 1940–42, Wrangler, 1942, BA Cantab 1943. Junior Scientific Officer, Min. of Aircraft Prod., 1942–45; BA Scholar, at Sidney Sussex Coll., 1945–47; MA Cantab 1946; Mayhew Prizeman, 1946, PhD Cantab 1950. FRAS 1949. Lectr in Astronomy, Univ. of Glasgow, 1947–52; Lectr in Astronomy and Asst Director of the Observatory, Univ. of London, 1952–59; Dean, Faculty of Science, Univ. of Glasgow, 1973–75. Visiting Asst Professor of Astronomy, Univ. of California, Berkeley, 1957–58; Vis. Sen. Res. Fellow, NASA Inst. for Space Studies, NY, 1965–66. *Publications:* papers on Stellar Evolution, Cosmic Magnetism, and Solar Flares in Monthly Notices of Royal Astronomical Soc., etc. *Recreations:* music, gardening. *Address:* 17 Westbourne Crescent, Glasgow G61 4HB. *T:* 041–942 4425.

SWEETING, William Hart, CMG 1969; CBE 1961; Chairman, Board of Directors, Bank of London and Montreal, 1970–79; *b* 18 Dec. 1909; *s* of late Charles Cecil Sweeting, Nassau, Bahamas; *m* 1950, Isabel Jean (*née* Woodall). *Educ:* Queen's Coll., Nassau; London Univ. Entered Bahamas Public Service as Cadet, 1927; served in Colonial Secretary's Office, 1927–37; acted as Asst Colonial Sec. for short periods in 1928 and 1936; transferred to Treasury, 1937; Cashier, Public Treasury, 1941; Asst Treasurer and Receiver of Crown Dues, 1946; seconded as Financial Sec., Dominica, 1950–52; Receiver-Gen. and Treasurer, Bahamas, 1955; MLC, Bahamas, 1960–64; Chairman: Bahamas Currency Comrs, 1955–63; Bahamas Broadcasting and Television Commn, 1957–62; Bahamas Public Disclosure Commn, 1978–84. Acted as Governor various periods 1959, 1964, 1965, 1966, 1968, 1969; acted as Colonial Secretary various periods, 1962–63; Chief Secretary, Bahamas 1964; Dep. Governor, Bahamas, 1969, retired 1970. Member: Bahamas Music Soc.; Elder, St Andrew's Presbyterian Church; Trinity Coll. of Music Local Exams Cttee, 1961–86; United World Colleges Local Cttee, 1970–87. *Recreations:* swimming, painting, music, bird watching. *Address:* PO Box N 573, Nassau, Bahamas. *T:* 39–31518. *Club:* Corona.

SWEETMAN, Jennifer Joan, (Mrs Ronald Andrew); *see* Dickson, J. J.

SWEETMAN, John Francis, CB 1991; TD 1964; Clerk of Committees of the House of Commons, since 1990; *b* 31 Oct. 1930; *s* of late Thomas Nelson Sweetman and Mary Monica (*née* D'Arcy-Reddy); *m* 1st, 1959, Susan Margaret Manley; one *s* one *d*; 2nd, 1983, Celia Elizabeth, *yr d* of Sir William Nield, *qv*; two *s*. *Educ:* Cardinal Vaughan Sch.; St Catharine's Coll., Cambridge (MA Law). Served RA, Gibraltar, 1949–51; TA (City of London RA) and AER, 1951–65. A Clerk, House of Commons, 1954–: Second Clerk of Select Cttees, 1979–83; Clerk of the Overseas Office, 1983–87; Clerk Asst of H of C, 1987–90. Mem., Oxford and Cambridge Catholic Educn Bd, 1964–84. *Publications:* contrib. to: Erskine May's Parliamentary Practice; Halsbury's Laws of England, 4th edn; Council of Europe, Procedure and Practice of the Parliamentary Assembly, 9th edn 1990. *Address:* House of Commons, SW1A 0AA. *T:* 071–219 3313. *Club:* MCC.

SWEETNAM, (David) Rodney, CBE 1990; MA; FRCS; Orthopaedic Surgeon to the Queen, since 1982; Consultant Surgeon to: The Middlesex Hospital, since 1960; King Edward VII Hospital for Officers, London, since 1964; *b* 5 Feb. 1927; second *s* of late Dr William Sweetnam and Irene (*née* Black); *m* 1959, Patricia Ann, *er d* of late A. Staveley Gough, OBE, FRCS; one *s* one *d*. *Educ:* Clayesmore; Peterhouse, Cambridge (Titular Scholar; BA 1947, MA 1951); Middlesex Hosp. Med. Sch. (MB, BChir 1950). FRCS 1955. Surg. Lieut RNVR, 1950–52. Jun. appts, Mddx Hosp., London Hosp. and Royal National Orthopaedic Hosp. Hon. Civil Consultant in Orth. Surgery to the Army, 1974–; Hon. Consultant Orthopaedic Surgeon, Royal Hosp., Chelsea, 1974–. Consultant Advisor in Orth. Surgery to DHSS, 1981–90; Hon. Consultant Surgeon, Royal Nat. Orthopaedic Hosp., 1983–. Dir, Medical Sickness Annuity and Life Assce Soc. Ltd, 1982–; Dir and Vice-Chm., Permanent Insurance Co., 1989–. Chairman: DHSS Adv. Gp on Orthopaedic Implants, 1973–81; MRC's Working Party on Bone Sarcoma, 1980–85. Member: Council, RCS, 1985–; Exec. Cttee, Arthritis and Rheumatism Council, 1985–. Royal College of Surgeons: Jacksonian Prize, 1966; Hunterian Prof., 1967; Gordon Taylor Meml Lectr, 1982; Stanford Cade Meml Lectr, 1986. President: Combined Services Orthopaedic Soc., 1983–86; British Orthopaedic Assoc., 1984–85. Mem. Res. Adv. Cttee, Royal Hosp. for Incurables, Putney, 1985–. Trustee: Develt Trust, Queen Elizabeth Foundn for the Disabled, 1984–; Smith & Nephew Charitable Trust 1988–. Dir (Sec. and Treas.), British Editorial Soc. of Bone and Joint Surgery, 1975–. *Publications:* (ed jtly) The Basis and Practice of Orthopaedics, 1980; contrib. med. books and jls in field of gen. orth. surgery, trauma and bone tumours. *Recreation:* gardening. *Address:* 23 Wimpole Street, W1M 7AD. *T:* 071–580 5409.

SWEETT, Cyril, CEng, AIStructE; FRICS; FCIArb; Founder Partner, Cyril Sweett & Partners, Chartered Quantity Surveyors, 1928; *b* 7 April 1903; *s* of William Thomas Sweett; *m* 1931, Barbara Mary, *d* of late Henry Thomas Loft, Canterbury and London; one *d*. *Educ:* Whitgift Sch.; Coll. of Estate Management. Artists Rifles, TA, 1923–27. Army Service: RE, 1939–43, France, N Africa and Italy; demob. as Lt-Col. Member: Council, RICS, 1959–61, 1970–72; Management Cttee, Royal Instn of GB, 1962–65 (Vice-Pres., 1964–65); Cttee, London Library, 1973–86; Chm., Nat. Jt Consultative Cttee of Architects, Quantity Surveyors and Builders, 1962–63. Master, Worshipful Co. of Painter Stainers, 1964–65, 1966–67; Sheriff of City of London, 1965–66. Jordanian Star, 1966; Silver Star of Honour, Austria, 1966. *Address:* 14 Princes Crescent, Hove, East Sussex BN3 4GS. *T:* Brighton (0273) 777292. *Clubs:* Garrick, MCC; Royal Thames Yacht, Royal Burnham Yacht (Cdre, 1963–65).

SWIFT, John Anthony; QC 1981; *b* 11 July 1940; *s* of late Jack Swift and Clare Medcalf; *m* 1972, Jane Carol Sharples; one *s* one *d*. *Educ:* Birkenhead Sch.; University Coll., Oxford (MA); Johns Hopkins Univ.; Bologna. Called to the Bar, Inner Temple, 1965. *Address:* Wittenham House, Little Wittenham, Abingdon, Oxon OX14 4RA.

SWIFT, Lionel, QC 1975; JD; Barrister, since 1961; a Recorder of the Crown Court, since 1979; *b* Bristol, 3 Oct. 1931; *s* of late Harris and of Bessie Swift, Hampstead; *m* 1966, Elizabeth (*née* Herzig) (Liz E, London fashion writer); one *d*. *Educ:* Whittingehame Coll., Brighton; University Coll., London (LLB 1951); Brasenose Coll., Oxford (BCL 1959); Univ. of Chicago (Juris Doc, 1960). Solicitor, Natal, S Africa, 1954; called to the Bar, Inner Temple, 1959, Bencher, 1984. British Commonwealth Fellow, Univ. of Chicago Law Sch., 1960; Amer. Social Science Res. Council Grant for work on admin of criminal justice, 1960. Jun. Counsel to Treasury in Probate Matters, 1974. Chm., Inst. of Laryngology and Otology, 1985–86. *Publication:* The South African Law of Criminal Procedure (Gen. Editor, A. B. Harcourt, QC), 1957. *Address:* (chambers) 4 Paper Buildings, Temple, EC4Y 7EX.

SWIFT, Malcolm Robin; QC 1988; a Recorder, since 1987; *b* 19 Jan. 1948; *s* of Willie Swift and Heather May Farquhar Swift, OBE (*née* Nield); *m* 1969, Anne Rachael (*née* Ayre); one *s* two *d*. *Educ:* Colne Valley High Sch., Yorks; King's Coll. London (LLB, AKC). Called to the Bar, Gray's Inn, 1970. Co-opted Mem., Remuneration Cttee of Bar Council, 1978–89 (rep. NE Circuit). *Recreations:* squash, music ("Count One and the t.i.cs"), theatre, cycling, re-cycling, DIY. *Address:* Park Court Chambers, Park Cross Street, Leeds LS1 2QH. *T:* Leeds (0532) 433277.

SWIFT, Michael Charles, MC 1943; Member, Economic and Social Committee of the European Communities, 1983–86; Secretary-General, British Bankers' Association, 1978–82; *b* 29 Aug. 1921; *s* of late Comdr C. C. Swift, OBE, RN; *m* 1957, Dorothy Jill, *d* of late R. G. Bundey; one *s* one *d*. *Educ:* Radley College. Served War, Royal Artillery (Captain), 1940–45. Bank of England, 1946–58; Committee of London Clearing Bankers, 1958–75; Dep. Sec., British Bankers' Assoc., 1975–78. UK Rep., European Communities Banking Fedn Central Cttee, 1978–82, Chm. 1980–82. Gen. Comr for City of London, 1982–87. *Recreations:* golf, birdwatching. *Club:* Royal West Norfolk Golf.

SWIFT, Reginald Stanley, CB 1969; Under-Secretary, Ministry of Social Security, 1962–68, Department of Health and Social Security, 1968–76, retired; *b* 2 Nov. 1914; *e s* of Stanley John and Annie Swift; *m* 1940, Mildred Joan Easter; no *c*. *Educ:* Watford Grammar School; Christ's College, Cambridge. BA Cantab (1st Cl. Hons in Classics) 1936; MA Cantab 1940; BSc (Econ.) London 1944. Entered Civil Service as Asst Comr, National Savings Cttee, 1938; transferred to Min. of National Insurance as Principal, 1947; Principal Private Secretary to Minister, 1953–54; Assistant Secretary, 1954; Under-Secretary, 1962. *Recreations:* gardening, golf. *Address:* 16 Beechfield, Banstead, Surrey SM7 3RG. *T:* Burgh Heath (0737) 361773. *Club:* Kingswood Golf.

SWINBURN, Lt-Gen. Sir Richard (Hull), KCB 1991; General Officer Commanding South East District, since 1990; *b* 30 Oct. 1937; *s* of late Maj.-Gen. H. R. Swinburn, CB, OBE, MC and of Naomi Barbara Swinburn, *d* of late Maj.-Gen. Sir Amyatt Hull, KCB, and *sister* of Field Marshal Sir Richard Hull, KG, GCB, DSO; *m* 1964, Jane Elise Brodie, *d* of late Antony Douglas Brodie and of Juliane (*née* Falk). *Educ:* Wellington Coll.; RMA Sandhurst. Commnd 17th/21st Lancers, 1957; Adjt, Sherwood Rangers Yeomanry and 17th/21st Lancers, 1963–65; sc 1968–69; MA to VCGS, 1971–72; Instructor, Staff Coll., 1975–76; MA to COS AFCENT, 1976–78; Comdr 17th/21st Lancers, UK and BAOR, 1979–81; Col ASD 2, MoD, Falklands Campaign, 1982; Comdr, 7th Armoured Bde, BAOR, 1983–84; rcds 1985; Dir Army Plans, 1986–87; GOC 1st Armoured Div., BAOR, 1987–89; ACGS, MoD, 1989–90. Mem. Council, RUSI, 1991–. Huntsman: RMA Sandhurst Beagles, 1956–57; Dhekelia Draghounds, Cyprus, 1971; (and Master) Staff Coll. Draghounds, 1975–76; Chm., Army Beagling Assoc., 1988. *Recreations:* hunting, country pursuits, lurchers. *Clubs:* Cavalry and Guards; Hampshire Hunt.

SWINBURNE, Hon. Ivan Archie, CMG 1973; Member of Legislative Council of Victoria, Australia, 1946–76, retired; *b* 6 March 1908; *s* of George Arthur and Hilda Maud Swinburne; *m* 1950, Isabella Mary, *d* of James Alexander Moore; one *d*. *Educ:* Hurdle Creek West and Milawa State Schs; Wangaratta and Essendon High Schs. MLC, for NE Prov., 1946–76; Dep. Leader of Country Party, 1954–69; Leader of Country Party in Legislative Council, 1969–76; Minister of Housing and Materials, 1950–52; Mem., Subordinate Legislation Cttee, 1961–67 and 1973. Councillor, Shire of Bright, 1940–47 (Pres., 1943–44). Mem., Bush Nursing Council of Victoria, 1948–84; Chm. Cttee of Management, Mount Buffalo National Park, 1963–84. *Recreation:* football administration. *Address:* PO Box 340, Myrtle Street, Myrtleford, Victoria 3737, Australia. *T:* 057 521167. *Clubs:* RACV (Melbourne); Wangaratta (Wangaratta).

SWINBURNE, Nora; actress; retired from stage and films, 1975; *b* Bath, 24 July 1902; *d* of H. Swinburne Johnson; *m* 1st, Francis Lister (marr. diss.); one *s*; 2nd, Edward Ashley-Cooper (marr. diss.); 3rd, 1946, Esmond Knight (*d* 1987). *Educ:* Rossholme College, Weston-super-Mare; Royal Academy of Dramatic Art. First West End appearance, 1916; went to America, 1923; returned to London stage, 1924; New York, again, 1930; continuous successes in London, from 1931; went into management, 1938, in addition to acting. Played as Diana Wentworth in The Years Between (which ran for more than a year), Wyndhams, 1945; Red Letter Day, Garrick; A Woman of No Importance, Savoy, 1953; The Lost Generation, Garrick, 1955; Fool's Paradise, Apollo, 1959; Music at Midnight, Westminster, 1962; All Good Children, Hampstead, 1964; Family Reunion, 1973, The Cocktail Party, 1975, Royal Exchange, Manchester. *Films include:* Jassy, Good Time Girl, The Blind Goddess, Fanny by Gaslight, They Knew Mr Knight, Quartet, Christopher Columbus, My Daughter Joy, The River (made in India), Quo Vadis, also Helen of Troy (made in Italy), Third Man on the Mountain, Conspiracy of Hearts, Music at Midnight, Interlude, Anne of the Thousand Days. Has appeared on television (incl. Forsyte Saga, Post Mortem, Kate serial, Fall of Eagles). *Address:* 52 Cranmer Court, SW3.

SWINBURNE, Prof. Richard Granville; Nolloth Professor of Philosophy of Christian Religion, University of Oxford, since 1985; *b* 26 Dec. 1934; *s* of William Henry Swinburne and Gladys Edith Swinburne (*née* Parker); *m* 1960, Monica Holmstrom; two *d*. *Educ:* Exeter College, Oxford (Scholar). BPhil 1959, MA 1961, DipTheol 1960. Fereday Fellow, St John's Coll., Oxford, 1958–61; Leverhulme Res. Fellow in Hist. and Phil. of Science, Univ. of Leeds, 1961–63; Lectr in Philosophy, then Sen. Lectr, Univ. of Hull, 1963–72; Prof. of Philosophy, Univ. of Keele, 1972–84. Vis. Associate Prof. of Philosophy, Univ. of Maryland, 1969–70; Vis. Prof. of Philosophy, Syracuse Univ., 1987; Lectures: Wilde, Oxford Univ., 1975–78; Forwood, Liverpool Univ., 1977; Marrett Meml, Exeter Coll., Oxford, 1980; Gifford, Univ. of Aberdeen, 1982–84; Edward Cadbury, Univ. of Birmingham, 1987; Dist. Vis. Scholar, Univ. of Adelaide, 1982. *Publications:* Space and Time, 1968, 2nd edn 1981; The Concept of Miracle, 1971; An Introduction to Confirmation Theory, 1973; The Coherence of Theism, 1977; The Existence of God, 1979; Faith and Reason, 1981; (with S. Shoemaker) Personal Identity, 1984; The Evolution of the Soul, 1986; Responsibility and Atonement, 1989; Revelation, 1992; articles and reviews in learned jls. *Address:* Oriel College, Oxford OX1 4EW. *T:* Oxford (0865) 276589.

SWINBURNE, Dr Terence Reginald; Senior Research Fellow, Wye College, London University; *b* 17 July 1936; *s* of Reginald and Gladys Swinburne; *m* 1958, Valerie Parkes; two *s*. *Educ:* Imperial Coll., Univ. of London (DSc, ARCS, DIC, PhD); FIHort. Plant Pathology Res. Div., Min., later Dept, of Agriculture for NI, 1960–80; Scientific Officer, 1960–62; Sen. Scientific Officer, 1962–71; PSO, 1971–79; SPSO, 1979–80; Queen's University, Belfast: Asst Lectr, Faculty of Agriculture, 1961–64; Lectr, 1965–77; Reader, 1977–80; Head of Crop Protection Div., E Malling Res. Stn, 1980–85; Dir, Inst. of Hortl Res., AFRC, 1985–90. Kellogg Fellow, Oregon State Univ., 1964–65; Vis. Prof., Dept of Pure and Applied Biology, Imperial Coll., London, 1986–. *Publication:* Iron Siderophores and Plant Diseases, 1986. *Recreation:* sailing. *Address:* Tan House, 15 Frog Lane, West Malling, Kent ME19 6LN. *T:* West Malling (0732) 846090. *Club:* Farmers'.

SWINDELLS, Maj.-Gen. (George) Michael (Geoffrey), CB 1985; Controller, Army Benevolent Fund, since 1987; *b* 15 Jan. 1930; *s* of late George Martyn Swindells and Marjorie Swindells; *m* 1955, Prudence Bridget Barbara Tully; one *s* two *d*. *Educ:* Rugby School. Nat. Service Commission, 5th Royal Inniskilling Dragoon Guards, 1949; served in Germany, Korea and Canal Zone; Adjutant, Cheshire Yeomanry, 1955–56; Staff Coll., 1960; transfer to 9th/12th Royal Lancers, to command, 1969–71; Comdr 11th Armd Brigade, 1975–76; RCDS course, 1977; Dir of Op. Requirements (3), MoD, 1978–79;

Chief of Jt Services Liaison Organisation, Bonn, 1980–83; Dir of Management and Support of Intelligence, 1983–85. Chairman: Royal Soldiers' Daughters Sch., 1985–89; BLESMA, 1991–. *Recreations:* country life, gardening. *Club:* Cavalry and Guards.

SWINDEN, (Thomas) Alan, CBE 1971; Executive Chairman, Institute of Manpower Studies, 1978–86; *b* 27 Aug. 1915; *s* of Thomas and Ethel Swinden; *m* 1941, Brenda Elise Roe; one *d. Educ:* Rydal Sch.; Sheffield Univ. (BEng). With Rolls-Royce, 1937–55; seconded to AFV Div., Min. of Supply, 1941–45; with Engrg Employers Fedn, 1955–65, Dir, 1964–65; Dir, Engrg Industry Trng Bd, 1965–70; Confederation of British Industry: Dep. Dir Gen. (Industrial Relations), 1970–74; Chief Advr, Social Affairs, 1974–78; Consultant, 1978–81; Chm., 1974–85, Dir, 1980–84, Kingston Regional Management Centre. Chm., Derby No 1 HMC, 1953–55. Council Member: British Employers Confedn, 1955–65; ACAS, 1974–84; British Assoc. for Commercial and Industrial Educn, 1982–; Inst. of Manpower Studies, 1986–; Mem., BBC Consultative Gp on Industrial and Business Affairs, 1977–83. *Address:* 85 College Road, Epsom, Surrey KT17 4HH. *T:* Epsom (0372) 720848. *Club:* Royal Automobile.

SWINDLEHURST, Rt. Rev. Owen Francis; Bishop Auxiliary of Hexham and Newcastle, (RC), since 1977; Titular Bishop of Chester-le-Street; *b* 10 May 1928; *s* of Francis and Ellen Swindlehurst. *Educ:* Ushaw College, Durham; English College, Rome. PhL, STL, LCL (Gregorian Univ., Rome). Assistant Priest: St Matthew's, Ponteland, 1959–67; St Bede's, Denton Burn, Newcastle, 1967–72; Parish Priest at Holy Name, Jesmond, Newcastle, 1967–77. *Recreations:* walking, geriatric squash, reading. *Address:* Oaklea, Tunstall Road, Sunderland SR2 7JR. *T:* Sunderland (091) 41158.

SWINDON, Archdeacon of; *see* Clark, Ven. K. J.

SWINFEN, 3rd Baron *cr* 1919; **Roger Mynors Swinfen Eady;** *b* 14 Dec. 1938; *s* of 2nd Baron Swinfen and of Mary Aline (*see* M. A. Siepmann); *S* father, 1977; *m* 1962, Patricia Anne, *o d* of late F. D. Blackmore, Dundrum, Dublin; one *s* three *d. Educ:* Westminster; RMA, Sandhurst. ARICS 1970. Mem., Direct Mail Services Standards Bd, 1983–. Chm., Parly Gp, Video Enquiry Working Party, 1983–85. Pres. SE Reg., British Sports Assoc. for the Disabled, 1986–. Fellow, Industry and Parlt Trust. *Heir: s* Hon. Charles Roger Peregrine Swinfen Eady, *b* 8 March 1971. *Address:* House of Lords, SW1A 0PW.

SWINGLAND, Owen Merlin Webb, QC 1974; Barrister-at-Law; *b* 26 Sept. 1919; *er s* of Charles and Maggie Eveline Swingland; *m* 1941, Kathleen Joan Eason (*née* Parry), Newport, Mon; one *s* two *d. Educ:* Haberdashers' Aske's Hatcham Sch.; King's Coll., London. LLB 1941, AKC. Called to Bar, Gray's Inn, 1946, Bencher, 1985; practice at Chancery Bar, 1948–88; Barrister of Lincoln's Inn, 1977. A Church Comr, 1982–90. Past Pres., British Insurance Law Assoc. Mem., Court of Assts, Haberdashers' Co. (Master, 1987–88); Freeman of the City of London. *Recreations:* music, theatre, fishing, reading; interested in competitive sports. *Address:* Redwings House, Bayleys Hill, Weald, Sevenoaks, Kent TN14 6HS. *T:* Sevenoaks (0732) 451667.

SWINGLER, Bryan Edwin, CBE 1979; British Council Representative in France, 1980–84, retired; *b* 20 Sept. 1924; *s* of late George Edwin Swingler, Birmingham, and Mary Eliza Frayne; *m* 1954, Herta, *er d* of late Edwin Jaeger, Schoenlinde; one *d. Educ:* King Edward's Sch., Birmingham; Peterhouse, Cambridge (Sen. Schol.); Charles Univ., Prague. BA 1948, MA 1953. Served War, Royal Navy (Leading Signalman), 1943–46. Apptd to British Council, 1949; Vienna, 1949–52; Lahore, 1952–55; Karachi, 1955–56; Oslo, 1956–59; Berlin, 1959–61; Cologne, 1961–63; Dir, Scholarships, 1963–67; Dep. Controller, Commonwealth Div., 1967–68; Rep. Indonesia, Djakarta, 1968–71; Controller Finance, 1972–73; Controller, Home, 1973–75; Asst Dir-Gen., 1975–77; Head of British Council Div., India, and Minister (Educn), British High Commn, New Delhi, 1977–80. Vice-Chm., British Council Staff Assoc., 1965–67; Member: British-Austrian Mixed Commn, 1973–77; British-French Mixed Commn, 1976–77, 1980–84. *Recreations:* music, painting, oriental ceramics, contemplating sailing. *Address:* 5 quai Commandant Mages, 34300 Agde, France. *T:* 67–94–46–21. *Club:* Travellers'.

SWINGLER, Raymond John Peter; Assistant Director, Press Complaints Commission, since 1991; *b* 8 Oct. 1933; *s* of Raymond Joseph and Mary Swingler; *m* 1960, Shirley (*d* 1980), *e d* of Frederick and Dorothy Wilkinson, Plymouth; two *d. Educ:* St Bede's Coll., Christchurch, NZ; Canterbury Univ. Journalist, The Press, Christchurch, NZ, 1956–57; Marlborough Express, 1957–59; Nelson Mail, 1959–61; freelance Middle East, 1961–62; Cambridge Evening News, 1962–79. Press Council: Mem., 1975–78; Mem., Complaints Cttee, 1976–78; Sec. and conciliator, 1980–91; Asst Dir, 1989–91. Member: Nat. Exec. Council, Nat. Union of Journalists, 1973–75, 1978–79; Provincial Newspapers Industrial Council, 1976–79; Chm., General Purposes Cttee (when journalists' Code of Professional Conduct (revised) introduced), 1974–75. *Recreations:* horses, and horsewomen. *Address:* 11A Church Path, E17 9QR.

SWINLEY, Margaret Albinia Joanna, OBE 1980; British Council Service, retired; *b* 30 Sept. 1935; *er* twin *d* of late Captain Casper Silas Balfour Swinley, DSO, DSC, RN and of Sylvia Jocosa Swinley, 4th *d* of late Canon W. H. Carnegie. *Educ:* Southover Manor Sch., Lewes; Edinburgh Univ. (MA Hons Hist.). English Teacher/Sec., United Paper Mills, Jämsänkoski, Finland, 1958–60; joined British Council, 1960; Birmingham Area Office, 1960–63; Tel Aviv, 1963; Lagos, 1963–66; seconded to London HQ of VSO, 1966–67; New Delhi, 1967–70; Dep. Rep., Lagos, 1970–73; Dir, Tech. Assistance Trng Dept, 1973–76; Rep., Israel, 1976–80; Asst, then Dep., Controller, Educn, Medicine and Science Div., 1980–82; Controller, Africa and Middle East Div., 1982–86; Controller, Home Div., 1986–89. Trustee, Lloyd Foundn; Mem., Internat. Cttee and Adviser on Overseas Projects, Help the Aged; Mem., Council of Govs, Internat. Students' House, London; Governor: Westbury-on-Severn C of E Primary Sch. (Chm., 1990–); Hosting for Overseas Students. *Recreations:* theatre-going, country life, keeping dogs and Shire horses. *Clubs:* Commonwealth Trust, Soroptimist International of Greater London (Pres., 1988–89).

SWINNERTON-DYER, Prof. Sir (Henry) Peter (Francis), 16th Bt *cr* 1678; KBE 1987; FRS 1967; Chief Executive, Universities Funding Council, 1989–91; *b* 2 Aug. 1927; *s* of Sir Leonard Schroeder Swinnerton Dyer, 15th Bt, and Barbara (*d* 1990), *d* of Hereward Brackenbury, CBE; *S* father, 1975; *m* 1983, Dr Harriet Crawford, *er d* of Rt Hon. Sir Patrick Browne, *qv. Educ:* Eton; Trinity College, Cambridge (Hon. Fellow 1981). University of Cambridge: Research Fellow, 1950–54, Fellow, 1955–73, Dean, 1963–73, Trinity Coll.; Master, St Catharine's Coll., 1973–83 (Hon. Fellow, 1983); Univ. Lectr, 1960–71 (at Mathematical Lab., 1960–67); Prof. of Maths, 1971–88; Vice-Chancellor, 1979–81. Commonwealth Fund Fellow, Univ. of Chicago, 1954–55. Vis. Prof., Harvard Univ., 1971. Hon. Fellow, Worcester Coll., Oxford, 1980. Chairman: Cttee on Academic Organisation, Univ. of London, 1980–82; Meteorological Cttee, 1983–; UGC, 1983–89. Hon. DSc Bath, 1981. *Publications:* numerous papers in mathematical journals. *Recreation:* gardening. *Heir: kinsman* Richard Dyer-Bennet [*b* 6 Oct. 1913; *m* 1st, 1936, Elizabeth Hoar Pepper (marr. diss. 1941); two *d*; 2nd, 1942, Melvene Ipcar; two *d*]. *Address:* The Dower House, Thriplow, Royston, Herts. *T:* Fowlmere (0763) 208220.

SWINSON, Christopher, FCA; National Managing Partner, BDO Binder Hamlyn, since 1989; *b* 27 Jan. 1948; *s* of Arthur Montagu Swinson and Jean Swinson; *m* 1972, Christine Margaret Hallam; one *s. Educ:* Wadham Coll., Oxford (MA). FCA 1979. Price Waterhouse, 1970–77; with Binder Hamlyn, 1979–. Mem. Bd, Museum Trng Inst., 1990–; Treasurer: Navy Records Soc., 1987–; Soc. for Nautical Res., 1991–. *Publications:* Companies Act 1989, 1990; Regulation of Auditors, 1990; Group Accounts, 1991. *Recreation:* model railway construction. *Address:* 2 Seymour Close, Hatch End, Pinner, Mddx HA5 4SB. *T:* 081–421 0951; (business) 071–489 6261. *Club:* Athenæum.

SWINSON, Sir John (Henry Alan), Kt 1984; OBE 1974; Commercial Director (Ireland), Trusthouse Forte plc, since 1965; *b* 12 July 1922; *s* of Edward Alexander Stanley Swinson and Mary Margaret McLeod; *m* 1944, Margaret Sturgeon Gallagher; two *s. Educ:* Royal Belfast Academical Institution. Founded J. H. A. Swinson and Co. Ltd, 1946; Man. Dir (also of associated cos), until 1959; merged with Lockhart Gp, 1959, which merged with Trust Houses (later Trusthouse Forte plc), 1965. Chairman: Catering Industry Training Board, 1966–75; NI Training Executive, 1975–83; Livestock Marketing Commn (NI), 1970–85; NI Tourist Bd, 1979–88 (Mem., 1970–88); Member: Council, NIHCA, 1961– (Past Pres.); Catering Wages Council, 1965–82; NI Economic Council, 1977–81; Industrial Forum for NI, 1980–83. *Recreation:* sailing. *Address:* 10 Circular Road East, Cultra, Co. Down BT18 0HA. *T:* (office) Belfast (0232) 612101; (home) Holywood (02317) 2494.

SWINTON, 2nd Earl of, *cr* 1955; **David Yarburgh Cunliffe-Lister,** JP; DL; Viscount Swinton, 1935; Baron Masham, 1955; Director, Leeds Permanent Building Society, since 1987; Member, Countyside Commission, since 1987; *b* 21 March 1937; *s* of Major Hon. John Yarburgh Cunliffe-Lister (*d* of wounds received in action, 1943) and Anne Irvine (*d* 1961), *yr d* of late Rev. Canon R. S. Medlicott (she *m* 2nd, 1944, Donald Chapple-Gill); *S* grandfather, 1972; *m* 1959, Susan Lilian Primrose Sinclair (*see* Baroness Masham of Ilton); one *s* one *d* (both adopted). *Educ:* Winchester; Royal Agricultural College. Member: N Riding Yorks CC, 1961–74; N Yorks CC, 1973–77. Captain of the Yeoman of the Guard (Dep. Govt Chief Whip), 1982–86. JP North (formerly NR) Yorks, 1971; DL North Yorks, 1978. *Heir: b* Hon. Nicholas John Cunliffe-Lister [*b* 4 Sept. 1939; *m* 1966, Hon. Elizabeth Susan, *e d* of Viscount Whitelaw, *qv*; two *s* one *d*]. *Address:* Dykes Hill House, Masham, N Yorks HG4 4NS. *T:* Ripon (0765) 689241; 46 Westminster Gardens, SW1. *T:* 071–834 0700. *Clubs:* White's, Pratt's; Leyburn Market (N Yorks).

SWINTON, Countess of; *see* Masham of Ilton, Baroness.

SWINTON, Maj.-Gen. Sir John, KCVO 1979; OBE 1969; JP; Lord-Lieutenant of Berwickshire, since 1989; *b* 21 April 1925; *s* of late Brig. A. H. C. Swinton, MC, Scots Guards; *m* 1954, Judith, *d* of late Harold Killen, Merribee, NSW; three *s* one *d. Educ:* Harrow. Enlisted, Scots Guards, 1943, commissioned, 1944; served NW Europe, 1945 (twice wounded); Malaya, 1948–51 (despatches); ADC to Field Marshal Sir William Slim, Governor-General of Australia, 1953–54; Staff College, 1957; DAA&QMG 1st Guards Brigade, 1958–59; Regimental Adjutant Scots Guards, 1960–62; Adjutant, RMA Sandhurst, 1962–64; comd 2nd Bn Scots Guards, 1966–68; AAG PS12 MoD, 1968–70; Lt Col Comdg Scots Guards, 1970–71; Comdr, 4th Guards Armoured Brigade, BAOR, 1972–73; RCDS 1974; Brigadier Lowlands and Comdr Edinburgh and Glasgow Garrisons, 1975–76; GOC London Dist and Maj.-Gen. Comdg Household Divn, 1976–79; retired 1979. Brigadier, Queen's Body Guard for Scotland (Royal Co. of Archers), 1977–; Hon. Col 2nd Bn 52nd Lowland Volunteers, 1983–90. Nat. Chm., Royal British Legion Scotland, 1986–89 (Nat. Vice-Chm., 1984–86); Trustee, Housing Assoc., 1989–); Mem. Council, British Commonwealth Ex-Services League, 1984–. Mem., Central Adv. Cttee on War Pensions, 1986–89. Trustee: Army Museums Ogilby Trust, 1978–90; Scottish Nat. War Meml, 1984– (Vice-Chm., 1987–); Chm., Thirlestane Castle Trust, 1984–90. Borders Liaison Officer, Duke of Edinburgh's Award Scheme, 1982–84. Chairman: Jt Management Cttee, St Abb's Head National Nature Reserve, 1991–. Berwicks Civic Soc., 1982–; Roxburgh and Berwickshire Cons. Assoc., 1983–85. DL, 1980–89, JP, 1989–, Berwickshire. *Address:* Kimmerghame, Duns, Berwickshire. *T:* Duns (0361) 83277.

SWIRE, Sir Adrian (Christopher), Kt 1982; DL; Chairman, John Swire and Sons Ltd, since 1987 (Director, 1961; Deputy Chairman, 1966–87); Director: Swire Pacific Ltd, Cathay Pacific Airways; *b* 15 Feb. 1932; *yr s* of late John Kidston Swire and Juliet Richenda, *d* of Theodore Barclay, Fanshaws, Hertford; *m* 1970, Lady Judith Compton, *e d* of 6th Marquess of Northampton, DSO; two *s* one *d. Educ:* Eton; University Coll., Oxford (MA). Coldstream Guards, 1950–52; RAFVR and Royal Hong Kong AAF (AE 1961). Joined Butterfield & Swire in Far East, 1956. Director: Brooke Bond Gp, 1972–82; NAAFI, 1972–87 (Dep. Chm., 1982–85); Chm., China Navigation Co. Ltd, 1968–88; Mem., London Adv. Cttee, Hongkong and Shanghai Banking Corp., 1990–. Mem., Gen. Cttee, Lloyd's Register, 1967–. Pres., General Council of British Shipping, 1980–81; Chm., Internat. Chamber of Shipping, 1982–87. Elder Brother, Trinity House, 1990. Vis. Fellow, Nuffield Coll., Oxford, 1981–89. Trustee, RAF Museum, 1983–. Hon. Air Cdre, No 1 (Co. Hertford) Maritime HQ Unit, RAuxAF, 1987–. Mem. Council, Wycombe Abbey Sch., 1988–. DL Oxon, 1989. *Address:* Swire House, 59 Buckingham Gate, SW1E 6AJ. *Clubs:* White's, Brooks's, Pratt's; Hong Kong (Hong Kong).
See also Sir J. A. Swire.

SWIRE, Sir John (Anthony), Kt 1990; CBE 1977; Hon. President, since 1987, and Director, since 1955, John Swire & Sons Ltd (Chairman, 1966–87); *b* 28 Feb. 1927; *er s* of late John Kidston Swire and Juliet Richenda, *d* of Theodore Barclay; *m* 1961, Moira Cecilia Ducharne; two *s* one *d. Educ:* Eton; University Coll., Oxford (MA). Served Irish Guards, UK and Palestine, 1945–48. Joined Butterfield & Swire, Hong Kong, 1950; Director: Swire Pacific Ltd, 1965–; Royal Insurance plc, 1975–80; British Bank of the Middle East, 1975–79; James Finlay plc, 1976–; Ocean Transport & Trading plc, 1977–83; Shell Transport and Trading Co., 1990–. Chairman: Hong Kong Assoc., 1975–87; Cook Soc., 1984. Member: London Adv. Cttee, Hongkong and Shanghai Banking Corp., 1969–89; Euro-Asia Centre Adv. Bd, 1980–91; Adv. Council, Sch. of Business, Stanford Univ., 1981–90; Council, Univ. of Kent, 1989–. Hon. Fellow: St Antony's Coll., Oxford, 1987; University Coll., Oxford, 1989. Hon. LLD Hong Kong Univ., 1989. *Address:* Swire House, 59 Buckingham Gate, SW1E 6AJ. *T:* 071–834 7717. *Clubs:* Brooks's, Pratt's, Cavalry and Guards, Flyfishers' (Pres., 1988–89); Union (Sydney); Hong Kong (Hong Kong).
See also Sir A. C. Swire.

SWISS, Sir Rodney (Geoffrey), Kt 1975; OBE 1964; JP; FDSRCS; President, General Dental Council, 1974–79 (Member, 1957–79); *b* 4 Aug. 1904; *e s* of Henry H. Swiss, Devonport, Devon, and Emma Jane Swiss (*née* Williams); *m* 1928, Muriel Alberta Gledhill (*d* 1985). *Educ:* Plymouth Coll.; Dean Close Sch., Cheltenham; Guy's Hosp. LDSRCS 1926, FDSRCS 1978. General dental practice, Harrow, Mddx, 1930–69 (Hon. dental surgeon, Harrow Hosp., 1935–67). NHS Mddx Exec. Council, 1947–74 (Chm., 1970–71); Chm., Visiting Cttee and Bd of Visitors, Wormwood Scrubs Prison, 1958–63; Mem., Central Health Services Council, 1964–74; Chairman: Standing Dental Advisory Cttee, 1964–74; Hendon Juvenile Court, 1959–64; Gore Petty Sessional Div., 1965–67 and 1970–74; Management Cttee, Sch. for Dental Auxiliaries, 1972–74. JP Mddx area, 1949. *Publications:* contribs to dental press. *Recreation:* philately. *Address:* Shrublands, 23 West Way, Pinner, Mddx HA5 3NX.

SWITZER, Barbara; Assistant General Secretary, Manufacturing Science Finance, since 1988; *b* 26 Nov. 1940; *d* of Albert and Edith McMinn; *m* 1973, John Michael Switzer. *Educ:* Chorlton Central Sch., Manchester; Stretford Technical Coll. City & Guilds Final Cert. for Electrical Technician. Engrg apprentice, Metropolitan Vickers, 1957–62; Draughtswoman: GEC, Trafford Park, 1962–70; Cableform, Romiley, 1970–71; Mather & Platt, 1972–76; Divisional Organiser 1976–79, National Organiser 1979–83, AUEW (TASS); Dep. Gen. Sec., TASS—The Manufacturing Union, 1983–87. Associate Mem., Women's Engineering Soc. TUC Women's Gold Badge for services to Trade Unionism, 1976. *Address:* 16 Follett Drive, Abbots Langley, Herts WD5 0LP. *T:* Garston (0923) 674662.

SWORD, John Howe; Director, Oral History Project, University of Toronto, 1981–90; a Vice-President, Associated Medical Services Inc., since 1984; *b* Saskatoon, Saskatchewan, 22 Jan. 1915; *m* 1947, Constance A. Offen; one *s* one *d*. *Educ:* public and high schs, Winnipeg; Univ. of Manitoba (BA); Univ. of Toronto (MA). Served War, RCAF, Aircrew navigation trg and instr in Western Canada. Taught for six years, before War, in Roland, Teulon and Winnipeg, Manitoba. Secretary, Manitoba Royal Commn on Adult Educn, 1945–46. Univ. of Toronto: Asst Sec. and Sec., Sch. of Grad. Studies, 1947–60; Exec. Asst to the President, 1960–65; Vice-Provost, 1965–67; Actg Pres., 1967–68; Exec. Vice-Pres. (Academic), and Provost, 1968–71; Actg Pres., 1971–72; Vice-Pres., Institutional Relations and Planning, 1972–74; Special Asst to the President, Institutional Relations, 1974–80, retired; Acting Dir, Sch. of Continuing Studies, 1980–81 and 1983–84. Chm., Art Cttee, 1980–83, Finance Cttee, 1983–88, Mem. Bd of Stewards, 1988–, Hart House, Univ. of Toronto; Chm., Certificate Review Adv. Cttee, Min. of Educn, 1984–; Member: Bd, Addiction Res. Foundn of Ont, 1981–88; Council, Royal Canadian Inst., Toronto, 1981–. Dir, Toronto Dist Heating Corp., 1983–87. Mem. Management Bd, Geneva Park YMCA, 1972–85; Trustee: Toronto Sch. of Theology, 1978–83; Wychwood Pk Heritage Conservation Dist, 1986–90. Mem., United Church. Hon. LLD: Univ. of Manitoba, 1970; Univ. of Toronto, 1988. Silver Jubilee Medal, 1977. *Recreations:* tennis, swimming. *Address:* 8 Wychwood Park, Toronto, Ontario M6G 2V5, Canada. *T:* 6565876. *Clubs:* Faculty (Univ. of Toronto); Arts and Letters, Queen's.

SWYER, Dr Gerald Isaac Macdonald, FRCP; Consultant Endocrinologist, Department of Obstetrics and Gynæcology, University College Hospital, London, 1951–78, retired; Councillor, London Borough of Camden, 1982–86; *b* 17 Nov. 1917; *s* of Nathan Swyer; *m* 1945, Lynda Irene (*née* Nash); one *s* one *d*. *Educ:* St Paul's School; Magdalen College and St John's College, Oxford; University of California; Middlesex Hospital Medical School. Foundation Schol. and Leaving Exhib., St Paul's School, 1931–36; Open Exhib. and Casberd Schol., St John's Coll., Oxford, 1936–39; Welsh Memorial Prize, 1937; Theodore Williams Schol. in Anatomy, 1938; 1st Cl. Final Honour School of Animal Physiology, 1939; Senior Demy, Magdalen Coll., 1940; Rockefeller Medical Student, Univ. of Calif, 1941. MA, DPhil, BM Oxon 1943; MD Calif, 1943; DM Oxon 1948; MRCP 1945; FRCP 1964; FRCOG *ad eundem* 1975. Mem. of Scientific Staff, Nat. Inst. for Med. Res., 1946–47; Endocrinologist, UCH Med. Sch., 1947. 1st Sec., formerly Chm., Soc. for the Study of Fertility; formerly Mem. Council, Soc. for Endocrinology (Hon. Mem.); formerly Pres., Sect. of Endocrinology, Roy. Soc. Med.; formerly Sec.-Gen., Internat. Fedn of Fertility Societies and Mem. Exec. Sub-Cttee Internat. Endocrine Soc. *Publications:* Reproduction and Sex, 1954; papers in medical and scientific journals. *Recreations:* golf, music, making things. *Address:* Flat 4, 71 Fitzjohn's Avenue, NW3 6PD. *T:* 071–435 4723.

SWYNNERTON, Sir Roger (John Massy), Kt 1976; CMG 1959; OBE 1951; MC 1941; former consultant in tropical agriculture and development; Director, Booker Agriculture International Ltd, 1976–88; *b* S Rhodesia, 16 Jan. 1911; *s* of late C. F. M. Swynnerton, CMG, formerly Dir, Tsetse Research, Tanganyika, and Mrs N. A. G. Swynnerton (*née* Watt Smyth); *m* Grizel Beryl Miller, *d* of late R. W. R. Miller, CMG, formerly Member for Agriculture and Natural Resources, Tanganyika; two *s*. *Educ:* Lancing Coll.; Gonville and Caius Coll., Cambridge (BA Hons 1932; DipAgric 1933); Imperial Coll. of Tropical Agriculture, Trinidad. AICTA 1934. O/c CUOTC Artillery Bty, 1932–33; TARO, 1933–60. Entered Colonial Agricultural Service as Agric. Officer and Sen. Agric. Officer, 1934–50, in Tanganyika Territory. Served War, 1939–42, with 1/6 Bn KAR (Temp. Capt. and Adjt, 1941–42); Abyssinian Campaign. Seconded to Malta on Agric. duty, 1942–43. Transferred to Kenya on promotion, Asst Director of Agric., 1951, Dep. Dir, 1954, Director, 1956. Nominated Member of Kenya Legislative Council, 1956–61; Permanent Sec., Min. of Agriculture, 1960–62; Temp. Minister for Agriculture, Animal Husbandry and Water Resources, 1961, retd 1963. Mem. Advisory Cttee on Development of Economic Resources of S Rhodesia, 1961–62; Agric. Adviser and Mem. Exec. Management Bd, Commonwealth Develt Corp., 1962–76. Vis. Lectr, 1977–, and Mem. Adv. Bd, Inst. of Irrigation Studies, 1980–88, Southampton Univ. President: Swinnerton Family Soc., 1982–; Tropical Agriculture Assoc., 1983–. *Publications:* All About KNCU Coffee, 1948; A Plan to Intensify the Development of African Agriculture in Kenya, 1954; various agricultural and scientific papers. *Address:* Cherry House, 2 Vincent Road, Stoke D'Abernon, Cobham, Surrey KT11 3JB. *Clubs:* Commonwealth Trust, Royal Over-Seas League.

SYDNEY, Archbishop of, and Metropolitan of New South Wales, since 1982; **Most Rev. Donald William Bradley Robinson,** AO 1984; *b* 9 Nov. 1922; *s* of Rev. Richard Bradley Robinson and Gertrude Marston Robinson (*née* Ross); *m* 1949, Marie Elizabeth Taubman; three *s* one *d*. *Educ:* Sydney Church of England Gram. Sch.; Univ. of Sydney (BA); Queens' Coll., Cambridge (MA). Australian Army, 1941–45, Lieut Intell. Corps, 1944. Deacon 1950, Sydney; priest 1951; Curate, Manly, NSW, 1950–52; St Philip's, Sydney, 1952–53; Lecturer: Moore Coll., 1952–81 (Vice-Principal, 1959–72); Sydney Univ., 1964–81; Asst Bishop, Diocese of Sydney (Bishop in Parramatta), 1973–82. Hon. ThD Aust. Coll. of Theology, 1979. *Address:* St Andrew's House, Sydney Square, NSW 2000, Australia. *T:* (02) 265 1555.

SYDNEY, Archbishop of, (RC), since 1983; **His Eminence Cardinal Edward Bede Clancy,** AO 1984; *b* 13 Dec. 1923; *s* of John Bede Clancy and Ellen Lucy Clancy (*née* Edwards). *Educ:* Marist Brothers Coll., Parramatta, NSW; St Patrick's Coll., Manly, NSW; Biblical Inst., Rome (LSS); Propaganda Fide Univ., Rome (DD). Ordained to priesthood, 1949; parish ministry, 1950–51; studies in Rome, 1952–54; parish ministry, 1955–57; seminary staff, 1958–61; studies in Rome, 1962–64; seminary staff, Manly, 1966–73; Auxiliary Bishop, Sydney, 1974–78; Archbishop of Canberra and Goulburn, 1979–82. Cardinal, 1988. *Publications:* The Bible—The Church's Book, 1974; contribs to Australian Catholic Record. *Recreation:* golf. *Address:* St Mary's Cathedral, Sydney, NSW 2000, Australia. *T:* 264–7211 (02).

SYDNEY, NORTH, Bishop of; *see* Barnett, Rt Rev. P. W.

SYDNEY, SOUTH, Bishop of; *see* Reid, Rt Rev. J. R.

SYDNEY, Assistant Bishops of; *see* Barnett, Rt Rev. P. W.; Cameron, Rt Rev. E. D.; Goodhew, Rt Rev. R. H.; Reid, Rt Rev. J. R.; Watson, Rt Rev. P. R.

SYDNEY, (St Andrew's Cathedral), Dean of; *see* Short, Rt Rev. K. H.

SYKES, Lt-Col Arthur Patrick, MBE 1945; JP; DL; *b* 1 Sept. 1906; *e s* of late Herbert R. Sykes, JP; *m* 1936, Prudence Margaret, *d* of late Maj.-Gen. D. E. Robertson, CB, DSO, Indian Army (marr. diss. 1966); one *s* one *d*; *m* 1968, Katharine Diana, *d* of Lt-Col. A. J. N. Bartlett, DSO, OBE. *Educ:* Eton; Magdalene College, Cambridge. 2nd Lt 60th Rifles, 1929; served India, Burma, Palestine; ADC to Governor of Bengal, 1933–35; War of 1939–45, Middle East (wounded); Lt-Col 1944. JP 1951, DL 1951, High Sheriff, 1961, Shropshire. *Address:* Lydham Manor, Bishop's Castle, Shropshire SY9 5HA. *T:* Bishop's Castle (0588) 638486.

SYKES, Bonar Hugh Charles; farmer; formerly Counsellor in HM Diplomatic Service; *b* 20 Dec. 1922; *s* of late Sir Frederick Sykes, GCSI, GCIE, GBE, KCB, CMG, and of Isabel, *d* of Andrew Bonar Law; *m* 1949, Mary, *d* of late Sir Eric Phipps, GCB, GCMG, GCVO, and of Frances Phipps; four *s*. *Educ:* Eton; The Queen's Coll., Oxford. War service in Navy (Lieut RNVR), 1942–46. Trainee with Ford Motor Co. (Tractor Div.), 1948–49. Joined Foreign Service, 1949: served in Prague, Bonn, Tehran, Ottawa, FCO; retired 1970. Pres., Wiltshire Archaeological and Natural History Soc., 1975–85 (Trustee, 1947–). Chm., Bd of Visitors of Erlestoke Prison, 1983–85 (Mem., 1977–87); Member: Area Museums Council (SW), 1976–86; Council, Museums Assoc., 1981–84. FSA 1986. High Sheriff, Wilts, 1988. *Address:* Conock Manor, Devizes, Wiltshire. *T:* Devizes (0380) 840227.

SYKES, Dr Donald Armstrong; Principal of Mansfield College, Oxford, 1977–86; *b* 13 Feb. 1930; *s* of late Rev. Leonard Sykes and Edith Mary Sykes (*née* Armstrong); *m* 1962, Marta Sproul Whitehouse; two *s*. *Educ:* The High Sch. of Dundee; Univ. of St Andrews (MA 2nd cl. Classics 1952; Guthrie Scholar); Mansfield Coll., Oxford (BA 1st cl. Theol. 1958; MA 1961; DPhil 1967); Univ. of Glasgow (DipEd). Fellow in Theology, 1959–77, Senior Tutor, 1970–77, and Sen. Res. Fellow, 1986–89, Mansfield Coll., Oxford. Vis. Professor, St Olaf Coll., Northfield, Minn: in Religion, 1969–70; in Classics and Religion, 1987; Hon. DD St Olaf, 1979. *Publications:* (contrib.) Studies of the Church in History: essays honoring Robert S. Paul, ed Horton Davies, 1983; articles and reviews in Jl Theological Studies, Studia Patristica, Byzantinische Zeitschrift. *Recreations:* gramophone records, walking. *Address:* 23 Weyland Road, Headington, Oxford OX3 8PE. *T:* Oxford (0865) 61576.

SYKES, Edwin Leonard, CMG 1966; *b* 1 May 1914; *m* 1st, 1946, Margaret Elizabeth McCulloch (*d* 1973); 2nd, 1976, Dorothy Soderberg. *Educ:* Leys School, Cambridge (Schol.); Trinity Coll., Cambridge (Senior Schol.). Entered Dominions Office, 1937; Asst Priv. Sec. to Secretary of State, 1939. Served War, 1939–45 (despatches). Served in British High Commissions, Canada, 1945–47, India, 1952–54; idc 1955; Dep. UK High Commissioner in Federation of Rhodesia and Nyasaland, 1956–59; Asst Under-Sec. of State, CRO, 1964–65; Dep. UK High Commissioner in Pakistan, 1965–66; Sec., Office of the Parly Comr for Administration, 1967–74. *Address:* 7 Upper Rose Hill, Dorking, Surrey RH4 2EB.

SYKES, Sir (Francis) John (Badcock), 10th Bt *cr* 1781, of Basildon, Berkshire; Partner, Townsends, solicitors, Swindon and Newbury, since 1972; *b* 7 June 1942; *s* of Sir Francis Godfrey Sykes, 9th Bt and Lady Eira Betty Sykes (*née* Badcock) (*d* 1970); *S* father, 1990; *m* 1966, Susan Alexandra, *er d* of Adm. of the Fleet Sir E. B. Ashmore, *qv*; three *s*. *Educ:* Shrewsbury; Worcester Coll., Oxford (MA). Admitted solicitor, 1968; Assistant Solicitor: Gamlens, Lincoln's Inn, 1968–69; Townsends, 1969–71. Pres., Swindon Chamber of Commerce, 1981. Governor: Swindon Coll., 1982–90; Swindon Enterprise Trust, 1982–89. Trustee: Roman Research Trust, 1990–; Merchant's House (Marlborough) Trust, 1991–. Mem., HAC. *Recreations:* local and Anglo-Indian history, tennis, sailing. *Heir:* *s* Francis Charles Sykes, *b* 18 June 1968. *Address:* Kingsbury Croft, Kingsbury Street, Marlborough, Wilts SN8 1HU. *T:* Marlborough (0672) 512115.

SYKES, (James) Richard, QC 1981; *b* 28 May 1934; *s* of late Philip James and Lucy Barbara Sykes; *m* 1959, Susan Ethne Patricia Allen, *d* of late Lt-Col J. M. and Mrs E. M. B. Allen, Morrinsville, NZ; one *s* three *d*. *Educ:* Charterhouse; Pembroke Coll., Cambridge. BA 1957, MA 1971. Nat. Service, 2nd Lieut RASC, 1952–54. Called to the Bar, Lincoln's Inn, 1958, Bencher, 1989. Member: City Company Law Cttee, 1974–79; City Capital Markets Cttee, 1980–; Chairman: Judging Panel, Accountant and Stock Exchange Annual Awards, 1982–90; Judging Panel, Stock Exchange and Inst. of Chartered Accountants Awards, 1990–. Mem. Management Cttee, Internat. Exhibn Co-operative Wine Soc. Ltd, 1986–. Mem. Council and Exec., VSO, 1987–. *Publications:* (Consultant Editor) Gore-Browne on Companies, 42nd edn 1972, 43rd edn 1977, 44th edn 1986; (ed jtly) The Conduct of Meetings, 20th edn 1966, 21st edn 1975. *Address:* Vassars, Langley, Hitchin, Herts SG4 7PH. *T:* Stevenage (0438) 352271.

SYKES, Sir John; *see* Sykes, Sir F. J. B.

SYKES, Dr John Bradbury; General Editor, New Shorter Oxford English Dictionary, Oxford University Press, since 1989; *b* Folkestone, Kent, 26 Jan. 1929; *s* of late Stanley William Sykes and late Eleanor Sykes Sykes (*née* Bradbury); *m* 1955, Avril Barbara Hart (marr. diss. 1988); one *s*. *Educ:* Wallasey Grammar Sch.; Rochdale High Sch.; St Lawrence Coll.; Wadham Coll., Oxford (BA Maths 1950); Balliol Coll., Oxford (Skynner Sen. Student); Merton Coll., Oxford (Harmsworth Sen. Schol., MA and DPhil Astrophysics 1953). AERE, Harwell, 1953–71 (Head of Translations Office 1958, Principal Scientific Officer 1960); Member, Internat. Astronomical Union, 1958 (Pres., Commn for Documentation, 1967–73). Editor, Concise and Pocket Oxford Dictionaries, 1971–81, Hd of German Dictionaries, 1981–89, OUP. Mem. Bd, Translators' Guild, 1980–88 (Chm., 1984–88). Fellow: Inst. of Linguists, 1960–86 (Mem. Council, 1977–86; Editor, Incorporated Linguist, 1980–86); Inst. of Translation and Interpreting, 1988 (Chm. Council, 1986–91). FRSA. Hon. DLitt City, 1984. *Publications:* (with B Davison) Neutron Transport Theory, 1957; (ed) Technical Translator's Manual, 1971; (ed) Concise Oxford Dictionary, 6th edn, 1976, 7th edn, 1982; (ed) Pocket Oxford Dictionary, 6th edn, 1978; (ed jtly) Oxford–Duden German Dictionary, 1990; translations of many Russian textbooks in physics and astronomy; contribs to Incorporated Linguist. *Recreation:* crossword-solving (National Champion 1958, 1972–75, 1977, 1980, 1983, 1985, 1989, 1990). *Address:* 68 Woodstock Close, Oxford OX2 8DD. *T:* Oxford (0865) 57532. *Club:* PEN.

SYKES, Sir John (Charles Anthony le Gallais), 3rd Bt *cr* 1921; *b* 19 April 1928; *s* of Stanley Edgar Sykes (*d* 1963) (2nd *s* of 1st Bt) and Florence Anaise le Gallais (*d* 1955); *S* uncle, 1974; *m* (marr. diss.). *Educ:* Churchers College. Export merchant. Mem., British Epicure Soc. *Recreations:* wine, food, travel. *Heir:* *nephew* David Michael Sykes [*b* 10 June 1954; *m* 1st 1974, Susan Elizabeth (marr. diss. 1987), 3rd *d* of G. W. Hall; one *s*; 2nd, 1987, Margaret Lynne, *o d* of J. McGreavy; one *d*]. *Address:* 58 Alders View Drive, East Grinstead, Sussex RH19 2DN. *T:* East Grinstead (0342) 322027.

SYKES, Joseph Walter, CMG 1962; CVO 1953; Chairman, Fiji Public Service Commission, 1971–80, retired 1981; *b* 10 July 1915; *s* of Samuel Sykes and Lucy M. Womack; *m* 1940, Elima Petrie, *d* of late Sir Hugh Hall Ragg; three *s* two *d*. *Educ:* De La Salle Coll., Sheffield; Rotherham Gram. Sch.; Jesus Coll., Oxford. Colonial Administrative Service, Fiji; Cadet, 1938; Dist Officer, 1940; District Commissioner, 1950; Deputy Secretary for Fijian Affairs, 1952; Assistant Colonial Secretary, 1953; transferred to Cyprus as Dep. Colonial Sec., Nov. 1954; Admin. Sec., Cyprus. 1955–56; Colonial Sec., Bermuda, 1956–68; Chief Sec., Bermuda, 1968–71; retired. *Publication:* The Royal Visit to Fiji 1953, 1954. *Recreations:* gardening, carpentry. *Address:* 8 Dorking Road, City Beach, Perth, WA 6015, Australia.

SYKES, Prof. Keble Watson; Vice-Principal, 1978–86, Professor of Physical Chemistry, 1956–86, Queen Mary College, University of London; now Emeritus Professor; *b* 7 Jan. 1921; *s* of Watson and Victoria May Sykes; *m* 1950, Elizabeth Margaret Ewing Forsyth; three *d* (and one *s* decd). *Educ:* Seascale Preparatory Sch.; St Bees Sch.; The Queen's Coll., Oxford, MA, BSc, DPhil (Oxon.). ICI Research Fellow, Physical Chemistry Lab., Oxford, 1945–48; Lecturer, 1948–51, and Senior Lecturer in Chemistry, 1951–56, University Coll. of Swansea, Univ. of Wales; Head of Chemistry Dept, 1959–78, and Dean, Fac. of Science, 1970–73, QMC, London (Fellow, 1987). Hon. Sec. Chemical Soc. of London, 1960–66, Vice-Pres., 1966–69, Mem. Council, 1977–80. Member Council, Westfield College, University of London, 1962–77; Governor, Highgate Sch., 1986–91. *Publications:* scientific papers in journals of Royal Society, Faraday Soc. and Chem. Soc. *Address:* 58 Wood Vale, Muswell Hill, N10 3DN. *T:* 081–883 1502.

SYKES, Sir Keith; *see* Sykes, Sir M. K.

SYKES, Sir (Malcolm) Keith, Kt 1991; Nuffield Professor of Anaesthetics, University of Oxford, 1980–91, Emeritus Professor since 1991; Supernumary Fellow of Pembroke College, Oxford, since 1992 (Fellow, 1980–91); *b* 13 Sept. 1925; *s* of Joseph and Phyllis Mary Sykes; *m* 1956, Michelle June (*née* Ratcliffe); one *s* three *d*. *Educ:* Magdalene Coll., Cambridge (MA, MB, BChir); University Coll. Hosp., London (DA; FFARCS). RAMC, 1950–52. House appointments, University Coll. and Norfolk and Norwich Hosps, 1949–50; Sen. House Officer, Registrar and Sen. Registrar in anaesthetics, UCH, 1952–54 and 1955–58; Rickman Godlee Travelling Scholar and Fellow in Anesthesia, Mass. General Hosp., Boston, USA, 1954–55; RPMS and Hammersmith Hosp., 1958–80: Lectr and Sen. Lectr, 1958–67; Reader, 1967–70; Prof. of Clinical Anaesthesia, 1970–80. Vis. Prof., univs in Canada, USA, Australia, NZ, Malaysia, Europe. Eponymous lectures: Holme, 1970; Clover, 1976; Weinbren, 1976; Rowbottom, 1978; Gillespie, 1979; Gillies, 1985; Wesley Bourne, 1986; Husfeldt, 1986; Della Briggs, 1988; E. M. Papper, 1991. Mem. Bd, Fac. of Anaesthetists, 1969–85; Pres., Section of Anaesthetics, RSM, 1989–90; Vice Pres., Assoc. of Anaesthetists, 1990–Sept. 1992 (Mem. Council, 1967–70); Senator and Vice Pres., European Acad. of Anaesthesiology, 1978–85. Hon. FFARACS 1979; Hon. FFA (SA) 1989. Dudley Buxton Prize, Fac. of Anaesthetists, 1980; Fac. of Anaesthetists Medal, 1987. *Publications:* Respiratory Failure, 1969, 2nd edn 1976; Principles of Measurement for Anaesthetists, 1970; Principles of Clinical Measurement, 1980; Principles of Measurement and Monitoring in Anaesthesia and Intensive Care, 1991; chapters and papers on respiratory failure, intensive care, respiratory and cardiovascular physiology applied to anaesthesia, etc. *Recreations:* sailing, walking, birdwatching, gardening, music. *Address:* 10 Fitzherbert Close, Iffley, Oxford OX4 4EN. *T:* Oxford (0865) 771152.

SYKES, Richard; *see* Sykes, J. R.

SYKES, Rt. Rev. Stephen Whitefield; *see* Ely, Bishop of.

SYKES, Sir Tatton (Christopher Mark), 8th Bt *cr* 1783; landowner; *b* 24 Dec. 1943; *s* of Sir (Mark Tatton) Richard Tatton-Sykes, 7th Bt and Virginia (*d* 1970), *d* of late John Francis Grey Gilliat; *S* father, 1978; granted use of additional arms of Tatton, 1980. *Educ:* Eton; Univ. d'Aix-Marseille; Royal Agric. Coll., Cirencester. *Heir:* *b* Jeremy John Sykes [*b* 8 March 1946; *m* 1982, Pamela June, *o d* of Thomas Wood]. *Address:* Sledmere, Driffield, East Yorkshire.

SYLVESTER, (Anthony) David (Bernard), CBE 1983; writer on art, etc; editing catalogue raisonné of René Magritte; *b* 21 Sept. 1924; *s* of Philip Silvester and Sybil Rosen; *m* Pamela Briddon; three *d*. *Educ:* University Coll. Sch. Arts Council of Great Britain: Mem., 1980–82; Mem., Art Panel, 1962–70, 1972–77, Chm., 1980–82. Mem., BFI Prodn Bd, 1966–69; Mem., Commn d'Acquisitions, Musée Nat. D'Art Moderne, Paris, 1984–; Trustee, Tate Gall., 1967–69. Vis. Lecturer: Slade Sch. of Fine Art, 1953–57; RCA, 1960–70; Swarthmore Coll., Pa, 1967–68. Hon. FRA 1986. *Exhibitions:* Henry Moore, Tate, 1951; Alberto Giacometti, Arts Council, 1955; Chaim Soutine, Tate, 1963; Giacometti, Tate, 1965; Moore, Tate, 1968; René Magritte, Tate, 1969; (with M. Compton) Robert Morris, Tate, 1971; (with J. Drew) Henri Laurens, Hayward, 1971; Joan Miró bronzes, Hayward, 1972; Islamic carpets, Hayward, 1972; Willem de Kooning, Serpentine, 1977; Dada and Surrealism Reviewed (Chm. of Cttee), Hayward, 1978; Moore, Serpentine, 1978; Magritte, Palais des Beaux-Arts, Brussels, and Musée National d'Art Moderne, Paris, 1978–79; Giacometti, Serpentine, 1981; (with D. King) The Eastern Carpet in the Western World, Hayward, 1983, etc; *films and TV:* Ten Modern Artists (writer/presenter of series), 1964; Giacometti (writer/producer), 1967; Matisse and His Model (writer), 1968; Magritte: The False Mirror (dir), 1970, etc; *radio:* many interviews, talks and discussions for BBC. *Publications:* Henry Moore, 1968; Magritte, 1969; Interviews with Francis Bacon, 1975, enlarged edn 1980; exhibn catalogues; articles, incl. some on films or sport, 1942–, in Tribune, New Statesman, Burlington Mag., Listener, Encounter, The Times, Observer, Sunday Times Mag., etc. *Fax:* 071–229 4078.

SYLVESTER, George Harold, CBE 1967; retired 1967 as Chief Education Officer for Bristol; *b* 26 May 1907; *s* of late George Henry and Martha Sylvester; *m* 1936, Elsie Emmett; one *s*. *Educ:* Stretford Grammar School; Manchester University. BA Manchester 1928; MA Bristol 1944. Teaching, Manchester, 1929–32; Administrative posts (Education) in Wolverhampton and Bradford, 1932–39; Assistant Education Officer, Bristol, 1939–42; Chief Education Officer, Bristol, 1942–67. Hon. MEd Bristol, 1967. *Recreations:* golf, music. *Address:* 43 Hill View, Henleaze, Bristol BS9 4QE. *T:* Bristol (0272) 629287.

SYLVESTER-EVANS, Alun, CB 1975; Deputy Chief Executive, Property Services Agency, Department of the Environment, 1973–78, retired; Member, Chairman's Panel of Assessors, Civil Service Selection Boards, 1980–88; *b* 21 April 1918; *o c* of Daniel Elias Evans and Esther Evans, Rhymney, Mon.; *m* 1945, Joan Maureen, *o c* of A. J. Sylvester, CBE; two *s*. *Educ:* Lewis' School, Pengam; University of Wales, Aberystwyth. Armed services, 1940–46. Asst Research Officer, Min. of Town and Country Planning, 1946–47; Asst Principal, 1947–48; Principal Private Sec. to Minister of Housing and Local Govt, 1954–57; Asst Secretary, 1957–66, Under-Sec., 1966–73, Min. of Housing and Local Govt, later DoE. *Recreation:* golf. *Address:* Rudloe Cottage, Rudloe, Corsham, Wilts SN13 0PG. *T:* Hawthorn (0225) 810375. *Club:* Commonwealth Trust.

SYME, Dr James, FRCP, FRCPE, FRCPGlas; Consultant Paediatrician, Edinburgh, since 1965; *b* 25 Aug. 1930; *s* of James Wilson Syme and Christina Kay Syme (*née* Marshall); *m* 1956, Pamela McCormick; one *s* one *d*. *Educ:* University of Edinburgh (MB ChB). FRCPE 1967; FRCPGlas 1978; FRCP 1991. House Officer posts, 1954–55; Captain, RAMC, 1955–57; Royal Infirmary, Edinburgh, 1957–62; Senior Registrar in Paediatrics, Glasgow, 1962–65. Royal College of Physicians of Edinburgh: Secretary, 1971–75; Mem. Council, 1976–85; Vice-Pres., 1985–89. Chm., Part II MRCP Bd of three Royal Colls of Physicians of UK, 1989–. External examnr, London, Glasgow, Dundee, Nigeria, Hong Kong, Dublin, Singapore. *Publications:* contribs to Textbook of Paediatrics (Forfar & Arneil), 1st edn, 1973 to 3rd edn, 1984; papers in med. jls on paediatric topics. *Recreations:* travel, visiting churches, gardening. *Address:* 13 Succoth Park, Edinburgh EH12 6BX. *T:* 031–337 6069. *Clubs:* New, Aesculapian, Harveian Society (Edinburgh).

SYMES, (Lilian) Mary; Clerk to Justices, 6 Divisions in Suffolk, 1943–74; Chairman, Norfolk and Suffolk Rent Tribunal, 1974–83; *b* 18 Oct. 1912; *d* of Walter Ernest and Lilian May Hollowell; *m* 1953, Thomas Alban Symes (*d* 1984); one *s*. *Educ:* St Mary's Convent, Lowestoft; Great Yarmouth High School. Articled in Solicitor's Office; qualified as Solicitor, 1936. Became first woman Clerk to Justices (Stowmarket), 1942; first woman Deputy Coroner, 1945; Clerk to the Justices, Woodbridge, 1946, Bosmere and Claydon, 1951; first woman Coroner, 1951; Deputy Coroner, Northern District, Suffolk, 1956–82. *Recreations:* Worcester porcelain, gardening. *Address:* Leiston Old Abbey, Leiston, Suffolk.

SYMINGTON, Prof. Sir Thomas, Kt 1978; MD; FRSE; Director, 1970–77, and Professor of Pathology, 1970–77, Institute of Cancer Research, Royal Cancer Hospital; *b* 1 April 1915; *m* 1943, Esther Margaret Forsyth, MB, ChB; two *s* one *d*. *Educ:* Cumnock Academy. BSc 1936; MB ChB, 1941; MD 1950. Maj., RAMC (Dep. Asst Dir Pathology, Malaya, 1947–49). St Mungo (Notman) Prof. of Pathology, Univ. of Glasgow, 1954–70. Visiting Prof. of Pathology, Stanford Univ., Calif., 1965–66. Member, Medical Research Council, 1968–72. FRSE, 1956; FRIC, 1958 (ARIC, 1951); FRCP(G), 1963; FRFPS (G), 1958; FRCPath, 1964. Hon. MD Szeged Univ., Hungary, 1971; Hon. DSc McGill Univ., Canada, 1983. *Publications:* Functional Pathology of the Human Adrenal Gland, 1969; Scientific Foundations of Oncology, 1976; numerous papers on problems of adrenal glands in Journals of Endocrinology and Pathology. *Recreation:* golf. *Address:* Greenbriar, 2 Lady Margaret Drive, Troon KA10 7AL. *T:* Troon (0292) 315707.

SYMMERS, Prof. William St Clair, senior; MD; retired; Emeritus Professor of Histopathology, University of London, since 1986; *b* 16 Aug. 1917; *s* of William St Clair Symmers, Columbia, S Carolina (Musgrave Professor of Pathology and Bacteriology, QUB) and Marion Latimer (*née* Macredie), Sydney, NSW; *m* 1941, Jean Noble (*d* 1990), *d* of Kenyon and Elizabeth Wright, Paisley, Renfrewshire; one *s*. *Educ:* Royal Belfast Academical Instn; Queen's Univ. of Belfast (MB, BCh, BAO 1939; Johnson Symington Medal in Anatomy, 1936; Sinclair Medal in Surgery, 1939; MD 1946); Univ. of Freiburg, Breisgau, Germany. PhD Birmingham, 1953; DSc London, 1979; FRCP, FRCPI, FRCPE, FRCS; FRCPA; FRCPath; FFPath, RCPI. Surg.-Lieut, RNVR, 1940–46. Demonstrator in Pathology and pupil of Prof. G. Payling Wright, Guy's Hosp. Med. Sch., 1946–47; Registrar in Clinical Pathology, Guy's Hosp., 1946–47; Deptl Demonstrator of Pathology, Univ. of Oxford, 1947; Sen. Asst Pathologist, 1947–48, Consultant, 1948, Radcliffe Infirmary, Oxford; Sen. Lectr in Pathology, Univ. of Birmingham, England, 1948–53; Hon. Consultant Pathologist: United Birmingham Hosps, 1948–53; Birmingham Regional Hosp. Bd, 1949–53; Prof. of Morbid Anatomy, later of Histopathology, Univ. of London at Charing Cross Hosp. Med. Sch., 1953–82; Hon. Consultant Pathologist, Charing Cross Hosp., 1953–82, Hon. Consulting Pathologist, 1983–. Pres., Section of Pathology, RSM, 1969–70. Hon. FRCPA 1980; Hon. FACP 1982. Hon. DSc QUB, 1990. Dr Dhayagude Meml Prize, Seth GS Med. Sch., Univ. of Bombay, 1967; Yamagiwa Medal, Univ. of Tokyo, 1969; Scott-Heron Medal, Royal Victoria Hosp., Belfast, 1975; Morgagni Medal, Univ. of Padua, 1979. *Publications:* Systemic Pathology, 1966 (ed with late Prof. G. Payling Wright), (ed) 2nd edn, 6 vols, 1976–80, (gen. editor) 3rd edn, 15 vols, 1986–; Curiosa, 1974; Exotica, 1984. *Address:* Woodbine Cottage, 10 Kingsmeadows Road, Peebles EH45 9EN.

SYMMONDS, Algernon Washington, GCM 1980; solicitor and attorney-at-law; *b* 19 Nov. 1926; *s* of late Algernon F. Symmonds and Olga Ianthe (*née* Harper); *m* 1954, Gladwyn Ward; one *s* one *d*. *Educ:* Combermere Sch.; Harrison Coll.; Codrington Coll., Barbados. Solicitor, Barbados, 1953, enrolled in UK, 1958; in practice as Solicitor, Barbados, 1953–55; Dep. Registrar, Barbados, 1955–59; Crown Solicitor, Barbados, 1959–66; Permanent Secretary: Min. of Home Affairs, 1966–72; Min. of Educn, 1972–76; Min. of External Affairs and Head of Foreign Service, 1976–79; appointed to rank of Ambassador, 1977; High Comr in UK, 1979–83 and non-resident Ambassador to Denmark, Finland, Iceland, Norway and Sweden, 1981–83, and to the Holy See, 1982–83; Perm. Sec., Prime Minister's Office, Barbados, 1983–86; Head of CS, 1986. President: Barbados CS Assoc., 1958–65; Fedn of British CS Assocs in Caribbean, 1960–64; Dep. Mem. Exec., Public Services Internat., 1964–66. Dep. Chm., Caribbean Examinations Council, 1973–76. Past Pres., Barbados Lawn Tennis Assoc. *Recreations:* tennis, cricket broadcasting (represented Barbados in football, lawn tennis, basketball). *Address:* Melksham, Margaret Terrace, Pine, St Michael, Barbados, WI; Equitas Chambers, Pinfold Street, Bridgetown, Barbados, WI. *Clubs:* Bridgetown, Empire (Cricket and Football) (Life Mem. and Past Vice-Pres.), Summerhayes Tennis (Past Pres.) (Barbados).

SYMON, Prof. Lindsay, TD 1967; FRCS, FRCSE; Professor of Neurological Surgery, Institute of Neurology, London University and the National Hospital, Queen Square, since 1978; *b* 4 Nov. 1929; *s* of William Lindsay Symon and Isabel Symon; *m* 1954, Pauline Barbara Rowland; one *s* two *d*. *Educ:* Aberdeen Grammar Sch.; Aberdeen Univ. (MB, ChB Hons). FRCSE 1957; FRCS 1959. House Physician and Surgeon, Aberdeen Royal Infirmary, 1952–53; Jun. Specialist in Surgery, RAMC, 1953–55; Surgical Registrar, Aberdeen Royal Infirmary, 1956–58; Neurosurgical Registrar, Middlesex and Maida Vale Hosps, 1958–61, Sen. Neurosurgical Registrar, 1962–65; Mem., External Scientific Staff, MRC, 1965–78; Consultant Neurosurgeon: Nat. Hosp. for Nervous Diseases, Queen Square and Maida Vale, 1965–78; St Thomas' Hosp., 1970–78. Hon. Consultant Neurological Surgeon, St Thomas' Hosp., Hammersmith Hosp., Royal Nose, Throat and Ear Hosp., 1978–; Civilian Advr in Neurological Surgery to RN, 1979–. Adjunct Prof., Dept of Surgery, Southwestern Med. Sch., Dallas, 1982–. Rockefeller Travelling Fellow in Medicine, Wayne State Univ., Detroit, 1961–62. Pres., World Fedn Neurosurgical Socs, 1989–. *Publications:* Operative Surgery/Neurosurgery, 1976, 2nd edn 1986; Advances and Technical Standards in Neurosurgery, 1972, 18th edn 1991; numerous papers on cerebral circulation and metabolism, brain tumours, general neurosurgical topics, etc. *Recreation:* golf. *Address:* Department of Neurological Surgery, Institute of Neurology, Queen Square, WC1N 3BG. *T:* 071–278 1091; Cairngorm, 42 Granville Road, Barnet, Herts. *T:* 081–449 5842. *Clubs:* Caledonian; Royal & Ancient (St Andrews).

SYMONDS, Ann Hazel S.; *see* Spokes Symonds.

SYMONDS, Jane Ursula; *see* Kellock, J. U.

SYMONDS, (John) Richard (Charters); Senior Associate Member, St Antony's College, Oxford, since 1979; Senior Research Associate, Queen Elizabeth House, Oxford, since 1979; Hon. Director, United Nations Career Records Project, since 1989; *b* 2 Oct. 1918; *s* of Sir Charles Putnam Symonds, KBE, CB, DM, FRCP, and Janet (*née* Poulton); *m* 1980, Ann Hazel Spokes (*see* A. H. Spokes Symonds); two *s* by a previous marriage. *Educ:* Rugby Sch.; Corpus Christi Coll., Oxford (Scholar in Mod. History, MA); Secretary Elect, Oxford Union, 1939. Friends Amb. Unit, 1939–44; Dep. Dir Relief and Rehab., Govt of Bengal, 1944–45; UNRRA, Austria, 1946–47; Friends Service Unit, Punjab and Kashmir, 1947–48; UN Commn for India and Pakistan (Kashmir), 1948–49; UN Technical Assistance Board: New York, 1950–51; Liaison Officer in Europe, 1952–53; Resident Rep., Ceylon, 1953–55, Yugoslavia, 1955–58; Rep. in Europe, 1959–62; Reg. Rep., E Africa, 1961. Sen. Res. Officer, Oxford Univ. Inst. of Commonwealth Studies, 1962–65; Reg. Rep. in Southern Africa, UNTAB, 1964–65; Professorial Fellow, IDS, Univ. of Sussex, 1966–69, later Vis. Prof.; Consultant, UN Population Div., 1968–69; Rep. in Europe, UNITAR, 1969–71; UNDP Resident Rep. in Greece, 1972–75, and in Tunisia, 1975–78; Sen. Adviser, UNDP and UN Fund for Population Activities, NY, 1978–79; Consultant: Commonwealth Foundn, 1980; WHO, 1981. Mem. Council, Royal Commonwealth Soc., 1983–86. *Publications:* The Making of Pakistan, 1950; The British and their Successors, 1966; (ed) International Targets for Development, 1970; (with M. Carder) The United Nations and the Population Question, 1973; Oxford and Empire—the last lost cause?, 1986; Alternative Saints: the post Reformation British people commemorated by the Church of England, 1988. *Recreations:* walking, travel. *Address:* 43 Davenant Road, Oxford OX2 8BU. *T:* Oxford (0865) 515661. *Club:* Commonwealth Trust.
See also R. C. Symonds.

SYMONDS, Matthew John; Deputy Editor, The Independent, since 1986 and Executive Editor, since 1989; *b* 20 Dec. 1953; *s* of Lord Ardwick, *qv*, and Anne Symonds; *m* 1981, Alison Mary Brown; one *s* one *d*. *Educ:* Holland Park, London; Balliol College, Oxford (MA). Graduate trainee, Daily Mirror, 1976–78; Financial Times, 1978–81; economics and defence leader writer, economics columnist, Daily Telegraph, 1981–86; Director, The Independent, 1986–. *Recreations:* history, looking at churches and pictures, novels, boating, tennis, family. *Address:* The Independent, 40 City Road, EC1Y 2DB. *T:* 071–253 1222.

SYMONDS, Richard; *see* Symonds, J. R. C.

SYMONDS, Ronald Charters, CB 1975; *b* 25 June 1916; *e s* of Sir Charles Symonds, KBE, CB, and late Janet (*née* Poulton); *m* 1939, Pamela Painton; two *s* one *d*. *Educ:* Rugby Sch.; New Coll., Oxford. British Council, 1938–39 and 1946–51. Military Service, 1939–45. War Office, later MoD, 1951–76, retired. Advr, Royal Commn on Gambling, 1976–78. Consultant, ICI Ltd, 1978–81. United States Bronze Star, 1948. *Recreations:* walking, ornithology. *Address:* 10 Bisham Gardens, N6 6DD.
See also J. R. C. Symonds.

SYMONS, Christopher John Maurice; QC 1989; *b* 5 Feb. 1949; *s* of Clifford Louis Symons and Pamela Constance Symons; *m* 1974, Susan Mary Teichmann; one *s* one *d*. *Educ:* Sherborne Prep. Sch.; Clifton Coll.; Kent Univ. (BA Hons (Law)). Called to the Bar, Middle Temple, 1972; called to the Bar of Gibraltar, 1985, to the Irish Bar, 1988, to the NI Bar, 1990. Jun. Crown Counsel (Common Law), 1985–89; Asst Recorder, 1990. *Recreation:* hitting balls. *Address:* 3 Gray's Inn Place, Gray's Inn, WC1R 5EA. *T:* 071–831 8441. *Clubs:* Hurlingham, Roehampton; Sotogrande (Spain).

SYMONS, Elizabeth Conway; General Secretary, Association of First Division Civil Servants, since 1989; *b* 14 April 1951; *d* of Ernest Vize Symons, CB and of Elizabeth Megan Symons (*née* Jenkins); partner, Philip Alan Bassett; one *s*. *Educ:* Putney High Sch. for Girls; Girton Coll., Cambridge (MA). Research, Girton Coll., Cambridge, 1972–74; Administration Trainee, DoE, 1974–77; Asst Sec. 1977–78, Dep. Gen. Sec., 1988–89, Inland Revenue Staff Fedn. Member: Gen. Council, TUC; Council, RIPA; Exec. Council, Campaign for Freedom of Information. Hon. Associate, Nat. Council of Women. Governor, Polytechnic of North London. *Recreations:* reading, gardening, friends, entertaining unruly six-year old. *Address:* Association of First Division Civil Servants, 2 Caxton Street, SW1H 0QH. *T:* 071–222 6242.

SYMONS, Julian Gustave, FRSL; author; *b* 30 May 1912; *y s* of M. A. Symons and Minnie Louise Bull; *m* 1941, Kathleen Clark; one *s* (one *d* decd). Editor, Twentieth Century Verse, 1937–39. Sunday Times Reviewer, 1958–. Chairman: Crime Writers Association, 1958–59; Cttee of Management, Soc. of Authors, 1970–71. President: Detection Club, 1976–85; Conan Doyle Soc., 1989–. Mem. Council, Westfield Coll., Univ. of London, 1972–75. Grand Master: Swedish Acad. of Detection, 1977; Mystery Writers of America, 1982; Internat. Crime Writers, 1991. FRSL 1975. *Publications:* Confusions About X, 1938; (ed) Anthology of War Poetry, 1942; The Second Man, 1944; A. J. A. Symons, 1950; Charles Dickens, 1951; Thomas Carlyle, 1952; Horatio Bottomley, 1955; The General Strike, 1957; A Reasonable Doubt, 1960; The Thirties, 1960, with additions, as The Thirties and the Nineties, 1990; The Detective Story in Britain, 1962; Buller's Campaign, 1963; England's Pride, 1965; Critical Occasions, 1966; A Picture History of Crime and Detection, 1966; (ed) Essays and Biographies by A. J. A. Symons, 1969; Bloody Murder: from the detective story to the crime novel, a history, 1972 (MWA Edgar Allan Poe Award), rev. edn 1985; Notes from Another Country, 1972; Between the Wars, 1972; The Hungry Thirties, 1976; The Tell-Tale Heart, 1978; Conan Doyle, 1979; The Great Detectives, 1981; Critical Observations, 1981; The Tigers of Subtopia (short stories), 1982; (ed) New Poetry 9, 1983; Dashiell Hammett, 1985; (ed) Tchekov's The Shooting Party, 1986; Makers of the New, 1987; author of 26 crime novels, including: The 31st of February, 1950; The Broken Penny, 1952; The Colour of Murder, 1957 (CWA Critics Award); The Progress of a Crime, 1960 (MWA Edgar Allan Poe Award); The End of Solomon Grundy, 1964; The Man Who Killed Himself, 1967; The Man Whose Dreams Came True, 1968; The Man Who Lost His Wife, 1970; The Players and the Game, 1972; A Three Pipe Problem, 1975; The Blackheath Poisonings, 1978; Sweet Adelaide, 1980; The Detling Murders, 1982; The Name of Annabel Lee, 1983; (ed) The Penguin Classic Crime Omnibus, 1984; The Criminal Comedy of the Contented Couple, 1985; The Kentish Manor Murders, 1988; (ed) The Essential Wyndham Lewis, 1989; Death's Darkest Face, 1990; Portraits of the Missing, 1991; several plays for television. *Recreations:* watching cricket, snooker and Association football, wandering in cities. *Address:* Groton House, 330 Dover Road, Walmer, Deal, Kent CT14 7NX. *T:* Deal (0304) 365209.

SYMONS, Prof. Martyn Christian Raymond, FRS 1985; Research Professor of Chemistry, Cancer Research Campaign Senior Fellow, and Director, Cancer Research Campaign Electron Spin Resonance Research Group, Leicester University, since 1988; *b* 12 Nov. 1925; *s* of Marjorie LeBrasseur and Stephen White Symons; *m* 1st, 1950, Joy Lendon (decd); one *s* one *d*; 3rd, 1970, Janice O'Connor. *Educ:* Battersea Polytechnic (BSc, PhD, DSc London); CChem, FRSC. Army, 1945–48. Lecturer: Battersea Polytechnic, 1948–53; Southampton Univ., 1953–60; Prof. of Physical Chem., Leicester Univ., 1960–88. Royal Soc. of Chemistry: Vice Pres., Faraday Div., 1985–87; Bruker Lectr (first), 1986; R. A. Robinson Lectr, 1987. FRSA. *Publications:* The Structure of Inorganic Radicals (with P. W. Atkins), 1967; Chemical and Biochemical Aspects of Electron Spin Resonance Spectroscopy, 1978; over 900 scientific articles mainly in chem. jls. *Recreations:* watercolour landscape painting, piano playing. *Address:* 144 Victoria Park Road, Leicester LE2 1XD. *T:* Leicester (0533) 700314.

SYMONS, Vice-Adm. Sir Patrick (Jeremy), KBE 1986; Supreme Allied Commander Atlantic's Representative in Europe, since 1988; *b* 9 June 1933; *s* of Ronald and Joanne Symons; *m* 1961, Elizabeth Lawrence; one *s* one *d*. *Educ:* Dartmouth Royal Naval College. Commissioned 1951; in command, HMS Torquay, 1968–70, HMS Birmingham, 1976–77, HMS Bulwark, 1980–81; Naval Attaché, Washington, 1982–84; C of S to Comdr, Allied Naval Forces Southern Europe, 1985–88. *Recreations:* sailing, skiing, swimming. *Address:* c/o Lloyds Bank, Cox's and King's Branch, 6 Pall Mall, SW1. *Clubs:* Commonwealth Trust; Royal Naval Sailing Association (Portsmouth).

SYMONS, Patrick Stewart, RA 1991 (ARA 1983); Painter in oils; teacher, Chelsea School of Art, 1959–86; *b* 24 Oct 1925; *s* of Norman H. Symons and Nora Westlake. *Educ:* Bryanston Sch.; Camberwell Sch. of Arts and Crafts. One-man exhibitions: New Art Centre, 1960; William Darby Gall., 1975–76; Browse and Darby, 1982, 1989. *Address:* 20 Grove Hill Road, Camberwell, SE5 8DG. *T:* 071–274 2373.

SYMONS, Prof. Robert Henry, FRS 1988; FAA 1983; Professor, Department of Plant Science, University of Adelaide, since 1991 (Professor of Biochemistry, 1987–90); *b* 20 March 1934; *s* of Irene Olivette Symons (*née* Wellington) and Henry Officer Symons; *m* 1958, Verna Helen Lloyd; two *s* two *d*. *Educ:* Univ. of Melbourne (BAgSc 1956; PhD 1963). Senior Demonstrator, Univ. of Melbourne, 1958–60 ; Post-Doctoral Fellow, UK, 1961–62; Lectr, Sen. Lectr, Reader, Dept of Biochemistry, Univ. of Adelaide, 1962–87. Lemberg Medal, Aust. Biochem. Soc., 1985. *Publications:* papers to learned jls on nucleic acid biochemistry and allied subjects. *Recreations:* gardening, tennis, wine. *Address:* Department of Plant Science, Waite Agricultural Research Institute, University of Adelaide, Glen Osmond, SA 5064, Australia. *T:* 61–8 372 2423, *Fax:* 61–8 338 1757.

SYMS, John Grenville St George, OBE 1981; QC 1962; Barrister-at-Law; a Recorder of the Crown Court, 1972–80; *b* 6 Jan. 1913; *s* of late Harold St George Syms and Margaret (*née* Wordley); *m* 1st, 1951, Yvonne Yolande Rigby (marr. diss. 1971); one *s*; 2nd, 1971, Anne Jacqueline, *d* of Brig. J. B. P. Willis-Fleming, CBE, TD. Educ: Harrow; Magdalen College, Oxford (BA). Called to the Bar, 1936. Dep. Chm., Huntingdon and Peterborough QS, 1965–71. Chm., SE Agricultural Land Tribunal, 1972–83. Served in RAFVR, 1940–45 (despatches); Wing Commander, 1944. *Recreations:* shooting and fishing. *Address:* Brook Lodge, Brook, Albury, near Guildford, Surrey GU5 9DJ. *T:* Shere (048641) 2393.

SYNGE, Henry Millington; Chairman, Union International Co. Ltd, 1969–88 (Director 1955–88); Consultant, Charterhouse Tilney (Stockbrokers); *b* 3 April 1921; *s* of Richard Millington Synge, MC, Liverpool and Eileen Hall; *m* 1947, Joyce Helen, *d* of Alexander Ross Topping and Mrs Topping (*née* Stileman); two *s* one *d*. *Educ:* Shrewsbury School. Mercantile Marine: Radio Officer, 1941; Purser, Bibby Line, 1943; demobilised, 1946. Partner, Sing White & Co. (Stockbrokers), 1947. Manager, Liverpool Trustee Savings Bank, 1957, Chm. 1968–69; Regional Bd Mem., Trustee Savings Bank, England and Wales, 1970–85. *Recreations:* private flying, fishing, amateur radio. *Address:* Lake Cottage, Llynclys Hill, Oswestry, Shropshire SY10 8LL. *T:* Oswestry (0691) 830845.

SYNGE, John Lighton, FRS 1943; MA, ScD Dublin; MRIA, FRSC (Tory Medal, 1943); Senior Professor, School of Theoretical Physics, Dublin Institute for Advanced Studies, 1948–72, now Emeritus; *b* Dublin, 1897; *y s* of Edward Synge; *m* 1918, Elizabeth Allen (*d* 1985); three *d*. *Educ:* St Andrew's Coll., Dublin; Trinity Coll., Dublin. Senior Moderator and Gold Medallist in Mathematics and Experimental Science, 1919; Lecturer in Mathematics, Trinity College, Dublin, 1920; Assistant Professor of Mathematics, University of Toronto, 1920–25; Secretary to the International Mathematical Congress, Toronto, 1924; Fellow of Trinity College, Dublin, and University Professor of Natural Philosophy, 1925–30; Treas., Royal Irish Academy, 1929–30. Sec., 1949–52. Pres., 1961–64; Professor of Applied Mathematics, Univ. of Toronto, 1930–43; Professor of Mathematics and Chm. of Dept, Ohio State Univ., 1943–46; Prof. of Mathematics and Head of Dept, Carnegie Inst. of Technology, 1946–48; Visiting Lecturer, Princeton Univ., 1939; Vis. Prof.: Brown Univ., 1941–42; Inst. for Fluid Dynamics and Applied Maths, University of Maryland, 1951. Ballistics Mathematician, United States Army Air Force, 1944–45. Hon. FTCD. Hon. LLD St Andrews, 1966; Hon. ScD: QUB, 1969; NUI, 1970. Boyle Medal, RDS, 1972. *Publications:* Geometrical Optics, 1937; (with B. A. Griffith) Principles of Mechanics, 1942; (with A. E. Schild) Tensor Calculus, 1949; Science: Sense and Nonsense, 1951; Geometrical Mechanics and de Broglie Waves, 1954; Relativity: the Special Theory, 1956; The Hypercircle in Mathematical Physics, 1957; The Relativistic Gas, 1957; Kandelman's Krim, 1957; Relativity: the General Theory, 1960; Talking about Relativity, 1970; papers on geometry and applied mathematics; Ed. Sir W. R. Hamilton's Mathematical Papers, Vol. I. *Address:* Torfan, 8 Stillorgan Park, Blackrock, Co. Dublin. *T:* 01–2881251.

SYNGE, Richard Laurence Millington, FRS 1950; Hon. Professor of Biology, University of East Anglia, Norwich, 1968–84; *b* 28 Oct. 1914; *s* of late Laurence M. Synge and Katharine C. Synge (*née* Swan), Great Barrow, Chester; *m* 1943, Ann, *d* of late Adrian L. Stephen and Karin Stephen (*née* Costelloe), both of London; three *s* four *d*. *Educ:* Winchester College; Trinity College, Cambridge (Hon. Fellow, 1972). International Wool Secretariat Research Student, University of Cambridge, 1938; Biochemist: Wool Industries Research Assoc., Leeds, 1941; Lister Institute of Preventive Medicine, London, 1943; Rowett Research Inst., Bucksburn, Aberdeen, 1948; Food Research Inst., Norwich, 1967–76. Editorial Board, Biochemical Journal, 1949–55. Hon. MRIA 1972; Hon. DSc: East Anglia, 1977; Aberdeen, 1987; Hon. PhD Uppsala, 1980. (Jtly) Nobel Prize for Chemistry, 1952. *Publications:* papers in biochemical and chemical journals, etc, 1937–. *Address:* 19 Meadow Rise Road, Norwich NR2 3QE. *T:* Norwich (0603) 53503.

SYNGE, Sir Robert Carson, 8th Bt, *cr* 1801; Manager and Owner, Rob's Furniture; *b* 4 May 1922; *s* of late Neale Hutchinson Synge (2nd *s* of 6th Bt) and Edith Elizabeth Thurlow (*d* 1933), Great Parndon, Essex; *m* 1944, Dorothy Jean Johnson, *d* of T. Johnson, Cloverdale; two *d*. *S* uncle, 1942. *Heir: cousin* Neale Francis Synge [*b* 28 Feb. 1917; *m* 1939, Kathleen Caroline Bowes; one *s* one *d*]. *Address:* 19364 Fraser Highway, RR4, Langley, British Columbia, Canada.

SYNNOT, Adm. Sir Anthony (Monckton), KBE 1979 (CBE 1972); AO 1976; Hon. JMN 1965; Hon. PSM 1982; *b* 5 Jan. 1922; *m* 1st, 1959, M. Virginia (*d* 1965), *d* of late Dr W. K. Davenport; two *d*; 2nd, 1968, E. Anne, *d* of late E. W. Manifold, MC. *Educ:* Geelong Grammar School. Joined RAN, 1939; served War of 1939–45 in HMA Ships Canberra, Stuart, Quiberon; HM Ships Barham, Punjabi; CO HMAS Warramunga, 1956–57; HMAS Vampire, 1961–62; OC Royal Malaysian Navy, 1962–65; CO HMAS Sydney, 1966, HMAS Melbourne, 1967; IDC 1968; Chief of Naval Personnel, 1970;

Dep. Chief of Naval Staff, 1971–72; Commanding HM Australian Fleet, 1973; Director Joint Staff, 1974–76; Chief of Naval Staff, 1976–79; Chief of Defence Force Staff, 1979–82, retired. Chm., Australian War Meml Council, 1982–85. *Recreations:* tennis, golf, horse-driving. *Address:* Ballymoyer, Barton Highway, Yass, NSW 2582, Australia. *Clubs:* Commonwealth (Canberra); Melbourne (Melbourne).

SYNNOTT, Hilary Nicholas Hugh; HM Diplomatic Service; Head of Security Co-ordination Department, Foreign and Commonwealth Office, since 1991; *b* 20 March 1945; *s* of late Commander Jasper Nicholas Netterville Synnott, DSC, RN and Florence England Synnott (*née* Hillary); *m* 1973, Anne Penelope Clarke; one *s* decd. *Educ:* Beaumont College; Dartmouth Naval College (scholar); Peterhouse, Cambridge (MA); RN Engineering College. CEng; MIEE 1971–76. RN 1962–73 (HM Submarines, 1968–73). Joined HM Diplomatic Service, FCO, 1973; UK Delegn to OECD, Paris, 1975; Bonn, 1978; FCO, 1981; Head of Chancery, Amman, 1985; Head of Western European Dept, FCO, 1989. *Recreations:* sub-aqua diving, squash. *Address:* c/o Foreign and Commonwealth Office, King Charles Street, SW1 2AH. *Club:* United Oxford & Cambridge University.

SYSONBY, 3rd Baron, *cr* 1935, of Wonersh; **John Frederick Ponsonby;** *b* 5 Aug. 1945; *s* of late Baron Sysonby, DSO and Sallie Monkland, *d* of Dr Leonard Sanford, New York; *S* father 1956. *Address:* c/o Friars, White Friars, Chester.

SYTHES, Percy Arthur, CB 1980; retired 1980; Comptroller and Auditor General for Northern Ireland, 1974–80; *b* 21 Dec. 1915; *s* of William Sythes and Alice Maud Grice; *m* 1941, Doreen Smyth Fitzsimmons; three *d. Educ:* Campbell Coll., Belfast; Trinity Coll., Dublin. Exhibr, Scholar; BA (Mod. Lit.), 1st cl. hons Gold Medal 1938; Vice-Chancellor's Prizeman 1939. Asst Master: Royal Sch., Dungannon, 1939; Portadown Coll., 1940. Royal Artillery, 1940–46 (Major); GSO2, 1946. Asst Principal, NI Civil Service, 1946; Asst Sec. 1963; Dep. Sec. 1971. Chm., Bd of Governors, Strathearn Sch., 1982–91 (Mem., 1966–91). *Recreations:* gardens, family. *Address:* Malory, 37 Tweskard Park, Belfast BT4 2JZ. *T:* Belfast (0232) 63310.

SZASZY, Dame Miraka Petricevich, DBE 1990 (CBE 1976); QSM 1975; JP; *b* Aug. 1921; *d* of Lovré (Lawrence) Cvitanov Petricevich and Mákeretá Raharuhi; *m* Albert Szaszy (decd); two *s. Educ;* Te Hapua Primary Sch.; Queen Victoria Coll.; Auckland Girls' Grammar Sch.; Auckland Teachers' Training Coll.; Auckland Univ. (BA); Univ. of Hawaii (Dip. Soc. Sci.). Teacher's Cert. Teacher, 1945–70; Lecturer: Teachers' Training Coll., 1972 and 1974–79; Ardmore Trng Coll., 1973; Dir, Community Dept, Ngatapuwae Sec. Sch., 1980–84. Member: Wellington UN Club; SE Asian and Pacific Women's Assoc.; Board of Trustees, Queen Victoria and St Stephen's Schs; Anglican Church and Soc. Commn, 1970; Bishopric of Aotearoa, 1988–; NZ Anglican Synod, 1989–; NZ Race Relations Council, 1969–70; Bd, NZ Broadcasting Council (Mem., Northern NZ Broadcasting Council, 1969–70; Dep. Chm., Radio NZ); NZ Council, Protection Citizens Rights (Vice-Pres.); Social Welfare Commn, 1988–90; Maori Educn Foundn Trust Board; Maori Fisheries Commn, 1990–; Women's Adv. Cttee on estabt of Ministry of Women's Affairs; Maori Women's Gp which estabd Te Ohu Whakatupu (Maori Women's Secretariat) within Women's Ministry; Maori Women's Develt Trust, 1988; Muriwhenua Runanga, 1986; Muriwhenua Incorporation, 1991; Te Orangikaupapa Trust, 1987–; Telethon Family Trust Cttee, 1982–85; Maori Women's Welfare League:

Rep., 1962–70; 1st Vice-Pres., 1971; Pres., 1974–76; Mem., 1st Delegn to Govt on Equal Pay for Women; Delegate: Maori Congress, 1990; Taitokerau Forum, 1990. Pres., Three Combined Tribes, 1988. Silver Jubilee Medal, 1977. *Recreations:* tennis, basketball (rep. Auckland Univ., rep. North Island). *Address:* Ngataki, RD4, Kaitaia, New Zealand. *T:* 0889–58–558.

SZEMERÉNYI, Prof. Oswald John Louis, DrPhil (Budapest); FBA 1982; Professor of Indo-European and General Linguistics, University of Freiburg-im-Breisgau, 1965–81, now Emeritus Professor; *b* London, 7 Sept. 1913; *m* 1940, Elizabeth Kövér; one *s. Educ:* Madách Imre Gimnázium; University of Budapest. Classics Master in Beregszász and Mátyásföld, 1939–41; Lecturer in Greek, 1942–45, Reader, 1946, Professor of Comparative Indo-European Philology in University of Budapest, 1947–48. Came to England, Oct. 1948; employed in industry, 1949–52; Research Fellow, Bedford Coll., London, 1952–53; Asst Lecturer, 1953–54, Lecturer, 1954–58, Reader, 1958–60, in Greek at Bedford College; Professor of Comparative Philology, University College, London, 1960–65. Collitz Prof., Linguistic Inst., USA, 1963; Vis. Prof., Seattle, 1964. Corresp. Mem., Hungarian Acad., 1948 (restitution, 1989); Hon. Mem., Linguistic Soc. of Amer., 1989. *Publications:* The Indo-European liquid sonants in Latin, 1941; Studies in the Indo-European System of Numerals, 1960; Trends and Tasks in Comparative Philology, 1962; Syncope in Greek and Indo-European, 1964; Einführung in die vergleichende Sprachwissenschaft, 1970 (trans. Spanish, 1978, Russian, 1980, Italian, 1985), 4th edn 1991; Richtungen der modernen Sprachwissenschaft, part I, 1971 (trans. Spanish, 1979), part II, 1982 (trans. Spanish, 1986); (contrib.) Comparative Linguistics in: Current Trends in Linguistics 9, 1972; The Kinship Terminology of the Indo-European Languages, 1978; Four Old Iranian Ethnic Names, 1980; An den Quellen des Lateinischen Wortschatzes, 1989; Scripta Minora: selected essays in Indo-European, Greek and Latin, I–III, 1987; contribs to British and foreign learned jls; Studies in Diachronic, Synchronic and Typological Linguistics, Festschrift for Oswald Szemerényi (ed Bela Brogyanyi), I-II, 1979. *Recreation:* motoring. *Address:* Caspar Schrenk Weg 14, D-7800 Freiburg-im-Breisgau, Germany. *T:* (0761) 66117.

SZWARC, Michael M., FRS 1966; Distinguished Professor of Chemistry of the State University of New York, 1966–79, now Professor Emeritus; *b* 9 June 1909; Polish; *m* 1933, Marja Frenkel; one *s* two *d. Educ:* Warsaw Inst. of Technology (Chem. Eng. 1933); Hebrew Univ., Jerusalem (PhD 1942). University of Manchester (Lecturer), 1945–52; PhD (Phys. Chem.) 1947; DSc 1949; State University Coll. of Environmental Scis at Syracuse, NY, 1952–82: Prof. of Physical and Polymer Chemistry; Research Prof.; Distinguished Prof. of Chemistry; Dir, Polymer Research Inst. Baker Lectr, Cornell Univ., 1972. Nobel Guest Prof., Univ. of Uppsala, 1969; Visiting Professor: Univ. of Leuven, 1974; Univ. of Calif, San Diego, 1979–80. Foreign Mem., Polish Acad. of Scis, 1988. Hon. Dr: Leuven, Belgium, 1974; Uppsala, Sweden, 1975; Louis Pasteur Univ., France, 1978. Amer. Chem. Soc. Award for Outstanding Achievements in Polymer Chemistry, 1969; Gold Medal, Soc. of Plastic Engrs, 1972; Gold Medal, Benjamin Franklin Inst., 1978; Herman Mark Award, Amer. Chem. Soc., 1990. *Publications:* Carbanions, Living Polymers and Electron Transfer Processes, 1968; Ions and Ion-pairs in Organic Chemistry, Vol. I, 1972, Vol. II, 1974; numerous contribs to Jl Chem. Soc., Trans Faraday Soc., Proc. Royal Soc., Jl Am. Chem. Soc., Jl Chem. Phys., Jl Phys. Chem., Jl Polymer Sci., Nature, Chem. Rev., Quarterly Reviews, etc. *Address:* 1176 Santa Luisa Drive, Solana Beach, Calif 92075, USA. *T:* (619) 481–1863.

T

TABACHNIK, Eldred, QC 1982; *b* 5 Nov. 1943; *s* of Solomon Joseph Tabachnik and Esther Tabachnik; *m* 1966, Jennifer Kay Lawson; two *s* one *d*. *Educ:* Univ. of Cape Town (BA, LLB); Univ. of London (LLM). Called to the Bar, Inner Temple, 1970, Bencher, 1988. Lectr, UCL, 1969–72. *Recreation:* reading. *Address:* 3 Drax Avenue, SW20 0EG. *T:* 081–947 0699. *Club:* Reform.

TABBARA, Hani Bahjat; Hon. GCVO 1984; Ambassador of the Hashemite Kingdom of Jordan to Yugoslavia, since 1987; *b* 10 Feb. 1939; *s* of Bahjat and Nimat Tabbara; *m* 1980, Wafa; three *s*. *Educ:* University of Alexandria. Entered Govt service, 1963; Jordan Embassy, London, 1971–73; Counsellor, Foreign Ministry, Amman, 1973; Minister Plenipotentiary, Jordan Embassy, London, 1973–76; Private Sec. to Prime Minister, Amman, 1976–77; Ambassador: Morocco, 1977–80; Romania, 1980–82; Saudi Arabia, 1982–84; UK, 1984–85; Turkey, 1985–87. Al Istiklal decoration, 1988. *Address:* c/o Ministry of Foreign Affairs, Amman, Jordan.

TABONE, Dr Vincent, (Censu), FRCSE; President of Malta, since 1989; *b* 30 March 1913; *s* of Elisa Calleja and Nicolo Tabone; *m* 1948, Maria Wirth; four *s* five *d* (and one *c* decd). *Educ:* St Aloysius Coll.; Univ. of Malta. Dip. Opth. Oxford 1946; FRCSE 1948; Dip. RCP; Dip. RCS; Dip. in Med. Jurisp., Soc. of Apothecaries of London 1963. Surgeon Captain, Royal Malta Artillery (campaign medals), 1939–45 War. WHO Consultant on Trachoma in Taiwan, Indonesia, Iraq; Dep., Internat. Panel of Trachoma Experts, WHO, 1956; Lectr in Clinical Ophthalmology. Dept of Surgery, Univ. of Malta, 1960. MP; Minister of Labour, Employment and Welfare, 1966–71; Minister of Foreign Affairs, 1987–89. Mem., Council of Europe Cttees; Chm., Council of Ministers, 1988. Founded Medical Officers Union of Malta, 1954. Hon. LLD Univ. of Malta, 1989. Awarded UN Testimonial for service to UN Programme on Aging, 1989. *Recreations:* reading, watch repairing, travel. *Address:* Office of the President, The Palace, Valletta, Malta. *T:* 221221 *Clubs:* Casino Maltese (1852), Sliema Band.

TABOR, Prof. David, PhD, ScD; FRS 1963; Professor of Physics in the University of Cambridge, 1973–81, now Emeritus; Head of Physics and Chemistry of Solids, Cavendish Laboratory, 1969–81; Fellow of Gonville and Caius College, Cambridge, since 1957; *b* 23 Oct. 1913; *s* of Charles Tabor and Rebecca Weinstein; *m* 1943, Hannalene Stillschweig; two *s*. *Educ:* Regent St Polytechnic; Universities of London and Cambridge. BSc London 1934; PhD Cambridge 1939; ScD Cambridge 1956. Reader in Physics, Cambridge Univ., 1964–73. Vis. Prof., Imperial Coll., London, 1981–. Hon. DSc Bath, 1985. Inaugural Gold Medal of Tribology, Instn of Engrs, 1972; Guthrie Medal, Inst. Physics, 1975. *Publications:* The Hardness of Metals, 1951; Gases, Liquids and Solids, 1969, 2nd edn 1979; (with F. P. Bowden) Friction and Lubrication of Solids, Part I, 1950, rev. edn 1954, repr. 1986; Part II, 1964; contributions to learned jls on friction, adhesion, lubrication and hardness. *Recreation:* Judaica. *Address:* Cavendish Laboratory, Madingley Road, Cambridge CB3 0HE; Gonville and Caius College, Cambridge; 8 Rutherford Road, Cambridge. *T:* Cambridge (0223) 841336.

TABOR, Maj.-Gen. David John St Maur, CB 1977; MC 1944; late Royal Horse Guards; GOC Eastern District, 1974–77, retired; *b* 5 Oct. 1922; *y s* of late Harry Tabor, Hitchin, Herts; *m* 1st 1955, Hon. Pamela Roxane (*d* 1987), 2nd *d* of 2nd Baron Glendyne; two *s*; 2nd, 1989, Marguerite, *widow* of Col Peter Arkwright. *Educ:* Eton; RMA, Sandhurst. Served War: 2nd Lieut, RHG, 1942; NW Europe, 1944–45 (wounded, 1944); Major, 1946. Lt-Col Comdg RHG, 1960; Lt-Col Comdg Household Cavalry, and Silver Stick in Waiting, 1964; Col, 1964; Brig., 1966; Comdr Berlin Infty Bde, 1966; Comdr, British Army Staff and Mil. Attaché, Washington, 1968; RCDS, 1971; Maj.-Gen., 1972; Defence Attaché, Paris, 1972–74. *Recreations:* shooting, fishing, sailing, golf, gardening. *Address:* Willersey House, Willersey, Broadway, Worcs WR12 7PQ. *T:* Broadway (0386) 852211; Lower Farm, Compton Abdale, Cheltenham, Glos GL54 4DS. *T:* Withington (024289) 234. *Clubs:* Turf, Royal Automobile, MCC.

See also Baron Glendyne.

TACKABERRY, John Antony, QC 1982; FCIArb, FFB; a Recorder, since 1988; *b* 13 Nov. 1939; *s* of late Thomas Raphael Tackaberry and Mary Catherine (*née* Geoghegan); *m* 1966, Penelope Holt (separated); two *s*. *Educ:* Downside; Trinity Coll., Dublin; Downing Coll., Cambridge (MA, LLB). Called to the Bar, Gray's Inn, 1967. FCIArb 1973; FFB 1979. Teacher in China, 1963–64 and in London, 1965–66. Adjunct Prof. of Law, Qld Univ. of Technology, 1989. Mem. Council, CIArb, 1985–; President: Soc. of Construction Law, 1983–85; Eur. Soc. of Construction Law, 1985–87. *Recreations:* good food, good wine, good company; and if there's any time left, wind-surfing and photography. *Address:* 22 Willes Road, NW5 3DS. *T:* 071–267 2137; 1 Atkin Building, Gray's Inn, WC1R 5BQ. *Club:* Athenæum.

TACON, Air Cdre Ernest William, CBE 1958; DSO 1944; LVO 1950; DFC 1940 (Bar 1944); AFC 1942 (Bar 1953); *b* 6 Dec. 1917; *s* of Ernest Richard Tacon, Hastings, New Zealand; *m* 1st, 1949, Clare Keating (*d* 1956), *d* of late Michael Keating, Greymouth, NZ; one *s* two *d*; 2nd, 1960, Bernardine, *d* of Cecil Leamy, Wellington, NZ; three *s*. *Educ:* St Patrick's College, Silverstream, New Zealand. Joined RNZAF, 1938. Served with RAF, 1939–46. Transferred to RAF, 1946. CO, King's Flight, Benson, 1946–49. Overseas Services since War: Canal Zone, 1951–53; Cyprus, 1956–58; Persian Gulf, 1961–63; Commandant, Central Fighter Establishment, 1963–65; Air Cdre, Tactics, HQ Fighter Comd, 1966–67; AOC Military Air Traffic Ops, 1968–71, retired. MBIM. *Address:* 69 McLeans Road, Bucklands Beach, Auckland, NZ.

TADIÉ, Prof. Jean-Yves, Chevalier de l'Ordre National du Mérite, 1974; Officier des Palmes académiques, 1988; Professor of French Literature, Université de Paris-Sorbonne, since 1991; *b* 7 Sept. 1936; *s* of Henri Tadié and Marie (*née* Férester); *m* 1962, Arlette Khoury; three *s*. *Educ:* St Louis de Gonzague, Paris; Lycée Louis-le-Grand; Ecole Normale Supérieure (Agrégé de lettres); DèsL Sorbonne 1970; MA Oxford 1988. Lectr, Univ. of Alexandria, 1960–62; Asst Prof., Faculté des Lettres de Paris, 1964; Professor: Univ. de Caen, 1968–69; Univ. de Tours, 1969–70; Univ. de la Sorbonne nouvelle, Paris III, 1970; Hd of French Dept, Cairo Univ., 1972–76; Dir, French Inst., London, 1976–81; Marshal Foch Prof. of French Literature, and Fellow, All Souls Coll., Oxford Univ., 1988–91. Corresp. FBA, 1991. Grand Prix de l'Acad. française, 1988. Officier de l'Ordre de la Couronne de Belgique, 1979. *Publications:* Introduction à la vie littéraire du XIXe Siècle, 1970; Lectures de Proust, 1971; Proust et le Roman, 1971; Le Récit poétique, 1978; Le Roman d'aventures, 1982; Proust, 1983; La Critique littéraire au XXe Siècle, 1987; (ed) M. Proust, A la Recherche du Temps perdu (Bibl. de la Pléiade), 1987–89; Portrait de l'Artiste, 1990; Le Roman du XXe Siècle, 1990. *Recreations:* tennis, opera, cinema. *Address:* Université de Paris-Sorbonne, 1 rue Victor Cousin, 75005 Paris, France; La Croix d'Ouault, 37310 Tauxigny, France. *T:* (16) 47.92.15.93. *Club:* Reform.

TAFT, William Howard, IV; United States Permanent Representative on North Atlantic Council, since 1989; *b* 13 Sept. 1945; *s* of William Howard Taft, III and Barbara Bradfield Taft; *m* 1974, Julia Ann Vadala; one *s* two *d*. *Educ:* St Paul's Sch., Concord, Mass; Yale Coll. (BA 1966); Harvard Univ. (JD 1969). Attorney, Winthrop, Stimson, Putnam & Roberts, NY, 1969–70; Attorney Advr to Chm., Federal Trade Commn, 1970; Principal Asst to Dep. Dir, Office of Management and Budget, 1970–72, Exec. Asst to Dir, 1972–73; Exec. Asst to Sec., Health, Educn and Welfare, 1973–76; Gen. Counsel, Dept of Health, Educn and Welfare, 1976–77; Partner, Leva, Hawes, Symington, Martin & Oppenheimer, 1977–81; General Counsel 1981–84, Dep. Sec. of Defense 1984–85, US Dept of Defense. Mem., DC Bar Assoc., Washington. Bd Mem., Washington Opera, 1977–81. Woodrow Wilson Vis. Teaching Fellow, Woodrow Wilson Foundn, 1977–81. US Dept of Defense Distinguished Public Service Award, 1987. *Publication:* contrib. Indiana Law Jl. *Recreation:* tennis. *Address:* (business) Avenue Leopold III, OTAN-NATO, 1110 Brussels, Belgium; (home) Truman Hall, Waalsebaan 4, 3080 Tervuren, Belgium. *T:* (2) 242–5280. *Clubs:* Cosmos, Leo, Literary Society (Washington, DC).

TAFTI, Rt. Rev. Hassan Barnaba D.; *see* Dehqani-Tafti.

TAGG, Alan; freelance designer/theatre designer; *b* 13 April 1928; *s* of Thomas Bertram Tagg and Edith Annie Hufton. *Educ:* Mansfield Coll. of Art; Old Vic Theatre Sch. Worked as asst to Cecil Beaton, Oliver Messel, etc; first play, Charles Morgan's The River Line, 1952; worked for H. M. Tennent Ltd; Founder Mem., English Stage Co., 1956: designed first prodn of Look Back in Anger, 1956; designed The Entertainer (with Laurence Olivier), 1957; also 15 other prodns at Royal Court Theatre; designed 4 prodns for RSC, including Graham Greene's The Return of A. J. Raffles, 1975; designed 12 prodns at Chichester Festival Theatre, including: Dear Antoine (with Edith Evans), 1971; Waters of the Moon (with Ingrid Bergman), 1977; 9 plays by Alan Ayckbourn; designed: 10 prodns for NT; 93 West End prodns, including: Billy Liar, 1959; How the Other Half Loves, 1970; The Constant Wife, 1973; Alphabetical Order, 1975; Donkeys Years, 1976; The Kingfisher, 1977; Candida, 1977; The Millionairess, 1978; Peter Shaffer's Lettice and Lovage (with Maggie Smith), 1987; 11 prodns on Broadway, including Peter Shaffer's Black Comedy, 1967, Lettice and Lovage, 1990; Look Back in Anger, Moscow Arts Theatre, 1957; Sleuth, Berlin, 1991; directors worked with include Lindsay Anderson, Michael Blakemore, John Dexter, John Gielgud, Tony Richardson and Michael Rudman; exhibitions designed include: Shakespeare, Stratford-upon-Avon, 1964; Hector Berlioz, 1969; 25 Years of Covent Garden, V&A Museum, 1971; Byron, 1974. *Recreation:* living in France. *Address:* 19 Parsons Green, SW6 4UL. *T:* 071–731 2787; Chemin de Masmolène, Vallabrix, 30700 Uzès, France. *T:* 66.22.63.93. *Club:* Groucho.

TAHOURDIN, John Gabriel, CMG 1961; HM Diplomatic Service, retired; *b* 15 Nov. 1913; *s* of late John St Clair Tahourdin; *m* 1957, Margaret Michie; one *s* one *d*. *Educ:* Merchant Taylors' School; St John's College, Oxford. Served HM Embassy, Peking, 1936–37; Private Secretary to HM Ambassador at Shanghai, 1937–40; BoT, 1940–41; Vice-Consul, Baltimore, 1941; Foreign Office, 1942; Private Secretary to Parliamentary Under-Secretary of State, 1943, and to Minister of State, 1945; Athens, 1946; returned to Foreign Office, 1949; Counsellor, British Embassy, The Hague, 1955; Foreign Office, 1957; Minister, UK Delegn to 18 Nation Disarmament Conf., Geneva, 1963–66; HM Ambassador to: Senegal, 1966–71, and concurrently to Mauritania, 1968–71, to Mali, 1969–71, and to Guinea, 1970–71; Bolivia, 1971–73. Mem., Internat. Inst. for Strategic Studies. Price Commission, 1975–77; Kleinwort Benson, 1977–79. *Recreations:* music cinematography, foreign languages, travel. *Address:* Diana Lodge, Little Kineton, Warwick CV35 0DL. *T:* Kineton (0926) 640276; Le Clos des Oliviers, 1007 Bar-sur-Loup, 06620 France. *Clubs:* Athenæum, Travellers', Beefsteak; Norfolk.

TAIT, Dr Alan Anderson; Deputy Director, Fiscal Affairs Department, International Monetary Fund, Washington, since 1982; *b* 1 July 1934; *s* of Stanley Tait and Margaret Ruth (*née* Anderson); *m* 1963, Susan Valerie Somers; one *s*. *Educ:* Heriot's Sch., Edinburgh; Univ. of Edinburgh (MA); Trinity Coll., Dublin (PhD). Lectr, Trinity Coll., Dublin, 1959–71 (Fellow, 1968, Sen. Tutor, 1970); Visiting Prof., Univ. of Illinois, 1965–66. Economic adviser to Irish Govt on industrial develt and taxation and chief economic adviser to Confedn of Irish Industry, 1967–71; economic consultant to Sec. of State for Scotland, 1972–77; International Monetary Fund: Visiting Scholar, 1972; Consultant, 1973 and 1974; Chief, Fiscal Analysis Div., 1976–79; Asst Dir, 1979–82. Prof. of Money and Finance, Univ. of Strathclyde, 1971–77. *Publications:* The Taxation of Personal Wealth, 1967; (with J. Bristow) Economic Policy in Ireland, 1968; (with J. Bristow) Ireland: some problems of a developing economy, 1971; The Value Added Tax, 1972; The Value Added Tax: international practice and problems, 1988; articles on public finance in Rev. of Economic Studies, Finanzarchiv, Public Finance, Staff Papers, etc.

Recreations: sailing, painting. *Address:* 4284 Vacation Lane, Arlington, Va 22207, USA. *T:* 202–623–8725. *Clubs:* Cosmos (Washington DC); Royal Irish Yacht (Dun Laoghaire).

TAIT, Adm. Sir (Allan) Gordon, KCB 1977; DSC 1943; Chief of Naval Personnel and Second Sea Lord, 1977–79; Chairman, Lion Nathan Ltd (formerly Lion Breweries Ltd, then Lion Corporation Ltd), since 1984; *b* 30 Oct. 1921; *s* of Allan G. Tait and Ann Gordon, Timaru, NZ; *m* 1952, Philippa, *d* of Sir Bryan Todd; two *s* two *d*. *Educ:* Timaru Boys' High Sch.; RNC Dartmouth; War Service, Atlantic and N Russia Convoys, 1939–42; Submarines, Mediterranean and Far East, 1942–45 (despatches); Commanded HM Submarines: Teredo, 1947; Solent, 1948; ADC to Governor-General of New Zealand (Lt-Gen. Lord Freyberg, VC), 1949–51; commanded HM Submarines: Ambush, 1951; Aurochs, 1951–53; Tally Ho, 1955; Sanguine, 1955–56; Asst Naval Adviser, UK High Commn, Canada, 1957–59; commanded HM Ships: Caprice, 1960–62; Ajax, 1965–66; Maidstone, 1967; commanded: 2nd Destroyer Squadron (Far East), 1965–66; 3rd Submarine Sqdn, 1967–69; Chief of Staff, Submarine Comd, 1969–70; commanded, Britannia RNC, 1970–72; Rear-Adm., 1972; Naval Secretary, MoD, 1972–74; Vice-Adm., 1974; Flag Officer, Plymouth, Port Admiral, Devonport, NATO Comdr, Central Sub Area, Eastern Atlantic, 1975–77; Adm., 1978. Naval ADC to the Queen, 1972. Director: The Todd Corp. Ltd (Dep. Chm.); NZ Bd, Westpac Banking Corp., 1988–; AGC (NZ) Ltd; Owens Group Ltd; Pres., and Chm. of Trustees, NZ Sports Foundn, 1981–86; Chairman: NZ Family Trust; NZ Internat. Yachting Trust; Mem., Spirit of Adventure Trust Board. *Address:* 22 Orakei Road, Auckland 5, New Zealand; Hiwiroa Farm, PO Box 2, Tokaanu, New Zealand. *Clubs:* White's; Royal Yacht Squadron; Northern (Auckland).

TAIT, Andrew Wilson, OBE 1967; Chairman: New Homes Environmental Group, since 1988; National House-Building Council, 1984–87 (Director-General, 1967–84); *b* 25 Sept. 1922; *s* of late Dr Adam and Jenny Tait; *m* 1954, Elizabeth Isobel Maclennan; three *d*. *Educ:* George Watson's Coll., Edinburgh; Edinburgh Univ. (MA 1st Class Hons History). Served Army, 1942–45. Leader writer, The Scotsman, 1947–48; Scottish Office, 1948–64; Chm., Housing Res. Foundn, 1969–85. Chairman: Internat. Housing and Home Warranty Assoc., 1984–87; Jt Land Requirements Cttee, 1981–87; Home Buyers Adv. Service, 1985–; Bridging the Gap, 1986–; New Homes Mktg Bd, 1988–89; Johnson Fry Property, 1988–. Mem., Lloyd's, 1985–. Dir, Barratt plc, 1988–. *Recreations:* golf, tennis, chess. *Address:* Orchard Croft, Grimmshill, Great Missenden, Bucks HP16 9BA. *T:* Great Missenden (02406) 2061. *Club:* Caledonian.

TAIT, Eric, MBE 1980; Director of European Operations, Pannell Kerr Forster, Chartered Accountants, since 1989; *b* 10 Jan. 1945; *s* of William Johnston Tait and Sarah Tait (*née* Jones); *m* 1967, Agnes Jean Boag (*née* Anderson); one *s* one *d*. *Educ:* George Heriot's Sch., Edinburgh; RMA Sandhurst; RMCS Shrivenham (BSc Eng); Churchill Coll., Cambridge (MPhil); 2nd Lieut, Royal Engineers, 1965; despatches 1976; student, RAF Staff Coll., Bracknell, 1977; OC 7 Field Sqn, RE, 1979–81; Lt-Col 1982; Directing Staff, Staff Coll., Camberley, 1982–83, retired, at own request, 1983; Sec., Inst. of Chartered Accountants of Scotland, 1984–89. Mem. of Exec., Scottish Council (Develt and Industry), 1984–89. Editor in Chief, The Accountant's Magazine, 1984–89. *Recreations:* swimming, hill walking, reading. *Address:* Pannell Kerr Forster, New Garden House, 78 Hatton Garden, EC1N 8JA. *T:* 071–831 7393. *Club:* New (Edinburgh).

TAIT, Prof. James Francis, PhD; FRS 1959; engaged in theoretical research on mathematical modelling of endocrine systems; Emeritus Professor, University of London, since 1982; *b* 1 December 1925; *s* of Herbert Tait and Constance Levinia Brotherton; *m* 1956, Sylvia Agnes Simpson (*née* Wardropper) (*see* S. A. S. Tait). *Educ:* Darlington Grammar Sch.; Leeds Univ. Lectr in Medical Physics, Middlesex Hospital Medical School, 1948–55; External Scientific Staff, Medical Research Council, Middlesex Hospital Medical School, 1955–58; Senior Scientist, Worcester Foundation for Experimental Biology, USA, 1958–70; Joel Prof. of Physics as Applied to Medicine, Univ. of London, 1970–82; Co-Dir, Biophysical Endocrinology Unit, Physics Dept, Middlesex Hosp. Med. Sch., 1970–85. (With S. A. S. Tait) R. Douglas Wright Lectr and Medallion, Univ. of Melbourne, 1989. Hon. DSc Hull, 1979. Society for Endocrinology: Medal, 1969 and Sir Henry Dale Medal, 1979; Tadens Reichstein Award, Internat. Soc. of Endocrinology, 1976; CIBA Award, Amer. Heart Assoc. for Hypertension Research, 1977. *Publications:* papers on medical physics, biophysics and endocrinology. *Recreations:* gardening, photography, chess. *Address:* Moorlands, Main Road, East Boldre, near Brockenhurst, Hants SO42 7WT. *T:* East End (059065) 312.

TAIT, Sir James (Sharp), Kt 1969; DSc, LLD, PhD, BSc(Eng), CEng, FIEE; Vice-Chancellor and Principal, The City University, 1966–74, retired (formerly Northampton College of Advanced Technology, London, of which he was Principal, 1957–66); *b* 13 June 1912; *s* of William Blyth Tait and Helen Sharp; *m* 1939, Mary C. Linton; two *s* one *d*. *Educ:* Royal Technical College, Glasgow; Glasgow Univ. (BSc (Eng.), PhD). Lecturer, Royal Technical Coll., Glasgow, 1935–46; Head of Electrical Engineering Department: Portsmouth Municipal Coll., 1946–47; Northampton Polytechnic, EC1, 1947–51; Principal, Woolwich Polytechnic, SE18, 1951–56. Member: Adv. Council on Scientific Policy, 1959–62; National Electronics Council, 1964–76, Hon. Mem., 1976. Pres., Inst. of Information Scientists, 1970–72. Hon. Fellow: Inst. of Measurement and Control, 1970; Inst. of Inf. Scientists, 1973. Hon. LLD Strathclyde, 1967; Hon. DSc City, 1974. *Recreation:* open-air pursuits. *Address:* 23 Trowlock Avenue, Teddington, Mddx TW11 9QT. *T:* 081–977 6541.

TAIT, Michael Logan, CMG 1987; LVO 1972; HM Diplomatic Service; Assistant Under-Secretary of State with responsibility for Soviet Union and Eastern Europe, since 1990; *b* 27 Sept. 1936; *s* of William and Dorothea Tait; *m* 1968, Margaret Kirsteen Stewart (marr. diss. 1990); two *s* one *d*. *Educ:* Calday Grange Grammar Sch.; New College, Oxford. Nat. service, 2nd Lieut Royal Signals, 1955–57. Foreign Office, 1961; served MECAS, 1961; Bahrain, 1963; Asst Political Agent, Dubai, Trucial States, 1963; FO, 1966; Private Sec. to Minister of State, FO, later FCO, 1968; First Sec. and Hd of Chancery, Belgrade, 1970; First Sec. (Political), Hd of Chancery and Consul, Amman, 1972; FCO, 1975; Counsellor and Hd of Chancery, Baghdad, 1977; Counsellor, FCO, 1978; Dep. Hd of Delegn, CSCE, Madrid, 1980; Dep. Hd of Delegn and Counsellor (Econ. and Finance), OECD, Paris, 1982; Hd of Economic Relns Dept, FCO, 1984; Ambassador to UAE, 1986–89. *Recreations:* languages, mountains, sailing. *Address:* c/o Foreign and Commonwealth Office, SW1A 2AH. *Clubs:* Garrick; Vanderbilt; Wimbleball Sailing (Brompton Regis).

TAIT, Sir Peter, KBE 1975 (OBE 1967); JP; financial consultant, New Zealand; *b* Wellington, NZ, 5 Sept. 1915; *s* of John Oliver Tait and Barbara Ann Isbister; *m* 1946, Lilian Jean Dunn; one *s* one *d*. *Educ:* Wellington Coll., NZ. MP, New Zealand National Party, 1951–54; Mayor, City of Napier, 1956–74; Pres., NZ Municipal Assoc., 1968–69. Chairman: Napier Fire Bd, 1956–75; Hawke's Bay Airport Authority, 1962–74. Freeman, City of Napier. JP 1956–. *Recreations:* bowls, gardening. *Address:* 1 Avon Terrace, Taradale, Napier, New Zealand. *T:* 8445266. *Clubs:* Lions, (Hon.) Cosmopolitan (Napier).

TAIT, Mrs Sylvia Agnes Sophia, (Mrs James F. Tait), FRS 1959; Honorary Research Associate and Co-Director, Biophysical Endocrinology Unit, Physics Department, Middlesex Hospital Medical School, 1982; biochemist; distinguished for her work on the hormones controlling the distribution of salts in the body; *m* 1956, James Francis Tait, *qv*. Research Asst, Courtauld Inst. of Biochemistry, Middlesex Hosp. Med. Sch., 1944–45; External Scientific Staff, MRC, Middlesex Hosp. Med. Sch., 1955–58; Senior Scientist, Worcester Foundn for Experimental Biology, USA, 1958–70; Research Associate and Co-Director, Biophysical Endocrinology Unit, Dept of Physics as Applied to Medicine, Middlesex Hosp. Med. School, 1970–82. (With Prof. J. F. Tait) R. Douglas Wright Lecture and Medallion, Univ. of Melbourne, 1989. Hon. DSc Hull, 1979. Tadeus Reichstein Award, Internat. Endocrine Society, 1976; Gregory Pincus Meml Medal, 1977; CIBA Award, American Heart Assoc. for Hypertension Research, 1977; Sir Henry Dale Medal of Soc. for Endocrinology, 1979. *Address:* Moorlands, Main Road, East Boldre, Brockenhurst, Hants SO42 7WT. *T:* East End (059065) 312.

TAK; *see* Drummond, T. A. K.

TALBOT OF MALAHIDE, 10th Baron *cr* 1831 (Ire.); **Reginald John Richard Arundell;** DL; Hereditary Lord Admiral Malahide and Adjacent Seas; *b* 9 Jan. 1931; *s* of Reginald John Arthur Arundell (*g g g s* of 1st Baroness) (who assumed by Royal Licence, 1945, names and arms of Arundell in lieu of Talbot, and *d* 1953), and Winifred (*d* 1954), *d* of R. B. S. Castle; *S* cousin, 1987; *m* 1955, Laura Duff (*d* 1989), *d* of late Group Captain Edward John Tennant, DSO, MC; one *s* four *d*. *Educ:* Stonyhurst. DL Wilts. KStJ 1988 (CStJ 1983; OStJ 1978); Chm., St John Council for Wilts, 1976–. Knight of Malta, 1977. Hon. Citizen, State of Maryland, USA, 1984. *Heir:* *s* Hon. Richard John Tennant Arundell [*b* 28 March 1957; *m* 1984, Jane Catherine, *d* of Timothy Heathcote Unwin; four *d*]. *Address:* Hook Manor, Donhead, Shaftesbury, Dorset. *Club:* Farmers'.

TALBOT, Vice-Adm. Sir (Arthur Allison) FitzRoy, KBE 1964; CB 1961; DSO 1940 and Bar 1942; DL; Commander-in-Chief, Plymouth, 1965–67; retired; *b* 22 October 1909; *s* of late Henry FitzRoy George Talbot, Captain Royal Navy, and of Susan Blair Athol Allison; *m* 1st, 1940, Joyce Gertrude Linley (*d* 1981); two *d*; 2nd, 1983, Lady (Elizabeth) Durlacher. *Educ:* RN College, Dartmouth. Served War of 1939–45: Comd 10th A/S Striking Force, North Sea, 1939, and 3rd MGB Flotilla, Channel, 1940–41 (DSO); Comd HMS Whitshed, East Coast, 1942 (Bar to DSO); Comd HMS Teazer, Mediterranean, 1943–44. Comdr 1945; Chief Staff Officer, Commodore Western Isles, 1945; Staff Officer Ops to C-in-C Brit. Pacific Fleet and Far East Station, 1947–48; Comd HMS Alert, 1949. Capt. 1950; Naval Attaché, Moscow and Helsinki, 1951–53. Imperial Defence College, 1954. Capt. (D) 3rd Destroyer Squadron, 1955–57; Commodore RN Barracks Portsmouth, 1957–59; Rear-Adm. 1960; Flag Officer: Arabian Seas and Persian Gulf, 1960–61; Middle East, 1961–62; Vice-Adm. 1962; Commander-in-Chief, S Atlantic and S America, 1963–65. DL Somerset, 1973. *Recreations:* riding, shooting. *Address:* Wootton Fitzpaine Manor, Bridport, Dorset, DT6 6NF. *T:* Charmouth (0297) 60455. *Club:* Army and Navy.

TALBOT, Maj.-Gen. Dennis Edmund Blaquière, CB 1960; CBE 1955; DSO 1945; MC 1944; DL; *b* 23 Sept. 1908; *s* of late Walter Blaquière Talbot, St John, Jersey and The White House, Hadlow, Kent; *m* 1939, Barbara Anne, *o d* of late Rev. R. B. Pyper, Rector of Pluckley, Kent; three *s* two *d*. *Educ:* Tonbridge; RMC Sandhurst. 2nd Lieut Roy. West Kent Regt, 1928; served India, 1928–37. Served War of 1939–45 (despatches, DSO, MC); Brigade Major: 30th Infantry Bde, BEF; 141 Inf. Bde; GSO 2, HQ 1st Corps; GSO 2 and 1, Combined Ops; 2nd i/c 5th Bn Dorset Regt; in command, 7th Bn Hampshire Regt, NW Europe, 1944–45. I/c 2nd Bn Royal W Kent Regt, 1945–46; GSO 1, HQ, Far ELF, 1947–48; Senior UK Army Liaison Officer, NZ, 1948–51; Lt-Col 1949; AAG (Col), War Office, 1951–53; Col 1952; i/c 18th Inf. Bde and 99th Gurkha Inf. Bde, Malaya, 1953–55; Brig. 1956; BGS, HQ, BAOR, 1957–58; Maj.-Gen. 1958; GOC, E Anglian Dist and 54th Inf. Div. (TA), 1958–61; Dep. Comdr, BAOR, and Comdr British Army Group Troops, 1961–63; Chief of Staff, BAOR, and GOC Rhine Army Troops, 1963–64, retired; Civil Service, 1964–73. Chm., Kent Cttee, Army Benev. Fund, 1964–84. Graduate of: Staff Coll., Camberley; RN Staff Coll., Greenwich; Joint Services Staff Coll., Latimer; Imperial Defence College, London; Civil Defence Staff Coll., Sunningdale. Col, The Queen's Own Royal West Kent Regt, 1959–61; Dep. Colonel, The Queen's Own Buffs, The Royal Kent Regt, 1961–65; Hon. Col, 8 Queen's Cadre (formerly 8 Bn The Queen's Regt (West Kent)), 1968–71. Pres., local horticultural soc.; Vice-Pres., local br., Royal British Legion. DL Kent, 1964. Knight Commander 1962, Grand Cross 1965, Order of the Dannebrog (Denmark). *Recreations:* gardening, regimental history. *Address:* Oast Court, Barham, near Canterbury, Kent CT4 6PG.

TALBOT, Vice-Adm. Sir FitzRoy, *see* Talbot, Vice-Adm. Sir A. A. F.

TALBOT, Godfrey Walker, LVO 1960; OBE 1946; author, broadcaster, lecturer, journalist; Senior News Reporter and Commentator on staff of British Broadcasting Corporation, 1946–69; official BBC observer accredited to Buckingham Palace, 1948–69; *b* 8 Oct. 1908; *s* of Frank Talbot and Kate Bertha Talbot (*née* Walker); *m* 1933, Bess, *d* of Robert and Clara Owen, Bradford House, Wigan; one *s* (and one *s* decd). *Educ:* Leeds Grammar School. Joined editorial staff on The Yorkshire Post, 1928; Editor of The Manchester City News, 1932–34; Editorial Staff, Daily Dispatch, 1934–37. Joined BBC, 1937; War of 1939–45: BBC war correspondent overseas, 1941–45 (despatches, OBE); organised BBC Home Reporting Unit, as Chief Reporter, after the war. BBC Commentator, Royal Commonwealth Tour, 1953–54, and other overseas visits by HM the Queen. Pres., Queen's English Soc., 1982–. *Publications:* Speaking from the Desert, 1944; Ten Seconds from Now, 1973; Queen Elizabeth the Queen Mother, 1973; Permission to Speak, 1976; Royal Heritage, 1977; Royalty Annual, 1952, 1953, 1954, 1955, 1956; The Country Life Book of Queen Elizabeth The Queen Mother, 1978, 3rd edn 1989; The Country Life Book of the Royal Family, 1980, new edn 1983. *Recreation:* keeping quiet. *Address:* Holmwell, Hook Hill, Sanderstead, Surrey CR2 0LA. *T:* 081–657 3476. *Club:* Royal Over-Seas League (Vice-Chm., 1985–).

TALBOT, Sir Hilary Gwynne, Kt 1968; a Judge of the High Court of Justice, Queen's Bench Division, 1968–83; Judge of the Employment Appeals Tribunal, 1978–81; *b* 22 Jan. 1912; *s* of late Rev. Prebendary A. T. S. Talbot, RD, and Mrs Talbot; *m* 1963, Jean Whitworth (JP Wilts), *o d* of late Mr and Mrs Kenneth Fisher. *Educ:* Haileybury Coll.; Worcester Coll., Oxford. MA Oxon. Served War of 1939–45; Captain, RA. Called to Bar by Middle Temple Jan. 1935, Bencher, 1968. Dep. Chm., Northants QS, 1948–62; Chm., Derbyshire QS, 1958–63; Dep. Chm. Hants QS, 1964–71; Judge of County Courts, 1962–68; a Presiding Judge, Wales and Chester Circuit, 1970–74. Mem., Parole Bd, 1980–82. Dep. Chm., Boundary Commn for Wales, 1980–83. Formerly Dep. Chm., Agricultural Land Tribunals. *Recreations:* fishing, walking, bird-watching. *Address:* Old Chapel House, Little Ashley, Bradford-on-Avon, Wilts BA15 2PN.

TALBOT, Commandant Mary (Irene), CB; Director, Women's Royal Naval Service, 1973–76; *b* 17 Feb. 1922. *Educ:* Bristol Univ. BA Hons, Philosophy and Economics. Joined WRNS as a Naval recruiting asst, Nov. 1943; Officer training course, 1944, and apptd to HMS Eaglet, in Liverpool, as an Educn and Resettlement Officer; served on staffs of C-in-Cs: Mediterranean; the Nore; Portsmouth, 1945–61; First Officer, and apptd to staff of Dir Naval Educn Service, 1952; subseq. served HMS Condor, Dauntless and Raleigh; Chief Officer, and apptd Sen. WRNS Officer, the Nore, 1960; on staff of Dir Naval Manning, 1963–66, and then became Asst Dir, WRNS; Superintendent, and served on staff of C-in-C Naval Home Command, 1969; Supt in charge, WRNS training estabt, HMS Dauntless, near Reading, 1972–73. Hon. ADC, 1973–76. *Recreations:* bridge, gardening, racing. *Address:* Sonning Cottage, Pound Lane, Sonning-on-Thames RG4 0XE. *T:* Reading (0734) 693323; Flat 2, 35 Buckingham Gate, SW1. *T:* 071–834 2579.

TALBOT, Very Rev. Maurice John; Dean Emeritus of Limerick; *b* 29 March 1912; 2nd *s* of late Very Rev. Joseph Talbot, sometime Dean of Cashel; *m* 1942, Elisabeth Enid Westropp (*d* 1975); four *s*; 2nd, 1980, Reta Soames. *Educ:* St Columba's College; Trinity College, Dublin (MA). Curate of Nantenan, 1935; Rector of Rathkeale, 1942; Rector of Killarney, 1952; Dean of Limerick, 1954–71; Prebendary of Taney, St Patrick's Nat. Cathedral, Dublin; Bishop's Curate, Kilmallock Union of Parishes, 1971–73; Rector of Drumcliffe, 1980–84. *Publications:* Pictorial Guide to St Mary's Cathedral, Limerick, 1969; contrib. to North Munster Studies, 1967; The Monuments of St Mary's Cathedral, 1976. *Recreations:* tennis, shooting, fishing. *Address:* 4 Meadow Close, Caherdavin, Limerick, Ireland.

TALBOT, Prof Michael Owen, FBA 1990; James and Constance Alsop Professor of Music, University of Liverpool, since 1986; *b* 4 Jan. 1943; *s* of Alan and Annelise Talbot; *m* 1970, Shirley Ellen Mashiane; one *s* one *d*. *Educ:* Welwyn Garden City Grammar Sch.; Royal Coll. of Music (ARCM); Clare Coll., Cambridge (Open, later Meml Scholar; MusB Hons 1963; MA; PhD 1968). Lectr in Music, 1968, Sen. Lectr, 1979, Reader, 1983–86, Univ. of Liverpool. Corresp. Mem., Ateneo Veneto, Venice, 1986. Order of Merit (Italy), 1980. *Publications:* Vivaldi, 1978 (Italian, German and Polish edns); Vivaldi, 1979 (Japanese, Brazilian and Spanish edns); Albinoni: Leben und Werk, 1980; Antonio Vivaldi: a guide to research, 1988 (Italian edn); Tomaso Albinoni: the Venetian composer and his world, 1990. *Recreations:* chess, reading novels, travel. *Address:* 36 Montclair Drive, Liverpool L18 0HA. *T:* 051–722 3328.

TALBOT, Patrick John; QC 1990; *b* 28 July 1946; *s* of John Bentley Talbot, MC, and Marguerite Maxwell Talbot (*née* Townley); *m* 1976, Judith Anne Urwin; one *s* two *d*. *Educ:* Charterhouse (Foundn Schol.); University Coll., Oxford (MA). Called to Bar, Lincoln's Inn, 1969; in practice at Chancery Bar, 1970–. Member: Senate of Inns of Court and the Bar, 1976–78; Council of Legal Educn, 1977–. Affiliate British Trustee, British Amer. Educnl Foundn, 1984–. Hon. Life Mem., Nat. Union of Students, 1982. *Recreations:* cricket, ski-ing, collecting toys. *Address:* 22 West Park Road, Kew, Richmond, Surrey TW9 4DA. *T:* 081–878 3516. *Clubs:* MCC, Wimbledon Wanderers CC.

TALBOT, His Honour Richard Michael Arthur Chetwynd; a Circuit Judge, 1972–83; *b* 28 Sept. 1911; 3rd *s* of late Reverend Prebendary A. H. Talbot and late Mrs E. M. Talbot; unmarried. *Educ:* Harrow; Magdalene College, Cambridge (MA). Called to Bar by Middle Temple, 1936, Bencher, 1962. Mem. Bar Council, 1957–61. Dep. Chm., 1950–67, Chm., 1967–71, Shropshire QS; Recorder of Banbury, 1955–71, Hon. Recorder, 1972–. Served War of 1939–45, in Army; Major, King's Shropshire Light Infantry. *Address:* 7 St Leonard's Close, Bridgnorth, Salop WV16 4EJ. *T:* Bridgnorth (0746) 763619.

TALBOT, Thomas George, CB 1960; QC 1954; *b* 21 Dec. 1904; *s* of late Rt Hon. Sir George John Talbot and late Gertrude Harriet, *d* of late Albemarle Cator, Woodbastwick Hall, Norfolk; *m* 1933, Hon. Cynthia Edith Guest; one *s* three *d*. *Educ:* Winchester; New Coll., Oxford. Called to Bar, Inner Temple, 1929; Bencher, 1960. RE (TA), 1938; Scots Guards, 1940–44 (Hon. Captain). Assistant, subsequently Deputy, Parliamentary Counsel to Treasury, 1944–53; Counsel to Chm. of Cttees, H of L, 1953–77; Asst Counsel to Chm. of Cttees, H of L, 1977–82. *Address:* Falconhurst, Edenbridge, Kent. *T:* Cowden (034286) 850641. *Club:* Brooks's.

TALBOYS, Rt. Hon. Sir Brian Edward, Hon. AC 1982; CH 1981; KCB 1991; PC 1977; Chairman: Board, Indosuez New Zealand Ltd, since 1982; Genestock New Zealand, since 1983; Ericsson Communications, since 1983; *b* Wanganui, 1921; *m*; two *s*. *Educ:* Wanganui Collegiate Sch.; Univ. of Manitoba; Victoria Univ., Wellington (BA). Served war of 1939–45, RNZAF. MP for Wallace, NZ, 1957–81; Dep. Leader, National Party, 1974–81; Parly Under-Sec. to Minister of Trade and Industry, 1960; Minister of Agriculture, 1962–69; Minister of Science, 1964–72; Minister of Education, 1969–72; Minister of Overseas Trade and Trade and Industry, 1972; Minister of Nat. Develt, 1975–77; Dep. Prime Minister and Minister of For. Affairs and Overseas Trade, 1975–81. Leader of a number of NZ delegns to overseas confs. Owns 500 acre sheep farm, Heddon Bush. Grand Cross 1st Class, Order of Merit, Fed. Republic of Germany, 1978. Hon. DSc Massey Univ., 1981; Hon. DLitt Chung-Ang Univ., Seoul, 1981. *Address:* 1 Hamilton Avenue, Winton, New Zealand.

TALINTYRE, Douglas George; Director, Office of Manpower Economics, since 1989; *b* 26 July 1932; *o s* of late Henry Matthew Talintyre and of Gladys Talintyre; *m* 1956, Maureen Diana Lyons; one *s* one *d*. *Educ:* Harrow County Grammar School; London School of Economics. BSc (Econ.) 1956; MSc (Industrial Relns and Personnel Management) 1983. Joined National Coal Board, 1956: Administrative Assistant, 1956–59; Marketing Officer, Durham Div., 1959–61; Head of Manpower Planning and Intelligence, HQ, 1961–62; Dep. Head of Manpower, HQ, 1962–64; Head of Wages and Control, NW Div., 1964–66. Entered Civil Service, 1966: Principal, Naval Personnel (Pay) Div., MoD, 1966–69; Senior Industrial Relations Officer, CIR, 1969–71; Director of Industrial Relations, CIR, 1971–74; Asst Secretary, Training Services Agency, 1974–75; Counsellor (Labour), HM Embassy, Washington DC, 1975–77; Head of Policy and Planning, Manpower Services Commn, 1977–80; Department of Employment: Hd of Health and Safety Liaison, 1980–83; Asst Sec., Industrial Relations Div., 1983–86; Under Sec., 1986; Dir of Finance and Resource Management, and Principal Finance Officer, 1986–89. Freeman, Co. of Cordwainers, Newcastle upon Tyne, 1952. *Address:* Woodwards, School Lane, Cookham Dean, Berks SL6 9PQ. *Club:* Reform.

See also P. A. Rowan.

TALLBOYS, Richard Gilbert, CMG 1981; OBE 1974; FCA; FCIS; FCPA; Chief Executive, World Coal Institute, London, since 1988; *b* 25 April 1931; *s* of late Harry Tallboys; *m* 1954, Margaret Evelyn, *d* of late Brig. H. W. Strutt, DSO, ED, Hobart; two *s* two *d*. *Educ:* Palmer's School. LLB (London), BCom (Tasmania). Lt-Comdr RANR. Merchant Navy apprentice, 1947–51; Third/Second Mate, Australian coast, 1952–55; accounting profession in Australia, 1955–62; Alderman, Hobart City Council, 1958–62; Australian Govt Trade Commissioner, Johannesburg, Singapore, Jakarta, 1962–68. HM Diplomatic Service, 1968–88: First Secretary i/c Brasilia, 1969; Head of Chancery, Phnom Penh, 1972 (Chargé d'Affaires *ai* 1972, 1973); FO, 1973; Counsellor Commercial, Seoul, 1976–80 (Chargé d'Affaires *ai* 1977, 1978, 1979); Consul-General, Houston, 1980–85; Ambassador to Vietnam, 1985–87. Mem., Internat. Trade Cttee, 1990–, and Mem. Council, London Chamber of Commerce and Industry. Freeman, City of London, 1985. *Recreations:* squash, ski-ing, cautious adventuring. *Address:* 7 Chapel Side, W2 4LG; 5/14 Henrietta Street, Double Bay, Sydney, NSW 2028, Australia. *Clubs:* Travellers', Naval; Tasmanian (Hobart); Royal Australian Naval Sailing Assoc.

TALLING, John Francis, DSc; FRS 1978; Research Associate, Freshwater Biological Association, since 1990; *b* 23 March 1929; *s* of Frank and Miriam Talling; *m* 1959, Ida Björnsson; one *s* one *d*. *Educ:* Sir William Turner's Sch., Coatham; Univ. of Leeds. BSc, PhD, DSc. Lecturer in Botany, Univ. of Khartoum, 1953–56; Visiting Research Fellow, Univ. of California, 1957; Plant Physiologist (SPSO), Freshwater Biological Assoc., 1958–89; Hon. Reader, Univ. of Lancaster, 1979–84. *Publications:* co-author, Water Analysis: some revised methods for limnologists, 1978; papers in various learned jls. *Recreation:* country walking. *Address:* 18 Brow Crescent, Windermere, Cumbria LA23 2EZ. *T:* Windermere (09662) 2836.

TAMBLIN, Air Cdre Pamela Joy, CB 1980; retired; Director, Women's Royal Air Force, 1976–80; *b* 11 Jan. 1926; *d* of late Albert Laing and Olga Victoria Laing; *m* 1970, Douglas Victor Tamblin; one step *s* one step *d*. *Educ:* James Gillespie's High Sch., Edinburgh; Heaton High Sch., Newcastle upon Tyne; Durham Univ. (BA Hons). ATS, 1943–45. Essex County Council Planning Officer, 1949–51. Joined Royal Air Force, 1951; served Education Branch, 1951–55: RAF Locking; RAF Stanmore Park; RAF Wahn, Germany; Secretarial (now Administrative) Branch, 1955–76; Schools Liaison Recruiting, 1955–59; Accountant Officer, RAF St Mawgan and RAF Steamer Point, Aden, 1959–61; Staff College, 1962–63; MoD, Air Secretary's Dept, 1963–66; Sen. Trng Officer, RAF Spitalgate, 1966–68; Admin. Plans Officer, HQ Maintenance Comd, 1968–69; Command WRAF Admin. Officer, HQ Strike Comd, 1969–71; Station Comdr, RAF Spitalgate, 1971–74; Command Accountant, HQ Strike Comd, 1974–76. Chm., Cttee on Women in Nato Forces, 1977–79. Pres., E Cornwall Branch, RAFA, 1984–; Chm., S Western Area Council, RAFA, 1991– (Mem., 1986–; Vice-Chm., 1988–91). FBIM 1977, CBIM 1979; FRSA 1979. *Recreations:* various charitable works, tapestry work, handbell ringing. *Address:* Trecairne, 3 Plaidy Park Road, Looe, Cornwall PL13 1LG. *Club:* Royal Air Force.

TAME, William Charles, CB 1963; Deputy Secretary, Ministry of Agriculture, Fisheries and Food, 1967–71; *b* 25 June 1909; *s* of late Charles Henry Tame, Wimbledon, Surrey; *m* 1935, Alice Margaret, *o d* of late G. B. Forrest, Witherslack, Cumbria; one *s* one *d*. *Educ:* King's College School, Wimbledon; Hertford College, Oxford. Entered Ministry of Agriculture as Assistant Principal, 1933. Chairman: International Whaling Commission, 1966–68; Fisheries R&D Bd, 1972–78. Member: Council, Royal Veterinary Coll., Univ. of London, 1972–80 (Vice-Chm., 1973–80); Governing Body, Animal Virus Res. Inst., 1972–76. *Recreation:* music. *Address:* Windrush, Walton Lane, Bosham, Chichester. *T:* Bosham (0243) 573217.

TAMMADGE, Alan Richard; Headmaster, Sevenoaks School, 1971–81; *b* 9 July 1921; *m* 1950, Rosemary Anne Broadribb; two *s* one *d*. *Educ:* Bromley County Sch.; Dulwich Coll.; Emmanuel Coll., Cambridge. BA (Maths) 1950; MA 1957. Royal Navy Special Entry, 1940; resigned, 1947 (Lt); Cambridge, 1947–50; Lectr, RMA Sandhurst, 1950–55; Asst Master, Dulwich College, 1956–58; Head of Mathematics Dept, Abingdon School, 1958–67; Master, Magdalen College School, Oxford, 1967–71. Pres., Mathematical Assoc., 1978–79. Chm, Battle Fest., 1984–. FIMA 1965. *Publications:* Complex Numbers, 1965; (jtly) School Mathematics Project Books 1–5, 1965–69; (jtly) General Education, 1969; Parents' Guide to School Mathematics, 1976; articles in Mathemat. Gazette, Mathematics Teacher (USA), Aspects of Education (Hull Univ.). *Recreations:* music, gardens. *Address:* 20 Claverham Way, Battle, East Sussex.

TAMUNO, Prof. Tekena Nitonye, PhD; Research Professor in History, National Institute for Policy and Strategic Studies, Kuru, Nigeria; *b* 28 Jan. 1932; *s* of late Chief Mark Tamuno Igbiri and Mrs Ransoline I. Tamuno; *m* 1963, Olu Grace Tamuno (*née* Esho); two *s* two *d*. *Educ:* University Col Ibadan; Birkbeck Coll., Univ. of London; Columbia Univ., New York City. BA (Hons) History, PhD History (London). University of Ibadan: Professor of History, 1971; Head, Dept of History, 1972–75; Dean of Arts, 1973–75; Chairman, Cttee of Deans, 1974–75; Vice-Chancellor, 1975–79; Res. Prof. in History, Inst. of African Studies, 1979. Principal, University Coll., Ilorin, Oct-Nov. 1975; Pro-Chancellor and Chm. Council, Rivers State Univ. of Sci. and Technol., Port-Harcourt, 1981–88; Vis. Prof. in History, Nigerian Defence Acad., Kaduna, 1989–90. Chairman: Presidential Panel on Nigeria Since Independence History Project, 1980–; Bd of Dirs, New Nigerian Newspapers Ltd, 1984–89. Nat. Vice-Pres., Historical Soc. of Nigeria, 1974–78. JP Ibadan, 1976. *Publications:* Nigeria and Elective Representation, 1923–1947, 1966; The Police in Modern Nigeria, 1961–1965, 1970; The Evolution of the Nigerian State: The Southern Phase, 1898–1914, 1972; (ed, with Prof. J. F. A. Ajayi) The University of Ibadan, 1948–1973: A History of the First Twenty-Five Years, 1973; History and History-makers in Modern Nigeria, 1973; Herbert Macaulay, Nigerian Patriot, 1975; (ed with E. J. Alagoa) Eminent Nigerians of the Rivers State, 1980; (ed) Ibadan Voices: Ibadan University in Transition, 1981; Songs of an Egg-Head (poems), 1982; (ed) National Conference on Nigeria since Independence: addresses at the formal opening, 1983; (ed) Proceedings of the National Conference on Nigeria since Independence, Zaria, March 1983, Vol. III: The Civil War Years, 1984; Nigeria Since Independence: The First Twenty-Five Years: (ed with J. A. Atanda) Vol. III, Education, 1989; (ed with J. A. Atanda) Vol. IV, Government and Public Policy, 1989; (ed with S. C. Ukpabi) Vol. VI, The Civil War Years, 1989; (ed with E. J. Alagoa) Land and People of Nigeria: Rivers State, 1989. *Recreations:* music, photography, swimming, horse-riding, gardening, domestic pets. *Address:* National Institute for Policy and Strategic Studies, Kuru, PMB 2024, Bukuru, Plateau State, Nigeria. *T:* 073 80730. *Club:* National Institute (Kuru).

TAMWORTH, Viscount; Robert William Saswalo Shirley, FCA; Director, Norseman Holdings Ltd (formerly Ashby Securities Ltd), since 1987 and of associated companies, since 1988; *b* 29 Dec. 1952; *s* and *heir* of 13th Earl Ferrers, *qv*; *m* 1980, Susannah, *y d* of late C. E. W. Sheepshanks, Arthington Hall, Yorks; two *s* one *d*. *Educ:* Ampleforth. Teaching in Kenya, under CMS's Youth Service Abroad Scheme, 1971–72. Articled to Whinney Murray & Co, CA, 1972–76; employed at Ernst & Whinney, 1976–82, Asst Manager, 1981–82; Gp Auditor, 1982–85, Sen. Treasury Analyst, 1986, BICC plc; Dir, Viking Property Gp Ltd, 1987–88 (Financial Controller and Company Sec., 1986–87). Admitted to Inst. of Chartered Accountants of England and Wales, 1976. *Recreations:* the countryside and related activities, gardening. *Heir:* *s* Hon. William Robert Charles Shirley, *b* 10 Dec. 1984. *Address:* The Old Vicarage, Shirley, Derby DE6 3AZ. *T:* Ashbourne (0335) 60815. *Club:* Boodle's.

TANBURN, Jennifer Jephcott; research consultant, since 1984; *b* 6 Oct. 1929; *d* of late Harold Jephcott Tanburn and Elise Noel Tanburn (*née* Armour). *Educ:* St Joseph's Priory, Dorking; Settrington Sch., Hampstead; University Coll. of the South West, Exeter (BSc (Econ)). Market Research Dept, Unilever Ltd, 1951–52; Research and Information, Lintas Ltd, 1952–66, Head of Div., 1962–66, Head of Special Projects, 1966–74; British Airways Board, 1974–76; Head of Res. and Consumer Affairs, Booker McConnell Food Distbn Div., 1975–76 (a Dir, 1976–83). Member: Marketing Policy Cttee, 1977–80, and Potato Product Gp, 1980–82, Central Council for Agricl and Hortl Co-operation; Market

Research Soc.; Marketing Gp of GB; Packaging Council, 1978–82; Chm., Consumers' Cttees for GB and England and Wales under Agricl Marketing Act of 1958, 1982–. Hon. Fellow, Durham Univ. (Business Sch.), 1991. FRSA 1991. *Publications:* Food, Women and Shops, 1968; People, Shops and the '70s, 1970; Superstores in the '70s, 1972; Retailing and the Competitive Challenge: a study of retail trends in the Common Market, Sweden and the USA, 1974; Food Distribution: its impact on marketing in the '80s, 1981; articles on retailing and marketing subjects. *Recreations:* travel, golf, gardening, dressmaking, television viewing, reading. *Address:* 8 Ellwood Rise, Vache Lane, Chalfont St Giles, Bucks HP8 4SU. *T:* Chalfont St Giles (02407) 5205. *Club:* Beaconsfield Golf.

TANCRED, Sir H. L.; *see* Lawson-Tancred.

TANDY, Jessica; actress, stage and screen; *b* London, 7 June 1909; *d* of Harry Tandy and Jessie Helen (*née* Horspool); *m* 1st, 1932, Jack Hawkins (marr. diss.); one *d;* 2nd, 1942, Hume Cronyn; one *s* one *d. Educ:* Dame Owen's Girls' Sch.; Ben Greet Acad. of Acting. Birmingham Repertory Theatre, 1928; first London appearance, 1929; first New York appearance, 1930; subsequently alternated between London and New York. *New York plays include:* The Matriarch, 1930; The Last Enemy, 1930; Time and the Conways, 1938; The White Steed, 1939; Geneva, 1940; Jupiter Laughs, 1940; Anne of England, 1941; Yesterday's Magic, 1942; A Streetcar Named Desire, 1947–49 (Antoinette Perry Award, 1948); Hilda Crane, 1950; The Fourposter, 1951–53 (Comœdia Matinee Club Bronze Medallion, 1952); Madame Will You Walk?, 1953; Face to Face, 1954; the Honeys, 1955; A Day by the Sea, 1955; The Man in the Dog Suit, 1957–58; Triple Play, 1959; Five Finger Exercise, 1959 (New York League's Delia Austria Medal, 1960); The Physicists, 1964; A Delicate Balance, 1966–67; Camino Real, 1970; Home, 1971; All Over, 1971; Promenade All (tour), 1972; Happy Days, Not I (Samuel Beckett Festival), 1972 (Drama Desk Award, 1973); Rose, 1981; Foxfire, 1982–83 (Antoinette Perry, Drama Desk, Outer Critics Circle awards, 1983); Glass Menagerie, 1983; Salonika, 1985; The Petition, 1986; Tours: Not I, 1973; Many Faces of Love, 1974, 1975 and 1976; Noel Coward in Two Keys, 1974, 1975; The Gin Game, 1977 (US and USSR Tour, 1978–79; Sarah Siddons Award, Chicago and Los Angeles Critics' Award). *London plays include:* The Rumour, 1929; Autumn Crocus, Lyric, 1931; Children in Uniform, Duchess, 1932; Hamlet, New, 1934; French without Tears, Criterion, 1936; Anthony and Anna, Whitehall, 1935; The Gin Game, Lyric, 1979. Open-Air Theatre, London, 1933 and 1939; Old Vic, 1937 and 1940, leading Shakespearian rôles, etc. Toured Canada, 1939; tour of US with husband, (poetry and prose readings), 1954; they also toured Summer Theatres (in plays), 1957. Opening Season of the Tyrone Guthrie Theatre Minneapolis, USA: Hamlet, Three Sisters, Death of A Salesman, 1963; The Way of the World, The Cherry Orchard, The Caucasian Chalk Circle, 1965; Foxfire, 1981. The Miser, Los Angeles, 1968; Heartbreak House, Shaw Festival, Niagara-on-the-Lake, Ontario, 1968; Tchin-Tchin, Chicago, 1969; Eve, The Way of the World and A Midsummer Night's Dream, Stratford, Ontario Festival, 1976; Long Day's Journey Into Night, London, Ontario, 1977, Stratford, Ont, 1980; The Gin Game, Long Wharf Theatre, New Haven, Conn, 1977 (Drama Desk Award, 1977–78; Antoinette Perry Award, 1978); Foxfire, Stratford, Ont, 1980, Ahmanson, LA, 1985–86. *Films include:* The Indiscretions of Eve, The Seventh Cross, The Valley of Decision, Dragonwyck, The Green Years, A Woman's Vengeance, Forever Amber, September Affair, Rommel-Desert Fox, A Light in the Forest, Adventures of a Young Man, The Birds, Butley; Honky Tonk Freeway, 1980; Still of the Night, 1981; Garp, 1981; Best Friends, 1982; The Bostonians, 1984; Cocoon, 1985; The House on Carroll Street; Batteries Not Included; Cocoon: the return, 1988; Driving Miss Daisy, 1990 (Academy Award, 1990; BAFTA Award, 1991). *Television:* all major American dramatic programs. Obie Award, 1972–73; Brandeis Theatre Arts Medal, 1978; Elected to Theatre Hall of Fame, 1979; Commonwealth Award for distinguished service in dramatic arts, 1983; Honoree, Kennedy Center Honors, 1986. Hon. LLD Univ. of Western Ontario, 1974; Hon. DHL Fordham Univ., 1985.

TANGAROA, Hon. Sir Tangaroa, Kt 1987; MBE 1984; Queen's Representative, Cook Islands, since 1984; *b* 6 May 1921; *s* of Tangaroa and Mihiau; *m* 1941; two *s* seven *d. Educ:* Avarua Primary School, Rarotonga. Radio operator, 1939–54; Shipping Clerk, A. B. Donald Ltd and J. & P. Ingram Ltd, 1955–63; MP for Penrhyn, 1958–84; Minister of Educn, Works, Survey, Printing and Electric Power Supply; Minister of Internal Affairs, 1978–80; retired from politics, 1984. Pres., Cook Is Crippled Children's Soc., 1966–; Deacon, Cook Is Christian Church (served 15 years in Penrhyn, 28 years in Avarua); former community positions: Mem., Tereora Coll. Sch. Cttee for 20 years and 10 as Sec./Treasurer; Pres., Cook Is Boys Brigade for 15 years; delegate to Cook Is Sports Assoc. *Address:* Government House, Rarotonga, Cook Islands. *T:* 23499. *Clubs:* Rarotonga Rotary; Avatiu (formerly Treasurer).

TANGE, Sir Arthur (Harold), AC 1977; Kt 1959; CBE 1955 (OBE 1953); retired civil servant; *b* 18 August 1914; 2nd *s* of late Charles L. Tange, Solicitor, Gosford, New South Wales; *m* 1940, Marjorie Florence, 2nd *d* of late Professor Edward O. G. Shann; one *s* one *d. Educ:* Gosford High School; Western Australia University (BA; 1st Cl. Hons Economics). Joined Bank of NSW, 1931; Economist, Bank of NSW, 1938; Economic Research in Commonwealth Depts, Canberra, 1942–46. Entered Australian Diplomatic Service, 1946; First Secretary, Australian Mission to United Nations, 1946–48; Counsellor, United Nations Division, Canberra, 1948–50; Assistant Secretary, Department of External Affairs, Canberra, 1950–53; Minister at Australian Embassy, Washington, 1953–54; Secretary of Dept of External Affairs, Canberra, 1954–65; High Comr in India and Ambassador to Nepal, 1965–70; Sec., Dept of Defence, 1970–79. Represented Australia at many international diplomatic, economic, trade and defence conferences, 1944–79. *Publication:* (jointly) Australia Foots the Bill, 1942. *Recreation:* stream fishing. *Address:* 32 La Perouse Street, Griffith, ACT 2603, Australia. *T:* 295–8879. *Club:* Commonwealth (Canberra).

TANKERVILLE, 10th Earl of, *cr* 1714; **Peter Grey Bennet;** Baron Ossulston, 1682; *b* 18 Oct. 1956; *s* of 9th Earl of Tankerville, and of Georgiana Lilian Maude, *d* of late Gilbert Wilson, MA, DD, PhD; *S* father, 1980. *Educ:* Oberlin Conservatory, Ohio (Bachelor of Music); San Francisco State Univ. (Master of Music). Working as musician, San Francisco. *Heir: uncle* Rev. the Hon. George Arthur Grey Bennet [*b* 12 March 1925; *m* 1957, Hazel Glyddon, *d* of late E. W. G. Judson; two *s* one *d*]. *Address:* 139 Olympia Way, San Francisco, California 94131, USA. *T:* 415–826–6639.

TANLAW, Baron *cr* 1971 (Life Peer), of Tanlawhill, Dumfries; **Simon Brooke Mackay;** Chairman and Managing Director, Fandstan Ltd, since 1973; *b* 30 March 1934; *s* of 2nd Earl of Inchcape; *m* 1st, 1959, Joanna Susan, *d* of Major J. S. Hirsch; one *s* two *d* (and one *s* decd); 2nd, 1976, Rina Siew Yong Tan, *d* of late Tiong Cha Tan and Mrs Tan; one *s* one *d. Educ:* Eton College; Trinity College, Cambridge (MA 1966). Served as 2nd Lt XII Royal Lancers, Malaya. Inchcape Group of Companies, India and Far East, 1960–66; Managing Director, Inchcape & Co., 1967–71, Dir 1971–; Chm., Thwaites & Reed Ltd, 1971–74; Chm. and Man. Dir, Fandstan Group of private cos, 1973–. Chm., Building Cttee, Univ. of Buckingham (formerly UC at Buckingham), 1973–78, Mem. Council of Management 1973–, Hon. Fellow, 1981, DUniv 1983; Mem. Ct of Governors, LSE, 1980–. Mem., Lord Chancellor's Inner London Adv. Cttee on Justices of the Peace, 1972–83. Contested (L) Galloway, by-election and gen. election, 1959, and gen. election, 1964. Mem., EC Cttee Sub-Cttee F (Energy, Transport Technology and Research), 1980–83; Chm., Parly Liaison Gp for Alternative Energy Strategies, 1981–83. Joint Treasurer, 1971–72, Dep. Chm., 1972, Scottish Liberal Party. Pres., Sarawak Assoc., 1973–75. Chm., Nat. Appeal, Elizabeth FitzRoy Homes for the mentally handicapped, 1985–. Mem. Consultative Panel, Horological Inst. *Publications:* article, The Case for a British Astro-physical Master Clock; paper, Horology and Space-Time. *Recreations:* normal. *Address:* Tanlawhill, Eskdalemuir, By Langholm, Dumfriesshire. *T:* Eskdalemuir (03873) 73273; 31 Brompton Square, SW3 2AE. *Clubs:* White's, Oriental, Buck's; Puffin's (Edinburgh).

TANNER, Dr Bernice Alture, FRCGP; General Practitioner in London W11 area, 1948–85, retired; *b* 23 Sept. 1917; *m* 1942, Prof. James M. Tanner, MD, DSc, FRCP; one *d* (one *s* decd). *Educ:* Cornell Univ., USA; New York Univ.; McGill Univ., Canada; Medical Coll. of Pennsylvania, USA. BA 1939; MD 1943 (Med. Coll., Pa); FRCGP 1980. Convenor, Educational Cttee, London NW Faculty RCGP; Course organizer, St Charles Hosp. Vocational Trng Scheme for Gen. Practice; Mem., AHA Cttee paediatric care, London NW Area. Mem., Supplementary Benefits Commn, 1976–79. *Publications:* (ed) Language and Communication in General Practice, 1976; Signposts for the Future of General Practice: health, human biology and primary care, 1991. *Recreations:* music, postgraduate medical education. *Address:* 127 Oakwood Court, Abbotsbury Road, W14. *T:* 071–603 7881.

TANNER, Brian Michael; Chief Executive, Somerset County Council, since 1990; *b* 15 Feb. 1941; *s* of Gerald Evelyn Tanner and Mary Tanner; *m* 1963, June Ann Walker; one *s* one *d. Educ:* Acklam Hall Grammar Sch., Middlesbrough; Bishop Vesey Grammar Sch., Sutton Coldfield; Bristol Univ. (BA 1st class Hons). CIPFA. Trainee Accountant, Birmingham CBC, 1962–66; Economist, Coventry CBC, 1966–69; Chief Accountant, Teesside CBC, 1969–71; Warwickshire County Council: Asst County Treasurer, 1971–73; Asst Chief Exec., 1973–75; County Treasurer, Somerset CC, 1975–90; Treasurer, Avon and Somerset Police Authy, 1975–91. Advr, ACC Cttees on agric, educn, nat. parks, finance, policy, police, 1976–91; Mem., Accounting Standards Cttee, 1982–85; Chief Negotiator with Central Govt on Rate Support Grant, 1985–88; Mem., Investment Cttee, Nat. Assoc. of Pension Funds, 1988–91. Trustee, Central Bureau for Educnl Visits and Exchanges, 1981–91. Governor, Millfield Sch., 1989–91. Freeman, City of London, 1990. *Publication:* Financial Management in the 1990's, 1989. *Recreations:* squash, gardening, philately, antiques. *Address:* County Hall, Taunton, Somerset. *T:* Taunton (0823) 255000; 8 Broadlands Road, Taunton, Somerset TA1 4HQ. *T:* Taunton (0823) 337826. *Club:* Sloane.

TANNER, David Williamson, DPhil; Under Secretary, Head of Science Branch, Department of Education and Science, 1981–89; *b* 28 Dec. 1930; *s* of late Arthur Bertram Tanner, MBE and of Susan (*née* Williamson); *m* 1960, Glenis Mary (*née* Stringer); one *s* two *d. Educ:* Raynes Park County Grammar Sch.; University Coll., Oxford. MA, DPhil (Oxon). Univ. of Minnesota (post-doctoral research), USA, 1954–56; Dept of Scientific and Industrial Research (Fuel Research Station and Warren Spring Lab.), 1957–64; Dept of Educn and Science, 1964–89. *Publications:* papers on physical chem. in Trans. Faraday Soc., Jl Applied Chem., Jl Heat and Mass Transfer, etc. *Recreations:* family, philosophy. *Address:* The Limes, Market Place, Kenninghall, Norwich, Norfolk NR16 2AH. *T:* Quidenham (095387) 666.

See also P. A. Tanner.

TANNER, Dr John Ian, CBE 1979; Founding Director: Royal Air Force Museum, 1963–88; Battle of Britain Museum, 1978–88; Cosford Aero-Space Museum, 1978–88; Bomber Command Museum, 1982–88; Hon. Archivist, since 1980, Senior Research Fellow, since 1982, Pembroke College, Oxford; *b* London, 2 Jan. 1927; *o s* of R. A. and I. D. M. Tanner; *m* 1st, 1953, April Rothery (marr. diss. 1972, and subseq. by RC Tribunal); one *d;* 2nd, 1991, Andrea Isobel Duncan. *Educ:* City of London Library Sch.; Universities of London, Nottingham (MA, PhD) and Oxford (MA). Reading Public Library, 1950; Archivist-Librarian, Kensington Library, 1950–51; Leighton House Art Gall. and Museum, 1951–53; Curator, Librarian and Tutor, RAF Coll., 1953–63; Hon. Sec., Old Cranwellian Assoc., 1956–64; Extra-mural Lectr in History of Art, Univ. of Nottingham, 1959–63. Walmsley Lectr, City Univ., 1980. Vis. Fellow, Wolfson Coll., Cambridge, 1983–; Prof., The Polish Univ., 1987–. Mem., Adv. Council, Inst. of Heraldic and Genealogical Studies. Chm., Internat. Air Museum Cttee; Vice-President: Guild of Aviation Artists; Croydon Airport Museum Soc.; Trustee, Manchester Air and Space Museum; Mem. Founding Cttee, All England Lawn Tennis Museum; Mem. Br. Cttee, Caen Musée pour la Paix; President: Anglo-American Ecumenical Assoc; USAF European Meml Foundn; Mem. Bd of Advrs, Battle Harbour Foundn's Anglican Service, Training and Religious Orgn. Life Vice-Pres., Friends of RAF Mus. FLA, FMA, FRHistS, FRAeS, FSA. Hon. DLitt City, 1982; Hon. LLD, The Polish Univ., 1989. Freeman, City of London, 1966; Liveryman: Worshipful Co. of Gold and Silver Wyre Drawers, 1966; Scriveners' Co., 1978. Freeman, Guild of Air Pilots and Air Navigators, 1979. Hon. Mem. Collegio Araldico of Rome, 1963; Tissandier Award, Fedn Aeronautique Internat., 1977. KStJ 1978 (OStJ 1964; St John Service Medal, 1985); KCSG 1977; KCSG, with Star, 1985; Cross of Merit, Order of Malta, 1978. Grand Comdr, OM Holy Sepulchre (Vatican); Order of Polonia Restituta (Poland), 1985; Nile Gold Medal (Egypt), 1987. *Publications:* (ed) List of Cranwell Graduates, 2nd edn, 1963; (jtly) Encyclopedic Dictionary of Heraldry, 1968; How to trace your Ancestors, 1971; Man in Flight (limited edn), 1973; The Royal Air Force Museum: one hundred years of aviation history, 1973; (with W. E. May and W. Y. Carman) Badges and Insignia of the British Armed Services, 1974; Charles I, 1974; Who's Famous in Your Family: a Reader's Digest guide to genealogy, 1975, 2nd edn 1979; Wings of the Eagle (exhibition catalogue), 1976; (ed) They Fell in the Battle, 1980 (limited edn, to commemorate 40th anniv. of Battle of Britain); Sir William Rothenstein: an RAF Museum exhibition catalogue, 1985; RAF Museum — a combined guide, 1987; Editor, RAF Museum Air Publication series, 10 vols; General Editor: Museums and Libraries (Internat. Series); Studies in Air History; reviews and articles in professional and other jls. *Recreations:* cricket, opera, reading. *Address:* Flat One, 57 Drayton Gardens, SW10 9RU. *Clubs:* Athenæum, Beefsteak, Reform, MCC, Royal Air Force.

TANNER, John W., CBE 1983; FRIBA, FRTPI; Director, United Nations Relief and Works Agency for Palestine Refugees, Jordan, 1971–83 (accorded rank of Ambassador to Hashemite Kingdom of Jordan, 1973); *b* 15 Nov. 1923; *s* of Walter George Tanner and Elizabeth Wilkes Tanner (*née* Humphreys); *m* 1948, Hazel Harford Harford-Jones; one *s* two *d. Educ:* Clifton Coll.; Liverpool Univ. Sch. of Architecture and Dept of Civic Design. MCD, BArch (Hons). Sen. Planning Officer, Nairobi, 1951; Architect, Nairobi, 1953; Hon. Sec., Kenya Chapter of Architects, 1954; UN Relief and Works Agency: Architect and Planning Officer, Beirut, 1955; Chief Techn. Div., 1957. Past Mem. Cttee, Fedn of Internat. Civil Servants Assoc., 1968–70. *Buildings:* vocational and teacher training centres, schools; low cost housing and health centres; E African Rugby Union HQ, Nairobi; training centres: Damascus, Syria; Siblin, Lebanon; Ramallah; Wadi Seer;

Amman, Jordan. *Publications:* The Colour Problem in Liverpool: accommodation or assimilation, 1951; Building for the UNRWA/UNESCO Education and Training Programme, 1968. *Recreations:* formerly: Rugby football (Waterloo, Lancs, 1950; Kenya Harlequins, Kenya and E Africa); skiing, board sailing. *Address:* 69B La Pleta, Ordino, Andorra. *Club:* Royal Automobile.

TANNER, Meg; *see* Beresford, M.

TANNER, Prof. Paul Antony, (Tony); Professor of English and American Literature, since 1989, and Fellow of King's College, since 1960, University of Cambridge; *b* 18 March 1935; *s* of late Arthur Bertram Tanner, MBE and of Susan Williamson; *m* 1979, Nadia Fusini. *Educ:* Raynes Park County Grammar Sch.; Jesus Coll., Cambridge (MA, PhD). ACLS Fellow, Univ. of California, Berkeley, 1962–63; Univ. Lectr, Cambridge, 1966–80; Fellow, Center for Advanced Studies in Behavioral Sciences, Stanford, 1974–75; Reader in Amer. Lit., Cambridge Univ., 1980–89. *Publications:* The Reign of Wonder, 1965; City of Words, 1970; Adultery in the Novel, 1979; Thomas Pynchon, 1982; Henry James, 1985; Jane Austen, 1986; Scenes of Nature, Signs of Men, 1987. *Recreations:* travelling, talking. *Address:* King's College, Cambridge. *T:* Cambridge (0223) 350411.
See also D. W. Tanner.

TANSLEY, Sir Eric (Crawford), Kt 1953; CMG 1946; Chairman, Pacol, 1962–72; formerly Director: Bank of West Africa; Standard Bank Ltd; Standard & Chartered Banking Group Ltd; Gill & Duffus Ltd; *b* 25 May 1901; *o s* of William and Margaret Tansley; *m* 1931, Iris, *yr d* of Thomas Richards; one *s* one *d*. *Educ:* Mercers' Sch. Formerly: Mem., Colonial, now Commonwealth, Development Corporation, 1948–51, 1961–68; Chairman: London Cocoa Terminal Market Assoc., 1932; Cocoa Assoc. of London, 1936–37; Marketing Director, West African Produce Control Board (Colonial Office), 1940–47. Retired, 1961 as Managing Director, Ghana Cocoa Marketing Co. and Adviser, Nigerian Produce Marketing Co. *Address:* 11 Cadogan Square, SW1. *T:* 071–235 2752.

TANZANIA, Archbishop of, since 1984; **Most Rev. John Acland Ramadhani;** Bishop of Zanzibar and Tanga, since 1980; *b* 1932. *Educ:* Univ. of Birmingham (DipTh 1975); Univ. of Dar-es-Salaam (BA 1967); Queen's Coll., Birmingham. Deacon 1975, Birmingham; priest 1976, Dar-es-Salaam; Asst Chaplain, Queen's Coll., Birmingham, 1975–76; Warden, St Mark's Theol Coll., Dar-es-Salaam, 1976–80. *Address:* PO Box 35, Korogwe, Tanzania.

TAPPER, Colin Frederick Herbert; All Souls Reader in Law, since 1979, and Fellow of Magdalen College, since 1965, Oxford University; Special Consultant on Computer Law to Messrs Masons (Solicitors), since 1990; *b* 13 Oct. 1934; *s* of Herbert Frederick Tapper and Florence Gertrude Tapper; *m* 1961, Margaret White; one *d*. *Educ:* Bishopshalt Grammar Sch.; Magdalen Coll., Oxford. Lectr, LSE, 1959–65. Visiting Professor, Universities of: Alabama, 1970; NY, 1970; Stanford, 1975; Monash, 1984; Northern Kentucky, 1986; Sydney, 1989. *Publications:* Computers and the Law, 1973; Computer Law, 1978, 4th edn 1990; (ed) Crime Proof and Punishment, 1981; (ed) Cross on Evidence, 6th edn 1985, 7th edn 1990; (ed) Cross and Wilkins Introduction to Evidence, 6th edn 1986. *Recreations:* reading, computing, writing. *Address:* Corner Cottage, Stonesfield, Oxford OX7 2QA. *T:* Stonesfield (099389) 284.

TAPPS GERVIS MEYRICK; *see* Meyrick.

TAPSELL, Sir Peter (Hannay Bailey), Kt 1985; MP (C) East Lindsey (Lincs), since 1983 (Nottingham West, 1959–64; Horncastle, Lincs, 1966–83); *b* Hove, Sussex, 1 Feb. 1930; *s* of late Eustace Bailey Tapsell (39th Central India Horse) and of Jessie Maxwell (*née* Hannay); *m* 1st, 1963, Hon. Cecilia Hawke (marr. diss. 1971), 3rd *d* of 9th Baron Hawke; one *s* decd; 2nd, 1974, Mlle Gabrielle Mahieu, *e d* of late Jean and Bathelde Mahieu, Normandy, France. *Educ:* Tonbridge Sch.; Merton Coll., Oxford (1st Cl. Hons Mod. Hist., 1953; Hon. Postmaster, 1953; MA 1957; Hon. Fellow, 1989). Nat. Service, Subaltern, Royal Sussex Regt, 1948–50 (Middle East). Librarian of Oxford Union, 1953; Rep. Oxford Union on debating tour of United States, 1954 (Trustee, Oxford Union, 1985–). Conservative Research Department, 1954–57 (Social Services and Agriculture). Personal Asst to Prime Minister (Anthony Eden) during 1955 General Election Campaign. Contested (C) Wednesbury, bye-election, Feb. 1957. Opposition front bench spokesman on Foreign and Commonwealth affairs, 1976–77, on Treasury and economic affairs, 1977–78. London Stock Exchange, 1957–. Internat. investment advr to several central banks, foreign banks and trading cos; Hon. Mem., Brunei Gout Investment Adv. Bd, 1976–83; Hon. Dep. Chm., Mitsubishi Trust Oxford Foundn, 1988–; Member: Council, Inst. for Fiscal Studies; Court, Univ. of Nottingham, 1959–64; Univ. of Hull, 1966–. Chm., Coningsby Club, 1957–58. Jt Chm., British-Caribbean Assoc., 1963–64. Mem. Organising Cttee, Zaire River Expedn, 1974–75. Vice Pres., Tennyson Soc., 1966–. Hon. Life Mem., 6th Sqdn RAF, 1971. Brunei Dato, 1971. *Recreations:* travel in Third World, walking in mountains, reading history. *Address:* c/o House of Commons, SW1A 0AA. *T:* 071–219 3000. *Clubs:* Athenæum, Carlton, Hurlingham.

TARBAT, Viscount; Colin Ruaridh Mackenzie; *b* 7 Sept. 1987; *s* and *heir* of Earl of Cromartie, *qv*.

TARGETT, Prof. Geoffrey Arthur Trevor, PhD, DSc; Professor of Immunology of Protozoal Diseases, since 1983 and Head of Department of Medical Parasitology, since 1988, London School of Hygiene and Tropical Medicine; *b* 10 Dec. 1935; *s* of Trevor and Phyllis Targett; *m* 1958, Sheila Margaret Gibson (*d* 1988); two *s* three *d*. *Educ:* Nottingham Univ. (BSc Hons Zool. 1957); London Univ. (PhD 1961; DSc 1982). Research Scientist: MRC Bilharzia Res. Gp, 1957–62; Nat. Inst. for Med. Res., 1962–64; Lectr, Dept of Natural History, St Andrews Univ., 1964–70; London School of Hygiene and Tropical Medicine: Sen. Lectr, 1970–76; Reader, 1976–83. *Publications:* numerous papers in internat. med. and scientific jls. *Recreations:* golf, music, travel. *Address:* London School of Hygiene and Tropical Medicine, Keppel Street, WC1E 7HT. *T:* 071–636 8636.

TARJANNE, Pekka; Secretary General, International Telecommunication Union, since 1989; *b* 19 Sept. 1937; *s* of P. K. Tarjanne and Annu Tarjanne; *m* 1962, Aino Kairamo; two *s* one *d* (and one *d* decd). *Educ:* Helsinki Univ. of Technology (Dr Tech. 1962). Prof. of Theoretical Physics, Univ. of Oulu, 1965–66, Univ. of Helsinki, 1967–77. MP, Finland, 1970–77; Minister of Communications, 1972–75; Dir. Gen., Posts and Telecommunications, 1977–89. Commander, Order of White Rose of Finland. *Address:* International Telecommunication Union, Place des Nations, CH-1211 Geneva 20, Switzerland. *T:* 41 22 730 5115

TARN, Prof. John Nelson; Roscoe Professor of Architecture, since 1974 and Acting Vice-Chancellor, 1991, University of Liverpool (Pro-Vice-Chancellor, 1988–91); *b* 23 Nov. 1934; *s* of Percival Nelson Tarn and Mary I. Tarn (*née* Purvis); unmarried. *Educ:* Royal Grammar Sch., Newcastle upon Tyne; Univ. of Durham (BArch); Univ. of Cambridge (PhD). 1st cl. hons Dunelm; FRIBA, FRSA, FRHistS, FSA. Lectr in Architecture, Univ. of Sheffield, 1963–70; Prof. of Architecture, Univ. of Nottingham, 1970–73. Member: Professional Literature Cttee, RIBA, 1968–77; RIBA Educn Cttee, 1978– (Vice-Chm., 1983–; Chm., Moderators and Examiners Cttee, 1975–); Council, RIBA, 1987–; Council, ARCUK, 1980– (Vice-Chm., 1986–87; Chm., 1987–90; Vice-Chm., Bd of Educn, 1981–83, Chm., 1983–86); Technology Sub-Cttee, UGC, 1974–84; Adv. Cttee on Architectural Educn to EEC, Brussels, 1987–; CNAA Built Environment Bd, 1987–; Ministerial nominee, Peak Park Jt Planning Bd, 1973–82, a rep. of Greater Manchester Council, PPJPB, 1982–86 (Vice-Chm. of Bd, 1981–86; co-opted Mem., Planning Control Cttee and Park Management Cttee, 1986–; Chm., Planning Control Cttee, 1979–); Mem., National Parks Review Cttee, 1990. Member: Design and Planning Cttee, Central Council for Care of Churches, 1981–86; Diocesan Adv. Cttee for Derby, 1979–. *Publications:* Working Class Housing in Nineteenth Century Britain, 1971; The Peak District National Park: its architecture, 1971; Five Per Cent Philanthropy, 1974; (adv. ed.) Sir Banister Fletcher's History of Architecture, 19th edn, 1987. *Recreations:* music, cooking. *Address:* University of Liverpool, PO Box 147, Liverpool L69 3BX. *Club:* Athenæum.

TARR, Robert James; Director General, Centro (The West Midlands Passenger Transport Executive), since 1987; *b* 8 June 1944; *s* of Jack William Tarr; *m* 1966, Linda Andrews. *Educ:* Whytemead and Downsbrook Schools, Worthing; Worthing High Sch. for Boys. IPFA 1967; BSc(Econ) Hons London, 1977; BA Open Univ.,1979. FCIT 1989. W Sussex CC, Worthing BC, Denbighshire CC, Sunderland Met. BC to 1975; Corporate Planning Co-ordinator and Head of Policy Unit, Bradford Met. Council, 1975–81; Chief Exec., Royal Borough of Kingston upon Thames, 1981–83; Chief Exec. and Town Clerk, Coventry City Council, 1983–87. Chm., Adv. Council, BBC CWR. *Publications:* contribs to jls and conf. papers. *Recreations:* soaking up sun and scenery, the Pre-Raphaelites and Victorian architecture, mountains and alpine flowers, canal-boating, photography, computing, amateur radio (call sign G3PUR), keeping fit. *Address:* Centro, 16 Summer Lane, Birmingham B19 3SD. *T:* 021–214 7001, *Fax:* 021–214 7004. *Club:* Birmingham Press.

TARUA, Ilinome Frank, CBE 1988 (OBE 1980); Consultant Lawyer with Gadens Ridgeway Lawyers, Sydney, Melbourne, Brisbane and Port Moresby, since 1991; *b* 21 Sept. 1941; *s* of Peni Frank Tarua and Anaiele Tarua; *m* 1970, Susan Christine (*née* Reeves); two *d*. *Educ:* Sydney University; University of Papua New Guinea (BL 1971). Legal Officer, Dept of Law, 1971–72; Legal Constitutional Advisor to Prime Minister, 1972–76; Dep. Perm. Head, Prime Minister's Dept, 1977–78; Secretary to Cabinet, 1978–79; High Commissioner to NZ, 1980; Ambassador to UN, 1980–81; Perm. Head, Dept of Public Service, 1982; Perm. Head, Prime Minister's Dept, 1982–83; High Comr in London, 1983–89, concurrently Ambassador to Greece, Israel and Italy; Consul Gen., Sydney, 1989–91. *Recreations:* cricket, squash, golf. *Address:* c/o Gadens Ridgeway Lawyers, Skygarden Building, 77 Castlereagh Street, Sydney, NSW 2000, Australia.

TASMANIA, Bishop of, since 1982; **Rt. Rev. Phillip Keith Newell;** *b* 30 Jan. 1930; *s* of Frank James and Ada Miriam Newell; *m* 1959, Merle Edith Callaghan; three *s*. *Educ:* Univ. of Melbourne; Trinity Coll., Melbourne. BSc 1953; DiplEd(Hons) 1954; ThL(Hons) 1959; BEd 1960; MEd 1969; FACE 1990. Mathematics Master: Melbourne High School, 1954–56; University High School, 1957–58; Tutor in Physics, Secondary Teachers' Coll., 1957; Assistant Curate: All Saints, East St Kilda, Melbourne, 1960–61; S Andrew's, Brighton, Melbourne, 1962–63; Asst Priest, S James, King Street, Sydney, 1963–67; Chaplain, Sydney Hosp., 1963–67; Rector, Christ Church, St Lucia, Brisbane, 1967–82; Residentiary Canon, S John's Cathedral, Brisbane, 1973–82; Archdeacon of Lilley, Brisbane, 1976–82. KStJ 1981. *Recreations:* education; music (classical and light opera); singing; choral conducting; wine making; travel; cricket (spectator); tennis (occasional game). *Address:* GPO Box 748H, Hobart, Tas 7001, Australia. *T:* 238811. *Club:* Tasmanian (Hobart).

TATA, Dr Jamshed Rustom, FRS 1973; Head, Laboratory of Developmental Biochemistry, National Institute for Medical Research, since 1973; *b* 13 April 1930; *s* of Rustom and Gool Tata; *m* 1954, Renée Suzanne Zanetto; two *s* one *d*. *Educ:* Univ. of Bombay (BSc); Univ. of Paris, Sorbonne (D-ès-Sc). Post-doctoral Fellow, Sloan-Kettering Inst., New York, 1954–56; Beit Memorial Fellow, Nat. Inst. for Med. Research, 1956–60; Vis. Scientist, Wenner-Gren Inst., Stockholm, 1960–62; Mem., Scientific Staff, MRC, Nat. Inst. for Med. Research, 1962–. Visiting Prof.: King's Coll., London, 1968–69, and 1970–77; Univ. of California, Berkeley, 1969–70; Vis. Senior Scientist, Nat. Institutes of Health, USA, 1977; Fogarty Scholar, NIH, USA, 1983, 1986, 1989; Fellow, Indian Nat. Science Acad., 1978. Van Meter Award, 1954; Colworth Medal, 1966; Medal of Soc. for Endocrinology, 1973; Jubilee Medal, Indian Inst. of Sci., 1985. *Publications:* (jtly): The Thyroid Hormones, 1959; The Chemistry of Thyroid Diseases, 1960; papers in jls of: Biochemistry; Developmental Biology. *Address:* 15 Bittacy Park Avenue, Mill Hill, NW7 2HA. *T:* 081–346 6291.

TATE, Ellalice; *see* Hibbert, Eleanor.

TATE, Francis Herbert; Vice-Chairman, Tate & Lyle Ltd, 1962–78; *b* 3 April 1913; 2nd *s* of late Alfred Herbert Tate and late Elsie Tate (*née* Jelf Petit); *g g s* of Sir Henry Tate, Bt, founder of Henry Tate & Sons (now Tate & Lyle, Ltd) and donor of the Tate Gallery; *m* 1937, Esther, *d* of late Sir John Bromhead-Matthews, KC, JP, and late Lady Matthews, JP; one *s* two *d*. *Educ:* Private Tutor; Christ Church Oxford (BA 1934, MA 1963). Called to the Bar, Inner Temple, 1937. War Service, 1940–46, Royal Corps of Military Police (Lt-Col). Joined Tate & Lyle Ltd, 1946; Man. Dir, 1949. Chairman: British Sugar Bureau, 1966–78; Council, London Chamber of Commerce, 1962–64 (Vice-Pres., 1964–); Federation of Commonwealth Chambers of Commerce, 1964–69. Dir, Lloyds Bank, Southern Region, 1977–83; a Managing Trustee, Bustamente Foundn, 1979–. General Comr for Income Tax, Woking Div., 1980–88. Dep. Chm., Royal Commonwealth Soc. for the Blind, 1984–89; Chm. Central Council, Royal Commonwealth Soc., 1969–72; Mem. Council, Australia Soc., 1974–78. Governor, Commonwealth Inst., 1975–88. Master of Mercers' Company, 1967–68. *Recreations:* golf (played for Oxford, 1934–35); motoring. *Address:* Little Wissett, Hook Heath, Woking, Surrey GU22 0QG. *T:* Woking (0483) 760532. *Club:* Woking Golf (Pres., 1986–).

TATE, Lt-Col Sir Henry, 4th Bt, *cr* 1898; TD; DL; late Royal Welch Fusiliers TA; *b* 29 June 1902; *s* of Sir Ernest Tate, 3rd Bt and Mildred Mary, 2nd *d* of F. H. Gossage of Camp Hill, Woolton, Liverpool; *S* father, 1939; *m* 1927, Nairne (*d* 1984), *d* of late Saxon Gregson-Ellis, JP; two *s*; *m* 1988, Edna Stokes. Sometime Lt Grenadier Guards. Joint Master Cottesmore Hounds, 1946–58. Councillor Rutland CC, 1958–69, 1970–74; High Sheriff of Rutland, 1949–50. Commanding 1st Bn Rutland Home Guard, 1954–57. DL, Co. of Rutland, 1964. *Heir:* *s* Henry Saxon Tate, *qv*. *Address:* Preston Lodge, Withcote, Oakham, Rutland, Leics LE15 8DP. *Club:* Buck's.

TATE, (Henry) Saxon, CBE 1991; Chairman, London Futures and Options Exchange (formerly London Commodity Exchange Co. Ltd), since 1985; Director, Tate & Lyle Ltd, since 1956; *b* 28 Nov. 1931; *s* and *heir* of Lt-Col Sir Henry Tate, Bt, *qv*; *m* 1st, 1953, Sheila Ann (marr. diss. 1975; she *d* 1987), *e d* of Duncan Robertson; four *s* (incl. twin *s*); 2nd, 1975, Virginia Sturm. *Educ:* Eton; Christ Church, Oxford. FBIM 1975. National Service, Life Guards (Lieut), 1949–50. Joined Tate & Lyle Ltd, 1952, Director, 1956; Pres. and Chief Executive Officer, Redpath Industries Ltd, Canada, 1965–72; Tate & Lyle Ltd:

Chm., Executive Cttee, 1973–78; Man. Dir., 1978–80; Vice Chm., 1980–82. Chief Executive, Industrial Development Bd of NI, 1982–85. Fellow, Amer. Management Assoc., 1972. *Recreations*: various. *Address*: London FOX, 1 Commodity Quay, St Katharine Docks, E1 9AX. *Club*: Buck's.

TATE, Dr Jeffrey Philip, CBE 1990; Principal Conductor, English Chamber Orchestra, since 1985; Chief Conductor and Artistic Director, Rotterdam Philharmonic Orchestra, since 1991; Chief Guest Conductor, Geneva Opera, since 1983; *b* 28 April 1943; *s* of Cyril Henry Tate and Ivy Ellen Naylor (*née* Evans). *Educ*: Farnham Grammar Sch.; Christ's Coll., Cambridge (MA; MB, BChir; Hon. Fellow, 1989); St Thomas' Hosp., London. Trained as doctor of medicine, 1961–67; left medicine for London Opera Centre, 1969; joined Covent Garden Staff, 1970; assisted conductors who included Kempe, Krips, Solti, Davies, Kleiber, for performances and recordings; records made as harpsichordist, 1973–77; Assistant to Boulez for Bayreuth Ring, 1976–81; joined Cologne Opera as assistant to Sir John Pritchard, 1977; conducted Gothenberg Opera, Sweden, 1978–80; NY Metropolitan Opera début, USA, 1979; Covent Garden début, 1982; Salzburg Fest. début (world première Henze/Monteverdi), 1985; Principal Conductor, Royal Opera House, Covent Garden, 1986–91, Principal Guest Conductor, 1991–; Principal Guest Conductor, Orchestre National de France, 1989–. Appearances with major symph. orchs in Europe and Amer.; numerous recordings with English Chamber Orch. Pres., ASBAH, 1989–. Chevalier de l'Ordre des Arts et des Lettres, France, 1990. *Recreation*: church-crawling, with gastronomic interludes. *Address*: c/o Royal Opera House, Covent Garden, WC2E 7QA. *T*: 071–240 1200.

TATE, Prof. Robert Brian, FBA 1980; FRHistS; Professor and Head of Department of Hispanic Studies, Nottingham University, 1958–83, retired; *b* 27 Dec. 1921; *s* of Robert and Jane Grantie Tate; *m* 1951, Beth Ida Lewis; one *s* one *d*. *Educ*: Royal Belfast Academical Instn; Queen's Univ. Belfast (MA, PhD). FRHistS 1990. Asst Lectr, Manchester Univ., 1949–52; Lectr, QUB, 1952–56; Reader in Hispanic Studies, Nottingham Univ., 1956–58. Vis. Prof., Univs of Harvard, Cornell, SUNY at Buffalo, Texas and Virginia. Corresponding Fellow: Institut d'Estudis Catalans, Barcelona, 1964; Real Academia de Historia, Madrid, 1974; Real Academia de Buenas Letras de Barcelona, 1980. *Publications*: Joan Margarit i Pau, Cardinal Bishop of Gerona: a biographical study, 1954; Ensayos sobre la historiografía peninsular del siglo XV, 1970; The Medieval Kingdoms of the Iberian Peninsula, in P. E. Russell, Spain: a companion to Spanish studies, 1973; El Cardenal Joan Margarit, vida i obra, 1976; (with Marcus Tate) The Pilgrim Route to Santiago, 1987; Pilgrimages to St James of Compostella from the British Isles during the Middle Ages, 1990; *edited*: (with A. Yates) Actes del Colloqui internacional de llengua i literatura catalanes, 1976; Essays on Narrative Fiction in the Iberian Peninsula, 1982; *edited with introduction and notes*: Fernán Pérez de Guzmán, Generaciones y Semblanzas, 1965; Fernando del Pulgar, Claros varones de Castilla, 1971, rev. edn 1985; (with I. R. Macpherson) Don Juan Manuel, Libro de los estados, 1974, rev. edn 1991; Anon, Directorio de príncipes, 1977; Alfonso de Palencia, Epistolario, 1983; contrib. articles in numerous learned jls. *Recreations*: architecture and the history of art, jazz. *Address*: 11 Hope Street, Beeston, Nottingham NG9 1DJ. *T*: Nottingham (0602) 251243.

TATE, Saxon; *see* Tate, H. S.

TATHAM, David Everard, CMG 1991; HM Diplomatic Service; Ambassador to Lebanese Republic, since 1990; *b* 28 June 1939; *s* of Lt-Col Francis Everard Tatham and Eileen Mary Wilson; *m* 1963, Valerie Ann Mylechreest; three *s*. *Educ*: St Lawrence Coll., Ramsgate; Wadham Coll., Oxford (BA History). Entered HM Diplomatic Service, 1960; 3rd Sec., UK Mission to the UN, New York, 1962–63; Vice-Consul (Commercial), Milan, 1963–67; ME Centre for Arabic Studies, 1967–69; Jeddah, 1969–70; FCO, 1971–74; Muscat, 1974–77; Asst Head of ME Dept, FCO, 1977–80; Counsellor, Dublin, 1981–84; Ambassador to Yemen Arab Republic, also accredited to Republic of Djibouti, 1984–87; Hd of Falkland Is Dept, FCO, 1987–90. *Recreation*: walking uphill. *Address*: c/o Foreign and Commonwealth Office, SW1A 2AH. *Club*: Athenæum.

TATHAM, Francis Hugh Currer; Editor of Whitaker's Almanack, 1950–81; *b* 29 May 1916; *s* of late Harold Lewis Tatham, Gravesend, Kent, and late Frances Eva (*née* Crook); *m* 1945, Nancy Margaret, *d* of John Robins, Newton Abbot; two *s*. *Educ*: Charterhouse; Christ Church, Oxford. Missioner, Shrewsbury School Mission, Liverpool, 1939–42; Sub-Warden, Mary Ward Settlement, 1942–45; Army Cadet Force, 1943–45; Editor, Church of England Newspaper, 1945–47. Vice-Pres., Harrow RFC. *Recreations*: watching cricket, travel. *Address*: 27 Montacute Road, Lewes, East Sussex BN7 1EN. *T*: Lewes (0273) 473585. *Clubs*: Lansdowne, MCC.

TATLOW, John Colin, PhD, DSc (Birmingham); CChem; FRSC; consultant; Professor of Organic Chemistry, University of Birmingham, 1959–82, now Emeritus; *b* 19 Jan. 1923; *s* of Thomas George and Florence Annie Tatlow, Cannock, Staffs; *m* 1946, Clarice Evelyn Mabel, *d* of Eric Millward and Mabel Evelyn Joiner, Sutton Coldfield; two *d*. *Educ*: Rugeley Grammar School, Staffs; University of Birmingham. Scientific Officer, Min. of Supply, 1946–48; University of Birmingham: Lectr in Chemistry, 1948–56; Sen. Lectr, 1956–57; Reader in Organic Chemistry, 1957–59; Head of Dept of Chemistry, 1974–81. Council of Chemical Society, 1957–60. Examiner, Royal Inst. of Chemistry, 1963–67. ACS Award for creative work in fluorine chemistry, 1990. *Publications*: over 300 scientific papers on fluorine chemistry, mainly in Jl of Chem. Soc., Tetrahedron, Nature, and Jl of Fluorine Chem.; Editor, Jl of Fluorine Chemistry. *Address*: 30 Grassmoor Road, King's Norton, Birmingham B38 8BP. *T*: 021–458 1260.

TATTON BROWN, William Eden, CB 1965; ARIBA; retired architect; *b* 13 Oct. 1910; *m* 1936, Aileen Hope Johnston Sparrow; two *s* one *d* (and one *d* decd). *Educ*: Wellington Coll.; King's Coll., Cambridge (MA); Architectural Association School, London; School of Planning, London. Special Final Examination of Town Planning Institute. Chief Design Asst, Messrs Tecton, Architects, 1934–38; private practice, 1938–40; Finsbury Borough Council, 1940–41. Served in HM Forces, Major, Royal Engineers, 1941–46. Asst Regional Planning Officer, Min. of Town and Country Planning, 1946–48; Dep. County Architect, Herts CC, 1948–59; Chief Architect, Min. of Health, later Dept of Health and Social Security, 1959–71. Steuben-Corning Research Fellowship, Travelling Scholarship to USA, 1957. Guest Lectr, Internat. Hosp. Confs: Finland, 1966; Holland, 1967; Australia, 1967; Düsseldorf, 1969; Tunisia, 1969; Sweden, 1970; Canada, 1970; S Africa, 1971; WHO Commn to Madrid, 1968. Lecturer and broadcaster. *Publications*: (with Paul James) Hospitals: design and development, 1986; contributor to technical and national press. *Recreation*: painting. *Address*: 47 Lansdowne Road, W11 2LG. *T*: 071–727 4529.

TAUBE, Prof. Henry, PhD; Professor, Department of Chemistry, Stanford Univeristy, since 1962; *b* 30 Nov. 1915; *s* of Samuel and Albertina (Tiledetski) Taube; *m* 1952, Mary Alice Wesche; two *s* two *d*. *Educ*: Univ. of Saskatchewan (BS 1935, MS 1937); Univ. of California, Berkeley (PhD 1940). Instructor, Univ. of California, Berkeley, 1940–41; Instructor and Asst Prof., Cornell Univ., 1941–46; Asst Prof., Associate Prof., Prof., Univ. of Chicago, 1946–61; Chm., Dept. of Chemistry, Univ. of Chicago, 1956–59; Chm., Stanford Univ., 1972–74 and 1978–79. Foreign Mem., Royal Soc., 1988; Hon. Member:

Canadian Soc. for Chemistry, 1986; Hungarian Acad. of Scis, 1988; Corresponding Member: Brazilian Acad. of Scis, 1991; Australian Acad. of Sci.; Foreign Associate, Engrg Acad. of Japan. Hon. FRSC 1989; Hon. Fellow, Indian Chem. Soc., 1989. Hon. LLD Saskatchewan, 1973; Hon. PhD Hebrew Univ. of Jerusalem, 1979; Hon. DSc: Chicago, 1983; Polytechnic Inst., NY, 1984; State Univ. of NY, 1985; Guelph Univ., 1987; Seton Hall Univ., 1988; Lajos Kossuth Univ., Debrecen, Hungary, 1988. Guggenheim Fellow, 1949, 1955. ACS Award for Nuclear Applications in Chemistry, 1955; ACS Award for Distinguished Service in the Advancement of Inorganic Chemistry, 1967; Willard Gibbs Medal, Chicago Section, ACS, 1971; Nat. Medal of Science, Washington DC, 1977; T. W. Richards Medal of the Northwestern Section, ACS, 1980; ACS Award in Inorganic Chemistry of the Monsanto Co., 1981; Nat. Acad. of Sciences Award in Chemical Sciences, 1983; Robert A. Welch Foundn Award in Chemistry, 1983; Nobel Prize for Chemistry, 1983; Priestly Medal, ACS, 1985; Dist. Achievement Award, Internat. Precious Metals Inst., 1986. *Publications*: numerous papers in scientific jls on the reactivity of coordination compounds. *Recreations*: gardening, collecting classical vocal records. *Address*: 441 Gerona Road, Stanford, Calif 94305, USA. *T*: (415) 328–2759.

TAUKALO, Sir (David) Dawea, Kt 1985; MBE 1970; Independence Medal, Solomon Islands, 1984; Doctor, retired 1975; *b* 24 Feb. 1920; *s* of J. Paiyom and H. Tevio; *m* 1951, Anne Kamamara; three *s* five *d* (and one *s* decd). *Educ*: Church School, The Solomons; Govt School, Fiji (Dip. in Medicine and Surgery; Cert. in Public Health). General practitioner, Central Hosp. sanitary and mosquito control inspection, Honiara Town, 1947; MO i/c Eastern District Hosp. and clinics, 1951; postgrad. course, Fiji, 1960; returned to Central Hosp., i/c medical patients; rural hosp., eastern Solomons, 1969, to advise Council and field med. workers that good health could not be achieved by building huge hosp. and employing numerous doctors, but by telling people to develop their lands and seas. Premier in Provincial Assembly until 1984. *Publication*: booklet on health of Solomon Islands. *Recreations*: soccer fan; farming, sailing. *Address*: Rocky Hill, Lata, Santa Cruz Temotu Province, Solomon Islands.

TAUNTON, Bishop Suffragan of, 1986–92; **Rt. Rev. Nigel Simeon McCulloch**; Bishop of Wakefield, from Feb. 1992; *b* 17 Jan. 1942; *s* of late Pilot Officer Kenneth McCulloch, RAFVR, and of Audrey Muriel McCulloch; *m* 1974, Celia Hume Townshend, *d* of Canon H. L. H. Townshend; two *d*. *Educ*: Liverpool College; Selwyn Coll., Cambridge (Kitchener Schol., BA 1964, MA 1969); Cuddesdon Coll., Oxford. Ordained, 1966; Curate of Ellesmere Port, 1966–70; Chaplain of Christ's Coll., Cambridge, 1970–73; Director of Theological Studies, Christ's Coll., Cambridge, 1970–75; permission to officiate, dio. of Liverpool, 1970–73; Diocesan Missioner for Norwich Diocese, 1973–78; Rector of St Thomas' and St Edmund's, Salisbury, 1978–86; Archdeacon of Sarum, 1979–86. Prebendary of Ogbourne, Salisbury Cathedral, 1979–86, of Wanstrow, Wells Cathedral, 1986; Canon Emeritus of Salisbury Cathedral, 1989. Mem., House of Bishops, Gen. Synod of C of E, 1990–. Chm., Decade of Evangelism Steering Gp, 1989–. Pres., Somerset Rural Music Sch., 1986–; Mem. Council, RSCM, 1984–. Chairman: Somerset County Scout Assoc., 1988–; Finance Cttee, ACCM, 1988–. *Recreations*: music, walking in the Lake District. *Address*: (until Feb. 1992) Sherford Farm House, Sherford, Taunton TA1 3RF. *T*: Taunton (0823) 288759; (from Feb. 1992) Bishop's Lodge, Woodthorpe Lane, Wakefield, W Yorks WF2 6JJ. *Club*: Commonwealth Trust.

TAUNTON, Archdeacon of; *see* Olyott, Ven. L. E.

TAUNTON, Doidge Estcourt, CB 1951; DSO and bar 1945; DL; Secretary, Northamptonshire TA and AFA, 1952–68; *b* 9 Nov. 1902; *s* of late J. G. C. Taunton, Launceston, Cornwall; *m* 1930, Rhona Caroline Wetherall (*d* 1951); one *s* (and one *s* decd). *Educ*: Cheltenham College; RMC Sandhurst; 2nd Lt Northamptonshire Regt, 1923; Lt 1925; Capt. 1935, and Adjt TA, 1932–36; Major 1940; Lt-Col 1941; Col 1948; Temp. Brig. 1945–47 and 1948–52. Served NWF India, 1936–38 (Medal and 2 clasps); War of 1939–45, India and Burma, 1936–45; French Indo-China and Netherlands East Indies, 1945–46 (Medal and clasp); Comd Somaliland Area, 1948–50; Comd 2nd Inf. Brigade, 1950–51; retired pay, 1951. DL Northants, 1969. *Address*: Great Hayne, Duston, Northampton.

TAUSKY, Vilem, CBE 1981; FGSM 1968; Director of Opera, Guildhall School of Music, since 1966; Artistic Director, Phoenix Opera Co., since 1967; BBC Conductor since 1950; *b* 20 July 1910; *s* of Emil Tausky, MD, Prerov, Czechoslovakia, and Josefine Ascher, opera singer; *m* 1948, Margaret Helen Powell (*d* 1982). *Educ*: Univ. of Brno; Janáček Conservatoire, Brno; Meisterschule, Prague. Military Service in France and England, 1939–45. National Opera House, Brno, Czechoslovakia, 1929–39; Musical Director, Carl Rosa Opera, 1945–49. Guest Conductor: Royal Opera House, Covent Garden, 1951–; Sadler's Wells Opera, 1953–. Freeman, City of London, 1979. Czechoslovak Military Cross, 1944; Czechoslovak Order of Merit, 1945. *Publications*: Czechoslovak Christmas Carols, 1942; Oboe Concerto, 1957; Concertino for harmonica and orchestra, 1963; Divertimento for strings, 1966; Soho: Scherzo for orchestra, 1966; Concert Overture for Brass Band, 1969; Cakes and Ale: Overture for Brass Band, 1971; Ballad for Cello and Piano; From Our Village: orchestral suite, 1972; Sonata for Cello and Piano, 1976; Suite for Violin and Piano, 1979; String Quartet, 1981; (book) Vilem Tausky Tells his Story, 1979; Leoš Janáček, Leaves from his Life, 1982; contribs to: Tension in the Performance of Music, 1979; The Spectator, 1979. *Recreation*: country life. *Address*: 44 Haven Green Court, W5. *T*: 081–997 6512.

TAVAIQIA, Ratu Sir Josaia (Nasorowale), KBE 1986; JP; Minister of State for Forests, Fiji, since 1977; *b* 25 Dec. 1930; *s* of Ratu Josaia Tavaiqia and Adi Lusiana Ratu; *m* 1955, Adi Lady Merewalesi Naqei; three *d*. *Educ*: Queen Victoria Sch.; Natabua Indian Secondary Sch., Fiji (Sen. Cambridge Examination). Custom Officer, Custom Dept, Fiji, 1949–59; Hotel Manager, 1961–75. Pres., Rural Youth Council of Fiji, 1979–. Traditional role as Tui (Chief) of Vuda, with tradit. title of Tui Vuda (Chief of Vuda). *Recreation*: Rugby management. *Address*: (office) Ministry of Forests, Box 2218, Suva, Fiji. *T*: 313439; (home) Viseisei, Vuda, Fiji. *T*: 61273. *Clubs*: Commonwealth Trust, Union.

TAVARÉ, Andrew Kenneth; Special Commissioner of Income Tax, 1976–88 (Deputy Special Commissioner, April–Oct. 1988); *b* 10 Jan. 1918; *s* of late L. A. Tavaré, Bromley, Kent; *m* 1950, June Elinor Attwood, Beckenham, Kent; three *s*. *Educ*: Chatham House School, Ramsgate; King's College, London University. LLB (London). Solicitor of the Supreme Court. Served War with 79th HAA Regt (Hertfordshire Yeomanry), RA, 1940–45; N Africa and Italy, rank of Captain. Admitted Solicitor, 1948; Solicitor's Office, Inland Revenue, 1953–; Assistant Solicitor, 1965–75. Consultant Editor of Sergeant on Stamp Duties, 4th edition 1963, to 8th edition 1982. *Publications*: (contrib.) Simon's Taxes, 2nd edn, 1965, and 3rd edn, 1970.
See also Sir J. Tavaré.

TAVARÉ, Sir John, Kt 1989; CBE 1983; CEng; Chairman: Mersey Basin Campaign, Department of the Environment, since 1983; Luxonic Lighting plc, since 1986; *b* 12 July 1920; *s* of Leon Alfred Tavaré and Grace Tavaré; *m* 1949, Margaret Daphne Wray; three *s* (and one *s* decd). *Educ*: Chatham House, Ramsgate; Bromley Grammar Sch.; King's

Coll., London (BScEng 1946). MIMechE 1954; FInstD 1983. Trainee, Thames Board Mills Ltd, 1938–43; Works Manager, Wm C. Jones. Ltd, 1946–48; Personnel Administration Ltd, UK, Australia and NZ, 1949–58; Thames Board Mills Ltd (Unilever), 1958–68: Sales and Marketing Dir, 1960–65; Vice-Chm., 1966–68; Paper, Plastics and Packaging Bd, Unilever, 1968–70; Whitecroft plc, 1970–85: Gp Man. Dir, 1973–76; Chm. and Gp Man. Dir, 1976–85. Member: Nat. Council, CBI, 1978–85 (Chm., NW Reg., 1980–82); Nat. Rivers Authy Adv. Bd, NW Region, 1989–. *Recreations:* golf, garden, environment, business. *Address:* The Gables, 4 Macclesfield Road, Prestbury, Macclesfield, Cheshire SK10 4BN. *T:* Macclesfield (0625) 829778.
See also A. K. Tavaré.

TAVENER, John; composer; Professor of Music at Trinity College of Music since 1969; *b* 28 Jan. 1944. *Educ:* Highgate Sch.; Royal Academy of Music (LRAM). Hon. FRAM, Hon. FTCL. Russian Orthodox religion. *Publications:* compositions: Piano Concerto; Three Holy Sonnets (Donne); Cain and Abel (1st Prize, Monaco); Chamber Concerto; The Cappe-makers; Three Songs of T. S. Eliot; Grandma's Footsteps; In Memoriam Igor Stravinsky; Responsorium in memory of Annon Lee; The Whale; Introit for March 27th; Three Surrealist Songs; In Alium; Celtic Requiem; Ultimos Ritos; Thérèse (opera); A Gentle Spirit (opera); Kyklike Kinesis; Palin; Palintropos: Canticle of the Mother of God; Divine Liturgy of St John Chrysostom; The Immurement of Antigone; Lamentation, Last Prayer and Exaltation; Six Abbasid Songs; Greek Interlude; Akhmatova: Rékviem; Sappho: Lyrical Fragments; Prayer for the World; The Great Canon of St Andrew of Crete; Trisăgion; Risen!; Mandelion; The Lamb (a Christmas carol); Mandoodles; Towards the Son; 16 Haiku of Seferis; Ikon of Light; All-Night Vigil Service of the Orthodox Church; Eis Thanaton (a ritual); Two Hymns to the Mother of God; Ikon of St Cuthbert; Akathist (Glory to God for everything); Meditation on the Light; Panikhida (Orthodox Burial Service); The Protecting Veil; Ikon of St Seraphim; Let not the Prince be silent; The Tyger; Resurrection; The Uncreated Eros; Lament of the Mother of God; The Hidden Treasure (string quartet); Today the Virgin; Eonia; Psalm 121, I Will Lift Up Mine Eyes unto the Hills; Resurrection; Thunder Entered Her (a divine allegory); Ikon of the Trinity; Do Not Move; A Christmas Round; The Repentant Thief (dance-lament); Threnos (for solo 'cello); Mary of Egypt (chamber opera). *Address:* c/o Chester Music, 8–9Frith Street, W1V 5TZ.

TAVERNE, Dick, QC 1965; Director, PRIMA Europe Ltd, since 1987; *b* 18 Oct. 1928; *s* of Dr N. J. M. and Mrs L. V. Taverne; *m* 1955, Janice Hennessey; two *d*. *Educ:* Charterhouse School; Balliol College, Oxford (First in Greats). Oxford Union Debating tour of USA, 1951. Called to Bar, 1954. MP (Lab) Lincoln, March 1962–Oct. 1972, resigned; MP (Democratic Lab) Lincoln, March 1973–Sept. 1974; Parliamentary Under-Secretary of State, Home Office, 1966–68; Minister of State, Treasury, 1968–69; Financial Secretary to the Treasury, 1969–70. Chm., Public Expenditure (General) Sub-Cttee, 1971–72. Institute for Fiscal Studies: First Dir, 1970; Dir-Gen., 1979–81; Chm., 1981–82; Chm., Public Policy Centre, 1984–87. Chm., OLIM Investment Trust, 1989–; Director: Equity and Law; BOC Group. Mem., Internat. Ind. Review Body to review workings of European Commn, 1979. Member: Nat. Cttee, SDP, 1981–87; Federal Policy Cttee, Liberal Democrats, 1989–90. Contested (SDP): Southwark, Peckham, Oct. 1982; Dulwich, 1983. *Publication:* The Future of the Left: Lincoln and after, 1973. *Recreations:* marathon running, sailing. *Address:* 60 Cambridge Street, SW1V 4QQ.

TAVISTOCK, Marquess of; Henry Robin Ian Russell, DL; a Director, TR Property Investment Trust, since 1982 (Chairman, 1977–89); *b* 21 Jan. 1940; *s* and *heir* of 13th Duke of Bedford, *qv*; *m* 1961, Henrietta Joan, *d* of Henry F. Tiarks, *qv*; three *s*. *Educ:* Le Rosey, Switzerland; Harvard University. Partner, De Zoete and Bevan, 1970–82; Chairman: Cedar Investment Trust, 1977–82; Berkeley Develt Capital Ltd, 1984–; Director: Touche, Remnant Holdings, 1977–88; Trafalgar House Ltd, 1977–91; United Racecourses, 1977–; Berkeley Govett & Co. Ltd, 1985–. Hon. Trustee, Kennedy Memorial Trust (Chm., 1985–90). Pres., Woburn Golf and Country Club. DL Beds, 1985. *Heir: s* Lord Howland, *qv*. *Address:* Woburn Abbey, Woburn, Bedfordshire MK43 0TP. *T:* Woburn (0525) 290666. *Clubs:* White's; Jockey Club Rooms; The Brook (New York).

TAYLER, Harold Clive, QC 1979; **His Honour Judge Tayler;** a Circuit Judge, since 1984; *b* 4 Nov. 1932; *m* 1959, Catherine Jane (*née* Thomas); two *s* one *d*. *Educ:* Solihull Sch.; Balliol Coll., Oxford. BCL and BA (Jurisprudence). Called to the Bar, Inner Temple, 1956; in practice, Birmingham, 1958–84, and London, 1979–84; a Recorder of the Crown Court, 1974–84; Midland and Oxford Circuit. *Address:* c/o Midland and Oxford Circuit Administrators' Office, 2 Newton Street, Birmingham B4 7LU.

TAYLOR; *see* Suenson-Taylor, family name of Baron Grantchester.

TAYLOR, family name of **Barons Ingrow, Taylor of Blackburn, Taylor of Gryfe** and **Taylor of Hadfield.**

TAYLOR, Lady, (Charity), MB, BS, MRCS, LRCP; retired as Assistant Director and Inspector of Prisons (Women), (1959–66); Member, BBC General Advisory Council, 1964–67; President, Newfoundland and Labrador Social Welfare Council, 1968–71; *b* Sept. 1914; *d* of W. George and Emma Clifford; *m* 1939, Stephen J. L. Taylor (later Lord Taylor) (*d* 1988); two *s* one *d*. *Educ:* The Grammar School, Huntingdon; London (Royal Free Hospital) School of Medicine for Women. HS Royal Free Hospital; HS Elizabeth Garrett Anderson Hospital; Assistant Medical Officer HM Prison, Holloway; Medical Officer, HM Prison Holloway; Governor, HM Prison, Holloway, 1945–59. *Recreation:* conversation. *Address:* Flat 10, Clover Court, Church Road, Haywards Heath, West Sussex RH16 3UF.

TAYLOR OF BLACKBURN, Baron *cr* 1978 (Life Peer), of Blackburn in the County of Lancashire; **Thomas Taylor,** CBE 1974 (OBE 1969); JP; Consultant, Shorrock Security Systems Ltd, and other companies, since 1976; Director and Vice Chairman, Themes International PLC, since 1989; *b* 10 June 1929; *s* of James and Edith Gladys Taylor; *m* 1950, Kathleen Nurton; one *s*. *Educ:* Mill Hill Primary Sch.; Blakey Moor Elementary Sch. Mem., Blackburn Town Council, 1954–76 (Leader, chm. of cttees and rep. on various bodies). Chm., Electricity Cons. Council for NW and Mem. Norweb Bd, 1977–80; Member: NW Econ. Planning Council; NW AHA (Chm. Brockhall HMC, 1972–74, Vice-Chm. Blackburn HMC, 1964–74); Council for Educational Technology in UK; Nat. Foundn for Educn Research in Eng. and Wales; Schools Council; Regional Rent Tribunal. Chairman: Govt Cttee of Enquiry into Management and Govt of Schools; Nat. Foundn for Visual Aids. Former Mem., Public Schools Commn; past Pres., Assoc. of Educn Cttees. Dir, Councils and Education Press. Univ. of Lancaster: Founder Mem. and Mem. Council; author of Taylor Report on problems; Dep. Pro-Chancellor. Former Dep. Dir, Central Lancs Family and Community Project. JP Blackburn, 1960; former Chm., Juvenile Bench. Elder, URC; Pres., Free Church Council, 1962–63. *Address:* 34 Tower Road, Feniscliffe, Blackburn BB2 5LE. *T:* Blackburn (0254) 202808.

TAYLOR OF GRYFE, Baron *cr* 1968 (Life Peer), of Bridge of Weir; **Thomas Johnston Taylor;** DL; FRSE 1977; Chairman, Morgan Grenfell (Scotland) Ltd, 1973–85; *b* 27 April 1912; *m* 1943, Isobel Wands; two *d*. *Educ:* Bellahouston Acad., Glasgow. Member: British Railways Bd, 1968–80 (Chm., Scottish Railways Board, 1971–80); Board of Scottish Television Ltd, 1968–82; Forestry Commn, 1963–76 (Chm., 1970–76). President, Scottish CWS, 1965–70; Mem., Scottish Economic Council, 1971–74. Director: Whiteaway Laidlaw & Co. Ltd, 1971–; Friends' Provident Life Office, 1972–82; Scottish Metropolitan Property Co. Ltd, 1972–88; BR Property Bd, 1972–82; Mem., Internat. Adv. Council, Morgan Grenfell. Chm., Economic Forestry Group, 1976–81. Trustee, Dulverton Trust, 1980–; Chm., Scottish Action on Dementia, 1989–. DL Renfrewshire, 1970. Hon. LLD Strathclyde, 1974. *Recreations:* theatre, golf, walking. *Address:* 33 Seagale, Kingsbarns, Fife KY16 8SR. *T:* Boarhills (033488) 430. *Clubs:* Caledonian; Royal and Ancient (St Andrews).

TAYLOR OF HADFIELD, Baron *cr* 1982 (Life Peer), of Hadfield in the County of Derbyshire; **Francis Taylor;** Kt 1974; Founder, 1921, and Life President and Executive Director, since 1979, Taylor Woodrow Group (Managing Director, 1935–79; Chairman, 1937–74); Director, Taylor Woodrow of Canada Ltd since 1953; *b* 7 Jan. 1905; *s* of late Francis Taylor and late Sarah Ann Earnshaw; *m* 1st, 1929 (marr. diss.); two *d*; 2nd, 1956, Christine Enid Hughes; one *d*. Founded, 1921, Taylor Woodrow, Building, Civil & Mechanical Engineering Contractors, which became Public Company, in 1935. Member of Advisory Council to Minister of State, 1954–55; Chm. Export Group for Constructional Industries, 1954–55; President Provident Institution of Builders' Foremen and Clerks of Works, 1950; Dir, Freedom Federal Savings and Loan Assoc., Worcester, Mass, 1972–82. Director: BOAC, 1958–60; Monarch Investments Ltd, Canada, 1954–84. Pres., Aims of Industry, 1990–. Vice-Pres., Aims, 1978–. Governor, Queenswood School for Girls, 1948–77. Hon. DSc Salford, 1973. Fellow, Chartered Inst. of Building, Hon. Fellow 1979; Hon. FFB 1986; Hon. FICE 1987. *Recreations:* tennis, swimming, riding. *Address:* 10 Park Street, W1Y 4DD. *Clubs:* Royal Automobile, Queen's, Hurlingham, All England.

TAYLOR, Alan; *see* Taylor, Robert A.

TAYLOR, Alan Broughton; barrister-at-law; a Recorder of the Crown Court (Midland and Oxford Circuit), since 1979; *b* 23 Jan. 1939; *yr s* of Valentine James Broughton Taylor and Gladys Maud Taylor; *m* 1964, Diana Hindmarsh; two *s*. *Educ:* Malvern Coll.; Geneva Univ.; Birmingham Univ. (LLB); Brasenose Coll., Oxford (BLitt, re-designated MLitt 1979). Called to the Bar, Gray's Inn, 1961; barrister on Oxford Circuit, subseq. Midland and Oxford Circuit, 1963–. Gov., St Matthew's Sch., Sandwell, 1988–. *Publication:* (contrib.) A Practical Guide to the Care of the Injured, ed P. S. London, 1967. *Recreations:* philately, fell walking. *Address:* 94 Augustus Road, Edgbaston, Birmingham B15 3LT. *T:* 021–454 8600.

TAYLOR, Lt-Gen. Sir Allan (Macnab), KBE 1972; MC 1944; Deputy Commander-in-Chief, United Kingdom Land Forces, 1973–76, retired; *b* 26 March 1919; *s* of Alexander Lawrence Taylor and Winifred Ethel (*née* Nisbet); *m* 1945, Madeleine Turpin (marr. diss. 1963); two *d*. *Educ:* Fyling Hall School, Robin Hood's Bay. Joined TA, 1938; Troop Leader, 10th R Tank Regt, 1940; Squadron Leader, 7th R Tank Regt, 1942; 6th R Tank Regt, 1946; Staff College, 1948; GSO, 2, 56 London Armoured Div., 1949; Bde Major 20 Armoured Bde, 1952; Instructor, Staff College, 1954; Squadron Leader, 1st R Tank Regt, 1957; Second in Comd 5th RTR, 1959; Comdg Officer: 5th RTR, 1960 and 3rd, 1961; AA & QMG, 1st Div., 1962; Commandant, RAC Gunnery School, 1963; Comd Berlin Brigade, 1964; Imperial Defence College, 1967; Comdr, 1st Div., 1968; Commandant, Staff College, Camberley, 1969–72; GOC South East District, April-Dec. 1972. Chm., Cttee on Regular Officer Training, 1972–. Col Comdt, RTR, 1973–77. *Recreation:* golf. *Address:* 4 Mill Close, Middle Assendon, Henley-on-Thames, Oxon RG9 6BA. *T:* Henley (0491) 575167.

TAYLOR, Andrew James, CBE 1965; Chairman, British Manufacturing and Research Co., Grantham, Lincs, 1968–73; *b* 1902; *s* of late Alfred George Ralph Meston Taylor, Broughty Ferry, Dundee; *m* 1925, Mary Ann Symmers, *d* of George Cowie, Aberdeen; one *s* one *d* (and two *s* decd). *Educ:* Robert Gordon's Coll., Aberdeen. Dir of Manufacture and Exec. Dir, Ford Motor Co. Ltd, 1962–65; Deputy Managing Director, 1965–67. *Recreations:* photography, fishing. *Address:* 2 Drummond Road, Blairgowrie, Perthshire PH10 6PD. *T:* Blairgowrie (0250) 3358. *Club:* Royal Automobile.
See also R. O. Taylor.

TAYLOR, Ann; *see* Taylor, (Winifred) Ann.

TAYLOR, Arnold Joseph, CBE 1971; DLitt, MA; Docteur *hc* Caen; FBA 1972; FSA; Hon. Vice-President, Society of Antiquaries, since 1978 (Vice-President, 1963–64; Secretary, 1964–70; Director, 1970–75; President, 1975–78); *b* 24 July 1911; *y s* of late John George Taylor, Headmaster of Sir Walter St John's School, Battersea; *m* 1940, Patricia Katharine, *d* of late S. A. Guilbride, Victoria, BC; one *s* one *d*. *Educ:* Merchant Taylors' School; St John's College, Oxford (MA). Assistant master, Chard School, Somerset, 1934; Assistant Inspector of Ancient Monuments, HM Office of Works, 1935. Served War of 1939–45, Intelligence Officer, RAF, 1942–46. Inspector of Ancient Monuments for Wales, Min. of Works, 1946–54, Asst Chief Inspector, 1954–61; Chief Inspector of Ancient Monuments and Historic Buildings, MPBW, later DoE, 1961–72. Commissioner: Royal Commissions on Ancient and Historical Monuments (Wales and Monmouthshire), 1956–83; Historical Monuments (England), 1963–78; Mem., Ancient Monuments Board: for England, 1973–82; for Scotland, 1974–79; for Wales, 1974–82. Member: Cathedrals Advisory Cttee, 1964–80; Adv. Bd for Redundant Churches, 1973–82 (Chm., 1975–77); Westminster Abbey Architectural Adv. Panel, 1979; Vice-Pres., English Place-Name Soc., 1986–; Hon. Vice-President: Flintshire Hist. Soc., 1953; Royal Archaeol. Inst., 1979– (Vice-Pres., 1968–72); Surrey Archaeol. Soc., 1979; President: Cambrian Archaeolog. Assoc., 1969; London and Mddx Archaeolog. Soc., 1971–74; Soc. for Medieval Archaeology, 1972–75; Friends of Lydiard Tregoze, 1983–86; Sir Walter St John's Old Boys' Assoc., 1969–70; Old Merchant Taylors' Soc., 1985–86. Mem., Sir Walter St John's Schools Trust, 1970. Reckitt Lectr, British Acad., 1977. Hon. Corres. Mem., Société Jersiaise, 1983. Hon. DLitt Wales, 1970; Docteur *hc* Caen, 1980. Reginald Taylor Prize, British Archaeol Assoc., 1949; G. T. Clark Prize, Cambrian Archaeol Assoc., 1956; Gold Medal, Soc. of Antiquaries, 1988. Médaille d'Honneur de la Ville de Saint-Georges d'Espéranche, 1988. Silver Jubilee Medal, 1977. *Publications:* Records of the Barony and Honour of the Rape of Lewes, 1940; official guides to various historical monuments in care Ministry of Works (now DoE), 1939–80; chapter on Military Architecture, in vol. Medieval England, 1958; (part author) History of the King's Works, 1963; Four Great Castles, 1983; Studies in Castles and Castle-Building, 1986; contribs on medieval architectural history in Eng. Hist. Rev., Antiquaries Jl, Archaeologia Cambrensis, etc. *Recreations:* reading and using records, resisting iconoclasts. *Address:* Rose Cottage, Lincoln's Hill, Chiddingfold, Surrey GU8 4UN. *T:* Wormley (042868) 2069.

TAYLOR, Sir (Arthur) Godfrey, Kt 1980; DL; Chairman, London Residuary Body, since 1985; *b* 3 Aug. 1925; *s* of Fred and Lucy Taylor; *m* 1945, Eileen Dorothy Daniel; one *s* three *d*. *Educ:* Stockport Secondary School. Sutton and Cheam Borough Council: Councillor, 1951–62; Alderman, 1962–65; London Bor. of Sutton: Alderman, 1964–78; Councillor, 1978–82; Hon. Freeman, 1978. Managing Trustee, Municipal Mutual Insurance Ltd, 1979–86; Chm., Southern Water Authority, 1981–85. Chm., Assoc. of

Metropolitan Authorities, 1978–80. Chm., London Bor. Assoc., 1968–71. High Sheriff, 1984, DL, 1988, Greater London. *Recreation:* golf. *Address:* 23 Somerhill Lodge, Somerhill Road, Hove, E Sussex BN3 1RU. *T:* Brighton (0273) 776161.

TAYLOR, Prof. Arthur John; Professor of Modern History, Leeds University, 1961–84, now Emeritus; University Archivist, Leeds, 1984–89; *b* 29 Aug. 1919; *s* of Victor Henry and Mary Lydia Taylor, Manchester; *m* 1955, Elizabeth Ann Jeffries; one *s* two *d*. *Educ:* Manchester Grammar School; Manchester University. Assistant Lecturer in History, University Coll. London, 1948; Lecturer, 1950. Pro-Vice Chancellor, Leeds Univ., 1971–73. Chm., Jt Matriculation Bd, 1970–73. *Publications:* Laissez-faire and State Intervention in Nineteenth Century Britain, 1973; The Standard of Living in Britain in the Industrial Revolution, 1975; (with P. H. J. H. Gosden) Studies in the History of a University: Leeds 1874–1974, 1975; contrib. to books and learned journals. *Address:* Redgarth, Leeds Road, Collingham, Wetherby, West Yorks LS22 5AA. *T:* Collingham Bridge (0937) 572930.

TAYLOR, Arthur Robert; Chairman, Arthur Taylor & Co., Inc., since 1977; Dean, Graduate School of Business, Fordham University, since 1985; *b* 6 July 1935; *s* of Arthur Earl Taylor and Marian Hilda Scott; *m* Kathryn Pelgrift; three *d* by previous marriage. *Educ:* Brown Univ., USA (AB, MA). Asst Dir, Admissions, Brown Univ., June 1957–Dec. 1960; Vice-Pres./Dir, The First Boston Co., Jan. 1961–May 1970; Exec. Vice-Pres./Director, Internat. Paper Co., 1970–72; Pres., CBS Inc., 1972–76. Director: Louisiana Land & Exploration Co.; Pitney Bowes; The Forum; Eastern Air Lines; Nomura Pacific Basin Fund, Inc.; Trustee, Drucker Foundn; Trustee Emeritus, Brown Univ. Hon. degrees: Dr Humane Letters: Simmons Coll., 1975; Rensselaer Polytechnic Inst., 1975; Dr of Humanities, Bucknell Univ., 1975. *Publications:* contrib. chapter to The Other Side of Profit, 1975; articles on US competitiveness and corporate responsibility in jls. *Recreations:* sailing, tennis, riding. *Address:* (office) 113 West 60th Street, New York, NY 10023, USA. *Clubs:* The Brook, Century (New York); Metropolitan (Washington); California (Los Angeles).

TAYLOR, Arthur Ronald, MBE (mil.) 1945; Chairman, Willis Faber plc, 1978–81; Vice-Chairman, Legal and General Group plc, 1984–86 (Director, 1982–86); *b* 13 June 1921; *yr s* of late Arthur Taylor and Kathleen Frances (*née* Constable Curtis); *m* 1949, Elizabeth Josephine Kiek; three *s*. *Educ:* Winchester Coll.; Trinity Coll., Oxford. Served Grenadier Guards, 1940–53 (despatches); sc; Bde Major 32nd Guards Bde. Laurence Philipps & Co. (Insurance) Ltd, 1953–58; Member of Lloyd's, 1955; Director, Willis, Faber and Dumas Ltd, 1959; Dep. Chm., Willis Faber Ltd, 1974. Vice-President: Corporation of Insurance Brokers, 1967–78; British Insurance Brokers Assoc., 1978–81. *Recreations:* golf, shooting. *Address:* Coutts & Co., 15 Lombard Street, EC3V 9AU.

TAYLOR, Arthur William Charles, CBE 1981; PhD; CChem, FRSC; Chairman, Heavy Organics (Petrochemical Division), Imperial Chemical Industries Ltd, 1972–75; *b* 4 Jan. 1913; *s* of Edward Charles Taylor and Alice (*née* Lucas); *m* 1936, Rosina Peggy (*née* Gardner); one *s* one *d*. *Educ:* Brighton Hove and Sussex Grammar Sch.; University Coll. London (BSc, PhD). FInstPet. Imperial Chemical Industries Ltd: Billingham Division: Research Chemist, 1935–45; Jt Research Manager, 1945–57; Plastics Division: Technical and Research Director, 1958–64; Heavy Organics (Petrochemical Division): Technical Dir, 1964–66; Dep. Chm., 1966–72. Chairman: British Ports Assoc., 1978–80; Tees and Hartlepool Port Authority, 1976–82 (Mem., 1974–83); Tees Pilotage Authority, 1978–83; Mem., Nat. Ports Council, 1978–80; Chm., NE Industrial Develt Bd, 1979–81. Chm. of Governors, Teesside Polytechnic, 1975–78. Fellow, University Coll. London, 1977; FRSA 1976. *Publications:* papers in Chemistry and Industry, particularly the Holroyd Meml Lecture, 1976. *Address:* 35 The Grove, Marton, Middlesbrough, Cleveland TS7 8AF. *T:* Middlesbrough (0642) 315639.

TAYLOR, Bernard David; Chairman, Medeva plc, since 1990; *b* 17 Oct. 1935; *s* of Thomas Taylor and Winifred (*née* Smith); *m* 1959, Nadine Barbara; two *s* two *d*. *Educ:* Univ. of Wales, Bangor (BSc Zoology). Science Teacher, Coventry Educn Authority, 1958; Sales and Marketing, SK&F, 1960; Sales and Marketing Manager, Glaxo NZ, 1964; New Products Manager, Glaxo UK, 1967; Man. Dir, Glaxo Australia, 1972; Dir, Glaxo Holdings plc, and Man. Dir, Glaxo Pharmaceuticals UK, 1984; Chief Exec., Glaxo Holdings, 1986–89. Councillor and Vice-Pres., Aust. Pharm. Manufrs' Assoc., 1974–79; Councillor, Victorian Coll. of Pharmacy, 1976–82. Member: CBI Europe Cttee, 1987–89; BOTB, 1987–. CBIM 1986; Fellow, London Business Sch., 1988. *Address:* Medeva plc, 10 St James's Street, SW1A 1EF.

TAYLOR, Brian Hyde; Secretary General, Committee of Vice-Chancellors and Principals, 1983–88; *b* 18 Aug. 1931; *s* of late Robert E. Taylor and late Ivy Taylor (*née* Wash), Woodford, Essex; *m* 1960, Audrey Anne Barnes; two *s*. *Educ:* Buckhurst Hill County High Sch.; SW Essex Technical Coll.; LSE (BSc (Econ)). Nat. Service, commnd RASC, 1954–56. Clerk, Corp. of Lloyd's, 1947–48; Personal Asst to Principal, Univ. of London, 1956–59; administrative posts, Univ. of London, 1959–66; Asst Sec., ACU (and Vice-Chancellors Cttee), 1966; Exec. Sec., Cttee of Vice-Chancellors and Principals, 1973; Sec., Univ. Authorities Panel, 1980. Mem., Bd of Dirs, Busoga Trust, 1990–; Treasurer, Council for Educn in Commonwealth, 1991–. *Recreations:* walking, travel, browsing in bookshops. *Address:* Sylverstone, Ashley Park Road, Walton-on-Thames, Surrey KT12 1JN. *T:* Walton-on-Thames (0932) 225397. *Club:* Athenæum.

TAYLOR, Brian William; Under Secretary, Civil Service Commission; Resident Chairman, Recruitment and Assessment Services, Office of Minister for Civil Service, since 1990; *b* 29 April 1933; *s* of late Alan Taylor and Betty Taylor; *m* 1959, Mary Evelyn Buckley; two *s* two *d*. *Educ:* Emanuel School. Entered Ministry of Nat. Insurance (subseq. DHSS, then DSS) as Exec. Officer, 1952; Higher Exec. Officer, 1963; Principal, 1968; Asst Sec., 1976; Under Sec., 1982; on loan from DSS, 1990–. *Recreations:* music, theatre, literature, tennis. *Address:* Civil Service Selection Board, 24 Whitehall, SW1A 2ED. *Club:* Commonwealth Trust.

TAYLOR, Cavan; Senior Partner, Lovell White Durrant, since 1991; *b* 23 Feb. 1935; *s* of Albert William Taylor and of late Constance Muriel (*née* Horncastle); *m* 1962, Helen Tinling; one *s* two *d*. *Educ:* King's Coll. Sch., Wimbledon; Emmanuel Coll., Cambridge (BA 1958; LLM 1959). 2nd Lieut, RASC, 1953–55. Articled with Herbert Smith & Co., 1958–61; qualified as solicitor, 1961; Legal Dept, Distillers' Co. Ltd, 1962–65; Asst Solicitor, Piesse & Sons, 1965–66, Partner, 1966; by amalgamation, Partner, Durrant Piesse and Lovell White Durrant; Dep. Sen. Partner, Lovell White Durrant, 1990–91. Gov., King's Coll. Sch., Wimbledon, 1970– (Chm., 1973–90). *Publications:* articles in legal jls. *Recreations:* reading, gardening, conversation with my children. *Address:* (office) 65 Holborn Viaduct, EC1A 2DY. *T:* 071–236 0066, *Fax:* 071–248 4212.

TAYLOR, Dr Charity; *see* Taylor, Lady.

TAYLOR, Prof. Charles Margrave, DPhil; FBA 1979; Professor of Political Science, McGill University, since 1982; *b* 5 Nov. 1931; *s* of Walter Margrave Taylor and Simone Beaubien; *m* 1956, Alba Romer; five *d*. *Educ:* McGill Univ. (BA History); Oxford Univ. (BA PPE, MA, DPhil). Fellow, All Souls Coll., Oxford, 1956–61; McGill University: Asst Prof., later Associate Prof., later Prof. of Polit. Science, Dept of Polit. Science, 1961–76; Prof. of Philosophy, Dept. of Philos., 1973–76; Chichele Prof. of Social and Political Theory, and Fellow of All Souls Coll., Oxford Univ., 1976–81; Mem., Sch. of Social Science, Inst. for Advanced Study, Princeton, 1981–82. Prof. asst, later Prof. agrégé, later Prof. titulaire, Ecole Normale Supérieure, 1962–64, Dept de Philos., 1963–71, Univ. de Montréal. Vis. Prof. in Philos., Princeton Univ., 1965; Mills Vis. Prof. in Philos., Univ. of Calif, Berkeley, 1974. For. Hon. Mem., Amer. Acad. of Arts and Scis, 1986. *Publications:* The Explanation of Behavior, 1964; Pattern of Politics, 1970; Hegel, 1975; Erklarung und Interpretation in den Wissenschaften vom Menschen, 1975; Social Theory as Practice, 1983; Philosophical Papers, 1985; Negative Freiheit, 1988; Sources of the Self, 1989. *Recreations:* skiing, swimming. *Address:* 344 Metcalfe Avenue, Montréal, PQ H3Z 2J3 Canada.

TAYLOR, Clifford; Director, Resources Television, BBC, since 1988 (Deputy Director, 1987–88); *b* 6 March 1941; *s* of Fred Taylor and Annie Elisabeth (*née* Hudson); *m* 1962, Catherine Helen (*née* Green); two *d*. *Educ:* Barnsley and District Holgate Grammar Sch.; Barnsley College of Mining and Technology. ACMA. NCB, 1957–65; Midlands Counties Dairies, 1965–68; BBC: Radio Cost Accountant, 1968–71; Television Hd of Costing, 1971–76; Chief Accountant, Corporate Finance, 1976–77 and 1982–84; Chief Acct, Engineering, 1977–82; Dep. Dir, Finance, 1984–86. *Recreations:* sport — plays squash, enjoys horse racing. *Address:* 35 Hare Hill Close, Pyrford, near Woking, Surrey GU22 8UH. *T:* Byfleet (09323) 48301. *Clubs:* MCC (Associate Mem.), Rugby, BBC (Chm.).

TAYLOR, Sir Cyril (Julian Hebden), Kt 1989; Chairman: City Technology Colleges Trust, since 1987; American Institute for Foreign Study, since 1964; *b* 14 May 1935; *s* of Cyril Eustace Taylor and Margaret Victoria (*née* Hebden); *m* 1965, June Judith Denman; one *d*. *Educ:* St Marylebone Grammar Sch.; Trinity Hall, Cambridge (MA); Harvard Business Sch. (MBA). National Service, Officer with KAR in Kenya during Mau Mau Emergency, 1954–56 (seconded from E Surrey Regt). Brand Manager in Advertising Dept, Proctor & Gamble, Cincinnati, Ohio, 1961–64; Founder Chm., American Institute for Foreign Study, 1964–: group cos include: Amer. Inst. for Foreign Study; Richmond Coll.; English Language Services; Amer. Council for Internat. Studies; Camp America; Au Pair in America. Advr to Sec. of State for Educn and Science, 1987–. Mem. for Ruislip Northwood, GLC, 1977–86: Chm., Professional and Gen. Services Cttee, 1979–81; Opposition spokesperson for employment, 1981–82, transport, 1982–85, policy and resources, 1985–86; Dep. Leader of the Opposition, 1983–86; Mem., Wkg Party reviewing legislation to abolish GLC and MCCs, 1983–86. Pres., Ruislip Northwood Cons. Assoc., 1986–; contested (C): Huddersfield E, Feb. 1974; Keighley, Oct. 1974. Member: Bd of Dirs, Centre for Policy Studies, 1984–; Council, Westfield Coll., Univ. of London, 1983–89; Council, RCM, 1988–; Bd of Governors, Holland Park Comprehensive Sch., 1971–74. Chm., Lexham Gdns Residents' Assoc., 1986–. Pres., Harvard Business Sch. Club, London. FRSA 1990. Hon. PhD New England, 1991. *Publications:* (jtly) The New Guide to Study Abroad, USA 1969, 4th edn 1976; Peace has its Price, 1972; No More Tick, 1974; The Elected Member's Guide to Reducing Public Expenditure, 1980; A Realistic Plan for London Transport, 1982; Reforming London's Government, 1984; Quangoes Just Grow, 1985; London Preserv'd, 1985; Bringing Accountability Back to Local Government, 1985; Employment Examined: the right approach to more jobs, 1986; Raising Educational Standards, 1990. . *Recreations:* keen tennis player, swimmer, gardener, theatre-goer. *Address:* 1 Lexham Walk, W8 5JD. *T:* 071–370 2081; American Institute for Foreign Study, 37 Queen's Gate, SW7 5HR. *T:* 071–581 2733. *Clubs:* Carlton, Hurlingham, Chelsea Arts; Harvard, Racquet (New York).

TAYLOR, Dr Daniel Brumhall Cochrane; JP; Vice-Chancellor, Victoria University of Wellington, New Zealand, 1968–82; Referee of the Small Claims Tribunal, Wellington, 1985–88; *b* 13 May 1921; *s* of Daniel Brumhall Taylor, Coleraine, NI and Anna Martha Taylor (*née* Rice); *m* 1955, Elizabeth Page, Christchurch, NZ; one *s* one *d*. *Educ:* Coleraine Academical Instn, NI; Queen's Univ., Belfast. BSc (Mech. Engrg) 1942, BSc (Elec. Engrg) 1943, MSc 1946, PhD 1948, QUB; MA Cantab 1956; FIMechE 1968. Lecturer in Engineering: Liverpool Univ., 1948–50; Nottingham Univ., 1950–53; ICI Fellow, Cambridge Univ., 1953–56; Lectr in Mechanical Sciences, Cambridge Univ., 1956–68; Fellow of Peterhouse, 1958–68, Fellow Emeritus, 1968; Tutor of Peterhouse, 1958–65, Senior Tutor, 1965–68. Member: NZ/USA Educnl Foundn, 1970–82; Council, Assoc. of Commonwealth Univs, 1974–77 (Chm., 1975–76); Chm., NZ Vice-Chancellors' Cttee, 1975–77. JP New Zealand, 1985. Hon. LLD Victoria Univ. of Wellington, 1983. *Publications:* numerous engrg and metallurgical papers. *Recreation:* golf. *Address:* PO Box 40895, Upper Hutt, New Zealand. *T:* Wellington 267904. *Clubs:* Athenæum; Leander (Henley-on-Thames); Wellington (NZ).

TAYLOR, David George Pendleton; Governor of Montserrat, West Indies, since 1990; *b* 5 July 1933; *s* of George James Pendleton Taylor and Dorothy May Taylor (*née* Williams). *Educ:* Clifton College; Clare College, Cambridge (MA). Nat. Service as Sub-Lieut (Special) RNVR, 1952–54; Admin. Officer, HMOCS Tanganyika, 1958–63; joined Booker McConnell, 1964; Chm. and Chief Exec., Bookers (Malaŵi) Ltd, 1976–77; Director: Consumer Buying Corp. of Zambia, 1978; National Drug Co., Zambia, 1978; Bookers (Zambia), 1978; Minvielle & Chastanet Ltd, St Lucia, 1979; United Rum Merchants Ltd, 1981; Estate Industries Ltd, Jamaica, 1981; seconded full time to Falkland Is Govt, Dec. 1983; Chief Exec., Falkland Islands Govt and Exec. Vice Chm., FI Develt Corp., 1983–87 and 1988–89 (sometime acting Governor). Dir, Booker Agric. Internat., 1987–88. Member: Royal African Soc., 1986–; RIIA, 1988–. Governor, Clifton Coll., 1987–. FRGS 1990. *Recreations:* water colour painting, travel, rural France, pandas. *Address:* Government House, Plymouth, Montserrat, West Indies; 53 Lillian Road, Barnes, SW13 9JF. *Clubs:* United Oxford & Cambridge Universities, Commonwealth Trust, MCC.

TAYLOR, David John; Editor, Business Life, since 1988; *b* 17 March 1947; *s* of John Whitfield Taylor and Alice Elaine Oldacre; *m* 1972, Ann Robinson; two *d*. *Educ:* High Sch., Newcastle-under-Lyme; Magdalene Coll., Cambridge (MA (English)). Reporter, Staffordshire Evening Sentinel, 1966; Editor, Varsity, 1969; BBC TV, Late Night Line-Up, 1969; Asst Editor, 1970–78, Dep. Editor, 1978–87, Editor, 1988, Punch. Radio and TV broadcaster; columnist, Daily Telegraph. *Recreations:* fast cars, golf, personal computers. *Address:* c/o Business Life, Headway Publications, Greater London House, Hampstead Road, NW1 7QQ.

TAYLOR, Derek; Managing Director, NNC Ltd (formerly National Nuclear Corporation), since 1987; Chairman, FASTEC Ltd, since 1987; *b* 25 April 1930; *s* of Ambrose and Joyce Taylor; *m* 1955, Lorna Margaret Ross; two *s* one *d*. *Educ:* Egerton Boys' School, Knutsford; Salford Royal Tech. Coll. MIMechE; FEng 1988. Engineer, Ministry of Supply, 1951; UKAEA, 1955; Asst Chief Engineer, UKAEA, 1968; Eng. Manager, Nuclear Power Gp, 1969; Project Gen. Manager, Nuclear Power Co., 1980; Project Dir, Nat. Nuclear Corp., 1984–87. Non-exec. Dir, PWR Power Projects Ltd,

1988–. *Publications:* papers on nuclear engineering. *Recreations:* golf, gardening. *Address:* 68 Glebelands Road, Knutsford, Cheshire WA16 9DZ. *T:* Knutsford (0565) 633907.

TAYLOR, Desmond S.; *see* Shawe-Taylor.

TAYLOR, Douglas Hugh Charles, PhD; FEng; Group Managing Director, Ricardo International plc, since 1990; *b* 4 April 1938; *s* of Richard Hugh Taylor and Alice Mary Davies; *m* 1970, Janet Elizabeth Scott; two *d. Educ:* King Edward VI Grammar Sch., Lichfield; Loughborough University of Technology. PhD, BTech; FEng, 1987; FIMechE. Ruston & Hornsby/GEC Ruston Diesels, 1962–72, Chief Research Engineer, 1968; Ricardo Consulting Engineers, 1972–90: Head of Large Engines, 1973; Dir, 1977; Man. Dir, 1984–90; Chm., 1987–90. *Recreations:* campanology, flying. *Address:* Ellington House, 20 Coombe Drove, Bramber, Steyning, Sussex BN4 3PW. *T:* Steyning (0903) 813566.

TAYLOR, Sir Edward Macmillan, (Sir Teddy), Kt 1991; MP (C) Southend East, since March 1980; journalist, consultant and company director; *b* 18 April 1937; *s* of late Edward Taylor and of Minnie Hamilton Taylor; *m* 1970, Sheila Duncan; two *s* one *d. Educ:* Glasgow High School and University (MA (Hons) Econ. and Politics). Commercial Editorial Staff of Glasgow Herald, 1958–59; Industrial Relations Officer on Staff of Clyde Shipbuilders' Assoc., 1959–64. Director: Shepherds Foods, 1968–; Ansvar (Temperance) Insurance, 1970–; Adviser: John Lawrence (Glasgow) Ltd, 1970–; Port of London Police Fedn, 1972–. MP (C) Glasgow, Cathcart, 1964–79; Parly Under-Sec. of State, Scottish Office, 1970–71, resigned; Parly Under-Sec. of State, Scottish Office, 1974; Opposition spokesman on Trade, 1977, on Scotland affairs, 1977–79. Sec., Cons. Parly Party Home Affairs Cttee, 1984–. *Publications:* (novel) Hearts of Stone, 1968; contributions to the press. *Address:* 12 Lynton Road, Thorpe Bay, Southend-on-Sea, Essex.

TAYLOR, Prof. Edwin William, FRS 1978; Professor of Molecular Genetics and Cell Biology, University of Chicago, since 1984 (Professor, Department of Biophysics, since 1975; Professor and Chairman, Department of Biology, 1979); *b* Toronto, 8 June 1929; *s* of William Taylor and Jean Taylor (*née* Christie); *m* 1956, Jean Heather Logan; two *s* one *d. Educ:* Univ. of Toronto (BA 1952); McMaster Univ. (MSc 1955); Univ. of Chicago (PhD 1957). Asst Prof., 1959–63, Associate Prof., 1963–67, Prof., 1967–72, Univ. of Chicago; Prof. of Biology, King's College and MRC Unit, London, 1972–74; Associate Dean, Div. of Biol Sci and Medicine, Chicago Univ., 1977–79. Rockefeller Foundn Fellow, 1957–58; Nat. Insts of Health Fellow, 1958–59, cons. to NIH, 1970–72, 1976–80. Member: Amer. Biochem. Soc.; Biophysical Soc. *Address:* Cummings Life Sciences Center, University of Chicago, 920 East 58th Street, Chicago, Ill 60637, USA. *T:* (312) 962–1660; 5634 South Harper Avenue, Chicago, Ill 60637, USA. *T:* (312) 955–2441.

TAYLOR, Elizabeth (Rosemond); film actress; *b* London, 27 Feb. 1932; *d* of Francis Taylor and Sara (*née* Sothern); *m* 1st, 1950, Conrad Nicholas Hilton, Jr (marr. diss.; he *d* 1969); 2nd, 1952, Michael Wilding, *qv* (marr. diss.; he *d* 1979); two *s*; 3rd, 1957, Mike Todd (*d* 1958); one *d*; 4th, 1959, Eddie Fisher (marr. diss.); 5th, 1964, Richard Burton, CBE (*d* 1984) (marr. diss.; remarried 1975; marr. diss. 1976); 7th, 1976, Senator John Warner (marr. diss. 1982). *Educ:* Byron House, Hampstead; Hawthorne School, Beverly Hills; Metro-Goldwyn-Mayer School; University High School, Hollywood. First film, There's One Born Every Minute, 1942. *Films include:* Lassie Come Home, 1943; Jane Eyre, National Velvet, 1944; Courage of Lassie, 1946; Little Women, The Conspirator, Father of the Bride, 1950; A Place in the Sun, 1951; Ivanhoe, 1952; Beau Brummel, 1954; Giant, 1956; Raintree County, 1957; Cat on a Hot Tin Roof, 1958; Suddenly Last Summer, 1959; Butterfield 8 (Academy Award for Best Actress), 1960; Cleopatra, The VIPs, 1963; The Sandpiper, 1965; Who's Afraid of Virginia Woolf? (Academy Award for Best Actress), 1966; The Taming of the Shrew, Doctor Faustus, 1967; Boom!, The Comedians, Reflections in a Golden Eye, Secret Ceremony, 1968; The Only Game in Town, 1970; Under Milk Wood, Zee and Co., Hammersmith is Out, 1972; Night Watch, 1973; Blue Bird, 1975; A Little Night Music, 1977; The Mirror Crack'd, 1980; Winter Kills, 1985; Young Toscanini, 1988. Stage debut as Regina in The Little Foxes, NY, 1981, London stage debut, Victoria Palace, 1982; Private Lives, NY, 1983. Founded American Foundn for AIDS Res., 1985. Legion of Honour (France), 1987. *Publications:* Elizabeth Taylor, 1966; Elizabeth Takes Off, 1988. *Address:* c/o Chen Sam, Chen Sam & Associates, 315 East 72nd Street, New York, NY 10021, USA. *Fax:* 212–439–9438.

TAYLOR, Eric; a Recorder of the Crown Court, since 1978; *b* 22 Jan. 1931; *s* of Sydney Taylor and Sarah Helen (*née* Lea); *m* 1958, Margaret Jessie Taylor, *qv. Educ:* Wigan Grammar Sch.; Manchester Univ. (LLB 1952; Dauntesey Sen. Legal Scholar; LLM 1954). Admitted solicitor, 1955. Partner, Temperley Taylor, Middleton, Manchester, 1957–. Part-time Lectr in Law, Manchester Univ., 1958–80, Hon. Special Lectr in Law, 1980–. Examr (Old) Law Soc. Final Exams, 1968–81, Chief Examr (New) Law Soc. Final Exams, 1978–83. Pres., Oldham Law Assoc., 1970–72. Chairman: Manchester Young Solicitors' Gp, 1963; Manchester Nat. Insurance Appeal Tribunal, 1967–73; Disciplinary Cttee, Architects Registration Council, 1989–. Member: Council, Law Soc., 1972–91 (Chm., Educn and Trng Cttee, 1980–83; Chm., Criminal Law Cttee, 1984–87); CNAA Legal Studies Bd, 1975–84; Lord Chancellor's Adv. Cttee on Trng of Magistrates, 1974–79. Governor, Coll. of Law, 1984–. *Publications:* Modern Conveyancing Precedents, 1964, 2nd edn 1989; Modern Wills Precedents, 1969, 2nd edn 1987; contrib. legal jls. *Recreations:* equestrian sports. *Address:* 10 Mercers Road, Heywood, Lancs OL10 2NP. *T:* Heywood (0706) 66630. *Club:* Farmers'.

TAYLOR, Eric Scollick, PhD; Presiding Bishop, Liberal Catholic Church, since 1984; Clerk of Committee Records, House of Commons, 1975–83; *b* 16 April 1918; *s* of late Percy Scollick Taylor and Jessie Devlin. *Educ:* Durham Univ. (MA); Edinburgh Univ. (PhD 1942). Asst Clerk, House of Commons, 1942; Dep. Principal Clerk, 1962; Principal Clerk, 1972. Clerk to: Cttee of Privileges, 1949–57; Estimates Cttee, 1957–64; Cttee of Public Accounts, 1964–68; Clerk of the Journals, 1972–75. Ordained priest, Liberal Catholic Church, 1943; consecrated Bishop, 1977; Regionary Bishop, Great Britain and Ireland, 1985. *Publications:* The House of Commons at Work, 1951, 9th rev. edn 1979; The Liberal Catholic Church—what is it?, 1966, 2nd edn 1979 (also foreign trans); The Houses of Parliament, 1976; contribs to Times Lit. Supp., etc. *Recreations:* walking, listening to music, preaching to the converted, worship. *Address:* 113 Beaufort Street, SW3 6BA. *T:* 071–351 1765; 71 Woodbine Road, Gosforth, Newcastle upon Tyne NE3 1DE. *T:* Newcastle upon Tyne (091) 857040.

TAYLOR, Eric W., RE 1948 (ARE 1935); ARCA 1934; ASIA (Ed) 1965; printmaker, painter and sculptor; *b* 6 Aug. 1909; *s* of Thomas John and Ethel Annie Taylor; *m* 1939, Alfreda Marjorie Hurren; one *s* one *d. Educ:* William Ellis School, Hampstead; Royal College of Art, South Kensington. Worked for 3 years in London Studio; then as a free-lance illustrator; won British Inst. Scholarship, 1932; runner-up in Prix de Rome, 1934, while at Royal College of Art. Exhibited: Royal Academy; Royal Scottish Academy; Doncaster Art Gallery; New York; Brooklyn; Chicago; London Group; New English Art Club. Pictures in permanent Collections of Stockholm Art Gallery, Art Inst. of Chicago, Washington Art Gallery, War Museum, London, V&A and British Museum Print Rooms, Leeds Art Gall., Bradford Art Gall. Logan Prize for best Etching in International Exhibition of Etching and Engraving at Art Institute of Chicago, 1937. Selected by British Council to exhibit in Scandinavian Exhibition, 1940, S America, 1942–44, Spain and Portugal, 1942–44, Turkey, 1943–45, Iceland, 1943, Mexico, 1943–45, China, 1945, Czechoslovakia, 1948, and Rotterdam, 1948. Associate Chicago Society of Etchers, 1937. War pictures bought by National Gallery Advisory Committee for Imperial War Museum, 1945. Volunteered for RA, Nov. 1939. Instructor at Northern Command Camouflage School, 1941–43; Royal Engineers, France and Germany, 1943–45; Normandy Landing, Battle of Caen, crossings of Rhine and Maas. Instructing for Educational Corps Germany, 1946; Art Instructor Camberwell School of Art, 1936–39; Willesden School of Art, 1936–49; Central School of Art, 1948–49; Examiner: Bristol Univ., 1948–51; Durham Univ., 1971–74; Min. of Education NDD Pictorial Subjects, 1957–59. Designer and Supervisor of Lubeck School of Art for the Services, 1946. Head of the Design School, Leeds Coll. of Art, 1949–56, Principal, 1956–69, Organiser and Administrator of revolutionary Leeds Basic Course which played considerable part in changing whole direction of British art education; Asst Dir, Leeds Polytechnic, 1969–71; disagreed with organization of Art Faculties in Polytechnics and returned to work as full-time artist, 1971. Leverhulme Research Awards, 1958–59, visiting Colleges of Art in Austria, Germany, Holland, Denmark and Italy. Study of Mosaics, Italy, 1965, prior to execution of large mural on Leeds building. Representative Exhibitions: Wakefield Art Gall., 1960; Goosewell Gall., Menston, 1972, 1973, 1976; Middlesbrough Art Gall., 1972; Northern Artists Gall., Harrogate, 1977; Linton Ct Gall., Settle, 1983. Extensive experimental ceramic work, 1980–. British Representative Speaker, International Design Conference, Karachi, 1962. Print selected by Royal Soc. of Painter Etchers for Presentation to Print Collections Club, 1947. Mem. of Senefelder Club, 1947. Picture purchased by British Council, 1948. *Publications:* etching published in Fine Prints of the Year, 1935, 1936, 1937, and in 1939 and 1940 issues of Print Collectors Quarterly. *Address:* Linton Springs Farm, Sicklinghall Road, near Wetherby, W Yorks LS22 4AQ.

TAYLOR, Ernest Richard; Headmaster of Wolverhampton Grammar School, 1956–April 1973; *b* Oldham, 9 Aug. 1910; *e s* of late Louis Whitfield Taylor and Annie Taylor; *m* 1936, Muriel Hardill; twin *s. Educ:* Hulme Grammar School, Oldham; Trinity College, Cambridge. Hist. Tripos, Class I, 1931; Sen. Schol. and Earl of Derby Research Student (Trinity), 1931–32; Thirlwall and Gladstone Prizes, 1933; MA 1935. Asst Master, Culford School, 1932–36; Moseley Gram. Sch., Birmingham, 1936–39; Manchester Gram. Sch., 1939–47. War Service in RA and AEC, 1940–46. Headmaster of Quarry Bank High School, Liverpool, 1947–56; Member, Schools Council for Curriculum and Examinations (formerly Secondary Schools Examinations Council), 1962–84. Walter Hines Page Scholar, HMC, 1964. Pres. Incorporated Assoc. of Head Masters, 1965; Chm. Central Exec., Jt Four Secondary Assocs, 1970–72. Member: President's Council of Methodist Church, 1976–79; Churches' Council for Covenanting, 1978–82. Hon. Life Mem., Secondary Heads Assoc., 1979. Hon. Fellow, Selly Oak Colls, Birmingham, 1989. *Publications:* Methodism and Politics, (1791–1851), 1935; Padre Brown of Gibraltar, 1955; Religious Education of pupils from 16 to 19 years, 1962. *Recreation:* golf. *Address:* Highcliff, Whitcliffe, Ludlow, Shropshire SY8 2HD. *T:* Ludlow (0584) 872093.

TAYLOR, Frank, CBE 1969; QFSM 1965; fire consultant; Chief Fire Officer, Merseyside County Fire Brigade, 1974–76, retired (Liverpool Fire Brigade, 1962–74); *b* 6 April 1915; *s* of Percy and Beatrice Taylor; *m* 1940, Nancy (*née* Hefford); two *s* two *d*; *m* 1976, Florence Mary Latham. *Educ:* Council Sch., Sheffield. Fireman, Sheffield Fire Bde, 1935–41; Instr, NFS West Riding, 1941–42; Company Officer up to Station Officer (ops), NFS in Yorkshire, 1942–49; Chief Officer, Western Fire Authority, NI, 1949–51; Divl Officer NI Fire Authority, 1951–57; Belfast: Dep. Chief Officer, 1958–60; Chief Officer, 1960–62. *Recreations:* football, gardening. *Address:* Onchan, Hall Lane, Wrightington, near Wigan, Lancs.

TAYLOR, Dr Frank; Deputy Director and Principal Keeper, The John Rylands University Library of Manchester, 1972–77; Hon. Lecturer in Manuscript Studies, University of Manchester, 1967–77. *Educ:* Univ. of Manchester (MA, PhD). FSA. Served with RN, 1942–46: Lieut, RNVR, 1943–46. Research for Cttee on History of Parlt, 1934–35; Keeper of Western Manuscripts, 1935–49, Keeper of Manuscripts, 1949–72, Librarian, 1970–72, John Rylands Library. Jt. Hon. Sec., Lancs Parish Record Soc., 1937–56, Hon. Sec., 1956–82; Registrar of Research, Soc. of Architectural Historians, 1978–82. Member: British Acad. Oriental Documents Cttee, 1974–80; British Acad. Medieval Latin Dictionary Cttee, 1973–83. Editor, Bulletin of the John Rylands Univ. Lib. of Manchester, 1948–87. *Publications:* various Calendars of Western Manuscripts and Charter Room collections in the Rylands Library, 1937–77; The Chronicle of John Strecche for the Reign of Henry 5, 1932; An Early Seventeenth Century Calendar of Records Preserved in Westminster Palace Treasury, 1939; The Parish Registers of Aughton, 1541–1764, 1942; contrib. to Some Twentieth Century Interpretations of Boswell's Life of Johnson (ed J. L. Clifford), 1970; The Oriental Manuscript Collections in the John Rylands Library, 1972; (ed with J. S. Roskell) Gesta Henrici Quinti, 1975; (with G. A. Matheson) Hand-List of Personal Papers from the Muniments of the Earl of Crawford and Balcarres, 1976; revised edn of M. R. James's Descriptive Catalogue of Latin Manuscripts in the John Rylands Library (1921), 1980; (ed) Society of Architectural Historians, Research Register No 5, 1981; The John Rylands University Library of Manchester, 1982; articles in Bulletin of John Rylands Library, Indian Archives. *Recreations:* cricket, walking.

TAYLOR, Frank Henry; Principal, Frank H. Taylor & Co., City of London, Chartered Accountants; *b* 10 Oct. 1907; 2nd *s* of George Henry Taylor, Cambridgeshire; *m* 1936, Margaret Dora Mackay (*d* 1944), Invernesshire; one *d*; *m* 1948, Mabel Hills (*d* 1974), Hertfordshire; two *s*; *m* 1978, Glenys Mary Edwards, MBE, Bethesda, N Wales. *Educ:* Rutlish School, Merton, Surrey, FCIS 1929; FCA 1930. Commenced in practice as Chartered Accountant, 1930; Ministry of Food Finance Director of Tea, Coffee, Cocoa and Yeast, 1942; Min. of War Transport Finance Rep. overseas, 1944; visited over 40 countries on financial and political missions. Lt-Colonel comdg 1st Caernarvonshire Bn Home Guard, 1943. Contested (C) Newcastle under Lyme, 1955, Chorley, 1959; MP (C) Manchester, Moss Side, Nov. 1961–Feb. 1974. Chm., Wimbledon & South West Finance PLC, 1959–. Mem. Council, London World Trade Centre, 1982–. Governor of Rutlish School, 1946–. Liveryman, City of London. Master, Bakers' Co., 1981–82; Mem., Guild of Air Pilots. *Recreations:* numerous including Rugby (for Surrey County), sculling (Thames Championship), punting (several Thames championships), golf (Captain RAC 1962). *Address:* 4 Barrie House, Lancaster Gate, W2. *T:* 071–262 5684; Tinker Taylor, Sennen Cove, Cornwall. *T:* Sennen (0736) 871220. *Clubs:* City Livery, Royal Automobile, British Sportsman's.

TAYLOR, Dr Frank Henry; Director, Libraries, Books and Information Division, British Council, 1990–91; *b* 20 Jan. 1932; *s* of Frank Taylor and Norah (*née* Dunn). *Educ:* Frimley and Camberley Co. Grammar Sch.; King's Coll., London (BSc 1953; PhD 1957). Beit Meml Fellow for Med. Res., Imperial Coll., London and Pasteur Inst., Paris, 1957–60; British Council, 1960–91: Science Officer, 1960–61; Asst Cultural Attaché, Cairo, 1961–64; Asst Regl Rep., Calcutta, 1965–69; Science Officer, Rio de Janeiro, 1970–74; Dir, Science and Technology Dept, 1974–78; Rep., Saudi Arabia, 1978–81; Head

Operations, Technical Educn and Trng in Overseas Countries, and Dep. Controller, Science, Technology and Education Div., 1981–84; Counsellor, British Council and Cultural Affairs, Ankara, 1984–87; Dep. Controller, Asia and Pacific Div., then S and W Asia Div., 1987–88; Controller, Africa and ME Div., 1989–90. *Publications:* articles on surface chemistry and reviews in Proc. Royal Soc., etc. *Recreations:* music, bridge, travel, Middle East. *Address:* c/o British Council, 10 Spring Gardens, SW1A 2BN. *T:* 071–930 8466.

TAYLOR, Prof. Fredric William, DPhil; Professor of Atmospheric Physics, since 1990, Head of Department, since 1979, Oxford University; Fellow, Jesus College, Oxford, since 1979; *b* 24 Sept. 1944; *s* of William Taylor and Ena Lloyd (*née* Burns); *m* 1969, Doris Jean Buer. *Educ:* Duke of Northumberland's Sch.; Univ. of Liverpool (BSc 1966): Univ. of Oxford (DPhil 1970; MA 1983). Resident Res. Associate, US Nat. Res. Council, 1970–72; Sen. Scientist, Jet Propulsion Lab., CIT, 1972–79; Reader in Atmospheric Physics, Oxford Univ., 1983–89. *Publications:* Cambridge Atlas of the Planets, 1982, 2nd edn 1986 (trans. German 1984, Italian 1988); Remote Sounding of Atmospheres, 1984, 2nd edn 1987; contrib. to learned jls. *Recreations:* walking, theatre, opera, literature, history, railways. *Address:* Clarendon Laboratory, Oxford OX1 3PU; Jesus College, Oxford OX1 3DW. *T:* Oxford (0865) 272903.

TAYLOR, Geoffrey H.; *see* Handley-Taylor.

TAYLOR, Geoffrey William, FCIB; Chairman, Daiwa Europe Bank PLC, since 1987; *b* 4 Feb. 1927; *s* of late Joseph William and Doris Taylor; *m* 1951, Joyce (*née* Walker); three *s* one *d*. *Educ:* Heckmondwike Grammar School; Univ. of London. BComm. Joined Midland Bank Ltd, 1943; Gen. Man. and Man. Dir, Midland Bank Finance Corp. Ltd, 1967–76; Asst Chief General Manager, 1974–80, Dep. Group Chief Exec., 1980–82, Group Chief Exec., 1982–86, Dir, 1982–87, Vice-Chm., 1986–87, Midland Bank Plc. Dir, Y. J. Lovell (Hldgs) PLC, 1987–. Member: Review Cttee on Banking Services Law, 1987–; Internat. Adv. Council, Wells Fargo & Co., 1987–; Internat. Adv. Bd, Govt of Malta, 1989–. Gilbart Banking Lectr, 1973. *Recreations:* golf, reading, music. *Address:* Daiwa Europe Bank PLC, City Tower, 40 Basinghall Street, EC2V 5DE. *Clubs:* Buck's, Overseas Bankers.

TAYLOR, Sir George, Kt 1962; DSc; FRS 1968, FRSE, FLS; Director, Royal Botanic Gardens, Kew, 1956–71; *b* 15 February 1904; *o s* of George William Taylor and Jane Sloan; *m* 1st, 1929, Alice Helen Pendrich (*d* 1977); two *s*; 2nd, Norah English (*d* 1967); 3rd, 1969, Beryl, Lady Colwyn (*d* 1987); 4th, 1989, June Maitland. *Educ:* George Heriot's Sch., Edinburgh; Edinburgh Univ. BSc (1st class hons Botany), 1926; Vans Dunlop Scholar. Member of Botanical Expedition to South Africa and Rhodesia, 1927–28; Joint Leader of British Museum Expedition to Ruwenzori and mountains of East Africa, 1934–35; Expedition to SE Tibet and Bhutan, 1938. Principal in Air Ministry, 1940–45. Deputy Keeper of Botany, British Museum (Natural History), 1945–50; Keeper of Botany, 1950–56; Dir, 1970–89, Consultant, 1989–, Stanley Smith Horticultural Trust. Vis. Prof., Reading Univ., 1969–. Botanical Sec. Linnean Soc., 1950–56; Vice-Pres. 1956. Percy Sladen Trustee, 1951–81. Royal Horticultural Soc.: Mem. Council, 1951–73, Vice-Pres., and Prof. of Botany, 1974–; Council Member: National Trust (Chm. Gardens Cttee), 1961–72; RGS 1957–61 (Vice-Pres. 1964); Mem. Min. of Transport Adv. Cttee on Landscaping Treatment of Trunk Roads, 1956–81 (Chm. 1969–81). Editor, Curtis's Botanical Magazine, 1962–71. Gen. Sec., Brit. Assoc. for the Advancement of Science, 1951–58. Hon. Botanical Adviser, Commonwealth War Graves Commn, 1956–77. President: Botanical Society of British Isles, 1955; Division of Botany, Internat. Union Biol Sci., 1964–69; Internat. Assoc. for Plant Taxonomy, 1969–72. Member Royal Society Science, Uppsala, 1956; Corr. Member Royal Botanical Soc. Netherlands; Hon. Mem., Botanical Soc. of S Africa; Hon. Mem., American Orchid Soc. Hon. FRHS 1948. Hon. Freeman, Worshipful Co. of Gardeners, 1967. Hon. LLD Dundee, 1972. VMH 1956; Veitch Gold Medal, Royal Horticultural Soc., 1963; Bradford Washburn Award, Museum of Science, Boston, USA, 1969; Scottish Horticultural Medal, Royal Caledonian Horticultural Soc., 1984. Hon. DrPhil Gothenburg, 1958. *Publications:* An Account of the Genus Meconopsis, 1934; contributions on flowering plants to various periodicals. *Recreations:* angling, gardening, music. *Address:* Belhaven House, Dunbar, East Lothian EH42 1NS. *T:* Dunbar (0368) 62392, 63546. *Clubs:* Athenæum; New (Edinburgh).

TAYLOR, Prof. Gerard William, MS, FRCS; Hon. FACS; Professor of Surgery, University of London, 1960–84; Surgeon and Director Surgical Professorial Unit, St Bartholomew's Hospital, London; Honorary Consultant in Vascular Surgery to the Army since 1962; *b* 23 September 1920; *s* of William Ivan Taylor; *m* 1951, Olivia Gay; one *s* one *d*. *Educ:* Bemrose School, Derby; St Bartholomew's Hospital Medical College. Served War of 1939–45, Capt. RAMC, 1944–47. Fellow in Surgery, Asst Resident, Fulbright Schol., Stanford Univ. Hosp., San Francisco, Calif., 1950–51; Surgeon, St Bartholomew's Hosp., London, Reader in Surgery, Univ. of London, 1955; Hunterian Prof., RCS, 1962; Vis. Prof. of Surgery: Univ. of Calif., Los Angeles, 1965; Univ. of Melbourne, 1969; Sir James Wattie Prof., NZ, 1972. Examiner in Surgery: Univ. of London, 1960; NUI, 1966; Univ. of Cambridge, 1966; Trinity Coll., Dublin, 1969; Univ. of Liverpool, 1974; Univ. of Birmingham, 1978. Governor, St Bartholomew's Hosp., 1971; Mem. Council, Epsom Coll., 1972. President: Vascular Surgical Soc. of GB and Ireland, 1975; Surgical Res. Soc., 1976; Assoc. of Surgeons of GB and Ireland, 1979. *Publications:* articles on general and arterial surgery in scientific journals. *Recreation:* motoring. *Address:* Maple Farm, Shantock Lane, Bovingdon, Herts. *T:* Hemel Hempstead (0442) 833170.

TAYLOR, Sir Godfrey; *see* Taylor, Sir A. G.

TAYLOR, Gordon; Chief Executive, Professional Footballers' Association, since 1981; *b* 28 Dec. 1944; *s* of Alec and Mary Taylor; *m* 1968, Catharine Margaret Johnston; two *s*. *Educ:* Ashton-under-Lyne Grammar Sch.; Bolton Technical Coll.; Univ. of London (BScEcon Hons (ext.)). Professional footballer with: Bolton Wanderers, 1960–70; Birmingham City, 1970–76; Blackburn Rovers, 1976–78; Vancouver Whitecaps (N American Soccer League), 1977; Bury, 1978–80, retd. Professional Footballers Association: Mem., Management Cttee, 1971; Chm., 1978–80; (full-time) Asst Sec., 1980; Sec./Treasurer, 1981. Hon. MA Loughborough Univ. of Technol., 1986 (for services to football). *Recreations:* theatre, dining-out, squash, watching football, reading. *Address:* (office) 2 Oxford Court, Bishopsgate, Manchester M2 3WQ. *T:* 061–236 0575.

TAYLOR, Dr Gordon William; Managing Director, Firemarket Ltd, since 1988; *b* 26 June 1928; *s* of William and Elizabeth Taylor; *m* 1954, Audrey Catherine Bull; three *s* two *d*. *Educ:* J. H. Burrows Sch., Grays, Essex; Army Apprentice Sch.; London Univ. (BScEng Hons, PhDEng). MICE, MIMechE, AMIEE. Kellogg Internat. Corp., 1954–59; W. R. Grace, 1960–62; Gen. Man., Nalco Ltd, 1962–66; BTR Industries, 1966–68; Managing Director: Kestrel Chemicals, 1968–69; Astral Marketing, 1969–70; Robson Refractories, 1970–87. Greater London Council: Alderman, 1972–77; Mem. for Croydon Central, 1977–80; Chairman: Public Services Cttee, 1977–78; London Transp. Cttee, 1978–79. *Recreations:* theatre, reading, tennis. *Address:* 33 Royal Avenue, Chelsea, SW3 4QE. *Club:* Holland Park Lawn Tennis.

TAYLOR, Graham; Manager, England Football Team, since 1990; *b* Worksop, Notts, 15 Sept. 1944; *s* of Tommy Taylor; *m* Rita; two *d*. *Educ:* Scunthorpe Grammar Sch. Professional football player: Grimsby Town, 1963–68; Lincoln City, 1968–72; Manager: Lincoln City, 1972–77; Watford, 1977–87; Aston Villa, 1987–90. *Address:* c/o Football Association, 16 Lancaster Gate, W2 3LW.

TAYLOR, Greville Laughton; company director; *b* 23 Oct. 1902; *s* of Rowland Henry and Edith Louise Taylor; *m* 1947, Mary Eileen Reece Mahon; one *s* one *d*. *Educ:* Lodge School, Barbados; St John's College, Oxford. Called to the Bar, Lincoln's Inn, 1927. Clerk to the House of Assembly, Barbados, 1930–36; Police Magistrate, Barbados, 1936–44; Army 1940–44 (UK, N Africa, Italy); Registrar, Barbados, 1944–46; Judge of the Assistant Court of Appeal, Barbados, 1947–57; Puisne Judge, Windward Islands and Leeward Islands, 1957–64. *Recreations:* reading, shooting, fishing. *Address:* Frangipani, No 9 Long Bay, St Philip, Barbados, West Indies. *T:* 207. *Club:* Barbados Yacht.

TAYLOR, Harold Joseph, CBE 1966; Chief Director, Prison Department, Home Office, 1965–68, retired; *b* 7 May 1904; *s* of Herbert Taylor and Gertrude Mary Taylor; *m* 1940, Olive Alice Slade, *d* of Harry Slade, Honor Oak Park, SE; one adopted *s* decd. *Educ:* Blandford Sec. Gram. Sch.; Southampton University. Teacher, Brighton Education Authority, 1924–28; Asst Housemaster, Prison Commission, HM Borstal, Portland, 1928; Housemaster, Portland Borstal, 1930; Superintendent, Borstal Training School, Thayetmyo, Burma, 1933–37; Governor, HM Borstal: Feltham, Middx, 1938–41; Lowdham Grange, 1941–46; Governor, HM Prison: Camp Hill, IoW, 1946–49; Sudbury, Derby, 1949–51; Asst Comr, HM Prison Commission, 1951–57; Comr and Director of Borstal Administration, 1958–65. *Recreations:* fishing, country lore, tinkering. *Address:* 45 Church Way, Pagham, Bognor Regis, West Sussex PO21 4QQ. *T:* Pagham (0243) 263750.

TAYLOR, Harold McCarter, CBE 1955; TD 1945; retired, 1967; *b* Dunedin, New Zealand, 13 May 1907; *s* of late James Taylor, and late Louisa Urquhart Taylor; *m* 1st, 1933, Joan (*d* 1965), *d* of late George Reginald Sills, Lincoln; two *s* two *d*; 2nd, 1966, Dorothy Judith, *d* of late Charles Samuel, Liverpool. *Educ:* Otago Boys' High School and Univ. of Otago, NZ; Clare Coll., Cambridge. MSc New Zealand, 1928; MA, PhD Cambridge, 1933. Allen Scholar and Smith's Prizeman, 1932. Fellow of Clare College, Cambridge, 1933–61; Hon. Fellow, 1961–; Lecturer in Mathematics, University of Cambridge, 1934–45; Treasurer of the University, 1945–53; Secretary General of the Faculties, 1953–61; Vice-Chancellor, University of Keele, 1962–67 (Principal, University College of North Staffordshire, 1961–62); Rede Lecturer, Cambridge University, 1966. Mem., Royal Commn on Historical Monuments (England), 1972–78. Pres., Royal Archaeol Inst., 1972–75; Vice-Pres., Soc. of Antiquaries of London, 1974–77 (Frend Medal, 1981). Hon. LLD Cambridge, 1967; Hon. DLitt: Keele, 1968; Birmingham, 1983. Commissioned in TA, NZ, 1925; served War of 1939–45 as Major and Lieut-Col RA; Instructor and Senior Instructor in Gunnery at School of Artillery, Larkhill; J. H. Lefroy Medal, RA, 1946. *Publications:* Anglo-Saxon Architecture, vols I and II (with Joan Taylor), 1965, vol. III, 1978; many articles in nat. and county archaeological jls. *Recreations:* mountaineering and ski-ing; Anglo-Saxon art and architecture; photography. *Address:* 192 Huntingdon Road, Cambridge CB3 0LB. *T:* Cambridge (0223) 276324.

TAYLOR, Henry George, DSc(Eng); Director of Electrical Research Association, 1957–69, retired; *b* 4 Nov. 1904; *m* 1931, Gwendolyn Hilda Adams; one *s* two *d*. *Educ:* Taunton School; Battersea Polytechnic Inst., City and Guilds Engineering College. Metropolitan Vickers, 1929–30; Electrical Research Assoc., 1930–38; Copper Development Assoc., 1938–42; Philips Lamps Ltd, 1942–47; British Welding Research Assoc., 1947–57. *Publications:* contribs to: Instn of Electrical Engineers Jl, Jl of Inst. of Physics, etc. *Recreation:* walking.

TAYLOR, Sir Henry Milton, Kt 1980; JP; Acting Governor-General, Commonwealth of the Bahamas, since 1988; Editor of Hansard, Bahamas House of Assembly, since 1979; *b* 4 Nov. 1903; adopted *s* of Joseph and Evelyn Taylor; *m* 1962, Eula Mae Sisco; three step *c*; four *d* by previous marriage. *Educ:* Govt Grade Sch.; privately. Teacher; Headmaster, Public Sch. at Pompey Bay, Acklins Island, 1925–26. Elected Mem., House of Assembly, 1949; Co-founded and organized estabt of Progressive Liberal Party of Bahamas (first political party of Bahamas), 1953–64; Nat. Party Chm., 1953–64, Hon. Chm. for life, 1963; MP for 10 yrs; Leader of delegns to Westminster: to upgrade antiquated Acts of Parliament, 1956; in interest of Women's Suffrage, 1960. Temp. Dep. Governor-General of The Bahamas, July-Aug. and Nov. 1981, Aug.-Nov. 1982 and June 1984. Mem., Develt Bd (Tourist), 1960–62; successfully toured Britain, Eire, W Germany and Sweden in interests of tourism and financial investments; officially visited Nassau/Lahn. (First) Dir, Princess Margaret Hosp. Blood Bank, 1954–55. Organised Bahamas Soc. of Arms and Awards, 1984. Letters Patent for Armorial Bearing approved by Duke of Norfolk, 1981. JP Bahama Isles, 1984. *Publications:* (compiled and ed) United Bahamian Party Annual Handbook, 1967, 1968; My Political Memoirs, 1986. *Address:* PO Box N10846, Nassau, Bahamas; Lucaya at Brentwood, 221 NE 44 Street, Miami, Fla 33137, USA. *Club:* British Floridian (Miami).

TAYLOR, Hermon, MA, MD, MChir, FRCS; retired; formerly Consulting Surgeon: London Hospital, E1; King George Hospital, Ilford; *b* 11 May 1905; *s* of Enoch Oliver Taylor and L. M. Taylor (*née* Harrison); *m* 1st, 1932, Méarie Amélie Pearson (*d* 1981); three *s* two *d*; 2nd, 1983, Mrs Noreen Cooke. *Educ:* Latymer School, Edmonton; St John's Coll., Cambridge (scholar); St Bartholomew's Hospital (Entrance Scholar). BA 1926; MRCS, LRCP 1929; MB, ChB Cantab. 1930; FRCS Eng. 1930. House Surgeon, Demonstr of Pathology, St Bart's Hosp.; Res. Surgical Officer: Hertford Co. Hosp., Lincoln Co. Hosp.; Surgical Registrar, Prince of Wales' Hosp., Tottenham. MChir Cantab 1932; MD Cantab 1934; Horton Smith Prize, Univ. Cantab; Luther Holden Research Scholar, St Bartholomew's Hospital; BMA Research Scholar, Surgical First Assistant London Hospital. Moynihan Fellow, Assoc. of Surgeons of GB and Ireland; Hunterian Professor, RCS. Past President, British Society of Gastro-enterology; Hon. Member Amer. Gastro-enterological Assoc. Hon. Fellow, London Hosp. Med. Coll., 1988. *Publications:* Carcinoma of the Stomach, in Modern Trends in Gastro-Enterology, 1952; contrib. to BMJ, Lancet, etc, 1942–. *Address:* Coppice Field, Bosham Hoe, Chichester, West Sussex PO18 8ET. *T:* Chichester (0243) 573385. *Club:* Athenæum.
See also J. Hermon-Taylor.

TAYLOR, Rt. Rev. Humphrey Vincent; *see* Selby, Bishop Suffragan of.

TAYLOR, Ian Colin, MBE 1974; MP (C) Esher, since 1987; *b* 18 April 1945; *s* of Horace Stanley Taylor and late Beryl Taylor (*née* Harper); *m* 1974, Hon. Carole Alport, *d* of Baron Alport, *qv*; two *s*. *Educ:* Whitley Abbey Sch., Coventry; Keele Univ. (BA); London School of Economics (Res. Schol.). Associate, Soc. of Investment Analysts. Corporate financial adviser; Dir, Mathercourt Securities Ltd, 1980–90; non-exec. Dir of several cos. Nat. Chm., Fedn of Cons. Students, 1968–69; Chm., Europ. Union of Christian Democratic and Cons. Students, 1969–70; Hon. Sec., Brit. Cons. Assoc. in France, 1976–78; Chairman: Commonwealth Youth Exchange Council, 1980–84; Cons. Foreign and Commonwealth Council, 1990–; Nat. Chm., Cons. Gp for Europe, 1985–88.

Contested (C) Coventry SE, Feb. 1974. Parliamentary Private Secretary: FCO, 1990; to Sec. of State for Health, 1990–. Mem., Select Cttee on Foreign Affairs, 1987–90; Chm., Cons. Parly European Affairs Cttee, 1988–89. Vice-Chm., Assoc. of Cons. Clubs, 1988–. *Publications:* various pamphlets; contrib. to various jls, etc, on politics and business. *Recreations:* cricket, opera, lawnmowing, shooting. *Address:* House of Commons, SW1A 0AA. *T:* 071–219 5221. *Clubs:* Carlton; Molesey Working Men's (Pres.).

TAYLOR, Prof. Ian Galbraith, CBE 1987; Ellis Llwyd Jones Professor of Audiology and Education of the Deaf, University of Manchester, 1964–88, now Emeritus; *b* 24 April 1924; *s* of David Oswald Taylor, MD, and Margaret Ballantine Taylor; *m* 1954, Audrey Wolstenholme; two *d.* *Educ:* Manchester Grammar Sch.; Univ. of Manchester. MB, ChB, DPH Manchester; MD (Gold Medal) Manchester 1963; MRCP 1973; FRCP 1977. Ho. Surg., Manchester Royal Infirm., 1948; DAD, Army Health of N Regional Canal Zone, and OC Army Sch. of Hygiene, ME, 1949–51; Asst MO, City of Manchester, 1951–54. Univ. of Manchester: Hon. Special Lectr and Ewing Foundn Fellow, Dept of Education of the Deaf, 1956–60; Lectr in Clinical Audiology, 1963–64. Consultant in Audiological Medicine, United Manchester Hosps, 1968. *Publication:* Neurological Mechanisms of Hearing and Speech in Children, 1964. *Recreations:* gardening, fishing. *Address:* Croft Cottage, The Beeches, Whitegate, near Northwich, Cheshire CW8 2BL.

TAYLOR, Ivor Ralph, QC 1973; **His Honour Judge Taylor;** a Circuit Judge, since 1976; *b* 26 Oct. 1927; *s* of late Abraham and Ruth Taylor; *m* 1st, 1954, Ruth Cassel (marr. diss. 1974); one *s* one *d* (and one *d* decd); 3rd, 1984, (Audrey) Joyce Goldman (*née* Wayne). *Educ:* Stand Grammar Sch., Whitefield; Manchester Univ. Served War of 1939–45, AC2 in RAF, 1945. Called to Bar, Gray's Inn, 1951. Standing Counsel to Inland Revenue, N Circuit, 1969–73; a Recorder of the Crown Court, 1972–76. Chm., Inquiry into Death of Baby Brown at Rochdale Infirmary, 1974. Chm., PTA, Dept of Audiology, Manchester Univ., 1966–67. Pres., Manchester and District Medico Legal Soc., 1974, 1975. Gov., Royal Manchester Children's Hosp., 1967–70; Mem. Management Cttee, Salford Hosp., 1967–70. *Recreations:* walking, indifferent golfing. *Address:* 5 Eagle Lodge, 19 Harrop Road, Hale, Altrincham, Cheshire WA15 9DA. *T:* 061–941 5591.

TAYLOR, Sir James, Kt 1966; MBE 1945; DSc, FRSC, Hon. FInstP, Hon. MIMinE; Director, Surrey Independent Hospital plc, 1981–86; Deputy Chairman: Royal Ordnance Factories Board, 1959–72 (Member, 1952–72); Chairman, Chloride Silent Power Ltd, 1974–81; *b* 16 Aug. 1902; *s* of James and Alice Taylor; *m* 1929, Margaret Lennox Stewart (*d* 1990); two *s* one *d.* *Educ:* Bede College, Sunderland; Rutherford College, Newcastle upon Tyne; Universities of Durham, Sorbonne, Utrecht, Cambridge. BSc (1st cl. Hons Physics) 1923; PhD 1925; Dr of Physics and Maths (*cum laude*) Utrecht, 1927; DSc Dunelm, 1931. ICI Ltd: joined Nobel Div. 1928; Research Dir, 1946; Jt Man. Dir, 1951; Director, 1952–64. Chairman: Yorkshire Imperial Metals Ltd, 1958–64; Imperial Aluminium Co. Ltd, 1959–64; Imperial Metal Industries Ltd, 1962–64; Fulmer Res. Institute, 1976–78. Director: Nuclear Developments Ltd, 1961–64; European Plumbing Materials Ltd, 1962–64; BDH Group Ltd, 1965–67; Oldham & Son Ltd, 1965–69; Oldham (International) Ltd, 1969–72. Member: Adv. Coun. on Scientific Research and Tech. Develt, MoD, 1965–68; NPL Steering Committee, 1966; Adv. Coun. on Calibration and Measurement, 1966; Chm., Glazebrook Cttee, NPL, 1966. Member: Court, Brunel Univ., 1967–82; Council, British Non-Ferrous Metals Research Assoc., 1954–67 (Vice-Chm. 1961–67); Council, City and Guilds of London, 1969–71; Court, RCA, 1969–71; Pres. Section B British Assoc. 1960, Council 1965; Pres. Inst. of Physics and Physical Society, 1966–68 (Hon. Treas. 1957–66); FRIC 1945; MIMinE 1947 (Hon. Member, 1960); FInstP 1948 (Hon. FInstP 1972). FRSA 1962 (Member Council 1964–86, Vice-Pres., 1969, Chm., 1969–71, Vice-Pres. Emeritus, 1988, Silver Medal, 1969); Hon. Pres., Research and Development Soc., 1970; Hon. Mem., Newcomen Soc. in N America, 1970. Mem., Inst. of Dirs, 1964–. Hon. DSc Bradford, 1968; Hon. DCL Newcastle, 1969. Medal, Society Chemical Industry, 1965; Silver Medal, Chem. Soc., 1972. *Publications:* On the Sparking Potentials of Electric Discharge Tubes, 1927; Detonation in Condensed Explosives, 1952; British Coal Mining Explosives, 1958; Solid Propellent and Exothermic Compositions, 1959; The Modern Chemical Industry in Great Britain (Cantor Lectures, Jl of Roy. Soc. Arts), 1961; Restrictive Practices (Soc. of Chem. Ind. Lecture), 1965; Monopolies and Restrictive Practices (RSA), 1967; The Scientist and The Technologist in Britain today (Pres. Address, IPPS), 1967; Britain's Technological Future (IOP Jubilee Address), 1968; Arts, Crafts and Technology (RSA), 1969; Cobalt, Madder and Computers (RSA), 1969; The Seventies and the Society (RSA), 1970; The American Dream and the RSA, 1971; New Horizons in Research and Development (RSA), 1971; The Scientific Community, 1973; numerous contribs to Proc. Roy. Soc., Phil. Mag., Trans Inst. Min. Eng., Advancement of Science, ICI Magazine. *Recreations:* gardening, cooking and writing. *Address:* Culvers, Seale, near Farnham, Surrey GU10 1JN. *T:* Runfold (02518) 2210. *Clubs:* Institute of Directors; RNVR Carrick (Hon.) (Glasgow).

TAYLOR, Dame Jean (Elizabeth); DCVO 1978 (CVO 1976; MVO 4th Cl. 1971, 5th Cl. 1964); retired; *b* 7 Nov. 1916; *d* of late Captain William Taylor (killed in action, 1917). *Educ:* Tunbridge Wells High School (GPDST). Entered Office of Private Secretary to the Queen, 1958; Chief Clerk, 1961–78. *Recreations:* music, walking, looking at old buildings. *Address:* Church Cottage, Frittenden, Cranbrook, Kent TN17 2DD.

TAYLOR, Jessie; *see* Taylor, M. J.

TAYLOR, His Honour John Barrington, MBE 1945; TD 1957; JP; a Circuit Judge, 1977–89; *b* 3 Aug. 1914; *y s* of Robert Edward Taylor, Bath; *m* 1941, Constance Aleen, *y d* of J. Barkly Macadam, Edinburgh and Suffolk; two *s* three *d* (and one *s* decd). *Educ:* King Edward's Sch., Bath. LLB (London). Admitted a Solicitor, 1936, and practised at Bath until 1960. Enlisted Somerset LI, 1939; overseas service 1942–46: DAAG, HQ 5 Corps, 1943; demobilised, Lieut-Col, 1946. HM Coroner, City of Bath, 1958–72; Registrar, Bath Gp of County Courts, 1960–77; a Recorder of the Crown Court, 1972–77. JP Somerset, 1962, Essex, 1978. *Recreation:* gardening. *Address:* The White House, Panfield, Braintree, Essex CM7 5AW.

TAYLOR, Rt. Rev. John Bernard; *see* St Albans, Bishop of.

TAYLOR, Prof. John Bryan, FRS 1970; Fondren Professor of Plasma Theory, University of Texas at Austin, since 1989; *b* 26 Dec. 1928; *s* of Frank and Ada Taylor, Birmingham; *m* 1951, Joan M. Hargest; one *s* one *d.* *Educ:* Oldbury Grammar Sch.; Birmingham Univ., 1947–50 and 1952–55. RAF, 1950–52. Atomic Weapons Research Establishment, Aldermaston, 1955–59 and 1960–62; Harkness Fellow, Commonwealth Fund, Univ. of California (Berkeley), 1959–60; Culham Laboratory (UKAEA), 1962–69 and 1970–89 (Head of Theoretical Physics Div., 1963–81; Chief Physicist, 1981–89); Inst. for Advanced Study, Princeton, 1969. FInstP 1969. Fellow, Amer. Phys. Soc., 1984. Maxwell Medal, IPPS, 1971; Max Born Medal, German Phys. Soc., 1979; Award for Excellence in Plasma Physics Res., Amer. Phys. Soc., 1986. *Publications:* contribs to scientific learned jls. *Recreations:* gliding, model engineering. *Address:* Institute for Fusion Studies, University of Texas at Austin, Austin, Texas 78712, USA. *T:* 512–471–1322.

TAYLOR, John Charles; QC 1983; *b* 22 April 1931; *s* of late Sidney Herbert and Gertrude Florence Taylor, St Ives, Cambs; *m* 1964, Jean Aimée Monteith; one *d.* *Educ:* Palmers Sch., Grays, Essex; Queens' Coll., Cambridge (MA, LLB); Harvard Law School (LLM). Called to the Bar, Middle Temple, 1958. Mem., Stephens Cttee on Minerals Planning Control, 1972–74. Contested (C) Kettering, 1970. *Recreations:* country pursuits, art, boardsailing, motorcycling. *Address:* Clifton Grange, Clifton, Shefford, Beds SG17 5EW. *Clubs:* Athenæum, Travellers'.

TAYLOR, Prof. John Clayton, PhD; FRS 1981; Professor of Mathematical Physics, Cambridge University, and Fellow of Robinson College, since 1980; *b* 4 Aug. 1930; *s* of Leonard Taylor and Edith (*née* Tytherleigh); *m* 1959, Gillian Mary (*née* Schofield); two *s.* *Educ:* Selhurst Grammar Sch., Croydon; Cambridge Univ. (MA). Lectr, Imperial Coll., London, 1956–60; Lectr, Cambridge Univ., and Fellow of Peterhouse, 1960–64; Reader in Theoretical Physics, Oxford Univ., and Fellow of University Coll., Oxford, 1964–80 (Hon. Fellow, 1989). *Publication:* Gauge Theories of Weak Interactions, 1976. *Recreation:* pottering about. *Address:* 9 Bowers Croft, Cambridge CB1 4RP.

TAYLOR, Rt. Hon. John David, PC (N Ire.) 1970; MP (UU) Strangford, since 1983 (resigned seat Dec. 1985 in protest against Anglo-Irish Agreement; re-elected Jan. 1986); *b* 24 Dec. 1937; *er s* of George D. Taylor and Georgina Baird; *m* 1970, Mary Frances Todd; one *s* five *d.* *Educ:* Royal Sch., Armagh; Queen's Univ. of Belfast (BSc). CEng; AMInstHE, AMICEI. MP (UU) S Tyrone, NI Parlt, 1965–73; Mem. (UU), Fermanagh and S Tyrone, NI Assembly, 1973–75; Mem. (UU), North Down, NI Constitutional Convention, 1975–76; Parly Sec. to Min. of Home Affairs, 1969–70; Minister of State, Min. of Home Affairs, 1970–72; Mem. (UU), North Down, NI Assembly, 1982–86. Mem. (UU) NI, Europ. Parlt, 1979–89. Partner, G. D. Taylor and Associates, Architects and Civil Engineers, 1966–74; Director: Bramley Apple Restaurant Ltd, 1974–; West Ulster Estates Ltd, 1968–; West Ulster Hotels Co. Ltd, 1976–86; Gosford Housing Assoc. Ltd, 1977–; Tontine Rooms Ltd, 1978–; Ulster Gazette (Armagh) Ltd, 1983–; Cerdac (Belfast) Ltd, 1986–; Tyrone Printing Co. Ltd, 1986–. *Publication:* (jtly) Ulster—the facts, 1982. *Recreation:* foreign travel. *Address:* Mullinure, Portadown Road, Armagh, Northern Ireland BT61 9EL. *T:* Armagh (0861) 522409. *Clubs:* Farmers'; Armagh County (Armagh).

TAYLOR, John D.; *see* Debenham Taylor.

TAYLOR, Prof. John Gerald; Professor of Mathematics, King's College, University of London, since 1971; *b* 18 Aug. 1931; *s* of William and Elsie Taylor; *m* Pamela Nancy (*née* Cutmore); two *s* three *d.* *Educ:* King Edward VI Grammar Sch., Chelmsford; Mid-Essex Polytechnic, Chelmsford; Christ's Coll., Cambridge. Fellow, Inst. for Advanced Study, Princeton, NJ, USA, 1956–58 (Mem., 1961–63); Fellow, Christ's Coll., Cambridge, 1958–60; Asst Lectr, Faculty of Mathematics, Univ. of Cambridge, 1959–60. Dir, Centre for Neural Networks, KCL, 1990–. Member: Inst. des Hautes Etudes Scient., Paris, 1960; Res. Inst. Advanced Study, Baltimore, Md, USA, 1960. Sen. Res. Fellow, Churchill Coll., Cambridge, 1963–64; Prof. of Physics, Rutgers Univ., New Brunswick, NJ, 1964–66; Fellow, Hertford Coll., Oxford, and Lectr, Math. Inst., Oxford, 1966–67; Reader in Particles and Fields, Queen Mary Coll., London, 1967–69; Prof. of Physics, Univ. of Southampton, 1969–71. Chm., 1982–87, Vice-Chm., 1988–, Mathematical Physics Gp, Inst. of Physics. Chm., Jt European Neural Net Initiative, 1990–; Convener, British Neural Networks Soc., 1989–. *Publications:* Quantum Mechanics, an Introduction, 1969; The Shape of Minds to Come, 1970; The New Physics, 1972; Black Holes: the end of the Universe?, 1973; Superminds, 1975; Special Relativity, 1975; Science and the Supernatural, 1980; The Horizons of Knowledge, 1982; *edited:* Supergravity, 1981; Supersymmetry and Supergravity, 1982; Tributes to Paul Dirac, 1987; Recent Developments in Neural Computation, 1990; also scientific papers in Proc. Royal Soc., Phys. Rev., Proc. Camb. Phil. Soc., Jl Math. Phys. etc. *Recreations:* listening to music, walking. *Address:* 33 Meredyth Road, Barnes, SW13 0DS. *T:* 081–876 3391.

TAYLOR, John H.; *see* Hermon-Taylor.

TAYLOR, Sir John Lang, (Sir Jock Taylor), KCMG 1979 (CMG 1974); HM Diplomatic Service, retired; Chairman: Klöckner INA Industrial Plants Ltd, since 1985; Siemens Ltd, since 1986; Director, Schering Holdings Ltd, since 1986; *b* 3 Aug. 1924; *y s* of Sir John William Taylor, KBE, CMG; *m* 1952, Molly, *o d* of James Rushworth; five *s* three *d.* *Educ:* Prague; Vienna; Imperial Services Coll., Windsor; Baltimore Polytechnic Inst., Md; Cornell Univ.; Trinity Coll., Cambridge. RAFVR, 1944–47 (Flt-Lt 1946). Joined HM Foreign (now Diplomatic) Service, 1949; served in: FO, 1949–50 and 1957–60; Saigon, 1950–52; Hanoi, 1951; Beirut, 1952–55; Prague, 1955–57; Montevideo, 1960–64; Bonn, 1964–69; Minister (Commercial), Buenos Aires, 1969–71; RCDS, 1972; Head of Industry, Science and Energy Dept, FCO, 1972–73; Asst Under-Sec. of State, FCO, 1973–74; Under-Sec., Dept of Energy, 1974–75; Ambassador to: Venezuela, 1975–79; the Netherlands, 1979–81; FRG, 1981–84. Chm., Latin Amer. Trade Adv. Gp, BOTB, 1986–89. Vice-Chm., Hispanic and Luso-Brazilian Councils (Canning House), 1987; Trustee, Anglo-German Foundn for the Study of Industrial Soc., 1988. *Address:* The Old Flint, Boxgrove, near Chichester, W Sussex. *Club:* Travellers'.

TAYLOR, John Mark; MP (C) Solihull, since 1983; Vice-Chamberlain of HM Treasury, since 1990; *b* 19 Aug. 1941; *s* of Wilfred and Eileen Martha Taylor; *m* 1979, Catherine Ann Hall. *Educ:* Eversfield Prep. School; Bromsgrove School and College of Law. Admitted Solicitor, 1966; Senior Partner, John Taylor & Co., 1983–88. Member: Solihull County Borough Council, 1971–74; W Midlands Metropolitan County Council, 1973–86 (Opposition (Conservative) Leader, 1975–77; Leader, 1977–79). PPS to Chancellor of Duchy of Lancaster and Minister for Trade and Industry, 1987–88; an Asst Govt Whip, 1988–89; a Govt Whip, 1989–90. Mem., Select Cttee on the Environment, 1983–87; Sec., Cons. Back-bench Cttee on Eur. Affairs, 1983–86 (Vice-Chm., 1986–87); Vice-Chm., Cons. Back-bench Cttee on Sport, 1986–87. Vice-Pres., AMA, 1979– (Dep. Chm., 1978–79). Mem., W Midlands Economic Planning Council, 1978–79; Governor, Univ. of Birmingham, 1977–81. Contested (C) Dudley East, Feb. and Oct. 1974. Mem. (C) Midlands E, European Parlt, 1979–84; European Democratic Group spokesman on Community Budget, 1979–81, Group Dep. Chm., 1981–82. *Recreations:* fellowship, cricket, golf, reading. *Address:* 211 St Bernards Road, Solihull, West Midlands B92 7DL. *T:* 021–707 1076; (office) 021–704 3071. *Clubs:* Carlton, MCC.

TAYLOR, Rt. Rev. John Mitchell; *see* Glasgow and Galloway, Bishop of.

TAYLOR, John Russell; Art Critic, The Times, since 1978; *b* 19 June 1935; *s* of Arthur Russell and Kathleen Mary Taylor (*née* Picker). *Educ:* Dover Grammar Sch.; Jesus Coll., Cambridge (MA); Courtauld Inst. of Art, London. Sub-Editor, Times Educational Supplement, 1959; Editorial Asst, Times Literary Supplement, 1960; Film Critic, The Times, 1962–73. Lectr on Film, Tufts Univ. in London, 1970–71; Prof., Div. of Cinema, Univ. of Southern California, 1972–78. Editor, Films and Filming, 1983–90. *Publications:* Anger and After, 1962; Anatomy of a Television Play, 1962; Cinema Eye, Cinema Ear, 1964; Penguin Dictionary of the Theatre, 1966; The Art Nouveau Book in Britain, 1966; The Rise and Fall of the Well-Made Play, 1967; The Art Dealers, 1969; Harold Pinter,

1969; The Hollywood Musical, 1971; The Second Wave, 1971; David Storey, 1974; Directors and Directions, 1975; Peter Shaffer, 1975; Hitch, 1978; The Revels History of Drama in English, vol. VII, 1978; Impressionism, 1981; Strangers in Paradise, 1983; Ingrid Bergman, 1983; Alec Guinness, 1984; Vivien Leigh, 1984; Portraits of the British Cinema, 1985; Hollywood 1940s, 1985; Orson Welles, 1986; Edward Wolfe, 1986; Great Movie Moments, 1987; Post-war Friends, 1987; Robin Tanner, 1989; Bernard Meninsky, 1990; Impressionist Dreams, 1990. *Address:* c/o The Times, 1 Pennington Street, E1.

TAYLOR, Rt. Rev. John Vernon; *b* 11 Sept. 1914; *s* of late Bishop J. R. S. Taylor and Margaret Irene Taylor (*née* Garrett); *m* 1940, Margaret Wright; one *s* two *d*. *Educ:* St Lawrence Coll., Ramsgate; Trinity Coll., Cambridge (Hon. Fellow, 1987); St Catherine's Soc., Oxford; Wycliffe Hall, Oxford; Institute of Education, London. Curate, All Souls, Langham Place, W1, 1938–40; Curate in Charge, St Andrew's Church, St Helens, Lancs, 1940–43; Warden, Bishop Tucker College, Mukono, Uganda, 1945–54; Research Worker, Internat. Missionary Council, 1955–59; Africa Sec., CMS, 1959–63; Gen. Sec., CMS, 1963–74; Bishop of Winchester, 1975–85. Chm., Doctrine Commn of C of E, 1978–85. Examng Chap. to Bishop of Truro, 1974–75. Hon. Canon of Namirembe Cathedral, 1963–74. Hon. Fellow: New Coll., Oxford, 1985; Magdalen Coll., Oxford, 1986; Selly Oak Colls, Birmingham, 1987. Hon. DD (Wycliffe Coll., Toronto), 1964. *Publications:* Man in the Midst, 1955; Christianity and Politics in Africa, 1957; The Growth of the Church in Buganda, 1958; African Passion, 1958; Christians of the Copperbelt, 1961; The Primal Vision, 1963; For All the World, 1966; Change of Address, 1968; The Go-Between God, 1972; Enough is Enough, 1975; Weep not for Me, 1986; A Matter of Life and Death, 1986; Kingdom Come, 1989. *Recreations:* theatre, music. *Address:* 65 Aston Street, Oxford OX4 1EW. *T:* Oxford (0865) 248502.

TAYLOR, John William Ransom, OBE 1991; author; Editor Emeritus, Jane's All the World's Aircraft, since 1990; *b* 8 June 1922; *s* of late Victor Charles Taylor and late Florence Hilda Taylor (*née* Ransom); *m* 1946, Doris Alice Haddrick; one *s* one *d*. *Educ:* Ely Cathedral Choir Sch., Soham Grammar Sch., Cambs. FRAeS, FRHistS, AFAIAA. Design Dept, Hawker Aircraft Ltd, 1941–47; Editorial Publicity Officer, Fairey Aviation Gp, 1947–55; Jane's All the World's Aircraft: Editl Asst, 1955; Asst Compiler, 1956–59; Editor, 1959–84; Editor-in-Chief, 1985–89. Air Corresp., Meccano Magazine, 1943–72; Editor, Air BP Magazine, British Petroleum, 1956–72; Jt Editor, Guinness Book of Air Facts and Feats, 1974–83; Contributing Editor: Air Force Magazine (USA), 1971–; Jane's Defence Weekly (formerly Jane's Defence Review), 1980–87; Specialist Correspondent, Jane's Soviet Intelligence Review, 1989–. Member: Académie Nat. de l'Air et de l'Espace, France, 1985–; CFS Assoc. (Hon. Mem., 1987–). Pres., Chiltern Aviation Soc.; Vice-President: Horse Rangers Assoc.; Guild of Aviation Artists; Croydon Airport Soc., Surbiton Scout Assoc. Warden, Christ Church, Surbiton Hill, 1976–80. Freeman, 1983, Liveryman, 1987, GAPAN; Freeman, City of London, 1987. C. P. Robertson Memorial Trophy, 1959; Cert. of Honour, Commn of Bibliography, History and Arts, Aero Club de France, 1971; Order of Merit, World Aerospace Educn Organization, 1981; Tissandier Diploma, FAI, 1990; Lauren D. Lyman Award, Aviation Space Writers Assoc., USA, 1990. *Publications:* Spitfire, 1946; Aircraft Annual, 1949–75; Civil Aircraft Markings, 1950–78; Wings for Tomorrow, 1951; Military Aircraft Recognition, 1952–79; Civil Airliner Recognition, 1953–79; Picture History of Flight, 1955; Science in the Atomic Age, 1956; Rockets and Space Travel, 1956; Best Flying Stories, 1956; Jane's All the World's Aircraft, 1956–89; Helicopters Work Like This, 1957; Royal Air Force, 1957; Fleet Air Arm, 1957; Jet Planes Work Like This, 1957; Russian Aircraft, 1957; Rockets and Missiles, 1958; CFS, Birthplace of Air Power, 1958, rev. edn 1987; Rockets and Spacecraft Work Like This; British Airports, 1959; US Military Aircraft, 1959; Warplanes of the World, 1959, rev. as Military Aircraft of the World; BP Book of Flight Today, 1960; Combat Aircraft of the World, 1969; Westland 50, 1965; Pictorial History of the Royal Air Force, 3 vols 1968–71, rev. 1980; Aircraft Aircraft, 1967, 4th edn 1974; Encyclopaedia of World Aircraft, 1966; The Lore of Flight, 1971; Rockets and Missiles, 1971; Light Plane Recognition, 1970; Civil Aircraft of the World, 1970–79; British Civil Aircraft Register, 1971; (with M. J. H. Taylor) Missiles of the World, 1972–79; (with D. Mondey) Spies in the Sky, 1972; (with K. Munson) History of Aviation, 1973, 2nd edn, 1978; Jane's Aircraft Pocket Books, 1973–87; History of Aerial Warfare, 1974; (with S. H. H. Young) Passenger Aircraft and Airlines, 1975; Jets, 1976; (with M. J. H. Taylor) Helicopters of the World, 1976–79; (with Air Vice-Marshal R. A. Mason) Aircraft, Strategy and Operations of the Soviet Air Force, 1986; Soviet Wings, 1991. *Recreations:* historical studies, travel. *Address:* 36 Alexandra Drive, Surbiton, Surrey KT5 9AF. *T:* 081–399 5435. *Clubs:* City Livery, Royal Aero, Royal Air Force (Hon.); Avro 504 (Manchester).

TAYLOR, Jonathan Francis; Chief Executive, Booker plc, since 1984; *b* 12 Aug. 1935; *s* of Sir Reginald Taylor, CMG and Lady Taylor; *m* 1965, Anthea Gail Proctor; three *s*. *Educ:* Winchester College; Corpus Christi College, Oxford (Schol.; BA Mod. Hist.; MA). Joined Booker, 1959; Chm., Agricultural Div., 1976–80; Dir, Booker plc, 1980; Pres., Ibec Inc. (USA), 1980–84; Dir, Arbor Acres Farm Inc., 1980– (Dep. Chm., 1985–90; Chm., 1990). Director: Sifida Investment Bank, Geneva, 1978–90; Tate & Lyle, 1988–. Mem., Adv. Council, UNIDO, 1986–; Dir, Foundn for Develt of Polish Agric., 1991–. Governor, SOAS, London Univ., 1988–; Curator, Bodleian Library, 1989–. *Recreations:* collecting water colours, ski-ing, travel. *Address:* Booker plc, Portland House, Stag Place, SW1E 5AY. *Clubs:* Travellers'; Knickerbocker (NY).

TAYLOR, Judy, (Julia Marie), (Judy Hough), MBE 1971; writer and publisher; *b* 12 Aug. 1932; adopted *d* of Gladys Spicer Taylor; *m* 1980, Richard Hough, *qv*. *Educ:* St Paul's Girls' Sch. Joined The Bodley Head, 1951, specialising in children's books; Director: The Bodley Head Ltd, 1967–84 (Dep. Man. Dir, 1971–80); Chatto, Bodley Head & Jonathan Cape Ltd, 1973–80; Chatto, Bodley Head & Jonathan Cape Australia Pty Ltd, 1977–80. Publishers Association: Chm., Children's Book Gp, 1969–72; Mem. Council, 1972–78; Member: Book Develt Council, 1973–76; Unicef Internat. Art Cttee, 1968–70, 1976, 1982–83; UK Unicef Greeting Card Cttee, 1982–85. Consultant to Penguin (formerly to Frederick Warne) on Beatrix Potter, 1981–87, 1989–; Associate Dir, Weston Woods Inst., USA, 1984–; Consulting Ed., Reinhardt Books, 1988–. FRSA 1991. *Publications:* Sophie and Jack, 1982; Sophie and Jack Help Out, 1983; My First Year: a Beatrix Potter baby book, 1983; Sophie and Jack in the Snow, 1984; Beatrix Potter: artist, storyteller and countrywoman, 1986; Dudley and the Monster, 1986; Dudley Goes Flying, 1986; Dudley in a Jam, 1986; Dudley and the Strawberry Shake, 1986; That Naughty Rabbit: Beatrix Potter and Peter Rabbit, 1987; My Dog, 1987; My Cat, 1987; Dudley Bakes a Cake, 1988; Beatrix Potter and Hawkshead, 1988; Sophie and Jack in the Rain, 1989; Beatrix Potter and Hill Top, 1989; Beatrix Potter's Letters: a selection, 1989; numerous professional articles. *Recreations:* collecting early children's books, gardening. *Address:* 31 Meadowbank, Primrose Hill, NW3 1AY. *T:* 071–722 5663.

TAYLOR, Keith Breden, MA, DM; FRCP; Vice-Chancellor, St George's University School of Medicine, 1989–90, retired; George de Forest Barnett Professor of Medicine, Stanford University, 1966–81 and 1982–89, now Emeritus; *b* 16 April 1924; *yr s* of

Francis Henry Taylor and Florence (*née* Latham); *m* 1st, 1949, Ann Gaynor Hughes Jones (*d* 1971); three *s* one *d* (and one *s* decd); 2nd, 1972, Kym Williams, Adelaide, Aust. *Educ:* King's College Sch., Wimbledon; Magdalen Coll., Oxford (Exhibnr; BA Hons Physiology 1946, BM BCh 1949). Member, SHAEF Nutrition Survey Team, 1945; RAMC (Major), 1951–53; Dir Gen., Health Educn Council, 1981–82. Late Hon. Consultant, Central Middlesex Hosp.; Mem., MRC Gastroenterology Research Unit; Asst in Nuffield Dept Clin. Med., Oxford. Radcliffe Travelling Fellow, 1953; Rockefeller Foundn Fellow, 1959; Guggenheim Fellow, 1971; Fogarty Sen. Fellow, USPHS, 1978–79. Cons., US National Insts of Health; Mem., USPHS Trng Grants Cttee in Gastroenterology and Nutrition, 1965–70; Chm., Stanford Univ. Cttee on Human Nutrition, 1974–81; Vis. Professorships include: Rochester, NY, 1966; Columbia-Presbyterian, NY, 1969; Univ. of Adelaide, 1971; Academic Medical Unit, Royal Free Hosp., 1978–79. *Publications:* contribs to scientific jls, also texts, espec. in biochemistry and physiology of vitamin B12, immunological and other aspects of gastrointestinal disease and nutrition. *Recreations:* theatre, tennis, walking, gardening. *Address:* 131 Peter Coutts Circle, Stanford, Calif 94305, USA. *Club:* Athenæum.

TAYLOR, Keith Henry, PhD; Managing Director, Esso UK plc, since 1985; *b* 25 Oct. 1938; *s* of George Henry Philip Taylor and Vera May (*née* Jones); *m* 1964, Adelaide Lines; one *s* one *d*. *Educ:* King Edward VI Sch., Stratford upon Avon; Birmingham Univ. (BSc, PhD Chem. Engrg). Joined Esso, 1964, holding variety of positions in Refining, Research, Marine and Planning Functions of Co., 1964–80; Division Operations Man., Exxon Co. USA, New Orleans, 1980; Production Man., Esso Exploration and Production UK Ltd, London, 1982; Exec. Asst to Chm., Exxon Corp., New York, 1984. Pres., UKOOA, 1988–89; Vice Pres., Inst. of Petroleum, 1991–; Mem., Offshore Industry Adv. Bd, 1989–. *Address:* Esso House, Victoria Street, SW1E 5JW *T:* 071–245 3280.

TAYLOR, Kenneth, OBE 1981; FEng, FIMechE, FIEE; FCIT; consultant on railway mechanical and electrical engineering; Director of Mechanical and Electrical Engineering, British Railways Board, 1977–82; *b* 29 Sept. 1921; *s* of Charles Taylor and Amy (*née* Booth); *m* 1945, Elsie Armitt; one *d*. *Educ:* Manchester Coll. of Technol. FIMechE, FIEE 1971; FCIT 1977; FEng 1981. Principal appts with British Railways: Electric Traction Engr, Manchester, 1956; Electrical Engr, LMR, 1963; Chief Mech. and Elec. Engr, LMR, 1970; Traction Engr, BR Bd HQ, 1971. *Recreations:* golf, gardening. *Address:* 137 Burley Lane, Quarndon, Derby DE6 4JS. *T:* Derby (0332) 550123.

TAYLOR, Kenneth John; His Honour Judge Kenneth Taylor; a Circuit Judge, since 1977; *b* 29 March 1929; *s* of Hereford Phillips Taylor and Florence Gertrude Taylor; *m* 1953, Joan Cattermole; one *s* one *d*. *Educ:* William Hulme's Grammar Sch., Manchester; Manchester Univ. (LLB). Called to Bar, Middle Temple, 1951. A Recorder of the Crown Court, 1972–77. *Recreations:* reading, music. *Address:* 25 Mill Lane, off The Bank, Scholar Green, Stoke-on-Trent ST7 3LD. *T:* Stoke-on-Trent (0782) 512102.

TAYLOR, Prof. Kenneth MacDonald, MD; FRCSE, FRCSGlas; FSAScot; British Heart Foundation Professor of Cardiac Surgery, University of London, since 1983, and Professor and Chief of Cardiac Surgery, Royal Postgraduate Medical School, Hammersmith Hospital, since 1983; *b* 20 Oct. 1947; *s* of Hugh Baird Taylor and late Mary Taylor; *m* 1971, Christine Elizabeth (*née* Buchanan); one *s* one *d*. *Educ:* Jordanhill College School; Univ. of Glasgow (MB ChB, MD; Cullen Medal, 1968; Gairdner Medal, 1969; Allan Hird Prize, 1969). Univ. of Glasgow: Hall Fellow in Surgery, 1971–72, Lectr and Sen. Lectr in Cardiac Surgery, 1975–83; Consultant Cardiac Surgeon, Royal Infirmary and Western Infirmaries, Glasgow, 1979–83. Mem., Specialist Adv. Cttee in Cardiothoracic Surgery, 1986–; Dir, UK Heart Valve Registry, 1986–; Clin. Dir, UK Sch. of Perfusion Science, 1987–; Pres., Soc. of Perfusionists of GB and Ire., 1989–. Member: British Cardiac Soc., 1983–; Amer. Soc. of Thoracic Surgeons, 1984–; Amer. Assoc. for Thoracic Surgery, 1988–; European Assoc. for Cardiothoracic Surgery, 1988–; Pres., Soc. of Perfusionists of GB and Ire., 1989–. Governor, Drayton Manor High Sch., London, 1989–. Editor, Perfusion, 1986–; Mem., Adv. Editl Bd, Annals of Thoracic Surgery, 1990–. Peter Allen Prize, Soc. of Thoracic and Cardiovascular Surgeons, 1975; Patey Prize, Surgical Res. Soc., 1977; Fletcher Prize, RCSG, 1977; Watson Prize, RCSG, 1982. *Publications:* Pulsatile Perfusion, 1979, 2nd edn 1982; Handbook of Intensive Care, 1984; Cardiopulmonary Bypass, 1986; Cardiac Surgery, 1987; Principles of Surgical Research, 1989; numerous articles on cardiac surgery. *Recreations:* family, church, music. *Address:* 129 Argyle Road, Ealing, W13 0DB.

TAYLOR, Kim; see Taylor, L. C.

TAYLOR, Prof. Laurie, (Laurence John); Professor of Sociology, University of York, since 1974; *s* of Stanley Douglas Taylor and Winifred Agnes (*née* Cooper); marr. diss.; one *s*. *Educ:* St Mary's Coll., Liverpool; Rose Bruford College of Drama, Kent; Birkbeck Coll., Univ. of London (BA); Univ. of Leicester (MA). Librarian, 1952–54; Sales Asst, 1954–56; Professional Actor, 1960–61; English Teacher, 1961–64; Lectr in Sociology, 1965–73, Reader in Sociology, 1973–74, Univ. of York. *Publications:* Deviance and Society, 1971; (jtly) Psychological Survival, 1972; (jtly) Crime, Deviance and Socio-Legal Control, 1972; (ed jtly) Politics and Deviance, 1973; Man's Experience of the World, 1976; (jtly) Escape Attempts, 1976; (jtly) Prison Secrets, 1978; (jtly) In Whose Best Interests?, 1980; In the Underworld, 1984; (jtly) Uninvited Guests, 1986; Professor Lapping Sends His Apologies, 1987; The Tuesday Afternoon Time Immemorial Committee, 1989; articles, reviews, broadcasts, TV series. *Address:* c/o Department of Sociology, University of York, Heslington, York YO1 5DD. *T:* York (0904) 430000.

TAYLOR, Len Clive, (Kim); Director, Calouste Gulbenkian Foundation (UK Branch), 1982–88, retired; *b* 4 Aug. 1922; *s* of late S. R. Taylor, Calcutta, India; *m* 1951, Suzanne Dufault, Spencer, Massachusetts, USA; one *s* two *d*. *Educ:* Sevenoaks School; New College, Oxford; Chicago University. New College, Oxford; 1st Cl. Hons Mod. Hist.; Commonwealth Fund Fellowship. Assistant Master, St Paul's School, Darjeeling, India, 1940–42 and 1945–46; Indian Army Intelligence Corps, 1942–45; New College, Oxford, 1946–49; Chicago University, 1949–50; Senior History Master, Repton School, 1950–54; Headmaster, Sevenoaks School, 1954–68; Dir, Nuffield Foundn 'Resources for Learning' Project, 1966–72; Principal Administrator, Centre for Educnl Res. and Innovation, OECD, Paris, 1972–77; Head of Educnl Prog. Services, IBA, 1977–82. Comdr, Order of Henry the Navigator (Portugal), 1989. *Publications:* Experiments in Education at Sevenoaks, 1965; Resources for Learning, 1971. *Address:* 43 The Drive, Sevenoaks, Kent TN13 3AD. *T:* Sevenoaks (0732) 451448.

TAYLOR, Leon Eric Manners; Research Analyst; *b* 28 Oct. 1917; *s* of late Leon Eric Taylor and Veronica Dalmahoy (*née* Rogers); *m* 1963, Margaret Betty Thompson; no *c*. *Educ:* Fettes Coll., Edinburgh; Oriel Coll., Oxford. Captain RA (Service, 1939–46). Asst Principal, 1945, Principal, 1948, in Bd of Trade until 1963. First Sec., UK Delegn to the European Communities, 1963–66; Econ. Counsellor, British High Commn, Kuala Lumpur, 1966–70. Called to Bar, Inner Temple, 1951. Attended Joint Services Staff College, 1952. Hon. Visiting Fellow, Centre for Contemporary European Studies, University of Sussex, 1970–71; Counsellor (Commercial), The Hague, 1971–72; Research Fellow, Univ. of Sussex, 1973–75. *Recreations:* walking, amateur theatre, golf. *Address:*

Sam's Hill Cottage, 47 North Street, Middle Barton, Oxford OX5 4BH. *T:* Steeple Aston (0869) 47256.

TAYLOR, Malcolm; *see* McDowell, M.

TAYLOR, (Margaret) Jessie, OBE 1989; Headmistress, Whalley Range High School for Girls, 1976–88; *b* 30 Nov. 1924; *d* of Thomas Brown Gowland and Ann Goldie Gowland; *m* 1958, Eric Taylor, *qv*. *Educ:* Queen Elizabeth's Grammar Sch., Middleton; Manchester Univ. (BA Hons, DipEd). Jun. Classics Teacher, Cheadle Hulme Sch., 1946–49; North Manchester Grammar School for Girls: Sen. Classics Teacher, 1950; Sen. Mistress, 1963; Actg Headmistress, Jan.-July 1967; Dep. Head Teacher, Wright Robinson Comprehensive High Sch., 1967–75. Voluntary worker, UNICEF, 1988–. Dir, Piccadilly Radio, 1979–. Chm., Manchester High Sch. Heads Gp, 1984–88; Member: Council and Exams Cttee, Associated Lancs Schs Examining Bd, 1976–91 (Mem. Classics Panel, 1968–72); Exams Cttee, Northern Exams Assoc., 1988–; Nursing Educn Cttee, S Manchester Area, 1976–84; Home Office Cttee on Obscenity and Film Censorship, 1977–79; Consultant Course Tutor, NW Educnl Management Centre, Padgate, 1980–82. Mem. Court, Salford Univ., 1982–88; Gov., William Hulme's Grammar Sch., 1989–. FRSA 1980. *Recreations:* music, riding. *Address:* 10 Mercers Road, Hopwood, Heywood, Lancs OL10 2NP. *T:* Heywood (0706) 66630.

TAYLOR, Mark Christopher; Director, Museums Association, since 1989; *b* 24 Nov. 1958; *s* of Norman and June Taylor; *m* 1989, Debra Howes; one *s*. *Educ:* Loughborough Grammar Sch.; Birmingham Univ. (BA Medieval and Modern Hist.); Leeds Poly. (postgrad. Hotel Management qualification). Hotel Management, Norfolk Capital Hotels, 1981–84; Conf. Manager, Museums Assoc., 1984–89. Dir, Museum Enterprises Ltd, 1989–. Mem. Council, Nat. Campaign for the Arts, 1990–. *Recreations:* sport, films, cookery. *Address:* 78 George Street, Bedford, Beds MK40 3SQ; Museums Association, 34 Bloomsbury Way, WC1A 2SF. *T:* 071–404 4767.

TAYLOR, Matthew Owen John; MP Truro, since March 1987 (L 1987–88, Lib Dem since 1988); *b* 3 Jan. 1963; *s* of Ken Taylor and Jill Taylor (*née* Black). *Educ:* Treliske School, Truro; University College School; Lady Margaret Hall, Oxford (Scholar; BA Hons). Pres., Oxford Univ. Student Union, 1985–86. Economic policy researcher to Parly Liberal Party (attached to David Penhaligon, MP), 1986–87. Parly spokesman on energy, 1987–88, on local govt, 1988–89, on trade and industry, 1989–90, on educn, 1990–. Communications Chm. for Lib Dems, 1989–. *Address:* House of Commons, SW1. *T:* 071–219 3483.

TAYLOR, Rt. Rev. Maurice; *see* Galloway, Bishop of, (RC).

TAYLOR, Rev. Michael Hugh; JP; Director, Christian Aid, since 1985; *b* 8 Sept. 1936; *s* of Albert Ernest and Gwendoline Louisa Taylor; *m* 1960, Adèle May Dixon; two *s* one *d*. *Educ:* Northampton Grammar School; Univ. of Manchester (BA, BD, MA); Union Theological Seminary, NY (STM). Baptist Minister, N Shields, 1961–66, Birmingham Hall Green, 1966–69; Principal, Northern Baptist Coll., Manchester, 1970–85; Lectr, Univ. of Manchester, 1970–85. JP Manchester, 1980. *Publications:* Variations on a Theme, 1973; Sermon on the Mount, 1982; (ed) Christians and the Future of Social Democracy, 1982; Learning to Care, 1983; Good for the Poor, 1990; contribs to books and jls. *Recreations:* walking, cooking, theatre. *Address:* c/o Christian Aid, PO Box 100, SE1 7RT.

TAYLOR, Neville, CB 1989; Principal Associate, Defence Public Affairs Consultants Ltd, since 1989; freelance writer, since 1989; *b* 17 Nov. 1930; *y s* of late Frederick Taylor and of Lottie Taylor; *m* 1954, Margaret Ann, *y d* of late Thomas Bainbridge Vickers and Gladys Vickers; two *s*. *Educ:* Sir Joseph Williamson's Mathematical Sch., Rochester; Coll. of Commerce, Gillingham, Kent. Junior Reporter, Chatham News Group, 1947; Royal Signals, 1948–50; Journalism, 1950–58; Asst Information Officer, Admiralty, 1958; Information Officer (Press), Admiralty, 1960; Fleet Information Officer, Singapore, 1963; Chief Press Officer, MoD, 1966; Information Adviser to Nat. Economic Develt Office, 1968; Dep. Dir, Public Relns (Royal Navy), 1970; Head of Information, Min. of Agriculture, Fisheries and Food, 1971; Dep. Dir of Information, DoE, 1973–74, Dir of Information, 1974–79; Dir of Information, DHSS, 1979–82; Chief of Public Relations, MOD, 1982–85; Dir-Gen., COI and Hd of Govt Inf. Service, 1985–88. *Recreation:* fishing. *Address:* Crow Lane House, Crow Lane, Rochester, Kent ME1 1RF. *T:* Medway (0634) 842990.

TAYLOR, Nicholas George Frederick, CMG 1970; FIPR 1973; Development Director, East Caribbean; Higgs & Hill (UK) Ltd, 1973–80; Chairman: Higgs & Hill (St Kitts) Ltd, 1973–80; West Indies General Insurance Co., since 1979; Caribbean (East) Currency Authority, 1983 (Director, since 1981); Director, Cariblue Hotels Ltd, St Lucia, since 1968; Local Adviser, Barclays Bank International, St Lucia, since 1974; *b* 14 Feb. 1917; 3rd *s* of Louis Joseph Taylor and Philipsie (*née* Phillip); *m* 1952, Morella Agnes, *e d* of George Duncan Pitcairn and Florence (*née* La Guerre); two *s* two *d*. *Educ:* St Mary's Coll., St Lucia; LSE, London; Gonville and Caius Coll., Cambridge. Clerk, various Depts, St Lucia, 1937–46; Asst Social Welfare Officer, 1948–49; Public Relations and Social Welfare Officer, 1949–54; District Officer, and Authorised Officer, Ordnance Area, St Lucia, 1954–57; Dep. Dir St Lucia Br., Red Cross Soc., 1956–57; Perm. Sec., Min. of Trade and Production, 1957–58 (acted Harbour Master in conjunction with substantive duties); Commn for W Indies in UK: Administrative Asst, 1959; Asst Sec.-Chief Community Development Officer, Migrants Services Div., 1961; Commn in UK for Eastern Caribbean Govts: Officer-in-Charge, 1962–63; Actg Comr, 1964–66; Comr for E Caribbean Govts in UK, 1967–73. Dir, St Lucia (Co-operative) Bank Ltd, 1973–74. Mem., Civil Service Appeals Bd, 1973–77. Vice-Chm. Commonwealth Assoc., Bexley, Crayford and Erith, 1965–67; a Patron, British-Caribbean Assoc., 1962–73. Member: West India Committee Executive, 1968–; Bd of Governors, Commonwealth Inst., 1968–73. Assoc. Mem. 1951, Mem. 1962, Fellow, 1973, (British) Inst. of Public Relations. Chairman: Central Library Bd, 1973–81, Nat. Insurance Scheme, 1979–81, St Lucia; Central Housing Authority, St Lucia, 1975–77; Income Tax Comrs Appeals Bd, 1980–; St Lucia Boy Scouts Assoc., 1977–79. Vice-Chm., Nat. Develt Corp., 1979–. Founder Life Mem., Cambridge Soc., 1976. JP 1948. Coronation Medal, 1953; British Red Cross Medal, 1949–59. *Recreations:* cricket, lawn tennis, reading. *Address:* PO Box 816, Castries, St Lucia, West Indies. *T:* 8513. *Clubs:* Commonwealth Trust, Travellers'.

TAYLOR, Sir Nicholas Richard S.; *see* Stuart Taylor.

TAYLOR, Peter, BScEcon, FCIS; Clerk of the Senate, University of London, 1977–89; *b* 5 Jan. 1924; *s* of late Frederick and Doris Taylor; *m* 1948, Jeannette (*née* Evans); two *d*. *Educ:* Salt Boys' High Sch., Saltaire, Yorks; Bradford Technical Coll. BSc(Econ) London, 1949. FCIS 1959. Served War, FAA, 1942–46. WR Treasurer's Dept, 1940–50; Registrar, Lincoln Technical Coll., 1950–58; Secretary: Wolverhampton and Staffs Coll. of Technol., 1959–60; Chelsea Coll., Univ. of London, 1961–77. Pres., Assoc. of Coll. Registrars, 1970–72. Treas., Soc. for Promotion of Hellenic Studies, 1989–. Hon. FKC, 1985. *Recreations:* walking, painting, sailing. *Address:* April Cottage, 52 Wattleton Road, Beaconsfield, Bucks.

TAYLOR, Rt. Hon. Sir Peter (Murray), Kt 1980; PC 1988; **Rt. Hon. Lord Justice Taylor;** a Lord Justice of Appeal, since 1988; *b* 1 May 1930; *s* of Herman Louis Taylor, medical practitioner and Raie Helena Taylor (*née* Shockett); *m* 1956, Irene Shirley, *d* of Lionel and Mary Harris; one *s* three *d*. *Educ:* Newcastle upon Tyne Royal Gram. Sch.; Pembroke Coll., Cambridge (Exhibr). Called to Bar, Inner Temple, 1954, Bencher, 1975; QC 1967; Vice-Chm. of the Bar, 1978–79, Chm., 1979–80. Recorder of: Huddersfield, 1969–70; Teesside, 1970–71; Dep. Chm., Northumberland QS, 1970–71; a Recorder of the Crown Court, 1972–80; a Judge of the High Court of Justice, QBD, 1980–88. North Eastern Circuit: Leader, 1975–80; Presiding Judge, 1984–88. Pres., Inns of Court Council, 1990–. Chm., Inquiry into Hillsborough Football Club Disaster, 1989. Controller, Royal Opera House Develt Land Trust, 1990–. Hon. Member: Amer. Bar Assoc., 1980–; Canadian Bar Assoc., 1980–. Hon. LLD Newcastle upon Tyne, 1990. *Recreation:* music. *Address:* Royal Courts of Justice, Strand, WC2A 2LL. *Club:* Garrick.

TAYLOR, Peter William Edward, QC 1981; *b* 27 July 1917; *s* of late Peter and Julia A. Taylor; *m* 1948, Julia Mary Brown, *d* of Air Cdre Sir Vernon Brown, CB, OBE; two *s*. *Educ:* Peter Symonds' Sch., Winchester; Christ's Coll., Cambridge (MA; Wrangler, Math. Tripos, Part II; 1st Class, Law Tripos, Part II). Served RA, 1939–46: France and Belgium, 1939–40; N Africa, 1942–43; NW Europe, 1944–45 (mentioned in dispatches); Actg Lt-Col 1945; transferred to TARO as Hon. Major, 1946. Called to the Bar, Inner Temple, 1946; Lincoln's Inn, *ad eundem*, 1953 (Bencher, 1976); practice at the Bar, 1947–; Occasional Lectr, LSE, 1946–56; Lectr in Construction of Documents, Council of Legal Educn, 1952–70; Conveyancing Counsel of the Court, 1974–81. Member: General Council of the Bar, 1971–74; Senate of Inns of Court and the Bar, 1974–75; Inter-Professional Cttee on Retirement Provision, 1974–; Land Registration Rule Cttee, 1976–81; Standing Cttee on Conveyancing, 1985–87; Incorporated Council of Law Reporting, 1977– (Vice-Chm., 1987–); Council, Selden Soc., 1977–. *Recreations:* sailing, shooting, music. *Address:* 46 Onslow Square, SW7 3NX. *T:* 071–589 1301; Carey Sconce, Yarmouth, Isle of Wight.

TAYLOR, Philippe Arthur; Chief Executive, Birmingham Convention and Visitor Bureau Ltd, since 1982; *b* 9 Feb. 1937; *s* of Arthur Peach Taylor and Simone Vacquin; *m* 1973, Margaret Nancy Wilkins; two *s*. *Educ:* Trinity College, Glenalmond; St Andrews University. Procter & Gamble, 1963; Masius International, 1967; British Tourist Authority, 1970; Chief Executive, Scottish Tourist Board, 1975–80; Man. Dir, Taylor and Partners, 1980–82. Vice-Chm., Ikon Gall.; Chm., British Assoc. of Conf. Towns. *Publications:* childrens' books; various papers and articles on tourism. *Recreations:* sailing, making things, tourism, reading. *Address:* Cadogan House, Beauchamp Avenue, Leamington Spa, Warwickshire. *Clubs:* Royal Yachting Association; Royal Northumberland Yacht (Blyth); Orford Sailing.

TAYLOR, Phyllis Mary Constance, MA; Honorary Associate, Institute of Education, London, 1983–85; *b* 29 Sept. 1926; *d* of Cecil and Constance Tedder; *m* 1949, Peter Royston Taylor; one *s*. *Educ:* Woodford High Sch.; Sudbury High Sch., Suffolk; Girton Coll., Cambridge (State Scholar; BA Hons History, 1948; MA 1951). Asst Hist. Mistress, Loughton High Sch., 1948–51, Head of Hist., 1951–58; Teacher of Hist. and Religious Educn, Lancaster Royal Grammar Sch. for Boys, 1959; Head of Hist., Casterton Sch. (private boarding), Kirby Lonsdale, 1960; Teacher of Gen. Subjects, Lancaster Girls' Grammar Sch., 1960–61, Head of Hist., 1961–62; Dep. Headmistress, Carlisle Sch., Chelsea, 1962–64; Headmistress: Walthamstow High Sch. for Girls, 1964–68; Walthamstow Sen. High Sch., 1968–75; Wanstead High Sch., London Borough of Redbridge, 1976–82. Consultant Head to NE London Polytechnic (Counselling/Careers sect.), 1974–78; Moderator, Part-time Diploma, Pastoral Care and Counselling, 1979–85. Pres., Essex Sector, Secondary Heads' Assoc., 1978–79. Member: UGC, 1978–83 (Mem., Educn Sub-Cttee, 1978–85, and Wkg Party on Continuing Educn, 1983); Teacher Trng Sub-Cttee, Adv. Cttee on Supply and Educn of Teachers, 1980–85; former Mem., Nat. Exec., Assoc. of Head Mistresses. Mem., RAM Foundn Appeals Cttee, 1985–86. Chm., Dunmow Liberals, 1986–88. Governor, Rodings Primary Sch., 1988–. *Publications:* (as Julianne Royston) The Penhale Saga: The Penhale Heiress, 1988; The Penhale Fortune, 1989. *Recreations:* music, theatre, bridge, horses, country life, ecology. *Address:* White Horses, High Roding, Great Dunmow, Essex CM6 1NS. *T:* Great Dunmow (0371) 873161.

TAYLOR, Prof. Richard Edward; Professor, Stanford Linear Accelerator Center, Stanford University, since 1968; *b* 2 Nov. 1929; *s* of Clarence Richard Taylor and Delia Alena Taylor (*née* Brunsdale); *m* 1951, Rita Jean Bonneau; one *s*. *Educ:* Univ. of Alberta (BS 1950; MS 1952); Stanford Univ. (PhD 1962). Boursier Lab. de l'Accelerateur Linéaire, France, 1958–61; physicist, Lawrence Berkeley Lab., Berkeley, Calif., 1961–62; staff mem., 1962–68, Associate Dir, 1982–86, Stanford Linear Accelerator Center. Fellow: Guggenheim Foundn, 1971–72; Amer. Phys. Soc (W. K. H. Panofsky Prize, Div. of Particles and Fields, 1989); FRSC; Mem., AAAS. Hon DSc: Univ. of Paris-Sud, 1980; Univ. of Alberta, 1991. Von Humboldt Award, 1982; Nobel Prize in Physics, 1990. *Address:* Stanford Linear Accelerator Center, PO Box 4349-MS 96, Stanford, Calif 94309, USA. *T:* (415) 926–2417.

TAYLOR, (Robert) Alan; Chief Executive and Town Clerk, Royal Borough of Kensington and Chelsea, since 1990; *b* 13 Sept. 1944; *s* of Alfred Taylor and Hilda Mary (*née* Weekley); *m* 1st, 1965, Dorothy Joan Walker (*d* 1986); two *s*; 2nd, 1987, Margaret Susanne Barnes. *Educ:* Thornbury Grammar Sch., Thornbury, Glos.; King's Coll., Univ. of London (LLB). Solicitor. Asst Solicitor, Plymouth CBC, 1970–74; Plymouth City Council: Dep. City Solicitor and Sec., 1974–76; Asst Town Clerk, 1976–81; Chief Exec., London Borough of Sutton, 1981–90. Clerk, NE Surrey Crematorium Bd, 1983–90; Director: Sutton Enterprise Agency Ltd, 1987–90; S London TEC, 1989–90. *Recreations:* theatre, books, walking, painting very badly. *Address:* 2 Morden Grange Cottages, The Street, Betchworth, Surrey RH3 7OJ. *T:* Betchworth (0737) 843237.

TAYLOR, Robert Carruthers; His Honour Judge Robert Taylor; a Circuit Judge, since 1984; *b* 6 Jan. 1939; *o s* of late John Taylor, CBE and of Barbara Mary Taylor; *m* 1968, Jacqueline Marjorie, *er d* of Nigel and Marjorie Chambers; one *s* one *d*. *Educ:* Wycliffe Coll.; St John's Coll., Oxford. MA 1967. Called to Bar, Middle Temple, 1961; Member, NE Circuit, 1962–84; a Recorder, 1976–84. Chm., Agricl Land Tribunal, Yorks and Lancs, Yorks and Humberside Areas, 1979–; Liaison Judge, Kirklees Magistrates, 1986–; Chm., Kirklees Juvenile Justice Forum, 1987–. Member: Leeds Family Conciliation Service Management Cttee, 1986–; W Yorks Probation Cttee, 1991–. *Recreations:* reading, music, spectating, gardening, domestic life. *Address:* The Courthouse, 1 Oxford Row, Leeds LS1 3BE. *T:* Leeds (0532) 451616.

TAYLOR, Robert Martin, OBE 1976; Editorial Director, The Croydon Advertiser Ltd, 1967–76; *b* 25 Nov. 1914; *s* of Ernest H. and Charlotte Taylor; *m* 1947, Ray Turney; one *s* one *d*. *Educ:* Simon Langton, Canterbury. Croydon Advertiser: Editor, 1950–58; Managing Editor, 1958–74; Dir, 1967–76. Mem., Nat. Council for the Training of Journalists, 1967–71; Pres., Guild of British Newspaper Editors, 1971–72, Hon. Vice-Pres., 1976; Mem., Press Council, 1974–76. Sec., Glenurquhart Community Council,

1982–86; Hon. Treasurer, Glenurquart Rural Community Assoc., 1984–86, Chm., 1988–. Founded Glenurquart Newsletter, 1985. *Publications:* Editor and co-author, Essential Law for Journalists, 1954, 6th edn 1975; Glenurquhart Official Guide, 1980. *Address:* Glengarry, Milton, Drumnadrochit, Inverness-shire. *T:* Drumnadrochit (04562) 291.

TAYLOR, Robert Richardson, QC (Scotland) 1959; MA, LLB, PhD; Sheriff-Principal of Tayside Central and Fife, 1975–90; *b* 16 Sept. 1919; *m* 1949, Märtha Birgitta Björkling; two *s* one *d*. *Educ:* Glasgow High School; Glasgow University. Called to Bar, Scotland, 1944; called to Bar, Middle Temple, 1948. Lectr in Internat. Private Law, Edinburgh Univ., 1947–69; Sheriff-Principal, Stirling, Dunbarton and Clackmannan, 1971–75. Chm., Sheriff Ct Rules Council, 1982–89. Contested (U and NL): Dundee East, 1955; Dundee West, 1959 and Nov. 1963. Chm., Central and Southern Region, Scottish Cons. Assoc., 1969–71. Chm., Northern Lighthouse Bd, 1985–86. *Recreations:* lapidary, mineral collecting. *Address:* 51 Northumberland Street, Edinburgh. *T:* 031–556 1722.

TAYLOR, (Robert) Ronald, CBE 1971; Director, Robert Taylor (Holdings) Ltd (formerly Robert Taylor Ironfounders (Holdings) Ltd); *b* 25 Aug. 1916; *e s* of late Robert Taylor, ironfounder, Larbert; *m* 1941, Margaret, *d* of late William Purdie, Coatbridge; two *s* two *d*. *Educ:* High Sch., Stirling. Chm., Glenrothes Develt Corp., 1964–78. *Recreations:* fishing, shooting, golf. *Address:* Beoraid, Caledonian Crescent, Auchterarder, Perthshire. *Club:* Army and Navy.

TAYLOR, Most Rev. Robert Selby, CBE 1983; Archbishop Emeritus of Cape Town, 1987; *b* 1 March 1909; *s* of late Robert Taylor, Eden Bank, Wetheral, Cumberland; unmarried. *Educ:* Harrow; St Catharine's Coll., Cambridge; Cuddesdon Coll. Ordained deacon, 1932; priest, 1933; served as a curate at St Olave's, York; went out to Diocese of Northern Rhodesia in 1935 as a Mission priest; Principal of Diocesan Theological Coll., 1939; Bishop of Northern Rhodesia, 1941–51; Bishop of Pretoria, 1951–59; Bishop of Grahamstown, 1959–64; Archbishop of Cape Town, 1964–74; Bishop of Central Zambia, 1979–84. Hon. Fellow, St Catharine's Coll., Cambridge, 1964. DD (Hon.) Rhodes Univ., 1966. *Address:* Braehead House, Auburn Road, Kenilworth 7700, South Africa. *T:* 77 1440. *Clubs:* Commonwealth Trust; City and Civil Service (Cape Town).

TAYLOR, Dr Robert Thomas, CBE 1990; Assistant Director-General, British Council, since 1990; *b* 21 March 1933; *s* of George Taylor and Marie Louise Fidler; *m* 1965, Rosemary Janet Boileau; three *s* one *d*. *Educ:* Boteler Grammar Sch., Warrington; University Coll., Oxford (Open Exhbnr; BA 1954, MA 1957; DPhil 1957). Fulbright Scholar. Research Associate, Randall Lab. of Physics, Univ. of Michigan, USA, 1957–58; ICI Research Fellow, 1958–59, Lectr, Physics Dept, 1959–61, Univ. of Liverpool; Chief Examr for NUJMB, GCE Physics (Scholarship Level), 1961; British Council: Asst Regional Rep., Madras, 1961–64; Science Officer, Madrid, 1964–69; Dir, Staff Recruitment Dept, 1969–73; Regional Educn Advr, Bombay, 1973–77; Rep., Mexico, 1977–81; Controller, Personnel, 1981–86; Rep., Greece, 1986–90. *Publications:* contrib. to Chambers Encyclopaedia, 1967 edn; papers in scientific jls. *Recreations:* making harpsichords, war gaming, music, theatre. *Address:* Mark Haven, High Street, Cranbrook, Kent TN17 3EW. *T:* Cranbrook (0580) 714212.

TAYLOR, Roger Miles Whitworth; Chief Executive, Birmingham City Council, since 1988; *b* 18 May 1944; *s* of Richard and Joan Taylor; *m* 1969, Georgina Lucy Tonks; two *s* two *d*. *Educ:* Repton School; Birmingham University (LLB). Solicitor, admitted 1968; Asst Sol., Cheshire CC, 1969–71; Asst County Clerk, Lincs parts of Lindsey, 1971–73; Dep. County Secretary, Northants CC, 1973–79; Dep. Town Clerk, 1979–85, Town Clerk and Chief Exec., 1985–88, City of Manchester. Mem., Farrand Cttee on Conveyancing, 1983–84; Clerk, Greater Manchester Passenger Transport Authy, 1986–88. Sec., W Midlands Jt Cttee, 1988–. Director: Foundn for IT in Local Govt, 1990–; Birmingham TEC, 1990–. Mancunian of the Year, Manchester Jun. Chamber of Commerce, 1988. *Publications:* contribs to Local Govt Chronicle, Municipal Review, Municipal Jl. *Recreations:* sailing, walking. *Address:* The Council House, Victoria Square, Birmingham, B1 1BB.

TAYLOR, Ronald; *see* Taylor, R. R.

TAYLOR, Ronald George, CBE 1988; Director-General, Association of British Chambers of Commerce, since 1984; *b* 12 Dec. 1935; *s* of Ernest and May Taylor; *m* 1960, Patricia Stoker; one *s* two *d*. *Educ:* Jesus College, Oxford (BA Modern Langs). Commnd Royal Signals, 1957–59. Leeds Chamber of Commerce and Industry: joined, 1959; Asst Sec., 1964–74; Director, 1974–84. Reg. Sec., Assoc. of Yorks and Humberside Chambers of Commerce, 1974–84. FRSA; FSAE. *Recreations:* Rugby Union, bridge. *Address:* 2 Holly Bush Lane, Harpenden, Herts. *T:* Harpenden (0582) 712139.

TAYLOR, Ronald Oliver; Managing Director, Vickers, 1988–90; *b* 12 Aug. 1931; *s* of Andrew James Taylor, *qv*; *m* 1961, Frances Sylvia Howcroft; three *s* one *d*. *Educ:* Grove Academy, Dundee. Mem., Inst. of Chartered Accountants of Scotland. Joined Vickers as Accountant, 1958: Managing Dir, Printing Machinery Group, 1969–72; Chief Exec., Howson-Algraphy Group, 1972–85; Director, 1977; Jt Dep. Managing Dir, 1984; Jt Managing Dir, 1987. Mem., CBI Europe Cttee, 1987–89. *Recreations:* golf, walking. *Address:* Stang Hall, Stang Lane, Farnham, near Knaresborough, N Yorks HG5 9JW. *T:* Harrogate (0423) 868053.

TAYLOR, Prof. Ronald Wentworth, MD; FRCOG; Professor of Obstetrics and Gynaecology, United Medical and Dental Schools of Guy's and St Thomas' Hospitals; *b* 28 Oct. 1932; *s* of George Richard and Winifred Taylor; *m* 1962, Mary Patricia O'Neill; three *s* one *d*. *Educ:* St Mary's Coll., Crosby; Liverpool Univ. (MB ChB 1958; MD 1972). MRCOG 1965, FRCOG 1975. Jun. House Officer posts, Liverpool, 1958–59; Sen. House Officer posts, Preston, 1960, Manchester, 1962; GP, Ormskirk, Lancs, 1962–63; Registrar, Whittington Hosp., London, 1963–64; St Thomas' Hospital: Lectr, 1965–67; Sen. Lectr, 1968–76; Prof., 1977–, subseq. at UMDS of Guy's and St Thomas' Hosps. *Publications:* Gynaecological Cancer, 1975; "Ten Teachers" Obstetrics and Gynaecology, 14th edn 1985; (ed) Confidential Enquiry into Perinatal Deaths, 1988; Endometrial Cancer, 1988. *Recreations:* fell walking, sailing, silversmithing, restoration of furniture, photography. *Address:* 26 Hale Lane, NW7 3PN. *Club:* Royal Society of Medicine.

TAYLOR, Selwyn Francis, DM, MCh, FRCS; Dean Emeritus and Fellow, Royal Postgraduate Medical School, London; Senior Lecturer in Surgery, and Surgeon, Hammersmith Hospital; Emeritus Consultant to Royal Navy; Member, Armed Forces Medical Advisory Board; Examiner in Surgery, Universities of Oxford, London, Manchester, Leeds, National University of Ireland, West Indies, Makerere and Society of Apothecaries; *b* Sale, Cheshire, 16 Sept. 1913; *s* of late Alfred Petre Taylor and Emily Taylor, Salcombe, Devon; *m* 1939, Ruth Margaret, 2nd *d* of late Sir Alfred Howitt, CVO; one *s* one *d*. *Educ:* Peter Symonds, Winchester; Keble College, Oxford; King's College Hospital. BA (Hons) Oxford, 1936; Burney Yeo Schol., King's Coll. Hosp., 1936; MA Oxon; MRCS, LRCP, 1939; FRCS 1940; MCh, 1946; DM 1959. Surgical Registrar, King's Coll. Hosp., 1946–47; Oxford Univ. George Herbert Hunt Travelling Schol., Stockholm, 1947; Rockefeller Travelling Fellow in Surgery, 1948–49; Research Fellow, Harvard Univ., and Fellow in Clin. Surgery, Massachusetts Gen. Hosp., Boston, Mass, USA, 1948–49. RNVR, 1940–46; Surgeon Lt-Comdr; Surgeon Specialist, Kintyre, East Indies, Australia; Surgeon: Belgrave Hosp. for Children, 1946–65; Hammersmith Hosp., 1947–78; King's Coll. Hospital, 1951–65. Bradshaw Lectr, RCS, 1977; Legg Meml Lectr, KCH, 1979; Keats Lectr, Soc. of Apothecaries, 1987. President: Harveian Soc., 1969; Internat. Assoc. Endocrine Surgeons, 1979–81; Member: Council, RCS, 1966– (Senior Vice-Pres., 1976–77 and 1977–78; Joll Prize, 1976); GMC, 1974–83; Surgical Research Soc.; Internat. Soc. for Surgery; Fellow Assoc. Surgeons of GB; FRSM; Hon. FRCSE 1976; Hon. FCS (S Africa) 1978; Corresp. Fellow Amer. Thyroid Assoc.; Pres., London Thyroid Club and Sec., Fourth Internat. Goitre Conference. Mem., Senate of London Univ., 1970–75. Chm., Heinemann Medical Books, 1972–83. *Publications:* books and papers on surgical subjects and thyroid physiology. *Recreations:* sailing, tennis, wine. *Address:* Trippets, Bosham, West Sussex PO18 8JE. *T:* Bosham (0243) 573387. *Clubs:* Garrick, Hurlingham; Bosham Sailing (Trustee).

TAYLOR, Sir Teddy; *see* Taylor, Sir E. M.

TAYLOR, Maj.-Gen. Walter Reynell, CB 1981; European Consultant, Lone Star Industries, Inc.; *b* 5 April 1928; *s* of Col Richard Reynell Taylor and Margaret Catherine Taylor (*née* Holme); *m* 1st, 1954, Doreen Myrtle Dodge; one *s* one *d*; 2nd, 1982, Mrs Rosemary Gardner (*née* Breed); one *s*. *Educ:* Wellington; RMC, Sandhurst. Commanded: 4th/7th Royal Dragoon Guards, 1969–71; 12 Mechanised Bde, 1972–74; rcds 1975; Brig., Mil. Operations, MoD, 1976–78; Administrator, Sovereign Base Areas of Cyprus, 1978–80; COS, HQ BAOR, 1980–84. Dir, ME Centre for Management Studies, Nicosia, Cyprus, 1984–86. *Recreations:* sailing, golf. *Address:* c/o C. Hoare & Co., 37 Fleet Street, EC4P 4DQ. *Clubs:* Special Forces; Royal Armoured Corps Yacht; West Dorset Golf.

TAYLOR, Wendy Ann, CBE 1988; sculptor; Member, Royal Fine Art Commission, since 1981; Specialist Adviser, since 1985 and Committee Member, Fine Art Board, Council of National Academic Awards (Member, 1980–85); Specialist Adviser, Committee for Arts Design, since 1988; *b* 29 July 1945; *d* of Edward Philip Taylor and Lilian Maude Wright; *m* 1982, Bruce Robertson; one *s*. *Educ:* St Martin's School of Art. LDAD (Hons). One-man exhibitions: Axiom Gall., London, 1970; Angela Flowers Gall., London, 1972; 24th King's Lynn Fest., Norfolk, and World Trade Centre, London, 1974; Annely Juda Fine Art, London, 1975; Oxford Gall., Oxford, 1976; Oliver Dowling Gall., Dublin, 1976 and 1979; Building Art—the process, Building Centre Gall., 1986. Shown in over 100 group exhibitions, 1964–82. Represented in collections in GB, USA, Eire, NZ, Germany, Sweden, Qatar, Switzerland, Seychelles. Major commissions: The Travellers 1969, London; Gazebo (edn of 4) 1970–72, London, New York, Suffolk, Oxford; Triad 1971, Oxford; Timepiece 1973, London; Calthae 1977, Leicestershire; Octo 1979, Milton Keynes; Counterpoise 1980, Birmingham; Compass Bowl 1980, Basildon; Sentinel 1981, Reigate; Bronze Relief 1981, Canterbury; Equatorial Sundial 1982, Bletchley; Essence 1982, Milton Keynes; Opus 1983, Morley Coll., London; Gazebo 1983, Golder's Hill Park, London; Network, 1984, London; Geo I & Geo II, 1985, Stratford-Upon-Avon; Landscape, and Tree of the Wood 1986, Fernhurst, Surrey; Pharos 1986, Peel Park, E Kilbride; Ceres 1986, Fernhurst, Surrey; Nexus 1986, Corby, Northants; Globe Sundial 1987, Swansea Maritime Quarter; Spirit of Enterprise 1987, Isle of Dogs, London; Roundacre Improvement Scheme Phase I, 1987–89, Basildon; Silver Fountain 1988, Continuum, 1990, Guildford, Surrey; The Whirlies, 1988, Pharos II, 1989, Phoenix, 1989–90, E Kilbride; Pilot Kites, 1988, Norwich Airport; Fireflow, 1988, Strathclyde Fire Brigade HQ, Hamilton; Armillary Sundial, 1989, The New Towns, Essex; Globe Sundial, London Zool Gdns, 1990. Consultant, New Town Commn (Basildon) (formerly Basildon Develt Corp.), 1985–; Mem., Design Adv. Gp, LDDC, 1989–; Design Consultant, London Borough of Barking and Dagenham, 1989–. Mem., Adv. Gp, PCFC, 1989–. Examiner, Univ. of London, 1982–83; Mem. Court, RCA, 1982–; Mem. Council, Morley Coll., 1984–88. FZS 1989. Awards: Walter Neurath, 1964; Pratt, 1965; Sainsbury, 1966; Arts Council, 1977; Duais Na Riochta (Kingdom Prize) Gold Medal, Eire, 1977; 1st Prize Silk Screen, Barcham Green Print Comp., 1978. *Recreation:* gardening. *Address:* 73 Bow Road, Bow E3 2AN. *T:* 081–981 2037.

TAYLOR, Sir William, Kt 1990; CBE 1982; Chairman, Council for the Accreditation of Teacher Education, since 1984; *b* 31 May 1930; *s* of Herbert and Maud E. Taylor, Crayford, Kent; *m* 1954, Rita, *d* of Ronald and Marjorie Hague, Sheffield; one *s* two *d*. *Educ:* Erith Grammar Sch.; London Sch. of Economics; Westminster Coll., Oxford (Hon. Fellow, 1990); Univ. of London Inst. of Educn. BSc Econ 1952, PhD 1960. Teaching in Kent, 1953–56; Deputy Head, Slade Green Secondary Sch., 1956–59; Sen. Lectr, St Luke's Coll., Exeter, 1959–61; Head of Educn Dept, Bede Coll., Durham, 1961–64; Tutor and Lectr in Educn, Univ. of Oxford, 1964–66; Prof. of Educn and Dir of Sch. of Educn, Univ. of Bristol, 1966–73; Dir, Univ. of London Inst. of Educn, 1973–83; Principal, Univ. of London, 1983–85; Vice-Chancellor, Univ. of Hull, 1985–91. Research Consultant, Dept of Educn and Science (part-time), 1968–73; Chairman: European Cttee for Educnl Research, 1969–71; UK Nat. Commn for UNESCO, 1975–83 (Mem., 1973–83); Educnl Adv. Council, IBA, 1974–82; UCET, 1976–79; Cttee on Training of Univ. Teachers, 1981–88; NFER, 1983–88; Univs Council for Adult and Continuing Educn, 1986–90; N of England Univs Management and Leadership Prog., 1987–. Member: UGC Educn Cttee, 1971–80; British Library Res. and Develt Cttee, 1975–79; Open Univ. Academic Adv. Cttee, 1975–82; SSRC Educnl Research Board, 1976–80 (Vice-Chm., 1978–80); Adv. Cttee on Supply and Training of Teachers, 1976–79; Working Gp on Management of Higher Educn, 1977–78; Steering Cttee on Future of Examinations at 16+, 1977–78; Cttee of Vice-Chancellors and Principals, 1980–91; Adv. Cttee on Supply and Educn of Teachers (Sec. of State's nominee), 1980–83. UK Rep., Permanent Educn Steering Cttee, Council of Europe, 1971–73; Rapporteur, OECD Review of Educn in NZ, 1982–83. Member: Senate, Univ. of London, 1977–85; Cttee of Management, Inst. of Advanced Legal Studies, 1980–83; Council, Open Univ., 1984–88; Council, Coll of Preceptors, 1987–89. Commonwealth Vis. Fellow, Australian States, 1975; NZ UGC Prestige Fellowship, 1977. President: Council for Educn in World Citizenship, 1979–90; English New Educn Fellowship, 1979–86; Comparative Educn Soc. of GB, 1981–84; Assoc. of Colls of Further and Higher Educn, 1984–88; European Assoc. for Institnl Res., 1990–; Univs of N of England Consortium for Internat. Develt, 1991–; N of England Educn Conference, 1992; Vice President: Soc. for Research in Higher Educn, 1983–; British Educnl Admin, and Management Soc., 1985–. Chm., NFER/Nelson Publishing Co., 1985–86, 1987–; Dir, Fenner plc, 1988–. Governor: Wye Coll., 1981–83; Hymers Coll., Hull, 1985–; Westminster Coll., Oxford, 1991–. Freeman, City of London, 1985. Trustee, Forbes Trust, 1987–88. Hon. DSc Aston (Birmingham), 1977; Hon. LittD Leeds, 1979; Hon. DCL Kent, 1981; DUniv Open, 1983; Hon. DLitt Loughborough, 1984. Hon. FCP 1977. Hon. FCCEA 1980. Yeoman, 1982–87, Liveryman, 1988–, Worshipful Soc. of Apothecaries of London. *Publications:* The Secondary Modern School, 1963; Society and the Education of Teachers, 1969; (ed with G. Baron) Educational Administration and the Social Sciences, 1969; Heading for Change, 1969; Planning and Policy in Post Secondary Education, 1972; Theory into Practice, 1972; Research Perspectives in Education, 1973; (ed with R. Farquhar and R. Thomas) Educational Administration in Australia and Abroad, 1975; Research and Reform in Teacher Education, 1978; (ed with B. Simon) Education in the Eighties: the central issues, 1981;

(ed) Metaphors of Education, 1984; Universities Under Scrutiny, 1987; Policy and Strategy for Higher Education: collaboration between business and higher eduction, 1989; articles and papers in professional jls. *Recreations:* writing, walking. *Address:* Council for the Accreditation of Teacher Education, Elizabeth House, York Road, SE1 7PH. *T:* 071–934 0936, *Fax:* 071–934 0946.

TAYLOR, William, QPM 1991; Assistant Commissioner, Specialist Operations, Metropolitan Police, since 1990; *b* 25 March 1947; *s* of William Taylor and late Margaret Taylor; *m* 1978, Denise Lloyd; two step *s*. *Educ:* Blairgowrie High Sch.; Nat. Police Coll. (8th Special Course and 16th Sen. Command Course). Joined Metropolitan Police Service, 1966; served Central London locations as Det. Constable, Sergeant and Inspector, and Chief Inspector, 1966–76; New Scotland Yard: Community Relations Branch, 1976–78; Det. Supt, Central Drugs Squad, 1978–79; Staff Officer to Comr of Police, 1980–82 (Det. Chief Supt); Comdr CID NE London, then Uniform Comdr, Hackney; Comdr Robbery Squad (Flying Squad) and Regional Crime Squad, 1982–85; Asst Comr, City of London Police, 1985–89; Dep. Chief Constable, Thames Valley Police, 1989–90. Police Long Service and Good Conduct Medal, 1988. *Recreations:* reading (travel, management and historical), hill walking, horse riding, collecting some Dalton ware. *Address:* New Scotland Yard, The Broadway, SW1H 0BG. *T:* 071–230 1212.

TAYLOR, William Bernard; Public Sector Specialist Adviser to Ernst & Young, Lombard North Central PLC, MIM Ltd and Sedgwick UK Ltd, since 1986; Underwriting Member, Lloyd's, since 1988; *b* 13 Dec. 1930; *s* of Frank and Elizabeth Taylor; *m* 1956, Rachel May Davies; one *s* two *d*. *Educ:* Dynevor Sch., Swansea; Univ. of Kent. MA; IPFA, FRSA. Nat. Service, RN, 1949–51; commnd RNVR; served in coastal forces. District Audit Service, 1951–61; Llwchwr UDC, 1961–70; Asst Educn Officer, Manchester Corp., 1970–72; Asst County Treasurer, 1972–73, Dep. County Treasurer, 1973–80, County Treasurer, 1980–86, Kent. Financial Adviser: Social Servs, ACC, 1983–86; Standing Conf. of Planning Auths in SE England, 1983–86; Hon. Treas., SE England Tourist Bd, 1980–86; Chm., wkg party of Council of Europe on borrowing by municipalities of member states, 1982–84. Dir, Interlake DRC Ltd., 1989–. Gov., and Chm. Finance Cttee, Kent Inst. of Art and Design, 1989–; Non-exec. Mem., and Chm. Finance and Rev. Cttee, Medway HA, 1990. Mem., Rotary Club. *Publications:* The Management of Assets: terotechnology in the pursuit of economic life cycle costs, 1980; contribs to local govt and other learned journals. *Recreations:* cricket, rugby, public speaking. *Address:* Selby Shaw, Heath Road, Boughton Monchelsea, near Maidstone, Kent ME17 4JE. *T:* Maidstone (0622) 745022. *Club:* Maidstone (Maidstone).

TAYLOR, William Edward Michael; His Honour Judge William Taylor; a Circuit Judge, Western Circuit, since 1989; Resident Judge for Plymouth and Cornwall; *b* 27 July 1944; *s* of William Henry Taylor and Winifred Mary (*née* Day); *m* 1969, Caroline Joyce Gillies; two *d*. *Educ:* Denstone Coll., Uttoxeter, Staffs; Council of Legal Educn. Called to the Bar, Inner Temple, 1968. Practised from 2 Harcourt Bldgs, Temple; a Recorder, 1987–89. Lectr, Council of Legal Educn, 1976–89. *Recreations:* music, opera, fishing, vintage cars, wine. *Address:* 63 Bridgend, Noss Mayo, Plymouth, Devon PL8 1DX. *T:* Plymouth (0752) 872934. *Club:* Royal Western Yacht (Plymouth).

TAYLOR, Lt-Comdr William Horace, GC 1941; MBE 1973; Commissioner of the Scout Association, since 1946; *b* 23 Oct. 1908; *s* of William Arthur Taylor; *m* 1946, Joan Isabel Skaife d'Ingerthorpe; one *s* three *d*. *Educ:* Manchester Grammar Sch. Junior Partner, 1929; Managing Dir, 1937. Served War: Dept of Torpedoes and Mines, Admiralty, 1940 (despatches, 1941); Founder Mem., Naval Clearance Divers, HMS Vernon (D), 1944. Travelling Commissioner for Sea Scouts of UK, 1946; Field Commissioner for SW England, Scout Association, 1952–74, Estate Manager, 1975–84. *Recreations:* scouting, boating, music. *Address:* The Bungalow, Carbeth, Blanefield, near Glasgow. *T:* Blanefield (0360) 70847. *Clubs:* Naval; Manchester Cruising Association.

TAYLOR, William James; QC (Scot) 1986; *b* 13 Sept. 1944; *s* of Cecil Taylor and Ellen Taylor (*née* Daubney). *Educ:* Robert Gordon's College, Aberdeen; Aberdeen Univ. (MA Hons 1966; LLB 1969); Glasgow Univ. (Cert. in European Law (French) 1990). Admitted Faculty of Advocates, 1971; called to the Bar, Inner Temple, 1990. Standing Junior Counsel to DHSS, 1978–79, to FCO, 1979–86. Contested (Lab) Edinburgh W, Feb. and Oct. 1974; Regional Councillor (Lab), 1973–82. *Recreations:* the arts, ski-ing, sailing, Scottish mountains, swimming, travel. *Address:* Hill House, 69 Direlton Avenue, North Berwick, E Lothian EH39 4QL. *T:* North Berwick (0620) 5111; 307 Ben Jonson House, Barbican, EC2Y 8DL. *T:* 071–588 1453. *Club:* Traverse Theatre (Edinburgh).

TAYLOR, William McCaughey; Chairman, Northern Ireland Coal Importers Association, 1986–91, retired; *b* 10 May 1926; *s* of William and Georgina Lindsay Taylor; *m* 1955, June Louise Macartney; two *s* two *d*. *Educ:* Campbell College, Belfast; Trinity College, Oxford (MA 1950). Lieut, Royal Inniskilling Fusiliers, 1944–47. International Computers Ltd, 1950–58; Lobitos Oilfields Ltd, 1958–60; HM Vice Consul, New York, 1960–63, HM Consul, 1963–65; NI Dept of Commerce, 1965–79; Sec. and Chief Exec., NI Police Authy, 1979–86. *Recreations:* golf, bridge, gardening, music. *Club:* Royal Belfast Golf.

TAYLOR, William Rodney E.; *see* Eatock Taylor.

TAYLOR, Mrs (Winifred) Ann; MP (Lab) Dewsbury, since 1987; *b* Motherwell, 2 July 1947; *m* 1966, David Taylor; one *s* one *d*. *Educ:* Bolton Sch.; Bradford Univ.; Sheffield Univ. Formerly teaching. Past part-time Tutor, Open Univ.; interested in housing, regional policy, and education. Monitoring Officer, Housing Corp., 1985–87. Member: Association of Univ. Teachers; APEX; Holmfirth Urban District Council, 1972–74. MP (Lab) Bolton W, Oct. 1974–1983; PPS to Sec. of State for Educn and Science, 1975–76; PPS to Sec. of State for Defence, 1976–77; an Asst Govt Whip, 1977–79; Opposition spokesman on Education, 1979–81, on Housing, 1981–83, on Home Affairs, 1987–90, Frontbench spokesman on Environment, 1990–; Shadow Water Minister, 1988–. Contested (Lab): Bolton W, Feb. 1974; Bolton NE, 1983. Hon. Fellow, Birkbeck Coll. *Address:* Glyn Garth, Stoney Bank Road, Thongsbridge, Huddersfield, Yorks.

TAYLOR-SMITH, Prof. Ralph Emeric Kasope; Professor of Chemistry, Fourah Bay College, University of Sierra Leone, 1980–84, (formerly Associate Professor, on leave, as Ambassador of Sierra Leone to Peking, 1971–74, High Commissioner in London for Sierra Leone, and Ambassador to Norway, Sweden and Denmark, 1974–78); *b* 24 Sept. 1924; *m* 1953, Sarian Dorothea; five *s*. *Educ:* CMS Grammar Sch., Sierra Leone; Univ. of London (BSc (2nd Cl. Hons Upper Div.); PhD (Org. Chem.)). CChem, FRSC. Analytical chemist, 1954; Demonstrator, Woolwich Polytechnic, 1956–59; Lectr, Fourah Bay Coll., Sierra Leone, 1959–62 and 1963; post-doctoral Fellow, Weizmann Inst. of Sci., 1962–63; Research Associate, Princeton Univ., 1965–69; Fourah Bay College: Sen. Lectr, 1965; Dean, Faculty of Pure and Applied Sci., 1967; Associate Prof., 1968 and 1969; Visiting Prof., Kalamazoo Coll., Mich, 1969. Service in academic and public cttees, including: Mem. Council, Fourah Bay Coll., 1963–65 and 1967–69; Member: Senate, 1967–69, Court, 1967–69, Univ. of Sierra Leone; Mem., Student Welfare Cttee, 1967–69; Univ. Rep., Sierra Leone Govt Schol. Cttee, 1965–68; Mem., Bd of Educn, 1970. Pres., Teaching Staff Assoc., Fourah Bay Coll., 1971. Chm., Sierra Leone Petroleum Refining Co., 1970. Delegate or observer to academic confs, 1958–69, incl. those of W African Science Assoc., and Commonwealth Univ. Conf., Sydney, Aust., 1968. Fellow, Thames Polytechnic, 1975; FRSA 1979. *Publications:* papers to learned jls, especially on Investigations on Plants of West Africa. *Recreations:* tennis, swimming. *Address:* c/o Department of Chemistry, Fourah Bay College, University of Sierra Leone, Private Mail Bag, Freetown, Sierra Leone.

TAYLOR THOMPSON, John Derek, CB 1985; Commissioner of Inland Revenue, 1973–87; Secretary, Churches' Main Committee, since 1990; *b* 6 Aug. 1927; *o s* of John Taylor Thompson and Marjorie (*née* Westcott); *m* 1954, Helen Laurie Walker; two *d*. *Educ:* St Peter's Sch., York; Balliol Coll., Oxford. MA. Asst Principal, Inland Revenue, 1951; Private Sec. to Chm., 1954; Private Sec. to Minister without Portfolio, 1962; Asst Sec., Inland Revenue, 1965. Chm., Fiscal Affairs Cttee, OECD, 1984–89. *Recreations:* rural pursuits, reading. *Address:* Jessops, Nutley, Sussex. *Club:* United Oxford & Cambridge University.

TAYLORSON, John Brown; Chairman and Managing Director, International Service Industry Search, since 1990; Managing Director: John Taylorson Associates, since 1990; Inflight Marketing Services, since 1990; *b* 5 March 1931; *s* of John Brown Taylorson and Edith Maria Taylorson; *m* 1st, 1960, Barbara June (*née* Hagg) (marr. diss.); one *s* one *d*; 2nd, 1985, Helen Anne (*née* Parkinson); one *s*. *Educ:* Forest School, Snaresbrook; Hotel School, Westminster. Sales Director, Gardner Merchant Food Services Ltd, 1970–73; Managing Director: International Division, Gardner Merchant Food Services, 1973–77; Fedics Food Services, 1977–80; Chief Executive, Civil Service Catering Organisation, 1980–81; Hd of Catering Servs, British Airways, 1981–89. Pres., Internat. Flight Catering Assoc., 1983–85; Chm., Inflight Services Gp, Assoc. of European Airlines, 1983–85. *Recreations:* golf, theatre, crossword puzzles. *Address:* Deer Pond Cottage, Highfields, East Horsley, Surrey KT24 5AA. *Clubs:* Old Foresters; Burhill Golf.

TAYLOUR, family name of **Marquess of Headfort.**

TEAR, Robert, CBE 1984; concert and operatic tenor; first Professor of International Singing, Royal Academy of Music, since 1985; *b* 8 March 1939; *s* of Thomas Arthur and Edith Tear; *m* 1961, Hilary Thomas; two *d*. *Educ:* Barry Grammar Sch.; King's Coll., Cambridge (MA; Hon. Fellow 1989). Hon. RCM, RAM. Mem., King's Coll. Choir, 1957–60; subseq. St Paul's Cathedral and solo career; joined English Opera Group, 1964. By 1968 worked with world's leading conductors, notably Karajan, Giulini, Bernstein and Solti; during this period created many rôles in operas by Benjamin Britten. Has appeared in all major festivals; close association with Sir Michael Tippett, 1970–; Covent Garden: début, The Knot Garden, 1970, closely followed by Lensky in Eugène Onégin; Fledermaus, 1977; Peter Grimes, 1978; Rake's Progress, 1979; Thérèse, 1979; Loge in Rheingold, 1980; Admetus in Alceste, 1981; David in Die Meistersinger, 1982; Captain Vere in Billy Budd, 1982; appears regularly with Royal Opera. Started relationship with Scottish Opera (singing in La Traviata, Alceste, Don Giovanni), 1974. Paris Opera: début, 1976; Lulu 1979. Début as conductor with Thames Chamber Orchestra, QEH, 1980. Has conducted Minneapolis Orch., ECO, LSO, Philharmonia, London Mozart Players. Has worked with every major recording co. and made numerous recordings (incl. solo recital discs). Sermon, King's Coll. Chapel, Cambridge Univ., 1990. *Publications:* Victorian Songs and Duets, 1980; Tear Here (autobiog.), 1990. *Recreations:* any sport; interested in 18th and 19th century English water colours. *Club:* Garrick.

TEARE, Andrew Hubert; Group Chief Executive, ECC Group, since 1990; *b* 8 Sept. 1942; *s* of Arthur Hubert Teare and Rosalind Margaret Baker; *m* 1964, Janet Nina Skidmore; three *s*. *Educ:* Kingswood School, Bath; University College London (BA Hons Classics 1964). Turner & Newall, 1964–72; CRH, 1972–83 (Gen. Manager Europe, 1978–83); Rugby Group, 1983–90 (Asst Man. Dir, 1983–84; Man. Dir, 1984–90). Non-Executive Director: Heiton Holdings, 1984–90; NFC, 1989–. Pres., Nat. Council of Building Material Producers, 1990–. CBIM. *Recreations:* ski-ing, mountain walking, reading. *Address:* ECC Group, 125 Wood Street, EC2V 7AQ. *T:* 071–696 9229. *Club:* Hibernian United Service (Dublin).

TEARE, Nigel John Martin; QC 1991; *b* 8 Jan. 1952; *s* of Eric John Teare and Mary Rackham Teare; *m* 1975, Elizabeth Jane Pentecost; two *s* one *d*. *Educ:* King William's Coll., Isle of Man; St Peter's Coll., Oxford (BA 1973; MA 1975). Called to the Bar, Lincoln's Inn, 1974; practising barrister, 1975–; Jun. Counsel to Treasury in Admiralty matters, 1989–91. *Recreations:* collecting Manx paintings, squash, tennis. *Address:* 2 Essex Court, Temple, EC4Y 9AP. *T:* 071–583 8381. *CLub:* Royal Automobile.

TE ATAIRANGIKAAHU, Arikinui, ONZ 1987; DBE 1970; Arikinui and Head of Maori Kingship, since 1966; *b* 23 July 1931; *o d* of King Koroki V; *m* 1952, Whatumoana; two *s* five *d*. *Educ:* Waikato Diocesan School, Hamilton, NZ. Elected by the Maori people as Head of the Maori Kingship on the death of King Koroki, the fifth Maori King, with title of Arikinui (Queen), in 1966. Hon. Dr Waikato, 1979. OStJ 1986. *Recreation:* the fostering of all aspects of Maori culture and traditions. *Address:* Turongo House, Turangawaewae Marae, Ngaruawahia, New Zealand.

TEBALDI, Renata; Italian Soprano; *b* Pesaro, Italy, 1 Feb. 1922; *o c* of Teobaldo and Giuseppina (Barbieri) Tebaldi. Studied at Arrigo Boito Conservatory, Parma; Gioacchino Rossini Conservatory, Pesaro; subsequently a pupil of Carmen Melis and later of Giuseppe Pais. Made professional début as Elena in Mefistofele, Rovigo, 1944. First sang at La Scala, Milan, at post-war reopening concert (conductor Toscanini), 1946. Has sung at Covent Garden and in opera houses of Naples, Rome, Venice, Pompeii, Turin, Cesana, Modena, Bologna and Florence; toured England, France, Spain and South America. American début in title rôle Aïda, San Francisco, 1950; Metropolitan Opera House Season, New York, 1955. Recordings of complete operas include: Otello; Adriana Lecouvreur; Il Trittico; Don Carlo; La Gioconda; Un Ballo in Maschera; Madame Butterfly; Mefistofele; La Fanciulla Del West; La Forza Del Destino; Andrea Chenier; Manon Lescaut; La Tosca; Il Trovatore; Aida, La Bohème. *Address:* c/o S. A. Gorlinsky Ltd, 33 Dover Street, W1X 4NJ; 1 Piazza della Guastella, Milan, Italy.

TEBBIT, Sir Donald (Claude), GCMG 1980 (KCMG 1975; CMG 1965); HM Diplomatic Service, retired; *b* 4 May 1920; *m* 1947, Barbara Margaret Olson Matheson; one *s* three *d*. *Educ:* Perse School; Trinity Hall, Cambridge (MA). Served War of 1939–45, RNVR. Joined Foreign (now Diplomatic) Service, 1946; Second Secretary, Washington, 1948; transferred to Foreign Office, 1951; First Secretary, 1952; transferred to Bonn, 1954; Private Secretary to Minister of State, Foreign Office, 1958; Counsellor, 1962; transferred to Copenhagen, 1964; Commonwealth Office, 1967; Asst Under-Sec. of State, FCO, 1968–70; Minister, British Embassy, Washington, 1970–72; Chief Clerk, FCO, 1972–76; High Comr in Australia, 1976–80. Chairman: Diplomatic Service Appeals Bd, 1980–87; E-SU, 1983–87; Mem., Appeals Bd, Council of Europe, 1981–. Dir, RTZ Corp., 1980–90. Dir Gen., British Property Fedn, 1980–85. Pres. (UK), Australian-British Chamber of Commerce, 1980–90; Chairman: Zimbabwe Tech. Management Training Trust, 1983–; Marshall Aid Commemoration Commn, 1985–; Jt Commonwealth Socs

Council, 1985–. Governor, Nuffield Hospitals, 1980–90, Dep. Chm., 1985–90. President: Old Persean Soc., 1981–82; Trinity Hall Assoc., 1984–85. *Address:* Priory Cottage, Toft, Cambridge CB3 7RH.

TEBBIT, Rt. Hon. Norman (Beresford), CH 1987; PC 1981; MP (C) Chingford, since 1974 (Epping, 1970–74); Director: Sears (Holdings) PLC, since 1987; British Telecom, since 1987; BET, since 1987; Spectator (1828) Ltd, since 1989; Golden Globe plc, since 1989; Onix Ltd, since 1990; journalist; *b* 29 March 1931; 2nd *s* of Leonard and Edith Tebbit, Enfield; *m* 1956, Margaret Elizabeth Daines; two *s* one *d*. *Educ:* Edmonton County Grammar Sch. Embarked on career in journalism, 1947. Served RAF: commissioned GD Branch; qualif. Pilot, 1949–51; Reserve service RAuxAF, No 604 City of Mddx Sqdn, 1952–55. Entered and left publishing and advertising, 1951–53. Civil Airline Pilot, 1953–70 (Mem. BALPA; former holder various offices in that Assoc.). Active mem. and holder various offices, Conservative Party, 1946–. PPS to Minister of State, Dept of Employment, 1972–73; Parly Under Sec. of State, Dept of Trade, 1979–81; Minister of State, Dept of Industry, 1981; Secretary of State for: Employment, 1981–83; Trade and Industry, 1983–85; Chancellor of the Duchy of Lancaster, 1985–87; Chm., Conservative Party, 1985–87. Former Chm., Cons. Members Aviation Cttee; former Vice-Chm. and Sec., Cons. Members Housing and Construction Cttee; Sec. House of Commons New Town Members Cttee. Dir, J. C. Bamford Excavators, 1987–91. Co-presenter, Target, Sky TV, 1989–. *Publication:* Upwardly Mobile (autobiog.), 1988. *Address:* House of Commons, SW1A 0AA.

TEBBLE, Norman, DSc; FRSE; CBiol, FIBiol; Director, Royal Scottish Museum, 1971–84; *b* 17 Aug. 1924; 3rd *s* of late Robert Soulsby Tebble and Jane Ann (*née* Graham); *m* 1954, Mary Olivia Archer, *o d* of H. B. and J. I. Archer, Kenilworth; two *s* one *d*. *Educ:* Bedlington Grammar School; St Andrews Univ.; BSc 1950, DSc 1968; MA, Merton Coll., Oxford, 1971. FIBiol 1971, CBiol 1986; FRSE 1976. St Andrews Univ. Air Squadron, 1942–43; Pilot, RAFVR, Canada, India and Burma, 1943–46. Scientific Officer, British Museum (Natural History), 1950, Curator of Annelida; John Murray Travelling Student in Oceanography, Royal Soc., 1958; Vis. Curator, Univ. of California, Scripps Inst. of Oceanography, 1959; Curator of Molluscs, British Museum, 1961; Univ. Lecturer in Zoology and Curator, zoological collection, Univ. of Oxford, 1968; Curator, Oxford Univ. Museum, 1969. Member Council: Marine Biological Assoc., UK, 1963–66; Scottish Marine Biological Assoc., 1973–78; Museums Assoc., 1972–75 (Vice-Pres., 1976–77; Pres., 1977–78); Mem., Tyne and Wear Museums Cttee, 1986–. *Publications:* (ed jtly) Speciation in the Sea, 1963; British Bivalve Seashells, 1966, 2nd edn 1976; (ed jtly) Bibliography British Fauna and Flora, 1967; scientific papers in Systematics of Annelida and Distribution in the World Oceans. *Recreations:* Tebbel-Tebble genealogy, ornithology, walking grandson in Arizona desert. *Address:* 4 Bright's Crescent, Edinburgh EH9 2DB. *T:* 031–667 5260.

TEDDER, family name of **Baron Tedder.**

TEDDER, 2nd Baron, *cr* 1946, of Glenguin; **John Michael Tedder,** MA, ScD, PhD, DSc; Purdie Professor of Chemistry, St Salvator's College, University of St Andrews, 1969–89, now Emeritus; *b* 4 July 1926; 2nd and *er* surv. *s* of 1st Baron Tedder, GCB, and Rosalinde (*née* Maclardy); *S* father, 1967; *m* 1952, Peggy Eileen Growcott; two *s* one *d*. *Educ:* Dauntsey's School, Wilts; Magdalene College, Cambridge (MA 1951; ScD 1965); University of Birmingham (PhD 1951; DSc 1961). Roscoe Professor of Chemistry, University of Dundee, 1964–69. Mem., Ct of Univ. of St Andrews, 1971–76. Vice-Pres., Perkin Div., RSC, 1980–83. FRSE; FRSC. *Publications:* Valence Theory, 1966; Basic Organic Chemistry, 1966; The Chemical Bond, 1978; Radicals, 1979; papers in Jl of RSC and other scientific jls. *Heir: s* Hon. Robin John Tedder [*b* 6 April 1955; *m* 1st, 1977, Jennifer Peggy (*d* 1978), *d* of John Mangan, NZ; 2nd, 1980, Rita Aristeia, *yr d* of John Frangidis, Sydney, NSW; two *s* one *d*]. *Address:* Little Rathmore, Kennedy Gardens, St Andrews, Fife KY16 9DJ. *T:* St Andrews (0334) 73546.

TEELOCK, Dr Boodhun; High Commissioner for Mauritius in London, since 1989; *b* 20 July 1922; *s* of Ramessur Teelock and Sadny Teelock; *m* 1956, Riziya; three *d*. *Educ:* Edinburgh Univ. (MB ChB 1950); Liverpool Univ. (DTM&H 1951). DPH. Ministry of Health, Mauritius: School MO, 1952–58; Senior School MO, 1958–59; Principal MO, 1960–68; World Health Organisation: Regional Adviser, Public Health Administration, Brazzaville, 1968–71; Chief of Mission, Tanzania, 1971–74, Kenya and Seychelles, 1974–79; Immunisation MO, Air Mauritius, 1980–88. *Recreation:* reading. *Address:* Mauritius High Commission, 32/33 Elvaston Place, SW7 5NW. *T:* 071–581 0294.

TEESDALE, Edmund Brinsley, CMG 1964; MC 1945; DPhil; *b* 30 Sept. 1915; *s* of late John Herman Teesdale and late Winifred Mary (*née* Gull); *m* 1947, Joyce, *d* of late Walter Mills and of Mrs J. T. Murray; three *d*. *Educ:* Lancing; Trinity College, Oxford. DPhil CNAA, 1987. Entered Colonial Administrative Service, Hong Kong, 1938. Active Service in Hong Kong, China, India, 1941–45. Subsequently various administrative posts in Hong Kong; Colonial Secretary, Hong Kong, 1963–65. Dir, Assoc. of British Pharmaceutical Industry, 1965–76. *Publication:* The Queen's Gunstonemaker, 1984. *Recreations:* gardening, swimming, reading. *Address:* The Hogge House, Buxted, East Sussex TN22 4AY.

TEGNER, Ian Nicol, CA; Director: Wiggins Teape Appleton, since 1990; Control Risks Group, since 1990; President, Institute of Chartered Accountants of Scotland, 1991–April 1992 (Vice President, 1990–91); *b* 11 July 1933; *s* of Sven Stuart Tegner, OBE, and Edith Margaret Tegner (*née* Nicol): *m* 1961, Meriel Helen, *d* of Brig. M. S. Lush, CB, CBE, MC; one *s* one *d*. *Educ:* Rugby School. CA. Clarkson Gordon & Co., Toronto, 1958–59; Manager 1959–65, Partner 1965–71, Barton Mayhew & Co., Chartered Accts; Finance Dir, Bowater Industries, 1971–86; Chm., Cayzer Steel Bowater, 1981–86; Dir, Gp Finance, Midland Bank, 1987–89. Dir, Opera 80, 1991–. Institute of Chartered Accountants of Scotland: Mem. Council 1981–86; Vice Pres., 1986–87; Mem., Accounting Standards Cttee of CCAB, 1984–86; Chm., Hundred Gp of Finance Dirs, 1988–90. *Publications:* articles on accountancy in various jls and pubns. *Recreations:* book collecting, travel, hill-walking, choral singing, family life. *Address:* 44 Norland Square, W11 4PZ. *T:* 071–229 8604.

TE HEUHEU, Sir Hepi (Hoani), KBE 1979; New Zealand sheep and cattle farmer; Paramount Chief of Ngati-Tuwharetoa tribe of Maoris; *b* 1919; *m*; six *c*. Chairman: Tuwharetoa Maori Trust Board; Puketapu 3A Block (near Taupo); Rotoaira Lake Trust; Rotoaira Forest Trust; Tauranga-Taupo Trust; Motutere Point Trust; Turamakina Tribal Cttee; Lake Taupo Forest Trust; Oraukura 3 Block; Hauhungaroa 1C Block; Waihi Pukawa Block; Mem., Tongariro National Park Board (great grandson of original donor). OStJ. *Address:* Taumarunui, New Zealand.

TEI ABAL, Sir, Kt 1976; CBE 1974; MHA, PNG; *b* 1932; *m*; six *c*. Became a tea-planter and trader in Papua New Guinea; a Leader of the Engi Clan in Western Highlands. Member for Wabag, open electorate, PNG; Former Member (Ministerial) in 1st, 2nd and 3rd Houses of Assembly; Leader of the Opposition, UP, and later Minister of Public Utilities, 1979–80, in Somare Govt. *Address:* c/o PO Box 3534, Port Moresby, Papua New Guinea; Wabag, Papua New Guinea.

TEJAN-SIE, Sir Banja, GCMG 1970 (CMG 1967); Governor-General of Sierra Leone, 1970–71 (Acting Governor-General, 1968–70); international business and legal consultant; *b* 7 Aug. 1917; *s* of late Alpha Ahmed Tejan-Sie; *m* 1946, Admira Stapleton; three *s* one *d*. *Educ:* Bo Sch., Freetown; Prince of Wales Sch., Freetown; LSE, London University. Called to Bar, Lincoln's Inn, 1951. Station Clerk, Sierra Leone Railway, 1938–39; Nurse, Medical Dept, 1940–46; Ed., West African Students' Union, 1948–51; Nat. Vice-Pres., Sierra Leone People's Party, 1953–56; Police Magistrate: Eastern Province, 1955; Northern Province, 1958; Sen. Police Magistrate Provinces, 1961; Speaker, Sierra Leone House of Representatives, 1962–67; Chief Justice of Sierra Leone, 1967–70. Mem. Keith Lucas Commn on Electoral Reform, 1954. Hon. Sec. Sierra Leone Bar Assoc., 1957–58. Chm. Bd of Management, Cheshire Foundn, Sierra Leone, 1966. Has led delegations and paid official visits to many countries throughout the world. Hon. Treasurer, Internat. African Inst., London, 1978–. Pres., Freetown Golf Club, 1970–. GCON (Nigeria), 1970; Grand Band, Order of Star of Africa (Liberia), 1969; Special Grand Cordon, Order of propitious clouds (Taiwan), 1970; Grand Cordon, Order of Knighthood of Pioneers (Liberia), 1970; Order of Cedar (Lebanon), 1970. *Recreations:* music, reading. *Address:* 3 Tracy Avenue, NW2. *T:* 081–452 2324. *Club:* Commonwealth Trust.

TE KANAWA, Dame Kiri (Janette), DBE 1982 (OBE 1973); opera singer; *b* Gisborne, New Zealand, 6 March 1944; *m* 1967, Desmond Stephen Park; one *s* one *d*. *Educ:* St Mary's Coll., Auckland, NZ; London Opera Centre. Major rôles at Royal Opera House, Covent Garden, include: the Countess, in Marriage of Figaro; Elvira, in Don Giovanni; Mimi, in La Bohème; Desdemona, in Otello; Marguerite, in Faust; Amelia, in Simon Boccanegra; Fiordiligi, in Cosi Fan Tutti; Tatiana, in Eugene Onegin; title rôle in Arabella; Rosalinde, in Die Fledermaus; Violetta, in La Traviata; Manon, in Manon Lescaut. Has sung leading rôles at Metropolitan Opera, New York, notably, Desdemona, Elvira, and Countess; also at the Paris Opera, Elvira, Fiordiligi and Pamina in Magic Flute, title rôle in Tosca; at San Francisco Opera, Amelia and Pamina; at Sydney Opera House, Mimi, Amelia, and Violetta in La Traviata; Elvira, with Cologne Opera; Amelia at la Scala, Milan; Countess in Le Nozze di Figaro at Salzburg fest. Hon. Fellow, Somerville Coll., Oxford, 1983; Hon. DMus Oxford, 1983. *Publication:* Land of the Long White Cloud: Maori myths and legends, 1989. *Recreations:* golf, swimming. *Address:* c/o Jack Mastroianni, Cami, 165 W 57th Street, New York, NY 1009, USA.

TELFER, Robert Gilmour Jamieson, (Rab), CBE 1985; PhD; Executive Chairman, BSI Standards, since 1989; Director, Manchester Business School, 1984–88; *b* 22 April 1928; *s* of late James Telfer and Helen Lambie Jamieson; *m* 1953, Joan Audrey Gunning; three *s*. *Educ:* Bathgate Academy (Dawson Trust Bursary); Univ. of Edinburgh (Mackay-Smith Prize; Blandfield Prize; BSc (Hons 1st cl.) 1950, PhD 1953). Shift Chemist, AEA, 1953–54; Imperial Chemical Industries Ltd: Res. Chemist, Billingham Div., 1954–58; Heavy Organic Chemicals Div., 1958–71; Fibre Intermediates Dir and R & D Dir, 1971–75; Div. Dep. Chm., 1975–76, Div. Chm., 1976–81, Petrochemicals Div.; Chm. and Man. Dir, 1981–84, Dir, 1984, Mather & Platt Ltd; Chm., European Industrial Services Ltd, 1988–89. Mem. Bd, Philips-Imperial Petroleum Ltd, 1975–81; Director: Renold PLC, 1984–; Volex PLC, 1986–. Sen. Vis. Fellow, Manchester Business Sch., 1988–. Group Chm., Duke of Edinburgh's Study Conf., 1974; Mem., ACORD for Fuel and Power, 1981–87; Chm., Adv. Council on Energy Conservation, 1982–84. Personal Adviser to Sec. of State for Energy, 1984–87. British Standards Institution: Mem. Main Bd, 1988–, and Finance Cttee, 1988–; non-exec. Chm., Standards Bd and Testing Bd, 1988–89. Mem., Civil Service Coll. Adv. Council, 1986–89; Governor, Teesside Polytechnic, 1989– (Chm., Resources Cttee, 1989–). CBIM. Hon. MBA Manchester, 1989. *Publications:* papers in Jl Chem. Soc. and Chemistry and Industry. *Recreations:* walking, swimming, poetry, decorative egg collecting, supporting Middlesborough FC. *Address:* Downings, Upleatham Village, Redcar, Cleveland TS11 8AG. *Club:* Caledonian.

TELFORD, Sir Robert, Kt 1978; CBE 1967; DL; FEng, FIEE, FIProdE, CBIM, FRSA; Life President, The Marconi Company Ltd, 1984 (Managing Director, 1965–81; Chairman, 1981–84, retired); Chairman, Prelude Technology Investments Ltd, since 1985; *b* 1 Oct. 1915; *s* of Robert and Sarah Annie Telford; *m* 1st, 1941 (marr. diss. 1950); one *s*; 2nd, 1958, Elizabeth Mary (*née* Shelley); three *d*. *Educ:* Quarry Bank Sch., Liverpool; Queen Elizabeth's Grammar Sch., Tamworth; Christ's Coll., Cambridge (MA). Manager, Hackbridge Works, The Marconi Co. Ltd, 1940–46; Man. Dir, Companhia Marconi Brasileira, 1946–50; The Marconi Company Ltd: Asst to Gen. Manager, 1950–53; Gen. Works Manager, 1953–61; Gen. Manager, 1961–65; Man. Dir, GEC-Marconi Electronics Ltd, 1968–84; Chm., GEC Avionics Ltd, 1982–86; Director: The General Electric Co., 1973–84; Canadian Marconi Co., Montreal, 1968–84; Ericsson Radio Systems AB (formerly SRA Communications, AB), Stockholm, 1969–85. Chairman: DRI Hldgs Ltd, 1984–88; CTP Investments, 1987–90; Diametric, 1988–89; Dir, BAJ Hldgs, 1985–87. Visitor, Hatfield Polytech., 1986–. President: Electronic Engrg Assoc., 1963–64; IProdE, 1982–83; Chairman: Electronics and Avionics Requirement Bd, DTI, 1980–85; Alvey Steering Cttee, 1983–88; SERC Teaching Company Management Cttee, 1984–87; Commonwealth Engineers' Council, 1989–; Member: Electronics EDC, 1964–67, 1981–85; Engrg Industry Trng Bd, 1968–82; Council, Industrial Soc., 1982–86; Council, Fellowship of Engrg, 1983–86; BTEC, 1984–86; SERC Engrg Bd, 1985–88; Engrg Council, 1985–89; IT Adv. Gp, DTI, 1985–88. Advr to Comett Programme of European Community, 1987–; Mem., Industrial R & D Adv. Cttee to European Community, 1988–. Mem., Council, 1981–88, and Court, 1981–, Univ. of Essex. DL Essex, 1981. Freeman, City of London, 1984. Hon. FIMechE, 1983; Hon. FIEE, 1987. Hon. DSc: Salford, 1981; Cranfield, 1983; Bath, 1984; Aston, 1985; Hon. DEng: Bradford, 1986; Birmingham, 1986; Hon. DTech Anglia Inst., 1989. *Address:* Rettendon House, Rettendon, Chelmsford, Essex CM3 8DW. *T:* Wickford (0268) 733131. *Club:* Royal Air Force.

TELFORD BEASLEY, John, CBE 1988; Chairman: Docklands Light Railway, since 1989; London Buses Ltd, since 1985; Director, London Regional Transport, since 1984; *b* 26 March 1929; *s* of James George and Florence Telford Beasley; *m* (marr. diss.); one *s* two *d*. *Educ:* Watford Grammar School; Open Univ. (BA). Dep. Chm., Cadbury Ltd, 1970–73; Chm., Cadbury Schweppes Food Ltd, 1973–75; Dir, Cadbury Schweppes, 1973–77; Chm., Schweppes Ltd, 1975–77; Regional Pres., Warner Lamber Co., 1977–84. *Recreations:* squash, flying, bus driving. *Address:* 3 Monmouth Square, Winchester, Hants SO22 4HY.

TELLER, Prof. Edward; Senior Research Fellow, Hoover Institution, since 1975; University Professor, University of California, Berkeley, 1971–75, now Emeritus (Professor of Physics, 1960–71); Chairman, Department of Applied Science, University of California, 1963–66; Associate Director, Lawrence Radiation Laboratory, University of California, 1954–75, now Emeritus; *b* Budapest, Hungary, 15 January 1908; *s* of a lawyer; became US citizen, 1941; *m* 1934, Augusta Harkanyi; one *s* one *d*. *Educ:* Karlsruhe Technical Inst., Germany; Univ. of Munich; Leipzig (PhD). Research Associate, Leipzig, 1929–31; Research Associate, Göttingen, 1931–33; Rockefeller Fellow, Copenhagen,

1934; Lectr, Univ. of London, 1934–35; Prof. of Physics, George Washington Univ., Washington, DC, 1935–41; Prof. of Physics, Columbia Univ., 1941–42; Physicist, Manhattan, Engineer District, 1942–46, Univ. of Chicago, 1942–43; Los Alamos Scientific Laboratory, 1943–46; Prof. of Physics, Univ. of Chicago, 1946–52; Asst Dir, Los Alamos (on leave, Chicago), 1949–52; Consultant, Livermore Br., Univ. of Calif, Radiation Laboratory, 1952–53; Prof. of Physics, Univ. of Calif, 1953–60; Dir, Livermore Br., Lawrence Livermore Lab., Univ. of Calif, 1958–60. Mem. Nat. Acad. of Sciences, etc. Holds several hon. degrees, 1954–. Has gained awards, 1957–, incl. Enrico Fermi Award, 1962; Harvey Prize, Israel, 1975; Gold Medal, Amer. Coll. of Nuclear Med., 1980; Man of the Year, Achievement Rewards for College Scientists, 1980; Nat. Medal of Science, 1983. *Publications:* The Structure of Matter, 1949; Our Nuclear Future, 1958; The Legacy of Hiroshima, 1962; The Reluctant Revolutionary, 1964; The Constructive Uses of Nuclear Explosives, 1968; Great Men of Physics, 1969; Nuclear Energy in a Developing World, 1977; Energy from Heaven and Earth, 1979; Pursuit of Simplicity, 1980; Better a Shield than a Sword, 1987. *Address:* Stanford, Calif 94305, USA.

TELLO, Manuel, CMG (Hon.) 1975; Mexican Ambassador to France, since 1989; *b* 15 March 1935; *s* of late Manuel Tello and Guadalupe M. de Tello; *m* 1983, Rhonda M. de Tello. *Educ:* schools in Mexico City; Georgetown Univ.; Sch. for Foreign Service, Washington, DC; Escuela Libre de Derecho; Institut de Hautes Etudes Internationales, Geneva. Equivalent of BA in Foreign Service Studies; post-grad. studies in Internat. Law. Joined Mexican Foreign Service, 1957; Asst Dir Gen. for Internat. Organizations, 1967–70, Dir Gen., 1970–72; Dir for Multilateral Affairs, 1972–74; Dir for Political Affairs, 1975–76; Ambassador to UK, 1977–79; Under Sec., Dept of Foreign Affairs, Mexico, 1979–82; Perm. Rep. of Mexico to Internat. Orgns, Geneva, 1983–89. Alternate Rep. of Mexico to: OAS, 1959–63; Internat. Orgs, Geneva, 1963–65; Conf. of Cttee on Disarmament, Geneva, 1963–66; Rep. of Mexico to: Org. for Proscription of Nuclear Weapons in Latin America, 1970–73; 3rd UN Conf. on Law of the Sea, 1971–76 and 1982. Has attended 13 Sessions of UN Gen. Assembly. Holds decorations from Chile, Ecuador, Egypt, France, Italy, Jordan, Panama, Senegal, Sweden, Venezuela, Yugoslavia. *Publications:* contribs to learned jls in the field of international relations. *Recreations:* tennis, theatre, music. *Address:* Mexican Embassy, 9 rue de Longchamp, 75116 Paris, France.

TEMIN, Prof. Howard M(artin), PhD; Professor of Oncology, since 1969, Harry Steenbock Professor of Biological Science, since 1982, Harold P. Rusch Professor of Cancer Research, since 1980 and American Cancer Society Professor of Viral Oncology and Cell Biology, since 1974, University of Wisconsin-Madison; *b* 10 Dec. 1934; *s* of Henry Temin and Annette Lehman Temin; *m* 1962, Rayla Greenberg; two *d*. *Educ:* Swarthmore Coll., Swarthmore, Pa (BA 1955); Calif Inst. of Technol., Pasadena (PhD 1959). Postdoctoral Fellow, Calif Inst. of Technol., Pasadena, 1959–60; Asst Prof. of Oncology, Univ. of Wis-Madison, 1960–64, Associate Prof. of Oncol., 1964–69, Wisconsin Alumni Res. Foundn Prof. of Cancer Res, 1971–80. Foreign Mem., Royal Soc., 1988. Hon. DSc: Swarthmore Coll., 1972; NY Med. Coll., 1972; Univ. of Pa, 1976; Hahnemann Med. Coll., 1976; Lawrence Univ., 1976; Temple Univ., 1979; Medical Coll., Wisconsin, 1981; Colorado State Univ., 1987; Univ. Paris V, 1988; Univ. Med. Dent., NJ, 1989. US Public Health Service Res. Career Develt Award, National Cancer Inst., 1964–74; (jtly) Nobel Prize for Physiology or Medicine, 1975. *Publications:* articles on viruses and cancer, on RNA-directed DNA synthesis, on evolution of viruses from cellular movable genetic elements, on retrovirus vectors, and on retrovirus genetics. *Address:* McArdle Laboratory, University of Wisconsin-Madison, Madison, Wis 53706, USA. *T:* 608–262–1209.

TEMKO, Edward James, (Ned); Editor, Jewish Chronicle, since 1990; *b* 5 Nov. 1952; *s* of Stanley L. Temko and Francine (*née* Salzman); *m* 1st, 1980, Noa Weiss (marr. diss. 1984); 2nd, 1986, Astra Bergson Kook; one *s*. *Educ:* Williams Coll., USA (BA Hons Pol Sci. and Econs). Reporter, Associated Press, Lisbon, 1976; United Press International: Europe, ME and Africa Editl Desk, Brussels, 1977; Correspondent, ME Office, Beirut, 1977–78; Christian Science Monitor: Chief ME Correspondent, Beirut, 1978–80; Moscow Correspondent, 1981–83; ME Correspondent, Jerusalem, 1984–85; SA Correspondent, Johannesburg, 1986–87; Sen. TV Correspondent for Europe, ME and Africa in London, World Monitor TV, 1989–90. *Publications:* To Win or To Die: a biography of Menachem Begin, 1987. *Recreations:* tennis, reading, computers, travel. *Address:* 25 Furnival Street, EC4A 1JT. *T:* 071–405 9252.

TEMPANY, Myles McDermott, OBE 1984; Vice-Principal (External Affairs), King's College London, 1986–88; *b* 31 March 1924; *y s* of late Martin Tempany and Margaret (*née* McDermott); *m* 1951, Pamela Allan; one *s* one *d*. *Educ:* St Muredach's College, Ballina, Co. Mayo; Intermediate and University College, Dublin. Military service, 1944–47. King's College London: Asst Acct, 1948–70; Acct, 1970–73; Finance Officer and Acct, 1973–77; FKC 1975; Bursar, 1977–81; Head of Admin and Bursar, 1981–83; Secretary, 1983–85; Mem. Council, 1986–89. Mem. Delegacy, King's Coll. Sch. of Medicine and Dentistry, 1986–88; Founder Chm., St Raphael's Training Centre Develt Trust, 1978–; Mem., Governing Body, Hatfield Polytechnic, 1985–; Chm., Bd of Governors, Pope Paul Sch., Potters Bar, 1986–. KHS 1972, KCHS 1978; KSG 1983. President's Award, Develt Bd, Univ. of Texas Health Science Center, Houston, 1986. *Recreations:* golf, watching Association Football. *Address:* 18 Tiverton Road, Potters Bar, Herts EN6 5HY. *T:* Potters Bar (0707) 56860. *Clubs:* Institute of Directors; Brookman's Park Golf.

TEMPLE OF STOWE, 8th Earl *cr* 1822; **Walter Grenville Algernon Temple-Gore-Langton;** *b* 2 Oct. 1924; *s* of Comdr Hon. Evelyn Arthur Temple-Gore-Langton, DSO, RN (*d* 1972) (*y s* of 4th Earl) and Irene (*d* 1967), *d* of Brig.-Gen. Cavendish Walter Gartside-Spaight; *S* cousin, 1988; *m* 1st, 1954, Zillah Ray (*d* 1966), *d* of James Boxall; two *s* one *d*; 2nd, 1968, Margaret Elizabeth Graham, *o d* of late Col H. W. Scarth. *Heir:* *s* Hon. James Grenville Temple-Gore-Langton, *b* 11 Sept. 1955.

TEMPLE, Anthony Dominic Afamado; QC 1986; a Recorder, since 1989; *b* 21 Sept. 1945; *s* of Sir Rawden Temple, *qv*; *m* 1st, 1975 (marr. diss.); 2nd, 1983, Suzie Bodansky; two *d*. *Educ:* Haileybury and ISC; Worcester College, Oxford (Hon. Sec., OU Modern Pentathlon Assoc.). Called to the Bar, Inner Temple, 1968; Crown Law Office, Western Australia, 1969; Assistant Recorder, 1982. *Recreations:* modern pentathlon, travel, history. *Address:* 4 Pump Court, EC4.

TEMPLE, Sir (Ernest) Sanderson, Kt 1988; MBE; MA; QC 1969; **His Honour Judge Temple;** a Circuit Judge, since 1977; Honorary Recorder of Kendal, since 1972, of Liverpool, since 1978, and of Lancaster, since 1987; *b* 23 May 1921; *o s* of Ernest Temple, Oxenholme House, Kendal; *m* 1946, June Debonnaire, *o d* of W. M. Saunders, JP, Wennington Hall, Lancaster; one *s* two *d*. *Educ:* Kendal School; Queen's Coll., Oxford. Served in Border Regt in India and Burma, attaining temp. rank of Lt-Col (despatches, 1945). Barrister-at-Law, 1943. Joined Northern Circuit, 1946; Dep. Recorder of Salford, 1962–65; Dep. Chm., Agricultural Land Tribunal (Northern), 1966–69; Chm., Westmorland QS, 1969–71 (Dep. Chm., 1967); a Recorder of the Crown Court, 1972–77; Mem., Bar Council, 1965. Chairman: Arnside/Silverdale Landscape Trust, 1987–; NW Area Point-to-Point Assoc., 1987–; Dep. Chm., British Harness Racing Club, 1983–. Jt Master, Vale of Lune Hunt, 1963–85. Hon. FICW. *Recreations:* farming and horses. *Address:* Yealand Hall, Yealand Redmayne, near Carnforth, Lancs LA5 9TD. *T:* Burton (Cumbria) (0524) 781200. *Club:* Racquet (Liverpool).

TEMPLE, Rt. Rev. Frederick Stephen; Honorary Assistant Bishop, Diocese of Bristol, since 1983; *b* 24 Nov. 1916; *s* of Frederick Charles and Frances Temple; *m* 1947, Joan Catharine Webb; one *s* one *d* (and one *s* decd). *Educ:* Rugby; Balliol Coll., Oxford; Trinity Hall, Cambridge; Westcott House, Cambridge. Deacon, 1947, Priest, 1948; Curate, St Mary's, Arnold, Notts, 1947–49; Curate, Newark Parish Church, 1949–51; Rector, St Agnes, Birch, Manchester, 1951–53; Dean of Hong Kong, 1953–59; Senior Chaplain to the Archbishop of Canterbury, 1959–61; Vicar of St Mary's, Portsea, 1961–70; Archdeacon of Swindon, 1970–73; Bishop Suffragan of Malmesbury, 1973–83. Proctor, Canterbury Convocation, 1964; Hon. Canon, Portsmouth Cathedral, 1965. *Publication:* (ed) William Temple, Some Lambeth Letters, 1942–44, 1963. *Recreations:* gardening, theatre, television. *Address:* 7 The Barton, Wood Street, Wootton Bassett, Wilts SN4 7BG. *T:* Swindon (0793) 851227.

TEMPLE, George, CBE 1955; PhD, DSc, MA; FRS 1943; Sedleian Professor of Natural Philosophy, University of Oxford, 1953–68; now Professor Emeritus; Hon. Fellow of Queen's College, Oxford, 1970; *b* 2 Sept. 1901; *o s* of late James Temple, London; *m* 1930, Dorothy Lydia (*d* 1979), *e d* of late Thomas Ellis Carson, Liverpool. *Educ:* Ealing County School; Birkbeck College, University of London; Trinity College, Cambridge. Research Assistant and Demonstrator, Physics Dept, Birkbeck College, 1922–24; Assistant Lecturer, Maths Dept, City and Guilds (Eng.) College, 1924–28; Keddey Fletcher Warr Studentship, 1928; 1851 Exhibition Research Student, 1928–30; Assistant Professor in Maths Dept, Royal College of Science, 1930–32; Professor of Mathematics, University of London, King's College, 1932–53. Seconded to Royal Aircraft Establishment, Farnborough, 1939–45. Chairman, Aeronautical Research Council, 1961–64. Professed as Benedictine monk, 1982. Leverhulme Emeritus Fellowship, 1971–73. Hon. DSc: Dublin, 1961; Louvain, 1966; Reading, 1980; Hon. LLD W Ontario, 1969. Sylvester Medal (Royal Soc.), 1970. *Publications:* An Introduction to Quantum Theory, 1931; Rayleigh's Principle, 1933; General Principles of Quantum Theory, 1934; An Introduction to Fluid Dynamics, 1958; Cartesian Tensors, 1960; The Structure of Lebesgue Integration Theory, 1971; papers on Mathematical Physics, Relativity, Quantum Theory, Aerodynamics, Distribution Theory, History of Mathematics. *Address:* Quarr Abbey, Ryde, Isle of Wight.

TEMPLE, Ven. George Frederick; Archdeacon of Bodmin, 1981–89, Archdeacon Emeritus since 1989; *b* 16 March 1933; *s* of George Frederick and Lilian Rose Temple; *m* 1961, Jacqueline Rose Urwin; one *s* one *d*. *Educ:* St Paul's, Jersey; Wells Theological College. Deacon 1968, priest 1969, Guildford; Curate: St Nicholas, Great Bookham, 1968–70; St Mary the Virgin, Penzance, 1970–72; Vicar of St Just in Penwith with Sancreed, 1972–74; Vicar of St Gluvias, Penryn, 1974–81; Vicar of Saltash, 1982–85. Mem., General Synod of C of E, 1981–85; Chm., House of Clergy, Truro Diocesan Synod, 1982–85; Diocesan Dir of Ordinands, 1985–87. Hon. Canon of Truro, 1981–89. *Recreations:* poetry, history, walking. *Address:* 50 Athelstan Park, Bodmin, Cornwall PL31 1DT.

TEMPLE, Sir John (Meredith), Kt 1983; JP; DL; *b* 1910; *m* 1942, Nancy Violet, *d* of late Brig.-Gen. Robert Wm Hare, CMG, DSO, DL, Cobh, Eire, and Norwich; one *s* one *d*. *Educ:* Charterhouse; Clare College, Cambridge (BA). Served War of 1939–45 (despatches). ADC to Governor of S Australia, 1941. MP (C) City of Chester, Nov. 1956–Feb. 1974. Pres., Ellesmere Port and Neston Cons. Assoc.; Vice-Pres., Chester Conservative Club; Vice-Pres., Army Benevolent Fund (Chester Branch); Vice-Chairman: British Group, IPU, 1973–74; Cons. Finance Cttee, 1966–68; Vice-President: Anglo-Colombian Society; Cerro Galan Expedn, Argentina, 1981; Salmon and Trout Assoc. JP Cheshire 1949, DL 1975; High Sheriff of Cheshire, 1980–81. Great Officer: Order of San Carlos, Colombia, 1973; Order of Boyacà, Colombia, 1974; Order of the Liberator, Venezuela, 1974. *Address:* Picton Gorse, Chester CH2 4JU. *T:* Mickle Trafford (0244) 300239. *Clubs:* Carlton, Army and Navy; Racquet (Liverpool).

TEMPLE, Sir Rawden (John Afamado), Kt 1980; CBE 1964; QC 1951; Chief Social Security (formerly National Insurance) Commissioner, 1975–81 (a National Insurance Commissioner, 1969); a Referee under Child Benefit Act, 1975, since 1976; *b* 1908; *m* 1936, Margaret Jessie Wiseman (*d* 1980), *d* of late Sir James Gunson, CMG, CBE; two *s*. *Educ:* King Edward's School, Birmingham; The Queen's College, Oxford. BA 1930; BCL, 1931; called to Bar, 1931; Master of the Bench, Inner Temple, 1960 (Reader, 1982; Treasurer, 1983); Vice-Chairman, General Council of the Bar, 1960–64. Mem., Industrial Injuries Adv. Council, 1981–84. War Service, 1941–45. Liveryman Worshipful Company of Pattenmakers, 1948. *Recreations:* fishing; collecting portraits and oriental rugs. *Address:* 3 North King's Bench Walk, Temple, EC4Y 7DQ.

See also A. D. A. Temple, V. B. A. Temple.

TEMPLE, Reginald Robert, CMG 1979; HM Diplomatic Service, retired; Oman Government Service, 1979–85; *b* 12 Feb. 1922; *s* of Lt-Gen. R. C. Temple, CB, OBE, RM, and Z. E. Temple (*née* Hunt); *m* 1st, 1952, Julia Jasmine Anthony (marr. diss. 1979); one *s* one *d*; 2nd, 1979, Susan McCorquodale (*née* Pick); one *d* (one step *s* one step *d*). *Educ:* Wellington College; Peterhouse, Cambridge. HM Forces, 1940–46, RE and Para Regt; Stockbroking, 1947–51; entered HM Foreign Service, 1951; Office of HM Comr Gen. for SE Asia, 1952–56; 2nd Sec., Beirut, 1958–62; 1st Sec., Algiers, 1964–66, Paris, 1967–69; FCO, 1969–79; Counsellor 1975. Dir, Shearwater Securities Ltd, I of M, 1989–. American Silver Star, 1944; Order of Oman, 3rd Class, 1985. *Recreation:* sailing. *Address:* Scarlett House, near Castletown, Isle of Man. *Clubs:* Army and Navy, Royal Cruising, Royal Ocean Racing.

TEMPLE, Sir Richard Anthony Purbeck, 4th Bt, *cr* 1876; MC 1941; *b* 19 Jan. 1913; *s* of Sir Richard Durand Temple, 3rd Bt, DSO; *S* father, 1962; *m* 1st, 1936, Lucy Geils (marr. diss., 1946), 2nd *d* of late Alain Joly de Lotbinière, Montreal; two *s*; 2nd, 1950, Jean, *d* of late James T. Finnie, and *widow* of Oliver P. Croom-Johnson; one *d*. *Educ:* Stowe; Trinity Hall, Cambridge; Lausanne University. Served War of 1939–45 (wounded, MC). Sometime Major, KRRC. *Recreation:* sailing. *Heir:* *s* Richard Temple [*b* 17 Aug. 1937; *m* 1964, Emma Rose, 2nd *d* of late Maj.-Gen. Sir Robert Laycock, KCMG, CB, DSO; three *d*]. *Address:* c/o National Westminster Bank, 94 Kensington High Street, W8.

TEMPLE, Sir Sanderson; *see* Temple, Sir E. S.

TEMPLE, Victor Bevis Afoumado; 6th Senior Prosecuting Counsel to the Crown, Central Criminal Court, since 1991; a Recorder of the Crown Court, since 1989; *b* 23 Feb. 1941; *s* of Sir Rawden Temple, CBE, QC and of late Lady Temple; *m* 1974, Richenda Penn-Bull; two *s*. *Educ:* Shrewsbury Sch.; Inns of Court Sch. of Law. TA, Westminster Dragoons, 1960–61. Marketing Exec., 1960–68. Called to the Bar, Inner Temple, 1971; Jun. Prosecuting Counsel to the Crown, CCC, 1985–91. *Recreations:* rowing, carpentry.

Address: 6 King's Bench Walk, Temple, EC4Y 7DR. *T:* 071–583 0410. *Club:* Thames Rowing.
See also A. D. A. Temple.

TEMPLE-GORE-LANGTON, family name of **Earl Temple of Stowe.**

TEMPLE-MORRIS, Peter; MP (C) Leominster since Feb. 1974; Solicitor, Payne Hicks Beach, since 1989; *b* 12 Feb. 1938; *o s* of His Honour Sir Owen Temple-Morris, QC and Lady (Vera) Temple-Morris (*née* Thompson); *m* 1964, Taheré, *e d* of HE Senator Khozeimé Alam, Teheran; two *s* two *d. Educ:* Hillstone Sch., Malvern; Malvern Coll.; St Catharine's Coll., Cambridge (MA). Chm., Cambridge Univ. Conservative Assoc., 1961; Mem. Cambridge Afro-Asian Expedn, 1961. Called to Bar, Inner Temple, 1962. Judge's Marshal, Midland Circuit, 1958; Mem., Young Barristers' Cttee, Bar Council, 1962–63; in practice on Wales and Chester Circuit, 1963–66; London and SE Circuit, 1966–76; 2nd Prosecuting Counsel to Inland Revenue, SE Circuit, 1971–74; admitted a solicitor, 1989. Contested (C): Newport (Mon), 1964 and 1966; Norwood (Lambeth), 1970. PPS to Minister of Transport, 1979. Member: Select Cttee on Agriculture, 1982–83; Select Cttee on Foreign Affairs, 1987–90. Chairman: British-Lebanese Parly Gp, 1983–; British-Netherlands Parly Gp, 1988–; British-Iranian Parly Gp, 1989– (Sec., 1974–89); Co-Chm., Working Party to establish British-Irish Inter-Parly Body, 1988–90, first British Co-Chm., 1990–; Secretary: Conservative Parly Transport Cttee, 1976–79; Cons. Parly Legal Cttee, 1977–78; Vice-Chairman: Cons. Parly Foreign and Commonwealth Affairs Cttee, 1982–90 (Sec., 1979–82); Cons. Parly NI Cttee, 1989–; British-USSR Parly Gp, 1987–; British-Southern Africa Parly Gp, 1987–; British-Argentina Parly Gp, 1990–. Mem. Exec. British Branch, IPU, 1977– (Chm., 1982–85); British delegate, IPU fact-finding mission on Namibia, 1977; Mem., 1980, Leader, 1984, Parly Delegation to UN Gen. Assembly; Mem., Argentine-British Conf., 1991. Chm., Hampstead Conservative Political Centre, 1971–73; Mem. Exec. Cttee, Soc. of Cons. Lawyers, 1968–71, 1990– (Vice-Chm., Standing Cttee on Criminal Law, 1976–79); Chm., Bow Gp Standing Cttee on Home Affairs, 1975–79. Chm., Afghanistan Support Cttee, 1981–82; Council Member: Iran Soc., 1968–80; GB-USSR Assoc., 1982–. Mem., RIIA. Nat. Treas., UNA, 1987–. Freeman, City of London; Liveryman, Basketmakers' Co. Governor, Malvern Coll., 1975– (Council Mem., 1978–). Hon. Associate, BVA, 1976. Chevalier du Tastevin, 1991. *Recreations:* shooting; wine and food; family relaxation. *Address:* House of Commons, SW1A 0AA. *T:* 071–219 4181. *Clubs:* Carlton, Buck's; Cardiff and County.

TEMPLEMAN, family name of **Baron Templeman.**

TEMPLEMAN, Baron *cr* 1982 (Life Peer), of White Lackington in the County of Somerset; **Sydney William Templeman;** Kt 1972; MBE 1946; PC 1978; a Lord of Appeal in Ordinary, since 1982; *b* 3 March 1920; *s* of late Herbert William and Lilian Templeman; *m* 1946, Margaret Joan (*née* Rowles) (*d* 1988); two *s. Educ:* Southall Grammar School; St John's College, Cambridge (Schol.; MA 1944; Hon. Fellow 1982). Served War of 1939–45: commnd 4/1st Gurkha Rifles, 1941; NW Frontier, 1942; Arakan, 1943; Imphal, 1944; Burma with 7 Ind. and 17 Ind. Divisions, 1945 (despatches; Hon. Major). Called to the Bar, 1947; Harmsworth and MacMahon schols; Mem., Middle Temple and Lincoln's Inn; Mem., Bar Council, 1961–65, 1970–72; QC 1964; Bencher, Middle Temple, 1969 (Treasurer, 1987). Attorney Gen. of the Duchy of Lancaster, 1970–72; a Judge of the High Court of Justice, Chancery Div., 1972–78; a Lord Justice of Appeal, 1978–82. Member: Tribunal to inquire into matters relating to the Vehicle and General Insurance Co., 1971; Adv. Cttee on Legal Education, 1972–74; Royal Commn on Legal Services, 1976–79. Treasurer, Senate of the Four Inns, 1972–74; Pres., Senate of the Inns of Court and the Bar, 1974–76. President: Bar Assoc. for Commerce, Finance and Industry, 1982–85; Bar European Gp, 1987–. Pres., Holdsworth Club, 1983–84. Hon. Member: Canadian Bar Assoc., 1976; Amer. Bar Assoc., 1976; Newfoundland Law Soc., 1984. Hon. DLitt Reading, 1980; Hon. LLD Birmingham, 1986; Hon. LLD CNAA, 1990. *Address:* Manor Heath, Knowl Hill, Woking, Surrey. *T:* Woking (0483) 761930.

TEMPLER, Maj.-Gen. James Robert, CB 1989; OBE 1978 (MBE 1973); retired; *b* 8 Jan. 1936; *s* of Brig. Cecil Robert Templer, DSO and Angela Mary Templer (*née* Henderson); *m* 1963 (marr. diss. 1979); two *s* one *d*; 2nd, 1981, Sarah Ann Evans (*née* Rogers). *Educ:* Charterhouse; RMA Sandhurst. RCDS, psc. Commissioned Royal Artillery, 1955; Instructor, Staff Coll., 1974–75; Comd 42nd Regt, 1975–77; Comd 5th Regt, 1977–78; CRA 2nd Armd Div., 1978–82; RCDS 1983; ACOS Training, HQ UKLF, 1983–86; ACDS (Concepts), MoD, 1986–89. Mem., British Cross Country Ski Team, 1958; European 3 Day Event Champion, 1962; Mem., British Olympic 3 Day Event Team, 1964. FBIM 1988. *Recreations:* sailing, ski-ing, riding, gardening, fishing, beekeeping, DIY. *Address:* c/o Lloyds Bank, Crediton, Devon.

TEMPLETON, Prof. (Alexander) Allan, FRCOG; Professor of Obstetrics and Gynaecology, University of Aberdeen, since 1985; *b* 28 June 1946; *s* of Richard and Minnie Templeton; *m* 1980, Gillian Constance Penney; three *s* one *d. Educ:* Aberdeen Grammar School; Univ. of Aberdeen (MB ChB 1969; MD Hons 1982); MRCOG 1974, FRCOG 1987. Resident and Registrar, Aberdeen Hosps, 1969–75; Lectr and Sen. Lectr, Dept of Obst. and Gyn., Univ. of Edinburgh, 1976–85. *Publications:* clinical and sci. articles on human infertility and *in vitro* fertilisation. *Recreation:* mountaineering. *Address:* Knapperna House, Udny, Aberdeenshire AB4 0SA. *T:* Udny (06513) 2481.

TEMPLETON, Darwin Herbert, CBE 1975; *b* 14 July 1922; *s* of Malcolm and Mary Templeton; *m* 1950; two *s* one *d. Educ:* Rocavan Sch.; Ballymena Academy. FICAI. Qualified as Chartered Accountant, 1945. Partner, Ashworth Rowan, 1947; Senior Partner, Price Waterhouse Northern Ireland (formerly Ashworth Rowan Craig Gardner), 1967–82. Chm., Ulster Soc. of Chartered Accountants, 1961–62; Pres., ICAI, 1970–71. Mem., Royal Commn on Legal Services, 1976–79. Chairman: Northern Publishing Office (UK) Ltd; Ballycassidy Sawmills Ltd; NI Local Govt Officers Superannuation Fund; Director: Larne Harbour Ltd; Boxmore International plc. *Recreations:* music, golf, motor racing. *Address:* 4 Cashel Road, Broughshane, Ballymena, Co. Antrim, Northern Ireland BT42 4PL. *T:* Broughshane (0266) 861017. *Club:* Royal Scottish Automobile.

TEMPLETON, Mrs Edith; author, since 1950; *b* 7 April 1916; *m* Edmund Ronald, MD; one *s. Educ:* Prague and Paris; Prague Medical University. During War of 1939–45 worked in American War Office, in office of Surgeon General. Conference (1945–46) and Conference Interpreter for British Forces in Germany, rank of Capt. *Publications:* Summer in the Country, 1950 (USA 1951), repr. 1985; Living on Yesterday, 1951, repr. 1986; The Island of Desire, 1952, repr. 1985; The Surprise of Cremona, 1954 (USA 1957), repr. 1985; This Charming Pastime, 1955; (as Louise Walbrook) Gordon, 1966; Three (USA 1971); contributor to The New Yorker, Holiday, Atlantic Monthly, Vogue, Harper's Magazine. *Recreation:* travel, with the greatest comfort possible. *Address:* 76 Corso Europa, 18012 Bordighera, Italy.

TEMPLETON, Sir John (Marks), Kt 1987; Chairman, Templeton, Galbraith and Hansberger Ltd, since 1986; chartered financial analyst, since 1965; *b* 29 Nov. 1912; *s* of Harvey Maxwell Templeton and Vella Templeton (*née* Handly); *m* 1st, 1937, Judith Dudley Folk (*d* 1950); two *s* one *d*; 2nd, 1958, Irene Reynolds Butler; one step *s* one step *d. Educ:* Yale Univ. (BA *summa cum laude*); Balliol Coll., Oxford (MA; Rhodes Scholar). Vice Pres., Nat. Geophysical Co., 1937–40; President: Templeton Dobbrow and Vance Inc., 1940–60; Templeton Growth Fund Ltd, 1954–85; Templeton Investment Counsel Ltd of Edinburgh, 1976–; Templeton World Fund Inc., 1978–87; Sec., Templeton Foundn, 1960–; Founder: Templeton Prizes for Progress in Religion, 1972; Templeton UK Project Trust, 1984. Pres., Bd of Trustees, Princeton Theol Seminary, 1967–73 and 1979–85; Mem. Council, Templeton College (formerly Oxford Centre for Management Studies), 1983– (Hon. Fellow, 1991). Hon. LLD: Beaver Coll., 1968; Marquette Univ., 1980; Jamestown Coll., 1983; Maryville Coll., 1984; Hon. LHD Wilson Coll., 1974; Hon. DD Buena Vista Coll., 1979; Hon. DCL Univ. of the South, 1984; Hon. DLitt Manhattan Coll., 1990. *Publications:* The Humble Approach, 1982; articles in professional jls. *Recreations:* swimming, gardening. *Address:* Lyford Cay, Nassau, Bahamas. *T:* 809–362–4295. *Clubs:* Athenæum, United Oxford & Cambridge University; University (NY); Lyford Cay (Bahamas).

TEMPLETON-COTILL, Rear-Adm. John Atrill, CB 1972; retired; *b* 4 June 1920; *s* of late Captain Jack Lionel Cottle, Tank Corps. *Educ:* Canford Sch.; New Coll., Oxford. Joined RNVR, 1939; served war 1939–45; HMS Crocus, 1940–41; British Naval Liaison Officer, French warship Chevreuil, 1941–42; staff, GOC New Caledonia (US), 1942; US Embassy, London, 1943; Flag Lieutenant to Vice-Adm., Malta, 1943–44; 1st Lieut, MTB 421, 1944–45; ADC to Governor of Victoria, 1945–46; served in HMS London, Loch Quoich, Whirlwind, Jutland, Barrosa and Sparrow, 1946–55; Comdr 1955; comd HMS Sefton and 108th Minesweeping Sqdn, 1955–56; jssc 1956; Comdr-in-Charge, RN School of Work Study, 1957–59; HMS Tiger, 1959–61; Captain 1961; British Naval Attaché, Moscow, 1962–64; comd HMS Rhyl and Captain (D), 23rd Escort Sqdn, 1964–66; Senior Naval Mem., Defence Operational Analysis Estabt, 1966–68; comd HMS Bulwark, 1968–69; Rear-Adm. Jan. 1970; Chief of Staff to Comdr Far East Fleet, 1970–71; Flag Officer, Malta, and NATO Comdr, SE Area Mediterranean, 1971–73; Comdr, British Forces Malta, 1972–73. Director: Sotheby Parke Bernet (France), 1974–81; Sotheby Parke Bernet (Monaco), 1975–81. *Recreations:* gardening, riding, shooting, travel, skiing. *Address:* Moulin de Fontvive, Ribas, par 30290 Laudun, France. *T:* 66.79.47.37.

TENBY, 3rd Viscount *cr* 1957, of Bulford; **William Lloyd-George;** Chairman, St James Public Relations, since 1990; *b* 7 Nov. 1927; 2nd *s* of 1st Viscount Tenby, TD, PC, and Edna Gwenfron (*d* 1971), *d* of David Jones, Gwynfa, Denbigh; *S* brother, 1983; *m* 1955, Ursula Diana Ethel, *y d* of late Lt-Col Henry Edward Medlicott, DSO; one *s* two *d. Educ:* Eastbourne College; St Catharine's Coll., Cambridge (Exhibnr; BA 1949). Captain, Royal Welch Fusiliers, TA. Dir, Williams Lea & Co., 1988–. JP Hants (Chm., Odiham Bench, 1990–). *Heir: s* Hon. Timothy Henry Gwilym Lloyd-George, *b* 19 Oct. 1962. *Address:* Triggs, Crondall, near Farnham, Surrey.

TENCH, David Edward, OBE 1987; Legal Adviser, since 1969, Head of Legal Department, since 1988, Director of Legal Affairs, since 1991, Consumers' Association (publishers of Which?); *b* 14 June 1929; *s* of late Henry George Tench and Emma Rose (*née* Orsborn); *m* 1st, 1957, Judith April Seaton Gurney (*d* 1986); two *s* one *d*; 2nd, 1988, Elizabeth Ann Irvine Macdonald. *Educ:* Merchant Taylors' Sch., Northwood, Mddx. Solicitor, 1952. Private practice, 1954–58; Office of Solicitor of Inland Revenue, 1958–69. Chm., Domestic Coal Consumers' Council, 1976–87; Energy Comr, 1977–79. Broadcaster on consumer affairs, 1964–. *Publications:* The Law for Consumers, 1962; The Legal Side of Buying a House, 1965 (2nd edn 1974); Wills and Probate, 1967 (6th edn 1977); How to Sue in the County Court, 1973; Towards a Middle System of Law, 1981. *Recreations:* music, amateur re-upholstery, bland gardening. *Address:* Pleasant View, The Platt, Amersham, Bucks HP7 0HX. *T:* Amersham (0494) 724974.
See also W. H. Tench.

TENCH, William Henry, CBE 1980; Special Adviser on Air Safety to the EEC Commissioner for Transport, 1986–88; *b* 2 Aug. 1921; *s* of Henry George Tench and Emma Rose Tench (*née* Orsborn); *m* 1944, Margaret Ireland; one *d. Educ:* Portsmouth Grammar School. CEng, FRAeS. Learned to fly in Fleet Air Arm, 1940; pilot with oil co. in S America, 1947 and 1948; joined KLM Royal Dutch Airlines, W Indies Div., 1948; transf. to Holland, 1951, flying N and S Atlantic, S African, ME and European routes; joined Min. of Transport and Civil Aviation as Inspector of Accidents, 1955; Chief Inspector of Accidents, DoT, 1974–81. *Publication:* Safety is no Accident, 1985. *Recreations:* music, sailing. *Address:* Seaways, Restronguet Point, Feock, Cornwall TR3 6RB.
See also D. E. Tench.

TENISON; *see* Hanbury-Tenison.

TENISON; *see* King-Tenison.

TENNANT, family name of **Baron Glenconner.**

TENNANT, Anthony John; Chairman, Guinness plc, since 1989 (Group Chief Executive, 1987–89); *b* 5 Nov. 1930; *s* of late Major John Tennant, TD and Hon. Antonia, *d* of 1st Baron Charnwood and later Viscountess Radcliffe; *m* 1954, Rosemary Violet Stockdale; two *s. Educ:* Eton; Trinity College, Cambridge (BA). National Service, Scots Guards (Malaya). Mather & Crowther, 1953–66 (Dir, 1959); Marketing Consultancy, 1966–70; Dir, 1970, then Dep. Man. Dir, Truman Ltd; Dir, Watney Mann & Truman Brewers, 1972–76; Man. Dir, 1976–82, Chm., 1983–87, International Distillers & Vintners Ltd; Director: Exploration Co. plc, 1967–89; El Oro Mining and Exploration Co. plc, 1967–89; Grand Metropolitan PLC, 1977–87; Close Brothers Group plc, 1980–90; Guardian Royal Exchange, 1989–; Guardian Assurance, 1989–; BNP UK Hldgs Ltd, 1990–; Mem., Supervisory Bd, LVMH Moet Hennessy Louis Vuitton, Paris, 1988–. Mem. Council, Food From Britain, 1983–86. *Address:* 18 Hamilton House, Vicarage Gate, W8. *T:* 071–937 6203. *Club:* Boodle's.
See also M. I. Tennant of Balfluig.

TENNANT, Bernard; Director General, National Chamber of Trade, since 1987; *b* 14 Oct. 1930; *s* of Richard and Phyllis Tennant; *m* 1956, Marie (*née* Tonge); two *s* one *d. Educ:* Farnworth Grammar Sch.; Open Univ. (BA Govt and Modern European Hist.). Nat. Service, RAF, 1949. Local authority admin, Worsley and Bolton, 1950; Secretary: Bolton Chamber of Trade, 1960–74; Bolton Chamber of Commerce and Industry, and numerous trade associations, 1968–74; National Chamber of Trade, 1975–. Member: Retail Consortium Council, 1986–; Home Office Standing Cttee on Crime Prevention, 1986–; Dept of Employment Retail Price Index Adv. Cttee, 1988–. Magistrate, Bolton, 1968–75; Reading, 1975–78. Founder Sec., Moorside Housing Gp of charitable housing assocs, 1964–75. Editor, NCT News, 1986–. *Publications:* articles in professional and trade jls. *Recreations:* film musicals, opera, photography, collating historical chronology.

TENNANT, Emma Christina, FRSL 1982; writer; *b* 20 Oct. 1937; *d* of 2nd Baron Glenconner and Elizabeth Lady Glenconner; one *s* two *d. Educ:* St Paul's Girls' School. Freelance journalist to 1973; became full time novelist, 1973; founder Editor, Bananas, 1975–78; general editor: In Verse, 1982–; Lives of Modern Women, 1985–. TV film script, Frankenstein's Baby, 1990. *Publications:* The Colour of Rain (pseud. Catherine Aydy), 1963; The Time of the Crack, 1973; The Last of the Country House Murders,

1975; Hotel de Dream, 1976; (ed) Bananas Anthology, 1977; (ed) Saturday Night Reader, 1978; The Bad Sister, 1978; Wild Nights, 1979; Alice Fell, 1980; Queen of Stones, 1982; Woman Beware Woman, 1983; Black Marina, 1985; Adventures of Robina by Herself, ed Emma Tennant, 1986; Cycle of the Sun: The House of Hospitalities, 1987, A Wedding of Cousins, 1988; The Magic Drum, 1989; Two Women of London, 1989; Sisters and Strangers, 1990; (contrib.) Novelists in Interview (ed John Haffenden), 1985; (contrib.) Women's Writing: a challenge to theory (ed Maria Monteith), 1986; *for children:* The Boggart (with Mary Rayner), 1979; The Search for Treasure Island, 1981; The Ghost Child, 1984; contribs to Guardian. *Recreation:* walking in Dorset. *Address:* c/o Faber & Faber, 3 Queen Square, WC1. *T:* 071–465 0045.

TENNANT, Harry; Commissioner of Customs and Excise, 1975–78; *b* 10 Dec. 1917; *s* of late Robert and Mary Tennant; *m* 1944, Bernice Baker; one *s. Educ:* Oldham High School. Appointed Officer of Customs and Excise, 1938; Inspector, 1960; Principal Inspector, 1970; Asst Sec., 1971; Dep. Chief Inspector, 1973; Mem., CS Appeal Bd, 1980–87. *Publications:* Back to the Bible, 1962, repr. 1984; Moses My Servant, 1966, repr. 1990; The Man David, 1968, repr. 1983; The Christadelphians: what they believe and preach, 1986. *Recreations:* walking, travel. *Address:* Strathtay, Alexandra Road, Watford, Herts WD1 3QY. *T:* Watford (0923) 222079.

TENNANT, Sir Iain (Mark), KT 1986; JP; Lord-Lieutenant of Morayshire, since 1963; Crown Estate Commissioner, 1970–90; Lord High Commissioner to General Assembly, Church of Scotland, 1988–89; *b* 11 March 1919; *e s* of late Col Edward Tennant, Innes, Elgin and Mrs Georgina Tennant; *m* 1946, Lady Margaret Helen Isla Marion Ogilvy, 2nd *d* of 12th Earl of Airlie, Kt, GCVO, MC; two *s* one *d. Educ:* Eton College; Magdalene College, Cambridge. Scots Guards, 1939–46. Caledonian Cinemas, 1947; Chm., Grampian Television Ltd, 1968–89; Director: Times Publishing Co. Ltd, 1962–66; Clydesdale Bank Ltd, 1968–89; The Seagram Co. Ltd, Montreal, 1978–81; Moray Enterprise Trust Ltd, 1986–; Chairman: The Glenlivet Distillers Ltd, 1964–84; Seagram Distillers, 1979–84. Mem. Newspaper Panel, Monopolies and Mergers Commn, 1981–86. Chm. Bd of Governors, Gordonstoun School, 1954–71. Lieut, Queen's Body Guard for Scotland (Royal Company of Archers), 1981–. FRSA 1971; CBIM 1983. DL Moray, 1954; JP Moray, 1961. *Recreations:* shooting, fishing; formerly rowing (rowed for Eton, 1937). *Address:* (home) Lochnabo, Lhanbryde, Moray. *T:* Lhanbryde (034384) 2228; (office) Innes House, Elgin, Moray. *T:* Lhanbryde (034384) 2410.

TENNANT of Balfluig, Mark Iain; Master of the Supreme Court, Queen's Bench Division, since 1988; Baron of Balfluig; *b* 4 Dec. 1932; *s* of late Major John Tennant, TD, KStJ and Hon. Antonia Mary Roby Benson, *d* of 1st Baron Charnwood and later Viscountess Radcliffe; *m* 1965, Lady Harriot Pleydell-Bouverie, *y d* of 7th Earl of Radnor; one *s* one *d. Educ:* Eton College; New College, Oxford (MA 1959). Lieut, The Rifle Brigade (SRO). Called to the Bar, Inner Temple, 1958, Bencher, 1984; Recorder, 1987. Restored Balfluig Castle, 1967. Chm., Royal Orchestral Soc. for Amateur Musicians, 1989–. *Recreations:* music, architecture, books, shooting. *Address:* Royal Courts of Justice, Strand, WC2A 2LL. *Club:* Brooks's.
See also A. J. Tennant.

TENNANT, Maj.-Gen. Michael Trenchard; Director Royal Artillery, since 1991; *b* 3 Sept. 1941; *s* of Lt-Col Hugh Trenchard Tennant, MC and Mary Isobel Tennant (*née* Wilkie); *m* 1964, Susan Daphne, *d* of Lt-Col Frank Beale, LVO; three *s. Educ:* Wellington College. psc†. Commissioned RA 1961; served Bahrain, Aden, BAOR, Hong Kong, UK, 1962–71; Staff College, 1972–73; MoD, 1974–75; Bty Comdr, 127 (Dragon) Bty, BAOR, 1976–78; Directing Staff, Staff Coll., 1978–80; CO, 1 RHA, UK and BAOR, 1980–83; Comdr British Training Team, Nigeria, 1983–85; CRA 3 Armd Div., BAOR, 1985–87; CRA UKLF, 1988–91. *Recreations:* bridge, golf, tennis. *Address:* c/o Lloyds Bank (Cox's & King's), 7 Pall Mall, SW1Y 5NA. *Club:* Army and Navy.

TENNANT, Sir Peter (Frank Dalrymple), Kt 1972; CMG 1958; OBE 1945; Director-General, British National Export Council, 1965–71; Industrial Adviser, Barclays Bank International Ltd, 1972–81; Director: Prudential Assurance Company Ltd, 1973–81; Prudential Corporation plc, 1979–86; C. Tennant Sons & Company Ltd, 1972–80; Anglo-Romanian Bank, 1973–81; Northern Engineering Industries (International) Ltd, 1979–82; International Energy Bank, 1981–84; *b* 29 Nov. 1910; *s* of G. F. D. Tennant and Barbara Tennant (*née* Beck); *m* 1st, 1934 (marr. diss. 1952), Hellis, *d* of Professor Fellenius, Stockholm; one *s* two *d*; 2nd, 1953, Galina Bosley, *d* of K. Grunberg, Helsinki; one step *s. Educ:* Marlborough; Trinity College, Cambridge. Sen. Mod. Languages Scholar, Trinity College, Cambridge, 1929; Cholmondely Studentship, Lincoln's Inn; 1st Cl. Hons Mod. Langs Tripos, 1931; BA 1931, MA 1936, Cambridge. Cambridge Scandinavian Studentship, Oslo, Copenhagen, Stockholm, 1932–33; Fellow Queens' College, Cambridge, and University Lecturer, Scandinavian Languages, 1933; Press Attaché, British Legation, Stockholm, 1939–45; Information Counsellor, British Embassy, Paris, 1945–50; Deputy Commandant, British Sector, Berlin, 1950–52; resigned Foreign Service to become Overseas Director, FBI, 1952–63. Deputy Director-General, FBI, 1963–65. Special Advr, CBI, 1964–65. Former Mem., Council of Industrial Design; past acting Chm., Wilton Park Academic Council; former Mem. Bd, Centre for Internat. Briefing, Farnham Castle; past Chm., Gabbitas Thring Educational Trust; Pres., London Chamber of Commerce and Industry, 1978–79 (Chm., 1976–78); Chm., British Cttee, European Cultural Foundn, 1975–90. Vis. Fellow, St Cross Coll., Oxford, 1982. MA Oxford, 1982. *Publications:* Ibsen's Dramatic Technique, 1947; The Scandinavian Book, 1952; (in Swedish) Touchlines of War, 1989. *Recreations:* writing, talking, painting, travel, languages, sailing, country life. *Address:* Blue Anchor House, Linchmere Road, Haslemere, Surrey GU27 3QF. *T:* Haslemere (0428) 3124. *Club:* Travellers'.

TENNEKOON, Victor; Chairman, Law Commission of Sri Lanka, since 1978; *b* 9 Sept. 1914; *s* of Loku Banda Tennekoon and Nandu Menike Tennekoon (*née* Rambukwella); *m* 1946, Semitha Murie Wijeyewardene; one *s* two *d. Educ:* St Anthony's Coll., Kandy; University Coll., Colombo. BA London Univ. (External) 1935. Called to Sri Lanka Bar, 1942. QC 1965. Practised at Kegalle, 1943–46; Crown Counsel, 1946; Solicitor-General, 1964; Attorney-General, 1970; Judge of Court of Appeal, Sri Lanka, 1973; Chief Justice of Sri Lanka, 1974–77. Chancellor, Univ. of Peradeniya, 1979–84. *Recreations:* tennis, golf, billiards, bridge, chess. *Address:* 40/1 Ananda Coomaraswamy Nawata, Green Path, Colombo 3, Sri Lanka. *T:* 20853. *Club:* Orient (Colombo).

TENNSTEDT, Klaus; Principal Conductor and Music Director, The London Philharmonic, 1983–87, now Conductor Laureate; *b* 6 June 1926; *s* of Hermann and Agnes Tennstedt; *m* 1960, Ingeborg Fischer. *Educ:* Leipzig Conservatory (violin, piano). Conductor at: Landersoper, Dresden, 1958–62; Staatstheater, Schwerin, 1962–70; Operhaus, Kiel, 1972–76; guest conductor with Boston, Chicago, New York Philharmonic, Cleveland, Philadelphia, Berlin and Israel Philharmonic Orchestras. Hon. RAM, 1990. Hon. DMus Colgate Hamilton, NY State, 1984. Officer's Cross, Order of Merit (FRG), 1986. *Recreations:* astronomy, hot air ballooning. *Address:* c/o The London Philharmonic, 35 Doughty Street, WC1N 2AA. *T:* 071–833 2744.

TENNYSON, family name of **Baron Tennyson.**

TENNYSON, 4th Baron *cr* 1884; **Harold Christopher Tennyson;** *b* 25 March 1919; *e s* of 3rd Baron and Hon. Clarissa Tennant (*d* 1960), *o d* of 1st Baron Glenconner; *S* father 1951. *Educ:* Eton; Trinity Coll., Cambridge. BA 1940. Employed War Office, 1939–46. Co-founder, Tennyson Research Centre, Lincoln. Hon. Freeman, City of Lincoln, 1964. *Heir: b* Hon. Mark Aubrey Tennyson, DSC 1943; RN retd [*b* 28 March 1920; *m* 1964, Deline Celeste Budler. *Educ:* RN College, Dartmouth. Served War of 1939–45 (despatches, DSC); Comdr RN, 1954]. *Address:* 18 Rue Galilée, 75016 Paris, France. *Clubs:* White's, Royal Automobile; Royal and Ancient.

TENNYSON-d'EYNCOURT, Sir Mark (Gervais), 5th Bt *cr* 1930, of Carter's Corner Farm, Herstmonceux; *b* 12 March 1967; *o s* of Sir Giles Gervais Tennyson-d'Eyncourt, 4th Bt and of Juanita, *d* of late Fortunato Borromeo; *S* father, 1989. *Heir:* none. *Educ:* Charterhouse; Kingston Polytechnic (BA Hons Fashion). Freeman, City of London. *Address:* 775 Wandsworth Road, SW8 3JG. *T:* 071–978 2562.

TENZIN GYATSO; The Dalai Lama XIV; spiritual and temporal leader of Tibet, since 1940; *b* 6 July 1935; named Lhamo Thondup; *s* of Chokyong Tsering and Diki Tsering. *Educ:* Monasteries of Sera, Drepung and Gaden, Lhasa; traditional Tibetan degree equivalent to Dr in Buddhist philosophy, 1959. Enthroned Dalai Lama, Lhasa, 1940; given name Jetsun Jampel Ngawang Losang Yeshi Tenzin Gyatso Sisum Wang-gyur Tsungpa Mepai De Pel Sangpo. Fled to Chumbi, South Tibet, on Chinese invasion, 1950; negotiated with China, 1951; fled to India after abortive revolt of Tibetan people against Communist Chinese, 1959, and established govt-in-exile in Dharamsala. Awards include: Magsaysay, Philippines, 1959; Lincoln, USA, 1960; Albert Schweitzer Humanitarian, USA, 1987; numerous other awards, hon. doctorates, hon. citizenships from France, Germany, India, Mongolia, Norway, USA; Nobel Peace Prize, 1989. *Publications:* My Land and My People, 1962; The Opening of the Wisdom Eye, 1963; An Introduction to Buddhism, 1965; Key to the Middle Way, 1971; Universal Responsibility and Good Heart, 1977; Four Essential Buddhist Commentaries, 1982; A Human Approach to World Peace, 1984; Kindness, Clarity and Insight, 1987; Freedom in Exile, 1990. *Address:* Thekchen Choeling, Mcleod Ganj 176219, Dharamsala, HP, India.

TEŌ, Sir (Fiatau) Penitala, GCMG 1979; GCVO 1982; ISO 1970; MBE 1956; Governor-General of Tuvalu, 1978–86; *b* 23 July 1911; *s* of Teō Veli, Niutao, and Tilesa Samuelu, Funafuti; *m* 1st, 1931, Muniara Apelu, Vaitupu; one *d* (one *s* decd); 2nd, 1949, Uimai Tofiga, Nanumaga; eight *s* three *d* (and one *d* decd). *Educ:* Elisefou, Vaitupu, Tuvalu. Asst Sch. Master, Elisefou, 1930–32; Clerk and Ellice Interpreter: Dist Admin, Funafuti, 1932–37; Resident Comr's Office, Ocean Is., 1937–42; under Japanese Occupation (Ocean Is. and Tarawa), 1942–43 (1939–45 Star, Pacific Star and War Medal); re-joined Res. Comr's Office, 1943 (i/c Labour Force), Special Clerk 1944; Asst Admin. Officer and Mem., Gilbert and Ellice Is Defence Force (2nd Lieut), 1944; Asst and Actg Dist Officer for Ellice Is, 1944–50; transf. to Tarawa to re-organise Information Office, 1953; Dep. Comr for Western Pacific, 1960; Lands Officer for Gilbert and Ellice Is, 1960–62; Dist Commissioner: Ocean Is., 1963; Ellice Is, 1967–69; Asst and Actg Supt of Labour, British Phosphate Comrs, Ocean Is., 1971–78. ADC to High Comr of Western Pacific during tours, 1954 and 1957; Dist Officer for visit of Prince Philip to Vaitupu Is., Ellice Is, 1959. Represented Gilbert and Ellice Is at confs, and Festival of Britain, 1951. Coronation Medal, 1953. *Recreations:* formerly fishing, cricket, football, Rugby, local games. *Address:* Alapi, Funafuti, Tuvalu.

TERESA, Mother, (Agnes Gonxha Bojaxhiu), MC; Hon. OM 1983; Hon. OBE 1978; Padma Shri, 1962; Bharat Ratna (Jewel of India), 1980; Roman Catholic nun; *b* Skopje, Yugoslavia, 27 Aug. 1910; *d* of Albanian parents. *Educ:* government school in Yugoslavia. Joined Sisters of Loretto, Rathfarnam, Ireland, 1929; trained at Loretto insts in Ireland and India; came to Calcutta, 1929; Principal, St Mary's High School, Calcutta. Founded the Missionaries of Charity (Sisters), 1950, Missionary Brothers of Charity, 1963, the Internat. Co-Workers of Mother Teresa, 1969, Missionaries of Charity, Sisters Contemplatives, 1976, Brothers of the Word Contemplatives, 1979, and Missionaries of Charity Fathers, 1983, to give free service to the poor and the unwanted, irrespective of caste, creed, nationality, race or place; she has set up: slum schools; orphanages; Nirmol Hridoy (Pure Heart) Homes for sick and dying street cases; Shishu Bhavan Homes for unwanted, crippled and mentally-retarded children; mobile gen. clinics and centres for malnourished; mobile clinics and rehabilitation centres for leprosy patients; homes for drug addicts and alcoholics; night shelters for the homeless. Hon. DD Cambridge, 1977; Hon. DrMed: Catholic Univ. of Sacred Heart, Rome, 1981; Catholic Univ. of Louvain, 1982. Ramón Magsaysay Internat. Award, 1962; Pope John XXIII Peace Prize, 1971; Kennedy Internat. Award, 1971; Jawaharlal Nehru Internat. Award, 1972; Templeton Foundation Prize, 1973; first Albert Schweitzer Internat. Prize, 1975; Nobel Peace Prize, 1979, and many other awards too numerous to mention. Hon. Citizen, Assisi, 1982. *Publication:* Gift for God, 1975; *relevant publications* include: Something Beautiful for God, by Malcolm Muggeridge; Mother Teresa, her people and her works, by Desmond Doig; Such a Vision of the Street, by Eileen Egan. *Address:* 54A Acharya Jagadish Chandra Bose Road, Calcutta 700016, India. *T:* 29.7115.

TERESHKOVA, Valentina N.; *see* Nikolayeva-Tereshkova.

TERLEZKI, Stefan; *b* Ukraine, 29 Oct. 1927; *s* of late Oleksa Terlezki and Olena Terlezki; *m* 1955, Mary; two *d. Educ:* Cardiff Coll. of Food Technol. and Commerce. Member: Hotel and Catering Inst., 1965–80; Chamber of Trade, 1975–80. Member: Cardiff CC, 1968–83 (Press Officer, 1970–83; Chairman: Licensing Cttee, 1975–78; Environment Services Cttee, 1978–80; Housing Liaison Cttee, 1978–80); S Glam CC, 1973–85; S Wales Police Auth., 1975–80; Welsh Jt Educn Cttee, 1975–85; Chm., Jt Consultative Cttee, S Glam Health Auth., 1978–79; Member: Educn Authority for Cardiff CC and S Glam CC, 1969–85; Planning, Finance and Policy Cttee, 1965–83. Member: Welsh Tourist Council, 1965–80; Welsh Games Council, 1974–80. Contested (C): Cardiff South East, Feb. and Oct. 1974; Cardiff West, 1987; South Wales, European Parly elecn, 1979. MP (C) Cardiff West, 1983–87. Mem., Parly Select Cttee on Welsh Affairs, 1983–87. Chairman: Keep Britain in Europe Campaign, 1973–75; Cons. Gp for European Movement, 1973–75; Foreign Affairs Forum, 1974–. Vice-Pres., Wales Area Young Conservatives, 1975–80; Member: Central Council, CPC, 1979–83; Official Nat. Speaking Panels of Cons. Party, European Movement, and Eur. Parlt; British delegn, Council of Europe, 1985–87 (Mem. Convention Cttee for the Prevention of Torture and In-Human or Degradation Treatment and Punishment, 1989–); WEU, 1985–87; UK Br., CPA; Industry and Parlt Trust; British Gp, IPU, 1987–; UN Temple of Peace, Cardiff, 1979–87; Rapporteur, Assembly of Western European Community for Parly and Public Relns, 1986–87. Chairman: Cardiff City Football Club, 1975–77; Cardiff High Sch. Bd of Governors, 1975–83. Languages: Ukrainian, Polish, Russian, German (basic). Radio and television broadcasts; occasional journalism. Silver Jubilee Medal, 1977. *Recreations:* foreign affairs, defence, European Community, East-West Relations, glasnost and perestroika, law and order, senior citizens, debates, sport, travel. *Address:* 16 Bryngwyn Road, Cyncoed, Cardiff CF2 6PQ. *T:* Cardiff (0222) 759524.

TERRAINE, John Alfred, FRHistS; author; *b* 15 Jan. 1921; *s* of Charles William Terraine and Eveline Holmes; *m* 1945, Joyce Eileen Waite; one *d. Educ:* Stamford Sch.;

Keble Coll., Oxford (Hon. Fellow, 1986). Joined BBC, 1944; Pacific and S African Programme Organiser, 1953–63; resigned from BBC, 1964. Associate producer and chief scriptwriter of The Great War, BBC TV, 1963–64; part-scriptwriter The Lost Peace, BBC TV, 1965; scriptwriter, The Life and Times of Lord Mountbatten, Rediffusion/Thames TV, 1966–68; scriptwriter, The Mighty Continent, BBC TV, 1974–75. Founder Pres., Western Front Assoc., 1980–; Mem. Council, RUSI, 1976–84. FRHistS 1987. Chesney Gold Medal, RUSI, 1982. C. P. Robertson Meml Trophy, Air Public Relations Assoc., 1985. *Publications:* Mons: The Retreat to Victory, 1960; Douglas Haig: The Educated Soldier, 1963; The Western Front, 1964; General Jack's Diary, 1964; The Great War: An Illustrated History, 1965 (NY), unillustrated reprint, The First World War, 1983; The Life and Times of Lord Mountbatten, 1968; Impacts of War 1914 and 1918, 1970; The Mighty Continent, 1974; Trafalgar, 1976; The Road to Passchendaele, 1977; To Win a War: 1918 The Year of Victory, 1978; The Smoke and the Fire, 1980; White Heat: The New Warfare 1914–1918, 1982; The Right of the Line: the Royal Air Force in the European War 1939–45, 1985 (Yorkshire Post Book of the Year Award, 1985); Business in Great Waters: the U-Boat Wars 1916–1945, 1989. *Recreation:* convivial and congenial conversation. *Address:* 74 Kensington Park Road, W11 2PL. *T:* 071–229 8152.

TERRELL, Colonel Stephen, OBE 1952; TD; QC 1965; DL. Called to the Bar, Gray's Inn, 1946; Bencher, Gray's Inn, 1970. South Eastern Circuit. Pres., Liberal Party, 1972. Contested (L) Eastbourne, Feb. 1974. DL Middlesex, 1961.

TERRINGTON, 4th Baron, *cr* 1918, of Huddersfield; **James Allen David Woodhouse;** former Member, Stock Exchange; Partner in Sheppards and Chase, 1952–80; *b* 30 December 1915; *er s* of 3rd Baron Terrington, KBE, and Valerie (*née* Phillips) (*d* 1958), Leyden's House, Edenbridge, Kent; *S* father, 1961; *m* 1942, Suzanne, *y d* of Colonel T. S. Irwin, DL, JP, late Royal Dragoons, Justicetown, Carlisle, and Mill House, Holton, Suffolk; three *d*. *Educ:* Winchester; Royal Military College, Sandhurst. Commnd Royal Norfolk Regiment, TA, 1936. Farming in Norfolk, 1936–39. Served War of 1939–45 in India, North Africa and Middle East (wounded); ADC to GOC Madras, 1940; Staff Coll., Haifa, 1944; psc 1944; GSOII, Allied Force HQ Algiers, Ninth Army, Middle East, and War Office, Military Operations; retired as Major, 1948; joined Queen's Westminster Rifles (KRRC), TA. Joined Messrs Chase Henderson and Tennant, 1949 (now Sheppards and Chase). Deputy Chairman of Cttees, House of Lords, 1961–63. Member: Ecclesiastical Cttee, 1979–; Exec. Cttee, Wider Shareownership Council, 1981– (former Dep. Chm. of Council); Dep. Chm., Nat. Listening Library (Talking Books for the Disabled), 1977–. Vice-Pres., Small Farmers' Assoc., 1986–. Mem. Internat. Adv. Bd, American Univ., Washington DC, 1985–. *Recreations:* fishing, gardening. *Heir:* *b* Hon. Christopher Montague Woodhouse, *qv*. *Address:* The Mill House, Breamore, near Fordingbridge, Hampshire SP6 2AF. *Clubs:* Boodle's, Pratt's.

See also Earl Alexander of Tunis.

TERRY, Sir George (Walter Roberts), Kt 1982; CBE 1976; QPM 1967; DL; Chief Constable of Sussex, 1973–83; *b* 29 May 1921; *s* of late Walter George Tygh Terry and Constance Elizabeth Terry; *m* 1942, Charlotte Elizabeth Kresina; one *s*. *Educ:* Peterborough, Northants. Served War, Northamptonshire Regt, in Italy, 1942–46 (Staff Captain). Chief Constable: Pembrokeshire, 1958–65; East Sussex, 1965–67; Dep. Chief Constable, Sussex, 1968–69; Chief Constable, Lincolnshire, 1970–73. Chm., Traffic Cttee, 1976–79, Pres., 1980–81, Assoc. of Chief Police Officers; Dir, Police Extended Interviews, 1977–83. Dir, Terrafix Ltd, 1984–. Trustee: Disabled Housing Trust, 1985–; Coll. of Driver Educn, 1989–. CStJ. DL E Sussex, 1983. *Recreations:* horticulture, motoring. *Address:* c/o National Westminster Bank, 173 High Street, Lewes, Sussex BN7 1XD.

TERRY, Sir John Elliott, Kt 1976; Consultant with Denton Hall & Burgin; Managing Director, National Film Finance Corporation, 1958–78; *b* 11 June 1913; *s* of Ernest Fairchild Terry, OBE, FRICS, and Zabelle Terry (*née* Costikyan), Pulborough, Sussex; *m* 1940, Joan Christine, *d* of Frank Alfred Ernest Howard Fell and Ethel Christine Fell (*née* Nilson), Stoke D'Abernon, Surrey; one *s* one *d*. *Educ:* Mill Hill School; Univ. of London (LLB). Articled with Denton Hall & Burgin, London; admitted solicitor, 1938. London Fire Service, 1939–40; Friends' Ambulance Unit, 1941–44; Nat. Council of Social Service, 1944–46; Film Producers' Guild, 1946–47; The Rank Organisation's Legal Dept, 1947–49; joined Nat. Film Finance Corp. as Solicitor, 1949, also Sec., 1956. Governor: Nat. Film Sch., 1970–81; London Internat. Film Sch., 1982–90; Royal Nat. Coll. for the Blind, 1980–; Pres., Copinger Soc., 1981–83. *Address:* Still Point, Branscombe, Devon. *Club:* Savile.

TERRY, (John) Quinlan, FRIBA 1962; architect in private practice, since 1967; *b* 24 July 1937; *s* of late Philip and of Phyllis Terry; *m* 1961, Christine de Ruttié; one *s* four *d*. *Educ:* Bryanston School; Architectural Association; Rome Scholar. Assistant to Raymond Erith, RA, FRIBA, 1962, Partner 1967–, Erith & Terry; work includes: new country houses in classical style; Ionic, Veneto and Gothick Villas, Regent's Park for Crown Estate Comrs; Common Room Building, Gray's Inn; offices, shops, flats and public gardens at Richmond Riverside; new Lecture Theatre and new Library, Downing Coll., Cambridge; new Brentwood Cathedral; restoration of the three State Drawing Rooms, 10 Downing Street. *Recreation:* the Pauline epistles. *Address:* Old Exchange, High Street, Dedham, Colchester, Essex CO7 6HA. *T:* Colchester (0206) 323186.

TERRY, Sir Michael Edward Stanley I.; *see* Imbert-Terry.

TERRY, Air Chief Marshal Sir Peter (David George), GCB 1983 (KCB 1978; CB 1975); AFC 1968; QCVSA 1959 and 1962; *b* 18 Oct. 1926; *s* of James George Terry and Laura Chilton Terry (*née* Powell); *m* 1946, Betty Martha Louisa Thompson; one *s* one *d* (and one *s* decd). *Educ:* Chatham House Sch., Ramsgate. Joined RAF, 1945; commnd in RAF Regt, 1946; Pilot, 1953. Staff Coll., 1962; OC, No 51 Sqdn, 1966–68; OC, RAF El Adem, 1968–70; Dir, Air Staff Briefing, MoD, 1970–71; Dir of Forward Policy for RAF, 1971–74; ACOS (Policy and Plans), SHAPE, 1975–77; VCAS, 1977–79; C-in-C RAF Germany and Comdr Second Allied Tactical Air Force, 1979–81; Dep. C-in-C, Allied Forces Central Europe, Feb.-April 1981; Dep. Supreme Allied Commander, Europe, 1981–84; Governor and C-in-C, Gibraltar, 1985–89. Trustee, Imperial War Museum, 1989–. Vice-Pres., Re-Solv, 1985–. KStJ 1986. *Recreation:* golf. *Address:* 17 Main Road, Milford, Stafford ST17 0UL. *T:* Stafford (0785) 661168. *Club:* Royal Air Force.

TERRY, Quinlan; *see* Terry, J. Q.

TESH, Robert Mathieson, CMG 1968; HM Diplomatic Service, retired; Ambassador to Ethiopia, 1979–82; *b* 15 Sept. 1922; *s* of late E. Tesh, Hurst Green, Surrey; *m* 1950, Jean Bowker; two *s* one *d*. *Educ:* Queen Elizabeth's, Wakefield; Queen's College, Oxford (MA). Oxford, 1940–42 and 1945–47; Rifle Brigade, 1942–45; HM Foreign Service, 1947: New Delhi, 1948–50; FO, 1950–53 and 1957–60; Delegation to NATO, Paris, 1953–55; Beirut, 1955–57; Bangkok, 1960–64; Dep. High Comr, Ghana, 1965–66; Lusaka, 1966; Consul-General British Interests Section, Canadian Embassy, Cairo, 1966–67; Counsellor, British Embassy, Cairo, 1968; IDC, 1969; Head of Defence Dept, FCO, 1970–72; Ambassador to Bahrain, 1972–75; Ambassador to: the Democratic Republic of Vietnam, 1976; the Socialist Republic of Vietnam, 1976–78; FCO, 1978–79. *Recreations:* singing, acting, golf. *Address:* Ashenden, 10 Albany Close, Esher, Surrey KT10 9JR. *T:* Esher (0372) 64192. *Club:* Travellers'.

TESLER, Brian, CBE 1986; Deputy Chairman, LWT (Holdings) plc, since 1990; Chairman: London Weekend Television Ltd, since 1984 (Managing Director, 1976–90; Deputy Chairman, 1982–84; Deputy Chief Executive, 1974–76); The London Studios Ltd (formerly LWT Production Facilities Ltd), since 1989; LWT International Ltd, since 1990; LWT Programmes Ltd, since 1990; *b* 19 Feb. 1929; *s* of late David Tesler and of Stella Tesler; *m* 1959, Audrey Mary Maclean; one *s*. *Educ:* Chiswick County School for Boys; Exeter Coll., Oxford (State Schol.; MA). Theatre Editor, The Isis, 1950–51; Pres., Oxford Univ. Experimental Theatre Club, 1951–52. British Forces Broadcasting Service, 1947–49; Producer/Director: BBC Television, 1952; ATV, 1957; ABC Television: Head of Features and Light Entertainment, 1960; Programme Controller, 1961; Dir of Programmes, 1962; Dir of Programmes, Thames Television, 1968. Chairman: ITV Superchannel Ltd, 1986–88; ITCA, 1980–82; Indep. TV Network Prog. Cttee, 1976–78, 1986–88; ITCA Cable and Satellite Television Wkg Party, 1981–88; ITV Film Purchase Cttee, 1989–90. Director: ITN, 1979–90; Channel Four Television Ltd, 1980–85; Oracle Teletext Ltd, 1980–; Services Sound and Vision Corp. (formerly Services Kinema Corp.), 1981–. Member: Lord Chancellor's Adv. Cttee on JPs, 1991–; British Screen Adv. Council, 1985– (Wkg Party on Future of British Film Industry, 1975–77; Interim Action Cttee on Film Industry, 1977–85); TRIC, 1979– (Pres., 1979–80); Vice-Pres., RTS, 1984–. Governor: Nat. Film and TV Sch. (formerly Nat. Film Sch.), 1977–; BFI, 1986–. Daily Mail Nat. TV Award, 1954; Guild of Television Producers and Directors Award, 1957; Lord Willis Trophy for Outstanding Services to Television, Pye Television Award, 1986; TRIC President's Award, 1991. *Recreations:* books, theatre, cinema, music. *Address:* LWT (Holdings) plc, The London Studios, Kent House, Upper Ground, SE1 9LT. *T:* 071–620 1620.

TESTAFERRATA, Marquis; *see* San Vincenzo Ferreri, Marquis of.

TETLEY, Glen; choreographer, since 1948; *b* 3 Feb. 1926; *s* of Glenford Andrew Tetley and Mary Eleanor (*née* Byrne). *Educ:* Franklyn and Marshal Coll., Lancaster, USA (pre-med); New York Univ. (BSc). Studied medicine, then dance with Hanya Holm, Antony Tudor, Martha Graham. Danced with Holm's Co., 1946–51; New York City Opera, 1952–54; John Butler Dance Theatre, 1955; Joffrey Ballet, 1956–57; Martha Graham Co., 1958; American Ballet Theatre, 1960; Robbins Ballets USA, 1961. Joined Netherlands Dance Theatre as dancer and choreographer, 1962, eventually becoming artistic co-director; directed own company, 1969; Dir, Stuttgart Ballet, 1974–76. *Choreography:* Pierrot Lunaire, own company, 1962, Ballet Rambert, 1985; Netherlands Dance Theatre: The Anatomy Lesson, 1964; Circles, 1968; Imaginary Film, 1970; Mutations, 1970; Summer's End, 1980; American Ballet Company: Ricercare, 1966; Nocturne, 1977; Sphinx, 1977; Contredances, 1979; Ballet Rambert: Freefall, 1967; Ziggurat, 1967; Embrace Tiger and Return to Mountain, 1968; Rag Dances, 1971; Praeludium, 1978; The Tempest, first full-length work, 1979; Murderer, Hope of Women, 1983; Royal Ballet: Field Figures, 1970; Laborintus, 1972; Dances of Albion, 1980; Stuttgart Ballet: Voluntaries, 1973; Daphnis and Chloe, 1975; Greening, 1975; Nat. Ballet of Canada: Alice, 1986; La Ronde, 1987; Tagore, 1989; also: Le Sacre du Printemps, Munich State Opera Ballet, 1974; Tristan, Paris Opera, 1974; Firebird, Royal Danish Ballet, 1981; Revelation and Fall, Australian Dance Theatre, 1984; Pulcinella, Festival Ballet, 1984; Dream Walk of the Shaman, Aterballetto, 1985; Orpheus, Australian Ballet, 1987; Dialogues, Dance Theatre of Harlem, 1991. Queen Elizabeth Coronation Award, Royal Acad. of Dancing, 1980; Prix Italia, 1982; Ohioana Career Medal, 1986; NY Univ. Achievement Award, 1988. *Address:* 15 West Ninth Street, New York, NY 10011, USA. *T:* (212) 475 4604.

TETLEY, Sir Herbert, KBE 1965; CB 1958; Government Actuary, 1958–73; *b* 23 April 1908; *s* of Albert Tetley, Leeds; *m* 1941, Agnes Maclean Macfarlane Macphee; one *s*. *Educ:* Leeds Grammar School; The Queen's College, Oxford. Hastings Scholar, Queen's College, 1927–30; 1st Cl. Hons Mods (Mathematics), 1928; 1st Cl. Final Hons School of Mathematics, 1930. Fellow of Institute of Actuaries, 1934; Fellow of Royal Statistical Society; served with London Life Assoc., 1930–36; Scottish Provident Instn, 1936–38; National Provident Instn, 1938–51 (Joint Actuary). Joined Government Actuary's Dept as Principal Actuary, 1951; Deputy Government Actuary, 1953; Chairman: Civil Service Insurance Soc., 1961–73; Cttee on Economics Road Research Board, 1962–65; Cttee on Road Traffic Research, 1966–73. Pres., Inst. of Actuaries, 1964–66. *Publications:* Actuarial Statistics, Vol. I, 1946; (jtly) Statistics, An Intermediate Text Book, Vol. I, 1949, Vol. II, 1950. *Recreations:* gardening, music, fell-walking. *Address:* 37 Upper Brighton Road, Surbiton, Surrey KT6 6QX. *T:* 081–399 3001.

TETLEY, Air Vice-Marshal John Francis Humphrey, CB 1987; CVO 1978; *b* 5 Feb. 1932; *s* of Humphrey and Evelyn Tetley; *m* 1960, Elizabeth, *d* of Wing Comdr Arthur Stevens; two *s*. *Educ:* Malvern College. RAF Coll., Cranwell, 1950–53; served No 249 Sqn, No 204 Sqn and HQ Coastal Command, 1955–64; RAF Staff Coll., 1964; HQ Middle East Command, 1965–67; OC No 24 Sqn, 1968–70; JSSC 1970; MoD (Air), 1971–72; RAF Germany, 1973–75; Dir Air Staff Briefing, MoD (Air), 1975–76; Silver Jubilee Project Officer, 1977; RCDS, 1978; SASO HQ 38 Group, 1979–82; Dir of Ops (Air Support), RAF, 1982–83; AO Scotland and NI, 1983–86; Sen. Directing Staff (Air), RCDS, 1986–87; retired 1987. Mem. Cttee of Management, RNLI, 1987–. *Recreations:* gardening, photography, boating. *Club:* Royal Air Force.

TETLEY, Kenneth James; a Recorder of Crown and County Courts, since 1972; *b* Ashton-under-Lyne, Lancs, 17 Oct. 1921; *o s* of William Tetley, Dukinfield, Cheshire, and Annie Lees, Oldham; *m* 1945, Edna Rita, *e d* of Peter Charles Spurrin Gray and Annie Gray, Audenshaw, Manchester; one *s* three *d*. *Educ:* Ashton-under-Lyne Grammar Sch.; Manchester Univ. Served War of 1939–45: joined RN, 1941; Lieut RNVR (attached Combined Ops); discharged, 1945. Admitted Solicitor, 1947; Councillor, Ashton-under-Lyne Borough Council, 1955; Alderman, 1967. *Recreations:* Rugby Union football, fell-walking, photography. *Address:* 6 Pine Lodge, 28 London Road South, Poynton, Stockport, Cheshire SK12 1NJ. *T:* (home) Poynton (0625) 859126; (office) 061–330 2865. *Clubs:* Rugby (Ashton-under-Lyne); Romiley Golf; Lancashire County RFU.

TETT, Sir Hugh (Charles), Kt 1966; ARCS, BSc, DIC; *b* Exeter, Devon, 28 Oct. 1906; *e s* of late James Charles Tett and late Florence Tett (*née* Lihou); *m* 1st, 1931, Katie Sargent (*d* 1948); one *d*; 2nd, 1949, Joyce Lilian (*née* Mansell) (*d* 1979); one *d*; 3rd, 1980, Barbara Mary (*née* Mackenzie). *Educ:* Hele's School, Exeter; University College, Exeter; Royal College of Science (Kitchener's Scholar). Joined Esso Petroleum Co. Ltd, 1928; Technical Advisory Committee, Petroleum Board, 1940–45; Lieut-Colonel, Combined Intelligence Objectives Sub-Cttee, 1944–45; Chairman of Council, Institute of Petroleum, 1947–48; Managing Director, Esso Research Ltd, 1947–49; Director, Esso Petroleum Co. Ltd, 1951, Chairman, 1959–67. Member: Council for Scientific and Industrial Research, 1961–64; Advisory Council, Ministry of Technology, 1964–67. Chairman, Economic Development Cttee for Motor Manufacturing Industry, 1967–69. Pro-Chancellor, Univ. of

Southampton, 1967–79. Fellow, Imperial Coll. of Science and Technology, 1964. Hon. DSc: Southampton, 1965; Exeter, 1970. *Address:* Primrose Cottage, Bosham, Chichester, West Sussex PO18 8HZ. *T:* Bosham (0243) 572705. *Club:* Athenæum.

TEUSNER, Hon. Berthold Herbert, CMG 1972; JP; Solicitor since 1931; Speaker, South Australian Parliament, 1956–62; *b* 16 May 1907; *s* of Carl Theodor Teusner and Agnes Sophie Elisabeth Teusner (*née* Christian); *m* 1934, Viola Hilda Kleeman; two *s. Educ:* Immanuel Coll., Adelaide; Univ. of Adelaide (LLB). Legal Practice at Tanunda, SA, 1932–. MP for Angas, S Australian Parlt, 1944–70; Govt Whip, 1954–55; Dep. Speaker and Chm. of Cttees: 1955–56, 1962–65 and 1968–70. Councillor, Dist. Council of Tanunda, 1936–56 (Chm. for 17 years); JP, 1939–. Member: Bd of Governors, Adelaide Botanical Gdns, 1956–70; SA Nat. Fitness Council, 1953–70; Royal Adelaide Hosp. and Queen Elizabeth Hosp. Advisory Cttees (Chm., 1962–65); Immanuel Coll. Council, 1933–71; Hon. Assoc. Life Mem., SA Br. of Commonwealth Parly Assoc.; Mem., Transport Control Bd of SA, 1971–74. *Recreations:* bowls, gardening. *Address:* 18 Elizabeth Street, Tanunda, SA 5352, Australia. *T:* 632422.

TEVIOT, 2nd Baron, *cr* 1940, of Burghclere; **Charles John Kerr;** genealogist; *b* 16 Dec. 1934; *s* of 1st Baron Teviot, DSO, MC, and Florence Angela (*d* 1979), *d* of late Lt-Col Charles Walter Villiers, CBE, DSO; *S* father, 1968; *m* 1965, Patricia Mary Harris; one *s* one *d. Educ:* Eton. Bus Conductor and Driver; genealogical and historical record agent. Director: Debrett's Peerage Ltd, 1977–83; Burke's Peerage Research, 1983–85; Burke's Peerage Ltd, 1984–85. Mem., Adv. Council on Public Records, 1974–83. Fellow, Soc. of Genealogists, 1975. *Recreations:* reading, walking. *Heir: s* Hon. Charles Robert Kerr, *b* 19 Sept. 1971. *Address:* The Knoll, Stockcroft Road, Balcombe, West Sussex RH17 6LG. *T:* Haywards Heath (0444) 811654.

TEW, Prof. John Hedley Brian, OBE 1988; PhD; External Professor, Economics Department, University of Loughborough, since 1982; Midland Bank Professor of Money and Banking, University of Nottingham, 1967–82; *b* 1 Feb. 1917; *s* of Herbert and Catherine Mary Tew; *m* 1944, Marjorie Hoey Craigie; one *s* one *d. Educ:* Mill Hill School, Leicester; University College, Leicester; Peterhouse, Cambridge. BSc (Econ.) London; PhD Cantab. Iron and Steel Control, 1940–42; Ministry of Aircraft Production, 1942–45; Industrial and Commercial Finance Corp., 1946; Professor of Economics, Univ. of Adelaide (Australia), 1947–49; Professor of Economics, University of Nottingham, 1950–67. Part-time Member: Iron and Steel Board, 1964–67; East Midlands Electricity Board, 1965–76; Tubes Div., BSC, 1969–73; Mem., Cttee of Enquiry on Small Firms, Dept of Trade and Industry, 1969–71. *Publications:* Wealth and Income, 1950; International Monetary Co-operation 1952; (jt editor) Studies in Company Finance, 1959; Monetary Theory, 1969; The Evolution of the International Monetary System, 1977. *Address:* 121 Bramcote Lane, Wollaton, Notts NG8 2NJ.

TEWKESBURY, Bishop Suffragan of, since 1986; **Rt. Rev. Geoffrey David Jeremy Walsh;** *b* 7 Dec. 1929; *s* of late Howard Wilton Walsh, OBE and Helen Maud Walsh (*née* Lovell); *m* 1961, Cynthia Helen, *d* of late F. P. Knight, FLS, VMH, and H. I. C. Knight, OBE; two *s* one *d. Educ:* Felsted Sch., Essex; Pembroke Coll., Cambridge (MA Econ.); Lincoln Theological Coll. Curate, Christ Church, Southgate, London, 1955–58; Staff Sec., SCM, and Curate, St Mary the Great, Cambridge, 1958–61; Vicar, St Matthew, Moorfields, Bristol, 1961–66; Rector of Marlborough, Wilts, 1966–76; Rector of Elmsett with Aldham, 1976–80; Archdeacon of Ipswich, 1976–86. Hon. Canon, Salisbury Cathedral, 1973–76. *Recreations:* gardening, golf, bird-watching. *Address:* Green Acre, 166 Hempsted Lane, Gloucester GL2 6LG. *T:* Gloucester (0452) 521824.

TEYNHAM, 20th Baron *cr* 1616; **John Christopher Ingham Roper-Curzon;** *b* 25 Dec. 1928; *s* of 19th Baron Teynham, DSO, DSC, and Elspeth Grace (who *m* 2nd, 1958, 6th Marquess of Northampton, DSO, and *d* 1976), *e d* of late William Ingham Whitaker; *S* father, 1972; *m* 1964, Elizabeth, *yr d* of Lt-Col the Hon. David Scrymgeour-Wedderburn, DSO, Scots Guards (killed on active service 1944), and of Patricia, Countess of Dundee; five *s* five *d* (of whom one *s* one *d* are twins). *Educ:* Eton. A Land Agent. Late Captain, The Buffs (TA), formerly Coldstream Guards; active service in Palestine, 1948. ADC to Governor of Bermuda, 1953 and 1955; ADC to Governor of Leeward Islands, 1955; Private Secretary and ADC, 1956; ADC to Governor of Jamaica, 1962. Pres., Inst. of Commerce, 1972–; Vice Pres., Inst. of Export. Member of Council, Sail Training Association, 1964–. OStJ. Lord of the Manors of South Baddesley and Sharpricks. *Recreations:* shooting and fishing. *Heir: s* Hon. David John Henry Ingham Roper-Curzon [*b* 5 Oct. 1965; *m* 1985, Lydia Lucinda, *d* of Maj.-Gen. Sir Christopher Airy, *qv*; one *s*]. *Address:* Pylewell Park, Lymington, Hants. *Clubs:* Turf; House of Lords Yacht; Ocean Cruising; Puffin's (Edinburgh).

THAIN, Eric Malcolm, PhD; FRSC; Director, Tropical Development and Research Institute, Overseas Development Administration, 1983–86; Hon. Research Fellow, Chemistry Department, University College London, since 1986; *b* 29 Nov. 1925; *s* of late Arthur Robert Thain and Olive Grace (*née* Parsons); *m* 1954, Nancy Garbutt Key *d* of late Mr and Mrs T. G. Key; one *s* one *d. Educ:* St Dunstan's Coll., Catford; Univ. of London (BSc, PhD). Lister Institute of Preventive Medicine, 1949: ICI Research Fellow, 1953–54; Royal Society/National Academy of Science Research Fellow, Univ. of California, Berkeley, 1954–55; ICI Research Fellow, University Coll. London, 1955–57; Tropical Products Institute: Member, Scientific Staff, 1957; Asst Director, 1963; Dep. Director, 1969; Director, 1981–83. Member: WHO and FAO Expert Committees on Pesticides, 1961–; Executive Cttee, Essex Bird Watching and Preservation Soc., 1950– (Chm. 1970–73); Queckett Microscopical Club (Pres., 1980–81). *Publications:* research papers on organic chemistry and pesticides in jls of various learned societies. *Recreations:* natural history, visiting museums. *Address:* 36 Friars Quay, Norwich, Norfolk NR3 1ES. *T:* Norwich (0603) 625017. *Club:* Savage.

THALMANN, Dr Ernesto; retired Swiss Ambassador; *b* 14 Jan. 1914; *s* of Friedrich Thalmann and Clara (*née* Good) *m* 1943, Paula Degen; two *s* one *d. Educ:* Gymnasium, Zürich; Univ. of Zürich (LLD). Entered Federal Dept of Public Economy, 1941; Federal Political Dept (Swiss Foreign Office), 1945; Minister/Counsellor and Dep. Head of Mission, Swiss Embassy, Washington, 1957–61; Permanent Observer to UN, New York (Ambassador Extraordinary and Plenipotentiary), 1961–66; Head of Internat. Organizations Div., Fed. Political Dept, Berne, 1966–71; Special Mission in Jerusalem, after 6–day war, as Personal Rep. of UN Secretary-General, U Thant, 1967; Secretary-General, Fed. Political Dept and Director of Political Affairs, 1971–75; Swiss Ambassador to the Court of St James's, 1976–79. Pres., Nat. Swiss Unesco Commn, 1981–85. *Address:* 8 Anshelmstrasse, 3005 Berne, Switzerland.

THATCHER, Anthony Neville, CEng, FIMechE; President and Chief Executive, Thyssen-Bornemisza Group, since 1991; *b* 10 Sept. 1939; *s* of Edwin Neville Thatcher and Elsie May Webster; *m* 1968, Sally Margaret Clark. *Educ:* Sir John Lawes Sch., Harpenden; Luton Tech. Coll.; Manchester Univ. (MSc). Student apprentice, Haywards Tyler & Co., Luton, 1956–64; Project Engineer, Smiths Industries, 1964–77; Ultra Electronics: Operations Res. Asst, Acton, 1967–69; Vice-Pres., Sales, USA, 1970–72; Marketing Dir, Acton, 1973–77; Managing Dir, Ultra Electronic Controls, 1977; Managing Director: Dowty Electronic Controls, 1978–82; Electronics Div., Dowty Gp, 1982; Dir, 1983–91, Chief Exec., 1986–91, Dowty Gp. Member: Avionics Cttee, Electronics and Avionics Requirements Bd, DTI, 1981–85; Council, Electronics Engineering Assoc., 1983–91 (Pres., 1986–87); RARDE Management Bd (Indust.), 1986–91; Innovation Adv. Bd, DTI, 1988–91; Engrg Markets Adv. Bd, DTI, 1988–90; Engrg Council, 1989–91. Council Mem., Cheltenham Ladies' Coll., 1988–91. Freeman, City of London; Liveryman, Glass Sellers' Co. *Recreations:* art, jazz piano, opera, fishing, gardening, bird watching. *Address:* 12 Gayfere Street, SW1P 3HP.

THATCHER, Arthur Roger, CB 1974; Director, Office of Population Censuses and Surveys, and Registrar General for England and Wales, 1978–86; *b* 22 Oct. 1926; *s* of Arthur Thatcher and Edith Mary Ruth (*née* Dobson); *m* 1950, Mary Audrey Betty (*née* Street); two *d. Educ:* The Leys Sch.; St John's Coll., Cambridge (MA). Instr Lieut, Royal Navy, 1947–49. North Western Gas Board, 1949–52; Admiralty, 1952–61; Cabinet Office, 1961–63; Ministry of Labour, 1963–68; Director of Statistics, Dept of Employment, 1968–78, Dep. Sec., 1972–78. *Publications:* official publications; articles in jls. *Address:* 129 Thetford Road, New Malden, Surrey KT3 5DS. *Club:* Army and Navy.

THATCHER, Sir Denis, 1st Bt *cr* 1991, of Scotney in the County of Kent; MBE (mil.) 1944; TD 1946; company director; *b* 10 May 1915; *m* 1951, Margaret Hilda Roberts (*see* Rt Hon. Margaret Thatcher); one *s* one *d* (twins). *Educ:* Mill Hill Sch. Major, RA, 1938–46. Man. Dir, Atlas Preservative Co., 1949; Director: Castrol, 1963; Burmah Oil Trading Ltd, 1969–; non-exec. Dir, various cos, 1975–. *Recreation:* golf. *Heir: s* Mark Thatcher [*b* 15 Aug. 1953; *m* 1987, Diane Bergdorf, Dallas, Texas; one *s*]. *Clubs:* Carlton, Buck's, Pratt's.

THATCHER, Rt. Hon. Margaret (Hilda), OM 1990; PC 1970; FRS 1983; MP (C) Finchley, since 1959; Prime Minister and First Lord of the Treasury, 1979–90; Chancellor, University of Buckingham, from March 1992; *b* 13 Oct. 1925; *d* of late Alfred Roberts, Grantham, Lincs; *m* 1951, Denis Thatcher (*see* Sir Denis Thatcher, Bt); remains known as Mrs Thatcher; one *s* one *d* (twins). *Educ:* Kesteven and Grantham Girls' School; Somerville College, Oxford (MA, BSc). Research Chemist, 1947–51; called to the Bar, Lincoln's Inn, 1954, Hon. Bencher, 1975. Joint Parly Sec., Min. of Pensions and National Insurance, Oct. 1961–64; Sec. of State for Educn and Sci., 1970–74; Leader of the Opposition, 1975–79. Co-Chm., Women's Nat. Commn, 1970–74. Hon. Fellow, Somerville Coll., Oxford, 1970. Freedom of Borough of Barnet, 1980, of City of London, 1989. Donovan Award, USA, 1981. *Publication:* In Defence of Freedom, 1986. *Recreations:* music, reading. *Address:* House of Commons, SW1A 0AA. *Club:* Carlton.

THAW, John; actor; *b* 3 Jan. 1942; *s* of John Edward Thaw and Dorothy (*née* Abblott); *m* 1st (marr. diss.); one *d*; 2nd, 1973, Sheila Hancock, *qv*; one *d* one step *d. Educ:* Ducie Technical High Sch., Manchester; RADA (Vanbrugh Award; Liverpool Playhouse Award). *Theatre* appearances include: A Shred of Evidence, Liverpool Playhouse, 1960; The Fire Raisers, Royal Court, 1961; Women Beware Women, Arts, 1962; Semi-Detached, Saville, 1962; So What About Love?, Criterion, 1969; Random Happenings in the Hebrides, Edinburgh Fest., 1970; The Lady from the Sea, Greenwich, 1971; Collaborators, Duchess, 1973; Absurd Person Singular (tour), 1976; Night and Day, Phoenix, 1978; Sergeant Musgrave's Dance, NT, 1982; Twelfth Night, The Time of Your Life, Henry VIII, RSC, 1983; Pygmalion, Shaftesbury, 1984; All My Sons, Royal Exchange, Manchester, 1988; *Television* appearances include: Redcap, 1965–66; Thick As Thieves, 1973; The Sweeney, 1974–78; Sir Francis Drake, 1981; Mitch, 1983; The Life and Death of King John, 1984; Home to Roost, 1985–89; Inspector Morse, 1986–; *Films* include: The Bofors Gun, 1968; The Sweeney, 1976; The Sweeney II, 1977; The Grass is Singing, 1982; Cry Freedom, 1987. *Address:* c/o John Redway Associates, 5 Denmark Street, WC2H 8LP.

THAW, Sheila, (Mrs John Thaw); *see* Hancock, S.

THELLUSSON, family name of **Baron Rendlesham.**

THELWELL, Norman; freelance artist-cartoonist since 1957; *b* Birkenhead, 3 May 1923; *s* of Christopher Thelwell and Emily (*née* Vick); *m* 1949, Rhona Evelyn Ladbury; one *s* one *d. Educ:* Rock Ferry High Sch., Birkenhead; Liverpool Coll. of Art. Nat. Diploma of Art; ATD. Teacher of Art, Wolverhampton Coll. of Art, 1950–57. Regular contributor to Punch, 1952–; cartoonist for: News Chronicle, 1956–60; Sunday Dispatch, 1960–61; Sunday Express, 1962–. Drawings for general publications, advertising, book jackets, illustrations, etc. *Publications:* Angels on Horseback, 1957; Thelwell Country, 1959; A Place of Your Own, 1960; Thelwell in Orbit, 1961; A Leg at Each Corner, 1962; The Penguin Thelwell, 1963; Top Dog, 1964; Thelwell's Riding Academy, 1965; Drawing Ponies, 1966; Up the Garden Path, 1967; Thelwell's Compleat Tangler, 1967; Thelwell's Book of Leisure, 1968; This Desirable Plot, 1970; The Effluent Society, 1971; Penelope, 1972; Three Sheets in the Wind, 1973; Belt Up, 1974; Thelwell Goes West, 1975; Thelwell's Brat Race, 1977; A Plank Bridge by a Pool, 1978; Thelwell's Gymkhana, 1979; Thelwell Annual, 1980; A Millstone Round My Neck, 1981; Thelwell Annual, 1981; Pony Cavalcade, 1981; How to Draw Ponies, 1982; Some Damn Fool's Signed the Rubens Again, 1982; Thelwell's Magnificat, 1983; Thelwell's Sporting Prints, 1984; Wrestling with a Pencil: the life of a freelance artist, 1986; Play It As It Lies: Thelwell's golfing manual, 1987; Penelope Rides Again, 1988. *Recreations:* trout and salmon angling, painting. *Address:* Herons Mead, Timsbury, Romsey, Hants SO51 0NE. *T:* Braishfield (0794) 68238.

THEOBALD, George Peter, JP; company director, since 1958; *b* 5 Aug. 1931; *s* of late George Oswald Theobald and Helen (*née* Moore); *m* 1955, Josephine Mary (*née* Boodle); two *s* three *d. Educ:* Betteshanger Sch.; Harrow. National Service commission, 5 Regt RHA, 1950–52; 290 (City of London) RA (TA), 1953–59. Robert Warner Ltd, 1953–74: Director, 1958; Man. Dir, Chm. Gp subsidiaries, 1965; Director: of four private companies, 1974–; Tea Clearing House, 1959–72 (Chm., 1970–72); Moran Tea Holdings plc, 1980–; Moran Tea (India) plc, 1981–. City of London (Queenhithe Ward): Chm., Ward Club, 1966–68; Common Councilman, 1968–74; Alderman, 1974–79. Member: Transport Users' Consultative Cttee for London, 1969–84 (Dep. Chm. 1978); London Regional Passengers Cttee, 1984–90. Governor: Bridewell Royal Hosp., 1974–; King Edward's Sch., Witley, 1974– (Trustee, Educational Trust, 1977–); Donation Governor, Christ's Hosp., 1976–; Governor, St Leonards-Mayfield Sch., 1982–88; Chm., St John's Sch., Northwood, 1990–; Mem. Cttee, Langford Cross Children's Home, 1976–90; Trustee: National Flood and Tempest Distress Fund, 1977–; Harrow Club W10, 1978–. Church Commissioner for England, 1978–79. Master, Merchant Taylors' Co., 1989–90, 1991–92. JP City of London, 1974. *Recreations:* gardening, transport, walking. *Address:* Towerhill Manor, Gomshall, Guildford, Surrey GU5 9LP. *T:* Shere (048641) 2381. *Clubs:* Oriental, City Livery, Guildhall, MCC.

THEOCHARUS, Archbishop Gregory; His Eminence The Most Rev. Gregorios; Greek Orthodox Archbishop of Thyateira and Great Britain, since 1988; *b* 1929. *Educ:* High Sch., Lefkoniko, Famagusta; Pan Cyprian Gymnasium, Nicosia; Theol Sch., Univ. of Athens. Monk in the Sacred Monastery, Stavrovouni, Cyprus; ordained: deacon;

presbyter, 1959; asst parish priest and later parish priest, All Saints, London, 1959–69; Archdiocese of Thyateira: Chancellor, 1965; Privy Counsellor to Archbishop Athenagoras, 1969–79; locum tenens on death of Archbishop Athenagoras, 1979; Bishop of Tropaeou, 1970–88; spiritual oversight of Community of St Barnabas, Wood Green, 1970–88. *Address:* The Secretariat, The Greek Archdiocese, 5 Craven Hill, W2 3EN. *T:* 071–723 4787.

THEROUX, Paul Edward, FRSL; FRGS; writer; *b* 10 April 1941; *s* of Albert Eugene Theroux and Anne Dittami Theroux; *m* 1967, Anne Castle; two *s*. *Educ:* Univ. of Massachusetts (BA). Lecturer: Univ. of Urbino, 1963; Soche Hill Coll., Malawi, 1963–65; Makerere Univ., Kampala, Uganda, 1965–68; Univ. of Singapore, 1968–71; Writer-in-Residence, Univ. of Virginia, 1972. Mem., AAIL, 1984. Hon. DLitt: Trinity Coll., Washington DC, 1980; Tufts Univ., Mass, 1980; Univ. of Mass, 1988. *Publications: novels:* Waldo, 1967; Fong and the Indians, 1968; Girls at Play, 1969; Murder in Mount Holly, 1969; Jungle Lovers, 1971; Sinning with Annie, 1972; Saint Jack, 1973 (filmed, 1979); The Black House, 1974; The Family Arsenal, 1976; Picture Palace, 1978 (Whitbread Award, 1978); A Christmas Card, 1978; London Snow, 1980; The Mosquito Coast, 1981 (James Tait Black Prize, 1982; filmed, 1987); Doctor Slaughter, 1984 (filmed as Half Moon Street, 1987); O-Zone, 1986; My Secret History, 1989; Chicago Loop, 1990; Doctor de Marr, 1990; *short stories:* The Consul's File, 1977; World's End, 1980; The London Embassy, 1982 (televised, 1987); *play:* The White Man's Burden, 1987; *criticism:* V. S. Naipaul, 1972; *travel:* The Great Railway Bazaar, 1975; The Old Patagonian Express, 1979; The Kingdom by the Sea, 1983; Sailing through China, illus. Patrick Procktor, 1983; Sunrise with Seamonsters: travels and discoveries 1964–84, 1985; The Imperial Way, 1985; Riding the Iron Rooster, 1988; Travelling The World, 1990; *screenplay:* Saint Jack, 1979; reviews in The Sunday Times, New York Times, etc. *Recreation:* rowing. *Address:* c/o Hamish Hamilton Ltd, 27 Wrights Lane, W8 5TZ.

THESIGER, family name of **Viscount Chelmsford.**

THESIGER, Roderic Miles Doughty; Director, P. & D. Colnaghi and Co. Ltd, 1955–71; *b* 8 Nov. 1915; *y s* of late Hon. Wilfred Thesiger, DSO, and Mrs Reginald Astley, CBE; *m* 1st, 1940, Mary Rose (marr. diss. 1946; she *d* 1962), *d* of Hon. Guy Charteris; 2nd, 1946, Ursula, *d* of A. W. Whitworth, Woollas Hall, Pershore; one *s* one *d*. *Educ:* Eton; Christ Church, Oxford; Courtauld Institute. Served War of 1939–45, Welsh Guards, 1939–41; 1st Parachute Bde, 1941–44 (twice wounded, POW). Assistant, Tate Gallery, 1945–46; afterwards worked with Messrs Sotheby and privately until 1954. *Recreations:* visiting Italy and France. *Address:* The Paddocks, Lucton, Leominster, Herefordshire. *T:* Yarpole (056885) 327.

See also W. P. Thesiger.

THESIGER, Wilfred Patrick, CBE 1968; DSO 1941; MA Oxon; *b* 3 June 1910; *e s* of late Hon. Wilfred Thesiger, DSO, and Mrs Reginald Astley, CBE. *Educ:* Eton; Magdalen College, Oxford (MA; Hon. Fellow, 1982). Repres. Oxford at boxing, 1930–33; Captain Oxford Boxing Team, 1933; Hon. Attaché Duke of Gloucester's Mission to Abyssinia, 1930; served Middle East, 1941 (DSO); explored Danakil country of Abyssinia and the Aussa Sultanate, 1933–34 (awarded Back Grant by RGS, 1935); Sudan Political Service, Darfur-Upper Nile, 1935–40; served in Ethiopian, Syrian and Western Desert campaigns with SDF and SAS regiment with rank of Major; explored in Southern Arabia, 1945–49; twice crossed the Empty Quarter. Founder's Medal, RGS, 1948; Lawrence of Arabia Medal, RCAS, 1955; Livingstone Medal, RSGS, 1962; W. H. Heinemann Award (for 1964), RSL, 1965; Burton Memorial Medal, Roy. Asiatic Soc., 1966. FRSL; Hon. FBA 1982; Hon. DLitt Leicester, 1967. 3rd Class Star of Ethiopia, 1930. *Publications:* Arabian Sands, 1959; The Marsh Arabs, 1964; Desert, Marsh and Mountain: the world of a nomad, 1979; The Life of my Choice (autobiog.), 1987; Visions of a Nomad, 1987. *Recreations:* travelling, photography. *Address:* 15 Shelley Court, Tite Street, SW3. *T:* 071–352 7213. *Clubs:* Travellers', Beefsteak.

See also R. M. D. Thesiger.

THETFORD, Bishop Suffragan of; *no new appointment at time of going to press.*

THIAN, Robert Peter; Group Chief Executive, North West Water Group plc, since 1990; *b* 1 Aug. 1943; *s* of Clifford Peter Thian and Frances Elizabeth (*née* Stafford-Bird); *m* 1964, Liselotte Borges; two *d*. *Educ:* Geneva Univ. (Lic. en Droit 1967). Called to the Bar, Gray's Inn, 1971. Glaxo Group plc: Legal Advr, 1967–71; Man. Dir, Portugal, 1972–80; Abbott Laboratories (USA): European Business Develt Dir, 1981–84; Regional Dir, Europe, 1985–87; Vice Pres., Internat. Operations, Novo Industri A/S (Denmark), 1987–89. *Recreations:* horses, golf, reading. *Address:* (office) Dawson House, Warrington, Cheshire WA5 3LW. *Clubs:* East India and Sports, Lansdowne.

THIESS, Sir Leslie Charles, Kt 1971; CBE 1968; Chairman of Directors: Thiess Watkins Group of Companies, 1982–88; Breakwater Island Ltd, since 1984; Governing Director, Drayton Investments Pty Ltd, since 1953; *b* 8 April 1909; *m* 1929, Christina Mary (*née* Erbacher) (decd); two *s* three *d*. *Educ:* Drayton, Queensland. Founded Thiess Bros as a private company, 1933; Managing Dir, Thiess Holdings Ltd when it was formed in 1950; also when firm became a public company, 1958; Chairman: Thiess Group of Cos, 1968–80; Thiess Consortium, 1981–82; Chm. of Dirs, 1971–86, Hon. Chm., 1986–, Thiess Toyota Pty Ltd; Chairman of Directors: Daihatsu Australia Pty Ltd, 1975–86; Queensland Metals Corp., 1983–87 (Dir, 1987–). Dir, Thiess Watkins White Gp of Cos, 1988–. FCIT (London), 1971. Total Community Development Award, 1982. Order of the Sacred Treasure (third class), Japan, 1972. *Publication:* Thiess Story. *Recreation:* deep sea fishing. *Address:* 121 King Arthur Terrace, Tennyson, Qld 4105, Australia. *Clubs:* Tattersalls, Royal Queensland Yacht (Brisbane); Huntington, NSW Sports (NSW).

THIMANN, Prof. Kenneth Vivian; Professor of Biology, 1965–72, and Provost of Crown College, 1966–72, Emeritus Professor, recalled to duty since 1972, University of California, Santa Cruz, Calif, USA; *b* 5 Aug. 1904; *s* of Phoebus Thimann and Muriel Kate Thimann (*née* Harding); *m* 1929, Ann Mary Bateman, Sutton Bridge, Lincs; three *d*. *Educ:* Caterham Sch., Surrey; Imperial Coll., London. BSc, ARCS 1924; DIC 1925; PhD 1928. Beit Memorial Res. Fellow, 1927–29; Demonstr in Bacteriology, King's Coll. for Women, 1926–28; Instr in Biochem., Calif Inst. of Techn., 1930–35; Harvard University: Lectr on Botany, 1935; (Biology): Asst Prof., 1936, Associate Prof., 1939, Prof., 1946, and Higgins Prof., 1962–65, now Prof. Emeritus. Vis. Professor: Sorbonne, 1954; Univ. of Massachusetts, 1974; Univ. of Texas, 1976. Scientific Consultant, US Navy, 1942–45. Dir, Amer. Assoc. for Adv. of Science, 1968–71. Pres., XIth Internat. Botanical Congress, Seattle, USA, 1969; 2nd Nat. Biol Congress, Miami, 1971. Hon. AM Harvard, 1940; PhD (Hon.) Univ. of Basle, 1959; Doctor (Hon.) Univ. of Clermont-Ferrand, 1961; DSc (Hon.) Brown Univ., 1989. Fellow: Nat. Acad. of Scis (Councillor, 1967–71); Amer. Acad. of Arts and Scis; Amer. Philosophical Soc. (Councillor, 1973–76); and professional biological socs in USA and England; Foreign Member: Royal Society (London); Institut de France (Acad. des Sciences, Paris); Académie d'Agriculture; Accademia Nazionale dei Lincei (Rome); Leopoldina Akademie (Halle); Roumanian Academy (Bucharest); Botanical Societies of Japan and Netherlands. Silver Medal, Internat. Plant Growth Substance Assoc.; Balzan Prize, 1983. *Publications:* (in USA) Phytohormones (with F. W. Went), 1937; The Action of Hormones in Plants and Invertebrates, 1948; The Life of Bacteria, 1955, 2nd edn 1963 (German edn 1964); L'Origine et les Fonctions des Auxines, 1956; The Natural Plant Hormones, 1972; Hormones in the Whole Life of Plants, 1977; (ed) Senescence in Plants, 1980; (with J. Langenheim) Botany: Plant Biology in relation to Human Affairs, 1981; about 300 papers in biological and biochemical jls. *Recreations:* music (piano), gardening. *Address:* The Quadrangle, 3300 Darby Road, Apt 3314, Haverford, Pa 19041, USA. *Clubs:* Harvard Faculty (Cambridge, Mass); Harvard (San Francisco).

THIMONT, Bernard Maurice, CB 1979; Secretary, Churches' Main Committee, 1981–90; *b* 1 July 1920; *s* of Georges André Thimont; *m* 1949, Joy Rowe; one *s* one *d*. *Educ:* St Ignatius Coll., London. Served War of 1939–45, in Army (Major), 1939–48. Foreign Office, 1948–50; HM Treasury, 1950–65; IDC, 1966; Cabinet Office, 1967; HM Treasury, 1967–68; Civil Service Dept, 1968–77; Controller, HM Stationery Office and Queen's Printer of Acts of Parlt, 1977–80. MA Lambeth, 1990. *Recreations:* music, building. *Address:* Trusham, Kingsnorth Close, Bridport, Dorset DT6 4BZ. *T:* Bridport (0308) 25426.

THIRD, Rt. Rev. Richard Henry McPhail; *see* Dover, Bishop Suffragan of.

THIRKETTLE, (William) Ellis, CBE 1959; Principal, London College of Printing, 1939–67; *b* 26 July 1904; *s* of William Edward Thirkettle; *m* 1930, Alva (*d* 1987), *d* of Thomas Tough Watson; two *s*. *Educ:* Tiffin School. Principal, Stow College of Printing, Glasgow, 1936–39. *Address:* 21 Astley Close, Hollybush Lane, Pewsey, Wilts SN9 5BD.

THIRLWALL, Air Vice-Marshal George Edwin, CB 1976; retired; *b* 24 Dec. 1924; *s* of Albert and Clarice Editha Thirlwall; *m* 1st, 1949, Daphne Patricia Wynn Giles (*d* 1975); 2nd, 1977, Louisa Buck Russell (*née* Cranston). *Educ:* Sheffield Univ.; Cranfield Inst. of Technology. BEng, MSc. Joined RAF, 1950; OC RAF Sealand, 1969; Dir Air Guided Weapons, MoD, 1972; AO Ground Trng, RAF Trng Comd, 1974–76; AO Engineering, Strike Command, 1976–79. Director: Ceramics, Glass and Mineral ITB, 1979–82; Sand and Gravel Assoc., 1983–89. *Recreations:* gardening, golf. *Address:* Che Sara Sara, Gosmore Road, Hitchin, Herts SG4 9AR. *T:* Hitchin (0462) 434182. *Club:* Royal Air Force.

THIRSK, Dr (Irene) Joan, FBA 1974; Reader in Economic History in the University of Oxford, and Fellow of St Hilda's College, Oxford, 1965–83 (Hon. Fellow, 1983); *b* 19 June 1922; *d* of William Henry Watkins and Daisy (*née* Frayer); *m* 1945, James Wood Thirsk; one *s* one *d*. *Educ:* Camden School for Girls, NW5; Westfield Coll., Univ. of London. BA, PhD London; MA Oxford. Subaltern, ATS, Intelligence Corps, 1942–45. Asst Lectr in Sociology, LSE, 1950–51; Sen. Res. Fellow in Agrarian History, Dept of English Local History, Leicester Univ., 1951–65. Ford Lectr in English History, Oxford, 1975. Sen. Mellon Fellow, Nat. Humanities Centre, 1986–87. Member: Royal Commn on Historical Monuments (England), 1977–86; Econ. and Social Hist. Cttee, SSRC, 1978–82; Royal Commn on Historical Manuscripts, 1989–. Mem. Council, Economic Hist. Soc., 1955–83; Vice-Chm., Standing Conf. for Local Hist., 1965–82; President: British Agricl Hist. Soc., 1983–86 (Mem. Exec. Cttee, 1953–83, Chm. Exec. Cttee, 1974–77); Edmonton Hundred Historical Soc., 1978–; Oxfordshire Local Hist. Assoc., 1981–86 (Vice-Pres., 1980–81); Conf. of Teachers of Regional and Local Hist. in Tertiary Educn, 1981–82; British Assoc. for Local Hist., 1986–; Kent Hist. Fedn, 1990–; Vice-Pres., Soc. for Lincs Hist. and Archaeol., 1979–; Foreign Mem., Amer. Philos. Soc., 1982–; Corresp. Mem., Colonial Soc. of Massachusetts, 1983–. Editor, Agricultural History Review, 1964–72; Gen. Editor, The Agrarian History of England and Wales, 1974– (Dep. Gen. Ed., 1966–74); Mem. Editorial Bd, Past and Present, 1956–. Hon. DLitt: Leicester, 1985; East Anglia, 1990; DUniv Open, 1991. *Publications:* English Peasant Farming, 1957; Suffolk Farming in the Nineteenth Century, 1958; Tudor Enclosures, 1959; The Agrarian History of England and Wales: vol. IV, 1500–1640, 1967; vol. V, 1640–1750, 1984; (with J. P. Cooper) Seventeenth-Century Economic Documents, 1972; The Restoration, 1976; Economic Policy and Projects, 1978; The Rural Economy of England (collected essays), 1985; England's Agricultural Regions and Agrarian History 1500–1750, 1987; articles in Economic History Rev., Agric. History Rev., Past and Present, History, Jl Modern History, etc. *Recreations:* gardening, sewing, machine-knitting. *Address:* 1 Hadlow Castle, Hadlow, Tonbridge, Kent TN11 0EG.

THISELTON, Rev. Dr Anthony Charles; Principal, St John's College with Cranmer Hall, University of Durham, since 1988; *b* 13 July 1937; *s* of Eric Charles Thiselton and Hilda Winifred (*née* Kevan); *m* 1963, Rosemary Stella Harman; two *s* one *d*. *Educ:* City of London School; King's Coll., London. BD, MTh (London); PhD (Sheffield). Curate, Holy Trinity, Sydenham, 1960–63; Lectr and Chaplain, Tyndale Hall, Bristol, 1963–67, Sen. Tutor, 1967–70; Recognised Teacher in Theology, Univ. of Bristol, 1965–71; University of Sheffield: Sir Henry Stephenson Fellow, 1970–71; Lectr in Biblical Studies, 1971–79; Sen. Lectr, 1979–86; Principal, St John's Coll., Nottingham and Special Lectr in Theology, Univ. of Nottingham, 1986–88. Visiting Professor: Calvin Coll., Grand Rapids, USA, 1982–83; Regent Coll., Vancouver, 1983; Fuller Theolog. Seminary, Pasadena, Calif, 1984; North Park Coll. and Seminary, Chicago, 1984. Exam. Chaplain to Bishop of Sheffield, 1977–80, to Bishop of Leicester 1979–. Member: C of E Faith and Order Adv. Group, 1971–81, 1987–90; Doctrine Commn, 1977–90 (Vice-Chm., 1987–90). Council for National Academic Awards: Vice-Chm., Bd of Theol and Religious Studies, 1984–87; Mem., Cttee for Humanities, 1987–89. Mem., Working party on Revised Catechism, 1988–89. Adv. Editor, Jl for Study of NT, 1981–91. *Publications:* The Two Horizons: New Testament Hermeneutics and Philosophical Description, 1980; (with C. Walhout and R. Lundin) The Responsibility of Hermeneutics, 1985; New Horizons in Hermeneutics: theory and practice of transforming biblical reading, 1992; contribs to learned jls and other books on New Testament, doctrine, and philosophical hermeneutics. *Recreation:* choral and organ music. *Address:* St John's College, Durham DH1 3RJ. *T:* Durham (091) 3743561.

THISTLETHWAITE, Prof. Frank, CBE 1979; Emeritus Professor, University of East Anglia; founding Vice-Chancellor, 1961–80; *b* 24 July 1915; *s* of late Lee and Florence Nightingale Thistlethwaite; *m* 1940, Jane, *d* of H. Lindley Hosford, Lyme, Connecticut, USA; one *s* three *d* (and one *s* decd). *Educ:* Bootham School; St John's College, Cambridge (Exhibitioner and Scholar). BA 1938, MA 1941. FRHistS. Editor, The Cambridge Review, 1937. Commonwealth Fund Fellow, University of Minnesota, 1938–40; British Press Service, New York, 1940–41. RAF, 1941–45; seconded to Office of War Cabinet (Joint-Amer. Secretariat), 1942–45. Fellow, St John's College, Cambridge, 1945–61; at various times, Tutor, Praelector, Steward; University Lecturer in Faculty of Economics and Politics, 1949–61. Visiting Prof. of American Civilization, Univ. of Pennsylvania, 1956; Vis. Fellow, Henry E. Huntington Library, Calif, 1973; Leverhulme Emeritus Fellow, 1981; Hill Vis. Prof., Univ. of Minnesota, 1986. Chairman: British Assoc. for Amer. Studies, 1955–59; Cttee of Management, Inst. of US Studies, Univ. of London, 1966–80; IUPC (formerly IUC), 1977–81 (Mem., 1962–81); Member: Inst. for Advanced Study, Princeton, 1954; Academic Adv. Cttee, Open Univ., 1969–74; Provisional Council, Univ. of Zambia, 1965–69; Univ. of Malaŵi, 1971–75; Univ. of

Mauritius, 1974–84; Marshall Aid Commemoration Commn, 1964–80; US-UK Educnl (Fulbright) Commn, 1964–79; European Adv. Council, Salzburg Seminar in Amer. Studies, 1969–74; Bd, British Council, 1971–82; British Cttee of Award, Harkness Fellowships, 1974–80; Adviser to Nat. Council of Higher Educn, Ceylon, 1967. Governor, Sedbergh Sch., 1958–73. Pres., Friends of Cambridge Univ. Library, 1983–. Hon. Fellow, St John's Coll., Cambridge, 1974. Hon. Prof. of History, Univ. of Mauritius, 1981. Hon. FRIBA 1985. Hon. LHD Colorado, 1972; Hon. DCL East Anglia, 1980. *Publications*: The Great Experiment: An Introduction to the History of the American People, 1955 (trans. 14 languages); The Anglo-American Connection in the Early Nineteenth Century, 1958; Dorset Pilgrims: the story of West Country pilgrims who went to New England in the 17th century, 1989; A Century of European Migrations 1830–1930, 1991; contrib. New Cambridge Modern History and other historical works and journals; New Universities in the Modern World (ed M. G. Ross). *Recreation*: music. *Address*: 15 Park Parade, Cambridge CB5 8AL; Island Cottage, Winson, Glos. *Club*: Athenæum.

　　See also M. E. Pellew.

THODAY, Prof. John Marion, BSc Wales, PhD, ScD Cantab; FRS 1965; Arthur Balfour Professor of Genetics, Cambridge University, 1959–83, now Emeritus; Life Fellow of Emmanuel College, 1983 (Fellow, 1959); *b* 30 Aug. 1916; *s* of Professor D. Thoday, FRS; *m* 1950, Doris Joan Rich, PhD (Fellow, Lucy Cavendish College); one *s* one *d*. *Educ*: Bootham School, York; University Coll. of N Wales, Bangor; Trinity College, Cambridge. Photographic Intelligence, Royal Air Force, 1941–46; Cytologist, Mount Vernon Hospital, 1946–47; Asst Lectr, then Lectr for Cytogenetics, Departments of Botany and Zoology, University of Sheffield, 1947–54; Head of Department of Genetics: Sheffield, 1954–59; Cambridge, 1959–82. Leverhulme Emeritus Res. Fellow, 1984–86. Director, OECD Project for reform of secondary school Biology teaching 1962, 1963. Chm., UK Nat. Cttee for Biology, 1982–88. Pres., Genetical Soc., 1975–78. *Publications*: (with J. N. Thompson) Quantitive Genetics, 1979; articles on radiation cytology, experimental evolution, the genetics of continuous variables, biological progress and on genetics and society. *Address*: 7 Clarkson Road, Cambridge CB3 0EH.

THODE, Dr Henry George, CC (Canada) 1967; MBE 1946; FRS 1954; FRSC 1943; FCIC 1948; Professor Emeritus, McMaster University, Canada, since 1979; *b* 10 September 1910; Canadian; *m* 1935, Sadie Alicia Patrick; three *s*. *Educ*: University of Saskatchewan (BSc 1930, MSc 1932); University of Chicago (PhD 1934). Research Asst, Columbia Univ., 1936–38; Research Chemist, US Rubber Co., 1938; McMaster University: Asst Prof. of Chem., 1939–42; Assoc. Prof. of Chem., 1942–44; Prof. of Chem., 1944–79; Head, Department of Chemistry, 1948–52; Dir of Res., 1947–61; Principal of Hamilton Coll., 1944–63; Vice-Pres., 1957–61; Pres. and Vice-Chancellor, 1961–72. California Inst. of Technology, Pasadena, Calif: Nat. Science Foundn Sen. Foreign Res. Fellow, 1970; Sherman Fairchild Distinguished Scholar, 1977. National Research Council, War Research-Atomic Energy, 1943–45. Member: Nat. Research Council, 1955–61; Defence Research Bd, 1955–61; Commn on Atomic Weights (SAIC), IUPAC, 1963–79; Board of Governors, Ontario Research Foundn, 1955–82; Director: Atomic Energy of Canada Ltd, 1966–81; Stelco Inc., 1969–85. Hon. Fellow, Chemical Inst. of Canada, 1972; Shell Canada Merit Fellowship, 1974. Hon. DSc: Universities: Toronto, 1955; BC, Acadia, 1960; Laval, 1963; RMC, 1964; McGill, 1966; Queen's, 1967; York, 1972; McMaster, 1973. Hon. LLD: Sask., 1958; Regina, 1983. Medal of Chemical Inst. of Canada, 1957; Tory Medal, 1959, Centenary Medal, 1982, Sir William Dawson Medal, 1989, Royal Soc. of Canada; Arthur L. Day Medal, Geological Soc. of America, 1980. Order of Ontario, 1989. *Publications*: numerous publications on nuclear chemistry, isotope chemistry, isotope abundances in terrestrial and extraterrestrial material, separation of isotopes, magnetic susceptibilities, electrical discharges in gases, sulphur concentrations and isotope ratios in lunar materials. *Recreations*: swimming, farming. *Address*: Department of Chemistry, Nuclear Research Building, McMaster University, 1280 Main Street West, Hamilton, Ontario L8S 4K1, Canada. *T*: (416) 525–9140. *Club*: Rotary (Hamilton, Ont.).

THODY, Prof. Philip Malcolm Waller; Professor of French Literature, University of Leeds, since 1965; *b* Lincoln, 21 March 1928; *s* of Thomas Edwin Thody and Florence Ethel (*née* Hart); *m* 1954, Joyce Elizabeth Woodin; two *s* two *d*. *Educ*: Lincoln Sch.; King's Coll., Univ. of London. FIL 1982. Temp. Asst Lectr, Univ. of Birmingham, 1954–55; Asst Lectr, subseq. Lectr, QUB, 1956–65; Chairman: Dept of French, Univ. of Leeds, 1968–72, 1975–79, 1982–85, 1987–; Bd of Faculties of Arts, Social Studies and Law, Univ. of Leeds, 1972–74. Visiting Professor: Univ. of Western Ontario, Canada, 1963–64; Berkeley Summer Sch., 1964; Harvard Summer Sch., 1968; Virginia Summer Sch., 1990; Centenary Vis. Prof., Adelaide Univ., 1974; Canterbury Vis. Fellow, Univ. of Canterbury, NZ, 1977, 1982; Vis. Fellow, Univ. of WA, 1988. Pres., Modern Languages Assoc., 1980, 1981. Officer dans l'Ordre des Palmes Académiques, 1981. *Publications*: Albert Camus, a study of his work, 1957; Jean-Paul Sartre, a literary and political study, 1960; Albert Camus, 1913–1960, 1961; Jean Genet, a study of his novels and plays, 1968; Jean Anouilh, 1968; Choderlos de Laclos, 1970; Jean-Paul Sartre, a biographical introduction, 1971; Aldous Huxley, a biographical introduction, 1973; Roland Barthes: a conservative estimate, 1977; A True Life Reader for Children and Parents, 1977; Dog Days in Babel (novel), 1979; (jtly) Faux Amis and Key Words, 1985; Marcel Proust, novelist, 1987; Albert Camus, novelist, 1989; French Caesarism from Napoleon 1er to Charles de Gaulle, 1989; contribs to French Studies, Times Literary Supplement, Times Higher Educational Supplement, Modern Languages Review, London Magazine, Twentieth Century, Encounter, Yorkshire Post. *Recreations*: talking, golf, Wodehouse inter-war first editions. *Address*: 6 The Nook, Primley Park, Alwoodley, Leeds LS17 7JU. *T*: Leeds (0532) 687350.

THOM, Kenneth Cadwallader; HM Diplomatic Service, retired; *b* 4 Dec. 1922; *m* 1948, Patience Myra (*née* Collingridge); three *s* one *d*. *Educ*: University College School, London; St Andrews Univ.; MA(Hons). Army Service, 1942–47; Assistant District Officer, then District Officer, Northern Nigerian Administration, 1950–59; 1st Secretary: FO, 1959; UK Mission to UN, NY, 1960–63; FO, 1963–66; Budapest, 1966–68; FCO, 1968–72; Counsellor, Dublin, 1972–74; Counsellor, FCO, 1974–78; Consul-General: Hanover, 1978–79; Hamburg, 1979–81; retired, and re-employed, FCO, 1981–85. FIL 1981. *Address*: Prospect House, Bruton, Somerset BA10 0AZ.

THOMAS, family name of **Viscount Tonypandy** and **Barons Thomas of Gwydir** and **Thomas of Swynnerton.**

THOMAS OF GWYDIR, Baron *cr* 1987 (Life Peer), of Llanrwst in the county of Gwynedd; **Peter John Mitchell Thomas;** PC 1964; QC 1965; a Recorder of the Crown Court, 1974–88; *b* 31 July 1920; *o s* of late David Thomas, Solicitor, Llanrwst, Denbighshire, and Anne Gwendoline Mitchell; *m* 1947, Frances Elizabeth Tessa (*d* 1985), *o d* of late Basil Dean, CBE and Lady Mercy Greville; two *s* two *d*. *Educ*: Epworth College, Rhyl; Jesus College, Oxford (MA). Served War of 1939–45, in RAF; Prisoner of War (Germany), 1941–45. Called to Bar, 1947, Middle Temple, Master of the Bench 1971, Member of Wales and Chester Circuit; Deputy Chairman: Cheshire QS, 1966–70; Denbighshire QS, 1968–70. Arbitrator, Court of Arbitration, Internat. Chamber of

Commerce, Paris, 1974–88. MP (C): Conway Div. of Caernarvonshire, 1951–66; Hendon South, 1970–87; PPS to the Solicitor-General, 1954–59; Parly Secretary, Min. of Labour, 1959–61; Parly Under-Sec. of State, Foreign Office, 1961–63; Minister of State for Foreign Affairs, 1963–64; Opp. Front Bench Spokesman on Foreign Affairs and Law, 1964–66; Sec. of State for Wales, 1970–74. Member: Select Cttee on Conduct of Members, 1976–77; Select Cttee on Procedure (Supply), 1981–83; Select Cttee on Foreign Affairs, 1983–87; Select Cttee on Privileges, 1984–87; Chairman: Select Cttee on Members' Salaries, 1981–82; Select Cttee on Revision of Standing Orders, 1982–83. Chm., Cons. Party Organisation, 1970–72. Pres., Nat. Union of Conservative and Unionist Assocs, 1974 and 1975. Mem., Council of Europe and WEU, 1957–59. Member, Historic Buildings Council for Wales, 1965–67. *Address*: 37 Chester Way, SE11. *T*: 071–735 6047; Millicent Cottage, Elstead, Surrey. *T*: Elstead (0252) 702052. *Club*: Carlton.

THOMAS OF SWYNNERTON, Baron *cr* 1981 (Life Peer), of Notting Hill in Greater London; **Hugh Swynnerton Thomas;** historian; *b* 21 Oct. 1931; *s* of Hugh Whitelegge Thomas, CMG, Colonial Service, Gold Coast (Ghana) and Margery Swynnerton; *m* 1962, Vanessa Jebb, *d* of 1st Baron Gladwyn, *qv*; two *s* one *d*. *Educ*: Sherborne; Queens' Coll., Cambridge (Scholar); Sorbonne, Paris. Pres. Cambridge Union, 1953. Foreign Office, 1954–57; Sec. to UK delegn to UN Disarmament Sub-Cttee, 1955–56; Lectr at RMA Sandhurst, 1957; Prof. of History, 1966–76, and Chm., Grad. Sch. of Contemp. European Studies, 1973–76, Univ. of Reading. Chm., Centre for Policy Studies, 1979–91. Somerset Maugham Prize, 1962; Arts Council prize for History (1st Nat. Book Awards), 1980. Commander, Order of Isabel la Católica, Spain, 1986. *Publications*: (as Hugh Thomas) The World's Game, 1957; The Spanish Civil War, 1961, rev. edn 1977, rev. illustrated edn, Spain, 1979; The Story of Sandhurst, 1961; The Suez Affair, 1967; Cuba, or the Pursuit of Freedom, 1971; (ed) The selected writings of José Antonio Primo de Rivera, 1972; Goya and The Third of May 1808, 1972; Europe, the Radical Challenge, 1973; John Strachey, 1973; The Cuban Revolution, 1977; An Unfinished History of the World, 1979, rev. edn 1982 (US 1979, A History of the World); The Case for the Round Reading Room, 1983; Havannah (novel), 1984; Armed Truce, 1986; A Traveller's Companion to Madrid, 1988; Klara (novel), 1988; Ever Closer Union: Britain's destiny in Europe, 1991. *Address*: c/o House of Lords, SW1A 0PW. *Clubs*: Garrick; Travellers' (Paris).

THOMAS, Prof. Adrian Tregerthen; Hamilton Harty Professor of Music, Queen's University of Belfast, since 1985; Head of Music, BBC Radio 3, since 1990; *b* 11 June 1947; *s* of Owen George Thomas and Jean Tregerthen. *Educ*: Univ. of Nottingham (BMus 1969); University Coll., Cardiff (MA 1971). Lectr in Music, 1972–82, Sen. Lectr, 1982–85, QUB. Medal of Polish Composers' Union, for Distinguished Service to Contemporary Polish Music, 1989. *Publications*: Grazyna Bacewicz: chamber and orchestral music, USA 1985; (contrib.) Cambridge Companion to Chopin, 1992; contrib. Music Rev., THES, Contemp. Music Rev., Music and Letters. *Recreations*: poetry, oriental arts, hill-walking. *Address*: BBC, 16 Langham Street, W1A 1AA. *T*: 071–927 4435.

THOMAS, Alan; see Thomas J. A.

THOMAS, Alston Havard Rees; Finance and Property Writer, Bristol Evening Post, 1985 (Diary Editor, 1970–85); *b* Dinas, Pembrokeshire, 8 July 1925. Trainee and reporter, West Wales Guardian, 1939–44; Dist Reporter, Wilts Times, 1944–46; joined Bristol Evening Post, 1946, successively Industrial, Speedway, Municipal, Ecclesiastical, Crime and Med. correspondent. Institute of Journalists: Mem., 1974–; Chm. Nat. Exec., 1981–84; Pres., 1985–86; Chm. SW Region, 1975–; Mem., Press Council, 1979–90. Mem., St John Council (Avon Co., 1974–). *Recreations*: rugby union, music, travel, gardening. *Address*: Havene, Maysmead Lane, Langford, Avon BS18 7HX. *T*: Weston-super-Mare (0934) 862515. *Club*: Savages (Bristol).

THOMAS, Ambler Reginald, CMG 1951; Under-Secretary, Ministry of Overseas Development, retired 1975; *b* 12 Feb. 1913; *s* of late John Frederick Ivor Thomas, OBE, MICE, MIME and Elizabeth Thomas; *m* 1943, Diana Beresford Gresham; two *s* three *d*. *Educ*: Gresham's School, Holt; Corpus Christi College, Cambridge. Entered Home Civil Service as Asst Principal and apptd to Ministry of Agriculture and Fisheries, 1935; transferred to Colonial Office, 1936. Asst Private Sec. to Sec. of State for Colonies, 1938–39; Principal, Colonial Office, 1939; Asst Sec., 1946; Chief Sec. to Govt of Aden, 1947–49; Establishment and Organization Officer, Colonial Office, 1950–52; Assistant Under-Sec. of State, Colonial Office, 1952–64; Under-Sec., Min. of Overseas Develt, and Overseas Develt Administration, 1964–73. Member, Exec. Cttee, British Council, 1965–68. Chairman: Commn of Inquiry into Gilbert Is Develt Authority, 1976; Corona Club. *Address*: Champsland, North Chideock, Bridport, Dorset. *Club*: United Oxford & Cambridge University.

THOMAS, Aneurin Morgan; Director, Welsh Arts Council, 1967–84; *b* 3 April 1921; *s* of Philip Thomas and Olwen Amy Thomas (*née* Davies); *m* 1947, Mary Dineen; one *s* one *d*. *Educ*: Ystalyfera Intermediate Sch., Glamorgan; Swansea School of Art and Crafts. British and Indian Armies, 1941–46 (Major). Lecturer, later Vice-Principal, Somerset College of Art, 1947–60; Vice-Principal, Hornsey College of Art, 1960–67. Member, Board of Governors: Loughborough Coll. of Art and Design, 1980–89; S Glamorgan Inst. of Higher Educn, 1985–89 (Chm., Faculty of Art and Design Adv. Cttee, 1985–90); Carmarthenshire Coll. of Tech. and Art, 1985– (Chm., Faculty of Art and Design Adv. Cttee, 1985–); Vice-President: Nat. Soc. for Art Educn, 1967–68; Llangollen Internat. Music Eisteddfod, 1970–. Chm., Assoc. of Art Instns, 1977–78. *Publications*: periodic contribs to books and professional jls. *Recreation*: observing with interest and humour. *Address*: Netherwood, 8 Lower Cwrt-y-vil Road, Penarth, South Glamorgan CF6 2HQ. *T*: Penarth (0222) 702239.

THOMAS, Prof. (Antony) Charles, CBE 1991; DL; DLitt; FSA; FBA 1989; Professor of Cornish Studies, University of Exeter, and Director, Institute of Cornish Studies, since 1971; *b* 24 April 1928; *s* of late Donald Woodroffe Thomas and Viva Warrington Thomas; *m* 1959, Jessica Dorothea Esther, *d* of F. A. Mann, CBE, FBA; two *s* two *d*. *Educ*: Winchester; Corpus Christi Coll., Oxon (BA Hons Jurisp.); Univ. of London (Dipl. Prehist. Archaeol.). DLitt Oxon, 1983. Lectr in Archaeology, Univ. of Edinburgh, 1957–67; Prof. of Archaeology, Univ. of Leicester, 1967–71. Leverhulme Fellowship, 1965–67; Sir John Rhys Fellow, Univ. of Oxford, and Vis. Sen. Res. Fellow, Jesus Coll., 1985–86. President: Council for British Archaeology, 1970–73; Royal Instn of Cornwall, 1970–72; Cornwall Archaeol. Soc., 1984–88; Soc. for Medieval Archaeology, 1986–89; Chairman: BBC SW Reg. Adv. Council, 1975–80; DoE Area Archaeol Cttee, Cornwall and Devon, 1975–79; Cornwall Cttee Rescue Archaeol., 1976–88; Mem., Royal Commn on Historical Monuments (England), 1983– (Acting Chm., Feb. 1988–Oct. 1989; Vice Chm., 1991–). Hon. Archaeol Consultant, National Trust, 1970–. Hon. Mem., Royal Irish Acad., 1973; Hon. Fellow, RSAI, 1975. DL Cornwall, 1988. William Frend Medal, Soc. of Antiquaries, 1982. *Publications*: Christian Antiquities of Camborne, 1967; The Early Christian Archaeology of North Britain, 1971; Britain and Ireland in Early Christian Times, 1971; (with A. Small and D. Wilson) St Ninian's Isle and its Treasure, 1973; (with D. Ivall) Military Insignia of Cornwall, 1974; Christianity in Roman Britain to AD 500, 1981; Exploration of a Drowned Landscape, 1985; Celtic Britain, 1986; Views and Likenesses: photographers in Cornwall and Scilly 1839–70, 1988. *Recreations:* military history, archaeological fieldwork. *Address:* Lambessow, St Clement, Truro, Cornwall TR1 1TB.

THOMAS, Brinley, CBE 1971 (OBE 1955); MA, PhD; FBA 1973; Hon. Research Associate, Department of Economics, University of California, Berkeley, since 1987; Professor of Economics, University College, Cardiff, 1946–73, Director, Manpower Research Unit, 1974–76; *e s* of late Thomas Thomas and Anne Walters; *m* 1943, Cynthia, *d* of late Dr Charles T. Loram, New Haven, Connecticut; one *d. Educ:* Port Talbot County School; University College of Wales, Aberystwyth; London School of Economics. MA (Wales) (with distinction), 1928; Fellow of the University of Wales, 1929–31; Social Science Research Training Scholar, 1929–31; PhD (London), 1931; Hutchinson Silver Medal, London School of Economics, 1931; Acland Travelling Scholar in Germany and Sweden, 1932–34; Lecturer in Economics, London School of Economics, 1931–39; War Trade Department, British Embassy, Washington, 1941–42; Dir, Northern Section, Political Intelligence Dept of Foreign Office, 1942–45. Member: National Assistance Bd, 1948–53; Anderson Cttee on Grants to Students, 1958–60; Dept of Employment Retail Prices Index Advisory Cttee; Prince of Wales Cttee, 1969–76. Chairman: Welsh Advisory Cttee of British Council, 1966–74; Welsh Council, 1968–71; Assoc. of Univ. Teachers of Econs, 1965–68; Mem. Exec. Cttee, British Council, 1966–74; Pres., Atlantic Economic Soc. Nat. Science Foundn Fellow, 1971. University of California, Berkeley: Ford Vis. Res. Prof., 1976–77; Vis. Prof., 1978–79 and 1979–83; Visiting Professor: Queen's Univ., Canada, 1977–78; Univ. of California, Davis, 1984–86. Governor, Centre for Environmental Studies, 1972–74. *Publications:* Monetary Policy and Crises, A Study of Swedish Experience, 1936; Migration and Economic Growth, A Study of Great Britain and the Atlantic Economy, 1954, 2nd edn 1973; International Migration and Economic Development: A Trend Report and Bibliography, 1961; Migration and Urban Development, 1972; (ed) Economics of International Migration, 1958; (ed) The Welsh Economy: Studies in Expansion, 1962; articles in various journals. *Address:* 44a Church Road, Whitchurch, Cardiff CF4 2EA. *T:* Cardiff (0222) 693835.

THOMAS, Cedric Marshall, CBE 1991 (OBE 1983); Director and Chief Executive, Engineering Employers' West Midlands Association, since 1984; *b* 26 May 1930; *s* of David J. Thomas and Evis (*née* Field); *m* 1st, 1954, Dora Ann Pritchard (*d* 1975); one *s* one *d*; 2nd, 1976, Margaret Elizabeth (*née* Crawley); one step *s* three step *d. Educ:* King Edward's Sch., Birmingham; Univ. of Birmingham (BSc Hons, PhD). CEng; FIMinE; FMES (Pres., 1969–71); MIPM. NCB, 1954–60; Johnson Progress Group, 1961–77 (Chief Exec., 1970–77); Business Consultant, 1977–80; Benjamin Priest Group, 1980–84 (Chief Exec., 1983). Member: Management Bd, Engrg Employers' Fedn, 1974–80, 1983–84; HSC, 1980–90; Chairman: Special Programmes Area Bd, 1978–83; Area Manpower Bd, 1986–88. Pres., Engineering Employers' W Midlands Assoc., 1976–78. Governor, N Staffs Polytechnic, 1973–80. *Recreations:* Rugby football, tennis, theatre, walking. *Address:* Parkfields House, Tittensor, Staffs ST12 9HQ. *T:* Barlaston (078139) 3677.

THOMAS, Charles; *see* Thomas, A. C.

THOMAS, Ven. Charles Edward; Archdeacon of Wells, since 1983; *b* 1927. *Educ:* St David's College, Lampeter (BA 1951); College of the Resurrection, Mirfield. Deacon 1953, priest 1954; Curate of Ilminster, 1953–56; Chaplain and Asst Master, St Michael's Coll., Tenbury, 1956–57; Curate of St Stephen's, St Albans, 1957–58; Vicar, St Michael and All Angels, Boreham Wood, 1958–66; Rector, Monksilver with Elworthy, 1966–74, with Brompton Ralph and Nettlecombe, 1969–74 (Curate-in-charge of Nettlecombe, 1968–69); Vicar of South Petherton with the Seavingtons, 1974–83. RD of Crewkerne, 1977–82. *Address:* 6 The Liberty, Wells, Som BA5 2SU. *T:* Wells (0749) 72224.

THOMAS, Christopher Sydney; QC 1989; *b* 17 March 1950; *s* of late John Raymond Thomas and of Daphne May Thomas; *m* 1979, Patricia Jane Heath; one *s* one *d. Educ:* King's Sch., Worcester; Univ. of Kent at Canterbury (BA Hons); Faculté International de Droit Comparé, Paris (Diplôme de Droit Comparé (avec mérite), 1972). Hardwick Scholar and Jenkins Scholar, Lincoln's Inn; called to the Bar, Lincoln's Inn, 1973. *Recreation:* farming. *Address:* 10 Essex Street, Outer Temple, WC2R 3AA. *T:* 071–240 6981.

THOMAS, Colin Agnew; chartered accountant; *b* 14 Feb. 1921; *s* of Harold Alfred Thomas and Nora (*née* Williams); *m* 1947, Jane Jardine Barnish, *d* of Leonard Barnish, FRIBA; one *s* one *d. Educ:* Oundle School. Lieut, RNVR, 1941–46. Finance Comptroller, Lloyd's, 1964–75, Sec.-Gen., 1976–79. *Recreations:* golf, sailing, gardening, sketching. *Address:* 33 Cobham Road, Leatherhead, Surrey KT22 9AY. *T:* Leatherhead (0372) 374335; 15 Ravenspoint, Trearddur Bay, Anglesey LL65 2AJ. *T:* Trearddur Bay (0407) 860091. *Clubs:* Effingham Golf, Holyhead Golf, Trearddur Bay Sailing.

THOMAS, Dafydd Elis; MP (Plaid Cymru) Meirionnydd Nant Conwy, since 1983 (Merioneth, Feb. 1974–1983); President, Plaid Cymru, 1984–91; *b* 18 Oct. 1946; *m* 1970, Elen M. Williams (separated 1986); three *s. Educ:* Ysgol Dyffryn Conwy; UC North Wales. Research worker, Bd of Celtic Studies, 1970; Tutor in Welsh Studies, Coleg Harlech, 1970; Lectr, Dept of English, UC North Wales, 1974. Part-time freelance broadcaster, BBC Wales, HTV, 1970–73. *Recreations:* hill walking, camping. *Address:* Maes y Bryner Isaf, Dolgellau, Gwynedd. *T:* (constituency office) Dolgellau (0341) 422661; (London) 071–219 4172/5021. *Club:* Sport and Social (Trawsfynydd).

THOMAS, Rev. David; Vicar of St Peter's, Newton, Swansea, since 1987; *b* 22 July 1942; *s* of Rt Rev. John James Absalom Thomas, *qv*; *m* 1967, Rosemary Christine Calton; one *s* one *d. Educ:* Christ College, Brecon; Keble College, Oxford; St Stephen's House, Oxford. MA Oxon. Curate of Hawarden, 1967–69; Tutor, St Michael's College, Llandaff, Cardiff, 1969–70, Chaplain 1970–75; Secretary, Church in Wales Liturgical Commn, 1970–75; Vice-Principal, St Stephen's House, Oxford, 1975–79; Vicar of Chepstow, 1979–82; Principal, St Stephen's House, Oxford, 1982–87. *Publication:* (contrib.) The Ministry of the Word (ed G. J. Cuming), 1979. *Recreations:* music, walking. *Address:* The Vicarage, Mary Twill Lane, Newton, Swansea SA3 4RB. *T:* Swansea (0792) 368348.

THOMAS, Prof. David; Professor of Geography, since 1978, and Head of School of Geography, since 1991, University of Birmingham; *b* 16 Feb. 1931; *s* of William and Florence Grace Thomas; *m* 1955, Daphne Elizabeth Berry; one *s* one *d. Educ:* Bridgend Grammar School; University College of Wales, Aberystwyth (BA, MA); PhD London. Asst Lectr, Lectr, Reader, University College London, 1957–70; Prof. and Head of Dept, St David's University College, Lampeter, 1970–78; Birmingham University: Head of Dept of Geography, 1978–86; Pro Vice-Chancellor, 1984–89. Pres., IBG, 1988 (Hon. Sec., 1976–78); Mem., Council, RGS, 1988–91. *Publications:* Agriculture in Wales during the Napoleonic Wars, 1963; London's Green Belt, 1970; (ed) An Advanced Geography of the British Isles, 1974; (with J. A. Dawson) Man and his world, 1975; (ed) Wales: a new study, 1977; (with P. T. J. Morgan) Wales: the shaping of a nation, 1984; articles in learned jls. *Recreations:* music, wine, spectating. *Address:* 6 Plymouth Drive, Barnt Green, Birmingham B45 8JB. *T:* 021–445 3295.

THOMAS, David Bowen, PhD; Keeper, Department of Physical Sciences, Science Museum, 1984–87 (Keeper, Department of Physics, 1978–84); *b* 28 Dec. 1931; *s* of Evan Thomas and Florence Annie Bowen. *Educ:* Tredegar Grammar Sch.; Manchester Univ. (BSc). Research Fellow, Wayne Univ., Detroit, USA, 1955–57; Research Scientist, Min. of Agriculture, Fisheries and Food, Aberdeen, 1957–61; Asst Keeper, Science Museum, Dept of Chemistry, 1961–73; Keeper, Dept of Museum Services, 1973–78. *Publications:* The First Negatives, 1964; The Science Museum Photography Collection, 1969; The First Colour Motion Pictures, 1969. Hon. FRPS 1985. *Recreation:* country walking. *Address:* Tanglewood, Moushill Lane, Milford, Godalming, Surrey GU8 5BQ.

THOMAS, David Churchill, CMG 1982; HM Diplomatic Service, retired; Assistant Under Secretary of State, Foreign and Commonwealth Office, 1984–86; *b* 21 Oct. 1933; *o s* of late David Bernard Thomas and Violet Churchill Thomas (*née* Quicke); *m* 1958, Susan Petronella Arrow; one *s* two *d. Educ:* Eton Coll.; New Coll., Oxford (Exhibnr). Mod. Hist. 1st Cl., 1957. Army, 2nd Lieut, Rifle Brigade, 1952–54. Foreign Office, 1958; 3rd Sec., Moscow, 1959–61; 2nd Sec., Lisbon, 1961–64; FCO, 1964–68; 1st Sec. (Commercial), Lima, 1968–70; FCO, 1970–73; Head of South West European Dept, 1974; Asst Sec., Cabinet Office, 1973–78; Counsellor (Internal Affairs), Washington, 1978–81; Ambassador to Cuba, 1981–84. Advr on Overseas Scholarships Funding, FCO, 1989–. Mem. Council, RIIA, 1988–. Mem. Bd, Inst. of Latin American Studies, Univ. of London, 1988–. Associate Fellow, Centre for Caribbean Studies, Warwick Univ., 1990–. *Publications:* essays and review articles on Latin American affairs. *Recreations:* photography, listening to music. *Address:* 11 Crookham Road, SW6 4EG. *T:* 071–736 9096.
See also D. W. P. Thomas.

THOMAS, David Emrys; management and personnel consultant, since 1991; *b* Ewell, 9 July 1935; *s* of Emrys and Elsie Florence Thomas; *m* 1957, Rosemary, *d* of Alexander and Kathleen De'Ath of Hampton, Middx; two *s* one *d. Educ:* Tiffin Grammar Sch., Kingston upon Thames. Dip. Mun. Admin; FIPM. Local Govt Administrator, 1951–63; Indust. Relations Officer, LACSAB, 1963–68; Chief Admin. Officer, LGTB, 1968–69; Dep. Estab. Officer, Surrey CC, 1969–70; County Personnel Officer, Surrey, 1970–77; Under-Sec. (Manpower), AMA, 1977–81; Dep. Sec., 1981–87, Sec., 1987–91, LACSAB; Employers' Sec. to nat. jt negotiating councils in local govt, 1987–91; Official Side Sec., Police Negotiating Bd, 1987–91; Sec., UK Steering Cttee on Local Govt Superannuation, 1987–91. Founder Pres., Soc. of Chief Personnel Officers in Local Govt, 1975. *Recreations:* unskilled gardening, the musical theatre. *Address:* The White House, Three Pears Road, Merrow, Guildford, Surrey GU1 2XU. *T:* Guildford (0483) 69588.

THOMAS, David Hamilton Pryce, CBE 1977; solicitor, retired; Chairman, Land Authority for Wales, 1980–86 (Deputy Chairman, 1975–80); President, Rent Assessment Panel for Wales, 1971–89 (Member, 1966); *b* 3 July 1922; *s* of Trevor John Thomas and Eleanor Maud Thomas; *m* 1948, Eluned Mair Morgan; two *s* one *d. Educ:* Barry County Sch.; University College, Cardiff. Served War of 1939–45; British and Indian Armies, terminal rank T/Captain (GSO III), 1941–46. Qualified as Solicitor, 1948, with hons; Partner in J. A. Hughes & Co., Solicitors, Barry, 1950–75; Notary Public, 1953. Director 1962–67, Vice-Chm. 1967–71, Chm. 1971–78, Barry Mutual Building Society; Vice Chm., 1978, Chm., 1982–84, Glam. Building Soc.; Chm., Wales Area Bd, Bradford and Bingley Bldg Soc., 1984–87; Vice-Chm., Building Socs Assoc. for Wales, 1983; Mem., Adv. Cttee on Fair Rents, 1973; Chm., E Glam. Rent Tribunal, 1967–71; District Comr of Scouts, Barry and District, 1963–70; Chm., Barry District Scout Assoc. 1971–81; Vice-Chm., S Glam. Scout Council, 1975–81. *Recreations:* books, music, gardening. *Address:* 34 Camden Road, Brecon, Powys LD3 7RT.
See also R. L. Thomas.

THOMAS, David Monro; retired; *b* 31 July 1915; *s* of late Henry Monro and Winifred Thomas, East Hagbourne, Berks; *m* 1948, Ursula Mary, *d* of late H. W. Liversidge; two *s* one *d. Educ:* St Edward's School, Oxford; St Edmund Hall, Oxford. Oxford House, 1937; Army, 1939, Major, Royal Welch Fusiliers; Head of Oxford House, 1946–48; Secretary of Greek House, 1948–51; Legal & General Assurance Soc. Ltd, 1951–75; YWCA, 1975–80; Co. Sec., YWCA, 1977–80. *Address:* Watcombe Corner, Watlington, Oxford OX9 5QJ. *T:* Watlington (049161) 2403.

THOMAS, David Owen, QC 1972; a Recorder of the Crown Court, since 1972; *b* 22 Aug. 1926; *s* of late Emrys Aeron Thomas and Dorothy May Thomas; *m* 1967, Mary Susan Atkinson; three *d* (and one *d* decd). *Educ:* Queen Elizabeth's, Barnet; John Bright Sch., Llandudno; Queen's Univ., Belfast. Served War, HM Forces, 1943–45 and to 1948. Called to the Bar, Middle Temple, 1952, Bencher, 1980; Dep. Chairman, Devon QS, 1971. Mem., Criminal Injuries Compensation Bd, 1987. *Recreations:* acting, cricket, Rugby football. *Address:* 2 King's Bench Walk, Temple, EC4Y 7DE. *T:* 071–353 1746; Briar Cottage, Church Lane, Kings Worthy, Winchester, Hants SO23 7QS. *T:* Winchester (0962) 882141. *Clubs:* Garrick, MCC; Hampshire (Winchester); Western (Glasgow).

THOMAS, David William Penrose; Editor of Punch, since 1989; *b* 17 Jan. 1959; *s* of David Churchill Thomas, *qv*; *m* 1986, Clare Jeremy; two *d. Educ:* Eton; King's College, Cambridge (BA History of Art). Freelance journalist, 1980–84; Editor, The Magazine, 1984–85; Editor, Extra Magazine, Sunday Today, 1986; Asst Editor and Chief Feature Writer, You Magazine, Mail on Sunday, 1986–89. Young Journalist of the Year (British Press Awards), 1983; Columnist of the Year (Magazine Publishing Awards), 1989. *Publications:* (all with Ian Irvine) Bilko: the Fort Baxter Story, 1985; Fame and Fortune, 1988; Sex and Shopping, 1988. *Recreations:* working out and staying in. *Address:* c/o Punch Magazine, Ludgate House, Blackfriars Road, SE1. *Clubs:* Groucho, Hogarth.

THOMAS, Derek John, IPFA; Chief Executive, Surrey County Council, since 1988; *b* 3 Dec. 1934; *s* of late James Llewellyn Thomas and Winifred Mary Thomas; *m* 1st (marr. diss.); three *d*; 2nd, 1978, Christine (*née* Brewer); one *s. Educ:* Hele's Sch., Exeter. Formerly: Treasurer's Depts: Devon CC; Corby Development Corporation; Bath CC; Taunton Bor. Council; Sen. Asst Bor. Treasurer, Poole Bor. Council; Asst County Treasurer, Gloucestershire CC; Principal Asst County Treasurer, Avon CC; County Treasurer, Surrey CC. CIPFA: Mem. Council, 1977–78, 1985–87; Chm., Local Management in Schools Initiative, 1988–. *Address:* County Hall, Penrhyn Road, Kingston upon Thames, Surrey. *T:* 081–541 9000.

THOMAS, Sir Derek (Morison David), KCMG 1987 (CMG 1977); consultant and company director; *b* 31 Oct. 1929; *s* of K. P. D. Thomas and Mali McL. Thomas; *m* 1956, Lineke van der Mast; two *c. Educ:* Radley Coll., Abingdon; Trinity Hall, Cambridge (MA). Mod. Langs Tripos. Articled apprentice, Dolphin Industrial Developments Ltd, 1947. Entered HM Foreign Service, 1953; Midshipman 1953, Sub-Lt 1955, RNVR; FO, 1955; 3rd, later 2nd, Sec., Moscow, 1956–59; 2nd Sec., Manila, 1959–61; UK Delegn to Brussels Conf., 1961–62; 1st Sec., FO, 1962; Sofia, 1964–67; Ottawa, 1967–69; seconded to Treasury, 1969–70; Financial Counsellor, Paris, 1971–75; Head of N American Dept, FCO, 1975–76; Asst Under Sec. of State, FCO, 1976–79; Minister Commercial and later

Minister, Washington, 1979–84; Dep. Under Sec. of State for Europe and Political Dir, FCO, 1984–87; Amb. to Italy, 1987–89. European Advr to N M Rothschild & Sons, 1990–; Director: Rothschild Italia, 1990–; Christow Consultants, 1990–; Associate, CDP Nexus, 1990–. Mem., Reading Univ. Council, 1991–. *Recreations:* listening to people and music; being by, in or on water. *Address:* Flat 1, 12 Lower Sloane Street, SW1W 8BJ. *Clubs:* United Oxford & Cambridge University; Leander.

See also Sir E. W. Gladstone, Bt.

THOMAS, His Honour Dewi Alun, MBE; a Circuit Judge, 1972–90; *b* 3 Dec. 1917; *e s* of late Joshua and Martha Ann Thomas; *m* 1952, Doris Maureen Smith, Barrister; one *s* one *d*. *Educ:* Christ Coll., Brecon; Jesus Coll., Oxford (MA). Served War of 1939–45 (MBE, despatches): mobilised with TA (RA), 1939; served Sicily, Italy, the Balkans; Major, No 2 Commando. Called to Bar, Inner Temple, 1951, Bencher 1969. *Recreations:* golf, watching Rugby football. *Address:* c/o Law Courts, Barker Road, Maidstone, Kent.

THOMAS, Donald Martin; *see* Thomas, Martin.

THOMAS, Donald Michael; poet and novelist; *b* Redruth, Cornwall, 27 Jan. 1935; *s* of Harold Redvers Thomas and Amy (*née* Moyle); two *s* one *d* *Educ:* Redruth Grammar Sch.; Univ. High Sch., Melbourne; New Coll., Oxford (BA 1st cl. Hons in English; MA). School teacher, Teignmouth Grammar Sch., 1959–63; Lectr, Hereford Coll. of Educn, 1964–78; full-time author, 1978–. *Publications: poetry:* Penguin Modern Poets 11, 1968; Two Voices, 1968; Logan Stone, 1971; Love and Other Deaths, 1975; The Honeymoon Voyage, 1978; Dreaming in Bronze, 1981; Selected Poems, 1983; *novels:* The Flute-Player, 1979; Birthstone, 1980; The White Hotel, 1981; Russian Nights, a quintet (Ararat, 1983; Swallow, 1984; Sphinx, 1986; Summit, 1987; Lying Together, 1990); *translations:* Requiem and Poem without a Hero, Akhmatova, 1976; Way of All the Earth, Akhmatova, 1979; Bronze Horseman, Pushkin, 1982; *memoirs:* Memories and Hallucinations, 1988. *Recreations:* travel, Russia and other myths, the culture and history of Cornwall, the life of the imagination. *Address:* The Coach House, Rashleigh Vale, Truro, Cornwall TR1 1TJ.

THOMAS, Donnall; *see* Thomas, Edward D.

THOMAS, Dudley Lloyd; Metropolitan Stipendiary Magistrate, since 1990; *b* 11 Jan. 1946; *s* of late Myrddin Lloyd Thomas and Marjorie Emily (*née* Morgan); *m* 1970, Dr Margaret Susan Early; three *s*. *Educ:* King Edward's Sch., Bath; Coll. of Law, London. Justices Clerk's Asst, 1966–71; admitted as solicitor, 1971; Partner, Trump & Partners, Bristol, 1973–88; called to the Bar, Gray's Inn, 1988; Mem., Western Circuit; in practice at the Bar, 1988–90. Mem., British Medico-Legal Soc. *Recreations:* Rugby football, cricket, music, theatre, India, dogs and walking, classic motor cars. *Address:* Old Street Magistrates' Court, 335 Old Street, EC1V 9LJ. *T:* 071–739 2373.

THOMAS, Prof. (Edward) Donnall, MD; Professor Emeritus of Medicine, University of Washington School of Medicine, Seattle, since 1990; *b* Mart, Texas, 15 March 1920; *m* Dorothy; two *s* one *d*. *Educ:* Univ. of Texas, Austin (BA 1941; MA 1943); Harvard Medical Sch. (MD 1946). Assignments in internal medicine, US Army, 1948–50; Nat. Res. Council Postdoctoral Fellow in Medicine, Dept of Biol., MIT, 1950–51; Chief Med. Resident and Sen. Asst Resident, Peter Bent Brigham Hosp., Seattle, 1951–53, Hematologist, 1953–55; Instructor in Medicine, Harvard Med. Sch. and Res. Associate, Cancer Res. Foundn, Children's Med. Center, Boston, 1953–55; Physician-in-Chief, Mary Imogene Bassett Hosp., Cooperstown, NY and Associate Clinical Prof. of Medicine, Coll. of Physicians and Surgeons, Columbia Univ., NY, 1955–63; Prof. of Medicine, Univ. of Washington Sch. of Medicine, Seattle, 1963–90, Hd, Div. of Oncology, 1963–85; Mem., Fred Hutchinson Cancer Res. Center, Seattle, 1974– (Dir, Med. Oncology, 1974–89, Associate Dir, Clinical Res. Programs, 1982–89). Consulting Physician, Children's Orthopedic Hosp. and Med. Center, Seattle, 1963–; Attending Physician, Seattle: Univ. of Washington Hosp., 1963–; Harborview Med. Center, 1963–; Veterans Admin Hosp., 1963–; Providence Med. Center, 1973–; Swedish Hosp., 1975–. Member Editorial Board: Blood, 1962–75, 1977–82; Transplantation, 1970–76; Procs Soc. Exptl Biol. and Medicine, 1974–81; Leukemia Res., 1977–; Hematological Oncology, 1982–; Jl Clinical Immunology, 1982–; Amer. Jl Hematology, 1985–; Bone Marrow Transplantation, 1986–. Member: Amer. Assoc. Cancer Res.; Amer. Assoc. Physicians; Amer. Fedn Clinical Res.; Amer. Soc. Clinical Oncology; Amer. Soc. Clinical Investigation; Amer. Soc. Hematology (Pres., 1987–88); Nat. Acad. Scis and other foreign socs on related subjects. Lectures in US and UK on hematology and cancer res. Numerous awards from instns in N America and abroad incl. Nobel Prize for Physiology or Medicine, 1990; Presidential Medal of Science, 1990. *Recreations:* hunting, fishing, hiking. *Address:* c/o Fred Hutchinson Cancer Research Center, Room 227, 1124 Columbia Street, Seattle, WA 98104, USA.

THOMAS, Elizabeth; *see* Thomas, M.E.

THOMAS, Elizabeth Marjorie; Secretary General, 1979–83, Literary Consultant, 1984–85, The Authors' Lending and Copyright Society; *b* 10 Aug. 1919; *d* of Frank Porter and Marjorie Porter (*née* Pascall); *m* 1941, George Thomas; one *s* one *d*. *Educ:* St George's Sch., Harpenden; Girton Coll., Cambridge (BA 1st Cl.). Journalist, 1951–59 and Literary Editor, 1959–71, Tribune; Asst Literary Editor, New Statesman, 1971–76; Political Adviser to Rt Hon. Michael Foot, MP, Lord Pres. of the Council and Leader of the House of Commons, 1976–79. Mem., Arts Council, 1974–77 (Mem., Literature Panel, 1971–77); Chm., Literature Panel, Eastern Arts Assoc., 1978–84; Member: Ethnic Minority Arts Cttee, Commission for Racial Equality, 1979–82; British Council Bd, 1982–88. *Publication:* (ed) Tribune 21, 1959. *Address:* 27 Delavale Road, Winchcombe, Glos GL54 5YL. *T:* Cheltenham (0242) 602788.

THOMAS, Emyr, CBE 1980; LLB, LMTPI; DL; General Manager, Telford New Town Development Corporation, 1969–80; Chairman, Telford Community Council, 1980–84; *b* 25 April 1920; *s* of late Brinley Thomas, MA, Aldershot; *m* 1947, Barbara J. May; one *d*. *Educ:* Aldershot County High School. Served War of 1939–45, RASC. Admitted Solicitor, 1947. Asst Solicitor, Exeter City Council, 1947–50; Sen. Asst Solicitor, Reading County Borough Council, 1950–53; Dep. Town Clerk, West Bromwich County Borough Council, 1953–64; Sec. and Solicitor, Dawley (later Telford) Development Corp., 1964–69. First Hon. Sec., 1968–89, Hon. Curator and Vice-Pres., 1989–, Ironbridge Gorge Museum Trust. DL Salop, 1979. *Recreation:* industrial archaeology. *Address:* 8 Kynnersley Lane, Leighton, near Shrewsbury, Shropshire SY5 6RS.

THOMAS, Rt. Rev. Eryl Stephen; Hon. Assistant Bishop of Swansea and Brecon, since 1988; *b* 20 Oct. 1910; *s* of Edward Stephen and Margaret Susannah Thomas; *m* 1939, Jean Mary Alice Wilson; three *s* one *d*. *Educ:* Rossall Sch.; St John's Coll., Oxford; Wells Theological Coll. BA 2nd Class Hon. Theology, Oxford, 1932; MA 1935. Curate of Colwyn Bay, 1933–38, of Hawarden, 1938–43; Vicar of Risca, Mon, 1943–48; Warden of St Michael's Theological Coll., Llandaff, 1948–54; Dean of Llandaff, 1954–68; Bishop of Monmouth, 1968–71, of Llandaff, 1971–75. Chaplain and Sub-Prelate, Order of St John of Jerusalem, 1969. *Address:* 17 Orchard Close, Gilwern, Abergavenny, Gwent NP7 0EN. *T:* Gilwern (0873) 831050.

THOMAS, Frank; *see* Thomas, J. F. P.

THOMAS, Franklin Augustine; President, Ford Foundation, since 1979; *b* 27 May 1934; *s* of James Thomas and Viola Thomas (*née* Atherley); *m* (mar diss.); two *s* two *d*. *Educ:* Columbia College, New York (BA 1956); Columbia Univ. (LLB 1963). Admitted to NY State Bar, 1964; Attorney, Fed. Housing and Home Finance Agency, NYC, 1963–64; Asst US Attorney for Southern District, NY, 1964–65; Dep. Police Comr, charge legal matters, NYC, 1965–67; Pres., Chief Exec. Officer, Bedford Stuyvesant Restoration Corp., Brooklyn, 1967–77. Hon. LLD: Yale, 1970; Fordham, 1972; Pratt Institute, 1974; Pace, 1977; Columbia, 1979. *Address:* The Ford Foundation, 320 East 43rd Street, New York, NY 10017, USA. *T:* (212) 573–5383.

THOMAS, Sir Frederick William, Kt 1959; Councillor, City of Melbourne, 1953–65 (Lord Mayor, 1957–59); *b* 27 June 1906; *s* of F. J. Thomas; *m* 1968, Dorothy Alexa Gordon; three *s* by former marr. *Educ:* Melbourne Grammar School. Served War of 1939–45, RAAF (Air Efficiency Award, two bars); Group Captain. Comdr Order of Orange Nassau with swords (Holland), 1943. *Recreation:* golf. *Address:* 35 Hitchcock Avenue, Barwon Heads, Victoria 3227, Australia. *Clubs:* Naval and Military, Royal Automobile of Victoria (Melbourne); Barwon Heads Golf, Melbourne Cricket, Victoria Racing.

THOMAS, Air Vice-Marshal Geoffrey Percy Sansom, CB 1970; OBE 1945; retired; *b* 24 April 1915; *s* of Reginald Ernest Sansom Thomas, New Malden; *m* 1940, Sally, *d* of Horace Biddle, Gainsborough; one *s* one *d*. *Educ:* King's College School, Wimbledon. Commissioned RAF, 1939; served India and Ceylon, 1942–45; on loan to Turkish Air Force, 1950–52; Group Captain, 1958; served with RAAF, 1960–62; Air Commodore, 1965; Director of Movements, 1965; Air Vice-Marshal, 1969; SASO, Maintenance Comd, 1969–71. *Address:* Elms Wood House, Elms Vale, Dover, Kent CT15 7AR. *T:* Dover (0304) 206375.

THOMAS, Maj.-Gen. George Arthur, CB 1960; CBE 1957; retired; *b* 2 May 1906; *s* of Colonel F. H. S. Thomas, CB, and Diana Thomas; *m* 1936, Diana Zaidee Browne; one *s* one *d*. *Educ:* Cheltenham College; Royal Military Academy, Woolwich. Commissioned, Royal Artillery, 1926; served in UK and Egypt; Staff College, 1940; CO 17 Field Regt, 1st Army, 1942–43; GSO1, 4 Division, 1943–44; BGS 8th Army, 1944–45; Commanding Officer, 1945–46: 138 Field Regt; 17 Medium Regt; 7 RHA; CRA 16 Airborne Div., 1947–48; Imperial Defence Coll., 1952; BGS, MELF, 1955–57; Chief of Staff, HQ Northern Command, 1958–60; Chief of Staff, GHQ Far ELF, 1960–62. Retired, 1962. *Recreations:* games and sports of all kinds. *Address:* Fishing Cottage, Upper Clatford, Andover, Hants. *T:* Andover (0264) 52120. *Club:* Army and Navy.

THOMAS, Sir (Godfrey) Michael (David), 11th Bt, *cr* 1694; Member of Stock Exchange, London, 1959–88; *b* 10 Oct. 1925; *o s* of Rt Hon. Sir Godfrey Thomas, PC, GCVO, KCB, CSI, 10th Bt, and Diana, *d* of late Ven. B. G. Hoskyns (*d* 1985); *S* father 1968; *m* 1956, Margaret Greta Cleland, *yr d* of John Cleland, Stormont Court, Godden Green, Kent; one *s* two *d*, of whom one *s* one *d* are twins. *Educ:* Harrow. The Rifle Brigade, 1944–56. *Heir: s* David John Godfrey Thomas, *b* 11 June 1961. *Address:* 2 Napier Avenue, SW6 3PT. *T:* 071–736 6896. *Clubs:* MCC, Hurlingham.

See also Sir Peter Hutchison, Bt.

THOMAS, Graham Stuart, OBE 1975; VMH 1969; Gardens Consultant to National Trust, since 1974; *b* 3 April 1909; *s* of W. R. Thomas and L. Thomas. *Educ:* horticultural and botanical training, Cambridge Univ. Botanic Garden, 1926–29. Six Hills Nursery, Stevenage, 1930; Foreman, later Manager, T. Hilling & Co., Chobham, 1931–55; Manager, Sunningdale Nurseries, Windlesham, 1956, Associate Dir, 1968–71; Gardens Adviser, National Trust, 1955–74. Vice-President: RHS; Garden History Soc.; British Hosta and Hemerocallis Soc.; Vice-Patron, Royal Nat. Rose Soc. (Dean Hole Medal, 1976); Hon. Mem., Irish Garden Plant Soc. Veitch Meml Medal, RHS, 1966. *Publications:* The Old Shrub Roses, 1955, 5th edn 1978; Colour in the Winter Garden, 1957, 3rd edn 1984; Shrub Roses of Today, 1962, rev. edn 1980; Climbing Roses Old and New, 1965, new edn 1983; Plants for Ground Cover, 1970, rev. edn 1989; Perennial Garden Plants, 1976, rev. and enlarged edn 1990; Gardens of the National Trust, 1979; Three Gardens, 1983; Trees in the Landscape, 1983; The Art of Planting, 1984; A Garden of Roses, 1987; The Complete Flower Paintings and Drawings of Graham Stuart Thomas, 1987; The Rock Garden and its Plants, 1989; An English Rose Garden, 1991. *Recreations:* horticulture, music, painting and drawing plants. *Address:* 21 Kettlewell Close, Horsell, Woking, Surrey GU21 4HY.

THOMAS, Gwyn Edward Ward; *see* Ward Thomas.

THOMAS, Harvey; *see* Thomas, J. H. N.

THOMAS, Prof. Howard Christopher, FRCP; FRCPGlas; Professor of Medicine, St Mary's Hospital Medical School and Imperial College of Science, Technology and Medicine, London University, since 1987; *b* 31 July 1945; *s* of Harold Thomas and Hilda Thomas; *m* 1975, Dilys Ferguson; one *s* one *d*. *Educ:* Univ. of Newcastle (BSc Physiol; MB, BS); PhD Glasgow. MRCPath 1983; MRCP 1969, FRCP 1983; FRCPGlas 1984. Lectr in Immunology, Glasgow Univ., 1971–74; Royal Free Hospital Medical School, London: Lectr in Medicine, 1974–78; Sen. Wellcome Fellow in Clin. Sci., 1978–83; Reader in Medicine, 1983–84; Titular Prof. of Medicine, 1984–87. Humphry Davy Rolleston Lectr, RCP, 1986. British Soc. of Gastroenterology Res. Medal, 1984; Hans Popper Internat. Prize for Distinction in Hepatology, 1989. *Publications:* Clinical Gastrointestinal Immunology, 1979; (ed jtly) Recent Advances in Hepatology, Vol. 1, 1983, vol. 2, 1986; pubns in Hepatology. *Recreations:* fishing, golf. *Address:* Department of Medicine, St Mary's Hospital Medical School, Praed Street, W2 1PG. *T:* 071–725 1606.

THOMAS, Hugh; *see* Thomas of Swynnerton, Baron.

THOMAS, Ivor B.; *see* Bulmer-Thomas.

THOMAS, Prof. Jean Olwen, ScD; FRS 1986; Professor of Macromolecular Biochemistry, University of Cambridge, since 1991; Fellow, New Hall, Cambridge, since 1969; *b* 1 Oct. 1942; *o c* of John Robert Thomas and Lorna Prunella Thomas (*née* Harris). *Educ:* Llwyn-y-Bryn High School for Girls, Swansea; University Coll., Swansea, Univ. of Wales (BSc and Ayling Prize, 1964; PhD and Hinkel Research Prize, 1967 (Chem.)); MA Cantab 1969; ScD Cantab 1985. CChem, MRSC. Beit Meml Fellow, MRC Lab. of Molecular Biology, Cambridge, 1967–69; Demonstrator in Biochemistry, 1969–73, Lectr, 1973–87, Reader in the Biochemistry of Macromolecules, 1987–91, Univ. of Cambridge; Tutor, 1970–76, Vice-Pres., 1983–87, Coll. Lectr, 1969–91, New Hall, Cambridge. Member: EMBO, 1982; SERC, 1990–; Council, Royal Soc., 1990–. Mem., Academia Europaea, 1991. Hon. Fellow, UCW, Swansea, 1987. K. M. Stott Research Prize, Newnham Coll., Cambridge, 1976. *Publications:* Companion to Biochemistry: selected topics for further study, vol. 1, 1974, vol. 2, 1979 (ed jtly and contrib.); papers in sci. jls, esp. on histones and chromatin structure. *Recreations:* reading, music, walking. *Address:* Department of Biochemistry, Tennis Court Road, Cambridge CB2 1QW. *T:*

Cambridge (0223) 333670; 26 Eachard Road, Cambridge CB3 0HY. *T:* Cambridge (0223) 62620.

THOMAS, Jenkin; HM Diplomatic Service; Deputy UK Permanent Representative and Counsellor (Economic and Financial), OECD, Paris, since 1990; *b* 2 Jan. 1938; *s* of late William John Thomas and of Annie Muriel (*née* Thomas). *Educ:* Maesydderwen Sch.; University Coll. London (BA Hons); Univ. of Michigan, Ann Arbor (MA). Joined HM Foreign (subseq. Diplomatic) Service, 1960; Foreign Office, 1960–63; Pretoria/Cape Town, 1963–66; Saigon, 1966–68; FCO, 1968–73; Washington, 1973–77; FCO, 1977–79; Cabinet Office, 1979–80; Tokyo, 1980–82; Athens, 1982–87; Head of Claims Dept, FCO, 1987–90. *Recreations:* reading, music. *Address:* c/o Foreign and Commonwealth Office, SW1.

THOMAS, Sir Jeremy (Cashel), KCMG 1987 (CMG 1980); HM Diplomatic Service, retired; Ambassador to Greece, 1985–89; *b* 1 June 1931; *s* of Rev. H. C. Thomas and Margaret Betty (*née* Humby); *m* 1957, Diana Mary Summerhayes; three *s*. *Educ:* Eton; Merton Coll., Oxford. 16th/5th Lancers, 1949–51. Entered FO, 1954; served Singapore, Rome and Belgrade; Dep. Head, Personnel Ops Dept, FCO, 1970–74; Counsellor and Head of Chancery, UK Mission to UN, NY, 1974–76; Head of Perm. Under-Sec.'s Dept, FCO, 1977–79; Ambassador to Luxembourg, 1979–82; Asst Under-Sec. of State, FCO, 1982–85. *Recreations:* sailing, fishing. *Address:* East Manor Farm, Pook Lane, East Lavant, near Chichester, West Sussex PO18 0AH. *T:* Chichester (0243) 531661. *Clubs:* United Oxford & Cambridge University; Itchenor Sailing.

THOMAS, (John) Alan; seconded to Ministry of Defence as Head of Defence Export Services, since 1989; *b* 4 Jan. 1943; *s* of Idris Thomas and Ellen Constance Noakes; *m* 1966, Angela Taylor; two *s*. *Educ:* Dynevor Sch.; Nottingham Univ. (Industrial Schol.; BSc Hons). FCMA (Prizewinner); CEng; MIEE. Chief Exec., Data Logic, 1973–85; Vice Pres., Raytheon Co. (US), 1985; Pres. and Chief Exec. Officer, Raytheon Europe, 1985–89; Chm., Tag Semi-Conductors (US), 1985–89; Dir, Eur. subsids, 1978–89. Vis. Prof., 1981–, Gov., 1989–, Polytechnic of Central London. Pres., Computing Services Assoc., 1980–81. Freeman, City of London, 1988. *Recreations:* music, sport. *Address:* c/o Ministry of Defence, Main Building, Whitehall, SW1. *T:* 071–218 3042. *Clubs:* Athenæum, Annabel's.

THOMAS, John David, PhD; FBA 1989; Professorial Fellow and Tutor in Palaeography, University of Durham, since 1990; *b* 23 June 1931; *s* of Henry Thomas and Elsie Thomas (*née* Bruin); *m* 1956, Marion Amy Peach; two *s*. *Educ:* Wyggeston Grammar Sch., Leicester; Worcester Coll., Oxford (MA); PhD Wales. Lectr in Classics, UCW, Aberystwyth, 1955–66; University of Durham: Lectr, then Sen. Lectr in Palaeography, 1966–77; Reader in Papyrology, 1977–90. Vis. Fellow, Wolfson Coll., Oxford, 1981. Member: Inst. for Advanced Study, Princeton, 1972; Comité Internat. de Papyrologie, 1983–. *Publications:* Greek Papyri in the Collection of W. Merton III, 1967; The Epistrategos in Ptolemaic and Roman Egypt, Pt I 1975, Pt II 1982; (with A. K. Bowman) Vindolanda: the Latin writing tablets, 1983; contribs to the Oxyrhynchus Papyri XXXVIII, XLIV, XLVII, L, LVII; articles and reviews in learned jls. *Recreations:* music, bird watching, fell walking. *Address:* Archives and Special Collections, University of Durham, 5 The College, Durham DH1 3EQ. *T:* Durham (091) 3743610.

THOMAS, (John) Frank (Phillips); Telecommunications Consultant to British Telecom, international industry and commerce; *b* 11 April 1920; *s* of late John and Catherine Myfanwy Phillips Thomas; *m* 1942, Edith V. Milne; one *s* one *d*. *Educ:* Christ's Coll., Finchley; Univ. of London (BSc). CEng, MIEE. Joined Post Office Research Dept, 1937; trans-oceanic telephone cable system develt, 1947–63; planning UK inland telephone network, 1963–69; Dep. Dir London Telephone Region, 1969–71; Dep. Dir Engrg, Network Planning Dept, 1971; Dir, Network Planning Dept, 1972–79; Dir, Overseas Liaison and Consultancy Dept, Post Office, 1979–81. *Publications:* contrib. scientific and technical jls on telecommunications subjects. *Recreations:* fly fishing, automated horticulture. *Address:* 24 Moneyhill Road, Rickmansworth, Herts. *T:* Rickmansworth (0923) 772992. *Club:* Rickmansworth Lawn Tennis (Vice-Pres.).

THOMAS, (John) Harvey (Noake), CBE 1990; international public relations consultant, since 1976; Consultant Director of Presentation, Conservative Party, 1986–91; *b* 10 April 1939; *s* of John Humphrey Kenneth Thomas and Olga Rosina Thomas (*née* Noake); *m* 1978, Marlies (*née* Kram); two *d*. *Educ:* Westminster School; Northwestern Bible College, Minneapolis; Univs of Minnesota and Hawaii. Billy Graham Evangelistic Assoc., 1960–75; Internat. Public Relations and Project Consultant, 1976–; Dir of Press and Communications, Conservative Party, 1985–86. Mem., Bd of Dirs, London Cremation Co., 1984–. FIPR, FJI, MACE. *Publications:* In the Face of Fear, 1985; Making an Impact, 1989. *Recreations:* travel, family. *Address:* 23–24 The Service Road, Potters Bar, Herts EN6 1QA. *T:* Potters Bar (0707) 49910. *Club:* Institute of Directors.

THOMAS, Rt. Rev. John James Absalom, DD Lambeth 1958; *b* 17 May 1908; *s* of William David and Martha Thomas; *m* 1941, Elizabeth Louise, *d* of Very Rev. H. L. James, DD, former Dean of Bangor; one *s*. *Educ:* University College of Wales, Aberystwyth; Keble College, Oxford. Curate of Llanguicke, 1931–34; Curate of Sketty, 1934–36; Bishop's Messenger and Examining Chaplain, 1936–40; Warden of Church Hostel, Bangor, and Lecturer in University Coll. of N Wales, 1940–44; Vicar of Swansea, 1945–58, also Chaplain to Bishop of Swansea and Brecon; Canon of Brecon Cathedral, 1946; Precentor, 1952; Rural Dean of Swansea, 1952–54; Archdeacon of Gower, 1954–58; Bishop of Swansea and Brecon, 1958–76. Chm. of Governors, Christ Coll., Brecon, 1961–. Chaplain and Sub-Prelate, Order of St John of Jerusalem, 1965. *Address:* Woodbine Cottage, St Mary Street, Tenby, Dyfed.

See also Rev. David Thomas.

THOMAS, Sir (John) Maldwyn, Kt 1984; President, Welsh Liberal Party, 1985–86; *b* 17 June 1918; *s* of Daniel and Gwladys Thomas; *m* 1975, Maureen Elizabeth. *Educ:* Porth Rhondda Grammar Sch. FCIS. Called to Bar, Gray's Inn, 1953; Solicitor, 1965; readmitted to Gray's Inn, 1987. Lewis & Tylor Ltd, Cardiff, 1940–56; Signode Ltd, Swansea, 1956–59; Commercial Agreements Manager, UKAEA, 1959–63; Rank Xerox Ltd: Sec., 1964–70; Man. Dir, 1970–72; Chm., 1972–79; Chm., European Govt Business Relations Council, 1978–79; Dir, Westland PLC, 1985–. Contested (L) Aberavon, 1950. Mem. Council, Richmond Fellowship, 1984–. Vice-President: London Welsh Rugby Football Club; London Welsh Trust. Trustee, London Welsh Sch. *Address:* 9 Chester Terrace, Regent's Park, NW1 4ND. *Club:* Reform.

THOMAS, Sir John Meurig, Kt 1991; MA, PhD, DSc; FRS 1977; Fullerian Professor of Chemistry, Royal Institution of Great Britain, since 1988 (Resident Professor, 1986–88); Deputy Pro-Chancellor, University of Wales, since 1991; Director of the Royal Institution of Great Britain, and Director of the Davy Faraday Research Laboratory, 1986–91; *b* Llanelli, Wales, 15 Dec. 1932; *s* of David John and Edyth Thomas; *m* 1959, Margaret (*née* Edwards); two *d*. *Educ:* Gwendraeth Grammar Sch. (State Scholar); University College of Swansea (Hon. Fellow, 1985); Queen Mary Coll., London. Scientific Officer, UKAEA, 1957–58; Asst Lectr 1958–59, Lectr 1959–65, Reader 1965–69, in Chemistry, UCNW, Bangor; Prof. and Head of Dept of Chemistry, UCW, Aberystwyth, 1969–78; Prof. and Head of Dept of Physical Chemistry, and Fellow of King's Coll., Univ. of Cambridge, 1978–86. Visiting appointments: Tech. Univ. Eindhoven, Holland, 1962; Penna State Univ., USA, 1963, 1967; Tech. Univ. Karlsruhe, Germany, 1966; Weizmann Inst., Israel, 1969; Univ. of Florence, Italy, 1972; Amer. Univ. in Cairo, Egypt, 1973; IBM Res. Center, San José, 1977. Ind. Mem., Radioactive Waste Management Cttee, 1978–80; Member: Chem. SRC, 1976–78; SERC, 1986–; Adv. Cttee, Davy-Faraday Labs, Royal Instn, 1978–80; Scientific Adv. Cttee, Sci. Center, Alexandria, 1979–; ACARD (Cabinet Office), 1982–85; Cttee for Public Understanding of Sci., 1986–; Bd of Governors, Weizmann Inst., 1982–; Academia Europaea, 1989. Chm., Chemrawn (Chem. Res. Applied to World Needs), IUPAC, 1987–; President: Chem. Section, BAAS, 1988–89; London Internat. Youth Sci. Fortnight, 1989–91. Trustee: BM (Natural Hist.), 1987–; Science Mus., 1990–. Hon. Visiting Professor: in Physical Chem., QMC, 1986–; of Chem., Imperial Coll., London, 1986–; Academia Sinica, Beijing; Inst. of Ceramic Sci., Shanghai, 1986–; Winegard Vis. Prof., Guelph Univ., 1982; Sloan Vis. Prof., Harvard, 1983; Vis. Prof., Ecole Nat. Sup. de Chimie de Paris, 1991. Lectures: BBC Welsh Radio Annual, 1978; Gerhardt Schmidt Meml, Weizmann Inst., 1979; Distinguished Vis., London Univ., 1980; Royal Soc.-British Assoc., 1980; Baker, Cornell Univ., 1982–83; Dist. Vis., Univ. of Notre Dame, Indiana, 1986; Schuit, Inst. of Catalysis, Univ. of Delaware, 1986; Battista, Clarkson Univ., USA, 1987; Hund-Klemm, Max Planck Ges., Stuttgart, 1987; Christmas Lectures, Royal Instn, 1987 (televised, 1988); (part-time) First Kenneth Pitzer, Coll. of Chem., Univ. of Calif, Berkeley, 1988; Van't Hoff, Royal Dutch Acad. of Arts and Scis, 1988; Public, RSC, 1988–89; Forum, Brigham Young Univ., Utah, 1989; Bakerian, Royal Soc., 1990; Pierre et Marie Curie Univ., Paris 1991; Bruce Preller Prize, RSE, 1990; Sir Krishnan Meml, Delhi, 1991; Watson Centennial, CIT, 1991. Hon. Fellow: Indian Acad. of Science, 1980; UMIST, 1984; UCNW, Bangor, 1988; RMS, 1989; Queen Mary and Westfield Coll., London, 1990; Foreign Fellow, INA, 1985; Hon. For. Mem., Amer. Acad. of Arts and Scis, 1990; Hon. For. Assoc., Engrg Acad. of Japan, 1991. Hon. Bencher, Gray's Inn, 1987. Hon. LLD Wales, 1984; Hon. DLitt CNAA, 1987; Hon. DSc: Heriot-Watt, 1989; Birmingham, 1991; DUniv Open, 1991. Corday Morgan Silver Medal, Chem. Soc., 1967; first Pettinos Prize, American Carbon Soc., 1969; Tilden Medal and Lectr, Chem. Soc., 1973; Chem. Soc. Prizewinner in Solid State Chem., 1978; Hugo Müller Medal, RSC, 1983; Faraday Medal and Lectr, RSC, 1989; Messel Medal, SCI, 1992. Crystals and Lasers, TV series, 1987; Dylanwadau, radio series, 1990. *Publications:* (with W. J. Thomas) Introduction to the Principles of Heterogeneous Catalysis, 1967 (trans. Russian, 1970); Pan edrychwyf ar y nefoedd, 1978; (with K. I. Zamaraev) Perspectives in Catalysis, 1990; Heterogeneous Catalysis: theory and practice, 1991; Michael Faraday and the Royal Institution: the genius of man and place, 1991; numerous articles on solid state and surface chemistry, catalysis and influence of crystalline imperfections, in Proc. Royal Soc., Jl Chem. Soc., etc. *Recreations:* ancient civilizations, bird watching, hill walking, Welsh literature. *Address:* The Royal Institution, 21 Albemarle Street, W1X 4BS; University Registry, University of Wales, Cathays Park, Cardiff CF1 3NS.

THOMAS, Keith Henry Westcott, CB 1982; OBE 1962; FEng, FRINA, FIIM; RCNC; Chief Executive, Royal Dockyards, 1979–83; *b* 20 May 1923; *s* of Henry and Norah Thomas; *m* 1946, Brenda Jeanette Crofton; two *s*. *Educ:* Portsmouth Southern Secondary Sch.; HM Dockyard Sch., Portsmouth; RNC, Greenwich. Asst Constructor, Admiralty Experiment Works, Haslar, 1947–49; Constructor: Admty, London, 1949–56; Large Carrier Design Section, Admty, Bath, 1956–60; Submarines and New Construction, HM Dockyard, Portsmouth, 1960–63; Project Leader, Special Refit HMS Hermes, Devonport, 1963–66; Dep. Planning Manager, HM Dockyard, Devonport, 1966–68; Project Man., Ikara Leanders, MoD(N), 1968–70; Dir-Gen. of Naval Design, Dept of Navy, Canberra, Aust. (on secondment), 1970–73; Planning Man., 1973–75, Gen. Man., 1975–77, HM Dockyard, Rosyth; Gen. Manager, HM Dockyard, Devonport, 1977–79. Pres., Portsmouth Royal Dockyard Historical Soc., 1988–. *Recreations:* music, lapidary, painting. *Address:* 6 Wyborn Close, Hayling Island, Hants PO11 9HY. *T:* Hayling Island (0705) 463435.

THOMAS, Sir Keith (Vivian), Kt 1988; FBA 1979; President of Corpus Christi College, Oxford, since 1986; *b* 2 Jan. 1933; *s* of Vivian Jones Thomas and Hilda Janet Eirene Thomas (*née* Davies); *m* 1961, Valerie Little; one *s* one *d*. *Educ:* Barry County Grammar Sch.; Balliol Coll., Oxford (Brackenbury Schol.; 1st Cl. Hons Mod. History, 1955; Hon. Fellow 1984). Oxford University: Senior Scholar, St Antony's Coll., 1955; Fellow of All Souls Coll., 1955–57; Fellow of St John's Coll., 1957–86 (Tutor, 1957–85; Hon. Fellow, 1986); Reader in Modern Hist., 1978–85; Prof. of Modern Hist., Jan.–Sept. 1986; Pro-Vice-Chancellor, 1988–; Mem., Hebdomadal Council, 1988–. Vis. Professor, Louisiana State Univ., 1970; Vis. Fellow, Princeton Univ., 1978. Joint Literary Director, Royal Historical Soc., 1970–74, Mem. Council, 1975–78, Vice-Pres., 1980–84. Member: ESRC, 1985–89; Reviewing Cttee on Export of Works of Art, 1989–; Trustee, Nat. Gall., 1991–. Delegate, OUP, 1980–. Lectures: Stenton, Univ. of Reading, 1975; Raleigh, British Acad., 1976; Neale, University Coll. London, 1976; G. M. Trevelyan, Univ. of Cambridge, 1978–79; Sir D. Owen Evans, University Coll. of Wales, Aberystwyth, 1980; Kaplan, Univ. of Pennsylvania, 1983; Creighton, Univ. of London, 1983; Ena H. Thompson, Pomona Coll., 1986; Prothero, RHistS, 1986; Merle Curti, Univ. of Wisconsin-Madison, 1989. For. Hon. Mem., Amer. Acad. of Arts and Scis, 1983. Hon. DLitt: Kent, 1983; Wales, 1987; Hon. LLD Williams Coll., Mass, 1988. Cavaliere Ufficiale, Ordine al Merito della Repubblica Italiana, 1991. Gen. Editor, Past Masters Series, OUP, 1979–. *Publications:* Religion and the Decline of Magic, 1971 (Wolfson Lit. Award for History, 1972); Rule and Misrule in the Schools of Early Modern England, 1976; Age and Authority in Early Modern England, 1977; ed (with Donald Pennington), Puritans and Revolutionaries, 1978; Man and the Natural World, 1983; contribs to historical books and jls. *Recreation:* visiting secondhand bookshops. *Address:* Corpus Christi College, Oxford OX1 4JF. *T:* Oxford (0865) 276700.

THOMAS, Kenneth Rowland; General Secretary, Civil and Public Services Association, 1976–82; *b* 7 Feb. 1927; *s* of William Rowland Thomas and Anne Thomas; *m* 1955, Nora (*née* Hughes); four *s*. *Educ:* St Joseph's Elementary Sch., Penarth; Penarth Grammar Sch. Trainee Reporter, South Wales Echo and Western Mail, 1943–44; Civil Servant, 1944–54; Asst Sec., Civil and Public Services Assoc., 1955, Dep. Gen. Sec., 1967. Mem., TUC Gen. Council, 1977–82. Member: Occupational Pensions Bd, 1981–; CSAB, 1984–91; Law Soc. Professional Purposes Cttee, 1984–86; Solicitors Complaints Bureau, 1986–; Trustee: London Develt Capital Fund, 1984–; British Telecommunications Fund, 1983–; Charity Aid Foundn, 1982–; Director: Postel, 1982–; West Midlands Enterprise Bd, 1982–; Univ. of Warwick Sci. Park, 1986–; Warwickshire Venture Capital Fund, 1988–91; Coventry Venture Capital Fund, 1988–91. *Recreations:* music, anything Welsh. *Address:* Penycoed Hall, Dolgellau, Gwynedd LL40 2YP. *T:* Dolgellau (0341) 423403.

THOMAS, Leslie John; author; *b* 22 March 1931; *s* of late David James Thomas and late Dorothy Hilda Court Thomas, Newport (Mon); *m* 1st, 1956, Maureen Crane (marr. diss.); two *s* one *d*; 2nd, 1970, Diana Miles; one *s*. *Educ:* Dr Barnardo's, Kingston-upon-Thames; Kingston Technical Sch.; SW Essex Technical Coll., Walthamstow. Local Newspapers, London area, 1948–49 and 1951–53; Army, 1949–51 (rose to Lance-

Corporal); Exchange Telegraph News Agency, 1953–55; Special Writer, London Evening News, 1955–66; subseq. author. *Publications: autobiography:* This Time Next Week, 1964; In My Wildest Dreams, 1984; *novels:* The Virgin Soldiers, 1966; Orange Wednesday, 1967; The Love Beach, 1968; Come to the War, 1969; His Lordship, 1970; Onward Virgin Soldiers, 1971; Arthur McCann and All His Women, 1972; The Man with Power, 1973; Tropic of Ruislip, 1974; Stand up Virgin Soldiers, 1975; Dangerous Davies, 1976; Bare Nell, 1977; Ormerod's Landing, 1978; That Old Gang of Mine, 1979; The Magic Army, 1981; The Dearest and the Best, 1984; The Adventures of Goodnight and Loving, 1986; Dangerous in Love, 1987; Orders For New York, 1989; The Loves and Journeys of Revolving Jones, 1991; *short stories:* The Boundary Book, 1986; *non-fiction:* Some Lovely Islands, 1968; The Hidden Places of Britain, 1981; A World of Islands, 1983; Short Singles, 1986; TV Plays and Documentaries, etc, incl. Channel Four series, Great British Isles (also presented), 1989. *Recreations:* islands, antiques, cricket. *Address:* The Walton Canonry, The Close, Salisbury, Wilts. *Clubs:* Wig and Pen, Lord's Taverners; Press.

THOMAS, Sir Maldwyn; *see* Thomas, Sir J. M.

THOMAS, Margaret, Women's International Art Club, 1940; RBA 1947; NEAC 1950; Contemporary Portrait Society, 1970; RWA 1971; Practising Artist (Painter); *b* 26 Sept. 1916; *d* of late Francis Stewart Thomas and of Grace Whetherly. *Educ:* privately; Slade Sch.; RA Schools. Slade Scholar, 1936. Hon. Sec. Artists International Assoc., 1944–45; FRSA 1971. Group exhibitions, Wildensteins, 1946, 1949 and 1962; First one-man show at Leicester Galls, 1949, and subsequently at same gallery, 1950; one-man shows in Edinburgh (Aitken Dotts), 1952, 1955, 1966, and at Outlook Tower, Edinburgh, during Internat. Fest., 1961; RBA Galleries, London, 1953; at Canaletto Gall. (a barge, at Little Venice), 1961; Exhibition of Women Artists, Wakefield Art Gall., 1961; Howard Roberts Gallery Cardiff, 1963, The Minories, Colchester, 1964, QUB, 1967, Mall Galls, London, 1972; Octagon Gall., Belfast, 1973; Court Lodge Gallery, Kent, 1974; Gallery Paton, Edinburgh, 1977; Scottish Gall., Edinburgh (major retrospective), 1982; Sally Hunter, London, 1988 and 1991; regular exhibitor Royal Academy and Royal Scottish Academy. Official purchases: Prince Philip, Duke of Edinburgh; Chantrey Bequest; Arts Council; Exeter College, Oxford; Min. of Education; Min. of Works; Wakefield, Hull, Paisley and Carlisle Art Galleries; Edinburgh City Corporation; Nuffield Foundation Trust; Steel Co. of Wales; Financial Times; Mitsukoshi Ltd, Tokyo; Scottish Nat. Orchestra; Robert Flemming collection; Lloyd's of London; Sock Shop Internat.; GLC and county education authorities in Yorks, Bucks, Monmouth, Derbyshire, Hampshire and Wales. Coronation painting purchased by Min. of Works for British Embassy in Santiago. Winner, Hunting Gp Award for best oil painting of the year, 1981. *Publications:* work reproduced in: Daily Telegraph, News Chronicle, Listener, Studio, Scottish Field, Music and Musicians, The Lady, Arts Review, Western Mail; Illustrated London News, The Artist, The Spectator, Eastern Daily Press. *Recreations:* antique collecting, gardening, vintage cars. *Address:* Ellingham Mill, near Bungay, Suffolk NR35 2EP. *T:* Kirby Cane (050845) 656; 8 North Bank Street, Edinburgh EH1 2LP. *T:* 031–225 3343; 13A North Road, Highgate Village, N6 4BD. *T:* 081–340 2527.

THOMAS, Martin, OBE 1982; QC 1979; a Recorder of the Crown Court, since 1976; *b* 13 March 1937; *s* of Hywel and Olwen Thomas; *m* 1961, Nan Thomas (*née* Kerr); three *s* one *d.* *Educ:* Grove Park Grammar Sch., Wrexham; Peterhouse, Cambridge. MA, LLB (Cantab). Solicitor at Wrexham, 1961–66; Lectr in Law, 1966–68; called to the Bar, Gray's Inn, 1967, Bencher, 1989; Barrister, Wales and Chester Circuit, 1968–; Dep. Circuit Judge, 1974–76. Contested (L): W Flints, 1964, 1966, 1970; Wrexham, Feb. and Oct. 1974, 1979, 1983, 1987; Vice Chm., Welsh Liberal Party, 1967–69, Chm. 1969–74; President: Wrexham Liberal Assoc., 1975–; Welsh Liberal Party, 1977, 1978, 1979. Vice Chm., Marcher Sound (ind. local radio for NE Wales and Cheshire), 1983–. *Recreations:* Rugby football, rowing, golf, music-making, fishing. *Address:* Glasfryn, Gresford, Wrexham, Clwyd. *T:* Gresford (097883) 2205. *Clubs:* Reform; Western (Glasgow); Wrexham Rugby Football, Bristol Channel Yacht.

THOMAS, (Mary) Elizabeth; Director, West Midlands Board, Central Television plc, since 1982; *b* 22 March 1935; *d* of Kathleen Mary Thomas (*née* Dodd) and David John Thomas; *m* 1962, Brian Haydn Thomas; two *d.* *Educ:* Dr Williams' School, Dolgellau; Talbot Heath School, Bournemouth; Royal Acad. of Music. ARCM, GRSM. Head of Music, High Sch., Totnes, 1958–61; Music Lectr, Ingestre Hall, Stafford, 1962; Berkshire Music Schs, 1964–66; Adult Educn Lectr, Bridgnorth Coll. of Further Educn, 1966–69. Chm., Pentabus Arts Ltd, 1983–87. Arts Council of Great Britain: Member, 1984–88; Chm., Regl Adv. Cttee, 1984–86; Chm., Planning and Develt Bd, 1986–88. Chairman: W Midlands Arts, 1980–84; Council, Regional Arts Assocs, 1982–85; Nat. Assoc. of Local Arts Councils, 1980–82 (Vice-Pres., 1982); City of Birmingham Touring Opera, 1987–. *Recreations:* collecting antique glass, gardening, string quartet playing. *Address:* Cutters House, 48 Shineton Street, Much Wenlock, Shropshire TF13 6HU.

THOMAS, Rt. Rev. Maxwell McNee, ThD; Warden of St Paul's College, Sydney, since 1985; Lecturer in History and Thought of Christianity, University of Sydney, since 1986; *b* 23 Aug. 1926; *s* of Rev. Charles Elliot Thomas, ThL, and Elsie Frances Thomas (*née* McNee); *m* 1952, Elaine Joy Walker; two *s* one *d.* *Educ:* St Paul's Coll., Univ. of Sydney (MA, BD); General Theological Seminary, New York (ThD). Lectr in Theology and Greek, St John's Coll, Morpeth, NSW, 1950; deacon, 1950; priest, 1952; Curate: St Peter's, E. Maitland, 1951–52; St Mary Magdalene, Richmond, Surrey, 1952–54; All Saints', Singleton, NSW, 1955. Priest-in-Charge and Rector, The Entrance, NSW, 1955–59; Fellow and Tutor, General Theol. Seminary, NY, 1959–63; Hon. Chaplain to Bishop of New York, 1959–63, Chaplain, 1963–64; Chaplain, Univ. of Melbourne and of Canterbury Fellowship, 1964–68; Consultant Theologian to Archbishop of Melbourne, Stewart Lectr in Divinity, Trinity Coll. and Chaplain of Canterbury Fellowship, 1968–75; Bishop of Wangaratta, 1975–85. Member: Gen. Synod's Commn on Doctrine, 1970– (Chm., 1976–); Faith and Order Commn, WCC, 1977–; Anglican-Orthodox Jt Doctrinal Discussion Gp, 1978. *Address:* St Paul's College, Sydney, NSW 2006, Australia. *Clubs:* Melbourne, Royal Automobile of Victoria; Australian (Sydney).

THOMAS, Sir Michael, 3rd Bt; *see* Thomas, Sir W. M. M.

THOMAS, Sir Michael, 11th Bt; *see* Thomas, Sir G. M. D.

THOMAS, Michael David, CMG 1985; QC 1973; barrister in private practice; Attorney-General of Hong Kong, 1983–88; Member, Executive and Legislative Councils, Hong Kong, 1983–88; Chairman, Law Reform Commission, Hong Kong, 1983–88; *b* 8 Sept. 1933; *s* of late D. Cardigan Thomas and Kathleen Thomas; *m* 1st, 1958, Jane Lena Mary (marr. diss. 1978), *e d* of late Francis Neate; two *s* two *d*; 2nd, 1981, Mrs Gabrielle Blakemore (marr. diss. 1986); 3rd, 1988, Hon. Lydia Dunn (*see* Baroness Dunn). *Educ:* Chigwell Sch., Essex; London Sch. of Economics. LLB (Hons) 1954. Called to Bar, Middle Temple, 1955 (Blackstone Entrance Schol., 1952; Harmsworth Schol., 1957); Bencher, 1981. Nat. Service with RN, Sub-Lt RNVR, 1955–57. In practice at Bar from 1958. Junior Counsel to Minister of Defence (RN) and to Treasury in Admty matters, 1966–73. Wreck Commissioner under Merchant Shipping Act 1970; one of Lloyd's salvage arbitrators, 1974. Governor, Chigwell Sch., 1971–83. *Publications:* (ed jtly) Temperley: Merchant Shipping Acts, 6th edn 1963 and 7th edn 1974. *Recreations:* music, travel. *Address:* Temple Chambers, 16F One Pacific Place, Hong Kong. *Clubs:* Garrick; Hong Kong (Hong Kong).

THOMAS, Col Michael John Glyn, LRAMC; Commanding Officer, Army Blood Supply Depot, since 1987; *b* 14 Feb. 1938; *s* of Glyn Pritchard Thomas and Mary Thomas (*née* Moseley); *m* 1969, Sheelagh Thorpe; one *d.* *Educ:* Haileybury and ISC; Trinity College, Cambridge; St Bartholomew's Hosp. MA, MB, BChir, LMSSA, DTM&H. Qualified 1962; House Surgeon, Essex County Hosp. and House Physician, St James, Balham, 1963; Regtl MO, 2nd Bn The Parachute Regt, 1965; Trainee Pathologist, BMH Singapore, 1968; Specialist in Pathology, Colchester Mil. Hosp., 1971; Senior Specialist in Pathology, Army Blood Supply Depot, 1977; Exchange Pathologist, Walter Reed Army Inst. of Research, 1982–84; Officer in Charge of Leishman Lab., Cambridge Mil. Hosp., 1985–87. Hon. Consultant Haemotologist, UCH/Middlesex Hosp., 1987. Member: Council, BMA, 1974–82 (Chm., Junior Mems Forum, 1974–75; Chm., Central Ethical Cttee, 1978–82; Mem., expert panel on AIDS, 1986–; Mem., Bd of Sci. and Educn, 1987–); Cttee on Transfusion Equipment, BSI; Economic and Social Cttee, EEC, 1989–. *Publications:* contribs to ref. books, reports and jls on Medical Ethics, Haematology and Blood Banking, Malariology and subjects of general medical interest. *Recreations:* sailing, travel, photography, philately. *Address:* Army Blood Supply Depot, Ordnance Road, Aldershot, Hants GU11 2AF. *Club:* Tanglin (Singapore).

THOMAS, Michael Stuart, (Mike Thomas); Chairman and Managing Director, Corporate Communications Strategy, since 1988; Chairman, Media Audits Ltd, since 1990; *b* 24 May 1944; *s* of Arthur Edward Thomas. *Educ:* Latymer Upper Sch.; King's Sch., Macclesfield; Liverpool Univ. (BA). Pres., Liverpool Univ. Guild of Undergraduates, 1965–66; Past Mem. Nat. Exec., NUS. Head of Research Dept, Co-operative Party, 1966–68; Sen. Res. Officer, Political and Economic Planning (now PSI), 1968–73; Dir, Volunteer Centre, 1973–74; Dir of Public Relations and Public Affairs, Dewe Rogerson, 1984–88; Mem., BR Western Reg. Bd, 1985–90. MP (Lab and Co-op 1974–81, SDP 1981–83) Newcastle upon Tyne E, Oct. 1974–1983. Mem., Select Cttee on Nationalised Industries, 1975–79; Chm., PLP Trade Gp, 1979–81; SDP spokesman on health and social services, 1981–83; Member: SDP Nat. Cttee, 1981–90; SDP Policy Cttee, 1981–90; Chairman: Organisation Cttee of SDP, 1981–88; By-election Cttee, SDP, 1984–88; SDP Finance Working Gp, 1988–90; a Vice-Pres., SDP, 1988–90; Mem., Alliance Strategy Cttee, 1983–87. Contested: (SDP) Newcastle upon Tyne East, 1983; (SDP/Alliance) Exeter, 1987. Mem., USDAW; founder of parly jl The House Magazine. *Publications:* Participation and the Redcliffe Maud Report, 1970; (ed) The BBC Guide to Parliament, 1979, 1983; various PEP pamphlets, contribs, etc, 1971–; various articles, reviews, etc. *Recreations:* theatre, music, cooking. *Address:* 45 St Mary's Grove, W4 3LN. *T:* 071–995 8803.

THOMAS, Michael T.; *see* Tilson Thomas.

THOMAS, Neville; *see* Thomas, R. N.

THOMAS, Norman, CBE 1980; HM Chief Inspector of Schools, 1973–81; Specialist Professor in Primary Education, University of Nottingham, 1987–90; *b* 1 June 1921; *s* of Bowen Thomas and Ada Thomas (*née* Redding); *m* 1942, Rose Henshaw; one *s* one *d.* *Educ:* Latymer's Sch., Edmonton; Camden Coll. Qual. Teacher. Commerce and Industry, then primary schs in London and Herts, 1948–56; Head, Longmeadow Sch., Stevenage, 1956–61; HM Inspector of Schools, Lincs and SE England, 1962–68; HMI, Staff Inspector for Primary (Junior and Middle) Schs, 1969–73. Chm., Cttee of Enquiry on Primary Educn in ILEA, 1983–84. Adviser to Parly Cttee on Educn, Science and Art, 1984–86. Visiting Professor: NE London Polytechnic, 1984–86; Hatfield Polytechnic, 1991–; Hon. Prof., Univ. of Warwick, 1986–. Hon. FCP, 1988. *Publications:* Primary Education from Plowden to the 1990s, 1990; articles in professional jls. *Recreations:* photography, reading. *Address:* 19 Langley Way, Watford, Herts WD1 3EJ. *T:* Watford (0923) 223766.

THOMAS, Patricia Anne; Commissioner for Local Administration in England, since 1985; *b* 3 April 1940; *d* of Frederick S. Lofts and Ann Elizabeth Lofts; *m* 1968, Joseph Glyn Thomas; one *s* two *d.* *Educ:* King's College London. LLB, LLM. Lectr in Law, Univ. of Leeds, 1962–63, 1964–68; Teaching Fellow, Univ. of Illinois, 1963–64; Sen. Lectr, then Principal Lectr, Head of Sch. of Law and Prof., Lancashire Polytechnic, 1973–85. Mem., 1976–84, Vice-Pres., 1984, Pres., 1985, Greater Manchester and Lancashire Rent Assessment Panel; Chm., Blackpool Supplementary Benefit Appeal Tribunal, 1980–85. *Publication:* Law of Evidence, 1972. *Recreations:* walking, cooking, reading, travel. *Address:* Commission for Local Administration in England, Beverley House, Shipton Road, York YO3 6FZ. *T:* York (0904) 630151.

THOMAS, Prof. Phillip Charles; Principal, Scottish Agricultural College, and Professor of Agriculture, University of Glasgow, since 1987; *b* 17 June 1942; *s* of William Charles Thomas and Gwendolen (*née* Emery); *m* 1967, Pamela Mary Hirst; one *s* one *d.* *Educ:* University College of North Wales, Bangor (BSc, PhD). Lectr in animal nutrition and physiology, Univ. of Leeds, 1966–71; progressively, SSO to SPSO, Hannah Research Inst., 1971–87. *Publications:* (with J. A. F. Rook) Silage for Milk Production, 1982; (with J. A. F. Rook) Nutritional Physiology of Farm Animals, 1983. *Recreation:* Rugby coaching. *Address:* Scottish Agricultural College, Cleeve Gardens, Oakbank Road, Perth PH1 1HF. *T:* Perth (0738) 36611. *Club:* Farmers'.

THOMAS, Quentin Jeremy; Deputy Secretary, Northern Ireland Office, since 1991; *b* 1 Aug. 1944; *s* of late Arthur Albert Thomas and Edith Kathleen Thomas (*née* Bigg); *m* 1969, Anabel Jane, *d* of J. H. Humphreys, *qv*; one *s* two *d.* *Educ:* Perse School, Cambridge; Gonville and Caius College, Cambridge. Home Office, 1966; Private Sec. to Perm. Under-Sec. of State, 1970; Crime Policy Planning Unit, 1974–76; Sec. to Royal Commn on Gambling, 1976–78; Civil Service (Nuffield and Leverhulme) Travelling Fellowship, 1980–81; Head, Broadcasting Dept, Home Office, 1984–88; Under Sec., NI Office, 1988–91. *Address:* Northern Ireland Office, Whitehall, SW1A 2AZ.

See also R. C. Thomas.

THOMAS, Ralph Philip, MC 1942; Film Director; *b* Hull, Yorks, 10 Aug.; *m* 1944, Joy Spanjer; one *s* one *d.* *Educ:* Tellisford School, Clifton. Entered film industry, 1932, and worked in all production depts, particularly editing, until 1939. Served War of 1939–45, as Regimental Officer 9th Lancers until 1944; thereafter Instructor Royal Military College. Returned to Film Industry, in Rank Organisation Trailer Dept, 1946; Joined Gainsborough Pictures, 1948, and directed Once Upon a Dream, Traveller's Joy. Films directed at Pinewood Studios: The Clouded Yellow, Appointment with Venus, The Venetian Bird, A Day to Remember, Doctor in the House, Mad About Men, Above Us The Waves, Doctor at Sea, The Iron Petticoat, Checkpoint, Doctor at Large, Campbell's Kingdom, A Tale of Two Cities, The Wind Cannot Read, The 39 Steps, Upstairs and Downstairs, Conspiracy of Hearts, Doctor in Love, No My Darling Daughter, No Love for Johnnie, The Wild and the Willing, Doctor in Distress, Hot enough for June, The High Bright Sun, Doctor in Clover, Deadlier than the Male, Nobody Runs Forever, Some Girls Do,

Doctor in Trouble, Quest, Percy, It's a 2 foot 6 inch Above the Ground World, Percy's Progress, A Nightingale Sang in Berkeley Square, Doctors' Daughters, Pop Pirates. *Address:* Kirrin House, Blyton Close, Beaconsfield, Bucks HP9 2LX. *T:* Beaconsfield (0494) 671856. *Club:* Garrick.

THOMAS, Dr Reginald; Ambassador; Inspector General in the Ministry of Foreign Affairs, Vienna, since 1988; *b* 28 Feb. 1928; *s* of Dr Leopold Thomas and Irma Thomas (*née* von Smekal); *m* 1960, Ingrid Renate Leitner; three *s* one *d*. *Educ:* Univ. of Vienna (Dr jur 1950). Entered Austrian Foreign Service, 1951; Austrian Legation, Bern, 1952–56; Dep. Legal Adviser on Internat. Law, Min. of Foreign Affairs, Vienna, 1956–59; Austrian Embassy, Tokyo, 1959–62; Head of Office of Sec. Gen. for Foreign Affairs, Vienna, 1962–68; Ambassador to Pakistan and concurrently accredited to Union of Burma, 1968–71; Ambassador to Japan and concurrently accredited to Republic of Korea, 1971–75; Head of Dept of Administration, Min. of Foreign Affairs, Vienna, 1975–82; concurrently Dep. Sec. Gen. for Foreign Affairs, Vienna, 1978–82; Austrian Ambassador to UK, 1982–87. Mem., Austrian Assoc. for Foreign Policy and Internat. Relations, Vienna, 1978–82. Foreign orders include: Grand Cross: Order of the Rising Sun (Japan); Order of Diplomatic Service (Korea); Independence Order (Jordan); Order of F. de Miranda (Venezuela); Hilal-i-Qaid-i-Azam (Pakistan). *Recreation:* sports. *Address:* Schwarzenbergstrasse 8, A-1010 Wien, Austria. *Club:* Queen's.

THOMAS, Adm. Sir Richard; *see* Thomas, Adm. Sir W. R. S.

THOMAS, Richard, CMG 1990; HM Diplomatic Service; Ambassador to Bulgaria, since 1989; *b* 18 Feb. 1938; *s* of Anthony Hugh Thomas, JP and Molly Thomas, MBE; *m* 1966, Catherine Jane Hayes, Sydney, NSW; one *s* two *d*. *Educ:* Leighton Park; Merton Coll., Oxford (MA). Nat. Service, 2nd Lt, RASC, 1959–61. Asst Principal, CRO, 1961; Private Sec. to Parly Under Sec., 1962–63; Second Secretary: Accra, 1963–65; Lomé, 1965–66; (later First Sec.) UK Delegn NATO, Paris and Brussels, 1966–69; First Secretary: FCO, 1969–72; (Economic), New Delhi, 1972–75; and Asst Head of Dept, FCO, 1976–78; FCO Visiting Res. Fellow, RIIA, 1978–79; Counsellor, Prague, 1979–83; Ambassador, Iceland, 1983–86; Overseas Inspector, 1986–89. *Publication:* India's Emergence as an Industrial Power: Middle Eastern Contracts, 1982. *Recreations:* foreign parts, gossip, skiing. *Address:* c/o Foreign and Commonwealth Office, SW1A 2AH. *Club:* United Oxford & Cambridge University.

THOMAS, Richard James, LLB; Under Secretary, and Director of Consumer Affairs, Office of Fair Trading, since 1986; *b* 18 June 1949; *s* of Daniel Lewis Thomas, JP, and Norah Mary Thomas; *m* 1974, Julia Delicia, *d* of Dr E. G. W. Clarke; two *s* one *d*. *Educ:* Bishop's Stortford Coll.; Univ. of Southampton (LLB Hons); College of Law. Admitted Solicitor, 1973. Articled clerk and Asst Solicitor, Freshfields, 1971–74; Solicitor, CAB Legal Service, 1974–79; Legal Officer and Hd of Resources Gp, Nat. Consumer Council, 1979–86. Chm., British Univs N America Club, 1970–71; Trustee, W London Fair Housing Gp, 1976–79; Member: Management Cttee, Gtr London CAB Service, 1977–79; Legal Services Gp, Nat. Assoc. of CABx, 1978–86; London Electricity Cons. Council, 1979–84; European Consumer Law Gp, 1981–86; European Commn Working Party on Access to Justice, 1981–82; Cttee of City of Westminster Law Soc., 1984–86; Lord Chancellor's Adv. Cttee on Civil Justice Rev., 1985–88. *Publications:* reports, articles and broadcasts on range of legal and consumer issues. *Recreations:* family, maintenance of home and garden, travel. *Address:* Office of Fair Trading, Field House, Bream's Buildings, EC4A 1PR. *T:* 071–269 8821.

THOMAS, Sir Robert (Evan), Kt 1967; DL, JP; Leader, Greater Manchester Metropolitan County Council, 1973–77; Deputy Chairman, Manchester Ship Canal, 1971–74; *b* 8 Oct. 1901; *s* of Jesse and Anne Thomas; *m* 1924, Edna Isherwood; one *s* one *d*. *Educ:* St Peter's, Leigh, Lancs. Miner, 1914; served Army, 1919–21; Bus Driver, 1924–37; Trade Union Official, 1937–66; Member, Manchester City Council, 1944–74; Lord Mayor of Manchester, 1962–63. Chairman: Assoc. of Municipal Corps, 1973–74; Assoc. of Metropolitan Authorities, 1974–77; British Sector, Internat. Union of Local Authorities, 1974–77. JP Manchester, 1948; DL: County Palatine of Lancaster, 1967–73, County Palatine of Greater Manchester, 1974. Hon. MA Manchester, 1974. *Recreations:* dancing, gardening, golf. *Address:* 29 Milwain Road, Manchester M19 2PX. *T:* 061–224 5778.

THOMAS, (Robert) Neville, QC 1975; barrister-at-law; a Recorder of the Crown Court, 1975–82; *b* 31 March 1936; *s* of Robert Derfel Thomas and Enid Anne Thomas; *m* 1970, Jennifer Anne Brownrigg; one *s* one *d*. *Educ:* Ruthin Sch.; University Coll., Oxford (MA, BCL). Called to Bar, Inner Temple, 1962, Bencher, 1985. *Recreations:* fishing, walking, reading. *Address:* Glansevern, Berriew, Welshpool, Powys SY21 8AH. *Club:* Garrick.

THOMAS, Prof. Roger Christopher, FRS 1989; Professor of Physiology, University of Bristol, since 1986; *b* 2 June 1939; *e s* of late Arthur Albert Thomas and Edith Kathleen (*née* Bigg); *m* 1964, Monica Mary, *d* of late Lt-Comdr William Peter Querstret, RN; two *s*. *Educ:* Perse Sch., Cambridge; Univ. of Southampton (BSc, PhD). Res. Associate, Rockefeller Univ., NY, 1964–66; Hon. Res. Asst, Biophysics, UCL, 1966–69; Bristol University: Lectr, 1969–77; Reader in Physiology, 1977–86; Hd of Dept of Physiology, 1985–90. Vis. Prof., Yale Univ., 1979–80. *Publications:* Ion-Sensitive Intracellular Microelectrodes, 1978; many papers on ion transport in learned jls. *Recreations:* cooking, ski-ing. *Address:* Department of Physiology, School of Medical Sciences, The University, Bristol BS8 1TD. *T:* Bristol (0272) 303473.

See also Q. J. Thomas.

THOMAS, Dr Roger Gareth; Family Medical Practitioner, since 1952; *b* 14 Nov. 1925; *m* 1958, Indeg Thomas; one *s* one *d*. *Educ:* Amman Valley Grammar Sch.; London Hosp. Med. Coll. Captain, RAMC, 1949–52. MP (Lab) Carmarthen, 1979–87. *Recreation:* music. *Address:* Ffynnon Wên, Capel Hendre, Ammanford, Dyfed SA18 3SD. *T:* Cross Hands (0269) 843093.

THOMAS, Roger John Laugharne; QC 1984; a Recorder, since 1987; *b* 22 Oct. 1947; *s* of Roger Edward Laugharne Thomas and Dinah Agnes Thomas; *m* 1973, Elizabeth Ann Buchanan; one *s* one *d*. *Educ:* Rugby School; Trinity Hall, Cambridge (BA); Univ. of Chicago (Commonwealth Fellow; JD). Called to Bar, Gray's Inn, 1969. Asst Teacher, Mayo College, Ajmer, India, 1965–66. Faculty Fellow, Law Sch., Univ. of Southampton, 1990. *Publications:* papers and articles on maritime law and insurance and reinsurance law. *Recreations:* gardens, opera, walking, travel. *Address:* 4 Essex Court, Temple, EC4Y 9AJ. *T:* 071–583 9191.

THOMAS, Roger Lloyd; Senior Clerk (Acting), Committee Office, House of Commons, 1979–84 and Clerk, Select Committee on Welsh Affairs, 1982–84, retired; *b* 7 Feb. 1919; *er s* of Trevor John Thomas and Eleanor Maud (*née* Jones), Abercarn, Mon; *m* 1945, Stella Mary, *d* of Reginald Ernest Willmett, Newport, Mon; three *s* one *d*. *Educ:* Barry County Sch.; Magdalen Coll., Oxford (Doncaster Schol.; Heath Harrison Trav. Schol.). BA 2nd Mod. Langs, 1939; MA 1946. Pres., OU Italian Soc., 1938–39. Served 1939–46, RA and Gen. Staff (Major GSO2) in India, Middle East, N Africa, Italy and Germany. Civil Servant, 1948–70: Min. of Fuel and Power, Home Office, Treasury, Welsh Office and Min. of Housing and Local Govt; Private Sec. to Perm. Under-Sec. of State, Home Office, 1950 and to successive Parly Under-Secs of State, 1951–53; Sec., Interdeptl Cttee on powers of Subpoena, 1960; Asst Sec., 1963; Sec., Aberfan Inquiry Tribunal, 1966–67; Chm., Working Party on Building by Direct Labour Organisations, 1968–69; Gen. Manager, The Housing Corporation, 1970–73; Asst Sec., DoE, 1974–79. *Publications:* sundry reports. *Recreation:* growing flowers. *Address:* 5 Park Avenue, Caterham, Surrey CR3 6AH. *T:* Caterham (0883) 342080. *Club:* Union (Oxford).

See also D. H. P. Thomas.

THOMAS, Roger R.; *see* Ridley-Thomas, R.

THOMAS, Ronald Richard; *b* March 1929. *Educ:* Ruskin Coll. and Balliol Coll., Oxford (MA). Sen. Lectr, Econ. and Indust. Studies, Univ. of Bristol. Contested (Lab): Bristol North-West, Feb. 1974; Bristol East, 1987; MP (Lab) Bristol NW, Oct. 1974–1979. Former Mem., Bristol DC. Mem. ASTMS. *Address:* 64 Morris Road, Lockleaze, Bristol BS7 9TA.

THOMAS, Rev. Ronald Stuart; poet; *b* 29 March 1913; *m* Mildred E. Eldridge; one *s*. *Educ:* University of Wales (BA); St Michael's College, Llandaff. Ordained deacon, 1936; priest, 1937. Curate of Chirk, 1936–40; Curate of Hanmer, in charge of Talarn Green, 1940–42; Rector of Manafon, 1942–54; Vicar of Eglwysfach, 1954–67; Vicar of St Hywyn, Aberdaron, with St Mary, Bodferin, 1967–78, and Rector of Rhiw with Llanfaelrhys, 1972–78. First record, reading his own poems, 1977. Queen's Gold Medal for Poetry, 1964; Cholmondeley Award, 1978. *Publications:* poems: Stones of the Field (privately printed), 1947; Song at the Year's Turning, 1955 (Heinemann Award of the Royal Society of Literature, 1956); Poetry for Supper, 1958; Tares, 1961; Bread of Truth, 1963; Pieta, 1966; Not That He Brought Flowers, 1968; H'm, 1972; Selected Poems 1946–1968, 1974; Laboratories of the Spirit, 1976; Frequencies, 1978; Between Here and Now, 1981; Later Poems 1972–1982, 1983; Experimenting with an Amen, 1986; The Echoes Return Slow, 1988; edited A Book of Country Verse, 1961; George Herbert, A Choice of Verse, 1967; A Choice of Wordsworth's Verse, 1971; Welsh Airs, 1987; Counterpoint, 1990. *Address:* Sarn-y-Plas, Y Rhiw, Pwllheli, Gwynedd.

THOMAS, Roydon Urquhart; QC 1985; a Recorder, since 1986; *b* 17 May 1936; *s* of Rowland Daniel Thomas and Jean Milne Thomas; *m* 1984, Caroline; one *s* one *d* (and one *s* decd). *Educ:* Fettes College; Sidney Sussex College, Cambridge (BA). Called to the Bar, Middle Temple, 1960; South Eastern Circuit. *Publication:* (Asst Editor) Tolstoy on Divorce, 1964. *Recreations:* golf, fishing. *Address:* 1 Essex Court, Temple, EC4Y 9AR. *T:* 071–583 2000. *Club:* Hurlingham.

THOMAS, Hon. Sir Swinton (Barclay), Kt 1985; **Hon. Mr Justice Swinton Thomas;** a Judge of the High Court of Justice, Queen's Bench Division, since 1990 (Family Division, 1985–90); *b* 12 Jan. 1931; *s* of late Brig. William Bain Thomas, CBE, DSO, and Mary Georgina Thomas; *m* 1967, Angela, Lady Cope; one *s* one *d*. *Educ:* Ampleforth Coll.; Lincoln Coll., Oxford (Scholar) (MA). Served with Cameronians (Scottish Rifles), 1950–51, Lieut. Called to Bar, Inner Temple, 1955 (Bencher, 1983); QC 1975; a Recorder of the Crown Court, 1975–85. A Presiding Judge, Western Circuit, 1987–90. Member: General Council of the Bar, 1970–74; Criminal Injuries Compensation Bd, 1984–85. *Recreations:* reading, travel. *Address:* Royal Courts of Justice, Strand, WC2A 2LL. *T:* 071–936 6884. *Club:* Garrick.

THOMAS, Trevor, BA; artist, author; retired; *b* Ynysddu, Gwent, 8 June 1907; 2nd *s* of William Thomas and Mary Richards; *m* 1947; two *s*. *Educ:* Sir Alfred Jones Scholar, University Coll. of Wales, Aberystwyth. Demonstrator, Dept of Geography and Anthropology, University Coll. of Wales, Aberystwyth, 1929–30; Secretary and Lecturer-Assistant, Department of Geography, Victoria University, Manchester, 1930–31; Cartographer to Geographical Association, Manchester, 1930–31; Keeper, Departments of Ethnology and Shipping, Liverpool Public Museums, 1931–40; Rockefeller Foundation Museums Fellow, USA, 1938–39; Director, Museum and Art Gallery, Leicester, 1940–46; Surveyor, Regional Guide to Works of Art, Arts Council of Great Britain, 1946–48; Designer of Exhibitions for the British Institute of Adult Education, 1946–48; Director, Crafts Centre of Great Britain, 1947–48; Programme Specialist for Education through the Arts, UNESCO, Paris, 1949–56; Visiting Prof. of Art Education, Teachers' Coll., Columbia Univ., NY, USA, 1956; Prof. of Art, State Univ. of New York, College for Teachers, Buffalo, 1957–58; Prof. of Art Hist., University of Buffalo, and Art Critic, Buffalo Evening News, 1959–60; Art Editor, Gordon Fraser Gall. Ltd, 1960–72. Exhibitions: The Gall., Wellingborough, Bowen-West Gall., Bedford, 1988. Mem. Exec. Cttee, Campaign for Homosexual Equality, 1976–78, 1979–82; Hon. Sec., Gaydaid, 1980–87; Hon. Mem., United Soc. of Artists, 1980–; Mem., Bedford Soc. of Artists, 1988–. *Publications:* Penny Plain Twopence Coloured: the Aesthetics of Museum Display (Museums Jl, April 1939); Educations and Art: a Symposium (jt Editor with Edwin Ziegfeld), Unesco, 1953; Creating with Paper: basic forms and variations (Foreword and associate writer with Pauline Johnson), 1958; Sylvia Plath: Last Encounters, 1989; contribs to: Museums Journal, Dec. 1933, April 1935, April 1939, Oct. 1941; Parnassus, Jan. and April 1940; Unesco Educn Abstracts, Feb. 1953. *Recreations:* art, music, theatre, gardening. Research: Art. *Address:* 36 Pembroke Street, Bedford MK40 3RH. *T:* Bedford (0234) 358879.

THOMAS, Maj.-Gen. Walter Babington, CB 1971; DSO 1943; MC and Bar, 1942; Commander, HQ Far East Land Forces, Nov. 1970–Nov. 1971 (Chief of Staff, April–Oct. 1970); retired Jan. 1972; *b* Nelson, NZ, 29 June 1919; *s* of Walter Harington Thomas, Farmer; *m* 1947, Iredale Edith Lauchlan (*née* Trent); three *d*. *Educ:* Motueka Dist High Sch., Nelson, NZ. Clerk, Bank of New Zealand, 1936–39. Served War of 1939–45 (despatches, MC and Bar, DSO): 2nd NZEF, 1940–46, in Greece, Crete, Western Desert, Tunis and Italy; Comd 23 (NZ) Bn, 1944–45; Comd 22 (NZ) Bn, in Japan, 1946; transf. to Brit. Army, Royal Hampshire Regt, 1947; Bde Major, 39 Inf. Bde Gp, 1953–55 (despatches); GSO2, UK JSLS, Aust., 1958–60; AA&QMG, HQ 1 Div. BAOR, 1962–64; Comd 12 Inf. Bde Gp, 1964–66; IDC, 1967; GOC 5th Div., 1968–70. Silver Star, Medal, 1945 (USA). *Publications:* Dare to be Free, 1951; Touch of Pitch, 1956. *Recreation:* riding. *Address:* Kerry Road, M/S 413, Beaudesert, Qld 4285, Australia.

THOMAS, William David; Stipendiary Magistrate for South Yorkshire, since 1989; *b* 10 Oct. 1941; *s* of Arnold and Ada Thomas; *m* 1966, Cynthia Janice Jackson; one *s* two *d*. *Educ:* Whitcliffe Mount Grammar Sch., Cleckheaton; LSE (LLB Hons 1963); Part II, Law Society Finals, 1964. Admitted Solicitor, 1966. Asst Solicitor 1966, Partner, 1967–89, Finn Gledhill & Co., Halifax. *Publications:* contribs to Yorkshire Ridings Magazine and Pennine Radio, Bradford. *Recreations:* Rugby, theatre, ballet, gardening. *Address:* Rotherham Magistrate's Court, 26 Moorgate Street, PO Box 15, Rotherham S60 2DQ. *T:* Rotherham (0709) 377451. *Club:* Halifax Rugby Union Football.

THOMAS, William Fremlyn Cotter; His Honour Judge Thomas; a Circuit Judge, since 1990; *b* 18 March 1935; *s* of Stephen Kerr Thomas and Nâdine Dieudonnée Thomas (*née* March); *m* 1st, 1960, Mary Alanna Mudie; one *d*; 2nd, 1968, Thalia Mary Edith Myers; 3rd, 1978, Ursula Nancy Eden; one *s* one *d*. *Educ:* Bryanston Sch., Dorset; University Coll., Oxford. National Service in 1st NRR, Malaya, 2nd Lieut, 1954–56.

Called to the Bar, Inner Temple, 1961; SE Circuit; a Recorder, 1986. *Recreations:* music, carpentry, architecture. *Address:* The Crown Court, Canbury Park Road, Kingston upon Thames, Surrey KT2 6JU.

THOMAS, Sir William James Cooper, 2nd Bt, *cr* 1919; TD; JP; DL; Captain RA; *b* 7 May 1919; *er s* of Sir William James Thomas, 1st Bt, and Maud Mary Cooper, Bexhill-on-Sea; *S* father 1945; *m* 1947, Freida Dunbar (*d* 1990), *yr d* of late F. A. Whyte; two *s* one *d*. *Educ:* Harrow; Downing Coll., Cambridge. Barrister, Inner Temple, 1948. Member TA, 1938. Served War of 1939–45. Monmouthshire: JP 1958; DL 1973; High Sheriff, 1973. *Heir: s* William Michael Thomas, *b* 5 Dec. 1948. *Address:* Tump House, Llanrothal, Monmouth, Gwent NP5 3QL. *T:* Monmouth (0600) 712757. *Club:* Army and Navy.

THOMAS, Ven. William Jordison; Archdeacon of Northumberland, since 1983; *b* 16 Dec. 1927; *s* of Henry William and Dorothy Newton Thomas; *m* 1954, Kathleen Jeffrey Robson, *d* of William Robson, Reaveley, Powburn, Alnwick. *Educ:* Holmwood Prep. School, Middlesbrough; Acklam Hall Grammar School, Middlesbrough; Giggleswick School; King's Coll., Cambridge (BA 1951, MA 1955); Cuddesdon College. National Service, RN, 1946–48. Assistant Curate: St Anthony of Egypt, Newcastle upon Tyne, 1953–56; Berwick Parish Church, 1956–59; Vicar: Alwinton with Holystone and Alnham and the Lordship of Kidland, 1959–70; Alston with Garrigill, Nenthead and Kirkhaugh, 1970–80, i/c Knaresdale, 1973–80; Team Rector of Glendale, 1980–82; RD of Bamburgh and Glendale, 1980–82. Harbour Comr, N Sunderland, 1990. *Recreations:* sailing own dinghy and other people's yachts, making pictures, travelling and making magic. *Address:* 80 Moorside North, Fenham, Newcastle upon Tyne NE4 9DU. *T:* 091–273 8245. *Club:* Victory Services.

THOMAS, Sir (William) Michael (Marsh), 3rd Bt *cr* 1918; *b* 4 Dec. 1930; *s* of Sir William Eustace Rhyddlad Thomas, 2nd Bt, and Enid Helena Marsh; *S* father 1957; *m* 1957, Geraldine Mary, *d* of Robert Drysdale, Anglesey; three *d*. *Educ:* Oundle School, Northants. Formerly Man. Dir, Gors Nurseries Ltd. *Address:* Belan, Rhosneigr, Gwynedd LL64 5JE.

THOMAS, Adm. Sir (William) Richard (Scott), KCB 1987; OBE 1974; Gentleman Usher of the Black Rod, and Serjeant-at-Arms, House of Lords, since 1992; *b* 22 March 1932; *s* of late Comdr William Scott Thomas, DSC, RN and Mary Hilda Bertha Hemelryk, Findon, Sussex; *m* 1959, Patricia (Paddy) Margaret, *d* of late Dr and Mrs J. H. Cullinan, Fressingfield, Suffolk; three *s* four *d* (and one *s* decd). *Educ:* Penryn Sch., Ross-on-Wye; Downside Sch., Bath. psc 1963, jssc 1966, rcds 1979. Midshipman, 1951–52; Sub-Lt and Lieut, 1953–62 (CO HM Ships Buttress, Wolverton and Greetham); CO HMS Troubridge, 1966–68; Staff Officer Ops to Flag Officer First Flotilla and Flag Officer Scotland and NI, 1970–74; Directorate of Naval Plans, MoD, 1974–77; CO HMS Fearless, 1977–78; Dir of Office Appts (Seamen), 1980–83; Naval Sec., 1983–85; Flag Officer Second Flotilla, 1985–87; Dep. SACLANT, 1987–89; UK Mil. Rep. to NATO, 1989–92. *Recreations:* family, gardening, golf. *Address:* c/o National Westminster Bank, Emsworth, Hants.

THOMAS, Wyndham, CBE 1982; Chairman, Inner City Enterprises, since 1983; *b* 1 Feb. 1924; *s* of Robert John Thomas and Hannah Mary; *m* 1947, Elizabeth Terry Hopkin; one *s* three *d*. *Educ:* Maesteg Grammar School. Served Army (Lieut, Royal Welch Fusiliers), 1943–47. Schoolmaster, 1950–53; Director, Town and Country Planning Association, 1955–67; Gen. Manager, Peterborough New Town Develt Corp., 1968–83. Member: Land Commission, 1967–68; Commission for the New Towns, 1964–68; Property Adv. Gp, DoE, 1978–90; London Docklands Develt Corp., 1981–88. Chm., House Builders' Fedn Commn of Inquiry into Housebuilding and the Inner Cities, 1986–87 (report published 1987). Mayor of Hemel Hempstead, 1958–59. Hon. MRTPI 1979 (Mem. Council, 1989–). Officer of the Order of Orange-Nassau (Netherlands), 1982. *Publications:* many articles on town planning, housing, etc, in learned jls. *Recreations:* collecting old furniture, work, golf. *Address:* 8 Westwood Park Road, Peterborough PE3 6JL. *T:* Peterborough (0733) 64399.

THOMASON, Prof. George Frederick, CBE 1983; Montague Burton Professor of Industrial Relations, University College, Cardiff, 1969–85, now Emeritus; *b* 27 Nov. 1927; *s* of George Frederick Thomason and Eva Elizabeth (*née* Walker); *m* 1953, Jean Elizabeth Horsley; one *s* one *d*. *Educ:* Kelsick Grammar Sch.; Univ. of Sheffield (BA); Univ. of Toronto (MA); PhD (Wales). CIPM, FBIM; FCIT. University College, Cardiff: Research Asst, 1953; Asst Lectr, 1954; Research Associate, 1956; Lectr, 1959; Asst Man. Dir, Flex Fasteners Ltd, Rhondda, 1960; University College, Cardiff: Lectr, 1962; Sen. Lectr, 1963; Reader, 1969; Dean, Faculty of Economics, 1971–73; Dep. Principal (Humanities), 1974–77. Member: Doctors' and Dentists' Pay Review Body, 1979–; Pay Rev. Body for Nurses, Midwives, Health Service Visitors and Professions allied to Medicine, 1983–. Director: Enterprise Develt and Trng Ltd; Family Care Housing Assoc. *Publications:* Welsh Society in Transition, 1963; Personnel Manager's Guide to Job Evaluation, 1968; Professional Approach to Community Work, 1969; The Management of Research and Development, 1970; Improving the Quality of Organization, 1973; Job Evaluation: Objectives and Methods, 1980; Textbook of Industrial Relations Management, 1984; Textbook of Human Resource Management, 1988. *Recreation:* gardening. *Address:* Ty Gwyn, 149 Lake Road West, Cardiff CF2 5PJ. *T:* Cardiff (0222) 754236. *Clubs:* Athenæum; Cardiff and County (Cardiff).

THOMASON, (Kenneth) Roy, OBE 1986; solicitor; Senior Partner, Horden & George, Bournemouth, since 1979 (Partner, 1970); Chairman, Association of District Councils, since 1987; *b* 14 Dec. 1944; *s* of Thomas Roger and Constance Dora Thomason; *m* 1969, Christine Ann (*née* Parsons); two *s* two *d*. *Educ:* Cheney Sch., Oxford; London Univ. (LLB). Admitted Solicitor, 1969. Dir of private cos. Mem., Bournemouth Council, 1970– (Leader, 1974–82; past Chm. Policy, Ways and Means, and Finance Cttees). Association of District Councils: Mem. Council, 1979–; Leader, 1981–87; Chm., Housing and Environmental Health Cttee, 1983–87. Mem., Cons. Nat. Local Govt Adv. Cttee, 1981–; Various Cons. Party positions at constituency and area level, 1966– (Constituency Chm., 1981–82); contested (C) Newport E, 1983. *Recreations:* walking, reading, architectural history. *Address:* Culross House, 18 Wellington Road, Bournemouth BH8 8JN. *T:* Bournemouth (0202) 292113; Association of District Councils, 9 Buckingham Gate, SW1E 6LE. *T:* 071–828 7931. *Club:* Commonwealth Trust.

THOMPSON, Alan, CB 1978; Chairman, Review Group on the Youth Service, 1981–82; *b* 16 July 1920; *s* of Herbert and Esther Thompson; *m* 1944, Joyce Nora Banks; two *s* one *d*. *Educ:* Carlisle Grammar Sch.; Queen's Coll., Oxford. Joined Min. of Education, 1946; Private Sec. to Minister of Education, 1954–56; Asst Sec., Further Education Br., 1956–64; Under Sec., UGC, 1964–71; Under Sec., Science Br., DES, 1971–75; Dep. Sec., DES, 1975–80. *Address:* 1 Haven Close, Wimbledon, SW19 5JW.

THOMPSON, Prof. Alan Eric; Professor of the Economics of Government, 1972–87, Professor Emeritus, since 1988, Heriot-Watt University (Professor, School of Business and Financial Studies, 1987–88); *b* 16 Sept. 1924; *o c* of late Eric Joseph Thompson and of Florence Thompson; *m* 1960, Mary Heather Long; three *s* one *d*. *Educ:* University of Edinburgh (MA 1949, MA (Hons Class I, Economic Science), 1951, PhD 1953, Carnegie Research Scholar, 1951–52). Served army (including service with Central Mediterranean Forces), World War II. Asst in Political Economy, 1952–53, Lectr in Economics (formerly Political Economy), 1953–59, and 1964–71, Univ. of Edinburgh. Parly Adviser to Scottish Television, 1966–76; Scottish Governor, BBC, 1976–79. Visiting Professor, Graduate School of Business, Stanford Univ., USA, 1966, 1968. Contested (Lab) Galloway, 1950 and 1951; MP (Lab) Dunfermline, 1959–64. Mem., Speaker's Parly Delegn to USA, 1962. Chm., Adv. Bd on Economics Educn (Esmée Fairbairn Research Project), 1970–76; Jt Chm., Scottish-Soviet Co-ordinating Cttee for Trade and Industry, 1985–; Member: Scottish Cttee, Public Schools Commn, 1969–70; Cttee enquiring into conditions of service life for young servicemen, 1969; Scottish Council for Adult Educn in HM Forces, 1973–; Jt Mil. Educn Cttee, Edinburgh and Heriot-Watt Univs, 1975–; Local Govt Boundary Commn for Scotland, 1975–82; Royal Fine Art Commn for Scotland, 1975–80; Adv. Bd, Defence Finance Unit, Heriot-Watt Univ., 1986–; Chm., Northern Offshore (Maritime) Resources Study, 1974–77; Chm., Edinburgh Cttee, Peace Through NATO, 1984–. Parly Adviser, Pharmaceutical Gen. Council (Scotland), 1984–. Hon. Vice-Pres., Assoc. of Nazi War Camp Survivors, 1960–; Pres., Edinburgh Amenity and Transport Assoc., 1970–75; Dir, Scottish AIDS Res. Appeal, 1988–. Chm. of Governors, Newbattle Abbey Coll., 1980–82 (Governor, 1975–82); Governor, Leith Nautical Coll., 1981–;85 Trustee, Bell's Nautical Trust, 1981–85. Has broadcast and appeared on TV (economic and political talks and discussions) in Britain and USA. FRSA 1972. *Publications:* Development of Economic Doctrine (jtly), 1980; contribs to learned journals. *Recreations:* writing children's stories and plays, bridge, croquet. *Address:* 11 Upper Gray Street, Edinburgh EH9 1SN. *T:* 031–667 2140; Ardtrostan Cottage, St Fillans, Perthshire. *T:* St Fillans (076485) 275. *Clubs:* New, Edinburgh University Staff (Edinburgh); Loch Earn Sailing.

THOMPSON, Anthony Arthur Richard; QC 1980; a Recorder, since 1985; *b* 4 July 1932; *s* of late William Frank McGregor Thompson and Doris Louise Thompson (*née* Hill); *m* 1958, Françoise Alix Marie Reynier; two *s* one *d* (and one *s* decd). *Educ:* Latymer; University Coll., Oxford; La Sorbonne. FCIArb 1991. Called to the Bar, Inner Temple, 1957, Bencher, 1986; admitted to Paris Bar, 1988. Chm., Bar European Gp, 1984–86 (Vice-Chm., 1982–84); Mem., Internat. Relations Cttee, Bar Council, 1984–86. QC, St Vincent and the Grenadines, 1986. Contested (Lab) Arundel and Shoreham, Oct. 1964. *Recreations:* food and wine, lawn tennis, theatre, cinema, 19th century music, 20th century painting. *Address:* 1 Essex Court, Temple, EC4Y 9AR. *T:* 071–583 2000; Lafarge Flecheux, 17 avenue de Lamballe, 75016 Paris, France. *Club:* Roehampton.

THOMPSON, Aubrey Gordon D.; *see* Denton-Thompson.

THOMPSON, Charles Allister; HM Diplomatic Service, retired; *b* 21 July 1922; *yr s* of late Herbert Ivie and Margaret (*née* Browne-Webber) Thompson, Managua, Nicaragua; *m* 1950, Jean Margaret, *er d* of late Alexander Bruce Dickson; one *s* two *d* (and one *s* decd). *Educ:* Haileybury; Hertford Coll., Oxford (MA, BLitt). War Service, 1942–46, 1st King's Dragoon Guards. Joined Foreign Service (now Diplomatic Service), 1947, and served in FO until 1949; 3rd Sec., Prague, 1949–50; 2nd Sec. (Commercial), Mexico City, 1950–53; FO 1953–56; 1st Sec., Karachi, 1956–59; Head of Chancery, Luxembourg, 1959–62; FO, 1962–65; Counsellor, 1965; Dep. Consul-Gen., New York, 1965–67; Dep. High Comr, Port of Spain, 1967–70; HM Consul-Gen., Philadelphia, 1970–74; Vis. Fellow, Centre for Internat. Studies, LSE, 1974–75; Head of Training Dept, FCO, and Dir, Diplomatic Service Language Centre, 1975–76. *Recreations:* gardening, golf, gerontology. *Address:* C/Carrasquetes 17, MGCA 212, Jávea, 03737 Alicante, Spain. *T:* (96) 5792283.

THOMPSON, Charles Norman, CBE 1978; CChem; FRSC; Head of Research and Development Liaison, and Health, Safety and Environment Administration, Shell UK Ltd, 1978–82, retired; Consultant to Shell UK Ltd, since 1982; *b* 23 Oct. 1922; *s* of Robert Norman Thompson and Evelyn Tivendale Thompson (*née* Wood); *m* 1946, Pamela Margaret Wicks; one *d*. *Educ:* Birkenhead Institute; Liverpool Univ. (BSc). Research Chemist, Thornton Research Centre (Shell Refining & Marketing Co. Ltd), 1943; Lectr, Petroleum Chemistry and Technology, Liverpool Coll. of Technology, 1947–51; Personnel Supt and Dep. Associate Manager, Thornton Research Centre, Shell Research Ltd, 1959–61; Dir (Res. Admin), Shell Research Ltd, 1961–78. Mem. Council, 1976–82, Vice Pres., 1977–80, 1981–82, Inst. of Petroleum (Chm., Res. Adv. Cttee, 1973–82). Pres., RIC, 1976–78. Chairman: Professional Affairs Bd, 1980–84, Water Chemistry Forum, 1987–90, RSC; Council of Science and Technology Insts, 1981–83 (Chm., Health Care Scientific Adv. Cttee, 1986–); Bd Mem., Thames Water Authority, 1980–87; Member: Technician Educn Council, 1980–83; Ct, Univ. of Surrey, 1980–; Parly and Scientific Cttee, 1976–. *Publications:* Reviews of Petroleum Technology, vol. 13: insulating and hydraulic oils, 1953; numerous papers in Jl Inst. Petroleum, Chem. and Ind., Chem. in Brit., on hydrocarbon dielectrics, insulating oils, diffusion as rate-limiting factor in oxidation, antioxidants in the oil industry, mechanism of copper catalysis in insulating oil oxidation, scientific manpower, etc. *Recreation:* golf. *Address:* Delamere, Horsell Park, Woking, Surrey GU21 4LW. *T:* Woking (0483) 714939.

THOMPSON, Maj.-Gen. Christopher Noel, CB 1988; *b* 25 Dec. 1932; *s* of late Brig. William Gordon Starkey Thompson and Kathleen Elizabeth (*née* Craven); *m* 1964, Margaret (*née* Longsworth); one *s* twin *d*. *Educ:* Wellington College; RMA Sandhurst; Sidney Sussex College, Cambridge (BA); University College London. Commissioned RE, 1953; served BAOR, 1957–59; Bomb Disposal, UK, 1959–62; Aden, 1963–66; Canada, 1966–68; OC 13 Field Survey Sqn, 1969–70; USA, 1971–75; CO 42 Survey Engr Regt, 1975–77; Dep. Dir, Planning and Develt, Ordnance Survey, 1978–79; Dir, Surveys and Production, Ordnance Survey, 1980–83; Dir of Mil. Survey, MoD, 1984–87. Col Comdt, RE, 1987–. Pres., Commission D, European Organisation for Experimental Photogrammetric Research, 1980–87. *Publications:* articles on surveying and mapping in Chartered Surveyor, Photogrammetric Record. *Recreations:* sailing, tennis, gardening, house restoration. *Address:* Burgh House, Burgh-by-Sands, Carlisle CA5 6AN.

THOMPSON, Lt-Col Sir Christopher (Peile), 6th Bt *cr* 1890; Equerry, since 1989, and Private Secretary, since 1990, to HRH Prince Michael of Kent; *b* 21 Dec. 1944; *s* of Sir Peile Thompson, 5th Bt, OBE, and of Barbara Johnson, *d* of late H. J. Rampling; *S* father, 1985; *m* 1969, Anna Elizabeth, *d* of Major Arthur Callander; one *s* one *d*. *Educ:* Marlborough; RMA Sandhurst. Commnd 11th Hussars (PAO), 1965; Tank Troop Leader and Reconnaissance Troop Leader, 11th Hussars, 1965–69; Gunnery Instructor, RAC Gunnery Sch., 1970–72; Sqdn Second i/c, A Sqdn, Royal Hussars, 1972–75; GSO 3 Intelligence, Allied Staff, Berlin, 1975–76; RMCS Shrivenham, 1977; Staff Coll., Camberley, 1978; DAAG (a) M2 (A) (Officer Manning), MoD, 1978–81; C Sqdn Ldr, Royal Hussars, 1981–83; GSO 2 (Operational Requirements), HQ DRAC, 1983–85; CO, Royal Hussars (PWO), 1985–87; SO1, Sen. Officers Tactics Div., 1988–90, retd. *Recreations:* fishing, shooting, windsurfing, skiing, reading, gardening, sailing, Cresta Run. *Heir: s* Peile Richard Thompson, *b* 3 March 1975. *Address:* Old Farm, Augres, Trinity, Jersey. *Clubs:* Cavalry and Guards, Royal Automobile; St Moritz Tobogganing.

THOMPSON, Christopher Ronald; Senior Partner, Aldenham Business Services Ltd, since 1984; *b* 14 Dec. 1927; *s* of late Col S. J. Thompson, DSO, DL and Margaret

Thompson (née Green); *m* 1949, Rachael Meynell; one *s* one *d* (and one *s* decd). *Educ:* Shrewsbury School; Trinity College, Cambridge. 1st Bn KSLI (Lieut), 1946–48. Dir, John Thompson Ltd, 1954–68, Chm., 1969; Dir, Rockwell-Thompson Ltd, 1973–74; Vice-Pres., Rockwell Europe, 1974–78. Chairman: NEI Internat., 1979–84; Wynn Electronics, 1983–87; Hoccum Developments Ltd, 1985–; John Sutcliffe Shipping Ltd, 1986–89; Director: Barclays Bank Birmingham Bd, 1974–87; G. T. Japan Investment Trust, 1983–; Isotron plc, 1984–; Saraswati Syndicate pte India, 1954–; Plessey Co. plc, 1988–89. Member: Overseas Projects Bd, BOTB, 1981–84; Sino-British Trade Council, 1983–85.; Indo-British Industrial Forum, 1987–. Pres., BEAMA, 1984–85. Mem., CLA Council for Shropshire, 1990–. Chm., Anglo-Venezuelan Soc., 1981–85. Trustee: Hereford Cathedral Trust, 1984–; Mappa Mundi Trust, 1990–. High Sheriff, Shropshire, 1984–85. *Recreations:* flyfishing, shooting, forestry. *Address:* Aldenham Park, near Bridgnorth, Shropshire. *T:* Morville (074631) 218. *Club:* Boodle's.

THOMPSON, Colin Edward, CBE 1983; FRSE 1978; Director, National Galleries of Scotland, 1977–84; *b* 2 Nov. 1919; *s* of late Edward Vincent Thompson, CB, and Jessie Forbes Cameron; *m* 1950, Jean Agnes Jardine O'Connell; one *s* one *d*. *Educ:* Sedbergh Sch.; King's College, Cambridge; Chelsea Polytechnic Sch. of Art. MA (Cantab). FMA. FS Wing CMP, 1940–41; Foreign Office, 1941–45. Lectr, Bath Acad. of Art, Corsham, 1948–54; Asst Keeper, 1954, Keeper, 1967, National Gall. of Scotland. Sen. Adviser, Res. Centre in Art Educn, Bath Acad. of Art, 1962–65; Chm., Scottish Museums Council, 1984–87; Member: Scottish Arts Council, 1976–83; Edinburgh Fest. Council, 1979–82 (Chm., Art Adv. Panel, 1979–); Bd of Governors, Edinburgh Coll. of Art, 1985–91 (Chm., 1989–91). DUniv Edinburgh, 1985. *Publications:* (with Lorne Campbell) Hugo van der Goes and the Trinity Panels in Edinburgh, 1974; Exploring Museums: Scotland, 1990; guide books, catalogues and a history of the National Gallery of Scotland; articles in Burlington Magazine, Museums Jl, etc. *Address:* Edenkerry, Lasswade, Midlothian EH18 1LW. *T:* 031–663 7927. *Club:* New.
See also D. C. Thompson.

THOMPSON, David Brian; Chairman, Union Square plc, since 1987; *b* 4 April 1936; *s* of Bernard Thompson and Rosamund Dee; *m* 1962, Patricia Henchley; one *s* two *d*. *Educ:* Haileybury and ISC. Jt Man. Dir, B. Thompson Ltd, 1960–70; Chm. and co-founder, 1974–84, Jt Chm., 1984–87, Dir, 1987–89, Hillsdown Holdings plc. *Recreations:* family, business, breeding and racing of bloodstock, swimming. *Address:* 1 Dover Street, W1. *T:* 071–491 8839.

THOMPSON, David Richard, CB 1974; QC 1980; Master of the Crown Office and Queen's Coroner and Attorney, Registrar of Criminal Appeals and of the Courts Martial Appeal Court, 1965–88; *b* 11 Feb. 1916; *s* of William George Thompson; *m* 1952, Sally Jennifer Rowntree Thompson (*née* Stockton); two *s* four *d*. *Educ:* Alleyn's Sch., Dulwich; Jesus Coll., Oxford. BA Physics 1938. Royal Corps of Signals, 1939–46 (despatches). Called to Bar, Lincoln's Inn, 1946, Bencher, 1982. Office of DPP, 1948–54; Dep. Asst Registrar, then Asst Registrar, Court of Criminal Appeal, 1954–65. *Publications:* (with H. W. Wollaston) Court of Appeal Criminal Division, 1969; (with Morrish and McLean) Proceedings in the Criminal Division of the Court of Appeal, 1979. *Recreation:* personal computer word processor. *Address:* 54 Highbury Grove, N5 2AG. *T:* 071–226 6514.

THOMPSON, David Robin Bibby, TD 1987; Director, Bibby Line Ltd, 1974–87; Member, Rural Development Commission, since 1986; *b* 23 July 1946; *s* of Noel Denis Thompson and Cynthia Joan (*née* Bibby); *m* 1971, Caroline Ann Foster; one *s* one *d*. *Educ:* Uppingham Sch.; Mons Officer Cadet Sch. Short service commn, QRIH, 1965; comd Queen's Own Yeomanry (TA), 1984–87; Col (TA), RAC, 1987–90; Hon. ADC to the Queen, 1987–90. Chm., NAC Housing Assoc., 1983–87; Vice-Chm., NAC Rural Trust, 1983–; Member: Council, Royal Agricl Soc. of England, 1985–; Bd, Housing Corp., 1989–. High Sheriff, Shropshire, 1989. *Recreations:* ski-ing, horses, conservation. *Address:* Sansaw Hall, Clive, Shrewsbury, Shropshire SY4 3JR. *Club:* Cavalry and Guards.

THOMPSON, Dennis Cameron, FCIArb; Founder, 1967, Consulting Editor, since 1987, Journal of World Trade (formerly Journal of World Trade Law) (Editor, 1977–86); Consulting Editor, Journal of International Arbitration, since 1985; *b* 25 Oct. 1914; *s* of late Edward Vincent Thompson, CB, and late Jessie Forbes; *m* 1959, Maria von Skramlik; one *d*. *Educ:* Oundle; King's Coll., Cambridge. Nat. Sci. Tripos Pt I, Law Pt II; MA 1949. RAF, 1940–45: Sqdn-Ldr, personnel staff, Desert Air Force, and Germany. Called to Bar, Inner Temple, 1939; practised London and Midland Circuit, 1946–63; Asst Dir (European Law), British Inst. of Internat. and Comparative Law, 1963–66; Legal Adviser, Secretariat of EFTA, Geneva, 1967–73; participated in negotiations for European Patent Convention, 1969–73; Dir, Restrictive Practices and Dominant Positions, EEC, 1973–76; Consultant to UNCTAD on Restrictive Business Practices and Transfer of Technol., 1977–82. Vis. Prof., Georgia Univ. Sch. of Law, Athens, GA, 1978. Trustee, Federal Trust, 1962–71. Member: Assoc. Suisse de L'Arbitrage; Panel of Arbitrators, Amer. Arbitration Assoc. *Publications:* (ed) Kennedy, CIF Contracts, 3rd edn 1959; (with Alan Campbell) Common Market Law, 1962; The Proposal for a European Company, 1969; articles in Internat. and Compar. Law Quarterly; (ed jtly) Common Market Law Review, 1963–67. *Recreations:* walking, Antarctic studies. *Address:* 8 rue des Belles Filles, 1299 Crans, Switzerland. *T:* (22) 776 16 87. *Club:* United Oxford & Cambridge University.
See also C. E. Thompson.

THOMPSON, Donald; MP (C) Calder Valley, since 1983 (Sowerby, 1979–83); *b* 13 Nov. 1931; *s* of Geoffrey and Rachel Thompson; *m* 1957, Patricia Ann Hopkins; two *s*. Formerly Dir, Halifax Farmers' Trading Assoc.; Man. Dir, Armadillo Plastics (Glass Fibre Manufacturers), 1974–79, Dir, 1979–. Member: WR CC, 1967–74; W Yorks CC, 1974–75; Calderdale Dist Council, 1975–79. Contested (C): Batley and Morley, 1970; Sowerby, Feb. and Oct. 1974. An Asst Govt Whip, then a Lord Comr of HM Treasury, 1981–86; Parly Sec., MAFF, 1986–89. A Govt Whip, Council of Europe and WEU, 1990–. Chm., Cons. Candidates' Assoc., 1972–74. *Recreations:* Rugby football, poor golf, conversation. *Address:* Moravian House, Lightcliffe, near Halifax, West Yorks. *T:* Halifax (0422) 202920. *Clubs:* Beefsteak, St Stephen's Constitutional; Brodleians (Hipperholme); Octave (Elland).

THOMPSON, Donald Henry, MA Oxon; Headmaster, Chigwell School, Essex, 1947–71; *b* 29 Aug. 1911; *s* of H. R. Thompson, solicitor, Swansea; *m* 1942, Helen Mary Wray; four *s*. *Educ:* Shrewsbury School; Merton College, Oxford. Postmaster in Classics, Merton Coll., Oxford, 1930; 1st Class Hon. Mod., 1932; 1st Class Literae Humaniores, 1934; Asst Master Haileybury Coll., Hertford, 1934–46. Served War of 1939–45, RA, 1940–45. Chm., Frome Area, Somerset Trust for Nature Conservation. JP Essex, 1955–81. *Recreations:* cricket, bird-watching, conservation. *Address:* Glasses Farm, Holcombe Bath, Somerset BA3 5EQ. *T:* Stratton-on-Fosse (0761) 232322.

THOMPSON, Prof. Edward Arthur, FBA 1964; Professor of Classics, University of Nottingham, 1948–79; *b* 22 May 1914; *s* of late Robert J. Thompson and late Margaret Thompson, Waterford. *Educ:* Trinity Coll., Dublin. Lecturer in Classics: Dublin, 1939–41; Swansea, 1942–45; King's College, London, 1945–48. Vis. Bentley Prof. of History, Univ. of Michigan, 1969–71; H. F. Johnson Res. Prof., Univ. of Wisconsin (Madison), 1979–80. *Publications:* The Historical Work of Ammianus Marcellinus, 1947; A History of Attila and The Huns, 1948; A Roman Reformer and Inventor, 1952; The Early Germans, 1965; The Visigoths in the Time of Ulfila, 1966; The Goths in Spain, 1969; Romans and Barbarians, 1982; St Germanus of Auxerre and the End of Roman Britain, 1984; Who was St Patrick?, 1985. *Address:* 32A Mapperley Hall Drive, Mapperley Park, Nottingham NG3 5EY.

THOMPSON, Sir Edward (Hugh Dudley), Kt 1967; MBE 1945; TD; DL; Director: Allied Breweries Ltd, 1961–78; P-E Consulting Group Ltd, 1968–73 (Chm., 1971–73); *b* 12 May 1907; *s* of Neale Dudley Thompson and Mary Gwendoline Scutt; *m* 1st, 1931, Ruth Monica, 3rd *d* of Charles Henry Wainwright, JP; two *s*; 2nd, 1947, Doreen Maud (*d* 1990), *d* of George Tibbitt; one *s* one *d*. *Educ:* Uppingham; Lincoln Coll., Oxford. Served War of 1939–45 (despatches twice, MBE); 1st Derbyshire Yeomanry, 1939–43, in N Africa; General Staff, 1943–45, in Italy and Germany. Solicitor, 1931–36. Asst Man. Dir, Ind Coope & Allsopp Ltd, 1936–39, Managing Director, 1939; Chairman: Ind Coope & Allsopp Ltd, Burton on Trent, 1955–62; Allied Breweries Ltd (formerly Ind Coope Tetley Ansell Ltd), 1961–68. Director: Sun Insurance Ltd, 1946–59; Sun Alliance & London Insurance Ltd, 1959–77. Chm., Brewers' Soc., 1959–61; Trustee, Civic Trust; Mem. Northumberland Foot and Mouth Cttee. Mem. Council, Nottingham Univ., 1969–87. Mem. Council, RASE, 1972–85 (Hon. Vice Pres., 1985–). High Sheriff of Derbyshire, 1964; DL Derbyshire, 1978. Hon. LLD Nottingham, 1984. *Recreations:* farming, sailing, ski-ing. *Address:* Culland Hall, Brailsford, Derby DE6 3BW. *T:* Ashbourne (0335) 60247. *Club:* Boodle's.

THOMPSON, Eric John; Deputy Director, Office of Population Censuses and Surveys, since 1989; *b* Beverley, E Yorks, 26 Sept. 1934; *o s* of Herbert William Thompson and Florence Thompson (*née* Brewer). *Educ:* Beverley Grammar Sch.; London School of Economics (BScEcon). National Service: Pilot Officer in Dept of Scientific Adviser to Air Ministry, 1956–58. Operations Planning Dept, International Computers and Tabulators Ltd, 1958–60; Supply and Planning Dept, Shell International Petroleum Co. Ltd, 1960–65; Head of Regional Demography Unit, General Register Office, 1965–67; Head of Population Studies Section, 1967–72, Asst Dir of Intelligence, 1972–74, GLC Research and Intelligence Unit; Head of Social Monitoring Branch, Central Statistical Office, 1975–80; Dir of Statistics, Dept of Transport, 1980–89. Royal Statistical Society: Fellow, 1956, Mem. Council 1981–85, Vice-Pres., 1982–83; ESRC (formerly SSRC): Assessor, Statistics Cttee, 1979–80; Mem., Research Resources and Methods Cttee, 1982–84; Mem., British Computer Soc., 1959–76 (MBCS 1968). Member: East Yorkshire Local History Soc., 1974–; Housman Soc., 1976–; Richard III Soc., 1979– (Mem. Cttee, 1984–); Friends of Nat. Libraries, 1981–; Selden Soc., 1987–; Friends of British Library, 1989–; Trustee, Richard III and Yorkist Hist. Trust, 1985–. *Publications:* ed, Social Trends, Nos 6–10, 1975–80; contrib. chapters in three books on regional and urban planning; articles and reviews in GLC Intelligence Unit's quarterly bulletin and various statistical jls; article on historical bibliography in The Ricardian. *Recreations:* reading and collecting books, British mediæval history, English literature. *Address:* Office of Population Censuses and Surveys, St Catherine's House, WC2B 6JP.

THOMPSON, Prof. Francis Michael Longstreth, FBA 1979; Director, Institute of Historical Research, and Professor of History in the University of London, 1977–90, now Emeritus Professor; *b* 13 Aug. 1925; *s* of late Francis Longstreth-Thompson, OBE; *m* 1951, Anne Challoner; two *s* one *d*. *Educ:* Bootham Sch., York; Queen's Coll., Oxford (Hastings Schol.; MA, DPhil). ARICS 1968. War service, with Indian Artillery, 1943–47; James Bryce Sen. Schol., Oxford, 1949–50; Harmsworth Sen. Schol., Merton Coll., Oxford, 1949–51; Lectr in History, UCL, 1951–63; Reader in Economic History, UCL, 1963–68; Prof. of Modern Hist., Univ. of London, and Head of Dept of Hist., Bedford Coll., London, 1968–77. Joint Editor, Economic History Review, 1968–80. Sec., British Nat. Cttee of Historical Scis, 1978–; British Mem., Standing Cttee for Humanities, European Sci. Foundn, 1983–; President: Economic Hist. Soc., 1983–86; RHistS, 1988– (Fellow, 1964); British Agricl Hist. Soc., 1989–. Member: Senate and Academic Council, Univ. of London, 1970–78; Senate and Collegiate Council, 1981–89. *Publications:* English Landed Society in the Nineteenth Century, 1963; Chartered Surveyors: the growth of a profession, 1968; Victorian England: the horse-drawn society, 1970; Countrysides, in The Nineteenth Century, ed Asa Briggs, 1970; Hampstead: building a borough, 1650–1964, 1974; introd. to General Report on Gosford Estates in County Armagh 1821, by William Greig, 1976; Britain, in European Landed Elites in the Nineteenth Century, ed David Spring, 1977; Landowners and Farmers, in The Faces of Europe, ed Alan Bullock, 1980; 2 chapters in The Victorian Countryside, ed G. E. Mingay, 1981; (ed) The Rise of Suburbia, 1982; (ed) Horses in European Economic History, 1983; Towns, Industry and the Victorian Landscape, in The English Landscape, ed S. R. J. Woodell, 1985; Private Property and Public Policy, in Salisbury: The Man and his Policies, ed Lord Blake and Hugh Cecil, 1987; Rise of Respectable Society: a social history of Victorian Britain, 1988; (ed) The Cambridge Social History of Britain 1750–1950, vol. 1 Regions and Communities, vol. 2 People and their Environment, vol. 3 Social Agencies and Social Institutions, 1990; (ed) The University of London and the World of Learning 1836–1986, 1990; numerous articles in Economic History Review, History, English Historical Review, etc. *Recreations:* gardening, walking, carpentry, tennis. *Address:* Holly Cottage, Sheepcote Lane, Wheathampstead, Herts AL4 8NJ. *T:* Wheathampstead (058283) 3129.

THOMPSON, Dr Frank Derek, FRCP; Senior Consultant Nephrologist, St Peter's group of Hospitals, since 1981; Dean, Institute of Urology, London University, since 1985; *b* 18 May 1939; *s* of Frank and Irene Thompson; *m* 1964, Elizabeth Ann Sherwood; two *s* one *d*. *Educ:* St Catharine's College, Cambridge (MA, MB BChir); St Mary's Hosp., London. FRCP 1983. Sen. Lectr, Inst. of Urology, 1974; Consultant Nephrologist to Harefield and Mount Vernon Hosps, 1979; Hon. Consultant Nephrologist to Nat. Heart Hosp., 1980; Vice-Dean, Faculty of Clinical Science, University College and Middx Sch. of Medicine, 1990. *Publications:* Disorders of the Kidney and Urinary Tract, 1987; contribs to BMJ, Clinical Nephrology. *Recreations:* golf, gardening, ornithology. *Address:* 27 Moor Park Road, Northwood, Middx HA6 2DL. *T:* Northwood (09274) 27361. *Club:* Moor Park Golf.

THOMPSON, Air Commodore Frederick William, CBE 1957; DSO 1944; DFC 1942; AFC 1944; Director, Air Weapons, British Aerospace Dynamics Group, 1977–80, retired; *b* 9 July 1914; *s* of William Edward Thompson, Winster, Poulton-le-Fylde, Lancs; *m* 1941, Marian, *d* of Wm Bootyman, Hessle, E Yorks; two *d*. *Educ:* Baines's Grammar School; Liverpool University. BSc 2nd Cl. Hons Maths; Advanced Diploma in General Hygiene (Hons). Joined RAF, 1935, invalided 1936. S Rhodesian Education Dept, 1936–39. Served War of 1939–45 (despatches, DFC, AFC, DSO): S Rhodesian Air Force, 1940, Pilot Officer; seconded to RAFVR, 4 Gp Bomber Command, 1940; Flight Comdr 10 Sqdn Bombers, 1941; 1658 HCU, 1942; CO 44 Bomber Sqdn, 1944; Bomber Command Instructor's School, 1944; Station Commander, RAF Heany, 1945; HQ Mid Med., 1946–47; Min. of Defence, 1947–50; HQ CC, 1950–53; OC ASWDU, 1953; Group Capt., CO Luqa, 1954; Deputy Director Operational Requirements (1), Air Ministry, 1957–60. Air Cdre Imperial Defence Coll., 1960; Director of Guided Weapons

(Trials), Ministry of Aviation, 1961. Retired from RAF at own request to join de Havilland Aircraft Co. Ltd as Representative of the Company on the West Coast of America; Engrg Manager, Hawker Siddeley Dynamics Co. Ltd, 1964, Divisional Manager, Air Weapons Div., 1972–77. idc, jssc, psc, cfs. *Recreations:* tennis, swimming. *Address:* Westwick, Lye Green Road, Chesham, Bucks HP5 3NH. *T:* Chesham (0494) 785413. *Club:* Royal Air Force.

THOMPSON, Rt. Rev. Geoffrey Hewlett; *see* Exeter, Bishop of.

THOMPSON, Rev. George H.; Assistant Priest, St Teresa's, Dumfries, since 1989; *b* Sept. 1928. *Educ:* Dalry Sch.; Kirkcudbright Acad.; Edinburgh Univ. Teacher, modern languages, Kirkcudbright Academy; Principal Teacher of French, 1979–85, Principal Teacher of Modern Languages, 1985–86, Annan Acad., Dumfriesshire. Contested (SNP): Galloway, Feb. 1974, 1979; Galloway and Upper Nithsdale, 1983. Former SNP Asst Nat. Sec.; MP (SNP) Galloway, Oct. 1974–1979; SNP Spokesman: on health, Oct. 1974–79; on forestry, 1975. Deacon, RC dio. of Galloway, 1989, priest 1989. *Address:* St Teresa's, Glasgow Road, Dumfries DG2 9DE. *T:* Dumfries (0387) 52603.

THOMPSON, Gerald Francis Michael Perronet; Chairman, Kleinwort Benson Ltd, 1971–75, retired (Director 1961, Vice-Chairman 1970); Member, Accepting Houses Committee, 1971–75; *b* 10 Oct. 1910; *s* of late Sir John Perronet Thompson, KCSI, KCIE, and Ada Lucia Tyrrell; *m* 1944, Margaret Mary Bodenham Smith; two *s* one *d*. *Educ:* Repton; King's Coll., Cambridge (Scholar, MA); London Sch. of Economics (post graduate). Kleinwort Sons & Co., 1933. Served War, RAFVR, 1939–46 (despatches): in France, UK, and Middle East, Wing Comdr. Director: Kleinwort Sons & Co., 1960; Kleinwort Benson Lonsdale Ltd, 1970–82. Lectures and broadcasts on monetary and internat. affairs, 1957–; lecture on merchant banking, RSA, 1966 (FRSA). Received into RC Church, 1939; Hon. Treasurer, Westminster Cathedral Appeal Fund, 1978–84; Trustee, Tablet Trust, 1977–. Governor, New Hall Sch., 1977–83. *Publication:* contrib. Festschrift presented to Fernand Collin, 1972. *Recreations:* travel, garden. *Address:* Whitewebs, Margaretting, Essex CM4 9HX. *T:* Ingatestone (0277) 352002. *Club:* United Oxford & Cambridge University.
See also Rear-Adm. J. Y. Thompson, Sir E. H. T. Wakefield, Bt.

THOMPSON, Godfrey; *see* Thompson, W. G.

THOMPSON, Sir Godfrey James M.; see Milton-Thompson.

THOMPSON, Rt. Rev. Hewlett; *see* Thompson, Rt Rev. G. H.

THOMPSON, Howard; *see* Thompson, James H.

THOMPSON, Vice-Adm. Sir Hugh (Leslie Owen), KBE 1987; FEng 1989; FIMechE; Deputy Controller of the Navy and Chief Above-Water Systems Executive (formerly Deputy Controller Warships), Ministry of Defence, 1986–89; Chief Naval Engineer Officer, 1987–89; retired; *b* 2 April 1931; *s* of Hugh Thompson and Elsie Standish (*née* Owen); *m* 1st, 1957, Sheila Jean Finch (*d* 1974); one *s* two *d*; 2nd, 1977, Rosemary Ann (*née* Oliver). *Educ:* Royal Belfast Academical Institution; RNC Dartmouth; RNEC Manadon. Asst Dir, Submarines Mechanical, 1976–79; RCDS, 1980; Dep. Dir, Systems 1, 1981–83; Dir Gen., Marine Engineering, 1983–84; Dir Gen. Surface Ships, MoD, 1984–86. *Recreations:* railways, woodwork. *Club:* Army and Navy.

THOMPSON, (Hugh) Patrick; MP (C) Norwich North, since 1983; *b* 21 Oct. 1935; *s* of Gerald Leopold Thompson and Kathleen Mary Landsdown Thompson; *m* 1962, Kathleen Howson. *Educ:* Felsted Sch., Essex; Emmanuel Coll., Cambridge (MA). MInstP 1964. Nat. Service, 2nd Lieut, KOYLI, 1957–59; TA, Manchester, 1960–65; Gresham's Sch., CCF, 1965–82 (CFM 1980); Major, retd. Engr, English Electric Valve Co., Chelmsford, 1959–60; Sixth Form Physics Master: Manchester Grammar Sch., 1960–65; Gresham's Sch., Holt, 1965–83. PPS to Minister of State for Transport, 1987–88, to Minister of State, Dept of Social Security, 1988–89. Mem., Parly and Scientific Cttee, 1983–; Founder Mem., All Party Gp for Engrg Develt, 1985–; Sec., Cons. Back Bench Energy Cttee, 1986–87. *Publication:* Elementary Calculations in Physics, 1963. *Recreations:* travel, music, gardening. *Address:* The Cottage, Swanton Novers, Norfolk NR24 2RB. *T:* Melton Constable (0263) 860529. *Club:* Norfolk (Norwich).

THOMPSON, Sir (Humphrey) Simon M.; *see* Meysey-Thompson.

THOMPSON, Dr (Ian) McKim; Deputy Secretary, British Medical Association, since 1985 (Senior Under Secretary, 1969–85); *b* 19 Aug. 1938; *s* of late J. W. Thompson and of Dr E. M. Thompson; *m* 1962, Dr Veronica Jane Richards; two *s* one *d*. *Educ:* Epsom Coll.; Birmingham Univ. (MB, ChB 1961). FRSM 1987. Lectr in Pathology, Univ. of Birmingham, 1964–67; Sen. Registrar, Birmingham RHB, 1967–69. Consulting Forensic Pathologist to HM Coroner, City of Birmingham, 1966–. Part time Tutor, Dept of Adult and Continuing Educn, Keele Univ., 1985–. Member: GMC, 1979–; Birmingham Med. Inst. Hon. Collegian, Med. Colls of Spain, 1975. *Publications:* (ed) The Hospital Gazeteer, 1972; (ed) BMA Handbook for Hospital Junior Doctors, 1977, 5th edn 1990; (ed) BMA Handbook for Trainee Doctors in General Practice, 1982, 3rd edn 1985; various medical scientific papers. *Recreations:* inland waterways, rambling. *Address:* Weir Cottage, Millbank, Fladbury, Pershore, Worcs WR10 2QA. *T:* Evesham (0386) 860668.

THOMPSON, James Craig; Chairman and Managing Director: Maidstone United Football Club Ltd, since 1970; Harvest Publications Ltd, since 1983; *b* 27 Oct. 1933; *s* of Alfred Thompson and Eleanor (*née* Craig); *m* 1957, Catherine (*née* Warburton); one *s* one *d*. *Educ:* Heaton Grammar Sch., Newcastle upon Tyne; Rutherford Coll., Newcastle upon Tyne. Commercial Exec., Belfast Telegraph, Newcastle Chronicle and Journal, Scotsman Publications, Liverpool Post and Echo, 1960–76; Advertising and Marketing Manager, Kent Messenger Gp, 1976–79, Dir, 1972–79; Man. Dir, South Eastern Newspapers, 1975–79; Chm. and Man. Dir, 1973–89, Consultant Dir, 1989–, Adverkit Internat. Ltd. Dir, Weekly Newspaper Advtg Bureau, 1977. Dir, Ad Builder Ltd, 1971–89. Life Governor, Kent County Agricl Soc., 1976. Hon. Life Mem., Kent CCC, 1978; Mem., Catenian Assoc. (Pres., Maidstone Circle, 1974–75). Chm., Southern Football League, 1977–79 (Life Mem., 1985); President: Eastern Professional Floodlight League, 1976–89; Kent League, 1984–89; The Football Conf., 1989–; Mem. Council, Football Assoc., 1982–. FInstD; MInstM; MBIM. Liveryman, Worshipful Co. of Stationers and Newspaper Makers; Freeman, City of London. Distinguished Service Award, Internat. Classified Advertising Assoc., Baltimore, 1968. *Publications:* numerous articles on commercial aspects of newspaper publishing and Association football. *Recreations:* walking, Northumbrian history. *Address:* Prescott House, Otham, Kent ME15 8RL. *T:* Maidstone (0622) 861606. *Clubs:* MCC; Maidstone (Maidstone).

THOMPSON, (James) Howard, OBE 1984; British Council Director (formerly Representative) in Indonesia, since 1989; *b* 26 March 1942; *s* of James Alan Thompson and Edna (*née* Perkins); *m* 1965, Claire Marguerite Dockrell; one *s* one *d*. *Educ:* Northampton Grammar Sch.; Magdalene Coll., Cambridge (BA); Stanford Univ. (MA). English Language Officer, British Council, Yugoslavia, 1966–69; Associate Prof., Punjab Univ., 1970–73; Dep. Representative, British Council, Kenya, 1974–78; Advr, Schs and Further Educn Dept, 1978–80; Educn Attaché, British Embassy, Washington, 1980–84; Dep. Controller, 1984–87, Controller, 1987–89, Science, Technology and Educn Div., British Council. Chm., Educn and Trng Export Cttee, 1988–89. *Publication:* Teaching English, 1972. *Recreations:* photography, travel. *Address:* 1 Homefield Road, W4 2LN; c/o British Council, 10 Spring Gardens, SW1A 2BN.

THOMPSON, Rt. Rev. James Lawton; *see* Bath and Wells, Bishop of.

THOMPSON, Sir John, Kt 1961; Judge of the High Court of Justice, Queen's Bench Division, 1961–82; *b* Glasgow, 16 Dec. 1907; *e s* of Donald Cameron Thompson and Jeanie Dunn Thompson (*née* Nisbet); *m* 1934, Agnes Baird, (Nancy), *o d* of John and Jeanie Drummond, Glasgow; two *s*. *Educ:* Bellahouston Academy; Glasgow University; Oriel College, Oxford (Neale Schol.). Glasgow University: MA and Arthur Jones Memorial Prize, 1928; Ewing Gold Medal, 1929; Oxford University: BA, 1930; MA 1943. Barrister-at-Law, Powell Prize, Middle Temple, 1933. QC 1954; Bencher, Middle Temple, 1961; Lent Reader, 1977; Dep. Treasurer, 1977; Treasurer, 1978. Vice-Chm., Gen. Council of the Bar, 1960–61 (Mem. 1958–61). Commissioner of Assize (Birmingham) 1961. *Publications:* (edited with H. R. Rogers) Redgrave's Factories, Truck and Shops Acts. *Recreation:* golf. *Address:* 73 Sevenoaks Road, Orpington, Kent BR6 9JN. *T:* Orpington (0689) 822339. *Clubs:* Royal & Ancient Golf, Sundridge Park Golf (Capt., 1958–59).

THOMPSON, John; MP (Lab) Wansbeck, since 1983; *b* 27 Aug. 1928; *s* of Nicholas and Lilian Thompson; *m* 1952, Margaret Clarke; one *s* one *d*. *Educ:* Bothal Sch.; Ashington Mining Coll. Electrical Engr, 1966–83. Councillor: Wansbeck DC, 1974–79; Northumberland CC, 1974–85 (Leader, and Chm., Policy and Resources, and Employment Cttees, 1981–83). An Opposition Whip, 1990–. Mem., Select Cttee on Educn, Science and Arts, 1985–87; Sec., Northern Labour MPs, 1985–90. Alternate Mem., Council of Europe and WEU. *Address:* 20 Falstone Crescent, Ashington, Northumberland NE63 0TY. *T:* Ashington (0670) 817830.

THOMPSON, John, MBE 1975; HM Diplomatic Service; High Commissioner to Vanuatu, since 1988; *b* 28 May 1945; *s* of Arthur Thompson and Josephine (*née* Brooke); *m* 1966, Barbara Hopper; one *d*. *Educ:* Whiteheath County Primary Sch., Ruislip, Mddx; St Nicholas Grammar Sch., Northwood, Mddx; Polytechnic of Central London (DMS). Joined FO, 1964; Vice-Consul, Düsseldorf, 1966–69; Consular Officer, later Vice-Consul, Abu Dhabi, 1969–72; Vice-Consul, Phnom Penh, 1972–74; seconded to DTI, 1975–77; First Sec., FCO, 1977–79; First Sec., Hd of Chancery and Consul, Luanda, 1979–81; Consul (Commercial), São Paulo, 1981–85; Assistant Head: S Pacific Dept, FCO, 1985–87; Aid Policy Dept, FCO, 1987–88. *Recreations:* philately, walking, reading, bridge. *Address:* c/o Foreign and Commonwealth Office, King Charles Street, SW1A 2AH. *Club:* Royal Commonwealth Trust.

THOMPSON, John Alan, CMG 1974; HM Diplomatic Service, retired; *b* 21 June 1926; *m* 1956, Maureen Sayers. *Educ:* Bromsgrove Sch.; Brasenose Coll., Oxford. Control Commission for Germany, 1952; Vice-Consul, Hanoi, 1954; Second Sec., Saigon, 1956; Warsaw, 1959; Foreign Office, 1961; First Sec. (Commercial), Havana, 1964; First Sec., FO (later FCO), 1966–75; Counsellor, 1973. *Recreations:* music, mountains. *Address:* Sun House, Hall Street, Long Melford, Suffolk CO10 9HZ. *T:* Sudbury (0787) 78252.

THOMPSON, John Brian, CBE 1980; Editor, The Viewer, since 1988; *b* 8 June 1928; *y s* of late John and Lilian Thompson; *m* 1957, Sylvia, *d* of late Thomas Waterhouse, CBE, and of Doris Waterhouse (*née* Gough); two *s* one *d*. *Educ:* St Paul's; Pembroke College, Oxford (BA; MA). Eileen Power Studentship, LSE, 1950; Glaxo Laboratories Ltd, 1950–54; Masius & Fergusson Ltd, 1955; Asst Editor, Truth, 1956–57; Daily Express, 1957–59 (New York Correspondent; Drama Critic); ITN, 1959–60 (Newscaster/Reporter); Editor, Time and Tide, 1960–62; News Editor, The Observer, 1962–66; Editor, Observer Colour Magazine, 1966–70; Publisher and Editorial Dir, BPC Publishing Ltd, 1971; Dir of Radio, IBA, 1973–87. Vis. Prof., Sch. of Media, Lancashire Poly., 1987–90. Sen. Advr on Radio to Minister of Posts and Telecommunications, 1972; Mem., MoD Study Group on Censorship, 1983. Director: Worlds End Productions Ltd, 1987–; The Observer, 1989–; Dep. Chm., Zabaxe Gp, 1988–90. Vice-Chm. (radio), EBU, 1986–88. Mem. Delegacy, Goldsmiths' Coll., London, 1986–. Associate Mem., Nuffield Coll., Oxford, 1988–90. Judge, Booker Fiction Prize, 1987. Sony Radio special award, 1983. *Address:* 1 Bedwyn Common, Great Bedwyn, Marlborough, Wilts SN8 3HZ. *T:* Marlborough (0672) 870641; 46 Holland Road, W14 8BB. *T:* 071–602 5276. *Clubs:* Garrick, Groucho.
See also Hon. Sir R. G. Waterhouse.

THOMPSON, John Derek T.; *see* Taylor Thompson.

THOMPSON, Prof. John Griggs, PhD; FRS 1979; Rouse Ball Professor of Mathematics, University of Cambridge, since 1971; Fellow of Churchill College, since 1968; *b* Kansas, 13 Oct. 1932; *s* of John and Eleanor Thompson; *m* 1960, Diane Oenning; one *s* one *d*. *Educ:* Yale (BA 1955); Chicago (PhD 1959); MA Cantab 1972. Prof. of Mathematics, Chicago Univ., 1962–68; Vis. Prof. of Mathematics, Cambridge Univ., 1968–70. Hon. DSc Oxon, 1987. Cole Prize, 1966; Field Medal, 1970; Berwick Prize, London Math. Soc., 1982; Sylvester Medal, Royal Soc., 1985. *Address:* 16 Millington Road, Cambridge CB3 9HP.

THOMPSON, John Handby, CB 1988; Ceremonial Officer, Cabinet Office, since 1988; *b* 21 Feb. 1929; *s* of late Rev. John Thomas Thompson and Clara Handby; *m* 1957, Catherine Rose, *d* of Charles Bowman Heald; two *s* one *d*. *Educ:* Silcoates Sch., Wakefield; St John's Coll., Oxford (MA); Sheffield Univ. (PhD 1991). Served Intell. Corps, 1947–49. HM Inspector of Taxes, 1953–63; Dept of Educn and Science, 1964–88: Schs Council, 1971–73; Asst Sec., 1973; Mem., Prep. Cttee of European Univ. Inst., 1973–75; Dep. Accountant-Gen., 1976–78; Under Sec., 1978; Head of Schs Br. 1, 1978–80; Head of Further and Higher Educn Br. 1, 1980–84; Dir of Estabts and Orgn, 1985–88. Gov., Polytechnic of N London, 1989–. *Recreations:* reading about Albania, Nonconformist history. *Club:* Reform.

THOMPSON, Prof. John Jeffrey, CBE 1989; PhD; CChem, FRSC; Professor of Education, University of Bath, since 1979 (Pro-Vice-Chancellor, 1986–89); *b* 13 July 1938; *s* of John Thompson and Elsie May Thompson (*née* Wright); *m* 1963, Kathleen Audrey Gough; three *d*. *Educ:* King George V Sch., Southport; St John's Coll., Cambridge (MA); Balliol Coll., Oxford (MA); PhD (CNAA); DipEd (Oxon). Asst Master, Blundell's Sch., 1961–65; Head of Chemistry, Watford Grammar Sch., 1965–69; Lectr in Educn, KCL, 1968–69; Shell Fellow, UCL, 1969–70; Lectr and Tutor, Dept of Educnl Studies, Oxford Univ., 1970–79; Lectr in Chemistry, Keble Coll., Oxford, 1970–76. Chief Examnr, Internat. Baccalaureate, 1970– (Chm., Bd of Chief Examnrs, 1985–89). Chairman: Assoc. for Science Educn, 1981; Nat. Curriculum Science Working Gp, 1987–88. Mem., Council, 1988–, Dep. Chm., 1989–, School Exams and Assessment Council; Mem., Nat. Commn on Educn, 1991–. Pres., Educn Div., Royal Soc. of Chemistry, 1983–85; Vice-Pres. and Gen. Sec., BAAS, 1985–91 (Chm., Council 1991–). Mem., Educn Cttee, Royal Soc., 1989–. Mem. Council, Wildfowl Trust, 1981–91. FRSA

1983. *Publications:* Introduction to Chemical Energetics, 1967; European Curriculum Studies; Chemistry, 1972; (ed) Practical Work in Sixthform Science, 1976; Foundation Course in Chemistry, 1982; Modern Physical Chemistry, 1982; (ed) Dimensions of Science, 1986; The Chemistry Dimension, 1987. *Recreations:* music (brass bands and blue grass), North Country art, collecting sugar wrappers. *Address:* University of Bath, Claverton Down, Bath BA2 7AY.

THOMPSON, John Keith Lumley, CMG 1982; MBE (mil.) 1965; TD 1961; President, Lumley Associates, since 1983; *b* 31 March 1923; *s* of late John V. V. and Gertrude Thompson; *m* 1950, Audrey Olley; one *s*. *Educ:* Wallsend Grammar Sch.; King's Coll., Durham Univ. (BSc). FBIM (MBIM 1975); MSAE 1983. Served War of 1939–45: Officer in REME, 1942–47, NW Europe; BEME 44 Para Bde (V), 1948–70. Dep. Inspector, REME (V) Southern Comd, 1970–72 (Lt-Col); Dep. Comdr, 44 Para Bde (V), 1972–75 (Col). Road Research Lab., DSIR, 1948–55; AWRE, Aldermaston, 1955–64; Staff of Chief Scientific Adviser, MoD, 1964–65; Head of E Midlands Regional Office, Min. Tech., 1965–70; Head, Internat. Affairs, Atomic Energy Div., Dept of Energy, 1972–74; Regional Dir, W Midlands and Northern Regional Offices, DoI, 1970–72 and 1974–78; Counseller (Sci. and Tech.), Washington, 1978–83. ADC to the Queen (TAVR), 1974–78. *Publications:* papers on vehicle behaviour, crash helmets and implosion systems; numerous articles on American science and technology. *Recreations:* outdoor activities, reading. *Address:* c/o Lumley Associates, 7 School Lane, Baston, Peterborough PE6 9PD. *T:* Greatford (077836) 374.

THOMPSON, John Leonard C.; *see* Cloudsley-Thompson.

THOMPSON, Air Commodore John Marlow, CBE 1954; DSO 1943; DFC 1940 (and Bar 1942); AFC 1952; RAF retired; *b* 16 Aug. 1914; *s* of late John Thompson and Florence Thompson (*née* Marlow); *m* 1938, Margaret Sylvia Rowlands; one *s* one *d* (and one *s* decd). *Educ:* Bristol Grammar School. Joined RAF 1934; comd 111 Sqdn, Battle of Britain; Spitfire Wing, Malta, 1942–43; SASO 11 Group, 1952–54; comd RAF Leeming, 1956–57; Dir of Air Defence, Air Ministry, 1958–60; Graduate Imperial Defence Coll., 1961; AOC, Military Air Traffic Ops, 1962–65; Gen. Manager, Airwork Services, Saudi Arabia, 1966–68. Belgian MC 1st Class, 1942; Danish Order of Dannebrog, 1951. *Recreation:* golf. *Address:* Flat 3, 35 Adelaide Crescent, Hove, East Sussex BN3 2JJ. *T:* Brighton (0273) 722859. *Clubs:* Royal Air Force; Monte-Carlo; Moor Park Golf, Monte Carlo Golf (Dir, 1973–83).

THOMPSON, John Michael Anthony, FMA; Director, Art Galleries and Museums, Tyne and Wear County Museums, since 1975; *b* 3 Feb. 1941; *s* of George Thompson and Joan Smith; *m* 1965, Alison Sara Bowers; two *d*. *Educ:* William Hulme's Grammar Sch., Manchester; Univ. of Manchester. BA, MA; FMA 1980. Research Asst, Whitworth Art Gall., 1964–66; Keeper, Rutherston Collection, City Art Gall., Manchester, 1966–68; Director: North Western Museum and Art Gall. Service, 1968–70; Arts and Museums, Bradford City Council, 1970–74; Chief Arts and Museums Officer, Bradford Metropolitan Council, 1974–75. Councillor, Museums Assoc., 1977–80, 1984–87 (Chm., Accreditation Cttee, 1978–80); Advisor to Arts and Recreation Cttee, AMA, 1981–; Pres., Museums North, 1977, and 1991–92; Chm., Soc. of County Museum Dirs, 1982–86; Founder Mem. and Hon. Sec., Gp of Dirs of Museums in the British Isles, 1985–. *Publications:* (ed) The Manual of Curatorship: a guide to museum practice, 1984, 2nd edn 1992; articles in Museums Jl, Penrose Annual, Connoisseur. *Recreations:* classical guitar, long distance running, walking. *Address:* 21 Linden Road, Gosforth, Newcastle upon Tyne NE3 4EY. *T:* 091–284 2797.

THOMPSON, Prof. John Michael Tutill, FRS 1985; Professor of Structural Mechanics, Department of Civil Engineering, since 1977, and Director, Centre for Nonlinear Dynamics and Its Applications, since 1991, University College London; Senior Fellow, Science and Engineering Research Council, since 1988; *b* 7 June 1937; *s* of John Hornsey Thompson and Kathleen Rita Thompson (*née* Tutill); *m* 1959, Margaret Cecilia Chapman; one *s* one *d*. *Educ:* Hull Grammar Sch.; Clare Coll., Cambridge (MA, PhD, ScD). FIMA. Research Fellow, Peterhouse, 1961–64; Vis. Res. Associate, Stanford (Fulbright grant), 1962–63; Lectr, 1964–68, Reader, 1968–77, UCL; Chm., Bd of Studies in Civil and Mech. Eng., Univ. of London, 1984–86. Vis. Prof., Faculté des Sciences, Univ. Libre de Bruxelles, 1976–78; Vis. Mathematician, Brookhaven Nat. Lab., 1984; Vis. Res. Fellow, Centre for Nonlinear Studies, Univ. of Leeds, 1987–89. Mem. Council, IMA, 1989– (Organizer, Conf. on Chaos, UCL, 1990). OMAE Award, ASME, 1985. Organizer and Editor, IUTAM Symp. on Collapse: the buckling of structures in theory and practice, 1982; Actg Ed., Phil. Trans Roy. Soc., Series A, 1990 (Ed. and Organizer, first Theme Issue, 1990); sci. contribs to radio and TV, 1975–. *Publications:* (with G. W. Hunt) A general theory of elastic stability, 1973; Instabilities and catastrophes in science and engineering, 1982; (with G. W. Hunt) Elastic instability phenomena, 1984; (with H. B. Stewart) Nonlinear dynamics and chaos, 1986; articles in learned jls (and mem., editl bds). *Recreations:* walking, music, tennis, table tennis. *Address:* 31 Hillside Road, Bushey, Herts WD2 2HB. *T:* Watford (0923) 229803.

THOMPSON, (John) Peter (Stuart); Director, Solicitors' Complaints Bureau, 1986–90; *b* 6 July 1925; *s* of Frederick Charles Victor Thompson and Hilda Mary (*née* Hampton); *m* 1956, Valerie Merriel (*née* Harman). *Educ:* Burton Grammar Sch.; Royal Naval Coll., Dartmouth; Royal Naval Engineering Coll., Devonport; Univ. of Birmingham, 1952–55 (LLB). Admitted Solicitor, 1966. Served Royal Navy, 1943–47. Arts Council Drama Dept and associated theatres: Actor/Stage Dir, 1947–52. Asst Company Sec., Saunders-Roe Ltd, Aircraft Manufrs, 1955–61; articled clerk, Helder Roberts & Co., Solicitors, London, 1961–66, Partner 1966–70; Law Soc. Professional Purposes Dept, 1971–86. *Recreations:* gardening, marine technology, 18th Century music, flora and fauna of tropical islands. *Address:* Parkhurst Lodge, Abinger Common, Dorking, Surrey RH5 6LL. *T:* Dorking (0306) 730522.

THOMPSON, John William McWean, CBE 1986; Editor, Sunday Telegraph, 1976–86; *b* 12 June 1920; *s* of Charles and Charlotte Thompson; *m* 1947, Cynthia Ledsham; one *s* one *d*. *Educ:* Roundhay Sch., Leeds. Previously on staffs of Yorkshire Evening News, Evening Standard, London, and The Spectator (Dep. Editor); joined Sunday Telegraph, 1970; Asst Editor, 1975. *Publication:* (as Peter Quince) Country Life, 1975. *Address:* Corner Cottage, Burnham Norton, King's Lynn, Norfolk PE31 8DS. *T:* Fakenham (0328) 738396. *Club:* Travellers'.

THOMPSON, Rear-Adm. John Yelverton, CB 1960; DL; retired 1961; *b* 25 May 1909; *s* of late Sir John Perronet Thompson, KCSI, KCIE, and Ada Lucia, Lady Thompson (*née* Tyrrell); *m* 1934, Barbara Helen Mary Aston Key; two *s*. *Educ:* Mourne Grange, Kilkeel, Co. Down; RN College, Dartmouth. Midshipman: HMS Repulse and Berwick, 1926–29; Sub-Lieutenant: HMS Warspite, 1931; Lieutenant: HMS Queen Elizabeth, 1931–32, Restless 1933, Excellent 1933–34, Queen Elizabeth 1935, Glasgow 1936–39; Lieut-Commander: HMS Excellent 1939–41, Anson 1941–43; Commander: Admiralty, Naval Ordnance Dept, 1943–45; US Fifth Fleet, 1946; HMS Liverpool, 1947; HMS Newcastle, 1948; Captain: Ordnance Board, 1948–50; HMS Unicorn, 1951–52; Director, Gunnery Division, Naval Staff, 1952–54; Imperial Defence College, 1955; Commodore: Royal Naval Barracks, Portsmouth, 1956–57; Rear-Admiral: Admiralty Interview Boards, 1958; Adm. Superintendent, HM Dockyard, Chatham, 1958–61. ADC to the Queen, 1957. Governor, Aldenham Sch., 1967–73. DL: Hertfordshire, 1966–73; Cornwall, 1973. American Legion of Merit, 1953. *Address:* The Old Vicarage, Moulsford, Wallingford OX10 9JB.

See also G. F. M. P. Thompson.

THOMPSON, Julian; *see* Thompson, R. J. de la M.

THOMPSON, Maj.-Gen. Julian Howard Atherden, CB 1982; OBE 1978; Senior Research Fellow in Logistics and Armed Conflict in the Modern Age, King's College London, since 1987; *b* 7 Oct. 1934; *s* of late Major A. J. Thompson, DSO, MC and Mary Stearns Thompson (*née* Krause); *m* 1960, Janet Avery, *d* of late Richard Robinson Rodd; one *s* one *d*. *Educ:* Sherborne School. 2nd Lieut RM, 1952; served 40, 42, 43, 45 Commandos RM, 1954–69; Asst Sec., Chiefs of Staff Cttee, 1970–71; BM, 3 Cdo Brigade, 1972–73; Directing Staff, Staff Coll., Camberley, 1974–75; CO 40 Cdo RM, 1975–78; Comdr 3 Cdo Brigade, 1981–83, incl. Falklands campaign (CB); Maj.-Gen. Comdg Trng Reserve Forces and Special Forces RM, 1983–86, retired. Pres., British Assoc. for Physical Training, 1988–. *Publications:* No Picnic: 3 Commando Brigade in the South Atlantic 1982, 1985; Ready for Anything: The Parachute Regiment at War 1940–1982, 1989; (contrib.) Military Strategy in a Changing Europe, 1991; (contrib.) Fallen Stars, 1991; The Lifeblood of War, 1991. *Recreations:* sailing, shooting, history, cross-country ski-ing, ballet, opera, jazz. *Address:* c/o Lloyds Bank, Royal Parade, Plymouth, Devon. *Clubs:* Army and Navy; Royal Marines Sailing.

THOMPSON, Julian O.; *see* Ogilvie Thompson.

THOMPSON, Keith Bruce; Director, Staffordshire (formerly North Staffordshire) Polytechnic, since 1987 (Deputy Director, 1978–86); *b* 13 Sept. 1932; *m* 1956, Kathleen Reeves; one *s* one *d*. *Educ:* Bishopshalt School, Hillingdon; New College, Oxford (Sec./Librarian, Oxford Union). PPE 1955, Dip Educn (distn), 1956, MA 1959; MEd Bristol, 1968. Schoolmaster, City of Bath Boys' School, 1956–62; Lectr, Newton Park Coll., Bath, 1962–67; Head of Dept, Philippa Fawcett Coll., Streatham, 1967–72; Principal, Madeley Coll. of Educn, 1972–78. Chairman: Standing Conf. on Studies in Educn, 1980–82; Undergraduate Initial Training Bd (Educn), CNAA, 1981–85; Chm., Polytechnics Central Admissions System, 1989–; Member: Bd, Nat. Adv. Body for Public Sector Higher Educn, 1983–88 (Chm., Teacher Educn Gp, 1983–85). Editor, Educn for Teaching, 1968–74. *Publications:* Education and Philosophy, 1972; (jtly) Curriculum Development, 1974; articles on educn, philosophy, physical educn. *Recreations:* sport, music. *Address:* Staffordshire Polytechnic, Beaconside, Stafford ST18 0AD. *T:* Stafford (0785) 52331.

THOMPSON, Hon. Lindsay Hamilton Simpson, AO 1990; CMG 1975; Premier of Victoria, 1981–82; Leader of the Opposition, Victoria, 1982; *b* 15 Oct. 1923; *s* of Arthur K. Thompson and Ethel M. Thompson; *m* 1950, Joan Margaret Poynder; two *s* one *d*. *Educ:* Caulfield Grammar Sch., Victoria (Captain and Dux 1941); Melbourne Univ. (BA Hons, BEd). MACE. AIF, New Guinea, 1942–45. MP (Lib.) in Victorian Legislative Council: Higinbotham Prov., 1955–67; Monash Prov., 1967–70; MLA Malvern, 1970–82; Member of Cabinet, 1956–82; Parly Sec. of Cabinet, 1956–58; Asst Chief Sec. and Asst Attorney-Gen., 1958–61; Asst Minister of Transport, 1960–61; Minister of Housing and Forests, 1961–67; Dep. Leader of Govt in Legislative Council, 1962–70; Minister in charge of Aboriginal Welfare, 1965–67; Minister of Educn, 1967–79 (longest term ever in this portfolio); Leader of Legislative Assembly, 1972–79; Dep. Premier of Victoria, 1972–81; Minister for Police and Emergency Services, 1979–81; Treasurer, 1979–82; served longest period as Cabinet Minister in history of Victoria. Director: Mutual Friendly Soc., 1986–; Composite Benefits Soc., 1986–. State Govt Rep., Melbourne Univ. Council, 1955–59. Dep. Chm., Aust. Advertising Standards Council, 1990– (Mem., 1988–90). Pres., Royal Life Saving Soc., 1970–. Trustee: Melb. Cricket Ground, 1967– (Chm., 1987–); Nat. Tennis Centre Trust, 1986–; Patron: Victorian Cricket Assoc.; Prahran CC; Aust. Quadriplegic Assoc.; Richmond FC. Bronze Medal, Royal Humane Soc., 1974. *Publications:* Australian Housing Today and Tomorrow, 1965; Looking Ahead in Education, 1969; A Fair Deal for Victoria, 1981; I Remember, 1989. *Recreations:* cricket, golf, tennis. *Address:* 19 Allenby Avenue, Glen Iris, Victoria 3146, Australia. *T:* 25 6191. *Clubs:* Melbourne (Melbourne), Kingston Heath Golf, Sorrento Golf.

THOMPSON, Sir Lionel; *see* Thompson, Sir T. L. T., Bt.

THOMPSON, Major Lloyd H.; *see* Hall-Thompson.

THOMPSON, McKim; *see* Thompson, I. McK.

THOMPSON, Marjorie Ellis; Chair, Campaign for Nuclear Disarmament, since 1990; *b* St Louis, Mo, 8 June 1957; *d* of John William Thompson, III and Janet Ann (*née* Neubeiser); *m* 1982, Kevin Mark Williams (separated 1986). *Educ:* Woodrow Wilson High Sch., Long Beach, California; Colorado Coll., Colorado Springs (BSc Hons History 1978); LSE (MSc Econ W European Politics 1979). Volunteer, Georgetown Centre for Strategic and Internat. Studies, Washington, DC, 1980; Personal Asst, Energy and Lang. Services Depts, World Bank, Washington, 1980–81; Legislative Corresp., office of Congressman Gerald B. Solomon, 1981–82; Lobbyist, Nat. Energy Educn Day Project, 1982; Administrator, Boston Univ. Overseas Educn Prog., US Naval Support Facility, Holy Loch, Scotland, 1982–83; Asst to political reporters, Harlech TV, General Election, 1983; Volunteer, Medical Campaign Against Nuclear Weapons, CBC Radio Action Line, Cardiff, 1983; Campaign for Nuclear Disarmament: Parly Officer, 1983–86; Hd of Press and Public Relns, 1986–87; Researcher for Ann Clwyd, MP, 1987; Vice-Chair, 1987–90; Parly Officer, 1988–91, Advr, Dept of Nursing Policy and Practice, 1991, RCN. Co-Chair, Cttee to Stop War in the Gulf, 1990–91; Hon. Pres., Cttee for Just Peace in ME, 1991. Fellow, British–American Project, 1990. *Publications:* contrib. Nursing Standard, Tribune, Sanity. *Recreations:* friends, swimming, winter sports, travel, biography and contemporary fiction, theatre, cinema. *Address:* c/o Campaign for Nuclear Disarmament, 162 Holloway Road, N7 8DQ. *T:* 071–700 2393, *Fax:* 071–700 2357.

THOMPSON, Michael Harry Rex, FCIB; Deputy Chairman, Lloyds Bank Plc, since 1991 (Director, since 1986); *b* 14 Jan. 1931; *s* of William Henry Thompson and late Beatrice Hilda Thompson (*née* Heard); *m* 1958, Joyce (*née* Redpath); one *s* one *d*. *Educ:* St John's Sch., Leatherhead, Surrey. Joined Lloyds Bank, 1948; Dep. Chief Exec., 1987–91; Director: National Bank of New Zealand; Lloyds Abbey Life; Lloyds Merchant Bank Hldgs; Chm., German Investment Trust; Dep. Chm., Lloyds Bank Stockbrokers. *Recreation:* Rugby football. *Address:* Lloyds Bank, 71 Lombard Street, EC3P 3BS. *T:* 071–626 1500.

THOMPSON, Michael Jacques, CMG 1989; OBE 1977; HM Diplomatic Service; Counsellor, Foreign and Commonwealth Office, since 1985; *b* 31 Jan. 1936; *s* of late Christopher Thompson and of Colette Jeanne-Marie Thompson; *m* 1967, Mary Susan (*née* Everard); one *s* one *d*. *Educ:* Uppingham; Christ's Coll., Cambridge (Law Tripos, 1956–60; MA). National Service, Kenya, Aden and Cyprus, 1954–56. HMOCS, Kenya, 1960–63; FCO, 1964; served Kuala Lumpur, Saigon, Lusaka and FCO, 1965–79;

Counsellor, Kuala Lumpur, 1979–82; seconded to Comdr, British Land Forces, Hong Kong, 1982–85. Mem., Royal Asia Soc. Mem., Co. of Barbers. *Recreations:* squash, tennis, golf, gardening. *Address:* c/o Foreign and Commonwealth Office, SW1. *Clubs:* United Oxford & Cambridge University; Hong Kong; Huntercombe Golf.

THOMPSON, Prof. Sir Michael (Warwick), Kt 1991; DSc; FInstP; Vice-Chancellor and Principal, University of Birmingham, since 1987; *b* 1 June 1931; *s* of Kelvin Warwick Thompson and Madeleine Thompson; *m* Sybil (*née* Spooner); two *s*. *Educ:* Rydal Sch.; Univ. of Liverpool (BSc, DSc). Research scientist, AERE, Harwell, 1953–65; Sussex University: Prof. of Experimental Physics, 1965–80; Pro-Vice-Chancellor, 1973–77, actg Vice-Chancellor, 1976; Vis. Prof., 1980–; Vice-Chancellor, UEA, 1980–86. Chm., Physics Cttee, SRC, 1975–79; Member: E Sussex AHA, 1974–79; E Sussex Educn Cttee, 1973–78; W Midlands RHA, 1987–. Member: Council, CNAA, 1989–; Council for Internat. Co-operation in Higher Educn, 1989–; Council, CVCP, 1990–. Dir, Alliance & Leicester Building Soc., 1985– (Dir, Alliance Building Soc., 1979–85). Mem. Council, Eastbourne Coll., 1977–. Oliver Lodge Prizewinner, Univ. of Liverpool, 1953; Prizewinner, Materials Science Club, 1970; C. V. Boys Prizewinner, Inst. of Physics, 1972. *Publications:* Defects and Radiation Damage in Metals, 1969; (jtly) Channelling, 1973; over 90 papers in sci. jls. *Recreations:* the arts, navigation in small ships. *Address:* University of Birmingham, Edgbaston, Birmingham B15 2TT. *Clubs:* Athenæum; Royal Fowey Yacht.

THOMPSON, Nicolas de la Mare; Director: Octopus Publishing Group Plc, since 1985; Reed International Books Ltd, since 1990; Chairman: Heinemann Educational Books Ltd, since 1985; Ginn & Co. Ltd, since 1985; *b* 4 June 1928; *s* of Rupert Spens Thompson and Florence Elizabeth Thompson (*née* de la Mare); *m* 1956, Erica Pennell; two *s* one *d*. *Educ:* Eton; Christ Church, Oxford (MA). Managing Director, George Weidenfeld and Nicolson, 1956–70; Publishing Dir, Pitman, 1970–85; Managing Dir, Heinemann Gp of Publishers, 1985–87; Director: Heinemann Professional Publishing, 1986–90; George Philip & Son, 1988–90; Mitchell Beazley, 1988–90. Chm., Book Development Council, 1984–86; Treas., Publishers Assoc., 1986–88. *Address:* 8 Ennismore Gardens, SW7 1NL.

THOMPSON, Dr Noel Brentnall Watson; Chief Executive, National Council for Educational Technology, since 1988; *b* 11 Dec. 1932; *s* of George Watson Thompson and Mary Henrietta Gibson; *m* 1957, Margaret Angela Elizabeth Baston; one *s*. *Educ:* Manchester Grammar School; Cambridge Univ. (MA); Imperial College, London (MSc Eng, PhD). National Service, RN (Sub-Lieut), 1951–53. Research, Imperial Coll., 1958–61; Lectr in Physical Metallurgy, Univ. of Birmingham, 1961–65; Dept of Education and Science, 1966–67, 1969–77 and 1979–88 (Under Sec., 1980–88; Head of Higher and Further Educn III Br., 1980–86; Head of Schools 2 Br. and Internat. Relations, 1986–88); Secretary, National Libraries Cttee, 1967–69; Cabinet Office, 1977–79. *Publications:* papers in professional journals. *Recreations:* railways of all sizes, mechanics, music, modern history, photography, walking. *Address:* c/o National Council for Educational Technology, 3 Devonshire Street, W1N 2BA. *T:* 071–636 4186. *Clubs:* other people's.

THOMPSON, Norman Sinclair, CBE 1980; Chairman: Vaile & Co. (Dorset) Ltd, since 1991; Horsemaster Ltd, since 1991; *b* 7 July 1920; *s* of Norman Whitfield Thompson and Jane Thompson (*née* Robinson); *m* 1945, Peggy Sivil; two *s* (one *d* decd). *Educ:* Middlesbrough High Sch. Qual. Chartered Accountant, 1947 (FCA); Cost and Management Accountant (ACMA), 1949. Served War, Merchant Seaman, 1940–45. Asst Sec., Paton's and Baldwin's Ltd, 1947; Commercial Manager, Cowan's Sheldon & Co. Ltd, 1955; Group Secretary, Richardson's Westgarth & Co. Ltd, 1957; Financial Dir, David Brown & Sons (Huddersfield) Ltd, 1961; Gen. Manager, Malta Drydocks, Swan Hunter Group Ltd, 1963; apptd Swan Hunter Bd, 1964; Overseas Dir, 1967; Dep. Managing Dir, 1969; The Cunard Steam-Ship Co. Ltd: Man. Dir, Cargo Shipping, 1970; Man. Dir, 1971–74; Chairman: Mass Transit Railway Corp., Hong Kong, 1975–83; Poole Harbour Comrs, 1984–86; Dep. Chm., New Hong Kong Tunnel Co., 1986–91; Director: Hong Kong and Shanghai Banking Corp., 1978–86; British Shipbuilders, 1983–86. *Recreations:* sailing, music. *Address:* Shadrach House, Burton Bradstock, Bridport, Dorset DT6 4QG. *Clubs:* Oriental, Royal Ocean Racing; Hong Kong, Royal Hong Kong Yacht, Royal Hong Kong Jockey.

THOMPSON, Oliver Frederic, OBE 1945; Pro-Chancellor of The City University, 1966–72; *b* 26 Jan. 1905; 3rd *s* of late W. Graham Thompson and late Oliveria C. Prescott; *m* 1939, Frances Phyllida, *d* of late F. H. Bryant; one *s* three *d*. *Educ:* Tonbridge. Mem. Shell Gp of Cos, 1924–64: managerial posts in USA, Caribbean, London. Head of Oil Sect., Min. of Econ. Warfare, and Mem. War Cabinet Sub-Cttee on Oil, 1942–46; rep. UK, Suez Canal Users Assoc.; rep. UK on various UN and OECD Cttees; Mem. Parly and Sci. Cttee, 1955–65. Past Master and Mem. Ct, Worshipful Co. of Skinners. Chm. Governing Body, Northampton Coll. of Advanced Technology, 1956–66 (now City University); Governor, Tonbridge Sch. FInstP (Past Mem. Council); Chm. Qualifications Cttee, British Computer Society, 1968 (Hon. Fellow, 1972). County Councillor, Surrey, 1965–77 (Majority Leader, 1970–73). Hon. DSc, City Univ., 1967. *Publications:* various papers on economics of energy and petroleum. *Recreation:* country pursuits. *Address:* 32 Park Road, Aldeburgh, Suffolk IP15 5EU. *T:* Aldeburgh (0728) 452424.

THOMPSON, Patrick; *see* Thompson, H. P.

THOMPSON, Sir Paul (Anthony), 2nd Bt *cr* 1963; company director; *b* 6 Oct. 1939; *s* of Sir Kenneth Pugh Thompson, 1st Bt, and of Nanne, *yr d* of Charles Broome, Walton, Liverpool; *S* father, 1984; *m* 1971, Pauline Dorothy, *d* of Robert O. Spencer, Bolton, Lancs; two *s* two *d*. *Educ:* Aldenham School, Herts. *Heir:* *s* Richard Kenneth Spencer Thompson, *b* 27 Jan. 1976. *Address:* 28 Dowhills Road, Blundellsands, Liverpool.

THOMPSON, Prof. Paul Richard, DPhil; social historian; Research Professor in Social History, University of Essex, since 1988; Director, National Life Story Collection, since 1987; *b* 1935; *m* 1st, Thea Vigne; one *s* one *d*; 2nd, Natasha Burchardt; one *d*. *Educ:* Bishop's Stortford Coll., Corpus Christi Coll., Oxford; The Queen's Coll., Oxford (Junior Research Fellow, 1961–64). MA, DPhil 1964. University of Essex: Lectr in Sociology, 1964–69; Sen. Lectr, 1969–71; Reader, 1971–88; Sen. Res. Fellow, Nuffield Coll., Oxford, 1968–69; Vis. Prof. of Art History, Johns Hopkins Univ., 1972; Hoffman Wood Prof. of Architecture, Univ. of Leeds, 1977–78; Benjamin Meaker Prof., Univ. of Bristol, 1987. Editor: Victorian Soc. Conf. Reports, 1965–67; Oral History, 1970–; Life Stories, 1985–. *Publications:* History of English Architecture (with Peter Kidson and Peter Murray), 1965, 2nd edn 1979; The Work of William Morris, 1967, 3rd edn 1991; Socialists, Liberals and Labour: the struggle for London 1880–1914, 1967; The Edwardians: the remaking of British Society, 1975; The Voice of the Past: Oral History, 1978, 2nd edn 1988; Living the Fishing, 1983; I Don't Feel Old: the experience of later life, 1990; The Myths We Live By, 1990. *Recreations:* cycling, drawing, music, friendship, travel. *Address:* 18 Lonsdale Road, Oxford OX2 7EW. *T:* Oxford (0865) 510840.

THOMPSON, Peter; *see* Thompson, J. P. S.

THOMPSON, Sir Peter (Anthony), Kt 1984; FCIT; President, NFC plc, since 1991; Chairman: Community Hospitals plc, since 1981; Child Base Ltd, since 1989; FI Group plc, since 1990; M–31, since 1991; M–33, since 1991; *b* 14 April 1928; *s* of late Herbert Thompson and of Sarah Jane Thompson; *m* 1st, 1958, Patricia Anne Norcott (*d* 1983); one *s* two *d*; 2nd, 1986, Lydia Mary Kite (*née* Hodding); two *d*. *Educ:* Royal Drapers Sch.; Bradford Grammar Sch.; Leeds Univ. (BA Econ). Unilever, 1952–62; GKN, 1962–64; Transport Controller, Rank Organisation, 1964–67; Head of Transport, BSC, 1967–72; Group Co-ordinator, BRS Ltd, 1972–75; Exec. Vice-Chm. (Operations), Nat. Freight Corp., 1975–77; Chief Exec., Nat. Freight Corp., later Nat. Freight Co., 1977–80; Dep. Chm. and Chief Exec., 1980–82, Chm. and Chief Exec., 1982–84, Exec. Chm., 1984–90, NFC. Dir, 1989–90, Dep. Chm., 1989–90, Chm., March–July 1990, British & Commonwealth Hldgs; Director: Granville & Co. Ltd, 1984–90; Pilkington plc, 1985–; Kenning Motor Group, 1985–86; Smiths Industries PLC, 1986–; Meyer International, 1988–. Mem., Nat. Trng Task Force, 1989–. President: Inst. of Freight Forwarders, 1982–83; Inst. of Logistics and Distribn Management (formerly Inst. of Physical Distribn Management), 1988– (Chm., 1985–88); Vice-Pres., CIT, 1982–85; Chm., CBI Wider Share Ownership Task Force, 1990. CBIM. Hambro Businessman of the Year, 1983. *Publication:* Sharing the Success: the story of the NFC, 1990. *Recreations:* golf, walking, music. *Address:* The Mill House, Mill Street, Newport Pagnell, Bucks MK16 8ER. *Club:* Royal Automobile.

THOMPSON, Prof. Peter John; Chief Executive, National Council for Vocational Qualifications, since 1986; *b* 17 April 1937; *s* of late George Kenneth Thompson and Gladys Pamela (*née* Partington), W Midlands; *m* 1961, Dorothy Ann Smith; one *s* one *d*. *Educ:* Aston Univ. (Tube Investments Schol.; BSc 1st Cl. Hons MechEngrg; MSc); CNAA (DTech). Whitworth Soc. Prize. CEng, FIMechE, FIProdE, FIPlantE; FITD. With Tube Investments, 1952–61; Lectr 1961, Sen. Lectr 1968–70, Harris Coll., Preston; Sen. Sci. Officer, UKAEA, Preston, 1965–68; Prin. Lectr, Sheffield City Poly., 1970–77; Hd of Dept and Dean of Engrg, Trent Poly., Nottingham, 1977–83; Pro Rector, then Dep. Rector, Poly. of Central London, 1983–86; Professor: Trent Poly., 1980–83; Poly. of Central London, 1983–. Mem., then Chm., Manufacturing Bd, CNAA, 1978–86; Mem., Cttee for Sci. and Technology, CNAA, 1982–86; Mem. then Chm., Cttee for Engrg in Polytechnics, 1981–86; Member: Engrg Adv. Cttee, NAB, 1980–84; Engrg Scis Divl Bd of IMechE, 1984–86; Chm., Materials Tech. Activities Cttee, IMechE, 1984–86; Mem., Council, Open Coll., 1987–. FRSA. *Publications:* numerous papers on engrg manufacture and vocational educn and trng, 1968–, incl. papers on hydrostatic extension, lubrication, cutting tool wear and mechanics and metal forming; patents. *Recreations:* genealogy, numismatics, golf. *Address:* 222 Euston Road, NW1 2BZ. *T:* 071–387 9898.

THOMPSON, Peter Kenneth James; Solicitor to Departments of Health and of Social Security, since 1989; *b* 30 July 1937; *s* of Kenneth George Thompson and Doreen May Thompson; *m* 1970, Sandy Lynne Harper; two *d*. *Educ:* Worksop Coll.; Christ's Coll., Cambridge (MA, LLB). Called to the Bar, Lincoln's Inn, 1961; practised at Common Law Bar, 1961–73; Lawyer in Govt Service: Law Commission, 1973–78; Lord Chancellor's Dept, 1978–83; Under Sec., DHSS, 1983. *Publications:* The Unfair Contract Terms Act 1977, 1978; The Recovery of Interest, 1985; *radio plays:* A Matter of Form, 1977; Dormer and Grand-Daughter, 1978. *Recreation:* writing. *Address:* Departments of Health and Social Security, Richmond House, 79 Whitehall, SW1A 2NS.

THOMPSON, Pratt; *see* Thompson, W. P.

THOMPSON, Sir Ralph (Patrick), Kt 1980; Barrister and Solicitor of the High Court of New Zealand, since 1938; *b* 19 June 1916; *m* 1st, 1940, Dorothy Maud Simes (*d* 1982); one *s* two *d*; 2nd, 1988, Dorothy Maisie Collins. *Educ:* Napier Boys High Sch.; Dannevirke High Sch.; Canterbury Univ. (LLB 1937). Admitted barrister and solicitor, 1938; in practice in Christchurch. Former Chairman: United Building Soc; Waitaki NZ Refrigerating Ltd; M. O'Brien & Co. Ltd; Director: New Zealand Refining Co. Ltd, 1967–86; Waitaki International Ltd (formerly Waitaki NZ Ltd), 1975–86; Barclays Bank New Zealand Ltd (formerly New Zealand United Corp. Ltd), 1976–86. *Recreations:* reading, racing, walking. *Address:* 115 Heaton Street, Christchurch 5, New Zealand. *T:* 557.490. *Clubs:* Canterbury, Canterbury University (Hon. Life Mem.), Canterbury Jockey; New Zealand Metropolitan Trotting (Christchurch).

THOMPSON, Prof. Raymond, CBE 1988; PhD; FRSC; FEng 1985, FIMM; Deputy Chairman, Borax Research Ltd, 1986–90 (Managing Director, 1980–86); Director: RTZ Chemicals (formerly Borax Consolidated) (Borides) Ltd, 1986–89; Boride Ceramics and Composites Ltd, since 1990; *b* 4 April 1925; *s* of late William Edward Thompson and Hilda Thompson (*née* Rowley). *Educ:* Longton High Sch.; Univ. of Nottingham (MSc 1950, PhD 1952); Imperial Coll., Univ. of London (DIC 1953). Research Manager, Borax Consolidated, 1961; Res. Dir, 1969–86, Business Develt Dir, 1986–87, Scientific Advr, 1987–, RTZ Borax and Minerals Ltd (formerly Borax Hldgs Ltd). Consultant: RTZ Chemicals Ltd, 1988–89; CRA Ltd, 1988–; Rhône-Poulenc, 1989–. Special Professor of Inorganic Chemistry, Univ. of Nottingham, 1975–; Hon. Prof., Molecular Sciences, Univ. of Warwick, 1975–. Member Council: Royal Inst. of Chemistry, 1969–72; Chemical Soc., 1977–80 (Chm., Inorganic Chemicals Gp, 1972–83); RSC, 1983–88 (Vice-Pres., Industrial Div., 1981–83, Pres., 1983–85 and 1988–89). Governor, Kingston-upon-Thames Polytechnic, 1978–88. Hon. Associate, RHC, London Univ., 1984. Liveryman: Glass Sellers' Co.; Engineers' Co. Freeman, City of London. FRSA. Industrial Chemistry Award, Chem. Soc., 1976. *Publications:* (ed) The Modern Inorganic Chemicals Industry, 1977; (ed) Mellors Comprehensive Treatise, Boron Supplement, Part A, 1979, Part BI, 1981; (ed) Speciality Inorganic Chemicals, 1981; (ed) Energy and Chemistry, 1981; (ed) Trace Metal Removal From Aqueous Solution, 1986; (ed) The Chemistry of Wood Preservation, 1991; various papers on inorganic boron and nitrogen chemistry. *Recreation:* gardening. *Address:* The Garth, Winchester Close, Esher, Surrey KT10 8QH. *T:* Esher (0372) 464428.

THOMPSON, Reginald Aubrey, CMG 1964; *b* 22 Nov. 1905; *s* of John and Alice Thompson, Mansfield; *m* 1932, Gwendoline Marian Jackson (*d* 1978); one *s*. *Educ:* Brunts Sch., Mansfield; University Coll., Nottingham. BSc London (1st Cl. Hons Chemistry), 1927. Research, Organic Chemistry, 1927–29; Science Master, various grammar schools, 1929–41; Scientific Civil Service, Min. of Supply, 1941–46; transf. to Admin. Class (Principal), 1946; Asst Sec., 1953; Assistant Secretary, Department of Education and Science (formerly Office of Minister of Science), 1956–64; Ministry of Technology, 1964; retd, 1966. Led UK Delegn at Confs on: liability of operators of nuclear ships, Brussels Convention, 1962; liability for nuclear damage, Vienna Convention, 1963. *Recreations:* reading, music, crosswords. *Address:* 81 Bentsbrook Park, North Holmwood, Dorking, Surrey RH5 4JL. *T:* Dorking (0306) 882289.

THOMPSON, Reginald Harry; Chairman, National Dock Labour Board, 1983; *b* 26 Oct. 1925; *s* of late Ernest and Phyllis Thompson; *m* 1951, Winifred (*née* Hoyle); one *s* one *d*. *Educ:* Ecclesfield Grammar School, Sheffield. Thorncliffe Collieries, 1940; Yorkshire Mineworkers Assoc., 1941; RN, 1942; Admin. and Conciliation Officer, NUM (Yorks Area), 1946; National Coal Board: Labour Officer, S Barnsley Area, 1955; Area Ind.

Relations Officer, N Barnsley Area, 1962, N Yorks Area, 1967; Dep. Area Dir, N Yorks Area, 1970; Dir of Wages, HQ, 1973; Dep. Dir Gen., 1974, Dir Gen., 1975–83, Ind. Relations. Member: Industrial Tribunals, 1983–; Solicitors Disciplinary Tribunal, 1985–. FBIM 1978. *Publications:* articles in technical jls. *Recreations:* local government affairs; golf. *Address:* Rowley Road, Priory Hill, St Neots, Huntingdon, Cambs PE19 1UF. *T:* Huntingdon (0480) 73691.

THOMPSON, (Reginald) Stanley; Headmaster of Bloxham School, 1952–65, retired; *b* 23 Sept. 1899; *s* of late Reverend Canon C. H. Thompson, formerly Vicar of Eastleigh, Hants, and of Newport, Isle of Wight; *m* 1938, Phyllis Barbara, *y d* of Henry White, Solicitor, Winchester, Hants; one *s* two *d*. *Educ:* Hereford Cathedral School; Lancing College; Oriel College, Oxford. Assistant Master at Sherborne School, 1922–52 (Housemaster, 1936–52). *Recreations:* music, books, cricket. *Address:* Davenham, Graham Road, Malvern, Worcs WR14 2HY.

THOMPSON, Sir Richard (Hilton Marler), 1st Bt *cr* 1963; *b* Calcutta, India, 5 Oct. 1912; *s* of late Richard Smith Thompson and Kathleen Hilda (*née* Marler); *m* 1939, Anne Christabel de Vere, *d* of late Philip de Vere Annesley, MA, and of Mrs Annesley, BEM; one *s*. *Educ:* Malvern College. In business in India, Burma and Ceylon, 1930–40; travelled in Tibet, Persia, Iraq, Turkey, etc. Served in RNVR, 1940–46, volunteering as ordinary seaman; commissioned, 1941 (despatches, 1942); Lieut-Comdr 1944. MP (C) Croydon West, 1950–55; Assistant-Government Whip, 1952; Lord Commissioner of the Treasury, 1954; MP (C) Croydon South, 1955–66 and 1970–Feb. 1974; Vice-Chamberlain of HM Household, 1956; Parly Sec., Ministry of Health, 1957–59; Under-Secretary of State, CRO, 1959–60; Parly Sec., Ministry of Works, Oct. 1960–July 1962. Mem., Public Accounts Cttee, 1973–74. A Cottonian family Trustee of the British Museum, 1951–63, a Prime Minister's Trustee, 1963–84; Trustees' representative on Council of Nat. Trust, 1978–84. Chm., Overseas Migration Bd, 1959; led UK delegation to ECAFE in Bangkok, 1960; signed Indus Waters Agreement with India, Pakistan and World Bank for UK, Sept. 1960; led UK Parly Delegn to Tanganyika, to present Speaker's chair, Jan. 1963. Chm., Capital and Counties Property Co., 1971–77, retired; Pres., British Property Fedn, 1976–77; Director, British Museum Publications Ltd. Chm., British Museum Society, 1970–74. *Recreations:* gardening, collecting, study of history. *Heir:* *s* Nicholas Annesley Marler Thompson [*b* 19 March 1947; *m* 1982, Venetia, *y d* of Mr and Mrs John Heathcote, Conington; three *s* one *d*]. *Address:* Rhodes House, Sellindge, Kent TN25 6JA. *Clubs:* Carlton, Army and Navy.

THOMPSON, Richard Paul Hepworth, DM; FRCP; Physician to the Royal Household, since 1982; Consultant Physician, St Thomas' Hospital, since 1972; Physician, King Edward VII Hospital for Officers, since 1982; *b* 14 April 1940; *s* of Stanley Henry and Winifred Lilian Thompson; *m* 1974, Eleanor Mary Hughes. *Educ:* Epsom Coll.; Worcester Coll., Oxford (MA, DM); St Thomas's Hosp. Med. Sch. MRC Clinical Res. Fellow, Liver Unit, KCH, 1967–69; Fellow, Gastroenterology Unit, Mayo Clinic, USA, 1969–71; Lectr, Liver Unit, KCH, 1971–72. Mem., Lambeth, Southwark and Lewisham AHA, 1979–82. Examiner in Medicine: Soc. of Apothecaries, 1976–80; Faculty of Dental Surgery, RCS, 1980–86. Governor, Guy's Hosp. Med. Sch., 1980–82; Member Cttee of Management: Inst. of Psychiatry, 1981–; King Edward VII Hosp. Fund, 1985–89 (Mem., Gen. Council, 1985–). *Publications:* Physical Signs in Medicine, 1980; Lecture Notes on the Liver, 1986; papers and reviews in med. jls. *Address:* 36 Dealtry Road, SW15. *T:* 081–789 3839.

THOMPSON, Sir Robert Grainger Ker, KBE 1965; CMG 1961; DSO 1945; MC 1943; *b* 12 April 1916; *s* of late Canon W. G. Thompson; *m* 1950, Merryn Newboult; one *s* one *d*. *Educ:* Marlborough; Sidney Sussex College, Cambridge (MA). Cadet, Malayan Civil Service, 1938. Served War of 1939–45 (MC, DSO), RAF, 1941–46. Asst Commissioner of Labour, Perak, 1946; despatches 1948; jssc 1948–49; Staff Officer (Civil) to Director of Operations, 1950; Co-ordinating Officer, Security, 1955; Dep. Sec. for Def., Fedn of Malaya, 1957; Perm. Sec. for Def., 1959–61; Head, British Advisory Mission to Vietnam, 1961–65. Author and consultant. Johan Mangku Negara (JMN), Malaya, 1958. *Publications:* Defeating Communist Insurgency, 1966; The Royal Flying Corps, 1968; No Exit from Vietnam, 1969; Revolutionary War in World Strategy, 1945–1969, 1970; Peace Is Not At Hand, 1974; (ed) War in Peace: an analysis of warfare since 1945, 1981; Make for the Hills, 1989. *Recreations:* all country pursuits. *Address:* Pitcott House, Winsford, Minehead, Som. TA24 7JE.

THOMPSON, Robert Henry Stewart, CBE 1973; MA, DSc, DM, BCh; FRS 1974; FRCP; FRCPath; Courtauld Professor of Biochemistry, Middlesex Hospital Medical School, University of London, 1965–76; now Emeritus Professor; Trustee, Wellcome Trust, 1963–82; *b* 2 Feb. 1912; *s* of Dr Joseph Henry Thompson and Mary Eleanor Rutherford; *m* 1938, Inge Vilma Anita Gebert; one *s* two *d*. *Educ:* Epsom College; Trinity College, Oxford; Guy's Hospital Medical School. Millard Scholar, Trinity College, Oxford, 1930; Theodore Williams Scholar in Physiology, Oxford, 1932; 1st Class Animal Physiology, Oxford, 1933; Senior Demy, Magdalen College, Oxford, 1933; Univ. Scholar, Guy's Hosp. Med. School, 1933; Adrian Stokes Travelling Fellowship to Hosp. of Rockefeller Inst., New York, 1937–38; Gillson Research Scholar in Pathology, Soc. of Apothecaries of London, 1938; Fellow of University Coll., Oxford, 1938–47, Hon. Fellow, 1983; Demonstrator in Biochemistry, Oxford, 1938–47; Dean of Medical School, Oxford, 1946–47; Prof. of Chemical Pathology, Guy's Hosp. Medical School, Univ. of London, 1947–65; Secretary-General International Union of Biochemistry, 1955–64; Hon. Sec. Royal Society of Medicine, 1958–64; Mem. of Medical Research Council, 1958–62; Mem., Bd of Governors, Middlesex Hosp., 1972–74. Governor, Epsom Coll., 1982–. Hon. Mem., Biochemical Soc., 1986. Radcliffe Prize for Medical Research, Oxford, 1943. Served War of 1939–45, Major, RAMC, 1944–46. *Publications:* (with C. W. Carter) Biochemistry in relation to Medicine, 1949; Joint Editor (with E. J. King) Biochemical Disorders in Human Disease, 1957; numerous papers on biochemical and pathological subjects in various scientific journals. *Recreation:* gardening. *Address:* 7 The Cedars, Milford, Godalming, Surrey GU8 5DH. *T:* Godalming (0483) 427516. Orchard's Almshouses, Launcells, N Cornwall EX23 9NG. *T:* Bude (0288) 353817. *Club:* Athenæum.

THOMPSON, Major Robert Lloyd H.; *see* Hall-Thompson.

THOMPSON, (Rupert) Julian (de la Mare); Deputy Chairman, Sotheby's, since 1987 (Chairman, 1982–86); *b* 23 July 1941; *s* of Rupert Spens Thompson and Florence Elizabeth (*née* de la Mare); *m* 1965, Jacqueline Mary Ivimy; three *d*. *Educ:* Eton Coll.; King's Coll., Cambridge (MA). Joined Sotheby's, 1963; appointed a Director, 1969; Chm., Sotheby's International, 1982–85, 1987–88. *Address:* 43 Clarendon Road, W11 4JD. *T:* 071–727 6039.

See also N. de la M. Thompson.

THOMPSON, Stanley; *see* Thompson, Reginald S.

THOMPSON, Sir (Thomas) Lionel (Tennyson), 5th Bt, *cr* 1806; Barrister-at-Law; *b* 19 June 1921; *s* of Lt-Col Sir Thomas Thompson, 4th Bt, MC, and of Milicent Ellen Jean, *d* of late Edmund Charles Tennyson-d'Eyncourt, Bayons Manor, Lincolnshire; *S* father, 1964; *m* 1955, Mrs Margaret van Beers (marr. diss. 1962), *d* of late Walter Herbert Browne; one *s* one *d*. *Educ:* Eton. Served War of 1939–45: Royal Air Force Volunteer Reserve, 1940; Flying Officer, 1942 (invalided, 1944); Able Seaman, Royal Fleet Auxiliary, 1944–46. Awarded 1939–45 Star, Aircrew (Europe) Star, Defence and Victory Medals. Called to the Bar, Lincoln's Inn, 1952. *Recreations:* shooting, sailing, photography. *Heir:* *s* Thomas d'Eyncourt John Thompson, *b* 22 Dec. 1956. *Address:* 16 Old Buildings, Lincoln's Inn, WC2. *T:* 071–405 7929.

THOMPSON, Vernon Cecil, MB, BS London; FRCS; retired 1970 as Surgeon to Department of Thoracic Surgery, The London Hospital; Surgeon, London Chest Hospital; Hon. Consulting Thoracic Surgeon to: West London Hospital, Hammersmith; King Edward VII Hospital, Windsor; Harefield Hospital, Middlesex; Broomfield and Black Notley Hospitals, Essex; *b* 17 Sept. 1905; 2nd *s* of Dr C. C. B. Thompson, Tidenham, Glos; *m* 1942, Jean, *d* of late H. J. Hilary; one *s* one *d*. *Educ:* Monmouth School; St Bartholomew's Hospital. Resident House appointments followed by First Assistant to a Surgical Unit, St Bartholomew's Hospital, 1929–37. Dorothy Temple Cross Travelling Fellowship, Vienna, and University Hosp., Ann Arbor, Michigan, USA, 1937. President, Soc. of Thoracic Surgeons of Great Britain and Ireland, 1966; Hon. Mem. Amer. Soc. for Thoracic Surgery, 1967. *Publications:* contrib. on surgical diseases of the chest to jls and text books. *Recreations:* fishing, shooting, gardening. *Address:* Vicarage House, Llowes, Hereford HR3 5JA. *T:* Glasbury (04974) 323.

THOMPSON, William Bell, MA, PhD; Professor of Physics, University of California, since 1965; Chairman, Department of Physics, University of California at San Diego, 1969–72; *b* N Ireland, 27 Feb. 1922; *m* 1953, Gertrud Helene Goldschmidt, PhD (marr. diss. 1972); one *s* one *d*; *m* 1972, Johanna Elzelina Ladestein Korevaar. *Educ:* Universities of British Columbia and Toronto, Canada. BA 1945, MA 1947, Univ. of BC; PhD Toronto, 1950. AERE Harwell: Senior Research Fellow, 1950; Deputy Chief Scientist, 1959. Visiting Prof., Univ. of California, 1961; Head, Theoretical Physics Division, Culham Laboratory, UKAEA, 1961–63; Prof. of Theoretical Plasma Physics, Oxford Univ., 1963–65. *Publications:* Introduction to Plasma Physics, 1962; numerous papers in learned journals, on controlled thermonuclear research, plasma physics, kinetic theory, etc. *Recreations:* music, walking. *Address:* Physics Department, University of California at San Diego, La Jolla, California 92093, USA.

THOMPSON, (William) Godfrey, MA; FSA, FLA, FRSA; library planning consultant, since 1983; *b* 28 June 1921; *s* of late A. and E. M. Thompson, Coventry; *m* 1946, Doreen Mary Cattell; one *s*. *Educ:* King Henry VIII Sch., Coventry. MA Loughborough, 1977. Served with Royal Signals, 1941–46. Entered Library Service, Coventry, 1937; Dep. Borough Librarian, Chatham, 1946; Dep. City Librarian: Kingston-upon-Hull, 1952; Manchester, 1958; City Librarian, Leeds, 1963; Guildhall Librarian, Director of Libraries and Art Galleries, City of London, 1966–83; Cultural Consultant, UAE, Abu Dhabi, 1983–86. Hon. Librarian to Clockmakers' Co., Gardeners' Co., Charles Lamb Soc.; Pres., Assoc. of Assistant Librarians, 1962. Member: Council, Library Assoc., 1968–81 (Hon. Treasurer, 1974–77; Pres., 1978); Council, Aslib, 1968–71; Founding Hon. Sec. Internat. Assoc. Metropolitan Libraries, 1968–70; Adv. Bd, New Library World. Member: Adv. Panel to Sec. of State on allocation of books received under Capital Transfer Tax; Adv. Panel to Sec. of State on Export of Works of Art. Mem. Exec. Cttee, Friends of the Nat. Libraries. Governor, St Bride Foundn. Consultant on libraries to several overseas governments, including the planning of eight nat. libraries. *Publications:* London's Statues, 1971; Planning and Design of Library Buildings, 1972, 3rd edn 1989; (ed) London for Everyman, 1969; (ed) Encyclopædia of London, 1969. *Address:* Southdown, Down Lane, Compton, Surrey GU3 1DN.

THOMPSON, (William) Pratt; Managing Director, Unitech plc, since 1989 (Executive Director, since 1987); Chairman, Gallex Ltd, since 1989; *b* 9 Feb. 1933; *s* of Philip Amos Thompson and Regina Beatrice (*née* Kirby); *m* 1963, Jenny Frances Styles; two *d*. *Educ:* Princeton Univ.; Columbia Univ. (BA Econ *magna cum laude*, Phi Beta Kappa); University of Geneva (MBA). AMF Incorporated, 1959–73: executive assignments in NYC, Geneva, Tokyo, Hong Kong and London; Vice Pres., 1968; Dep. Managing Director, Bowthorpe Holdings Ltd, 1973–78; BL Limited, 1978–81: Man. Dir, Jaguar Rover Triumph Ltd, 1978–79; Chm., BL Internat. Ltd, 1979–81; Dir, Metalurgica de Santa Ana SA (Madrid), 1978–81; Vice-Chm., Colbert Gp (Geneva), 1981–84; Chairman: AIDCOM International plc, 1983–86 (Dir, 1982–); AIDCOM Technology Ltd, 1982–86; Husky Computers Ltd, 1982–86. Member: Council, SMM&T, 1978–81; Council on Foreign Relations (USA), 1980–89. Advisor, Internat. Centre for Child Studies, Bristol Univ., 1982–84. Mem., Adv. Cttee, Barnardos, 1989–. *Recreations:* various. *Address:* 29 Palace Gardens Terrace, W8 4SB. *Clubs:* Brooks's, Hurlingham; Knickerbocker (New York); Hong Kong (Hong Kong).

THOMPSON, Willoughby Harry, CMG 1974; CBE 1968 (MBE 1954); *b* 3 Dec. 1919; *m* 1963, Sheelah O'Grady; no *c*. Served War: RA, and E African Artillery, 1939–47. Kenya Govt Service, 1947–48; Colonial Administrative Service, Kenya, 1948–63; Colonial Sec., Falkland Islands, 1963–69 (Actg Governor, 1964 and 1967); Actg Judge, Falkland Islands and Dependencies Supreme Court, 1965–69; Actg Administrator, British Virgin Islands, May-July 1969; HM Commissioner in Anguilla, July 1969–71; Governor of Montserrat, 1971–74.

THOMPSON HANCOCK, P(ercy) E(llis); *see* Hancock.

THOMPSON-McCAUSLAND, Benedict Maurice Perronet, FCA; Group Managing Director, National & Provincial Building Society, 1987–90; *b* 5 Feb. 1938; *s* of late Lucius P. Thompson-McCausland, CMG and of Helen Laura McCausland; *m* 1964, Frances Catherine Fothergill Smith; three *d*. *Educ:* Eton Coll.; Trinity Coll., Cambridge (MA; Rowing Blue). FCA 1974. Articled to Coopers & Lybrand, Chartered Accountants, 1961–64; Arbuthnot Latham & Co. Ltd, 1964–80: Asst to Dirs, 1964; Banking Manager, 1967; Dir, 1968; Dep. Chm., 1978; London Life Association Ltd: Dir, 1976–81; Vice-Pres., 1979–87; Chief Exec., 1981–87. Formerly Director: Western Trust & Savings Ltd; Concord Internat.; First National Finance Corp. plc. Chm., Lombard Assoc., 1979–81. Mem. Council, 1987–, and Mem. Exec. Cttee, 1988–, Industrial Soc. Mem., Council of Management, Arnolfini Gall., 1983–86. *Publications:* (with Derek Biddle) Change, Business Performance and Values, 1985; articles in business jls. *Recreations:* windsurfing, ski-ing, walking. *Address:* 91 Blenheim Crescent, W11 2EQ. *T:* 071–727 1266. *Clubs:* Leander (Henley-on-Thames); Hawks (Cambridge).

THOMSON, family name of **Barons Thomson of Fleet** and **Thomson of Monifieth.**

THOMSON OF FLEET, 2nd Baron *cr* 1964; **Kenneth Roy Thomson;** newspaper proprietor; Chairman of the Board, The Thomson Corporation; Chairman of the Board and Director: The Thomson Corporation; The Thomson Corporation Plc; Woodbridge Co. Ltd; Thomson Newspapers Hldgs Inc.; Thomson US Inc.; *b* Toronto, Ont., 1 Sept. 1923; *s* of 1st Baron Thomson of Fleet, GBE, founder of Thomson Newspapers, and Edna Alice (*d* 1951), *d* of John Irvine, Drayton, Ont.; *S* father, 1976; *m* 1956, Nora Marilyn, *d* of A. V. Lavis; two *s* one *d*. *Educ:* Upper Canada Coll.; Univ. of Cambridge, England (MA). Served War of 1942–45 with RCAF. Began in editorial dept of Timmins Daily Press, Timmins, Ont., 1947; Advertising Dept, Galt Reporter, Cambridge, Ont, 1948–50, General Manager, 1950–53; returned to Toronto Head Office of Thomson Newspapers to take over direction of Company's Canadian and American operations. Pres. and Dir: Thomson Works of Art Ltd; Director: Hudson's Bay Co.; IBM Canada; Markborough Properties Inc.; Toronto-Dominion Bank. Dep. Chm., 1966–67, Chm., 1968–70, Co-Pres., 1971–81, Times Newspapers Ltd. Member, Baptist Church. *Recreations:* collecting paintings and works of art, walking. *Heir: s* Hon. David Kenneth Roy Thomson, *b* 12 June 1957. *Address:* (home) 8 Castle Frank Road, Toronto, Ont M4W 2Z4, Canada; 8 Kensington Palace Gardens, W8; (office) The Thomson Corporation, 65 Queen Street West, Toronto, Ont. M5H 2M8, Canada; The Thomson Corporation Plc, The Quadrangle, PO Box 4YG, 180 Wardour Street, W1A 4YG. *Clubs:* York Downs, National, Toronto, Granite, York, Toronto Hunt (Toronto).

THOMSON OF MONIFIETH, Baron *cr* 1977 (Life Peer), of Monifieth, Dundee; **George Morgan Thomson,** KT 1981; PC 1966; Chairman, Independent Broadcasting Authority, 1981–88 (Deputy Chairman, 1980); Chancellor, Heriot Watt University, 1977–91; *b* 16 Jan. 1921; *s* of late James Thomson, Monifieth; *m* 1948, Grace Jenkins; two *d*. *Educ:* Grove Academy, Dundee. Served War of 1939–45, in Royal Air Force, 1940–46. Assistant Editor, Forward, 1946, Editor, 1948–53. Contested (Lab) Glasgow, Hillhead, 1950; MP (Lab) Dundee East, July 1952–72. Joint Chm., Council for Education in the Commonwealth, 1959–64; Adviser to Educational Institute of Scotland, 1960–64. Minister of State, Foreign Office, 1964–66; Chancellor of the Duchy of Lancaster, 1966–67; Joint Minister of State, Foreign Office, 1967; Secretary of State for Commonwealth Affairs, Aug. 1967–Oct. 1968; Minister Without Portfolio, 1968–69; Chancellor of the Duchy of Lancaster, 1969–70; Shadow Defence Minister, 1970–72. Chm., Labour Cttee for Europe, 1972–73; Commissioner, EEC, 1973–Jan. 1977. Chairman: European Movement in Britain, 1977–80; Advertising Standards Authority, 1977–80; European TV and Film Forum, 1989–. First Crown Estate Comr, 1978–80. Director: Royal Bank of Scotland Gp, 1977–90; ICI plc, 1977–89; Woolwich Equitable Building Soc., 1979–91 (Dep. Chm., 1988–91). President: Hist. of Advertising Trust, 1985–; Prix Italia, 1989–; Dir, ENO, 1987–. Chm., Suzy Lamplugh Trust, 1990–; Dep. Chm., Ditchley Foundn, 1983–87; Pilgrims Trustee, 1977–; Trustee: Thomson Foundn, 1977–; Leeds Castle Foundn, 1978–. Mem., SLD, 1989–. FRSE 1985; FRTS 1990 (Vice-Pres., 1982–89). Hon. LLD Dundee, 1967; Hon. DLitt: Heriot-Watt, 1973; New Univ. of Ulster, 1984; Hon. DSc Aston, 1976. *Address:* House of Lords, SW1A 0PW. *Club:* Brooks's.

THOMSON, Sir Adam, Kt 1983; CBE 1976; Chairman, Gold Stag, since 1988; Chairman and Chief Executive, British Caledonian Group (formerly The Caledonian Aviation Group plc), 1970–88 (formerly Airways Interests (Thomson) Ltd, Chairman and Managing Director, 1964–70); Chairman and Chief Executive, British Caledonian Airways Ltd, 1970–88; *b* 7 July 1926; *s* of Frank Thomson and Jemina Rodgers; *m* 1948, Dawn Elizabeth Burt; two *s*. *Educ:* Rutherglen Acad.; Coatbridge Coll.; Royal Technical Coll., Glasgow. Pilot; Fleet Air Arm, 1944–47; Flying Instructor/Commercial Pilot, 1947–50; BEA, West African Airways, Britavia, 1951–59. Caledonian Airways: Man. Dir, 1961–64; Chm. and Man. Dir, 1964–70; Chairman: Caledonian Airmotive Ltd, 1978–87; Caledonian Hotel Holdings, 1971–87. Dep. Chm., Martin Currie Pacific Trust PLC, 1985–; Director: Williams & Glyn's Bank Ltd, 1978–82; Royal Bank of Scotland Gp, 1982–; Otis Elevators Ltd, 1978–84; MEPC plc, 1982–89. Chairman: Assoc. of European Airlines, 1977–78; Inst. of Directors, 1988– (Mem., 1977–). FRAeS; FCIT; FBIM. Hon. LLD: Glasgow, 1979; Sussex, 1984; Strathclyde, 1986. Businessman of the Year, Hambro Award, 1970; first Scottish Free Enterprise Award, Aims for Freedom and Enterprise, 1976. *Publication:* High Risk: the politics of the air, 1990. *Recreations:* golf, sailing. *Address:* 154 Buckswood Drive, Crawley, West Sussex. *Clubs:* Caledonian; Royal & Ancient Golf (St Andrews); Walton Heath Golf.

THOMSON, Brian Harold, TD 1947; DL; Chairman, since 1974, Joint Managing Director, since 1948, D. C. Thomson & Co. Ltd; *b* 21 Nov. 1918; *e s* of late William Harold Thomson of Kemback and Helen Irene, *d* of Sir Charles Ballance; *m* 1947, Agnes Jane Patricia Cunninghame (*d* 1991); one *s* four *d*. *Educ:* Charterhouse. Served War of 1939–45: 1st Fife and Forfar Yeomanry, and on Staff, DAQMG 1st Armoured Div., N Africa and Italy, 1943–44. GS02 Instructor, Staff Coll., Haifa, 1944–46; Lt-Col Comdg Fife and Forfar Yeomanry TA, 1953–56. Entered D. C. Thomson & Co. Ltd, 1937. Director: John Leng & Co. Ltd, 1948–; Southern Television, 1959–88; Alliance Trust and Second Alliance Trust, 1961–89. DL Fife, 1988. *Recreations:* golf, shooting. *Club:* Royal and Ancient Golf (St Andrews).

THOMSON, Bryden; Orchestral Conductor; Artistic Director, since 1977, and Principal Conductor, 1977–85 (now Conductor Emeritus) Ulster Orchestra; Principal Conductor, RTE Symphony Orchestra, since 1984; *b* Ayr, Scotland. *Educ:* Ayr Academy; Royal Scottish Academy of Music; Staatliche Hochschule für Musik, Hamburg. BMus Dunelm; DipMusEd (Hons); RSAM; LRAM; ARCM; FRSAMD. Asst Conductor, BBC Scottish Orchestra, 1958; Conductor: Royal Ballet, 1962; Den Norske Opera, Oslo, 1964; Stora Teatern, Göteborg, Sweden, 1965; Royal Opera, Stockholm, 1966; NI Opera Trust, 1981 and 1982; Associate Conductor, Scottish National Orch., 1966; Principal Conductor: BBC Northern Symphony Orch., 1968–73; BBC Welsh Symphony Orch., 1978–83; Prin. Conductor and Music Dir, Scottish National Orch., subseq. Royal Scottish Orch., 1988–91. Guest Conducting: Norway; Sweden; Denmark; Canada; Germany; S Africa; France; Italy; Principal Guest Conductor, Trondheim Symphony Orch., 1977. Recordings of many works by British and foreign composers. Hon. DLitt NUU, 1984. Award for services to contemporary Scottish music, Scottish Soc. of Composers, 1985. *Recreations:* golf, learning about music. *Address:* Garinish, 19a Greenfield Park, Donnybrook, Dublin 4.

THOMSON, Air Marshal Sir (Charles) John, KCB 1991; CBE 1984; AFC 1979; Air Officer Commanding-in-Chief, RAF Support Command, since 1991; *b* 7 June 1941; *e s* of Dr Charles Thomson and Elizabeth Susan (*née* McCaughey); *m* 1972, Jan Hart Bishop; two *d* (and one *d* decd). *Educ:* Campbell College; RAF College; psc, rcds. Commissioned 1962; flying and staff appts include: 43 Sqn, Aden; 2 Sqn, Germany; USAF 67 TRW, Texas; OC 41 Sqn, 1976–78; Personal Staff Officer to Chief of Air Staff, 1979–81; Station Comdr, RAF Bruggen, 1982–83; Dir, Defence Concepts Staff, 1985–86; AOC No 1 Gp, 1987–89; Asst Chief of Air Staff, 1989–91. *Recreations:* sailing, shooting, ski-ing, reading. *Address:* c/o Royal Bank of Scotland, Kirkland House, Whitehall, SW1A 3EB. *Club:* Royal Air Force.

THOMSON, Sir David; *see* Thomson, Sir F. D. D.

THOMSON, David Kinnear, CBE 1972 (MBE 1945); TD 1945; JP, DL; Former President, Peter Thomson (Perth) Ltd, whisky blenders and exporters; Chairman, Tayside Health Board, 1973–77; *b* Perth, 26 March 1910; *s* of Peter Thomson, whisky blender, and Jessie Kinnear; unmarried. *Educ:* Perth Academy; Strathallan School. Mem., Perth Local Authority, 1949–72; Chm. Bd of Management, Perth Technical Coll., 1972–75; Mem., ITA (Scottish Br.), 1968–73; Mem., Scottish Economic Council, 1968–75; Director: Scottish Transport Gp, 1972–76; Scottish Opera, 1973–81; Chm., Perth Festival of the Arts, 1973–85 (Pres., 1985–90). Mem. Court, Dundee Univ., 1975–79. Chm., Scottish Licensed Trade, 1981–82. Lord Provost of Perth, 1966–72, and Hon. Sheriff of Perth; DL 1966–72, 1980–, JP 1955, Perth and Kinross; Freeman, Perth and Kinross District, 1982. CStJ 1984. *Recreations:* golf, walking, listening to music. *Address:* Fairhill, Oakbank Road, Perth PH1 1HD. *T:* Perth (0738) 26593. *Club:* Royal Perth Golfing Society.

THOMSON, David Paget, RD 1969; Member, Monopolies and Mergers Commission, since 1984; Chairman, F & C Germany Investment Trust, since 1990; Director General, British Invisible Exports Council, 1987–90; *b* 19 March 1931; *s* of Sir George Paget Thomson, FRS, Nobel Laureate, and Kathleen Buchanan Smith; *m* 1959, Patience Mary, *d* of Sir William Lawrence Bragg, CH, OBE, MC, FRS, Nobel Laureate; two *s* two *d*. *Educ:* Rugby Sch.; Grenoble Univ.; Trinity Coll., Cambridge (scholar; BA 1953, MA 1957). Nat. Service, RN (Sub-Lieut), 1953–55; subseq. Lieut-Comdr RNR. Senior Scholar, Trinity Coll., Cambridge, 1955; Lazard Bros & Co., 1956, Director, 1965–86; seconded to HM Diplomatic Service, 1971–73, as Counsellor (Economic), Bonn. Dep. Chm., City Communications Centre, 1987–89. Chm., Jufcrest, 1984–89; Director: Finance Co. Viking, Zurich, 1969–87; Richard Daus & Co., bankers, Frankfurt, 1974–81; Applied Photophysics, 1976–87; Medical Sickness Annuity and Life Assurance Soc. Ltd, 1990–. Member: Council, Brunel Univ., 1974–85; Court of Governors, Henley Management Coll. (formerly Admin. Staff Coll.), 1979–; Dir, Henley Distance Learning Ltd, 1985. Hon. Treasurer, British Dyslexia Assoc., 1984–86. Chm., Fitzwilliam Mus. Trust, 1988–; Trustee, Portsmouth Naval Base Property Trust, 1985–; Royal Institution: Treasurer, 1976–81; Chm. Council, 1985. CC Oxon 1985–89. Master, Plumbers' Co., 1980–81. *Recreations:* hill-walking, gardening, historical biography. *Address:* Little Stoke House, Wallingford, Oxon OX10 6AX. *T:* Wallingford (0491) 37161. *Club:* Athenæum.

See also S. L. Bragg, Sir J. A. Thomson.

THOMSON, Rt. Hon. David Spence, MC 1942; ED; PC 1981; *b* Stratford, 14 Nov. 1915; *s* of Percy Thomson, MBE; *m* 1942, June Grace Adams; one *s* three *d*. *Educ:* Stratford Primary and High Sch. Territorial Army, 1931–; served Middle East, 19th Inf. Bat. 1st Echelon, 1939–42; 2nd NZED, 1939–45; POW 1942; Hon. Col, 5 RNZIR, 1955–81; Brigadier (Reserve of Officers), 2nd Inf. Brig., 1959–60. Dairy farmer; Pres., NZ Federated Farmers Central Taranaki Exec., 1959–63. MP (Nat.) Stratford/Taranaki, 1963–84; Minister of Defence, War Pensions and Rehabilitation, 1966–72, and 1980–84; Minister of Tourism, 1966–69; Minister of Police, 1969–72; Minister of Labour and Immigration, 1972; Minister of Justice, 1975–78; Minister of State Services and Leader, House of Reps, 1978–84. *Recreations:* golf, gardening, classical music. *Address:* 22 Bird Road, Stratford, New Zealand.

THOMSON, Duncan, PhD; Keeper, Scottish National Portrait Gallery, since 1982; *b* 2 Oct. 1934; *s* of Duncan Murdoch Thomson and Jane McFarlane Wilson; *m* 1964, Julia Jane Macphail; one *d*. *Educ:* Airdrie Acad.; Univ. of Edinburgh (MA 1956, PhD 1970); Edinburgh Coll. of Art (Cert. of Coll.; Post-Dip. Scholarship); Moray House Coll. of Educn. Teacher of Art, 1959–67; Asst Keeper, Scottish National Portrait Gall., 1967–82. Scottish Arts Council: Mem., Art Cttee, 1983–89; Chm., Exhibn Panel, 1985–89. *Publications:* The Life and Art of George Jamesone, 1974; *exhibition catalogues:* A Virtuous and Noble Education, 1971; Painting in Scotland 1570–1650, 1975; Eye to Eye, 1980; (jtly) John Michael Wright, 1982; (jtly) The Queen's Image, 1987. *Recreation:* reading poetry (and thinking about writing it). *Address:* 3 Eglinton Crescent, Edinburgh EH12 5DH. *T:* 031–225 6430.

THOMSON, Sir Evan (Rees Whitaker), Kt 1977; FRCS, FRACS, FACS; Hon. Consultant Surgeon, Princess Alexandra Hospital, Brisbane; *b* 14 July 1919; *s* of Frederick Thorpe Thomson and Ann Margaret Thomson (*née* Evans); *m* 1955, Mary Kennedy. *Educ:* Brisbane Boys' Coll.; Univ. of Queensland (MB BS). Full time staff, Brisbane General Hospital, 1942–48; RAAF Reserve, 1942–45; Visiting Surgeon: Brisbane General Hospital, 1950–56; Princess Alexandra Hospital, 1956–71; Clinical Lectr in Surgery, Univ. of Queensland, 1951–71. Qld Branch, Australian Medical Association: Councillor, 1966–78; Pres., 1967–68; a Vice-Pres., 1980–; Chm. of Council; Chm. of Ethics Cttee. Pres., 4th Aust. Med. Congress, 1971. Member: Med. Bd of Queensland; Wesley Hospital Bd, etc.; Pres., Qld Council of Professions, 1970–72; Vice-Patron, Medico-Legal Soc. of Qld; Governor, Univ. of Qld Foundn; Life Governor, Aust. Postgrad. Fedn in Medicine. Patron, Aust. Nat. Flag Assoc. (Qld). Silver Jubilee Medal, 1977. *Publications:* Future Needs for Medical Education in Queensland (ed), 1981; (jtly) Ernest Sandford Jackson: the life and times of a pioneer Australian surgeon, 1987; papers in medical and allied jls. *Recreations:* golf, swimming. *Address:* 19/104 Station Road, Indooroopilly, Qld 4068, Australia. *Clubs:* Queensland, University of Queensland Staff and Graduates (Life Mem.); Mooloolaba Yacht.

THOMSON, Francis Paul, OBE 1975; CEng, MIEE; Consultant on Post Office and Bank Giro Systems, 1968–85; Founder, Charity Law Reform Campaign, 1985; *b* Corstorphine, Edinburgh, 17 Dec. 1914; *y s* of late William George and Elizabeth Hannah Thomson, Goring-by-Sea; *m* 1954, E. Sylvia, *e d* of late Lokförare J. Erik Nilsson, Bollnäs, Sweden. *Educ:* Friends' Sch., Sibford Ferris; Sch. of Engrg, Polytechnic, London; in Denmark and Sweden. TV and radar research, 1935–42; Special Ops Exec., 1942–44; Sen. Planning Engr, Postwar research and reconstruction, communications industry; founded British Post Giro Campaign, 1946 and conducted Campaign to victory in Parlt, 1965; Lectr, Stockholm Univ. Extension, 1947–49; Founder, and Man. Editor, English Illustrated, 1950–61; techn. exports promotion with various firms, esp. electronic equipment, 1950–60; pioneered electronic language laboratory equipment and methods, 1930, subseq. joined consultancy-production groups; Bank Computerisation Consultant, 1967–80. Governor, Watford Coll. of Technology, 1965–70 (Engrg and Sci. Dept Adv. Cttee, 1972–91); Mem., Communication of Technical Information Adv. Cttee, CGLI; Advr to PO Users' Nat. Council's Giro Sub Cttee, 1975; Founder and first Hon. Sec., SW Herts Post Office Adv. Cttee, 1976; First British Cttee Mem., Internat. Centre for Ancient and Modern Tapestry (CITAM), Lausanne, 1974–80. Founder and Hon. Sec., St Andrews Residents' Assoc. (Watford). Mem., Soc. of Authors, 1990–; MBIM; FIQA 1978. Hon. Fellow, Inst. of Scientific and Technical Communicators, 1975. Life Member: Corstorphine Trust; Anglo-Swedish Soc. *Publications:* Giro Credit Transfer Systems, 1964; Money in the Computer Age, 1968; (ed jtly) Banking Automation, 1971; (ed with E. S. Thomson) rev. repr. of A History of Tapestry (2nd edn), by W. G. Thomson, 1973; Tapestry: mirror of history, 1979; originated Household Directory, Personal Record books, Home and Car Emergency Card series; numerous papers in European and other learned jls. *Recreations:* gardening, archaeology, walking, campaigning to prohibit smoking in public places.

THOMSON, Sir (Frederick Douglas) David, 3rd Bt *cr* 1929; Chairman: Jove Investment Trust, since 1983; Britannia Steam Ship Insurance Association Ltd, since 1986 (Director, since 1965); Through Transport Marine Mutual Assurance Association (Burmuda), since 1983 (Director, since 1973); The Castle Cairn Investment Trust Co., since 1990; Abtrust New European Investment Trust, since 1990; *b* 14 Feb. 1940; *s* of Sir James Douglas Wishart Thomson, 2nd Bt, and of Evelyn Margaret Isabel, (Bettina), *d* of Lt-Comdr D. W. S. Douglas, RN; *S* father, 1972; *m* 1967, Caroline Anne, *d* of Major Timothy Stuart Lewis; two *s* one *d*. *Educ:* Eton; University College, Oxford (BA Agric). Worked for Ben Line, 1961–89. Director: Life Assoc. of Scotland Ltd, 1970–; Cairn Energy, 1971–; Danae Investment Trust, 1979–; Martin Currie Pacific Trust, 1985–; G. & G. Kynoch, 1990–; The Murrayfield, 1991–. Member: Queen's Body Guard for Scotland, Royal Company of Archers. *Recreations:* shooting, ski-ing, music. *Heir: s* Simon Douglas Charles Thomson, *b* 16 June 1969. *Address:* Old Caberston, Walkerburn, Peeblesshire EH43 6AA. *T:* Walkerburn (089687) 206.

THOMSON, Garry, CBE 1983; Scientific Adviser to the Trustees and Head of the Scientific Department, National Gallery, London, 1960–85; *b* 13 Sept. 1925; *s* of late Robert Thomson and Mona Spence; *m* 1954, M. R. Saisvasdi Svasti; four *s*. *Educ:* Charterhouse; Magdalene College, Cambridge (MA). Editorial Staff of A History of Technology, 1951; Research Chemist, National Gallery, 1955; Hon. Editor, Studies in Conservation, 1959–67; Pres., Internat. Inst. for Conservation of Historic and Artistic Works, 1983–86. Vice-Pres., Buddhist Soc., London, 1978–88. Trustee, Nat. Museums and Galls on Merseyside, 1986–91. *Publications:* Recent Advances in Conservation (ed), 1963; Museum Climatology (ed), 1967; The Museum Environment, 1978; Reflections on the Life of the Buddha, 1982. *Address:* Squire's Hill, Tilford, Surrey. *T:* Runfold (02518) 2206.

THOMSON, George Malcolm, OBE 1990; author and journalist; *b* Leith, Scotland, 2 Aug. 1899; *e s* of Charles Thomson, journalist, and Mary Arthur, *d* of John Eason; *m* 1926, Else (*d* 1957), *d* of Harald Ellefsen, Tœnsberg, Norway; one *s* one *d*; *m* 1963, Diana Van Cortlandt Robertson. *Educ:* Daniel Stewart's College, Edinburgh; Edinburgh University. Journalist. *Publications:* Caledonia, or the Future of the Scots, 1927; A Short History of Scotland, 1930; Crisis in Zanat, 1942; The Twelve Days, 1964; The Robbers Passing By, 1966; The Crime of Mary Stuart, 1967; Vote of Censure, 1968; A Kind of Justice, 1970; Sir Francis Drake, 1972; Lord Castlerosse, 1973; The North-West Passage, 1975; Warrior Prince: Prince Rupert of the Rhine, 1976; The First Churchill: the life of John, 1st Duke of Marlborough, 1979; The Prime Ministers, 1980; The Ball at Glenkerran, 1982; Kronstadt '21, 1985. *Address:* 5 The Mount Square, NW3. *T:* 071–435 8775. *Club:* Garrick.

THOMSON, Very Rev. Ian; *see* White-Thomson.

THOMSON, Ian Mackenzie, WS; President, Industrial Tribunals (Scotland), 1989–91; *b* 16 Feb. 1926; *s* of Donald Hugh Thomson and Doris Emma (*née* Moseley); *m* 1950, Elizabeth Marie Wallace; two *s* one *d*. *Educ:* George Watson's Coll.; Edinburgh Univ., 1947–50 (BL). Served Royal Navy, 1944–47. Admitted: Solicitor, 1951; Writer to the Signet, 1958; Partner, Davidson and Syme, WS, and after merger, Dundas and Wilson, CS, 1958–75; full-time Chm., Industrial Tribunals, 1975; Regl Chm., 1978; Temp. Sheriff, 1987. *Recreations:* swimming, walking, reading, occasional fishing. *Club:* Drumsheugh Baths (Edinburgh).

THOMSON, Prof. James Leonard, CBE 1955; Professor Emeritus in Civil Engineering, Royal Military College of Science, Shrivenham, since 1970; *b* 9 Aug. 1905; *s* of James Thomson, Liverpool. *Educ:* University of Manchester; St John's College, Cambridge. Mather & Platt, Ltd, Manchester, 1923–26; Univ. of Manchester, 1926–30 (BSc (Tech.) 1st Cl. Hons and Stoney Prizeman); Lecturer, Technical College, Horwich, 1930–32; Whitworth Senior Scholar, 1931; St John's Coll., Cambridge, 1932–34 (BA 1934, MA 1938); Research Engineer, ICI, Billingham-on-Tees, 1934–38; Lecturer, Dept of Civil and Mechanical Engineering, Univ. of London, King's College, 1938. Seconded for War-time Service: Managing Engineer, HM Royal Ordnance Factory, Pembrey, Carms, 1940–42; Principal Technical Officer, School of Tank Technology, 1942–46. Royal Military College of Science, Shrivenham: Prof. of Mechanical Engrg and Head of Dept of Civil and Mechanical Engrg, 1946–61; Prof. of Civil Engrg and Head of Dept of Civil Engrg, 1965–70; seconded to ME Technical Univ., Ankara, Turkey, 1961–65 : Consultant Dean and Mechanical Engrg Specialist; later Chief Technical Adviser for UNESCO project in Turkey. *Publications:* various scientific papers dealing with High Pressure Techniques. *Recreations:* mountaineering, sailing. *Address:* Astral House, Netherbury, Bridport, Dorset DT6 5LU.

THOMSON, Air Marshal Sir John; *see* Thomson, Air Marshal Sir C. J.

THOMSON, Sir John, KBE 1972; TD 1944; MA; Chairman, Morland and Co. Ltd, 1979–83; Director: Barclays Bank Ltd, 1947–78 (Chairman, 1962–73); Union Discount Company of London Ltd, 1960–74; *b* 1908; *s* of late Guy Thomson, JP, Woodperry, Oxford; *m* 1st, 1935, Elizabeth, JP (*d* 1977), *d* of late Stanley Brotherhood, JP, Thornhaugh Hall, Peterborough; no *c*; 2nd, 1979, Eva Elizabeth, *d* of Marcus Ralph Russell, and *widow* of Tom Dreaper. *Educ:* Winchester; Magdalen College, Oxford. Commanded Oxfordshire Yeomanry Regt, RATA, 1942–44 and 1947–50. Deputy High Steward of Oxford University; a Curator of Oxford University Chest, 1949–74; Chairman: Nuffield Medical Benefaction, 1951–82 (Trustee, 1947–82); Nuffield Orthopædic Centre Trust, 1949–81. President, British Bankers' Association, 1964–66 (Vice-President, 1963–64); FIB. Mem. Royal Commn on Trade Unions and Employers' Assocs, 1965–68; Mem. BNEC, 1968–71. Hon. Fellow St Catherine's Coll., Oxford. Hon. Colonel: 299 Fd Regt RA (TA), 1964–67; Oxfordshire Territorials, 1967–75; Bt Col, 1950. DL Oxfordshire, 1947–57; High Sheriff of Oxfordshire, 1957; Vice-Lieut, 1957–63; Lord-Lieut, 1963–79. A Steward, Jockey Club, 1974–77. Hon. DCL Oxford, 1957. KStJ 1973. *Address:* Manor Farm House, Spelsbury, Oxford OX7 3LG. *T:* Charlbury (0608) 810266. *Clubs:* Cavalry and Guards, Overseas Bankers' (Vice-Pres., 1969–; Pres., 1968–69).

THOMSON, Sir John (Adam), GCMG 1985 (KCMG 1978; CMG 1972); MA; HM Diplomatic Service, retired; Director, ANZ Grindlays Bank, since 1987; *b* 27 April 1927; *s* of late Sir George Thomson, FRS, Master of Corpus Christi Coll., Cambridge, 1952–62 (*s* of Sir J. J. Thomson, OM, FRS, Master of Trinity Coll., Cambridge, 1919–40), and late Kathleen, *d* of Very Rev. Sir George Adam Smith, DD, LLD, Principal of Aberdeen Univ., 1909–35; *m* 1953, Elizabeth Anne McClure (*d* 1988), *d* of late Norman McClure, Pres. of Ursinus Coll., Penn, USA; three *s* one *d*. *Educ:* Phillips Exeter Acad., USA; Univ. of Aberdeen; Trinity Coll., Cambridge. Foreign Office, 1950; Third Sec., Jedda, 1951; Damascus, 1954; FO, 1955; Private Sec. to Permanent Under-Secretary, 1958–60; First Sec., Washington, 1960–64; FO, 1964; Acting Head of Planning Staff, 1966; Counsellor, 1967; Head of Planning Staff, FO, 1967; seconded to Cabinet Office as Chief of Assessments Staff, 1968–71; Minister and Dep. Permanent Rep. to N Atlantic Council, 1972–73; Head of UK Delegn to MBFR Exploratory Talks, Vienna, 1973; Asst Under-Sec. of State, FCO, 1973–76; High Comr to India, 1977–82; UK Perm. Rep. to UN, 1982–87. Principal Dir, 21st Century Trust, 1987–90; Chm., Minority Rights Gp, 1991–; Member: Council, IISS, 1987–; Council, ODI, 1987–; Governing Body, IDS, 1987–. Associate Mem., Nuffield Coll., Oxford, 1987–. Hon. LLD: Ursinus Coll., Penn, 1984; Aberdeen, 1986; Hon. DHL Allegheny Coll., Penn, 1985. *Publication:* Crusader Castles (with R. Fedden), 1956. *Recreations:* carpets, castles, walking. *Clubs:* Athenæum; Century (New York).

See also Janet Adam Smith (Mrs John Carleton), D. P. Thomson.

THOMSON, Sir John Sutherland, (Sir Ian), KBE 1985 (MBE (mil.) 1944); CMG 1968; retired, 1987; *b* 8 Jan. 1920; *s* of late William Sutherland Thomson and of Jessie McCaig Malloch; *m* 1st, 1945, Nancy Marguerite Kearsley (*d* 1988), Suva, Fiji; seven *s* one *d*; 2nd, 1989, Nancy Caldwell (*née* McColl). *Educ:* High Sch. of Glasgow; Univ. of Glasgow (MA Hons). Served War of 1939–45: Black Watch, 1940; Fiji Military Forces, 1941–45 (Captain). Appointed Cadet, Colonial Administrative Service, Fiji and Western Pacific, 1941; District Administration and Secretariat, Fiji, 1946–54; Seconded to Colonial Office, 1954–56; Dep. Comr, Native Lands and Fisheries, Fiji, 1957–58; Comr of Native Reserves and Chairman, Native Lands and Fisheries Commission, Fiji, 1958–62; Divisional Commissioner, Fiji, 1963–66; Administrator, British Virgin Islands, 1967–71; Acting Governor-Gen., Fiji, 1980–83 on occasions. Indep. Chm., Fiji Sugar Industry, 1971–84; Chairman: Fiji Coconut Bd, 1973–83; Economic Develt Bd, Fiji, 1980–86; Fiji Liquor Laws Review Cttee, 1985; Fiji Nat. Tourism Assoc., 1984–87; Chairman: Sedgwick (Fiji) Ltd, 1984–87; Air Pacific Ltd, 1984–87; Thomson Pacific Resources Ltd, 1988–. *Recreations:* golf, gardening. *Address:* Sonas, Ardentallen, by Oban, Argyll PA34 4SF. *T:* Oban (0631) 62846.

THOMSON, Prof. Joseph McGeachy; Regius Professor of Law, University of Glasgow, since 1991; *b* 6 May 1948; *s* of James Thomson and Catherine (*née* McGeachy). *Educ:* Keil Sch., Dumbarton; Univ. of Edinburgh (LLB 1970). Lectr in Law, Univ. of Birmingham, 1970–74; Lectr in Laws, King's Coll., London, 1974–84; Prof. of Law, Univ. of Strathclyde, 1984–90. Dep. General Editor, Stair Meml Encyclopaedia of Laws of Scotland, 1984–. *Publications:* Family Law in Scotland, 1987, 2nd edn 1991; contribs to Law Qly Review, Modern Law Review, Juridical Review, Scots Law Times, etc. *Recreations:* opera, ballet, wine and food. *Address:* Department of Private Law, Stair Building, The University, Glasgow G12 8QQ. *T:* 041–339 8855; 140 Hyndland Road, Glasgow G12 9PN.

THOMSON, Malcolm George; QC (Scot.) 1987; *b* 6 April 1950; *s* of late George Robert Thomson, OBE, and of Daphne Ethel Thomson; *m* 1978, Susan Gordon Aitken; two *d*. *Educ:* Edinburgh Acad.; Edinburgh Univ. (LLB). Advocate 1974; called to the Bar, Lincoln's Inn, 1991. Standing Junior Counsel to Dept of Agriculture and Fisheries for Scotland and Forestry Commn in Scotland, 1982–87. *Recreations:* sailing, ski-ing. *Address:* 10 Avon Grove, Edinburgh EH4 6RF. *T:* 031–336 5261. *Club:* New (Edinburgh).

THOMSON, Sir Mark (Wilfrid Home), 3rd Bt *cr* 1925, of Old Nunthorpe, Co. York; *b* 29 Dec. 1939; *s* of Sir Ivo Wilfrid Home Thomson, 2nd Bt and Sybil Marguerite, *yr d* of C. W. Thompson; *S* father, 1991; *m* 1976, Lady Jacqueline Rufus Isaacs, *o d* of 3rd Marquess of Reading, MBE, MC; three *s* one *d* (incl. twin *s*). *Heir: s* Albert Mark Home Thomson, *b* 3 Aug. 1979. *Address:* 42 Glebe Place, SW3 5JE.

THOMSON, Nigel Ernest Drummond; Sheriff of Lothian and Borders, at Edinburgh and Peebles, since 1976; *b* 19 June 1926; *y s* of late Rev. James Kyd Thomson, and late Joan Drummond; *m* 1964, Snjólaug Magnússon, *yr d* of late Consul-General Sigursteinn Magnússon; one *s* one *d*. *Educ:* George Watson's College, Edinburgh; Univs of St Andrews and Edinburgh. Served with Scots Guards and Indian Grenadiers, 1944–47. MA (St Andrews) 1950; LLB (Edin.) 1953. Called to Scottish Bar, 1953. Standing Counsel to Scottish Educn Dept, 1961–66; Sheriff of Lanarkshire, later S Strathclyde, Dumfries and Galloway, at Hamilton, 1966–76. Chm., Music Cttee, Scottish Arts Council, 1978–83; Chm., Edinburgh Youth Orchestra. Pres., Speculative Soc., Edinburgh, 1960. Hon. President: Tenovus, Edinburgh; Scottish Assoc. for Counselling, 1978–88. *Recreations:* music, woodwork, golf. *Address:* 50 Grange Road, Edinburgh. *T:* 031–667 2166. *Clubs:* New (Edinburgh); Arts (Strathaven); Bruntsfield Golf (Edinburgh); Golfklúbbur (Reykjavik).

THOMSON, Peter Alexander Bremner, CVO 1986; HM Diplomatic Service; Counsellor, Foreign and Commonwealth Office, since 1991; *b* 16 Jan. 1938; *s* of Alexander Thomson, financial journalist, and Dorothy (*née* Scurr); *m* 1965, Lucinda Sellar; three *s*. *Educ:* Canford School; RN College, Dartmouth; Sch. of African and Oriental Studies, London (BA 1970; MPhil 1975). Sub Lieut and Lieut RN in HM Ships Albion, Plover, Tiger, Ark Royal, Eagle; Lt Comdr ashore in Taiwan and Hong Kong; joined Diplomatic Service, 1975; First Sec., FCO, Lagos, Hong Kong, 1975–84; Counsellor, Peking, 1984–87; High Comr, Belize, 1987–90. *Recreations:* sailing, walking. *Address:* c/o Foreign and Commonwealth Office, SW1A 2AH; The Red House, Charlton Horethorne, near Sherborne. *T:* Corton Denham (096322) 301. *Clubs:* Travellers'; Thames Barge Sailing; Hong Kong.

THOMSON, Robert Howard Garry; *see* Thomson, Garry.

THOMSON, Robert John Stewart, CMG 1969; MBE 1955; Ministry of Defence, 1969–81; *b* 5 May 1922; *s* of late John Stewart Thomson, FRIBA, and late Nellie Thomson (*née* Morris). *Educ:* Bromsgrove Sch.; Worcester Coll., Oxford. Service with Sudan Defence Force, 1943–45. Sudan Political Service, 1943–54 (District Commissioner, 1950–54). Attached Ministry of Defence, 1955–56; First Sec., British High Commission, Accra, 1956–60, 1962–64, Counsellor, 1966–69. *Recreations:* gardening, singing. *Address:* Ardgowan, 119 Lenthay Road, Sherborne, Dorset DT9 6AQ. *Clubs:* Royal Over-Seas League; Polo (Accra).

THOMSON, Robert Norman; Executive Director, Royal Society of Medicine, since 1982; Director, since 1984, Vice-President, since 1988, Royal Society of Medicine Foundation Inc., New York; *b* 14 Nov. 1935. *Educ:* Wells Cathedral School; Clare College, Cambridge (MA). Royal Society of Medicine: Assistant Executive Director, 1973; Deputy Executive Director, 1977. Freedom, Apothecaries' Soc., 1991. *Recreations:* music, cooking. *Address:* 9 Downside Lodge, 29 Upper Park Road, NW3 2UY. *T:* 071–722 7176. *Clubs:* Athenæum; University (New York).

THOMSON, Prof. Robert William, PhD; Mashtots Professor of Armenian Studies, Harvard University, 1969–June 1992; Calouste Gulbenkian Professor of Armenian Studies and Fellow of Pembroke College, Oxford, from July 1992; *b* 24 March 1934; *s* of late David William Thomson and Lilian (*née* Cramphorn); *m* 1963, Judith Ailsa Cawdry; two *s*. *Educ:* George Watson's Boys' Coll., Edinburgh; Sidney Sussex Coll., Cambridge (BA 1955); Trinity Coll., Cambridge (PhD 1962). Halki Theol Coll., Istanbul, 1955–56; Jun. Fellow, Dumbarton Oaks, Washington, 1960–61; Louvain Univ., 1961–62; Harvard University: Instructor, then Asst Prof. of Classical Armenian, Dept of Near Eastern Langs, 1963–69; Chm., Dept of Near Eastern Langs, 1973–78, 1980–81. Dir, Dumbarton Oaks, Washington DC, 1984–89. *Publications:* (ed with J. N. Birdsall) Biblical and Patristic Studies in Memory of Robert Pierce Casey, 1963; Athanasiana Syriaca, 4 parts, 1965–77; Athanasius: Contra Gentes and De Incarnatione, 1971; The Teaching of Saint Gregory, 1971; Introduction to Classical Armenian, 1975; Agathangelos: history of the Armenians, 1977; (with K. B. Bardakjian) Textbook of Modern Western Armenian, 1977; Moses Khorenatsi: history of the Armenians, 1978; Elishe: history of Vardan, 1982; (ed with N. G. Garsoian and T. J. Mathews) East of Byzantium, 1982; (with B. Kendall) David the

Invincible Philosopher, 1983; Thomas Artsruni: history of the Artsruni House, 1985; The Armenian Version of Dionysius the Areopagite, 2 vols, 1987; Lazar Parpetsi: history of the Armenians, 1991; contribs to Jl Theol Studies, Le Muséon, Revue des études arméniennes, Oxford Dictionary of Byzantium, Encyclopedia Iranica. *Address:* (until June 1992) Department of Near Eastern Languages, 6 Divinity Avenue, Cambridge, Mass 02138, USA; (from July 1992) Oriental Institute, Pusey Lane, Oxford OX1 2LE.

THOMSON, Sir Thomas James, Kt 1991; CBE 1984 (OBE 1978); FRCPGlas, FRCP, FRCPEd, FRCPI; Chairman, Greater Glasgow Health Board, since 1987; Consultant Physician and Gastroenterologist, Stobhill General Hospital, Glasgow, 1961–87; Hon. Lecturer, Department of Materia Medica, University of Glasgow, 1961–87; *b* 8 April 1923; *s* of Thomas Thomson and Annie Jane Grant; *m* 1948, Jessie Smith Shotbolt; two *s* one *d*. *Educ:* Airdrie Acad.; Univ. of Glasgow (MB, ChB 1945). FRCPGlas 1964 (FRFPSG 1949); FRCP 1969 (MRCP 1950); FRCPEd 1982; FRCPI 1983. Lectr, Dept of Materia Medica, Univ. of Glasgow, 1953–61; Postgrad. Adviser to Glasgow Northern Hosps, 1961–80. Hon. Sec., RCPGlas, 1965–73; Sec., Specialist Adv. Cttee for Gen. Internal Medicine for UK, 1970–74; Chairman: Medico-Pharmaceutical Forum, 1978–80 (Chm., Educn Adv. Bd, 1979–84); Conf. of Royal Colls and Faculties in Scotland, 1982–84; National Med. Consultative Cttee for Scotland, 1982–87; Pres., RCP Glas., 1982–84; active participation in postgrad. med. educnl cttees, locally, nationally and in EEC. Hon. FACP 1983. Hon. LLD Glasgow, 1988. *Publications:* (ed jtly) Dilling's Pharmacology, 1969; Gastroenterology—an integrated course, 1972, 3rd edn 1983; pubns related to gen. medicine, gastroent. and therapeutics. *Recreations:* swimming, golfing. *Address:* 1 Varna Road, Glasgow G14 9NE. *T:* 041–959 5930. *Club:* Royal Air Force.

THOMSON, William Oliver, MD, DPH, DIH; Chief Administrative Medical Officer, Lanarkshire Health Board, 1973–88; *b* 23 March 1925; *s* of William Crosbie Thomson and Mary Jolie Johnston; *m* 1956, Isobel Lauder Glendinning Brady; two *s*. *Educ:* Allan Glen's Sch., Glasgow; Univ. of Glasgow (MB ChB, MD). DPA; FFCM; FRCPGlas 1988 (MRCPGlas 1986). Chronic student of Gray's Inn, London. Captain, RAMC, 1948–50. Hospital appointments, 1951–53; appointments in Public Health, Glasgow, 1953–60; Admin. MO, Western Regional Hospital Bd, 1960–70; Group Medical Superintendent, Glasgow Maternity and Women's Hospitals, 1970–73; Mem., Health Services Ind. Adv. Cttee, 1980–86. Visiting Lecturer: Univ. of Michigan, Ann Arbor; Ministry of Health, Ontario; Hon. Lectr, Univ. of Glasgow. Diploma of Scottish Council for Health Educn (for services to health educn), 1979. *Publications:* articles on clinical medicine, community medicine, general practice, occupational health and health education, in various medical jls; humorous pieces in The Lancet, BMJ, etc. *Recreations:* walking, talking, writing. *Address:* Flat 7, Silverwells Court, Silverwells Crescent, Bothwell, Glasgow G71 8LT. *T:* Bothwell (0698) 852586.

THONEMANN, Peter Clive, MSc, DPhil; Professor Emeritus, Department of Physics, University College, Swansea (Professor and Head of Department, 1968–84); *b* 3 June 1917. *Educ:* Melbourne Church of England Grammar Sch., Melbourne; Sydney and Oxford Univs. BSc Melbourne, 1940; MSc Sydney, 1945; DPhil Oxford, 1949. Munition Supply Laboratories, Victoria, Australia, 1940; Amalgamated Wireless, Australia, 1942; University of Sydney, Commonwealth Research Fellow, 1944; Trinity Coll. and Clarendon Laboratory, Oxford, ICI Research Fellow, 1946; initiated research for controlled fusion power, 1947–49; United Kingdom Atomic Energy Authority: Head of Controlled Fusion Res., 1949–60; Chief Scientist, 1964; Dep. Dir, Culham Laboratory, 1967–68. *Publications:* many contributions to learned journals. *Address:* Department of Physics, University College of Swansea, Singleton Park, Swansea, Wales; 130 Bishopston Road, Swansea SA3 3EU. *T:* Bishopston (044128) 2669.

THORBURN, Andrew, BSc; FRTPI; FTS; Chairman: Thorburns, since 1990; Hardway, since 1991; Principal, Andrew Thorburn Associates, since 1985; *b* 20 March 1934; *s* of James Beresford Thorburn and Marjorie Clara Burford; *m* Margaret Anne Crack; one *s* two *d*. *Educ:* Bridport Grammar Sch.; Univ. of Southampton (BSc). MRTPI 1959, FRTPI 1969. National Service, RN, 1954–56. Planning Asst, Kent CC, 1957–59; Planning Officer, Devon CC, 1959–63; Asst County Planning Officer, Hampshire CC, 1963–68; Dir, Notts and Derbyshire Sub-Region Study, 1968–70; Dep. County Planning Dir, Cheshire CC, 1970–73; County Planning Officer, E Sussex CC, 1973–83; Chief Exec., English Tourist Bd, 1983–85; Head of Tourism and Leisure Div., Grant Thornton, 1986–90. Pres., RTPI, 1982; Mem. Exec., Town and Country Planning Assoc., 1969–81; Founder Trustee, Sussex Heritage Trust, 1978–; Fellow, Tourism Soc., 1983–. *Publication:* Planning Villages, 1971. *Recreations:* sailing, countryside appreciation. *Address:* Hyde Manor, Kingston, Lewes, East Sussex BN7 3PB.

THORLEY, Charles Graham; *b* 4 Jan. 1914; *s* of Charles Lord Thorley; *m* 1958, Peggy Percival Ellis (*née* Boor); one step *s* one step *d*. *Educ:* Manchester Grammar Sch.; King's Coll., Cambridge (Mod. Lang. Scholar). Served War of 1939–45, Eritrea and Cyrenaica (Lt-Col). Entered Civil Service as Economist, Bd of Trade, 1936; attached to British Embassy, China, 1936–38; Mem. British Economic Mission to Belgian Congo, 1940–41; HM Treasury, 1940–57; served on UK financial delegns and missions in Japan, US, Egypt, France, Switzerland, W Germany, etc; Min. of Power, 1957; Under-Secretary and Head of Coal Div., 1965–69; Acct-Gen. and Dir of Finance, 1969. Chm., NATO Petroleum Planning Cttee, 1962–65; Under-Sec., Min. of Technology and DTI, 1969–74. Specialist Advr, House of Lords, 1975–79. *Recreation:* travel. *Address:* Preston House, Corton Denham, Sherborne, Dorset DT9 4LS. *T:* Corton Denham (096322) 269.

THORLEY, Simon Joe; QC 1989; *b* 22 May 1950; *s* of Sir Gerald Bowers Thorley, TD and of Beryl, *d* of G. Preston Rhodes; *m* 1983, Jane Elizabeth Cockcroft; two *s* one *d*. *Educ:* Rugby Sch.; Keble Coll., Oxford (MA Jurisprudence). Called to the Bar, Inner Temple, 1972. Pupilled to William Aldous; in practice at Patent Bar. *Publication:* (co-ed) Terrell on The Law of Patents, 13th edn 1982. *Recreations:* family, tennis, walking, shooting, opera. *Address:* 6 Pump Court, Temple, EC4Y 7AR. *T:* 071–353 8588.

THORN, E. Gaston; Politician, Luxembourg; President: Banque Internationale, Luxembourg, since 1985; Mouvement Européen International, since 1985; President—Director General, RTL Luxembourg, since 1987; Member, Public Review Board, Arthur Andersen & Co.; *b* 3 Sept. 1928; *s* of Edouard Thorn and Suzanne Weber; *m* 1957, Liliane Petit; one *s*. *Educ:* Univs of Montpellier, Lausanne, and Paris. DenD. Admitted to Luxembourg Bar; Pres., Nat. Union of Students, Luxembourg, 1959; Member, European Parlt, 1959–69, Vice-Pres., Liberal Group; Pres., Democratic Party, Luxembourg, 1969; Minister of Foreign Affairs and of Foreign Trade, also Minister of Physical Educn and Sport, 1974–77; Prime Minister and Minister of State, 1974–79; Minister of Nat. Econ. and Middle Classes, 1977; of Justice, 1979; Dep. Prime Minister, and Minister of Foreign Affairs, July 1979–1980; Pres., EEC, 1981–85. Pres., 30th Session of UN Gen. Assembly, 1975–76. President: Liberal International, 1970–82; Fedn of Liberal and Democratic Parties of European Community, 1976–80. Decorations include Grand Cross of Orders of Adolphe de Nassau, Couronne de Chêne, and Mérite (Luxembourg), Grand Cross of Légion d'Honneur (France), GCVO and GCMG (GB) and other Grand Crosses. *Recreations:* tennis, reading. *Address:* 1 rue de la Forge, Luxembourg.

THORN, John Leonard, MA; writer and educational consultant; Headmaster of Winchester College, 1968–85; *b* 28 April 1925; *s* of late Stanley and Winifred Thorn; *m* 1955, Veronica Laura, *d* of late Sir Robert Maconochie, OBE, QC; one *s* one *d*. *Educ:* St Paul's School; Corpus Christi College, Cambridge. Served War of 1939–45, Sub-Lieutenant, RNVR, 1943–46. 1st Class Historical Tripos, Parts I and II. Asst Master, Clifton Coll., 1949–61; Headmaster, Repton School, 1961–68. Dir, Winchester Cathedral Trust, 1986–89. Dir, Royal Opera House, Covent Garden, 1971–76. Chm., Headmasters' Conference, 1981. Member: Bd, Securities Assoc., 1987–91; Exec. Cttee, Cancer Res. Campaign, 1987–90; Vice-Chm., Hants Bldgs Preservation Trust, 1989–; Trustee: British Museum, 1980–85; Oakham Sch., 1985–89. Governor, Stowe Sch., 1985–90; Chm. of Governors, Abingdon Sch., 1991–. *Publications:* (joint) A History of England, 1961; The Road to Winchester (autobiog.), 1989; various articles. *Address:* 6 Chilbolton Avenue, Winchester SO22 5HD. *T:* Winchester (0962) 855990. *Club:* Garrick.

THORN, Sir John (Samuel), Kt 1984; OBE 1977; Member, since 1950, Mayor, since 1956, Port Chalmers Borough Council; *b* 19 March 1911; *s* of J. S. Thorn; *m* 1936, Constance Maud, *d* of W. T. Haines; one *s*. *Educ:* Port Chalmers School; King Edward Technical College. Served 1939–45 war, 3rd Div. Apprentice plumber, later plumbing contractor and land agent; Manager, Thorn's Bookshop, 1950–. Chairman: Municipal Insce Co.; Coastal N Otago United Council. Pres., Municipal Assoc., 1974–; Dep. Chm., Nat. Roads Board, 1974–83. *Address:* Dalkeith, Port Chalmers, New Zealand.

THORN, Roger Eric; QC 1990; *b* 23 March 1948; twin *s* of James Douglas 'Pat' Thorn and Daphne Elizabeth (*née* Robinson). *Educ:* Mill Hill Sch.; Newcastle Univ. (LLB Hons). Called to the Bar, Middle Temple, 1970 (Harmsworth Schol. and Major Exhibn); NE Circuit, 1970–. Mem., Bd of Faculty of Law, Newcastle Univ., 1990–. *Publications:* A Practical Guide to Road Traffic Accident Claims, 1987, 2nd edn 1991; legal contributor to Negotiating Better Deals, by J. G. Thorn (twin *b*), 1988. *Recreations:* theatre, music, walking, local Amenity Society (Chairman). *Address:* Whitton Grange, Rothbury, via Morpeth, Northumberland NE65 7RL. *Club:* Durham County.

THORNBURGH, Richard Lewis; Attorney General of the United States, 1988–91; *b* 16 July 1932; *s* of Charles G. and Alice S. Thornburgh; *m* 1955, Virginia Hooton (decd); *m* 1963, Virginia Judson; four *s*. *Educ:* Yale Univ. (BEng 1954); Univ. of Pittsburgh Sch. of Law (LLB 1957). Staff Counsel, Aluminum Co. of America, 1957–59; Associate, Kirkpatrick, Pomeroy, Lockhart & Johnson, 1959–69; US Attorney, Western District, Pennsylvania, 1969–75; Asst Attorney General, Criminal Div., US Dept of Justice, 1975–77; Partner, Kirkpatrick Lockhart, Johnson & Hutchison, 1977–79; Governor, Commonwealth of Pennsylvania, 1979–87; Partner, Kirkpatrick & Lockhart, 1987–88; Dir, Inst. of Politics, John F. Kennedy Sch. of Govt, 1987–88. Numerous hon. degrees. *Publications:* articles in professional jls. *Address:* 1500 Oliver Building, Pittsburgh, Pa 15222, USA. *T:* (412) 355–6341.

THORNE, Benjamin, CMG 1979; MBE 1966; consultant on Far East trade; *b* 19 June 1922; *m* 1949, Sylvia Una (*née* Graves); one *s* two *d*. *Educ:* St Marylebone Grammar Sch.; Regent Street Polytechnic. Served War, RAF, 1940–46. Joined Civil Service, 1946; British Trade Commission: India, 1950–54; Ghana, 1954–58; Nigeria, 1958–61; Hong Kong, 1964–68; Dir, British Week in Tokyo, 1968–69; Commercial Counsellor, Tokyo, 1973–79, retd. Japanese Order of the Sacred Treasure, 3rd cl., 1975. *Recreations:* cricket, travel, gardening, reading. *Address:* 34 Quarry Hill Road, Borough Green, Sevenoaks, Kent TN15 8RH. *T:* Borough Green (0732) 882547. *Clubs:* Civil Service; Hong Kong (Hong Kong); Foreign Correspondents' (Tokyo); Yokohama Country and Athletic.

THORNE, Prof. Christopher Guy, DLitt; FBA 1982; Professor of International Relations, University of Sussex, since 1977; *b* 17 May 1934; *s* of Reginald Harry Thorne and late Alice Thorne (*née* Pickard); *m* 1958, Beryl Lloyd Jones; two *d*. *Educ:* King Edward VI Royal Grammar Sch., Guildford; St Edmund Hall, Oxford (Hon. Fellow 1989). BA 1958; MA 1962; DLitt 1980. Nat. Service, RN, 1953–55. Teacher, St Paul's Sch., London, 1958–61; Sen. Hist. Master, Charterhouse, 1961–66; Head of Further Educn, BBC Radio, 1966–68; Lectr in Internat. Relations, 1968, Reader, 1972, Univ. of Sussex. Resident Fellow, Netherlands Inst. for Advanced Study, 1979–80. Lectures: Lees-Knowles, Cambridge, 1977; Raleigh, British Acad., 1980; Phillips, British Acad., 1986; Becker, Cornell, 1988; Shaw, Johns Hopkins, 1991. *Publications:* Ideology and Power, 1965; Chartism, 1966; The Approach of War 1938–39, 1967; The Limits of Foreign Policy: the West, the League, and the Far Eastern Crisis of 1931–33, 1972; Allies of a Kind: the United States, Britain, and the war against Japan 1941–1945, 1978 (Bancroft Prize, 1979); Racial Aspects of the Far Eastern War of 1941–45, 1982; The Issue of War: states, societies and the Far Eastern conflict of 1941–45, 1985, repr. as The Far Eastern War, 1986; American Political Culture and the Asian Frontier 1943–1973, 1988; Border Crossings: studies in international history, 1988. *Recreations:* music, Crete. *Address:* School of English and American Studies, University of Sussex, Brighton, Sussex BN1 9QN. *T:* Brighton (0273) 606755.

THORNE, Maj.-Gen. Sir David (Calthrop), KBE 1983 (CBE 1979; OBE 1975); Director General, Commonwealth Trust, since 1989; *b* 13 Dec. 1933; *s* of Richard Everard Thorne and Audrey Ursula (*née* Bone); *m* 1962, Susan Anne Goldsmith; one *s* two *d*. *Educ:* St Edward's Sch., Oxford; RMA, Sandhurst. Staff Coll., Camberley, 1963; jssc 1967; Defence Intelligence Staff, MoD, 1968–70; Instructor, RAF Staff Coll., 1970–72; CO 1 Royal Anglian, 1972–74; Col, General Staff, MoD, 1975–77; Comdr, 3rd Inf. Bde, 1978–79; RCDS 1980; VQMG, 1981–82; Comdr, British Forces Falkland Islands, July 1982–April 1983; Comdr, 1st Armoured Div., 1983–85. Dep. Col, Royal Anglian Regt, 1981–86; Col Comdt, Queen's Div., 1986–88; Dir of Infantry, 1986–88. *Recreations:* cricket, squash, butterfly collecting. *Address:* c/o Barclays Bank, 52 Abbeygate Street, Bury St Edmunds, Suffolk IP33 1LL. *Clubs:* Army and Navy, MCC.

THORNE, Rear-Adm. (retd) Edward Courtney, CB 1975; CBE 1971; FNZIM; Chairman, Manuahi Enterprises (representatives of TRT, AEG, AI West Germany in New Zealand); Chairman, New Zealand Fire Service Commission, 1977–88; Chief of Naval Staff, New Zealand, 1972–75; *b* 29 Oct. 1923; *s* of Ernest Alexander Thorne and Ethel Violet Thorne; *m* 1949, Fay Bradburn (*née* Kerr); three *s*. *Educ:* Nelson Coll., NZ. Chm., Nat. Council, United World Colls, 1982–; Mem., Nat. Council, Duke of Edinburgh Award Scheme; Chm., NZ Sea Cadet Council, 1982–. FNZIM 1980; Hon. FIFireE 1983. *Recreations:* golf, gardening. *Address:* 75 Hatton Street, Karori, Wellington 5, New Zealand. *Club:* Wellington (New Zealand).

THORNE, Neil Gordon, OBE 1980; TD 1969; DL; MP (C) Ilford South, since 1979; *b* 8 Aug. 1932; *s* of late Henry Frederick Thorne and Ivy Gladys Thorne. *Educ:* City of London Sch.; London Univ. BSc. FRICS. Asst Adjt, 58 Med. Regt, RA, BAOR, 1957–59. Sen. Partner, Hull & Co., Chartered Surveyors, 1962–76. Councillor, London Borough of Redbridge, 1965–68, Alderman, 1975–78; Mem., GLC and Chm., Central Area Bd, 1967–73. Chairman: Unpaired Members Gp, 1982–85; British Nepalese Parly Gp, 1983–; British Korean Parly Gp, 1988–; Vice Chm., UK Br., IPU, 1987–90; Member: Defence Select Cttee, 1983–; Court of Referees, 1987–. Chm., H of C Motor Club, 1985–91; Founder and Chm., Armed Forces Parly Scheme, 1988–. Mem., TA, 1952–82;

CO, London Univ. OTC, 1976–80. Fellow, Industry and Parliament Trust, 1980 and 1990. Chairman: Nat. Council for Civil Defence, 1982–86; St Edward's Housing Assoc., 1986–; Ilford Age Concern, 1984–87; President: Redbridge Parkinson's Disease Soc., 1982–; Ilford Arthritis Care, 1986–; Ilford St John Ambulance Cadets, 1991–; Vice Pres., Ilford Tuberculosis and Chest Care Assoc., 1987–; Patron, Jubilee Club for Visually Handicapped, 1986–. DL Greater London, 1991. OStJ 1988. Silver Jubilee Medal, 1977. *Publications*: Pedestrianised Streets: a study of Europe and America, 1973; Highway Robbery in the Twentieth Century: policy reform for compulsory purchase, 1990. *Address*: House of Commons, SW1A 0AA. *T*: 071–219 4123. *Clubs*: Carlton; Ilford Conservative.

THORNE, Sir Peter (Francis), KCVO 1981; CBE 1966; ERD; Serjeant at Arms, House of Commons, 1976–82; *b* 1914; *y s* of late Gen. Sir Andrew Thorne, KCB, CMG, DSO; *m* 1959, Lady Anne Pery, MA, DPhil, Senior Lecturer, Imperial College of Science and Technology, *d* of 5th Earl of Limerick, GBE, CH, KCB, DSO, TD; one *s* three *d*. *Educ*: Eton; Trinity Coll., Oxford. Served War of 1939–45: with 3rd Bn Grenadier Guards (wounded), 1939–41; HQ 2nd Div., 1941–42; Staff College, Quetta, 1942; on staff of India Command and HQ, SACSEA, 1943–45; demobilised with rank of Hon. Lieut-Col, 1946. With Imperial Chemical Industries Ltd, 1946–48. Assistant Serjeant at Arms, House of Commons, 1948–57, Dep. Serjeant at Arms, 1957–76. *Publications*: The Royal Mace in the House of Commons, 1990; various HMSO pamphlets and articles in parly and historical pubns. *Address*: Chiddinglye Farmhouse, West Hoathly, East Grinstead, West Sussex RH19 4QS. *T*: Sharpthorne (0342) 810338. *Clubs*: Cavalry and Guards; Royal Yacht Squadron.

THORNE, Robin Horton John, CMG 1966; OBE 1963; HM Overseas Service, retired; *b* 13 July 1917; *s* of late Sir John Anderson Thorne; *m* 1946, Joan Helen Wadman; one *s*. *Educ*: Dragon Sch., Oxford; Rugby (open scholar); Exeter College, Oxford (open scholar; MA). War Service, Devonshire Regiment and King's African Rifles, 1939–46. Colonial Administrative Service (now HM Overseas Civil Service), 1946–67; Tanganyika Administration, 1946–58; Aden, 1958–67; Asst Chief Sec. (Colony), MLC and Mem. of Governor's Exec. Coun., 1959–63; Ministerial Sec. to Chief Minister, 1963–65; Assistant High Commissioner, 1966–67. With Vice-Chancellors' Cttee, 1967–77; part-time admin. work, Univ. of Sussex, 1978–81. Trustee of Aden Port Trust, 1959–66; Chm., Staines Trust, 1979–85; Mem., Management Cttee, Sussex Housing Assoc. for the Aged, 1983–87. *Recreations*: various. *Address*: The Old Vicarage, Old Heathfield, East Sussex. *T*: Heathfield (04352) 3160. *Club*: Commonwealth Trust.

THORNE, Stanley George; *b* 22 July 1918; *s* of postman and dressmaker; *m* Catherine Mary Rand; two *s* three *d*. *Educ*: Ruskin Coll., Oxford; Univ. of Liverpool. Dip. Social Studies Oxon 1968; BA Hons Liverpool 1970. 30 yrs in industry and commerce: coal-miner, semi-skilled fitter, chartered accountant's clerk, rly signalman, office manager, auditor, commercial manager, etc; lectr in govt and industrial sociology. MP (Lab): Preston South, Feb. 1974–1983; Preston 1983–87. *Recreations*: chess, bridge, golf. *Address*: 26 Station Road, Gateacre, Liverpool L25 3PZ.

THORNELY, Gervase Michael Cobham; Headmaster of Sedbergh School, 1954–75; *b* 21 Oct. 1918; *er s* of late Major J. E. B. Thornely, OBE, and late Hon. Mrs M. H. Thornely; *m* 1954, Jennifer Margery, *d* of late Sir Hilary Scott, Knowle House, Addington, Surrey; two *s* two *d*. *Educ*: Rugby Sch.; Trinity Hall, Cambridge. Organ Scholar; 2nd Cl. Hons, Modern and Mediæval Languages Tripos; BA, 1940; MA, 1944. FRSA 1968. Assistant Master, Sedbergh School, 1940. *Recreations*: music, fly-fishing. *Address*: High Stangerthwaite, Killington, Sedbergh, Cumbria. *T*: Sedbergh (05396) 20444.

THORNEYCROFT, family name of **Baron Thorneycroft.**

THORNEYCROFT, Baron *cr* 1967 (Life Peer), of Dunston; **(George Edward) Peter Thorneycroft,** CH 1980; PC 1951; Barrister-at-law; late RA; Chairman of the Conservative Party, 1975–81; President: Pirelli General plc (formerly Pirelli General Cable Works Ltd), since 1987 (Chairman, 1967–87); Pirelli plc, since 1987 (Chairman, 1969–87); Pirelli UK plc, since 1989 (Chairman, 1987–89); Trusthouse Forte Ltd, since 1982 (Chairman, 1969–81); *b* 26 July 1909; *s* of late Major George Edward Mervyn Thorneycroft, DSO, and Dorothy Hope, *d* of Sir W. Franklyn, KCB; *m* 1st, 1938, Sheila Wells Page (who obtained a divorce, 1949); one *s*; 2nd, 1949, Countess Carla Roberti; one *d*. *Educ*: Eton; Roy. Mil. Acad., Woolwich. Commissioned in Royal Artillery, 1930; resigned Commission, 1933; called to Bar, Inner Temple, 1935; practised Birmingham (Oxford Circuit); MP (C) Stafford, 1938–45, Monmouth, 1945–66. Parliamentary Secretary, Ministry of War Transport, 1945. President of the Board of Trade, October 1951–January 1957; Chancellor of the Exchequer, Jan. 1957–Jan. 1958, resigned; Minister of Aviation, July 1960–July 1962; Minister of Defence, 1962–64; Secretary of State for Defence, Apr.–Oct. 1964. Chairman: SITPRO, 1968–75; BOTB, 1972–75; Pye of Cambridge Ltd, 1967–79; British Reserve Insurance Co. Ltd, 1980–87; Gil, Carvajal & Partners Ltd, 1981–; Cinzano UK Ltd, 1982–85; Director: Riunione Adriatica di Sicurta, 1981–89; Banca Nazionale del Lavoro, 1984–. Exhibitions of paintings: Trafford Gallery, 1961, 1970; Café Royal, 1981, 1989; Mall Galls, 1984; Cadogan Gall., 1987. Mem., Royal Soc. of British Artists, 1978. *Publication*: The Amateur: a companion to watercolour, 1985. *Address*: House of Lords, SW1A 0PW. *T*: (personal secretary) 081–748 5843. *Club*: Army and Navy.

THORNHILL, Andrew Robert; QC 1985; *b* 4 Aug. 1943; *s* of Edward Percy Thornhill and Amelia Joy Thornhill; *m* 1971, Helen Mary Livingston; two *s* two *d*. *Educ*: Clifton Coll. Prep. Sch.; Clifton Coll.; Corpus Christi Coll., Oxford. Called to the Bar, Middle Temple, 1969; entered chambers of H. H. Monroe, QC, 1969. *Publications*: (ed) Potter & Monroe: Tax Planning with Precedents, 7th edn 1974, to 9th edn 1982; (jtly) Tax Planning Through Wills, 1981, 1984; (jtly) Passing Down the Family Farm, 1982; (jtly) Passing Down the Family Business, 1984. *Recreations*: dinghy sailing, squash, walking. *Address*: 37 Canynge Road, Clifton, Bristol. *T*: Bristol (0272) 744015. *Clubs*: United Oxford & Cambridge University; Tamesis (Teddington).

THORNHILL, Lt-Col Edmund Basil, MC 1918; *b* 27 Feb. 1898; *e s* of late E. H. Thornhill, Manor House, Boxworth, Cambridge; *m* 1934, Diana Pearl Day Beales (*d* 1983), *d* of late Hubert G. D. Beales, Hambleden and Cambridge; two *s* one *d*. *Educ*: St Bees School; Royal Military Academy. 2nd Lieut Royal Artillery, 1916; served European War, 1914–18, France and Belgium (wounded, MC); served War of 1939–45, France, Western Desert (Eighth Army) and Italy (despatches); psc 1934; Lt-Col 1945; retd 1948. Chm., Cambs and I of Ely TA & AFA, 1957–62. DL Cambs and Isle of Ely, 1956, Vice-Lieut, 1965–75. *Address*: Manor House, Boxworth, Cambridge CB3 8NF. *T*: Elsworth (09547) 209. *Club*: Army and Navy.

THORNING-PETERSEN, Rudolph; Commander, Order of the Dannebrog, 1981; Ambassador of Denmark to the Court of St James's, since 1989; *b* 17 July 1927; *s* of Erik Thorning-Petersen, FRDanAA, architect, and Helga (*née* Westergaard); *m* 1949, Britta Leyssac; one *s* one *d*. *Educ*: Copenhagen Univ. (LLM 1952). Entered Royal Danish Foreign Service, 1952; alternating service, Min. of Foreign Affairs and at Danish Embassies in Cairo, Moscow and Stockholm, 1952–75; Ambassador to Lebanon, Syria, Jordan, Iraq and Cyprus (resident Beirut), 1975; to People's Republic of China, 1980, to USSR, 1983–89 Knight Grand Order of Cedar of Lebanon; Order of Independence (Jordan); Comdr, Order of Polar Star (Sweden). *Recreations*: modern history, genealogy, history of art. *Address*: Royal Danish Embassy, 55 Sloane Street, SW1X 9SR. *T*: 071–333 0200. *Clubs*: Travellers', Royal Automobile.

THORNTON, Allan Charles; a Director, Greenpeace UK, since 1988 (Executive Director, 1977–81, and 1986–88); Chairman, Environmental Investigation Agency, since 1988 (Co-Founder and Director, 1984–86); *b* 17 Nov. 1949; *s* of Robert Charles Thornton and Jessie (Waldram) Thornton. *Educ*: Banff Centre of Fine Art, Banff, Canada. Co-ordinator of Banff Centre Creative Writing Programme, 1976, 1977; established Greenpeace UK, 1977; co-founder of Greenpeace vessel, Rainbow Warrior, 1978; Internat. Project Co-ordinator with Greenpeace International, 1981. *Recreation*: saving African elephants and viewing them in the wilds of Tanzania and other African countries. *Address*: c/o Greenpeace UK, 30–31 Islington Green, N1 8XE. *T*: 071–354 5100.

THORNTON, Anthony Christopher Lawrence; QC 1988; *b* 18 Aug. 1947; *s* of Richard Thornton and Margery Alice (*née* Clerk); *m* 1983, Lyn Christine Thurlby; one *s*. *Educ*: Eton Coll.; Keble Coll., Oxford (BCL, MA). AIArb. Called to the Bar, Middle Temple, 1970. Chairman: Fulham Legal Advice Centre, 1973–78; Hammersmith and Fulham Law Centre, 1975–78; an Asst Recorder, 1988–. External Moderator, Centre of Construction and Project Management, KCL, 1987–; Hon. Sen. Vis. Fellow, Centre for Commercial Law Studies, QMC, 1987–. Mem., Gen. Council of the Bar, 1988– (Treas., 1990–). Dir, Apex Trust, 1991–. Jt Editor, Construction Law Jl, 1984–. *Publications*: (ed jtly) Building Contracts, in Halsbury's Laws of England, vol. 4, 1973; (contrib.) Construction Disputes: liability and the expert witness, 1989; contribs to Construction Law Jl. *Recreations*: family, cricket, opera. *Address*: 1 Cannons Field, Old Marston, Oxford OX3 0QR. *T*: Oxford (0865) 725038; 1 Atkin Building, Gray's Inn, WC1R 5BQ. *T*: 071–404 0102. *Club*: Royal Automobile.

THORNTON, Clive Edward Ian, CBE 1983; LLB (Lond); FInstLEx, FCBSI; Chairman: Universe Publications Ltd, since 1986; LHW Futures, since 1988; Burgon Hall Ltd, since 1988; Melton Mowbray Building Society, since 1988; Armstrong Capital Holdings Ltd, since 1988; *b* 12 Dec. 1929; *s* of Albert and Margaret Thornton; *m* 1956, Maureen Carmine (*née* Crane); one *s* one *d*. *Educ*: St Anthony's Sch., Newcastle upon Tyne; Coll. of Commerce, Newcastle upon Tyne; College of Law, London; LLB London. Solicitor. FInstLEx 1958; FCBSI 1970. Associate, Pensions Management Inst. Articled to Kenneth Hudson, solicitor, London, 1959; admitted solicitor of Supreme Court, 1963. Asst Solicitor, Nationwide Building Soc., 1963; Solicitor, Cassel Arenz Ltd, Merchant Bankers, 1964–67; Abbey National Building Society: Chief Solicitor, 1967; Dep. Chief Gen. Man., 1978; Chief Gen. Manager, 1979–83; Dir, 1980–83; Partner, Stoneham Langton and Passmore, Solicitors, 1985–88. Chm., Metropolitan Assoc. of Building Socs, 1981–82. Chairman: Mirror Group Newspapers, 1984; Financial Weekly, 1985–87; Thamesmead Town Ltd, 1986–90; Dir, Investment Data Services Ltd, 1986–90; Proprietor, Thorndale Devon Cattle, 1983–. Member: Law Soc. (Chm., Commerce and Industry Gp, 1974); Council, Chartered Bldg Socs Inst., 1973–81; Council, Building Socs Assoc., 1979–83; Bd, Housing Corp., 1980–86. Chairman: SHAC, 1983–86; Belford Hall Management Co. Ltd, 1990–. Mem. Council, St Mary's Hosp. Med. Sch., 1984–. Freeman, City of London; Liveryman, Worshipful Co. of Bakers. *Publication*: Building Society Law, Cases and Materials, 1969 (3rd edn 1988). *Recreations*: antique collecting, music, reading, farming. *Address*: The Old Rectory, Creeton, Grantham, Lincs. *Club*: City Livery.

THORNTON, Ernest, MBE 1951; JP; DL; *b* Burnley, Lancs, 18 May 1905; *s* of Charles Thornton and Margaret (*née* Whittaker); *m* 1930, Evelyn, *d* of Fred Ingham, Blacko, Nelson; one *s* (and one *s* decd). *Educ*: Walverden Council Sch., Nelson, Lancs. Cotton weaver, 1918–26; costing clerk, 1926–29. Rochdale Weavers and Winders' Assoc.; Asst Secretary, 1929–40, Secretary, 1940–70. President, Amalgamated Weavers' Assoc., 1960–65. Secretary, United Textile Factory Workers' Assoc., 1943–53. Member: Lord President's Advisory Council for Scientific and Industrial Research, 1943–48; Council of British Cotton Industry Research Assoc., 1948–53. MP (Lab) Farnworth, 1952–70; Joint Parliamentary Secretary, Min. of Labour, 1964–66. Member: UK Trade Mission to China, 1946; Anglo-American Cotton Textile Mission to Japan, 1950; Cotton Board's Mission to India, 1950. Mayor of County Borough of Rochdale, 1942–43. Comp. TI 1966. JP 1944, DL Manchester Metropolitan County (formerly Lancaster), 1970. *Address*: 31 Lynnwood Drive, Rochdale, Lancs. *T*: Rochdale (0706) 31954.

THORNTON, (George) Malcolm; MP (C) Crosby, since 1983 (Liverpool, Garston, 1979–83); *b* 3 April 1939; *s* of George Edmund and Ethel Thornton; *m* 1st, 1962; one *s*; 2nd, 1972, Shirley Ann, (Sue) (*née* Banton) (*d* 1989); 3rd, 1990, Rosemary (*née* Hewitt). *Educ*: Wallasey Grammar Sch.; Liverpool Nautical Coll. Liverpool Pilot Service, 1955–79 (Sen. 1st cl. Licence holder). Member: Wallasey County Borough Council, 1965–74 (Chm., Transport Cttee, 1968–69); Wirral Metropolitan Council, 1973–79 (Council Leader, 1974–77); Chairman: Merseyside Metropolitan Districts Liaison Cttee, 1975–77; Educn Cttee, AMA, 1978–79 (Mem., 1974–79); Council of Local Educn Authorities, 1978. Mem., Burnham (Primary and Secondary) Cttee, 1975–79. PPS to Sec. of State for Industry, 1981–83, for the Environment, 1983–84. Chm., Select Cttee on Educn, Sci. and the Arts, 1989– (Mem., 1985–). *Recreations*: fishing, sailing, cooking. *Address*: House of Commons, SW1A 0AA. *T*: 071–219 4489. *Club*: Wyresdale Anglers.

THORNTON, Helen Ann Elizabeth, (Mrs J. E. C. Thornton); *see* Meixner, H. A. E.

THORNTON, Jack Edward Clive, CB 1978; OBE 1964 (MBE 1945); *b* 22 Nov. 1915; *s* of late Stanley Henry Thornton and Elizabeth Daisy (*née* Baxter); *m* 1st, Margaret, JP, *d* of late John David and Emily Copeland, Crewe, Cheshire; 2nd, Helen Ann Elizabeth Meixner, *qv*. *Educ*: Solihull Sch.; Christ's Coll., Cambridge (Open Exhibnr 1936; BA 1938). Cert. Educn 1939; MA 1942. Served in RASC, 1939–46 (despatches, 1946); Lt-Col 1944. Teaching in UK, 1946–47; Asst, then Dep. Educn Officer, City of York, 1947–51; Asst Educn Officer, WR Yorks, 1951–54; Dep. Dir of Educn, Cumberland, 1954–62; Sec., Bureau for External Aid for Educn, Fed. Govt of Nigeria, 1962–64; Educn Consultant, IBRD, 1964–65; Adviser on Educn in W Africa and Controller Appts Div., British Council, 1965–68; Dep. Educn Adviser, 1968–70, Chief Educn Adviser and Under Sec., 1970–77, Ministry of Overseas Develt (now Overseas Develt Admin in FCO). Lectr, Dept of Educn in Developing Countries, Inst. of Educn, Univ. of London, 1978–79. Chm., PNEU World-wide Educn Service, 1979–; Member: Exec. Cttee, Council for Educn in the Commonwealth (Chm., 1979–85; Dep. Chm., 1985–90); Lloyd Foundn (Vice-Chm., 1988–); Educational Panel, Independent Schs Tribunal; Charlotte Mason Coll. Higher Educn Corp.; Trustee, Christopher Cox Meml Fund. *Recreations*: books, conservation, gardens, mountains, music, railways, travel. *Address*: 131 Dalling Road, W6 0ET. *T*: 081–748 7692.

THORNTON, John Henry, OBE 1987; QPM 1980; Deputy Assistant Commissioner, Metropolitan Police, 1981–86; *b* 24 Dec. 1930; *s* of late Sidney Thornton and Ethel Thornton (*née* Grinnell); *m* 1st, 1952, Norma Lucille, *d* of Alfred and Kate Scrivenor (marr. diss. 1972); two *s*; 2nd, 1972, Hazel Ann, *d* of William and Edna Butler; one *s* one *d* (and one *s* decd). *Educ*: Prince Henry's Grammar School. Evesham. RN 1949–50. Metropolitan Police, 1950; Head of Community Relations, 1977–80; RCDS, 1981; Dep. Asst Commissioner, 1981; Dir of Information, 1982–83; Hd of Training, 1983–85; NW Area, 1985–86. Vice-Pres., British Section, Internat. Police Assoc., 1969–79. Chm., Breakaway Theatre Co., St Albans, 1987–; Chm., St Albans Internat. Organ Fest., 1988. Lay Canon and Cathedral Warden, St Albans, 1988–. Liveryman, Glaziers' Co., 1983. CStJ 1984. *Recreations*: music, gardening, classics. *Address*: c/o Barclays Bank, 16 High Street, Harpenden, Herts AL5 2TD.

THORNTON, Lt-Gen. Sir Leonard (Whitmore), KCB 1967 (CB 1962); CBE 1957 (OBE 1944); *b* Christchurch, 15 Oct. 1916; *s* of late Cuthbert John Thornton and Frances Caverhill Thornton; *m* 1942, Gladys Janet Sloman, Wellington; three *s*; *m* 1971, Ruth Leicester, Wellington. *Educ*: Christchurch Boys' High Sch.; Royal Military Coll., Duntroon, Australia. Commissioned in New Zealand Army, 1937. Served War of 1939–45 (despatches twice, OBE), Middle East and Italy in 2nd New Zealand Expeditionary Force; Commander, Royal Artillery, 2 New Zealand Division. Commander, Tokyo Sub-area, 1946; Deputy Chief of General Staff, 1948; idc 1952; Head, New Zealand Joint Service Liaison Staff, 1953 and 1954; QMG, New Zealand, 1955; AG, 1956–58; Chief, SEATO Planning Office, Thailand, 1958–59; Chief of General Staff, NZ, 1960–65; Chief of Defence Staff, NZ, 1965–71; Ambassador for New Zealand in S Vietnam and Khmer Republic, 1972–74. Chm., Alcoholic Liquor Adv. Council, 1977–83. *Recreation*: fishing. *Address*: 20 Beauchamp Street, Wellington 5, New Zealand. *Club*: Wellington (Wellington).

THORNTON, Malcolm; *see* Thornton, G. M.

THORNTON, Neil Ross; Head, Internal European Policy Division, Department of Trade and Industry, since 1990; *b* 11 Feb. 1950; *s* of George and Kay Thornton; *m* 1977, Christine Anne Boyes; two *d*. *Educ*: Sedbergh Sch.; Pembroke Coll., Cambridge (BA Eng. 1971). Private Sec. to Perm. Sec., DoI, 1975; HM Treasury, 1979; Asst Sec., DTI, 1984; Principal Private Sec. to Lord Young of Graffham and Rt Hon. Nicholas Ridley, Sec. of State for Trade and Industry, 1988–90; Under Sec., 1990. *Recreations*: literature, choral singing, golf. *Address*: Department of Trade and Industry, 1–19 Victoria Street, SW1H 0ET. *T*: 071–215 7877.

THORNTON, Sir Peter (Eustace), KCB 1974 (CB 1971); Director, Laird Group, since 1978; Permanent Secretary, Department of Trade, 1974–77; *b* 28 Aug. 1917; *s* of Douglas Oscar Thornton and Dorothy (*née* Shepherd); *m* 1946, Rosamond Hobart Myers, US Medal of Freedom, Sewanee, Tennessee; two *s* one *d*. *Educ*: Charterhouse; Gonville and Caius Coll., Cambridge. Served with RA, mainly in Middle East and Italy, 1940–46. Joined Board of Trade, 1946. Secretary, Company Law Cttee (Jenkins Cttee), 1959–62; Assistant Under-Secretary of State, Department of Economic Affairs, 1964–67; Under-Sec., 1967–70, Dep. Sec., 1970–72, Cabinet Office, with central co-ordinating role during British negotiations for membership of EEC; Dep. Sec., DTI, March-July 1972; Sec. (Aerospace and Shipping), DTI, 1972–74; Second Permanent Sec., Dept of Trade, 1974. Director: Hill Samuel Gp, 1977–83; Rolls Royce, 1977–85; Courtaulds, 1977–87; Superior Oil, 1980–84. Mem., Megaw Cttee of Inquiry into Civil Service Pay, 1981–82. Pro-Chancellor, Open Univ., 1979–83(D Univ 1984). Governor, Sutton's Hosp., Charterhouse, 1980–89. *Address*: 22 East Street, Alresford, Hants SO24 9EE.

THORNTON, Peter Kai, FSA 1976; Curator of Sir John Soane's Museum, since 1984; *b* 8 April 1925; *s* of Sir Gerard Thornton, FRS, and of Gerda, *d* of Kai Nørregaard, Copenhagen; *m* 1950, Mary Ann Rosamund, *d* of E. A. P. Helps, Cregane, Rosscarbery, Co. Cork; three *d*. *Educ*: Bryanston Sch.; De Havilland Aeronautical Technical Sch.; Trinity Hall, Cambridge. Served with Army, Intelligence Corps, Austria, 1945–48; Cambridge, 1948–50; Voluntary Asst Keeper, Fitzwilliam Museum, Cambridge, 1950–52; Joint Secretary, National Art-Collections Fund, London, 1952–54; entered Victoria and Albert Museum as Asst Keeper, Dept of Textiles, 1954; transf. to Dept of Woodwork, 1962; Keeper, Dept of Furniture and Woodwork, 1966–84. Sen. Vis. Res. Fellow, St John's Coll., Oxford, 1985–86; Leverhulme Emeritus Res. Fellow, 1988–89. Chm., Furniture History Soc., 1974–84; Member: Council, Nat. Trust, 1983–85; London Adv. Cttee, English Heritage, 1986–88. *Publications*: Baroque and Rococo Silks, 1965; Seventeenth Century Interior Decoration in England, France and Holland, 1978 (Alice Davis Hitchcock Medallion, Soc. of Architectural Historians of GB, 1982); (jtly) The Furnishing and Decoration of Ham House, 1981; Musical Instruments as Works of Art, 1982; Authentic Décor: the domestic interior 1620–1920, 1984 (Sir Bannister Fletcher Prize, RIBA, 1985); numerous articles on interior decoration, furniture and textiles. *Address*: 15 Cheniston Gardens, W8. *T*: 071–937 8868; Cahergal, Union Hall, Co. Cork; Phillips Farm Cottage, Eaton Hastings, Faringdon, Oxon. *Club*: Kilmacabea and Castlehaven Gun (Co. Cork).

See also Hon. P. Jay.

THORNTON, Richard Eustace, OBE 1980; JP; HM Lord Lieutenant of Surrey, since 1986; *b* 10 Oct. 1922; *m* 1954, Gabrielle Elizabeth Sharpe; four *d*. *Educ*: Eton Coll.; Trinity Coll., Cambridge (MA). Member: Royal Commission on Environmental Pollution, 1977–84; Governing Body, Charterhouse Sch. (Chm., 1981–89). Surrey: DL; High Sheriff 1978–79; JP. KStJ 1986. *Address*: Hampton, Seale, near Farnham, Surrey. *T*: Guildford (0483) 810208.

THORNTON, Robert John, CB 1980; Assistant Under Secretary of State and Director General of Supplies and Transport (Naval), Ministry of Defence, 1977–81; *b* 23 Dec. 1919; *s* of Herbert John Thornton and Ethel Mary Thornton (*née* Dunning); *m* 1944, Joan Elizabeth Roberts; three *s*. *Educ*: Queen Elizabeth Grammar School, Atherstone. MBIM 1970. Joined Naval Store Dept, Admiralty, as Asst Naval Store Officer, 1938; Singapore, 1941; Dep. Naval Store Officer, Colombo, 1942; Support Ship Hong Siang, 1943; Naval Store Officer, Admiralty, 1945; Gibraltar, 1951; Asst Dir of Stores, 1955; Superintending Naval Store Officer, Portsmouth, 1960; Dep. Dir of Stores, 1964; Dir of Victualling, 1971; Dir of Supplies and Transport (General Stores and Victualling), 1971. *Recreations*: bowls, fly fishing, gardening.

THORNTON, Robert Ribblesdale, CBE 1973; DL; solicitor; Deputy Chairman, Local Government Boundary Commission for England, 1982 (Member, 1976–82); *b* 2 April 1913; *s* of Thomas Thornton and Florence Thornton (*née* Gatenby); *m* 1940, Ruth Eleonore Tuckson; one *s* one *d*. *Educ*: Leeds Grammar Sch.; St John's Coll., Cambridge (MA, LLM). Asst Solicitor, Leeds, 1938–40 and 1946–47. Served War, 1940–46. Asst Solicitor, Bristol, 1947–53; Dep. Town Clerk, Southampton, 1953–54; Town Clerk: Salford, 1954–66; Leicester, 1966–73; Chief Exec., Leicestershire CC, 1973–76. Pres., Soc. of Town Clerks, 1971. Treasurer, Leicester Univ., 1980–85. Hon. LLD Leicester, 1987. DL Leicestershire, 1974–85. French Croix de Guerre, 1946. *Recreations*: music, sport. *Address*: 16 St Mary's Close, Winterborne Whitechurch, Blandford Forum, Dorset DT11 0DJ. *T*: Milton Abbas (0258) 880980. *Club*: National Liberal.

THORNTON, Sally; *see* Burgess, Sally.

THORNTON, Dr William Dickson, CB 1990; Deputy Chief Medical Officer, Department of Health and Social Services, Northern Ireland, 1978–90, retired; *b* 9 July 1930; *s* of late William J. Thornton and of Elfreda Thornton (*née* Dickson); *m* 1957, Dr Maureen Gilpin; one *s* three *d*. *Educ*: Portora Royal School; Trinity College Dublin (BA, MD). FFPHM. General medical practitioner, 1955–65; NI Hospitals Authy, 1966–72; Dept of Health and Social Services (NI), 1973–90. Civil QHP, 1990–. *Recreations*: yachting, reading, gardening. *Address*: 54 Deramore Park South, Belfast BT9 5JY. *T*: Belfast (0232) 660186.

THOROGOOD, Alfreda, (Mrs D. R. Wall), ARAD (PDTC); Artistic Advisor, Royal Academy of Dancing, since 1989; *b* 17 Aug. 1942; *d* of Alfreda and Edward Thorogood; *m* 1967, David Wall, *qv*; one *s* one *d*. *Educ*: Lady Eden's Sch.; Royal Ballet Sch., Jun. and Sen. Royal Ballet Company, 1960–80: Soloist, Aug. 1965; Principal Dancer, 1968; Bush Davies School: Sen. Teacher, 1982–84; Dep. Ballet Principal, 1984–89; Dir, 1988–89. *Recreations*: listening to music, cooking, interior design, art, painting. *Address*: 34 Croham Manor Road, S Croydon CR2 7BE.

THOROGOOD, Rev. Bernard George; General Secretary, United Reformed Church, 1980–July 1992; *b* 21 July 1927; *s* of Frederick and Winifred Thorogood; *m* 1952, Jannett Lindsay Paton (*née* Cameron) (*d* 1988); two *s*. *Educ*: Glasgow Univ. (MA); Scottish Congregational College. Ordained in Congregational Church, 1952; missionary appointment under London Missionary Society in South Pacific Islands, 1953–70; Gen. Sec., Council for World Mission, 1971–80. Moderator, Exec. Cttee, BCC, 1984–90; Mem., Central Cttee, WCC, 1984–91. *Publications*: Not Quite Paradise, 1960; Guide to the Book of Amos, 1971; Our Father's House, 1983; Risen Today, 1987; The Flag and The Cross, 1988; No Abiding City, 1989; On Judging Caesar, 1990; One Wind Many Flames, 1991. *Recreation*: sketching. *Address*: c/o Church House, 86 Tavistock Place, WC1H 9RT. *T*: 071–837 7661.

THOROGOOD, Kenneth Alfred Charles; Chairman, Ardil (Holdings) UK Ltd, since 1984; Director: Welbeck Finance plc, since 1984; Trade and Industry Acceptance Corporation (London) Ltd, since 1984; *b* 1924; *s* of Albert Jesse and Alice Lucy Thorogood; *m* 1st, 1947, José Patricia Smith; two *d*; 2nd, 1979, Mrs Gaye Lambourne. *Educ*: Highbury County Grammar School. Pilot, RAF, 1941–46. Pres., Deepsoval Services Ltd; Chm., Tozer Kemsley & Millbourn (Holdings) plc, 1972–82; Director: Alexanders Discount Co. Ltd, to 1983; Royal Insurance Co. Ltd; Abelson Plant (Holdings) Ltd; Spicer-Firgos Ltd. Chairman, Brit. Export Houses Assoc., 1968–70; Mem., Cttee of Invisibles, 1968–70. *Recreations*: aviation, music. *Address*: Flat 1, 18 Lowndes Square, SW1X 9HB; Kimmer Farm, Faccombe, Hants. *Clubs*: Travellers', City of London, Royal Air Force; Wanderers (Johannesburg).

THOROLD, Captain Sir Anthony (Henry), 15th Bt, *cr* 1642; OBE 1942; DSC 1942, and Bar 1945; DL; JP; RN Retired; *b* 7 Sept. 1903; *s* of Sir James (Ernest) Thorold, 14th Bt; *S* father, 1965; *m* 1939, Jocelyn Elaine Laura, *er d* of late Sir Clifford Heathcote-Smith, KBE, CMG; one *s* two *d*. *Educ*: Royal Naval Colleges Osborne and Dartmouth. Entered RN 1917; qualified as Navigating Officer, 1928; psc 1935; Commander, 1940; served in Mediterranean and Home Fleets, 1939–40; Staff Officer Operations to Flag Officer Commanding Force 'H', 1941–43; in command of Escort Groups in Western Approaches Comd, 1944–45; Captain, 1946; Naval Assistant Secretary in Cabinet Office and Ministry of Defence, 1945–48; Sen. Officer, Fishery Protection Flotilla, 1949–50; Captain of HMS Dryad (Navigation and Direction Sch.), 1951–52; Commodore in Charge, Hong Kong, 1953–55; ADC to the Queen, 1955–56; retired, 1956. DL Lincs, 1959; JP Lincolnshire (Parts of Kesteven), 1961; High Sheriff of Lincolnshire, 1968. Chairman: Grantham Hospital Management Cttee, 1963–74; Lincoln Diocesan Trust and Board of Finance, 1966–71; Community Council of Lincs, 1974–81; CC Kesteven, 1958–74; Leader, Lincs County Council, 1973–81. *Recreation*: shooting. *Heir*: *s* (Anthony) Oliver Thorold [*b* 15 April 1945; *m* 1977, Genevra M., *y d* of John Richardson, Midlothian; one *s* one *d*]. *Address*: Syston Old Hall, Grantham, Lincs NG32 2BX. *T*: Loveden (0400) 50270. *Club*: Army and Navy.

THORP, Jeremy Walter; HM Diplomatic Service; Deputy Head of Mission, Dublin, since 1988; *b* 12 Dec. 1941; *s* of Walter and Dorothy Bliss Thorp; *m* 1973, Estela Lessa de Guyer. *Educ*: Corpus Christi Coll., Oxford (MA). HM Treasury, 1963–67; DEA, 1967–69; HM Treasury, 1969–71; First Sec. (Financial), HM Embassy, Washington, 1971–73; HM Treasury, 1973–78; FCO, 1978–82; Head of Chancery, Lima, 1982–86; FCO, 1986–88. *Recreations*: music, travel, reading, walking. *Address*: c/o Foreign and Commonwealth Office, King Charles Street, SW1A 2AH. *Club*: Kildare Street and University (Dublin).

THORPE, Adrian Charles, MA; HM Diplomatic Service; Deputy High Commissioner, Kuala Lumpur, since 1989; *b* 29 July 1942; *o s* of late Prof. Lewis Thorpe and of Dr Barbara Reynolds, *qv*; *m* 1968, Miyoko Kosugi. *Educ*: The Leys Sch., Cambridge; Christ's Coll., Cambridge (MA). HM Diplomatic Service, 1965–: Tokyo, 1965–70; FCO, 1970–73; Beirut, 1973–76 (Head of Chancery, 1975–76); FCO, 1976; Tokyo, 1976–81; FCO, 1981–85, Hd of IT Dept, 1982–85; Counsellor (Econ.), Bonn, 1985–89. FRSA. *Publications*: articles in journals. *Recreations*: opera, travel, bookshops, comfort. *Address*: c/o Foreign and Commonwealth Office, SW1A 2AH. *Clubs*: Tokyo (Japan); Bankers, Royal Selangor Golf (Kuala Lumpur).

THORPE, Anthony Geoffrey Younghusband; His Honour Judge Thorpe; a Circuit Judge, since 1990; *b* 21 Aug. 1941; *s* of G. J. Y. Thorpe, MBE; *m* 1966, Janet Patricia; one *s* one *d*. *Educ*: Highgate School; Britannia Royal Naval College (scholarship); King's College London. Royal Navy: served HM Ships Hermes, Ark Royal, Vidal, Blake; Captain 1983; Chief Naval Judge Advocate, 1983–86; retired from RN 1990. Called to the Bar, Inner Temple, 1972 (Treasurer's Prize). *Publications*: articles in learned jls. *Recreations*: sailing. *Address*: c/o Lloyds Bank, 4 West Street, Havant PO9 1PE. *Club*: Naval.

THORPE, Brian Russell, CBE 1987; Deputy Chairman, Southern Water (formerly Southern Water Authority), since 1983 (Chief Executive, 1973–88); *b* 12 July 1929; *s* of late Robert and Florrie Thorpe; *m* 1955, Ann Sinclair Raby; three *d*. *Educ*: Rastrick Grammar Sch. LLB London, LLM Leeds. Solicitor, 1952. Asst Prosecuting Solicitor, Bradford CC, 1954–55; Asst Solicitor, later Asst Town Clerk, Southampton CC, 1955–61; Dep. Town Clerk, Blackpool, 1961–65; Gen. Man., Sussex River Authority, 1965–73. Churchill Fellow, 1972. *Recreations*: golf, gardening, foreign travel. *Address*: Southern Water, Southern House, Yeoman Road, Worthing, West Sussex BN13 3NX. *T*: Worthing (0903) 64444. *Clubs*: Worthing Golf; Seaview Yacht.

THORPE, Rt. Hon. (John) Jeremy, PC 1967; Chairman, Jeremy Thorpe Associates (Development Consultants in the Third World), since 1984; *b* 29 April 1929; *s* of late J. H. Thorpe, OBE, KC, MP (C) Rusholme, and Ursula, *d* of late Sir John Norton-Griffiths, Bt, KCB, DSO, sometime MP (C); *m* 1st, 1968, Caroline (*d* 1970), *d* of Warwick Allpass, Kingswood, Surrey; one *s*; 2nd, 1973, Marion, *d* of late Erwin Stein. *Educ*: Rectory Sch., Connecticut, USA; Eton Coll.; Trinity Coll., Oxford. Hon. Fellow, 1972. President,

Oxford Union Society, Hilary, 1951; Barrister, Inner Temple, 1954. Member Devon Sessions. Contested (L) N Devon, 1955; MP (L) Devon N, 1959–79. Hon. Treasurer, Liberal Party Organisation, 1965–67; Leader, Liberal Party, 1967–76; Pres., N Devon Liberal Democrats (formerly N Devon Liberal Assoc.), 1987–. United Nations Association: Chm., Exec., 1976–80; Chm., Political Cttee, 1977–85. FRSA. Hon. LLD Exeter, 1974. *Publications:* (jtly) To all who are interested in Democracy, 1951; Europe: the case for going in, 1971; contrib. to newspapers and periodicals. *Recreations:* music; collecting Chinese ceramics. *Address:* 2 Orme Square, W2. *Clubs:* National Liberal; N Devon Liberal.

THORPE, Hon. Sir Mathew Alexander, Kt 1988; **Hon. Mr Justice Thorpe;** a Judge of the High Court of Justice, Family Division, since 1988; *b* 1938; *s* of late Michael Alexander Thorpe and of Dorothea Margaret Lambert; *m* 1st, 1966, Lavinia Hermione Buxton (marr. diss. 1989); three *s*; 2nd, 1989, Mrs Carola Millar. *Educ:* Stowe; Balliol Coll., Oxford. Called to the Bar, Inner Temple, 1961, Bencher, 1985; QC 1980; a Recorder, 1982–88. *Address:* Royal Courts of Justice, Strand, WC2A 2LL.

THORPE, Nigel James; HM Diplomatic Service; Deputy High Commissioner, Harare, since 1989; *b* 3 Oct. 1945; *s* of Ronald Thorpe and Glenys (*née* Robilliard); *m* 1969 (marr. diss. 1976); two *s*; *m* 1978, Susan Banforth; two *d*. *Educ:* East Grinstead Grammar Sch.; University Coll. of S Wales and Monmouthshire (BA Hons). Clerical Asst, Library Assoc., 1968; Res. Asst, British Sulphur Corp., 1968–69; joined HM Diplomatic Service, 1969; Warsaw, 1970–72; Dacca, 1973–74; FCO, 1975–79; Ottawa, 1979–81; seconded to Dept of Energy, 1981–82; Asst Hd of Southern Africa Dept, FCO, 1982–85; Counsellor, Warsaw, 1985–88. *Recreations:* my family, keeping fit, carpentry. *Address:* c/o Foreign and Commonwealth Office, King Charles Street, SW1A 2AH; 171 Leathwaite Road, SW11 6RW. *T:* 071–223 7562. *Club:* Harare (Zimbabwe).

THORPE, Sir Ronald Laurence G.; *see* Gardner-Thorpe.

THORPE-TRACEY, Stephen Frederick; management consultant; Controller, Newcastle Central Office, Department of Social Security (formerly of Health and Social Security), 1986–89, retired; *b* 27 Dec. 1929; *s* of Rev. and Mrs J. S. V. Thorpe-Tracey; *m* 1955, Shirley Byles; one *s* two *d*. *Educ:* Plymouth Coll. Emergency Commn, 1948; Short Service Commn, 1950; Regular Commn, DLI, 1952; Staff Coll., Camberley, 1960 (psc); GS02, Defence Operational Res. Estabt, 1961–64; Training Major, 8 DLI (TA), 1964–65; Major, 1 DLI, 1965–66; GSO2, MoD, 1966–70; direct entry, Home Civil Service, 1970; Principal, DHSS, 1970; Asst Sec., 1977; Under Sec., 1986. Chm., Northern Gp, RIPA, 1988–90. Mem., Prescription Pricing Authy, 1990–; Vice Chm., Carr-Gomm (Tyneside) Housing Assoc. Ltd, 1990–. Hon. Sec., Civil Service Chess Assoc., 1974–77; Cdre, Goring Thames Sailing Club, 1981–82. *Publications:* T^2 series of articles in military jls. *Recreations:* chess, golf, fell-walking. *Address:* 12 Woodbine Avenue, Gosforth, Newcastle upon Tyne NE3 4EU. *T:* 091–284 5491. *Clubs:* Naval and Military; Gosforth Golf.

THOULESS, Prof. David James, FRS 1979; Professor of Physics, University of Washington, since 1980; *b* 21 Sept. 1934; *s* of late Robert Henry Thouless; *m* 1958, Margaret Elizabeth Scrase; two *s* one *d*. *Educ:* Winchester Coll.; Trinity Hall, Cambridge (BA); Cornell Univ. (PhD). Physicist, Lawrence Radiation Laboratory, Berkeley, Calif, 1958–59; ICI Research Fellow, Birmingham Univ., 1959–61; Lecturer, Cambridge Univ., and Fellow of Churchill Coll., 1961–65; Prof. of Mathematical Physics, Birmingham Univ., 1965–78; Prof. of Applied Science, Yale Univ., 1979–80; Royal Soc. Res. Prof., and Fellow of Clare Hall, Cambridge Univ., 1983–86. Wolf Prize for Physics, Wolf Foundn, Israel, 1990. *Publication:* Quantum Mechanics of Many-Body Systems, 1961, 2nd edn 1972. *Address:* Department of Physics FM-15, University of Washington, Seattle, Wash 98195, USA.

THOURON, Sir John (Rupert Hunt), KBE 1976 (CBE 1967); *b* 10 May 1908; *m* 1st, 1930, Lorna Ellett (marr. diss. 1939); one *s*; 2nd, 1953, Esther duPont (*d* 1984). *Educ:* Sherborne School, Dorset. Served War of 1939–45; Major, Black Watch. With Lady Thouron, Founder of the Thouron University of Pennsylvania Fund for British-American Student Exchange, 1960. *Recreations:* shooting, fishing, golf, gardening. *Address:* Unionville, Chester County, Pa 19375, USA. *T:* (215) 384–5542; (winter) 416 South Beach Road, Hobe Sound, Fla 33455, USA. *T:* 305–546–3577. *Clubs:* White's; Brook (NY); Sunningdale Golf; Royal St George Golf; Wilmington, Wilmington Country, Vicmead (all Delaware); Pine Valley, British Officers Club of Philadelphia (Pennsylvania); Seminole Golf, Island Club of Hobe Sound (Florida).

THRELFALL, David; actor; *b* 12 Oct. 1953; *m* 1990, Harriet Robinson. *Educ:* Wilbraham Comprehensive Sch.; Sheffield Art Coll.; Manchester Polytechnic Sch. of Theatre. *Stage:* Bed of Roses, Royal Court; 3 years with RSC, incl. Savage Amusement, Nicholas Nickleby, 1980 (Clarence Derwent Award, British Theatre Assoc., SWET Award); Not Quite Jerusalem, Royal Court, 1982; Hamlet, Edinburgh Fest., 1986; Bussy D'Ambois, Old Vic, 1988; Wild Duck, Phoenix, 1990; *television:* The Kiss of Death, 1976; Nicholas Nickleby, 1984; Paradise Postponed, 1985; The Marksman, 1988; Jumping the Queue, 1989; Nightingales, 1990–; Titmuss Regained, 1991; *films:* When the Whales Came, 1989; The Russia House, 1990. Plays and Players Promising Newcomer, 1978. *Recreations:* motor bike, squash, gym, friends. *Address:* c/o James Sharkey Associates, 15 Golden Square, W1R 8RU.

THRELFALL, Richard Ian, QC 1965; *b* 14 Jan. 1920; *s* of William Bernhard and Evelyn Alice Threlfall; *m* 1948, Annette, *d* of George C. H. Matthey; two *s* three *d* (and one *s* decd). *Educ:* Oundle; Gonville and Caius Coll., Cambridge. War service, 1940–45 (despatches twice); Indian Armoured Corps (Probyn's Horse) and Staff appointments. Barrister, Lincoln's Inn, 1947, Bencher 1973. FSA, 1949. Member: Court of Assistants, Worshipful Co. of Goldsmiths (Prime Warden, 1978–79); British Hallmarking Council. *Address:* Pebble Hill House, Limpsfield, Surrey RH8 0EA. *T:* Oxted (0883) 712452.

THRING, Rear-Adm. George Arthur, CB 1958; DSO 1940 and Bar 1952; DL; *b* 13 Sept. 1903; *s* of late Sir Arthur Thring, KCB; *m* 1929, Betty Mary (*d* 1983), *er d* of Colonel Stewart William Ward Blacker, DSO; two *s* two *d*. *Educ:* Royal Naval Colleges, Osborne and Dartmouth. Commander, 1941; Captain, 1946; Rear-Admiral, 1956; retired, 1958. Commanded: HMS Deptford, 1940–41; 42nd and 20th Escort Groups, Atlantic, 1943–45; HMS Ceylon, 1951–52; Flag Officer, Malayan Area, 1956–58. Officer, Legion of Merit (USA), 1945. DL Somerset, 1968. *Recreations:* golf, shooting and fishing. *Address:* Alford House, Castle Cary, Somerset BA7 7PN. *T:* Wheathill (096324) 329.

THRING, Prof. Meredith Wooldridge, ScD; FEng; Professor of Mechanical Engineering, Queen Mary College, London University, 1964–81; *b* 17 Dec. 1915; *s* of Captain W. H. C. S. Thring, CBE, RN, and Dorothy (*née* Wooldridge); *m* 1940, Alice Margaret Hooley (*d* 1986), two *s* one *d*. *Educ:* Malvern Coll., Worcs; Trinity Coll., Cambridge (Senior Scholar, 1937). Hons Degree Maths and Physics, 1937; ScD, 1964. Student's Medal, Inst. of Fuel, for work on producer gas mains, 1938; British Coal Utilisation Research Assoc.: Asst Scientific Officer, 1937; Senior Scientific Officer and Head of Combustion Research Laboratory, 1944; British Iron and Steel Research Assoc.: Head of Physics Dept, 1946; Superintendent, 1950; Assistant Director, 1953; Prof. of Fuel Technology and Chemical Engineering, Sheffield Univ., 1953–64. General Superintendent International Flame Radiation Research Foundn, 1951–76. Visitor: Production Engineering Research Assoc., 1967; Machine Tool Industry Research Assoc., 1967. Member Clean Air Council, 1957–62; Fuel Research Board, 1957–58; Fire Research Board, 1961–64; BISRA Council, 1958–60; President, Inst. of Fuel, 1962–63 (Vice-President, 1959–62); Member: Adv. Council on Research and Development, Ministry of Power, 1960–66; Acad. Adv. Council, University of Strathclyde, 1962–67; Education Cttee, RAF, 1968–76; Unesco Commn to Bangladesh, 1979. FInstP 1944; FInstF 1951; FIChemE 1972 (MIChemE 1956); FIMechE 1968 (MIMechE 1964); FIEE 1968 (MIEE 1964); FEng 1976; FRSA 1964; MRI 1965; FRAeS 1969. Elected Mem., Royal Norwegian Scientific Soc., 1974; Corresp. Mem., Nat. Acad. of Engineering of Mexico, 1977. Lectures: Parsons Meml on Magnetohydrodynamics, 1961; First Wenca, Lagos, 1989. DUniv Open, 1982. Sir Robert Hadfield medal of Iron and Steel Inst. for studies on open hearth furnaces, 1949. *Publications:* The Science of Flames and Furnaces, 1952, 2nd edn, 1960; (with J. H. Chesters) The Influence of Port Design on Open Hearth Furnace Flames (Iron and Steel Institute Special Report 37), 1946; (with R. Edgeworth Johnstone) Pilot Plants, Models and Scale-up Methods in Chemical Engineering, 1957; (ed.) Air Pollution, 1957; Nuclear Propulsion, 1961; Man, Machines and Tomorrow, 1973; Machines—Masters or Slaves of Man?, 1973; (ed with R. J. Crookes) Energy and Humanity, 1974; (with E. R. Laithwaite) How to Invent, 1977; The Engineer's Conscience, 1980; Robots and Telechirs, 1983. *Recreations:* arboriculture, wood-carving. *Address:* Bell Farm, Brundish, Suffolk IP13 8BL. *Club:* Athenæum.

THROCKMORTON, Sir Anthony (John Benedict), 12th Bt *cr* 1642, of Coughton, Warwickshire; *b* 9 Feb. 1916; *s* of Herbert Throckmorton (*d* 1941) (3rd *s* of 10th Bt) and Ethel (*d* 1929), *d* of late Frederick Stapleton-Bretherton; *S* cousin, 1989; *m* 1972, Violet Virginia, *d* of late Anders Anderson. *Educ:* Beaumont Coll., Old Windsor, Berks. Ordained 1943, dio. Northampton; served Bury St Edmunds, Cambridge, Oundle; archdio. Seattle, 1952; retired 1963. Univ. of Washington Mailing Services, 1966–82. *Heir:* none. *Address:* 2006 Oakes Avenue, Everett, Washington 98201, USA. *T:* 206–258–1394.

THROCKMORTON, Clare McLaren, (Mrs Andrew McLaren); *see* Tritton, E. C.

THRUSH, Prof. Brian Arthur, FRS 1976; Professor of Physical Chemistry, since 1978, Head of Department of Chemistry, since 1988, University of Cambridge; Fellow, Emmanuel College, Cambridge, since 1960; *b* Hampstead Garden Suburb, 23 July 1928; *s* of late Arthur Albert Thrush and late Dorothy Charlotte Thrush (*née* Money); *m* 1958, Rosemary Catherine Terry, *d* of late George and Gertrude Terry, Ottawa; one *s* one *d*. *Educ:* Haberdashers' Aske's Sch.; Emmanuel Coll., Cambridge (Schol. 1946–50). BA 1949, MA, PhD 1953, ScD 1965. University of Cambridge: Demonstrator in Physical Chemistry, 1953; Asst Dir of Research, 1959; Lectr in Physical Chemistry, 1964, Reader, 1969; Hd of Dept of Physical Chemistry, 1986–88; Tutor, 1963–67, Dir of Studies in Chemistry, 1963–78, Vice-Master, 1986–90 and Acting Master, 1986–87, Emmanuel Coll. Consultant Physicist, US Nat. Bureau of Standards, Washington, 1957–58; Sen. Vis. Scientist, Nat. Res. Council, Ottawa, 1961, 1971, 1980. Tilden Lectr, Chem. Soc., 1965; Vis. Prof., Chinese Acad. of Science, 1980–; Member: Faraday Council, Chem. Soc., 1976–79; US Nat. Acad. of Scis Panel on Atmospheric Chemistry, 1975–80; Lawes Agric. Trust Cttee, 1979–89; NERC, 1985–90; Council, Royal Soc., 1989–91; NATO Panel on Global Change, 1989–. Pres., Chemistry Sect., BAAS, 1986. Mem., Academia Europaea, 1990. M. Polanyi Medal, RSC, 1980. *Publications:* papers on gas kinetics and spectroscopy in Proc. Royal Soc., Trans Faraday Soc., etc. *Recreations:* wine, fell-walking. *Address:* Brook Cottage, Pemberton Terrace, Cambridge CB2 1JA. *T:* Cambridge (0223) 357637. *Club:* Athenæum.

THUBRON, Colin Gerald Dryden; travel writer and novelist, since 1966; *b* 14 June 1939; *s* of Brig. Gerald Ernest Thubron, DSO, OBE, and Evelyn (*née* Dryden). *Educ:* Eton Coll. Editorial staff, Hutchinson & Co., 1959–62; freelance television film maker, Turkey, Japan, Morocco, 1962–64; Editorial staff, Macmillan Co., New York, 1964–65. FRSL 1969. *Publications:* non-fiction: Mirror to Damascus, 1967; The Hills of Adonis, 1968, 2nd edn 1987; Jerusalem, 1969, 2nd edn 1986; Journey into Cyprus, 1975; The Royal Opera House, 1982; Among the Russians, 1983; Behind the Wall, 1987 (Thomas Cook Award, Hawthorden Prize, 1988); novels: The God in the Mountain, 1977; Emperor, 1978; A Cruel Madness, 1984 (Silver Pen Award, 1985); Falling, 1989; Turning Back the Sun, 1991; contribs The Times, TLS, The Independent, The Spectator, Sunday Telegraph. *Address:* Garden Cottage, 27 St Ann's Villas, W11 4RT. *T:* 071–602 2522.

THUILLIER, Maj.-Gen. Leslie de Malapert, (Pete), CB 1958; CVO 1966; OBE 1944; *b* 26 Sept. 1905; *s* of late Lt-Col L. C. Thuillier, Indian Army; *m* 1936, Barbara Leonard Rawlins; one *s* two *d*. *Educ:* Berkhamsted Sch.; Royal Military Academy, Woolwich. Commissioned as 2nd Lieut, Royal Corps of Signals, 1926; Lieut, 1929; Captain, 1937; Staff Coll., Camberley, 1939; Temp. Major, 1940; Temp. Lt-Col, 1941; Temp. Colonel, 1945; Colonel, 1949, Brigadier, 1951; Maj.-Gen., 1955. War Office, 1940–41; Middle East and Italy, 1941–45; Chief Signal Officer, Northern Ireland District, 1945–46; British Troops in Egypt, 1951–53; Northern Command, 1954–55; Director of Telecommunications, War Office, 1955–58; Asst Sec., Cabinet Office, 1958–67. Leader, UK Govtl Mission to USA to discuss experimental civil mil. satellite communications systems, 1960; Mem., UK Delegn to Internat. Conf. in Paris, Rome and London to discuss estabt of internat. communication satellite systems, 1963–65. Consultant, Airwork Services Ltd, 1969–84. *Recreation:* gardening. *Address:* The Red Barn, Patney, Devizes, Wilts SN10 3RA. *T:* Chirton (038084) 669. *Club:* Naval and Military.

THURBURN, Gwynneth Loveday, OBE 1956; Hon. FCST; Principal, Central School of Speech and Drama, 1942–67; *b* 17 July 1899; *d* of Robert Augustus Thurburn and Bertha Loveday. *Educ:* Birklands, St Albans; Central School of Speech and Drama. Vice-Pres., Central Sch. of Speech and Drama. *Publication:* Voice and Speech. *Address:* Leiston Old Abbey, Leiston, Suffolk IP16 4RP.

THURLOW, 8th Baron *cr* 1792; **Francis Edward Hovell-Thurlow-Cumming-Bruce,** KCMG 1961 (CMG 1957); Governor and C-in-C of the Bahamas, 1968–72; *b* 9 March 1912; *s* of 6th Baron Thurlow and Grace Catherine, *d* of Rev. Henry Trotter; *S* brother, 1971; *m* 1949, Yvonne Diana Aubyn Wilson, CStJ 1969 (*d* 1990); one *s* two *d* (and one *s* decd). *Educ:* Shrewsbury Sch.; Trinity Coll., Cambridge. Asst Principal, Dept of Agriculture for Scotland, 1935; transferred to Dominions Office, 1937; Asst Private Sec. to Sec. of State, 1939; Asst Sec., Office of UK High Comr in NZ, 1939; Asst Sec., Office of UK High Comr in Canada, 1944; Secretariat, Meeting of Commonwealth Prime Ministers in London, 1946; served with UK Delegn at Paris Peace Conf., 1946, and at UN Gen. Assemblies, 1946 and 1948; Principal Private Sec. to Sec. of State, 1946; Asst Sec., CRO, 1948; Head of Political Div., Office of UK High Comr in New Delhi, 1949; Establishment Officer, CRO, 1952; Head of Commodities Dept, CRO, 1954; Adviser on External Affairs to Governor of Gold Coast, 1955; Deputy High Comr for the UK in Ghana, 1957; Asst Under-Sec. of State, CRO, April 1958; Deputy High Comr for the UK in Canada, 1958; High Comr for UK: in New Zealand, 1959–63; in Nigeria, 1964–67; Dep. Under-Sec. of State, FCO, 1964. KStJ 1969. *Heir:* *s* Hon. Roualeyn Robert

Hovell-Thurlow-Cumming-Bruce [*b* 13 April 1952; *m* 1980, Bridget Anne, *o d* of H. B. Ismay Cheape, Fossoway Lodge, Kinross; two *s* one *d*]. *Address:* 102 Leith Mansions, Grantully Road, W9 1LJ. *T:* 071–289 9664. *Club:* Travellers'.
See also Rt Hon. Sir J. R. H.-T.-Cumming-Bruce.

THURNHAM, Peter Giles; MP (C) Bolton North-East, since 1983; Chairman, Wathes Group of Cos (formerly First and Third Securities Ltd), since 1972; *b* 21 Aug. 1938; *s* of Giles Rymer Thurnham and Marjorie May (*née* Preston); *m* 1963, Sarah Janet Stroude; one *s* three *d* and one adopted *s*. *Educ:* Oundle Sch.; Peterhouse, Cambridge (MA 1967); Cranfield Inst. of Technol. (Dip. in Advanced Engrg, 1967); SRC/NATO Scholarship, Harvard Business Sch., Harvard Univ. (MBA 1969). CEng 1967; FIMechE 1985. Design Engr, NEI Parsons Ltd, 1957–66; Divl Dir, British Steam Specialties Ltd, 1967–72. Parliamentary Private Secretary: to Sec. of State for Employment, 1987–90; to Eric Forth, MP and Robert Jackson, MP, 1991–. Mem., Select Cttee on Employment, 1983–87. Treas., All-Party Parly Gp, Chemical Industry, 1985–87; Vice Chm., All-Party Parly Gp for Children, 1986–. Conservative Back Bench 1922 Committees: Vice-Chairman: Smaller Business Cttee, 1985–87; Home Improvement Sub-Cttee, 1986–87; Secretary: Employment Cttee, 1986–87; Social Security Cttee, 1990–91. Mem. Council, PSI, 1985–89. Founder Mem., 1985 and Mem. Cttee, 1985–, Progress, Campaign for Res. into Reproduction; Vice Pres., Campaign for Inter Country Adoption, 1991–. *Publications:* discussion papers; contrib. technical jls. *Recreation:* Lake District family life. *Address:* Hollin Hall, Crook, Kendal, Cumbria LA8 9HP. *T:* Staveley (0539) 821382; 4 North Court, Great Peter Street, SW1P 3LL. *T:* 071–799 5859.

THURSO, 2nd Viscount *cr* 1952, of Ulbster; **Robin Macdonald Sinclair;** Bt 1786; Baron of Thurso; JP; Lord-Lieutenant of Caithness, since 1973; Founder and first Chairman, Caithness Glass Ltd; Chairman: Sinclair Family Trust Ltd; Lochdhu Hotels Ltd; Thurso Fisheries Ltd; Director: Stephens (Plastics) Ltd; Ulbster Estates (Sporting) Ltd; *b* 24 Dec. 1922; *s* of 1st Viscount Thurso, KT, PC, CMG, and Marigold (*d* 1975), *d* of late Col J. S. Forbes, DSO; *S* father, 1970; *m* 1952, Margaret Beaumont Brokensha, *widow* of Lieut G. W. Brokensha, DSC, RN, and *d* of Col J. J. Robertson, DSO, DL, TD; two *s* one *d*. *Educ:* Eton; New College, Oxford; Edinburgh Univ. Served RAF, 1941–46; Flight Lieut 684 Sqdn, 540 Sqdn, commanded Edinburgh Univ. Air Sqdn, 1946; Captain of Boats, Edinburgh Univ. Boat Club, 1946–47, Green 1946, Blue, 1947. Caithness CC, 1949, 1952, 1955, 1958; Thurso Town Council, 1957, 1960, resigned 1961, re-elected 1965, 1968, 1971, Dean of Guild 1968, Baillie 1960, 1969, Police Judge 1971. President: North Country Cheviot Sheep Soc., 1951–54; Assoc. of Scottish Dist Salmon Fishery Bds (Chm., Caithness Dist Salmon Fishery Bd); Mem., Red Deer Commn, 1965–74. Chm. Caithness and Sutherland Youth Employment Cttee, 1957–75; Brigade Pres., Boys Brigade, 1985–. Mem. Council, Royal Nat. Mission to Deep Sea Fishermen, 1983–84. Pres., Highland Soc. of London, 1980–82. DL 1952, JP 1959, Vice-Lieutenant, 1964–73, Caithness. *Recreations:* fishing, shooting, amateur drama. *Heir:* *s* Hon. John Archibald Sinclair [*b* 10 Sept. 1953; *m* 1976, Marion Ticknor, *d* of Louis D. Sage, Connecticut, USA, and of Mrs A. R. Ward; two *s* one *d*]. *Address:* Thurso East Mains, Thurso, Caithness KW14 8HW. *T:* Thurso (0847) 62600. *Clubs:* Royal Air Force; New (Edinburgh).
See also A. M. Lyle.

THURSTON, Thea; *see* King, T.

THWAITE, Ann Barbara, FRSL 1987; writer; *b* London, 4 Oct. 1932; *d* of A. J. Harrop, LittD, PhD and H. M. Valentine of New Zealand; *m* 1955, Anthony Simon Thwaite, *qv*; four *d*. *Educ:* Marsden School, Wellington, NZ; Queen Elizabeth's Girls' Grammar Sch., Barnet; St Hilda's Coll., Oxford (MA 1959). Vis. Prof., Tokyo Women's Univ., 1985–86; Helen Stubbs Meml Lectr, Toronto Public Library, 1990. Regular reviewer of children's books; TLS, 1963–85; Guardian; TES. Governor, St Mary's Middle Sch., Long Stratton, Norfolk, 1990–. *Publications:* Waiting for the Party: the life of Frances Hodgson Burnett, 1974; (ed) My Oxford, 1977; Edmund Gosse: a literary landscape, 1984 (Duff Cooper Meml Prize, 1985); A. A. Milne: his life, 1990 (Whitbread Biography Award); (ed) Portraits from Life: essays by Edmund Gosse, 1991; *children's books include:* The Camelthorn Papers, 1969; Tracks, 1978; (ed) Allsorts 1–7, 1968–75; Allsorts of Poems, 1978. *Recreations:* other people's lives, messing about on the river. *Address:* The Mill House, Low Tharston, Norfolk NR15 2YN. *T:* Fundenhall (050841) 569. *Club:* Society of Authors.

THWAITE, Anthony Simon, OBE 1990; FRSL 1978; poet; Director, André Deutsch Ltd, since 1986; *b* 23 June 1930; *s* of Hartley Thwaite, JP, FSA, and Alice Evelyn Mallinson; *m* 1955, Ann Barbara Harrop (*see* A. B. Thwaite); four *d*. *Educ:* Kingswood Sch.; Christ Church, Oxford (MA). Vis. Lectr in English, Tokyo Univ., 1955–57; Producer, BBC, 1957–62; Literary Editor, The Listener, 1962–65; Asst Prof. of English, Univ. of Libya, 1965–67; Literary Editor, New Statesman, 1968–72; co-editor, Encounter, 1973–85. Henfield Writing Fellow, Univ. of East Anglia, 1972; Vis. Prof., Kuwait Univ., 1974; Japan Foundn Fellow, Tokyo Univ., 1985–86. Chm. of Judges, Booker Prize, 1986. Hon. Fellow, Westminster Coll., Oxford, 1990. Hon. DLitt Hull, 1989. Cholmondeley Poetry Award, 1983. *Publications: poetry:* Home Truths, 1957; The Owl in the Tree, 1963; The Stones of Emptiness, 1967 (Richard Hillary Memorial Prize, 1968); Inscriptions, 1973; New Confessions, 1974; A Portion for Foxes, 1977; Victorian Voices, 1980; Poems 1953–1983, 1984; Letter from Tokyo, 1987; Poems 1953–1988, 1989; *criticism:* Contemporary English Poetry, 1959; Poetry Today, 1973, rev. and expanded, 1985; Twentieth Century English Poetry, 1978; Six Centuries of Verse, 1984 (companion to Thames TV/Channel 4 series); *travel:* (with Roloff Beny) Japan, 1968; The Deserts of Hesperides, 1969; (with Roloff Beny and Peter Porter) In Italy, 1974; (with Roloff Beny) Odyssey: Mirror of the Mediterranean, 1981; *editor:* (with Geoffrey Bownas) Penguin Book of Japanese Verse, 1964; (with Peter Porter) The English Poets, 1974; (with Fleur Adcock) New Poetry 4, 1978; Larkin at Sixty, 1982; (with John Mole) Poetry 1945 to 1980, 1983; Collected Poems of Philip Larkin, 1988; *for children:* Beyond the Inhabited World, 1976. *Recreations:* archaeology, travel. *Address:* The Mill House, Low Tharston, Norfolk NR15 2YN. *T:* Fundenhall (050841) 569.

THWAITES, Prof. Sir Bryan, Kt 1986; MA, PhD; FIMA; Hon. Professor, Southampton University, since 1983; *b* London, 6 December 1923; *e s* of late Ernest James and Dorothy Marguerite Thwaites; *m* 1948, Katharine Mary, 4th *c* of late H. R. Harries and late Mrs L. Harries, Longhope, Glos; four *s* two *d*. *Educ:* Dulwich College; Winchester College; Clare College, Cambridge (Wrangler, 1944). Scientific Officer, National Physical Laboratory, 1944–47; Lecturer, Imperial College, London, 1947–51; Assistant Master, Winchester College, 1951–59; Professor of Theoretical Mechanics, Southampton Univ., 1959–66; Principal, Westfield Coll., London, 1966–83 (Hon. Fellow, 1983; Hon. Fellow, QMW, 1990). Gresham Prof. in Geometry, City Univ., 1969–72. Co-founder and Co-Chm., Education 2000, 1982–86. Hon. Sec. and Treas., Dulwich College Mission, 1946–57; inventor of the Thwaites Flap, 1947. Chm. and Mem. ARC Cttees, 1948–69. Special Lecturer, Imperial College, 1951–58. Chm., Southampton Mathematical Conf., 1961. Founding Director of the School Mathematics Project, 1961–75, Chm. of Trustees, 1966–83, Life Pres., 1984; Chm. of Internat. Mathematical Olympiad, first in UK, 1979; Chm. Adv. Council, ICL/CES, 1968–84. Member: Approved Sch. Cttee, Hampshire CC, 1954–58, 1961–66; US/UK (Fulbright) Commn, 1966–76; Davies Cttee on CSSB, 1969–70; Council, Kennedy Inst. of Rheumatology, 1969–71; Ct of London Univ., 1975–81; Council, Middlesex Hosp. Med. Sch., 1975–83; Court, Southampton Univ., 1981–. Chairman: Collegiate Council, London Univ., 1973–76; Delegacy, Goldsmiths' Coll., 1975–80. Mem. Acad. Advisory Committee: Univ. of Bath, 1964–71; Open Univ., 1969–75. Chairman of: Council of C of E Colleges of Education, 1969–71; Church of England Higher Educn Cttee, 1974–76; Northwick Park Hosp. Management Cttee, 1970–74; Brent and Harrow AHA, 1973–82; Wessex RHA, 1982–88; King's Fund Enquiry into Sen. Management Trng in NHS, 1975–76; Nat. Staff Cttee for Admin. and Clerical Staff, NHS, 1983–86; Enquiry into Radiotherapy Incident, Exeter Hosp., 1988. Chairman: Govs, Heythrop Coll., 1978–82; Friends of Winchester Coll., 1989–; Trustee: Westfield Coll. Develt Trust, 1979–83; Southampton Med. Sch. Trust, 1982–88; Richmond Coll., 1987–; City Tech. Colls, 1987–; Forbes Trust, 1987–; Patron, Winchester Detached Youth Project, 1990–. Mercier Lectr, Whitelands Coll., 1973; Foundn Lectr, Inst. of Health Policy Studies, Southampton Univ., 1987; 25th Anniv. Lectr, Nuffield Inst., Leeds Univ., 1988. Shadow Vice-Chancellor, Independent Univ., July-Nov. 1971. Hon. Life Mem., Math. Assoc., 1962. JP, Winchester City Bench, 1963–66. A Vice-Pres., Friends of GPDST, 1975–. Life. Mem. Council, 1964–, Pres., 1966–67, Institute of Mathematics and its Applications. Sponsor, Family and Youth Concern (formerly The Responsible Society), 1979–. *Publications:* (ed) Incompressible Aerodynamics, 1960; (ed) On Teaching Mathematics, 1961; The SMP: the first ten years, 1973; (ed) Hypotheses for Education in AD 2000, 1983; numerous contributions to Proc. Royal Soc., Reports and Memoranda of Aeronautical Research Council, Quart. Jl of Applied Mech., Jl of Royal Aeronautical Soc., etc. *Recreations:* music, sailing. *Address:* Milnthorpe, Winchester, Hants SO22 4NF. *T:* Winchester (0962) 852394. *Club:* Institute of Directors.

THWAITES, Jacqueline Ann, JP; Principal of Inchbald Schools of Design and Fine Arts since 1960; *b* 16 Dec. 1931; *d* of Mrs Donald Whitaker; *m* 1st, 1955, Michael Inchbald, *qv* (marr. diss. 1964); one *s* one *d*; 2nd, 1974, Brig. Peter Trevenen Thwaites (*d* 1991). *Educ:* Convent of the Sacred Heart, Brighton; House of Citizenship, London. Founded: Inchbald Sch. of Design, 1960; Inchbald Sch. of Fine Arts, 1970; Inchbald Sch. of Garden Design, 1972. Member: Monopolies Commn, 1972–75; Whitford Cttee on Copyright and Design, 1974–76; London Electricity Cons. Council, 1973–76; Westminster City Council (Warwick Ward), 1974–78. Mem., Vis. Cttee, RCA, 1986–90; International Society of Interior Designers: Acting Pres., London Chapter, 1987–90; Chm., 1990–. Trustee, St Peters' Research Trust, 1987–90. JP South Westminster, 1976. *Publications:* Directory of Interior Designers, 1966; Bedrooms, 1968; Design and Decoration, 1971. *Recreations:* fishing, travel. *Address:* The Manor, Ayot St Lawrence, Herts; (office) 32 Eccleston Square, SW1.

THWAITES, Ronald; QC 1987; *b* 21 Jan. 1946; *e s* of Stanley Thwaites and Aviva Thwaites; *m* 1972, Judith Myers; three *s* one *d*. *Educ:* Richard Hind Secondary Tech. Sch.; Grangefield Grammar Sch., Stockton-on-Tees; Kingston Coll. of Technol. (now Polytechnic); LLB London (external) 1968. Called to the Bar, Gray's Inn, 1970. *Recreations:* squash, swimming, lighting bonfires. *Address:* (chambers) 10 King's Bench Walk, Temple, EC4Y 7EB. *T:* 071–353 2501.

THWAITES, Roy; Director, SYT Ltd, Sheffield; *b* 13 Aug. 1931; *s* of Walter and Emily Alice Thwaites; *m* 1954, Margaret Anne (*née* Noble); one *s*. *Educ:* Southey Green Secondary Sch.; Sheffield Central Technical Sch. City Councillor, Sheffield, 1965, Chief Whip and Chm. of Transport Cttee, 1969–74; South Yorkshire County Council: Councillor, 1973–86; Chief Whip and Chm. Passenger Transport Authority, 1973–78; Dep. Leader, 1978–79; Leader, and Chm. of Policy Cttee, 1979–86. Mem., E Midlands Airport Consultative Gp, 1982–86. Chm., Yorks and Humberside County Councils Assoc., 1983–86; Vice-Chm., Assoc. of Metropolitan Authorities, 1984–86 (Dep. Chm., 1979–84); Mem., Local Authorities' Conditions of Service Adv. Bd, 1979–86; Vice-Chm., NJC Local Govt Manual Workers Employers, 1982. Mem., Special Employment Measures Adv. Gp, MSC, 1983–86. Trustee: Yorks Mining Museum Trust; S Yorks Apprentice Racing Trng Sch. *Recreation:* reading. *Address:* 14 Foxhill Drive, Sheffield S6 1GD. *T:* Sheffield (0742) 311222.

THYATEIRA AND GREAT BRITAIN, Archbishop of; *see* Theocharus, Archbishop Gregory.

THYNE, Malcolm Tod, MA; Headmaster, Fettes College, Edinburgh, since 1988; *b* 6 Nov. 1942; *s* of late Andrew Tod and Margaret Melrose Thyne; *m* 1969, Eleanor Christine Scott; two *s*. *Educ:* The Leys Sch., Cambridge; Clare Coll., Cambridge (MA Nat. Scis with Pt II in Chem.; Cert. of Educn). Asst Master, Edinburgh Acad., 1965–69; Asst Master, Oundle Sch., 1969–72, Housemaster, 1972–80; Headmaster, St Bees School, 1980–88. *Publications:* Periodicity, Atomic Structure and Bonding (Revised Nuffield Chemistry), 1976; contrib: Revised Nuffield Chemistry Handbook for Pupils, 1978; Revised Nuffield Chemistry Teachers' Guides, Vols II and III, 1978. *Recreation:* mountaineering. *Address:* The Lodge, Fettes College, Edinburgh EH4 1QX. *T:* 031–332 2281. *Club:* New (Edinburgh).

THYNN, Alexander; *see* Weymouth, Viscount.

THYNNE, family name of **Marquess of Bath.**

THYNNE, John Corelli James, CB 1990; PhD, DSc; Director General, Electronic Components Industry Federation, since 1991; *b* 27 Nov. 1931; *s* of Corelli James Thynne and Isabel Ann (*née* Griffiths). *Educ:* Milford Haven Grammar Sch.; Nottingham Univ. (BSc, PhD); Edinburgh Univ. (DSc). Res. Chemist, English Electric Co. (Guided Missile Div.), 1956–58; Fellow: Nat. Res. Council, Ottawa, 1958–59; UCLA, 1959–60; Univ. of Leeds, 1960–63; Lectr in Chemistry and Dir of Studies, Univ. of Edinburgh, 1963–70; Principal, DTI, 1970–73; Counsellor (Scientific), British Embassy, Moscow, 1974–78; Asst Sec., IT Div., DoI, 1978–83; Regl Dir, NW Reg., DTI, 1983–86; Under Sec., Electronic Applications Div., DTI, 1986–87; Under Sec., IT Div., DTI, 1987–89; Dir, Information Engrg Directorate, DTI, 1989–90; Under Sec. and Head, IT Div., DTI, 1990. Dir, Camrose Consultancy Services; Consultant: Ensigma Ltd; CSK Corp.; Sen. Advr, InterMatrix Gp. Member: Exec. Cttee, Nat. Electronics Council, 1986–90; NEDO Electronics Industries Sector Gp, 1986–90; Council, Nat. Interactive Video Centre, 1987–89; Management Bd, Science and Engrng Policy Studies Unit, 1991–; IT Adv. Bd, Welsh Develt Agency, 1991–. Mem. Council, Salford Univ., 1984–87; Vice Chm. Trustees, Mus. of Sci. and Industry, 1991–. *Publications:* contribs on physical chemistry to scientific journals. *Recreation:* cricket. *Address:* Romano House, 399–401 Strand, WC2R 0LT. *T:* 071–497 2311; 5 Eldon Grove, NW3 5PS. *T:* 071–794 1356. *Clubs:* Athenæum, Lansdowne, MCC.

THYSSEN BORNEMISZA de KASZON, Baron Hans Heinrich; Swiss industrialist and administrator; *b* The Hague, 13 April 1921; *s* of Dr Heinrich Thyssen-Bornemisza and Margit Bornemisza de Kaszon; *m* 1985, Carmen Cervera; three *s* one *d* by former marrs. *Educ:* Realgymnasium, The Hague; Fribourg Univ. Chm., Supervisory Bd,

Thyssen-Bornemisza Gp; Member: Trustee Council, Nat. Gallery of Art, Washington DC; Sotheby's Holdings Adv. Bd; Trustee, Mus. of Modern Art, NY; Hon. Pres., Mauritshuis, The Hague. Corresp. Mem., Acad. of Fine Arts, San Fernando, Madrid; owner of collection of paintings and works of art partially housed in Villa Favorita, Lugano. Gran Cruz, Orden Carlo III (Spain), 1988. *Address:* 56 Chester Square, SW1W 9AE; Villa Favorita, CH-6976, Castagnola, Switzerland. *Clubs:* Corviglia (St Moritz); Knickerbocker (NY).

TIARKS, Henry Frederic, FRAS; *b* 8 Sept. 1900; *e s* of late Frank Cyril Tiarks, OBE and Emmy Maria Franziska Brodermann; *m* 1st, 1930, Lady Millicent Olivia Taylour (marr. diss. 1936), *d* of 4th Marquess of Headfort; (one *s* decd); 2nd, 1936, Joan (*d* 1989), *d* of Francis Marshman-Bell; one *d* (one *s* decd). *Educ:* Eton College. Served European War 1914–19; Midshipman RNVR 1918; Sqdn Ldr AAF, 1940; Wing Commander, 1942–43, Retd (invalided). Mem., pre-war German Standstill Cttee (to negotiate repayment of German Debt); Negotiating Mem., British Banking Cttee for German Affairs, 1948–62. Former directorships: J. Henry Schroder & Co., Partner 1926–57, J. Henry Schroder & Co. Ltd, 1957–62, J. Henry Schroder Wagg & Co. Ltd, 1962 (May to Sept.), Schroders Ltd, 1962–65; J. Henry Schroder Banking Corpn, NY, 1945–62; Antofagasta (Chili) and Bolivia Railway Co. Ltd, 1926–67 (Chairman 1966–67); Securicor Ltd (founder) 1939–68; Pressed Steel Co. Ltd, 1936–66; Joseph Lucas Ltd, 1946–68; Bank of London & South America Ltd, 1958–68; Bank of London & Montreal Ltd, Nassau, 1959–69; Anglo-Scottish Amalgamated Corpn Ltd, 1935–68. Member: Dollar Exports Council, 1952–60; Western Hemisphere Exports Council, 1960–64; European League for Economic Co-operation (European Central Council); Internat. EFTA Action Cttee, 1967–75; Vice-Pres., European-Atlantic Gp. Mem., The Wildfowl Trust; Trustee, World Wildlife Fund (International), Morges, Switzerland, 1966–76; Founder Mem., WWF. Adena, Spain. Mem. Cttee of Managers, Royal Institution, 1960–62; Mem., British Astronomical Assoc.; Founder Mem., Sociedad Malagueña de Astronomia, Spain. Gran Oficial, Order of Merit, Chile. *Recreations:* golf, observational astronomy, photography, travel. *Address:* Casa Ina, Marbella Club, Marbella (Málaga), Spain. *T:* (52) 772650, *Fax:* (52) 860049. *Clubs:* Overseas Member: White's, Royal Thames Yacht; Royal and Ancient Golf (St Andrews), Swinley Forest Golf (Ascot), Royal St George's Golf (Sandwich); Woburn Golf and Country; Political Economy; Valderrama Golf (Sotogrande, Cadiz); The Brook (New York), Lyford Cay (Nassau, Bahamas); Royal Bermuda Yacht.

See also Marquess of Tavistock.

TIBBER, Anthony Harris; His Honour Judge Tibber; a Circuit Judge, since 1977; *b* 23 June 1926; *s* of Maurice and Priscilla Tibber; *m* 1954, Rhona Ann Salter; three *s*. *Educ:* University College School, London; Magdelen College School, Brackley. Served in Royal Signals, 1945–48; called to the Bar, Gray's Inn, 1950; a Recorder of the Crown Court, 1976. Member: Matrimonial Causes Rule Cttee, 1980–84; Matrimonial Causes Procedure Cttee (Booth Cttee), 1983–85. *Recreations:* cultivating, idling, pottering. *Address:* c/o Edmonton County Court, 59 Fore Street, N18 2TM. *T:* (home) 081–348 3605.

TIBBITS, Captain Sir David (Stanley), Kt 1976; DSC 1942; FNI; RN retired; Deputy Master and Chairman of Board, Trinity House, 1972–76; *b* 11 April 1911; *s* of late Hubert Tibbits, MB, BCh, Warwick, and Edith Lucy (*née* Harman) Tibbits; *m* 1938, Mary Florence Butterfield, Hamilton, Bermuda; two *d*. *Educ:* Wells House, Malvern Wells; RNC, Dartmouth. RN Cadet 1925; navigation specialist, 1934; served War, 1939–45, HMS York, Devonshire and Anson; Comdr 1946; Captain 1953; Dir, Radio Equipment Dept, Admty, 1953–56; in comd, HM Ships Manxman, Dryad and Hermes, 1956–61; retd. Trinity House: Elder Brother, 1961; Warden, 1969. Hon. Sec., King George's Fund for Sailors, 1974–80; Lay Vice-Pres., Missions to Seamen, 1972–. Engaged in various voluntary activities in Bermuda including: Mem., Marine Board and Port Authy, 1978–; Chm., Pilotage Commn, 1978–; Pres., Sea Cadet and Sail Trng Assoc., 1978–87; Chm. and Jt Pres., Bermuda Soc. for Blind, 1982– (Mem. Cttee, 1977–). Mem. Court, Worshipful Co. of Shipwrights, 1976–. Trustee, National Maritime Museum, 1974–77. Governor, Pangbourne Coll., 1973–78. Founder Mem., 1972, Fellow 1979–, Nautical Inst. *Recreations:* sailing, colour photography, classical music. *Address:* Harting Hill, PO Box HM 1419, Hamilton, Bermuda HM FX; c/o Trinity House, Tower Hill, EC3N 4DH. *Clubs:* Army and Navy, Hurlingham; Royal Yacht Squadron (Naval Mem.); Royal Bermuda Yacht (Bermuda).

TIBBS, Craigie John, FRICS; Head of Estates and Planning Department, BBC, 1980; *b* 17 Feb. 1935; *s* of Arthur and Gladys Tibbs; *m* 1959, Carol Ann (*née* Linsell); two *d* *Educ:* King George V School, Southport; Heaton Grammar School, Newcastle upon Tyne; RMA Sandhurst; London University. BSc; FRICS. Trainee Estates Officer, London Transport, 1959–62; Valuer and Senior Valuer, Luton Corp., 1962–67; Chief Valuer and Surveyor, London Borough of Newham, 1967–71; Development Officer, City of Birmingham, 1971–73; County Estates Officer, Hants County Council, 1973–76; Under Sec. (Dir of Land Economy), Depts of Environment and Transport, 1976–80. *Recreations:* music, reading, writing, walking, swimming, golf, the Well Game.

TIBBS, (Geoffrey) Michael (Graydon), OBE 1987; Secretary of the Royal College of Physicians, 1968–86 (Secretary of Joint Faculty of Community Medicine, 1971–72 and of Faculty of Occupational Medicine, 1978–86); *b* 21 Nov. 1921; *s* of Rev. Geoffrey Wilberforce Tibbs, sometime Chaplain RN and Vicar of Lynchmere, Sussex, and Margaret Florence Tibbs (*née* Skinner); *m* 1951, Anne Rosemary Wortley; two *s*. *Educ:* Berkhamsted Sch.; St Peter's Hall, Oxford. BA Hons Geography, 1948; MA 1952. FInstAM; MIPM; FRGS. Served RNVR, Ordinary Seaman/Lieut, 1940–46 (despatches), HMS Cottesmore, HMS Sheffield, HM S/M Tantalus, HM S/M Varne. Sudan Political Service, Kordofan Province, 1949–55: seconded to MECAS, 1950; Dist Comr, Dar Messeria District, 1953. Various appointments in personnel, organisation and overseas services depts, Automobile Assoc., 1955–68. Hon. Mem., Soc. of Occupational Medicine, 1983; Hon. FRCP 1986; Hon. FFOM 1986; Hon. FFCM 1987. Freeman, City of London, 1986. *Publication:* A Look at Lynchmere, 1990. *Recreations:* producing pantomimes, parish affairs, making bonfires. *Address:* Welkin, Lynchmere Ridge, Haslemere, Surrey GU27 3PP. *T:* Haslemere (0428) 643120, 642176. *Club:* Naval.

TICEHURST, Maj.-Gen. Arthur Christopher; Commander Medical, HQ UK Land Forces, since 1990; *b* 22 April 1933; *s* of late Arthur William Ticehurst and of Edith Violet Ticehurst (*née* Adams); *m* 1959, Valerie Jean Hughes; four *s*. *Educ:* Chichester High Sch.; King's Coll. London; Westminster Hosp. (MB BS 1955). MFCM 1977; FFPHM 1990. House appointments, Westminster Hosp., 1955–56; National Service, RAMC, 1958–60; Regular Commn, 1961; Medical Officer: Kent, Cyprus, 1958–61; Singapore, Brunei, Thailand, 1962–65; CO, 11 Field Dressing Station, BAOR, 1965–67; Instructor, RAMC Trng Centre, 1967–68; Army Staff Coll., 1968–69; MoD, 1970–72; CO, 4 Armoured Field Ambulance, 1972–74; ndc, 1974–75; Army Med. Directorate, MoD, 1976–80; Chief Instructor, RAMC Trng Centre, 1980–83; Comdr, Med. HQ, NE Dist, 1983–84; Dep. Comdr, Med. HQ, BAOR, 1984–87; Asst Surgeon Gen., MoD, 1987–90; Dir, Med. Ops and Plans, MoD, 1990. OStJ 1972. *Publications:* articles on use of medical services in disaster relief to professional jls. *Recreations:* tennis, squash, board sailing, military history, maps, water colours. *Address:* c/o Lloyds Bank, 19 Obelisk Street, Camberley, Surrey.

TICKELL, Sir Crispin (Charles Cervantes), GCMG 1989; KCVO 1983 (MVO 1958); HM Diplomatic Service, retired; Warden, Green College, University of Oxford, since 1990; President, Royal Geographical Society, since 1990; *b* 25 Aug. 1930; *s* of late Jerrard Tickell and Renée (*née* Haynes); *m* 1st, 1954, Chloë (marr. diss. 1976), *d* of late Sir James Gunn, RA, PRP; two *s* one *d*; 2nd, 1977, Penelope, *d* of late Dr Vernon Thorne Thorne. *Educ:* Westminster (King's Schol.); Christ Church, Oxford (Hinchliffe and Hon. Schol.). 1st Cl. Hons Mod. Hist. 1952. Served with Coldstream Guards, 1952–54; entered HM Diplomatic Service, 1954. Served at: Foreign Office, 1954–55; The Hague, 1955–58; Mexico, 1958–61; FO (Planning Staff), 1961–64; Paris, 1964–70; Private Sec. to successive Ministers responsible for negotiations for British entry into the European Communities, 1970–72; Head of Western Organisations Dept, FCO, 1972–75; Fellow, Center for Internat. Affairs, Harvard Univ., 1975–76; Chef de Cabinet to Pres. of Commn of European Communities, 1977–81; Vis. Fellow, All Souls Coll., Oxford, 1981; Ambassador to Mexico, 1981–83; Dep. Under-Sec. of State, FCO, 1983–84; Perm. Sec., ODA, 1984–87; British Perm. Rep. to UN, 1987–90. Director: IBM (UK), 1990–; BOC Envmtl Foundn, 1990–; Mexican Horizons, 1991–. Chairman: Internat. Inst. for Envmt and Develt, 1990–; Climate Inst. of Washington, 1990–; Earthwatch (Europe), 1990; Pres., Marine Biol. Assoc., 1990–. FRGS 1985; FZS 1986. Mem. (Dr *hc*), Mexican Acad. of Internat. Law, 1983 (Orden Academico del Derecho, de la Cultura y de la Paz, 1989). Hon. LLD: Massachusetts, 1990; Bristol, 1991; Birmingham, 1991; Hon. DSc: UEA, 1990; Sussex, 1991; Dr *hc*: Central London Poly., 1990; Stirling, 1990. Officer, Order of Orange Nassau (Netherlands), 1958. *Publications:* (contrib.) The Evacuees, 1968; (contrib.) Life After Death, 1976; Climatic Change and World Affairs, 1977, 1986 (contrib.) The United Kingdom/The United Nations, 1990; (contrib.) Sustaining Earth, 1990. *Recreations:* climatology; palæohistory; art, especially pre-Columbiana; mountains. *Address:* Warden's Lodgings, Green College, Oxford OX2 6HG. *Club:* Brooks's.

TICKELL, Maj.-Gen. Marston Eustace, CBE 1973 (MBE 1955); MC 1945; CEng, FICE; Commandant Royal Military College of Science, 1975–78, retired; *b* 18 Nov. 1923; *er s* of late Maj.-Gen. Sir Eustace Tickell, KBE, CB, MC; *m* 1961, Pamela Vere, *d* of Vice-Adm. A. D. Read, CB; no *c*. *Educ:* Wellington Coll.; Peterhouse, Cambridge (MA). Commnd in RE, 1944; NW Europe Campaign and Middle East, 1944–45; psc 1954; Mil. Ops, MoD, 1955–57; served in Libya, Cyprus and Jordan, 1958–59; US Armed Forces Staff Coll. and Instructor RMCS and Staff Coll., 1959–62; Defence Planning Staff, MoD, 1962–64; CRE 4th Div., 1964–66; comd 12 Engr Bde, 1967–69; Indian Nat. Defence Coll., 1970; COS Northern Ireland, 1971–72; E-in-C, MoD, 1972–75. Col Comdt, RE, 1978–83. Hon. Col, Engr and Transport Staff Corps, 1983–88. Pres., Instn of Royal Engrs, 1979–82. FICE 1974. *Recreation:* sailing. *Address:* The Old Vicarage, Branscombe, Seaton, Devon EX12 3DW. *Clubs:* Army and Navy; Royal Ocean Racing.

TICKLE, Brian Percival, CB 1985; Senior Registrar of the Family Division, High Court of Justice, 1982–88 (Registrar, 1970–88); *b* 31 Oct. 1921; *s* of late William Tickle and Lucy (*née* Percival); *m* 1945, Margaret Alice Pendrey; one *s* one *d*. *Educ:* The Judd Sch., Tonbridge. Entered Civil Service, 1938. Served War, Royal Signals, 1941–46. Civil Service, 1946–70. Member: Matrimonial Causes Rules Cttee, 1982–88; Independent Schs Tribunal, 1988–. *Publications:* Rees Divorce Handbook, 1963; Atkins Court Forms and Precedents (Probate), 1974, 2nd edn 1984. *Recreation:* golf. *Address:* Hillbrow Court, 1A Royal Chase, Tunbridge Wells, Kent TN4 8AX.

TICKLE, Rt. Rev. Gerard William; Titular Bishop of Bela; *b* 2 Nov. 1909; 2nd *s* of William Joseph Tickle and Rosanna Kelly. *Educ:* Douai School; Venerable English College, Rome. Priest, 1934. Curate at St Joseph's Church, Sale, 1935–41; Army Chaplain, 1941–46; Vice-Rector, 1946, Rector, 1952, Venerable English College, Rome. Bishop-in-Ordinary to HM Forces, 1963–78; Apostolic Administrator, 1978–79. Privy Chamberlain to Pope Pius XII, 1949; Domestic Prelate to Pope Pius XII, 1953. *Address:* Ty Mair, 115 Mwrog Street, Ruthin, Clwyd LL15 1LE.

TIDBURY, Sir Charles (Henderson), Kt 1989; DL; Chairman, William and Mary Tercentenary Trust Ltd, since 1986; *b* 26 Jan. 1926; *s* of late Brig. O. H. Tidbury, MC, and Beryl (*née* Pearce); *m* Anne, *d* of late Brig. H. E. Russell, DSO, and of Lady O'Connor; two *s* three *d*. *Educ:* Eton Coll. Served KRRC, 1943–52: Palestine, 1946–48 (despatches); Queen's Westminsters TA, 1952–60. Joined Whitbread & Co. Ltd, 1952; a Man. Dir, 1959; Chief Exec., 1974; Dep. Chm., 1977; Chm., 1978–84; Dir, 1984–88. Chm., Brickwoods Brewery Ltd, 1966–71. Director: Whitbread Investment Co. PLC; Barclays PLC; Barclays Bank PLC; Mercantile Gp plc (formerly Mercantile Credit Co.), 1985–91; Nabisco Gp Ltd, 1985–88; Vaux Gp plc, 1985–91; ICL (Europe, formerly UK), 1985–; Pearl Assurance PLC, 1986–. Pres., Inst. of Brewing, 1976–78; Chm., 1982–84, Vice-Pres., 1985–, Brewers' Soc.; President: Shire Horse Soc., 1985–87 (Jt Vice-Pres., 1988–); British Inst. of Innkeeping, 1985–. Chairman: Mary Rose Development Trust, 1980–86; Brewing Res. Foundn, 1985–. Trustee, Nat. Maritime Museum, 1984–. Member, Board of Governors: Nat. Heart and Chest Hosps, 1988–90; Portsmouth Polytechnic, 1988–. Master, Brewers' Co., 1988–89. DL Hampshire, 1989. *Recreations:* my family, sailing, countryside. *Address:* Crocker Hill Farm, Forest Lane, Wickham, Hants PO17 5DW; 22 Ursula Street, SW11 3DW; (office) 20 Queen Anne's Gate, SW1H 9AA. *T:* 071–222 7060. *Clubs:* Brooks's; Royal Yacht Squadron, Island Sailing, Bembridge Sailing.

TIDY, Morley David; Assistant Under-Secretary of State (Personnel) (Air), Ministry of Defence, since 1990; *b* 23 April 1933; *s* of James Morley and Winnie Tidy; *m* 1957, Wendy Ann Bennett; one *s* two *d*. *Educ:* Hove County Grammar School; Magdalene College, Cambridge (MA). National Service, RAF, 1951–53. Dept of Employment, 1956–57; HM Inspector of Taxes, Inland Revenue, 1957–66; MoD, 1966; Manchester Business School, 1967; First Sec. (Defence), UK Delegn to NATO, 1969–72; MoD, 1973; RCDS, 1977; Chief Officer, SBAA, Cyprus, 1980–83; Asst Under-Sec., Air Staff, MoD, 1984; Asst Under Sec. (Ordnance), MoD, 1985; Asst Under Sec., Defence Export Services, Administration, MoD, 1988. *Recreations:* tennis, cricket, golf, jigsaws.

TIDY, William Edward, (Bill); freelance cartoonist, since 1958; writer, playwright, television and radio presenter; Managing Director, Bill Tidy Ltd, since 1980; *b* 9 Oct. 1933; *s* of William Edward Tidy and Catherine Price; *m* 1960, Rosa Colotti; two *s* one *d*. *Educ:* Anfield Road Jun. Sch., Liverpool; St Margaret's Sen. Sch., Anfield, Liverpool. Shipping office boy, R. P. Houston, Liverpool, 1950–51. Served RE, 1952–55. Layout artist, Pagan Smith Advertising Agency, 1956–58. Presented for BBC TV: Tidy Up Walsall; Tidy Up Naples; My City; radio broadcasting includes: The News Quiz (also Guest Presenter); Midweek (also Guest Presenter); I'm Sorry I Haven't a Clue; Back to Square One; radio adaptation, The Fosdyke Saga (with John Junkin). *Publications: (written and illustrated):* Sporting Chance, 1961; O Cleo, 1962; Laugh with Bill Tidy, 1966; Up the Reds, Up the Blues, 1968; Tidy's World, 1969; The Cloggies, 1969; Tidy Again, 1970; The Fosdyke Saga (14 vols), 1972–85; The Cloggies Dance Back, 1973; The Great Eric Ackroyd Disaster, 1976; The Cloggies Are Back, 1977; Mine's a Pint, What's Yours (The Kegbuster Story), 1981; Robbie and the Blobbies, 1982; Bill Tidy's Little Rude

Book, 1984; A Day at Cringemound School, 1985; Bill Tidy's Book of Classic Cockups, 1985; The World's Worst Golf Club, 1987; The Incredible Bed, 1990; has also illustrated over seventy other books; contrib. to New Scientist, Gen. Practioner. *Recreation:* cricket (Lord's Taverners'). *Address:* The Yews, 59 High Street, Kegworth, Derby DE7 2DA. *T:* Kegworth (05097) 3939. *Clubs:* Cartoonist of Great Britain; Nottinghamshire County Cricket.

TIERNEY, Dom Francis Alphonsus, OSB; MA; Parish Priest since 1977; *b* 7 March 1910; *s* of James Francis Tierney and Alice Mary Claypoole. *Educ:* Douai; St Benet's Hall, Oxford. Headmaster of: Douai Junior School, Ditcham Park, 1948–52; Douai Sch., 1952–73. Prior of Douai Abbey, 1973–77. *Address:* St Gregory's Priory, 10 St James Square, Cheltenham, Glos GL50 3PR. *T:* Cheltenham (0242) 523737.

TIERNEY, Sydney; JP; President, 1977–81, and 1983–91, and National Officer, since 1979, Union of Shop, Distributive and Allied Workers; Chairman, Labour Party, 1986–87 (Vice-Chairman, 1985–86); *b* Sept. 1923; *m* Margaret Olive (*née* Hannah). *Educ:* Secondary Modern Sch., Dearne; Plater Coll., Oxford. Mem., Co-operative Party; an Official and Member, USDAW. Vice-Chm., W Midlands Labour Gp of MPs, 1974–79; Mem., Labour Party NEC, to 1990. MP (Lab) Birmingham, Yardley, Feb. 1974–1979; PPS to Min. of State for Agriculture, 1976–79. JP Leicester, 1966. *Address:* Rocklands, 56 Priory Lane, Kents Bank, Grange Over Sands, Cumbria LA11 7BJ.

TIKARAM, Sir Moti, KBE 1980; **Hon. Justice Sir Moti Tikaram;** Justice of the Court of Appeal, Fiji, since 1988; *b* 18 March 1925; *s* of Tikaram and Singari; *m* 1944, Satyawati (*d* 1981); two *s* one *d*. *Educ:* Marist Brothers High Sch., Suva; Victoria Univ., Wellington, NZ (LLB 1954). Started law practice, 1954; Stipendiary Magistrate, 1960; Puisne Judge, 1968; acted as Chief Justice, 1971 and 1990. Ombudsman, Fiji, 1972–87. Patron, Fiji Lawn Tennis Assoc. Scouting Medal of Merit, 1986. *Publications:* articles in The Pacific Way and in Recent Law 131. *Recreation:* tennis. *Address:* (home) PO Box 514, 45 Domain Road, Suva, Fiji. *T:* 302005; (office) PO Box 2215, Government Buildings, Suva. *T:* 211489. *Clubs:* Fiji, Fiji Golf (Suva).

TILBERIS, Elizabeth Jane; Editor in Chief, Vogue Magazine, since 1987; *b* 7 Sept. 1947; *d* of Thomas Stuart-Black Kelly and Janet Storrie Kelly; *m* 1971, Andrew Tilberis; two *s*. *Educ:* Malvern Girl's Coll.; Jacob Kramer Coll., Leeds; Leicester College of Art (BA Art and Design). Vogue Magazine: Fashion Asst, 1970; Fashion Editor, 1973; Exec. Fashion Editor, 1985; Fashion Dir, 1986. *Recreations:* gardening, music. *Address:* Vogue House, Hanover Square, W1R 0AD. *T:* 071–499 9080.

TILEY, Arthur, CBE 1972; JP; retired as Insurance Broker and Marine Underwriter; *b* 17 January 1910; *m* 1936, Mary, *d* of late Craven and Mary Tankard, Great Horton; one *s* one *d*. *Educ:* Grange High School, Bradford. Treasurer, Young Women's Christian Association, Bradford, 1934–50. Contested (C and Nat. L) Bradford Central, 1951. MP (C and Nat. L) Bradford West, 1955–66. Opposition front bench spokesman on pensions and national insurance, 1964–66. Served War of 1939–45 as Senior Company Officer, National Fire Service. Mem. Council, Churchill Memorial Trust, 1965–76. Hon. MA Bradford, 1981. JP Bradford, 1967. *Address:* 40 The Majestic, North Promenade, St Annes-on-Sea, Lancs FY8 2LZ.

TILEY, Prof. John; Professor of the Law of Taxation, University of Cambridge, since 1990; Fellow, since 1967, Vice-President, since 1988, Queen's College, Cambridge; a Recorder of the Crown Court, since 1989; *b* 25 Feb. 1941; *s* of William Arthur Tiley, OBE and Audrey Ellen (*née* Burton); *m* 1964, Jillinda Millicent Draper; two *s* one *d*. *Educ:* Winchester Coll.; Lincoln Coll., Oxford (BA 1962; BCL 1963; MA 1967). Called to the Bar, Inner Temple, 1964. Lecturer: Lincoln Coll., Oxford, 1963–64; Univ. of Birmingham, 1964–67; University of Cambridge: Asst Lectr, 1967–72; Lectr, 1972–87; Reader in Law of Taxation, 1987–90. Visiting Professor: Dalhousie Univ., 1972–73; Univ. of W Ontario, 1978–79; Univ. of Melbourne, 1979; Case Western Reserve Univ., 1985–86. *Publications:* Revenue Law, 1976, 3rd edn 1981; author and editor, various legal texts; contrib. to legal jls. *Recreations:* walking, cricket, music. *Address:* Queen's College, Cambridge CB3 9ET. *T:* Cambridge (0223) 335546.

TILL, Barry Dorn; Principal of Morley College, London, 1965–86; Adviser, 1973–86, Director, since 1986, Baring Foundation; *b* 1 June 1923; *s* of John Johnson and Hilda Lucy Till; *m* 1st, 1954, Shirley Philipson (marr. diss. 1965); two *s*; 2nd, 1966, Antonia, *d* of Sir Michael Clapham, *qv*; two *d*. *Educ:* Harrow; Jesus College and Westcott House, Cambridge. 1st Class Theology Pt III, 1949; Lightfoot Scholar, 1949. Served War, Coldstream Guards, 1942–46; Italian campaign. Deacon, 1950; Priest, 1951; Asst Curate, Bury Parish Church, Lancs, 1950–53; Fellow of Jesus Coll., Cambridge, 1953–60, Chaplain, 1953–56, Dean, 1956–60, Tutor, 1957–60; Univ. Preacher, Cambridge, 1955; Examining Chaplain to Bishop of Lichfield, 1957–60; Dean of Hong Kong, 1960–64. Chm., Asia Christian Colleges Assoc., 1968–76, Vice-Pres., 1976–. Governor, British Inst. of Recorded Sound, 1967–72; Mem., Adv. Council, V&A Museum, 1977–83. Chairman: Greater London AACE, 1976–82; Work-Out, 1986–89; Mary Ward Settlement, 1987–. Founder Mem., Exec. Cttee, Assoc. of Charitable Foundns, 1989–. Governor, St Olaf's Grammar Sch., 1973–82 (Chm., 1980–82); Mem., Cultural Cttee, European Culture Foundn, 1976–78. Trustee: Thomas Cubitt Trust, 1978–; LentA Educnl Trust, 1987– (Chm., 1990–). *Publications:* contrib. to The Historic Episcopate, 1954; Change and Exchange, 1964; Changing Frontiers in the Mission of the Church, 1965; contrib. to A Holy Week Manual, 1967; The Churches Search for Unity, 1972. *Recreations:* travel, gardening, opera. *Address:* 44 Canonbury Square, N1 2AW. *T:* 071–359 0708. *Club:* Brooks's.

TILL, Ven. Michael Stanley; Archdeacon of Canterbury, since 1986; *b* 19 Nov. 1935; *s* of Stanley Brierley Till and Mary Till; *m* 1965, Tessa, *d* of Capt. Stephen Roskill; one *s* one *d*. *Educ:* Brighton, Hove and Sussex Grammar School; Lincoln Coll., Oxford (BA, History 1960, Theology 1962; MA 1967); Westcott House, Cambridge. Curate, St John's, St John's Wood, NW8, 1964–67; Chaplain 1967–70, Dean and Fellow 1970–81, King's College, Cambridge; Vicar of All Saints', Fulham, 1981–86; Area Dean, Hammersmith and Fulham, 1984–86. *Address:* 29 The Precincts, Canterbury, Kent CT1 2EP. *T:* Canterbury (0227) 463036.

TILLARD, Maj.-Gen. Philip Blencowe, CBE 1973; (OBE 1966); Chairman, East Sussex British Field Sports Society, since 1988; *b* 2 Jan. 1923; *s* of late Brig. John Arthur Stuart Tillard, OBE, MC and of Margaret Penelope (*née* Blencowe); *m* 1953, Patricia Susan (*née* Robertson) (*d* 1988); three *s* one *d*. *Educ:* Winchester College. Commnd into 60th Rifles, 1942; served Syria, Italy and Greece, 1943–45; ADC to GOC 2 Div. and to Army Comdr Malaya, 1946; ADC to GOC N Midland Dist, 1947; transf. to 13th/18th Royal Hussars (QMO), 1947; served in Libya, Malaya (despatches, 1950) and Germany, comd Regt, 1964–66; psc 1956; jssc 1962; Comdr RAC 3rd Div., 1967–69; BGS (Army Trng), MoD, 1970–73 (produced: Tillard Report on RMA Sandhurst course for young officers; Suffield Report setting up Army tank trng area in Canada); ADC to the Queen, 1970–73; COS, BAOR, 1973–76. With Borough of Brighton, 1977–87. *Recreations:* normal family pursuits; shooting. *Address:* Church House, Chailey Green, Lewes, East Sussex BN8 4DA. *T:* Newick (082572) 2759. *Clubs:* Farmers'; Sussex.

TILLER, Rev. Canon John; Chancellor and Canon Residentiary of Hereford Cathedral, since 1984; Diocesan Director of Training, Hereford, since 1991; *b* 22 June 1938; *s* of Harry Maurice Tiller and Lucille Maisie Tiller; *m* 1961, Ruth Alison (*née* Watson); two *s* one *d*. *Educ:* St Albans Sch.; Christ Church, Oxford (MA, 2nd Cl. Mod. Hist.); Bristol Univ. (MLitt). Ordained deacon 1962, priest 1963, St Albans. Asst Curate: St Cuthbert, Bedford, 1962–65; Widcombe, Bath, 1965–67; Chaplain and Tutor, Tyndale Hall, Bristol, 1967–71; Lectr in Church History and Worship, Trinity Coll., Bristol, 1971–73; Priest-in-Charge, Christ Church, Bedford, 1973–78; Chief Sec., ACCM, 1978–84. Hon. Canon of St Albans Cathedral, 1979–84. *Publications:* The Service of Holy Communion and its Revision (with R. T. Beckwith), 1972; A Modern Liturgical Bibliography, 1974; The Great Acquittal, 1980; Puritan, Pietist, Pentecostalist, 1982; A Strategy for the Church's Ministry, 1983; The Gospel Community, 1987; contribs to: The New International Dictionary of the Christian Church, 1974; Anglican Worship Today, 1980; New Dictionary of Christian Theology, 1988; The Parish Church?, 1988. *Recreations:* walking, bird-watching, spuddling. *Address:* Canon's House, 3 St John Street, Hereford HR1 2NB. *T:* Hereford (0432) 265659.

TILLEY, John Vincent; Parliamentary Secretary of the Co-operative Union, since 1988; *b* June 1941; *m* Kathryn Riley; two *d*. Mem., Wandsworth Borough Council, 1971–78. Mem., Co-operative Party. MP (Lab) Lambeth Central, Apr. 1978–83. Contested (Lab): Kensington Div. of Kensington and Chelsea, Feb. and Oct. 1974; Southwark and Bermondsey, 1983. Chief Economic Advisor, London Borough of Hackney, 1983–88. *Address:* 35 Point Hill, SE10.

TILLING, George Henry Garfield; Chairman, Scottish Postal Board, 1977–84, retired; *b* 24 Jan. 1924; *s* of late Thomas and Anne Tilling; *m* 1956, Margaret Meriel, *d* of late Rear-Adm. Sir Alexander McGlashan, KBE, CB, DSO; two *s* two *d*. *Educ:* Hardye's Sch., Dorchester; University Coll., Oxford (Open Exhibnr, Kitchener Schol., Farquharson Prizeman, MA). Served War of 1939–45, NW Europe: Captain, Dorset Regt, 1943–46. Post Office: Asst Principal, 1948; Principal, 1953; Private Sec. to Postmaster General, 1964; Dep. Dir of Finance, 1965; Dir, Eastern Postal Region, 1967; Sec. of the Post Office, 1973–75; Dir of Postal Ops, 1975–77. Mem. Council, Lord Kitchener Nat. Meml Fund, 1979–90. Mem. Council, Order of St John for London, 1975–77, Mem. Cttee of the Order for Edinburgh, 1978–87. Trustee, Bield Retirement Housing Trust, 1988–. Hon. Mem., St Andrew's Ambulance Assoc., 1980. CStJ. FSAScot; FCIT. *Recreations:* orders and medals, heraldry, uniforms. *Address:* Standpretty, Gorebridge, Midlothian EH23 4QG. *T:* Gorebridge (0875) 22409.

TILLINGHAST, Charles Carpenter, Jr; aviation and financial consultant; *b* 30 Jan. 1911; *s* of Charles Carpenter Tillinghast and Adelaide Barrows Shaw; *m* 1935, Elizabeth (Lisette) Judd Micoleau; one *s* three *d*. *Educ:* Horace Mann Sch.; Brown Univ. (PhB); Columbia Univ. (JD). Associate, Hughes, Schurman & Dwight, 1935–37; Dep. Asst Dist Attorney, NY County, 1938–40; Associate, Hughes, Richards, Hubbard & Ewing, 1940–42; Partner, Hughes, Hubbard and Ewing (and successor firm, Hughes, Hubbard, Blair & Reed), 1942–57; Vice-Pres. and Dir, The Bendix Corp., 1957–61; Pres. and Chief Exec. Officer, Trans World Airlines Inc., 1961–69 (Director, 1961–81; Chm. and Chief Exec. Officer, 1969–76); Vice-Chm., White, Weld & Co. Inc., 1977–78; Man. Dir, Merrill Lynch White Weld Capital Markets Gp, 1978–83; Vice-Pres., Merrill Lynch Pierce Fenner & Smith Inc., 1978–84; Director: Amstar Corp., 1964–83; Merck & Co., 1962–83; Trustee: Mutual Life Ins. Co. of NY, 1966–84; Brown Univ., 1954–61, 1965–79 (Chancellor, 1968–79; Fellow, 1979–); Mem. IATA Executive Cttee, 1969–76. Hon. Degrees: LHD, South Dakota Sch. of Mines and Tech., 1959; LLD: Franklin Coll., 1963; Univ. of Redlands, 1964; Brown Univ., 1967; Drury Coll., 1967; William Jewell Coll., 1973. *Recreations:* golf, shooting, gardening, woodworking, reading, Philharmonic and opera. *Address:* 25 John Street, Providence, RI 02906, USA. *T:* 401–861–6676. *Clubs:* Blind Brook, Brown Univ., Wings (NY); Hope (RI); Sakonnet Golf (all in USA).

TILLOTSON, Maj.-Gen. Henry Michael, CB 1983; CBE 1976 (OBE 1970, MBE 1956); *b* 12 May 1928; *er s* of Henry Tillotson, Keighley, Yorks; *m* 1956, Angela, *d* of Bertram Wadsworth Shaw, E Yorks; two *s* one *d*. *Educ:* Chesterfield Sch.; RMA Sandhurst. Commnd E Yorks Regt, 1948; served: Austria, 1948–50; Germany, 1951–52; Indo-China (attached French Union Forces), 1953; Malaya, 1953–55; Staff Coll., Camberley, 1958; JSSC, Latimer, 1963–64; Malaysia, 1964–65; S Arabia, 1965–67 (Queen's Commendation); GSO 1 Defence Intelligence, MoD, 1967–69; CO 1st Bn Prince of Wales's Own Regt of Yorks, Cyprus, 1969–71; Col GS, Hong Kong, 1974–76; Chief of Staff UN Force, Cyprus, and Comdr British Contingent, 1976–78; Dep. Dir, Army Staff Duties, MoD, 1978–79; Chief of Staff to C-in-C UKLF, 1980–83. Col, Prince of Wales's Own Regt of Yorks, 1979–86. Regl Dir, SE Asia, Internat. Mil. Services Ltd, 1983–86. Associate Mem., Council for Arms Control, 1989–. Fellow, RSPB, 1981. *Recreations:* travel, birds, listening to music. *Address:* c/o Lloyds Bank, 8/10 Waterloo Place, SW1. *Club:* Army and Navy.

TILLOTSON, Prof. Kathleen Mary, CBE 1991 (OBE 1983); MA, BLitt; FRSL 1984; FBA 1965; Hildred Carlile Professor of English in the University of London, at Bedford College, 1958–71, now Emeritus; *b* 3 April 1906; *e d* of late Eric A. Constable, BLitt (Durham), journalist, and Catherine H. Constable, Berwick-on-Tweed and Birmingham; *m* 1933, Geoffrey Tillotson, FBA (*d* 1969); two adopted *s*. *Educ:* Ackworth School; Mount School, York; Somerville College, Oxford (Exhibitioner and Shaw Lefevre Scholar). Charles Oldham Shakespeare Scholarship, 1926; BA 1927; temporary tutor, Somerville College, 1928–29; BLitt 1929; teaching at Somerville and St Hilda's Colleges, 1929–39; part-time Assistant, later Junior Lecturer, 1929, Lecturer, 1939, Fellow, 1971, Bedford College; Reader in the University of London at Bedford College, 1947–58. Vice-President: Dickens Fellowship; Brontë Soc.; Trustee: Wordsworth Trust; Bosanquet Trust. Warton Lecture, British Academy, 1956; Annual Brontë Lecture, 1966, 1986; Dickens Meml Lecture, 1970; Annual Tennyson Lecture, 1974; Robert Spence Watson Lecture, 1978. James Bryce Memorial Lecturer, Somerville College, Oxford, 1963, Hon. Fellow, 1965. Hon. DLit Belfast, 1972; Hon. DLitt: Oxon, 1982; London, 1982. Rose Mary Crawshay prize, British Academy, 1943, 1988. *Publications:* (with J. W. Hebel and B. H. Newdigate) Works of Michael Drayton, vol. V, 1941; Novels of the Eighteen-Forties, 1954; Matthew Arnold and Carlyle (Warton Lecture), 1957; (with John Butt) Dickens at Work, 1957; Introductions to Trollope's Barsetshire novels, 1958–75; The Tale and the Teller (inaug. lect.), 1959; Vanity Fair (ed with G. Tillotson), 1963; Mid-Victorian Studies (with G. Tillotson), 1965; Letters of Charles Dickens, vol. 1, 1965, vol. 2, 1969, vol. 3, 1974 (Associate Editor), vol. 4, 1977, vol. 5, 1981, vol. 6, 1988 (Joint Editor) (General Editor, 1978–); Oliver Twist, 1966; (General Editor, Clarendon Dickens, 1957–, seven novels published by 1986); (ed with A. Trodd) The Woman in White, 1969; (ed) Oliver Twist (World's Classics), 1982; James Kinsley (memoir, British Acad.), 1989; contributions to periodicals. *Address:* 23 Tanza Road, NW3 2UA. *T:* 071–435 5639. *Club:* University Women's.

TILNEY, Charles Edward, CMG 1956; Minister for Finance and Economics, Tanganyika, 1957–60; *b* 13 April 1909; *yr s* of late Lt-Col N. E. Tilney, CBE, DSO, and Mrs Tilney; *m* 1952, Rosalind Hull, *e d* of late Lt-Col E. C. de Renzy-Martin, CMG, DSO, MC, and Mrs de Renzy-Martin; two *s*. *Educ:* Rugby School; Oriel College, Oxford. Ceylon Civil Service, 1932; Tanganyika: Asst Chief Secretary (Finance), 1948; Dep. Financial Secretary, 1948; Secretary for Finance, 1950; Member for Finance and Economics, 1953. Retd from E Africa, 1960. *Address:* 8 Butts Close, Biddestone, Chippenham, Wilts SN14 7DZ. *T:* Corsham (0249) 714770.

TILNEY, Dame Guinevere, DBE 1984; Adviser to Rt Hon. Margaret Thatcher, MP, 1975–83; UK Representative on United Nations Commission on Status of Women, 1970–73; *b* 8 Sept. 1916; *y d* of late Sir Hamilton Grant, 12th Bt, KCSI, KCIE, and late Lady Grant; *m* 1st, 1944, Captain Lionel Hunter (*d* 1947), Princess Louise Dragoon Guards; one *s*; 2nd, 1954, Sir John Tilney, *qv*. *Educ:* Westonbirt. WRNS, 1941–45; Private Sec. to Earl of Selborne, 1949–54; Vice-Chm., SE Lancs Br., British Empire Cancer Campaign, 1957–64; Founder Mem., 1st Chm., 1st Pres., Merseyside Conservative Ladies Luncheon Club, 1957–75, now 1st Hon. Life Mem.; Nat. Council of Women of Great Britain: Vice-Pres., 1958–61, Pres., 1961–68, Liverpool and Birkenhead Br.; Sen. Nat. Vice-Pres., 1966–68; Nat. Pres., 1968–70; Co-Chm., Women's Nat. Commn, 1969–71; Mem., North Thames Gas Consultative Council, 1967–69; Mem., BBC Gen. Adv. Council, 1967–76. Co-Chm., Women Caring Trust, 1972–75. DL: Co. Palatine of Lancaster, 1971–74; Co. Merseyside, 1974–76. *Recreations:* reading, making soup, writing. *Address:* 3 Victoria Square, SW1W 0QZ. *T:* 071–828 8674.

TILNEY, Sir John (Dudley Robert Tarleton), Kt 1973; TD; JP; *b* 19 Dec. 1907; *yr s* of late Col R. H. Tilney, DSO; *m* 1954, Dame Guinevere Tilney, *qv*; one step *s*. *Educ:* Eton; Magdalen College, Oxford. Served during War of 1939–45 (despatches), with 59th (4th West Lancs) Medium Regt, RA, and 11th Medium Regt, RA; commanded 47/49 359 (4th West Lancs), Medium Regt RATA; Hon. Col 470 (3 W Lancs), LAA Regt, 1957–61. MP (C) Wavertree, Liverpool, 1950–Feb. 1974; Parliamentary Private Sec. to: Sec. of State for War, 1951–55; Postmaster-General, 1957–59; Chm. Inter-Parly Union, Brit. Gp, 1959–62; Chm. Conservative Commonwealth Council W Africa Cttee, 1954–62; PPS to Minister of Transport, 1959–62; Parly Under-Sec. of State for Commonwealth Relations, 1962–64 and for the Colonies, 1963–64; Member: Select Cttee on Expenditure; Exec. Cttee, Nat. Union of Conservative and Unionist Assocs, 1965–73; Chm. Merseyside Conservative MPs, 1964–74 (Vice-Chm., NW Area Cttee); Treasurer, UK Branch, Commonwealth Parly Assoc., 1968–70; Mem., Exec. Cttee, Cons. Political Centre, 1972–81. Chairman: Liverpool Luncheon Club, 1948–49; Liverpool Branch, Royal Commonwealth Soc., 1955–60 (Pres., 1965); Sir Winston Churchill Meml Statue Cttee; Pres., Airey Neave Meml Trust, 1983– (Chm., 1979–83); Pres., Victoria Square Assoc. (Chm., 1959–83). Member: Liverpool Cathedral Gen. Council; Exec. Cttee, Westminster Soc., 1975–91; Council, Imperial Soc. of Knights Bachelor, 1978–90. Pres., Assoc. of Lancastrians in London, 1980–81. Trustee, Bluecoat Sch.; Governor, Liverpool Coll. JP Liverpool, 1946. Croix de Guerre with Gilt Star, 1945; Legion of Honour, 1960. *Recreations:* gardening, travel. *Address:* 3 Victoria Square, SW1W 0QZ. *T:* 071–828 8674. *Clubs:* Pratt's; Jesters; Liverpool Racquet.

TILSON, Joseph Charles, (Joe), RA 1991 (ARA 1985); painter, sculptor and printmaker; *b* 24 Aug. 1928; *s* of Frederick Albert Edward Tilson and Ethel Stapley Louise Saunders; *m* 1956, Joslyn Morton; one *s* two *d*. *Educ:* St Martin's School of Art; Royal Coll. of Art (ARCA); British School at Rome (Rome Scholar). RAF, 1946–49. Worked in Italy and Spain, 1955–59; Vis. Lectr, Slade Sch., Univ. of London and King's Coll., Univ. of Durham, 1962–63; taught at Sch. of Visual Arts, NY, 1966; Vis. Lectr, Staatliche Hochschule für Bildende Kunste, Hamburg, 1971–72. Mem., Arts Panel, Arts Council, 1966–71. Exhib. Venice Biennale, 1964; work at Marlborough Gall., 1961–77, later at Waddington Galls; retrospective exhibitions: Boymans Van Beuningen Mus., Rotterdam, 1973; Vancouver Art Gall., 1979; Volterra, 1983. Biennale Prizes: Krakow, 1974; Ljubljana, 1985. Subject of TV films, 1963, 1968, 1974. *Recreation:* planting trees. *Address:* The Old Rectory, Christian Malford, Wilts SN15 4BW. *T:* Seagry (0249) 720223; Woolley Dale, 44 Broomwood Road, SW11 6HT. *T:* 071–223 4078.

TILSON THOMAS, Michael; Principal Conductor, London Symphony Orchestra, since 1988; Artistic Director, New World Symphony, since 1988; concert pianist; *b* 21 Dec. 1944; *s* of Theodore and Roberta Thomas; *g s* of Boris and Bessie Thomashefsky, founders of Yiddish Theater, United States. *Educ:* Univ. of Southern California (Master of Music). Conductor, Young Musicians' Foundn Orchestra, LA, and conductor and pianist, Monday Evening Concerts, 1963–68; musical asst, Bayreuth, 1966–67; Koussevitzky Prize, Tanglewood, 1968; Asst then Principal Guest Conductor, Boston Symphony, 1969–74; NY début, 1969; London début, with LSO, 1970; Music Director: Buffalo Philharmonic, 1971–79; televised NY Philharmonic Young Peoples' Concerts, 1971–77; Principal Guest Conductor, LA Philharmonic, 1981–85; Music Dir, Great Woods Festival, 1985; guest conductor with orchestras and opera houses in US and Europe; numerous recordings (now exclusively Sony Classical). *Address:* c/o Columbia Artists, 7A Fitzroy Park, N6 6HS. *Club:* St Botolph (Boston).

TILSTON, Col Frederick Albert, VC 1945; CD; *b* Toronto, Ontario, 11 June 1906; *s* of late Fred Tilston, English birth, and late Agnes Estelle Le May, Cdn birth; *m* 1946; one *s*. *Educ:* De La Salle Collegiate, Toronto; Ontario College of Pharmacy (graduated 1929). Salesman for Sterling Products Ltd, Windsor, Ont., manufacturers of nationally advertised drug products, 1930–36; Canadian Sales Manager for Sterling Products Ltd, 1937–40; Vice-Pres. in charge of sales, Sterling Products Ltd, Windsor, Ontario, 1946–57; Pres., Sterling Drug Ltd, 1957–70; retired 1971. Canadian Army, 1941–46. KStJ 1984. Hon. Dr Laws Windsor, 1977. *Recreations:* swimming, ice hockey, golf; amateur pianist. *Address:* 188 Douglas Avenue, Toronto, Ont M5M 1G6, Canada. *T:* (416)–482 6482. *Clubs:* New Windsor, Essex County Golf and Country (Windsor, Ont); Royal Canadian Military Institute (Toronto); Summitt Golf and Country (Oak Ridges).

TIMBERLAKE, Herman Leslie Patterson, (Tim); Director, Abbey National Building Society, 1972–84 (Chief General Manager, 1971–79; Deputy Chairman, 1976–79); *b* 3 Feb. 1914; *s* of William Walter and Mabel Timberlake; *m* 1940, Betty (*née* Curtis); two *s*. *Educ:* Watford Grammar Sch. FCIS; FCBSI; CBIM. Served War of 1939–45. Joined Abbey Road Building Soc., 1930; Asst Branch Manager, Watford, 1936; became Abbey National Building Soc., 1944; Branch Manager appts, 1946–59; Manager: Branches Admin. Dept, 1959; Investments Admin. Dept, 1964; Branches and Agencies, 1966; Jt General Manager, 1968. Mem. Council, Building Societies Assoc., 1975–79; Pres., Building Societies Institute, 1977–78. *Address:* 1 Rochester Drive, Pinner, Mddx HA5 1DA. *T:* 081–866 1554.

TIMBURY, Dr Morag Crichton, FRSE; FRCPGlas, FRCPath; Director, Central Public Health Laboratory, Public Health Laboratory Service, since 1988; *b* 29 Sept. 1930; *d* of William McCulloch and Dr Esther Sinclair McCulloch (*née* Hood); *m* 1954, Dr Gerald Charles Timbury, FRCPE, FRCPGlas, FRCPsych (decd); one *d*. *Educ:* St Bride's Sch.; Univ. of Glasgow (MB ChB; MD; PhD). MRCPath 1964, FRCPath 1976; MRCPGlas

1972, FRCPGlas 1974; FRSE 1979. University of Glasgow: Maurice Bloch Res. Fellow in Virology, 1960–63; Lectr in Bacteriology, 1963–65; Sen. Lectr in Virology, 1966–76; Reader, 1976–78; Prof. of Bacteriology and William Teacher Lectr, 1978–88. Hon. Cons., 1966–88; External examiner in med. microbiol., 1973–88, variously at QUB, Univs of Aberdeen, Cambridge, Dundee, Edinburgh, Newcastle. Vis. Associate Prof. in Virology, Baylor College of Medicine, Houston, Texas, 1975; Vis. Mayne Guest Prof., Univ. of Queensland, Brisbane, 1990; Hon. Vis. Prof. (Virology) RPMS, 1990–; Hon. Sen. Lectr, Royal Free Hosp. and Hon. Lectr in Virology, St Bartholomew's Hosp., 1990–. Mem., RSM, 1986–. *Publications:* Notes on Medical Virology, 1967, 9th edn 1991; (with J. D. Sleigh) Notes on Medical Bacteriology, 1981, 3rd edn 1990; (co-ed) vol. 4, Virology, Topley and Wilson's Principles of Bacteriology, Virology and Immunity, 1929, 8th edn 1990; sci. papers on bacterial and viral infections, genetics of herpes simplex virus type 2. *Recreations:* military history, theatre. *Address:* Central Public Health Laboratory, 61 Colindale Avenue, NW9 5HT. *T:* 071–200 4400.

TIMMINS, Col John Bradford, OBE (mil.) 1973; TD 1968 (1st Clasp 1974); JP; Lord Lieutenant of Greater Manchester, since 1987; Chairman, Warburton Properties Ltd, since 1973; *b* 23 June 1932; *s* of John James Timmins and Janet Gwendoline (*née* Legg); *m* 1956, Jean Edwards; five *s* one *d*. *Educ:* Dudley Grammar Sch.; Wolverhampton Technical Coll.; Univ. of Aston-in-Birmingham (MSc). MCIOB. Building and Civil Engrg Industry, 1949–80; NW Regional Pres., Nat. Fedn of Building Trade Employers, 1974–75. Commnd RE, 1954; National Service, 1954–56; TA, 1956–80; comd 75 Eng. Regt(V), 1971–73; Hon. Col of the Regt, 1980–; Vice Pres., TA&VRA for NW England, 1987– (Vice-Chm., 1983–87). ADC to the Queen, 1975–80. Mem., Literary and Philosophical Soc., Manchester, 1987–. High Sheriff of Gtr Manchester, 1986–87. JP Trafford, 1987. KStJ 1988. Hon. DSc Salford, 1990. *Recreations:* sailing, good food and good wine. *Address:* The Old Rectory, Warburton, Lymm WA13 9SS. *Clubs:* Army and Navy; St James's (Manchester); Royal Engineer Yacht.

TIMMS, Dr Cecil, DEng, CEng, FIMechE, FIProdE; Former Engineering Consultant, Department of Trade and Industry, later Department of Industry, retired; *b* 13 Dec. 1911; *m*; no *c*. *Educ:* Liverpool Univ. Head of Metrology, Mechanisms and Noise Control Div., 1950–61, Supt of Machinery Group, 1961–65, National Engrg Laboratory; Head of Machine Tools Branch, Min. of Technology, later DTI, 1965–73. *Publications:* contribs to Proc. IMechE, Metalworking Prod. and Prod. Engr. *Address:* Broom House, Ballsdown, Chiddingfold, Surrey. *T:* Wormley (042879) 2014.

TIMMS, Ven. George Boorne; Archdeacon of Hackney, 1971–81, now Emeritus; Vicar of St Andrew, Holborn, 1965–81; *b* 4 Oct. 1910; *s* of late George Timms and Annie Elizabeth Timms (*née* Boorne); unmarried. *Educ:* Derby Sch.; St Edmund Hall, Oxford; Coll. of the Resurrection, Mirfield. MA Oxon. Deacon, 1935; Priest, 1936; Curate: St Mary Magdalen, Coventry, 1935–38; St Bartholomew, Reading, 1938–49; Oxford Diocesan Inspector of Schools, 1944–49; Sacrist of Southwark Cath., 1949–52; Vicar of St Mary, Primrose Hill, NW3, 1952–65; Rural Dean of Hampstead, 1959–65; Prebendary of St Paul's Cathedral, 1964–71. Proctor in Conv., 1955–59, 1965–70, 1974–80; Member: Standing Cttee Church Assembly, 1968–70; Anglican-Methodist Unity Commn, 1965–69. Dir of Ordination Trg, and Exam. Chap. to Bp of London, 1965–81; Chm., Alcuin Club, 1968–87. Pres., Sion Coll., 1980–81. Papal Medallion for services to Christian Unity, 1976. *Publications:* Dixit Cranmer, 1946; The Liturgical Seasons, 1965; (jtly) The Cloud of Witnesses, 1982; contributor to A Manual for Holy Week, 1967; (ed) English Praise, 1975; (ed) The New English Hymnal, 1985. *Address:* Cleve Lodge, Minster-in-Thanet, Ramsgate, Kent CT12 4BA. *T:* Thanet (0843) 821777.

TIMMS, Prof. Noel Walter; Professor of Social Work and Director, School of Social Work, University of Leicester, 1984–89, now Emeritus Professor; *b* 25 Dec. 1927; *s* of Harold John Timms and Josephine Mary Cecilia Timms; *m* 1956, Rita Caldwell; three *s* three *d*. *Educ:* Cardinal Vaughan School; Univ. of London (BA Hons History; MA Sociology); Univ. of Oxford. Social Worker, Family Service Units, 1952–54; Psychiatric social worker, 1955–57; Lectr, Dept of Social Science, Cardiff University Coll., 1957–61; Lectr, LSE, 1963–69; Prof. of Applied Social Studies, Bradford Univ., 1969–75; Prof. of Social Studies, Newcastle upon Tyne Univ., 1975–84. Trustee, Bar Convent Museum, York, 1988–. *Publications:* Social Casework, Principles and Practice, 1964; Language of Social Casework, 1968; (with John Mayer) The Client Speaks, 1970; (with Rita Timms) Dictionary of Social Welfare, 1982; Social Work Values: an enquiry, 1983. *Recreations:* Evensong; looking at old furniture and at performances of Don Giovanni. *Address:* 1/2 Church Cottages, Honiley Road, near Kenilworth, Warwicks CV8 1NP. *T:* Haseley Knob (0926) 484401.

TIMMS, Vera Kate, (Mrs E. W. Gordon); Minister (Agriculture), Office of the UK Permanent Representative, Brussels, since 1990; *b* 8 Oct. 1944; *d* of late Kenneth Timms and of Elsie Timms (*née* Cussans); *m* 1977, Ernest William Gordon; one step *d*. *Educ:* Queen Anne Grammar School, York; St Hilda's College, Oxford (PPE hons). Economic Asst, NEDO, 1966–70; Ministry of Agriculture, Fisheries and Food, 1970; Asst Private Sec. to Minister of Agric., 1974–75; seconded to European Secretariat of Cabinet Office, 1976–79; Principal Private Sec. to Minister of Agric. 1980–82; Asst Sec. responsible for marketing policy, MAFF, 1982–84; Counsellor, Paris, seconded to HM Diplomatic Service, 1984–88; Asst Sec. and Head of Sugar and Oilseeds Div., MAFF, 1988–89; Under Sec., Arable Crops Gp, MAFF, 1989–90. Ordre du Mérite Agricole (France), 1988. *Address:* Holly House, 62A London Street, Swaffham, Norfolk. *T:* Swaffham (0760) 23034; 42 The Foreshore, SE8. *T:* 081–691 0823.

TIMPSON, John Harry Robert, OBE 1987; writer and broadcaster; *b* 2 July 1928; *s* of late John Hubert Victor Timpson and Caroline (*née* Willson); *m* 1951, (Muriel) Patricia Whale; two *s*. *Educ:* Merchant Taylors' Sch. National Service, RASC, 1946–49. Reporter: Wembley News, 1945–46 and 1949–51; Eastern Daily Press, 1951–59; BBC News Staff, 1959–87; BBC Dep. Court Correspondent, 1962–67 (reporting Australian, Ethiopian and other Royal tours); Presenter: Newsroom, BBC-2, 1968–70; Tonight, BBC-1, 1976–78; Today, BBC Radio 4, 1970–76, 1978–86; Chm., Any Questions, BBC Radio 4, 1984–87. Hon. MA UEA, 1991. Sony Gold Award for outstanding services to radio, 1986. *Publications:* Today and Yesterday (autobiog.), 1976; The Lighter Side of Today, 1983; The Early Morning Book, 1986; Timpson's England—A Look beyond the Obvious, 1987; Paper Trail (novel), 1989; Timpson's Towns, 1989; Timpson's Travels in East Anglia, 1990; Sound Track (novel), 1991; Timpson's English Eccentrics, 1991. *Recreation:* enjoying Norfolk. *Address:* Ark Cottage, Wellingham, Weasenham St Peter, King's Lynn, Norfolk PE32 2TH.

TIMSON, Penelope Anne Constance; *see* Keith, P. A. C.

TINBERGEN, Dr Jan; Officer, Order of The Lion; Commander, Order of Orange Nassau; Professor Emeritus, Erasmus University, Rotterdam; *b* 12 April 1903; *s* of Dirk Cornelis Tinbergen and Jeannette Van Eek; *m* 1929, Tine Johanna De Wit; three *d* (and one *d* decd). *Educ:* Leiden University. On Staff, Central Bureau of Statistics, 1929–45; Prof., Netherlands Sch. of Economics (now Erasmus Univ.), 1933–73; Staff, League of Nations, 1936–38; Director, Central Planning Bureau (Dutch Government), 1945–55;

Advisor to various governments and international organisations, 1955–; Chm., UN Develt Planning Cttee, 1965–72. Hon. Degrees from 20 Universities, 1954–. (Jointly) Prize in Economics to the memory of Alfred Nobel, 1969. *Publications:* Economic Policy, Principles and Design, 1956; Selected Papers, 1959; Shaping the World Economy, 1962; Income Distribution, 1975; (with D. Fischer) Warfare and Welfare, 1987; World Security and Equity, 1990; articles. *Recreations:* languages, drawing. *Address:* Haviklaan 31, 2566XD The Hague, Netherlands. *T:* 070–3644630.

TINDAL-CARILL-WORSLEY, Air Commodore Geoffrey Nicolas Ernest, CB 1954; CBE 1943; Royal Air Force, retired; *b* 8 June 1908; *s* of late Philip Tindal-Carill-Worsley; *m* 1st, 1937, Berys Elizabeth Gilmour (marr. diss., 1951; she *d* 1962); one *s*; 2nd, 1951, Dorothy Mabel Murray Stanley-Turner. *Educ:* Eton; RAF Coll., Cranwell. Commanding Officer, RAF Station, Halton, Bucks, 1954–56; Sen. Technical Staff Officer, Far East Air Force, 1956–59; Director of Technical Training, Air Ministry, 1959; retired 1960. *Recreation:* country life.

TINDALE, Gordon Anthony, OBE 1983; Cultural Attaché, British Embassy, Washington, since 1989; *b* 17 March 1938; *s* of George Augustus Tindale and Olive Sarah Collier; *m* 1960, Sonia Mary Soper; one *s* one *d*. *Educ:* Highgate Sch.; Trinity Coll., Oxford (BA (Mod. Hist)); Birkbeck Coll., London (MA (Int. Relations)). Nat. Service, 1956–58. Joined British Council, 1961; postings in Iraq, Jordan, London and Egypt; Representative: Lesotho, Botswana and Swaziland, 1975–78; Zambia, 1979–83; Controller, Management Div., 1984–87; Representative, Egypt, 1987–89. *Recreations:* music, golf. *Address:* c/o British Embassy, 3100 Massachusetts Avenue, NW, Washington, DC 20008, USA. *T:* (202) 8984330; 23 Heath Hurst Road, Hampstead, NW3. *Club:* Hendon Golf.

TINDALE, Lawrence Victor Dolman, CBE 1971; CA; Deputy Chairman, 3i Group plc (formerly Investors in Industry Group plc, and FFI), since 1974; *b* 24 April 1921; *s* of late John Stephen and Alice Lilian Tindale; *m* 1946, Beatrice Mabel (Betty) Barton; one *s* one *d*. *Educ:* Latymer Upper Sch., Hammersmith; Inst. of Chartered Accountants of Scotland. Apprenticed McClelland Ker, 1938. Served War, Army, in E Africa and Burma, 1941–45. Returned to McClelland Ker, and qualified, 1946; Partner, 1951. Invited to join ICFC Ltd as Asst Gen. Manager, 1959; Dir and Gen. Manager, 1966–72. On secondment, DTI, as Dir of Industrial Development, 1972–74. Member: DTI Cttee of Inquiry on Small Firms, 1969–71; Adv. Council on Energy Conservation, 1977–80; British Technology Gp (NRDC, 1974–; NEB, 1981–); Chm., EDC for Mechanical Engrg Industry, 1968–72. Director: Commodore Shipping Co. Ltd, 1969–; Guernsey Gas Light Co. Ltd, 1970–; Investment Trust of Guernsey Ltd, 1970–; Edbro plc (Chm.), 1974–; Northern Engineering Industries plc, 1974–89 (Dep. Chm., 1986–89); Flextech (Holdings) Ltd, 1975– (Chm., 1984–86); London Atlantic Investment Trust plc (Chm.), 1977–91; N British Canadian Investment Trust Ltd (Chm.), 1979–; Transpec Holdings Ltd, 1980–87; Dewrance MacNeil Ltd, 1980–88; British Caledonian Gp (formerly Caledonian Airways) plc, 1980–88; BNOC, 1980–84; Britoil, 1984–88; Penspen Ltd, 1985–89; Polly Peck (International) plc, 1985–; Shandwick plc, 1985–; C. & J. Clark, 1986–91 (Chm., 1986–91). Mem. Council: Consumers' Assoc., 1970–87 (Vice Chm., 1981–85); BIM, 1974– (Chm. 1982–84; Vice-Pres., 1984–); Soc. for Protection of Ancient Buildings (Hon. Treasurer), 1974–. CA; CBIM; FRSA 1989. *Recreation:* opera. *Address:* 3 Amyand Park Gardens, Twickenham, TW1 3HS. *T:* 081–892 9457; Le Bouillon House, St George's Esplanade, St Peter Port, Guernsey. *T:* Guernsey (0481) 21688. *Clubs:* Reform; St James's (Manchester).

TINDALE, Patricia Randall; architect; Chief Architect, Department of the Environment, 1982–86; *b* 11 March 1926; *d* of Thomas John Tindale and May Tindale (*née* Uttin). *Educ:* Blatchington Court, Seaford, Sussex; Architectural Assoc. Sch. of Architecture (AADip.). ARIBA. Architect, Welsh Dept, Min. of Educn, 1949–50; Min. of Educn Develt Gp, 1951–60; Min. of Housing and Local Govt R&D Gp, 1960–70; DoE Housing Develt Gp, 1970–72; Head, Building Regulations Professional Div., DoE, 1972–74; Dir, Housing Develt Directorate, DoE, 1974–81; Dir, Central Unit of Built Environment, DoE, 1981–82. Mem., AA Council, 1965–68. *Publication:* Housebuilding in the USA, 1966. *Recreations:* weaving, sailing. *Address:* 34 Crescent Grove, SW4 7AH. *T:* 071–622 1926. *Club:* Reform.

TINDALL, Rev. Canon Frederick Cryer, BD 1923; FKC 1950 (AKC 1922); Principal Emeritus of Salisbury Theological College since 1965; Canon and Prebendary Emeritus of Salisbury Cathedral since 1981; *b* 2 July 1900; *s* of late Frederick and Frances Tindall, Hove, Sussex; *m* 1942, Rosemary Phyllis, *d* of late Frank and Katharine Alice Newman, Woking; one *s* (one *d* decd). *Educ:* Brighton Grammar Sch.; King's Coll., London; Ely Theological College. Curate of S Cyprian, S Marylebone, 1924–28; Lecturer and Bursar, Chichester Theological College, 1928–30, Vice-Principal, 1930–36; Warden of Connaught Hall and Lecturer in Theology, Southampton Univ., 1936–39; Vicar of St Augustine, Brighton, 1939–50; Principal, Salisbury Theological Coll., 1950–65 (Sabbatical Year 1965–66). Proctor in Convocation for Diocese of Chichester, 1936–45, 1949–50; Examining Chaplain to Bishop of Chichester, 1941–50, Canon and Prebendary of Chichester Cathedral, 1948–50; Canon and Prebendary of Salisbury Cathedral, 1950–81; Proctor in Convocation for Diocese of Salisbury, 1950–75; Vice-Pres. and Chm. House of Clergy, Salisbury Diocesan Synod, 1970–76; Chm., Salisbury Diocesan Liturgical Cttee, 1973–81; Member: Commn for Revision of the Catechism, 1958; Church Assembly Standing Orders Cttee, 1963; Archbishop's Commn on London and SE England, 1965; Greater London Area Liaison Cttee, 1968; Pastoral Measure Appeal Tribunal, 1969–75; General Synod Standing Orders Cttee, 1970–75. Clerical Judge, Court of Arches, Canterbury, 1969–80. Pro-Prolocutor, Lower House of Convocation of Canterbury, 1959–75. Trustee, St John's Hosp., Heytesbury, 1968–83. *Publications:* England Expects, 1946; a History of S Augustine's Brighton, 1946; Christian Initiation, Anglican Principles and Practice, 1951; contributor to: History of Christian Thought, 1937; Encyclopædia Britannica Year Book, 1939; Baptism To-Day, 1949; Theology, Church Quarterly Review, Guardian, etc. *Recreations:* music, travelling, golf, gardening. *Address:* 16 The Close, Salisbury, Wilts SP1 2EB. *T:* Salisbury (0722) 322373. *Clubs:* Athenæum, Commonwealth Trust, Ski Club of Great Britain.

TINDALL, Gillian Elizabeth; novelist, biographer, historian; *b* 4 May 1938; *d* of D. H. Tindall and U. M. D. Orange; *m* 1963, Richard G. Lansdown; one *s*. *Educ:* Univ. of Oxford (BA 1st cl., MA). Freelance journalism: occasional articles and reviews for Observer, Guardian, New Statesman, London Evening Standard, The Times, Encounter, New Society, and Independent. Occasional broadcasts, BBC. *Publications: novels:* No Name in the Street, 1959; The Water and the Sound, 1961; The Edge of the Paper, 1963; The Youngest, 1967; Someone Else, 1969, 2nd edn 1975; Fly Away Home, 1971 (Somerset Maugham Award, 1972); The Traveller and His Child, 1975; The Intruder, 1979; Looking Forward, 1983; To the City, 1987; Give Them All My Love, 1989; *short stories:* Dances of Death, 1973; The China Egg and Other Stories, 1981; Journey of a Lifetime and Other Stories, 1990; *biography:* The Born Exile (George Gissing), 1974; *other non-fiction:* A Handbook on Witchcraft, 1965; The Fields Beneath, 1977; City of Gold: the biography of Bombay, 1981; Rosamond Lehmann: an Appreciation, 1985; (contrib.) Architecture of the British Empire, 1986; Countries of the Mind: the meaning of place to writers, 1991. *Recreations:* keeping house, foreign travel. *Address:* c/o Curtis Brown Ltd, 162–168 Regent Street, W1.

TINDALL, Prof. Victor Ronald, FRCSE, FRCOG; Professor of Obstetrics and Gynaecology, University of Manchester at St Mary's Hospital, since 1972; *b* 1 Aug. 1928; *m* 1955, Brenda Fay; one *s* one *d*. *Educ:* Wallasey Grammar Sch.; Liverpool Univ. (MB ChB; MD); Manchester Univ. (MSc). Sen. Lectr and Consultant, Welsh Nat. Sch. of Medicine, Cardiff, 1965–70; Consultant Obstetrician and Gynaecologist, Univ. Hosp. of Wales, 1970–72. Sen. Vice-Pres., RCOG, 1990–. Hon. FRCS, 1991. *Publications:* MCQ Tutor, MRCOG Part I, 1977, 2nd edn 1985, combined edn 1987; (jtly) Practical Student Obstetrics, 1980; Colour Atlas of Clinical Gynaecology, 1981; Essential Sciences for Clinicians, 1981; Clinical Gynaecology, 1986; (ed) Jeffcoates' Principles of Gynaecology, 5th edn 1987; Diagnostic Picture Tests in Obstetrics and Gynaecology, 1986; (ed jtly) Current Approaches to Endometrial Carcinoma, 1988; (jtly) Preparations and Advice for the Members of the Royal College of Obstetricians and Gynaecologists, 1989; Illustrated Textbook of Gynaecology, 1991; reports for DHSS on maternal deaths in the UK. *Recreations:* ex Rugby international, international sporting activities. *Address:* 4 Planetree Road, Hale, Altrincham, Cheshire WA15 9JL. *T:* 061–980 2680; St Mary's Hospital, Whitworth Park, Manchester M13 0JH. *Clubs:* Royal Society of Medicine, Royal College of Obstetricians and Gynaecologists.

TINDEMANS, Leo; Member (EPP) European Parliament, 1979–81, and since 1989; Member (Christian Democratic Party), House of Representatives, Belgium, 1961–89; Minister of Foreign Relations, 1981–89; Professor in the Faculty of Social Sciences, Catholic University, Louvain; *b* Zwijndrecht, 16 April 1922; *m* 1960, Rosa Naesens; two *s* two *d*. *Educ:* State Univ., Ghent; Catholic Univ., Louvain. Minister: for Community Relations, 1968–71; of Agriculture and Middle Class Affairs, 1972–73; Dep. Prime Minister and Minister for the Budget, 1973–74; Prime Minister of Belgium, 1974–78. Mayor of Edegem, 1965–76. President: Christian Democratic Party, 1979–81; European People's Party, 1976–85. Hon. DLitt: City Univ., 1976; Heriot-Watt Univ., 1978; Georgetown Univ., Washington, 1984; Univ. de Deusto, Bilbao, 1991. Charlemagne Prize, 1976; St Liborius Medaille für Einheit und Frieden, 1977; Stresemann Medaille, 1979; Schuman Prize, 1980. *Publications:* L'autonomie culturelle, 1971; Een handvest voor woelig België, 1972; Dagboek van de werkgroep Eyskens, 1973; European Union, 1975; Europe, Ideal of our Generation, 1976; Atlantisch Europa, 1981; Europa zonder Kompas, 1987; L'Europe de l'Est vue de Bruxelles, 1989. *Recreations:* reading, writing, walking. *Address:* Jan Verbertlei 24, B-2650 Edegem, Belgium.

TINDLE, David, RA 1979 (ARA 1973); RE 1988; painter; Dealer and Agent, Fischer Fine Art Ltd, since 1985; *b* 29 April 1932; *m* 1969, Janet Trollope; one *s* two *d*. *Educ:* Coventry Sch. of Art. MA Oxon 1985. Worked as scene painter and commercial artist, 1946–51; subseq. taught at Hornsey Coll. of Art; Vis. Tutor, Royal Coll. of Art, 1972–83, Fellow, 1981, Hon. FRCA, 1984; Ruskin Master of Drawing, Oxford Univ., and Professorial Fellow, St Edmund Hall, Oxford, 1985–87 (Hon. Fellow, 1988). Hon. RBSA 1989. First showed work, Archer Gall., 1952 and 1953; regular one-man exhibns, Piccadilly Gall., from 1954; one-man exhibns at many public and private galleries in Gt Britain incl. Fischer Fine Art, 1985, 1989; Galerie du Tours, San Francisco and Los Angeles, 1964; Gallerie Vinciana, Milan, 1968; Galleria Carbonesi, Bologna, 1968; Gallery XX, Hamburg, 1974, 1977, 1980; rep. in exhibns at: Piccadilly Gall., 1954–; Royal Acad.; Internat. Biennale of Realist Art, Bruges, 1958 and Bologna, 1967; British Exhibn Art, Basel, 1958; John Moores, 1959 and 1961; Arts Council Shows: British Self-Portraits; Painters in East Anglia; Thames in Art; The British Art Show, 1979–80; Salon de la Jeune Peinture, Paris, 1967; Mostra Mercato d'Arte Contemporanea, Florence, 1967; British Painting 1974, Hayward Gall.; British Painting 1952–77, RA; Six English Painters—Eros in Albion, Arezzo, Italy, 1989. Set of 3 Mural decorations for Open Univ., Milton Keynes, 1977–78. Designed sets for Iolanta, Aldeburgh Fest., 1988. Work rep. in numerous public and private collections, incl. Nat. Portrait Gall.; Chantrey Bequest purchases, 1974 and 1975, now in Tate Gall. Critic Prize, 1962; Europe Prize for Painting, 1969; Critics' Choice, Tooths, 1974; Waddington Prize, Chichester Nat. Art Exhibn, 1975; Johnson Wax Award, RA, 1983. *Address:* Fischer Fine Art, 30 King Street, SW1Y 6RJ.

TINDLE, Ray Stanley, CBE 1987 (OBE 1973); DL; Chairman: Tindle Newspapers Ltd, since 1972; Surrey Advertiser Newspaper Holdings Ltd, since 1978; *b* 8 Oct. 1926; *s* of late John Robert Tindle and Maud Tindle; *m* 1949, Beryl Julia (*née* Ellis), MA, DipEd; one *s*. *Educ:* Torquay Grammar Sch.; Strand Sch. FCIS; FCIArb. War service, Devonshire Regt (Captain), 1944–47. Asst to Dir, Newspaper Soc., 1952–58; Managing Director: Surrey Mirror Newspapers, 1959–63; Surrey Advertiser Newspapers, 1963–78. Pres., Newspaper Soc., 1971–72; Member: Newspaper Panel, Monopolies and Mergers Commn, 1987–; Council, CPU, 1987–. Founder, Tindle Enterprise Centres for the Unemployed, 1984–. Master, Stationers' and Newspaper Makers' Co., 1985–86. DL Surrey, 1989. *Publication:* The Press Today and Tomorrow, 1975. *Recreations:* veteran cars, newspapers, boating. *Address:* Devonshire House, 92 West Street, Farnham, Surrey GU9 7EN. *Clubs:* Veteran Car, City Livery Yacht.

TING, Prof. Samuel Chao Chung; Thomas D. Cabot Institute Professor, Massachusetts Institute of Technology, since 1977; *b* 27 Jan. 1936; *s* of K. H. Ting and late T. S. Wang; *m*; two *d*; *m* 1985, Susan Carol Marks; one *s*. *Educ:* Univ. of Michigan (PhD). Ford Fellow, CERN, Geneva, 1963; Asst Prof. of Physics, Columbia Univ., 1965; Prof. of Physics, MIT, 1969. Assoc. Editor, Nuclear Physics B, 1970; Mem. Editorial Board: Nuclear Instruments and Methods, 1977; Mathematical Modeling, 1980. Hon. Professor: Beijing Normal Coll., 1984; Jiatong Univ., Shanghai, 1987. Member: US Nat. Acad. of Science, 1976; European Physical Soc.; Italian Physical Soc.; Foreign Member: Pakistan Acad. of Science, 1984; Academia Sinica (Republic of China), 1975; Soviet Acad. of Science, 1988; Fellow, Amer. Acad. of Arts and Science, 1975. Hon. ScD: Chinese Univ. of Hong Kong, 1987; Bologna, 1988. Nobel Prize for Physics (jt), 1976; Ernest Orlando Lawrence Award, US Govt, 1976; A. E. Eringen Medal, Soc. of Engineering Science, USA, 1977; Gold Medal in Science, City of Brescia, Italy, 1988; De Gasperi Prize, Italian Republic, 1988. Hon. ScD Michigan, 1978. *Publications:* articles in Physical Review and Physical Review Letters. *Address:* 51 Vassar Street, Cambridge, Mass 02139, USA. *Club:* Explorers' (NY).

TINKER, Prof. Hugh Russell; Professor of Politics, University of Lancaster, 1977–82, now Emeritus; *b* 20 July 1921; *s* of late Clement Hugh Tinker and Gertrude Marian Tinker; *m* 1947, Elisabeth McKenzie (*née* Willis); two *s* (and one *s* killed in action). *Educ:* Taunton Sch.; Sidney Sussex Coll., Cambridge (BA Scholar). Indian Army, 1941–45; Indian civil admin, 1945–46. Lectr, Reader and Prof., SOAS, 1948–69; Dir, Inst. of Race Relations, 1970–72; Sen. Fellow, Inst. of Commonwealth Studies, Univ. of London, 1972–77. Prof., Univ. of Rangoon, 1954–55; Prof., Cornell Univ., USA, 1959. Vice-Pres., Ex-Services Campaign for Nuclear Disarmament. Trustee, Noel Buxton Trust. Contested (L): Barnet, gen. elecs 1964 and 1966; Morecambe and Lonsdale, 1979. *Publications:* The Foundations of Local Self-Government in India, Pakistan and Burma,

1954; The Union of Burma, a Study of the First Years of Independence, 1957 (4th edn 1967); India and Pakistan, a Political Analysis, 1962; Ballot Box and Bayonet, People and Government in Emergent Asian Countries, 1964; Reorientations, Studies on Asia in Transition, 1965; South Asia, a Short History, 1966; Experiment with Freedom, India and Pakistan 1947, 1967; (ed and wrote introduction) Henry Yule: Narrative of the Mission to the Court of Ava in 1855, 1969; A New System of Slavery: the export of Indian labour overseas 1830–1920, 1974; Separate and Unequal: India and the Indians in the British Commonwealth 1920–1950, 1976; The Banyan Tree: overseas emigrants from India, Pakistan and Bangladesh, 1977; Race, Conflict and the International Order: from Empire to United Nations, 1977; The Ordeal of Love: C. F. Andrews and India, 1979; A Message from the Falklands: the life and gallant death of David Tinker, 1982; (ed) Burma: the struggle for independence, vol. I 1944–1946, 1983, vol. II 1946–1948, 1984; Men Who Overturned Empires: fighters, dreamers, schemers, 1987. *Recreations:* writing, walking. *Address:* Montbegon, Hornby, near Lancaster LA2 8JZ.

TINKER, Dr Jack, FRCP, FRCSGlas; Postgraduate Medical Dean, University of London, since 1988; *b* 20 Jan. 1936; *s* of Lawrence and Jessie Tinker; *m* 1961, Maureen Ann Crawford; two *s*. *Educ:* Manchester Univ. (BSc (Hons), MB ChB); DIC. Dir, Intensive Therapy Unit, Middlesex Hosp., 1974–88; Hon. Cons. Physician, Middlesex Hosp., 1988–; Hon. Sec. Clin. Lectr, UCMSM, 1988–. Sen. Med. Cons. Sun Life of Canada, 1983–; Med. Advr, RTZ Gp, 1986–. FRSM, 1988. Editor in Chief, British Jl of Hospital Medicine, 1985– Man. Editor, Intensive Care Medicine, 1973–88. *Publications:* A Course in Intensive Therapy Nursing, 1980; Care of the Critically Ill Patient, 1982, 2nd edn 1991; A Pocket Book for Intensive Care, 1986, 2nd edn 1990; contribs to intensive care and cardiological jls. *Recreations:* road running, cricket. *Address:* 1 Rectory Road, Barnes, SW13 9HH. *T:* 081–878 0159. *Clubs:* Royal Automobile; Scarborough.

TINKER, Dr Philip Bernard Hague, FIBiol, FRSC; Director of Terrestrial and Freshwater Science, Natural Environment Research Council, since 1985; *b* 1 Feb. 1930; *s* of Philip and Gertrude Tinker; *m* 1955, Maureen Ellis; one *s* one *d*. *Educ:* Rochdale High Sch.; Sheffield Univ. (BSc); PhD 1955; MA, DSc 1984, Oxon. FIBiol 1974; FRSC 1985. Overseas Res. Service, 1955–62; Sen. Scientific Officer, Rothamsted Experimental Stn, 1962–65; Lectr, Oxford Univ., 1965–71; Prof. of Agricultural Botany, Leeds Univ., 1971–77; Head of Soils Div., 1977–85, and Dep. Dir, 1981–85, Rothamsted Experimental Stn. Fellow, 1969–72, Sen. Res. Fellow, 1988–, St Cross Coll., Oxford. Lectures: Regents, Univ. of California, 1979; Hannaford Meml, Adelaide, 1990; Francis New Meml and Medal, Fertilizer Soc., 1991. Pres., British Soil Sci. Soc., 1983–84; Gov., Macaulay Land Use Res. Inst., Aberdeen, 1990–. Fellow, Norwegian Acad. of Science and Letters, 1987; Hon. FRASE, 1990. *Publications:* (with F. E. Sanders and B. Mosse) Endomycorrhisas, 1975; (with P. H. Nye) Solute Movement in the Soil-root System, 1977; Soil and Agriculture—Critical Reviews, 1980; (with A. Läuchli) Advances in Plant Nutrition, vol. I, 1984, vol. II, 1986, vol. III, 1988; *c* 140 papers. *Recreations:* reading, gardening, map collecting. *Address:* The Glebe House, Broadwell, Lechlade, Glos GL7 3QS. *T:* Faringdon (0367) 860436. *Club:* Farmers'.

TINN, James; *b* 23 Aug. 1922; *s* of James Tinn and Nora (*née* Davie). *Educ:* Consett Elementary School; Ruskin College; Jesus College, Oxford. Cokeworker until 1953; Branch official, Nat. Union of Blastfurnacemen. Full-time study for BA (PPE Oxon). Teacher, secondary modern school, 1958–64. MP (Lab): Cleveland, 1964–74; Redcar, 1974–87. PPS to Sec. of State for Commonwealth (formerly for Commonwealth Relations), 1965–66, to Minister for Overseas Development, 1966–67; an Asst Govt Whip, 1976–79; an Opposition Whip, 1979–82. Mem. Exec. Cttee, CPA. *Address:* 1 Norfolk Road, Moorside, Consett, Co. Durham. *T:* Consett (0207) 509313. *Club:* United Oxford & Cambridge University.

TINNISWOOD, Maurice Owen; *b* 26 March 1919; *y s* of late Robert Tinniswood, OBE; *m* 1946, Anne Katharine, *yr d* of late Rev. J. Trevor Matchett; one *s* one *d*. *Educ:* Merchant Taylors' School. Served with Royal Hampshire Regt, 1939–46 (Major). Joined PO, 1938 as Executive Officer, Principal, 1949; Asst Secretary, 1958; Imperial Defence College, 1963; Director of Establishments and Organisation, 1965; Director of Reorganization, 1966; Secretary to the Post Office, 1969–70; Dir of Personnel, BBC, 1970–77. Chm., Kingston, Richmond and Esher Community Health Council, 1980–81; Mem., Kingston and Esher HA, 1982–85. CBIM. *Address:* Little Croft, Weston Green Road, Thames Ditton, Surrey KT7 0HY. *T:* 081–398 4561.

TINSLEY, Charles Henry, FRICS; Deputy Chief Valuer, Inland Revenue Valuation Office, 1974–78; *b* 3 March 1914; *s* of Arthur William and Teresa Tinsley; *m* 1938, Solway Lees; two *s* one *d*. *Educ:* Ratcliffe Coll., Leicester. Served War: joined TA, 1939; commn in Royal Artillery, 1941; with Lanarkshire Yeomanry, RA, in ME, Sicily and Italy; GSOII, in ME Supply Centre, Tehran, 1945–46. Nottinghamshire and W Riding of Yorkshire County Valuation Depts, 1929–39; Co. Valuer, N Riding of Yorkshire, 1948. Re-joined TA, 1948, and retd as Lt-Col, 1955. Joined Valuation Office, 1949; Suptg Valuer (Rating) Northern Region, 1949–68; Asst Chief Valuer, 1968. *Recreations:* the violin, travel, reading. *Address:* 44 Belgrave Manor, Brooklyn Road, Woking, Surrey GU22 7TW. *T:* Woking (0483) 767444.

TINSLEY, Rt. Rev. Ernest John; *b* 22 March 1919; *s* of Ernest William and Esther Tinsley; *m* 1947, Marjorie Dixon (*d* 1977); two *d*. *Educ:* St John's Coll., Univ. of Durham (BA, MA, BD); Westcott House, Cambridge. Priest, 1942; Curate: S Mary-le-Bow, Durham, 1942–44; South Westoe, 1944–46. Lectr in Theology, University Coll. of Hull, 1946–61; Sen. Lectr and Head of Dept of Theology, Univ. of Hull, 1961–62; Lectr of St Mary, Lowgate, Hull, 1955–62; Prof. of Theology, 1962–75, and Dean of Faculty of Arts, 1965–67, Univ. of Leeds; Bishop of Bristol, 1976–85; Special Lectr in Theology, Univ. of Bristol, 1976–84. Hulsean Preacher, Cambridge Univ., 1982; Bishop John Prideaux Lectr, Exeter Univ., 1982. Examining Chaplain: to Archbp of York, 1957–63; to Bp of Sheffield, 1963–75. Hon. Canon of Ripon Cath., 1966–75. Jt Chm., Gen. Synod's Bd of Educn and of Nat. Soc. for Promoting Religious Educn, 1979–82; Member: Doctrine Commn, 1967–69; Home Office Cttee on obscenity and film censorship, 1977–79. *Publications:* The Imitation of God in Christ, 1960; The Gospel according to Luke, 1965; (ed) Modern Theology, 1979; Tragedy, Irony and Faith, 1985; Tell it slant, 1990; contributor to: The Church and the Arts, 1960; Vindications, 1966; A Dictionary of Christian Ethics, 1967; A Dictionary of Christian Theology, 1969; Art and Religion as Communication, 1974; Dictionary of Christian Spirituality, 1983; In Search of Christianity, 1986. *Recreations:* France, Romanesque art. *Address:* 100 Acre End Street, Eynsham, Oxford OX8 1PD. *T:* Oxford (0865) 880822.

TINSON, Dame Susan (Myfanwy), DBE 1990; Head of Special Events, Independent Television News, since 1990; *b* 15 Jan. 1943; *d* of John and Kathleen Thomas; *m* 1968, Trevor James Tinson (marr. diss. 1979). *Educ:* South Hampstead High Sch.; Hull Univ. (BA Hons Social Studies). Independent Television News: trainee, 1964; Sub-editor, field co-ordinator, 1967; editor of news, 1975; Senior Editor, News at Ten and Asst Editor, ITN, 1982; Associate Editor, ITN, 1989; programmes include: elections, UK, USA, European, Rhodesian; Parly TV; space; Royal occasions; revolutions and wars; Falklands, Berlin, Czechoslovakia, Romania, Saudi Arabia, Kuwait, Iraq. *Address:* c/o ITN, 200 Gray's Inn Road, WC1X 8XZ. *T:* 071–430 4546.

TIPPET, Vice-Adm. Sir Anthony (Sanders), KCB 1984; CBIM; General Manager, Hospitals for Sick Children, London, since 1987; *b* 2 Oct. 1928; *s* of W. K. R. Tippet and H. W. P. Kitley (*née* Sanders); *m* 1950, Lola Bassett; two *s* one *d* (and one *s* decd). *Educ:* West Buckland Sch., Devon. Called to the Bar, Gray's Inn, 1959. Entered RN, 1946; Lieut 1950; HM Ships Ceres, Superb, Staff C-in-C Mediterranean; Lt Comdr 1958; HMS Trafalgar, Britannia RNC; Comdr 1963; Secretary: to Director of Naval Intelligence; to Flag Officer Middle East; CO HMS Jufair, Supply Officer, HMS Eagle; Captain 1970: Asst Director Naval Plans (Warfare), 1970–72; CSO (Administration) to Flag Officer Plymouth, 1972–74; Director of Naval Officers' Appointments (Supply and WRNS Officers), 1974–76; Captain HMS Pembroke and Flag Captain to Flag Officer Medway, 1976–79; Rear-Adm. 1979; Asst Chief of Fleet Support, MoD, 1979–81; Flag Officer and Port Admiral, Portsmouth, and Chief Naval Supply and Secretariat Officer, 1981–83; Chief of Fleet Support, 1983–86. Vice-Chm., RN Benevolent Soc., 1983–; Chm. of Govs, West Buckland Sch., 1989. *Recreations:* sailing, hill walking. *Clubs:* Anchorites; Royal Naval Sailing Association (Portsmouth).

TIPPETT, Sir Michael (Kemp), OM 1983; CH 1979; Kt 1966; CBE 1959; Composer; *b* 2 Jan. 1905; *s* of Henry William Tippett and Isabel Kemp. *Educ:* Stamford Grammar Sch.; Royal College of Music (Foley Scholar; FRCM 1961). Ran Choral and Orchestral Society, Oxted, Surrey, and taught French at Hazelwood School, till 1931. Entered Adult Education work in music (LCC and Royal Arsenal Co-operative Soc. Educn Depts), 1932. Director of Music at Morley College, London, 1940–51. Sent to prison for 3 months as a conscientious objector, June 1943. A Child of Our Time first performed March 1944, broadcast Jan. 1945. 1st Symphony performed Nov. 1945 by Liverpool Philharmonic Society. Artistic Dir, Bath Festival, 1969–74. President: Kent Opera Company, 1979–; London Coll. of Music, 1983–. Hon. Mem., Amer. Acad. of Arts and Letters, 1973; Extraordinary Mem., Akad. der Künste, Berlin, 1976. Cobbett Medal for Chamber Music, 1948; Gold Medal, Royal Philharmonic Society, 1976; Prix de Composition Musicale, Fondation Prince Pierre de Monaco, 1984. Honorary degrees include: MusD Cambridge, 1964; DMus: Trinity Coll., Dublin, 1964; Leeds, 1965; Oxford, 1967; London, 1975; Keele, 1986; DUniv York, 1966; DLitt Warwick, 1974. Commandeur de l'Ordre des Arts et des Lettres (France), 1988. *Works include:* String Quartet No 1, 1935; Piano Sonata, 1937; Concerto for Double String Orchestra, 1939; A Child of Our Time, Oratorio, 1941; Fantasia on a theme of Handel for Piano and Orchestra, 1942; String Quartet, No 2, 1943; Symphony No 1, 1945; String Quartet No 3, 1946; Little Music for Strings, 1946; Suite in D, 1948; Song Cycle, The Heart's Assurance, 1951; Opera, The Midsummer Marriage, 1952 (first performed 1955); Ritual Dances, excerpts from the Opera for Orchestra, 1952; Fantasia Concertante on a Theme of Corelli for String Orchestra, 1953 (commnd for Edinburgh Festival); Divertimento, 1955; Concerto for piano and orchestra, 1956 (commnd by City of Birmingham Symphony Orch.); Symphony No 2, 1957 (commnd by BBC); Crown of the Year (commnd by Badminton School), 1958; Opera, King Priam (commnd by Koussevitsky Foundation of America), 1961; Magnificat and Nunc Dimittis (commnd by St John's Coll., Cambridge), 1961; Piano Sonata No 2, 1962; Incidental music to The Tempest, 1962; Praeludium for Brass etc (commnd by BBC), 1962; Cantata, The Vision of St Augustine, 1966; The Shires Suite, 1970; Opera, The Knot Garden, 1970; Songs for Dov, 1970; Symphony No 3, 1972; Piano Sonata no 3, 1973; Opera, The Ice Break, 1977; Symphony No 4, 1977 (commnd by Chicago SO); String Quartet No 4, 1979; Triple Concerto, 1979 (commnd by LSO with Ralph Vaughan Williams Trust); The Mask of Time, 1983 (commnd by Boston SO); The Blue Guitar, 1983 (commnd by Ambassador Internat. Cultural Foundn); Festal Brass with Blues, 1983 (commnd by Hong Kong Fest.); Piano Sonata No 4, 1984 (commnd by LA Philharmonic Assoc.); Opera, New Year, 1989 (commnd by Houston Grand Opera, Glyndebourne Fest. Opera and BBC); Byzantium, for soprano solo and orchestra, 1989 (commnd by Chicago Symphony Orch. and Carnegie Hall for their centennials); String Quartet No 5, 1991. *Publications:* Moving into Aquarius, 1959, rev. edn 1974; Music of the Angels, 1980. *Recreation:* walking. *Address:* c/o Schott & Co., 48 Great Marlborough Street, W1Y 2BN. *TA:* Shotanco, London. *T:* 071–439 2640.

TIPPETTS, Rutherford Berriman; *b* 8 Feb. 1913; *s* of late Percy William Berriman Tippetts and Katherine Brown Rutherford; *m* 1948, Audrey Helen Wilson Cameron; one *s* one *d*. *Educ:* Rugby; Trinity Coll., Oxford (MA). Asst Principal, BoT, 1936; Principal Private Sec. to Ministers of Supply and Presidents of BoT, 1941–45; idc 1954; Chief Exec., Dollar Exports Council, 1959–61; served in Commercial Relations and Exports, Industry and Tourism Divs of BoT; Under-Sec., Export Services Div., DTI, 1970–73. Mem., Council, CGLI. Master, Worshipful Co. of Armourers and Brasiers, 1975–76. *Address:* 74 Ebury Mews East, SW1W 9QA. *T:* 071–730 6464. *Clubs:* Carlton, Royal Wimbledon.

TIPPLER, John; Director, Network, British Telecom, UK Communications Division, 1986–89, retired; *b* 9 Aug. 1929; *s* of George Herbert and Sarah Tippler, Spalding, Lincs; *m* 1952, Pauline Taylor (marr. diss. 1983); two *s*. *Educ:* Spalding Grammar School. Architect's Dept, Spalding RDC, 1945; Post Office Telephone Service, 1947; Royal Signals, 1949–50; Staff Mem., PO Central Engineering Sch., 1954–59; PO Engineering Develt, 1960–80; Dir, Exchange and Data Systems Op. and Develt, 1980; Dir of Engrg, BT, 1982–86. *Recreations:* music, country walking, motor-cycling, cinema, theatre. *Address:* 227 Broadgate, Weston Hills, Spalding, Lincs.

TIRVENGADUM, Sir Harry (Krishnan), Kt 1987; Chevalier, Ordre National de la Légion d'Honneur 1986; Chairman and Managing Director, Air Mauritius, since 1981; *b* 2 Sept. 1933; *s* of Govinden Tirvengadum and Meenatchee Sangeelee; *m* 1970, Elahe Amin Amin; three *d*. *Educ:* Royal College, Mauritius; Oxford Univ. Principal Assistant Secretary: Min. of Works, 1952–67; Min. of Communications, in charge of Depts of Civil Aviation, Telecommunications, Marine Services, Posts & Telegraphs and Meteorological Services, 1968–72; Min. of Commerce and Industry, 1970; Air Mauritius: Gen. Manager, 1972–78; Dep. Chm. and Dep. Man. Dir, 1978–81. Chairman: Rodrigues Hotel, 1981–; New Airport Catering Services, 1988–; Chm. and Man. Dir, Mauritius Shopping Paradise Ltd, 1984–; Director: Mauritius Hotels Gp, 1973–81; Plaisance Airlift Catering Unit, 1980–; Mauritius Estate Development & Co., 1986–; Mauritius Commercial Bank, 1989–; State Bank Internat., 1990–. Dir of Overseas Telecommunication Services and Dir of Telecommunication Services, 1984–. Chm., Municipal Commn, Quatre-Bornes, 1974–77. Chief delegate of Mauritius, Triennial Assembly, ICAO, 1971–; Rep. of Employers on Employment of Disabled Persons Bd, 1988–. Member: Exec. Cttee, IATA, 1988–91; Nat. Educn Award Panel, 1988. FCIT; FInstD. Citoyen d'Honneur, Town of Beau Bassin/Rose Hill, Mauritius, 1986. Chevalier, Légion d'Honneur (France), 1986. *Recreations:* bridge, swimming, walking. *Address:* Dr Arthur De Chazal Lane, Floréal, Mauritius. *T:* 86–3037. *Club:* Mauritius Gymkhana.

TITCHELL, John, RA 1991 (ARA 1986); ARCA; professional painter, since 1951; *b* 1926; *s* of Arthur Titchell and Elsie Catt; *m* 1947, Audrey Ward; one *s* one *d*. *Educ:*

Crayford Elem. Sch.; Sidcup Sch. of Art; Royal Coll. of Art (ARCA 1951). *Recreations:* reading, listening to music. *Address:* Frith Farm, Pluckley, Ashford, Kent TN27 0SY.

TITCHENER, Alan Ronald; Under Secretary, Enterprise Initiative Division, Department of Trade and Industry, since 1987; *b* 18 June 1934; *s* of Edmund Hickman Ronald Titchener and Minnie Ellen Titchener; *m* 1959, Joyce Blakesley; two *s*. *Educ:* Harrow County Grammar Sch.; London School of Economics. BSc(Econ) 1962. RAF, 1952. Colonial Office, 1954; Min. of Transport, 1962; Board of Trade, 1964; HM Consul New York, 1969; Dept of Trade, 1973; HM Consul-Gen., Johannesburg, 1978; Under Sec., Overseas Trade Div., DTI, 1982. *Address:* c/o Department of Trade and Industry, 1 Victoria Street, SW1H 0ET. *Club:* Royal Air Force.

TITCHENER, (John) Lanham (Bradbury), CMG 1955; OBE 1947; *b* 28 Nov. 1912; *s* of late Alfred Titchener and late Alicia Marion Leonora Bradbury; *m* 1937, Catherine Law Clark (*decd*) (marr. diss. 1958); no *c*; *m* 1958, Rikke Marian Lehmann (*née* Bendixsen), *e d* of late Frederik Carl Bendixsen and Kammerherreinde Nina Grandjean of Vennerslund, Falster, Denmark; two step *s*. *Educ:* City of London Sch.; Royal College of Music. Nat. Council of Education of Canada, 1934; BBC 1938–43; War of 1939–45: served HM Forces, Jan.-Aug. 1943; Psychological Warfare Branch, Allied Force HQ, Algiers, 1943; 15th Army Group HQ, Italy, 1944–45; Asst Dep. Director, Political Warfare Div., SACSEA, 1945; Political Warfare Adviser to C-in-C, Netherlands East Indies, 1945–46; First Secretary, HM Foreign Service, 1947; served in FO until 1950, when transferred to HM Embassy, Moscow; then at HM Embassy, Ankara, 1953–54; Economic Counsellor, HM Embassy, Tehran, 1954–56, Chargé d'Affaires, 1955. Resigned HM Foreign Service, 1957. *Recreations:* music, gardening, fishing. *Address:* 3 Impasse du Château, 06190 Roquebrune Village, France. *T:* 93 350785. *Club:* Travellers'.

TITCHENER-BARRETT, Sir Dennis (Charles), Kt 1981; TD 1953, 2 bars; Chairman, Woodstock (London) Ltd (industrial minerals), 1962–89; *m* 1940, Joan Wilson; one *s* three *d*. Served War, RA, 1939–46; commanded 415 Coast Regt RA (TA), 1950–56; Mem., Kent T&AFA, 1950–56. An Underwriting Member of Lloyd's, 1977–. ILEA School Governor, 1956–73; Member: Gtr London Central Valuation Panel, 1964–75; Cons. Bd of Finance, 1968–75; Cons. Policy Gp for Gtr London, 1975–78; National Union of Conservative Associations: Mem., Central Council and Exec. Cttee, 1968–81; Treasurer, 1968–75, Chm., 1975–78, Vice-Pres., 1978–, Gtr London Area; Vice-Pres., Nat. Soc. of Cons. Agents, Gtr London Area, 1975–; Chm., S Kensington Cons. Assoc., 1954–57; Trustee, Kensington Cons. Assoc., 1975– (Pres., 1975–89). Mem., RUSI, 1947–. Fellow, Inst. of Dirs, 1952. High Sheriff of Greater London, 1977–78. *Address:* 8 Launceston Place, W8 5RL. *T:* 071–937 0613. *Club:* Carlton.

TITE, Prof. Michael Stanley, DPhil; FSA; Edward Hall Professor of Archaeological Science, Director of Research Laboratory for Archaeology and History of Art, and Fellow of Linacre College, University of Oxford, since 1989; *b* 9 Nov. 1938; *s* of late Arthur Robert Tite and Evelyn Frances Violet Tite (*née* Endersby); *m* 1967, Virginia Byng Noel; two *d*. *Educ:* Trinity Sch. of John Whitgift, Croydon; Christ Church, Oxford (MA, DPhil). FSA 1977. Research Fellow in Ceramics, Univ. of Leeds, 1964–67; Lectr in Physics, Univ. of Essex, 1967–75; Keeper, Dept of Scientific Res. (formerly Res. Lab.), British Museum, 1975–89. *Publications:* Methods of Physical Examination in Archaeology, 1972; papers on scientific methods applied to archaeology in various jls. *Recreations:* travelling with "The Buildings of England", gardening. *Address:* 7 Kings Cross Road, Oxford OX2 7EU. *T:* Oxford (0865) 58422; Research Laboratory for Archaeology and History of Art, 6 Keble Road, Oxford.

TITFORD, Rear-Adm. Donald George, CEng, FRAeS; retired 1978; Deputy Controller of Aircraft, Ministry of Defence, 1976–78; *b* 15 June 1925; *s* of late Percy Maurice Titford and Emily Hannah Titford (*née* McLaren). *Educ:* Highgate Sch Royal Naval Engineering Coll.; Coll. of Aeronautics, Cranfield. MSc. Entered RN as Cadet, 1943; Comdr 1959; Air Engr Officer, HMS Victorious, 1965; Captain 1967; comd, RN Air Station, Lee-on-Solent, 1972–74; Comd Engr Officer, Naval Air Comd, 1974–76. *Recreations:* modern pentathlon, old English watercolours. *Address:* Merry Hill, North Road, Bath BA2 6HD. *T:* Bath (0225) 462132. *Club:* Army and Navy.

TITHERIDGE, Roger Noel, QC 1973; a Recorder of the Crown Court since 1972; Barrister-at-Law; *b* 21 Dec. 1928; *s* of Jack George Ralph Titheridge and Mabel Titheridge (*née* Steains); *m* 1963, Annabel Maureen (*née* Scott-Fisher); two *d*. *Educ:* Midhurst Grammar Sch.; Merton Coll., Oxford (Exhibnr). MA (History and Jurisprudence). Called to the Bar, Gray's Inn, 1954; Holker Sen. Scholar, Gray's Inn, 1954; Bencher, Gray's Inn, 1985; Leader, Western Circuit, 1989–92. *Recreations:* tennis, sailing. *Address:* 1 Paper Buildings, Temple, EC4. *T:* 071–353 3728; 13 The Moat, Traps Lane, New Malden, Surrey. *T:* 081–942 2747.

TITLEY, Gary; Member (Lab) Greater Manchester West, European Parliament, since 1989; *b* 19 Jan. 1950; *s* of Wilfred James and Joyce Lillian Titley; *m* 1975, Maria, (Charo), Rosario; one *s* one *d*. *Educ:* York Univ. (BA Hons Hist./Educn, 1973; PGCE 1974). TEFL, Bilbao, 1973–75; taught History, Earls High Sch., Halesowen, 1976–84; Personal Assistant to MEP, 1984–89. Mem., W Midlands CC, 1981–86 (Vice-Chair: EDC, 1981–84; Consumer Services Cttee, 1984–86). Dir, W Midlands Enterprise Bd, 1982–89; Chairman: W Midlands Co-op Finance Co., 1982–89; Black Country Co-op Develt Agency, 1982–88. Contested (Lab): Bromsgrove, 1983; Dudley W, 1987. *Recreations:* family, reading, sport. *Address:* (office) 16 Spring Lane, Radcliffe, Manchester M26 9TQ. *T:* 061–724 4008. *Clubs:* Halesowen Labour (W Midlands); Springvale Sports and Social (Bilston); Little Lever (Bolton).

TITLEY, Principal Nursing Officer Jane, RRC 1990 (ARRC 1986); QHNS 1990; Matron-in-Chief, Queen Alexandra's Royal Naval Nursing Service, since 1990; *b* 22 April 1940; *d* of Louis and Phyllis Myra (Josephine) Titley. *Educ:* St Catherine's Convent, Nottingham; St Bartholomew's Hosp.; Sussex Maternity Hosp. SRN 1962; SCM 1963. Joined QARNNS, 1965; served in Naval hosps and estabts in UK, Malta, Singapore, Naples and Gibraltar; Matron, 1986; Dep. Matron-in-Chief, 1988. OStJ 1990. *Recreations:* 'to stand and stare', personal correspondence, gardening, dress-making. *Address:* c/o Naval Secretary, Ministry of Defence, Old Admiralty Building, Whitehall, SW1A 2BE.

TITMAN, Sir John (Edward Powis), KCVO 1991 (CVO 1982; LVO 1966; MVO 1957); JP; DL; Secretary of the Lord Chamberlain's Office, 1978–91; Serjeant-at-Arms to the Queen, 1982–91; *b* 23 May 1926; *s* of late Sir George Titman, CBE, MVO, sometime Secretary, Lord Chamberlain's Office, and Lady Titman; *m* 1953, Annabel Clare (*née* Naylor); two *s*. *Educ:* City of London School. Entered Lord Chamberlain's Office, 1947; State Invitations Asst, 1956; Asst Sec., 1976; retired 1991. Master, Wax Chandlers' Co., 1984. JP Surrey, 1971, DL Surrey, 1991. *Address:* Friars Garth, The Parade, Epsom, Surrey KT18 5DH. *T:* Epsom (0372) 722302. *Clubs:* Royal Automobile, MCC.

TIVERTON, Viscount; *see* Giffard, A. E.

TIWARI, Narayan Datt; Chief Minister, Uttar Pradesh, 1976–77, 1984–85, March–Sept. 1985 and since 1988; MLA (Socialist), Uttar Pradesh, since 1952; *b* Balyuti, UP, 18 Oct. 1925; *s* of Poorna Nand Tiwari and Chandrawati Devi Tiwari; *m* 1954, Dr Sushila Tiwari. *Educ:* Allahabad Univ., UP (Golden Jubilee Schol. 1948; MA Diplomacy and Internat. Affairs; LLB; Pres., Students' Union). Studied Scandinavian Econ. and Budgetary Systems in Sweden, 1959; Congressional Practices and Procedures in USA, 1964; Whitley Council System, UK, and Co-op. Banking System in Germany, Dairy Develt in Denmark. Joined Freedom Movement, 1938, and Quit India Movement, 1942, resulting in 15 months in jail, 1942. State Govt appts, 1969–: Chm., Public Accts Cttee; Minister for Finance, Heavy Industry, Sugar Cane Develt; Dep. Chm., State Planning Commn, 1980. Leader of Opposition in UP, 1977; MP (Lower House), Union Minister for Planning and Labour and Dep. Chm., Planning Commn, India, 1980; Union Minister: for Industry and Steel and Mines, 1981–84; of Industry, Petroleum and Natural Gas, Ext. Affairs, Finance and Commerce, 1985–87; of Finance and Commerce, India, 1987–88. Editor, Prabhat (a Hindi Monthly magazine). *Publications:* European Miscellany; hundreds of articles as a journalist. *Recreations:* playing cricket, hockey, chess; reading. *Address:* 2 Jantar Mantar Road, New Delhi; Village Padampuri, PO Padampuri, Dist Nainital (UP); 338-C, Sector B-1, Mahanagar, Lucknow, UP. *T:* 3015510, 3015223, 384098, 382693.

TIZARD, Prof. Barbara, PhD, FBPsS; Professor of Education, Institute of Education, University of London, 1982–90, now Emeritus; Director, Thomas Coram Research Unit, Institute of Education, 1980–90; *b* 16 April 1926; *d* of late Herbert Parker and Elsie Parker (*née* Kirk); *m* 1947, Jack Tizard (*d* 1979); one *s* two *d* (and two *s* decd). *Educ:* St Paul's Girls' School; Somerville College, Oxford. BA Oxon, PhD London. Lectr, Dept of Experimental Neurology, Inst. of Psychiatry, 1963–67; Res. Officer then Senior Res. Fellow, Inst. of Education, 1967–77, Reader in Education, 1978–80. Chm., Assoc. of Child Psychology and Psychiatry, 1976–77. Co-editor, British Jl of Psychology, 1975–79; Mem., Editorial Bd, Jl of Child Psychology and Psychiatry, 1979–. *Publications:* Early Childhood Education, 1975; Adoption: a second chance, 1977; (with J. Mortimore and B. Burchell) Involving Parents in Nursery and Infant Schools, 1981; (with M. Hughes) Young Children Learning, 1984; (jtly) Young Children at School in the Inner City, 1988; articles on transracial and intercountry adoption, children in care, child development and early education. *Address:* The Garden Flat, 6 Hampstead Hill Gardens, NW3 2PL.
See also M.C. Parker.

TIZARD, Dame Catherine (Anne), GCMG 1990; DBE 1985; Governor-General of New Zealand, since 1990; *b* 4 April 1931; *d* of Neil Maclean and Helen Montgomery Maclean; *m* 1951, Hon. Robert James Tizard, *qv* (marr. diss. 1983); one *s* three *d*. *Educ:* Matamata College; Auckland University (BA). Tutor in Zoology, Univ. of Auckland, 1967–84. Member: Auckland City Council, 1971–83 (Mayor of Auckland, 1983–90); Auckland Regional Authy, 1980–83. *Recreations:* music, reading, drama, scuba diving. *Address:* Government House, Wellington, New Zealand. *T:* (09) 898 055.

TIZARD, Sir (John) Peter (Mills), Kt 1982; Professor of Pædiatrics, University of Oxford, and Fellow of Jesus College, Oxford, 1972–83, Hon. Fellow 1983, now Professor Emeritus; Hon. Consultant Children's Physician, Oxfordshire Health Authority, 1972–83; *b* London, 1 April 1916; *e s* of late Sir Henry Thomas Tizard, GCB, AFC, FRS, and late Lady (Kathleen Eleanor) Tizard; *m* 1945, Elisabeth Joy, *yr d* of late Clifford John Taylor, FRCSE; two *s* one *d*. *Educ:* Rugby Sch.; Oriel Coll., Oxford; Middlesex Hospital. BA Oxon 1938 (3rd cl. Hons Honour Sch. of Natural Science); Oxford and Cambridge Schol. (Biochemistry and Physiology), Middlesex Hospital, 1938; MA, BM, BCh Oxon 1941; MRCP 1944; FRCP 1958; DCH England 1947. Served War of 1939–45 with RAMC, 1942–46 (Temp. Major). Med. Registrar and Pathologist, Hospital for Sick Children, Great Ormond Street, 1947; Asst Director, Pædiatric Unit, St Mary's Hospital Medical Sch., 1949; Physician, Paddington Green Children's Hospital, 1949; Nuffield Foundation Medical Fellow, 1951; Research Fellow in Pediatrics, Harvard Univ., 1951; Reader in Child Health, 1954–64, Prof. of Pædiatrics, Inst. of Child Health, Royal Postgraduate Med. Sch., Univ. of London, 1964–72; Hon. Cons. Children's Physician, Hammersmith Hosp., 1954–72. Chm., Med. Cttee, Hammersmith Hosp., 1970–71; Mem., Oxford AHA, 1979–82; Chm., Exec. Cttee, British Pædiatric Surveillance Unit, 1985–89. McLaughlin Gallie Vis. Prof., Royal Coll. of Physicians and Surgs of Canada, 1984. Lectures: Blackfan Meml, Harvard Univ., 1963; Samuel Gee, RCP, 1972; Carl Fridericksen, Danish Paediatric Soc., 1972; Perlstein, Louisville Univ., 1973; Clausen Meml, Rochester Univ., NY, 1975; Choremis Meml, Hellenic Paediatric Soc., 1975; Croonian, RCP 1978; Woolmer Meml, Biol Engrg Soc., 1982; Orator, Reading Pathological Soc., 1973. Mem. Ct of Assistants, 1971–, Master, 1983–84, Soc. of Apothecaries of London. FRSocMed 1941 (Pres., Sect. of Paediatrics, 1980–81, Hon. Fellow, 1984); Second Vice-Pres., RCP, 1977–78; Member: British Pædiatric Assoc., 1953 (Pres. 1982–85; Hon. Mem., 1987); European Pædiatric Research Soc., 1959 (Pres., 1970–71); Neonatal Society, 1959–83 (Hon. Sec. 1964–66; Pres., 1975–78; Hon. Mem., 1983); Assoc. Physicians of Great Britain and Ireland, 1965; Assoc. British Neurologists, 1969; German Acad. of Scientists, Leopoldina, 1972; Harveian Soc., 1974– (Pres., 1977); British Pædiatric Neurol. Assoc., 1975– (Pres., 1979–82; Hon. Mem., 1991); Corresp. Member: Société française de Pédiatrie, 1969; Pædiatric Soc. of Chile, 1968; Austrian Paediatric Soc., 1972; Swiss Paediatric Soc., 1973; Hon. Member: Pædiatric Soc. of Concepcion, 1968; Czechoslovak Med. Assoc. J. E. Purkyně, 1971; Dutch Pædiatric Soc., 1971; Amer. Pediatric Soc., 1976; Hellenic Soc. Perinatal Medicine, 1979; Deutsche Ges. für Kinderheilkunde, 1984. Dawson Williams Meml Prize, BMA, 1982; James Spence Medal, BPA, 1986. *Publications:* Medical Care of Newborn Babies (jtly), 1972; papers in scientific and medical journals. *Address:* Holly Cottage, Court Drive, Hillingdon, Uxbridge, Mddx UB10 0BN. *T:* Uxbridge (0895) 811055; Jesus College, Oxford OX1 3DW. *Club:* Athenæum.

TIZARD, Rt. Hon. Robert James, PC (NZ) 1985; MP for Tamaki, Otahuhu, Pakuranga, and Panmure, New Zealand, 1957–90; Minister of Defence, Science and Technology, 1987–90; retired; *b* 7 June 1924; *s* of Henry James and Jessie May Tizard; *m* 1951, Catherine Anne Maclean (*see* Dame Catherine Tizard) (marr. diss. 1983); one *s* three *d*; *m* 1983, Mary Christina Nacey; one *s*. *Educ:* Auckland Grammar Sch.; Auckland Univ. MA, Hons Hist., 1949. Served War: RNZAF, 1943–46, incl. service in Canada and Britain; (commnd as a Navigator, 1944). Pres., Students' Assoc., Auckland Univ., 1948; Lectr in History, Auckland Univ., 1949–53; teaching, 1954–57 and 1961–62. MP 1957–60 and 1963–90; Minister of Health and State Services, 1972–74; Dep. Prime Minister and Minister of Finance, 1974–75; Dep. Leader of the Opposition, 1975–79; Minister of Energy, Science and Technol., and Statistics, and Minister i/c Audit Dept, 1984–87. *Recreation:* golf. *Address:* 8 Glendowie Road, Auckland 5, New Zealand.

TOBIN, Prof. James, PhD; Sterling Professor of Economics, Yale University, 1957–88, now Emeritus; *b* 5 March 1918; *s* of Louis Michael and Margaret Edgerton Tobin; *m* 1946, Elizabeth Fay Ringo; three *s* one *d*. *Educ:* Harvard Univ. AB 1939 (*summa cum laude*); MA 1940; PhD 1947. Economist, Office of Price Admin, and Civilian Supply and War Production Bd, Washington, 1941–42; line officer, destroyer, USN, 1942–46. Teaching Fellow in Econs, 1946–47, Jun. Fellow, Soc. of Fellows, 1947–50, Harvard Univ.; Yale University: Associate Prof. of Econs, 1950–55; Prof. of Econs, 1955–88; Dir, Cowles Foundn for Res. in Econs, 1955–61; Chm., Dept of Econs, 1968–69, 1974–78.

Vis. Prof., Univ. of Nairobi, 1972–73; Ford Vis. Res. Prof. of Econs, Univ. of Calif. Berkeley, 1983. Mem., Pres.'s Council of Econ. Advrs, 1961–62. Corresp. FBA 1984. LLD *hc*: Syracuse Univ., 1967; Univ. of Illinois, 1969; Dartmouth Coll., 1970; Swarthmore Coll., 1980; New Sch. for Social Res., and New York Univ., 1982; Univ. of Hartford, 1984; Colgate Univ., 1984; Western Maryland Coll., 1984; Univ. of New Haven, 1986; Sacred Heart Univ., 1990; DEcon *hc* New Univ. of Lisbon, 1980; Hon. DHL: Bates Coll., 1982; Hofstra Univ., 1983; Gustavus Adolphus Coll., 1986; DSocSc *hc* Helsinki, 1986. Foreign Associate, Acad. of Sciences, Portugal, 1980. Nobel Prize in Economics, 1981; Centennial Medal, Harvard Univ. Graduate Sch., 1989. Grand Cordon, Order of the Sacred Treasure (Japan), 1988. *Publications:* (jtly) The American Business Creed, 1956; National Economic Policy, 1966; Essays in Economics: vol. 1, Macroeconomics, 1971; vol. 2, Consumption and Econometrics, 1975; vol. 3, Theory and Policy, 1982; The New Economics One Decade Older, 1974; Asset Accumulation and Economic Activity, Reflections on Contemporary Macroeconomic Theory, 1980; Policies for Prosperity, 1987; contribs to professional jls. *Recreations:* tennis, ski-ing, sailing, canoeing, fishing, chess. *Address:* Yale University, Box 2125 Yale Station, New Haven, Conn 06520, USA. *T:* 203–432–3720. *Clubs:* Yale (New York); Mory's Association, The Club (New Haven).

TOD, Sir John Hunter H.; *see* Hunter-Tod.

TOD, Rear-Adm. Jonathan James Richard, CBE 1982; Assistant Chief of Defence Staff (Policy and Nuclear), Ministry of Defence, since 1990; *b* 26 March 1939; *e s* of late Col Richard Logan Tod and Elizabeth Allan Tod; *m* 1962, Claire Elizabeth Russell Dixon; two *s*. *Educ:* Gordonstoun Sch. BRNC, Dartmouth, 1957–59; Flying trng, 1961; Hal Far (Malta), 1963; HM Ships: Ark Royal, Hermes, Eagle, RNAS, Lossiemouth, 1962–70; BRNC, Dartmouth, 1970–72; Exec. Officer, HMS Devonshire, 1972–74; Naval Staff, 1975–77; Comd HMS Brighton, 1978–80; Cabinet Office, 1980–82; RCDS 1983; Comd HMS Fife, 1984–85; Dir, Defence Programme, 1986–88; Comd HMS Illustrious, 1988–89; Flag Officer Portsmouth and Naval Base Comdr Portsmouth, 1989–90. *Recreations:* sailing, driving pony and trap. *Address:* Ministry of Defence, Main Building, Whitehall, SW1A 2HB.

TODD, family name of **Baron Todd.**

TODD, Baron, *cr* 1962, of Trumpington (Life Peer); **Alexander Robertus Todd,** OM 1977; Kt 1954; FRS 1942; DSc Glasgow; Dr Phil nat Frankfurt; DPhil Oxon; MA Cantab; FRSC; Master of Christ's College, Cambridge, 1963–78 (Fellow, 1944); Professor of Organic Chemistry, University of Cambridge, 1944–71; (first) Chancellor, University of Strathclyde, Glasgow, 1965–91 (Fellow, 1990); *b* Glasgow, 2 Oct. 1907; *e s* of Alexander Todd, JP, Glasgow; *m* 1937, Alison Sarah (*d* 1987), *e d* of Sir H. H. Dale, OM, GBE, FRS; one *s* two *d*. *Educ:* Allan Glen's Sch.; University of Glasgow. Carnegie Research Scholar, University of Glasgow, 1928–29; Univ. of Frankfurt a M, 1929–31; 1851 Exhibition Senior Student, Univ. of Oxford, 1931–34; Assistant in Medical Chemistry, 1934–35, and Beit Memorial Research Fellow, 1935–36, University of Edinburgh; Member of Staff, Lister Institute of Preventive Medicine, London, 1936–38; Reader in Biochemistry, University of London, 1937–38; Visiting Lecturer, California Institute of Technology, USA, 1938; Sir Samuel Hall Professor of Chemistry and Director of Chemical Laboratories, University of Manchester, 1938–44. Visiting Professor: University of Chicago, 1948; University of Sydney, 1950; Mass. Inst. Tech., 1954. Chemical Society, Tilden Lecturer, 1941, Pedler Lecturer, 1946; Meldola Medal, 1936; Leverhulme Lecturer, Society of Chemical Industry, 1948; Visitor, Hatfield Polytechnic, 1978–86. Dir, Fisons Ltd, 1963–78. President: Chemical Soc., 1960–62; Internat. Union of Pure and Applied Chemistry, 1963–65; BAAS, 1969–70; Royal Soc., 1975–80; Soc. of Chem. Industry, 1981–82. Chairman: Adv. Council on Scientific Policy, 1952–64; Royal Commn on Medical Education, 1965–68; Board of Governors, United Cambridge Hospitals, 1969–74. Member Council, Royal Society, 1967–70; Mem., NRDC, 1968–76. Hon. Member French, German, Spanish, Belgian, Swiss, Japanese Chemical Societies; Foreign Member: Nat. Acad. Sciences, USA; American Acad. of Arts and Sciences; Akad. Naturf. Halle; American Phil. Soc.; Australian, Austrian, Indian, Iranian, Japanese, New York, Soviet and Polish Academies of Science. Hon. Fellow: Australian Chem. Institute; Manchester College Technology; Royal Society Edinburgh. Chairman, Managing Trustees, Nuffield Foundation, 1973–79 (Trustee, 1950–79); Pres., Croucher Foundn (Hong Kong), 1988– (Trustee, 1979–; Chm., Trustees, 1980–88); Pres., Parly and Scientific Cttee, 1983–86. Lavoisier Medallist, French Chemical Society, 1948; Davy Medal of Royal Society, 1949; Bakerian Lecturer, 1954; Royal Medal of Royal Society, 1955; Nobel Prize for Chemistry, 1957; Cannizzaro Medal, Italian Chemical Society, 1958; Paul Karrer Medal, Univ. Zürich, 1962; Stas Medal, Belgian Chemical Society, 1962; Longstaff Medal, Chemical Society, 1963; Copley Medal, Royal Society, 1970; Lomonosov Medal, USSR Acad. Sci., 1979; Copernicus Medal, Polish Acad. Sci., 1979; Hanbury Medal, Pharmaceutical Soc., 1986. Hon. FRCP 1975; Hon. FRCPS(Glas) 1980; Hon. FIMechE 1976. Hon. Fellow: Oriel Coll., Oxford, 1955; Churchill Coll., Cambridge, 1971; Darwin Coll., Cambridge, 1981. Hon. LLD: Glasgow, Melbourne, Edinburgh, Manchester, California, Hokkaido, Chinese Univ. of Hong Kong; Hon. Dr rer nat Kiel; Hon. DSc: London, Madrid, Exeter, Leicester, Aligarh, Sheffield, Wales, Yale, Strasbourg, Harvard, Liverpool, Adelaide, Strathclyde, Oxford, ANU, Paris, Warwick, Durham, Michigan, Cambridge, Widener, Philippines, Tufts, Hong Kong; Hon. DLitt Sydney. Pour le Mérite, German Federal Republic, 1966; Order of Rising Sun (Japan), 1978. Master, Salters' Company, 1961. *Publications:* A Time to Remember (autobiog.), 1983; numerous scientific papers in chemical and biochemical journals. *Recreations:* fishing, golf. *Address:* 9 Parker Street, Cambridge. *T:* Cambridge (0223) 356688.

TODD, Rev. Alastair, CMG 1971; *b* 21 Dec. 1920; *s* of late Prof. James Eadie Todd, MA, FRHistS (formerly Prof. of History, Queen's University, Belfast) and Margaret Simpson Johnstone Maybin; *m* 1952, Nancy Hazel Buyers; two *s* two *d*. *Educ:* Royal Belfast Academical Institution; Fettes Coll., Edinburgh; Corpus Christi Coll., Oxford; London Univ. (External); Salisbury and Wells Theological Coll. BA (Oxon), DipTheol (London). Served War, Army, 1940–46, Capt. RHA. Apptd Colonial Administrative Service, Hong Kong, 1946; Joint Services Staff Coll., 1950; Defence Sec., Hong Kong, 1957–60; Dep. Colonial Sec., Hong Kong, 1963–64; Dir of Social Welfare, also MLC, 1966–68; and, again, Defence Sec., 1968–71, retd. Ordained Deacon by Bishop of Chichester, 1973 and Priest, 1974; Asst Curate, Willingdon, 1973–77; Vicar, St Augustine's, Brighton, 1978–86. *Recreations:* reading, walking, embroidery, gardening. *Address:* 59 Park Avenue, Eastbourne BN21 2XH. *T:* Eastbourne (0323) 505843.

TODD, Ann; Actress; *m* 1933, Victor Malcolm; one *s*; *m* 1939, Nigel Tangye; one *d*; *m* 1949, Sir David Lean, *qv* (marr. diss.). Stage plays and films include: *Plays:* Peter, in Peter Pan, Winter Garden, 1942–43; Lottie, in Lottie Dundass, Vaudeville, 1943; Madeleine Smith, in The Rest is Silence, Prince of Wales, 1944; Francesca Cunningham in The Seventh Veil, Princes, 1951; Foreign Field, 1953; Old Vic Season, 1954–55; Macbeth; Love's Labour's Lost; Taming of the Shrew; Henry IV, Parts I and II; Jennifer Dubedat in The Doctor's Dilemma, Saville, 1956; Four Winds, New York, 1957; Duel of Angels, London, 1958; *Films:* The Seventh Veil, 1945; Daybreak, 1948; The Paradine Case, 1948; So Evil My Love, 1948; The Passionate Friends, 1949; Madeleine, 1950; The Sound Barrier, 1952; The Green Scarf, 1954; Time Without Pity, 1956; Taste of Fear, 1960; Son of Captain Blood, 1961; 90 Degrees in the Shade, 1964; The Vortex, 1965; Beware my Brethren, 1970; The Fiend, 1971; The Human Factor, 1980; Persian Fairy Tale; produced, wrote and appeared in Diary Documentaries, 1964–76: Thunder in Heaven (Kathmandu); Thunder of the Gods (Delphi); Thunder of the Kings (Egypt); Free in the Sun (Australia); Thunder of Silence (Jordan); Thunder of Light (Scotland); Hebrides (Scotland). TV appearances include: The Last Target, BBC, 1972; Maelstrom (series) Norway, 1983; The McGuffin, 1985; frequent radio and television appearances both in USA and GB. Hon. DLitt Durham, 1989. *Publications:* two novels; The Eighth Veil (autobiog.), 1980.

TODD, Hon. Sir Garfield; *see* Todd, Hon. Sir R. S. G.

TODD, Sir Ian (Pelham), KBE 1989; FRCS; Consulting Surgeon: King Edward VII Hospital for Officers, since 1989 (Consultant Surgeon, 1972–89); St Bartholomew's Hospital, since 1981 (Consultant Surgeon, 1958–61); St Mark's Hospital, since 1986 (Consultant Surgeon, 1954–86); *b* 23 March 1921; *s* of Alan Herepath and Constance Todd; *m* 1946, Jean Audrey Ann Noble; two *s* three *d*. *Educ:* Sherborne Sch.; St Bartholomew's Hosp. Med. Coll. (DCH 1947); Toronto Univ. (Rockefeller studentship, 1941–43; MD 1945; MS 1956). MRCS, LRCP 1944; FRCS 1949. Served RAMC, Captain (AER Major). Wellcome Res. Fellow, 1955–56. Lectures: Wilson-Hay Meml, Perth, 1978; Howard H. Frykman Meml, Minneapolis, 1979; Patrick Hanley Meml, New Orleans, 1982; Gordon Watson, St Bart's Hosp., 1982; Purdue Frederick, New Orleans, 1984; Zachary Cope Meml, RCS, 1985; Henry Floyd Meml, Stoke Mandeville, 1986; John Clive Meml, Calif., 1986; Pybus Meml, Durham, 1988; Chesledon, St Thomas' Hosp., 1988; Cutait Oration, Brazil, 1991. Visiting Professorships incl.: Montevideo; Ribeirao Preto; La Paz; Vellore; New Orleans; Minneapolis; Madras; Detroit. Examiner in Surgery: Univ. of London, 1958–64; Cambridge Univ., 1988; Ex-civilian Cons. (Proctology), RN, 1970–86. President: Sect. Colo-proctology, RSM, 1970–71; Med. Soc. of London, 1984–85; RCS, 1986–89 (Mem. Council, 1975–89; Hunterian Prof., 1953; Arris and Gale Lectr, 1957–58); Vice-President: Imperial Cancer Res. Fund, 1986–89; Internat. Fedn of Surgical Colls, 1990–. Founder, Leeds Castle Polyposis Gp, 1983. Fellow, Assoc. of Surgeons of GB and Ire., 1960; Founder Mem., Surgical Sixty Club; Hon. Member: Amer. Soc. of Colon and Rectal Surgs, 1974; RACS, 1974; Soc. Gastroent. Belge, 1964; Surgical Res. Soc. of SA; Hellenic Surgical Assoc.; Assoc. of Surgs of India; Acad. of Medicine of Malaysia; NY State Surgical Soc., and S Amer. socs. FRGS 1986; Hon. FCMSA 1987; Hon. FRACS 1988; Hon. FACS 1988; Hon. FRCSCan 1989; Hon. FRCPSGlas 1989; Hon. Fellow, Colo-rectal Soc. of Sydney. Lister Prize in Surgery, Toronto, 1956. Star of Jordan, 1973. *Publications:* Intestinal Stomas, 1978; (ed) Rob and Smith, Operative Surgery, vol. 3, 1982; many articles on surgery of colon and rectum in Brit. and Amer. jls. *Recreations:* ski-ing, travel, philately, music. *Address:* 34 Chester Close North, NW1 4JE. *T:* 071–486 7776; Pumphill Cottage, Brent Pelham, Buntingford, Herts SG9 0HQ. *T:* Brent Pelham (0279) 777316.

TODD, John Arthur, FRS 1948; PhD; Emeritus Reader in Geometry in the University of Cambridge; Fellow of Downing College, 1958–73, Hon. Fellow 1973; *b* 23 Aug. 1908; *s* of John Arthur and Agnes Todd. *Educ:* Liverpool Collegiate School; Trinity Coll., Cambridge. Assistant Lecturer in Mathematics, University of Manchester, 1931–37; Lecturer in Mathematics in the University of Cambridge, 1937–60, Reader in Geometry 1960–73. *Publications:* Projective and Analytical Geometry, 1947; various mathematical papers. *Address:* 10 Reddington Close, Sanderstead, South Croydon, Surrey CR2 0QZ. *T:* 081–657 4994.

TODD, Prof. John Francis James, PhD; CEng; CChem, FRSC; Professor of Mass Spectroscopy, and Director, University Chemical Laboratory, University of Kent at Canterbury, since 1991; *b* 20 May 1937; *o s* of late Eric Todd and Annie Lewin Todd (*née* Tinkler); *m* 1963, Mavis Georgina Lee; three *s*. *Educ:* Leeds Grammar Sch.; Leeds Univ. (BSc, Cl. I Hons Chem.). FInstMC; MIEnvSci; CEng. Research Fellow: Leeds Univ., 1962–63; Yale Univ., USA, 1963–65; University of Kent at Canterbury: Asst Lectr in Chemistry, 1965–66; Lectr in Chemistry, 1966–73; Sen. Lectr, 1973–89; Reader in Physical Chemistry, Faculty of Natural Scis, 1990; Master of Rutherford Coll., 1975–85. CIL Distinguished Vis. Lectr, Trent Univ., Canada, 1988. J. B. Cohen Prizeman, Leeds Univ., 1963; Fulbright Research Scholar, 1963–65. Chm., Canterbury and Thanet HA, 1982–86. Chairman: Kent Section of Chem. Soc., 1975; British Mass Spectroscopy Soc., 1980–81; Treas., British Mass Spectrometry Soc., 1990–; Titular Mem., IUPAC Commn on Molecular Structures and Spectroscopy, 1979–91. Mem., Kent Educn Cttee, 1983–88. Member: Clergy Orphan Corp., 1985–; Council, Strode Park Foundn for the Disabled, 1986–90. Governor, S Kent Coll. of Technology, 1977–89. Mem., Amer. Soc. of Sigma Xi, Yale Chapter. Jt Editor, Internat. Jl of Mass Spectrometry and Ion Processes, 1985–. *Publications:* Dynamic Mass Spectrometry, vol. 4, 1975, vol. 5, 1978, vol. 6, 1981; Advances in Mass Spectrometry 1985, 1986; reviews and papers, mainly on mass spectrometry, in Jl of Chem. Soc. and Jl of Physics, etc. *Recreations:* music, travel. *Address:* University Chemical Laboratory, University of Kent at Canterbury, CT2 7NH. *T:* Canterbury (0227) 764000 (ext. 3518); West Bank, 122 Whitstable Road, Canterbury, Kent CT2 8EG. *T:* Canterbury (0227) 69552.

TODD, John Rawling, CVO 1972; OBE 1985; Secretary for Housing, Hong Kong Government, 1986–88; *b* 15 Feb. 1929; *s* of William Rawling Todd and Isabella May Todd; *m* 1960, Ingrid von Rothermann; one *s* one *d*. *Educ:* Durham Univ. (BSc). Nat. Service, RA, 1952. Joined HMOCS; Admin. Officer, Gambia, 1955; New Hebrides, 1962; Administrator, British Indian Ocean Territory, 1966; Dep. Governor, Seychelles, 1970; seconded to FCO, 1974; Hong Kong: Dep. Sec., 1976; Dir of Lands, 1982. Chm., Special Cttee on Compensation under Town Planning Ordinance, Hong Kong, 1991. *Recreations:* reading, gardening, walking, croquet. *Address:* A2822, Erlach, NO, Gut Harrathof, Austria. *Club:* Commonwealth Trust.

TODD, Prof. Malcolm, FSA 1970; Professor of Archaeology, University of Exeter, since 1979; *b* 27 Nov. 1939; *s* of Wilfrid and Rose Evelyn Todd; *m* 1964, Molly Tanner; one *s* one *d*. *Educ:* Univ. of Wales (BA, DLitt); Brasenose Coll., Oxford (Dip. Class. Archaeol (Dist.)). Res. Assistant, Rheinisches Landesmus., Bonn, 1963–65; Lectr 1965–74, Sen. Lectr 1974–77, Reader in Archaeology 1977–79, Univ. of Nottingham. Vis. Prof., New York Univ., 1979; Visiting Fellow: All Souls Coll., Oxford, 1984; Brasenose Coll., Oxford, 1990–91; Sen. Res. Fellow, British Acad./Leverhulme Trust, 1990–91. Vice-Pres., Roman Soc., 1985–; Member: RCHM, 1986–; Council, National Trust, 1987–. Corr. Mem., German Arch. Inst., 1977–. Editor, Britannia, 1984–89. *Publications:* The Northern Barbarians, 1975, 2nd edn 1987; The Walls of Rome, 1978; Roman Britain, 1981, 2nd edn 1985; The South-West to AD 1000, 1987; (ed) Research on Roman Britain, 1960–89, 1989; Les Germains: aux frontières romaines, 1990; papers in Germania, Britannia, Antiquaries Jl, Antiquity, Amer. Jl of Arch. *Recreations:* reading, writing, travel on foot. *Address:* The University, Exeter, Devon EX4 4QH. *T:* Exeter (0392) 264351.

TODD, Mary Williamson Spottiswoode, MA; Headmistress of Harrogate College, 1952–73; *b* 11 June 1909; *d* of John and Mary Todd, Oxford. *Educ:* Oxford High School;

Lady Margaret Hall, Oxford. MA Hons Oxon. Final Hon. Sch.: Mathematics, 1932, Nat. Science, 1933; London Diploma in Theology, 1941. Various teaching posts: St Felix School, Southwold, 1933–37; Clifton High School, Bristol, 1937–39; Westonbirt School, Glos, 1939–46; Headmistress of Durham, 1946–52. *Address:* 93 Oakdale, Harrogate, North Yorks. *T:* Harrogate (0423) 566411.

TODD, Hon. Sir (Reginald Stephen) Garfield, Kt 1986; *b* 13 July 1908; *s* of late Thomas and Edith C. Todd; *m* 1932, Jean Grace Wilson; three *d. Educ:* Otago Univ.; Glen Leith Theol Coll., NZ; University of Witwatersrand. Superintendent Dadaya Mission, 1934–53, Chm. Governing Bd 1963–85. MP for Shabani, 1946–58; Prime Minister of S Rhodesia, 1953–58; Mem. Senate, Parlt of Zimbabwe, 1980–85. First Vice-President, World Convention of Churches of Christ, 1955–60; awarded Citation for Christian Leadership in Politics and Race Relations; former Member Executive: United Coll. of Educn, Bulawayo; Rhodesian Christian Council. Arrested by Smith regime in 1965 and confined to Hokonui Ranch for one year; arrested by Smith regime in 1972 and imprisoned, then detained, Jan 1972–June 1976. Received medal acknowledging efforts for peace and justice in Rhodesia, from Pope Paul, 1973. Holds hon. doctorates, NZ and USA. Knighted for services to NZ and Africa. *Address:* PO Dadaya, Zimbabwe. *Club:* Bulawayo.
  See also Baron Acton.

TODD, Richard, (Richard Andrew Palethorpe-Todd); actor; *b* 11 June 1919; *s* of Major A. W. Palethorpe-Todd, Castlederg, Co. Tyrone, and Marvil Agar-Daly, Ballymalis Castle, Kerry; *m* 1st, 1949, Catherine Stewart Crawford Grant-Bogle (marr. diss. 1970); one *s* one *d*; 2nd, 1970, Virginia Anne Rollo Mailer; two *s. Educ:* Shrewsbury; privately. Entered the theatre in 1937. Served in King's Own Yorkshire Light Infantry and The Parachute Regt, 1940–46; GSO iii (Ops), 6 Airborne Div., 1944–45. Films since War of 1939–45 include: The Hasty Heart, 1949; Stage Fright, 1950; Robin Hood, 1952; Rob Roy, 1953; A Man Called Peter, 1954; The Dambusters, 1954; The Virgin Queen, 1955; Yangtse Incident, 1957; Chase a Crooked Shadow, 1957; The Long and the Short and the Tall, 1960; The Hellions, 1961; The Longest Day, 1962; Operation Crossbow, 1964; Coast of Skeletons, 1964; The Love-Ins (USA), 1967; Subterfuge, 1968; Dorian Grey, 1969; Asylum, 1972; Secret Agent 008, 1976; The House of the Long Shadows, 1982; The Olympus Force, 1988. Stage appearances include: An Ideal Husband, Strand, 1965–66; Dear Octopus, Haymarket, 1967; USA tour, The Marquise, 1972; Australia tour, Sleuth, 1973; led RSC N American tour, 1974; Equus, Australian Nat. Theatre Co., 1975; On Approval (S Africa), 1976; nat. tour of Quadrille, and The Heat of the Moment, 1977; Nightfall (S Africa), 1979; This Happy Breed (nat. tour), 1980; The Business of Murder, Duchess, 1981, Mayfair, 1982–88. Formed Triumph Theatre Productions, 1970. Past Grand Steward, Past Master, Lodge of Emulation No 21. *Publications:* Caught in the Act (autobiog.), 1986; In Camera (autobiog.), 1989. *Recreations:* shooting and farming. *Address:* Chinham Farm, Faringdon, Oxon; Little Ponton House, near Grantham, Lincs. *Club:* Army and Navy.

TODD, Ronald; General Secretary, Transport and General Workers' Union, 1985–March 1992; *b* 11 March 1927; *s* of late George Thomas Todd and of Emily Todd; *m* 1945, Josephine Tarrant; one *s* two *d. Educ:* St Patrick's Sch., Walthamstow, E17. Served with Royal Marine Commandos; spent considerable time in China. Joined TGWU: worked at Ford Motor Co., 1954–62, latterly Dep. Convener; full-time officer of TGWU, 1962; Regional Officer, 1969; Reg. Sec., 1976; Nat. Organiser, 1978. Mem., TUC Gen. Council, 1984–92; Chm., TUC Internat. Cttee, 1985–92. Chm. (TU side), Ford Nat. Jt Council, 1978–85; Jt Sec., Nat. Jt Council for Stable Staff (Workpeople's side), 1978–85. Member: NEDC, 1985–; MSC, 1986–88. Member: Unity Trust, 1986– (Pres., 1986–89); Council for Charitable Support, 1988–. Hon. Vice-Pres., CND. *Recreations:* collecting Victorian music covers, archaeology. *Address:* 20 Manor Road, Walthamstow, E17.

TOFT, Dr Anthony Douglas, FRCPE; Consultant Physician, Royal Infirmary, Edinburgh, since 1978; *b* 29 Oct. 1944; *s* of William Vincent Toft and Anne Laing; *m* 1968, Maureen Margaret Darling; one *s* one *d. Educ:* Perth Academy; Univ. of Edinburgh (BSc Hons, MD). FCPS(Pak) 1990. House Physician and House Surgeon, Royal Infirmary, Edinburgh, 1969–70. Chief Medical Adviser, Scottish Equitable Life Assurance Soc., 1989–. Royal Coll. of Physicians of Edinburgh: Chm., Collegiate Members' Cttee, 1977; Mem. Council, 1986–88; Vice-Pres., 1990–; Mem., Assoc. of Physicians of GB and Ireland, 1983–; Sec., Harveian Soc., 1980–. *Publications:* Diagnosis and Management of Endocrine Diseases, 1982; papers on thyroid disease. *Recreations:* golf, gardening, hill-walking. *Address:* 41 Hermitage Gardens, Edinburgh EH10 6AZ. *T:* 031–447 2221.

TOGANIVALU, Ratu Josua Brown, CBE 1980; JP; Chairman: Fiji Broadcasting Commission, since 1988; Fiji Public Service Commission, since 1989; *b* Fiji, 2 May 1930; *m;* two *s* one *d. Educ:* Levuka Public Sch.; Marist Brothers Sch., Suva; Queensland Agricultural Coll.; Royal Agricultural Coll., Cirencester. With Native Lands Trust Board, 1953–71; MP Fiji, 1966–77: Minister for Lands, Mines and Mineral Resources, 1972–73; Minister for Agriculture, Fisheries and Forests, 1974–77; High Commissioner for Fiji: to New Zealand, 1978–81; in London, 1981–85. Represented Fiji at ACP Meeting, Guyana, 1975, ACP Meeting, Malawi, 1976, ACP/EEC Sugar Meetings, Brussels, 1976. JP (Fiji) 1968. *Recreations:* cricket, Rugby, boxing. *Address:* Box 13326, Suva, Fiji. *Clubs:* United, Defence (Fiji).

TOH CHIN CHYE, BSc, PhD, DipSc; *b* 10 Dec. 1921; *m. Educ:* Raffles Coll., Singapore; University College, London; Nat. Inst. for Medical Research, London. Reader in Physiology, 1958–64, Research Associate 1964, Vice-Chancellor, 1968–75, Univ. of Singapore. Chm., People's Action Party, 1954–81 (a Founder Mem.); MP, Singapore, 1959–88; Dep. Prime Minister of Singapore, 1959–68; Minister for Science and Technology, 1968–75; Minister for Health, 1975–81. Chm. Board of Governors: Singapore Polytechnic, 1959–75; Regional Inst. of Higher Educn and Develt, 1970–74; Mem. Admin. Bd, Assoc. of SE Asian Insts of Higher Learning, 1968–75. DLitt (*hc*) Singapore, 1976. *Publications:* papers in Jl of Physiology and other relevant jls. *Address:* 23 Greenview Crescent, Singapore 1128.

TOKATY, Prof. Grigori Alexandrovich; Professor Emeritus, City University; *b* North Caucasus, Russia; Ossetian by mother tongue. *Educ:* Leningrad Rabfak, 1929–30; Rykov Rabfak, Moscow Higher Technical Coll. MVTU, 1930–32; Zhukovsky Air Force Academy of Aeronautics, Moscow, 1932–37. DEng, PhD, DAeSc, CEng, CanTechSc. Lt Col, Air Force. Zhukovsky Academy: Aeronautical Research Engineer, 1937–38; Head of Aeronautics Laboratory, 1938–41; Dep. Head of Res. Dept, 1941; Lectr in Aerodynamics and Aircraft Design, 1941–45; Acting Prof. of Aviation, Moscow Engrg Inst, 1939–45; Rocket research and development, 1944–45; Rocket scientist, Berlin, 1945–47. Varied work for HM Govt, London, 1948–52; Imperial Coll., and Coll. of Aeronautics, Cranfield, 1953–56; work on theoretical rocket dynamics and orbital flight mechanics associated with Apollo programme, 1956–68; Reader in Aeronautics and Astronautics, Northampton Coll. of Advanced Technology, 1960–61; Head, 1961–75, and Prof., 1967–75, Dept of Aeronautics and Space Technology, Northampton Coll. of Advanced Technology and City Univ. Chief Scientific Adviser, WTI, 1976–78. Visiting Professor: Univs of the US,

Jordan, Nigeria, Iran, Turkey, Holland. FRAeS, FAIAA, FIMA. *Publications:* numerous, including seven books: Rocketdynamics, 1961; The History of Rocket Technology (jt), 1964; A History and Philosophy of Fluid Mechanics, 1971; Cosmonautics-Astronautics, 1976; Higher Education, 1982; Scientific Technol Education for the shape of things to come, 1988; Theoretic Principles of Spaceship Design, 1989; articles and booklets (alone or jointly) in the fields of fluid mechanics, gasdynamics, rocketdynamics, theory and philosophy of educn, and non-scientific subjects. *Recreations:* writing, broadcasting, travelling. *Address:* The City University, St John Street, EC1V 4PB. *Club:* National Liberal.

TOLER; *see* Graham-Toler, family name of Earl of Norbury.

TOLER, Maj.-Gen. David Arthur Hodges, OBE 1963; MC 1945; DL; *b* 13 Sept. 1920; *s* of Major Thomas Clayton Toler, DL, JP, Swettenham Hall, Congleton; *m* 1951, Judith Mary, *d* of James William Garden, DSO, Aberdeen; one *s* one *d. Educ:* Stowe; Christ Church, Oxford (MA). 2nd Lieut Coldstream Guards, 1940; served War of 1939–45, N Africa and Italy; Regimental Adjt, Coldstream Guards, 1952–54; Bde Major, 4th Gds Bde, 1956–57; Adjt, RMA Sandhurst, 1958–60; Bt Lt-Col 1959; comd 2nd Bn Coldstream Guards, 1962–64; comd Coldstream Guards, 1964–65; comd 4th Guards Bde, 1965–68; Dep. Comdt, Staff Coll., Camberley, 1968–69; GOC E Midland Dist, 1970–73; retired 1973. Dep. Hon. Col, Royal Anglian Regt (Lincolnshire) TAVR, 1979–84. Emergency Planning Officer, Lincolnshire CC, 1974–77. Chm., Lincoln Dio. Adv. Cttee, 1981–86. Pres., SSAFA, Lincs, 1978–. DL Lincs, 1982. *Recreations:* shooting, fishing, gardening. *Address:* Rutland Farm, Fulbeck, Grantham, Lincs NG32 3LG. *Club:* Army and Navy.

TOLLEMACHE, family name of **Baron Tollemache.**

TOLLEMACHE, 5th Baron *cr* 1876; **Timothy John Edward Tollemache;** DL; Chairman: NRG Holdings (UK) Ltd, since 1987; Victory NRG Holdings Ltd, since 1990; Director, AMEV (UK) Ltd, since 1980, and other companies; farmer and landowner; *b* 13 Dec. 1939; *s* of 4th Baron Tollemache, MC, DL, and of Dinah Susan, *d* of late Sir Archibald Auldjo Jamieson, KBE, MC; *S* father, 1975; *m* 1970, Alexandra Dorothy Jean, *d* of late Col Hugo Meynell, MC; two *s* one *d. Educ:* Eton. Commissioned into Coldstream Guards, 1959; served Kenya, Persian Gulf and Zanzibar, 1960–62; Course of Estate Management at Sandringham, Norfolk, 1962–64. President: Suffolk Assoc. of Local Councils, 1978–; NW Agronomy, 1983–; E Anglian Productivity Assoc., 1984–88; Suffolk Agricl Assoc., 1988; Chairman: Historic Houses Assoc. (East Anglia Region), 1979–83; CLA, Suffolk, 1990–. Vice Pres., Cheshire Red Cross, 1980–; Chm., St John's Council for Suffolk, 1982–89. President: Friends of Ipswich Museums, 1980–; Suffolk Family History Soc., 1988–; Chm., Bury St Edmunds Cathedral Appeal, 1986–90. Patron, Suffolk Accident Rescue Service, 1983–. DL Suffolk, 1984. CStJ 1988. *Recreations:* shooting, fishing, natural history. *Heir: s* Hon. Edward John Hugo Tollemache, *b* 12 May 1976. *Address:* Helmingham Hall, Stowmarket, Suffolk IP14 6EF. *T:* Helmingham (0473) 890217. *Clubs:* White's, Pratt's, Special Forces.

TOLLEMACHE, Sir Lyonel (Humphry John), 7th Bt *cr* 1793, of Hanby Hall; JP; DL; *b* 10 July 1931; *s* of Maj.-Gen. Sir Humphry Tollemache, 6th Bt, CB, CBE and Nora Priscilla (*d* 1990), *d* of John Taylor; *S* father, 1990; *m* 1960, Mary Joscelyne, *d* of William Henry Whitbread, *qv;* two *s* two *d. Educ:* Uppingham Sch.; RMA Sandhurst; RAC Cirencester. FRICS. Major, Coldstream Guards, retd 1963. Mem., Leics CC, 1985–. Gov., Royal Star and Garter Home, Richmond, 1985–. High Sheriff 1978–79, JP 1978, DL 1980, Leics. *Heir: s* Lyonel Thomas Tollemache, *b* 23 Jan. 1963. *Address:* Buckminster Park, Grantham NG33 5RU.

TOLLEY, Rev. Canon George; Hon. Canon, since 1976, and Hon. Assistant, since 1990, Sheffield Cathedral; *b* 24 May 1925; *s* of George and Elsie Tolley, Old Hill, Staffordshire; *m* 1947, Joan Amelia Grosvenor; two *s* one *d. Educ:* Halesowen Grammar Sch.; Birmingham Central Tech. Coll. (part-time); Princeton Univ., USA; Lincoln Theol Coll., 1965–67. BSc, MSc, PhD (London); FRSC; FPRI; CBIM. Rotary Foundation Fellow, Princeton Univ., 1949–50. Head, Department of Chemistry, College of Advanced Technology, Birmingham, 1954–58; Head of Research and Experimental Dept, Allied Ironfounders Ltd, 1958–61; Principal, Worcester Tech. College, 1961–65; Senior Director of Studies, Royal Air Force Coll., Cranwell, 1965–66; Principal, Sheffield Coll. of Technology, 1966–69, Sheffield City Polytechnic, 1969–82; Manpower Services Commission: Dir, Open Tech Unit, 1983–84; Head, Quality Branch, 1984–85; Chief Officer, Review of Vocational Qualifications, 1985–86; Advr, NCVQ, 1986–88; Advr, Trng Commn, then Trng Agency, 1988–90. Ordained deacon, 1967, priest, 1968; Curate, St Andrew's, Sharrow, 1967–90. Chairman: Council, Plastics Inst., 1959–61; Further Educn Adv. Cttee, Food, Drink and Tobacco Ind. Trng Bd, 1974–78; Bd, Further Educn Curriculum Unit, 1978–82; BTec Continuing Educn Cttee, 1983–85; Council of the Selly Oak Colls, Birmingham, 1984–; Adv. Bd, Pitman Exams Inst., 1987–; Pres., Inst. of Home Economics, 1987–90; Vice-Pres., Educn 2000, 1990–; Hon. Sec., Assoc. of Colleges of Further and Higher Educn, 1975–82; Member: CNAA (Chm., Cttee for Business and Management Studies, 1972–83); Yorks and Humberside Economic Planning Council, 1976–79; RAF Trng and Educn Cttee, 1975–80; Governing Body, Derbyshire Coll. of Higher Educn, 1984–87. Member Council: PSI, 1981–89; RSA. Dep. Chm., S Yorks Foundn, 1986–. Sheffield Church Burgess. Hon. FCP; Hon. Fellow: Sheffield City Polytechnic, 1982; Columbia—Pacific Univ., 1983; CGLI, 1984; Inst. of Trng and Develt, 1989. Hon. DSc: Sheffield, 1984; CNAA, 1986; DUniv Open, 1984. *Publications:* Meaning and Purpose in Higher Education, 1976; many papers relating to plastics and education in British and foreign journals. *Recreations:* music, hill walking, bird watching. *Address:* 74 Furniss Avenue, Dore, Sheffield S17 3QP. *Club:* Athenæum.

TOLLEY, Leslie John, CBE 1973; FEng 1977; Chairman, Excelsior Industrial Holdings Ltd (formerly Wheatfield Engineering Holdings), 1983–90, retired; *b* Oxford, 11 Nov. 1913; *s* of late Henry Edward Charles and Gertrude Eleanor Tolley; *m* 1939, Margaret Butterfield, *d* of late Walter Bishop and Nellie May Butterfield; one *s* one *d. Educ:* Oxford Sch. of Technology. FIProdE; CBIM. Gen. Manager, Nuffield Metal Products, 1941–52; Gen. Works Manager, 1952, Works Dir, 1954, Renold Chains Ltd; Gp Man. Dir, 1962, Chm., 1972–82, Renold Ltd; Chairman: Fodens Ltd, 1975–80; Francis Shaw & Co. Ltd, 1977–81; Dir, NW Regional Bd, Lloyds Bank Ltd, 1975–84. A Vice-Chm., 1973–78, Chm., 1978–80, BIM. *Recreation:* golf. *Address:* 5 The Redlands, Manor Road, Sidmouth, Devon EX10 8RT.

TOLOLO, Sir Alkan, KBE 1985 (CBE); High Commissioner for Papua New Guinea in Malaysia, since 1986; *m* Nerrie Tololo, MBE; two *s* two *d.* Teaching, 1957–61; supervisory teacher, 1963–65; Superintendent of Schools, 1967–69; Mem., Public Service Board, 1969–70; First Comr, PNG Teaching Service, 1971–73; Dir of Education, 1973–79; Chm., Public Services Commn, 1979–80; Consul-General Sydney, 1981; High Comr in Australia, 1983–86. Former Mem. or Chm. of numerous Boards and Cttees on education, culture and employment, PNG. Hon. LLD 1982, Hon. DTech 1982, Univ. of Papua New Guinea. *Address:* Papua New Guinea High Commission, 1 Lorong Ru Kedua, off Jalan Ru, Ampang, Kuala Lumpur, Malaysia.

TOLSTOY, Dimitry, (Dimitry Tolstoy-Miloslavsky), QC 1959; Barrister-at-Law; *b* 8 Nov. 1912; *s* of late Michael Tolstoy-Miloslavsky and Eileen May Hamshaw; *m* 1st, 1934, Frieda Mary Wicksteed (marr. diss.); one *s* one *d*; 2nd, 1943, Natalie Deytrikh; one *s* one *d*. *Educ:* Wellington; Trinity Coll., Cambridge. President of Cambridge Union, 1935. Called to Bar, Gray's Inn, 1937. Lecturer in Divorce to Inns of Court, 1952–68. *Publications:* Tolstoy on Divorce, 1946–7th edn 1971; articles in legal periodicals.

TOMALIN, Claire; writer; *b* 20 June 1933; *d* of Emile Delavenay and Muriel Herbert; *m* 1955, Nicholas Osborne Tomalin (*d* 1973); one *s* two *d* (and one *s* one *d* decd). *Educ:* Hitchin Girls' Grammar Sch.; Dartington Hall Sch.; Newnham Coll., Cambridge (MA). Publishers' reader and editor, Messrs Heinemann, Hutchinson, Cape, 1955–67; Evening Standard, 1967–68; New Statesman: Asst Literary Editor, 1968–70; Literary Editor, 1974–77; Literary Editor, Sunday Times, 1979–86. Stage play, The Winter Wife, Nuffield, Southampton, 1991. FRSL. *Publications:* The Life and Death of Mary Wollstonecraft, 1974, paperback 1977; Shelley and his World, 1980; Parents and Children, 1981; Katherine Mansfield: a secret life, 1987; The Invisible Woman, 1990 (NCR Prize, 1991); literary journalism. *Address:* 57 Gloucester Crescent, NW1 7EG. *T:* 071–485 6481.

TOMBS, family name of **Baron Tombs.**

TOMBS, Baron *cr* 1990 (Life Peer), of Brailes in the county of Warwickshire; **Francis Leonard Tombs,** Kt 1978; FEng 1977; Chairman, Rolls-Royce, since 1985 (Director, since 1982); Director: N. M. Rothschild & Sons, since 1981; Shell-UK, since 1983; *b* 17 May 1924; *s* of Joseph and Jane Tombs; *m* 1949, Marjorie Evans; three *d*. *Educ:* Elmore Green Sch., Walsall; Birmingham Coll. of Technology. BSc (Econ) Hons, London. FIMechE; FIEE; FInstE. GEC, 1939–45; Birmingham Corp., 1946–47; British Electricity Authority, Midlands, then Central Electricity Authority, Merseyside and N Wales, 1948–57; Gen. Man., GEC, Erith, 1958–67; Dir and Gen. Man., James Howden & Co., Glasgow, 1967–68; successively Dir of Engrg, Dep. Chm., Chm., South of Scotland Electricity Bd, 1969–77; Chm., Electricity Council, 1977–80. Chairman: Weir Group, 1981–83; Turner & Newall, subseq. T & N, 1982–89; Director: Turner & Newall Internat., 1982–89; Turner & Newall Welfare Trust Ltd, 1982–89. Chm., Molecule Theatre Ltd, 1985–. Member: Nature Conservancy Council, 1978–82; Standing Commn on Energy and the Environment, 1978–; SERC, 1982–85; Chairman: Engrg Council, 1985–88; ACARD, 1985–87 (Mem., 1984–87); ACOST, 1987–90. Pres., IEE, 1981–82; formerly Vice-Pres., Fellowship of Engrg; Vice-Pres., Engineers for Disaster Relief, 1985–. Chm., Assoc. of British Orchestras, 1982–86. Hon. FIChemE 1985; Hon. FICE 1986; Hon. FIProdE 1986; Hon. FIMechE 1989; Hon. FIEE 1991; Hon. Mem., British Nuclear Energy Soc. Pro-Chancellor and Chm. Council, Cranfield Inst. of Technol., 1985–91; Chancellor, 1991–, Vis. Prof., 1979–, Strathclyde Univ. (Hon. LLD, 1976; DUniv). Freeman, City of London, 1980; Liveryman, 1981–, and Asst Warden, Goldsmiths' Co. Hon. DTech Loughborough, 1979; Hon. DSc: Aston, 1979; Lodz, Poland, 1980; Cranfield, 1985; Bradford, 1986; City, 1986; Surrey, 1988; Nottingham, 1989; Warwick, 1990; Cambridge, 1990; DSc(Eng) QUB, 1986; DEd CNAA, 1989. *Recreations:* music, golf, sailing. *Address:* Honington Lodge, Honington, Shipston-upon-Stour, Warwickshire CV36 5AA.

TOMKINS, Sir Edward Emile, GCMG 1975 (KCMG 1969; CMG 1960); CVO 1957; Grand Officiér, Légion d'Honneur, 1984; HM Diplomatic Service, retired; HM Ambassador to France, 1972–75; *b* 16 Nov. 1915; *s* of late Lt-Col E. L. Tomkins; *m* 1955, Gillian Benson; one *s* two *d*. *Educ:* Ampleforth Coll.; Trinity Coll., Cambridge. Foreign Office, 1939. Military service, 1940–43. HM Embassy, Moscow, 1944–46; Foreign Office, 1946–51; HM Embassy, Washington, 1951–54; HM Embassy, Paris, 1954–59; Foreign Office, 1959–63; HM Embassy, Bonn, 1963–67; HM Embassy, Washington, 1967–69; Ambassador to the Netherlands, 1970–72. Mem., Bucks CC, 1977–85. *Address:* Winslow Hall, Winslow, Bucks. *T:* Winslow (029671) 2323. *Club:* Garrick.

TOMKINS, Rt. Rev. Oliver Stratford, MA, DD, LLD; *b* 9 June 1908; *s* of Rev. Leopold Charles Fellows Tomkins and Mary Katie (*née* Stratford); *m* 1939, Ursula Mary Dunn; one *s* three *d*. *Educ:* Trent Coll; Christ's Coll, Cambridge; Westcott House, Cambridge. Asst Gen. Sec., Student Christian Movement, 1933–40, and Editor, Student Movement Magazine, 1937–40. Deacon, 1935; Priest, 1936; Vicar of Holy Trinity, Millhouses, Sheffield, 1940–45; an Associate Gen. Sec. World Council of Churches and Sec. of its Commission on Faith and Order, 1945–52; Warden of Lincoln Theological College (Scholae Cancellarii) and Canon and Prebend, Lincoln Cathedral, 1953–59; Bishop of Bristol, 1959–75. Mem. Central Cttee, World Council of Churches, 1968–75. DD (*hon. causa*) Edinburgh University, 1953; Hon. LLD Bristol, 1975. *Publications:* The Wholeness of the Church, 1949; The Church in the Purpose of God, 1950. Editor and contributor The Universal Church in God's Design, 1948; Intercommunion, 1951; (ed) Faith and Order (Lund Conference Report), 1953; Life of E. S. Woods, Bishop of Lichfield, 1957; A Time for Unity, 1964; Guarded by Faith, 1971; Prayer for Unity, 1987. *Recreation:* simply being. *Address:* 23 St Paul's Road West, Dorking, Surrey RH4 2HT. *T:* Dorking (0306) 885536.

See also Very Rev. T. W. I. Cleasby.

TOMKINSON, John Stanley, CBE 1981; FRCS; Hon. Secretary General, International Federation of Gynaecology and Obstetrics (Secretary General, 1976–85); Obstetric Surgeon, Queen Charlotte's Maternity Hospital, 1953–79; Obstetric and Gynæcological Surgeon, Guy's Hospital, 1953–79; Gynæcological Surgeon, Chelsea Hospital for Women, 1971–79; *b* 8 March 1916; *o s* of Harry Stanley and Katie Mills Tomkinson, Stafford; *m* 1954, Barbara Marie Pilkington; one *s* one *d* (and one *s* decd). *Educ:* Rydal Sch.; Birmingham University Medical Sch.; St Thomas' Hospital. MRCS, LRCP 1941; MB, ChB Birmingham 1941; FRCS 1949; MRCOG 1952; FRCOG 1967. Medal in Surgery and Priestley-Smith Prize, Birmingham. Demonstrator of Anatomy, Birmingham Medical School, 1946; appointments in General Surgery, Obst. and Gynæcol., at Birmingham and Midland Hosp. for Women, Birmingham Maternity Hospital, and Queen Elizabeth Hospital, Birmingham, 1941–42 and 1947–52; Registrar, Professorial Unit in General Surgery and Professorial Unit in Obst. and Gynæcol., Birmingham; Chief Asst, Chelsea Hospital for Women, 1952–53; Resident Obstetrician and Tutor in Obstetrics (Postgrad. Inst. of Obst. and Gynæcol. of University of London), Queen Charlotte's Maternity Hospital, 1952–53. Travelling Fellow (Guy's Hospital), USA and Canada, 1954. Vis. Prof., Spanish Hospital, Mexico City, 1972. Consultant Advr in Obstetrics and Gynæcol., Min. of Health, later DHSS, 1966–81; Consultant, WHO, 1981–. Lectures: William Hawksworth Meml, 1969; Sir Winston Churchill Meml, Canterbury, 1970; Edward Sharp Meml, 1977; Foundn Amer. Assoc. of Gynaecol. and Obstetrics, 1978; Charter Day, Nat. Maternity Hosp. Dublin, 1979; John Figgis Jewett Meml, Mass Med. Soc., USA, 1988; Bert B. Hershenson Meml, Brigham and Women's Hosp., Boston, Mass, 1988. Examiner for: Univs of Oxford, Cambridge, London, Birmingham, QUB; Univs of Haile Selassie I in Ethiopia, East Africa in Uganda, El Fateh in Tripoli, Singapore; RCOG; Conjoint Examining Bd, Central Midwives Bd. FRSM. Member: Gynæcological Club of Great Britain; Birmingham and Midland Obst. and Gynæcol. Society; Central Midwives Board; Member Council: RCOG; RCS; section of Obstetrics and Gynæcology, RSM; Mem. Exec. Council, Internat. Fedn of Obstetrics and Gynaecology; Past Chm., Jt Study Working Gp of Internat. Confedn of Midwives and Internat. Fedn of Gynaecology and Obstetrics. Jt Editor, Report on Confidential Enquiries into Maternal Deaths in England and Wales, 1964–66, 1967–69, 1970–72, 1973–75, 1976–78. Foreign Member, Continental Gynæcol. Society (of America). Hon. Fellow: Soc. of Gynaecologists and Obstetricians of Colombia, 1972; Nigerian Soc. Obst. and Gynaecol., 1977; Italian Soc. Obst. and Gynaecol., 1978; Romanian Soc. Obst. and Gynaecol., 1978; South African Soc. Obst. and Gynaecol., 1980; Spanish Soc. Obst. and Gynaecol., 1981.; Polish Soc. Obst. and Gynaecol., 1984 (Hon. Mem. 1985); Canadian Soc. Obst. and Gynaecol., 1984; Brazilian Soc. Obst. and Gynaecol., 1985; Jordanian Soc. Obst. and Gynaecol., 1985; Korean Soc. Obst. and Gynaecol., 1986. Surgeon Lieut, RNVR, 1942–46. Copernicus Medal, Copernicus Acad. of Medicine, Cracow, 1985; Medal of Polish Nation for Aid and Co-operation in Medicine, 1985. *Publications:* (ed) Queen Charlotte's Textbook of Midwifery; papers of general surgical, obstetric and gynæcological interest. *Recreations:* fly-fishing, painting, and the arts generally. *Address:* Keats House, Guy's Hospital, SE1. *T:* 071–955 5000, ext. 5570; 3 Downside, St John's Avenue, SW15 2AE. *T:* 081–789 9422; Rose Cottage, Up Somborne, Hants SO20 6QY. *T:* Romsey (0794) 388837. *Clubs:* Athenæum, Flyfishers', MCC.

TOMKYS, Sir (William) Roger, KCMG 1991 (CMG 1984); HM Diplomatic Service; High Commissioner, Kenya, since 1990; *b* 15 March 1937; *s* of late William Arthur and Edith Tomkys; *m* 1963, Margaret Jean Abbey; one *s* one *d*. *Educ:* Bradford Grammar Sch.; Balliol Coll., Oxford (Domus Scholar; 1st cl. Hons Lit. Hum.). Entered Foreign Service, 1960; MECAS, 1960; 3rd Sec., Amman, 1962; 2nd Sec., FCO, 1964; 1st Sec., Head of Chancery, Benghazi, 1967; Planning Staff, FCO, 1969; Head of Chancery, Athens, 1972; Counsellor, seconded to Cabinet Office, 1975; Head of Near East and North Africa Dept, FCO, 1977–80; Counsellor, Rome, 1980–81; Ambassador: to Bahrain, 1981–84; to Syria, 1984–86; Asst Under Sec. of State and Principal Finance Officer, FCO, 1987–89; Dep. Under Sec. of State, FCO, 1989–90. Commendatore dell'Ordine al Merito, 1980; Order of Bahrain, 1st cl., 1984. *Address:* c/o Foreign and Commonwealth Office, SW1A 2AH. *Clubs:* United Oxford & Cambridge University; Royal Blackheath Golf.

TOMLINSON, Prof. (Alfred) Charles, FRSL; Professor of English, University of Bristol, since 1982; *b* 8 Jan. 1927; *s* of Alfred Tomlinson and May Lucas; *m* 1948, Brenda Raybould; two *d*. *Educ:* Longton High School; Queens' Coll., Cambridge (MA); Royal Holloway and Bedford Colls, Univ. of London (MA; Hon. Fellow RHBNC, 1991). Lecturer, 1957–68, Reader in English poetry, 1968–82, Bristol Univ. Visiting Prof., Univ. of New Mexico, 1962–63; O'Connor Prof., Colgate Univ., NY, 1967–68 and 1989; Vis. Fellow, Princeton Univ., 1981; Lamont Prof., Union Coll., NY, 1987; Vis. Prof., McMaster Univ., Canada, 1987; Hon. Prof. of English, Keele Univ., 1989. Arts Council Poetry Panel, 1964–66. Lectures: Witter Bynner, Univ. of New Mexico, 1976; Clark, Cambridge, 1982; Edmund Blunden, Hong Kong, 1987. Exhibition of Graphics: Ely House, OUP, London, 1972; Clare Coll., Cambridge, 1975; Arts Council touring exhibn, 1978–80; Poetry Soc., 1983; Regent's Coll. Gall., 1986; in Surrealism in English Art, touring exhibn, 1986–87; Colby Coll., Maine, USA, 1987; McMaster Univ. Gall., Canada, 1987. Hon. Fellow, Queens' Coll., Cambridge, 1974. FRSL 1974. Hon. DLitt: Keele, 1981; Colgate, 1981; New Mexico, 1986. Cholmondeley Award, 1979. *Publications: poetry:* Relations and Contraries, 1951; The Necklace, 1955, repr. 1966; Seeing is Believing, 1960 (US 1958); A Peopled Landscape, 1963; Poems, 1964; American Scenes, 1966; The Poem as Initiation, (US) 1968; The Way of a World, 1969; Poems, in Penguin Modern Poets, 1969; Renga (France) 1970, (US) 1972, (England) 1979; Written on Water, 1972; The Way In, 1974; Selected Poems, 1978; The Shaft, 1978; (with Octavio Paz) Air Born, 1981 (Mexico 1979); The Flood, 1981; Notes from New York and other Poems, 1984; Collected Poems, 1985, expanded repr., 1987; The Return, 1987; Annunciations, 1989; Selected Poems, 1989; *prose:* Some Americans: a personal record, 1980 (US); Poetry and Metamorphosis, 1983; *graphics:* Words and Images, 1972; In Black and White, 1975; Eden, 1985; *translations:* (with Henry Gifford): Versions from Fyodor Tyutchev, 1960; Castilian Ilexes: Versions from Antonio Machado, 1963; Ten Versions from Trilce by César Vallejo, (US) 1970; Translations, 1983; *edited:* Marianne Moore: A Collection of Critical Essays, (US) 1969; William Carlos Williams: A Collection of Critical Essays, 1972; William Carlos Williams: Selected Poems, 1976, rev. edn (US) 1985; Octavio Paz: Selected Poems, 1979; The Oxford Book of Verse in English Translation, 1980; George Oppen: selected poems, 1990; Eros Englished: erotic poems from the Greek and Latin, 1991; contribs to: Essays in Criticism, Hudson Review, Modern Painters, Poetry (Chicago), Poetry Nation Review, Sewanee Review, Times Lit. Supp. *Recreations:* music, walking. *Address:* c/o English Department, University of Bristol, Bristol BS8 1TB.

TOMLINSON, Sir Bernard (Evans), Kt 1988; CBE 1981; DL; MD; FRCP, FRCPath; Chairman, Northern Regional Health Authority, 1982–90; Emeritus Professor of Pathology, University of Newcastle upon Tyne, since 1985; Consultant Neuropathologist, Newcastle Health Authority (formerly Area Health Authority), since 1976; *b* 13 July 1920; *s* of James Arthur Tomlinson and Doris Mary (*née* Evans); *m* 1944, Betty Oxley; one *s* one *d*. *Educ:* Brunts Sch., Mansfield; University Coll. and University Coll. Hosp., London (BS 1943, MD 1962). FRCP 1965; FRCPath 1964. Trainee Pathologist, EMS, 1943–47; served RAMC as Specialist Pathologist, 1947–49 (Major). Newcastle upon Tyne General Hospital: Sen. Registrar, Pathology, 1949–50; Consultant Pathologist, 1950–53; Sen. Consultant Pathologist, 1953–82; Hon. Lectr in Path., Univ. of Newcastle upon Tyne, 1960–71, Hon. Prof., 1973–85. Hon. Mem. Scientific Staff, MRC Neurochemical Pathology Unit, 1987–. Chm., Jt Planning Appts Cttee, DHSS, 1986–90; Mem., Disablement Services Authority, 1987–91. Privy Council Mem., RPharmS, 1990–. Pres., NE Alzheimer Disease Soc., 1985–. Chm., Friends of Durham Cathedral, 1991–. DL Tyne and Wear 1988. *Publications:* articles and book chapters on neuropath., partic. on path. of brain injury, brain changes in old age and on dementia. *Recreations:* gardening, golf, music, walking. *Address:* Greyholme, Wynbury Road, Low Fell, Gateshead, Tyne and Wear NE9 6TS.

TOMLINSON, Charles; *see* Tomlinson, A. C.

TOMLINSON, David (Cecil MacAlister); actor; *b* 7 May 1917; *s* of C. S. Tomlinson, Solicitor, Folkestone, Kent, and F. E. Tomlinson (*née* Sinclair-Thomson); *m* Audrey Freeman, actress; four *s*. *Educ:* Tonbridge Sch. Guardsman, Grenadier Guards, 1935–36; served War of 1939–45, Flight Lieut, Pilot, RAF; demobilised, 1946. Chief roles include: Henry, in The Little Hut, Lyric, Aug. 1950–Sept. 1953; Clive, in All for Mary, Duke of York's, June 1954–May 1955; David, in Dear Delinquent, Westminster and Aldwych, June 1957–July 1958; Tom, in The Ring of Truth, Savoy, July 1959; Robert in Boeing Boeing, Apollo, 1962; acted and directed: Mother's Boy (Nero), Globe, 1964; A Friend Indeed, Cambridge, 1966; The Impossible Years, Cambridge, 1966; On the Rocks (Prime Minister), Dublin Festival, 1969; A Friend Indeed, and A Song at Twilight, South Africa, 1973–74; The Turning Point, Duke of York's, 1974. First appeared in films, 1939; since then has appeared, in leading roles, in over 50 films. *Publication:* Luckier than Most (autobiog.), 1990. *Recreation:* putting my feet up. *Address:* Brook Cottage, Mursley, Bucks MK17 0RS. *T:* Mursley (029672) 213. *Club:* Travellers'.

TOMLINSON, Sir (Frank) Stanley, KCMG 1966 (CMG 1954); HM Diplomatic Service, retired; *b* 21 March 1912; *m* 1959, Nancy, *d* of late E. Gleeson-White and Mrs Gleeson-White, Sydney, Australia. *Educ:* High Pavement Sch., Nottingham; University College, Nottingham. Served in various consular posts in Japan, 1935–41; Saigon, 1941–42; United States, 1943; Washington, 1945; Acting Consul-General, Manila, 1945, Chargé d'Affaires, 1946; Foreign Office, 1947; Washington, 1951; Imperial Defence Coll., 1954; Counsellor and Head, SE Asia Dept, 1955; Dep. Commandant, Berlin, 1958; Minister, UK Permanent Delegation to NATO, 1961–64; Consul General, New York, 1964–66; British High Comr, Ceylon, 1966–69; Dep. Under-Sec. of State, FCO, 1969–72. Hon. LLD Nottingham, 1970. *Recreations:* trout fishing, oenophily, reading. *Address:* 32 Long Street, Devizes, Wilts. *Club:* Oriental.

TOMLINSON, John; operatic bass; *b* 22 Sept. 1946; *s* of Rowland and Ellen Tomlinson; *m* 1969, Moya (*née* Joel); one *s* two *d*. *Educ:* Manchester Univ. (BSc Civil Engrg); Royal Manchester Coll. of Music. Since beginning career with Glyndebourne in 1970, has sung over 100 operatic bass roles with ENO and Royal Opera House, Covent Garden, and in Geneva, Lisbon, Milan, Copenhagen, Amsterdam, Stuttgart, Bayreuth, Berlin, Tokyo, Vienna, Paris, Bordeaux, Avignon, Aix-en-Provence, Orange, San Diego, San Francisco, Pittsburgh and Vancouver. *Address:* c/o Music International, 13 Ardilaun Road, Highbury, N5 2QR. *T:* 071–359 5183.

TOMLINSON, John Edward; Member (Lab) Birmingham West, since 1984, Socialist Group Spokesman on Budgetary Control, and Member, Bureau of Socialist Group, since 1989, European Parliament; *b* 1 Aug. 1939; *s* of Frederick Edwin Tomlinson, headmaster, and Doris Mary Tomlinson; *m* 1963, Marianne Solveig Sommar, Stockholm; three *s* one *d*. *Educ:* Westminster City Sch.; Co-operative Coll., Loughborough; Nottingham Univ. (Dip. Polit. Econ. Social Studies); MA (Industrial Relations) Warwick, 1982. Sec., Sheffield Co-operative Party, 1961–68; Head of Research Dept, AUEW, 1968–70; Lectr in Industrial Relations, 1970–74. MP (Lab) Meriden, Feb. 1974–1979; PPS to Prime Minister, 1975–76; Parly Under-Sec. of State, FCO, 1976–79, and ODM, 1977–79. Sen. Lectr in Industrial Relations and Management, later Hd of Social Studies, Solihull Coll. of Tech., 1979–84. Contested (Lab) Warwicks N, 1983. *Publication:* Left, Right: the march of political extremism in Britain, 1981. *Address:* 42 Bridge Street, Walsall, WS1 1JQ. *Club:* West Bromwich Labour.

TOMLINSON, Prof. John Race Godfrey, CBE 1983; MA; Professor of Education and Director, Institute of Education, University of Warwick, since 1985; *b* 24 April 1932; *s* of John Angell Tomlinson and Beatrice Elizabeth Race Godfrey; *m* 1954, Audrey Mavis Barrett; two *s* two *d*. *Educ:* Stretford Grammar Sch.; Manchester Univ. (MA); London Inst. of Historical Research. Flt Lt, RAF, 1955–58. Teaching, 1958–60; Admin. Asst, Salop LEA, 1960–63; Asst Educn Officer, Lancs LEA, 1963–67; Dep. Dir of Educn, Cheshire LEA, 1967–72; Dir of Educn, Cheshire CC, 1972–84. Chairman: Schools Council, 1978–81; NICEC, 1985–89; Arts in Education Project, SCDC, 1985–90. Member: Court Cttee on Child Health Services, 1973–76; Gulbenkian enquiries into Drama, Music and Dance, 1974–78; Founder Chm., Further Educn Curriculum Review and Develt Unit, 1976; Member: Special Programmes Bd, MSC, 1977–82; Delegacy for Continuing Educn, Open Univ., 1978–81; Study Commn on the Family, 1978–83; Adv. Cttee on Supply and Trng of Teachers, 1979–82; Council, Foundn for Educn Business Partnerships, 1990–; Educn Advr, RNCM, 1972–85. Chairman: Exec. Cttee and Trustees, Nat. Schs Curriculum Award, 1982–; MSC TVEI Quality and Standards Gp, 1986–88; Enquiry into Freedom of Information, ILEA, 1986–87; Mem., Educn Cttee, Goldsmiths' Co., 1982–. Royal Society of Arts: Vice-Pres., 1986; Chm., Exams Bd, 1986–89; Chm. Council, 1989–91 (Mem. Council, 1982–); FRSA 1976. Pres., Soc. of Educn Officers, 1982; Trustee, Community Service Volunteers, 1981–89; Governor: Chetham's Sch., Manchester, 1984–; Menuhin Sch., 1987–89. Hon. Prof., Dept of Educn, Keele Univ., 1981–84. Lectures: Wilfred Fish Meml, GDC, 1978; Charles Gittens Meml, Univ. of Wales, 1980; Lockyer, RCP, 1980; Schools Council, BAAS, 1981; Standing Conf. on Schools' Science and Technology Annual, 1987; Barry and Tye Meml, 1987. FBIM (MBIM 1976); FCP 1980. Hon. RNCM 1980. Freeman, City of London, 1989. *Publications:* Additional Grenville Papers 1763–65, 1962; (ed) The Changing Government of Education, 1986; Teacher Appraisal: a nationwide approach, 1989; articles in various jls. *Recreations:* family and garden, music and walking, a relentless search for good bitter. *Address:* Institute of Education, University of Warwick, Coventry CV4 7AL; Barn House, 76 Birmingham Road, Allesley, Coventry CV5 9GX. *Clubs:* Athenæum, Army and Navy, Royal Over-Seas League.

TOMLINSON, Maj.-Gen. Michael John, CB 1981; OBE 1973 (MBE 1964); Secretary, The Dulverton Trust, since 1984; Director Royal Artillery, 1981–84, retired; *b* 20 May 1929; *s* of late Sidney Tomlinson and Rose Hodges; *m* 1955, Patricia, *d* of late Lt-Col A. Rowland; one *s* one *d*. *Educ:* Skinners' Sch.; Royal Military Academy. Commissioned, RA, 1949; served in Brunei (despatches, 1962); GSO2 to Dir of Ops Borneo, 1962–64; DAMS, MoD, 1966–68; GSO1, Staff Coll. Camberley, 1968–70; CO, 2 Field Regt RA, 1970–72; Col GS, Staff Coll. Camberley, 1972–73; CRA 3rd Div., 1973–75; Student, RCDS, 1976; Dep. Mil. Sec. (B), MoD, 1976–78; Dir of Manning, Army, 1978–79; Vice-Adjt Gen., 1979–81. Col Comdt, RA, 1982–; Hon. Colonel: 2 Field Regt, RA, 1985–89; 104 Regt RA (Volunteers), 1985–87. FBIM 1984; FRSA 1985. *Recreations:* music, gardening. *Address:* The Dulverton Trust, 5 St James's Place, SW1A 1NP. *Club:* Army and Navy.

TOMLINSON, Michael John; Chief Inspector (Schools), HM Inspectorate of Schools, since 1989; *b* 17 Oct. 1942; *s* of Edith Cresswell and Jack Tomlinson; *m* 1965, Maureen Janet; one *s* one *d*. *Educ:* Oakwood Technical High Sch., Rotherham; Bournemouth Boys' Sch.; Durham Univ. (BSc Hons Chem.); Nottingham Univ. (post-grad. Cert Ed (First Div.)). Chemistry teacher, Henry Mellish GS, Nottingham, 1965–69; Head of Chemistry, Ashby-de-la-Zouch GS, 1969–77; School/Industry Liaison Officer, ICI (secondment), 1977. Chem. Soc. Award in Chem. Educn (Bronze Medal), 1975. Silver Jubilee Medal, 1977. *Publications:* New Movements in the Study and Teaching of Chemistry, 1975; Organic Chemistry: a problem-solving approach, 1977; Mechanisms in Organic Chemistry: case studies, 1978; BP educn service contribs, 1974–78; articles in professional jls. *Recreations:* gardening, food and wine, reading. *Address:* Brooksby, Mayhall Lane, Chesham Bois, Amersham, Bucks HP6 5NR. *T:* Amersham (0494) 726967.

TOMLINSON, Prof. Richard Allan, FSA; Professor of Ancient History and Archaeology since 1971, and Head of School of Antiquity since 1988, University of Birmingham; *b* 25 April 1932; *s* of James Edward Tomlinson and Dorothea Mary (*née* Grellier); *m* 1957, Heather Margaret Murphy; three *s* one *d*. *Educ:* King Edward's Sch., Birmingham; St John's Coll., Cambridge (BA, MA). FSA 1970. Asst, Dept of Greek, Univ. of Edinburgh, 1957; Asst Lectr 1958, Lectr 1961, Sen. Lectr 1969, Dept of Ancient History and Archaeology, Univ. of Birmingham. British School at Athens: Editor, Annual, 1978–91; Chm. Managing Cttee, 1991–. *Publications:* Argos and the Argolid, 1972; Greek Sanctuaries, 1976; Epidaurus, 1983; (ed) Greek Architecture, by A. W. Lawrence, 4th edn 1983; (contrib.) Sir Banister Fletcher, A History of Architecture, 19th edn, 1987; Greek Architecture, 1989; The Athens of Alma-Tadema, 1991; articles in Annual of British Sch. at Athens, Jl of Hellenic Studies, Amer. Jl of Archaeology, etc. *Recreations:* architecture, walking. *Address:* Department of Ancient History and Archaeology, University of Birmingham, PO Box 363, Birmingham B15 2TT. *T:* 021–414 5497.

TOMLINSON, Sir Stanley; *see* Tomlinson, Sir F. S.

TOMLINSON, Stephen Miles; QC 1988; *b* 29 March 1952; *s* of Enoch Tomlinson and Mary Marjorie Cecilia Tomlinson (*née* Miles); *m* 1980, Joanna Kathleen Greig; one *s* one *d*. *Educ:* King's Sch., Worcester; Worcester Coll., Oxford (Eldon Law Schol.; MA). Called to the Bar, Inner Temple, 1974, Bencher, 1990. Lectr in Law, Worcester Coll., Oxford, 1974–76. *Recreations:* gardening, family, cricket. *Address:* 7 King's Bench Walk, Temple, EC4Y 7DS. *T:* 071–583 0404. *Clubs:* Travellers', MCC.

TOMPKINS, Prof. Frederick Clifford, FRS 1955; Professor in Physical Chemistry, Imperial College of Science and Technology, SW7, 1959–77, now Emeritus; Editor and Secretary of Faraday Division of The Chemical Society (formerly The Faraday Society), 1950–77, President, 1978; *b* 29 Aug. 1910; *m* 1936, Catherine Livingstone Macdougal; one *d*. *Educ:* Yeovil Sch.; Bristol Univ. Asst Lectr, King's Coll., Strand, 1934–37; Lectr and Senior Lectr, Natal Univ., Natal, S Africa, 1937–46; ICI Fellow, King's College, Strand, 1946–47; Reader in Physical Chemistry, Imperial College of Science and Technology, 1947; Hon. ARCS 1964. Hon. DSc Bradford, 1975. *Publications:* Chemisorption of Gases on Metals, 1978; contributions to Proc. Royal Society, Journal Chem. Soc., Trans Faraday Soc., Jl Chem. Physics, Zeitung Elektrochem. *Address:* 9 St Helens Close, Southsea, Portsmouth, Hants. *T:* Portsmouth (0705) 731901.

TOMPKINS, (Granville) Richard (Francis); Founder, Chairman and Managing Director: Green Shield Trading Stamp Co. Ltd, since 1958; Argos Distributors Ltd, 1973–79; *b* 15 May 1918; *s* of late Richard and Ethel May Tompkins; *m* 1970, Elizabeth Nancy Duke (Cross of Merit with Crown Order, Order Pro Merito Melitensi SMO Malta; Comdr, Order of Holy Cross of Jerusalem, Bailiwick of St Louis); one *d* (and two *d* of a former marriage). *Educ:* Pakeman St LCC Sch., London, N7. Engineering Draughtsman, Home Forces, 1939–46; founded several companies in printing and advertising, 1945. Patron: The Tompkins Foundn, 1980; Regimental Museum of the Buffs—the East Kent Regt, 1985; Floral Lunch, Forces Help Soc. and Lord Roberts Workshops, 1985; SSAFA Centenary Dinner, London, 1985; Friend, Duke of Edinburgh's Award, 1986. Vice-Pres., City of London Lifeboat and RNLI Selsey, 1985. Liveryman, Glaziers' and Painters of Glass Co., 1986; Hon. Freeman, Painter–Stainers' Co., 1984. Hon. DH Lewis Univ., Chicago, 1985. Hon. FRCP, 1985. CStJ 1988; Knight Grand Cross of Merit, Order Pro Merito Melitensi SMO Malta, 1984; Grand Cross, Order of Holy Cross of Jerusalem, Bailiwick of Saint Louis, 1985; Knight Grand Comdr, Noble Companions of the Swan, 1987. *Recreations:* travel, theatre, golf. *Address:* 7 Belgrave Square, SW1.

TOMS, Carl, OBE 1969; First Head of Design, and Associate Director, for the Young Vic at the National Theatre, since 1970; *b* 29 May 1927. *Educ:* High Oakham Sch., Mansfield, Nottingham; Mansfield College of Art; Royal Coll. of Art; Old Vic Sch. Designing for theatre, films, opera, ballet, etc, on the London stage, 1957–; also for productions at Glyndebourne, Edinburgh Festival, Chichester Festival, and Aldeburgh (world première of Midsummer Night's Dream, 1960). Theatre designs include: Vivat! Vivat Regina!, Chichester and London, 1970, NY 1972; Sherlock Holmes, London, 1974, NY 1974 (Tony Award and Drama Desk Award for Theatre Design); Travesties, London, 1974, NY 1975, Vienna Burgtheater, 1976; Long Day's Journey into Night, LA 1977; Man and Superman, Malvern Festival and London, 1977; The Devil's Disciple, LA 1977, NY 1978; Look After Lulu, Chichester, 1978, Haymarket, 1978; Night and Day, Phoenix, 1978, NY, 1979; Stage Struck, Vaudeville, 1979; Windy City, Victoria Palace, 1982; The Real Thing, Strand, 1982; The Winslow Boy, Lyric, 1983; A Patriot for Me, Chichester and Haymarket, 1983, LA, 1984 (Hollywood Dramalogue Critics Award); The Hothouse, Vienna Burgtheater, 1983; Jeeves Takes Charge, NY, 1983; Hay Fever, Queen's, 1983; The Aspern Papers, 1984; Jumpers, Aldwych, 1985; The Dragon's Tail, Apollo, 1985; Blithe Spirit, Vaudeville, 1986; Wildfire, Phoenix, 1986; The Importance of Being Earnest, Royalty, 1987; Hapgood, Aldwych, 1988; The Browning Version, Royalty, 1988; Artist Descending a Staircase, Duke of York's, 1988; Richard II, Phoenix, 1988; Richard III, Phoenix, 1989; Hapgood, LA, 1989; Noël and Gertie, Comedy, 1989; Thark, Lyric, Hammersmith, 1989; Look Look!, Aldwych, 1990; The Silver King, Chichester, 1990; Private Lives, Aldwych, 1990. Designs for the Royal Opera House, Covent Garden, include: Gala perf. for State Visit of King and Queen of Nepal, 1960; Iphigénie en Tauride, 1961; Ballet Imperial, 1963; Swan Lake, 1963; Die Frau ohne Schatten (costumes), 1967; Fanfare for Europe, 1973; Queen's Silver Jubilee Gala, 1977; Fanfare for Elizabeth, 1986; for London Festival Ballet: Swan Lake, 1982; for Sadler's Wells: Cenerentola, 1959; The Barber of Seville, 1960; Our Man in Havana, 1963; for Nat. Theatre: Edward II, Love's Labour's Lost, 1968; Cyrano de Bergerac, 1970; For Services Rendered, 1979; Playbill, The Provok'd Wife, 1980 (SWET Designer of the Year award); The Second Mrs Tanqueray, On the Razzle, 1981; Rough Crossing, 1984; Brighton Beach Memoirs, Dalliance, The Magistrate, 1986; Six Characters in Search of an Author, Fathers and Sons, The Ting Tang Mine, 1987; for RSC: The Happiest Days of Your Life, 1984; The Man Who Came to Dinner, 1989; for Vienna Nat. Theatre: Travesties, 1977; She Stoops to Conquer, 1978; Betrayal, 1978; The Guardsman, 1979; Night and Day, 1980; for Vienna State Opera: Macbeth, 1982; Faust, 1985; for NY City Opera: Die Meistersinger von Nürnberg, 1975; The Marriage of Figaro, 1977; The Voice of Ariadne, 1977; Der Freischutz, 1981; Rigoletto, 1988; for NY Metropolitan Opera: Thais, 1978; for San Diego Opera Co.: Norma, 1976; La Traviata, 1976; The Merry Widow, 1977; Hamlet, 1978; Romeo and Juliet, 1982; for San Francisco Opera: Peter Grimes, 1973; Thais, 1976; The Italian Girl in Algiers (costumes), Geneva, 1984; Lucia di Lammermoor (costumes), Cologne Opera, 1985; Oberon, Edinburgh Fest. and Frankfurt, 1986; The Importance of Being Earnest, Royal Th., Copenhagen, 1987. Other companies and theatres designed for include Old Vic, Young Vic, Welsh Nat. Opera, NY State Opera. Completed re-designing of Theatre Royal, Windsor, 1965; re-designing of Theatre Royal, Bath, 1982; design consultant for Investiture of Prince of Wales, Caernarvon Castle, 1969. Has designed sets and costumes for numerous films; work has incl. decoration of restaurants, hotels, houses, etc; has also designed exhibns, programmes, cards, etc. FRSA 1987. *Publications:* Winter's Tale (designs for stage prod.), 1975; Scapino (designs for stage prod.), 1975. *Recreations:* gardening, travel. *Address:* The White House, Beaumont, near Wormley, Broxbourne, Herts EN10 7QJ. *T:* Hoddesdon (0992) 63961.

TOMS, Edward Ernest; Director, Porcelain & Pictures Ltd, since 1983; *b* 10 Dec. 1920; *s* of Alfred William and Julia Harrington Toms; *m* 1946, Veronica Rose, Dovercourt, Essex; three *s* one *d*. *Educ:* St Boniface's Coll.; Staff Coll., Camberley (psc), Nat. Defence Coll. (jssc). War service 1939–45; Captain Seaforth Highlanders; Special Forces, W Desert, Italy, Balkans, NW Europe; Regular Army, 1946, Seaforth Highlanders and QO Highlanders; Brigade Major, Berlin, 1959–61; Col GS (UK Cs-in-C Cttee), 1967–69. Principal, Home Civil Service, 1969; Asst Sec., Dept of Employment, 1973; seconded to

Diplomatic Service as Counsellor, Bonn and Vienna, 1977–81; Internat. Labour Advr, FCO, 1981–83. *Publications:* infrequent contribs to Punch and Pick of Punch. *Recreation:* hill-walking (founder Mem., Aberdeen Mountain Rescue Assoc., 1964). *Address:* c/o Clydesdale Bank, 5 Castle Street, Aberdeen. *Club:* Special Forces.

TOMSETT, Alan Jeffrey, OBE 1974; Director, Associated British Ports Holdings PLC (Finance Director, 1983–87); chartered accountant; *b* 3 May 1922; *s* of Maurice Jeffrey Tomsett and Edith Sarah (*née* Mackelworth); *m* 1948, Joyce May Hill; one *s* one *d. Educ:* Trinity School of John Whitgift, Croydon; Univ. of London (BCom). JDipMA. Hodgson Harris & Co., Chartered Accountants, London, 1938. Served War, with RAF, 1941–46 (Middle East, 1942–45). Smallfield Rawlins & Co., Chartered Accountants, London, 1951; Northern Mercantile & Investment Corp. Ltd, 1955; William Baird & Co. Ltd, 1962–63. British Transport Docks Board, later Associated British Ports: Dep. Chief Accountant, 1963; Chief Accountant, 1964; Financial Controller, 1970; Bd Mem., 1974–87 (Finance Dir, 1974–85). FCA, FCMA, IPFA, FCIS, FCIT (Hon. Treasurer, 1982–88). *Address:* 102 Ballards Way, Croydon, Surrey CR0 5RG. *T:* 081–657 5069.

TONBRIDGE, Bishop Suffragan of, since 1982; **Rt. Rev. David Henry Bartleet;** *b* 11 April 1929; *s* of Edmund Arthur Bartleet and Helen Bartleet (*née* Holford); *m* 1956, Jean Mary (*née* Rees); one *s* two *d. Educ:* St Edward's School, Oxford; AA School of Architecture, London; St Peter's Hall, Oxford; Westcott House, Cambridge. Curate: St Mary-le-Tower, Ipswich, 1957–60; St George's, Doncaster (in charge of St Edmund's), 1960–64; Vicar: Edenbridge, Kent, 1964–73; Bromley, Kent, 1973–82. *Recreations:* music, woodturning, beekeeping; architecture; icons. *Address:* Bishop's Lodge, 48 St Botolph's Road, Sevenoaks, Kent TN13 3AG. *T:* Sevenoaks (0732) 456070.

TONBRIDGE, Archdeacon of; *see* Mason, Ven. R. J.

TONČIĆ-SORINJ, Dr Lujo; Secretary-General, Council of Europe, 1969–74; *b* Vienna, 12 April 1915; *s* of Dušan Tončić-Sorinj (formerly Consul-Gen. in service of Imperial Ministry for Foreign Affairs), and Mabel (*née* Plason de la Woesthyne); *m* 1956, Renate Trenker; one *s* four *d. Educ:* Secondary sch. (Gymnasium), Salzburg. Studied law and philosophy at Univs of Vienna and Agram (Zagreb), 1934–41, also medicine and psychology (LLD Vienna); political science, Institut d'Etudes Politiques, Paris. Head of Polit. Dept of Austrian Research Inst. for Economics and Politics in Salzburg and Editor of Berichte und Informationen (political periodical published by Austrian Research Inst. for Economics and Politics), 1946–49. MP for Land Salzburg, 1949–66; Chairman: Legal Cttee of Austrian Parl., 1953–56; For. Affairs Cttee, 1956–59; in charge of For. Affairs questions, Austrian People's Party, 1959–66. Austrian Parly Observer to Consultative Assembly of Council of Europe, 1953–56; Austrian Mem., Consultative Assembly, 1956–66; Vice-Pres., Council of Europe; Vice-Pres., Political Commn, 1961–62; Minister for Foreign Affairs, Austria, 1966–68. Permanent Rep. of Austrian People's Party to Christian-Democratic Gp, European Parlt, 1980–; Hon. Rep. of Republic of Croatia to European Parlt. Chm., Austrian Assoc. of UN, 1978–; Pres., Union Internationale de la Propriété Immobilière, 1987–. Grand Cross of several orders including Order of St Michael and St George, Great Britain (Hon. GCMG). *Publications:* Erfüllte Träume (autobiog.), 1982; over 350 articles and essays on politics, economics, internat. law and history. *Recreations:* swimming, diving, history, geography. *Address:* 5020 Salzburg, Schloss Fürberg, Pausingerstrasse 11, Austria. *T:* 0662–672886.

TONEGAWA, Prof. Susumu; Professor of Biology, Center for Cancer Research and Department of Biology, Massachusetts Institute of Technology, since 1981; *b* Nagoya, 5 Sept. 1939; *s* of Tsutomo and Miyoko Tonegawa; *m* 1985, Mayumi Yoshinari; one *s. Educ:* Kyoto Univ. (BS); Univ. of San Diego (PhD). Postgraduate work: Univ. of California, San Diego, 1968–69; Salk Inst., San Diego, 1969–70; Mem., Basel Inst. of Immunology, 1971–81. Avery Landsteiner Prize, Ges. für Immunologie, 1981; Gairdner Foundn Internat. Award, 1983; Nobel Prize for Physiology or Medicine, 1987. *Address:* Massachusetts Institute of Technology, 77 Massachusetts Avenue, Cambridge, Mass 02139, USA.

TONGA, HM the King of; **King Taufa'ahau Tupou IV,** Hon. GCMG 1977 (Hon. KCMG 1968); Hon. GCVO 1970; Hon. KBE 1958 (Hon. CBE 1951); *b* 4 July 1918; *s* of Prince Uiliami Tupoulahi Tungi and Queen Salote Tupou of Tonga; *S* mother, 1965; *m* 1947, Halaevalu Mata'aho 'Ahome'e; three *s* one *d. Educ:* Tupou College, Tonga; Newington College, Sydney; Wesley College, Sydney University. Minister for Health and Education, Tonga, 1943–50; Prime Minister, 1950–65. *Heir: s* HRH Prince Tupouto'a, *b* 4 May 1948. *Address:* The Palace, Nukualofa, Tonga. *T:* 21–000.

See also HRH Prince Fatafehi Tu'ipelehake.

TONGE, Brian Lawrence, PhD; Director, Oxford Polytechnic, 1981–85; *b* 19 April 1933; *s* of Lawrence and Louisa Tonge; *m* 1955, Anne Billcliff; one *d. Educ:* Bury High Sch.; London Univ. (BSc 1st Cl. Chemistry); Manchester Univ. (PhD). FRIC 1964. Scientific Officer, Hirst Research Centre, GEC Ltd, 1956–59; Chemist, Medical Research Council Carcinogenic Substances Research Unit, Exeter Univ., 1959; Lectr in Chemistry, Plymouth Coll. of Technology, 1960–63; Research Manager, Pure Chemicals Ltd, 1963–65; Principal Lectr in Chemistry, West Ham Coll. of Technology, 1965–67; Head of Dept of Applied Science and Dean of Faculty of Science, Wolverhampton Polytechnic, 1967–71; Dep. Director, Oxford Polytechnic, 1971–81. Member, Wolfson Coll., Oxford, 1975–85. *Publications:* numerous contribs to learned jls and articles in scientific and educnl press. *Recreations:* gardening, reading, music. *Address:* 2 Pullens Field, Oxford OX3 0BU. *T:* Oxford (0865) 69666.

TONGE, Prof. Cecil Howard, TD; DDSc; FDSRCS; Professor of Oral Anatomy, 1964–81, Professor Emeritus 1981, and Dental Postgraduate Sub-Dean, 1968–82, University of Newcastle upon Tyne; *b* 16 Dec. 1915; *s* of Norman Cecil Tonge and Gladys Marian (*née* Avison); *m* 1946, Helen Wilson Currie. *Educ:* Univ. of Durham. DDSc, MB, BS, BDS (Dunelm); FDSRCS. House Surg., later Asst Resident MO, Royal Victoria Inf., 1939; Demonstrator in Anatomy, Medical Sch., Newcastle upon Tyne, 1940; Lectr in Anatomy, 1944, Sen. Lectr, 1952, Reader in Oral Anatomy, 1956, Univ. of Durham. Lieut RAMC (TA), 1941; Lt-Col RAMC (TA) Comdg 151 (N) Field Ambulance, 1954–58; Hon. Col, Northumbrian Univ. OTC, 1974–82. Chairman, Council of Military Educn Cttees of Univs of UK, 1968–82; Pres., British Div. Internat. Assoc. for Dental Research, 1968–71; Northern Regional Adviser in Postgrad. Dental Educn of RCS, 1970–83; Chm., Dental Cttee, Council for Postgrad. Medical Educn, 1978–84; British Dental Association: Pres., 1981–82; (Life) Vice-Pres., 1983–; Member: Representative Bd, 1970–; Council, 1970–82; Chm., Central Cttee for Univ. Teachers and Res. Workers, 1976–81. Member, Sunderland AHA, 1973–82; Vice-Chm., Sunderland DHA, 1982–87. Consultant to several commns estabd by FDI, 1976–89. *Publications:* chapters in: Scientific Foundations of Dentistry, 1976; Handbook of Microscopic Anatomy, vol. V/6: Teeth, 1989; papers in Dental Anatomy and Embryology; contribs to Brit. Jl of Nutrition, Jl of Anatomy, Jl of Dental Res., Jl of RCSE, Brit. Dental Jl, Dental Update, Nature, Internat. Dental Jl. *Recreation:* history.

TONGE, Rev. David Theophilus; Chaplain to the Queen, since 1984; Vicar of St Godwald's, Finstall, Bromsgrove, since 1976; *b* 15 Sept. 1930; *s* of Magdalene Tonge and late Robert Tonge; *m* 1952, Christobelle Augusta Richards; three *d. Educ:* Johnson's Point Public School, Antigua; Teacher's Certificate (Leeward); General Ordination Certificate. Pupil teacher, 1944; uncertificated teacher, 1952; postman, 1956; postal and telegraph officer, 1960. Wells Theol. Coll., 1968; deacon 1970, priest 1971; Curate of Kidderminster, 1970–75; Asst C of E Chaplain, Brockhill Remand Centre, Redditch, 1983. *Recreations:* gardening, music. *Address:* The Vicarage, 15 Finstall Road, Bromsgrove, Worcs B60 2EA. *T:* Bromsgrove (0527) 72459.

TONGUE, Carole; Member (Lab) London East, European Parliament, since 1984; *b* 14 Oct. 1955; *d* of Muriel Esther Lambert and Walter Archer Tongue; *m* 1990, Chris Pond. *Educ:* Brentwood County High School; Loughborough University of Technology (BA Govt (Hons) and French). Asst Editor, Laboratory Practice, 1977–78; courier/guide in France with Sunsites Ltd, 1978–79; Robert Schuman scholarship for research in social affairs with European Parlt, Dec. 1979–March 1980; sec./admin. asst., Socialist Group of European Parlt, 1980–84. Member: CND; World Disarmament Campaign; Quaker Council for European Affairs; Co-operative Party; Fabian Soc.; World Women Parliamentarians for Peace; Vice-Pres., Socialist Envmt and Resources Assoc. *Recreations:* piano, cello, tennis, squash, horse riding, cinema, theatre, opera. *Address:* London East European Constituency Office, 97A Ilford Lane, Ilford, Essex IG1 2RJ. *T:* 081–514 0198.

TONKIN, Hon. David Oliver, FRACO; Secretary-General, Commonwealth Parliamentary Association, since 1986; *b* 20 July 1929; *s* of Oliver Athelstone Prisk Tonkin and Bertha Ida Louise (*née* Kennett); *m* 1954, Prudence Anne Juttner; three *s* three *d. Educ:* St Peter's Coll., Adelaide; Univ. of Adelaide (MB, BS 1953); Inst. of Ophthalmology, London (DO 1958). FRACO 1974. In private ophthalmic practice, 1958–70. Vis. staff, Royal Adelaide Hosp., 1958–68. Mem., Social Adv. Council, SA Govt, 1968–70; MLA (L) for Bragg, SA, 1970–83; Leader, Liberal Party of SA, 1975–82; Leader of the Opposition, 1975–79; Premier, Treasurer, Minister of State Development and of Ethnic Affairs, SA, 1979–82. Chm., Patient Care Review Cttee, Adelaide Children's Hosp., 1984–86. Chm., State Opera of SA, 1985. Hon. Consul of Belgium for SA and NT, 1984–85. Governor, Queen Elizabeth House, Oxford, 1986–. Freeman, City of London, 1981. FRSA. *Publication:* Patient Care Review: quality assurance in health care, 1985. *Recreations:* the family, music and theatre. *Address:* 7 Old Palace Yard, Westminster, SW1P 3JY. *T:* 071–799 1460; Kenilworth Court, Lower Richmond Road, Putney, SW15 1HB. *T:* 081–788 2208. *Club:* Adelaide.

TONKIN, Derek, CMG 1982; HM Diplomatic Service, retired; Ambassador to Thailand, 1986–89, and concurrently Ambassador to Laos, 1986–89; Director, Thai Holdings Ltd, since 1990; *b* 30 Dec. 1929; *s* of Henry James Tonkin and Norah Wearing; *m* 1953, Doreen Rooke; one *s* two *d* (and one *s* decd). *Educ:* High Pavement Grammar Sch., Nottingham; St Catherine's Society, Oxford (MA). HM Forces, 1948–49; FO, 1952; Warsaw, 1955; Bangkok, 1957; Phnom Penh, 1961; FO, 1963; Warsaw, 1966; Wellington, 1968; FCO, 1972; East Berlin, 1976; Ambassador to Vietnam, 1980–82; Minister, Pretoria, 1983–86. Chairman: Ockenden Venture Gen. Cttee, 1990; Adv. Bd, Centre for SE Asia Studies, SOAS, 1990; Thai–British Business Assoc., 1991. *Recreations:* tennis, music. *Address:* Heathfields, Berry Lane, Worplesdon, Guildford, Surrey GU3 3PU. *Club:* Royal Bangkok Sports.

TONYPANDY, 1st Viscount *cr* 1983, of Rhondda in the County of Mid Glamorgan; **Thomas George Thomas;** PC 1968; *b* 29 Jan. 1909; *s* of Zacharia and Emma Jane Thomas. *Educ:* University Coll., Southampton. Schoolmaster. MP (Lab): Cardiff Central, 1945–50; Cardiff West, 1950–83; Speaker of the House of Commons, 1976–83; PPS, Min. of Civil Aviation, 1951; Mem., Chairman's Panel, H of C, 1951–64; Jt Parly Under-Sec. of State, Home Office, 1964–66; Minister of State: Welsh Office, 1966–67; Commonwealth Office, 1967–68; Secretary of State for Wales, 1968–70; Dep. Speaker and Chm. of Ways and Means, House of Commons, 1974–76. First Chm., Welsh Parly Grand Cttee, 1951; Chairman: Welsh PLP, 1950–51; Jt Commonwealth Societies' Council, 1984–87. Chm., Bank of Wales, 1985–91. Vice-Pres., Methodist Conf., 1960–61; President: Nat. Brotherhood Movement, 1955; Luton Methodist Industrial Coll., 1982; College of Preceptors, 1984–87; National Children's Home, 1990– (Chm., 1983–89). Hon. Mem., Ct of Assts, Blacksmiths' Co., 1980. Freeman: Borough of Rhondda, 1970; City of Cardiff, 1975; City of London, 1980; Hon. Freeman: Paphos, Cyprus, 1989; Port Talbot, 1990. Hon. Master Bencher, Gray's Inn, 1982; Hon. Fellow: UC Cardiff, 1972; College of Preceptors, 1977; Polytechnic of Wales, 1982; St Hugh's Coll., Oxford, 1983; Hertford Coll., Oxford, 1983; Faculty of Bldg, 1983; Westminster Coll., Oxford, 1990; Hon. Companion, Leicester Polytechnic, 1989. Hon. DCL Oxford, 1983; Hon. LLD: Asbury Coll., Kentucky, 1976; Southampton, 1977; Wales, 1977; Birmingham, 1978; Oklahoma, 1981; Liverpool, 1982; Leeds, 1983; Keele, 1984; Warwick, 1984; DUniv Open, 1984; Hon. DD Centenary Univ., Louisiana, 1982. Dato Setia Negara, Brunei, 1971; Grand Cross of the Peruvian Congress, 1982; Gold Medal for Democratic Services, State of Carinthia, Austria, 1982; William Hopkins Bronze Medal, St David's Soc., New York, 1982; Silver Medal of St Paul and St Barnabas, Cyprus, 1989. *Publications:* The Christian Heritage in Politics, 1960; George Thomas, Mr Speaker, 1985; My Wales, 1986. *Heir:* none. *Address:* House of Lords, SW1A 0AA. *Clubs:* Travellers', Reform, English-Speaking Union, United Oxford & Cambridge University; County (Cardiff).

TOOHEY, Mrs Joyce, CB 1977; Under-Secretary, Department of the Environment, 1970–76; *b* 20 Sept. 1917; *o d* of Louis Zinkin and Lena Zinkin (*née* Daiches); *m* 1947, Monty I. Toohey, MD, MRCP, DCH (*d* 1960); two *d. Educ:* Brondesbury and Kilburn High Sch.; Girton Coll., Cambridge; London Sch. of Economics. BA 1938, MA 1945, Cambridge. Asst Principal, Min. of Supply, 1941; transferred to Min. of Works, 1946; Principal, 1948; Asst Secretary, MPBW, 1956; Under-Secretary, 1964. Harvard Business Sch., 1970. *Recreations:* reading, walking. *Address:* 11 Kensington Court Gardens, W8 5QE. *T:* 071–937 1559. *Club:* Hurlingham.

TOOK, John Michael Exton, MBE 1964; Controller, Europe and North Asia Division, British Council, 1983–86, retired; *b* 15 Sept. 1926; *s* of George Took, Dover, and of late Ailsa Clowes (*née* Turner); *m* 1964, Judith Margaret, *d* of late Brig. and Mrs W. J. Birkle; two *d. Educ:* Dover Coll.; Jesus Coll., Cambridge (MA, Mod. and Med. Langs Tripos). Served Indian Army, 1944–47, Captain. HM Colonial Admin. Service (later HMOCS), N Rhodesia, 1950–57; Min. of External Affairs, Fedn of Rhodesia & Nyasaland, 1957–63; Min. of External Affairs, Republic of Zambia, 1964–65; joined British Council, 1965; Asst Reg. Dir, Frankfurt, 1965–67; Reg. Dir, Cape Coast, 1967–69; Rep., Cyprus, 1971–74; Cultural Attaché, British Embassy, Budapest, 1974–77; Dep. Controller, European Div., 1977–80; Rep., Greece, 1980–83. *Publications:* Common Birds of Cyprus, 1973, 3rd edn 1983; contribs to ornithological jls. *Recreations:* ornithology, fishing, natural history. *Address:* Pilgrims, Appledore, near Ashford, Kent. *T:* Appledore (023383) 215. *Club:* United Oxford & Cambridge University.

TOOKER, H. C. W.; *see* Whalley-Tooker.

TOOKEY, Richard William, CBE 1984; Director, since 1984 and Group Public Affairs Co-ordinator, since 1984, Shell International Petroleum Co. Ltd; *b* 11 July 1934; *s* of Geoffrey William Tookey, QC and Rosemary Sherwell Tookey (*née* Clogg); *m* 1956, Jill (*née* Ransford); one *s* one *d* (and one *s* decd). *Educ:* Charterhouse. National Service, 2nd Lieut, 1st King's Dragoon Guards, 1952–54; Lanarkshire Yeomanry (TA), 1954–56; Inns of Court Regt/Inns of Court and City Yeomanry (TA), 1957–64. Joined Royal Dutch/Shell Group, 1954; posts in internat. oil supply and trading, 1954–73; Head of Supply Operations, 1973–75; Vice-Pres., Shell Internat. Trading Co., 1975–77; Man. Dir, Shell Tankers (UK) Ltd, 1978–79, Chm., 1980–84; Man. Dir, Shell Internat. Marine Ltd, 1980–84; Marine Co-ordinator, Shell Internat. Petroleum Co. Ltd, 1980–84. Part-time Mem., BRB, 1985–90; Mem., Gen. Cttee, Lloyd's Register of Shipping, 1978–85; Pres., Gen. Council of British Shipping, 1983–84. Liveryman, Shipwrights' Co., 1983–, Mem. Ct of Assts, 1987–. *Recreations:* home, garden. *Address:* Shell Centre, SE1 7NA. *T:* 071–934 5522.

TOOLEY, Sir John, Kt 1979; Chairman, ARMA Insurance Brokers Ltd, since 1990; General Director, Royal Opera House, Covent Garden, 1980–88; *b* 1 June 1924; *yr s* of late H. R. Tooley; *m* 1st, 1951, Judith Craig Morris (marr. diss., 1965); three *d*; 2nd, 1968, Patricia Janet Norah Bagshawe (marr. diss. 1990), 2nd *d* of late G. W. S. Bagshawe; one *s*. *Educ:* Repton; Magdalene Coll., Cambridge. Served The Rifle Brigade, 1943–47. Sec., Guildhall School of Music and Drama, 1952–55; Royal Opera House, Covent Garden: Asst to Gen. Administrator, 1955–60; Asst Gen. Administrator, 1960–70; Gen. Administrator, 1970–80. Chm., Nat. Music Council Executive, 1970–72. Chm., Almeida Th.; Director: Artists Risk Management & Investment Co. Ltd, 1988–; Britten Estate Ltd, 1989–; Consultant: Internat. Management Gp, 1988–; Ballet Opera House, Toronto, 1989–90; Trustee: Wigmore Hall; SPNM; Purcell Sch.; Britten Pears Foundn, 1989–; Pres., Salisbury Festival, 1988–; Chm., Salisbury Cathedral Fabric Cttee, 1990. Governor, Repton Sch., 1984–. Hon. FRAM; Hon. GSM; Hon. RNCM. Commendatore, Italian Republic, 1976. *Recreations:* walking, theatre. *Address:* 32 First Street, SW3 2LD. *Clubs:* Garrick, Arts.

TOOMEY, Ralph; Under-Secretary, Department of Education and Science, 1969–78; *b* 26 Dec. 1918; *s* of late James and Theresa Toomey; *m* 1951, Patricia Tizard; two *d*. *Educ:* Cyfarthfa Grammar Sch., Merthyr Tydfil; University Coll., London; Univ. of Caen. Served British and Indian Army, 1940–46. Teacher, Enfield Grammar Sch., 1947; Lecturer, Univ. of London, at Sch. of Oriental and African Studies, 1948. Min. of Education, 1948–60 and 1963–78 (seconded to Govt of Mauritius, 1960–63, Principal Asst Sec. in Colonial Secretary's Office and Min. of Local Govt and Co-operative Develt). A UK Rep., High Council, European Univ. Inst., Florence, 1974–78. DUniv Open, 1979. *Address:* 8 The Close, Montreal Park, Sevenoaks, Kent TN13 2HE. *T:* Sevenoaks (0732) 452553. *Club:* Knole Park Golf (Sevenoaks).

TOOTH, Geoffrey Cuthbert, MD, MRCP, DPM; Visiting Scientist, National Institute of Mental Health, USA, 1968–71; *b* 1 Sept. 1908; *s* of late Howard Henry Tooth, CB, CMG, MD, FRCP, and late Helen Katherine Tooth, OBE (*née* Chilver); *m* 1st, 1934, Princess Olga Galitzine (*d* 1955), *d* of Prince Alexander Galitzine, MD; 2nd, 1958, HSH Princess Xenia of Russia, *d* of Prince Andrew of Russia. *Educ:* Rugby Sch.; St John's Coll., Cambridge; St Bartholomew's Hosp.; Johns Hopkins Hosp., Baltimore, Md, USA. MRCS, LRCP 1934, MA Cantab 1935, MD Cantab 1946, DPM 1944; MRCP 1965. Asst Psychiatrist, Maudsley Hosp., 1937–39. Surg. Lt-Comdr, RNVR, Neuropsychiatric Specialist, 1939–45. Colonial Social Science Research Fellow, 1946–53; Comr, Bd of Control, 1954–60; transf. to Min. of Health, and retd as Sen. PMO, Head of Mental Health Section, Med. Div., 1968. Mem. Expert Advisory Panel (Mental Health), WHO. *Publications:* Studies in Mental Illness in the Gold Coast, 1950; various reports to learned societies; articles and papers in med. jls. *Recreations:* sailing, gardening, metal work, photography. *Address:* Grand Prouillac, Plazac, 24580 Rouffignac, France.

TOOTH, Sir (Hugh) John L.; *see* Lucas-Tooth.

TOPE, Graham Norman, CBE 1991; Deputy General Secretary, Voluntary Action Camden, 1975–90; *b* 30 Nov. 1943; *s* of late Leslie Tope, Plymouth and Winifred Tope (*née* Merrick), Bermuda; *m* 1972, Margaret East; two *s*. *Educ:* Whitgift Sch., S Croydon. Company Sec., 1965–72; Insce Manager, 1970–72. Pres., Nat. League of Young Liberals, 1973–75 (Vice-Chm., 1971–73); Mem., Liberal Party Nat. Council, 1970–76; Exec. Cttee, London Liberal Party, 1981–84. Sutton Council: Councillor 1974–; Leader, Soc & Lib Dem Group, 1988– (Liberal Gp, 1974–83, Liberal/SDP Alliance Gp, 1983–88); Leader of Opposition, 1984–86; Leader of Council, 1986–. MP (L) Sutton and Cheam, 1972–Feb. 1974; Liberal Party spokesman on environment, Dec. 1972–1974; contested (L) Sutton and Cheam, Oct. 1974. Mem., Policy Cttee, AMA, 1989–. Pres., London Lib. Democrats, 1991–. *Publication:* (jtly) Liberals and the Community, 1974. *Address:* 88 The Gallop, Sutton, Surrey SM2 5SA. *T:* 081–642 1459.

TOPHAM, Surgeon Captain Lawrence Garth, RN (Retd); Consultant Physician in Geriatric Medicine, Central Hampshire District Winchester and Andover Hospitals, 1974–83; *b* 14 Nov. 1914; *s* of late J. Topham and late Mrs Topham; *m* 1943, Olive Barbara Marshall (VAD), *yr d* of late J. Marshall and late Mrs Marshall; one *s* one *d*. *Educ:* Bradford Grammar Sch.; Univ. of Leeds. MB, ChB 1937; MD 1946; MRCPE 1957; FRCPE 1967; MRCP 1969. Joined RN 1938. Served War: HMS Newcastle and HMS Milford, 1939–41; USN Flight Surgeon's Wings, 1943; RN Fleet Air Arm Pilot's Wings, 1944. Pres., Central Air Med. Bd, 1949; HMS Sheffield, 1951; Med. Specialist and Consultant in Medicine, at RN Hosps, Trincomalee, Haslar and Plymouth, 1952–66; Prof. of Med., RN, and RCP, 1966–71; QHP 1970; retd at own request, from RN, 1971. House Governor and Medical Superintendent, King Edward VII Convalescent Home for Officers, Osborne, IoW, 1971–74. Member: British Nat. Cttee, Internat. Soc. of Internal Medicine; British Geriatric Soc.; Wessex Physicians Club. OStJ (Officer Brother) 1970. *Publications:* several articles in med. jls, especially on subject of diseases of the chest. *Recreations:* Rugby football refereeing, rowing, photography, Oriental cookery. *Address:* Tilings, 3 Holt Close, Wickham, Hants PO17 5EY. *T:* Wickham (0329) 832072.

TOPLEY, Keith; *see* Topley, W. K.

TOPLEY, Kenneth Wallis Joseph, CMG 1976; retired; *b* 22 Oct. 1922; *s* of William Frederick Topley, MC and Daisy Elizabeth (*née* Wellings); *m* 1st, 1949, Marjorie Doreen Wills (marr. diss.); two *s* two *d*; 2nd, 1989, Barbara Newman Hough. *Educ:* Dulwich Coll.; Aberdeen Univ.; London Sch. of Econs and Pol. Science (BScEcon 1949). Served War, RAFVR, 1941–46 (Flt Lieut). Westminster Bank, 1939–41; Mass-Observation, 1941; Malayan Civil Service, 1950–55: Econ. Affairs Secretariat, Comr Gen.'s Office, and Labour Dept; Hong Kong Civil Service, 1955–83: various appts, 1955–62; Comr for Co-operative Develt and Fisheries, 1962–64; Sec., UGC, 1965–67; Comr for Census and Statistics, 1970–73; Dir of Social Welfare, 1973–74; Dir of Educn, 1974–80; Chm., Cttee to Review Post-Secondary and Technical Educn, 1980–81; Sec. for Educn and Manpower, Hong Kong, 1981–83, retired. Secretary: Univ. of E Asia, Macau, 1984–88; E Asia Open Inst, 1988–90. Commandeur de l'Ordre des Arts et des Lettres (France), 1987. *Recreations:* walking, study of society. *Address:* Merens-les-Vals, 09580 Ariège, France. *Club:* Royal Hong Kong Jockey (Hong Kong).

TOPLEY, (William) Keith, MA; Senior Master of the Supreme Court (Queen's Bench Division) and Queen's Remembrancer, since 1990; Admiralty Registrar of the Supreme Court, since 1986; *b* 19 Jan. 1936; *s* of late Bryan Topley and Grizel Hester (*née* Stirling); *m* 1980, Clare Mary Pennington; one *s* by former marriage. *Educ:* Bryanston School; Trinity Coll., Oxford (MA). Called to Bar, Inner Temple, 1959, Bencher, 1990; Master of Supreme Court, QBD, 1980–90. Mem., Bar Council, 1967–68. *Publication:* (ed jtly) Supreme Court Practice, 1988, 1990. *Recreations:* golf, sailing. *Address:* Basset Shaw, Checkendon, near Reading, Berks RG8 0TD. *T:* Checkendon (0491) 680244. *Clubs:* Garrick; Royal Yacht Squadron, Royal London Yacht (Cowes); Huntercombe Golf.

TOPP, Air Commodore Roger Leslie, AFC 1950 (Bar 1955, 2nd Bar 1957); independent consultant, aviation and defence; *b* 14 May 1923; *s* of William Horace Topp and Kathleen (*née* Peters); *m* 1945, Audrey Jane Jeffery; one *s* one *d*. *Educ:* North Mundham Sch.; RAF, Cranwell. Served War: Pilot trg, Canada, 1943–44, commissioned 1944; 'E' Sqdn Glider Pilot Regt, Rhine Crossing, 1945. Nos 107 and 98 Mosquito Sqdns, Germany, 1947–50; Empire Test Pilots' Sch. and RAE Farnborough, 1951–54; Commanded No 111 Fighter Sqdn (Black Arrows) Aerobatic Team, 1955–58; Allied Air Forces Central Europe, Fontainbleau, 1959; Sector Operational Centre, Brockzetel, Germany, 1959–61; jssc, Latimer, 1961–62; commanded Fighter Test Sqdn, Boscombe Down, 1962–64; Station Cmdr, RAF Coltishall, 1964–66; Nat. Def. Coll., Canada, 1966–67; Opl Requirements, MoD (Air), London, 1967–69; Multi-role Combat Aircraft Project, Munich, 1969–70; HQ No 38 Gp, Odiham, 1970; Commandant, Aeroplane and Armament Experimental Estabt, Boscombe Down, 1970–72; Dep. Gen. Man., Multi-role Combat Aircraft Develt and Production Agency, Munich, 1972–78; retd from RAF, 1978. Consultant to Ferranti Defence Systems Ltd, Scotland (Aviation and Defence, FRG), 1978–88. *Recreations:* golf, sailing. *Address:* Cedar Lodge, Meadow Drive, Hoveton St John, Norfolk NR12 8UN. *Clubs:* Royal Air Force; Royal Fowey Yacht.

TOPPING, Rev. Frank; Chaplain, Kent College, since 1988; author and broadcaster; Hon. National Chaplain of Toc H, since 1986 (National Chaplain, 1984–86); *b* 30 March 1937; *s* of late Frank and Dorothy Topping; *m* 1958, June Berry; two *s* one *d*. *Educ:* St Anne's Convent Sch., Birkenhead; St Anselm's Christian Brother Coll., Birkenhead; North West School of Speech and Drama; Didsbury Coll., Bristol. Served RAF, in Cyprus during EOKA and Suez crisis, 1955–57. Stage manager, electrician, asst carpenter and actor, Leatherhead Rep. Th., 1957–59; played Krishna in Dear Augustine, Royal Court, Chelsea, 1959; tour of Doctor in the House, 1959; stage manager/actor, Wolverhampton Rep. Th., 1959; stage-hand with zoological film unit, Granada TV, 1960; TV Studio Floor Man., 1960; 1st Asst Film Dir, 1962; read Theology at Didsbury Coll., Bristol, 1964–67; asst minister at Dome Methodist Mission, Brighton, and methodist univ. chaplain at Sussex, 1967–70; also freelance broadcaster, BBC Radio Brighton, 1967–70; ordained 1970. Producer, BBC Radio Bristol, responsible for religious and farming progs, a music magazine, a comedy record prog., and was short-story editor, 1970–72; asst religious progs organizer for network progs, BBC N Region, 1972–73; network series editor and producer, London, 1973–80; many progs, incl. Pause for Thought and Thought for the Day; has written and presented Pause for Thought progs, 1973–. Began making progs and writing songs with Donald Swann, 1973; became freelance, 1980; in partnership with Donald Swann wrote two man show, Swann with Topping, played in London fringe theatre, then at Ambassadors; presented three one-man plays, Frank Topping 1 Man–3 Shows, Edinburgh Fest. Fringe, 1986. Many TV appearances; own series, Sunday Best, 1981, and Topping on Sunday, 1982–84; The 5 Minute Show (weekday series), TVS, 1989–90; has written radio plays: On the Hill, 1974 (Grace Wyndham Goldie UNDA Dove award, 1975); A Particular Star, 1977. *Publications:* Lord of the Morning, 1977; Lord of the Evening, 1979; Lord of my Days, 1980; Working at Prayer, 1981; Pause for Thought with Frank Topping, 1981; Lord of Life, 1982; The Words of Christ: forty meditations, 1983; God Bless You—Spoonbill, 1984; Lord of Time, 1985; An Impossible God, 1985; Wings of the Morning, 1986; Act Your Age, 1989. *Recreations:* sailing, painting (watercolours), photography, conversation into the small hours. *Address:* Kent College, Pembury, Tunbridge Wells, Kent TN2 4AX. *T:* Pembury (089282) 3870. *Clubs:* Naval; Hurst Castle Sailing (Keyhaven, Hants).

TOPPING, Prof. James, CBE 1977; MSc, PhD, DIC, FInstP; FIMA; Vice-Chancellor, Brunel University, 1966–71; Emeritus Professor, 1971; *b* 9 Dec. 1904; 3rd *s* of James and Mary A. Topping, Ince, Lancashire; *m* 1934, Muriel Phyllis Hall (*d* 1963); one *s*; *m* 1965, Phyllis Iles. *Educ:* Univ. of Manchester; Imperial Coll. of Science and Technology. BSc (Manchester), 1924; PhD (London), 1926; Beit Scientific Research Fellow, 1926–28. Asst Lectr, Imperial Coll., 1928–30; Lectr Chelsea Polytechnic, 1930–32; Lectr, Coll. of Technology, Manchester, 1932–37; Head, Dept of Maths and Physics, Polytechnic, Regent St, 1937–53; Principal, Technical Coll., Guildford, 1953–54; Principal, Brunel College, W3, 1955–66. Vice-Pres., Inst. of Physics, 1951–54, 1960–63; Chairman: Nuffield Secondary Science Consultative Cttee, 1965–71; Hillingdon Gp Hosp. Management Cttee, 1971–74; London Conf. on Overseas Students, 1971–81; Council, Roehampton Inst. of Higher Educn, 1975–78; Council, Polytechnic of the S Bank, 1975–81; Vis. Cttee, Cranfield Inst. of Technol., 1970–78; Member: Anderson Cttee on Student Grants, 1958–60; Nat. Council for Technological Awards, 1955–64; CNAA, 1964–70. Hon. DTech Brunel, 1967; Hon. DSc CNAA, 1969. *Publications:* Shorter Intermediate Mechanics (with D. Humphrey), 1949; Errors of Observation, 1955; The Beginnings of Brunel University, 1981; papers in scientific jls. *Address:* Forge Cottage, Forest Green, near Dorking, Surrey RH5 5SF. *T:* Forest Green (030670) 358.

TORDOFF, family name of **Baron Tordoff.**

TORDOFF, Baron *cr* 1981 (Life Peer), of Knutsford in the County of Cheshire; **Geoffrey Johnson Tordoff;** President of the Liberal Party, 1983–84; Lib Dem Chief Whip, House of Lords, since 1988 (Liberal Chief Whip, 1984–88; Deputy Chief Whip, 1983–84); *b* 11 Oct. 1928; *s* of Stanley Acomb Tordoff and Annie Tordoff (*née* Johnson); *m* 1953, Mary Patricia (*née* Swarbrick); two *s* three *d*. *Educ:* North Manchester School; Manchester Grammar School; Univ. of Manchester. Contested (L), Northwich 1964, Knutsford 1966, 1970. Chairman: Liberal Party Assembly Cttee, 1974–76; Liberal Party, 1976–79 (and its Campaigns and Elections Cttee, 1980, 1981); Member, Liberal Party Nat. Executive, 1975–84. Chm., ME Cttee, Refugee Council, 1990–. *Address:* House of Lords, SW1A 0PW.

TORLESSE, Rear-Adm. Arthur David, CB 1953; DSO 1946; retired; Regional Director of Civil Defence, North Midlands Region, 1955–Jan. 1967; *b* 24 Jan. 1902; *e s* of Captain A. W. Torlesse, Royal Navy, and H. M. Torlesse (*née* Jeans); *m* 1933, Sheila Mary Susan, *d* of Lt-Col Duncan Darroch of Gourock; two *s* one *d*. *Educ:* Stanmore Park; Royal Naval Colleges, Osborne and Dartmouth. Served as midshipman, Grand Fleet, 1918; specialised as observer, Fleet Air Arm, 1926; Commander, 1935; staff appointments in HMS Hood and at Singapore and Bangkok (Naval Attaché), 1936–39; Executive officer, HMS Suffolk, 1939–40; aviation staff appointments at Lee on Solent and

Admiralty, 1940–44; Captain, 1942; commanded HMS Hunter, 1944–45; Director of Air Equipment, Admiralty, 1946–48; Imperial Defence College, 1949; commanded HMS Triumph, Far East, 1950, taking part in first 3 months of Korean War (despatches); Rear-Admiral, 1951; Flag Officer, Special Squadron and in command of Monte Bello atomic trial expedition, 1952; Flag Officer, Ground Training, 1953–54, retired Dec. 1954. Officer, US Legion of Merit, 1954. *Recreations:* formerly fishing, entomology. *Address:* 1 Sway Lodge, Sway, Lymington, Hants SO41 6EB. *T:* Lymington (0590) 682550. *Club:* Naval and Military.

TORNARITIS, Criton George, QC (Cyprus); LLB (Hons, Athens); Attorney-General of the Republic of Cyprus, 1960–84 (Attorney-General, Cyprus, 1952); seconded as Commissioner for Consolidation of the Cyprus Legislation, 1956; Special Legal Adviser of the President of the Republic of Cyprus; *b* 27 May 1902; *m* 1934, Mary (*née* Pitta) (*d* 1973); one *s*. *Educ:* Gymnasium of Limassol; Athens University; Gray's Inn. Advocate of the Supreme Court of Cyprus, 1924; District Judge, Cyprus, 1940; President District Court, Cyprus, 1942; Solicitor-General, Cyprus, 1944; Attorney-General, Cyprus, 1952. Attached to Legal Div. of the Colonial Office, 1955. Legal Adviser to Greek-Cypriot Delegation on the Mixed Constitutional Commission, 1959; Greek-Cypriot delegate to Ankara for initialling of Constitution of Republic of Cyprus, 1960. Prize of Academy of Athens, 1984. *Publications:* The Laws of Cyprus, rev. edn, 1959; The individual as a subject of international law, 1972; The Turkish invasion of Cyprus and legal problems arising therefrom, 1975; The European Convention of Human Rights in the Legal Order of the Republic of Cyprus, 1975; The Ecclesiastical Courts especially in Cyprus, 1976; Cyprus and its Constitutional and other Legal Problems, 1977, 2nd edn 1980; Federalism and Regionalism in the Contemporary World, 1979; The State Law of the Republic of Cyprus, 1982; Constitutional Review of the Laws in the Republic of Cyprus, 1983; The Legal System in the Republic of Cyprus, 1984; The Legal Position of the Church in the Republic of Cyprus, 1989; contributions to legal journals and periodicals. *Recreations:* walking, reading. *Address:* 11 Penelope Delta Street, Nicosia, Cyprus. *T:* 77242.

TORNEY, Thomas William; JP; *b* London, 2 July 1915; *m*; one *d*. *Educ:* elementary school. Joined Labour Party, 1930; Election Agent: Wembley North, 1945; Derbyshire West, 1964. Derby and Dist Area Organizer, USDAW, 1946–70. Member: (Past Chm.) North Midland Regional Joint Apprenticeship Council for catering industry, 1946–68; Local Appeals Tribunal, Min. of Social Security, 1946–68. MP (Lab) Bradford South, 1970–87. Member: Parly Select Cttee on Race Relations and Immigration, 1970–79; Parly Select Cttee on Agriculture, 1979–87; Chm., PLP Gp on Agriculture, Fish and Food, 1981–87. Especially interested in education, social security, industrial relations, agriculture and food. JP Derby, 1969. Chevalier, Commanderie of GB, Confrérie des Chevaliers du Sacavan d'Anjou, 1976.

ToROBERT, Sir Henry Thomas, KBE 1981; Governor and Chairman of the Board of the Bank of Papua New Guinea since its formation in 1973; Chairman, Management Board, PNG Bankers' College, since 1973; President, PNG Amateur Sports Federation, and PNG Olympic and Commonwealth Games Committees, since 1980; *b* Kokopo, 1942. *Educ:* primary educn in East New Britain; secondary educn in Qld, Australia; Univ. of Sydney, Aust. (BEcon. 1965). Asst Research Officer, Reserve Bank of Australia, Port Moresby, 1965 (one of first local officers to join the bank); Dep. Manager, Port Moresby Branch, 1971; Manager of the Reserve Bank, 1972 (the first Papua New Guinean to hold such a position at a time when all banks were branches of the Aust. commercial banks). Member of the cttee responsible for working out a PNG banking system which came into effect by an act of parliament in 1973; Chairman: PNG Currency Working Group advising the Govt on arrangements leading to the introduction of PNG currency, the Kina; ToRobert Cttee to look into problems of administration in PNG Public Service, 1979 (ToRobert Report, 1979); Council, PNG Inst. of Applied Social and Econ. Res., 1975–82. *Address:* PO Box 898, Port Moresby, Papua New Guinea.

TORONTO, Bishop of, since 1989; **Rt. Rev. Terence Edward Finlay;** *b* 19 May 1937; *s* of Terence John Finlay and Sarah McBryan; *m* 1962, Alice-Jean Cracknell; two *d*. *Educ:* Univ. of Western Ontario (BA); Huron Coll., London, Ont (BTh); Cambridge Univ., Eng. (MA). Deacon1961, priest 1962; Dean of Residence, Renison Coll., Waterloo, Canada; Incumbent: All Saints, Waterloo, 1964–66; St Aidan's, London, Canada, 1966–68; Rector: St John the Evangelist, London, 1968–78; Grace Church, Brantford, 1978–82; Archdeacon of Brant, 1978–82; Incumbent, St Clement's, Eglinton, Toronto, 1982–86; a Suffragan Bishop, Diocese of Toronto, 1986; Coadjutor Bishop, 1987. DD: (*jure dignitatis*) Huron Coll., 1987; (*hc*) Wycliffe Coll., 1988; (*hc*) Trinity Coll., 1989. *Recreations:* music, ski-ing, travel. *Address:* Synod Office, 135 Adelaide Street E, Toronto, Ont M5C 1L8, Canada. *T:* 416 363 6021.

TORONTO, Bishops Suffragan of; *see* Blackwell, Rt Rev. D. C.; Brown, Rt Rev. A. D.; Fricker, Rt Rev. J. C.; Pryce, Rt Rev. J. T.

TORPHICHEN, 15th Lord *cr* 1564; **James Andrew Douglas Sandilands;** *b* 27 Aug. 1946; *s* of 14th Lord Torphichen, and Mary Thurstan, *d* of late Randle Henry Neville Vaudrey; *S* father, 1975; *m* 1976, Margaret Elizabeth, *o d* of late William A. Beale and of Mrs Margaret Patten Beale, Peterborough, New Hampshire, USA; three *d*. *Heir: cousin* Douglas Robert Alexander Sandilands [*b* 31 Aug. 1926; *m* 1949, Ethel Louise Burkitt; one *s*; *m* Suzette Véva (*née* Pernet); two *s*]. *Address:* Calder House, Mid-Calder, West Lothian EH53 0HN.

TORRANCE, Rev. Professor James Bruce; Professor of Systematic Theology, King's College, University of Aberdeen, and Christ's College, Aberdeen, 1977–89 (Dean of the Faculty of Divinity, 1978–81), now Professor Emeritus; *b* 3 Feb. 1923; *s* of late Rev. Thomas Torrance and Annie Elizabeth Sharp; *m* 1955, Mary Heather Aitken, medical practitioner; one *s* two *d*. *Educ:* Royal High School, Edinburgh; Edinburgh Univ. (MA Hons Philosophy, 1st Cl.); New Coll., Edinburgh (BD Systematic Theol., Distinction); Univs of Marburg, Basle and Oxford. Licensed Minister of Church of Scotland, 1950; parish of Invergowrie, Dundee, 1954; Lectr in Divinity and Dogmatics in History of Christian Thought, New Coll., Univ. of Edinburgh, 1961; Sen. Lectr in Christian Dogmatics, New Coll., 1972. Visiting Professor: of New Testament, Union Theol. Seminary, Richmond, Va, 1960; of Theology, Columbia Theol. Seminary, Decatur, Ga., 1965, and Vancouver Sch. of Theology, BC, 1974–75; Fuller Theol Seminary, Pasadena, 1982, 1984, 1987, 1989, 1991; S Africa, 1980, 1984, 1986; univs and theol schs in Melbourne, Adelaide and Sydney, 1990. *Publications:* (trans. jtly) Oscar Cullmann's Early Christian Worship, 1953; contribs: Essays in Christology for Karl Barth (Karl Barth's Festschrift), 1956; Where Faith and Science Meet, 1954; Calvinus Ecclesiae Doctor, 1978; Incarnation (on Nicene-Constantinopolitan Creed, 381 AD), 1981; The Westminster Confession in the Church Today, 1982; Calvinus Reformator, 1982; articles to Biblical and Biographical Dictionaries, Scottish Jl of Theology, Interpretation, Church Service Society Annual, and other symposia; *festschrift:* Christ in Our Place (ed T. Hart and D. Timell), 1991. *Recreations:* beekeeping, fishing, gardening, swimming. *Address:* 3 Greenbank Crescent, Edinburgh EH10 5TE. *T:* 031–447 3230.

See also Very Rev. Prof. T. F. Torrance.

TORRANCE, Very Rev. Prof. Thomas Forsyth, MBE 1945; DLitt, DTh, DThéol, Dr Teol, DD, DSc; FRSE 1979; FBA 1983; Professor of Christian Dogmatics, University of Edinburgh, and New College, Edinburgh, 1952–79; Moderator of General Assembly of Church of Scotland, May 1976–77; *b* 30 Aug. 1913; *e s* of late Rev. T. Torrance, then of Chengtu, Szechwan, China; *m* 1946, Margaret Edith, *y d* of late Mr and Mrs G. F. Spear, The Brow, Combe Down, Bath; two *s* one *d*. *Educ:* Chengtu Canadian School; Bellshill Academy; Univs of Edinburgh, Oxford, Basel. MA Edinburgh 1934; studies in Jerusalem and Athens, 1936; BD Edinburgh 1937; post-grad. studies, Basel, 1937–38; DLitt Edinburgh 1971. Prof. of Theology, Auburn, NY, USA, 1938–39; post-grad. studies, Oriel Coll., Oxford, 1939–40; ordained minister of Alyth Barony Parish, 1940; Church of Scotland chaplain (with Huts and Canteens) in MEF and CMF, 1943–45; returned to Alyth; DTh Univ. of Basel, 1946; minister of Beechgrove Church, Aberdeen, 1947; Professor of Church History, Univ. of Edinburgh, and New Coll., Edinburgh, 1950–52. Participant, World Conf. on Faith and Order, Lund, 1952; Evanston Assembly of WCC, 1954; Faith and Order Commn of WCC, 1952–62; Participant in Conversations between: Church of Scotland and Church of England, 1950–58; World Alliance of Reformed Churches and Greek Orthodox Church, 1979–. Lectures: Hewett, 1959 (NY, Newton Center and Cambridge, Mass); Harris, Dundee, 1970; Anderson, Presbyterian Coll., Montreal, 1971; Taylor, Yale, 1971; Keese, Univ. of Mississippi, Chattanooga, 1971; Cummings, McGill Univ., Montreal, 1978; Richards, Univ. of Virginia at Charlottesville, 1978; Staley, Davidson Coll., NC, 1978; Cosgrove, Glasgow, 1981; Warfield, Princeton, 1981; Payton, Pasadena, 1981; Didsbury, Manchester, 1982; Staley, Regent Coll., Vancouver, 1982; William Lyall Meml, Montreal, 1990. Mem., Académie Internationale des Sciences Religieuses, 1965 (Pres., 1972–81); For. Mem., Société de l'Histoire du Protestantisme Français, 1968; Mem. Soc. Internat. pour l'Etude de la Philosophie Médiévale, 1969; Hon. President: Soc. for Study of Theology, 1966–68; Church Service Soc. of the Church of Scotland, 1970–71; New Coll. Union, 1972–73. Vice-Pres., Inst. of Religion and Theology of GB and Ireland, 1973–76 (Pres., 1976–78); Mem., Center of Theol Inquiry, Princeton, 1982–. Protopresbyter of Greek Orthodox Church (Patriarchate of Alexandria), 1973. Curator: Deutsches Institut für Bildung und Wissen, 1982–; Europäische Akademie für Umweltfragen, 1986–. Membre d'honneur, Acad. Internat. de Philosophie des Scis, 1976. DD (*hc*) Presbyterian Coll., Montreal, 1950; DThéol (*hc*) Geneva, 1959; DThéol (*hc*) Paris, 1959; DD (*hc*) St Andrews, 1960; Dr Teol (*hc*) Oslo, 1961; Hon. DSc Heriot-Watt, 1983. Templeton Foundn Prize, 1978. Cross of St Mark (first class), 1970. *Publications:* The Modern Theological Debate, 1942; The Doctrine of Grace in the Apostolic Fathers, 1949; Calvin's Doctrine of Man, 1949; Royal Priesthood, 1955; Kingdom and Church, 1956; When Christ Comes and Comes Again, 1957; The Mystery of the Lord's Supper (Sermons on the Sacrament by Robert Bruce), 1958; ed Calvin's Tracts and Treatises, Vols I-III, 1959; The School of Faith, 1959; Conflict and Agreement in the Church, Vol. I, Order and Disorder, 1959; The Apocalypse Today, 1959; Conflict and Agreement in the Church, Vol. II, The Ministry and the Sacraments of the Gospel, 1960; Karl Barth: an Introduction to his Early Theology, 1910–1930, 1962; ed (with D. W. Torrance) Calvin's NT Commentaries, 1959–73; Theology in Reconstruction, 1965; Theological Science, 1969 (Collins Religious Book Award; trans. French, 1990); Space, Time and Incarnation, 1969; God and Rationality, 1971; Theology in Reconciliation: Essays towards Evangelical and Catholic Unity in East and West, 1975; The Centrality of Christ, 1976; Space, Time and Resurrection, 1976; The Ground and Grammar of Theology, 1980; Christian Theology and Scientific Culture, 1980; (ed) Belief in Science and in Christian Life, 1980; (ed) The Incarnation: ecumenical studies in the Nicene Constantinopolitan Creed, 1981; Divine and Contingent Order, 1981; Reality and Evangelical Theology, 1982; Juridical Law and Physical Law, 1982; (ed) James Clerk Maxwell: A Dynamical Theory of the Electromagnetic Field, 1982; The Meditation of Christ, 1983, new enlarged edn 1992; Transformation and Convergence in the Frame of Knowledge, 1984; The Christian Frame of Mind, 1985, 2nd enlarged edn (subtitled Reason, Order and Openness in Theology and Natural Science), 1989; Reality and Scientific Theology, 1985; (ed) Theological Dialogue between Orthodox and Reformed Churches, 1985; The Trinitarian Faith: the Evangelical Theology of the Ancient Catholic Church, 1988; The Hermeneutics of John Calvin, 1988; (ed) Thomas Torrance, China's First Missionaries, Ancient Israelites, 1988; Karl Barth, Biblical and Evangelical Theologian, 1990; Editor, Theology and Science at the Frontiers of Knowledge, series, 1985–91; Jt Editor, Church Dogmatics, Vols 1, 2, 3 and 4, by Karl Barth, 1956–69; Emeritus Editor: Scottish Jl Theology; SJT Monographs. *Recreations:* golf, fishing. *Address:* 37 Braid Farm Road, Edinburgh EH10 6LE. *Clubs:* New, University (Edinburgh).

See also Rev. Prof. J. B. Torrance.

TORRENS-SPENCE, Captain (Frederick) Michael (Alexander), DSO 1941; DSC 1941; AFC 1944; Royal Navy retired; Lord Lieutenant of County Armagh, 1981–89; *b* 10 March 1914; *s* of Lt-Col Herbert Frederick Torrens-Spence and Mrs Eileen Torrens-Spence; *m* 1944, Rachel Nora Clarke; three *s* one *d*. *Educ:* RNC, Dartmouth. Commnd Sub Lieut, 1934; specialised as pilot, 1936; Battle of Taranto, 1940; commanded 815 Naval Air Sqdn, 1941; Battle of Matapan, 1941; Chief Instructor, Empire Test Pilots Sch., 1947–48; Dep. Dir, Air Warfare Div., Naval Staff, 1952–54; commanded HMS Delight, 1955–56, HMS Albion, 1959–61; ADC to the Queen, 1961. Comdr 1946, Captain 1952. Co. Comdt, Ulster Special Constabulary, 1961–70; commanded 2nd (Co. Armagh) Bn, Ulster Defence Regt, 1970–71. High Sheriff, Co. Armagh, 1979. DFC, Greece, 1941. *Address:* Drumcullen House, Ballydugan, Downpatrick, Co. Down BT30 8HZ. *Club:* MCC.

TORRINGTON, 11th Viscount, *cr* 1721; **Timothy Howard St George Byng;** Bt 1715; Baron Byng of Southill, 1721; *b* 13 July 1943; *o s* of Hon. George Byng, RN (*d* on active service, 1944; *o s* of 10th Viscount) and Anne Yvonne Wood (she *m* 2nd, 1951, Howard Henry Masterton Carpenter); *S* grandfather, 1961; *m* 1973, Susan, *d* of M. G. T. Webster, *qv*; three *d*. *Educ:* Harrow; St Edmund Hall, Oxford. Mem., Select Cttee on EEC, H of L, 1984– (Chm., Sub-Cttee B (Energy, Transport and Broadcasting), 1985–87). Chm., Moray Firth Exploration plc, 1987–; Dir, Flextech plc, 1987–. *Recreation:* travel. *Heir: kinsman,* John Launcelot Byng, MC [*b* 18 March 1919; *m* 1955, Margaret Ellen Hardy; one *s* two *d*]. *Address:* Great Hunts Place, Owslebury, Winchester, Hants. *Clubs:* White's, Pratt's; Muthaiga (Nairobi).

TORY, Sir Geofroy (William), KCMG 1958 (CMG 1956); HM Diplomatic Service, retired; *b* 31 July 1912; *s* of William Frank Tory and Edith Wreghitt; *m* 1st, 1938, Emilia Strickland; two *s* one *d*; 2nd, 1950, Hazel Winfield (*d* 1985). *Educ:* King Edward VII Sch., Sheffield; Queens' Coll., Cambridge. Apptd Dominions Office, 1935; Private Sec. to Perm. Under-Sec. of State, 1938–39; served War, 1939–43, in Royal Artillery; Prin. Private Sec. to Sec. of State, 1945–46; Senior Sec., Office of UK High Comr, Ottawa, 1946–49; Prin. Sec., Office of UK Rep. to Republic of Ireland, 1949–50; Counsellor, UK Embassy, Dublin, 1950–51; idc 1952; Dep. High Comr for UK in Pakistan (Peshawar), 1953–54, in Australia, 1954–57; Asst Under-Sec. of State, CRO, 1957; High Comr for UK in Fedn of Malaya, 1957–63; Ambassador to Ireland, 1964–66; High Commissioner to Malta, 1967–70. PMN (Malaysia) 1963. *Recreation:* painting. *Address:* 17 Barrowgate Road, W4 4QX.

TOSELAND, Ronald James, OBE 1991; Deputy Controller, National Air Traffic Services, 1988–91, retired; *b* 7 March 1933; *s* of W. M. and E. M. Toseland; *m* 1954, J. M. Toseland; two *s*. *Educ:* Kettering Boys' School. RAF Navigator, 1951–61; Air Traffic Control Officer, 1961–91; i/c Heathrow ATC, 1981–83; Dir, Civil Air Traffic Ops, 1983–87; Joint Field Commander, NATS, 1987–88. *Recreations:* music, walking. *Address:* 1 Marshall Place, Oakley Green, Windsor SL4 4QD. *T:* Windsor (0753) 863313.

TOTNES, Archdeacon of; *see* Tremlett, Ven. A. F.

TOTTENHAM, family name of **Marquess of Ely.**

TÖTTERMAN, Richard Evert Björnson, Kt Comdr, Order of the White Rose of Finland; Hon. GCVO 1976 (Hon. KCVO 1969); Hon. OBE 1961; DPhil; Finnish Ambassador, retired; *b* 10 Oct. 1926; *s* of Björn B. Tötterman and Katharine C. (*née* Wimpenny); *m* 1953, Camilla Susanna Veronica Huber; one *s* one *d*. *Educ:* Univ. of Helsinki (LLM); Brasenose Coll., Oxford (DPhil; Hon. Fellow, 1982). Entered Finnish Foreign Service, 1952: served Stockholm, 1954–56; Moscow, 1956–58; Ministry for Foreign Affairs, Finland, 1958–62; Berne, 1962–63; Paris, 1963–66; Dep. Dir, Min. for For. Affairs, Helsinki, 1966; Sec.-Gen., Office of the President of Finland, 1966–70; Sec. of State, Min. for For. Aff., 1970–75; Ambassador: UK, 1975–83; Switzerland, 1983–90, and (concurrently) to the Holy See, 1988–90. Chm. or Mem. of a number of Finnish Govt Cttees, 1959–75, and participated as Finnish rep. in various internat. negotiations; Chm., Multilateral Consultations preparing Conf. on Security and Co-operation in Europe, 1972–73. Holds numerous foreign orders (Grand Cross, Kt Comdr, etc). *Recreations:* music, outdoor life. *Address:* Parkgatan 9 A 11, 00140 Helsinki, Finland.

TOTTLE, Prof. Charles Ronald; Professor of Medical Engineering, University of Bath, 1975–78, now Emeritus, a Pro Vice-Chancellor, 1973–77; Director, Bath Institute of Medical Engineering, 1975–78; Editor, Materials Science, Research Studies Press, since 1977; *b* 2 Sept. 1920; *m* 1944, Eileen P. Geoghegan; one *s* one *d*. *Educ:* Nether Edge Grammar School; University of Sheffield (MMet). English Electric Co. Ltd, 1941–45; Lecturer in Metallurgy, University of Durham, King's College, 1945–50; Ministry of Supply, Atomic Energy Division, Springfields Works, 1950–51; Culcheth Laboratories, 1951–56 (UKAEA); Head of Laboratories, Dounreay, 1956–57; Deputy Director, Dounreay, 1958–59; Prof. of Metallurgy, 1959–67, Dean of Science, 1966, Univ. of Manchester; Prof. and Head of School of Materials Science, Univ. of Bath, 1967–75; Man. Dir, South Western Industrial Research Ltd, 1970–75. Resident Research Associate, Argonne Nat. Laboratory, Illinois, USA, 1964–65. Vice-Pres., Instn of Metallurgists, 1968–70; Jt Editor, Institution of Metallurgists Series of Textbooks, 1962–70. Governor, Dauntsey's Sch., 1979–88. CEng 1978; FIM; FInstP 1958, CPhys 1985. Hon. MSc Manchester. *Publications:* The Science of Engineering Materials, 1965; An Encyclopaedia of Metallurgy and Materials, 1984; various contribs to metallurgical and engineering jls. *Recreations:* music, model making, gardening. *Address:* Thirdacre, Hilperton, Trowbridge, Wilts BA14 7RL.

TOUCH, Dr Arthur Gerald, CMG 1967; Chief Scientist, Government Communications Headquarters, 1961–71; *b* 5 July 1911; *s* of A. H. Touch, Northampton; *m* 1938, Phyllis Wallbank, Birmingham; one *s*. *Educ:* Oundle; Jesus College, Oxford. MA, DPhil 1937. Bawdsey Research Station, Air Ministry, 1936; Radio Dept, RAE, Farnborough, 1940; British Air Commn, Washington, DC, 1941; Supt, Blind Landing Experimental Unit, RAE, 1947; Director: Electronic R and D (Air), Min. of Supply, 1953; Electronic R and D (Ground), Min. of Supply, 1956–59; Imperial Defence College, 1957; Head, Radio Dept, RAE, 1959; Min. of Defence, 1960. *Recreations:* fly fishing, horticulture (orchids). *Address:* Yonder, Ideford, Newton Abbot, Devon TQ13 0BG. *T:* Chudleigh (0626) 852258.

TOUCHE, Sir Anthony (George), 3rd Bt *cr* 1920; Deputy Chairman, Friends' Provident Life Office, since 1983; *b* 31 Jan. 1927; *s* of Donovan Meredith Touche (*d* 1952) (2nd *s* of 1st Bt) and of Muriel Amy Frances (*d* 1983), *e d* of Rev. Charles R. Thorold Winckley; *S* uncle, 1977; *m* 1961, Hester Christina, *er d* of Dr Werner Pleuger; two *s* one *d* (and one *s* decd). *Educ:* Eton College. FCA. Partner in George A. Touche & Co. (later Touche Ross & Co.), 1951; Director of investment trust companies, 1952–90; retired from Touche Ross & Co., 1968; Touche, Remnant Holdings Ltd, 1965–89. Dir, 1968–90, Dep. Chm., 1977–87, National Westminster Bank. Chairman, Assoc. of Investment Trust Companies, 1971–73. Prime Warden, Goldsmiths' Co., 1987. *Recreations:* music, reading, walking. *Heir:* *s* William George Touche [*b* 26 June 1962; *m* 1987, Elizabeth Louise, *y d* of Allen Bridges]. *Address:* Stane House, Ockley, Dorking, Surrey RH5 5TQ. *T:* Oakwood Hill (030679) 397.

TOUCHE, Sir Rodney (Gordon), 2nd Bt *cr* 1962; *b* 5 Dec. 1928; *s* of Rt Hon. Sir Gordon Touche, 1st Bt, and of Ruby, Lady Touche (formerly Ruby Ann Macpherson) (*d* 1989); *S* father 1972; *m* 1955, Ouida Ann, *d* of F. G. MacLellan, Moncton, NB, Canada; one *s* three *d*. *Educ:* Marlborough; University Coll., Oxford. *Heir:* *s* Eric MacLellan Touche, *b* 22 Feb. 1960. *Address:* 2403 Westmount Place, 1100 8th Avenue SW, Calgary, Alta T2P 3T9, Canada. *T:* 403–233–8800.

TOULMIN, John Kelvin, QC 1980; barrister-at-law; a Recorder, since 1984; *b* 14 Feb. 1941; *s* of Arthur Heaton Toulmin and of late B. Toulmin (*née* Fraser); *m* 1967, Carolyn Merton (*née* Gullick), barrister-at-law; one *s* two *d*. *Educ:* Winchester Coll.; Trinity Hall, Cambridge (Patterson Law Scholar, 1959; BA 1963, MA 1966); Univ. of Michigan (Ford Foundn Fellow and Fulbright Scholar, 1964; LLM 1965). Middle Temple: Harmsworth Exhibnr, 1960; Astbury Scholar, 1965; called to the Bar, 1965; Bencher, 1986; Western Circuit; called to Bar of NI, 1989, to Irish Bar, 1991. Cambridge Univ. Debating Tour, USA, 1963. Chm., Young Barristers, 1973–75; Member: Bar Council, 1971–77, 1978–81 and 1987–90 (Chm., Internat. Practice Cttee, 1987); Supreme Court Rules Cttee, 1976–80; Council of Legal Educn, 1981–83; DHSS Enquiry into Unnecessary Dental Treatment in NHS (Report, 1986); Council of Bars and Law Societies of Europe: Mem. UK delegn, 1983–90, Leader, 1987–90; Chm. of the cttee at European Courts of Justice, 1990–; Vice-Pres., CCBE, 1991. Member: Bd of Governors, Maudsley and Bethlem Royal Hosps, 1979–82; SHA, 1982–87; Cttee of Management, Inst. of Psychiatry, 1982–. *Publications:* (contrib.) The Influence of Litigation in Medical Practice, 1977; European Ed., Encyclopaedia of Banking Law, 1990. *Recreations:* cricket, theatre. *Address:* 3 Gray's Inn Place, Gray's Inn, WC1R 5EA. *T:* 071–831 8441, *Fax:* 071–831 8479. *Clubs:* Pilgrims, MCC; Surrey County Cricket.

TOULMIN, Stephen Edelston, MA, PhD; Avalon Foundation Professor in the Humanities, Northwestern University, since 1986; *b* 25 March 1922; *s* of late G. E. Toulmin and Mrs E. D. Toulmin; *m*; two *s* two *d*. *Educ:* Oundle School; King's College, Cambridge. BA 1943; MA 1946; PhD 1948; MA (Oxon) 1948. Junior Scientific Officer, Ministry of Aircraft Production, 1942–45; Fellow of King's College, Cambridge, 1947–51; University Lecturer in the Philosophy of Science, Oxford, 1949–55; Acting Head of Department of History and Methods of Science, University of Melbourne, Australia, 1954–55; Professor of Philosophy, University of Leeds, 1955–59; Visiting Prof. of Philosophy, NY Univ. and Stanford Univ. (California) and Columbia Univ. (NY), 1959–60; Director, Nuffield Foundation Unit for History of Ideas, 1960–64; Prof. of Philosophy, Brandeis Univ., 1965–69, Michigan State Univ., 1969–72; Provost, Crown College, Univ. of California, Santa Cruz, 1972–73; Prof. in Cttee on Social Thought, Chicago Univ., 1973–86. Counsellor, Smithsonian Institution, 1966–75; Mem., Consejo Cientifico, Instituto Internacional de Estudios Avanzados, Carácas, 1985–. *Publications:* The Place of Reason in Ethics, 1950; The Philosophy of Science: an Introduction, 1953; Metaphysical Beliefs (3 essays: author of one of them), 1957; The Uses of Argument, 1958; Foresight and Understanding, 1961; The Ancestry of Science, Vol. I (The Fabric of the Heavens) 1961, Vol. II (The Architecture of Matter), 1962, Vol. III (The Discovery of Time), 1965; Night Sky at Rhodes, 1963; Human Understanding, vol. 1, 1972; Wittgenstein's Vienna, 1973; Knowing and Acting, 1976; An Introduction to Reasoning, 1979; The Return to Cosmology, 1982; The Abuse of Casuistry, 1987; Cosmopolis, 1989; also films, broadcast talks and contribs to learned jls and weeklies. *Address:* Northwestern University, Department of Philosophy, 1818 Hinman, Evanston, Ill 60208, USA.

See also M. E. P. Jones.

TOULSON, Roger Grenfell; QC 1986; a Recorder, since 1987; *b* 23 Sept. 1946; *s* of Stanley Kilsha Toulson and late Lilian Mary Toulson; *m* 1973, Elizabeth, *d* of Henry Bertram Chrimes, *qv*; two *s* two *d*. *Educ:* Mill Hill School; Jesus College, Cambridge (MA, LLB). Called to the Bar, Inner Temple, 1969. *Recreations:* ski-ing, tennis, gardening. *Address:* Billhurst Farm, Wood Street Village, near Guildford, Surrey GU3 3DZ. *T:* Worplesdon (0483) 235246. *Club:* Old Millhillians.

TOUT, Herbert, CMG 1946; MA; Reader in Political Economy, University College, London, 1947–68, retired; *b* Manchester, 20 April 1904; *e s* of Professor T. F. Tout, Manchester University, and Mary Johnstone; unmarried. *Educ:* Sherborne School; Hertford College, Oxford. Instructor in Economics, University of Minnesota, USA, 1929–35; Assistant Lecturer, University College, London, 1936; Colston Research Fellow and Director of University of Bristol Social Survey, 1936–38; Lecturer, University of Bristol, 1938–47; Temp. Principal, Board of Trade, 1940–41; Assistant Secretary, 1941–45. *Recreations:* walking, gardening. *Address:* Little Greeting, West Hoathly, East Grinstead, West Sussex RH19 4PW. *T:* Sharpthorne (0342) 810400.

TOVELL, Laurence, FCA, IPFA; Chief Inspector of Audit, Department of the Environment, 1977–79; *b* 6 March 1919; *s* of William Henry Tovell and Margaret Tovell (*née* Mahoney); *m* 1945, Iris Joan (*née* Lee); two *s* one *d*. *Educ:* Devonport High School. Entered Civil Service as Audit Assistant, District Audit Service, 1938. Served War, 1940–46; Lieut RNVR, 1942–46. District Auditor, No 4 Audit District, Birmingham, 1962. *Recreation:* do-it-yourself. *Address:* White Lions, Links Road, Bramley, Guildford, Surrey. *T:* Guildford (0483) 892702.

TOVEY, Sir Brian (John Maynard), KCMG 1980; Chairman: Cresswell Associates Ltd, since 1988; Fujitsu Telecoms R & D Centre Ltd, since 1990; Res Publica Ltd, since 1991; *b* 15 April 1926; *s* of Rev. Collett John Tovey (Canon, Bermuda Cathedral, 1935–38) and Kathleen Edith Maud Tovey (*née* Maynard); *m* 1989, Mary Helen (*née* Lane). *Educ:* St Edward's Sch., Oxford; St Edmund Hall, Oxford, 1944–45; School of Oriental and African Studies, London, 1948–50. BA Hons London. Service with Royal Navy and subseq. Army (Intelligence Corps and RAEC), 1945–48. Joined Government Communications Headquarters as Jun. Asst, 1950; Principal, 1957; Asst Sec., 1967; Under Sec., 1975; Dep. Sec., 1978; Dir, 1978–83, retired. Defence Systems Consultant, 1983–85, and Defence and Political Adviser, 1985–88, Plessey Electronic Systems Ltd; Dir, Plessey Defence Systems Ltd; 1983–85. *Recreations:* music, walking, history of art (espec. 16th Century Italian). *Address:* 8 Cresswell Gardens, SW5 0BJ. *Club:* Naval and Military.

TOVUE, Sir Ronald, Kt 1987; OBE 1981; Premier, Provincial Government of East New Britain Province, Papua New Guinea, since 1981; Member of Provincial Assembly, since 1979; *b* 14 Feb. 1933; *s* of Apmeledi To Palanga and Rachael Waruruai; *m* 1969, Suluet Tinvil; two *s* one *d*. *Educ:* Pilapila Community Sch.; Kerevat High Sch. Teacher, 1957–65; Magistrate, 1965–74; Commissioner, 1974–76. *Recreations:* golf, reading, gardening, church activities. *Address:* Ratavul, Rabaul, Papua New Guinea. *T:* 92 1301 B/H; PO Box 354, Rabaul, Papua New Guinea. *T:* 92 7216 A/H. *Club:* Rabaul Golf (Rabaul).

TOWER, Maj.-Gen. Philip Thomas, CB 1968; DSO 1944; MBE 1942; National Trust Administrator, Blickling Hall, 1973–82; *b* 1 March 1917; *s* of late Vice-Admiral Sir Thomas Tower, KBE, CB and late Mrs E. H. Tower; *m* 1943, Elizabeth, *y d* of late Thomas Ralph Sneyd-Kynnersley, OBE, MC and late Alice Sneyd-Kynnersley. *Educ:* Harrow; Royal Military Acad., Woolwich. 2nd Lt Royal Artillery, 1937; served in India, 1937–40; served War of 1939–45 (despatches); Middle East, 1940–42; POW Italy, 1942–43; escaped, 1943; Arnhem, 1944; Norway, 1945; Staff Coll., 1948; Instructor at RMA Sandhurst, 1951–53; comd J (Sidi Rezegh) Bty RHA in Middle East, 1954–55; Joint Services Staff Coll., 1955–56; GSO1 Plans, BJSM Washington, DC, 1956–57; comd 3rd Regt RHA, 1957–60; Imperial Defence Coll., 1961; Comd 51 Inf. Bde Gp, 1961–62; Comd 12 Inf. Bde Gp, BAOR, 1962–64; Director of Public Relations (Army), 1965–67; GOC Middle East Land Forces, 1967 (despatches); Comdt, RMA Sandhurst, 1968–72, retd 1972. Col Comdt, Royal Regt of Artillery, 1970–80. County Comr (Norfolk), SJAB, 1975–78. OStJ 1977. *Recreations:* shooting, gardening. *Address:* Hall Farm, East Raynham, Fakenham, Norfolk NR21 7EE. *T:* Fakenham (0328) 864904; Studio A, 414 Fulham Road, SW6 1EB. *T:* 071–385 8538. *Club:* Army and Navy.

TOWNDROW, Ven. Frank Noel; Archdeacon of Oakham, 1967–77, now Archdeacon Emeritus; Residentiary Canon of Peterborough, 1966–77, now Canon Emeritus; a Chaplain to the Queen, 1975–81; *b* 25 Dec. 1911; *e s* of F. R. and H. A. Towndrow, London; *m* 1947, Olive Helen Weinberger (*d* 1978); one *d* (one *s* decd). *Educ:* St Olave's Grammar Sch.; King's Coll., Cambridge; Coll. of Resurrection, Mirfield. Curate, Chingford, E4, 1937–40; Chaplain, RAFVR, 1940–47; Rector of Grangemouth, Stirlingshire, 1947–51; Vicar of Kirton Lindsey, Lincs, 1951–53; Rector of Greenford, Middx, 1953–62; Vicar of Ravensthorpe, E Haddon and Rector of Holdenby, 1962–66. *Recreation:* modern history. *Address:* 17 Croake Hill, Swinstead, Grantham, Lincs NG33 4PE. *T:* Corby Glen (047684) 478.

TOWNELEY, Simon Peter Edmund Cosmo William; Lord-Lieutenant and Custos Rotulorum of Lancashire, since 1976; *b* 14 Dec. 1921; *e s* of late Col A. Koch de Gooreynd, OBE and Baroness Norman, CBE; assumed surname and arms of Towneley by royal licence, 1955, by reason of descent from *e d* and senior co-heiress of Col Charles Towneley of Towneley; *m* 1955, Mary, 2nd *d* of Cuthbert Fitzherbert; one *s* six *d*. *Educ:* Stowe; Worcester Coll., Oxford (MA, DPhil; Ruffini Scholar). Served War of 1939–45, KRRC. Lectr in History of Music, Worcester Coll., Oxford, 1949–55. Mem., Agricultural Lands Tribunal, 1960–. Dir, Granada Television, 1981–. CC Lancs, 1961–64; JP 1956; DL 1970; High Sheriff of Lancashire, 1971. Mem. Council, Duchy of Lancaster, 1986–. Patron, Nat. Assoc. for Mental Health (North-West). President: Community Council of Lancashire; Mid-Pennine Assoc. for the Arts; Lancashire Playing Field Assoc.; NW of England and IoM TA&VRA; Chm., Northern Ballet Theatre, 1969–86; Vice-Chm., Bd of Governors, Royal Northern Coll. of Music; Mem., Court and Council, Univ. of

Manchester; Vice-Pres., NW Arts; Trustee: Historic Churches Preservation Trust, 1984–; British Museum, 1988–. Hon. Col, Duke of Lancaster's Own Yeomanry, 1979–88. Hon. CRNCM 1990; Hon. Fellow, Lancashire Polytechnic, 1987. KStJ; KCSG. *Publications:* Venetian Opera in the Seventeenth Century, 1954 (repr. 1968); contribs to New Oxford History of Music. *Address:* Dyneley, Burnley, Lancs. *T:* Burnley (0282) 23322. *Clubs:* Boodle's, Pratt's, Beefsteak.

See also Sir P. G. Worsthorne.

TOWNEND, James Barrie Stanley; QC 1978; a Recorder of the Crown Court, since 1979; *b* 21 Feb. 1938; *s* of late Frederick Stanley Townend and Marjorie Elizabeth Townend (*née* Arnold); *m* 1970, Airelle Claire (*née* Nies); one step *d. Educ:* Tonbridge Sch.; Lincoln Coll., Oxford (MA). National Service in BAOR and UK, 1955–57: 2nd Lieut, 18th Medium Regt, RA. Called to Bar, Middle Temple, 1962, Bencher, 1987. Chairman: Sussex Crown Court Liaison Cttee, 1978–89; Family Law Bar Assoc., 1986–88; Member: Kingston and Esher DHA, 1983–86; Bar Council, 1984–88; Supreme Court Procedure Cttee, 1986–88. *Recreations:* sailing, fishing. *Address:* 1 King's Bench Walk, Temple, EC4Y 2DB. *T:* 071–583 6266. *Club:* Bar Yacht.

TOWNEND, John Ernest; MP (C) Bridlington, since 1979; *b* 12 June 1934; *s* of Charles Hope Townend and Dorothy Townend; *m* 1963, Jennifer Ann; two *s* two *d. Educ:* Hymers Coll., Hull. FCA (Plender Prize). Articled Clerk, Chartered Accountants, 1951–56; National Service: Pilot Officer, RAF, 1957–59; J. Townend & Sons Ltd (Hull) Ltd: Co. Sec./Dir, 1959–67; Man. Dir, 1967–77; Chm., 1977–; Vice-Chm., Surrey Building Soc., 1984–; Dir, AAH Hldgs, 1984–. Mem., Hull City Council, 1966–74 (Chm., Finance Cttee, 1968–70); Chm., Humber Bridge Bd, 1969–71; Member, Humberside County Council, 1973–79: Cons. Leader of Opposition, 1973–77; Leader, 1977–79; Chm., Policy Cttee, 1977–79. Mem., Policy Cttee, Assoc. of County Councils, 1977–79. PPS to Minister of State for Social Security, 1981–83. Mem., Treasury and Civil Service Select Cttee, 1983–; Chm., Cons. Small Business Cttee, 1988–; Vice-Chm., Cons. backbench Finance Cttee, 1983–. *Recreations:* swimming, tennis. *Address:* Sigglesthorne Hall, Sigglesthorne, Hull, North Humberside. *Club:* Carlton.

TOWNEND, John Philip; His Honour Judge Townend; a Circuit Judge, since 1987; *b* 20 June 1935; *o s* of Luke and Ethel Townend; *m* 1st, 1959; two *s* one *d*; 2nd, 1981, Anne Glover; one step *s* one step *d. Educ:* St Joseph's Coll., Blackpool; Manchester Univ. (LLB). National Service, 1957–58. Called to the Bar, Gray's Inn, 1959; Lectr in Law, Gibson and Weldon College of Law, 1960–65; Asst Legal Advr, Pilkington Bros, 1966–68; Legal Advr, Honeywell Ltd and G. Dew Ltd, 1968–70; joined chambers of Mr Stewart Oakes, Manchester, 1970. *Publications:* articles in various jls on legal topics. *Recreations:* classical music, jazz, food and wine, a decreasing number of active games, mountain walking. *Address:* c/o The Crown Court, Crown Square, Manchester. *Clubs:* Fairhaven Golf; Lytham Tennis and Hockey.

TOWNES, Charles Hard; University Professor of Physics, University of California, USA, 1967–86, now Emeritus; *b* Greenville, South Carolina, 28 July 1915; *s* of Henry Keith Townes and Ellen Sumter (*née* Hard); *m* 1941, Frances H. Brown; four *d. Educ:* Furman Univ. (BA, BS); Duke Univ. (MA); California Institute of Technology (PhD). Assistant in Physics, California Inst. of Technology, 1937–39; Member Techn Staff, Bell Telephone Labs, 1939–47; Associate Prof. of Physics, Columbia Univ., 1948–50; Prof. of Physics, Columbia Univ., 1950–61; Exec. Director, Columbia Radiation Lab., 1950–52; Chairman, Dept of Physics, Columbia Univ., 1952–55; Vice-President and Director of Research, Inst. for Defense Analyses, 1959–61; Provost and Professor of Physics, MIT, 1961–66; Institute Professor, MIT, 1966–67. Guggenheim Fellow, 1955–56; Fulbright Lecturer, University of Paris, 1955–56, University of Tokyo, 1956; Lecturer, 1955, 1960, Dir, 1963, Enrico Fermi Internat. Sch. of Physics; Scott Lecturer, University of Cambridge, 1963. Centennial Lecturer, University of Toronto, 1967. Director: Perkin-Elmer Corp.; Bulletin of Atomic Scientists, 1964–69. Board of Editors: Review of Scientific Instruments, 1950–52; Physical Review, 1951–53; Journal of Molecular Spectroscopy, 1957–60; Columbia University Forum, 1957–59. Fellow: American Phys. Society (Richtmyer Lecturer, 1959; Member Council, 1959–62, 1965–71; President, 1967); Inst. of Electrical and Electronics Engrs; Chairman, Sci. and Technology Adv. Commn for Manned Space Flight, NASA, 1964–69; Member: President's Science Adv. Cttee, 1966–69 (Vice-Chm., 1967–69); Scientific Adv. Bd, US Air Force, 1958–61; Soc. Française de Physique (Member Council, 1956–58); Nat. Acad. Scis (Mem. Council, 1969–72); American Acad. Arts and Sciences; American Philos. Society; American Astron. Society; American Assoc. of Physics Teachers; Société Royale des Sciences de Liège; Pontifical Acad., 1983; Foreign Mem., Royal Society, 1976; Hon. Mem., Optical Soc. of America. Trustee: Salk Inst. for Biological Studies, 1963–68; Rand Corp., 1965–70; Carnegie Instn of Washington, 1965–; Calif Inst. of Technol., 1979–. Chairman: Space Science Bd, Nat. Acad. of Sciences, 1970–73; Science Adv. Cttee, General Motors Corp., 1971–73; Bd of Dirs, General Motors, 1973–86; Perkin-Elmer Corp., 1966–85. Trustee: Pacific Sch. of Religion, 1983–; California Acad. of Scis, 1987–; Enshrinee, Engrg and Sci. Hall of Fame, Ohio, 1983. Holds numerous honorary degrees. Nobel Prize for Physics (jointly), 1964. Research Corp. Annual Award, 1958; Comstock Prize, Nat. Acad. of Sciences, 1959; Stuart Ballantine Medal, Franklin Inst., 1959, 1962; Rumford Premium, Amer. Acad. of Arts and Sciences, 1961; Thomas Young Medal and Prize, Inst. of Physics and Physical Soc., England, 1963; Medal of Honor, Inst. of Electrical and Electronics Engineers, 1967; C. E. K. Mees Medal, Optical Soc. of America, 1968; Churchman of the Year Award, Southern Baptist Theological Seminary, 1967; Distinguished Public Service Medal, NASA, 1969; Michelson-Morley Award, 1970; Wilhelm-Exner Award (Austria), 1970; Medal of Honor, Univ. of Liège, 1971; Earle K. Plyler Prize, 1977; Niels Bohr Internat. Gold Medal, 1979; Nat. Medal of Sci., 1983. National Inventors Hall of Fame, 1976; S Carolina Hall of Fame, 1977. *Publications:* (with A. L. Schawlow) Microwave Spectroscopy, 1955; (ed) Quantum Electronics, 1960; (ed with P. A. Miles) Quantum Electronics and Coherent Light, 1964; many scientific articles on microwave spectroscopy, molecular and nuclear structure, quantum electronics, radio and infra-red astrophysics; fundamental patents on masers and (with A. L. Schawlow) lasers. *Address:* Department of Physics, University of California, Berkeley, California 94720, USA. *T:* 642–1128. *Clubs:* Cosmos (Washington, DC); Bohemian (San Francisco).

TOWNSEND, Albert Alan, FRS 1960; PhD; Reader (Experimental Fluid Mechanics), Cavendish Laboratory, University of Cambridge, 1961–85 (Assistant Director of Research, 1950–61); Fellow of Emmanuel College, Cambridge, since 1947; *b* 22 Jan. 1917; *s* of A. R. Townsend and D. Gay; *m* 1950, V. Dees; one *s* two *d. Educ:* Telopea Park IHS; Melbourne and Cambridge Universities. PhD 1947. *Publications:* The Structure of Turbulent Shear Flow, 1956; papers in technical journals. *Address:* Emmanuel College, Cambridge.

TOWNSEND, Bryan Sydney; Chairman, since 1986, and Chief Executive, since 1990, Midlands Electricity plc (formerly Midlands Electricity Board); *b* 2 April 1930; *s* of Sydney and Gladys Townsend; *m* 1951, Betty Eileen Underwood; one *s* two *d. Educ:* Wolverton Technical Coll. CEng, FIEE; FBIM. Trainee, Northampton Electric Light & Power Co., 1946–50; successive appts, E Midlands, Eastern and Southern Electricity Bds, 1952–66; Southern Electricity Board: Swindon Dist Manager, 1966–68; Newbury Area Engr, 1968–70; Asst Chief Engr, 1970–73; Dep. Chief Engr, SE Electricity Bd, 1973–76; Chief Engr, S Wales Electricity Bd, 1976–78; Dep. Chm., SW Electricity Bd, 1978–86. *Recreation:* golf. *Address:* Midlands Electricity plc, Mucklow Hill, Halesowen, West Midlands B62 8BP. *T:* 021-423 2345.

TOWNSEND, Cyril David; MP (C) Bexleyheath since Feb. 1974; *b* 21 Dec. 1937; *s* of Lt-Col Cyril M. Townsend and Lois (*née* Henderson); *m* 1976, Anita, MA, *d* of late Lt-Col F. G. W. Walshe and of Mrs Walshe; two *s. Educ:* Bradfield Coll.; RMA Sandhurst. Commnd into Durham LI; served in Berlin and Hong Kong; active service in Cyprus, 1958 and Borneo, 1966; ADC to Governor and C-in-C Hong Kong, 1964–66; Adjt 1DLI, 1966–68. A Personal Asst to Edward Heath, 1968–70; Mem. Conservative Research Dept, 1970–74. PPS to Minister of State, DHSS, 1979; Member: Select Cttee on Violence in the Family, 1975; Select Cttee on Foreign Affairs, 1982–83; Vice-Chm., Cons. Parly Defence Cttee, 1985– (Jt Sec., 1982–85); Chairman: Select Cttee on Armed Forces Bill, 1981; British-Cyprus Parly Gp, 1983–; All-Party Freedom for Rudolf Hess Campaign, 1977–87; Bow Gp Standing Cttee on Foreign Affairs, 1977–84; (and Co-Founder) South Atlantic Council, 1983–; Organizing Cttee, Argentine-British Conference, 1988–90; Jt Chm., Council for Advancement of Arab-British Understanding, 1982–; Vice-Chairman: Friends of Cyprus, 1980–; Cons. ME Council, 1988– (formerly Hon. Sec.); Hansard Soc., 1988–; Mem., SE London Industrial Consultative Gp, 1975–83. Fellow, Industry and Parliament Trust, 1982. Introduced Protection of Children Act, 1978. *Publications:* Helping Others to Help Themselves: voluntary action in the eighties, 1981; contribs to Contemporary Review and political jls. *Recreations:* books, music, exercise, exploring Cornwall. *Address:* House of Commons, SW1A 0AA.

TOWNSEND, Mrs Joan, MA, MSc; Headmistress, Oxford High School, GPDST, since 1981; *b* 7 Dec. 1936; *d* of Emlyn Davies and Amelia Mary Davies (*née* Tyrer); *m* 1960, Prof. William Godfrey Townsend, RMCS, Shrivenham; two *d. Educ:* Somerville Coll., Oxford (Beilby Schol.; BA (Cl.I), MA); University College of Swansea, Univ. of Wales (MSc). School teaching and lecturing of various kinds, including: Tutor, Open University, 1971–75; Lectr, Oxford Polytechnic, 1975–76; Head of Mathematics, School of S Helen and S Katharine, Abingdon, 1976–81. FRSA. *Publication:* paper in Qly Jl Maths and Applied Mech., 1965. *Address:* Silver Howe, 62 Iffley Turn, Oxford OX4 4HN. *T:* Oxford (0865) 715807.

TOWNSEND, Mrs Lena Moncrieff, CBE 1974; Member, Race Relations Board, 1967–72; *b* 3 Nov. 1911; twin *d* of late Captain R. G. Westropp, Cairo, Egypt; *m* (twice); two *s* one *d. Educ:* Downe House, Newbury; Somerville Coll., Oxford; Heidelberg Univ., Germany. During War of 1939–45 was an Organiser in WVS and in Women's Land Army, and then taught at Downe House. Mem. for Hampstead, LCC, 1955–65; Alderman, London Borough of Camden, 1964–67; Mem. for Camden, GLC, 1967–70; Alderman, GLC, 1970–77, and Dep. Chm., 1976–77; Inner London Education Authority: Dep. Leader, later Leader, 1967–70; Leader of the Opposition, 1970–71; Chm., Management Panel, Burnham Cttee, 1967–70; Mem., Women's European Cttee, 1972–75. Pres., Anglo-Egyptian Assoc., 1961–87 (when wound-up); Exec. Member: British Section, European Union of Women, 1970–81; National Council, European Movement (British Council), 1970–86 (Mem., Speaker's Panel); Cons. Gp for Europe, 1967–88 (Founder Mem.); British Section, Internat. Union of Local Authorities and Council of European Municipalities, 1975– (rep. on Jt Twinning Cttee, 1975–83); London Europe Soc., 1977– (Vice-Pres. 1981–); Arkwright Arts Trust, 1971–84 (Chm., 1971–73). Mem., House Cttee, New End Hosp., then Hampstead Cttee, Royal Free Hosp., 1953–65. Contemporary Dance Trust, 1968–75. Chm., Students' Accommodation Cttee, Univ. of London, 1977–86 (and Mem., Intercollegiate Halls Management Cttee); Member: Council, Westfield Coll., London Univ., 1965–89; Cons Nat. Adv. Cttee on Education, 1976–82; Governor: Barrett Street Coll., later London Coll. of Fashion, 1958–86 (Chm., 1967–86); Old Vic Trust, 1976–88; Hampstead Parochial Primary Sch., 1979–. First Patron, Lewis Carroll Soc. Hon. Fellow, QMW (Hon. Fellow, Westfield Coll., 1983). *Recreations:* foreign languages, travel, the arts, gardening. *Address:* 16 Holly Mount, NW3 6SG. *T:* 071–435 8555.

TOWNSEND, Rear-Adm. Sir Leslie (William), KCVO 1981; CBE 1973; Member, Lord Chancellor's Panel of Independent Inspectors, since 1982; *b* 22 Feb. 1924; *s* of Ellen (*née* Alford) and William Bligh Townsend; *m* 1947, Marjorie Bennett; one *s* three *d. Educ:* Regent's Park School, Southampton. Joined RN, 1942; served in HMS Durban, 1942–43; Commissioned, 1943; HM Ships Spurwing, Astraea, Liverpool, Duke of York, Ceres, 1944–53; HMS Ceylon, 1956–58; Secretary to ACNS, 1959, to VCNS, 1967, to First Sea Lord, 1970; MA to CDS, 1971–73, to Chm. NATO Mil. Cttee, 1974; Dir, Naval and WRNS Officers' Appointments, 1977; Rear-Adm. 1979; Defence Services Sec., 1979–82. *Recreations:* fishing, cooking. *Address:* 21 Osborne View Road, Hill Head, near Fareham, Hants. *T:* Stubbington (0329) 663446. *Clubs:* Army and Navy; Hill Head Sailing.

TOWNSEND, Prof. Peter Brereton; Professor of Social Policy, University of Bristol, since 1982; *b* 6 April 1928; *s* of late Philip Brereton Townsend and Alice Mary Townsend (*née* Southcote); *m* 1st, 1949, Ruth (*née* Pearce); four *s*; 2nd, 1977, Joy (*née* Skegg); one *d*; 3rd, 1985, Jean (formerly Corston); one step *s* one step *d. Educ:* Fleet Road Elementary Sch., London; University Coll. Sch., London; St John's Coll., Cambridge Univ.; Free Univ., Berlin. Research Sec., Political and Economic Planning, 1952–54; Research Officer, Inst. of Community Studies, 1954–57; Research Fellow and then Lectr in Social Administration, London Sch. of Economics, 1957–63; Prof. of Sociology, 1963–81, Pro-Vice-Chancellor (Social Policy), 1975–78, Univ. of Essex; Dir, Sch. of Applied Social Studies, Bristol Univ., 1983–85 and 1988–. Vis. Prof. of Sociology, Essex Univ., 1982–86. Chm., 1965–66, Vice Pres., 1989–, Fabian Society (Chairman: Social Policy Cttee, 1970–82; Res. and Pubns Cttee, 1983–86). President: Psychiatric Rehabilitation Assoc., 1968–83; Child Poverty Action Gp, 1989– (Chm., 1969–89); SW Region, MENCAP, 1989–; Chm., Disability Alliance, 1974–. Member: Chief Scientist's Cttee, DHSS, 1976–78; Govt Working Gp on Inequalities and Health, 1977–80; MSC Working Gp on Quota Scheme for Disabled, 1983–85. UNESCO consultant on poverty and development, 1978–80; Consultant: to GLC on poverty and the labour market in London, 1985–86; to Northern RHA on Inequalities of Health, 1985–86; to a consortium of 7 metropolitan boroughs on deprivation and shopping centres in Greater Manchester, 1987–88; to Islington Borough Council on deprivation and living standards, 1987–88. DU Essex, 1990. *Publications:* The Family Life of Old People, 1957; National Superannuation (co-author), 1957; Nursing Homes in England and Wales (co-author), 1961; The Last Refuge: a survey of residential institutions and homes for the aged in England and Wales, 1962; The Aged in the Welfare State (co-author), 1965; The Poor and the Poorest (co-author), 1965; Old People in Three Industrial Societies (co-author), 1968; (ed) The Concept of Poverty, 1970; (ed) Labour and Inequality, 1972; The Social Minority, 1973; Sociology and Social Policy, 1975; Poverty in the United Kingdom: a survey of household resources and standards of living, 1979; (ed) Labour and Equality, 1980; Inequalities in Health (co-author), 1980; Manifesto (co-author), 1981; (ed jtly) Disability in Britain, 1981; The

Family and Later Life, 1981; (ed jtly) Responses to Poverty: lessons from Europe, 1984; (jtly) Inequalities of Health in the Northern Region, 1986; Poverty and Labour in London, 1987; (jtly) Health and Deprivation: inequalities and the North, 1987; (jtly) Service Provision and Living Standards in Islington, 1988; (jtly) Inequalities in Health: the Black report and the health divide, 1988; Home from Hospital: a study of elderly people leaving hospital in Bristol, 1990. *Recreation:* athletics.

TOWNSEND, Group Captain Peter Wooldridge, CVO 1947; DSO 1941; DFC and Bar, 1940; *b* 22 Nov. 1914; *s* of late Lt-Col E. C. Townsend; *m* 1959, Marie Luce, *d* of Franz Jamagne, Brussels, Belgium; one *s* two *d* (two *s* by former marriage). *Educ:* Haileybury; Royal Air Force Coll., Cranwell. Royal Air Force, 1933; served War of 1939–45, Wing Commander, 1941 (despatches, DFC and Bar, DSO). Equerry to King George VI, 1944–52; Deputy Master of HM Household, 1950; Equerry to the Queen, 1952–53; Air Attaché, Brussels, 1953–56. *Publications:* Earth, My Friend, 1959; Duel of Eagles, 1970; The Last Emperor, 1975; Time and Chance (autobiog.), 1978; The Smallest Pawns in the Game, 1979; The Girl in the White Ship, 1981; The Postman of Nagasaki, 1984; Duel in the Dark, 1986. *Address:* La Mare aux Oiseaux, Route des Grands Coins, 78610 Saint Léger-en-Yvelines, France.

TOWNSEND, Susan, (Sue); writer; *b* 2 April 1946. *Educ:* South Wigston Girls' High Sch. *Publications:* The Secret Diary of Adrian Mole Aged 13¾, 1982; The Growing Pains of Adrian Mole, 1984; Bazaar and Rummage, Groping for Words, and Womberang (plays), 1984; The Great Celestial Cow (play), 1985; The Secret Diary of Adrian Mole (play), 1985; Rebuilding Coventry, 1988; Mr Bevans Dream, 1989; Ten Tiny Fingers, Nine Tiny Toes (play), 1989. *Recreations:* mooching about, reading, looking at pictures, canoeing. *Address:* Bridge Works, Knighton Fields Road West, Leicester LE2 6LH. *T:* Leicester (0533) 831176. *Club:* Groucho.

TOWNSHEND, family name of **Marquess Townshend.**

TOWNSHEND, 7th Marquess *cr* 1787; **George John Patrick Dominic Townshend;** Bt 1617; Baron Townshend of Lynn Regis, 1661; Viscount Townshend of Raynham, 1682; *b* 13 May 1916; *s* of 6th Marquess and Gladys Ethel Gwendolen Eugenie (*d* 1959), *e d* of late Thomas Sutherst, barrister; *S* father, 1921; *m* 1st, 1939, Elizabeth (marr. diss. 1960; she *m* 1960, Brig. Sir James Gault, KCMG, MVO, OBE; she *d* 1989), *o d* of Thomas Luby, ICS; one *s* two *d*; 2nd, 1960, Ann Frances (*d* 1988), *d* of Arthur Pellew Darlow; one *s* one *d*. Norfolk Yeomanry TA, 1936–40; Scots Guards, 1940–45. Chairman: Anglia Television Gp plc, 1971–86; Anglia Television Ltd, 1958–86; Survival Anglia, 1971–86; Anchor Enterprises Ltd, 1967–88; AP Bank Ltd, 1975–87; East Coast Grain Ltd, 1982–90; D. E. Longe & Co. Ltd, 1982–90; Norfolk Agricultural Station, 1973–87; Raynham Farm Co. Ltd, 1957–; Vice-Chairman: Norwich Union Life Insurance Society Ltd, 1973–86; Norwich Union Fire Insurance Society Ltd, 1975–86; Director: Scottish Union & National Insurance Co., 1968–86; Maritime Insurance Co. Ltd, 1968–86; London Merchant Securities plc, 1964–; Norwich Union (Holdings) plc, 1981–86; Napak Ltd, 1982–90; Riggs Nat. Corp., Washington, 1987–89. Chairman, Royal Norfolk Agricultural Association, 1978–85. Hon. DCL East Anglia, 1989. DL Norfolk, 1951–61. *Heir: s* Viscount Raynham, *qv*. *Address:* Raynham Hall, Fakenham, Norfolk NR21 7EP. *T:* Fakenham (0328) 862133. *Clubs:* White's, MCC; Norfolk (Norwich).

TOWNSING, Sir Kenneth (Joseph), Kt 1982; CMG 1971; ISO 1966; Director: Western Mining Corporation Ltd, 1975–87; Central Norseman Gold Corporation, 1982–87; *b* 25 July 1914; *s* of J. W. and L. A. Townsing; *m* 1942, Frances Olive Daniel; two *s* one *d*. *Educ:* Perth Boys' Sch.; Univ. of Western Australia. Treasury Officer, 1933–39. Served War, AIF (Middle East), 1940–46, Major. Public Service Inspector, 1946–49; Sec., Public Service Commissioner's Office, 1949–52; Dep. Under Treasurer, 1952–57; Public Service Comr, 1958–59; Under Treasurer (Permanent Head), 1959–75. Chm., Salaries and Allowances Tribunal, 1975–84. Mem. Senate, Univ. of Western Australia, 1954–70 (Chm. Finance Cttee, 1956–70; Pro-Chancellor, 1968–70); Comr, Rural and Industries Bank, 1959–65; Member: Jackson Cttee on Tertiary Educn, 1967; Tertiary Educn Commn, 1971–74; Past Mem. numerous other Bds and Cttees. Fellow, W Australian Museum, 1975; Hon. Zoo Associate, 1979. FCPA. Hon. LLD Univ. of W Australia, 1971; DUniv Murdoch, 1982. *Recreation:* gardening. *Address:* 22 Robin Street, Mount Lawley, WA 6050, Australia. *T:* (09) 272 1393. *Club:* University House (Perth).

TOWRY, Peter; *see* Piper, Sir D. T.

TOY, Rev. Canon John, PhD; Chancellor of York Minster, since 1983 (also Librarian and Guestmaster); Prebendary of Tockerington, since 1983; *b* 25 Nov. 1930; *e s* of late Sidney Toy, FSA and late Violet Mary (*née* Doudney); *m* 1963, Mollie *d* of Eric and Elsie Tilbury; one *s* one *d*. *Educ:* Epsom County Grammar Sch.; Hatfield Coll., Durham (BA 1st cl. Hons. Theol. 1953, MA 1962). PhD Leeds, 1982. Ordained deacon, 1955, priest, 1956; Curate, St Paul's, Lorrimore Sq., Southwark, 1955–58; Student Christian Movement Sec. for S of England, 1958–60; Chaplain: Ely Theol Coll., 1960–64; St Andrew's Church, Gothenburg, Sweden, 1965–69; St John's College, York: Lectr in Theology, 1969; Sen. Lectr, 1972; Principal Lectr, 1979–83. *Publications:* Jesus, Man for God, 1988; contrib. to learned jls and cathedral booklets. *Recreations:* music, history, architecture. *Address:* 10 Precentor's Court, York YO1 2EJ. *T:* York (0904) 620877. *Club:* Yorkshire (York).

TOY, Sam; Chairman and Managing Director, Ford Motor Co. Ltd, 1980–86; Chairman, Norman Cordiner Ltd, Inverness, since 1991; *b* 21 Aug. 1923; *s* of Edward and Lillian Toy; *m* 1st, 1944, Jean Balls; one *s*; 2nd, 1950, Joan Franklin Rook; two *s* one *d*; 3rd, 1984, Janetta McMorrow. *Educ:* Falmouth Grammar Sch.; Fitzwilliam Coll., Cambridge (MA; Hon. Fellow, 1984). Pilot (Flt Lieut), RAF, 1942–48. Graduate trainee, Ford Motor Co. Ltd, 1948; thereafter, all business career with Ford Motor Co. Ltd. Mem. Council, SMMT, 1975– (Vice-Pres., 1982–86; Pres., 1986–87; Dep. Pres., 1987–88). Chm., UK 2000 Scotland, 1988–. *Recreations:* trout and salmon fishing, golf. *Address:* 1 Primrose Bay, Invermoriston, Inverness IV3 6YD; 35 Stanhope Terrace, Lancaster Gate, W2 2UA. *Clubs:* Lord's Taverners', Eccentric.

TOYE, Prof. John Francis Joseph; Director, Institute of Development Studies, University of Sussex, since 1987; *b* 7 Oct. 1942; *s* of John Redmond Toye and Adele Toye (*née* Francis); *m* 1967, Janet Reason; one *s* one *d*. *Educ:* Christ's Coll., Finchley; Jesus Coll., Cambridge (schol.; MA); Harvard Univ. (Frank Knox Vis. Fellow); Sch. of Oriental and African Studies, Univ. of London (MScEcon; PhD). Asst Principal, HM Treasury, 1965–68; Res. Fellow, SOAS, Univ. of London, 1970–72; Fellow (later Tutor), Wolfson Coll., Cambridge, 1972–80, and Asst Dir of Develt Studies, Cambridge Univ., 1977–80; Dir, Commodities Res. Unit Ltd, 1980–85; Prof. of Develt Policy and Planning and Dir, Centre for Develt Studies, University Coll. of Swansea, 1982–87. Hon. Fellow, Univ. of Birmingham, Inst. of Local Govt Studies, 1986. Member: Council, ODI, 1988–; Adv. Cttee on Econ. and Social Res., ODA, 1989–. *Publications:* (ed) Taxation and Economic Development, 1978; (ed) Trade and Poor Economies, 1979; Public Expenditure and Indian Development Policy 1960–70, 1981; Dilemmas of Development, 1987; (jtly) Does Aid Work in India?, 1990; (jtly) Aid and Power, 1991; numerous articles in acad. jls. *Recreations:* walking, music. *Address:* c/o Institute of Development Studies, University of Sussex, Falmer, Brighton, Sussex BN1 9RE. *T:* Brighton (0273) 606261. *Club:* Commonwealth Trust.

TOYE, Wendy; theatrical and film director; choreographer, actress, dancer; *b* 1 May 1917. First professional appearance as Peasblossom in A Midsummer Night's Dream, Old Vic, 1929; principal dancer in Hiawatha, Royal Albert Hall, 1931; Marigold, Phœbe in Toad of Toad Hall and produced dances, Royalty, Christmas, 1931–32; in early 1930s performed and choreographed for the very distinguished Carmargo Society of Ballet; guest artist with Sadler's Wells Ballet and Mme Rambert's Ballet Club; went to Denmark as principal dancer with British Ballet, organized by Adeline Genée, 1932; danced in C. B. Cochran's The Miracle, Lyceum, 1932; masked dancer in Ballerina, Gaiety, 1933; member of Ninette de Valois' original Vic Wells Ballet, principal dancer for Ninette de Valois in The Golden Toy, Coliseum, 1934; toured with Anton Dolin's ballet (choreog. for divertissements and short ballets), 1934–35; in Tulip Time, Alhambra, then Markova-Dolin Ballet as principal dancer and choreog., 1935; in Love and How to Cure It, Globe, 1937. Arranged dances and ballets for many shows and films including most of George Black's productions for next 7 years, notably Black Velvet in which also principal dancer, 1939. Shakespearean season, Open Air Theatre, 1939. *Theatre productions:* Big Ben, Bless the Bride, Tough at the Top (for C. B. Cochran), Adelphi; The Shepherd Show, Prince's; Co-Director and Choreographer, Peter Pan, New York; And So To Bed, New Theatre; Co-Director and Choreographer, Feu d'Artifice, Paris; Night of Masquerade, Q; Second Threshold, Vaudeville; Choreography for Three's Company in Joyce Grenfell Requests the Pleasure, Fortune; Wild Thyme, Duke of York's; Lady at the Wheel, Lyric, Hammersmith; Majority of One, Phœnix; Magic Lantern, Saville; As You Like It, Old Vic; Virtue in Danger, Mermaid and Strand; Robert and Elizabeth, Lyric; On the Level, Saville; Midsummer Night's Dream, Shakespeare quatercentenary Latin American tour, 1964; Soldier's Tale, Edinburgh Festival, 1967; Boots with Strawberry Jam, Nottingham Playhouse, 1968; The Great Waltz, Drury Lane, 1970; Showboat, Adelphi, 1971; She Stoops to Conquer, Young Vic, 1972; Cowardy Custard, Mermaid, 1972; Stand and Deliver, Roundhouse, 1972; R loves J, Chichester, 1973; The Confederacy, Chichester, 1974; The Englishman Amused, Young Vic, 1974; Follow The Star, Chichester, 1974, Westminster Theatre, 1976; Made in Heaven, Chichester, 1975; Make Me a World, Chichester, 1976; Once More with Music (with Cicely Courtneidge and Jack Hulbert), 1976; Oh, Mr Porter, Mermaid, 1977; Dance for Gods, Conversations, 1979; Colette, Comedy, 1980; Gingerbread Man, Water Mill, 1981; This Thing Called Love, Ambassadors, 1983; (Associate Prod.) Singin' in the Rain, Palladium, 1983; (dir and narr.) Noel and Gertie, Monte Carlo and Canada; (Associate Prod.) Barnham, Manchester, 1984, Victoria Palace, 1985; Birds of a Feather, 1984, and Mad Woman of Chaillot, 1985, Niagara-on-the-Lake; Gala for Joyce Grenfell Tribute, 1985; (Associate Prod.) Torvill and Dean World Tour, 1985; Once Upon a Mattress, Watermill Theatre, 1985; Kiss Me Kate, Aarhus and Copenhagen, 1986; Unholy Trinity, Stephenville Fest., 1986; Laburnam Grove, Palace Th. Watford, 1987; Miranda, Chichester Fest., 1987; Get the Message, Molecule, 1987; Songbook, Watermill, 1988; Mrs Dot, Watford, 1988; When That I Was, Manitoba, 1988; Oh! Coward, Hong Kong, 1989; Cinderella, Palace Th., Watford, 1989; Penny Black, Wavendon, 1990; Moll Flanders, Watermill, 1990; Heaven's Up, Playhouse, 1990; Mrs Pat's Profession (workshop with Cleo Laine), Wavendon, 1991; The Drummer, Watermill, 1991. *Opera Productions:* Bluebeard's Castle (Bartok), Sadler's Wells and Brussels; The Telephone (Menotti), Sadler's Wells; Russalka (Dvořák), Sadler's Wells; Fledermaus, Coliseum and Sadler's Wells; Orpheus in the Underworld, Sadler's Wells and Australia; La Vie Parisienne, Sadler's Wells; Seraglio, Bath Festival, 1967; The Impresario, Don Pasquale (for Phoenix Opera Group), 1968; The Italian Girl in Algiers, Coliseum, 1968; La Cenerentola; Merry Widow, 1979, Orpheus in the Underworld, 1981, ENO North; The Mikado, Nat. Opera Co., Ankara, 1982; Italian Girl in Algiers, ENO, 1982; La Serva Pachona and Apotoker, Aix-en-Provence Fest., 1991. *Films directed:* The Stranger Left No Card; The Teckman Mystery; Raising a Riot; The Twelfth Day of Christmas; Three Cases of Murder; All for Mary; True as a Turtle; We Joined the Navy; The King's Breakfast; Cliff in Scotland; A Goodly Manor for a Song; Girls Wanted—Istanbul; Trial by Jury (TV). Retrospectives of films directed: Festival de Films des Femmes International, Créteil, Paris, 1990; Tokyo Film Fest., 1991. Productions for TV, etc, inc. Golden Gala, ATV, 1978; Follow the Star, BBC2, 1979; Stranger in Town, Anglia, 1981. Dir concert, Till We Meet Again, RFH, 1989. Advisor, Arts Council Trng Scheme, for many years; Member: Council, LAMDA; (original) Accreditation Bd instig. by Nat. Council of Drama Training for acting courses, 1981–84; Grand Council, Royal Acad. of Dancing; 1st directors' rep. on Equity Council, 1974– (Dir, Sub-Cttee, 1971–). Committee Member: Wavendon All Music Scheme; Vivian Ellis Award Scheme; Richard Stilgoe Award Scheme. Trained with Euphen MacLaren, Karsavina, Dolin, Morosoff, Legat, Rambert. Silver Jubilee Medal, 1977.

TOYN, Richard John; His Honour Judge Toyn; a Circuit Judge since 1972; *b* 24 Jan. 1927; *s* of Richard Thomas Millington Toyn and Ethel Toyn; *m* 1955, Joyce Evelyn Goodwin; two *s* two *d*. *Educ:* Solihull Sch.; Bristol Grammar Sch.; Bristol Univ. (LLB). Royal Army Service Corps, 1948–50. Called to the Bar, Gray's Inn, 1950. Mem., Parole Bd, 1978–80. Contributing Ed., Butterworths County Court Precedents and Pleadings, 1985. *Recreations:* music, drama, photography. *Address:* c/o Queen Elizabeth II Law Courts, Newton Street, Birmingham.

TOYNBEE, Polly; Social Affairs Editor, News and Current Affairs, BBC, since 1988; writer; *b* 27 Dec. 1946; *d* of late Philip Toynbee, and of Anne Powell; *m* 1970, Peter Jenkins, *qv*; one *s* two *d* and one step-*d*. *Educ:* Badminton Sch.; Holland Park Comprehensive; St Anne's Coll., Oxford. Reporter, The Observer, 1968–71; Editor, The Washington Monthly, USA, 1972–73; Feature Writer, The Observer, 1974–76; Columnist, The Guardian, 1977–88. Contested (SDP) Lewisham E, 1983. Catherine Pakenham Award for Journalism, 1975; British Press Award, 1977, 1982, 1986 (Columnist of the Year). *Publications:* Leftovers, 1966; A Working Life, 1970 (paperback 1972); Hospital, 1977 (paperback 1979); The Way We Live Now, 1981; Lost Children, 1985. *Address:* 1 Crescent Grove, SW4 7AF. *T:* 071–622 6492.

TOYNE, Prof. Peter, DL; Rector, Liverpool Polytechnic, since 1986; *b* 3 Dec. 1939; *s* of Harold and Doris Toyne; *m* 1969, Angela Wedderburn; one *s*. *Educ:* Ripon Grammar Sch.; Bristol Univ. (BA); The Sorbonne. FRSA; FBIM. Res. Asst, Univ. of Lille, 1964; Univ. of Exeter: Lectr in Geography, 1965–76; Sen. Lectr in Geography and Sub Dean of Social Studies, 1976–78; Dir, DES Credit Transfer Feasibility Study, 1978–80; Hd of Bishop Otter Coll., Chichester, and Dep. Dir (Academic), W Sussex Inst. of Higher Educn, 1980–83; Dep. Rector, NE London Polytechnic, 1983–86. Dir, Liverpool Playhouse, 1987–91. Chairman: Initial Training Panel, Council for Educn and Training in Youth and Community Work, 1984–87; Credit Accumulation and Transfer Scheme Cttee, CNAA, 1986–90; CNAA/DES Cttee on Recognition of Access Courses, 1988–; ECCTIS 2000 Adv. Gp, 1990–; BBC Radio Merseyside Adv. Council, 1988–; Vice-Chm., Cttee of Dirs of Polytechnics, 1990–; Member: BBC NW Regional Council, 1988–; Merseyside Enterprise Forum, 1986–; Business Opportunities on Merseyside, 1986–; Bd, Merseyside Innovation Centre, 1987–; Council, Merseyside Chamber of Commerce and Industry, 1990–; Further and Higher Educn Cttee, Gen. Synod Bd of Educn, 1985–; Central

Services Unit, Careers in Higher Educn, 1989–; Theol Coll. Inspector, House of Bishops, 1980–; Trustee: Farringdon Trust, 1982–; St Luke's Trust, 1984–89; Higher Educn Foundn, 1988–. DL Merseyside, 1990. *Publications:* World Problems, 1970; Techniques in Human Geography, 1971; Organisation, Location and Behaviour, 1974; Recreation and Environment, 1974; Toyne Report: Credit Transfer, 1979; numerous articles in geographical, educnl jls, festschriften and popular press. *Recreations:* railways (model and real), liturgy, music (especially sacred), gardening. *Address:* Rodney House, 70 Mount Pleasant, Liverpool L3 5UX. *T:* 051–709 3676. *Club:* Athenæum (Liverpool).

TOYNE SEWELL, Maj.-Gen. Timothy Patrick; Commandant, Royal Military Academy, Sandhurst, since 1991; *b* 7 July 1941; *s* of late Brig. E. P. Sewell, CBE and of E. C. M. Sewell, MBE (*née* Toyne); *m* 1965, Jennifer Lesley Lunt; one *s* one *d*. *Educ:* Bedford Sch.; RMA, Sandhurst. psc 1973; jsdc 1985; rcds 1988. Commnd KOSB, 1961; ADC to Governor of Aden, 1962–63; helicopter pilot, 2 RGJ and 2 Para, 1966–69; Staff College, 1973; GSO 1, staff of CDS, 1979–81; CO, 1 KOSB, 1981–83; CoS, British Forces Falkland Is, 1983–84; Sen. Directing Staff (Army), JSDC, 1984–85; Comdr, 19 Infantry Bde, 1985–87; RCDS, 1988; Comdr, British Mil. and Adv. Team, Zimbabwe, 1989–91. *Recreations:* racquet sports, golf, fishing, music. *Address:* c/o Lloyds Bank, Cox's & King's Branch, PO Box 1190, 7 Pall Mall, SW1Y 5NA. *Club:* Army and Navy.

TRACEY, Richard Patrick, JP; MP (C) Surbiton, since 1983; *b* 8 Feb. 1943; *o s* of late P. H. (Dick) Tracey and of Hilda Tracey; *m* 1974, Katharine Gardner; one *s* three *d*. *Educ:* King Edward VI Sch., Stratford-upon-Avon; Birmingham Univ. (LLB Hons). Leader Writer, Daily Express, 1964–66; Presenter/Reporter, BBC Television and Radio, 1966–78: internat. news and current affairs (The World at One, PM, Today, Newsdesk, 24 Hours, The Money Prog.); feature programmes (Wheelbase, Waterline, Motoring and the Motorist, You and Yours, Checkpoint); also documentaries; Public Affairs Consultant/Advisor, 1978–83. Member: Econ. Res. Council, 1981–; ISIS Assoc., 1981–. Various Conservative Party Offices, 1974–81; Dep. Chm., Greater London Cons. Party, 1981–83; Mem., Cons. National Union Exec. Cttee, 1981–83. PPS to Min. of State for Trade and Industry (IT), 1984–85; Parly Under Sec. of State, DoE (with special responsibility for sport), 1985–87. Mem., Select Cttee on Televising H of C, 1988–. Chm., Cons. Parly Greater London MP's Cttee, 1990– (Jt Sec., 1983–84); Sec., Cons. Parly Media Cttee, 1983–84. Contested (C) Northampton N, Oct. 1974. JP SW London (Wimbledon PSD), 1977. Freeman, City of London, 1984. *Publications:* (with Richard Hudson-Evans) The World of Motor Sport, 1971; (with Michael Clayton) Hickstead—the first twelve years, 1972; articles, pamphlets. *Recreations:* riding, boating, debating. *Address:* House of Commons, SW1A 0AA. *T:* 071–219 5196. *Club:* Wig and Pen.

TRACEY, Stanley William, OBE 1986; professional pianist, composer and arranger, since 1943; *b* 30 Dec. 1926; *s* of Stanley Clark Tracey and Florence Louise Tracey; *m* 1st, 1946, Joan; 2nd, 1954, Jean; 3rd, 1960, Florence Mary, (Jackie); one *s* one *d*. *Educ:* Tooting, Graveney and Ensham Schools. Leading own small group, 1965–, orchestra, 1969–. Hon. RAM 1984. Numerous records of own compositions and arrangements; compositions include: Under Milk Wood suite, 1965; Genesis, 1986; 500 other titles. Awards include: BASCA Award, 1984; voted best jazz composer, Wire/Guardian, 1989; voted best album of year, Big Band, 1989. *Address:* 12 Cotlandswick, London Colney, Herts AL2 1EE. *T:* Bowmansgreen (0727) 23286.

TRACEY, Stephen Frederick T.; *see* Thorpe-Tracey.

TRACY; *see* Hanbury-Tracy, family name of Baron Sudeley.

TRACY, Rear-Adm. Hugh Gordon Henry, CB 1965; DSC 1945; *b* 15 Nov. 1912; *e s* of Comdr A. F. G. Tracy, RN; *m* 1938, Muriel, *d* of Maj.-Gen. Sir R. B. Ainsworth, CB, DSO, OBE; two *s* one *d*. *Educ:* Nautical Coll., Pangbourne. Joined RN, 1929; Lieut, 1934; served in HMS Shropshire, Hawkins and Furious, in Admiralty and attended Advanced Engineering course before promotion to Lt-Comdr, 1942; Sen. Engineer, HMS Illustrious, 1942–44; Asst to Manager, Engineering Dept, HM Dockyard Chatham, 1944–46; Comdr 1946; served in HMS Manxman, Admiralty, RN Engineering Coll. and HM Dockyard Malta; Captain, 1955; Asst Director of Marine Engineering, Admiralty, 1956–58; CO HMS Sultan, 1959–60; Imperial Defence Coll., 1961; CSO (Tech.) to Flag Officer, Sea Training, 1962–63; Rear-Admiral, 1963; Director of Marine Engineering, Ministry of Defence (Navy), 1963–66; retired, 1966. Chm., Wilts Gardens Trust, 1985–89. *Recreations:* gardening, plant ecology. *Address:* Orchard House, Claverton, Bath BA2 7BG. *T:* Bath (0225) 465650.

TRACY, Walter Valentine, RDI; *b* 14 Feb. 1914; *s* of Walter and Anne Tracy; *m* 1942, Muriel Frances Campbell. *Educ:* Central Sch. of Arts and Crafts. Apprentice compositor, Wm Clowes Ltd, 1930–35; typographic studio, Baynard Press, 1935–38; Notley Advertising, 1938–46; freelance, 1946–47; on staff of (British) Linotype Co., editor Linotype Matrix, i/c typographic design, 1947–73; Linotype-Paul, 1973–78. In 1965, assisted Editor of The Times in re-designing the paper for news on front page, May 1966; designed newspaper types: Jubilee, 1953; Adsans, 1959; Maximus, 1967; Telegraph Modern, 1969; Times-Europa, 1972; Argus 1989; also designed: Hebrew types Gold, Silver, 1975 (under pseudonym David Silver) for Linotype-Paul; Arabic types Kufic Light, Med., Bold, 1979 for Letraset; Qadi, 1983 for Linotype-Paul; Oasis, 1985 for Kroy; Malik, Sharif and Medina, 1988 for Bitstream. RDI 1973. *Publications:* Letters of Credit: a view of type design, 1986; The Typographic Scene, 1988; contribs to Penrose Annual, Alphabet, Motif, Typographica. *Address:* 2 Cedar Court, The Drive, Finchley Way, N3 1AE. *T:* 081–349 3785. *Club:* Double Crown (Hon. Mem.).

TRAFFORD; *see* de Trafford.

TRAFFORD, Ian Colton, OBE 1967; Publisher, The Times Supplements, 1981–88, retired; *b* 8 July 1928; *s* of Dr Harold Trafford and late Laura Dorothy Trafford; *m* 1st, 1949, Nella Georgara (marr. diss. 1964); one *d*; 2nd, 1972, Jacqueline Carole Trenque. *Educ:* Charterhouse; St John's Coll., Oxford. Feature writer and industrial correspondent, The Financial Times, 1951–58; UK Correspondent, Barrons Weekly, New York, 1954–60; Director, Industrial and Trade Fairs Holdings Ltd, 1958–71, Managing Director, 1966–71; Director-General British Trade Fairs in: Peking, 1964; Moscow, 1966; Bucharest, 1968; Sao Paulo, 1969; Buenos Aires, 1970; Man. Dir, Economist Newspaper, 1971–81; Chm., Economist Intelligence Unit, 1971–79; Dep. Chm., Times Books Ltd, 1981–86. Local Dir, W London Board, Commercial Union Assce, 1974–83. OBE awarded for services to exports. *Address:* Grafton House, Westhall Road, Warlingham, Surrey CR6 9HF. *T:* Upper Warlingham (0883) 622048.

TRAHAIR, John Rosewarne, CBE 1990; DL; Chairman, Plymouth District Health Authority, 1981–90; *b* 29 March 1921; *s* of late Percy Edward Trahair and Edith Irene Trahair; *m* 1948, Patricia Elizabeth (*née* Godrich); one *s* one *d*. *Educ:* Leys Sch.; Christ's Coll., Cambridge (MA). FCIS. Served with Royal Artillery, 1941–46 (Captain). Finance Dir, Farleys Infant Food Ltd, 1948–73; Dir 1950–74, Dep. Chm. 1956–74, Western Credit Holdings Ltd. Chairman: Moorhaven HMC, 1959–66; Plymouth and District HMC, 1966–74; Member: SW Regional Hosp. Bd, 1965–74 (Vice-Chm. 1971–73, Chm. 1973–74); South Western RHA, 1974–81. Mem., Devon CC, 1977–81. High Sheriff, Devon, 1987–88; DL Devon, 1989. *Recreations:* sailing, walking. *Address:* West Park, Ivybridge, South Devon PL21 9JP. *T:* Plymouth (0752) 892466. *Club:* Royal Western Yacht.

TRAHERNE, Sir Cennydd (George), KG 1970; Kt 1964; TD 1950; MA; HM Lord-Lieutenant of Mid, South and West Glamorgan, 1974–85 (HM Lieutenant for Glamorgan, 1952–74); *b* 14 Dec. 1910; *er s* of late Comdr L. E. Traherne, RN, of Coedarhydyglyn, near Cardiff, and Dorothy, *d* of G. F. S. Sinclair; *m* 1934, Olivera Rowena, OBE, BA, JP, DStJ (*d* 1986), *d* of late James Binney, and late Lady Marjory Binney, Pampisford Hall, Cambridgeshire. *Educ:* Wellington; Brasenose Coll., Oxford. Barrister, Inner Temple, 1938 (Hon. Bencher, 1983). 81st Field Regt RA (TA), 1934–43; 102 Provost Coy, Corps of Military Police, 1943–45 (despatches); Dep. Asst Provost Marshal, Second British Army, 1945; 53rd Div. Provost Company, Royal Military Police, 1947–49, TA; Hon. Colonel: 53 Div. Signal Regt, 1953–58; 282 (Glamorgan Yeomanry) Field Regt RA (TA), 1958–61; 282 (Glam and Mon) Regt RA (TA), 1962–67; 37 (Wessex and Welsh) Signal Regt, T&AVR, 1971–75; Glamorgan ACF, 1982. DL 1946, JP 1946, Glamorgan. Deputy Chairman Glamorgan Quarter Sessions, 1949–52; President: Welsh College of Advanced Technology, 1957–65; Welsh Nat. Sch. of Medicine, 1970–83; Univ. of Wales Coll. of Medicine, 1983–87 (Hon. Fellow, 1989). Chairman, Rep. Body of the Church in Wales, 1965–77. Director: Cardiff Building Society, 1953–85 (Chm., 1964–85); Wales Gas Board, 1958–71; Commercial Bank of Wales, 1972–88; Chm., Wales Gas Consultative Council, 1958–71. Member, Gorsedd of the Bards of Wales. Honorary Freeman: Borough of Cowbridge, 1971; Borough of Vale of Glamorgan, 1984; City of Cardiff, 1985. Hon. LLD University of Wales. GCStJ 1991 (Sub Prior, Priory of Wales, 1978–90). *Address:* Coedarhydyglyn, near Cardiff, S Wales CF5 6SF. *T:* Peterston-super-Ely (0446) 760321. *Clubs:* Athenæum; Cardiff and County (Cardiff).

TRAILL, Sir Alan Towers, GBE 1984; QSO 1990; Managing Director, Colburn Traill Ltd, since 1989; Underwriting Member of Lloyd's, since 1963; *b* 7 May 1935; *s* of George Traill and Margaret Eleanor (*née* Matthews); *m* 1964, Sarah Jane (*née* Hutt); one *s*. *Educ:* St Andrew's Sch., Eastbourne; Charterhouse; Jesus Coll., Cambridge (MA). Dir, Saltire Insurance Investments plc, 1988–. Mem. Council, British Insurance Brokers Assoc., 1978–79; Chairman: Reinsurance Brokers Cttee of the Assoc., 1978–; UK/NZ 1990 Cttee, 1989–90. Member, Court of Common Council, City of London, 1970; Alderman for Langbourn Ward, 1975–; Sheriff, 1982–83; Lord Mayor of London, 1984–85. Master, Worshipful Co. of Cutlers, 1979–80; Director: City Arts Trust, 1980–; Historic Arts Trust, 1988–; Chm. Trustees, Waitangi Foundn. Governor: Royal Shakespeare Co., 1982–; King Edward's Sch., Witley, 1980–; St Paul's Cathedral Choir Sch., 1986–; Treloar Coll., 1986–; Almoner, Christ's Hosp. Foundn, 1980–. KStJ 1985. *Recreations:* shooting, skiing, DIY, travel, opera, assisting education. *Address:* 19/21 Great Tower Street, EC3R 5AQ. *T:* 071–626 5644. *Club:* City Livery.

TRAIN, Christopher John, CB 1986; Deputy Under Secretary of State, Home Office, and Director-General, Prison Service, 1983–91; *b* 12 March 1932; *s* of late Keith Sydney Sayer Train and of Edna Ashby Train; *m* 1957, Sheila Mary Watson; one *s* one *d*. *Educ:* Nottingham High Sch.; Christ Church Oxford (BA Lit. Hum., MA). Served Royal Navy, 1955–57; Assistant Master, St Paul's Sch., W Kensington, 1957–67; Principal, Home Office, 1968; Asst Sec., Home Office, 1972; Secretary, Royal Commn on Criminal Procedure, 1978–80; Asst Under Sec. of State, Home Office, 1980–83. Pres., Suffolk Horse Soc., 1989–90. *Recreations:* cricket and collecting cricket books, jogging, cooking. *Clubs:* Reform; Vincent's (Oxford).

TRAIN, David, MC 1945; PhD; FCGI, FRPharmS, FRSC; FEng, FIChemE; Senior Consultant, Cremer and Warner, Consulting Engineers and Scientists, since 1982 (Senior Partner, 1980–82); *b* 27 Feb. 1919; *s* of Charles and Elsie Louisa Train; *m* 1943, Jeanne Catherine, *d* of late William R. and M. M. Edmunds; two *s*. *Educ:* Lady Hawkins' Grammar Sch., Kington; School of Pharmacy, Univ. of London; Northampton Coll. of Advanced Technology; Imperial Coll., Univ. of London. Fairchild Schol. 1940, MPS 1941, Hewlett Exhibn 1941; BPharm 1942, PhC 1942; BScChemEng 1949, PhD 1956, DIC 1956. ARIC 1949; FRSH 1972; FCGI 1982 (ACGI 1949); FEng 1983. Apprenticed to F. T. Roper and Daughter, Kington, 1935–38. War service: St John's Hosp. Reserve, 1939; RAMC (non-med.), NW Europe, 1942–45; 212 Fd Amb. 53rd Welsh (Lieut). Lectr in Pharmaceutical Engrg Science, 1949–59, Reader, 1959–61, Sch. of Pharmacy, London; Vis. Prof., Univ. of Wisconsin, 1959. Partner, Cremer and Warner, 1961–82. Examiner: for Pharm. Soc. of Gt Brit., 1949–56; IChemE, 1956–66; Mem. Bd of Studies in Chem. Engrg, Univ. of London, 1958–; External Examr, PhD Theses, 1956–75; Jt Hon. Secretary: Brit. Pharm. Conf., 1958–64; IChemE, 1972–77; Member: Adv. Cttee on Oil Pollution of the Sea, 1973–84; Air Pollution Control Assoc., USA, 1971–84; Fédn Internat. Pharmaceutique, 1970–82. Liveryman: Worshipful Soc. of Apothecaries, 1975–; Worshipful Co. of Engineers, 1983–. *Publications:* various, on compression of powders, protection of the environment, acidic emissions, hazards in medicaments, preventative toxicology. *Recreations:* gardening, travelling. *Address:* 3 Grayland Close, Bromley, Kent BR1 2PA. *T:* 081–464 4701. *Club:* Athenæum.

TRANMIRE, Baron *cr* 1974 (Life Peer), of Upsall, North Yorkshire; **Robert Hugh Turton,** PC 1955; KBE 1971; MC 1942; JP; DL; *b* 8 Aug. 1903; *s* of late Major R. B. Turton, Kildale Hall, Kildale, Yorks; *m* 1928, Ruby Christian, *d* of late Robert T. Scott, Beechmont, Sevenoaks; two *s* one *d* (and one *s* decd). *Educ:* Eton; Balliol Coll., Oxford. Called to Bar, Inner Temple, 1926; joined 4th Bn of Green Howards at outbreak of war, 1939; served as DAAG 50th (N) Division, AAG GHQ MEF. MP (C) Thirsk and Malton, 1929–Feb. 1974. Parly Sec., Min. of Nat. Insurance, 1951–53. Min. of Pensions and Nat. Insce, 1953–54; Joint Parly Under-Sec. of State for Foreign Affairs, Oct. 1954–Dec. 1955; Minister of Health, Dec. 1955–Jan. 1957; Chm., Select Cttee on Procedure, 1970–74. Chm., Commonwealth Industries Assoc., 1963–74. JP 1936, DL 1962, N Riding, Co. York. Hon. Colonel, 4/5th Bn The Green Howards (TA), 1963–67. *Address:* Upsall Castle, Thirsk, N Yorks YO7 2QJ. *T:* Thirsk (0845) 537202; 15 Grey Coat Gardens, SW1P 2QA. *T:* 071–834 1535.

TRANT, Gen. Sir Richard (Brooking), KCB 1982 (CB 1979); Chairman: Hunting Engineering Ltd, since 1988; Defence Division, Hunting Plc, since 1989; Deputy Chairman, Wilson's Hogg Robinson Ltd, since 1988; *b* 30 March 1928; *s* of Richard Brooking Trant and Dora Rodney Trant (*née* Lancaster); *m* 1957, Diana Clare, 2nd *d* of Rev. Stephen Zachary and Ruth Beatrice Edwards; one *s* two *d*. Commissioned RA 1947; served Korean War, 1952–53; Defence Services Staff Coll., India, 1961–62; S Arabia, 1962–65; Jt Services Staff Coll., 1965; commanded 3rd Regt RHA, 1968–71, 5th Airportable Brigade, 1972–74; Dep. Mil. Sec., MoD (Army), 1975–76; Comdr Land Forces, NI, 1977–79; Dir, Army Staff Duties, 1979–82; GOC South East District, 1982–83, Land Dep. C-in-C Fleet during S Atlantic Campaign, 1982; QMG, 1983–86. Col Comdt: RAEC, 1979–86; RA, 1982–87; RAOC, 1984–88; HAC (TA), 1984–. Special Comr, Duke of York's Royal Mil. Sch., Dover, 1987–; Comr, Royal Hosp. Chelsea, 1988–. Defence Advisor, Short Bros, 1987–88; Dir, Eastern Region Technology Centre. Member: Armed Forces Pay Rev. Body, 1988–; Council, SBAC, 1988–; Vice Pres., Defence Manufacturers' Assoc., 1989–. Pres., RA Hunt and RA Saddle Club,

1984–90; Admiral, Army Sailing Assoc., 1984–87. CBIM 1985; MInstD 1987. Freeman, City of London, 1984. Order of South Arabia, 3rd Class, 1965. *Recreations:* golf, field sports, natural history, sailing. *Address:* c/o Lloyds Bank, Newquay, Cornwall. *Clubs:* Army and Navy; Royal Fowey Yacht.

TRANTER, Professor Clement John, CBE 1967 (OBE 1953); Bashforth Professor of Mathematical Physics, Royal Military College of Science, Shrivenham, 1953–74, now Emeritus; *b* 16 Aug. 1909; *s* of late Archibald Tranter, and Mrs Tranter, Cirencester, Glos.; *m* 1937, Joan Louise Hatton, *d* of late J. Hatton, MBE, and Mrs Hatton, Plumstead, SE18. *Educ:* Cirencester Grammar Sch.; Queen's Coll., Oxford (Open Math. Scholar; 1st Class Hons Mathematical Mods, 1929; 1st Class Hons Final Sch. of Maths, 1931; MA (Oxon) 1940; DSc (Oxon) 1953). Commissioned RA, TA, 1932; Captain, 1938. Junior Assistant Research Dept, Woolwich, 1931–34; Senior Lecturer, Gunnery and Mathematics Branch, Military College of Science, Woolwich, 1935–40; Asst Professor 1940–46; Assoc. Professor of Mathematics, Royal Military College of Science, Shrivenham, 1946–53. *Publications:* Integral Transforms in Mathematical Physics, 1951; Advanced Level Pure Mathematics, 1953; Techniques of Mathematical Analysis, 1957; (with C. G. Lambe) Differential Equations for Engineers and Scientists, 1961; Mathematics for Sixth Form Scientists, 1964; (with C. G. Lambe) Advanced Level Mathematics, 1966; Bessel Functions with some Physical Applications, 1968; mathematical papers in various journals. *Recreations:* painting, golf, fly-fishing. *Address:* Flagstones, Stanton Fitzwarren, near Swindon, Wilts SN6 7RZ. *T:* Swindon (0793) 762913.

TRANTER, Nigel Godwin, OBE 1983; novelist and author since 1936; *b* Glasgow, 23 Nov. 1909; *yr s* of Gilbert T. Tranter and Eleanor A. Cass; *m* 1933, May Jean Campbell Grieve (*d* 1979); one *d* (one *s* decd). *Educ:* St James Episcopal Sch., Edinburgh; George Heriot's Sch., Edinburgh. Served War of 1939–45, RASC and RA. Accountancy trng, then in small family insce co., until could live on writing, after war service; much and actively interested in Scottish public affairs; Chm., Scottish Convention, Edinburgh Br., 1948–51; Vice-Convener, Scottish Covenant Assoc., 1951–55; Pres., E Lothian Liberal Assoc., 1960–76; Chm., Nat. Forth Road Bridge Cttee, 1953–57; Pres., Scottish PEN, 1962–66, Hon. Pres., 1973–; Chm., Soc. of Authors, Scotland, 1966–72; Pres., E Lothian Wildfowlers' Assoc., 1952–73; Chm., St Andrew Soc. of E Lothian, 1966–; Chm., Nat. Book League, Scotland, 1972–77; Hon. Vice-Pres., Scottish Assoc. of Teachers of History, 1989; Mem., Cttee of Aberlady Bay Nature Reserve, 1953–76, etc. Hon. Mem., Mark Twain Soc. of Amer., 1976. Hon. Freeman, Blackstone, Va, 1980. Hon. MA Edinburgh, 1971; Hon. DLitt Strathclyde, 1990. Scot of the Year, BBC Radio Scotland, 1989. Chevalier, Order of St Lazarus of Jerusalem, 1961 (Vice-Chancellor of the Order, Scotland, 1980, Chancellor, 1986). *Publications: fiction:* 72 novels, from Trespass, 1937, including: Bridal Path, 1952; Macgregor's Gathering, 1957; the Master of Gray trilogy: The Master of Gray, 1961; The Courtesan, 1963; Past Master, 1965; Chain of Destiny, 1964; the Robert the Bruce trilogy: The Steps to the Empty Throne, 1969; The Path of the Hero King, 1970; The Price of the King's Peace, 1971; The Young Montrose, 1972; Montrose: the Captain General, 1973; The Wisest Fool, 1974; The Wallace, 1975; Lords of Misrule, 1976; A Folly of Princes, 1977; The Captive Crown, 1977; Macbeth the King, 1978; Margaret the Queen, 1979; David the Prince, 1980; True Thomas, 1981; The Patriot, 1982; Lord of the Isles, 1983; Unicorn Rampant, 1984; The Riven Realm, 1984; James, By the Grace of God, 1985; Rough Wooing, 1986; Columba, 1987; Cache Down, 1987; Flowers of Chivalry, 1988; Mail Royal, 1989; Warden of the Queen's March, 1989; Kenneth, 1990; Crusader, 1991; 12 children's novels; *non-fiction:* The Fortalices and Early Mansions of Southern Scotland, 1935; The Fortified House in Scotland (5 vols), 1962–71; Pegasus Book of Scotland, 1964; Outlaw of the Highlands: Rob Roy, 1965; Land of the Scots, 1968; Portrait of the Border Country, 1972; Portrait of the Lothians, 1979; The Queen's Scotland Series: The Heartland: Clackmannan, Perth and Stirlingshire, 1971; The Eastern Counties: Aberdeen, Angus and Kincardineshire, 1972; The North East: Banff, Moray, Nairn, East Inverness and Easter Ross, 1974; Argyll and Bute, 1977; Nigel Tranter's Scotland, 1981; Scottish Castles: tales and traditions, 1982; Scotland of Robert the Bruce, 1986; The Story of Scotland, 1987; contribs to many jls, on Scots history, genealogy, topography, castellated architecture, knighthood, etc. *Recreations:* walking, historical research, helping to restore Scottish castles. *Address:* Quarry House, Aberlady, East Lothian EH32 0QB. *T:* Aberlady (08757) 258. *Club:* PEN.

TRAPNELL, Barry Maurice Waller, CBE 1982; DL; MA, PhD Cantab; Headmaster of Oundle School, 1968–84; Chairman, Cambridge Occupational Analysts, since 1986; Director, Thomas Wall Trust, since 1984; *b* 18 May 1924; *s* of Waller Bertram and late Rachel Trapnell; *m* 1951, Dorothy Joan, *d* of late P. J. Kerr, ICS; two *d*. *Educ:* University College Sch., Hampstead; St John's Coll., Cambridge (Scholar). Research in physical chemistry in Department of Colloid Science, Cambridge, 1945–46, and Royal Institution, London, 1946–50; Commonwealth Fund Fellow, Northwestern Univ., Ill., 1950–51; Lecturer in chemistry: Worcester Coll., Oxford, 1951–54; Liverpool Univ., 1954–57; Headmaster, Denstone Coll., 1957–68. Visiting Lecturer, American Association for Advancement of Science, 1961. Pres., Independent Schools Assoc. Inc., 1984–; Member: Adv. Cttee on Supply and Training of Teachers; C of E Commn on Religious Education. E Anglian Regl Dir, Index, 1985–. Mem. Governing Body, Roedean Sch., 1987–. DL: Staffs, 1967; Northants, 1974–84. Hon. Liveryman, Worshipful Co. of Grocers, 1984. *Publications:* Chemisorption, 1955 (Russian edition, 1958; 2nd English edition, 1964); Learning and Discerning, 1966; papers in British and American scientific journals. *Recreations:* several games (represented Cambridge *v* Oxford at cricket and squash rackets, and Gentlemen *v* Players at cricket; won Amateur Championships at Rugby Fives); English furniture and silver. *Address:* 6 Corfe Close, Cambridge CB2 2QA. *T:* Cambridge (0223) 249278. *Club:* East India, Devonshire, Sports and Public Schools.

TRAPNELL, John Arthur; Under-Secretary, Departments of Trade and Industry, 1973–77; *b* 7 Sept. 1913; *s* of Arthur Westicote Trapnell and Helen Trapnell (*née* Alles); *m* 1939, Winifred Chadwick Rushton; two *d*. *Educ:* privately; Law Soc.'s Sch. of Law. Admitted Solicitor 1938; private practice until 1940; served HM Army, 1940–46: commnd Som. LI, 1943; served with 82nd W African Div. (Major). Civil Service from 1946: Board of Trade, Solicitors Dept. Mem. Law Soc. *Recreations:* golf, bridge. *Address:* 29 Connaught Road, New Malden, Surrey. *T:* 081–942 3183.

TRAPP, Rt. Rev. Eric Joseph; *b* 17 July 1910; *s* of late Archibald Edward Trapp and Agnes Trapp, Leicester and Coventry; *m* 1937, Edna Noreen Thornton, SRN; two *d*. *Educ:* Alderman Newton's Sch., Leicester; Leeds Univ.; College of the Resurrection, Mirfield. BA 1st Class, philosophy. Asst Curate, St Olave's, Mitcham, Surrey, 1934–37; Director, Masite Mission, Basutoland, 1937–40; Rector, St Augustine's Bethlehem, Orange Free State, 1940–43; Rector, St John's, Maseru and Director of Maseru Mission, Basutoland, 1943–47; Canon of Bloemfontein Cathedral, 1944–47; Bishop of Zululand, 1947–57; Sec., Soc. for the Propagation of the Gospel, 1957–64, United Soc. for the Propagation of the Gospel, 1965–70; Bishop of Bermuda, 1970–75; Hon. Asst Bishop, Dio. St Albans, 1976–final retirement in 1980. Hon. DD Trinity College, Toronto, 1967. *Address:* Flat 15, Manormead, Tilford Road, Hindhead, Surrey GU26 6RA. *T:* Hindhead (0428) 607301.

TRAPP, Prof. Joseph Burney, CBE 1990; FSA; FBA 1980; Director, Warburg Institute (University of London) and Professor of the History of the Classical Tradition, 1976–90; *b* 16 July 1925; *s* of H. M. B. and Frances M. Trapp; *m* 1953, Elayne M. Falla; two *s*. *Educ:* Dannevirke High Sch. and Victoria University Coll., Wellington, NZ (MA). FSA 1978. Alexander Turnbull Library, Wellington, 1946–50; Jun. Lectr, Victoria University Coll., 1950–51; Asst Lectr, Reading Univ., 1951–53; Warburg Institute: Asst Librarian, 1953–66; Librarian, 1966–76; Hon. Fellow, 1990. Visiting Professor: Univ. of Toronto, 1969; Univ. of Melbourne, 1980. Member: Advisory Council: V&A Museum, 1977–83; British Library, 1980–87; Exec. Cttee, British Sch. at Rome, 1983–87, Council, 1984–; Foreign Sec., British Academy, 1988– (Vice-Pres., 1983–85). *Publications:* (ed) The Apology of Sir Thomas More, 1979; Essays in the Renaissance and the Classical Tradition, 1990; articles in learned jls. *Address:* c/o Warburg Institute, Woburn Square, WC1H 0AB.

TRASENSTER, Michael Augustus Tulk, CVO 1954; Photographer, ARPS 1979; *b* 26 Jan. 1923; *er s* of late Major William Augustus Trasenster, MC, and late Brenda de Courcy Trasenster; *m* 1950, Fay Norrie Darley, *d* of late Thomas Bladworth Darley, Cantley Hall, Yorkshire; two *d*. *Educ:* Winchester. Served with 4th/7th Royal Dragoon Guards, 1942–; NW Europe, 1944; Middle East, 1946; ADC to Governor of South Australia, 1947–49; School of Tank Technology, 1951; Military Secretary and Comptroller to the Governor General of New Zealand, 1952–55. Chevalier of Order of Leopold II of Belgium, with palm, 1944; Belgian Croix de Guerre, with palm, 1944. *Recreations:* painting, tennis. *Address:* c/o Royal Bank of Scotland, High Street, Winchester, Hants SO23 9DA.

TRASLER, Prof. Gordon Blair, PhD; FBPsS; JP; first Professor of Psychology, University of Southampton, since 1964; *b* 7 March 1929; *s* of Frank Ferrier Trasler and Marian (*née* Blair); *m* 1953, Kathleen Patricia Fegan. *Educ:* Isleworth Grammar Sch.; Bryanston Sch.; University Coll., Exeter (MA); London Univ. (BSc, PhD). FBPsS 1963; CPsychol. Tutorial Asst, UC, Exeter, 1952–53; Psychologist, HM Prisons, Wandsworth and Winchester, 1955–57; Lectr, Southampton Univ., 1957–64. Visiting Lecturer: LSE, 1962–63; Inst. of Criminology, Cambridge Univ., 1968–; Vis. Prof., Univ. of Alberta at Edmonton, 1977. Mem., Winchester Health Authority, 1981–89. Vice-Pres., Inst. for Study and Treatment of Delinquency, 1987– (Chm., 1981–87); Chm., Div. of Criminolog. and Legal Psychol., BPsS, 1980–83. Chief Scientist's Advr, DHSS, 1977–80 and 1983–; Member: Adv. Council on Penal System, 1968–74; Wootton Cttee on Non-custodial penalties, 1968–70; Younger Cttee on Young Adult Offenders, 1970–74; Lord Chancellor's Adv. Cttee for Southampton, 1988–. Editor-in-chief, British Jl of Criminology, 1980–85. JP Hants, 1978. Sellin-Glueck Award (for outstanding scholarly contribs to criminology), Amer. Soc. of Criminology, 1990. *Publications:* In Place of Parents, 1960; The Explanation of Criminality, 1962; The Shaping of Social Behaviour, 1967; (jtly) The Formative Years, 1968; (with D. P. Farrington) Behaviour Modification with Offenders, 1980; many papers in jls and chapters on psychology and criminology. *Recreations:* reading, photography, writing. *Address:* Fox Croft, Old Kennels Lane, Oliver's Battery, Winchester SO22 4JT. *T:* Winchester (0962) 52345.

TRAVERS, Basil Holmes, AM 1983; OBE 1943; BA (Sydney); MA (Oxon); BLitt (Oxon); FACE; FRSA; FAIM; Headmaster of Sydney Church of England Grammar School, North Sydney, NSW, 1959–84; *b* 7 July 1919; *m* 1942, Margaret Emily Marr; three *d*. *Educ:* Sydney Church of England Grammar Sch.; Sydney Univ.; New Coll., Oxford Univ. Rhodes Scholar for NSW, 1940. Served War of 1939–45 (despatches, OBE); AIF, 2/2 Australian Infantry Battalion; ADC to Maj.-Gen. Sir I. G. Mackay, 1940; Brigade Major, 15 Aust. Inf. Bde, 1943–44; psc 1944; GSO 2, HQ, 2 Aust. Corps, 1944–45. Assistant Master, Wellington Coll., Berks, England, 1948–49; Assistant Master, Cranbrook Sch., Sydney, 1950–52; Headmaster, Launceston Church Grammar Sch., Launceston, Tasmania, 1953–58. Chm., Headmasters' Conf. of Australia, 1971–73. Lt-Col commanding 12 Inf. Bn (CMF), 1955–58. Member: Soldiers' Children Education Board, 1959–; NSW Cttee, Duke of Edinburgh's Award Scheme in Australia, 1959– (Chm., 1979–84). Col Comdt, Royal Australian Army Educn Corps, 1984–88. *Publications:* Let's Talk Rugger, 1949; The Captain General, 1952. *Recreations:* cricket (Oxford Blue, 1946, 1948), swimming, rugby (Oxford Blue, 1946, 1947), athletics (Half Blue, 1947); also Sydney Blue, football, cricket; Rugby Union International for England, 1947, 1948, 1949; represented NSW, 1950. *Address:* 19 Edward Street, Gordon, NSW 2072, Australia. *T:* 498 4661. *Clubs:* Union, Rugby Union (Sydney); Elanora Country.

TRAVERS, Rt. Rev. Mgr. Brendan; *b* 21 March 1931; *s* of Dr Charles Travers and Eileen Travers (*née* Gordon). *Educ:* Belmont Abbey Sch.; Venerable English College, Rome; Gregorian Univ., Rome. (STL, JCL, PhL). Ordained priest, 1955; Curate, Salford diocese, 1957–72; Bishop's Secretary, 1961–64; Chm., Manchester Catholic Marriage Adv. Council, 1966–71; Rector, Pontifical Beda College, Rome, 1972–78; Parish Priest, All Souls, Salford, 1978–. *Recreation:* golf. *Address:* All Souls Presbytery, Liverpool Street, Weaste, Salford M5 2HQ. *Club:* Worsley Golf (Manchester).

TRAVERS, Sir Thomas (à Beckett), Kt 1972; Consulting Ophthalmologist, Royal Melbourne Hospital, since 1962; *b* 16 Aug. 1902; *s* of late Walter Travers, Warragul, Vic and late Isabelle Travers; *m* Tone, *widow* of late R. S. Burnard; no *c*. *Educ:* Melbourne Grammar School. MB, BS 1925, DSc 1941, Melbourne; MRCP 1928; DOMS London 1928; FRACS. *Publications:* various on strabismus. *Recreation:* gardening. *Address:* 55 Victoria Parade, Fitzroy, Vic 3065, Australia. *T:* 417 1722. *Club:* Melbourne (Melbourne).

TRAVERSE-HEALY, Thomas Hector, (Tim), OBE 1989; FIPR, FPA; corporate affairs counsel; Senior Partner, Traverse-Healy Ltd, since 1947; Professional Adviser, Corporate Communications plc, since 1990; *b* 25 March 1923; *s* of John Healy, MBE, and Gladys Traverse; *m* 1946, Joan Thompson; two *s* three *d*. *Educ:* Stonyhurst Coll.; St Mary's Hosp., London Univ. DipCAM. Served War, Royal Marines Commandos and Special Forces, 1941–46. Chairman: Traverse-Healy & Regester Ltd, 1985–87; Charles Barker Traverse-Healy, 1987–89; Non-exec. Dir, Charles Barker Hldgs, 1990–. Mem., Public and Social Policy Cttee, National Westminster Bank, 1974–; Specialist Advr, CNAA, 1990–. Vis. Prof., Baylor Univ., Texas, 1988–; Hon. Professor: Stirling Univ., 1988–; Univ. of Wales, 1990–. President: Internat. PR Res. and Educn Foundn, 1983–86; Internat. Foundn for PR Studies, 1987–89; Chm., (UK) PR Educn Trust, 1990–; Mem., Professional Practices Cttee, PR Consultants Assoc., 1987–. Inst. of Public Relations: Mem. 1948, Fellow 1956; Pres. 1967–68; Tallents Gold Medal, 1985; Hon. Fellow 1988; European PR Federation: Vice-Pres. 1965–69; Internat. PR Assoc.: Sec. 1950–61, Pres. 1968–73, Mem. Emeritus, 1982; Presidential Gold Medal, 1985. FRSA 1953; FIPA 1957. Member, US Public Affairs Council, 1975–; Board Mem., Centre for Public Affairs Studies, 1969–; Pres., World PR Congress: Tel Aviv, 1970; Geneva, 1973. Congress Foundn Lecture: Boston, 1976; Bombay, 1982; Melbourne, 1988. PR News Award, 1983; PR Week Award, 1987; Page Soc. Award, 1990. *Publications:* numerous published lectures and articles in professional jls. *Recreations:* French politics, Irish Society. *Address:* PO Box LDN 810, SE24 9NQ. *T:* 071–738 3044. *Clubs:* Athenæum, Royal Automobile, Norwegian; Philippics.

TREACHER, Adm. Sir John (Devereux), KCB 1975; Director, Meggitt PLC, since 1989; *b* Chile, 23 Sept. 1924; *s* of late Frank Charles Treacher, Bentley, Suffolk; *m* 1st,

1953, Patcie Jane (marr. diss. 1968), *d* of late Dr F. L. McGrath, Evanston, Ill; one *s* one *d*; 2nd, 1969, Kirsteen Forbes, *d* of late D. F. Landale; one *s* one *d*. *Educ:* St Paul's School. Served in HM Ships Nelson, Glasgow, Keppel and Mermaid in Mediterranean, Russian convoys; qual. Fleet Air Arm pilot, 1947; CO: 778 Sqdn 1951, 849 Sqdn 1952–53; CO, HMS Lowestoft, 1964–66; CO, HMS Eagle, 1968–70; Flag Officer Carriers and Amphibious Ships and Comdr Carrier Striking Gp 2, 1970–72; Flag Officer, Naval Air Comd, 1972–73; Vice-Chief of Naval Staff, 1973–75; C-in-C Fleet, and Allied C-in-C Channel and Eastern Atlantic, 1975–77. Chief Exec., 1977–81, and Dir, 1977–85, Nat. Car Parks; Chm., Westland Inc., 1983–89; Dep. Chm., Westland Gp, 1986–89 (Dir. 1978–89). Non-press Mem., Press Council, 1978–81; Dir, SBAC, 1983–89. FRAeS 1973. *Recreations:* shooting, photography. *Address:* 22 Newton Road, W2 5LT. *Clubs:* Boodle's, Institute of Directors.

TREACY, Colman Maurice; QC 1990; a Recorder, since 1991; *b* 28 July 1949; *s* of Dr Maurice Treacy and Mary Treacy; *m* 1976, Laura Elizabeth Daniels; one *s* one *d*. *Educ:* Stonyhurst Coll.; Jesus Coll., Cambridge (MA). Called to the Bar, Middle Temple, 1971; an Asst Recorder, 1988–91. *Address:* 3 Fountain Court, Steelhouse Lane, Birmingham B4 6DR. *T:* 021–236 5854.

TREADGOLD, Hazel Rhona; JP; Central President of the Mothers' Union, 1983–88; *b* 29 May 1936; *m* 1959, John David Treadgold, *qv*; two *s* one *d*. Mothers' Union: has held office, Dioceses of Southwell and Durham, and at HQ; Chm., Central Young Families Cttee, 1971–76; a Central Vice-Pres., 1978–83. Archbishop of Canterbury's Co-ordinator, Bishops' Wives Conf., Lambeth, 1988; Member: Women's Nat. Commn, 1980–83; Exec., Women's Council, 1989–; Deanery Synod, Chichester, 1990–. Gov., Bishop Luffa C of E Comprehensive Sch., 1990–. JP, 1973–81, 1991–. *Recreations:* travel, reading, cookery. *Address:* The Deanery, Chichester, West Sussex PO19 1PX. *T:* Chichester (0243) 783286.

TREADGOLD, Very Rev. John David, LVO 1990; Dean of Chichester, since 1989; Chaplain to the Queen, 1983–89; *b* 30 Dec. 1931; *s* of Oscar and Sybil Treadgold; *m* 1959, Hazel Rhona Bailey (*see* H. R. Treadgold); two *s* one *d*. *Educ:* Nottingham Univ. (BA); Wells Theological College. Deacon 1959, priest 1960; Vicar Choral, Southwell Minster, 1959–64; Rector of Wollaton, Nottingham, 1964–74; Vicar of Darlington, 1974–81; Canon of Windsor and Chaplain to Windsor Great Park, 1981–89. Chaplain, TA, 1962–67; TAVR, 1974–78; Chaplain to High Sheriff: of Nottinghamshire, 1963–64 and 1975–76; of Durham, 1978–79. *Recreations:* musical appreciation; church architecture. *Address:* The Deanery, Chichester, West Sussex PO19 1PX. *T:* Chichester (0243) 783286.

TREADGOLD, Sydney William, FCA; Secretary, Financial Reporting Council, since 1990; *b* 10 May 1933; *s* of Harold Bryan Treadgold and Violet Gladys Watson; *m* 1961, Elizabeth Ann White; two *s*. *Educ:* Larkmead Sch., Abingdon. Chartered accountant (ACA 1960, FCA 1970). Served RAF, 1951–53 (Navigator). Wenn Townsend & Co., Chartered Accountants, 1954–62; Asst Finance Officer, Univ. of Liverpool, 1963–65; Principal: Min. of Aviation, 1965–67; Min. of Technol., 1967–71; Asst Sec., DTI, 1972–78; Under Secretary: Price Commn, 1978–79; Depts of Industry and Trade, 1979–83; DTI, 1983–; Gen., subseq. Competition, Policy Div., 1985–89; Mem., Accounting Standards Task Gp, 1989–90. FRSA 1988.

TREADWELL, Charles James, CMG 1972; CVO 1979; HM Diplomatic Service, retired; *b* 10 Feb. 1920; *s* of late C. A. L. Treadwell, OBE, Barrister and Solicitor, Wellington, NZ. *Educ:* Wellington Coll., NZ; University of New Zealand (LLB). Served with HM Forces, 1939–45. Sudan Political Service and Sudan Judiciary, 1945–55; FO, 1955–57; British High Commn, Lahore, 1957–60; HM Embassy, Ankara, 1960–62; HM Embassy, Jedda, 1963–64; British Dep. High Comr for Eastern Nigeria, 1965–66; Head of Joint Information Services Department, Foreign Office/Commonwealth Office, 1966–68; British Political Agent, Abu Dhabi, 1968–71; Ambassador, United Arab Emirates, 1971–73; High Comr to Bahamas, 1973–75; Ambassador to Oman, 1975–79. *Address:* Cherry Orchard Cottage, Buddington Lane, Midhurst, W Sussex GU29 0QP.

TREASE, Geoffrey; *see* Trease, R. G.

TREASE, (Robert) Geoffrey, FRSL 1979; *b* 11 Aug. 1909; *s* of George Albert Trease and Florence (*née* Dale); *m* 1933, Marian Haselden Granger Boyer (*d* 1989); one *d*. *Educ:* Nottingham High Sch.; Queen's Coll., Oxford (schol.). Chm., 1972–73, Mem. Council, 1974–, Society of Authors. *Publications:* Walking in England, 1935; Such Divinity, 1939; Only Natural, 1940; Tales Out of School, 1949; Snared Nightingale, 1957; So Wild the Heart, 1959; The Italian Story, 1963; The Grand Tour, 1967; (ed) Matthew Todd's Journal, 1968; Nottingham, a biography, 1970; The Condottieri, 1970; A Whiff of Burnt Boats, an early autobiography, 1971; Samuel Pepys and his World, 1972; Laughter at the Door, a continued autobiography, 1974; London, a concise history, 1975; Portrait of a Cavalier: William Cavendish, first Duke of Newcastle, 1979; *for young readers:* Bows Against the Barons, 1934; Cue for Treason, 1940; The Hills of Varna, 1948; No Boats on Bannermere, 1949; The Seven Queens of England, 1953; This Is Your Century, 1965; The Red Towers of Granada, 1966; Byron, A Poet Dangerous to Know, 1969; A Masque for the Queen, 1970; Horsemen on the Hills, 1971; D. H. Lawrence: the Phoenix and the Flame, 1973; Popinjay Stairs, 1973; Days to Remember, 1973; The Iron Tsar, 1975; The Chocolate Boy, 1975; When the Drums Beat, 1976; Violet for Bonaparte, 1976; The Field of the Forty Footsteps, 1977; Mandeville, 1980; A Wood by Moonlight and Other Stories, 1981; Saraband for Shadows, 1982; The Cormorant Venture, 1984; The Edwardian Era, 1986; Tomorrow is a Stranger, 1987; The Arpino Assignment, 1988; A Flight of Angels, 1988; Shadow Under the Sea, 1990; Calabrian Quest, 1990; Aunt Augusta's Elephant, 1991, and many others; *plays:* After the Tempest, 1938 (Welwyn Fest. award); Colony, 1939. *Recreations:* walking, the theatre. *Address:* 1 Yomede Park, Newbridge Road, Bath BA1 3LS.

TREASURE, Prof. John Albert Penberthy, PhD; Consultant to Saatchi & Saatchi Advertising Ltd, since 1989; *b* 20 June 1924; *s* of Harold Paul Treasure and Constance Frances Treasure; *m* 1954, Valerie Ellen Bell; three *s*. *Educ:* Cardiff High Sch.; University Coll., Cardiff (BA 1946); Univ. of Cambridge (PhD 1956). Joined British Market Research Bureau Ltd, 1952, Man. Dir 1957; Marketing Dir, J. Walter Thompson Co. Ltd, 1960, Chm. 1967; Dir, J. Walter Thompson Co. USA, 1967, Vice Chm. 1974; Vice-Chm., Saatchi & Saatchi Advertising Ltd (formerly Saatchi & Saatchi Compton Ltd), 1983–89. Director: Rowntree Mackintosh plc, 1976–88; AFIH Ltd, 1984–; Household Mortgage Corp. plc, 1986–. Dean and Prof. of Marketing, City Univ. Business Sch., 1978–82. President: Inst. of Practitioners in Advertising, 1975–77; Market Res. Soc., 1975–78; Nat. Advertising Benevolent Soc., 1977–78; Chm., History of Advertising Trust, 1985–90. *Publications:* articles on marketing, market research and economics in Financial Times, Times, New Soc., Econ. Jl, Commentary, and Advertising Qly. *Recreations:* golf, tennis. *Address:* Cholmondeley Lodge, Friars Lane, Richmond, Surrey TW9 1NS. *T:* (office) 071–636 5060. *Clubs:* Queen's, Hurlingham; Royal Mid-Surrey Golf (Richmond).

TREDINNICK, David Arthur Stephen; MP (C) Bosworth, since 1987; *b* 19 Jan. 1950; *m* 1983, Rebecca Jane Shott; one *s* one *d*. *Educ:* Ludgrove Sch., Wokingham; Eton; Mons Officer Cadet Sch.; Graduate Business Sch., Capetown Univ. (MBA); St John's Coll., Oxford (MLitt 1987). Trainee, E. B. Savoury Milln & Co, Stockbrokers, 1972; Account Exec., Quadrant International, 1974; Salesman, Kalle Infotec UK, 1976; Sales Manager, Word Processing, 1977–78; Consultant, Baird Communications, NY, 1978–79; Marketing Manager, Q1 Europe Ltd, 1979–81; Res. asst to Kenneth Warren, MP, and Angela Rumbold, CBE, MP, 1981–87; Manager, Malden Mitcham Properties (family business), 1985–. PPS to Minister of State for Wales, 1991–. Secretary: Cons. backbench Defence Cttee, 1990–; Cons. backbench Foreign Affairs Cttee, 1990–. Contested (C) Cardiff S and Penarth, 1983. *Address:* House of Commons, SW1A 0AA. *T:* 071–219 3000.

TREFGARNE, family name of **Baron Trefgarne.**

TREFGARNE, 2nd Baron, *cr* 1947, of Cleddau; **David Garro Trefgarne;** PC 1989; *b* 31 March 1941; *s* of 1st Baron Trefgarne and of Elizabeth (who *m* 1962, Comdr A. T. Courtney (from whom she obt. a divorce, 1966); *m* 1971, H. C. H. Ker (*d* 1987), Dundee), *d* of C. E. Churchill; *S* father, 1960; *m* 1968, Rosalie, *d* of Baron Lane of Horsell, *qv*; two *s* one *d*. *Educ:* Haileybury; Princeton University, USA. Opposition Whip, House of Lords, 1977–79; a Lord in Waiting (Govt Whip), 1979–81; Parly Under Sec. of State, DoT, 1981, FCO, 1981–82, DHSS, 1982–83, (Armed Forces) MoD, 1983–85; Minister of State: for Defence Support, 1985–86; for Defence Procurement, 1986–89; DTI, 1989–90. Hon. Pres., METCOM, 1990–. Awarded Royal Aero Club Bronze Medal (jointly) for flight from England to Australia and back in light aircraft, 1963. *Recreation:* photography. *Heir:* *s* Hon. George Garro Trefgarne, *b* 4 Jan. 1970. *Address:* House of Lords, SW1A 0PW.

TREFUSIS; *see* Fane Trefusis, family name of Baron Clinton.

TREGARTHEN JENKIN, Ian Evers; *see* Jenkin.

TREGEAR, Mary, FBA 1985; Keeper of Eastern Art, Ashmolean Museum, Oxford, 1987–91; *b* 11 Feb. 1924; *d* of late Thomas R. and Norah Tregear. *Educ:* Sidcot Sch., Somerset; West of England Coll. of Art (ATD 1946); London Univ. (BA); MA Oxon. Taught Art, Wuhan, China, 1947–50; Curator/Lectr, Hong Kong Univ., 1956–61; Sen. Asst Keeper, Chinese, Ashmolean Museum, 1961–87. *Publications:* Arts of China, vol. 1 (co-ordinating ed.), 1968; Catalogue of Chinese Greenwares in the Ashmolean Museum, 1976; Chinese Art, 1980; Song Ceramics, 1982; contribs to Oriental Art, Connoisseur, Burlington Magazine.

TREGLOWN, Jeremy Dickinson; Honorary Research Fellow, University College London, since 1991; Contributing Editor, Grand Street, New York, since 1991; *b* 24 May 1946; *s* of late Rev. Geoffrey and of Beryl Treglown; *m* 1st, 1970, Rona Bower (marr. diss. 1982); one *s* two *d*; 2nd, 1984, Holly Eley (*née* Urquhart). *Educ:* Bristol Grammar Sch.; St Peter's Coll., Oxford. MA, BLitt Oxon; PhD London. Lecturer: Lincoln Coll., Oxford, 1974–77; University College London, 1977–80; Times Literary Supplement: Asst Editor, 1980–82; Editor, 1982–90. Vis. Fellow: All Souls Coll., Oxford, 1986; Huntington Library, San Marino, Calif, 1988; Mellon Vis. Associate, Calif Inst. of Technol., 1988; Ferris Vis. Prof., Princeton Univ., 1991–92. Mem. Council, RSL, 1989–; FRSL 1991 (Hon. FRSL 1989). FRSA 1990. Chm. of Judges, Booker Prize, 1991. *Publications:* edited: The Letters of John Wilmot, Earl of Rochester, 1980; Spirit of Wit, 1982; The Lantern Bearers, Essays by Robert Louis Stevenson, 1988; various articles and book introductions. *Address:* 102 Savernake Road, NW3 2JR.

TREHANE, Sir (Walter) Richard, Kt 1967; Chairman of the Milk Marketing Board, 1958–77; *b* 14 July 1913; *s* of James Trehane and Muriel Yeoman Cowl; *m* 1948, Elizabeth Mitchell; two *s*. *Educ:* Monkton Combe School, Somerset; University of Reading (BSc (Agric.)). On staff of School of Agriculture, Cambridge, 1933–36; Manager of Hampreston Manor Farm, Dorset, 1936–. Member Dorset War Agric. Exec. Cttee, 1942–47, Chm., 1957–. Mem., 1947–77, Vice-Chm., 1952–58, MMB; Dep. Chm. Dorset Agric. Exec. Cttee, 1947–52; Mem. (later Vice-Chm.) Avon and Stour Catchment Bd, subseq. Avon & Dorset Rivers Bd, 1944–53; Mem. Dorset County Council and Chm. Secondary Education Cttee, 1946–49; Chm. Dorset National Farmers' Union, 1947–48; Member, Nat. Milk Publicity Council, 1954–77 (1st Pres. 1954–56); Chm. English Country Cheese Council, 1955–77; Pres. British Farm Produce Council, 1963–78 (Chm. 1960–63). Chm. Govg Body, Grassland Research Institute, Hurley, Berks, 1959–78 (Hon. Fellow, 1981); Chm. and Pres. European Cttee on Milk/Butterfat Recording, 1957–60; Director of British Semen Exports Ltd, 1960–77; Vice-President: World Assoc. Animal Production, 1965–68; President: European Assoc. Animal Prodn, 1961–67 (Hon. Pres., 1967–); British Soc. Animal Prodn, 1954, 1961; British Friesian Cattle Soc., 1969–70; Royal Assoc. British Dairy Farmers, 1968, 1977; Internat. Dairy Fedn, 1968–72, Hon. Pres., 1972–76. Chm., UK Dairy Assoc., 1963–69. Chm., Alfa-Laval Co. Ltd, 1982–84 (Dir, 1977–84); Director: Southern Television, 1969–81; The Rank Organisation Ltd, 1970–84; Beaumont UK, 1980–83. Trustee, UK Farming Scholarship Trust, 1970. Governor: Monkton Combe School, 1957–83; British Nutrition Foundn, 1975–77. FRAgSs 1970. Hon. DSc Reading, 1976. Justus-von-Liebig Prize, Kiel Univ., 1968; Gold Medal, Soc. of Dairy Technology, 1969; Massey-Fergusson Award, 1971. Comdr du Mérite Agricole, 1964. *Address:* Hampreston Manor Farm, Wimborne, Dorset BH21 7LX. *Clubs:* Farmers'; Royal Motor Yacht (Poole).

TREITEL, Prof. Guenter Heinz, DCL; FBA 1977; QC 1983; Vinerian Professor of English Law, Oxford University, since 1979; Fellow of All Souls College, Oxford, since 1979; *b* 26 Oct. 1928; *s* of Theodor Treitel and Hanna Lilly Treitel (*née* Levy); *m* 1957, Phyllis Margaret Cook; two *s*. *Educ:* Kilburn Grammar School; Magdalen College, Oxford. BA 1949, BCL 1951, MA 1953, DCL 1976. Called to the Bar, Gray's Inn, 1952, Hon. Bencher, 1982. Asst Lectr, LSE, 1951–53; Lectr, University Coll., Oxford, 1953–54; Fellow, Magdalen Coll., Oxford, 1954–79, Fellow Emeritus, 1979; All Souls Reader in English Law, Univ. of Oxford, 1964–79. Vis. Lectr, Univ. of Chicago, 1963–64; Visiting Professor: Chicago, 1968–69 and 1971–72; W Australia, 1976; Houston, 1977; Southern Methodist, 1978 and 1988–89; Virginia, 1978–79 and 1983–84; Santa Clara, 1981; Vis. Scholar, Ernst von Caemmerer Gedächtnisstiftung, 1990. Trustee, British Museum, 1983–; Mem. Council, National Trust, 1984–. *Publications:* The Law of Contract, 1962, 8th edn 1991; An Outline of the Law of Contract, 1975, 4th edn 1989; Remedies for Breach of Contract: a comparative account, 1988; edited jointly: Dicey's Conflict of Laws, 7th edn 1958; Dicey and Morris, Conflict of Laws, 8th edn 1967; Chitty on Contracts, 23rd edn 1968 to 26th edn 1989; Benjamin's Sale of Goods, 1974, 3rd edn 1987. *Recreations:* music, reading. *Address:* All Souls College, Oxford OX1 4AL. *T:* Oxford (0865) 279379.

TRELAWNY, Sir John Barry Salusbury-, 13th Bt *cr* 1628; Director, Goddard Kay Rogers and Associates Ltd, since 1984; *b* 4 Sept. 1934; *s* of Sir John William Robin Maurice Salusbury-Trelawny, 12th Bt and of his 1st wife, Glenys Mary (*d* 1985), *d* of John Cameron Kynoch; *S* father, 1956; *m* 1958, Carol Knox, *yr d* of late C. F. K. Watson,

The Field, Saltwood, Kent; one *s* three *d*. *Educ:* HMS Worcester. Subseq. Sub-Lt RNVR (National Service). Dir, The Martin Walter Group Ltd, 1971–74; various directorships, 1974–; Dir, 1978–83, Jt Dep. Man. Dir 1981–83, Korn/Ferry Internat. Inc. FInstM 1974. JP 1973–78. *Heir: s* John William Richard Salusbury-Trelawny [*b* 30 March 1960; *m* 1st, 1980, Anita (marr. diss. 1986), *d* of Kenneth Snelgrove; one *s* one *d*; 2nd, 1987, Sandra, *d* of Joseph Thompson; one *s*]. *Address:* Beavers Hill, Rectory Lane, Saltwood, Kent. *T:* Hythe (0303) 266476. *Clubs:* Army and Navy, Buck's.

TRELFORD, Donald Gilchrist; Editor of The Observer, since 1975; Director, The Observer Ltd, since 1975; *b* 9 Nov. 1937; *s* of Thomas and Doris Trelford (*née* Gilchrist); *m* 1st, 1963, Janice Ingram; two *s* one *d*; 2nd, 1978, Katherine Louise, *d* of Mr and Mrs John Mark, Guernsey, and *g d* of late John Mark and Louisa (*née* Hobson); one *d*. *Educ:* Bablake Sch., Coventry (School Captain, 1956); Selwyn Coll., Cambridge; MA; University rugby and cricket. Pilot Officer, RAF, 1956–58. Reporter and Sub-Editor, Coventry Standard and Sheffield Telegraph, 1960–63; Editor, Times of Malawi, 1963–66; Correspondent in Africa for The Observer, The Times, and BBC, 1963–66; Dep. News Editor, The Observer, 1966, Asst Man. Editor, 1968, Dep. Editor, 1969. Director: Optomen Television, 1988–; Observer Films, 1989–; Central Observer TV, 1990–. Mem. Editorial Adv. Gp, Bloomsbury Publishing, 1987–. Member: British Executive Cttee, IPI, 1976–; Assoc. of British Editors, 1984–; Guild of British Newspaper Editors, 1985– (Mem., Parly and Legal Cttee, 1987–91); Patron: Milton Keynes Civic Forum, 1977–; Internat. Centre for Child Studies, 1984–; Sponsor: Educn for Capability, 1983–; Educnl Trust for Southern Africa, 1986–; Vice-Pres., British Sports Trust, 1988–; Member: Council, Media Soc., 1981–; judging panel, British Press Awards, 1981–; judging panel, Scottish Press Awards, 1985; Olivier Awards Cttee, SWET, 1984–; Defence, Press and Broadcasting Cttee, 1986–. External Examiner in Journalism, Stradbroke Coll., Sheffield Univ., 1988–. Liveryman, Worshipful Co. of Stationers and Newspaper Makers, 1986; Freeman, City of London, 1986. FRSA 1988. Hon. DLitt Sheffield, 1990. Granada Newspaper of the Year Award, 1983; commended, Internat. Editor of the Year, World Press Rev., NY, 1984. Frequent broadcasts (writer, interviewer and panellist) on TV and radio; presenter: Running Late (C4); LBC Newstalk Breakfast, 1990–; TV interviews include: Rajiv Gandhi, Lord Goodman, Sir Leonard Hutton, Gromyko; speaker at internat. media confs in Spain, Egypt, W Germany, USA, India, Turkey, S Africa, Argentina, Kenya and Canada. *Publications:* Siege, 1980; (ed) Sunday Best, 1981, 1982, 1983; (contrib.) County Champions, 1982; Snookered, 1986; (contrib.) The Queen Observed, 1986; (with Garry Kasparov) Child of Change, 1987; (contrib.) Saturday's Boys, 1990; (contrib.) Fine Glances, 1991. *Recreations:* golf, snooker. *Address:* c/o The Observer, Chelsea Bridge House, Queenstown Road, SW8 4NN. *T:* 071–350 3306. *Clubs:* Garrick, Beefsteak, Groucho, Royal Air Force, MCC (Mem., Cttee, 1988–91).
See also J. Mark, Sir R. Mark.

TREMAIN, Rose, FRSL 1983; novelist and playright; part-time Lecturer, University of East Anglia, since 1984; *b* 2 Aug. 1943; *d* of Viola Mabel Thomson and Keith Nicholas Home Thomson; *m* 1st, 1971, Jon Tremain (marr. diss.); one *d*; 2nd, 1982, Jonathan Dudley. *Educ:* Sorbonne, Paris; Univ. of East Anglia (BA Hons Eng. Lit.). Dylan Thomas Prize, 1984; Giles Cooper Award, Best Radio Play, 1984. *Publications: novels:* Sadler's Birthday, 1976; Letter to Sister Benedicta, 1978; The Cupboard, 1981; The Swimming Pool Season, 1984; Restoration, 1989 (Sunday Express Book of the Year Award); *short stories:* The Colonel's Daughter, 1982; The Garden of the Villa Mollini, 1986; *for children:* Journey to the Volcano, 1985. *Recreations:* gardening, swimming, yoga. *Address:* 2 High House, South Avenue, Thorpe St Andrew, Norwich NR7 0EZ. *T:* Norwich (0603) 39682.

TREMBLAY, Dr Marc-Adélard, OC 1981; Professor of Anthropology, Université Laval, Québec, since 1956; *b* Les Eboulements, Qué., 24 April 1922; *s* of Willie Tremblay and Lauretta (*née* Tremblay); *m* 1949, Jacqueline Cyr; one *s* five *d*. *Educ:* Montréal Univ. (AB, LSA (Agricl Sci.)); Laval (MA Sociol.); Cornell Univ. (PhD Anthropol.). Research Associate, Cornell Univ., 1953–56; Université Laval: Vice-Dean, Faculty Social Scis, 1969–71; Head, Anthropology Dept, 1970; Dean, Graduate Sch., 1971–79. Pres., RSC, 1982–85. Hon. LLD: Ottawa, 1982; Guelph, 1984. Innis-Gerin Medal, RSC, 1979; Centennial Medal, RSC, 1982; Molson Prize, Canada Council, 1987; Marcel Vincent Medal, French Canadian Assoc. for Advancement of Science, 1988; Internat. Order of Merit, 1990. *Publications:* The Acadians of Portsmouth, 1954; (jtly) People of Cove and Woodlot, 1960; (jtly) Les Comportements économiques de la famille salariée, 1964; Les Fondements Sociaux de la Maturation chez l'enfant, 1965; (jtly) Rural Canada in Transition, 1966; (jtly) A Survey of Contemporary Indians of Canada, 1967; Initiation à la recherche dans les sciences humaines, 1968; (jtly) Etude sur les Indiens contemporains du Canada, 1969; (jtly) Les Changements socio-culturels à Saint-Augustin, 1969; (jtly) Famille et parenté en Acadie, 1971; (jtly) Communautés et Culture, 1973 (Eng. trans. 1973); (jtly) Patterns of Amerindian Identity, 1976; (jtly) The Individual, Language and Society in Canada, 1977; L'Identité Québécoise en péril, 1983; (jtly) Conscience et Enquête, 1983; L'Anthropologie à l'Université Laval: fondements historiques, pratiques académiques, dynamismes d'évolution, 1989; Les fondements historiques et théoriques de la practique professionnelle en anthropologie, 1990; over one hundred and seventy-five scientific articles. *Recreations:* gardening, cross-country skiing. *Address:* 835 Nouvelle-Orléans, Sainte Foy, Québec G1X 3J4, Canada. *T:* (418) 653–5411.

TREMLETT, Ven. Anthony Frank; Archdeacon of Totnes, since 1988; *b* 25 Aug. 1937; *s* of Frank and Sally Tremlett; *m* 1958, Patricia Lapthorn; two *s* one *d*. *Educ:* Plymouth College. Certificated Transport Manager; MBIM. Clerk, Management Trainee (Traffic Apprentice), Area Manager, 1953–68, British Rail; Traffic Manager, District Manager, Operations Director, 1968–80, National Carriers (Nat. Freight Corporation). Asst Curate, Southway, Plymouth, 1981–82; Priest-in-Charge, 1982–84; Vicar, 1984–88; RD of Moorside, Plymouth, 1986–88. *Recreations:* music, home and family. *Address:* 38 Huxhams Cross, Dartington, Totnes TQ9 6NT. *T:* Staverton (080426) 263.

TREMLETT, Rt. Rev. Anthony Paul; *b* 14 May 1914; *s* of late Laurence and Nyda Tremlett; unmarried. *Educ:* King's Sch., Bruton; King's Coll., Cambridge; Cuddesdon Theological Coll. Ordained, 1938; Curate of St Barnabas, Northolt Park, Middx. Chaplain to the Forces (Emergency Commission), 1941–46 (despatches). Domestic Chaplain to the Bishop of Trinidad, BWI, 1946–49; Chaplain of Trinity Hall, Cambridge, 1949–58; Vicar of St Stephen with St John, Westminster, 1958–64; Bishop Suffragan of Dover, 1964–80. *Address:* Doctors Commons, The Square, Northleach, Gloucestershire. *T:* Cotswold (0451) 60426.

TREMLETT, George William, OBE 1981; author, journalist and bookseller; Director, Corran Books Ltd, since 1981; Founder Chairman, George Tremlett Ltd, since 1965; *b* 5 Sept. 1939; *s* of late Wilfred George and of Elizabeth Tremlett; *m* 1971, Jane, *o c* of late Benjamin James Mitchell and Mrs P. A. Mitchell; three *s*. *Educ:* Taunton School; King Edward VI School, Stratford upon Avon. Member of Richmond upon Thames Borough Council, 1963–74; Chairman: Further Education Cttee, 1966–68; Barnes School Governors, 1967–73; Schools Cttee, 1972–73; Shene VIth Form Coll. Governors, 1973–74; Housing Cttee, 1972–74; Thames Water Authority, 1973–74. Greater London Council: Mem. for Hillingdon, 1970–73, for Twickenham, 1973–86; Opposition Housing Spokesman, 1974–77; Leader of Housing Policy Cttee, 1977–81. Consultant: Nat. Assoc. of Voluntary Hostels, 1980–84; Local Govt Inf. Unit, 1985–86; Appeal Dir, SHAC and Help the Homeless National Appeal, 1985–. Member: Housing Minister's Adv. Cttee on Co-operatives, 1977–79; Housing Consultative Council for England, 1977–81; Northampton Develt Corp., 1979–83; Stonham Housing Assoc., 1978–; Chiswick Family Rescue Appeal Fund, 1979–80; Bd, Empty Property Unit, 1985–86; Adv. Panel, BBC Community Prog. Unit, 1985–. Founder Chm., Dylan Thomas Meml Trust, 1985–90. Governor, Kingston Polytechnic and Twickenham Coll. of Technology, 1967–70; Court of City Univ., 1968–74. *Publications:* 17 biographies of rock musicians, 1974–77—on John Lennon, David Bowie, 10cc, Paul McCartney, The Osmonds, Alvin Stardust, Cat Stevens, Cliff Richard, Slade, The Who, David Essex, Slik, Gary Glitter, Marc Bolan, Rod Stewart, Queen and the Rolling Stones (published in many different countries); Living Cities, 1979; (with Caitlin Thomas) Life with Dylan Thomas, 1986; Clubmen, 1987; Homeless but for St Mungo's, 1989; Little Legs, 1989; Rock Gold, 1990; Dylan Thomas: in the mercy of his means, 1991. *Recreations:* ornithology, exploring old churches, local history, rock 'n' roll music. *Address:* Corran House, Laugharne, Carmarthen, Dyfed SA33 4SJ. *T:* Laugharne (0994) 427444. *Clubs:* Carlton, Wig and Pen, United and Cecil; Laugharne RFC.

TRENAMAN, Nancy Kathleen, (Mrs M. S. Trenaman); Principal of St Anne's College, Oxford, 1966–84 (Hon. Fellow, since 1984); *b* 1919; *d* of Frederick Broughton Fisher and Edith Fisher; *m* 1967, M. S. Trenaman. *Educ:* Bradford Girls' Grammar School; Somerville College, Oxford (Hon. Fellow, 1977). Board of Trade, 1941–51; Assistant Secretary, Ministry of Materials, 1951–54; Counsellor, British Embassy, Washington, 1951–53; Board of Trade, 1954–66, Under-Sec. 1962–66. Mem., Commn on the Constitution, 1969–73. *Address:* 4 Fairlawn End, Oxford OX2 8AR. *T:* Oxford (0865) 57723. *Club:* United Oxford & Cambridge University.

TRENCH, family name of **Baron Ashtown.**

TRENCH, *see* Le Poer Trench, family name of Earl of Clancarty.

TRENCH, John; Master of the Supreme Court, Queen's Bench Division, since 1986; *b* 15 Sept. 1932; *s* of late Prince Constantine Lobanow-Rostovsky and Princess Violette Lobanow-Rostovsky (*née* Le Poer Trench); *m* 1st, 1955, Roxane Bibica-Rosetti (marr. diss.); two *s* one *d*; 2nd 1980, Patricia Margaret Skitmore. *Educ:* Oundle; Christ's College, Cambridge (MA). Nat. Service, 1950–52; commissioned The Duke of Wellington's Regt. Called to the Bar, Lincoln's Inn, 1956, practised at the Bar, in London and on the Oxford Circuit, 1956–86. *Recreations:* opera, collecting antique handwriting equipment. *Address:* Royal Courts of Justice, Strand WC2.

TRENCH, Sir Peter (Edward), Kt 1979; CBE 1964 (OBE (mil.) 1945); TD 1949; *b* 16 June 1918; *s* of James Knights Trench and Grace Sim; *m* 1940, Mary St Clair Morford; one *s* one *d*. *Educ:* privately; London Sch. of Economics, London Univ.; St John's Coll., Cambridge Univ. BSc (Econ.) Hons. Served in The Queen's Royal Regt, 1939–46: Staff Coll., 1942; AAG, HQ 21 Army Gp, 1944–45 (OBE). Man. Dir, Bovis Ltd, 1954–59; Director: Nat. Fedn of Bldg Trades Employers, 1959–64; Nat. Bldg Agency, 1964–66; Part-time Mem., Nat. Bd for Prices and Incomes, 1965–68. Chm., Y. J. Lovell (Holdings) plc, 1972–83; Director: LEP plc; Haden plc; Capital & Counties plc; Builder Gp plc; Crendon Ltd; Nationwide Building Soc., 1970–83. Vis. Prof. in Construction Management, Reading Univ., 1981–88. Chm., Construction and Housing Res. Adv. Council, 1973–79; Pres., Construction Health Safety Gp, 1974–80; Vice-President: NHBC, 1984– (Chm., 1978–84); Building Centre, 1976–; Member: Review of Housing Finance Adv. Gp, 1975–76; Council, CBI, 1981–83; Council, RSA, 1981–83. Mem. Court of Governors, LSE; Hon. Mem., Architectural Assoc.; Hon. Treasurer, St Mary's Hosp. Med. Sch. JP Inner London, 1963–71. Hon. FCIOB; Hon. FFB; FCIArb; FRSA; CBIM; Hon. FRIBA; Hon. DSc Reading, 1986. *Recreations:* tennis, swimming, travelling. *Address:* 4 Napier Close, Napier Road, W14 8LG. *T:* 071–602 3936. *Club:* MCC.

TRENCHARD, family name of **Viscount Trenchard.**

TRENCHARD, 3rd Viscount *cr* 1936, of Wolfeton; **Hugh Trenchard;** Bt 1919; Baron 1930; Director, Kleinwort Benson Ltd, since 1986; *b* 12 March 1951; *s* of 2nd Viscount Trenchard, MC and of Patricia, *d* of Admiral Sir Sidney Bailey, KBE, CB, DSO; *S* father, 1987; *m* 1975, Fiona Elizabeth, *d* of Hon. James Morrison, *qv*; two *s* two *d*. *Educ:* Eton; Trinity Coll., Cambridge. Captain, 4th Royal Green Jackets, TA, 1973–80. Entered Kleinwort Benson Ltd, 1973; Chief Rep. in Japan, 1980–85; Gen. Man., Kleinwort Benson Internat. Inc., Tokyo Br., 1985–88; Pres., Kleinwort Benson Internat. Incorporated, 1988–; Director: KB Berkeley Japan Development Capital Ltd, 1987–; Dover Japan Inc., 1985–87. Member: Gen. Affairs Cttee, Japan Security Dealers' Assoc., 1987–88; Japan Assoc. of Corporate Executives, 1987–. *Heir: s* Hon. Alexander Thomas Trenchard, *b* 26 July 1978. *Address:* 85 Thurleigh Road, SW12 8TY. *T:* 081–673 6399.

TRENDALL, Prof. Arthur Dale, AC 1976; CMG 1961; MA, LittD; FSA; FBA; FAHA; Resident Fellow, Menzies College, La Trobe University; Emeritus Professor, University of Sydney, 1954; *b* Auckland, NZ, 28 March 1909; *s* of late Arthur D. Trendall and late Iza W. Uttley-Todd; unmarried. *Educ:* King's College, Auckland; Univs of Otago (MA 1929, LittD 1936) and Cambridge (MA 1937, LittD 1968). NZ Post-Graduate Scholar in Arts, 1931; Rome Scholar in Archæology, 1934–35; Fellow of Trinity Coll., Cambridge, 1936–40; Librarian British School at Rome, 1936–38; FSA 1939; Professor of Greek, Univ. of Sydney, 1939–54; Dean, Faculty of Arts, 1947–50; Chairman Professorial Board, 1949–50, 1952; Acting Vice-Chancellor, 1953; Master of Univ. House, ANU, 1954–69, retd; Hon. Fellow, 1969. Hon. Curator, Greek and Roman Section, Nicholson Museum, 1954, and Hon. Consultant, National Gallery of Victoria, 1957; Deputy Vice-Chancellor, ANU, 1958–64; Mem. Royal Commn on Univ. of Tas., 1955. Geddes-Harrower Professor of Greek Art and Archæology, Aberdeen Univ., 1966–67; Guest Scholar, J. Paul Getty Mus., 1985. Chm. Aust. Humanities Research Council, 1957–59. Mem., Nat. Capital Planning Cttee, 1958–67; Mem. Australian Universities Commission, 1959–70. Member: Accademia dei Lincei, Rome, 1971; Athens Acad., 1973; Corresp. Mem., Pontifical Acad. of Archaeology, Rome, 1973; Life Mem., Nat. Gall. of Victoria, 1976; For. Mem., Royal Netherlands Acad., 1977; Hon. Member: Hellenic Soc., 1982; Archaeol Inst. of Amer., 1987. Hon. Fellow: Athens Archaeological Soc., 1975; British School at Rome, 1983. FBA 1968. Hon. LittD: Melbourne, 1956; ANU 1970; Hon. DLitt: Adelaide, 1960; Sydney, 1972; Tasmania, 1979; Hon. Dott. in Lettere Lecce, 1981. For. Galileo Galilei Prize for Archaeology, 1971; Cassano Gold Medal for Magna Graecia Studies, 1971; Britannica Award (Australia), 1973; Kenyon Medal, British Acad., 1983. KCSG, 1956; Commendatore, Ordine al Merito, Republic of Italy, 1965 (Cav. Uff. 1961). *Publications:* Paestan Pottery, 1936; Frühitaliotische Vasen, 1938; Guide to the Cast Collection of the Nicholson Museum, Sydney, 1941; The Shellal Mosaic, 1942, 4th edn 1973; Handbook to the Nicholson Museum (editor), 2nd edn 1948; Paestan Pottery, Supplement, 1952; Vasi Italioti del Vaticano, vol. i, 1953; vol. ii, 1955; The Felton Greek Vases, 1958; Phlyax Vases, 1959, 2nd edn 1967; Paestan Addenda, 1960; Apulian Vase Painters of the Plain Style (with A. Cambitoglou), 1962; South Italian

Vase Painting (British Museum Guide), 1966, 2nd edn 1976; The Red-figured Vases of Lucania, Campania and Sicily, 1967, Supplement I, 1970, Supplement II, 1973, Supplement III, 1983; Greek Vases in the Felton Collection, 1968, 2nd edn 1978; Greek Vases in the Logie Collection, Christchurch, NZ, 1971; Illustrations of Greek Drama (with T. B. L. Webster), 1971; Early South Italian Vase-painting, 1974; Eine Gruppe Apulischer Grabvasen in Basel (with M. Schmidt and A. Cambitoglou), 1976; Vasi antichi dipinti del Vaticano—Collezione Astarita: (iii) Vasi italiòti, 1976; (with A. Cambitoglou) The Red-figured Vases of Apulia, 2 vols, 1978, 1982, Supplement I, 1983, Supplement II, 1991; (with Ian McPhee) Greek Red-figured Fish-plates, 1987; The Red-figured Vases of Paestum, 1987; Red-figure Vases of South Italy and Sicily, 1989, German edn 1991; several articles in learned periodicals. *Address:* Menzies College, La Trobe University, Bundoora, Vic 3083, Australia.

TRENTHAM, Dr David Rostron, FRS 1982; Head of Physical Biochemistry Division, National Institute for Medical Research, Mill Hill, since 1984; *b* 22 Sept. 1938; *s* of John Austin and Julia Agnes Mary Trentham; *m* 1966, Kamalini; two *s*. *Educ:* Univ. of Cambridge (BA Chemistry, PhD Organic Chemistry). Biochemistry Dept, University of Bristol: Jun. Research Fellow (Medical Research Council), 1966–69; Research Associate, 1969–72; Lectr in Biochemistry, 1972–75; Reader in Biochemistry, 1975–77; Edwin M. Chance Prof., Biochemistry and Biophysics Dept, Univ. of Pennsylvania, 1977–84. Colworth Medal (an annual award), Biochemical Soc., UK, 1974; Wilhelm Feldberg Prize, 1990. *Publications:* numerous research papers in scientific jls. *Address:* Physical Biochemistry Division, National Institute for Medical Research, The Ridgeway, Mill Hill, NW7 1AA. *T:* 081–959 3666.

TREPTE, Paul, FRCO; Organist and Master of the Choristers, Ely Cathedral, since 1990; *b* 24 April 1954; *s* of Harry and Ruth Trepte; *m* 1981, Sally Lampard; one *d*. *Educ:* New College, Oxford (MA). Asst Organist, Worcester Cathedral, 1976; Dir of Music, St Mary's, Warwick, 1981; Organist and Master of the Choristers, St Edmundsbury Cathedral, 1985. *Publications:* choral works. *Address:* The Old Sacristy, The College, Ely CB7 4JU. *T:* Ely (0353) 665669.

TRESCOWTHICK, Sir Donald (Henry), AC 1991; KBE 1979; Chairman: Charles Davis Ltd and subsidiaries, since 1971; Investment & Merchant Finance Corporation Ltd and subsidiaries, since 1976; Perpetual Insurance and Securities (Aust.) Ltd, since 1979; McEwans Ltd and subsidiaries; Signet Group Pty Ltd, since 1968; *b* 4 Dec. 1930; *s* of Thomas Patrick Trescowthick; *m* 1952, Norma Margaret Callaghan; two *s* two *d*. FASA. Member, Lloyd's of London. Dep. Chm., Nat. Olympic Fund, 1980–91; Director: DOXA Youth Welfare Foundn; Minus Children's Fund; Aust. Ballet Develt Fund Appeal; Melbourne to Hobart Yacht Race Cttee; Chm., Sir Donald and Lady Trescowthick Foundn. CLJ, 1982; Knight of Magistral Grace, SMO, Malta, 1984. *Recreations:* tennis, swimming, reading. *Address:* GPO Box 2139T, Melbourne, Vic. 3000, Australia. *T:* (03) 62 7658; 38A Lansell Road, Toorak, Vic. 3142, Australia. *T:* (03) 241 5099. *Clubs:* Les Ambassadeurs; Athenæum, Victoria Racing, Victorian Amateur Turf (Melbourne); Moonee Valley Racing, Tasmanian Turf, Tasmanian Racing (Hobart); Geelong Football.

TRESIDDER, Gerald Charles, FRCS; Lecturer, Department of Anatomy, University of Leicester; *b* Rawalpindi, 5 Dec. 1912; *s* of late Lt-Col A. G. Tresidder, CIE, MD, MS, FRCS; *m* 1940, Marguerite Bell; one *s* two *d*. *Educ:* Haileybury College; Queen Mary College and The London Hospital Medical College, Univ. of London. LRCP, MRCS 1937; MB, BS London 1938; FRCS 1946. Surgical Specialist, Major, Indian Medical Service, 1940–46. Surgeon, 1951–64, Urologist, 1964–76, at The London Hospital; Lectr in Surgery and part-time Sen. Lectr in Anatomy, The London Hosp. Med. Sch., 1951–76; Senior Lectr, Human Morphology, Univ. of Southampton, 1976–80. Past Pres., Section of Urology, RSocMed; Senior Mem., British Assoc. of Urological Surgeons; Sen. Fellow, British Assoc. of Clinical Anatomists; formerly Examr in Anatomy for Primary FRCSEng and Ed. *Publications:* contributions to: Rob and Smith's Operative Surgery; Smith and Aitkenhead's Textbook of Anaesthesia, 1985; British Jl of Surgery; British Jl of Urology; Lancet; BMJ. *Recreations:* walking and talking. *Address:* Woodspring, 4 Penny Long Lane, Derby DE3 1AW. *T:* Derby (0332) 558026.

TRESS, Ronald Charles, CBE 1968; BSc (Econ.) London, DSc Bristol; Director, The Leverhulme Trust, 1977–84; *b* Upchurch, Sittingbourne, Kent, 11 Jan. 1915; *er s* of S. C. Tress; *m* 1942, Josephine Kelly, *d* of H. J. Medland; one *s* two *d*. *Educ:* Gillingham (Kent) County School; Univ. College, Southampton. Gladstone Student, St Deiniol's Library, Hawarden, 1936–37; Drummond Fraser Research Fellow, Univ. of Manchester, 1937–38; Asst Lecturer in Economics, Univ. Coll. of the S West, Exeter, 1938–41; Economic Asst, War Cabinet Offices, 1941–45; Economic Adviser, Cabinet Secretariat, 1945–47; Reader in Public Finance, Univ. of London, 1947–51; Prof. of Political Economy, Univ. of Bristol, 1951–68; Master of Birkbeck Coll., 1968–77, Fellow, 1977–; Mem., Univ. of London Senate, 1968–77, and Court, 1976–77. Managing Editor, London and Cambridge Economic Service, 1949–51; Member: Reorganisation Commn for Pigs and Bacon, 1955–56; Nigeria Fiscal Commn, 1957–58; Departmental Cttee on Rating of Charities, 1958; Develt Commn, 1959–81; Financial Enquiry, Aden Colony, 1959; East Africa Economic and Fiscal Commn, 1960, Uganda Fiscal Commn, 1962; Kenya Fiscal Commn (Chm.), 1962–63; National Incomes Commn, 1963–65; Chm., SW Economic Planning Council, 1965–68; Mem., Cttee of Inquiry into Teachers' Pay, 1974; Chm., Cttee for Univ. Assistance to Adult Educn in HM Forces, 1974–79; Lay Mem., Solicitors' Disciplinary Tribunal, 1975–79; Chm., Lord Chancellor's Adv. Cttee on Legal Aid, 1979–84. Trustee, City Parochial Foundn, 1974–77, 1979–89; Governor, Christ Church Coll., Canterbury, 1975–91; Mem. Council, Kent Univ., 1977–. Royal Economic Society: Council, 1960–70, Sec.-Gen., 1975–79, Vice-Pres., 1979–. Hon. LLD: Furman Univ., S Carolina, 1973; Exeter, 1976; DUniv Open Univ., 1974; Hon. DSc (SocSc) Southampton, 1978; Hon. DCL Kent, 1984. *Publications:* articles and reviews in Economic Journal, Economica, LCES Bulletin, etc. *Address:* 22 The Beach, Walmer, Deal, Kent CT14 7HJ. *T:* Deal (0304) 373254. *Club:* Athenæum.

TRETHOWAN, Prof. Sir William (Henry), Kt 1980; CBE 1975; FRCP, FRACP; Professor of Psychiatry, University of Birmingham, 1962–82, Emeritus since 1983; Hon. Consultant Psychiatrist: Hollymoor Hospital, 1964–82; Midland Centre for Neurosurgery, 1975–82; Central Birmingham Health District, since 1983; *b* 3 June 1917; *s* of William Henry Trethowan and Joan Durham Trethowan (*née* Hickson); *m* 1st, 1941, Pamela Waters (*d* 1985); one *s* two *d*; 2nd, 1988, Heather Dalton (*née* Gardiner). *Educ:* Oundle Sch.; Clare Coll., Cambridge; Guy's Hosp. Med. Sch. MA, MB, BChir (Cantab) 1943; MRCP 1948; FRACP 1961; FRCP 1963; FRCPsych 1971 (Hon. Fellow 1983). Served War, RAMC: Major, Med. Specialist, 1944–47. Psychiatric Registrar, Maudsley Hosp., 1948–50; Psychiatric Resident, Mass Gen. Hosp., and Hon. Teaching Fellow, Harvard, 1951; Lectr and Sen. Lectr in Psychiatry, Univ. of Manchester, 1951–56; Prof. of Psychiatry, Univ. of Sydney, and Hon. Consultant Psychiatrist, Royal Prince Alfred and Royal North Shore Hosps, Sydney, 1956–62. Mem. GMC, 1969–81 (Treasurer, 1978–81); Cons. Adviser in Psychiatry, DHSS, 1964–78; Dean, Univ. of Birmingham Med. Sch., 1968–74; Chm., Standing Mental Health Adv. Cttee, 1968–74; Mem., UGC Med. Subcttee, 1974–81. Member: Birmingham Reg. Hosp. Bd, 1964–74; Standing Med. Adv. Cttee, 1966–82 (Chm., 1976); Central Health Services Council, 1966–80 (Vice-Chm., 1976–80); W Midlands Regional Health Authority, 1974–76. Chm., Med. Acad. Adv. Cttee, Chinese Univ. of Hong Kong, 1976–86. FRSocMed; Hon. Fellow, Royal Aust. and NZ Coll. of Psychiatry (FRANZCP 1962); Corresp. Fellow, Amer. Psychiatric Assoc. Hon. DSc Chinese Univ. of Hong Kong, 1979. Hon. FRCPsych. *Publications:* Psychiatry, 2nd edn (with Prof. E. W. Anderson), 1967, 5th edn (with Prof. A. C. P. Sims), 1983; Uncommon Psychiatric Syndromes, 1967, 3rd edn (with M. D. Enoch), 1991; numerous scientific and other articles in various jls; book reviews, etc. *Recreations:* music, cooking, natural history. *Address:* 99 Bristol Road, Edgbaston, Birmingham B5 7TX.

TREUHERZ, Julian Benjamin; Keeper of Art Galleries, National Museums and Galleries on Merseyside (Walker Art Gallery, Lady Lever Art Gallery and Sudley), since 1989; *b* 12 March 1947; *s* of Werner Treuherz and Irmgard (*née* Amberg). *Educ:* Manchester Grammar Sch.; Christ Church, Oxford (MA); Univ. of East Anglia (MA). Dip. Museums Assoc. 1974. Manchester City Art Gallery: Trainee, 1971; Asst Keeper, 1972–74, Keeper, 1974–89, of Fine Art. Member: Victorian Soc. (Hon. Sec., Manchester Gp, 1972–79, Chm., 1980–83); Cttee, Contemporary Art Soc., 1989–; Fine Arts Sub-Gp, Liverpool Univ., 1989–. *Publications:* Pre-Raphaelite Paintings from the Manchester City Art Gallery, 1981; Hard Times: social realism in Victorian art, 1987; (with Peter de Figueiredo) Country Houses of Cheshire, 1988; articles in art-historical jls. *Recreations:* playing the piano, cooking, opera. *Address:* Walker Art Gallery, William Brown Street, Liverpool L3 8EL.

TREVELYAN, Dennis John, CB 1981; MA; FIPM; Principal, Mansfield College, Oxford, since 1989; *b* 21 July 1929; *s* of John Henry Trevelyan; *m* 1959, Carol Coombes; one *s* one *d*. *Educ:* Enfield Grammar Sch.; University Coll., Oxford (Scholar). Entered Home Office, 1950; Treasury, 1953–54; Sec. to Parly Under-Sec. of State, Home Office, 1954–55; Principal Private Sec. to Lord President of Council and Leader of House, 1964–67; Asst Sec., 1966; Asst Under-Sec. of State, NI Office, 1972–76; Home Office: Asst Under-Sec. of State, Broadcasting Dept, 1976–77; Dep. Under-Sec. of State and Dir-Gen., Prison Service, 1978–83; First CS Comr and Dep. Sec., Cabinet Office, 1983–89, retd. Secretary: Peppiatt Cttee on a Levy on Betting on Horse Races, 1960; Lord Radcliffe's Cttee of Privy Counsellors to inquire into D Notice Matters, 1967. Vice-Chm., CS Sports Council, 1981–; Vice-Pres., Industrial Participation Assoc., 1987–; Member: Bd of Management, Eur. Inst. of Public Admin, Maastricht, 1984–89; Council, City Univ. Business Sch., 1986–89; ECCTIS Adv. Group, 1990–; Governor: Ashridge Management Coll., 1985–89; Contemporary Dance Trust, 1986–89; Trustee, Dancers Resettlement Fund, 1987–. FRSA 1986. *Recreations:* sailing, music. *Address:* Mansfield College, Mansfield Road, Oxford OX1 3TF. *Clubs:* Athenæum, United Oxford & Cambridge University, MCC.

TREVELYAN, Sir George (Lowthian), 4th Bt, *cr* 1874; Hon. President, Wrekin Trust (Founder, 1971; Director, 1971–86); *b* 5 Nov. 1906; *e s* of Rt Hon. Sir C. P. Trevelyan, 3rd Bt; *S* father 1958; *m* 1940, Editha Helen, *d* of Col John Lindsay-Smith; one adopted *d*. *Educ:* Sidcot School; Trinity College, Cambridge (MA). Worked as artist-craftsman with Peter Waals workshops, fine furniture, 1929–31. Trained and worked in F. M. Alexander re-education method, 1932–36. Taught at Gordonstoun School and Abinger Hill School, 1936–41. Served War, 1941–45, Captain, Home Guard Training. Taught No 1 Army Coll., Newbattle Abbey, 1945–47. Principal, Shropshire Adult College, Attingham Park, Shrewsbury, 1947–71; mounted and ran Wrekin Trust courses, 1971–86; now lecture tours on holistic themes. *Publications:* A Vision of the Aquarian Age, 1977; The Active Eye in Architecture, 1977; Magic Casements, 1980; Operation Redemption, 1981; Summons to a High Crusade, 1986; Exploration into God, 1991. *Heir:* *b* Geoffrey Washington Trevelyan [*b* 4 July 1920; *m* 1947, Gillian Isabel, *d* of late Alexander Wood; one *s* one *d*]. *Address:* The Barn, Hawkesbury, near Badminton, Avon GL9 1BW. *T:* Didmarton (045423) 359.

TREVELYAN, Sir Norman Irving, 10th Bt *cr* 1662; *b* 29 Jan. 1915; *s* of Edward Walter Trevelyan (*d* 1947), and of Kathleen E. H., *d* of William Irving; *S* kinsman, Sir Willoughby John Trevelyan, 9th Bt, 1976; *m* 1951, Jennifer Mary, *d* of Arthur E. Riddett, Burgh Heath, Surrey; two *s* one *d*. *Educ:* The Cate School, Carpinteria, California (grad. 1932); Harvard Univ., Cambridge, Mass (grad. 1936). *Heir: s* Edward Norman Trevelyan, *b* 14 Aug. 1955. *Address:* 1041 Adella Avenue, Coronado, California 92118, USA.

[*But his name does not, at the time of going to press, appear on the Roll of the Baronetage.*]

TREVELYAN OMAN, Julia; *see* Oman.

TREVES, Vanni Emanuele; Senior Partner, Macfarlanes, Solicitors, since 1987; Chairman: BBA Group PLC, since 1989; McKechnie plc, since 1991; *b* 3 Nov. 1940; *s* of Giuliano Treves (killed in action, 1944), and of Marianna Treves (*née* Baer); *m* 1971, Angela Veronica Fyffe; two *s* one *d*. *Educ;* St Paul's Sch.; University Coll. Oxford (MA); Univ. of Illinois (LLM). Articled clerk and Solicitor, Macfarlanes, 1963–68; Vis. Attorney, White & Case, New York, 1968–69; Partner, Macfarlanes, 1970–87. Director: Oceonics Group, 1984–, Saatchi & Saatchi, 1987–90. Trustee: J. Paul Getty Jr Charitable Trust, 1985–; 29th May 1961 Charitable Trust, 1970–. Hon. Treas., London Fedn of Boys Clubs, 1976–. Gov., Hall Sch., Hampstead, 1983–. *Recreations:* walking, eating, English watercolours. *Address:* 10 Norwich Street, EC4A 1BD. *T:* 071–831 9222. *Clubs:* Boodle's, City of London.

TREVETHIN, 4th Baron **AND OAKSEY,** 2nd Baron; *see under* Oaksey, 2nd Baron.

TREVOR, 4th Baron *cr* 1880; **Charles Edwin Hill-Trevor,** JP; *b* 13 Aug. 1928; *e s* of 3rd Baron and Phyllis May, 2nd *d* of J. A. Sims, Ings House, Kirton-in-Lindsey, Lincolnshire; *S* father, 1950; *m* 1967, Susan Janet Elizabeth, *o d* of Dr Ronald Bence; two *s*. *Educ:* Shrewsbury. Royal Forestry Society: Mem. Council and Trustee; Chm., N Wales Div. Trustee, Robert Jones and Agnes Hunt Orthopaedic Hosp. Inst. Cttee. JP Clwyd (formerly Denbighshire) 1959; Chm., Berwyn PSD. CStJ. *Recreations:* shooting, fishing. *Heir:* *s* Hon. Marke Charles Hill-Trevor, *b* 8 Jan. 1970. *Address:* Brynkinalt, Chirk, Wrexham, Clwyd LL14 5NS. *T:* Chirk (0691) 773425; Auch, Bridge of Orchy, Argyllshire. *T:* Tyndrum (08384) 282. *Clubs:* East India, Flyfishers'.

TREVOR, Elleston; author; *b* Bromley, Kent, 17 Feb.; *m* 1st, Jonquil Burgess (*d* 1986); one *s*; 2nd, 1987, Chaille Anne Groom. *Educ:* Sevenoaks. Apprenticed as a racing driver upon leaving school, 1938. Served in Royal Air Force, War of 1939–45. Began writing professionally in 1945. Member: Writers' Guild of GB; Authors' Guild of America. Amer. Mystery Writers' award, 1965; French Grand Prix de Littérature Policière, 1965. *Plays:* Touch of Purple, Globe, London, 1972; Just Before Dawn, Murder by All Means, 1972. *Publications:* Chorus of Echoes, 1950 (filmed); Tiger Street, 1951; Redfern's Miracle, 1951; A Blaze of Roses, 1952; The Passion and the Pity, 1953; The Big Pick-up, 1955 (filmed); Squadron Airborne, 1955; The Killing-Ground, 1956; Gale Force, 1956 (filmed); The Pillars of Midnight, 1957 (filmed); The VIP, 1959 (filmed); The Billboard Madonna, 1961; The Burning Shore (The Pasang Run, USA), 1962; Flight of the Phœnix, 1964 (filmed); The Shoot, 1966; The Freebooters, 1967 (filmed); A Place for the Wicked,

1968; Bury Him Among Kings, 1970; The Theta Syndrome, 1977 (filmed); Blue Jay Summer, 1977; Deathwatch, 1985. Under pseudonym Warwick Scott: Image in the Dust, 1951; The Domesday Story, 1951; Naked Canvas, 1952. Under pseudonym Simon Rattray: Knight Sinister, Queen in Danger, Bishop in Check, Dead Silence, Dead Circuit (all 1951–53). Under pseudonym Adam Hall: Volcanoes of San Domingo, 1964; The Berlin Memorandum, 1964 (filmed as The Quiller Memorandum); The 9th Directive, 1966; The Striker Portfolio, 1969; The Warsaw Document, 1971; The Tango Briefing, 1973; The Mandarin Cypher, 1975; The Kobra Manifesto, 1976; The Sinkiang Executive, 1978; The Scorpion Signal, 1979; The Pekin Target, 1981; Northlight, 1985; Quiller's Run, 1988; Quiller KGB, 1989; Quiller Barracuda, 1991. Under pseudonym Caesar Smith: Heatwave, 1957 (filmed). Under pseudonym Roger Fitzalan: A Blaze of Arms, 1967. Under pseudonym Howard North: Expressway, 1973; The Paragon (Night Stop, USA), 1974; The Sibling, 1979; The Damocles Sword, 1981; The Penthouse, 1982; Deathwatch, 1986. Under pseudonym Lesley Stone: Siren Song, 1985; Riviera Story, 1987. *Recreations:* astronomy, metaphysics; first degree black belt in Shotokan karate, 1984. *Address:* 6902 E Dynamite Boulevard, Cave Creek, Arizona 85331, USA. *T:* (602)585–3686.

TREVOR, Brig. Kenneth Rowland Swetenham, CBE 1964 (OBE 1952); DSO 1945; Brigadier (retired 1966); *b* 15 April 1914; 2nd *s* of late Mr and Mrs E. S. R. Trevor, formerly of The Acres, Upton Heath, Chester; *m* 1st, 1941, Margaret Baynham (*d* 1988), *er d* of late Reverend J. H. Baynham, ACG; two *s*; 2nd, 1989, Jeanne Alexander (*née* Holmes Henderson). *Educ:* Rossall; RMC, Camberley. Joined 22nd (Cheshire) Regt, 1934; served in India and with RWAFF in Nigeria. War of 1939–45 (despatches and DSO): No. 1 Commando, N Africa and Burma, 1941–45, as CO, 1943–45; Staff College, Camberley, 1945–46; Bde Major, 29 Infantry Brigade Group, 1949–51; served Korea, 1950–51 (despatches, OBE); GSO1 and Chief Instructor, RMA, Sandhurst, 1954–56; Commanded 1st Bn Cheshire Regt, 1956–58; Malaya, 1957–58 (despatches); Deputy Commander, 50 Infantry Brigade Group/Central Area, Cyprus, 1959; Brigade Col Mercian Brigade, 1960–61; Commander, 2 Infantry Brigade Group and Devon/Cornwall Sub District, 1961–64; Commander, British Guiana Garrison, 1963; Inspector of Boys' Training (Army), 1964–66. With Runcorn Develt Corp., 1966–78. Vice-Pres., The Commando Assoc. *Address:* Barrelwell Hill, Chester CH3 5BR. *Club:* Army and Navy.

TREVOR, Meriol; Author; *b* 15 April 1919; *d* of Lt-Col Arthur Prescott Trevor and Lucy M. E. Trevor (*née* Dimmock). *Educ:* Perse Girls' Sch., Cambridge; St Hugh's Coll., Oxford. FRSL. *Publications: novels:* The Last of Britain, 1956; The New People, 1957; A Narrow Place, 1958; Shadows and Images, 1960; The City and the World, 1970; The Holy Images, 1971; The Fugitives, 1973; The Two Kingdoms, 1973; The Marked Man, 1974; The Enemy at Home, 1974; The Forgotten Country, 1975; The Fortunate Marriage, 1976; The Treacherous Paths, 1976; The Civil Prisoners, 1977; The Fortunes of Peace, 1978; The Wanton Fires, 1979; The Sun with a Face, 1984; The Golden Palaces, 1986; *poems:* Midsummer, Midwinter, 1957; *biography:* Newman: The Pillar of the Cloud, 1962; Newman: Light in Winter, 1962 (James Tait Black Meml Prize); Apostle of Rome, 1966; Pope John, 1967; Prophets and Guardians, 1969; The Arnolds, 1973; The Shadow of a Crown: the life story of James II of England and VII of Scotland, 1988; also books for children. *Address:* 70 Pulteney Street, Bath, Avon BA2 4DL.

TREVOR, William, (William Trevor Cox), CBE (Hon.) 1977; writer; *b* 24 May 1928; *er s* of J. W. Cox; *m* 1952, Jane, *yr d* of C. N. Ryan; two *s*. *Educ:* St Columba's College, Co. Dublin; Trinity College, Dublin. Mem., Irish Acad. Letters. Television plays include: The Mark-2 Wife; O Fat White Woman; The Grass Widows; The General's Day; Love Affair; Last Wishes; Matilda's England; Secret Orchards; Autumn Sunshine. Radio plays include: The Penthouse Apartment; Beyond the Pale (Giles Cooper award, 1980); Travellers; Autumn Sunshine (Giles Cooper award, 1982); Events at Drimaghleen. Allied Irish Banks Award for Literature, 1976. Hon. DLitt: Exeter, 1984; TCD, 1986; Cork, 1990; Hon. DLit Belfast, 1989. *Publications:* A Standard of Behaviour, 1956; The Old Boys, 1964 (Hawthornden Prize; as play, produced Mermaid, 1971); The Boarding-House, 1965; The Love Department, 1966; The Day We Got Drunk on Cake, 1967; Mrs Eckdorf in O'Neill's Hotel, 1969; Miss Gomez and the Brethren, 1971; The Ballroom of Romance, 1972 (adapted for BBC TV, 1982); Going Home (play), 1972; A Night with Mrs da Tanka (play), 1972; Marriages (play), 1973; Elizabeth Alone, 1973; Angels at the Ritz, 1975 (RSL award); The Children of Dynmouth, 1976 (Whitbread Award; televised, 1987); Lovers of Their Time, 1978; Other People's Worlds, 1980; Beyond the Pale, 1981 (televised, 1989); Scenes from an Album (play), 1981; Fools of Fortune, 1983 (Whitbread Award); A Writer's Ireland, 1984; The News from Ireland and other stories, 1986; Nights at the Alexandra, 1987; The Silence in the Garden, 1988; (ed) The Oxford Book of Irish Short Stories, 1989; Family Sins and other stories, 1989; Two Lives, 1991. *Address:* c/o A. D. Peters, 5th Floor, The Chambers, Chelsea Harbour, SW10.

TREVOR COX, Major Horace Brimson; *o s* of late C. Horace Cox, Roche Old Court, Winterslow, Wilts and formerly of Whitby Hall, nr Chester; *m* 1957, Gwenda Mary, *d* of Alfred Ellis, Woodford, Essex; one *d*. *Educ:* Eton (played football for Eton Field and Wall game, 1926 and 1927, boxed for Eton, 1925, 1926, 1927); Germany and USA. Major late Welsh Guards (SR); served in France with BEF, 1939–40, and on General Staff, 1940–44; Major AA Comd. HQ, 1944–46, RARO, 1946–61. Studied commercial and political conditions in Germany, 1927–29, in America and Canada, 1929–30, and in Near East (Egypt and Palestine), 1934; contested (C) NE Derbyshire, 1935, Stalybridge and Hyde, 1937; MP (C) County of Chester, Stalybridge and Hyde, 1937–45; Parliamentary Private Secretary to: Rt Hon. Sir Ronald Cross when Under-Secretary Board of Trade, 1938–39, and when Minister of Economic Warfare, 1939–40; Minister of Health Rt Hon. H. U. Willink, 1945. Hon. Treasr, Russian Relief Assoc., 1945–47. Contested (C) Stalybridge and Hyde, 1945, Birkenhead, 1950; Parly Candidate (C) for Romford and Brentwood, Essex, 1953–55; contested (Ind) Salisbury by-election, 1965; later joined Labour Party; contested (Lab): RDC, Wilts, 1970; Wilts CC, 1973. Member of Exec. County Committee, British Legion, Wilts, 1946–62; Chairman: Salisbury and S Wilts Branch, English-Speaking Union, 1957–63; Salisbury Road Safety Cttee, 1985 (Mem., 1977–85); Mem. Exec. Cttee, CLA, for Wilts, Hants, IoW and Berks. Farmer and landowner. Lord of Manor of East Winterslow. *Address:* Roche Old Court, Winterslow, Wilts. *Club:* Brooks's.

TREVOR-ROPER, family name of **Baron Dacre of Glanton.**

TREVOR-ROPER, Patrick Dacre, MA, MD, BChir Cantab; FRCS, DOMS England; FCOphth; FZS; FRGS; Consultant Ophthalmic Surgeon: Westminster Hospital, 1947–82; Moorfields Eye Hospital, 1961–81; King Edward VII Hospital for Officers, 1964–86; Teacher of Ophthalmology, University of London, 1953–82; *b* 1916; *yr s* of Dr B. W. E. Trevor-Roper, Alnwick, Northumberland; unmarried. *Educ:* Charterhouse (senior classical schol.); Clare Coll., Cambridge (exhibitioner); Westminster Hospital Medical Sch. (scholar). Served as Captain, NZ Medical Corps, 1943–46, in Central Mediterranean Forces. Held resident appointments, Westminster Hospital and Moorfields Eye Hospital. Vice-Pres., Ophthalmol Soc. of UK; Chm., Ophth. Qualifications Cttee, 1974–; Founder Mem., Internat. Acad. of Ophthalmology, 1976; FRSocMed (Pres., Ophthalmol Sect., June 1978–80). Formerly: Examnr for Diploma of Ophthalmology, RCS; Mem., Ophth. Group Cttee, BMA; Mem., London Med. Cttee. Hon. Member: Brazilian Society of Ophthalmology, 1958; Ophthalmological Soc. of NZ, 1975; Hon. dipl., Peruvian and Columbian Societies of Otolaryngology and Ophthalmology, 1958; President, etc., of various clubs in connection with sports, music and drama, both hospital and county. Freeman, City of London; Liveryman, Soc. of Spectaclemakers. Doyne medal, 1980; (first) de Lancey medal, RSocMed. Editor, Trans Ophthalmol Soc., UK, 1949–88; Member Editorial Board: Modern Medicine, 1975–; Annals of Ophth., 1972–86; The Broadway, 1946–83. *Publications:* (ed) Music at Court (Four 18th century studies by A. Yorke-Long), 1954; Ophthalmology, a Textbook for Diploma Students, 1955, new edn 1962; Lecture-notes in Ophthalmology, 1960, 7th edn 1986 (trans. French, Spanish, Portuguese, Malay); (ed) International Ophthalmology Clinics VIII, 1962; The World Through Blunted Sight: an inquiry into the effects of disordered vision on character and art, 1971, 2nd edn 1988; The Eye and Its Disorders, 1973, new edn 1984; (ed) Recent Advances in Ophthalmology, 1975; (ed) The Bowman Lectures, 1980; (ed) Procs 6th Congress of European Ophth. Soc., 1980; Ophthalmology (pocket consultant series), 1981, 2nd edn 1985; miscellaneous articles in medical and other journals. *Recreations:* music, travel. *Address:* 3 Park Square West, Regent's Park, NW1 4LJ. *T:* 071–935 5052; Long Crichel House, near Wimborne, Dorset. *Clubs:* Athenæum, Beefsteak.

See also Baron Dacre of Glanton.

TREW, Francis Sidney Edward, CMG 1984; HM Diplomatic Service, retired; Ambassador to Bahrain, 1984–88; *b* 22 Feb. 1931; *s* of Harry Francis and Alice Mary Trew; *m* 1958, Marlene Laurette Regnery; three *d*. *Educ:* Taunton's Sch., Southampton. Served Army, 1949–51; 2nd Lieut, Royal Hampshire Regt. FO, 1951; Lebanon, 1952; Amman, 1953; Bahrain, 1953–54; Jedda, 1954–56; Vice-Consul, Philadelphia, 1956–59; Second Sec., Kuwait, 1959–62; FO, 1962; seconded as Sec., European Conf. on Satellite Communications, 1963–65; Consul, Guatemala City, 1965–70; First Sec., Mexico City, 1971–74; FCO, 1974–77; Consul, Algeciras, 1977–79; FCO, 1980–81; High Comr at Belmopan, Belize, 1981–84. Order of Aztec Eagle (Mexico), 1975. *Recreations:* carpentry, fishing. *Address:* The Orchard, Higher Trickeys, Morebath, Devon.

TREW, Peter John Edward, FCIS, FCT, FCIArb, MICE; Director, Rush & Tompkins Group plc, 1973–90 (Chairman of Executive Committee, 1986–87); *b* 30 April 1932; *s* of Antony Trew, DSC; *m* 1st, 1955, Angela (marr. diss. 1985), *d* of Kenneth Rush, CBE; two *s* one *d*; 2nd, 1985, Joan, *d* of Allan Haworth. *Educ:* Diocesan Coll., Rondebosch, Cape. Royal Navy, 1950–54; served HMS Devonshire, Unicorn and Charity. Chartered Inst. of Secretaries Sir Ernest Clarke Prize, 1955. Contested (C) Dartford, 1966; MP (C) Dartford, 1970–Feb. 1974; Jt Sec., Cons. Parly Finance Cttee, 1972–74; Mem., Select Cttee on Tax Credits, 1972–73. Chm., Kent West Cons. European Constituency Council, 1978–80. Mem. Council, CBI, 1975–83 (Mem., Econ. and Fin. Policy Cttee, 1980–86). Foundn FCT, 1979; FCIArb 1989. *Address:* 1 Painshill House, Cobham, Surrey KT11 1DL. *T:* Cobham (0932) 863315.

TREWBY, Vice-Adm. Sir (George Francis) Allan, KCB 1974; FEng 1978; retired; *b* Simonstown, S Africa, 8 July 1917; *s* of late Vice-Admiral G. Trewby, CMG, DSO, and Dorothea Trewby (*née* Allan); *m* 1942, Sandra Coleridge Stedham; two *s*. *Educ:* RNC, Dartmouth; RNEC, Keyham; RNC, Greenwich. Naval Cadet, Dartmouth, 1931 (King's Dirk, 1934). Served in HMS: Frobisher, Barham, Nelson, Duke of York, Dido, Cadiz, Albion. Comdg Officer, HMS Sultan, 1963–64; IDC, 1965; Captain of Naval Base, Portland, 1966–68; Asst Controller (Polaris), MoD, 1968–71; Chief of Fleet Support and Member of Board of Admiralty, 1971–74. Commander, 1950; Captain, 1959; Rear-Adm., 1968; Vice-Adm., 1971. Naval ADC to HM the Queen, 1968. FIMechE; FIMarE; CBIM. Akroyd Stuart Award of InstMarE for 1954–55. *Publications:* papers on naval marine engineering, in UK, USA, Sweden and Italy. *Address:* 2 Radnor Close, Henley-on-Thames RG9 2DA. *T:* Henley (0491) 577260. *Clubs:* MCC, Ebury Court; Phyllis Court (Henley).

TRIBE, Geoffrey Reuben, OBE 1968; Controller, Higher Education Division, British Council, 1981–83, retired; *b* 20 Feb. 1924; *s* of late Harry and Olive Tribe; *m* 1st, 1946, Sheila Mackenzie (marr. diss. 1977); 2nd, 1978, Malvina Anne Butt. *Educ:* Southern Grammar Sch., Portsmouth; University Coll. London (BA). Served War, Royal Hampshire Regt (Lieut), 1942–45. Teaching, 1948–58. Appointed to British Council, 1958; Asst Regional Rep., Madras, 1958–63; Regional Dir, Mwanza, 1963–65; Regional Rep., E Nigeria, 1965–67; Asst Controller, Personnel and Staff Recruitment, 1968–73; Controller, Arts Div., 1973–79; Representative, Nigeria, 1979–81. *Recreation:* gardening. *Address:* Chelmer, Aston Court, Iwerne Minster, Blandford Forum, Dorset DT11 8QN. *T:* Fontmell Magna (0747) 811258.

TRIBE, Rear-Admiral Raymond Haydn, CB 1964; MBE 1944; DL; *b* 9 April 1908; *s* of Thomas and Gillian Ada Tribe; *m* 1938, Alice Mary (*née* Golby); no *c*. Served War of 1939–45 (MBE, despatches twice). Commander, 1947; Captain, 1955; Rear-Admiral, 1962. Inspector-General, Fleet Maintenance, and Chief Staff Officer (Technical) to C-in-C Home Fleet, 1962–65; retired from Royal Navy, Sept. 1965. Distinguished Battle Service Medal of Soviet Union, 1943. CC Berks, 1970–77. DL Berks, 1975. *Recreations:* gardening, painting. *Address:* Oak Cottage, Compton, near Newbury, Berks. *T:* Compton (0635) 578253.

TRICKER, Prof. Robert Ian, DLitt; FCA; FCMA; Professor of Finance and Accounting, University of Hong Kong, since 1986; Director, Corporate Policy Group, Oxford, since 1979; *b* 14 Dec. 1933; *s* of Ralph Edward Tricker, Coventry; *m* 1st, 1958, Doreen Murray (marr. diss. 1982); two *d*; 2nd, 1982, Gretchen Elizabeth Bigelow. *Educ:* King Henry VIII Sch., Coventry; Harvard Business Sch., USA. MA, JDipMA; DLitt CNAA, 1983. Articled Clerk, Daffern & Co., 1950–55; Sub-Lt, RNVR, 1956–58; Controller, Unbrako Ltd, 1959–64; Directing Staff, Iron & Steel Fedn Management Coll., 1965; Barclays Bank Prof. of Management Information Systems, Univ. of Warwick, 1968–70. Director, Oxford Centre for Management Studies, 1970–79, Professorial Fellow, 1979–84 (P. D. Leake Res. Fellow, 1966–67); Res. Fellow, Nuffield Coll., Oxford, 1979–84 (Vis. Fellow, 1971–79); Dir, Management Develt Centre of Hong Kong, 1984–86. Institute of Chartered Accountants in England and Wales: Mem. Council, 1979–84; Mem. Educn and Trng Directorate, 1979–82; Chairman: Examination Cttee, 1980–82; Tech. and Res. Cttee, 1982–84. Member: Council, ICMA, 1969–72; Management and Industrial Relations Cttee, SSRC, 1973–75; Chm., Independent Inquiry into Prescription Pricing Authority for Minister for Health, 1976. Member: Nuffield Hosp. Management Cttee, 1972–74; Adv. Panel on Company Law, Dept of Trade, 1980–83; Company Affairs Cttee, Inst. of Directors, 1980–84; Standing Commn on CS Salaries and Conditions of Service, Hong Kong, 1989–. *Publications:* The Accountant in Management, 1967; Strategy for Accounting Research, 1975; Management Information and Control Systems, 1976, 2nd edn 1982; The Independent Director, 1978; Effective Information Management, 1982; Governing the Institute, 1983; Corporate Governance, 1984; The Effective Director, 1986; The Director's Manual, 1990. *Address:* University of Hong Kong Business School, Hong Kong.

TRICKETT, Jon Hedley; Leader, Leeds City Council, since 1989; *b* 2 July 1950; *s* of Lawrence and Rose Trickett; *m* 1969 (separated); one *s* one *d*. *Educ:* Hull Univ. (BA Politics); Leeds Univ. (MA Pol Sociol). Builder/plumber, to 1985. Joined Labour Party, 1971; Leeds City Council: Councillor, Beeston Ward, 1985; Chair: Finance Cttee, 1986–89; Housing Cttee, 1988–89. Chm., Leeds City Development Co., 1989–; Director: Leeds/Bradford Airport, 1988–; Leeds Playhouse, 1988–; Leeds Theatre Co., 1988–. Mem., GMBATU. *Recreations:* cycling, Leeds United. *Address:* 268 Cross Flatts Grove, Leeds LS11 7BS. *T:* Leeds (0532) 773108. *Clubs:* Cyclists Touring, Youth Hostels Association.

TRICKETT, (Mabel) Rachel; Principal, St Hugh's College, Oxford, 1973–91; *b* 20 Dec. 1923. *Educ:* Lady Margaret Hall, Oxford, 1942–45. BA Hons 1st Cl. in English; MA 1947; Hon. Fellow, 1978. Asst to Curator, Manchester City Art Galleries, 1945–46; Asst Lectr in English, Univ. of Hull, 1946–49; Commonwealth Fund Fellow, Yale Univ., 1949–50; Lectr in English, Hull Univ., 1950–54; Fellow and Tutor in English, St Hugh's Coll., Oxford, 1954–73. *Publications:* The Honest Muse (a study in Augustan verse), 1967; *novels:* The Return Home, 1952; The Course of Love, 1954; Point of Honour, 1958; A Changing Place, 1962; The Elders, 1966; A Visit to Timon, 1970. *Address:* Flat 4, 18 Norham Gardens, Oxford OX2 6QB.

TRICKEY, Edward Lorden, FRCS; Dean, Institute of Orthopaedics, London University, 1981–87, retired; Consultant Orthopaedic Surgeon, Royal National Orthopaedic Hospital, London, and Edgware General Hospital, 1960–85, retired; *b* 22 July 1920; *s* of E. G. W. Trickey and M. C. Trickey; *m* 1944, Ivy Doreen Harold; two *s* one *d*. *Educ:* Dulwich College; King's College, London Univ. (MB BS). Consultant Orthopaedic Surgeon, Ashton under Lyne, 1957–60. *Publications:* various articles on orthopaedic trauma and knee joint surgery. *Recreations:* cricket, bridge. *Address:* 43 Beverley Gardens, Stanmore, Mddx. *T:* 081–863 6964. *Clubs:* MCC, Middlesex CC.

TRIER, Peter Eugene, CBE 1980; MA; FEng, FIEE; FInstP, FIMA; Pro-Chancellor, Brunel University, since 1980; Director of Research and Development, Philips Electronics UK, 1969–81, retired; *b* Darmstadt, 12 Sept. 1919; *s* of Ernst and Nellie Trier; *m* 1946, Margaret Nora Holloway; three *s*. *Educ:* Mill Hill Sch.; Trinity Hall, Cambridge (Wrangler 1941). Royal Naval Scientific Service, 1941–50; Mullard Research Labs, 1950–69, Dir, 1953–69. Dir, Mullard Ltd and other Philips subsidiaries, 1957–85; Main Bd Dir, Philips Electronics, 1969–85. Specialist Advr, House of Lords Select Cttee on Sci and Technol., 1982–84; Member: Electronics Res. Council, MoD, 1963–80 (Chm., 1976–80); Defence Scientific Adv. Council, 1975–85 (Chm., 1981–85); ACARD Working Party on IT, 1980; ACARD sub-group on Annual Review of Govt-funded R&D, 1984–86. (Chm., 1985–86). IEE: Vice-Pres., 1974–77; Faraday Lectr, 1968–69; Chm., Electronics Div. Bd, 1971–72; Pres., IMA, 1982–83. FEng 1978 (Hon. Sec. for Electrical Engrg, 1985–87; Chm., Membership Cttee, 1987–90); Pres., Electronic Engrg Assoc., 1980–81; Member: Management Cttee, Royal Instn, 1978–81; Adv. Bd, RCDS, 1980–90. Brunel University: Mem. Council, 1968– (Chm., 1973–78); Chm., Supervisory Bd, Brunel Inst. of Bio-Engineering, 1983–; Chm., Bute Engrg Adv. Cttee, UWIST, 1983–86; External Examr in Maths: Polytechnic of Central London, 1983–86; Coventry Polytechnic, 1986–. Mem. Editorial Bd, Interdisciplinary Science Reviews, 1975–. Mem., Management Cttee, The Wine Soc., 1977–. Liveryman, Co. of Scientific Instrument Makers, 1968–. Hon. DTech Brunel, 1975. Glazebrook Medal and Prize, Inst. of Physics, 1984. *Publications:* Strategic Implications of Micro-electronics, 1982; Mathematics and Information, 1983; papers in scientific and technical jls. *Recreations:* travel, mathematical games, Trier family history, railway history. *Address:* Yew Tree House, Bredon, Tewkesbury, Glos GL20 7HF. *T:* Bredon (0684) 72200. *Club:* Savile.

TRILLO, Rt. Rev. Albert John, MTh; *b* 4 July 1915; *s* of late Albert Chowns and late Margaret Trillo; *m* 1942, Patricia Eva Williams; two *s* one *d*. *Educ:* The Quintin Sch.; King's Coll., University of London. Business career, 1931–36; University, 1936–38, BD (1st Class Hons) and AKC (1st Class Hons), 1938; MTh 1943. Asst Curate, Christ Church, Fulham, 1938–41; Asst Curate, St Gabriel's, Cricklewood (in charge of St Michael's), 1941–45; Secretary, SCM in Schools, 1945–50; Rector of Friern Barnet and Lecturer in New Testament Greek, King's Coll., London, 1950–55; Principal, Bishops' Coll., Cheshunt, 1955–63; Bishop Suffragan of Bedford, 1963–68; Bishop Suffragan of Hertford, 1968–71; Bishop of Chelmsford, 1971–85. Examining Chaplain to Bishop of St Edmundsbury and Ipswich, 1955–63, to Bishop of St Albans, 1963–71. Hon. Canon, Cathedral and Abbey Church at St Albans, 1958–63; Canon Residentiary, 1963–65. Fellow of King's Coll., London, 1959. Proctor in Convocation for Dean and Chapter of St Albans, 1963–64; Proctor-in-Convocation for the Clergy, 1965. Governor: Aldenham Sch., 1963–71; Harper Trust Schs, Bedford, 1963–68; Queenswood Sch., 1969–71; Forest Sch., 1976–. Chairman: Church of England Youth Council, 1970–74; Exec. Cttee, British Council of Churches, 1974–77 (Chm., Fund for Ireland, 1978–); Church of England's Cttee on Roman Catholic Relations, 1975–85; Jt Chm., English Anglican/Roman Catholic Commn. *Recreations:* reading and walking. *Address:* Copperfield, Back Road, Wenhaston, Halesworth, Suffolk.

TRIMBLE, David; *see* Trimble, W. D.

TRIMBLE, Jenifer, (Mrs M. R. Trimble); *see* Wilson-Barnett, J.

TRIMBLE, (William) David; MP (UU) Upper Bann, since May 1990; *b* 15 Oct. 1944; *s* of William and Ivy Trimble; *m* 1978, Daphne Orr; two *s* one *d*. *Educ:* Bangor Grammar Sch.; Queen's University Belfast (LLB). Called to the Bar of Northern Ireland, 1969; Lectr, 1968, Sen. Lectr, 1977, Faculty of Law, QUB. Mem., Constitutional Convention, 1975–76. *Publications:* Northern Ireland Housing Law, 1986; NI Law Reports, 1975–. *Recreations:* music, reading. *Address:* House of Commons, SW1A 0AA.

TRIMLESTOWN, 20th Baron *cr* 1461 (Ire.); **Anthony Edward Barnewall;** *b* 2 Feb. 1928; *s* of 19th Baron and Muriel (*d* 1937), *d* of Edward Oskar Schneider; *S* father, 1990; *m* 1st, 1963, Lorna Margaret Marion (marr. diss. 1973; she *d* 1988), *d* of late Douglas Ramsay; 2nd, 1977, Mary Wonderly, *e d* of late Judge Thomas F. McAllister. *Educ:* Ampleforth. Irish Guards, 1946–48. Naval architect with Jack Jones, 1949–53; European Sales Exec., P&O Shipping Co., 1965–74. *Recreation:* travel. *Heir:* *b* Hon. Raymond Charles Barnewall, *b* 29 Dec. 1930. *Address:* PO Box 35, Ada, Michigan 49301, USA.

TRINDER, Frederick William; Charity Commissioner, 1984–85; Member, BBC and IBA Central Appeals Advisory Committee, since 1986; *b* 18 Nov. 1930; *s* of Charles Elliott Trinder and Grace Johanna Trinder (*née* Hoadly); *m* 1964, Christiane Friederike Brigitte Dorothea (*née* Hase); one *s*. *Educ:* LSE, Univ. of London (BSc). Admitted Solicitor, 1966; Legal Asst/Sen. Legal Asst, Charity Commn, 1966–74; Dep. Charity Comr, 1974–84. Trustee, Charities Official Investment Fund, 1988–. *Recreations:* travel, gardening, music. *Address:* 37 The Common, West Wratting, Cambridge CB1 5LR. *T:* Cambridge (0223) 290469. *Club:* Royal Over-Seas League.

TRIPP, Rt. Rev. Howard George; an Auxiliary Bishop in Southwark, (RC), since 1980; Titular Bishop of Newport, since 1980; *b* 3 July 1927; *s* of late Basil Howard Tripp and Alice Emily Tripp (*née* Haslett). *Educ:* John Fisher School, Purley; St John's Seminary, Wonersh. Priest, 1953; Assistant Priest: Blackheath SE3, 1953–56; East Sheen, 1956–62; Asst Diocesan Financial Sec., 1962–68; Parish Priest, East Sheen, 1965–71; Director, Southwark Catholic Children's Soc., 1971–80. *Recreation:* vegetable gardening. *Address:* 8 Arterberry Road, SW20 8AJ. *T:* 081–946 4609.

TRIPP, (John) Peter, CMG 1971; Consultant, Al-Tajir Bank, since 1986; *b* 27 March 1921; *s* of Charles Howard and Constance Tripp; *m* 1948, Rosemary Rees Jones; one *s* one *d*. *Educ:* Bedford Sch.; Sutton Valence Sch.; L'Institut de Touraine. Served War of 1939–45: Royal Marines, 1941–46. Sudan Political Service, 1946–54. Foreign (subsequently Diplomatic) Service, 1954–81; Political Agent, Trucial States, 1955–58; Head of Chancery, Vienna, 1958–61; Economic Secretary, Residency Bahrain, 1961–63; Counsellor 1963; Political Agent, Bahrain, 1963–65; sabbatical year at Durham Univ., 1965; Amman, 1966–68; Head of Near Eastern Dept, FCO, 1969–70; Ambassador to Libya, 1970–74; High Comr in Singapore, 1974–78; Ambassador to Thailand, 1978–81. Political Adviser, Inchcape Gp, 1981–86; Chm., Private Investment Co. for Asia (UK), 1981–84. Chm., Anglo-Thai Soc., 1983–88. County Councillor (Ind.), Powys, 1985–87. *Recreations:* theatre, gardening. *Address:* Tanyffridd, Llanfechain, Powys SY22 6UE.

TRIPPIER, David Austin; RD 1983; JP; MP (C) Rossendale and Darwen, since 1983 (Rossendale, 1979–83); Minister of State (Minister for the Environment and Countryside) Department of the Environment, since 1989; *b* 15 May 1946; *s* of Austin Wilkinson Trippier, MC and late Mary Trippier; *m* 1975, Ruth Worthington, Barrister; three *s*. *Educ:* Bury Grammar School. Commnd Officer, Royal Marines Reserve, 1968. Member of Stock Exchange, 1968–. Mem., Rochdale Council, 1969–78, Leader Cons. Gp, 1974–76. Secretary: All Party Parly Footwear Cttee, 1979–83; Cons. Parly Defence Cttee, 1980–82; PPS to Minister for Health, 1982–83; Parly Under-Sec. of State, DTI, 1983–85, Dept of Employment, 1985–87; Parly Under-Sec. of State, DoE, 1987–89; Dep. Chm., Cons. Party, 1990. Nat. Vice Chm., Assoc. of Cons. Clubs, 1980–84. JP Rochdale, 1975. *Publications:* Defending the Peace, 1982; New Life for Inner Cities, 1989. *Recreation:* gardening. *Address:* House of Commons, SW1A 0AA. *Club:* Army and Navy.

TRISTRAM, William John, CBE 1965; JP; FRPharmS; Pharmaceutical Chemist; Liverpool City Council, 1934–55 (Alderman, 1944–55); appointed Hon. Alderman, 1964; *b* 6 Oct. 1896; *s* of late Rev. W. J. Tristram and Elizabeth Critchlow; *m* 1966, Philomena Mary Moylan (*d* 1986), Drogheda. *Educ:* Scarborough High Sch.; Leeds Central High Sch.; Liverpool College of Pharmacy. Member Council Pharmaceutical Society of Great Britain, 1944–67 (President, 1952–53, FPS, 1966, Gold Medal, 1968); Hon. Treasurer and Member Executive National Pharmaceutical Union, 1936–68 (Chairman, 1943–44); Chairman, Joint Cttee for the Pharmaceutical Service, 1946–52; Member Central Health Services Council (Min. of Health), 1948–64. Vice-Chairman, Standing Pharmaceutical Advisory Cttee (Min. of Health), 1946–48 (Chairman, 1948–59); Chairman, Liverpool Licensing Cttee, 1965–70; Dep. Chairman, South Liverpool Hospitals Management Cttee, 1965–70; Mem., Liverpool Exec. Council (Min. of Health), 1948–70 (Chairman, 1960–64); Chairman, Liverpool Homœopathic Hospital, 1960–70. Pres., Heswall Br., Royal British Legion. JP Liverpool, 1938; Lord Mayor of Liverpool, 1953–54; Dep. Lord Mayor, 1954–55. *Recreations:* cricket-watching, walking. *Address:* Fairfield Nursing Home, 10 Quarry Road East, Heswall, Wirral, Merseyside L61 6XD. *T:* 051–342 7618. *Clubs:* National Liberal; Lyceum (Liverpool).

TRITTON, Alan George; Director: Barclays Bank Ltd, since 1974; Mercantile Credit Co. Ltd, since 1973; a Vice-President, Equitable Life Assurance Society, since 1983 (Director, since 1976); *b* 2 Oct. 1931; *s* of George Henton Tritton, Lyons Hall, Essex, and Iris Mary Baillie, Lochloy; *m* 1st, 1958, Elizabeth Clare d'Abreu, QC (marr. diss.) (*see* E. C. McLaren-Throckmorton); two *s* one *d*; 2nd, 1972, Diana Marion Spencer. *Educ:* Eton. Member of British Schools Exploring Soc. Expedn, N Norway, 1949. Served with 1st Batt. Seaforth Highlanders, Malaya, 1950–52 (wounded in action, Pahang). Falkland Islands Dependencies Survey, 1952–54; entered Barclays Bank Ltd, 1954; local Dir, 54 Lombard Street, 1964; Dir, Barclays Bank UK Management Ltd, 1972. A Vice-Pres., Royal Geographical Soc., 1983– (Mem. Council, 1975–, Hon. Treas., 1984–). Member: Cttee, British Trans-Arctic Expedn, 1966–69; Cttee, British Everest SW Face Expedn, 1974–75; Cttee of Management, Mount Everest Foundn, 1976–; Friends' Cttee, Scott Polar Research Inst., 1976–80. Commissioner, Public Works Loan Bd, 1970–74; Chairman: Westminster Abbey Investment Cttee, 1976–; Calcutta Tercentenary Trust, 1989–; Member: Governing Body, British Nat. Cttee, Internat. Chamber of Commerce, 1975– (Hon. Treas. 1985); Council, Essex Agricl Soc., 1973–76. *Recreations:* travelling, shooting. *Address:* 54 Lombard Street, EC3. *T:* 071–283 2161. *Clubs:* Boodle's, Pratt's, Antarctic, Geographical, Essex.

TRITTON, Major Sir Anthony (John Ernest), 4th Bt *cr* 1905; *b* 4 March 1927; *s* of Sir Geoffrey Ernest Tritton, 3rd Bt, CBE, and Mary Patience Winifred (*d* 1960), *d* of John Kenneth Foster; *S* father, 1976; *m* 1957, Diana, *d* of Rear-Adm. St J. A. Micklethwait, CB, DSO, and of Clemence Penelope Olga Welby-Everard; one *s* one *d*. *Educ:* Eton. Commissioned 3rd Hussars, Oct. 1945; retired as Major, 1962, The Queen's Own Hussars. *Recreations:* shooting, fishing. *Heir:* *s* Jeremy Ernest Tritton, *b* 6 Oct. 1961. *Address:* River House, Heytesbury, Wilts. *Club:* Cavalry and Guards.

TRITTON, (Elizabeth) Clare, (Clare McLaren-Throckmorton; Mrs Andrew McLaren); QC 1988; Senior Partner, Throckmorton Estates; *b* 18 Aug. 1935; *d* of Prof. Alfonsus d'Abreu and Elizabeth d'Abreu (*née* Throckmorton); *m* 1st, 1958, Alan Tritton, *qv* Marr. diss. 1971); two *s* one *d*; 2nd, 1973, Andrew McLaren; name changed to McLaren-Throckmorton by deed poll, 1991. *Educ:* Convent of the Holy Child Jesus, Mayfield, St Leonards; Univ. of Birmingham (BA Hons English). Called to the Bar, Inner Temple, 1968. Lived and worked in USA, France, Germany and Italy, intermittently, 1952–86; Centre Organiser, WVS, 1963–64; Charlemagne Chambers, Brussels, 1985–89; founded own Chambers, practising overseas as European Law Chambers, 1987. Chm., Bar European Group, 1982–84; Vice Chm., Internat. Practice Cttee, Gen. Council of the Bar, 1988–. Member: Council, Bow Gp, 1963–65; Eur. Cttee, British Invisible Exports Council, 1989–. Dir, Severn Trent plc, 1991–. Indep. Mem., Council, FIMBRA, 1991–. Founder, Bar European News, 1983. *Publications:* articles in law magazines on EEC and private internat. law. *Recreations:* reading, gardening, theatre, travel, cooking, walking, children. *Address:* Coughton Court, Alcester, Warwicks B49 5JA. *T:* Alcester (0789) 762542; Manor House, Molland, South Molton, North Devon. *T:* South Molton (07697) 325; 18 Battersea Square, SW11 3JF. *T:* 071–228 7140; (chambers) 5 Paper Buildings, Temple, EC4Y 7HB. *T:* 071–583 4555.

TROLLOPE, Andrew David Hedderwick; QC 1991; a Recorder of the Crown Court, since 1989; *b* 6 Nov. 1948; *s* of Arthur George Cecil Trollope and Rosemary (*née* Hodson); *m* 1978, Anne Forbes; two *s*. *Educ:* Charterhouse. Called to the Bar, Inner Temple, 1971; Asst Recorder, 1985–89. *Recreations:* opera, jazz, swimming, tennis, sailing, travel. *Address:* 1 Middle Temple Lane, Temple, EC4Y 9AA. *T:* 071–583 0659. *Club:* Hurlingham.

TROLLOPE, Sir Anthony (Simon), 17th Bt *cr* 1642, of Casewick, Lincolnshire; Marketing Executive with Ricegrowers Co-operative Ltd; *b* 31 Aug. 1945; *s* of Sir

Anthony Owen Clavering Trollope, 16th Bt and of Joan Mary Alexis, *d* of Alexis Robert Gibbs; *S* father, 1987; *m* 1969, Denise, *d* of Trevern and Vida Thompson; two *d. Educ:* Univ. of Sydney (BA 1969). Breeder, in partnership with his wife, of Anglo-Arabian horses and Rhodesian Ridgeback dogs. Mem., Australian Marketing Inst. *Heir: b* Hugh Irwin Trollope [*b* 31 March 1947; *m* 1971, Barbara Anne, *d* of William Ian Jamieson; one *s* two *d*]. *Address:* 28 Midson Road, Oakville, NSW 2765, Australia. *Clubs:* Gordon Rugby, Rhodesian Ridgeback, Arab Horse Society of Australia, Castle Hill RSL (Sydney).

TROTMAN-DICKENSON, Sir Aubrey (Fiennes), Kt 1989; PhD, DSc; Principal, University of Wales College of Cardiff, since 1988 (University of Wales Institute of Science and Technology, Cardiff, 1968–88, University College Cardiff, 1987–88); *b* 12 Feb. 1926; *s* of late Edward Newton Trotman-Dickenson and Violet Murray Nicoll; *m* 1953, Danusia Irena Hewell; two *s* one *d. Educ:* Winchester Coll.; Balliol Coll., Oxford. MA Oxon, BSc Oxon; PhD Manchester; DSc Edinburgh. Fellow, National Research Council, Ottawa, 1948–50; Asst Lecturer, ICI Fellow, Manchester Univ., 1950–53; E. I. du Pont de Nemours, Wilmington, USA, 1953–54; Lecturer, Edinburgh Univ., 1954–60; Professor, University College of Wales, Aberystwyth, 1960–68. Vice-Chancellor, Univ. of Wales, 1975–77 and 1983–85. Chm., Job Creation Programme, Wales, 1975–78. Member: Welsh Council, 1971–79; Planning and Transport Res. Adv. Council, DoE, 1975–79. Tilden Lectr, Chem. Soc., 1963. *Publications:* Gas Kinetics, 1955; Free Radicals, 1959; Tables of Bimolecular Gas Reactions, 1967; (ed) Comprehensive Inorganic Chemistry, 1973; contrib. to learned journals. *Address:* Radyr Chain, Llantrisant Road, Cardiff CF5 2PW. *T:* Cardiff (0222) 563263.

TROTTER, Neville Guthrie, JP; FCA; MP (C) Tynemouth, since Feb. 1974; *b* 27 Jan. 1932; *s* of Captain Alexander Trotter and Elizabeth Winifred Trotter (*née* Guthrie); *m* 1983, Caroline, *d* of Captain John Farrow, RN retd and Oona Farrow (*née* Hall); one *d. Educ:* Shrewsbury; King's Coll., Durham (BCom). Short service commn in RAF, 1955–58. Partner, Thornton Baker & Co., Chartered Accountants, 1962–74, now Consultant with Grant Thornton; Dir, Romag Plc; Consultant: Bowring; Northern General Transport; British Marine Equipment Council. Mem., Newcastle City Council, 1963–74 (Alderman, 1970–74; Chm., Finance Cttee, Traffic Highways and Transport Cttee, Theatre Cttee). Mem., CAA Airline Users Cttee, 1973–79. Mem., Tyne and Wear Metropolitan Council, 1973–74; Vice-Chm., Northumberland Police Authority, 1970–74. Chm., Cons. Party Shipping and Shipbuilding Cttee, 1979–85 (Vice-Chm., 1976–79); Secretary: Cons. Party Industry Cttee, 1981–83; Cons. Party Transport Cttee, 1983–84; Mil. Sec., Cons. Party Aviation Cttee, 1976–79; Member: Industry Sub-Cttee, Select Cttee on Expenditure, 1976–79; Select Cttee on Transport, 1983–; Parly Defence Study Group, 1980–. Private Member's Bills: Consumer Safety, 1978; Licensing Amendment, 1980; Intoxicating Substances Supply (Glue Sniffing), 1985. Former Member: Northern Economic Planning Council; Tyne Improvement Commn; Tyneside Passenger Transport Authority; Industrial Relations Tribunal; Council, RUSI. Member: British Maritime League; US Naval Inst. Freeman, City of London, 1978; Mem., Worshipful Co. of Chartered Accountants, 1978. JP Newcastle upon Tyne, 1973. *Recreations:* aviation, gardening, fell-walking, study of foreign affairs, defence and industry. *Address:* (office) c/o Grant Thornton, Higham House, Higham Place, Newcastle upon Tyne NE1 8EE. *T:* 091–261 2631. *Clubs:* Royal Air Force; Northern Counties (Newcastle upon Tyne); Tynemouth and Whitley Bay Conservative.

TROTTER, Sir Ronald (Ramsay), Kt 1985; FCA; New Zealand business executive; Chairman, Fletcher Challenge Ltd, since 1981 (Chief Executive, 1981–87); *b* Hawera, 9 Oct. 1927; *s* of Clement George Trotter, CBE and Annie Euphemia Trotter (*née* Young); *m* 1955, Margaret Patricia, *d* of James Rainey; three *s* one *d. Educ:* Collegiate School, Wanganui; Victoria Univ. of Wellington; Lincoln Coll., Canterbury (BCom, Cert. in Agric.). FCA 1976. Wright Stephenson & Co., 1958–72: Dir, 1962–68; Man. Dir, 1968–70; Chm. and Man. Dir, 1970–72; Chm. and Man. Dir, Challenge Corp., 1972–81. Chairman: Telecom Corp. of New Zealand Ltd, 1987–90; Post Office Bank, 1989; Ciba-Geigy New Zealand Ltd, 1990–; Director: Reserve Bank of NZ, 1986–88; Australia and New Zealand Banking Gp, 1988– (Inaugural Mem., Internat. Bd of Advice, 1986–); Air New Zealand Ltd, 1989–; Toyota New Zealand Ltd, 1990–; Ciba-Geigy Australia Ltd, 1991–. Trustee and Chm., NZ Inst. of Economic Research, 1973–86; Chairman: Overseas Investment Commn, 1974–77; NZ Business Roundtable, 1985–90; Pacific Basin Econ. Council, 1985–90 (Internat. Pres., 1986–88). Mem., Project Develt Bd, Museum of NZ, 1988–. Hon. LLD Victoria Univ. of Wellington, 1984. Bledisloe Medal, Lincoln Coll., 1988. Silver Jubilee Medal, 1977; NZ Commemoration Medal, 1990. *Address:* 16 Wesley Road, Wellington 1, New Zealand. *T:* (4) 472–6628, *Fax:* (4) 499–0051; Fletcher Challenge Ltd, 87–91 The Terrace, PO Box 1696, Wellington 1. *T:* (4) 473–8267, *Fax:* (4) 472–1856. *Club:* Wellington (Wellington, NZ).

TROTTER, Thomas Andrew, FRCO; Organist, St Margaret's Church, Westminster, since 1982; Organist to the City of Birmingham, since 1983; *b* 4 April 1957; *s* of late His Honour Richard Stanley Trotter and Ruth Elizabeth Trotter. *Educ:* Malvern Coll.; Royal Coll. of Music, 1974–76 (schol.; ARCM) (organ schol., St George's Chapel, Windsor, 1975–76); King's Coll., Cambridge (organ schol., 1976–79; MA). John Stewart of Rannock Schol. in Sacred Music, Cambridge Univ., 1979; Countess of Munster schol. for further organ studies with Marie-Claire Alain in Paris. Début at Royal Fest. Hall, 1980; Prom. début, 1986; regular broadcasts for Radio 2 and Radio 3; has performed at fests throughout UK and in Europe; concert tours to Australia, USA and Far East; organ recordings. Walford Davies Prize, RCM, 1976; First prize and Bach prize, St Albans Internat. Organ Competition, 1979; Prix de Virtuosité, Conservatoire Rueil-Malmaison, 1981. *Address:* c/o The Town Hall, Birmingham B3 3DQ. *T:* 021–235 3942.

TROUBRIDGE, Sir Thomas (Richard), 7th Bt *cr* 1799, of Plymouth; FCA; Partner, Price Waterhouse, since 1989; *b* 23 Jan. 1955; *s* of Sir Peter Troubridge, 6th Bt and of Hon. Venetia Daphne, *d* of 1st Baron Weeks; *S* father, 1988; *m* 1984, Hon. Rosemary Douglas-Pennant, *yr d* of Baron Penrhyn, *qv*; one *s* one *d. Educ:* Eton College; Durham Univ. (BSc Eng). ACA 1980, FCA 1991. Joined Price Waterhouse, 1977. *Recreations:* sailing, ski-ing. *Heir: s* Edward Peter Troubridge, *b* 10 Aug. 1989. *Address:* 28 Lilyville Road, SW6 5DW. *T:* 071–736 5739. *Clubs:* White's, Royal Automobile; Itchenor Sailing.

TROUGHTON, Henry Lionel, BSc(Eng), CEng, FIMechE, MIEE; Deputy Director, Projects and Research, Military Vehicles and Engineering Establishment, Ministry of Defence, 1970–74; *b* 30 March 1914; *o s* of late Henry James Troughton; *m* 1940, Dorothy Janet Louie (*née* Webb); one *d. Educ:* Mill Hill Sch.; University Coll., London. War of 1939–45: commissioned REME (Major), 1940–47; Fighting Vehicles Research and Development Estabt, 1947 (now Mil. Vehicles and Engineering Estabt); Asst Dir (Electrical), later Asst Dir (Power Plant), and Dep. Dir (Vehicles), 1960, retired 1974. *Recreations:* gardening, travel. *Address:* 10 Brookside Close, Feltham, Mddx TW13 7HR.

TROUGHTON, Peter, PhD; Managing Director and Chief Executive Officer, Telecom Corporation of New Zealand, since 1988; *b* 26 Aug. 1943; *s* of late Frank Sydney Troughton and of Joan Vera Troughton (*née* Root); *m* 1967, Joyce Uncles; two *s. Educ:* City Univ. (BSc Eng); University College London (PhD). Technical apprentice, Plessey Co., then Post Office apprentice, 1959; PO scholarship, 1964; research for PhD, 1967; develt of microprocessor techniques for control of telephone switching systems, 1970; Dep. Gen. Manager, South Central Telephone Area, 1977; Head of Ops, Prestel, with special responsibility for establishing Prestel network, 1979; Gen. Manager, City Telephone Area, 1980; Regional Dir, British Telecom London, 1983; Man. Dir, British Telecom Enterprises, 1984–86; Dir and Partner, Alan Patricof Associates, 1986–88, non-exec. Dir, 1988–; non-exec. Chm., Trans Power (NZ National Power Grid) Estabt Bd, 1990–. NZ Commemoration Medal, 1990. *Publications:* articles and papers on microwave systems, computers and communications. *Recreations:* travel, archaeology, bridge. *Address:* Telecom Headquarters, 13/27 Manners Street, PO Box 570, Wellington, New Zealand. *T:* 4 823000. *Clubs:* Wellesley, Wellington (NZ).

TROUNSON, Rev. Ronald Charles, MA; Rector, Easton-on-the-Hill and Collyweston with Duddington and Tixover, since 1989; *b* 7 Dec. 1926; *s* of Edwin Trounson and Elsie Mary Trounson (*née* Bolitho); *m* 1952, Leonora Anne Keate; two *s* three *d. Educ:* Plymouth Coll.; Emmanuel Coll., Cambridge (Schol.); Ripon Hall, Oxford (MA). Deacon, 1956; Priest, 1957. National Service, RAF, 1948–50. Asst Master, Scaitcliffe Sch., Englefield Green, Surrey, 1950–52; Sixth Form Classics Master, Plymouth Coll., 1953–58; Asst Curate, St Gabriel's, Plymouth, 1956–58; Chaplain, Denstone Coll., 1958–76; Second Master, 1968–76, Bursar, 1976–78; Principal of St Chad's College and Lectr in Classics, Univ. of Durham, 1978–88. Chm., of Governors, Durham High Sch., 1990. Fellow, Woodard Corporation, 1983. FRSA 1984. *Address:* The Rectory, Easton-on-the-Hill, Stamford PE9 3LS. *T:* Stamford (0780) 62616.

TROUP, Alistair Mewburn; His Honour Judge Troup; a Circuit Judge, since 1980; *b* 23 Nov. 1927; *y s* of late William Annandale Troup, MC, MD, and Margaret Loïs Troup (*née* Mewburn); *m* 1969, Marjorie Cynthia (*née* Hutchinson); one *s* three *d* by previous marriages. *Educ:* Merchant Taylor's School; New College, Oxford (BA). Served Army, 1946–48. Called to the Bar, Lincoln's Inn, 1952; Crown Counsel, Tanganyika, 1955–62, Sen. Crown Counsel, 1962–64; returned to practice at English bar, 1964; Dep. Circuit Judge, 1975–77; a Recorder of the Crown Court, 1977–80. Member Panel of Counsel: for Courts Martial Appeals Court, 1970–80; for Comrs of Customs and Excise at VAT Tribunals, 1973–80; Inspector for Dept of Trade, Hartley-Baird Ltd Inquiry, 1974–76. *Recreations:* golf, gardening. *Address:* c/o Lewes Crown Court, The Law Courts, High Street, Lewes, East Sussex BN7 1YB. *Clubs:* Sloane; Wildernesse (Sevenoaks); Seaford Golf.

TROUP, Sir Anthony; *see* Troup, Sir J. A. R.

TROUP, Vice-Adm. Sir (John) Anthony (Rose), KCB 1975; DSC and Bar; *b* 18 July 1921; *s* of late Captain H. R. Troup, RN and N. M. Troup (*née* Milne-Thompson); *m* 1st, 1943, B. M. J. Gordon-Smith (marr. diss. 1952); two *s* one *d*; 2nd, 1953, C. M. Hope; two *s* one *d. Educ:* Naut. Trng Coll., HMS Worcester, 1934; RNC Dartmouth, 1936; service includes: Submarines Turbulent and Strongbow, 1941–45 (dispatches, 1942); HMS Victorious, 1956–59; Comd 3rd Submarine Sqdn, 1961–63; HMS Intrepid, 1966–68; Flag Officer Sea Training, 1969–71; Comdr Far East Fleet, 1971; Flag Officer Submarines and NATO Comdr Submarines, Eastern Atlantic, 1972–74; Flag Officer, Scotland and NI, and NATO Comdr Norlant, 1974–77. *Recreations:* sailing, shooting, gardening. *Address:* Bridge Gardens, Hungerford, Berks RG17 0DL. *Clubs:* Army and Navy; Royal Yacht Squadron.

TROWBRIDGE, George William Job, CBE 1969; CEng; Chairman, AMT (Birmingham) Ltd, since 1981; *b* 21 July 1911; *s* of George Clarke Trowbridge and Thirza Lampier Trowbridge (*née* Dingle); *m* 1938, Doris Isobel Morrison (decd); one *s. Educ:* Southall Technical Coll. Works Manager, Gays (Hampton) Ltd, 1938–45; Works Dir, Kingston Instrument Co. Ltd, 1945–52; Wickman Ltd, Coventry, 1952–79: London Area Manager, 1952–57; General Sales Manager, 1957–62; General Sales Dir, 1962–64; Dep. Man. Dir, 1966–79; Man. Dir, Machine Tool Sales Ltd, 1964–79; Director: John Brown & Co. Ltd, 1969–79; Machine Tools (India) Ltd, Calcutta, 1976–79; Drury Wickman Ltd, Johannesburg, 1976–79; Wickman (Australia) Ltd, Melbourne, 1976–79; Chairman: Wickman Machine Tools Inc., USA; Wickman Machine Tools SA, France. President: Machine Tool Trades Assoc., 1975–77; Comité Européen de Coopération des Industries de la Machine-Outil, 1975–77; Mem., Economic Develt Cttee for Machine Tools, 1968–79. MIProdE. *Publications:* A Handbook for Marketing Machinery, 1970; A Financial Study of British Machine Tool Companies, 1974. *Recreations:* walking, fishing. *Address:* 6 Moultrie Road, Rugby CV21 3BD. *T:* Rugby (0788) 60946. *Club:* Institute of Directors.

TROWBRIDGE, Martin Edward O'Keeffe, CBE 1987; CEng; FIChemE; FRSA; EEC and public affairs counsellor; Chairman, since 1973, and Chief Executive, since 1987, Martin Trowbridge Ltd; *b* 9 May 1925; *s* of late Edward Stanley Trowbridge and Ida Trowbridge (*née* O'Keeffe); *m* 1946, Valerie Ann Glazebrook; one *s. Educ:* Royal College of Science; Imperial Coll. of Science and Technology, London Univ. (BSc Eng (Chem. Eng); ACGI 1946, FCGI 1990); Amer. Management Assoc. Coll., NYC (Dip. Bus. Studies). Technical Officer, ICI (Billingham Div.) Ltd, 1946–48; Division Manager, HWP/Fluor, 1948–53; Technical Dir, Sharples Co., 1953–57; Man. Dir, Sharples Co., 1957–59; Internat. Man. Dir, Sharples Corp., 1959–63; Group Managing Director: Pennwalt International Corp., 1963–72; Pegler-Hattersley Ltd, 1972–73; Dir Gen., Chemical Industries Assoc., 1973–87. Member: Process Plant Working Party, NEDO, 1970–77; Chemicals EDC, NEDO, 1973–87; Process Plant EDC, NEDO, 1977–80; CBI Council; CBI Heads of Sector Group; CBI Europe Cttee; Eur. Chem. Ind. PR Cttee, Brussels; CEFIC R&D Cttee, Brussels; Anglo-German Gp for Chem. Ind.; Anglo-French Gp for Chem. Ind.; ESRC Govt Industry Relns Cttee, 1973–87; Adv. Cttee, Eur. Business Inst., 1984–90; Bd, NRPB, 1987–90; IMRO Ltd, 1988–. Chairman: NEDO Task-Group on Tech., Research and Develt; Conseil d'Administration/CEFIC, Brussels, 1984–87 (Mem., 1973–87). Chm., Professional Develt Cttee, IChemE; Mem. Council, IChemE, 1987–89. Trustee, Chemical Ind. Museum, 1985–89. Hinchley Medal, IChemE, 1946; Internat. Medal, SCI, 1987. *Publications:* Purification of Oils for Marine Service, 1960; Scaling Up Centrifugal Separation Equipment, 1962; Collected Poems, 1963; Centrifugation, 1966; Exhibiting for Profit, 1969; Market Research and Forecasting, 1969; The Financial Performance of Process and Plant Companies, 1970; Poems for the Second Half, 1975; The Particular World of the Directors General, 1987. *Recreations:* writing, shooting, mineralogy, print making, kitsch, wooden containers. *Address:* 51A Moreton Terrace, SW1V 2NS. *Club:* Frensham Gun.

TROWBRIDGE, Rear-Adm. Sir Richard (John), KCVO 1975; Governor of Western Australia, 1980–83; *b* 21 Jan. 1920; *s* of A. G. Trowbridge, Andover, Hants; *m* 1955, Anne Mildred Perceval; two *s. Educ:* Andover Grammar Sch.; Royal Navy. Joined RN as Boy Seaman, 1935. War of 1939–45: commissioned as Sub Lieut, Dec. 1940 (despatches Aug. 1945). Comdr, 1953; commanded Destroyer Carysfort, 1956–58; Exec. Officer, HMS Bermuda, 1958–59, and HMS Excellent, 1959–60; Captain, 1960; commanded Fishery Protection Sqdn, 1962–64; completed course IDC, 1966; commanded HMS

Hampshire, 1967–69; Rear-Adm., 1970; Flag Officer Royal Yachts, 1970–75. An Extra Equerry to the Queen, 1970–. Younger Brother of Trinity Hse, 1972. KStJ 1980. *Recreations:* fishing, sailing, golf; most outdoor pursuits. *Address:* Old Idsworth Garden, Finchdean, Portsmouth. *T:* Rowlands Castle (0705) 412714. *Club:* Army and Navy.

TROWELL, Prof. Brian Lewis, PhD; Heather Professor of Music and Fellow of Wadham College, University of Oxford, since 1988; *b* 21 Feb. 1931; *s* of Richard Lewis and Edith J. R. Trowell; *m* 1958, Rhianon James; two *d. Educ:* Christ's Hospital; Gonville and Caius Coll., Cambridge. MA 1959; PhD 1960. Asst Lectr, later Lectr, in Music, Birmingham Univ., 1957–62; freelance scholar, conductor, opera producer, lecturer and editor, 1962–67; Head of BBC Radio opera, 1967–70; Reader in Music, 1970, Professor of Music, 1973, King Edward Prof. of Music, 1974–88, KCL. Regents' Prof., Univ. of California at Berkeley, 1970; Vis. Gresham Prof. of Music, City Univ., 1971–74. Pres., Royal Musical Assoc., 1983–88. Hon. RAM, 1972; Hon. FGSM, 1972; FRCM 1977; FTCL 1978; Fellow, Curwen Inst., 1987. Chm., Editorial Cttee, Musica Britannica, 1983–. *Publications:* The Early Renaissance, Pelican History of Music vol. ii, 1963; Four Motets by John Plummer, 1968; (ed jtly) John Dunstable: Complete Works, ed M. F. Bukofzer, 2nd edn, 1970; (ed) Invitation to Medieval Music, vol. 3 1976, vol. 4 1978; opera translations; contrib. dictionaries of music and articles in learned journals. *Recreations:* theatre, reading, gardening. *Address:* Faculty of Music, St Aldate's, Oxford OX1 1DB; 15 Crescent East, Hadley Wood, near Barnet, Herts EN4 0EY.

TROYAT, Henri; Légion d'Honneur; writer; Member of the French Academy, 1959; *b* Moscow, 1 Nov. 1911; *m* 1948, Marguerite Saintagne; one *s* one *d. Educ:* Paris. *Publications:* novels: l'Araigne (Prix Goncourt, 1938) (The Web, 1984); Les Semailles et les Moissons (5 vols), 1957; Tant que la Terre durera (3 vols), 1960; La Lumière des Justes (5 vols), 1963; Viou, 1980; Le Pain de l'Etranger, 1982 (The Children, 1983); Le Bruit solitaire du Coeur, 1985; A demain, Sylvie, 1986; Le Troisième Bonheur, 1987; Treachery, 1990; Aliocha, 1991; biographies: Pushkin, Dostoievsky, Tolstoi, Gogol, Catherine la Grande, Pierre le Grand, Alexandre 1er, Ivan le Terrible, Tchekhov, Gorki, Flambert, Turgenev, Maupassant. *Address:* Académie Française, Quai de Conti, Paris.

TRUBSHAW, (Ernest) Brian, CBE 1970 (OBE 1964); MVO 1948; FRAeS; consultant; *b* 29 Jan. 1924; *s* of late Major H. E. Trubshaw, DL, and Lumly Victoria (*née* Carter); *m* 1973, Mrs Yvonne Edmondson, *widow* of Richard Edmondson, and *d* of late J. A. Clapham, Harrogate, Yorks. *Educ:* Winchester College. Royal Air Force, 1942–50: Bomber Command, 1944; Transport Command, 1945–46; The King's Flight, 1946–48; Empire Flying School, 1949; RAF Flying Coll., 1949–50. Joined Vickers-Armstrongs (Aircraft) Ltd as Experimental Test Pilot, 1950; Dep. Chief Test Pilot, 1953; Chief Test Pilot, 1960; Dir of Flight Test, 1966–80; Divl Dir and Gen. Man. (Filton), Civil Aircraft Div., BAe plc, 1980–86. Mem. Bd (part-time), CAA, 1986–. Warden, Guild of Air Pilots, 1958–61; Fellow, Society Experimental Test Pilots, USA. Hon. DTech Loughborough, 1986. Derry and Richards Memorial Medal, 1961 and 1964; Richard Hansford Burroughs Memorial Trophy (USA), 1964; R. P. Alston Memorial Medal, 1964; Segrave Trophy, 1970; Air League Founders' Medal, 1971; Iven C. Kinchloe Award, USA, 1971; Harmon Aviation Trophy, 1971; Bluebird Trophy, 1973; French Aeronautical Medal, 1976. *Recreations:* cricket, golf. *Address:* The Garden House, Dodington, Chipping Sodbury, Avon BS17 6SG. *T:* Chipping Sodbury (0454) 323951. *Club:* Royal Air Force.

TRUDEAU, Rt. Hon. Pierre Elliott, CH 1984; PC (Can.); QC (Can.) 1969; FRSC; MP (L) Mount Royal, Montreal, 1965–84; Prime Minister of Canada, 1968–79 and 1980–84; Leader of Liberal Party of Canada, 1968–84; Senior Consultant, Heenan Blaikie, since 1984; *b* Montreal, 18 Oct. 1919; *s* of Charles-Emile Trudeau and late Grace Elliott; *m* 1971, Margaret (marr. diss. 1984), *d* of late James Sinclair and of Kathleen Bernard; three *s. Educ:* Jean-de-Brébeuf College, Montreal; University of Montreal; Harvard University; Ecole des Sciences Politiques, Paris; London School of Economics. Called to Bar: Quebec, 1943; Ontario 1967; practised law, Quebec; co-founder of review Cité Libre; Associate Professor of Law, University of Montreal, 1961–65. Parliamentary Secretary to Prime Minister, Jan. 1966–April 1967; Minister of Justice and Attorney General, April 1967–July 1968; Leader of the Opposition, 1979. Mem., Bars of Provinces of Quebec and Ontario. Founding Member, Montreal Civil Liberties Union. Freeman of City of London, 1975. Hon. Dean, Faculty of Law, Univ. of Poitiers, 1975. Hon. Fellow, LSE, 1969. Hon. degrees and awards from many universities in Canada, US, Japan, Macau. *Publications:* La Grève de l'Amiante, 1956; (with Jacques Hébert) Deux Innocents en Chine Rouge, 1961 (Two Innocents in Red China, 1969); Le Fédéralisme et la Société canadienne-française, 1968 (Federalism and the French Canadians, 1968); Réponses, 1968. *Recreations:* swimming, ski-ing, flying, scuba diving, canoeing. *Address:* c/o Heenan Blaikie, Suite 1400, 1001 Maisonneuve Boulevard W, Montreal, Que H3A 3C8, Canada.

TRUDGILL, Prof. Peter John, FBA 1989; Professor of Sociolinguistics, Department of Language and Linguistics, University of Essex, since 1987 (Reader, 1986–87); *b* 7 Nov. 1943; *s* of John Trudgill and Hettie Jean Trudgill (*née* Gooch), *m* 1980, Jean Marie Hannah. *Educ:* City of Norwich Sch.; King's Coll., Cambridge (BA; MA 1966); Edinburgh Univ. (Dip Gen Linguistics 1967; PhD 1971). Asst Lectr, Lectr, Reader, Prof., Dept of Linguistic Sci., Univ. of Reading, 1970–86. Vis. Prof. at Univs of Hong Kong, Bergen, Aarhus, Illinois, Stanford, Osmania, Tokyo International Christian, ANU, Texas Austin, Toronto, Canterbury (NZ). *Publications:* The Social Differentiation of English in Norwich, 1974; Sociolinguistics: an introduction, 1974, 2nd edn 1983; Accent, Dialect and the School, 1975; Sociolinguistic Patterns in British English, 1978; (with A. Hughes) English Accents and Dialects, 1979; (with J. K. Chambers) Dialectology, 1980; (with J. M. Hannah) International English, 1982, 2nd edn 1985; On Dialect, 1983; Coping with America, 1983, 2nd edn 1985; Language in the British Isles, 1984; Applied Sociolinguistics, 1984; Dialects in Contact, 1986; The Dialects of England, 1990; (with J. K. Chambers) English Dialects: studies in grammatical variation, 1991; (with L. Andersson) Bad Language, 1991. *Recreations:* Norwich City FC, playing the 'cello. *Address:* Department of Language and Linguistics, University of Essex, Wivenhoe Park, Colchester CO4 3SQ. *T:* Colchester (0206) 872228.

TRUEMAN, Prof. Edwin Royden; Beyer Professor of Zoology, University of Manchester, 1974–82, now Emeritus; *b* 7 Jan. 1922; *s* of late Sir Arthur Trueman, KBE, FRS, and late Lady (Florence Kate) Trueman (*née* Offler); *m* 1945, Doreen Burt; two *d. Educ:* Bristol Grammar Sch.; Univ. of Glasgow. DSc Glasgow, MSc Manchester. Technical Officer (Radar), RAF, 1942–46. Asst Lectr and Lectr, Univ. of Hull, 1946–58, Sen. Lectr and Reader, 1958–68; Dean, Faculty of Science, Univ. of Hull, 1954–57; Prof. of Zoology, Univ. of Manchester, 1969–74. R. T. French Vis. Prof., Univ. of Rochester, NY, 1960–61; Nuffield Travelling Fellowship in Tropical Marine Biology, Univ. of West Indies, Jamaica, 1968–69; Leverhulme Emeritus Fellowship, 1983–85. *Publications:* Locomotion of Soft-bodied Animals, 1975; (ed) Aspects of Animal Movement, 1980; (ed) vols 10–12 of series The Mollusca, 1985–88; articles on animal locomotion, littoral physiology and Mollusca. *Address:* Heron's Creek, Yealm View Road, Newton Ferrers, Plymouth, Devon. *T:* Plymouth (0752) 872775.

TRUEMAN, Frederick Sewards, OBE 1989; writer and broadcaster; *b* Stainton, Yorks, 6 Feb. 1931; *s* of late Alan Thomas Trueman; *m* 1st, 1955, Enid (marr. diss.); one *s* two *d* (incl. twin *s* and *d*); 2nd, Veronica. *Educ:* Maltby Secondary Sch. Apprentice bricklayer, 1946; worked in tally office of Maltby Main pit, 1948–51; Nat. service, RAF, 1951–53. Played club cricket, 1945–48; Yorks Fedn cricket tour, 1948; played for Yorks CCC, 1949–68 (took 2304 wickets in first class games, incl. 100 wickets in a season twelve times; also made 3 centuries); county cap, 1951; captained Yorkshire 31 times, 1962–68; played 6 one day matches for Derby CCC, 1972; first Test series, against India, 1952; MCC tours to WI, 1953–54, 1959–60, and to Australia, 1958–59, 1962–63 (took a total of 307 Test wickets, 1952–65, incl. 10 in a match and 7 in an innings three times, and was first bowler to take 300 Test wickets, 1963). Journalist, Sunday People, 1957–; anchorman, Indoor League series, Yorks TV; cricket commentator for BBC. *Publications:* Fast Fury, 1961; Cricket, 1963; Book of Cricket, 1964; The Freddie Trueman Story, 1966; Ball of Fire (autobiog.), 1976; (with John Arlott) On Cricket, 1977; Thoughts of Trueman Now, 1978; (with Frank Hardy) You Nearly Had Him That Time, 1978; My Most Memorable Matches, 1982; (with Trevor Bailey) From Larwood to Lillee, 1983; (with Don Mosey) Fred Trueman's Yorkshire, 1984; (with Trevor Bailey) The Spinners' Web, 1988; (with Peter Grosvenor) Fred Trueman's Cricket Masterpieces: classic tales from the pavilion, 1990. *Recreations:* ornithology, working for children's charities. *Address:* c/o BBC, Broadcasting House, W1A 1AA. *Clubs:* Yorkshire County Cricket (Hon. Life Mem.), MCC (Hon. Life Mem.), Lord's Taverners, Variety of GB, Forty, Saint Cricket; Ilkley Golf.

TRUMPINGTON, Baroness *cr* 1980 (Life Peer), of Sandwich in the County of Kent; **Jean Alys Barker;** Minister of State, Ministry of Agriculture, Fisheries and Food, since 1989; *d* of late Arthur Edward Campbell-Harris, MC and late Doris Marie Robson; *m* 1954, William Alan Barker (*d* 1988); one *s. Educ:* privately in England and France. Land Girl to Rt Hon. David Lloyd George, MP, 1940–41; Foreign Office, Bletchley Park, 1941–45; European Central Inland Transport Orgn, 1945–49; Sec. to Viscount Hinchingbrooke, MP, 1950–52. Conservative Councillor, Cambridge City Council, Trumpington Ward, 1963–73; Mayor of Cambridge, 1971–72; Deputy Mayor, 1972–73; Conservative County Councillor, Cambridgeshire, Trumpington Ward, 1973–75; Hon. Councillor of the City of Cambridge, 1975–. Baroness in Waiting (Government Whip), 1983–85; Parly Under-Sec. of State, DHSS, 1985–87, MAFF, 1987–89. UK Delegate to UN Status of Women Commn, 1979–82. Member: Air Transport Users' Cttee, 1972–80 (Dep. Chairman 1978–79, Chm. 1979–80); Bd of Visitors to HM Prison, Pentonville, 1975–81; Mental Health Review Tribunal, 1975–81. Gen. Commissioner of Taxes, 1976–83. Pres., Assoc. of Heads of Independent Schs, 1980–89. Steward, Folkestone Racecourse, 1980–. Hon. Fellow, Lucy Cavendish Coll., Cambridge, 1980. JP Cambridge, 1972–75, South Westminster, 1976–82. *Recreations:* bridge, racing, collecting antiques, needlepoint. *Address:* House of Lords, SW1.

TRURO, Bishop of, since 1990; **Rt. Rev. Michael Thomas Ball,** CGA; *b* 14 Feb. 1932; *s* of Thomas James Ball and Kathleen Bradley Ball *Educ:* Lancing Coll., Sussex; Queens' Coll., Cambridge (BA 1955, MA 1959). Schoolmastering, 1955–76; Co-Founder, Community of the Glorious Ascension, 1960; Prior at Stroud Priory, 1963–76; Curate, Whitehall, Stroud, Glos, 1971–76; Priest-in-charge of Stanmer with Falmer, and Senior Anglican Chaplain to Higher Education in Brighton, including Sussex Univ., 1976–80; Bishop Suffragan of Jarrow, 1980–90. *Recreations:* music, sport, housework. *Address:* Lis Escop, Truro, Cornwall TR3 6QQ. *T:* Truro (0872) 862657.
See also Bishop of Lewes.

TRURO, Dean of; *see* Shearlock, Very Rev. D. J.

TRUSCOTT, Sir George (James Irving), 3rd Bt *cr* 1909; *b* 24 Oct. 1929; *s* of Sir Eric Homewood Stanham Truscott, 2nd Bt, and Lady (Mary Dorcas) Truscott (*née* Irving) (*d* 1948); *S* father, 1973; *m* 1962, Yvonne Dora (*née* Nicholson); one *s* one *d. Educ:* Sherborne School. *Heir: s* Ralph Eric Nicholson Truscott, *b* 21 Feb. 1966. *Address:* BM QUILL, London WC1N 3XX.

TRUSTRAM EVE; *see* Eve, family name of Baron Silsoe.

TRUSWELL, Prof. (Arthur) Stewart, MD, FRCP, FFCM, FRACP; Boden Professor of Human Nutrition, University of Sydney, since 1978; *b* 18 Aug. 1928; *s* of George Truswell and Molly Truswell (*née* Stewart-Hess); *m* 1st, 1956, Sheila McGregor (marr. diss. 1983); four *s*; 2nd, 1986, Catherine Hull; two *d. Educ:* Ruthin Sch., Clwyd; Liverpool and Cape Town Univs. MB, ChB 1952, MD 1959; FRCP 1975; FFCM 1979; FRACP 1980. Registrar in Pathology, Cape Town Univ., 1954; Registrar in Med., Groote Schuur Hosp., 1955–57; Research Bursar, Clin. Nutrition Unit, Dept. of Med., Cape Town Univ., 1958 and 1959; Adams Meml Trav. Fellowship to London, 1960; Sen. Fellow, Clin. Nutrition, Tulane Univ., USA, 1961; Res. Officer, Clin. Nutrition Unit, Cape Town Univ., 1962; Sen. Mem., Scientific Staff, MRC Atheroma Research Unit, Western Infirmary, Glasgow, 1963 and 1964; full-time Lectr, then Sen. Lectr in Med. and Consultant Gen. Physician, Cape Town Univ. and Groote Schuur Hosp., 1965–71; Warden of Med. Students' Residence, Cape Town Univ., 1967–69; Prof. of Nutrition and Dietetics, Queen Elizabeth Coll., London Univ., 1971–78. Vice-Pres., Internat. Union of Nutritional Sciences, 1985–; Member, numerous cttees, working parties, editorial bds and socs related to nutrition. *Publications:* Human Nutrition and Dietetics, 7th edn (with S. Davidson, R. Passmore, J. F. Brock), 1979; ABC of Nutrition, 1986; numerous research papers in sci. jls on various topics in human nutrition and medicine. *Recreations:* gardening, walking (esp. on mountains), running. *Address:* 23 Woonona Road, Northbridge, NSW 2063, Australia; Human Nutrition Unit, Department of Biochemistry, Sydney University, Sydney, NSW 2006, Australia. *T:* 692–3726.

TRYON, family name of **Baron Tryon.**

TRYON, 3rd Baron *cr* 1940, of Durnford; **Anthony George Merrik Tryon;** *b* 26 May 1940; *s* of 2nd Baron Tryon, PC, GCVO, KCB, DSO, and of Etheldreda Josephine, *d* of Sir Merrik Burrell, 7th Bt, CBE; *S* father, 1976; *m* 1973, Dale Elizabeth, *d* of Barry Harper; two *s* two *d* (of whom one *s* one *d* are twins). *Educ:* Eton. Page of Honour to the Queen, 1954–56. Captain Wessex Yeomanry, 1972. Dir, Lazard Bros & Co. Ltd, 1976–83; Chairman: English & Scottish Investors Ltd, 1977–88; Swaine Adeney Brigg, 1991–. Chm., Salisbury Cathedral Spire Trust, 1985–. Pres., Anglers Co-op. Assoc., 1985–. *Recreations:* fishing and shooting. *Heir: s* Hon. Charles George Barrington Tryon, *b* 15 May 1976. *Address:* Ogbury House, Great Durnford, near Salisbury, Wilts. *T:* Middle Woodford (072273) 225. *Clubs:* White's, Pratt's.

TRYON-WILSON, Brig. Charles Edward, CBE 1945 (MBE 1943); DSO 1944; Vice Lord-Lieutenant of Cumbria, 1980–83; *b* 20 Sept. 1909; 2nd *s* of late Charles Robert Tryon; *m* 1st, 1937, Cicely Joan (*d* 1969), *y d* of Captain Henry Whitworth; one *d* (and one *d* decd); 2nd, 1975, Rosemary Lucas. *Educ:* Shawnigan Lake School, BC; Trinity Coll., Glenalmond. Served 60th Rifles, 1927–30, Royal Fusiliers, 1930–36 and 1938–45 (N Africa, Italy, Austria; despatches twice). DL Westmorland (later Cumbria), 1971–85. *Recreations:* shooting, fishing. *Address:* Dallam Tower, Milnthorpe, Cumbria LA7 7AG. *T:* Milnthorpe (05395) 63368. *Clubs:* Army and Navy, Lansdowne; Flyfishers' (Buck's).

TRYPANIS, Constantine Athanasius, MA (Oxon); DLitt (Oxon) 1970; DPhil (Athens); FRSL; Secretary-General, 1981–85, President, 1986, Academy of Athens; Minister of Culture and Science, Government of Greece, 1974–77; *b* Chios, 22 Jan. 1909; *s* of Athanasius G. Trypanis and Maria Zolota; *m* 1942, Alice Macri; one *d*. *Educ*: Chios Gymnasium; Universities of Athens, Berlin and Munich. Classical Lecturer, Athens Univ., 1939–47; Bywater and Sotheby Professor of Byzantine and Modern Greek Language and Literature, and Fellow of Exeter Coll., Oxford, 1947–68; Emeritus Fellow, 1968–; Univ. Prof. of Classics, Chicago Univ., 1968–74, Emeritus Prof., 1974–. Gray Lectr, Cambridge Univ., 1947. Mem. Poetry Panel, Arts Council of GB, 1962–65. FRSL, 1958; Hon. FBA 1978; Life Fellow, International Institute of Arts and Letters, 1958; Member Institute for Advanced Study, Princeton, USA, 1959–60; Visiting Professor: Hunter Coll., New York, 1963; Harvard Univ., 1963, 1964; Univ. of Chicago, 1965–66; Univ. of Cape Town, 1969; Univ. of Vienna, 1971. Corresp. Mem., Inst. for Balkan Studies (Greece); Member: Athens Academy, 1974 (Corres. Mem., 1971); Medieval Acad. of America; Accademia Tiburina, Rome, 1982. Hon. Fellow, Internat. Poetry Soc., 1977; Fellow: Greek Archaeol Soc., 1985; Soc. for Promotion of Greek Letters, 1985; Hon. Mem., Soc. for Promotion of Hellenic Studies, 1979; Hon. MRIA 1988. Dr of Humane Letters *hc*: MacMurray Coll., USA, 1974; Assumption Coll., 1977. Gottfried von Herder Prize, Vienna Univ., 1983. Ordre des Arts et des Lettres; Ordre National du Mérite. Archon Megas Hieromnemon of the Oekumenical Patriarchate. *Publications*: Influence of Hesiod upon Homeric Hymn of Hermes, 1939; Influence of Hesiod upon Homeric Hymn on Apollo, 1940; Alexandrian Poetry, 1943; Tartessos, 1945; Medieval and Modern Greek Poetry, 1951; Pedasus, 1955; Callimachus, 1956; The Stones of Troy, 1956; The Cocks of Hades, 1958; (with P. Maas) Sancti Romani Melodi Cantica, 1963, vol. II, 1970; Pompeian Dog, 1964; The Elegies of a Glass Adonis, 1967; Fourteen Early Byzantine Cantica, 1968; (ed) The Penguin Book of Greek Verse, 1971; The Glass Adonis, 1973; The Homeric Epics, 1975; Greek Poetry: from Homer to Seferis, 1981; Atticism and the Greek Language Question, 1984; Skias Onar (poems in Greek), 1986; (trans.) Sophocles, Three Theban Plays, 1986; Katalepton (poems in Greek), 1990; articles in Enc. Brit., Oxford Classical Dictionary and in classical and literary periodicals. *Recreations*: walking, tennis, painting. *Address*: 3 Georgiou Nikolaou Kefisia, 14561 Athens, Greece. *Clubs*: Athenæum; Athens.

TRYTHALL, Maj.-Gen. Anthony John, CB 1983; Director of Army Education, 1980–84; Executive Deputy Chairman, Brassey's (UK) Ltd, since 1988 (Managing Director, 1984–87); *b* 30 March 1927; *s* of Eric Stewart Trythall and Irene (*née* Hollingham); *m* 1952, Celia Haddon; two *s* one *d*. *Educ*: Lawrence Sheriff Sch., Rugby; St Edmund Hall, Oxford (BA Hons Mod. Hist., 1947, DipEd 1951); Institute of Education, London Univ. (Academic DipEd 1962); King's College, London (MA in War Studies, 1969). National Service as RAEC Officer, UK, Egypt and Akaba, 1947–49; teaching, 1951–53; Regular RAEC Officer, 1953; seconded to Malay Regt for service at Fedn Mil. Coll., Port Dickson, 1953–56; WO, 1957–62; BAOR, 1962–66; Inspector, 1967–68; Educn Adviser, Regular Commns Bd, 1969–71; Head of Officer Educn Br., 1971–73; Chief Inspector of Army Educn, and Col Res., 1973–74; MoD, 1974–76; Chief Educn Officer, UKLF, 1976–80. Col Comdt, RAEC, 1986–89. Member: Council, Royal United Services Instn for Def. Studies, 1978–84; London Univ. Bd of War Studies, 1983–; Chm., Gallipoli Meml Lecture Trust, 1986–89. 1st Prize, Trench-Gascoigne Essay Competition, 1969. *Publications*: Boney Fuller: the intellectual general, 1977 (USA, as Boney Fuller: soldier, strategist and writer); (contrib.) The Downfall of Leslie Hore-Belisha in the Second World War, 1982; Fuller and the Tanks in Home Fires and Foreign Fields, 1985; articles in Army Qly, Jl of RUSI, British Army Rev., and Jl of Contemp. Hist. *Address*: c/o Royal Bank of Scotland, Holt's Whitehall Branch, Kirkland House, Whitehall, SW1A 2EB. *Club*: Naval and Military.

TS'ONG, Fou; *see* Fou Ts'ong.

TSUI, Prof. Lap-Chee, PhD; FRS 1991; FRSC 1989; Staff Geneticist and Senior Research Scientist, since 1983, Sellers Professor in Cystic Fibrosis Research, since 1989, Hospital for Sick Children, Toronto; Professor, Department of Molecular and Medical Genetics, University of Toronto, since 1990; *b* 21 Dec. 1950; *s* of Jing-Lue Hsue and Hui-Ching Wang; *m* 1977, Lan Fong (Ellen); two *s*. *Educ*: Chinese Univ. of Hong Kong (BSc Biol. 1972; MPhil 1974); Univ. of Pittsburgh (PhD Biol Scis 1979). Asst Prof. 1983–88, Associate Prof. 1988–90, Depts of Med. Genetics and Med. Biophysics, Univ. of Toronto. Trustee, Educn Foundn, Fedn of Chinese Canadian Professionals, Ontario. Paul di Sant'Agnese Distinguished Scientific Achievement Award, Cystic Fibrosis Foundn, USA, 1989; Gold Medal of Honor, Pharmaceutical Manufacturers' Assoc., Canada, 1989; Centennial Award, RSCan, 1989; Maclean's Honor Roll, 1989; Award of Excellence, Genetic Soc. Canada, 1990; Couvoisier Leadership Award, 1990; Gairdner Internat. Award, 1990. *Publications*: numerous papers in learned jls and invited papers and reviews. *Recreations*: cooking, travel, sightseeing. *Address*: Department of Genetics, Hospital for Sick Children, 555 University Avenue, Toronto, Ont M5G 1X8, Canada. *T*: (416) 598–6015, *Fax*: (416) 591–4931.

TUAM, Archbishop of, (RC), since 1987; **Most Rev. Joseph Cassidy;** *b* 29 Oct. 1933; *s* of John Cassidy and Mary Gallagher. *Educ*: St Nathy's College, Maynooth; University College, Galway. Professor, Garbally College, Ballinasloe, 1959–77, President 1977–79; Coadjutor Bishop of Clonfert, 1979–82; Bishop of Clonfert, 1982–87; Spokesman for Irish Bishops' Conference, 1980–88. *Publications*: plays, articles and homilies. *Address*: Archbishop's House, Tuam, Co. Galway, Ireland. *T*: Tuam 24166.

TUAM, KILLALA AND ACHONRY, Bishop of, since 1986; **Rt. Rev. John Robert Winder Neill;** *b* 17 Dec. 1945; *s* of Eberto Mahon Neill and Rhoda Anne Georgina Neill; *m* 1968, Betty Anne (*née* Cox); three *s*. *Educ*: Sandford Park School, Dublin; Trinity Coll., Dublin (Foundation Schol., BA 1st Cl., MA); Jesus Coll., Cambridge (MA, Gardiner Memorial Schol., Univ. of Cambridge); Ridley Hall, Cambridge (GOE). Curate Asst, St Paul's, Glenageary, Dublin, 1969–71; Lectr (Old Testament) in Divinity Hostel, 1970–71; Bishop's Vicar and Dio. Registrar, Kilkenny, 1971–74; Rector of Abbeystrewry, Skibbereen, Co. Cork, 1974–78; Rector of St Bartholomew's, and Leeson Park, Dublin, 1978–84; Lectr (Liturgy) in Theological Coll., 1982–84; Exam. Chaplain to Archbishop of Dublin, 1982–84; Dean of Christ Church Cathedral, Waterford, 1984–86; Archdeacon of Waterford, 1984–86. Sec., Irish House of Bishops, 1988–; Pres., Council of Churches for Britain and Ireland, 1990–. *Publications*: contribs to Theology, New Divinity, Search, Doctrine and Life and Intercom. *Recreations*: photography, travel. *Address*: Bishop's House, Knockglass, Crossmolina, Co. Mayo, Ireland. *T*: Ballina 31317.

TUBBS, Oswald Sydney, FRCS; Consulting Surgeon: in Cardiothoracic Surgery, St Bartholomew's Hospital; to Brompton Hospital; *b* 21 March 1908; *s* of late Sydney Walter Tubbs, The Glebe, Hadley Common, Hertfordshire; *m* 1934, Marjorie Betty Wilkins (*d* 1976); one *s* one *d*. *Educ*: Shrewsbury School; Caius College, Cambridge; St Bartholomew's Hospital. MA, MB, BCh, FRCS. Surgical training at St Bartholomew's Hosp. and Brompton Hosp. Dorothy Temple Cross Fellowship, spent as Surgical Fellow at Lahey Clinic, Boston, USA. Served War of 1939–45, in EMS. Consulting Chest Surgeon to Royal Navy, Papworth Village Settlement and to various Local Authorities. President: Soc. of Thoracic and Cardiovascular Surgeons of GB and Ireland, 1971–72;

Thoracic Soc., 1973. *Publications*: papers on surgical subjects. *Recreations*: fishing and gardening. *Address*: The White Cottage, 136 Coast Road, West Mersea, Colchester, Essex CO5 8PA. *T*: Colchester (0206) 382355.

TUBBS, Ralph, OBE 1952; FRIBA; architect; *b* 9 Jan. 1912; *s* of late Sydney W. Tubbs and Mabel Frost; *m* 1946, Mary Taberner; two *s* one *d*. *Educ*: Mill Hill School; Architectural Assoc. School (Hons Dip.). Sec. MARS Group (Modern Architectural Research), 1939; Member: Council and Executive Committee of RIBA, 1944–50, re-elected Council, 1951; Vice-Pres. Architectural Assoc., 1945–47; Associate Institute of Landscape Architects, 1942–. Member Presentation Panel and Design Group for 1951 Festival of Britain, and architect of Dome of Discovery in London Exhibn (then the largest dome in world, 365 ft diam.). Other works include: Baden-Powell House for Boy Scouts' Assoc., London; Indian Students' Union building, Fitzroy Sq., London; Granada TV Centre and Studios, Manchester; Cambridge Inst. Educn; Halls of residence for University Coll., London, Residential Areas at Harlow and Basildon New Towns; Industrial Buildings. Architect for new Charing Cross Hospital and Med. Sch., London; Consultant for Hospital Develt, Jersey, CI. Pres., British Entomological and Natural Hist. Soc., 1977; Vice-Pres., Royal Entomol Soc. of London, 1982–84. *Publications*: Living in Cities, 1942; The Englishman Builds (Penguin), 1945. *Recreation*: study of the natural world. *Address*: 9 Lingfield Road, Wimbledon, SW19 4QA. *T*: 081–946 2010.

TUCK, Anthony; *see* Tuck, J. A.

TUCK, Sir Bruce (Adolph Reginald), 3rd Bt, *cr* 1910; *b* 29 June 1926; *o s* of Major Sir (William) Reginald Tuck, 2nd Bt, and Gladys Emily Kettle (*d* 1966), *d* of late N. Alfred Nathan, Wickford, Auckland, New Zealand, and *widow* of Desmond Fosberry Kettle, Auckland Mounted Rifles; *S* father 1954; *m* 1st, 1949, Luise (marr. diss., in Jamaica, 1964), *d* of John C. Renfro, San Angelo, Texas, USA; two *s*; 2nd, 1968, Pamela Dorothy Nicholson, *d* of Alfred Nicholson, London; one *d*. *Educ*: Canford School, Dorset. Lieutenant, Scots Guards, 1945–47. *Heir*: *s* Richard Bruce Tuck, *b* 7 Oct. 1952. *Address*: PO Box 274, Montego Bay, Jamaica.

TUCK, Clarence Edward Henry; Civil Service Commissioner, 1977–83; *b* 18 April 1925; *s* of Frederick and May Tuck; *m* 1950, Daphne Robinson; one *s* one *d*. *Educ*: Rendcomb Coll., Cirencester; Merton Coll., Oxford. BA 1949. Served in Royal Signals, 1943–47. Inland Revenue, 1950; Min. of Supply, 1950–55; seconded to Nigerian Federal Govt, Lagos, 1955–57; Ministry of Supply, 1957–59; Aviation, 1959–60; Defence, 1960–62; Aviation, 1962–66; IDC, 1967; Min. of Technology, 1968–70; Trade and Industry, 1970; CSD, 1971; Trade and Industry, 1973; Dept of Energy, 1974; Civil Service Dept, 1976; Management and Personnel Office, 1981; Dir, Civil Service Selection Board, 1977–81. Asst Principal, 1950; Principal, 1953; Asst Sec., 1962; Under-Sec., 1970.

TUCK, Prof. (John) Anthony, MA, PhD; FRHistS; Professor of Medieval History, University of Bristol, since 1990; *b* 14 Nov. 1940; *s* of Prof. John Philip Tuck, *qv*; *m* 1976, Amanda, *d* of Dr L. J. Cawley, Carlton Husthwaite, near Thirsk, Yorks; two *s*. *Educ*: Newcastle upon Tyne Royal Grammar Sch.; Jesus Coll., Cambridge (BA, MA, PhD). FRHistS 1987. Lecturer in History, 1965–75, Sen. Lectr, 1975–78, Univ. of Lancaster; Master of Collingwood Coll., and Hon. Lectr in History, Univ. of Durham, 1978–87; Reader in Medieval History, Univ. of Bristol, 1987–90. *Publications*: Richard II and the English Nobility, 1973; Crown and Nobility 1272–1461, 1985; contribs to English Historical Rev., Northern History, etc. *Recreations*: walking, gardening. *Address*: 66A Hill View, Henleaze, Bristol BS9 4PU. *T*: Bristol (0272) 622953.

TUCK, Prof. John Philip; Professor of Education, University of Newcastle upon Tyne (formerly King's College, University of Durham) 1948–76, now Emeritus; *b* 16 April 1911; *s* of late William John and Annie Tuck, Uplyme, Lyme Regis; *m* 1936, Jane Adelaide (*née* Wall); two *s*. *Educ*: Strand School; Jesus College, Cambridge. BA Hons English and History, Class I, 1933; Cambridge certificate in Education, 1934; Adelaide Stoll Bachelor Research Scholar, Christ's College, 1935; MA 1937. English Master: Gateshead Grammar School, 1936; Manchester Central High School, 1938; Wilson's Grammar School, 1939 and 1946. Served War of 1939–45, East Surrey Regt, and Army Education Corps, N Africa, Sicily, Italy, Austria. Lecturer in Education, King's College, Newcastle upon Tyne, 1946–48. Mem. Council, GPDST, 1976–84. FRSA 1970. Hon. Fellow, Coll. of Speech Therapists, 1966. *Address*: 7 Chesterford House, Southacre Drive, Chaucer Road, Cambridge CB2 2TZ. *T*: Cambridge (0223) 324655.

See also J. A. Tuck.

TUCK, Prof. Ronald Humphrey; Professor of Agricultural Economics, University of Reading, 1965–86 (part-time, 1982–86), now Emeritus; *b* 28 June 1921; *s* of Francis Tuck and Edith Ann Tuck (*née* Bridgewater); *m* Margaret Sylvia Everley (*d* 1990); one *s* two *d*. *Educ*: Harrow County Sch.; Corpus Christi Coll., Oxford. War Service, RAOC and REME, mainly N Africa and Italy, 1941–45 (despatches). Univ. of Reading, Dept of Agric. Economics: Research Economist, 1947–49; Lecturer, 1949–62; Reader, 1962–65; Head of Dept of Agricultural Economics and Management, Univ. of Reading, and Provincial Agricultural Economist (Reading Province), 1965–81; Dean, Faculty of Agriculture and Food, Univ. of Reading, 1971–74. *Publications*: An Essay on the Economic Theory of Rank, 1954; An Introduction to the Principles of Agricultural Economics, 1961 (Italian trans., 1970); reviews etc in Jl of Agric. Economics and Economic Jl. *Recreations*: reading, music, drawing, walking. *Address*: 211 Kidmore Road, Caversham, Reading, Berks. *T*: Reading (0734) 473426.

TUCKER, Brian George, CB 1976; OBE 1963; Deputy Secretary, Department of Energy, 1974–81; Member, UKAEA, 1976–81; *b* 6 May 1922; *s* of late Frank Ernest Tucker and May Tucker; *m* 1948, Marion Pollitt; three *d*. *Educ*: Christ's Hospital. Entered Home Civil Service, 1939, as Clerical Officer, Admty; successive postings at home, in Africa, the Middle East, Ceylon and Hong Kong till 1953; promoted Executive Officer, 1945; Higher Executive Officer, 1949. Min. of Power, Asst Principal, 1954, Principal, 1957; seconded to HMOCS, 1957–62, Asst Sec., Govt of Northern Rhodesia; returned to MOP, 1962, Principal Private Sec. to Minister, 1965–66, Asst Sec., 1966, Under-Sec., Ministry of Technology, 1969–70, Cabinet Office, 1970–72, DTI, 1972–73; Dep. Sec., 1973. *Recreations*: gardening, music. *Address*: 1 Sondes Place Drive, Dorking, Surrey RH4 3ED. *T*: Dorking (0306) 884720.

TUCKER, Clive Fenemore; Under Secretary, Department of Employment, since 1987; *b* 13 July 1944; *s* of William Frederick Tucker and Joan Tucker; *m* 1978, Caroline Elisabeth Macready; two *d*. *Educ*: Cheltenham Grammar Sch.; Balliol Coll., Oxford (BA). Entered Ministry of Labour, 1965; Private Sec. to Perm. Sec., 1968–70; Department of Employment: Principal, 1970; Asst Sec., 1978; Grade 4, 1986. Non-exec. Dir, RTZ Chemicals, 1987–90. *Recreations*: opera, looking at pictures, tennis. *Address*: c/o Department of Employment, Caxton House, Tothill Street, SW1H 9NF.

TUCKER, Rt. Rev. Cyril James, CBE 1975; *b* 17 Nov. 1911; British; *s* of Henry Castledine and Lilian Beatrice Tucker; *m* 1936, Kathleen Mabel, *d* of Major Merry; one *s* two *d*. *Educ*: Highgate Sch.; St Catharine's Coll., Cambridge (MA; athletics blue, 1934); Ridley Hall, Cambridge. MA Oxford (by Incorporation), 1951. Deacon, 1935; Priest,

1936; Curate, St Mark's, Dalston (in charge Highgate Sch. Mission), 1935; Curate, St Barnabas, Cambridge, 1937; Youth Sec., British and Foreign Bible Soc., 1938. Chaplain, RAFVR, 1939–46. Warden of Monmouth Sch., 1946; Chaplain, Wadham Coll., Oxford, and Chaplain of the Oxford Pastorate, 1949; Vicar of Holy Trinity, Cambridge, 1957–63; Rural Dean of Cambridge, 1959–63; Chaplain of the Cambridge Pastorate, 1957–63; Bishop in Argentina and Eastern S America, 1963–75; Bishop of the Falkland Islands, 1963–76. Hon. Exec. Dir, Argentine Dio. Assoc., 1976–83. *Recreations:* walking, fishing. *Address:* 202 Gilbert Road, Cambridge CB4 3PB. *T:* Cambridge (0223) 358345. *Clubs:* Hawks (Cambridge); Hurlingham (Buenos Aires).

TUCKER, Edward William, CB 1969; Head of Royal Naval Engineering Service, 1966–70; Director of Dockyards, Ministry of Defence, at Bath, 1967–70, retired; *b* 3 Nov. 1908; *s* of Henry Tucker, Plymouth; *m* 1935, Eva (*d* 1986), *d* of Arthur Banks, Plymouth. *Educ:* Imperial Coll. of Science and Technology, London Univ.; Royal Naval Coll., Greenwich. BSc (Eng). Electrical Engineer in Admiralty service, at Plymouth, London, Hong Kong and Bath, 1935–64; General Manager of HM Dockyard, Chatham, 1964–66. *Recreation:* bridge. *Address:* 18 Salt Quay Moorings, Embankment Road, Kingsbridge, Devon. *T:* Kingsbridge (0548) 856894.

TUCKER, Elizabeth Mary; Head Mistress, Headington School, Oxford, since 1982; *b* 20 July 1936; *d* of Harold and Doris Tucker. *Educ:* Cheltenham Ladies' College; Newnham College, Cambridge (MA Classical Tripos); King's College London (PGCE). Assistant Mistress, Queen Anne's School, Caversham, 1959–64; Head of Classics, Notting Hill and Ealing High School, GPDST, 1964–72; Head Mistress, Christ's Hospital, Hertford, 1972–82. Mem. Council, St Hugh's Sch., Faringdon. Trustee, Bloxham Project, 1982–. *Recreations:* music (piano, spinet, singing), art and architecture (sketching), fell walking, travel. *Address:* Headington School, Oxford OX3 7TD. *T:* Oxford (0865) 62711. *Club:* University Women's.

TUCKER, (Henry John) Martin, QC 1975; **His Honour Judge Tucker;** a Circuit Judge, since 1981; *b* 8 April 1930; *s* of late P. A. Tucker, LDS, RCS and Mrs Dorothy Tucker (*née* Hobbs); *m* 1957, Sheila Helen Wateridge, LRAM; one *s* four *d*. *Educ:* St Peter's Sch., Southbourne; Downside Sch.; Christ Church, Oxford (MA). Called to Bar, Inner Temple, 1954; Dep. Chm., Somerset QS, 1971; a Recorder of the Crown Court, 1972–81. *Recreations:* walking occasionally; gardening gently; listening to music. *Address:* Chingri Khal, Sleepers Hill, Winchester, Hants SO22 4NB. *T:* Winchester (0962) 853927. *Club:* Hampshire (Winchester).

TUCKER, Herbert Harold, OBE 1965; HM Diplomatic Service, retired; Secretary, Roberts Centre; Consultant, Dulverton Trust, since 1989; *b* 4 Dec. 1925; *o s* of late Francis Tucker and late Mary Ann Tucker; *m* 1948, Mary Stewart Dunlop; three *s*. *Educ:* Queen Elizabeth's, Lincs; Rossington Main, Yorks. Western Morning News, Sheffield Telegraph, Nottingham Journal, Daily Telegraph, 1944–51; Economic Information Unit, Treasury, 1948–49; FO, later FCO, 1951; Counsellor (Information) and Dir, British Information Services, Canberra, 1974–78; Consul-General, Vancouver, 1979–83; Disarmament Information Coordinator, FCO, 1983–84. Consultant, Centre for Security and Conflict Studies, 1986–89. *Publication:* (ed) Combating the Terrorists, 1988. *Recreations:* gardening, reading, watercolouring. *Address:* Pullens Cottage, Leigh Hill Road, Cobham, Surrey KT11 2HX. *T:* Cobham (0932) 864461. *Clubs:* Travellers', Commonwealth Trust.

TUCKER, Martin; *see* Tucker, H. J. M.

TUCKER, Peter Louis; practising barrister, Sierra Leone; Commissioner/Chairman, Sierra Leone Population Census, since 1984; *b* 11 Dec. 1927; *s* of Peter Louis Tucker and Marion Tucker; *m* 1st, 1955, Clarissa Mary Harleston; three *s* one *d* (and one *d* decd); 2nd, 1972, Teresa Josephine Ganda; one *s*. *Educ:* Fourah Bay Coll., Sierra Leone (MA Latin, Dunelm); Jesus Coll., Oxford (MA Jurisp.); DipEd. Called to Bar, Gray's Inn, 1970. Teacher, 1952–57; Education Officer, 1957–61; Secretary, Training and Recruitment, Sierra Leone Civil Service, 1961–63; Establishment Sec., 1963–66; Sec. to the Prime Minister and Head of Sierra Leone Civil Service, 1966–67; Asst Director, UK Immigrants Advisory Service, 1970–72; Principal Admin. Officer, Community Relations Commn, 1972–74, Dir of Fieldwork and Admin., 1974–77; Dir of Legal and Gen. Services, and Sec., 1977, Chief Exec., 1977–82, CRE; Special Envoy on Foreign Aid to Sierra Leone and Chm., Nat. Aid Co-ordinating Cttee, 1986; Chm., National Constitutional Review Commn, 1990–91. DCL (*hc*) Sierra Leone. Papal Medal Pro Ecclesia et Pontifice, 1966. *Publications:* miscellaneous booklets, articles and reports for Community Relations Commission and Govt of Sierra Leone. *Recreations:* photography, listening to music. *Address:* 1 Forest Road Hill Station, Free Town, Sierra Leone. *T:* Sierra Leone 24868; (home) 236414.

TUCKER, Hon. Sir Richard (Howard), Kt 1985; **Hon. Mr Justice Tucker;** a Judge of the High Court of Justice, Queen's Bench Division, since 1985; *b* 9 July 1930; *s* of Howard Archibald Tucker, later His Honour Judge Tucker, and Margaret Minton Tucker; *m* 1st, 1958, Paula Mary Bennett Frost (marr. diss. 1974); one *s* two *d*; 2nd, 1975, Wendy Kate Standbrook (*d* 1988); 3rd, 1989, Jacqueline Suzanne Rossvell, *widow* of William Thomson, artist. *Educ:* Shrewsbury Sch.; The Queen's Coll., Oxford (MA). Called to Bar, Lincoln's Inn, 1954; Bencher, 1979. QC 1972; a Recorder, 1972–85; Mem. Senate, Inns of Court and the Bar, 1984–86; Dep. Leader, 1984–85, and Presiding Judge, 1986–90, Midland and Oxford Circuit. Mem., Employment Appeal Tribunal, 1986–. *Recreations:* sailing, shooting, gardening. *Address:* Royal Courts of Justice, Strand, WC2. *Clubs:* Garrick; Leander (Henley-on-Thames); Bar Yacht.

TUCKER, Robert St John P.; *see* Pitts-Tucker.

TUCKEY, Andrew Marmaduke Lane; Chairman, Baring Brothers & Co., Ltd, since 1989; Deputy Chairman, Barings plc, since 1989; *b* 28 Aug. 1943; *s* of late Henry Lane Tuckey and of Aileen Rosemary Newson Tuckey; *m* 1967, Margaret Louise (*née* Barnes); one *s* two *d*. *Educ:* Plumtree Sch., Zimbabwe. Chartered Accountant, 1966. Dixon Wilson, Chartered Accountants, 1962–66; British American Tobacco, 1966–68; Baring Brothers & Co., Ltd, 1968–: Dir, 1973–81; Man. Dir, 1981–89. Dir and Treasurer, Friends of Covent Garden, 1981–; Trustee, Esmée Fairbairn Charitable Trust, 1986–. *Recreations:* music, tennis. *Address:* 36 Lonsdale Road, SW13 9EB. *T:* 081–748 9893. *Clubs:* City of London, Roehampton.

See also S. L. Tuckey.

TUCKEY, Simon Lane, QC 1981; a Recorder, since 1984; *b* 17 Oct. 1941; *s* of late Henry Lane Tuckey and of Aileen Rosemary Newsom Tuckey; *m* 1964, Jennifer Rosemary (*née* Hardie); one *s* two *d*. *Educ:* Plumtree School, Zimbabwe. Called to Bar, Lincoln's Inn, 1964, Bencher, 1989. Chm., Review Panel, Financial Reporting Council, 1990–. *Recreations:* sailing, tennis. *Address:* 6 Regent's Park Terrace, NW1. *T:* 071–485 8952.

See also A. M. L. Tuckey.

TUCKMAN, Frederick Augustus, (Fred), OBE 1990; FCIS, FIPM; *b* 9 June 1922; *s* of Otto and Amy Tina Tuchmann (*née* Adler); *m* 1966, Patricia Caroline Myers; two *s* one *d*. *Educ:* English and German schools; London School of Economics, 1946–49 (BScEcon). Served RAF, 1942–46. Commercial posts, 1950–65; Management Consultant and Partner, HAY Gp, 1965–85; Managing Director, HAY GmbH, Frankfurt, 1970–80; Partner, HAY Associates, 1975–85; Chm., Suomen HAY, OY, Helsinki, 1973–81; consultant assignments in Europe, Africa and N America. Hon. Sec., Bow Gp, 1958–59; Councillor, London Borough of Camden, 1965–71 (Chm., Library and Arts, 1968–71). Mem. (C) Leicester, European Parliament, 1979–89; contested (C) Leicester, Eur. Parly elecn, 1989. Mem. Council, Inst. of Personnel Management, 1963–70. Chm., Greater London Area, CPC, 1968–70. European Parliament: Budget Cttee, 1979–81; Social and Employment Cttee, 1981–89 (Cons. spokesman, 1984–89); substitute Mem., Economic and Monetary Cttee, 1979–87; substitute Mem., Budgetary Control Cttee, 1984–87; First Vice Pres., Latin American Delegn, 1982–85; Mem., Israel Delegn, 1987–89; Chm., Internat. Gp on Small Business, 1985–86. UK Chm., European Year of Small Business, 1983; Vice Chm., Small Business Bureau, London, 1985–89. Pres., Anglo-Jewish Assoc., 1989– (Vice-Pres., 1988–89); Vice Pres., Eur. Medium and Small Units, 1985–. Cross, Order of Merit (FRG), 1989. *Recreations:* reading, arguing, travel, swimming; priority—family. *Address:* 6 Cumberland Road, Barnes, SW13 9LY. *T:* 081–748 2392. *Clubs:* Athenæum, Carlton.

TUCKWELL, Barry Emmanuel, OBE 1965; horn soloist; conductor; Conductor and Music Director, Maryland Symphony Orchestra, since 1982; *b* 5 March 1931; *s* of Charles Tuckwell, Australia; married twice; two *s* one *d*. *Educ:* various schs, Australia; Sydney Conservatorium. Melbourne Symph. Orch., 1947; Sydney Symph. Orch., 1947–50; Hallé Orch., 1951–53; Scottish Nat. Orch., 1953–54; Bournemouth Symphony Orch., 1954–55; London Symph. Orch., 1955–68; founded Tuckwell Wind Quintet, 1968; Conductor, Tasmanian Symphony Orch., 1979–83. Mem. Chamber Music Soc. of Lincoln Center, 1974–81; Horn Prof., Royal Academy of Music, 1963–74; Pres., Internat. Horn Soc., 1969–77. Plays and conducts annually throughout Europe, Gt Britain, USA and Canada; has appeared at many internat. festivals, incl. Salzburg and Edinburgh; took part in 1st Anglo-Soviet Music Exchange, Leningrad and Moscow, 1963; toured: Far East, 1964 and 1975; Australia, 1970–; S America, 1976; USSR, 1977; People's Republic of China, 1984. Many works dedicated to him; has made numerous recordings. Editor, complete horn literature for G. Schirmer Inc. Hon. RAM, 1966; Hon. GSM, 1967. Harriet Cohen Internat. Award for Solo Instruments, 1968; Grammy Award Nominations. *Publications:* Playing the Horn, 1978; The Horn, 1981. *Club:* Athenæum.

TUDHOPE, David Hamilton, CMG 1984; DFC 1944, and Bar 1944; Chairman, National Bank of New Zealand, since 1983; Director, Steel & Tube Ltd, since 1986; *b* 9 Nov. 1921; *s* of William and Sybil Tudhope; *m* 1946, Georgina Charity Lee; two *s* two *d*. *Educ:* Wanganui Collegiate Sch., NZ; King's Coll., Cambridge (MA, LLB). Served War, 1941–45: Pilot RNZAF, UK (Flt Lieut) (DFC and Bar, Pathfinder Force, Bomber Comd). Barrister and Solicitor, NZ, 1947–49; Shell Oil, NZ, 1949–60; Gen. Manager, Shell Oil Rhodesia, N Rhodesia and Nyasaland, 1960–62; Area Co-ordinator, Shell London, 1962–67; Chm. and Chief Exec., Shell Interests in NZ, 1967–81; Chm., Shell BP & Todd Oil Services, 1967–81; Chm. (in rotation), NZ Oil Refinery, 1969, 1974, 1980, and Maui Development, 1975, 1980; Chm., National Mutual Life Assoc., 1983–88; Director: Shell Holdings Ltd, 1981–87; Commercial Union Insurance, 1982–88. Dep. Chm., Crown Corp., 1984–86. Chm., Pukeiti Rhododendron Trust, 1981–90. *Recreations:* gardening, golf. *Address:* 7 Cluny Avenue, Kelburn, Wellington, New Zealand. *T:* Wellington 759–358. *Club:* Wellington.

TUDHOPE, James Mackenzie, CB 1987; Chairman of Social Security Appeal Tribunals, since 1987; *b* 11 Feb. 1927; *m* Margaret Willock Kirkwood, MA Glasgow; two *s*. *Educ:* Dunoon Grammar School; Univ. of Glasgow (BL 1951). Admitted Solicitor, 1951. Private legal practice, 1951–55; Procurator Fiscal Depute, 1955, Senior PF Depute, 1962, Asst PF, 1968–70, Glasgow; PF, Kilmarnock, 1970–73, Dumbarton, 1973–76; Regional Procurator Fiscal: S Strathclyde, Dumfries and Galloway at Hamilton, 1976–80; for Glasgow and Strathkelvin, 1980–87. Hon. Sheriff, N Strathclyde, 1989–. Mem. Council, Law Soc. of Scotland, 1983–86. *Recreation:* serendipity.

TUDOR, Sir James Cameron, KCMG 1987 (CMG 1970); Minister of Foreign Affairs and Leader of the Senate, Barbados, since 1986; *b* St Michael, Barbados, 18 Oct. 1919; *e s* of James A. Tudor, JP, St Michael, Barbados; unmarried. *Educ:* Roebuck Boys' Sch.; Combermere Sch.; Harrison Coll., Barbados; Lodge Sch.; (again) Harrison Coll.; Keble Coll., Oxford, 1939–43. BA Hons (Mod. Greats), 1943, MA 1948; Pres., Oxford Union, 1942. Broadcaster, BBC: Lobby Correspondent (Parliament); Overseas Service, 1942–44; Lectr, Extra-Mural Dept, Reading Univ., 1944–45; History Master, Combermere Sch., Barbados, 1946–48; Civics and History Master, Queen's Coll., British Guiana, 1948–51; Sixth Form Master, Modern High Sch., Barbados, 1952–61, also free-lance Journalist, Lectr, Broadcaster, over the same period. Mem., Barbados Lab. Party, 1951–52; MLC, Barbados, 1954–72; Foundn Mem., Democratic Lab. Party, 1955 (Gen. Sec., 1955–63; Third Vice-Chm., 1964–65 and 1965–66). Minister: of Educn, 1961–67; of State for Caribbean and Latin American Affairs, 1967–71 (Leader of the House, 1965–71); of External Affairs, 1971–72 (Leader of the Senate, 1971–72); High Comr for Barbados in UK, 1972–75; Perm. Rep. of Barbados to UN, 1976–79. Mem. Council, Univ. of the West Indies, 1962–65; awarded US State Dept Foreign Leader Grant, to study US Educn Instns, 1962. Silver Star, Order of Christopher Columbus (Dominican Republic), 1969. *Recreations:* reading, lecturing; keen on Masonic and other fraternities. *Address:* Lemon Grove, Westbury New Road, St Michael, Barbados.

TUDOR, Rev. Dr (Richard) John, BA; Superintendent Minister, Westminster Central Hall, London, since 1981; *b* 8 Feb. 1930; *s* of Charles Leonard and Ellen Tudor; *m* 1956, Cynthia Campbell Anderson; one *s* one *d*. *Educ:* Clee Grammar Sch., Grimsby; Queen Elizabeth's, Barnet; Univ. of Manchester, 1951–54 (BA Theology). Served RAF, 1948–51. Junior Methodist Minister, East Ham, London, 1954–57; Ordained, Newark, 1957; Minister, Thornton Cleveleys, Blackpool, 1957–60; Superintendent Minister: Derby Methodist Mission, 1960–71: Chaplain to Mayor of Derby, Factories and Association with Derby Football Club; Coventry Methodist Mission, 1971–75; Chaplain to Lord Mayor; Brighton Dome Mission, 1975–81; Free Church Chaplain, Westminster Hosp., 1982–; Chaplain to Ancient Order of Foresters Charity Stewards, 1989–. Hon. DD Texas Wesleyan Univ., Fort Worth, USA, 1981; Hon. Texan, 1965; Freeman of Fort Worth, 1970. *Recreations:* motoring, cooking, photography, the delights of family life. *Address:* The Methodist Church, Central Hall, Westminster, SW1. *T:* 071–222 8010.

TUDOR EVANS, Hon. Sir Haydn, Kt 1974; **Hon. Mr Justice Tudor Evans;** a Judge of the High Court of Justice, Queen's Bench Division, since 1978 (Family Division, 1974–78); a Judge of the Employment Appeal Tribunal, since 1982; *b* 20 June 1920; 4th *s* of John Edgar Evans and Ellen Stringer; *m* 1947, Sheilagh Isabella Pilkington; one *s*. *Educ:* Cardiff High Sch.; West Monmouth School; Lincoln College, Oxford. RNVR, 1940–41. Open Scholar, Lincoln Coll., Oxford (Mod. History), 1940; Stewart Exhibitioner, 1942; Final Hons Sch., Mod. History, 1944; Final Hons Sch., Jurisprudence, 1945. Cholmeley Scholar, Lincoln's Inn, 1946; called to the Bar, Lincoln's Inn, 1947, Bencher 1970. QC 1962; Recorder of Crown Court, 1972–74. *Recreation:* watching

Rugby, racing and cricket. *Address:* c/o Royal Courts of Justice, Strand, WC2A 2LL. *Clubs:* Garrick, Royal Automobile, MCC.

TUDWAY QUILTER, David C.; *see* Quilter.

TUFFIN, Alan David; General Secretary, Union of Communication Workers, since 1982; *b* 2 Aug. 1933; *s* of Oliver Francis and Gertrude Elizabeth Tuffin; *m* 1957, Jean Elizabeth Tuffin; one *s* one *d. Educ:* Eltham Secondary Sch., SE9. Post Office employment, London, 1949–69; London Union Regional Official for UCW, 1957–69; National Official, 1969; Deputy General Secretary, 1979. Member: TUC Gen. Council, 1982–; Council, NIESR, 1985–; HSC, 1986–. Director: Unity Trust, 1984–; Trade Union Unit Trust, 1985–. *Recreations:* reading, squash, West Ham United FC. *Address:* UCW House, Crescent Lane, SW4 9RN.

TUFTON, family name of **Baron Hothfield.**

TUGENDHAT, Sir Christopher (Samuel), Kt 1990; Chairman, Abbey National plc, since 1991; Director: The BOC Group, since 1985; LWT (Holdings) plc, since 1991; *b* 23 Feb. 1937; *er s* of late Dr Georg Tugendhat; *m* 1967, Julia Lissant Dobson; two *s. Educ:* Ampleforth Coll.; Gonville and Caius Coll., Cambridge (Pres. of Union). Financial Times leader and feature writer, 1960–70. MP (C) City of London and Westminster South, 1974–76 (Cities of London and Westminster, 1970–74); Mem., 1977–85, a Vice-Pres., 1981–85, EEC Commn. Director: Sunningdale Oils, 1971–76; Phillips Petroleum International (UK) Ltd, 1972–76; National Westminster Bank, 1985–91 (Dep. Chm., 1990–91); Commercial Union Assce, 1988–91. Chm., CAA, 1986–91. Chm., RIIA (Chatham House), 1986–; Member: Council, Centre for Eur. Policy Studies, Brussels, 1985–; Council, Hughenden Foundn, 1986–; Governor, Council of Ditchley Foundn, 1986–; Vice-Pres., Council of British Lung Foundn, 1986–. *Publications:* Oil: the biggest business, 1968; The Multinationals, 1971 (McKinsey Foundn Book Award, 1971); Making Sense of Europe, 1986; (with William Wallace) Options for British Foreign Policy in the 1990s, 1988; various pamphlets and numerous articles. *Recreations:* being with his family, reading, conversation. *Address:* 35 Westbourne Park Road, W2 5QD. *Clubs:* Carlton, Buck's, Anglo-Belgian.
See also M. G. Tugendhat.

TUGENDHAT, Michael George; QC 1986; *b* 21 Oct. 1944; *s* of Georg Tugendhat and Maire Littledale; *m* 1970, Blandine de Loisne; four *s. Educ:* Ampleforth Coll.; Gonville and Caius Coll., Cambridge (MA); Yale Univ. Henry Fellowship. Called to the Bar, Inner Temple, 1969, Bencher, 1988. *Address:* 10 South Square, Gray's Inn, WC1R 5EU. *T:* 071–242 2902. *Club:* Brooks's.
See also Sir C. S. Tugendhat.

TU'IPELEHAKE, HRH Prince Fatafehi, Hon. KBE 1977 (Hon. CBE); Prime Minister of Tonga, since 1965; also Minister for Agriculture, Fisheries and Forests, and Marine Affairs; *b* 7 Jan 1922; *s* of HRH Prince Viliami Tupoulahi Tungi and HM Queen Salote of Tonga; *m* 1947, Princess Melenaite Topou Moheofo; two *s* four *d. Educ:* Newington College, Sydney; Gatton Agricultural College, Queensland. Governor of Vava'u, 1949–51. Chm., Commodities Board. 'Uluafi Medal, 1982. *Address:* Office of the Prime Minister, Nuku'alofa, Tonga.
See also HM King of Tonga.

TUITE, Sir Christopher (Hugh), 14th Bt *cr* 1622; Accounting Systems Manager, The Nature Conservancy; *b* 3 Nov. 1949; *s* of Sir Dennis George Harmsworth Tuite, 13th Bt, MBE, and of Margaret Essie, *d* of late Col Walter Leslie Dundas, DSO; *S* father, 1981; *m* 1976, Deborah Anne, *d* of A. E. Martz, Pittsburgh, Pa; two *s. Educ:* Univ. of Liverpool (BSc Hons); Univ. of Bristol (PhD). Research Officer, The Wildfowl Trust, 1978–81. *Publications:* contribs to Jl of Animal Ecology, Jl of Applied Ecology, Freshwater Biology, Wildfowl. *Heir: s* Thomas Livingstone Tuite, *b* 24 July 1977. *Address:* c/o The Midland Bank, 33 The Borough, Farnham, Surrey.

TUIVAGA, Hon. Sir Timoci (Uluiburotu), Kt 1981; **Hon. Mr Justice Tuivaga;** Chief Justice of Fiji, 1980–87, and since 1988; *b* 21 Oct. 1931; *s* of Isimeli Siga Tuivaga and Jessie Hill; *m* 1958, Vilimaina Leba Parrott Tuivaga; three *s* one *d. Educ:* Univ. of Auckland (BA). Called to Bar, Gray's Inn, 1964, and NSW, 1968. Native Magistrate, 1958–61; Crown Counsel, 1965–68; Principal Legal Officer, 1968–70; Acting Director of Public Prosecutions, 1970; Crown Solicitor, 1971; Puisne Judge, 1972; Acting Chief Justice, 1974; sometime Acting Gov.-Gen., 1983–87. *Recreations:* golf, gardening. *Address:* 228 Ratu Sukuna Road, Suva, Fiji. *T:* 301–782. *Club:* Fiji Golf (Suva).

TUKE, Sir Anthony (Favill), Kt 1979; Chairman, Savoy Hotel, since 1984 (Director, since 1982); Director, Barclays Bank International, since 1966 (Chairman, 1972–79; Vice-Chairman, 1968–72); *b* 22 Aug. 1920; *s* of late Anthony William Tuke; *m* 1946, Emilia Mila; one *s* one *d. Educ:* Winchester; Magdalene Coll., Cambridge. Scots Guards, 1940–46. Barclays Bank Ltd, 1946–90 (Dir, 1965–90; Vice-Chm, 1972–73; Chm., 1973–81); Dir, Barclays Bank UK, 1971–81. Dep. Chm., Royal Insurance, 1985– (Dir, 1978–); Director: Merchants Trust, 1969–; RTZ Corp., 1980–91 (Chm., 1981–85); Whitbread Investment Company PLC, 1984–. Vice-President: Inst. of Bankers, 1973–81; British Bankers' Assoc., 1977–81; Chm., Cttee of London Clearing Bankers, 1976–78 (Dep. Chm., 1974–76); Pres., Internat. Monetary Conference, 1977–78. Mem., Trilateral Commn, 1973–91. Chm., 1980 British Olympic Appeal; Pres., MCC, 1982–83. Mem., Stevenage Develt Corp., 1959–64. Governor, Motability, 1978–85. Mem. Council, Warwick Univ., 1966–73; Treas., English-Speaking Union, 1969–73. *Recreation:* gardening. *Address:* Freelands, Wherwell, near Andover, Hants. *Club:* MCC.

TUKE, Comdr Seymour Charles, DSO 1940; Royal Navy; *b* 20 May 1903; 3rd *s* of late Rear-Adm. J. A. Tuke; *m* 1928, Marjorie Alice Moller (*d* 1985); one *s* one *d. Educ:* Stonyhurst; RNC, Osborne and Dartmouth. Midshipman, 1921; Lieutenant, 1926; Acting Commander, 1945; FAA, 1927–29; Local Fishery Naval Officer, English Channel, 1935–37; served War of 1939–45 (DSO, 1939–45 Medal, Atlantic Star, Italy Star, War Medal); in command of SS Hannah Boge (first prize of the war), 1939; Senior Officer Res. Fleet, Harwich, 1946; Maintenance Comdr to Senior Officer Res. Fleet, 1947–48; retired, 1948. *Address:* c/o National Westminster Bank, 32 Market Place, Cirencester, Glos GL7 2NW.

TULLIS, Major Ramsey; Vice Lord-Lieutenant of Clackmannanshire, since 1974; farmer, retired 1987; *b* 16 June 1916; *s* of late Major J. Kennedy Tullis, Tullibody, Clackmannanshire; *m* 1943, Daphne Mabon, *d* of late Lt-Col H. L. Warden, CBE, DSO, Edinburgh; three *s. Educ:* Trinity Coll., Glenalmond; Worcester Coll., Oxford (BA). 2nd Lieut, Cameronians, 1936. Served War, 1939–45: Cameronians, Parachute Regt; Major 1943; psc 1949; retired, 1958. Income Tax Comr, 1964–90. County Comr for Scouts, Clackmannanshire, 1958–73; Mem. Cttee, Council of Scout Assoc., 1967–72; Activities Comr, Scottish HQ, Scout Assoc., 1974. Chm. Visiting Cttee, Glenochil Young Offenders Instn and Detention Centre, 1974–83. Clackmannanshire: JP 1960, DL 1962. *Recreations:* golf and gardening. *Address:* Woodacre, Pool of Muckhart, by Dollar, Clackmannanshire FK14 7JW. *Club:* Senior Golfers' Society.

TULLY, (William) Mark, OBE 1985; Chief of Bureau, British Broadcasting Corporation, Delhi, since 1972; *b* 24 Oct. 1935; *s* of late William Scarth Carlisle Tully, CBE and of Patience Treby Tully; *m* 1960, Frances Margaret (*née* Butler) two *s* two *d. Educ:* Twyford School, Winchester; Marlborough College; Trinity Hall, Cambridge (MA). Regional Dir, Abbeyfield Soc., 1960–64; BBC, 1964–: Asst, Appointments Dept, 1964–65; Asst, then Actg Rep., New Delhi, 1965–69; Prog. Organiser and Talks Writer, Eastern Service, 1969–71. *Publications:* (with Satish Jacob) Amritsar: Mrs Gandhi's last battle, 1985; (with Z. Masani) From Raj to Rajiv, 1988. *Recreations:* fishing, bird watching, reading. *Address:* 1 Nizamuddin (East), New Delhi 110 013, India. *T:* Delhi 616108/616102. *Clubs:* Oriental; Press, India International, Gymkhana (Delhi).

TUMIM, Stephen; His Honour Judge Tumim; a Circuit Judge, since 1978; HM's Chief Inspector of Prisons for England and Wales, since 1987; *b* 15 Aug. 1930; *yr s* of late Joseph Tumim, CBE (late Clerk of Assize, Oxford Circuit) and late Renée Tumim; *m* 1962, Winifred, *er d* of late Col A. M. Borthwick; three *d. Educ:* St Edward's Sch., Oxford; Worcester Coll., Oxford (Scholar). Called to Bar, Middle Temple, 1955, Bencher, 1990. A Recorder of the Crown Court, 1977–78; a Judge of Willesden County Court, 1980–87. Chm., Nat. Deaf Children's Soc., 1974–79 (Vice-Chm., 1966–74). Mem. Cttee, Contemp. Art Soc.; Chairman: Friends of Tate Gall., 1983–90; British Art Market Standing Cttee, 1990–; Pres., Royal Lit. Fund, 1990–. *Publications:* Great Legal Disasters, 1983; Great Legal Fiascos, 1985; occasional reviews. *Recreations:* books and pictures. *Address:* c/o Home Office, Queen Anne's Gate, SW1H 9AT. *Clubs:* Garrick, Beefsteak.

TUNC, Prof. André Robert; Croix de Guerre 1940; Officier de la Légion d'Honneur 1984; Professor, University of Paris, since 1958; *b* 3 May 1917; *s* of Gaston Tunc and Gervaise Letourneur; *m* 1941, Suzanne Fortin. *Educ:* Law Sch., Paris. LLB 1937, LLM 1941. Agrégé des Facultés de Droit, 1943. Prof., Univ. of Grenoble, 1943–47; Counsellor, Internat. Monetary Fund, 1947–50; Prof., Univ. of Grenoble, 1950–58; Legal Adviser, UN Economic Commn for Europe, 1957–58. Hon. Doctorates: Free Univ. of Brussels, 1958; Cath. Univ. of Louvain, 1968; LLD Cambridge, 1986; DCL: Oxford, 1970; Stockholm, 1978; Geneva, 1984; Gent, 1986; Saarbrück, 1988; MA Cantab, 1972; Corr. FBA (London), 1974; Corresp. Fellow, Royal Acad. of Belgium, 1978; Foreign Member: Royal Acad. of the Netherlands, 1980; Amer. Acad. of Arts and Scis. Officier de l'Ordre d'Orange-Nassau, 1965. *Publications:* Le contrat de garde, 1941; Le particulier au service de l'ordre public, 1942; (with Suzanne Tunc) Le Système constitutionnel des Etats-Unis d'Amérique, 2 vols, 1953, 1954; (with Suzanne Tunc) Le droit des Etats-Unis d'Amérique, 1955; (with François Givord) (tome 8) Le louage: Contrats civils, du Traité pratique de droit civil français de Planiol et Ripert, 2nd edn 1956; Traité théorique et pratique de la responsabilité civile de Henri et Léon Mazeaud, vols, 1957, 1958, 1960, 5th edn, and 6th edn (Vol. I) 1965; Les Etats-Unis—comment ils sont gouvernés, 1958, 3rd edn 1974; Dans un monde qui souffre, 1962, 4th edn 1968; Le droit des Etats-Unis (Que sais-je?), 1964, 5th edn 1989; La sécurité routière, 1965; Le droit anglais des sociétés anonymes, 1971, 3rd edn 1987; Traffic Accident Compensation: Law and Proposals (Internat. Encycl. of Comparative Law, Vol. XI: Torts, chap. 14), 1971; Introd. to Vol. XI: Torts (Internat. Encycl. of Comparative Law), 1974; La cour judiciaire suprême: une enquête comparative, 1978; La responsabilité civile, 1981, 2nd edn 1990; Pour une loi sur les accidents de la circulation, 1981; Le droit américain des sociétés anonymes, 1985; Jalons, dits et écrits d'André Tunc, 1991; articles in various legal periodicals. *Address:* 112 rue de Vaugirard, 75006 Paris, France.

TUNNELL, Hugh James Oliver Redvers; HM Diplomatic Service; Consul General, Jedda, since 1989; *b* 31 Dec. 1935; *s* of Heather and Oliver Tunnell; *m* 1st, 1958, Helen Miller (marr. diss.); three *d*; 2nd, 1979, Margaret, *d* of Sir Richard John Randall; two *d. Educ:* Chatham House Grammar School, Ramsgate. Royal Artillery, 1954–56. FO, 1956–59; Amman, 1959–62; Middle East Centre for Arab Studies, 1962–63; served FO, Aden, CRO, Damascus and FO, 1964–67; UK Delegn to European Communities, 1968–70; FCO, 1970–72; Kuwait, 1972–76; FCO, 1976–79; Head of Chancery, Muscat, 1979–83; Consul Gen., Brisbane, 1983–88; Comr-Gen., British Section, EXPO 88, 1987–88. *Recreations:* water sports, tennis. *Address:* c/o Foreign and Commonwealth Office, SW1A 2AH. *Clubs:* Brisbane, Tattersalls (Brisbane).

TUNNICLIFFE, Denis; Managing Director, London Underground Ltd, since 1988; *b* 17 Jan. 1943; *s* of Arthur Harold and Ellen Tunnicliffe; *m* 1968, Susan Dale; two *s. Educ:* Henry Cavendish Sch., Derby; University Coll. London (State Schol.; BSc (Special)); College of Air Training, Hamble. Pilot, BOAC, 1966–72; British Airways, 1972–86; Chief Exec., International Leisure Group, Aviation Div., 1986–88. Co. Councillor, Royal County of Berkshire, 1978–82; Dist Councillor, Bracknell, 1979–83. FCIT; CBIM. *Recreations:* flying, boating, church, travelling. *Address:* 18 Octavia, Bracknell, Berks RG12 4YZ. *T:* Bracknell (0344) 54283. *Clubs:* Royal Air Force, Royal Automobile.

TUOHY, John Francis, (Frank Tuohy); FRSL 1965; novelist; short story writer; *b* 2 May 1925; *s* of late Patrick Gerald Tuohy and Dorothy Marion (*née* Annandale). *Educ:* Stowe Sch.; King's College, Cambridge. Prof. of English Language and Literature, Univ. of São Paulo, 1950–56; Contract Prof., Jagiellonian Univ., Cracow, Poland, 1958–60; Visiting Professor: Waseda Univ., Tokyo, 1964–67; Rikkyo Univ., Tokyo, 1983–89; Writer-in-Residence, Purdue Univ., Indiana, 1970–71, 1976, 1980. Hon. DLitt Purdue, 1987. *Publications:* The Animal Game, 1957; The Warm Nights of January, 1960; The Admiral and the Nuns, short stories (Katherine Mansfield Memorial Prize), 1962; The Ice Saints (James Tait Black and Geoffrey Faber Memorial Prizes), 1964; Portugal, 1970; Fingers in the Door, short stories (E. M. Forster Meml Award, 1972), 1970; Yeats: a biographical study, 1976; Live Bait, short stories (Heinemann Award, 1979), 1978.; Collected Stories, 1984. *Recreation:* travel. *Address:* Shatwell Cottage, Yarlington, near Wincanton, Somerset.

TUOHY, Thomas, CBE 1969; Managing Director, British Nuclear Fuels Ltd, 1971–73; *b* 7 Nov. 1917; *s* of late Michael Tuohy and Isabella Tuohy, Cobh, Eire; *m* 1949, Lilian May Barnes (*d* 1971); one *s* one *d. Educ:* St Cuthberts Grammar Sch., Newcastle; Reading Univ. (BSc). Chemist in various Royal Ordnance Factories, 1939–46. Manager: Health Physics, Springfields Nuclear Fuel Plant, Dept Atomic Energy, 1946; Health Physics, Windscale Plutonium Plant, 1949; Plutonium Piles and Metal Plant, Windscale, 1950; Works Manager: Springfields, 1952; Windscale, UKAEA, 1954; Windscale and Calder Hall: Dep. Gen. Manager, 1957; Gen. Manager, 1958; Man. Dir, Production Gp, UKAEA, 1964–71. Managing Director: Urenco, 1973–74; Vorsitzender der Geschäftsführung Centec GmbH, 1973–74; Dep. Chm., Centec, 1973–74; former Dir, Centec-Algermann Co. Mem. Council, Internat. Inst. for Management of Technology, 1971–73. *Publications:* various technical papers on reactor operation and plutonium manufacture. *Recreations:* golf, gardening, travel. *Address:* Ingleberg, Beckermet, Cumbria CA21 2XX. *T:* Beckermet (094684) 226.

TUPMAN, William Ivan, DPhil; Director General of Internal Audit, Ministry of Defence, 1974–81; *b* 22 July 1921; *s* of Leonard and Elsie Tupman; *m* 1945, Barbara (*née* Capel); two *s* one *d. Educ:* Queen Elizabeth's Hosp., Bristol; New Coll., Oxford (Exhibnr; MA, DPhil). Served War, 1942–45, RN (Lieut RNVR). Entered Admiralty as Asst

Principal, 1948; Private Sec. to Parly Sec., 1950–52; Principal, 1952; Civil Affairs Adviser to C-in-C, Far East Station, 1958–61; Private Sec. to First Lord of the Admiralty, 1963; Asst Sec., 1964; IDC, 1967.

TUPPER, Sir Charles Hibbert, 5th Bt *cr* 1888, of Armdale, Halifax, Nova Scotia; *b* 4 July 1930; *o s* of Sir James Macdonald Tupper, 4th Bt, formerly Assistant Commissioner, Royal Canadian Mounted Police, and of Mary Agnes Jean Collins; *S* father, 1967; *m* (marr. diss. 1976); one *s*. *Heir: s* Charles Hibbert Tupper, [*b* 10 July 1964; *m* 1987, Elizabeth Ann Heaslip]. *Address:* 955 Marine Drive, Apt 1101, West Vancouver, BC V7T 1A9, Canada.

TURBERVILLE, Geoffrey, MA; Principal, Leulumoega High School, Samoa, 1959–62, (retired); *b* 31 Mar. 1899; *o s* of A. E. Turberville, FCA, Stroud Green, London; *m* Jane Campbell Lawson. *Educ:* Westminster Sch. (King's Scholar); Trinity College, Cambridge (Exhibitioner). 2nd Lieut, Queen's Royal West Surrey Regt, 1917–19; Senior Classical Master, Liverpool Collegiate School, 1921–25; Senior Classical Master, Epsom College, 1925–30; Headmaster of Eltham College, 1930–59. Chm. Dorset Congregational Assoc., 1970–71. *Publications:* Cicero and Antony; Arva Latina II; Translation into Latin. *Address:* 4 Spiller's House, Shaftesbury, Dorset SP7 8EP.

TURBOTT, Sir Ian (Graham), Kt 1968; CMG 1962; CVO 1966; Foundation Chancellor, University of Western Sydney, since 1989; *b* Whangarei, New Zealand, 9 March 1922; *s* of late Thomas Turbott and late E. A. Turbott, both of New Zealand; *m* 1952, Nancy Hall Lantz, California, USA; three *d*. *Educ:* Takapuna Grammar School, Auckland, NZ; Auckland University; Jesus College, Cambridge; London University. NZ Forces (Army), 1940–46: Solomon Is area and 2 NZEF, Italy. Colonial Service (Overseas Civil Service): Western Pacific, Gilbert and Ellice Is, 1948–56; Colonial Office, 1956–58; Administrator of Antigua, The West Indies, 1958–64; also Queen's Representative under new constitution, 1960–64; Administrator of Grenada and Queen's Representative, 1964–67; Governor of Associated State of Grenada, 1966–68. Partner, Spencer Stuart and Associates Worldwide, 1973–84; Chairman: Spencer Stuart and Associates Pty Ltd, 1970–84; Chloride Batteries Australia Ltd, 1978–85; TNT Security Pty Ltd; Stuart Brooke Consultants Pty Ltd, Sydney, 1974–82; 2MMM Broadcasting Co. Pty Ltd; Melbourne F/M Radio Pty Ltd; Penrith Lakes Devel Corp.; Essington Ltd, 1984–89; New World Pictures (Aust.) Ltd, 1986–89; Triple M FM Radio Group, 1986–; Cape York Space Agency Ltd, 1987–89; Dep. Chm., Hoyts Media Ltd, 1986–; Dir, Hoyts Entertainment Ltd, 1990; Dep. Chm., Adv. Bd, Amer. Internat. Underwriting (Aust.) Ltd; Director: Standard Chartered Bank Australia Ltd; Capita Financial Gp, 1979–90. Chairman: Internat. Piano Competition Ltd, Sydney, 1977–84; Duke of Edinburgh's Award Scheme, NSW. Governor, NSW Conservatorium of Music, 1974–89. FRSA, JP. Silver Jubilee Medal, 1977. Holds 1939–45 Star, Pacific Star, Italy Star, Defence Medal, War Medal, New Zealand Service Medal. CStJ 1964. *Publications:* various technical and scientific, 1948–51, in Jl of Polynesian Society (on Pacific area). *Recreations:* boating, farming, cricket, fishing. *Address:* 27 Amiens Road, Clontarf, NSW 2093, Australia; 38 MacMasters Parade, MacMasters Beach, NSW 2250, Australia. *Clubs:* Australian (Sydney); Royal Sydney Yacht.

TURCAN, Henry Watson; a Recorder of the Crown Court, since 1985; *b* 22 Aug. 1941; *s* of late Henry Hutchison Turcan and Lilias Cheyne; *m* 1969, Jane Fairrie Blair; one *s* one *d*. *Educ:* Rugby School; Trinity College, Oxford (BA, MA). Called to the Bar, Inner Temple, 1965. Legal Assessor to General Optical Council, 1983. *Recreations:* hunting, shooting, fishing, golf. *Address:* 4 Paper Buildings, Temple, EC4. *T:* 01–353 3420. *Clubs:* Royal and Ancient Golf (St Andrews); Hon. Company of Edinburgh Golfers (Muirfield).

TURECK, Rosalyn; concert artist (Bach specialist); conductor; writer; *b* Chicago, 14 Dec. 1914; *d* of Samuel Tureck and Monya (*née* Lipson); *m* 1964, George Wallingford Downs (*d* 1964). *Educ:* Juilliard Sch. of Music, NY. Member Faculty: Philadelphia Conservatory of Music, 1935–42; Mannes School, NYC, 1940–44; Juilliard School of Music, 1943–53; Lecturer in Music: Columbia University, NY, 1953–55; London Univ., 1955–56. Visiting Professor, Washington University, St Louis, 1963–64; Regents Professorship, University of California, San Diego, 1966; Professor of Music: 4th Step, Univ. of California, San Diego, 1966–72; Univ. of Maryland, 1982–; Vis. Fellow, St Hilda's Coll., Oxford, 1974 and 1976–, Hon. Life Fellow, 1974; Vis. Fellow, Wolfson Coll., Oxford, 1975. Lectures: Univ. of Winnipeg, Canada, 1989; Yale Univ., and Brandeis Univ., 1990; (also Chairperson) Symposium on Structure, Menendez Pelayo Internat. Univ., Santander, Spain, 1990. Has appeared as soloist and conductor of leading orchestras in US, Europe and Israel, and toured US, Canada, South Africa, South America; since 1947 has toured extensively in Europe, and played at festivals in Edinburgh, Venice, Holland, Wexford, Schaffhausen, Bath, Brussels World Fair, Glyndebourne, Barcelona, etc, and in major Amer. festivals including Mostly Mozart Festival, NY, Caramoor, Detroit, etc; extensive tours: India, Australia and Far East, 1971; guest soloist, White House, at state dinner for the Prime Minister of Canada, 1986. Formed: Composers of Today, 1951–55; Tureck Bach Players, 1959; Internat. Bach Soc., Inc., 1966 (Lectr, 1967–72); Inst. for Bach Studies, 1968; Tureck Bach Inst. Inc., 1982 (Lectr, 1983–90). Hon. Member, Guildhall School of Music and Drama, London, 1961; Member: Royal Musical Assoc., London; Inc. Soc. of Musicians, London; Amer. Musicological Soc; Amer. Br., New Bach Soc. Editor, Tureck/Bach Urtext series, 1979–. Numerous recordings. Hon. Dr of Music, Colby Coll., USA, 1964; Hon. DMus: Roosevelt Univ., 1968; Wilson Coll., 1968; Oxon, 1977; Music and Art Inst. of San Francisco, 1987. Has won several awards. Officer's Cross, Order of Merit, Fed. Republic of Germany, 1979. *Television films:* Fantasy and Fugue: Rosalyn Tureck plays Bach, 1972; Rosalyn Tureck plays on Organ and Harpsichord, 1977; Joy of Bach, 1978; Bach and Tureck at Ephesus, 1985. *Publications:* An Introduction to the Performance of Bach, 1960; (ed) Bach: Sarabande, C minor, 1950; (transcribed) Paganini: Moto Perpetuo, 1950; (Urtext and performance edns) Bach: Italian Concerto, 1983; J. S. Bach, Lute Suite in E minor, set for classical guitar, 1984, Lute Suite in C minor, 1985; many articles.

TURING, Sir John Dermot, 12th Bt *cr* 1638 (NS), of Foveran, Aberdeenshire; *b* 26 Feb. 1961; *s* of John Ferrier Turing (*d* 1983) and of Beryl Mary Ada, *d* of late Herbert Vaughan Hann; *S* kinsman, Sir John Leslie Turing, 11th Bt, 1987; *m* 1986, Nicola J., *er d* of M. D. Simmonds; two *s*. *Educ:* Sherborne School, Dorset; King's College, Cambridge; New College, Oxford. *Heir: s* John Malcolm Ferrier Turing, *b* 5 Sept. 1988. *Address:* 35 Tavistock Avenue, E17 6HP.

TURMEAU, Dr William Arthur, CBE 1989; PhD; FRSE; CEng, FIMechE; Principal, Napier Polytechnic of Edinburgh (formerly Napier College), since 1982; *b* 19 Sept. 1929; *s* of Frank Richard Turmeau and Catherine Lyon Linklater; *m* 1957, Margaret Moar Burnett, MA, BCom; one *d*. *Educ:* Stromness Acad., Orkney; Univ. of Edinburgh (BSc); Moray House Coll. of Educn; Heriot-Watt Univ. (PhD). FIMechE, CEng, 1971; FRSE 1990. Royal Signals, 1947–49. Research Engr, Northern Electric Co. Ltd, Montreal, 1952–54; Mechanical Engr, USAF, Goose Bay, Labrador, 1954–56; Contracts Manager, Godfrey Engrg Co. Ltd, Montreal, 1956–61; Lectr, Bristo Technical Inst., 1962–64; Napier College: Lectr and Sen. Lectr, 1964–68; Head, Dept of Mechanical Engrg, 1968–75; Asst Principal and Dean, Faculty of Technology, 1975–82. Member: Manpower Policy Cttee, Scottish Council for Develt and Industry, 1985–; Scottish Econ. Council, 1987–; Edinburgh Chamber of Commerce, 1989–; Scottish Exams Bd, 1988–; Council, Soc. Européenne pour la Formation des Ingénieurs, 1983–; CICHE, British Council, 1982–; Cttee of Dirs of Polytechnics, 1982–; Standing Conf. of Rectors and Vice-Chancellors of European Univs, 1990–. *Publications:* various papers relating to higher educn. *Recreations:* modern jazz, Leonardo da Vinci. *Address:* 71 Morningside Park, Edinburgh EH10 5EZ. *T:* 031–447 4639. *Club:* Caledonian.

TURNBULL, Andrew, CB 1990; Principal Private Secretary to the Prime Minister, since 1988; *b* 21 Jan. 1945; *s* of Anthony and Mary Turnbull; *m* 1967, Diane Clarke; two *s*. *Educ:* Enfield Grammar Sch.; Christ's Coll., Cambridge (BA). ODI Fellow working as economist, Govt of Republic of Zambia, Lusaka, 1968–70; Asst Principal, HM Treasury, 1970; Principal, 1972; on secondment to staff of IMF, 1976–78; Asst Sec., HM Treasury, 1978; Private Sec. to the Prime Minister, 1983–85; Under Sec., 1985; Hd of Gen. Expenditure Policy Gp, HM Treasury, 1985–88. *Recreations:* walking, running, cricket, opera. *Address:* c/o 10 Downing Street, SW1A 2AA. *Club:* Tottenham Hotspur.

TURNBULL, Rt. Rev. (Anthony) Michael (Arnold); *see* Rochester, Bishop of.

TURNBULL, Sir George (Henry), Kt 1990; BSc (Hons), CEng, FIMechE, FIProdE; Chairman and Chief Executive, Inchcape PLC, since 1986 (Group Managing Director, 1984–86; Group Chief Executive, 1985–86); *b* 17 Oct. 1926; *m* 1950, Marion Wing; one *s* two *d*. *Educ:* King Henry VIII Sch., Coventry; Birmingham Univ. (BSc (Hons)). PA to Techn. Dir, Standard Motors, 1950–51; Liaison Officer between Standard Motors and Rolls Royce, 1951–53; Exec., i/c Experimental, 1954–55; Works Manager, Petters Ltd, 1955–56; Standard Motors: Divl Manager Cars, 1956–59; Gen. Man., 1959–62; Standard Triumph International: Dir and Gen. Man., 1962; Dep. Chm., 1969; British Leyland Motor Corporation Ltd: Dir, 1967; Dep. Man. Dir, 1968–73; Man. Dir, 1973; Man. Dir, BL Austin Morris Ltd, 1968–73; Chm., Truck & Bus Div., BL, 1972–73; Vice-Pres. and Dir, Hyundai Motors, Seoul, South Korea, 1974–77; Consultant Advr to Chm. and Man. Dir, Iran Nat. Motor Co., Tehran, 1977–78, Dep. Man. Dir, 1978–79; Chm., Talbot UK, 1979–84. Director: Bank in Liechtenstein (UK) Ltd, 1988–90; Kleinwort Benson Group plc, 1988–; Westland Group plc, 1991–. Pres., SMMT, 1982–84 (Dep. Pres., 1984–); Chairman: Industrial Soc., 1987–90; Korea-Europe Fund Ltd, 1987–; Dir, Euro-Asia Centre, 1987–; Mem. Council, Birmingham Chamber of Commerce and Industry, 1972 (Vice-Pres., 1973); past Member: Careers Adv. Bd, Univ. of Warwick; Management Bd, Engineering Employers' Assoc.; Engineering Employers' Fedn; Engrg Industry Trng Bd. Governor, Bablake Sch., Coventry. FIMI; Fellow, Inst. of Directors. *Recreations:* golf, tennis, fishing. *Address:* Inchcape plc, St James's House, 23 King Street, SW1Y 6QY. *T:* 071–321 0110; *Telex:* 885395; *Fax:* 071–321 0604.

TURNBULL, Jeffrey Alan, CBE 1991; CEng, FICE, FIHT; Chairman and Director, Mott MacDonald Group Ltd, since 1989; *b* 14 Aug. 1934; *s* of Alan Edward Turnbull and Alice May (*née* Slee); *m* 1957, Beryl (*née* Griffith); two *s* one *d*. *Educ:* Newcastle upon Tyne Royal Grammar Sch.; Liverpool Coll. of Technology. DipTE 1964; CEng; FIHT 1966; FICE 1973. National Service, RE, 1956–58. Jun. Engr, Cheshire CC, 1951–55; Engr, Herefordshire CC, 1955–59; Resident Engr, Berks CC, 1959–66; Mott Hay & Anderson, 1966–: Chief Designer (Roads), 1968; Associate, 1973; Dir, Mott Hay & Anderson International Ltd, 1975–88; Dir, Mott Hay & Anderson, 1978–88; Dir, 1983–88, Chief Exec., 1987–88, Mott Hay & Anderson Holdings Ltd. FInstD. *Publication:* (contrib.) Civil Engineer's Reference Book, 4th edn 1988. *Recreations:* cricket, walking, France. *Address:* c/o Mott MacDonald Group Ltd, 20/26 Wellesley Road, Croydon, Surrey CR9 2UL. *T:* 081–686 5041; 63 Higher Drive, Banstead, Surrey SM1 1PW. *T:* 081–393 1054. *Clubs:* Royal Automobile, Institute of Directors.

TURNBULL, Malcolm Bligh; Managing Director, Turnbull & Partners Ltd, Investment Bankers, Sydney, since 1987; Principal, Turnbull & Co., Solicitors, since 1987; *b* 24 Oct. 1954; *s* of Bruce Bligh Turnbull and late Coral (*née* Lansbury); *m* 1980, Lucinda Mary Forrest Hughes; one *s* one *d*. *Educ:* Sydney Grammar Sch.; Sydney Univ. (BA, LLB); Brasenose Coll., Oxford (Rhodes Schol. (NSW) 1978, BCL 1980). Journalist, Nation Review, 1975; Political Correspondent: TCN–9, Sydney, 1976; The Bulletin, 1977–78; Journalist, Sunday Times, London, 1979; admitted to NSW Bar, 1980; Barrister, Sydney, 1980–82; Gen. Counsel and Secretary, Consolidated Press Holdings Ltd, 1983–85; Partner, Turnbull McWilliam, Solicitors, Sydney, 1986–87; Jt Man. Dir, Whitlam Turnbull & Co. Ltd, Investment Bankers, Sydney, 1987–90. Director: Muswellbrook Energy and Minerals Ltd, 1985–87; Communications and Entertainment Ltd, 1986–87. Chm., Centre for Immunology, St Vincent's Hosp., Sydney. *Publication:* The Spycatcher Trial, 1988. *Recreations:* riding, swimming. *Address:* Turnbull & Partners Ltd, 8th Floor, 1 Chifley Square, Sydney, NSW 2000, Australia. *T:* (02) 2235899. *Clubs:* Australian, Tattersall's, University and Schools (Sydney).

TURNBULL, Rt. Rev. Michael; *see* Rochester, Bishop of.

TURNBULL, Reginald March; *b* 10 Jan. 1907; *s* of late Sir March and Lady (Gertrude) Turnbull; *m* twice; one *s*. *Educ:* Horton Sch.; Eton; Cambridge Univ. (MA). Family shipping firm, Turnbull, Scott & Co., 1928–77. *Recreations:* teaching golf, motoring, New River, water mills. *Address:* Sarum, Church Lane, Worplesdon, Surrey GU3 3RU.

TURNBULL, Sir Richard (Gordon), GCMG 1962 (KCMG 1958, CMG 1953); *b* 7 July 1909; *s* of Richard Francis Turnbull; *m* 1939, Beatrice (*d* 1986), *d* of John Wilson, Glasgow; two *s* one *d*. *Educ:* University College School, London; University College, London; Magdalene Coll., Cambridge. Colonial Administrative Service, Kenya: District Officer, 1931–48; Provincial Comr, 1948–53; Minister for Internal Security and Defence, 1954; Chief Secretary, Kenya, 1955–58; Governor and C-in-C, Tanganyika, 1958–61; Governor-General and Commander-in-Chief, 1961–62; Chairman, Central Land Board, Kenya, 1963–64; High Commissioner for Aden and the Protectorate of South Arabia, 1965–67. Fellow of University College, London; Hon. Fellow, Magdalene College, Cambridge, 1970–. KStJ 1958. *Address:* Friars Neuk, Jedburgh, Roxburghshire TD8 6BN. *T:* Jedburgh (0835) 62589.

TURNER, family name of **Baron Netherthorpe** and **Baroness Turner of Camden.**

TURNER OF CAMDEN, Baroness *cr* 1985 (Life Peer), of Camden in Greater London; **Muriel Winifred Turner;** *b* 1927; *m* Reginald T. F. Turner. Asst Gen. Sec., ASTMS, 1970–87. Member: Occupational Pensions Board, 1978–; Central Arbitration Cttee, 1980–90; TUC General Council, 1981–87; Equal Opportunities Commission, 1982–88. Junior Spokesperson on Social Security, 1986–, Principal Opposition Spokesperson on Employment, 1988–, H of L. *Address:* House of Lords, SW1A 0PW.

TURNER, Alan B.; *see* Brooke Turner.

TURNER, Rt. Hon. Sir Alexander (Kingcome), PC 1968; KBE 1973; Kt 1963; *b* Auckland, New Zealand, 18 Nov. 1901; *s* of J. H. Turner; *m* 1934, Dorothea F., *d* of Alan Mulgan; two *s* one *d*. *Educ:* Auckland Grammar Sch.; Auckland Univ. (Scholar). BA

1921; MA 1922; LLB 1923. Served War of 1939–45, National Military Reserve, New Zealand. Barrister and Solicitor, 1923; QC (NZ) 1952. Carnegie Travelling Fellowship, 1949. Judge of the Supreme Court of New Zealand, 1953–62; Senior Resident Judge at Auckland, 1958–62; Judge of Court of Appeal, 1962–71, Pres., 1972–73. President, Auckland University Students' Assoc., 1928; President, Auckland District Court of Convocation, 1933; Member, Auckland Univ. Council, 1935–51; Vice-President, Auckland Univ., 1950–51; a Governor, Massey Agricultural Coll., 1944–53. Hon. LLD Auckland, 1965. *Publications:* (with George Spencer Bower) The Law of Estoppel by Representation, 1966; Res Judicata, 1969; The Law of Actionable Misrepresentation, 1974. *Recreations:* gardening, golf, Bush conservation, agriculture. *Address:* 14 St Michael's Crescent, Kelburn, Wellington 5, New Zealand. *T:* 757768. *Clubs:* Wellington; Auckland.

TURNER, Amédée Edward, QC 1976; Member (C) Suffolk, European Parliament, since 1979; *b* 26 March 1929; *s* of Frederick William Turner and Ruth Hempson; *m* 1960, Deborah Dudley Owen; one *s* one *d. Educ:* Temple Grove, Heron's Ghyll, Sussex; Dauntsey Sch., Wilts; Christ Church, Oxford (MA). Called to Bar, Inner Temple, 1954; practised patent bar, 1954–57; Associate, Kenyon & Kenyon, patent attorneys, NY, 1957–60; London practice, 1960–. Contested (C) Norwich N, gen. elections, 1964, 1966, 1970. European Parliament: EDG spokesman on energy res. and technol., 1984–89; Chief Whip, EDG, 1989–; Vice Chm., Legal Cttee, 1979–84; Member: Economic and Monetary Cttee, 1979–84; ACP Jt Cttee, 1980–; Transport Cttee, 1981–84; Energy Cttee, 1984–; Legal Affairs Cttee, 1984–89. *Publications:* The Law of Trade Secrets, 1962, supplement, 1968; The Law of the New European Patent, 1979; many Conservative Party study papers on defence, oil and Middle East. *Recreations:* garden design, art deco collection, fish keeping, oil painting, Annexe 3A Royal Festival Hall. *Address:* 3 Montrose Place, SW1X 7DU. *T:* 071–235 2894, 071–235 3191; 1 Essex Court, Temple, EC4. *T:* 071–353 8507; The Barn, Westleton, Saxmundham, Suffolk IP17 3AN. *T:* Westleton (072873) 235; La Combe de la Boissière, St Maximin, Uzès 30700, France. *Clubs:* Carlton, Coningsby, United & Cecil.

TURNER, Ven. Antony Hubert Michael; Archdeacon of the Isle of Wight, since 1986; *b* 17 June 1930; *s* of Frederick George and Winifred Frances Turner; *m* 1956, Margaret Kathleen (*née* Phillips); one *s* two *d. Educ:* Royal Liberty Grammar School, Romford, Essex; Tyndale Hall, Bristol. FCA 1963 (ACA 1952); DipTh (Univ. of London), 1956. Deacon, 1956; Priest, 1957; Curate, St Ann's, Nottingham, 1956–59; Curate in Charge, St Cuthbert's, Cheadle, Dio. Chester, 1959–62; Vicar, Christ Church, Macclesfield, 1962–68; Home Sec., Bible Churchmen's Missionary Soc., 1968–74; Vicar of St Jude's, Southsea, 1974–86; RD of Portsmouth, 1979–84. Church Commissioner, 1983–. Vice Chm., C of E Pensions Bd, 1988–. *Recreations:* photography, caravanning. *Address:* 3 Beech Grove, Ryde, Isle of Wight PO33 3AN. *T:* Isle of Wight (0983) 65522.

TURNER, Adm. Sir (Arthur) Francis, KCB 1970 (CB 1966); DSC 1945; Chief of Fleet Support, Ministry of Defence, 1967–71; *b* 23 June 1912; *s* of Rear-Admiral A. W. J. Turner and Mrs A. M. Turner (*née* Lochrane); *m* 1963, Elizabeth Clare de Trafford; two *s. Educ:* Stonyhurst Coll. Entered RN, 1931; Commander, 1947; Captain, 1956; Rear-Admiral, 1964; Vice-Admiral, 1968; Admiral, 1970. Dir.-Gen. Aircraft (Navy), MoD, 1966–67. *Recreations:* cricket, golf. *Address:* Plantation House, East Horsley, Surrey. *Clubs:* Army and Navy; Union (Malta).

TURNER, Air Vice-Marshal Cameron Archer, CB 1968; CBE 1960 (OBE 1947); Royal New Zealand Air Force, retired; *b* Wanganui, NZ, 29 Aug. 1915; *s* of James Oswald Turner and Vida Cathrine Turner; *m* 1941, Josephine Mary, *d* of George Richardson; two *s. Educ:* New Plymouth Boys' High Sch.; Victoria University of Wellington; Massey Univ., Palmerston North, NZ. CEng, FIEE, FRAeS. Commn RAF, 1936–39; commn RNZ Air Force, 1940; served War of 1939–45, UK, NZ, and Pacific; comd RNZAF Station Nausori, Fiji, 1944; comd RNZAF Station, Guadalcanal, Solomon Islands, 1944; Director of Signals, 1945–47; psa 1947; RNZAF Liaison Officer, Melbourne, Australia, 1948–50; comd RNZAF Station, Taieri, NZ, 1950–52; Director of Organization, HQ, RNZAF, 1953–56; comd RNZAF Station Ohakea, NZ, 1956–58; Asst Chief of Air Staff, HQ, RNZAF, 1958; Air Member for Personnel, HQ, RNZAF, 1959; idc 1960; AOC HQ, RNZAF, London, 1961–63; Air Member for Supply, HQ, RNZAF, 1964–65; Chief of Air Staff, HQ RNZAF, 1966–69. Dir, NZ Inventions Devclt Authority, 1969–76. Pres., RNZAF Assoc., 1972–81. *Recreations:* fishing, Polynesian and religious studies. *Address:* 37a Parkvale Road, Wellington 5, New Zealand. *T:* 4766063. *Clubs:* Wellington (Wellington); Taranaki (New Plymouth).

TURNER, Prof. Cedric Edward, CBE 1987; FEng 1989; Professor of Materials in Mechanical Engineering, Imperial College, London, since 1975; *b* 5 Aug. 1926; *s* of Charles Turner and Mabel Evelyn (*née* Berry); *m* 1953, Margaret Dorothy (*née* Davies); one *s* two *d. Educ:* Brockenhurst Grammar Sch.; University Coll., Southampton (now Univ. of Southampton) (BScEng); DScEng, PhD London. CEng, FIMechE. Res. Asst, Imperial Coll., 1948–52; Academic Staff, Imperial Coll., 1952–76 and 1979–; seconded NPL and Brit. Aerospace, 1976–78. Hon. Prof., Shenyang Inst. of Aeronautical Engrg, Shenyang, China, 1987. Silver Medal, Plastics Inst., 1963; James Clayton Prize, IMechE, 1981. *Publications:* Introduction to Plate and Shell Theory, 1965; (jtly) Post Yield Fracture Mechanics, 1979, 2nd edn 1984; contribs to Proc. Royal Soc., Proc. IMechE, Jl Strain Anal., Amer. Soc. Test & Mat., etc. *Recreations:* fracture mechanics, travel, reading. *Address:* The Corner House, 17 Meadway, Epsom, Surrey KT19 8JZ. *T:* Epsom (03727) 22989.

TURNER, Christopher Gilbert; Headmaster, Stowe School, 1979–89; *b* 23 Dec. 1929; *s* of late Theodore F. Turner, QC; *m* 1961, Lucia, *d* of late Prof. S. R. K. Glanville (Provost of King's Coll., Cambridge); one *s* one *d* (and one *d* decd). Educ: Winchester Coll. (Schol.); New Coll., Oxford (Exhibnr), MA. Asst Master, Radley Coll., 1952–61; Senior Classics Master, Charterhouse, 1961–68; Headmaster, Dean Close Sch., 1968–79. Schoolmaster Student at Christ Church, Oxford, 1967. Foundation Member of Council, Cheltenham Colleges of Educn, 1968. Mem., HMC Cttee, 1974–75, 1987–88; Chm., Common Entrance Cttee, 1976–80; Governor, Monkton Combe Sch.; Chm. of Governors: Aldro Sch.; Beachborough Sch; Elstree Sch.; Great Rollright Sch. Lay Reader. FRSA. *Publications:* chapter on History, in Comparative Study of Greek and Latin Literature, 1969; chapter on Dean Close in the Seventies, in The First Hundred Years, 1986. *Recreations:* music (violin-playing), reading, walking, different forms of manual labour; OUBC 1951. *Address:* Rosemullion, Great Rollright, near Chipping Norton, Oxon OX7 5RQ. *T:* Chipping Norton (0608) 737359; 78 Vista Green, King's Norton, Birmingham B38 9PD. *T:* 021–459 3863.

See also Hon. Sir M. J. Turner.

TURNER, Christopher John, CBE 1990 (OBE 1977); consultant to McLane (Wal Mart) on regional business development, Santa Domingo, since 1990; Governor of Montserrat, West Indies, 1987–90; *b* 17 Aug. 1933; *s* of Arthur Basil Turner and Joan Meddows (*née* Taylor); *m* 1961, Irene Philomena de Souza; two *d* (one *s* decd). *Educ:* Truro Cathedral Sch.; Jesus Coll., Cambridge (MA). Served RAF, Pilot Officer (Navigator), 1951–53. Tanganyika/Tanzania: Dist Officer, 1958–61; Dist Comr, 1961–62; Magistrate and Regional Local Courts Officer, 1962–64; Sec., Sch. Admin, 1964–69; Anglo-French Condominium of New Hebrides: Dist Agent, 1970–73; Devclt Sec., 1973; Financial Sec., 1975; Chief Sec., 1977–80; Admin. Officer (Staff Planning), Hong Kong, 1980–82; Governor, Turks and Caicos Islands, 1982–87. Vanuatu Independence Medal, 1981. *Recreations:* ornithology, photography, diving, tropical gardening. *Address:* 98 Christchurch Road, Winchester SO23 9TE. *T:* Winchester (0962) 61318.

TURNER, Air Cdre Clifford John, CB 1973; MBE 1953; *b* 21 Dec. 1918; *s* of J. E. Turner; *m* 1942, Isabel Emily Cormack; two *s. Educ:* Parkstone Grammar Sch.; RAF Techn. College. Engrg Apprentice, 1935–38; various RAF engrg appts, 1938–64; Group Dir, RAF Staff Coll., 1965–67; Stn Comdr, RAF Colerne, 1968–69; AO Engineering, Training Comd, 1969–73. *Address:* Garnet Drive, Vernon, RR4, BC V1T 6L7, Canada.

TURNER, Colin Francis; Senior District Judge (formerly Senior Registrar), Family Division of High Court, 1988–91 (Registrar, 1971–88); *b* 11 April 1930; *s* of Sidney F. and Charlotte C. Turner; *m* 1951, Josephine Alma Jones; two *s* one *d. Educ:* Beckenham Grammar Sch.; King's Coll., London. LLB 1955. Entered Principal Probate Registry, 1949; District Probate Registrar, York, 1965–68. *Publications:* (ed jtly) Rayden on Divorce, 9th, 11th, 12th and 13th edns, consulting editor to 14th edn; an editor of Supreme Court Practice, 1972–90; (jtly) Precedents in Matrimonial Causes and Ancillary Matters, 1985. *Recreations:* birding, fishing. *Address:* Lakers, Church Road, St Johns, Redhill, Surrey RH1 6QA. *T:* Redhill (0737) 761807.

TURNER, Colin William; Rector, Glasgow Academy, since 1983; *b* 10 Dec. 1933; *s* of William and Joyce Turner; *m* 1958, Priscilla Mary Trickett; two *s* two *d. Educ:* Torquay Grammar Sch.; King's Coll., London (BSc; AKC). Edinburgh Academy: Asst Master, 1958–82; OC CCF, 1960–74; Head, Maths Dept, 1973–75; Housemaster, 1975–82. *Recreations:* mountaineering, caravanning. *Address:* 11 Kirklee Terrace, Glasgow G12 0TH. *T:* 041–357 1776.

TURNER, Colin William Carstairs, CBE 1985; DFC 1944; President, The Colin Turner Group, International Media Representatives and Marketing Consultants, since 1988 (Chairman, 1985–88); *b* 4 Jan. 1922; *s* of late Colin C. W. Turner, Enfield; *m* 1949, Evelyn Mary, *d* of late Claude H. Buckard, Enfield; three *s* one *d. Educ:* Highgate Sch. Served War of 1939–45 with RAF, 1940–45, Air observer; S. Africa and E Africa, 223 Squadron; Desert Air Force, N. Africa, 1942–44; commissioned, 1943; invalided out as Flying Officer, 1945, after air crash; Chm., 223 Squadron Assoc., 1975–; Pres., RAFA (Enfield Br.), 1979–. Mem., Enfield Borough Council, 1956–58. Pres., Overseas Press and Media Association, 1965–67, Life Pres., 1982 (Hon. Secretary, 1967; Hon. Treasurer, 1974–82; Editor, Overseas Media Guide, 1968, 1969, 1970, 1971, 1972, 1973, 1974); Chm., PR Cttee, Commonwealth Press Union, 1970–87; Chm., Cons. Commonwealth and Overseas Council, 1976–82 (Dep. Chm. 1975); Vice-Pres., Cons. Foreign and Commonwealth Council (formerly Cons. Commonwealth and Overseas Council), 1985–88; Mem., Nat. Exec., Cons. Party, 1946–53, 1968–73, 1976–82; Pres., Enfield North Cons. Assoc., 1984– (Chm., 1979–84); Chm., Cons. Europ. Constituency Council, London N, 1984–89. Contested (C) Enfield (East), 1950 and 1951; MP (C) Woolwich West, 1959–64. Editor, The Cholmeleian, 1982– (Pres., Old Cholmeleian Soc., 1985–86). *Recreations:* gardening, do-it-yourself, sailing, fishing. *Address:* 55 Rowantree Road, Enfield, Mddx. *T:* 081–363 2403.

TURNER, David Andrew; QC 1991; a Recorder of the Crown Court, since 1990; *b* 6 March 1947; *s* of James and Phyllis Turner; *m* 1978, Mary Christine Moffatt; two *s* one *d. Educ:* King George V Sch., Southport; Queens' Coll., Cambridge (MA, LLM). Called to the Bar, Gray's Inn, 1971; Asst Recorder, 1987–90. *Recreations:* squash, music. *Address:* Pearl Assurance House, Derby Square, Liverpool L2 9XX. *T:* 051–236 7747. *Club:* Liverpool Racquet.

TURNER, Prof. David Warren, FRS 1973; Fellow of Balliol College, Oxford, since 1967; Professor of Electron Spectroscopy, Oxford, since 1985; *b* 16 July 1927; *s* of Robert Cecil Turner and Constance Margaret (*née* Bonner); *m* 1954, Barbara Marion Fisher; one *s* one *d. Educ:* Westcliff High Sch.; Univ. of Exeter. MA, BSc, PhD, DIC. Lectr, Imperial Coll., 1958; Reader in Organic Chemistry, Imperial Coll., 1965; Oxford University: Lectr in Physical Chem., 1968; Reader in Physical Chemistry, 1978; Reader in Electron Spectroscopy, 1984. Lectures: Kahlbaum, Univ. of Basle, 1971; Van Geuns, Univ. of Amsterdam, 1974; Harkins, Chicago Univ., 1974; Kistiakowski, Harvard, 1979; Liversidge, RSC, 1981–82. Tilden Medal, Chemical Soc., 1967; Harrison Howe Award, Amer. Chem. Soc., 1973. Hon. DTech, Royal Inst., Stockholm, 1971; Hon. DPhil Basle, 1980. *Publications:* Molecular Photoelectron Spectroscopy, 1970; contrib. Phil. Trans Royal Soc., Proc. Royal Soc., Jl Chem. Soc., etc. *Recreations:* music, gardening, tinkering with gadgets. *Address:* Balliol College, Oxford OX1 3BJ.

TURNER, Dennis; MP (Lab) Wolverhampton South East, since 1987; *b* 26 Aug. 1942; *s* of Mary Elizabeth Peasley and Thomas Herbert Turner; *m* 1976, Patricia Mary Narroway; one *s* one *d. Educ:* Stonefield Secondary Modern School, Bilston; Bilston College of Further Education; Bilston Black Country. Office boy, salesman, market trader, steel worker, partner in worker co-operative. *Address:* House of Commons, SW1A 0AA. *T:* 071–219 4210; Ambleside, King Street, Bradley, Bilston, W Midlands WV14 8PQ. *Club:* Springvale Sports and Social (Bilston).

TURNER, Donald William, CEng, FICE; Partner, Turner Associates, since 1986; Director: London Underground, since 1985; Lydd Airport Group, since 1987; *b* 17 Aug. 1925; *s* of William John Turner and Agnes Elizabeth Jane (*née* Bristow); *m* 1947, Patricia (*née* Stuteley); one *s* one *d. Educ:* Wanstead County High Sch.; Birmingham Univ. Served War, Army, 1943–45. Subseq. completed engrg trng in Britain; then took up post in Australia with Qld Railways, 1949. Left Qld, 1954; joined firm of UK consulting engrs and then worked in W Africa on rly and highway construction until 1960. Returned to UK, but remained with consultants until 1966, when joined BAA; Chief Engr, Heathrow Airport, 1970; Dir of Planning and Bd Mem., 1973; Dir of Privatisation, 1985–86; Chm., British Airports International, 1984–87. *Address:* 18 Osborne Villas, Hove, Sussex BN3 2RE.

TURNER, Dudley Russell Flower, CB 1977; Secretary, Advisory, Conciliation and Arbitration Service, 1974–77; *b* 15 Nov. 1916; *s* of Gerald Flower Turner and Dorothy May Turner (*née* Gillard), Penang; *m* 1941, Sheila Isobel Stewart; one *s* one *d. Educ:* Whitgift Sch.; London Univ. (BA Hons). Served RA (Captain), 1940–46. Entered Ministry of Labour, 1935; HM Treasury, 1953–56; Principal Private Secretary to Minister of Labour, 1956–59; Assistant Secretary: Cabinet Office, 1959–62; Ministry of Labour, 1962–64, 1966; Under-Sec., Ministry of Labour, 1967; Asst Under-Sec. of State, Dept of Employment and Productivity, 1968–70; Under-Sec., Trng Div., 1970–72, Manpower Gen. Div., 1972–73, Dept of Employment; Sec., Commn on Industrial Relations, 1973–74. Imperial Defence Coll., 1965. Pres., East Surrey Decorative and Fine Arts Soc., 1986– (Chm., 1980–86). *Recreations:* music, gardening. *Address:* 9 Witherby Close, Croydon, Surrey CR0 5SU. *Club:* Civil Service.

TURNER, Captain Ernest John Donaldson, CBE 1968; DSO 1942; DSC 1941, RN retd; French Croix de Guerre 1941; Vice Lord-Lieutenant of Dunbartonshire, since 1986; *b* 21 March 1914; *s* of Ernest Turner (*d* 1916, HMS Hampshire) and Margaret Donaldson; *m* 1940, Catherine Chalmers; one *d*. *Educ:* Hermitage Academy; Glasgow Technical College; Royal Navy; sowc, IDC. Joined Merchant Navy as Cadet, 1930; RN from RNR, 1937; specialised in submarines, 1939; served in submarines, 1941–68; Commodore, Submarines, 1964; Captain i/c Clyde, 1965–68, during building of Faslane Polaris Base; officer recruitment (after retiring), 1968–80; PA to Chm., Whyte & Mackay Distillers Ltd, 1980–82. *Recreations:* hockey and golf, holidays abroad. *Address:* Langcroft, Buchanan Castle, Drymen, by Glasgow G63 0HX. *T:* Drymen (0360) 60274. *Clubs:* Victory; Buchanan Castle Golf.

TURNER, Brig. Dame Evelyn Marguerite; *see* Turner, Brig. Dame Margot.

TURNER, Sir Francis; *see* Turner, Sir Arthur Francis.

TURNER, Prof. Grenville, FRS 1980; Professor of Isotope Geochemistry, Manchester University, since 1988; *b* 1 Nov. 1936; *o s* of Arnold and Florence Turner, Todmorden, Yorks; *m* 1961, Kathleen, *d* of William and Joan Morris, Rochdale, Lancs; one *s* one *d*. *Educ:* Todmorden Grammar Sch.; St John's Coll., Cambridge (MA); Balliol Coll., Oxford (DPhil). Asst Prof., Univ. of Calif at Berkeley, 1962–64; Lectr, Sheffield Univ., 1964–74, Sen. Lectr, 1974–79, Reader, 1979–80, Prof. of Physics, 1980–88. Vis. Associate in Nuclear Geophysics, Calif Inst. of Technol., 1970–71. Mem. Council, Royal Soc., 1990–. *Publications:* scientific papers. *Recreation:* photography. *Address:* The Royd, Todmorden, Lancs OL14 8DW. *T:* Todmorden (0706) 818621.

TURNER, Harry Edward; Managing Director, Television South West PLC, since 1985; *b* 28 Feb. 1935; *s* of Harry Turner and Bessie Elizabeth Jay; *m* 1956, Carolyn Bird; one *s* one *d*. *Educ:* Sloane Grammar Sch., Chelsea. Served Middlesex Regt, Austria, 2nd Lieut, 1953–55. Sales Representative, Crosse & Blackwell Foods, 1955–56; Advertising Executive: Daily Herald, 1956–58; Kemsley Newspapers, 1958–60; Feature Writer and Advtsg Manager, TV International Magazine, 1960–62; Sales Dir, Westward Television, 1962–80; Dir of Marketing, Television South West, 1980–85; Dir, ITN, 1987–. Dir, Prince of Wales Trust, 1988–. FRSA 1986. *Publications:* The Man Who Could Hear Fishes Scream (short stories), 1978; The Gentle Art of Salesmanship, 1985; So You Want To Be a Sales Manager, 1987; Innocents in the Boardroom, 1991. *Recreations:* tennis, riding, ski-ing, literature, travel. *Address:* Four Acres, Lake Road, Deepcut, Surrey GU16 6RB. *T:* Deepcut (0252) 835527; Derry's Cross, Plymouth. *Clubs:* English-Speaking Union, White Elephant, Tramp.

TURNER, Rev. Professor Henry Ernest William, DD; Canon Residentiary, Durham Cathedral, 1950–73; Treasurer, 1956–73; Sub-Dean, 1959–73; Acting Dean, 1973; Van Mildert Professor of Divinity, Durham University, 1958–73, now Emeritus; *b* 14 Jan. 1907; *o s* of Henry Frederick Richard and Ethel Turner, Sheffield; *m* 1936, Constance Parker, *d* of Dr E. P. Haythornthwaite, Rowrah, Cumberland; two *s*. *Educ:* King Edward VII Sch., Sheffield; St John's Coll., Oxford; Wycliffe Hall, Oxford. MA 1933; BD 1940; DD 1955. Curate, Christ Church, Cockermouth, 1931–34; Curate, Holy Trinity, Wavertree, 1934–35; Fellow, Chaplain and Tutor, Lincoln Coll., Oxford, 1935–50; Chaplain, RAFVR, 1940–45; Librarian, Lincoln Coll., 1945–48; Senior Tutor, Lincoln Coll., 1948–50; Lightfoot Prof. of Divinity, Durham Univ., 1950–58. Select Preacher, Oxford Univ., 1950–51; Bampton Lectr, Oxford, 1954. Member: Anglican delegation to Third Conference of World Council of Churches, Lund, 1952; Doctrine Commn of the Church of England, 1967–76; formerly Mem., Anglican-Presbyterian Conversations; Theological Consultant to Anglican Roman Catholic Conversations, 1970. *Publications:* The Life and Person of Jesus Christ, 1951; The Patristic Doctrine of Redemption, 1952; Jesus Master and Lord, 1953; The Pattern of Christian Truth (Bampton Lectures), 1955; Why Bishops?, 1955; The Meaning of the Cross, 1959; (jt author with H. Montefiore) Thomas and the Evangelists, 1962; Historicity and the Gospels, 1963; Jesus the Christ, 1976; contributions to the Guardian, Theology and Church Quarterly Review. *Address:* Realands, Eskdale, near Holmrook, Cumbria CA19 1TW. *T:* Eskdale (09403) 321.

TURNER, Prof. Herbert Arthur (Frederick), BSc Econ London, PhD Manchester, MA Cantab; Montague Burton Professor of Industrial Relations, University of Cambridge, 1963–83, now Professor Emeritus; Fellow of Churchill College, Cambridge, since 1963; *b* 11 Dec. 1919; *s* of Frederick and May Turner. *Educ:* Henry Thornton Sch., Clapham; LSE (Leverhulme Schol., then Leverhulme Res. Student, 1936–40; BSc (Econ) 1939); PhD Manchester, 1960. Army, then naval staff, 1940–44. Member, Trades Union Congress Research and Economic Department, 1944; Assistant Education Secretary, TUC, 1947; Lecturer, 1950, Senior Lecturer, 1959, University of Manchester; Council of Europe Res. Fellow, 1957–58; Montague Burton Professor of Industrial Relations, University of Leeds, 1961–63. Mem., NBPI, 1967–71. Visiting Professor: Lusaka, 1969; Harvard and MIT, 1971–72; Sydney Univ., 1976–77; Hong Kong Univ., 1978–79 and 1985–87; Monash Univ., 1982; Bombay and Lucknow Univs, 1983; South China Univ. of Technology, 1986; Zhongshan Univ., 1987; Leverhulme Sen. Res. Fellow, 1985–88. Sometime Adviser to Govts of Congo, Zaïre, Egypt, Tanzania, Fiji, Papua New Guinea, Zambia and other developing countries; Chm., Incomes Policies Commn of E African Community, 1973; ILO Adviser: Malawi, 1967; Iran, 1975; Labour Adviser, UNECA, 1980; World Bank Consultant, China, 1988. *Publications:* Arbitration, 1951; Wage Policy Abroad, 1956; Trade Union Growth, Structure and Policy, 1962; Wages: the Problems for Underdeveloped Countries, 1965, 2nd edn 1968; Prices, Wages and Incomes Policies, 1966; Labour Relations in the Motor Industry, 1967; Is Britain Really Strike-Prone?, 1969; Do Trade Unions Cause Inflation?, 1972, 3rd edn 1978; Management Characteristics and Labour Conflict, 1978; The Last Colony: labour in Hong Kong, 1980; The ILO and Hong Kong, 1986; Between Two Societies: Hong Kong labour in transition, 1990; various reports of ILO, monographs, papers and articles on labour economics and statistics, industrial relations, developing countries. *Recreations:* minimal but mostly excusable. *Address:* Churchill College, Cambridge CB3 0DS; La Sandrais, Pleudihen 22698, France. *Club:* United Oxford & Cambridge University.

TURNER, Hugh Wason, CMG 1980; Director, National Gas Turbine Establishment, 1980–83, retired; *b* 2 April 1923; *s* of Thomas W. Turner and Elizabeth P. Turner (*née* Pooley); *m* 1950, Rosemary Borley; two *s* two *d*. *Educ:* Dollar Academy; Glasgow University. BSc Hons (Mech. Eng); CEng; FRAeS. Aeroplane and Armament Experimental Establishment, 1943–52; Chief Tech. Instructor, Empire Test Pilots School, 1953; A&AEE (Prin. Scientific Officer), 1954–64; Asst Director, RAF Aircraft, Min. of Technology, 1965–68; Superintendent, Trials Management, A&AEE, 1968–69; Division Leader, Systems Engineering, NATO MRCA Management Agency (NAMMA), Munich, 1969–74; Chief Superintendent, A&AEE, 1974–75; DGA1 (Dir Gen., Tornado), MoD (PE), 1976–80. *Recreations:* ski-ing, model building, photography, DIY. *Address:* Lavender Cottage, 1 Highcliff Road, Lyme Regis, Dorset DT7 3EW. *T:* Lyme Regis (0297) 442310.

TURNER, Prof. James Johnson; Professor of Inorganic Chemistry, since 1979, and Head of Department, since 1991, University of Nottingham (Pro-Vice-Chancellor, 1986–90); *b* 24 Dec. 1935; *s* of Harry Turner and Evelyn Turner (*née* Johnson); *m* 1961, Joanna Margaret Gargett; two *d*. *Educ:* Darwen Grammar Sch.; King's Coll., Cambridge (MA, PhD 1960; ScD 1985). CChem; FRSC. Research Fellow, King's Coll., Cambridge, 1960; Harkness Fellow, Univ. of Calif, Berkeley, 1961–63; University of Cambridge: Univ. Demonstrator, 1963–68; Univ. Lectr, 1968–71; College Lectr, 1963–71, Admissions Tutor, 1967–71, King's Coll.; Prof. and Head of Dept of Inorganic Chemistry, Univ. of Newcastle upon Tyne, 1972–78. Visiting Professor: Univ. of Western Ontario, 1975; Texas, 1977; MIT, 1984; Chicago, 1986. Science and Engineering Research Council (formerly SRC): Mem., 1974–77, Chm., 1979–82, Chemistry Cttee; Mem., Science Bd, 1979–86; Mem. Council, 1982–86. Royal Society of Chemistry: Mem., 1974–77, Vice-Pres., 1982–84, Dalton Council; Tilden Lectr, 1978; Liversidge Lectr, 1991. *Publications:* papers mainly in jls of Chem. Soc. and Amer. Chem. Soc. *Recreation:* walking. *Address:* Department of Chemistry, University of Nottingham, University Park, Nottingham NG7 2RD. *T:* Nottingham (0602) 506101.

TURNER, Hon. Joanna Elizabeth, (Hon. Mrs Turner), MA; Classics Teacher, Ellesmere College, Salop, 1975–80; *b* 10 Jan. 1923; 2nd *d* of 1st Baron Piercy, CBE, and Mary Louisa, *d* of Hon. Thomas Pelham; *m* 1968, James Francis Turner (*d* 1983), *er s* of late Rev. P. R. Turner. *Educ:* St Paul's Girls' Sch.; Somerville Coll., Oxford (Sen. Classics Schol.). Asst Classics Mistress: Downe House, Newbury, 1944–46; Gordonstoun Sch., 1947–48; Badminton Sch., Bristol, 1948–65, Headmistress, Badminton Sch., Bristol, 1966–69. JP Inner London (Juvenile Courts), 1970–75. *Publications:* B. M. Sanderson and Badminton School 1947–1966, 1988; Quarries and Craftsmen of the Windrush Valley, 1988. *Address:* The Old Coach House, Burford, Oxon OX8 4RE. *T:* Burford (099382) 2368.

TURNER, John; Under Secretary, Employment Department Group (formerly Department of Employment), since 1988; Deputy Chief Executive, Employment Service, since 1989; *b* 22 April 1946; *s* of William Cecil Turner and late Hilda Margaret Turner; *m* 1971, Susan Georgina Kennedy; two *s* one *d*. *Educ:* Ramsey Abbey Grammar Sch.; Northwood Hills Grammar Sch. Entered Civil Service, 1967; Principal, DoI, 1979; MSC, 1981–84; Asst Sec., Dept of Employment, 1985; Prin. Pvte Sec. to Rt. Hon. Lord Young of Graffham and Rt. Hon. Norman Fowler, 1986–87; Small Firms and Tourism Div., Dept of Employment, 1989. *Recreations:* music, motoring, the outdoors. *Address:* 24 Rutland Park, Sheffield S10 2PB. *T:* Sheffield (0742) 661067.

TURNER, Prof. John Derfel; Sarah Fielden Professor of Education, since 1985, and Pro Vice-Chancellor, since 1991, University of Manchester; *b* 27 Feb. 1928; *s* of Joseph Turner and Dorothy Winifred Turner; *m* 1951, Susan Broady Hovey; two *s*. *Educ:* Manchester Grammar Sch.; Univ. of Manchester. BA 1948, MA 1951, Teacher's Diploma 1951. Education Officer, RAF, 1948–50; teacher, Prince Henry's Grammar Sch., Evesham, 1951–53; Lectr in English, 1953–56, Sen. Lectr in Educn, 1956–61, Nigerian Coll. of Arts, Science and Technology; Lectr in Educn, Univ. of Exeter Inst. of Education, 1961–64; Prof. of Educn and Dir, Sch. of Educn, 1964–70, and Pro-Vice-Chancellor, 1966–70, Univ. of Botswana, Lesotho and Swaziland, Emeritus Prof., 1970; University of Manchester: Prof. of Educn and Dir of Sch. of Educn, 1970–76; Dean, Faculty of Educn, 1972–74 and 1986–91; Prof. of Adult and Higher Educn, 1976–85. Rector, University Coll. of Botswana, Univ. of Botswana and Swaziland, 1981–82 and Vice-Chancellor, Univ. of Botswana, 1982–84. Chairman: Univs Council for Educn of Teachers, 1979–81 and 1988–91 (Vice-Chm., 1976–79); Council of Validating Univs, 1990–; Presidential Commn on Higher Educn in Namibi, 1991–; Member: UK Nat. Commn for UNESCO, 1975–81; IUC Working Parties on East and Central Africa and on Rural Development, 1975–81; Educn Sub-Cttee, UGC, 1980–81; Educn Cttee and Further Educn Bd, CNAA, 1979–81; Chm., European Develt Fund/IUC Working Party on Academic Develt of Univ. of Juba, 1977–78; Chm. and Mem. Council, Social Studies Adv. Cttee, Selly Oak Colleges, 1975–81. Chm., Bd of Governors, Abbotsholme Sch., 1980–. Chm., Editl Bd, Internat. Jl of Educn and Develt, 1978–81. Hon. FCP 1985. Hon. LLD Ohio Univ., 1982. *Publications:* Introducing the Language Laboratory, 1963; (ed with A. P. Hunter) Educational Development in Predominantly Rural Countries, 1968; (ed with J. Rushton) The Teacher in a Changing Society, 1974; (ed with J. Rushton) Education and Deprivation, 1975; (ed with J. Rushton) Education and Professions, 1976; school text books and contribs to edited works and to jls. *Recreations:* reading, music, theatre, walking; Methodist local preacher. *Address:* 13 Firswood Mount, Gatley, Cheadle, Cheshire SK8 4JY. *T:* 061–428 2734. *Club:* Commonwealth Trust.

TURNER, Rt. Hon. John Napier, PC (Can.) 1965; QC (Can.); MP; Leader of the Liberal Party of Canada, and Leader of the Opposition, 1984–90; *b* 7 June 1929; *s* of Leonard Turner and Phyllis Turner (*née* Gregory); *m* 1963, Geills McCrae Kilgour; three *s* one *d*. *Educ:* Norman Model Public Sch., Ottawa, Ont.; Ashbury Coll., 1939–42; St Patrick's Coll., 1942–45; Univ. of BC; Oxford Univ. BA (PolSci, Hons) BC, 1949; Rhodes Scholar, Oxford Univ., BA (Juris.) 1951; BCL 1952; MA 1957. Joined Stikeman, Elliott, Tamaki, Mercier & Turner, Montreal, Quebec; practised with them after being called to English Bar, 1953, Bar of Quebec, 1954 and Bar of Ont., 1968; QC (Ont and Que) 1968; with McMillan Binch, Toronto, 1976–84. MP for Montreal-St Lawrence-St Georges, 1962–68, Ottawa-Carleton, 1968–76, Vancouver Quadra, 1984–; Parly Sec. to Minister of Northern Affairs and Nat. Resources, 1963–65; Minister without Portfolio, Dec. 1965–April 1967; Registrar-Gen. of Canada, April 1967–Jan. 1968; Minister of Consumer and Corporate Affairs, Dec. 1967–July 1968; Solicitor-Gen., April-July 1968; Minister of Justice and Attorney-Gen. of Canada, July 1968–Jan. 1972; Minister of Finance, Jan. 1972–Sept. 1975; resigned as MP, Feb. 1976; Prime Minister of Canada, June–Sept. 1984. Barbados Bar, 1969; Yukon and Northwest Territories, 1969; Trinidad Bar, 1969; British Columbia, 1969. Hon. Dr of Laws: Univ. of New Brunswick, 1968; York Univ., Toronto, 1969; Hon. Dr of Civil Law, Mt Allison Univ., NB, 1980. *Publications:* Senate of Canada, 1961; Politics of Purpose, 1968. *Recreations:* tennis, canoeing, ski-ing; Canadian Track Field Champion 1948, Mem. English Track and Field Team. *Address:* (office) House of Commons, Ottawa, Ont K1A 0A6, Canada; (home) 27 Dunloe Road, Toronto, Ont M4W 2W4, Canada.

TURNER, Prof. John Stewart, FAA 1979; FRS 1982; Professor of Geophysical Fluid Dynamics, Australian National University, since 1975; *b* Sydney, Aust., 11 Jan. 1930; *s* of Ivan Stewart Turner and Enid Florence (*née* Payne); *m* 1959, Sheila Lloyd Jones; two *s* one *d*. *Educ:* North Sydney Boys' High Sch.; Wesley Coll., Univ. of Sydney (BSc, MSc); Trinity Coll., Univ. of Cambridge (PhD). FInstP 1969. Research Officer, CSIRO cloud physics group, 1953–54 and 1960–61; 1851 Exhibition Overseas Schol., 1954–57; postdoctoral research post, Univ. of Manchester, 1958–59; Rossby Fellow, then Associate Scientist, Woods Hole Oceanographic Instn, 1962–66; Asst Director of Research, then Reader, Dept of Applied Mathematics and Theoretical Physics, Univ. of Cambridge, 1966–75; Fellow of Darwin Coll., Cambridge, 1974; Foundation Prof. of Geophysical Fluid Dynamics in the Research Sch. of Earth Sciences, ANU, 1975–; Overseas Fellow, Churchill Coll., Cambridge, 1985. Matthew Flinders Lectr, Aust. Acad. of Science, 1990. Member, Australian Marine Sciences and Technologies Adv. Cttee (AMSTAC), 1979–84. Associate Editor, Journal of Fluid Mechanics, 1975–; Mem. Editorial Adv. Board, Deep-Sea Research, 1974–84. *Publications:* Buoyancy Effects in Fluids, 1973, paperback 1979;

papers in various scientific jls. *Recreations:* bushwalking, photography, home handyman. *Address:* (office) Research School of Earth Sciences, Australian National University, GPO Box 4, Canberra, ACT 2601, Australia. *T:* (06) 249 4530; (home) 2/28 Black Street, Yarralumla, ACT 2600, Australia.

TURNER, John Turnage; His Honour Judge Turner; a Circuit Judge, since 1976; Resident Judge at Ipswich, since 1984; *b* 12 Nov. 1929; *s* of Wilfrid Edward and May Martha Turner; *m* 1956, Gillian Mary Rayner; two *d*. *Educ:* Earls Colne Grammar School. Called to the Bar, Inner Temple, 1952. *Recreations:* music appreciation, travelling, watching cricket. *Address:* The Crown Court, Ipswich, Suffolk. *Club:* MCC.

TURNER, Lloyd Charles; livestock farmer, Kent, since 1986; Director, Messenger Nationwide, since 1988; Assistant Editor, Today, since 1990; *b* 2 Oct. 1938; *s* of Charles Thomas and Lily Turner; *m* 1st, 1961, Rosemary Munday (marr. diss. 1966); 2nd, 1967, Jennifer Anne Cox (marr. diss. 1972); 3rd, 1973, Jill Marguerite King. *Educ:* Giants Creek Primary Sch., Australia; The Armidale Sch., Armidale, Australia. Newcastle Morning Herald, Australia: Cadet journalist, 1956; Chief Crime Reporter, 1960; Features Editor, 1961; Picture Editor, 1962; Asst Editor, 1964; Industrial Correspondent, Manchester Evening News, 1968; Daily Express: Sub-Editor, 1968; Asst Chief Sub-Editor, 1974; Dep. Chief Sub-Editor, 1975; Asst Night Editor, 1976; Dep. Night Editor, 1977; Night Editor, 1979; Editor: The Daily Star, subseq. The Star, 1980–87; The Post, 1988; Editor-in-Chief, Messenger TV, 1988; Director: Express Newspapers plc, 1982–87; Daily Star plc, 1982–87. CPU Scholar, 1966. Pres., Australian Journalists Assoc. (Provincial), 1962–65; Chm., (Father), Daily Express/Sunday Express NUJ Chapel, 1969–74. Hon. Mem., NSPCC, 1989. *Recreations:* gardening, horse-racing. *Address:* 1 Virginia Street, E1 9BS. *Clubs:* St James's; Journalists' (Sydney).

TURNER, Brig. Dame Margot, (E. M. Turner), DBE 1965 (MBE 1946); RRC 1956; Matron-in-Chief and Director Army Nursing Service, 1964–68; *b* 10 May 1910; *d* of late Thomas Frederick Turner and late Molly Cecilia (*née* Bryan). *Educ:* Finchley County Sch., Middlesex. Trained at St Bartholomew's Hospital, London, 1931–35. Joined QAIMNS, 1937 (became QARANC, 1949). Served in UK, India, Malaya, Hong Kong, Bermuda, Germany and Near East. POW Sumatra, Feb. 1942–Aug. 1945. Col Comdt, QARANC, 1969–74. CStJ 1966. *Relevant Publication:* Sir John Smyth, Will to Live: the story of Dame Margot Turner, 1970. *Recreations:* reading, photography, golf, tennis. *Address:* 2 Chantry Court, Frimley, Surrey. *T:* Camberley (0276) 22030.

TURNER, Hon. Sir Michael (John); Hon. Mr Justice Turner; Kt 1985; a Judge of the High Court of Justice, Queen's Bench Division, since 1985; *b* 31 May 1931; *s* of late Theodore F. Turner, QC; *m* 1st, 1956, Hon. Susan Money-Coutts (marr. diss. 1965); one *s* one *d*; 2nd, 1965, Frances Deborah, *d* of Rt. Hon. Sir David Croom-Johnson, *qv*; two *s*. *Educ:* Winchester; Magdalene Coll., Cambridge (BA). Called to Bar, Inner Temple, 1954 (Bencher 1981); a Recorder, 1972–85; QC 1973–85. Chm., E Mids Agricultural Tribunal, 1979–82. Mem., Judicial Studies Bd, 1988– (Co-Chm., Civil and Family Cttee, 1988–). *Recreations:* horses, listening to music. *Address:* Royal Courts of Justice, Strand, WC2A 2LL.

See also C. G. Turner.

TURNER, Michael Ralph, FRSA; Chairman, Book Trust, since 1990; Group Managing Director, 1976–88, Chief Executive, 1982–88, Associated Book Publishers PLC; Chairman, Associated Book Publishers (UK) Ltd, 1977–90; *b* 26 Jan. 1929; *s* of Ralph Victor Turner and May Turner; *m* 1955, Ruth Baylis; two *s* two *d*. *Educ:* Newport Sch., Essex; Trinity Coll., Cambridge (BA Hons). Served RAF, Transport Comd, 1947–49. Jun. Editor, J. M. Dent & Sons, 1949–50; Methuen & Co.: Jun. Editor, 1953; subseq. Publicity and Promotion Manager, and Dir; Associated Publishers Ltd: Marketing Dir, 1973; Asst Gp Man. Dir, 1975; Gp Man. Dir, 1976. Chm., Methuen Inc., New York, 1981–88; Pres., Carswell Co. Ltd, Toronto, 1982–84; Dir, ABP Investments (Aust.) Pty Ltd, 1976–88; Sen. Vice-Pres., Publishing Information Gp, Internat. Thomson Orgn Ltd, 1987–89. Chm., Book Marketing Council, 1981–84; Member: Book Trade Working Party, 1973–74; Council, Publishers Assoc., 1981–90 (Vice-Pres., 1985–87 and 1989–90; Pres., 1987–89; Chm., Home Trade and Services Council, 1989–90); National Council and Exec., NBL, 1980–87; British Library Adv. Council, 1989–; Centre for the Book Adv. Cttee, 1990–; Publishing Bd, Design Council, and Chm., books and videos operation, 1991–. FRSA 1984. *Publications:* The Bluffer's Guide to the Theatre, 1967; Parlour Poetry, 1967; (with Antony Miall) The Parlour Song Book, 1972; (with Antony Miall) Just a Song at Twilight, 1975; (with Antony Miall) The Edwardian Song Book, 1982; (with Michael Geare) Gluttony, Pride and Lust and Other Sins from the World of Books, 1984; (with Leslie Lonsdale-Cooper) translations of Hergé's Tintin books, 1958–91. *Recreations:* reading, music, theatre, maritime painting and models. *Address:* Paradise House, Boscastle, Cornwall PL35 0BL. *T:* Boscastle (08405) 250. *Club:* Garrick.

TURNER, Norman Henry, CBE 1977; Official Solicitor to the Supreme Court of Judicature, 1970–80; *b* 11 May 1916; *s* of late Henry James Turner, MA and Hilda Gertrude Turner; *m* 1939, Dora Ardella (*née* Cooper) (*d* 1990); three *s* two *d*; *m* 1991, Mona Florence Mackenzie. *Educ:* Nottingham High School. Articled, Nottingham, 1933; admitted Solicitor (Hons), 1938; joined Official Solicitor's Dept, 1948; Asst Official Solicitor, 1958. *Address:* 48 Rushington Avenue, Maidenhead, Berks SL6 1BZ. *T:* Maidenhead (0628) 22918.

TURNER, Patricia, OBE 1981; Head of National Equal Rights Department, and National Industrial Officer, General, Municipal, Boilermakers and Allied Trades Union (formerly General and Municipal Workers' Union), 1971–89; Member, General Council, TUC, 1981–89; *b* 14 May 1927; *d* of John Richard and Maire Collins; *m* 1954, Donald Turner, BSc (Econ). *Educ:* London School of Economics (BSc (Econ), MSc (Econ)). Industrial Sociology Lectr, 1965–69; Consultant, Manpower and Productivity Service (Dept of Employment and Productivity), 1969–70; Sen. Industrial Relations Officer, Commn on Industrial Relations, 1970–71. Member: Confedn of Shipbuilding and Engineering Unions Exec. Council, 1971–89 (Pres., 1982–83); Engineering Industry Training Bd, 1971–89; Women's Nat. Commn, 1973–89; Central Arbitration Cttee, 1976–; Dept of Employment Adv. Cttee on Women's Employment, 1980–89; Equal Opportunities Commn, 1985–91; Employment Appeal Tribunal, 1987–. *Recreations:* reading, theatre. *Address:* 22 Kenilworth Road, Edgware, Middlesex HA8 8YG.

TURNER, Peter; *see* Turner, T. P.

TURNER, Air Vice-Marshal Peter, CB 1979; MA; Bursar and Steward, Wolfson College, Cambridge, 1979–89; *b* 29 Dec. 1924; *s* of late George Allen and of Emma Turner; *m* 1949, Doreen Newbon; one *s*. *Educ:* Tapton House Sch., Chesterfield. Served War of 1939–45; 640 Sqdn, 1943–45; Nos 51, 242 and 246 Sqdns, 1945–48; psa 1961; NATO staff, 1963–67; jssc 1967; Chief Equipment and Secretarial Instructor, RAF Coll., Cranwell, 1967–68; Comd Accountant, HQ Air Support Comd, 1968–69; Station Comdr, RAF Uxbridge, 1969–71; RCDS, 1972; Dir of Personnel (Ground) (RAF), MoD, 1973–75; AOA, HQ RAF Support Command, 1975–79, and Head of RAF Admin. Branch, 1976–79. MA Cantab 1979. *Recreation:* retrospective contemplation. *Address:* Hedge End, Potton Road, Hilton, Cambs PE18 9NG. *Club:* Royal Air Force.

TURNER, Peter William; District Secretary, Transport and General Workers' Union, to 1991, retired; *m* Maureen Ann Turner (*née* Hill), Councillor, JP. *Educ:* Bordesley Green Infant and Junior Sch.; Saltley Grammar Sch. (until 1940); various Trade Union weekend courses. Appointed District Officer, TGWU, 1969; District Sec., CSEU, 1974–76; seconded as Industrial Advr to DoI, 1976–78. Member of various cttees including: Chemical Industry Area Productivity Cttee, 1969–76 (Vice-Chm., 1970–72, Chm., 1972–74); TUC Regional Educn Adv. Cttee, 1970–76; Birmingham Crime Prevention Panel, 1973–76; W Midlands Consultative Cttee on Race Relations, 1974–76; DoE Working Party on Race Relations, 1974–76; Teaching Co. Management Cttee, 1977–82. Member: Birmingham Trades Council, 1956–76; Local Appeals Tribunal, 1969–74. *Recreations:* motoring, motor cycling, caravanning, do-it-yourself, reading, electronics. *Address:* c/o Transport and General Workers' Union, 8 Severn Street, Worcester WR1 2ND.

TURNER, Phil; *b* 7 June 1939; *s* of William Morris Turner and Eileen Lascelles Turner; *m* 1963, Gillian Sharp (*d* 1988); one *s* two *d* (and one *s* decd). *Educ:* Beckenham and Penge Grammar School for Boys; University Coll. London (BScEcon). National Coal Board, later British Coal: Management Trainee, 1961–63; Hd of Information, Purchasing and Stores, 1963–65; O & M Officer, 1965–66; Hd of Admin, R & D Dept, 1966–68; Hd of Manpower Planning, 1968–73; Staff Manager, Opencast Exec., 1973–78; Hd of Conditions of Service, 1978–80; Dep. Dir of Staff Pay and Conditions, 1980–86; Head of Employment Policy, 1986–89. Joined Labour Party, 1963; Chairman, Hampstead Labour Party, 1968–70; Councillor, Camden Bor. Council, 1971–: Chm., Building Works and Services Cttee, 1978–80 and 1986–89; Chair, Staff and Management Services Cttee, 1990–; Leader of Council, 1982–86. Member: Assoc. of London Authorities, 1983–86; Policy Cttee, AMA, 1984–86. Contested (Lab): Cities of London and Westminster South, Feb. and Oct. 1974; (Lab) Hampstead and Highgate, 1987. *Recreations:* family, conversation at the Blenheim Arms, collecting books. *Address:* 33 Minster Road, NW2 3SH. *T:* 071–794 8805.

TURNER, Philip, CBE 1975; LLB (London); in private practice with Infields, Hampton Wick, Surrey; *b* 1 June 1913; *er s* of late George Francis and late Daisy Louise Turner (*née* Frayn), Alverstoke, Hants; *m* 1938, Hazel Edith, *d* of late Douglas Anton and late Edith Ada Benda; one *d* (one *d* decd). *Educ:* Peter Symonds, Winchester. Admitted Solicitor, 1935. Entered General Post Office Solicitor's Dept, 1935. Served in Royal Navy, 1940–46 (Lt-Comdr). Asst Solicitor to General Post Office, 1953; Principal Asst Solicitor, 1962–72, Solicitor to the Post Office, 1972–75; temp. mem. of legal staff, DoE, 1976–77. Chm., Civil Service Legal Soc., 1957–58; Chm., Internat. Bar Assoc.'s Cttee on Public Utility Law, 1972–77. FBSA 1955. *Recreations:* piano, golf. *Address:* 8 Walters Mead, Ashtead, Surrey KT21 2BP. *T:* Ashtead (0372) 273656. *Clubs:* Naval, Royal Automobile, Law Society; Hampshire County Cricket, Surrey County Cricket.

TURNER, Surgeon Rear-Admiral (D) Philip Stanley, CB 1963; QHDS 1960–64; Director of Dental Services, RN, Admiralty, Nov. 1961–64; *b* 31 Oct. 1905; *s* of Frank Overy Turner and Ellen Mary Turner, Langton Green, Tunbridge Wells; *m* 1934, Marguerite Donnelly (*d* 1990); one *d* (and one *s* decd). *Educ:* Cranbrook Coll.; Guy's Hospital. LDS, RCS 1927. Surgeon Lieut (D) Royal Navy, 1928; Surgeon Captain (D) 1955; Surgeon Rear-Admiral (D), 1961; Senior Specialist in Dental Surgery, 1946–61. Served in: HMS Ramillies, Vanguard, Implacable, Indomitable; HMHS Maine, Tjitjalengka; RN Hospitals Haslar, Plymouth; RN Barracks Portsmouth, etc; Naval HQ, Malta. Foundation Fellow, British Assoc. of Oral Surgeons, 1962. *Address:* Woodhurst, Warren Lane, Cross-in-Hand, Heathfield, East Sussex. *T:* Heathfield (04352) 3532.

TURNER, Raymond C.; *see* Clifford-Turner.

TURNER, Richard, CMG 1956; LRIBA; consultant architect, retired 1983; *b* 2 May 1909; *m* 1933, Annie Elizabeth, *d* of late Rev. R. W. Gair; one *d*. *Educ:* Dame Alice Owen's School. Entered Office of Works, 1929; in charge of ME Office, 1938–47, centred in Istanbul and, later, Cairo; Asst Chief Architect, Min. of Works, 1951; Dir of Works (Overseas), 1960–65; Dir, Overseas Svcs, MPBW, 1965–69, retired. Mem., Esher UDC, 1969–72. *Address:* Flat 3, Western Field, Manor Road, Sidmouth, Devon EX10 8RR. *T:* Sidmouth (0395) 3805. *Club:* Travellers'.

TURNER, Dr Richard Wainwright Duke, OBE 1945; Senior Research Fellow in Preventive Cardiology, University of Edinburgh, 1974–84, retired (Reader in Medicine, 1960–74); Senior Physician and Physician in Charge of the Cardiac Department, Western General Hospital, Edinburgh, 1946–74; *b* Purley, Surrey, 30 May 1909; *s* of Sydney Duke Turner, MD (General Practitioner), and Lilian Maude, *d* of Sir James Wainwright; *m* Paula, *d* of Henry Meulen, Wimbledon; three *s* one *d*. *Educ:* Epsom Coll.; Clare Coll., Cambridge; St Thomas' Hosp., London. 1st Class Hons Nat. Sci. Tripos, Cambridge, 1934. MA, MB, BChir Cantab 1934; MRCS, LRCP 1935; MRCP 1936; MD Cantab 1940; FRCP 1950; FRCPE 1952. Served in RAMC, 1939–45: UK, Egypt and Italy (Lt-Col); officer i/c Med. Div. 31st and 92nd British General Hospitals. Examiner in Medicine: Univs of Edinburgh and Leeds; RCP; RCPE. Chm., Coronary Prevention Group, 1978–. Member: Assoc. Physicians of GB; British Cardiac Soc.; Hon. Member, Cardiol Socs of India and Pakistan. *Publications:* Diseases of Cardiovascular System in Davidson's Principles and Practice of Medicine, vols 1–11, 1952–65; Electrocardiography, 1963; Auscultation of the Heart, 1st edn 1963 to 6th edn 1984; contribs to British Heart Jl, Lancet, BMJ, Quarterly Jl of Med., American Heart Jl, etc. *Recreations:* travel, climbing, gardening, photography. *Address:* Cotterlings, Ditchling, Sussex BN6 8TS. *T:* Hassocks (07918) 3392; Cardiac Department, Western General Hospital, Edinburgh EH4 2XU. *T:* 031–332 2525. *Clubs:* Royal Over-Seas League; University Staff (Edinburgh).

TURNER, Robert Lockley; Master of the Supreme Court, Queen's Bench Division, since 1984; *b* 2 Sept. 1935; *s* of James Lockley Turner and Maud Beatrice Turner; *m* 1963, Jennifer Mary Leather; one *s* one *d*. *Educ:* Clifton Coll.; St Catharine's Coll., Cambridge (BA 1957, MA 1973). Called to the Bar, Gray's Inn, 1958. Commnd Gloucestershire Regt (28th/61st), 1959 (2nd Lieut); transf. to Army Legal Services, 1960 (Captain); Major 1962; retd from Army, 1966 (GSM with clasp South Arabia, 1966). Practised at Common Law Bar in London and on Midland and Oxford Circuit, 1967–84; a Recorder of the Crown Court, 1981–84. Hon. Steward, Westminster Abbey, 1985–; Churchwarden, St Matthew's, Midgham, 1990–. *Recreations:* gardening, gothic churches. *Publications:* (ed jtly) Supreme Court Practice; The Office of the Queen's Bench Master, 1990. *Address:* Royal Courts of Justice, WC2; Midgham Green, Berks. *Club:* Royal Fowey Yacht (Fowey).

TURNER, Stephen Gordon; General Secretary, National Union of Journalists, since 1990; *b* 27 July 1935; *s* of John Turner and Lillian Turner (*née* Wiseman); *m* 1st, 1955, Jean Florence Watts (marr. diss. 1978); two *s* one *d*; 2nd, 1979, Deborah Diana Thomas; one *d*. *Educ:* Triptons Secondary Modern Sch., Dagenham; Royal Liberty Grammar Sch., Romford. Royal Signals radio mechanic, 1953–55. Reporter: Romford Times, 1955–56;

Ilford Recorder, 1956; Bristol Evening World, 1957; freelance journalist, 1958–68; News sub-editor: Ipswich Evening Star, 1969; Daily Mail, 1969–71; Features sub-editor, 1971–73, Public Opinion Editor, 1973–90, Daily Mirror. Independent Councillor, Colchester BC, 1967–68. Mem., NUJ, 1955–; Father of the Chapel, Daily Mirror, 1976–78, 1986–90. *Address:* 1 Priory Grove, Dover, Kent CT17 0AB.

TURNER, Theodora, OBE 1961; ARRC 1944; retired as Matron of St Thomas' Hospital and Superintendent Nightingale Training School (1955–65); *b* 5 Aug. 1907; *er d* of H. E. M. Turner. *Educ:* Godolphin School, Salisbury; Edinburgh School of Domestic Economy. Ward Sister, St Thomas' Hosp., 1935–38; Administrative Course, Florence Nightingale Internat. Foundn, 1938–39. QAIMNS Reserve, 1939–45. Administrative Sister, St Thomas' Hosp., 1946–47; Matron Royal Infirmary, Liverpool, 1948–53; Education Officer, Educn Centre, Royal College of Nursing, Birmingham, 1953–55. President: Florence Nightingale Internat. Nurses Assoc., 1971–74; Royal Coll. of Nursing and Nat. Council of Nurses of UK, 1966–68. Mem., Argyll and Clyde Health Bd, 1974–75. *Recreations:* gardening and painting.

TURNER, (Thomas) Peter; Evaluation Consultant, since 1985; *b* 8 May 1928; *s* of Thomas Turner and Laura Crawley; *m* 1952, Jean Rosalie Weston; one *s* one *d.* *Educ:* Ilford County High Sch.; London University. BSc (1st Class Hons), Maths and Physics. GEC, North Wembley, 1947–50; Armament Design Establishment, 1950–54; Air Ministry (Science 3), 1954–58 and 1962–63; Chief Research Officer, RAF Maintenance Command, 1958–62; Police Research and Development Branch, Home Office, 1963–68; Civil Service Dept (OR), 1968–73; Head of Treasury/CSD Joint Operational Research Unit, 1973–76; Head of Operational Res., CSD, 1977–81, HM Treasury, 1981–84. *Address:* 8 Waring Drive, Green St Green, Orpington, Kent BR6 6DW. *T:* Farnborough (Kent) (0689) 851189.

TURNER, Wilfred, CMG 1977; CVO 1979; HM Diplomatic Service, retired; Director, Transportation Systems and Market Research Ltd (Transmark), 1987–90; *b* 10 Oct. 1921; *s* of late Allen Turner and Eliza (*née* Leach); *m* 1947, June Gladys Tite; two *s* one *d.* *Educ:* Heywood Grammar Sch., Lancs; London Univ. BSc 1947. Min. of Labour, 1938–42. Served War, REME, 1942–47. Min. of Labour, 1947–55; Brit. High Commn, New Delhi (Asst Lab. Adviser), 1955–59; Senior Wages Inspector, Min. of Labour, 1959–60; Min. of Health (Sec., Cttee on Safety of Drugs, 1963–66), 1960–66. Joined HM Diplomatic Service, 1966; Commonwealth Office, 1966; First Sec.: Kaduna, Nigeria, 1966–69; Kuala Lumpur, 1969–73; Dep. High Comr, and Commercial/Economic Counsellor, Accra, 1973–77; High Comr to Botswana, 1977–81. Dir, Southern Africa Assoc., 1983–88. Member: Cttee, Zambia Soc., 1983–; Central Council, Royal Commonwealth Soc., 1987–91; RIIA, 1987–; Royal African Soc., 1987–. *Recreation:* hill walking. *Address:* 44 Tower Road, Twickenham TW1 4PE. *T:* 081–892 1593. *Club:* Commonwealth Trust.

TURNER, Dr William; Regional Medical Officer, Yorkshire Regional Health Authority, 1976–86, retired; *b* 23 Feb. 1927; *s* of Clarence and Mabel Turner; *m* 1950, Patricia Bramham Wilkinson; one *s* two *d.* *Educ:* Prince Henry's Grammar Sch., Otley, Yorks; Leeds Univ. MB, ChB; DPH, FFCM; LLB. House Officer, Leeds Gen. Infirmary, 1950–51; RAMC, 1951–53; Gen. Practitioner, 1953–55; Public Health Trng, 1955–60; Medical Officer of Health: Hyde, 1960–63; Huddersfield, 1963–67; Bradford, 1967–74; Area MO, Bradford, 1974–76. Member: Standing Med. Adv. Cttee, 1978–82; NHS Steering Gp on Health Services Inf., 1979–84. *Publications:* contrib. BMJ, Medical Officer. *Address:* Bentcliffe, 1 Premiere Park, Ilkley, West Yorks LS29 9RQ. *T:* Ilkley (0943) 600114.

TURNER CAIN, Maj.-Gen. George Robert, CB 1967; CBE 1963; DSO 1945; President, Anglia Maltings (Holdings) Ltd, since 1982 (Chairman, 1976–82); Chairman: Anglia Maltings Ltd, 1976–82; F. & G. Smith Ltd, 1962–82; Walpole & Wright Ltd, 1968–82; Director: Crisp Maltings Ltd, 1967–82; Crisp Malt Products Ltd, 1968–82; Edme Ltd, 1972–82; *b* 16 Feb. 1912; *s* of late Wing Comdr G. Turner Cain; *m* 1938, Lamorna Maturin, *d* of late Col G. B. Hingston; one *s* one *d.* *Educ:* Norwich Sch.; RMC Sandhurst. 2nd Lt Norfolk Regt, 1932; 1st Bn Royal Norfolk Regt, India, 1933–38; Waziristan Campaign, 1937. Served War of 1939–45 with 1st Royal Norfolk and 1st Hereford Regt, BLA, 1944–45. Comd 1st Royal Norfolk Regt, Berlin, 1947–48; Hong Kong and UK, 1953–55; Comd Tactical Wing, School of Infantry, 1955–57; Comd 1st Fed. Inf. Bde, Malaya, in operations in Malaya, 1957–59; BGS, HQ, BAOR, 1961; Maj.-Gen. Administration, GHQ FARELF, 1964–67, retired; ADC, 1961–64. Dep. Col, Royal Anglian Regt, 1971–74. Croix de Guerre avec Palm, 1945; Star of Kedah (Malaya), 1959. *Recreation:* shooting. *Address:* Holbreck, Hollow Lane, Stiffkey, Wells-next-the-Sea, Norfolk NR23 1QG.

TURNER-SAMUELS, David Jessel, QC 1972; Barrister-at-Law; *b* 5 April 1918; *s* of late Moss Turner-Samuels, QC, MP, and Gladys Deborah Turner-Samuels (*née* Belcher); *m* 1939, Norma Turner-Samuels (*née* Verstone) (marr. diss. 1975); one *s* one *d*; *m* 1976, Norma Florence Negus, *qv.* *Educ:* Westminster Sch. Called to Bar, Middle Temple, 1939 (Bencher 1980); admitted to Trinidad bar, 1976. Served War of 1939–45, in Army, 1939–46. *Publication:* (jointly) Industrial Negotiation and Arbitration, 1951. *Recreation:* getting away from it all. *Address:* Cherry Tree Cottage, Petworth Road, Anstead Brook, Haslemere, Surrey GU27 3BG. *T:* Haslemere (0428) 51970; New Court, Temple, EC4Y 9BE. *T:* 071–353 7613.

TURNER-SAMUELS, Norma Florence, (Mrs D. J. Turner-Samuels); *see* Negus, N. F.

TURNER-WARWICK, Dame Margaret (Elizabeth Harvey), DBE 1991; MA, DM, PhD; FRCP; FRACP; FFOM; FRCPE; President, Royal College of Physicians, since 1989; Consultant Physician, Brompton Hospital, since 1965 (Professor of Medicine (Thoracic Medicine), 1972–87, Dean, 1984–87, Cardiothoracic Institute); *b* 19 Nov. 1924; *d* of William Harvey Moore, QC, and Maud Baden-Powell; *m* 1950, Richard Trevor Turner-Warwick, *qv*; two *d.* *Educ:* St Paul's Sch.; Lady Margaret Hall (Open Schol. 1943), Oxford. University Coll. Hosp., 1947–50: Tuke silver medal, Filliter exhibn in Pathology, Magrath Schol. in Medicine, Atchison Schol.; Postgrad. trng at UCH and Brompton Hosp., 1950–61; Cons. Physician: (Gen. Med.), Elizabeth Garrett Anderson Hosp., 1961–67; Brompton and London Chest Hosps, 1967–72. Sen. Lectr, Inst. of Diseases of the Chest, 1961–72. Lectures: Marc Daniels, 1974, Phillip Ellman, 1980, Tudor Edwards, 1985, RCP; Lettsomian, Med. Soc. of London, 1982. Pres., British Thoracic Soc., 1982–85; Chairman: Central Academic Council, BPMF, 1982–85; Asthma Res. Council (Chm., Med, Res. Cttee, 1982–); Conf. of Colleges and their Faculties in UK, 1990–; UKCCCR, 1991–; Member: MRC Systems Bd (DHSS nomination), 1982–85; Council, British Lung Foundn, 1984–; Gen. Council, King's Fund, 1991; Mem. Council and Vice-Pres., ASH, 1990–. University of London: Mem. Senate, 1983–87; Mem., Academic Council, 1983–87; Mem., Scholarships Cttee, 1984–87; Mem., Cttee of Extramural Studies, 1984–. Fellow, UCL, 1991. FRCPE 1988; FFPHM 1990; FRCGP 1990; Hon. FACP 1988; Hon. FRCP&S (Canada) 1990; Hon. Bencher, Middle Temple, 1990. Hon. Mem., Assoc. of Physicians of GB and Ireland, 1991. Hon. DSc: New York, 1985; Exeter, 1990; London, 1990; Hull, 1991. *Publications:* Immunology of the Lung, 1978; (jtly) Occupational Lung Diseases: research approaches and methods, 1981; chapters in various textbooks on immunology and thoracic medicine, particularly fibrosing lung disorders and asthma; contrib. original articles: Lancet, BMJ, Quarterly Jl Med., Thorax, Tubercle, Jl Clin. Experimental Immunology, etc. *Recreations:* her family and their hobbies, gardening, country life, watercolour painting, music. *Address:* 55 Fitzroy Park, Highgate, N6 6JA. *T:* 081–340 6339.

TURNER-WARWICK, Richard Trevor, CBE 1991; MA, BSc, DM Oxon, MCh; Hon. DSc; FRCP, FRCS, FRCOG, FACS; Hon. FRACS; specialist in reconstruction and functional restoration of the urinary tract; Senior Surgeon and Urologist to the Middlesex Hospital, W1, since 1961; Senior Urological Surgeon to: St Peter's Hospital Group and Royal National Orthopædic Hospital; King Edward VII Hospital for Officers; Senior Lecturer, London University Institute of Urology, since 1962; Hon. Consultant Urologist, Royal Prince Alfred Hospital, Sydney, since 1980; Robert Luff Foundation Fellow in Reconstrucive Surgery, since 1990; *b* 21 Feb. 1925; *s* of W. Turner Warwick, FRCS; *m* 1950, Margaret Elizabeth Harvey Moore (*see* Dame Margaret Turner-Warwick); two *d.* *Educ:* Bedales School; Oriel Coll., Oxford; Middlesex Hosp. Medical School. Pres. OUBC, 1946; Mem. Univ. Boat Race Crew, Isis Head of River crew and Univ. Fours, 1946; Winner OU Silver Sculls, 1946; BSc thesis in neuroanatomy, 1946. Sen. Broderip Schol., Lyell Gold Medallist and Freeman Schol., Middx Hosp., 1949; surgical trng at Middx Hosp. and St Paul's Hosp., London, and Columbia Presbyterian Med. Centre, NY, 1959. Hunterian Prof. of RCS, 1957, 1976; Comyns Berkeley Travelling Fellowship to USA, 1959. British Assoc. of Urological Surgeons: Mem. Council, 1975–78 and 1982–; Pres., 1988–90; Fellow, 1961; St Peter's Medal, 1978. Fellow: Assoc. of Surgeons of GB and Ireland, 1960; Australasian Soc. Urology, 1989; Member: Council, Royal Coll. of Surgeons, 1980–; RCOG, 1990–; Internat. Soc. of Urology, 1966–; European Soc. of Urology; Soc. of Pelvic Surgeons, 1963; Founder Mem., 1969, Pres., 1985, Internat. Continence Soc.; Corresp. Member: Amer. Assoc. of Genito Urinary Surgeons, 1972; American, Australasian and Belgian Urological Assocs. Hon. FRACS, 1981. Hon. DSc New York, 1985. Moynihan Prize of Assoc. of Surgeons, 1957; Victor Bonney Prize, RCOG, 1987. *Publications:* various articles in scientific jls, contributing to surgery, to develt of operative procedures for the reconstruction and restoration of function of the urinary tract, and to design of surgical instruments. *Recreation:* water. *Address:* 61 Harley House, NW1. *T:* 071–935 2550; Tirnanog, 55 Fitzroy Park, Highgate, N6. *T:* 081–340 6339. *Clubs:* Vincent's (Oxford); The Houghton (Stockbridge); Leander (Henley); Ottery St Mary Fly Fishers; Royal Motor Yacht (Poole).

TURNEY, Alan Harry, CB 1991; Assistant Under Secretary of State, Fire and Emergency Planning Department, Home Office, since 1986; *b* 20 Aug. 1932; *s* of late Harry Landry Turney and of Alice Theresa Turney (*née* Bailey); *m* 1957, Ann Mary Dollimore. *Educ:* St Albans Grammar Sch.; London School of Economics (BScEcon). Asst Principal, Home Office, 1961; Asst Private Sec. to Home Sec., 1962–65; Principal, 1965; Asst Sec., Broadcasting Dept, 1976; Rayner Review of Forensic Science Service, 1981; Criminal Dept, 1981–82; Prison Dept, 1982–86. *Recreations:* Rugby Union football, touring provincial France, enjoying the garden. *Address:* 74 Kimpton Road, Blackmore End, Wheathampstead, Herts AL4 8LX. *T:* Kimpton (0438) 832636.

TURNOUR, family name of **Earl Winterton.**

TURPIN, James Alexander, CMG 1966; HM Diplomatic Service, retired; business consultant, since 1977; *b* 7 Jan. 1917; *s* of late Samuel Alexander Turpin; *m* 1942, Kathleen Iris Eadie; one *d.* *Educ:* King's Hosp., Dublin; Trinity Coll., Dublin (schol., 1st cl. Hons, Gold Medal, MA). Asst Lectr, Trinity College, Dublin, 1940. Served Army (Royal Irish Fusiliers), 1942–46. Joined Foreign Service, 1947; Mem., UK Delegn to OEEC, Paris, 1948; 1st Sec., 1949; FO, 1950; Warsaw, 1953; Tokyo, 1955; Counsellor, 1960; seconded to BoT, 1960–63; Counsellor (Commercial), The Hague, 1963–67; Minister (Economic and Commercial), New Delhi, 1967–70; Asst Under-Sec. of State, FCO, 1971–72; Ambassador to the Philippines, 1972–76; retired, 1977. Chm., British-Philippine Soc., 1986–88. *Publications:* New Society's Challenge in the Philippines, 1980; The Philippines: problems of the ageing New Society, 1984. *Recreations:* tennis, music, swimming, wine, cookery. *Address:* 12 Grimwood Road, Twickenham, Middlesex TW1 1BX.

TURPIN, Kenneth Charlton; Provost of Oriel College, Oxford, 1957–80, and Hon. Fellow since 1980; Vice-Chancellor, Oxford University, 1966–69 (Pro-Vice Chancellor, 1964–66, 1969–79); Member, Hebdomadal Council, 1959–77; *b* 13 Jan. 1915; *e s* of late Henry John Turpin, Ludlow. *Educ:* Manchester Grammar Sch.; Oriel College, Oxford. Treasury, 1940–43; Asst Private Sec. to C. R. Attlee, Lord President and Dep. Prime Minister, 1943–45; 2nd Asst Registrar, University Registry, Oxford, 1945–47; Sec. of Faculties, Univ. of Oxford, 1947–57; professorial fellow, Oriel Coll., 1948; Hon. Fellow Trinity Coll., Dublin, 1968. A Church Commissioner, 1984–89. *Recreations:* gardening, walking. *Address:* 13 Apsley Road, Oxford OX2 7QX. *Clubs:* Athenæum; Vincent's (Oxford).

TURPIN, Maj.-Gen. Patrick George, CB 1962; OBE 1943; FCIT; *b* 27 April 1911; 3rd *s* of late Rev. J. J. Turpin, MA, BD, late Vicar of Misterton, Somerset; *m* 1947, Cherry Leslie Joy, *d* of late Major K. S. Grove, York and Lancaster Regiment; one *s* one *d.* *Educ:* Haileybury Coll., Hertford; Exeter College, Oxford (Sen. Classical Schol.). BA (Hons) Oxford (Lit. Hum.), 1933; MA 1963. Commd RASC, 2nd Lt, 1933; Lt 1936; Capt. 1941; Major 1946; Lt-Col 1949; Col 1953; Brig. 1959; Maj.-Gen. 1960. Served War of 1939–45 (despatches twice, OBE): Adjt, 1939–40; AQMG, 30 Corps, W Desert, 1943; AA&QMG, 5th Div., Italy, 1943–44; DA&QMG (Brig.), 1 Corps, BLA, 1945; Brig. A, 21 Army Gp, 1945–46; Comd 6 Training Bn, RASC, 1947; ADS&T, WO, 1948; AA&QMG (Plans), HQ, BTE (Egypt), 1950; GSO1 (instructor), Jt Services Staff Coll., 1951–53; ADS&T (Col), WO, 1953–54; DAG, HQ, BAOR, 1956–59; Brig. i/c Adm., 17 Gurkha Div., Malaya, 1959–60; DST, 1960–63; Dir of Movements, MoD (Army), 1963–66; psc 1941; jssc 1949; idc 1955; Col Comdt, Royal Corps of Transport, 1965–71; Col Gurkha Army Service Corps, 1960–65; Col Gurkha Transport Regt, 1965–73. Sec.-Gen., Assoc. of British Travel Agents, 1966–69. Pres., Army Lawn Tennis Assoc., 1968–73. Governor, Royal Sch. for Daughters of Officers of the Army, Bath, 1963–83. FCIT (MInstT 1961). *Publication:* The Turn of the Wheel, 1988. *Recreations:* lawn tennis (Somerset County Champion, 1948, Army Colours, 1952); squash rackets (Bucks County Colours, 1952); golf. *Clubs:* Oxford Union Society; All England Lawn Tennis; International Lawn Tennis; Escorts Squash Rackets.

TURTON, family name of **Baron Tranmire.**

TURTON, Eugenie Christine, (Genie); Deputy Secretary, Department of the Environment, since 1991; *b* 19 Feb. 1946; *d* of Arthur Turton and Georgina (*née* Fairhurst); *m* 1st, 1968, Richard Gordon (marr. diss. 1972); 2nd, 1974, Gerry Flanagan (marr. diss. 1978). *Educ:* Nottingham Girls' High Sch. (GPDST); Girton Coll., Cambridge (schol.; MA). Research student (G. C. Winter Warr Studentship), Univ. of Cambridge, 1967–70; joined CS as Asst Principal, MoT (later DoE), 1970; Private Sec. to Parly Under Sec. of State, 1973–74; Principal, 1974–80; Prin. Private Sec. to successive Secretaries of State for Transport, 1978–80; Asst Sec., 1980–86; seconded to Midland Bank International,

1981–82, and to Cabinet Office/MPO (Machinery of Govt Div.), 1982–85; Under Sec., DoE, 1986–91; Dir, Heritage and Royal Estate (formerly Ancient Monuments and Historic Bldgs), 1987–90. Non-Exec. Dir, Woolwich Building Soc., 1987–91. Trustee, Pilgrim Trust, 1991–. *Recreations:* books, music, shopping, gardening. *Address:* c/o Department of the Environment, 2 Marsham Street, SW1P 3EB.

TURTON, Victor Ernest; Managing Director: V. E. Turton (Tools) Ltd; V. E. Turton (Wholesalers) Ltd; *b* 29 June 1924; *s* of H. E. Turton; *m* 1951, Jean Edith Murray; two *d*. *Educ:* Paget Secondary Modern Sch.; Aston Techn. Coll.; Birmingham Central Techn. Coll. Birmingham City Councillor (Lab) Duddeston Ward, 1945–63; Saltley Ward, 1970–71; Alderman, Birmingham, 1963–70 and 1971–74, Hon. Alderman, 1974–; Lord Mayor of Birmingham, 1971–72, Dep. Lord Mayor, 1972–73; West Midlands County Council: Mem., 1974–77, 1981–86; Vice-Chm., 1983–84, Chm., 1984–85; Chm., Airport Cttee, 1974–77; Member: Airport and Fire Bde Cttee; Transportation Cttee. Chm., Birmingham Airport, 1959–66; Dir, Birmingham Exec. Airways, 1983–89. Chairman: Smallholdings and Agric. Cttee, 1954–58; West Midlands Regional Adv. Cttee for Civil Aviation, 1966–72; Jt Airports Cttee of Local Authorities, 1975–77. Vice Pres., Heart of England Tourist Bd, 1977– (Chm., 1975–77). Chm., Hall Green Div. Labour Party, 1957–59. Former Governor, Coll. of Technology (now Univ. of Aston in Birmingham). *Recreations:* football, cricket, table tennis, philately. *Address:* 121 Maypole Lane, King's Heath, Birmingham B14 4PF. *Club:* Rotary (Birmingham).

TURTON-HART, Sir Francis (Edmund), KBE 1963 (MBE 1942); *b* 29 May 1908; *s* of David Edwin Hart and Zoe Evelyn Turton; *m* 1947, Margaret Greaves; one *d*. *Educ:* Uppingham. Served with Royal Engineers, 1939–46 (Hon. Major, 1946). East Africa, 1924–38; Portugal, 1939; West Africa, 1946–65; Federal House of Representatives, Nigeria, 1956–60; President, Lagos Chamber of Commerce, 1960–63. *Recreations:* shooting, fishing, golf. *Address:* 28 Vincent Road, Kingsbridge, South Devon TQ7 1RP. *T:* Kingsbridge (0548) 2872. *Club:* Thurlestone Golf.

TURVEY, Garry, CBE 1991; Director-General, Freight Transport Association, since 1984; *b* 11 Oct. 1934; *s* of Henry Oxley Turvey and Annie Maud Braley; *m* 1960, Hilary Margaret Saines; three *s*. *Educ:* Morecambe Grammar School. FCIS; FCIT; FILDM. Metropolitan Vickers Ltd, Manchester, 1956–58; AEI Manchester Ltd, 1958–60; Asst Sec., 1960–67, Sec., 1967–69, Traders' Road Transport Assoc.; Sec., 1969–84 and Dep. Dir-Gen., 1974–84, Freight Transport Assoc. *Recreations:* cricket, gardening. *Address:* 139 Imberhorne Lane, East Grinstead, West Sussex. *T:* East Grinstead (0342) 325829. *Club:* Royal Automobile.

TURVEY, Ralph, DSc (Econ); economist; Visiting Professor of Economics, London School of Economics, 1973–75 and since 1990; *b* 1 May 1927; *s* of John and Margaret Turvey; *m* 1957, Sheila Bucher (*d* 1987); one *s* one *d*. *Educ:* Sidcot School; London School of Economics; Uppsala University. Lectr, then Reader, in Economics, at London School of Economics, 1948–64, with interruptions. Vis. Lectr, Johns Hopkins Univ., 1953; Ford Foundation Vis. Res. Prof., Univ. of Chicago, 1958–59; Economic Section, HM Treasury, 1960–62; Center of Economic Research, Athens, 1963. Chief Economist, The Electricity Council, 1964–67. Member, NBPI, 1967–71, Jt Dep. Chm. 1968–71; Economic Advr, Scientific Control Systems Ltd, 1971–75; Economic Advr, then Chief Statistician, ILO, 1975–89; Dir, Dept of Labour Information and Statistics, ILO, until 1989; Res. Fellow, Statistics Canada, 1989–90. Mem., Nat. Water Council, 1974–75. Governor, Kingston Polytechnic, 1972–75. Mem., Inflation Accounting Cttee, 1974–75. *Publications:* The Economics of Real Property, 1957; Interest Rates and Asset Prices, 1960; (joint author) Studies in Greek Taxation, 1964; Optimal Pricing and Investment in Electricity Supply, 1968; Economic Analysis and Public Enterprises, 1971; Demand and Supply, 1971; (joint author) Electricity Economics, 1977; Consumer Price Indices, 1989; (ed and joint author) Developments in International Labour Statistics, 1989; papers on applied welfare economics in Economic Jl, Amer. Economic Review, etc. *Recreations:* computing, piano, walking. *Address:* 30 Sloane Gardens, SW1W 8DJ. *Club:* Reform.

TUSA, John; Managing Director, World Service, BBC, since 1986; *b* 2 March 1936; *s* of John Tusa and Lydia Sklenarova; *m* 1960, Ann Hilary Dowson; two *s*. *Educ:* Trinity Coll., Cambridge (BA 1st Cl. Hons History). BBC general trainee, 1960; Producer, BBC External Services, 1962; freelance radio journalist, 1965; Presenter: BBC Radio 4 The World Tonight, 1968; BBC2 Newsnight, 1979–86. Trustee, Nat. Portrait Gall., 1988–. Member: Council, RIIA, 1984–90; Adv. Council, Inst. of Contemp. British Hist., 1986–; Governing Body, Imperial Coll., London, 1991–. TV Journalist of the Year, RTS 1983; Richard Dimbleby Award, BAFTA, 1984. Mem., Editorial Board, Political Quarterly, 1978–. *Publications:* Conversations with the World, 1990; (with Ann Tusa): The Nuremberg Trial, 1983; The Berlin Blockade, 1988. *Recreations:* squash, opera, talking. *Address:* 21 Christchurch Hill, NW3 1JY. *T:* 071–435 9495. *Club:* United Oxford & Cambridge University.

TUSHINGHAM, Rita; actress; *b* 14 March 1942; *d* of John Tushingham; *m* 1962, Terence William Bicknell (marr. diss. 1976); two *d*; *m* 1981, Ousama Rawi. *Educ:* La Sagesse Convent, Liverpool. Student, Liverpool Playhouse, 1958–60. BBC Personality of the Year, Variety Club of GB, 1988. *Stage appearances:* Royal Court Theatre: The Changeling, 1960; The Kitchen, 1961; A Midsummer Night's Dream, 1962; Twelfth Night, 1962; The Knack, 1962; other London theatres: The Giveaway, 1969; Lorna and Ted, 1970; Mistress of Novices, 1973; My Fat Friend, 1981; Children, Children, 1984. *Films:* A Taste of Honey, 1961 (Brit. Film Acad. and Variety Club awards for Most Promising Newcomer, 1961; NY Critics, Cannes Film Festival and Hollywood Foreign Press Assoc. awards); The Leather Boys, 1962; A Place to Go, 1963; Girl with Green Eyes, 1963 (Variety Club award); The Knack, 1964 (Silver Goddess award, Mexican Assoc. of Film Corresps); Dr Zhivago, 1965; The Trap, 1966; Smashing Time, 1967; Diamonds For Breakfast, 1967; The Guru, 1968; The Bed-Sitting Room, 1970; Straight on till Morning, 1972; Situation, 1972; Instant Coffee, 1973; Rachel's Man, 1974; The Human Factor, 1976; Pot Luck, 1977; State of Shock, 1977; Mysteries, 1978; Incredible Mrs Chadwick, 1979; The Spaghetti House Siege, 1982; Flying, 1984; A Judgement in Stone, 1986; Single Room, 1986; Resurrected, 1989; Dante and Beatrice in Liverpool, 1989; Hard Days' Hard Nights, 1990. *TV appearances include:* Red Riding Hood (play), 1973; No Strings (own series), 1974; Don't Let Them Kill Me on Wednesday, 1980; Confessions of Felix Krull, 1980; Seeing Red, 1983; Pippi Longstocking, 1984; The White Whale — The Life of Ernest Hemingway (film), 1987; cameo appearance in Bread, 1988; Sunday Pursuit. *Recreations:* interior decorating, cooking, watercolour painting. *Address:* c/o Michael Anderson, ICM, 388–396 Oxford Street, W1.

TUSTIN, Arnold; Professor Emeritus, MSc, FIEE, retired; *b* 16 July 1899; *m* 1948, Frances Tustin; no *c*. *Educ:* King's Coll., Univ. of Durham. Subsequently Chief Asst Engineer, Metropolitan-Vickers Electrical Co., until 1945. Visiting Webster Prof., Massachusetts Inst. of Technology, 1953–54; Prof. of Electrical Engineering, Univ. of Birmingham, 1947–55; Prof. of Heavy Electrical Engineering, Imperial Coll., Univ. of London, 1955–64. Chm. Measurement and Control Section, IEE, 1959–60; Chm. Research Adv. Council, Transport Commn, 1960. Hon. DTech Bradford, 1968. *Publications:* Direct Current Machines for Control Systems, 1952; The Mechanism of Economic Systems, 1953; (ed) Automatic and Manual Control, 1951. *Address:* 17 Orchard Lane, Amersham-on-the-Hill, Bucks HP6 5AA.

TUSTIN, Rt. Rev. David; *see* Grimsby, Bishop Suffragan of.

TUTI, Rt. Rev. Dudley, KBE 1988 (OBE 1974); Paramount Chief of Santa Ysabel, since 1975, and Chairman, Solomon Islands Credit Union, since 1982; *b* 1919; *s* of John Tariniu and Daisy Mele Pago; *m* 1957, Naomi Tate; one *s* seven *d* (and one *s* decd). *Educ:* St John's Coll., Auckland, NZ. Deacon, 1946; priest, 1954. Headmaster, Vureas Boys' Sch., 1954–56; District Priest and Rural Dean of Santa Ysabel, 1956–63; consecrated Bishop (by the Archbishop of NZ), 1963; Asst Bishop, dio. of Melanesia, 1963–75; Bishop and Archdeacon, Central Solomons, 1968–75; Vicar-General, dio. of Melanesia, 1971–75; Bishop of Santa Ysabel, 1975–82. *Address:* Jejevo, Santa Ysabel, Solomon Islands. *T:* 35135.

TUTIN, Dorothy, CBE 1967; actress (stage and films); *b* 8 April 1931; *d* of late John Tutin, DSc, and of Adie Evelyn Tutin; *m* 1963, Derek Barton-Chapple (stage name Derek Waring); one *s* one *d*. *Educ:* St Catherine's, Bramley, Surrey; RADA. Began career, 1950; Stratford Festival, 1958, 1960. *Parts include:* Rose, in The Living Room; Katherine, in Henry V; Sally Bowles, in I am a Camera; St Joan, in The Lark; Catherine, in The Gates of Summer; Hedwig, in The Wild Duck; Viola, in Twelfth Night; Juliet, in Romeo and Juliet; Ophelia, in Hamlet; during Shakespeare Memorial Theatre tour of Russia, 1958, played parts of Ophelia, Viola and Juliet; Dolly, in Once More, With Feeling (New), 1959; Portia, Viola, Cressida (S-on-A), 1960; Sister Jeanne, in The Devils (Aldwych), 1961, 1962; Juliet, Desdemona (S-on-A), 1961; Varya, in The Cherry Orchard (S-on-A, and Aldwych), 1961; Cressida, Prioress, in The Devils (Edinburgh), 1962; Polly Peachum, in The Beggar's Opera (Aldwych), 1963; The Hollow Crown (New York), 1963; Queen Victoria, in Portrait of a Queen, Vaudeville, 1965; Rosalind, As You Like It, Stratford, 1967, Los Angeles, 1968; Portrait of a Queen, NY, 1968; Play on Love, St Martin's, 1970; Old Times, Aldwych, 1971; Peter Pan, Coliseum, 1971, 1972; What Every Woman Knows, 1973, Albery, 1974; Natalya Petrovna, in A Month in the Country, Chichester, 1974, Albery, 1975; Cleopatra, in Antony and Cleopatra, Edinburgh, 1977; Madame Ranevsky, The Cherry Orchard, Lady Macbeth, in Macbeth, Lady Plyant, in The Double Dealer (SWET Award, 1978), Nat. Theatre, 1978; Undiscovered Country, Nat. Theatre, 1979; Reflections, Theatre Royal, Haymarket, 1980; The Provok'd Wife, Nat. Theatre, 1980; Hester, in The Deep Blue Sea, Greenwich, 1981; After the Lions, Royal Exchange, Manchester, 1982; Ballerina, Churchill Theatre, Bromley, 1984; A Kind of Alaska, Duchess Theatre, 1985; The Chalk Garden, Chichester, 1986; Are you sitting comfortably, Watford, 1986; Brighton Beach Memoirs, Aldwych, 1987; Thursday's Ladies, Apollo, 1987; Harlequinade and The Browning Version (double-bill), Royalty, 1988; A Little Night Music, Chichester Fest., transf. Piccadilly, 1989; Henry VIII, Chichester, 1991. *Films:* Polly Peachum, in The Beggar's Opera; Cecily, in The Importance of Being Earnest; Lucie Manette, in A Tale of Two Cities; Henrietta Maria in Cromwell; Sophie Breska in Savage Messiah (Variety Club of GB Film Actress Award, 1972); The Shooting Party. Has appeared on television. *Recreations:* music; Isle of Arran. *Address:* c/o Michael Whitehall, 125 Gloucester Road, SW7 4TE.

TUTIN, Mrs Winifred Anne, (Winifred Pennington), PhD; FRS 1979; Principal Scientific Officer, Freshwater Biological Association, 1967–81, retired; *b* 8 Oct. 1915; *d* of Albert R. Pennington and Margaret S. Pennington; *m* 1942, Thomas Gaskell Tutin, FRS (*d* 1987); one *s* three *d*. *Educ:* Barrow-in-Furness Grammar Sch.; Reading Univ. (BSc, PhD). Research posts with Freshwater Biological Assoc., 1940–45; Demonstrator and Special Lectr, Univ. of Leicester, 1947–67; Hon. Reader in Botany, Univ. of Leicester, 1971–79, Hon. Professor, 1980–. Foreign Member, Royal Danish Academy, 1974. *Publications:* (as Winifred Pennington): The History of British Vegetation, 1969, 2nd edn 1974; (with W. H. Pearsall) The Lake District, 1973; papers in New Phytologist, Jl of Ecology, Phil. Trans of Royal Society, and others. *Recreations:* gardening, plain cooking. *Address:* Priory Cottage, North Street, Kingsclere, Newbury, Berks RG15 8QY.

TUTT, Prof. Norman Sydney; Director of Social Services, Leeds City Council, since 1989; Professor of Applied Social Studies, University of Lancaster, since 1979 (on leave of absence); *b* 8 June 1944; *s* of Sydney Robert Tutt and Stella May Tutt; *m* 1966, Diana Patricia Hewitt; two *s*. *Educ:* Chislehurst and Sidcup Grammar Sch.; Univ. of Keele (BA); Univ. of Leeds (MSc); Univ. of Nottingham (PhD). Clin. Psychologist, Nottingham, 1966–69; Resident Psychologist, St Gilbert's Approved Sch., 1969–73; Professional Advr, Northampton Social Services, 1973–74; Sen. Develt Officer, London Boroughs Children Reg. Planning Cttee, 1974–75; Principal Social Work Services Officer, DHSS, 1975–79. *Publications:* Care or Custody, 1975; (ed) Violence, 1975; (ed) Alternative Strategies for Coping with Crime, 1978; (ed) A Way of Life for the Handicapped, 1983; Children in Custody, 1987; contributor to other pubns. *Recreations:* work, wine, walks, cracking jokes. *Address:* Northolme, 8 Church View, Thorner, Leeds LS14 3ED. *T:* Leeds (0532) 892539. *Clubs:* as with Groucho Marx he would not join a club which would have him as a member.

TUTTE, Prof. William Thomas, FRS 1987; FRSC 1958; Professor of Mathematics, University of Waterloo, Ontario, 1962–85, Professor Emeritus since 1985; *b* 14 May 1917; *s* of William John Tutte and Annie Tutte (*née* Newell); *m* 1949, Dorothea Geraldine Mitchell. *Educ:* Cambridge and County High Sch.; Cambridge Univ. (BA, MA, PhD). Fellow of Trinity Coll., Cambridge, 1942–49; Lectr to Associate Prof., Univ. of Toronto, 1948–62. *Publications:* Connectivity in Graphs, 1966; Introduction to the Theory of Matroids, 1971; Graph Theory, 1984; papers in mathematical jls. *Address:* 16 Bridge Street, West Montrose, Ont N0B 2V0, Canada. *T:* (519) 669.2475.

TUTU, Most Rev. Desmond Mpilo; *see* Cape Town, Archbishop of.

TUZO, Gen. Sir Harry (Craufurd), GCB 1973 (KCB 1971); OBE 1961; MC 1945; DL; *b* 26 Aug. 1917; *s* of John Atkinson Tuzo and Annie Katherine (*née* Craufurd); *m* 1943, Monica Patience Salter; one *d*. *Educ:* Wellington Coll.; Oriel Coll., Oxford (Hon. Fellow 1977). BA Oxon 1939, MA 1970. Regimental Service, Royal Artillery, 1939–45; Staff appts, Far East, 1946–49; Royal Horse Artillery, 1950–51 and 1954–58; Staff at Sch. of Infantry, 1951–53; GSO1, War Office, 1958–60; CO, 3rd Regt, RHA, 1960–62; Asst Comdt, Sandhurst, 1962–63; Comdr, 51 Gurkha Infantry Bde, 1963–65; Imp. Def. Coll., 1966; Maj.-Gen. 1966; Chief of Staff, BAOR, 1967–69; Director, RA, 1969–71; Lt-Gen. 1971; GOC and Dir of Operations, NI, 1971–73; Gen. 1973; Comdr Northern Army Gp and C-in-C BAOR, 1973–76; Dep. Supreme Allied Comdr, Europe, 1976–78. ADC (Gen.) to the Queen, 1974–77. Colonel Commandant: RA, 1971–83; RHA, 1976–83; Master Gunner, St James's Park, 1977–83. Chm., Marconi Space and Defence Systems, 1979–83; Dir, Oceonics, 1988–91. Chm., RUSI, 1980–83; Member: Council, IISS, 1978–87; Council, Inst. for Study of Conflict, later Res. Inst. for Study of Conflict and Terrorism, 1979–. Chairman: Fermoy Centre Foundn, Kings Lynn, 1982–87; Imperial War Mus. Redevelt Appeal, 1984–88. Pres., Norfolk Soc., CPRE, 1987–. DL Norfolk,

1983. Dato Setia Negeri Brunei, 1965. *Recreations:* shooting, gardening, music, theatre. *Club:* Army and Navy.

See also Sir William Garthwaite, Bt.

TWEEDDALE, 13th Marquis of, *cr* 1694; **Edward Douglas John Hay;** Lord Hay of Yester, 1488; Earl of Tweeddale, 1646; Viscount Walden, Earl of Gifford, 1694; Baron Tweeddale (UK), 1881; Hereditary Chamberlain of Dunfermline; insurance broker; *b* 6 Aug. 1947; *s* of 12th Marquis of Tweeddale, GC, and of Sonia Mary, *d* of 1st Viscount Ingleby; *S* father, 1979. *Educ:* Milton Abbey, Blandford, Dorset; Trinity Coll., Oxford (BA Hons PPE). *Heir:* yr twin *b* Lord Charles David Montagu Hay, *b* 6 Aug. 1947. *Address:* House of Lords, SW1.

TWEEDIE, Jill Sheila; author, journalist, scriptwriter; *b* 1936; *d* of late Patrick Graeme Tweedie, CBE and of Sheila (*née* Whittall); *m* 1954, Count Bela Cziraky; one *s* one *d*; 1963, Robert d'Ancona; one *s*; *m* 1973, Alan Brien, *qv*. *Educ:* eight girls' schools, ranging from PNEU to GPDST and Switzerland. Columnist with the Guardian newspaper, 1969–88; freelance writer for Press, radio and television. Woman Journalist of the Year, IPC Nat. Press Awards, 1971; Granada TV Award, 1972. *Publications:* In The Name Of Love, 1979; It's Only Me, 1980; Letters from a Faint-hearted Feminist, 1982; More from Martha, 1983; Bliss (novel), 1984; Internal Affairs (novel), 1986. *Recreations:* getting out of London, getting back to London. *Address:* 15 Marlborough Yard, Marlborough Road, N19 4ND.

TWEEDSMUIR, 2nd Baron, *cr* 1935, of Elsfield; **John Norman Stuart Buchan,** CBE 1964 (OBE (mil.) 1945); CD 1964; FRSE; Lt-Col Canadian Infantry Corps, retired; *b* 25 November 1911; *e s* of 1st Baron and Susan Charlotte (*d* 1977), *d* of Hon. Norman Grosvenor; *S* father, 1940; *m* 1st, 1948, Priscilla Jean Fortescue, later Baroness Tweedsmuir of Belhelvie, PC (*d* 1978); one *d*; 2nd, 1980, Jean Margherita, *widow* of Sir Francis Grant, 12th Bt. *Educ:* Eton; Brasenose Coll., Oxford (BA 1933; MA 1987). Asst District Comr, Uganda Protectorate, 1934–36; joined Hudson's Bay Company, 1937; wintered in their service at Cape Dorset, Baffin Land, Canadian Arctic, 1938–39; served War of 1939–45 in Canadian Army (wounded, despatches twice, OBE (mil.) 1945, Order of Orange-Nassau, with swords); comd Hastings and Prince Edward Regt in Sicily and Italy, 1943; Hon. Col, 1955–60. Rector of Aberdeen Univ., 1948–51; Chm., Joint East and Central African Board, 1950–52; UK Delegate: UN Assembly, 1951–52; Council of Europe, 1952; Pres., Commonwealth and British Empire Chambers of Commerce, 1955–57; a Governor: Commonwealth Inst., 1958–77, Trustee, 1977–; Ditchley Foundn; Pres., Inst. of Export, 1964–67; Mem. Board, BOAC, 1955–64; Chairman: Advertising Standards Authority, 1971–74; Council on Tribunals, 1973–80. Mem., Scottish Cttee, Nature Conservancy, 1971–73. President: Institute of Rural Life at Home and Overseas, 1951–85; British Schools Exploring Society, 1964–85; Chm., British Rheumatism and Arthritis Assoc., 1971–78, Pres., 1978–86. Chancellor, Primrose League, 1969–75. FRSA. Hon. LLD: Aberdeen, 1949; Queen's (Canada) 1955. *Publications:* (part author) St Kilda papers, 1931; Hudson's Bay Trader, 1951; Always a Countryman, 1953; One Man's Happiness, 1968. *Recreations:* fishing, shooting, falconry. *Heir:* *b* Hon. William de l'Aigle Buchan, RAFVR [*b* 10 Jan. 1916; *m* 1st, Nesta (marr. diss. 1946), *o d* of Lt-Col C. D. Crozier; one *d*; 2nd, 1946, Barbara (marr. diss. 1960), 2nd *d* of E. N. Ensor, late of Hong Kong; three *s* three *d*; 3rd, 1960, Sauré Cynthia Mary, *y d* of late Major G. E. Tatchell, Royal Lincolnshire Regt; one *s*. *Educ:* Eton; New College, Oxford]. *Address:* Kingston House, Kingston Bagpuize, Oxon OX13 5AX. *T:* Longworth (0865) 820259. *Clubs:* Carlton, Travellers', Pratt's, Flyfishers'.

See also Lord James Douglas-Hamilton

TWEEDY, Colin David; Director General, Association for Business Sponsorship of the Arts, since 1983; *b* 26 Oct. 1953; *s* of Clifford Harry Tweedy, of Abbotsbury, Dorset and Kitty Audrey (*née* Matthews). *Educ:* City of Bath Boys' Sch.; St Catherine's Coll., Oxford (MA). Manager, Thorndike Theatre, Leatherhead, 1976–78; Corporate Finance Officer, Guinness Mahon, 1978–80; Asst Dir, Streets Financial PR, 1980–83. Mem. Council, Japan Festival, 1991; Trustee, Crusaid; Director: Art Advisers Ltd; Covent Garden Festival; Oxford Stage Co.; Mem., UK Nat. Cttee, European Cinema and TV Year, 1988–89. Freeman, City of London, 1978. FRSA. *Publication:* A Celebration of Ten Years' Business Sponsorship of the Arts, 1987. *Recreations:* the arts in general, opera, theatre and contemporary art in particular, food, travel. *Address:* Association for Business Sponsorship of the Arts, Nutmeg House, 60 Gainsford Street, SE1 2NY. *T:* 071–378 8143. *Club:* United Oxford & Cambridge University.

TWELVETREE, Eric Alan; designer silversmith; County Treasurer, Essex County Council, 1974–87; *b* 26 Dec. 1928; *m* 1953, Patricia Mary Starkings; two *d*. *Educ:* Stamford Sch., Lincs; qualif. IPFA and ACCA. Served with Borough Councils: Gt Yarmouth, Ipswich, Stockport, Southampton; County Councils: Gloucestershire, Kent. Pres., Soc. of County Treasurers, 1986–87. *Address:* 17 Bishopscourt Gardens, Chelmsford, Essex CM2 6AZ.

TWIGG, Patrick Alan; QC 1986; a Recorder, since 1987; *b* 19 May 1943; *s* of Alan Oswald Twigg and Gwendoline Mary Twigg; *m* 1974, Gabrielle Madeline Bay Green; one *s* one *d*. *Educ:* Repton Sch., Derbyshire; Universities of: The Sorbonne, Paris; Perugia, Italy; Bristol (LLB); Virginia, USA (LLM). Called to the Bar, Inner Temple, 1967; Mem., Western Circuit. *Recreations:* family, landscape and other gardening, music (particularly piano and chamber music), musical composition, amateur dramatics (Mem. Old Stagers 1969–), travel, lawn tennis. *Address:* 2 Temple Gardens, Temple, EC4Y 9AY. *T:* 071–583 6041, *Fax:* 071–583 2094. *Club:* Delta Theta Phi Fraternity (Charlottesville, Virginia).

TWIGGY, (Lesley Lawson); actress and singer; *b* 19 Sept. 1949; *y d* of (William) Norman Hornby and Nell (Helen) Hornby (*née* Reeman); *m* 1st, 1977, Michael Whitney Armstrong (*d* 1983); one *d*; 2nd, 1988, Leigh Lawson. Started modelling in London, 1966; toured USA and Canada, 1967; world's most famous model, 1966–71. *Films:* The Boy Friend, 1971; W, 1973; There Goes the Bride, 1979; Blues Brothers, 1981; The Doctor and the Devils, 1986; Club Paradise, 1986; Madame Sousatzka, 1989; Harem Hotel, Istanbul, 1989; *stage:* Cinderella, 1976; Captain Beaky, 1982; My One and Only, 1983, 1984; *television:* numerous appearances and series, UK and USA; numerous recordings. Many awards and honours including Hon. Col, Tennessee Army, 1977. *Publications:* Twiggy, 1975; An Open Look, 1985. *Recreations:* daughter Carly, music, design. *Address:* c/o Neville Shulman, Manager, 4 St George's House, 15 Hanover Square, W1R 9AJ. *T:* 071–486 6363, *Fax:* 071–408 1388.

TWINING, Prof. William Lawrence; Quain Professor of Jurisprudence, University College London, since 1983; *b* 22 Sept. 1934; *s* of Edward Francis Twining and Helen Mary Twining (*née* Dubuisson); *m* 1957, Penelope Elizabeth Wall Morris; one *s* one *d*. *Educ:* Charterhouse School; Brasenose College, Oxford (BA 1955; MA 1960; DCL 1990); Univ. of Chicago (JD 1958). Lectr in Private Law, Univ. of Khartoum, 1958–61; Sen. Lectr in Law, University Coll., Dar-es-Salaam, 1961–65; Prof. of Jurisprudence, The Queen's Univ., Belfast, 1965–72; Prof. of Law, Univ. of Warwick, 1972–82. Mem., Cttee on Legal Educn in N Ireland, 1972–74; President: Soc. of Public Law Teachers of Law, 1978–79; UK Assoc. for Legal and Social Philosophy, 1980–83; Chairman: Bentham Cttee, 1982–; Commonwealth Legal Educn Assoc., 1983–; vis. appts in several Univs. Hon. LLD Univ. of Victoria, BC, 1980. General Editor: Law in Context series, 1966–; Jurists series, 1979–. *Publications:* The Karl Llewellyn Papers, 1968; Karl Llewellyn and the Realist Movement, 1973; (with David Miers) How to Do Things with Rules, 1976, 3rd edn 1991; (with J. Uglow) Law Publishing and Legal Information, 1981; (ed) Facts in Law, 1983; Theories of Evidence, 1985; (ed) Legal Theory and Common Law, 1986; (ed with R. Tur) Essays on Kelsen, 1986; (ed jtly) Learning Lawyers' Skills, 1989; (ed jtly) Access to Legal Education and the Legal Profession, 1989; Rethinking Evidence, 1990; (ed) Issues of Self-determination, 1991; (with T. Anderson) Analysis of Evidence, 1991. *Address:* 10 Mill Lane, Iffley, Oxford OX4 4EJ.

TWINN, Ian David, PhD; MP (C) Edmonton, since 1983; *b* 26 April 1950; *s* of David Twinn and Gwynneth Irene Twinn; *m* 1973, Frances Elizabeth Holtby; two *s*. *Educ:* Netherhall Secondary Modern School, Cambridge; Cambridge Grammar School; University College of Wales, Aberystwyth (BA hons); University of Reading (PhD). Senior Lecturer in Planning, Polytechnic of the South Bank, 1975–83. PPS to Minister of State for Industry, 1985–86, to Dep. Chm. of Cons. Party, 1986–88, to Minister of State for Energy, 1987–90, and to Minister of State for the Environment, 1990–. Vice Chm., British Caribbean Assoc., 1986–. FRSA 1989. *Publications:* papers on planning matters. *Recreations:* collecting secondhand books, renovating antique furniture. *Address:* House of Commons, SW1A 0AA. *T:* 071–219 3000.

TWINN, John Ernest; Director General Guided Weapons and Electronics, Ministry of Defence, 1978–81, retired; *b* 11 July 1921; *s* of late Col Frank Charles George Twinn, CMG and Lilian May Twinn (*née* Tomlinson); *m* 1950, Mary Constance Smallwood; three *d*. *Educ:* Manchester Grammar Sch.; Christ's Coll., Cambridge (MA). FIEE 1981. Air Min., 1941; Telecommunications Research Estabt (later Royal Radar Estabt), 1943; Head of Guided Weapons Gp, RRE, 1965; Head of Space Dept, RAE, 1968; Head of Weapons Dept, RAE, 1972; Asst Chief Scientific Advr (Projects), MoD, 1973; Dir Underwater Weapons Projects (Naval), 1976. *Recreations:* sailing, music, genealogy. *Address:* Timbers, 9 Woodway, Merrow, Guildford, Surrey GU1 2TF. *T:* Guildford (0483) 68993.

TWISK, Russell Godfrey; Editor-in-Chief, British Reader's Digest, since 1988; *b* 24 Aug. 1941; *s* of K. Y. Twisk of Twisk, Holland, and Joyce Brunning; *m* 1965, Ellen Elizabeth Banbury; two *d*. *Educ:* Salesian Coll., Farnborough. Harmsworth Press, Dep. Editor, Golf Illustrated, 1960; Sub Editor, Sphere; freelance journalist, 1962; joined BBC, editorial staff Radio Times, 1966; Deputy Editor, Radio Times, 1971; Development Manager, BBC, 1975; Editor, The Listener, 1981–87. Has edited numerous BBC publications; radio critic for The Observer; Publisher, BBC Adult Literacy Project; devised Radio Times Drama Awards. Governor, London College of Printing, 1967–87 (Chm., 1974, 1978). Member, Advisory Council: ASH. Chm., Reader's Digest Trust, 1988–. Chm., National Leadership Cttee, Charities Aid Foundn, 1991. *Recreations:* running, map reading, watching horses race. *Address:* 20 Elm Grove Road, W5 3JJ. *T:* 081–567 5125. *Clubs:* Reform, Groucho.

TWISLETON-WYKEHAM-FIENNES; *see* Fiennes.

TWISLETON-WYKEHAM-FIENNES, Sir John (Saye Wingfield), KCB 1970 (CB 1953); QC 1972; First Parliamentary Counsel, 1968–72, retired; *b* 14 April 1911; *s* of Gerard Yorke Twisleton-Wykeham-Fiennes and Gwendolen (*née* Gisborne); *m* 1937, Sylvia Beatrice, *d* of Rev. C. R. L. McDowall; two *s* one *d*. *Educ:* Winchester; Balliol College, Oxford. Called to Bar, Middle Temple, 1936; Bencher, 1969. Joined parliamentary counsel office, 1939; Second Parly Coun., Treasury, 1956–68. Parliamentary Counsel, Malaya, 1962–63 (Colombo Plan). With Law Commission, 1965–66. *Address:* Mill House, Preston, Sudbury, Suffolk CO10 9ND.

TWISS, Adm. Sir Frank (Roddam), KCB 1965 (CB 1962); KCVO 1978; DSC 1945; Gentleman Usher of the Black Rod, House of Lords, 1970–78; Serjeant-at-Arms, House of Lords, and Secretary to the Lord Great Chamberlain, 1971–78; *b* 7 July 1910; *s* of Col E. K. Twiss, DSO; *m* 1st, 1936, Prudence Dorothy Hutchison (*d* 1974); two *s* one *d*; 2nd, 1978, Rosemary Maitland (*née* Howe), *widow* of Captain Denis Chilton, RN. *Educ:* RNC Dartmouth. Cadet 1924; Midshipman 1928; Lieut 1931; Comdr 1945; Captain 1950; Rear-Adm. 1960; Vice-Adm. 1963; Adm. 1967. Naval Sec., Admty, 1960–62; Flag Officer, Flotillas, Home Fleet, 1962–64; Comdr Far East Fleet, 1965–67; Second Sea Lord and Chief of Naval Personnel, 1967–70. Mem., Commonwealth War Graves Commn, 1970–79. *Recreations:* fishing, walking. *Address:* East Marsh Farm, Bratton, near Westbury, Wilts BA13 4RG. *Club:* Army and Navy.

TWISS, (Lionel) Peter; OBE 1957; DSC 1942 and Bar 1943; marine consultant; Director and General Manager, Hamble Point Marina Ltd, 1978–88; formerly Chief Test Pilot of Fairey Aviation Ltd; *b* 23 July 1921; *m* 1950, Mrs Vera Maguire (marr. diss.); one *d* (and one *d* decd), one step *s* one step *d*; *m* 1960, Cherry (marr. diss.), *d* of late Sir John Huggins, GCMG, MC; one *d*; *m* 1964, Mrs Heather Danby (*d* 1988), Titchfield; one step *s* one step *d*. *Educ:* Sherborne Sch. Joined Fleet Air Arm, 1939; served on catapult ships, aircraft-carriers, 1941–43; night fighter development, 1943–44; served in British Air Commn, America, 1944. Empire Test Pilots School, Boscombe Down, 1945; Test Pilot, Fairey Aviation Co. Ltd, 1946, Chief Test Pilot, 1957–60. Dir, Fairey Marine Ltd, 1968–78. Holder of World's Absolute Speed Record, 10 March 1956. *Publication:* Faster than the Sun, 1963. *Address:* Nettleworth, 33 South Street, Titchfield, Hants. *T:* Titchfield (0329) 43146. *Clubs:* Royal Southern Yacht, Island Sailing.

TWIST, Henry Aloysius, CMG 1966; OBE 1947; company director; *b* 18 June 1914; *s* of John Twist, Preston; *m* 1941, Mary Monica, *yr d* of Nicholas Mulhall, Manchester; one *s* one *d*. *Educ:* Liverpool Univ. (BA). Senior Classics Master, St Chad's Coll., Wolverhampton, 1936–40; Lecturer in English, South Staffordshire High School of Commerce, 1939–40. Served War of 1939–45 with RASC and RAEC, 1940–46; released with rank of Lt-Col, 1946. Principal, Dominions Office, 1946; Official Secretary, British High Commission in Ceylon, 1948–49; British High Commission in Australia, 1949–52; Commonwealth Relations Office, 1952–54; Secretariat, Commonwealth Economic Conference, London, 1952; Deputy High Commissioner for the United Kingdom in Bombay, 1954–57; Assistant Secretary, Commonwealth Relations Office, 1957–60; British Deputy High Commissioner, Kaduna, Northern Region, Federation of Nigeria, 1960–62; Commonwealth Service representative on the 1963 Course at Imperial Defence College; Commonwealth Office, 1964; Asst Under-Sec., 1966; Dep. High Comr, 1966–70, Minister (Commercial), 1968–70, Rawalpindi; retired 1970. Dir of Studies, RIPA, 1973–82. *Recreation:* gardening. *Address:* Pine Lodge, Woodham Lane, Woking, Surrey GU21 5SP. *Club:* Commonwealth Trust.

TWITCHETT, Prof. Denis Crispin, FBA 1967; Gordon Wu Professor of Chinese Studies, Princeton University, since 1980; *b* 23 Sept. 1925; *m* 1956, Umeko (*née* Ichikawa); two *s*. *Educ:* St Catharine's Coll., Cambridge. Lectr in Far-Eastern History, Univ. of London, 1954–56; Univ. Lectr in Classical Chinese, Univ. of Cambridge, 1956–60; Prof. of Chinese, SOAS, London Univ., 1960–68; Prof. of Chinese, Univ. of Cambridge, 1968–80. Vis. Prof., Princeton Univ., 1973–74, 1978–79. Principal Editor, Cambridge

History of China, 1977–. *Publications:* (ed with A. F. Wright) Confucian Personalities, 1962; The Financial Administration under the T'ang dynasty, 1963, 2nd edn 1971; (ed with A. F. Wright) Perspectives on the T'ang, 1973; (ed with P. J. M. Geelan) The Times Atlas of China, 1975; (ed) Cambridge History of China, Vol. 10 1978, Vol. 3 1979, Vol. 11 1980, Vol. 12 1983, Vol. 1 1986; Vol. 13 1986; Vol. 7 1987; Printing and Publishing in Medieval China, 1983; Reader in T'ang History, 1986. *Address:* 24 Arbury Road, Cambridge; 14 College Road, Princeton, NJ 08540, USA.

TWITE, Robin, OBE 1982; Advisor to Chairman, Research Authority, Hebrew University, Jerusalem, since 1988; *b* 2 May 1932; *s* of Reginald John Twite and May Elizabeth Walker; *m* 1st, 1958, Sally Randall (marr. diss.); 2nd, 1980, Sonia Yaari; one *s* three step *d*. *Educ:* Lawrence Sheriff School, Rugby; Balliol College, Oxford (BA History 1955). Asst Editor, Schoolmaster, weekly jl of NUT, 1956–58; British Council, 1958–73: served in Israel and London as Sec., Overseas Students Fees Awards Scheme; Sec., Open Univ. of Israel, 1973–76; British Council, 1976–88: adviser on adult and further educn, 1977–79; regional rep., Calcutta, 1980–84; Controller, Books, Libraries and Inf. Div., 1984–88. *Recreations:* travel, local history. *Address:* 36 Ezor Gimel, Ein Kerem, Jerusalem, Israel. *T:* Jerusalem 4100–23.

TWYFORD, Donald Henry, CB 1990; Under Secretary, Export Credits Guarantee Department, 1981–89, Director and Chairman of Project Group Board, 1986–89; *b* 4 Feb. 1931; *s* of Henry John Twyford and Lily Hilda (*née* Ridler). *Educ:* Wembley County School. Joined Export Credits Guarantee Dept, 1949; Principal, 1965; seconded to Dept of Trade: Principal (Commercial Relations with East Europe), 1972–75; Asst Secretary (Country Policy), 1976; Establishment Officer, 1979–81; Under Secretary, Head of Services Group (internat. and country policy), ECGD, 1981–85; Hd of Project Underwriting Gp, 1985–89. Chairman, European Policy Coordination Group, 1981. *Recreations:* gardening (especially growing exhibition daffodils), music, travel. *Address:* 2 Beehive Close, Ferring, Worthing, Sussex; Cansala Lluca 16, Javea, Spain.

TWYMAN, Paul Hadleigh; management consultant; Executive Chairman, Political Strategy Ltd, since 1988; Director: Nationwide (formerly Nationwide Anglia) Building Society, since 1987 (Anglia Building Society, 1983–87); D'Arcy Masius Benton & Bowles, since 1990; *b* 24 July 1943; *s* of late Lawrence Alfred Twyman and of Gladys Mary (*née* Williams). *Educ:* Leyton County High Sch.; Chatham House Sch., Ramsgate; Univ. of Sheffield (BAEcon); London Sch. of Econs and Pol Science (MScEcon). Schoolteacher, 1964; Asst Principal, BoT, 1967; Secretariat, Commn on Third London Airport, 1969; Private Sec. to Sec. of State for Trade and Industry, 1971; Dept of Industry, 1975; Anti-Dumping Unit, Dept of Trade, 1976; Asst Sec., and Head of Overseas Projects Group, Dept of Trade, 1978; Dept of Transport, 1983; Cabinet Office, 1984; Under Sec., and Dir, Enterprise and Deregulation Unit, Dept of Employment, 1985. Contested (C) Greater Manchester W, European Parly elecn, 1989. Econ. Adviser to Chm. of Conservative Party, and Head of Econ. Section, Cons. Res. Dept, 1987. Chm., N Thanet Conservative Assoc., 1989–91; Mem., SE Area Council and Gen. Purposes Cttee, Cons. Nat. Union, 1990–. *Recreations:* gardening, hill walking, observing gorillas.

TYACKE, Maj.-Gen. David Noel Hugh, CB 1970; OBE 1957; Controller, Army Benevolent Fund, 1971–80; *b* 18 Nov. 1915; *s* of Capt. Charles Noel Walker Tyacke (killed in action, March 1918) and late Phoebe Mary Cicely (*née* Coulthard), Cornwall; *m* 1940, Diana, *d* of Aubrey Hare Duke; one *s*. *Educ:* Malvern Coll.; RMC Sandhurst. Commissioned DCLI, 1935; India, 1936–39; France and Belgium, 1939–40; India and Burma, 1943–46; Instructor, Staff Coll., Camberley, 1950–52; CO 1st Bn DCLI, 1957–59; Comdr 130 Inf. Bde (TA), 1961–63; Dir of Administrative Planning (Army), 1963–64; Brig. Gen. Staff (Ops), Min. of Defence, 1965–66; GOC Singapore Dist., 1966–70, retired. Col, The Light Infantry, 1972–77. Mem., Malvern Coll. Council, 1978–88. *Recreations:* walking, motoring, bird-watching. *Address:* c/o Lloyds Bank, Cox's & King's Branch, 7 Pall Mall, SW1.

See also S. J. Tyacke.

TYACKE, Sarah Jacqueline, (Mrs Nicholas Tyacke), FSA; Chief Executive designate, Jan.–April 1992, Chief Executive and Keeper of Public Records, from April 1992, Public Record Office; *b* 29 Sept. 1945; *d* of late Colin Walton Jeacock and Elsie Marguerite Stanton; *m* 1971, Nicholas, *s* of Maj.-Gen. D. N. H. Tyacke, *qv*; one *d*. *Educ:* Chelmsford County High Sch.; Bedford Coll., London (BA Hons History). FSA 1985. Asst Keeper, Map Room, BM, 1968; Dep. Map Librarian, British Liby, 1973–85; undertook govt scrutiny of British Liby preservation (under Efficiency Unit, Cabinet Office), 1985–86; Director of Special Collections, British Library, 1986–91: Manuscript Collections, Map Liby, Music Liby, and Philatelic Collections, 1986–91; Oriental and India Office Collections, 1990–91. Trustee, Soc. for Nautical Res., 1982–89; Jt Hon. Sec., Hakluyt Soc., 1985–; Vice-Chm., Professional Bd, IFLA, 1987–89. Dir, Imago Mundi, 1987–. *Publications:* Copernicus and the New Astronomy (with H. Swiderska), 1973; (ed jtly with H. M. Wallis) My Head is a Map: essay and memoirs in honour of R. V. Tooley, 1973; (ed) Sir Francis Drake: a commemorative catalogue (prepared jtly with H. M. Wallis, P. Higgins), 1977; London Map-Sellers 1660–1720, 1978; (with John Huddy) Christopher Saxton and Tudor map-making, 1980; The Map of Rome 1625 by Paul Maupin (a facsimile reprodn of original in the Pepys Liby, Magdalene Coll., Cambridge, with accompanying text), 1982; (ed) English map-making 1500–1650: historical essays, 1983; Catalogue of maps, charts and plans in the Pepys Library, Magdalene College, Cambridge, 1989; contribs to professional liby and cartographic jls, incl. The Library, Imago Mundi, Cartographic Jl, Word and Image. *Recreations:* the sea, travel, hill-walking. *Address:* 1a Spencer Rise, NW5 1AR.

TYBULEWICZ, Albin, FInstP; Editor: Soviet Physics—Semi-conductors, since 1967; Soviet Journal of Quantum Electronics, since 1970; Soviet Physics—Solid State (jointly with Professor L. Azaroff), since 1982; *b* Poland, 1 March 1929; *s* of Julian and Elżbieta Tybulewicz (*née* Świgost); *m* 1959, Tuliola Sylwina Bryl; one *s* one *d*. *Educ:* schools in Poland, Russia, Iran, India; St Mary's High Sch., Bombay. BSc London 1952. Research Officer, BICC, 1953–56; Asst Editor, 1956–63, Editor, 1963–67, Physics Abstracts and Current Papers in Physics. Founder and Chm., Food for Poland Fund, 1980–84. FIL; FIInfSc; Fellow: Amer. Phys. Soc.; Inst. of Translation and Interpreting (Mem. Council, 1986–). Natthorst Non-Literary Prize, Fedn Internat. des Traducteurs, 1990. *Publications:* American Institute of Physics Translation Manual, 1983; trans of numerous Russian physics monographs; contribs to physics and professional jls on language and translation. *Recreations:* theatre, reading, Polish community affairs in England, politics in Poland. *Address:* 2 Oak Dene, W13 8AW. *T:* 081–997 8822. *Club:* Wig and Pen.

TYDEMAN, Col Frank William Edward, CMG 1966; CIE 1945; Port Consultant; *b* 20 January 1901; *s* of Harvey James and Kate Mary Anne Tydeman; *m* 1924, Jessie Sarah Mann (*d* 1947); two *s*. *Educ:* London University. BSc (Eng) London 1920. Chartered Civil Engineer. FICE, FIMechE, FIStructE, FIEAust, FCIT. Served Palestine; Haifa Harbour, 1930; Jaffa Port, 1934; Singapore Harbour Board, 1937; Colonel, Deputy Director Transportation, India, Burma and Malaya, 1947; Port Consultant, Australia, to Commonwealth and WA govts and port authorities, on develt of ports of Fremantle, Bunbury, Townsville, Davenport, Mackay, Lae, Tjilatjap; retired 1965. *Recreation:* golf. *Address:* c/o ANZ Banking Group Ltd, 77 St George's Terrace, Perth, WA 6000, Australia. *Clubs:* Naval and Military, West Australian Golf (Perth).

TYDEMAN, John Peter; Head of BBC Radio Drama, since 1986; *b* 30 March 1936; *s* of George Alfred Tydeman and Gladys (*née* Johnson). *Educ:* Feltonfleet; Hertford GS; Trinity Coll., Cambridge (MA). Nat. Service, 2 Lieut RA, 1954–56. Joined BBC, 1959; producer, 1962–80; Asst Head, Radio Drama, 1980–86. Dir of stage, radio and television plays. Prix Italia, 1970; Prix Futura, 1979 and 1983; Broadcasting Press Guild Award, 1983. *Recreations:* theatre, travel, reading, the company of friends. *Address:* Flat 7, 88 Great Titchfield Street, W1P 7AG. *T:* 071–636 3886. *Clubs:* Garrick, Rugby.

TYE, Alan Peter, RDI 1986; Partner, Alan Tye Design (Industrial & Product Designers), since 1962; *b* 18 Sept. 1933; *s* of Chang Qing Tai and Emily Tai (*née* Thompson); *m* 1966, Anita Birgitta Göethe Tye; three *s* two *d*. *Educ:* Regent Street Polytechnic Sch. of Architecture. RIBA 1959; FCSD (FSIAD 1979). Qualified as architect, 1958; with Prof. Arne Jacobsen, Copenhagen, 1960–62; formed Alan Tye Design, 1962. Mem., Selection Cttee, Council of Industrial Design, 1967; Civic Trust Award Assessor, 1968, 1969; Vis. Tutor, RCA, 1978–83, External Examr, 1987–90; Specialist Adviser on Industrial Design, CNAA, 1980; London Region Assessor, RIBA, 1981 and 1988; RSA Bursary Judge, 1983–87. Internat. Design Prize, Rome, 1962; Council of Industrial Design Award, 1965, 1966, 1981; British Aluminium Design Award, 1966; 1st Prize, GAI Award, 1969; Observer (London) Design Award, 1969; Ringling Mus. of Art (Fla) Award, 1969; Gold Medal, Graphic Design, 1970; 1st Prize, GAI Award, Internat. Bldg Exhibn, 1971; British Aluminium Eros Trophy, 1973; 4 Awards for Design Excellence, Aust., 1973; Commendation for Arch., 1977; Internat. Award, Inst. of Business Designers (NY), 1982; Internat. Bldg Exhibits Top Design Award, 1983, 1985; Resources Council of America Design Award, 1987; other design awards. FRSA (Convenor, Faculty of RDI, 1991). *Recreations:* tai chi, aikido, badminton, fly-fishing. *Address:* Great West Plantation, Tring, Herts HP23 6DA. *T:* Tring (044282) 5353.

TYE, James; Director-General, British Safety Council, since 1968; *b* 21 Dec. 1921; *s* of late Benjamin Tye and Rose Tye; *m* 1950, Mrs Rosalie Hooker; one *s* one *d*. *Educ:* Upper Hornsey LCC Sch. Served War of 1939–45; RAF, 1940–46. Advertising Agent and Contractor, 1946–50; Managing Dir, 1950–62: Sky Press Ltd; Safety Publications Ltd. Joined British Safety Council as Exec. Dir, 1962. Chm., Bd of Governors, Internat. Inst. of Safety Management, 1975–. FBIM; Associate, Inst. of Occupational Safety and Health; Member: Amer. Soc. of Safety Engineers; Amer. Safety Management Soc.; Vice-Pres., Jamaica Safety Council; Fellow, Inst. of Accident Prevention, Zambia. FRSA. Freeman, City of London, 1976; Liveryman, Worshipful Co. of Basketmakers; Mem., Guild of Freemen of City of London. *Publications:* Communicating the Safety Message, 1968; Management Introduction to Total Loss Control, 1971; Safety-Uncensored (with K. Ullyett, JP), 1971; (with Bowes Egan) The Management Guide to Product Liability, 1979; *handbooks:* Industrial Safety Digest, 1953; Skilful Driving, 1952; Advanced Driving, 1954; International Nautical Safety Code (with Uffa Fox), 1961; Why Imprison Untrained Drivers?, 1980; Workplace Wellness; Papers and Reports to Parly Groups and British Safety Council Members on: product liability, training safety officers, vehicle seat belts, anti-jack knife devices for articulated vehicles, lifejackets and buoyancy aids, motorway safety barriers, Britain's filthy beaches, back pain, insurance costs, dangers of: mini fire extinguishers, safety in fairgrounds, drip feed oil heaters, children's flammable nightwear, vehicle recall procedures, need for a nat. vehicle defects hotline, brain injuries caused by boxing and recommendations to improve the rules, pollution caused by diesel engines, safe toys, introduction of defensive driving techniques, risk management — stress at work, incr. risk of accidents thereof, use of colour in envmt to promote safety and productivity, dangers of smoke masks, fire prevention — recommendations to industry. *Recreations:* squash, badminton, ski-ing, golf, sailing. *Address:* 55 Hartington Road, Chiswick, W4 3TS. *T:* 081–995 3206. *Clubs:* City Livery, Royal Automobile.

TYE, Dr Walter, CBE 1966; CEng; *b* 12 Dec. 1912; *s* of Walter and Alice Tye; *m* 1939, Eileen Mary Whitmore; one *s* one *d*. *Educ:* Woodbridge Sch.; London Univ. (BScEng). Fairey Aviation Co., 1934; RAE, 1935–38; Air Registration Bd, 1938–39; RAE, 1939–44; Air Registration Bd, 1944–72 (Chief Techn. Officer, 1946, Chief Exec., 1969); Mem., CAA (Controller Safety), 1972–74. Hon. FRAeS; Hon. DSc Cranfield Inst. of Technology, 1972. *Publications:* articles, lectures and contrib. Jl RAeS. *Address:* 12 Bramble Rise, Cobham, Surrey KT11 2HP. *T:* Cobham (0932) 863692.

TYLER, Brig. Arthur Catchmay, CBE 1960; MC 1945; DL; a Military Knight of Windsor, since 1978; *b* 20 Aug. 1913; 4th *s* of Hugh Griffin Tyler and Muriel Tyler (*née* Barnes); *m* 1938, Sheila, *d* of James Kinloch, Meigle, Perthshire; three *s* one *d*. *Educ:* Allhallows Sch.; RMC, Sandhurst. Commissioned, The Welch Regt, 1933. Served War of 1939–45: Africa, India and Burma (despatches). Staff Coll., 1946; JSSC, 1951; Sec., BJSM, Washington, 1952–54; Bt Lt-Col, 1953; Comd 4th (Carms) Bn The Welch Regt, 1954–57; Col, 1957; AAG, War Office, 1957–60; Brig. 1960; Senior UK Liaison Officer and Military Adviser to High Commissioner, Canada, 1960–63; Asst Chief of Staff (Ops and Plans), Allied Forces Central Europe, 1963–65. Sec., Council, TA&VR Assocs, 1967–72. Hon. Col., 7th(V) Bn, The Queen's Regt, T&AVR, 1971–75. Governor, Allhallows Sch., 1968, Chm., 1977–80. DL Surrey, 1968. *Address:* 19 Lower Ward, Windsor Castle, Berks SL4 1NJ.

TYLER, Maj.-Gen. Christopher, CB 1989; CEng, FIMechE, FRAeS; Resident Governor and Keeper of the Jewel House, HM Tower of London, since 1989; *b* 9 July 1934; *s* of Maj.-Gen. Sir Leslie Tyler, *qv* and late Louie Teresa Tyler (*née* Franklin); *m* 1958, Suzanne, *d* of Eileen Whitcomb and late Patrick Whitcomb; one *s* three *d*. *Educ:* Beaumont College; RMA Sandhurst; Trinity Coll., Cambridge (MA). Commissioned REME, 1954; served UK and BAOR, 1959–65; Army Staff Course, 1966–67; Weapons Staff, 1968–70 and 1972–74; CO 1st Parachute Logistic Regt, 1974–76; MoD, 1976–80; Chief Aircraft Engineer, Army Air Corps, 1980–82; DEME (Management Services), Logistic Exec., 1982–83; Comd Maint., HQ 1 (BR) Corps, 1983–85; Dep. Comdt, RMCS, 1985–87; DCS (Support), HQ Allied Forces N Europe, 1987–89. Col Comdt, REME, 1989–. FBIM. *Recreations:* Rugby football (RFU Panel Referee, 1957–59 and 1967–73 and Chm., Army and Combined Services, 1985–86), tennis, squash. *Address:* Queen's House, HM Tower of London, EC3N 4AB. *Clubs:* Lansdowne; Hawks (Cambridge).

TYLER, Cyril, DSc, PhD, FRSC; Professor of Physiology and Biochemistry, University of Reading, 1958–76, now Emeritus; Deputy Vice-Chancellor, 1968–76; *b* 26 Jan. 1911; *er s* of John and Annie Tyler; *m* 1st, 1939, Myra Eileen (*d* 1971), *d* of George and Rosa Batten; two *s* one *d*; 2nd, 1971, Rita Patricia, *d* of Sidney and Lilian Jones. *Educ:* Ossett Grammar Sch.; Univ. of Leeds. BSc 1st Class Hons 1933, PhD 1935, DSc 1959, Leeds. Lectr in Agricultural Chemistry. RAC, Cirencester, 1935–39; Univ. of Reading: Lecturer in Agricultural Chemistry, 1939–47; Professor, 1947–58; Dean of the Faculty of Agriculture, 1959–62. Playing Mem., Glos CCC, 1936–39. *Publications:* Organic Chemistry for Students of Agriculture, 1946; Animal Nutrition (2nd edn), 1964; Wilhelm von Nathusius 1821–1899 on Avian Eggshells, 1964; numerous papers on poultry metabolism and egg shells in scientific journals. *Recreations*: gardening, history of animal nutrition. *Address*: 22 Belle Avenue, Reading, Berks RG6 2BL.

TYLER, Ven. Leonard George; Rector of St Michael and St Mary Magdalene, Easthampstead, 1973–85, retired; *b* 15 April 1920; *s* of Hugh Horstead Tyler and Mabel Adam Stewart Tyler; *m* 1946, Sylvia May Wilson; one *s* two *d*. *Educ*: Darwen Grammar School; Liverpool University; Christ's College, Cambridge; Westcott House. Chaplain, Trinity College, Kandy, Ceylon, 1946–48; Principal, Diocesan Divinity School, Colombo, Ceylon, 1948–50; Rector, Christ Church, Bradford, Manchester, 1950–55; Vicar of Leigh, Lancs, 1955–66 (Rural Dean, 1955–62); Chaplain, Leigh Infirmary, 1955–66; Archdeacon of Rochdale, 1962–66; Principal, William Temple College, Manchester, 1966–73. Anglican Adviser to ABC Television, 1958–68. *Publications*: contributor to Theology. *Address*: 11 Ashton Place, Kintbury, Newbury, Berks RG15 0XS. *T*: Kintbury (0488) 58510.

TYLER, Maj.-Gen. Sir Leslie (Norman), KBE 1961 (OBE 1942); CB 1955; BScEng; CEng; FIMechE; *b* 26 April 1904; *s* of late Major Norman Tyler, Addiscombe, Surrey; *m* 1st, 1930, Louie Teresa Franklin (*d* 1950); one *s* one *d*; 2nd, 1953, Sheila, *widow* of Maj.-Gen. L. H. Cox, CB, CBE, MC; two *s* two step *d*. *Educ*: Diocesan Coll., Rondebosch, SA; RN Colleges Osborne and Dartmouth; King's College, Univ. of London. Commissioned Lieut, RAOC, 1927; served War of 1939–45, Malta and NW Europe; transferred to REME, 1942; DDME, Second Army, 1945; Comdt REME Training Centre, 1945–47; AAG, War Office, 1948–49; DME, MELF, 1949–50; DDME, War Office, 1950–53; DME, MELF, 1953–55; Commandant, Headquarters Base Workshop Group, REME, 1956–57; Director of Electrical and Mechanical Engineering, War Office, 1957–60; retd 1960. Regional Dir, MPBW, Central Mediterranean Region, 1963–69. Chm., Royal Hosp. and Home for Incurables, Putney, 1971–76. Colonel Commandant, REME, 1962–67. Freeman, City of London; Liveryman, 1961, Master, 1982–83, Worshipful Company of Turners. FKC 1969. FRSA 1984. *Address*: 51 Chiltley Way, Liphook, Hants GU30 7HE. *T*: Liphook (0428) 722335. *Club*: Army and Navy.
See also Maj.-Gen. C. Tyler.

TYLER, Paul Archer, CBE 1985; politician and public affairs consultant; Managing Director, Western Approaches Public Relations Ltd, Plymouth, since 1987; Senior Consultant, Good Relations Ltd, since 1987; *b* 29 Oct. 1941; *s* of Oliver Walter Tyler and Ursula Grace Gibbons Tyler (*née* May); *m* 1970, Nicola Mary Ingram; one *s* one *d*. *Educ*: Mount House Sch., Tavistock; Sherborne Sch.; Exeter Coll., Oxford (MA). Pres., Oxford Univ. Liberal Club, 1962. Royal Inst. of British Architects: Admin. Asst, 1966; Asst Sec., 1967; Dep. Dir Public Affairs, 1971; Dir Public Affairs, 1972. Man. Dir, Cornwall Courier newspaper gp, 1976–81; Exec. Dir, Public Affairs Div., Good Relations plc, 1982–84; Chief Exec., 1984–86; Chm., 1986–87, Good Relations Public Affairs Ltd; Dir, Good Relations plc, 1985–88. County Councillor, Devon, 1964–70; Mem., Devon and Cornwall Police Authority, 1965–70; Vice-Chm., Dartmoor Nat. Park Cttee, 1965–70; Chm., CPRE Working Party on the Future of the Village, 1974–81; Mem. Bd of Shelter (Nat. Campaign for the Homeless), and rep. in Devon and Cornwall, 1975–76. Sec., L/SDP Jt Commn on Employment and Industrial Recovery, 1981–82. Chm., Devon and Cornwall Region Liberal Party, 1981–82; Chm., Liberal Party NEC, 1983–86. Campaign Adviser to Rt Hon. David Steel, and Mem., Alliance Campaign Planning Gp, 1986–87. Contested (L): Totnes, 1966; Bodmin, 1970, 1979; Beaconsfield, 1982; contested (Soc & Lib Dem) Cornwall and Plymouth, European Parly Election, 1989; Parly Cand. (Lib Dem), N Cornwall, 1990–; MP (L) Bodmin, Feb.–Sept. 1974; Parly Liberal Spokesman on Housing and Transport, 1974; Parly Adviser to RIBA, 1974. *Publication*: A New Deal for Rural Britain (jtly), 1978. *Recreations*: sailing, gardening, walking. *Address*: Tregrove House, Rilla Mill, Callington, Cornwall PL17 7NA. *Clubs*: National Liberal; Launceston Liberal (Cornwall); Saltash Sailing.

TYNAN, Prof. Michael John, MD, FRCP; Professor of Paediatric Cardiology, Guy's Hospital, since 1982; *b* 18 April 1934; *s* of late Jerry Joseph Tynan and Florence Ann Tynan; *m* 1958, Eirlys Pugh Williams. *Educ*: Bedford Modern School; London Hospital. MD, BS. Senior Asst Resident, Children's Hosp., Boston, Mass, 1962; Registrar, Westminster Hosp., 1964; Registrar, later Lectr, Hosp. for Sick Children, Great Ormond St, 1966; consultant paediatric cardiologist, Newcastle Univ. Hospitals, 1971, Guy's Hosp., 1977. *Publications*: (jtly) Paediatric Cardiology, a textbook, vol. 5, 1983; articles on nomenclature and classification of congenital heart disease and on heart disease in children. *Recreations*: singing, watching cricket, playing snooker. *Address*: 5 Ravensdon Street, SE11 4AQ. *T*: 071-735 7119. *Clubs*: Athenæum; Borth and Ynyslas Golf.

TYNDALE-BISCOE, Rear-Adm. Alec Julian, CB 1959; OBE 1946; lately Chairman of Blaw Knox Ltd; *b* 10 Aug. 1906; *s* of late Lt-Col A. A. T. Tyndale-Biscoe, Aubrey House, Keyhaven, Lymington, Hants; *m* 1st, 1939, Emma Winifred Haselden (*d* 1974); four *d*; 2nd, 1974, Hugolyne Cotton Cooke, *widow* of Captain Geoffrey Cotton Cooke. *Educ*: RN Colleges Osborne and Dartmouth. Entered RN, 1920. Served War, 1939–46; HMS Vanguard, 1947–49; Captain, 1949; Asst Engineer-in-Chief, Fleet, 1950–53; Comdg RN Air Station, Anthorn, 1953–55; Fleet Engr Officer, Mediterranean, 1955–57; Rear-Adm. 1957; Flag-Officer Reserve Aircraft, 1957–59, retired. *Address*: Bunces Farm Gardens, Birch Grove, Haywards Heath, West Sussex RH17 7BT.

TYNDALL, Nicholas John; Training Officer, Cruse-Bereavement Care, since 1987; *b* 15 Aug. 1928; *s* of Rev. Edward Denis Tyndall and Nora Mildred Tyndall; *m* 1953, Elizabeth Mary (*née* Ballard); two *s* two *d*. *Educ*: Marlborough College; Jesus College, Cambridge. BA. HM Prison and Borstal Service, 1952–68; Chief Officer, National Marriage Guidance Council, 1968–86. Dir, Council of Europe Co-ordinated Research Fellowship on Marriage Guidance and Family Counselling, 1973–75; Mem., Home Office/DHSS Working Party on Marriage Guidance, 1976–78; Chairman: British Assoc. for Counselling, 1976–78; Marriage and Marriage Guidance Commn of Internat. Union of Family Organisations, 1971–86. Mem., Gen. Synod of Church of England, 1981–88. *Recreations*: folk dancing, children. *Address*: 18 Stanford Road, Faringdon, Oxon SN7 7AQ; (office) Cruse House, 126 Sheen Road, Richmond TW9 1UR. *T*: 081-940 4818.
See also Rev. T. Tyndall.

TYNDALL, Rev. Canon Timothy; Chief Secretary, Advisory Council for the Church's Ministry, 1985–90; *b* 24 April 1925; *s* of Rev. Denis Tyndall and Nora Tyndall; *m* 1953, Dr Ruth Mary Turner; two *s* twin *d*. *Educ*: Jesus Coll., Cambridge (BA). Parish Incumbent: Newark, 1955; Nottingham, 1960; Sunderland, 1975. *Address*: 27 Beverley Road, Chiswick, W4 2LP. *T*: 081-944 4516.
See also N. J. Tyndall.

TYREE, Sir (Alfred) William, Kt 1975; OBE 1971; electrical engineer, chief executive and chairman; *b* Auckland, NZ, 4 Nov. 1921; *s* of J. V. Tyree and A. Hezeltine (who migrated to Australia, 1938); *m* 1946, Joyce, *d* of F. Lyndon; two *s* one *d*. *Educ*: Auckland Grammar School; Sydney Technical Coll. (Dip. in Elec. Engrg). FIE (Aust) 1968 (Peter Nicol Russell Mem. Award 1985); FIProdE 1983 (James N. Kirby Medal 1980). Founded Tyree Industries Ltd and Westralian Transformers and subsids, 1956; retired, 1981. Founder and Chairman: Alpha Air (Sydney) Pty Ltd; C. P. R. Constructions Pty Ltd; C.

P. R. Investments Pty Ltd; C. P. R. Properties Pty Ltd; Technical Components Pty Ltd; Tycan Australia Pty Ltd; Tyree Holdings Pty Ltd; Tyronsea Plastics Pty Ltd; A. W. Tyree Transformers Pty Ltd; Wirex Pty Ltd; A. W. Tyree Foundation (incorporating Medicheck Referral Centre, Sydney Square Diagnostic Breast Clinic, Tyree Chair of Electrical Engineering, Univ. of NSW, Chair of Otolaryngology, Univ. of Sydney); Centre for Corporate Engrg, All Sydney Univs, 1991. Dir, Sydney Cttee; Member: CIGRE, Aust.; Inst. of Dirs in Aust.; Councillor: Metal Trades Industries Assoc.; Aust. Chamber of Manufrs. Hon. Fellow, Univ. of Sydney, 1985; Hon. Life Governor, Aust. Postgrad. Fedn in Medicine, 1985. Hon. DSc Univ. of NSW, 1986. IEEE Centennial Medal and Cert., 1984. *Recreations*: ski-ing, private flying, water ski-ing, yachting, tennis, music, golf, sail board riding. *Address*: 60 Martin Place, Sydney, NSW 2000, Australia; (home) 3 Lindsay Avenue Darling Point, NSW. *Clubs*: Royal Aero, American National, Royal Automobile (NSW); Royal Prince Alfred Yacht, Royal Motor Yacht, Cruising Yacht, Kosciusko Alpine, Australian Alpine, RAC, Australian Golf.

TYRELL-KENYON; *see* Kenyon.

TYRER, Christopher John Meese; His Honour Judge Tyrer; a Circuit Judge, since 1989; *b* 22 May 1944; *s* of Jack Meese Tyrer and Margaret Joan Tyrer (*née* Wyatt); *m* 1974, Jane Beckett, JP, LLB, MA, barrister; one *s* one *d*. *Educ*: Wellington College; Bristol University. LLB hons. Called to the Bar, Inner Temple, 1968. Asst Recorder, 1979–83; a Recorder, 1983–89. Governor: St John's Sch., Lacey Green, 1984–; Speen Sch., 1984– (Chm., 1989–). Mem., Bucks Assoc. of Govs of Primary Schs, 1989–. *Recreations*: music, growing fuchsias, photography. *Address*: Randalls Cottage, Loosley Row, Princes Risborough, Bucks. *T*: Princes Risborough (08444) 4650.

TYRIE, Peter Robert; Managing Director, Balmoral International Ltd, since 1989; *b* 3 April 1946; *m* 1972, Christine Mary Tyrie; three *s* (and one *d* decd). *Educ*: Westminster College Hotel Sch. (BSc Hotel Admin). Manager, Inverurie Hotel, Bermuda, 1969–71; Resident Man., Portman Hotel, London, 1971–73; Project Dir, Pannell Kerr Forster, 1973–77; Operations Dir, Penta Hotels, 1977–80; Managing Director: Gleneagles Hotels plc, 1980–86; Mandarin Oriental Hotel Gp, 1986—89. Dir, Bell's Whisky, 1983. FHCIMA 1977. *Recreations*: squash, shooting, fishing, Rugby, classic cars. *Address*: Balmoral International Hotels, Princes Street, Edinburgh EH2 2EQ. *T*: 031-557 8688, *Fax*: 031-557 6333.

TYRONE, Earl of; Henry Nicholas de la Poer Beresford; *b* 23 March 1958; *s* and *heir* of 8th Marquess of Waterford, *qv*; *m* 1986, Amanda, *d* of Norman Thompson; two *s*. *Educ*: Harrow School. *Heir*: *s* Baron Le Poer, *qv*.

TYROR, John George, JP; Director of Safety, United Kingdom Atomic Energy Authority, since 1990; *b* 5 Nov. 1930; *s* of John Thomas Tyror and Nora Tyror (*née* Tennant); *m* 1956, Sheila Wylie; one *s* one *d*. *Educ*: Manchester Univ. (BSc 1st cl. Hons Maths, MSc); Trinity Hall, Cambridge. FInstP. Asst Lectr, Univ. of Leeds, 1955–56; AEA Harwell, 1956–59; Atomic Energy Estabt, Winfrith, 1959–63; Reactor Develt Lab., Windscale, 1963–66; Winfrith, 1966–87 (Asst Dir, 1979–87); Dir, Safety and Reliability Directorate, Culcheth, 1987–90. JP Macclesfield, 1976. *Publication*: An Introduction to the Neutron Kinetics of Nuclear Power Reactors, 1970. *Recreations*: tennis, golf, food and wine, antique map collecting, grandfather. *Address*: AEA Technology, Safety and Reliability Directorate, Wigshaw Lane, Culcheth, Cheshire WA3 4NE. *T*: Culcheth (0925) 254206. *Clubs*: Lancashire CC, Knutsford Golf, Broadstone Golf, East Dorset Lawn Tennis and Croquet.

TYRRELL, Alan Rupert, QC 1976; a Recorder of the Crown Court, since 1972; Barrister-at-Law; *b* 27 June 1933; *s* of Rev. T. G. R. Tyrrell, and Mrs W. A. Tyrrell, MSc; *m* 1960, Elaine Eleanor Ware, LLB; one *s* one *d*. *Educ*: Bridport Grammar Sch.; London Univ. (LLB). Called to the Bar, Gray's Inn, 1956, Bencher, 1986; Chm. of the Bar Eur. Gp, 1986–88; Chm. of the Internat. Practice Cttee, Bar Council (co-opted to Bar Council), 1988. Lord Chancellor's Legal Visitor, 1990–. Council Mem., Med. Protection Soc., 1990–. Chm. London Reg., and Mem. Nat. Exec., Nat. Fedn of Self-Employed, 1978–79. Mem. (C) London E, European Parlt, 1979–84; contested same seat, 1984, 1989. *Publications*: (ed) Moore's Practical Agreements, 10th edn 1965; Students' Guide to Europe, 1984. *Recreations*: bridge, budgerigars. *Address*: 15 Willifield Way, Hampstead Garden Suburb, NW11 7XU. *T*: 081-455 5798; Francis Taylor Building, Temple, EC4Y 7BY. *T*: 071-353 2182; 42 rue du Taciturne, 1040 Brussels, Belgium. *T*: Brussels 2305059. *Clubs*: Hampshire (Winchester); Exeter and County (Exeter).

TYRRELL, Dr David Arthur John, CBE 1980; FRCP, FRCPath; FRS 1970; Director, MRC Common Cold Unit, 1982–90, retired; *b* 19 June 1925; *s* of Sidney Charles Tyrrell and Agnes Kate (*née* Blewett); *m* 1950, Betty Moyra Wylie; two *d* (one *s* decd). *Educ*: Sheffield University. FRCP 1965. Junior hosp. appts, Sheffield, 1948–51; Asst, Rockefeller Inst., New York, 1951–54; Virus Research Lab., Sheffield, 1954–57; MRC Common Cold Unit, Salisbury, 1957–90; Dep. Dir of Clin. Res. Centre, Northwick Park, Harrow, and Head of Div. of Communicable Diseases, 1970–84. Chairman: (first), Adv. Cttee on Dangerous Pathogens, 1981–; Consultative Cttee on Res. into Spongiform Encephalopathies, 1989–90; Biol Sub-Cttee, Cttee on Safety of Medicines, 1989–. Managing Trustee, Nuffield Foundn, 1977–. Sir Arthur Sims Commonwealth Travelling Prof., 1985. Hon. DSc Sheffield, 1979; Hon. DM Southampton, 1990. Stewart Prize, BMA, 1977; Ambuj Nath Bose Prize, 1983, Conway Evans Prize, 1986, RCP. *Publications*: Common Colds and Related Diseases, 1965; Interferon and its Clinical Potential, 1976; (jtly) Microbial Diseases, 1979; The Abolition of Infection: hope or illusion?, 1982; numerous papers on infectious diseases and viruses. *Recreations*: music-making, gardening, sailing, walking; various Christian organizations. *Address*: (office) Public Health Laboratory Service, Centre for Applied Microbiology and Research, Porton Down, Salisbury SP4 0JG. *T*: Idmiston (0980) 610391; Ash Lodge, Dean Lane, Whiteparish, Salisbury, Wilts SP5 2RN. *T*: Whiteparish (07948) 84352.

TYRRELL, Gerald Fraser; former Buyer, Stewart Dry Goods Co., Louisville, USA, and London; retired 1974; *b* London, 7 March 1907; *s* of late Lt-Col G. E. Tyrrell, DSO, RA, and C. R. Tyrrell (*née* Fraser); *m* 1937, Virginia Lee Gettys, Louisville, Kentucky; three *s* one *d*. *Educ*: Eton; Magdalene Coll., Cambridge. Student Interpreter, China Consular Service, 1930; served in Tientsin, Chungking, Shanghai, Foochow, Canton; Vice-Consul at San Francisco, 1941; Vice-Consul, Boston, 1942, Acting Consul-General, 1944; 1st Secretary, Washington, 1945; Consul at Cincinnati, 1946; Acting Consul-General, New Orleans, 1947; Consul-General, Canton, 1948; Foreign Office, 1949, resigned, 1950. *Address*: 2333 Glenmary Avenue, Louisville, Kentucky 40204, USA.

TYRRELL, Prof. (Henry John) Valentine, FRSC; Vice-Principal, King's College London (KQC), 1985–87, retired; *b* 14 Feb. 1920; *s* of John Rice Tyrrell and Josephine (*née* McGuinness); *m* 1st, 1947, Sheila Mabel (*née* Straw) (*d* 1985); three *s* three *d*; 2nd, 1986, Dr Bethan Davies. *Educ*: state schools; Jesus Coll., Oxford. DSc. Chemical Industry, 1942–47; Sheffield Univ., 1947–65; Chelsea College: Professor of Physical and Inorganic Chemistry, 1965–84; Head of Dept, 1972–82; Vice-Principal, 1976–84; Principal, 1984–85. Sec., 1978–84, Vice-Pres., 1978–84 and 1987–89, and Chm. of Council,

1987–89, Royal Instn of GB. *Publications:* Diffusion and Heat Flow in Liquids, 1961; Thermometric Titrimetry, 1968; Diffusion in Liquids, 1984; papers in chemical and physical jls. *Recreations:* foreign travel, gardening. *Address:* Fair Oaks, Coombe Hill Road, Kingston-on-Thames KT2 7DU. *Clubs:* Athenæum, Royal Institution.

TYRRELL, Sir Murray (Louis), KCVO 1968 (CVO 1954); CBE 1959; JP; Official Secretary to Governor-General of Australia, 1947–73; *b* 1 Dec. 1913; *s* of late Thomas Michael and Florence Evelyn Tyrrell; *m* 1939, Ellen St Clair, *d* of late E. W. St Clair Greig; one *s* two *d. Educ:* Orbost and Melbourne Boys' High Schools, Victoria. Central Office, Postmaster General's Department, Melbourne, 1929–39; Asst Private Secretary to Minister for Air and Civil Aviation, 1940; Private Secretary to Minister for Air, 1940, to Minister for Munitions, 1940; Personal Asst to Secretary, Min. of Munitions, 1942; Private Secretary: Commonwealth Treas. and Min. for Post-War Reconstruction, 1943, to Prime Minister and Treasurer, 1945; Official Secretary and Comptroller to Governor-General, 1947; resigned Comptrollership, 1953. Attached Royal Household, Buckingham Palace, May-Aug. 1962. Director: Nat. Heart Foundn of Australia, 1970–; Canberra C of E Girls' Grammar Sch., 1952–65; Canberra Grammar Sch., 1954–65; Registrar, Order of St John of Jerusalem in Australia, 1976; Mem., Buildings and Grounds Cttee, ANU, 1974–. Alderman, Queanbeyan CC, 1974; Mem., Southern Tablelands CC, 1974. KStJ (CStJ 1969). Australian of the Year, 1977. *Recreation:* fishing. *Address:* 136 Learmonth Drive, Kambah, ACT 2902, Australia.

TYRRELL, Valentine; *see* Tyrrell, H. J. V.

TYRWHITT, Brig. Dame Mary (Joan Caroline), DBE 1949 (OBE 1946); TD; *b* 27 Dec. 1903; *d* of Admiral of the Fleet Sir Reginald Tyrwhitt, 1st Bt, GCB, DSO; unmarried. Senior Controller, 1946 (rank altered to Brigadier, 1950); Director, ATS, 1946–49, Women's Royal Army Corps, 1949–50, retired Dec. 1950; Hon. ADC to the King, 1949–50. *Address:* 14 Manor Court, Pewsey, Wilts.

TYRWHITT, Sir Reginald (Thomas Newman), 3rd Bt, *cr* 1919; *b* 21 Feb. 1947; *er s* of Admiral Sir St John Tyrwhitt, 2nd Bt, KCB, DSO, DSC and Bar (*d* 1961), and of Nancy (Veronica) Gilbey (who *m* 1965, Sir Godfrey Agnew, *qv*), *S* father, 1961; *m* 1972, Sheila Gail (marr. diss. 1980 and annulled 1984), *d* of William Alistair Crawford Nicoll, Liphook, Hants; *m* 1984, Charlotte, *o d* of Captain and Hon. Mrs Angus Hildyard, The White Hall, Winestead, Kingston-upon-Hull; one *s* one *d. Educ:* Downside. 2nd Lieut, RA, 1966, Lieut 1969; RARO 1969. *Recreations:* shooting, fishing, drawing. *Heir: s* Robert St John Hildyard Tyrwhitt, *b* 15 Feb. 1987.
See also Dame Mary Tyrwhitt.

TYSON, Dr Alan Walker, CBE 1989; FBA 1978; musicologist and psychoanalyst; Fellow of All Souls College, Oxford, since 1952, Senior Research Fellow, since 1971; *b* 27 Oct. 1926; *e s* of Henry Alan Maurice Tyson and Dorothy (*née* Walker). *Educ:* Rugby School; Magdalen College, Oxford; University College Hospital Medical School, London. BA 1951, MA 1952; MB, BS 1965; MRCPsych 1972. Vis. Lectr in Psychiatry, Montefiore Hosp., NY, 1967–68; Lectr in Psychopathology and Developmental Psychology, Oxford Univ., 1968–70. Vis. Prof. of Music, Columbia Univ., 1969; James P. R. Lyell Reader in Bibliography, Oxford Univ., 1973–74; Ernest Bloch Prof. of Music, Univ. of California at Berkeley, 1977–78; Mem., Inst. for Advanced Study, Princeton, 1983–84; Vis. Prof. of Music, Graduate Center, City Univ. of New York, 1985. Hon. Mem., British Psychoanalytical Soc., 1989–. Hon. DLitt St Andrews, 1989. On editorial staff, Standard Edition of Freud's Works, 1952–74. *Publications:* The Authentic English Editions of Beethoven, 1963; (with O. W. Neighbour) English Music Publishers' Plate Numbers, 1965; (ed) Selected letters of Beethoven, 1967; Thematic Catalogue of the Works of Muzio Clementi, 1967; (ed) Beethoven Studies, Vol. 1, 1973, Vol. 2, 1977, Vol. 3, 1982; (with D. Johnson and R. Winter) The Beethoven Sketchbooks, 1985; Mozart: studies of the autograph scores, 1987; (with A. Rosenthal) Mozart's Thematic Catalogue: a facsimile, 1990. *Address:* 7 Southcote Road, N19 5BJ. *T:* 071–609 2981.

TYSON, Monica Elizabeth; Editor, A La Carte, 1986–87, retired; *b* 7 June 1927; *d* of F. S. Hill and E. Hill; *m* R. E. D. Tyson; one *d. Educ:* George Watson's Ladies Coll.; Edinburgh Coll. of Domestic Science (Dip. in Dom. Sci.). Asst Home Editor, Modern Woman, 1958–60; Ideal Home: Domestic Planning Editor, 1960–64; Asst Editor, 1964–68; Editor, 1968–77; Editor: Woman's Realm, 1977–82; Special Assignments, IPC Magazines, 1982–84; Mother, 1984–86. *Recreations:* travelling, reading, cooking. *Address:* 29 Fisher Street, Sandwich, Kent.

TYTLER, Christian Helen F.; *see* Fraser-Tytler.

TYTLER, Rt. Rev. Donald Alexander; *see* Middleton, Bishop Suffragan of.

TYZACK, Margaret Maud, OBE 1970; *b* 9 Sept. 1931; *d* of Thomas Edward Tyzack and Doris Moseley; *m* 1958, Alan Stephenson; one *s. Educ:* St Angela's Ursuline Convent; Royal Academy of Dramatic Art. Trained at RADA (Gilbert Prize for Comedy). First engagement, Civic Theatre, Chesterfield. Vassilissa in The Lower Depths, Royal Shakespeare Co., Arts Theatre, 1962; Lady MacBeth, Nottingham, 1962; Miss Frost in The Ginger Man, Royal Court, London, 1964; Madame Ranevsky in The Cherry Orchard, Exeter and Tour, 1969; Jacqui in Find Your Way Home, Open Space Theatre, London, 1970; Queen Elizabeth in Vivat! Vivat Regina!, Piccadilly, 1971; Tamora in Titus Andronicus, Portia in Julius Caesar and Volumnia in Coriolanus, Royal Shakespeare Co., Stratford-on-Avon, 1972; Portia in Julius Caesar, and Volumnia in Coriolanus, RSC, Aldwych, 1973; Maria Lvovna in Summerfolk, RSC, Aldwych, and NY, 1974–75; Richard III, All's Well That Ends Well, Ghosts, Stratford, Ont., 1977; People Are Living There, Manchester Royal Exchange, 1979; Martha, in Who's Afraid of Virginia Woolf?, Nat. Theatre, 1981 (SWET Best Actress in a Revival Award); Countess of Rossilion, in All's Well That Ends Well, RSC Barbican and NY, 1983; An Inspector Calls, Greenwich, 1983; Tom and Viv, Royal Court, 1984, also New York, 1985; Mornings at Seven, Westminster, 1984; Night Must Fall, Greenwich, 1986; Lettice and Lovage, Globe, 1987 (Variety Club of GB Award for Best Stage Actress), and New York, 1990 (Tony award). *Films:* Ring of Spies, 2001: A Space Odyssey, The Whisperers, A Clockwork Orange, The Legacy, The King's Whore. *Television series include:* The Forsyte Saga; The First Churchills; Cousin Bette, 1970–71; I, Claudius, 1976; Quatermass, 1979; A Winter's Tale. Actress of the Year Award (BAFTA) for Queen Anne in The First Churchills, 1969. *Address:* c/o Representation Joyce Edwards, 275 Kennington Road, SE11 6BY. *T:* 071–735 5736, *Fax:* 071–820 1845.

U

UATIOA, Dame Mere, DBE 1978; *b* 19 Jan. 1924; *d* of Aberam Takenibeia and Bereti Bamatang; *m* 1950, Reuben K. Uatioa, MBE (*d* 1977); three *s* one *d*. *Educ:* Hiram Bingham High School, Beru Island. Widow of Reuben K. Uatioa, MBE, a leading Gilbertese nationalist and former Speaker, House of Assembly, Gilbert Islands; supported her husband throughout his long public service, demonstrating those qualities of wife and mother which are most admired in the Pacific. After his death, she devoted herself to her family. *Recreations:* social and voluntary work for Churches. *Address:* Erik House, Antebuka, Tarawa, Gilbert Islands.

UBEE, Air Vice-Marshal Sydney Richard, CB 1952; AFC 1939; Royal Air Force; retired as Air Officer Commanding, No 2 Group, 2nd Tactical Air Force, Germany (1955–58); *b* 5 March 1903; *s* of late Edward Joseph Ubee, London; *m* 1942, Marjorie Doris (*d* 1954), *d* of George Clement-Parker, Newport, Mon; two step *s*. *Educ:* Beaufoy Technical Institute. Joined RAF, 1927, with short service commission; permanent commission, 1932; test pilot, Royal Aircraft Establishment, Farnborough, 1933–37; served in India, Iraq, Burma, and Ceylon, 1937–43; Airborne Forces Experimental Establishment, 1943–45; Comdg Officer, Experimental Flying, RAE Farnborough, 1946–47; Commandant Empire Test Pilots' Sch., Cranfield, Bucks, and Farnborough, 1947–48; Deputy Director Operational Requirements, Air Min., 1948–51; Commandant RAF Flying Coll., Manby, 1951–54; Director-General of Personnel (II), Air Ministry, 1954–55. *Address:* Harwood Lodge, 100 Lodge Hill Road, Lower Bourne, Farnham, Surrey GU10 3RD. *Club:* Royal Air Force.

ud-DIN, Rt. Rev. Khair-; Church Missionary Society Mission Partner in Britain, since 1990; *b* 7 Feb. 1921; *s* of Sharam-ud-Din and Barkat Bibi; *m* 1963, Daphne Dionys. *Educ:* Punjab Univ., Lahore (BA Hons Oriental Langs); theol studies in India, Canada, UK. Ordained Deacon, 1948, priest, 1949. Mem., St John's Divinity Sch., 1952. Pattoki, Okara and Clarkabad mission dists, Punjab, 1948–64; Vicar: St John's, Peshawar, 1964–68; Cath. Church of the Resurrection, Lahore, 1968–77; Associate Priest, St Martin in the Bullring, Birmingham, 1973; Archdeacon of Lahore and Dean of Frontier Regions, Lahore Dio., 1977–82; Bishop of Peshawar, 1982–90. Official rep. of Danish Missionary Soc. in Pakistan, as Dean of Frontier Regions. Radio and TV broadcaster in Pakistan. Reviewer of books of poetry and prose in oriental lit., 1969–85. Hon. DD Theol Seminary, Gujranwala, Pakistan, 1987. Gold Medallist for outstanding servs in Dio. Lahore, 1979. *Publications:* Guidebook for Youth Workers, 1966; ed. Sunday Sch. courses, 1962–66. *Recreations:* gardening, antiques. *Address:* The Flat, St Clement's Family Centre, Cross Street, Oxford OX4 1DA. *T:* Oxford (0865) 725160. *Club:* St Clement's Family Centre (Oxford).

UDOMA, Hon. Sir (Egbert) Udo, CFR 1978; Kt 1964; Justice, Supreme Court of Nigeria, Lagos, 1969–82, retired; Commissioner for Law Reform, Cross River State, Nigeria, 1985–88; *b* 21 June 1917; *s* of Chief Udoma Inam of Ibekwe Ntanaran Akama of Opobo (now Ikot Abasi, Akwa Ibom State), Nigeria; *m* 1950, Grace Bassey; six *s* one *d*. *Educ:* Methodist Coll., Uzuakoli, Nigeria; Trinity Coll., Dublin; St Catherine's Coll., Oxford. BA 1942; LLB 1942; PhD 1944; MA 1945. President, Dublin Univ. Philosophical Society, 1942–43. Called to Bar, Gray's Inn, 1945; practised as Barrister-at-Law in Nigeria, 1946–61; Member, House of Representatives, Nigeria, 1952–59; Judge of High Court of Federal Territory of Lagos, Nigeria, 1961–63. Member Nigeria Marketing Board and Director Nigeria Marketing Co. Board, 1952–54; Member Managing Cttee, West African Inst. for Oil Palm Research, 1953–63; Nat. President, Ibibio State Union, 1947–61; Vice-President, Nigeria Bar Assoc., 1957–61; Member: Internat. Commn of Jurists; World Assoc. of Judges; Chief Justice, High Court, Uganda, 1963–69; Acting Gov.-Gen., Uganda, 1963; Vice-President, Uganda Sports Union, 1964; Chairman, Board of Trustees, King George V Memorial Fund, 1964–69; Chancellor, Ahmadu Bello Univ., Zaria, 1972–75. Chm., Constituent Assembly for Nigerian Constitution, 1977–78; Dir, Seminar for Judges, 1980–82. Patron, Nigerian Soc. of Internat. Law, 1968–82; Mem., Nigerian Inst. of Internat. Affairs, 1979–. LLD (*hc*): Ibadan, 1967; Zaria, 1972; TCD, 1973. Awarded title of Obong Ikpa Isong Ibibio, 1961. *Publications:* The Lion and the Oil Palm and other essays, 1943; (jtly) The Human Right to Individual Freedom—a Symposium on World Habeas Corpus, ed by Luis Kutner, 1970; The Story of the Ibibio Union, 1987. *Recreations:* billiards, tennis, gardening. *Address:* Mfut Itiat Enin, 8 Dr Udoma Street, PO Box 47, Ikot Abasi, Akwa Ibom State, Nigeria, West Africa. *Clubs:* Island, Metropolitan (Lagos); Yoruba Tennis (Vice-Patron, 1982–) (Lagos).

UFF, John Francis, QC; PhD, CEng, FICE, FCIArb; arbitrator, advocate and consulting engineer; Visiting Professor, since 1985 and Director, Centre of Construction Law and Project Management, since 1987, King's College London; *b* 30 Jan. 1942; *s* of Frederick and Eva Uff; *m* 1967, Diana Muriel Graveson; two *s* one *d*. *Educ:* Stratton Sch.; King's College London. BSc (Eng), PhD. Asst engineer, Rendel Palmer & Tritton, 1966–70; Vis. Lectr in civil engineering, 1963–68; called to the Bar, Gray's Inn, 1970; practice at Bar in construction cases, 1970–; arbitrator in construction disputes; Lectr to professional bodies in engineering law and arbitration. Mem. Council, ICE, 1982–85. *Publications:* Construction Law, 1974, 5th edn 1991; Commentary on ICE Conditions of Contract, 1978, 1991; (jtly) ICE Arbitration Practice, 1986; (jtly) Methods of Procurement in the Ground Investigation Industry, 1986; technical papers in civil engineering; papers and articles in engineering law and procedure. *Recreations:* playing and making violins, farming. *Address:* 6 Southwood Lane, Highgate, N6. *T:* 081–340 5127; Ashtead Farm, Selside, Cumbria. *T:* Selside (053983) 266. *Club:* Ronnie Scott's.

UFFEN, Kenneth James, CMG 1977; HM Diplomatic Service, retired; Ambassador and UK Permanent Representative to OECD, Paris, 1982–85; *b* 29 Sept. 1925; *s* of late Percival James Uffen, MBE, former Civil Servant, and late Gladys Ethel James; *m* 1954, Nancy Elizabeth Winbolt; one *s* two *d*. *Educ:* Latymer Upper Sch.; St Catharine's Coll., Cambridge. HM Forces (Flt-Lt, RAFVR), 1943–48; St Catharine's Coll., 1948–50; 3rd Sec., FO, 1950–52; Paris, 1952–55; 2nd Sec., Buenos Aires, 1955–58; 1st Sec., FO, 1958–61; 1st Sec. (Commercial), Moscow, 1961–63; seconded to HM Treasury, 1963–65; FCO, 1965–68; Counsellor, Mexico City, 1968–70; Economic Counsellor, Washington, 1970–72; Commercial Counsellor, Moscow, 1972–76; Res. Associate, IISS, 1976–77; Ambassador to Colombia, 1977–82. *Recreations:* music, gardens. *Address:* 40 Winchester Road, Walton-on-Thames, Surrey KT12 2RH.

UGANDA, Archbishop of, since 1984; **Most Rev. Yona Okoth;** Bishop of Kampala, since 1984; *b* 15 April 1927; *s* of Nasanairi Owora and Tezira Akech; *m* Jessica Naome Okoth; four *s* five *d*. Bishop's clerk, 1947; Ordination Class, 1953–54 (certificate); deacon 1954, priest 1955; Parish Priest, Nagongera, 1956–60; St Augustine's Coll., Canterbury, 1963 (Diploma); Diocesan Treasurer, Mbale Diocese, 1961–65; Provincial Sec., Kampala, 1965–66; studies, Wycliffe Coll., Toronto Univ., 1966–68 (Dip. and LTh); Provincial Sec., Kampala, 1968–72; Diocesan Bishop of Bukedi, 1972–83. Hon. DD Wycliffe Coll., Toronto, 1978. *Recreation:* interest in farming. *Address:* PO Box 14123, Kampala, Uganda. *T:* 70218.

ULANOVA, Galina Sergeyevna; Order of Lenin, 1953, 1970; Hero of Socialist Labour, 1974, 1980; People's Artist of the USSR, 1951; Order of Red Banner of Labour, 1939, 1951, 1959, 1967; Order of People's Friendship, 1986; Badge of Honour, 1940; Prima Ballerina, Bolshoi Theatre, Moscow, 1944–60, retired; ballet-mistress at the Bolshoi Theatre since 1963; *b* 8 Jan. 1910; *d* of Sergei Nikolaevich Ulanov and Maria Feodorovna Romanova (dancers at Mariinsky Theatre, Petersburg). *Educ:* State School of Choreography, Leningrad. Kirov Theatre of Opera and Ballet, Leningrad, 1928–44 (début, 1928); danced Odette-Odile in Swan Lake, 1929; Raimonda, 1931; Solweig in The Ice Maiden, 1931; danced Diane Mirelle in first performance of Flames of Paris, 1932; Giselle, 1933; Masha in The Nutcracker Suite, 1933; The Fountain of Bakhchisarai, as Maria, 1934; Lost Illusions, as Coralie, 1936; Romeo and Juliet, as Juliet, 1940; with Bolshoi: Cinderella, as Cinderella, 1945; Parasha in The Bronze Horseman, 1949; Tao Hua in The Red Poppy, 1950; Katerina in The Stone Flower, 1954. Visited London with the Bolshoi Theatre Ballet, 1956. Member, Academies of Arts of USA, GB and France. Winner of first Anna Pavlova Prize; awarded State Prize, 1941; for Cinderella, 1946; for Romeo and Juliet, 1947; for Red Poppy, 1950. Awarded Lenin prize for outstanding achievement in ballet, 1957. FRAD 1963. *Address:* Bolshoi Theatre, Moscow. *Clubs:* Union of Theatrical Workers, Central House of Workers in the Arts.

ULLENDORFF, Prof. Edward, MA Jerusalem, DPhil Oxford; FBA 1965; Professor of Semitic Languages, School of Oriental and African Studies, University of London, 1979–82, now Professor Emeritus (Professor of Ethiopian Studies, 1964–79; Head of Africa Department, 1972–77); *b* 25 Jan. 1920; *s* of late Frederic and Cilli Ullendorff; *m* 1943, Dina Noack. *Educ:* Gymnasium Graues Kloster; Universities of Jerusalem and Oxford. Chief Examiner, British Censorship, Eritrea, 1942–43; Editor, African Publ., British Ministry of Information, Eritrea-Ethiopia, 1943–45; Assistant Political Secretary, British Military Admin, Eritrea, 1945–46; Asst Secretary, Palestine Government, 1947–48; Research Officer and Librarian, Oxford Univ. Inst. of Colonial Studies, 1948–49; Scarbrough Senior Research Studentship in Oriental Languages, 1949–50; Reader (Lectr, 1950–56) in Semitic Languages, St Andrews Univ., 1956–59; Professor of Semitic Languages and Literatures, University of Manchester, 1959–64. Carnegie Travelling Fellow to Ethiopia, 1958; Research Journeys to Ethiopia, 1964, 1966, 1969. Catalogued Ethiopian Manuscripts in Royal Library, Windsor Castle. Chairman: Assoc. of British Orientalists, 1963–64; Anglo-Ethiopian Soc., 1965–68 (Vice-Pres. 1969–77); Pres., Soc. for Old Testament Study, 1971; Vice-Pres., RAS, 1975–79, 1981–85. Joint Organizer, 2nd Internat. Congress of Ethiopian Studies, Manchester, 1963. Chm., Editorial Bd, Bulletin of SOAS, 1968–78; Mem., Adv. Bd, British Library, 1975–83. Vice-Pres., British Acad., 1980–82; Schweich Lectr, British Acad., 1967. FRAS; Hon. Fellow, SOAS, 1985. Imperial Ethiopian Gold Medallion, 1960; Haile Sellassie Internat. Prize for Ethiopian studies, 1972. MA Manchester, 1962; Hon. DLitt St Andrews, 1972; Hon. Dr Phil Hamburg, 1990. *Publications:* The definite article in the Semitic languages, 1941; Exploration and Study of Abyssinia, 1945; Catalogue of Ethiopian Manuscripts in the Bodleian Library, Oxford, 1951; The Semitic Languages of Ethiopia, 1955; The Ethiopians, 1959, 3rd edn 1973; (with Stephen Wright) Catalogue of Ethiopian MSS in Cambridge University Library, 1961; Comparative Semitics in Linguistica Semitica, 1961; (with S. Moscati and others) Introduction to Comparative Grammar of Semitic Languages, 1964; An Amharic Chrestomathy, 1965, 2nd edn 1978; The Challenge of Amharic, 1965; Ethiopia and the Bible, 1968; (with J. B. Pritchard and others) Solomon and Sheba, 1974; annotated and trans., Emperor Haile Sellassie, My Life and Ethiopia's Progress (autobiog.), 1976; Studies in Semitic Languages and Civilizations, 1977; (with M. A. Knibb) Book of Enoch, 1978; The Bawdy Bible, 1979; (jtly) The Amharic Letters of Emperor Theodore of Ethiopia to Queen Victoria, 1979; (with C. F. Beckingham) The Hebrew Letters of Prester John, 1982; A Tigrinya Chrestomathy, 1985; Studia Aethiopica et Semitica, 1987; The Two Zions, 1988; From the Bible to Enrico Cerulli, 1990; Joint Editor of Studies in honour of G. R. Driver, 1962; Joint Editor of Ethiopian Studies, 1964; articles and reviews in journals of learned societies; contribs to Encyclopaedia Britannica, Encyclopaedia of Islam, etc; Joint Editor, Journal of Semitic Studies, 1961–64. *Recreations:* music, motoring in Scotland. *Address:* 4 Bladon Close, Oxford OX2 8AD.

ULLMANN, Liv (Johanne); actress; *b* Tokyo, 16 Dec. 1938; *d* of late Viggo Ullmann and of Janna (*née* Lund), Norway; *m* 1960, Dr Gappe Stang (marr. diss. 1965). *Educ:* Norway; London (dramatic trng). Stage début, The Diary of Anne Frank (title role), Stavanger, 1956; major roles, National Theatre and Norwegian State Theatre, Oslo; Amer. stage début, A Doll's House, New York Shakespeare Festival, 1974–75; Anna

Christie, USA, 1977; The Bear, La Voix humaine, Australia, 1978; I Remember Mama, USA, and Ghosts (Ibsen), Broadway, 1979; British theatre début, Old Times, Guildford, 1985. Wrote and dir. short film, Parting, 1981. Eight Hon. doctorates, including Brown, Smith Coll., Tufts and Haifa. *Films:* Pan, 1965; The Night Visitor, 1971; Pope Joan, 1972; The Emigrants, 1972 (Golden Globe Award); The New Land, 1973 (Best Actress, Nat. Soc. of Film Critics, USA); Lost Horizon, 1973; 40 Carats, 1973; Zandy's Bride, 1973; The Abdication, 1974; The Wild Duck, 1983; The Bay Boy, 1985; Let's Hope it's a Girl, 1987; Mosca Addio, 1987; Time of Indifference, 1987; La Amiga, 1987; *(dir. by Ingmar Bergman):* Persona, 1966; The Hour of the Wolf, 1968 (Best Actress, Nat. Soc. of Film Critics, USA); Shame, 1968 (Best Actress, Nat. Soc. of Film Critics, USA); The Passion of Anna, 1969; Cries and Whispers, 1972; Scenes from a Marriage, 1974; Face to Face, 1976; The Serpent's Egg, 1977; The Autumn Sonata, 1978. Peer Gynt Award, Norway (1st female recipient). Order of St Olav (Norway), 1979. *Publications:* (autobiog.) Changing, 1977; Choices, 1984. *Address:* c/o Robert Lantz, 888 Seventh Avenue, New York, NY 10106, USA; c/o London Management, 235 Regent Street, W1.

ULLSWATER, 2nd Viscount *cr* 1921, of Campsea Ashe, Suffolk; **Nicholas James Christopher Lowther;** Parliamentary Under Secretary of State, Department of Employment, since 1990; *b* 9 Jan. 1942; *s* of Lieut John Arthur Lowther, MVO, RNVR (*d* 1942), and Priscilla Violet (*d* 1945), *yr d* of Reginald Everitt Lambert; *S* great-grandfather, 1949; *m* 1967, Susan, *d* of James Howard Weatherby; two *s* two *d*. *Educ:* Eton; Trinity Coll., Cambridge. Captain, Royal Wessex Yeomanry, T&AVR, 1973–78. A Lord in Waiting (Govt Whip), H of L, 1989–90. *Heir: s* Hon. Benjamin James Lowther, *b* 26 Nov. 1975. *Address:* Barrow Street House, near Mere, Warminster, Wilts. *T:* Mere (0747) 860621.

ULRICH, Walter Otto; Deputy Secretary, Department of Education and Science, 1977–87; *b* 1 April 1927. Ministry of Works: Asst Principal, 1951; Principal, 1955; Treasury 1958–60; Principal Private Sec. to Minister of Public Building and Works, 1963–65; Asst Sec., 1965; Min. of Housing and Local Govt, 1966; DoE, 1970; Under-Sec., 1972; Cabinet Office, 1974–76. *Address:* 41 Beechwood Avenue, St Albans, Herts AL1 4XR. *T:* St Albans (0727) 834024.

ULSTER, Earl of; Alexander Patrick Gregers Richard Windsor; *b* 24 Oct. 1974; *s* of HRH the Duke of Gloucester and HRH the Duchess of Gloucester.
See under Royal Family.

UNDERHILL, family name of **Baron Underhill.**

UNDERHILL, Baron *cr* 1979 (Life Peer), of Leyton in Greater London; **Henry Reginall Underhill,** CBE 1976; *b* 8 May 1914; *s* of Henry James and Alice Maud Underhill; *m* 1937, Flora Janet Philbrick; two *s* one *d*. *Educ:* Norlington Road Elementary School; Tom Hood Central School, Leyton. Junior Clerk, C. A. Hardman & Sons Ltd, Lloyd's Underwriters, 1929; joined Labour Party Head Office as Junior Accounts Clerk, 1933. National Fire Service, 1939–45. Assistant to Mr Morgan Phillips, Labour Party Gen. Sec., 1945; Admin. Assistant to National Agent, 1945; Propaganda Officer, 1947; Regional Organiser, W Midlands, 1948; Assistant National Agent, 1960; National Agent, 1972–79. Pres., AMA, 1982–. Joined Labour Party, 1930; Vice-Chm. 1933, Hon. Sec. 1937–48, Leyton West Constituency Labour Party. House of Lords: Dep. Leader of the Opposition, 1982–89; Opposition front bench spokesman on transport, 1980–90, and on electoral affairs, 1983–. Member: APEX, 1931– (Life Mem. and Gold Badge); Nat. Union of Labour Organisers, 1945– (Hon. Mem.); Fire Bdes Union, 1939–45 (Br. Sec. and Chm., Dist, Div. and Area Cttees). Member: HO Electoral Adv. Cttee, 1970–79; Houghton Cttee on Financial Aid to Political Parties, 1975–76; Parly delegn to Zimbabwe, 1980 and to USSR, 1986; Kilbrandon Ind. Inquiry into New Ireland Forum, 1984. Hon. Sec., British Workers' Sports Assoc., 1935–37. *Recreations:* golf, life-long support of Leyton Orient FC, countryside rambling. *Address:* 94 Loughton Way, Buckhurst Hill, Essex IG9 6AH. *T:* 081–504 1910.

UNDERHILL, Herbert Stuart; President, Victoria (BC) Press, 1978–79; Publisher, Victoria Times, 1971–78, retired; *b* 20 May 1914; *s* of Canon H. J. Underhill and Helena (*née* Ross); *m* 1937, Emma Gwendolyn MacGregor; one *s* one *d*. *Educ:* University Sch., Victoria, BC. Correspondent and Editor, The Canadian Press, Vancouver, BC, Toronto, New York and London, 1936–50; Reuters North American Editor, 1950; Asst General Manager, Reuters, 1958; Managing Editor, 1965–68; Dep. Gen. Manager, with special responsibility for North and South America and Caribbean, 1963–70. Director: Canadian Daily Newspaper Publishers' Assoc., 1972–76; The Canadian Press, 1972–78. *Publication:* The Iron Church, 1984. *Recreations:* travel, reading. *Address:* 308 Beach Drive, Victoria, BC, V8S 2M2, Canada.

UNDERWOOD, John Morris; Director of Campaigns and Communications, Labour Party, 1990–91; *s* of John Edward Underwood and Ella Lillian Morris Underwood; *m* 1987, Susan Clare Inglish; two *s*. *Educ:* Univ. of Sheffield (BSc hons); University Coll., Cardiff (Graduate Dip. in Journalism). BBC trainee journalist, 1976–78; regional TV reporter, 1978–80; TV reporter, ITN, 1980–82; home affairs corresp., ITN, 1982–83; freelance TV producer and presenter, 1983–89; Exec. Producer, House of Commons Cttee TV, 1989–90. *Publication:* The Will to Win: John Egan and Jaguar, 1989. *Recreations:* theatre, walking. *Address:* 100 Fawnbrake Avenue, SE24 0BZ. *T:* 071–738 7789.

UNDERWOOD, Michael; *see* Evelyn, J. M.

UNGER, Michael Ronald; Editor, Manchester Evening News, since 1983; Director, The Guardian and Manchester Evening News plc, since 1983; Trustee, Scott Trust, since 1986; *b* 8 Dec. 1943; *s* of Ronald and Joan Maureen Unger; *m* 1966, Eunice Dickens; one *s* (one *d* decd). *Educ:* Wirral Grammar School. Trainee journalist, Thomson Regional Newspapers, Stockport, 1963; Reading Evening Post, 1965–67; Perth Daily News, W Australia, 1967–71; Daily Post, Liverpool, 1971, Editor, 1979–82; Editor, Liverpool Echo, 1982–83. Chm., NW Arts Bd, 1991–. *Publication:* (ed) The Memoirs of Bridget Hitler, 1979. *Recreation:* reading. *Address:* 164 Deansgate, Manchester M60 2RD. *T:* 061–832 7200. *Club:* Press (Manchester).

UNGERER, Tomi; writer and graphic artist; Attaché de Mission, Jack Lang, Ministre de la Culture, commission inter-ministérielle Franco-Allemande, since 1987; *b* Strasbourg, 28 Nov. 1931; *s* of Theo Ungerer and Alice (*née* Essler); *m* 1970, Yvonne Wright; two *s* one *d*. *Educ:* Colmar; Ecole Municipale des Arts Décoratifs, Strasbourg. Window dresser and commercial artist, 1956; moved to USA, 1956; joined Harper's, 1957; worked for Amer. magazines and in advertising; moved to Nova Scotia, 1971, to Ireland, 1976; exhibitions: (first) Berlin, 1962; Strasbourg, 1975; Louvre, Paris, 1981; RFH, London, 1985. Pres., Culture Bank, Strasbourg. Commandeur des Arts et des Lettres (France), 1985; Légion d'Honneur (France), 1990; numerous other prizes and awards. *Films include:* The Three Robbers, 1972; Beast of Monsieur Racine, 1975. *Publications:* over 100 books, including: Horrible, 1958; Inside Marriage, 1960; The Underground Sketchbook, 1964; The Party, 1966; Fornicon, 1970; Compromises, 1970; The Poster Art of Tomi Ungerer, 1971; Testament, 1985; Once in a Lifetime, 1985; Far Out is not Far Enough, 1985; Joy of Frogs, 1985; *for children:* The Mellops series: The Mellops go Diving for Treasure; Crictor, 1958; Adelaide, 1959; Christmas Eve at the Mellops', 1960; Emile, 1960; Rufus, 1961; The Three Robbers, 1962; Snail, Where Are You?, 1962; One, Two, Where's My Shoe?, 1964; The Brave Vulture Orlando, 1966; Moon Man, 1967; Zeralda's Ogre, 1967; Ask Me a Question, 1968; The Hat, 1970; The Beast of Monsieur Racine, 1971; I am Papa Snap and These are My Favourite No Such Stories, 1971; No Kiss for Mother, 1973; Allumette, 1974. *Address:* Diogens Verlag AG, Sprecherstrasse 8, CH-8032 Zürich, Switzerland.

UNSWORTH, Sir Edgar (Ignatius Godfrey), Kt 1963; CMG 1954; QC (N Rhodesia) 1951; *b* 18 April 1906; *yr s* of John William and Minnie Unsworth; *m* 1964, Eileen, *widow* of Raymond Ritzema. *Educ:* Stonyhurst Coll.; Manchester Univ. (LLB Hons). Barrister-at-Law, Gray's Inn, 1930; private practice, 1930–37. Parly Cand. (C) for Farnworth, General Election, 1935. Crown Counsel: Nigeria, 1937; N Rhodesia, 1942; Solicitor-General: N Rhodesia, 1946; Fedn of Malaya, 1949; Chm. of Cttees, N Rhodesia, 1950; Attorney-General, N Rhodesia, 1951–56. Acting Chief Sec. and Dep. to Governor of N Rhodesia for periods during 1953, 1954 and 1955; Attorney-General, Fedn of Nigeria, 1956–60; Federal Justice of Federal Supreme Court of Nigeria, 1960–62; Chief Justice, Nyasaland, 1962–64; Director of a Course for Government Officers from Overseas, 1964–65; Chief Justice of Gibraltar, 1965–76; Justice of Appeal, Gibraltar, 1976–81. Member Rhodesia Railways Arbitration Tribunal, 1946; Chm., Commn of Enquiry into Central African Airways Corp., 1947; Mem., British Observers' Group, Independence Elections, Rhodesia, 1980 (submitted independent report). *Publication:* Laws of Northern Rhodesia (rev. edn), 1949. *Recreations:* gardening, bridge. *Address:* Pedro El Grande 9, Sotogrande, Provincia de Cadiz, Spain. *Club:* Royal Gibraltar Yacht.

UNWIN, Sir Brian; *see* Unwin, Sir J. B.

UNWIN, Rev. Canon Christopher Philip, TD 1963; MA; Archdeacon of Northumberland, 1963–82; *b* 27 Sept. 1917; *e s* of Rev. Philip Henry and Decima Unwin. *Educ:* Repton Sch.; Magdalene Coll., Cambridge; Queen's Theological Coll., Birmingham. Deacon, 1940, Priest, 1941. Asst Curate of: Benwell, 1940–43; Sugley, 1944–47; Vicar of: Horton, Northumberland, 1947–55; Benwell, 1955–63. *Recreations:* reading, walking. *Address:* 60 Sandringham Avenue, Benton, Newcastle upon Tyne NE12 8JX. *T:* 091–270 0418.

UNWIN, David Storr; author; *b* 3 Dec. 1918; *e s* of late Sir Stanley Unwin, KCMG; *m* 1945, Periwinkle, *yr d* of late Captain Sidney Herbert, RN; twin *s* and *d*. *Educ:* Abbotsholme. League of Nations Secretariat, Geneva, 1938–39; George Allen & Unwin Ltd, Publishers, 1940–44. *Publications:* The Governor's Wife, 1954 (Authors' Club First Novel Award, 1955); A View of the Heath, 1956; Fifty Years with Father: a Relationship (autobiog.), 1982; *for children:* (under pen name David Severn) Rick Afire!, 1942; A Cabin for Crusoe, 1943; Waggon for Five, 1944; Hermit in the Hills, 1945; Forest Holiday, 1946; Ponies and Poachers, 1947; Dream Gold, 1948; The Cruise of the Maiden Castle, 1948; Treasure for Three, 1949; My Foreign Correspondent through Africa, 1950; Crazy Castle, 1951; Burglars and Bandicoots, 1952; Drumbeats!, 1953; The Future Took Us, 1958; The Green-eyed Gryphon, 1958; Foxy-boy, 1959; Three at the Sea, 1959; Clouds over the Alberhorn, 1963; Jeff Dickson, Cowhand, 1963; The Girl in the Grove, 1974; The Wishing Bone, 1977. *Recreations:* travel, gardening. *Address:* Garden Flat, 31 Belsize Park, NW3 4DX. *Club:* PEN.
See also R. S. Unwin.

UNWIN, Eric Geoffrey; Executive Chairman, Hoskyns Group, since 1988; *b* 9 Aug. 1942; *s* of Maurice Doughty Unwin and Olive Milburn (*née* Watson); *m* 1967, Margaret Bronia Element; one *s* one *d*. *Educ:* Heaton Grammar School, Newcastle upon Tyne; King's College, Durham Univ. (BSc Hons Chemistry). Cadbury Bros, 1963–68; joined John Hoskyns & Co., 1968; Managing Dir, Hoskyns Systems Development, 1978; Dir, 1982, Man. Dir, 1984, Hoskyns Group. Pres., Computing Services Assoc., 1987–88. Mem., ITAB, 1988–. CBIM, 1984 (Mem., Bd., 1990–). Freeman, City of London, 1987; Founder Mem., and Freeman, Co. of Information Technologists, 1987. *Recreations:* golf, riding, ski-ing, sailing. *Address:* 17 Park Village West, NW1 4AE. *Club:* Royal Automobile.

UNWIN, Sir (James) Brian, KCB 1990 (CB 1986); Chairman, Board of HM Customs and Excise, since 1987; *b* 21 Sept. 1935; *s* of Reginald Unwin and Winifred Annie Walthall; *m* 1964, Diana Susan, *d* of Sir D. A. Scott, *qv*; three *s*. *Educ:* Chesterfield School; New College, Oxford (MA); Yale University (MA). Asst Principal, CRO, 1960; Private Sec. to British High Commissioner, Salisbury, 1961–64; 1st Secretary, British High Commission, Accra, 1964–65; FCO, 1965–68; transferred to HM Treasury, 1968; Private Sec. to Chief Secretary to Treasury, 1970–72; Asst Secretary, 1972; Under Sec., 1976; seconded to Cabinet Office, 1981–83; Dep. Sec., HM Treasury, 1983–85; Dir, Eur. Investment Bank, 1983–85; Dep. Sec., Cabinet Office, 1985–87. Sec., Bd of Dirs, ENO, 1987–. Chm., Civil Service Sports Council, 1989–. Mem., IMPACT Adv. Bd, 1990–. *Recreations:* opera, bird watching, Wellingtoniana, cricket. *Address:* HM Customs and Excise, New King's Beam House, 22 Upper Ground, SE1 9PJ. *Clubs:* Reform; Kingswood Village (Surrey).

UNWIN, Ven. Kenneth; Archdeacon of Pontefract, since 1981; *b* 16 Sept. 1926; *s* of Percy and Elsie Unwin; *m* 1958, Beryl Riley; one *s* four *d*. *Educ:* Chesterfield Grammar School; St Edmund Hall, Oxford (MA Hons); Ely Theological Coll. Assistant Curate: All Saints, Leeds, 1951–55; St Margaret, Durham City (in charge, St John's, Neville's Cross), 1955–59; Vicar: St John Baptist, Dodworth, Barnsley, 1959–69; St John Baptist, Royston, Barnsley, 1969–73; St John's, Wakefield, 1973–82. Hon. Canon, Wakefield Cathedral, 1980–; RD of Wakefield, 1980–81. Proctor in Convocation, 1972–82. *Address:* Pontefract House, 19a Tithe Barn Street, Horbury, Wakefield WF4 6LJ. *T:* Wakefield (0924) 263777.

UNWIN, Dr (Peter) Nigel (Tripp), FRS 1983; Joint Head of Structural Studies, Medical Research Council Laboratory of Molecular Biology, Cambridge, since 1987; Senior Research Fellow, Trinity College, Cambridge, since 1988; *b* 1 Nov. 1942; *s* of Peter Unwin and Cara Unwin (*née* Pinckney); *m* 1968, Janet Patricia Ladd; one *s* one *d*. *Educ:* Univ. of Otago, NZ (BE); Univ. of Cambridge (PhD 1968). Scientist, MRC Lab. of Molecular Biology, Cambridge, 1968–80 and 1987–; Prof. of Structural Biol., then Cell Biol., Stanford Univ. Sch. of Medicine, Calif, 1980–87. *Recreation:* mountaineering. *Address:* 19/20 Portugal Place, Cambridge.

UNWIN, Peter William, CMG 1981; Deputy Secretary General (Economic) of the Commonwealth, since 1989; *b* 20 May 1932; *s* of Arnold and Norah Unwin; *m* 1955, Monica Steven; two *s* two *d*. *Educ:* Ampleforth; Christ Church, Oxford (MA). Army, 1954–56; FO, 1956–58; British Legation, Budapest, 1958–61; British Embassy, Tokyo, 1961–63; FCO, 1963–67; British Information Services, NY, 1967–70; FCO, 1970–72; Bank of England, 1973; British Embassy, Bonn, 1973–76; Head of Personnel Policy Dept, FCO, 1976–79; Fellow, Center for Internat. Affairs, Harvard, 1979–80; Minister (Economic), Bonn, 1980–83; Ambassador to: Hungary, 1983–86; Denmark, 1986–88.

Publication: Voice in the Wilderness: Imre Nagy and the Hungarian Revolution, 1991. *Address:* 30 Kew Green, Richmond, Surrey TW9 3BH. *T:* 081–940 8037; c/o Commonwealth Secretariat, 2 Carlton Gardens, SW1. *Clubs:* Commonwealth Trust, United Oxford & Cambridge University.

UNWIN, Rayner Stephens, CBE 1977; Chairman, Unwin Enterprises, since 1986; Director, Allen and Unwin Australia, since 1990; *b* 23 Dec. 1925; *s* of late Sir Stanley Unwin and Mary Storr; *m* 1952, Carol Margaret, *d* of Harold Curwen; one *s* three *d*. *Educ:* Abbotsholme Sch.; Trinity Coll., Oxford (MA); Harvard, USA (MA). Sub-Lt, RNVR, 1944–47. Entered George Allen & Unwin Ltd, 1951; Chm., 1968–86; Chm., 1986–88, Vice-Chm., 1988–90, Unwin Hyman. Mem. Council, Publishers' Assoc., 1965–85 (Treasurer, 1969; Pres., 1971; Vice-Pres., 1973); Chm., British Council Publishers' Adv. Cttee, 1981–88. Pres., Book Trade Benevolent Soc., 1989–. Chm., Little Missenden Festival, 1981–88. *Publications:* The Rural Muse, 1954; The Defeat of John Hawkins, 1960. *Recreations:* mountains, birds and gardens. *Address:* Limes Cottage, Little Missenden, near Amersham, Bucks HP7 0RG. *T:* Great Missenden (02406) 2900. *Club:* Garrick.

See also D. S. Unwin.

UPDIKE, John Hoyer; freelance writer; *b* 18 March 1932; *s* of Wesley R. and Linda G. Updike; *m* 1st, 1953, Mary E. Pennington (marr. diss.); two *s* two *d*; 2nd, 1977, Martha Bernhard. *Educ:* Harvard Coll. Worked as journalist for The New Yorker magazine, 1955–57. *Publications: poems:* Hoping for a Hoopoe (in America, The Carpentered Hen), 1958; Telephone Poles, 1968; Midpoint and other poems, 1969; Tossing and Turning, 1977; Facing Nature, 1985; *novels:* The Poorhouse Fair, 1959; Rabbit, Run, 1960; The Centaur, 1963; Of the Farm, 1966; Couples, 1968; Rabbit Redux, 1972; A Month of Sundays, 1975; Marry Me, 1976; The Coup, 1979; Rabbit is Rich (Pulitzer Prize), 1982; The Witches of Eastwick, 1984 (filmed 1987); Roger's Version, 1986; S., 1988; Rabbit at Rest, 1990 (Pulitzer Prize 1991); *short stories:* The Same Door, 1959; Pigeon Feathers, 1962; The Music School, 1966; Bech: A Book, 1970; Museums and Women, 1973; Problems, 1980; Bech is Back, 1982; (ed) The Year's Best American Short Stories, 1985; Trust Me, 1987; *miscellanies:* Assorted Prose, 1965; Picked-Up Pieces, 1976; Hugging the Shore, 1983; Just Looking: essays on art, 1989; *autobiography:* Self-Consciousness: Memoirs, 1989; *play:* Buchanan Dying, 1974. *Address:* Beverly Farms, Mass 01915, USA.

UPHAM, Captain Charles Hazlitt, VC 1941 and Bar, 1943; JP; sheep-farmer; *b* Christchurch, New Zealand, 21 Sept. 1908; *s* of John Hazlitt Upham, barrister, and Agatha Mary Upham, Christchurch, NZ; *m* 1945, Mary Eileen, *d* of James and Mary McTamney, Dunedin, New Zealand; three *d* (incl. twins). *Educ:* Waihi Prep. School, Winchester; Christ's Coll., Christchurch, NZ; Canterbury Agric. Coll., Lincoln, NZ (Diploma). Post-grad. course in valuation and farm management. Farm manager and musterer, 1930–36; govt valuer, 1937–39; farmer, 1945–. Served War of 1939–45 (VC and Bar, despatches): volunteered, Sept. 1939; 2nd NZEF (Sgt 1st echelon advance party); 2nd Lt; served Greece, Crete, W Desert (VC, Crete; Bar, Ruweisat); Captain; POW, released 1945. *Relevant Publication:* Mark of the Lion: The Story of Captain Charles Upham, VC and Bar (by Kenneth Sandford), 1962. *Recreations:* rowing, Rugby (1st XV Lincoln Coll., NZ). *Address:* Lansdowne, Hundalee, North Canterbury, NZ. *Clubs:* Canterbury, Christchurch, RSA (all NZ).

UPJOHN, Maj.-Gen. Gordon Farleigh, CB 1966; CBE 1959 (OBE 1955); *b* 9 May 1912; *e s* of late Dudley Francis Upjohn; *m* 1946, Rita Joan, *d* of late Major Clarence Walters; three *d*. *Educ:* Felsted School; RMC Sandhurst. 2nd Lieut, The Duke of Wellington's Regt; RWAFF, 1937; Adjt 3rd Bn The Nigeria Regt, 1940; Staff Coll., 1941; GSO2 Ops GHQ Middle East, 1941; Bde Maj. 3 WA Inf. Bde, 1942 (despatches); Lt-Col Comd 6 Bn The Nigeria Regt, 1944 (despatches); DAA&QMG Southern Comd India, 1946; GSO2 Mil. Ops Directorate WO, 1948; Lt-Col Chief Instructor RMA Sandhurst, 1951; Lt-Col Comd WA Inf. Bn, 1954; Bde Comdr 2 Inf. Bde Malaya, 1957 (despatches; Meritorious Medal (Perak Malaya)); Provost Marshal WO, 1960; GOC Yorkshire District, 1962–65. Automobile Assoc., 1965–76. *Recreations:* golf, cricket, field sports. *Address:* c/o Lloyds Bank, Grayshott, Hindhead, Surrey GU26 6LG. *Club:* Army and Navy.

UPWARD, Mrs Janet; Quality Assurance Review Officer, Birmingham Family Health Services Authority, since 1991. *Educ:* Newnham College, Cambridge. BA (Geog. Hons) 1961, MA 1966. Sec., National Fedn of Consumer Gps, 1972–82; Mem., 1978–84, Dep. Chm., 1978–83, Domestic Coal Consumers' Council; Chm., National Consumer Congress, 1981–83; Chief Officer, S Birmingham CHC, 1983–90. *Address:* 61 Valentine Road, Birmingham B14 7AJ. *T:* 021–444 2837.

URE, James Mathie, OBE 1969; British Council Representative, India, and Minister (Education), British High Commission, New Delhi, 1980–84; *b* 5 May 1925; *s* of late William Alexander Ure, and of Helen Jones; *m* 1950, Martha Walker Paterson; one *s* one *d*. *Educ:* Shawlands Acad., Glasgow; Glasgow Univ. (MA); Trinity Coll., Oxford (BLitt). Army Service, 1944–47. Lectr, Edinburgh Univ., 1953–59; British Council: Istanbul, 1956–57; India, 1959–68; Dep. Controller, Arts Div., 1968–71; Rep., Indonesia, 1971–75; Controller, Home Div., 1975–80. *Publications:* Old English Benedictine Office, 1952; (with L. A. Hill) English Sounds and Spellings, 1962; (with L. A. Hill) English Sounds and Spellings—Tests, 1963; (with J. S. Bhandari and C. S. Bhandari) Read and Act, 1965; (with C. S. Bhandari) Short Stories, 1966.

URE, Sir John (Burns), KCMG 1987 (CMG 1980); LVO 1968; HM Diplomatic Service, retired; UK Commissioner General to Expo 92, since 1990; Director, Thomas Cook Group, since 1991; *b* 5 July 1931; *s* of late Tam Ure; *m* 1972, Caroline, *d* of Charles Allan, Roxburghshire; one *s* one *d*. *Educ:* Uppingham Sch.; Magdalene Coll., Cambridge (MA); Harvard Business Sch. (AMP). Active Service as 2nd Lieut with Cameronians (Scottish Rifles), Malaya, 1950–51; Lieut, London Scottish (Gordon Highlanders) TA, 1952–55. Book publishing with Ernest Benn Ltd, 1951–53; joined Foreign (subseq. Diplomatic) Service, 1956; 3rd Sec. and Private Sec. to Ambassador, Moscow, 1957–59; Resident Clerk, FO, 1960–61; 2nd Sec., Leopoldville, 1962–63; FO, 1964–66; 1st Sec. (Commercial), Santiago, 1967–70; FCO, 1971–72; Counsellor, and intermittently Chargé d'Affaires, Lisbon, 1972–77; Head of South America Dept, FCO, 1977–79; Ambassador to Cuba, 1979–81; Asst Under-Sec. of State, FCO, 1981–84; Ambassador to Brazil, 1984–87, to Sweden, 1987–91. Life Fellow and Mem. Council, RGS, 1982–84. Thomas Cook lecture on Literary Travellers, RGS, 1988. Comdr, Mil. Order of Christ, Portugal, 1973. *Publications:* Cucumber Sandwiches in the Andes, 1973 (Travel Book Club Choice); Prince Henry the Navigator, 1977 (History Guild Choice); The Trail of Tamerlane, 1980 (Ancient History Club Choice); The Quest for Captain Morgan, 1983; Trespassers on the Amazon, 1986; RGS History of World Exploration (Central and South America sections), 1990; book reviews in TLS. *Recreation:* travelling uncomfortably in remote places and writing about it comfortably afterwards. *Address:* Netters Hall, Hawkhurst, Kent TN18 5AT. *T:* Hawkhurst (0580) 752191. *Clubs:* White's, Beefsteak.

URIE, Wing Comdr John Dunlop, AE 1942; bar 1945; *b* 12 Oct. 1915; *s* of late John Urie, OBE, Glasgow; *m* 1939, Mary Taylor, *d* of Peter Bonnar, Dunfermline; one *s* two *d*. *Educ:* Sedbergh; Glasgow Univ. Served War of 1939–45: with RAuxAF, in Fighter Command and Middle East Command; Wing Comdr, 1942. DL Co. of Glasgow, 1963. OStJ. *Address:* 80 Westbrook Avenue, Wahroonga, NSW 2076, Australia. *Club:* Royal Northern and Clyde Yacht.

URMSON, James Opie, MC 1943; Emeritus Professor of Philosophy, Stanford University; Emeritus Fellow of Corpus Christi College, Oxford; *b* 4 March 1915; *s* of Rev. J. O. Urmson; *m* 1940, Marion Joyce Drage; one *d*. *Educ:* Kingswood School, Bath; Corpus Christi College, Oxford. Senior Demy, Magdalen College, 1938; Fellow by examination, Magdalen College, 1939–45. Served Army (Duke of Wellington's Regt), 1939–45. Lecturer of Christ Church, 1945–46; Student of Christ Church, 1946–55; Professor of Philosophy, Queen's College, Dundee, University of St Andrews, 1955–59; Fellow and Tutor in Philosophy, CCC, Oxford, 1959–78. Visiting Associate Prof., Princeton Univ., 1950–51. Visiting Lectr, Univ. of Michigan, 1961–62, 1965–66, and 1969; Stuart Prof. of Philosophy, Stanford, 1975–80. *Publications:* Philosophical Analysis, 1956; The Emotive Theory of Ethics, 1968; Berkeley, 1982; Aristotle's Ethics, 1988; The Greek Philosophical Vocabulary, 1990; edited: Encyclopedia of Western Philosophy, 1960; J. L. Austin: How to Do Things with Words, 1962; (with G. J. Warnock) J. L. Austin: Philosophical Papers, 2nd edn, 1970; articles in philosophical jls. *Recreations:* gardening, music. *Address:* Standfast, Tumbledown Dick, Cumnor, Oxford OX2 9QE. *T:* Oxford (0865) 862769.

URQUHART, Sir Brian (Edward), KCMG 1986; MBE 1945; Scholar-in-Residence, Ford Foundation, since 1986; an Under-Secretary-General, United Nations, 1974–86; *b* 28 Feb. 1919; *s* of Murray and Bertha Urquhart; *m* 1st, 1944, Alfreda Huntington (marr. diss. 1963); two *s* one *d*; 2nd, 1963, Sidney Damrosch Howard; one *s* one *d*. *Educ:* Westminster; Christ Church, Oxford (Hon. Student, 1985). British Army: Dorset Regt and Airborne Forces, N Africa, Sicily and Europe, 1939–45; Personal Asst to Gladwyn Jebb, Exec. Sec. of Preparatory Commn of UN, London, 1945–46; Personal Asst to Trygve Lie, 1st Sec.-Gen. of UN, 1946–49; Sec., Collective Measures Cttee, 1951–53; Mem., Office of Under-Sec.-Gen. for Special Political Affairs, 1954–71; Asst Sec.-Gen., UN, 1972–74; Exec. Sec., 1st and 2nd UN Conf. on Peaceful Uses of Atomic Energy, 1955 and 1958; active in organization and direction of UN Emergency Force in Middle East, 1956; Dep. Exec. Sec., Preparatory Commn of Internat. Atomic Energy Agency, 1957; Asst to Sec.-Gen.'s Special Rep. in Congo, July-Oct. 1960; UN Rep. in Katanga, Congo, 1961–62; responsible for organization and direction of UN peace-keeping ops and special political assignments. Hon. LLD: Yale, 1981; Tufts, 1985; Grinnell, 1986; State Univ. NY, 1986; Warwick, 1989; DUniv: Essex, 1981; City Univ. NY, 1986; Hon. DCL Oxford, 1986; Hon. DHL Colorado, 1987; Hon. DLitt Keele, 1987. *Publications:* Hammarskjold, 1972; A Life in Peace and War (autobiog.), 1987; Decolonization and World Peace, 1989; (with Erskine Childers) A World in Need of Leadership: tomorrow's United Nations, 1990; various articles and reviews on internat. affairs. *Address:* 131 East 66th Street, New York, NY 10021, USA; Howard Farm, Tyringham, Mass 01264. *T:* 535–0805. *Club:* Century (New York).

URQUHART, Donald John, CBE 1970; Director General, British Library Lending Services, 1973–74; *b* 27 Nov. 1909; *s* of late Roderick and Rose Catherine Urquhart, Whitley Bay; *m* 1939, Beatrice Winefride, *d* of late W. G. Parker, Sheffield; two *s*. *Educ:* Barnard Castle School; Sheffield University (BSc, PhD). Research Dept, English Steel Corp., 1934–37; Science Museum Library, 1938–39; Admiralty, 1939–40; Min. of Supply, 1940–45; Science Museum Library, 1945–48; DSIR Headquarters, 1948–61; Dir, Nat. Lending Library for Science and Technology, 1961–73. Hon. Lectr, Postgrad. Sch. of Librarianship and Information Science, Sheffield Univ., 1970–; Vis. Prof., Loughborough Univ. Dept of Library and Information Studies, 1973–80. Chm., Standing Conf. of Nat. and Univ. Libraries, 1969–71. FLA, Pres., Library Assoc., 1972. Hon. DSc: Heriot-Watt, 1974; Sheffield, 1974; Salford, 1974. Hon. Citation, Amer. Library Assoc., 1978. *Publications:* The Principles of Librarianship, 1981; Mr Boston Spa, 1990; papers on library and scientific information questions. *Recreation:* gardening. *Address:* Wood Garth, First Avenue, Bardsey, near Leeds. *T:* Collingham Bridge (0937) 573228. *Club:* Athenæum.

URQUHART, James Graham, CVO 1983; FCIT, FIMH; Chairman, Fiox Ltd, since 1990 (Director, 1988–90); Director: Systems Connection Group PLC, since 1988; Electronics Ltd, since 1987; CVC Ltd, since 1988; *b* 23 April 1925; *s* of James Graham Urquhart and Mary Clark; *m* 1949, Margaret Hutchinson; two *d*. *Educ:* Berwickshire High Sch. Served War, RAF, 1941–44. Management Trainee, Eastern Region, BR, 1949–52; Chief Controller, Fenchurch Street, 1956–59; Dist Traffic Supt, Perth, 1960–62; Divl Operating Supt, Glasgow, 1962–64; Divl Manager, Glasgow and SW Scotland, 1964–67; Asst Gen. Man., Eastern Reg., 1967–69; BR Bd HQ: Chief Ops Man., 1969–72; Exec. Dir, Personnel, 1972–75; Gen. Manager, London Midland Reg., BR, 1975–76; BR Bd: Exec. Mem., Operations and Productivity, 1977–83; Mem., Exports, 1983–85; Chairman: British Transport Police, 1977–86; BRE-Metro, 1978–86; BR Engrg Ltd, 1979–85; Freightliners, 1983–85; Transmark, 1983–86. Director: Waterslides PLC, 1987–; Sonic Tape PLC, 1988–90. Mem., Industrial Tribunal, 1987. MIPM, MInstM, CBIM. *Recreations:* golf, travel, gardening. *Address:* 10 Wychcotes, Caversham, Reading RG4 7DA. *T:* Reading (0734) 479071.

URQUHART, Lawrence McAllister, CA; Chairman since 1990, and Chief Executive since 1988, Burmah Castrol (formerly Burmah Oil) plc; *b* 24 Sept. 1935; *s* of Robert and Josephine Urquhart; *m* 1961, Elizabeth Catherine Burns; three *s* one *d*. *Educ:* Strathallan; King's Coll., London (LLB). Price Waterhouse & Co., 1957–62; Shell International Petroleum, 1962–64; P. A. Management Consultants, 1964–68; Charterhouse Gp, 1968–74; TKM Gp, 1974–77; Burmah Oil, subseq. Burmah Castrol, 1977–: Gp Man. Dir, 1985–88. *Recreations:* golf, music. *Address:* Burmah Castrol plc, Burmah Castrol House, Pipers Way, Swindon, Wilts SN3 1RE. *T:* Swindon (0793) 511521. *Clubs:* Frilford Heath Golf; Lilley Brook Golf (Cheltenham).

URSELL, Prof. Fritz Joseph, FRS 1972; Emeritus Professor of Applied Mathematics, Manchester University, since 1990 (Beyer Professor of Applied Mathematics, 1961–90); *b* 28 April 1923; *m* 1959, Katharina Renate (*née* Zander); two *d*. *Educ:* Clifton; Marlborough; Trinity College, Cambridge. BA 1943, MA 1947, ScD 1957, Cambridge. Admiralty Service, 1943–47; ICI Fellow in Applied Mathematics, Manchester Univ., 1947–50. Fellow (Title A), Trinity Coll., Cambridge, 1947–51; Univ. Lecturer in Mathematics, Cambridge, 1950–61; Stringer Fellow in Natural Sciences, King's Coll., Cambridge, 1954–60. Georg Weinblum Lectr in Ship Hydrodynamics, Hamburg and Washington, 1986; Stewartson Lectr in Fluid Mechanics, 1991. FIMA 1964. MSc (Manchester), 1965. *Address:* 28 Old Broadway, Manchester M20 9DF. *T:* 061–445 5791.

URSELL, Rev. Philip Elliott; Principal of Pusey House, Oxford, since 1982; *b* 3 Dec. 1942; *o s* of Clifford Edwin Ursell and Hilda Jane Ursell (*née* Tucker). *Educ:* Cathays High Sch.; University Coll. Cardiff (Craddock Wells Exhibnr; BA); St Stephen's House, Oxford. MA Oxon. Curate of Newton Nottage, Porthcawl, 1968–71; Asst Chaplain of University Coll. Cardiff, 1971–77; Chaplain of Polytechnic of Wales, 1974–77; Chaplain, Fellow and Dir of Studies in Music, Emmanuel Coll., Cambridge, 1977–82. Select

Preacher, Harvard Univ., 1982, 1983; Univ. Preacher, Harvard Summer Sch., 1985. Warden, Soc. of Most Holy Trinity, Ascot Priory, 1985–. Examining Chaplain to the Bishop of London, 1987–. Mem. Governing Body, Church in Wales, 1971–77. *Recreations:* gardening, painting, sailing. *Address:* Pusey House, Oxford OX1 3LZ. *T:* Oxford (0865) 278415; Ascot Priory, Berks SL5 8RT. *T:* Ascot (0344) 885157.

URUGUAY, Bishop of, since 1988; **Rt. Rev. (Harold) William Godfrey;** Assistant Presiding Bishop, Province of the Southern Cone of America, since 1989; *b* 21 April 1948; *s* of Charles Robert Godfrey and Irene Eva Godfrey (*née* Kirk); *m* 1968, Judith Moya (*née* Fenton); one *s* two *d*. *Educ:* Chesterfield School; King's Coll., Univ. of London (AKC); St Augustine's Coll., Canterbury. VSO, Isfahan, Iran, 1966–67; Asst Curate, Warsop with Sookholme, Diocese of Southwell, 1972–75; Team Vicar of St Peter and St Paul, Hucknall Torkard, 1975–86; Bishop of Southwell's Ecumenical Officer, 1981–82; Rector of Montevideo, 1986–88, Archdeacon of Montevideo, 1986–87; Asst Bishop of Argentina and Uruguay, 1987–88. Founder Mem., Jesus Caritas Fraternity (Anglican Communion), 1974. *Recreations:* walking, guitar, bird watching, hockey (University, Derbyshire and Midland colours). *Address:* Casa Episcopal, Francisco Araúcho 1287, 11300 Montevideo, Uruguay. *T:* 78.38.85.

URWICK, Sir Alan (Bedford), KCVO 1984; CMG 1978; Serjeant at Arms, House of Commons, since 1989; *b* 2 May 1930; *s* of late Col Lyndall Fownes Urwick, OBE, MC and Joan Wilhelmina Saunders (*née* Bedford); *m* 1960, Marta, *o d* of Adhemar Montagne; three *s*. *Educ:* Dragon Sch.; Rugby (Schol.); New Coll., Oxford (Exhibr). 1st cl. hons Mod. History 1952. Joined HM Foreign (subseq. Diplomatic) Service, 1952; served in: Brussels, 1954–56; Moscow, 1958–59; Baghdad, 1960–61; Amman, 1965–67; Washington, 1967–70; Cairo, 1971–73; seconded to Cabinet Office as Asst Sec., Central Policy Review Staff, 1973–75; Head of Near East and N Africa Dept, FCO, 1975–76; Minister, Madrid, 1977–79; Ambassador to Jordan, 1979–84; Ambassador to Egypt, 1985–87; High Comr to Canada, 1987–89. KStJ 1982. Grand Cordon, first class, Order of Independence (Jordan), 1984. *Address:* c/o House of Commons, Westminster, SW1A 0AA.

URWIN, Harry, (Charles Henry); Associate Fellow, Industrial Relations Research Unit, Warwick University, since 1981; Member, TUC General Council, 1969–80; Deputy General-Secretary, Transport and General Workers Union, 1969–80; Chairman, TUC Employment Policy and Organisation Committee, 1973–80; *b* 24 Feb. 1915; *s* of Thomas and Lydia Urwin; *m* 1941, Hilda Pinfold; one *d*. *Educ:* Durham County Council Sch. Convenor, Machine Tool Industry, until 1947; Coventry Dist Officer, TGWU, 1947–59; Coventry Dist Sec., Confedn of Shipbuilding and Engineering Unions, 1954–59; Regional Officer, TGWU, 1959–69; Member: Industrial Develt Adv. Bd, Industry Act, 1972–79; Sir Don Ryder Inquiry, British Leyland Motor Corp., 1974–75; Manpower Services Commn, 1974–79; Nat. Enterprise Bd, 1975–79; Energy Commn, 1977–79; Council, ACAS, 1978–80; Standing Cttee on Pay Comparability, 1979–80. *Recreation:* swimming. *Address:* 4 Leacliffe Way, Aldridge, Walsall WS9 0PW.

URWIN, (Terence) Peter; County Secretary and Solicitor, Northumberland County Council, since 1990; *b* 28 Oct. 1948; *s* of John Robson Urwin; *m* 1971, Mary Theresa Smith; one *d*. *Educ:* Durham Johnston Sch.; Liverpool Univ. (LLB Hons). Solicitor. Durham County Council: Asst Solicitor, 1973–74; Asst Clerk of the Council, 1974–86; Dep. County Solicitor, 1986–90. Clerk to the Lieutenancy, Northumberland, 1990–. Secretary, Northumberland Advisory Committee: Justices of the Peace, 1990–; Gen. Comrs of Income Tax, 1990–. *Recreations:* Rugby, walking, crosswords. *Address:* 6 Ryedale, Belmont, Durham City DH1 2AL. *T:* Durham (091) 3869208.

USBORNE, Henry Charles, MA; Founder, Parliamentary Group for World Government, 1946; *b* 16 Jan. 1909; *s* of Charles Frederick Usborne and Janet Lefroy; *m* 1936; two *s* two *d*. *Educ:* Bradfield; Corpus Christi, Cambridge. MP (Lab) Yardley Div. of Birmingham, 1950–59 (Acock's Green Div. of Birmingham, 1945–50). JP Worcs, 1964–79. *Address:* Totterdown, Evesham, Worcs WR11 5JP.
See also R. A. Usborne.

USBORNE, Richard Alexander; writer; *b* 16 May 1910; *s* of Charles Frederick Usborne, ICS, and Janet Muriel (*née* Lefroy); *m* 1938, Monica (*d* 1986), *d* of Archibald Stuart MacArthur, Wagon Mound, New Mexico, USA; one *s* one *d*. *Educ:* Summer Fields Preparatory Sch.; Charterhouse; Balliol Coll., Oxford. BA Mods and Greats; MA 1981. Served War, 1941–45: Army, SOE and PWE, Middle East, Major, Gen. List. Advertising agencies, 1933–36; part-owner and Editor of What's On, 1936–37; London Press Exchange, 1937–39; BBC Monitoring Service, 1939–41; Asst Editor, Strand Magazine, 1946–50; Dir, Graham & Gillies Ltd, Advertising, retd, 1970; Custodian, National Trust, 1974–81. *Publications:* Clubland Heroes, 1953 (rev. 1975, 1983); (ed) A Century of Summer Fields, 1964; Wodehouse at Work, 1961, rev. edn, as Wodehouse at Work to the End, 1977; (ed) Sunset at Blandings, 1977; (ed) Vintage Wodehouse, 1977; A Wodehouse Companion, 1981; (ed) Wodehouse 'Nuggets', 1983; (ed) The Penguin Wodehouse Companion, 1988; After Hours with P. G. Wodehouse, 1991; adaptations of Wodehouse novels and stories for BBC radio serials. *Recreations:* reading, writing light verse. *Address:* The Charterhouse, Charterhouse Square, EC1M 6AN. *T:* 071–608 0140.
See also H. C. Usborne.

USHER, Sir Leonard (Gray), KBE 1986 (CBE 1971); JP; Secretary, Fiji Press Council, since 1985; Chairman, Suva Stock Exchange, since 1978; *b* 29 May 1907; *s* of Robert Usher and Mary Elizabeth (*née* Johnston); *m* 1st, 1940, Mary Gertrude Lockie; one *s* one *d*; 2nd, 1962, Jane Hammond Derné (*d* 1984). *Educ:* Auckland Grammar Sch., NZ; Auckland Training Coll. (Trained Teachers Cert. B); Auckland Univ. (BA). Headmaster, Levuka Public Sch., Provincial Schs, Queen Victoria Sch., 1930–43; Fiji Govt PRO, 1943–56; Exec. Dir, Fiji Times and Herald Ltd, 1957–73; Editor, Fiji Times, 1958–73; Org. Dir, Pacific Is News Assoc., 1974–85 (Councillor and Life Mem., 1985–). Chm., Fiji Develt Bank, 1978–82; Dep. Chm., Nat. Bank of Fiji, 1974–83. Mem., Suva CC, 1962–71, 1975–77; Mayor of Suva, 1966–70, 1975–76. *Publications:* Satellite Over The Pacific, 1975; 50 Years in Fiji, 1978; (jtly) Suva—a history and guide, 1978; Levuka School Century, 1979; (jtly) This is Radio Fiji, 1979; The Lodge of Fiji 1882–1982, 1982; (ed) Pacific News Media, 1986; Mainly About Fiji, 1987; 60 Years in Fiji, 1988. *Recreations:* reading, computer programmes, conversation. *Address:* 22 Des Voeux Road, Suva, Fiji. *T:* 302–025, *Fax:* 303–025; PO Box 14432, Suva, Fiji. *Clubs:* Defence, Fiji, United, Ex-Servicemen's (Fiji); Royal Automobile (Sydney); Grammar (Auckland).

USHER, Sir Robert (Edward), 6th Bt *cr* 1899, of Norton, Midlothian, and of Wells, Co. Roxburgh; *b* 18 April 1934; *yr s* of Sir (Robert) Stuart Usher, 4th Bt, and Gertrude Martha (*d* 1984), 2nd *d* of Lionel Barnard Sampson; *S* brother, 1990. *Heir: kinsman* (William) John Tevenar Usher [*b* 18 April 1940; *m* 1962, Rosemary Margaret, *d* of Col Sir Reginald Houldsworth, 4th Bt, OBE, TD; two *s* one *d*].

USTINOV, Sir Peter (Alexander), Kt 1990; CBE 1975; FRSA, FRSL; actor, dramatist, film director; Rector of the University of Dundee, 1968–74; Goodwill Ambassador for UNICEF, 1969; *b* London, 16 April 1921; *s* of late Iona Ustinov and Nadia Benois, painter; *m* 1st, 1940, Isolde Denham (marr. diss. 1950); one *d*; 2nd, 1954, Suzanne Cloutier (marr. diss. 1971); one *s* two *d*; 3rd, 1972, Hélène du Lau d'Allemans. *Educ:* Westminster School. Served in Army, Royal Sussex Regt and RAOC, 1942–46. Author of plays: House of Regrets, 1940 (prod Arts Theatre 1942); Blow Your Own Trumpet, 1941 (prod Playhouse [Old Vic] 1943); Beyond, 1942 (prod Arts Theatre, 1943); The Banbury Nose, 1943 (prod Wyndham's 1944); The Tragedy of Good Intentions, 1944 (prod Old Vic, Liverpool, 1945); The Indifferent Shepherd (prod Criterion, 1948); Frenzy (adapted from Swedish of Ingmar Bergman, prod and acted in St Martin's, 1948); The Man in the Raincoat (Edinburgh Festival, 1949); The Love of Four Colonels (and acted in, Wyndham's, 1951); The Moment of Truth (Adelphi, 1951); High Balcony, 1952 (written 1946); No Sign of the Dove (Savoy, 1953); The Empty Chair (Bristol Old Vic, 1956); Romanoff and Juliet (Piccadilly, 1956, film, 1961; musical, R loves J, Chichester, 1973); Photo Finish (prod and acted in it, Saville, 1962); The Life in My Hands, 1963; The Unknown Soldier and his Wife, 1967 (prod and acted in it, Chichester, 1968, New London, 1973); Halfway up the Tree (Queen's), 1967; compiled, prod and acted in The Marriage, Edinburgh, 1982; wrote and acted in Beethoven's Tenth (Vaudeville, 1983, 1987–88); An Evening with Peter Ustinov, (Haymarket), 1990, 1991. Co-Author of film: The Way Ahead, 1943–44. Author and Director of films: School for Secrets, 1946; Vice-Versa, 1947. Author, director, producer and main actor in film Private Angelo, 1946; acted in films: One of Our Aircraft is Missing, 1941; The Way Ahead, 1944; Odette, Quo Vadis, Hotel Sahara, 1950; Beau Brummell, The Egyptian, We're No Angels, 1954; Lola Montez, 1955; The Spies, 1955; I Girovaghi, 1956; An Angel Flew Over Brooklyn, 1957; Spartacus, 1960 (Academy Award, Best Supporting Actor, 1961); The Sundowners, 1961; Romanoff and Juliet, 1961; Topkapi (Academy Award, Best Supporting Actor), 1964; John Goldfarb, Please Come Home, 1964; Blackbeard's Ghost, 1967; The Comedians, 1968; Hot Millions, 1968; Viva Max, 1969; Big Truck and Poor Clare, 1971; One of our Dinosaurs is Missing, 1974; Logan's Run, 1975; Treasure of Matecumbe, 1977; Un Taxi Mauve, 1977; The Last Remake of Beau Geste, 1977; Death on the Nile, 1978 (Best Film Actor, Variety Club of GB); Ashanti, The Thief of Baghdad, 1979; Charlie Chan and the Curse of the Dragon Queen, 1981; Evil under the Sun, 1981; Appointment with Death, 1988; The French Revolution, 1989; director, producer and actor in film Billy Budd, 1961; director and actor in films: Hammersmith is Out, 1971; Memed My Hawk, 1984. Directed operas at: Covent Garden, 1962; Hamburg Opera, 1968; Paris Opera, 1973; Edinburgh Fest., 1973, 1981; Berlin Opera, 1978; Piccola Scala, Milan, 1981, 1982; Hamburg Opera, 1985, 1987. Master's Course (opera direction), Salzburg, 1986. Acted in: revues: Swinging the Gate, 1940, Diversion, 1941; plays: Crime and Punishment, New Theatre, 1946; Love in Albania, St James's, 1949; King Lear, Stratford, Ont, 1979; Beethoven's Tenth, Berlin, 1987; directed Lady L, 1965; *television:* Omnibus: the life of Samuel Johnson (Emmy Award), 1957–58; Barefoot in Athens (Emmy Award), 1966; Storm in Summer (Emmy Award), 1970; The Mighty Continent (series), 1974; Einstein's Universe (series), 1979; 13 at Dinner, 1985; Dead Man's Folly, 1985; World Challenge (series), 1985; Peter Ustinov's Russia (series), 1987; Peter Ustinov in China, 1987 (ACE Award, 1988); Around the World in 80 Days, 1988–89; Secret Identity of Jack the Ripper, 1989. Member: British Film Academy; Acad. of Fine Arts, Paris, 1988. Mem., British USA Bicentennial Liaison Cttee, 1973–. Hon. DHL Georgetown Univ., 1988. Benjamin Franklin Medal, Royal Society of Arts, 1957; Medal of the Greek Red Cross, 1990; Grammy Award. Order of the Smile (for dedication to idea of internat. assistance to children), Warsaw, 1974; Commandeur des Arts et des Lettres, France, 1985; Order of El Istiqlal, Jordan; Order of Yugoslav Flag, Yugoslavia. *Publications:* House of Regrets, 1943; Beyond, 1944; The Banbury Nose, 1945; Plays About People, 1950; The Love of Four Colonels, 1951; The Moment of Truth, 1953; Romanoff and Juliet (Stage and Film); Add a Dash of Pity (short stories), 1959; Ustinov's Diplomats (a book of photographs), 1960; The Loser (novel), 1961; The Frontiers of the Sea, 1966; Krumnagel, 1971; Dear Me (autobiog.), 1977; Overheard (play), 1981; My Russia, 1983; Ustinov in Russia, 1987; The Disinformer, 1989; The Old Man and Mrs Smith, 1990; contributor short stories to Atlantic Monthly. *Recreations:* lawn tennis, squash, collecting old masters' drawings, music. *Address:* 11 rue de Silly, 92100 Boulogne, France. *Clubs:* Garrick, Savage, Royal Automobile, Arts Theatre, Queen's.

UTIGER, Ronald Ernest, CBE 1977; Director: British Alcan Aluminium, since 1982; Ultramar, since 1983; National Grid Co., since 1990; *b* 5 May 1926; *s* of Ernest Frederick Utiger and Kathleen Utiger (*née* Cram); *m* 1953, Barbara Anna von Mohl; one *s* one *d*. *Educ:* Shrewsbury Sch.; Worcester Coll., Oxford (2nd cl. Hons PPE 1950; MA). Economist, Courtaulds Ltd, 1950–61; British Aluminium Ltd: Financial Controller, 1961–64; Commercial Dir, 1965–68; Man. Dir, 1968–79; Chm., 1979–82; BNOC: Dir, 1976–80, Chm., 1979–80; Tube Investments, subseq. TI Group: Dir, 1979–89; Dep. Chm. and Gp Man. Dir, 1982–84; Man. Dir, 1984–86; Chm., 1984–89. Member: NEDC, 1981–84; BBC Consultative Gp on Industrial and Business Affairs, 1985–. Chm., Internat. Primary Aluminium Inst., 1976–78; Pres., European Primary Aluminium Assoc., 1976–77. Chm., CBI Economic and Financial Policy Cttee, 1980–83; Mem., British Library Bd, 1987–; Governor, NIESR, 1983– (Pres., 1986–). FRSA; CBIM 1975. *Recreations:* music, gardening. *Address:* 9 Ailsa Road, St Margaret's-on-Thames, Twickenham, Mddx. *T:* 081–892 5810.

UTLEY, (Clifton) Garrick; journalist and broadcaster, since 1964; *b* 19 Nov. 1939; *s* of late Clifton Maxwell Utley and of Frayn Garrick Utley; *m* 1973, Gertje Rommeswinkel. *Educ:* Carleton Coll., Northfield, Minn, USA (BA 1961); Free Univ., Berlin. Correspondent, NBC News: Saigon, Vietnam, 1964–65; Berlin, Germany, 1966–68; Paris, France, 1969–71; NY, 1971–72; London (Senior European Correspondent), 1973–79; New York, 1980– (Chief Foreign Correspondent). Numerous documentary films on foreign affairs. Hon. LLD, Carleton Coll., 1979. *Recreations:* music, conversation, languages. *Address:* c/o NBC News, 30 Rockefeller Plaza, New York, NY 10112, USA. *T:* 664–4444.

UTLEY, Prof. James Henry Paul; Professor of Organic Chemistry, since 1983, and Dean, Faculty of Physical and Biological Sciences, since 1991, Queen Mary and Westfield College (formerly at Queen Mary College), University of London; *b* 11 Sept. 1936; *s* of Victor Eric Utley and Lena Beatrice Utley; *m* 1959, Hazel Wendler (*née* Brown); two *s* two *d*. *Educ:* E. P. Collier Sch., Reading; Univ. of Hull (BSc, PhD); Technische Hogeschool, Delft; University College London; DSc London. CChem, FRSC. NATO Research Fellowships, 1961–62; Queen Mary, later Queen Mary and Westfield College, London: Lectr, 1963–76; Reader in Organic Chemistry, 1976–83; Head of Chemistry, 1987–91. Guest Professor: Univ. of Aarhus, 1973; Univ. of Münster, 1985. *Publications:* research and review articles in internat. learned jls. *Recreations:* walking, bowls, jazz. *Address:* 23 Frewin Road, Wandsworth Common, SW18 3LR. *T:* 081–874 2939. *Club:* Heathfield (Wandsworth Common).

UTTING, Sir William (Benjamin), Kt 1991; CB 1985; Chief Inspector, Social Services Inspectorate, Department of Health (formerly of Health and Social Security), 1985–91; *b* 13 May 1931; *s* of John William Utting and Florence Ada Utting; *m* 1954, Mildred Jackson; two *s* one *d*. *Educ:* Great Yarmouth Grammar Sch.; New Coll., Oxford; Barnett House, Oxford. MA Oxon. Probation Officer: Co. Durham, 1956–58; Norfolk, 1958–61;

Sen. Probation Officer, Co. Durham, 1961–64; Principal Probation Officer, Newcastle upon Tyne, 1964–68; Lectr in Social Studies, Univ. of Newcastle upon Tyne, 1968–70; Dir of Social Services, Kensington and Chelsea, 1970–76; Chief Social Work Officer, DHSS, 1976–85. Member: Chief Scientist's Res. Cttee, DHSS, 1973–76; SSRC, 1979–83; ESRC, 1984. Trustee: Mental Health Foundn, 1988–; Joseph Rowntree Foundn, 1991–. *Publications:* contribs to professional jls. *Recreations:* literature, music, art. *Address:* 76 Great Brownings, College Road, SE21 7HR. *T:* 081–670 1201.

UVAROV, Dame Olga (Nikolaevna), DBE 1983 (CBE 1978); DSc, FRCVS; Vice-President, Universities Federation for Animal Welfare, 1986; *d* of Nikolas and Elena Uvarov. *Educ:* Royal Vet. Coll. (Bronze Medals for Physiol. and Histol.). MRCVS 1934; FRCVS 1973. Asst in gen. mixed practice, 1934–43; own small animal practice, 1944–53; licence to practice and work at greyhound stadium, 1945–68; clinical res., Pharmaceutical industry, 1953–70; Head of Vet. Adv. Dept, Glaxo Laboratories, 1967–70; BVA Technical Inf. Service, 1970–76; Advr on Tech. Inf., BVA, 1976–78; Mem. MAFF Cttees under Medicines Act (1968), 1971–78. RCVS: Mem. Council, 1968–88; Chm. Parly Cttee, 1971–74; Jun. Vice-Pres., 1975; Pres., 1976–77; Sen. Vice-Pres., 1977–78; President: Soc. Women Vet. Surgeons, 1947–49 (Sec., 1946); Central Vet. Soc., 1951–52; Assoc. Vet. Teachers and Res. Workers, 1967–68 (Pres. S Reg., 1967–68); Section of Comparative Medicine, RSocMed, 1967–68 (Sec., 1965–67; Sec. for Internat. Affairs, 1971–78, 1983–); Lab. Animal Science Assoc., 1984–86 (Vice-Pres., 1983–84); Vice-Pres., Inst. of Animal Technicians, 1983–; Member Council: BVA, 1944–67; RSocMed, 1968–70 (Hon. Fellow, 1982); Res. Defence Soc., 1968–82 (Hon. Sec., 1978–82; Vice-Pres., 1982–); Member: Medicines Commn, 1978–82; Vet. Res. Club, 1967–; British Small Animal Vet. Assoc.; British Codex Sub-Cttee, Pharmaceutical Soc., 1970–71. FRVC 1979; Hon. FIBiol, 1983; Hon. DSc Guelph, 1976. Victory Gold Medal, Central Vet. Soc., 1965. *Publications:* contribs to: The Veterinary Annual; International Encyclopaedia of Veterinary Medicine, 1966; also papers in many learned jls. *Recreations:* work, travel, literature, flowers. *Address:* 76 Elm Park Court, Elm Park Road, Pinner, Middx HA5 3LL. *Club:* Royal Society of Medicine.

UXBRIDGE, Earl of; Charles Alexander Vaughan Paget; *b* 13 Nov 1950; *s* and *heir* of 7th Marquess of Anglesey, *qv*; *m* 1986, Georganne Elizabeth Elliott, *d* of Col John Alfred Downes, MBE, MC; one *s*. *Educ:* Dragon School, Oxford; Eton; Exeter Coll., Oxford. *Heir: s* Lord Paget de Beaudesert, *qv*. *Address:* Plâs-Newydd, Llanfairpwll, Gwynedd.

UZIELL-HAMILTON, Adrianne Pauline; Her Honour Judge Uziell-Hamilton; a Circuit Judge, since 1990; *b* 14 May 1932; *e d* of late Dr Marcus and Ella Grantham; *m* 1952, Mario Reginald Uziell-Hamilton (*d* 1988); one *s* one *d*. *Educ:* Maria Gray's Academy for Girls and privately. Called to the Bar, Middle Temple, 1965; *ad eundem* Mem., Inner Temple, 1976–; Head of Chambers, 1976–90; a Recorder, 1985–90. Member: Legal Aid Panel, 1969–; General Council of the Bar, 1970–74 (Exec. Cttee, 1973–74). Pres., Mental Health Review Tribunals, 1988. Gov., Polytechnic of N London, 1986–. FRSA. *Publications:* articles on marriage contracts. *Recreations:* collecting ballet and theatre costume design, cooking for friends, conversation. *Clubs:* Lloyds, Maccabaeans.

V

VACHON, His Eminence Cardinal Louis-Albert; *see* Quebec, Archbishop of, (RC).

VAEA, Baron of Houma; Minister for Labour, Commerce and Industries, Tonga, since 1973; *b* 15 May 1921; *s* of Viliami Vilai Tupou and Tupou Seini Vaea; *m* 1952, Tuputupu Ma'afu; three *s* three *d*. *Educ:* Wesley College, Auckland, NZ. RNZAF, 1942–45; Tonga Civil Service, 1945–53; ADC to HM Queen Salote, 1954–59; Governor of Haapai, 1959–68; Commissioner and Consul in UK, 1969; High Comr in UK, 1970–72; Actg Dep. Prime Minister, 1986. Given the title Baron Vaea of Houma by HM The King of Tonga, 1970. *Recreations:* Rugby, cricket, fishing. *Heir: e s* Albert Tuivanuavou Vaea, *b* 19 Sept. 1957. *Address:* PO Box 262, Nuku'alofa, Tonga. *T:* (home) 21–340; (office) 21–888.

VAES, Baron Robert, Hon. KCMG 1966; LLD; Grand Officer, Order of Leopold, Belgium; Director of Sotheby's, since 1984; *b* Antwerp, 9 Jan. 1919; created Baron, 1985; *m* 1947, Anne Albers; one *d*. *Educ:* Brussels Univ. (LLD; special degree in Commercial and Maritime Law). Joined Diplomatic Service, 1946: postings to Washington, Paris, Hong Kong, London, Rome and Madrid; Personal Private Sec. to Minister of Foreign Trade, 1958–60; Dir-Gen. of Polit. Affairs, 1964–66; Permanent Under-Sec., Min. of For. Affairs, For. Trade and Develt Cooperation, 1966–72; Ambassador: to Spain, 1972–76; to UK, 1976–84. Numerous foreign decorations including: Grand Officer, Legion of Honour (France); Grand Cross, Order of Isabela la Católica (Spain). *Recreation:* bridge. *Address:* 45 Gloucester Square, W2 2TQ. *Clubs:* White's, Beefsteak, Anglo-Belgian; Royal Yacht of Belgium.

VAISEY, David George, FSA; FRHistS; Bodley's Librarian, Oxford, since 1986; Professorial Fellow, Exeter College, Oxford, since 1975; *b* 15 March 1935; *s* of William Thomas Vaisey and Minnie Vaisey (*née* Payne); *m* 1965, Maureen Anne (*née* Mansell); two *d*. *Educ:* Rendcomb Coll., Glos (schol.); Exeter Coll., Oxford (Exhibnr; BA Mod. Hist., MA). 2nd Lieut, Glos Regt and KAR, 1955–56. Archivist, Staffordshire CC, 1960–63; Asst then Sen. Asst Librarian, Bodleian Liby, 1963–75; Dep. Keeper, Oxford Univ. Archives, 1966–75; Keeper of Western Manuscripts, Bodleian Liby, 1975–86. Vis. Prof., Liby Studies, UCLA, 1985. Hon. Res. Fellow, Dept of Library, Archive and Information Studies, UCL, 1987–. Member: Royal Commn on Historical Manuscripts, 1986–; Adv. Council on Public Records, 1989–; Chm., Nat. Council on Archives, 1988–. FRHistS 1973; FSA 1974. Encomienda, Order of Isabel the Catholic (Spain), 1989. *Publications:* Staffordshire and The Great Rebellion (jtly), 1964; Probate Inventories of Lichfield and District 1568–1680, 1969; (jtly) Victorian and Edwardian Oxford from old photographs, 1971; (jtly) Oxford Shops and Shopping, 1972; (jtly) Art for Commerce, 1973; Oxfordshire: a handbook for students of local history, 1973, 2nd edn 1974; The Diary of Thomas Turner 1754–65, 1984; articles in learned jls and collections. *Address:* Bodleian Library, Oxford OX1 3BG. *T:* Oxford (0865) 277000.

VAIZEY, Lady; Marina Vaizey; Art Critic of the Sunday Times, since 1974; *b* 16 Jan. 1938; *o d* of Lyman Stansky and late Ruth Stansky; *m* 1961, Lord Vaizey (*d* 1984); two *s* one *d*. *Educ:* Brearley Sch., New York; Putney Sch., Putney, Vermont; Radcliffe Coll., Harvard Univ. (BA Medieval History and Lit.); Girton Coll., Cambridge (BA, MA). Art Critic, Financial Times, 1970–74; Dance Critic, Now!, 1979–81; Mem. Arts Council, 1976–78 (Mem. Art Panel, 1973–78, Dep. Chm., 1976–78); Member: Advisory Cttee, DoE, 1975–81; Paintings for Hospitals, 1974–; Cttee, Contemporary Art Soc., 1975–79, 1980– (Hon. Sec., 1988–); Hist. of Art and Complementary Studies Bd, CNAA, 1978–82; Photography Bd, CNAA, 1979–81; Fine Art Bd, CNAA, 1980–83; Passenger Services Sub-Cttee, Heathrow Airport, 1979–83; Fine Arts Adv. Cttee, British Council, 1987–; Crafts Council, 1988–; Art Wkg Gp, National Curriculum, DES, 1990–91; Trustee: Nat. Museums and Galleries on Merseyside, 1986–; Geffrye Museum, London, 1990–; Imperial War Museum, 1991–; Exec. Dir, Mitchell Prize for the Hist. of Art, 1976–87. Governor: Camberwell Coll. of Arts and Crafts, 1971–82; Bath Acad. of Art, Corsham, 1978–81. Broadcaster, occasional exhibition organiser and lecturer; organised Critic's Choice, Tooth's, 1974; Painter as Photographer, touring exhibn, UK, 1982–85. Co-Sec., Radcliffe Club of London, 1968–74. *Publications:* 100 Masterpieces of Art, 1979; Andrew Wyeth, 1980; The Artist as Photographer, 1982; Peter Blake, 1985; Christo, 1990; articles in various periodicals, anthologies, exhibition catalogues. *Address:* 24 Heathfield Terrace, W4 4JE. *T:* 081–994 7994.

VAJPAYEE, Atal Bihari; Member, Rajya Sabha, 1962–67 and since 1986; Leader, Bharatiya Janata Party Parliamentary Party, 1980–84 and since 1986; *b* Gwalior, Madhya Pradesh, 25 Dec. 1926; *s* of Shri Krishna Bihari; unmarried. *Educ:* Victoria Coll., Gwalior; D.A.V. Coll., Kanpur (MA). Journalist and social worker. Arrested in freedom movement, 1942; Founder Mem., Jana Sangh, 1951–77; Leader, Jana Sangh Parly Party, 1957–77; Pres., Bharatiaya Jana Sangh, 1968–73; detained 26 June 1975, during Emergency; Founder Member: Janata Party, 1977–80; Bharatiya Janata Party, 1980– (Pres., 1980–86). Mem., Lok Sabha, 1957–62 and 1967–84; Minister of External Affairs, 1977–79; Chairman: Cttee on Govt Assurances, 1966–67; Public Accounts Cttee, 1969–70. Member: Parly Goodwill Mission to E Africa, 1965; Parly Delegns to Australia, 1967, Eur. Parlt, 1983; Indian Delegn to CPA meetings in Canada, 1966, Zambia, 1980, IOM, 1984; Indian Delegn to IPU Confs in Japan, 1974, Sri Lanka, 1975, Switzerland, 1984. Mem., Nat. Integration Council, 1958–62, 1967–73, 1986. President: All India Station Masters and Asst Station Masters Assoc., 1965–70; Pandit Deen Dayal Upadhyay Smarak Samiti, 1968–84; Pandit Deen Dayal Upadhyaya Janma Bhumi Smarak Samiti, 1979–. Formerly Editor: Rashtra-dharma; Panchajanya; Veer Arjun. *Publications:* Lok Sabha Men Atalji (collection of speeches); Qaidi Kavirai ki Kundaliyan; New Dimensions of India's Foreign Policy. *Address:* Shinde ki Chhawni, Gwalior, MP, India; 6 Raisina Road, New Delhi 110001, India. *T:* 385166.

VALDAR, Colin Gordon; Consultant Editor; *b* 18 Dec. 1918; 3rd *s* of Lionel and Mary Valdar; *m* 1st, 1940, Evelyn Margaret Barriff (marr. diss.); two *s*; 2nd, Jill, (*née* Davis). *Educ:* Haberdashers' Aske's Hampstead School. Free-lance journalist, 1936–39. Served War of 1939–45, Royal Engineers, 1939–42. Successively Production Editor, Features Editor, Asst Editor, Sunday Pictorial, 1942–46; Features Editor, Daily Express, 1946–51; Asst Editor, Daily Express, 1951–53; Editor, Sunday Pictorial, 1953–59; Editor, Daily Sketch, 1959–62. Director, Sunday Pictorial Newspapers Ltd, 1957–59; Director, Daily Sketch and Daily Graphic Ltd, 1959–62; Chm., Bouverie Publishing Co., 1964–83. Founded UK Press Gazette, 1965. *Address:* 2A Ratcliffe Wharf, 18–22 Narrow Street, E14 8DQ. *T:* 071–791 2155.

VALDIVIESO-BELAUNDE, Felipe; Grand Cross, Order Al Merito por Servicios Distinguidos (Peru), 1980; Peruvian Ambassador to the Court of St James's since 1989; *b* 21 Nov. 1928; *s* of Francisco Valdivieso and Rosario Belaunde de Valdivieso; *m* 1973, Samija de Valdivieso-Belaunde. *Educ:* Pontificia Universidad Católica, Peru. Joined Foreign Ministry, 1947; served: Holy See, 1952–54; Argentina, 1954–56; Brasil, 1956; USA, Washington, 1957–59; OAS, Washington, 1960–61; Costa Rica, 1961–62; Head, Foreign Minister's Cabinet, 1962–63; Counsellor, France, 1963–67; Foreign Ministry: Chief, UN Dept, 1967–69; Minister, Dir of Inf. and Planning, 1969; Ambassador: Morocco, 1970–71; Egypt, 1971–75; Dir Gen., Protocol, Foreign Ministry, 1975; Ambassador, Argentina, 1975–79; Perm. Rep., UN Internat. Orgs, Geneva, 1979–82; Ambassador, Ecuador, 1982–87; Under Sec. for Bilateral Affairs, Foreign Ministry, 1987—88, Sec. Gen. and Vice-Minister of Foreign Affairs, 1988–89. Holds numerous foreign decorations. *Recreation:* tennis. *Address:* 34 Porchester Terrace, W2 3TP. *T:* 071–262 5045. *Clubs:* Travellers', Canning; Nacional (Lima); Lima Golf.

VALE, Brian, OBE 1977; British Council Director, Spain, since 1991; *b* 26 May 1938; *s* of Leslie Vale and May (*née* Knowles); *m* 1966, Margaret Mary Cookson; two *s*. *Educ:* Sir Joseph Williamson's Mathematical Sch., Rochester; Keele Univ. (BA, DipEd); King's Coll., London (MPhil). HMOCS, N Rhodesia, 1960–63; Assistant to Comr for N Rhodesia, London, 1963–64; Educn Attaché, Zambia High Commn, London, 1964–65; British Council: Rio de Janeiro, 1965–68; Appts Div., 1968–72; Educn and Sci. Div., 1972–75; Rep., Saudi Arabia, 1975–78; Dep. Controller, Educn and Sci. Div., 1978–80; Dir Tech. Educn and Trng Orgn for Overseas Countries, 1980–81; Controller, Sci., Technol. and Educn Div., 1981–83; Rep. in Egypt, and Cultural Counsellor, British Embassy, Cairo, 1983–87; Asst Dir Gen., 1987–90. FRSA. *Publications:* contribs to specialist jls on educnl subjects and naval hist. *Recreations:* reading, talking, naval history. *Address:* c/o 10 Spring Gardens, SW1A 2BN. *T:* 071–930 8466. *Club:* Travellers'.

VALENTIA, 15th Viscount *cr* 1622 (Ireland); **Richard John Dighton Annesley**; Bt 1620; Baron Mountnorris 1628; farmer in Zimbabwe, since 1957; *b* 15 Aug. 1929; *s* of 14th Viscount Valentia, MC, MRCS, LRCP, and Joan Elizabeth (*d* 1986), *d* of late John Joseph Curtis; *S* father, 1983; *m* 1957, Anita Phyllis, *o d* of William Arthur Joy, Bristol; two *s* one *d* (and one *s* decd). *Educ:* Marlborough; RMA Sandhurst. BA Univ. of S Africa. Commnd RA, 1950; retd, rank of Captain, 1957. Schoolmaster, Ruzawi Prep. Sch., Marondera, Zimbabwe, 1977–83. *Recreations:* sport, shooting, fishing, leisure riding. *Heir: s* Hon. Francis William Dighton Annesley [*b* 29 Dec. 1959; *m* 1982, Shaneen Hobbs]. *Address:* East Range Farm, PO Chinhoyi, Zimbabwe.

VALENTINE, Rt. Rev. Barry, MA, BD, LTh, DD; Rector, Parish of Salt Spring Island, British Columbia, since 1989; *b* 26 Sept. 1927; *s* of Harry John Valentine and Ethel Margaret Purkiss; *m* 1st, 1952, Mary Currell Hayes; three *s* one *d*; 2nd, 1984, Shirley Carolyn Shean Evans. *Educ:* Brentwood Sch.; St John's Coll., Cambridge; McGill Univ., Montreal. Curate, Christ Church Cath., Montreal, 1952; Incumbent, Chateauguay-Beauharnois, 1954; Dir, Religious Educn, Dio. Montreal, 1957; Rector of St Lambert, PQ, 1961; Exec. Officer, Dio. Montreal, 1965; Dean of Montreal, 1968; Bishop Coadjutor of Rupert's Land, 1969; Bishop of Rupert's Land, 1970–82; Chaplain, Univ. of British Columbia, 1984–85; Asst Bishop of Maryland, 1986–89. Chancellor, 1970, Res. Fellow, 1983, St John's Coll., Winnipeg. Hon. DD: St John's Coll., Winnipeg, 1969; Montreal Dio. Theol Coll., 1970. *Publication:* The Gift that is in you, 1984. *Recreations:* music, theatre, walking, reading. *Address:* Box 214, 120 Park Drive, Ganges, BC V0S 1E0, Canada. *Club:* Taverners Cricket.

VALIANT, Prof. Leslie Gabriel, PhD; FRS 1991; Gordon McKay Professor of Computer Science and Applied Mathematics, Harvard University, since 1982; *b* 28 March 1949; *s* of Leslie Valiant and Eva Julia (*née* Ujlaki); *m* 1977, Gayle Lynne Dyckoff; two *s*. *Educ:* Tynemouth High Sch.; Latymer Upper Sch.; King's Coll., Cambridge (MA); Imperial Coll., London (DIC); Warwick Univ. (PhD). Vis. Asst Prof., Carnegie Mellon Univ., Pittsburgh, 1973–74; Lecturer: Leeds Univ., 1974–76; Edinburgh Univ., 1977–81, Reader 1981–82. Vis. Prof., Harvard Univ., 1982; Vis. Fellow, Oxford Univ. Computing Lab. and Merton Coll., Oxford, 1987–88. Guggenheim Fellow, 1985–86. Nevanlinna Prize, IMU, 1986. *Publications:* research papers in scientific jls. *Address:* Division of Applied Sciences, Harvard University, 33 Oxford Street, Cambridge, Mass 02138, USA. *T:* (617) 495–5817.

VALIN, Reginald Pierre; Deputy Chairman, The VPI Group (formerly Valin Pollen International plc), 1989–90 (Chairman, 1984–89); Non-Executive Director, Valin Pollen, since 1991; *b* 8 March 1938; *s* of Pierre Louis Valin and Molly Doreen Valin; *m* 1960, Brigitte Karin Leister; one *d*. *Educ:* Emanuel School. Trainee Exec., Bank of America, 1959–60; Charles Barker & Sons Ltd, later Charles Barker City: Account Management, 1960–69; Associate Dir, 1970–71; Dir, 1971–73; Man. Dir, 1973–76; Chief Exec., 1976–79; Founder Dir, Valin Pollen, 1979. *Address:* 11 Sheffield Terrace, W8 7NG. *T:* 071–371 1872; (office) Valin Pollen Ltd, 18 Grosvenor Gardens, SW1. *T:* 071–730 3456.

VALIOS, Nicholas Paul; QC 1991; a Recorder of the Crown Court, since 1986; *b* 5 May 1943; *s* of Nicholas William and Elizabeth Joan Valios; *m* 1967, Cynthia Valerie Horton; one *s* one *d*. *Educ:* Stonyhurst Coll., Lancs. Called to the Bar, Inner Temple, 1964; Mem., SE Circuit. *Recreations:* windsurfing, golf, reading, computers. *Address:* Francis Taylor Building, Temple, EC4Y 7BY. *T:* 071–353 7768.

VALLANCE, Iain David Thomas; Chairman, British Telecommunications plc, since 1987 (a Corporate Director, since 1984); *b* 20 May 1943; *s* of Edmund Thomas Vallance and Janet Wright Bell Ross Davidson; *m* 1967, Elizabeth Mary McGonnigill; one *s* one *d*. *Educ:* Edinburgh Acad.; Dulwich Coll.; Glasgow Acad.; Brasenose Coll., Oxford; London Graduate School of Business Studies (MSc). Joined Post Office, 1966; Director: Central Finance, 1976–78; Telecommunications Finance, 1978–79; Materials Dept, 1979–81; British Telecommunications: Board Mem. for Orgn and Business Systems, 1981–83; Man. Dir, Local Communications Services Div., 1983–85; Chief of Operations, 1985–86; Chief Exec., 1986–87. Fellow, London Business School, 1989. *Recreations:* hill walking, music. *Address:* c/o 81 Newgate Street, EC1A 7AJ.

VALLANCE, Michael Wilson; Headmaster of Bloxham School 1982–91; *b* 9 Sept. 1933; *er s* of late Vivian Victor Wilson Vallance and Kate Vallance, Wandsworth and Helston; *m* 1970, Mary Winifred Ann, *d* of John Steele Garnett; one *s* two *d*. *Educ:* Brighton Coll.; St John's Coll., Cambridge (MA). On staff of United Steel Companies Ltd, 1952–53; awarded United Steel Companies Scholarship (held at Cambridge), 1953; Asst Master, Abingdon School, 1957–61; Asst Master, Harrow School, 1961–72; Headmaster, Durham Sch., 1972–82. Chairman: Cttee of Northern Isis, 1976–77; NE Div., HMC, 1981–82. Trustee, Bloxham Project, 1971–91. *Recreations:* reading, cricket, gardening, the sea. *Address:* 22 Foxholes Hill, Exmouth, Devon EX8 2DQ. *T:* Exmouth (0395) 271633. *Clubs:* MCC, Jesters.

VALLANCE, Philip Ian Fergus; QC 1989; *b* 20 Dec. 1943; *o s* of Aylmer Vallance and Helen Gosse; *m* 1973, Wendy, *d* of J. D. Alston; one *s* one *d*. *Educ:* Bryanston; New Coll., Oxford (BA Mod. Hist). Called to the Bar, Inner Temple, 1968. *Recreations:* cooking, drystone walling. *Address:* (chambers) 1 Crown Office Row, Temple, EC4Y 7HH. *T:* 071–353 1801. *Club:* Travellers'.

VALLANCE-OWEN, Prof. John, MA, MD, FRCP, FRCPI, FRCPath; Visiting Professor, Royal Postgraduate Medical School, Hammersmith Hospital; Consultant Physician, London Independent Hospital, since 1988; *b* 31 Oct. 1920; *s* of late Prof. E. A. Owen; *m* 1950, Renee Thornton; two *s* two *d*. *Educ:* Friar's Sch., Bangor; Epsom Coll.; St John's Coll., Cambridge (de Havilland Schol. from Epsom); London Hosp. (Schol.). BA 1943; MA, MB, BChir Cantab, 1946; MD Cantab 1951; FRCP 1962; Hon. FRCPI 1970; FRCPath 1971; FRCPI 1973. Various appts incl. Pathology Asst and Med. 1st Asst, London Hosp., 1946–51; Med. Tutor, Royal Postgrad. Med. Sch., Hammersmith Hosp., 1952–55 and 1956–58; Rockefeller Trav. Fellowship, at George S. Cox Med. Research Inst., Univ. of Pennsylvania, 1955–56; Cons. Phys. and Lectr in Medicine, Univ. of Durham, 1958–64; Cons. Phys., Royal Victoria Infirmary and Reader in Medicine, Univ. of Newcastle upon Tyne, 1964–66; Prof. of Medicine, QUB, 1966–82; Consultant Physician: Royal Victoria Hosp., Belfast, 1966–82 (Chm., Med. Div., 1979–81); Belfast City Hosp., 1966–82; Forster Green Hosp., Belfast, 1975–82 (Chm., Med. Staff Cttee, 1979–82); Dir of Med. Services, Maltese Is, 1981–82; Chinese University of Hong Kong: Foundation Prof. and Chm., Dept of Medicine, 1983–88; Associate Dean, Faculty of Medicine, 1984–88. Hon. Consultant in Medicine: to Hong Kong Govt, 1984–88; to the British Army in Hong Kong, 1985–88. Member: Standing Med. Adv. Cttee, Min. of Health and Social Services, NI, 1970–73; Specialist Adv. Cttee (General Internal Medicine) to the Govt; Northern Health and Social Services Bd, Dept of Health and Soc. Services, NI; Mem., Exec. Cttee, Assoc. of Physicians of GB and Ireland, 1976–79; Regional Adviser for N Ire, to RCP, 1970–75 and Councillor, RCP, 1976–79 (Oliver-Sharpey Prize, RCP, 1976); Councillor, RCPI, 1978–82; Mem. Research Cttee, Brit. Diabetic Assoc.; Brit. Council Lectr, Dept Medicine, Zürich Univ., 1963; 1st Helen Martin Lectr, Diabetic Assoc. of S Calif, Wm H. Mulberg Lectr, Cincinnati Diabetes Assoc., and Lectr, Brookhaven Nat. Labs, NY, 1965; Brit. Council Lectr, Haile Selassie Univ., Makerere UC and S African Univs, 1966; Guest Lectr: Japan Endocrinological Soc., 1968; Madrid Univ., 1969; Endocrine Soc. of Australia, 1970, Bologna Univ., 1976. *Publications:* Essentials of Cardiology, 1961 (2nd edn 1968); Diabetes: its physiological and biochemical basis, 1976; papers in biochem., med., and scientific jls on carbohydrate and fat metabolism and aetiology of diabetes mellitus and related conditions, with special reference to insulin antagonism. *Recreations:* tennis, golf, music. *Address:* 10 Spinney Drive, Great Shelford, Cambridge CB2 5LY. *T:* Cambridge (0223) 842767; 17 St Matthews Lodge, Oakley Square, NW1 1NB. *T:* 071–388 3644. *Clubs:* East India, Royal Society of Medicine; Gog Magog Golf (Cambridge); United Services Recreation (Hong Kong).

VALLANCE WHITE, James Ashton; Principal Clerk, Judicial Office and Fourth Clerk at the Table, House of Lords, since 1983; *b* 25 Feb. 1938; *s* of Frank Ashton White and Dieudonnée Vallance; *m* 1987, Anne O'Donnell. *Educ:* Allhallows School; Albert Schweitzer College, Switzerland; St Peter's College, Oxford (MA). Clerk, House of Lords, 1961; Clerk of Committees, 1971–78; Chief Clerk, Public Bill Office, 1978–83. *Address:* 14 Gerald Road, SW1. *T:* 071–730 7658; Biniparrell, San Luis, Menorca. *T:* 366369. *Club:* Brooks's.

VALLAT, Prof. Sir Francis Aimé, GBE 1982; KCMG 1962 (CMG 1955); QC 1961; Barrister-at-Law; Emeritus Professor of International Law, University of London; *b* 25 May 1912; *s* of Col Frederick W. Vallat, OBE; *m* 1st, 1939, Mary Alison Cockell (marr. diss. 1973); one *s* one *d*; 2nd, 1988, Patricia Maria Morton Anderson. *Educ:* University College, Toronto (BA Hons); Gonville and Caius Coll., Cambridge (LLB). Called to Bar, Gray's Inn, 1935, Bencher, 1971; Assistant Lecturer, Bristol Univ., 1935–36; practice at Bar, London, 1936–39; RAFVR (Flt Lieut), 1941–45; Asst Legal Adviser, Foreign Office, 1945–50; Legal Adviser, UK Permanent Deleg. to UN, 1950–54; Deputy Legal Adviser, FO, 1954–60, Legal Adviser, 1960–68. (On leave of absence) Actg Director, Inst. of Air and Space Law, and Vis. Prof. of Law, McGill Univ., 1965–66. Dir of International Law Studies, King's Coll. London, 1968–76 (Reader, 1969–70, Prof., 1970–76). Dir of Studies, Internat. Law Assoc., 1969–73. UK Mem., UN Fact Finding Panel, 1969–. Associate Mem., Institut de Droit International, 1965, elected Mem. 1977; Member: Internat. Law Commn, 1973–81 (Chm. 1977–78); Permanent Court of Arbitration, 1980–; Curatorium, Hague Acad., 1982–. Expert Consultant, UN Conf. on Succession of States in respect of Treaties, 1977–78. Dr en dr. *hc*, Lausanne Univ., 1979. *Publications:* International Law and the Practitioner, 1966; Introduction to the Study of Human Rights, 1972; articles in British Year Book of International Law and other journals. *Recreation:* restoration of antiques. *Address:* 17 Ranelagh Grove, SW1W 8PA. *T:* 071–730 6656; 3 Essex Court, Temple, EC4. *T:* 071–583 9294. *Club:* Hurlingham.

VALLINGS, Vice-Adm. Sir George (Montague Francis), KCB 1986; Secretary, Chartered Institute of Management Accountants, since 1987; *b* 31 May 1932; *s* of Robert Archibald Vallings and Alice Mary Joan Vallings (*née* Bramsden); *m* 1964, Tessa Julia Cousins; three *s*. *Educ:* Belhaven Hill, Dunbar; Royal Naval College, Dartmouth. Midshipman, HMS Theseus, 1950–51; HMS Scarborough, 1961–65; HMS Defender, 1967–68; HMS Bristol, 1970–73; Naval Adviser and RNLO Australia, 1974–76; Captain F2, HMS Apollo, 1977–78; Dir, Naval Ops and Trade, 1978–80; Commodore, Clyde, 1980–82; Flag Officer: Gibraltar, 1983–85; Scotland and NI, 1985–87. Chm., STA Race Cttee, 1988–. *Recreations:* family and sport. *Address:* c/o Midland Bank, Charing Cross Branch, 455 Strand, WC2. *Club:* Royal Ocean Racing.

VALLIS, Rear-Adm. Michael Anthony, CB 1986; FEng 1987; Director, Darchem Ltd, since 1987; consultant engineer; *b* 30 June 1929; *s* of R. W. H. Vallis and S. J. Dewsnup; *m* 1959, Pauline Dorothy Abbott, Wymondham, Leics; three *s* one *d*. *Educ:* RN College, Dartmouth; RN Engineering College, Plymouth; RN College, Greenwich. CEng, MIMechE, FIMarE. RN Service, 1943–86. *Recreations:* fishing, gardening, walking, food and wine, theatre. *Address:* Holly Lodge, 54 Bloomfield Park, Bath, Avon BA2 2BX. *Club:* Royal Over-Seas League.

VALOIS, Dame Ninette de; *see* de Valois.

VAN ALLAN, Richard; principal bass; Director, National Opera Studio, since 1986; *b* 28 May 1935; *s* of Joseph Arthur and Irene Hannah Van Allan; *m* 1976, Elisabeth Rosemary (marr. diss. 1986); two *s* one *d*. *Educ:* Worcester College of Education (DipEd Science); Birmingham School of Music. Glyndebourne, 1964; Welsh National Opera, 1968; English National Opera, 1969; Royal Opera House, Covent Garden, 1971; performances also: l'Opéra de Paris, Bordeaux, Nice, Toulouse, Rome, Brussels; USA: Boston, San Diego, Phoenix, Houston, Austin, San Antonio, New Orleans, NY; Argentina: Buenos Aires; Spain: Madrid and Barcelona; Hong Kong. Recordings incl. Don Giovanni (Grammy nomination), Così fan tutte (Grammy Award), Luisa Miller, L'Oracolo. Hon. RAM 1987. *Recreations:* shooting, tennis, golf. *Address:* 18 Octavia Street, SW11 3DN.

VAN ALLEN, Prof. James Alfred; Professor of Physics and Head of Department of Physics (of Physics and Astronomy, 1959–85), 1951–85, Carver Professor of Physics, 1972–85, now Emeritus, University of Iowa, USA; *b* Iowa, 7 Sept. 1914; *s* of Alfred Morris and Alma Olney Van Allen; *m* 1945, Abigail Fithian Halsey II; two *s* three *d*. *Educ:* Public High School, and Iowa Wesleyan Coll., Mount Pleasant, Iowa (BSc); University of Iowa, Iowa City (MSc, PhD). Research Fellow, then Physicist, Carnegie Instn of Washington, 1939–42; Physicist, Applied Physics Lab., Johns Hopkins Univ., Md, 1942. Ordnance and Gunnery Officer and Combat Observer, USN, 1942–46, Lt-Comdr 1946. Supervisor of High-Altitude Research Group and of Proximity Fuze Unit, Johns Hopkins Univ., 1946–50. Leader, various scientific expeditions to Central and S Pacific, Arctic and Antarctic, for study of cosmic rays and earth's magnetic field, using Aerobee and balloon-launched rockets, 1949–57. Took part in promotion and planning of International Geophysical Year, 1957–58; developed radiation measuring equipment on first American satellite, Explorer I, and subseq. satellites (discoverer of Van Allen Radiation Belts of the earth, 1958); has continued study of earth's radiation belts, aurorae, cosmic rays, energetic particles in interplanetary space, planetary magnetospheres. Research Fellow, Guggenheim Memorial Foundation, 1951; Research Associate (controlled thermonuclear reactions), Princeton Univ., Project Matterhorn, 1953–54; Regents' Fellow, Smithsonian Inst., 1981. Mem., Space Science Bd of Nat. Acad. of Sciences, 1958–70, 1980–83; Fellow: American Phys. Society; Amer. Geophysical Union (Pres., 1982–84), etc; Member: Nat. Acad. of Sciences; RAS; Royal Swedish Acad. of Sciences; Founder Member, International Acad. of Astronautics, etc. Holds many awards and hon. doctorates; Gold Medal, RAS, 1978; US Nat. Medal of Sci., 1987; Crafoord Prize, Royal Swedish Acad. of Scis, 1989. *Publications:* numerous articles in learned journals and contribs to scientific works. *Address:* Department of Physics and Astronomy, University of Iowa, Iowa City, Iowa 52242, USA; 5 Woodland Mounds Road, Iowa City, Iowa 52245, USA.

van ANDEL, Dr Katharine Bridget, (Mrs T. H. van Andel); *see* Pretty, Dr K. B.

van BELLINGHEN, Jean-Paul; Grand Officer, Order of Leopold; Grand Officer, Order of the Crown; Grand Officer, Order of Leopold II; Belgian Ambassador to the Court of St James's, 1984–90, retired; *b* 21 Oct. 1925; *s* of Albert and Fernande van Bellinghen; *m* Martine Vander Elst (*d* 1991); one *s* one *d* (and one *s* decd). *Educ:* Catholic University of Leuven. Fellow, Centre for Internat. Affairs, Harvard Univ.; Lectr, Univ. of Grenoble. Joined Diplomatic Service, 1953; served Cairo, Washington, New York (UN), Min. of Foreign Affairs, Geneva, 1968–74; Chef de Cabinet to Minister of Foreign Affairs, 1974–77, to Minister of Foreign Trade, 1977–79; Ambassador in Kinshasa, 1980–83. Holds numerous foreign decorations. *Publication:* Servitude in the Sky (Harvard Centre for Internat. Affairs), 1967. *Recreations:* golf, ski-ing, filming. *Address:* 8 Avenue de l'Orée, 1050 Brussels, Belgium. *Club:* Anglo-Belgian.

VAN CAENEGEM, Prof. Raoul Charles Joseph; Ordinary Professor of Medieval History and of Legal History, University of Ghent, Belgium, since 1964; *b* 14 July 1927; *s* of Joseph Van Caenegem and Irma Barbaix; *m* 1954, Patricia Mary Carson; two *s* one *d*. *Educ:* Univ. of Ghent (LLD 1951; PhD 1953); Univ. of Paris; London Univ. Ghent University: Assistant to Prof. of Medieval Hist., 1954; Lectr, 1960. Vis. Fellow, UC, Cambridge, 1968; Arthur L. Goodhart Prof. in Legal Science, and Vis. Fellow of Peterhouse, Cambridge Univ., 1984–85; Erasmus Lectr on the History and Civilization of the Netherlands, Harvard Univ., 1991. Corresp. Fellow, Medieval Acad. of Amer., 1971; Corresp. FBA 1982; Sir Henry Savile Fellow, Merton Coll., Oxford, 1989. Mem. Acad. of Scis, Brussels, 1974; For. Mem., Acad. of Scis, Amsterdam, 1977. Hon. Dr: Tübingen, 1977; Catholic Univ., Louvain, 1984; Paris, 1988. Francqui Prize, Brussels, 1974; Solvay Prize, Brussels, 1990. *Publications:* Royal Writs in England from the Conquest to Glanvill: studies in the early history of the common law, 1959; The Birth of the English Common Law, 1973, 2nd edn 1988; Geschiedenis van Engeland: van Stonehenge tot het tijdperk der vakbonden (History of England: from Stonehenge to the era of the trade unions), 1982; Judges, Legislators and Professors: chapters in European legal history, 1987; (contrib.) International Encyclopaedia of Comparative Law, 1973. *Recreations:* wine (Bordeaux, Alsace), swimming, classical music, bridge. *Address:* Veurestraat 47, 9051 Afsnee, Belgium. *T:* 091–226211. *Club:* Universitaire Stichting (Brussels).

VANCE, Charles Ivan; actor, director and theatrical producer; *b* 6 Dec. 1929; *s* of Eric Goldblatt and Sarah (*née* Freeman); *m* 1959, Hon. Imogen Moynihan; one *d*. *Educ:* Royal Sch., Dungannon; Queen's Univ., Belfast. FInstD 1972; FRSA 1975. Early career as broadcaster; acting debut with Anew MacMaster Co., Gaiety, Dublin, 1949; dir, first prodn, The Glass Menagerie, Arts, Cambridge, 1960; founded Civic Theatre, Chelmsford, 1962; i/c rep. cos, Tunbridge Wells, Torquay, Whitby and Hastings, 1962–; as Dir of Charles Vance Prodns, created Eastbourne Theatre Co., 1969; dir. own adaptation of Wuthering Heights, 1972; wrote and staged four pantomimes, 1972–75; devised and dir. The Jolson Revue, 1974 (staged revival, Australia, 1978; world tour, 1981); played Sir Thomas More in A Man for All Seasons, and dir, Oh! What a Lovely War, Greenwood, 1975; prod and dir. world tour of Paddington Bear, 1978; produced: Cinderella, Stafford, 1981; Aladdin, Bognor, 1981. Purchased Leas Pavilion Theatre, Folkestone, 1976 (HQ of own theatre organisation until 1985). Produced (London and national tours): Stop the

World—I Want to Get Off (revival), 1976; Salad Days (revival), 1977; (also dir.) In Praise of Love, 1977; Witness for the Prosecution, (revival), 1979; Hallo Paris, 1980; This Happy Breed (revival), 1980; Starlite Spectacular, 1981; The Kingfisher (revival), 1981; The Hollow (revival), 1982 (also dir.); The Little Hut, Australia (also dir.), 1982; Cinderella, Aladdin, 1982 (also wrote); Lady Chatterley's Lover, 1983; The Mating Game, 1983; Cinderella, The Sleeping Beauty, The Gingerbread Man, The Wizard of Oz, 1983; Dick Whittington, Jack and the Beanstalk, Cinderella, Pinocchio, Jesus Christ Superstar (revival), 1984; Mr Cinders (revival), 1985; Policy for Murder, 1984 (also dir.); Jane Eyre, 1985 (also wrote and dir.); Oh Calcutta! (revival), 1985–86; Wuthering Heights (own adaptation), 1987; directed: Verdict (revival), 1984; Alice in Wonderland, 1985 (also wrote); Dick Whittington, Aladdin, Jack and the Beanstalk, Cinderella, 1986–87 (also wrote); Dénouement (also prod), 1988; Spiders Web (Agatha Christie Centenary Prodn) (also prod), 1990; The Mousetrap, USA (also prod), 1990; Daisy Pulls it Off (also prod), 1991; Gaslight (also prod), 1991; Time and Time Again (also prod), 1991. Controlled: Floral Hall Th., Scarborough, 1984–86; Beck Th., Hillingdon, 1986–90; Grand Opera House York, 1988–89; controls Summer Th., Manor Pavilion, Sidmouth, 1987–; launched first UK Dinner Theatre, Imperial Hotel, Torquay, 1990. Theatrical Management Association: Mem. Council, 1969; Pres., 1971–73 and 1973–76; Exec. Vice-Pres., 1976– (also of Council of Reg. Theatre). Advisor to Govt of Ghana on bldg Nat. Theatre, 1969. Director: Theatres Investment Fund, 1975–83; Entertainment Investments Ltd, 1980–82; International Holiday Investments, 1980–87; Southern Counties Television, 1980–87; Channel Radio, 1981–86; Gateway Broadcasting Ltd, 1982; Prestige Plays Ltd, 1987–; Trustee Dir, Folkestone Theatre Co., 1979–85. Chairman: Provincial Theatre Council, 1971–87; Standing Adv. Cttee on Local Authority and the Theatre, 1977–90 (Vice-Chm., 1975–77); Gala and Fund-raising Cttee, British Theatre Assoc., 1986–89; Standing Adv. Cttee on Local Authority and the Performing Arts, 1990–. Vice-Chairman: Theatres Adv. Council, resp. for theatres threatened by develt, 1974–; (also dir.) Festival of Brit. Theatre, 1975–. Member: Theatres Nat. Cttee, 1971–; Drama Adv. Panel, SE Arts Assoc., 1974–85; Prince of Wales' Jubilee Entertainments Cttee, 1977; Entertainment Exec. Cttee, Artists' Benev. Fund, 1980–; Variety Club of GB, 1984–; Rotary Internat., 1971–; Vice-Pres., E Sussex Br., RSPCA, 1975–; Rotary Club of London, 1986–. Founded Vance Offord (Publications) Ltd, publishers of British Theatre Directory, British Theatre Review, and Municipal Entertainment, 1971; Chm., Platform Publications Ltd, 1987–; Editor in Chief, Team Publishing, 1986–87; Editor, Amateur Stage, and Preview, 1987–. *Publications:* British Theatre Directory, 1972, 1973, 1974, 1975; (ed) Amateur Theatre Yearbook, 1989, and 1991; Agatha Christie, The Theatrical Celebration, 1990; . *Recreations:* sailing (crossed Atlantic single-handed, 1956), cooking (Cordon Bleu, 1957), travelling, animals. *Address:* Oak Lodge, Perry Hill, Farway, near Colyton, East Devon EX13 6DH. *Clubs:* Hurlingham, Royal Automobile, Directors', Kennel (Mem. Cttee, 1989–), Green Room, Dorchester.

VANCE, Cyrus Roberts; Secretary of State, USA, 1977–80; barrister-at-law; *b* Clarksburg, W Va, 27 March 1917; *m* 1947, Grace Elsie Sloane; one *s* four *d*. *Educ:* Kent Sch.; Yale Univ. (BA 1939); Yale Univ. Law Sch. (LLB 1942). Served War, USNR, to Lieut (s.g.), 1942–46. Asst to Pres., The Mead Corp., 1946–47; admitted to New York Bar, 1947; Associate and Partner of Simpson Thacher & Bartlett, New York, 1947–60, Partner, Jan. 1956–60, 1967–77 and 1980–. Special Counsel, Preparedness Investigation Sub-cttee of Senate Armed Services Cttee, 1957–60; Consulting Counsel, Special Cttee on Space and Astronautics, US Senate, 1958; Gen. Counsel, Dept of Defense, 1961–62; Sec. of the Army, 1962–64; Dep. Sec. of Defense, 1964–67; Special Rep. of the President: in Civil Disturbances in Detroit, July-Aug. 1967 and in Washington, DC, April 1968; in Cyprus, Nov.-Dec. 1967; in Korea, Feb. 1968; one of two US Negotiators, Paris Peace Conf. on Vietnam, May 1968–Feb. 1969; Mem., Commn to Investigate Alleged Police Corruption in NYC, 1970–72. Chm., Bd of Govs, Federal Reserve Bank of NY, 1989. Pres., Assoc. of Bar of City of New York, 1974–76. Mem. Bd of Trustees: Rockefeller Foundn, 1970–77, 1980–82 (Chm., 1975–77); Yale Univ., 1968–78, 1980–87; Amer. Ditchley Foundn, 1980– (Chm., 1981–); Mayo Foundn, 1980–90. Hon. degrees: Marshall, 1963; Trinity Coll., 1966; Yale, 1968; West Virginia, Bowling Green, 1969; Salem Coll., 1970; Brandeis, 1971; Amherst, W Virginia Wesleyan, 1974; Harvard, Colgate, Gen. Theol Seminary, Williams Coll., 1981. Medal of Freedom (US), 1969. *Publications:* The Choice is Ours, 1983; Hard Choices, 1983. *Address:* Simpson Thacher & Bartlett, 425 Lexington Avenue, New York, NY 10017–3909, USA. *T:* 212/455–7190.

VAN CULIN, Rev. Canon Samuel; Secretary General, Anglican Consultative Council, since 1983; *b* 20 Sept. 1930; *s* of Samuel Van Culin and Susie (*née* Mossman). *Educ:* High School, Honolulu; Princeton University (AB); Virginia Theological Seminary (BD). Ordained 1955; Curate, St Andrew's Cathedral, Honolulu, 1955–56; Canon Precentor and Rector, Hawaiian Congregation, 1956–58; Asst Rector, St John, Washington DC, 1958–60; Gen. Sec., Laymen International, Washington, 1960–61; Asst Sec., Overseas Dept, Episcopal Church, USA, 1962–68; Sec. for Africa and Middle East, Episcopal Church, USA, 1968–76; Executive, World Mission, 1976–83. Hon. Canon: Canterbury Cathedral, 1983; Ibadan, Nigeria, 1983; Jerusalem, 1984; Southern Africa, 1989. Hon. DD: Virginia Seminary, 1977; Gen. Theol Seminary, 1983. *Recreations:* music, swimming. *Address:* Anglican Consultative Council, 157 Waterloo Road, SE1. *T:* 071–620 1110. *Clubs:* Athenæum; Princeton, Huguenot Society (New York).

VANDEN-BEMPDE-JOHNSTONE; *see* Johnstone.

van den BERGH, Prof. Sidney, FRS 1988; FRSC 1970; Astronomer, Dominion Astrophysical Observatory, Victoria, British Columbia, since 1977; *b* 20 May 1929; *s* of S. J. van den Bergh and S. M. van den Berg; widowed; one *s* two *d*. *Educ:* Princeton Univ. (AB); Ohio State Univ. (MSc); Göttingen Univ. (Dr rer. nat.). Asst Prof., Ohio State Univ., 1956–58; progressively, Asst Prof., Associate Prof., Prof., Univ. of Toronto, 1958–77; Dir, Dominion Astrophys. Observatory, 1977–86. Res. Associate, Mt Wilson and Palomar Observatories, 1967–68. ARAS 1984. NRCC President's Research Medal, 1988. *Publications:* approx. 400 articles in various scholarly jls. *Recreation:* photography. *Address:* Dominion Astrophysical Observatory, 5071 West Saanich Road, Victoria, BC V8X 4M6, Canada.

VAN DEN BOGAERDE, Derek Niven, (Dirk Bogarde); actor; *b* 28 March 1921. *Educ:* University College School; Allan Glen's (Scotland). Served War of 1939–45: Queen's Royal Regt, 1940–46, Europe and Far East, and Air Photographic Intelligence. Hon. DLitt St Andrews, 1985. Chevalier de l'Ordre des Arts et des Lettres, 1982. Films include (since 1947): Hunted, Appointment in London, They Who Dare, The Sleeping Tiger, Doctor in the House, Doctor at Sea, Doctor at Large, Simba, The Spanish Gardener, Cast a Dark Shadow, Ill Met by Moonlight, The Blue Lamp, So Long at the Fair, Quartet, A Tale of Two Cities (Sidney Carton), The Wind Cannot Read, The Doctor's Dilemma, Libel, Song Without End, The Angel Wore Red, The Singer Not The Song, Victim, HMS Defiant, The Password is Courage, The Lonely Stage, The Mindbenders, The Servant, Doctor in Distress, Hot Enough for June, The High Bright Sun, King and Country, Darling . . ., Modesty Blaise, Accident, Our Mother's House, Mister Sebastian, The Fixer, Oh What A Lovely War, Götterdämmerung, Justine, Death in Venice, Upon This Rock, Le Serpent, The Night Porter, Permission To Kill, Providence, A Bridge Too Far, Despair, These Foolish Things; *television:* The Patricia Neal Story (USA), 1981 (film); May We Borrow Your Husband? (also adapted), 1986 (play); The Vision, 1987 (film); *radio* includes Galsworthy in serial, The Forsyte Chronicles, 1990–91. *Theatre:* Cliff, in Power Without Glory, 1947; Orpheus, in Point of Departure, 1950; Nicky, in The Vortex, 1953; Alberto, in Summertime, 1955–56; Jezebel, Oxford Playhouse, 1958, etc. *Publications: autobiography:* A Postillion Struck by Lightning, 1977; Snakes and Ladders, 1978; An Orderly Man, 1983; Backcloth, 1986; A Particular Friendship, 1989; *novels:* A Gentle Occupation, 1980; Voices in the Garden, 1981; West of Sunset, 1984. *Address:* Duncan Heath Associates, 162 Wardour Street, W1.

VAN DEN HOVEN, Helmert Frans; *see* Hoven.

VANDERFELT, Sir Robin (Victor), KBE 1973 (OBE 1954); Secretary-General, Commonwealth Parliamentary Association, 1961–86; *b* 24 July 1921; *y s* of late Sydney Gorton Vanderfelt, OBE, and Ethel Maude Vanderfelt (*née* Tremayne); *m* 1962, Jean Margaret Becker, *d* of John and Eve Steward; two *s* (and one step *s* one step *d*). *Educ:* Haileybury; Peterhouse, Cambridge. Served War in India and Burma, 1941–45. Asst Secretary, UK Branch, CPA, 1949–59; Secretary, 1960–61. Secretary, UK Delegn, Commonwealth Parly Conf., India, 1957; as Sec.-Gen., CPA, served as Secretary to Parliamentary Conferences throughout Commonwealth, 1961–85, also attended many area and regional confs and Confs of Commonwealth Speakers and Clerks. Mem. Internat. Services Bd, RIPA, 1986–89; Governor: Queen Elizabeth House, Oxford, 1980–87; E-SU, 1984–89. *Recreation:* gardening. *Address:* No 6 Saddler's Mead, Wilton, Salisbury, Wilts SP2 0DE. *T:* Salisbury (0722) 742637. *Clubs:* Commonwealth Trust, Royal Over-Seas League.

VAN DER KISTE, Wing Commander Robert Edgar Guy, DSO 1941; OBE 1957; Royal Auxiliary Air Force, retired; Director, Plymouth Incorporated Chamber of Trade and Commerce, 1974–80 (Secretary, 1964–74); *b* 20 July 1912; *y s* of late Lt-Col F. W. Van der Kiste, DSO; *m* 1939, Nancy Kathleen, *er d* of Alec George Holman, MRCS, LRCP, and Grace Kathleen Brown; one *s* two *d* (and one *s* decd). *Educ:* Cheltenham College. Commissioned Royal Air Force, Nov. 1936. Served War of 1939–45 (despatches, DSO); retired, 1959. Commanded No 3 MHQ Unit, Royal Auxiliary Air Force. *Recreation:* caravanning. *Address:* Lavandou, Moorland Park, South Brent, Devon TQ10 9AR.

van der LOON, Prof. Piet; Professor of Chinese, University of Oxford, and Fellow of University College, Oxford, 1972–87, now Emeritus Professor and Emeritus Fellow; *b* 7 April 1920; *m* 1947, Minnie C. Snellen; two *d*. *Educ:* Univ. of Leiden. Litt. Drs Leiden, MA Cantab. Univ. Asst Lectr, Cambridge, 1948; Univ. Lectr, Cambridge, 1949. *Publications:* Taoist Books in the Libraries of the Sung Period, 1984; articles in Asia Major, T'oung Pao, Jl Asiatique. *Recreations:* travel, gardening. *Address:* Midhurst, Old Boars Hill, Oxford OX1 5JQ. *T:* Oxford (0865) 739318.

VANDERMEER, (Arnold) Roy; QC 1978; a Recorder of the Crown Court, since 1972; *b* London, 26 June 1931; *o s* of late William Arnold Vandermeer and Katherine Nora Vandermeer; *m* 1964, Caroline Veronica (*née* Christopher); one *s* two *d*. *Educ:* Dame Alice Owen's Sch., Islington; King's Coll., London (LLB). Called to Bar, Gray's Inn, 1955, Bencher, 1988. Flt-Lt, RAF, 1955–58. Chairman: Greater Manchester Structure Plan Examination in Public, 1978; County of Avon Structure Plan Examination in Public, 1983. *Recreations:* reading, cricket. *Address:* The Field House, Barnet Lane, Elstree, Herts. *T:* 081–953 2244. *Club:* MCC.

van der MEER, Dr Simon; Ridder Nederlandse Leeuw, 1985; Senior Engineer, CERN, Geneva (European Organisation for Nuclear Research), 1956–90; *b* 24 Nov. 1925; *s* of Pieter van der Meer and Jetske Groeneveld; *m* 1966, Catharina M. Koopman; one *s* one *d*. *Educ:* Technical University, Delft, Netherlands; physical engineer. Philips Research Laboratories, Eindhoven, 1952–56. Hon. degrees: Univ. of Geneva, 1983; Amsterdam, 1984; Genoa, 1985. Nobel Prize for Physics (jtly), 1984. *Recreation:* literature. *Address:* 4 chemin des Corbillettes, 1218 Grand-Saconnex, Switzerland. *T:* 798 43 05.

van der POST, Sir Laurens (Jan), Kt 1981; CBE 1947; writer, farmer, soldier, explorer, conservationist; Trustee, World Wilderness Foundation, since 1974; *b* Philippolis, S Africa, 13 Dec. 1906; *s* of late C. W. H. Van Der Post, Chairman of Orange Free State Republic Volksraad, and late M. M. Lubbe, Boesmansfontein, Wolwekop, and Stilton; *m* 1928, Marjorie Wendt; one *d* (one *s* decd); *m* 1949, Ingaret Giffard. Served War of 1939–45: Ethiopia; North Africa; Syria; Dutch East Indies; Java; commanded 43 Special Military Mission, Prisoner of War 1943–45, thereafter Lord Mountbatten's Military-Political Officer, attached to 15 Indian Army Corps, Java, and subseq. to British Minister, Batavia, until 1947. Since then has undertaken several missions for British Government and Colonial Development Corp. in Africa, including Government Mission to Kalahari, 1952. FRSL. Hon. DLitt: Univ. of Natal, 1964; Univ. of Liverpool, 1976; Rhodes Univ., 1978; St Andrews, 1980; DUniv Surrey, 1971. *Films:* Lost World of Kalahari, 1956; A Region of Shadow, 1971; The Story of Carl Gustav Jung, 1971; All Africa Within Us, 1975; Shakespeare in Perspective—The Tempest, 1976; Zulu Wilderness: Black Umfolozi Re-discovered, 1979. *Publications:* In a Province, 1934; Venture to the Interior, 1952 (Book Society choice and Amy Woolf Memorial Prize); A Bar of Shadow, 1952 (repr., 1972); The Face Beside the Fire, 1953; Flamingo Feather, 1955 (German Book Society choice); The Dark Eye in Africa, 1955; Creative Pattern in Primitive Man, 1956; The Lost World of the Kalahari, 1958 (American Literary Guild Choice), rev. edn with long epilogue, The Great and Little Memory, 1988; The Heart of the Hunter, 1961; The Seed and the Sower, 1963 (South African CNA Award for best work published in 1963; filmed, 1983, as Merry Christmas, Mr Lawrence); Journey into Russia, 1964; A Portrait of all The Russias, 1967; The Hunter and the Whale, 1967 (CNA and Yorkshire Post Fiction Awards); A Portrait of Japan, 1968; The Night of the New Moon, 1970; A Story like the Wind, 1972; A Far Off Place, 1974; A Mantis Carol, 1975; Jung and the Story of Our Time, 1976; First Catch Your Eland: a taste of Africa, 1977; Yet Being Someone Other, 1982; (with Jane Taylor) Testament to the Bushmen, 1984; *relevant publication:* A Walk with a White Bushman: Laurens van der Post in conversation with Jean-Marc Pottiez, 1986. *Recreations:* walking, climbing, ski-ing, tennis, studying grasses and cooking in winter. *Address:* lives London and Aldeburgh, Suffolk.

van der WATEREN, Jan Floris; Keeper and Chief Librarian, National Art Library, since 1988; *b* 14 May 1940; *s* of late Jacob van der Wateren and of Wilhelmina (*née* Labuschagne). *Educ:* Potchefstroom Univ., S Africa (MA); University Coll. London (Postgrad. Dip. Librarianship). Lectr in Philosophy, Potchefstroom Univ., 1962–64; Asst Librarian, Univ. of London Inst. of Educn, 1967–71; Dep. Librarian, Sir Banister Fletcher Liby, RIBA, 1971–78; British Architectural Library: Managing Librarian, 1978–83; Dir and Sir Banister Fletcher Librarian, 1983–88. Sec., British Architectural Liby Trust, 1983–88. *Publications:* articles, reviews for librarianship jls. *Address:* 52 Blenheim Crescent, W11 1NY. *T:* 071–221 6221.

van der WERFF, Jonathan Ervine; His Honour Judge van der Werff; a Circuit Judge, since 1986; Resident Judge, Croydon Law Courts, since 1989; *b* 23 June 1935; *s* of H. H. J. van der Werff; *m* 1968, Katharine Bridget, *d* of Major J. B. Colvin; two *d. Educ:* St Piran's Sch., Maidenhead; Harrow; RMA, Sandhurst. Commnd in Coldstream Guards, 1955; Adjt 1st Bn, 1962–63; Major 1967, retired 1968. Called to Bar, Inner Temple, 1969; a Recorder, 1986. *Address:* The Law Courts, Altyre Road, Croydon CR9 5AB. *Clubs:* Pratt's, Something.

VANDER ZALM, Hon. William N.; Premier of the Province of British Columbia, 1986–91; MLA (Social Credit Party) for Richmond, British Columbia; *b* Noordwykerhout, Holland, 29 May 1934; *s* of Wilhelmus Nicholaas van der Zalm and Agatha C. Warmerdam; *m* 1956, Lillian Mahalick; two *s* two *d. Educ:* Phillip Sheffield Sen. Secondary Sch., Abbotsford, BC. Purchased Art Knapp Nurseries Ltd, and became Co. Pres., 1956. Alderman 1965, Mayor 1969, Surrey Municipal Council. Minister of Human Resources, BC, 1975; Minister of Municipal Affairs and Minister responsible for Urban Transit Authority, 1978; Minister of Educn and Minister responsible for BC Transit, 1982; Leader, BC Social Credit Party, 1986–. Established Fantasy Garden World, major tourist attraction in Richmond, BC, 1983–. *Publication:* The Northwest Gardener's Almanac, 1982. *Recreations:* gardening, fishing, soccer. *Address:* 10800 No 5 Road, Richmond, British Columbia V7A 4E5, Canada. *T:* 271–9325. *Clubs:* Union (Victoria, BC); Hon. Member: Victoria Golf, Royal Vancouver Yacht, Royal Victoria Yacht.

VANDORE, Peter Kerr; QC (Scot.) 1982; *b* 7 June 1943; *s* of James Vandore and Janet Kerr Fife; *m* 1970, Hilary Ann Davies; two *d. Educ:* Berwickshire High Sch., Duns; Edinburgh Univ. (MA Hons Hist.; LLB). Called to the Scottish Bar, 1968; Standing Counsel to Sec. of State for Scotland, for private legislation procedure, 1975–86. Mem., Legal Aid Central Cttee, 1972–85. *Publications:* contribs to Juridical Rev. *Address:* 26 India Street, Edinburgh. *T:* 031–225 1980.

VANDYK, Neville David, PhD; Editor, Solicitors' Journal, 1968–88; *b* 6 Sept. 1923; *yr s* of late Arthur Vandyk, solicitor, and Constance Vandyk (*née* Berton); *m* 1956, Paula (*née* Borchert); one *d. Educ:* St Paul's Sch.; London School of Economics, Univ. of London (BCom 1947, PhD 1950). Admitted Solicitor, 1957. HM Forces, incl. service in India, Burma and Japan, 1942–46; research asst, LSE, 1951–52; with Herbert Oppenheimer, Nathan & Vandyk, Solicitors, 1953–58; Asst Editor, 1958, Managing Editor, 1963, Solicitors' Journal; Member for its duration, Law Society's Constitution Cttee prior to the adoption in 1969 of their revised Bye-Laws, 1966–68. Founder Mem., W London Law Soc. (Pres., 1970–71); Mem. Council, Medico-Legal Soc., 1963–66, Vice-Pres. 1966–67, and 1985–90, Hon. Treas. 1967–85; Founder Mem., Assoc. of Disabled Professionals, Vice-Chm. 1972–80; Mem. for its duration, Royal Bor. of Kensington and Chelsea's Working Gp on the Disabled and their Families, 1980–81. Governor (nominated by Univ. of London) William Blake County Secondary Sch., 1957–70. Freeman 1962, Liveryman 1963, Worshipful Co. of Solicitors of City of London. Founder's Meml Lecture, Brit. Council for Rehabilitation of the Disabled, 1971; Hon. Prof. of Legal Ethics, Univ. of Birmingham, 1981–83. Hon. Life Mem., British Legal Assoc., 1989. *Publications:* Tribunals and Inquiries, 1965; Accidents and the Law, 1975, 2nd edn 1979; (title) National Health Service, in Halsbury's Laws of England, 3rd edn 1959, 4th edn 1982. *Address:* c/o Law Society Records Office, Ipsley Court, Berrington Close, Redditch, Worcs B98 0TD.

VANE; *see* Fletcher-Vane, family name of Baron Inglewood.

VANE, family name of **Baron Barnard.**

VANE, Sir John (Robert), Kt 1984; FRS 1974; Chairman, William Harvey Research Institute, since 1990 (Director, 1986–90); Professor of Pharmacology and of Medicine, New York Medical College, since 1986; *b* 29 March 1927; *s* of Maurice Vane and Frances Florence Vane (*née* Fisher); *m* 1948, Elizabeth Daphne Page; two *d. Educ:* Birmingham Univ. (BSc Chemistry, 1946); St Catherine's Coll., Oxford (BSc Pharmacology, 1949; DPhil 1953; DSc 1970; Hon. Fellow, 1983). Stothert Research Fellow of Royal Soc., 1951–53; Asst Prof. of Pharmacology, Yale Univ., 1953–55; Sen. Lectr in Pharmacology, Inst. of Basic Medical Sciences, RCS, 1955–61; Reader in Pharmacology, RCS, Univ. of London, 1961–65; Prof. of Experimental Pharmacology, RCS, Univ. of London, 1966–73; Gp Res. and Develt Dir, Wellcome Foundn, 1973–85. Visiting Professor: King's Coll., London, 1976; Charing Cross Hosp. Med. Sch., 1979; Harvard Univ., 1979. British Pharmacological Soc.: Meetings Sec., 1967–70; Gen. Sec., 1970–73; For. Sec., 1979–85; Hon. Mem., 1985; a Vice Pres., Royal Soc., 1985–87. Mem., Royal Acad. of Medicine, Belgium, 1978 (Hon. Foreign Mem., 1983). Foreign Member: Royal Netherlands Acad. of Arts and Scis, 1979; Polish Acad. of Scis, 1980; For. Associate, US Nat. Acad. of Scis, 1983; For. Hon. Mem., Amer. Acad. of Arts and Scis, 1982; Hon. Member, Polish Pharmacological Soc., 1973; Alpha Omega Alpha Honor Med. Soc., USA, 1990; Hon. FACP, 1978; Hon. FRCP, 1983; Hon. FRCPath, 1990; Hon. Fellow, Swedish Soc. of Medical Scis, 1982. Hon. DM Krakow, 1977; Hon. Dr René Descartes Univ., Paris, 1978; Hon. DSc: Mount Sinai Med. Sch., NY, 1980; Aberdeen, 1983; NY Med. Coll., 1984; Birmingham, 1984. (Jtly) Albert Lasker Basic Med. Res. Award, 1977; Baly Medal, RCP, 1977; (jtly) Peter Debye Prize, Univ. of Maastricht, 1980; Feldberg Foundn Prize, 1980; Ciba Geigy Drew Award, Drew Univ., 1980; Dale Medal, Soc. for Endocrinol., 1981; Nobel Prize for Physiology or Medicine (jtly), 1982; Galen Medal, Apothecaries' Soc., 1983; Biol Council Medal, 1983; Louis Pasteur Foundn Prize, Calif, 1984; Royal Medal, Royal Soc., 1989. *Publications:* (ed jtly) Adrenergic Mechanisms, 1960; (ed jtly) Prostaglandin Synthetase Inhibitors, 1974; (ed jtly) Metabolic Functions of the Lung, Vol. 4, 1977; (ed jtly) Handbook of Experimental Pharmacology, 1978; (ed jtly) Prostacyclin, 1979; (ed jtly) Interactions Between Platelets and Vessel Walls, 1981; numerous papers in learned jls. *Recreations:* photography, travel, underwater swimming. *Address:* William Harvey Research Institute, St Bartholomew's Hospital Medical College, Charterhouse Square, EC1M 6BQ. *Clubs:* Athenæum, Garrick.

VANE-TEMPEST-STEWART, family name of **Marquess of Londonderry.**

van EYCK, Aldo Ernest; Officer, Order of House of Orange; architect in private practice; *b* 16 March 1918; *s* of Peter Nicolaas van Eyck and Nellie Estelle van Eyck-Benjamins; *m* 1943, Hannie van Roojen; one *s* one *d. Educ:* Federal Sch. of Technology, Zürich. Private practice, 1951–, with wife Hannie, 1983–; Prof. of Architecture, Delft Univ. of Technology, 1966–85; Paul Philip Cret Prof. of Architecture, 1979–84. Hon. FAIA 1981; Hon. RIAS 1985; Hon. Fellow, Bund Deutscher Arch. 1983; Hon. RIBA 1988; Hon. Fellow, Royal Acad., Belgium 1981. Hon. degrees from Dutch, Canadian and US Univs. Wihuri Internat. Culture Prize, Finland, 1982; Royal Gold Medal for Arch., RIBA, 1990; Medal for Science and Art, Austria, 1991. *Publications:* Steps towards a configurative discipline, 1962; Miracles of moderation, 1968; Rats, Posts and other Pests, 1981 (RIBA annual discourse). *Recreations:* world-wide travel, lecturing. *Address:* Entrepotdok 23–24, 1018 AD Amsterdam, Holland. *T:* 020 230947.

van HASSELT, Marc; Headmaster, Cranleigh School, 1970–84; *b* 24 April 1924; *s* of Marc and Helen van Hasselt; *m* 1949, Geraldine Frances Sinclair; three *s* one *d. Educ:* Sherborne; Selwyn Coll., Cambridge (MA); Corpus Christi Coll., Oxford (DipEd). Served War of 1939–45 (despatches): commissioned in Essex Yeomanry, RHA, 1944; served North-West Europe. Lecturer in Commonwealth Studies, RMA, Sandhurst, 1950–58; Asst Master, Oundle School, 1959–70 (Housemaster, Sanderson House, 1963–70). *Publications:* occasional articles in Yachting World. *Recreations:* cruising under sail, interviewing, governing schools. *Address:* Blue Cedars, 12 Solent Avenue, Lymington, Hants SO41 9SD. *Clubs:* Royal Cruising; Royal Lymington Yacht.

van LENNEP, Jonkheer Emile; Commander, Order of the Netherlands Lion; Commander, Order of Orange Nassau; Minister of State, since 1986; Secretary-General, OECD, 1969–84; *b* 20 Jan. 1915; *s* of Louis Henri van Lennep and Catharina Hillegonda Enschede; *m* 1941, Alexa Alison Labberton; two *s* two *d. Educ:* Univ. of Amsterdam. Foreign Exchange Inst., 1940–45; Netherlands Bank, 1945–48; Financial Counsellor, High Representative of the Crown, Indonesia, 1948–50; Netherlands Bank, 1950–51. Treasurer-General, Ministry of Finance, The Netherlands, 1951–69. Chairman: Monetary Cttee, EEC, 1958–69; Working Party No 3, OECD, 1962–69; Mem., Board Directors, KLM (Airline), 1951–69. KStJ. Grand Cross or Grand Officer in various foreign orders. *Address:* Ruychrocklaan 444, 2597 EJ The Hague, Netherlands. *Club:* Haagsche (The Hague).

van MAURIK, Ernest Henry, OBE 1944; HM Diplomatic Service, retired; *b* 24 Aug. 1916; *s* of late Justus van Maurik and Sybil van Maurik (*née* Ebert), BEM; *m* 1945, Winifred Emery Ritchie Hay (*d* 1984); one *s* one *d. Educ:* Lancing Coll.; Ecole Sup. de Commerce, Neuchatel, Switzerland. Worked in Tea Export, Mincing Lane, 1936–39. Commnd as 2nd Lt, in Wiltshire Regt, 1939; seconded to Special Ops Exec., 1941–46; demob. with hon. rank of Lt-Col (subst. Major), 1946. Joined Foreign Office, 1946; Moscow, 1948–50; West Germany and West Berlin, 1952–56; Buenos Aires, 1958–62; Copenhagen, 1965–67; Rio de Janeiro, 1968–71; FCO, 1971–75. Officier de la Couronne (Belgium), 1944. *Recreations:* golf, gardening, languages. *Address:* Parkside, The Common, Sevenoaks, Kent TN13 1SQ. *T:* Sevenoaks (0732) 452173. *Club:* Special Forces.

van MIERT, Karel; Member for Belgium, Commission of the European Communities, since 1989; *b* 17 Jan. 1942; *m* 1971, Annegret Sinner; one *s. Educ:* Univ. of Ghent; European Univ. Centre, Nancy. With Sicco Mansholt, 1968–70; Asst in Internat. Law, New Univ. of Brussels, 1971–73; Office of Vice-Pres. of EC, 1973–75; Head of Private Office of Minister of Economic Affairs, Belgium, 1977; part-time Lectr on European Instns, New Univ. of Brussels, 1978; Mem., European Parlt, 1979–85; Mem., Belgian Chamber of Reps, 1985–88. Vice-Chm., Socialist Internat., 1986. *Publications:* papers on European integration. *Address:* Commission of the European Communities, rue de la Loi 200, B1049 Brussels, Belgium.

VANN, (William) Stanley, DMus(Lambeth); *b* 15 Feb. 1910; *s* of Frederick and Bertha Vann; *m* 1934, Frances Wilson; one *s* one *d. Educ:* privately. BMus London; FRCO; ARCM. Asst Organist, Leicester Cath., 1931–33; Chorus Master, Leicester Phil. Soc., 1931–36; Organist and Choirmaster, Gainsborough Parish Ch., Dir of Music, Queen Elizabeth Grammar Sch. and High Sch., Gainsborough, Conductor, Gainsborough Mus. and Orch. Socs, also Breckin Choir, Doncaster, 1933–39; Organist and Choirmaster, Holy Trinity PC, Leamington Spa, Founder-Conductor, Leamington Bach Choir and Warwicks Symph. Orch., and Dir of Music, Emscote Lawn Sch., Warwick, 1939–49. Served War of 1939–45, RA, final rank Captain. Master of Music, Chelmsford Cath., Conductor, Chelmsford Singers, Founder Conductor, Essex Symph Orch., Prof., Trinity Coll. of Music, London, 1949–53; Master of Music, Peterborough Cath., Conductor, Peterborough Phil. Choir and Orch., 1953–77, retired. Examiner, TCL, 1953–77; Mem. Council and Examr RCO, 1972–; Mem., ISM; Adjudicator, Brit. Fed. of Festivals, Canadian Fed. Fest. and Hong Kong Fest., 1950–84; Chairman: Peterborough Music Fest., 1953–; Eastern Area Council, British Fedn of Music Festivals, 1982–; Pres., Essex Symph. Orch., 1990–. Hon. DMus Lambeth 1971 (for eminent services to church music); Hon. FTCL 1953. *Publications:* seven settings of Missa Brevis; two settings of Rite A Communion Service; Evening Services in E minor and C major and for Rochester, Gloucester, Hereford, Lincoln, Peterborough, Chester, Salisbury, York, Chichester and Worcester Cathedrals; anthems, motets, carols and choral arrangements of folk-songs and of Handel; four sets of Preces and Responses and a Collection of Anglican Chants. *Recreations:* railway modelling, painting, gardening. *Address:* Holly Tree Cottage, Wansford, Peterborough PE8 6PL. *T:* Stamford (0780) 782192.

VANNECK, family name of **Baron Huntingfield.**

VANNECK, Air Commodore Hon. Sir Peter Beckford Rutgers, GBE 1977 (OBE (mil.) 1963); CB 1973; AFC 1955; AE 1954; MA, DSc; JP; DL; *b* 7 Jan. 1922; *y s* of 5th Baron Huntingfield, KCMG and Margaret Eleanor, *d* of Judge Ernest Crosby, NY; *m* 1st, 1943, Cordelia (marr. diss. 1984), *y d* of Captain R. H. Errington, RN (retd); one *d* (and one *d* decd); 2nd, 1984, Mrs Elizabeth Forbes; one step *s* one step *d. Educ:* Geelong Grammar Sch.; Stowe Sch. (Scholar); Trinity Coll., Cambridge (MA); Harvard; IEng; MIAgrE. Cadet, RN, 1939; served in Nelson, King George V, Eskimo, 55th LCA Flot., Wren, MTB 696 (in comd), 771 Sqdn and 807 Sqdn FAA, resigned 1949; Cambridge Univ. Air Sqdn, 1949; 601 (Co. of London) Sqdn RAuxAF, 1950–57 (101 Sqdn Mass. Air Nat. Guard, 1953); 3619 (Co. of Suffolk) Fighter Control Unit, 1958–61 (in comd 1959–61); No 1 Maritime HQ Unit, 1961–63; Group Captain, 1963; Inspector RAuxAF, 1963–73, Hon. Inspector-General 1974–83; ADC to the Queen, 1963–73; Hon. Air Cdre, No 1 (Co. Hertford) Maritime HQ Unit, RAuxAF, 1973–87. Gentleman Usher to the Queen, 1967–79. Mem., Stock Exchange Council, 1968–79 (Dep. Chm., 1973–75). Mem. (C) Cleveland, 1979–84, Cleveland and Yorks N, 1984–89, contested (C) Cleveland and Yorks N, 1989, European Parliament; Mem., Energy, Res. and Technology Cttee, 1979–89; Vice-Chm., Political Affairs Cttee, 1984–89. Prime Warden, Fishmongers' Co., 1981–82; Past Master: Gunmakers' Co., 1977 and 1988; Guild of Air Pilots and Air Navigators, 1976–77; Freeman, Watermen's and Lightermen's Co., 1978; Alderman of Cordwainer Ward, City of London, 1969–79; Sheriff, City of London, 1974–75; Lord Mayor of London, 1977–78. Member: Ipswich Gp Hosps Bd, 1956–62; City and E London AHA, 1973–77; Gov. Body, Brit. Post Graduate Medical Fedn, Univ. of London, 1963–71; St Bartholomew's Hosp. Bd of Governors, 1971–73; Special Trustee, St Bartholomew's Hosp., 1974–82. Pres., Anglo-Netherlands Soc., 1989–. Trustee: RAF Museum, 1976–87; Royal Academy Trust, 1981–87; Governor, RSC, 1974–87. President: Gun Trades Assoc., 1976–87; Stock Exchange Ski Club, 1977–87. KStJ (Mem. Chapter General). Hon. DSc City Univ. DL Greater London, 1970; High Sheriff, Suffolk, 1979. Churchwarden of St Mary-le-Bow, 1969–84. Supernumerary JP, City of London. Commander, Legion of Honour (France), 1981; Grand Officer, Order of the Crown (Belgium), 1983. *Recreations:* sailing, shooting, ski-ing, bad bridge. *Address:* 2/10 Brompton Square, SW3 2AA; Red House, Sudbourne, Woodbridge, Suffolk IP12 2AT. *Clubs:* White's, Pratt's; Royal Yacht Squadron, Royal London Yacht (Commodore, 1977–78); Bembridge Sailing, Island Sailing, Orford Sailing; Seawanhaka Corinthian Yacht (US).

See also Baron Huntingfield, H. D. Stevenson.

VAN OSS, (Adam) Oliver, MA; FSA; Master of the London Charterhouse, 1973–84; *b* 28 March 1909; *s* of S. F. Van Oss, The Hague, newspaper proprietor; *m* 1945, Audrey (*d* 1960), *widow* of Capt. J. R. Allsopp; two *d*. *Educ:* Dragon Sch., Oxford; Clifton; Magdalen Coll., Oxford. Housemaster and Head of Modern Language Dept, Eton Coll.; Lower Master, Eton Coll., 1959–64, Acting Headmaster, 1964; Headmaster of Charterhouse, 1965–73. Mem. Council, City Univ. Chevalier de la Légion d'Honneur. *Publications:* Eton Days, 1976; (ed jtly) Cassell's French Dictionary, 8th edn; articles on ceramics, travel and education. *Recreations:* all forms of art and sport. *Address:* 7 Park Lane, Woodstock OX7 1UD. *Clubs:* Pratt's, Beefsteak.

van PRAAG, Louis, CBE 1986; FCSD; Senior Partner, Design Resource, since 1989; Chairman, Sabre International Group, 1976–88; Director, Sabre Group, 1958–88; *b* 9 Aug. 1926; *s* of Barend van Praag and Rosalie (*née* Monnickendam); *m* 1st, 1947, Angela McCorquodale; two *s* one *d*; 2nd, 1964, Kathy Titelman; one *s* two *d*. *Educ:* Owen's Sch.; Univ. of Paris, Sorbonne (LèsL). Member: Nat Council for Diplomas in Art and Design, 1971–74; CNAA, 1974–83; Chairman: Design Res. Cttee, 1976–79; Nat. Adv. Body, Art and Design Bd, 1981–83; DTI Wkg Party on Management of Design, 1980–84; DTI Steering Gp for in-co. management of design, 1989–; DoE Wkg Party, Industry Lead Body for Design, 1989–; Member: Financial Times Design Management Awards Cttee, 1987–; Adv. Bd, Music at Oxford, 1988–; Design Adv. Cttee, London Business Sch., 1989–; Corporate Adv. Cttee, Design Mus., 1989–. Royal College of Art: Chm., RCA Enterprises, 1979–83; Member: Council, 1979–83; Court, 1980–; Hon. Fellow, 1980. Chm., Mus. of Modern Art, Oxford, 1984–88; Mem. Adv. Bd, Ashmolean Museum, 1988–; Mem. Council, Ecole Nat. Sup. de Création Industrielle, Paris, 1986–; Gov., Winchester Coll. of Art, 1976–79. Hon. Dr Des CNAA, 1987. Bicentenary Medal, RSA, 1989. *Publications:* various papers and articles on management of design. *Recreations:* walking, ski-ing, listening to traditional and modern jazz, opera and, sometimes, Schoenberg. *Address:* 53 St John Street, Oxford OX1 2LQ.

van RIEMSDIJK, John Theodore, CIMechE; Keeper of Mechanical and Civil Engineering, Science Museum, 1976–84; author and broadcaster; *b* 13 Nov. 1924; *s* of late Adrianus Kors van Riemsdijk and Nora Phyllis van Riemsdijk (*née* James); *m* 1957, Jocelyn Kilma Arfon-Price. *Educ:* University College Sch.; Birkbeck Coll. (BA). Served SOE, 1943–46. Manufacturer of gearing, 1946–54; Science Museum: Asst, 1954; Lectr, 1961; Educn Officer, 1969. Engaged in setting up Nat. Railway Mus., York, 1973–75. *Publications:* Pregrouping Railways, 1972; Pictorial History of Steam Power, 1980; Compound Locomotives, 1982; Science Museum Books; contribs to: BBC Publications; Newcomen Soc. Trans, Procs of IMechE. *Recreations:* oil painting, making models. *Address:* Le Moulin du Gavot, St Maximin, 30700 Uzès, Gard, France. *T:* 66–22–73–78.

van STRAUBENZEE, Sir William (Radcliffe), Kt 1981; MBE 1954; *b* 27 Jan. 1924; *o s* of late Brig. A. B. van Straubenzee, DSO, MC and late Margaret Joan, 3rd *d* of A. N. Radcliffe, Kensington Square, W8, and Bag Park, Widecombe-in-the-Moor, Newton Abbot, S Devon. *Educ:* Westminster. Served War of 1939–45: five years with Royal Artillery (Major); Regimental and Staff Appointments, including two years in Far East. Admitted a Solicitor, 1952. Chairman, Young Conservative Nat. Advisory Cttee, 1951–53. Contested Wandsworth (Clapham), 1955. MP (C) Wokingham, 1959–87. PPS to Minister of Educn (Sir David Eccles), 1960–62; Jt Parly Under-Sec. of State, Dept of Educn and Science, 1970–72; Minister of State, NI Office, 1972–74. Chairman: Select Cttee on Assistance to Private Members, 1975–77; Select Cttee on Educn and the Arts, 1984–87; Cons. Parly Educn Cttee, 1979–83. Mem. Exec. Cttee, 1922 Cttee, 1979–87. Member of Richmond (Surrey) Borough Council, 1955–58. Chairman: United and Cecil Club, 1965–68 (Hon. Sec., 1952–59); Westminster House Boys' Club, Camberwell, 1965–68 (Hon. Sec., 1952–65); Nat. Council for Drama Training, 1976–81. Hon. Sec., Fedn of Conservative Students, 1965–71, Vice-Pres., 1974. Mem. House of Laity, Church Assembly, 1965–70, Mem. General Synod, 1975–85; Chairman: Dioceses Commn, 1978–86; Commn on Sen. Church Appts, 1988–; Second Church Estates Commissioner, 1979–87. Patron of Living of Rockbourne, Hants. *Recreations:* walking, reading. *Address:* 199 Westminster Bridge Road, SE1. *T:* 071–928 6855. *Clubs:* Carlton, Garrick.

van WACHEM, Lodewijk Christiaan; Knight, Order of the Netherlands Lion, 1981; Commander, Order of Orange-Nassau, 1990; Hon. KBE 1988 (Hon. CBE 1977); mechanical engineer, Netherlands; Chairman, Committee of Managing Directors of Royal Dutch/Shell Group of Companies, since 1985; President, Royal Dutch Petroleum Co., The Hague, since 1982 (Managing Director, 1976–82); Member, Presidium of Board of Directors of Shell Petroleum NV; Managing Director, The Shell Petroleum Co. Ltd; Director, Shell Canada Ltd, since 1982; Chairman, Shell Oil Co., USA, since 1982; *b* Pangkalan Brandan, Indonesia, 31 July 1931; *m* 1958, Elisabeth G. Cristofoli; two *s* one *d*. *Educ:* Technological Univ., Delft (mech. engr). Joined BPM, The Hague, 1953; Mech. Engr, Compania Shell de Venezuela, 1954–63; Shell-BP Petr. Develt Co. of Nigeria: Chief Engr, 1963–66; Engrg Manager, 1966–67; Brunei Shell Petr. Co. Ltd: Head of Techn. Admin., 1967–69; Techn. Dir, 1969–71; Head of Prod. Div., SIPM, The Hague, 1971–72; Chm. and Managing Dir, Shell-BP Petr. Develt Co. of Nigeria, 1972–76; Co-ordinator, Exploration and Prod., SIPM, The Hague, 1976–79. *Address:* Carel van Bylandtlaan 30, 2596 HR The Hague, Holland. *T:* 070–377.21.18.

VARAH, (Doris) Susan, OBE 1976; *b* 29 Oct. 1916; *d* of Harry W. and Matilda H. Whanslaw; *m* 1940, Rev. (Edward) Chad Varah, *qv*; four *s* (three of them triplets) one *d*. *Educ:* Trinity Coll. of Music. Mothers' Union: Diocesan Pres., Southwark, 1956–64; Vice-Chm., Central Young Members' Cttee, 1962–64; Central Vice-Pres., 1962–70; Vice-Chm., Central Social Problems Cttee, 1965–67, Chm., 1970–76; Chm., Central Overseas Cttee, 1968–70, 1977–82; Central Pres., 1970–76. *Recreations:* music, gardening, reading. *Address:* 42 Hillersdon Avenue, SW13 0EF. *T:* 081–876 5720.

VARAH, Rev. Dr (Edward) Chad, OBE 1969; Rector, Lord Mayor's Parish Church of St Stephen Walbrook, in the City of London, since 1953; a Prebendary of St Paul's Cathedral, since 1975; Founder, The Samaritans (to befriend the suicidal and despairing), 1953, President of London Branch, 1974–86 (Director, 1953–74); President, Befrienders International (Samaritans Worldwide), 1983–86 (Chairman 1974–83); *b* 12 Nov. 1911; *e s* of Canon William Edward Varah, Vicar of Barton-on-Humber, and Mary (*née* Atkinson); *m* 1940, Doris Susan Whanslaw (*see* D. S. Varah); four *s* (three of them triplets) one *d*. *Educ:* Worksop Coll., Notts; Keble Coll., Oxford (Hon. Fellow 1981); Lincoln Theol. Coll.; Exhibnr in Nat. Sci. (Keble); BA Oxon (Hons in PPE), 1933, MA 1943. Secretary: OU Russian Club, 1931; OU Slavonic Club, 1932; Founder Pres., OU Scandinavian Club, 1931–33. Deacon, 1935, Priest, 1936. Curate of: St Giles, Lincoln, 1935–38; Putney, 1938–40; Barrow-in-Furness, 1940–42; Vicar of: Holy Trinity, Blackburn, 1942–49; St Paul, Clapham Junction, 1949–53. Staff Scriptwriter-Visualiser for Eagle and Girl, 1950–61; Sec., Orthodox Churches Aid Fund, 1952–69; Pres., Cttee for Publishing Russian Orthodox Church Music, 1960–76; Chm., The Samaritans (Inc.), 1963–66; Pres., Internat. Fedn for Services of Emergency Telephonic Help, 1964–67. Consultant, Forum Magazine, 1967–87. Patron, Outsiders' Club, 1984–; Terrence Higgins Trust, 1987–. Hon. Liveryman, Worshipful Co. of Carmen, 1977. Hon. LLD Leicester, 1979. Roumanian Patriarchal Cross, 1968. Albert Schweitzer Gold Medal, 1972; Louis Dublin Award, Amer. Assoc. Suicidology, 1974; with Befrienders International, Prix de l'Institut de la Vie, 1978; Honra ao Mérito Medal, São Paulo TV, Brazil, 1982. *Publications:* Notny Sbornik Russkogo Pravoslavnogo Tserkovnogo Peniya, vol. 1 Bozhestveniya Liturgia, 1962, vol. 2 Pt 1 Vsenoshchnaya, 1975; (ed) The Samaritans, 1965; Samariter: Hilfe durchs Telefon, 1966; Vänskap som hjälp, 1971; (TV play) Nobody Understands Miranda, 1972; (ed) The Samaritans in the 70s, 1973, rev. edn 1977; Telephone Masturbators, 1976; (ed) The Samaritans in the 80s, 1980, rev. edn as The Samaritans: befriending the suicidal, 1984, 2nd edn 1988; Before I Die Again (autobiog.), 1991. *Recreations:* reading, listening to music, watching videos of nature programmes on television. *Address:* St Stephen's Church, Walbrook, EC4N 8BN. *T:* 071–283 4444. *Clubs:* Sion College (EC4); Oxford Union.

VARAH, Susan; *see* Varah, Doris S.

VARCOE, (Christopher) Stephen; baritone; *b* 19 May 1949; *s* of Philip William and Mary Northwood Varcoe; *m* 1972, Melinda Davies; two *s* two *d* (and one *s* decd). *Educ:* King's School, Canterbury; King's College, Cambridge (MA). Freelance concert and opera singer, 1970–; Calouste Gulbenkian Foundation Fellowship, 1977. *Recreations:* painting, gardening, building. *Address:* Ansells Farm, Alphamstone, Bures, Suffolk. *T:* Twinstead (078729) 570.

VARCOE, Jeremy Richard Lovering Grosvenor, CMG 1989; HM Diplomatic Service; Assistant Under-Secretary of State, Foreign and Commonwealth Office, since 1990; *b* 20 Sept. 1937; *s* of Ronald Arthur Grosvenor Varcoe and late Zoe Elizabeth Varcoe (*née* Lovering); *m* 1961, Wendy Anne Moss (*d* 1991); two *d*. *Educ:* Charterhouse; Lincoln Coll., Oxford (MA). National Service, Royal Tank Regt, 2nd Lieut, 1956–58. HMOCS: District Officer, Swaziland, 1962–65. Called to the Bar, Gray's Inn, 1966; Lectr in Law, Univ. of Birmingham, 1967–70; resigned to enter HM Diplomatic Service, 1970; FCO, 1970–72; Dep. Secretary General, Pearce Commn on Rhodesian Opinion, 1972; First Sec. (Information), Ankara, 1972–74; First Sec. and Head of Chancery, Lusaka, 1974–78; FCO, 1978–79; Commercial Counsellor, Kuala Lumpur, 1979–82; Head of Southern African Dept, FCO, 1982–84; Counsellor, Ankara, 1984–85; on special leave with Standard Chartered Bank, Istanbul, 1985–87; Ambassador to Somalia, 1987–89; Minister/Dep. High Comr, Lagos, 1989–90. Co-ordinator, London Economic Summit, 1991. *Publication:* Legal Aid in Criminal Proceedings—a Regional Survey (Birmingham Univ.), 1970. *Recreations:* sailing, golf. *Address:* 2 Neate House, 52 Lupus Street, SW1V 3EE. *Club:* Commonwealth Trust.

VARCOE, Stephen; *see* Varcoe, C. S.

VAREY, Prof. John Earl, PhD, LittD; FBA 1985; Principal, Westfield College, 1984–89, and Professor of Spanish, 1963–89, now Emeritus, London University; *b* 26 Aug. 1922; *s* of Harold Varey and Dorothy Halstead Varey; *m* 1948, Cicely Rainford Virgo; two *s* one *d* (and one *s* decd). *Educ:* Blackburn Grammar Sch.; Emmanuel Coll., Cambridge. MA 1948; PhD 1951; LittD 1981. Served Bomber and Transport Commands, RAF, 1942–45. Westfield College: Lectr in Spanish, 1952; Reader, 1957; Actg Principal, 1983. Leverhulme Trust Fellow, 1970–71 and 1976; Visiting Professor: Univ. of Indiana, 1970, 1971; Purdue Univ., 1977. Pres., Assoc. of Hispanists of GB and Ireland, 1979–81. Corresp. Mem., Spanish Royal Acad., 1981; Hon. Mem., Instituto de Estudios Madrileños, 1988. Hon. Fellow, QMW, 1989. Hijo ilustre de Madrid, 1980. Co-founder, Tamesis Books Ltd, 1963; Gen. Editor, Colección Támesis, 1963–. Hon. Dr Univ. Valencia, 1989. *Publications:* Historia de los títeres en España, 1957; (with N. D. Shergold) Los autos sacramentales en Madrid en la época de Calderón: 1637–1681, 1961; (ed) Galdós Studies, 1970; (ed with N. D. Shergold and Jack Sage) Juan Vélez de Guevara: Los celos hacen estrellas, 1970; Pérez Galdós: Doña Perfecta, 1971 (Spanish trans., 1989); (with N. D. Shergold and others) Fuentes para la historia del teatro en España, 11 vols, 1971–; (with D. W. Cruickshank) The Comedias of Calderón, 19 vols, 1973; (ed with J. M. Ruano) Lope de Vega: Peribáñez y el Comendador de Ocaña, 1980; Cosmovisión y escenografía: el teatro español en el Siglo de Oro, 1988; contrib. Bull. of Hispanic Studies, etc. *Recreation:* travel. *Address:* 38 Platt's Lane, NW3 7NT. *T:* 071–435 1764.

VARFIS, Grigoris; Member (Socialist), European Parliament, 1984–89; *b* 1927. *Educ:* Univ. of Athens; Univ. of Paris. Journalist, Paris, 1953–58; OECD, 1958–62; Econ. Adviser to permt Greek delegn to EEC, 1963–74; Dir-Gen., Econ. Min. of Co-ordination, 1974–77; Man. Dir in chemical industry, 1977–81; Vice-Minister of Foreign Affairs, 1981–84; Greek Comr to EC, 1985–88 (responsible for structural funds and consumer protection, 1986–88). *Address:* Spefsipou 35, 10676 Athens, Greece.

VARLEY, family name of **Baron Varley.**

VARLEY, Baron *cr* 1990 (Life Peer), of Chesterfield in the County of Derbyshire; **Eric Graham Varley,** PC 1974; DL; Director: Ashgate Hospice Ltd, since 1987; Cathelco Ltd, since 1989; Laxgate Ltd, since 1991; *b* 11 Aug. 1932; *s* of Frank Varley, retired miner, and Eva Varley; *m* 1955, Marjorie Turner; one *s*. *Educ:* Secondary Modern and Technical Schools; Ruskin Coll., Oxford. Apprentice Engineer's Turner, 1947–52; Engineer's Turner, 1952–55; Mining Industry (Coal) Craftsman, 1955–64. National Union of Mineworkers: Branch Sec., 1955–64; Mem. Area Exec. Cttee, Derbyshire, 1956–64. MP (Lab) Chesterfield, 1964–84; Asst Govt Whip, 1967–68; PPS to the Prime Minister, 1968–69; Minister of State, Min. of Technology, 1969–70; Chm., Trade Union Gp of Labour MPs, 1971–74; Secretary of State: for Energy, 1974–75; for Industry, 1975–79; Principal Opposition Spokesman on employment, 1979–83; Treasurer, Labour Party, 1981–83. Chm., and Chief Exec., Coalite Gp, 1984–89; N and E Midlands Regional Dir, 1987–89, Midlands and N Wales Regl Dir, 1989–91, Lloyds Bank PLC. Vis. Fellow, Nuffield Coll., 1977–81. DL Derbys, 1989. *Recreations:* reading, gardening, music, sport. *Address:* c/o House of Lords, SW1A 0PW.

VARLEY, Dame Joan (Fleetwood), DBE 1985 (CBE 1974); Director, Local Government Organisation, Conservative Central Office, 1976–84; *b* 22 Feb. 1920; *d* of late F. Ireton and Elizabeth Varley. *Educ:* Cheltenham Ladies' College; London School of Economics (BSc Econ). Section Officer, WAAF, 1944–46. Conservative Agent, Shrewsbury, 1952–56; Dep. Central Office Agent, NW Area, 1957–65; Dep. Dir Orgn, 1966–74, Dir, Central Admin, 1975–76, Cons. Central Office. Chm., Friends of St James Norlands Assoc., 1986–; Chm., Thames Polytechnic Court of Governors, 1991– (Vice-Chm., 1986–91); pt-time Mem., Panel of VAT Tribunals, 1986–. *Recreations:* gardening, walking. *Address:* 9 Queensdale Walk, W11 4QQ. *T:* 071–727 1292. *Club:* St Stephen's Constitutional.

VARMUS, Prof. Harold Eliot, MD; Professor of Microbiology and Immunology, since 1979, Department of Biochemistry and Biophysics, since 1982, University of California Medical Center, San Francisco; *b* 18 Dec. 1939; *s* of Frank Varmus and Beatrice Barasch Varmus; *m* 1969, Constance Louise Casey; two *s*. *Educ:* Freeport High Sch., NY; Amherst Coll., Mass (BA 1961); Harvard Univ. (MA 1962); Columbia Univ., NY (MD 1966). Surgeon, US Public Health Service, 1968–70; Dept of Microbiology, Univ. of California Medical Center, San Francisco: Lectr, 1970–72; Asst Prof., 1972–74; Associate Prof., 1974–79; Amer. Cancer Soc. Prof. of Molecular Virology, 1984–. Scientific Consultant,

Chiron Corp., 1982–87; Member, Scientific Adv. Bd: Merck Corp., 1985–88; Gilead Corp., 1988–. Associate Editor: Cell, 1974–78, 1979–; Virology, 1974–84; Genes and Develt, 1986–; Editor, Molecular and Cellular Biol., 1984–88; Mem., Editl Bd, Trends in Genetics, 1989–. Member: Special Grants Cttee, Calif. Div., Amer. Cancer Soc., 1973–76; Breast Cancer Virus Wkg Gp, Virus Cancer Program, 1973–74. Bd of Scientific Counselors, Div. of Cancer Biol. and Diagnosis, 1983–87, Nat. Cancer Inst.; Virology Study Section, NIH, 1976–80. Member: AAAS; Amer. Soc. Microbiology; Amer. Soc. Biochem. and Molecular Biol; Amer. Soc. Virology; Nat. Acad. Scis, 1984; Amer. Acad. Arts and Scis, 1988. Hon. DSc: Amherst Coll., 1984; Columbia Univ., 1990. Numerous awards and prizes incl. (jtly) Nobel Prize for Physiology or Medicine, 1989. *Address:* c/o Department of Microbiology and Immunology, University of California Medical Center, San Francisco, Calif 94143, USA.

VARNAM, Ivor; Deputy Director, Royal Armament Research and Development Establishment, 1974–82, retired; *b* 12 Aug. 1922; *s* of Walter Varnam and Gertrude Susan Varnam (*née* Vincent); *m* 1942, Doris May Thomas; two *s. Educ:* Alleyn's Coll., Dulwich; University Coll., Cardiff; Birkbeck Coll., London. BSc Wales 1944; BSc (Hons) London 1952. Served War, RAF, 1940–46 (commnd 1944). Joined Tannoy Products, 1946; Atomic Energy Research Estabt, 1947; Siemens Bros., 1948; Royal Armament Research and Development Estabt, 1953–60 and 1962–82 (Defence Research Staff, Washington, USA, 1960–62), as: Supt Mil. ADP Br., 1964; Supt GW Br., 1967; Prin. Supt Systems Div., 1969; Head, Applied Physics Dept, 1972. *Publications:* official reports. *Recreations:* gardening, photography, bridge, music.

VASARY, Tamàs; pianist and conductor; Joint Musical Director, Northern Sinfonia Orchestra, since 1979; *b* 8 Nov. 1933; *s* of Jozsef Vàsàry and Elizabeth (*née* Baltazàr); *m* 1967, Ildiko (*née* Kovàcs). *Educ:* Franz Liszt Music Academ Budapest. First concert at age of 8 in Debrecen, Hungary; First Prize, Franz Liszt Competition, Budapest, 1947; prizes at internat. competitions in Warsaw, Paris, Brussels, Rio de Janeiro; Bach and Paderewski medals, London, 1961; début in London, 1961, in Carnegie Hall, NY, 1961; plays with major orchestras and at festivals in Europe, USA, Australasia and Far East; 3 world tours. Conducting debut, 1970; conducts in Europe and USA. Records Chopin, Debussy, Liszt, Rachmaninov (in Germany). *Recreations:* yoga, writing, sports. *Address:* 9 Village Road, N3. *T:* 081–346 2381.

VASCONCELLOS, Josefina Alys Hermes de, MBE 1985; Hon. DLitt; FRBS; Founder, The Harriet Trust, Beached Trawler adapted for Nature-observation Base for Young Disabled; *d* of late H. H. de Vasconcellos, Brazilian Consul-General in England, and Freda Coleman; *m* 1930, Delmar Banner (*d* 1983), painter. *Educ:* sculpture: London, Paris, Florence; Royal Academy Schools. Mem., IPI. Works: High Altar and Statue, Varengeville, Normandy, 1925; Bronze St Hubert, Nat. Gall. of Brazil, 1926; Music in Trees, in stone, Southampton Gall., 1933; Ducks, in marble, Glasgow Art Gall., 1946; Refugees, in stone, Sheffield Art Gall., 1949; Episcopal Crozier, in perspex, for Bristol Cathedral, 1948. Exhibits RA, Leicester Galls. Exhibn with husband, of 46 sculptures in 20 materials at RWS Gall., 1947; Last Chimera, Canongate Kirk, Edinburgh; 8ft Christ (in Portland Stone), Nat. War Meml to Battle of Britain, Aldershot, 1950. Two works, Festival of Britain, Lambeth Palace, 1951; Sculpture Exhibn, with husband, RWS Galls, 1955; War Memorial, St Bees School, 1955; two figures, St Bees Priory, 1955; life-size Mary and Child and design group of 11 sculptures by 11 collaborators, for Nativity, St Paul's Cathedral, Christmas 1955; Mary and Child bought for St Paul's, 1956; life-size Resurrection for St Mary, Westfield, Workington, 1956–57; Madonna and Child, St James's, Piccadilly, (now in Burrswood, Dorothy Kerin Trust), 1957; Rising Christ in St Bartholomew the Great, Smithfield; Winter, carving in Perspex, Oldham Gallery, 1958; Nativity (for ruins of Coventry Cathedral), 1958; Flight into Egypt, for St Martin-in-the-Fields, 1958 (now in Cartmel Priory); War Memorial, Reredos of carved oak, Rossall School Chapel, 1959; Nativity Set, life-size figures, St Martin-in-the-Fields, annually in Trafalgar Sq.; Winged Victory Crucifix, Clewer Church, 1964, and Canongate Kirk, Edinburgh; life-size Holy Family, Liverpool Cathedral and Gloucester Cathedral, 1965; life-size Virgin and Child, Blackburn Cathedral, 1974; Reunion, Bradford Univ., 1977; Return of the Carpenter, group of 10 life-size children, Samlesbury Hall, 1978; life-size Holy Family, for St Martin-in-the-Fields, 1983; life-size Holy Family, in cold cast stone, Norwich Cathedral, 1985; Revelation XXI, 'and God shall wipe the tears from their eyes', life-size two figure group, in plaster, for Lake Artists Exhibn, Grasmere, 1986; life-size Virgin and Child, Ambleside Parish Church, 1988; Reredos, Wordsworth Chapel, 1988; life-size Mary and Babe, Carlisle Cathedral, 1989; Sea Legend, in bronze, Hutton in the Forest, 1990; Childline to God, life-size figures of Christ, angels and 4 children, the Fratery, Carlisle Cathedral, 1990; one man exhibn: A Christmas Exhibition of Sculpture, Painting and Poems, Manchester Cath., 1991–92, Rydal Hall, 1992; sculptures at Dallas, Tulsa, Chicago, USA; Portraits: bronze of Lord Denning, 1969; Bishop Fleming; Rev. Austen Williams; Mario Borelli; and Rev. Dr M. S. Israel. Documentary film Out of Nature (on her work), 1949; BBC programme, Viewpoint TV, 1968. Pres., Guild of Lakeland Craftsmen, 1971–73; Brother, Art Workers Guild. Mem., Inst. of Patentees and Inventors; Hon. Member, Glider Pilots Regimental Assoc. Hon. DLitt Bradford, 1977. *Publications:* Woodcut illustrations for The Cup (Poems by F. Johnson), 1938; contrib. to They Became Christians (ed Dewi Morgan), 1966. *Recreations:* musical composition, dance. *Address:* Old Wash House Studio, Peggy Hill, Ambleside, Cumbria LA22 9EG. *T:* Ambleside (05394) 33794. *Club:* Royal Over-Seas League.

VASQUEZ, Hon. Sir Alfred (Joseph), Kt 1988; CBE 1974; QC (Gibraltar) 1986; Speaker, Gibraltar House of Assembly, 1970–89; *b* 2 March 1923; *s* of Alfred Joseph Vasquez and Maria Josefa (*née* Rugeroni); *m* 1950, Carmen, *o d* of Lt-Col Robert Sheppard-Capurro, OBE, JP; three *s* one *d. Educ:* Mount St Mary's Sch., Millfield; Fitzwilliam Coll., Cambridge (MA). Gibraltar Defence Force, 1943–45; The Gibraltar Regt, 1957–64, Captain. Called to the Bar, Inner Temple, 1950; called to Gibraltar Bar, 1950; Sen. Partner, Vasquez Benady & Co., barristers and solicitors, 1950–. Mayor of Gibraltar, 1970–76. *Recreations:* golf, shooting, gardening, bridge. *Address:* 2 St Bernards Road, Gibraltar. *T:* Gibraltar 73710. *Clubs:* Royal Gibraltar Yacht; Sotogrande Golf (Spain).

VASSAR-SMITH, Major Sir Richard Rathborne, 3rd Bt, *cr* 1917; TD; RA; Partner at St Ronan's Preparatory School, since 1957; *b* 24 Nov. 1909; *s* of late Major Charles Martin Vassar-Smith (2nd *s* of 1st Bt); *S* uncle, 1942; *m* 1932, Mary Dawn, *d* of late Sir Raymond Woods, CBE; one *s* one *d. Educ:* Lancing; Pembroke College, Cambridge. Employed by Lloyds Bank Ltd, 1932–37; Schoolmaster, 1938–39. War of 1939–45, Major, RA. *Recreation:* Association football (Cambridge, 1928–31). *Heir: s* John Rathborne Vassar-Smith [*b* 23 July 1936; *m* 1971, Roberta Elaine, *y d* of Wing Comdr N. Williamson; two *s*]. *Address:* Orchard House, Hawkhurst, Kent TN18 5DT. *T:* Hawkhurst (05805) 2300. *Clubs:* MCC; Hawks (Cambridge); Kent County Cricket; Rye Golf.

VASSILIOU, Dr George; President of Cyprus, since 1988; *b* 20 May 1931; *s* of Vassos Vassiliou and Fofo Vassiliou; *m* Androulla Georgiades; one *s* two *d. Educ:* Univs of Geneva, Vienna and Budapest (DEcon). Market researcher, Reed Paper Group, UK; Founder: Middle East Marketing Research Bureau, 1962 (Chm. and Man. Dir); Middle East Centres for Management and Computing Studies, 1984; Cyprus Branch, Inst. of Directors (Hon. Sec.). Vis. Prof., Cranfield School of Management, 1985–. Member: Bd and Exec. Cttee, Bank of Cyprus, 1984–88; Econ. Adv. Council, Church of Cyprus, 1980–88; Educn Adv. Council, 1986–88. Dr *hc:* Univ. of Athens; Univ. of Econs, Budapest. Grand Cross, Legion of Honour (France); Grand Cross, Order of the Saviour (Greece); Standard (Flag) Order (Hungarian People's Republic). *Publications:* Marketing in the Middle East, 1976, etc. *Address:* Office of the President, Nicosia, Cyprus.

VAUGHAN, family name of **Earl of Lisburne.**

VAUGHAN, Viscount; David John Francis Malet Vaughan; artist; *b* 15 June 1945; *e s* of 8th Earl of Lisburne, *qv*; *m* 1973, Jennifer Jane Sheila Fraser Campbell, artist, *d* of James and Dorothy Campbell, Invergarry; one *s* one *d. Educ:* Ampleforth Coll.

VAUGHAN, Rt. Rev. Benjamin Noel Young; Hon. Assistant Bishop, Swansea and Brecon, since 1988; *b* 25 Dec. 1917; *s* of late Alderman and Mrs J. O. Vaughan, Newport, Pembs; *m* 1st, 1945, Nesta Lewis (*d* 1980); 2nd, 1987, Magdalene Reynolds. *Educ:* St David's Coll., Lampeter (BA; Hon. Fellow, 1990); St Edmund Hall, Oxford (MA); Westcott House, Cambridge. Deacon, 1943; Priest, 1944. Curate of: Llannon, 1943–45; St David's, Carmarthen, 1945–48; Tutor, Codrington Coll., Barbados, 1948–52; Lecturer in Theology, St David's Coll., Lampeter, and Public Preacher, Diocese of St David's, 1952–55; Rector, Holy Trinity Cathedral, Port of Spain, and Dean of Trinidad, 1955–61; Bishop Suffragan of Mandeville, 1961–67; Bishop of British Honduras, 1967–71; Assistant Bishop and Dean of Bangor, 1971–76; Bishop of Swansea and Brecon, 1976–87. Examining Chaplain to Bishop of Barbados, 1951–52, to Bishop of Trinidad, 1955–61; Commissary for Barbados, 1952–55. Formerly Chairman: Nat. Council for Educn in British Honduras; Govt Junior Secondary Sch.; Provincial Commn on Theological Educn in WI; Provincial Cttee on Reunion of Churches, Christian Social Council of British Honduras; Ecumenical Commn of British Honduras; Agric. Commn of Churches of British Honduras. Chairman: Provincial Cttee on Missions, Church in Wales; Church and Society Dept, Council of Churches for Wales; Adv. Cttee on Church and Society, Church in Wales, 1977; Judge of Provincial Court, Church in Wales. Pres., Council of Churches for Wales, 1980–82. Member: Council, St David's Univ. Coll., Lampeter, 1976–89 (Sub-Visitor, 1987–); Council and Ct, Swansea Univ. Coll., 1976–89; Ct, Univ. of Wales, 1986–89. Sub-Prelate, OStJ, 1977; Order of Druids, Gorsedd y Beirdd. *Publications:* Structures for Renewal, 1967; Wealth, Peace and Godliness, 1968; The Expectation of the Poor, 1972. *Address:* 4 Caswell Drive, Caswell, Swansea, West Glamorgan SA3 4RJ. *T:* Swansea (0792) 360646.

VAUGHAN, David Arthur John; QC 1981; QC (NI) 1981; *b* 24 Aug. 1938; *s* of late Captain F. H. M. Vaughan, OBE, RN and J. M. Vaughan; *m* 1st, 1967, Philippa Mary Maclure (marr. diss.); 2nd, 1985, Leslie Anne Fenwick Irwin; one *s* one *d. Educ:* Eton Coll.; Trinity Coll., Cambridge (MA). 2nd Lieut, 14th/20th King's Hussars, 1958–59. Called to the Bar, Inner Temple, 1962, Bencher, 1988. Vis. Prof. in Law, Durham Univ., 1989–. Member: Bar Council, 1968–72, 1984–86; Bar Cttee, 1987–88; International Relations Committee of Bar Council, 1968–86 (Chm., 1984–86); Bar/Law Soc. Working Party on EEC Competition Law, 1977– (Chm., 1978–88); UK Delegation to Consultative Committee of the Bars and Law Societies of the European Communities, 1978–81 (Chm., Special Cttee on EEC Competition Law, 1978–81); Law Adv. Cttee, British Council, 1982–85; Bar European Gp, 1978– (Founder and Chm., 1978–80, Hon. Vice-Pres., 1990–); EEC Section, Union Internationale des Avocats, 1987– (Chm., 1987–91). Bronze Medal, Bar of Bordeaux, 1985. *Publications:* co-ordinating editor, vols on European Community Law, Halsbury's Laws of England, 1986; (ed) Vaughan on Law of the European Communities, 1986. *Recreations:* fishing, tennis. *Address:* 50 Oxford Gardens, W10. *T:* 081–960 5865; 081–969 0707; Brick Court Chambers, 15/19 Devereux Court, WC2R 3JJ. *T:* 071–583 0777. *Clubs:* Brooks's, Flyfishers'.

VAUGHAN, Sir Edgar; *see* Vaughan, Sir G. E.

VAUGHAN, Elizabeth, (Mrs Ray Brown), FRAM; international operatic soprano; *b* Llanfyllin, Montgomeryshire; *m* 1968, Ray Brown (Gen. Administrator, Wren Orchestra of London); one *s* one *d. Educ:* Llanfyllin Grammar Sch.; RAM (ARAM, LRAM); Kathleen Ferrier Prize. Joined Royal Opera House; rôles in: Benvenuto Cellini; La Bohème; Midsummer Night's Dream; Madame Butterfly; Rigoletto; Simon Boccanegra; La Traviata; Il Trovatore; Turandot; Don Giovanni; Un Ballo in Maschera; Ernani; Nabucco; Aida; Cassandra; La Forza del Destino; Tosca; Idomeneo; Macbeth; Gloriana. Frequent appearances with: ENO; WNO; Opera North; Scottish Opera; Vienna State Opera; Deutsche Oper, Berlin; Hamburg State Opera; Metropolitan Opera, NY; Paris Opera. Professor of Singing: Welsh Coll. of Music and Drama, 1987–; Guildhall School of Music, 1989–. Has toured in: Europe; USA; Australia; Canada; Japan; S America. Hon. DMus Univ. of Wales. *Recreations:* tennis, driving, cookery. *Address:* c/o Music International, 13 Ardilaun Road, Highbury, N5 2QR.

VAUGHAN, Sir (George) Edgar, KBE 1963 (CBE 1956; OBE 1937); *b* 24 Feb. 1907; *s* of late William John Vaughan, BSc, of Cardiff, and Emma Kate Caudle; *m* 1st, 1933, Elsie Winifred Deubert (*d* 1982); one *s* two *d*; 2nd, 1987, Mrs Mary Sayers. *Educ:* Cheltenham Grammar Sch.; Jesus Coll., Oxford (Exhibitioner and later Hon. Scholar; Hon. Fellow, 1966). 1st Cl. Honour School of Mod. Hist., 1928; 1st Cl. Honour School of Philosophy, Politics and Economics, 1929; Laming Travelling Fellow of the Queen's College, Oxford, 1929–31. Entered Consular Service, 1930; Vice-Consul at: Hamburg, 1931; La Paz, 1932–35; Barcelona, 1935–38; Buenos Aires, 1938–44; Chargé d'Affaires, Monrovia, 1945–46; Consul at Seattle, Washington, 1946–49; Consul-General at Lourenço Marques, 1949–53, Amsterdam, 1953–56; Minister and Consul-General at Buenos Aires, 1956–60; Ambassador, 1960–63 and Consul-General, 1963, at Panama; Ambassador to Colombia, 1964–66. Retired from Diplomatic Service, 1966. Univ. of Saskatchewan, Regina Campus: Special Lectr, 1966–67; Prof. of History, 1967–74; Dean of Arts and Science, 1969–73. FRHistS 1965. Order of Andrés Bello, First Class (Venezuela), 1990. *Publication:* Joseph Lancaster en Caracas 1824–1827 y sus relaciones con el Libertador Simón Bolívar, vol. 1 1987, vol. 2 1989. *Address:* 9 The Glade, Sandy Lane, Cheam, Surrey SM2 7NZ. *T:* 081–643 1958. *Clubs:* Travellers', Royal Automobile.

VAUGHAN, Sir Gerard (Folliott), Kt 1984; FRCP; MP (C) Reading East, since 1983 (Reading, 1970–74; Reading South, 1974–83); *b* Xinavane, Portuguese E Africa, 11 June 1923; *s* of late Leonard Vaughan, DSO, DFC, and Joan Vaughan (*née* Folliott); *m* 1955, Joyce Thurle (*née* Laver); one *s* one *d. Educ:* privately in E Africa; London Univ.; Guy's Hosp. MB, BS 1947; MRCP 1949; Academic DPM London 1952; FRCP 1966; FRCPsych 1972. Consultant Staff, Guy's Hosp., 1958–79, now Consultant Emeritus. Minister for Health, DHSS, 1979–82; Minister of State (Consumer Affairs), Dept of Trade, 1982–83. Parly Mem., MRC, 1973–76; Alderman: LCC, 1955–61; LCC Streatham, 1961–64; GLC Lambeth, 1966–70; Alderman, GLC, 1970–72; Chm., Strategic Planning Cttee GLC, 1968–71; Mem., SE Economic Planning Council, 1968–71. Governor, UCL, 1959–68. Liveryman, Worshipful Co. of Barbers (Upper Warden, 1991–92). Contested (C) Poplar, 1955. Hon. FASI (FFAS 1978). *Publications:* various professional and general literary publications. *Recreations:* painting, fishing. *Address:* House of Commons, SW1. *Club:* Carlton.

VAUGHAN, Dame Janet (Maria), DBE 1957 (OBE 1944); DM, FRCP; FRS 1979; Principal of Somerville College, Oxford, 1945–67, Hon. Fellow since 1967; *b* 18 October 1899; *d* of William Wyamar Vaughan and Margaret Symonds; *m* 1930, David Gourlay (*d* 1963); two *d. Educ:* North Foreland Lodge; Somerville College, Oxford; University College Hospital (Goldsmith Entrance Scholar). Asst Clinical Pathologist, Univ. Coll. Hosp.; Rockefeller Fellowship, 1929–30; Beit Memorial Fellowship, 1930–33; Leverhulme Fellow, RCP, 1933–34; Asst in Clinical Pathology, British Post-Graduate Medical School, 1934–39; Mem. Inter-Departmental Cttee on Medical Schools, 1942; Nuffield Trustee, 1943; late Medical Officer in charge North-West London Blood Supply Depot for Medical Research Council. Mem., Royal Commn on Equal Pay, 1944; Chm., Oxford Regional Hosp. Board, 1950–51 (Vice-Chm. 1948); Member: Cttee on Economic and Financial Problems of Provision for Old Age, 1953–54; Medical Adv. Cttee of University Grants Cttee; University Grants Cttee on Libraries; Commonwealth Scholarship Commn in the UK. Fogarty Scholar, NIH, 1973. Hon. FRSM, 1980. Osler Meml Medal, Univ. of Oxford. Hon. Fellow: Wolfson Coll., Oxford, 1981; Girton Coll., Cambridge, 1986. Hon. DSc: Wales, 1960; Leeds, 1973; Hon. DCL: Oxford, 1967; London, 1968; Bristol, 1971. *Publications:* The Anæmias, 1st edn 1934, 2nd edn 1936; The Physiology of Bone, 1969, 3rd edn 1981; The Effects of Irradiation on the Skeleton, 1973; numerous papers in scientific jls on blood diseases, blood transfusion and metabolism of strontium and plutonium isotopes; section on leukæmias, Brit. Ency. Med. Pract.; section on blood transfusion in British Surgical Practice, 1945. *Recreations:* travel, gardening. *Address:* 5 Fairlawn Flats, First Turn, Wolvercote, Oxford. *T:* Oxford (0865) 514069.

VAUGHAN, Prof. Leslie Clifford, FRCVS; Professor of Veterinary Surgery, since 1974, and Vice-Principal, since 1982, Royal Veterinary College; *b* 9 Jan. 1927; *s* of Edwin Clifford and Elizabeth Louise Vaughan; *m* 1951, Margaret Joyce Lawson; one *s* one *d. Educ:* Bishop Gore Grammar School, Swansea; Royal Veterinary College, Univ. of London (DVR 1967, DSc 1970). FRCVS 1957. Lectr in Veterinary Surgery, RVC, 1951; Reader, London Univ., 1968; Prof. of Vet. Orthopaedics, 1972. Junior Vice-Pres., 1986, Pres., 1987–88, Senior Vice-Pres., 1988–89, 1989–90, RCVS. Francis Hogg Prize for contribs to small animal medicine and surgery, RCVS, 1962; Simon Award for small animal surgery, 1966, Bourgelat Prize, 1975, British Small Animal Vet. Assoc.; Victory Medal, Central Vet. Soc., 1982. *Publications:* papers in sci jls. *Recreations:* gardening, watching rugby football. *Address:* Royal Veterinary College, Hawkshead Lane, North Mymms, near Hatfield, Herts. *T:* Potters Bar (0707) 55486.

VAUGHAN, Rt. Rev. Peter St George; *see* Ramsbury, Area Bishop of.

VAUGHAN, Prof. Robert Charles, FRS 1990; Professor of Pure Mathematics, Imperial College of Science, Technology and Medicine, since 1980; *b* 1945. Imperial College, 1972–. *Publication:* The Hardy-Littlewood Method, 1981. *Address:* Department of Mathematics, Huxley Building, Imperial College, 180 Queen's Gate, SW7 2BZ. *T:* 071–589 5111.

VAUGHAN, Roger, PhD; FEng; FRINA; Joint Chief Executive: Swan Hunter Ltd, since 1988; Swan Hunter Shipbuilding and Engineering Ltd, since 1991; Chairman and Chief Executive, Swan Hunter Shipbuilders, since 1988; *b* 14 June 1944; *s* of Benjamin Frederick Vaughan and Marjorie (*née* Wallace); *m* 1st, 1968 (marr. diss.); three *s* two *d*; 2nd, 1987, Valerie (*née* Truelove); two step *s. Educ:* Newcastle Univ. (BSc Hons Naval Architecture and Shipbuilding 1966, PhD 1971). Student apprentice, Vickers Gp, 1962; Shipbuilding Develt Engr, Swan Hunter Shipbuilders Ltd, 1970–71; Dir, 1971–81, Man. Dir, 1978–81, A&P Appledore Ltd; Dir, Performance Improvement and Productivity, British Shipbuilders, 1981–86; took part in privatisation of Swan Hunter, 1986. Shipbuilding Gold Medal, NECInst, 1969. *Recreations:* music, theatre, ballet, opera, sailing, walking, reading. *Address:* Swan Hunter Ltd, Wallsend, Newcastle upon Tyne NE28 6EQ. *T:* Tyneside 091–295 0295.

VAUGHAN, Roger Davison, OBE 1986; FEng 1981; General Manager, Fast Reactor Projects, National Nuclear Corporation Ltd, 1977–88, retired; Director, Fast Reactor Technology Ltd, 1984–88; *b* 2 Oct. 1923; *s* of late David William and Olive Marion Vaughan; *m* 1951, Doreen Stewart; four *s. Educ:* University High Sch., Melbourne; Univ. of Melbourne, Aust. BMechE; FIMechE. Engineer Officer, RAAF, 1945–46. Chemical Engr, Commonwealth Serum Laboratories, 1946–47; Works apprenticeship, C. A. Parsons & Co., 1948–49; Chief Engr, C. A. Parsons Calcutta, 1950–53; AERE, Harwell, 1954; Chief Engineer: Nuclear Power Plant Co., 1955–59 (Director, 1958); The Nuclear Power Group, 1960–75; Manager, Technology Div., Nuclear Power Co., 1976–77. Chm., Gas-cooled Breeder Reactor Assoc., Brussels, 1970–; Mem. Bd, BSI, 1989– (Chm., BSI Engineering Council, 1983–88). Mem. Council, IMechE, 1977–81, 1985–89 (Chm., Power Industries Div., 1985–89). *Publications:* papers in jls of IMechE, Brit. Nuc. Energy Soc., World Energy Conf. *Recreations:* skiing, mountain walking; questionable performer on piano and clarinet. *Address:* Otterburn House, Manor Park South, Knutsford, Cheshire WA16 8AG. *T:* Knutsford (0565) 632514. *Clubs:* Ski of Great Britain; Himalayan (Bombay).

VAUGHAN, William Randal; Founder and Proprietor, W. R. Vaughan Associates Ltd (formerly W. R. Vaughan Ltd), since 1945; *b* 11 March 1912; *m* 1945, K. A. Headland; three *s* one *d. Educ:* Centaur Trade School, Coventry. FIProdE. Apprenticed, Alfred Herbert Ltd, 1926; Coventry Gauge & Tool Co. Ltd, 1933; A. C. Wickman Ltd, 1934; A. Pattison Ltd, 1942; C. G. Wade Ltd, London, 1943. Chairman, Machine Tool Industry Research Assoc., 1974–83 (Vice-Pres., 1983–); President, Machine Tool Trades Assoc., 1977–79. Member of Lloyd's. *Recreations:* squash, skiing, sailing, flying. *Address:* Rowley Bank, Rowley Lane, Arkley, Barnet, Herts EN5 3HS. *T:* 081–441 4800. *Clubs:* Lansdowne, Royal Automobile.

VAUGHAN-JACKSON, Oliver James, VRD 1951; FRCS; Consulting Orthopaedic Surgeon to London Hospital, since 1971; *b* 6 July 1907; *e s* of Surgeon Captain P. Vaughan-Jackson, RN, Carramore, Ballina, County Mayo; *m* 1939, Joan Madeline, *er d* of E. A. Bowring, CBE, St Johns, Newfoundland; two *s. Educ:* Berkhamsted School; Balliol Coll., Oxford; The London Hospital. Kitchener Scholar; BA, BM, BCh Oxon, 1932; MRCS, LRCP, 1932; FRCS 1936. House Physician, Demonstrator of Pathology, House Surgeon, Resident Accoucheur, and Surgical Registrar at The London Hosp. Surgeon Lieut-Comdr RNVR, Retd, Surgical specialist, Roy. Naval Hosp., Sydney, Australia. Sen. Registrar (Orthopædic), The London Hosp.; Orthopædic Surgeon to: The London Hosp., 1946–71; St Bartholomew's Hosp., Rochester, 1947–70; Medway Hosp., 1970–71; Claybury Mental Hosp., 1946–64; Halliwick Cripples Sch., 1946–71; Cons. In Orthopaedics to Royal Navy, 1956–71; Vis. Prof. of Orthopaedics, Memorial Univ. of Newfoundland, 1971–73; Senior Consultant in Orthopaedics at St John's Gen. Hosp., St Clare Mercy Hosp. and Janeway Child Health Centre, St John's, Newfoundland, 1971–73. Fellow: British Orthopædic Assoc.; RSM (Pres., Section of Orthopædics, 1968–69); Med. Soc. London; Member: Soc. Internat. de Chirurgie Orthopédique et de Traumatologie; British Soc. for Surgery of the Hand. Trustee, Meml Univ. of Newfoundland's Harlow Campus Trust, 1988–91. Former Mem., Editorial Board of Jl of Bone and Joint Surgery. Hon. DSc Memorial Univ. of Newfoundland, 1973. *Publications:* Sections on: Arthrodesis (Maingot's Techniques in British Surgery), 1950; Arthrodesis of the Hip, and Osteotomy of the Upper End of Femur (Operative Surgery, ed Rob and Smith), 1958; Surgery of the Hand; Orthopædic Surgery in Spastic conditions; Peripheral Nerve Injuries (Textbook of British Surgery, ed Sir Henry Souttar and Prof. J. C. Goligher), 1959; The Rheumatoid Hand; Carpal Tunnel Compression of the Median Nerve (Clinical Surgery, ed Rob and Smith), 1966; Surgery in Arthritis of the Hand, in Textbook of Rheumatic Diseases, 1968; The Rheumatoid Hand, in Operative Surgery, 2nd edn, 1971; contribs to Jl of Bone and Joint Surgery, etc. *Recreations:* gardening, photography. *Address:* The White Cottage, Bowesden Lane, Shorne, near Gravesend, Kent DA12 3LA. *T:* Shorne (047482) 2321. *Club:* Naval and Military.

VAUGHAN-MORGAN, family name of **Baron Reigate.**

VAUX OF HARROWDEN, 10th Baron *cr* 1523; **John Hugh Philip Gilbey;** *b* 4 Aug. 1915; 2nd *s* of William Gordon Gilbey (*d* 1965) and Grace Mary Eleanor, 8th Baroness Vaux of Harrowden (*d* 1958); *S* brother, 1977; *m* 1939, Maureen Pamela, *e d* of Hugh Gilbey; three *s* one *d. Educ:* Ampleforth College; Christ Church, Oxford (BA 1937). Formerly Major, Duke of Wellington's Regt; served War of 1939–45. *Heir: s* Hon. Anthony William Gilbey [*b* 25 May 1940; *m* 1964, Beverley Anne, *o d* of Charles Alexander Walton; two *s* two *d*]. *Address:* Cholmondeley Cottage, 2 Cholmondeley Walk, Richmond, Surrey TW9 1NS.

VAUX, Maj.-Gen. Nicholas Francis, CB 1989; DSO 1982; Major General Royal Marines Commando Forces, 1987–90; *b* 15 April 1936; *s* of late Harry and of Penelope Vaux; *m* 1966, Zoya Hellings; one *s* two *d. Educ:* Stonyhurst College. Commissioned RM, 1954; served Suez, 1956; Far East, 1958–61; West Indies Frigate, 1962–64; Staff Coll., Camberley, 1969; MoD (Army), 1975–77; Special Advisor, USMC, 1979–81; CO 42 Commando RM, 1981–83; Falklands, 1982; RCDS, 1985. *Publication:* March to the South Atlantic, 1986. *Recreations:* field sports. *Address:* National Westminster Bank, Old Town Street, Plymouth PL1 1DG. *Club:* Farmers'.

VAVASOUR, Comdr Sir Geoffrey William, 5th Bt *cr* 1828; DSC 1943; RN (retired); a Director of W. M. Still & Sons, 1962–80, retired; *b* 5 Sept. 1914; *s* of Captain Sir Leonard Vavasour, 4th Bt, RN, and Ellice Margaret Nelson; *S* father, 1961; *m* 1st, 1940, Joan Robb (marr. diss. 1947); two *d*; 2nd, 1971, Marcia Christine, *d* of late Marshall Lodge, Batley, Yorks. *Educ:* RNC Dartmouth. *Heir: kinsman* Hugh Bernard Moore Vavasour [*b* 4 July 1918; *m* 1950, Monique Pauline Marie Madeleine (*d* 1982), *d* of Maurice Erick Beck; one *s* one *d*]. *Address:* 8 Bede House, Manor Fields, Putney, SW15 3LT. *Club:* All England Lawn Tennis.

VAZ, (Nigel) Keith (Anthony Standish); MP (Lab) Leicester East, since 1987; *b* Aden, 26 Nov. 1956. *Educ:* St Joseph's Convent, Aden; Latymer Upper Sch., Hammersmith; Gonville and Caius Coll., Cambridge; Coll. of Law, Lancaster Gate. Senior Solicitor, Islington Borough Council, 1982–85; Solicitor, Highfields and Belgrave Law Centre, Leicester, 1985–87. Contested (Lab): Richmond and Barnes (gen. election), 1983; Surrey W (European Parlt election), 1984. Mem., Home Affairs Select Cttee, H of C, 1987–; Secretary: Indo-British Parly Gp; PLP Wool and Textiles Gp. Clothing and Footwear Inst., 1988. Chairman: All-Party Footwear & Leather Industries Gp; PLP Legal Services Gp. Member: NUPE, 1985–; Nat. Adv. Cttee, Crime Concern, 1989–. Patron, Gingerbread, 1990–; Pres., Leicester and S Leics RSPCA, 1988–. Columnist: Tribune; Catholic Herald; New Life (Gujarat Samachar). President: Hillcroft FC; Thurnby Lodge Boys' Club FC. *Address:* 144 Uppingham Road, Leicester LE5 0QF. *T:* Leicester (0533) 768834.

VEAL, Group Captain John Bartholomew, CBE 1956; AFC 1940; Civil Aviation Safety Adviser, Department of Trade and Industry, 1972–74, retired; *b* 28 September 1909; *er s* of John Henry and Sarah Grace Veal; *m* 1933, Enid Marjorie Hill (*d* 1987); two *s. Educ:* Christ's Hosp. Special trainee, Metropolitan-Vickers, 1926–27; commissioned in RAF as pilot officer, 1927; served in Nos 4 and 501 Squadrons and as flying Instructor at Central Flying School, transferring to RAFO, 1932; Flying-Instructor, Chief Flying Instructor, and Test Pilot, Air Service Training Ltd, 1932–39; recalled to regular RAF service, 1939; commanded navigation and flying training schools, 1939–43; Air Staff No. 46 Transport Group, 1944 and Transport Command, 1945–46 (despatches); released from RAF, 1946, to become Deputy Director of Training, Ministry of Civil Aviation; Director of Air Safety and Training, 1947; Director of Operations, Safety and Licensing, 1952; Deputy Director-General of Navigational Services, Ministry of Transport and Civil Aviation, 1958; Director-General of Navigational Services, Ministry of Aviation, 1959–62; Chief Inspector of Accidents, Civil Aviation Department, Board of Trade (formerly Min. of Aviation), 1963–68; Dir Gen. of Safety and Operations, DTI (formerly BOT), 1968–72. FRAeS 1967 (AFRAeS 1958). *Recreation:* trout fishing. *Address:* Woodacre, Horsham Road, Cranleigh, Surrey GU6 8DZ. *T:* Cranleigh (0483) 274490. *Club:* Royal Air Force.

VEALE, Sir Alan (John Ralph), Kt 1984; FEng 1980; Chairman: Rossmore Warwick Ltd, 1986–88; RFS Industries Ltd, since 1987; *b* 2 Feb. 1920; *s* of Leslie H. Veale and Eleanor Veale; *m* 1946, Muriel Veale; two *s* (and one *s* decd). *Educ:* Exeter School; Manchester College of Technology. AMCT, FIMechE, FIProdE. Manufacturing Dir, AEI Turbine Generators Ltd, 1963; Director and General Manager: Heavy Plant Div., AEI, 1966; Motor Control Group, AEI, 1967; Managing Director: GEC Diesels Ltd, 1969; GEC Power Engineering Ltd, 1970–85; Dir, GEC plc, 1973–85; Chm., Fairey Gp, 1987; Dir, Throgmorton Trust PLC, 1986–90. Pres., IProdE, 1985–86. CBIM. Hon. DSc Salford, 1984. *Recreations:* sailing, walking. *Address:* 41 Northumberland Road, Leamington Spa CV32 6HF. *T:* Leamington Spa (0926) 424349.

VEASEY, Josephine, CBE 1970; opera singer (mezzo soprano), retired; teaching privately, since 1982; vocal consultant to English National Opera, since 1985; *b* London, 10 July 1930; *m* (marr. diss.); one *s* one *d*. Joined chorus of Royal Opera House, Covent Garden, 1949; a Principal there, 1955– (interval on tour, in opera, for Arts Council). Teacher of voice production, RAM, 1983–84. Has sung at Royal Opera House, Glyndebourne, Metropolitan (NY), La Scala, and in France, Germany, Spain, Switzerland, South America; operatic Roles include: Octavian in Der Rosenkavalier; Cherubino in Figaro; name role in Iphigenie; Dorabella in Cosi fan Tutte; Amneris in Aida, Fricka in Die Walküre; Fricka in Das Rheingold; name role in Carmen; Dido and Cassandra in the Trojans; Marguerite in The Damnation of Faust; Charlotte in The Sorrows of Werther; Eboli, Don Carlos; name role, Orfeo; Adalgesa in Norma; Rosina in The Barber of Seville; Kundry in Parsifal; Gertrude in Hamlet, 1980. Concerts, 1960–70 (Conductors included Giulini, Bernstein, Solti, Mehta, Sargent). Verdi's Requiem; Monteverdi's Combattimento di Tancredi e Clorinda, Aix Festival, 1967; various works of Mahler; two tours of Israel (Solti); subseq. sang in Los Angeles (Mehta); then Berlioz: Death of Cleopatra, Royal Festival Hall, and L'enfance du Christ, London and Paris; Rossini's Petite Messe Solennelle, London and Huddersfield (with late Sir Malcolm Sargent); Handel's Messiah, England,

Munich, Oporto, Lisbon; Berlioz' Romeo and Juliette, London, and Bergen Festival; Rossini's Stabat Mater, Festival d'Angers and London, 1971; Berlioz' Beatrice and Benedict, NY, and London; Emperor in 1st perf. Henze's We Come to the River, Covent Garden, 1976. Has sung Elgar's Dream of Gerontius all over England. Frequently makes recordings. Hon. RAM, 1972. *Recreations:* reading, gardening. *Address:* 2 Pound Cottage, St Mary Bourne, Andover, Hants SP11 6EQ. *T:* St Mary Bourne (0264) 738282.

VEEDER, Van Vechten; QC 1986; *b* 14 Dec. 1948; *s* of John Van Vechten Veeder and Helen Letham Townley; *m* 1970; one *s* one *d*. *Educ:* Ecole Rue de la Ferme, Neuilly, Paris; Clifton College, Bristol; Jesus College, Cambridge. Called to the Bar, Inner Temple, 1971. *Recreations:* sailing, travelling, reading. *Address:* 4 Essex Court, Temple, EC4Y 9AJ. *T:* 071–583 9191.

VEGA TREJOS, Guillermo; Ambassador of Panama to the Court of St James's, 1984–90; *b* 14 Aug. 1927; *s* of late Simon Vega and Onofre Trejos de Vega; *m* Lesley Ann de Vega; three *s* two *d*. *Educ:* National Institute, Panama; British College, Buenos Aires; Univ. of La Plata, Argentina. Licenciado. Editor: La Hora, 1952–55; La Nación, 1955–58; Pres., Sindicate of Journalists, 1958–60; Sec. Gen., Housing Inst., Panama, 1960–64; Pres., Municipal Council, Panama, 1964–68; Pres., Nat. Municipalities Assoc., 1964–68; Editor, Panama America, 1969–73; Ambassador to France and Switzerland, 1973–84. *Publications:* Muchos son los Llamados; Cuentos para una Esquina Redonda. *Recreations:* theatre, music. *Address:* c/o Ministry for Foreign Affairs, Panama 4.

VEIL, Simone Annie, Chevalier de l'Ordre national du Mérite; Magistrate; Member, European Parliament, since 1979 (President, 1979–82; Chairman, Liberal and Democratic Reformist Group, 1984–89); *b* Nice, 13 July 1927; *d* of André Jacob and Yvonne (*née* Steinmetz); *m* 1946, Antoine Veil, Inspecteur des Finances, President of International Aeroplane Co. and Chief Exec. Officer, La Compagnie Internationale des Wagons Lits et du Tourisme; three *s*. *Educ:* Lycée de Nice; Lic. en droit, dipl. de l'Institut d'Etudes Politiques, Paris; qualified as Magistrate, 1956. Deported to Auschwitz and Bergen-Belsen, March 1944–May 1945. Ministry of Justice, 1957–69; Technical Advr to Office of Minister of Justice, 1969; Gen.-Sec., Conseil Supérieur de la magistrature, 1970–74. Minister of Health, France, 1974–76; Minister of Health and Social Security, France, 1976–79. Monismanie Prize, 1978; Onassis Foundn Prize, Athens, 1980; Charlemagne Prize, Prix Louise Weiss, 1981; Louise Michel Prize, 1983; Jabotinsky Prize, 1983; Prize for Everyday Courage, 1984; Special Freedom Prize, Eleanor and Franklin Roosevelt Foundn, 1984; Fiera di Messina Prize, 1984; Living Legacy Award, San Diego, Univ. d'Acadie, 1987; Johanna Lowenherz Prize, Neuwied, 1987; Thomas Dehler Prize, Munich, 1988. *Dhc:* Princeton, 1975; Institut Weizmann, 1976; Yale, Cambridge, Edinburgh, Jerusalem, 1980; Georgetown, Urbino, 1981; Yeschiva, Sussex, 1982; Free Univ., Brussels, 1984; Brandeis, 1989. *Publication:* (with Prof. Launay and Dr Soulé) les Données psycho-sociologiques de l'Adoption, 1969. *Address:* 11 place Vauban, 75007 Paris, France.

VEIRA, Sir Philip (Henry), KBE 1988 (OBE); merchant, since 1942; *b* 14 Aug. 1921; *s* of Benedict and Mary Veira; *m* 1943, Clara Lauretta; one *s* seven *d*. *Educ:* St Mary's Roman Catholic Sch., St Vincent. *Recreations:* fishing, reading. *Address:* Kingstown Park, St Vincent, West Indies.

VENABLES, (Harold) David (Spenser); Official Solicitor to the Supreme Court, since 1980; *b* 14 Oct. 1932; *s* of late Cedric Venables and Gladys Venables (*née* Hall); *m* 1964, Teresa Grace, *d* of late J. C. Watts; one *d* one *s*. *Educ:* Denstone College. Admitted Solicitor, 1956. Pilot Officer, Royal Air Force, 1957–58. Legal Assistant, Official Solicitor's Office, 1960; Secretary, Lord Chancellor's Cttee on the Age of Majority, 1965–67; Asst Official Solicitor, 1977–80. *Publications:* A Guide to the Law Affecting Mental Patients, 1975; The Racing Fifteen-Hundreds: a history of voiturette racing 1931–40, 1984; contributor, Halsbury's Laws of England, 4th edn. *Recreations:* vintage cars, motoring and military history. *Address:* 81 Chancery Lane, WC2A 1DD. *T:* 071–911 7116.

VENABLES, Richard William Ogilvie; Member of Council and Board, Direct Mail Services Standards Board, since 1983; *b* 23 Feb. 1928; *s* of late Canon and Mrs E. M. Venables; *m* 1952, Ann Richards; three *s* two *d*. *Educ:* Marlborough Coll.; Christ Church, Oxford (BA, MA). Joined former Mather and Crowther Ltd, as trainee, 1952; Account Group Director, 1965; Board Member, 1966; Mem. Executive Cttee, 1972; Managing Director, 1974; joined Board of Ogilvy and Mather International, 1975; Chm., Ogilvy Benson and Mather Ltd, 1978–81; retired early, 1981, to pursue new career in the making of violins, violas, lutes, harpsichords. Chm., Apple and Pear Develt Council, 1980–83; Council and Bd Mem., Direct Mail Services Standards Bd, 1983–. *Recreation:* fly fishing. *Address:* First Field, Combe Hay, Bath, Avon BA2 8RD. *T:* Bath (0225) 833694.

VENABLES, Robert; QC 1990; *b* 1 Oct. 1947; *s* of Walter Edwin Venables, MM, and Mildred Daisy Robson Venables. *Educ:* Merton Coll., Oxford (MA); London School of Economics (LLM). FTII. Called to Bar, Middle Temple, 1973; private practice as barrister, 1976–. Lecturer: Merton Coll., Oxford, 1972–75; UCL, 1973–75; Official Fellow and Tutor in Jurisprudence, St Edmund Hall, Oxford, and CUF Lectr, Oxford Univ., 1975–80. *Publications:* Inheritance Tax Planning, 1986, 2nd edn 1988; Preserving the Family Farm, 1987, 2nd edn 1989; Non-Resident Trusts, 1988, 4th edn 1991; Tax Planning and Fundraising for Charities, 1989; Tax Planning Through Trusts—Inheritance Tax, 1990; National Insurance Contributions Planning, 1990; Hold-Over Relief, 1990; The Company Car, 1990; Capital Gains Tax Planning for Non-UK Residents, 1991. *Recreation:* music making. *Address:* 24 Old Buildings, Lincoln's Inn, WC2A 3UJ. *T:* 071–242 2744, *Fax:* 071–831 8095. *Club:* Travellers'.

VENABLES, Robert Michael Cochrane; Charity Commissioner, since 1989; *b* 8 Feb. 1939; *s* of late Cdre Gilbert Henry Venables, DSO, OBE, RN and Muriel Joan Haes; *m* 1972, Hazel Lesley Gowing, BSc; two *s* two *d*. *Educ:* Portsmouth Grammar Sch. Admitted solicitor, 1962; in private practice, London, Petersfield and Portsmouth, 1962–70; Treasury Solicitor's Department: Legal Asst, 1970; Sen. Legal Asst, 1973; Asst Treasury Solicitor, 1980. *Recreations:* opera, collecting domestic anachronisms. *Address:* St Albans House, 57–60 Haymarket, SW1Y 4QX. *T:* 071–210 4410.

VENABLES-LLEWELYN, Sir John (Michael) Dillwyn-, 4th Bt *cr* 1890; farmer, since 1975; *b* 12 Aug. 1938; *s* of Sir Charles Michael Dillwyn-Venables-Llewelyn, 3rd Bt, MVO, and of Lady Delia Mary Dillwyn-Venables-Llewelyn, *g d* of 1st Earl St Aldwyn; *S* father, 1976; *m* 1st, 1963, Nina (marr. diss. 1972), *d* of late Lt J. S. Hallam; two *d*; 2nd, 1975, Nina Gay Richardson Oliver; one *d* decd. *Recreation:* racing vintage cars. *Address:* Llysdinam, Newbridge-on-Wye, Llandrindod Wells, Powys LD1 6NB.

VENKATARAMAN, Ramaswamy; President of India, since 1987 (Vice-President, 1984–87); *b* 4 Dec. 1910; *s* of Ramaswami Iyer; *m* 1938, Janaki; three *d*. *Educ:* Madras Univ. (MA, LLB). Formerly in practice as a lawyer, Madras High Court and Supreme Court; prominent trade union leader, also political and social worker. Mem., Provisional Parlt, 1950; Mem., Lok Sabha, 1952–57 and (for Madras S), 1977–84; Leader of the House, Madras Legislative Council, and Minister of Industries, 1957–67; Mem., Planning Commn, Madras, 1967–71. Minister of: Finance and Industry, 1980–82; Defence, 1982–84. Sec., Madras Provincial Bar Fedn, 1947–50. Chm., Nat. Research and Develt Corp. Leader, Indian delegation to Internat. Labour Organisation, 1958, and delegate, UN Gen. Assembly, 1953–61. *Address:* Rashtrapati Bhavan, New Delhi 110004, India.

VENNING, Philip Duncombe Riley, FSA; Secretary, Society for the Protection of Ancient Buildings, since 1984; *b* 24 March 1947; *s* of late Roger Venning and of Rosemary (*née* Mann); *m* 1987, Elizabeth Frances Ann, *d* of M. A. R. Powers. *Educ:* Sherborne Sch.; Trinity Hall, Cambridge (MA). Times Educational Supplement, 1970–81 (Asst Editor, 1978–81); freelance journalist and writer, 1981–84. Sec., William Morris Craft Fellowship Cttee, 1986–. Member: Council on Occupational Standards and Qualifications in Envmtl Conservation, 1988–; Conf. on Training in Architectural Conservation, 1988–. FSA 1989; FRSA 1990. *Publications:* contribs to books and other pubns on educn and on historic buildings. *Recreations:* archaeology, book collecting. *Address:* 17 Highgate High Street, N6 5JT. *T:* 081–341 0925.

VENNING, Robert William Dawe; Under Secretary, Health Authority Personnel Division, Department of Health, since 1990; *b* 25 July 1946; *s* of Tom William Dawe and Elsie Lillian Venning; *m* 1969, Jennifer Mei-Ling Jackson; one *s* one *d*. *Educ:* Midhurst Sch.; Univ. of Birmingham (BA Special Hons Philosophy 1968). Tutor in Philosophy, Univ. of Birmingham, 1968; Lectr in Logic and Scientific Method, Lanchester Polytechnic, 1969; Admin. Trainee, DHSS, 1971; Private Sec. to Minister for Disabled, 1974; Principal, 1975; Private Sec. to Minister for Health, 1981; Asst Sec., 1983. Non-Exec. Dir, Compel plc, 1990–. *Recreations:* playing classical and flamenco guitar; electronics and computing. *Address:* Department of Health, Hannibal House, Elephant and Castle, SE1 6TE.

VENTRY, 8th Baron *cr* 1800 (Ire.); **Andrew Wesley Daubeny de Moleyns;** Bt 1797; Director: Burgie Lodge Farms Ltd, since 1970; C. & R. Briggs Commercials Ltd, since 1986; Glenscott Motor Controls Inc., since 1987 (Vice-President); *b* 28 May 1943; *s* of Hon. Francis Alexander Innys Eveleigh Ross de Moleyns (*d* 1964) (2nd *s* of 6th Baron) and of Joan (now Joan Springett), *e d* of Harold Wesley; assumed by deed poll, 1966, surname of Daubeny de Moleyns; *S* uncle, 1987; *m* 1st, 1963, Nelly Renée (marr. diss. 1979), *d* of Abel Chaumillon; one *s* two *d*; 2nd, 1983, Jill Rosemary, *d* of C. W. Oramon; one *d*. *Educ:* Edge Grove; Aldenham. Farmer, 1961–; in electronics, 1986–. *Recreations:* shooting, stalking, photography, sailing, ski-ing. *Heir:* *s* Hon. Francis Wesley Daubeny de Moleyns, *b* 1 May 1965.

VENTURI, Robert; architect; Principal, Venturi, Scott Brown and Associates, Inc., since 1989 (Venturi, Rauch and Scott Brown, 1980–89); *b* 25 June 1925; *s* of Robert Charles Venturi and Vanna Venturi (*née* Lanzetta); *m* 1967, Denise Scott Brown; one *s*. *Educ:* Princeton Univ. (AB 1947, MFA 1950). Designer, Oskar Stonorov, 1950, Eero Saarinen & Assoc., 1950–53; Rome Prize Fellow, Amer. Acad. in Rome, 1954–56; designer, Louis I Kahn, 1957; Principal: Venturi, Cope and Lippincott, 1958–61; Venturi and Short, 1961–64; Venturi and Rauch, 1964–80. Associate Prof., Univ. of Pennsylvania, 1957–65; Charlotte Shepherd Davenport Prof. of Architecture, Yale, 1966–70. Works include: Vanna Venturi House, 1961, Guild House, 1961, Franklin Court, 1972, Inst. for Sci. Inf. Corp. HQ, 1978 (all Philadelphia); Allen Meml Art Museum Addition (Oberlin, Ohio), 1973; Gordon Wu Hall (Princeton), 1980; Seattle Art Mus., 1984; Sainsbury Wing, Nat. Gall., London, 1986; Philadelphia Orchestra Hall, 1987. Fellow: Amer. Inst. of Architects; Amer. Acad. in Rome; Accad. Nazionale di San Luca; Amer. Acad. of Arts and Scis; Hon. FFRIAS. Hon. DFA: Oberlin Coll., 1977; Yale, 1979; Univ. of Pennsylvania, 1980; Princeton Univ., 1983; Philadelphia Coll. of Art, 1985; Hon. LHD NJ Inst. of Technology, 1984. James Madison Medal, Princeton Univ., 1985; Thomas Jefferson Meml Foundn Medal, Univ. of Virginia, 1983; Pritzker Architecture Prize, Hyatt Foundn, 1991. *Publications:* A View from the Campidoglio: selected essays, 1953–84 (with Denise Scott Brown), 1984; Complexity and Contradiction in Architecture, 1966, 2nd edn 1977; Learning from Las Vegas (with Denise Scott Brown and Steven Izenour), 1972, 2nd edn 1977; articles in periodicals. *Recreation:* travel. *Address:* Venturi, Scott Brown and Associates, Inc., 4236 Main Street, Philadelphia, Pa 19127, USA. *T:* (215) 487–0400.

VENUGOPAL, Dr Sriramashetty; Principal in General Practice, Aston, Birmingham, since 1967; *b* 14 May 1933; *s* of Satyanarayan and Manikyamma Sriramashetty; *m* 1960, Subhadra Venugopal; one *s* one *d*. *Educ:* Osmania Univ., Hyderabad, India (BSc, MB BS); Madras Univ. (DMRD). Medical posts, Osmania Hosp., State Med. Services, Hyderabad, Singareni Collieries, 1959–65; Registrar, Radiology, Selly Oak Hosp., Birmingham, 1965–66; Registrar, Chest Medicine, Springfield Hosp., Grimsby, 1966–67; Hosp. Practitioner, Psychiatry, All Saints Hosp., Birmingham, 1972–. Member: Working Group, DHSS, 1984–; Local Med. Cttee, 1975–; Dist. Med. Cttee, 1978–; GMC, 1984–; West Birmingham HA, 1982– (Chm., sub-cttee on needs of ethnic minorities, 1982–85); Birmingham FPC, 1984–; Birmingham Community Liaison Adv. Cttee, 1985. Vice-Chm., Birmingham Div., BMA, 1986–87 (Chm., 1985–86). Mem., Local Review Cttee for Winson Green Prison, 1981–83. Founder Mem., Overseas Doctors' Assoc., 1975–81 (Dep. Treasurer, 1975–81; Nat. Vice-Chm., 1981–87; Inf. and Adv. Service, 1981–; Nat. Chm., 1987–); Founder Mem. and Chm., Link House Council, 1975–. Founder Mem., Osmania Grad. Med. Assoc. in UK, 1984–. Vice-Chm., Hyderabad Charitable Trust, 1985–. FRSocMed 1986; FRIPHH 1988; MRCGP 1990. *Publications:* contribs to learned jls on medico-political topics. *Recreations:* medical politics, music, gardening. *Address:* Aston Health Centre, 175 Trinity Road, Aston, Birmingham B6 6JA. *T:* 021–328 3597; 24 Melville Road, Edgbaston, Birmingham B16 9JT. *T:* 021–454 1725. *Club:* Aston Rotary (Pres., 1984–85).

VERCO, Sir Walter (John George), KCVO 1981 (CVO 1970; MVO 1952); OStJ 1954; Secretary of the Order of the Garter, 1974–88; Secretary to the Earl Marshal, since 1961; Surrey Herald of Arms Extraordinary, since 1980; *b* 18 January 1907; *s* of late John Walter Verco, Chelsea; *m* 1929, Ada Rose (*d* 1989), *d* of late Bertram Leonard Bennett, Lymington, Hants; one *s* one *d*. Served War, 1940–45, with RAFVR, Flight Lt. Secretary to Garter King of Arms, 1949–60; Rouge Croix Pursuivant of Arms, 1954–60; Chester Herald, 1960–71; Norroy and Ulster King of Arms, 1971–80. Hon. Genealogist to Royal Victorian Order, 1968–88; Inspector, RAF Badges, 1970–, RAAF Badges, 1971–; Adviser on Naval Heraldry, 1970–. *Address:* College of Arms, Queen Victoria Street, EC4. *T:* 071–248 6185; 8 Park Court, Linkfield Lane, Redhill, Surrey. *T:* Redhill (0737) 771794.

VERCOE, Rt. Rev. Whakahuihui; *see* Aotearoa, Bishop of.

VERDON-SMITH, Sir (William) Reginald, Kt 1953; DL; Pro-Chancellor, Bristol University, 1965–86; Vice Lord-Lieutenant, Avon, 1980–88; *b* 5 Nov. 1912; *s* of late Sir William G. Verdon Smith, CBE, JP; *m* 1946, Jane Margaret, *d* of late V. W. J. Hobbs; one *s* one *d*. *Educ:* Repton School; Brasenose College, Oxford (Scholar), 1st class School of Jurisprudence, 1935; BCL 1936 and Vinerian Law Scholar; Barrister-at-law, Inner Temple. Bristol Aeroplane Co., 1938–68: Dir., 1942; Jt Asst Man. Dir., 1947; Jt Man. Dir., 1952; Chm. 1955. Vice-Chm., Rolls Royce Ltd, 1966–68; Chm., British Aircraft Corp. (Hldgs) Ltd, 1969–72; Dir, Lloyds Bank Ltd, 1951–83; Chairman: Lloyds Bank Internat., 1973–79; Lloyds Bank Bristol Region, 1976–83. Pres. SBAC, 1946–48; Chm., Fatstock and Meat Marketing Committee of Enquiry, 1962–64; Mem. of Council, Univ.

of Bristol, 1945–86 (Chm., 1949–56). Mem. Cttee on the Working of the Monetary System (Radcliffe Cttee), 1957–59. Mem., Review Body on Remuneration of Doctors and Dentists, 1964–68. Master, Worshipful Co. of Coachmakers and Coach Harness Makers, 1960–61; Master, Soc. of Merchant Venturers, 1968–69. FRSA. DL Avon, 1974. Hon. LLD Bristol, 1959; Hon. DSc Cranfield Inst. of Technology, 1971; Hon. Fellow: Brasenose Coll., Oxford, 1965; Bristol Univ., 1986. *Recreations:* golf and sailing. *Address:* Flat 3, Spring Leigh, Church Road, Leigh Woods, Bristol BS8 3PG. *Clubs:* United Oxford & Cambridge University, Royal Cruising; Royal Yacht Squadron, Royal Lymington Yacht.

See also Sir G. S. J. White, Bt.

VEREKER, family name of **Viscount Gort.**

VEREKER, John Michael Medlicott; Deputy Secretary, Department of Education and Science, since 1988; Chairman, Student Loans Company Ltd, since 1989; *b* 9 Aug. 1944; *s* of Comdr C. W. M. Vereker and late M. H. Vereker (*née* Whatley); *m* 1971, Judith Diane, *d* of Hobart and Alice Rowen, Washington, DC; one *s* one *d*. *Educ:* Marlborough Coll.; Keele Univ. (BA Hons 1967). Asst Principal, ODM, 1967–69; World Bank, Washington, 1970–72; Principal, ODM, 1972; Private Sec. to successive Ministers of Overseas Develt, 1977–78; Asst Sec., 1978; Prime Minister's Office, 1980–83; Under Sec., 1983–88, and Principal Finance Officer, 1986–88, ODA, FCO. Council Mem., Inst. of Manpower Studies, 1989–. *Address:* c/o Department of Education and Science, Sanctuary Buildings, Great Smith Street, SW1P 3BT.

See also P. W. M. Vereker.

VEREKER, Peter William Medlicott; HM Diplomatic Service; Head of Arms Control and Disarmament Department, Foreign and Commonwealth Office, since 1991; *b* 13 Oct. 1939; *s* of Comdr Charles William Medlicott Vereker and late Marjorie Hughes Whatley; *m* 1967, Susan Elizabeth, *d* of Maj.-Gen. A. J. Dyball, CBE, MC; three *s*. *Educ:* Elstree Sch.; Marlborough Coll.; Trinity Coll., Cambridge (MA); Harvard Univ. (Henry Fellow, 1962). CUAS (RAFVR), 1958–61. Assistant d'Anglais, Paris, 1963; joined FO, 1963; Bangkok, 1964; Chiang Mai, 1967; FCO, 1968; Canberra, 1971; Head of Chancery, Athens, 1975; Asst Head, W European Dept, FCO, 1978; RCDS, 1982; Counsellor and Consul-Gen., Bangkok, 1983 (acted as Chargé d'Affaires, 1984, 1986); Dep. Perm. Rep., UK Mission at Geneva, 1987. *Recreations:* writing, sport. *Address:* c/o Foreign and Commonwealth Office, SW1A 2AH.

See also J. M. M. Vereker.

VEREY, David John; Chief Executive, Lazard Brothers, since 1990; *b* 8 Dec. 1950; *s* of Michael John Verey, *qv*; *m* 1st, 1974, Luise Jaschke (marr. diss. 1990); two *s* one *d*; 2nd, 1990, Emma Katharine Broadhead (*née* Laidlaw). *Educ:* Eton College; Trinity College, Cambridge (MA). Lazard Brothers: joined 1972; Dir, 1983; Dep. Chief Exec., 1985. *Recreations:* stalking, bridge, gardening, travel. *Address:* Lazard Brothers & Co., 21 Moorfields, EC2P 2HT. *T:* 071–588 2721.

VEREY, Michael John, TD 1945; *b* 12 Oct. 1912; *yr s* of late Henry Edward and late Lucy Alice Verey; *m* 1947, Sylvia Mary, *widow* of Charles Bartlet and *d* of late Lt-Col Denis Wilson and late Mrs Mary Henrietta Wilson; two *s* one *d*. *Educ:* Eton; Trinity College, Cambridge (MA). Joined Helbert, Wagg & Co. Ltd, 1934. Served War of 1939–45, Middle East, Italy, Warwickshire Yeomanry (Lt-Col). Chairman: J. Henry Schroder Wagg & Co. Ltd, 1972–73 (Dep. Chm., 1966–72); Schroders Ltd, 1973–77; Accepting Houses Cttee, 1974–77; Broadstone Investment Trust Ltd, 1962–83; Brixton Estate Ltd 1971–83; Trustees, Charities Official Investment Fund, 1974–83; American Energy Investments Ltd, 1981–83; Director: British Petroleum Co. Ltd, 1974–82; The Boots Co. (Vice-Chm., 1978–83); Commercial Union Assurance Co. Ltd (Vice-Chm., 1975–78; Dep. Chm., 1978–82); BI International, and other cos; Mem., Covent Garden Market Authority, 1961–66. High Sheriff of Berkshire, 1968. Pres., Warwickshire Yeomanry Regtl Assoc., 1976–86. *Recreations:* gardening, travel. *Address:* The Lodge, Little Bowden, Pangbourne, Berks. *T:* Pangbourne (0734) 842210. *Club:* Boodle's.

See also D. J. Verey.

VERITY, Anthony Courtenay Froude, MA; Master of Dulwich College, since 1986; *b* 25 Feb. 1939; *s* of Arthur and Alice Kathleen Verity; *m* 1962, Patricia Ann Siddall; one *s* one *d*. *Educ:* Queen Elizabeth's Hosp., Bristol; Pembroke Coll., Cambridge (MA). Assistant Master: Dulwich Coll., 1962–65; Manchester Grammar Sch., 1965–69; Head of Classics, Bristol Grammar Sch., 1969–76; Headmaster, Leeds Grammar Sch., 1976–86. Editor, Greece and Rome, 1971–76. *Publications:* Latin as Literature, 1971; contribs to Jl of Arabic Lit. *Recreations:* music, fell-walking, squash, cricket. *Address:* Elm Lawn, Dulwich Common, SE21 7EW. *Clubs:* United Oxford & Cambridge University, Academy.

VERMES, Prof. Geza, FBA 1985; Professor of Jewish Studies, 1989–91, now Professor Emeritus, and Fellow of Wolfson College, 1965–91, now Fellow Emeritus, Oxford University; Director, Oxford Forum for Qumran Research, Oxford Centre for Postgraduate Hebrew Studies, since 1991; *b* 22 June 1924; *s* of late Ernö Vermes and Terézia Riesz; *m* 1958, Mrs Pamela Curle (*née* Hobson). *Educ:* Univ. of Budapest; Coll. St Albert de Louvain, Louvain Univ. Licencié en Histoire et Philologie Orientales (avec la plus grande distinction), 1952; DTheol 1953; MA Oxon 1965, DLitt 1988. Asst Editor, Cahiers Sioniens, Paris, 1953–55; research worker, CNRS, Paris, 1955–57; Lectr, later Sen. Lectr in Divinity, Newcastle Univ., 1957–65; Reader in Jewish Studies, Oxford Univ., 1965–89; Chm. of Curators of Oriental Inst., Oxford, 1971–74; Chm. Bd of Faculty of Oriental Studies, Oxford, 1978–80; Governor, Oxford Centre for Postgrad. Hebrew Studies, 1972–. Vis. Prof. in Religious Studies, Brown Univ., 1971; Rosenstiel Res. Fellow, Univ. of Notre Dame, 1972; Margaret Harris Lectr in Religion, Dundee Univ., 1977; Riddell Meml Lectr, Newcastle Univ., 1981; Dist. Vis. Prof. in Judeo-Christian Studies, Tulane Univ., 1982; Igor Kaplan Vis. Lectr, Toronto Sch. of Theology, 1985, 1987. Pres., British Assoc. for Jewish Studies, 1975, 1988; Pres., European Assoc. for Jewish Studies, 1981–84. Editor, Jl of Jewish Studies, 1971–. Hon. DD: Edinburgh, 1989; Durham, 1990. *Publications:* Les manuscrits du désert de Juda, 1953; Discovery in the Judean Desert, 1956; Scripture and Tradition in Judaism, 1961; The Dead Sea Scrolls in English, 1962, rev. edn 1987 (trans. Portuguese); Jesus the Jew, 1973 (trans. Spanish, French, Japanese, Italian, German); Post-Biblical Jewish Studies, 1975; (with Pamela Vermes) The Dead Sea Scrolls: Qumran in perspective, 1977 (trans. Spanish); The Gospel of Jesus the Jew, 1981; (ed jtly) Essays in Honour of Y. Yadin, 1982; Jesus and the World of Judaism, 1983; (ed and rev., with F. G. B. Millar and M. D. Goodman) E. Schürer, The History of the Jewish People in the Age of Jesus Christ I–III, 1973–87 (trans. Spanish, Italian); (with M. D. Goodman) The Essenes according to the Classical Sources, 1989. *Recreations:* watching wild life, correcting proofs. *Address:* Oriental Institute, Pusey Lane, Oxford OX1 2LE; West Wood Cottage, Foxcombe Lane, Boars Hill, Oxford OX1 5DH. *T:* Oxford (0865) 735384.

VERMEULE, Prof. Emily Dickinson Townsend, FSA; Zemurray-Stone-Radcliffe Professor, Harvard University, since 1970; Fellow for Research, Museum of Fine Arts, Boston, since 1963; *b* 11 Aug. 1928; *d* of Clinton Blake Townsend and Eleanor Mary Meneely; *m* 1957, Cornelius Clarkson Vermeule III; one *s* one *d*. *Educ:* The Brearley Sch.; Bryn Mawr Coll. (BA, PhD); Radcliffe Coll. (MA). Instructor in Greek: Bryn Mawr, 1956–57; Wellesley Coll., 1957–58; Asst Prof. of Classics, 1958–61, Associate Prof. of Classics, 1961–64, Boston Univ.; Prof. of Greek and Fine Arts, Wellesley, 1965–70. James Loeb Vis. Prof. of Classical Philology, Harvard Univ., 1969; Sather Prof. of Classical Literature, Univ. of California, Berkeley, 1975; Geddes-Harrower Prof. of Greek Art and Archaeology, Univ. of Aberdeen, 1980–81; Bernhard Vis. Prof., Williams Coll., 1986. Corresp. Member: German Archaeological Inst., 1964; British Academy, 1982. Member: Archaeological Inst. of America, 1950; Soc. for Preservation of Hellenic Studies, 1954; Amer. Philosophical Soc., 1971; Amer. Acad. of Arts and Scis, 1970; Bd of Scholars, Library of Congress, 1982–87; Smithsonian Council, 1983–90. National Endowment for the Humanities Jefferson Lectr, 1981. Hon. degrees: DLitt: Douglass Coll., Rutgers, 1968; Smith Coll., 1971; Wheaton Coll., 1973; Tufts, 1980; Univ. of Pittsburgh, 1983; Bates Coll., 1983; DFA, Univ. of Massachusetts at Amherst, 1970; LLD: Regis Coll., 1970; LHD: Trinity Coll., Hartford, Conn., 1974; Emmanuel Coll., Boston, 1980; Princeton, 1989. Gold Medal, Radcliffe Coll., 1968; Charles Goodwin Award of Merit, American Philological Assoc., 1980. *Publications:* Euripides' Electra, 1959; Greece in the Bronze Age, 1964, 7th edn 1980; The Trojan War in Greek Art, 1964; Götterkult, Archaeologia Homerica V, 1974; The Mound of Darkness, 1974; The Art of the Shaft Graves, 1975; Death in Early Greek Art and Poetry, 1979; (with V. Karageorghis) Mycenaean Pictorial Vase-Painting, 1982; Toumba tou Skourou, A Bronze Age Potters' Quarter on Morphou Bay in Cyprus, 1990; contribs to Jl of Hellenic Studies, American Jl of Archaeology, Jahrbuch des d.Arch. Insts, Classical Philology, etc. *Recreations:* dogs, gardening. *Address:* 47 Coolidge Hill Road, Cambridge, Mass 02138, USA. *T:* (617) UN 4–1879. *Club:* Cosmopolitan (New York City).

VERNEY, family name of **Baron Willoughby de Broke.**

VERNEY, Sir John, 2nd Bt, *cr* 1946; MC 1944; TD 1970; painter, illustrator, author; *b* 30 Sept. 1913; *s* of Sir Ralph Verney, 1st Bt (Speaker's Secretary, 1921–55); *S* father, 1959; *m* 1939, Lucinda, *d* of late Major Herbert Musgrave, DSO; one *s* five *d* (and one *s* decd). *Educ:* Eton; Christ Church, Oxford. Served War of 1939–45 with N. Somerset Yeomanry, RAC and SAS Regt in Palestine, Syria, Egypt, Italy, France and Germany (despatches twice, MC). Exhibitor: RBA; London Group; Leicester, Redfern, New Grafton Gall., etc. Légion d'Honneur, 1945. *Publications:* Verney Abroad, 1954; Going to the Wars, 1955; Friday's Tunnel, 1959; Look at Houses, 1959; February's Road, 1961; Every Advantage, 1961; The Mad King of Chichiboo, 1963; ismo, 1964; A Dinner of Herbs, 1966; Fine Day for a Picnic, 1968; Seven Sunflower Seeds, 1968; Samson's Hoard, 1973; A John Verney Collection, 1989; periodic contributor to Cornhill etc; annually, The Dodo Pad (the amusing telephone diary). *Heir:* *s* John Sebastian Verney, *b* 30 Aug. 1945. *Address:* The White House, Clare, Suffolk CO10 8NP. *T:* Clare (0787) 277494.

VERNEY, Lawrence John, TD 1955; DL; **His Honour Judge Verney;** Recorder of London, since 1990; *b* 19 July 1924; *y s* of Sir Harry Verney, 4th Bt, DSO; *m* 1972, Zoë Auriel, *d* of Lt-Col P. G. Goodeve-Docker. *Educ:* Harrow; Oriel Coll., Oxford. Called to Bar, Inner Temple, 1952, Bencher, 1990. Dep. Chm., Bucks QS, 1962–71; Dep. Chm., Middlesex Sessions, then a Circuit Judge, 1971–90. Editor, Harrow School Register, 1948–; Governor, Harrow Sch., 1972–87. Master, Co. of Pattenmakers, 1988. DL Bucks 1967. *Address:* Central Criminal Court, EC4M 7EH.

See also Sir R. B. Verney, Bt, Rt Rev. S. E. Verney.

VERNEY, Sir Ralph (Bruce), 5th Bt *cr* 1818; KBE 1974; JP; Landowner; Vice-Lord-Lieutenant (formerly Vice-Lieutenant) of Buckinghamshire, 1965–84; *b* 18 Jan. 1915; *e s* of Sir Harry Calvert Williams Verney, 4th Bt, DSO, and Lady Rachel Bruce (*d* 1964), *d* of 9th Earl of Elgin; *S* father, 1974; *m* 1948, Mary Vestey; one *s* three *d*. *Educ:* Canford; Balliol Coll., Oxford. 2nd Lieut Bucks Yeomanry, 1940; Major, Berks Yeomanry, 1945 and Bucks Yeomanry, 1946. Pres., Country Landowners' Assoc., 1961–63; Vice-President for Great Britain, Confédération Européenne de L'Agriculture, 1965–71, Counsellor, 1971–; Chairman, Forestry Commn Cttee for England, 1967–80; Member: Forestry Commn, 1968–80; Milton Keynes New Town Corporation, 1967–74; BBC Adv. Cttee on Agriculture, 1970–78; Royal Commn on Environmental Pollution, 1973–79; Chm., Nature Conservancy Council, 1980–83 (Mem., 1966–71); Chm., Sec. of State for the Environment's Adv. Cttee on Aggregates for Construction Industry, 1972–77. Trustee: Radcliffe Trust; Ernest Cook Trust; Chequers Trust; Sch. of Water Sciences, Cranfield, 1982–87. Member, Council: Buckingham Univ., 1983–87; Royal Soc. of Arts, 1983–87 (FRSA 1972). Buckinghamshire County Council: Member, 1951; Chairman, Finance Cttee, 1957; Planning Cttee, 1967; CA 1961; JP Bucks, 1954; High Sheriff of Buckinghamshire, 1957–58; DL Bucks, 1960; High Steward of Buckingham, 1966. Prime Warden, Worshipful Co. of Dyers, 1969–70. Hon. Fellow: RIBA, 1977; Green Coll., Oxford, 1980. DUniv Buckingham, 1991. Chevalier de Tastevin, Clos Vougeot, 1978. *Recreation:* shooting. *Heir:* *s* Edmund Ralph Verney [*b* 28 June 1950; *m* 1982, Daphne Fausset-Farquhar; one *s* one *d*]. *Address:* Claydon House, Middle Claydon, Buckingham MK18 2EX. *T:* Aylesbury (0296) 730297; Plas Rhôscolyn, Holyhead LL65 2NZ. *T:* Trearddur Bay (0407) 860288. *Club:* Cavalry and Guards.

See also L. J. Verney, Rt Rev. S. E. Verney.

VERNEY, Rt. Rev. Stephen Edmund, MBE 1945; *b* 17 April 1919; 2nd *s* of late Sir Harry Verney, 4th Bt, DSO and Lady Rachel Verney (*née* Bruce); *m* 1st, 1947, Priscilla Avice Sophie Schwerdt (*d* 1974); one *s* three *d*; 2nd, 1981, Sandra Ann Bailey; (one *s* decd). *Educ:* Harrow School; Balliol College, Oxford (MA). Curate of Gedling, Nottingham, 1950; Priest-in-charge and then first Vicar, St Francis, Clifton, Nottingham, 1952; Vicar of Leamington Hastings and Diocesan Missioner, Dio. Coventry, 1958; Canon Residentiary, Coventry Cathedral, 1964; Canon of Windsor, 1970; Bishop Suffragan of Repton, 1977–85. *Publications:* Fire in Coventry, 1964; People and Cities, 1969; Into the New Age, 1976; Water into Wine, 1985; The Dance of Love, 1989. *Recreations:* conversation and aloneness; music, gardening, travel. *Address:* Charity School House, Church Road, Blewbury, Oxon OX11 9PY. *Club:* English-Speaking Union.

See also L. J. Verney, Sir R. B. Verney, Bt.

VERNIER-PALLIEZ, Bernard Maurice Alexandre; Commandeur de la Légion d'Honneur; Croix de Guerre; Médaille de la Résistance; Ambassadeur de France, 1984; *b* 2 March 1918; *s* of Maurice Vernier and Marie-Thérèse Palliez; *m* 1952, Denise Silet-Pathe; one *s* three *d*. *Educ:* Ecole des Hautes Etudes Commerciales; Ecole Libre des Sciences Politiques. Licencié en Droit. Joined Régie Nationale des Usines, Renault, 1945 (dealing with personnel and trade unions); Sécretaire Général, RNUR, 1948–67; Directeur Général Adjoint, RNUR, 1967–71; Président Directeur Général, SAVIEM, 1967–74; Délégué Général aux Vehicules Industriels, Cars et Bus à la RNUR, Président du Directoire de Berliet, and Vice-Président du Conseil de Surveillance de SAVIEM, Jan.-Dec. 1975; Président Directeur Général, RNUR, Dec. 1975–1981; Ambassador to Washington, 1982–84. Dir, Public Affairs for Europe, International Distillers and Vintners, 1987–; Pres., Adv. Bd, Case-Poclain (formerly Poclain SA), 1985–; Pres. Bd, Bureau d'Information et de prévisions économiques, 1989–; Member: American International Gp Adv. Bd, 1985–; Tenneco European Adv. Council, 1985–; Byrnes Internat. Center Adv. Bd, 1985–. *Address:* 25 Grande Rue, 78170 La Celle St-Cloud, France. *T:* (1) 39 69 30 11.

VERNON, family name of **Barons Lyveden** and **Vernon.**

VERNON, 10th Baron, *cr* 1762; **John Lawrance Vernon;** *b* 1 Feb. 1923; *s* of 9th Baron, and Violet (*d* 1978), *d* of Colonel Clay; *S* father, 1963; *m* 1st, 1955, Sheila Jean (marr. diss. 1982), *d* of W. Marshall Clark, Johannesburg; one *d* (and one *d* decd); 2nd, 1982, Sally, *d* of Robin Stratford, QC. *Educ:* Eton; Magdalen Coll., Oxford. Served in Scots Guards, 1942–46, retiring with rank of Captain. Called to Bar, Lincoln's Inn, 1949. Served in various Government Departments, 1950–61; attached to Colonial Office (for service in Kenya), 1957–58. Chm., Population Concern, 1984–89. JP Derbyshire, 1965–77. *Heir: kinsman* Col William Ronald Denis Vernon-Harcourt, OBE [*b* 4 May 1909; *m* 1937, Nancy Everil, *d* of Lt-Col Bertram Henry Leatham, DSO; one *s* one *d*]. *Address:* Sudbury House, Sudbury, Derbyshire DE6 5HT. *Club:* Boodle's.

VERNON, David Bowater; Under Secretary, Inland Revenue, 1975–84; *b* 14 Nov. 1926; *s* of Lt-Col Herbert Bowater Vernon, MC, and Ivy Margaret Vernon; *m* 1954, Anne de Montmorency Fleming; three *s* three *d*. *Educ:* Marlborough Coll.; Oriel Coll., Oxford (MA). RA, 1945–48 (Lieut). Inland Revenue, 1951–84. *Recreation:* gardening. *Address:* The Oast, Gedges Farm, Matfield, Tonbridge, Kent. *T:* Brenchley (089272) 2400.

VERNON, Sir James, AC 1980; Kt 1965; CBE 1962 (OBE 1960); Director, O'Connell Street Associates Pty Ltd, since 1976; *b* 13 June 1910; *s* of Donald Vernon, Tamworth, New South Wales; *m* 1935, Mavis, *d* of C. Lonsdale Smith; two *d*. *Educ:* Sydney Univ. (BSc); University College, London (PhD). CSR Ltd: Chief Chemist, 1938–51; Senior Exec. Officer, 1951–56; Asst General Manager, 1956–57; Gen. Manager, 1958–72; Dir, 1958–82; Chm., 1978–80. Chairman: Commonwealth Cttee of Economic Enquiry, 1963–65; Australian Post Office Commn of Inquiry, 1973; Internat. Pres., Pacific Basin Econ. Council, 1980–82. FRACI; FAIM; FTS. Hon. DSc: Sydney, 1965; Newcastle, 1969. Leighton Medal, Royal Australian Chemical Inst., 1965; John Storey Medal, Aust. Inst. of Management, 1971. Order of Sacred Treasure, 1st cl. (Japan), 1983. *Address:* 27 Manning Road, Double Bay, NSW 2028, Australia. *Clubs:* Australian, Union, Royal Sydney Golf (Sydney).

VERNON, James William, CMG 1964; retired; *b* 19 Nov. 1915; *s* of late John Alfred Vernon; *m* 1941, Betty Désirée, *d* of Gordon E. Nathan; one *s* one *d*. *Educ:* Wallasey Grammar Sch.; Emmanuel Coll., Cambridge (Scholar). BA 1937 (Senior Wrangler); MA 1940. Entered Civil Service, Ministry of Food, 1939; Flt Lieut, RAF, 1943; Wing Comdr (despatches), 1945; Principal Scientific Officer, Ministry of Works, 1945; Assistant Secretary, Colonial Office, 1954–64; Economic Adviser, British High Commission, Lusaka, 1966; Asst Under-Sec. of State, DEA, 1966–69; Under-Sec., Min. of Housing and Local Govt, later DoE, 1969–72. Called to Bar, Inner Temple, 1975. Queen's Commendation for Brave Conduct, 1955. *Recreations:* gardening, computer science, chaos. *Address:* 20 Grove Hill, Topsham, Devon.

VERNON, Kenneth Robert, CBE 1978; Deputy Chairman and Chief Executive, North of Scotland Hydro-Electric Board, 1973–88; *b* 15 March 1923; *s* of late Cecil W. Vernon and Jessie McGaw, Dumfries; *m* 1946, Pamela Hands, Harrow; one *s* three *d* (and one *d* decd). *Educ:* Dumfries Academy; Glasgow University. BSc, FEng, FIEE, FIMechE. BTH Co., Edinburgh Corp., British Electricity Authority, 1948–55; South of Scotland Electricity Bd, 1955–56; North of Scotland Hydro-Electric Bd, 1956: Chief Electrical and Mech. Engr, 1964; Gen. Man., 1966; Bd Mem., 1970. Dir, British Electricity International Ltd, 1976–88; Mem. Bd, Northern Ireland Electricity Service, 1979–85. *Publications:* various papers to technical instns. *Recreation:* fishing. *Address:* 10 Keith Crescent, Edinburgh EH4 3NH. *T:* 031–332 4610. *Club:* Commonwealth Trust.

VERNON, Prof. Magdalen Dorothea, MA (Cantab) 1926; ScD (Cantab) 1953; Professor of Psychology in the University of Reading, 1956–67; *b* 25 June 1901; *d* of Dr Horace Middleton Vernon and Katharine Dorothea Ewart. *Educ:* Oxford High Sch.; Newnham Coll., Cambridge. Asst Investigator to the Industrial Health Research Board, 1924–27; Research Investigator to the Medical Research Council, in the Psychological Laboratory, Cambridge, 1927–46; Lecturer in Psychology, 1946–51, Senior Lecturer in Psychology, 1951–55, Reader in Psychology, 1955–66, University of Reading. President, British Psychological Society, 1958 (Hon. Fellow, 1970); President, Psychology Section, British Assoc., 1959. *Publications:* The Experimental Study of Reading, 1931; Visual Perception, 1937; A Further Study of Visual Perception, 1952; Backwardness in Reading, 1957; The Psychology of Perception, 1962; Experiments in Visual Perception, 1966; Human Motivation, 1969; Perception through Experience, 1970; Reading and its Difficulties, 1971; numerous papers on Perception, etc. in British Journal of Psychology and British Journal of Educational Psychology. *Recreations:* walking, gardening. *Address:* 50 Cressingham Road, Reading, Berks. *T:* Reading (0734) 871088. *Club:* University Women's.

VERNON, Michael; *see* Vernon, William M.

VERNON, Sir Nigel (John Douglas), 4th Bt, *cr* 1914; Consultant, HRGM UK Division (formerly Hogg Robinson), since 1984; *b* 2 May 1924; *s* of Sir (William) Norman Vernon, 3rd Bt, and Janet Lady Vernon (*d* 1973); *S* father, 1967; *m* 1947, Margaret Ellen (*née* Dobell); one *s* one *d* (and one *s* decd). *Educ:* Charterhouse. Royal Naval Volunteer Reserve (Lieutenant), 1942–45. Spillers Ltd, 1945–65; Director: Castle Brick Co Ltd, 1965–71; Deeside Merchants Ltd, 1971–74; Travel Finance Ltd, 1971–87. Consultant, Hogg Insurance Brokers, 1986–. *Recreations:* golf, shooting, gardening. *Heir: s* James William Vernon, FCA [*b* 2 April 1949; *m* 1981, Davinia, *er d* of Christopher David Howard, Ryton, Shrewsbury; one *s* one *d*]. *Address:* Top-y-Fron Hall, Kelsterton, near Flint, N Wales. *T:* Deeside (0244) 830010. *Club:* Naval.

VERNON, (William) Michael; Chairman, Royal National Lifeboat Institution, since 1989 (Deputy Chairman, 1980–89, and Vice-President, since 1975); Chairman, Granville Meat Co. Ltd, since 1981; *b* 17 April 1926; *o* surv. *s* of late Sir Wilfred Vernon; *m* 1st, 1952, Rosheen O'Meara; one *s*; 2nd, 1977, Mrs Jane Colston (*née* Kilham-Roberts). *Educ:* Marlborough Coll.; Trinity Coll., Cambridge. MA 1948. Lieut, Royal Marines, 1944–46. Joined Spillers Ltd, 1948: Dir 1960; Jt Man. Dir 1962; Chm. and Chief Exec., 1968–80; Director: EMI Ltd, 1973–80; Strong & Fisher (Hldgs), 1980–90; Chm., Famous Names Ltd, 1981–85. Pres., Nat. Assoc. of British and Irish Millers, 1965; Vice-Chm., Millers' Mutual Assoc., 1968–80; Pres., British Food Export Council, 1977–80. CBIM. *Recreations:* sailing, shooting, ski-ing. *Address:* Fyfield Manor, Andover, Hants SP11 8EN. *Clubs:* Hurlingham; Royal Ocean Racing (Cdre 1964–68); Royal Yacht Squadron.

VERULAM, 7th Earl of, *cr* 1815; **John Duncan Grimston;** Bt 1629; Baron Forrester (Scot.), 1633; Baron Dunboyne and Viscount Grimston (Ire.), 1719; Baron Verulam (Gt. Brit.), 1790; Viscount Grimston (UK), 1815; *b* 21 April 1951; *s* of 6th Earl of Verulam, and of Marjorie Ray, *d* of late Walter Atholl Duncan; *S* father, 1973; *m* 1976, Dione Angela, *e d* of Jeremy Smith, *qv*; three *s* one *d*. *Educ:* Eton; Christ Church, Oxford (MA 1976). Dir, Baring Brothers & Co. Ltd, 1987–. *Heir: s* Viscount Grimston, *qv*. *Address:* Gorhambury, St Albans, Herts AL3 6AH. *T:* St Albans (0727) 55000. *Clubs:* White's, Beefsteak, Turf.

VESEY, family name of **Viscount de Vesci.**

VESEY, Sir Henry; *see* Vesey, Sir N. H. P.

VESEY, Sir (Nathaniel) Henry (Peniston), Kt 1965; CBE 1953; Chairman, H. A. & E. Smith Ltd, since 1939; Chairman, Bank of N. T. Butterfield & Son Ltd, 1970–86; Member of House of Assembly, Bermuda, 1938–72; *b* 1 June 1901; *s* of late Hon. Nathaniel Vesey, Devonshire, Bermuda; *m* 1920, Louise Marie, *d* of late Captain J. A. Stubbs, Shelly Bay, Bermuda; two *s*. *Educ:* Saltus Grammar Sch. Chairman: Food and Supplies Control Board, 1941–42; Board of Trade, 1943; Finance Cttee of House of Assembly, 1943–44; Bermuda Trade Development Board, 1945–56, 1960–69; Board of Civil Aviation, 1957–59; Board of Agriculture, 1957–59. MEC, 1948–57, Mem. Executive Council for Tourism and Trade, 1968–69. *Recreations:* fishing, golf. *Address:* Windward, Shelly Bay, Bermuda FL BX. *T:* (809) 293–0186. *Clubs:* Naval and Military; Royal Bermuda Yacht, Mid Ocean, Coral Beach (Bermuda).

VESSEY, Prof. Martin Paterson, FRS 1991; Professor of Social and Community Medicine, University of Oxford, since 1974; Fellow of St Cross College, Oxford, since 1973; *b* 22 July 1936; *s* of Sidney J. Vessey and Catherine P. Vessey (*née* Thomson); *m* 1959, Anne Platt; two *s* one *d*. *Educ:* University College Sch., Hampstead; University Coll. London; University Coll. Hosp. Med. Sch., London. MB, BS London 1959; MD London 1971; FFCM RCP 1972; MA Oxon 1974; MRCPE 1978; FRCPE 1979; FRCGP 1983; FRCP 1987; FRCOG 1989. Scientific Officer, Dept of Statistics, Rothamsted Exper. Stn, 1960–65; House Surg. and House Phys., Barnet Gen. Hosp., 1965–66; Mem. Sci. Staff, MRC Statistical Research Unit, 1966–69; Lectr in Epidemiology, Univ. of Oxford, 1969–74. Chm., Adv. Cttee on Breast Cancer Screening, DHSS, subseq. Dept of Health, 1987–; Member: Cttee on Safety of Medicines, 1980–; Royal Commn on Environmental Pollution, 1984–89. *Publications:* many sci. articles in learned jls, notably on med. aspects of fertility control, safety of drugs, and epidemiology of cancer. *Recreations:* motoring, fine arts, conservation. *Address:* 8 Warnborough Road, Oxford OX2 6HZ. *T:* Oxford (0865) 52698.

VESTEY, family name of **Baron Vestey.**

VESTEY, 3rd Baron, *cr* 1922, of Kingswood; **Samuel George Armstrong Vestey;** Bt, *cr* 1913; DL; *b* 19 March 1941; *s* of late Captain the Hon. William Howarth Vestey (killed in action in Italy, 1944; *o s* of 2nd Baron Vestey and Frances Sarah Howarth) and of Pamela Helen Fullerton, *d* of George Nesbitt Armstrong; *S* grandfather, 1954; *m* 1st, 1970, Kathryn Mary (marr. diss. 1981), *er d* of John Eccles, Moor Park, Herts; two *d*; 2nd, 1981, Celia Elizabeth, *d* of Major Guy Knight, MC, Lockinge Manor, Wantage, Oxon; two *s*. *Educ:* Eton. Lieut, Scots Guards. Director, Union International plc and associated companies. President: London Meat Trade and Drovers Benevolent Assoc., 1973; Three Counties Agricl Soc., 1978; Inst. of Meat, 1978–83. Pres., Glos Assoc. of Boys' Clubs; Liveryman, Butchers' Co. DL Glos, 1982. GCStJ 1987 (Chancellor of the Order, 1988–91, Lord Prior, 1991–). *Recreations:* racing, shooting. *Heir: s* Hon. William Guy Vestey, *b* 27 Aug. 1983. *Address:* Stowell Park, Northleach, Glos. *Clubs:* White's; Jockey (Newmarket); Melbourne (Melbourne).

VESTEY, Edmund Hoyle, DL; Chairman: Lamport & Holt Line, since 1970; Albion Insurance Co., since 1970; Blue Star Line, since 1971; Union International PLC and associated companies, since 1988; *b* 1932; *o s* of late Ronald Arthur Vestey and Florence Ellen McLean, *e d* of Col T. G. Luis, VD; *m* 1960, Anne Moubray, *yr d* of Gen. Sir Geoffry Scoones, KCB, KBE, CSI, DSO, MC; four *s*. *Educ:* Eton. 2nd Lieut Queen's Bays, 1951; Lieut, City of London Yeomanry. Chm., Associated Container Transportation (Australia), 1979–82, 1985–88. Pres., Gen. Council of British Shipping, 1981–82. FRSA; FCIT, 1982. Joint Master, Puckeridge and Thurlow Foxhounds; Pres., Essex County Scout Council, 1979–87. High Sheriff, Essex, 1977; DL Essex, 1978. *Address:* Little Thurlow Hall, Haverhill, Suffolk CB9 7LQ; Glencanisp Lodge, Lochinver, Sutherland; Sunnyside Farmhouse, Hawick, Roxburghshire. *Clubs:* Cavalry and Guards, Carlton.

VESTEY, Sir (John) Derek, 2nd Bt, *cr* 1921; *b* 4 June 1914; *s* of John Joseph Vestey (*d* 1932) and Dorothy Mary (*d* 1918), *d* of John Henry Beaver, Gawthorpe Hall, Bingley, Yorkshire; *g s* of Sir Edmund Vestey, 1st Bt; *S* grandfather 1953; *m* 1938, Phyllis Irene, *o d* of H. Brewer, Banstead, Surrey; one *s* one *d*. *Educ:* Leys Sch., Cambridge. Served War of 1939–45: Flt-Lieut, RAFVR, 1940–45. *Heir: s* Paul Edmund Vestey [*b* 15 Feb. 1944; *m* 1971, Victoria Anne Scudamore, *d* of John Salter, Tiverton, Devon; three *d*. *Educ:* Radley]. *Address:* Park Penthouse, 355 Kings Road, Chelsea, SW3. *T:* 071–352 5940. *Clubs:* MCC, Royal Automobile.

VIAL, Sir Kenneth Harold, Kt 1978; CBE 1969; chartered accountant; retired; *b* 11 Aug. 1912; *s* of G. O. Vial, Melbourne; *m* 1937, Adele, *d* of R. G. R. Ball; one *s* two *d*. *Educ:* Scotch Coll., Melbourne. Served RAAF, 1941–46 (Flight Lieut). Partner, Arthur Andersen & Co. (formerly Fuller King & Co.), 1946–69; Chairman: Yarra Falls Ltd, 1969–74; Rocke Tompsitt & Co. Ltd, 1975–79; Director: Michaelis Bayley Ltd, 1969–81 (Chm., 1975–81); Mono Pumps (Aust.) Pty Ltd, 1969–81; F. H. Faulding & Co. Ltd, 1978–84; Hortico Ltd, 1981–84 (Chm., 1981–84). Member: Aust. Nat. Airlines Commn, 1956–79 (Chm., 1975–79); Aviation Industry Adv. Council, 1978–79; Council, Aust. Services Canteens Organisation, 1959–76 (Chm., Bd of Management, 1971–76); Council, La Trobe Univ., 1966–74 (Dep. Chancellor, 1970–72); Melbourne Underground Rail Loop Authority, 1971–81. *Address:* 54 The Parade, Ocean Grove, Vic 3226, Australia. *Clubs:* Athenæum, Naval and Military (Melbourne).

VICARY, Rev. Douglas Reginald; Canon Residentiary and Precentor of Wells Cathedral, 1975–88; *b* 24 Sept. 1916; *e s* of R. W. Vicary, Walthamstow; *m* 1947, Ruth, *y d* of late F. J. L. Hickinbotham, JP, and of Mrs Hickinbotham, Edgbaston; two *s* two *d*. *Educ:* Sir George Monoux Grammar Sch., Walthamstow; Trinity Coll., Oxford (Open Scholar), Wycliffe Hall, Oxford. 1st Class Nat. Sci. 1939; BSc 1939, MA 1942; Diploma in Theology with distinction, 1940; deacon, 1940; priest, 1941. Curate of St Peter and St Paul, Courteenhall, and Asst Chaplain and House Master, St Lawrence Coll., Ramsgate, while evacuated at Courteenhall, Northampton, 1940–44; Chaplain, Hertford Coll., Oxford, 1945–48; Tutor at Wycliffe Hall, 1945–47, Chaplain 1947–48; Dir of Religious Education, Rochester Diocese, 1948–57; Sec., CACTM Exams Cttee and GOE, 1952–57; Dir, Post-Ordination Training, 1952–57, Headmaster of King's School, Rochester, 1957–75; Chaplain to HM the Queen, 1977–86. Minor Canon, Rochester Cathedral, 1949–52; Canon Residentiary and Precentor, 1952–57; Hon. Canon, 1957–75. Exam. Chaplain to Bishop of Rochester, 1950–88, to Bishop of Bath and Wells, 1975–87. Mem. Court, Kent Univ., 1965–75. FRSA 1970. *Publication:* contrib. Canterbury Chapters, 1976. *Recreations:* music, architecture, hill-walking, reading. *Address:* 8 Tor Street, Wells, Somerset BA5 2US. *T:* Wells (0749) 679137.

VICK, Arnold Oughtred Russell; QC 1980; **His Honour Judge Russell Vick;** a Circuit Judge, since 1982; *b* 14 Sept. 1933; *yr s* of late His Honour Judge Sir Godfrey Russell Vick, QC and late Lady Russell Vick, JP, *d* of J. A. Compston, KC; *m* 1959, Zinnia Mary, *e d* of Thomas Brown Yates, Godalming; two *s* one *d*. *Educ:* The Leys Sch., Cambridge; Jesus Coll., Cambridge (MA). Pilot, RAF, 1952–54. Called to Bar, Inner

Temple, 1958; Mem. Gen. Council of the Bar, 1964–68; Prosecuting Counsel to the Post Office, 1964–69; Dep. Recorder, Rochester City QS, 1971; a Recorder of the Crown Court, 1972–82; Principal Judge for Civil Matters in Kent, 1990–. Mem., Lord Chancellor's County Court Rules Cttee, 1972–80; Recorder, SE Circuit Bar Mess, 1978–80. Gov., New Beacon Sch., Sevenoaks, 1982–. Master, Curriers' Co., 1976–77. *Publication:* A Hundred Years of Golf at Wildernesse, 1990. *Recreations:* golf, cricket. *Address:* The Law Courts, Barker Road, Maidstone. *T:* Maidstone (0622) 754966. *Clubs:* MCC; Hawks (Cambridge); Wildernesse (Captain 1978) (Sevenoaks); Royal Worlington and Newmarket Golf.

VICK, Sir (Francis) Arthur, Kt 1973; OBE 1945; PhD; FIEE, FInstP; MRIA; President and Vice-Chancellor, Queen's University of Belfast, 1966–76; Pro-Chancellor, University of Warwick, since 1977 (Chairman of Council, 1977–90); *b* 5 June 1911; *s* of late Wallace Devenport Vick and late Clara (*née* Taylor); *m* 1943, Elizabeth Dorothy Story (*d* 1989); one *d*. *Educ:* Waverley Grammar School, Birmingham; Birmingham Univ. Asst Lectr in Physics, University Coll., London, 1936–39, Lectr, 1939–44; Asst Dir of Scientific Research, Min. of Supply, 1939–44; Lectr in Physics, Manchester Univ., 1944–47, Sen. Lectr, 1947–50; Prof. of Physics, University Coll. of N Staffs, 1950–59 (Vice-Principal, 1950–54, Actg Principal, 1952–53); Dep. Dir, AERE, Harwell, 1959–60, Dir, 1960–64; Dir of Research Group, UKAEA, 1961–64; Mem. for Research, 1964–66. Institute of Physics: Mem. Bd, 1946–51; Chm., Manchester and District Branch, 1948–51; Vice-Pres., 1953–56; Hon. Sec., 1956–60. Chairman: Manchester Fedn of Scientific Societies, 1949–51; Naval Educn Adv. Cttee, 1964–70; Academic Adv. Council, MoD, 1969–76; Standing Conf. on Univ. Entrance, 1968–75. Pres., Assoc. of Teachers in Colls and Depts of Educn, 1964–72, Hon. Mem., 1972; Vice-Pres., Arts Council of NI, 1966–76. Member: Adv. Council on Bldg Research, Min. of Works, 1955–59; Scientific Adv. Council, Min. of Supply, 1956–59; UGC, 1959–66; Colonial Univ. Grants Adv. Cttee, 1960–65; Adv. Council on Research and Develt, Min. of Power, 1960–63; Nuclear Safety Adv. Cttee, Min. of Power, 1960–66; Governing Body, Nat. Inst. for Research in Nuclear Science, 1964–65. MRIA 1973. Hon. DSc: Keele, 1972; NUI, 1976; Birmingham, 1988; Hon. LLD: Dublin, 1973; Belfast, 1977; Hon. DCL Kent, 1977. Kt Comdr, Liberian Humane Order of African Redemption, 1962. *Publications:* various scientific papers and contributions to books. *Recreations:* music, gardening, using tools. *Address:* Fieldhead Cottage, Fieldhead Lane, Myton Road, Warwick CV34 6QF. *T:* Warwick (0926) 491822. *Clubs:* Athenæum, Savile.

VICK, His Honour Richard (William); a Circuit Judge (formerly County Court Judge), 1969–89; Senior Circuit Judge in England and Wales, 1987–89; Judge, Wandsworth County Court, 1985–89; Honorary Recorder of Guildford, since 1973; *b* 9 Dec. 1917; *s* of late Richard William Vick, JP, and Hilda Josephine (*née* Carlton), Windsor, Berks; *m* 1st, 1947, Judith Jean Warren (*d* 1974); one *s* two *d*; 2nd, 1975, Mrs Joan Chesney Frost, BA, *d* of Arthur Blaney Powe, MA, Sydney, Australia. *Educ:* Stowe; Jesus Coll., Cambridge (BA Hons). Served in RNVR, 1939–46: i/c Coastal Forces, Western Approaches, Mediterranean and N Sea. Called to Bar, Inner Temple, 1940. Partner, R. W. Vick Jr & Co., Lloyd's Insurance Brokers, 1944–46; Associate Mem. of Lloyd's, 1944–46; Deputy Chairman: W Kent QS, 1960–62; Kent QS, 1962–65; QS for Middx Area of Gtr London, 1965–69; Resident Judge, 1978–83, Liaison Judge for Magistrates, 1979–83, Kingston Gp of Courts. Chm., London Gp of County Court Judges, 1983–89. Vice-Chm., Surrey Magistrates Soc., 1972–83; Member: Magistrates' Courts Cttee; Probation Cttee, 1972–83; Circuit Adviser, Judicial Studies Bd, 1981–83. *Publication:* The Administration of Civil Justice in England and Wales, 1967. *Recreations:* sailing, swimming, bridge. *Address:* 18 Ibis Lane, Chiswick, W4 3UP. *Clubs:* Savage; Hawks (Cambridge); Bar Yacht; Royal Naval Sailing Association (Portsmouth).

VICKERMAN, Prof. Keith, FRS 1984; FRSE 1971; Regius Professor of Zoology, University of Glasgow, since 1984; *b* 21 March 1933; *s* of Jack Vickerman and Mabel Vickerman (*née* Dyson); *m* 1961, Moira Dutton, LLB; one *d*. *Educ:* King James' Grammar School, Almondbury; University College London (Fellow, 1985). BSc 1955; PhD 1960; DSc 1970. Wellcome Trust Lectr, Zoology Dept, UCL, 1958–63; Royal Soc. Tropical Res. Fellow, UCL, 1963–68; Glasgow University: Reader in Zoology, 1968–74; Prof., 1974–; Head of Dept of Zoology, 1979–85. Mem., WHO Panel of Consultant Experts on Parasitic Diseases, 1973–. *Publications:* The Protozoa (with F. E. G. Cox), 1967; numerous papers on protozoa (esp. trypanosomes) in scientific and med. jls. *Recreations:* sketching, gardening. *Address:* Department of Zoology, University of Glasgow, Glasgow G12 8QQ. *T:* 041–339 8855, *Fax:* 041–307 8016; 16 Mirrlees Drive, Glasgow G12 0SH. *T:* 041–334 2794.

VICKERS, family name of **Baroness Vickers.**

VICKERS, Baroness *cr* 1974 (Life Peer), of Devonport; **Joan Helen Vickers,** DBE 1964 (MBE 1946); *e d* of late Horace Cecil Vickers and late Lilian Monro Lambert Grose. *Educ:* St Monica's Coll., Burgh Heath, Surrey. Member, LCC, Norwood Division of Lambeth, 1937–45. Contested (C) South Poplar, 1945. Served with British Red Cross in SE Asia (MBE); Colonial Service in Malaya, 1946–50. MP (C) Plymouth, Devonport, 1955–Feb. 1974; UK Delegate (C), Council of Europe and WEU, 1967–74. Chairman: Anglo-Indonesian Society; UK Delegate, UK Status of Women Commn, 1960–64; President: Status of Women Cttee; Internat. Friendship League; Inst. of Qualified Private Secretaries; Europe China Assoc. Chm., National Centre for Cued Speech. Netherlands Red Cross Medal. *Address:* The Manor House, East Chisenbury, Pewsey, Wilts.

VICKERS, Eric, CB 1979; Director of Defence Services, Department of the Environment, 1972–81; *b* 25 April 1921; *s* of late Charles Vickers and late Ida Vickers; *m* 1945, Barbara Mary Jones; one *s* one *d*. *Educ:* King's School, Grantham. Joined India Office, 1938; RAF (Fl/Lt Coastal Command), 1941–46; Ministry of Works, 1948; Principal, 1950; Assistant Secretary, 1962; Imperial Defence College, 1969; Dir of Home Estate Management, DoE, 1970–72. *Recreation:* photography, caravanning. *Address:* 46 Stamford Road, Oakham, Rutland, Leicestershire LE15 6JA. *T:* Oakham (0572) 724166.

VICKERS, James Oswald Noel, OBE 1977; General Secretary, Civil Service Union, 1963–77 (Deputy General Secretary, 1960–62); *b* 6 April 1916; *s* of Noel Muschamp and Linda Vickers; *m* 1940, Winifred Mary Lambert; one *s* one *d*. *Educ:* Stowe Sch.; Queens' Coll., Cambridge. Exhibnr, BA Hons Hist., MA. Served War, HM Forces, 1939–45. Warden, Wedgwood Memorial Coll., 1946–49; Educn Officer, ETU, and Head of Esher Coll., 1949–56. Member: Civil Service Nat. Whitley Council, 1962–77 (Chm. Staff Side, 1975–77); TUC Inter-Union Disputes Panel, 1970–77; TUC Non-Manual Workers Adv. Cttee, 1973–75; Fabian Soc. Trade Union and Industrial Relations Cttee, 1964–81 (Chm. 1973–78; Vice-Chm., 1978–79); UCL Coll. Cttee, 1974–79; Council, Tavistock Inst., 1976–80; Employment Appeal Tribunal, 1978–86; CS Appeal Bd, 1978–86. *Publications:* contrib. to Fabian pamphlets. *Recreations:* bird-watching, gardening, travel. *Address:* 5 The Butts, Brentford, Mddx TW8 8BJ. *T:* 081–560 3482; Heber Vale Cottage, Timberscombe, near Minehead, Som.

VICKERS, Prof. John Stuart; Drummond Professor of Political Economy, Oxford University, and Fellow of All Souls College, since 1991; *b* 7 July 1958; *s* of Aubrey and Kay Vickers; *m* 1991, Maureen Freed. *Educ:* Eastbourne Grammar Sch.; Oriel Coll., Oxford (BA PPE 1979); MPhil Econs Oxon 1983; DPhil Econs Oxon 1985. Financial Analyst, Shell UK, 1979–81; Fellow, All Souls Coll., Oxford, 1979–84; Roy Harrod Fellow in Economics of Business and Public Policy, Nuffield Coll., Oxford, 1984–90. Vis. Fellow, Princeton, 1988; Vis. Lectr, Harvard, 1989, 1990. Asst Editor, Review of Economic Studies, 1988–. *Publications:* (jtly) Privatisation and the Natural Monopolies, 1985; (ed jtly) The Economics of Market Dominance, 1987; (jtly) Privatization: an economic analysis, 1988; (ed jtly) The Politics of Privatisation in Western Europe, 1989; articles in econ. jls on industrial organisation, regulation, technological competition. *Address:* All Souls College, Oxford. *T:* Oxford (0865) 279379; 33 Folly Bridge Court, Oxford.

VICKERS, Jon, CC (Canada) 1968; dramatic tenor; *b* Prince Albert, Saskatchewan, 1926; *m* 1953, Henrietta Outerbridge; three *s* two *d*. Studied under George Lambert, Royal Conservatory of Music, Toronto. Made debut with Toronto Opera Company, 1952; Stratford (Ontario) Festival, 1956. Joined Royal Opera House, Covent Garden, 1957. First sang at: Bayreuth Festival, 1958; Vienna State Opera, San Francisco Opera, and Chicago Lyric, 1959; Metropolitan, New York, and La Scala, Milan, 1960; Buenos Aires, 1962; Salzburg Festival, 1966; appeared in other opera houses of Argentina, Austria, Brazil, France, Germany, Greece, Mexico and USA. *Films:* Carmen; Pagliacci; Otello; Norma; Peter Grimes; Fidelio; Samson et Delilah. Has made many recordings. Presbyterian. Hon. Dr: University of Saskatchewan, 1963; Bishop's Univ., 1965; Univ. West Ontario, 1970; Brandon Univ., 1976; Laval Univ., 1977; Univ. of Guelph, 1978; Illinois, 1983; Queens, Canada, 1984; Toronto, 1987. RAM 1977. Canada Centennial Medal, 1967; Critics' Award, London, 1978; Grammy Award, 1979. *Address:* c/o Co-Concert, 376/9 Strand, WC2R 0LR.

VICKERS, Prof. Michael Douglas Allen; Professor of Anaesthetics, University of Wales College of Medicine (formerly Welsh National School of Medicine), since 1976; *b* 11 May 1929; *s* of George and Freda Vickers; *m* 1959, Ann Hazel Courtney; two *s* one *d*. *Educ:* Abingdon Sch.; Guy's Hosp. Med. Sch. MB, BS; FFARCS; FRSM. Lectr, RPMS, 1965–68; Consultant Anaesthetist, Birmingham AHA, 1968–76. Mem. Bd, Faculty of Anaesthetists, 1971–85; President: Assoc. of Anaesthetists of GB and Ireland, 1982–84 (Hon. Sec., 1974–76; John Snow Lectr, 1982); European Acad. of Anaesthesiology, 1988– (Sec., 1982–84, Pres., 1988–91); Chm., Exec. Cttee, World Fedn of Socs of Anaesthesiologists, 1988–92. Hon. FFARACS. Editor, European Journal of Anaesthesiology, 1983–. *Publications:* (jtly) Principles of Measurement for Anaesthetists, 1970 (2nd edn, as Principles of Measurement, 1981, 3rd edn 1991); (jtly) Drugs in Anaesthetic Practice, 3rd edn 1968, to 7th edn 1991; Medicine for Anaesthetists, 1977, 3rd edn 1989. *Recreations:* music, theatre. *Address:* Department of Anaesthetics, University of Wales College of Medicine, Heath Park, Cardiff CF4 4XN. *T:* Cardiff (0222) 755944.

VICKERS, Rt. Rev. Michael Edwin; *see* Colchester, Area Bishop of.

VICKERS, Lt-Gen. Sir Richard (Maurice Hilton), KCB 1983; LVO 1959; OBE 1970 (MBE 1964); Director General Winston Churchill Memorial Trust, since 1983; a Gentleman Usher to the Queen, since 1986; *b* 21 Aug. 1928; *s* of Lt-Gen. W. G. H. Vickers, CB, OBE; *m* 1957, Gaie, *d* of Maj.-Gen. G. P. B. Roberts, *qv*; three *d*. *Educ:* Haileybury and Imperial Service Coll.; RMA. Commissioned Royal Tank Regt, 1948; 1st RTR, BAOR, Korea, Middle East, 1948–54; Equerry to HM The Queen, 1956–59; Brigade Major, 7 Armd Bde, 1962–64; 4th RTR, Borneo and Malaysia, 1964–66; CO The Royal Dragoons, 1967–68, The Blues and Royals, 1968–69; Comdr, 11th Armd Brigade, 1972–74; Dep. Dir of Army Training, 1975–77; GOC 4th Armoured Div., 1977–79; Comdt, RMA, 1979–82; Dir-Gen. of Army Training, 1982–83. *Recreations:* squash, flyfishing. *Club:* Cavalry and Guards.

VICKERS, Thomas Douglas, CMG 1956; *b* 25 Sept. 1916; 2nd *s* of late Ronald Vickers, Scaitcliffe, Englefield Green, Surrey; *m* 1951, Margaret Awdry, *o c* of late E. A. Headley, Wagga, NSW; one *s* one *d*. *Educ:* Eton; King's Coll., Cambridge (MA Hons). Cadet, Colonial Administrative Service, 1938. Served War of 1939–45; Coldstream Guards, 1940–45. Colonial Office, 1938–40 and 1945–50; Gold Coast, 1950–53; Colonial Secretary, British Honduras, 1953–60; Chief Secretary, Mauritius, 1960–67, Dep. Governor, 1967–68; retired from HMOCS, Oct. 1968. Head of Personnel Services, Imperial Cancer Research Fund, 1969–81. *Address:* Wood End, Worplesdon, Surrey GU3 3RJ. *T:* Worplesdon (0483) 233468. *Club:* Army and Navy.

VICKERS, Dr Tony; Project Manager, UK Human Genome Mapping Project, since 1990; *b* 6 July 1932; *s* of Harry and Frances Vickers; *m* 1964, Anne Dorothy Wallis (marr. diss. 1986); two *d*. *Educ:* Manchester Grammar Sch.; Sidney Sussex Coll., Cambridge (MA, PhD). University of Cambridge: Demonstrator, 1956; Lectr in Physiology, 1961–72; Fellow, Sidney Sussex Coll., 1956–70; Headquarters Office, MRC, 1972–84 (Head of Medical Div., 1980–84); UK Administrator, Ludwig Inst. for Cancer Res., 1985–89. Member of Council: BAAS, 1969–72, 1982–85 (Pres., Biomed. Scis Sect., 1977); Cancer Res. Campaign, 1980–85 (Mem., Scientific Cttee, 1979–85); Paterson Labs, Manchester, 1984–85. Chm., Tenovus Sci. Adv. Cttee, 1987–. Governor, Beatson Inst., Glasgow, 1983–85. *Address:* HGMP Resource Centre, Clinical Research Centre, Watford Road, Harrow, Middx HA1 3UJ. *T:* 081–869 3446.

VICKERY, Prof. Brian Campbell, FLA, FIInfSc; Professor of Library Studies and Director, School of Library Archive and Information Studies, University College London, 1973–83, now Professor Emeritus; *b* 11 Sept. 1918; *s* of Adam Cairns McCay and Violet Mary Watson; *m* 1st, 1945, Manuletta McMenamin; one *s* one *d*; 2nd, 1970, Alina Gralewska. *Educ:* King's Sch., Canterbury; Brasenose Coll., Oxford. MA. Chemist, Royal Ordnance Factory, Somerset, 1941–45; Librarian, ICI Ltd, Welwyn, 1946–60; Principal Scientific Officer, Nat. Lending Library for Sci. and Technology, 1960–64; Librarian, UMIST, 1964–66; Head of R&D, Aslib, 1966–73. *Publications:* Classification and Indexing in Science, 1958, 3rd edn 1975; On Retrieval System Theory, 1961, 2nd edn 1965; Techniques of Information Retrieval, 1970; Information Systems, 1973; Information Science, 1987; articles in professional jls. *Recreations:* reading history, poetry, philosophy; music and theatre; personal computing. *Address:* 138 Midhurst Road, W13 9TP. *T:* 081–567 6544.

VICTOR, Ed; Chairman and Managing Director, Ed Victor Ltd, since 1977; *b* 9 Sept. 1939; *s* of Jack Victor and Lydia Victor; *m* 1st, 1963, Michelene Dinah Samuels (marr. diss.); two *s*; 2nd, 1980, Carol Lois Ryan; one *s*. *Educ:* Dartmouth Coll. USA (BA *summa cum laude* 1961); Pembroke Coll., Cambridge (MLitt 1963). Began as art books editor, later editorial Dir, Weidenfeld & Nicolson, 1964–67; editorial Dir, Jonathan Cape Ltd, 1967–71; Senior Editor, Alfred A. Knopf Inc., NY, 1972–73; literary agent and Dir, John Farquharson Ltd (lit. agents), 1974–76; founded Ed Victor Ltd (lit. agency), 1977. Dir, Groucho Club PLC, 1988–. *Recreations:* running, tennis, travel, opera. *Address:* 10 Cambridge Gate, Regent's Park, NW1. *T:* 071–224 3030; The South Cottage, Sissinghurst Castle, Sissinghurst, Kent. *Club:* Groucho.

VICUÑA, Francisco O.; *see* Orrego-Vicuña.

VIDAL, Gore; author; *b* 3 Oct. 1925; *s* of Eugene and Nina Gore Vidal. *Educ:* Phillips Exeter Academy, New Hampshire, USA (grad. 1943). Army of the US, 1943–46: Private to Warrant Officer (jg) and First Mate, Army FS-35, Pacific Theatre Ops. Democratic-Liberal candidate for US Congress, 1960; candidate for Democratic nomination for election to US Senate from California, 1982. Apptd to President Kennedy's Adv. Council of the Arts, 1961–63. *Publications: novels:* Williwaw, 1946; In a Yellow Wood, 1947; The City and the Pillar, 1948; The Season of Comfort, 1949; A Search for the King, 1950; Dark Green, Bright Red, 1950; The Judgment of Paris, 1952; Messiah, 1954; Julian, 1964; Washington, DC, 1967; Myra Breckinridge, 1968 (filmed 1969); Two Sisters, 1970; Burr, 1973; Myron, 1975; 1876, 1976; Kalki, 1978; Creation, 1981; Duluth, 1983; Lincoln, 1984; Empire, 1987; Hollywood, 1989; *essays:* Rocking the Boat, 1962; Reflections upon a Sinking Ship, 1969; Homage to Daniel Shays (collected essays 1952–72), 1972; Matters of Fact and of Fiction, 1977; The Second American Revolution (UK title, Pink Triangle and Yellow Star and other essays (1976–1982)), 1982; Armageddon?, 1987; At Home, 1988; *short stories:* A Thirsty Evil, 1956; *travel:* Vidal in Venice, 1987; *plays:* Visit to a Small Planet (NY prod.), 1957; The Best Man (NY prod.), 1960; Romulus (adapted from F. Dürrenmatt) (NY prod.), 1962; Weekend (NY prod.), 1968; On the March to the Sea (German prod.), 1962; An Evening with Richard Nixon (NY prod.), 1972; *screenplays,* from 1955: Wedding Breakfast, 1957; Suddenly Last Summer, 1958; The Best Man, 1964, etc; *television plays:* 1954–56: The Death of Billy the Kid (translated to screen as The Lefthanded Gun, 1959, and as Gore Vidal's Billy the Kid, 1989), etc; *literary and political criticism for:* NY Review of Books, Esquire, Partisan Review, TLS, etc. *Recreations:* as noted above. *Address:* La Rondinaia, Ravello, (Salerno), Italy. *Club:* Athenæum.

VIDIC, Dobrivoje, Order of Yugoslav Flag 1st class; Order of Service to the People; Order of Brotherhood and Unity 1st class; Order for Bravery; Partisan Remembrance Medal 1941; Member of Presidium, 1982–90, and Chairman of the Commission for International Relations, 1986–90, Central Committee of League of Communists of Yugoslavia; *b* 24 Dec. 1918; *m* 1941, Mrs Vukica; one *s. Educ:* Skoplje University. Diplomatic Service, 1951–86: served as: Minister Counsellor, London; Ambassador to Burma; Ambassador to USSR; Under-Sec. of State for Foreign Affairs; Perm. Rep. to UN, New York; Chm., Commn for Internat. Relations of Socialist Alliance of Yugoslavia; Ambassador to USSR; Ambassador of Yugoslavia to the Court of St James's, 1970–73. Mem. Exec. Cttee of Presidium, Central Cttee of League of Communists of Yugoslavia, 1974–79; Pres. of Presidium, Socialist Republic of Serbia, 1978–82; Chm., Commn for Internat. Relations, League of Communists of Yugoslavia, 1986–. *Address:* Central Committee of League of Communists of Yugoslavia, Bulaver Lengina 6, Belgrade, Yugoslavia.

VIELER, Geoffrey Herbert, FCA; Member of Board, Post Office Corporation, 1969–71; *b* 21 Aug. 1910; *s* of late Herbert Charles Stuart Vieler, Huddersfield, and Emily Mary; *m* 1934, Phyllis Violet; one *d. Educ:* Fairway Sch., Bexhill-on-Sea. With Vale & West, Chartered Accountants, Reading, 1927–41 (qual. 1932); War Service, 1941–46: commnd RAOC, 1943, Major 1945; joined Binder Hamlyn, Chartered Accountants, 1946, Partner 1959–69; Managing Dir, Posts and National Giro, 1969–71. Member: Techn. Adv. Cttee, Inst. of Chartered Accountants in England and Wales, 1967–74; Special Cttee, Tax Law Consultative Bodies, 1986–. Chm., London Chartered Accountants, 1976–77; Chm., Taxation Cttee, ABCC, 1985–91. *Address:* Robins Wood, Monks Drive, South Ascot, Berks SL5 9BB; Riversmeet, Mill Lane, Lower Shiplake RG9 3LY.

VIERTEL, Deborah Kerr; see Kerr, D. J.

VIGARS, Della, (Mrs Paul Vigars); see Jones, D.

VIGARS, Robert Lewis; *b* 26 May 1923; *s* of late Francis Henry Vigars and Susan Laurina May Vigars (*née* Lewis); *m* 1962, Margaret Ann Christine, *y d* of late Sir John Walton, KCIE, CB, MC, and Lady Walton; two *d. Educ:* Truro Cathedral Sch.; London Univ. (LLB (Hons)). Served War of 1939–45: RA and Royal Corps of Signals, 1942–47; attached Indian Army (Captain), 1944–47; Captain, Princess Louise's Kensington Regt, TA, 1951–54. Qualified as solicitor (Hons), 1948. Partner, Simmons & Simmons, London, EC2, 1951–75. Member: Kensington Borough Council, 1953–59; London and Home Counties Traffic Adv. Cttee, 1956–58; London Roads (Nugent) Cttee, 1958–59; LCC and GLC Kensington (formerly South Kensington), 1955–86; Environmental Planning Cttee, GLC, 1967–71 (Chm.); Strategic Planning Cttee, GLC, 1971–73 (Chm.); Leader of Opposition, ILEA, 1974–79; Chm. of the GLC, 1979–80; Mem., Standing Conf. on London and SE Regional Planning and SE Economic Planning Council, 1968–75. Gen. Comr of Income Tax (Highbury), 1988–; Mem., Central London Valuation and Community Charge Tribunal, 1989–. Mem., Historic Buildings and Monuments Commn for England, 1986–88 (Mem., London Adv. Cttee, 1986– (Chm. 1986–88)). Mem. Court, London Univ., 1977–82. *Recreation:* mountain walking. *Address:* 24 Cope Place, Kensington, W8 6AA. *Club:* Hurlingham.

VIGGERS, Peter John; MP (C) Gosport, since Feb. 1974; *b* 13 March 1938; *s* of late J. S. Viggers and E. F. Viggers (later Mrs V. E. J. Neal), Gosport; *m* 1968, Jennifer Mary McMillan, MB, BS, LRCP, MRCS, DA, *d* of late Dr R. B. McMillan, MD, FRCP, Guildford, and late Mrs J. T. C. McMillan, MA, MIB; two *s* one *d. Educ:* Portsmouth Grammar Sch.; Trinity Hall, Cambridge (MA). Solicitor 1967. Trained as RAF Pilot with Royal Canadian Air Force, awarded Wings 1958. Cambridge, 1958–61; Chm. Cambridge Univ. Conservative Assoc., 1960. Commnd in 457 (Wessex) Regt Royal Artillery (TA), 1963. PPS to Solicitor-General, 1979–83, to Chief Sec. of HM Treasury, 1983–85; Parly Under-Sec. of State (Industry Minister), NI Office, 1986–89. Chm., Select Cttee on Armed Forces Bill, 1986. Atlantic Assembly, 1981–86; Vice-Chm., Cons. Energy Cttee, 1977–79 (a Sec., 1975–76). Dir, Premier Consolidated Oilfields Ltd, 1973–86, and others cos; Chm., Britannia Cablesystems Solent, 1989–, and other cos. Underwriting Member of Lloyd's. Chairman: Campaign for Defence and Multilateral Disarmament, 1984–86; Cttee for Peace with Freedom, 1984–86; UK Deleg., Jt IPU and UN Conf. on Conventional Disarmament, Mexico City, 1985. Mem., Management Cttee, RNLI, 1979–89, Vice-Pres., 1989——. *Recreations:* walking, reading, country pursuits. *Address:* House of Commons, SW1A 0AA.

VIGNOLES, Roger Hutton, ARCM; pianoforte accompanist; *b* 12 July 1945; *s* of late Keith Hutton Vignoles and of Phyllis Mary (*née* Pearson); *m* 1st, 1972, Teresa Ann Elizabeth Henderson (marr. diss. 1982); 2nd, 1982, Jessica Virginia, *d* of Prof. Boris Ford, *qv*; one *d. Educ:* Canterbury Cathedral Choir Sch.; Sedbergh Sch.; Magdalene Coll., Cambridge (BA, BMus); Royal College of Music, London (ARCM). Accompanist of national and internat. reputation, regularly appearing with the most distinguished internat. singers and instrumentalists, both in London and provinces and at major music festivals (eg Aldeburgh, Cheltenham, Edinburgh, Brighton, Bath, Salzburg, Prague, etc) and broadcasting for BBC Radio 3 and television. International tours incl. USA, Canada, Australia-New Zealand, Hong Kong, Scandinavia, and recitals at Opera Houses of Cologne, 1982, Brussels, 1983, Frankfurt, 1984, Lincoln Center, NY, 1985, San Francisco, 1986, Tokyo, 1985 and 1987, Carnegie Hall, NY, 1988. Repetiteur: Royal Opera House,

Covent Garden, 1969–71; English Opera Group, 1968–74; Australian Opera Company, 1976. Professor of Accompaniment, RCM, 1974–81. Gramophone records include English songs and works by Schumann, Brahms, Dvorak, Britten, Gershwin, Dankworth, Franck, Grieg, and Parry and the première recording of Nicholas Maw's The Voice of Love. Hon. RAM 1984. *Recreations:* drawing, painting, looking at pictures, swimming, sailing. *Address:* 1 Ascham Street, Kentish Town, NW5 2PB. *T:* 071–267 3187.

VILE, Prof. Maurice John Crawley; Director of British Programmes, Boston University, since 1989; Professor Emeritus of Political Science, University of Kent at Canterbury; *b* 23 July 1927; *s* of Edward M. and Elsie M. Vile; two *s. Educ:* London Sch. of Economics. BSc (Econ) 1951; PhD London, 1954; MA Oxford, 1962. FRHistS 1989. Lectr in Politics, Univ. of Exeter, 1954–62; Fellow of Nuffield Coll., Oxford, 1962–65; University of Kent: Reader in Politics and Govt, 1965–68; Prof. of Political Sci., 1968–84; Dir of Internat. Progs, 1984–87; Dean of Faculty of Social Scis, 1969–75; Pro-Vice-Chancellor, 1975–81; Dep. Vice-Chancellor, 1981–84. Visiting Professor: Univ. of Massachusetts, 1960; Smith College, Mass., 1961. Royer Lectr, Univ. of Calif., Berkeley, 1974. *Publications:* The Structure of American Federalism, 1961; Constitutionalism and the Separation of Powers, 1967; Politics in the USA, 1970, 4th edn 1987; Federalism in the United States, Canada and Australia (Res. Paper No 2, Commn on the Constitution), 1973; The Presidency (Amer. Hist. Documents Vol. IV), 1974. *Address:* Little Cob, Garlinge Green, Petham, Canterbury, Kent CT4 5RT. *T:* Canterbury (0277) 70432. *Club:* United Oxford & Cambridge University.

VILJOEN, Marais, DMS 1976; State President of the Republic of South Africa, 1979–84; *b* 2 Dec. 1915; *s* of Gabriel François Viljoen and Magdalena Debora (*née* de Villiers); *m* 1940, Dorothea Maria Brink; one *d. Educ:* Jan van Riebeeck High Sch., Cape Town; Univ. of Cape Town. After leaving school, employed in Dept of Posts and Telegraphs, 1932–37; on editorial staff, Die Transvaler newspaper, 1937–40; manager, Transvaler book trade business, Potchefstroom, 1940; co-founder and provincial leader of Nat. Youth League, 1940–45; organiser of Transvaal National Party, 1945–49; Member, Provincial Council, Transvaal, 1949–53; Information Officer, Transvaal National Party, several years from 1951; Chairman, Inf. Service of Federal Council, National Party of S Africa, 1969–74; Dep. Chm., Nat. Party, Transvaal, 1966–75. MP Alberton, 1953–76; Dep. Minister of Labour and of Mines, 1958–61; various other ministerial offices, incl. Interior and Immigration, until 1966; Cabinet appointments, 1966–: Minister of Labour and of Coloured Affairs, 1966–69, also of Rehoboth Affairs, 1969–70; Minister of Labour and of Posts and Telecommunications, 1970–76. President of the Senate, 1976–79. Special Cl., Grand Collar, Order of Good Hope, Republic of S Africa, 1981. *Recreations:* golf, bowls, reading. *Address:* PO Box 5555, Pretoria, 0001, Republic of South Africa.

VILLIERS; see Child Villiers, family name of Earl of Jersey.

VILLIERS; see de Villiers.

VILLIERS, family name of **Earl of Clarendon.**

VILLIERS, Viscount; George Henry Child Villiers; guitarist and composer; *b* 29 Aug. 1948; *s* and *heir* of 9th Earl of Jersey, *qv*; *m* 1st, 1969, Verna (marr. diss. 1973), 2nd *d* of K. A. Stott, St Mary, Jersey; one *d*; 2nd, 1974, Sandra (marr. diss. 1988), step *d* of H. Briginshaw, Feremina, St Martin, Guernsey; one *s* two *d. Educ:* Eton; Millfield. Late The Royal Hussars (PWO). Leader, George Villiers Express. *Publication:* (ed) Classic Duets for Guitar. *Heir: s* Hon. George Francis William Child Villiers, *b* 5 Feb. 1976. *Address:* Little Forder, Cott Road, Dartington, Devon TQ9 6HQ; Radier Manor Cottage, Longueville, Jersey, CI.

VILLIERS, Sir Charles (Hyde), Kt 1975; MC 1945; Director: W. C. Norris Institute, Minneapolis, since 1989; Chairman, Theatre Royal, Windsor; *b* 14 Aug. 1912; *s* of Algernon Hyde Villiers (killed in action, 1917) and Beatrix Paul (later Lady Aldenham) (*d* 1978); *m* 1st, 1938, Pamela Constance Flower (*d* 1943); one *s*; 2nd, 1946, Marie José, *d* of Count Henri de la Barre d'Erquelinnes, Jurbise, Belgium; two *d. Educ:* Eton; New Coll., Oxford. Asst to Rev. P. B. Clayton, of Toc H, 1931; Glyn Mills, Bankers, 1932. Grenadier Guards (SRO), 1936; served at Dunkirk, 1940 (wounded, 1942); Special Ops Exec., London and Italy, 1943–45; parachuted into Yugoslavia and Austria, 1944; Lt-Col and Comd 6 Special Force Staff Section, 1945 (MC). A Man. Dir, Helbert Wagg, 1948, and J. Henry Schroder Wagg, 1960–68; Managing Director, Industrial Reorganisation Corporation, 1968–71; Chm., Guinness Mahon & Co. Ltd, 1971–76; Exec. Dep. Chm., Guinness Peat Gp, 1973–76; Chairman: British Steel Corp., 1976–80; BSC (Industry), 1977–89. Formerly Director: Bass Charrington; Courtaulds; Sun Life Assurance; Banque Belge; Financor SA; Darling & Co. (Pty); European Industrial Equity Co. SA, 1986–; W. C. Norris Inst., Minneapolis; Formerly Chm., Ashdown Trans-Europe and Trans-Australian Investment Trusts. Chairman: Federal Trust Gp on European Monetary Integration, 1972; Northern Ireland Finance Corp., 1972–73. Chm., 13th Internat. Small Business Congress, 1986–87; Co-Chairman: Europalia Festival, 1973; British-American Project, 1990–. Member: Inst. Internat. d'Etudes Bancaires, 1959–76 (Pres. 1964); Minister of Labour's Resettlement Cttee for London and SE, 1958 (Chm. 1961–68); Review Body for N Ireland Economic Develt, 1971; NEDC, 1976–80. Lubbock Meml Lectr, Oxford, 1971. Mem., Chelsea Borough Council, 1950–53. Order of the People, Yugoslavia, 1970; Grand Officier de l'Ordre de Léopold II (Belgium), 1974; Gold Medal of IRI, Italy, 1975. *Publication:* Start again, Britain, 1984. *Recreation:* gardening. *Address:* Blacknest House, Sunninghill, Berks SL5 0PS. *T:* Ascot (0344) 22137.

VILLIERS, Charles Nigel, FCA; Managing Director of Corporate Development, Abbey National plc (formerly Abbey National Building Society), since 1988; Director (non executive), Conder Group plc, since 1989; *b* 25 Jan. 1941; *s* of Robert Alexander and Elizabeth Mary Villiers; *m* 1970, Sally Priscilla Magnay; one *s* one *d. Educ:* Winchester Coll.; New Coll., Oxford (MA German and Russian). Arthur Andersen & Co., 1963–67; ICFC, 1967–72; County Bank Ltd, 1972–86; Dir, 1974; Dep. Chief Exec., 1977; Chm. and Chief Exec., 1984–85; Exec. Chm., 1985–86; Exec. Dir, National Westminster Bank, 1985–88; Chief Exec., NatWest Investment Bank Ltd (estab. June 1986 incorporating the business of County Bank Ltd), 1986–88; Chm., County NatWest Ltd, 1986–88. *Recreations:* opera, squash, ski-ing, tennis. *Clubs:* Hurlingham, Institute of Directors.

VINCENT, Anthony Lionel; Australian Ambassador to the Czech and Slovak Federal Republic, since 1990; *b* 18 Oct. 1933; *s* of Harold Francis Vincent and Lesley Allison Vincent; *m* 1958, Helen Frances Beasley; one *s* one *d. Educ:* Univ. of Western Australia, Perth (LLB); Univ. of Oxford (BCL). Joined Dept of Foreign Affairs, Aust., 1958; served: Karachi, 1959–61; Hong Kong, 1963–66; Singapore, 1966–69; Belgrade, 1972–74; Paris, 1977–80; Australian Ambassador to: Iraq, 1981–83; GDR, 1984; Dep. High Comr in London, 1984–87; Asst Sec., Treaties and Sea Law Br., 1987–89, Intelligence and Defence Br., 1989–90, Dept of Foreign Affairs and Trade, Canberra. *Recreations:* walking, cycling, reading. *Address:* c/o Department of Foreign Affairs and Trade, Canberra, ACT 2600, Australia. *Club:* Canberra Yacht.

VINCENT, Maj.-Gen. Douglas, CB 1969; OBE 1954; Director, Alcatel Australia, since 1987; *b* Australia, 10 March 1916; *s* of William Frederick Vincent, civil engineer, and

Sarah Jane Vincent; *m* 1947, Margaret Ector, *d* of N. W. Persse, Melbourne; two *s* one *d.* *Educ*: Brisbane State High School; Royal Military Coll., Duntroon. Commissioned, Dec. 1938; Middle East (7 Div.), 1940–42; BLA, 1944; NW Europe (30 Corps); Borneo Campaign, 1945; Brit. Commonwealth Forces, Korea, 1954; Dir of Signals, 1954–58; Dir of Staff Duties, 1958–60; Chief of Staff, Eastern Command, 1960–62; Commander, Aust. Army Force, 1962–63 (Singapore, Malaya); idc 1964; Commander: 1 Task Force, 1965; 1st Div., 1966; Aust. Force, Vietnam, 1967–68; Head, Aust. Jt Services Staff, Washington, DC, USA, 1968–70; Adjutant General, Australian Army, 1970–73. Mem. Nat. Exec., RSL (Defence Adviser, 1975–). SMIREE(Aust). *Recreations*: golf, swimming. *Address*: 41 Hampton Circuit, Yarralumla, Canberra, ACT 2600, Australia.

VINCENT, Prof. Ewart Albert; Professor of Geology, and Fellow of University College, Oxford, 1967–86, now Emeritus; *b* 23 Aug. 1919; *o s* of Albert and Winifred Vincent, Aylesbury; *m* 1944, Myrtle Ablett; two *d. Educ*: Reading Sch.; Univ. of Reading. BSc (Reading) 1940; PhD 1951; MA (Oxon) 1952; MSc (Manch.) 1966. FGS. Chemist, Min. of Supply, 1940–45; Geologist, Anglo-Iranian Oil Co., 1945–46; Lectr in Mineralogy and Crystallography, Univ. of Durham, 1946–51; Lectr in Geology, Oxford Univ., 1951–56; Reader in Mineralogy, Oxford Univ., 1956–62; Prof. of Geology, Manchester Univ., 1962–66. Mem. NERC, 1975–78. Vice-Pres., Internat. Assoc. of Volcanology, 1968–71; Pres., Mineralogical Soc. of GB, 1974–76; Mem. Council, Geol Soc., 1973–76. Fellow, Mineralogical Soc. of Amer. Hon. Corresp. Mem., Soc. Géol. de Belgique. Awarded Wollaston Fund, Geol Soc. London, 1961. *Publications*: scientific papers in learned jls. *Recreations*: music, photography. *Address*: 2 Linch Farm, Wytham, Oxford OX2 8QP. *T*: Oxford (0865) 723170; Department of Earth Sciences, Parks Road, Oxford OX1 3PR. *T*: Oxford (0865) 272000.

VINCENT, Rev. Irvin James; Minister, Temple Methodist Church, Taunton, since 1986; *b* 22 July 1932; *s* of Amy Mary Catharine Vincent (*née* Nye) and Vince Thomas Vincent; *m* 1959, Stella Margaret (*née* Chaplin); one *s* two *d. Educ*: Mitcham Grammar School; Didsbury College (Methodist), Bristol. BA Open Univ. Accountancy, 1948; National Service, RAF, 1950–52; Local Govt, 1952–55; theological training, 1955–59; Methodist Circuit, Stonehouse and Dursley, 1959–61; entered RN as Chaplain, 1961; Malta, 1968–72; exchange with USN, 1976–78; Principal Chaplain, Church of Scotland and Free Churches (Navy), 1984–86; QHC, 1984–86. *Recreations*: soccer, cricket, drama, music, gardening. *Address*: Temple Methodist Church, Upper High Street, Taunton, Somerset TA1 3PY. *T*: Taunton (0823) 288662.

VINCENT, Ivor Francis Sutherland, CMG 1966; MBE 1945; HM Diplomatic Service, retired; Hon. Secretary, The Andean Project, since 1983; *b* 14 Oct. 1916; *s* of late Lt-Col Frank Lloyd Vincent and Gladys Clarke; *m* 1949, Patricia Mayne; three *d* (and one *d* decd). *Educ*: St Peter's Coll., Radley; Christ Church, Oxford. Served Indian Army, Royal Garhwal Rifles, 1941–46. Entered HM Foreign Service, 1946; Second Secretary, Foreign Office, 1946–48; First Sec., Buenos Aires, 1948–51; UK Delegn, NATO, Paris, 1951–53; FO, 1954–57; Rabat, 1957–59; Geneva (Disarmt Delegn), 1960; Paris (UK Delegn to OECD), 1960–62; Counsellor, FO, 1962–66; Baghdad, Jan.-June, 1967; Caracas, Oct. 1967–70; Ambassador to Nicaragua, 1970–73; Consul-Gen., Melbourne, 1973–76, retired. Dir, Fairbridge Soc. (Inc.), 1978–83. *Recreations*: music, walking. *Address*: c/o Lloyds Bank plc, 7 Pall Mall, SW1Y 5NA. *Club*: Lansdowne.

VINCENT, Rev. Dr John James; Methodist Minister; Superintendent, Sheffield Inner City Ecumenical Mission, and Director, Urban Theology Unit, since 1970; President of the Methodist Conference, 1989–90; *b* 29 Dec. 1929; *s* of late David Vincent and of Ethel Beatrice (*née* Gadd); *m* 1958, Grace Johnston, *d* of Rev. Wilfred Stafford, Bangor, Co. Down; two *s* one *d. Educ*: Manchester Grammar Sch.; Richmond Coll.; London Univ. (BD 1954); Drew Univ., USA (STM 1955); Basel Univ., Switzerland (DTheol 1960). Sgt, RAMC, 1948–49. Minister, Manchester and Salford Mission, 1956–62; Supt, Rochdale Mission, 1962–69; Founder and Leader, The Ashram Community, 1967–. Visiting Professor of Theology: Boston Univ., and New York Theol Seminary, 1969–70; Drew Univ., 1977; Adjunct Prof. of Theol., New York Theol Seminary, 1979–88. Hon. Lectr in Biblical Studies, Sheffield Univ., 1990–. Chairman: NW Campaign for Nuclear Disarmament, 1957–63; Alliance of Radical Methodists, 1970–76; Urban Mission Trng Assoc., 1982–; Trustee Savings Bank Depositors Assoc. (also litigant in High Court and H of L, TSB *v* Vincent), 1986; Director: British Liberation Theol. Project, 1984–; Doctor of Ministry Programme of GB, 1988–; Member: Studiorum Novi Testamenti Societas, 1961–; Council, Christian Orgns for Social, Political and Econ. Change, 1981–91; Exec., Assoc. of Centres of Adult Theol. Educn, 1984–90. *Publications*: Christ in a Nuclear World, 1962; Christian Nuclear Perspective, 1964; Christ and Methodism, 1965; Here I Stand, 1967; Secular Christ, 1968; The Race Race, 1970; The Jesus Thing, 1973; Stirrings: essays Christian and Radical, 1975; Alternative Church, 1976; Disciple and Lord: discipleship in the Synoptic Gospels, 1976; Starting All Over Again, 1981; Into the City, 1982; OK, Let's Be Methodists, 1984; Radical Jesus, 1986; Mark at Work, 1986; Britain in the Nineties, 1989; Discipleship in the Nineties, 1991. *Recreations*: jogging, writing. *Address*: 239 Abbeyfield Road, Sheffield S4 7AW. *T*: Sheffield (0742) 436688, (Urban Theology Unit) Sheffield (0742) 435342.

VINCENT, Prof. John Joseph, MSc, MSc Tech., CText, FTI; Professor of Textile Technology, University of Manchester Institute of Science and Technology, 1957–74, now Emeritus; *b* 29 June 1907; 2nd *s* of J. H. Vincent, MA, DSc; *m* 1935, M. Monica Watson, MSc, PhD, of Sheffield; one *s* one *d. Educ*: County Grammar Sch., Harrow; University Coll., London. Mathematics Dept, University Coll., London, 1927–29; Shirley Inst., Manchester, 1929–42 and 1945–57. Ministry of Aircraft Production, 1942–45. Hon. Life Mem., Textile Institute, 1976 (Mem. Council, 1959–74; Vice-Pres., 1971–74); Pres., British Assoc. of Managers of Textile Works, 1963–64; Mem., Cotton and Allied Textiles Industry Training Bd, 1966–74. Textile Inst. Medal, 1968; Leverhulme Emeritus Fellowship, 1976. *Publications*: Shuttleless Looms, 1980; papers on textile technology. *Recreations*: gardening, reading, listening to music. *Address*: The White House, Perranarworthal, Truro, Cornwall TR3 7QE. *T*: Truro (0872) 863504.
See also J. R. Vincent.

VINCENT, Prof. John Russell; Professor of History, University of Bristol, since 1984; *b* 20 Dec. 1937; *s* of Prof. J. J. Vincent, *qv*; *m* 1972, Nicolette Elizabeth Kenworthy; one *s* (and one *s* decd). *Educ*: Bedales Sch.; Christ's Coll., Cambridge. Lectr in Modern British History, Cambridge Univ., 1967–70; Prof. of Modern History, Univ. of Bristol, 1970–84. Chm., Bristol Br., NCCL, 1972–74. *Publications*: The Formation of the Liberal Party, 1966 (2nd edn as The Formation of the British Liberal Party 1857–68, 1980); Poll Books: How Victorians voted, 1967; (ed with A. B. Cooke) Lord Carlingford's Journal, 1971; (ed with M. Stenton) McCalmont's Parliamentary Poll Book 1832–1918, 1971; (with A. B. Cooke) The Governing Passion: Cabinet Government and party politics in Britain 1885–86, 1974; (ed) Disraeli, Derby and the Conservative Party: the political journals of Lord Stanley 1849–69, 1978; Gladstone and Ireland (Raleigh Lecture), 1979; (ed) The Crawford Papers: the journals of David Lindsay, Twenty-Seventh Earl of Crawford and Tenth Earl of Balcarres during the years 1892 to 1940, 1984; Disraeli, 1990. *Recreation*: journalism. *Address*: History Department, The University, Bristol BS8 1TH.

VINCENT, Leonard Grange, CBE 1960; FRIBA, FRTPI, Distinction Town Planning (RIBA); formerly architect and town planner, and Principal Partner, Vincent and Gorbing, Architects and Planning Consultants; *b* 13 April 1916; *s* of late Godfrey Grange Vincent; *m* 1942, Evelyn (*née* Gretton); twin *s* one *d. Educ*: Forest House School. Trained as architect in London, 1933, and subsequently as a town planner; experience in private practice and local government. Served War of 1939–45: Royal Engineers (Major); mostly overseas, in Western Desert, and Italian campaigns with 8th Army, 1940–45. Formerly Chief Architect and Planner, Stevenage Development Corporation. *Publications*: various technical and planning articles in technical press. *Recreations*: archaeology, painting. *Address*: Medbury, Rectory Lane, Stevenage, Hertfordshire. *T*: Stevenage (0438) 351175.

VINCENT, Field Marshal Sir Richard (Frederick), GBE 1990; KCB 1984; DSO 1972; FIMechE; FRAeS; Chief of the Defence Staff, since 1991; *b* 23 Aug. 1931; *s* of Frederick Vincent and late Frances Elizabeth (*née* Coleshill); *m* 1955, Jean Paterson, *d* of Kenneth Stewart and Jane (*née* Banks); one *s* one *d* (and one *s* decd). *Educ*: Aldenham Sch.; RMCS. Commnd RA, National Service, 1951; Germany, 1951–55; Gunnery Staff, 1959; Radar Res. Estabt, Malvern, 1960–61; BAOR, 1962; Technical Staff Training, 1963–64; Staff Coll., 1965; Commonwealth Bde, Malaysia, 1966–68; MoD, 1968–70; Comd 12th Light Air Def. Regt, Germany, UK and NI, 1970–72; Instr, Staff Coll., 1972–73; Mil. Dir of Studies, RMCS, 1974–75; Comd 19 Airportable Bde, 1975–77; RCDS, 1978; Dep. Mil. Sec., 1979–80; Comdt, Royal Military College of Science, 1980–83; Master-Gen. of the Ordnance, MoD, 1983–87; VCDS, 1987–91. Col Commandant: REME, 1981–87; RA, 1983–; Hon. Colonel: 100 (Yeomanry) Field Regt RA, TA, 1982–91; 12th Air Defence Regt, 1987–91. President: Combined Services Winter Sports Assoc., 1983–90; Army Ski-ing Assoc., 1983–87. Kermit Rooosevelt Lectr, 1988. Member: Court, Cranfield Inst. of Technol., 1981–83; Adv. Council, RMCS, 1983–91; Gov., Aldenham Sch., 1987–. FRAeS 1990; FIMechE 1990. Hon. DSc Cranfield, 1985. *Publications*: contrib. mil. jls and pubns. *Recreations*: travel, reading, film making, theatre. *Address*: c/o Midland Bank, Shaftesbury, Dorset SP7 8JX.

VINCENT, Sir William (Percy Maxwell), 3rd Bt, *cr* 1936; Joint Managing Director, since 1987, and Investment Director, since 1986, Touche, Remnant & Co. and Touche Remnant Holdings; *b* 1 February 1945; *o s* of Sir Lacey Vincent, 2nd Bt, and of Helen Millicent, *d* of Field Marshal Sir William Robert Robertson, 1st Bt, GCB, GCMG, GCVO, DSO; *S* father, 1963; *m* 1976, Christine Margaret, *d* of Rev. E. G. Walton; three *s. Educ*: Eton College. 2nd Lieutenant, Irish Guards, 1964–67. Director: Save and Prosper Investment Management, 1980–85; Touche Remnant & Co., 1985–; Touche Remnant Holdings, 1987–; Société Générale Touche Remnant Asset Management, 1989; Chm., Société Générale Touche Remnant Corp., NY, 1990. *Recreations*: water ski-ing, sailing. *Heir*: *s* Edward Mark William Vincent, *b* 6 March 1978. *Address*: Whistlers, Buriton, Petersfield, Hampshire. *T*: Petersfield (0730) 63532.

VINCENT BROWN, Kenneth; see Brown.

VINCENT-JONES, Captain Desmond, DSC; Royal Navy; retired 1964; *b* 13 Feb. 1912; *s* of late Sir Vincent Jones, KBE; *m* 1944, Jacqueline, *e d* of Col Sloggett, DSO; two *d. Educ*: Beacon School, Crowborough; Royal Naval College, Dartmouth. Served in Royal Navy, 1929–64; War of 1939–45, in aircraft carrier operations in Atlantic and Mediterranean (DSC and Bar); Served in Air Staff appointments and in Command of HM Ships, 1946–64. Graduate of US Armed Forces and British Services Staff Colleges. Naval and Military Attaché to Buenos Aires and Montevideo, 1958–60. On retirement from RN joined Marine Consortiums as consultant. *Recreations*: golf, tennis, fishing, cruising. *Address*: 8 High Street, Chobham, Surrey. *T*: Chobham (0276) 857274. *Clubs*: Free Foresters; Sunningdale Golf.

VINCZE, Paul, FRBS, FRNS; *b* Hungary, 15 August 1907; *s* of Lajos Vincze; British subject, 1948; *m* 1958, Emilienne Chauzeix. *Educ*: High School of Arts and Crafts, Budapest, later under E. Telcs. Won a travelling scholarship to Rome, 1935–37; came to England, 1938. *Exhibited*: Royal Academy, Rome, Budapest, Paris, etc; *works represented in*: British Museum, London; Museum of Fine Arts, Budapest; Ashmolean Museum, Oxford; Swedish Historical Museum; Danish Nat. Museum; Museum of Amer. Numismatic Soc.; Smithsonian Instn, Washington; Cabinet des Medailles, Paris, etc. *Works include*: Aga Khan Platinum Jubilee Portrait; Sir Bernard Pares Memorial Tablet, Senate House, London Univ.; President Truman, portrait medallion; Pope Paul VI, portrait medallion; official medal to commemorate 400th Anniversary of birth of William Shakespeare; medal to commemorate Independence of Ghana; official seal of Ghana Govt; (designed) Smithsonian Instn Award Medal (1965); Nat. Commemorative Society (USA) Winston Churchill Medal; Florence Nightingale Medal for Société Commemorative de Femmes Célèbres; E. and J. De Rothschild Medal for inauguration of Knesset, 1966; Yehudi Menuhin 50th Birthday Medal, 1966; Prince Karim Aga Khan 10th Anniversary Medal, 1968; Cassandra Memorial Tablet for Internat. Publishing Corp. Bldg, 1968; Shakespeare-Garrick Medal, 1969; Medal to commemorate 100th Anniversary of birth of Sir Henry J. Wood, 1969; Dickens 100th Anniversary Medal for Dickens Fellowship, 1970; Medal to commemorate J. B. Priestley's 80th birthday, 1974; Internat. Shakespeare Assoc. Congress Medal, USA, 1976; Self-portrait Medal to commemorate 70th birthday, 1978; Wall Panel illustrating all Shakespeare's plays for new Shakespeare Centre, Stratford-upon-Avon, 1981; Archie F. Carr award medal for Conservation for Florida State Museum, USA; (designed) Amer. Numismatic Assoc. 90th Anniversary Medal, 1981; Karim Aga Khan Silver Jubilee Medal, 1983; portrait-tablets: Harry Guy Bartholomew, Cecil H. King, Lord Cudlipp, for the Mirror's headquarters, 1985. *Coin designs*: obverse and reverses, Libya, 1951; obverses, Guatemala, 1954; reverses, threepence, sixpence and shilling, Cen. African Fedn, 1955; obverses, Ghana, 1958; reverses, Guernsey, 1957; threepence and florin, Nigeria, 1960; Guinea, obverse and reverses, Malawi, 1964; reverse, Uganda crown, 1968; Bustamante Portrait for obverse of Jamaican Dollar, 1969; reverses for decimal coins, Guernsey, 1970, etc. Awarded Premio Especial, Internat. Exhib., Madrid, 1951; Silver Medal, Paris Salon, 1964; first gold Medal of Amer. Numismatic Assoc., 1966. *Address*: Villa La Méridienne, 81 avenue de la Bastide, 06520 Magagnosc, France. *T*: (93) 36.47.54.

VINE, Prof. Frederick John, FRS 1974; Professor of Environmental Sciences, University of East Anglia, since 1974; *b* 17 June 1939; *s* of Frederick Royston Vine and Ivy Grace Vine (*née* Bryant); *m* 1964, Susan Alice McCall; one *s* one *d. Educ*: Latymer Upper Sch., Hammersmith; St John's Coll., Cambridge (BA, PhD). Instructor, 1965–67, and Asst Professor, 1967–70, Dept of Geological and Geophysical Sciences, Princeton Univ., NJ, USA; Reader, School of Environmental Sciences, Univ. of E Anglia, 1970–74. *Publications*: (jtly) Global Tectonics, 1990; articles in Nature, Science, Phil. Trans Roy. Soc. London, etc. *Recreations*: walking, camping. *Address*: 144 Christchurch Road, Norwich NR2 3PG. *T*: Norwich (0603) 53875.

VINE, Philip Mesban, CBE 1981; DL; Member, since 1976, Chairman, 1977–90, New Towns Staff Commission; Member, New Towns Commission, since 1978; *b* 26 Oct. 1919; *s* of late Major George H. M. Vine and Elsie Mary (*née* Shephard), London; *m* 1944, Paulina, JP, *d* of late Arthur Oyler, Great Hormead Hall, Herts; one *s* one *d. Educ*:

Sherborne Sch.; Taft Sch., USA; Sidney Sussex Coll., Cambridge (MA, LLM); Nottingham Univ. (MPhil 1981, PhD 1987). Served in Royal Artillery, 1939–45; Adjutant 90th Field Regt, RA. Articled to W. H. Bentley, Town Clerk of Paddington; admitted Solicitor, 1948; Asst Solicitor, Paddington, 1948–50; Chief Asst Solicitor, Birkenhead, 1950–53; Deputy Town Clerk: Wallasey, 1953–59; Southend-on-Sea, 1959–62; Town Clerk, Cambridge, 1963–66; Town Clerk and Chief Exec. Officer, Nottingham, 1966–74. Chairman: Notts Local Valuation Panel, 1974–85; London Housing Staff Commn, 1979–86; Mem., Local Radio Council for BBC Radio Nottingham, 1970–76; Indep. Chm., Home Sec.'s Adv. Cttee, Wireless and Telegraphy Act 1949, 1975–89; Member: Panel of Asst Comrs of Local Govt Boundary Commn, 1974–89; Panel of Indep. Inspectors, DoE, 1974–89; Bd Telford (New Town) Develt Corp., 1975–89; Police Complaints Bd, 1977–80; Ind. Review of the Radio Spectrum (30–960 MHz), 1982–83. Gen. Comr of Income Tax, 1975–. Mem., Bd, English Sinfonia, 1980–. Gov., Derbyshire Coll. of Higher Educn, 1985–89; Mem. Court, Nottingham Univ., 1966–74. Liveryman, Clockmakers' Co. (Mem. Court, 1981; Master, 1988). DL Notts, 1974. *Publication:* The Neolithic and Bronze Age Cultures of the Middle and Upper Trent Basin (British Archaeological Reports, British Series 105), 1982. *Recreations:* fishing, archaeology, enjoyment of music. *Address:* 42 Magdala Road, Mapperley Park, Nottingham NG3 5DF. *T:* Nottingham (0602) 621269. *Clubs:* Army and Navy; United Services (Nottingham).

VINE, Col (Roland) Stephen, FRCPath, FZS; Chief Inspector, Cruelty to Animals Act (1876), Home Office, 1962–75; *b* 26 Dec. 1910; *s* of late Joseph Soutter Vine and of Josephine Vine (*née* Moylan); *m* 1935, Flora Betty, *d* of Charles Strutton Brookes, MBE, Dovercourt; three *d. Educ:* Southend-on-Sea High Sch.; Guy's Hosp. BSc; MRCS, LRCP, FRCPath, FZS(Scientific). Royal Army Medical Corps, 1934–60 (incl. War of 1939–45). Home Office, 1960–75. Former Mem., Council, Res. Defence Soc., 1977–85. *Publications:* chapter in: Biomedical Technology in Hospital Diagnosis, 1972; Animals in Scientific Research, 1983; articles in RAMC Jl. *Recreations:* gardening, bowling. *Address:* Shola, Fielden Road, Crowborough, Sussex TN6 1TR. *T:* Crowborough (0892) 661381. *Club:* Civil Service.

VINE, Roy; Director: First National Finance Corporation plc, since 1984; First National Commercial Bank Ltd, since 1990; *b* 1923; *m* 1945, Dorothy A. Yates; one *s* one *d. Educ:* Taunton's Sch., Southampton. Served RAF (Flt Lieut), 1942–46 and 1951–53. Vice-Chm., Barclays Bank UK Ltd, 1982–84; Dir, Barclays Bank plc, 1979–84 (Gen. Man., 1972; Senior Gen. Man., 1979–81). Dir, First National Bank Plc (formerly First National Securities Ltd), 1985–90. FCIB 1951. *Recreations:* golf, football, music. *Address:* Summerfold, Itchen Abbas, Winchester SO21 1AX.

VINELOTT, Hon. Sir John (Evelyn), Kt 1978; **Hon. Mr Justice Vinelott;** Judge of the High Court of Justice, Chancery Division, since 1978; *b* 15 Oct. 1923; *s* of George Frederick Vine-Lott and Vera Lilian Vine-Lott (*née* Mockford); *m* 1956, Sally Elizabeth, *d* of His Honour Sir Walker Kelly Carter, QC; two *s* one *d. Educ:* Queen Elizabeth's Gram. Sch., Faversham, Kent; Queens' Coll., Cambridge (MA). War Service, Sub-Lieut RNVR, 1942–46. Called to Bar, Gray's Inn, 1953 (Atkin Scholar); QC 1968; Bencher, 1974; practised at the Chancery Bar. Chm., Insolvency Rules Adv. Cttee, 1984–. Président, L'association de Bousquetara, 1989–. *Publications:* essays and articles on Revenue and Administration Law, in specialist periodicals. *Address:* 22 Portland Road, W11. *T:* 071–727 4778. *Club:* Garrick.

VINEN, William Frank, FRS 1973; Poynting Professor of Physics, University of Birmingham, since 1974 (Professor of Physics, 1962–74); *b* 15 Feb. 1930; *o s* of Gilbert Vinen and Olive Maud Vinen (*née* Roach); *m* 1960, Susan-Mary Audrey Master; one *s* one *d. Educ:* Watford Grammar Sch.; Clare College, Cambridge. Research Fellow, Clare College, 1955–58. Royal Air Force, 1948–49. Demonstrator in Physics, Univ. of Cambridge and Fellow of Pembroke Coll., 1958–62. Hon. Life Fellow, Coventry Polytechnic, 1989. Simon Meml Prize, Inst. of Physics, 1963; Holweck Medal and Prize, Inst. of Physics and French Physical Soc., 1978; Rumford Medal, Royal Soc., 1980. *Recreation:* good food. *Address:* 52 Middle Park Road, Birmingham B29 4BJ. *T:* 021–475 1328.

VINER, Monique Sylvaine, (Mrs M. S. Gray), QC 1979; **Her Honour Judge Viner;** a Circuit Judge, since 1990; *b* 3 Oct. 1926; *d* of late Hugh Viner and Eliane Viner; *m* 1958, Dr Pieter Francis Gray; one *s* three *d. Educ:* Convent of the Sacred Heart, Roehampton; St Hugh's Coll., Oxford (MA; Hon. Fellow, 1990). Called to the Bar, Gray's Inn, 1950, Bencher, 1988. In teaching, publishing, factory and shop work, 1947–50. A Recorder, 1986–90. Chm. or Ind. Mem. of Wages Councils (various), 1952–; Mem., Industrial Court, 1976. *Recreations:* talking, reading, tennis, golf, sailing, walking, gardening, cooking, bird watching, history, sketching, painting. *Address:* Old Glebe, Waldron, Heathfield, East Sussex TN21 0RB. *T:* Heathfield (04352) 3865; 2 Mitre Court Buildings, Temple, EC4Y 7BX. *T:* 071–353 2246.

VINES, Prof. David Anthony, PhD; Adam Smith Professor of Political Economy, University of Glasgow, since 1985; *b* 8 May 1949; *s* of Robert Godfrey and Vera Frances Vines; *m* 1979, Susannah Lucy; three *s. Educ:* Scotch Coll., Melbourne; Melbourne Univ. (BA 1971); Cambridge Univ. (BA 1974; MA 1977; PhD 1984). Cambridge University: Fellow, Pembroke Coll., 1976–85; Res. Officer and Sen. Res. Officer, Dept of Applied Econs, 1979–85. Board Member: Channel 4 Television, 1987–; Glasgow Local Enterprise Co., 1990–. Economic Consultant to Sec. of State for Scotland, 1987–; Consultant, IMF, 1988–. Member: Econ. Affairs Cttee, ESRC, 1985–87; Academic Panel, HM Treasury, 1986–. Mem. Council, Royal Economic Soc., 1988–. *Publications:* (with J. E. Meade and J. M. Maciejowski) Stagflation, Vol. II: Demand Management, 1983; (with D. A. Currie) Macroeconomic Interactions Between North and South, 1988; (jtly) Macroeconomic Policy: inflation, wealth and the exchange rate, 1989; (with G. Hughes) Deregulation and the Future of Commercial Television, 1989; (with A. Stevenson) Information, Strategy, and Public Policy, 1991; papers on international macroeconomics, balance of payments and economic policy, in professional jls. *Recreations:* hillwalking, music. *Address:* 1 Ralston Road, Bearsden, Glasgow G61 3SS.

VINES, Eric Victor, CMG 1984; OBE 1971; HM Diplomatic Service; Staff Assessor, since 1991; Trustee, Centre for Southern African Studies, York University, since 1989; *b* 28 May 1929; *s* of late Henry E. Vines; *m* 1953, Ellen-Grethe Ella Küppers; one *s. Educ:* St Dunstan's Coll., London; St Catharine's Coll., Cambridge (MA). Army service, 1947–49. Joined Commonwealth Relations Office, 1952; Colombo, 1954–55; 1st Sec., Singapore, 1958–61; Canberra, 1961–65; Diplomatic Service Administration Office, 1965–68; 1st Sec., Information, Mexico City, 1968–70; Counsellor, Exec. Sec.-Gen., SEATO Conf., London, 1971; Head, Cultural Exchange Dept, FCO, 1971–74; Counsellor (Commercial), Tel Aviv, 1974–77, Stockholm, 1977–80; Consul-Gen., Barcelona, 1980–83; Ambassador to Mozambique, 1984–85; Ambassador to Uruguay, 1986–89. *Recreations:* opera, archaeology, walking. *Address:* c/o Foreign and Commonwealth Office, King Charles Street, SW1A 2AH. *Club:* Commonwealth Trust.

VINES, Sir William (Joshua), AC 1987; Kt 1977; CMG 1969; FASA, ACIS; psc; Chairman, ANZ Banking Group, 1982–89 (Director, since 1976); Director, Dalgety Australia Ltd, 1980–91 (Chairman, 1970–80); grazier at Tara, Queensland, 1965–82 and Cliffdale, Currabubula, NSW, since 1982; *b* 27 May 1916; *s* of P. V. Vines, Canterbury, Victoria, Australia; *m* 1939, Thelma J. (*d* 1988), *d* of late F. J. Ogden; one *s* two *d*; *m* 1990, Judith Anne Ploeg, *d* of late T. E. Raynsford. *Educ:* Haileybury College, Brighton Beach, Victoria. Managing Director: Internat. Wool Secretariat, 1961–69 (Board Mem., 1969–79); Berger, Jenson & Nicholson Ltd, 1960 (Dir, 1961–69); Dalgety Australia Ltd, 1971–76 (Chm., 1970–80); Group Managing Director, Lewis Berger & Sons Ltd, 1955–61; Director: Lewis Berger & Sons (Aust.) Pty Ltd & Sherwin Williams Co. (Aust.) Pty Ltd, 1952–55; Goodlass Wall & Co. Pty Ltd, 1947–49; Dalgety Ltd; Dalgety New Zealand Ltd, 1969–80; Port Phillip Mills Pty Ltd, 1969–88; Wiggins Teape Ltd (UK), 1970–79; Tubemakers of Australia Ltd, 1970–86 (Dep. Chm., 1973–86); Associated Pulp & Paper Mills Ltd, 1971–83 (Dep. Chm. 1977, Chm. 1979–83); Conzinc Rio Tinto of Australia, 1977–84; Grindlays Hldgs, subseq. ANZ UK Hldgs, 1985–89; Grindlays Bank, 1987–89; Chm., Thorn Holdings Pty Ltd, 1969–74. Vice-President Melbourne Legacy, 1949–51; Pres. Building Industry Congress, Vic., 1954–55. Chm., Aust. Wool Commn, 1970–72; Mem. Exec., CSIRO, 1973–78; Chm. Council, Hawkesbury Agric. Coll., 1975–85. Mem., Australia New Zealand Foundn, 1979–84. Chm., The Sir Robert Menzies Meml Trust. Served War of 1939–45 (despatches, C-in-C's commendation for gallantry, El Alamein), 2nd AIF, 2/23 Aust. Inf. Bn, Middle East, New Guinea and Borneo, Capt. *Address:* Cliffdale, Currabubula, NSW 2342, Australia. *T:* (067) 689109. *Clubs:* Union (Sydney); Australian, Melbourne (Melbourne).

VINEY, Hon. Anne Margaret, (Hon. Mrs Viney), JP; barrister; Part-time Chairman, Social Security Appeal Tribunals, since 1987; *b* 14 June 1926; *d* of late Baron Morton of Henryton, PC, MC, and Lady Morton of Henryton; *m* 1947, Peter Andrew Hopwood Viney; one *s* two *d. Educ:* Priorsfield, Godalming, Surrey. Left school after matriculation, 1943; worked in publicity dept of Internat. Wool Secretariat, 1945–47. Called to the Bar, Lincoln's Inn, 1979. Councillor, Kensington and Chelsea BC, 1960–62. JP, 1961. Mem., Inner London Juvenile Court panel, 1961–87 (Chm. 1970). Helped to found London Adventure Playground Assoc., 1962 (Sec. 1962–69); Chm., Consumer Protection Adv. Cttee, 1973–82. *Recreations:* conversation, playing poetry game. *Address:* Worth House, Worth Matravers, near Swanage, Dorset BH19 3LQ.

VINEY, Elliott (Merriam), DSO 1945; MBE 1946; TD; JP; DL; FSA; Director: British Printing Corporation Ltd, 1964–75; Hazell, Watson & Viney Ltd, 1947–78; *b* 21 Aug. 1913; *s* of late Col. Oscar Viney, TD, DL, and Edith Merriam; *m* 1950, Rosamund Ann Pelly; two *d. Educ:* Oundle; Univ. Coll., Oxford. Bucks Bn, Oxford and Bucks Light Infantry (TA), 1932–46. Governor and Trustee, Museum of London, 1972–88. Pres., British Fedn of Master Printers, 1972–73. Master, Grocers' Company, 1970–71. County Dir, Bucks St John Amb. Assoc., 1953–55; Trustee, Bucks Historic Churches Trust, 1957; Pres., Bucks Archaeol. Soc., 1979 (Hon. Sec., 1954–79); Pres., CPRE (Bucks), 1990 (Chm., 1976–90); Chm., Bucks Record Soc., 1986. JP 1950, DL 1952, High Sheriff, 1964, Buckinghamshire. OStJ 1953. Editor: Oxford Mountaineering, 1935; Climbers' Club Jl, 1936–39; (jt) Records of Bucks, 1947–74. *Publications:* The Sheriffs of Buckinghamshire, 1965; (jtly) Old Aylesbury, 1976. *Recreations:* conservation, music, walking. *Address:* Cross Farmhouse, Quainton, Aylesbury, Bucks HP22 4AR. *Clubs:* Alpine; County Hall (Aylesbury).

VINING, Rowena Adelaide, OBE 1979 (MBE 1964); HM Diplomatic Service, retired; *b* 25 Sept. 1921; *er d* of late Col Percival Llewellyn Vining and Phyllis Servante Vining. *Educ:* privately, and at Chiddingstone Castle, Edenbridge, Kent. Foreign Office, 1941–52 (war service in Italy, Indonesia, 1943–45). Commonwealth Relations Office, 1952–55; Second Secretary: Karachi, 1955–58; Sydney, 1958–62; First Sec.: CRO, 1962–65; Canberra, 1965–67; Commonwealth Office (later Foreign and Commonwealth Office), 1967–71; Vienna, 1972–74; Consul, Florence and Consul-General, San Marino, 1974–78; Dep. UK Permanent Rep. to the Council of Europe, 1978–81; Consul-General, Strasbourg, 1979–80. Staff Assessor, FCO, 1983–86. *Recreations:* gardening, music. *Address:* Dorchester Cottage, Greywell, near Basingstoke RG25 1BT.

VINSON, family name of **Baron Vinson.**

VINSON, Baron *cr* 1985 (Life Peer), of Roddam Dene in the County of Northumberland; **Nigel Vinson,** LVO 1979; DL; Inventor; Deputy Chairman, Electra Investment Trust, since 1990 (Director, since 1975); Chairman, Institute of Economic Affairs, since 1989 (Trustee, since 1972); *b* Nettlestead Place, Kent, 27 Jan. 1931; *s* of late Ronald Vinson and Bettina Vinson (*née* Southwell-Sander); *m* 1972, Yvonne Ann Collin; three *d. Educ:* Pangbourne Naval Coll. Lieut, Queen's Royal Regt, 1949–51. Chm., 1952–72, and Founder, Plastic Coatings Ltd (started in a Nissen hut, 1952, flotation, 1969; Queen's Award to Industry, 1971). Member: Crafts Adv. Cttee, 1971–77; Design Council, 1973–80; Dep. Chm., CBI Smaller Firms Council, 1979–; Chairman: CoSIRA, 1980–82; Rural Develt Commn, 1980–90 (Mem., 1978–90); Industry Year Steering Cttee, RSA, 1985–; Pres., Industrial Participation Assoc., 1979–89 (Chm., 1971–78). Director: British Airports Authority, 1973–80; Centre for Policy Studies, 1974–80; Hon. Dir, Queen's Silver Jubilee Appeal, 1976–78; Dir, Fleming High Income Growth Trust (formerly Fleming Tech. Trust), 1972–; Dir, Barclays Bank UK, 1982–88. Member: Northumbrian Nat. Parks Countryside Cttee, 1977–89; Regional Cttee, Nat. Trust, 1977–84. Council Mem., St George's House, Windsor Castle, 1990–. FRSA, CBIM. DL Northumberland, 1990. *Publication:* Personal and Portable Pensions for All, 1984. *Recreations:* fine art and craftmanship, horses, farming. *Address:* 34 Kynance Mews, SW7 4QR. *T:* Wooperton (06687) 230. *Club:* Boodle's.

VINTER, (Frederick Robert) Peter, CB 1965; *b* 27 March 1914; *e s* of P. J. Vinter (Headmaster, Archbishop Holgate's Grammar Sch., York, 1915–37) and Harriet Mary (*née* Cammack); *m* 1938, Margaret, *d* of S. I. Rake, Pembroke; two *s. Educ:* Haileybury Coll.; King's Coll., Cambridge (MA). Min. of Economic Warfare, 1939; Cabinet Office, 1943; HM Treasury, 1945–69, Third Sec., 1965–69; Dep. Sec., Min. of Technology and DTI, 1969–73. Overseas Adviser to CEGB, 1973–79; Dir (non-Exec.), Vickers Ltd, 1974–80. Nuffield Travelling Fellowship (in India), 1950–51. *Address:* 3 Sunnyside, Wimbledon, SW19 4SL. *T:* 081–946 4137. *Club:* United Oxford & Cambridge University.

VINTER, Peter; *see* Vinter, F. R. P.

VINTON, Alfred Merton; Chief Operating Officer, N. M. Rothschild & Sons, since 1988; *b* 11 May 1938; *s* of Alfred Merton Vinton and Jean Rosalie Vinton (*née* Guiterman); *m* 1st, 1963, Mary Bedell Weber; two *s* one *d*; 2nd, 1983, Anna-Maria Hawser (*née* Dugan-Chapman); one *s* one *d. Educ:* Harvard College (AB Econs 1960). US Navy Lieut (JG), 1960–62. J. P. Morgan, 1962–88. *Recreations:* tennis, riding, music. *Address:* Stoke Albany House, Market Harborough, Leics LE16 8PT. *T:* Dingley (085885) 227. *Clubs:* Mark's; Queen's; Harvard (NY).

VIOT, Jacques Edmond; Commandeur de la Légion d'Honneur; Commandeur de l'Ordre National du Mérite; President, France-Great Britain Association, since 1987; *b* 25 Aug. 1921; *m* 1950, Jeanne de Martimprey de Romécourt. *Educ:* Bordeaux and Paris Lycées; Ecole Normale Supérieure; Ecole Nationale d'Administration. Foreign Office (European Dept), 1951–53; Second Sec., London, 1953–57; First Sec., Rabat, 1957–61; Tech. Advisor to Foreign Minister, 1961–62; Head of Technical Co-operation, FO, 1962–68; Dir for Personnel and Gen. Admin, 1968–72; Ambassador to Canada, 1972–77; Gen. Inspector for Foreign Affairs, 1977–78; Directeur de Cabinet to Foreign Minister, 1978–81; Gen. Inspector for Foreign Affairs, 1981–84; Ambassador to the Court of St James's, 1984–86; Ambassadeur de France, 1986; Chm., Review Cttee on Foreign Affairs, Paris, 1986–87. Chm. Entrance Examination Bd, Ecole Nat. d'Admin, 1987. Fellow, St Antony's College, Oxford. *Address:* 19 rue de Civry, 75016 Paris, France.

VIRANI, Nazmudin Gulamhusein; Chairman and Chief Executive, Control Securities PLC, property and leisure company, since 1985; *b* 2 March 1948; *s* of Gulamhusein Virani and Fatma Virani; *m* 1970, Yasmin Abdul Rasul Ismail; two *s* one *d. Educ:* Aga Khan Sch., Kampala, Uganda. Left Uganda for UK, 1972; founded Virani gp of companies, 1972 (Chm. and Chief Exec.); Chm. and Chief Exec., Belhaven PLC, 1983–86. *Recreations:* cricket, travel, philanthropy. *Address:* Control House, 47/51 Gillingham Street, Westminster, SW1V 1PS. *T:* 071–828 6405.

VISHNEVSKAYA, Galina; soprano; *b* 25 Oct. 1926; *m* 1955, Mstislav Rostropovich, *qv*; two *d. Educ:* studied with Vera Garina. Toured with Leningrad Light Opera Co., 1944–48, with Leningrad Philharmonic Soc., 1948–52; joined Bolshoi Theatre, 1952. Concert appearances in Europe and USA, 1950–; first appeared at Metropolitan Opera, NY, 1961. Rôles include: Leonora in Fidelio, Tatiana in Eugene Onegin, Iolanta. Has sung in Britain at Festival Hall, Aldeburgh Festival, Edinburgh Festival, Covent Garden, Rostropovich Festival, Snape; Dir, Iolanta, Aldeburgh Fest., 1988. Makes concert tours with her husband. Has made many recordings. *Publication:* Galina (autobiog.), 1984. *Address:* c/o Victor Hochhauser, 4 Oak Hill Way, NW3 7LR.

VISSER, John Bancroft; Director of Administration, Science and Engineering Research Council (formerly Science Research Council), 1974–88; *b* 29 Jan. 1928; *o s* of late Gilbert and Ethel Visser; *m* 1955, Astrid Margareta Olson; two *s* one *d. Educ:* Mill Hill Sch.; New Coll., Oxford (Exhibnr). Entered Civil Service, Asst Principal, Min. of Supply, 1951; Principal, 1956; Min. of Aviation, 1959; Admin. Staff Coll., 1965; Asst Sec., 1965; Min. of Technology, 1967; Royal Coll. of Defence Studies, 1970; Civil Service Dept, 1971; Procurement Exec., MoD, 1971; Under-Sec., 1974; Sec. of Nat. Defence Industries Council, 1971–74. *Recreations:* sport, music, gardening, walking. *Address:* Rosslyn, 3 Berkeley Road, Cirencester, Glos GL7 1TY. *T:* Cirencester (0285) 652626. *Club:* Old Millhillians.

VIVENOT, Baroness de, (Hermine Hallam Hipwell), OBE 1967; free lance writer; *b* Buenos Aires, 23 April 1907; *d* of late Humphrey Hallam Hipwell and Gertrude Hermine Isebrée-Moens tot Bloois; *m* 1931, Baron Raoul de Vivenot (*d* 1973), *e s* of Baron de Vivenot and Countess Kuenburg, Vienna; one *s. Educ:* Northlands, Buenos Aires. Staff of Buenos Aires Herald, 1928–31. Joined Min. of Information, 1941; transferred Foreign Office, 1946; appointed to Foreign (subseq. Diplomatic) Service, Jan. 1947; Vice-Consul, Bordeaux, 1949–52, Nantes, 1952–53; Foreign Office, 1953–55; First Secretary (Information), HM Embassy, Brussels, 1955–59; Foreign Office, 1959–62; First Secretary (Information), HM Embassy, The Hague, 1962–66; retired 1967. External Examiner in Spanish, Univ. of London. *Publications:* The Niñas of Balcarce, a novel, 1935; Younger Argentine Painters; Argentine Art Notes; Buenos Aires Vignettes; articles in La Nación and Buenos Aires Herald. *Recreations:* Whippet racing and coursing, gardening, grandchildren. *Address:* The Flat, Aughton House, Collingbourne Kingston, Marlborough, Wilts SN8 3SA. *T:* Collingbourne Ducis (026485) 0682.

VIVIAN, family name of **Barons Swansea** and **Vivian.**

VIVIAN, 6th Baron *cr* 1841; **Nicholas Crespigny Laurence Vivian;** Bt 1828; *b* 11 Dec. 1935; *s* of 5th Baron Vivian and Victoria (*d* 1985), *er d* of late Captain H. G. L. Oliphant, DSO, MVO; *S* father, 1991; *m* 1st, 1960, Catherine Joyce (marr. diss. 1972), *y d* of late James Kenneth Hope, CBE; one *s* one *d*; 2nd, 1972, Carol, *e d* of F. Alan Martineau, MBE; two *d. Educ:* Eton; Madrid Univ. CO 16th/5th The Queen's Royal Lancers, 1976–79; Col, MoD, 1980–84; Dep. Comdr Land Forces and Chief of Staff, Cyprus, 1984–87; Brig., 1987; Comdr, British Communication Zone (Antwerp), 1987–90. *Recreation:* travel. *Heir: s* Hon. Charles Hussey Crespigny Vivian, *b* 20 Dec. 1966. *Clubs:* White's, Cavalry and Guards.

VIVIAN, Michael Hugh; Full-time Board Member, 1974–80, and Deputy Chairman, 1978–80, Civil Aviation Authority; *b* 15 Dec. 1919; *s* of Hugh Vivian and Mary (*née* Gilbertson); *m* 1st, 1951, June Stiven; one *s* one *d*; 2nd, Joy D. Maude. *Educ:* Uppingham; Oxford. Served War: RAF (139 Sqdn), Flying Instructor, Test Pilot, 1940–44. Min. of Civil Aviation, 1945; Private Sec. to Parly Sec. for Civil Aviation, 1945–46; various operational appts, 1947–61; Dep. Dir of Flight Safety, 1961–66; Dir of Flight Safety, 1966–67; Dir of Advanced Aircraft Ops, 1967–71; Civil Aviation Authority, 1972: Dir-Gen. Safety Ops, 1972–74; Gp Dir, Safety Services, 1974–78; Dir, CSE Aviation Ltd, 1980–82. *Recreations:* golf, vintage cars. *Address:* Willow Cottage, The Dickredge, Steeple Aston, Oxfordshire OX5 3RS. *T:* Steeple Aston (0869) 47171. *Club:* Royal Air Force.

VOCKLER, Rt. Rev. John Charles, (Rt. Rev. Brother John Charles); engaged in writing and research and active preaching and teaching ministry; Bishop Protector, Poor Clares of Reparation, Mt Sinai, NY, since 1987 (Warden, 1982–83); Vicar, Trinity Church, Monmouth, Illinois, since 1990; Founder, and Superior, Franciscan Order of the Divine Compassion, since 1990; *b* 22 July 1924; *e s* of John Thomas Vockler and Mary Catherine Vockler (*née* Widerberg), Sydney, New South Wales. *Educ:* Sydney Boys' High Sch.; after studying accountancy, matriculated by private study and correspondence (Metropolitan Business Coll. and Internat. Correspondence Schs, Sydney) to the University of Sydney; University of Queensland; Moore Theological Coll.; St John's Theological College, Morpeth, NSW; General Theological Seminary, New York. LTheol, Australian College of Theology, 1948; received Hey Sharp Prize for NT Greek. Junior Clerk, W. R. Carpenter & Co. Ltd, Sydney, NSW, 1939–43. Deacon, 1948; priest, 1948; Asst Deacon, Christ Church Cathedral, Newcastle, 1948; Asst Priest, 1948–50; Vice-Warden of S John's Coll., within University of Queensland, 1950–53; Acting Chaplain, C of E Grammar School for Boys, Brisbane, 1953. BA (1st Class Hons History) University of Queensland, 1953; University Gold Medal for outstanding achievement, 1953; BA University of Adelaide, aegr, 1961; Walter and Eliza Hall Foundation Travelling Scholarship, University of Queensland, 1953; Fulbright Scholar, 1953. Acting Vice-Warden, S John's Coll., Morpeth and Lecturer in Old Testament, 1953; Graduate Student, General Theological Seminary, New York, 1954. MDiv (General Seminary), 1954. Asst Priest, Cathedral of S John the Divine, NY and Chaplain, St Luke's Home for Aged Women and the Home for Old Men and Aged Couples, 1953–54; Australian Delegate to Anglican Congress, 1954; Fellow and Tutor Gen. Theol. Seminary, 1954–56; STM Gen. Theol. Seminary, 1956. Asst Priest, St Stephen's Church, West 69th Street, NY, 1955; Priest-in-charge, St Stephen's, New York, 1956; Asst Priest, parish of Singleton, NSW, 1956–59; Lecturer in Theology, St John's Theological College, Morpeth, NSW, 1956–59; Secretary, Newcastle Diocesan Board of Education, 1958–59. Titular Bishop of Mount Gambier and Assistant Bishop of Adelaide (Coadjutor, 1959; title changed to Assistant, 1961), until 1962; also Archdeacon of Eyre Peninsula, 1959–62; Vicar-General, Examining Chaplain to Bishop of Adelaide, 1960–62; Bishop of Polynesia, 1962–68. Warden: Community of St Clare, Newcastle, NSW, 1975–80; Soc. of Sacred Advent, 1976–80; Spiritual Dir, Community of the Holy Spirit, NY, 1988–89; Spiritual Advr, Order of the Incarnation, NY, 1988–; Confessor Extraordinary, Soc. of St John the Evangelist, Cambridge, Mass, 1987–89; Chaplain to: Episcopal Students, Monmouth Coll., 1990–; Monmouth Community Hosp., 1990–. Collegial Mem., House of Bishops, Episcopal Church, USA, 1983–; Member: House of Bishops' Cttee on Religious Life, 1986–89; Episcopal Synod of America, 1989–. President, Harry Charman's All Races Sports and Social Club, Suva, Fiji, 1962–68, Hon. Life Vice-Pres., 1968; Chairman: S Pacific Anglican Council, 1963–68; Council of Pacific Theological Coll., 1963–68; President: Fiji Council of Social Services, 1964–68; Fiji Branch, Royal Commonwealth Soc., 1966–68. Writing Grant, Literature Bd of Australia Council, 1979, 1981. Member: Soc. of Authors; Australian Soc. of Authors; PEN (International), Sydney Br. and New York Br.; Guild of Writers Inc., NY; Christian Writers' Fellowship (USA); Aust. Professional Writers' Services; Penman Club (UK); National Writers' Club (USA); Federated Clerks Union of Aust., 1978–81; Internat. Center for Integrative Studies, NY 1983–; Internat. Ecumenical Fellowship; Guild of All Souls; Confraternity of the Blessed Sacrament; Soc. of Mary; Catholic and Evangelical Mission; Anglican Pacifist Fellowship; Fellowship of Reconciliation; Integrity USA; Gay Christian Movement; Fellowship of S Alban and S Sergius; Anglican Fellowship of Prayer, USA; Fellowship of Three Kings, Haddington, Scotland; Amnesty Internat., USA (Mem., Urgent Action Gp); SSC. Priest Associate, Shrine of Our Lady, Walsingham and Priory of Our Lady of Pew, Westminster Abbey; Associate, Guild of St Vincent, 1985–; Priest Member, Oratory of the Good Shepherd, 1952–75. Society of St Francis: entered Soc., 1969, to test vocation to religious life; professed, 1972; Chaplain to Third Order, European Province, 1972–74; made life profession, 1975; Guardian, Friary of St Francis, Brisbane, 1975–77, Islington, NSW, 1978–79; Minister Provincial, Pacific Province, 1976–81; Archivist, Amer. Province, 1985–89; left SSF, 1990. Sec., Adv. Council for Religious Communities in Aust. and Pacific, 1976–80. Permission to officiate: dio. Salisbury, 1969–70; dio. Fulham and Gibraltar, with Episcopal Commn, 1971–73; dio. Newcastle, NSW, 1975–81; dio. Auckland, NZ, 1976–81; dio. Long Island, 1981–; dio. of NY, 1981–; dio. of Quincy, USA, 1988–90 (Assisting Bishop, 1990). Vice-Pres. and Mem. Council, USPG, 1973–74; Vice-Pres., Missions to Seamen, 1963–69; Hon. Asst Bp of Worcester, 1972–73; Assistant Bishop: Chelmsford, 1973–74; Southwark, 1974–75; Hon. Canon of Southwark, 1975, Canon Emeritus 1975; Hon. Mission Chaplain, dio. Brisbane, 1975–79, permission to officiate, 1979–81. Examnr for Aust. Coll. of Theology, 1975–76 and 1979. ThD (*jure dig.*) ACT, 1961; STD (*hc*) Gen. Theological Seminary, NY, 1961; BD (*ad eund.*) Melbourne College of Divinity, 1960. Bishop's Cross, dio. of Long Is, 1989. *Publications:* Can Anglicans Believe Anything—The Nature and Spirit of Anglicanism, 1961 (NSW); Forward Day by Day, 1962; (ed) Believing in God (by M. L. Yates), 1962 (Australian edn), revd edn 1983 (US). One Man's Journey, 1972; St Francis: Franciscanism and the Society of St Francis, 1980; contributions to: Preparatory Volume for Anglican Congress, Toronto, 1963; Anglican Mosaic, 1963; Mutual Responsibility: Questions and Answers, 1964; All One Body (ed T. Wilson), 1968; Australian Dictionary of Biography (4 articles); St Mark's Review, Australian Church Quarterly, The Anglican, The Young Anglican, Pacific Journal of Theology, New Zealand Theological Review, weekly feature, Newcastle Morning Herald, NSW; book reviews in Amer. theol jls; Aust. corresp. to New Fire, 1980–81; book review Editor, New York Episcopalians, 1986–. *Recreations:* classical music, detective stories, theatre, films, prints and engravings. *Address:* The Friar's Lodgings, PO Box 281, Monmouth, Ill 61462–0281, USA. *T:* 309–734–7429. *Clubs:* Tonga (Nukualofa); St John's Coll. (Brisbane) (Hon Mem., 1976–).

VOELCKER, Christopher David, TD 1967; Metropolitan Stipendiary Magistrate, since 1982; a Recorder, since 1989; *b* 10 May 1933; *s* of Eric Voelcker and Carmen Muriel Lyon Voelcker (*née* Henstock); *m* 1st, 1964, Sybil Russell Stoneham (marr. diss. 1985); two *d*; 2nd, 1991, Petrina Alexandra Keany (*née* Holdsworth). *Educ:* Wellington Coll., Berks. Called to Bar, Middle Temple, 1955. National Service, 8th King's Royal Irish Hussars, 1952–53. 3/4 County of London Yeomanry (Sharpshooters) TA, 1953–60; Kent and County of London Yeomanry (Sharpshooters) TA, 1960–67. Member: Inner London Probation Cttee, 1986–; Recruitment and Trng Cttee, Central Council of Probation for England and Wales, 1988–. *Recreations:* military history, gardening. *Address:* 6 Pump Court, Temple, EC4Y 7AR. *T:* 071–353 7242. *Club:* Cavalry and Guards.

VOGEL, Hans-Jochen, Hon. CBE; Dr jur; Chairman, Social Democratic Party (SPD), Federal Republic of Germany, since 1987; Member, Bundestag, since 1972 (Social Democratic Party); Leader of the Opposition, since 1983; *b* 3 Feb. 1926; *s* of Dr Hermann Vogel and Caroline (*née* Brinz); *m* 1st, 1951, Ilse Leisnering (marr. diss. 1970); one *s* two *d*; 2nd, 1972, Liselotte Sonnenholzer. *Educ:* Göttingen and Giessen; Univs of Marburg and Munich (Dr jur 1950). Army service, 1943–45 (PoW). Admitted Bavarian Bar, 1951; Legal Asst, Bavarian Min. of Justice, 1952–54; District Court Counsel, Traunstein, 1954–58; staff of Bavarian State Chancellery, 1955–58; Munich City Council, 1958, Oberbürgermeister (Chief Executive), Munich, 1960–72 (re-elected, 1966); Vice-Pres., Org. Cttee, Olympic Games, 1972. Chm., Bavarian SDP, 1972–77; Minister of regional planning, housing and urban develt, 1972–74; Minister of Justice, 1974–81; Mayor of West Berlin, Jan.–June 1981, leader of opposition, 1981–83. Bundesverdienstkreuz; Bavarian Verdienstorden. *Publications:* Städte im Wandel, 1971; Die Amtskette: Meine 12 Münchner Jahre, 1972; Reale Reformen, 1973. *Recreations:* mountaineering, swimming, reading history. *Address:* c/o Bundeshaus, 5300 Bonn 1, Federal Republic of Germany.

VOGELPOEL, Pauline, (Mrs R. D. Mann), MBE 1962; Vice-President, Contemporary Art Society, since 1984; *d* of late Pieter Vogelpoel and Yvonne Vogelpoel, Mozambique; *m* 1975, Richard David Mann, *s* of F. A. Mann, CBE, FBA. *Educ:* Herschel School, Cape Town; University of Cape Town (BA). Joined Contemporary Art Society, 1954, as Organising Secretary; Director 1976–82. Zurich Editor, Harpers & Queen Magazine, 1982–86. Mem., Adv. Council, Victoria and Albert Museum, 1977–82. *Publications:* occasional journalism. *Recreations:* cooking, music, junkshops, pugs. *Address:* Hebelstrasse 15, CH-4056, Basle, Switzerland.

VOGT, Dr Marthe Louise, FRS 1952; Dr med Berlin, Dr phil Berlin; PhD Cantab; *b* 1903; *d* of Oskar Vogt and Cécile Vogt (*née* Mugnier). *Educ:* Auguste Viktoria-Schule, Berlin; University of Berlin. Research Assistant, Department of Pharmacology, Berlin Univ., 1930; Research Assistant and head of chemical division, Kaiser Wilhelm Institut für Hirnforschung, Berlin, 1931–35; Rockefeller Travelling Fellow, 1935–36; Research Worker, Dept of Pharmacology, Cambridge Univ., 1935–40; Alfred Yarrow Research Fellow of Girton Coll., 1937–40; Member Staff of College of Pharmaceutical Society, London, 1941–46; Lecturer, later Reader, in Pharmacology, University of Edinburgh, 1947–60; Head of Pharmacology Unit, Agricultural Research Council Institute of Animal

Physiology, 1960–68. Vis. Associate Prof. in Pharmacology, Columbia Univ., New York, 1949; Vis. Prof., Sydney 1965, Montreal 1968. Life Fellow, Girton Coll., Cambridge, 1970. For. Hon. Mem., Amer. Acad. of Arts and Scis, 1977. Hon. Fellow RSM 1980. Corresp. Mem., Deutsche Physiologische Gesellschaft, 1976; Hon. Member: Physiological Soc., 1974; British Pharmacological Soc., 1971; Hungarian Acad. of Scis, 1981; British Assoc. for Psychopharmacol., 1983. Hon. DSc: Edinburgh, 1974; Cambridge, 1983. Royal Medal, Royal Soc., 1981. *Publications:* papers in neurological, physiological and pharmacological journals. *Address:* Chateau La Jolla Terrace, 7544 La Jolla Boulevard, La Jolla, Calif 92037, USA.

VOLCKER, Paul A.; Chairman, James D. Wolfensohn, since 1988; Frederick H. Schultz Professor of International Economic Policy, Princeton University, since 1988; *b* Cape May, New Jersey, 5 Sept. 1927; *s* of Paul A. Volcker and Alma Louise Klippel; *m* 1954, Barbara Marie Bahnson; one *s* one *d. Educ:* Princeton Univ. (AB *summa cum laude*); Harvard Univ. (MA); LSE. Special Asst, Securities Dept, Fed. Reserve Bank, NY, 1953–57; Financial Economist, Chase Manhattan Bank, NYC, 1957–62; Vice-Pres. and Dir of Forward Planning, 1965–69; Dir, Office of Financial Analysis, US Treasury Dept, 1962–63; Dep. Under-Sec. for Monetary Affairs, 1963–65; Under-Sec. for Monetary Affairs, 1969–74; Senior Fellow, Woodrow Wilson Sch. of Public and Internat. Affairs, Princeton Univ., 1974–75; Pres. NY Federal Reserve Bank, 1975–79; Chairman: American Federal Reserve Board, 1979–87; Commn on the Public Service, 1987–90. *Address:* 151 E 79th Street, New York, NY 10021, USA.

VOLGER, Dr Hendrik Cornelis; Manager, Sittingbourne Research Centre, and Director, Shell Research Ltd, since 1989; *b* 6 March 1932; *s* of Ferdinand Pieter and Marijtje Spaans Volger; *m* 1959, Aaltje Roorda; two *d. Educ:* Univ. of Groningen (PhD). Lieut, Special Branch, Royal Dutch Air Force, 1958–59; Shell Research BV, Amsterdam, 1960 and 1969–75; Shell Development Co., USA, 1968–69; Director: Shell Milstead Lab., 1975–77; Shell Biotech. Res., 1977–83; Product Res. Lab., Amsterdam, 1983–89. Mem., Royal Dutch Akademie of Science, 1987. AKZO Prize, 1972. *Publications:* Organic Chemistry, 1956; Organometal Complexes, 1961; Homogenous Catalysis, 1965. *Recreations:* tennis, gardening. *Address:* Shell Research Ltd, Sittingbourne Research Centre, Sittingbourne, Kent ME9 8AG. *T:* Sittingbourne (0795) 424444.

VOLLRATH, Prof. Lutz Ernst Wolf; Professor of Histology and Embryology, University of Mainz, Germany, since 1974; *b* 2 Sept. 1936; *s* of Pastor Richard Hermann Vollrath and Rita (*née* Brügmann); *m* 1963, Gisela (*née* Dialer); three *d. Educ:* Ulrich von Hutten-Schule, Berlin; Univs of Berlin, Kiel and Tübingen. Dr med Kiel, 1961. Wissenschaftlicher Assistent, Dept of Anatomy, Würzburg, Germany, 1963; Res. Fellow, Dept of Anatomy, Birmingham, 1964; Wissenschaftlicher Assistent, Dept of Anatomy, Würzburg, 1965–71 (Privatdozent, 1968; Oberassistent, 1969; Universitätsdozent, 1970); King's College London: Reader in Anatomy, 1971; Prof. of Anatomy, 1973–74. *Publications:* (co-editor) Neurosecretion: the final neuroendocrine pathway, 1974; The Pineal Organ, 1981; (editor) Cell & Tissue Research; Handbuch der mikr. Anat. des Menschen; research publications on histochemistry and ultrastructure of organogenesis and various aspects of neuroendocrinology, in Z Zellforsch., Histochemie, Phil. Trans Royal Society B, Erg. Anat. Entw.gesch. *Recreations:* gardening, tennis. *Address:* c/o Anatomisches Institut, 65 Mainz, Saarstr. 19/21, Germany.

von BITTENFELD; *see* Herwarth von Bittenfeld.

von CLEMM, Michael; Executive Vice President, Merrill Lynch & Co. Inc., since 1986; *b* 18 March 1935; *s* of Werner Conrad Clemm von Hohenberg and Veronica Rudge Green; *m* 1956, Louisa Bronson Hunnewell; two *d. Educ:* Harvard College (AB *cum laude* 1956); Harvard Graduate School of Arts and Sciences; Corpus Christi College, Oxford (MLitt 1959, DPhil 1962). Staff journalist, Boston Globe, 1959–60; First National City Bank, 1962–67; Faculty, Harvard Graduate Sch. of Business Administration, 1967–71; Pres., Roux Restaurants, 1990– (Chm., 1971–89); White Weld & Co.: Exec. Dir, 1971–75; Man. Dir, 1975–78; Dep. Chm., 1976; Chm., Credit Suisse First Boston Ltd, 1978–86. Member Advisory Board: E African Develt Bank, 1979–; Creditanstalt Bankverein, Vienna, 1986–. President: Foundn for Preservation of the Archaeol Heritage, USA, 1979–87; ESU of US, 1991–; Vice-Pres., City of London Archaeol Trust, 1979–; Member: Court of The Mary Rose, 1982–; Adv. Bd, Royal Acad. of Arts, 1986–; Council, Compton Verney Opera Project, 1986–; Corp., Massachusetts Gen. Hosp., 1980–; Nat. Tanglewood Cttee, 1986–; US–Japan Business Council, 1982–; US–Korea Business Council, 1988– (also Vice-Chm.); Vis. Cttee, Harvard Univ. Grad. Sch. of Design, 1983–86 (Co-Chm., Resources Council, 1985–89); Univ. Resources, Harvard Univ., 1986–; Vis. Cttee, Harvard Univ. Sch. of Public Health, 1990–; Bd of Fellows, Harvard Med. Sch., 1990–; Trustee and Hon. Treasurer, British Museum Develt Trust, 1979–; Trustee: Gen. Hosp. Corp., 1988–; NY Historical Soc., 1989–. *Publications:* contribs to Economic Botany, 1963, and Harvard Business Review, 1971. *Recreations:* collecting Michelin Guide stars (with Albert and Michel Roux), collecting airline boarding cards. *Address:* (office) 2 Drayson Mews, W8 4LY. *T:* 071–499 7812. *Clubs:* White's, Boodle's; Porcellian (Trustee, 1988–) (Cambridge, Mass); Brook (NY).

von HASE, Karl-Günther, Hon. GCVO 1972; Hon. KCMG 1965; Chairman, Deutsch-Englische Gesellschaft, Düsseldorf, since 1982; *b* 15 Dec. 1917; *m* 1945, Renate Stumpff; five *d. Educ:* German schools. Professional Soldier, 1936–45; War Academy, 1943–44; Training College for Diplomats, 1950–51; Georgetown Univ., Washington DC, 1952. German Foreign Service: German Embassy, Ottawa, 1953–56; Spokesman, Foreign Office Bonn, 1958–61; Head, West European Dept, 1961–62; Spokesman of German Federal Government, 1962–67; State Secretary, Min. of Defence, German Federal Govt, 1968–69; German Ambassador to the Court of St James's, 1970–77; Dir-Gen., Zweites Deutsches Fernsehen, 1977–82. Hon. LLD Manchester, 1987. Holds German and other foreign decorations. *Recreations:* shooting, music. *Address:* Am Stadtwald 60, 5300 Bonn 2, West Germany.

von KLITZING, Prof. Klaus, PhD; Director, Max-Planck-Institut für Festkörperforschung, Stuttgart, since 1985; *b* 28 June 1943; *s* of Bogislav and Anny von Klitzing; *m* 1971, Renate Falkenberg; two *s* one *d. Educ:* Technische Univ., Braunschweig (Dipl Phys); Univ. of Würzburg (PhD; Habilitation (univ. teaching qual.). Prof., Technische Univ., München, 1980–84; Hon. Prof., Univ. of Stuttgart, 1985. Nobel Prize for Physics, 1985. *Address:* Max-Planck-Institut für Festkörperforschung, Heisenbergstrasse 1, D-7000 Stuttgart 80, Federal Republic of Germany. *T:* (0711) 6860–570.

von KÜNHEIM, Eberhard; Chairman, Executive Board, BMW AG, Munich, since 1970; *b* 2 Oct. 1928, E Prussia. *Educ:* Stuttgart Technical Univ. (Diplom-Ingenieur; MSc). Technical Dir, Machine tool factory, Hanover, 1954–65; joined QUANDT Gp, 1965; Dep. Chm., Exec. Bd., Industriewerke Karlsruhe Augsburg AG, 1968–70. Mem. Supervisory Board: Bayerische Vereinsbank, Munich; Royal Dutch Petroleum Co.; Münchner Rückversicherungsges. Pres., Assoc. Bavarian Ind.; Vice-Pres., German Motor Ind. Assoc. Mem. Senate, Max Planck Soc. for Advancement of Scis. Hon. Senator, Munich Technical Univ. Hon. doctorates: Clausthal-Zellerfeld Technical Univ.; Munich Technical Univ. *Address:* 8000 Munich 40, Petuelring 130, Germany.

von MALLINCKRODT, Georg Wilhelm; Executive Chairman, Schroders plc, since 1984 (Director, since 1977); Chairman and Chief Executive Officer, Schroders Incorporated, New York, since 1985; Chairman, J. Henry Schroder Bank AG, Zurich, since 1984; *b* 19 Aug. 1930; *s* of Arnold Wilhelm von Mallinckrodt and Valentine von Mallinckrodt (*née* von Joest); *m* 1958, Charmaine Brenda Schroder; two *s* two *d. Educ:* Salem, West Germany. Agfa AG Munich, 1948–51; Münchmeyer & Co., Hamburg, 1951–53; Kleinwort Sons & Co., London, 1953–54; J. Henry Schroder Banking Corp., New York, 1954–55; Union Bank of Switzerland, Geneva 1956; J. Henry Schroder Banking Corp., NY, 1957–60; J. Henry Schroder & Co., subseq. J. Henry Schroder Wagg & Co., London, 1960–85, Director, 1967–; Chm. and Chief Exec. Officer, J. Henry Schroder Bank & Trust Co., NY, 1984–86. Director: Schroder Asseily & Co., 1981–; Schroders Australia Hldgs Ltd, Sydney, 1984–; Wertheim Schroder Hldgs Inc., NY, 1986–; Wertheim Schroder & Co. Inc., NY, 1986–; NM UK, 1986–90; Euris SA, Paris, 1987–; Singapore Internat. Merchant Bankers, 1988–; Siemens UK, 1989–. Vice-Pres., German Chamber of Industry and Commerce in UK, 1971–; Mem., Europ. Adv. Cttee, McGraw Hill Inc., USA, 1986–89; Dir, Europ. Arts Foundn, 1987–. Member: British N American Cttee, 1988–; City Adv. Gp, CBI, 1990–. Pres., German YMCA, London, 1961–; Mem., Ct of Benefactors, Oxford Univ., 1990–. FRSA 1986; CBIM 1986. Verdienstkreuz am Bande des Verdienstordens (FRG), 1986; Verdienstkreuz 1 Klasse des Verdienstordens (FRG), 1990. *Recreations:* shooting, ski-ing. *Address:* 120 Cheapside, EC2V 6DS. *T:* 071–382 6000. *Club:* River (New York).

VONNEGUT, Kurt, Jr; writer; *b* Indianapolis, 11 Nov. 1922; *m* 1st, 1945, Jane Marie Cox (marr. diss. 1979; decd); one *s* two *d;* 2nd, 1979, Jill Krementz. *Educ:* Cornell Univ.; Carnegie Inst. of Technol.; Univ. of Chicago. Served War, US Army, 1942–45 (POW). Reporter, Chicago City News Bureau, 1945–47; PRO, GEC, Schenectady, 1947–50; freelance writer, 1950–65; Lectr, Writers' Workshop, Univ. of Iowa, 1965–67; Guggenheim Fellow, 1967–68; Lectr in English, Harvard, 1970; Dist. Prof., City Coll., New York, 1973–74. Mem., National Inst. of Arts and Letters. *Publications:* Player Piano, 1951; The Sirens of Titan, 1959; Mother Night, 1961; Cat's Cradle, 1963; God Bless You, Mr Rosewater, 1964; Welcome to the Monkey House (short stories), 1968; Slaughterhouse-Five, 1969; Happy Birthday, Wanda June (play), 1970; Between Time and Timbuktu or Prometheus-5 (TV script), 1972; Breakfast of Champions, 1973; Wampeters, Foma and Granfalloons (essays), 1974; Slapstick, or Lonesome No More, 1976; Jailbird, 1979; (with Ivan Chermayeff) Sun Moon Star, 1980; Palm Sunday (autobiog.), 1981; Deadeye Dick, 1982; Galapagos, 1985; Bluebeard, 1988; Hocus Pocus, 1990; Fates Worse Than Death (essays and speeches), 1991. *Address:* c/o Donald C. Farber Esq., Tanner Propp Fersko & Sterner, 99 Park Avenue, 25th Floor, New York, NY 10016, USA.

von REITZENSTEIN, Hans-Joachim Freiherr; *see* Leech, John.

von RICHTHOFEN, Baron Hermann; Ambassador of the Federal Republic of Germany to the Court of St James's, since 1988; *b* 20 Nov. 1933; *s* of Baron Herbert von Richthofen and Baroness Gisela von Richthofen (*née* Schöller); *m* 1966, Christa, Countess von Schwerin; one *s* two *d. Educ:* Univs of Heidelberg, Munich and Bonn; Dr in law Cologne Univ. 1963. Joined Diplomatic Service of FRG, 1963; served Boston, Mass, 1963–64; FO, 1964–66; Saigon, 1966–68; Jakarta, 1968–70; FO, 1970–74; Dep. Hd, Sect. for Internat. Law, FO, 1974; Hd, Sect. for For. Policy, Perm. Mission to GDR, 1975–78; Hd of Dept for German and Berlin Affairs, FO, 1978–80; seconded to Fed. Chancellery as Hd of Intra-German Policy Unit, 1980–86; Dir Gen. of Legal Div., 1986, of Political Div., and Political Dir, 1986–88, FO. KStJ, ER 1961, RR 1985; Officer's Cross, Order of the Knights of Malta, 1967; Commander's Cross: Order of Merit (Italy), 1979; Legion of Honour (France), 1987; Grand Officer's Cross, Order of Infante D. Henrique (Portugal), 1988; Knight's Commander's Cross, Order of Merit (Luxembourg), 1988; Knight Commander's Cross, 2nd class (Austria), 1989. *Recreations:* ski-ing, swimming, gardening, reading history, arts. *Address:* Embassy of the Federal Republic of Germany, 23 Belgrave Square, SW1X 8PZ. *T:* 071–235 5033. *Clubs:* Travellers', Royal Automobile.

von SCHRAMEK, Sir Eric (Emil), Kt 1982; FRIBA; Chairman, von Schramek and Dawes Pty Ltd, 1963–91; Consultant to Hames Sharley International, Architects and Planners, since 1989; *b* 4 April 1921; *s* of Emil and Annie von Schramek; *m* Edith, *d* of Dipl. Ing. W. Popper; one *s* two *d. Educ:* Stefans Gymnasium, Prague; Technical Univ., Prague. DiplIngArch; Life Fellow RAIA, FIArbA, Affiliate FRAPI. Town Planner, Bavaria, 1946–48; Sen. Supervising Architect, Dept of Works and Housing, Darwin, NT, 1948–51; Evans, Bruer & Partners (now von Schramek and Dawes), 1951–91: work includes multi-storey office buildings in Adelaide (Nat. Mutual Centre; State Govt Insce Bldg; Wales House; TAA Bldg, etc); Wesley House, Melbourne; Westpac House, Hobart; AMP Bldg and TAA Bldg, Darwin; numerous churches throughout Australia and New Guinea. National Pres., Building Science Forum of Aust., 1970–72; President: RAIA (SA Chapter), 1974–76; Inst. of Arbitrators, Aust. (SA Chapter), 1977–80. Vis. Lectr, Univ. of Adelaide; Vis. Lectr, S Australian Inst. of Technol. Past National Dep. Chm., Austcare; past Councillor, Council of Professions; past Chm., Commn on Worship and other Depts, Lutheran Church of Australia. Hon. Associate (Arch.), SA Inst. of Technology, 1989. *Publications:* contribs and articles in architectural pubns. *Recreations:* music, reading, golf. *Address:* 4/118 Brougham Place, North Adelaide, SA 5006, Australia. *T:* (08) 267 4352; The Olives, Yankalilla, South Australia 5203. *T:* (085) 58 2205.

von WECHMAR, Baron Rüdiger, Hon. GCVO 1986; Ambassador of Federal Republic of Germany to the Court of St James's, 1983–88, retired; Member (FDP) for Germany, European Parliament, since 1989; *b* 15 Nov. 1923; *s* of Irnfried von Wechmar and Ilse (*née* von Binzer); *m* 1961, Dina-Susanne (Susie) (*née* Woldenga); one *d* (one *s* one *d* of previous marr.). *Educ:* Oberrealschule, Berlin; Univ. of Minnesota, USA (as prisoner of war). MA Journalism. Army, 3rd Reconnaissance Battalion, Western Desert and PoW Camp, 1941–46. Journalist, 1946–58; joined German Foreign Service as Consul, New York, 1958; Dir, German Inf. Centre, NY; Dep. Head, Govt Press and Inf. Office, Bonn, 1969; State Sec. and Chief Govt Spokesman, 1972; Perm. Rep. to UN, 1974–81; Pres., UN Security Council, 1977–78; Pres., 35th Gen. Assembly, UN, 1980–81; Ambassador to Italy, 1981–83. Member: North-South Round Table, Deutsche Ges. für Auswärtige Politik; UNA Presidium. Commander's Cross, Order of Merit (FRG), 1980; decorations from UK, Sweden, Norway, Japan, Netherlands, Egypt, Mexico, Italy, Romania. Paul Klinger Award, DAG, 1973; UN Peace Gold Medal, 1980. *Recreations:* stamp collecting, ski-ing. *Address:* Amalienstrasse 45, 8000 München 40, Germany.

von WEIZSÄCKER, Freiherr Carl-Friedrich, Dr Phil; University Professor Emeritus; *b* Kiel, 28 June 1912; *m* 1937, Gundalena (*née* Wille); three *s* one *d. Educ:* Universities of Leipzig, Göttingen, Copenhagen, 1929–33. Dr.phil 1933, Dr.phil.habil, 1936, Univ. Leipzig; Asst., Inst. of Theor. Physik, Univ. of Leipzig, 1934–36; Wissenschaftl. Mitarb., Kaiser Wilhelm Inst., Berlin, 1936–42; Dozent, Univ. of Berlin, 1937–42; pl. ao. Prof. Theor. Physik, Univ. of Strassburg, 1942–44; Kaiser-Wilhelm-Inst., Berlin and Hechingen, 1944–45; Hon. Prof., Univ. Göttingen and Abt. Leiter, Max Planck Inst. für Physik, Göttingen, 1946–57; Hon. Prof. of Theor. Physik, Univ. of Göttingen, 1946–57; Ord. Prof. of Philosophy, Univ. of Hamburg, 1957–69. Hon. Prof., Univ. of Munich, and Dir,

Max-Planck-Institut on the preconditions of human life in the modern world, 1970–80. Gifford Lecturer, Glasgow Univ., 1959–61. Member: Deutsche Akademie der Naturforscher Leopoldina, Halle (DDR); Akademie der Wissenschaften, Göttingen; Joachim-Jungius-Gesellschaft der Wissenschaften, Hamburg; Bayerische Akademie der Wissenschaften, München; sterreichische Akademie der Wissenschaften, Wien; Sächsische Akademie der Wissenschaften zu Leipzig. Verdienstorden der Bundesrepublik Deutschland, 1959–73; Orden Pour le Mérite für Wissenschaften und Künste, 1961; Wiss. Mitglied der Max-Planck-Gesellschaft, München. Max Planck Medal, 1957; Goethe Prize (Frankfurt) 1958; Friedenspreis des deutschen Buchhandels, 1963; Erasmus Prize (with Gabriel Marcel), 1969; Templeton Prize for Progress in Religion (jtly), 1989. Hon. Dr theol, Univ. Tübingen, 1977; Hon. Dr iur Free Univ., Amsterdam, 1977. Hon. LLD Alberta, Canada; Hon. Dr rer. nat. Karl-Marx-Univ., Leipzig, 1987; Dr.phil *hc* Technische Univ., Berlin, 1987. *Publications:* Die Atomkerne, 1937; Zum Weltbild der Physik, 11th edn, 1970 (English, London, 1952); Die Geschichte der Natur, 7th edn, 1970 (English, Chicago, 1949); Physik der Gegenwart (with J. Juilfs), 2nd edn, 1958 (Engl., 1957); Die Verantwortung der Wissenschaft im Atomzeitalter, 5th edn, 1969; Atomenergie und Atomzeitalter, 3rd edn, 1958; Bedingungen des Friedens, 1963, 5th edn, 1970; Die Tragweite der Wissenschaft, 1964; Der ungesicherte Friede, 1969; Die Einheit der Natur, 1971, 3rd edn, 1972; (ed) Kriegsfolgen und Kriegsverhütung, 1970, 3rd edn, 1971; Voraussetzungen der naturwissenschaftlichen Denkens, 1972, 2nd edn, 1972; Fragen zur Weltpolitik, 1975; Wege in der Gefahr, 1976; Der Garten des Menschlichen, Beiträge zur geschichtlichen Anthropologie, 1977; Deutlichkeit, Beiträge zu politischen und religiösen Gegenwartsfragen, 1978; Der bedrohte Friede, 1981; Wahrnehmung der Neuzeit, 1983; Aufbau der Physik, 1985; Die Zeit drängt — Eine Weltversammlung der Christen für Gerechtigkeit, Frieden und die Bewahrung der Schöpfung, 1986; Bewusstseinswandel, 1988; *relevant Publication:* bibliography in Einheit und Vielheit, Festschrift…ed Scheibe and Süssmann, 1973. *Recreations:* hiking, chess. *Address:* D-813(0) Starnberg, Maximilianstrasse 15, Germany.
See also R. von Weizsäcker.

von WEIZSÄCKER, Richard, Dr jur; President of the Federal Republic of Germany, since 1984; *b* 15 April 1920; *s* of late Baron Ernst von Weizsäcker; *m* 1953, Marianne von Kretschman; three *s* one *d. Educ:* Berlin and Bern; Univs of Oxford, Grenoble and Göttingen (Dr jur). Army service, 1938–45 (Captain, wounded). Formerly with Allianz Lebensversicherung, Stuttgart and Robeco-Gruppe, Amsterdam. Member: Robert Bosch Foundn, Stuttgart; Synod and Council, German Evangelical Church, 1969– (Pres., Congress). Joined Christian Democratic Union, 1954: Mem., Fed. Board; Chm., Gen. Policy Commn, 1971–74; Chm., Basic Prog. Commn, 1974–77; Dep. Chm., CDU/CSU Parlt Gp, 1972–79; Presidential candidate, 1974; First Chm., Berlin CDU, 1981–83. Mem., Bundestag, 1969–81, Vice-Pres., 1979–81; Governing Mayor of West Berlin, 1981–84. *Address:* Villa Hammerschmidt, 5300 Bonn, Adenauer-Allee 135, Federal Republic of Germany.
See also Carl-Friedrich von Weizsäcker.

von WINTERFELDT, (Hans) Dominik; Director (Public Affairs), Hoechst AG, Frankfurt, since 1987; *b* 3 July 1937; *s* of late Curt von Winterfeldt and Anna Franziska Margaretha Luise (*née* Petersen); *m* 1966, Cornelia Waldthausen; one *s* one *d. Educ:* German schools; Stanford-INSEAD, Fontainebleau (Industriekaufmann). DipICC. Joined Hoechst AG, Frankfurt/Main, 1957; Asst Manager, Hoechst Colombiana Ltda, 1960; Commercial Manager, Pharmaceuticals, Hoechst Peruana SA, 1963; General Manager, Hoechst Dyechemie W. L. L., Iraq, 1965; Man. Dir, Hoechst Pakistan Ltd and Hoechst Pharmaceuticals Ltd, 1967; Hoechst UK Ltd: Dep. Man. Dir, 1972; Man. Dir and Chief Exec., 1975; Exec. Chm., 1984; Dir, 1987–. Member: British Inst. of Directors, 1975–; Anglo-German Assoc., 1975–; British Deer Soc., 1979–; British Assoc. for Shooting and Conservation, 1979–. *Recreations:* music, deer stalking, golf. *Address:* Hoechst AG, Brueningstrasse, PO Box 800320, D–6230 Frankfurt (M) 80, Germany. *T:* (01049)–69–3050.

VOS, Geoffrey Michael; His Honour Judge Vos; a Circuit Judge, since 1978; *b* 18 Feb. 1927; *s* of Louis and Rachel Eva Vos; *m* 1955, Marcia Joan Goldstone (marr. diss. 1977); two *s* two *d*; *m* 1981, Mrs Anne Wilson. *Educ:* St Joseph's College, Blackpool; Gonville and Caius College, Cambridge. MA, LLB. Called to the Bar, Gray's Inn, 1950. A Recorder of the Crown Court, 1976–78. *Recreations:* swimming, walking. *Address:* c/o The Crown Court, Kenton Bar, Ponteland Road, Newcastle-upon-Tyne. *T:* Newcastle-upon-Tyne (091) 864023.

VOWLES, Paul Foster; Academic Registrar, University of London, 1973–82; *b* 12 June 1919; *s* of late E. F. Vowles and G. M. Vowles, Bristol; *m* 1948, Valerie Eleanor Hickman; one *s* two *d. Educ:* Bristol Grammar Sch.; Corpus Christi Coll., Oxford (schol.; MA). Served Gloucestershire Regt and King's African Rifles, 1939–46 (despatches, Major). Asst Secretary: Appts Bd, Univ. of Birmingham, 1947–48; Inter-University Council for Higher Educn Overseas, 1948–51; Registrar, Makerere University Coll., E Africa, 1951–63; Sen. Asst to Principal, Univ. of London, 1964–68; Warden, Lillian Penson Hall, 1965–69; External Registrar, 1968–73. Mem., 1983–89, Vice-Chm., 1986–89, Westfield Coll. Council. Fellow, Queen Mary and Westfield Coll., 1990. *Address:* 13 Dale Close, Oxford OX1 1TU. *T:* Oxford (0865) 244042. *Club:* Athenæum.

VOYSEY, Reginald George, FIMechE; Consultant; Deputy Director, National Physical Laboratory, 1970–77; *s* of Richard Voysey and Anne Paul; *m* 1943, Laidley Mary Elizabeth Barley (*d* 1987); one *s* three *d* (and one *s* decd). *Educ:* Royal Dockyard Sch., Portsmouth; Imperial Coll. of Science. ACGI, DIC, WhSch. Dep. Develt Manager, Power Jets Ltd, 1940–45; Gas Turbine Dept Manager, C. A. Parsons & Co., 1945–48; Engineering Asst to Chief Scientist, Min. of Fuel and Power, 1948–66; IDC 1963; Scientific Counsellor, British Embassy, and Dir, UK Sci. Mission to Washington, 1966–69. *Publications:* patents and articles in jls. *Recreations:* swimming, sailing, painting. *Address:* 16 Beauchamp Road, East Molesey, Surrey KT8 0PA. *T:* 081–979 3762.

VREDELING, Hendrikus, (Henk); Member of Supervisory Board: DSM, since 1981; UCN, since 1982; Weekbladpers, since 1983; *b* 20 Nov. 1924. *Educ:* Agricultural Univ., Wageningen. Member: Second Chamber of States-General, Netherlands, 1956–73; European Parliament, 1958–73; Socio-Economic Adviser to Agricultural Workers' Union, Netherlands, 1950–73; Minister of Defence, 1973–76; Mem. and Vice-Pres. of Commn of European Communities (for Employment and Social Affairs), 1977–80. Member: Dutch Emancipation Council, 1981–85; Dutch Council on Peace and Security, 1987–. *Address:* Rembrandtlaan 13A, 3712 AJ Huis ter Heide, Netherlands.

VULLIAMY, Shirley, (Mrs J. S. P. Vulliamy); *see* Hughes, S.

VYSE, Lt-Gen. Sir Edward D. H.; *see* Howard-Vyse.

VYVYAN, Sir John (Stanley), 12th Bt *cr* 1645; Owner of Trelowarren Estate, since 1950 (property acquired by marriage in 1427); *b* 20 Jan. 1916; *s* of Major-General Ralph Ernest Vyvyan, CBE, MC (*d* 1971) and Vera Grace (*d* 1956), *d* of Robert Arthur Alexander; *S* cousin, 1978; *m* 1958, Jonet Noël, *d* of Lt-Col Alexander Hubert Barclay, DSO, MC; one *s* one *d* (and one *d* (decd) of former marriage). *Educ:* Charterhouse; and British-American Tobacco Co. Ltd, who sent him to London School of Oriental Studies. With British-American Tobacco Co. Ltd in England and China until War. Commissioned RCS in India, 1940 and served, 1940–46, in Arakan, Bangalore, etc; Temp. Major; GSO II Signals, Southern Army, 1944. *Recreations:* gardening, photography and books; travel when possible. *Heir: s* Ralph Ferrers Alexander Vyvyan, [*b* 21 Aug. 1960; *m* 1986, Victoria, *y d* of M. B. Ogle, Skerraton, Buckfastleigh, Devon; three *s*]. *Address:* Trelowarren Mill, Mawgan, Helston, Cornwall. *T:* Mawgan (032622) 505. *Clubs:* Army and Navy; Royal Cornwall Yacht (Falmouth).

W

WADDELL, Sir Alexander (Nicol Anton), KCMG 1959 (CMG 1955); DSC 1944; HM Overseas Civil Service, retired; *b* 8 Nov. 1913; *yr s* of late Rev. Alexander Waddell, Eassie, Angus, Scotland, and late Effie Thompson Anton Waddell; *m* 1949, Jean Margot Lesbia, *d* of late W. E. Masters. *Educ:* Fettes Coll., Edinburgh; Edinburgh Univ. (MA); Gonville and Caius Coll., Cambridge. Colonial Administrative Service, 1937; British Solomon Islands Protectorate: Cadet, 1937; District Officer, 1938; District Commissioner, 1945; Acting Resident Commissioner, 1945; Malayan Civil Service, 1946; Principal Asst Secretary, North Borneo, 1947–52 (Acting Dep. Chief Secretary, periods, 1947–51). Colonial Secretary, Gambia, 1952–56; Colonial Secretary, Sierra Leone, 1956–58; Dep. Governor, Sierra Leone, 1958–60; Governor and Commander-in-Chief of Sarawak, 1960–63; UK Comr, British Phosphate Commissioners, 1965–77. Mem., Panel of Independent Inspectors, Dept of the Environment, 1979–85. On Naval Service (Coastwatcher), 1942–44. Lieut, RANVR; on Military Service, 1945–47, Lt-Col, Gen. List (British Mil. Administration). *Recreations:* hill walking, golf, gardening. *Address:* Pilgrim Cottage, Ashton Keynes, Wilts. *Clubs:* Commonwealth Trust, East India, Devonshire, Sports and Public Schools.

WADDELL, Gordon Herbert; Chairman, Fairway (London) plc, since 1989; Director, E. Oppenheimer & Son Ltd, 1965–87; Executive Director, Anglo American Corporation of South Africa Ltd, 1971–87; *b* Glasgow, 12 April 1937; *s* of late Herbert Waddell; *m* 1st, 1965, Mary (marr. diss. 1971), *d* of H. F. Oppenheimer, *qv*; 2nd, 1973, Kathy May, *d* of W. S. Gallagher. *Educ:* St Mary's Sch., Melrose; Fettes Coll., Edinburgh; Cambridge Univ. (BA); Stanford Univ. (MBA). Rugby Blue, Cambridge Univ., 1959, 1960, 1961; Member, British Isles Rugby Touring Team: to Australia and NZ, 1959; to South Africa, 1962; eighteen rugby caps for Scotland. MP (Progressive Party) for Johannesburg North, April 1974–Nov. 1977. Chairman: Johannesburg Consolidated Investment Co. Ltd, 1981–87; Rustenburg Platinum Mines Ltd, 1981–87; South African Breweries Ltd, 1984–87; Digger, 1991. Director: Cadbury Schweppes, 1988–; Scottish Nat. Trust, 1988–; London and Strathclyde Trust, 1989–. *Recreation:* golf. *Address:* 14 Thurloe Square, SW7 2TE; Corbet Tower, Morebattle, Kelso TD5 8AQ. *Clubs:* Hawks (Cambridge); Honourable Company of Edinburgh Golfers; Royal and Ancient (St Andrews).

WADDELL, Sir James (Henderson), Kt 1974; CB 1960; Deputy Chairman, Police Complaints Board, 1977–81; *b* 5 Oct. 1914; *s* of D. M. Waddell and J. C. Fleming; *m* 1940, Dorothy Abbie Wright; one *s* one *d*. *Educ:* George Heriot's Sch.; Edinburgh Univ. Assistance Board, 1936; Ministry of Information, 1940; Reconnaissance Corps, 1942; Ministry of Housing and Local Government, 1946; Under-Secretary, 1955; Under-Secretary, Cabinet Office, 1961–63; Dep.-Secretary, Min. of Housing and Local Government, 1963–66; Dep. Under-Sec., Home Office, 1966–75. *Recreation:* sailing. *Address:* Long Meadow, East Lavant, Chichester, W Sussex PO18 0AH. *T:* Chichester (0243) 527129.

WADDELL, Rear-Adm. William Angus, CB 1981; OBE 1966; *b* 5 Nov. 1924; *s* of late James Whitefield Waddell and Christina Waddell (*née* Maclean); *m* 1950, Thelma Evelyn Tomlins; one *s* one *d*. *Educ:* Glasgow University. BSc (Hons) Maths and Nat. Phil.; CEng; FIEE. Midshipman, Sub Lieut RNVR (Special Branch), HMS Ranee, HMS Collingwood, 1945–47; Instr Lieut, HMS Collingwood, HMS Glasgow, HMS Siskin, HMS Gambia, 1947–59 (RMCS 1956–57); Instr Comdr, HMS Albion, 1959–61; Staff of Dir, Naval Educn Service, 1961–63; Sen. British Naval Officer, Dam Neck, Virginia, 1963–66; Officer i/c RN Polaris Sch., 1966–68; Instr Captain, Staff of SACLANT (Dir, Inf. Systems Gp), 1969–72; Dean, RN Coll., Greenwich, 1973–75; Dir Naval Officer Appointments (Instr), 1975–78; Rear-Adm. 1979; Chief Naval Instructor Officer, 1978–81 and Flag Officer, Admiralty Interview Bd, 1979–81. ADC to HM the Queen, 1976–79. Assoc. Teacher, City Univ., 1973–75; Sec. and Chief Exec., RIPH & H, 1982–90. Hon. FRIPHH. *Publication:* An Introduction to Servomechanisms (with F. L. Westwater), 1961, repr. 1968. *Address:* c/o National Westminster Bank, 1 Lee Road, Blackheath, SE3 9RM.

WADDILOVE, Lewis Edgar, CBE 1978 (OBE 1965); JP; Deputy Chairman, Housing Corporation, 1978–83 (Member since 1968); Director, Joseph Rowntree Memorial Trust, 1961–79 (Executive Officer of the Trust, 1946–61); *b* 5 Sept. 1914; *s* of Alfred and Edith Waddilove; *m* 1st, 1940, Louise Power (*d* 1967); one *s* one *d*; 2nd, 1969, Maureen Piper. *Educ:* Westcliff High Sch.; Univ. of London (DPA). Admin. Officer, LCC Educn Dept, 1936–38; Govt Evacuation Scheme, Min. of Health, 1938–43; Friends Ambulance Unit, Middle East, 1943–45 (Exec. Chm., 1946); Chairman, Friends Service Council, 1961–67. Chm., Nat. Fedn of Housing Assocs (formerly Socs), 1965–73 and 1977–79 (Vice-Pres., 1982–90); Member: Cttee on Housing in Greater London (Milner Holland), 1963–65; Nat. Cttee for Commonwealth Immigrants, 1966–68; Social Science Research Council, 1967–71; Public Schools Commn, 1968–70; Central Housing Advisory Cttee, 1960–75; Standing Cttee, Centre for Socio-Legal Studies at Oxford, 1972–75; Legal Aid Advisory Cttee, 1972–78; Adv. Cttee on Rent Rebates and Rent Allowances, 1975–81; Cttee on Voluntary Organisations, 1974–78; Working Party on Housing Cooperatives, 1974–76; Central Appeals Adv. Cttee (BBC and IBA), 1974–84 (Chm., 1978–84); Chairman: Advisory Cttee on Fair Rents, 1973–74; Advisory Cttee on Housing Cooperatives, 1976–79; York City Charities, 1957–65 and 1972–88; York Univ. Council, 1977–87; Personal Social Services Council, 1977–80; Coal Mining Subsidence Compensation Review Cttee, 1983–84; Trustee, Shelter, 1966–74 (Chm. 1970–72). Presiding Clerk, 4th World Conf. of Friends, in N Carolina, 1967. Governor, Co. of Merchant Adventurers, City of York, 1978–79. Governor: Leighton Park Sch., 1951–71; Bootham and The Mount Schs., 1972–81 (Chm. 1974–81). JP York, 1968. DUniv: Brunel, 1978; York, 1987. *Publications:* One Man's Vision, 1954; Housing Associations (PEP), 1962; Private Philanthropy and Public Welfare, 1983; various articles in technical jls. *Address:* Red Oaks, Hawthorn Terrace, New Earswick, York YO3 8AJ. *T:* York (0904) 768696.

WADDINGTON, family name of **Baron Waddington.**

WADDINGTON, Baron *cr* 1990 (Life Peer), of Read in the County of Lancashire; **David Charles Waddington;** PC 1987; DL; QC 1971; Lord Privy Seal and Leader of the House of Lords, since 1990; a Recorder of the Crown Court, since 1972; *b* 2 Aug. 1929; *o s* of late Charles Waddington and of Mrs Minnie Hughan Waddington; *m* 1958, Gillian Rosemary, *d* of late Alan Green, CBE; three *s* two *d*. *Educ:* Sedbergh; Hertford Coll., Oxford. President, Oxford Univ. Conservative Assoc., 1950. 2nd Lieut, XII Royal Lancers, 1951–53. Called to Bar, Gray's Inn, 1951, Bencher, 1985. Contested (C): Farnworth Div., 1955; Nelson and Colne Div., 1964; Heywood and Royton Div., 1966; MP (C): Nelson and Colne, 1968–Sept. 1974; Clitheroe, March 1979–1983; Ribble Valley, 1983–90; a Lord Comr, HM Treasury, 1979–81; Parly Under-Sec. of State, Dept of Employment, 1981–83; Minister of State, Home Office, 1983–87; Parly Sec., HM Treasury and Govt Chief Whip, 1987–89; Sec. of State, Home Office, 1989–90. DL Lancs 1991. *Address:* House of Lords, SW1A 0PW. *Club:* Cavalry and Guards.

WADDINGTON, Prof. David James; Head of Department of Chemistry, University of York, since 1984 (Pro-Vice-Chancellor, 1985–91); *b* 27 May 1932; *s* of Eric James and Marjorie Edith Waddington; *m* 1957, Isobel Hesketh; two *s* one *d*. *Educ:* Marlborough College; Imperial College, Univ. of London (BSc, ARCS, DIC, PhD). Head of Chemistry Dept, 1959, Head of Science Dept, 1961, Wellington College; Sen. Lectr, 1965, Prof. of Chemical Educn, 1978, Univ. of York. Pres., Educn Div., Royal Soc. of Chem., 1981–83; Sec., 1977, Chm., 1981–86, Cttee on Teaching of Chemistry, IUPAC; Sec., 1986–89, Chm., 1990–, Cttee on Teaching of Science, ICSU. Nyholm Medal, RSC, 1985. *Publications:* Organic Chemistry, 1962; (with H. S. Finlay) Organic Chemistry Through Experiment, 1965; (with R. O. C. Norman) Modern Organic Chemistry, 1972; (with A. Kornhauser and C. N. R. Rao) Chemical Education in the 70s, 1980; (ed) Teaching School Chemistry, 1985; (ed) Education, Industry and Technology, 1987; (jtly) Introducing Chemistry: the Salters' approach, 1989; Chemists: the Salters' approach, 1990. *Recreations:* golf, gardening. *Address:* Murton Hall, York YO1 3UQ. *Club:* Tang Hall Horticultural Society (York).

WADDINGTON, Gerald Eugene, CBE 1975; QC (Cayman Islands) 1971; Attorney General of the Cayman Islands, 1970–April 1977; *b* 31 Jan. 1909; *o s* of Walter George Waddington and Una Blanche Waddington (*née* Hammond); *m* 1935, Hylda Kathleen (*née* Allen); one *s* one *d*. *Educ:* Jamaica Coll.; Wolmer's Schl., Jamaica. Solicitor, Supreme Court, Jamaica, 1932; LLB (London) 1949; Solicitor, Supreme Court, England, 1950; called to the Bar, Gray's Inn, 1957. Deputy Clerk of Courts, Jamaica, 1939; Asst Crown Solicitor, Jamaica, 1943–48; Resident Magistrate, 1948–58; Puisne Judge, 1959–64; Judge of the Court of Appeal, Jamaica, 1964–70, retired. Joint ed. West Indian Law Reports. Vice-Pres. Nat. Rifle Assoc. Chm. St John Council for Jamaica. CStJ 1962, KStJ 1970. *Recreation:* shooting (Member of Jamaica Rifle Team to Bisley, 1937, 1950, 1953, 1956, 1957, 1960, 1963, 1965, 1967, 1968; Captain, 1950, 1953, 1957, 1967; Captain, WI Rifle Team, 1960). *Address:* PO Box 864, Stittsville, Ontario K2S 1A9, Canada.

WADDINGTON, Very Rev. John Albert Henry, MBE 1945; TD 1951; MA (Lambeth) 1959; Provost of Bury St Edmunds, 1958–76, now Provost Emeritus; a Church Commissioner, 1972–76; *b* 10 Feb. 1910; *s* of H. Waddington, Tooting Graveney, Surrey; *m* 1938, Marguerite Elisabeth (*d* 1986), *d* of F. Day, Wallington, Surrey; two *d*. *Educ:* Wandsworth Sch.; London Univ.; London College of Divinity. BCom London Univ., 1929. Deacon, 1933; priest, 1934; Curate of St Andrew's, Streatham, 1933–35; Curate of St Paul's, Furzedown, 1935–38; Rector of Great Bircham, 1938–45; Vicar of St Peter Mancroft, Norwich, 1945; Chaplain to High Sheriff of Norfolk, 1950; Proctor in Convocation of Canterbury, 1950; Hon. Canon of Norwich, 1951. Chaplain to Forces (TA) 1935–58; Staff Chaplain, Eighth Army, 1943 (despatches twice); DACG XIII Corps, 1945, Eastern Command TA, 1951. *Recreations:* travel, theatre and cinema, religious journalism. *Address:* The Chantry, 67 Churchgate Street, Bury St Edmunds, Suffolk IP33 1RL. *T:* Bury St Edmunds (0284) 754494.

WADDINGTON, Leslie; Managing Director, Waddington Galleries, since 1966; *b* Dublin, 9 Feb. 1934; *s* of late Victor and Zelda Waddington; *m* 1st, 1967, Ferriel Lyle (marr. diss. 1983); two *d*; 2nd, 1985, Clodagh Frances Fanshawe. *Educ:* Portora Royal School; Sorbonne; Ecole du Louvre (Diplômé). Formed Waddington Galleries with father, 1957. *Recreations:* chess, backgammon, reading. *Address:* 11 Cork Street, W1X 1PD. *T:* 071–437 8611.

WADDINGTON, Very Rev. Robert Murray; Dean of Manchester, since 1984; *b* 24 Oct. 1927; *s* of Percy Nevill and Dorothy Waddington. *Educ:* Dulwich Coll.; Selwyn Coll., Cambridge; Ely Theological Coll. MA (2nd cl. Theol.). Asst Curate St John's, Bethnal Green, 1953–55; Chaplain, Slade Sch., Warwick, Qld, Aust., 1955–59; Curate, St Luke's, Cambridge, 1959–61; Headmaster, St Barnabas Sch., Ravenshoe, N Qld, Aust., 1961–70; Oxford Univ. Dept of Education, 1971–72; Residentiary Canon, Carlisle Cathedral, and Bishop's Adviser for Education, 1972–77; Gen. Sec., C of E Bd of Education and Nat. Soc. for Promoting Religious Education, 1977–84. Superior, Oratory of the Good Shepherd, 1987–90. *Recreations:* cooking, films, sociology. *Address:* The Cathedral, Manchester M3 1SX. *T:* 061–833 2220; The Deanery, 44 Shrewsbury Road, Prestwich, Manchester M25 8GQ. *T:* 061–773 2959. *Club:* St James's (Manchester).

WADDS, Mrs Jean Casselman, OC 1982; Member, Royal Commission on Economic Union and Development Prospects for Canada, 1983–85; *b* 16 Sept. 1920; *d* of Hon. Earl Rowe and Treva Lennox Rowe; *m* 1st, 1946, Clair Casselman; one *s* one *d*; 2nd, 1964,

Robert Wadds (marr. diss. 1977). *Educ:* Univ. of Toronto (BA); Weller Business Coll. First elected to Canadian House of Commons (Riding Grenville-Dundas), 1958; re-elected: 1962, 1963, 1965; defeated (Riding Grenville-Carlton), 1968. Member, Canada's Delegn to United Nations, 1961; Parliamentary Sec. to Minister of Health and Welfare, 1962. National Sec., Progressive Conservative Party, 1971–75; Member, Ontario Municipal Bd, 1975–79. Canadian High Comr to UK, 1980–83. Director: Bell Canada; Royal Trustco Ltd; Air Canada. Adv. Bd, Norman Paterson Sch. of Internat. Affairs, Carleton Univ., Ont. Freeman, City of London, 1981. Hon. DCL Acadia Univ., NS, 1981; Hon. LLD St Thomas Univ., NB, 1983; hon. degrees: Univ. of Toronto, 1985; Dalhousie Univ., NS, 1985. Hon. Fellowship Award, Bretton Hall Coll., W Yorks, 1982; Hon. Patron, Grenville Christian Coll., Brockville, 1981. *Recreations:* walking, swimming. *Address:* PO Box 579, Prescott, Ont K0E 1T0, Canada. *Clubs:* Albany (Toronto); Rideau (Ottawa).

WADDY, Rev. Lawrence Heber; retired; Lecturer, University of California, San Diego, 1970–80; Hon. Assistant, St James', La Jolla, since 1974; *b* 5 Oct. 1914; *s* of late Archdeacon Stacy Waddy, Secretary of SPG, and Etheldred (*née* Spittal). *Educ:* Marlborough Coll.; Balliol Coll., Oxford. Domus Exhibitioner in Classics, Balliol, 1933; 1st Class Hon. Mods., Oxford, 1935; de Paravicini Scholar, 1935; Craven Scholar, 1935; 2nd Class Lit. Hum., 1937; BA 1937; MA 1945; Asst Master: Marlborough Coll., 1937–38; Winchester Coll., 1938–42 and 1946–49 (Chaplain, 1946). Headmaster, Tonbridge Sch., 1949–62. Select Preacher, Cambridge Univ., 1951; Oxford Univ., 1954–56. Examining Chaplain to the Bishop of Rochester, 1959–63; Hon. Canon of Rochester, 1961–63; Hon. Chaplain to the Bishop of Rochester, 1963. Deacon, 1940; Priest, 1941; Chaplain, RNVR, 1942–46. Lecturer in Classics, University of California, 1961. Education Officer, School Broadcasting Council, 1962–63; Chaplain to The Bishop's School, La Jolla, California, 1963–67; Headmaster, Santa Maria Internat. Acad., Chula Vista, Calif, 1967–70; Vicar, Church of the Good Samaritan, University City, 1970–74. *Publications:* Pax Romana and World Peace, 1950; The Prodigal Son (musical play), 1963; The Bible as Drama, 1974; Faith of Our Fathers, 1975; Symphony, 1977; Drama in Worship, 1978; Mayor's Race, 1980; A Parish by the Sea, 1988. *Recreations:* cricket and other games. *Address:* 5910 Camino de la Costa, La Jolla, California 92037, USA.

WADE, family name of **Baron Wade.**

WADE OF CHORLTON, Baron *cr* 1990 (Life Peer), of Chester in the County of Cheshire; **(William) Oulton Wade,** Kt 1982; JP; farmer and cheese master; company director; consultant; Chairman: Marlow Wade and Partners Ltd, Consultants; William Wild & Son (Mollington), farmers and landowners; Joint Treasurer, Conservative Party, 1982–90; *b* 24 Dec. 1932; *s* of Samuel Norman Wade and Joan Ferris Wade (*née* Wild); *m* 1959 Gillian Margaret Leete, Buxton, Derbys; one *s* one *d. Educ:* Birkenhead Sch.; Queen's Univ., Belfast. Dir, Chester Developments Ltd. JP Cheshire 1967. Freeman, City of London, 1980; Liveryman, Farmers' Co., 1980–. *Publications:* contribs to Dairy Industries Internat., Jl of Soc. of Dairy Technol. *Recreations:* politics, reading, shooting, food, travel. *Address:* Chorlton Lodge, Chorlton-by-Backford, Chester CH2 4DB. *T:* Chester (0244) 381451. *Clubs:* Carlton, Farmers'; Chester City (Chester); St James's (Manchester).

WADE, Maj.-Gen. (Douglas) Ashton (Lofft), CB 1946; OBE 1941; MC 1918; BA; CEng; MIEE; *b* 13 March 1898; 2nd *s* of C. S. D. Wade, Solicitor, Saffron Walden, Essex; *m* 1st, 1926, Heather Mary Patricia Bulmer (*d* 1968), Sowerby, Thirsk, Yorkshire; one *d*; 2nd, 1972, Cynthia Halliday (*née* Allen). *Educ:* St Lawrence Coll., Ramsgate; Royal Military Acad., Woolwich; Clare Coll., Cambridge. Commnd into Royal Artillery, 1916; served European War, France, Italy and S Russia; seconded RE 1918–21; transferred to Royal Signals, 1921; Staff Coll., Camberley, 1933–34; DAQMG India, 1937–40; GSO 1, GHQ, BEF and GHQ Home Forces, 1940–41; AA and QMG 2nd Division, 1941–42; Dep. Ajt.-General, India, 1942–44; Comdr, Madras Area, India, 1944–47; GOC Malaya District, 1947–48; Mem., Indian Armed Forces Nationalisation Cttee, 1947; Special Appointment War Office, 1948–49; retired, 1950; Telecommunications Attaché, British Embassy, Washington, 1951–54; Sen. Planning Engineer, Independent Television Authority, 1954–60; Regional Officer, East Anglia, Independent Television Authority, 1960–64. Technical Consultant: Inter-University Research Unit, Cambridge, 1965–69; WRVS Headquarters, 1970–75. Chm., South East Forum for closed circuit TV in educn, 1967–73. Chm., Royal Signals Institute, 1957–63; National Vice-Chairman Dunkirk Veterans' Association, 1962–67, National Chairman, 1967–74. *Publications:* A Life on the Line (autobiog.), 1988; contributed to various Services publications, including RUSI Journal, United Services Journal (India), and Brassey's Annual. *Recreations:* gardening, writing. *Address:* Phoenix Cottage, 6 Church Street, Old Catton, Norwich NR6 7DS. *T:* Norwich (0603) 425755.

WADE, Prof. Sir (Henry) William (Rawson), Kt 1985; QC 1968; FBA 1969; MA; LLD (Cantab); DCL (Oxon); Master of Gonville and Caius College, Cambridge, 1976–88; Barrister-at-Law; *b* 16 Jan. 1918; *s* of late Colonel H. O. Wade and of E. L. Rawson-Ackroyd; *m* 1st, 1943, Marie (*d* 1980), *d* of late G. E. Osland-Hill; two *s*; 2nd, 1982, Marjorie, *d* of late Surgeon-Capt. H. Hope-Gill, RN, and *widow* of B. C. Browne. *Educ:* Shrewsbury Sch. (Governor, 1977–85); Gonville and Caius Coll., Cambridge. Henry Fellow, Harvard Univ., 1939; temp. officer, Treasury, 1940–46. Called to the Bar, Lincoln's Inn, 1946; Hon. Bencher, 1964. Fellow of Trinity Coll., Cambridge, 1946–61, Hon. Fellow, 1991; University Lecturer, 1947; Reader, 1959; Prof. of English Law, Oxford Univ., 1961–76; Fellow, St John's College, Oxford, 1961–76, Hon. Fellow, 1976; Rouse Ball Prof. of English Law, Cambridge Univ., 1978–82. Lectr, Council of Legal Education, 1957; British Council Lectr in Scandinavia, 1958, and Turkey, 1959; Cooley Lectr, Michigan Univ., 1961; Vithalbai Patel Lectr, New Delhi, 1971; Chettyar Lectr, Madras, 1974; Chitaley Lectr, New Delhi, 1982; Cassel Lectr, Stockholm, 1987. Vice-Pres., British Acad., 1981–83. Member: Council on Tribunals, 1958–71; Relationships Commn, Uganda, 1961; Royal Commn on Tribunals of Inquiry, 1966. *Publications:* The Law of Real Property, 1957 (with Rt Hon. Sir Robert Megarry), 5th edn 1984; Administrative Law, 1961, 6th edn 1988; Towards Administrative Justice, 1963; (with Prof. B. Schwartz) Legal Control of Government, 1972; Constitutional Fundamentals (Hamlyn Lectures), 1980, rev. edn 1989; articles in legal journals; broadcast talks. *Recreations:* climbing, gardening. *Address:* 1A Ludlow Lane, Fulbourn, Cambridge CB1 5BL. *T:* Cambridge (0223) 881745; Gonville and Caius College, Cambridge CB2 1TA. *T:* Cambridge (0223) 332400, *Fax:* (0223) 332456. *Clubs:* Alpine, United Oxford & Cambridge University.

WADE, Joseph Frederick; General Secretary, National Graphical Association, 1976–84; Visiting Professor, University of Strathclyde, 1985–88; *b* 18 Dec. 1919; *s* of James and Ellen Wade; *m* Joan Ann; two *s. Educ:* elementary sch., Blackburn, Lancs. Trained as compositor, The Blackburn Times, 1934–40; served UK and overseas, East Lancs Regt and RAOC, 1940–46; newspaper compositor, 1946–56. Full-time Trade Union official, Typographical Assoc., 1956; Nat. Officer, NGA, 1964; Asst Gen. Sec., NGA, 1968; Gen. Sec., NGA, 1976, NGA '82 (after amalgamation) 1982. Member: Exec. Cttee, Printing and Kindred Trades Fedn, 1971–74; Exec. Cttee, Internat. Graphical Fedn, 1976–85 (Vice-Pres.); TUC Printing Industries Cttee, 1976–84; TUC Gen. Council, 1983–84; Printing and Publishing Industry Training Bd, 1977–82; Printing Industries EDC, 1979–84. Mem., Blackburn County Borough Council, 1952–56. *Recreations:* walking, Scrabble, gardening. *Address:* 3 Westmore Close, Newbiggin, Ulverston, Cumbria LA12 0TZ.

WADE, Prof. Kenneth, FRS 1989; CChem, FRSC; Professor of Chemistry, Durham University, since 1983; *b* Sleaford, Lincs, 13 Oct. 1932; 2nd *s* of Harry Kennington Wade and Anna Elizabeth (*née* Cartwright); *m* 1962, Gertrud Rosmarie Hetzel; one *s* two *d. Educ:* Carre's Grammar Sch., Sleaford; Nottingham Univ. (BSc, PhD; DSc 1970). Postdoctoral research assistant: Cambridge Univ., 1957–59; Cornell Univ., 1959–60; Lectr in Inorganic Chemistry, Derby Coll. of Technology, 1960–61; Durham University: Lectr 1961–71, Sen. Lectr 1971–77, Reader 1977–83, in Chemistry; Chm., Dept of Chemistry, 1986–89. Visiting Professor: Technical Univ., Warsaw, 1974; Free Univ., Amsterdam, 1977–78; Univ. of S California, 1979 and 1984–85; Notre Dame Univ., 1983; McMaster Univ., 1984; Western Ontario Univ., 1991. Tilden Lectr, RSC, 1987–88. Main Gp Element Award, RSC, 1982. *Publications:* (jtly) Organometallic Compounds: the main group elements, 1967; (jtly) Principles of Organometallic Chemistry, 1968; Electron Deficient Compounds, 1971; (jtly) The Chemistry of Aluminium, Gallium, Indium and Thallium, 1973; (jtly) Organometallic Chemistry, 1976; Hypercarbon Chemistry, 1987; Electron Deficient Boron and Carbon Clusters, 1990; many papers (res. and rev. articles) in learned jls. *Recreations:* (a) musing, (b) musing, (c) walking. *Address:* Chemistry Department, Durham University Science Laboratories, South Road, Durham DH1 3LE. *T:* Durham (091) 3743122.

WADE, Prof. Owen Lyndon, CBE 1983; MD; FRCP; FRCPI; FFPM; Professor of Therapeutics and Clinical Pharmacology, 1971–86, now Emeritus, and Pro-Vice-Chancellor and Vice-Principal, 1985–86, University of Birmingham; *b* 17 May 1921; *s* of J. O. D. Wade, MS, FRCS, and Kate Wade, Cardiff; *m* 1948, Margaret Burton, LDS; three *d. Educ:* Repton; Cambridge; University College Hospital, London. Senior Scholar, Emmanuel Coll., Cambridge, 1941; Achison and Atkinson Morley Schol., UCH, 1945; Resident Medical Officer, UCH, 1946; Clinical Assistant, Pneumoconiosis Research Unit of the Medical Research Council, 1948–51; Lecturer and Sen. Lecturer in Medicine, Dept of Medicine, University of Birmingham, 1951–57; Whitla Prof. of Therapeutics and Pharmacology, Queen's Univ., Belfast, 1957–71; Dean, Faculty of Medicine and Dentistry, Univ. of Birmingham, 1978–84. Rockefeller Travelling Fellowship in Medicine, 1954–55; Research Fellow, Columbia Univ. at Department of Medicine, Presbyterian Hospital, New York, 1954–55; Consultant, WHO. Chm., Cttee on the Review of Medicines, 1978–84; Chm., Jt Formulary Cttee for British Nat. Formulary, 1978–86. Mem. GMC, 1981–84. Hon. MD QUB, 1989. *Publications:* (with J. M. Bishop) The Cardiac Output and Regional Blood Flow, 1962; Adverse Reactions to Drugs, 1970, 2nd edn with L. Beeley, 1976; papers on cardiorespiratory research, adverse reactions to drugs and drug use in the community, in Jl Physiology, Clinical Science, Brit. Med. Bull., Jl Clin. Invest. *Recreations:* books, travel and sailing. *Address:* c/o The Medical School, Birmingham University. *Club:* Athenæum.

WADE, R(obert) Hunter; New Zealand diplomat, retired; *b* 14 June 1916; *s* of R. H. Wade, Balclutha, NZ; *m* 1941, Avelda Grace Petersen (*d* 1990); two *s* two *d. Educ:* Waitaki; Otago Univ. NZ Treasury and Marketing Depts, 1939; NZ Govt diplomatic appts, Delhi, Simla, Sydney, Canberra, 1941–49; Head of Eastern Political Div., Dept of External Affairs, Wellington, NZ, 1949; NZ Embassy, Washington, 1951; NZ High Commn, Ottawa, 1956; Director of Colombo Plan Bureau, Colombo, 1957; Dir, External Aid, Wellington, 1959; Comr for NZ in Singapore and British Borneo, 1962; High Comr in Malaya/Malaysia, 1963–67; Dep. High Comr in London, 1967–69; NZ Ambassador to Japan and Korea, 1969–71; Dep. Sec.-Gen. of the Commonwealth, 1972–75; NZ Ambassador to Federal Republic of Germany and to Switzerland, 1975–78. Represented New Zealand at Independence of: Uganda, 1962; Botswana, 1966; Lesotho, 1966. Pres., Asiatic Soc. of Japan, 1971. *Address:* 12 Pleasant Place, Howick, Auckland, New Zealand. *Club:* Northern (Auckland).

WADE, Major-General Ronald Eustace, CB 1961; CBE 1956; retired; *b* 28 Oct. 1905; *s* of late Rev. E. V. Wade and Marcia Wade; *m* 1933, Doris, *d* of late C. K. Ross, Kojonup, WA; one *s* one *d. Educ:* Melbourne Church of England Grammar Sch.; RMC, Duntroon. ACT. Commissioned, 1927; attached 4/7 DG (India), 1928–29; Adjutant 10 LH and 9 LH, 1930–38; Captain, 1935; Major, 1940; served War of 1939–45, Lieut-Colonel (CO 2/10 Aust. Armd Regt), 1942; Colonel (Colonel A, Adv. LHQ, Morotai), 1945; Colonel Q, AHQ, Melbourne, 1946; idc 1948; Director of Cadets, 1949; Director of Quartering, 1950–51; Director of Personal Services, 1951–52; Military Secretary, 1952–53; Comd 11 Inf. Bde (Brig.), 1953–55; Maj.-General (Head Aust. Joint Service Staff, Washington), 1956–57; Adjutant-General, 1957–60; GOC Northern Command, 1961–62, retired, 1962. *Address:* Windsor, 1/20 Comer Street, Como, WA 6152, Australia.

WADE, Air Chief Marshal Sir Ruthven (Lowry), KCB 1974 (CB 1970); DFC 1944; Chief of Personnel and Logistics, Ministry of Defence, 1976–78, retired 1978; Director, Acatos and Hutcheson, since 1979; *b* 1920. *Educ:* Cheltenham Coll.; RAF Coll., Cranwell. RAF, 1939; served War of 1939–45, UK and Mediterranean (DFC); psa, 1953; HQ 2nd Tactical Air Force, Germany; RAF Flying Coll.; Gp Captain 1960; Staff Officer, Air HQ, Malta; Comdr, Bomber Comd station, RAF Gaydon, 1962–65; Air Cdre, 1964; idc 1965; Air Exec. to Deputy for Nuclear Affairs, SHAPE, 1967–68; AOC No 1 (Bomber) Gp, Strike Comd, 1968–71; Air Vice-Marshal, 1968; Dep. Comdr, RAF Germany, 1971–72; ACAS (Ops), 1973; Vice Chief of Air Staff, 1973–76; Air Marshal, 1974; Air Chief Marshal, 1976. *Address:* White Gables, Westlington, Dinton, Aylesbury, Bucks HP17 8UR. *T:* Aylesbury (0296) 748884.

WADE, (Sarah) Virginia, OBE 1986 (MBE 1969); tennis player; commentator, BBC Television; *b* 10 July 1945; *d* of late Eustace Holland Wade and of Joan Barbara Wade. *Educ:* Sussex Univ. (BSc). Won tennis championships: US Open, 1968; Italian, 1971; Australian, 1972; Wimbledon, 1977; played for GB in Wightman Cup and Federation Cup 20 times (record); Captain, GB team. Mem. Cttee, All England Lawn Tennis Club, 1983–. Hon. LLD Sussex, 1985. *Publications:* Courting Triumph, 1978; Ladies of the Court, 1984. *Address:* Sharsted Court, near Sittingbourne, Kent. *T:* 081–994 1444.

WADE, Sir William; see Wade, Sir H. W. R.

WADE-GERY, Sir Robert (Lucian), KCMG 1983 (CMG 1979); KCVO 1983; Executive Director, Barclays de Zoete Wedd, since 1987; *b* 22 April 1929; *o s* of late Prof. H. T. Wade-Gery; *m* 1962, Sarah, *er d* of A. D. Marris, CMG; one *s* one *d. Educ:* Winchester; New Coll., Oxford. 1st cl. Hon. Mods 1949 and Lit. Hum. 1951; Hon. Fellow, 1985. Fellow, All Souls Coll., Oxford, 1951–73, 1987–89. Joined HM Foreign (now Diplomatic) Service, 1951; FO (Economic Relations Dept), 1951–54; Bonn, 1954–57; FO (Private Sec. to Perm. Under-Sec., later Southern Dept), 1957–60; Tel Aviv, 1961–64; FO (Planning Staff), 1964–67; Saigon, 1967–68; Cabinet Office (Sec. to Duncan Cttee), 1968–69; Counsellor 1969; on loan to Bank of England, 1969; Head of Financial Policy and Aid Dept, FCO, 1969–70; Under-Sec., Central Policy Review Staff, Cabinet Office, 1971–73; Minister, Madrid, 1973–77; Minister, Moscow, 1977–79; Dep.

Sec. of the Cabinet, 1979–82; High Comr to India, 1982–87. Hon. Treas., IISS, 1991–. Chm. of Govs, SOAS, 1990–. *Recreations:* walking, sailing, travel, history. *Address:* 7 Rothwell Street, NW1 8YH. *T:* 071–722 4754; Church Cottage, Cold Aston, Cheltenham GL54 3BN. *T:* Cotswold (0451) 21115. *Club:* Athenæum.

WADHAMS, Dr Peter, FRGS; Director, Scott Polar Research Institute, since 1988, and Senior Research Fellow, Churchill College, since 1983, Cambridge University; *b* 14 May 1948; *s* of late Frank Cecil Wadhams and of Winifred Grace Wadhams (*née* Smith); *m* 1980, Maria Pia Casarini. *Educ:* Palmer's Sch., Grays, Essex; Churchill Coll., Cambridge (BA Phys. 1969; MA 1972); graduate res., Scott Polar Res. Inst. (PhD 1974). Res. Scientist, Bedford Inst. of Oceanography, Dartmouth, Canada, 1969–70 (asst to Sen. Scientist on Hudson '70 expedn, first circumnavigation of Americas); Fellow, NRC Canada, 1974–75 (Inst. Ocean Scis, Victoria, BC); Scott Polar Res. Inst., 1976–: leader, Sea Ice Gp, 1976; Asst Dir of Res., 1981; Dep. Dir, 1983–88. Sen. Res. Fellow, Churchill Coll., Cambridge, 1983–. Leader, 18 field ops in Arctic, 4 in Antarctic; UK Deleg., Arctic Ocean Scis Bd, 1984–89; Member: NERC Polar Scis Cttee; Nat. Arctic Res. Forum; IAPSO Commn on Sea Ice; Royal Soc. Cttee, Antactic Res. SCAR Gp of specialists in Antarctic Sea Ice. Vis. Prof., Naval Postgrad. Sch., Monterey, 1980–81; Green Schol Scripps Instn, 1987–88; Walker-Ames Vis. Prof., Univ. of Washington, WA, 1988. W. S. Bruce Prize, RSE 1977; Polar Medal, 1987; Italgas Prize for Envmtl Scis, 1990. *Publications:* (contrib.) The Nordic Seas, 1986; (contrib.) The Geophysics of Sea Ice, 1986; (ed) Ice Technology for Polar Operations, 1990; numerous sci. papers on glaciology and polar oceanography. *Recreations:* painting, music, sailing. *Address:* 40 Grafton Street, Cambridge CB1 1DS. *T:* Cambridge (0223) 359433. *Clubs:* Arctic, Antarctic.

WADSWORTH, James Patrick, QC 1981; barrister; a Recorder of the Crown Court, since 1980; *b* 7 Sept. 1940; *s* of Francis Thomas Bernard Wadsworth, Newcastle, and Geraldine Rosa (*née* Brannan); *m* 1963, Judith Stuart Morrison, *e d* of Morrison Scott, Newport-on-Tay; one *s* one *d*. *Educ:* Stonyhurst; University Coll., Oxford (MA). Called to the Bar, Inner Temple, 1963, Bencher, 1988. *Recreations:* eating, idling. *Address:* 4 Paper Buildings, Temple, EC4. *T:* 071–353 3366.

WADSWORTH, Vivian Michael, DSc; former Chairman of several public and private companies, retired 1986; *b* 12 April 1921; *s* of Frank Wadsworth and Tillie Wadsworth (*née* Widdop); *m* 1943, Ethel Mary Rigby; three *s* four *d*. *Educ:* Univs of Reading (BScAgric), Bristol, Leeds, and Natal, S Africa (MA, DSc). Economics Lectr, Bristol, Leeds and Natal Univs, 1942–49; Economic Adviser to Govt of S Rhodesia, 1949–55; Under Secretary for Agriculture, Fedn of Rhodesia and Nyasaland, 1955–61; Asst Sec. to Industrial Division, and Principal Economic Adviser, Distillers Co., 1961–63; Man. Dir, Fabrica Nacional de Margerina (SARL), Lisbon, Portugal (food company and former Distillers subsidiary), 1963–68; Tanganyika Concessions: Dir, Chief Exec. and Chm. of all UK subsidiaries, of which Elbar Group Industrial Holding Co. was the principal, 1968–83; Dir, Benguela Railway, Angola, 1974–83; Chm., Harland and Wolff Ltd, Belfast, 1981–83. CBIM. *Recreations:* gardening, travel, walking. *Address:* High Walls, Houndscroft, near Stroud, Glos GL5 5DG. *T:* Amberley (045387) 2434.

WAGNER, Sir Anthony (Richard), KCB 1978; KCVO 1961 (CVO 1953); DLitt, MA, Oxon; FSA; Clarenceux King of Arms, since 1978; Director, Heralds' Museum, Tower of London, 1978–83; Kt Principal, Imperial Society of Knights Bachelor, 1962–83; Secretary of Order of the Garter, 1952–61; Joint Register of Court of Chivalry, since 1954; Editor, Society of Antiquaries' Dictionary of British Arms, since 1940; *b* 6 Sept. 1908; *o s* of late Orlando Henry Wagner, 90 Queen's Gate, SW7, and late Monica, *d* of late Rev. G. E. Bell, Henley in Arden; *m* 1953, Gillian Mary Millicent (*see* G. M. M. Wagner); two *s* one *d*. *Educ:* Eton (King's Scholar); Balliol Coll., Oxford (Robin Hollway Scholar; Hon. Fellow, 1979). Portcullis Pursuivant, 1931–43. Richmond Herald, 1943–61; Garter King of Arms, 1961–78; served in WO, 1939–43; Ministry of Town and Country Planning, 1943–46; Private Secretary to Minister, 1944–45; Secretary (1945–46), member, 1947–66, Advisory Cttee on Buildings of special architectural or historic interest. Registrar of College of Arms, 1953–60; Genealogist: the Order of the Bath, 1961–72; the Order of St John, 1961–75. Inspector of Regtl Colours, 1961–77. President: Chelsea Soc., 1967–73; Aldeburgh Soc., 1970–83. Mem. Council, Nat. Trust, 1953–74; Trustee, Nat. Portrait Gallery, 1973–80; Chm. of Trustees, Marc Fitch Fund, 1971–77. Master, Vintners' Co., 1973–74. Hon. Fellow, Heraldry Soc. of Canada, 1976. KStJ. *Publications:* Catalogue of the Heralds' Commemorative Exhibition, 1934 (compiler); Historic Heraldry of Britain, 1939, repr. 1972; Heralds and Heraldry in the Middle Ages, 1939; Heraldry in England, 1946; Catalogue of English Mediæval Rolls of Arms, 1950; The Records and Collections of the College of Arms, 1952; English Genealogy, 1960, 1983; English Ancestry, 1961; Heralds of England, 1967; Pedigree and Progress, 1975; Heralds and Ancestors, 1978; Stephen Martin Leake's Heraldo-Memoriale (Roxburghe Club), 1982; The Wagners of Brighton, 1983 (jt author); How Lord Birkenhead Saved the Heralds, 1986; A Herald's World, 1988; genealogical and heraldic articles, incl. in Chambers's Encyclopædia. *Address:* College of Arms, Queen Victoria Street, EC4V 4BT. *T:* 071–248 4300; 10 Physic Place, Royal Hospital Road, SW3 4HQ. *T:* 071–352 0934; Wyndham Cottage, Aldeburgh, Suffolk. *T:* Aldeburgh (0728) 452596. *Clubs:* Athenæum, Garrick, Beefsteak.

WAGNER, Gerrit Abram, KBE (Hon.) 1977 (CBE (Hon.) 1964); Kt, Order of Netherlands Lion, 1969; Grand Officer, Order of Oranje Nassau, 1983 (Commander 1977); Chairman, Supervisory Board, Royal Dutch Petroleum Co., 1977–88 (President, 1971–77); *b* 21 Oct. 1916; *m* 1946, M. van der Heul; one *s* three *d*. *Educ:* Leyden Univ. LLM 1939. After a period in a bank in Rotterdam and in Civil Service in Rotterdam and The Hague, joined Royal Dutch Shell Group, 1946; assignments in The Hague, Curaçao, Venezuela, London and Indonesia; apptd Man. Dir, Royal Dutch Petroleum Co. and Shell Petroleum Co. Ltd; Mem. Presidium of Bd of Directors of Shell Petroleum NV, 1964; Dir, Shell Canada Ltd, 1971–77; Chm., Cttee of Man. Dirs, Royal Dutch/Shell Group, 1972–77; Chm., Shell Oil USA, 1972–77. Chairman: De Nederlandsche Bank NV; Gist-Brocades NV; Supervisory Bd, KLM; Vice-Chm., Supervisory Bd, Hoogovens Gp BV, Beverwijk; Member, International Advisory Committee: Chase Manhattan Bank, NY; Robert Bosch, Stuttgart. Order of Francisco de Miranda, Grand Officer (Venezuela), 1965; Officier Légion d'Honneur (France), 1974. *Address:* c/o Royal Dutch Petroleum Company, 30 Carel van Bylandtlaan, The Hague, The Netherlands.

WAGNER, Gillian Mary Millicent, (Lady Wagner), OBE 1977; Chairman, Volunteer Centre, 1984–89; *b* 25 Oct. 1927; *e d* of late Major Henry Archibald Roger Graham, and of Hon. Margaret Beatrix, *d* of 1st Baron Roborough; *m* 1953, Sir Anthony Wagner, *qv*; two *s* one *d*. *Educ:* Cheltenham Ladies' Coll.; Geneva Univ. (Licence ès Sciences Morales); London Sch. of Economics (Dip. Social Admin). PhD London 1977. Mem. Council, Dr Barnardo's, 1969– (Chm., Exec./Finance Cttee, 1973–78; Chm. Council, 1978–84); Chm., Review of Residential Care, 1986–88; Chm., Ct of Govs, Thomas Coram Foundation for Children, 1990–; President: Skill: Nat. Bureau for Students with Disabilities, 1978–; IAPS, 1985–90 (Gov., 1974–). Mem. Exec. Cttee, Georgian Gp, 1970–78. Chm. of Governors, Felixstowe Coll., 1980–87; Gov., Nat. Inst. for Social Work, 1988– (Vice-Chm.). Trustee, Carnegie UK Trust, 1980–. Hon. DSc Bristol, 1989; Hon. LLD Liverpool, 1990. *Publications:* Barnardo, 1979; Children of the Empire, 1982; The Chocolate Conscience, 1987; various articles on residential care. *Recreations:* sailing, gardening, travelling. *Address:* 10 Physic Place, Royal Hospital Road, SW3 4HQ. *T:* 071–352 0934; Wyndham Cottage, Crespigny Road, Aldeburgh, Suffolk. *T:* Aldeburgh (0728) 452596. *Club:* Aldeburgh Yacht.

WAGNER, Jean; Luxembourg Ambassador to the Holy See, since 1981; *b* 31 May 1924; *m* 1957, Laura Wissiak; one *s* two *d*. *Educ:* Univs of Bâle, Lausanne and Paris; Collège d'Europe, Bruges (LLD). Luxembourg Bar, 1951–55; Foreign Ministry, 1954; Delegate to 11th session, UN Gen. Assembly, 1956–57; Counsellor, Paris, 1959–64; Perm. Rep. to Council of Europe, 1964–69; Dir, Political Affairs, Foreign Ministry, 1965–69; Ambassador: to USA (also accredited to Mexico and Canada), 1969–74; to Italy, 1974–81; Sec. Gen., Foreign Affairs, 1981–84; Ambassador: to Belgium (and NATO), 1984–86; to the UK, 1986–89. Commandeur de l'Ordre National de la Couronne de Chêne; Commandeur avec Couronne de l'Ordre de Mérite civil et militaire d'Adolphe de Nassau (Cour grand-ducale); Grand Officier de l'Ordre national du Mérite; several foreign orders and decorations. *Address:* 54 boulevard Napoléon 1er, L 2210 Luxembourg, Grand Duchy of Luxembourg.

WAGNER, Leslie, MA; Director, Polytechnic of North London, since 1987; *b* 21 Feb. 1943; *s* of Herman and Toby Wagner; m 1967, Jennifer Jean Fineberg; one *s* one *d*. *Educ:* Salford Grammar Sch.; Manchester Univ. (MAEcon). Economic Asst and Economic Advr, DEA, 1966–69; Economic Advr, Min. of Technology, 1969–70; Lectr in Econs, Open Univ., 1970–76; Hd of Social Sciences, Polytechnic of Central London, 1976–82; Asst Sec. (Academic), Nat. Adv. Body for Local Authy Higher Educn, 1982–85; Dep. Sec., Nat. Adv. Body for Public Sector Higher Educn, 1985–87. Councillor (Lab) London Bor. of Harrow, 1971–78, Chm., Educn Cttee, 1972–74. Contested (Lab) Harrow W, Feb. 1974. *Publications:* (ed) Readings in Applied Microeconomics, 1973, 2nd edn 1981; (ed) Agenda for Institutional Change in Higher Education, 1982; The Economics of Educational Media, 1982; (jtly) Choosing to Learn: a study of mature students, 1987. *Address:* Polytechnic of North London, Holloway Road, N7 8DB. *T:* 071–753 5181. *Club:* Reform.

WAGSTAFF, Ven. Christopher John Harold; Archdeacon of Gloucester, since 1982; *b* 25 June 1936; *s* of Harold Maurice Wagstaff and Kathleen Mary Wagstaff (*née* Bean); *m* 1964, Margaret Louise (*née* Macdonald); two *s* one *d*. *Educ:* Bishop's Stortford College, Herts; Essex Inst. of Agriculture, Chelmsford (Dipl. in Horticulture 1959); St David's Coll., Lampeter (BA 1962, Dipl. in Theol. 1963). Deacon 1963, priest 1964; Curate, All Saints, Queensbury, 1963–68; Vicar, St Michael's, Tokyngton, Wembley, 1968–73; Vicar of Coleford with Staunton, 1973–83; RD, South Forest, 1975–82. Diocese of Gloucester: Chairman: House of Clergy, 1983–; Bd of Social Responsibility, 1983–; Diocesan Trust, 1983–; Diocesan Assoc. for the Deaf, 1983–; Diocesan Adv. Cttee, 1988–. Mem., General Synod, 1988–. Freeman, City of London; Liveryman, Worshipful Co. of Armourers and Brasiers. *Recreations:* gardening, swimming, travel. *Address:* Christchurch Vicarage, Montpellier, Gloucester GL1 1LB. *T:* Gloucester (0452) 28500.

WAGSTAFF, David St John Rivers; a Recorder of the Crown Court, since 1974; barrister; *b* 22 June 1930; *s* of late Prof. John Edward Pretty Wagstaff and Dorothy Margaret (*née* McRobie); *m* 1970, Dorothy Elizabeth Starkie; two *d*. *Educ:* Winchester Coll. (Schol.); Trinity Coll., Cambridge (Schol., MA, LLB). Called to Bar, Lincoln's Inn, 1954. *Recreations:* mountaineering, fencing. *Address:* 8 Breary Lane East, Bramhope, Leeds. *Clubs:* Alpine; Fell and Rock Climbing (Lake District), Leeds (Leeds).

WAGSTAFF, Edward Malise Wynter; HM Diplomatic Service; Counsellor, Foreign and Commonwealth Office, since 1982; *b* 27 June 1930; *s* of Col Henry Wynter Wagstaff, *qv* and Jean Mathieson, MB, BS; *m* 1957, Eva Margot, *d* of Erik Hedelius; one *s* two *d*. *Educ:* Wellington Coll.; RMA Sandhurst; Pembroke Coll., Cambridge (MA; Mech Scis Tripos); Staff Coll., Camberley; psc. Commissioned RE, 1949; served in UK, Germany and Gibraltar, 1950–62; seconded to Federal Regular Army, Fedn of S Arabia, 1963–65; Asst Mil. Attaché, Amman, 1967–69 (Major, 1962; GSM; South Arabia Radfan bar). Joined FCO, 1969; served Saigon, 1973, FCO, 1975, Oslo, 1976, Copenhagen, 1978, FCO, 1981. Kt, First Degree, Order of Dannebrog, 1979. *Recreations:* God, concern for the bewildered, plumbing. *Address:* c/o Lloyds Bank PLC, 32 Commercial Way, Woking, Surrey GU21 1ER. *Club:* Travellers'.

WAGSTAFF, Colonel Henry Wynter, CSI 1945; MC 1917; FCIT; RE (retired); *b* 19 July 1890; *s* of Edward Wynter Wagstaff and Flora de Smidt; *m* 1st, 1918, Jean, MB, BS, *d* of George Frederick Mathieson; two *s*; 2nd, 1967, Margaret, *o d* of late Sir John Hubert Marshall, CIE. *Educ:* Woodbridge; RMA, Woolwich. Commissioned RE 1910; served in India and Mesopotamia in European War, 1914–18 (despatches, MC); Captain, 1916; seconded Indian State Railways, 1921; Major, 1927; Lieut-Colonel, 1934; Colonel, 1940. 1929–46, employed on problems connected with Labour in general and Railway Labour in particular. Member, Railway Board, Government of India, New Delhi, 1942–46; retired, 1948. *Publication:* Operation of Indian Railways in Recent Years, 1931. *Recreations:* reading and writing. *Address:* c/o Lloyds Bank, 7 Pall Mall, SW1.

See also E. M. W. Wagstaff.

WAHLSTRÖM, General Jarl Holger; International Leader of The Salvation Army, 1981–86; *b* 9 July 1918; *s* of Rafael Alexander Wahlström and Aina Maria Wahlström (*née* Dahlberg); *m* 1944, Maire Helfrid Nyberg; two *s* one *d*. *Educ:* Salvation Army International Training Coll. Salvation Army, Finland: Corps Officer, 1939–45; Scout Organizer, 1945–52; Private Sec. to Territorial Commander, 1952–54; Youth Sec., 1954–60; Divisional Comdr, 1960–63; Principal, Training Coll., 1963–68; Chief Secretary, 1968–72; Territorial Comdr, 1976–80; Salvation Army, Canada and Bermuda: Chief Secretary, 1972–76; Salvation Army, Sweden: Territorial Comdr, 1981. Hon. DHL Western Illinois, 1985. Cross of Liberty, IV cl., Finland, 1941; Knight, Order of Lion of Finland, 1964; Order of Civil Merit, Mugunghwa Medal, Republic of Korea, 1983; Comdr, Order of White Rose, Finland, 1989. *Publications:* (autobiog.) Matkalaulu (Finnish edn), En Vallfartssång (Swedish edn), 1989; contribs to Salvation Army papers and magazines, English, Finnish, Swedish. *Recreation:* music. *Address:* Borgströminkuja 1 A 10, 00840 Helsinki, Finland. *T:* 90–698 2413. *Club:* Rotary.

WAIARU, Most Rev. Amos Stanley; *see* Melanesia, Archbishop of.

WAIDE, (Edward) Bevan, OBE 1988; Partner, Coopers & Lybrand Deloitte, since 1988; *b* 14 Sept. 1936; *s* of William Leathley Waide and Louisa Winifred Waide (*née* Evershed); *m* 1961, Pu-Chin; one *s* one *d*. *Educ:* Farnham Grammar Sch.; Emmanuel Coll., Cambridge (BA); Univ. of California, Berkeley (MA). Teaching Asst, Univ. of California, 1959–61; Sen. Economist, Asia, World Bank, 1962–69; Chief Advisor, Min. of Economic Affairs and Develt Planning, Govt of Tanzania, 1969–73; Dir, N Region Strategy Team, DoE, 1973–76; World Bank: Chief Economist, S Asia, 1976–79; Dir, Develt Policy, 1979–82; Dir, Country Policy Dept, 1982–84; Dir, New Delhi Office, 1984–88. Mem., Commonwealth Develt Corp., 1990–. *Publications:* (jtly) India: an industrialising economy in transition, 1989; World Develt Reports, World Bank; articles on develt and regional planning issues; country reports. *Recreations:* tennis, car restoration. *Address:* 16 St Paul's Place, N1 2QE. *T:* 071–226 3744. *Clubs:* Reform; Vintage Sports Car.

WAIGEL, Theodor; Minister of Finance, Germany, since 1989; *b* 22 April 1939; *s* of August Waigel and Genoveva Konrad; *m* 1966, Karin Hönig; one *s* one *d*. *Educ:* Univ. of Munich; Univ. of Würzburg. Lawyer, 1967–69; posts in Min. of Finance, Min. of Economy, and Min. of Transport, Bavaria, 1969–72; Mem. of Bundestag, 1972–. Chm., CSU, 1988– (Chm., Bavarian CSU Parly Gp, 1982–89). *Address:* Ministry of Finance, 5300 Bonn 1, Graurheindorfer Strasse 108, Germany.

WAIKATO, Bishop of, since 1986; **Rt. Rev. Roger Adrian Herft;** *b* 11 July 1948; *s* of Richard Clarence and Esmie Marie Herft; *m* 1976, Cheryl Oranee Jayasekera; two *s*. *Educ:* Royal College, Colombo; Theological Coll. of Lanka. BTh, BD (Serampore). Employed at Carson Cumberbatch & Co. Ltd, 1966–69; theol coll., 1969–73; deacon 1972, priest 1973; Assistant Curate: Holy Emmanuel Church, Moratuwa, 1972; St Luke's Church, Borella, with chaplaincy to Colombo Prison, 1973; Vicar: Holy Emmanuel, Moratuwa, 1976; SS Mary and John Nugegoda, 1979; Parish Consultant, Diocese of Waikato, 1983. *Publication:* (co-ed) Encounter with Reality, 1971. *Recreations:* reading, avid follower of cricket. *Address:* PO Box 21, Hamilton, New Zealand. *T:* (office) 82–309, (home) 393–696.

WAIN, John Barrington, CBE 1984; author; Professor of Poetry, University of Oxford, 1973–78; *b* 14 March 1925; *e* surv. *s* of Arnold A. Wain and Anne Wain, Stoke-on-Trent; *m* 1st, 1960, Eirian (*d* 1988), *o d* of late T. E. James; three *s*; 2nd, 1989, Patricia, *o d* of R. F. Dunn. *Educ:* The High Sch., Newcastle-under-Lyme; St John's Coll., Oxford (Hon. Fellow, 1985). Fereday Fellow, St John's Coll., Oxford, 1946–49; Lecturer in English Literature, University of Reading, 1947–55; resigned to become freelance author and critic. Churchill Visiting Prof., University of Bristol, 1967; Vis. Prof., Centre Universitaire Expérimentale de Vincennes, Paris, 1969. First Fellow in creative arts, Brasenose College, Oxford, 1971–72, Supernumerary Fellow, 1973–. Pres., Johnson Soc. of Lichfield, 1976–77. FRSL 1960, resigned 1961. Hon. DLitt: Keele, 1985; Loughborough, 1985. Radio plays: You Wouldn't Remember, 1978; Frank, 1983; Good Morning Blues, 1986. *Publications include: fiction:* Hurry On Down, 1953, repr. 1978; Living in the Present, 1955; The Contenders, 1958; A Travelling Woman, 1959; Nuncle and other stories, 1960; Strike the Father Dead, 1962; The Young Visitors, 1965; Death of the Hind Legs and other stories, 1966; The Smaller Sky, 1967; A Winter in the Hills, 1970; The Life Guard and Other Stories, 1971; The Pardoner's Tale, 1978; Lizzie's Floating Shop, 1981; Young Shoulders, 1982 (Whitbread Prize) (televised, BBC, 1984); Where the Rivers Meet, 1988; Comedies, 1990; *plays:* Harry in the Night, 1975; Frank, 1984 (radio); *poetry:* A Word Carved on a Sill, 1956; Weep Before God, 1961; Wildtrack, 1965; Letters to Five Artists, 1969; Feng, 1975; Poems 1949–79, 1981; Open Country, 1987; *criticism:* Preliminary Essays, 1957; Essays on Literature and Ideas, 1963; The Living World of Shakespeare, 1964, new edn 1979; A House for the Truth, 1972; Professing Poetry, 1977; *biography:* Samuel Johnson, 1974, new edn 1980 (James Tait Black Meml Prize; Heinemann Award, 1975); *autobiography:* Sprightly Running, 1962; Dear Shadows: portraits from memory, 1986; much work as editor, anthologist, reviewer, broadcaster, etc. *Recreations:* wet country walks; travelling by train, especially in France. *Address:* c/o Curtis Brown Ltd, 164–168 Regent Street, W1R 5TB.

WAIN, Prof. (Ralph) Louis, CBE 1968; DSc, PhD; FRS 1960, FRSC; Hon. Professor of Chemistry, University of Kent, since 1977 and Emeritus Professor, University of London, since 1978; Professor of Agricultural Chemistry, University of London, 1950–78, and Head of Department of Physical Sciences at Wye College (University of London), 1945–78; Hon. Director, Agricultural Research Council Unit on Plant Growth Substances and Systemic Fungicides, 1953–78; Fellow of Wye College, since 1981; *b* 29 May 1911; 2nd *s* of late G. Wain, Hyde, Cheshire; *m* 1940, Joan Bowker; one *s* one *d*. *Educ:* County Grammar Sch., Hyde, Cheshire; University of Sheffield (First Class Hons Chemistry, 1932; MSc 1933; PhD 1935; Hon. DSc 1977); DSc London, 1949; Town Trustees Fellow, University of Sheffield, 1934; Research Assistant, University of Manchester, 1935–37; Lecturer in Chemistry, Wye Coll., 1937–39; Research Chemist, Long Ashton Research Station (University of Bristol), 1939–45; Rockefeller Fellow, 1950 and 1962. Vice-President, Royal Institute of Chemistry, 1961–64, 1975–78; Member: Governing Body, Glasshouse Crops Res. Inst., 1953–71; E African Natural Resources Res. Council, 1963–; Manager, Royal Instn, 1971–74. Chm., AFRC Wain Fellowships Cttee, 1976–. Nuffield Vis. Prof., Ibadan Univ., 1959; Vis. Prof., Cornell Univ., 1966; NZ Prestige Fellowship, 1973; Leverhulme Emeritus Fellowship, 1978–. Elected to Académie Internationale de Lutèce, 1980. Lectures: Sir Thomas Middleton Meml, London, 1955; Frankland Meml, Birmingham, 1965; Benjamin Minge Duggar Meml, Alabama, 1966; Amos Meml, E Malling, 1969; Masters Meml, London, 1973; Sir Jesse Boot Foundn, Nottingham, 1974; Ronald Slack Meml, London, 1975; Extramural Centenary, London Univ., 1976; Vis. Lectr, Pontifical Acad. Scis, 1976; Douglas Wills, Bristol, 1977; Gooding Meml, London, 1978; Drummond Meml, London, 1979; John Dalton, Manchester, 1979; Holden, Nottingham, 1984; Hannaford Meml, Adelaide, 1985. Royal Soc. Vis. Prof. to Czechoslovakia, 1968, Mexico, 1971, China, 1973 and 1982, Romania, 1974, Poland, 1976, Israel, 1979, Hungary, 1980, West Indies and Philippines, 1981, Hong Kong, 1984, 1988, Japan 1991. Pruthivi Gold Medal, 1957; RASE Research Medal, 1960; John Scott Award, 1963; Flintoff Medal, Chem. Soc., 1969; Internat. Award, Amer. Chem. Soc., 1972; Internat. Medal for Research on Plant Growth Substances, 1973; John Jeyes Gold Medal and Award, Chem. Soc., 1976; Royal Instn Actonian Award, 1977; Mullard Award and Medal, Royal Soc., 1988. Hon. DAgricSci, Ghent, 1963; Hon. DSc: Kent, 1976; Lausanne, 1977. *Publications:* numerous research publications in Annals of Applied Biology, Journal of Agric. Science, Journal of Chemical Society, Berichte der Deutschen Chemischen Gesellschaft, Proc. Royal Society, etc. *Recreations:* painting, travel. *Address:* Crown Point, Scotton Street, Wye, Ashford, Kent TN25 5BZ. *T:* Wye (0233) 812157.

WAINE, Dr Colin, OBE 1990; FRCGP; Chairman, Council, Royal College of General Practitioners, since 1990; General Manager, South West Durham Health Authority, since 1985; *b* 12 March 1936; *m* 1959, Gwendoline Jameson; two *d*. *Educ:* King James I Grammar Sch., Bishop Auckland; Medical Sch., King's Coll., Univ. of Durham (MB BS Hons). MRCGP (dist.) 1975, FRCGP 1976. Principal in general practice, Bishop Auckland, 1962–; Hosp. Practitioner in Paediatrics, Bishop Auckland General Hosp., 1963–88. Course Organiser (Continuing Educn), Regional Post Grad. Inst., Newcastle upon Tyne, 1978–86. Consultant and UK Delegate, European Health Cttee, Primary Care and Prevention Gp, Council of Europe, Strasbourg, 1983–85. *Publications:* (contrib.) Handbook of Preventative Care for Pre-School Children, 1984; Organisation of Prevention in Primary Care, 1986; Why not care for your diabetic patients?, 1986; (contrib.) Chronic Disease in Medical Audit in General Practice, 1990; contrib. to reports of working parties and papers and articles on diabetes, health care for children, asthma, etc in BMJ, The Practitioner, Cardiology in Practice, Members Reference Books, RCGP. *Recreations:* reading, gardening, music, cricket. *Address:* 42 Etherley Lane, Bishop Auckland, Co. Durham. *T:* Bishop Auckland (0388) 604429.

WAINE, Rt. Rev. John; *see* Chelmsford, Bishop of.

WAINWRIGHT, Edwin, BEM 1957; *b* 12 Aug. 1908; *s* of John Wainwright and Ellen (*née* Hodgson); *m* 1938, Dorothy Metcalfe; two *s* two *d*. *Educ:* Darfield Council School; Wombwell and Barnsley Technical Colleges. WEA student for 20 years. Started work at 14, at Darfield Main Colliery; Nat. Union of Mineworkers: Member Branch Cttee, 1933–39; Delegate, 1939–48; Branch Sec., 1948–59; Member, Nat. Exec. Cttee, 1952–59. Member, Wombwell UDC, 1939–59. Sec./Agent, Dearne Valley Labour Party, 1951–59. MP (Lab) Dearne Valley, S Yorks, Oct. 1959–1983; Mem., Select Cttee on Energy, 1979–83. Secretary: PLP Trade Union Gp, 1966–83; Yorkshire Gp of PLP, 1966–83. *Recreations:* gardening, reading. *Address:* 20 Dovecliffe Road, Wombwell, near Barnsley, South Yorks S73 8UE. *T:* Barnsley (0226) 752153.

WAINWRIGHT, Geoffrey John, MBE 1991; PhD; FSA; Chief Archaeologist, English Heritage, since 1990; *b* 19 Sept. 1937; *s* of Frederick and Dorothy Wainwright; *m* 1977, Judith; one *s* two *d*. *Educ:* Pembroke Docks Sch.; Univ. of Wales (BA); Univ. of London (PhD). Prof. of Archaeology, Univ. of Baroda, India, 1961–63; Inspectorate of Ancient Monuments, English Heritage (formerly part of DoE), 1963–; Principal Inspector, 1963–90. Dir, Soc. of Antiquaries, 1984–90. Mem., Royal Commn on Ancient and Historical Monuments in Wales, 1987–; President: Cornwall Archaeological Soc., 1980–84; Prehistoric Soc., 1982–86. Fellow, University Coll., Cardiff, 1985. FRSA 1991. *Publications:* Stone Age in North India, 1964; Coygan Camp, Carms, 1967; Durrington Walls, Wilts, 1971; Mount Pleasant, Dorset, 1979; Gussage All Saints, Dorset, 1979; The Henge Monuments, 1990; numerous articles in learned jls. *Recreations:* Rugby football, racing, food and drink. *Address:* 81 St Margaret's Road, Twickenham, TW1 2LJ. *T:* 081–891 2429; March Pres, Pontfaen, Dyfed SA65 9TT.

WAINWRIGHT, Richard Scurrah; *b* 11 April 1918; *o s* of late Henry Scurrah and Emily Wainwright; *m* 1948, Joyce Mary Hollis; one *s* two *d* (and one *s* decd). *Educ:* Shrewsbury Sch.; Clare Coll., Cambridge (Open Scholar). BA Hons (History), 1939. Friends Ambulance Unit, NW Europe, 1939–46. Retired Partner, Peat Marwick Mitchell & Co., Chartered Accountants. Pres., Leeds/Bradford Society of Chartered Accountants, 1965–66. MP (L) Colne Valley, 1966–70 and Feb. 1974–87, retired. Chm., Liberal Party Research Dept, 1968–70; Chm., Liberal Party, 1970–72; Mem., Select Cttee on Treasury, 1979–87; Liberal spokesman on the economy, 1979–85, on employment, 1985–87. Dep. Chm., Wider Share Ownership Council, 1968–; Member: Nat. Exec., Charter 88, 1989–; Council, Electoral Reform Soc., 1986–. *Recreations:* gardening, swimming. *Address:* 8 Dunstarn Lane, Leeds LS16 8EL. *T:* Leeds 673938.

WAINWRIGHT, Sam, CBE 1982; Member: Monopolies and Mergers Commission, 1985–91; Post Office Audit Committee, since 1989; Director, BICC, 1985–90; *b* 2 Oct. 1924; *m* Ruth Strom; three *s* one *d*. *Educ:* Regent Street Polytechnic; LSE (MSc Econ). Financial journalist, Glasgow Herald, 1950; Deputy City Editor, 1952–55; Director: Rea Brothers Ltd (Merchant Bankers), 1960–77 (Managing Dir, 1965–77); Furness Withy & Co. Ltd, 1971–77; Stothert & Pitt Ltd, 1970–77 (Chm., 1975–77); Aeronautical & General Instruments Ltd, 1968–77; Lancashire & London Investment Trust Ltd, 1963–77; Scottish Cities Investment Trust Ltd, 1961–77; Scottish & Mercantile Investment Co. Ltd, 1964–77; AMDAHL (UK), 1987–; Post Office Corporation: Mem. Bd, 1977–85; Dep. Chm., 1981–85; Man. Dir, Nat. Girobank, 1977–85; Dir Postel Investment Ltd, 1982–85; Dir, 1972–87, Dep. Chm., 1985–86, Chm., 1986–87, Manders (Hldgs). Mem. Council, Soc. of Investment Analysts, 1961–75, Fellow, 1980. Chm., Jigsaw Day Nurseries, 1991–. Hon. Editor, The Investment Analyst, 1961–74. *Publications:* articles in various Bank Reviews. *Recreations:* reading, bridge, walking. *Address:* 6 Heath Close, NW11 7DX. *T:* 081–455 4448. *Club:* Reform.

WAITE, Hon. Sir John (Douglas), Kt 1982; **Hon. Mr Justice Waite;** a Judge of the High Court of Justice, Family Division, since 1982; Presiding Judge, North Eastern Circuit, since 1990; *b* 3 July 1932; *s* of late Archibald Harvey Waite and Betty, *d* of late Ernest Bates; *m* 1966, Julia Mary, *er d* of late Joseph Tangye; three *s* two step *s*. *Educ:* Sherborne Sch.; Corpus Christi Coll., Cambridge (MA). President of Cambridge Union, 1955. Nat. Service, 2nd Lieut, RA, 1951–52. Called to Bar, Gray's Inn, 1956, Bencher, 1981; QC 1975. Junior Counsel to Registrar of Trade Unions, 1972–74. Pres., Employment Appeal Tribunal, 1983–85. *Recreations:* reading (haphazardly), sailing (uncertainly), gardening (optimistically). *Address:* Royal Courts of Justice, Strand, WC2A 2LL.

See also Maj.-Gen. Sir (E.) J. (H.) Bates.

WAITE, Terence Hardy, MBE 1982; Adviser to Archbishop of Canterbury on Anglican Communion Affairs, since 1980; *b* 31 May 1939; *s* of Thomas William Waite and Lena (*née* Hardy); *m* 1964, Helen Frances Watters; one *s* three *d*. *Educ:* Wilmslow and Stockton Heath, Cheshire; Church Army Coll., London; privately in USA and Europe. Lay training adviser to Bishop and Diocese of Bristol, 1964–68; Adviser to Archbishop of Uganda, Rwanda and Burundi, 1968–71; Internat. Consultant working with Roman Catholic Church, 1972–79. Member, National Assembly, Church of England, 1966–68 (resigned on moving to Africa); Co-ordinator, Southern Sudan Relief Project, 1969–71. Founder-Chm., Y Care International, 1985–. Mem., Royal Inst. of International Affairs, 1980–. Paul Harris Fellow, Internat. Rotarian Organisation, 1983–. Member: World Wildlife Council, 1985–; Council, Internat. Year of Shelter for the Homeless, 1987; Council, Uganda Soc. for Disabled Children. Trustee, Butler Trust. Patron: Strode Park Foundn for the Disabled, Herne, Kent, 1985; Friends of the Commonwealth Inst. Templeton UK Project Award, 1985. Hon. DCL: City, 1986; Kent at Canterbury, 1986; Hon. LLD Liverpool, 1986. *Recreations:* music, walking, travel (esp. in remote parts of the world), Jungian studies, international affairs and politics, Left-Handed Society, preservation of old Blackheath. *Address:* Lambeth Palace, SE1 7JU. *T:* 01–928 8282. *Club:* Travellers'.

WAJDA, Andrzej; Polish film and theatre director; Managing Director, Teatr Powszechny, Warsaw, since 1989; Senator, Polish People's Republic, since 1989; *b* 6 March 1926; *s* of Jakub Wajda and Aniela Wajda; *m* 1st, 1967, Beata Tyszkiewicz (marr. diss.); one *d*; 2nd, 1975, Krystyna Zachwatowicz. *Educ:* Acad. Fine Arts, Cracow; Film Acad., Łódź. Asst Stage Manager, 1953; film dir, 1954–; Stage Manager, Teatr Stary, Cracow, 1973. Pres., Polish Film Assoc., 1978–83. Hon. Mem., Union of Polish Artists and Designers, 1977. Dr *hc*: American, Washington, 1981; Bologna, 1988; Jagiellonian, Cracow, 1989. British Acad. Award for Services to Film, 1982; BAFTA Fellowship, 1982. Order of Banner of Labour, 1975; Officer's Cross of Polonia Restituta; Officier, Légion d'Honneur (France), 1982; Order of Kirill and Methodius (Bulgaria). *Films:* Generation, 1954; I'm Going to the Sun, 1955; Kanal, 1956 (Silver Palm, Cannes, 1957); Ashes and Diamonds, 1957; Lotna, 1959; Innocent Sorcerers, 1959; Samson, 1960; Serbian Lady Macbeth, 1961; Love at Twenty, 1961; Ashes, 1965; Gates of Paradise, 1967; Everything For Sale, 1968; Jigsaw Puzzle (for TV), 1969; Hunting Flies, 1969; Macbeth (TV), 1969; Landscape After Battle, 1970; The Birch Wood, 1970; Pilatus (TV), 1971; Master and Margaret (TV), 1972; The Wedding, 1972 (Silver Prize, San Sebastian, 1973); The Promised Land, 1974 (Grand Prix, Moscow Film Festival, 1975); The Shadow Line, 1976; A Dead Class (TV), 1976; Man of Marble, 1977; Rough Treatment, 1978; The Orchestral Conductor,

1979; The Maids of Wilko, 1979 (Oscar nomination, 1980); Man of Iron, 1981 (Palme D'Or, Cannes, 1981); Danton, 1982; Love in Germany, 1985; Chronicle of Love Affairs, 1986; The Possessed, 1987; Korczak, 1990; *plays*: Hatful of Rain, 1959; Hamlet, 1960, 1980, 1989; Two on the Seesaw, 1960, 1990; The Wedding, 1962; The Possessed, 1963, 1971, 1975; Play Strindberg, 1969; Idiot, 1971, 1975; Sticks and Bones, Moscow, 1972; Der Mittmacher, 1973; November Night, 1974; The Danton Case, 1975, 1978; When Reason is Asleep, 1976; Emigrés, 1976; Nastasia Philipovna (improvisation based on Dostoyevsky's The Idiot), 1977; Conversation with the Executioner, 1977; Gone with the Years, Gone with the Days . . ., 1978; Antygone, 1984; Crime and Punishment, 1984, 1986, 1987; Miss Julia, 1988; Dybuk, 1988; Lesson of Polish Language, 1988; Nastasya (adapted from The Idiot), 1989; Hamlet IV, 1989; Romeo and Juliet, 1990; The Wedding, 1991. *Publication:* My Life in Film (autobiog.), 1989. *Address:* Film Polski, ul. Mazowiecka 6/8, Warsaw, Poland.

WAKE, Sir Hereward, 14th Bt *cr* 1621; MC 1942; Vice Lord-Lieutenant of Northamptonshire, since 1984; Major (retired) King's Royal Rifle Corps; *b* 7 Oct. 1916; *e s* of Sir Hereward Wake, 13th Bt, CB, CMG, DSO, and Margaret W. (*d* 1976), *er d* of R. H. Benson; *S* father, 1963; *m* 1952, Julia Rosemary, JP, *yr d* of late Capt. G. W. M. Lees, Falcutt House, Nr Brackley, Northants; one *s* three *d*. *Educ:* Eton; RMC, Sandhurst. Served War of 1939–45 (wounded, MC). Retired from 60th Rifles, 1947, and studied Estate Management and Agriculture. High Sheriff, 1955, DL 1969, Northants. *Heir: s* Hereward Charles Wake [*b* 22 Nov. 1952; *m* 1977, Lady Doune Ogilvy, *e d* of Earl of Airlie, *qv*; two *s* one *d* (and one *s* decd)]. *Address:* Courteenhall, Northampton. *Club:* Brooks's.

WAKEFIELD, Bishop of, from Feb. 1992, Rt Rev. N. S. McCulloch (*see* Taunton, Bishop Suffragan of).

WAKEFIELD, Provost of; *see* Allen, Very Rev. J. E.

WAKEFIELD, Derek John, CB 1982; Under Secretary, Government Communications Headquarters, 1978–82; *b* 21 Jan. 1922; *s* of Archibald John Thomas and Evelyn Bessie Wakefield; *m* 1951, Audrey Ellen Smith; one *d*. *Educ:* The Commonweal School. Air Ministry, 1939–42 and 1947–52. Served War, Lieut, Royal Pioneer Corps, 1942–47. Government Communications Headquarters, 1952–82. Mem., Airship Assoc. Governor, Barnwood House Trust, Gloucester, 1973–90. *Recreation:* airships. *Club:* Naval and Military.

WAKEFIELD, Sir (Edward) Humphry (Tyrrell), 2nd Bt *cr* 1962; *b* 11 July 1936; *s* of Sir Edward Birkbeck Wakefield, 1st Bt, CIE, and of Constance Lalage, *e d* of late Sir John Perronet Thompson, KCSI, KCIE; *S* father, 1969; *m* 1st, 1960, Priscilla (marr. diss. 1964), *e d* of O. R. Bagot; 2nd, 1966, Hon. Elizabeth Sophia (from whom he obt. a divorce, 1971), *e d* of 1st Viscount De L'Isle, VC, KG, PC, GCMG, GCVO, and former wife of G. S. O. A. Colthurst; one *s*; 3rd, 1974, Hon. Katharine Mary Alice Baring, *d* of 1st Baron Howick of Glendale, KG, GCMG, KCVO, and of Lady Mary Howick; one *s* one *d* (and one *s* decd). *Educ:* Gordonstoun; Trinity Coll., Cambridge (MA Hons). Formerly Captain, 10th Royal Hussars. Exec. Vice-Pres., Mallett, America Ltd, 1970–75; Chairman: Tyrrell & Moore Ltd, 1978–; Nicolai Patricia Co. Ltd, 1978–86; Director: Mallett & Son (Antiques) Ltd, 1971–78; Tree of Life Foundn 1976–. Dir, Spoleto Fest. of Two Worlds, USA and Italy, 1973–80. Appeals Consultant, London Br., British Red Cross Soc. Mem., Standing Council of Baronetage. Fellow, Pierrepont Morgan Library. *Recreations:* riding, writing, music, shooting. *Heir: s* Maximilian Edward Vereker Wakefield, 2nd Lieut, Royal Hussars (PWO) [*b* 22 Feb. 1967. *Educ:* Milton Abbey; RMA Sandhurst]. *Address:* Chillingham Castle, Alnwick, Northumberland; c/o Barclays Bank, St James' Street, Derby DE1 1QU. *Clubs:* Cavalry and Guards, Turf; Harlequins Rugby Football (Twickenham).

WAKEFIELD, Rev. Gordon Stevens; Principal of the Queen's College, Birmingham, 1979–87; Director, Alister Hardy Research Centre, Oxford, since 1989; *b* 15 Jan. 1921; *s* of Ernest and Lucy Wakefield; *m* 1949, Beryl Dimes; one *s* three *d*. *Educ:* Crewe County Sec. School; Univ. of Manchester; Fitzwilliam Coll. and Wesley House, Cambridge; St Catherine's Coll., Oxford. MA (Cantab); MLitt (Oxon). Methodist Circuit Minister in Edgware, Woodstock, Stockport, Newcastle upon Tyne, Bristol, 1944–63; Methodist Connexional Editor, 1963–72; Chairman, Manchester and Stockport Methodist District, 1971–79; Chaplain, Westminster Coll., Oxford, 1988–89. Fernley-Hartley Lectr, 1957; Select Preacher: Univ. of Oxford, 1971 and 1982; Cambridge, 1988. Recognized Lectr, Univ. of Birmingham, 1979–87. Member, Joint Liturgical Group (Chairman, 1978–84). DD Lambeth, 1986. *Publications:* Puritan Devotion, 1957; (with Hetley Price) Unity at the Local Level, 1965; Methodist Devotion, 1966; The Life of the Spirit in the World of Today, 1969; On the Edge of the Mystery, 1969; Robert Newton Flew, 1971; Fire of Love, 1976; (ed, with biographical introdns of E. C. Hoskyns and F. N. Davey) Crucifixion—Resurrection, 1981; (ed) Dictionary of Christian Spirituality, 1983; Kindly Light, 1984; The Liturgy of St John, 1985; John Wesley, 1990; contribs to theological jls and symposia. *Recreations:* watching and talking cricket; churches and cathedrals. *Address:* 56 Wissage Road, Lichfield WS13 6SW. *T:* Lichfield (0543) 414029.

WAKEFIELD, Sir Humphry; *see* Wakefield, Sir E. H. T.

WAKEFIELD, Sir Norman (Edward), Kt 1988; Chairman, Y. J. Lovell (Holdings) plc, 1987–90; *b* 30 Dec. 1929; *s* of Edward and Muriel Wakefield; *m* 1953, Denise Mary Bayliss; two *s* four *d*. *Educ:* Wallington County Sch.; Croydon and Brixton Technical Colls. Articled student, Wates Ltd, 1947; Man. Dir, Wates Construction Ltd, 1967; Pres., jt venture co., USA, between Wates and Rouse Co., 1970–73; Man. Dir, Holland, Hannen & Cubitts, 1973; Chief Exec., 1977–83, Chm. and Chief Exec., 1983–87, Y. J. Lovell (Holdings). Dep. Chm., Housing Corp., 1990–. Director: Lloyds Abbey Life, 1986–; English Estates, 1990–. Pres., CIOB, 1985–86. *Recreations:* opera, walking, gardening. *Address:* Bovey End, Brownshill, Stroud, Glos GL6 8AS. *T:* Brimscombe (0453) 884366. *Club:* Arts.

WAKEFIELD, Sir Peter (George Arthur), KBE 1977; CMG 1973; HM Diplomatic Service, retired; Director, National Art-Collections Fund, since 1982; *b* 13 May 1922; *s* of John Bunting Wakefield and Dorothy Ina Stace; *m* 1951, Felicity Maurice-Jones; four *s* one *d*. *Educ:* Cranleigh Sch.; Corpus Christi Coll., Oxford. Army Service, 1942–47; Military Govt, Eritrea, 1946–47; Hulton Press, 1947–49; entered Diplomatic Service, 1949; Middle East Centre for Arab Studies, 1950; 2nd Sec., Amman, 1950–52; Foreign Office, 1953–55; 1st Sec., British Middle East Office, Nicosia, 1955–56; 1st Sec. (Commercial), Cairo, 1956; Administrative Staff Coll., Henley, 1957; 1st Sec. (Commercial), Vienna, 1957–60; 1st Sec. (Commercial), Tokyo, 1960–63; Foreign Office, 1964–66; Consul-General and Counsellor, Benghazi, 1966–69; Econ. and Commercial Counsellor, Tokyo, 1970–72; Econ. and Commercial Minister, Tokyo, 1973; seconded as Special Adviser on the Japanese Market, BOTB, 1973–75; Ambassador to the Lebanon, 1975–78, to Belgium, 1979–82. Chm., Richmond Theatre Trust, 1989–; Gov. European Cultural Foundn, 1988–. *Recreations:* ceramics and restoring ruins. *Address:* Lincoln House, 28 Montpelier Row, Twickenham, Mddx TW1 2NQ. *T:* 081–892 6390; La Molineta, Frigiliana, near Malaga, Spain. *Club:* Travellers'.

WAKEFIELD, William Barry, CB 1990; Director of Statistics, Department of Education and Science, 1979–90; *b* 6 June 1930; *s* of Stanley Arthur and Evelyn Grace Wakefield; *m* 1953, Elizabeth Violet (*née* Alexander); three *s* one *d*. *Educ:* Harrow County Grammar Sch.; University Coll., London. BSc; FSS. Statistician, NCB, 1953–62; DES, 1962–67; Chief Statistician, MoD, 1967–72, CSO, 1972–75; Asst Dir, CSO, Cabinet Office, 1975–79. Member, United Reformed Church. *Recreations:* horse racing, gardening. *Address:* Egg Hall Cottage, 14 Birch Street, Nayland, Colchester CO6 4JA.

WAKEFORD, Geoffrey Michael Montgomery; Clerk to the Worshipful Company of Mercers, since 1974; Barrister-at-Law; *b* 10 Dec. 1937; *o s* of Geoffrey and late Helen Wakeford; *m* 1966, Diana Margaret Loy Cooper; two *s* two *d*. *Educ:* Downside; Clare Coll., Cambridge (Classical Schol., MA, LLB). Called to Bar, Gray's Inn and South Eastern Circuit, 1961; practised at Common Law Bar until 1971. Apptd Dep. Clerk to the Mercers Co., 1971. Clerk to: Governors St Paul's Schs; Joint Grand Gresham Cttee; City & Metropolitan Welfare Trustees; Collyers Foundn Trustees; Council of Gresham Coll., 1980–84 (Mem. Council, 1988–). Trustee, Lord Mayor's 800th Anniv. Awards Trust. Member: Small Firms Cttee, London Enterprise Agency, 1986–; Council, City Technology Colls Trust, 1988–. Hon. Sec., GBA, 1991–. Governor: London Internat. Film Sch., 1981–85, 1990–; Molecule Theatre, 1986–; The Hall Sch., 1990–; Thomas Telford Sch., 1990–. *Address:* Mercers' Hall, Ironmonger Lane, EC2V 8HE. *T:* 071–726 4991. *Club:* Travellers'.

WAKEFORD, Air Marshal Sir Richard (Gordon), KCB 1976; LVO 1961; OBE 1958; AFC 1952; Director, RAF Benevolent Fund, Scotland, 1978–89; *b* 20 April 1922; *s* of Charles Edward Augustus Wakeford; *m* 1948, Anne Butler; two *s* one *d* (and one *d* decd). *Educ:* Montpelier Sch., Paignton; Kelly Coll., Tavistock. Joined RAF, 1941; flying Catalina flying boats, Coastal Comd, operating out of India, Scotland, N Ireland, 1942–45; flying Liberator and York transport aircraft on overseas routes, 1945–47; CFS 1947; Flying Instructor, RAF Coll. Cranwell; CFS Examining Wing; ground appts, incl. 2 years on staff of Dir of Emergency Ops in Malaya, 1952–58; comdg Queen's Flight, 1958–61; Directing Staff, RAF Staff Coll., 1961–64; subseq.: comdg RAF Scampton; SASO, HQ 3 Group Bomber Comd; Asst Comdt (Cadets), RAF Coll. Cranwell; idc 1969; Comdr N Maritime Air Region, and Air Officer Scotland and N Ireland, 1970–72; Dir of Service Intelligence, MoD, 1972–73; ANZUK Force Comdr, Singapore, 1974–75; Dep. Chief of Defence Staff (Intell.), 1975–78; HM Comr, Queen Victoria Sch., Dunblane; Vice-Chm. (Air), Lowland T&AVR. Trustee, McRobert Trusts (Chm., 1982–); Director: Thistle Foundn; Cromar Nominees. CStJ 1986. *Recreations:* golf, fishing. *Address:* Earlston House, Forgandenny, Perth PH2 9DE. *T:* Bridge of Earn (0738) 812392. *Clubs:* Flyfishers', Royal Air Force.

WAKEHAM, Rt. Hon. John, PC 1983; JP; FCA; MP (C) Colchester South and Maldon, since 1983 (Maldon, Feb. 1974–1983); Secretary of State for Energy, since 1989; *b* 22 June 1932; *s* of late Major W. J. Wakeham and late Mrs E. R. Wakeham; *m* 1st, 1965, Anne Roberta Bailey (*d* 1984); two *s*; 2nd, 1985, Alison Bridget Ward, MBE, *d* of Ven. E. J. G. Ward, *qv*; one *s*. *Educ:* Charterhouse. Chartered Accountant. Asst Govt Whip, 1979–81; a Lord Comr of HM Treasury (Govt Whip), 1981; Parly Under-Sec. of State, DoI, 1981–82; Minister of State, HM Treasury, 1982–83; Parly Sec. to HM Treasury and Govt Chief Whip, 1983–87; Lord Privy Seal, 1987–88; Leader of the H of C, 1987–89; Lord Pres. of the Council, 1988–89; responsible for co-ordinating develt of presentation of govt policies, 1990–. JP Inner London 1972. *Recreations:* farming, sailing, racing, reading. *Address:* House of Commons, SW1A 0AA. *Clubs:* Carlton, St Stephen's Constitutional, Buck's, Garrick; Royal Yacht Squadron.

WAKEHURST, 3rd Baron *cr* 1934, of Ardingly; **(John) Christopher Loder;** Chairman: Anglo & Overseas Trust PLC (formerly Anglo-American Securities Corporation), since 1980 (Director, since 1968); The Overseas Investment Trust PLC (formerly North Atlantic Securities Corporation), since 1980; Deputy Chairman, London and Manchester Group PLC (Director, since 1966); *b* 23 Sept. 1925; *s* of 2nd Baron Wakehurst, KG, KCMG, and of Dowager Lady Wakehurst, *qv*; *S* father, 1970; *m* 1956, Ingeborg Krumbholz-Hess (*d* 1977); one *s* one *d*; *m* 1983, Brigid, *yr d* of William Noble, Cirencester. *Educ:* Eton; King's School, nr Sydney, NSW; Trinity College, Cambridge (BA 1948, LLB 1949, MA 1953). Served War as Sub Lieut RANVR and RNVR; West Pacific, 1943–45. Barrister, Inner Temple, 1950. Director: Mayfair & City Properties plc, 1984–87; The Nineteen Twenty-Eight Investment Trust plc, 1984–86; Chairman and Director: Hampton Gold Mining Areas, 1981–86; Continental Illinois Ltd, 1973–84; Chm., Philadelphia National, 1985–90. Trustee: The Photographers' Gallery Ltd, 1979–90; Photographers' Trust Fund, 1986–91. CStJ. *Heir: s* Hon. Timothy Walter Loder, *b* 28 March 1958. *Address:* 26 Wakehurst Road, SW11 6BY. *T:* 071–247 2000. *Clubs:* City of London, Chelsea Arts.

WAKEHURST, Dowager Lady; Dame Margaret Wakehurst, DBE 1965; *b* 4 Nov. 1899; *d* of Sir Charles Tennant, Bt and of Marguerite (*née* Miles); *m* 1920, John de Vere Loder (later 2nd Baron Wakehurst, KG, KCMG) (*d* 1970); three *s* one *d*. Founder, Northern Ireland Assoc. for Mental Health; Founder Mem., National Schizophrenia Fellowship (Pres., 1984–86); Vice-Pres., Royal College of Nursing, 1958–78. Hon. LLD Queen's Univ., Belfast; Hon. DLitt New Univ. of Ulster, 1973. DStJ 1959; GCStJ 1970. *Address:* 31 Lennox Gardens, SW1. *T:* 071–589 0956.

WAKELEY, Sir John (Cecil Nicholson), 2nd Bt *cr* 1952; FRCS; Consultant Surgeon, West Cheshire Group of Hospitals, since 1961; *b* 27 Aug. 1926; *s* of Sir Cecil Pembrey Grey Wakeley, 1st Bt, KBE, CB, MCh, FRCS, and Elizabeth Muriel (*d* 1985), *d* of James Nicholson-Smith; *S* father, 1979; *m* 1954, June Leney; two *s* one *d*. *Educ:* Canford School. MB, BS London 1950; LRCP 1950, FRCS 1955 (MRCS 1950), FACS 1973. Lectr in Anatomy, Univ. of London, 1951–52. Sqdn Ldr, RAF, 1953–54. Councillor, RCS, 1971–83; Member: Mersey Regional Health Authority, 1974–78; Editorial Bd, Health Trends, DHSS, 1968–71; Examiner for Gen. Nursing Council for England and Wales, 1954–59; Consultant Adviser in Surgery to RAF, 1981–89, Hon. Consultant Advr, 1990–. Liveryman: Worshipful Soc. of Apothecaries; Worshipful Co. of Barbers; Freeman of City of London. FACS 1973. CStJ 1959. *Publications:* papers on leading med. jls, incl. British Empire Cancer Campaign Scientific Report, Vol. II: Zinc 65 and the prostate, 1958; report on distribution and radiation dosimetry of Zinc 65 in the rat, 1959. *Recreations:* music, photography, bird-watching. *Heir: s* Nicholas Jeremy Wakeley, [*b* 17 Oct. 1957; *m* 1991, Sarah Ann, *d* of Air Vice-Marshal B. L. Robinson, *qv*]. *Address:* Mickle Lodge, Mickle Trafford, Chester CH2 4EB. *T:* Mickle Trafford (0244) 300316. *Club:* Council Club of Royal College of Surgeons.

WAKELING, Rt. Rev. John Denis, MC 1945; *b* 12 Dec. 1918; *s* of Rev. John Lucas Wakeling and Mary Louise (*née* Glover); *m* 1941, Josephine Margaret, *d* of Dr Benjamin Charles Broomhall and Marion (*née* Aldwinckle); two *s*. *Educ:* Dean Close Sch., Cheltenham; St Catharine's Coll., Cambridge. MA Cantab 1944. Commnd Officer in Royal Marines, 1939–45 (Actg Maj.). Ridley Hall, Cambridge, 1946–47. Deacon, 1947;

Priest, 1948. Asst Curate, Barwell, Leics, 1947; Chaplain of Clare Coll., Cambridge, and Chaplain to the Cambridge Pastorate, 1950–52; Vicar of Emmanuel, Plymouth, 1952–59; Prebendary of Exeter Cathedral, 1957, Prebendary Emeritus, 1959; Vicar of Barking, Essex, 1959–65; Archdeacon of West Ham, 1965–70; Bishop of Southwell, 1970–85. Entered House of Lords, June 1974. Chairman: Archbishops' Council on Evangelism, 1976–79; Lee Abbey Council, 1976–84. Hon. DD Nottingham, 1985. *Recreations:* formerly cricket and hockey (Cambridge Univ. Hockey Club, 1938, 1939, 1945, 1946, English Trials Caps, 1939, 1946–49), gardening, water colours, fly fishing. *Address:* The Maples, The Avenue, Porton, Salisbury, Wilts SP4 0NT. *T:* Idmiston (0980) 610666. *Club:* Hawks (Cambridge).

WAKELY, Leonard John Dean, CMG 1965; OBE 1945; *b* 18 June 1909; *s* of Sir Leonard Wakely, KCIE, CB; *m* 1938, Margaret Houssemayne Tinson; two *s*. *Educ:* Westminster School; Christ Church, Oxford; School of Oriental Studies, London. Indian Civil Service, 1932–47. Served in the Punjab and in the Defence Co-ordination, Defence and Legislative Departments of the Government of India. Appointed to Commonwealth Relations Office, 1947; Office of UK High Commissioner in the Union of South Africa, 1950–52; Dep. UK High Comr in India (Madras), 1953–57; Asst Sec., 1955; Dep. UK High Comr in Ghana, 1957–60; Dep. British High Comr in Canada, 1962–65; British Ambassador in Burma, 1965–67. *Address:* Long Meadow, Forest Road, East Horsley, Surrey.

WAKEMAN, Sir Edward Offley Bertram, 6th Bt *cr* 1828, of Perdiswell Hall, Worcestershire; *b* 31 July 1934; *s* of Captain Sir Offley Wakeman, 4th Bt, CBE and of his 2nd wife, Josceline Ethelreda, *e d* of Maj.-Gen. Bertram Revely Mitford, CB, CMG, DSO; *S* half-brother, 1991. *Heir:* none.

WAKERLEY, Richard MacLennon; QC 1982; a Recorder of the Crown Court, since 1982; *b* 7 June 1942; *s* of late Charles William Wakerley and Gladys MacLennon Wakerley; *m* Marian Heather Dawson; two *s* two *d*. *Educ:* De Aston Sch., Market Rasen; Emmanuel Coll., Cambridge (MA), Called to the Bar, Gray's Inn, 1965. Dep. Leader, Midland and Oxford Circuit, 1989–. *Recreations:* theatre, bridge, gardening. *Address:* Croft House, Grendon, Atherstone, Warwicks CV9 3DP. *T:* Atherstone (0827) 712329.

WAKLEY, Bertram Joseph, MBE 1945; **His Honour Judge Wakley;** a Circuit Judge, since 1973; *b* 7 July 1917; *s* of Major Bertram Joseph Wakley and Hon. Mrs Dorothy Wakley (*née* Hamilton); *m* 1953, Alice Margaret Lorimer. *Educ:* Wellington Coll.; Christ Church, Oxford. BA 1939, MA 1943. Commnd S Lancs Regt, 1940; Captain 1941; Major 1943; served N Africa, Italy, Greece (despatches). Called to Bar, Gray's Inn, 1948. A Recorder of the Crown Court, 1972–73. Reader, Diocese of Southwark, 1977–. *Publications:* History of the Wimbledon Cricket Club, 1954; Bradman the Great, 1959; Classic Centuries, 1964. *Recreations:* cricket, golf. *Address:* 4 The Watergardens, Warren Road, Kingston Hill, Surrey KT2 7LF. *T:* 081–546 7587. *Clubs:* Carlton, MCC, Roehampton.

WALBANK, Frank William, FBA 1953; MA; Rathbone Professor of Ancient History and Classical Archæology in the University of Liverpool, 1951–77, now Professor Emeritus; Dean, Faculty of Arts, 1974–77; *b* 10 Dec. 1909; *s* of A. J. D. and C. Walbank, Bingley, Yorks; *m* 1935, Mary Woodward (*d* 1987), *e d* of O. C. A. and D. Fox, Shipley, Yorks; one *s* two *d*. *Educ:* Bradford Grammar School; Peterhouse, Cambridge (Hon. Fellow, 1984). Scholar of Peterhouse, 1928–31; First Class, Parts I and II Classical Tripos, 1930–31; Hugo de Balsham Research Student, Peterhouse, 1931–32; Senior Classics Master at North Manchester High School, 1932–33; Thirlwall Prize, 1933; Asst Lecturer, 1934–36, Lecturer, 1936–46, in Latin, Professor of Latin, 1946–51, University of Liverpool; Public Orator, 1956–60; Hare Prize, 1939. J. H. Gray Lectr, Univ. of Cambridge, 1957; Andrew Mellon Vis. Prof., Univ. Pittsburgh, 1964; Myres Memorial Lectr, Univ. of Oxford, 1964–65; Sather Prof., Univ. of Calif (Berkeley), 1971. Pres., Cambridge Phil Soc., 1982–84; Member Council: Classical Assoc., 1944–48, 1958–61 (Pres. 1969–70); Roman Soc., 1948–51 (Vice-Pres., 1953–; Pres., 1961–64); Hellenic Soc., 1951–54, 1955–56; Classical Journals Bd, 1948–66; British Acad., 1960–63; British Sch. at Rome, 1979–87. Mem., Inst. for Advanced Study, Princeton, 1970–71; Foreign Mem., Royal Netherlands Acad. of Arts and Sciences, 1981–; Corresp. Mem., German Archaeol Inst., 1987–. Hon. DLitt Exeter, 1988. Kenyon Medal, British Acad., 1989; Steven Runciman Prize, Anglo-Hellenic Soc., 1989. *Publications:* Aratos of Sicyon, 1933; Philip V of Macedon, 1940; Latin Prose Versions contributed to Key to Bradley's Arnold, Latin Prose Composition, ed J. F. Mountford, 1940; The Decline of the Roman Empire in the West, 1946; A Historical Commentary on Polybius, Vol. i, 1957, Vol. ii, 1967, Vol. iii, 1979; The Awful Revolution, 1969; Polybius, 1972; The Hellenistic World, 1981; Selected Papers: Studies in Greek and Roman history and historiography, 1985; (with N. G. L. Hammond) A History of Macedonia, Vol. III: 336–167 BC, 1988; chapters in: The Cambridge Economic History of Europe, Vol. II, 1952, 2nd edn 1987; A Scientific Survey of Merseyside, 1953; (ed jtly and contrib.) Cambridge Ancient History, Vol. II pt 1, 1984, pt 2, 1989, Vol VIII 1989; contribs to: the Oxford Classical Dictionary, 1949; Chambers' Encyclopædia, 1950; Encyclopædia Britannica, 1960 and 1974; English and foreign classical books and periodicals. *Address:* 64 Grantchester Meadows, Cambridge CB3 9JL. *T:* Cambridge (0223) 64350.

WALCOTT, Prof. Richard Irving, PhD; FRS 1991; FRSNZ; Professor of Geology, Victoria University, Wellington, New Zealand, since 1985; *b* 14 May 1933; *s* of James Farrar Walcott and Lilian Stewart (*née* Irving); *m* 1960, Genevieve Rae Lovatt; one *s* two *d*. *Educ:* Victoria Univ., Wellington (BSc Hons 1962; PhD 1965). Meteorological Asst, Falkland Is Dependencies Survey, 1955–58; Post-doctoral Fellow, Geophysics Dept, Univ. of BC, 1966–67; Research Scientist: Earth Physics Br., Dept of Energy, Mines and Resources, Ottawa, 1967–74; Geophysics Div., Dept Sci. and Industrial Res., Wellington, NZ, 1975–84. FRSNZ 1982. *Recreations:* tramping, gardening. *Address:* 24 Mahoe Street, Eastbourne, Wellington, New Zealand. *T:* (644) 628040.

WALD, Prof. George; Higgins Professor of Biology, Harvard University, 1968–77, now Emeritus Professor; *b* 18 Nov. 1906; *s* of Isaac Wald and Ernestine (*née* Rosenmann); *m* 1st, 1931, Frances Kingsley (marr. diss.); two *s*; 2nd, 1958, Ruth Hubbard; one *s* one *d*. *Educ:* Washington Square Coll. of New York Univ. (BS); Columbia Univ. (PhD). Nat. Research Coun. Fellowship, 1932–34. Harvard University: Instr and Tutor in Biology, 1934–39; Faculty Instr, 1939–44; Associate Prof., 1944–48; Prof. of Biology, 1948–77, Emeritus Prof., 1977–. Nobel Prize in Physiology and Medicine (jointly), 1967. Vice-Pres., People's Permanent Tribunal, Rome (Pres., internat. tribunals on El Salvador, Philippines, Afghanistan, Zaire, Guatemala). Writes and lectures on cold war, arms race, human rights, nuclear power and weapons; developed World-Third World relations. Has many hon. doctorates from univs in USA and abroad; Guest, China Assoc. for Friendship with Foreign Peoples, Jan.-Feb. 1972; US/Japan Distinguished Scientist Exchange, 1973. *Publications:* (co-author) General Education in a Free Society; (co-author) Twenty-six Afternoons of Biology. Many sci. papers (on the biochemistry and physiology of vision and on biochem. evolution) in: Jl of Gen. Physiology, Nature, Science, Jl of Opt. Soc. of Amer., etc. *Recreations:* art, archæology. *Address:* 21 Lakeview Avenue, Cambridge, Mass 02138, USA. *T:* (617) 868–7748.

WALD, Prof. Nicholas John, FRCP; Professor and Head of Department of Environmental and Preventive Medicine, and Chairman, Wolfson Institute of Preventive Medicine, St Bartholomew's Hospital Medical College, since 1983; Hon. Consultant, St Bartholomew's Hospital, since 1983; *b* 31 May 1944; *s* of Adolf Max Wald and Frieda (*née* Shatsow); *m* 1966, Nancy Evelyn Miller; three *s* one *d*. *Educ:* Owen's Sch., EC1; University Coll. London; University Coll. Hosp. Med. Sch. (MB BS); DSc (Med) London 1987. FRCP 1986 (MRCP 1971); FFPHM (FFCM 1982; MFCM 1980). VSO, India, 1966. Ho. appts, UCH and Barnet Gen. Hosp., 1968–69; Med. Registrar, UCH, 1970; Member: MRC Sci. Staff, MRC Epidemiology and Med. Care Unit, 1971; Sci. Staff, ICRF (formerly DHSS) Cancer Epidem. and Clin. Trials Unit, 1972–82, Dep. Dir, 1982–83; Wellcome Vis. Prof. in Basic Med. Scis, at Foundn for Blood Res., USA, 1980, then Hon. Sen. Res. Scientist. Chairman: MRC Smoking Res. Rev. Cttee, 1986–; MRC Study Monitoring Cttee of Randomised Trial of Colo-rectal Cancer Screening, 1986–; MRC Volatile Substance Abuse Wkg Party, 1985–87; NE Thames Reg. Breast Cancer Res. Cttee, 1988–; Nat. Inst. of Child Health and Human Develt Wkg Gp on Quality Control of Alpha-fetoprotein Measurement, 1978; Member: MRC Neurosciences Bd, 1962–86; MRC Steering Cttee of Randomised Trial of Multivitamins and Neural Tube Defects, 1983–; DHSS Adv. Cttee on Breast Cancer, 1988–; DHSS Cttee on Med. Aspects of Air, Soil and Water, 1985–; DHSS Cttee on Carcinogenicity of Chemicals in Food, Consumer Products and the Environment, 1984–89; DHSS Indep. Sci. Cttee on Smoking and Health, 1983–; RCP Cttee on Ethical Issues in Medicine, 1986–; Sub-Cttee on Ethical Issues in Clin. Genetics, 1984–, and Computer Cttee, 1988–; Cttee on Environmental Tobacco Smoke, Nat. Acad. of Sci., USA, 1985–86. William Julius Mickle Fellow, 1990. *Publications:* (ed) Antenatal and Neonatal Screening, 1984; (ed with Sir Richard Doll) Interpretation of Negative Epidemiological Evidence for Carcinogenicity, 1985; (ed jtly) UK Smoking Statistics, 1988; (ed with Sir Peter Froggatt) Nicotine, Smoking and the Low Tar Programme, 1989; (ed with J. Baron) Smoking and Hormone Related Disorders, 1990; articles in sci. jls on screening for neural tube defects, Down's Syndrome and other disorders, on health effects of tobacco, on the aetiology and prevention of cancer, cardiovascular disease and congenital malformations. *Recreations:* ski-ing, boating, economics. *Address:* Department of Environmental and Preventive Medicine, St Bartholomew's Hospital Medical College, Charterhouse Square, EC1M 6BQ; 9 Park Crescent Mews East, W1N 5HB. *T:* 071–636 2721. *Club:* Athenæum.

WALDEGRAVE, family name of **Earl Waldegrave.**

WALDEGRAVE, 12th Earl, *cr* 1729, **Geoffrey Noel Waldegrave,** KG 1971; GCVO 1976; TD; DL; Bt 1643; Baron Waldegrave, 1685; Viscount Chewton, 1729; Member of the Prince's Council of the Duchy of Cornwall, 1951–58 and 1965–76, Lord Warden of the Stannaries, 1965–76; *b* 21 Nov. 1905; *o s* of 11th Earl and Anne Katharine (*d* 1962), *d* of late Rev. W. P. Bastard, Buckland Court and Kitley, Devon; *S* father, 1936; *m* 1930, Mary Hermione, *d* of Lt-Col A. M. Grenfell, DSO; two *s* five *d*. *Educ:* Winchester; Trinity Coll., Cambridge (BA). Served War of 1939–45, Major RA (TA). Chm., Som AEC, 1948–51; Liaison Officer to Min. of Agriculture, Fisheries and Food (formerly Min. of Agriculture and Fisheries), for Som, Wilts and Glos, 1952–57; Jt Parly Sec., Min. of Agriculture, Fisheries and Food, 1958–62; Chairman: Forestry Commn, 1963–65; Adv. Cttee on Meat Research, 1969–73. Director: Lloyds Bank Ltd, 1964–76 (Chm., Bristol Regional Bd, 1966–76); Bristol Waterworks Co., 1938–58 and 1963–78. Pres., Somerset Trust for Nature Conservation, 1964–80. Mem., BBC Gen. Adv. Council, 1963–66. Mem. Council and Trustee, Royal Bath and W Southern Counties Soc. (Pres., 1974); Trustee, Partis Coll., Bath, 1935–88; formerly Mem. Court and Council, and Chm. Agricl Cttee, Bristol Univ. Chm., Friends of Wells Cathedral, 1970–84. Hon. LLD Bristol, 1976. Former Governor: Wells Cathedral Sch.; Nat. Fruit and Cider Inst., Long Ashton. Mem. Som CC, 1937–58; CA, 1949–58; DL Somerset, 1951; Vice-Lieutenant Somerset, 1955–60. Officer, Legion of Merit, USA. *Heir: s* Viscount Chewton, *qv*. *Address:* House of Lords, SW1A 0PW. *Club:* Travellers'.

See also Sir J. D. Boles, Baron Forteviot, M. J. Hussey, Lady Susan Hussey, Baron Strathcona and Mount Royal, Rt Hon. William Waldegrave.

WALDEGRAVE, Rt. Hon. William (Arthur), PC 1990; MP (C) Bristol West, since 1979; Secretary of State for Health, since 1990; *b* 15 Aug. 1946; *yr s* of Earl Waldegrave, *qv*; *m* 1977, Caroline, *y d* of Major and Mrs Richard Burrows, Kemsing, Kent; one *s* three *d*. *Educ:* Eton (Newcastle Schol.); Corpus Christi Coll., Oxford (Open Schol.; 1st Cl. Lit. Hum. 1969; Hon. Fellow, 1991) (President, Oxford Union and Oxford Univ. Conservative Assoc.); Harvard Univ. (Kennedy Fellow). Fellow, All Souls Coll., Oxford, 1971–86. Central Policy Review Staff, Cabinet Office, 1971–73; Political Staff, 10 Downing Street, 1973–74; Head of Leader of Opposition's Office, 1974–75. Parly Under-Sec. of State, DES, 1981–83, DoE, 1983–85. Minister of State for the Environment and Countryside, 1985–87, for Planning, 1986–88, and for Housing, 1987–88, DoE; Minister of State, FCO, 1988–90. GEC Ltd, 1975–81. JP Inner London Juvenile Court, 1975–79. Mem., IBA Adv. Council, 1980–81. *Publication:* The Binding of Leviathan, 1977. *Address:* House of Commons, SW1A 0AA. *T:* 071–219 4574. *Clubs:* Beefsteak, Pratt's; Clifton (Bristol).

WALDEN, (Alastair) Brian; television presenter and journalist; *b* 8 July 1932; *s* of W. F. Walden; *m* Hazel Downes, *d* of William A. Downes; one *s* (and three *s* of former marriages). *Educ:* West Bromwich Grammar School; Queen's College and Nuffield College, Oxford; Pres., Oxford Union, 1957. University Lecturer. MP (Lab): Birmingham, All Saints, 1964–74; Birmingham, Ladywood, 1974–77. Mem., W Midland Bd, Central TV, 1981–84. Columnist: London Standard, 1983–86; Thomson Regional Newspapers, 1983–86; Sunday Times, 1986–90. Presenter: Weekend World, LWT, 1977–86; The Walden Interview, ITV, 1988 and 1989; Walden, LWT, 1990–. Shell International Award, 1982; BAFTA Richard Dimbleby Award, 1985; Aims of Industry Special Free Enterprise Award, 1990; TV Times Favourite TV Current Affairs Personality, 1990; Television and Radio Industries Club ITV Personality of the Year, 1991. *Publication:* The Walden Interviews, 1990. *Recreations:* chess, gardening. *Address:* Landfall, Fort Road, St Peter Port, Guernsey.

WALDEN, George Gordon Harvey, CMG 1981; MP (C) Buckingham, since 1983; *b* 15 Sept. 1939; *s* of G. G. Walden; *m* 1970, Sarah Nicolette Hunt; two *s* one *d*. *Educ:* Latymer Upper Sch.; Jesus Coll., Cambridge; Moscow Univ. (post-graduate). Research Dept, Foreign Office, 1962–65; Chinese Language Student, Hong Kong Univ., 1965–67; Second Secretary, Office of HM Chargé d'Affaires, Peking, 1967–70; First Sec., FCO (Soviet Desk), 1970–73; Ecole Nationale d'Administration, Paris, 1973–74; First Sec., HM Embassy, Paris, 1974–78; Principal Private Sec. to Sec. of State for Foreign and Commonwealth Sec., 1978–81; sabbatical year, Harvard, 1981; Head of Planning Staff, FCO, 1982–83; retired from HM Diplomatic Service, 1983. PPS to Sec. of State for Educn and Science, 1984–85; Parly Under-Sec. of State, DES, 1985–87. Columnist, Daily Telegraph, 1987–. *Publications:* The Shoeblack and the Sovereign, 1988; Ethics and Foreign Policy, 1990. *Address:* House of Commons, SW1.

WALDEN, Rt. Rev. Graham Howard; *see* Murray, Bishop of The.

WALDEN, Herbert Richard Charles, CBE 1986; part-time Member, Building Societies Commission, since 1986; *b* 6 Oct. 1926; *s* of Reginald George Walden and Matilda Ethel Walden; *m* 1950, Margaret Walker; two *d*. *Educ:* Westgate Sch., Warwick. FCIS; FCBSI. War service, 1944–47, Royal Warwickshire Regt and Royal Leicestershire Regt (UK and Gold Coast) (Captain). Asst Sec., Warwick Building Soc., 1955, Gen. Manager 1962; Gen. Manager, Rugby and Warwick Building Soc. (on merger), 1967; Gen. Manager, Heart of England Building Soc. (on merger), 1974, Dir and Gen. Manager, 1974–86. Mem. Bd, Housing Corp., 1985–88. Chm., Midland Assoc. of Building Socs, 1972–73, Vice-Pres., 1986; Mem. Council, Building Societies Assoc., 1974–86, Dep. Chm. 1981–83, Chm., 1983–85; Vice Pres., CBSI, 1988–. Mem., Warwick BC, 1955–63; Chm., S Warwickshire HMC, 1964–72; Mem., Warwick Schs Foundn, 1962–90 (Chm., 1986–90); Trustee, various Warwick Charities; Founder Pres., Rotary Club of Warwick, 1965; Vice Pres., Warwickshire Scout Assoc. (former County Treasurer). Commissioner of Taxes. *Recreation:* watching cricket and soccer. *Address:* Fieldgate House, 24 Hill Wootton Road, Leek Wootton, Warwick CV35 7QL. *T:* Kenilworth 54291. *Club:* Naval and Military.

WALDER, Edwin James, CMG 1971; management consultant and company director, since 1981; *b* 5 Aug. 1921; *s* of Edwin James Walder and Dulcie Muriel Walder (*née* Griffiths); *m* 1944, Norma Cheslin; two *d*. *Educ:* North Newtown High Sch.; Univ. of Sydney (BEc). FRAIPA 1983. Apptd NSW Civil Service, 1938; NSW State Treasury: 1945; Asst Under-Sec. (Finance), 1959–61; Dep. Under-Sec., 1961–63; Under-Sec. and Comptroller of Accounts, 1963–65; Pres., Metrop. Water, Sewerage and Drainage Bd, Sydney, 1965–81. Member: State Pollution Control Commn, 1971–81; Metropolitan Waste Disposal Authority (Sydney), 1971–81. *Recreations:* lawn bowls, fishing, swimming. *Address:* 44 Del Monte Place, Copacabana, NSW 2251, Australia. *Clubs:* City Tattersall's (Sydney); Central Coast League's; Avoca Beach Bowling; Avoca Beach Probus.

WALDER, Ruth Christabel, (Mrs Wesierska), OBE 1956; *b* 15 Jan. 1906; *d* of Rev. Ernest Walder; *m* 1955, Maj.-Gen. George Wesierski (*d* 1967), formerly Judge Advocate General of the Polish Forces. *Educ:* Cheltenham Ladies' College. General Organiser, National Federation of Women's Institutes, 1934–40; Admiralty, 1940–41; Relief Department, Foreign Office, 1942–44; UNRRA, Sec. Food Cttee of Council for Europe, 1944–47; Secretary United Nations Appeal for Children (in the UK), 1948; National General Secretary, YWCA of Great Britain, 1949–67. Lectr for the European Community, 1970–. Defence Medal, 1946. Polish Gold Cross of Merit, 1969. *Publication:* (as Ruth Walder Wesierska) They built a Jolly Good Mess (memoirs, in Europe 1939–45), 1987. *Address:* Westhope, Langton Herring, Weymouth, Dorset DT3 4HZ. *T:* Abbotsbury (0305) 871233. *Clubs:* Naval and Military; Royal Dorset Yacht.

WALDHEIM, Dr Kurt; President of the Republic of Austria, 1986–July 1992; *b* 21 Dec. 1918; *m* 1944, Elisabeth Ritschel Waldheim; one *s* two *d*. *Educ:* Consular Academy, Vienna; Univ. of Vienna (Dr Jr 1944). Entered Austrian foreign service, 1945; served in Min. for Foreign Affairs; Mem., Austrian Delegn to Paris, London and Moscow for negotiations on Austrian State Treaty, 1945–47; 1st Sec., Embassy, Paris, 1948–51; apptd Counsellor and Head of Personnel Div., Min. of Foreign Affairs, 1951–55; Permanent Austrian Observer to UN, 1955–56; Minister Plenipotentiary to Canada, 1956–58; Ambassador to Canada, 1958–60; Dir-Gen. for Political Affairs, Min. of Foreign Affairs, 1960–64; Permanent Rep. of Austria to UN, 1964–68 (Chm., Outer Space Cttee of UN 1965–68 and 1970–71); Federal Minister for Foreign Affairs, 1968–70; Candidate for the Presidency of Republic of Austria, 1971; Permanent Rep. of Austria to UN, 1970–Dec. 1971; Sec.-Gen. of UN, 1972–81. Guest Prof. of Diplomacy, Georgetown Univ., Washington DC, 1982–84. Chm., InterAction Council for Internat. Co-operation, 1983–85. Hon. LLD: Chile, Carleton, Rutgers, Fordham, 1972; Jawaharlal Nehru, Bucharest, 1973; Wagner Coll., NY, Catholic Univ. of America, Wilfrid Laurier, 1974; Catholic Univ. of Leuven, Charles Univ., Hamilton Coll., Clinton, NY, 1975; Denver, Philippines, Nice, 1976; American Univ., Kent State, Warsaw, Moscow State Univ., Mongolian State Univ., 1977; Atlanta Univ., Humboldt Univ., Univ. of S Carolina, 1979; Notre Dame, USA, 1980. George Marshall Peace Award, USA, 1977; Dr Karl Renner Prize, City of Vienna, 1978. *Publications:* The Austrian Example, 1971, English edn 1973; The Challenge of Peace, 1977, English edn 1980; Building the Future Order, 1980; In the Eye of the Storm, 1985. *Recreations:* sailing, swimming, skiing, horseback riding. *Address:* (until July 1992) Präsidentschaftskanzlei, Hofburg, 1014 Vienna, Austria; (from July 1992) 1 Lobkowitz-Platz, 1010 Vienna, Austria.

WALDMANN, Prof. Herman, FRS 1990; Kay Kendall Professor of Therapeutic Immunology, Cambridge, since 1989; Fellow of King's College, Cambridge, since 1985; *b* 27 Feb. 1945; *s* of Leon and Rene Ryfka Waldmann; *m* 1971, Judith Ruth Young. *Educ:* Sir George Monoux Grammar Sch., Walthamstow; Sidney Sussex Coll., Cambridge (BA); London Hosp. Med Coll. (MB BChir); PhD Cantab. MRCPath, MRCP. Dept of Pathology, Cambridge, 1971–. Graham Bull Prize for Clinical Res., RCP, 1991. *Publications:* Limiting Dilution Analysis (with Dr I. Lefkovits), 1977; The Immune System (with Dr I. McConnell and A. Munro), 1981; (ed) Monoclonal Antibodies, 1988; many scientific papers. *Recreations:* family, food, friends, travel, music. *Address:* 11 Gurney Way, Cambridge CB4 2ED; Immunology Division, New Addenbrooke's Hospital, Hills Road, Cambridge CB2 2QQ. *T:* Cambridge (0223) 336900.

WALDRON, Brig. John Graham Claverhouse, CBE 1958 (OBE 1944); DSO 1945; *b* 15 Nov. 1909; *s* of William Slade Olver (*d* 1909), Falmouth; *m* 1933, Marjorie, *d* of Arthur Waldron (*d* 1953), Newbury; one *s* one *d*. *Educ:* Marlborough; RMC, Sandhurst. jssc, psc. 2nd Lieut, Gloucestershire Regt, 1929. Served War of 1939–45 (OBE, DSO): 5 British Division and 1st Bn Green Howards, in India, Middle East, Italy, NW Europe. Lt-Col, 10th Gurkha Rifles, 1951; Brigadier, 1958; ADC to the Queen, 1960–61; retired, 1961. *Address:* c/o Lloyds Bank, Cox's and Kings Branch, 6 Pall Mall, SW1Y 5NL. *Clubs:* Army and Navy, Royal Cruising.

WALDRON-RAMSEY, Waldo Emerson; Barrister and Attorney-at-Law; international consultant; *b* 1 Jan. 1930; *s* of Wyatt and Delcina Waldron-Ramsey; *m* 1954, Shiela Pamella Beresford, Georgetown, Guyana; one *s* two *d*. *Educ:* Barbados; Hague Academy; London Sch. of Economics; Yugoslavia. LLB Hons; BSc (Econ) Hons; PhD. Called to Bar, Middle Temple; practised London Bar and SW Circuit, 1957–60; Marketing Economist, Shell International, 1960–61; Tanzanian Foreign Service, 1961–70; High Comr for Barbados in UK, and Ambassador to France, Netherlands and Germany, 1970–71; Ambassador and Perm. Rep. for Barbados to UN, 1971–76. UN Legal Expert: in field of human rights, 1967–71; on Israel, 1968–71. Mem., National Exec., Barbados Labour Party, 1980–. Senator, Parlt of Barbados, 1983. Editor, Beacon Newspaper, 1982. Member: Amer. Acad. of Political and Social Sciences; Amer. Soc. of Internat. Law; Amer. Inst. of Petroleum (Marketing Div.). Hon. Fellow, Hebrew Univ. of Jerusalem, 1972. DSc (Pol. Econ.) Univ. of Phnom-Penh, 1973; Hon. LLD Chung-Ang Univ., Republic of Korea, 1975. Grand Officer (1st Class), Nat. Order of Honneur et Mérite, Republic of Haiti, 1968; Grand Officier, Ordre Nat. de l'Amitié et Mérite, Khymèr, 1973; Order of Distinguished Diplomatic Service Merit, Gwangwha (1st Class), Republic of Korea, 1974. *Recreations:* cricket, tennis, bridge, travel. *Address:* (chambers) 50 Swan Street, Bridgetown, Barbados. *T:* (809) 427–8280, 424–2021; (chambers) 26 Court Street, Brooklyn, New York 11225, USA; The Monticello, 30 Park Avenue, Mount Vernon, New York 10550, USA. *T:* (London) 071–229 4870; (N Carolina) (919) 765 0080. *Clubs:* Royal Automobile; Lincoln Lodge (Connecticut).

WALES, Archbishop of; *no new appointment at time of going to press.*

WALES, Daphne Beatrice; Chairman, Board for Mission and Unity, General Synod of the Church of England, 1983–88; *b* 6 Dec. 1917; *d* of Frederick James Wales and Lilian Frederica (*née* Whitnall). Principal, Bank of England, retd. Mem., General Synod, 1975–90 (Mem., Panel of Chairmen, 1983); Chm., St Albans Diocese House of Laity, 1979–85. Vice-Chm., Highway Trust, 1983–; Governor: Partnership for World Mission, 1978–90; S American Missionary Soc., 1983– (Vice-Chm., 1989–). Mem. Council, Oak Hill Theol Coll., 1981–. *Address:* 41 Park Road, Watford, Herts WD1 3QW. *T:* Watford (0923) 225643.

WAŁESA, Lech; Hon. GCB 1991; President of Poland, since 1990; *b* Popowo, 29 Sept. 1943; *s* of late Bolesław Wałesa and Feliksa Wałesa; *m* 1969, Danuta; four *s* four *d*. *Educ:* Lipno primary and tech. schools; trained as electrician. Lenin Shipyard, Gdańsk, 1966–76, 1980–90 (Chm., Strike Cttees, 1970, 1980); founder Chm., Nat. Co-ordinating Commn of Indep. Autonomous Trade Union Solidarity (NSZZ Solidarność), 1980–82; in custody, 1981–82. Dr *hc:* Alliance Coll., Cambridge, Mass, 1981; Harvard, 1983. Nobel Peace Prize, 1983. *Publication:* A Path of Hope: An Autobiography, 1987. *Address:* Kancelaria Prezydenta RP, ul. Wiejska 4/8, 00–902 Warsaw, Poland; ul. Pilotow 17D/3, Gdańsk-Zaspa, Poland.

WALEY, (Andrew) Felix, VRD 1960 and Clasp 1970; QC 1973; **His Honour Judge Waley;** a Circuit Judge, since 1982; Resident Judge, County of Kent, since 1985; Judge Advocate of the Fleet, since 1986; *b* 14 April 1926; *s* of Guy Felix Waley and Anne Elizabeth (*née* Dickson); *m* 1955, Petica Mary, *d* of Sir Philip Rose, 3rd Bt; one *s* three *d* (and one *d* decd). *Educ:* Charterhouse; Worcester Coll., Oxford (MA). RN, 1944–48; RNR, 1951–71, retd as Comdr. Oxford, 1948–51; called to the Bar, Middle Temple, 1953, Bencher, 1981; a Recorder of the Crown Court, 1974–82. Conservative Councillor, Paddington, 1956–59. Contested (C) Dagenham, 1959. *Recreations:* gardens, boats, birds. *Address:* c/o The Law Courts, Barker Road, Maidstone, Kent ME16 8EQ. *Clubs:* Garrick, Naval; Royal Naval Sailing Association.

WALEY, Daniel Philip, FBA 1991; PhD; Keeper of Manuscripts, British Library, 1973–86 (Keeper of Manuscripts, British Museum, 1972–73); *b* 20 March 1921; *er s* of late Hubert David Waley and Margaret Hendelah Waley; *m* 1945, Pamela Joan Griffiths; one *s* two *d*. *Educ:* Dauntsey's Sch.; King's Coll., Cambridge (MA, PhD). Historical Tripos, Cambridge, 1939–40 and 1945–46 (cl. 1). Served War, 1940–45. Fellow of King's Coll., Cambridge, 1950–54. Asst Lectr in Medieval History, London School of Economics and Political Science, Univ. of London, 1949–51, Lectr, 1951–61, Reader in History, 1961–70, Prof. of History, 1970–72. Hon. Res. Fellow, Westfield Coll., London, 1986; Emer. Fellow, Leverhulme Trust, 1986–87. British Acad. Italian Lectr, 1975. Serena Medal, British Acad., 1990. *Publications:* Mediaeval Orvieto, 1952; The Papal State in the 13th Century, 1961; Later Medieval Europe, 1964 (2nd edn 1985); The Italian City Republics, 1969 (3rd edn 1988); British Public Opinion and the Abyssinian War, 1935–36, 1975; (ed) George Eliot's Didier: A Commonplace-Book, 1980; (contrib.) Storia d'Italia, ed by G. Galasso, vol. 7, 1987; Siena and the Sienese in the Thirteenth Century, 1991; contributor to: Dizionario Biografico degli Italiani, English Hist. Review, Trans Royal Hist. Soc., Papers of British Sch. at Rome, Jl of Ecclesiastical Hist., Jl of the History of Ideas, Rivista Storica Italiana, Rivista di Storia della Chiesa in Italia, Procs Brit. Acad., British Library Jl, Bull. of John Rylands Liby, etc. *Recreation:* walking. *Address:* The Croft, 43 Southover High Street, Lewes, E Sussex BN7 1HX.

WALEY, Felix; *see* Waley, A. F.

WALEY-COHEN, Hon. Joyce Constance Ina, MA; **(Hon. Lady Waley-Cohen);** President, Independent Schools Information Service Council, 1981–85 (Member, 1972–80); *b* 20 Jan. 1920; *o d* of 1st Baron Nathan, PC, TD, and Eleanor Joan Clara, *d* of C. Stettauer; *m* 1943, Sir Bernard Nathaniel Waley-Cohen, 1st Bt, (*d* 1991); two *s* two *d*. *Educ:* St Felix Sch., Southwold; Girton Coll., Cambridge (MA). Member: Governing Body, St Felix Sch., 1945–83 (Chm., 1970–83); Westminster Hosp. Bd of Governors, 1952–68; Chairman: Westminster Children's Hosp., 1952–68; Gordon Hosp., 1961–68; Governing Bodies of Girls' Schools' Assoc., 1974–79 (Mem., 1963); Ind. Schs Jt Council, 1977–80. Governor: Taunton Sch., 1978–90; Wellington Coll., 1979–90. JP Mddx 1949–59, Somerset 1959–86. *Recreations:* hunting, spinning, family life. *Address:* Honeymead, Simonsbath, Minehead, Somerset TA24 7JX. *T:* Exford (064383) 242.

WALEY-COHEN, Sir Stephen (Harry), 2nd Bt *cr* 1961, of Honeymead, Co. Somerset; Managing Director, Victoria Palace, since 1989; *b* 22 June 1946; *s* of Sir Bernard Nathaniel Waley-Cohen, 1st Bt and Hon. Joyce Constance Ina Waley-Cohen, *qv*; *S* father, 1991; *m* 1st, 1972, Pamela Elizabeth (marr. diss.), *yr d* of J. E. Doniger; two *s* one *d*; 2nd, 1986, Josephine Burnett, *yr d* of late Duncan M. Spencer; two *d*. *Educ:* Wellesley House Sch.; Eton (Oppidan Scholar); Magdalene Coll., Cambridge (MA Hons). Financial journalist, Daily Mail, 1968–73; Publisher, Euromoney, 1969–83; Chief Exec., Maybox Theatres, 1984–89; Chm., Thorndike Holdings, management training, 1989–; Director: Badgworthy Land Co., 1982–; Willis Faber & Dumas (Agencies) Ltd, 1988–; St Martin's Theatre, 1989–. Mem., SWET, 1984– (Mem., Finance Cttee, 1989–). Mem. Council, Jewish Colonisation Assoc., 1985–; Chm. Exec. Cttee, British American Project for Successor Generation, 1986–. Member: Public Affairs Cttee, British Field Sports Soc., 1972–; Cttee, Devon & Somerset Staghounds, 1974–. Governor, Wellesley House Sch., 1974–. Contested (C) Manchester, Gorton, Feb. and Oct. 1974. *Recreations:* family, theatre, hunting. *Heir:* *s* Lionel Robert Waley-Cohen, *b* 7 Aug. 1974. *Address:* 1 Wallingford Avenue, W10 6QA. *T:* 081–968 6268; Honeymead, Simonsbath, Minehead, Somerset TA24 7JX. *T:* Exford (064383) 584. *Club:* Garrick.

WALFORD, Christopher Rupert, TEM 1972; Partner, Allen & Overy, since 1970; *b* 15 Oct. 1935; *s* of John Rupert Charles Walford, MBE and Gladys Irene Walford (*née* Sperrin); *m* 1967, Anne Elizabeth Viggars; two *s* (and one *s* decd). *Educ:* Charterhouse; Oriel College, Oxford (MA). Solicitor (Hons). National Service, commissioned RA, 1954–56; HAC 1957–72 (to Warrant Officer). Allen & Overy, 1959–. Councillor, Kensington, 1962–65, Kensington & Chelsea, 1964–82, Dep. Mayor, 1974–75, Mayor, 1979–80; Alderman, Ward of Farringdon Within, 1982–; Sheriff, City of London, 1990–Sept. 1991. Member: Council, CGLI, 1984–; Council, Policy and Exec., and Company Laws Cttees, Inst. of Directors, 1986–; Court of Assistants and Finance Cttee, Corp. of Sons of the Clergy, 1989–; Trustee, St Paul's Cathedral Choir Sch. Foundn, 1985–. Governor, Bridewell Royal Hosp., 1984–. Freeman, City of London, 1964; Liveryman: Makers of Playing Cards Co., 1978 (Master, 1987–88); City of London Solicitors Co., 1983– (Jun. Warden, 1990). FRSA. *Recreations:* listening to music (especially opera), kitchen bridge, watching Rugby football and cricket, hill walking. *Address:* Allen

& Overy, 9 Cheapside, EC2V 6AD. *T*: 071–248 9898. *Clubs*: MCC, City Livery, United Wards, Farringdon Ward (Patron); Berkhamsted Golf, Craigendarroch Country.

WALFORD, Dr Diana Marion; Deputy Chief Medical Officer, Department of Health, since 1989; Hon. Consultant Haematologist, Central Middlesex Hospital, 1977–87; *b* 26 Feb. 1944; *d* of Lt-Col Joseph Norton, LLM, and Thelma Norton (*née* Nurick); *m* 1970, Arthur David Walford, LLB; one *s* one *d*. *Educ*: Calder High Sch. for Girls, Liverpool; Liverpool Univ. (George Holt Medal, Physiol.; J. H. Abram Prize, Pharmacol.; BSc (1st Cl. Hons Physiol.) 1965; MB ChB 1968; MD 1976); London Univ. (MSc (Epidemiology) 1987). FRCP 1990 (MRCP 1972); FRCPath 1986 (MRCPath 1974); MFPHM 1989. Ho. Officer posts, Liverpool Royal Inf., 1968–69; Sen. Ho. Officer posts and Sen. Registrar, St Mary's Hosp., Paddington, and Northwick Park Hosp., Harrow, 1969–75; MRC Research (Training) Fellow, Clin. Res. Centre, 1975–76; Sen. MO 1976–79, PMO 1979–83, SPMO (Under Sec.), 1983–89, DHSS, subseq. Dept of Health. Mem., British Soc. for Haematology, 1978–; Founder Mem., British Blood Transfusion Soc., 1983–; FRSM. *Publications*: chapters on haematological side effects of drugs in: Meyler's Side Effects of Drugs, 9th edn 1980; Side Effects of Drugs Annual, 1980; Drug-Induced Emergencies, 1980; articles on alpha-thalassaemia. *Recreations*: theatre, painting, travel. *Address*: Richmond House, 79 Whitehall, SW1A 2NS. *T*: 071–210 5593.

WALFORD, John Howard; President, Solicitors' Disciplinary Tribunal, 1979–88; *b* 16 May 1927; *s* of Henry Howard Walford and Marjorie Josephine Solomon; *m* 1953, Peggy Ann Jessel; two *s* two *d*. *Educ*: Cheltenham College; Gonville and Caius College, Cambridge; MA (Hons). Solicitor, 1950; Senior Partner, Bischoff & Co., 1979–88. Mem. Council, Law Society, 1961–69; Governor, College of Law, 1967–88; Senior Warden, City of London Solicitors' Co., 1980–81, Master, 1981–82. Governor, St John's Hosp. for Diseases of the Skin, 1960–82; Chairman: Appeal Cttee, Skin Disease Research Fund; Bd of Management, Petworth Cottage Nursing and Convalescent Home. Mem., Arbitration Panel, The Securities and Futures Authority Consumer Arbitration Scheme, 1988–. Commander, Order of Bernardo O'Higgins, Chile, 1972. *Address*: Pheasant Court, Northchapel, near Petworth, W Sussex GU28 9LJ; 9 Palliser Court, Palliser Road, W14. *Clubs*: Garrick, City Law; Leconfield Flyfishing.

WALFORD, John Thomas, OBE 1985; DL; General Secretary, Multiple Sclerosis Society of Great Britain and Northern Ireland, since 1977 (Deputy General Secretary, 1965–77); *b* 6 Feb. 1933; *s* of Frederick Thomas Walford and Rose Elizabeth Walford; *m* 1955, June Muriel Harding (marr. diss. 1970); two *s* one *d*. *Educ*: Richmond and East Sheen County Grammar Sch. Served RAF, 1951–53. C. C. Wakefield & Co. Ltd, 1949–51 and 1953–55; Stanley Eades & Co., 1955–60; Moo Cow Milk Bars Ltd, 1960–64. DL Greater London, 1988. Editor, MS News (qly jl of Multiple Sclerosis Soc.), 1977–. *Recreation*: collecting Victorian fairings. *Address*: 109B Holland Road, W14 8AS. *T*: 071–603 6903; Church House, Talley, Llandeilo, Dyfed SA19 7AX. *T*: Llandeilo (0558) 685744. *Club*: Royal Society of Medicine.

WALKER, Rev. Sir Alan, Kt 1981; OBE 1955; Principal, Pacific College for Evangelism, since 1989; *b* 1911; *s* of Rev. Alfred Edgar Walker, former Pres., NSW Methodist Conf., and Violet Louise Walker; *m* 1938, Winifred Garrard Walker (*née* Channon); three *s* one *d*. *Educ*: Leigh Theological Coll., Sydney; Univ. of Sydney (BA, MA); Bethany Biblical Seminary, Chicago. Minister, Cessnock, NSW, 1939–44; Supt, Waverley Methodist Mission, 1944–54; Dir, Australian Mission to the Nation, 1953–56; Vis. Professor: of Evangelism, Boston Sch. of Theology, 1957; of Evangelism and Preaching, Claremont Sch. of Theol., USA, 1973; Supt, Central Methodist Mission, Sydney, 1958–78; Dir, World Evangelism, World Methodist Council, 1978–89. Deleg. to First Assembly of WCC, Amsterdam, 1948; Adviser to: Aust. Delegn at UN, 1949; Third Ass. of WCC, New Delhi, 1962; Fourth Ass., WCC, Uppsala, 1968; Missions to: Fiji, S Africa, S America, Singapore and Malaysia, Sri Lanka, 1962–75; Founder, Sydney Life Line Tel. Counselling Centre, 1963 (Pres., Life Line Internat., 1966–); Sec., NSW Methodist Conf., 1970, Pres., 1971; lectures, various times, USA. Hon. DD Bethany Biblical Sem., 1954. Inst. de la Vie award, Paris, for services to humanity, 1978; (with Lady Walker) World Methodist Peace Award, 1986. *Publications include*: There is Always God, 1938; Everybody's Calvary, 1943; Coal Town, 1944; Heritage Without End, 1953; The Whole Gospel for the Whole World, 1957; The Many Sided Cross of Jesus, 1962; How Jesus Helped People, 1964; A Ringing Call to Mission, 1966; The Life Line Story, 1967 (USA, As Close as the Telephone); Breakthrough, 1969; God, the Disturber, 1973 (USA); Jesus, the Liberator, 1973 (USA); The New Evangelism, 1974 (USA); Love in Action, 1977; Life Grows with Christ, 1981; Life Ends in Christ, 1983; Standing Up To Preach, 1983; Your Life Can Be Changed, 1985; Life in the Holy Spirit, 1986; Try God, 1990. *Recreations*: swimming, tennis. *Address*: 14 Owen Stanley Avenue, Beacon Hill, NSW 2100, Australia. *T*: 451 3923.

WALKER, Alexander; Film Critic, London Evening Standard, since 1960; *b* Portadown, N Ireland, 22 March 1930; *s* of Alfred and Ethel Walker. *Educ*: Portadown Grammar Sch.; The Queen's Univ., Belfast (BA); Collège d'Europe, Bruges; Univ. of Michigan, Ann Arbor. Lecturer in political philosophy and comparative govt, Univ. of Michigan, 1952–54. Features editor, Birmingham Gazette, 1954–56; leader writer and film critic, The Birmingham Post, 1956–59; columnist, Vogue magazine, 1974–86. Frequent broadcaster on the arts on radio and television; author: TV series Moviemen; BBC Radio series Film Star; author and co-producer of TV programmes on History of Hollywood, Garbo and Chaplin. Member: British Screen Adv. Council (formerly Wilson Interim Action Cttee on the Film Industry), 1977–; Bd of Govs, BFI, 1989–. Chevalier de l'Ordre des Arts et des Lettres, 1981. Twice named Critic of the Year, in annual British Press awards, 1970, 1974, commended, 1985; Award of Golden Eagle, Philippines, for services to internat. cinema, 1982. *Publications*: The Celluloid Sacrifice: aspects of sex in the movies, 1966; Stardom: the Hollywood phenomenon, 1970; Stanley Kubrick Directs, 1971; Hollywood, England: the British film industry in the sixties, 1974; Rudolph Valentino, 1976; Double Takes: notes and afterthoughts on the movies 1956–76, 1977; Superstars, 1978; The Shattered Silents: how the talkies came to stay, 1978; Garbo, 1980; Peter Sellers: the authorized biography, 1981; Joan Crawford, 1983; Dietrich, 1984; (ed) No Bells on Sunday: journals of Rachel Roberts, 1984; National Heroes: British cinema industry in the seventies and eighties, 1985; Bette Davis, 1986; trans., Benayoun, Woody Allen: beyond words, 1986; Vivien: the life of Vivien Leigh, 1987; It's Only a Movie, Ingrid: encounters on and off screen, 1988; Elizabeth: the life of Elizabeth Taylor, 1990; Rex Harrison: a biography, 1992; contributor to Encounter and other British and for. publications. *Recreations*: ski-ing, persecuting smokers. *Address*: 1 Marlborough, 38–40 Maida Vale, W9 1RW. *T*: 071–289 0985.

WALKER, (Alfred) Cecil, JP; MP (OUP) Belfast North, since 1983 (resigned seat Dec. 1985 in protest against Anglo-Irish Agreement; re-elected Jan. 1986); *b* 17 Dec. 1924; *s* of Alfred George Walker and Margaret Lucinda Walker; *m* 1953, Ann May Joan Verrant; two *s*. *Educ*: Methodist College. Senior Certificate. In timber business with James P. Corry & Co. Ltd, Belfast, 1941–, Departmental Manager, 1952. JP Belfast, 1966. *Recreations*: sailing, sea angling. *Address*: 1 Wynnland Road, Newtownabbey, Northern Ireland. *T*: Glengormley (02313) 3463. *Club*: Down Cruising.

WALKER, Sir Allan (Grierson), Kt 1968; QC (Scotland); Sheriff Principal of Lanarkshire, 1963–74; *b* 1 May 1907; *er s* of late Joseph Walker, merchant, London, and Mary Grierson; *m* 1935, Audrey Margaret, *o d* of late Dr T. A. Glover, Doncaster; one *s*. *Educ*: Whitgift Sch., Croydon; Edinburgh Univ. Practised at Scottish Bar, 1931–39; Sheriff-Substitute of Roxburgh, Berwick, and Selkirk at Selkirk and of the County of Peebles, 1942–45; Sheriff-Substitute of Stirling, Dumbarton and Clackmannan at Dumbarton, 1945–50; Sheriff-Substitute of Lanarkshire at Glasgow, 1950–63; Member, Law Reform Cttee for Scotland, 1964–70; Chm., Sheriff Court Rules Council, 1972–74. Hon. LLD Glasgow, 1967. *Publications*: The Law of Evidence in Scotland (joint author); Purves' Scottish Licensing Laws (7th, 8th edns). *Recreations*: walking, gardening. *Address*: 24 Moffat Road, Dumfries DG1 1NJ. *T*: Dumfries (0387) 53583.

WALKER, Angus Henry; Managing Director, A. T. Kearney, since 1991; *b* 30 Aug. 1935; *s* of late Frederick William Walker and of Esther Victoria (*née* Wrangle); *m* 1st, 1968, Beverly Phillpotts (marr. diss. 1976); 2nd, 1979, Ann Snow (*née* Griffiths); two *d* and two step *d*. *Educ*: Erith Grammar Sch., Kent; Balliol Coll., Oxford (Domus Scholar; 1st Cl. Hons BA Mod. Hist. 1959; Stanhope Prize, 1958; MA 1968). Nat. Service, 1954–56 (2nd Lieut RA). Senior Scholar, St Antony's Coll., Oxford, 1959–63; HM Diplomatic Service, 1963–68: FO, 1963–65; First Sec., Washington, 1965–68. Lectr, SSEES, London Univ., 1968–70; Univ. Lectr in Russian Social and Political Thought, Oxford, and Lectr, Balliol Coll., 1971–76; Fellow, Wolfson Coll., Oxford, 1971–76; Dir, SSEES, London Univ., 1976–79; British Petroleum Co. Plc, 1979–84; Dir, Corporate Strategy, British Telecom PLC, 1985–88; Man. Dir, Strategic Planning Associates, 1988–91. Co-opted Mem., Arts Sub-Cttee, UGC, for enquiry into Russian in British Univs, 1978–79; Governor, Centre for Economic Policy Res., 1986–. CompIEE 1988. *Publications*: trans. from Polish: Political Economy, by Oskar Lange, vol. 1, 1963; Marx: His Theory in its Context, 1978, 2nd edn 1989. *Address*: 5 North Square, NW11 7AA. *T*: 081–455 2726. *Club*: Reform.

WALKER, Gen. Sir Antony (Kenneth Frederick), KCB 1987; Commandant, Royal College of Defence Studies, 1990–92; *b* 16 May 1934; *o s* of late Kenneth Walker and Iris Walker; *m* 1961, Diana Merran Steward (marr. diss. 1983); one *s* one *d*; *m* 1991, Hannah Watts. *Educ*: Merchant Taylors' School; RMA Sandhurst. Commissioned into Royal Tank Regt, 1954; served BAOR, Libya, Ghana, Northern Ireland, Hong Kong, Cyprus; Instructor, Staff Coll., 1971–73; CO 1st Royal Tank Regt, 1974–76 (despatches); Col GS HQ UK Land Forces, 1976–78; Comdr Task Force Golf (11 Armd Bde), 1978–80; Dep. Mil. Sec. (A), 1980–82; Comdr, 3rd Armoured Div., 1982–84; Chief of Staff, HQ UKLF, 1985–87; Dep. CDS (Commitments), MoD, 1987–89. Col Comdt, Royal Tank Regt, 1983– (Rep., 1985–91). Mem. Council, RUSI, 1982–85 and 1990–. Chm., Army Bobsleigh Assoc., 1983–; Governor, Centre for Internat. Briefing, Farnham Castle, 1987–91. Mem. Council, British Bobsleigh Assoc., 1989–. Mem., Council of Management, Salisbury Festival, 1988– (Vice-Chm., 1990–). Pres., Services' Dry Fly Fishing Assoc., 1988–. *Recreations*: bird watching, fly-fishing, music, practical study of wine. *Address*: c/o National Westminster Bank plc, 151 The Parade, High Street, Watford, Herts WD1 1NQ. *Club*: Travellers'.

WALKER, Arthur Geoffrey, FRS 1955; Professor of Pure Mathematics, Liverpool University, 1952–74, now Emeritus; *b* 17 July 1909; 2nd *s* of late A. J. Walker, Watford, Herts; *m* 1939, Phyllis Ashcroft, *d* of late Sterry B. Freeman, CBE. *Educ*: Watford Grammar Sch.; Balliol Coll., Oxford. MA (Oxon); PhD, DSc (Edinburgh); FRSE; Lectr at Imperial Coll. Science and Technology, 1935–36; at Liverpool Univ., 1936–47; Prof. of Mathematics in the Univ. of Sheffield, 1947–52. Mem. of Council, Royal Soc., 1962–63. Pres., London Mathematical Soc., 1963–65. Junior Berwick Prize of London Mathematical Soc., 1947; Keith Medal of Royal Society of Edinburgh, 1950. *Publication*: Harmonic Spaces (with H. S. Ruse and T. J. Willmore), 1962. *Address*: Beechcroft, Roundabout Lane, West Chiltington, Pulborough, W Sussex RH20 2RL. *T*: West Chiltington (0798) 812412.

WALKER, Sir Baldwin Patrick, 4th Bt, *cr* 1856; *b* 10 Sept. 1924; *s* of late Comdr Baldwin Charles Walker, *o s* of 3rd Bt and Mary, *d* of F. P. Barnett of Whalton, Northumberland; *S* grandfather, 1928; *m* 1948, Joy Yvonne (marr. diss. 1954); *m* 1954, Sandra Stewart; *m* 1966, Rosemary Ann, *d* of late Henry Hollingdrake; one *s* one *d*; *m* 1980, Vanessa Hilton. *Educ*: Gordonstoun. Served Royal Navy, Fleet Air Arm, 1943–58. Lieut, RN, retired. *Heir*: *s* Christopher Robert Baldwin Walker, *b* 25 Oct. 1969. *Address*: 8 Sweet Valley Road, Bergvliet, Cape Town, 7945, South Africa.

WALKER, Bill; *see* Walker, W. C.

WALKER, Bobby; *see* Walker, W. B. S.

WALKER, Brian Wilson; Executive Director, Earthwatch Europe, since 1989; *b* 31 Oct. 1930; *s* of Arthur Walker and Eleanor (*née* Wilson); *m* 1954, Nancy Margaret Gawith; one *s* five *d*. *Educ*: Heversham Sch., Westmorland; Leicester Coll. of Technology; Faculty Technology, Manchester Univ. Management Trainee, Sommerville Bros, Kendal, 1952–55; Personnel Man., Pye Radio, Larne, 1956–61; Bridgeport Brass Ltd, Lisburn: Personnel Man., 1961–66; Gen. Man. (Develt), 1966–69; Gen. Man. (Manufrg), 1969–74; Dir Gen., Oxfam, 1974–83; Dir, Independent Commn on Internat. Humanitarian Issues, 1983–85; Pres., Internat. Inst. for Envmt and Develt, 1985–89. Chm., Band Aid—Live Aid Projects Cttee, 1985–90. Founder Chm., New Ulster Movt, 1969–74; Founder Pres., New Ulster Movt Ltd, 1974. Member: Standing Adv. Commn on Human Rights for NI, 1975–77; World Commn on Food and Peace, 1989–. Mem., Editl Cttee, World Resources Report, 1985–. Hon. MA Oxon, 1983. Kt, Sov. Order of St Thomas of Acre; Kentucky Colonel, 1966. *Publications*: Authentic Development—Africa, 1986; various political/religious papers on Northern Ireland problem and Third World subjects. *Recreations*: gardening, Irish politics, classical music, active Quaker. *Address*: 14 Upland Park Road, Oxford OX2 7RU; (office) Belsyre Court, 57 Woodstock Road, Oxford OX2 6HU. *T*: Oxford (0865) 311600. *Club*: Athenæum.

WALKER, Carl, GC 1972; Police Inspector, 1976–82; *b* 31 March 1934; English; *m* 1955, Kathleen Barker; one *s*. *Educ*: Kendal Grammar Sch., Westmorland. RAF Police, 1952–54 (Corporal). Lancashire Police, Oct. 1954–March 1956, resigned; Blackpool Police, 1959–82 (amalgamated with Lancashire Constabulary, April 1968); Sergeant, 1971. Retired 1982, as a result of the injuries sustained from gunshot wounds on 23 Aug. 1971 during an armed raid by thieves on a jeweller's shop in Blackpool (GC). *Recreations*: Rugby; Cumberland and Westmorland wrestling. *Address*: 9 Lawnswood Avenue, Poulton-Le-Fylde, Blackpool FY6 7ED.

WALKER, Cecil; *see* Walker, A. C.

WALKER, Sir (Charles) Michael, GCMG 1976 (KCMG 1963; CMG 1960); HM Diplomatic Service, retired; Chairman, Commonwealth Scholarship Commission in the UK, 1977–87; *b* 22 Nov. 1916; *s* of late Col C. W. G. Walker, CMG, DSO; *m* 1945, Enid Dorothy, *d* of late W. A. McAdam, CMG; one *s* one *d*. *Educ*: Charterhouse; New Coll., Oxford. Clerk of House of Lords, June 1939. Enlisted in Army, Oct. 1939, and served in RA until 1946 when released with rank of Lt-Col. Dominions Office, 1947; First Sec.,

British Embasssy, Washington, 1949–51; Office of United Kingdom High Comr in Calcutta and New Delhi, 1952–55; Establishment Officer, Commonwealth Relations Office, 1955–58. Imperial Defence Coll., 1958; Asst Under-Sec. of State and Dir of Establishment and Organisation, CRO, 1959–62; British High Commissioner in: Ceylon, 1962–65 (concurrently Ambassador to Maldive Islands, July-Nov. 1965), Malaysia, 1966–71; Sec., ODA, FCO, 1971–73; High Comr, India, 1974–76. Chm., Festival of India Trust, 1980–83. Hon. DCL City, 1980. *Recreations:* fishing, gardening, golf. *Address:* Herongate House, West Chiltington Common, Pulborough, Sussex RH20 2NL. *T:* West Chiltington (0798) 813473. *Club:* Oriental.

WALKER, Charls E., PhD; Consultant, Washington, DC, since 1973; *b* Graham, Texas, 24 Dec. 1923; *s* of Pinkney Clay and Sammye McCombs Walker; *m* 1949, Harmolyn Hart, Laurens, S Carolina; one *s* one *d.* *Educ:* Univ. of Texas (MBA); Wharton Sch. of Finance, Univ. of Pennsylvania (PhD). Instructor in Finance, 1947–48, and later Asst and Associate Prof., 1950–54, at Univ. of Texas, in the interim teaching at Wharton Sch. of Finance, Univ. of Pennsylvania; Associate Economist, Fed. Reserve Bank: of Philadelphia, 1953, of Dallas, 1954 (Vice-Pres. and Economic Advr, 1958–61); Economist and Special Asst to Pres. of Republic Nat. Bank of Dallas, 1955–56 (took leave to serve as Asst to Treasury Sec., Robert B. Anderson, April 1959–Jan. 1961); Exec. Vice-Pres., Amer. Bankers Assoc., 1961–69. Under-Sec. of the Treasury, 1969–72, Dep. Sec., 1972–73. Chm., American Council for Capital Formation; Mem. Council on Foreign Relations; Co-Chm., Bretton Woods Cttee. Adjunct Prof. of Finance and Public Affairs, Univ. of Texas at Austin, 1985–. Hon. LLD Ashland Coll., 1970. Co-editor of The Banker's Handbook, 1988–. *Publications:* New Directions in Federal Tax Policy, 1983; The Consumption Tax, 1987; The US Savings Challenge, 1990; contribs to learned jls, periodicals. *Recreations:* golf, fishing, music. *Address:* 10120 Chapel Road, Potomac, Md 20854, USA. *T:* 301/299–5414. *Clubs:* Congressional Country, Burning Tree Golf (Bethesda, Md); Hills of Lakeway Golf and Tennis (Austin, Texas).

WALKER, (Christopher) Roy; Deputy Head of Science and Technology Secretariat, Cabinet Office, since 1989; *b* 5 Dec. 1934; *s* of Christopher Harry Walker and late Dorothy Jessica Walker; *m* 1961, Hilary Mary Biddiscombe; two *s.* *Educ:* Sir George Monoux Grammar Sch., E17; Sidney Sussex Coll., Cambridge (BA); Université Libre de Bruxelles. National Service, Essex Regt, 1952–54. BoT, 1958; CSD, 1968; Private Sec. to Lord Privy Seal, 1968–71; Treasury, 1973; DTI, 1973; Dept of Energy, 1974; Cabinet Office, 1974; Dept of Energy, 1975; Under Secretary: DES, 1977; Dept. of Employment, 1986; seconded as Dir, Business in the Cities, 1989. *Recreations:* hill walking, sailing. *Address:* c/o Cabinet Office, 70 Whitehall, SW1A 2AS. *Club:* Medway Yacht (Rochester).

WALKER, Sir Colin (John Shedlock), Kt 1991; OBE 1981; Chairman, East Anglian Regional Health Authority, since 1987; *b* 7 Oct. 1934; *s* of Arthur John Walker and Olave Gertrude Walker; *m* 1963, Wendy Elizabeth Ellis; two *s.* *Educ:* St Edward's Sch., Oxford; Royal Agricultural Coll., Cirencester. Landowner, farmer and businessman. Chm., Harwich Harbour Bd, 1988–. Chairman: All Party European Movement in Suffolk, 1979–81; E Suffolk HA, 1986–87; Member: E Anglian RHA, 1983–86; Central Blood Labs Authority, 1985–88. Various posts, incl. Chm., of Constituency Cons. Assoc., 1986–88. Mem., Suffolk CC, 1976–80. *Recreations:* shooting, gardening, reading, forestry, conservation. *Address:* Blomvyle Hall, Hacheston, Woodbridge, Suffolk IP13 0DY. *T:* Wickham Market (0728) 746756. *Club:* Royal Over-Seas League.

WALKER, Prof. David Alan, PhD, DSc; FRS 1979; Professor of Photosynthesis, University of Sheffield, since 1988; *b* 18 Aug. 1928; *s* of Cyril Walker and Dorothy Walker (*née* Dobson); *m* 1956, Shirley Wynne Walker (*née* Mason); one *s* one *d.* *Educ:* King's Coll., Univ. of Durham (BSc, PhD, DSc). Royal Naval Air Service, 1946–48. Lecturer, 1958–63, Reader, 1963–65, Queen Mary Coll., Univ. of London; Reader, Imperial Coll., Univ. of London, 1965–70; University of Sheffield: Prof. of Biology, 1970–84; Prof. and Dir, Res. Inst. for Photosynthesis, 1984–88. Corres. Mem., Amer. Soc. Plant Physiol., 1979. *Publications:* Energy Plants and Man, 1979; (with G. E. Edwards) C3, C4—Mechanisms, Cellular and Environmental Regulation of Photosynthesis, 1983; The Use of the Oxygen Electrode and Fluorescence Probes in Simple Measurements of Photosynthesis, 1987; papers, mostly in field of photosynthesis. *Recreation:* singing the Sheffield Carols. *Address:* The Robert Hill Institute, The University, Sheffield S10 2TN. *T:* Sheffield (0742) 78555.

WALKER, Sir David (Alan), Kt 1991; Chairman, Securities and Investments Board, since 1988; Director, Bank of England, since 1982 (non-executive, since 1988); *b* 31 Dec. 1939; *s* of Harold and Marian Walker; *m* 1963, Isobel Cooper; one *s* two *d.* *Educ:* Chesterfield Sch.; Queens' Coll., Cambridge (MA; Hon. Fellow, 1989). Joined HM Treasury, 1961; Private Sec. to Joint Permanent Secretary, 1964–66; seconded to Staff of International Monetary Fund, Washington, 1970–73; Asst Secretary, HM Treasury, 1973–77; joined Bank as Chief Adviser, then Chief of Economic Intelligence Dept, 1977; Chm., Johnson Matthey Bankers, later Minories Finance, 1985–88. Chm., Steering Gp, Financial Markets Gp, LSE, 1987–. Pt-time Mem. of Bd, CEGB, 1987–89; non-exec. Dir, National Power, 1990. Nominated Mem., Council of Lloyd's, 1988–. FRSA; CBIM. *Recreations:* music, long-distance walking. *Address:* Securities and Investments Board, Gavrelle House, 2–14 Bunhill Row, EC1Y 8RA. *Club:* Reform.

WALKER, David Bruce; Chairman: Sun International Exploration and Production Co., since 1988; Sun Oil Britain Ltd, since 1988; Member (part-time), British Coal Corporation, since 1988; *b* 30 Aug. 1934; *s* of Noel B. Walker and June R. Walker (*née* Sutherland); *m* 1961, Leonora C. Freeman; two *s.* *Educ:* Knox Grammar Sch., Wahroonga, NSW; Univ. of Sydney (BSc (Hons), MSc, Geology). Demonstrator in Geology: Univ. of Sydney, 1956–58; Bristol Univ., 1958–59; British Petroleum Co., 1959–85: worked as geologist in UK, Gambia, Algeria, Libya, Colombia, Kuwait, Iran and US; Vice-Pres., Production Planning, USA, 1974–77; Regional Coordinator, Western Hemisphere, 1977–79; Controller, BP Exploration, 1979–80; Chief Executive, BP Petroleum Development (UK), 1980–82; Dir, Resources Development, BP Australia, 1982–85; Chief Exec., Britoil plc, 1985–88. Distinguished Lectr, Soc. of Petroleum Engineers, 1976. President, UK Offshore Operators Assoc., 1982. CBIM 1985. *Recreations:* music, gardening. *Address:* Whippletrees, Chetnole, Sherborne, Dorset DT9 6PD. *T:* Sherborne (0935) 872604.

WALKER, David Critchlow, CVO 1988 (MVO 1976); HM Diplomatic Service; Counsellor, Foreign and Commonwealth Office, since 1989; *b* 9 Jan. 1940; *s* of John Walker and Mary Walker (*née* Cross); *m* 1965, Tineke van der Leek; three *s.* *Educ:* Manchester Grammar Sch.; St Catharine's Coll., Cambridge (BA,MA,DipEd). Assistant Lecturer, Dept of Geography, Manchester Univ., 1962; Commonwealth Relations Office, 1963; Third Secretary, British Embassy, Mexico City, 1965; Second Secretary, Brussels, 1968; First Secretary: FCO, 1970; Washington, 1973; First Sec., later Counsellor, FCO, 1978–83; Consul General, São Paulo, 1983–86; Minister, Madrid, 1986–89. *Address:* c/o Foreign and Commonwealth Office, SW1.

WALKER, Major David Harry, CM 1987; MBE 1946; author; *b* 9 Feb. 1911; *s* of Harry Giles Walker and Elizabeth Bewley (*née* Newsom); *m* 1939, Willa Magee, Montreal; four *s.* *Educ:* Shrewsbury; Sandhurst. The Black Watch, 1931–47 (retired); ADC to Gov.-Gen. of Canada, 1938–39; Comptroller to Viceroy of India, 1946–47. Member: Queen's Bodyguard for Scotland; Canada Council, 1957–61; Chm., Roosevelt-Campobello Internat. Park Commn, 1970–72 (Canadian Comr, 1965). Hon. DLitt, Univ. of New Brunswick, 1955. FRSL. *Publications: novels:* The Storm and the Silence, 1950 (USA 1949); Geordie, 1950 (filmed 1955); The Pillar, 1952; Digby, 1953; Harry Black, 1956 (filmed, 1957); Sandy was a Soldier's Boy, 1957; Where the High Winds Blow, 1960; Storms of Our Journey and Other Stories, 1962; Dragon Hill (for children), 1962; Winter of Madness, 1964; Mallabec, 1965; Come Back, Geordie, 1966; Devil's Plunge (USA, Cab-Intersec), 1968; Pirate Rock, 1969; Big Ben (for children), 1970; The Lord's Pink Ocean, 1972; Black Dougal, 1973 (USA 1974); Ash, 1976; Pot of Gold, 1977; *non-fiction:* Lean, Wind, Lean: a few times remembered (memoirs), 1984. *Address:* Strathcroix, St Andrews, NB E0G 2X0, Canada. *Club:* Royal and Ancient.

WALKER, Prof. David Maxwell, CBE 1986; QC (Scot.) 1958; FBA 1976; FRSE 1980; Regius Professor of Law, Glasgow University, 1958–90, now Professor Emeritus and Senior Research Fellow; Dean of the Faculty of Law, 1956–59; Senate Assessor on University Court, 1962–66; *b* 9 April 1920; *o s* of James Mitchell Walker, Branch Manager, Union Bank of Scotland, and Mary Paton Colquhoun Irvine; *m* 1954, Margaret Knox, OBE, MA, *yr d* of Robert Knox, yarn merchant, Brookfield, Renfrewshire. *Educ:* High School of Glasgow (Mackindlay Prizeman in Classics); Glasgow, Edinburgh and London Universities. MA (Glasgow) 1946; LLB (Distinction), Robertson Schol., 1948; Faulds Fellow in Law, 1949–52; PhD (Edinburgh), 1952; Blackwell Prize, Aberdeen Univ., 1955; LLB (London), 1957; LLD (Edinburgh), 1960; LLD (London), 1968; LLD (Glasgow), 1985. Served War of 1939–45, NCO Cameronians; commissioned HLI, 1940; seconded to RIASC, 1941; served with Indian Forces in India, 1942, Middle East, 1942–43, and Italy, 1943–46, in MT companies and as Brigade Supply and Transport Officer (Captain). HQ 21 Ind. Inf. Bde, 8 Ind. Div. Advocate of Scottish Bar, 1948; Barrister, Middle Temple, 1957; QC (Scotland) 1958; practised at Scottish Bar, 1948–53; studied at Inst. of Advanced Legal Studies, Univ. of London, 1953–54; Prof. of Jurisprudence, Glasgow Univ., 1954–58. Dir, Scottish Univs' Law Inst., 1974–80. Trustee, Hamlyn Trust, 1954–. Vice-Pres., RSE, 1985–88. Governor: Scottish College of Commerce, 1957–64; High School of Glasgow (and Chm., Educational Trust), 1974–. Hon. Sheriff of Lanarkshire at Glasgow, 1966–82. FSAScot; FRSA. Hon. LLD Edinburgh, 1974. *Publications:* (ed) Faculty Digest of Decisions, 1940–50, Supplements, 1951 and 1952; Law of Damages in Scotland, 1955; The Scottish Legal System, 1959, 5th edn 1981; Law of Delict in Scotland, 1966, 2nd edn 1981; Scottish Courts and Tribunals, 1969, 5th edn 1985; Principles of Scottish Private Law (2 vols), 1970, 4th edn (4 vols), 1988–89; Law of Prescription and Limitation in Scotland, 1973, 4th edn 1990; Law of Civil Remedies in Scotland, 1974; Law of Contracts in Scotland, 1979, 2nd edn 1985; Oxford Companion to Law, 1980; (ed) Stair's Institutions (6th edn), 1981; (ed) Stair Tercentenary Studies, 1981; The Scottish Jurists, 1985; Legal History of Scotland, vol. I, 1988, vol. II, 1990; Scottish Part of Topham and Ivamy's Company Law, 12th edn 1955, to 16th edn 1978; contribs to collaborative works; articles in legal periodicals; *festschrift:* Obligations in Context, ed A. J. Gamble, 1990. *Recreations:* motoring, book collecting, Scottish history. *Address:* 1 Beaumont Gate, Glasgow G12 9EE. *T:* 041–339 2802. *Club:* Royal Scottish Automobile (Glasgow).

WALKER, Maj.-Gen. Derek William Rothwell; Manager, CBI Overseas Scholarships, 1980–89, retired; *b* 12 Dec. 1924; *s* of Frederick and Eileen Walker; *m* 1950, Florence Margaret Panting; two *s* (and one *s* decd). *Educ:* Mitcham County Grammar Sch.; Battersea Polytechnic. FIMechE 1970–89; FIEE 1971–89. Commissioned REME, 1946; served: Middle East, 1947–50 (despatches 1949); BAOR, 1951–53; Far East, 1954–56 (despatches 1957); Near East, 1960–62; Far East, 1964–67; psc 1957. Lt-Col 1964, Col 1970, Brig. 1973. Appts include: Comdr, REME Support Group, 1976–77; Dir, Equipment Engineering, 1977–79. Mem. Council, IEE, 1975–79; Pres., SEE, 1979–81. *Recreations:* fishing, sailing, wine-making. *Address:* 26 Cranford Drive, Holybourne, Alton, Hants GU34 4HJ. *T:* Alton (0420) 84737.

WALKER, Prof. Donald, FRS 1985; Professor of Biogeography, Institute of Advanced Studies, Australian National University, Canberra, 1969–88; *b* 14 May 1928; *s* of Arthur Walker and Eva (*née* Risdon); *m* 1959, Patricia Mary Smith; two *d.* *Educ:* Morecambe Grammar School; Sheffield Univ. (BSc); MA, PhD Cantab. Commission, RAF (Nat. Service), 1953–55. Research Scholar and Asst in Res., later Sen. Asst, Sub-Dept of Quaternary Res., Cambridge Univ., 1949–60; Fellow of Clare College, 1952–60 (Asst Tutor, 1955–60); Reader in Biogeography, ANU, 1960–68; Head of Dept of Biogeography and Geomorphology, ANU, 1969–88. Hon. Prof., Chinese Acad. of Science, 1986–. *Publications:* articles on plant ecology, palaeoecology and related topics in sci. jls. *Recreations:* pottery, architecture, prehistory. *Address:* 8 Galali Place, Aranda, ACT 2614, Australia. *T:* 06–2513136.

WALKER, Esme; *see* Scott, Esme, (Lady Scott).

WALKER, Prof. Frederick, MD; FRCPath; Regius Professor of Pathology, University of Aberdeen, since 1984; Consultant Pathologist, Grampian Health Board, since 1984; *b* 21 Dec. 1934; *s* of Frederick James Walker and Helen Stitt Halliday; *m* 1963, Cathleen Anne Gordon, BSc; two *d.* *Educ:* Kirkcudbright Academy; Univ. of Glasgow. MB ChB 1958; PhD 1964; MD 1971; MRCPath 1966, FRCPath 1978. Lectr in Pathology, Univ. of Glasgow, 1962–67; Vis. Asst Prof., Univ. of Minnesota, 1964–65; Sen. Lectr in Pathology, Univ. of Aberdeen, 1968–73; Foundation Prof. of Pathology, Univ. of Leicester, 1973–84. Chm., NEQAS Adv. Panel (Histopathology and Cytology), 1991–; Council, RCPath, 1990–; Cttee, Pathol Soc. of GB and Ireland, 1990–. Gen. Editor, Biopsy Pathology Series, 1978–; Editor, Jl of Pathology, 1983–. *Publications:* papers in scientific and med. jls, esp. on connective tissues. *Recreations:* writing, walking. *Address:* Department of Pathology, University Medical Buildings, Foresterhill, Aberdeen AB9 2ZD. *T:* Aberdeen (0224) 681818.

WALKER, George Alfred; Chairman and Chief Executive, Brent Walker Group PLC, 1982–91; Managing Director, Brent Walker Ltd, 1974–91; Chairman, William Hill Group, 1989–91; *b* 14 April 1929; *s* of William James Walker and Ellen (*née* Page); *m* 1957, Jean Maureen Walker (*née* Hatton); one *s* two *d.* *Educ:* Jubilee Sch., Bedford, Essex. Formerly boxer and boxing manager; Amateur Boxing Champion, GB, 1951; proprietor of garages and restaurants. Projects include: Brent Cross Shopping Centre; Brighton Marina; Trocadero; Cardiff World Trade Centre; Basildon Astrodome. Freeman, City of London, 1978. *Recreations:* ski-ing, ocean racing, climbing. *Address:* Brent Walker House, 19 Rupert Street, W1V 7FS. *T:* 071–465 0111. *Club:* Royal Automobile.

WALKER, Dr George Patrick Leonard, FRS 1975; G. A. Macdonald Professor of Volcanology, University of Hawaii, since 1981; *b* 2 March 1926; *s* of Leonard Richard Thomas Walker and Evelyn Frances Walker; *m* 1958, Hazel Rosemary (*née* Smith); one *s* one *d.* *Educ:* Wallace High Sch., Lisburn, N Ire.; Queen's Univ., Belfast (BSc, MSc); Univ. of Leeds (PhD); Univ. of London (DSc 1982). Research, Univ. of Leeds, 1948–51; Asst Lectr and Lectr, Imperial Coll., 1951–64; Reader in Geology, Imperial Coll., 1964–79;

Captain J. Cook Res. Fellow, Royal Soc. of NZ, 1978–80. Fellow: Geol Soc. of America, 1987; Amer. Geophysical Union, 1988. Awarded moiety of Lyell Fund of Geological Soc. of London, 1963, Lyell Medal, 1982. Hon. Member: Vísindafjelag Íslendinga, (Iceland), 1968; Royal Soc. of NZ, 1987. Hon. DSc Iceland, 1988. McKay Hammer Award, Geol Soc. of NZ, 1982. Icelandic Order of the Falcon, Knight's Class, 1980. *Publications:* scientific papers on mineralogy, the geology of Iceland, and volcanology. *Recreation:* visiting volcanoes. *Address:* Department of Geology and Geophysics, University of Hawaii at Manoa, 2525 Correa Road, Honolulu, Hawaii 96822, USA. *T:* (808) 956–7826.

WALKER, Sir Gervas (George), Kt 1979; JP; DL; Chairman and Leader, Avon County Council, 1973–81; *b* 12 Sept. 1920; *yr s* of late Harry James Walker and Susanna Mary Walker; *m* 1944, Jessie Eileen (*née* Maxwell); two *s*. *Educ:* Monmouth Sch. Bristol City Council: Councillor, 1956–74; Alderman, 1970–74; Leader of Council, 1966–72; Leader of Opposition Party, 1972–74; Chm., Planning and Transportation Cttee, 1960–63 and 1966–72; Chm., Bristol Avon River Authority, 1963–66. Member: SW Regional Economic Planning Council, 1972–79; Local Authorities' Conditions of Service Adv. Bd, 1974–81; Severn Barrage Cttee, 1978–81; British Rail (Western) Bd, 1979–85. Chm., Assoc. of County Councils, 1979–81 (Vice-Chm., 1978–79). Chairman, Bristol Conservative Assoc., 1975–79. JP Bristol, 1969; DL Avon, 1982. *Recreation:* fly-fishing. *Address:* Bulverton Well Farm, Sidmouth, Devon EX10 9DW. *T:* Sidmouth (0395) 516902; The Lodge, Cobblestone Mews, Clifton Park, Bristol BS8 3DQ. *T:* Bristol (0272) 737063.

WALKER, Rt. Hon. Harold, PC 1979; MP (Lab) Doncaster Central, since 1983 (Doncaster, 1964–83); Chairman of Ways and Means and Deputy Speaker, House of Commons, since 1983; *b* 12 July 1927; *s* of Harold and Phyllis Walker; *m* 1984, Mary Griffin; one *d* by former marriage. *Educ:* Manchester College of Technology. FAA, 1946–48. An Assistant Government Whip, 1967–68; Jt Parly Under-Sec. of State, Dept of Employment and Productivity, 1968–70; Opposition Front-Bench spokesman on Industrial Relations, 1970–74, on Employment, 1980–; Parly Under-Sec. of State, Dept of Employment, 1974–76; Minister of State, Dept of Employment, 1976–79. *Recreations:* reading, gardening. *Address:* House of Commons, SW1. *Clubs:* Westminster, Clay Lane, Doncaster Trades, RN, Catholic (all Doncaster).

WALKER, Sir Harold (Berners), KCMG 1991 (CMG 1979); HM Diplomatic Service, until 1992; *b* 19 Oct. 1932; *s* of late Admiral Sir Harold Walker, KCB, RN, and of Lady Walker (*née* Berners); *m* 1960, Jane, *d* of late Capt. C. J. L. Bittleston, CBE, DSC, RN; one *s* two *d*. *Educ:* Winchester (Exhibition 1946); Worcester Coll., Oxford (Exhibition 1952). BA 1955. 2nd Lieut RE, 1951–52. Foreign Office, 1955; MECAS, 1957; Asst Political Agent, Dubai, 1958; Foreign Office, 1960; Principal Instructor, MECAS, 1963; First Sec., Cairo, 1964; Head of Chancery and Consul, Damascus, 1966; Foreign Office (later FCO), 1967; First Sec. (Commercial), Washington, 1970; Counsellor, Jedda, 1973; Dep. Head, Personnel Operations Dept, FCO, 1975–76, Head of Dept, 1976–78; Corpus Christi Coll., Cambridge, 1978; Ambassador to Bahrein, 1979–81, to United Arab Emirates, 1981–86, to Ethiopia, 1986–90, to Iraq, 1990–91. *Recreation:* tennis. *Address:* c/o Barclays Bank, 1 Pall Mall East, SW1Y 5AX. *Club:* United Oxford & Cambridge University.

WALKER, His Honour Judge Harry; *see* Walker, P. H. C.

WALKER, Major Sir Hugh (Ronald), 4th Bt, *cr* 1906; *b* 13 Dec. 1925; *s* of Major Sir Cecil Edward Walker, 3rd Bt, DSO, MC, and Violet (*née* McMaster); *S* father, 1964; *m* 1971, Norna, *er d* of Lt-Cdr R. D. Baird, RNR; two *s*. *Educ:* Wellington Coll., Berks. Joined Royal Artillery, 1943; commissioned Sept. 1945; 2 iC, RA Range, Benbecula, Outer Hebrides, 1964–66; Commanding No 1 Army Information Team, in Aden and Hong Kong, 1966–68; Larkhill, 1969–73, retired. Mem., Assoc. of Supervisory and Executive Engineers. *Recreation:* horses. *Heir:* *s* Robert Cecil Walker, *b* 26 Sept. 1974. *Address:* Ballinamona, Hospital, Kilmallock, Co. Limerick, Ireland.

WALKER, Prof. James, CBE 1971; BSc, MD, FRCPGlas, FRCOG; Professor of Obstetrics and Gynæcology, University of Dundee, 1967–81 (University of St Andrews, 1956–67); *b* 8 March 1916; *s* of James Walker, FEIS; *m* 1940, Catherine Clark Johnston, *d* of George R. A. Johnston; one *s* two *d*. *Educ:* High Schs of Falkirk and Stirling; Univ. of Glasgow. BSc 1935; MB, ChB (Hons) 1938; Brunton Memorial Prize; MRCOG 1947; MD (Hons) 1954; FRCOG 1957; MRCPGlas 1963, FRCPGlas 1968. Blair Bell Memorial Lectr, Royal Coll. Obstetrics and Gynæcology, 1953. Served War of 1939–45, RAFVR, UK and India, 1941–46. Hon. Surgeon to Out Patients, Royal Infirmary, Glasgow, Hall Tutor in Midwifery, Univ. Glasgow, 1946; Sen. Lectr in Midwifery and Gynæcology, Univ. of Aberdeen, Consultant NE Regional Hospital Board (Scotland), 1948; Reader in Obst. and Gynæcology, Univ. of London, Consultant, Hammersmith Hospital, 1955. Consultant, Eastern Regional Hosp. Bd, Scotland, 1956–81; Chm., Nat. Medical Consultative Cttee, Scotland, 1979–81; Chm., Cttee on Annual Reports Records and Definition of Terms in Human Reproduction of the Internat. Fedn of Gynæcology and Obstetrics, 1976–88. Visiting Professor: New York State, 1957, 1970; Florida, 1965, 1970; McGill, 1967; Alexandria, 1979; Malaysia, 1981, 1984; Duke (USA), 1981; Stellenbosch, 1986; Prof. of Obst. and Gyn., Univ. Kebangsaan Malaysia, 1982–83. *Publications:* senior editor, Combined Textbook of Obstetrics and Gynæcology, 9th edn, 1976; contrib. on Obstetrics and Gynæcology to textbooks and learned jls. *Address:* 31 Ravenscraig Gardens, West Ferry, Dundee DD5 1LT. *T:* Dundee (0382) 79238. *Club:* Royal Air Force.

WALKER, Rev. Dr James Bernard; Principal of The Queen's College, Birmingham, since 1987; *b* 7 May 1946; *s* of Rev. Dr Robert B. W. Walker and Grace B. Walker; *m* 1972, Sheila Mary Easton; three *s*. *Educ:* Hamilton Academy, Lanarkshire; Edinburgh Univ. (MA 1st cl. Hons Mental Philosophy 1968; BD 1st cl. Hons Systematic Theol. 1971); Merton Coll., Oxford (DPhil 1981). Church of Scotland minister, ordained 1975, Dundee; Associate Minister, Mid Craigie Parish Church linked with Wallacetown Parish Church, Dundee, 1975–78; Minister, Old and St Paul's Parish Church, Galashiels, 1978–87. *Publications:* Israel — Covenant and Land, 1986; (contrib.) Politique et Théologie chez Athanase d' Alexandrie (ed C. Kannengiesser), 1974. *Recreations:* squash, tennis, swimming, hill walking. *Address:* The Queen's College, Somerset Road, Edgbaston, Birmingham B15 2QH. *T:* 021–454 1527.

WALKER, James Findlay, QPM 1964; Commandant, National Police College, 1973–76; *b* 20 May 1916; *m* 1941, Gertrude Eleanor Bell; one *s*. *Educ:* Arbroath High Sch., Angus, Scotland. Joined Metropolitan Police, 1936. Served War, 1943–46: commissioned Black Watch; demobilised rank Captain. Served in Metropolitan Police through ranks to Chief Supt, 1963; Staff of Police Coll., 1963–65; Asst Chief Constable: W Riding Constabulary, 1965–68; W Yorks Constabulary, 1968–70; Dep. Chief Constable, W Yorks Constabulary, 1970–73. *Recreations:* gardening, golf. *Address:* Mayfield, Quarry Hill, Horbury, Wakefield, W Yorks.

WALKER, Sir James (Graham), Kt 1972; MBE 1963; Part Owner of Cumberland Santa Gertrudis Stud and Camden Park, Greenwoods and Wakefield sheep properties; *b* Bellingen, NSW, 7 May 1913; *s* of late Albert Edward Walker and Adelaide Walker, Sydney, NSW; *m* 1939, Mary Vivienne Maude Poole; two *s* three *d*. *Educ:* New England Grammar Sch., Glen Innes, NSW. Councillor, Longreach Shire Council, 1953– (Chm., 1957–89); Vice-Pres., Local Authorities of Qld, 1966, Sen. Vice-Chm., 1972–89. Dep. Chm., Longreach Pastoral Coll., since inception, 1966–78, Chm. 1978–89. Exec. Mem., Central Western Queensland Local Authorities' Assoc. and Queensland Local Authorities' Assoc., 1964–79. Chm., Central Western Electricity Bd, 1966–76; Dep. Chm., Capricornia Electricity Bd, 1968–76, Chm., 1976–85; Dep. Chm., Longreach Printing Co. Chm., Santa Gertrudis Assoc., Australia, 1976–77. Past Asst Grand Master, United Grand Lodge of Qld, 1970. Session Clerk, St Andrews Church, Longreach, 1948–78. Nat. Chm., Stockman's Hall of Fame and Out Back Heritage Centre, 1983–89. Fellow, Internat. Inst. of Community Service, 1975; Paul Harris Rotary Fellow, Longreach Rotary Club, 1985. Hon. LLD Queensland Univ., 1985. *Recreations:* bowls, golf, surfing, painting. *Address:* Camden Park, Longreach, Queensland 4730, Australia. *T:* Longreach 074581–331. *Clubs:* Queensland, Tattersall's (Brisbane); Longreach, Longreach Rotary, Diggers (Longreach).

WALKER, Sir James Heron, 5th Bt, *cr* 1868; *b* 7 April 1914; *s* of 4th Bt and Synolda, *y d* of late James Thursby-Pelham; *S* father, 1930; *m* 1st, 1939, Angela Margaret, *o d* of Victor Alexandre Beaufort; one *s* (one *d* decd); 2nd, 1972, Sharrone, *er d* of David Read; one *s*. *Educ:* Eton Coll.; Magdalene Coll., Cambridge. *Recreations:* long haired Dachshunds and music. *Heir:* *s* Victor Stewart Heron Walker [*b* 8 Oct. 1942; *m* 1st, 1969, Caroline Louise (marr. diss. 1982), *d* of late Lt-Col F. E. B. Wignall; two *s* one *d*; 2nd, 1982, Svea, *o d* of late Captain Ernst Hugo Gothard Knutson Borg and of Mary Hilary Borg]. *Address:* Oakhill, Port Soderick, Isle of Man.

See also Baron Cornwallis.

WALKER, John; Director, National Gallery of Art, Washington, DC, 1956–69, now Director Emeritus; *b* 24 Dec. 1906; *s* of Hay Walker and Rebekah Jane Friend; *m* 1937, Lady Margaret Gwendolen Mary Drummond (*d* 1987); one *d* (and one *s* decd). *Educ:* Harvard Univ. (AB). Associate in charge Dept Fine Arts American Acad., Rome, 1935–39 (now Trustee); Chief Curator, National Gall., Washington DC, 1939–56. Connected with protection and preservation of artistic and historic monuments; John Harvard Fellow, Harvard Univ., 1930–31; American Federation of Arts; Board of Advisers, Dumbarton Oaks; Trustee: Andrew W. Mellon Educational and Charitable Trust; American Federation of Arts; Wallace Foundation, NY; National Trust for Historic Preservation; Mem., Art Adv. Panel, National Trust (UK); Member Advisory Council: Univ. of Notre Dame; New York Univ.; Hon. Dr Fine Arts: Tufts Univ., 1958; Brown Univ., 1959; La Salle Coll., 1962; LittD: Notre Dame, 1959, Washington and Jefferson Univs, 1960; LHD: Catholic Univ. of America, 1964; Univ. of New York, 1965; Maryland Inst.; Georgetown Univ., 1966; William and Mary Univ., 1967. Holds foreign decorations. *Publications:* (with Macgill James) Great American Paintings from Smibert to Bellows, 1943; (with Huntington Cairns) Masterpieces of Painting from National Gallery of Art, 1944; Paintings from America, 1951; (with Huntington Cairns) Great Paintings from the National Gallery of Art, 1952; National Gallery of Art, Washington, 1956; Bellini and Titian at Ferrara, 1957; Treasures from the National Gallery of Art, 1963; The National Gallery of Art, Washington, DC, 1964; (with H. Cairns) Pageant of Painting, 1966; Self-Portrait with Donors, 1974; National Gallery of Art, 1976; Turner, 1976; Constable, 1978. *Address:* 1729 H Street, NW, Washington, DC 20006, USA. *Clubs:* Turf, Dilettanti, Pilgrims'; Century Association (New York City); Chevy Chase, Metropolitan (Washington, DC).

WALKER, John; Under Secretary, Scottish Development Department, 1985, retired; *b* 16 Dec. 1929; *s* of John Walker and Elizabeth Whyte Fish; *m* 1952, Rena Robertson McEwan; two *d*. *Educ:* Falkirk High School. Entered Civil Service, Min. of Labour, as clerical officer, 1946. National Service, RAF, 1948–50. Asst Principal, Dept of Health for Scotland, 1958; Scottish Home and Health Dept: Principal, 1960; Secretary, Cttee on General Medical Services in the Highlands and Islands, 1964–67; Asst Sec., 1969; Scottish Development Dept, 1975–78; Under Sec., Scottish Home and Health Dept, 1978–85. Asst Comr, Scottish Local Govt Boundary Commn, 1987–91. *Recreations:* grandparenthood, being looked after by Rena. *Address:* 8/1 Back Dean, Ravelston Terrace, Edinburgh EH4 3UA. *T:* 031–343 3811.

WALKER, John David, DL; **His Honour Judge Walker;** a Circuit Judge, since 1972; *b* 13 March 1924; *y s* of late L. C. Walker, MA, MB (Cantab), BCh, and late Mrs J. Walker, Malton; *m* 1953, Elizabeth Mary Emma (*née* Owbridge); one *s* two *d*. *Educ:* Oundle (1937–42); Christ's Coll., Cambridge (1947–50); BA 1950, MA 1953. War of 1939–45: commissioned Frontier Force Rifles, Indian Army, 1943; demob., Captain, 1947. Called to the Bar, Middle Temple, 1951; a Recorder, 1972. A Pres., Mental Health Review Tribunals, 1986–. FRSA 1986. DL Humberside, 1985. *Recreations:* shooting, fishing. *Address:* Arden House, North Bar Without, Beverley, North Humberside HU17 7AG. *Club:* Lansdowne.

WALKER, John Malcolm; Principal Assistant Director of Public Prosecutions (Grade 3), 1985–86, retired; *b* 25 Feb. 1930; *s* of James and Mary Walker; *m* 1955, Barbara Anne Fawcett (*d* 1989); two *d*. *Educ:* St Edward's Sch., Oxford; Leeds Univ. (LLB). Served Royal Artillery, 1948–50. Called to Bar, Gray's Inn, 1955; joined Director of Public Prosecutions as Temp. Legal Asst, 1956; Legal Asst, 1958; Sen. Legal Asst, 1964; Asst Solicitor, 1974; Asst Director, 1977. *Recreations:* music, painting. *Address:* 86 Popes Grove, Twickenham, Middx TW1 4JX.

WALKER, Julian Fortay, CMG 1981; MBE 1960; HM Diplomatic Service; Special Adviser (Syria), Research Department, Foreign and Commonwealth Office, since 1987; *b* 7 May 1929; *s* of Kenneth Macfarlane Walker, FRCS, and Eileen Marjorie Walker (*née* Wilson); *m* 1983, Virginia Anne Austin (*née* Stevens); three step *d*. *Educ:* Harvey Sch., Hawthorne, New York; Stowe; Bryanston; Cambridge Univ. (MA). National Service, RN, 1947–49; Cambridge, 1949–52; London Univ. Sch. of African and Oriental Studies, 1952. Foreign Service: MECAS, 1953; Asst Political Agent, Trucial States, 1953–55; 3rd and 2nd Sec., Bahrain Residency, 1955–57; FCO and Frontier Settlement, Oman, 1957–60; 2nd and 1st Sec., Oslo, 1960–63; FCO News Dept Spokesman, 1963–67; 1st Sec., Baghdad, 1967; 1st Sec., Morocco (Rabat), 1967–69; FCO, 1969–71; Political Agent, Dubai, Trucial States, 1971, Consul-Gen. and Counsellor, British Embassy, Dubai, United Arab Emirates, 1971–72; Cambridge Univ. on sabbatical leave, 1972–73; Political Advr and Head of Chancery, British Mil. Govt, Berlin, 1973–76; NI Office, Stormont Castle, 1976–77; Dir, MECAS, 1977–78; Ambassador to Yemen Arab Republic and Republic of Jibuti, 1979–84; Ambassador to Qatar, 1984–87. *Recreations:* skiing, sailing, tennis, music, cooking. *Address:* c/o Foreign and Commonwealth Office, SW1.

WALKER, Julian Guy Hudsmith, CB 1991; Head of Royal Armament Research and Development Establishment, Chertsey, since 1989; *b* 10 Oct. 1936; *s* of Nathanial and Frieda Walker; *m* 1960, Margaret Burns (*née* Jamieson). *Educ:* Winchester College; Southampton Univ. (BSc Mech Eng). CEng, MIMechE. Hawker Aircraft Co., 1958–61; Logistic Vehicles, FVRDE, WO, subseq. MoD, 1961–69; Ministry of Defence: Special Projects, MVEE, 1970–80; Head, Vehicle Engrg Dept, 1980–84; Scientific Adviser

(Land), 1984–87; Dir, Estabts and Research (B), 1987–89. *Recreations:* vintage cars, photography, wood-turning, Wombling, solving practical problems. *Address:* RARDE, Chobham Lane, Chertsey, Surrey KT16 0EE.

WALKER, Malcolm Conrad; Chairman and Chief Executive, Iceland Frozen Foods plc, since 1973; *b* 11 Feb. 1946; *s* of Willie Walker and Ethel Mary Walker; *m* 1969, Nest Rhianydd; one *s* two *d. Educ:* Mirfield Grammar Sch. Trainee Manager, F. W. Woolworth & Co., 1964–71; Jt Founder, Iceland Frozen Foods, 1970. *Recreations:* ski-ing, shooting, stalking, business, home and family. *Address:* Iceland Frozen Foods plc, Second Avenue, Deeside Industrial Park, Deeside, Clwyd. *T:* Deeside (0244) 830100.

WALKER, Sir Michael; *see* Walker, Sir C. M.

WALKER, Michael; His Honour Judge Michael Walker; a Circuit Judge, since 1978; *b* 13 April 1931; *m* 1959, Elizabeth Mary Currie; two *s. Educ:* Chadderton Grammar Sch.; Sheffield Univ. (LLM). Called to the Bar, Gray's Inn, 1956. Joined North Eastern Circuit, 1958. A Recorder of the Crown Court, 1972–78.

WALKER, Sir Michael Leolin F.; *see* Forestier-Walker.

WALKER, Miles Rawstron, CBE 1991; Chief Minister, Isle of Man, since 1986; *b* 13 Nov. 1940; *s* of George Denis Walker and Alice (*née* Whittaker); *m* 1966, Mary Lilian Cowell; one *s* one *d. Educ:* Arbory Primary Sch.; Castle Rushen High Sch.; Shropshire Coll. of Agric. Company Dir, farming and retail dairy trade, 1960–. Mem. and Chm., Arbory Parish Comrs, 1970–76; Mem., House of Keys for Rushen, 1976–. *Address:* Chief Minister's Office, Government Offices, Buck's Road, Douglas, Isle of Man; Magher Feailley, Main Road, Colby, Isle of Man. *T:* Douglas (0624) 833728.

WALKER, Prof. Nigel David, CBE 1979; MA Oxon, PhD Edinburgh, DLitt Oxon; Wolfson Professor of Criminology and Fellow of King's College, Cambridge, 1973–84 (Director, Institute of Criminology, 1973–80); *b* 6 Aug. 1917; *s* of David B. Walker and Violet Walker (*née* Johnson); *m* 1939, Sheila Margaret Johnston; one *d. Educ:* Tientsin Grammar Sch.; Edinburgh Academy; Christ Church, Oxford (Hon. Scholar). Served War, Infantry officer (Camerons and Lovat Scouts), 1940–46. Scottish Office, 1946–61; Gwilym Gibbon Fellow, Nuffield Coll., 1958–59; University Reader in Criminology and Fellow of Nuffield Coll., Oxford, 1961–73. Visiting Professor: Berkeley, 1965; Yale, 1973; Stockholm, 1978; Cape Town, 1984. Chairman: Home Secretary's Adv. Council on Probation and After-care, 1972–76; Study Gp on Legal Training of Social Workers, 1972–73; President: Nat. Assoc. of Probation Officers, 1980–84; British Soc. of Criminology, 1984–87; Member: Home Sec.'s TV Research Cttee, 1963–69; Adv. Council on Penal System, 1969–; Cttee on Mentally Abnormal Offenders, 1972–75; Working Party on Judicial Training and Information, 1975–78; Floud Cttee on Dangerous Offenders; Hodgson Cttee on Profits of Crime; Parole Bd, 1986–89. Hon. LLD: Leicester, 1976, Edinburgh 1985. Hon. FRCPsych 1987. *Publications:* Delphi, 1936 (Chancellor's Prize Latin Poem); A Short History of Psychotherapy, 1957 (various trans); Morale in the Civil Service, 1961; Crime and Punishment in Britain, 1965; Crime and Insanity in England, 2 vols, 1968 and 1972; Sentencing in a Rational Society, 1969 (various trans.); Crimes, Courts and Figures, 1971; Explaining Misbehaviour (inaug. lecture), 1974; Treatment and Justice (Sandoz lecture), 1976; Behaviour and Misbehaviour, 1977; Punishment, Danger and Stigma, 1980; Sentencing Theory Law and Practice, 1985; Crime and Criminology, 1987; (jtly) Public Attitudes to Sentencing, 1988; Why Punish?, 1991; reports, articles, etc. *Recreations:* chess, hill-climbing. *Address:* King's College, Cambridge. *Club:* Royal Society of Medicine.

WALKER, Noel John; Deputy General Manager, Milton Keynes Development Corporation, 1987–92; General Manager, Commission for the New Towns, from April 1992; *b* 18 Dec. 1948; *s* of Robert and Nora Walker; *m* 1979, Pamela Gordon; two *s. Educ:* Liverpool Univ. (BSc 1970); Trent Polytechnic (DipTP 1972). Planning Officer, Hartlepool BC, 1972–74; Sen. Planner, Cleveland CC, 1974; travelled abroad, 1974–75; Milton Keynes Development Corporation: Employment Planner, 1975–76; Head of Policy Evaluation, 1976–78; Dep. Planning Manager, 1978–79; Planning Man., 1979–80; Dir of Planning, 1980–87. *Recreations:* squash, gardening, travelling, wine-tasting. *Address:* Fullers Barn, The Green, Loughton, Milton Keynes MK5 8AW.

WALKER, Patricia Kathleen Randall; *see* Mann, P. K. R.

WALKER, Sir Patrick (Jeremy), KCB 1990; *b* 25 Feb. 1932; *m* 1955, Susan Mary Hastings; two *s* one *d.* Ministry of Defence, 1963.

WALKER, Dr Paul Crawford, JP; Director of Public Health, Norwich Health Authority, since 1989; *b* 9 Dec. 1940; *s* of Joseph Viccars Walker and Mary Tilley (*née* Crawford); *m* 1962, Barbara Georgina Bliss; three *d. Educ:* Queen Elizabeth Grammar Sch., Darlington; Downing Coll., Cambridge (BA); University College Hospital (MB, BChir); Edinburgh Univ. (DipSocMed). FFCM; FRSM 1981; LHA 1985. Assistant Senior Medical Officer, Birmingham Regional Hosp. Bd, 1969–72; Dep. Medical Officer of Health and Dep. Principal Sch. MO, 1974, Wolverhampton County Borough Council; District Community Physician, N Staffs Health District, Staffordshire AHA, 1974–76; Area MO, Wakefield AHA, 1976–77; Regional MO, NE Thames RHA, 1978–85; Dist Gen. Manager, Frenchay HA, 1985–88; Hon. Consultant in Community Medicine, Bristol and Weston HA, 1988–89. Hon. Senior Lecturer: Dept of Community Medicine, LSHTM, 1983–; UEA; Co-Dir, Centre for Health Policy Res., UEA; Vis. Prof., QMC, London Univ., 1985–. Governor, Moorfields Eye Hosp., 1981–82; Vice-Chm. Professional Adv. Gp, NHS Trng Authy, 1986–; Member: Bd of Management, London Sch. of Hygiene and Trop. Med., 1983–85; Adv. Cttee on Drug Misuse, 1983–; Exec. Cttee, Greater London Alcohol Adv. Service, 1978–85; Editorial Bd, Jl of Med. Management; NHS Computer Policy Cttee, 1984–85; Program for Health Systems Management, Harvard Business Sch., 1980; Health Care Management Program, Yale Sch. of Organisation and Management, 1984; Frenchay Mental Handicap Trust, 1986–; Sec., Frenchay Mental Health Trust. JP Epping and Ongar, 1980–. Captain, RAMC (V). FBIM 1988. *Publications:* contribs to medical and health service jls. *Recreations:* music, railway history. *Address:* Chagford, 8 Church Avenue, Sneyd Park, Bristol BS9 1LD. *T:* Bristol (0272) 687378.

WALKER, Rt. Hon. Peter Edward, PC 1970; MBE 1960; MP (C) Worcester since March 1961; Secretary of State for Wales, 1987–90; *b* 25 March 1932; *s* of Sydney and Rose Walker; *m* 1969, Tessa, *d* of G. I. Pout; three *s* two *d. Educ:* Latymer Upper Sch. Member, National Executive of Conservative Party, 1956–; Nat. Chairman, Young Conservatives, 1958–60; Parliamentary Candidate (C) for Dartford, 1955 and 1959. PPS to Leader of House of Commons, 1963–64; Opposition Front Bench Spokesman: on Finance and Economics, 1964–66; on Transport, 1966–68; on Local Government, Housing, and Land, 1968–70; Minister of Housing and Local Govt, June-Oct. 1970; Secretary of State for: the Environment, 1970–72; Trade and Industry, 1972–74; Opposition Spokesman on Trade, Industry and Consumer Affairs, Feb.-June 1974, on Defence, June 1974–Feb. 1975; Minister of Agric., Fisheries and Food, 1979–83; Sec. of State for Energy, 1983–87. Chm., Thornton & Co., 1991–; Non-Executive Director:

British Gas, 1990–; Dalgety, 1990–; Smith New Court, 1990–; Tate & Lyle, 1990–. *Publications:* The Ascent of Britain, 1977; Trust The People, 1987. *Address:* Abbots Morton Manor, Gooms Hill, Abbots Morton, Worcester WR7 4LT. *Clubs:* Buck's, Pratt's; Worcestershire County Cricket, Union and County (Worcester).

WALKER, Rt. Rev. Peter Knight, DD; Bishop of Ely, 1977–89; *b* 6 Dec. 1919; *s* of late George Walker and Eva Muriel (*née* Knight); *m* 1973, Mary Jean, JP 1976, *yr d* of late Lt-Col J. A. Ferguson, OBE. *Educ:* Leeds Grammar Sch. (Schol.); The Queen's Coll., Oxford (Hastings schol.); Cl. 2 Classical Hon. Mods. 1940, Cl. 1 Lit. Hum. 1947; MA Oxon 1947; Hon. Fellow, 1981); Westcott House, Cambridge. MA Cantab by incorporation, 1958; Hon. DD Cantab, 1978. Served in RN (Lieut, RNVR), 1940–45. Asst Master: King's Sch., Peterborough, 1947–50; Merchant Taylors' Sch., 1950–56. Ordained, 1954; Curate of Hemel Hempstead, 1956–58; Fellow, Dean of Chapel and Lectr in Theology, Corpus Christi Coll., Cambridge, 1958–62 (Asst Tutor, 1959–62), Hon. Fellow, 1978; Principal of Westcott House, Cambridge, 1962–72; Commissary to Bishop of Delhi, 1962–66; Hon. Canon of Ely Cathedral, 1966–72; Bishop Suffragan of Dorchester, and Canon of Christ Church, Oxford, 1972–77. Select Preacher: Univ. of Cambridge, 1962, 1967 (Hulsean), 1986; Univ. of Oxford, 1975, 1980, 1990; Examining Chaplain to Bishop of Portsmouth, 1962–72. Chm., Hosp. Chaplaincies Council, 1982–86. Pres., British Sect., Internat. Bonhoeffer Soc., 1989–. A Governor, St Edward's Sch., Oxford. Hon. Fellow: St John's Coll., Cambridge, 1989; St Edmund's Coll., Cambridge, 1989. *Publications:* The Anglican Church Today: rediscovering the middle way, 1988; contrib. to: Classical Quarterly; Theology, etc. *Address:* Anchorage House, The Lanes, Bampton, Oxon OX18 2LA. *T:* Bampton Castle (0993) 850943. *Club:* Cambridge County.

WALKER, Prof. Peter Martin Brabazon, CBE 1976; FRSE; Honorary Professor and Director, MRC Mammalian Genome Unit, 1973–80; *b* 1 May 1922; *e s* of Major Ernest Walker and Mildred Walker (*née* Heaton-Ellis), Kenya; *m* 1943, Violet Norah Wright (*d* 1985); one *s* three *d; m* 1986, Joan Patricia Taylor; one *d. Educ:* Haileybury Coll.; Trinity Coll., Cambridge, 1945. BA, PhD. Tool and instrument maker, 1939 (during War); Scientific Staff, MRC Biophysics Research Unit, King's Coll., London, 1948; Royal Society Research Fellow, Edinburgh, 1958; Univ. of Edinburgh: Lectr in Zoology, 1962; Reader in Zoology, 1963; Professor of Natural History, 1966–73. Member: Biological Research Bd, MRC, 1967 (Chm., 1970–72); MRC, 1970–72; Ext. Scientific Staff, MRC, 1980–84; Chief Scientist Cttee, Scottish Home and Health Dept, 1973–85; Chm., Equipment Res. Cttee, Scottish Home and Health Dept, 1973–79; Mem. Council, Imp. Cancer Res. Fund, 1971–; Chm., Imp. Cancer Res. Fund Scientific Adv. Cttee, 1975–85; Mem., Scientific Adv. Cttee of European Molecular Biology Lab., 1976–81. General Editor, Chambers Science & Technology Dictionary, 1985–; Chambers Biology Dictionary, 1989; Air and Space Dictionary, 1990; Earth Sciences Dictionary, 1991. *Publications:* contribs to the molecular biology of the genetic material of mammals in: Nature; Jl of Molecular Biology, etc. *Recreations:* gardening, design of scientific instruments, railway history. *Address:* Drumlaggan, The Ross, Comrie, Perthshire. *T:* Comrie (0764) 70303.

WALKER, Philip Gordon, FCA; Chairman: Chapman Industries PLC, 1968–83; *b* 9 June 1912; *s* of late William and Kate Blanche Walker; *m* 1st, 1938, Anne May (marr. diss.); one *s* two *d*; 2nd, 1962, Elizabeth Oliver. *Educ:* Epworth Coll., Rhyl, North Wales. Bourner, Bullock & Co., Chartered Accountants, 1929–35; Walkers (Century Oils) Ltd, 1935–40; Layton Bennett, Billingham & Co., Chartered Accountants, 1940, Partner, 1944–51 (now Arthur Young McLelland Moore); Albert E. Reed & Co Ltd (now Reed International), Man. Dir, 1951–63; Chm. and Man. Dir, Philblack Ltd, 1963–71; Chm., Sun Life Assurance Soc. Ltd, 1971–82 (Exec.Chm. 1976–82). Part-time Mem. Monopolies Commn, 1963–65; Member: Performing Right Tribunal, 1971–83; Restrictive Practices Court, 1973–83. *Recreation:* golf. *Address:* The Garden Flat, Scotswood, Devenish Road, Sunningdale, Berks SL5 9QP. *Clubs:* Brooks's; Wildernesse (Sevenoaks); Rye; Berkshire.

WALKER, Philip Henry Conyers; His Honour Judge Harry Walker; a Circuit Judge, since 1979; *b* 22 Dec. 1926; *o c* of Philip Howard and Kathleen Walker; *m* 1953, Mary Elizabeth Ross; two *s* two *d. Educ:* Marlborough; Oriel Coll., Oxford. MA, BCL (Oxon); DipTh (London). Army (6 AB Sigs), 1944–48 (despatches, 1948). Solicitor in private practice, 1954–79; a Recorder of the Crown Court, 1972–79. Mem., Church Assembly, Nat. Synod of C of E, 1960–80. Chm., Agricultural Land Tribunal (Yorks & Lancs), 1977–79; Mem., Criminal Law Revision Cttee, 1981–. *Recreations:* fishing, shooting, sailing, walking. *Address:* Pond House, Askwith, Otley, West Yorks. *T:* Otley (0943) 463196.

WALKER, Raymond Augustus; QC 1988; *b* 26 Aug. 1943; *s* of Air Chief Marshal Sir Augustus Walker, GCB, CBE, DSO, DFC, AFC and Lady Walker; *m* 1976, June Rose Tunesi; one *s. Educ:* Radley; Trinity Hall, Cambridge (BA). Called to the Bar, Middle Temple, 1966. *Recreations:* golf, tennis, ski-ing, sailing, opera. *Address:* 1 Harcourt Buildings, Temple, EC4. *T:* 071–353 0375. *Clubs:* Garrick; Royal Dornoch; Royal West Norfolk Golf, Huntercombe Golf.

WALKER, Raymond James, OBE 1991; Chief Executive, Simpler Trade Procedures Board (formerly Simplification of International Trade Procedures Board), since 1983; *b* 13 April 1943; *s* of Cyril James Walker and Louie Walker; *m* 1969, Mary Eastwood Whittaker; one *d. Educ:* St Audreys, Hatfield; University of Lancaster. BA (Hons). Personnel Director, Saracen Ltd, 1971–73; Jt Man. Dir, Carrington Viyella Exports Ltd, 1973–78; Export Dir, Carrington Viyella Home Furnishings (DORMA), 1978–83. Co-Chm., Jt Electronic Data Interchange Cttee, UN Econ. Commn for Europe, 1985–87; Rapporteur for Western Europe, UN-Electronic Data Interchange for Admin, Commerce and Transport, 1987–. Amer. Nat. Standards Inst. Award, 1986; Electronic Data Interchange Award, Internat. Data Exchange Assoc., 1988. *Recreations:* collecting wine labels, a fascination for maps, growing clematis. *Clubs:* Royal Automobile; Belle Toute (Lancaster).

WALKER, Richard; His Honour Judge Richard Walker; a Circuit Judge, since 1989; *b* 9 March 1942; *s* of Edwin Roland Walker and Barbara Joan (*née* Swann); *m* 1969, Angela Joan Hodgkinson; two *d. Educ:* Epsom Coll.; Worcester Coll., Oxford (MA). Called to the Bar, Inner Temple, 1966; in practise at the Bar, 1966–89; Asst Boundary Comr, 1979–88; a Recorder, 1989. Mental Health Review Tribunal, 1991–. *Publication:* (ed jtly) Carter-Ruck on Libel and Slander, 3rd edn 1985. *Address:* c/o 1 Brick Court, Temple, EC4Y 9BY. *T:* 071–353 8845.

WALKER, Richard Alwyne F.; *see* Fyjis-Walker.

WALKER, Richard John Boileau, MA; FSA; picture cataloguer; *b* 4 June 1916; *s* of Comdr Kenneth Walker and Caroline Livingstone-Learmonth; *m* 1946, Margaret, *d* of Brig. Roy Firebrace, CBE; one *s* two *d. Educ:* Harrow; Magdalene Coll., Cambridge (MA); Courtauld Institute of Art. Active service, RNVR, 1939–45. British Council, 1946; Tate Gallery, 1947–48; Min. of Works Picture Adviser, 1949–76; Curator of the Palace of Westminster, 1950–76; Nat. Portrait Gallery Cataloguer, 1976–85; Royal Collection Cataloguer, 1985–91; Nat. Trust Cataloguer, 1990–. Trustee: Nat. Maritime

Museum, 1977–84; Army Museums Ogilby Trust, 1979–. *Publications:* Catalogue of Pictures at Audley End, 1950 and 1973; Old Westminster Bridge, 1979; Regency Portraits, 1985; Palace of Westminster: a catalogue, 4 vols, 1988; Royal Collection: the 18th century miniatures, 1991. *Recreations:* looking at pictures and finding quotations. *Address:* 31 Cadogan Place, SW1X 9RX. *T:* 071–235 1801. *Clubs:* Athenæum, United Oxford & Cambridge University.

WALKER, Robert; HM Diplomatic Service, retired; *b* 1 May 1924; *s* of Young and Gladys Walker, Luddendenfoot, Yorks; *m* 1949, Rita Thomas; one *s* one *d*. *Educ:* Sowerby Bridge Grammar Sch.; Peterhouse, Cambridge. Commissioned RNVR 1944; served in minesweepers in home waters. Cambridge, 1942–43 and 1946–48; BA Hons History, 1948; MA 1963. Joined CRO, 1948; served Peshawar and Karachi, 1949–51; New Delhi, 1955–59; Sen. First Sec., Accra, 1962–64; Dep. British High Comr, in Ghana, 1964–65; FCO, 1965–68. IDC, 1969; Commercial Counsellor, Ankara, 1970–71; Dep. High Comr, Nairobi, 1971–72. Dep. Registrar, Hull Univ., 1972–79. Mem., Craven DC, 1984– (Chm., 1991–92). Contested (L): Haltemprice, Feb. and Oct. 1974, 1979; Humberside, European election, 1979; South Ribble, 1983. Mem., Liberal Party Council, 1976–87; Chm., Yorkshire Liberal Fedn, 1977–81. Mem. Council, Lancaster Univ., 1986–. Founder Mem. and first Chm., Ribblesdale Trust, 1987–. *Recreations:* coarse golf, country wine making, interior decorating. *Address:* Manor Farm, Langcliffe, North Yorks BD24 9NQ. *T:* Settle (0729) 823205.

WALKER, Robert, QC 1982; *b* 17 March 1938; *s* of Ronald Robert Anthony Walker and Mary Helen Walker (*née* Welsh); *m* 1962, Suzanne Diana Leggi; one *s* three *d*. *Educ:* Downside Sch.; Trinity Coll., Cambridge (BA). Called to Bar, Lincoln's Inn, 1960, Bencher 1990; in practice at Chancery Bar, 1961–. *Recreations:* riding, running, skiing. *Address:* Freeman's Farm, Thaxted, Essex CM6 3PY. *T:* Thaxted (0371) 830577.

WALKER, Robert Scott, FRICS; City Surveyor, City of London Corporation, 1955–75; *b* 13 June 1913; *s* of Harold and Mary Walker; *m* 1946, Anne Armstrong; no *c*. *Educ:* West Buckland Sch., North Devon. War Service, 1939–45, Major RA. Assistant City Surveyor, Manchester, 1946–55. *Address:* 10 Woodcote Close, Epsom, Surrey KT18 7QJ. *T:* Epsom (0372) 721220.

WALKER, Comdr Roger Antony Martineau-, RN; Private Secretary to the Duke and Duchess of Kent, since 1990; *b* 15 Oct. 1940; *s* of Antony Philip Martineau-Walker and Sheila Hazeal Mayoh Wilson; *m* Inger Lene Brag-Nielsen; two *s*. *Educ:* Haileybury and Imperial Service College, Hertford; BRNC Dartmouth. Commissioned RN, 1962; served Malta, Singapore and Sarawak, 1962–65; Torpedo and Antisubmarine Course, HMS Vernon, 1968; HMS Galatea, 1973–76; NDC Latimer, 1977–78; Naval and Defence Staff, MoD, 1978–83; Naval Manpower Planning, with special responsibility for introd. of longer career for ratings (2nd Open Engagement), 1983–85; operational staff (UK commitments), 1985–87; Head, Naval Sec's Policy Staff, 1987–90; Promotion System Study, 1990. *Recreations:* fishing, wildlife photography, listening to music, enforced DIY. *Address:* York House, St James's Palace, SW1. *T:* 071–930 4832. *Club:* Army and Navy.

WALKER, Ronald Jack; QC 1983; a Recorder, since 1986; *b* 24 June 1940; *s* of Jack Harris Walker and Ann Frances Walker; *m* 1964, Caroline Fox; two *s*. *Educ:* Owen's School, London; University College London. LLB (Hons). Called to the Bar, Gray's Inn, 1962. *Publications:* English Legal System (with M. G. Walker), 1967, 6th edn 1985; contributing ed., Bullen & Leake & Jacob's Precedents of Pleadings, 13th edn 1990. *Address:* 12 King's Bench Walk, Temple, EC4Y 7EL. *T:* 071–583 0811; 45 Nassau Road, Barnes, SW13.

WALKER, Roy; *see* Walker, C. R.

WALKER, Sarah Elizabeth Royle, (Mrs R. G. Allum), CBE 1991; mezzo-soprano; *d* of Elizabeth Brownrigg and Alan Royle Walker; *m* 1972, Graham Allum. *Educ:* Pate's Grammar School for Girls, Cheltenham; Royal College of Music. ARCM, FRCM 1987; LRAM. Pres., Cheltenham Bach Choir, 1986–. Major appearances at concerts and in recital in Britain, America, Australia, New Zealand, Europe; operatic débuts include: Coronation of Poppea, Kent Opera, 1969, San Francisco Opera, 1981; La Calisto, Glyndebourne, 1970; Les Troyens, Scottish Opera, 1972, Wien Staatsoper, 1980; Principal Mezzo Soprano, ENO, 1972–77; Die Meistersinger, Chicago Lyric Opera, 1977; Werther, Covent Garden, 1979; Giulio Caesare, Le Grand Théâtre, Genève, 1983; Capriccio, Brussels, 1983; Teseo, Sienna, 1985; Samson, NY Metropolitan Opera, 1986; numerous recordings and video recordings, incl. title rôle in Britten's Gloriana. Hon. GSM 1988. *Recreations:* interior design, encouraging her husband with the gardening. *Address:* 152 Inchmery Road, SE6 1DF. *T:* 081–697 6152.

WALKER, Sheila Mosley, (Mrs Owen Walker), CBE 1981; JP; Chief Commissioner, Girl Guides Association, 1975–80; *b* 11 Dec. 1917; *yr d* of late Charles Eric Mosley Mayne, Indian Cavalry, and Evelyn Mary, *d* of Sir Thomas Skewes-Cox, MP; *m* 1st, 1940, Major Bruce Dawson, MC, Royal Berkshire Regt (killed, Arnhem, 1944); one *s* one *d*; 2nd, 1955, Henry William Owen, *s* of late Sir Henry Walker, CBE; one step *s* one step *d*. *Educ:* St Mary's Hall, Brighton; St James' Secretarial Coll., London. Midlands Regional Chief Comr, 1970–75, Vice-Pres., 1988–, Girl Guides Assoc. Vice-Chm., Nat. Exec. Cttee, CPRE, 1988–. JP Nottingham City, 1970. *Recreations:* children, animals, all country and nature preservation. *Address:* Dingley Hall, near Market Harborough, Leics. *T:* Dingley (085885) 388. *Club:* New Cavendish (Chm. Bd, 1983–).

WALKER, Stanley Kenneth; Director and Chief General Manager, Leeds Permanent Building Society, 1978–82; *b* 18 Feb. 1916; *s* of Robert and Gertrude Walker; *m* 1956, Diana, *d* of Fred Broadhead; one *s*. *Educ:* Cockburn Sch., Leeds. FCIS, FCBSI. Served War of 1939–45, Middle East (despatches, 1944). Leeds Permanent Building Society: Branch Manager, Newcastle upon Tyne, 1960–62; Asst Sec., 1962–66; Asst Gen. Manager, 1967–77; Gen. Manager, 1977–78. Member: Council, Building Societies Assoc., 1978–81; Vice-Pres., Leeds Centre, Chartered Building Socs Inst., 1983. *Recreations:* tennis, walking, theatre. *Club:* Royal Automobile.

WALKER, Dame Susan (Armour), DBE 1972 (CBE 1963); Vice-Chairman, 1970–74, Deputy Chairman, 1974–77, Women's Royal Voluntary Service; *b* 15 April 1906; *d* of James Walker, Bowmont, Dunbar; unmarried. *Educ:* Grammar School, Dunbar. Conservative Central Office Agent, Yorkshire, 1950–56; Deputy Chief Organisation Officer, Conservative Central Office, 1956–64; Vice-Chm., Cons. Party Organisation, 1964–68, retired 1968. *Recreations:* golf, walking. *Address:* The Glebe House, Hownam, Kelso, Roxburghshire. *T:* Morebattle (05734) 277.

WALKER, Terence William, (Terry Walker); *b* 26 Oct. 1935; *s* of William Edwin and Lilian Grace Walker; *m* 1959, Priscilla Dart; two *s* one *d*. *Educ:* Grammar Sch. and Coll. of Further Educn, Bristol. Employed by Courage (Western) Ltd at Bristol for 23 yrs, Mem. Chief Accountant's Dept. MP (Lab) Kingswood, Feb. 1974–1979; Second Church Estates Comr, 1974–79. Contested (Lab): Kingswood, 1983; Bristol NW, 1987. Mem., Avon CC, 1981–; Chm., Avon Public Protection Cttee, 1981–86. *Recreations:* cricket, football. *Address:* 28 Cherrington Road, Westbury-on-Trym BS10 5BJ. *T:* Bristol (0272) 623027.

WALKER, Ven. Thomas Overington; Archdeacon of Nottingham, since 1991; *b* 7 Dec. 1933; *m* 1957, Molly Anne Gilmour; one *s* two *d*. *Educ:* Keble Coll., Oxford (BA 1958; MA 1961); Oak Hill Theol Coll. Ordained 1960. Curate: St Paul, Woking, dio. of Guildford, 1960–62; St Leon, St Leonards, dio. of Chichester, 1962–64; Travelling Sec., Inter-Varsity Fellowship, 1964–67; Succentor, Birmingham Cathedral, 1967–70; Vicar, Harborne Heath, 1970–91; Priest-in-charge, St Germain, Edgbaston, 1983–91; Rural Dean, Edgbaston, 1989–91; Hon. Canon, Birmingham Cathedral, 1980–91. Proctor in Convocation, 1985–. *Publications:* Renew Us By Your Spirit, 1982; The Occult Web, 1987, 3rd edn 1989; From Here to Heaven, 1987; Small Streams Big Rivers, 1991. *Recreations:* sport, music, reading, dry stone walling. *Address:* 16 Woodthorpe Avenue, Woodthorpe, Nottingham NG5 4FD. *T:* Nottingham (0602) 267349.

WALKER, Prof. Thomas William, ARCS; DSc; DIC; Professor of Soil Science, Lincoln College, New Zealand, 1961–79, now Emeritus; *b* 22 July 1916; *m* 1940, Edith Edna Bott; four *d*. *Educ:* Loughborough Grammar School; Royal College of Science. Royal Scholar and Kitchener Scholar, 1935–39; Salter's Fellow, 1939–41; Lecturer and Adviser in Agricultural Chemistry, Univ. of Manchester, 1941–46. Provincial Advisory Soil Chemist, NAAS, 1946–51; Prof. of Soil Science, Canterbury Agric. Coll., New Zealand, 1952–58; Prof. of Agric., King's Coll., Newcastle upon Tyne, 1958–61. *Publications:* numerous research. *Recreations:* fishing, gardening. *Address:* 843 Cashmere Road, Christchurch 3, New Zealand.

WALKER, Timothy Edward; QC 1985; a Recorder of the Crown Court, since 1986; *b* 13 May 1946; *s* of George Edward Walker, solicitor, and Muriel Edith Walker; *m* 1968, Mary (*née* Tyndall); two *d*. *Educ:* Harrow Sch. (Entrance Schol., Leaving Schol.); University Coll., Oxford (MA). Plumptre Schol., 1965; 1st Cl. Hons Jurisprudence, 1967; Asst Lectr in Law, King's Coll., London, 1967–68; Profumo scholarship, Inner Temple, 1968; called to the Bar, Inner Temple, 1968; Eldon Law schol., 1969. *Address:* Fountain Court, Temple EC4Y 9DH. *T:* 071–583 3335; (home) 58 Lamont Road, SW10 0HX. *T:* 071–351 1429; Well House, Ham Road, Shalbourne, Marlborough, Wilts SNQ 3QN. *T:* Marlborough (0672) 870572.

WALKER, Timothy Edward Hanson; Head of Atomic Energy Division, Department of Energy, since 1989; *b* 27 July 1945; *s* of late Harris and of Elizabeth Walker; *m* 1st, 1969, Judith Mann (*d* 1976); one *d*; 2nd, 1983, Anna Butterworth; two *d*. *Educ:* Tonbridge Sch.; Brasenose Coll., Oxford (BA Chemistry, 1967; MA, DPhil 1969). Weir Jun. Res. Fellow, University Coll., Oxford, and Exhibnr of Royal Commn of 1851, Oxford and Paris, 1969; Harkness Fellow, Commonwealth Fund of New York, 1971, Univ. of Virginia, 1971 and Northwestern Univ., 1972; Strategic Planner, GLC, 1974; Principal, Dept of Trade, 1977; Sloan Fellow, London Business Sch., 1983; Department of Trade and Industry: Asst Sec., 1983; Dir (Admin), Alvey Programme, 1983; Head, Policy Planning Unit, 1985; Principal Private Sec. to successive Secs of State for Trade and Industry, 1986; Under Sec., 1987; Dir, Inf. Engrg Directorate, 1987. Non-exec. Dir, ICI Chemicals and Polymers Ltd, 1988–89. UK Gov., IAEA, 1989–. *Publications:* contribs to scientific jls. *Recreations:* cookery, gardening, collecting modern prints. *Address:* c/o Department of Energy, 1 Palace Street, SW1E 5HE.

WALKER, Walter Basil Scarlett, (Bobby Walker), MA; FCA; Deputy UK Senior Partner, Peat, Marwick, Mitchell & Co., 1979–82; *b* 19 Dec. 1915; *s* of James and Hilda Walker, Southport; *m* 1945, Teresa Mary Louise John; one *d* (and one *s* decd). *Educ:* Rugby Sch.; Clare Coll., Cambridge (MA). Joined Peat, Marwick, Mitchell & Co., 1937, leaving temporarily, 1939, to join RNVR; service in Home Fleet, incl. convoys to Russia and Malta, 1940–42; finally, Asst Sec. to British Naval C-in-C in Germany; Lt-Comdr. Returned to Peat, Marwick, Mitchell & Co., 1946, becoming a partner, 1956. Mem. (part-time), UKAEA, 1972–81. Governor, Royal Ballet, Covent Garden, 1980–90. *Recreations:* ballet, gardening, golf. *Address:* 11 Sloane Avenue, SW3 3JD. *T:* 071–589 4133; Coles, Privett, near Alton, Hants GU34 3PH. *T:* Privett (073088) 223. *Club:* Royal Automobile.

WALKER, Gen. Sir Walter (Colyear), KCB 1968 (CB 1964); CBE 1959 (OBE 1949); DSO 1946 and Bars, 1953 and 1965; Commander-in-Chief, Allied Forces Northern Europe, 1969–72, retired; *b* 11 Nov. 1912; *s* of late Arthur Colyear Walker; *m* 1938, Beryl (*d* 1990), *d* of late E.N.W. Johnston; two *s* one *d*. *Educ:* Blundell's; RMC, Sandhurst. Waziristan, 1939–41 (despatches twice); Burma, 1942, 1944–46 (despatches, DSO); Malaya, 1949–59 (despatches twice, OBE, Bar to DSO, CBE); Bt Lieut Col, 1952; Atomic Trials, Maralinga, SA, 1956; Dir of Operations, Borneo, 1962–65 (CB, Bar to DSO); Deputy Chief of Staff, HQ ALFCE, 1965; Acting Chief of Staff, 1966–67; GOC-in-C, Northern Command, 1967–69. psc† 1942; jssc 1950; idc 1960. Col, 7th Duke of Edinburgh's Own Gurkha Rifles, 1964–75. Dato Seri Setia, Order of Paduka Stia Negara, Brunei, 1964; Hon. Panglima Mangku Negara, Malaysia, 1965. *Publications:* The Bear at the Back Door, 1978; The Next Domino, 1980. *Recreations:* normal. *Address:* Haydon Farmhouse, Sherborne, Dorset DT9 5JB. *Club:* Army and Navy.

WALKER, William Connoll, (Bill Walker), FIPM; MP (C) Tayside North, since 1983 (Perth and East Perthshire, 1979–83); Chairman, Walker Associates, since 1975; Director, United Transport Malaŵi, since 1989; *b* 20 Feb. 1929; *s* of Charles and Williamina Walker; *m* 1956, Mavis Evelyn Lambert; three *d*. *Educ:* Logie Sch., Dundee; Trades Coll., Dundee; College for Distributive Trades. FIPM 1968; FBIM. Message boy, 1943–44; office boy, 1944–46. Commissioned RAF, 1946–49; Sqdn Leader, RAFVR, 1949–. Salesman, public service vehicle driver, general manager, 1949–59; civil servant, 1959–65; training and education officer, furnishing industry, 1965–67; company director, 1967–79; pt-time presenter, TV progs, 1969–75. FRSA 1970. *Recreations:* RAFVR, gliding, caravanning, walking, youth work. *Address:* Candletrees, Golf Course Road, Rosemount, Blairgowrie, Perthshire PH10 6LQ. *T:* Blairgowrie (0250) 2660. *Club:* Royal Air Force.

WALKER, William MacLelland, QC (Scot.) 1971; Social Security Commissioner, since 1988; *b* 19 May 1933; *s* of late Hon. Lord Walker; *m* 1957, Joan Margaret, *d* of late Charles Hutchison Wood, headmaster, Dundee; one *d*. *Educ:* Edinburgh Academy; Edinburgh Univ. (MA, LLB). Advocate, 1957; Flying Officer, RAF, 1957–59; Standing Junior Counsel: Min. of Aviation, 1963–68; BoT (Aviation), 1968–71; Min. of Technology, 1968–70; Dept of Trade and Industry (Power), 1971; Min. of Aviation Supply, 1971. Chairman: Industrial Tribunals in Scotland, 1972–88; VAT Tribunals, 1985–88. *Recreations:* shooting, travel, photography. *Address:* 17 India Street, Edinburgh EH3 6HE. *T:* 031–225 3846; Edenside, Gordon, Berwickshire TD3 6LB. *T:* Gordon (057381) 271. *Clubs:* Royal Air Force; New (Edinburgh).

WALKER-HAWORTH, John Liegh; Director, S. G. Warburg & Co., since 1981; *b* 25 Oct. 1944; *s* of William and Julia Walker-Haworth; *m* 1976, Caroline Mary Blair Purves; two *s*. *Educ:* Charterhouse; Pembroke College, Oxford. Called to the Bar, Inner Temple, 1967. Dir-Gen., City Panel on Take-overs and Mergers, 1985–87. Chm., Charities Effectiveness Review Trust, 1991–. *Address:* 23 Eldon Road, W8 5PT. *T:* 071–937 3883.

WALKER-OKEOVER, Sir Peter (Ralph Leopold), 4th Bt *cr* 1886; *b* 22 July 1947; *s* of Colonel Sir Ian Peter Andrew Monro Walker-Okeover, 3rd Bt, DSO, TD, and of Dorothy Elizabeth, *yr d* of Captain Josceline Heber-Percy; *S* father, 1982; *m* 1972, Catherine Mary Maule, *d* of Colonel George Maule Ramsay; two *s* one *d*. *Educ:* Eton; RMA Sandhurst. Captain, Blues and Royals, retired. *Heir: s* Andrew Peter Monro Walker-Okeover, *b* 22 May 1978. *Address:* Okeover Hall, Osmaston, Ashbourne, Derbyshire; House of Glenmuick, Ballater, Aberdeenshire.

WALKER-SMITH, family name of **Baron Broxbourne.**

WALKER-SMITH, John Jonah; a Recorder of the Crown Court, since 1980; *b* 6 Sept. 1939; *s* of Baron Broxbourne, *qv*; *m* 1974, Aileen Marie Smith; one *s* one *d*. *Educ:* Westminster School; Christ Church, Oxford. Called to Bar, Middle Temple, 1963. *Address:* 11 Doughty Street, WC1.

WALKINE, Herbert Cleveland, CMG 1990; OBE 1985; Secretary to the Cabinet, Bahamas, since 1987; *b* 28 Nov. 1929; *s* of late Herbert Granville Walkine and Rebecca Walkine; *m* 1966, Julliette Pam Maria Sherman; three *d*. *Educ:* Government High Sch., Nassau; Bahamas Teachers' Coll.; Univ. of Manchester. Started career as teacher; served as District Commissioner, 1958–68; Asst Sec., 1968 and Perm. Sec., 1974–87, Bahamas. *Recreations:* fishing, reading, watching boxing matches. *Address:* PO Box N7147, Nassau, Bahamas. *T:* 1–809–32–22805.

WALL, Alfreda, (Mrs D. R. Wall); *see* Thorogood, A.

WALL, (Alice) Anne, (Mrs Michael Wall), DCVO 1982 (CVO 1972; MVO 1964); Extra Woman of the Bedchamber to HM the Queen, since 1981; *b* 1928; *d* of late Admiral Sir Geoffrey Hawkins, KBE, CB, MVO, DSC and late Lady Margaret, *d* of 7th Duke of Buccleuch; *m* 1975, Commander Michael E. St Q. Wall, Royal Navy. *Educ:* Miss Faunce's PNEU School. Asst Press Sec. to the Queen, 1958–81. *Address:* Ivy House, Lambourn, Berks RG16 7PB. *T:* Lambourn (0488) 72348; 6 Chester Way, Kennington, SE11 4UT. *T:* 071-582 0692.

WALL, Brian Owen, CEng, FRINA; RCNC; Chief Naval Architect, Ministry of Defence, 1985–90; *b* 17 June 1933; *s* of Maurice Stanley Wall and Ruby Wall; *m* 1960, Patricia Thora Hughes; one *s*. *Educ:* Newport High School, Mon; Imperial Coll. of Science and Technology; RN Coll., Greenwich. BSc Eng. ACGI. MoD Bath: Ship Vulnerability, 1958–61; Submarine Design, 1961–66; Head of Propeller Design, Admiralty Experiment Works, Haslar, 1966–71; Staff of C-in-C Fleet, Portsmouth, 1971–73; Submarine Support and Modernisation Group, MoD Bath, 1973–77; RCDS 1977; MoD Bath: Ship Production Div., 1978–79; Project Director, Vanguard Class, 1979–84; Dir, Cost Estimating and Analysis, 1985. *Recreations:* photography, chess, music, walking, golf. *Address:* Wychwood, 39 High Bannerdown, Batheaston, Bath BA1 7JZ.

WALL, Prof. Charles Terence Clegg, FRS 1969; Professor of Pure Mathematics, Liverpool University, since 1965; *b* 14 Dec. 1936; *s* of late Charles Wall, schoolteacher; *m* 1959, Alexandra Joy, *d* of late Prof. Leslie Spencer Hearnshaw; two *s* two *d*. *Educ:* Marlborough Coll.; Trinity Coll., Cambridge. PhD Cantab 1960. Fellow, Trinity Coll., 1959–64; Harkness Fellow, Princeton, 1960–61; Univ. Lectr, Cambridge, 1961–64; Reader in Mathematics, and Fellow of St Catherine's Coll., Oxford, 1964–65. SERC Sen. Fellowship, 1983–88. Royal Soc. Leverhulme Vis. Prof., CIEA, Mexico, 1967. Pres., London Mathematical Soc., 1978–80 (Mem. Council, 1973–80). Fellow, Royal Danish Academy, 1990. Sylvester Medal, Royal Soc., 1988. *Publications:* Surgery on Compact Manifolds, 1970; A Geometric Introduction to Topology, 1972; papers on various problems in geometric topology, and related algebra. *Recreations:* gardening, home winemaking. *Address:* 5 Kirby Park, West Kirby, Wirral, Merseyside L48 2HA. *T:* 051–625 5063.

WALL, David (Richard), CBE 1985; Director, Royal Academy of Dancing, 1987–91 (Associate Director, 1984–87); formerly Senior Principal, Royal Ballet Co.; *b* 15 March 1946; *s* of Charles and Dorothy Wall; *m* 1967, Alfreda Thorogood, *qv*; one *s* one *d*. *Educ:* Royal Ballet Sch. Joined Royal Ballet Co., Aug. 1964. Promotion to: Soloist, Aug. 1966; Junior Principal Dancer, Aug. 1967; Senior Principal Dancer, Aug. 1968; during period of employment danced all major roles and had many ballets created for him; retired from dancing, 1984. Evening Standard Award for Ballet, 1977. *Recreations:* music, theatre. *Address:* 34 Croham Manor Road, South Croydon, Surrey CR2 7BE.

WALL, Rt. Rev. Eric St Quintin; *b* 19 April 1915; *s* of Rev. Sydney Herbert Wall, MA, and Ethel Marion Wall (*née* Wilkins); *m* 1942, Doreen Clare (*née* Loveley); one *s* one *d*. *Educ:* Clifton; Brasenose Coll., Oxford (MA); Wells Theol. College. Deacon, 1938; Priest, 1939; Curate of Boston, 1938–41; Chaplain, RAFVR, 1941–45; Vicar of Sherston Magna, 1944–53; Rural Dean of Malmesbury, 1951–53; Vicar of Cricklade with Latton, 1953–60; Hon. Chaplain to Bp of Bristol, 1960–66; Hon. Canon, Bristol, 1960–72; Diocesan Adviser on Christian Stewardship, Dio. Bristol, 1960–66; Proc. Conv., 1964–69; Vicar, St Alban's, Westbury Park, Bristol, 1966–72; Rural Dean of Clifton, 1967–72; Canon Residentiary of Ely, 1972–80; Bishop Suffragan of Huntingdon, 1972–80. *Recreation:* golf. *Address:* 7 Peregrine Close, Diss, Norfolk IP22 3PG. *T:* Diss (0379) 644331.

WALL, Hon. Sir Gerard (Aloysius), Kt 1987; medical practitioner; *b* 24 Jan. 1920; *m* 1951, Uru Raupo (Cameron); two *s* three *d*. *Educ:* St Bede's College, Christchurch; Canterbury Univ.; Otago Univ. MB ChB; FRCSE. House Surgeon, Christchurch Public Hosp., 1948–49; GP, Denniston, 1949–53; Mem., Buller Hosp. Bd, 1949–50; House Surgeon, Postgraduate Hosp., London, 1953; Royal Nat. Orthopaedic Hosp., London, 1955; Res. Surgical Officer, Hitchin Hosp., 1954–55; Sen. Plastic Surgical Registrar: Birmingham Accident Hosp., 1956–57; Norwich Hosp., 1957–59; Surgeon Dep. Supt, Wairau Hosp., 1960–69; Mem., Marlborough Hosp. Bd, 1965–68; Porirua Hosp., 1968–69. MP (Lab) Porirua, 1969–85; Speaker, House of Reps, NZ, 1984–85. Mem. Govt Select Committees: Maori Affairs, Health and Social Services, Local Govt, Statutes Revision, Foreign Affairs; Chm., Parly Service Comm, 1985. Mem., Blenheim Borough Council, 1962–68. *Recreations:* woodworking, building. *Address:* 39 Tangare Drive, Elsdon, Porirua, New Zealand. *T:* (04) 375 015.

WALL, (John) Stephen, CMG 1990; LVO 1983; HM Diplomatic Service; Private Secretary to the Prime Minister, since 1991; *b* 10 Jan. 1947; *s* of John Derwent Wall and Maria Laetitia Wall (*née* Whitmarsh); *m* 1975, Catharine Jane Reddaway; one *s*. *Educ:* Douai Sch.; Selwyn Coll., Cambridge (BA). FCO 1968; Addis Ababa, 1969–72; Private Sec. to HM Ambassador, Paris, 1972–74; First Sec., FCO, 1974–76; Press Officer, No 10 Downing Street, 1976–77; Asst Private Sec. to Sec. of State for Foreign and Commonwealth Affairs, 1977–79; First Sec., Washington, 1979–83; Asst Head, later Head, European Community Dept, FCO, 1983–88; Private Sec. to Foreign and Commonwealth Sec., 1988–90. *Recreations:* walking, photography. *Address:* c/o Foreign and Commonwealth Office, King Charles Street, SW1A 2AH. *Club:* Athenæum.

WALL, Mrs Michael; *see* Wall, A. A.

WALL, Nicholas Peter Rathbone; QC 1988; a Recorder, since 1990; *b* 14 March 1945; *s* of late Frederick Stanley Wall and of Margaret Helen Wall; *m* 1973, Margaret Sydee, JP; four *c*. *Educ:* Dulwich College; Trinity Coll., Cambridge (Scholar; MA). Pres., Cambridge Union Soc., 1967; Mem., combined univs debating tour, USA, 1968. Called to the Bar, Gray's Inn, 1969; Asst Recorder, 1988–90. *Publication:* (ed jtly) Rayden and Jackson on Divorce, 16th edn, 1991–. *Recreations:* collecting and binding books, attempting to grow vegetables, opera, walking. *Address:* 1 Mitre Court Buildings, Temple, EC4Y 7BS. *T:* 071–353 0434. *Club:* Athenæum.

WALL, Prof. Patrick David, MA, DM; FRCP; FRS 1989; Professor of Anatomy and Director, Cerebral Functions Research Group, University College, London, 1967–90, Professor Emeritus, 1990; *b* 5 April 1925; *s* of T. Wall, MC, and R. Wall (*née* Cresswell). *Educ:* St Paul's; Christ Church, Oxford. MA 1947; BM, BCh 1948; DM 1960. Instructor, Yale School of Medicine, 1948–50; Asst Prof., Univ. of Chicago, 1950–53; Instructor, Harvard Univ., 1953–55; Assoc. Prof., 1957–60, Professor 1960–67, MIT. Vis. Prof., Hebrew Univ., Jerusalem, 1973–. Founding Chm., Brain Research Assoc. Hon. MD Sienna, 1987. Bonica Award, Internat. Assoc. Study of Pain, 1987; Sherrington Medal, RSM, 1988; Wakeman Award, Duke Univ., 1988; Research on Pain Award, Bristol-Myers, 1988. First Editor in Chief, Pain. *Publications:* Trio, The Revolting Intellectuals' Organizations (novel), 1966 (US 1965); (with R. Melzack) The Challenge of Pain, 1982, 2nd edn 1989; The Textbook of Pain, 1983, 2nd edn 1989; many papers on anat. and physiol. of nervous system. *Recreation:* kibbitzing. *Address:* 141 Gray's Inn Road, WC1X 8UB.

WALL, Major Sir Patrick (Henry Bligh), Kt 1981; MC 1945; VRD 1957; RM (retd); *b* 19 Oct. 1916; *s* of Henry Benedict Wall and Gladys Eleanor Finney; *m* 1953, Sheila Elizabeth Putnam (*d* 1983); one *d*. *Educ:* Downside. Commissioned in RM 1935 (specialised in naval gunnery). Served in HM Ships, support craft, with RM Commandos and US Navy. Actg Major, 1943; RN Staff Coll., 1945; Joint Services Staff Coll., 1947; Major, 1949. CO 47 Commando RMFVR, 1951–57; Comr for Sea Scouts in London, 1950–66. Westminster City Council, 1953–62. Contested Cleveland Division (Yorks), 1951 and 1952. MP (C): Haltemprice Div. of Hull, Feb. 1954–55; Haltemprice Div. of E Yorks, 1955–83; Beverley, 1983–87. Parliamentary Private Secretary to: Minister of Agriculture, Fisheries and Food, 1955–57; Chancellor of the Exchequer, 1958–59. Mem., Select Cttee on Defence, 1980–83. Chm. Mediterranean Group of Conservative Commonwealth Council, 1954–67; Chm. Cons. Parly East and Central Africa Cttee, 1956–59; Vice-Chairman: Conservative Commonwealth Affairs Cttee, 1960–68; Cons. Overseas Bureau, 1963–73; Cons. Defence Cttee, 1965–77; Vice-Chm. or Treasurer, IPU, 1974–82 (Chairman: British-Maltese, Anglo-Bahrain, Anglo-South African, Anglo-Taiwan Groups; Vice-Chm., Anglo-Portuguese, Treasurer, Anglo-Korean Groups). North Atlantic Assembly: Leader, British Delegn, 1979–87; Pres., 1983–85; Chm., Mil. Cttee, 1978–81; Chm., Cons./Christian Democrat Gp, 1977–87. Mem. Defence Cttee, WEU and Council of Europe, 1972–75. Chairman: Cons. Fisheries Sub-Cttee, 1962–83; Africa Centre, 1961–65; Joint East and Central Africa Board, 1965–75; Cons. Southern Africa Group, 1970–78; Cons. Africa Sub-Cttee, 1979–83; RM Parly Group, 1956–87; British Rep. at 17th General Assembly of UN, 1962. Chm., Monday Club, 1978–80. Pres., Yorks Area Young Conservatives, 1955–60. Pres., British UFO Res. Assoc.; Vice-Pres., British Sub-Aqua Club, 1955–87. FIJ 1989. Freeman of Beverley, 1989. Kt, SMO Malta; USA Legion of Merit, 1945; Gold Star of Taiwan, 1988. *Publications:* Royal Marine Pocket Book, 1944; Student Power, 1968; Defence Policy, 1969; Overseas Aid, 1969; The Soviet Maritime Threat, 1973; The Indian Ocean and the Threat to the West, 1975; Prelude to Detente, 1975; Southern Oceans and the Security of the Free World, 1977; co-author of a number of political pamphlets. *Recreation:* ship and aircraft models. *Address:* 8 Westminster Gardens, Marsham Street, SW1 4JA. *T:* 071–828 1803; Brantinghamthorp, Brantingham, near Brough, North Humberside HU15 1QG. *T:* Hull (0482) 667248. *Clubs:* Royal Yacht Squadron; Royal Naval Sailing Association.

WALL, Maj.-Gen. Robert Percival Walter, CB 1978; JP; Member, North East Thames Regional Health Authority, since 1990; Chairman, Essex Family Health Services Authority, since 1990; *b* 23 Aug. 1927; *s* of Frank Ernest and Ethel Elizabeth Wall; *m* 1st, 1953 (marr. diss. 1985); two *s* one *d*; 2nd, 1986, Jennifer Hilary Anning. Joined Royal Marines, 1945; regimental soldiering in Commandos, followed by service at sea and on staff of HQ 3 Commando Bde RM, 1945–58; psc(M) 1959; jssc 1961; Asst Sec., Chiefs of Staff Secretariat, 1962–65; 43 Commando RM, 1965–66; Naval Staff, 1966–68; Directing Staff, JSS Coll., 1969–71; Col GS Commando Forces and Dept of Commandant General RM, 1971–74; course at RCDS, 1975; Chief of Staff to Commandant General, RM, 1976–79. Dir, Land Decade Educnl Council, 1982–90. Chm., Essex FPC, 1985–90. Vice-Pres., River Thames Soc., 1983– (Chm., 1978–83); Mem. Council, Thames Heritage Trust, 1980–83; Pres., Blackheath Football Club (RFU), 1983–85; Council, Officers' Pension Soc., 1980–91. Freeman of City of London, 1977; Freeman, Co. of Watermen and Lightermen of River Thames, 1979. FBIM; FRSA 1985. JP City of London, 1982. *Recreations:* cricket, rugby, walking, reading. *Address:* c/o Barclays Bank, 116 Goodmayes Road, Goodmayes, Ilford, Essex. *Clubs:* Army and Navy, MCC.

WALL, Sir Robert (William), Kt 1987; OBE 1980; Pro-Chancellor, University of Bristol, since 1990; Leader, Conservative Group, Bristol City Council, since 1974; *b* 27 Sept. 1929; *s* of William George and Gladys Perina Wall; *m* 1968, Jean Ashworth; one *d* (and one *s* decd). *Educ:* Monmouth School; Bristol Coll. of Technology. HND MechEng; AMRAeS, TechEng. Student apprentice, Bristol Aeroplane Co., 1947–52; commissioned RAF Eng. Branch, and Mountain Rescue Service, 1955–57; management posts with British Aircraft Corp., 1957–67, Chief Ratefixer, 1969–75, Manager, Cost Control, 1975–88. Bristol City Council: Councillor 1959; Alderman 1971; re-elected Councillor 1974; Chm., Public Works Cttee, 1968–72; Dep. Leader, 1971–72, Council Leader, 1983–84. Chairman: Bristol Cons. Assoc., 1979–88; Western Area Provincial Council, Nat. Union of Cons. and Unionist Assocs, 1988–. Mem. Council, Univ. of Bristol, 1974– (Chairman: GP Cttee, 1979–87; Buildings Cttee, 1987–91); Governor, Bristol Old Vic Theatre Trust, 1974–87; Mem. Council, SS Great Britain Project, 1975–; Chm., Transport Users' Cons. Cttee for W England, 1982–. Mem., Audit Commn, 1986–. Pres., Bristol Soc. of Model and Experimental Engrs, 1972–. Freeman, Co. of Watermen and Lightermen. Hon. MA Bristol, 1982. *Publications:* Bristol Channel Pleasure Steamers, 1973; Ocean Liners, 1978 (trans. German, French, Dutch), 2nd edn 1984; Air Liners, 1980; Bristol: maritime city, 1981; The Story of HMS Bristol, 1986. *Recreations:* writing maritime history, collecting postcards, hill walking. *Address:* 1 Ormerod Road, Stoke Bishop, Bristol BS9 1BA. *T:* Bristol (0272) 682910. *Clubs:* Bristol Savages, Clifton (Bristol).

WALL, Stephen; *see* Wall, J. S.

WALL, Prof. William Douglas, PhD, DLit; Professor of Educational Psychology, Institute of Education, University of London, 1972–78, now Professor Emeritus; *b* 22 Aug. 1913; *s* of late John Henry Wall and Ann McCulloch Wall, Wallington, Surrey; *m* 1st, 1936, Doris Margaret (*née* Satchel) (marr. diss. 1960); two *s* one *d*; 2nd, 1960, Ursula Maria (*née* Gallusser); one *s*. *Educ:* Univ. Coll. London, 1931–34 (BA Hons); Univ. Coll.

London/Univ. of Birmingham, 1944–48 (PhD (Psychol.)); DLit (London) 1979. FBPsS; CPsychol. Mem., Social Psych. Sect., Child and Educnl Psych. Sect., Univ. of Birmingham Educn Dept, 1945–53; Reader, 1948–53; Head, Educn and Child Develt Unit, UNESCO, Paris, 1951–56; Dir, Nat. Foundn for Educnl Res. in England and Wales, 1956–68; Dean, Inst. of Educn, Univ. of London, 1968–73; Scientific Advr, Bernard van Leer Foundn, 1978–82. Visiting Professor: Univ. of Michigan, 1957; Univ. of Jerusalem, 1962; Univ. of Tel Aviv, 1967. Chm., Internat. Project Evaluation of Educnl Attainment, 1958–62; Mem., Police Trng Council, 1970–78; Co-Dir, 1958–75, and Chm., Nat. Child Develt Study, 1958–78; Mem. Council, Internat. Children's Centre, Paris, 1970–78. *Publications:* (many trans. various langs): Adolescent Child, 1948 (2nd edn, 1952); Education and Mental Health, 1955; Psychological Services for Schools, 1956; Child of our Times, 1959; Failure in School, 1962; Adolescents in School and Society, 1968; Longitudinal Studies and the Social Sciences, 1970; Constructive Education for Children, 1975; Constructive Education for Adolescents, 1977; Constructive Education for Handicapped, 1979; contrib: British Jl Educnl Psych.; British Jl Psych., Educnl Res. (Editor, 1958–68), Educnl Rev., Enfance, Human Develt, Internat. Rev. Educn. *Recreations:* painting (one-man exhibitions: Windsor, 1986, 1988; London, 1987), gardening. *Address:* La Geneste, Rose Hill, Burnham, Bucks SL1 8LW.

WALLACE, family name of **Barons Wallace of Campsie** and **Wallace of Coslany.**

WALLACE OF CAMPSIE, Baron *cr* 1974 (Life Peer), of Newlands, Glasgow; **George Wallace,** JP; DL; Life President, Wallace, Cameron (Holdings) Ltd, since 1981 (President, 1977–81); Director, Smith & Nephew Associated Companies Ltd, 1973–77; *b* 13 Feb. 1915; *s* of John Wallace and Mary Pollock; *m* 1977, Irene Alice Langdon Phipps, *er d* of Ernest Phipps, Glasgow. *Educ:* Queen's Park Secondary Sch., Glasgow; Glasgow Univ. Estd Wallace, Cameron & Co. Ltd, 1948, Chm., 1950–77. Solicitor before the Supreme Courts, 1950–; Hon. Sheriff at Hamilton, 1971–. Chm., E Kilbride and Stonehouse Develt Corp., 1969–75; Mem. Bd, S of Scotland Electricity Bd, 1966–68; founder Mem. Bd, Scottish Develt Agency, 1975–78; Chm., E Kilbride Business Centre, 1984–. Pres., Glasgow Chamber of Commerce, 1974–76; Vice-Pres., Scottish Assoc. of Youth Clubs, 1971–; Chm., Adv. Bd (Strathclyde) Salvation Army, 1972–; Mem. Court, Univ. of Strathclyde, 1973–74; Hon. Pres., Town and Country Planning Assoc. (Scottish Sect.), 1969–; Chm., Scottish Exec. Cttee, Brit. Heart Foundn, 1973–76; Chm., Britannia Cttee, British Sailors' Soc., 1967–77; Vice-Chm., Scottish Retirement Council, 1975–; Hon. Pres., Lanarkshire Samaritans, 1984–. FRSA 1970; FSAScot 1990; FCIM (FInstM 1968); MBIM 1969. JP 1968, DL 1971, Glasgow. KStJ 1976. *Recreation:* reading. *Address:* 14 Fernleigh Road, Newlands, Glasgow G43 2UE. *T:* 041–637 3337. *Clubs:* Caledonian; Royal Scottish Automobile (Glasgow).

WALLACE OF COSLANY, Baron *cr* 1974 (Life Peer), of Coslany in the City of Norwich; **George Douglas Wallace;** *b* 18 April 1906; *e s* of late George Wallace, Cheltenham Spa, Gloucestershire; *m* 1932, Vera Randall, Guildford, Surrey; one *s* one *d*. *Educ:* Central School, Cheltenham Spa. Mem. of Management Cttee, in early years, of YMCA at East Bristol and Guildford; Mem. Chislehurst-Sidcup UDC, 1937–46; has been Divisional Sec. and also Chm., Chislehurst Labour Party; also Chm. of Parks and Cemeteries Cttee of UDC, Schools Manager and Member of Chislehurst, Sidcup and Orpington Divisional Education Executive; Mem., Cray Valley and Sevenoaks Hosp. Management Cttee; Chm., House Cttee, Queen Mary's Hosp.; Vice-Chm., Greenwich and Bexley AHA, 1974–77. Joined Royal Air Force, reaching rank of Sergeant. Served in No 11 Group Fighter Command, 1941–45. MP (Lab) Chislehurst Div. of Kent, 1945–50; Junior Govt Whip, 1947–50; MP (Lab) Norwich North, Oct. 1964–Feb. 1974; PPS: to Lord President of the Council, Nov. 1964–65; to Sec. of State for Commonwealth Affairs, 1965; to Minister of State, Min. of Housing and Local Govt, 1967–68; Mem. Speaker's Panel of Chairmen, 1970–74; a Lord in Waiting (Govt Whip), 1977–79; opposition spokesman and Whip, H of L, 1979–84. Delegate to Council of Europe and WEU, 1975–77. Member: Commonwealth Parly Assoc.; Commonwealth War Graves Commn, 1970–86; Kent CC, 1952–57. Pres., London Soc. of Recreational Gardeners, 1977–. *Recreations:* interested in Youth Movements and social welfare schemes. *Address:* 44 Shuttle Close, Sidcup, Kent DA15 8EP. *T:* 081–300 3634.

WALLACE, Albert Frederick, CBE 1963 (OBE 1955); DFC 1943; Controller of Manpower, Greater London Council, 1978–82; *b* 22 Aug. 1921; *s* of Major Frederick Wallace and Ada Wallace; *m* 1940, Evelyn M. White; one *s* one *d*. *Educ:* Roan School, Blackheath, SE3. MIPM, MBIM, MILGA. Regular Officer, Royal Air Force, 1939–69; retired in rank of Group Captain. Regional Advisory Officer, Local Authorities Management Services and Computer Cttee, 1969–71; Asst Clerk of the Council, Warwickshire CC, 1971–73; County Personnel Officer, W Midlands CC, 1973–78. *Recreations:* golf, bridge. *Address:* Rochester Close, Eastbourne BN20 7TW. *T:* Eastbourne (0323) 30668. *Club:* Royal Air Force.

WALLACE, Charles William, CMG 1983; CVO 1975; HM Diplomatic Service, retired; *b* 19 Jan. 1926; *s* of Percival Francis and Julia Wallace; *m* 1957, Gloria Regina de Ros Ribas (*née* Sanz-Agero). *Educ:* privately and abroad. HM Foreign (later Diplomatic) Service, 1949; served: Asuncion; Barcelona; Bari; Bahrain; Tegucigalpa; Guatemala; Panama; Foreign Office; Baghdad; Buenos Aires; Montevideo; FO, later FCO, Asst Head of American Dept; Counsellor 1969; Rome and Milan; Mexico City; Ambassador: Paraguay, 1976–79; Peru, 1979–83; Uruguay, 1983–86. Freeman, City of London, 1981. Order of Aztec Eagle, 1975. *Recreations:* sailing, fishing. *Address:* c/o Lloyds Bank, Private Banking Branch, 51 Grosvenor Street, W1X 9FH; Calle del Sol 5, 17121 Corsa, Girona, Spain. *Club:* Travellers'.

WALLACE, Prof. David James, FRS 1986; FRSE; Tait Professor of Mathematical Physics, University of Edinburgh, since 1979; *b* 7 Oct. 1945; *s* of Robert Elder Wallace and Jane McConnell Wallace (*née* Elliot); *m* 1970, Elizabeth Anne Yeats; one *d*. *Educ:* Hawick High Sch.; Univ. of Edinburgh (BSc, PhD). FRSE 1982. Harkness Fellow, Princeton Univ., 1970–72; Lecturer in Physics, 1972–78, Reader in Physics, 1978–79, Southampton Univ.; Hd of Physics, Edinburgh Univ., 1984–87. Director: Edinburgh Concurrent Supercomputer, 1987–89; Edinburgh Parallel Computing Centre, 1990–. Science and Engineering Research Council: Chm., Physics Cttee, 1987–90; Chm., Science Bd, 1990–; Mem. Council, 1990–. Frequent visiting scientist abroad, incl. Europe, Israel, North and South America. Maxwell Medal of Inst. of Physics, 1980. *Publications:* in research and review jls, in a number of areas of theoretical physics. *Recreations:* running, eating at La Potinière. *Address:* Physics Department, The University, Mayfield Road, Edinburgh EH9 3JZ. *T:* 031–667 1081 ext. 2850.

WALLACE, David Mitchell, CBE 1978 (OBE 1942); MS, FRCS; retired, 1978; Professor of Urology, Riyadh Medical College, Saudi Arabia, 1974–78; *b* 8 May 1913; *s* of F. David Wallace and M. I. F. Wallace; *m* 1940, Noel Wilson; one *s* three *d*. *Educ:* Mill Hill; University Coll., London, BSc 1934; MB, BS 1938; FRCS 1939; MS 1948. Served War of 1939–45, Wing Comdr, RAF (despatches). Hunterian Prof., Royal Coll. of Surgeons, London, 1956, 1978. Formerly: Surgeon, St Peter's Hospital; Urologist, Royal Marsden Hospital, Chelsea Hospital for Women, and Manor House Hospitals; Lecturer, Institute of Urology; Adviser on Cancer to WHO. Mem., Amer. Radium Soc., 1968. *Publications:* Tumours of the Bladder, 1957; contrib. to Cancer, British Jl of Urology, Proc. Royal Soc. Med. *Recreations:* cine photography, pistol shooting. *Address:* 45 Fort Picklecombe, Tor Point, Cornwall PL10 1JB.

WALLACE, (Dorothy) Jacqueline H.; *see* Hope-Wallace.

WALLACE, Fleming; *see* Wallace, J. F.

WALLACE, Ian Alexander; JP; Headmaster, Canford School, 1961–76; *b* 5 Oct. 1917; *s* of late Very Rev. A. R. Wallace and Winifred, *d* of late Rev. H. C. Sturges; *m* 1947, Janet Glossop; two *s* two *d*. *Educ:* Clifton; Corpus Christi College, Cambridge (open scholar). Classical Tripos, Part I, 1st Cl.; Theological Tripos Part I, 2nd Cl. Div. One. Served War of 1939–45, Mountain Artillery, NW Frontier, India, 1941; School of Artillery, India, 1942–43; Arakan, 1944; Mandalay, 1945 (despatches). Rossall School: Assistant Master, 1946; Housemaster, 1951–61. SW Regional Sec., Independent Schools Careers Organisation, 1976–84; Project Manager for India, GAP Activity Projects, 1984–89. Governor: Portsmouth Grammar Sch., 1977–89; King's Sch., Bruton, 1977–. JP Poole Borough, 1966. *Address:* Steeple Close, Hindon, Salisbury, Wilts.

WALLACE, Ian Bryce, OBE 1983; Hon. RAM; Hon. RCM; singer, actor and broadcaster; *b* London, 10 July 1919; *o s* of late Sir John Wallace, Kirkcaldy, Fife (one-time MP for Dunfermline), and Mary Bryce Wallace (*née* Temple), Glasgow; *m* 1948, Patricia Gordon Black, Edenwood, Cupar, Fife; one *s* one *d*. *Educ:* Charterhouse; Trinity Hall, Cambridge (MA). Served War of 1939–45, (invalided from) RA, 1944. London stage debut in The Forrigan Reel, Sadler's Wells, 1945. Opera debut, as Schaunard, in La Bohème, with New London Opera Co., Cambridge Theatre, London, 1946. Sang principal roles for NLOC, 1946–49, incl. Dr Bartolo in Il Barbiere di Siviglia. Glyndebourne debut, Masetto, Don Giovanni, Edin. Fest., 1948. Regular appearances as principal *buffo* for Glyndebourne, both in Sussex and at Edin. Fest., 1948–61, incl. perfs as Don Magnifico in La Cenerentola, at Berlin Festwoche, 1954. Italian debut: Masetto, Don Giovanni, at Parma, 1950; also Don Magnifico, La Cenerentola, Rome, 1955, Dr Bartolo, Il Barbiere di Siviglia, Venice, 1956, and Bregenz Fest., 1964–65. Regular appearances for Scottish Opera, 1965–, incl. Leporello in Don Giovanni, Pistola in Falstaff, Duke of Plaza Toro in The Gondoliers. Don Pasquale, Welsh Nat. Opera, 1967, Dr Dulcamara, L'Elisir d'Amore, Glyndebourne Touring Opera, 1968. Devised, wrote and presented three series of adult education programmes on opera, entitled Singing For Your Supper, for Scottish Television (ITV), 1967–70. Recordings include: Gilbert and Sullivan Operas with Sir Malcolm Sargent, and humorous songs by Flanders and Swann. Theatrical career includes: a Royal Command Variety Perf., London Palladium, 1952; Cesar in Fanny, Theatre Royal, Drury Lane, 1956; 4 to the Bar, Criterion, 1960; Toad in Toad of Toad Hall, Queen's, 1964. Regular broadcaster, 1944–: radio and TV, as singer, actor and compere; a regular panellist on radio musical quiz game, My Music; acted in series, Porterhouse Blue, Channel 4 TV, 1987. President: ISM, 1979–80; Council for Music in Hosps, 1988. Hon. DMus St Andrews, 1991. Sir Charles Santley Meml Award, Musicians' Co., 1984. *Publications:* Promise Me You'll Sing Mud (autobiog.), 1975; Nothing Quite Like It (autobiog.), 1982; Reflections on Scotland, 1988. *Recreations:* walking, reading, sport watching, photography; singing a song about a hippopotamus to children of all ages. *Address:* c/o Peters, Fraser & Dunlop, 5th floor, The Chambers, Chelsea Harbour, Lots Road, SW10 0XF. *T:* 071–352 4446. *Clubs:* Garrick, MCC; Stage Golfing Society.

WALLACE, Sir Ian (James), Kt 1982; CBE 1971 (OBE (mil.) 1942); Director, Coventry Motor and Sundries Co. Ltd, since 1986; Chairman, SNR Bearings (UK) Ltd, 1975–85; *b* 25 Feb. 1916; *s* of John Madder Wallace, CBE; *m* 1942, Catherine Frost Mitchell, *e d* of Cleveland S. Mitchell; one *s* one *d*. *Educ:* Uppingham Sch.; Jesus Coll., Cambridge (BA). Underwriting at Lloyd's, 1935–39. War Service, Fleet Air Arm: Cmdr (A) RNVR, 1939–46. Harry Ferguson Ltd from 1947: Dir 1950; later Massey Ferguson Ltd, Dir Holdings Board until 1970. Coventry Conservative Association: Treas., 1956–68; Chm., 1968–88; Pres., 1988–; Chm., W Midlands Cons. Council, 1967–70 (Treas., 1962–67); Pres., W Midlands Area Cons. Council. Member: Severn-Trent Water Authority, 1974–82; W Midlands Econ. Planning Council, 1965–75; Vice-Chm., Midland Regional Council, CBI, 1964, Chm., 1967–69; Pres., Coventry Chamber of Commerce, 1972–74. Pres., Hereford-Worcs County Rifle Assoc., 1983–. *Recreation:* shooting (rifle and game). *Address:* Little House, 156 High Street, Broadway, Worcs WR12 7AJ. *T:* Broadway (0386) 852414. *Clubs:* Carlton, Naval and Military, North London Rifle.

WALLACE, Ian Norman Duncan, QC 1973; *b* 21 April 1922; *s* of late Duncan Gardner Wallace, HBM Crown Advocate in Egypt, Paymaster-Comdr RNR and Eileen Agnes Wallace. *Educ:* Loretto; Oriel Coll., Oxford (MA). Served War of 1939–45: Ordinary Seaman RN, 1940; Lieut RNVR, 1941–46. Called to Bar, Middle Temple, 1948; Western Circuit, 1949. Vis. Scholar, Berkeley Univ., Calif, 1977–86; Vis. Prof., Centre of Construction Law, KCL, 1987–. Editl Bd, Construction Law Jl, 1984–. *Publications:* (ed) Hudson on Building and Civil Engineering Contracts, 8th edn 1959, 9th edn 1965 and 10th edn 1970, supplement 1979; Building and Civil Engineering Standard Forms, 1969; Further Building and Engineering Standard Forms, 1973; The International Civil Engineering Contract, 1974, supplement 1980; The ICE Conditions (5th edn), 1978; Construction Contracts: principles and policies in Tort and Contract, 1986; contrib. Law Qly Review, Jl of Internat. Law and Commerce, Construction Law Jl, Internat. Construction Law Rev., Arbitration Internat. *Recreations:* shooting, keeping fit, foreign travel. *Address:* 53 Holland Park, W11 3RS. *T:* 071–727 7640. *Clubs:* Lansdowne, Hurlingham.

WALLACE, Ivan Harold Nutt, CB 1991; Senior Chief Inspector, Department of Education, Northern Ireland, since 1979; *b* 20 Feb. 1935; *s* of late Harold Wallace and Annie McClure Wallace; *m* 1962, Winifred Ervine Armstrong; two *d*. *Educ:* Grosvenor High Sch., Belfast; QUB (BSc 1957). MRSC 1963. School Teacher: Leeds Central High Sch., 1957–60; Foyle Coll., Londonderry, 1960–69; Inspector of Schools, NI, 1969–75; Sen. Inspector, 1975–77; Staff Inspector, 1977–78; Chief Inspector, 1978–79. *Recreations:* music, walking. *Address:* c/o Department of Education for Northern Ireland, Rathgael House, Balloo Road, Bangor, Co. Down, N Ireland. *T:* Bangor (0247) 270077.

WALLACE, (James) Fleming; QC (Scot) 1985; Counsel to Scottish Law Commission, since 1979; *b* 19 March 1931; *s* of James F. B. Wallace, SSC and Margaret B. Gray, MA; *m* 1st, 1964, Valerie Mary (*d* 1986), *d* of Leslie Lawrence, solicitor, and Madge Lawrence, Ramsbury, Wilts; two *d*; 2nd, 1990, Linda Ann, solicitor, *d* of Robert Grant, civil engineer, and Alice Grant. *Educ:* Edinburgh Academy; Edinburgh University (MA 1951; LLB 1954). Served RA, 1954–56 (2nd Lieut); TA 1956–60. Admitted Faculty of Advocates, 1957; practised at Scottish Bar until 1960; Parly Draftsman and Legal Secretary, Lord Advocate's Dept, London, 1960–79. *Publication:* The Businessman's Lawyer (Scottish Section), 1965, 2nd edn 1973. *Recreations:* hill walking, choral singing, golf, badminton. *Address:* 24 Corrennie Gardens, Edinburgh EH10 6DB. *Club:* Royal Mid-Surrey Golf.

WALLACE, James Robert; MP Orkney and Shetland, since 1983 (L 1983–88, Lib Dem since 1988); *b* 25 Aug. 1954; *s* of John F. T. Wallace and Grace Hannah Wallace (*née* Maxwell); *m* 1983, Rosemary Janet Fraser; two *d. Educ:* Annan Academy; Downing College, Cambridge (BA 1975, MA 1979); Edinburgh University (LLB 1977). Chm., Edinburgh Univ. Liberal Club, 1976–77. Called to the Scots Bar, 1979; practised as Advocate, 1979–83. Contested Dumfriesshire (L), 1979; contested South of Scotland (L), European Parlt election, 1979. Mem., Scottish Liberal Exec., 1976–85; Vice-Chm. (Policy), Scottish Liberal Party, 1982–85; Hon. Pres., Scottish Young Liberals, 1984–85; Liberal spokesman on defence, 1985–87; Deputy Whip, 1985–87, Chief Whip, 1987–88; first Lib Dem Chief Whip, 1988–; Alliance spokesman on Transport, 1987; Lib Dem spokesman on employment, training and fisheries, 1988–. *Recreations:* golf, music, travel. *Address:* Northwood House, Tankerness, Orkney KW17 2QS. *T:* Tankerness (085686) 383. *Club:* Scottish Liberal (Edinburgh).

WALLACE, John Malcolm Agnew; JP; Vice Lord-Lieutenant, Dumfries and Galloway (District of Wigtown), since 1990; *b* 30 Jan. 1928; *s* of John Alexander Agnew Wallace and Marjory Murray Wallace; *m* 1955, Louise Haworth-Booth; one *s* two *d. Educ:* Harrow; West of Scotland Agricultural College. Farmer. JP Stranraer, 1970; DL Dumfries and Galloway, 1971. *Address:* Lochryan, Stranraer DG9 8QY. *T:* Cairnryan (05812) 284.

WALLACE, John Williamson; Principal Trumpet: Philharmonia Orchestra, since 1976; London Sinfonietta, since 1987; freelance soloist, composer, conductor; *b* 14 April 1949; *s* of Christopher Kidd Wallace and Ann Drummond Allan; *m* 1971, Elizabeth Jane Hartwell; one *s* one *d. Educ:* Buckhaven High Sch.; King's Coll., Cambridge (MA); York Univ.; Royal Acad. of Music (ARAM 1983; FRAM 1990). ARCM 1968; Hon. RCM 1985. Asst Principal Trumpet, LSO, 1974–76; founded The Wallace Collection (brass-interest music gp), 1986. Trumpet solo recordings. *Publications:* Five Easy Pieces, 1984; First Book of Trumpet Solos, 1985; Second Book of Trumpet Solos, 1985, 2nd edn 1987; Grieg's Seven Lyric Pieces, 1985; Kornukopia, 1986; Prime Number, 1990. *Recreations:* family life, worrying, holidaying in France. *Address:* 16 Woodstock Road, Croydon CR0 1JR. *T:* 081–688 1170.

WALLACE, Lawrence James, OC 1972; CVO 1983; Deputy Minister to the Premier of British Columbia, since 1980; *b* Victoria, BC, Canada, 24 April 1913; *s* of John Wallace and Mary Wallace (*née* Parker); *m* 1942, Lois Leeming; three *d. Educ:* Univ. of British Columbia (BA); Univ. of Washington, USA (MEd). Served War, Lt-Comdr, Royal Canadian Navy Voluntary Reserve, 1941–45. Joined British Columbia Govt, as Dir of Community Programmes and Adult Educn, 1953; Dep. Provincial Sec., 1959–77, Dep. to Premier, 1969–72; Agent-General for British Columbia in UK and Europe, 1977–80. General Chairman: four centennial celebrations, marking founding of Crown Colony of British Columbia in 1858, union of Crown Colonies of Vancouver Is. and British Columbia, 1866, Canadian Confedn, 1867, and joining into confedn by British Columbia in 1871. Dir, Provincial Capital Commn; Vice Chm., BC Press Council; Past Chm., Inter-Provincial Lottery Corp., Queen Elizabeth II Schol. Cttee, and Nancy Green Schol. Cttee; Hon. Trustee, British Columbia Sports Hall of Fame. Director: Sen. Citizens Lottery; BC Forest Museum; Adv. Bd, Salvation Army; Canadian Council of Christians and Jews; President: Duke of Edinburgh Awards Cttee, BC; McPherson Playhouse Foundn; Hon. Pres., Univ of Victoria Alumni. Named British Columbia Man of the Year, 1958, and Greater Vancouver Man of the Year, 1967; Canadian Centennial Medal, 1967; Comdr Brother, OStJ, 1969; City of Victoria Citizenship Award, 1971; Queen's Jubilee Medal, 1977. Freeman of City of London, 1978. Hon. LLD, Univ. of British Columbia, 1978. Hon. Member: BC High Sch. Basketball Assoc.; BC Recreation Assoc. Hon. Chief: Alberni, Gilford and Southern Vancouver Is Indian Bands. *Recreations:* gardening, community activities. *Address:* 1345 Fairfield Road, Victoria, BC V8S 1E4, Canada; Parliament Buildings, Victoria, British Columbia V8V 1R3, Canada.

WALLACE, Major Malcolm Charles Robarts; Director General, British Equestrian Federation, since 1985; *b* 12 June 1947; *s* of Lionel John Wallace and Maureen Winefride (*née* Robarts); *m* 1974, Caroline Anne Doyne-Ditmas (marr. diss. 1990); one *s* one *d*; *m* 1991, Mrs Jane Thelwall. *Educ:* Blackrock College, Co. Dublin. Student pupil with Lt-Col J. Hume-Dudgeon at Burton Hall, Co. Dublin, 1965–67; Mons Officer Cadet Sch.; commissioned RA, 1967; gun line officer, 18 Light Regt, Hong Kong; 3rd Regt RHA, 1969; King's Troop RHA, 1970 (long equitation course, RAVC Melton Mowbray); Troop Comdr, 19 Field Regt, 1974; Adjutant 101 Northumbrian Field Artillery, 1976; Staff Officer, HQ UKLF, 1978–82; Comd King's Troop RHA, 1982–85, retired. Chef d'Equipe to British Internat. and Olympic Three Day Event Teams, 1979–84; Chef de Mission, Equestrian Team, Seoul Olympic Games, 1988. Steward: Sandown Park; Warwick. Freeman, Saddlers' Co., 1985. *Publication:* The King's Troop Royal Horse Artillery, 1984. *Recreations:* field sports, National Hunt racing. *Address:* The Manor House, Stoke Albany, Market Harborough, Northants LE16 8PT. *T:* Dingley (085885) 250, *Fax:* Dingley (085885) 499. *Club:* Cavalry and Guards.

WALLACE, Reginald James, CMG 1979; OBE 1961; fiscal adviser; Chairman: Norwich Union Fire Insurance Society (Gibraltar) Ltd, since 1984; Abbey National Gibraltar Ltd, since 1987; *b* 16 Aug. 1919; *s* of James Wallace and Doris (*née* Welch); *m* 1st, 1943, Doris Barbara Brown, MD, FRCS, MRCOG (decd); one *d*; 2nd, 1973, Maureen Coady (*d* 1983); 3rd, 1983, Marilyn Ryan (*née* Gareze); one *d. Educ:* John Gulson Sch., Coventry; Tatterford Sch., Norfolk; Leeds Univ. (BA); Queen's Coll., Oxford. Served War, 1939–46, 7th Rajput Regt, Indian Army (Major). Gold Coast/Ghana Admin. Service, 1947–58; Sen. District Comr, 1955; Asst Chief Regional Officer, Northern Region, 1957; Regional Sec., 1958; Financial Sec., British Somaliland, 1958–60; War Office, 1961–66; HM Treasury, 1966–78; seconded to Solomon Is, as Financial Sec. (later Financial Adviser), 1973–76; seconded, as British Mem., Anglo/French Mission on Admin. Reform in the Condominium of the New Hebrides, 1977; Governor of Gilbert Is, 1978 to Independence, July 1979; Financial and Develt Sec., Gibraltar, 1979–83. *Recreations:* walking, music. *Club:* Commonwealth Trust.

WALLACE, Richard Alexander; Principal Finance Officer, Welsh Office, since 1990; *b* 24 Nov. 1946; *s* of Lawrence Mervyn and Norah Wallace; *m* 1970, Teresa Caroline Harington Smith; three *c* (and one *c* decd). *Educ:* Bembridge and Sandown C of E Primary Schools; Clifton Coll. Prep. Sch.; Clifton Coll.; King's Coll., Cambridge (MA). Asst Master, Woking County GS for Boys, 1967; Min. of Social Security, 1968; Principal, DHSS, 1972, Asst Sec., 1981; transf. to Welsh Office, 1986; Under Sec., 1988. *Recreation:* not working. *Address:* Welsh Office, Cathays Park, Cardiff CF1 3NQ.

WALLACE, Robert, CBE 1970; BL; JP; Chairman, Highland Health Board, 1973–81; *b* 20 May 1911; *s* of late John Wallace, Glespin, Lanarkshire, and late Elizabeth Brydson; *m* 1st, 1940, Jane Maxwell (decd), *d* of late John Smith Rankin, Waulkmill, Thornhill, Dumfriesshire and late Jane Maxwell; no *c*; 2nd, 1987, Mary Isobel, *d* of late Hector M. Macdonald, Conon Bridge, Ross-shire, and late Catherine Ross. *Educ:* Sanquhar Sch.; Glasgow University. Solicitor 1932; BL (Dist.) 1933. Private legal practice, 1932–40; Depute Town Clerk, Ayr Burgh, 1940–44; Civil Defence Controller, Ayr Burgh, 1941–44; Depute County Clerk and Treas., Co. Inverness, 1944–48; County Clerk, Treasurer and Collector of the County of Inverness, 1948–73; Temp. Sheriff, Grampian, Highland and Islands, 1976–84. Hon. Sheriff at Inverness, 1967–. JP Co. Inverness, 1951–. *Recreations:* bowling, fishing, gardening. *Address:* Eildon, School Road, Conon Bridge, Ross-shire IV7 8AE. *T:* Dingwall (0349) 63592.

WALLACE, Walter Ian James, CMG 1957; OBE 1943; retired; *b* 18 Dec. 1905; *e s* of late David Wallace, Sandgate, Kent; *m* 1940, Olive Mary (*d* 1973), 4th *d* of late Col Charles William Spriggs, Southsea; no *c. Educ:* Bedford Modern School; St Catharine's College, Cambridge. Entered ICS 1928, posted to Burma; Dep. Commissioner, 1933; Settlement Officer, 1934–38; Dep. Commissioner, 1939–42; Defence Secretary, 1942–44; Military Administration of Burma (Col and Dep. Director Civil Affairs), 1944–45 (despatches); Commissioner, 1946; Chief Secretary, 1946–47. Joined Colonial Office, 1947, Asst Sec., 1949–62; Asst Under-Sec. of State, 1962–66, retired. *Publication:* Revision Settlement Operations in the Minbu District of Upper Burma, 1939. *Recreation:* local history. *Club:* East India, Devonshire, Sports and Public Schools.

WALLACE, Walter Wilkinson, CVO 1977; CBE 1973 (OBE 1964); DSC 1944; Foreign and Commonwealth Office; *b* 23 Sept. 1923; *s* of late Walter Wallace and of Helen Wallace (*née* Douglas); *m* 1955, Susan Blanche, *d* of Brig. F. W. B. Parry, CBE; one *s* one *d. Educ:* George Heriot's, Edinburgh. Served War, Royal Marines, 1942–46 (Captain). Joined Colonial Service, 1946; Asst Dist Comr, Sierra Leone, 1948; Dist Comr, 1954; seconded to Colonial Office, 1955–57; Sen. Dist Comr, 1961; Provincial Comr, 1961; Develt Sec., 1962–64; Estabt Sec., Bahamas, 1964–67; Sec. to Cabinet, Bermuda, 1968–73; HM Commissioner, Anguilla, 1973; Governor, British Virgin Islands, 1974–78. Constitutional Comr, St Helena, 1987, Cayman Islands, 1991. *Recreation:* golf. *Address:* Becketts, Itchenor, Sussex. *T:* Birdham (0243) 512438. *Club:* Army and Navy.

WALLACE, William John Lawrence; Senior Research Fellow in European Studies, St Antony's College, Oxford, since 1990; *b* 12 March 1941; *s* of William E. Wallace and Mary A. Tricks; *m* 1968, Helen Sarah Rushworth; one *s* one *d. Educ:* Westminster Abbey Choir School (Sen. Chorister, 1954); St Edward's Sch., Oxford; King's Coll., Cambridge (Exhibnr, 1959; BA Hist 1962); Nuffield Coll., Oxford; Cornell Univ. (PhD Govt 1968). Lectr in Govt, Univ. of Manchester, 1967–77; Dep. Dir, RIIA, 1978–90. Contested (L): Huddersfield West, 1970; Manchester Moss Side, Feb. and Oct. 1974; Shipley, 1983 and 1987. Vice-Chm., Liberal Party Policy Cttee, 1982–87. Editor, Jl of Common Market Studies, 1974–78. *Publications:* Foreign Policy and the Political Process, 1972; The Foreign Policy Process in Britain, 1977; (with Christopher Tugendhat) Options for British Foreign Policy in the 1990s, 1988; The Transformation of Western Europe, 1990. *Address:* St Antony's College, Oxford OX2 6JF.

WALLEN, Ella Kathleen, MA (Oxon); Headmistress, St Mary's School, Wantage, 1977–80; *b* 15 Feb. 1914. *Educ:* Camden School for Girls; St Hugh's College, Oxford. History Mistress, Queen Victoria High School, Stockton-on-Tees, 1937–41; Senior History Mistress, High School for Girls, Gloucester, 1942–59; Headmistress: Queen Victoria High School, Stockton-on-Tees, 1959–65; Bedford High Sch., 1965–76. *Address:* 15 Lynn Close, Marston Road, Oxford OX3 0JH.

WALLENBERG, Peter, Order of Wasa, 1974; King's Medal 12th Class, 1983; Hon. KBE 1989; First Vice Chairman, Skandinaviska Enskilda Banken, since 1984 (Vice Chairman, 1980–84); Chairman: Atlas Copco AB, since 1974; Investor, since 1982; Providentia, since 1982; Wallenberg Foundation, since 1982; STORA, since 1985; *b* Stockholm, 26 May 1926; *s* of Marcus Wallenberg and Dorothy (*née* Mackay); *m* (marr. diss.); two *s* one *d. Educ:* Stockholm Univ. (LLB). Various positions within Atlas Copco Gp, 1953–68; Man. Dir, Atlas Copco MCT AB, 1968–70; Dep. Man. Dir, Atlas Copco AB, 1970–74; Industrial Advr to Skandinaviska Enskilda Banken, 1974–80. Vice Chairman: ASEA AB, 1976–; Ericsson, 1976–; AB Electrolux, 1978–; SKF, 1986–; Director: Scandinavian Airlines System, 1973–; Fedn of Swedish Industries, 1975–; ASEA Brown Boveri Ltd, ABB (Zürich), 1988–. Member of Board: Stockholm Sch. of Econs, 1976–; Per Jacobson Foundn (USA), 1983–; Joseph H. Lauder Inst. (USA), 1983–; Nobel Foundn, 1986–. Hon. Dr: Stockholm Sch. of Econ., 1984; Augustana Coll., Ill, 1985; Upsala Coll., NJ, 1989. Orden de Isabel la Católica (Spain), 1979; Comdr, Légion d'Honneur (France), 1987; Comdr 1st Cl. Order of Lion of Finland, 1988; Comdr l'Ordre de Léopold (Belgium), 1989. *Recreations:* hunting, sailing, tennis. *Address:* Skandinaviska Enskilda Banken, S–106 40 Stockholm, Sweden. *T:* 46–822 19 00.

WALLER, Gary Peter Anthony; MP (C) Keighley, since 1983 (Brighouse and Spenborough, 1979–83); *b* 24 June 1945; *s* of late John Waller and of Elizabeth Waller. *Educ:* Rugby Sch.; Univ. of Lancaster (BA Hons). Chairman: Lancaster Univ. Conservative Assoc., 1965; Spen Valley Civic Soc., 1978–80; Vice-Chm., Nat. Assoc. of Cons. Graduates, 1970–73 and 1976–77. Member: Exec. Cttee, Cons. Nat. Union, 1976–77; Management Cttee, Bradford and Dist Housing Assoc., 1976–90. Exec. Sec., Wider Share Ownership Council, 1973–76. Contested (C): Kensington, Bor. Council elecns, 1971, 1974; Leyton, GLC elecn, 1973; Rother Valley, parly elecn, Feb. and Oct. 1974. PPS to Sec. of State for Transport, 1982–83. Member: H of C Select Cttee on Transport, 1979–82; Jt Cttee on Consolidation Bills, 1982–; Chm., All Party Wool Textile Gp, 1984–89 (Sec., 1979–83); Vice-Chairman: Parly Food and Health Forum, 1985–; Parly IT Cttee, 1987– (Treas., 1981–87); Secretary: Cons. Parly Sport and Recreation Cttee, 1979–81; Yorkshire Cons. Members, 1979–83; Cons. Parly Transport Cttee, 1985–87, 1988–; All-Party Rugby League Gp, 1989–; Hon. Sec., Parly and Scientific Cttee, 1988–91. Pres., Brighouse Citizens Advice Bureau, 1979–83; Vice-President: Newham S Cons. Assoc., 1979– (Chm., 1971–74); Bethnal Green and Bow Cons. Assoc., 1982–83. Vice-President: Inst. of Trading Standards Admin, 1988–; Keighley Sea Cadets, 1984–; Friends of the Settle–Carlisle Railway, 1987–. Governor: George Green's Sch., Tower Hamlets, 1968–70; Isaac Newton Sch., N Kensington, 1971–73; Manager, Moorend C of E Primary Sch., Cleckheaton, 1977–80. *Recreations:* music, poetry, squash, football. *Address:* House of Commons, SW1A 0AA. *T:* 071–219 4010. *Clubs:* Keighley Conservative, Haworth Conservative, Silsden Conservative, Ilkley Constitutional.

WALLER, Hon. Sir (George) Mark, Kt 1989; **Hon. Mr Justice Waller;** a Judge of the High Court of Justice, Queen's Bench Division, since 1989; Presiding Judge, North-East Circuit, since 1992; *b* 13 Oct. 1940; *s* of Rt Hon. Sir George Waller, *qv*; *m* 1967, Rachel Elizabeth, *d* of His Honour Judge Beaumont, *qv*; three *s. Educ:* Oundle Sch.; Durham Univ. (LLB). Called to the Bar, Gray's Inn, 1964, Bencher, 1988; QC 1979; a Recorder, 1986–89. *Recreations:* tennis, golf. *Address:* Royal Courts of Justice, Strand, WC2. *Clubs:* Garrick, MCC.

WALLER, Rt. Hon. Sir George (Stanley), Kt 1965; OBE 1945; PC 1976; a Lord Justice of Appeal, 1976–84; *b* 3 Aug. 1911; *s* of late James Stanley and late Ann Waller; *m* 1936, Elizabeth Margery, *d* of 1st Baron Hacking; two *s* one *d. Educ:* Oundle; Queens' Coll., Cambridge (Hon. Fellow 1974). Called to the Bar, Gray's Inn, 1934, Bencher, 1961, Treasurer, 1978. RAFO, 1931–36; served War of 1939–45, in RAFVR, Coastal Command; 502 Sqdn, 1940–41; Wing Comdr, 1943 (despatches). Chm., Northern Dist Valuation Bd, 1948–55; QC 1954; Recorder of Doncaster, 1953–54, of Sunderland, 1954–55, of Bradford, 1955–57, of Sheffield, 1957–61, and of Leeds, 1961–65; a Judge of

the High Court, Queen's Bench Div., 1965–76; Presiding Judge, NE Circuit, 1973–76. Solicitor-General of the County Palatine of Durham, 1957–61; Attorney-General of the County Palatine of Durham, 1961–65; Member: Criminal Injuries Compensation Board, 1964–65; General Council of the Bar, 1958–62 and 1963–65; Parole Bd, 1969–72 (Vice-Chm., 1971–72); Adv. Council on the Penal System, 1970–73 and 1974–78; Criminal Law Revision Cttee, 1977–85; Chm., Policy Adv. Cttee on Sexual Offences, 1977–85. President: Inns of Court and Bar, 1979–80; British Acad. of Forensic Sciences, 1983–84. *Address:* Hatchway, Hatch Lane, Kingsley Green, Haslemere, Surrey GU27 3LJ. *T:* Haslemere (0428) 644629. *Clubs:* Army and Navy; Hawks (Cambridge).
See also G. M. Waller.

WALLER, Sir (John) Keith, Kt 1968; CBE 1961 (OBE 1957); Secretary, Department of Foreign Affairs, Canberra, 1970–74, retired; *b* 19 Feb. 1914; *s* of late A. J. Waller, Melbourne; *m* 1943, Alison Irwin Dent; two *d. Educ:* Scotch Coll., Melbourne; Melbourne Univ. Entered Dept of External Affairs, Australia, 1936; Private Sec. to Rt Hon. W. M. Hughes, 1937–40; Second Sec., Australian Legation, Chungking, 1941; Sec.-Gen., Australian Delegn, San Francisco Conf., 1945; First Sec., Australian Legation, Rio de Janeiro, 1945; Chargé d'Affaires, 1946; First Sec., Washington, 1947; Consul-Gen., Manila, 1948; Officer-in-Charge, Political Intelligence Div., Canberra, 1950; External Affairs Officer, London, 1951; Asst Sec., Dept of External Affairs, Canberra, 1953–57; Ambassador to Thailand, 1957–60; Ambassador to USSR, 1960–62; First Asst Sec., Dept of External Affairs, 1963–64; Ambassador to US, 1964–70. Member: Australian Council for the Arts, 1973; Interim Film Board, 1974. Chm., Radio Australia Inquiry, 1975. *Address:* 17 Canterbury Crescent, Deakin, ACT 2600, Australia. *Club:* Commonwealth (Canberra).

WALLER, Sir John Stanier, 7th Bt, *cr* 1815; author, poet, and journalist; *b* 27 July 1917; *s* of Capt. Stanier Edmund William Waller (*d* 1923), and of Alice Amy (who *m* 2nd, 1940, Gerald H. Holiday), *d* of J. W. Harris, Oxford; *S kinsman* Sir Edmund Waller, 6th Bt, 1954; *m* 1974, Anne Eileen Mileham (marr. diss.). *Educ:* Weymouth Coll.; Worcester Coll., Oxford (Exhibnr in History, 1936, BA in Eng. Lang. and Lit., 1939, OU DipEd (Teaching), 1940). Founder-Editor of Quarterly, Kingdom Come, first new literary magazine of war, 1939–41. Served 1940–46 with RASC (in Middle East, 1941–46); Adjt RASC, HQ, Cairo Area; Capt. 1942; Features Editor, Brit. Min. of Inf., Middle East, 1943–45; Chief Press Officer, Brit. Embassy, Bagdad, 1945; News and Features Editor, MIME, Cairo, 1945–46. Dramatic Critic Cairo Weekly, The Sphinx, 1943–46; Founder-Mem. Salamander Soc. of Poets, Cairo, 1942; lectured in Pantheon Theatre, Athens, 1945; Greenwood Award for Poetry, 1947; Keats Prize, 1974; FRSL 1948; Lectr and Tutor in English and Eng. Lit. at Carlisle and Gregson (Jimmy's), Ltd, 1953–54; Asst Master, London Nautical Sch., May-June 1954; Information Officer, Overseas Press Services Div., Central Office of Information, 1954–59. Director: Literature Ltd, 1940–42; Richard Congreve Ltd, 1948–50; Export Trade Ships Ltd, 1956; Bristol Stone and Concrete Ltd, 1974; Mercantile Land and Marine Ltd, 1979. *Publications:* The Confessions of Peter Pan, 1941; Fortunate Hamlet, 1941; Spring Legend, 1942; The Merry Ghosts, 1946; Middle East Anthology (Editor), 1946; Crusade, 1946; The Kiss of Stars, 1948; The Collected Poems of Keith Douglas (Editor), 1951 and 1966; Shaggy Dog, 1953; Alamein to Zem Zem by Keith Douglas (Editor), 1966; Goldenhair and the Two Black Hawks, 1971; Return to Oasis (co-editor), 1980; contrib. to numerous anthologies and periodicals at home and abroad. *Recreations:* portrait photography, teaching. *Heir:* none. *Address:* 21 Lyndhurst Road, Hove, Sussex BN3 6FA. *T:* Brighton (0273) 734836.

WALLER, Rt. Rev. John Stevens; *b* 18 April 1924; *m* 1951, Pamela Peregrine; two *s* three *d. Educ:* St Edward's School, Oxford; Peterhouse, Cambridge (MA); Wells Theol Coll. War service with RNVR, 1942–46. Deacon 1950, priest 1951, London; Leader, Strood Gp of Parishes, 1967–72, Team Rector of Strood 1972–73; Rector of St Nicholas, Harpenden, Herts, 1973–79; Bishop Suffragan of Stafford, 1979–87; Team Vicar, Long Sutton and Long Load, Som, 1987–89; an Asst Bishop, dio. of Bath and Wells, 1987–89. *Address:* Grey Cottage, The Green, Beaminster, Dorset DT8 3SD. *T:* Beaminster (0308) 862284.

WALLER, Sir Keith; *see* Waller, Sir J. K.

WALLER, Hon. Sir Mark; *see* Waller, Hon. Sir G. M.

WALLER, Sir Robert William, 9th Bt, *cr* 1780, of Newport, Co. Tipperary; employed by the General Electric Co. of America as an Industrial Engineer, since 1957; *b* 16 June 1934; *s* of Sir Roland Edgar Waller, 8th Bt, and Helen Madeline, *d* of Joseph Radl, Matawan, New Jersey, USA; *S* father 1958; is a citizen of the United States; *m* 1960 (marr. diss.); two *s* two *d* (and one *s* decd). *Educ:* St Peter's Prep. Sch.; Newark Coll. of Engrg; Fairleigh Dickinson University. *Heir: s* John Michael Waller [*b* 14 May 1962; *m* 1986, Maria Renee Gonzalez; one *d*]. *Address:* 5 Lookout Terrace, Lynnfield, Mass 01940, USA.

WALLEY, Dr Francis, CB 1978; FEng 1985; consulting engineer; Consultant to the Ove Arup Partnership; *b* 30 Dec. 1918; *s* of late Reginald M. Walley and Maria M. Walley; *m* 1946, Margaret, *yr d* of late Rev. Thomas and Margaret J. Probert; two *d. Educ:* Cheltenham Grammar Sch.; Bristol Univ. MSc, PhD; FICE (Mem. Council, 1978–81); FIStructE (Vice-Pres., 1982–83; Hon. Treasurer, 1981; Hon. Sec., 1979–81); Lewis Kent Award, IStructE, 1985. Entered Min. of Home Security as Engr, 1941: reported to CIGS on allied bombing of Pantellaria, 1943; Member: British Bombing Survey Unit, France, 1944–45; Jt UK/USA Survey Unit of Nagasaki and Hiroshima, 1945. Min. of Works, 1945; Suptg Civil Engr, 1963; Dep. Dir of Building Develt, 1965; Dir of Estate Management Overseas, 1969; Dir of Post Office Services, 1971; Under-Sec., Dir of Civil Engineering Services, DoE, 1973–78. I/c of Civil Defence Structures, British Atomic Trials, Aust., 1954; Mem., British Govt team looking at building construction in USSR, 1966. Mem., Standing Cttee on Structural Safety, 1977–88; Chairman: BSI Code Cttee for Structural Use of Concrete, 1987–; ISO Cttee of Design of Concrete Structures, 1989–. *Publications:* Prestressed Concrete Design and Construction, 1954; (with Dr S. C. C. Bate) A Guide to the Code of Practice CP 115, 1960; several papers to ICE and techn. jls. *Recreations:* gardening, furniture-making. *Address:* 13 Julien Road, Coulsdon, Surrey CR5 2DN. *T:* 081–660 3290.
See also Sir John Walley.

WALLEY, Joan Lorraine; MP (Lab) Stoke-on-Trent North, since 1987; *b* 23 Jan. 1949; *d* of late Arthur Walley and of Mary Walley; *m* 1980, Jan Ostrowski; two *s. Educ:* Biddulph Grammar School; Hull Univ. (BA); University Coll. Swansea (Dip. Community Work). Alcoholics Recovery Project, 1970–73; Swansea City Council, 1974–78; Wandsworth Borough Council, 1978–79; NACRO, 1979–82. Mem., Lambeth Borough Council, 1982–86 (Chair: Health and Consumer Services Cttee; Assoc. of London Authorities Public Protection Cttee). Opposition front-bench spokesman on envmtl protection, 1988–90, on transport, 1990–. Sponsored by COHSE. Vice-Pres., Inst. of Environmental Health Officers. *Address:* House of Commons, SW1A 0AA.

WALLEY, Sir John, KBE 1965; CB 1950; retired as Deputy Secretary, Ministry of Social Security, 1966 (Ministry of Pensions and National Insurance, 1958–66); *b* Barnstaple, Devon, 3 April 1906; *e s* of late R. M. Walley; *m* 1934, Elisabeth Mary, *e d* of late R. H. Pinhorn, OBE; two *s* two *d. Educ:* Hereford High Sch.; Hereford Cathedral Sch.; Merton Coll., Oxford; Postmaster, 1924–28; Hons Maths and Dip., Pol. and Econ. Sci. Ministry of Labour: Asst Principal, 1929; Sec., Cabinet Cttee on Unemployment, 1932; Principal, 1934; Asst Sec., Min. of National Service, 1941; promoted Under-Sec. to take charge of legislation and other preparations for Beveridge Nat. Insce Scheme, in new Min. of National Insurance, 1945; Chm., Dental Benefit Council, 1945–48. Chm., Hampstead Centre, National Trust, 1969–79, Pres., 1980–90. *Publications:* Social Security-Another British Failure?, 1972; contribs: to The Future of the Social Services, ed Robson and Crick, 1970; on Children's Allowances, in Family Poverty, ed David Bull, 1971; vol. in British Oral Archive of Political and Administrative History, 1980; articles in journals and the press on Social Security matters. *Address:* Brookland House, 24 High Street, Cottenham, Cambs CB4 4SA. *T:* Cottenham (0954) 50931.
See also F. Walley.

WALLEY, Keith Henry, FEng 1981; FIChemE; Chairman, International Military Services Ltd, since 1985 (Director, since 1984); Deputy Chairman, Johnson Matthey plc, since 1986 (Director, since 1985); *b* 26 June 1928; *s* of Eric Henry James Walley and Rose Walley; *m* 1950, Betty Warner; one *s* one *d. Educ:* Hinckley Grammar School; Loughborough College (Dip. Chem. 1949, Dip. Chem. Eng. 1952); FIChemE 1972. Commissioned RAOC 1949–51. Joined Royal Dutch/Shell Group, 1952; served in Holland, 1952–69; Works Manager, Shell Chemicals, Carrington, 1970–71; Head, Manufacturing Economic and Ops, The Hague, 1972–73; Gen. Man., Base Chemicals Shell International Chemicals, 1974–77; Jt Man. Dir, Shell UK Ltd, 1978–84; Man. Dir, Shell Chemicals UK Ltd, 1978–84. Non-executive Director: John Brown plc, 1984–86; Reckitt & Colman plc, 1986–90. Vis. Prof., UCL, 1986–. Pres., Soc. of Chemical Industry, 1984–86 (Vice-Pres., 1981–84); Member Council: Chem. Ind. Assoc., 1978–84 (Chm., Educn and Sci. Policy Cttee, 1980–84); IChemE, 1983– (Vice-Pres., 1985; Pres., 1987); Fellowship of Engineering, 1984–. CBIM 1982. Hon. DSc Loughborough, 1989. *Publications:* papers in chem. jls and planning jls. *Recreations:* the Pyrenees, opera, tennis, ski-ing. *Address:* International Military Services Ltd, 4 Abbey Orchard Street, SW1P 2JJ. *Club:* Athenæum.

WALLINGTON, Jeremy Francis; television producer; Chairman, Wallington, Irving, Jackson Ltd, since 1990; *b* 7 July 1935; *s* of Ernest Francis Wallington and Nell (*née* Howe); *m* 1955, Margaret Ivy Willment; three *s* one *d. Educ:* Royal Grammar Sch., High Wycombe, Bucks. Reporter on several Fleet Street newspapers, 1956–62; Managing Editor, Topic Magazine, 1962; Co-Founder of Insight, Sunday Times, 1963; Assistant Editor: Sunday Times, 1963–65; Daily Mail, 1965–67; Editor, Investigations Bureau, World in Action, Granada Television, 1967–68; Jt Editor, then Editor, World in Action, 1968–72; Head of Documentaries, Granada Television, 1972–77; Dir of Progs, Southern TV, 1977–81; Chief Exec., Limehouse Prodns, 1982–86. *Publication:* (jtly) Scandal '63, 1963. *Recreation:* canal barges. *Address:* 6B Newell Street, E14. *T:* 071–987 8484.

WALLIS, Edmund Arthur, CEng; Chief Executive, Powergen, since 1988; *b* 3 July 1939; *s* of Reuben Wallis and Iris Mary Cliff; *m* 1964, Gillian Joan Mitchell; two *s.* CEng 1978; MIEE 1971; MIMechE 1972. Central Electricity Generating Board: Trainee, Drakelow Power Stn, 1955–62; various appts in coal, oil and nuclear power stns, 1962–75; Dep. Stn Manager, Pembroke Power Stn, 1975–77; Stn Manager, Oldbury Power Stn, 1977–79; Industrial Safeguards Manager, SW Reg., 1979–80; various appts in system op., then Dir of System Op., 1981–86; Divl Dir of Ops, 1986–88. CBIM 1991. *Recreations:* photography, walking, theatre, boating, ski-ing. *Address:* Powergen plc, 53 New Broad Street, EC2M 1JJ. *T:* 071–826 2800.

WALLIS, Frederick Alfred John E.; *see* Emery-Wallis.

WALLIS, Jeffrey Joseph; Managing Director, Eastoken, since 1981; *b* 25 Nov. 1923; *s* of Nathaniel and Rebecca Wallis; *m* 1948, Barbara Brickman; one *s* one *d. Educ:* Owen's; Coll. Aeronautical Engrg. Man. Dir, Wallis Fashion Group, 1948–80. Mem., Monopolies and Mergers Commn, 1981–85. Formerly Member: CNAA; Clothing Export Council; NEDC (Textiles). Involved in art educn throughout career; various governorships. *Recreations:* motor racing, motor boating, industrial design. *Address:* 37 Avenue Close, NW8 6DA. *T:* 071–722 8665.

WALLIS, Peter Gordon, CMG 1990; HM Diplomatic Service; High Commissioner to Malta, since 1991; *b* 2 Aug. 1935; *s* of Arthur Gordon Wallis, DFC, BScEcon, and Winifred Florence Maud (*née* Dingle); *m* 1965, Delysia Elizabeth (*née* Leonard); three *s* one *d. Educ:* Taunton and Whitgift Schools; Pembroke Coll., Oxford (MA). Ministry of Labour and National Service, 1958; HM Customs and Excise, 1959 (Private Sec., 1961–64); HM Diplomatic Service, 1968; Tel Aviv, 1970; Nairobi, 1974; Counsellor (Econ. and Comm.), Ankara, 1977; RCDS, 1981; Cabinet Office, 1982; Hd, Perm. Under-Sec.'s Dept, FCO, 1983; Minister, Pretoria, 1987; Minister, British Liaison Office, 1989, and subseq. Acting High Comr, 1990, Windhoek, Namibia; Political Advr to Jt Comdr, British Forces in the Gulf, Jan.–April 1991, to Comdr, British Forces, SE Turkey and N Iraq, May–July 1991. *Recreations:* reading, writing, music, children. *Address:* c/o Foreign and Commonwealth Office, SW1A 2AH.

WALLIS, Peter Ralph; Deputy Controller, Aircraft Weapons and Electronics, Ministry of Defence, 1980–84; *b* 17 Aug. 1924; *s* of Leonard Francis Wallis and Molly McCulloch Wallis (*née* Jones); *m* 1949, Frances Jean Patricia Cowie; three *s* one *d. Educ:* University College Sch., Hampstead; Imperial Coll. of Science and Technology, London (BSc(Eng)). Henrici and Siemens Medals of the College, 1944. Joined Royal Naval Scientific Service 1944; work at Admty Signal and Radar Estab. till 1959, Admty Underwater Weapons Estab. till 1968; Asst Chief Scientific Advr (Research), MoD, 1968–71, Dir Gen. Research Weapons, 1971–75, Dir Gen. Guided Weapons and Electronics, 1975–78, Dir Gen. Research A (Electronics) and Dep. Chief Scientist (Navy), 1978–80. Marconi Award, IERE, 1964; FCGI, CEng, FIEE, FIMA. *Publications:* articles in Jl of IEE, IERE and Op. Res. Quarterly. *Recreations:* skiing, mountain walking, swimming, sailing, cycling, Hampstead Scientific Soc. *Address:* 22 Flask Walk, Hampstead, NW3 1HE. *Clubs:* Alpine Ski, Eagle Ski.

WALLIS, Victor Harry; Assistant Under Secretary of State, Police and Fire Department, Home Office, 1980–82; *b* 21 Dec. 1922; *s* of Harry Stewart Wallis, MBE, and Ada Elizabeth (*née* Jarratt); *m* 1948, Margaret Teresa (*née* Meadowcroft); one *s* three *d. Educ:* Wilson's Grammar School. Served Royal Scots and Indian Army (Major), 1941–47 (War, Burma and Defence medals); RARO, 1947–48; Territorial Army and TARO (Int. Corps), 1948–77. Entered Home Office, Immigration Service, 1947; Regional Officer, 1952; Policy Div., 1958; Chief Trng Officer, 1967; Establishments, 1968. Chm., various cttees, Fire Brigades Adv. Council, 1980–82. *Recreations:* philately, military history, painting. *Address:* 26 Lumley Road, Horley, Surrey RH6 7JL. *Clubs:* Civil Service, St Stephen's Constitutional, Royal British Legion.

WALLIS-JONES, His Honour Ewan Perrins; a Circuit Judge (formerly County Court Judge), 1964–84; *b* 22 June 1913; *s* of late William James Wallis-Jones, MBE, and late Ethel Perrins Wallis-Jones; *m* 1940, Veronica Mary (*née* Fowler); one *s* two *d*. *Educ:* Mill Hill Sch.; University Coll. of Wales, Aberystwyth; Balliol Coll., Oxford. LLB Hons Wales, 1934; BA Oxon 1936; MA Oxon 1941. Qualified Solicitor, 1935; called to Bar, Gray's Inn, 1938. Chm., Carmarthenshire QS, 1966–71 (Dep. Chm., 1965–66); Jt Pres., Council of Circuit Judges, 1982. ARPS. *Recreations:* music, reading and photography. *Address:* 25 Cotham Grove, Bristol BS6 6AN. *T:* Bristol (0272) 248908. *Club:* Royal Photographic Society.

WALLIS-KING, Maj.-Gen. Colin Sainthill, CBE 1975 (OBE 1971); retired; UK agent for Norsk Forsvarsteknologi A/S, since 1987; *b* 13 Sept. 1926; *s* of late Lt-Col Frank King, DSO, OBE, 4th Hussars, and Colline Ammabel, *d* of late Lt-Col C. G. H. St Hill; *m* 1962, Lisabeth, *d* of late Swan Swanstrøm, Oslo, Norway; two *d*. *Educ:* Stowe. Commissioned Coldstream Guards, 1945; Liaison Officer with Fleet Air Arm, 1954; Staff Coll., 1960; Regtl Adjutant, Coldstream Guards, 1961; seconded to Para. Regt, 1963; ACOS HQ Land Norway, 1965; Comdr 2nd Bn Coldstream Guards, 1969; Dep. Comdr 8 Inf. Brigade, 1972; Comdr 3 Inf. Brigade, 1973; BGS Intell., MoD, 1975; Dir of Service Intelligence, 1977–80. Dir, Kongsberg Ltd, 1982–87. *Recreations:* equitation, sailing, music, cross-country skiing, fishing. *Address:* c/o Royal Bank of Scotland, 19 Grosvenor Gardens, SW1. *Club:* Cavalry and Guards.

WALLOP, family name of **Earl of Portsmouth.**

WALLROCK, John; Chairman, Conocean International Consultants Group, Hong Kong, since 1984; *b* 14 Nov. 1922; *s* of Samuel and Marie Kate Wallrock; *m* 1967, Audrey Louise Ariow; one *s* two *d*. *Educ:* Bradfield Coll., Berks. Cadet, Merchant Navy, 1939; Lieut RNR, 1943; Master Mariner, 1949; J. H Minet & Co. Ltd, 1950, Dir, 1955–79, Chm., 1972–79; Chairman: Minet Holdings, 1972–82; St Katherine Insurance Co. Ltd, London, 1972–82; Dir, Tugu Insce Co. Ltd, Hong Kong, 1976–84. Underwriting Mem. of Lloyd's, 1951–86. Mem., Council of Management, White Ensign Assoc. Ltd, 1974–83. Liveryman, Master Mariners' Co., 1954–; Freeman, City of London, 1965. FCIB, MNI. *Recreations:* yachting, shooting. *Address:* 2B Belgravia Heights, 27 Tai Tam Road, Tai Tam, Hong Kong. *Clubs:* East India; Royal London Yacht, Royal Southern Yacht.

WALLS, Prof. Eldred Wright; Emeritus Professor of Anatomy in the University of London at Middlesex Hospital Medical School (Dean, Medical School, 1967–74); Hon. Consultant Anatomist, St Mark's Hospital; *b* 17 Aug. 1912; 2nd *s* of late J. T. Walls, Glasgow; *m* 1939, Jessie Vivien Mary Robb, MB, ChB, DPH, *o d* of late R. F. Robb and late M. T. Robb; one *s* one *d*. *Educ:* Hillhead High Sch.; Glasgow Univ. BSc, 1931; MB, ChB (Hons), 1934; MD (Hons), 1947, FRSE, FRCS, FRCSE; Struthers Medal and Prize, 1942. Demonstrator and Lectr in Anatomy, Glasgow Univ., 1935–41; Senior Lectr in Anatomy, University Coll. of S Wales and Monmouthshire, 1941–47; Reader in Anatomy, Middlesex Hospital Medical Sch. 1947–49, S. A. Courtauld Prof. of Anatomy, 1949–74; Lectr in Anatomy, Edinburgh Univ., 1975–82. Past President: Anatomical Soc. of GB and Ireland; Chartered Soc. of Physiotherapy. Lectures: West., UC Cardiff, 1965; Osler, Soc. of Apothecaries, 1967; Astor, Mddx Hosp., 1975; Gordon Taylor, RCS, 1976; Struthers, RCSE, 1983. Farquharson Award, RCSE, 1988. *Publications:* (co-editor) Rest and Pain (by John Hilton) (6th edn), 1950; (co-author) Sir Charles Bell, His Life and Times, 1958; contrib. Blood-vascular and Lymphatic Systems, to Cunningham's Textbook Anat., 1981; contrib. to Journal of Anatomy, Lancet, etc. *Recreation:* annual visit to Lord's. *Address:* 19 Dean Park Crescent, Edinburgh EH4 1PH. *T:* 031–332 7164. *Clubs:* MCC; New (Edinburgh); Royal Scottish Automobile (Glasgow).

WALLS, Geoffrey Nowell; Agent General for South Australia, since 1986; *b* 17 Feb. 1945; *s* of late Andrew Nowell Walls and Hilda Margaret Thompson; *m* 1975, Vanessa Bodger; one *s* three *d*. *Educ:* Trinity Grammar Sch., Melbourne; Univ. of Melbourne (BComm 1965). Australian Regular Army, 2nd Lieut RAAOC, 1966–69; Australian Trade Comr Service, 1970–79; served Jakarta, Singapore, Cairo, Beirut, Bahrain, Manila, Baghdad; Regional Dir, Adelaide, Commonwealth Dept of Trade, 1980–83; Gen. Manager, ATCO Industries (Aust) Pty Ltd, 1983–86. *Recreations:* golf, tennis, gardening. *Address:* 53 Chiddingstone Street, Fulham, SW6 3TQ. *T:* 071–371 5988. *Clubs:* Royal Automobile, East India.

WALLS, Rev. Brother Roland Charles; Member, Community of the Transfiguration, since 1965; *b* 7 June 1917; *s* of late Roland William Walls and late Tina Josephine Hayward. *Educ:* Sandown Grammar Sch.; Corpus Christi Coll., Cambridge; Kelham Theological Coll. Curate of St James', Crossgates, Leeds, 1940–42; Curate of St Cecilia's, Parson Cross, Sheffield, 1942–45; Licensed preacher, Diocese of Ely, 1945–48; Fellow of Corpus Christi Coll., Cambridge, 1948–62; Lecturer in Theology, Kelham Theological Coll., 1948–51; Chaplain and Dean of Chapel, Corpus Christi Coll., Cambridge, 1952–58; Canon Residentiary, Sheffield Cathedral, 1958–62; Chaplain of Rosslyn Chapel, Midlothian, 1962–68. Examining Chaplain to Bishop of Edinburgh. Lecturer at Coates Hall Theological Coll.; Lecturer in Dogmatics Dept, New Coll., Edinburgh, 1963–74. Received into RC Church, ordained priest, 1983. *Publications:* (contrib.) Theological Word Book (ed A. Richardson), 1950; Law and Gospel, 1980; (contrib.) Dictionary of Christian Spirituality, 1983; (contrib.) Dictionary of Pastoral Counsel, 1984; The Royal Mysteries, 1990. *Recreations:* botany, music, etc. *Address:* Community House, 23 Manse Road, Roslin, Midlothian.

WALLS, Stephen Roderick; Chief Executive, Arjo Wiggins Appleton (formerly Wiggins Teape Appleton) plc, since 1990 (Chairman, 1990–91); *b* 8 Aug. 1947; *s* of late R. W. Walls and of D. M. Walls; *m*; one *s*. Chartered Accountant. Senior Auditor, Deloitte & Co., 1969; Group Chief Accountant, Lindustries, 1971; Financial Planning Exec., Vernons, 1974; Chesebrough Ponds: Finance Dir, UK and Geneva, 1975; Internat. Finance Dir, Geneva, 1981; Vice-Pres., Finance, 1981–87; Dir of Finance, 1987, Man. Dir, 1988–89, Plessey Co. Non-Exec. Chm., Aviation Hldgs, 1991–. Mem., Financial Reporting Council. *Recreations:* running, tennis, music, theatre. *Address:* Arjo Wiggins Appleton, 25 St James's Street, SW1A 1HA. *T:* 071–839 7505. *Club:* Royal Automobile.

WALLWORK, John, FRCSE; Consultant Cardiothoracic Surgeon, Papworth Hospital, since 1981; *b* 8 July 1946; *s* of Thomas and Vera Wallwork; *m* 1973, Elizabeth Ann Medley; one *s* two *d*. *Educ:* Accrington Grammar Sch.; Edinburgh Univ. (BSc Hons Pharm. 1966; MB ChB 1970). MA Cantab 1986. FRCSE 1974. Surgical Registrar, Royal Infirmary, Edinburgh, 1975–76; Senior Registrar, Adelaide Hosp., SA, 1977–78; Royal Infirmary, Glasgow, 1978–79; St Bartholomew's Hosp., 1979–81; Chief Resident in Cardiovascular and Cardiac Transplant Surgery, Stanford Univ. Med. Sch., 1980–81. Lister Prof., RCSE, 1985–86. *Publications:* (with R. Stepney) Heart Disease: what it is and how it is treated, 1987; (ed) Heart and Heart-Lung Transplantation, 1989; numerous papers on cardiothoracic and cardiopulmonary topics. *Recreations:* tennis, conversation, making phone calls from the bath. *Address:* 3 Latham Road, Cambridge CB2 2EG. *T:* Cambridge (0223) 352827. *Club:* Caledonian.

WALLWORK, John Sackfield, CBE 1982; Director, Daily Mail and General Trust PLC, 1982–91; Managing Director, Northcliffe Newspapers Group Ltd, 1972–82 (General Manager, 1967–71); *b* 2 Nov. 1918; *s* of Peter Wallwork and Clara Cawthorne Wallwork; *m* 1945, Bessie Bray; one *s* one *d*. *Educ:* Leigh Grammar Sch., Leigh, Lancs. FCIS. General Manager, Scottish Daily Mail, Edinburgh, 1959–62; Asst Gen. Man., Associated Newspapers Gp Ltd, London, 1962–66, Dir, 1973–82. Chm., Press Association Ltd, 1973–74 (Dir, 1969–76); Director: Reuters Ltd, 1973–76; Reuters Founders Share Co. Ltd, 1984–87; Reuters Trustee, 1978–84; Member Press Council, 1974–75; Newspaper Society: Mem. Council, 1967–85; Jun. Vice-Pres. 1975; Sen. Vice-Pres., 1976, Pres., 1977–78. Commander, Order of Merit, Republic of Italy, 1973. *Recreations:* golf, motoring. *Address:* Greenfield, Manor Road, Sidmouth, Devon EX10 8RR. *T:* Sidmouth (0395) 513489.

WALLWORTH, Cyril; Assistant Under-Secretary of State, Ministry of Defence, 1964–76; Gwilym Gibbon Fellow, Nuffield College, Oxford, 1975–76; *b* 6 June 1916; *s* of Albert A. Wallworth and Eva (*née* Taylor); unmarried. *Educ:* Oldham High Sch.; Manchester Univ. BA (Hons) History, 1937. Asst Principal, Admiralty, 1939; Asst Private Secretary to First Lord, 1941–45, Principal, 1943; Asst Secretary, 1951; Under-Secretary, 1964. Liveryman: Basketmakers' Co., 1990; Upholders' Co., 1991. *Recreations:* music, wine, cooking, photography. *Address:* 5 Leinster Mews, W2 3EY. *Clubs:* Hurlingham, Lansdowne, United Wards, City Livery.

WALMSLEY, Arnold Robert, CMG 1963; MBE 1946; HM Diplomatic Service, retired; *b* 29 Aug. 1912; *s* of late Rev. Canon A. M. Walmsley; *m* 1944, Frances Councell de Mouilpied. *Educ:* Rossall Sch.; Hertford Coll., Oxford. 1st Class Maths Mods, 1st Class Modern Greats. Private Sec. to Julius Meinl, Vienna, 1935–38; Foreign Office, 1939–45; established in Foreign Service, 1946; Foreign Office, 1946–50; British Consul in Jerusalem, 1950–54; Foreign Office, 1954–63; Head of Arabian Dept, 1961; Counsellor, Khartoum, 1963–65; Dir, Middle East Centre of Arab Studies, Lebanon, 1965–69. Order of the Two Niles (Sudan), 1965. *Publications:* (as Nicholas Roland) The Great One, 1967; Natural Causes, 1969; Who Came by Night, 1971. *Address:* 10 Park Lane, Saffron Walden, Essex CB10 1DA. *Club:* Travellers'.

WALMSLEY, Brian; Under Secretary, Department of Social Security, since 1985; *b* 22 April 1936; *s* of late Albert Edward Walmsley and Ivy Doreen Walmsley (*née* Black); *m* 1956, Sheila Maybury; two *d*. *Educ:* Lily Lane School, Moston, Manchester; Page Moss Primary School, Huyton; Prescot Grammar School. National Service, RAF, 1955–57. Joined Min. of Pensions and Nat. Insurance, 1957, later Min. of Social Security and DHSS; served in local offices to 1970; North West (Merseyside) Regional Office, DHSS, Bootle, 1970–72; DHSS HQ, London, 1973–88; Sec. to Industrial Injuries Adv. Council, 1978–79; Asst Sec., 1979; Under Sec., 1985; Under Sec., Cabinet Office, and Civil Service Comr, 1988–90. *Recreations:* following cricket, playing golf, reading, gardening. *Address:* Department of Social Security, Richmond House, 79 Whitehall, SW1A 2NS. *Club:* MCC.

WALMSLEY, Rt. Rev. Francis Joseph, CBE 1979; Roman Catholic Bishop of the Forces, since 1979; Titular Bishop of Tamalluma; *b* 9 Nov. 1926; *s* of Edwin Walmsley and Mary Walmsley (*née* Hall). *Educ:* St Joseph's Coll., Mark Cross, Tunbridge Wells; St John's Seminary, Wonersh, Guildford. Ordained, 1953; Asst Priest, Woolwich, 1953; Shoreham-by-Sea, Sussex, 1958; Chaplain, Royal Navy, 1960; Principal RC Chaplain, RN, 1975; retired from RN, 1979. Prelate of Honour to HH Pope Paul VI, 1975; ordained Bishop, 1979. *Recreations:* photography, gardening.

WALMSLEY, Nigel Norman; Chief Executive, Carlton Television, since 1991; Board Member, South Bank Centre, since 1985; Director, The Builder Group, since 1986; *b* 26 Jan. 1942; *s* of Norman and Ida Walmsley; *m* 1969, Jane Walmsley, broadcaster and author; one *d*. *Educ:* William Hulme's Sch.; Brasenose Coll., Oxford (BA English). Joined the Post Office, 1964; Asst Private Secretary to Postmaster General, 1967; Asst Director of Marketing, Post Office, 1973–75; Asst Sec., Industrial Planning Division of Dept of Industry, 1975–76; Director of Marketing, Post Office, 1977–81, Board Mem. for Marketing 1981–82; Man. Dir, Capital Radio, 1982–91. Bd Mem., Ind. Radio News, 1983–91. Chm., GLAA, 1985–86. *Recreation:* intensive inactivity. *Address:* 26 Belsize Road, NW6 4RD. *T:* 071–586 1950.

WALMSLEY, Peter James, MBE 1975; Director-General (formerly Director) of Petroleum Engineering Division, Department of Energy, 1981–89; *b* 29 April 1929; *s* of George Stanley and Elizabeth Martin Walmsley; *m* 1970, Edna Fisher; three *s* one *d*. *Educ:* Caterham Sch., Surrey; Imperial Coll., London (BSc; ARSM). Geologist: Iraq Petroleum Co., 1951–59; BP Trinidad, 1959–65; BP London, 1965–72; Exploration Manager, BP Aberdeen, 1972–78; Dep. Chief Geologist, BP London, 1978–79; Regional Exploration Manager, BP London, 1979–81. Chairman, Petroleum Exploration Soc. of Gt Britain, 1971–72. *Publications:* contribs to various learned jls on North Sea geology. *Recreations:* home and garden. *Address:* Elm Tree Cottage, 10 Great Austins, Farnham, Surrey GU9 8JG.

WALMSLEY, Prof. Robert, TD 1984; MD; DSc; FRCPE, FRCSE, FRSE; formerly Bute Professor of Anatomy, University of St Andrews, 1946–73; *b* 24 Aug. 1906; *s* of late Thomas Walmsley, Supt Marine Engr; *m* 1939, Isabel Mary, *e d* of James Mathieson, Aberdeen; two *s*. *Educ:* Greenock Acad.; Univ. of Edinburgh; Carnegie Inst. of Embryology, Baltimore, USA. MB, ChB (Edinburgh); MD (Edinburgh) with Gold Medal, 1937. Demonstrator, Lectr and Senior Lectr on Anatomy, Univ. of Edinburgh, 1931–46; Goodsir Fellowship in Anatomy, 1933; Rockefeller Fellowship, 1935–36; served as Pathologist in RAMC in UK and MEF, 1939–44. Struthers Lectr, Royal Coll. of Surgeons, Edinburgh, 1952; Fulbright Advanced Scholarship, 1960; Pres., Edinburgh Harveian Soc., 1963–64. Vis. Prof. of Anatomy: George Washington Univ., USA, 1960; Auckland, NZ, 1967. Formerly: Master, St Salvator's Coll.; Chm., Council St Leonards and St Katherines Schs; Hon. Pres., British Medical Students Assoc.; External Examiner in Anatomy, Cambridge, Edinburgh, Durham, Glasgow, Aberdeen, Liverpool, Singapore, Kingston (WI), Accra, etc. Life Mem. Anatomical Soc. Hon. Fellow, British Assoc. of Clinical Anatomists, 1980. Hon. DSc St Andrews, 1972. First Farquharson Award, RCSEd, 1974. *Publications:* Co-author Manual of Surgical Anatomy, 1964; (jtly) Clinical Anatomy of the Heart, 1978; co-reviser, Jamieson's Illustrations Regional Anatomy, 1981; contribs to various jls, on Heart, Bone and Joints, and on Whales. *Recreation:* gardening. *Address:* 45 Kilrymont Road, St Andrews, Fife KY16 8DE. *T:* St Andrews (0334) 72879.

See also Rear-Adm. R. Walmsley.

WALMSLEY, Rear-Adm. Robert; Assistant Chief of Defence Staff (Communications, Command, Control and Information Systems), since 1990; *b* Aberdeen, 1 Feb. 1941; *s* of Robert Walmsley, *qv*; *m* 1967, Christina Veronica Melvill; one *s* two *d*. *Educ:* Fettes Coll.; RN Coll., Dartmouth; Queens' Coll., Cambridge (MA MechScis); RN Coll., Greenwich (MSc Nuclear Sci.). HMS Ark Royal, 1962–63; HMS Otus, 1964–66; HMS Churchill, 1968–72; Ship Dept, MoD, 1973–74; HM Dockyard, Chatham, 1975–78; MoD, PE, 1979–80; Chm., Naval Nuclear Technical Safety Panel, 1981–83; Naval Staff, 1984; MoD, PE, 1985–86; Dir Operational Requirements (Sea), 1987–89. *Recreations:* fly fishing, West Ham United FC, Scotland. *Address:* c/o Ministry of Defence, Main Building, Whitehall, SW1.

WALPOLE, family name of **Baron Walpole.**

WALPOLE, 10th Baron *cr* 1723, of Walpole; **Robert Horatio Walpole;** Baron Walpole of Wolterton, 1756; *b* 8 Dec. 1938; *s* of 9th Baron Walpole, TD and of Nancy Louisa, OBE, *y d* of late Frank Harding Jones; *S* father, 1989; *m* 1st, 1962, S. Judith Schofield (*see* S. J. Chaplin) (marr. diss. 1979); two *s* two *d*; 2nd, 1980, Laurel Celia, *o d* of S. T. Ball; two *s* one *d*. *Educ:* Eton; King's College, Cambridge (MA, Dip Agric). Member, Norfolk CC, 1970–81 (Chm. of various cttees). Chairman: Area Museums Service for South East England, 1976–79; Norwich School of Art, 1977–87; Textile Conservation Centre, 1981–88 (Pres. 1988); East Anglian Tourist Board, 1982–88. JP Norfolk, 1972. *Heir: s* Hon. Jonathan Robert Hugh Walpole, *b* 16 Nov. 1967. *Address:* Mannington Hall, Norwich NR11 7BB. *T:* Saxthorpe (026387) 763. *Clubs:* none on principle.

WALSER, Ven. David; Archdeacon of Ely, and Hon. Canon, since 1981; *b* 12 March 1923; *s* of William and Nora Walser; *m* 1975, Dr Elizabeth Enid Shillito. *Educ:* Clayesmore School; St Edmund Hall, Oxford (MA, DipTh); St Stephen's House, Oxford. Served RA and Royal Indian Mountain Artillery, 1942–46. Deacon 1950, priest 1951; Asst Curate, St Gregory the Great, Horfield, 1950–54; Vice-Principal, St Stephen's House, 1954–60; Asst Chaplain, Exeter Coll., Oxford, 1956–57; Junior Chaplain, Merton Coll., Oxford, 1957–60; Minor Canon, Ely Cathedral and Chaplain of King's School, 1961–71; Vicar of Linton, dio. Ely, 1971–81; Rector of Bartlow, 1973–81; RD of Linton, 1976–81; Rector of St Botolph's, Cambridge, 1981–89; Priest-in-Charge, St Clement's, Cambridge, 1985–89. *Recreations:* hill walking, music, reading, caravanning, crosswords, hymn writing for local use. *Address:* St Botolph's Rectory, Summerfield, Cambridge CB3 9HE. *T:* Cambridge (0223) 350684.

WALSH, Sir Alan, Kt 1977; DSc; FRS 1969; Consultant Spectroscopist; *b* 19 Dec. 1916; *s* of late Thomas Haworth and Betsy Alice Walsh, Hoddlesden, Lancs; *m* 1949, Audrey Dale Hutchinson; two *s*. *Educ:* Darwen Grammar Sch.; Manchester Univ. BSc 1938; MSc (Tech.) 1946; DSc 1960. FAA 1958. British Non-Ferrous Metals Research Assoc., 1939–42 and 1944–46; Min. of Aircraft Production, 1943; Div. of Chemical Physics, CSIRO, Melbourne, 1946–77 (Asst Chief of Div., 1961–77). Einstein Memorial Lectr, Australian Inst. of Physics, 1967; Pres., Australian Inst. of Physics, 1967–69. Hon. Member: Soc. of Analytical Chemistry, 1969; Royal Soc. NZ, 1975. Foreign Mem., Royal Acad. of Sciences, Stockholm, 1969. FTS 1982. Hon. FCS, 1973; Hon. FAIP, 1981; Hon. Mem., Japan Soc. of Analytical Chemistry, 1981. Hon. DSc: Monash, 1970; Manchester, 1984, Britannica Australia Science Award, 1966; Research Medal, Royal Soc. of Victoria, 1968; Talanta Gold Medal, 1969; Maurice Hasler Award, Soc. of Applied Spectroscopy, USA, 1972; James Cook Medal, Royal Soc. of NSW, 1975; Torbern Bergman Medal, Swedish Chem. Soc., 1976; Royal Medal, Royal Soc., 1976; John Scott Award, City of Philadelphia, 1977; Matthew Flinders Medal, Aust. Acad. of Science, 1980; Robert Boyle Medal, RSC, 1982; K. L. Sutherland Medal, Aust. Acad. of Technol Sciences, 1982. *Publications:* papers in learned jls. *Address:* 11 Norwood Avenue, Brighton, Victoria 3186, Australia. *T:* 03–592 4897. *Club:* Metropolitan Golf (Melbourne).

WALSH, Arthur Stephen, CBE 1979; FEng 1980; FIEE; Chairman, Northern Telecom Europe, since 1991 (Chief Executive, 1985–91, Chairman, 1989–91, STC); *b* 16 Aug. 1926; *s* of Wilfred and Doris Walsh; *m* 2nd, 1985, Judith Martha Westenborg. *Educ:* Selwyn Coll., Cambridge (MA). FIEE 1974. GEC Group, 1952–79: various sen. appts within the Group; Managing Director: Marconi Space and Defence Systems, 1969–86; Marconi Co., 1982–85; Dir, GEC, 1983. Dir, FKI plc. Hon. DSc Ulster, 1988. *Recreations:* sailing, ski-ing. *Address:* Aiglemont, Trout Rise, Loudwater, Rickmansworth, Herts WD3 4JS. *T:* Rickmansworth (0923) 770883. *Clubs:* Little Ship; Royal Southern Yacht.

WALSH, Brian, QC 1977; a Recorder of the Crown Court, since 1972; *b* 17 June 1935; *er s* of late Percy Walsh and Sheila (*née* Frais), Leeds; *m* 1964, Susan Margaret, *d* of late Eli (Kay) Frieze and of Doris Frieze; two *d*. *Educ:* Sheikh Bagh Sch., Srinagar, Kashmir; Leeds Grammar Sch. (Head Boy, 1954); Gonville and Caius Coll., Cambridge (BA, LLB). Pres., Cambridge Union Soc., 1959. Served RAF (Pilot Officer), 1954–56. Called to the Bar, Middle Temple, 1961 (Blackstone Scholar, Harmsworth Scholar); Bencher, 1986. Joined North Eastern Circuit, 1961; Leader, 1989–. Member: Circuit Exec. Cttee, 1980–; Gen. Council of the Bar, 1982–84; Mental Health Review Tribunal, 1986–. Member: Court, Leeds Univ., 1988–; Cttee, Yorks CCC, 1984– (Chm., 1986–91); Governor: Leeds Grammar Sch., 1977–; Leeds Girls' High Sch., 1978–; Pres., Old Leodiensian Assoc., 1983–85. *Recreations:* golf, cricket, eating. *Address:* Park Court Chambers, 40 Park Cross Street, Leeds LS1 2QH. *T:* Leeds (0532) 433277.

WALSH, Colin Stephen, FRCO; Organist and Master of the Choristers, Lincoln Cathedral, since 1988; *b* 26 Jan. 1955. *Educ:* Portsmouth Grammar Sch.; St George's Chapel, Windsor Castle (Organ Scholar); Christ Church, Oxford (Organ Scholar; MA 1980). DipEd 1978. ARCM 1973; FRCO 1976. Asst Organist, Salisbury Cathedral, 1978–85; Master of the Music, St Alban's Cathedral, 1985–88. Recitals in UK (incl. Royal Festival Hall), France, Scandinavia, Czechoslovakia and USA. Recordings incl. French organ music, esp. by Vierne. *Recreations:* walking, dining out. *Address:* 12 Minster Yard, Lincoln LN2 1PJ. *T:* Lincoln 532877.

WALSH, Surgeon Rear-Adm. (retired) Dermot Francis, CB 1960; OBE 1952; FRCSE; *b* 21 Jan. 1901; *s* of Dr J. A. Walsh. *Educ:* Belvedere Coll., Dublin; Trinity Coll., Dublin. BA 1927; MB, BCh, BAO, 1928; FRCSE 1943, QHS 1958. CStJ 1958. *Recreations:* golf, gardening, music. *Address:* 20 Hazelwood, Shankill, Co. Dublin, Eire. *T:* Dublin 2823653.

WALSH, Lt-Gen. Geoffrey, CBE 1944; DSO 1943; CD; *b* 1909; *s* of late H. L. Walsh; *m* 1935, Gwynn Abigail Currie; one *s*. *Educ:* Royal Military Coll., Kingston; McGill Univ. (BEngEE). DSc(Mil) RMC, Kingston, 1971. Chief Engineer, 1st Canadian Army, 1944–45 (mentioned in despatches (twice) 1945); DQMG, 1945–46; Comdr Northwest Highway System, 1946–48; Comdr Eastern Ontario Area, 1948–51; Comdr 27 Bde (Europe), 1951–52; DGMT 1953–55; QMG 1955–58; GOC, Western Command, 1958–61; Chief of the General Staff, Canada, 1961–64; Vice Chief of the Defence Staff, Canada, 1964–65. Col Comdt, Royal Canadian Army Cadets and Cadet Services of Canada, 1970–73. Legion of Merit (US); Comdr of Orange Order of Nassau (Netherlands). *Recreations:* golf, fishing, philately. *Address:* 201 Northcote Place, Rockcliffe Park, Ottawa, Ont K1M 0Y7, Canada. *Clubs:* RMC, Royal Ottawa Golf (Ottawa); USI (Ottawa and Edmonton).

WALSH, Rt. Rev. Geoffrey David Jeremy; *see* Tewkesbury, Bishop Suffragan of.

WALSH, Graham Robert, FCA; Managing Director, Bankers Trust Co., since 1988; *b* 30 July 1939; *s* of Robert Arthur Walsh and Ella Marian (*née* Jacks); *m* 1967, Margaret Ann Alexander; one *s* one *d*. *Educ:* Hurstpierpoint Coll., Sussex. Qualified as chartered accountant, 1962; joined Philip Hill Higginson Erlangers (now Hill Samuel & Co. Ltd), 1964; Director, Hill Samuel, 1970, resigned 1973; Dir, 1973–87, Head of Corporate Finance Div., and Mem. Management Cttee, 1981–87, Morgan Grenfell & Co. Ltd; Director: Morgan Grenfell Group plc (formerly Morgan Grenfell Holdings), 1985–87; Armitage Shanks Group Ltd, 1973–80; Phoenix Opera Ltd, 1970–87; Ward White Group plc, 1981–89; Moss Bros Gp plc, 1988–; Rush & Tompkins Gp plc, 1988–90; Haslemere Estates, 1989–. Dir Gen., Panel on Takeovers and Mergers, 1979–81; Chm., Issuing Houses Assoc., 1985–87 (Dep. Chm., 1979 and 1983–85). *Recreations:* opera, theatre, music, gardening, tennis. *Address:* 19 Alleyn Park, Dulwich, SE21 8AU. *T:* 081–670 0676.

WALSH, Henry George; Deputy Chairman, Building Societies Commission, since 1991; *b* 28 Sept. 1939; *s* of James Isidore Walsh and Sybil Bertha Bazeley; *m* 1968, Janet Ann Grainger; two *d*. *Educ:* West Hill High Sch., Montreal; McGill Univ.; Churchill Coll., Cambridge. HM Treasury, 1966–74; Private Secretary to Chancellor of the Duchy of Lancaster, 1974–76; HM Treasury, 1976–78; Cabinet Office Secretariat, 1978–80; Counsellor (Economic), Washington, 1980–85; HM Treasury: Hd of Monetary Policy Div., 1985–86; Hd of IMF and Debt Div., 1986–89; Hd of Financial Instns and Markets Gp, 1989–91. *Recreations:* golf, reading philosophical works, being taken for walks by Labrador retrievers. *Address:* 54 Burbage Road, SE24 9HE. *Club:* Dulwich and Sydenham Hill Golf.

WALSH, James Mark, CMG 1956; OBE 1948; HM Diplomatic Service; Consul-General, Zürich, 1962–68; *b* 18 Aug. 1909; *s* of Mark Walsh and Emily (*née* Porter); *m* 1st, 1937, Mireille Loir (*d* 1966); one *s*; 2nd, 1967, Bertha Hoch. *Educ:* Mayfield Coll., Sussex; King's Coll., London; Lincoln's Inn, London. BA (Hons), 1929; LLB, 1932; Barrister, 1932; passed an examination and appointed to Foreign Service, 1932; Vice-Consul: Paris, 1932–33, Rotterdam, 1933–34; Judge of HBM Provincial Court, Alexandria, Egypt, 1934–38; Acting Consul-General, Barcelona, 1939; Vice-Consul, Philadelphia, 1939–44; Consul, Antwerp, 1944–45. First Secretary, British Legation: Helsinki, 1945–46, Budapest, 1946–48; Dep. Consul-General, New York, 1948–50; Counsellor (Commercial), Ankara, 1950–54, and Berne, 1954–59; Consul-General, Jerusalem, 1959–62. *Recreations:* painting, golf. *Address:* Fairfield, The Paddock, Haslemere, Surrey GU27 1HB. *T:* Haslemere (0428) 652089.

WALSH, Jill P.; *see* Paton Walsh.

WALSH, John; Director, J. Paul Getty Museum, since 1983; *b* 9 Dec. 1937; *s* of John J. Walsh and Eleanor Walsh (*née* Wilson); *m* 1961, Virginia Alys Galston; two *s* one *d*. *Educ:* Yale Univ. (BA 1961); Univ. of Leyden, Netherlands; Columbia Univ. (MA 1965; PhD 1971). Lectr, Research Asst, Frick Collection, NY, 1966–68; Metropolitan Museum of Art, NY: Associate for Higher Educn, 1968–71; Associate Curator and Curator, 1970–75, Vice-Chm., 1974–75, Dept of European Paintings; Columbia University: Adjunct Associate Prof., 1972–75; Prof. of Art History, Barnard Coll., 1975–77; Mrs Russell W. Baker Curator of Paintings, Museum of Fine Arts, Boston, 1977–83. Vis Prof. of Fine Arts, Harvard, 1979. Member: Governing Bd, Yale Univ. Art Gallery, 1975–; Bd of Fellows, Claremont Grad. Sch. and Univ. Center, 1988–; Assoc. of Art Museum Dirs, 1983– (Trustee, 1986–; Pres., 1989); Amer. Antiquarian Soc., 1984–. *Publications:* exhibition catalogues, art bulletins, guides; numerous contribs to learned jls. *Address:* J. Paul Getty Museum, PO Box 2112, Santa Monica, Calif 90406, USA. *T:* (213) 459–7611. *Club:* Century Association (NY).

WALSH, Dr John James; Consultant to Paddocks Private Clinic, Aylesbury Road, Princes Risborough; *b* 4 July 1917; *s* of Dr Thomas Walsh and Margaret (*née* O'Sullivan); *m* 1946, Joan Mary, *d* of Henry Teasdale and Nita Birks; three *s* one *d*. *Educ:* Mungret Coll.; University Coll., Cork. MB, BCh 1940; MD 1963; MRCP 1968, FRCP 1975; FRCS 1969. Various hospital appointments, including Medical Officer, Spinal Injuries Centre, Stoke Mandeville Hospital, Aylesbury, 1947; Deputy Director, National Spinal Injuries Centre, Stoke Mandeville Hospital, 1957–66, Dir, 1966–77. *Publications:* Understanding Paraplegia, 1964; a number of publications on subjects pertaining to paraplegia in medical journals. *Recreation:* shooting. *Address:* Alena, Bridge Street, Great Kimble, Aylesbury, Bucks HP17 9TN. *T:* Princes Risborough (08444) 3347.

WALSH, John P.; *see* Pakenham-Walsh.

WALSH, Sir John (Patrick), KBE 1960; Professor of Dentistry and Dean and Director, University of Otago Dental School, 1946–72; *b* 5 July 1911; *s* of John Patrick Walsh and Lillian Jane (*née* Burbidge), Vic, Australia; *m* 1934, Enid Morris; one *s* three *d*. *Educ:* Ormond Coll.; Melbourne Univ. BDSc 1st Cl. Hons Melbourne; LDS Victoria, 1936; MB, BS Melbourne, 1943; DDSc Melbourne, 1950; FDSRCS 1950; FDSRCS Edinburgh, 1951; MDS NUI, 1952; FRSNZ 1961; FACD 1962; Hon. FACDS, 1967; Hon. DSc Otago, 1975. Hosp. and teaching appointments in Melbourne till 1946. MO, RAAF, 1945–46. Consultant, WHO Dental Health Seminars: Wellington, 1954; Adelaide, 1959. Speaker: 11th and 12th Internat. Dental Congresses, London and Rome; Centennial Congress of Amer. Dental Assoc., New York, 1959; 12th, 14th and 15th Australian Dental Congresses. Chairman: Dental Council of NZ, 1956–72; Mental Health Assoc. of Otago, 1960. Dominion Pres., UNA, 1960–64. Member: MRC of NZ, 1950–72 (Chm. Dental Cttee, 1947–60); Scientific Commn; Fedn Dentaire Internat., 1954–61; Council, Univ. of Otago, 1958–63; Nat. Commn for UNESCO, 1961–69; Educn Commn, 1961–; Expert Panel on Dental Health, WHO, 1962; Nat. Council, Duke of Edinburgh's Award, 1963–68. CC, Dunedin, 1968–73. Pres., Dunedin Rotary Club, 1960, Governor Dist 298, 1966–67. Paul Harris Fellow, 1981. Hon. Mem., American Dental Assoc., 1969–; List of Honour, FDI, 1969–. Holds hon. degrees. *Publications:* A Manual of Stomatology, 1957; Living with Uncertainty, 1968; Psychiatry and Dentistry, 1976; numerous articles in scientific literature. *Recreation:* retirement. *Address:* Unit 29, Hillsborough Heights Village, Dominion Road, Auckland 4, New Zealand. *T:* Auckland 676583.

WALSH, (Mary) Noëlle; Editor, Good Housekeeping, 1987–91 (Deputy Editor, 1986–87); *b* 26 Dec. 1954; *d* of Thomas Walsh and Mary Kate Ferguson; *m* 1988, David Heslam; one *s* one *d*. *Educ:* Univ. of East Anglia (BA Hons European Studies (History and German)). Editorial Asst, PR Dept, St Dunstan's Orgn for the War-Blinded, 1977–79; News Editor, Cosmopolitan, 1979–85; Editor, London Week newspaper, 1985–86; freelance writer, 1986. Member: Network; 300 Group; Forum UK. *Publications:* Hot Lips, the Ultimate Kiss and Tell Guide, 1985; (co-ed) Ragtime to Wartime: the best of Good Housekeeping 1922–39, 1986; (co-ed) The Home Front: the best of Good Housekeeping 1939–1945, 1987; (co-ed) The Christmas Book: the best of Good Housekeeping at Christmas 1922–1962, 1988; (ed jtly) Food Glorious Food: eating and drinking with Good Housekeeping 1922–1942, 1990; Things my Mother Should Have Told Me, 1991; Childhood Memories, 1991. *Recreations:* unofficial agony aunt, medieval Irish history. *Address:* 17 Mortimer Crescent, NW6 5NP. *Club:* Groucho.

WALSH, Maj.-Gen. Michael John Hatley, CB 1980; DSO 1968; DL; Director of Overseas Relations, St John's Ambulance, since 1989; *b* 10 June 1927; *s* of Captain Victor Michael Walsh, late Royal Sussex, and Audrey Walsh; *m* 1952, Angela, *d* of Col Leonard Beswick; two *d*. *Educ:* Sedbergh Sch. Commnd, KRRC, 1946; served in Malaya, Germany, Cyprus, Suez, Aden, Australia and Singapore; Bde Maj. 44 Parachute Bde, 1960–61; GSO1 Defence Planning Staff, 1966; CO 1 Para Bn, 1967–69; Col AQ 1 Div., 1969–71;

Comdr, 28 Commonwealth Bde, 1971–73; BGS HQ BAOR, 1973–76; GOC 3rd Armoured Div., 1976–79; Dir of Army Training, MoD, 1979–81. Hon. Col, 1st Bn Wessex Regt, TA, 1981–89. Chief Scout of the UK and Dependent Territories, 1982–88. Council Mem., Operation Raleigh, 1984; Royal National Life-boat Institution: Member: Cttee of Management, 1988–; Search and Rescue Sub-cttee, 1989–; Fund Raising Sub-cttee, 1991–. Kt Pres., Hon. Soc. of Knights of the Round Table, 1988– (Kt 1986–); Mem., St John Council, Wilts, 1989–. DL Greater London, 1986. Freeman, City of London, 1987. CStJ 1990. *Recreations:* athletics, boxing (Life Pres., Army Boxing Assoc., 1986), parachuting (Pres., Army Parachute Assoc., 1979–81), sailing, Australian Rules football. *Address:* c/o Barclays Bank, James Street, Harrogate. *Club:* Royal Yacht Squadron (Cowes).

WALSH, Michael Thomas; Secretary, International Department, Trades Union Congress, since 1980; *b* 22 Oct. 1943; *s* of Michael Walsh and Bridget (*née* O'Sullivan); *m* 1972, Margaret Patricia Blaxhall; two *s* two *d. Educ:* Gunnersbury Grammar Sch.; Exeter Coll., Oxford (Hons degree PPE). International Dept. TUC, 1966; Deputy Overseas Labour Adviser, FCO, 1977–79. Member, Economic and Social Committee of the European Community, 1976–77 and 1979–80. *Recreations:* cricket, Tudor history. *Address:* 77 Uvedale Road, Enfield EN2 6HD.

WALSH, Lt-Col Noel Perrings; Under Secretary, and Director of Home Regional Services, Department of the Environment, 1976–79; *b* 25 Dec. 1919; *s* of late John and Nancy Walsh; *m* 1st, 1945, Olive Mary (*d* 1987), *y d* of late Thomas Walsh, Waterford; three *s* one *d*; 2nd, 1988, Mary Ruth, *d* of late Rev. R. D. M. Hughes. *Educ:* Purbrook Park Grammar Sch.; Open Univ. Served Army, 1939–66; India, 1941–44; Arakan Campaign, 1944–45; DAQMG, 52 (L) Div., 1951–53; GSO2 RA, HQ BAOR, 1955–57; GSO1 PR, MoD Army, 1964–66; retired Lt-Col, RA, 1966. Entered Home Civil Service as Principal, MPBW, 1966; Regional Director: Far East, 1969–70; Midland Region, 1970–75. Vice-Chm., Midland Study Centre for Building Team, 1982–90; Regional Chm., W Midlands Council, CIOB, 1988–90. Chm., W Midlands Central SSAFA, 1991–. FCIOB 1972; FBIM 1978; FRSA 1987. *Recreations:* gardening, economic history, gauge O railway modelling. *Address:* 25 Oakfield Road, Selly Park, Birmingham B29 7HH. *T:* 021–472 2031. *Clubs:* Naval and Military; Birmingham, Edgbaston Priory (Birmingham).

WALSH, Most Rev. Patrick Joseph; *see* Down and Connor, Bishop of.

WALSH, Robin; Controller, BBC Northern Ireland, since 1991; *b* 6 Feb. 1940; *s* of Charles and Ellen Walsh; *m* 1964, Dorothy Beattie; two *d. Educ:* Foyle College, Londonderry; Royal Belfast Academical Inst. Reporter, Belfast Telegraph, 1958–65; Reporter/News Editor, Ulster TV, 1965–74; BBC: News Editor, NI, 1974–81; Dep. Editor, TV News, 1982–85; Managing Editor, News and Current Affairs—TV, 1985–88; Asst Controller, News and Current Affairs, Regions, 1988–90. *Recreations:* cricket, walking. *Address:* Holly Lodge, 3A Ballymullan Road, Crawfordsburn, Co. Down, NI. *T:* Holywood (0247) 852709.

WALSH, Prof. William; Professor of Commonwealth Literature, 1972–84, now Emeritus, and Acting Vice-Chancellor, 1981–83 University of Leeds; Douglas Grant Fellow in Commonwealth Literature in the School of English, since 1969; Chairman, School of English, 1973–78; *b* 23 Feb. 1916; *e s* of William and Elizabeth Walsh; *m* 1945, May Watson; one *s* one *d. Educ:* Downing Coll., Cambridge; University of London. Schoolmaster, 1943–51; Senior English Master, Raynes Park County Grammar Sch., 1945–51; Lecturer in Education, University Coll. of N Staffordshire, 1951–53; Lecturer in Education, Univ. of Edinburgh, 1953–57; Prof. of Education, and Head of Dept. of Education, Univ. of Leeds, 1957–72; Chm., Sch. of Education, 1969–72; Chm., Bd of combined Faculties of Arts, Economics, Social Studies and Law, Univ. of Leeds, 1964–66; Pro-Vice-Chancellor, Univ. of Leeds, 1965–67; Chm. Bd of Adult Educn, 1969–77; Member: IBA Adult Educn Cttee, 1974–76; IBA Educn Adv. Cttee, 1976–81; Bd of Foundn for Canadian Studies in UK, 1981–. Dir, Yorkshire TV, 1967–86; Trustee, Edward Boyle Meml Trust, 1981–. Vis. Prof., ANU, 1968; Australian Commonwealth Vis. Fellow, 1970; Vis. Prof., Canadian Univs, 1973; Leverhulme Emeritus Fellow, 1986–88. Hon. LLD Leeds, 1984. *Publications:* Use of Imagination, 1959; A Human Idiom, 1964; Coleridge: The Work and the Relevance, 1967; A Manifold Voice, 1970; R. K. Narayan, 1972; V. S. Naipaul, 1972; Commonwealth Literature, 1973; Readings in Commonwealth Literature, 1973; D. J. Enright: poet of humanism, 1974; Patrick White: Voss, 1976; Patrick White's Fiction, 1977; F. R. Leavis, 1981; Introduction to Keats, 1981; R. K. Narayan, 1982; Indian Literature in English, 1990; contributions to: From Blake to Byron, 1957; Young Writers, Young Readers, 1960; Speaking of the Famous, 1962; F. R. Leavis-Some Aspects of his Work, 1963; The Teaching of English Literature Overseas, 1963; Higher Education: patterns of change in the 1970s, 1972; Literatures of the World in English, 1974; Considerations, 1977; Indo-English Literature, 1977; Perspectives on Mulk Raj Anand, 1978; Awakened Conscience, 1978; The Study of Education, vol. 1, 1980; The Twofold Voice: essays in honour of Ramesh Mohan, 1982; Life by Other Means: essays on D. J. Enright, 1990; Edward Boyle: his life by his friends, 1991; papers and essays on literary and educational topics in British and American journals. *Address:* 27 Moor Drive, Headingley, Leeds LS6 4BY. *T:* Leeds (0532) 755705.

WALSH-ATKINS, Leonard Brian, CMG 1962; CVO 1961; *b* 15 March 1915; *o c* of late Leonard and Gladys Atkins; step *s* of late Geoffrey Walsh, CMG, CBE; *m* 1st, 1940, Marguerite Black (marr. diss. 1968); three *s*; 2nd, 1969, Margaret Lady Runcorn. *Educ:* Charterhouse (Scholar); Hertford Coll., Oxford (Scholar; BA 1937). Asst Principal, India Office, 1937. Fleet Air Arm, 1940–45; Lieut-Comdr (A), RNVR (despatches). Burma Office, 1945–47; Commonwealth Relations Office, 1947; Counsellor, Dublin, 1953–56; idc 1957; Dep. High Comr, Pakistan, 1959–61; Asst Under-Sec. of State, 1962; retired 1970. The Abbeyfield Society, 1971–89 (Nat. Vice Chm., 1984–88); Dep. Chm., Nat. Fedn of Housing Assocs, 1984–86. *Address:* Berkeley Cottage, Mayfield, E Sussex TN20 6AU.

WALSHAM, Rear-Adm. Sir John Scarlett Warren, 4th Bt, *cr* 1831; CB 1963; OBE 1944; RN, retired; Admiral Superintendent HM Dockyard, Portsmouth, 1961–64; *b* 29 Nov. 1910; *s* of Sir John S. Walsham, 3rd Bt, and Bessie Geraldine Gundreda (*d* 1941), *e d* of late Vice-Admiral John B. Warren; *S* father, 1940; *m* 1936, Sheila Christina, *o d* of Comdr B. Bannerman, DSO; one *s* two *d*. Rear-Admiral, 1961. *Heir: s* Timothy John Walsham [*b* 26 April 1939. *Educ:* Sherborne]. *Address:* Priory Cottage, Middle Coombe, Shaftesbury, Dorset.

WALSINGHAM, 9th Baron, *cr* 1780; **John de Grey,** MC 1952; Lieut-Colonel, Royal Artillery, retired, 1968; *b* 21 Feb. 1925; *s* of 8th Baron Walsingham, DSO, OBE, and Hyacinth (*d* 1968), *o d* of late Lt-Col Lambart Henry Bouwens, RA; *S* father, 1965; *m* 1963, Wendy, *er d* of E. Hoare, Southwick, Sussex; one *s* two *d. Educ:* Wellington Coll.; Aberdeen Univ.; Magdalen Coll., Oxford; RMCS. BA Oxon, 1950; MA 1959. Army in India, 1945–47; Palestine, 1947; Oxford Univ., 1947–50; Foreign Office, 1950; Army in Korea, 1951–52; Hong Kong, 1952–54; Malaya, 1954–56; Cyprus, Suez, 1956; Aden, 1957–58; Royal Military Coll. of Science, 1958–60; Aden, 1961–63; Malaysia, 1963–65. *Heir: s* Hon. Robert de Grey, *b* 21 June 1969. *Address:* Merton Hall, Thetford, Norfolk IP25 6QJ. *T:* Watton (Norfolk) (0953) 881226. *Clubs:* Army and Navy, Special Forces; Norfolk County (Norwich).

WALTER, Hon. Sir Harold (Edward), Kt 1972; QC (Mauritius) 1985; Barrister-at-Law; MLA 1959–82, Minister of External Affairs, Tourism and Emigration, 1976–82, Mauritius; *b* 17 April 1920; *e s* of Rev. Edward Walter and Marie Augusta Donat; *m* 1942, Yvette Nidza, MBE, *d* of James Toolsy; no *c. Educ:* Royal Coll., Mauritius. Served in HM Forces, 1940–48, Mauritius Sub-Area; E Africa Comd, GHQ MELF. Called to Bar, Lincoln's Inn, 1951. Village Councillor, 1952; Municipal Councillor, Port Louis, 1956. Minister: of Works and Internal Communications, 1959–65; of Health, 1965–67 and 1971–76; of Labour, 1967–71; mem. numerous ministerial delegns. Chm., Commonwealth Med. Conf., 1972–74; Dep. Leader, UN General Assembly, NY, 1973, 1974, 1975; Pres., Security Council, UN, 1979; Mem. Exec. Bd, WHO, 1973–75, Pres., 1975–76. Chm., Council of Ministers, Organisation of African Unity, 1976–77; Vice Pres., Internat. Cttee for the Communities of Democracy (Washington), 1985. Trustee, Child Alive Program (Geneva), 1984–. Hon. DCL Univ. of Mauritius, 1984. Commandeur de l'Ordre National Français des Palmes Académiques, 1974; Comdr de la Légion d'Honneur (France), 1980; Diplomatic Order of Merit (Korea), 1981. *Recreations:* shooting, fishing, swimming, gardening. *Address:* La Rocca, Eau Coulée, Mauritius. *T:* 860300. *Clubs:* Wings, Racing (Mauritius).

WALTER, Kenneth Burwood, CVO 1978; Full-time Member, British Airports Authority, 1975–77; *b* 16 Oct. 1918; *s* of late Leonard James Walter and Jesse Florence Walter; *m* 1940, Elsie Marjorie Collett; two *s. Educ:* St Dunstan's Coll., SE6. Dept of Civil Aviation, Air Ministry, 1936. Served War, Royal Artillery (Anti Aircraft and Field), home and Far East, 1940–46. Ministries of: Civil Aviation; Transport and Civil Aviation; Aviation, 1946–66; British Airports Authority: Dep. Dir Planning, 1966; Dir Planning, 1972; Airport Dir, Heathrow, 1973–77. MCIT, ARAeS. *Publications:* various papers on airports. *Recreations:* music, swimming, fishing, gardening. *Address:* 7 Willersley Avenue, Orpington, Kent BR6 9RT.

WALTER, Neil Douglas; New Zealand Ambassador to Indonesia, since 1990; *b* 11 Dec. 1942; *s* of Ernest Edward Walter and Anita Walter (*née* Frethey); *m* 1966, Berys Anne (*née* Robertson); one *s* two *d. Educ:* New Plymouth Boys' High School; Auckland University (MA). Second Sec., Bangkok, 1966–70; First Sec., NZ Mission to UN, NY, 1972–76; Official Sec., Tokelau Public Service, Apia, 1976–78; Minister, Paris and NZ Permt Deleg. to Unesco, 1981–85; Dep. High Comr for NZ in London, 1985–87; Asst Sec., Ministry of External Relations, NZ, 1987–90. *Recreations:* sport, reading. *Address:* New Zealand Embassy, PO Box 2439, Jakarta, Indonesia.

WALTERS, Sir Alan (Arthur), Kt 1983; Vice-Chairman and Director, AIG Trading Corp.; Professor of Economics, Johns Hopkins University, Maryland, 1976–91; *b* 17 June 1926; *s* of James Arthur Walters and Claribel Walters (*née* Heywood); *m* 1975, Margaret Patricia (Paddie) Wilson; one *d* of former marr. *Educ:* Alderman Newton's Sch., Leicester; University Coll., Leicester (BSc (Econ) London); Nuffield Coll., Oxford (MA). Lectr in Econometrics, Univ. of Birmingham, 1951; Visiting Prof. of Economics, Northwestern Univ., Evanston, Ill, USA, 1958–59; Prof. of Econometrics and Social Statistics, Univ. of Birmingham, 1961; Cassel Prof. of Economics, LSE, 1968–76. Vis. Prof. of Econs, MIT, 1966–67; Vis. Fellow, Nuffield Coll., Oxford, 1982–84; Sen. Fellow, Amer. Enterprise Inst., 1983– (Boyer Lectr, 1983). Economic Adviser to World Bank, 1976–80, 1984–88; Personal Econ. Advr to the Prime Minister (on secondment), 1981–84, 1989. Mem. Commission on Third London Airport (the Roskill Commission), 1968–70. Fellow, Econometric Soc., 1971. Hon. DLitt Leicester, 1981; Hon. DSocSc Birmingham, 1984. *Publications:* Growth Without Development (with R. Clower and G. Dalton), 1966 (USA); Economics of Road User Charges, 1968; An Introduction to Econometrics, 1969 (2nd edn 1971); Economics of Ocean Freight Rates (with E. Bennathan), 1969 (USA); Money in Boom and Slump, 1970 (3rd edn 1971); Noise and Prices, 1974; (with R. G. Layard) Microeconomic Theory, 1977; (with Esra Bennathan) Port Pricing and Investment Policy for Developing Countries, 1979; Britain's Economic Renaissance, 1986; Sterling in Danger, 1990. *Recreations:* music, Thai porcelain, tennis. *Address:* 2820 P Street NW, Washington, DC 20007, USA. *Club:* Political Economy.

WALTERS, Sir Dennis, Kt 1988; MBE 1960; MP (C) Westbury Division of Wiltshire since 1964; *b* Nov. 1928; *s* of late Douglas L. Walters and of Clara Walters (*née* Pomello); *m* 1st, 1955, Vanora McIndoe (marr. diss. 1969); one *s* one *d*; 2nd, 1970, Hon. Celia (*née* Sandys) (mar diss. 1979); one *s*; 3rd, 1981, Bridgett, *d* of J. Francis Shearer; one *s* one *d. Educ:* Downside; St Catharine's College (Exhibitioner), Cambridge (MA). War of 1939–45: interned in Italy; served with Italian Resistance Movement behind German lines after Armistice; repatriated and continued normal educn, 1944. Chm., Fedn of Univ. Conservative and Unionist Assocs, 1950; Personal Asst to Lord Hailsham throughout his Chairmanship of Conservative Party; Chm., Coningsby Club, 1959. Contested (C) Blyth, 1959 and Nov. 1960. Jt Hon. Sec., Conservative Parly Foreign Affairs Cttee, 1965–71, Jt Vice-Chm., 1974–78; Jt Chm., Euro-Arab Parly Assoc., 1978–81; Mem., UK Parly Delegn to UN, 1966; UK Deleg. to Council of Europe and Assembly of WEU, 1970–73. Introduced Children and Young Persons (Amendment) Bill, 1985 (Royal Assent, 1986). Chm., Cons. ME Council, 1980–. Director: Cluff Oil Inc.; The Spectator, 1983–84; Middle East Internat., 1971–90 (Chm., 1990–). Chm., Asthma Research Council, 1968–88; Vice Pres., Nat. Asthma Campaign, 1989–. Chm., UK/Saudi Jt Cultural Cttee, 1988–; Jt Chm., Council for Advancement of Arab British Understanding, 1970–82 (Jt Vice-Chm., 1967–70). Governor, British Inst. of Florence, 1965–. Comdr, Order of Cedar of Lebanon, 1969. *Publication:* Not Always with the Pack (autobiographical memoirs), 1989. *Address:* 43 Royal Avenue, SW3 4QE. *T:* 071–730 9431; Orchardleigh, Corton, Warminster, Wilts. *T:* Warminster 50369. *Club:* Boodle's.

WALTERS, Very Rev. Derrick; *see* Walters, Very Rev. R. D. C.

WALTERS, Sir Donald, Kt 1983; Deputy Chairman, Welsh Development Agency, since 1984 (Board Member, since 1980); *b* 5 Oct. 1925; *s* of Percival Donald and Irene Walters; *m* 1950, Adelaide Jean McQuistin; one *s. Educ:* Howardian High Sch., Cardiff; London School of Economics and Political Science (LLB). Called to Bar, Inner Temple, 1946; practised at Bar, Wales and Chester circuit, 1948–59. Dir, 1959–85, Dep. Man. Dir, 1975–85, Chartered Trust plc. Mem., Develt Bd for Rural Wales, 1984–; Dir, WNO, 1985–(Vice-Chm., 1990); Chairman: Wales Council for Voluntary Action, 1987–; Council, Univ. of Wales Coll. of Cardiff, 1988–. High Sheriff, S Glamorgan, 1987–88. Hon. LLD Wales, 1990. *Recreations:* politics, gardening, walking. *Address:* 120 Cyncoed Road, Cardiff CF2 6BL. *T:* Cardiff (0222) 753166.

WALTERS, Geraint Gwynn, CBE 1958; Director for Wales, Ministry of Public Building and Works and Department of the Environment, 1966–72, retired; *b* in the Welsh Colony in Patagonia, 6 June 1910; *s* of Rev. D. D. Walters; *m* 1st, 1942, Doreena Owen (*d* 1959); 2nd, 1968, Sarah Ann Ruth Price; no *c. Educ:* various schools in Argentina and Wales; University Coll., Bangor (BA). Gladstone Prizeman, Foyle Prizeman. Schoolmaster, 1933–35; political organizer on staff of Rt Hon. David Lloyd George, 1935–40; Min. of Information, 1940–45; Dep. Regional Dir of Inf., Bristol and Plymouth, 1942–45;

Principal, Min. of Works HQ, 1945–48; Dir for Wales, Min. of Works, 1948–63; Dir, Far East Region, Min. of Public Building and Works, 1963–66. Chm., Royal Inst. of Public Admin (S Wales Br.), 1960–61; Hon. Mem. of Gorsedd, 1961; Pres., St David's Soc. of Singapore, 1965; Leader of Welsh Overseas, at Nat. Eisteddfod of Wales, 1965; Chm., Argentine Welsh Soc., 1976–78, Pres., 1979–82. Chm., Civil Service Sports Council for Wales, 1970–72. Govt Housing Comr for Merthyr Tydfil, 1972–73; Member: Welsh Bd for Industry, 1948–62; Housing Production Bd for Wales; Cttee of Inquiry on Welsh Television, 1963. Mem. Council, Univ. of Wales Inst. of Science and Technology, 1970–87 (Vice-Chm., 1980–83); Mem. Court, Univ. of Wales, 1982–88; Life Mem. Court, Univ. of Wales Coll. of Cardiff, 1989–. *Recreations:* reading Talking Books, radio, travel. *Address:* 1 The Mount, Cardiff Road, Llandaff, Cardiff CF5 2AR. *T:* Cardiff (0222) 568739. *Clubs:* Civil Service; Cardiff and County (Cardiff).

WALTERS, Rear-Adm. John William Townshend, CB 1984; Chairman, Industrial Tribunals, Southampton, since 1987 (London Central, 1984–87); Deputy Chairman, Data Protection Tribunal, since 1985; *b* 23 April 1926; *s* of William Bernard Walters and Lilian Martha Walters (*née* Hartridge); *m* 1949, Margaret Sarah Patricia Jeffkins; two *s* one *d*. *Educ:* John Fisher Sch., Purley, Surrey. Called to Bar, Middle Temple, 1956. Special Entry to RN, 1944; HMS King George V, 1944–46; HMS London, 1946–49; RN Air Station, Arbroath, 1949–51; Staff of C-in-C Mediterranean, 1951–53; Office of Vice Chief of Naval Staff, 1954–56; Sqdn Supply Officer, 8th Destroyer Sqdn, 1957–59; Staff of C-in-C Mediterranean, 1959–62; Secretary: to Flag Officer Middle East, 1962–64; to Naval Secretary, 1964–66; jssc 1967; Supply Officer, HMS Albion, 1967–69; Secretary to Chief of Fleet Support, 1969–72; Chief Naval Judge Advocate, 1972–75; Captain Naval Drafting, 1975–78; Director Naval Administrative Planning, 1978–80; ACDS (Personnel and Logistics), 1981–84, retired. *Recreations:* sailing, gardening. *Address:* Good Holding, 5 Hollycombe Close, Liphook, Hants GU30 7HR. *T:* Liphook (0428) 723222. *Clubs:* Army and Navy, Royal Naval Sailing Association.

WALTERS, Joyce Dora; Headmistress, Clifton High School, Bristol, since 1985; *m* 1979, Lt-Col Howard C. Walters (*d* 1983); one *s*. *Educ:* St Anne's College, Oxford. Headmistress, St Mary's, Calne, 1972–85. *Recreations:* travelling, reading, cooking. *Address:* 4 Longwood House, Failand, Bristol BS8 3TL. *T:* Bristol (0275) 392092. *Club:* United Oxford & Cambridge University.

WALTERS, Julie; actress; *b* 22 Feb. 1950; *d* of Thomas and Mary Walters; one *d*. *Educ:* Holly Lodge Grammar Sch., Smethwick; Manchester Polytechnic (Teaching Certificate). *Theatre:* Educating Rita, 1980 (Drama Critics' Most Promising Newcomer Award; Variety Club Best Newcomer); Having a Ball, Lyric, Hammersmith, 1981; Fool for Love, NT, 1984; Macbeth, Leicester Haymarket, 1985; When I was a Girl I used to Scream and Shout, Whitehall, 1986; Frankie and Johnny in the Clair de Lune, Comedy, 1989; The Rose Tattoo, Playhouse, 1991. *Films:* Educating Rita, 1983 (Variety Club of GB's Award for best film actress; BAFTA Award for best actress; Hollywood Golden Globe Award); She'll be Wearing Pink Pyjamas, 1985; Car Trouble, 1986; Personal Services, 1987 (British Video Award, Best Actress); Prick Up Your Ears, 1987; Buster, 1988; Killing Dad, 1989. *Television:* series include: Wood and Walters, 1981–82; Victoria Wood as Seen on TV, 1984, 2nd series, 1986; The Secret Diary of Adrian Mole, 1985; Victoria Wood Series, 1989; GBH, 1991; also television plays, incl. monologue in series, Talking Heads, 1988. *Publication:* Baby Talk, 1990. *Recreations:* reading, television, travel. *Address:* ICM, 388–396 Oxford Street, W1N 9HE.

WALTERS, Prof. Kenneth, PhD, DSc; FRS 1991; Professor of Applied Mathematics, University College of Wales, Aberystwyth, since 1973; *b* 14 Sept. 1934; *s* of late Trevor Walters and of Lilian (*née* Price); *m* 1963, Mary Ross; two *s* one *d*. *Educ:* University Coll. of Swansea (BSc 1956; MSc 1957; PhD 1959; DSc 1984). Dept of Mathematics, University Coll. of Wales, Aberystwyth: Lectr, 1960–65; Sen. Lectr, 1965–70; Reader, 1970–73. Gold Medal, British Soc. of Rheology, 1984. *Publications:* Rheometry, 1975; (ed) Rheometry: industrial applications, 1980; (with M. J. Crochet and A. R. Davies) Numerical Simulation of non-Newtonian Flow, 1984; (with H. A. Barnes amd J. F. Hutton) An Introduction to Rheology, 1989. *Recreation:* golf. *Address:* Department of Mathematics, University College of Wales, Penglais, Aberystwyth, Dyfed SY23 3BZ. *T:* Aberystwyth (0970) 622750; 8 Pen y Graig, Aberystwyth, Dyfed SY23 2JA. *T:* Aberystwyth (0970) 615276.

WALTERS, Michael Quentin; Senior Partner, Theodore Goddard, Solicitors, 1983–89; *b* 14 Oct. 1927; *s* of Leslie Walters and Helen Marie Walters; *m* 1954, Lysbeth Ann Falconer. *Educ:* Merchant Taylors' School; Worcester College, Oxford. MA. Served Army, 1946–48, 2nd Lieut. Joined Theodore Goddard, 1951; admitted Solicitor, 1954. Chairman: EIS Group plc, 1977–; Tilbury Group plc, 1989–; Dep. Chm., Martonair International plc, 1980–86; Dir, Delta plc, 1980–. Mem., Management Cttee, Inst. of Neurology, 1986–. *Recreations:* fishing, gardening, reading. *Address:* Derryfield Cottage, Ashton Keynes, Swindon, Wilts. *T:* Cirencester (0285) 861362.

WALTERS, Peter Ernest, CMG 1965; Group Staff Manager, Courage Ltd, 1967–78; Member, London (South) Industrial Tribunal, 1978–82; *b* 9 Oct. 1913; *s* of Ernest Helm Walters and Kathleen Walters (*née* Farrer-Baynes); *m* 1943, Ayesha Margaret, *d* of Alfred and Winifred Bunker; three *d*. *Educ:* Windlesham House Sch. Emigrated to Kenya, 1931. Army Service, 1939–45; commissioned KAR, 1940; Major 1944. Cadet, Colonial Admin. Service, Kenya, 1945; Dist Comr, 1948; Provincial Comr, Northern Prov., 1959; Civil Sec., Eastern Region, Kenya, 1963–65; retd from Colonial Service, 1965. Principal, Min. of Aviation (London), 1965–67. Staff Manager, Courage, Barclay and Simonds Ltd, 1967. Member Management Committee: Coastal Counties Housing Assoc., 1983–; CAB, Dorking, 1986–. *Address:* Cherry Orchard, Ockley, near Dorking, Surrey RH5 5NS. *T:* Dorking (0306) 711119. *Club:* Nairobi (Kenya).

WALTERS, Peter (Hugh Bennetts) Ensor, OBE 1957; Public Relations and Fund Raising Consultant since 1959; *b* 18 July 1912; *yr s* of late Rev. C. Ensor Walters, a President of the Methodist Conference, and late Muriel Havergal, *d* of late Alderman J. H. Bennetts, JP, Penzance; *m* 1936, Marcia, *er d* of Percival Burdle Hayter; no *c*. *Educ:* Manor House Sch.; St Peter's Coll., Oxford. On staff of late Rt Hon. David Lloyd George, 1935–39; enlisted as volunteer in Army, 1940; commissioned in Royal Army Pay Corps, 1942; National Organizer, National Liberal Organization, 1944–51. General Sec., National Liberal Organization, Hon. Sec. and Treas., National Liberal Party Council, and Dir, National Liberal Forum, 1951–58. Vice-Chm., Nat. Liberal Club, 1972–74. Pres., Worthing Central Cons. Assoc., 1984–89. *Recreation:* travel. *Address:* 2 Hopedene Court, Wordsworth Road, Worthing, W Sussex BN11 1TB. *T:* Worthing (0903) 205678. *Club:* Union Society (Oxford).

WALTERS, Sir Peter (Ingram), Kt 1984; Chairman: Midland Bank, since 1991; Blue Circle Industries PLC, since 1990; Director, since 1989, and Deputy Chairman, since 1990, Thorn EMI; *b* 11 March 1931; *s* of late Stephen Walters and of Edna Walters (*née* Redgate); *m* 1960, Patricia Anne (*née* Tulloch) (marr. diss. 1991); two *s* one *d*. *Educ:* King Edward's Sch., Birmingham; Birmingham Univ. (BCom). NS Commn; RASC, 1952–54; British Petroleum Co., 1954–90: Man. Dir, 1973–90; Chm., 1981–90; Vice-Pres., BP North America, 1965–67; Chairman: BP Chemicals, 1976–81; BP Chemicals Internat., 1981. Dir, 1981–89, Dep. Chm., 1988–89, Nat. Westminster Bank; Dir, Smithkline Beecham plc, 1989–. Member: Indust. Soc. Council, 1975–90; Post Office Bd, 1978–79; Coal Industry Adv. Bd, 1981–85; Inst. of Manpower Studies, 1986–88 (Vice-Pres., 1977–80; Pres., 1980–86); Gen. Cttee, Lloyds Register of Shipping, 1976–90; President's Cttee, CBI, 1982–90; President: Soc. of Chem. Industry, 1978–80; Gen. Council of British Shipping, 1977–78; Inst. of Directors, 1986–. Chm. Governors, London Business Sch., 1987–91 (Governor, 1981–; Dep. Chm., 1986–); Governor Nat. Inst. of Economic and Social Affairs, 1981–90; Mem. Foundn Bd, 1982–83, Chm., 1984–86, Internat. Management Inst.; Trustee: Nat. Maritime Museum, 1983–90; E Malling Res. Station, 1983–; Police Foundn, 1985–; Inst. of Economic Affairs, 1986–. Hon. DSocSc Birmingham, 1986; D Univ Stirling, 1987. Comdr. Order of Leopold (Belgium), 1984. *Recreations:* golf, gardening, sailing. *Address:* 84 Eccleston Square, SW1V 1PX. *Club:* Athenæum.

WALTERS, Very Rev. (Rhys) Derrick (Chamberlain); Dean of Liverpool, since 1983; *b* 10 March 1932; *s* of Ivor Chamberlain Walters and Rosamund Grace Walters (*née* Jackson); 1959, Joan Trollope (*née* Fisher); two *s*. *Educ:* Gowerton Boys' Grammar School; London School of Economics; Ripon Hall, Oxford. BSc(Soc) Lond, 1955. Curate, Manselton, Swansea, 1957–58; Anglican Chaplain, University College, Swansea and Curate, St Mary's, 1958–62; Vicar of All Saints, Totley, 1962–67; Vicar of St Mary's, Boulton by Derby, 1967–74; Diocesan Missioner, Diocese of Salisbury, 1974–82; Vicar of Burcombe, 1974–79; Non-residentiary Canon of Salisbury, 1978; Residentiary Canon and Treasurer of Salisbury Cathedral, 1979–82. *Recreations:* escapist literature, croquet, classical music. *Address:* Liverpool Cathedral, L1 7AZ. *T:* 051–709 6271.

WALTERS, Sir Roger (Talbot), KBE 1971 (CBE 1965); FRIBA, FIStructE; architect in private practice, 1984–87; *b* 31 March 1917; 3rd *s* of Alfred Bernard Walters, Sudbury, Suffolk; *m* 1976, Claire Myfanwy Chappell. *Educ:* Oundle; Architectural Association School of Architecture; Liverpool University. Diploma in Architecture, 1939. Served in Royal Engineers, 1943–46. Office of Sir E. Owen Williams, KBE, 1936; Directorate of Constructional Design, Min. of Works, 1941–43; Architect to Timber Development Assoc., 1946–49; Principal Asst Architect, Eastern Region, British Railways, 1949–59; Chief Architect (Development), Directorate of Works, War Office, 1959–62; Dep. Dir-Gen., R&D, MPBW, 1962–67; Dir-Gen., Production, 1967–69; Controller General, 1969–71; Architect and Controller of Construction Services, GLC, 1971–78; Birkbeck Coll., 1978–80 (BA 1980); Principal, The Self-Employed Agency, 1981–83. Hon. FAIA. *Address:* 46 Princess Road, NW1 8JL. *T:* 071–722 3740. *Club:* Reform.

WALTERS, Stuart Max, ScD; VMH; Director, University Botanic Garden, Cambridge, 1973–83, retired; *b* 23 May 1920; *s* of Bernard Walters and Ivy Dane; *m* 1948, Lorna Mary Strutt; two *s* one *d*. *Educ:* Penistone Grammar Sch.; St John's Coll., Cambridge. 1st cl. hons Pt I Nat. Scis Tripos 1940 and Pt II Botany 1946; PhD 1949. Research Fellow, St John's Coll., 1947–50; Curator of Herbarium, Botany Sch., Cambridge, 1948–73; Lectr in Botany 1962–73; Fellow of King's Coll., Cambridge, 1964–84. VMH 1984. *Publications:* (with J. S. L. Gilmour) Wild Flowers, 1954; (with J. Raven) Mountain Flowers, 1956; (ed, with F. H. Perring) Atlas of the British Flora, 1962; (with F. H. Perring, P. D. Sell and H. L. K. Whitehouse) A Flora of Cambridgeshire, 1964; (with D. Briggs) Plant Variation and Evolution, 1969, 2nd edn 1984; The Shaping of Cambridge Botany, 1981. *Address:* Inland Close, 46 Mill Way, Grantchester, Cambridge CB3 9NB. *T:* Cambridge (0223) 841295.

WALTON, family name of **Baron Walton of Detchant.**

WALTON OF DETCHANT, Baron *cr* 1989 (Life Peer), of Detchant in the County of Northumberland; **John Nicholas Walton;** Kt 1979; TD 1962; FRCP; Warden, Green College, University of Oxford, 1983–89; *b* 16 Sept. 1922; *s* of Herbert Walton and Eleanor Watson Walton; *m* 1946, Mary Elizabeth Harrison; one *s* two *d*. *Educ:* Alderman Wraith Grammar Sch., Spennymoor, Co. Durham; Med. Sch., King's Coll., Univ. of Durham. MB, BS (1st Cl. Hons) 1945; MD (Durham) 1952; DSc (Newcastle) 1972; MA(Oxon) 1983; FRCP 1963 (MRCP 1950). Ho. Phys., Royal Victoria Inf., Newcastle, 1946–47; service in RAMC, 1947–49; Med. Registrar, Royal Vic. Inf., 1949–51; Research Asst, Univ. of Durham, 1951–56; Nuffield Foundn Fellow, Mass. Gen. Hosp. and Harvard Univ., 1953–54; King's Coll. Fellow, Neurological Res. Unit, Nat. Hosp., Queen Square, 1954–55; First Asst in Neurology, Newcastle upon Tyne, 1956–58; Cons. Neurologist, Newcastle Univ. Hosps, 1958–83; Prof. of Neurology, 1968–83, and Dean of Medicine, 1971–81, Univ. of Newcastle upon Tyne. Numerous named lectureships and overseas visiting professorships. Member: MRC, 1974–78; GMC, 1971–89 (Chm. Educn Cttee, 1975–82; Pres., 1982–89); President: BMA, 1980–82; Royal Soc. of Medicine, 1984–86 (Hon. Fellow, 1988); ASME 1982–; Assoc. of British Neurologists, 1987–88; World Fedn Neurol., 1989– (First Vice-Pres., 1981–89; Chm., Res. Cttee); UK Rep., EEC Adv. Cttee, Med. Educn, 1975–83; Editor-in-Chief, Jl of Neurological Sciences, 1966–77; Chm., Muscular Dystrophy Gp of GB, 1970–, etc. Col (late RAMC) and OC 1 (N) Gen. Hosp. (TA), 1963–66; Hon. Col 201(N) Gen. Hosp. (T&AVR), 1971–77. Foreign Mem., Norwegian Acad. of Sci. and Letters, 1987; Hon. Foreign Member: Amer. Neurological Assoc., Amer. Acad. of Neurology, Assoc. Amer. Phys., Amer. Osler Soc., Osler Soc. of London, Japan Osler Soc., and of Canadian, French, German, Australian, Spanish, Polish, Venezuelan, Thai, Japanese and Brazilian Neurological Assocs. Hon. FACP 1980; Hon. FRCPE 1981; Hon. FRCP (Can) 1984. Dr de l'Univ. (Hon.) Aix-Marseille, 1975; Hon. DSc: Leeds, 1979; Leicester, 1980; Hull, 1988; Hon. MD Sheffield, 1987; Hon. DCL Newcastle, 1988. Hon. Freeman, Newcastle upon Tyne, 1980. *Publications:* Subarachnoid Haemorrhage, 1956; (with R. D. Adams) Polymyositis, 1958; Essentials of Neurology, 1961, 6th edn 1989; Disorders of Voluntary Muscle, 1964, 5th edn 1988; Brain's Diseases of the Nervous System, 7th edn 1969, 9th edn 1985; (with F. L. Mastaglia) Skeletal Muscle Pathology, 1982, 2nd edn 1991, etc; (ed jtly) The Oxford Companion to Medicine, 1986; numerous chapters in books and papers in sci. jls. *Recreations:* cricket, golf and other sports, reading, music. *Address:* 13 Norham Gardens, Oxford OX2 6PS. *T:* Oxford (0865) 512492. *Clubs:* Athenæum, United Oxford & Cambridge University.

WALTON, Anthony Michael, QC 1970; *b* 4 May 1925; *y s* of Henry Herbert Walton and Clara Martha Walton, Dulwich; *m* 1955, Jean Frederica, *o d* of William Montague Hey, Bedford; one *s*. *Educ:* Dulwich College (sometime Scholar); Hertford College, Oxford (sometime Scholar); pupil to W. L. Ferrar (maths) and C. H. S. Fifoot (law). BA 1946; BCL 1950; MA 1950. Pres., Oxford Union Society, Trinity Term 1945. Nat. Service as physicist. Called to the Bar, Middle Temple, 1950; Bencher, 1978; pupil to Lord Justice Winn. Interested in education. Liveryman, Worshipful Co. of Gunmakers. Freeman, City of London, 1968. *Publications:* (ed) (Asst to Hon. H. Fletcher-Moulton) Digest of the Patent, Design, Trade Mark and Other Cases, 1959; (ed) Russell on Arbitration, 17th edn, 1963–20th edn, 1982; (with Hugh Laddie) Patent Law of Europe and the United Kingdom, 1978. *Address:* 62 Kingsmead Road, SW2 3JG.

WALTON, Arthur Halsall, FCA; Partner in Lysons, Haworth & Sankey, 1949–85; *b* 13 July 1916; *s* of Arthur Walton and Elizabeth Leeming (*née* Halsall); *m* 1958, Kathleen

Elsie Abram; three *s. Educ:* The Leys School. Articled in Lysons & Talbot, 1934; ACA 1940. Military Service, 1939–48: commnd Lancs Fusiliers, 1940. Inst. of Chartered Accountants: Mem. Council 1959; Vice-Pres., 1969; Dep. Pres. 1970; Pres. 1971. *Recreation:* reading. *Address:* 19 Cavendish Mews, Wilmslow SK9 1PW. *Club:* St James's (Manchester).

WALTON, Ernest Thomas Sinton, MA, MSc, PhD; Fellow of Trinity College, Dublin, 1934–74, Fellow emeritus 1974; Erasmus Smith's Professor of Natural and Experimental Philosophy 1947–74; *b* 6 October 1903; *s* of Rev. J. A. Walton, MA; *m* 1934, Winifred Isabel Wilson; two *s* two *d. Educ:* Methodist College, Belfast; Trinity College, Dublin; Cambridge University. 1851 Overseas Research Scholarship, 1927–30; Senior Research Award of Dept of Scientific and Industrial Research, 1930–34; Clerk Maxwell Scholar, 1932–34. Hon. Life Mem., RDS, 1981. Hon. FIEI 1985; Hon. FInstP 1988. Hon. DSc: QUB, 1959; Gustavus Adolphus Coll., Minn, USA, 1975; Ulster, 1988. Awarded Hughes Medal by Royal Society, 1938; (with Sir John Cockcroft) Nobel prize for physics, 1951. *Publications:* papers on hydrodynamics, nuclear physics and micro-waves. *Address:* Trinity College, Dublin 2; 26 St Kevin's Park, Dartry Road, Dublin 6. *T:* 971328.

WALTON, Ven. Geoffrey Elmer; Archdeacon of Dorset, since 1982; *b* 19 Feb. 1934; *s* of Harold and Edith Margaret Walton; *m* 1961, Edith Mollie O'Connor; one *s. Educ:* St John's Coll., Univ. of Durham (BA); Queen's Coll., Birmingham (DipTh). Asst Curate, Warsop with Sookholme, 1961–65; Vicar of Norwell, Notts, 1965–69; Recruitment and Selection Sec., ACCM, 1969–75; Vicar of Holy Trinity, Weymouth, 1975–82; RD of Weymouth, 1980–82; Non-Residentiary Canon of Salisbury, 1981–. *Recreations:* conjuring, religious drama. *Address:* The Vicarage, Witchampton, Wimborne, Dorset BH21 5AP. *T:* Witchampton (0258) 840422.

WALTON, Sir John Robert, Kt 1971; retired; Director, Waltons Ltd Group, Australia (Managing Director, 1951–72, Chairman, 1961–72); Chairman, FNCB-Waltons Corp. Ltd, Australia, 1966–75; *b* 7 Feb. 1904; *s* of John Thomas Walton; *m* 1938, Peggy Everley Gamble; one *s* one *d. Educ:* Scots Coll., Sydney. National Cash Register Co. Pty Ltd, 1930: NSW Manager, 1934, Managing Director in Australia, 1946–51. *Recreations:* gardening, swimming, golf, reading. *Address:* 9A Longwood, 5 Thornton Street, Darling Point, NSW 2027, Australia. *Clubs:* Rotary, Royal Sydney Golf, American National, Tattersall's (all in Sydney).

WALTON, John William Scott; Director of Statistics, Board of Inland Revenue, 1977–85; *b* 25 Sept. 1925; *s* of late Sir John Charles Walton, KCIE, CB, MC, and late Nelly Margaret, Lady Walton, *d* of late Prof. W. R. Scott. *Educ:* Marlborough; Brasenose Coll., Oxford. Army (RA), 1943–47. Mutual Security Agency, Paris, 1952; Inland Revenue, 1954; Central Statistical Office, 1958, Chief Statistician, 1967, Asst Dir, 1972. *Publications:* (contrib. jtly) M. Perlman, The Organization and Retrieval of Economic Knowledge, 1977; articles in The Review of Income and Wealth, Economic Trends, Business Economist, Statistical News. *Club:* United Oxford & Cambridge University.

WALTON, William Stephen; Research Fellow, University of Sheffield, since 1990; Chief Education Officer, Sheffield, 1985–90; *b* 28 March 1933; *s* of Thomas Leslie Walton and Ena Walton (*née* Naylor); *m* 1964, Lois Elicia Petts; three *d* (incl. twins). *Educ:* King's School, Pontefract; Univ. of Birmingham (BA). RAF, gen. duties (flying), 1951–55. Production Management, Dunlop Rubber Co., 1958–61; Derbyshire Local Educn Authy School Teacher, 1961–67; Educational Administration: Hull, 1967–70; Newcastle upon Tyne, 1970–79; Sheffield 1979–90. Visiting Professor: Univ. of Simon Fraser, BC; Univ. of Portland, Oregon. Pres., Soc. of Educn Officers, 1989–90; Chm., Sch. Curriculum Industry Partnership/Mini Enterprise Schs Project, 1990–. Dir, Outward Bound. FRSA. Hon. Fellow, Sheffield City Polytechnic, 1990. *Recreations:* golf, France. *Address:* 3 Bentham Road, Chesterfield, Derbyshire S40 4EZ. *T:* Chesterfield (0246) 203769. *Club:* Royal Air Force.

WALWYN, Peter Tyndall; racehorse trainer, since 1960; *b* 1 July 1933; *s* of late Lt-Col Charles Lawrence Tyndall Walwyn, DSO, OBE, MC, Moreton in Marsh, Glos; *m* 1960, Virginia Gaselee, *d* of A. S. Gaselee, MFH; one *s* one *d. Educ:* Amesbury Sch., Hindhead, Surrey; Charterhouse. Leading trainer on the flat, 1974, 1975; leading trainer, Ireland, 1974, 1975; a new record in earnings (£373,563), 1975. Major races won include: One Thousand Guineas, 1970, Humble Duty; Oaks Stakes, 1974, Polygamy; Irish Derby, 1974, English Prince, and 1975, Grundy; King George VI and Queen Elizabeth Stakes, Ascot, 1975, Grundy; Epsom Derby, 1975, Grundy. *Recreations:* foxhunting, shooting. *Address:* Seven Barrows, Lambourn, Berks RG16 7UJ. *T:* Lambourn (0488) 71347. *Clubs:* Turf; Jockey Club Rooms (Newmarket).

WANAMAKER, Sam; Actor; Director, Producer; *b* Chicago, 14 June 1919; *s* of Morris Wanamaker and Molly (*née* Bobele); *m* 1940, Charlotte Holland; three *d. Educ:* Drake University, Iowa, USA. Studied for the stage at Goodman Theatre, Chicago. Appeared in summer theatres, Chicago (acting and directing), 1936–39; joined Globe Shakespearian Theatre Group; first New York Appearance, Café Crown, 1941; Counter Attack, 1942. Served in United States Armed Forces, 1943–46. In several parts on New York stage, 1946–49; appeared in This, Too, Shall Pass, 1946; directed and played in: Joan of Lorraine, 1946–47; Goodbye My Fancy, 1948–49; directed: Caeser and Cleopatra, 1950; The Soldier and the Lady, 1954; created Festival Repertory Theatre, New York, 1950. First performance (also producer) on London stage as Bernie Dodd, in Winter Journey, St James's, 1952; presented and appeared in The Shrike, Prince's, 1953; produced: Purple Dust, Glasgow, 1953; Foreign Field, Birmingham, 1954; directed and appeared in One More River, Cat on a Hot Tin Roof, and The Potting Shed, 1957. In Liverpool, 1957, created New Shakespeare Theatre Cultural Center, where produced (appearing in some): Tea and Sympathy, A View from the Bridge, 1957 The Rose Tattoo, Finian's Rainbow, Bus Stop, The Rainmaker, and Reclining Figure (all in 1958). *Presented, prod and appeared in:* The Big Knife, Duke of York's 1954; The Lovers, Winter Garden, 1955; The Rainmaker, St Martin's 1956; A Hatful of Rain, Prince's, 1957; The Rose Tattoo, New, 1959; Iago, Stratford-on-Avon, 1959; Dr Breuer, in A Far Country, New York, 1961; The Watergate Tapes, Royal Court, 1974; *produced:* The World of Sholom Aleichem, Embassy, 1955; King Priam, Coventry Theatre and Royal Opera House, Covent Garden, 1962, 1967, and 1972; Verdi's La Forza del Destino, Royal Opera House, Covent Garden, 1962; John Player season, Globe, 1972–73; Southwark Summer Festival, 1974; Shakespeare Birthday Celebrations, 1974; *directed:* Children from their Games, New York, 1963; A Case of Libel, New York, 1963; A Murder Among Us, New York, 1964; Defenders, 1964; War and Peace (première), Sydney Opera House, 1973; The Ice Break, Royal Opera House, Covent Garden, 1977; Chicago Lyric Opera Gala, 1979; Stravinsky's Oedipus, Boston Symphony Orch., Tanglewood, 1982; *acted and directed* Macbeth, Goodman Theater, Chicago, 1964; *directed and wrote* This Wooden O, Carnegie Hall, Pittsburgh, 1983; *acted (films):* Give Us This Day; Taras Bulba; Those Magnificent Men in Their Flying Machines, 1964; The Winston Affair, 1964; The Spy Who Came in from the Cold, 1964; Warning Shot; The Law, 1974; Spiral Staircase, 1974; The Sell-Out, 1975; The Voyage of the Damned, 1975; Billy Jack goes to Washington, 1976; From Hell to Victory, 1978; Private Benjamin, 1980; The Competition, 1980; Irreconcilable Differences, 1983; The Aviator, 1983; (film for TV) Embassy, 1985; Raw Deal, 1985; Superman IV, 1986; Judgement in Berlin, 1987; Secret Ingredient, 1987; Baby Boom, 1988; Fear No Evil, 1990; *films directed:* Hawk, 1965; Lancer, 1966; Custer, 1967; File of the Golden Goose, 1968; The Executioner, 1969; Catlow, 1970; Sinbad and the Eye of the Tiger, 1975; The Killing of Randy Webster, 1981; *directed (opera):* Aida, San Francisco, 1981; Tosca, San Diego, 1987; *directed (television):* Colombo, 1977; Hawaii 5–0, 1978; Dark Side of Love, Man Undercover, Mrs Columbo, Hart to Hart, 1979; Grand Deception (Columbo series), 1989; *acted and directed (TV):* The Holocaust, 1977; The Return of the Saint, 1978; *acted (TV):* Blind Love, 1976; Charlie Muffin, 1979; The Family Business, 1981; The Ghost Writer, 1982; The Berrengers, 1984; Heartsounds, 1984; The Ferret, 1984; Two Mrs Grenvilles, 1986; Baby Boom (series), 1988. Founder and Executive Vice-Chairman: Globe Playhouse Trust Ltd, 1971; Internat. Shakespeare Globe Centre (formerly World Centre for Shakespeare Studies Ltd). Directs and acts in TV productions and feature films in UK and USA. Benjamin Franklin Medal, RSA, 1989. Hon. LLD New Brunswick, 1989; Hon. DLitt Roosevelt, 1990. *Address:* Bear Gardens, SE1.

WANDSWORTH, Archdeacon of; *see* Gerrard, Ven. D. K. R.

WANG Gungwu, Prof., CBE 1991; FAHA; Vice-Chancellor, University of Hong Kong, since 1986; *b* 9 Oct. 1930; *s* of Wang Fo Wen and Ting Yien; *m* 1955, Margaret Lim Ping-Ting; one *s* two *d. Educ:* Anderson Sch., Ipoh, Malaya; Nat. Central Univ., Nanking, China; Univ. of Malaya, Singapore (BA Hons, MA); Univ. of London (PhD 1957). University of Malaya, Singapore: Asst Lectr, 1957–59; Lectr, 1959; University of Malaya, Kuala Lumpur: Lectr, 1959–61; Sen. Lectr, 1961–63; Dean of Arts, 1962–63; Prof. of History, 1963–68; Australian National University: Prof. of Far Eastern History, 1968–86, Emeritus Prof., 1988; Dir, Res. Sch. of Pacific Studies, 1975–80. Rockefeller Fellow, 1961–62, Sen. Vis. Fellow, 1972, Univ. of London; Vis. Fellow, All Souls Coll., Oxford, 1974–75; John A. Burns Distinguished Vis. Prof. of History, Univ. of Hawaii, 1979; Rose Morgan Vis. Prof. of History, Univ. of Kansas, 1983. Dir, East Asian History of Science Foundation Ltd, 1987–. MEC, Hong Kong, 1990–. Chairman: Australia-China Council, 1984–86; Envmt Pollution Cttee, HK, 1988–; Council for the Performing Arts, HK, 1989–; Member: Commn of Inquiry on Singapore Riots, 1964–65; Internat. Adv. Panel, E-W Center, Honolulu, 1979–; Cttee on Aust.-Japan Relations, 1980–81; Regional Council, Inst. of SE Asian Studies, Singapore, 1982–; Admin. Bd, Assoc. of SE Asian Instns of Higher Learning, 1986–; Council, Chinese Univ. of Hong Kong, 1986–; Exec. Council, WWF, HK, 1987–; President: Internat. Assoc. of Historians of Asia, 1964–68, 1988–; Asian Studies Assoc. of Aust., 1979–80; Australian Acad. of the Humanities, 1980–83 (Fellow 1970); Hon. Corresp. Mem. for Hong Kong, RSA, 1987 (Fellow 1987). Editor: (also Councillor), Jl of Nanyang Hsueh-hui, Singapore, 1958–68; (also Vice-Pres.), Jl of RAS, Malaysian Br., 1962–68; Gen. Editor, East Asian Historical Monographs series for OUP, 1968–. *Publications:* The Nanhai Trade: a study of the early history of Chinese trade in the South China Sea, 1958; A Short History of the Nanyang Chinese, 1959; Latar Belakang Kebudayaan Pendudok di-Tanah Melayu: Bahagian Kebudayaan China (The Cultural Background of the Peoples of Malaysia: Chinese culture), 1962; The Structure of Power in North China during the Five Dynasties, 1963; (ed) Malaysia: a survey, 1964; (ed jtly) Essays on the Sources for Chinese History, 1974; (ed) Self and Biography: essays on the individual and society in Asia, 1975; China and the World since 1949: the impact of independence, modernity and revolution, 1977; (ed jtly) Hong Kong: dilemmas of growth, 1980; Community and Nation: essays on Southeast Asia and the Chinese, 1981; (ed jtly) Society and the Writer: essays on literature in modern Asia, 1981; Dongnanya yu Huaren (Southeast Asia and the Chinese), 1987; Nanhai Maoyi yu Nanyang Huaren (Chinese Trade and Southeast Asia), 1988; (ed with J. Cushman) Changing Indentities of Southeast Asian Chinese since World War II, 1988; Lishi di Gongneng (The Functions of History), 1990; China and the Chinese Overseas, 1991; The Chineseness of China: selected essays, 1991; contribs to collected vols on Asian history; articles on Chinese and Southeast Asian history in internat. jls. *Recreations:* music, reading, walking. *Address:* The Lodge, 1 University Drive, Hong Kong; Vice-Chancellor's Office, University of Hong Kong. *T:* 8592100.

WANGARATTA, Bishop of, since 1985; **Rt. Rev. Robert George Beal;** *b* 17 Aug. 1929; *s* of Samuel and Phyllis Beal; *m* 1956, Valerie Francis Illich; two *s* four *d. Educ:* Sydney Grammar School; St Francis' College, Brisbane, Qld; Newcastle Univ., NSW (BA, ThL). Ordained, 1953; Priest, Asst Curate, St Francis', Nundah, Brisbane, 1953–55; Rector: South Townsville, 1955–59; Auchenflower, Brisbane, 1959–65; Dean of Wangaratta, 1965–72; Rector of Ipswich, Brisbane, and Residentiary Canon of St John's Cathedral, 1974–75; Dean of Newcastle, NSW, 1975–83; Archdeacon of Albury, 1983–85. *Recreations:* tennis, gardening. *Address:* Bishop's Lodge, Ovens Street, Wangaratta, Victoria 3677, Australia. *T:* (057) 21 3643.

WANI, Most Rev. Silvanus; *b* July 1916; *s* of late Mana Ada Wani and late Daa Miriam; *m* 1936, Penina Yopa Wani; six *s* two *d* (and two *s* decd). *Educ:* Kampala Normal School, Makerere (Teacher's Cert.). Teaching, Arua Primary School, 1936–39; student, Buwalasi Theol. Coll., 1940–42; ordained as one of first two priests in West Nile District, 1943; Chaplain, King's African Rifles, 1944–46; Parish Priest: Arua, 1947–50; Koboko, 1951–60; Canon and Rural Dean, Koboko, 1953–60; attended Oak Hill Theological Coll., 1955–56; Diocesan Secretary/Treasurer, N Uganda Diocese, 1961–64; student (Christianity and Islam), St George's Coll., Jerusalem, 1963–64; Asst Bishop, later full Bishop, N Uganda, 1964; Bishop of Madi/West Nile Diocese, 1969; Dean, Province of Church of Uganda, Rwanda, Burundi and Boga Zaire, 1974–77; Archbishop of Uganda (also of Rwanda, Burundi and Boga Zaire, 1977–80) and Bishop of Kampala, 1977–83; retd, on health and age grounds, to home area, 1983. Chaplain Gen. to Uganda Armed Forces, 1964–78. *Recreations:* reading, walking, gardening. *Address:* c/o PO Box 370, Arua, Uganda.

WANNAMETHEE, Phan; Secretary General, Association of South East Asian Nations, 1984–86; *b* 30 Jan. 1924; *s* of Mr and Mrs Puhn Wannamethee; *m* 1958, M. L. Hiranyika Ladawan; three *s* one *d. Educ:* Oberlin Coll., Ohio, USA (BA); Univ. of Calif at Berkeley (MA). Entered Foreign Min., Bangkok, 1942; attached Royal Thai Embassy, Washington, 1945; Third Sec., Cairo, 1956; Private Sec. to Prime Minister, 1957; First Secretary: Karachi, 1958; Saigon, 1959; (later Counsellor), London, 1964; Foreign Min., Bangkok: Dep. Under-Sec. of State, 1972; Dir-Gen., Polit. Dept, 1973; Under-Sec. of State for Foreign Affairs, 1973; Ambassador to: Fed. Republic of Germany, 1976; UK, 1977–84. *Recreation:* swimming. *Address:* 66 Soi 10, Pibulwattana, Rama 6 Road, Bangkok, Thailand. *Clubs:* Athenæum, Travellers', Naval and Military, Special Forces, Hurlingham.

WANSTALL, Hon. Sir Charles Gray, Kt 1974; Chief Justice of Queensland, Australia, 1977–82; *b* 17 Feb. 1912; *m* 1938, Olwyn Mabel, *d* of C. O. John; one *d. Educ:* Roma and Gympie State Schs; Gympie High Sch., Queensland, Australia. Called to Queensland Bar, 1933. High Court, 1942. MLA (Liberal) for Toowong, 1944–50; Pres., Liberal Party of Australia (Qld Div.), 1950–53. QC 1956; Judge, Supreme Court, Qld, 1958; Sen. Puisne Judge, 1971. *Recreations:* reading, photography. *Address:* 26/36 Jerdanefield Road, St

Lucia, Brisbane, Queensland 4067, Australia. *Clubs:* Queensland (Brisbane); St Lucia Bowling.

WAPSHOTT, Nicholas Henry; Political Editor, The Observer, since 1988; *b* 13 Jan. 1952; *s* of Raymond Gibson Wapshott and Olivia Beryl Darch; *m* 1980, Louise Nicholson; two *s*. *Educ:* Dursley County Primary Sch.; Rendcomb Coll., Cirencester; Univ. of York (BA Hons). The Scotsman, 1973–76; The Times, 1976–84; The Observer, 1984–. *Publications:* Peter O'Toole, 1982; (with George Brock) Thatcher, 1983; The Man Between: a biography of Carol Reed, 1990; Sir Rex, 1991. *Recreations:* cinema, music, elephants. *Address:* The Observer, Chelsea Bridge House, Queenstown Road, Battersea, SW8 4NN. *T:* 071–350 3235; 35 Cross Street, Islington, N1. *T:* 071–226 5278. *Clubs:* Reform; Morton's.

WARBURTON, Col Alfred Arthur, CBE 1961; DSO 1945; DL; JP; Chairman, SHEF Engineering Ltd, 1970–75; Company Director since 1953; *b* 12 April 1913; *s* of late A. V. Warburton. *Educ:* Sedbergh. Served War of 1939–45, with Essex Yeomanry; Lt-Col comdg South Notts Hussars Yeomanry, 1953–58; Hon. Col 1966–76; Col DCRA 49th Inf. Div. TA, 1958–60; ADC to the Queen, 1961–66; Chm., Notts Cttee TA&VR Assoc. for E Midlands, 1970–78. Director, John Shaw Ltd, Worksop, 1953–66. President: East Midlands Area, Royal British Legion, 1976–77, 1981–82, 1986–87, 1991–92; Notts County Royal British Legion, 1979–. DL 1966, High Sheriff 1968, JP 1968, Notts. *Recreations:* shooting, fishing, gardening. *Address:* Wigthorpe House, Wigthorpe, Worksop, Notts S81 8BT. *T:* Worksop (0909) 730357. *Club:* Cavalry and Guards.

WARBURTON, Dame Anne (Marion), DCVO 1979 (CVO 1965); CMG 1977; HM Diplomatic Service, 1957–85; President, Lucy Cavendish College, Cambridge, since 1985; *b* 8 June 1927; *d* of Captain Eliot Warburton, MC and Mary Louise (*née* Thompson), US. *Educ:* Barnard Coll., Columbia Univ. (BA); Somerville Coll., Oxford (BA, MA); Hon. Fellow, 1977. Economic Cooperation Administration, London, 1949–52; NATO Secretariat, Paris, 1952–54; Lazard Bros, London, 1955–57; entered Diplomatic Service, Nov. 1957; 2nd Sec., FO, 1957–59; 2nd, then 1st Sec., UK Mission to UN, NY, 1959–62; 1st Sec., Bonn, 1962–65; 1st Sec., DSAO, London, 1965–67; 1st Sec., FO, then FCO, 1967–70; Counsellor, UK Mission to UN, Geneva, 1970–75; Head of Guidance and Information Policy Dept, FCO, 1975–76; Ambassador to Denmark, 1976–83; Ambassador and UK Permanent Rep. to UN and other internat. organisations, Geneva, 1983–85. Dep. Leader, UK Delegn to UN Women's Conf., Nairobi, 1985. Member: Equal Opportunities Commn, 1986–88; British Library Bd, 1989–; Council, UEA, 1991–. FRSA 1986. Hon. Fellow, Regent's Coll., London, 1989. Verdienstkreuz, 1st Class (West Germany), 1965; Grand Cross, Order of Dannebrog, 1979; Lazo de Dama, Order of Isabel la Católica (Spain), 1988. *Recreations:* travel, walking, ski-ing, the arts. *Address:* Lucy Cavendish College, Cambridge CB3 0BU. *Clubs:* United Oxford & Cambridge University, English-Speaking Union.

WARBURTON, David; National Officer: GMB (formerly General, Municipal, Boilermakers and Allied Trades Union), since 1982; APEX (white collar section of GMB), since 1990; *b* 10 Jan. 1942; *s* of Harold and Ada Warburton; *m* 1966, Carole Anne Susan Tomney; two *d*. *Educ:* Cottingley Manor Sch., Bingley, Yorks; Coleg Harlech, Merioneth, N Wales. Campaign Officer, Labour Party, 1964; Educn Officer, G&MWU, 1965–66, Reg. Officer, 1966–73; Nat. Industrial Officer, G&MWU, 1973–82. Secretary: Chemical Unions Council; Rubber Industry Jt Unions, 1980–86; Health Care Textile Unions, 1988–; Chm., Paper and Packaging Industry Unions, 1988–. Mem., Europ. Co-ord. Cttee, Chem., Rubber and Glass Unions, 1975–. Chm., Chem. and Allied Industries Jt Indust. Council, 1973–86; Mem., Govt Industrial Workers Jt Consultative Cttee, 1988–; Sec., Home Office Jt Indust. Council, 1989–; Treas., Electricity Supply Nat. Jt Council, 1990–. Vice-Pres., Internat. Fedn of Chemical, Energy and Gen. Workers, 1986–. Member: NEDC, 1973–86; Commonwealth Develt Corp., 1979–87; Chm., TUC Gen. Purposes Cttee, 1984–. *Publications:* Pharmaceuticals for the People, 1973; Drug Industry: which way to control, 1975; UK Chemicals: The Way Forward, 1977; Economic Detente, 1980; The Case for Voters Tax Credits, 1983; Forward Labour, 1985; Facts, Figures and Damned Statistics, 1987. *Recreations:* music, American politics, flicking through reference books, films of the thirties and forties. *Address:* 47 Hill Rise, Chorleywood, Rickmansworth, Herts. *T:* Rickmansworth (0923) 778726.

WARBURTON, Prof. Geoffrey Barratt, FEng 1985; Hives Professor of Mechanical Engineering, University of Nottingham, 1982–89; *b* 9 June 1924; *s* of Ernest McPherson and Beatrice Warburton; *m* 1952, Margaret Coan; three *d*. *Educ:* William Hulme's Grammar School, Manchester; Peterhouse, Cambridge (Open Exhibition in Mathematics, 1942; 1st cl. Hons in Mechanical Sciences Tripos, 1944; BA 1945; MA 1949); PhD Edinburgh, 1949. Junior Demonstrator, Cambridge Univ., 1944–46; Asst Lecturer in Engineering, Univ. Coll. of Swansea, 1946–47; Dept of Engineering, Univ. of Edinburgh: Assistant, 1947–48, Lecturer, 1948–50 and 1953–56; ICI Research Fellow, 1950–53; Head of Post-graduate School of Applied Dynamics, 1956–61; Nottingham University: Prof. of Applied Mechanics, 1961–82; a Pro-Vice-Chancellor, 1984–88. Vis. Prof., Dept of Civil Engrg, Imperial Coll., 1990–. FRSE 1960; FIMechE 1968. Rayleigh Medal, Inst. of Acoustics, 1982. Editor, Earthquake Engineering and Structural Dynamics, 1988– (Associate Editor, 1972–88); Member, Editorial Boards: Internat. Jl of Mechanical Sciences, 1967–; Internat. Jl for Numerical Methods in Engineering, 1969–; Jl of Sound and Vibration, 1971–; Communications in Applied Numerical Methods, 1985–. *Publications:* The Dynamical Behaviour of Structures, 1964, 2nd edn 1976; research on mechanical vibrations, in several scientific journals. *Address:* 18 Grangewood Road, Wollaton, Nottingham NG8 2SH.

WARBURTON, Ivor William; General Manager, British Rail London Midland Region, since 1990; *b* 13 Aug. 1946; *s* of late Dennis and of Edna Margaret Warburton; *m* 1969, Carole-Ann (*née* Ashton) (marr. diss. 1982); three *d*. *Educ:* Dulwich Coll.; Queens' Coll., Cambridge (MA); Univ. of Warwick (MSc). FCIT 1989; MCIM. British Railways, 1968–: graduate trainee, 1968–70; local ops posts, London Midland Region, 1970–73; Divl Passenger Manager, Bristol, 1974–78; Overseas Tourist Manager, 1978–82; Regional Passenger Manager, York, 1982–83; Dir, Passenger Marketing Services, 1984–85; Asst Gen. Manager, London Midland Region, 1985–87; Employee Relations Manager, 1987–88; Dir of Operations, 1988–90. *Recreations:* cooking Chinese style, music, opera, handicapped scouting, Marketors' Livery Company. *Address:* 34 St Clair's Road, Croydon CR0 5NE. *T:* 081–688 2742.

WARBURTON, John Kenneth, CBE 1983; Director, Birmingham Chamber of Industry and Commerce, since 1978; Regional Secretary, West Midlands Regional Group of Chambers of Commerce, since 1978; *b* 7 May 1932; *s* of Frederick and Eva Warburton; *m* 1960, Patricia Gordon; one *d*. *Educ:* Newcastle-under-Lyme High Sch.; Keble Coll., Oxford (MA Jurisprudence). Called to Bar, Gray's Inn, 1977. London Chamber of Commerce, 1956–59; Birmingham Chamber of Industry and Commerce, 1959–. President, British Chambers of Commerce Executives, 1979–81; Member: Steering Cttee, Internat. Bureau of Chambers of Commerce, 1976–; Nat. Council, Assoc. of British Chambers of Commerce, 1978–; European Trade Cttee and Business Link Gp, BOTB, 1979–87; E European Trade Council, BOTB, 1984–; Review Body on Doctors' and Dentists' Remuneration, 1982–; MSC Task Gp on Employment Trng, 1987; Disciplinary Panels, FIMBRA, 1989–; Chairman: Adv. Council, W Midlands Industrial Develt Assoc., 1983–86; Birmingham Chamber Trng Ltd, 1987–. Director: Birmingham Venture, 1980–; Business in the Community, 1981–; National Garden Festival 1986 Ltd, 1983–87; Birmingham Convention and Visitor Bureau Ltd, 1986–; Black Business in Birmingham, 1986–89; National Exhibition Centre Ltd, 1989–; Alternate Dir, Birmingham Heartlands Ltd, 1988–. Governor, Univ. of Birmingham, 1982–. FRSA. *Address:* 35 Hampshire Drive, Edgbaston, Birmingham B15 3NY. *T:* 021–454 6764.

WARBURTON, Richard Maurice, OBE 1987; Director General, Royal Society for the Prevention of Accidents, 1979–90; *b* 14 June 1928; *s* of Richard and Phylis Agnes Warburton; *m* 1952, Lois May Green; two *s*. *Educ:* Wigan Grammar Sch.; Birmingham Univ. (BA 1st Cl. Hons). Flying Officer, RAF, 1950–52. HM Inspector of Factories, 1952–79; Head of Accident Prevention Advisory Unit, Health and Safety Executive, 1972–79. *Recreations:* golf, gardening, fell walking. *Address:* Cornaa, Wyfordby Avenue, Blackburn, Lancs BB2 7AR. *T:* Blackburn (0254) 56824.

WARD, family name of **Earl of Dudley** and of **Viscount Bangor.**

WARD, Prof. Alan Gordon, CBE 1972 (OBE 1959); Procter Professor of Food and Leather Science, Leeds University, 1961–77, now Emeritus; *b* 18 April 1914; *s* of Lionel Howell Ward and Lily Maud Ward (*née* Morgan); *m* 1938, Cicely Jean Chapman; one *s* two *d*. *Educ:* Queen Elizabeth's Grammar Sch., Wimborne; Trinity Coll., Cambridge (schol.). BA (Cantab) 1935; MA (Cantab) 1940; FInstP 1946; FIFST 1966; CPhys; FSLTC 1986. Lectr in Physics and Mathematics, N Staffs Technical Coll., 1937–40; Experimental Officer, Min. of Supply, 1940–46; Sen. Scientific Officer, Building Research Station, 1946–48; Principal Scientific Officer, 1948–49; Dir of Research, The British Gelatine and Glue Research Assoc., 1949–59; Prof. of Leather Industries, Leeds Univ., 1959–61. Chm., Food Standards Cttee set up by Minister of Agriculture, 1965–79. Hon. FIFST 1979; Hon. FAIFST 1979. *Publications:* Nature of Crystals, 1938; Colloids, Their Properties and Applications, 1945; The Science and Technology of Gelatin, 1977; papers in Trans. Far. Soc., Jl Sci. Instr, Biochem. Jl, etc. *Recreation:* music. *Address:* 35 Templar Gardens, Wetherby, West Yorkshire LS22 4TG. *T:* Wetherby (0937) 584177.

WARD, Hon. Sir Alan Hylton, Kt 1988; **Hon. Mr Justice Ward;** a Judge of the High Court of Justice, Family Division, since 1988; Family Division Liaison Judge for Midland and Oxford Circuit, since 1990; *b* 15 Feb. 1938; *s* of late Stanley Victor Ward and of Mary Ward; *m* 1st, 1963 (marr. diss. 1982); one *s* two *d*; 2nd, 1983, Helen (*née* Gilbert); twin *d*. *Educ:* Christian Brothers Coll., Pretoria; Univ. of Pretoria (BA, LLB); Pembroke Coll., Cambridge (MA, LLB). Called to the Bar, Gray's Inn, 1964, Bencher, 1988; QC 1984; a Recorder, 1985–88. Formerly an Attorney of Supreme Court of South Africa. Mem., Matrimonial Causes Procedure Cttee, 1982–85. Consulting Editor, Childrens Law and Practice. *Recreations:* hitting or attempting to hit some ball or other. *Address:* Royal Courts of Justice, Strand, WC2. *Club:* MCC.

WARD, (Albert Joseph) Reginald; Chief Executive, ISLEF, since 1989; *b* 5 Oct. 1927; *s* of Albert E. and Gwendolene M. E. Ward, Lydbook, Glos; *m* 1954, Betty Anne Tooze; one *s* one *d*. *Educ:* East Dean Grammar Sch., Cinderford, Glos; Univ. of Manchester (BA Hons History). HM Inspector of Taxes, 1952–65; Chief Administrator, County Architects Dept, Lancashire CC, 1965–68; Business Manager, Shankland Cox & Associates, 1968–69; Corporation Secretary, Irvine New Town Development Corporation, 1969–72; Chief Executive: Coatbridge Borough Council, 1972–74; London Borough of Hammersmith, 1974–76; Hereford and Worcester CC, 1976–80; LDDC, 1981–88. Mem., Duke of Edinburgh's Commn into Housing, 1986–87. Hon. Fellow, QMC, 1987. FRSA. *Recreations:* walking, tennis, music, architecture and urban design. *Address:* Abbott's Court, Deerhurst, Gloucester GL19 4BX. *T:* Tewkesbury (0684) 292663; 12 Elephant Lane, SE16.

WARD, Mrs Ann Sarita; Board Member, International Shakespeare Globe Centre, since 1988; Chairman, Friends of the Southwark Globe, since 1987; *b* 4 Aug. 1923; *d* of Denis Godfrey and Marion Phyllis Godfrey; *m* Frank Ward (*d* 1991); one *s*. *Educ:* St Paul's Girls' Sch., Hammersmith. Professional photographer; photo journalist, Daily Mail, 1962–67, Daily Mirror, 1967–70; award winner, British Press Photographs of Year, 1967. Councillor, London Bor. of Southwark, 1971–86 (Dep. Leader, 1978–83); Chm., ILEA, 1981–82. Contested (Lab) Streatham, Gen. Election, 1970. Mem., Lambeth, Southwark, Lewisham FHSA, 1991–; Associate Mem., Camberwell HA, 1990– (Mem., 1982–90). Special Trustee, KCH, 1983–88. *Recreations:* theatre, gardening. *Address:* 204 Peckham Rye, SE22 0LU. *T:* 081–693 4251.

WARD, Ven. Arthur Frederick, BA; Archdeacon of Exeter, 1970–81, Archdeacon Emeritus since 1981; Canon Residentiary of Exeter Cathedral, 1970–81, Precentor, 1972–81; *b* 23 April 1912; *s* of William Thomas and Annie Florence Ward, Corbridge, Northumberland; *m* 1937, Margaret Melrose, Tynemouth, Northumberland; two *d*. *Educ:* Durham Choir School; Newcastle upon Tyne Royal Grammar School; Durham University; Ridley Hall, Cambridge. Curate, Byker Parish Church, Newcastle, 1935–40; Rector of Harpurhey, North Manchester, 1940–44; Vicar of Nelson, 1944–55; Vicar of Christ Church, Paignton, 1955–62; Archdeacon of Barnstaple and Rector of Shirwell with Loxhore, Devon, 1962–70. *Recreations:* gardening, cricket, touring. *Address:* Melrose, Christow, Devon EX6 7LY. *T:* Christow (0647) 52498.

WARD, Sir Arthur (Hugh), KBE 1979 (OBE 1962); ACA; FNZIAS; Chancellor, Massey University, 1975–81 (Pro-Chancellor, 1970–75); *b* 25 March 1906; *s* of Arthur Ward and Ada Elizabeth Ward; *m* 1936, Jean Bannatyne Mueller; one *s* three *d*. *Educ:* Middlesbrough High Sch., Yorks. ACA (NZ); FNZIAS 1969. Sec., NZ Co-op. Herd Testing Assoc., 1929–36; Dir, Herd Improvement, NZ Dairy Bd, 1945–54; Gen. Man., Dairy Bd, 1954–70. Chm., W. M. Angus & Co., 1970–75; Dep. Chm., Ivon Watkins Dow, 1971–76. Member: NZ Monetary and Econ. Council, 1970–79; Remuneration Authority, 1971–72; National Res. Adv. Council, 1970–72 (Chm., 1971–72); Council, Massey Univ., 1967–81. Hon. DSc Massey. Marsden Medal for services to science, 1975; Queen's Silver Jubilee Medal, 1977. *Publications:* A Command of Co-operatives, 1975; articles on dairy cattle husbandry and dairy cattle breeding. *Recreations:* writing, reading, gardening, golf. *Address:* 4 Pukeko Street, Woodlands, Waikanae, New Zealand. *T:* Waikanae 36466; PO Box 56, Waikanae.

WARD, Cecil, CBE 1989; JP; Town Clerk, Belfast City Council, 1979–89; *b* 26 Oct. 1929; *s* of William and Mary Caroline Ward. *Educ:* Technical High Sch., Belfast; College of Technology, Belfast. Employed by Belfast City Council (formerly Belfast County Borough Council), 1947–89; Asst Town Clerk (Administration), 1977–79. Mem., Local Govt Staff Commn, 1983–89. Member: Arts Council NI, 1980–85, 1987–89; Bd, Ulster Mus., 1989–; Dir, Ulster Orchestra Soc., 1980– (Chm., 1990–). Mem., Senate, QUB, 1990–. JP Belfast, 1988. Hon. MA QUB, 1988. *Recreations:* music, reading, hill walking. *Address:* 24 Thornhill, Malone, Belfast, Northern Ireland BT9 6SS. *T:* Belfast (0232) 668950.

WARD, Rev. Canon Charles Leslie; Canon Treasurer of Wells and Prebendary of Warminster in Wells Cathedral, 1978–85, now Canon Emeritus; pastoral care for Elmore and Longney, Gloucester, since 1990; *b* 11 June 1916; *s* of Amos Ward and Maude Hazeldine Ballard; *m* 1943, Barbara, *d* of George and Alice Stoneman; two *s*. *Educ:* Mexborough Grammar Sch.; Lichfield Theological Coll. (Potter-Selwyn Exhibnr). Underground Surveyor, Cadeby Colliery, S Yorks, 1933–36. Assistant Curate: Parkgate, 1939; Rossington, 1940; Taunton, 1942; Bishop of Blackburn's Youth Chaplain and Succentor of Blackburn Cathedral, 1945; Vicar: St Michael, Ashton on Ribble, 1948; St Peter, Cheltenham, 1951; Northleach, Stowell, Hampnett, Yanworth and Eastington, 1960; Holy Trinity, Yeovil, 1964; Minehead, 1967. Fellow, St Paul's and St Mary's Colls, Cheltenham, 1954–. *Recreations:* church spotting, driving motor cars, listening to music. *Address:* 23 Clover Drive, Hardwicke, Gloucester GL2 6TG. *T:* Gloucester (0452) 720015.

WARD, Christopher John; Editorial Director and Joint Founder, Redwood Publishing, since 1983; Director, Acorn Computer plc, since 1983; *b* 25 Aug. 1942; *s* of John Stanley Ward and Jacqueline Law-Hume Costin; *m* 1st, 1971 (marr. diss.); one *s* two *d*; 2nd, 1990, Nonie Niesewand (*née* Fogarty). *Educ:* King's Coll. Sch., Wimbledon. Successively on staff of Driffield Times, 1959, and Newcastle Evening Chronicle, 1960–63; reporter, sub-editor, then feature writer and columnist, 1963–76, Daily Mirror; Assistant Editor: Sunday Mirror, 1976–79; Daily Mirror, 1979–81; Editor, Daily Express, 1981–83. *Publications:* How to Complain, 1974; Our Cheque is in the Post, 1980. *Recreations:* competition pistol shooting, walking in the Cheviots. *Address:* 147 Marlborough, 61 Walton Street, SW3 2JZ. *Club:* Savile.

WARD, Christopher John Ferguson; solicitor; Managing Partner, Clarks, Reading, since 1990; *b* 26 Dec. 1942; *m* Janet Ward, JP, LLB; one *s* one *d* and two *s* one *d* by former marr. *Educ:* Magdalen College Sch.; Law Society Sch. of Law. MP (C) Swindon, Oct. 1969–June 1970; contested (C) Eton and Slough, 1979. Mem., Berks CC, 1965–81 (Leader of the Council and Chm., Policy Cttee, 1979–81). Chm., Assoc. of Nursery Trng Colls, 1990–; Gov., Chiltern Nursery Trng Coll., 1975– (Chm., 1988–91). Hon. Sec., United & Cecil Club, 1982–87. *Address:* Ramblings, Maidenhead Thicket, Berks SL6 3QE. *T:* Littlewick Green (0628) 822577; (office) Reading (0734) 604687. *Club:* Carlton.

WARD, (Christopher) John (William); Head of Development, Opera North, since 1988; *b* 21 June 1942; *s* of late Thomas Maxfield and of Peggy Ward; *m* 1970, Diane Lelliott (marr. diss. 1988). *Educ:* Oundle Sch.; Corpus Christi Coll., Oxford (BA LitHum); Univ. of East Anglia (Graduate DipEcon). Overseas and Economic Intelligence Depts, Bank of England, 1965; General Secretary, Bank of England Staff Organisation, 1973; Gen. Sec., Assoc. of First Div. Civil Servants, 1980. *Recreations:* opera, theatre, football. *Address:* Opera North, Grand Theatre, 46 New Briggate, Leeds LS1 6NU. *T:* Leeds (0532) 439999. *Club:* Swindon Town Supporters.

WARD, David; Partner, Atkinson & North, Solicitors, Carlisle, since 1964; President, The Law Society, 1989–90; *b* 23 Feb. 1937; *s* of Rev. Frank Ward, Darfield, Yorks, and Elizabeth Ward (*née* Pattinson), Appleby, Westmorland; *m* 1978, Antoinette, *d* of Maj.-Gen. D. A. B. Clarke, CB, CBE; two *s* one *d*. *Educ:* Dame Allan's Sch., Newcastle upon Tyne; Queen Elizabeth Grammar Sch., Penrith; St Edmund Hall, Oxford (BA). Admitted solicitor, 1962. Articled Clerk, 1959, Assistant, 1962, Atkinson & North. Mem., Lord Chancellor's Adv. Cttee on Legal Educn and Conduct, 1991–. Mem. Council, 1972–91, Vice-Pres., 1988–89, Law Soc.; Pres., Carlisle and District Law Soc., 1985–86. Pres., Carlisle Mountaineering Club, 1985–88. Methodist local preacher, 1955–. *Recreations:* mountaineering, choral and church music. *Address:* The Green, Caldbeck, Wigton, Cumbria. *T:* Caldbeck (06998) 220.

WARD, Rev. David Conisbee; Vicar of St Paul's, Hook, Surrey, since 1987; *b* 7 Jan. 1933; *s* of late Sydney L. Ward and Ivy A. Ward; *m* 1958, Patricia Jeanette (*née* Nobes); one *s* one *d*. *Educ:* Kingston Grammar Sch.; St John's Coll., Cambridge (Scholar, MA). Asst Principal, Nat. Assistance Bd, 1956, Principal, 1961; Asst Sec., DHSS, 1970, Under Sec., 1976–83. Southwark Ordination Course, 1977–80; Deacon, 1980; Priest, 1981; Non-Stipendiary Curate, St Matthew, Surbiton, 1980–83; Curate, Immanuel Church, Streatham Common, 1983–84, parish priest, 1984–87. Governor, Kingston GS, 1988–. *Recreations:* member Chelsea FC; Pitcairn Islands Study Group (philately) (Dir-at-Large, and Chm. UK Chapter). *Address:* The Vicarage, 278 Hook Road, Hook, Chessington, Surrey KT9 1PF. *T:* 081-397 3521. *Club:* Sion College.

WARD, Donald Albert; *b* 30 March 1920; *s* of Albert and Rosie Ward; *m* 1948, Maureen Molloy; five *s*. *Educ:* Brewery Road Elementary Sch.; Southend-on-Sea High Sch.; The Queen's Coll., Oxford. BA(Hons)(Maths); MA. Served War, Indian Army (RIASC), 10th Indian Div., Middle East and Italy, 1940–45 (despatches). Min. of Food, 1946–53; Export Credits Guarantee Dept, 1953–74 (Under-Sec., 1971–74); Sec. Gen., Internat. Union of Credit and Investment Insurers (Berne Union), 1974–86. *Address:* Lindisfarne, St Nicholas Hill, Leatherhead, Surrey KT22 8NE. *Club:* United Oxford & Cambridge University.

WARD, General Sir Dudley, GCB 1959 (KCB 1957; CB 1945); KBE 1953 (CBE 1945); DSO 1944; *b* 27 Jan. 1905; *s* of L. H. Ward, Wimborne, Dorset; *m* 1st, 1933, Beatrice Constance (*d* 1962), *d* of Rev. T. F. Griffith, The Bourne, Farnham, Surrey; one *d*; 2nd, 1963, Joan Elspeth de Pechell, *d* of late Colonel D. C. Scott, CBE, Netherbury, Dorset. *Educ:* Wimborne Grammar Sch.; Royal Military Coll., Sandhurst. 2nd Lieut, Dorset Regt, 1929; Captain, The King's Regt, 1937. Served War of 1939–45 (DSO, CBE, CB); Director of Military Operations, War Office, 1947–48; Commandant, Staff Coll., Camberley, 1948–51; Commander of the 1st Corps, 1951–52; Deputy Chief of Imperial General Staff, 1953–56; Commander, Northern Army Group and Commander-in-Chief, British Army of the Rhine, 1957–Dec. 1959; Comdr in Chief, British Forces, Near East, 1960–62; Governor and Commander in Chief of Gibraltar, 1962–65. Colonel, King's Regt, 1947–57; Colonel Commandant, REME, 1958–63; ADC General to the Queen, 1959–61. DL Suffolk, 1968–84. Order of Suvorov, USSR, 1944; Legion of Merit, USA, 1946. *Recreation:* golf. *Address:* Wynney's Farmhouse, Dennington, Woodbridge, Suffolk. *T:* Badingham (072875) 663. *Club:* Army and Navy.

WARD, Edmund Fisher, CBE 1972; Architect; Member, Royal Fine Art Commission, 1974–83; Consultant (formerly Partner), Gollins Melvin Ward Partnership. *Address:* White Cottage, The Street, Chipperfield, near Kings Langley, Hertfordshire WD4 9BH.

WARD, Edward; *see* Bangor, 7th Viscount.

WARD, Ven. Edwin James Greenfield, LVO 1963; Archdeacon of Sherborne, 1968–84; Archdeacon Emeritus and Canon Emeritus of Salisbury Cathedral, since 1985; Extra Chaplain to the Queen, since 1989 (Chaplain, 1955–89); *b* 26 Oct. 1919; *er s* of Canon F. G. Ward, MC, lately of Canberra, Australia; *m* 1946, Grizell Evelyn Buxton (*d* 1985); one *s* two *d*. *Educ:* St John's, Leatherhead; Christ's Coll., Cambridge (MA). Served King's Dragoon Guards, 1940; Reserve, 1946. Ordained 1948; Vicar of North Elmham, Norfolk, 1950–55; Chaplain, Royal Chapel, Windsor Great Park, 1955–67; Rector of West Stafford, 1967–84. Mem. of Council, Marlborough Coll., 1969–88; Visitor, Milton Abbey School, 1991– (Mem., Bd of Govs, 1983). *Recreation:* fishing. *Address:* 14 Arle Close, Alresford, Hants SO14 9BG. *T:* Alresford (0962) 735501.

See also Rt Hon. J. Wakeham.

WARD, Air Cdre Ellacott Lyne Stephens, CB 1954; DFC 1939; RAF, retired; *b* 22 Aug. 1905; *s* of late Lt-Col E. L. Ward, CBE, IMS; *m* 1929, Sylvia Winifred Constance Etheridge (*d* 1974), *d* of late Lt-Col F. Etheridge, DSO, IA, and late Mrs Etheridge; one *s* one *d*. *Educ:* Bradfield; Cranwell. No 20 Sqdn, India, 1926–30; Engineering Course, and Engineering duties, UK, 1930–34; Instr, Sch. of Army Co-operation, RAF Old Sarum, 1934–36; student, Army Staff Coll., Quetta, 1936–37; comd No 28 Sqdn, RAF, 1938–39; MAP, 1940–42; Instructor, RAF Staff Coll., 1942–43; commanded stns in 5 Gp, Bomber Comd, 1943–45; Dep. Head, RAF Mission to Chinese Air Force Staff Coll., Chengtu, China, 1945–46; SASO, Burma, 1946–47; Air Ministry, 1947–49; Flying Training Comd, 1949–52; Head of British Services Mission to Burma, 1952–54; AOC No 64 (N) Group, Royal Air Force, 1954–57. Chinese Cloud and Banner, 1946; Chinese Chenyuan, 1946. *Recreation:* (retired from) bookbinding. *Address:* Carousel, 37 Brownsea Road, Sandbanks, Poole, Dorset BH13 7QW. *T:* Canford Cliffs (0202) 709455.

WARD, Frank Dixon; *see* Dixon Ward.

WARD, Hubert, MA; JP; Headmaster of the King's School, Ely, 1970–Aug. 1992; *b* 26 Sept. 1931; *s* of Allan Miles Ward and Joan Mary Ward; *m* 1958, Elizabeth Cynthia Fearn Bechervaise; one *s* two *d*. *Educ:* Westminster Sch.; Trinity Coll., Cambridge. Asst Master (Maths), Geelong C of E Grammar Sch., Victoria, 1955–66; Asst Master (Maths), Westminster Sch., London, 1966–69. Mem. (L)·Cambs CC, 1985–89. JP Cambs, 1976. *Publication:* (with K. Lewis) Starting Statistics, 1969. *Recreations:* rowing, sailing, bird-watching. *Address:* (until Sept. 1992) The King's School, Ely, Cambridgeshire CB7 4DB. *T:* Ely (0353) 662824; (from Oct. 1992) 1 The Green, Mistley, Essex.

WARD, Prof. Ian Macmillan, FRS 1983; FInstP; Professor of Physics, University of Leeds, since 1970; *b* 9 April 1928; *s* of Harry Ward and Joan Moodie (*née* Burt); *m* 1960, Margaret (*née* Linley); two *s* one *d*. *Educ:* Royal Grammar Sch., Newcastle upon Tyne; Magdalen Coll., Oxford (MA, DPhil). FInstP 1965; FPRI 1974. Technical Officer, ICI Fibres, 1954–61; seconded to Division of Applied Mathematics, Brown Univ., USA, 1961–62; Head of Basic Physics Section, ICI Fibres, 1962–65, ICI Research Associate, 1964; Sen. Lectr in Physics of Materials, Univ. of Bristol, 1965–69; Chm., Dept of Physics, Univ. of Leeds, 1975–78, 1987–89. Dir, IRC in Polymer Science and Technol., 1989–. Secretary, Polymer Physics Gp, Inst. of Physics, 1964–71, Chm. 1971–75; Chairman, Macromolecular Physics Gp, European Physical Soc., 1976–81; Pres., British Soc. of Rheology, 1984–86. A. A. Griffith Medal, 1982; S. G. Smith Meml Medal, Textile Inst., 1984; Swinburne Medal, Plastics and Rubber Inst., 1988. *Publications:* Mechanical Properties of Solid Polymers, 1971, 2nd edn 1983; (ed) Structure and Properties of Oriented Polymers, 1975; (ed jtly) Ultra High Modulus Polymers, 1979; contribs to Polymer, Jl of Polymer Science, Jl of Materials Science, Proc. Royal Soc., etc. *Recreations:* music, walking. *Address:* Kirkskill, 2 Creskeld Drive, Bramhope, Leeds LS16 9EL. *T:* Leeds (0532) 673637.

WARD, Ivor William, (Bill), OBE 1968; independent televison producer and director, since 1982; Deputy Managing Director, Associated Television (Network) Ltd, 1974–77; *b* 19 Jan. 1916; *s* of Stanley James Ward and Emily Ward; *m* 1st, 1940, Patricia Aston; two *s* one *d*; 2nd, 1970, Betty Nichols; one step *s*; 3rd, 1988, Sandra Calkins Hastie. *Educ:* Hoe Grammar Sch., Plymouth. Asst Engr, BBC Radio Plymouth, 1932; Technical Asst, BBC Experimental TV Service, Alexandra Palace, 1936; Maintenance Engr, BBC TV London, 1937. Instructor Radar, REME and Military Coll. of Science, 1939–45. Studio Manager, BBC TV, 1946; Producer, BBC TV, 1947–55; Head of Light Entertainment, ATV (Network) ITV, 1955–61; Production Controller, ATV, 1961–63; Executive Controller and Production Controller, ATV, 1963–67; Director of Programmes, ATV, 1968–76. Chm., ITV Network Sports Cttee, 1972–77; Head of Ops Gp, EBU: World Cup 1978, 1977–78; Moscow Olympics 1980, 1978–82; Exec. producer, Highway series, ITV, 1983. FRTS 1989; FRSA. *Recreations:* sport, golf, fishing, motor sport and motor cars, photography, music. *Address:* 50 Frith Street, W1.

WARD, John; *see* Ward, C. J. W.

WARD, Most Rev. John Aloysius; *see* Cardiff, Archbishop of, (RC).

WARD, Prof. John Clive, FRS 1965; Professor, Macquarie University, Sydney, NSW, 1967–84, now Emeritus; *b* 1 Aug. 1924; *s* of Joseph William Ward and Winifred Palmer. *Educ:* Bishops Stortford Coll.; Merton Coll., Oxford. Member, Inst. for Advanced Study, Princeton, 1951–52, 1955–56, 1960–61; Professor of Physics, Carnegie Inst. of Technology, Pittsburgh, 1959–60; The Johns Hopkins University, Baltimore, 1961–66. Hughes Medal, Royal Soc., 1983. *Publications:* various articles on particle theory and statistical mechanics. *Recreations:* ski-ing, music. *Address:* 16 Fern Street, Pymble, NSW 2073, Australia.

WARD, John Devereux, CBE 1973; BSc; CEng, FICE, FIStructE; MP (C) Poole, since 1979; *b* 8 March 1925; *s* of late Thomas Edward and Evelyn Victoria Ward; *m* 1955, Jean Miller Aitken; one *s* one *d*. *Educ:* Romford County Technical Sch.; Univ. of St Andrews (BSc). Navigator, RAF, 1943–47; student, 1949–53. Employed, Consulting Engineers, 1953–58, Taylor Woodrow Ltd, 1958–79; Man. Dir, Taylor Woodrow Arcon, Arcon Building Exports, 1976–78. PPS to: Financial Sec. to Treasury, 1984–86; Sec. of State for Social Security, 1987–89. UK Rep. to Council of Europe and WEU, 1983–87, 1989–. Chm., Wessex Area Conservatives, 1966–69; Conservative Party: Mem., Nat. Union Exec., 1965–78 (Mem., Gen. Purposes Cttee, 1966–72, 1975–78); Mem., Central Bd of Finance, 1969–78; Vice-Chm., Cons. Trade and Industry Cttee, 1983–84. *Address:* 54 Parkstone Road, Poole, Dorset BH15 2PX. *T:* Poole (0202) 674771.

WARD, John Stanton, CBE 1985; RA 1965 (ARA 1956); RP 1952; *b* 10 Oct. 1917; *s* of Russell Stanton and Jessie Elizabeth Ward; *m* 1950, Alison Christine Mary Williams; four *s* twin *d*. *Educ:* St Owen's School, Hereford; Royal College of Art. Royal Engineers, 1939–46. Vogue Magazine, 1948–52. Former Vice-Pres., Royal Soc. of Portrait Painters. Mem. Exec., Nat. Art-Collections Fund, 1976–87. Trustee, Royal Acad. Has held exhibitions at Agnews Gallery and Maas Gallery. Hon. DLitt. *Recreation:* book illustration. *Address:* Bilting Court, Bilting, Ashford, Kent. *T:* Wye (0233) 812478. *Clubs:* Athenæum, Buck's, Harry's Bar.

WARD, Rev. Prof. (John Stephen) Keith; Regius Professor of Divinity, University of Oxford, since 1991; Canon of Christ Church, Oxford, since 1991; *b* 22 Aug. 1938; *s* of John George Ward and Evelyn (*née* Simpson); *m* 1963, Marian Trotman; one *s* one *d*. *Educ:* Universities of Wales and Oxford. BA Wales, BLitt Oxon; MA Cantab. Ordained priest of Church of England, 1972. Lecturer in Logic, Univ. of Glasgow, 1964–69; Lectr in Philosophy, Univ. of St Andrews, 1969–71; Lectr in Philosophy of Religion, Univ. of London, 1971–75; Dean of Trinity Hall, Cambridge, 1975–82. F. D. Maurice Prof. of Moral and Social Theology, Univ. of London, 1982–85; Prof. of History and Phil. of Religion, King's Coll. London, 1985–91. Jt editor, Religious Studies, 1990–. *Publications:* Ethics and Christianity, 1970; Kant's View of Ethics, 1972; The Divine Image, 1976; The

Concept of God, 1977; The Promise, 1981; Rational Theology and the Creativity of God, 1982; Holding Fast to God, 1982; The Living God, 1984; Battle for the Soul, 1985; Images of Eternity, 1987; The Rule of Love, 1989; Divine Action, 1990. *Recreations*: music, walking. *Address*: Christ Church, Oxford OX1 1DP. *T*: Oxford (0865) 276246.

WARD, Joseph Haggitt; *b* 7 July 1926; *s* of Joseph G. and Gladys Ward; *m* 1961, Anthea Clemo; one *s* one *d*. *Educ*: St Olave's Grammar School; Sidney Sussex College, Cambridge. Asst Principal, Min. of National Insurance, 1951; Private Sec. to Minister of Social Security, 1966–68; Asst Sec., 1968; Min. of Housing, later DoE, 1969–72; DHSS, 1972; Under-Sec. (pensions and nat. insce contributions), DHSS, 1976–86. *Recreations*: music, history of music. *Address*: 34 Uffington Road, SE27 0ND. *T*: 081–670 1732.

WARD, Sir Joseph James Laffey, 4th Bt *cr* 1911; *b* 11 Nov. 1946; *s* of Sir Joseph George Davidson Ward, 3rd Bt, and of Joan Mary Haden, *d* of Major Thomas J. Laffey, NZSC; *S* father, 1970; *m* 1968, Robyn Allison, *d* of William Maitland Martin, Rotorua, NZ; one *s* one *d*. *Heir*: *s* Joseph James Martin Ward, *b* 20 Feb. 1971.

WARD, Keith; *see* Ward, J. S. K.

WARD, Malcolm Beverley; His Honour Judge Malcolm Ward; a Circuit Judge, Midland and Oxford Circuit, since 1979; *b* 3 May 1931; *s* of Edgar and Dora Mary Ward; *m* 1958, Muriel Winifred, *d* of Dr E. D. M. Wallace, Perth; two *s* two *d*. *Educ*: Wolverhampton Grammar Sch.; St John's Coll., Cambridge (Open Mathematical Schol.; MA, LLM). Called to the Bar, Inner Temple, 1956; practised Oxford (later Midland and Oxford) Circuit; a Recorder of the Crown Court, 1974–79. Governor, Wolverhampton Grammar Sch., 1972– (Chm., 1981–). *Recreations*: golf, music, (in theory) horticulture. *Address*: 1 Fountain Court, Birmingham B4 6DR.

WARD, Malcolm Stanley; Director and Editor, Metro News, Birmingham, since 1986; *b* 24 Sept. 1951; *s* of Hugh Ward and Rebecca Ward (*née* Rogerson). *Educ*: Gilberd School, Colchester. Dep. Editor, Gulf News, Dubai, 1978–79; Editor, Woodham and Wickford Chronicle, Essex, 1979–81; Dep. Editor, Gulf Times, Qatar, 1981–84; Dep. Editor, Daily News, Birmingham, 1984–86. *Recreations*: writing, travel, soccer, driving, tennis. *Address*: 3 Rectory Park Avenue, Sutton Coldfield, West Midlands B75 7BL. *T*: 021–329 2589.

WARD, Martyn Eric; Hon. Mr Justice Ward; Judge of the Supreme Court of Bermuda, since 1987; *b* 10 Oct. 1927; 3rd *s* of Arthur George Ward, DSM and Dorothy Ward (*née* Perkins); *m* 1st, 1957, Rosaleen Iona Soloman; one *d*; 2nd, 1966, Rosanna Maria Giubarelli; two *s*. Royal Navy, 1945–48. Called to Bar, Lincoln's Inn, 1955. A Circuit Judge, 1972–87. *Recreations*: ski-ing, tennis, swimming. *Address*: c/o Supreme Court, 21 Parliament Street, Hamilton HL12, Bermuda.

WARD, Michael Jackson, CBE 1980; British Council Director, Germany, 1990–91, retired; *b* 16 Sept. 1931; *s* of late Harry Ward, CBE, and Dorothy Julia Ward (*née* Clutterbuck); *m* 1955, Eileen Patricia Foster; one *s* one *d*. *Educ*: Drayton Manor Grammar Sch.; University Coll. London (BA); Univ. of Freiburg; Corpus Christi Coll., Oxford. HM Forces, 1953–55; 2nd Lieut Royal Signals. Admin. Officer, HMOCS, serving as Dist Comr and Asst Sec. to Govt, Gilbert and Ellice Is; British Council, 1961–91: Schs Recruitment Dept, 1961–64; Regional Rep., Sarawak, 1964–68; Dep. Rep., Pakistan, 1968–70; Dir, Appointments Services Dept, 1970–72; Dir, Personnel Dept, 1972–75; Controller, Personnel and Appts Div., 1975–77; Representative, Italy, 1977–81; Controller, Home Div., 1981–85; Asst Dir-Gen., 1985–90. Hon. Mem., British Council, 1991. *Recreations*: music, golf. *Address*: 1 Knapp Rise, Haslingfield, Cambridge CB3 7LO. *Clubs*: National Liberal; Gog Magog Golf.

WARD, Michael John; Assistant General Secretary, Public Relations, Association of Chief Officers of Probation, since 1989; *b* 7 April 1931; *s* of late Stanley William Ward and Margaret Annie Ward; *m* 1953, Lilian Lomas; two *d*. *Educ*: Mawney Road Jun. Mixed Sch., Romford; Royal Liberty Sch., Romford; Bungay Grammar Sch.; Univ. of Manchester. BA (Admin). MIPR. Education Officer, RAF, 1953–57; Registrar, Chartered Inst. of Secretaries, 1958–60; S. J. Noel-Brown & Co. Ltd: O&M consultant to local authorities, 1960–61; Local Govt Officer to Labour Party, 1961–65; Public Relns consultant to local authorities, 1965–70; Press Officer, ILEA, 1970–74 and 1979–80; Public Relns Officer, London Borough of Lewisham, 1980–84; Dir of Information, ILEA, 1984–86; Public Affairs Officer, Gas Consumers Council, 1986–88; Exec. Officer to Rt Hon. Paddy Ashdown, MP, 1988–89. Contested: (Lab) Peterborough, 1966, 1970, Feb. 1974; (SDP/Alliance) Tonbridge and Malling, 1987. MP (Lab) Peterborough, Oct. 1974–1979; PPS to Sec. of State for Educn and Science, 1975–76, to Minister for Overseas Develt, 1976, to Minister of State, FCO, 1976–79. Sponsored Unfair Contract Terms Act, 1977. Councillor, Borough of Romford, 1958–65; London Borough of Havering: Councillor, 1964–78; Alderman, 1971–78; Leader of Council, 1971–74. Labour Chief Whip, London Boroughs Assoc., 1968–71; Member: Essex River Authority, 1964–71; Greenwich DHA, 1982–85; Greenwich and Bexley FPC, 1982–85; Hon. Treas., GLAA, 1969–71; Pres., London Govt Public Relations Assoc., 1977–79. *Recreations*: gardens, music, reading, travel. *Address*: 1A Vanbrugh Terrace, Blackheath, SE3 7AP. *Club*: National Liberal.

WARD, Michael Phelps, CBE 1983; FRCS; FRGS; Consultant Surgeon: City and East London Area Health Authority (Teaching), since 1964; St Andrew's Hospital, Bow, since 1964; Newham Hospital, since 1983; Lecturer in Clinical Surgery, London Hospital Medical College, since 1975; *b* 26 March 1925; *s* of late Wilfrid Arthur Ward, CMG, MC and Norah Anne Phelps; *m* 1957, Felicity Jane Ewbank; one *s*. *Educ*: Marlborough Coll., Wilts; Peterhouse, Cambridge (Ironmongers' Co. Exhibn); London Hosp. Med. Coll. BA Hons Cantab 1945, MA 1961; MB BChir 1949, MD 1968. FRCS 1955. Ho. Surg., Surgical Registrar, Sen. Surgical Registrar, London Hosp.; Asst Resident, Royal Victoria Hosp., Montreal, Canada; Consultant Surg., Poplar Hosp., E14, 1964–75; Hunterian Prof., RCS, 1954. Served RAMC, Captain, 1950–52. Fellow, Assoc. of Surgs of Gt Britain; FRSM. Mem., Court of Assts, Soc. of Apothecaries, 1986. Mount Everest Reconnaissance Expedn, 1951; Mount Everest Expedn, 1953 (1st Ascent); Scientific Expedn to Everest Region, 1960–61 (Leader, 1st Winter Ascents of Amadablam and other peaks); Scientific Expedns to Bhutan Himal, 1964 and 1965; scientific and mountaineering expedn to West Kun Lun, China, 1980–81; Royal Soc./Chinese Acad. of Sciences Tibet Geotraverse, 1985. FRGS 1964. Dickson Asia Lectr, RGS, 1966, 1985; Cuthbert Peek Award, RGS, 1973; Founder's (Royal) Medal, RGS, 1982; Cullum Medal, Amer. Geog. Soc., 1954. Chm., Mount Everest Foundn, 1978–80. *Publications*: Mountaineers' Companion, 1966; In this Short Span, 1972; Mountain Medicine, 1975; (jtly) High Altitude Medicine and Physiology, 1989; many scientific and medical papers on the effects of great altitude, exposure to cold, and on exercise; also on exploratory journeys to Nepal, Bhutan, Chinese Central Asia and Tibet. *Recreations*: mountaineering, ski-ing. *Clubs*: Athenæum, Alpine (Vice-Pres., 1968–69).

WARD, Air Vice-Marshal Peter Alexander; General Manager, Bromley Health Authority, 1985; *b* 26 Jan. 1930; *s* of Arthur Charles Ward and Laura Mary (*née* Squires); *m* 1963, Patricia Louise (*née* Robertson); two *s*. *Educ*: Woking Grammar School. Joined RAF, 1947; Flying and Staff appointments; OC 511 Sqdn, 1968–70; jssc 1970; ndc 1971; Station Comdr, RAF Brize Norton, 1974–75; Senior Air Staff Officer, HQ 38 Group, 1976–79; rcds 1979; Dir Gen., RAF Training, 1980–82; Dep. COS (Ops), HQ Allied Air Forces Central Europe, 1982–84. *Address*: Whiteladies, 49 Marlings Park Avenue, Chislehurst, Kent. *Club*: Royal Air Force.

WARD, Maj.-Gen. Sir Philip (John Newling), KCVO 1976; CBE 1972; Vice Lord Lieutenant for West Sussex, since 1990; *b* 10 July 1924; *s* of George William Newling Ward and Mary Florence Ward; *m* 1948, Pamela Ann Glennie; two *s* two *d*. Commnd Welsh Guards, 1943; Adjt, RMA Sandhurst, 1960–62; Bde Major, Household Bde, 1962–65; Comdg 1st Bn Welsh Guards, 1965–67; Comdr Land Forces, Gulf, 1969–71; GOC London Dist and Maj.-Gen. comdg Household Div., 1973–76; Comdt, RMA, 1976–79. Communar of Chichester Cathedral, 1980–83. Dir, Public Affairs, Internat. Distillers and Vintners (UK), 1980–89; Chm., Peter Hamilton Security Consultants, 1986–90; Director: W & A Gilbey (formerly Gilbey Vintners), 1983–89; Morgan Furze, 1983–89; Justerini & Brooks, 1987–89; Southern Reg., Lloyds Bank, 1983–90. Chairman: Queen Alexandra Hosp. Home; Royal Soldiers Daughters School, 1980–83; Governor and Comdt, Church Lads and Church Girls Bde., 1980–86. Freeman, City of London, 1976. DL West Sussex, 1981, High Sheriff, 1985–86. *Recreation*: gardening. *Address*: 15 Tarrant Wharf, Arundel, W Sussex BN18 9NY. *Clubs*: Cavalry and Guards (Chm., 1987–90), Buck's.

WARD, Reginald; *see* Ward, A. J. R.

WARD, Reginald George; Assistant Director, Central Statistical Office, since 1989; *b* 6 July 1942; *s* of Thomas George and Ada May Ward; *m* 1964, Chandan Mistry; two *s* one *d*. *Educ*: Leicester, Aberdeen and Oxford Universities; London Business Sch. Lectr in Economics, St Andrews Univ., 1965; Analyst, National Cash Register, 1969; Economist, ICL, 1970; DTI, 1971; Chief Statistician: HM Treasury, 1978; Cabinet Office, 1982; Dir, Business Statistics Office, DTI, 1986. *Recreation*: sailing. *Address*: Millbank Tower, Millbank, SW1P 4QP.

WARD, Maj.-Gen. Robert William, CB 1989; MBE 1972; *b* 17 Oct. 1935; *s* of late Lt-Col William Denby Ward and Monica Thérèse Ward (*née* Collett-White); *m* 1966, Lavinia Dorothy Cramsie; two *s* one *d*. *Educ*: Rugby School; RMA Sandhurst. Commissioned Queen's Bays (later 1st Queen's Dragoon Guards), 1955; served Jordan, Libya, BAOR, Borneo and Persian Gulf; MA to C-in-C BAOR, 1973–75; CO 1st Queen's Dragoon Guards, 1975–77; Col GS Staff Coll., 1977–79; Comdr 22 Armd Brigade, 1979–82; RCDS Canada, 1982–83; Asst Chief of Staff, Northern Army Group, 1983–86; GOC Western Dist, 1986–89, retd. *Recreations*: gardening, outdoor sports, country pursuits, travel, food, wine. *Address*: Lloyds Bank, Cox's & King's, PO Box 1190, 7 Pall Mall, SW1Y 5NA. *Clubs*: Cavalry and Guards, MCC, I Zingari.

WARD, Robin William; Director-General, West Yorkshire Passenger Transport Executive, 1976–82; *b* 14 Jan. 1931; *s* of William Frederick and Elsie Gertrude Ward; *m* 1974, Jean Catherine Laird; three *s*. *Educ*: Colston's Sch., Bristol; University Coll. London. BScEcon, 1st Cl. Hons. Pilot Officer/Flying Officer, RAF Educn Br., 1954–55. Various posts, London Transport Exec., 1955–67; seconded to Brit. Transport Staff Coll. as mem. staff and latterly Asst Principal (incl. course at Harvard Business Sch.), 1967–70; Industrial Relations Officer, London Transport Exec., 1970–74; Dir of Personnel, W Yorks Passenger Transport Exec., 1974–76. *Recreations*: Scottish country dancing; trying to learn the piano. *Address*: 29 Stanley Street, Palmwoods, Qld 4555, Australia.

WARD, Roy Livingstone, QC 1972; **His Honour Judge Roy Ward**; a Circuit Judge, since 1979; *b* 31 Aug. 1925; *m* 1972, Barbara Anne (*née* Brockbank) (marr. diss.); one *s* one *d*. *Educ*: Taunton Sch.; Pembroke Coll., Cambridge. BA(Hons). Served RAF, 1943–47 (commnd 1945). Called to Bar, Middle Temple, 1950. A Recorder of the Crown Court, 1972–79. *Address*: Tethers End, Shelsley Drive, Colwall, Worcs. *Club*: United Oxford & Cambridge University.

WARD, Rt. Rev. Simon B.; *see* Barrington-Ward.

WARD, Sir Terence George, Kt 1971; CBE 1961 (MBE 1945); Dean of the Faculty of Dental Surgery, Royal College of Surgeons, 1965–68; *b* 16 Jan. 1906; *m* 1931, Elizabeth Ambrose Wilson (*d* 1981); one *s* one *d*; *m* 1982, Sheila Elizabeth Lawry. *Educ*: Edinburgh. Mem., SE Metropolitan Regional Hosp. Bd; Exmr, DSRCSEd, FDRCSIre. Pres., Internat. Assoc. Oral Surgeons; Past Pres., British Association of Oral Surgeons; Consulting Oral Surgeon to the Royal Navy; Consulting Dental Surgeon: to the British Army, 1954–71; Emeritus 1971; to the Royal Air Force; to Dept of Health and Social Security; to the Queen Victoria Hospital, East Grinstead. LRCP, LRCSEd 1928; LRFPS, 1930; LDS (Edinburgh) 1928; FDSRCS 1948; FACD (USA) 1959; FACDSurgeons; FFDRCS Ire., 1964; Hon. FDSRCSE, 1966; Hon. FRCCD, 1966; FRCS 1970. DDSc, Melbourne, 1963; Dr Odontology, Lund Univ. Mem., SA Dental Assoc.; Hon. Member: Amer. Soc. Oral Surgeons; Dutch Soc. Oral Surgeons; Hon. Fellow: Scandinavian Assoc. Oral Surgeons; Spanish Assoc. Oral Surgeons. *Publication*: The Dental Treatment of Maxillo-facial Injuries, 1956. *Recreation*: golf. *Address*: 22 Marina Court Avenue, Bexhill-on-Sea, East Sussex. *T*: Bexhill-on-Sea (0424) 4760.

WARD, Thomas William, ARCA 1949; RE 1955; RWS 1957; sometime Course Director, Illustration, Harrow College of Technology and Art; painter in water colour and oil colour, draughtsman, engraver, illustrator; *b* 8 Nov. 1918; *s* of John B. Ward, Master Stationer, and Lilly B. Ward (*née* Hunt), Sheffield; *m* Joan Palmer, ARCA, *d* of F. N. Palmer, Blackheath; one *s* one *d*. *Educ*: Nether Edge Grammar Sch., Sheffield; Sheffield Coll. of Art (part-time); Royal Coll. of Art, 1946–49, Silver Medal, 1949, Postgrad. Scholarship, 1949–50. Cadet, Merchant Service, 1935–36; stationer, 1936–39; Military service, 1939–46: commissioned N Staffs Regt, 1942; GSO3 1944–46. *One Man Exhibitions include*: Walker Gall., 1957, 1960; Wakefield City Art Gall., 1962; Shipley Art Gall., 1962; Middlesbrough Art Gall., 1963; St John's Coll., York, 1965; Bohun Gall., Henley, 1974; Digby Gall., Colchester, 1981; Coach House Gall., CI, 1987. *Group Exhibitions include*: Leicester Gall.; Kensington Gall.; Zwemmer Gall.; Bohun Gall; Bankside Gall., 1987. *Open Exhibitions include*: RA, RSA, NEAC, London Group, RSMA, and in Japan, USA, S Africa, NZ. *Important purchases include*: S London Art Gall.; V&A; Nat. Gall. of NZ; Leicester, Oxford and Durham Univs; Arts Council; Contemp. Art Soc.; Bowes Mus.; Graves Art Gall.; Rochdale Art Gall.; Lord Clark. *Illustrations include*: Colman Prentis Varley; Shell Mex; Editions Lausanne; books for Country Life, Conway Maritime Press, MAP. Designer of theatre properties, Tom Arnold Ice Show. *Recreation*: sailing. *Address*: Hollydene, Ipswich Road, Holbrook, Ipswich IP9 2QT.

WARD, William Alan H.; *see* Heaton-Ward.

WARD, William Alec; HM Diplomatic Service, retired; *b* 27 Nov. 1928; *s* of William Leslie Ward and Gladys Ward; *m* 1955, Sheila Joan Hawking; two *s* two *d*. *Educ*: King's Coll. Sch., Wimbledon; Christ Church, Oxford. HM Forces, 1947–49. Colonial Office, 1952; Private Sec. to Permanent Under-Sec., 1955–57; Singapore, 1960–64; seconded to CRO, 1963; Karachi, 1964–66; Islamabad, 1966–68; joined HM Diplomatic Service,

1968; FCO, 1968–71; Salisbury, 1971–72; Dep. High Comr, Colombo, 1973–76; High Comr, Mauritius, 1977–81. *Recreations:* music, walking. *Address:* The Grange, Ellesmere, Shropshire SY12 9DE.

WARD, William Ernest Frank, CMG 1945; *b* 24 Dec. 1900; *s* of W. H. Ward, Borough Treasurer, Battersea; *m* 1926, Sylvia Grace, *d* of Arthur Clayton Vallance, Mansfield, Notts; no *c*. *Educ:* LCC elementary school; Mercers' Sch.; Dulwich Coll.; Lincoln Coll., Oxford (BLitt, MA); Ridley Hall, Cambridge (Diploma in Education). Master, Achimota Coll., Gold Coast, 1924; Director of Education, Mauritius, 1940; Deputy Educational Adviser, Colonial Office, 1945–56. Editor, Oversea Education, 1946–63. Member of UK delegation to seven general conferences of UNESCO and many other international meetings on education. *Publications:* History of Ghana, 1967 (originally published as History of the Gold Coast, 1948); Educating Young Nations, 1959; Fraser of Trinity and Achimota, 1965; The Royal Navy and the Slavers, 1969; various historical works and educational textbooks. *Recreations:* music, walking. *Address:* Roseacre, Holly Hill Drive, Banstead, Surrey SM7 2BD. *T:* Burgh Heath (0737) 353547.

WARD, William Kenneth, CMG 1977; Under-Secretary, Department of Trade, retired; *b* 20 Jan. 1918; *e s* of late Harold and Emily Ward; *m* 1949, Victoria Emily, *d* of late Ralph Perkins, Carcavelos, Portugal; three *s* one *d*. *Educ:* Queen Elizabeth's Grammar Sch., Ashbourne; Trinity Coll., Cambridge. 1st class Hons Modern and Medieval Langs Tripos. Entered Ministry of Supply, 1939; Board of Trade, 1955; HM Principal Trade Commissioner, Vancouver, BC, 1959–63; Under-Sec., BoT, 1966–69, Min. of Technology, later DTI and Dept of Trade, 1969–78; Sec., BOTB, 1973. *Recreation:* gardening. *Address:* 31 Plough Lane, Purley, Surrey CR8 3QG. *T:* 081–660 2462.

WARD-BOOTH, Maj.-Gen. John Antony, OBE 1971; DL; Consultant; Francis Graves and Partners, since 1989; Services Sound and Vision Corporation, since 1989; *b* 18 July 1927; *s* of Rev. J. Ward-Booth and Mrs E. M. Ward-Booth; *m* 1952, Margaret Joan Hooper; one *s* two *d* (and one *s* decd). *Educ:* Worksop College, Notts. Joined Army, 1945; commnd into Worcestershire Regt in India, 1946; served India and Middle East, 1946–48; regular commn Bedfordshire and Hertfordshire Regt, 1948; served BAOR, Far East, Nigeria and Congo, 1950–63, trans. to Parachute Regt, 1963; commanded 3rd Bn, Parachute Regt, 1967–69; Hong Kong, 1969–70; Comdr, 16 Parachute Bde, 1970–73; Nat. Defence Coll., Canada, 1973–74; DAG, HQ BAOR, 1974–75; Dir, Army Air Corps, 1976–79; GOC Western District, 1979–82. Dep. Col, Royal Anglian Regt, 1982–87. Sec., Eastern Wessex TAVRA, 1982–89. Governor: Enham Village Centre, 1982–; Clayesmore Sch., Dorset, 1985– (Chm., 1989–). DL Hants, 1988. *Recreations:* sailing, golf, cricket. *Address:* 22 Winchester Gardens, Andover, Hants SP10 2EH. *T:* Andover (0264) 54317. *Clubs:* Army and Navy, MCC.

WARD-JACKSON, Mrs (Audrey) Muriel; *b* 30 Oct. 1914; *d* of late William James Jenkins and Alice Jenkins (*née* Glyde); *m* 1946, George Ralph Norman Ward-Jackson (*d* 1982); no *c*. *Educ:* Queenswood, Hatfield, Herts; Lady Margaret Hall, Oxford (MA). Home Civil Service (Ministries of Works, Town and Country Planning, Housing and Local Government, and HM Treasury): Asst Principal, 1937; Principal, 1942; Asst Sec., 1946–55. A Director (concerned mainly with Finance), John Lewis Partnership, 1955–74; John Lewis Partnership Ltd: Dir, 1957–74; Dir, John Lewis Properties Ltd, 1969–74; Chm., John Lewis Partnership Pensions Trust, 1964–74. On Civil Service Arbitration Tribunal, 1959–64; Chm., Consumers Cttees (Agric. Marketing), 1971–75; Member: Nat. Savings Review Cttee, 1971–73; Royal Commn on Standards of Conduct in Public Life, 1974–76. A Governor, British Film Inst., 1962–65; Mem. Council, Bedford Coll., London Univ., 1967–72. *Recreation:* swimming. *Address:* 195 Cranmer Court, Whiteheads Grove, Chelsea SW3 3HG. *T:* 071–581 1926. *Club:* Lansdowne.

WARD-JONES, Norman Arthur, CBE 1990; VRD 1959; JP; Chairman, Gaming Board for Great Britain, since 1986; *b* 19 Sept. 1922; *s* of Alfred Thomas Ward-Jones and Claire Mayall Lees; *m* 1962, Pamela Catherine Ainslie (*née* Glessing). *Educ:* Oundle Sch.; Brasenose Coll., Oxford. Solicitor 1950. War service, Royal Marines (Captain), 1941–46; RM Reserve, 1948–64, Lt-Col and CO RMR (City of London), 1961–64; Hon. Col 1968–74. Solicitor, Lawrance Messer & Co., Sen. Partner, 1981–85, retired 1989. Hon. Solicitor, Magistrates' Assoc., 1960–85. Chm., East Anglian Real Property Co. Ltd, 1970–80, non-exec. Dir, 1980–89. Mem. Gaming Board, 1984–. JP N Westminster PSD, 1966–. *Recreation:* wine drinking. *Address:* The Cottage, Barnhorne Manor, 75 Barnhorn Road, Little Common, Bexhill-on-Sea, East Sussex TN39 4QB; 19 Irving Street, WC2. *Club:* East India.

WARD-THOMAS, Evelyn, (Mrs Michael Ward-Thomas); *see* Anthony, Evelyn.

WARD THOMAS, Gwyn Edward, CBE 1973; DFC; Chairman: Bulloch & Dunn Associates Ltd; Worldwide Television Associates; Director: Television Showcase Ltd; Tyne Tees Television; Robert Vince Advertising; *b* 1 Aug. 1923; *o s* of William J. and Constance Thomas; *m* 1945, Patricia Cornelius; one *d*. *Educ:* Bloxham Sch.; The Lycée, Rouen. Served RAF, 1 Group Bomber Command and 229 Group Transport Command, 1941–46. Granada Television, 1955–61; Man. Dir, Grampian Television, 1961–67; Man. Dir, 1967–73, Dep. Chm., 1973–81, Yorkshire Television; Man. Dir, 1970–84, Chm., 1976–84, Trident Television. Chairman: Castlewood Investments Ltd, 1969–83; Don Robinson Holdings Ltd, 1969–83; Watts & Corry Ltd, 1969–83; Trident Casinos, 1982–84; Pres., Trident Independent Television Enterprises SA, 1969–. British Bureau of Television Advertising: Dir, 1966; Chm., 1968–70; Mem. Council, Independent Television Companies Assoc., 1961–76 (Chairman: Labour Relations Cttee, 1967; Network Programme Cttee, 1971); Mem., British Screen Adv. Council, 1985–. *Recreations:* ski-ing, boats, photography. *Address:* 100 Park Lane, W1.

WARDALE, Sir Geoffrey (Charles), KCB 1979 (CB 1974); Second Permanent Secretary, Department of the Environment, 1978–80; *b* 29 Nov. 1919; *m* 1944, Rosemary Octavia Dyer; one *s* one *d*. *Educ:* Altrincham Grammar Sch.; Queens' Coll., Cambridge (Schol.). Army Service, 1940–41. Joined Ministry of War Transport as Temp. Asst Princ., 1942; Private Sec. to Perm. Sec., 1946; Princ., 1948; Asst Sec., 1957; Under-Sec., Min. of Transport, later DoE, 1966; Dep. Sec., 1972. Led inquiry: into the Open Structure in the Civil Service (The Wardale Report), 1981; into cases of fraud and corruption in PSA, 1982–83. Mem. Council, Univ. of Sussex, 1986–; Chm., Brighton Coll. Council, 1985–90. *Recreations:* transport history, painting, listening to music. *Address:* 89 Paddock Lane, Lewes, East Sussex BN7 1TW. *T:* Lewes (0273) 473468. *Club:* United Oxford & Cambridge University.

WARDE, His Honour John Robins; a Circuit Judge, 1977–90; *b* 25 April 1920; (Guardian) A. W. Ormond, CBE, FRCS; *m* 1941, Edna Holliday Gipson; three *s*. *Educ:* Radley Coll., Abingdon, Berks; Corpus Christi Coll., Oxford (MA). Served War, 1940–45: Lieut, RA; awarded C-in-C's cert. for outstanding good service in the campaign in NW Europe. Member: Devon CC, 1946–49; Devon Agricl Exec. Cttee, 1948–53; West Regional Advisory Council of BBC, 1950–53. Admitted a solicitor, 1950; Partner in Waugh and Co., Solicitors, Haywards Heath and East Grinstead, Sussex, 1960–70. A Recorder of the Crown Court, 1972–77. Registrar of Clerkenwell County Court, 1970–77. Liveryman, Gardeners' Co., 1983–. *Recreations:* mountaineering, watching cricket, listening to music. *Address:* 20 Clifton Terrace, Brighton, East Sussex BN1 3HA. *T:* Brighton (0273) 26642. *Clubs:* Law Society, MCC, Forty.

WARDELL, Gareth Lodwig; MP (Lab) Gower, since Sept. 1982; *b* 29 Nov. 1944; *s* of John Thomas Wardell and Jenny Ceridwen Wardell; *m* 1967, Jennifer Dawn Evans; one *s*. *Educ:* London Sch. of Econs and Pol. Science (BScEcon, MSc). Geography Master, Chislehurst and Sidcup Technical High Sch., 1967–68; Head of Econs Dept, St Clement Danes Grammar Sch., 1968–70; Sixth Form Econs Master, Haberdashers' Aske's Sch., Elstree, 1970–72; Educn Lectr, Bedford Coll. of Physical Educn, 1972–73; Sen. Lectr in Geography, Trinity Coll., Carmarthen, 1973–82. *Publications:* articles on regional issues in British Econ. Survey. *Recreations:* cycling, cross-country running. *Address:* 67 Elder Grove, Carmarthen, Dyfed SA31 2LH.

WARDINGTON, 2nd Baron, *cr* 1936, of Alnmouth in the County of Northumberland; **Christopher Henry Beaumont Pease;** *b* 22 Jan. 1924; *s* of 1st Baron and Hon. Dorothy Charlotte (*d* 1983), *er d* of 1st Baron Forster; *S* father, 1950; *m* 1964, Margaret Audrey Dunfee, *d* of John and Eva White; one *s* two *d* (adopted). *Educ:* Eton. Served War of 1939–45, in Scots Guards, 1942–47, Captain. Partner in Stockbroking firm of Hoare Govett Ltd, 1947–86. Alderman of Broad Street Ward, City of London, 1960–63. Mem., Council of Foreign Bondholders, 1967–. Comr, Public Works Loan Bd, 1969–73. Trustee, Royal Jubilee Trusts; Chm., Athlone Trust, 1983–. Chm., Friends of the British Library, 1988–. *Recreations:* cricket, golf, book collecting. *Heir:* *b* Hon. William Simon Pease [*b* 15 Oct. 1925; *m* 1962, Hon. Elizabeth Jane Ormsby-Gore, *d* of 4th Baron Harlech, KG, PC, GCMG]. *Address:* Wardington Manor, Banbury, Oxon. *T:* Banbury (0295) 750202; 29 Moore Street, SW3. *T:* 071–584 5245. *Clubs:* Royal Automobile, Garrick, Roxburghe; All England Lawn Tennis.

WARDLAW, Sir Henry (John), 21st Bt *cr* 1631, of Pitreavie; *b* 30 Nov. 1930; *s* of Sir Henry Wardlaw, 20th Bt, and Ellen (decd), *d* of John Francis Brady; *S* father, 1983; *m* 1962, Julie-Ann, *d* of late Edward Patrick Kirwan; five *s* two *d*. *Educ:* Melbourne Univ. (MB, BS). *Heir:* *s* (Henry) Justin Wardlaw, *b* 10 Aug. 1963. *Address:* 82 Vincent Street, Sandringham, Vic 3191, Australia.

WARDLE, Charles Frederick; MP (C) Bexhill and Battle, since 1983; *b* 23 Aug. 1939; *s* of late Frederick Maclean Wardle; *m* 1964, Lesley Ann, *d* of Sidney Wells; one *d*. *Educ:* Tonbridge Sch.; Lincoln Coll., Oxford; Harvard Business Sch. MA Oxon 1968; MBA Harvard. Asst to Pres., American Express Co., NY, 1966–69; Merchant Banking, London, 1969–72; Chairman: Benjamin Priest Gp plc, 1977–84 (Dir, 1972–74, Man. Dir, 1974–77); Warne, Wright and Rowland, 1978–84; Dir, Asset Special Situations Trust plc, 1982–84. CBI: Mem. Council, 1980–84; Mem., W Midlands Regional Council, 1980–84. PPS: to Minister of State (Health), 1984; to Sec. of State for Social Services, 1984–87; to Sec. of State for Scotland, 1990–. Mem., Select Cttee on Trade and Industry, 1983–84. Member: Commercial and Econ. Cttee, EEF, 1981–83; Midlands Cttee, InstD, 1981–83. FRGS 1977. *Recreations:* books, sport, travel. *Address:* House of Commons, SW1A 0AA. *T:* 071–219 3000; The Dodo House, Caldbec Hill, Battle, East Sussex.

WARDLE, (John) Irving; Drama Critic, The Independent on Sunday, since 1990; *b* 20 July 1929; *s* of John Wardle and Nellie Partington; *m* 1958, Joan Notkin (marr. diss.); *m* 1963, Fay Crowder (marr. diss.); two *s*; *m* 1975, Elizabeth Grist; one *s* one *d*. *Educ:* Bolton Sch.; Wadham Coll., Oxford (BA); Royal Coll. of Music (ARCM). Joined Times Educational Supplement as sub-editor, 1956; Dep. Theatre Critic, The Observer, 1960; Drama Critic, The Times, 1963–89. Editor, Gambit, 1973–75. Play: The Houseboy, prod Open Space Theatre, 1974, ITV, 1982. *Publication:* *biography:* The Theatres of George Devine, 1978. *Recreation:* piano playing. *Address:* 51 Richmond Road, New Barnet, Herts EN5 1SF. *T:* 081–440 3671.

WARDLE, Sir Thomas (Edward Jewell), Kt 1970; Lord Mayor of Perth, Western Australia, 1967–72; *b* 18 Aug. 1912; *s* of Walter Wardle and Lily Wardle (*née* Jewell); *m* 1940, Hulda May Olson; one *s* one *d*. *Educ:* Perth Boys' Sch., Western Australia. Member: King's Park Bd, 1970–81; Bd, Churchland Teachers Coll., 1973–78; Chairman: Trustees, WA Museum, 1973–82; Aboriginal Loans Commn, 1974–80; Pres., Nat. Trust of WA, 1971–82. Hon. LLD Univ. of WA, 1973. Commendatore, Order of Merit (Italy), 1970. *Recreations:* boating, fishing. *Address:* 3 Kent Street, Bicton, WA 6157, Australia. *Club:* Returned Services League (Western Australia).

WARDS, Brig. George Thexton, CMG 1943; OBE 1935; late IA; Historian, Cabinet Office, 1951–69. *Educ:* Heversham Sch., Westmorland. Served European War, 1914–18, with 7 London Regt, France and Belgium, 1917–18; 2nd Lieut, Indian Army, 1918; attached to HM Embassy, Tokyo, 1923–28; NW Frontier of India, 1930; Bt Major, 1933; Staff Officer to British Troops in North China, 1932–36; Lt-Col and Asst Military Attaché, Tokyo, 1937–41; Brig., Military Attaché, Tokyo, 1941; GSO1, GHQ India, 1942; Commandant Intelligence Sch., India, 1943–45; Commandant Intelligence Corps, Training Centre, India, 1945–47. Lt-Col, 1944; Col, 1945. Official Interpreter in Japanese to Govt of India, 1928–32, 1936, and 1944–47. Information Officer, Min. of Food, 1949; Chief Enforcement Officer, Min. of Food, 1950. Chm., Nat. Anti-Vivisection Soc., 1954–57; Mem. Council, RSPCA, 1956–67; Official visit to Japan, 1966. *Publications:* Joint author, Official History, The War against Japan, Vol. I 1955, Vol. II 1958, Vol. III 1962, Vol. IV 1965, Vol. V 1969. *Club:* Army and Navy.

WARE, Cyril George, CB 1981; Under-Secretary, Inland Revenue, 1974–82; *b* 25 May 1922; *s* of Frederick George Ware and Elizabeth Mary Ware; *m* 1946, Gwennie (*née* Wooding); two *s* one *d*. *Educ:* Leyton County High Sch. Entered Inland Revenue as Tax Officer, 1939; Inspector of Taxes, 1949; Sen. Principal Inspector, 1969. *Recreations:* music, woodwork, gardening, swimming. *Address:* 86 Tycehurst Hill, Loughton, Essex IG10 1DA. *T:* 081–508 3588.

WARE, Martin, FRCP; Editor, British Medical Journal, 1966–75; *b* 1 Aug. 1915; *o s* of late Canon Martin Stewart Ware and late Margaret Isabel (*née* Baker, later Baker Wilbraham); *m* 1938, Winifred Elsie Boyce; two *s* three *d*. *Educ:* Eton; St Bartholomew's Hospital. MB, BS (London) 1939; MRCP 1945; FRCP 1967; MSc (Wales) 1978; BA (Open) 1989. House-surgeon, St Bartholomew's Hosp., 1939; served with RAMC, attached to Royal W African Frontier Force, 1940–45; HQ staff, Medical Research Council, 1946–50; editorial staff, British Medical Jl, 1950–75; research in micropalaeontology, UCW, Aberystwyth, 1975–84. Vice-President: BMA; Internat. Union of Med. Press, 1966–75. *Recreations:* bird watching, reading, Alpines. *Address:* 4 Ellis Close, Cottenham, Cambs CB4 4UN. *T:* Cottenham (0954) 51428.

WARE, Michael John, CB 1985; QC 1988; barrister-at-law; Solicitor and Legal Adviser, Department of the Environment, since 1982; *b* 7 May 1932; *s* of Kenneth George Ware and Phyllis Matilda (*née* Joynes); *m* 1966, Susan Ann Maitland three *d*. *Educ:* Cheltenham Grammar Sch.; Trinity Hall, Cambridge (BA(Law), LLB). Called to Bar, Middle Temple. Nat. Service, 2/Lieut RASC, 1954–56. Board of Trade (later Dept of Trade and Industry): Legal Asst, 1957–64; Sen. Legal Asst, 1964–72; Asst Solicitor, 1972–73; Dir, Legal Dept,

Office of Fair Trading, 1973–77; Under Secretary: Dept of Trade, 1977–81; DoE, 1982. *Address:* 2 Marsham Street, SW1P 3EB.

WAREING, Prof. Philip Frank, OBE 1986; PhD, DSc London; FRS 1969; FLS; Professor of Botany, University College of Wales, Aberystwyth, 1958–81, now Emeritus; *b* 27 April 1914; *e s* of late Frank Wareing; *m* 1939, Helen Clark; one *s* one *d* (and one *d* decd). *Educ:* Watford Grammar School; Birkbeck Coll., Univ. of London. Exec. Officer, Inland Revenue, 1931–41. Captain, REME, 1942–46. Lectr, Bedford Coll., Univ. of London, 1947–50; Lectr, then Sen. Lectr, Univ. of Manchester, 1950–58. Member: Nature Conservancy, 1965–68; Water Resources Board, 1968–71; Chm. Res. Adv. Cttee, Forestry Commn, 1972–86. President: Sect. K, British Assoc., 1970; Internat. Plant Growth Substances Assoc., 1982–85; Mem. Council, Royal Soc., 1972. Mem., Leopoldina Acad. of Science, 1971. *Publications:* Control of Plant Growth and Differentiation, 1970; various papers on plant physiology in scientific journals. *Recreations:* gardening, hill walking. *Address:* Bryn Rhedyn, Caemelyn, Aberystwyth, Dyfed SY23 3DA. *T:* Aberystwyth (0970) 3910.

WAREING, Robert Nelson; MP (Lab) Liverpool, West Derby, since 1983; *b* 20 Aug. 1930; *s* of late Robert Wareing and late Florence Wareing (*née* Mallon); *m* 1962, Betty Coward (decd). *Educ:* Ranworth Square Sch., Liverpool; Alsop High Sch., Liverpool; Bolton Coll. of Educn. BSc (Econ) London Univ., 1956. RAF, 1948–50. Administrative Asst, Liverpool City Bldg Surveyor's Dept, 1946–56; Lecturer: Brooklyn Technical Coll., Birmingham, 1957–59; Wigan and Dist Mining and Technical Coll., 1959–63; Liverpool Coll. of Commerce, 1963–64; Liverpool City Inst. of Further Educn, 1964–72; Central Liverpool Coll. of Further Educn, 1972–83. Merseyside County Council: Mem., 1981–86; Chief Whip, Labour Gp, 1981–83; Chm., Economic Develt Cttee, 1981–83; Chm., Merseyside Economic Develt Co. Ltd, 1981–86. A Vice-Pres., AMA, 1984–. Joined Labour Party, 1947: Pres., Liverpool Dist Labour Party, 1974–81; Mem., MSF. Introduced Chronically Sick and Disabled Persons Bill, 1983; Asst Labour Whip, 1987–, now with responsibility for employment, disabled people, sport and overseas develt. Vice-Chm., British–Yugoslav Parly Gp, 1985–. *Recreations:* watching soccer (especially Everton FC), concert-going and ballet, motoring and travel. *Address:* House of Commons, SW1A 0AA. *Club:* Pirrie Ward Labour (Liverpool).

WARHURST, Alan, CBE 1990; Director, Manchester Museum, since 1977; *b* 6 Feb. 1927; *s* of W. Warhurst; *m* 1953, Sheila Lilian Bradbury; one *s* two *d*. *Educ:* Canon Slade Grammar Sch., Bolton; Manchester Univ. BA Hons History 1950. Commnd Lancashire Fusiliers, 1947. Asst, Grosvenor Museum, Chester, 1950–51; Asst Curator, Maidstone Museum and Art Gallery, 1951–55; Curator, Northampton Museum and Art Gallery, 1955–60; Director, City Museum, Bristol, 1960–70; Director, Ulster Museum, 1970–77. FSA 1958; FMA 1958. Pres., S Western Fedn Museums and Galleries, 1966–68; Chm., Irish Nat. Cttee, ICOM, 1973–75; Dep. Chm., NW Museum and Art Gallery Service, 1987–; President: Museums Assoc., 1975–76; N Western Fedn of Museums and Art Galls, 1979–80; Hon. Sec., Univ. Museums Gp, 1987–. Trustee, Boat Mus., Ellesmere Port, 1990–. Chm., Hulme Hall Cttee, Univ. of Manchester, 1986–. Hon. MA Belfast, 1982. *Publications:* various archaeological and museum contribs to learned jls. *Address:* The Manchester Museum, The University, Manchester M13 9PL. *T:* 061–275 2650.

WARING, Sir (Alfred) Holburt, 3rd Bt *cr* 1935; *b* 2 Aug. 1933; *s* of Sir Alfred Harold Waring, 2nd Bt, and of Winifred, *d* of late Albert Boston, Stockton-on-Tees; *S* father, 1981; *m* 1958, Anita, *d* of late Valentin Medinilla, Madrid; one *s* two *d*. *Educ:* Rossall School; Leeds College of Commerce. Director: SRM Plastics Ltd; Waring Investments Ltd; Property Realisation Co. Ltd. Governor, Med. Coll. of St Bartholomew's Hosp. *Recreations:* tennis, golf, squash, swimming. *Heir:* *s* Michael Holburt Waring, *b* 3 Jan. 1964. *Address:* Earls Croft, 30 Russell Road, Moor Park, Northwood, Middlesex HA6 2LR. *T:* Northwood (09274) 24570. *Club:* Moor Park Golf (Rickmansworth).

WARKE, Rt. Rev. Robert Alexander; *see* Cork, Cloyne and Ross, Bishop of.

WARMAN, Oliver Byrne, RBA 1984; ROI 1989; Chief Executive, Federation of British Artists, since 1984; *b* 10 June 1932. *Educ:* Stowe; Exeter Univ.; Balliol Coll., Oxford. Commissioned Welsh Guards, 1952; GSO3 Cabinet Office; Instructor, Intelligence Centre; Staff College; RMCS; retired 1970. Dir, Public Relations, Ship and Boat Builders Fedn, 1970; Director: Ashlyns, 1978; Tulsemead, 1983. First exhibited RA, 1980; exhib. at RBA, RWA, NEAC, RSMA, ROI; work in public collections, incl. US Embassy, Sultanate of Oman and Crown Commn. *Publications:* Arnhem 1944, 1970; articles on wine and military history, 1968–. *Recreations:* France, food, wine, sailing, painting, mongrel dogs. *Address:* Le Manoir de Lussac, 24320 Verteillac, Dordogne, France. *T:* 53 91 92 10. *Clubs:* Cavalry and Guards, Arts, Chelsea Arts; Royal Cornwall Yacht.

WARMINGTON, Lt-Comdr Sir Marshall George Clitheroe, 3rd Bt, *cr* 1908; Royal Navy, retired; *b* 26 May 1910; *o s* of Sir Marshall Denham Warmington, 2nd Bt, and Alice Daisy Ing; *S* father, 1935; *m* 1st, 1933, Mollie (from whom he obtained a divorce, 1941), *er d* of late Capt. M. A. Kennard, RN (retired); one *s* one *d*; 2nd, 1942, Eileen Mary (*d* 1969), *o d* of late P. J. Howes; two *s*. *Educ:* Charterhouse. *Heir:* *s* Marshall Denham Malcolm Warmington, *b* 5 Jan. 1934. *Address:* Swallowfield Park, near Reading, Berks RG7 1TG. *T:* Reading (0734) 882210. *Club:* MCC.

WARNE, Maj.-Gen. Antony M.; *see* Makepeace-Warne.

WARNE, (Ernest) John (David), CB 1982; Secretary, Institute of Chartered Accountants in England and Wales, 1982–90; *b* 4 Dec. 1926; *m* 1953, Rena Wolfe; three *s*. *Educ:* Univ. of London (BA(Hons)). Civil Service Commission, 1953; Asst Comr and Principal, Civil Service Commn, 1958; BoT, later DTI and Dept of Industry: Principal, 1962; Asst Sec., 1967; Under-Sec., 1972; Dir for Scotland, 1972–75; Under-Secretary: Personnel Div., 1975–77; Industrial and Commercial Policy Div., 1977–79; Dep. Sec., Dep. Dir-Gen., OFT, 1979–82. *Recreations:* reading, collecting prints, languages. *Address:* 3 Woodville Road, Ealing, W5. *T:* 081–998 0215. *Club:* Reform.

WARNER, Prof. Anne Elizabeth, FRS 1985; Royal Society Foulerton Research Professor, and Professor of Developmental Biology, University College London, since 1986; *b* 25 Aug. 1940; *d* of James Frederick Crompton Brooks and Elizabeth Marshall; *m* 1963, Michael Henry Warner. *Educ:* Pate's Grammar School for Girls, Cheltenham; University College London (BSc); Nat. Inst. for Med. Res. (PhD). Res. Associate, Middlesex Hosp. Med. Sch., 1968–71, Lectr in Physiology 1971–75, Sen. Lectr 1975–76, Royal Free Hosp Sch. of Medicine; Sen. Lectr in Anatomy, 1976–80, Reader in Anatomy, 1980–86, UCL. *Publications:* papers in Jl of Physiology and other learned jls. *Address:* University College London, Gower Street, WC1E 6BT.

WARNER, Deborah; free-lance theatre director, since 1980; *b* 12 May 1959; *d* of Ruth and Roger Warner. *Educ:* Sidcot Sch., Avon; St Clare's Coll., Oxford; Central Sch. of Speech and Drama. Founder, 1980, and Artistic Dir, 1980–86, Kick Theatre Co.; Resident Dir, RSC, 1987–89; Associate Dir, Royal Nat. Theatre, 1989–. *Productions:* Kick Theatre Co.: The Good Person of Szechwan, 1980; Woyzeck, 1981–82; The Tempest, 1983; Measure for Measure, 1984; King Lear, 1985; Coriolanus, 1986; Royal Shakespeare Co.: Titus Andronicus, 1987; King John, Electra, 1988; Royal National Theatre: The Good Person of Sichuan, 1989; King Lear, 1990; Hedda Gabler, Abbey Theatre, Dublin. *Recreation:* travelling. *Address:* c/o Jeremy Conway, 18–21 Jermyn Street, SW1Y 6HP. *T:* 071–287 0077.

WARNER, Sir (Edward Courtenay) Henry, 3rd Bt, *cr* 1910; *m*; three *s*. *Heir:* *s* Philip Courtenay Thomas Warner, *b* 3 April 1951.

WARNER, Sir Edward (Redston), KCMG 1965 (CMG 1955); OBE 1948; HM Diplomatic Service, retired; *b* 23 March 1911; *s* of late Sir George Redston Warner, KCVO, CMG, and Margery Catherine (*née* Nicol); *m* 1943, Grizel Margaret Clerk Rattray; three *s* one *d*. *Educ:* Oundle; King's College, Cambridge. Entered Foreign Office and Diplomatic Service, 1935; UK Delegation to OEEC, Paris, 1956–59; Minister at HM Embassy, Tokyo, 1959–62; Ambassador to Cameroon, 1963–66; UK Rep., Econ. and Social Council of UN, 1966–67; Ambassador to Tunisia, 1968–70. *Address:* The Old Royal Oak, High Street, Blockley, Glos GL56 9EX. *Clubs:* United Oxford & Cambridge University, Commonwealth Trust.

WARNER, Francis (Robert Le Plastrier); poet and dramatist; Sir Gordon White Fellow in English Literature and Senior English Tutor, St Peter's College, Oxford; *b* Bishopthorpe, Yorks, 21 Oct. 1937; *s* of Rev. Hugh Compton Warner and Nancy Le Plastrier (*née* Owen); *m* 1st, 1958, Mary Hall (marr. diss. 1972); two *d*; 2nd, 1983, Penelope Anne Davis; one *s* one *d*. *Educ:* Christ's Hosp.; London Coll. of Music; St Catharine's Coll., Cambridge (BA, MA). Supervisor, St Catharine's Coll., Cambridge, 1959–63; Staff Tutor in English, Cambridge Univ. Bd of Extra-Mural Studies, 1963–65; Oxford University: Fellow and Tutor, 1965–, Fellow Librarian, 1966–76, Dean of Degrees, 1984–, and Vice-Master, 1987–89, St Peter's Coll.; University Lectr (CUF), 1965–; Pro Sen. Proctor, 1989–90. Messing Internat. Award for distinguished contribns to Literature, 1972. *Publications: poetry:* Perennia, 1962; Early Poems, 1964; Experimental Sonnets, 1965; Madrigals, 1967; The Poetry of Francis Warner, USA 1970; Lucca Quartet, 1975; Morning Vespers, 1980; Spring Harvest, 1981; Epithalamium, 1983; Collected Poems 1960–84, 1985; *plays:* Maquettes, a trilogy of one-act plays, 1972; Requiem: Pt 1, Lying Figures, 1972, Pt 2, Killing Time, 1976, Pt 3, Meeting Ends, 1974; A Conception of Love, 1978; Light Shadows, 1980; Moving Reflections, 1983; Living Creation, 1985; Healing Nature: the Athens of Pericles, 1988; Byzantium, 1990; *edited:* Eleven Poems by Edmund Blunden, 1965; Garland, 1968; Studies in the Arts, 1968; *relevant publications:* by G. Pursglove: Francis Warner and Tradition, 1981; Francis Warner's Poetry: a critical assessment, 1988. *Recreations:* children, cathedral music, travel. *Address:* St Peter's College, Oxford OX1 2DL. *T:* Oxford (0865) 278900. *Club:* Athenæum.

WARNER, Sir Frederick Archibald, (Sir Fred Warner), GCVO 1975; KCMG 1972 (CMG 1963); HM Diplomatic Service, retired; consultant; Director, Loral International Inc.; *b* 2 May 1918; *s* of Frederick A. Warner, Chaguanas, Trinidad, and Marjorie Miller Winants, New Jersey, USA; *m* 1971, Mrs Simone Georgina de Ferranti, *d* of late Col. Hubert Jocelyn Nangle; two *s* and one step *d*. *Educ:* Wixenford; RNC Dartmouth; Magdalen Coll., Oxford; Sheffield Univ. Served War of 1939–45. Asst Principal, Foreign Office, Feb. 1946; Member of Foreign Service, April 1946; promoted 2nd Sec., May 1946; promoted 1st Sec., and transferred to Moscow, 1950; Foreign Office, Dec. 1951; Rangoon, 1956 (acted as Chargé d'Affaires, 1956); transferred to Athens, 1958; Head of South-East Asia Dept, Foreign Office, 1960; Imperial Defence College, 1964; Ambassador to Laos, 1965–67; Minister, NATO, 1968; Under-Secretary of State, FCO, 1969; Ambassador and Dep. Permanent UK Rep. to UN, 1969–72; Ambassador to Japan, 1972–75. Mem. (C) Somerset, European Parlt, 1979–84. Formerly Director: Mercantile and General Reinsurance Co. Ltd; Chloride Gp Ltd; Guinness Peat Gp. Chairman: Overseas Cttee, CBI, 1985–88; Wessex Region of National Trust, 1976–78. Order of the Rising Sun, 1st class (Japan). *Publication:* Anglo-Japanese Financial Relations, 1991. *Address:* Inkpen House, Newbury, Berks RG15 0DS. *T:* Inkpen (04884) 266; 3 Kelvin Court, Kensington Park Road, W2. *Clubs:* Beefsteak, Turf.

WARNER, Prof. Sir Frederick (Edward), Kt 1968; FRS 1976; FEng 1977; Visiting Professor, Essex University, since 1983; *b* 31 March 1910; *s* of Frederick Warner; *m* 1st, Margaret Anderson McCrea; two *s* two *d*; 2nd, Barbara Ivy Reynolds. *Educ:* Bancrofts Sch.; University Coll., London. Pres., Univ. of London Union, 1933. Chemical Engr with various cos, 1934–56; self-employed, 1956–. Joined Cremer and Warner, 1956, Senior Partner 1963–80. Inst. of Chemical Engrs: Hon. Sec., 1953; Pres., 1966; Mem. Council, Engrg Instns, 1962; President: Fedn Européenne d'Assocs nationales d'Ingénieurs, 1968–71 (European Engr, 1987); Brit. Assoc. for Commercial and Industrial Educn, 1977–89; Inst. of Quality Assurance, 1987–90; Vice- Pres., BSI, 1976–80 and 1983–89 (Chm., Exec. Bd, 1973–76; Pres., 1980–83). Missions and Consultations in India, Russia, Iran, Egypt, Greece, France. Assessor, Windscale Inquiry, 1977. Chairman: Cttee on Detergents, 1970–74; Process Plant Working Party, 1971–77; Sch. of Pharmacy, Univ. of London, 1971–79; CSTI, 1987–90; Member: Royal Commn on Environmental Pollution, 1973–76; Adv. Council for Energy Conservation, 1974–79; Treasurer, SCOPE (Scientific Cttee on Problems of Environment), 1982–88 (Chm., Environmental Consequences of Nuclear Warfare, 1983–88). Vis. Professor: Imperial Coll., 1970–78; UCL, 1970–86; Pro-Chancellor, Open Univ., 1974–79; Member Court: Cranfield Inst. of Technology; Essex Univ.; Fellow UCL, 1967. Hon. FRSC 1991; Hon. Fellow: UMIST, 1986; Sch. of Pharmacy, 1979. Ordinario, Accademia Tiberina, 1969. Hon. DTech, Bradford, 1969; Hon. DSc: Aston, 1970; Cranfield, 1978; Heriot-Watt, 1978; Newcastle, 1979; DUniv. Open, 1980. Gold Medal, Czecho-Slovak Soc. for Internat. Relations, 1969; Medal, Insinöö-riliitto, Finland, 1969; Leverhulme Medal, Royal Soc., 1978; Buchanan Medal, 1982; Environment Medal, Technical Inspectorate of the Rheinland, 1984; Gerard Piel Award, 1991. Hon. Mem., Koninklijk Instituut van Ingenieurs, 1972; Academico Correspondiente, AI Mexico, 1972. *Publications:* Problem in Chemical Engineering Design (with J. M. Coulson), 1949; Technology Today (ed de Bono), 1971; Standards in the Engineering Industries, NEDO, 1977; Risk Assessment, Royal Soc., 1982; papers on Kuwait oil fires, nuclear winter, underground gasification of coal, air and water pollution, contracts, planning, safety, professional and continuous education. *Recreations:* monumental brasses, ceramics, gardens. *Address:* Essex University, Colchester CO4 3SQ. *T:* Colchester (0206) 873370. *Club:* Athenæum.

WARNER, Gerald Chierici, CMG 1984; Deputy Secretary, Cabinet Office, since 1991; *b* 27 Sept. 1931; *s* of Howard Warner and Elizabeth (*née* Chierici-Kendall); *m* 1956, Mary Wynne Davies, DMath, Reader, City Univ.; one *s* two *d*. *Educ:* Univ. of Oxford (BA). Joined HM Diplomatic Service, 1954; 3rd Sec., Peking, 1956–58; 2nd Sec., Rangoon, 1960–61; 1st Sec., Warsaw, 1964–66, Geneva, 1966–68; Counsellor, Kuala Lumpur, 1974–76; FCO, 1976–90, retd. Mem., Police Complaints Authy, 1990. *Address:* c/o Coutts & Co., 440 Strand, WC2R 0QS.

WARNER, Sir Henry; *see* Warner, Sir E. C. H.

WARNER, Hon. Sir Jean-Pierre Frank Eugene, Kt 1981; **Hon. Mr Justice Warner;** Judge of the High Court of Justice, Chancery Division, since 1981; a Judge of the

Restrictive Practices Court, since 1982; *b* 24 Sept. 1924; *s* of late Frank Cloudesley ffolliot Warner and of Louise Marie Blanche Warner (*née* Gouet); *m* 1950, Sylvia Frances, *d* of Sir Ernest Goodale, CBE, MC; two *d*. *Educ:* Sainte Croix de Neuilly; Ecole des Roches; Harrow; Trinity Coll., Cambridge (MA). Served in Rifle Bde, 1943–47, Actg Major, GSO2 (Ops) GHQ Far East. Called to Bar, Lincoln's Inn, 1950 (Cassel Schol.), Bencher 1966, Treasurer 1985; Mem. Gen. Council of Bar, 1969–72. Junior Counsel: to Registrar of Restrictive Trading Agreements, 1961–64; to Treasury (Chancery), 1964–72; QC 1972; Advocate-Gen., Ct of Justice of European Communities, 1973–81. Councillor: Royal Borough of Kensington, 1959–65 (Chm., Gen. Purposes Cttee, 1963–65); Royal Borough of Kensington and Chelsea, 1964–68. Dir, Warner & Sons Ltd and subsids, 1952–70. Pres., UK Assoc. for European Law, 1983–89 (Vice-Pres., 1975–83). Hon. Mem., Soc. of Public Teachers of Law, 1982. Hon. LLD: Exeter, 1983; Leicester, 1984; Edinburgh, 1987. Liveryman, Worshipful Co. of Weavers, 1957. Chevalier du Tastevin, 1952, Commandeur 1960; Mem., Confrérie St Etienne d'Alsace, 1981. *Recreation:* sitting in the sun with a cool drink. *Address:* Royal Courts of Justice, WC2A 2LL. *T:* 071–936 6768; 32 Abingdon Villas, W8 6BX. *T:* 071–937 7023.

WARNER, Marina Sarah, (Mrs John Dewe Mathews), FRSL; writer and critic; *b* 9 Nov. 1946; *d* of Esmond Pelham Warner and Emilia (*née* Terzulli); *m* 1st, 1971, William Shawcross; one *s*; 2nd, 1981, John Dewe Mathews. *Educ:* Lady Margaret Hall, Oxford (MA Mod. Langs, French and Italian). FRSL 1985. Getty Schol., Getty Centre for Hist. of Art and Humanities, Calif, 1987–88; Vis. Fellow, BFI, 1991; Tinbergen Prof., Erasmus Univ., Rotterdam, 1991. Member Advisory Board: Royal Mint, 1986–; Inst. of Contemporary Arts, 1987–. *Publications:* The Dragon Empress, 1972; Alone of All Her Sex: the myth and the cult of the Virgin Mary, 1976; Queen Victoria's Sketchbook, 1980; Joan of Arc: the image of female heroism, 1981; Monuments and Maidens: the allegory of the female form, 1985; *fiction:* In a Dark Wood, 1977; The Skating Party, 1983; The Lost Father, 1988; Sea-Change, 1992; *children's books:* The Impossible Day, 1981; The Impossible Night, 1981; The Impossible Bath, 1982; The Impossible Rocket, 1982; The Wobbly Tooth, 1984; *juvenile:* The Crack in the Teacup, 1979; *libretto:* The Legs of the Queen of Sheba, 1991; pamphlet in Counterblasts series; short stories, arts criticism, radio and television broadcasting. *Recreations:* friends, travels, reading. *Address:* c/o Peters, Fraser & Dunlop, 5th Floor, The Chambers, Chelsea Harbour, Lots Road, SW10 0XF.

WARNER, Dr Michael Henry Charles; author, engaged on historical research; *b* 21 May 1927; *s* of Captain Herbert H. M. Warner, MA, RGA, and Mrs Jessie R. H. Warner; *m* 1971, Gillian Margaret (*née* Easby); one *s* (by previous *m*). *Educ:* Monkton Combe Sch., Bath; Queens' Coll., Cambridge (BA 1951, MA 1955); King's Coll., London (PhD 1973). Served RAF, 1945–48. Govt Communications HQ: Exec. Officer, 1952; Higher Exec. Officer, 1956; Deptl Specialist Officer, 1957; Min. of Defence: Principal, 1965; Asst Sec., 1974; Counsellor, FCO, 1979; Dep. Leader, UK Delegn to Comprehensive Test Ban Treaty Negotiations, Geneva, 1979–80; Hd ER3 Div., MoD, 1981–84. Leverhulme Fellow, 1971–72. *Publications:* contrib. Thomas Hardy Yearbook, Anglo-Welsh Rev., Envoi, and BBC 2. *Recreations:* tennis, bridge. *Address:* 62 Poulett Gardens, Twickenham, Mddx TW1 4QR. *T:* 081–892 1456. *Club:* Commonwealth Trust.

WARNER, Norman Reginald; Director of Social Services, Kent County Council, since 1985; *b* 8 Sept. 1940; *s* of Albert Henry Edwin Warner and Laura Warner; *m* 1961, Anne Lesley Lawrence; one *s* one *d* (marr. diss. 1981); *m* 1990, Suzanne Elizabeth Reeve, *qv*; one *s*. *Educ:* Dulwich College; University of California, Berkeley (MPH). Min. of Health, 1959; Asst Private Sec. to Minister of Health, 1967–68, to Sec. of State for Social Services, 1968–69; Executive Councils Div., DHSS, 1969–71; Harkness Fellowship, USA, 1971–73; NHS Reorganisation, DHSS, 1973–74; Principal Private Sec. to Sec. of State for Social Services, 1974–76; Supplementary Benefits Div., 1976–78; Management Services, DHSS, 1979–81; Regional Controller, Wales and S Western Region, DHSS, 1981–83; Gwilym Gibbon Fellow, Nuffield Coll., Oxford, 1983–84; Under Sec., Supplementary Benefits Div., DHSS, 1984–85. Sen. Fellow in European Social Welfare, Univ. of Kent. Non-Exec. Dir, Kent FHSA. *Publications:* articles in Jl of Public Admin. *Recreations:* reading, cinema, theatre, exercise. *Address:* 8 College Gardens, Dulwich SE21 7BE. *T:* 081–693 7663.

WARNER, Suzanne Elizabeth, (Mrs Norman Warner); *see* Reeve, S. E.

WARNOCK, family name of **Baroness Warnock.**

WARNOCK, Baroness *cr* 1985 (Life Peer), of Weeke in the City of Winchester; **Helen Mary Warnock,** DBE 1984; Mistress of Girton College, Cambridge, 1985–91; *b* 14 April 1924; *d* of late Archibald Edward Wilson, Winchester; *m* 1949, Sir Geoffrey Warnock, *qv*; two *s* three *d*. *Educ:* St Swithun's, Winchester; Lady Margaret Hall, Oxford (Hon. Fellow 1984). Fellow and Tutor in Philosophy, St Hugh's Coll., Oxford, 1949–66; Headmistress, Oxford High Sch., GPDST, 1966–72; Talbot Res. Fellow, Lady Margaret Hall, Oxford, 1972–76; Sen. Res. Fellow, St Hugh's Coll., Oxford, 1976–84 (Hon. Fellow, 1985). Member: IBA, 1973–81; Cttee of Inquiry into Special Educn, 1974–78 (Chm.); Royal Commn on Environmental Pollution, 1979–84; Adv. Cttee on Animal Experiments, 1979–85 (Chm.); SSRC, 1981–85; UK Nat. Commn for Unesco, 1981–84; Cttee of Inquiry into Human Fertilization, 1982–84 (Chm.); Cttee of Inquiry into Validation of Public Sector Higher Educn, 1984; Cttee on Teaching Quality, PCFC, 1990 (Chm.). Gifford Lectr, Univ. of Glasgow, 1991–92. FRCP 1979; FRSM 1989; Hon. FIC 1986. Hon. degrees: Open, Essex, Melbourne, Manchester, Bath, Exeter, Glasgow, York, Nottingham, Warwick, Liverpool and London Univs.; Leeds Polytechnic; Leicester Polytechnic. *Publications:* Ethics since 1900, 1960, 3rd edn 1978; J.-P. Sartre, 1963; Existentialist Ethics, 1966; Existentialism, 1970; Imagination, 1976; Schools of Thought, 1977; (with T. Devlin) What Must We Teach?, 1977; Education: a way forward, 1979; A Question of Life, 1985; Teacher Teach Thyself (Dimbleby Lect.), 1985; Memory, 1987; A Common Policy for Education, 1988; Universities: knowing our minds, 1989; The Uses of Philosophy, 1991. *Recreations:* music, gardening. *Address:* Brick House, Axford SN8 2EX. *T:* Marlborough (0672) 514686.

WARNOCK, Sir Geoffrey (James), Kt 1986; Principal, Hertford College, Oxford, 1971–88, Hon. Fellow, 1988; Vice-Chancellor, University of Oxford, 1981–85; *b* 16 Aug. 1923; *s* of James Warnock, OBE, MD; *m* 1949, Helen Mary Wilson (*see* Baroness Warnock); two *s* three *d*. *Educ:* Winchester Coll.; New Coll., Oxford (Hon. Fellow, 1973). Served War of 1939–45: Irish Guards, 1942–45 (Captain). Fellow by Examination, Magdalen Coll., 1949; Fellow and Tutor, Brasenose Coll., 1950–53; Fellow and Tutor in Philosophy, Magdalen Coll., 1953–71, Emeritus Fellow, 1972, Hon. Fellow, 1980. Visiting Lectr, Univ. of Illinois, 1957; Visiting Professor: Princeton Univ., 1962; Univ. of Wisconsin, 1966. Hon. DH Univ. of Hartford, 1986. *Publications:* Berkeley, 1953; English Philosophy since 1900, 1958, 2nd edn 1969; Contemporary Moral Philosophy, 1967; (ed with J. O. Urmson) J. L. Austin: Philosophical Papers, 2nd edn, 1970; The Object of Morality, 1971; Morality and Language, 1983; J. L. Austin, 1989; articles in: Mind, Proc. Aristotelian Soc., etc. *Recreation:* golf. *Address:* Brick House, Axford, Marlborough, Wilts SN8 2EX.

WARR, John James; Deputy Chairman, Clive Discount Co. Ltd, 1973–87, retired; President of the MCC, 1987–88; *b* 16 July 1927; *s* of late George and Florence May Warr; *m* 1957, Valerie Powell (*née* Peter); two *d*. *Educ:* Ealing County Grammar Sch.; Emmanuel Coll., Cambridge (BA Hons 1952). Served RN, 1945–48. Man. Dir, Union Discount Co., 1952–73. Chm., Racecourse Assoc., 1989–. Mem., Jockey Club, 1977–. Pres., Berks CCC, 1990–. *Recreations:* racing, cricket, golf, good music. *Address:* Orchard Farm, Touchen End, Maidenhead, Berks SL6 3TA. *T:* Maidenhead (0628) 22994. *Clubs:* Saints and Sinners (Chm., 1991–92), MCC, XL, Lord's Taverners; Temple Golf, Berkshire Golf.

WARRELL, Prof. David Alan, DM; DSc; FRCP; Professor of Tropical Medicine and Infectious Diseases, since 1987, and Director, Centre for Tropical Medicine, since 1991, University of Oxford; Fellow, St Cross College, Oxford, since 1977; *b* 6 Oct. 1939; *s* of Alan and Mildred Warrell; *m* 1975, Dr Mary Jean Prentice; two *d*. *Educ:* Portsmouth Grammar Sch.; Christ Church, Oxford (MA, BCh 1964; DM 1970; DSc 1990). MRCS 1965; FRCP 1977. Oxford Univ. Radcliffe Travelling Fellow, Univ. of Calif at San Diego, 1969–70; Sen. Lectr, Ahmadu Bello Univ., Zaria, Nigeria, 1970–74; Lectr, RPMS, London, 1974–75; Consultant Physician, Radcliffe Infirmary, Oxford, 1975–79; Founding Dir, Wellcome-Mahidol Univ. Oxford Tropical Medicine Research Programme in Bangkok, 1979–86. WHO Consultant on malaria and snake bite, 1979–. Chm., MRC's AIDS Therapeutic Trials Cttee, 1987–; Mem., MRC's Tropical Medicine Res. Bd, 1986–89. Hon. Consultant Malariologist to the Army, 1989–. Lectures: Marc Daniels, RCP, 1977; Bradshaw, RCP, 1989. Scientific FZS 1976; FRGS 1989. Hon. Fellow, Ceylon Coll. of Physicians, 1985. *Publications:* Rabies—the Facts, 1977, 2nd edn 1986; (ed) Oxford Textbook of Medicine, 1983, 2nd edn 1987; chapters in textbooks of tropical medicine; papers in learned jls (Lancet, New England Jl of Medicine, etc) on respiratory physiology, malaria, rabies, infectious diseases and snake bite. *Recreations:* book collecting, music, bird watching, hill walking. *Address:* University of Oxford, Nuffield Department of Clinical Medicine, John Radcliffe Hospital, Headington, Oxford OX3 9DU. *T:* Oxford (0865) 220968 and 60871. *Club:* Royal Society of Medicine.

WARRELL, Ernest Herbert, MBE 1991; Organist, King's College, London, since 1980 (Lecturer in Music, KCL, 1953–80); *b* 23 June 1915; *er s* of Herbert Henry Warrell and Edith Peacock; *m* 1952, Jean Denton Denton; two *s* one *d*. *Educ:* Loughborough School. Articled pupil (Dr E. T. Cook), Southwark Cath., 1938; Asst Organist, Southwark Cath., 1946–54; Organist, St Mary's, Primrose Hill, 1954–57; Lectr in Plainsong, RSCM, 1954–59; Organist, St John the Divine, Kennington, SW9, 1961–68; Organist and Dir of Music, Southwark Cathedral, 1968–76; Musical Dir, Gregorian Assoc., 1969–82. Chief Examiner in Music, Internat. Baccalaureate, 1984–89. Hon. FCTL 1977; FKC 1979; Hon. FGCM 1988. *Publications:* Accompaniments to the Psalm Tones, 1942; Plainsong and the Anglican Organist, 1943. *Recreation:* sailing. *Address:* 41 Beechhill Road, Eltham, SE9 1HJ. *T:* 081–850 7800. *Clubs:* Special Forces, Little Ship; Royal Scots (Edinburgh).

WARREN, Very Rev. Alan Christopher; Provost of Leicester, since 1978; *b* 1932; *s* of Arthur Henry and Gwendoline Catherine Warren; *m* 1957, Sylvia Mary (*née* Matthews); three *d*. *Educ:* Dulwich College; Corpus Christi Coll., Cambridge (Exhibnr, MA); Ridley Hall, Cambridge. Curate, St Paul's, Margate, 1957–59; Curate, St Andrew, Plymouth, 1959–62; Chaplain of Kelly College, Tavistock, 1962–64; Vicar of Holy Apostles, Leicester, 1964–72; Coventry Diocesan Missioner, 1972–78; Hon. Canon, Coventry Cathedral, 1972–78; Proctor in Convocation, 1977–78, 1980–85; Mem., Cathedral Statutes Commn, 1981–. Chm., Council of Christians and Jews, 1985–; President: Leicester Council of Churches, 1985–; Leicester Civic Soc., 1983–. Mem., MCC, 1960–76. Pres., Alleyn Club, 1991–July 1992 (Vice-Pres., 1990–91). *Publications:* Putting it Across, 1975; The Miserable Warren, 1991; articles on church music, evangelism and sport in Church Times and other journals. *Recreations:* music, golf, steam trains. *Address:* Provost's House, St Martin's East, Leicester LE1 5FX. *T:* Leicester (0533) 25294/5. *Clubs:* Free Foresters; Leicestershire (Leicester); Hunstanton Golf.

WARREN, Alastair Kennedy, TD 1953; Editor, Dumfries and Galloway Standard, 1976–86; *b* 17 July 1922; *s* of John Russell Warren, MC, and Jean Cousin Warren; *m* 1952, Ann Lindsay Maclean; two *s*. *Educ:* Glasgow Acad.; Loretto; Glasgow Univ. (MA Hons). Served War of 1939–45; HLI, 1940–46; Major, 1946. Served 5/6th Bn HLI (TA) 1947–63. Sales Clerk, Stewarts & Lloyds Ltd, 1950–53; joined editorial staff of The Glasgow Herald as Sub-Editor, 1954; Leader Writer, 1955–58; Features Editor, 1958–59; Commercial Editor, 1960–64; City Editor, 1964–65; Editor, 1965–74; Regional Editor, Scottish and Universal Newspapers Ltd, 1974–76. Provost of New Galloway and Kells Community Council, 1978–81; Chairman: Loch Arthur Village Community (Camphill Movt), 1985–; Nithsdale Council of Voluntary Service, 1988–. *Publications:* contribs to various periodicals. *Recreations:* swimming, hill walking, marathon running. *Address:* Rathan, New Galloway, Castle Douglas DG7 3RN. *T:* New Galloway (06442) 257.

WARREN, Dame (Alice) Josephine (Mary Taylor); *see* Barnes, Dame A. J. M. T.

WARREN, Sir Brian; *see* Warren, Sir H. B. S.

WARREN, Sir Brian Charles Pennefather, 9th Bt *cr* 1784; *b* 4 June 1923; *o s* of Sir Thomas Richard Pennefather Warren, 8th Bt, CBE; *S* father, 1961; *m* 1976, Cola, *d* of Captain E. L. Cazenove, Great Dalby, Leics. *Educ:* Wellington College. Served War of 1939–45; Lt, 1943–45, 2nd Bn Irish Guards. *Recreations:* hunting, squash. *Heir: cousin* Michael Blackley Warren [*b* 12 Nov. 1918; *m* 1941, Marie Noelle, *e d* of Ernest Marcel Laffaille; one *d*]. *Address:* The Wilderness, Castle Oliver, Kilmallock, Co. Limerick. *T:* Kilfinane 89. *Club:* Cavalry and Guards.

WARREN, Rt. Rev. Cecil Allan; Rector, Old Brampton and Loundsley Green, 1983–88; Assistant Bishop, Diocese of Derby, 1983–88; *b* 25 Feb. 1924; *s* of Charles Henry and Eliza Warren; *m* 1947, Doreen Muriel Burrows. *Educ:* Sydney Univ. (BA 1950); Queen's Coll., Oxford (MA 1959). Deacon 1950, Priest 1951, Dio. of Canberra and Goulburn; appointments in Diocese of Oxford, 1953–57; Canberra, 1957–63; Organising Sec. Church Society, and Director of Forward in Faith Movement, Dio. of Canberra and Goulburn, 1963–65; Asst Bishop of Canberra and Goulburn, 1965–72; Bishop of Canberra and Goulburn, 1972–83. *Address:* 34 Panorama Crescent, Prince Henry Heights, Toowoomba, Qld 4350, Australia.

WARREN, Douglas Ernest, CMG 1973; *b* 8 June 1918; *s* of late Samuel Henry Warren; *m* 1945, Constance Vera (*née* Nix); two *d*. *Educ:* High Storrs Grammar Sch., Sheffield; Sheffield Univ. (BSc). FRICS. Royal Corps of Signals, 1940–46 (Captain): POW Thailand, 1942–45. Joined Colonial Service (later HMOCS), Tanganyika, as Surveyor, 1946: Supt of Surveys, 1955; transf. to Kenya as Asst Dir of Surveys, 1957; Dir of Survey of Kenya, 1961–65; retd from HMOCS, 1965; joined UK Civil Service as Dep. to Dir of Overseas Surveys, Min. of Overseas Develt, 1965, Dir of Overseas Surveys and Survey Adviser, 1968–80. Member: Land Surveyors Council, RICS, 1965–72; Council, RGS, 1968–71; various Royal Society cttees; Pres., Photogrammetric Soc., 1969–71. Patron's Medal, RGS, 1982. *Recreations:* travel, golf. *Address:* Flat 2, 19 St John's Road, Eastbourne, East Sussex BN20 7NQ. *T:* Eastbourne 639320 (0323). *Club:* Royal Eastbourne Golf.

WARREN, Frederick Lloyd, MA, BSc (Oxon), PhD, DSc (London); Professor of Biochemistry, London Hospital Medical College, 1952–78, now Emeritus; *b* 2 Oct. 1911; *s* of Frederick James and Edith Agnes Warren; *m* 1st, 1949, Natalia Vera Peierls (*née* Ladan) (marr. diss., 1958); two *s* one *d*; 2nd, 1961, Ruth Natallé Jacobs. *Educ:* Bristol Grammar Sch.; Exeter Coll., Oxford. Demonstrator, Biochem. Dept, Oxford, 1932–34; Sir Halley Stewart Res. Fellow, Chester Beatty Research Institute, Royal Cancer Hospital, 1934–46; Laura de Saliceto Student, University of London, 1937–42; Anna Fuller Research Student, 1942–46; Senior Lecturer in Biochemistry, St Mary's Hospital Medical School, 1946–48; Reader in Biochemistry, University College, London, 1948–52. *Publications:* papers and articles in scientific journals. *Address:* 5 River View, Enfield, Mddx EN2 6PX. *T:* 081–366 0674.

WARREN, Sir Frederick Miles, KBE 1985 (CBE 1974); FNZIA; ARIBA; Senior Partner, Warren & Mahoney, Architects Ltd; *b* Christchurch, 10 May 1929. *Educ:* Christ's Coll., Christchurch; Auckland Univ. DipArch; ARIBA 1952; FNZIA 1965. Founded Warren & Mahoney, 1958. Award-winning designs include: Christchurch Town Hall and Civic Centre; NZ Chancery, Washington; Canterbury Public Library; Michael Fowler Centre, Wellington; St Patrick's Church, Napier; Ohinetahi, Governors Bay; Rotorua Dist Council Civic Offices; Mulholland Hse, Wanganui; Parkroyal Hotel, Christchurch. Pres., Canterbury Soc. of Arts, 1972–76. Gold Medal, NZIA, 1960, 1964, 1969, 1973; Nat. Awards, NZIA, 1980, 1981, 1983–86, 1988, 1989, 1990, 1991. *Publication:* Warren & Mahoney Architects, 1990. *Recreation:* making a garden. *Address:* 65 Cambridge Terrace, Christchurch 1, New Zealand.

WARREN, Dr Graham Barry; Principal Scientist, Imperial Cancer Research Fund, since 1989; *b* 25 Feb. 1948; *s* of Joyce Thelma and Charles Graham Thomas Warren; *m* 1966, Philippa Mary Adeline (*née* Temple-Cole); four *d*. *Educ:* Willesden County Grammar Sch.; Pembroke Coll., Cambridge (MA, PhD). MRC Fellow, Nat. Inst. for Med. Research, 1972–75; Royal Soc. Stothert Research Fellow, Dept of Biochemistry, Cambridge, 1975–77; Research Fellow, Gonville & Caius Coll., Cambridge, 1975–77; Group Leader then Senior Scientist, European Molecular Biology Lab., Heidelberg, 1977–85; Prof. and Hd of Dept of Biochemistry, Dundee Univ., 1985–88. Mem., EMBO, 1986–. *Publications:* papers in learned jls on cell biology. *Recreation:* woodworking. *Address:* 17 Grosvenor Road, N10 2DR. *T:* 081–444 5808.

WARREN, Sir (Harold) Brian (Seymour), Kt 1974; physician; *b* 19 Dec. 1914; *er s* of late Harold Warren, St Ives, Hunts and Marian Jessie Emlyn; *m* 1st, 1942, Dame Alice Josephine Mary Taylor Barnes, *qv* (marr. diss. 1964); one *s* two *d*; 2nd, 1964, Elizabeth Anne (*d* 1983), *y d* of late Walter William Marsh, Wordsley, Staffs; two *s*. *Educ:* Bishop's Stortford Coll.; University Coll. London; University Coll. Hosp. MRCS, LRCP. Pres., Univ. of London Union, 1937–38. House Phys. and House Surg., UCH, 1942. War service with RAMC, RMO 1st Bn Gren. Gds and DADMS Gds Div., 1942–46 (despatches). Mem., Westminster City Council, 1955–64 and 1968–78; rep. West Woolwich on LCC, 1955–58, County Alderman 1961–62. Contested (C) Brixton Div. of Lambeth, 1959. Personal Phys. to Prime Minister, 1970–74. Mem., Westminster, Chelsea and Kensington AHA, 1975–77. Visitor and Mem. Emergency Bed Service Cttee, King Edward's Hosp. Fund for London, 1966–72; Mem. Governing Body, Westminster Hosp., 1970–74; Mem. Council, King Edward VII's Hosp. for Officers (Surg.-Apothecary, 1952–80). Pres., Chelsea Clinical Soc., 1955–56. Mem., Develt Cttee, BTA, 1978–87. Liveryman, Apothecaries' Soc., 1950; Freeman, City of London. *Publications:* contrib. Encycl. Gen. Practice. *Recreations:* reading, gardening, travel, listening to music. *Address:* 94 Oakley Street, SW3 5NR. *T:* 071–351 6462. *Clubs:* Boodle's, Pratt's.
See also A. I. Holden, M. G. J. Neary.

WARREN, Ian Scott; Senior Master of the Supreme Court (Queen's Bench Division) and Queen's Remembrancer, 1988–90 (Master, 1970–90); *b* 30 March 1917; *er s* of Arthur Owen Warren and Margaret Cromarty Warren (*née* Macnaughton); *m* 1st, 1943, Barbara (marr. diss.), *er d* of Walter Myrick, Tillsonburg, Ont.; four *s* one *d*; 2nd, Jeanne Hicklin (marr. diss.), *d* of late Frederick and Lydia Shaw, Crosland Moor; 3rd, 1987, Olive Sybil, *d* of late James Charles Montgomerie Wilson. *Educ:* Charterhouse (Exhbnr); Magdalene Coll., Cambridge (Exhbnr); BA 1938, MA 1950. Colonial Administrative Service, 1938–41, serving Gold Coast (Asst DC, 1940); RAF, 1942–46; Flying Badge and commissioned, 1943; Flt Lieut, 1944. Called to Bar, Lincoln's Inn, 1947, Bencher 1967; practised at Common Law Bar, London, 1947–70. *Publications:* Verses from Lincoln's Inn (jtly), 1975; Aesop's Fables: a selection, 1982. *Recreations:* ski-ing, walking, poetry. *Clubs:* Garrick, MCC.

WARREN, Jack Hamilton, OC 1982; company director; principal trade policy advisor, Government of Quebec, since 1986; *b* 10 April 1921; *s* of Tom Hamilton Warren and Olive Sykes (*née* Horsfall); *m* 1953, Hilary Joan Titterington; two *s* two *d*. *Educ:* Queen's Univ., Kingston, (BA). Served War, with Royal Canadian Navy. Public Service, 1945–57: Dept of External Affairs; Dept of Finance; diplomatic postings in Ottawa, London, Washington, Paris and Geneva; Asst Dep. Minister of Trade and Commerce, 1958; Chm., Council of Representatives, 1960, and Chm., Contracting Parties, 1962 and 1964, GATT; Dep. Minister: Dept of Trade and Commerce, 1964; Dept of Industry, Trade and Commerce, 1969; High Comr for Canada in London, 1971–74; Ambassador to USA, 1975–77; Ambassador, and Canadian Co-ordinator for the Multilateral Trade Negotiations, 1977–79; Vice-Chm., Bank of Montreal, 1979–86 (Mem. Internat. Adv. Council, 1986–88); Chm., Bank of Montreal International Ltd, 1984–89; Director: Roins Holdings Ltd, 1980–91; Royal Insurance Co. of Canada, 1980–91; Western Assurance Co., 1980–91; Pratt and Whitney, Canada, 1983–; PACCAR of Canada Ltd, 1984–. Dep. Chm. (N America), Trilateral Commn, 1985–91. Hon. LLD Queen's, Ont, 1974. Outstanding Achievement Award, Public Service of Canada, 1975. *Recreations:* fishing, gardening, golf, ski-ing. *Address:* PO Box 282 RR1, Chelsea, Que J0X 1N0, Canada. *Clubs:* Rideau (Ottawa); White Pine Fishing, Larrimac Golf (Canada).

WARREN, Dame Josephine; *see* Barnes, Dame A. J. M. T.

WARREN, Kenneth Robin, CEng, FRAeS; FCIT; FRSA; MP (C) Hastings and Rye, since 1983 (Hastings, 1970–83); Consultant in Engineering; Director of a number of companies; *b* 15 Aug. 1926; *s* of Edward Charles Warren and Ella Mary Warren (*née* Adams); *m* 1962, Elizabeth Anne Chamberlain, MA Cantab and MA Lond; one *s* two *d*. *Educ:* Midsomer Norton; Aldenham; London Univ.; De Havilland Aeronautical Technical Sch. Fulbright Scholar, USA; Research Engineer, BOAC, 1951–57; Personal Asst to Gen. Manager, Smiths Aircraft Instruments Ltd, 1957–60; Elliott Automation Ltd, 1960–69; Military Flight Systems: Manager, 1960–63; Divisional Manager, 1963–66; Marketing Manager, 1966–69. Former branch officer, G&MWU. Mem., Select Cttee on Science and Technology, 1970–79 (Chm., Offshore Engrg Sub-Cttee, 1975–76); Mem., Council of Europe, 1973–80; Chm., WEU, Science, Technology and Aerospace Cttee, 1976–79; Chm., Cons. Parly Aviation Cttee, 1975–77; PPS to Sec. of State for Industry, 1979–81, to Sec. of State for Educn and Sci., 1981–83; Chairman: Select Cttee on Trade and Industry, 1983–; British Soviet Parly Gp, 1986–. Pres., British Resorts Assoc. Liveryman: Coachmakers' Co.; GAPAN; Freeman, City of London. *Publications:* various papers to technical confs on aeronautical engineering and management, in USA, UK, Netherlands and Japan. *Recreations:* mountaineering, flying, gardening. *Address:* Woodfield House, Goudhurst, Kent. *T:* Goudhurst (0580) 211590.

WARREN, Maurice Eric; Chief Executive, Dalgety PLC, since 1989 (Director, since 1982); *b* 21 June 1933; *s* of Frederick Leonard and Winifred Warren; *m* 1954, Molly Warren; one *s* one *d*. *Educ:* St Brendan's Coll., Bristol. Certified Accountant, FCCA. Crosfield & Calthrop, 1958–74 (Dir, 1970–74); Managing Director: Dalgety Crosfields, 1974–76; Dalgety Agriculture Ltd, 1976–81; Dalgety UK Ltd, 1981–87; Dalgety plc, 1987–89. *Recreation:* golf. *Address:* Dalgety PLC, 100 George Street, W1H 5RH. *T:* 071–486 0200. *Clubs:* Royal Automobile, Lansdowne.

WARREN, Prof. Michael Donald, MD, FRCP, FFCM; Emeritus Professor of Social Medicine, University of Kent, since 1983; *b* 19 Dec. 1923; *s* of late Charles Warren and Dorothy Gladys Thornton Reeks; *m* 1946, Joan Lavina Peacock; one *s* two *d*. *Educ:* Bedford Sch.; Guy's Hosp.; London Sch. of Hygiene and Tropical Medicine. MB 1946, MD 1952; DPH 1952, DIH 1952; MRCP 1969, FRCP 1975; FFCM 1972. Sqdn Ldr RAF, Med. Branch, 1947–51; Dep. MOH, Metropolitan Borough of Hampstead, 1952–54; Asst Principal MO, LCC, 1954–58; Sen. Lectr and Hon. Consultant in Social Medicine, Royal Free Hosp. Sch., Royal Free Hosp. and London Sch. of Hygiene and Tropical Medicine, 1958–64; Sen. Lectr in Social Medicine, LSHTM, 1964–67; Reader in Public Health, Univ. of London, 1967–71; Prof. of Community Health, Univ. of London, 1978–80; Dir, Health Services Res. Unit, and Prof. of Social Medicine, Univ. of Kent, 1971–83, jtly with Specialist in Community Medicine (Epidemiology and Health Services Res.), SE Thames RHA, 1980–83. Chm., Soc. of Social Medicine, 1982–83. Academic Registrar, Faculty of Community Medicine, Royal Colls of Physicians, 1972–77. Jt Editor, British Jl of Preventive and Social Medicine, 1969–72. *Publications:* (jtly) Public Health and Social Services, 4th edn 1957, 6th edn 1965; (ed jtly) Management and the Health Services, 1971; (jtly) Physiotherapy in the Community, 1977; (jtly) Physically Disabled People Living at Home, 1978; (ed jtly) Recalling the Medical Officer of Health, 1987; contribs to BMJ, Lancet, Internat. Jl of Epidemiology. *Recreations:* light gardening (crocuses, primroses, narcissi, irises and shrubs), genealogy, reading, listening to music. *Address:* 2 Bridge Down, Bridge, Canterbury, Kent CT4 5AZ. *T:* Canterbury (0227) 830233. *Clubs:* Royal Society of Medicine; Kent County Cricket.

WARREN, Ven. Norman Leonard; Archdeacon of Rochester, since 1989; *b* 19 July 1934; *s* of Arthur Henry Warren and Gwendoline Catharine Warren; *m* 1961, Yvonne Sheather; three *s* two *d*. *Educ:* Dulwich College; Corpus Christi Coll., Cambridge (MA). Asst Curate, Bedworth, 1960–63; Vicar, St Paul's, Leamington Priors, 1963–77; Rector of Morden, 1977–89; RD of Merton, 1984–88. Musical Editor: Hymns for Today's Church, 1982; Jesus Praise, 1982. *Publications:* Journey into Life, 1964; The Way Ahead, 1965; Directions, 1969; What's the Point?, 1986; The Path of Peace, 1988; A Certain Faith, 1988; Is God there?, 1990. *Recreations:* cricket, soccer and Rugby, walking, music. *Address:* The Archdeaconry, Rochester, Kent ME1 1SX. *T:* Medway (0634) 842527.

WARREN, Peter Francis; Chairman: The Ogilvy Group (Holdings) Ltd (formerly Ogilvy & Mather (Holdings) Ltd), 1981–90; Ogilvy & Mather Europe, 1988–90; Consultant, Ogilvy & Mather Worldwide, since 1991 (Director, 1985–90); *b* 2 Dec. 1940; *s* of Francis Joseph Warren and Freda Ruth Hunter; *m* 1962, Susan Poole; two *s* one *d*. *Educ:* Finchley Grammar School. Deputy Managing Director, Ogilvy Benson & Mather Ltd, 1977; Director, Ogilvy & Mather International Inc., 1978; Man. Dir, Ogilvy Benson & Mather Ltd, 1978. *Address:* Brettenham House, Lancaster Place, WC2E 7EZ.

WARREN, Prof. Peter Michael, PhD; FSA; Professor of Ancient History and Classical Archaeology, since 1977 and Pro-Vice-Chancellor, since 1991, University of Bristol (Dean, Faculty of Arts, 1988–90); *b* 23 June 1938; *s* of Arthur George Warren and Alison Joan Warren (*née* White); *m* 1966, Elizabeth Margaret Halliday; one *s* one *d*. *Educ:* Sandbach Sch.; Llandovery Coll.; University College of N Wales, Bangor (Ellen Thomas Stanford Schol.; BA 1st Cl. Hons Greek and Latin); Corpus Christi Coll., Cambridge (Exhibnr; BA Classical Tripos Pt II 1962; MA 1966; PhD 1966; Fellow, 1965–68); student, British Sch. at Athens, 1963–65. FSA 1973. Research Fellow in Arts, Univ. of Durham, 1968–70; Asst Director, British Sch. at Athens, 1970–72; University of Birmingham: Lectr in Aegean Archaeol., 1972–74; Sen. Lectr, 1974–76; Reader, 1976. Vis. Prof., Univ. of Minnesota, 1981; Geddes-Harrower Prof. of Greek Art and Archaeol., Univ. of Aberdeen, 1986–87; Neubergh Lectr, Univ. of Göteborg, 1986. Dir of excavations, Myrtos, Crete, 1967–68; Debla, Crete, 1971; Knossos, 1971–73, 1978–82. Member: Managing Cttee, British Sch. at Athens, 1973–77, 1978–79, 1986–90 (Chm., 1979–83); Council, Soc. for Promotion of Hellenic Studies, 1978–81; Vice-Chm. Council, Bristol and Glos Archaeol Soc., 1980–81, Chm., 1981–84, Vice-Pres., 1989–. Hon. Fellow, Archaeol Soc. of Athens, 1987. *Publications:* Minoan Stone Vases, 1969; Myrtos, an Early Bronze Age Settlement in Crete, 1972; The Aegean Civilizations, 1975, 2nd edn 1989; Minoan Religion as Ritual Action, 1988; (with V. Hankey) Aegean Bronze Age Chronology, 1989; articles on Aegean Bronze Age, particularly Minoan archaeology, in archaeol and classical jls. *Recreations:* South Balkan travel and Greek village life. *Address:* Claremont House, Merlin Haven, Wotton-under-Edge, Glos GL12 7BA. *T:* Dursley (0453) 842290.

WARREN, Peter Tolman, PhD; Executive Secretary, The Royal Society, since 1985; *b* 20 Dec. 1937; *s* of late Hugh Alan Warren and Florence Christine Warren (*née* Tolman); *m* 1961, Angela Mary (*née* Curtis); two *s* one *d*. *Educ:* Whitgift Sch., Croydon; Queens' Coll., Cambridge (MA, PhD); FIGeol. Geological Survey of GB, 1962; Chief Scientific Adviser's Staff, Cabinet Office, 1972; Private Sec. to Lord Zuckerman, 1973–76; Science and Technology Secretariat, Cabinet Office, 1974–76; Safety Adviser, NERC, 1976–77; Dep. Exec. Sec., Royal Soc., 1977–85. Mem. Council, GPDST, 1989–. Editor, Monographs of Palaeontographical Soc., 1968–77. *Publications:* (ed) Geological Aspects of Development and Planning in Northern England, 1970; (co-author) Geology of the Country around Rhyl and Denbigh, 1984; papers on geology in learned jls. *Recreations:* geology, gardening. *Address:* Flat One, 6 Carlton House Terrace, SW1Y 5AG. *T:* 071–839 5260. *Club:* Athenæum.

WARREN, Prof. Raymond Henry Charles, MusD; Stanley Hugh Badock Professor of Music, University of Bristol, since 1972; *b* 7 Nov. 1928; *m* 1953, Roberta Lydia Alice Smith; three *s* one *d*. *Educ:* Bancroft's Sch.; Corpus Christi Coll., Cambridge (MA, MusD). Music Master, Wolverstone Hall Sch., 1952–55; Queen's University Belfast: Lectr in Music, 1955–66; Prof. of Composition, 1966–72; Resident Composer, Ulster Orchestra, 1967–72. Compositions incl. 2 symphonies, 3 string quartets and 6 operas. *Publications: compositions:* The Passion, 1963; String Quartet No 1, 1967; Violin Concerto, 1967; Songs of Old Age, 1971. *Recreation:* walking. *Address:* 9 Cabot Rise, Portishead, Bristol BS20 9NX. *T:* Bristol (0272) 844289.

WARREN, Stanley Anthony Treleaven, CB 1984; CEng, FRINA, FIMechE; RCNC; Director General Submarines, Ministry of Defence (Procurement Executive), 1979–85, retired; *b* 26 Sept. 1925; *s* of Stanley Howard Warren and Mabel Harriett (*née* Ham); *m* 1950, Sheila Glo May (*née* Rowe); two *s* one *d*. *Educ:* King's Coll., Univ. of London (BSc

1st Cl. Hons Engrg); RNC, Greenwich (1st Cl. Naval Architecture). FRINA 1967; FIMechE 1970. Sub-Lieut, RN, 1945–47; Constructor Lieut, RCNC, 1947–51; Royal Yacht Britannia design, 1951–54; frigate modernisations, 1954–57; Constructor, HM Dockyard, Malta, 1957–60; Admiralty Constructor Overseer, John Brown and Yarrow, 1960–64; Polaris Submarine design, 1964–67; Chief Constructor and Principal Naval Overseer, Birkenhead, 1967–72; Asst Dir and Invincible Class Proj. Manager, 1972–76; Dep. Dir of Submarines (Polaris), MoD (PE), 1976–79. *Publications:* contribs to learned societies. *Recreations:* golf, motoring, gardening.

WARREN EVANS, (John) Roger, FCIOB; Regional Property Director, J. Sainsbury plc, since 1988; *b* 11 Dec. 1935; *s* of Thomas and Mary Warren Evans; *m* 1966, Elizabeth M. James; one *s* one *d.* *Educ:* Leighton Park Sch., Reading; Trinity Coll., Cambridge (BA History, 1st Cl.); London Sch. of Economics. Called to Bar, Gray's Inn, 1962. Television Interviewer, Anglia Television, 1960–61; Research Officer, Centre for Urban Studies, London, 1961; practice at Bar, 1962–69; Legal Correspondent, New Society, 1964–68; general management functions with Bovis Gp, in construction and develt, 1969–74, incl. Man. Dir, Bovis Homes Southern Ltd, 1971–74; Under-Secretary, DoE, 1975; Industrial Advr on Construction, DoE, 1975–76; Man. Dir, Barratt Develts (London), Ltd, 1977–79; Dir, Swansea Centre for Trade and Industry, 1979–85; Man. Dir, Demos Ltd, 1985–87; SavaCentre Property Develt Manager, 1987–88. London Borough Councillor (Hackney), 1971–73. FCIOB 1976. *Recreations:* tennis, talking, playing the guitar. *Address:* 23 St Peter's Road, Newton, Swansea SA3 4SB. *T:* Swansea (0792) 368003; J. Sainsbury plc, Stamford House, Stamford Street, SE1 9LL.

WARRENDER, family name of **Baron Bruntisfield.**

WARRENDER, Col the Hon. John Robert, OBE 1963; MC 1943; TD 1967; DL; *b* 7 Feb. 1921; *s* and *heir* of Baron Bruntisfield, *qv*; *m* 1st, 1948, (Anne) Moireen Campbell (*d* 1976), 2nd *d* of Sir Walter Campbell, KCIE; two *s* two *d*; 2nd, 1977, Mrs Shirley Crawley (*d* 1981), *o d* of E. J. L. Ross; 3rd, 1985, Mrs (Kathleen) Joanna Graham, *o d* of David Chancellor. *Educ:* Eton; RMC, Sandhurst. Royal Scots Greys (2nd Dragoons), 1939–48; ADC to Governor of Madras, 1946–48; comd N Somerset Yeomanry/44th Royal Tank Regt, 1957–62; Dep. Brigadier RAC (TA), Southern and Eastern Commands, 1962–67. Mem., Queen's Body Guard for Scotland (Royal Co. of Archers), 1973 (Brigadier, 1973–85). DL Somerset 1965. *Recreations:* shooting, fishing. *Address:* 18 Warriston Crescent, Edinburgh EH3 5LB. *T:* 031–556 3701. *Clubs:* Pratt's; New (Edinburgh).

See also Hon. R. H. Warrender.

WARRENDER, Hon. Robin Hugh; Chairman and Chief Executive, London Wall Holdings PLC, since 1986; *b* 24 Dec. 1927; 3rd *s* of Baron Bruntisfield, *qv*; *m* 1951, Gillian, *d* of Leonard Rossiter; one *s* two *d.* *Educ:* Eton; Trinity Coll., Oxford. Underwriting Member of Lloyd's, 1953; Tudor & Co. (Insurance) Ltd, 1958–62; Managing Director, Fenchurch Insurance Holdings Ltd, 1963–69; Dep. Chm., A. W. Bain & Sons Ltd, 1970; Chm., Bain Dawes PLC and other group companies, 1973–85. Director: Comindus S. A. (France), 1980–; Worms & Co., 1981–; Varity Corporation (Canada), 1982–; Varity Holdings Ltd, 1982–; Heritable Group Holdings Ltd, 1983–; Société Centrale Préservatrice Foncière Assurances, 1986–89; Gp Athena, 1989–. Mem. Council and Cttee of Lloyd's, 1983–86. Mem. Council, Bath Univ., 1979–; Hon. Treas., Governing Cttee, Royal Choral Soc., 1979–. *Recreations:* shooting, gardening, bridge. *Address:* Widcombe Manor, Bath BA2 6AZ. *T:* Bath (0225) 317116; 69 Whitehall Court, SW1 2EL. *T:* 071–839 3848. *Clubs:* City of London, Portland, White's.

See also Baron Colgrain, Col the Hon. J. R. Warrender.

WARRINGTON, Bishop Suffragan of, since 1976; **Rt. Rev. Michael Henshall;** *b* 29 Feb. 1928; *m* Ann Elizabeth (*née* Stephenson); two *s* one *d.* *Educ:* Manchester Grammar Sch.; St Chad's Coll., Durham (BA 1954, DipTh 1956). Deacon 1956, priest 1957, dio. York; Curate of Holy Trinity, Bridlington and of Sewerby, 1956–59; Priest-in-charge, All Saints, Conventional District of Micklehurst, 1959–62; Vicar, 1962–63; Vicar of Altrincham, 1963–75; Proctor in Convocation, 1964–75; Mem., Terms of Ministry Cttee, General Synod, 1970–75; Hon. Canon of Chester, 1972–75; Secretary, Chester Diocesan Advisory Board for Ministry, 1968–75; Canon Emeritus of Chester Cathedral, 1979. Chairman: Northern Ordination Course Council, 1985–; Churches Gp NW, Industry Year, 1985–. Editor for 12 years of local newspaper, Spearhead. *Recreations:* military history, old battlefields, etc. *Address:* Martinsfield, Elm Avenue, Great Crosby, Liverpool, Merseyside L23 2SX. *T:* 051–924 7004; (office) 051–709 9722.

WARRINGTON, Archdeacon of; *see* Woodhouse, Ven. C. D. S.

WARRINGTON, Prof. Elizabeth Kerr, FRS 1986; Professor of Clinical Neuropsychology, National Hospital, since 1982; *d* of late Prof. John Alfred Valentine Butler, FRS and Margaret Lois Butler; one *d.* *Educ:* University College London (BSc 1954; PhD 1960; DSc 1975). Research Fellow, Inst. of Neurology, 1956; National Hospital: Senior Clinical Psychologist, 1960; Principal Psychologist, 1962; Top Grade Clinical Psychologist, 1972–82. *Publications:* (with R. A. McCarthy) Cognitive Neuropsychology, 1990; numerous papers in neurological and psychological jls. *Recreations:* gardening, entertaining grandchildren. *Address:* National Hospital, Queen Square, WC1N 3BG. *T:* 071–837 3611.

WARSOP, Rear-Adm. John Charles, CB 1984; CEng, FIMechE; Flag Officer Portsmouth and Naval Base Commander Portsmouth, 1983–85; RN retired, 1986; *b* 9 May 1927; *s* of John Charles Warsop and Elsie Lily Warsop; *m* 1958, Josephine Franklin Cotterell; two *d.* *Educ:* Gateway Sch., Leicester; RN Coll., Eaton Hall, Chester; RN Engineering Coll., Keyham, Plymouth, 1945–48. CEng 1981; FIMechE 1983. HM Ships Theseus and Gambia, 1949–50; RNC Greenwich, 1950–52; HMS Superb, 1952–54; Staff, RNEC, 1954–56; Min. of Defence, 1956–59; Sen. Engr, HMS Ark Royal, 1959–61; MoD, 1961–65; British Defence Staff, Washington, USA, 1965–68; MoD, 1968–70; Engr Officer, HMS Blake, 1970–72; MoD, 1972–75; CO, HMS Fisgard, 1975–78; MoD, 1979–81; Rear-Adm. 1981; Port Adm., Rosyth, 1981–83. Hon. Engrg Adviser, HMS Warrior (1860), 1986–. Chm., Soc. of Friends, RN Mus. and HMS Victory, 1989. *Publications:* papers for Instn of Marine Engineers. *Recreations:* offshore cruising, Rugby. *Club:* Royal Naval Sailing Association.

WARTIOVAARA, Otso Uolevi, Hon. GCVO; Ambassador of Finland to the Court of St James's, 1968–74; retired; *b* Helsinki, 16 Nov. 1908; *s* of J. V. Wartiovaara, Dir-Gen. of Finnish Govt Accounting Office, and Siiri Nystén; *m* 1936, Maine Alanen, three *s.* *Educ:* Helsinki Univ. Master of Law, 1932; Asst Judge, 1934. Entered Foreign Service, 1934; Attaché, Paris, 1936–39; Sec. and Head of Section, Min. for For. Affairs, 1939–42; Counsellor, Stockholm, 1942–44; Consul, Haaparanta, Sweden, 1944–45; Head of Section, Min. for For. Affairs, 1945–49; Counsellor, Washington, 1949–52; Head of Admin. Dept, Min. for For. Affairs, 1952–54; Envoy and Minister, 1954; Head of Legal Dept, Min. for For. Affairs, 1954–56; Minister, Belgrade and Athens, 1956–58; Ambassador, Belgrade, and Minister to Athens, 1958–61; Ambassador to Vienna, 1961–68, and to Holy See, 1966–68, also Perm. Rep. to Internat. Atomic Energy Organization, 1961–68. Grand Cross, Order of Lion of Finland; Kt Comdr, Order of White Rose of Finland; Cross of Freedom; Silver Cross of Sport, Finland. Grand Gold Cross of Austria; Grand Cross, Orders of Phœnix (Greece), Pius IX, Flag (Yugoslavia); Comdr, Orders of Northern Star (Sweden), St Olav (Norway) and Vasa (Sweden). *Recreations:* golf, shooting. *Address:* Lutherinkatn 6. A, 00100 Helsinki 10, Finland.

WARTNABY, Dr John; Keeper, Department of Earth and Space Sciences, Science Museum, South Kensington, 1969–82; *b* 6 Jan. 1926; *o s* of Ernest John and Beatrice Hilda Wartnaby; *m* 1962, Kathleen Mary Barber, MD, MRCP, DPM; one *s* one *d.* *Educ:* Chiswick Grammar Sch.; Chelsea Coll. (BSc 1946); Imperial Coll. of Science and Technology (DIC 1950); University Coll., London (MSc 1967; PhD 1972). FInstP 1971. Asst Keeper, Dept of Astronomy and Geophysics, Science Museum, 1951; Deputy Keeper, 1960. *Publications:* Seismology, 1957; The International Geophysical Year, 1957; Surveying, 1968; papers in learned jls. *Recreations:* country walking, Zen. *Address:* 11 Greenhurst Lane, Oxted, Surrey RH8 0LD. *T:* Oxted (0883) 714461.

WARWICK; *see* Turner-Warwick.

WARWICK, 8th Earl of, *cr* 1759; **David Robin Francis Guy Greville;** Baron Brooke 1621; Earl Brooke 1746; *b* 15 May 1934; *s* of 7th Earl of Warwick, and Rose, *d* of late D. C. Bingham; *S* father, 1984; *m* 1956, Sarah Anne (marr. diss. 1967), *d* of late Alfred Chester Beatty and Mrs Pamela Neilson; one *s* one *d.* *Educ:* Eton. Life Guards, 1952; Warwicks Yeo. (TA), 1954. *Heir:* *s* Lord Brooke, *qv*. *Clubs:* White's; The Brook (NY); Eagle Ski (Gstaad).

WARWICK, Bishop Suffragan of, since 1990; **Rt. Rev. (George) Clive Handford;** *b* 17 April 1937; *s* of Cyril Percy Dawson Handford and Alice Ethel Handford; *m* 1962, Anne Elizabeth Jane Atherley; one *d.* *Educ:* Hatfield Coll., Durham (BA); Queen's Coll., Birmingham and Univ. of Birmingham (DipTh). Curate, Mansfield Parish Church, 1963–66; Chaplain: Baghdad, 1967; Beirut, 1967–73; Dean, St George's Cathedral, Jerusalem, 1974–78; Archdeacon in the Gulf and Chaplain in Abu Dhabi and Qatar, 1978–83; Vicar of Kneesall with Laxton, and Wellow and Rufford, 1983–84; RD of Tuxford and Norwell, 1983–84; Archdeacon of Nottingham, 1984–90. ChStJ 1976. *Address:* Warwick House, 139 Kenilworth Road, Coventry CV4 7AF. *T:* Coventry (0203) 416200.

WARWICK, Archdeacon of; *see* Paget-Wilkes, Ven. M. J. J.

WARWICK, Diana; General Secretary, Association of University Teachers, since 1983; Member, TUC General Council, since 1989; *b* 16 July 1945; *d* of Jack and Olive Warwick; *m* 1969. *Educ:* St Joseph's Coll., Bradford; Bedford Coll., Univ. of London (BA Hons). Technical Asst to the Gen. Sec., NUT, 1969–72; Asst Sec., CPSA, 1972–83. Member: Bd, British Council, 1985–; Employment Appeal Tribunal, 1987–; Exec. and Council, Industrial Soc., 1987–; Council, Foundn for Educn Business Partnerships, 1989–91; Exec. and Council, Inst. of Employment Rights, 1989–; Council, Duke of Edinburgh's Seventh Commonwealth Study Conf., 1991. Gov., Commonwealth Inst., 1988–. Trustee, Royal Anniversary Trust, 1991–. FRSA. *Recreations:* reading, riding, looking at pictures. *Address:* AUT, United House, 1 Pembridge Road, Notting Hill Gate, W11 3JY. *T:* 071–221 4370.

WARWICK, Hannah Cambell Grant; *see* Gordon, H. C. G.

WARWICK, Captain William Eldon, CBE 1971; RD; RNR retired; Commodore, Cunard Line Ltd, 1970–75; First Master, RMS Queen Elizabeth 2, 1966–72; *b* 12 Nov. 1912; *e s* of Eldon Warwick, architect and Gertrude Florence Gent; *m* 1939, Evelyn King (*née* Williams); three *s.* *Educ:* Birkenhead Sch.; HMTS Conway. Joined Merchant Service, 1928, serving in Indian Ocean and Red Sea; awarded Master Mariner's Certificate, 1936; joined Cunard White Star as Jun. Officer (Lancastria), 1937; commissioned in RNR, 1937. Mobilized in RN War Service, 1939, in Coastal Forces and Corvettes in North Atlantic, Russian Convoys and Normandy Landings, 1939–46 (despatches, 1946). First cargo command, Alsatia, 1954; first passenger command, Carinthia, 1958; followed by command of almost all the passenger liners in Cunard fleet. Promoted Captain RNR, 1960; retd RNR, 1965. Treas., Internat. Fedn of Shipmasters' Assocs. Younger Brother of Trinity House; Liveryman, Hon. Co. of Master Mariners (Master, 1976–77); Freeman of City of London. *Recreations:* reading, music, walking. *Address:* Greywell Cottage, Callow Hill, Virginia Water, Surrey. *T:* Wentworth (0344) 843361. *Club:* Naval.

WASS, Sir Douglas (William Gretton), GCB 1980 (KCB 1975; CB 1971); Chairman: Equity & Law Life Assurance Society plc, since 1986 (Director, since 1984); Nomura International Ltd, since 1986; Permanent Secretary to HM Treasury, 1974–83, and Joint Head of the Home Civil Service, 1981–83; *b* 15 April 1923; *s* of late Arthur W. and late Elsie W. Wass; *m* 1954, Dr Milica Pavičić; one *s* one *d.* *Educ:* Nottingham High Sch.; St John's Coll., Cambridge (MA; Hon. Fellow, 1982). Served War, 1943–46: Scientific Research with Admiralty, at home and in Far East. Entered HM Treasury as Asst Principal, 1946; Principal, 1951; Commonwealth Fund Fellow in USA, 1958–59; Vis. Fellow, Brookings Instn, Washington, DC, 1959; Private Sec.: to Chancellor of the Exchequer, 1959–61; to Chief Sec. to Treasury, 1961–62; Asst Sec., 1962; Alternate Exec. Dir, Internat. Monetary Fund, and Financial Counsellor, British Embassy, Washington, DC, 1965–67; HM Treasury: Under-Sec., 1968; Dep. Sec., 1970–73; Second Permanent Sec., 1973–74. Director: Barclays Bank, 1984–87; De La Rue Company plc, 1984–; Administrateur, Axa SA, 1987–; Consultant to Coopers & Lybrand, 1984–86. Chairman: British Selection Cttee of Harkness Fellowships, 1981–84; UN Adv. Gp on Financial Flows for Africa, 1987–88; Syndicate on the Government of Univ. of Cambridge, 1988–89. Pres., Market Res. Soc., 1987–91. Dep. Chm., Council of Policy Studies Inst, 1981–85; Vice-Pres., 1984–, and Mem. Adv. Bd, Constitutional Reform Centre; Vice Chm., Africa Capacity Building Foundn, 1991–; Governor, Ditchley Foundn, 1981–; Member, Council: Centre for Econ. Policy Res., 1983–90; Employment Inst., 1985–; Univ. of Bath, 1985–91; British Heart Foundn, 1990–. Lectures: Reith, BBC, 1983; Shell, St Andrews Univ., 1985; Harry Street Meml, Univ. of Manchester, 1987. Hon. DLitt Bath, 1985. *Publications:* Government and the Governed, 1984; articles in newspapers and jls. *Address:* 6 Dora Road, SW19 7HH. *T:* 081–946 5556. *Club:* Reform.

WASSERMAN, Gordon Joshua; Assistant Under Secretary of State, Home Office, since 1983; *b* Montreal, 26 July 1938; *s* of late John J. Wasserman, QC, and Prof. Rachel Chait Wasserman, Montreal; *m* 1964, Cressida Frances, *yr d* of late Rt Hon. Hugh Gaitskell, PC, CBE, MP, and Baroness Gaitskell; two *d.* *Educ:* Westmount High Sch., Montreal; McGill Univ. (BA); New Coll., Oxford (MA). Rhodes Scholar (Quebec and New Coll.), 1959; Sen. Research Scholar, St Antony's Coll., Oxford, 1961–64; Lectr in Economics, Merton Coll., Oxford, 1963–64; Research Fellow, New Coll., Oxford, 1964–67; joined Home Office as Economic Adviser, 1967, Sen. Econ. Adviser, 1972, Asst Sec., 1977–81; Head, Urban Deprivation Unit, 1973–77; Civil Service Travelling Fellowship in USA, 1977–78; Under Sec., Central Policy Review Staff, Cabinet Office, 1981–83. Vice-Pres., English Basket Ball Assoc., 1983–86. *Recreations:* gardening, walking, theatre, music. *Address:* c/o Home Office, SW1. *Clubs:* Reform, Beefsteak.

WASSERSTEIN, Prof. Abraham; Professor of Greek, Hebrew University of Jerusalem, 1969–89, now Emeritus; *b* Frankfurt/Main, Germany, 5 Oct. 1921; *s* of late Berl Bernhard Wasserstein and late Czarna Cilla (*née* Laub); *m* 1942, Margaret Eva (*née* Ecker); two *s* one *d*. *Educ:* Schools in Berlin and Rome; privately in Palestine; Birkbeck Coll., London Univ. BA 1949, PhD 1951. Assistant in Greek, 1951–52, Lecturer in Greek, 1952–60, Glasgow Univ.; Prof. of Classics, Leicester Univ., 1960–69, and Dean of Faculty of Arts, 1966–69. Visiting Fellow: Centre for Postgraduate Hebrew Studies, Oriental Inst., Univ. of Oxford, 1973–74; Wolfson Coll., Oxford, 1986; Vis. Professor: Hochschule für Jüdische Studien, Heidelberg, 1980–81; Univ. of Heidelberg, 1983. Mem. Inst. for Advanced Study, Princeton, 1975–76 and 1985–86. Fellow, Annenberg Res. Inst., Philadelphia, 1988. FRAS 1961; Pres., Classical Assoc. of Israel, 1971–74. *Publications:* Flavius Josephus, 1974; Galen, On Airs, Waters, Places (critical edn, with trans. and notes), 1982; contrib. to learned journals. *Recreations:* theatre, travel. *Address:* Department of Classics, The Hebrew University, Jerusalem, Israel.

WASTELL, Cyril Gordon, CBE 1975; Secretary General of Lloyd's, 1967–76, retired; *b* 10 Jan. 1916; *s* of Arthur Edward Wastell and Lilian Wastell; *m* 1947, Margaret Lilian (*née* Moore); one *d*. *Educ:* Brentwood Sch., Essex. Joined Staff of Corporation of Lloyd's, 1932; apart from war service (Lieut Royal Corps of Signals), 1939–46, progressed through various depts and positions at Lloyd's, until retirement. *Recreations:* reading, gardening under duress, golf, various trivial pursuits. *Address:* Candys, Burgmann's Hill, Lympstone, Devon EX8 5HP.

WASTIE, Winston Victor, CB 1962; OBE 1946 (MBE 1937); Under-Secretary, Ministry of Public Building and Works, Scotland, 1959–62, retired; *b* 5 March 1900; *s* of H. Wastie; *m* 1924, Charmbury Billows (*d* 1986); one *d*. *Educ:* Greenwich Secondary Sch. Civil Service, New Scotland Yard, 1915–42; Chief Licensing Officer, Civil Building Control, Ministry of Works, 1942–46; Assistant Secretary, Scottish HQ, Ministry of Works, 1946–59; Under-Secretary, 1959. *Recreations:* bridge, gardening and sport. *Address:* Dirleton, Hazelbank Close, Petersfield, Hants.

WATERFIELD, Giles Adrian, FSA; Director, Dulwich Picture Gallery, since 1979; *b* 24 July 1949; *s* of late Anthony and Honor Waterfield. *Educ:* Eton College; Magdalen College, Oxford (BA); Courtauld Institute (MA). Education Officer, Royal Pavilion, Art Gallery and Museums, Brighton, 1976–79. FRSA. *Publications:* Faces, 1983; Collection for a King (catalogue), 1985; Soane and After, 1987; Rich Summer of Art, 1988; articles in Apollo, Connoisseur, Country Life, TLS, Turner Studies. *Recreation:* sightseeing. *Address:* c/o Dulwich Picture Gallery, College Road, SE21 7AD. *Club:* Travellers'.

WATERFIELD, John Percival; *b* Dublin, 5 Oct. 1921; *er s* of late Sir Percival Waterfield, KBE, CB; *m* 1950, Margaret Lee Thomas (*d* 1990); two *s* one *d*. *Educ:* Dragon Sch.; Charterhouse (schol.); Christ Church, Oxford (schol.). Served War of 1939–45: 1st Bn, The King's Royal Rifle Corps (60th Rifles), Western Desert, Tunisia, Italy and Austria (despatches). Entered HM Foreign (subseq. Diplomatic) Service, 1946; Third Secretary, Moscow, 1947; Second Secretary, Tokyo, 1950; Foreign Office, 1952; First Secretary, Santiago, Chile, 1954; HM Consul (Commercial), New York, 1957; FO, 1960; Ambassador to Mali Republic, 1964–65, concurrently to Guinea, 1965; duties connected with NATO, 1966; Counsellor and Head of Chancery, New Delhi, 1966–68; Head of Western Organizations Dept, FCO, 1969; Man. Dir, BEAMA, 1971; Principal Estabs and Finance Officer, NI Office, 1973–79; on secondment to Internat. Military Services Ltd, 1979–80; retired from public service, 1980; company dir and consultant, 1980–84. *Address:* 5 North Street, Somerton, Somerset. *T:* Somerton (0458) 72389. *Club:* Boodle's.

WATERFIELD, Prof. Michael Derek, PhD; FRS 1991; Director of Research, Ludwig Institute for Cancer Research, University College London, since 1986; *b* 14 May 1941; *s* of Leslie N. Waterfield and Kathleen A. (*née* Marshall); *m* 1982, Sally E. James, MB BS, PhD; two *d*. *Educ:* Brunel Univ. (BSc 1963); Univ. of London (PhD 1967). Res. Fellow, Harvard Univ. Med. Sch., 1967–70; Sen. Res. Fellow, CIT, 1970–72; Hd, Protein Chem. Lab., ICRF Labs, 1972–86. Hon. MD Ferrara, Italy, 1991. *Publications:* numerous articles in scientific jls on biochem. and molecular biol. as applied to cancer research. *Recreation:* gardening. *Address:* Chantemerle, Speen Lane, Newbury, Berks RG13 1RN.

WATERFORD, 8th Marquess of, *cr* 1789; **John Hubert de la Poer Beresford;** Baron Le Poer, 1375; Baronet, 1668; Viscount Tyrone, Baron Beresford, 1720; Earl of Tyrone, 1746; Baron Tyrone (Great Britain), 1786; *b* 14 July 1933; *er s* of 7th Marquess and Juliet Mary (who *m* 2nd, 1946, Lieut-Colonel John Silcock), 2nd *d* of late David Lindsay; *S* father, 1934; *m* 1957, Lady Caroline Wyndham-Quin, *yr d* of 6th Earl of Dunraven and Mount-Earl, CB, CBE, MC; three *s* one *d*. *Educ:* Eton. Lieut, RHG Reserve. *Heir: s* Earl of Tyrone, *qv*. *Address:* Curraghmore, Portlaw, Co. Waterford. *T:* Waterford (51) 87102, *Fax:* Waterford (51) 87481. *Club:* White's.

WATERHOUSE, David Martin; Director, Germany, British Council, since 1991; *b* 23 July 1937; *s* of Rev. John W. Waterhouse and Dr Esther Waterhouse; *m* 1966, Verena Johnson; one *s* two *d*. *Educ:* Kingswood Sch., Bath; Merton Coll., Oxford (MA). Joined British Council, 1961; Enugu, Nigeria, 1962–65; Glasgow, 1965–68; Ndola, Zambia, 1968–71; Inst. of Educn, London Univ., 1971–72; Representative: Nepal, 1972–77; Thailand, 1977–80; Dir, Personnel Management Dept, 1980–85; Rep., Nigeria, 1985–89; Controller, Home Div., subseq. Dir, Exchanges and Training Div., British Council, 1989–91. *Recreations:* walking, music. *Address:* c/o The British Council, 10 Spring Gardens, SW1A 2BN. *T:* 071–930 8466.

WATERHOUSE, Dr Douglas Frew, AO 1980; CMG 1970; FRS 1967; FAA 1954; FRACI 1948; Chief of Division of Entomology, Commonwealth Scientific and Industrial Research Organization, 1960–81, Honorary Research Fellow, since 1981; *b* 3 June 1916; *s* of late Prof. E. G. Waterhouse, CMG, OBE, and Janet Frew Kellie, MA; *m* 1944, Allison D., *d* of J. H. Calthorpe; three *s* one *d*. *Educ:* Sydney C of E Grammar Sch.; Universities of Sydney and Cambridge. BSc Hons, University Medal, MSc, DSc, Sydney. Served War of 1939–45, Captain, AAMC Medical Entomology. Joined Research Staff, CSIRO, 1938; Asst Chief, Div. of Entomology, 1953–60. Biological Secretary, Australian Acad. of Science, 1961–66; Chairman: Council, Canberra Coll. of Advanced Educn, 1969–84; Council for Internat. Congresses of Entomology, 1980–84 (Hon. mem., 1984); Nat. Sci. Summer Sch., Aust. Industry Develt Corp., 1985–88; Pres., ACT Br., Nat. Trust of Australia, 1984–88. Corresp. Mem., Brazilian Acad. of Sciences, 1974. Hon. For. Mem., All-Union Entomological Soc. of USSR, 1979; For. Mem., USSR Acad. of Science, 1982; Foreign Assoc., US Nat. Acad. of Scis, 1983. Hon. FRES 1972. Hon. DSc ANU, 1978. David Syme Research Prize, 1953; Mueller Medal, ANZAAS, 1972; Farrer Medal, Farrer Meml Trust, 1973; Medal, 10th Internat. Congress of Plant Protection, 1983; Principal Bicentennial Contrib. to Agriculture Award, 1988. *Publications:* numerous articles on insect physiology, biochemistry, ecology and control of insects. *Recreations:* gardening, fishing, gyotaku. *Address:* 60 National Circuit, Deakin, ACT 2600, Australia. *T:* (06) 2731772. *Club:* Commonwealth (Canberra).

WATERHOUSE, Frederick Harry; Chief Accountant, Jelkeep Ltd, Deerhyde Ltd, Thawscroft Ltd, Selsey, since 1988; *b* 3 June 1932; *m* 1954, Olive Carter; two *d*. *Educ:* King Edward's, Aston, Birmingham; London Univ. (BScEcon). Associate Mem. Inst. of Cost and Management Accountants. Chief Accountant, Copper Div., Imperial Metal Industries, 1967–70; Asst Chief Accountant, Agricl Div., ICI, 1970–72; Chief Accountant, Plant Protection Div., ICI, 1972–78; Dir, Société pour la Protection d'Agriculture (SOPRA), France, 1976–78; Dir, Solplant SA, Italy, 1976–78; Bd Member, Finance and Corporate Planning, The Post Office, 1978–79; Treasurer's Dept, ICI Ltd, Millbank, 1979–82. Partner, Bognor Antiques, 1984–87. *Recreations:* golf, gardening, sailing. *Address:* 47 Grosvenor Road, Chichester PO19 2RT. *T:* Chichester (0243) 783745.

WATERHOUSE, Keith Spencer, CBE 1991; FRSL; writer; *b* 6 Feb. 1929; 4th *s* of Ernest and Elsie Edith Waterhouse; *m* 1984, Stella Bingham (marr. diss. 1989); one *s* two *d* by previous *m*. *Educ:* Leeds. Journalist in Leeds and London, 1950–; Columnist with: Daily Mirror, 1970–86; Daily Mail, 1986–; Contributor to various periodicals; Mem. Punch Table, 1979. Mem., Kingman Cttee on Teaching of English Language, 1987–88. Hon. Fellow, Leeds Polytechnic, 1991. Granada Columnist of the Year Award, 1970; IPC Descriptive Writer of the Year Award, 1970; IPC Columnist of the Year Award, 1973; British Press Awards Columnist of the Year, 1978, 1991; Granada Special Quarter Century Award, 1982. Films (with Willis Hall) include: Billy Liar; Whistle Down the Wind; A Kind of Loving; Lock Up Your Daughters. Plays: Mr and Mrs Nobody, 1986; Jeffrey Bernard is Unwell, 1989; Bookends, 1990; plays with Willis Hall include: Billy Liar, 1960 (from which musical Billy was adapted, 1974); Celebration, 1961; All Things Bright and Beautiful, 1963; Say Who You Are, 1965; Whoops-a-Daisy, 1968; Children's Day, 1969; Who's Who, 1972; The Card (musical), 1973; Saturday, Sunday, Monday (adaptation from de Filippo), 1973; Filumena (adaptation from de Filippo), 1977; Worzel Gummidge, 1981; Budgie (musical), 1988. TV series: Budgie, Queenie's Castle, The Upper Crusts, Billy Liar, The Upchat Line, The Upchat Connection, Worzel Gummidge, West End Tales, The Happy Apple, Charters and Caldicott, Andy Capp; TV films: Charlie Muffin, 1983; This Office Life, 1985; The Great Paper Chase, 1988. *Publications: novels:* There is a Happy Land, 1957; Billy Liar, 1959; Jubb, 1963; The Bucket Shop, 1968; Billy Liar on the Moon, 1975; Office Life, 1978; Maggie Muggins, 1981; In the Mood, 1983; Thinks, 1984; Our Song, 1988; Bimbo, 1990; *plays:* Jeffrey Bernard Is Unwell, 1991; (with Willis Hall) include: Billy Liar, 1960; Celebration, 1961; All Things Bright and Beautiful, 1963; Say Who You Are, 1965; Who's Who, 1974; Saturday, Sunday, Monday (adaptation from de Filippo), 1974; Filumena (adaptation from de Filippo), 1977; *general:* (with Guy Deghy) Café Royal, 1956; (ed) Writers' Theatre, 1967; The Passing of The Third-floor Buck, 1974; Mondays, Thursdays, 1976; Rhubarb, Rhubarb, 1979; Daily Mirror Style, 1980, rev. and expanded edn, Newspaper Style, 1989; Fanny Peculiar, 1983; Mrs Pooter's Diary, 1983; Waterhouse At Large, 1985; Collected Letters of a Nobody, 1986; The Theory and Practice of Lunch, 1986; The Theory and Practice of Travel, 1989; English Our English, 1991. *Recreation:* lunch. *Address:* 29 Kenway Road, SW5 0RP. *Clubs:* Garrick, Savile, PEN.

WATERHOUSE, Dame Rachel (Elizabeth), DBE 1990 (CBE 1980); PhD; Chairman, Consumers' Association, 1982–90 (Member Council, since 1966, Deputy Chairman, 1979–82); Member, Health and Safety Commission, since 1990; *b* 2 Jan. 1923; *d* of Percival John Franklin and Ruby Susanna Franklin; *m* 1947, John A. H. Waterhouse; two *s* two *d*. *Educ:* King Edward's High Sch., Birmingham; St Hugh's Coll., Oxford (BA 1944, MA 1948); Univ. of Birmingham (PhD 1950). WEA and Extra-mural tutor, 1944–47. Birmingham Consumer Group: Sec., 1964–65, Chm. 1966–68, Mem. Cttee, 1968–; Member: Nat. Consumer Council, 1975–86; Consumers' Consultative Cttee of EEC Commn, 1977–84; Price Commn, 1977–79; Council, Advertising Standards Authority, 1980–85; NEDC, 1981–91; BBC Consultative Gp on Industrial and Business Affairs, 1984–89; Richmond Cttee on Microbiol Safety of Food, 1989–90; HSC, 1990–; Adv. Cttee on Microbiological Safety of Food, 1991–. Ministerial nominee to Potato Marketing Bd, 1969–81; Chm., Council for Licensed Conveyancers, 1986–89; Member: Home Office Working Party on Internal Shop Security, 1971–73; Adv. Cttee on Asbestos, 1976–79; Council for the Securities Industry, 1983–85; Securities and Investments Board, 1985–; Organising Cttee, Marketing of Investments Bd, 1985–86; Council, Office of the Banking Ombudsman, 1985–; Duke of Edinburgh's Inquiry into British Housing, 1984–85; Adv. Bd, Inst. of Food Res., 1988–. Pres., Inst. of Consumer Ergonomics, Univ. of Loughborough, 1980– (Chm., 1970–80); Vice-Pres., Nat. Fedn of Consumer Gps, 1980–. Chm., Birmingham Gp, Victorian Soc., 1966–67, 1972–74. Trustee, Joseph Rowntree Foundn, 1990–. Hon. FGIA (Hon. CGIA 1988). Hon. DLitt Univ. of Technology, Loughborough, 1978; Hon. DSocSc Birmingham, 1990. *Publications:* The Birmingham and Midland Institute 1854–1954, 1954; A Hundred Years of Engineering Craftsmanship, 1957; Children in Hospital: a hundred years of child care in Birmingham, 1962; (with John Whybrow) How Birmingham became a Great City, 1976; King Edward VI High School for Girls 1883–1983, 1983. *Address:* 252 Bristol Road, Birmingham B5 7SL. *T:* 021–472 0427. *Club:* Commonwealth Trust.

WATERHOUSE, Hon. Sir Ronald (Gough), Kt 1978; **Hon. Mr Justice Waterhouse;** Judge of the High Court of Justice, Family Division, 1978–88, Queen's Bench Division, since 1988; *b* Holywell, Flintshire, 8 May 1926; *s* of late Thomas Waterhouse, CBE, and of Doris Helena Waterhouse (*née* Gough); *m* 1960, Sarah Selina, *d* of late Captain E. A. Ingram; one *s* two *d*. *Educ:* Holywell Grammar Sch.; St John's Coll., Cambridge. RAFVR, 1944–48. McMahon Schol., St John's Coll., 1949; Pres., Cambridge Union Soc., 1950; MA, LLM; called to Bar, Middle Temple, 1952 (Harmsworth Schol.); Wales and Chester Circuit; QC 1969; Bencher 1977. A Recorder of the Crown Court, 1972–77; Presiding Judge, Wales and Chester Circuit, 1980–84; a Judge, Employment Appeal Tribunal, 1979–87. Mem. Bar Council, 1961–65. Deputy Chairman: Cheshire QS, 1964–71; Flintshire QS, 1966–71. Contested (Lab) West Flintshire, 1959. Chairman: Inter-departmental Cttee of Inquiry on Rabies, 1970; Cttees of Investigation for GB and England and Wales, under Agricultural Mkting Act, 1971–78; Local Govt Boundary Commn for Wales, 1974–78. Mem. Council, Zoological Soc. of London, 1972–89 and 1991–, a Vice-Pres., 1981–84. Hon. LLD Wales, 1986. *Recreations:* music, golf. *Address:* Royal Courts of Justice, Strand, WC2A 2LL. *Clubs:* Garrick, MCC; Cardiff and County (Cardiff).

See also J. B. Thompson.

WATERLOW, Sir Christopher Rupert, 5th Bt *cr* 1873; *b* 12 Aug. 1959; *s* of (Peter) Rupert Waterlow (*d* 1969) and Jill Elizabeth (*d* 1961), *e d* of E. T. Gourlay; *S* grandfather 1973; *m* 1986, Sally-Ann, *o d* of Maurice and Betty Bitten. *Educ:* Stonyhurst Coll., Lancs. Professional Videographer with Crown Productions (own company). Mem., Inst. of Videographers. *Recreations:* pistol shooting, squash. *Heir: cousin* Nicholas Anthony Waterlow [*b* 30 Aug. 1941; *m* 1965, Rosemary, *o d* of W. J. O'Brien; two *s* one *d*]. *Address:* 26 Barfield Road, Bickley, Kent BR1 2HS. *Clubs:* Stonyhurst Association; Mayfair Gun.

WATERLOW, Sir (James) Gerard, 4th Bt *cr* 1930; consultant; *b* 3 Sept. 1939; *s* of Sir Thomas Gordon Waterlow, 3rd Bt, CBE and Helen Elizabeth (*d* 1970), *yr d* of Gerard A. H. Robinson; *S* father, 1982; *m* 1965, Diana Suzanne, *yr d* of Sir Thomas Skyrme, *qv*; one *s* one *d*. *Educ:* Marlborough; Trinity College, Cambridge. Previously employed in the computer industry; now consultant on computer aided prodn management. *Recreations:* tennis, bridge. *Heir: s* (Thomas) James Waterlow, *b* 20 March 1970. *Address:* Windmills House, Hurstbourne Tarrant, Hants SP11 0DQ. *T:* Hurstbourne Tarrant (026476) 547. *Club:* Lansdowne.

WATERLOW, Prof. John Conrad, CMG 1970; MD, ScD; FRCP; FRS 1982; FRGS; Professor of Human Nutrition, London School of Hygiene and Tropical Medicine, 1970–82, now Emeritus; *b* 13 June 1916; *o s* of Sir Sydney Waterlow, KCMG, CBE, HM Diplomatic Service; *m* 1939, Angela Pauline Cecil Gray; two *s* one *d*. *Educ:* Eton Coll.; Trinity Coll., Cambridge (MD, ScD); London Hosp. Med. College. Mem., Scientific Staff, MRC, 1942; Dir, MRC Tropical Metabolism Research Unit, Univ. of the West Indies, 1954–70. *Publications:* numerous papers on protein malnutrition and protein metabolism. *Recreation:* mountain walking. *Address:* 15 Hillgate Street, W8 7SP; Oare, Marlborough, Wilts. *Club:* Savile.

WATERMAN, Fanny, OBE 1971; FRCM; Chairman, Leeds International Pianoforte Competition, since 1963 (in association with Harveys of Bristol, since 1985); also Chairman of Jury, since 1981; *b* 22 March 1920; *d* of Myer Waterman and Mary Waterman (*née* Behrmann); *m* 1944, Dr Geoffrey de Keyser; two *s*. *Educ:* Allerton High Sch., Leeds; Tobias Matthay, Cyril Smith, Royal College of Music, London (FRCM 1972). Concert pianist, teacher of international reputation. Vice-Pres., European Piano-Teachers Assoc., 1975–; Trustee, Edward Boyle Meml Trust, 1981–. Governor, Harrogate Fest., 1983. Founded (with Marion Harewood) Leeds International Pianoforte Competition, 1961. Member of International Juries: Beethoven, Vienna, 1977; Casagrande, Terni, 1978; Munich, 1979, 1986; Bach, Leipzig, 1980, 1984; Leeds (Chm.), 1981, 1984, 1987; Calgary, 1982; Gina Bachauer, Salt Lake City, 1982, 1984; Viña del Mar (Chm.), 1982, 1987; Maryland, 1983; Cologne, 1983, 1986; Pretoria, 1984; Santander, 1984; Rubinstein, Israel (Vice-Pres.), 1986, 1989; Tchaikowsky, Moscow, 1986; Vladigerov, Bulgaria, 1986; Lisbon, 1987; Canadian Broadcasting Corp., Toronto, 1989. Piano Progress series on ITV Channel 4. Hon. MA Leeds, 1966. *Publications:* (with Marion Harewood): series of Piano Tutors, 1967–: 1st Year Piano lessons: 1st Year Repertoire; 2nd Year Piano lessons: 2nd Year Repertoire; 3rd Year Piano lessons: 3rd Year Repertoire; Duets and Piano Playtime, 1978; Recital Book for pianists, Book 1, 1981; Sonatina and Sonata Book, 1982; Four Study Books for Piano (Playtime Studies and Progress Studies), 1986; (with Paul de Keyser) Young Violinists Repertoire books, 1–4; Fanny Waterman on Piano Playing and Performing, 1983; Music Lovers Diary, 1984–86; Merry Christmas Carols, 1986; Christmas Carol Time, 1986; Nursery Rhyme Time, 1987; Piano for Pleasure, Bks 1 and 2, 1988; Me and my Piano, 1988, Book 2, 1989; Animal Magic, 1989; Monkey Puzzles, Books 1 and 2, 1990; (with Wendy Thompson) Piano Competition: the story of the Leeds, 1990. *Recreations:* travel, reading, voluntary work, cooking. *Address:* Woodgarth, Oakwood Grove, Leeds LS8 2PA. *T:* Leeds (0532) 655771.

WATERPARK, 7th Baron *cr* 1792; **Frederick Caryll Philip Cavendish,** Bt 1755; Deputy Chairman, since 1984 and Chief Executive, since 1990, CSE Aviation Ltd; Managing Director, CSE International Ltd, since 1985; *b* 6 Oct. 1926; *s* of Brig.-General Frederick William Laurence Sheppard Hart Cavendish, CMG, DSO (*d* 1931) and Enid, Countess of Kenmare (she *m* 3rd, 1933, as his 3rd wife, 1st Viscount Furness, who *d* 1940; 4th, as his 2nd wife, 6th Earl of Kenmare), *d* of Charles Lindeman, Sydney, New South Wales, and *widow* of Roderick Cameron, New York; *S* uncle 1948; *m* 1951, Daniele, *e d* of Roger Guirche, Paris; one *s* two *d*. *Educ:* Eton. Lieut. 4th and 1st Bn Grenadier Guards, 1944–46. Served as Assistant District Commandant Kenya Police Reserve, 1952–55, during Mau Mau Rebellion. *Heir: s* Hon. Roderick Alexander Cavendish [*b* 10 Oct. 1959; *m* 1989, Anne, *d* of Hon. Luke Asquith; one *s*]. *Address:* (office) CSE Aviation, Oxford Airport, Kidlington, Oxford; (home) 74 Elm Park Road, SW3. *Club:* Cavalry and Guards.

WATERS, Gen. Sir (Charles) John, KCB 1988; CBE 1981 (OBE 1977); Commander-in-Chief, United Kingdom Land Forces, since 1990; *b* 2 Sept. 1935; *s* of Patrick George Waters and Margaret Ronaldson Waters (*née* Clark); *m* 1962, Hilary Doyle Nettleton; three *s*. *Educ:* Oundle; Royal Military Academy, Sandhurst. Commissioned, The Gloucestershire Regt, 1955; GSO2, MO1 (MoD), 1970–72; Instructor, GSO1 (DS), Staff Coll., Camberley, 1973–74; Commanding Officer, 1st Bn, Gloucestershire Regt, 1975–77; Colonel General Staff, 1st Armoured Div., 1977–79; Comdr 3 Infantry Bde, 1979–81; RCDS 1982; Dep. Comdr, Land Forces, Falkland Islands, May–July 1982; Comdr 4th Armoured Div., 1983–85; Comdt, Staff Coll., Camberley, 1986–88; GOC and Dir of Ops, NI, 1988–90. Col, The Gloucestershire Regt, 1985–91; Col Comdt, POW Div., 1988–; Col, Wessex Yeomanry, 1991. Mem. Adv. Council, Victory Meml Mus., Arlon, Belgium; Mem. Council, Cheltenham Coll. Mem., Army Sailing Assoc. *Recreations:* sailing, skiing, painting. *Address:* c/o Lloyds Bank, Colyton, Devon EX13 6DY. *Clubs:* Army and Navy, Ski Club of Great Britain, Admiral; British Keil Yacht, Axe Yacht.

WATERS, David Watkin, Lt-Comdr RN; *b* 2 Aug. 1911; *s* of Eng. Lt William Waters, RN, and Jessie Rhena (*née* Whitemore); *m* 1946, Hope Waters (*née* Pritchard); one step *s* one step *d*. *Educ:* RN Coll., Dartmouth. Joined RN, 1925; Cadet and Midshipman, HMS Barham, 1929; specialised in Aviation (Pilot), 1935. Served War of 1939–45: Fleet Air Arm, Malta (PoW, Italy, Germany, 1940–45). Admlty, 1946–50; retd, 1950. Admlty Historian (Defence of Shipping), 1946–60; Head of Dept of Navigation and Astronomy, Nat. Maritime Museum, 1960–76, and Sec. of Museum, 1968–71; Dep. Dir, 1971–78. Pres., British Soc. for Hist. of Sci., 1976–78 (Vice-Pres., 1972–74, 1978–81). Vis. Prof. of History, Simon Fraser Univ., Burnaby, BC, 1978; Regents' Prof., UCLA, 1979; Caird Res. Fellow, Nat. Maritime Museum, 1979–83; Alexander O. Victor Res. Fellow, John Carter Brown Library, Brown Univ., Providence, RI, 1990. Chm., Japan Animal Welfare Soc., 1972–80. Gold Medal, Admiralty Naval History, 1936, and Special Award, 1946; FRHistS 1951; Fellow, Inst. Internac. da Cultura Portuguesa, 1966; FSA 1970. Hon. Member: Royal Inst. of Navigation, 1989 (Fellow 1959); Scientific Instrument Soc., 1989; Acad. de Marinha Portuguesa, 1989. *Publications:* The True and Perfect Newes of Syr Francis Drake, 1955; (with F. Barley) Naval Staff History, Second World War, Defeat of the Enemy attack on Shipping, 1939–1945, 1957; The Art of Navigation in England in Elizabethan and Early Stuart Times, 1958, 2nd edn 1978; The Sea—or Mariner's Astrolabe, 1966; The Rutter of the Sea, 1967; (with Hope Waters) The Saluki in History, Art, and Sport, 1969, 2nd edn 1984; (with G. P. B. Naish) The Elizabethan Navy and the Armada of Spain, 1975; Science and the Techniques of Navigation in the Renaissance, 1976; contrib.: Jl RIN; RUSI; Mariners' Mirror; American Neptune; Jl RN Scientific Service; Jl British Soc. of History of Science; Navy International; Revista da Universidade de Coímbra. *Recreations:* maritime history, history of technology (especially in the Renaissance and Scientific Revolution, and Chinese sailing craft). *Address:* c/o Cobwebs, Graffham, Petworth, West Sussex GU28 0PY. *Club:* English-Speaking Union.

WATERS, Donald Henry; Chief Executive and Director, Grampian Television PLC, since 1987; *b* 17 Dec. 1937; *s* of late Henry Lethbridge Waters, WS, and Jean Manson Baxter; *m* 1962, June Leslie, *d* of late Andrew Hutchison; one *s* two *d*. *Educ:* George Watson's, Edinburgh; Inverness Royal Acad. Mem. ICA(Scot.) 1961. Dir, John M.

Henderson and Co. Ltd, 1972–75; Grampian Television: Company Sec., 1975; Dir of Finance, 1979. Director: Glenburnie Properties, 1976–; Blenheim Travel, 1981–91; Moray Firth Radio, 1982–; Independent Television Publications Ltd, 1988–90; Cablevision (Scotland) PLC, 1988–91. FRSA. *Recreations:* gardening, travel. *Address:* Balquhidder, Milltimber, Aberdeen AB1 0JS. *T:* Aberdeen (0224) 867131. *Club:* Royal Northern (Aberdeen).

WATERS, Mrs Frank; *see* Brown, D. L.

WATERS, Garth Rodney; Under-Secretary, Lands and Environmental Affairs Group, Ministry of Agriculture, Fisheries and Food, since 1990; *b* 2 March 1944; *s* of Edmund Claude and Bertha May Waters; *m* 1st, 1967, Malin Essen-Möller (marr. diss. 1975); two *s*; 2nd, 1976, Ann Margaret Evans; one *s* one *d*. *Educ:* Perse Sch., Cambridge; Oriel Coll., Oxford. Teacher of English, British Centre, Sweden, 1966–67; joined MAFF, 1968; Private Sec. to Minister of State, 1971–73; Head of Pesticides Branch, 1973; Durham Office, 1974–75; Milk, 1975–78; Principal Private Sec. to Minister of Agriculture, 1979–80; Head, Beef Div., 1980; Head, Marine Envmt Protection Div., 1984; joined Glaxo Holdings as Head, Corporate Policy Unit, 1987; Dir, Glaxo Europe, 1989–90; rejoined MAFF, 1990, as Head, Agric. Resources Policy Div. *Address:* Ministry of Agriculture, Fisheries and Food, Nobel House, 17 Smith Square, SW1P 3JR. *T:* 071–238 5682. *Club:* Royal Automobile.

WATERS, Gen. Sir John; *see* Waters, Gen. Sir C. J.

WATERS, Montague, QC 1968; *b* 28 Feb. 1917; *s* of Elias Wasserman, BSc, and Rose Waters; *m* 1940, Jessica Freedman (*d* 1988); three *s*. *Educ:* Central Foundation Sch., City of London; London University. LLB (Hons) London, 1938. Solicitor of the Supreme Court, 1939. Military Service, KRRC, Intelligence Corps and Dept of HM Judge Advocate General, 1940–46 (Defence and Victory Medals, 1939–45 Star). Called to the Bar, Inner Temple, 1946; released from HM Forces with rank of Major (Legal Staff), 1946. Governor, Central Foundation Schools, 1968. Freeman, City of London, 1962. *Recreations:* theatre, sport. *Address:* 37 Middleway, NW11. *T:* 081–458 7510.

WATERSTON, Dr Charles Dewar, FRSE, FGS; formerly Keeper of Geology, Royal Scottish Museum; *b* 15 Feb. 1925; *s* of Allan Waterston and Martha Dewar (*née* Robertson); *m* 1965, Marjory Home Douglas. *Educ:* Highgate Sch., London; Univ. of Edinburgh (BSc 1st Cl. Hons 1947; Vans Dunlop Scholar, PhD 1949; DSc 1980). FRSE 1958; FGS 1949. Asst Keeper, Royal Scottish Museum, 1950–63, Keeper, 1963–85. Member: Scottish Cttee, Nature Conservancy, 1969–73; Adv. Cttee for Scotland, Nature Conservancy Council, 1974–82; Chairman's Cttee, 1978–80, Exec. Cttee, 1980–82, Council for Museums and Galleries in Scotland; Gen. Sec., RSE, 1986–91 (Mem. Council, 1967–70; Vice-Pres., 1980–83; Sec., 1985–86); Hon. Sec., Edinburgh Geol Soc., 1953–58 (Pres., 1969–71). Keith Prize, RSE, 1969–71; Clough Medal, Edinburgh Geol Soc., 1984–85. *Publications:* (with G. Y. Craig and D. B. McIntyre) James Hutton's Theory of the Earth: the lost drawings, 1978; (with H. E. Stace and C. W. A. Pettitt) Natural Science Collections in Scotland, 1987; technical papers in scientific jls, chiefly relating to extinct arthropods and the history of geology. *Address:* 30 Boswall Road, Edinburgh EH5 3RN. *Club:* New (Edinburgh).

WATERSTONE, David George Stuart, CBE 1991; Chief Executive, Energy and Technical Services Group plc, since 1990; *b* 9 Aug. 1935; *s* of Malcolm Waterstone and Sylvia Sawday; *m* 1st, 1960, Dominique Viriot (marr. diss.); ; one *s* two *d*; 2nd, 1988, Sandra Packer (*née* Willey). *Educ:* Tonbridge; St Catharine's Coll., Cambridge (MA). HM Diplomatic Service, 1959–70; Sen. Exec., IRC, 1970–71; BSC, 1971–81: Board Mem., 1976–81; Man. Dir, Commercial, 1972–77; subseq. Executive Chairman, BSC Chemicals, 1977–81, and Redpath Dorman Long, 1977–81; Chief Exec., Welsh Develt Agency, 1983–90. *Recreations:* sailing, walking, painting, furniture making. *Address:* (office) 8 Headfort Place, SW1X 7BH. *T:* 071–823 2288; (home) 1 Prior Park Buildings, Prior Park Road, Bath BA2 4NP. *T:* Bath (0225) 427346. *Club:* Reform.

See also T. J. S. Waterstone.

WATERSTONE, Timothy John Stuart; Founder and Chairman, Waterstone's Booksellers Ltd (formerly Waterstone & Co.), since 1982; *b* 30 May 1939; *s* of Malcolm Waterstone and Sylvia Sawday; *m* 1st, Patricia Harcourt-Poole (marr. diss.); two *s* one *d*; 2nd, Clare Perkins (marr. diss.); one *s* two *d*; 3rd, Mary Rose Alison. *Educ:* Tonbridge; St Catharine's College, Cambridge (MA). Carritt Moran, Calcutta, 1962–64; Allied Breweries, 1964–73; W. H. Smith, 1973–81; Chairman: The Principals Ltd, 1987–; Priory Investments Ltd, 1990–; Dep. Chm., Sinclair-Stevenson Ltd, 1989–. Chm., Shelter 25th Anniversary Appeal Cttee, 1991–92. Member: Bd of Trustees, English International (Internat. House), 1987–; Bd, London Philharmonic Orch., 1990–; Bd, Acad. of Ancient Music, 1990–; Chm., London Internat. Festival of Theatre, 1991. Adv. Mem., Booker Prize Management Cttee, 1986–; Chm. of Judges, Prince's Youth Business Trust Awards, 1990. *Recreations:* books, music. *Address:* 37 Ixworth Place, SW3 3QH. *T:* 071–584 4448. *Clubs:* Athenæum; Rye Golf.

See also D. G. S. Waterstone.

WATERTON, Sqdn Leader William Arthur, GM 1952; AFC 1942, Bar 1946; *b* Edmonton, Canada, 18 March 1916. *Educ:* Royal Military College of Canada; University of Alberta. Cadet Royal Military College of Canada, 1934–37; Subaltern and Lieut, 19th Alberta Dragoons, Canadian Cavalry, 1937–39; served RAF, 1939–46: Fighter Squadrons; Training Command; Transatlantic Ferrying Command; Fighter Command; Meteorological Flight; Fighter Experimental Unit; CFE High Speed Flight World Speed Record. Joined Gloster Aircraft Co. Ltd, 1946. 100 km closed circuit record, 1947; Paris/London record (618.5 mph), 1947; "Hare and Tortoise" Helicopter and jet aircraft Centre of London to Centre of Paris (47 mins), 1948. Chief Test Pilot Gloster Aircraft Co. Ltd, 1946–54. Prototype trials on first Canadian jet fighter, Canuck and British first operational delta wing fighter, the Javelin. *Publications:* The Comet Riddle, 1956; The Quick and The Dead, 1956; aeronautical and meteorological articles. *Recreations:* sailing, riding, photography, motoring, shooting. *Address:* c/o Royal Bank of Scotland, Kirkland House, Whitehall, SW1. *Club:* Royal Military College of Canada (Kingston, Ont.).

WATERWORTH, Alan William, JP; Vice Lord-Lieutenant of Merseyside, since 1989; *b* 22 Sept. 1931; *s* of late James and Alice Waterworth, Liverpool; *m* 1955, Myriam, *d* of late Edouard Baete and Magdelaine Baete, formerly of Brussels; three *s* one *d*. *Educ:* Uppingham Sch.; Trinity Coll., Cambridge (MA). National Service, commnd King's Regt, 1950. Waterworth Bros Ltd: progressively, Dir, Man. Dir, Chm., 1954–69. Member: Skelmersdale Develt Corp., 1971–85 (Dep. Chm., 1979–85); Merseyside Police Authority, 1984–. Chairman: Liverpool Boys' Assoc., 1967–75; Merseyside Youth Assoc., 1971–75; Everton FC, 1973–76 (Dir, 1970–). JP Liverpool 1961 (Chm., Juvenile Panel, 1974–83; Chm. of Bench, 1985–89); DL Co. Merseyside 1986. *Recreations:* local history, bibliomania, shooting. *Address:* Crewood Hall, Kingsley, Cheshire. *T:* Kingsley (0928) 88316. *Clubs:* Army and Navy; Athenæum (Liverpool).

WATES, Sir Christopher (Stephen), Kt 1989; BA; FCA; Chief Executive, Wates Holdings, since 1976 (Director, since 1973); Chairman: Criterion Holdings, since 1981;

Wates Building Group Ltd, since 1984; *b* 25 Dec. 1939; *s* of Norman Edward Wates and Margot Irene Sidwell; *m* 1965, Sandra Mouroutsos (marr. diss. 1975); three *d*. *Educ:* Stowe School; Brasenose College, Oxford. BA 1962; FCA 1965. Financial Director, Wates Ltd, 1970–76. Director: Electra Investment Trust, 1980–; Equitable Life Assurance Society, 1983–; North British Canadian Investment Co., 1983–; Wates City of London Properties PLC, 1984–; Mem., 1980–89, Chm., 1983–89, English Industrial Estates Corp.; Chm., Keymer Brick & Tile Co. Ltd, 1985–89. Governor of Council, 1984–, Dep. Chm., 1989–, London House for Overseas Graduates; Trustee: Chatham Historic Dockyard Trust, 1984–87; Science Museum, 1987–; Lambeth Palace Library, 1990–. FRSA 1988. Hon. Mem., RICS, 1990. *Address:* Tufton Place, Northiam, near Rye, East Sussex TN31 6HL. *T:* Northiam (07974) 2125.

WATES, Michael Edward, Chairman, Wates Ltd, since 1974; Chairman, British Bloodstock Agency plc, since 1986; *b* 19 June 1935; 2nd *s* of Sir Ronald Wallace Wates and of Phyllis Mary Wates (*née* Trace); *m* 1959, Caroline Josephine Connolly; four *s* one *d*. *Educ:* Oundle School; Emmanuel College, Cambridge (MA). Joined Wates 1959; Director: Wates Construction, 1963; Wates Built Homes, 1966. Mem., Nat. Housebuilding Council, 1974–80. Member: Council, Thoroughbred Breeders Assoc., 1978–82 (Chm., 1980–82); Horserace Betting Levy Bd, 1987–90. King's College Hospital: Deleg., Sch. of Medicine and Dentistry, 1983–; Chm., Equipment Cttee, 1983–91; Special Trustee, 1985 (Chm., Trustees, 1985). Hon. FRIBA. *Address:* Manor House, Langton Long, Blandford Forum, Dorset DT11 9HS. *T:* Blandford (0258) 455241.

WATHEN, Julian Philip Gerard; Chairman, Hall School Charitable Trust, since 1972; *b* 21 May 1923; *s* of late Gerard Anstruther Wathen, CIE, and Melicent Louis (*née* Buxton); *m* 1948 Priscilla Florence Wilson; one *s* two *d*. *Educ:* Harrow. Served War, 60th Rifles, 1942–46. Third Secretary, HBM Embassy, Athens, 1946–47. Barclays Bank DCO, 1948; Ghana Director, 1961–65; General Manager, 1966; Sen. Gen. Manager, Barclays Bank International, 1974; Vice Chm., 1976; Vice Chairman: Barclays Bank, 1979–84; Banque du Caire, Barclays International, 1976–83; Dep. Chm., Allied Arab Bank, 1977–84; Director: Barclays Australia International, 1973–84; Barclays Bank of Kenya, 1975–84; Mercantile & General Reinsurance Co., 1977–91. Pres., Royal African Soc., 1984–89 (Chm., 1978–84); Chm., City of London Endowment Trust for St Paul's Cathedral, 1983–; Vice Chm., London House for Overseas Graduates, 1984–89; Governor: St Paul's Schs, 1981–; SOAS, 1983–; Overseas Develt Inst., 1984–; Dauntsey's Sch., 1985–; Abingdon Sch., 1985–; Thomas Telford Sch., 1990–. Mem. Cttee, GBA, 1986–. Master, Mercers' Co., 1984–85. *Address:* Woodcock House, Owlpen, Dursley, Glos GL11 5BY. *T:* Dursley (0453) 860214; 1 Montagu Place, Marylebone, W1H 1RG. *T:* 071–935 8569. *Club:* Travellers'.

WATKIN, Rt. Rev. Abbot (Christopher) Aelred (Paul); titular Abbot of Glastonbury; Headmaster of Downside School, 1962–75; *b* 23 Feb. 1918; *s* of late Edward Ingram Watkin and Helena Watkin (*née* Shepheard). *Educ:* Blackfriars Sch., Laxton; Christ's Coll., Cambridge (1st class Parts I and II, historical Tripos). Ordained Priest, 1943. Housemaster at Downside Sch., 1948–62. Mayor of Beccles, 1979. FRHistS, 1946; FSA, 1950; FRSA, 1969. *Publications:* Wells Cathedral Miscellany, 1943; (ed) Great Chartulary of Glastonbury, 3 vols, 1946–58; (ed) Registrum Archidiaconatus Norwyci, 2 vols, 1946–48; Heart of the World, 1954; The Enemies of Love, 1958; Resurrection is Now, 1975; Through the Church's Year, 1991; articles in Eng. Hist. Rev., Cambridge Hist. Journal, Victoria County History of Wilts, etc. *Address:* Downside Abbey, Stratton-on-the-Fosse, Bath BA3 4RH. *T:* Stratton-on-the-Fosse (0761) 232295.

WATKIN, David John, MA, PhD; FSA; Fellow of Peterhouse, Cambridge, since 1970; University Lecturer in History of Art, since 1972 and Head of Department of History of Art, since 1989, Cambridge University; Member, Historic Buildings Advisory Committee, Historic Buildings and Monuments Commission for England, since 1984 (Member, Historic Buildings Council for England, 1980–84); *b* 7 April 1941; *o s* of Thomas Charles and Vera Mary Watkin. *Educ:* Farnham Grammar Sch.; Trinity Hall, Cambridge (Exhibnr; BA (1st Cl. Hons Fine Arts Tripos); PhD). Librarian, Fine Arts Faculty, Cambridge, 1967–72. *Publications:* Thomas Hope (1769–1831) and the Neo-Classical Idea, 1968; (ed) Sale Catalogues of Libraries of Eminent Persons, vol. 4, Architects, 1970; The Life and Work of C. R. Cockerell, RA, 1974 (Alice Davis Hitchcock medallion, 1975); The Triumph of the Classical, Cambridge Architecture 1804–34, 1977; Morality and Architecture, 1977; The Rise of Architectural History, 1980; English Architecture, a Concise History, 1980; (with Hugh Montgomery-Massingberd) The London Ritz, a Social and Architectural History, 1980; (with Robin Middleton) Neo-Classical and Nineteenth-century Architecture, 1980; (jtly) Burke's and Savills Guide to Country Houses, vol. 3, East Anglia, 1981; The Buildings of Britain, Regency: a Guide and Gazetteer, 1982; Athenian Stuart, Pioneer of the Greek Revival, 1982; The English Vision: The Picturesque in Architecture, Landscape and Garden Design, 1982; (contrib.) John Soane, 1983; The Royal Interiors of Regency England, 1984; Peterhouse: an architectural record 1284–1984, 1984; (contrib.) Grand Hotel: the golden age of palace hotels, an architectural and social history, 1984; (contrib.) A House in Town: 22 Arlington Street, its owners and builders, 1984; A History of Western Architecture, 1986; (with Tilman Mellinghoff) German Architecture and the Classical Ideal: 1740–1840, 1987; (contrib.) The Legacy of Rome, 1991. *Address:* Peterhouse, Cambridge. *Clubs:* Travellers', Beefsteak; University Pitt (Cambridge).

WATKIN WILLIAMS, Sir Peter, Kt 1963; *b* 8 July 1911; *s* of late Robert Thesiger Watkin Williams, late Master of the Supreme Court, and Mary Watkin Williams; *m* 1938, Jane Dickinson (*née* Wilkin); two *d*. *Educ:* Sherborne; Pembroke Coll., Cambridge. Partner in Hansons, legal practitioners, Shanghai, 1937–40; served War of 1939–45, Rhodesia and Middle East, 1940–46. Resident Magistrate, Uganda, 1946–55; Puisne Judge, Trinidad and Tobago, 1955–58; Puisne Judge, Sierra Leone, 1958–61; Plebiscite Judge, Cameroons, 1961; Chief Justice of Basutoland, Bechuanaland and Swaziland, and President of the Court of Appeal, 1961–65; High Court Judge, Malawi, 1967–69; Chief Justice of Malawi, 1969–70. *Recreation:* fishing. *Address:* Lower East Horner, Stockland, Honiton, Devon.

WATKINS, Dr Alan Keith; Managing Director and Chief Executive, Hawker Siddeley Group plc, since 1989; *b* 9 Oct. 1938; *s* of late Wilfred Victor Watkins and of Dorothy Hilda Watkins; *m* 1963, Diana Edith Wynne (*née* Hughes); two *s*. *Educ:* Moseley Grammar School, Birmingham; Univ. of Birmingham (BSc Hons, PhD). FIM (Mem. Council, 1990–); CEng; FIMfgE (Vice-Pres., 1991–). Lucas Research Centre, 1962; Lucas Batteries, 1969, subseq. Manufacturing Dir; Lucas Aerospace, 1975; Man. Dir, Aerospace Lucas Industries, 1987–89. Member: Council, SBAC, 1982–89 (Vice-Pres., 1988–89); DTI Aviation Cttee, 1985–89; Vice-Pres., EEF, 1989–. *Recreations:* tennis, golf, hot-air ballooning, photography. *Address:* Hawker Siddeley Group plc, 18 St James's Square, SW1Y 4LJ. *Club:* Olton Golf.

WATKINS, Alan (Rhun); journalist; Political Columnist, Observer, since 1976; *b* 3 April 1933; *o c* of late D. J. Watkins, schoolmaster, Tycroes, Dyfed, and Violet Harris; *m* 1955, Ruth Howard (*d* 1982); one *s* one *d* (and one *d* decd). *Educ:* Amman Valley Grammar Sch., Ammanford; Queens' Coll., Cambridge. Chm., Cambridge Univ. Labour Club, 1954. National Service, FO, Educn Br., RAF, 1955–57. Called to Bar, Lincoln's Inn, 1957. Research Asst, Dept of Govt, LSE, 1958–59; Editorial Staff, Sunday Express, 1959–64 (New York Corresp., 1961; Actg Political Corresp., 1963; Cross-Bencher Columnist, 1963–64); Political Correspondent: Spectator, 1964–67; New Statesman, 1967–76; Political Columnist, Sunday Mirror, 1968–69; Columnist, Evening Standard, 1974–75; Rugby Columnist: Field, 1984–86; Independent, 1986–. Mem. (Lab) Fulham Bor. Council, 1959–62. Dir, The Statesman and Nation Publishing Co. Ltd, 1973–76. Chm., Political Adv. Gp, British Youth Council, 1978–81. Awards: Granada, Political Columnist, 1973; British Press, Columnist, 1982, commended 1984. *Publications:* The Liberal Dilemma, 1966; (contrib.) The Left, 1966; (with A. Alexander) The Making of the Prime Minister 1970, 1970; Brief Lives, 1982; (contrib.) The Queen Observed, 1986; Sportswriter's Eye, 1989; A Slight Case of Libel, 1990. *Recreations:* reading, walking. *Address:* 54 Barnsbury Street, N1 1ER. *T:* 071–607 0812. *Clubs:* Garrick, Beefsteak.

WATKINS, Brian; HM Diplomatic Service; High Commissioner to Swaziland, since 1990; *b* 26 July 1933; *s* of late James Edward Watkins and late Gladys Anne Watkins (*née* Fletcher); *m* 1st, 1957 (marr. diss. 1978); one *s*; 2nd, 1982, Elisabeth, *d* of A. and M. Arfon-Jones; one *d*. *Educ:* London School of Economics (BSc Econ); Worcester College, Oxford. Solicitor. Flying Officer, RAF, 1955–58. HMOCS, Sierra Leone, 1959–63; Local Govt, 1963–66; Administrator, Tristan da Cunha, 1966–69; Lectr, Univ. of Manchester, 1969–71; HM Diplomatic Service, 1971; FCO, 1971–73; New York, 1973–75; seconded to N Ireland Office, 1976–78; FCO, 1978–81; Counsellor, 1981; Dep. Governor, Bermuda, 1981–83; Consul General and Counsellor (Economic, Commercial, Aid), Islamabad, 1983–86; Consul Gen., Vancouver, 1986–90. *Recreations:* reading history and spy stories, watching theatre, watching TV, dancing. *Address:* c/o Foreign and Commonwealth Office, King Charles Street, SW1A 2AH; c/o Royal Bank of Scotland, Holts Branch, Whitehall, SW1. *Club:* Royal Bermuda Yacht.

WATKINS, David John; Director, Council for the Advancement of Arab-British Understanding, 1983–90 (Joint Chairman, 1979–83); company director and consultant; *b* 27 Aug. 1925; *s* of Thomas George Watkins and Alice Elizabeth (*née* Allen); unmarried. *Educ:* Bristol. Member: Bristol City Council, 1954–57; Bristol Educn Cttee, 1958–66; Labour Party, 1950–; Amalgamated Engineering Union, 1942–; Sec., AEU Gp of MPs, 1968–77. Contested Bristol NW, 1964. MP (Lab) Consett, 1966–83; Mem., House of Commons Chairmen's Panel, 1978–83. Sponsored Employers Liability (Compulsory Insurance) Act, 1969, and Industrial Common Ownership Act, 1976 as Private Member's Bills; introd Drained Weight Bill, 1973, and Consett Steel Works Common Ownership Bill, 1980. Chm., Labour Middle East Council, 1974–83; Treas., Internat. Co-ord Cttee, UN Meeting of Non-Governmental Organisations on Question of Palestine, 1985–90. *Publications:* Labour and Palestine, 1975; Industrial Common Ownership, 1978; The World and Palestine, 1980; The Exceptional Conflict, 1984. *Recreations:* reading, listening to music, swimming. *Address:* 1 Carisbrooke House, Courtlands, Sheen Road, Richmond, Surrey TW10 5AZ. *Club:* Commonwealth Trust.

WATKINS, Rev. Gordon Derek; Secretary, London Diocesan Advisory Committee, since 1984; *b* 16 July 1929; *s* of Clifford and Margaret Watkins; *m* 1957, Beryl Evelyn Whitaker. *Educ:* St Brendan's College, Clifton. Nat. Service, RAOC, 1947–49. Staff of W. D. & H. O. Wills, 1944–51; deacon 1953, priest 1954; Curate, Grafton Cathedral, NSW, 1953–56; Vicar of Texas, Qld, 1957–61; Curate, St Wilfrid's, Harrogate, 1961–63; Vicar of Upton Park, 1963–67; Rector: Great and Little Bentley, 1967–73; Great Canfield, 1973–78; Pastoral Sec., Dio. London, 1978–84; Vicar, St Martin-within-Ludgate, City and Dio. of London, 1984–89; Priest Vicar, Westminster Abbey, 1984–90; Priest in Ordinary to the Queen, 1984–. Freeman, City of London, 1984. *Recreations:* reading, music, country life. *Address:* 30 Causton Street, SW1P 4AU. *T:* 071–821 9386. *Club:* Athenæum.

WATKINS, Maj.-Gen. Guy Hansard, CB 1986; OBE 1974; Chief Executive, Royal Hong Kong Jockey Club, since 1986; *b* 30 Nov. 1933; *s* of Col A. N. M. Watkins and Mrs S. C. Watkins; *m* 1958, Sylvia Margaret Grant; two *s* two *d*. *Educ:* The King's Sch., Canterbury; Royal Military Academy, Sandhurst. Commissioned into Royal Artillery, 1953; CO 39 Medium Regt RA, 1973; Comd Task Force 'B'/Dep. Comd 1 Armd Div., 1977; Director, Public Relations (Army), 1980; Maj. Gen. RA and GOC Artillery Div., 1982; Dir Gen., Army Manning and Recruiting, 1985; retd 1986. Col Comdt, RA, 1986–. *Recreations:* riding, fly fishing, skiing. *Address:* The Royal Hong Kong Jockey Club, Happy Valley, Hong Kong. *Clubs:* Army and Navy; Shek O (Hong Kong); Littlehampton Golf.

WATKINS, Prof. Jeffrey Clifton, PhD; FRS 1988; Hon. Professor of Pharmacology, Department of Pharmacology, School of Medical Sciences (formerly The Medical School), Bristol, since 1989 (Senior Research Fellow, 1983–89); *b* 20 Dec. 1929; *s* of Colin Hereward and Amelia Miriam Watkins; *m* 1973, Beatrice Joan Thacher; one *s* one *d*. *Educ:* Univ. of Western Australia (MSc 1954); Univ. of Cambridge (PhD 1954). Research Fellow, Chemistry Department: Univ. of Cambridge, 1954–55; Univ. of Yale, 1955–57; Res. Fellow, 1958–61, Fellow, 1961–65, Physiology Dept, ANU; Scientific Officer, ARC Inst. of Animal Physiology, Babraham, Cambridge, 1965–67; Res. Scientist, MRC Neuropsychiatry Unit, Carshalton, Surrey, 1967–73; Senior Research Fellow, Dept of Physiology, The Med. Sch., Bristol, 1973–83 (Leader of Excitatory Amino Acid Gp). *Publications:* The NMDA Receptor, 1989; approx. 150 pubns in learned jls, eg Jl of Physiol., Brit. Jl of Pharmacol., Nature, Brain Res., Exptl Brain Res., Eur. Jl of Pharmacol., Neuroscience, Neuroscience Letters, Jl of Neuroscience. *Address:* 8 Lower Court Road, Lower Almondsbury, Bristol, Avon BS12 4DX. *T:* Almondsbury (0454) 613829.

WATKINS, Peter Rodney; Deputy Chief Executive, National Curriculum Council, since 1988; *b* 8 Oct. 1931; *s* of Frank Arthur Watkins and Mary Gwyneth Watkins (neé Price); *m* 1971, Jillian Ann Burge; two *d*. *Educ:* Solihull Sch.; Emmanuel Coll., Cambridge (Exhibnr; Hist. Tripos Pts I and II 1952, 1953; Cert. in Educn 1954; MA 1957). Flying Officer, RAF, 1954–56; History Master, East Ham Grammar Sch., 1956–59; Sixth Form Hist. Master, Brentwood Sch., 1959–64; Sen. Hist. Master, Bristol Grammar Sch., 1964–69; Headmaster, King Edward's Five Ways Sch., Birmingham, 1969–74; Headmaster, Chichester High Sch. for Boys, 1974–79; Principal, Price's Sixth Form Coll., Fareham, 1980–84; Dep. Chief Exec., Sch. Curriculum Develt Cttee, 1984–88. Exec., SHA, 1980–84. Chm., Christian Educn Movement, 1980–87. *Publications:* The Sixth Form College in Practice, 1982; Modular Approaches to the Secondary Curriculum, 1986. *Recreations:* fell walking, local history, theology. *Address:* 43 St Andrewgate, York YO1 2BR. *T:* York (0904) 626299. *Club:* Commonwealth Trust.

WATKINS, Rt. Hon. Sir Tasker, VC 1944; GBE 1990; Kt 1971; PC 1980; DL; **Rt. Hon. Lord Justice Watkins;** a Lord Justice of Appeal, since 1980; Deputy Chief Justice of England, since 1988; *b* 18 Nov. 1918; *s* of late Bertram and Jane Watkins, Nelson, Glam; *m* 1941, Eirwen Evans; one *d* (one *s* decd). *Educ:* Pontypridd Grammar Sch. Served War, 1939–45 (Major, the Welch Regiment). Called to Bar, Middle Temple, 1948,

Bencher 1970; QC 1965; Deputy Chairman: Radnor QS, 1962–71; Carmarthenshire QS, 1966–71. Recorder: Merthyr Tydfil, 1968–70, Swansea, 1970–71; Leader, Wales and Chester Circuit, 1970–71; Judge of the High Court of Justice, Family Div., 1971–74, QBD, 1974–80; Presiding Judge, Wales and Chester Circuit, 1975–80; Sen. Presiding Judge for England and Wales, 1983–91. Counsel (as Deputy to Attorney-General) to Inquiry into Aberfan Disaster, 1966. Chairman: Mental Health Review Tribunal, Wales Region, 1960–71; Judicial Studies Bd, 1979–80. Pres., Univ. of Wales Coll. of Medicine, 1987–. Pres., British Legion, Wales, 1947–68; Mem., TA Assoc., Glamorgan and Wales, 1947–. Chm., Welsh RU Charitable Trust, 1975–. Hon. LLD Wales, 1979. DL Glamorgan, 1956–. *Address*: Royal Courts of Justice, Strand, WC2A 2LL; Fairwater Lodge, Fairwater Road, Llandaff, Glamorgan. *T*: Cardiff (0222) 563558; 5 Pump Court, Middle Temple, EC4. *T*: 071–353 1993. *Clubs*: Army and Navy; Cardiff and County (Cardiff); Glamorgan Wanderers Rugby Football (Pres., 1968–).
See also J. G. Williams.

WATKINS, Thomas Frederick; Director, Chemical Defence Establishment, Porton, 1972–74; *b* 19 Feb. 1914; *s* of late Edward and late Louisa Watkins; *m* 1939, Jeannie Blodwen Roberts; two *d*. *Educ*: Cowbridge Grammar Sch.; Univ. of Wales, Cardiff. BSc Hons Wales 1935; MSc Wales 1936; FRIC 1947. Joined Scientific Staff of War Dept, 1936; seconded to Govt of India, 1939–44; seconded to Dept of Nat. Defence, Canada, 1947–49; Head of Research Section, CDRE, Sutton Oak and Min. of Supply CDE, Nancekuke, 1949–56; Supt Chemistry Research Div., CDE, Porton, 1956; Asst Dir Chemical Research, CDE, Porton, 1963; Dep. Dir, CDE, Porton, 1966. *Publications*: various papers on organic chemistry. *Recreation*: gardening. *Address*: 34 Harnwood Road, Salisbury, Wilts. *T*: Salisbury (0722) 335135.

WATKINS, Dr Winifred May, FRS 1969; Head of Division of Immunochemical Genetics, Clinical Research Centre, Medical Research Council, 1976–89; Visiting Professor, Royal Postgraduate Medical School, University of London, since 1990; *b* 6 Aug. 1924; *d* of Albert E. and Annie B. Watkins. *Educ*: Godolphin and Latymer Sch., London; Univ. of London. PhD 1950; DSc 1963. Research Asst in Biochemistry, St Bartholomew's Hosp. Med. Sch., 1948–50; Beit Memorial Research Fellow, 1952–55; Mem. of Staff of Lister Inst. of Preventive Medicine, 1955–76; Wellcome Travelling Research Fellow, Univ. of California, 1960–61; Reader in Biochemistry, 1965; Prof. of Biochemistry, Univ. of London, 1968–76; William Julius Mickle Fellow, London Univ., 1971. Mem. Council, Royal Soc., 1984–86. Hon. Mem., Internat. Soc. of Blood Transfusion, 1982; Foreign Mem., Polish Acad. of Sciences, 1988. Hon. Mem., Japanese Biochemical Soc., 1990. FRCPath 1983. Hon. FRCP 1990. Hon. DSc Utrecht, 1990. Landsteiner Memorial Award (jtly), 1967; Paul Ehrlich-Ludwig Darmstädter Prize (jtly), 1969; Kenneth Goldsmith Award, British Blood Transfusion Soc., 1986; Royal Medal, Royal Soc., 1988; Franz Oehlecker Medal, German Soc. of Transfusion Medicine and Immunohaematology, 1989; (jtly) Philip Levine Award, Amer. Soc. of Clin. Pathologists, 1990. *Publications*: various papers in biochemical and immunological jls. *Address*: Department of Haematology, Royal Postgraduate Medical School, Hammersmith Hospital, Du Cane Road, W12 0NN. *T*: 081–1743 2030.

WATKINS-PITCHFORD, Dr John, CB 1968; Chief Medical Adviser, Department of Health and Social Security (formerly Ministry of Social Security and Ministry of Pensions and National Insurance), 1965–73; retired 1973; *b* 20 April 1912; *s* of Wilfred Watkins Pitchford, FRCS, first Director of South African Institute of Medical Research, and Olive Mary (*née* Nichol); *m* 1945, Elizabeth Patricia Wright; one *s*. *Educ*: Shrewsbury School; St Thomas's Hospital. MRCS, LRCP 1937; MB, BS 1939 (London); MD 1946 (London); DPH 1946; DIH 1949. Various hosp. appts War of 1939–45: served RAFVR, Sqdn Ldr. Med. Inspector of Factories, 1947–50; Sen. Med. Off., Min. of Nat. Insce, 1950. Mem., Industrial Injuries Adv. Council, 1975–84. QHP 1971–74. *Publications*: articles on occupational medicine. *Recreation*: gardening. *Address*: Hill House, Farley Lane, Westerham, Kent. *T*: Westerham (0959) 64448.

WATKINSON, family name of **Viscount Watkinson.**

WATKINSON, 1st Viscount *cr* 1964, of Woking; **Harold Arthur Watkinson,** PC 1955; CH 1962; President, Confederation of British Industry, 1976–77; Chairman of Cadbury Schweppes Ltd, 1969–74 (Group Managing Director, Schweppes Ltd, 1963–68); Director: British Insulated Callender's Cables, 1968–77; Midland Bank Ltd, 1970–83; *b* 25 Jan. 1910; *e s* of A. G. Watkinson, Walton-on-Thames; *m* 1939, Vera, *y d* of John Langmead, West Sussex; two *d*. *Educ*: Queen's College, Taunton; King's College, London. Family business, 1929–35; technical and engineering journalism, 1935–39. Served War of 1939–45, active service, Lieut-Comdr RNVR. Chairman Production Efficiency Panel for S England, Machine Tool Trades Association, 1948; Chairman (first) Dorking Div. Conservative Assoc., 1948–49. MP (C) Woking Division of Surrey, 1950–64; Parliamentary Private Secretary to the Minister of Transport and Civil Aviation, 1951–52; Parliamentary Secretary to Ministry of Labour and National Service, 1952–55; Minister of Transport and Civil Aviation, Dec. 1955–59; Minister of Defence, 1959–62; Cabinet Minister, 1957–62. Mem., Brit. Nat. Export Council 1964–70; Chairman: Cttee for Exports to the United States, 1964–67; Nat. Advisory Cttee on the Employment of Older Men and Women, 1952–55; Companies Cttee, CBI, 1972–; a Vice-Pres., Council, BIM, 1970–73, Pres., 1973–78 (Chm., 1968–70). President: Grocers' Inst., 1970–71; Inst. of Grocery Distribution, 1972–73; Member: Council, RSA, 1972–77; NEDC, 1976–77; Falkland Islands Review Cttee, 1982–83. President: RNVR Officers' Assoc., 1973–76; Weald and Downland Museum, 1982–88. Chairman: Council, Cranleigh and Bramley Schools, 1973–87; Recruitment Working Party, Duke of Edinburgh's 1974 Study Conf., 1972–74. *Publications*: Blueprint for Industrial Survival, 1976; Turning Points, 1986; The Mountain, 1988; Jewels and Old Shoes, 1990. *Recreations*: mountaineering, walking, sailing. *Heir*: none. *Address*: Tyma House, Bosham, near Chichester, Sussex. *Clubs*: Naval; Royal Southern Yacht (Southampton).

WATKINSON, John Taylor; solicitor; Principal, Watkinson & Co., since 1989; *b* 25 Jan. 1941; *s* of William Forshaw Watkinson; *m* 1969, Jane Elizabeth Miller; two *s* two *d*. *Educ*: Bristol Grammar Sch.; Worcester Coll., Oxford. Schoolmaster, Rugby Sch., Warwicks, 1964–71. Called to the Bar, Middle Temple, 1971; practised, Midland Circuit, 1972–74, South East Circuit, 1978–79; Solicitor of the Supreme Ct, 1976–. MP (Lab) Gloucestershire West, Oct. 1974–1979; PPS to Sec. of State, Home Office, 1975–79; Member: Public Accounts Cttee, 1976–79; Expenditure Cttee, 1978–79; Speakers' Conf. on Northern Ireland, 1979; Hon. Sec., Anglo-Swiss Parly Gp, 1977–79; Mem. and Rapporteur, Council of Europe and WEU, 1976–79; Rapporteur, first Europ. Declaration on the Police. Contested: (Lab) Warwick and Leamington, 1970; (SDP) Glos West, 1983, 1987. Financial Reporter, BBC TV, 1979–82; Director: Interconnect Communications Ltd, 1986–; Wyedean Review Ltd, 1987. Visitor, Onley Borstal, Warwicks, 1970–71. Mem., NUJ. Amateur Rugby Fives Champion (Singles 3 times, Doubles 4 times), 1964–70. *Publications*: (jtly) UK Telecommunications Approval Manual, 1987; Telecommunications Approval Report, 1987. *Recreations*: rackets, cricket, golf. *Address*: Clanna Lodge, Alvington, Lydney, Glos.

WATLING, (David) Brian, QC 1979; **His Honour Judge Watling;** a Circuit Judge, since 1981; *b* 18 June 1935; *o s* of late Russell and Stella Watling; *m* 1964, Noelle Bugden. *Educ*: Charterhouse; King's Coll., London (LLB). Sub-Lieut RNR. Called to Bar, Middle Temple, 1957; Advocate, Gibraltar, 1980. Various Crown appts, 1969–72; Treasury Counsel, Central Criminal Court, 1972–79; a Recorder of the Crown Court, 1979–81. Vis. Lectr, 1978–80, Vis. Prof. in Criminal Law, 1980–84, University Coll. at Buckingham (now Univ. of Buckingham). Diocese of St Edmundsbury and Ipswich: Reader 1985; Deacon 1987; Priest 1988. Chm., Mistley Bk Club, 1989–. *Publication*: (contrib.) Serving Two Masters, 1988. *Recreations*: sailing, langlauf, hill walking, theatre and ballet, fireside reading, the company of old friends. *Address*: The Crown Court, PO Box 9, Chelmsford CM1 1EL. *Club*: Garrick.

WATSON, family name of **Baron Manton.**

WATSON, Adam; *see* Watson, John Hugh A.

WATSON, Alan; *see* Watson, W. A. J.

WATSON, Prof. Alan Albert, JP; FRCPath; Regius Professor of Forensic Medicine, University of Glasgow, since 1985; *b* 20 Feb. 1929; *s* of Wilfrid Roy Watson and Gladys Cusden or Watson; *m* 1955, Jeannette Anne Pitts or Watson; three *s*. *Educ*: Reading Sch.; St Mary's. Hosp. Med. Sch., Univ. of London (MB BS); MA Cantab; FRCPGlas; DMJ; DTM&H (Antwerp). Director, Ntondo Hosp., Zaire, 1958; Lectr in Pathology, Glasgow Univ., 1964; Asst Pathologist, Cambridge Univ., 1969, Fellow, Queens' Coll., Cambridge, 1970; Sen. Lectr, Forensic Medicine, Glasgow, 1971. District Court Judge, 1982; JP Glasgow District, 1985. Fellow, Royal Belgian Acad. of Medicine, 1983. *Publications*: Legal Aspects of Dental Practice, 1975; Forensic Medicine, 1989; Lecture Notes on Forensic Medicine, 1989; contribs to Jls of Forensic Medicine, and Pathology. *Address*: 1 Cessnock Castle, Galston, KA4 8LJ. *T*: Galston (0563) 820980.

WATSON, Prof. Alan Andrew, FRAS; Professor of Physics, University of Leeds, since 1984; *b* 26 Sept. 1938; *s* of William John Watson and Elsie Robinson; *m* 1973, Susan Lorraine Cartman; one *s* one *d*. *Educ*: Daniel Stewart's College, Edinburgh; Edinburgh Univ. (BSc 1st cl. hons Physics 1960; PhD 1964). Asst Lectr, Univ. of Edinburgh, 1962–64; University of Leeds: Lectr, 1964–76; Reader in Particle Cosmic Physics, 1976–84. Science and Engineering Research Council: Member: Astronomy and Planetary Science Bd, 1986–90; Nuclear Physics Bd, 1987–90; Space Science Program Bd, 1990–. Mem., Cosmic Ray Commn, IUPAP, 1991–. *Publications*: contribs to Physical Review Letters, Astrophysical Jl, Jl of Physics, Nuclear Instruments and Methods, Nature. *Recreations*: malt whisky tasting, tennis, watching Scotland win Grand Slams, theatre. *Address*: Department of Physics, University of Leeds, Leeds LS2 9JT. *T*: Leeds (0532) 333888.

WATSON, Rear-Adm. Alan George, CB 1975. Served Royal Navy, 1941–77; Asst Chief of Naval Staff, 1974–77, retired. Chairman: Church of England Soldiers', Sailors' and Airmen's Clubs, 1979–; Church of England Soldiers', Sailors' and Airmen's Housing Assoc., 1979–.

WATSON, Alan John, CBE 1985; Chairman: City and Corporate Counsel Ltd, since 1987; Corporate Vision Ltd, since 1989; Director, Translink Services Ltd, since 1989; *b* 3 Feb. 1941; *s* of Rev. John William Watson and Edna Mary (*née* Peters); *m* 1965, Karen Lederer; two *s*. *Educ*: Diocesan Coll., Cape Town, SA; Kingswood Sch., Bath, Somerset; Jesus Coll., Cambridge (Open Schol. in History 1959, State Schol. 1959) (MA Hons). Vice-Pres., Cambridge Union; Pres., Cambridge Univ. Liberal Club. Research Asst to Cambridge Prof. of Modern History on post-war history of Unilever, 1962–64. General trainee, BBC, 1965–66; Reporter, BBC TV, The Money Programme, 1966–68; Chief Public Affairs Commentator, London Weekend Television, 1969–70; Reporter, Panorama, BBC TV, 1971–74; Presenter, The Money Programme, 1974–75; Head of TV, Radio, Audio-Visual Div., EEC, and Editor, European Community Newsreel Service to Lomé Convention Countries, 1975–79; Dir, Charles Barker City Ltd, 1980–85 (Chief Exec., 1980–83). Pres., Liberal Party, 1984–85. Presenter, You and 1992, BBC 1 series, 1990. Vis. Fellow, Louvanium Internat. Business Centre, Brussels, 1990–; Vis. Erasmus Prof. in European Studies, Louvain Univ., 1990–. Charities Mem., UK Bd of UNICEF, 1986–. Mem. Council, RTS, 1989–. Chm. of Governors, Westminster Coll., Oxford, 1989–; Governor, Kingswood Sch., 1983–. MIPR 1986. Grand Prix Eurodiaporama of European Community for Common Market Coverage, 1974. *Publication*: Europe at Risk, 1972. *Recreation*: historical biography. *Address*: Cholmondeley House, 3 Cholmondeley Walk, Richmond upon Thames, Surrey TW9 1NS; Somerset Lodge, Nunney, Somerset. *Clubs*: Brooks's, United Oxford & Cambridge University, Royal Automobile, Kennel.

WATSON, Sir Andrew; *see* Watson, Sir J. A.

WATSON, Maj.-Gen. Andrew Linton, CB 1981; Lieutenant Governor and Secretary, Royal Hospital, Chelsea, 1984–92; Colonel, The Black Watch, since 1981; *b* 9 April 1927; *s* of Col W. L. Watson, OBE, and Mrs D. E. Watson (*née* Lea); *m* 1952, Mary Elizabeth, *d* of Mr and Mrs A. S. Rigby, Warrenpoint, Co. Down; two *s* one *d*. *Educ*: Wellington Coll., Berks. psc, jssc, rcds. Commnd The Black Watch, 1946; served, 1946–66: with 1st and 2nd Bns, Black Watch, in UK, Germany, Cyprus and British Guiana; with UN Force, Cyprus; as GSO 2 and 3 on Staff, UK and Germany; GSO 1 HQ 17 Div./Malaya Dist, 1966–68; CO 1st Bn The Black Watch, UK, Gibraltar and NI, 1969–71; Comdr 19 Airportable Bde, Colchester, 1972–73; RCDS, 1974; Comdr British Army Staff, and Military Attaché, Washington, DC, 1975–77; GOC Eastern District, 1977–80; COS, Allied Forces, Northern Europe, 1980–82. *Recreations*: tennis, shooting, walking, classical music. *Address*: c/o Royal Bank of Scotland, 18 South Methven Street, Perth, Scotland. *T*: Perth (0738) 31441. *Club*: Army and Navy.

WATSON, (Angus) Gavin; Under Secretary, since 1986, and Head, Directorate of Environmental Policy and Analysis, since 1991, Department of the Environment; *b* 14 April 1944; *s* of late H. E. and M. Watson; *m* 1967, Susan Naomi Beal (marr. diss. 1991); two *s* (and one *d* decd). *Educ*: Carlisle Grammar School; Merton College, Oxford. MA. Joined Dept of the Environment, 1971; Private Office, Secretary of State, 1975–77; Asst Sec., 1980–86; Under Sec., Housing Policy, 1986–; Hd, Water Directorate, Jun.–July 1991. *Recreations*: looking at buildings, industrial archaeology, fell walking. *Address*: c/o Department of the Environment, Romney House, 43 Marsham Street, SW1P 3PY. *T*: 071–276 8636.

WATSON, Anthony Gerard; Editor, Yorkshire Post, since 1989; *b* 28 May 1955; *s* of George Maurice Watson and Ann (*née* McDonnell); *m* 1982, Susan Ann Gutteridge; two *s* two *d*. *Educ*: St John Fisher Sch., Peterborough. N Staffs Polytechnic (BA Pol. and Internat. Relns). Journalist with E. Midlands Allied Press, Peterborough, 1977–79; joined Westminster Press—Evening Despatch, Darlington, 1979, News Editor, 1983–84; Yorkshire Post, 1984–86; Researcher, World in Action, Granada TV, 1986–88; Dep. Editor, Yorkshire Post, 1988–89. Provincial Journalist of the Year, British Press Awards, 1987. *Address*: Yorkshire Post, Wellington Street, Leeds LS1 1RF; Oakwell Drive, Leeds LS8 4AE. *T*: Leeds (0532) 403099.

WATSON, Anthony Heriot, CBE 1965; *b* 13 April 1912; *s* of William Watson and Dora Isabel Watson (*née* Fisher); *m* 1946, Hilary Margaret Fyfe. *Educ:* St Paul's Sch.; Christ Church, Oxford; University Coll., London. Statistical Officer, British Cotton Industry Research Assoc., 1936. Min. of Supply, 1940: Statistician; Asst Dir of Statistics; Min. of Aircraft Production, 1942; Statistician, Dept of Civil Aviation, Air Ministry, 1945; Chief Statistician: Min. of Civil Aviation, 1951; Min. of Transport and Civil Aviation, 1954; Min. of Aviation, 1959; Min. of Transport, 1964, Dir of Statistics, 1966; DoE, 1970; retired 1973. *Recreations:* music, garden. *Address:* 9 Kirk Park, Edinburgh EH16 6HZ. *T:* 031–664 7428.

WATSON, Antony Edward Douglas; QC 1986; *b* 6 March 1945; *s* of William Edward Watson and Margaret Watson (*née* Douglas); *m* 1972, Gillian Mary Bevan-Arthur; two *d. Educ:* Sedbergh School; Sidney Sussex College, Cambridge (MA). Called to the Bar, Inner Temple, 1968. *Publication:* (jtly) Terrell on Patents (1884), 13th edn 1982. *Recreations:* wine, opera, country pursuits. *Address:* The Old Rectory, Milden, Suffolk IP7 7AF. *T:* Bildeston (0449) 740227.

WATSON, Arthur Christopher, CMG 1977; HM Diplomatic Service, retired; Governor of Montserrat, West Indies, 1985–87; *b* 2 Jan. 1927; *s* of late Dr A. J. Watson and Dr Mary Watson, Kunming, China, and Chinnor; *m* 1956, Mary Cecil Candler (*née* Earl); one *d*; and one step *s* one step *d. Educ:* Norwich Sch.; St Catharine's Coll., Cambridge. Naval Service, 1945–48 (commissioned RNVR, 1946). Colonial Administrative Service, Uganda, 1951; District Commissioner, 1959; Principal Asst Sec., 1960; Principal, Commonwealth Relations Office, 1963; HM Diplomatic Service, 1965; Karachi, 1964–67; Lahore, 1967; FCO, 1967–71; HM Comr in Anguilla, 1971–74; Governor, Turks and Caicos Islands, 1975–78; High Comr in Brunei, 1978–83; FCO, 1983–84. *Address:* Holmesdale, Oval Way, Gerrards Cross, Bucks SL9 8QB. *Club:* Commonwealth Trust.

WATSON, Sir Bruce (Dunstan), Kt 1985; Chairman, M.I.M. Holdings Limited, since 1983 (Chief Executive Officer, 1981–90); *b* 1 Aug. 1928; *s* of James Harvey and Edith Mary (Crawford); *m* 1952, June Kilgour; one *s* two *d. Educ:* University of Queensland (BE (Elec) 1949, BCom 1957). Engineer, Tasmanian Hydro Elecricity Commn, 1950–54, Townsville Regional Electricity Board, 1954–56; MIM Group of Companies: Engineer, Copper Refineries Pty Ltd, Townsville, 1956–69; Mount Isa Mines Ltd, 1970–73; Group Industrial Relations Manager, MIM Group, Brisbane, 1973–75; First Gen. Man., Agnew Mining Co., WA, 1975–77; M.I.M. Holdings Ltd, Brisbane: Director, 1977; Man. Dir. 1980; Man. Dir and Chief Exec. Officer, 1981. Director: Asarco Inc., 1985–90; National Australia Bank, 1984–91; Mem., Supervisory Bd, Metallgesellschaft AG, 1988–. Member: Business Council of Australia, 1983–; Exec. Cttee, Australian Mining Industry Council, 1980–. Bd Mem., Australian Management Coll., Mt Eliza. Hon. DEng Queensland, 1989. *Recreation:* golf. *Address:* M.I.M. Holdings Limited, 410 Ann Street, Brisbane, Qld 4000, Australia. *T:* 833 8000.

WATSON, (Daniel) Stewart, CB 1967; OBE 1958; *b* 30 Dec. 1911; *s* of Reverend Dr William Watson, DD, DLitt, and Mary Mackintosh Watson; *m* 1939, Isabel (*née* Gibson); one *s. Educ:* Robert Gordon's Coll.; Aberdeen University. Student Apprentice, British Thomson Houston, Rugby, 1933, Research Engr, 1936. Scientific Officer, Admiralty, 1938–; Dir, Admiralty Surface Weapons Establishment, 1961–68; Dep. Chief Scientist (Naval), MoD, 1968–72; Dir Gen. Establishments, Resources Programme A, MoD, 1972–73. *Publications:* contribs to IEEJ. *Recreations:* thoroughbred cars; caravanning. *Address:* 28 Longhope Drive, Wrecclesham, Farnham, Surrey GU10 4SN. *T:* Farnham (0252) 733126.

WATSON, Prof. David John; Director, Brighton Polytechnic, since 1990; *b* 22 March 1949; *s* of late Lewis James Watson and of Berenice Nichols; *m* 1975, Betty Pinto Skolnick; one *d* one *s. Educ:* Cheshunt Grammar School; Eton College; Clare College, Cambridge (MA); Univ. of Pennsylvania (PhD). Sen. Lectr, Principal Lectr in Humanities, Crewe and Alsager Coll. of Higher Educn, 1975–81; Dean, Modular Course, Asst Dir, Dep. Dir, Oxford Polytechnic, 1981–90. Member: Council, CNAA, 1989– (Mem., 1977–); PCFC, 1988–. *Publications:* Margaret Fuller, 1988; Managing the Modular Course, 1989; (jtly) Developing Professional Education, 1992; papers on history of American and British ideas, higher education policy. *Recreations:* family, music (piano and saxophone), cricket. *Address:* Brighton Polytechnic, Mithras House, Lewes Road, Brighton BN2 4AT. *T:* Brighton (0273) 6009000.

WATSON, Sir Duncan; *see* Watson, Sir N. D.

WATSON, Duncan Amos, CBE 1986; Principal Assistant Treasury Solicitor, Common Law, 1978–86; Chairman, Executive Council, Royal National Institute for the Blind, 1975–90; *b* 10 May 1926; *m* 1954, Mercia Casey, Auckland, NZ. *Educ:* Worcester College for the Blind; St Edmund Hall, Oxford (BA). Solicitor. Chm., Access Cttee for England, 1989–; Pres., World Blind Union, 1988–. *Address:* 19 Great Russell Mansions, WC1B 3BE. *Clubs:* Reform, MCC.

WATSON, Sir Francis (John Bagott), KCVO 1973 (CVO 1965; MVO 1959); BA Cantab; Hon. MA Oxon 1969; FBA 1969; FSA; Director, Wallace Collection, 1963–74; Surveyor of The Queen's Works of Art, 1963–72, retired; Advisor for Works of Art, since 1972; *b* 24 Aug. 1907; *s* of Hugh Watson, Blakedown, and Helen Marian Bagott, Dudley; *m* 1941, Mary Rosalie Gray (*d* 1969), *d* of George Strong, Bognor; one adopted *s. Educ:* Shrewsbury School; St John's College, Cambridge. Registrar, Courtauld Inst. of Art, 1934–38; Asst Keeper (later Dep. Dir), Wallace Collection, 1938–63; Deputy Surveyor of The Queen's (until 1952 The King's) Works of Art, 1947–63; Trustee, Whitechapel Art Gallery, 1949–74; Chairman: Furniture History Society, 1966–74; Walpole Society, 1970–76; Slade Prof. of Fine Art, Oxford, 1969–70; Wrightsman Prof., NY Univ., 1970–71; Vis. Lectr, Univ. of California, 1970; Kress Prof., National Gallery, Washington DC, 1975–76; Regent Fellow, Smithsonian Instn, 1982–84. Uff. del Ord. al Merito della Repubblica Italiana, 1961. New York University Gold Medal, 1966. *Publications:* Canaletto, 1949 (rev. 2nd edn, 1954); (jtly) Southill, A Regency House, 1951; Wallace Collection: Catalogue of Furniture, 1956; Louis XVI Furniture, 1959 (rev. French edn, 1963); The Choiseul Gold Box (Charlton Lecture), 1963; (jtly) Great Family Collections, 1965; The Guardi Family of Painters (Fred Cook Memorial Lecture), 1966; (jtly) Eighteenth Century Gold Boxes, 1966, 3rd rev. edn 1990; The Wrightsman Collection Catalogue, Vols 1 and 2: Furniture, 1966, Vols 3 and 4: Furniture, Goldsmith's Work and Ceramics, 1970, Vol. 5: Paintings and Sculpture; Giambattista Tiepolo, 1966; Fragonard, 1967; Chinese Porcelains in European Mounts, 1980; (jtly) Catalogue of the Mounted Oriental Porcelains in the J. Paul Getty Museum, 1983; (contrib.) Vergoldete Bronzen-Die Bronzearbeiten des Spätbarok zu Klassizmus: Einfurung, 1985; Oriental Porcelains in European Mounts, 1986; Systematic Catalogue of Seventeenth and Eighteenth Century French Furniture, National Gallery, Washington, 1990; numerous contribs to learned journals, in Europe, America and Asia. *Recreations:* sinology, Western Americana. *Address:* West Farm House, Corton, Wilts BA12 0SY. *Club:* Beefsteak.

WATSON, Gavin; *see* Watson, A. G.

WATSON, Gerald Walter; Partner, Financial Services Group, Ernst & Young (formerly Arthur Young), since 1989; *b* 13 Dec. 1934; *s* of Reginald Harold Watson and Gertrude Hilda Watson (*née* Ruffell); *m* 1961, Janet Rosemary (*née* Hovey); one *s* two *d. Educ:* King Edward VI, Norwich School; Corpus Christi Coll., Cambridge (MA). National Service, RAF Regt, 1953–55. War Office, 1958–64; MoD, 1964–69; Civil Service Dept, 1969–73; Northern Ireland Office, 1973–75; CSD, 1975–81; HM Treasury, 1981–86; Dir, Central Computer and Telecommunications Agency, 1978–82. Dep. Chm., Building Socs Commn, 1986–88. *Recreations:* opera and theatre going, equestrian sports. *Address:* c/o Holts Branch, Royal Bank of Scotland, Kirkland House, Whitehall, SW1.

WATSON, Henry, CBE 1969; QPM 1963; Chief Constable of Cheshire, 1963–74; *b* 16 Oct. 1910; *s* of John and Ann Watson, Preston, Lancs; *m* 1933, Nellie Greenhalgh; two *d. Educ:* Preston Victoria Junior Technical Coll. Admitted to Inst. of Chartered Accountants, 1934; joined Ashton-under-Lyne Borough Police, 1934; King's Lynn Borough Police, 1942; Norfolk County Constabulary, 1947; Asst Chief Constable, Cumberland and Westmorland, 1955, Chief Constable, 1959. CStJ 1973. *Recreation:* golf. *Address:* Gorgate Road, Hoe, Dereham, Norfolk.

WATSON, Maj.-Gen. (Henry) Stuart (Ramsay), CBE 1973 (MBE 1954); *b* 9 July 1922; *yr s* of Major H. A. Watson, CBE, MVO and Mrs Dorothy Bannerman Watson, OBE; *m* 1965, Susan, *o d* of Col W. H. Jackson, CBE, DL; two *s* one *d. Educ:* Winchester College. Commnd 2nd Lieut 13th/18th Royal Hussars, 1942; Lieut 1943; Captain 1945; Adjt 13/18 H, 1945–46 and 1948–50; psc 1951; GSO2, HQ 1st Corps, 1952–53; Instr RMA Sandhurst, 1955–57; Instr Staff Coll. Camberley, 1960–62; CO 13/18 H, 1962–64; GSO1, MoD, 1964–65; Col GS, SHAPE, 1965–68; Col, Defence Policy Staff, MoD, 1968; idc 1969; BGS HQ BAOR, 1970–73; Dir Defence Policy, MoD, 1973–74; Sen. Army Directing Staff, RCDS, 1974–76. Col, 13th/18th Royal Hussars, 1979–90. Exec. Dir, 1977–85, Dep. Dir Gen., 1985–88, Inst. of Dirs. *Recreations:* golf, shooting, gardening. *Address:* The Glebe House, Little Kimble, Aylesbury, Bucks HP17 0UE. *T:* Aylesbury (0296) 612200. *Clubs:* Cavalry and Guards; Huntercombe Golf.

WATSON, Sir (James) Andrew, 5th Bt, *cr* 1866; a Recorder, since 1989; *b* 30 Dec. 1937; *s* of 4th Bt and Ella Marguerite, *y d* of late Sir George Farrar, 1st Bt; *S* father, 1941; *m* 1965, Christabel Mary, *e d* of K. R. M. Carlisle and Hon. Mrs Carlisle; two *s* one *d. Educ:* Eton. Barrister-at-law. Contested (L) Sutton Coldfield, Feb. and Oct. 1974. *Heir: s* Roland Victor Watson, *b* 4 March 1966. *Address:* Talton House, Newbold on Stour, Stratford-upon-Avon, Warwickshire. *T:* Alderminster (078987) 212.

WATSON, Prof. James Dewey; Director: Cold Spring Harbor Laboratory, since 1968; National Center for Human Genome Research, National Institutes of Health, USA, since 1989; *b* 6 April 1928; *s* of James D. and Jean Mitchell Watson; *m* 1968, Elizabeth Lewis; two *s. Educ:* Univ. of Chicago (BS); Indiana Univ. (PhD); Clare Coll., Cambridge. Senior Res. Fellow in Biology, California Inst. of Technology, 1953–55; Harvard University: Asst Prof. of Biology, 1955–57; Associate Prof., 1958–61; Prof. of Molecular Biology, 1961–76. Member: US National Acad. Sciences, 1962–; Amer Acad. of Arts and Sciences, 1957; Royal Danish Acad. 1962; Amer. Philosophical Soc., 1976; Foreign Member: Royal Soc., 1981; Acad. of Scis, USSR, 1989. Hon. DSc: Chicago, 1961; Indiana, 1963; Long Island, 1970; Adelphi, 1972; Brandeis, 1973; Albert Einstein Coll. of Medicine, 1974; Hofstra, 1976; Harvard, 1978; Rockefeller, 1980; Clarkson Coll., 1981; SUNY, 1983; Rutgers, 1988; Hon. MD Buenos Aires, 1986; Hon. LLD Notre Dame, 1965. Hon. Fellow, Clare Coll., Camb., 1967. Nobel Award in Medicine and Physiology (jointly), 1962. Carty Medal, US National Acad. of Sciences, 1971; Presidential Medal of Freedom, 1977. *Publications:* Molecular Biology of the Gene, 1965, 4th edn 1986; The Double Helix, 1968; (with John Tooze) The DNA Story, 1981; (with others) The Molecular Biology of the Cell, 1983, 2nd edn 1989; (with John Tooze and David T. Kurtz) Recombinant DNA: a short course, 1984; scientific papers on the mechanism of heredity. *Recreation:* mountain walking. *Address:* Bungtown Road, Cold Spring Harbor, NY 11724, USA. *Clubs:* Athenæum; Piping Rock (New York).

WATSON, James Kay Graham, PhD; FRS 1987; FRSC 1990; Principal Research Officer, National Research Council of Canada, since 1987 (Senior Research Officer, 1982–87); *b* Denny, Stirlingshire, 20 April 1936; *s* of Thomas Watson and Mary Catherine (*née* Miller); *m* 1981, Carolyn Margaret Landon Kerr, *e d* of Robert Reid Kerr, *qv. Educ:* Denny High Sch.; High School of Stirling; Univ. of Glasgow (BScChem, PhD). Postdoctoral Fellow: UCL, 1961–63; Nat. Res. Council, Ottawa, 1963–65; Univ. of Reading, 1965–66; Lectr in Chem. Physics, Univ. of Reading, 1966–71; Vis. Associate Prof. of Physics, Ohio State Univ., Columbus, 1971–75; SRC Sen. Res. Fellow in Chemistry, Univ. of Southampton, 1975–82. Award for Theoretical Chemistry and Spectroscopy, Chemical Soc., 1974; Plyler Prize, Amer. Phys. Soc., 1986. *Publications:* 85 articles on molecular physics and spectroscopy in learned jls. *Recreations:* music, golf, tree-watching. *Address:* 183 Stanley Avenue, Ottawa, Ontario K1M 1P2, Canada. *T:* (613) 745–7928; (business) Herzberg Institute of Astrophysics, National Research Council of Canada, Ottawa, Ontario K1A OR6, Canada.

WATSON, James Kenneth, FCA; Chairman, National Freight Consortium, since 1991 (Finance Director, 1982–84; Deputy Chairman, 1985–90); *b* 16 Jan. 1935; *s* of James and Helen Watson; *m* 1959, Eileen Fay Waller; two *s* one *d. Educ:* Watford Grammar Sch.; Stanford Univ., California, USA. Baker Sutton & Co., Chartered Accountants, 1964; Financial Controller, Times Group, 1968; Finance Director: British Road Services Ltd, 1970–76; Nat. Freight Corp., later Nat. Freight Co., 1977–82. *Publications:* contribs to transport and financial press. *Recreations:* cricket, hockey, theatre, history. *Address:* Inglands, Lower Icknield Way, Buckland, Aylesbury, Bucks HP22 5LR. *Clubs:* Royal Automobile, MCC.

WATSON, Prof. James Patrick; Professor of Psychiatry, United Medical and Dental Schools of Guy's and St Thomas' Hospitals (formerly Guy's Hospital Medical School), since 1974; *b* 14 May 1936; *e s* of Hubert Timothy Watson and Grace Emily (*née* Mizen); *m* 1962, Dr Christine Mary Colley; four *s. Educ:* Roan Sch. for Boys, Greenwich; Trinity Coll., Cambridge; King's Coll. Hosp. Med. Sch., London. MA, MD; FRCP, FRCPsych, DPM, DCH. Qualified, 1960. Hosp. appts in Medicine, Paediatrics, Pathology, Neurosurgery, at King's Coll. Hosp. and elsewhere, 1960–64; Registrar and Sen. Registrar, Bethlem Royal and Maudsley Hosps, 1964–71; Sen. Lectr in Psychiatry, St George's Hosp. Med. Sch., and Hon. Consultant Psychiatrist, St George's Hosp., 1971–74. Member: British Assoc. for Behavioural Psychotherapy; British Psychological Soc.; Soc. for Psychotherapy Res.; Assoc. of Sexual and Marital Therapists. Mem., various bodies concerned with interfaces between counselling and psychotherapy, religion and medicine. *Publications:* (ed jtly) Personal Meanings, 1982; papers on gp, family, marital and behavioural psychotherapy, treatment of phobias, hospital ward environmental effects on patients, postnatal depression, community psychiatry, in BMJ, Lancet, British Jl of Psychiatry, British Jl of Med. Psychology, British Jl of Clin. Psychology, Behaviour Research and Therapy. *Recreations:* mountains; music, especially opera, especially Mozart. *Address:* 36 Alleyn Road, SE21 8AL. *T:* 081–670 0444.

WATSON, John, FRCS, FRCSE; Consultant Plastic Surgeon to: Queen Victoria Hospital, East Grinstead, 1950–77, now Hon. Consultant; King Edward VII Hospital for Officers, 1963–87; London Hospital, 1963–82; *b* 10 Sept. 1914; *s* of late John Watson; *m* 1941, June Christine Stiles; one *s* three *d. Educ:* Leighton Park, Reading; Jesus Coll., Cambridge; Guy's Hospital. MRCS, LRCP 1938; MA, MB, BChir (Cantab) 1939; FRCS(Ed.) 1946; FRCS 1963. Served as Sqdn Ldr (temp.) RAF, 1940–46 (despatches twice). Marks Fellow in Plastic Surgery, Queen Victoria Hosp., E Grinstead, 1947–50; Consultant Plastic Surgeon, Queen Victoria Hospital, East Grinstead, and Tunbridge Wells Gp of Hospitals, 1950–77. Trustee, E Grinstead Research Trust for Blond-McIndoe Research Centre, 1959–; Gen. Sec., Internat. Confedn for Plastic and Reconstructive Surgery, 1971–75; Hon. Mem. Brit. Assoc. of Plastic Surgeons, 1979– (Hon. Sec., 1960–62, Pres., 1969); Hon. FRSM. Chm., Stargazers Trust, 1989–. *Publications:* numerous articles on plastic surgery in techn. jls and scientific periodicals. Chapters in: Textbook of Surgery, Plastic Surgery for Nurses, Modern Trends in Plastic Surgery, Clinical Surgery. *Recreations:* fishing, astronomy. *Address:* Iddons, Henley's Down, Catsfield, Battle, East Sussex TN33 9BN. *T:* Crowhurst (042483) 226.

WATSON, Sir John Forbes I.; *see* Inglefield-Watson.

WATSON, Rear-Adm. John Garth, CB 1965; BSc(Eng); CEng, FICE, FIEE; Secretary, Institution of Civil Engineers, 1967–79; *b* 20 February 1914; *er s* of Alexander Henry St Croix Watson and Gladys Margaret Watson (*née* Payne); *m* 1943, Barbara Elizabeth Falloon; two *s* one *d. Educ:* Univ. Coll. School, Hampstead; Northampton Engineering Coll., Univ. of London. BSc (Eng.). 1st Bn Herts Regt (TA), 1932; resigned on joining Admiralty, 1939; HMS Vernon, 1939; Development of Magnetic Minesweepers, Dec. 1939; Warship Electrical Supt, London and SE Area, 1943; BJSM, Washington, DC, 1945; Admlty, 1948; transf. to Naval Elec. Branch, 1949; served in Destroyers and on Staff of Flag Officer, Flot., Home Fleet, 1950; Admlty, 1952; HM Dockyard Devonport, 1953; promoted Capt. 1955; Staff of C-in-C Home Fleet, Fleet Elec. Officer, 1955; Suptg Elec. Engr, HM Dockyard Gibraltar, 1957; Sen. Officers' War Course, 1960; Asst Dir of Elec. Engineering, Admlty, Nov. 1961; promoted Rear Adm. 1963; Adm. Superintendent, Rosyth, 1963–66. ADC to the Queen, 1962. Mem., Smeatonian Soc. of Civil Engineers, 1968 (Pres., 1987). Hon. Mem., Soc. of Civil Engrg Technicians, 1979. Chm., Queen's Jubilee Scholarship Trust, ICE, 1980–86; Vice-Chm., Civil Engineers' Club, 1980–86. Liveryman: Engineers' Co., 1986–; Guild of Freemen, 1986–. FInstD 1977; FRSA 1988. Hon DSc City Univ., 1984. *Publications:* A Short History: Institution of Civil Engineers, 1982; The Civils, 1987; The Smeatonians, 1989; contrib. 15th edn Encyc. Britannica, 1974. *Recreations:* sailing and light gardening. *Address:* Little Hall Court, Shedfield, near Southampton SO3 2HL. *T:* Wickham (0329) 833216. *Clubs:* Athenæum, Royal Thames Yacht; Royal Naval and Royal Albert Yacht (Portsmouth).
See also Vice-Adm. Sir P. A. Watson.

WATSON, John Grenville Bernard; Director, Goddard Kay Rogers (Northern) Ltd, since 1989; *b* 21 Feb. 1943; *s* of Norman V. Watson and Ruby E. Watson; *m* 1965, Deanna Wood; one *s* two *d. Educ:* Moorlands Sch., Leeds; Bootham Sch., York; College of Law, Guildford. Articled, 1962, qualified as solicitor, 1967; joined John Waddington Ltd as managerial trainee, 1968; Export Director, Plastona John Waddington Ltd, 1972; Marketing Dir, 1975, Man. Dir, 1977, Waddington Games Ltd, responsible for Security Printing Div., 1984–89, for Johnsen & Jorgensen, 1988–89; Dir, John Waddington PLC, 1979–89; Chm., Murray Luckett Communications Ltd, 1989–. Mem., Leeds Develt Corp., 1988–. Joined Young Conservatives, 1965; Chairman, Yorkshire YC, 1969; Personal Asst to Rt Hon. Edward Heath, 1970; Chm., Nat. YC, 1971; contested (C) York, general elections, Feb. and Oct. 1974. MP (C): Skipton, 1979–83; Skipton and Ripon, 1983–87. Chm., Conservative Candidates Assoc., 1975–79. Mem., Parly Select Cttee on Energy, 1980–82; PPS, NI Office, 1982–83; PPS, Dept of Energy, 1983–85. Chm., British Atlantic Gp of Young Political Leaders, 1982–84; Nat. Vice Pres., Young Conservative Orgn, 1984–86. Pres., British Youth Council, 1980–83. *Recreations:* walking, running, standing still. *Address:* Bay Horse Corner, Ling Lane, Scarcroft, Leeds LS14 3HY. *T:* Leeds (0532) 892209.
See also V. H. Watson.

WATSON, (John Hugh) Adam, CMG 1958; Professor, Center for Advanced Studies, University of Virginia, since 1980; *b* 10 Aug. 1914; *er s* of Joseph Charlton Watson and Alice (*née* Tate); *m* 1950, Katharine Anne Campbell; two *s* one *d. Educ:* Rugby; King's Coll., Camb. Entered the Diplomatic Service, 1937; Brit. Legation, Bucharest, 1939; Brit. Embassy, Cairo, 1940; Brit. Embassy, Moscow, 1944; FO, 1947; Brit. Embassy, Washington, 1950; Head of African Dept, Foreign Office, 1956–59; appointed British Consul-General at Dakar, 1959; British Ambassador: to the Federation of Mali, 1960–61; to Senegal, Mauritania and Togo, 1960–62; to Cuba, 1963–66; Under-Secretary, Foreign Office, 1966–68; Diplomatic Adviser, British Leyland Motor Corp., 1968–73. Gwilym Gibbon Fellow, Nuffield Coll., Oxford, Oct. 1962–Oct. 1963. Vis. Fellow, ANU, 1973; Vis. Prof., Univ. of Virginia, 1978. Dir Gen., Internat. Assoc. for Cultural Freedom, 1974. *Publications:* The War of the Goldsmith's Daughter, 1964; Nature and Problems of Third World, 1968; (ed) The Origins of History, 1981; Diplomacy: the dialogue between States, 1982; (with Hedley Bull) The Expansion of International Society, 1984; The Evolution of International Society, 1992; various plays broadcast by BBC. *Address:* Sharnden Old Manor, Mayfield, East Sussex TN20 6QA. *T:* Mayfield (0435) 872441; 1871 Field Road, Charlottesville, Virginia 22903, USA. *T:* 804.295.8295. *Club:* Brooks's.

WATSON, Rev. John T., BA (London); LTCL; General Secretary, British and Foreign Bible Society, 1960–69, retired; *b* 13 Jan. 1904; *s* of late F. Watson, Sutton Bridge, Lincs; *m* 1933, Gertrude Emily Crossley (*d* 1982), Farsley, Leeds; two *s* one *d. Educ:* Moulton Grammar School; Westminster Training College, London; Didsbury Training College, Manchester. School-master, 1924–26. Missionary (under Methodist Missionary Soc.) in Dahomey, W Africa, 1929–34; Methodist Minister: Plymouth, 1935–38; Golders Green, 1938–46; Bible Society: Secretary for Schools and Colleges, 1946–49; Asst Home Sec., 1949–54; Asst Gen. Sec., 1954–60. Hon. DD, West Virginia Wesleyan Coll., 1966. *Publications:* Seen and Heard in Dahomey, 1934; Daily Prayers for the Methodist Church, 1951. *Recreation:* music. *Address:* 16 Beverington Road, Eastbourne, East Sussex BN21 2SD. *T:* Eastbourne (0323) 29838.

WATSON, (Leslie) Michael (Macdonald) S.; *see* Saunders Watson.

WATSON, Michael Goodall; MP (Lab) Glasgow Central, since 1989; *b* 1 May 1949; *s* of Clarke Watson and late Senga (*née* Goodall); *m* 1986, Lorraine Therese, *d* of late William McManus and of Mary McManus. *Educ:* Invergowrie Primary Sch., Dundee; Dundee High Sch.; Heriot-Watt Univ., Edinburgh (BA 2nd Cl. Hons Econs and Industrial Relns). Development Officer, WEA, E Midlands Dist, 1974–77; full-time official, ASTMS, then MSF, 1977–89. Mem., Scottish Exec. Cttee, Labour Party, 1987–90. *Publications:* Rags to Riches: the official history of Dundee United Football Club, 1985. *Recreations:* supporting Dundee United FC, reading political biographies, squash, running. *Address:* (constituency office) 58 Fox Street, Glasgow G1 4AU. *T:* 041–204 4738.

WATSON, Sir Michael M.; *see* Milne-Watson.

WATSON, Prof. Newton Frank, RIBA; Haden/Pilkington Professor of Environmental Design and Engineering, and Head, Bartlett School of Architecture and Planning, University College London, 1985–88, now Emeritus Professor; Dean of the Faculty of Environmental Studies, 1986–88; *b* 29 July 1923; *s* of Frank Watson and Amy Watson (*née* Cole); *m* 1944, Bridget Williams; two *d. Educ:* Holywell Grammar Sch.; King's Coll., Univ. of Durham. BArch. Wartime service, RWF (Lieut). Asst architect in practice, 1951–55; Res. Fellow, Nuffield Foundn Div. for Architectural Studies, 1955–57; Lectr in Arch., Poly. of N London, 1957–60; Lectr/Sen. Lectr in Arch., UCL, 1960–69; Bartlett Prof. of Architecture, UCL, 1969–85. Vis. Prof., Dept. of Arch., Univ. of California at Berkeley, 1965–66; Vis. Scholar, Sch. of Design, N Carolina State Univ., 1989. Awards (jtly) by Illuminating Soc. of Amer. for lighting design of London Stock Exchange, 1974, and Tate Gall., 1980. *Publications:* (jtly) in Design for Research, 1986; contribs to professional jls on lighting design (CIBSE medal (jtly) 1982, for contrib. Preferred Lighting Levels for Viewing Works of Art. *Recreations:* etching, France. *Address:* 1b Oval Road, NW1 7EA. *T:* 071–485 4796. *Club:* Athenæum.

WATSON, Sir (Noel) Duncan, KCMG 1967 (CMG 1960); HM Diplomatic Service, retired; *b* 16 Dec. 1915; *s* of late Harry and Mary Noel Watson, Bradford, Yorks; *m* 1951, Aileen Bryans (*d* 1980), *d* of late Charles Bell, Dublin. *Educ:* Bradford Grammar School; New College, Oxford. Colonial Administrative Service: Admin. Officer, Cyprus, 1938–43; Assistant Colonial Secretary, Trinidad, 1943–45; Principal, Colonial Office (secondment), 1946; transferred to Home Civil Service, 1947; Principal Private Sec. to Sec. of State for the Colonies, 1947–50; Asst Sec.: CO, 1950–62, Cent. Af. Office, 1962–63; Under-Secretary, 1963; Asst Under-Sec. of State, CO and CRO, 1964–67; Political Adviser to C-in-C Far East, 1967–70; High Comr in Malta, 1970–72; Dep. Under-Sec. of State, FCO, 1972–75. Mem., Central Council, Royal Commonwealth Soc., 1975– (Dep. Chm., 1983–87). *Address:* Sconce, Steels Lane, Oxshott, Surrey. *Clubs:* Travellers', Commonwealth Trust; Leander.

WATSON, Dr Peter, OBE 1988; Technical Director, British Railways, since 1991; *b* 9 Jan. 1944; *m* 1966, Elizabeth Buttery; two *s. Educ:* Univ. of Leeds (BSc 1966); Univ. of Waterloo, Canada (MSc 1968; PhD 1971). PSO, British Railways Res., 1971–76; GKN Technology Ltd, 1976–89 (Chm., 1982–89); Chm., GKN Axles Ltd, 1986–91. *Publications:* numerous articles on metal fatigue and management. *Address:* 49 Suckling Green Lane, Codsall, Wolverhampton, W Midlands WV8 2BT. *T:* Codsall (09074) 5252. *Club:* Royal Automobile.

WATSON, Rt. Rev. Peter Robert; an Assistant Bishop of Sydney (Bishop of Parramatta), since 1989; *b* 1 Jan. 1936; *s* of Noel Frederick and Helen Elizabeth Watson; *m* 1962, Margo Elinor Deans; three *d. Educ:* Canterbury Boys' High Sch., Sydney; Sydney Univ. (BEc); Moore Theological Coll., Sydney (ThL). Asst Priest, St Paul's, Chatswood, 1961–63; Curate-in-Charge, Lalor Park and Seven Hills, 1963–73; Rector, Lalor Park and Seven Hills, 1973–74; RD of Prospect, 1968–74; Canon, Prov. Cathedral of St John, Parramatta, 1969–74; Rector: St Luke's, Miranda, 1974–84; St Thomas, North Sydney, 1984–89; Area Dean, North Sydney, 1986–89. *Recreations:* caravanning, squash, swimming. *Address:* Suite 2, St John's Building, 191 Church Street, Parramatta, NSW 2150, Australia; Stuart Lodge, 5 Keith Place, Baulkham Hills, NSW 2153, Australia. *T:* (office) 02.635.3186. *Club:* NSW Leagues.

WATSON, Vice-Adm. Sir Philip (Alexander), KBE 1976; LVO 1960; *b* 7 Oct. 1919; *yr s* of A. H. St C. Watson; *m* 1948, Jennifer Beatrice Tanner; one *s* two *d. Educ:* St Albans School. FIEE 1963; CBIM 1973. Sub-Lt RNVR, 1940; qual. Torpedo Specialist, 1943; transf. to RN, 1946; Comdr 1955; HM Yacht Britannia, 1957–59; Captain 1963; MoD (Ship Dept), 1963; Senior Officers' War Course, 1966; comd HMS Collingwood, 1967; Dep. Dir of Engrg (Ship Dept), MoD, 1969; Dir Gen. Weapons (Naval), MoD, 1970–77; Chief Naval Engineer Officer, 1974–77. Rear-Adm. 1970; Vice-Adm. 1974. Director: Marconi International Marine Co. Ltd, 1977–86; Marconi Radar Systems Ltd, 1981–86 (Chm., 1981–85); Consultant, GEC–Marconi Ltd, 1986–87. Mem. Council, IEE, 1975–78, 1982–91, Chm. South East Centre, 1982–83. Adm. Pres., Midland Naval Officers Assoc., 1979–85, Vice Pres., 1985–. *Address:* The Hermitage, Bodicote, Banbury, Oxon OX15 4BZ. *T:* Banbury (0295) 263300. *Club:* Army and Navy.
See also Rear-Adm. J. G. Watson.

WATSON, Dr Reginald Gordon Harry, (Rex), CB 1987; CChem, FRSC; Director, Building Research Establishment, Department of the Environment, 1983–88; *b* 3 Nov. 1928; *s* of Gordon Henry and Winifred Catherine Watson; *m* 1951, Molly Joyce Groom (*d* 1989); one *s* two *d. Educ:* Chislehurst and Sidcup Grammar Sch.; Imperial Coll., London (Royal Schol.). BSc (1st cl. Hons Chem.), PhD; DIC; ARCS. Res. Worker (Fuel Cells), Dept of Chemical Engrg, Univ. of Cambridge, 1951–56; joined Royal Naval Scientific Service, 1956, as Sen. Scientific Officer, Admty Materials Lab.; Head of Chemical Engrg Div., 1958–66; Naval Staff Course, 1962; Individual Merit Sen. Principal Scientific Officer, 1965; Director: Naval R&D Admin, 1967–69; Admty Materials Lab., 1969–74; Chemical Defence Estab., Porton Down, 1974–83. *Publications:* papers on electrochemistry, chemical engineering and materials science. *Recreations:* photography, natural history, sailing. *Address:* 20 Merriefield Drive, Broadstone, Dorset BH18 8BP. *T:* Broadstone (0202) 692128. *Club:* Civil Service.

WATSON, Rt. Rev. Richard Charles Challinor; Hon. Assistant Bishop, Diocese of Oxford, since 1988; *b* 16 Feb. 1923; *o s* of Col Francis W. Watson, CB, MC, DL, The Glebe House, Dinton, Aylesbury, Bucks; *m* 1955, Anna, *er d* of Rt Rev. C. M. Chavasse, OBE, MC, MA, DD, then Bishop of Rochester; one *s* one *d. Educ:* Rugby; New Coll., Oxford; Westcott House, Cambridge. Served Indian Artillery, Lt and Capt. RA, 1942–45. Oxford Hon. Sch. Lang. and Lit., 1948, Theology 1949; Westcott House, Cambridge, 1950–51. Curate of Stratford, London E, 1952–53; Tutor and Chaplain, Wycliffe Hall, Oxford, 1954–57; Chaplain of Wadham Coll. and Chaplain of Oxford Pastorate, 1957–61; Vicar of Hornchurch, 1962–70; Asst Rural Dean of Havering, 1967–70; Rector of Burnley, 1970–77; Bishop Suffragan of Burnley, 1970–87; Hon. Canon of Blackburn Cathedral, 1970–87. Examining Chaplain to Bishop Rochester, 1956–61, to Bishop of Chelmsford, 1962–70. *Recreations:* reading, gardening. *Address:* 6 Church Road, Thame, Oxon OX9 3AJ. *T:* Thame (084421) 3853.

WATSON, Richard (Eagleson Gordon) Burges, CMG 1985; HM Diplomatic Service, retired; Ambassador to Nepal, 1987–90; *b* 23 Sept. 1930; *er s* of late Harold Burges Watson and Marjorie Eleanor (*née* Gordon); *m* 1966, Ann Rosamund Clarke; two *s* three *d. Educ:* King Edward VI Sch., Bury St Edmunds; St John's Coll., Cambridge. RA, 1948–50. Joined HM Foreign (subseq. Diplomatic) Service, 1954; Tokyo, 1954–60; FO, 1960–63; Bamako (Mali), 1963–66; British Delegn to OECD, 1966–69; FCO, 1969–71; Vis. Student, Woodrow Wilson Sch., Princeton, 1971–72; Tokyo, 1972–76; Brussels, 1976–78; FCO, 1978–81; Foundn for Internat. Research and Studies, Florence, 1981–82; FCO, 1982–83; Minister (Commercial) and Consul-Gen., Milan, 1983–86. *Recreations:* ski-ing, swimming, walking. *Address:* 101 Howards Lane, Putney, SW15 6NZ. *T:* 081–785 9053. *Club:* Travellers'.

WATSON, Roderick Anthony, QC 1967; *b* 1920; *o s* of late O. C. Watson, CBE and Peggy (*née* Donnelly); *m* Ann, *o d* of late W. L. Wilson; three *s* one *d*. *Educ:* Christian Brothers, Beulah Hill; King's Coll., Univ. of London. Served War of 1939–45, Captain RASC. Called to the Bar, Lincoln's Inn, 1949, Bencher, 1975. Dir, Standard Chartered Bank (IOM) Ltd, 1977–90; Dep. Chm., Isle of Man Financial Supervision Commn, 1983–. *Address:* Merton House, 11 The Promenade, Castletown, Isle of Man. *Clubs:* Army and Navy, Garrick; Isle of Man Yacht.

WATSON, Roy William, CBE 1983; Director General, National Farmers' Union, 1979–85, retired; *b* 7 Feb. 1926; *s* of William and Eleanor Maud Watson; *m* 1st, 1947, Margaret Peasey; two *s*; 2nd, 1977, Phyllis Frances Brotherwood (*née* Farrer). *Educ:* Alleyn's Sch., Dulwich. National Farmers' Union, 1948–85: Asst Dir General, 1973–78; Dep. Dir General, 1978. *Recreations:* music, military history, golf, gardening. *Address:* Avalon, Exeter Road, Honiton, Devon EX14 8AU. *T:* Honiton (0404) 42586.

WATSON, Prof. Stephen Roger; Peat, Marwick Professor of Management Studies, Cambridge, since 1986; Fellow of Emmanuel College, Cambridge, since 1968; *b* 29 Aug. 1943; *s* of John C. Watson and Marguerite F. R. Watson; *m* 1969, Rosemary Victoria Tucker; one *s* one *d*. *Educ:* University College Sch., Hampstead; Emmanuel Coll., Cambridge (BA 1964, MA 1968, PhD 1969). Research Fellow, Emmanuel Coll., Cambridge, 1968–70; Shell International, 1970–71; Cambridge University: Univ. Lectr in Operational Research, Engineering Dept, 1971–86; Tutor, Emmanuel Coll., 1973–85; Dir, Judge Inst. of Management Studies, 1990–. Director: Cambridge Decision Analysts Ltd, 1984–; Environmental Resources Ltd, 1989–. *Publications:* Decision Synthesis (with D. M. Buede), 1987; papers in learned jls. *Recreations:* singing, development issues. *Address:* 120 Huntingdon Road, Cambridge CB3 0HL. *T:* Cambridge (0223) 62536.

WATSON, Stewart; *see* Watson, D. S.

WATSON, Maj.-Gen. Stuart; *see* Watson, Maj.-Gen. H. S. R.

WATSON, Thomas Frederick, FCA, FCIS; Governor, National Society for Epilepsy, 1971–81 (Chairman, 1974–78); *b* 18 April 1906; *s* of late Frederick Watson and Jane Lucy (*née* Britton); *m* 1932, Eveline Dorothy Strang; one *d*. *Educ:* Tiffins Sch., Kingston-on-Thames. FCIS 1957; FCA 1960. With Deloitte Co., Chartered Accountants, 1925–45; qual. as Chartered Sec., 1930; Incorporated Accountant, 1945. Chm. and Chief Exec., Exchange Telegraph Co. Ltd, 1961–68, retired. Mem. Council, Commonwealth Press Union, 1959–68. *Recreations:* gardening, bridge, theatre, charity work. *Address:* Byeways Bungalow, Barrack Lane, Aldwick, Bognor Regis, W Sussex. *T:* Pagham (0243) 263896.

WATSON, Thomas Yirrell, CMG 1955; MBE 1943; *b* 27 May 1906; *s* of William Scott Watson and Edith Rose Watson (*née* Yirrell); *m* 1st, 1935, Margaret Alice (*d* 1978), *d* of late J. J. Watson; one *d*; 2nd, 1984, Katharine Margaret, *widow* of W. J. Mill Irving, OBE and *d* of late James Kay. *Educ:* Aberdeen Grammar Sch.; Aberdeen Univ. (BSc); Cambridge Univ. (Diploma in Agricultural Science); Pretoria Univ., South Africa. Colonial Agricultural Scholar, 1929–31; Agricultural Officer, Kenya, 1931–43; Senior Agricultural Officer, Kenya, 1943–48; Dep. Director of Agriculture, Uganda, 1948–51; Director of Agriculture, Uganda, 1951–53; Secretary for Agriculture and Natural Resources, Uganda, 1954–55; Minister of Natural Resources, 1955–56. General Manager, Uganda Lint Cotton Marketing Board, 1951–53; MEC and MLC, Uganda, 1951–56. Member: Commission of Inquiry into Land and Population Problems, Fiji, 1959–60; Economic Development Commn, Zanzibar, 1961; Commission of Inquiry into Cotton Ginning Industry, Uganda, 1962; Commissioner, Burley Tobacco Industry Inquiry, Malawi, 1964. Coronation Medal, 1953. *Address:* 2 Lennox Milne Court, Haddington, East Lothian EH41 4DF. *T:* Haddington (062082) 4490.

WATSON, Victor Hugo, CBE 1987; Chairman: John Waddington PLC, since 1977; John Foster & Son PLC, since 1985; *b* 26 Sept. 1928; *s* of Norman Victor and Ruby Ernestine Watson; *m* 1952, Sheila May Bryan; two *d*. *Educ:* Clare Coll., Cambridge (MA). Served Royal Engineers (2nd Lieut), 1946–48. Joined John Waddington Ltd, 1951. Director: Yorkshire TV Ltd, 1987–; Yorkshire TV Holdings PLC, 1989; Leeds & Holbeck Building Soc., 1986– (Pres., 1989–91). Pres., Inst. of Packaging, 1984–. *Recreations:* music, golf, sailing. *Address:* Moat Field, Moor Lane, East Keswick, Leeds LS17 9ET.

WATSON, Prof. William, CBE 1982; MA; FBA 1972; FSA; Professor of Chinese Art and Archaeology in University of London, at the School of Oriental and African Studies, 1966–83, now Emeritus, and Head of the Percival David Foundation of Chinese Art, 1966–83; Trustee, British Museum, since 1980; *b* 9 Dec. 1917; *s* of Robert Scoular Watson and Lily Waterfield; *m* 1940, Katherine Sylvia Mary, *d* of Mr and Mrs J. H. Armfield, Ringwood, Hants; four *s*. *Educ:* Glasgow High Sch.; Herbert Strutt Sch.; Gonville and Caius Coll., Cantab (Scholar; tripos in Modern and Medieval Langs). Served Intelligence Corps, 1940–46, Egypt, N Africa, Italy, India, ending as Major. Asst Keeper, British Museum, first in Dept of British and Medieval Antiquities, then in Dept of Oriental Antiquities, 1947–66. Slade Prof. of Fine Art, Cambridge University, 1975–76. Pres., Oriental Ceramic Soc., 1981–84. Hon. DLitt Chinese Univ. of Hong Kong, 1984. Sir Percy Sykes Meml Medal, 1973. *Publications:* The Sculpture of Japan, 1959; Archaeology in China, 1960; China before the Han Dynasty, 1961; Ancient Chinese Bronzes, 1961; Jade Books in the Chester Beatty Library, 1963; Cultural Frontiers in Ancient East Asia, 1971; The Genius of China (catalogue of Burlington House exhibn), 1973; Style in the Arts of China, 1974; L'Art de l'Ancienne Chine, 1980; (ed) Catalogue of the Great Japan Exhibition (at Burlington House 1981–82); Tang and Liao Ceramics, 1984; Pre-Tang Ceramics of China, 1991. *Recreation:* exploring N Wales, Romanesque France and Spain. *Address:* Cefn y Maes, Parc, Bala, Gwynedd. *T:* Bala (0678) 4302. *Club:* Arts.

WATSON, William Albert, CB 1989; PhD; FRCVS; Director, Veterinary Laboratories, Ministry of Agriculture, Fisheries and Food, 1986–90; *b* 8 March 1930; *s* of Henry Watson and Mary Emily Watson; *m* 1956, Wilma, *d* of Rev. Theodorus Johannas Henricus Steenbeck; one *s* one *d*. *Educ:* Preston Grammar School; University of Bristol (PhD, BVSc). Private practice, Garstang, Lancs, 1954–55; Asst Vet. Investigation Officer, Weybridge, 1954–56, Leeds, 1956–66; Animal Health Expert, FAO, Turkey, 1966–67; Vet. Investigation Officer, Penrith, 1967–71; Dep. Regional Vet. Officer, Nottingham, 1971–75; Regional Vet. Officer, Edinburgh, 1975–77; Asst Chief Vet. Officer, Tolworth, 1977–84; Dep. Dir, Vet. Labs, Weybridge, 1984–86. External Examr, London, Liverpool, Dublin and Edinburgh Univs. *Publications:* contribs to vet. jls and textbooks. *Recreations:* fishing, gardening, restoration of listed property, farming.

WATSON, Prof. William Alexander Jardine; Ernest P. Rogers Professor of Law, University of Georgia, since 1989; *b* 27 Oct. 1933; *s* of James W. and Janet J. Watson; *m* 1st, 1958, Cynthia Betty Balls, MA, MLitt (marr. diss.); one *s* one *d*; 2nd, 1986, Harriett Camilla Emanuel, BA, MS, JD, LLM; one *d*. *Educ:* Univ. of Glasgow (MA 1954, LLB 1957); Univ. of Oxford (BA (by decree) 1957, MA 1958, DPhil 1960, DCL 1973). Lectr, Wadham Coll., Oxford, 1957–59; Lectr, 1959–60, Fellow, 1960–65, Oriel Coll., Oxford; Pro-Proctor, Oxford Univ., 1962–63; Douglas Prof. of Civil Law, Univ. of Glasgow, 1965–68; Prof. of Civil Law, Univ. of Edinburgh, 1968–79; University of Pennsylvania: Prof. of Law and Classical Studies, 1979–84; Dir, Center for Advanced Studies in Legal Hist., 1980–89; Nicholas F. Gallichio Prof. of Law, 1984–86; Univ. Prof. of Law, 1986–89. Visiting Professor of Law: Tulane Univ., 1967; Univ. of Virginia, 1970 and 1974; Univ. of Cape Town, 1974 and 1975; Univ. of Michigan, 1977. Mem. Council, Stair Soc., 1970–; Hon. Mem., Speculative Soc., 1975. *Publications:* (as Alan Watson): Contract of Mandate in Roman Law, 1961; Law of Obligations in Later Roman Republic, 1965; Law of Persons in Later Roman Republic, 1967; Law of Property in Later Roman Republic, 1968; Law of the Ancient Romans, 1970; Roman Private Law Around 200 BC, 1971; Law of Succession in Later Roman Republic, 1971; Law Making in Later Roman Republic, 1974; Legal Transplants, An Approach to Comparative Law, 1974; (ed) Daube Noster, 1974; Rome of the Twelve Tables, 1975; Society and Legal Change, 1977; The Nature of Law, 1977; The Making of the Civil Law, 1981; Sources of Law, Legal Change, and Ambiguity, 1984; The Evolution of Law, 1985; (ed) The Digest of Justinian (4 vols), 1986; Failures of the Legal Imagination, 1988; Slave Law of the Americas, 1989; Roman Law and Comparative Law, 1991; The State, Law and Religion: pagan Rome, 1991; Studies in Roman Private Law, 1991; Legal Origins and Legal Change, 1991; various articles. *Recreations:* Roman numismatics, shooting. *Address:* Law School, University of Georgia, Herty Drive, Athens, Ga 30602, USA.

WATT; *see* Gibson-Watt.

WATT, Very Rev. Alfred Ian; Rector of St Paul's, Kinross, since 1982; Dean of the United Diocese of St Andrews, Dunkeld and Dunblane, since 1989; *b* 1934. *Educ:* Edinburgh Theological College. Deacon, 1960, priest 1961, Diocese of Brechin; Curate, St Paul's Cathedral, Dundee, 1960–63; Precentor, 1963–66; Rector of Arbroath, 1966–69; Provost of St Ninian's Cathedral, Perth, 1969–82; Canon, 1982–89; Convenor, Mission Bd of General Synod, 1982–87. *Address:* St Paul's Rectory, 55 Muirs, Kinross KY13 7AU.

WATT, Andrew, CBE 1963; Forestry Commissioner, 1965–69; *b* 10 Nov. 1909; 2nd surv. *s* of late James Watt, LLD, WS, and late Menie Watt; *m* 1943, Helen McGuffog (*d* 1969); two *s* one *d*. *Educ:* Winchester; Magdalen Coll., Oxford. BA 1931. District Officer, Forestry Commn, 1934; Divisional Officer, 1940; Conservator, 1946; Director of Forestry for Scotland, 1957–63; Director of Forest Research, 1963–65. *Address:* 7A Ravelston Park, Edinburgh EH4 3DX. *T:* 031–332 1084.

WATT, Charlotte Joanne, (Mrs G. L. Watt); *see* Erickson, Prof. C. J.

WATT, Prof. Donald Cameron; *see* Cameron Watt.

WATT, Hamish, JP; Rector of Aberdeen University, since 1985; *b* 27 Dec. 1925; *s* of Wm Watt and Caroline C. Allan; *m* 1948, Mary Helen Grant; one *s* two *d*. *Educ:* Keith Grammar Sch.; St Andrews Univ. Engaged in farming (dairy and sheep). Subseq. company director, quarries. Contested (C), Caithness, 1966; contested (SNP): Banff, 1970; Moray, 1983. MP (SNP) Banff, Feb. 1974–1979. Regional and Dist Councillor (SNP), Moray, 1985– (Chm., Educn Cttee, 1986–). JP Moray, 1984. Hon. LLD Aberdeen, 1988. *Address:* Mill of Buckie, Buckie, Banffshire. *T:* Buckie (0542) 32591. *Clubs:* Farmers', Whitehall Court.

WATT, Surgeon Vice-Adm. Sir James, KBE 1975; MS, FRCS; Medical Director-General (Navy), 1972–77; *b* 19 Aug. 1914; *s* of Thomas Watt and Sarah Alice Clarkson. *Educ:* King Edward VI Sch., Morpeth; Univ. of Durham. MB, BS 1938; MS 1949; FRCS 1955; MD 1972; FRCP 1975. Surgical Registrar, Royal Vic. Infirm., Newcastle upon Tyne, 1947; Surgical Specialist: N Ire., 1949; RN Hosp., Hong Kong, 1954; Consultant in Surgery, RN Hospitals: Plymouth, 1956; Haslar, 1959; Malta, 1961; Haslar, 1963; Jt Prof. of Naval Surgery, RCS and RN Hosp., Haslar, 1965–69; Dean of Naval Medicine and MO i/c, Inst. of Naval Medicine, 1969–72. Chm., RN Clin. Research Working Party, 1969–77; Chm. Bd of Trustees, Naval Christian Fellowship, 1968–75; President: Royal Naval Lay Readers Soc., 1973–83; Inst. of Religion and Medicine, 1989–91. QHS 1969–77. Surg. Comdr 1956; Surg. Captain 1965; Surg. Rear-Adm. 1969; Surg. Vice-Adm. 1972. Mem., Environmental Medicine Res. Policy Cttee, MRC, 1974–77. Thomas Vicary Lectr, RCS, 1974; University House Vis. Fellow, ANU, 1986. FICS 1964; Fellow: Assoc. of Surgeons of GB and Ire.; Med. Soc. of London (Mem. Council, 1976; Lettsomian Lectr, 1979; Pres., 1980–81; Vice-Pres., 1981–83); FRSM (Pres., 1982–84); FSA 1991; Hon. FRCSE; Member: Brit. Soc. for Surgery of the Hand; Internat. Soc. for Burns Injuries; Corr. Mem., Surgical Research Soc., 1966–77; Mem. Editorial Bd, Brit. Jl of Surgery, 1966–77. FRGS 1982; Mem. Council, RGS, 1985–. Trustee: Marylebone Centre Trust, 1989–; Medical Soc. of London, 1986–. Gov., Epsom Coll., 1990–. Hon. Mem., Smeatonian Soc. of Civil Engineers, 1978–. Hon. Freeman, Co. of Barbers, 1978. Hon. DCh Newcastle, 1978. Errol-Eldridge Prize, 1968; Gilbert Blane Medal, 1971. CStJ 1972. *Publications:* papers on: burns, cancer chemotherapy, peptic ulceration, hyberbaric oxygen therapy, naval medical history. *Recreations:* mountain walking, music. *Address:* 7 Cambisgate, Church Road, Wimbledon, SW19 5AL. *Club:* Royal Over-Seas League.

WATT, Sir James H.; *see* Harvie-Watt.

WATT, Robert; His Honour Judge Watt; County Court Judge since 1971; *b* 10 March 1923; *s* of John Watt, schoolmaster, Ballymena, Co. Antrim; *m* 1951, Edna Rea; one *d*. *Educ:* Ballymena Academy; Queen's Univ., Belfast (LLB). Called to Bar, Gray's Inn, 1946; called to Bar of Northern Ireland, 1946; QC (NI) 1964; subseq. Sen. Crown Prosecutor Counties Fermanagh and Tyrone. *Recreation:* sailing. *Address:* 12 Deramore Drive, Belfast BT9 5JQ. *Club:* Royal North of Ireland Yacht.

WATT, Prof. W(illiam) Montgomery; Professor of Arabic and Islamic Studies, University of Edinburgh, 1964–79; *b* Ceres, Fife, 14 March 1909; *o c* of late Rev. Andrew Watt; *m* 1943, Jean Macdonald, *er d* of late Prof. Robert Donaldson; one *s* four *d*. *Educ:* George Watson's Coll., Edinburgh; University of Edinburgh; Balliol Coll., Oxford; University of Jena; Cuddesdon Coll. Warner Exhibition (Balliol), 1930; Ferguson Schol. in Classics, 1931; MA, PhD (Edinburgh); MA, BLitt (Oxon). Asst Lecturer, Moral Philosophy, University of Edinburgh, 1934–38; Curate, St Mary Boltons, London, 1939–41; Curate, Old St Paul's, Edinburgh, 1941–43; Arabic specialist to Bishop in Jerusalem, 1943–46; Lecturer, Ancient Philosophy, University of Edinburgh, 1946–47; Lectr, Sen. Lectr and Reader in Arabic, Univ. of Edinburgh, 1947–64. Visiting Professor: of Islamic Studies, University of Toronto, 1963; Collège de France, Paris, 1970; of Religious Studies, Univ. of Toronto, 1978; of Arab Studies, Georgetown Univ., 1978–79. Chairman, Assoc. of British Orientalists, 1964–65. Hon. DD Aberdeen, 1966. Levi Della Vida Medal, Los Angeles, 1981. *Publications:* Free Will and Predestination in Early Islam, 1949; The Faith and Practice of al-Ghazali, 1953; Muhammad at Mecca, 1953; Muhammad at Medina, 1956; The Reality of God, 1958; The Cure for Human Troubles, 1959; Islam and the Integration of Society, 1961; Muhammad Prophet and Statesman, 1961; Islamic Philosophy and Theology, 1962, new enlarged edn, 1986; Muslim Intellectual, 1963; Truth in the Religions, 1963; Islamic Spain, 1965; Islam (in Propyläen Weltgeschichte, XI), 1965; A Companion to the Qur'an, 1967; What is Islam?, 1968; Islamic Political Thought, 1968; Islamic Revelation and the Modern World, 1970; Bell's Introduction to the Qur'an, 1970; The Influence of Islam on Medieval Europe, 1972; The

Formative Period of Islamic Thought, 1973; The Majesty that was Islam, 1974; Der Islam, i, 1980, ii, 1985; Islam and Christianity Today, 1984; Muhammad's Mecca, 1988; Islamic Fundamentalism and Modernity, 1988; Early Islam, 1991; Muslim-Christian Encounters, 1991; (ed) Islamic Surveys; contribs learned journals. *Address:* 2 Bridgend, Dalkeith, Midlothian EH22 1JT. *T:* 031-663 3197.

WATT, Emeritus Prof. William Smith, MA (Glasgow and Oxon); FBA 1989; Regius Professor of Humanity in the University of Aberdeen, 1952–79, Vice-Principal, 1969–72; *b* 20 June 1913; *s* of John Watt and Agnes Smith; *m* 1944, Dorothea, *e d* of R. J. Codrington Smith; one *s. Educ:* University of Glasgow; Balliol Coll., Oxford (Snell Exhibitioner and Hon. Scholar). First Class Hons in Classics, Glasgow Univ., 1933; Ferguson Schol., 1934; Craven Schol., 1934; First Class, Classical Moderations, 1935; Hertford Schol., 1935; Ireland Schol., 1935; First Class, Lit. Hum., 1937. Lecturer in Greek and Greek History, University of Glasgow, 1937–38; Fellow and Tutor in Classics, Balliol Coll., Oxford, 1938–52. Civilian Officer, Admiralty (Naval Intelligence Div.), 1941–45. Convener, Scottish Univs Council on Entrance, 1973–77. Governor, Aberdeen Coll. of Educn, 1958–75 (Chm. of Governors 1971–75). Pres., Classical Assoc. of Scotland, 1983–88. *Publications:* (ed) Ciceronis Epistulae ad Quintum fratrem, etc, 1958, 1965; (ed) Ciceronis Epistularum ad Atticum Libri I-VIII, 1965; (ed) Ciceronis Epistulae ad familiares, 1982; (ed with P. J. Ford) George Buchanan's Miscellaneorum Liber, 1982; (ed) Vellei Paterculi Historiae, 1988; many articles in classical periodicals. *Address:* 38 Woodburn Gardens, Aberdeen AB1 8JA. *T:* Aberdeen (0224) 314369. *Club:* Business and Professional (Aberdeen).

WATTLEY, Graham Richard; Director, Driver and Vehicle Licensing Directorate, Department of Transport, 1985–90, retired; *b* 12 March 1930; *s* of R. C. H. Wattley and Sylvia Joyce Wattley (*née* Orman); *m* 1953, Yvonne Heale (*d* 1990); one *s* two *d. Educ:* Devonport High School. Pilot Officer, RAF, 1949–50. Min. of Works, 1950–71; Dept of the Environment, 1971–73; Department of Transport, 1973–90: Asst Sec., DVLC Computer Div., 1978–85; Under Sec., 1986. Treas., Dewi Sant Housing Assoc., 1991. Warden, St Paul's Church, Sketty, 1991. *Recreations:* walking, cooking, photography. *Address:* 36 The Ridge, Derwen Fawr, Swansea SA2 8AG. *T:* Swansea (0792) 290408. *Club:* Civil Service.

WATTON, Rt. Rev. James Augustus, BA, DD; *b* 23 Oct. 1915; *s* of Geo. A. Watton and Ada Wynn; *m* 1st, 1941, Irene A. Foster; one *s* two *d*; 2nd 1986, Janet Miller. *Educ:* Univ. of Western Ontario (BA); Huron Coll. (STh); Post graduate Univ. of Michigan. Deacon 1938; Priest 1939. Bishop of Moosonee, 1963–80; Archbishop of Moosonee and Metropolitan of Ontario, 1974–79; retired 1980. DD (*jure dig.*), 1955. *Address:* Box 803, Southampton, Ontario N0H 2L0, Canada.

WATTS, Prof. Anthony Brian, PhD; Professor of Marine Geology and Geophysics, University of Oxford, since 1990; *b* 23 July 1945; *s* of Dennis Granville Watts and of late Vera (*née* Fisher); *m* 1970, Mary Tarbit; two *d. Educ:* University Coll. London (BSc); Univ. of Durham (PhD). Post-Doctoral Fellow, Nat. Res. Council of Canada, 1970–71; Res. Scientist, Lamont-Doherty Geol Observatory, Palisades, NY, 1971–81; Arthur D. Storke Meml Prof. of Geol Scis, Columbia Univ., NY, 1981–90. Fellow, Amer. Geophysical Union, 1986. A. I. Levorsen Meml Award, Amer. Assoc. Petroleum Geologists, 1981; Rosentiel Award, Univ. of Miami, 1982. *Publications:* numerous articles in scientific jls. *Recreations:* travelling, carpentry. *Address:* Department of Earth Sciences, University of Oxford, Parks Road, Oxford OX2 3PR. T: Oxford (0865) 272032. *Club:* Geological Society.

WATTS, Sir Arthur (Desmond), KCMG 1989 (CMG 1977); QC 1988; barrister; *b* 14 Nov. 1931; *o s* of Col A. E. Watts, MA (Cantab); *m* 1957, Iris Ann Collier, MA (Cantab); one *s* one *d. Educ:* Haileybury and Imperial Service College; Royal Military Academy, Sandhurst; Downing Coll., Cambridge (Schol.). BA 1954; LLM (First Cl.) 1955; Whewell Schol. in Internat. Law, 1955; called to Bar, Gray's Inn, 1957; MA. Legal Asst, Foreign Office, 1956–59; Legal Adviser, British Property Commn (later British Embassy), Cairo, 1959–62; Asst Legal Adviser, FO, 1962–67; Legal Adviser, British Embassy, Bonn, 1967–69; Asst Solicitor, Law Officers Dept, 1969–70; Legal Counsellor, FCO, 1970–73; Counsellor (Legal Advr), Office of UK Permanent Rep. to EEC, 1973–77; Legal Counsellor, 1977–82, Dep. Legal Advr, 1982–87, Legal Advr, 1987–91, FCO. *Publications:* Legal Effects of War, 4th edn (with Lord McNair), 1966; (with C. and A. Parry and J. Grant) Encyclopaedic Dictionary of International Law, 1986; (contrib.) The Antarctic Treaty System—An Assessment, 1986; (contrib.) Antarctic Challenge II, 1986, III, 1988; (with Sir Robert Jennings) Oppenheim's International Law, vol. 1, 9th edn 1991; contribs to: British Year Book of Internat. Law; Internat. and Comparative Law Quarterly; Egyptian Review of Internat. Law. *Recreation:* cricket (County Cap, Shropshire, 1955; in Antarctica, 1985). *Address:* 3 Essex Court, Temple, EC4Y 9AL.

WATTS, Donald Walter, PhD; FTS; FRACI; FACE; FAIM; Chief Executive Officer, Trade Development Zone Authority, Darwin, Northern Territory, Australia; *b* 1 April 1934; *s* of late Horace Frederick Watts and Esme Anne Watts; *m* 1960, Michelle Rose Yeomans; two *s. Educ:* Hale Sch., Perth; University of Western Australia (BSc Hons, PhD); University College London. FRACI 1967. Post-Doctoral Fellow, UCL, 1959–61; University of Western Australia: Sen. Lectr, 1962; Reader, 1969; Associate Prof., 1971; Personal Chair in Physical and Inorganic Chemistry, 1977–79; Dir, W Australian Inst. of Tech., 1980–86, renamed Vice-Chancellor, Curtin Univ. of Tech., Jan.–June 1987; Pres. and Vice-Chancellor, Bond Univ., Australia, 1987–90, now Emeritus. Vis. Scientist, Univ. of S California, 1967; Visiting Professor: Australian National Univ., 1973; Univ. of Toronto, 1974; Japan Foundn Vis. Fellow, 1984. Chm., Aust. Cttee of Dirs and Principals in Advanced Education Ltd, 1986–87; Member: Aust. Science and Technol. Council, 1984–90; Technology Develt Authority of WA, 1984–87. Hon. Fellow, Marketing Inst. of Singapore. Hon. DTech Curtin, 1987. *Publications:* Chemical Properties and Reactions (jtly) (Univ. of W Aust.), 1978 (trans. Japanese, 1987); (jtly) Chemistry for Australian Secondary School Students (Aust. Acad. of Sci.), 1979; (jtly) The School Chemistry Project—a secondary school chemistry syllabus for comment, 1984; Earth, Air, Fire and Water, and associated manuals (Aust. Acad. of Sci. Sch. Chem. Project), 1984; numerous papers on phys. and inorganic chemistry in internat. jls; several papers presented at nat. and internat. confs. *Recreations:* tennis (Mem. Interstate Tennis Team, 1952–53), squash (Mem. Interstate Squash Team, 1957–66), golf. *Address:* Trade Development Zone, PMB88, Winnellie, Darwin, NT 0821, Australia. *T:* 61 89 470133, *Fax:* 61 89 843417. *Clubs:* Brisbane (Brisbane); Royal Kings Park Tennis (Perth); Nedlands Tennis (Nedlands); Lake Karrinyup Golf (Karrinyup); Southport Golf (Southport); Darwin Golf; Vines Resort.

WATTS, Edward, (Ted), FRICS; Chairman, Watts & Partners, since 1976; President, Royal Institution of Chartered Surveyors, 1991–July 1992; *b* 19 March 1940; *s* of Edward Samuel Window Watts and Louise Coffey; *m* 1960, Iris Josephine Frost; two *s* (one *d* decd). *Educ:* SW Essex Technical Coll. FRICS 1971 (ARICS 1962). Cotton Ballard & Blow, architects, 1959–62; E. Wookey & Co., gen. practice surveyors, 1962–64; Ian Fraser & Associates, architects and town planners, 1964–66; Team Leader with Housing Develt Br., GLC, 1966–67; established Watts & Partners, bldg surveyors, architects and project managers, 1967. Interested in business management; FBIM 1982. *Recreations:* sailing, cruising, racing offshore. *Address:* 11/12 Haymarket, SW1Y 4BP. *T:* 071–930 6652; 10 Solent Avenue, Lymington, Hants SO41 9SD. *T:* Lymington (0590) 672599. *Clubs:* Royal Automobile, Royal Ocean Racing; Royal Lymington Yacht (Hants); Island Sailing (Cowes, IoW).

WATTS, Helen Josephine, (Mrs Michael Mitchell), CBE 1978; Hon. FRAM; concert, lieder and opera singer (contralto), retired 1985; *b* 7 Dec. 1927; *d* of Thomas Watts and Winifred (*née* Morgan); *m* 1980, Michael Mitchell. *Educ:* St Mary and St Anne's Sch., Abbots Bromley; Royal Academy of Music (LRAM). Hon. FRAM 1961 (Hon. ARAM 1955); FRSA 1982. *Recreation:* gardening.

WATTS, John Arthur, FCA; MP (C) Slough, since 1983; *b* 19 April 1947; *s* of late Arthur and Ivy Watts; *m* 1974, Susan Jennifer Swan; one *s* three *d. Educ:* Bishopshalt Grammar Sch., Hillingdon; Gonville and Caius Coll., Cambridge (MA). Qual. as chartered accountant, 1972; FCA 1979. Chairman: Cambridge Univ. Cons. Assoc., 1968; Uxbridge Cons. Assoc., 1973–76; Mem., Hillingdon Bor. Council, 1973–86 (Leader, 1978–84). PPS: to Minister for Housing and Construction, 1984–85; to Minister of State, Treasury, 1985. Mem., Treasury and CS Select Cttee, 1986–. *Recreation:* reading. *Address:* House of Commons, SW1A 0AA. *T:* 071–219 3589.

WATTS, Colonel John Cadman, OBE 1959; MC 1946; FRCS 1949; first Professor of Military Surgery, Royal College of Surgeons, 1960–64; *b* 13 April 1913; *s* of John Nixon Watts, solicitor, and Amy Bettina (*née* Cadman); *m* 1938, Joan Lilian (*née* Inwood); three *s* one *d. Educ:* Merchant Taylors' Sch.; St Thomas's Hospital. MRCS, LRCP, 1936; MB, BS, 1938. Casualty Officer, Resident Anæsthetist, House Surgeon, St Thomas's Hospital, 1937; Surgical Specialist, RAMC, 1938–60, serving in Palestine, Egypt, Libya, Syria, Tunisia, Italy, France, Holland, Germany, Malaya, Java, Japan, and Cyprus. Hunterian Professor, RCS, 1960; Conslt Surgeon, Bedford Gen. Hosp., 1966–76. Co. Comr, St John Ambulance Brigade, 1970. British Medical Association: Chm., N Beds Div., 1971; Mem. Council, 1972–74; Chm., Armed Forces Cttee, 1978–82; Pres., Ipswich Div., 1982–83. OStJ 1970. *Publications:* Surgeon at War, 1955; Clinical Surgery, 1964; Exploration Medicine, 1964. *Recreations:* sailing, gardening. *Address:* Lowood Lodge, Hasketon, near Woodbridge, Suffolk IP13 6JL. *T:* Grundisburgh (047335) 326. *Clubs:* Deben Yacht (Woodbridge); United Hospitals Sailing (Burnham-on-Crouch).

WATTS, John Francis, BA; educational writer; Principal, Countesthorpe College, Leicestershire, 1972–81; *b* 18 Oct. 1926; *s* of John Weldon Watts and Norah K. Watts; *m* 1st, 1950, Elizabeth Hamilton (marr. diss.); four *s* one *d*; 2nd, 1985, Madeleine Marshall. *Educ:* West Buckland Sch.; Univ. of Bristol (BA). First Headmaster, Les Quennevais Sch., Jersey, CI, 1964–69; Lectr, Univ. of London, 1969–72. Chm., Nat. Assoc. for Teaching of English (NATE), 1974–76. *Publications:* Encounters, 1965, 2nd edn 1983; Contact, 1970 (Australia); Interplay, 1972; Teaching, 1974; The Countesthorpe Experience, 1977; Towards an Open School, 1980; contrib. to various publications. *Address:* 106 Kineton Green Road, Olton, Solihull, West Midlands B92 7EE.

WATTS, Lt-Gen. Sir John Peter Barry Condliffe, KBE 1988 (CBE 1979; OBE 1972); CB 1985; MC 1960; Chief of Defence Staff, Sultan of Oman's Armed Forces, 1984–87; *b* 27 Aug. 1930; *m*; seven *c. Educ:* Westminster Sch.; Andover Acad., USA; RMA Sandhurst. Commissioned, RUR, 1951 (Royal Irish Rangers, 1968); served Hong Kong, Malaya (despatches), Cyprus, Oman (MC), BAOR, Borneo and Saudi Arabia; 48 Gurkha Inf. Bde, 1967–69; CO 22 SAS Regt, 1970–72; Directing Staff, Staff Coll., 1972–74; MoD, 1974; Comdr, Sultan of Oman's Land Forces, 1979–84.

WATTS, Rachel Mary; *see* Rosser, R. M.

WATTS, Ronald George, CBE 1962; *b* 15 May 1914; *m* 1940, Ruth Hansen (*d* 1970); one *s* two *d*; *m* 1972, Margit Tester. *Educ:* Latymer Sch., Edmonton; St John's Coll., Cambridge. Entered Foreign Service, 1937; appointed Counsellor, Foreign Office, 1958; Consul-Gen., Osaka-Kobe, 1958–63; Head of Consular Dept, FO, 1963–65; Consul-Gen., Paris, 1966–67; FCO 1967–69, retired. *Recreation:* church organist.

WATTS, Roy, CBE 1978; Chairman: Thames Water Authority, since 1983; Lowndes Lambert Group Holdings Ltd, since 1988; Frank Graham Group Ltd, since 1991; *b* 17 Aug. 1925; *m* 1951, Jean Rosaline; one *s* two *d. Educ:* Doncaster Grammar Sch.; Edinburgh Univ. (MA). FIMTA, FRAeS, FCIT. Army, 1943–47: commnd Sandhurst; 8th RTR. Accountant in local govt until 1955; joined BEA, 1955: Head of Systems Study Section (O&M Br.); Chief Internal Auditor; Area Man., Sweden and Finland; Fleet Planning Man.; Regional Gen. Man., North and East Europe; Dir, S1–11 Div; Chief Exec. BEA British Airways, 1972–74 (Chm., Jan.–March 1974); Chief Exec., European Div., British Airways, 1974–77; Dir, Commercial Operations, British Airways, 1977, Dir, Finance and Planning, 1978–79, Chief Exec., 1979–82; Group Man. Dir, 1982–83; Jt Dep. Chm., BA Bd, 1980–83 (Mem., 1974–83); Chairman: WaterAid, 1984–88; Armstrong Equipment plc, 1986–89. Chm., Assoc. of European Airlines, 1982. Hon. DBA Internat. Management Centre, Buckingham, 1987. *Recreations:* walking, cricket. *Address:* 14 Cavendish Place, W1M 9DJ. *T:* 071–636 8686.

WATTS, Thomas Rowland, CBE 1978; Chartered Accountant; *b* 1 Jan. 1917; *s* of late Thomas William Watts and late Daisy Maud Watts (*née* Bultitude); *m* 1955, Hester Zoë Armitstead; one *s* two *d. Educ:* Gresham's Sch., Holt. Served War, TA, 1939–41, Royal Marines (Captain), 1941–46. Articled to Price Waterhouse & Co., 1934–39, Partner, 1963–82. Dir, Jarrold & Sons Ltd, Norwich, 1982–87. Chm., Accounting Standards Cttee (UK and Ireland), 1978–82; Mem. Council, Inst. of Chartered Accountants in England and Wales, 1974–82; Mem. City EEC Cttee, 1974–82; Adviser to Dept of Trade on EEC company law, 1974–83; Vice-Pres. d'honneur, Groupe d'Etudes des experts comptables de la CEE, 1979–88 (Vice-Pres., 1975–79); Chm., EEC Liaison Cttee of UK Accountancy Bodies, 1986–88; Chm., Dental Rates Study Gp, 1982–85. A Gen. Comr of Income Tax, 1986–. Hon. Vis. Prof., City of London Polytech., 1983–86. Chartered Accountants Founding Socs' Centenary Award, 1982. *Publications:* editor, various professional books; papers in professional jls. *Recreations:* travel, music, opera costume designs. *Address:* 13 Fitzwalter Road, Colchester, Essex CO3 3SY. *T:* Colchester (0206) 573520.

WATTS, Victor Brian; His Honour Judge Watts; a Circuit Judge, since 1980; *b* 7 Jan. 1927; *o s* of Percy William King Watts and Doris Millicent Watts; *m* 1965, Patricia Eileen (*née* Steer); one *s* one *d. Educ:* Colfe's Grammar Sch.; University Coll., Oxford. MA(Oxon): BCL. Called to the Bar, Middle Temple, 1950; subseq. Western Circuit; a Recorder of the Crown Court, 1972–80. Flying Officer, Royal Air Force, 1950–52. Churchwarden, St Peter's Church, Hammersmith, 1984–90. *Publications:* Landlord and Tenant Act, 1954; Leading Cases on the Law of Contract, 1955; occasional articles of a legal nature. *Recreations:* the arts, walking, tennis, riding. *Address:* 28 Abinger Road, W4 1EL. *T:* 081–994 4435. *Club:* Hurlingham.

WATTS, William Arthur, MA, ScD; Provost, Trinity College, Dublin, 1981–91; *b* 26 May 1930; *s* of William Low Watts and Bessie (*née* Dickinson); *m* 1954, Geraldine Mary

Magrath; two *s* one *d*. *Educ:* Trinity Coll., Dublin (MA, ScD). Lecturer in Botany, Univ. of Hull, 1953–55; Trinity College, Dublin: Lectr in Botany, 1955–65; Fellow, 1970; Professor of Botany, 1965–80; Prof. of Quaternary Ecology, 1980–81. Adjunct Prof. of Geology, Univ. of Minnesota, 1975–. Pres., RIA, 1982–85; Governor: National Gallery of Ireland, 1982–85; Marsh's Library, 1981–; Member: Dublin Inst. for Advanced Studies, 1981–; Scholarship Exchange Bd, Ireland, 1982–. Chairman: Federated Dublin Voluntary Hosps, 1983–; Mercer's Hosp., 1975–83; Mercer's Hosp. Foundn, 1983–; Health Res. Bd, Ireland, 1987–89. Hon. LLD QUB, 1990; Hon. DSc NUI, 1991. *Publications:* numerous articles on aspects of quaternary ecology. *Recreations:* walking, conservation studies, music. *Address:* Room 24.02, Trinity College, Dublin 2. *T:* 772941. *Club:* Kildare Street and University (Dublin).

WAUCHOPE, Sir Roger (Hamilton) Don-, 11th Bt *cr* 1667 (NS), of Newton Don; chartered accountant, South Africa; *b* 16 Oct. 1938; *s* of Sir Patrick George Don-Wauchope, 10th Bt and Ismay Lilian Ursula (who later *m* George William Shipman), *d* of Sidney Richard Hodges; *S* father, 1989; *m* 1963, Sallee, *yr d* of Lt-Col Harold Mill-Colman, OBE, AMICE, Durban; two *s* one *d*. *Educ:* Hilton Coll., Natal; Durban Univ. Higher Diploma in Taxation. *Heir: s* Andrew Craig Don-Wauchope, *b* 18 May 1966. *Address:* Newton, 53 Montrose Drive, Pietermaritzburg 3201, Natal, South Africa. *T:* 0331–471107; PO Box 365, Pietermaritzburg 3200, Natal, South Africa. *Clubs:* Victoria, Maritzburg Country (Pietermaritzburg); Durban Country (Durban).

WAUD, Christopher Denis George Pierre; barrister-at-law; a Recorder of the Crown Court, since Dec. 1974; full-time Chairman of Industrial Tribunals, since 1982 (part-time, 1977–82); *b* 5 Dec. 1928; *s* of late Christopher William Henry Pierre Waud and Vera Constance Maria Waud; *m* 1954, Rosemary Paynter Bradshaw Moorhead; one *s* four *d* (and one *s* decd). *Educ:* Charterhouse; Christ Church, Oxford. Called to Bar, Middle Temple, 1956. *Publications:* Redundancy and Unfair Dismissal, annually 1981–84; Guide to Employment Law, annually, 1985–. *Recreations:* sailing, walking. *Address:* 93 Ebury Bridge Road, SW1W 8RE. *Clubs:* Old Carthusian Yacht, Bar Yacht.

WAUGH, Auberon Alexander; Editor, The Literary Review, since 1986; Columnist: The Spectator, since 1976; The Daily Telegraph, since 1990; *b* 17 Nov. 1939; *e s* of late Evelyn Waugh, writer, and late Laura Waugh, Combe Florey House, Somerset; *m* 1961, Teresa, *o d* of 6th Earl of Onslow, KBE, MC, and *sister* of 7th Earl of Onslow, *qv*; two *s* two *d*. *Educ:* Downside (schol. in Classics); Christ Church, Oxford (exhibn in English, read PPE). Editorial staff, Daily Telgraph, 1960–63. Commissioned Royal Horse Guards, 1957; served Cyprus; retd with wounds, 1958. Weekly Columnist, Catholic Herald, 1963–64; special writer, Mirror group, 1964–67; Political Correspondent: Spectator, 1967–70; Private Eye, 1970–86; Weekly Columnist: The Times, 1970–71; New Statesman, 1973–76; Sunday Telegraph, 1981–90; Chief Fiction Reviewer: Spectator, 1970–73; Evening Standard, 1973–80; Daily Mail, 1981–86; Chief Book Reviewer, The Independent, 1986–89; monthly contributor, Books and Bookmen, 1973–80. Contested (Dog Lovers' Party) Devon North, 1979. Pres., British Croatian Soc., 1973–. Nat. Press 'Critic of the Year' commendations, 1976, 1978; 'What the Papers Say' Columnist of the Year, Granada TV, 1979, 1988. *Publications: novels:* The Foxglove Saga, 1960; Path of Dalliance, 1963; Who are the Violets Now?, 1966; Consider the Lilies, 1968; A Bed of Flowers, 1971; *non-fiction:* (with S. Cronje) Biafra: Britain's Shame, 1969; Four Crowded Years: the Diaries of Auberon Waugh, 1976; The Last Word: an Eyewitness Account of the Thorpe Trial, 1980; Auberon Waugh's Yearbook, 1981; The Diaries of Auberon Waugh: a turbulent decade 1976–85, 1985; Waugh on Wine, 1986; Will This Do? the first fifty years of Auberon Waugh (autobiog.), 1991; *essays:* Country Topics, 1974; In The Lion's Den, 1978; Another Voice, 1986; *anthology:* (ed) The Literary Review Anthology of Real Poetry, 1991. *Recreation:* gossip. *Address:* Combe Florey House, near Taunton, Somerset TA4 3JD; 7 Phoenix Lodge Mansions, Brook Green, W6; La Pesegado, 11320 Montmaur, France. *Clubs:* Beefsteak, Academy.

WAUGH, Rev. Eric Alexander; Minister of the City Temple, United Reformed Church, since 1986; *b* 9 May 1933; *s* of Hugh Waugh and Marion Waugh (*née* McLay); *m* 1955, Agnes-Jean Saunders; two *s*. *Educ:* Glasgow Univ.; Edinburgh Univ. (LTh). Local government officer, 1948–64. Assistant Minister, High Church, Bathgate, 1969–70; Missionary, Kenya Highlands, 1970–73; Minister, Mowbray Presbyterian Church, Cape Town, 1973–78; Missioner, Presbyterian Church of Southern Africa, 1978–85. *Recreations:* hill walking, gardening. *Address:* 124 Rotherfield Street, Islington, N1 3DA. *T:* 071–359 7961.

WAVERLEY, 3rd Viscount *cr* 1952, of Westdean; **John Desmond Forbes Anderson;** *b* 31 Oct. 1949; *s* of 2nd Viscount Waverley and of Myrtle Ledgerwood; *S* father, 1990. *Educ:* Malvern. *Address:* c/o Chanders, Aldworth, Berks.

WAY, Col Anthony Gerald, MC 1944; Member, HM Body Guard of the Honourable Corps of Gentlemen at Arms, 1972–90 (Standard Bearer, 1988–90); *b* 5 Nov. 1920; *s* of Roger Hill Way and Brenda Lathbury; *m* 1st, 1946, Elizabeth Leslie Richmond (*d* 1986); one *s* one *d*; 2nd, 1989, Mrs Anthea Methven, St Martin's Abbey, by Perth. *Educ:* Stowe Sch.; RMC Sandhurst. Joined Grenadier Guards, 1939, 2nd Lieut; served in N Africa and Italy; CO, 3rd Bn, 1960–61; Lt-Col comdg Grenadier Guards, 1961–64. *Recreations:* shooting, gardening. *Address:* Kincairney, Dunkeld, Perthshire PH8 0RE. *T:* Caputh (073871) 304. *Club:* Pratt's.

WAY, Sir Richard (George Kitchener), KCB 1961 (CB 1957); CBE 1952; Principal, King's College London, 1975–80; *b* 15 Sept. 1914; *s* of Frederick and Clara Way; *m* 1947, Ursula Joan Starr; one *s* two *d*. *Educ:* Polytechnic Secondary Sch., London. Joined Civil Service as Exec. Officer, 1933; Higher Executive Officer, 1940; Principal, 1942; Asst Secretary, 1946; Asst Under-Secretary of State, 1954; Deputy Under-Secretary of State, War Office, 1955–57; Dep. Secretary, Ministry of Defence, 1957–58; Dep. Secretary, Ministry of Supply, 1958–59; Permanent Under-Secretary of State, War Office, 1960–63; Permanent Secretary, Ministry of Aviation, 1963–66. Dep. Chm., Lansing Bagnall Ltd, 1966–67, Chm. 1967–69; Chm., LTE, 1970–74. Chairman, EDC Machine Tool Industry, 1967–70; Member (part-time) Board of: BOAC, 1967–73; Dobson Park Industries Ltd, 1975–85. Chm., Council of Roedean Sch., 1969–74; Chm., Royal Commn for the Exhibn of 1851, 1978–87. London Zoological Society: Mem. Council 1977–82 and 1984–87; Vice-Pres., 1979–82 and 1984–87; Treasurer, 1983–84. CST J 1974. FKC 1975. Hon. DSc Loughborough, 1986. Coronation Medal, 1953. American Medal of Freedom (with bronze palm), 1946. *Address:* The Old Forge, Shalden, Alton, Hants GU34 4DX. *T:* Alton (0420) 82383. *Club:* Brooks's.

WAYMOUTH, Charity, BSc (London), PhD (Aberdeen); Senior Staff Scientist, The Jackson Laboratory, Bar Harbor, Maine, 1963–81, now Emeritus; *b* 29 April 1915; *o d* of Charles Sydney Herbert Waymouth, Major, The Dorsetshire Regt, and Ada Curror Scott Dalgleish; unmarried. *Educ:* Royal School for Daughters of Officers of the Army, Bath; University of London; University of Aberdeen. Biochemist, City of Manchester General Hospitals, 1938–41; Research Fellow, University of Aberdeen, 1944; Beit Memorial Fellow for Medical Research, 1944–46; Member of scientific staff and head of tissue culture dept, Chester Beatty Research Institute for Cancer Research (University of London), 1947–52; British Empire Cancer Campaign-American Cancer Society Exchange Fellow, 1952–53; The Jackson Laboratory: Staff Scientist, 1952–63; Asst Dir (Training), 1969–72; Asst Dir (Research), 1976–77; Associate Dir (Scientific Affairs), 1977–80; Dir *ad interim*, 1980–81. Mem. Bd of Dirs, W. Alton Jones Cell Sci. Center, 1979–82. Rose Morgan Vis. Prof., Univ. of Kansas, 1971. Member: Tissue Culture Association (President, 1960–62, Editor-in-Chief 1968–75; Mem. Council, 1980–84); various British and American professional and learned societies. Hon. Life member and Hon. Director, Psora Society (Canada); Episcopal Church of the USA: Vice-Chm., Clergy Deployment Bd, 1971–79, and Exec. Council, 1967–70; Deputy, Gen. Convention, 1970, 1973, 1976, 1979, 1982, 1985, 1988; Member, Diocesan Council, 1962–70, 1971–76, and Standing Cttee, 1984–87, Dio. of Maine; Chm., Cttee on the State of the Church, 1976–79; Mem., Standing Commn on Health, 1988–. DD *hc* Gen. Theol Seminary, NY, 1979; Hon. ScD Bowdoin College, 1982. *Publications:* numerous papers in scientific journals, on nucleic acids and on tissue culture and cell nutrition. *Recreations:* reading, gardening. *Address:* 16 Atlantic Avenue, Bar Harbor, Maine 04609, USA. *T:* (207) 288–4008.

WAYWELL, Prof. Geoffrey Bryan, FSA 1979; Professor of Classical Archaeology, King's College, University of London, since 1987; *b* 16 Jan. 1944; *s* of Francis Marsh Waywell and Jenny Waywell; *m* 1970, Elisabeth Ramsden; two *s*. *Educ:* Eltham Coll.; St John's Coll., Cambridge (BA, MA, PhD). Walston Student, Cambridge Univ., 1965–67; School Student, British Sch. at Athens, 1966–67; Asst Lectr in Classics 1968, Lectr in Classics 1970, Reader in Classical Archaeology 1982, Hon. Curator, Ashmole Archive, 1985, KCL. *Publications:* The Free-Standing Sculptures of the Mausoleum at Halicarnassus in the British Museum, 1978; The Lever and Hope Sculptures, 1986; numerous articles and reviews in archaeol and classical jls. *Recreations:* music, excavating. *Address:* Department of Classics, King's College London, Strand, WC2R 2LS. *T:* 071–836 5454.

WEARE, Trevor John, OBE 1990; PhD; Managing Director, Hydraulics Research Ltd, since 1982; *b* 31 Dec. 1943; *s* of Trevor Leslie Weare and Edna Margaret (*née* Roberts); *m* 1964, Margaret Ann Wright; two *s*. *Educ:* Aston Technical Coll.; Imperial College of Science and Technology (BSc Physics, PhD). Post-doctoral Research Fellow: Dept of Mathematical Physics, McGill Univ., Montreal, 1968–70; Dept of Theoretical Physics, Univ. of Oxford, 1970–72; Sen. Scientific Officer, Hydraulics Res. Station, 1972; Principal Scientific Officer, 1975; Sen. Principal Scientific Officer, Head of Estuaries Div., 1978; Chief Scientific Officer, DoE, 1981. *Publications:* numerous contribs to scientific jls on theoretical High Energy Nuclear Physics, and on computational modelling in Civil Engineering Hydraulics; archaeological paper in Oxoniensia. *Recreations:* music, walking, archaeology. *Address:* Rose Cottage, Dunsomer Hill, North Moreton, Oxon. *T:* Didcot (0235) 818544.

WEATHERALL, Sir David (John), Kt 1987; MD, FRCP; FRCPE 1983; FRS 1977; Nuffield Professor of Clinical Medicine, 1974–Oct. 1992, Regius Professor of Medicine, from Oct. 1992, University of Oxford; Fellow, Magdalen College, Oxford, since 1974; Hon. Director: Molecular Haematology Unit, Medical Research Council, since 1980; Institute for Molecular Medicine, University of Oxford, since 1988; *b* 9 March 1933; *s* of late Harry and Gwendoline Weatherall; *m* 1962, Stella Mayorga Nestler; one *s*. *Educ:* Calday Grange Grammar Sch.; Univ. of Liverpool. MB, ChB 1956; MD 1962; FRCP 1967; FRCPath 1969; MA Oxon 1974. Ho. Officer in Med. and Surg., United Liverpool Hosps, 1956–58; Captain, RAMC, Jun. Med. Specialist, BMH, Singapore, and BMH, Kamunting, Malaya, 1958–60; Research Fellow in Genetics, Johns Hopkins Hosp., Baltimore, USA, 1960–62; Sen. Med. Registrar, Liverpool Royal Infirmary, 1962–63; Research Fellow in Haematology, Johns Hopkins Hosp., 1963–65; Consultant, WHO, 1966–70; Univ. of Liverpool: Lectr in Med., 1965–66; Sen. Lectr in Med., 1966–69; Reader in Med., 1969–71; Prof. of Haematology, 1971–74; Consultant Physician, United Liverpool Hosps, 1966–74. Mem. Soc. of Scholars, and Centennial Schol., Johns Hopkins Univ., 1976; Physician-in-Chief *pro tem.*, Peter Bent Brigham Hosp., Harvard Med. Sch., 1980. RSocMed Foundn Vis. Prof., 1981; Sims Commonwealth Vis. Prof., 1982; Phillip K. Bondy Prof., Yale, 1982. K. Diamond Prof., Univ. of Calif in San Francisco, 1986; HM Queen Elizabeth the Queen Mother Fellow, Nuffield Prov. Hosps Trust, 1982. Lectures: Watson Smith, RCP, 1974; Foundn, RCPath, 1979; Darwin, Eugenics Soc., 1979; Croonian, RCP, 1984; Fink Meml, Yale, 1984; Sir Francis Frazer, Univ. of London, 1985; Roy Cameron, RCPath, 1986; Hamm Meml, Amer. Soc. of Haematology, 1986; Still Meml, BPA, 1987. Pres., British Soc. for Haematology, 1980–; Chm., Med. and Scientific Adv. Panel, Leukaemia Res. Fund, 1985–89; Mem. Council, Royal Soc., 1989– (Vice Pres., 1990–91); Trustee, Wellcome Trust, 1990–. Foreign Member: Nat. Acad. of Scis, USA, 1990; Inst. of Medicine, Nat. Acad. of Scis, USA, 1991; Hon. Member: Assoc. of Physicians of GB and Ireland, 1968 (Pres., 1989); Assoc. of Amer. Physicians, 1976; Amer. Soc. of Haematology, 1982; Eur. Molecular Biology Orgn, 1983; Amer. Acad. of Arts and Scis, 1988; Hon. FACP 1986; Hon. FRCOG 1988; Hon. FIC 1989; Hon. FACP 1991. Hon. DSc: Manchester, 1988; Edinburgh, 1989; Leicester, 1991; Aberdeen, 1991; Hon. MD: Leeds, 1988; Sheffield, 1989; Hon. DHL Johns Hopkins, 1990. Ambuj Nath Bose Prize, RCP, 1980; Ballantyne Prize, RCPE, 1982; Stratton Prize, Internat. Soc. Haematology, 1982; Feldberg Prize, 1984; Royal Medal, Royal Soc., 1989. *Publications:* (with J. B. Clegg) The Thalassaemia Syndromes, 1965, 3rd edn 1981; (with R. M. Hardisty) Blood and its Disorders, 1973, 2nd edn 1981; The New Genetics and Clinical Practice, 1982, 3rd edn 1991; (ed, with J. G. G. Ledingham and D. A. Warrell) Oxford Textbook of Medicine, 1983, 2nd edn 1987; many papers on Abnormal Haemoglobin Synthesis and related disorders. *Recreations:* music, oriental food. *Address:* 8 Cumnor Rise Road, Cumnor Hill, Oxford. *T:* Oxford (0865) 862467.

WEATHERALL, Vice-Adm. Sir James (Lamb), KBE 1989; Deputy Supreme Allied Commander Atlantic, 1989–91; *b* 28 Feb. 1936; *s* of Alwyn Thomas Hirst Weatherall and Olive Catherine Joan Weatherall (*née* Cuthbert); *m* 1962, Hon. Jean Stewart Macpherson, *d* of 1st Baron Drumalbyn, PC, KBE; two *s* three *d*. *Educ:* Glasgow Academy; Gordonstoun School. Joined RN 1954; commanded HM Ships: Soberton, 1966–67; Ulster, 1970–72; Tartar, 1975–76; Andromeda, 1982–84 (incl. Falklands conflict); Ark Royal, 1985–87; with SACEUR, 1987–89. Mem., Ct of Assts, Shipwrights' Co., 1989–; Younger Brother, Corp. of Trinity House, 1986. *Recreations:* hockey, stamp collecting, fishing. *Address:* c/o Midland Bank, Winchester, Hants. *Club:* Royal Navy Club of 1765 and 1785.

WEATHERALL, Miles, MA, DM, DSc; FIBiol; *b* 14 Oct. 1920; *s* of Rev. J. H. and Mary Weatherall; *m* 1944, Josephine A. C. Ogston; three *d*. *Educ:* Dragon School and St Edward's School, Oxford; Oriel College, Oxford. BA, BSc 1941; BM 1943; MA 1945; DM 1951; DSc 1966. Open Schol. in Nat. Sci., Oriel Coll., 1938. Lecturer in Pharmacology, Edinburgh University, 1945; Head of Dept of Pharmacology, London Hosp. Med. Coll., 1949–66; Prof. of Pharmacology, Univ. of London, 1958–66; Wellcome Research Laboratories: Head, Therapeutic Res. Div., 1967–75; Dep. Dir, 1969–74; Dir of Estblt, 1974–79. Member: Adv. Cttee on Pesticides and other Toxic Chemicals, 1964–66; Council, Pharmaceutical Soc., 1966–70; Council, Roy. Soc. Med., 1972–82 (Hon. Sec. 1974–82); Comr, Medicines Commn, 1979–81. Chm., Sci. Co-ord. Cttee, Arthritis and Rheumatism Council, 1983–88. Chm., Council, Chelsea Coll., Univ.

of London, 1970–83. Hon. Lecturer: UCL, 1968–89; KCL, 1979–82; Hon. Fellow: Chelsea Coll., London, 1984; KCL (KQC), 1985. Mem. Cttee, Wine Soc., 1964–72. *Publications:* Statistics for Medical Students (jointly with L. Bernstein), 1952; Scientific Method, 1968; (ed jtly) Safety Testing of New Drugs, 1984; In Search of a Cure, 1990; papers in scientific and medical journals. *Recreations:* writing, gardening, cooking. *Address:* Willows, Charlbury, Oxford OX7 3PX. *Club:* Royal Society of Medicine.

WEATHERHEAD, Alexander Stewart, OBE 1985; TD; solicitor; Partner in Tindal Oatts (formerly Tindal Oatts & Rodger, then Tindal Oatts Buchanan and McIlwraith), Solicitors, Glasgow, since 1960; *b* Edinburgh, 3 Aug. 1931; *er s* of Kenneth Kilpatrick Weatherhead and Katharine Weatherhead (*née* Stewart); *m* 1972, Harriett Foye, *d* of Rev. Dr Arthur Organ, Toronto, Canada; two *d. Educ:* Glasgow Acad.; Glasgow Univ. MA 1955, LLB 1958. Served in RA, 1950–52, 2nd Lieut, 1950. Solicitor, 1958; Temp. Sheriff, 1985–. Hon. Vice-Pres., Law Society of Scotland, 1983–84 (Mem. Council, 1971–84); Mem. Council, Soc. for Computers and Law, 1973–86 (Vice-Chm., 1973–82; Chm., 1982–84; Hon. Mem., 1986); Mem., Royal Commn on Legal Services in Scotland, 1976–80. Trustee, Nat. Technol. and Law Trust (formerly Nat. Law Library Trust), 1979–86; Mem., Internat. Bar Assoc.; Examr in Conveyancing, Univ. of Aberdeen, 1984–86. Joined TA, 1952; Lt-Col Comdg 277 (A&SH) Field Regt, RA (TA), 1965–67; The Lowland Regt (RA(T)), 1967 and Glasgow & Strathclyde Univs OTC, 1971–73; Col 1974; TAVR Col Lowlands (West), 1974–76; ADC (TAVR) to the Queen, 1977–81; Member: TAVR Assoc. Lowlands, 1967– (Vice-Chm., 1987–90; Chm., 1990–); RA Council for Scotland, 1972–. Hon. Col, Glasgow and Strathclyde Univs OTC, 1982–. Vice Commodore, Royal Western Yacht Club, 1991– (Hon. Sec., 1981–84). *Recreations:* sailing, reading, music, tennis. *Address:* 52 Partickhill Road, Glasgow G11 5AB. *T:* 041–334 6277. *Clubs:* New (Edinburgh); Royal Highland Yacht (Oban); Royal Western Yacht, Clyde Cruising (Glasgow).

WEATHERHEAD, Rev. James Leslie; Principal Clerk, General Assembly of Church of Scotland, since 1985; Chaplain to the Queen in Scotland, since 1991; *b* 29 March 1931; *s* of Leslie Binnie Weatherhead, MBE, MM and Janet Hood Arnot Smith or Weatherhead; *m* 1962, Dr Anne Elizabeth Shepherd; two *s. Educ:* High Sch., Dundee; Univ. of Edinburgh (MA, LLB; Senior Pres., Students' Repr. Council, 1953–54); New Coll., Univ. of Edinburgh (Pres., Univ. Union, 1959–60). Temp. Acting Sub-Lieut RNVR (Nat. Service), 1955–56. Licensed by Presb. of Dundee, 1960; ordained by Presb. of Ayr, 1960; Asst Minister, Auld Kirk of Ayr, 1960–62; Minister, Trinity Church, Rothesay, 1962–69; Minister, Old Church, Montrose, 1969–85. Convener, Business Cttee of Gen. Assembly, 1981–84. Mem., Broadcasting Council for Scotland, BBC, 1978–82. *Recreations:* sailing, music. *Address:* (home) 28 Castle Terrace, Edinburgh EH1 2EL. *T:* 031–228 6460; (office) Church of Scotland Offices, 121 George Street, Edinburgh EH2 4YN. *T:* 031–225 5722. *Club:* RNVR Yacht.

WEATHERILL, Rt. Hon. (Bruce) Bernard, PC 1980; MP Croydon North-East; Speaker of the House of Commons, since 1983; *b* 25 Nov. 1920; *s* of late Bernard Weatherill, Spring Hill, Guildford, and Annie Gertrude (*née* Creak); *m* 1949, Lyn, *d* of late H. T. Eatwell; two *s* one *d. Educ:* Malvern College. Served War of 1939–45; commissioned 4/7th Royal Dragoon Guards, 1940; transferred to Indian Army, 1941 and served with 19th King George V's Own Lancers, 1941–45 (Captain). Man. Dir, Bernard Weatherill Ltd, 1957–70. First Chm., Guildford Young Conservatives, 1946–49; Chm., Guildford Cons. Assoc., 1959–63; Vice-Chm., SE Area Prov. Council, 1962–64; Member National Union of Cons. Party, 1963–64. MP (C) Croydon NE, 1964–83 (when elected Speaker); an Opposition Whip, 1967; a Lord Comr of HM Treasury, 1970–71; Vice-Chamberlain, HM Household, 1971–72; Comptroller of HM Household, 1972–73; Treasurer of HM Household and Dep. Chief Govt Whip, 1973–74; Opposition Dep. Chief Whip, 1974–79; Chm. of Ways and Means and Dep. Speaker, 1979–83. Chm., Commonwealth Speakers and Presiding Officers, 1986–88. Pres., CPA, 1986. High Bailiff of Westminster Abbey and Searcher of the Sanctuary, 1989–. Freeman of City of London, 1949; Freeman of Borough of Croydon, 1983. Hon. Bencher, Lincoln's Inn, 1988. Hon. LLD Coll. of William and Mary, Va, 1989; Hon. DCL Kent. *Recreation:* playing with grandchildren. *Address:* Speaker's House, Westminster, SW1A 0AA. *T:* 071–219 4188; Emmetts House, Ide Hill, Kent TN14 6BA.

WEATHERLEY, Prof. Paul Egerton, FRS 1973; Regius Professor of Botany in the University of Aberdeen, 1959–81, now Emeritus; *b* 6 May 1917; *o s* of late Leonard Roger Weatherley and late Ethel Maude (*née* Collin), Leicester; *m* 1942, Margaret Logan, *o d* of late John Pirie, JP, Castle of Auchry, Aberdeenshire; one *s* three *d. Educ:* Wyggeston School; Keble College (Open Schol.), Oxford. Final Sch. of Nat. Sci. (Hons Botany) 1939; Keble Research Schol., 1939–40, elected to Colonial Agric. Schol., 1940. Trained in RE, then Colonial Office cadet at Imperial Coll. of Tropical Agric. Trinidad, 1940–42. Govt Botanist in Dept of Agriculture, Uganda Protectorate, 1942–47; Asst Lectr, Univ. of Manchester, 1947–49; Lecturer in Botany, 1949–59 (Sen. Lectr 1956), Univ. of Nottingham. *Publications:* papers in (mainly) botanical journals. *Recreations:* music, sketching. *Address:* Greystones, Torphins, Aberdeenshire AB31 4HP.

WEATHERSTON, (William) Alastair (Paterson); Under Secretary, Scottish Office Education Department, since 1989; *b* 20 Nov. 1935; *s* of William Robert Weatherston and Isabella (*née* Paterson); *m* 1961, Margaret Jardine; two *s* one *d. Educ:* Peebles High Sch.; Edinburgh Univ. (MA Hons History). Asst Principal, Dept of Health for Scotland and Scottish Educn Dept, 1959–63; Private Sec. to Permanent Under Sec. of State, Scottish Office, 1963–64; Principal, Scottish Educn Dept, 1964–72, Cabinet Office, 1972–74; Assistant Secretary: SHHD, 1974–77; Scottish Educn Dept, 1977–79; Central Services, Scottish Office, 1979–82; Dir, Scottish Courts Admin, 1982–86; Fisheries Sec., Dept of Agric. and Fisheries for Scotland, 1986–89. *Recreations:* reading, music. *Address:* Scottish Office Education Department, 43 Jeffrey Street, Edinburgh EH1 1DN. *T:* 031–244 5322.

WEATHERSTONE, Sir Dennis, KBE 1990; Chairman and Chief Executive, J. P. Morgan & Co., New York, since 1990; *b* 29 Nov. 1930; *s* of Henry and Gladys Weatherstone; *m* 1959, Marion Blunsum; one *s* three *d. Educ:* Northwestern Polytechnic, London. Morgan Guaranty Trust Co., subseq. J. P. Morgan & Co.: Sen. Vice-Pres., 1972–77; Exec. Vice-Pres., 1977–79; Treas., 1977–79; Vice-Chm., 1979–80; Chm., Exec. Cttee, 1980–86; Pres., 1987–89. *Address:* J. P. Morgan & Co., 23 Wall Street, New York, NY 10015, USA.

WEATHERSTONE, Robert Bruce, TD 1962; CA; Chairman, Lothian Health Board, 1986–90; *b* 14 May 1926; *s* of Sir Duncan Mackay Weatherstone, MC, TD, and late Janet Pringle; *m* 1954, Agnes Elaine Jean Fisher; one *s* one *d. Educ:* Edinburgh and Dollar Academies. CA 1951. Served Royal Marines, 44 Commando, 1944–47. Dir/Sec., J. T. Salvesen Ltd, 1954–62; Dir and Mem., Management Cttee, Christian Salvesen Ltd, 1962–83; Dir, Lothian Region Transport plc, 1986–. Chm., Leith Enterprise Trust, 1983–88; Trustee, 1973–, Chm. Exec. Cttee, Leonard Cheshire Foundn, 1988–91; Chm., Mental Care Cttee, 1991–. *Recreations:* hill-walking, ornithology. *Address:* 27 Ravelston Garden, Edinburgh EH4 3LE. *T:* 031–337 4035. *Clubs:* Army and Navy; New (Edinburgh).

WEAVER, Leonard John, CBE 1990; Chairman: Polymark International, since 1982; Manifold Industries, since 1982; Jones & Shipman, since 1988; *b* 10 June 1936; *s* of A. W. Weaver and B. I. M. Weaver (*née* Geleyns); *m* 1963, Penelope Ann Sturge-Young; five *s* one *d. Educ:* St Mary's Sch.; Battersea Coll. of Advanced Technology (Surrey Univ.). CEng, FIEE, FIMfgE, FIMC. Served Kenya Regt, 1955–57. AEI, 1962–64; PYE-TMC, 1964–66; Consultant, Dir and Man. Dir, P-E Internat., 1966–82; Chm., Pearson Engineering, 1985–88. Member: Council, 1978–83, Bd of Companions, 1981–, BIM; Council, Inst. of Management Consultants, 1978–86 (Pres., 1983–84); Council, IProdE, 1980– (Pres., 1990–); NEDO Prod. Control Adv. Gp (Chm., 1980–82); NEDO Advanced Manfg Systems Gp, 1983–86; SERC Teaching Co. Mangt Cttee, 1983–86; Jt DTI/SERC Advanced Manfg Tech. Cttee, 1983–91 (Chm., 1987–91); SERC Engrg Bd, 1987–; Indust. Develt Adv. Bd, 1989–. Hon. Mem., Soc. of Manfg Engrs, USA, 1990. Freeman, City of London, 1984; Mem., Court of Assts, Co. of Engrs, 1991–. CBIM, FRSA. Sandforth Smith Award, Inst. of Management Consultants, 1984; Internat. Engineer of the Year, San Fernando Valley Engrs Council, 1985; Calif. State Legis. Commend., 1985. *Publications:* contribs to professional jls. *Recreations:* book collecting, cricket. *Address:* Crab Apple Court, Oxshott Road, Leatherhead, Surrey KT22 0DQ. *T:* Leatherhead (0372) 843637. *Clubs:* Reform, City Livery, MCC.

WEAVER, Oliver; QC 1985; *b* 27 March 1942; *s* of Denis Weaver and Kathleen (*née* Lynch); *m* 1964, Julia (*née* MacClymont); one *s* two *d. Educ:* Friends' Sch., Saffron Walden; Trinity Coll., Cambridge (MA, LLM). President, Cambridge Union Society, 1963. Called to the Bar, Middle Temple, 1965; Lincoln's Inn, 1969. Mem. Bar Council, 1981–84; Vice-Chm., Bar Law Reform Cttee, 1987–89; Member: Incorporated Council of Law Reporting, 1987–; Panel of Chairmen of Authorisation and Disciplinary Tribunals, Securities and Futures Assoc. (formerly Securities Assoc.), 1988–. *Recreations:* fishing, racing, gun dogs. *Address:* Kennel Farm, Albury End, Ware, Herts SG11 2HS. *T:* Albury (0279) 771331.

WEAVER, Sir Tobias Rushton, (Sir Toby Weaver), Kt 1973; CB 1962; *b* 19 July 1911; *s* of late Sir Lawrence Weaver, KBE, and late Lady Weaver (*née* Kathleen Purcell); *m* 1941, Marjorie, *d* of Rt Hon. Sir Charles Trevelyan, 3rd Bt, PC; one *s* three *d. Educ:* Clifton College; Corpus Christi College, Cambridge. Bank clerk, Toronto, 1932; teaching at Barking, 1935, Eton, 1936; Asst Director of Education: Wilts CC 1936, Essex CC 1939. Admiralty, 1941; War Office, 1942; Dept of Education and Science, 1946–73; Under-Secretary, 1956; Deputy Secretary, 1962. Visiting Professor of Education: Univ. of Southampton, 1973; Univ. of London Inst. of Educn, 1974; Open Univ., 1976–78. FIC 1986; Hon. Fellow: Manchester Poly., 1970; Huddersfield Poly., 1972; Hatfield Poly., 1973; NE London Poly., 1985. Hon. LLD CNAA, 1972. *Address:* 14 Marston Close, NW6 4EU. *T:* 071–624 4263.

WEBB, Anthony Michael Francis, CMG 1963; QC (Kenya) 1961; JP; *b* 27 Dec. 1914; *s* of late Sir (Ambrose) Henry Webb; *m* 1948, Diana Mary, *e d* of late Capt. Graham Farley, Indian Army, and Mrs Herbert Browne (*née* Pyper); one *s* one *d. Educ:* Ampleforth; Magdalen Coll., Oxford (MA). Barrister-at-Law, Gray's Inn, 1939. Served War, 1939–46, Maj. GSO2, The Queen's Bays. Colonial Legal Service (HMOCS), 1947–64 (Malaya; Kenya; MLC 1958–63; Attorney-General and Minister for Legal Affairs, 1961–63); Sec., Nat. Adv. Council on Trng of Magistrates, and Trng Officer, 1964–73, Dep. Sec. of Commns, 1969–75, Head of Court Business, 1975–77, Lord Chancellor's Office; retd 1977. A Chm. of Indust. Tribunals, 1978–87. Member of Council of Kenya Lawn Tennis Association, 1957–63. JP, Kent, 1966. *Publication:* The Natzweiler Trial (ed). *Address:* Yew Tree Cottage, Speldhurst Road, Langton Green, Tunbridge Wells, Kent TN3 0JH. *T:* Langton (0892) 862779. *Club:* Special Forces.

WEBB, Rear-Adm. Arthur Brooke, CB 1975; retired; *b* 13 June 1918; *m* 1949, Rachel Marian Gerrish; three *d.* Joined Royal Navy, 1936. Comdr 1954, Captain 1963, Rear-Adm. 1973. *Recreations:* gardening, walking, survival. *Address:* c/o National Westminster Bank, 68 Palmerston Road, Southsea, Hants PO5 3PN.

WEBB, Dr Colin Edward, FRS 1991; FInstP; Reader, Department of Physics, University of Oxford, since 1990; Senior Research Fellow, Jesus College, Oxford, since 1988; Founder and Chairman, Oxford Lasers Ltd, since 1977; *b* 9 Dec. 1937; *s* of Alfred Edward Webb and Doris (*née* Collins); *m* 1964, Pamela Mabel Cooper White; two *d. Educ:* Univ. of Nottingham (BSc 1960); Oriel Coll., Oxford (DPhil 1964). FInstP 1985. Mem., Technical Staff, Bell Labs, Murray Hill, NJ, 1964–68; University of Oxford: AEI Res. Fellow in Physics, Clarendon Lab., 1968–71; Univ. Lectr, 1971–90; Tutorial Fellow, Jesus Coll., 1973–88. Vis. Prof., Dept of Pure and Applied Physics, Univ. of Salford, 1987–. Fellow, Optical Soc. of America, 1988. Duddell Medal and Prize, Inst. of Physics, 1985. *Publications:* contribs on lasers, laser mechanisms and applications to learned jls. *Recreations:* travel, photography, music, reading. *Address:* Clarendon Laboratory, Parks Road, Oxford OX1 3PU. *T:* Oxford (0865) 272210.

WEBB, Colin Thomas; Editor-in-Chief, Press Association, since 1986 (Director, since 1989); *b* 26 March 1939; *e s* of late William Thomas and Ada Alexandra Webb; *m* 1970, Margaret Frances, *y d* of Maurice George and Joan Rowden Cheshire; two *s* one *d. Educ:* Portsmouth Grammar School. Reporter, Portsmouth Evening News, Surrey Mirror, Press Assoc., Daily Telegraph, The Times; Royal Army Pay Corps Short Service Commission (to Captain), 1960–64; Home News Editor, The Times, 1969–74; Editor, Cambridge Evening News, 1974–82; Dep. Editor, The Times, 1982–86; Journalist Dir, Times Newspaper Holdings, 1983–86. Member: Core Cttee, British Executive Internat. Press Inst., 1984–; Council, Commonwealth Press Union, 1985–. Hon. Fellow, Portsmouth Polytechnic (Business Sch.), 1991. *Publication:* (co-author with The Times News Team) Black Man in Search of Power, 1968. *Recreations:* family, walking, history books, ballet. *Address:* 49 Winterbrook Road, SE24. *T:* 071–274 4533. *Club:* Garrick.

WEBB, Prof. Edwin Clifford; Emeritus Professor, University of Queensland; Vice-Chancellor, Macquarie University, 1976–86; *b* 21 May 1921; *s* of William Webb and Nellie Webb; *m* 1st, 1942, Violet Sheila Joan (*née* Tucker) (marr. diss. 1987); one *s* four *d* (and one *s* decd); 2nd, 1988, Miriam Margaret Therese (*née* Armstrong). *Educ:* Poole Grammar Sch.; Cambridge Univ. (BA, MA, PhD). FRACI 1968. Cambridge University: Beit Meml Res. Fellow, 1944–46; Univ. Demonstrator in Biochem., 1946–50; Univ. Lectr in Biochem., 1950–62; University of Queensland: Foundn Prof. of Biochem. and Head of Dept, 1962–70; Dep. Vice-Chancellor (Academic), 1970–76. Hon. DSc: Queensland, 1978; Macquarie, 1988. *Publications:* Enzymes, 1959, 3rd edn 1979; 56 scientific papers. *Recreations:* photography, music, motoring, coin collecting. *Address:* 1/221 King's Road, Mundingburra, Townsville, Qld 4812, Australia.

WEBB, George Hannam, CMG 1984; OBE 1974; Senior Fellow, City University, London, since 1989 (Director, Management Development, 1985–89); *b* 24 Dec. 1929; *s* of late George Ernest Webb, HM Colonial Service, Kenya, and Mary Hannam (*née* Stephens); *m* 1956, Josephine (later MA Cantab; JP Surrey), *d* of late R. Chatterton, Horncastle; two *s* two *d. Educ:* Malvern Coll.; King's Coll., Cambridge (MA). Served 14/20th King's Hussars, 1948–49; Parachute Regt (TA), 1950–53. Joined Colonial Administration, Kenya, 1953: District Officer, Central Nyanza, 1954–56; N Nyanza,

1956–57; District Commissioner, Moyale, 1958–60; Secretariat, Nairobi, 1960–62; retired 1963 and joined HM Diplomatic Service; First Sec., Bangkok, 1964–67; Accra, 1969–73; Counsellor, Tehran, 1977–79, Washington, 1980–82; retd 1985. Member Council: Royal Soc. for Asian Affairs, 1984–91; Gresham Coll., 1988–; Friends of Nat. Army Museum, 1988–; Trustee: Hakluyt Soc., 1986–; Encounter, 1989–91. FRSA. Mem., Guild of Freemen of the City of London, 1986–; Liveryman, Scriveners' Co., 1989–. Editor, *Kipling Journal*, 1980–. *Publications:* The Bigger Bang: growth of a financial revolution, 1987; (ed with Sir Hugh Cortazzi) Kipling's Japan, 1988; contribs to learned jls. *Recreations:* books, travel. *Address:* Weavers, Danes Hill, Woking GU22 7HQ. *T:* Woking (0483) 761989. *Clubs:* Travellers', Beefsteak, Commonwealth Trust.

WEBB, Prof. John Stuart, FEng; Professor of Applied Geochemistry in the University of London, 1961–79, now Emeritus, and Senior Research Fellow, 1979–89, Imperial College of Science and Technology; *b* 28 Aug. 1920; *s* of Stuart George Webb and Caroline Rabjohns Webb (*née* Pengelly); *m* 1946, Jean Millicent Dyer; one *s*. *Educ:* Westminster City School; Royal School of Mines, Imperial College of Science and Technology, BSc, ARSM, 1941. Served War of 1939–45, Royal Engineers, 1941–43. Geological Survey of Nigeria, 1943–44; Royal School of Mines, Imperial Coll., 1945–; Beit Scientific Research Fellow, 1945–47; PhD, DIC, in Mining Geology, 1947; Lecturer in Mining Geology, 1947–55; Reader in Applied Geochemistry, 1955–61. DSc, 1967. Mem., Home Office Forensic Science Cttee, 1969–75. Mem. Council, Instn of Mining and Metallurgy, 1964–71, and 1974–83, Vice Pres., 1971–73, Pres., 1973–74; Mem. Bd, Council Engineering Instns, 1973–74; Reg. Vice-Pres. (Europe), Soc. of Econ. Geologists, USA, 1979–81. Mem., Royal Soc. Wkg Pty on Environmental Geochem. and Health, 1979–83. Hon. Mem., Assoc. Exploration Geochemists, USA, 1977; Hon. FIMM 1980. Consolidated Goldfields of SA Gold Medal, IMM, 1953; William Smith Medal, Geol Soc. of London, 1981. *Publications:* (with H. E. Hawkes) Geochemistry in Mineral Exploration, 1962, 2nd edn (with A. W. Rose) 1979; (jtly) Geochemical Atlas of Northern Ireland, 1973; (jtly) Wolfson Geochemical Atlas of England and Wales, 1978; contrib. to scientific and technical jls. *Recreations:* fishing, wild life photography, amateur radio. *Address:* Stone Cottage, Lyons Road, Slinfold, Horsham, Sussex RH13 7QT. *T:* Slinfold (0403) 790243.

WEBB, Prof. Joseph Ernest, PhD (London) 1944, DSc (London) 1949; CBiol, FIBiol; FLS; FZS; Professor of Zoology, 1960–80, and Vice-Principal, 1976–80, Westfield College, University of London, now Emeritus Professor (Hon. Fellow, 1986); *b* 22 March 1915; *s* of Joseph Webb and Constance Inman Webb (*née* Hickox); *m* 1940, Gwenlilian Clara Coldwell; three *s*. *Educ:* Rutlish School; Birkbeck College, London (BSc 1940). FZS 1943; CBiol, FIBiol 1963; FLS 1972. Research Entomologist and Parasitologist at The Cooper Technical Bureau, Berkhampsted, Herts, 1940–46; Lecturer, Univ. of Aberdeen, 1946–48; Senior Lecturer, 1948–50, Professor of Zoology, 1950–60, University Coll., Ibadan, Nigeria. CBiol; FIBiol. *Publications:* (jointly): Guide to Invertebrate Animals, 1975, 2nd edn 1978; Guide to Living Mammals, 1977, 2nd edn 1979; Guide to Living Reptiles, 1978; Guide to Living Birds, 1979; Guide to Living Fishes, 1981; Guide to Living Amphibians, 1981; various on insect physiology, insecticides, systematics, populations, tropical ecology, marine biology and sedimentology. *Recreations:* art, music, photography, gardening. *Address:* 43 Hill Top, NW11 6EA. *T:* 081–458 2571. *Club:* Athenæum.

WEBB, Kaye, MBE 1974; Chairman and Founder of Puffin Club (for children), since 1967; Director, Unicorn Children's Theatre, since 1972; Managing Director, Kaye Webb Ltd, since 1973; *d* of Arthur Webb and Kathleen Stevens, journalists; *m* 1st, Christopher Brierley; 2nd, Andrew Hunter; 3rd, 1946, Ronald Searle, *qv*; one *s* one *d*. Entered journalism via Picturegoer, 1931; joined Picture Post, 1938; Asst Editor, Lilliput, 1941–47; Theatre Corresp., The Leader, 1947–49; Feature Writer, News Chronicle, 1949–55; Editor of children's magazine Elizabethan, 1955–58; Theatre Critic to National Review, 1957–58; Children's Editor, Puffin Books, and Publishing Dir, Children's Div., Penguin Books Ltd, 1961–79; Editor, Puffin Post, 1967–81. Children's Advisor, Goldcrest TV, 1978–84; Mem. UK Branch, UNICEF. Eleanor Farjeon Award for services to Children's Literature, 1969. *Publications:* (ed) C. Fry: Experience of Critics; (ed) Penguin Patrick Campbell; (ed) The Friday Miracle; (ed) The St Trinian's Story; (with Ronald Searle): Looking at London; Paris Sketchbook; Refugees 1960; (with Treld Bicknell) 1st and 2nd Puffin Annuals; Puffins Pleasure; (ed) I Like This Poem, 1979; (ed) Lilliput Goes to War, 1985; (ed) I Like This Story, 1986; The Book of Six, 1991; Meet my Friends, 1991. *Recreations:* children and their interests, theatre. *Address:* 8 Lampard House, Maida Avenue, W2 1SS. *T:* 071–262 4695.

WEBB, Prof. Leslie Roy; Vice-Chancellor, Griffith University, since 1985; *b* 18 July 1935; *s* of Leslie Hugh Charles Webb and Alice Myra Webb; *m* 1966, Heather, *d* of late H. Brown; one *s* one *d*. *Educ:* Wesley College, Univ. of Melbourne (BCom 1957); Univ. of London (PhD 1962). FASSA 1986; FAIM 1989; MACE 1991. Sen. Lectr in Economics, Univ. of Melbourne, 1962–68; Reader in Economics, La Trobe Univ., 1968–72; University of Melbourne: Truby Williams Prof. of Economics, 1973–84, Prof. Emeritus, 1984; Pro-Vice-Chancellor, 1982–84; Chm., Academic Bd, 1983–84. Vis. Prof., Cornell, 1967–68. Chairman: Bd, Qld Tertiary Admissions Centre, 1986 and 1991– (Mem., 1985–); Australian-Amer. Educnl Foundn (Fulbright Program), 1986–90; Member: Conf. of Qld Vice-Chancellors, 1985– (Chm., 1988); Council, Qld Innovation Centre, 1989–; Cttee, Sir Robert Menzies Australian Studies Centre, Univ. of London, 1990–; Bd of Govs, Foundn for Develt Co-operation, 1990–. Consultant, UN Conf. on Trade and Develt, 1974–75; Chm., Cttee of Inquiry into S Australian Dairy Industry, 1977; Mem., Council of Advice, Bureau of Industry Economics, 1982–84; Pres., Victoria Branch, Econ. Soc. of Aust. and NZ, 1976. Award for outstanding achievement, US Inf. Agency, 1987. Joint Editor, The Economic Record, 1973–77. *Publication:* (ed jtly) Industrial Economics: Australian studies, 1982. *Recreations:* music, art. *Address:* Griffith University, Kessels Road, Nathan, Qld 4111, Australia. *T:* (07) 875–7340.

WEBB, Margaret Elizabeth Barbieri; *see* Barbieri, M. E.

WEBB, Maysie (Florence), CBE 1979; BSc; Deputy Director, British Museum, 1971–83 (Assistant Director 1968–71); *b* 1 May 1923; *d* of Charles and Florence Webb. *Educ:* Kingsbury County School; Northern Polytechnic. Southwark Public Libraries, 1940–45; A. C. Cossor Ltd, 1945–50; British Non-Ferrous Metals Research Assoc., 1950–52; Mullard Equipment Ltd, 1952–55; Morgan Crucible Co. Ltd, 1955–60; Patent Office Library, 1960–66; Keeper, National Reference Library of Science and Invention, 1966–68. General Comr in England and Wales, 1976–. Trustee of the Royal Armouries, 1984–90. *Recreations:* family and friends, homes and gardens, thinking.

WEBB, Pauline Mary, FKC; retired; author and broadcaster; *b* 28 June 1927; *d* of Rev. Leonard F. Webb. *Educ:* King's Coll., London Univ. (BA, AKC, FKC 1985); Union Theological Seminary, New York (STM). BA English Hons (King's), 1948; Teacher's Diploma, London Inst. of Educn, 1949. Asst Mistress, Thames Valley Grammar Sch., 1949–52; Editor, Methodist Missionary Soc., 1955–66; Vice-Pres., Methodist Conf., 1965–66; Dir, Lay Training, Methodist Church, 1967–73; Area Sec., Methodist Missionary Soc., 1973–79; Chm., Community and Race Relns Unit, BCC, 1976–79; Organiser, Religious Broadcasting, BBC World Service, 1979–87. Vice-Chm., Central Cttee, WCC, 1968–75; Jt Chm., World Conf. on Religion and Peace, 1989–. Hon. Dr: in Protestant Theology, Univ. of Brussels, 1984; of Sacred Letters, Victoria Univ., Toronto, Canada, 1985; of Humane Letters, Mt St Vincent Univ., Nova Scotia, 1987. *Publications:* Women of Our Company, 1958; Women of Our Time, 1960; Operation-Healing, 1964; All God's Children, 1964; Are We Yet Alive?, 1966; Agenda for the Churches, 1968; Salvation Today, 1974; Eventful Worship, 1975; Where are the Women?, 1979; Faith and Faithfulness, 1985; Celebrating Friendship, 1986; Evidence for the Power of Prayer, 1987; Candles for Advent, 1989; (ed jtly) Dictionary of the Ecumenical Movement, 1991. *Address:* 14 Paddocks Green, Salmon Street, NW9 8NH. *Club:* BBC.

WEBB, Lt-Gen. Sir Richard (James Holden), KBE 1974 (CBE 1970, MBE 1952); CB 1972; *b* 21 Dec. 1919; *s* of late George Robert Holden Webb and Jessie Muriel Hair; *m* 1950, Barbara, *d* of Richard Griffin; one *s* one *d*. *Educ:* Nelson Coll., NZ; Royal Military Coll., Duntroon (Aust.); Staff Coll., Haifa; US Artillery School, Oklahoma; Joint Services Staff Coll., Latimer; Imperial Defence Coll. Commissioned NZ Army 1941. Served War, with Divisional Artillery, 2nd NZ Expeditionary Force, in Middle East and Italy, 1942–45, and Korea, 1950–51 (despatches twice). Quartermaster-Gen., NZ Army, 1967; Dep. Chief of Gen. Staff, NZ Army, 1969–70; Chief of Gen. Staff, NZ Army, 1970–71; Chief of Defence Staff, NZ, 1971–76. Chm., Local Govt Commn, 1978–85. Comdr, Legion of Merit (US), 1971. *Address:* Pahangahanga, Waimate North, RD1 Ohaeawai, Bay of Islands, New Zealand. *Club:* Wellington (Wellington, NZ).

WEBB, Richard Murton Lumley; Chairman, Morgan Grenfell & Co. Ltd, since 1989; *b* 7 March 1939; *s* of Richard Henry Lumley Webb and Elizabeth Martin (*née* Munro Kerr); *m* 1966, Juliet Wendy English Devenish; one *s* one *d*. *Educ:* Winchester Coll.; New Coll., Oxford (BA Modern Hist.). Mem., Inst. Chartered Accountants of Scotland, 1965. Brown Fleming & Murray, 1961–68; Morgan Grenfell & Co. Ltd, 1968–; Morgan Grenfell Gp PLC, 1988–. *Address:* (office) 23 Great Winchester Street, EC2P 2AX. *T:* 071–588 4545. *Club:* Hurlingham.

WEBB, Robert Stopford; QC 1988; *b* 4 Oct. 1948; *s* of Robert Victor Bertram Webb, MC and Isabella Raine Webb; *m* 1975, Angela Mary Freshwater; two *s*. *Educ:* Wycliffe Coll.; Exeter Univ. (LLB 1970). Called to the Bar, Inner Temple, 1971; Western Circuit. Chm., Air Law Gp, RAeS, 1988– (MRAeS 1987). Mem., Internat. Assoc. of Defence Council, 1990. Fellow, Internat. Acad. of Trial Lawyers, 1990. *Recreations:* fly-fishing, golf. *Address:* 1 Harcourt Buildings, Temple, EC4Y 9DA. *T:* 071–353 9371, *Fax:* 071–583 1656. *Clubs:* Royal Wimbledon Golf, Royal Lytham St Anne's Golf, Prestbury Golf.

WEBB, Sir Thomas (Langley), Kt 1975; *b* 25 April 1908; *s* of Robert Langley Webb and Alice Mary Webb; *m* 1942, Jeannette Alison Lang; one *s* one *d*. *Educ:* Melbourne Church of England Grammar Sch. Joined Huddart Parker Ltd, 1926 (Man. Dir, 1955–61). Served War, AIF, 1940–45. Dir, Commercial Bank of Aust., 1960–78 (Chm., 1970–78); Dir, McIlwraith McEacharn Ltd (Vice-Chm.). *Recreations:* golf, tennis. *Address:* 6 Yarradale Road, Toorak, Victoria 3142, Australia. *T:* Melbourne 8275259. *Clubs:* MCC; Australian, Melbourne, Royal Melbourne Golf, Royal South Yarra Tennis (all Melbourne).

WEBB, William Grierson; Director, London College of Music, since 1991; freelance conductor; *b* 16 Oct. 1947; *s* of Horace James Harry Webb and Marjorie Cairns (*née* Grierson); *m* 1984, Elizabeth Jean Shannon; two *s*. *Educ:* Rugby School; Merton Coll., Oxford (MA); Salzburg Mozarteum (Dip.). Hon. FLCM. Conductor, Trier Opera House, Germany, 1973–76; Asst General Administrator, Scottish Nat. Orchestra, 1976–78; Founder Administrator, Nat. Youth Orchestra of Scotland, 1978–87; Dep. Dir, London Coll. of Music, 1987–90. Musical Dir, Aberdeen Internat. Youth Festival, 1989–91. *Publication:* (trans.) Tyrol through the Ages. *Address:* c/o London College of Music, Polytechnic of West London, St Mary's Road, Ealing, W5 5RF. *T:* 081–579 5000.

WEBBER; *see* Lloyd Webber.

WEBBER, Roy Seymour, IPFA, FCCA; Town Clerk and Chief Executive, Royal Borough of Kensington and Chelsea, 1979–90; *b* 8 April 1933; *s* of A. E. and A. M. Webber; *m* 1960, Barbara Ann (*née* Harries); one *s* three *d*. *Educ:* Ipswich School. Ipswich CBC, 1949–55; Coventry CBC, 1955–58; St Pancras BC, 1958–61; IBM (UK) Ltd, 1961–62; Woolwich BC, 1962–65; Greenwich LBC, 1965–68; Royal Borough of Kensington and Chelsea: Dep. Borough Treasurer, 1968–73; Director of Finance, 1973–79. *Recreations:* tennis, walking. *Address:* 11 River Park, Marlborough, Wilts SN8 1NH. *T:* Marlborough (0672) 511462.

WEBER, (Edmund) Derek (Craig); Editor, The Geographical Magazine, 1967–81; *b* 29 April 1921; 3rd *s* of late R. J. C. and B. M. Weber; *m* 1953, Molly Patricia, *d* of the late R. O. and Ellen Podger; one *s* four *d*. *Educ:* Bristol Grammar School. Journalist on newspapers in Swindon, Bristol and Bath, and on magazines in London from 1937 until 1953, except for War Service in RAF, 1940–46. The Geographical Magazine: Art Editor, 1953; Assoc. Editor, 1965. Hon. FRGS 1980. Hon. Life Member: IBG, 1981; NUJ, 1981. Hon. MA Open, 1982. *Address:* 32 London Road, Maldon, Essex CM9 6HD. *T:* Maldon (0621) 852871. *Club:* Savage.

WEBLIN, Harold; Chairman and Chief Executive, Liberty's, since 1984; *b* 10 April 1930; *s* of E. W. Weblin and B. Weblin; *m* 1954, June Weblin (decd); two *s*. *Educ:* Walpole Grammar School, London. General Manager, Way-In, Harrods, 1948–71; General Manager, Liberty's, 1971–84. *Recreation:* gardening. *Address:* 84 The Uplands, Gerrards Cross, Bucks. *T:* Gerrards Cross (0753) 887280.

WEBSTER, Very Rev. Alan Brunskill, KCVO 1988; Dean of St Paul's, 1978–87; *b* 1918; *s* of Reverend J. Webster; *m* 1951, M. C. F. Falconer; two *s* two *d*. *Educ:* Shrewsbury School; Queen's College, Oxford. MA, BD. Ordained, 1942; Curate of Attercliffe Parishes, Sheffield, 1942; Curate of St Paul's, Arbourthorne, Sheffield, 1944; Westcott House, 1946; Vicar of Barnard Castle, 1953; Warden, Lincoln Theol Coll., 1959–70; Dean of Norwich, 1970–78. Hon. DD City Univ., 1983. *Publications:* Joshua Watson, 1954; Broken Bones May Joy, 1968; Julian of Norwich, 1974 (rev. edn 1980). Contributor to The Historic Episcopate, 1954; Living the Faith, 1980; Strategist for the Spirit, 1985. *Recreation:* writing. *Address:* 20 Beechbank, Norwich, Norfolk NR2 2AL. *T:* Norwich (0603) 55833.

WEBSTER, Alec, FCCA; CIGasE; Regional Chairman, British Gas Wales, since 1989; *b* 22 March 1934; *s* of Clifford Webster and Rose Webster (*née* Proctor); *m* 1958, Jean Thompson; one *s* two *d*. *Educ:* Hull Univ. (BScEcon Hons). Chief Accountant, British Gas Southern, 1974; Controller of Audit and Investigations, British Gas, 1979; Treas., British Gas, 1981; Reg. Dep. Chm., British Gas Southern, 1984. Pres., Chartered Assoc. of Certified Accountants, 1989–90. FRSA 1990. *Recreations:* sailing, mountaineering, wood carving. *Address:* Tŷ Carreg, 2 Maillards Haven, Penarth, S Glam CF6 2RF.

WEBSTER, Maj.-Gen. Bryan Courtney, CB 1986; CBE 1981; Director of Army Quartering, 1982–86; *b* 2 Feb. 1931; *s* of Captain H. J. Webster, Royal Fusiliers (killed in action, 1940) and late M. J. Webster; *m* 1957, Elizabeth Rowland Waldron Smithers, *d* of Prof. Sir David Smithers, *qv*; two *s* one *d*. *Educ:* Haileybury College; RMA Sandhurst. Commissioned Royal Fusiliers, 1951; ADC to GOC, 16 Airborne Div., 1953–55; served Korea, Egypt, Malta, Gibraltar, Hong Kong; Directing Staff, Staff Coll., 1969–70; Comd 1st Bn Royal Regt of Fusiliers, 1971–73; Comd 8th Inf. Brigade, 1975–77 (Despatches); Dep. Col, Royal Regt of Fusiliers (City of London), 1976–89; Nat. Defence Coll., India, 1979; Staff appts, Far East, MoD, incl. Dir of Admin Planning (Army), 1980–82. Chm., Army Benevolent Fund, Surrey, 1988–. FBIM. Freeman, City of London, 1984. *Recreations:* ornithology, shooting. *Address:* Ewshot Lodge, Ewshot, Surrey GU10 5BS.

WEBSTER, Charles, DSc; FBA 1982; Senior Research Fellow, All Souls College, Oxford, since 1988. University Reader in the History of Medicine, University of Oxford, 1972–88; Director, Wellcome Unit for the History of Medicine, 1972–88; Fellow of Corpus Christi College, Oxford, 1972–88. *Publications:* The Great Instauration, 1975; From Paracelsus to Newton, 1982; Problems of Health Care: the British National Health Service before 1957, 1988. *Address:* All Souls College, Oxford OX1 4AL. *T:* Oxford (0865) 279379.

WEBSTER, Dr Cyril Charles, CMG 1966; Chief Scientific Officer, Agricultural Research Council, 1971–75 (Scientific Adviser, 1965–71); *b* 28 Dec. 1909; *s* of Ernest Webster; *m* 1947, Mary, *d* of H. R. Wimhurst; one *s* one *d*. *Educ:* Beckenham County Sch.; Wye Coll.; Selwyn Coll., Cambridge; Imperial Coll. of Tropical Agriculture, Trinidad. Colonial Agricultural Service, 1936–57: Nigeria, 1936–38; Nyasaland, 1938–50; Kenya (Chief Research Officer), 1950–55; Malaya (Dep. Dir of Agriculture), 1956–57; Prof. of Agriculture, Imperial Coll. of Tropical Agriculture, Univ. of W Indies, 1957–60; Dir, Rubber Research Inst. of Malaya, 1961–65; Dir-Gen., Palm Oil Research Inst. of Malaya, 1978–80. JMN, 1965. *Publications:* (with P. N. Wilson) Agriculture in the Tropics, 1966; (with W. J. Baulkwill) Rubber, 1989; scientific papers in agricultural jls. *Address:* 5 Shenden Way, Sevenoaks, Kent. *T:* Sevenoaks (0732) 453984.

WEBSTER, David; Senior Fellow, Annenberg Washington Program on Communications Policy Studies, since 1987; Chairman, Trans-Atlantic Dialogue on European Broadcasting, since 1988; consultant to international companies and institutions; *b* 11 Jan. 1931; *s* of Alec Webster and Clare Webster; *m* 1st, 1955, Lucy Law (marr. diss.), Princeton, NJ; two *s*; 2nd, 1981, Elizabeth Drew, author, Washington, DC. *Educ:* Taunton Sch.; Ruskin Coll., Oxford. British Broadcasting Corporation: Sub-Editor, External Services News Dept, 1953–59; Producer, Panorama, 1959–64; Exec. Producer, Enquiry, and Encounter, BBC-2, 1964–66; Dep. Editor, Panorama, 1966, Editor, 1967–69; Exec. Editor, Current Affairs Group, 1969, Asst Head, 1970; BBC Rep. in USA, 1971–76; Controller, Information Services, 1976–77; Dir, Public Affairs, 1977–80; Dir, US, BBC, 1981–85. Mem., Bd of Management, BBC, 1977–85. Resident Associate, Carnegie Endowment, 1985–87. Special Adviser, Communications Studies and Planning Internat., 1987; Chm., Internat. Disaster Communications Project, 1987–. Mem., Twentieth Century Fund Task Force on the Flow of the News, 1978. Mem. Adv. Council, Ditchley Foundn of US, 1981–; Mem., Nat. Adv. Cttee for the William Benton Fellowship Prog., Univ. of Chicago, 1983–89. Fellow, Internat. Council, National Acad. of Television Arts and Sciences, USA, 1980– (Chm., Internat. Council, 1974 and 1975). *Recreation:* coarse tennis. *Address:* 3000 Woodland Drive, Washington, DC 20008, USA. *T:* 202–342 7131. *Club:* Century Association (NY).

See also S. H. E. Kitzinger.

WEBSTER, David MacLaren, QC 1980; **His Honour Judge MacLaren Webster;** a Circuit Judge, since 1987; *b* 21 Dec. 1937; *s* of late John MacLaren Webster and Winning McGregor Webster (*née* Rough); *m* 1964, Frances Sally McLaren, RE, *o d* of late Lt-Col J. A. McLaren and Mrs H. S. Scammell; three *s*. *Educ:* Hutchesons', Glasgow; Christ Church, Oxford (MA (Eng Lang. and Lit.)); Conservatoire d'Art Dramatique and Sorbonne (French Govt Schol. 1960–61). Radio and television work in drama and current affairs, Scotland, 1949–64; called to the Bar, Gray's Inn, 1964; joined Western Circuit; a Dep. Circuit Judge, 1976–79; a Recorder, 1979–87. Member: Bar Council, 1972–74; Senate of Inns of Court and Bar, 1974–79, 1982–85 (Senate Representative, Commonwealth Law Conf., Edinburgh, 1977); Matrimonial Causes Rules Cttee, 1976–79; Crown Court Rules Cttee, 1983–87; Western Circuit Univs Liaison Cttee, 1978–84. Gold Medal, LAMDA, 1954; LRAM 1955. President, Oxford Univ. Experimental Theatre Club, 1958–59; Secretary, Mermaid's, 1958; Chm., Bar Theatrical Soc., 1976–86. Governor, Port Regis Sch., 1983–. *Recreations:* theatre, sailing, cricket, Scottish literature. *Address:* c/o The Law Courts, Winchester, Hants. *Clubs:* Garrick, MCC; Hampshire (Winchester); Bar Yacht, Island Sailing.

WEBSTER, Derek Adrian, CBE 1979; Chairman and Editorial Director, Scottish Daily Record and Sunday Mail Ltd, 1974–86; *b* 24 March 1927; *s* of James Tulloch Webster and Isobel Webster; *m* 1966, Dorothy Frances Johnson; two *s* one *d*. *Educ:* St Peter's, Bournemouth. Served RN, 1944–48. Reporter, Western Morning News, 1943; Staff Journalist, Daily Mail, 1949–51; joined Mirror Group, 1952; Northern Editor, Daily Mirror, 1964–67; Editor, Daily Record, 1967–72; Director: Mirror Gp Newspapers, 1974–86; Clyde Cable Vision, 1983–87. Mem., Press Council, 1981–84 (Jt Vice-Chm., 1982–83). Vice-Chm., Age Concern (Scotland), 1977–83; Hon. Vice-Pres., Newspaper Press Fund, 1983–; Mem. Council, CPU, 1984–86. *Recreations:* travel, boating. *Address:* 32 Athole Gardens, Dowanhill, Glasgow G12 9BD. *T:* Glasgow 041–339 6239.

WEBSTER, Henry George, CBE 1974; FSAE; Chairman, SKF Steel UK, 1982–87; retired; *b* Coventry, 27 May 1917; *s* of William George Webster; *m* 1943, Margaret, *d* of H. C. Sharp; one *d* decd. *Educ:* Welshpool County Sch.; Coventry Technical Coll. Standard Motor Co. Ltd: apprenticed, 1932; Asst Technl Engr, 1938–40; Dep. Chief Inspector, 1940–46; Asst Technl Engr, 1946–48; Chief Chassis Engr, 1948–55; Chief Engr, 1955–57; Dir and Chief Engr, Standard-Triumph Internat., 1957–68; Technical Dir, Austin Morris Div., British Leyland UK Ltd, 1968–74; Group Engineering Dir, Automotive Products, 1974–83. Joined original Instn of Automobile Engrs, as a grad., 1937 (Sec. of Grad. Section, Coventry Br. of Instn, 1941–45); transf. to Associate Mem., 1946, Mem., 1964. MSAE, 1958; FSAE, 1976; FRSA. Freeman, City of Coventry. *Recreation:* golf. *Address:* The Old School House, Barrowfield Lane, Kenilworth, Warwickshire CV8 1EP. *T:* Kenilworth (0926) 53363.

WEBSTER, Ian Stevenson; His Honour Judge Webster; a Circuit Judge, since 1981; *b* 20 March 1925; *s* of late Harvey Webster and late Annabella Stevenson Webster (*née* McBain); *m* 1951, Margaret (*née* Sharples); two *s*. *Educ:* Rochdale Grammar Sch.; Manchester Univ. Sub. Lieut (A), RNVR, 1944. Called to the Bar, Middle Temple, 1948. Asst Recorder: of Oldham, 1970; of Salford, 1971; a Recorder of the Crown Court, 1972–76, 1981; Chm., Industrial Tribunals for Manchester, 1976–81; Liaison Judge: for Burnley, Reedley and Accrington Benches, 1981–86; for Rochdale, Middleton and Heywood Benches, 1987–. Hon. Recorder, Burnley, 1991. *Recreations:* gardening, sailing. *Address:* 1 Higher Lodge, Norden, Rochdale, Lancs.

WEBSTER, Janice Helen, WS; Director General, Council of Bars and Law Societies of the European Community, since 1991; *b* 2 April 1944; *d* of James Bell Reid and Janet (*née* Johnston); *m* 1968, Hon. Mr Justice R. M. Webster, Puisne Judge, Tonga; two *d*. *Educ:* Edinburgh Univ. (LLB 1964). Solicitor and Notary Public. Apprenticeship, Cuchron Sayers and Cook, Glasgow, 1964–67; Legal Asst, then Sen. Solicitor, Falkirk Town Council, 1967–71; in private practice, Alston Nairn & Hogg, Edinburgh, 1971–74; Dep. Sec., Law Soc. of Scotland, 1974–80; Crown Counsel, then Magistrate, Govt of Seychelles, 1980–82; Law Society of Scotland, 1982–90 (Dep. Sec., Dir, European Affairs and Sec., Scottish Lawyers' European Gp). *Publications:* (with R. M. Webster) Professional Ethics and Practice for Scottish Solicitors, 2nd edn 1984, 3rd edn 1991; numerous articles in professional jls incl. Jl Law Soc. Scotland. *Recreations:* singing, French and German classes, walking, gardening. *Address:* 40 Rue Washington, B 1050 Brussels, Belgium. *T:* Brussels 640–422–74. *Club:* New (Edinburgh).

WEBSTER, John Alexander R.; *see* Riddell-Webster.

WEBSTER, John Lawrence Harvey, CMG 1963; *b* 10 March 1913; *s* of late Sydney Webster, Hindhead, and Elsie Gwendoline Webster (*née* Harvey); *m* 1st, 1940, Elizabeth Marshall Gilbertson (marr. diss., 1959); two *d*; 2nd, 1960, Jessie Lillian Royston-Smith. *Educ:* Rugby Sch.; Balliol College, Oxford (MA). District Officer, Colonial Administrative Service, Kenya, 1935–49; Secretary for Development, 1949–54; Administrative Sec., 1954–56; Sec. to Cabinet, 1956–58; Permanent Sec., Kenya, 1958–63; on retirement from HMOCS, with the British Council, 1964–80, in Thailand, Sri Lanka, Hong Kong, Istanbul and London. *Recreations:* travel, reading, swimming, golf. *Address:* Timbercroft, 11 Pevensey Road, West Worthing, Sussex BN11 5NP. *T:* Worthing (0903) 48617. *Clubs:* Commonwealth Trust; Leander; Nairobi (Kenya).

WEBSTER, Vice-Adm. Sir John (Morrison), KCB 1986; retired 1990; Flag Officer Plymouth, Naval Base Commander Devonport, Commander Central Sub Area Eastern Atlantic, and Commander Plymouth Sub Area Channel, 1987–90; *b* 3 Nov. 1932; *s* of late Frank Martin Webster and Kathleen Mary (*née* Morrison) *m* 1962, Valerie Anne Villiers; one *s* two *d*. *Educ:* Pangbourne College. Joined RN, 1951; specialised navigation, 1959; in command HMS Argonaut, 1969–71; MoD Navy, 1971–73; RNLO Ottawa, 1974–76; in command HMS Cleopatra and 4th Frigate Sqdn, 1976–78; MoD, Director Naval Warfare, 1980–82; Flag Officer Sea Trng, 1982–84; C of S to C-in-C Fleet, 1984–86. Lt-Comdr 1963, Comdr 1967, Captain 1973, Rear-Adm. 1982, Vice-Adm. 1985. Younger Brother of Trinity House, 1970–. Mem., Armed Forces Art Soc., 1967– (Chm., 1990–). One-man exhibitions of paintings: Canada, 1976; Winchester, 1980; London, 1982, 1984, 1986, 1988, 1991. Governor: Canford Sch., 1984–; Pangbourne College, 1990–. *Recreations:* painting, sailing. *Address:* c/o Royal Bank of Scotland, 62 Threadneedle Street, EC2. *Clubs:* Royal Naval Sailing Association, Royal Cruising.

WEBSTER, Prof. John Roger, OBE 1988; MA, PhD; Professor of Education, and Dean of Faculty of Education, University College of Wales, Aberystwyth, 1978–91, now Emeritus; *b* 24 June 1926; *s* of Samuel and Jessie Webster; *m* 1963, Ivy Mary Garlick; one *s* one *d*. *Educ:* Llangefni Secondary Sch.; University College of Wales, Aberystwyth. Lectr, Trinity Coll., Carmarthen, 1948; Lectr in Educn, University Coll., Swansea, 1951; Director for Wales, Arts Council of GB, 1961–66; Prof. of Educn, University Coll. of North Wales, Bangor, 1966–78. Member: Lloyd Cttee on Nat. Film Sch., 1965–66; James Cttee on Teacher Educn and Trng, 1971; Venables Cttee on Continuing Educn, 1974–76; Council, Open Univ. (Chm., Educ. Studies Adv. Cttee), 1969–78; Chm., Standing Conf. on Studies in Educn, 1972–76; Member: CNAA, 1976–79; British Council Welsh Adv. Cttee, 1982–; Post Office Users Nat. Council, 1981–88 (Chm., Wales, 1981–88); Chm., Wales Telecommunications Adv. Cttee, 1984–88. Governor, Commonwealth Inst., 1984–. *Publications:* Ceri Richards, 1961; Joseph Herman, 1962; School and Community in Rural Wales, 1991; contribs on educn and the arts to collective works and learned jls. *Address:* Bron y Glyn, Rhydyfelin, Aberystwyth, Dyfed SY23 4QD.

WEBSTER, Prof. Keith Edward, PhD; Professor of Anatomy and Human Biology (formerly Professor of Anatomy), King's College, University of London, since 1975; *b* 18 June 1935; *e s* of Thomas Brotherwick Webster and Edna Pyzer; 1st marr. diss. 1983; two *s*; 2nd marr. diss. 1990. *Educ:* UCL (BSc 1957, PhD 1960); UCH Med. Sch. (MB, BS 1962). University Coll. London: Lectr in Anatomy, 1962–66; Sen. Lectr in Anat., 1966–74; Reader in Anat., 1974–75. Symington Prize, British Anatomical Soc., 1966. *Publications:* A Manual of Human Anatomy, Vol. 5: The Central Nervous System (with J. T. Aitken and J. Z. Young), 1967; papers on the nervous system in Brain Res., Jl of Comp. Neurol., Neuroscience and Neurocytology. *Recreation:* Mozart, Wagner and language: the deification of the unspeakable. *Address:* Department of Anatomy and Human Biology, King's College London, Strand, WC2R 2LS. *T:* 071–836 5454.

WEBSTER, Maj. Michael; *see* Webster, R. M. O.

WEBSTER, Michael George Thomas; Chairman, DRG plc (formerly Dickinson Robinson Group), 1985–87 (Director, since 1976–87; Deputy Chairman, 1983–85); *b* 27 May 1920; *s* of late J. A. Webster, CB, DSO, and late Constance A. Webster, 2nd *d* of late Richard and Lady Constance Combe; *m* 1947, Mrs Isabel Margaret Bucknill, *d* of late Major J. L. Dent, DSO, MC; three *d*. *Educ:* Stowe; Magdalen Coll., Oxford (MA). Commnd Grenadier Guards, 1940–46: NW Europe Campaign, 1944–45 (despatches). Joined Watney Combe Reid & Co. Ltd, 1946; Chm., Watney Combe Reid, 1963–68; Watney Mann Ltd: Vice-Chm., 1965–70; Chm., 1970–72; Deputy Chm., 1972–74; Chm., Watney Mann & Truman Holdings, 1974; Director: Grand Metropolitan Ltd, 1972–74; National Provident Instn, 1973–85; Chm., Fitch Lovell PLC, 1977–83 (Vice-Chm., 1976). Master of Brewers' Co., 1964–65; a Vice-Pres., The Brewers' Soc., 1975–. Gov., Gabbitas Truman & Thring, 1986–90 (Chm., Truman and Knightley Educnl Trust, 1985–87; Gov., Gabbitas Thring, 1986–87). Chm., Aldenham Sch. Governing Body, 1977–84. High Sheriff, Berks, 1971; DL Berks, 1975–90. *Recreations:* fishing, shooting, golf. *Address:* Little Manor Farm, Dummer, Basingstoke, Hants RG25 2AD. *Clubs:* Cavalry and Guards, MCC.

See also Viscount Torrington.

WEBSTER, Patrick; Barrister-at-Law; a Recorder of the Crown Court, since 1972; Chairman, Industrial Tribunals, Cardiff Region, since 1976 (a part-time Chairman, 1965–75); *b* 6 January 1928; *s* of Francis Glyn Webster and late Ann Webster; *m* 1955, Elizabeth Knight; two *s* four *d*. *Educ:* Swansea Grammar Sch.; Rockwell Coll., Eire; St Edmund's Coll., Ware; Downing Coll., Cambridge (BA). Called to Bar, Gray's Inn, 1950. Practised at bar, in Swansea, 1950–75; Chm., Medical Appeals Tribunal (part-time), 1971–75. *Recreations:* listening to music, watching rowing and sailing. *Address:* 103 Plymouth Road, Penarth, South Glam CF6 2DE. *T:* Penarth (0222) 704758. *Clubs:* Penarth Yacht; Beechwood (Swansea).

WEBSTER, Hon. Sir Peter (Edlin), Kt 1980; **Hon. Mr Justice Webster;** a Judge of the High Court of Justice, Queen's Bench Division, since 1980; *b* 16 Feb. 1924; *s* of Herbert Edlin Webster and Florence Helen Webster; *m* 1955, Susan Elizabeth Richards (marr. diss.); one *s* two *d*; *m* 1968, Avril Carolyn Simpson, *d* of Dr John Ernest McCrae Harrisson. *Educ:* Haileybury; Merton Coll., Oxford (MA). RNVR, 1943–46 and 1950, Lieut (A). Imperial Tobacco Co., 1949; Lectr in Law, Lincoln Coll., Oxford, 1950–52;

called to Bar, Middle Temple, 1952; Bencher, 1972; Standing Jun. Counsel to Min. of Labour, 1964–67; QC 1967; a Recorder of the Crown Court, 1972–80. Mem., Council of Justice, 1955–60, 1965–70; Mem., General Council of the Bar, 1967–74, and of Senate of the Inns of Court and the Bar, 1974–81 (Vice-Chm. 1975–76; Chm., 1976–77), Chm., London Common Law Bar Assoc., 1975–79; Mem., Judicial Studies Bd, 1979–83, Chm., 1981–83. Dir, Booker McConnell, 1978–79. *Address:* Royal Courts of Justice, Strand, WC2.

WEBSTER, Maj. (Richard) Michael (Otley); Clerk of the Course: Kempton Park, since 1980; Epsom, since 1988; *b* 11 Aug. 1942; *s* of Brig. Frederick Richard Webster and Beryl Helena Sellars (*née* Otley): *m* 1971, Joanna Gay Enid Simpson, *d* of Lt-Col R. H. O. Simpson, DSO; two *s*. *Educ:* Charterhouse; RMA, Sandhurst. Commnd RA, 1962; CO, King's Troop, RHA, 1976–78. United Racecourses, 1979–; Clerk of the Course, Lingfield Park, 1986–87. Mem., Horseracing Adv. Council, 1987–90. *Recreations:* cricket, racing, shooting, walking.

WEBSTER, Prof. Robert Gordon, FRS 1989; Head of Department and Rose Marie Thomas Professor of Virology and Molecular Biology, St Jude Children's Research Hospital, Memphis, USA, since 1988; *b* 5 July 1932; *s* of Robert Duncan Webster and Mollie Sherriffs; *m* 1957, Marjorie Freegard; two *s* one *d*. *Educ:* Otago Univ., NZ (BSc, MSc); Australian Nat. Univ., Canberra (PhD). Virologist, NZ Dept of Agric., 1958–59; Postdoctoral Fellow, Sch. of Public Health, Univ. of Michigan, Ann Arbor (Fullbright Schol.), 1962–63; Res. Fellow, then Fellow, Dept of Microbiology, John Curtin Med. Sch., ANU, 1964–67; Associate Mem., then Mem., Dept of Virology and Molecular Biol., St Jude Children's Res. Hosp., 1968–88. Fogarty Internat. Sen. Fellow, Nat. Inst. for Med. Res., MRC, London, 1978–79. *Publications:* contribs on influenza viruses etc. to learned jls, incl. Virology, Nature, and Cell. *Recreations:* gardening, sea-fishing, walking. *Address:* Department of Virology and Molecular Biology, St Jude Children's Research Hospital, 332 N Lauderdale, PO Box 318, Memphis, Tenn 38101, USA. *T:* (901) 522–0403. *Club:* Royal Society of Medicine.

WEDD, George Morton, CB 1989; consultant; South-West Regional Director, Departments of the Environment and Transport, Bristol, 1983–90; *b* 30 March 1930; *s* of Albert Wedd and Dora Wedd; *m* 1953, Kate Pullin; two *s* one *d*. *Educ:* various schs in Derbyshire; St John's Coll., Cambridge (BA 1951). Joined Min. of Housing and Local Govt (later DoE), 1951; Principal, 1957; Asst Sec., 1966; Under Sec., 1976. *Address:* The Lodge, High Littleton, Avon; 1 Horsebrook Cottages, Avonwick, Devon.

WEDDERBURN, family name of **Baron Wedderburn of Charlton.**

WEDDERBURN OF CHARLTON, Baron *cr* 1977 (Life Peer), of Highgate; **(Kenneth) William Wedderburn,** FBA 1981; QC 1990; Cassel Professor of Commercial Law, London School of Economics, University of London, since 1964; *b* 13 April 1927; *o s* of Herbert J. and Mabel Wedderburn, Deptford; *m* 1st, 1951, Nina Salaman; one *s* two *d*; 2nd 1962, Dorothy E. Cole; 3rd, 1969, Frances Ann Knight; one *s*. *Educ:* Aske's Hatcham School; Whitgift School; Queens' College, Cambridge (MA 1951; LLB 1949). Royal Air Force, 1949–51. Called to the Bar, Middle Temple, 1953. Fellow, 1952–64, Tutor, 1957–60, Clare College, Cambridge; Asst Lectr, 1953–55, Lectr 1955–64, Faculty of Law, Cambridge University. Visiting Professor: UCLA Law Sch., 1967; Harvard Law Sch., 1969–70. Staff Panel Mem., Civil Service Arbitration Tribunal; Chm., Independent Review Cttee, 1976–; Mem., Cttee on Industrial Democracy, 1976–77. Pres., Inst of Employment Rights, 1989–. Independent Chm., London and Provincial Theatre Councils. Hon. Doctor of Jurisprudence, Pavia, 1987; Hon. Doctor of Econs, Siena, 1991. Gen. Editor, Modern Law Review, 1971–88. *Publications:* The Worker and the Law, 1965, 3rd edn 1986; Cases and Materials on Labour Law, 1967; (with P. Davies) Employment Grievances and Disputes Procedures in Britain, 1969; (ed) Contracts, Sutton and Shannon, 1956, 1963; Asst Editor: Torts, Clerk and Lindsell, 1969, 1975, 1982, 1989; Modern Company Law, Gower, 1969 (ed jtly 1979 edn); (ed with B. Aaron) Industrial Conflict, 1972; (with S. Sciarra *et al*) Democrazia Politica e Democrazia Industriale, 1978; (ed with Folke Schmidt) Discrimination in Employment, 1978; (with R. Lewis and J. Clark) Labour Law and Industrial Relations, 1983; (with S. Ghimpu and B. Veneziani) Diritto del Lavoro in Europa, 1987; Social Charter, European Company and Employment Rights, 1990; Employment Rights in Britain and Europe, 1991; articles in legal and other jls. *Recreation:* Charlton Athletic Football Club. *Address:* London School of Economics, Aldwych, WC2A 2AE. *T:* 071–405 7686.

WEDDERBURN, Sir Andrew John Alexander O.; *see* Ogilvy-Wedderburn.

WEDDERBURN, Prof. Dorothy Enid Cole; Senior Research Fellow, Imperial College, London, since 1981; Principal, Royal Holloway and Bedford New College, 1985–90, and a Pro-Vice-Chancellor, 1986–88, University of London; *b* 18 Sept. 1925; *d* of Frederick C. Barnard and Ethel C. Barnard. *Educ:* Walthamstow High Sch. for Girls; Girton Coll., Cambridge (MA). Research Officer, subseq. Sen. Res. Officer, Dept of Applied Economics, Cambridge, 1950–65; Imperial College of Science and Technology: Lectr in Industrial Sociology, 1965–70, Reader, 1970–77, Prof., 1977–81; Dir, Industrial Sociol. Unit, 1973–81; Head, Dept of Social and Economic Studies, 1978–81; Principal, Bedford Coll., 1981–85. Mem. Court, Univ. of London, 1981–Aug. 1990. Vis. Prof., Sloan Sch. of Management, MIT, 1969–70. Mem. SSRC, 1976–82; Chm., SERC/SSRC Jt Cttee, 1980–82. Member: Govt Cttee on the Pay and Condition of Nurses, 1974–75; (part-time), Royal Commn on the Distribution of Income and Wealth, 1974–78; Council, Advisory Conciliation and Arbitration Service, 1976–82; Cttee of Vice-Chancellors and Principals, 1988–90; Bd, Anglo-German Foundn, 1987–; Bd of Governors, City of London Polytechnic, 1989–; Council, Loughborough Univ., 1990–. Hon. Pres., Fawcett Soc., 1986–. Hon. Fellow Ealing Coll. of Higher Educn, 1985; Hon. FIC 1986. Hon. DLitt: Warwick, 1984; Loughborough, 1989; DUniv Brunel, 1990; Hon. LLD Cambridge, 1991. *Publications:* White Collar Redundancy, 1964; Redundancy and the Railwayman, 1964; Enterprise Planning for Change, 1968; (with J. E. G. Utting) The Economic Circumstances of Old People, 1962; (with Peter Townsend) The Aged in the Welfare State, 1965; (jtly) Old Age in Three Industrial Societies, 1968; (with Rosemary Crompton) Workers' Attitudes and Technology, 1972; (ed) Poverty, Inequality and Class Structure, 1974; contrib. Jl of Royal Statistical Soc.; Sociological Review; New Society, etc. *Recreations:* politics, walking, cooking. *Address:* Management School, Imperial College of Science, Technology and Medicine, 52/53 Princes Gate, Exhibition Road, SW7 2AZ; Flat 5, 65 Ladbroke Grove, W11 2PD.
See also Professor G. A. Barnard.

WEDDERSPOON, Very Rev. Alexander Gillan; Dean of Guildford, since 1987; *b* 3 April 1931; *s* of Rev. Robert John Wedderspoon and Amy Beatrice Woolley; *m* 1968, Judith Joyce Wynne Plumptre; one *s* one *d*. *Educ:* Westminster School; Jesus Coll., Oxford (MA, BD); Cuddesdon Theological Coll. Nat. Service, 1949–51; commnd, RA. Ordained 1961; Curate, Kingston Parish Church, 1961–63; Lectr in Religious Education, Univ. of London, 1963–66; Education Adviser, C of E Schools Council, 1966–69; Sec. of Commn on Religious Education, 1966–69; Priest in charge, St Margaret's, Westminster, 1969–70; Canon Residentiary, Winchester Cathedral, 1970–87. *Recreations:* walking, travel. *Address:* The Deanery, 1 Cathedral Close, Guildford GU2 5TL. *T:* Guildford (0483) 60328.

WEDEGA, Dame Alice, DBE 1982 (MBE 1962); retired; *b* 20 Aug. 1905; *d* of Wedega Gamahari and Emma; *Educ:* Kwato Mission School, Milne Bay, PNG; trained in domestic arts, bookbinding, teaching and nursing. Missionary and teacher among head-hunting tribes of SE Papua during 1930s; first Papuan woman to attend internat. conf., Unesco/Pan Pacific, NZ, 1952; first Papuan Girl Guide Comr, 1956; welfare worker with Agric. Dept, helping village women upgrade land and crops, 1958; developed Ahioma Trng Centre, Milne Bay, for village women to learn domestic arts and child care, 1960–68; Mem., Legislative Council, 1961 (first Papuan woman); sent by Govt to assist women in Bougainville during copper mining dispute, 1969–70; as worker with Moral Re-Armament visited and lectured in Asia and Europe, incl. N Ireland, Sweden, Lapland; attended MRA internat. confs in Ceylon, India, Switzerland, Australia and PNG. *Publication:* Listen My Country (autobiog.), 1981. *Recreation:* swimming. *Address:* K.B. Mission, Box 32, Alotau, Milne Bay Province, Papua New Guinea.

WEDELL, Prof. (Eberhard Arthur Otto) George; Professor of Communications Policy, University of Manchester and Director, European Institute for the Media, since 1983; *b* 4 April 1927; *er s* of late Rev. Dr H. Wedell and Gertrude (*née* Bonhoeffer); *m* 1948, Rosemarie (*née* Winckler); three *s* one *d*. *Educ:* Cranbrook; London School of Economics (BSc Econ., 1947). Ministry of Education, 1950–58; Sec., Bd for Social Responsibility, Nat. Assembly of Church of England, 1958–60; Dep. Sec., ITA, 1960–61, Secretary, 1961–64; Prof. of Adult Educn and Dir of Extra-Mural Studies, Manchester Univ., 1964–75, Vis. Prof. of Employment Policy, 1975–83; Senior Official, European Commn, 1973–82. Contested (L) Greater Manchester West, 1979, (L-SDP Alliance) Greater Manchester Central, 1984, European Parly elections; Chm., British Liberals in EEC, 1980–82; Vice-Pres., Greater Manchester Liberal Party, 1984–88. Chairman: Wyndham Place Trust, 1983–; Beatrice Hankey Foundn, 1984–. Director, Royal Exchange Theatre Company, 1968–89, Hon. Mem., 1989. FRSA; FRTS. Hon. MEd Manchester, 1968. Lord of the Manor of Clotton Hoofield in the County Palatine of Chester. Chevalier de l'Ordre des Arts et des Lettres (France), 1989; Verdienstkreuz (1 Klasse) des Verdienstordens (Germany), 1991. *Publications:* The Use of Television in Education, 1963; Broadcasting and Public Policy, 1968; (with H. D. Perraton) Teaching at a Distance, 1968; (ed) Structures of Broadcasting, 1970; (with R. Glatter) Study by Correspondence, 1971; Correspondence Education in Europe, 1971; Teachers and Educational Development in Cyprus, 1971; (ed) Education and the Development of Malawi, 1973; (with E. Katz) Broadcasting in the Third World, 1977 (Nat. Assoc. of Educational Broadcasters of USA Book Award, 1978); (with G. M. Luyken and R. Leonard) Mass Communications in Western Europe, 1985; (ed) Making Broadcasting Useful, 1986; (with G. M. Luyken) Media in Competition, 1986; (ed and contrib.) Europe 2000: what kind of television?, 1988; (with P. Crookes) Radio 2000, 1991; general editor, Media Monographs, 1985–. *Recreations:* gardening, theatre, reading. *Address:* 18 Cranmer Road, Manchester M20 0AW. *T:* 061–445 5106; Vigneau, Lachapelle, 47350 Seyches, France. *T:* (33) 53.83.88.71. *Clubs:* Athenæum; Fondation Universitaire (Brussels).
See also Ven. H. Lockley.

WEDGWOOD, family name of **Baron Wedgwood.**

WEDGWOOD, 4th Baron *cr* 1942, of Barlaston; **Piers Anthony Weymouth Wedgwood;** *b* 20 Sept. 1954; *s* of 3rd Baron Wedgwood and of Lady Wedgwood (Jane Weymouth, *d* of W. J. Poulton, Kenjockety, Molo, Kenya); *S* father, 1970; *m* 1985, Mary Regina Margaret Kavanagh Quinn, *d* of late Judge Edward Thomas Quinn and of Helen Marie Buchanan Quinn of Philadelphia; one *d*. *Educ:* Marlborough College; RMA Sandhurst. Royal Scots, 1973–80. GSM for N Ireland, 1976. *Heir: cousin* John Wedgwood, CBE, MD, FRCP [*b* 28 Sept. 1919; *m* 1st, 1943, Margaret (marr. diss. 1971), *d* of A. S. Mason; three *s* two *d*; 2nd, 1972, Joan, *d* of J. Ripsher]. *Address:* 152 Ashley Gardens, SW1.

WEDGWOOD, Dame (Cicely) Veronica, OM 1969; DBE 1968 (CBE 1956); FRHistS; FBA 1975; Hon. LLD Glasgow; Hon. LittD Sheffield; Hon. DLitt: Smith College; Harvard; Oxford; Keele; Sussex; Liverpool; Historian; *b* 20 July 1910; *d* of Sir Ralph Wedgwood, 1st Bt, CB, CMG. *Educ:* privately; Lady Margaret Hall, Oxford. 1st Class Mod. Hist. 1931. Mem., Royal Commn on Historical MSS, 1953–78. President: English Assoc., 1955–56; English Centre of Internat. Pen Club, 1951–57; Society of Authors, 1972–77; Member: Arts Council, 1958–61; Arts Council Literature Panel, 1965–67; Institute for Advanced Study, Princeton, USA, 1953–68; Adv. Council, V&A Museum, 1960–69; Trustee, Nat. Gall., 1962–68, 1969–76; Hon. Member: American Academy of Arts and Letters, 1966; American Acad. of Arts and Scis, 1973; Amer. Philosophical Soc., 1973. Special Lecturer, UCL, 1962–90. Hon. Fellow: Lady Margaret Hall, Oxford, 1962; UCL, 1965; LSE 1975. Hon. Bencher, Middle Temple, 1978. Officer, Order of Orange-Nassau, 1946; Goethe Medal, 1958. *Publications:* Strafford, 1935 (revd edn, as Thomas Wentworth, 1961); The Thirty Years' War, 1938; Oliver Cromwell 1939, rev. edn 1973; Charles V by Carl Brandi (trans.), 1939; William the Silent, 1944 (James Tait Black Prize for 1944); Auto da Fé by Elias Canetti (translation), 1946; Velvet Studies, 1946; Richelieu and the French Monarchy, 1949; Seventeenth Century Literature, 1950; Montrose, 1952; The King's Peace, 1955; The King's War, 1958; Truth and Opinion, 1960; Poetry and Politics, 1960; The Trial of Charles I, 1964 (in USA as A Coffin for King Charles, 1964); Milton and his World, 1969; The Political Career of Rubens, 1975; The Spoils of Time, vol. 1, 1984; History and Hope: collected essays, 1987. *Address:* c/o Messrs Collins, 8 Grafton Street, W1.

WEDGWOOD, Sir (Hugo) Martin, 3rd Bt *cr* 1942, of Etruria, Co. Stafford; *b* 27 Dec. 1933; *s* of Sir John Hamilton Wedgwood, 2nd Bt, TD and Diana Mildred (*d* 1976), *d* of late Col Oliver Hawkshaw, TD; *S* father, 1989; *m* 1963, Alexandra Mary Gordon Clark, *er d* of late Judge Alfred Gordon Clark; one *s* two *d*. *Educ:* Eton; Trinity Coll., Oxford. Mem., Stock Exchange, 1973–; Partner, Laurence, Prust and Co., 1973–84; Dir, Smith New Court Far East Ltd, 1986–91. *Heir: s* Ralph Nicholas Wedgwood, *b* 10 Dec. 1964. *Recreation:* ceramics. *Club:* Oriental.
See also Dame C. V. Wedgwood.

WEDGWOOD, John Alleyne, CBE 1984; MA, FCIS; Chairman, Southern Electricity Board, 1977–84; *b* 26 Jan. 1920; *s* of Rev. Charles Henry Wedgwood and Myrtle Winifred Perry; *m* 1st, 1942, Freda Mary Lambert (*d* 1963); 2nd, 1974, Lilian Nora Forey; one *s*. *Educ:* Monkton Combe Sch.; Queens' Coll., Cambridge (MA Hons Hist. Tripos). FCIS, CompIEE. Served War, Lincs Regt and Durham LI, 1940–46 (Actg Major). Asst Principal, Min. of Fuel and Power, 1946–48; Admin. Officer, British Electricity Authority, 1948–55; Dep. Sec., London Electricity Bd, 1955–58; Dep. Sec., Electricity Council, 1958–65, Sec., 1965–74; Dep. Chm., S Eastern Elec. Bd, 1974–77. President: Inst. of Chartered Secs and Administrators, 1976; Electric Vehicle Assoc., 1983–86; Chm. Bd of Management, Electrical and Electronics Industries Benevolent Assoc., 1977–83. Member: Worshipful Co. of Scriveners, 1973–; SE Econ. Planning Council, 1975–79. Founder Master, Worshipful Co. of Chartered Secs and Administrators, 1978. Freeman,

City of London, 1973. *Recreations:* gardening, music, railways, ornithology. *Address:* Pengethley, 16 Rotherfield Road, Henley-on-Thames, Oxon RG9 1NN. *T:* Henley-on-Thames (0491) 576804. *Club:* Phyllis Court (Henley).

WEDGWOOD, Dame Veronica; *see* Wedgwood, Dame C. V.

WEE CHONG JIN; Chief Justice of the Supreme Court, Singapore, 1963–90; *b* 28 Sept. 1917; *s* of late Wee Gim Puay and Lim Paik Yew; *m* 1955, Cecilia Mary Henderson; three *s* one *d*. *Educ:* Penang Free Sch.; St John's Coll., Cambridge. Called to Bar, Middle Temple, 1938; admitted Advocate and Solicitor of Straits Settlement, 1940; practised in Penang and Singapore, 1940–57; Puisne Judge, Singapore, 1957. Hon. DCL Oxon, 1987. *Recreation:* golf. *Address:* 1 Colombo Court #09–05, Singapore 0617.

WEE KIM WEE, Hon. GCB 1989; President of Singapore, since 1985; *b* 4 Nov. 1915; *m* 1936, Koh Sok Hiong; one *s* six *d*. *Educ:* Pearl's Hill School; Raffles Instn. Joined Straits Times, 1930; United Press Assoc., 1941 and 1945–59; Straits Times, 1959–73 (Dep. Editor, Singapore); High Comr to Malaysia, 1973–80; Ambassador to Japan, 1980–84 and to Republic of Korea, 1981–84; Chm., Singapore Broadcasting Corp., 1984–85. Formerly Member: Rent Control Bd; Film Appeal Cttee; Land Acquisition Bd; Bd of Visiting Justices; Nat. Theatre Trust; former Chm., Singapore Anti-Tuberculosis Assoc.; former Pres., Singapore Badminton Assoc. and Vice-Pres., Badminton Assoc. of Malaya. JP 1966. Public Service Star, 1963; Meritorious Service Medal, 1979. Most Esteemed Family Order Laila Utama (Brunei), 1990. *Address:* Office of the President, Istana, Singapore.

WEEDON, Prof. Basil Charles Leicester, CBE 1974; DSc; PhD; FRS 1971; FRSC; Vice-Chancellor, Nottingham University, 1976–88; Chm., Electricity Consumers' Committee, East Midlands Region, since 1990; *b* 18 July 1923; *s* of late Charles William Weedon; *m* 1959, Barbara Mary Dawe; one *s* one *d*. *Educ:* Wandsworth Sch.; Imperial Coll. of Science and Technology (ARCS; DIC). Research Chemist, ICI Ltd (Dyestuffs Div.), 1943–47; Lecturer in Organic Chemistry, Imperial Coll., 1947–55, Reader, 1955–60; Prof. of Organic Chemistry, QMC, 1960–76, Fellow, 1984. Chm., Food Additives and Contaminants Cttee, 1968–83; Mem., EEC Scientific Cttee for Food, 1974–81; Scientific Editor, Pure and Applied Chemistry, 1960–75. Mem., UGC, 1974–76; Chm. Council, National Stone Centre, 1985–91. Tilden Lecturer, Chemical Society, 1966. Hon. DTech Brunel Univ., 1975; Hon. LLD Nottingham, 1988. Meldola Medal, Roy. Inst. of Chemistry, 1952. *Publications:* A Guide to Qualitative Organic Chemical Analysis (with Sir Patrick Linstead), 1956; scientific papers, mainly in Jl Chem. Soc. *Address:* Sheepwash Grange, Heighington Road, Canwick, Lincoln LN4 2RJ. *T:* Lincoln (0522) 522488.

WEEDON, Dudley William, BSc(Eng), CEng, FIEE; retired; *b* 25 June 1920; *s* of Reginald Percy and Ada Kate Weedon; *m* 1951, Monica Rose Smith; two *s* one *d*. *Educ:* Colchester Royal Grammar Sch.; Northampton Polytechnic. Marconi's Wireless Telegraph Co., 1937–48; Cable & Wireless Ltd, 1949–82 (Dir, 1979–82); Chm., Energy Communications Ltd, 1980–82. *Recreation:* sailing. *Address:* 103 Lexden Road, Colchester, Essex CO3 3RB.

WEEKES, Rt. Rev. Ambrose Walter Marcus, CB 1970; FKC; Chaplain at Montreux, 1988–mid 1992; Auxiliary Bishop, Diocese in Europe, since 1988; *b* 25 April 1919; *s* of Lt-Comdr William Charles Tinnoth Weekes, DSO, RNVR, and Ethel Sarah Weekes, JP. *Educ:* Cathedral Choir Sch., Rochester; Sir Joseph Williamson's Sch., Rochester; King's Coll., London; AKC 1941, FKC 1972; Scholae Cancellarii, Lincoln. Asst Curate, St Luke's, Gillingham, Kent, 1942–44; Chaplain, RNVR, 1944–46, RN 1946–72; HMS: Ganges, 1946–48; Ulster, 1948–49; Triumph, 1949–51; Royal Marines, Deal, 1951–53; 3 Commando Bde, RM, 1953–55; HMS: Ganges, 1955–56; St Vincent, 1956–58; Tyne, 1958–60; Ganges, 1960–62; 40 Commando, RM, 1962–63; MoD, 1963–65; HMS: Eagle, 1965–66; Vernon, 1966–67; Terror, and Staff of Comdr Far East Fleet, 1967–68; HMS Mercury, 1968–69; Chaplain of the Fleet and Archdeacon for the Royal Navy, 1969–72; QHC, 1969–72; Chaplain of St Andrew, Tangier, 1972–73; Dean of Gibraltar, 1973–77; Assistant Bishop, Diocese of Gibraltar, 1977, until creation of new diocese, 1980; Suffragan Bishop of Gibraltar in Europe, 1980–86; Dean, Pro-Cathedral of the Holy Trinity, Brussels, 1980–86; Hon. Asst Bishop of Rochester, 1986–88; Hon. Canon of Rochester Cathedral, 1986–88. *Recreations:* yachting, music. *Address:* Montreux, Switzerland. *Clubs:* Royal Automobile, MCC.

WEEKES, Philip Gordon, OBE 1977; CEng, FIMinE; Chairman, 1992 Garden Festival Wales (Ebbw Vale) Ltd, since 1987; Area Director, South Wales Coalfield, 1973–85, retired; *b* 12 June 1920; *s* of Albert Edwin and Gwladys Magdaline Weekes; *m* 1944, Branwen Mair Jones; two *s* two *d*. *Educ:* Tredegar Sch.; University Coll., Cardiff (BSc Hons; Fellow, 1982). Jun. official, Tredegar Iron & Coal Co., 1939. Served War, RAF, 1942–44. Manager: Wyllie Colliery, Tredegar (Southern) Colliery Co., 1946; Oakdale Colliery, 1948; seconded to Colonial Office, 1950; Colliery Agent, S Wales, 1951; HQ Work Study Engr, 1952; Gp Manager, Dep. Prod. Manager, Area Prod. Manager, in various areas in S Wales, 1954; Dir of Studies, NCB Staff Coll., 1964; Dep. Dir (Mining), S Midlands Area, 1967; Chief Mining Engr, Nat. HQ, 1970; Dir-Gen. of Mining, Nat. HQ, 1971; part-time Mem., NCB, 1977–84. Director: B.W. Aviation Ltd, 1986–; Flectalon Ltd, 1986–; Barracudaverken (GB) Ltd, 1986–. Dir, Civic Trust for Wales, 1983–; Member: Prince of Wales' Cttee, 1978–89; IBA Wales Adv. Cttee, 1983–90. Gov., United World Coll. of the Atlantic, 1981–. OStJ 1977. *Publications:* articles in professional and techn. jls and transactions. *Address:* Hillbrow, Llantwit Major, South Glamorgan CF6 9RE. *T:* Llantwit Major (0446) 792125. *Club:* Cardiff and County; Cardiff Aero (Rhoose).

WEEKS, Alan Frederick; Governor, Sports Aid Foundation, since 1983; *b* 8 Sept. 1923; *s* of late Captain Frederick Charles Weeks, MN, and Ada Frances Weeks; *m* 1947, Barbara Jane (*née* Huckle); one *s* one *d* (and one *s* decd). *Educ:* Brighton, Hove and Sussex Grammar School. Served: MN, Cadet, 1939–41; RNR, Midshipman to Lieut, 1941–46. PRO, Sports Stadium, Brighton, 1946–65; Sec., Brighton Tigers Ice Hockey Club, 1946–65; Dir, London Lions Ice Hockey Club, 1973–74; first Director, Sports Aid Foundn, 1976–83; BBC Commentator: Ice Hockey, 1951–88; Football, 1956–78; Ice Skating, 1958–; Gymnastics, 1962–89; Swimming, 1971–90; Presenter: Summer Grandstand, 1959–62; Olympics, 1960, 1964; BBC Commentator: Winter Olympics: 1964, 1968, 1972, 1976, 1980, 1984, 1988; Olympics: 1968, 1972, 1976, 1980, 1984, 1988; World Cup: 1966, 1970, 1974, 1978; Commonwealth Games: 1970, 1974, 1978, 1982, 1986; Presenter, Pot Black, 1970–84. Life Mem., Nat. Skating Assoc. of GB, 1984; Mem. Council, British Ice Hockey Assoc., 1983–; inducted British Ice Hockey Hall of Fame, 1988. Life Pres., Brighton and Hove Entertainment Managers' Assoc., 1985. Hon. Mem., Amateur Swimming Assoc., 1990. *Recreation:* swimming. *Address:* c/o B.H.O., 141–143 Drury Lane, WC2B 5TB.

WEEKS, Sir Hugh (Thomas), Kt 1966; CMG 1946; Chairman: Leopold Joseph Holdings Ltd, 1966–78; London American Finance Corporation Ltd, 1970–78; Electrical Industrial Securities, 1971–77; *b* 27 April 1904; *m* 1929; one *d* (and one *s* decd); *m* 1949, Constance

Tomkinson; one *d*. *Educ:* Hendon Secondary and Kilburn Grammar Schools; Emmanuel College, Cambridge (MA). Research and Statistical Manager, Cadbury Bros, till 1939; Director of Statistics, Min. of Supply, 1939–42; Director-General of Statistics and Programmes and Member of Supply Council, 1942–43; Head of Programmes and Planning Division, Ministry of Production, 1943–45. Represented Ministries of Supply and Production on various Missions to N America, 1941–45; Director J. S. Fry & Sons, 1945–47; Mem. Economic Planning Bd, 1947–48, 1959–61; Joint Controller of Colonial Development Corporation, 1948–51; Chm., NIESR, 1970–74. Deputy Chairman: Truscon, 1951–60; Richard Thomas & Baldwins, 1965–68; Director: Finance Corp. for Industry, 1956–74; Industrial and Commercial Finance Corp., 1960–74; S Wales and Strip Mill Bds, BSC, 1968–72. UK Representative, UN Cttee for Industrial Development, 1961–63. Chairman: EDC for Distributive Trades, 1964–70; Econ. Cttees, FBI and CBI, 1957–72. Pres., British Export Houses Assoc., 1972–74. Medal of Freedom with Silver Palm (US). *Publications:* Market Research (with Paul Redmayne); various articles. *Address:* 14 St John's Street, Chichester, W Sussex PO19 1UU. *T:* Chichester (0243) 788631.

WEEKS, John Henry, QC 1983; **His Honour Judge Weeks;** a Circuit Judge, since 1991; *b* 11 May 1938; *s* of Henry James and Ada Weeks; *m* 1970, Caroline Mary, *d* of Lt Col J. F. Ross; one *s* two *d*. *Educ:* Cheltenham Coll.; Worcester Coll., Oxford (MA). Called to Bar, Inner Temple, 1963. *Publication:* Limitation of Actions, 1989. *Recreation:* walking the dog. *Address:* 31 The Terrace, SW13. *T:* 081–876 0991.

WEEPLE, Edward John; Under Secretary, Scottish Office Industry Department, since 1990; *b* 15 May 1945; *s* of Edward Weeple and Mary Catherine (*née* McGrath); *m* 1970, Joan (*née* Shaw); three *s* one *d*. *Educ:* St Aloysius' Coll., Glasgow; Glasgow Univ. (MA). Asst Principal, Min. of Health, 1968–71; Private Sec. to Minister of Health, 1971–73; Principal: DHSS, 1973–78; Scottish Econ. Planning Dept, 1978–80; Assistant Secretary: SHHD, 1980–85; Dept of Agriculture and Fisheries for Scotland, 1985–90. *Address:* (office) New St Andrew's House, Edinburgh EH1 3TD. *T:* 031–244 4605; 19 Lauder Road, Edinburgh EH9 2JG. *T:* 031–668 1150.

WEETCH, Kenneth Thomas; *b* 17 Sept. 1933; *s* of Kenneth George and Charlotte Irene Weetch; *m* 1961, Audrey Wilson; two *d*. *Educ:* Newbridge Grammar Sch., Mon; London School of Economics. MSc(Econ), DipEd (London Inst. of Educn). National Service: Sgt, RAEC, Hong Kong, 1955–57; Walthamstow and Ilford Educn Authorities and Research at LSE, 1957–64; Head of History Dept, Hockerill Coll. of Educn, Bishop's Stortford, 1964–74. Contested (Lab): Saffron Walden, 1970; Ipswich, 1987. MP (Lab) Ipswich, Oct. 1974–1987. PPS to Sec. of State for Transport, 1976–79. Member: Lab Select Cttee on Home Affairs, 1981–83; Select Cttee on Parly Comr for Administration, 1983–87. *Recreations:* walking, reading, watching Association football, playing the piano in pubs, eating junk food. *Address:* 4 Appleby Close, Ipswich, Suffolk. *Club:* Silent Street Labour (Ipswich).

WEEVERS, Theodoor, LitD (Leyden); Officier in de Orde van Oranje-Nassau; Professor of Dutch Language and Literature, University of London, 1945–71; *b* Amersfoort, 3 June 1904; *e s* of Prof. Theodorus Weevers and Cornelia Jeannette, *d* of J. de Graaff; *m* 1933, Sybil Doreen, 2nd *d* of Alfred Jervis; two *s*. *Educ:* Gymnasia at Amersfoort and Groningen; Universities of Groningen and Leyden. Lecturer in Dutch at University College and Bedford College, London, 1931–36; Reader in Dutch Language and Literature in University of London, 1937–45; Lecturer in Dutch at Birkbeck College (Univ. of London), 1942–45. During War of 1939–45 Language Supervisor and Announcer-Translator in European News Service of BBC (Dutch Section), 1940–44. Corr. mem. Koninklijke Nederlandse Akademie van Wetenschappen te Amsterdam; hon. mem. Koninklijke Academie voor Nederlandse Taal en Letterkunde, Gent; mem. Maatschappij der Nederlandse Letterkunde. *Publications:* Coornhert's Dolinghe van Ulysse, 1934; De Dolinge van Ulysse door Dierick Volckertsz Coornhert, 1939; The Idea of Holland in Dutch Poetry, 1948; Poetry of the Netherlands in its European Context, 1170–1930, 1960; Mythe en Vorm in de gedichten van Albert Verwey, 1965; Albert Verwey's Portrayal of the Growth of the Poetic Imagination, in Essays in German and Dutch Literature, 1973; Droom en Beeld: De Poëzie van Albert Verwey, 1978; Vision and Form in the Poetry of Albert Verwey, 1986; articles and reviews in Modern Language Review, Mededelingen Kon. Nederlandse Akademie van Wetenschappen, Tijdschrift v. Nederl. Taal en Letterkunde, De Nieuwe Taalgids, Neophilologus, Journal of English and Germanic Philology, German Life and Letters, Spiegel der Letteren, Publications of the English Goethe Society, English Studies. *Recreations:* music, walking. *Address:* Warnscale, 42 Pasture Lane, Clayton, Bradford, W Yorks BD14 6LN.

WEIDENBAUM, Murray Lew, PhD; Director, Center for the Study of American Business, Washington University, 1975–81 and since 1983; Mallinckrodt Distinguished University Professor, Washington University, 1971–81 and since 1982; *b* 10 Feb. 1927; *m* 1954, Phyllis Green; one *s* two *d*. *Educ:* City Coll., NY; Columbia Univ. (MA); Princeton Univ. (PhD 1958). Fiscal Economist, Budget Bureau, Washington, 1949–57; Corp. Economist, Boeing Co., Seattle, 1958–63; Sen. Economist, Stanford Res. Inst., 1963–64; Washington Univ., St Louis, 1964–81, 1982–, Prof. and Chm. of Dept of Econs, 1966–69; Asst Sec., Treasury Dept, Washington, 1969–71 (on secondment); Chairman, Council of Economic Advisers, USA, 1981–82. Hon. LLD: Baruch Coll., 1981; Evansville, 1983. Mem., Free Market Hall of Fame, 1983. Nat. Order of Merit, Republic of France, 1985. *Publications:* Federal Budgeting, 1964; Economic Impact of the Vietnam War, 1967; Modern Public Sector, 1969; Economics of Peacetime Defense, 1974; Government-Mandated Price Increases, 1975; Business, Government, and the Public, 1977, 4th edn 1990; The Future of Business Regulation, 1980; Rendezvous with Reality: the American economy after Reagan, 1988. *Address:* Center for the Study of American Business, Washington University, Campus Box 1208, St Louis, Missouri 63130–4899, USA.

WEIDENFELD, family name of **Baron Weidenfeld.**

WEIDENFELD, Baron *cr* 1976 (Life Peer), of Chelsea; **Arthur George Weidenfeld,** Kt 1969; Chairman: Weidenfeld & Nicolson Ltd since 1948, and associated companies; Wheatland Corporation, New York, 1985–90; Grove Press, New York, 1985–90; Wheatland Foundation, San Francisco and New York, since 1985; *b* 13 Sept. 1919; *o s* of late Max and Rosa Weidenfeld; *m* 1st, 1952, Jane Sieff; one *d*; 2nd, 1956, Barbara Connolly (*née* Skelton) (marr. diss. 1961); 3rd, 1966, Sandra Payson Meyer (marr. diss. 1976). *Educ:* Piaristen Gymnasium, Vienna; University of Vienna (Law); Konsular Akademie (Diplomatic College). BBC Monitoring Service, 1939–42; BBC News Commentator on European Affairs on BBC Empire & North American service, 1942–46. Wrote weekly foreign affairs column, News Chronicle, 1943–44; Founder: Contact Magazine and Books, 1945; Weidenfeld & Nicolson Ltd, 1948. One year's leave as Political Adviser and Chief of Cabinet of President Weizmann of Israel. Vice-Chm., Bd of Governors, Ben Gurion Univ. of the Negev, Beer-Sheva, 1976–; Governor: Univ. of Tel Aviv, 1980–; Weizmann Inst. of Science, 1964–; Bezalel Acad. of Arts, Jerusalem, 1985–; Member: Royal Opera House Trust, 1974–87; South Bank Bd, 1986–; ENO Bd, 1988–; Trustee: Aspen Inst., Colorado, 1985–; Nat. Portrait Gall., 1988–. Hon. PhD Ben Gurion Univ. of the Negev, 1984. *Publication:* The Goebbels Experiment, 1943 (also publ. USA). *Recreations:* travel, opera. *Address:* 9 Chelsea Embankment, SW3 4LE. *Club:* Garrick.

See also C. A. Barnett.

WEIGALL, Peter Raymond; Managing Director, P. R. Weigall & Co. Ltd, 1976–84; *b* 24 Feb. 1922; *s* of Henry Stuart Brome Weigall and Madeleine Bezard; *m* 1950, Nancy, *d* of Alexander Webster, CIE, and Margaret Webster; one *s* one *d*. *Educ:* Lycée Janson, Paris; Edinburgh Univ. (BSc). Served War, Captain, RE, 1942–46. Henry Wiggin & Co. Ltd, Birmingham, 1949–51; Petrochemicals Ltd, London, 1951–54; Chemical Industry Admin, Shell Petroleum Co., London, 1954–58; Chemicals Manager, Shell Sekiyu, Tokyo, 1958–63; Shell Internat. Chemical Co., London, 1964–69; Managing Dir, Monteshell, Milan, 1970–73; Industrial Advr to HM Govt, DTI, 1973–75. Member: Movement of Exports EDC, 1974–75; Chemicals EDC, 1974–75; Motor Vehicle Distribution and Repair EDC, 1974–75; Mergers Panel, Office of Fair Trading, 1974–75. *Recreations:* sailing, skiing. *Clubs:* Royal Engineer Yacht, Bosham Sailing.

WEIGH, Brian, CBE 1982; QPM 1976; HM Inspector of Constabulary for South-West England and part of East Anglia, 1983–88; *b* 22 Sept. 1926; *s* of late Edwin Walter Weigh and Ellen Weigh; *m* 1952, Audrey; one *d*. *Educ:* St Joseph's Coll., Blackpool, Lancs; Queen's Univ., Belfast. All ranks to Supt, Metrop. Police, 1948–67; Asst Chief Constable, 1967–69, Dep. Chief Constable, 1969–74, Somerset and Bath Constab.; Chief Constable: Gloucestershire Constab., 1975–79; Avon and Somerset Constab., 1979–83 (Dep. Chief Constable, 1974–75). President: County of Avon Special Olympics, 1982–; UK Br., Royal Life Saving Soc., 1989–. *Recreations:* walking, gardening, golf. *Address:* c/o Bridge House, Sion Place, Clifton Down, Bristol BS8 4XA.

WEIGHELL, Sidney; General Secretary, National Union of Railwaymen, 1975–Jan. 1983; Member, Trades Union General Council, 1975–83; *b* 31 March 1922; *s* of John Thomas and Rose Lena Weighell; *m* 1st, 1949, Margaret Alison Hunter (killed, 1956); one *s* (one *d*, killed, 1956); 2nd, 1959, Joan Sheila Willetts. *Educ:* Church of England Sch., Northallerton, Yorks. Joined LNER, Motive Power Dept, 1938. Elected to: NUR Exec., 1953; full-time NUR Official, 1954; Asst Gen. Sec., 1965. Labour Party Agent, 1947–52; Mem., Labour Party Exec., 1972–75. Non-exec. Dir, BAA plc (formerly BAA), 1987–88 (pt-time Bd Mem., 1983–87); Mem., Programme Consultative Panel, Tyne Tees TV Ltd, 1984–87. Pres., Great Yorks Rly Preservation Soc., 1986–; Mem. and Governor, Ditchley Foundn, 1983–. *Publications:* On the Rails, 1983; A Hundred Years of Railway Weighells (autobiog.), 1984. *Recreations:* trout fishing, swimming, gardening; professional footballer, Sunderland FC, 1945–47. *Address:* Blenheim, 2 Moor Park Close, Beckwithshaw, near Harrogate, North Yorkshire HG3 1TR.

WEIGHILL, Air Cdre Robert Harold George, CBE 1973; DFC 1944; Secretary, Rugby Football Union, 1973–86; *b* 9 Sept. 1920; *s* of late Harold James and Elsie Weighill, Heswall, Cheshire; *m* 1946, Beryl (*d* 1981), *d* of late W. Y. Hodgson, Bromborough, Cheshire; two *s* (one *d* decd). *Educ:* Wirral Grammar Sch., Bebington, Cheshire. Served War: RAF, 1941; No 2 F R Sqdn, 1942–44; No 19 F Sqdn, 1944–45. Sqdn Comdr, RAF Coll., Cranwell, 1948–52; Student, RAF Staff Coll., 1952; CO, No 2 FR Sqdn and 138 F Wing, 1953–57; Student, JSSC, 1959; Directing Staff, Imperial Defence Coll., 1959–61; CO, RAF, Cottesmore, 1961–64; Gp Captain Ops, RAF Germany, 1964–67; Asst Comdt, RAF Coll. of Air Warfare, 1967–68; Comdt, RAF Halton, 1968–73. ADC to the Queen, 1968–73. Hon. Sec., Internat. Rugby Football Bd, 1986–. *Recreations:* Rugby (Harlequins, Barbarians, Cheshire, RAF, Combined Services, England), squash, swimming. *Address:* 3 Bridle Manor, Halton, Aylesbury, Bucks HP22 5PQ. *T:* Wendover (0296) 625172. *Clubs:* Royal Air Force, East India, Devonshire, Sports and Public Schools.

WEIGHT, Prof. Carel Victor Morlais, CBE 1961; RA 1965 (ARA 1955); Hon. RBA 1972 (RBA 1934); Hon. RWS 1985; practising artist (painter); Professor Emeritus, since 1973, Senior Fellow, since 1984, Royal College of Art; *b* London, 10 Sept. 1908; *s* of Sidney Louis and Blanche H. C. Weight; British. *Educ:* Sloane School; Goldsmiths' Coll., Univ. of London (Sen. County Scholarship, 1933). First exhibited at Royal Acad., 1931; first one-man show, Cooling Galls, 1934; 2nd and 3rd exhibns, Picture Hire Ltd, 1936 and 1938. Official War Artist, 1945. Royal College of Art: Teacher of Painting, 1947; Fellow, 1956; Prof. of Painting, 1957–73. One-man Shows: Leicester Galls, 1946, 1952, 1968; Zwemmer Gall., 1956, 1959, 1961, 1965; Agnew's, 1959; Russell Cotes Gall., Bournemouth, 1962; Fieldbourne Galleries, 1972; New Grafton Gall., 1974, 1976; exhibited in: 60 Paintings for 1951; (by invitation) exhibns of Contemporary British Art in provinces and overseas, incl. USSR, 1957; Retrospective Exhibns: Reading Museum and Art Gallery, 1970; RCA, 1973; Royal Acad., 1982; Bernard Jacobson Gall., 1988. Work purchased by: Chantry Bequest for Tate Gall., 1955, 1956, 1957, 1963, 1968; Walker Art Gall., Liverpool; Southampton, Hastings and Oldham Art Galls, etc; Art Gall., Melbourne; Nat. Gall., Adelaide; Arts Council; New Coll., Oxford; Contemporary Art Soc.; V & A Museum. Mural for: Festival of Britain, 1951; Manchester Cathedral, 1963. Picture, Transfiguration, presented by Roman Catholics to the Pope. Member: London Group, 1950; West of England Acad.; Fine Arts Panel, Arts Council, 1951–57; Rome Faculty of Art, 1960. Mem., Cttee of Enquiry into the Economic Situation of the Visual Artist (Gulbenkian Foundn), 1978. Vice-Pres., Artists' Gen. Benevolent Inst., 1980. Trustee, RA, 1975–84. Hon. DUniv. Heriot-Watt, 1983. *Recreations:* music, reading. *Address:* 33 Spencer Road, SW18. *T:* 071–228 6928. *Club:* Chelsea Arts.

WEILER, Terence Gerard; *b* 12 Oct. 1919; *s* of Charles and Clare Weiler; *m* 1952, Truda, *d* of Wilfrid and Mary Woollen; two *s* two *d*. *Educ:* Wimbledon College; University College, London. Army (RA and Queen's Royal Regiment), 1940–45; UCL, 1937–39 and 1946–47; Home Office: Asst Principal, 1947; Principal, 1948; Asst Sec., 1958; Asst Under-Sec. of State, 1967–80; Mem., Prisons Board, 1962–66, 1971–80; Chm., Working Party: on Habitual Drunken Offenders, 1967–70; on Adjudication Procedures in Prisons, 1975. *Recreations:* cinema, crime fiction. *Address:* 4 Vincent Road, Isleworth, Mddx. *T:* 081–560 7822.

WEILL, Michel Alexandre D.; *see* David-Weill.

WEINBERG, Prof. Felix Jiri, FRS 1983; CPhys, FInstP; CEng, FInstE; Professor of Combustion Physics, Imperial College, University of London, since 1967; consultant to numerous industrial and government research organisations in UK and USA; *b* 2 April 1928; *s* of Victor Weinberg and Nelly Marie (*née* Altschul); *m* 1954, Jill Nesta (*née* Piggott); three *s*. *Educ:* Univ. of London (BSc, PhD, DIC, DSc). Lecturer 1956–60, Sen. Lectr 1960–64, Reader in Combustion, 1964–67, Dept of Chemical Engrg and Chem. Technology, Imperial Coll. Director, Combustion Inst., 1978–88 (Chm. British Sect., 1975–80); Founder and first Chm., Combustion Physics Gp, Inst. of Physics, 1974–77, and Rep. on Watt Cttee on Energy, 1979–85; Mem. Council, Inst. of Energy, 1976–79; Mem., Royal Institution. DSc *hc* Israel Inst. of Technol., Haifa, 1990. Combustion Inst. Silver Combustion Medal 1972, Bernard Lewis Gold Medal 1980; Rumford Medal, Royal Soc., 1988. *Publications:* Optics of Flames, 1963; Electrical Aspects of Combustion, 1969; (ed) Combustion Institute European Symposium, 1973; Advanced Combustion Methods, 1986; over 160 papers in Proc., jls and symposia of learned socs. *Recreations:* Eastern philosophies, motor cycling, travel. *Address:* Imperial College, SW7 2BY. *T:* 071–589 5111, ext. 4360; 59 Vicarage Road, SW14 8RY. *T:* 081–876 1540.

WEINBERG, Sir Mark (Aubrey), Kt 1987; Chairman, J Rothschild Assurance, since 1991; Joint Chairman, St James's Place Capital, since 1991; *b* 9 Aug. 1931; *s* of Philip and Eva Weinberg; *m* 1st, 1961, Sandra Le Roith (*d* 1978); three *d*; 2nd, 1980, Anouska Hempel; one *s*. *Educ:* King Edward VII Sch., Johannesburg; Univ. of the Witwatersrand (BCom, LLB); London Sch. of Econs (LLM). Called to the Bar, South Africa, 1955. Barrister, S Africa, 1955–61; Man. Dir, Abbey Life Assurance Co., 1961–70; Hambro Life Assurance, subseq. Allied Dunbar Assurance: Man. Dir, 1971–83; Chm., 1984–90; Chm., Microwriter Systems, 1982–. Chm., Organizing Cttee, Marketing of Investments Bd, 1985–86; Dep. Chm., Securities and Investment Bd, 1986–90 (Mem., 1985–90); Trustee, Tate Gall., 1985–. Hon. Treas., NSPCC, 1983–91. *Publication:* Take-overs and Mergers, 1962, 4th edn 1980. *Recreations:* ski-ing, tennis. *Address:* 15 St James's Place, SW1A 1NW. *T:* 071–493 8111.

WEINBERG, Prof. Steven, PhD; Josey Regental Professor of Science, University of Texas, since 1982; *b* 3 May 1933; *s* of Fred and Eva Weinberg; *m* 1954, Louise Goldwasser; one *d*. *Educ:* Cornell Univ. (AB); Copenhagen Institute for Theoretical Physics; Princeton Univ. (PhD). Instructor, Columbia Univ., 1957–59; Research Associate, Lawrence Berkeley Laboratory, 1959–60; Faculty, Univ. of California at Berkeley, 1960–69; full prof., 1964; on leave: Imperial Coll., London, 1961–62; Loeb Lectr, Harvard, 1966–67; Vis. Prof., MIT, 1967–69; Prof., MIT, 1969–73; Higgins Prof. of Physics, Harvard Univ., and concurrently Senior Scientist, Smithsonian Astrophysical Observatory, 1973–83 (Sen. Consultant, 1983–). Morris Loeb Vis. Prof., Harvard Univ., 1983–; Dir, Jerusalem Winter Sch. of Theoretical Physics, 1983–. Lectures: Richtmeyer, Amer. Assoc. of Physics Teachers, 1974; Scott, Cavendish Lab., 1975; Silliman, Yale Univ., 1977; Lauritsen, Calif. Inst. of Technol., 1979; Bethe, Cornell, 1979; Schild, Texas, 1979; de Shalit, Weizmann Inst., 1979; Henry, Princeton, 1981; Harris, Northwestern, 1981; Cherwell-Simon, Oxford, 1983; Bampton, Columbia, 1983; Einstein, Israel Acad. of Arts and Sciences, 1984; Hilldale, Wisconsin, 1985; Dirac, Cambridge, 1986; Klein, Stockholm, 1989. Mem., Science Policy Cttee, Superconducting Supercollider Lab., 1989–. Fellow, Amer. Acad. of Arts and Scis; Member: US Nat. Acad. of Scis; Amer. Philosophical Soc.; IAU; Amer. Medieval Acad.; Amer. Historical Assoc.; For. Mem., Royal Soc.; Hon. ScD: Knox Coll. 1978; Chicago, 1978; Rochester, 1979; Yale, 1979; City Univ. of New York, 1980; Clark, 1982; Dartmouth Coll., 1984; Columbia, 1990; Hon. PhD Weizmann Inst., 1985; Hon. DLitt, Washington Coll., 1985. J. R. Oppenheimer Prize, 1973; Heinemann Prize in Mathematical Physics, 1977; Amer. Inst. of Physics—US Steel Foundn Science Writing Award, 1977; Elliott Cresson Medal of Franklin Inst., 1979; (jtly) Nobel Prize in Physics, 1979; Madison Medal, Princeton, 1991. Co-editor, CUP Monographs on Mathematical Physics; Bd of Dirs, Daedalus. *Publications:* Gravitation and Cosmology: principles and applications of the general theory of relativity, 1972; The First Three Minutes: a modern view of the origin of the universe, 1977; The Discovery of the Subatomic Particles, 1982; (jtly) Elementary Particles and the Laws of Physics, 1988; numerous articles in learned jls. *Recreation:* reading history. *Address:* Physics Department, University of Texas, Austin, Texas 78712, USA. *T:* (512) 471 4394. *Clubs:* Saturday (Boston, Mass); Cambridge Scientific (Cambridge, Mass); Headliners, Tuesday (Austin, Texas).

WEINBERGER, Caspar Willard, Hon. GBE 1988; Secretary of Defense, United States of America, 1981–87; Counsel, Rogers & Wells International Law Firm, since 1988; Publisher, Forbes Magazine, since 1989; *b* San Francisco, Calif, 18 Aug. 1917; *s* of Herman and Cerise Carpenter (Hampson) Weinberger; *m* 1942, Jane Dalton; one *s* one *d*. *Educ:* Harvard Coll. (AB *magna cum laude*); Harvard Law Sch. (LLB). Member: Phi Beta Kappa; Amer. Bar Assoc.; State Bar of Calif; Dist of Columbia Bar. Served in Infantry, Private to Captain, AUS, 1941–45 (Bronze Star). Law Clerk to US Ct of Appeals Judge William E. Orr, 1945–47; with law firm Heller, Ehrman, White & McAuliffe, 1947–69, partner, 1959–69. Member, Calif Legislature from 21st Dist, 1952–58; Vice-Chm., Calif Republican Central Cttee, 1960–62, Chm. 1962–64; Chm., Commn on Calif State Govt Organization and Economy, 1967–68; Dir of Finance, Calif, 1968–69; Chm., Fed. Trade Commn, 1970; Dep. Dir, 1970–72, Dir 1972–73, Office of Management and Budget; Counsellor to the President, 1973; Sec., HEW, 1973–75. Gen. Counsel, Vice-Pres., Dir, Bechtel gp of companies, 1975–81; former Dir, Pepsi Co. Inc., Quaker Oats Co. Distinguished Vis. Prof., Edinburgh Univ., 1988. Formerly staff book reviewer, San Francisco Chronicle; moderator weekly TV prog., Profile, Bay area, station KQED, San Francisco, 1959–68. Frank Nelson Doubleday (Smithsonian) Lectr, 1974; Chm., Pres.'s Commn on Mental Retardation, 1973–75; Chm., USA–ROC Economic Council, 1991–; Member: Nat. Econ. Commn, 1988–89; Pres's For. Intelligence Adv. Bd, 1988–; former Member: Trilateral Commn; Adv. Council, Amer. Ditchley Foundn; Bd of Trustees, St Luke's Hosp., San Francisco; former Nat. Trustee, Nat. Symphony, Washington, DC. Hon. LLD Leeds, 1989. Medal of Freedom, with Distinction (USA), 1987; Grand Cordon, Order of Rising Sun (Japan), 1988; Order of Brilliant Star, with Grand Cordon (China), 1988; Hilal-i-Pakistan (Pakistan). *Publications:* contributed a semi-weekly column for a number of Calif newspapers. *Address:* 1737 H Street NW, Washington, DC 20006, USA. *T:* (202) 331–7760; Forbes Magazine, 60–5th Avenue, New York, NY 10011, USA. *Clubs:* Century (NY); Bohemian and Pacific-Union (San Francisco); Harvard (San Francisco/Washington DC).

WEINER, Edmund Simon Christopher; Co-Editor, Oxford English Dictionary, since 1984; *b* 27 Aug. 1950; *s* of Prof. Joseph Sidney Weiner and Marjorie Winifred (*née* Daw); *m* 1973, Christine Mary Wheeler; two *s* one *d*. *Educ:* Westminster; Christ Church, Oxford (BA Eng. Lang. and Lit.; MA). Lectr, Christ Church, Oxford, 1974–77; Mem. Staff, A Supplement to The Oxford English Dictionary, 1977–84. *Publications:* Oxford Guide to English Usage, 1983; (ed jtly) The Oxford English Dictionary, 2nd edn, 1989. *Recreations:* language, music, family life, the Church, history. *Address:* Oxford University Press, Walton Street, Oxford OX2 6DP. *T:* Oxford (0865) 56767.

WEINSTOCK, family name of **Baron Weinstock.**

WEINSTOCK, Baron *cr* 1980 (Life Peer), of Bowden in the County of Wiltshire; **Arnold Weinstock;** Kt 1970; BSc (Econ), FSS; Managing Director, General Electric Co. Ltd, since 1963; *b* 29 July 1924; *s* of Simon and Golda Weinstock; *m* 1949, Netta, *d* of Sir Michael Sobell, *qv*; one *s* one *d*. *Educ:* University of London. Degree in Statistics. Junior administrative officer, Admiralty, 1944–47; engaged in finance and property development, group of private companies, 1947–54; Radio & Allied Industries Ltd (later Radio & Allied Holdings Ltd), 1954–63 (Managing Director); General Electric Co. Ltd, Director 1961. Dir, Rolls-Royce (1971) Ltd, 1971–73. Trustee: British Museum, 1985–; Royal Philharmonic Soc., 1984–. Foundn Fund. Mem., Jockey Club. Hon. FRCR 1975. Hon. Fellow: Peterhouse, Cambridge, 1982; LSE, 1985. Hon. Bencher, Gray's Inn, 1982. Hon. DSc: Salford, 1975; Aston, 1976; Bath, 1978; Reading, 1978; Ulster, 1987; Hon. LLD: Leeds, 1978; Wales, 1985; Hon. DTech Loughborough, 1981. Commendatore nell' Ordine al Merito della Repubblica Italiana, 1991. *Recreations:* racing and music. *Address:* 7 Grosvenor Square, W1.

WEIR, family name of **Baron Inverforth** and **Viscount Weir.**

WEIR, 3rd Viscount *cr* 1938; **William Kenneth James Weir;** Chairman, The Weir Group PLC; Vice Chairman, St James's Place Capital (formerly J. Rothschild Holdings) plc, since 1985; Director: BICC Ltd, since 1977; Canadian Pacific Ltd, since 1989; *b* 9 Nov 1933; *e s* of 2nd Viscount Weir, CBE, and Lucy (*d* 1972), *d* of late James F. Crowdy, MVO; *S* father, 1975; *m* 1st, 1964, Diana (marr. diss.), *o d* of Peter L. MacDougall; one *s* one *d*; 2nd, 1976, Mrs Jacqueline Mary Marr (marr. diss.), *er d* of late Baron Louis de Chollet; 3rd, 1989, Marina, *d* of late Marc Sevastopoulo; one *s*. *Educ:* Eton; Trinity Coll., Cambridge (BA). Dir, BSC, 1972–76. Dir, 1970, Chm., 1975–82, Great Northern Investment Trust Ltd; Co-Chm., RIT and Northern plc, 1982–83. Member: London Adv. Cttee, Hongkong & Shanghai Banking Corp., 1980–; Court, Bank of England, 1972–84. Chm., Engrg Design Res. Centre, 1989. Chm., Patrons of Nat. Galls of Scotland, 1985–. Mem., Queen's Bodyguard for Scotland (Royal Co. of Archers). FRSA. *Recreations:* shooting, golf, fishing. *Heir: s* Hon. James William Hartland Weir, *b* 6 June 1965. *Address:* Rodinghead, Mauchline, Ayrshire. *T:* Fiveways (0563) 84233. *Club:* White's.

WEIR, Hon. Lord; David Bruce Weir; a Senator of the College of Justice in Scotland, since 1985; *b* 19 Dec. 1931; *yr s* of late James Douglas Weir and Kathleen Maxwell Weir (*née* Auld); *m* 1964, Katharine Lindsay, *yr d* of Hon. Lord Cameron, *qv*; three *s*. *Educ:* Kelvinside Academy; Glasgow Academy; The Leys Sch., Cambridge; Glasgow Univ. (MA, LLB). Royal Naval Reserve, 1955–64, Lieut RNR. Admitted to Faculty of Advocates, 1959; Advocate Depute for Sheriff Court, 1964; Standing Junior Counsel: to MPBW, 1969; to DoE, 1970; QC (Scot.) 1971; Advocate Depute, 1979–82. Chairman: Medical Appeal Tribunal, 1972–77; Pensions Appeal Tribunal for Scotland, 1978–84 (Pres., 1984–85); NHS Tribunal, Scotland, 1983–85; Member: Criminal Injuries Compensation Bd, 1974–79 and 1984–85; Transport Tribunal, 1979–85; Legal Adv. Cttee, British Council, 1988–; Parole Bd, Scotland, 1989–. Governor, Fettes Coll., 1986– (Chm., 1989–). *Recreations:* sailing, music. *Address:* Parliament House, Edinburgh EH1 1RQ. *T:* 031–225 2595. *Clubs:* New (Edinburgh); Royal Highland Yacht.

WEIR, Rear-Adm. Alexander Fortune Rose, CB 1981; JP; Senior Associate, Captain Colin McMullen and Associates, Marine Consultants, since 1982; *b* 17 June 1928; *s* of late Comdr Patrick Wylie Rose Weir and Minna Ranken Forrester Weir (*née* Fortune); *m* 1953, Ann Ross Hamilton Crawford, Ardmore, Co. Londonderry; four *d*. *Educ:* Royal Naval Coll., Dartmouth. FBIM 1979; AVCM 1982. Cadet, 1945–46; Midshipman, 1946–47; Actg Sub-Lieut under trng, HMS Zephyr, Portland, 1947; Sub-Lieut professional courses, 1947–48; Sub-Lieut and Lieut, HMS Loch Arkaig, Londonderry Sqdn, 1949–51; ADC to Governor of Victoria, Aust., 1951–53; HMS Mariner, Fishery Protection Sqdn, Home waters and Arctic, 1953–54; qual. as Navigating Officer, 1954; HMS St Austell Bay, WI, Navigating Officer, 1955–56; HMS Wave, Fishery Protection Sqdn, Home, Arctic and Iceland, 1956–58; Lt-Comdr, advanced navigation course, 1958; Staff ND Officer, Flag Officer Sea Trng at Portland, Dorset, 1958–61; HMS Plymouth, Staff Officer Ops, 4th Frigate Sqdn, Far East Station, 1961–62; Comdr 1962; Trng Comdr, BRNC Dartmouth, 1962–64; Comd, HMS Rothesay, WI Station, 1965–66; Staff of C-in-C Portsmouth, Staff Officer Ops, 1966–68; 2nd in Comd and Exec. Officer, HMS Eagle, 1968–69; Captain 1969; jssc 1969–70; Pres., Far East Comd Midshipman's Bd, 1970; Asst Dir Naval Operational Requirements, MoD(N), 1970–72; Captain (F) 6th Frigate Sqdn (8 ships) and HMS Andromeda, 1972–74; NATO Def. Coll., Rome, 1974–75; ACOS Strategic Policy Requirements and Long Range Objectives, SACLANT, 1975–77; Captain HMS Bristol, 1977–78; Rear-Adm. 1978; Dep. Asst Chief of Staff (Ops) to SACEUR, 1978–81. FBIM. Associate, Victoria Coll. of Music. Member: Nautical Inst.; Royal Inst. of Navigation. Licenced Royal Naval Lay Reader, 1981; Licensed Lay Reader, St Kew Parish, Dio. Truro, 1984–. JP: Chichester, 1982–84; Bodmin, 1985–. *Recreations:* sailing, shooting, golf. *Address:* Tipton, St Kew, Bodmin, Cornwall PL30 3ET. *T:* St Mabyn (020884) 289, *Fax:* (020884) 675; Yeoman House, Penge, SE20 7TP. *T:* 081–778 6060. *Clubs:* Royal Navy 1765 and 1785, Institute of Directors; Royal Yacht Squadron, Royal Yachting Association, Royal Naval Sailing Association.

WEIR, Very Rev. Andrew John, MSc; Clerk of Assembly and General Secretary, The Presbyterian Church in Ireland, 1964–85, Emeritus since 1985; *b* 24 March 1919; *s* of Rev. Andrew Weir and Margaret Weir, Missionaries to Manchuria of the Presbyterian Church in Ireland. *Educ:* Campbell Coll., Belfast; Queen's Univ., Belfast; New Coll., Edinburgh; Presbyterian Coll., Belfast. Ordained, 1944; Missionary to China, 1945–51; Minister, Trinity Presbyterian Church, Letterkenny, Co. Donegal, 1952–62; Asst Clerk of Assembly and Home Mission Convener, The Presbyterian Church in Ireland, 1962–64. Moderator of the General Assembly, The Presbyterian Church in Ireland, 1976–77. Hon. DD: Presbyterian Theol Faculty, Ireland, 1972; QUB, 1990. *Address:* 18 Cyprus Park, Belfast BT5 6EA. *T:* Belfast (0232) 651276.

WEIR, Rev. Cecil James Mullo, MA, DD, DPhil; Professor of Hebrew and Semitic Languages, University of Glasgow, 1937–68; *b* Edinburgh, 4 Dec. 1897; *e s* of late James Mullo Weir, SSC, FSAScot, Solicitor, Edinburgh; unmarried. *Educ:* Royal High School, Edinburgh; Universities of Edinburgh, Marburg, Paris and Leipzig; Jesus College, Oxford. Served World War I, 1917–19, with Expeditionary Force in France, Belgium and Germany; Tutor in Hebrew, University of Edinburgh, 1921–22; MA Edinburgh with 1st Class Honours in Classics, 1923; 1st Class Honours in Semitic Languages, 1925; BD Edinburgh, 1926; DPhil Oxford, 1930; Minister of Orwell, Kinross-shire, 1932–34; Rankin Lecturer and Head of Department of Hebrew and Ancient Semitic Languages, University of Liverpool, 1934–37; Lecturer in the Institute of Archæology, Liverpool, 1934–37. President, Glasgow Archæological Soc., 1945–48; Dean of Faculty of Divinity, Univ. of Glasgow, 1951–54; Hon. DD (Edinburgh), 1959; FRAS, FSAScot. *Publications:* A Lexicon of Accadian Prayers in the Rituals of Expiation, 1934; contributed to A Companion to the Bible (ed Manson), 1939; Fortuna Domus, 1952; Documents from Old Testament Times (ed Thomas), 1958; Hastings's Dictionary of the Bible, 1963; A Companion to the Bible (ed Rowley), 1963; Archæology and Old Testament Study (ed Thomas), 1967; edited Transactions of Glasgow University Oriental Soc., Studia Semitica et Orientalia, Transactions of Glasgow Archæological Soc.; articles and reviews of books. *Recreations:* golf, travel. *Address:* 4/17 Gillsland Road, Edinburgh EH10 5BW. *T:* 031–228 6965.

WEIR, David Bruce; *see* Weir, Hon. Lord.

WEIR, Gillian Constance, CBE 1989; concert organist; *b* 17 Jan. 1941; *d* of Cecil Alexander Weir and Clarice M. Foy Weir. *Educ:* Royal College of Music, London. LRSM, LRAM, LTCL; Hon. FRCO. Winner of St Albans Internat. Organ Competition, 1964; Début, 1965: Royal Festival Hall, solo recital; Royal Albert Hall, concerto soloist, opening night of Promenade Concerts; since then, worldwide career solely as touring concert organist; concerto appearances with all major British orchestras, also with Boston Symphony, Seattle Symphony, Württemberg Chamber Orch., and others; solo appearances at leading internat. Festivals, incl. Bath, Aldeburgh, Edinburgh, English Bach, Europalia, Europe and USA (AGO Nat. Conventions, RCCO Diamond Jubilee Nat. Convention, etc). Frequent radio and television appearances: BBC Third Prog., USA, Australasia, Europe; TV film, Toccata: two weeks in the life of Gillian Weir, 1981 (shown NZ TV 1982); presenter and performer, The King of Instruments, TV series BBC2 and Europe, 1989; many first performances, incl. major works by Fricker, Connolly, Camilleri, Messiaen. Master-classes, adjudicator internat. competitions, UK, France, N America, Japan. Hon. FRCO and Mem. Council, RCO, 1977– (first woman Mem.); President: Incorp. Assoc. of Organists, 1981–83 (first woman Pres.); ISM, April 1992–; Hon. RAM, 1989. Internat. Performer of the Year Award, NY Amer. Guild of Organists, 1981; Internat. Music Guide's Musician of the Year Award, 1982; Turnovsky Prize for outstanding achievement in the arts, Turnovsky Foundn for the Arts, NZ, 1985. Hon. Fellow, Royal Canadian Coll. of Organists, 1983; Hon. DMus, Victoria Univ. of Wellington, NZ, 1983. *Publications:* contributor to: Grove's Internat. Dictionary of Music and Musicians, 1980; musical jls and periodicals. *Recreation:* theatre. *Address:* 78 Robin Way, Tilehurst, Berks RG3 5SW. *Club:* University Women's.
See also Sir R. B. Weir.

WEIR, Judith; composer; *b* 11 May 1954; *d* of Jack and Ishbel Weir. *Educ:* King's Coll., Cambridge (MA). Cramb Fellow, Glasgow Univ., 1979–82; Fellow-Commoner, Trinity Coll., Cambridge, 1983–85; Composer-in-Residence, RSAMD, Glasgow, 1988–91. *Publications include: compositions:* King Harald's Saga, 1979; Several Concertos, 1980; The Consolations of Scholarship, 1985; Lovers, Learners and Libations, 1987; A Night at the Chinese Opera, 1987; Missa Del Cid, 1988; Distance and Enchantment, 1989; Heaven Ablaze In His Breast, 1989; The Vanishing Bridegroom, 1990 (opera); Ardnamurchan Point, 1990; Ox Mountain Was Covered By Trees, 1990; String Quartet, 1990. *Address:* c/o Chester Music, 8/9 Frith Street, W1V 5TZ. *T:* 071–434 0066.

WEIR, Sir Michael (Scott), KCMG 1980 (CMG 1974); HM Diplomatic Service, retired; Director, 21st Century Trust, since 1990; *b* 28 Jan. 1925; *s* of Archibald and Agnes Weir; *m* 1953, Alison Walker; two *s* two *d*; *m* 1976, Hilary Reid; two *s*. *Educ:* Dunfermline High School; Balliol College, Oxford. Served RAF (Flt Lt), 1944–47; subseq. HM Diplomatic Service; Foreign Office, 1950; Political Agent, Trucial States, 1952–54; FO, 1954–56; Consul, San Francisco, 1956–58; 1st Secretary: Washington, 1958–61; Cairo, 1961–63; FO, 1963–68; Counsellor, Head of Arabian Dept, 1966; Dep. Political Resident, Persian Gulf, Bahrain, 1968–71; Head of Chancery, UK Mission to UN, NY, 1971–73; Asst Under-Sec. of State, FCO, 1974–79; Ambassador, Cairo, 1979–85. Pres., Egypt Exploration Soc., 1988–; Chm., British Egyptian Soc., 1990–. *Recreations:* golf, music. *Address:* 37 Lansdowne Gardens, SW8 2EL. *Clubs:* Rye Golf, Royal Wimbledon Golf.

WEIR, Peter Lindsay, AM 1982; film director, since 1969; *b* 21 Aug. 1944; *s* of Lindsay Weir and Peggy Barnsley Weir; *m* 1966, Wendy Stites; one *s* one *d*. *Educ:* Scots Coll., Sydney; Vaucluse High Sch.; Sydney Univ. Short Film: Homesdale, 1971; Feature Films: The Cars That Ate Paris, 1973; Picnic at Hanging Rock, 1975; Last Wave, 1977; The Plumber (for TV), 1979; Gallipolli, 1980; The Year of Living Dangerously, 1982; Witness, 1985; The Mosquito Coast, 1986; Dead Poets Society, 1989; Green Card, 1991. *Address:* c/o Australian Film Commission, 8 West Street, North Sydney, NSW 2060, Australia.

WEIR, Richard Stanton; Director-General, Institutional Fund Managers' Association, since 1989; *b* 5 Jan. 1933; *o s* of Brig. R. A. Weir, OBE and Dr M. L. Cowan; *m* 1961, Helen Eugenie Guthrie; one *d*. *Educ:* Repton Sch., Derbys; Christ Church, Oxford (MA). Called to the Bar, Inner Temple, 1957. Commnd 3rd Carabiniers (Prince of Wales' Dragoon Guards), 1952. Head of Legal Dept, Soc. of Motor Mfrs and Traders Ltd, 1958–61; Exec., British Motor Corp. Ltd, 1961–64; Dep. Co. Sec., Rank Organisation Ltd, 1964–67; Head of Admin, Rank Leisure Services, 1967–69; Sec., CWS Ltd, 1969–74; Dir, 1975–81, Dir-Gen., 1987–89, Retail Consortium; Sec. Gen. (Chief Exec.), BSA, 1981–86; Dir, British Retailers' Assoc., 1987–89. Mem., Consumer Protection Adv. Cttee set up under Fair Trading Act, 1973, 1973–76. *Recreations:* reading, walking, shooting. *Address:* 2 Lamont Road, SW10. *T:* 071–352 4809. *Club:* United Oxford & Cambridge University.

WEIR, Sir Roderick (Bignell), Kt 1984; JP; Chairman, McKechnie Pacific Ltd, since 1983; *b* 14 July 1927; *s* of Cecil Alexander Weir and Clarice Mildred Foy; *m* 1952, Loys Agnes Wilson (*d* 1984); one *d*; *m* 1986, Anna Jane Mcfarlane. *Educ:* Wanganui Boys' Coll., NZ. Various positions to regional manager, Dalgety NZ Ltd, Wanganui, 1943–63; formed stock and station co., Rod Weir & Co. Ltd, 1963; formed Crown Consolidated Ltd, 1976; Chm., Amuri Corp. Ltd; Director: Rangatira; Sun Alliance Insurance Ltd; Sun Alliance Life Assurance Co.; Fluid Control; NZ Casing Co Ltd; Crown Meats Ltd; Bain Clarkson Ltd. Former Chm., Members Listed Cos Assoc.; Chm., Massey Coll. Business & Property Trust. Past President: NZ Stock and Station Agents' Assoc.; Asean Business Council. Mem., NZ Inst. of Econ. Res. Inc.; Board Member and Patron: Massey Univ. Foundn; Medic Alert; Wellington Sch. of Medicine; Wellington Med. Res. Foundn; Mem., Adv. Bd, Salvation Army. Trustee, Wanganui Old Boys' Assoc. JP NZ 1972. *Recreations:* fishing, shooting, boxing. *Address:* 78 Salamanca Road, Kelburn, Wellington, New Zealand. *T:* Wellington 724–033; The Grove, Main Road, Waikanae 36373, New Zealand. *Clubs:* Wellington (Wellington); Heretaunga (Lower Hutt); Levin (Levin).
See also Gillian Weir.

WEIR, Stuart Peter; Joint Editor, Democratic Audit of the United Kingdom, and Senior Research Fellow, Human Rights Centre, Essex University, since 1991; *b* 13 Oct. 1938; *e s* of Robert Hendry Weir, CB and Edna Frances (*née* Lewis); *m* 1st, 1963, Doffy Burnham; two *s*; 2nd, 1987, Elizabeth Ellen Bisset; one *s* two *d*. *Educ:* Peter Symonds Sch., Winchester; Brasenose Coll., Oxford (BA Hons Modern History). Feature writer, Oxford Mail, 1964–67; diarist, The Times, 1967–71; Dir, Citizens Rights Office, CPAG, 1971–75; Founding Editor, Roof magazine, 1975–77; Dep. Editor, New Society, 1977–84; Editor: New Socialist, 1984–87; New Statesman, 1987–88, New Statesman and Society, 1988–90 (Journalist and Associate Editor, 1990–). WEA and Adult Educn lectr, 1969–73. Founder Chair, Family Rights Gp, 1975; Co-founder, Charter 88, 1988; Chm., Charter 88 Trust, 1991–. Member: Exec., CPAG and Finer Jt Action Cttee, 1970–84; (Founding), Labour Co-ordinating Cttee, 1979. Active in anti-racist and community groups, Oxford and Hackney, 1964–72; Mem. (Lab), London Bor. of Hackney Council, 1972–76. Columnist: Community Care, 1973–75; London Daily News, 1987; script consultant: Spongers, BBC TV, 1977; United Kingdom, BBC TV, 1980–81. *Publications:* (contrib.) Towards Better Social Services, 1973; Social Insecurity, 1974; Supplementary Benefits: a social worker's guide, 1975; (ed and contrib.) Manifesto, 1981; (contrib.) The Other Britain, 1982; (contrib.) Consuming Secrets, 1982. *Recreations:* cooking, gardening, being with my children. *Address:* 15 Grazebrook Road, N16 0HU.

WEISKRANTZ, Lawrence, FRS 1980; Professor of Psychology, Oxford University, since 1967; Fellow, Magdalen College, Oxford; *b* 28 March 1926; *s* of Dr Benjamin Weiskrantz and Rose (*née* Rifkin); *m* 1954, Barbara Collins; one *s* one *d*. *Educ:* Girard College; Swarthmore; Univs of Oxford and Harvard. Part-time Lectr, Tufts University, 1952; Research Assoc., Inst. of Living, 1952–55; Sen. Postdoctoral Fellow, US Nat. Res. Coun., 1955–56; Research Assoc., Cambridge Univ., 1956–61; Asst Dir of Research,

Cambridge Univ., 1961–66; Reader in Physiological Psychology, Cambridge Univ., 1966–67. Member, US Nat. Acad. of Scis, 1987. Farrier Lectr, Royal Soc., 1989; Hughlings Jackson Lectr/Medallist, RSM, 1990. Kenneth Craik Research Award, St John's Coll., Cambridge, 1975–76. Dep. Editor, Brain, 1981–; Co-Editor, Oxford Psychology Series, 1979–. *Publications:* (jtly) Analysis of Behavioural Change, 1967; The Neuropsychology of Cognitive Function, 1982; Animal Intelligence, 1985; Blindsight, 1986; Thought Without Language, 1988; articles in Science, Nature, Quarterly Jl of Experimental Psychology, Jl of Comparative and Physiological Psychology, Animal Behaviour. *Recreations:* music, walking. *Address:* Department of Experimental Psychology, South Parks Road, Oxford OX1 3UD.

WEISMAN, Malcolm; Barrister-at-law; a Recorder of the Crown Court, since 1980; *s* of David and Jeanie Pearl Weisman; *m* 1958, Rosalie, *d* of Dr and Mrs A. Spiro; two *s*. *Educ:* Harrogate Grammar Sch.; Parmiter's Sch.; London School of Economics; St Catherine's Coll., Oxford (MA). Blackstone Pupillage Prize. Chaplain (Sqdn Ldr), Royal Air Force, 1956; called to Bar, Middle Temple, 1961; Head of Chambers, 1983–90. Senior Jewish Chaplain, HM Forces, 1972; Religious advisor to small congregations, and Hon. Chaplain, Oxford, Cambridge and new universities, 1963–; Chm. and Sec.-Gen., Allied Air Forces in Europe Chief of Chaplains Cttee, 1981–; Mem., Cabinet of the Chief Rabbi, 1967–. Asst Comr of Parly Boundaries, 1976–85. Mem., Senior Common Room, Essex, Kent and Lancaster Univs, 1964–; Member of Court: Univ. of Lancaster, 1970–; Warwick Univ., 1983–; Univ. of East Anglia, 1985–. Governor, Parmiter's Sch., 1980–. Editor, Menorah Jl, 1972–. *Recreations:* travelling, reading, doing nothing. *Address:* 1 Gray's Inn Square, WC1R 5AA. *T:* 071–405 8946.

WEISS, Mrs Althea McNish; *see* McNish, A. M.

WEISS, Prof. Nigel Oscar; Professor of Mathematical Astrophysics, since 1987 and Fellow of Clare College, since 1965, Cambridge University; Senior Fellow, Science and Engineering Research Council, 1987–Sept. 1992; *b* 16 Dec. 1936; *s* of Oscar and Molly Weiss; *m* 1968, Judith Elizabeth Martin; one *s* two *d*. *Educ:* Hilton College, Natal; Rugby School; Clare College, Cambridge (MA, PhD). Research Associate, UKAEA Culham Lab., 1962–65; Lectr, Dept of Applied Maths and Theoretical Physics, Cambridge, 1965–79; Reader in Astrophysics, 1979–87. Vis. Prof., Sch. of Math. Scis, QMC, London, 1986–; temporary appointments: MIT; Max Planck Inst. für Astrophysik, Munich; Nat. Solar Observatory, New Mexico; Harvard-Smithsonian Center for Astrophysics. *Publications:* papers on solar and stellar magnetic fields, astrophysical and geophysical fluid dynamics and nonlinear systems. *Recreation:* travel. *Address:* Department of Applied Mathematics and Theoretical Physics, Silver Street, Cambridge CB3 9EW. *T:* Cambridge (0223) 337910; 10 Lansdowne Road, Cambridge CB3 0EU. *T:* Cambridge (0223) 355032.

WEISS, Prof. Robert Anthony, (Robin), PhD; FRCPath; Head, Chester Beatty Laboratories, Institute of Cancer Research, since 1990 (Director, Institute of Cancer Research, 1980–89); *b* 20 Feb. 1940; *s* of Hans Weiss and Stefanie Löwensohn; *m* 1964, Margaret Rose D'Costa; two *d*. *Educ:* University College London (BSc, PhD). Lecturer in Embryology, University Coll. London, 1963–70; Eleanor Roosevelt Internat. Cancer Research Fellow, Univ. of Washington, Seattle, 1970–71; Visiting Associate Prof., Microbiology, Univ. of Southern California, 1971–72; Staff Scientist, Imperial Cancer Research Fund Laboratories, 1972–80, Gustav Stern Award in Virology, 1973. Researching into retroviruses causing leukaemia and AIDS. Hon. MRCP. *Publications:* RNA Tumour Viruses, 1982, 2nd edn (2 vols) 1985; various articles on cell biology, virology and genetics. *Recreations:* music, natural history. *Address:* Institute of Cancer Research, Chester Beatty Laboratories, Fulham Road, SW3 6JB. *T:* 071–352 8133.

WEISSKOPF, Prof. Victor Frederick; Professor of Physics at Massachusetts Institute of Technology, Cambridge, Mass, USA, since 1946 (on leave, 1961–65); Chairman, Department of Physics, MIT, 1967–73; *b* 19 Sept. 1908; *m* 1934, Ellen Margrete Tvede; one *s* one *d*. *Educ:* Göttingen, Germany. PhD 1931. Research Associate: Berlin Univ., 1932; Eidgenossiche Technische Hochschule (Swiss Federal Institute of Technology), Zürich, 1933–35; Inst. for Theoretical Physics, Copenhagen, 1936; Asst Professor of Physics, Univ. of Rochester, NY, USA, 1937–43; Dep. Division Leader, Manhattan Project, Los Alamos, USA, 1943–45; Director-Gen., CERN, Geneva, 1961–65. Chm., High Energy Physics Adv. Panel, AEC, 1967–75. Mem., Nat. Acad. of Sciences, Washington, 1954; Pres., Amer. Acad. of Arts and Sciences, 1976–79; Corresp. Member: French Acad. of Sciences, 1957; Scottish Acad. of Scis, 1959; Royal Danish Scientific Soc., 1961; Bavarian Acad. of Scis, 1962; Austrian Acad. of Scis, 1963; Spanish Acad. of Scis, 1964; Soviet Acad. of Scis, 1976; Pontifical Acad. of Scis, 1976. Hon. Fellow: Weizmann Inst., Rehovot, Israel, 1962; Inst. of Physics, France, 1980. Hon. PhD: Manchester, 1961; Uppsala, 1964; Yale, 1964; Chicago, 1967; Hon. DSc: Montreal, 1959; Sussex, 1961; Lyon, 1962; Basle, 1962; Bonn, 1963; Genève, 1964; Oxford, 1965; Vienna, 1965; Paris, 1966; Copenhagen, 1966; Torino, 1968; Yale, 1968; Upsala, 1969; Harvard, 1984; Graz, 1985. Cherwell-Simon Memorial Lecturer, Oxford, 1963–64. Planck Medal, 1956; Gamov Award, 1969; Prix Mondial Del Duca, 1972; Killian Award, 1973; Smoluchovski Medal, Polish Physical Soc., 1979; Nat. Medal of Science, 1979; Wolf Prize (Israel), 1981; Enrico Fermi Award, 1989. Légion d'Honneur (France), 1959; Pour le Mérite Order, Germany, 1978. *Publications:* Theoretical Nuclear Physics, 1952; Knowledge and Wonder, 1962; Physics in the XX Century, 1972; Concepts of Particle Physics, 1984; The Privilege of Being a Physicist, 1989; papers on theoretical physics in various journals. *Address:* 36 Arlington Street, Cambridge, Mass 02140, USA.

WEISSMÜLLER, Alberto Augusto, FCIB; Representative of Banca Commerciale Italiana, in Washington, DC, since 1983 and in Mexico City, since 1987; *b* 2 March 1927; *s* of late Carlos Weissmüller and Michela Cottura; *m* 1976, Joan Ann Freifrau von Süsskind-Schwendi (*née* Smithson); one *s* one *d* by previous *m*. *Educ:* Univ. of Buenos Aires, Argentina; Illinois Inst. of Technol., Chicago, USA. Civil Engr, 1952; FCIB (FIB 1977). The Lummus Co., New York, 1958–59; Office of Graham Parker, NY, 1960–62; Bankers Trust Co., NY, 1962–71: Edge Act subsid., 1962–64; Asst Treasurer, and Mem., Bd of Corporation Financiera Nacional, Colombia, 1964–65; Asst Vice-Pres., 1965–67; Vice-Pres., 1967–71; Rome Rep., 1968–71; Man. Dir, Bankers Trust Finanziaria, SpA, Rome, 1970–71; Crocker National Bank, San Francisco, seconded to United Internat. Bank (now Privatbanken Ltd), London, as Chief Exec., 1971–79; Chief Adviser, Bank of England, 1979–81; Chief Exec. (UK), Banca Commerciale Italiana, 1981–82; Chm., BCI Ltd, London, 1981–83; Dir, N American Bancorp Inc. (a subsid. of Banca Commerciale Italiana), 1982–87. *Publication:* Castles from the Heart of Spain, 1977. *Recreations:* medieval fortified architecture, photography (architectural). *Address:* Banca Commerciale Italiana, 1133 Twenty-first Street, NW, Washington, DC 20036, USA. *Club:* Board Room (New York).

WEITZ, Dr Bernard George Felix, OBE 1965; DSc; MRCVS; FIBiol; Chief Scientist, Ministry of Agriculture, Fisheries and Food, 1977–81; *b* London, 14 Aug. 1919; *m* 1945, Elizabeth Shine; one *s* one *d*. *Educ:* St Andrew, Bruges, Belgium; Royal Veterinary College, London. MRCVS 1942; DSc London 1961. Temp. Research Worker, ARC Field Station, Compton, Berks, 1942; Research Officer, Veterinary Laboratory, Min. of Agric. and Fisheries, 1942–47; Asst Bacteriologist, Lister Inst. of Preventive Medicine, Elstree, Herts, 1947; Head of Serum Dept, 1952; Dir, Nat. Inst. for Res. in Dairying, Univ. of Reading, Shinfield, Berks, 1967–77. Vis. Prof., Dept of Agriculture and Horticulture, Univ. of Reading, 1980–88. Member: ARC, 1978–81; NERC, 1978–81. Hon. FRASE, 1977. *Publications:* many contribs to scientific journals on Immunology and Tropical Medicine. *Recreations:* music, croquet. *Address:* Grazebrook, Brockhampton, Glos GL54 5XQ.

WEITZMAN, Peter, QC 1973; a Recorder of the Crown Court, since 1974; Leader, Midland and Oxford Circuit, since 1988 (Deputy Leader, 1985–88); *b* 20 June 1926; *s* of late David Weitzman, QC, and Fanny Weitzman; *m* 1954, Anne Mary Larkam; two *s* two *d*. *Educ:* Cheltenham Coll.; Christ Church, Oxford (MA). Royal Artillery, 1945–48. Called to Bar, Gray's Inn, 1952; Bencher, 1981. Mem., Senate of Inns of Court, 1980–81, 1984–. Member: Criminal Injuries Compensation Bd, 1986–; Mental Health Review Tribunal, 1986–. *Recreations:* hedging and ditching. *Address:* 21 St James's Gardens, W11; Little Leigh, Kingsbridge, Devon.

WELANDER, Rev. Canon David Charles St Vincent; Canon Residentiary, Gloucester Cathedral, 1975–91; *b* 22 Jan. 1925; *s* of late Ernest Sven Alexis Welander, Orebro and Uppsala, Sweden, and Louisa Georgina Downes Welander (*née* Panter) *m* 1952, Nancy O'Rorke Stanley; two *s* three *d*. *Educ:* Unthank Coll., Norwich: London Univ. (BD 1947, Rubie Hebrew Prize 1947); ALCD (1st Cl.) 1947; Toronto Univ., 1947–48 (Hon. Mem. Alumni, Wycliffe Coll., 1948). FSA 1981. Deacon 1948, Priest 1949; Asst Curate, Holy Trinity, Norwich, 1948–51; Chaplain and Tutor, London Coll. of Divinity, 1952–56; Vicar: of Iver, Bucks, 1956–62; of Christ Church, Cheltenham, 1963–75; Rural Dean of Cheltenham, 1973–75. Member: Council, St Paul's and St Mary's Colls of Educn, Cheltenham, 1963–78; Council, Malvern Girls' Coll., 1982–; Bishops' Cttee on Inspections of Theol Colls, 1967–81; Sen. Inspector of Theol Colls, 1970–84; Mem., Gen. Synod of C of E, 1970–85; Trustee, Church Patronage Trust, 1969–78. Canon-Librarian of Gloucester, 1975–. *Publications:* History of Iver, 1954; Gloucester Cathedral, 1979; The Stained Glass of Gloucester Cathedral, 1984; Gloucester Cathedral: its history, art and architecture, 1990; contrib. Expository Times, etc. *Recreations:* walking, church architecture, music. *Address:* 1 Sandpits Lane, Sherston Magna, near Malmesbury, Wilts SN16 0NN. *T:* Malmesbury (0666) 840103.

WELBOURN, Prof. Richard Burkewood, MA, MD, FRCS; Professor of Surgical Endocrinology, Royal Postgraduate Medical School, University of London, 1979–82, now Emeritus Professor; *b* 1919; *y s* of late Burkewood Welbourn, MEng, MIEE, and Edith Welbourn, Rainhill, Lancs; *m* 1944, Rachel Mary Haighton, BDS, Nantwich, Cheshire; one *s* four *d*. *Educ:* Rugby School; Emmanuel College, Cambridge; Liverpool University. MB, BChir 1942; FRCS 1948; MA, MD Cambridge, 1953. War of 1939–45: RAMC. Senior Registrar, Liverpool Royal Infirmary, 1948; Research Asst, Dept of Surgery, Liverpool Univ., 1949. Fellow in Surgical Research, Mayo Foundation, Rochester, Minn., 1951. Professor of Surgical Science, Queen's University of Belfast, 1958–63; Surgeon, Royal Victoria Hospital, Belfast, 1951–63 and Belfast City Hosp., 1962–63; Prof. of Surgery, Univ. of London and Dir, Dept of Surgery, RPMS and Hammersmith Hosp., 1963–79; Hon. Consultant Surgeon, Hammersmith Hosp., 1979–82. Consultant Adviser in Surgery to Dept of Health and Social Security, 1971–79; Consultant (Vis. Schol., res. in hist. of Endocrine Surgery), Dept of Surgery, Univ. of California, LA, 1983–89. Member: Council, MRC, 1971–75; Council, Royal Postgraduate Med. Sch, 1963–82. Hunterian Professor, RCS of England, 1958 (James Berry Prize, 1970). Member: Society of Sigma XI; British Medical Association; Internat. Assoc. of Endocrine Surgeons, 1979– (Peter Heimann Lectr, 1989); Internat. Surgical Soc., 1979–; British Soc. of Gastro-enterology and Assoc. of Surgeons; 58th Member King James IV Surgical Association Inc.; Fellow, West African Coll. of Surgeons; FRSM (Former Mem. Council, Section of Endocrinology, former Vice-Pres., Section of Surgery); Hon. Fellow Amer. Surgical Assoc.; Hon. Mem., Soc. for Surgery of the Alimentary Tract; formerly: Pres., Surgical Res. Soc. (Hon. Mem.); British Assoc. of Endocrine Surgeons (Hon. Mem.); Chm., Assoc. of Profs of Surgery; Mem., Jt Cttee for Higher Surgical Training; formerly Examr in Surgery, Univs of Manchester, Glasgow, Oxford, Sheffield, Edinburgh, QUB, and Liverpool; formerly Examr in Applied Physiology, RCS. Chm., Editorial Cttee, Journal of Medical Ethics, 1974–81; former Member: Editorial Cttee, Gut; Exec. Cttee, British Jl of Surgery. Formerly: Pres., Internat. Surgical Gp; Chm. Governing Body, Inst. of Medical Ethics; Pres., Prout Club. Hon. MD Karolinska Inst., Stockholm, 1974; Hon. Mem., Roy. Coll. of Surgeons of Univs of Denmark, 1978; Hon. FACS 1984. Hon. DSc QUB, 1985. *Publications:* (with D. A. D. Montgomery): Clinical Endocrinology for Surgeons, 1963, rev. edn, Medical and Surgical Endocrinology, 1975; (with A. S. Duncan and G. R. Dunstan) Dictionary of Medical Ethics, 1977, 2nd edn 1980, American edn 1981; The History of Endocrine Surgery, 1990; contrib. chaps to Textbook of British Surgery, ed Souttar & Goligher; Surgery of Peptic Ulcer, ed Wells & Kyle; Progress in Clinical Surgery, ed Rodney Smith; British Surgical Practice, ed Rock-Carling & Ross; Scientific Foundations of Surgery, ed Wells & Kyle; Scientific Foundations of Oncology, ed Symington and Carter; Scientific Foundations of Family Medicine, ed Fry, Gambrill & Smith; Surgical Management, ed Taylor, Chisholm, O'Higgins & Shields; Recent Advances in Surgery, etc; papers, mainly on gastro-intestinal and endocrine surgery and physiology, in med. and surg. jls. *Recreations:* reading, writing, gardening, music. *Address:* 2 The Beeches, Elsley Road, Tilehurst, Berks RG3 6RQ; 102 Gloucester Court, Kew Road, Kew, Richmond, Surrey TW9 3DZ.

WELBY, Sir Bruno; *see* Welby, Sir R. B. G.

WELBY, Sir (Richard) Bruno (Gregory), 7th Bt *cr* 1801; *b* 11 March 1928; *s* of Sir Oliver Charles Earle Welby, 6th Bt, TD, and Barbara Angela Mary Lind (*d* 1983), *d* of late John Duncan Gregory, CB, CMG; *S* father, 1977; *m* 1952, Jane Biddulph, *y d* of late Ralph Wilfred Hodder-Williams, MC; three *s* one *d*. *Educ:* Eton; Christ Church, Oxford (BA 1950). *Heir:* *s* Charles William Hodder Welby [*b* 6 May 1953; *m* 1978, Suzanna, *o d* of Major Ian Stuart-Routledge, Harston Hall, Grantham; two *d*]. *Address:* Denton Manor, Grantham, Lincs.

WELBY-EVERARD, Maj.-Gen. Sir Christopher Earle, KBE 1965 (OBE 1945); CB 1961; DL; *b* 9 Aug. 1909; *s* of late E. E. E. Welby-Everard, Gosberton House, near Spalding, Lincolnshire; *m* 1938, Sybil Juliet Wake Shorrock; two *s*. *Educ:* Charterhouse; CCC, Oxford. Gazetted The Lincolnshire Regt, 1930; OC 2 Lincolns, 1944; GSO1, 49 (WR) Inf. Div., 1944–46; GSO1 GHQ, MELF, 1946–48; OC 1 Royal Lincolnshire Regt, 1949–51; Comd 264 Scottish Beach Bde and 157 (L) Inf. Bde, 1954–57. BGS (Ops), HQ, BAOR, and HQ Northern Army Group, 1957–59; Chief of Staff, HQ Allied Forces, Northern Europe, 1959–61; GOC Nigerian Army, 1962–65; retd. DL Lincolnshire, 1966; High Sheriff of Lincolnshire, 1974. *Recreations:* shooting, cricket. *Address:* The Manor House, Sapperton, Sleaford, Lincolnshire NG34 0TB. *T:* Ingoldsby (047685) 273. *Clubs:* Army and Navy; Free Foresters.

WELCH, Anthony Edward, CB 1957; CMG 1949; formerly Under-Secretary, Board of Trade, 1946–66 (Ministry of Materials, 1951–54); *b* 17 July 1906; *s* of late Francis

Bertram Welch; *m* 1946, Margaret Eileen Strudwick (*d* 1978); no *c*. *Educ:* Cheltenham College; New College, Oxford. *Address:* Marlborough House, Southwold, Suffolk IP18 6LR. *T:* Southwold (0502) 724643.

WELCH, Colin; *see* Welch, J. C. R.

WELCH, Air Vice-Marshal Edward Lawrence C.; *see* Colbeck-Welch.

WELCH, (James) Colin (Ross); Columnist and Critic, The Spectator, since 1982; parliamentary sketch writer, Daily Mail, since 1984; *b* 23 April 1924; *s* of James William Welch and Irene Margherita (*née* Paton), Ickleton Abbey, Cambridgeshire; *m* 1950, Sybil Russell; one *s* one *d*. *Educ:* Stowe Sch. (schol.); Peterhouse, Cambridge (major schol., BA Hons). Commissioned Royal Warwickshire Regt, 1942; served NW Europe, twice wounded. Glasgow Herald, 1948; Colonial Office, 1949; Daily Telegraph: leader writer, columnist (Peter Simple, with Michael Wharton), Parliamentary sketch-writer, 1950–64; Dep. Editor, 1964–80; regular column, 1981–83; Editor-in-Chief, Chief Executive magazine, 1980–82. Specialist Writer, British Press Awards, 1986. Knight's Cross, Order of Polonia Restituta, 1972. *Publications:* (ed) Sir Frederick Ponsonby: Recollections of Three Reigns, 1951; (trans. with Sybil Welch) Nestroy: Liberty Comes to Krähwinkel, 1954 (BBC); articles in Encounter, Spectator, New Statesman, American Spectator, etc; contribs to symposia, incl. The Future that Doesn't Work, 1977 (New York). *Address:* 4 Goddard's Lane, Aldbourne, Wilts SN8 2DL. *T:* Marlborough (0672) 40010.

WELCH, John K.; *see* Kemp-Welch.

WELCH, Sir John (Reader), 2nd Bt *cr* 1957; Partner, Wedlake Bell, since 1972; Chairman, John Fairfax (UK) Ltd, 1977–90; *b* 26 July 1933; *s* of Sir (George James) Cullum Welch, 1st Bt, OBE, MC, and Gertrude Evelyn Sladin Welch (*d* 1966); *S* father, 1980; *m* 1962, Margaret Kerry, *o d* of K. Douglass, Killara, NSW; one *s* twin *d*. *Educ:* Marlborough College; Hertford Coll., Oxford (MA). National service in RCS, 1952–54. Admitted a solicitor, 1960. Partner, Bell Brodrick & Gray, 1961–71. Ward Clerk of Walbrook Ward, City of London, 1961–74, Common Councilman, 1975–86 (Chm., Planning and Communications Cttee, 1981, 1982); Registrar of Archdeaconry of London. Liveryman, Haberdashers' Co., 1955 (Court of Assistants, 1973; Master, 1990–91); Freeman, Parish Clerks' Co. (Master, 1967). Chm., Cttee of Management, London Homes for the Elderly, 1980–90. CStJ 1981. *Recreation:* piano. *Heir: s* James Douglass Cullum Welch, *b* 10 Nov. 1973. *Address:* 28 Rivermead Court, Ranelagh Gardens, SW6 3RU; 16 Bedford Street, Covent Garden, WC2E 9HF. *T:* 071–379 7266. *Clubs:* City Livery (Hon. Solicitor, 1983–90, Pres., 1986–87), Walbrook Ward (Chm., 1978–79), Hurlingham, MCC, Surrey County Cricket.

WELCH, Robert Radford, MBE 1979; RDI 1965; FCSD (FSIAD 1962); designer and silversmith, since 1955; *b* 21 May 1929; *m* 1959, Patricia Marguerite Hinksman; two *s* one *d*. *Educ:* Hanley Castle Grammar Sch.; Malvern Sch. of Art; Birmingham Coll. of Art; Royal Coll. of Art (DesRCA). FRSA 1967. Hon. Fellow RCA, 1972. Started own workshop in Chipping Campden, 1955; Design Consultant to Old Hall Tableware, 1955–. Vis. Lecturer: Central Sch. of Art and Design, 1957–63; RCA, 1963–71; visited India by invitation of All India Handicraft Bd, 1975. Silver commns for various clients, incl. civic plate, university colls, Goldsmiths' Hall, Canterbury Cathedral, V&A Museum, and British Govt Gift to St Lucia; tableware for British Ambassador's residence, Manila; British Museum; design commns in Denmark, Germany, USA and Japan. Liveryman, Goldsmiths' Co., 1982. *Publications:* Design in a Cotswold Workshop (with Alan Crawford), 1973; Hand and Machine, 1986. *Recreations:* drawing, painting. *Address:* The White House, Alveston Leys, Alveston, Stratford-on-Avon, Warwicks CV37 7QN. *T:* Stratford-on-Avon (0789) 4191.

WELCH, Rt. Rev. William Neville, MA; *b* 30 April 1906; *s* of Thomas William and Agnes Maud Welch; *m* 1935, Kathleen Margaret Beattie; two *s* two *d*. *Educ:* Dean Close Sch., Cheltenham; Keble Coll., Oxford; Wycliffe Hall, Oxford. Asst Curate: Kidderminster, 1929–32; St Michael's, St Albans, 1932–34; Organising Sec., Missions to Seamen, 1934–39; Vicar of Grays, 1939–43; Officiating Chaplain, Training Ship Exmouth, 1939–40; Vicar of Ilford, 1943–53; Rural Dean of Barking, 1948–53; Vicar of Great Burstead, 1953–56; Archdeacon of Southend, 1953–72; Bishop Suffragan of Bradwell, 1968–73. Proctor in Convocation, 1945 and 1950; Hon. Canon of Chelmsford, 1951–53. *Address:* 112 Earlham Road, Norwich NR2 3HE. *T:* Norwich (0603) 618192.

WELD, Col Sir Joseph William, Kt 1973; OBE 1946; TD 1947 (two Bars); JP; DL; Lord-Lieutenant of Dorset, 1964–84; Chairman, Wessex Regional Health Authority (formerly Wessex Regional Hospital Board), 1972–75; *b* 22 Sept. 1909; *s* of Wilfrid Joseph Weld, Avon Dassett, Warwickshire; *m* 1933, Elizabeth, *d* of E. J. Bellord; one *s* four *d* (and two *d* decd). *Educ:* Stonyhurst; Balliol College, Oxford. Served with Dorset Regt, TA, 1932–41; Staff College, Camberley, 1941; GSO2, General Headquarters Home Forces, 1942; Instructor, Staff College, Camberley, 1942–43; GSO1, Headquarters SEAC, 1943–46; commanded 4th Battalion Dorset Regt, 1947–51; Colonel, 1951. Hon. Colonel, 4th Battalion Dorset Regiment (TA). Chairman of Dorset Branch, County Landowners' Assoc., 1949–60; Chm. S Dorset Conservative Assoc., 1952–55 (Pres., 1955–59); Privy Chamberlain of Sword and Cape to Pope Pius XII. JP 1938, High Sheriff 1951, DL 1952, CC 1961, Dorset. KStJ 1967. *Address:* Lulworth Manor, East Lulworth, Dorset. *T:* West Lulworth (092941) 2352. *Club:* Royal Dorset Yacht.

WELD FORESTER, family name of **Baron Forester.**

WELDON, Sir Anthony (William), 9th Bt *cr* 1723; *b* 11 May 1947; *s* of Sir Thomas Brian Weldon, 8th Bt, and of Marie Isobel (now Countess Cathcart), *d* of Hon. William Joseph French; *S* father, 1979; *m* 1980, Mrs Amanda Wigan, *d* of Major Geoffrey and Hon. Mrs North; two *d*. *Educ:* Sherborne. Formerly Lieutenant, Irish Guards. *Recreations:* stalking, fishing, antiquarian books, champagne. *Heir: cousin* Kevin Nicholas Weldon [*b* 19 April 1951; *m* 1973, Catherine Main; one *s*]. *Clubs:* White's, Stranded Whales.

WELDON, Duncan Clark; theatrical producer; Chairman and Managing Director, Triumph Proscenium (formerly Triumph Theatre) Productions Ltd; *b* 19 March 1941; *s* of Clarence Weldon and Margaret Mary Andrew; *m* 1973, Janet Mahoney; one *d*. *Educ:* King George V School, Southport. Formerly a photographer; first stage production, A Funny Kind of Evening, with David Kossoff, Theatre Royal, Bath, 1965; co-founder, Triumph Theatre Productions, 1970; Director: Theatre Royal Haymarket Ltd; Strand Theatre; Triumph Proscenium Productions Ltd; Duncan C. Weldon Productions Ltd. First London production,Tons of Money, Mayfair Theatre, 1969; 150 productions in the West End: When We are Married, 1970; The Chalk Garden, Big Bad Mouse, The Wizard of Oz, 1971; Lord Arthur Savile's Crime, Bunny, The Wizard of Oz, 1972; Mother Adam, Grease, The King and I, 1973; Dead Easy, 1974; The Case in Question, Hedda Gabler, Dad's Army, Betzi, On Approval, 1975; 13 Rue de l'Amour, A Bedful of Foreigners, Three Sisters, The Seagull, Fringe Benefits, The Circle, 1976; Separate Tables, Stevie, Hedda Gabler, On Approval, The Good Woman of Setzuan, Rosmersholm, Laburnum Grove, The Apple Cart, 1977; Waters of the Moon, Kings and Clowns, The Travelling Music Show, A Family, Look After Lulu, The Millionairess, 1978; The Crucifer of Blood, 1979; Reflections, Rattle of a Simple Man, The Last of Mrs Cheyney, Early Days, 1980; Virginia, Overheard, Dave Allen, Worzel Gummidge, 1981; Murder In Mind, Hobson's Choice, A Coat of Varnish, Captain Brassbound's Conversion, Design for Living, Uncle Vanya, Key for Two, The Rules of the Game, Man and Superman, 1982; The School for Scandal, DASH, Heartbreak House, Call Me Madam, Romantic Comedy, Liza Minelli, Beethoven's Tenth, Edmund Kean, Fiddler on the Roof, A Patriot for Me, Cowardice, Great and Small, The Cherry Orchard, Dial 'M' for Murder, Dear Anyone, The Sleeping Prince, The School for Scandal, Hi-De-Hi!, 1983; Hello, Dolly!, The Aspern Papers, Strange Interlude, Serjeant Musgrave's Dance, Aren't We All?, American Buffalo, The Way of the World, Extremities, 1984; The Wind in the Willows, The Lonely Road, The Caine Mutiny Court-Martial, Other Places, Old Times, The Corn is Green, Waste, Strippers, Guys and Dolls, Sweet Bird of Youth, Interpreters, Fatal Attraction, The Scarlet Pimpernel, 1985; The Apple Cart, Across From the Garden of Allah, Antony and Cleopatra, The Taming of the Shrew, Circe and Bravo, Annie Get Your Gun, Long Day's Journey Into Night, Rookery Nook, Breaking the Code, Mr and Mrs Nobody, 1986; A Piece of My Mind, Court in the Act!, Canaries Sometimes Sing, Kiss Me Kate, Melon, Portraits, Groucho: a Life In Review, A Man for All Seasons, You Never Can Tell, Babes in the Wood, 1987; A Touch of the Poet, The Deep Blue Sea, The Admirable Crichton, The Secret of Sherlock Holmes, A Walk in the Woods, Richard II, Orpheus Descending, 1988; Richard III, The Royal Baccarat Scandal, Ivanov, Much Ado About Nothing, The Merchant of Venice, Veterans Day, Another Time, The Baker's Wife, London Assurance, 1989; Salome, Bent, An Evening with Peter Ustinov, Wild Duck, Henry IV, Kean, Love Letters, Time and the Conways, 1990; The Homecoming, The Philanthropist, The Caretaker, Becket, Tovarich, The Cabinet Minister, 1991; presented on Broadway: Brief Lives, 1974; Edmund Kean, Heartbreak House, 1983; Beethoven's Tenth, 1984; Strange Interlude, Aren't We All?, 1985; Wild Honey, 1986; Blithe Spirit, Pygmalion, Breaking the Code, 1987; Orpheus Descending, The Merchant of Venice, 1989; has also presented in Europe, Australia, Canada and Hong Kong. *Address:* Brackenhill, Munstead Park, near Godalming, Surrey. *T:* Godalming (0483) 415508.

WELDON, Fay; writer; *b* 22 Sept. 1931; *d* of Frank Birkinshaw and Margaret Jepson; *m* Ron Weldon; four *s*. *Educ:* Hampstead Girls' High Sch.; St Andrews Univ. Has written or adapted numerous television and radio plays, dramatizations, and series, and nine stage plays. Chm. of Judges, Booker McConnell Prize, 1983. *Libretto:* A Small Green Space, 1989. *Publications:* The Fat Woman's Joke, 1967; Down Among the Women, 1972; Female Friends, 1975; Remember Me, 1976; Little Sisters, 1977 (as Words of Advice, NY, 1977); Praxis, 1978 (Booker Prize Nomination); Puffball, 1980; Watching Me, Watching You (short stories), 1981; The President's Child, 1982; The Life and Loves of a She-Devil, 1984 (televised, 1986; filmed as She-Devil, 1990); Letters to Alice—on First Reading Jane Austen, 1984; Polaris and other Stories, 1985; Rebecca West, 1985; The Shrapnel Academy, 1986; Heart of the Country, 1987 (televised, 1987); The Hearts and Lives of Men, 1987; The Rules of Life, 1987; Leader of the Band, 1988; (for children) Wolf the Mechanical Dog, 1989; The Cloning of Joanna May, 1989; (for children) Party Puddle, 1989; Darcy's Utopia, 1990; (contrib.) Storia 4: Green, 1990; Moon over Minneapolis or Why She Couldn't Stay (short stories), 1991. *Address:* c/o Giles Gordon, Anthony Sheil Associates, 43 Doughty Street, WC1N 2LF; c/o Casarotto Co. Ltd, National House, 62/66 Wardour Street, W1V 3HP.

WELENSKY, Rt. Hon. Sir Roy, (Roland), PC 1960; KCMG 1959 (CMG 1946); Kt 1953; *b* Salisbury, Southern Rhodesia, 20 January 1907; *s* of Michael and Leah Welensky; *m* 1st, 1928, Elizabeth Henderson (*d* 1969); one *s* one *d*; 2nd, 1972, Valerie Scott; two *d*. *Educ:* Salisbury, S Rhodesia. Joined Railway service, 1924; Member National Council of the Railway Workers Union; Director of Manpower, Northern Rhodesia, 1941–46; formed N Rhodesia Labour Party, 1941; Member of Sir John Forster's commission to investigate the 1940 riots in Copperbelt; Chairman of various conciliation Boards and member of the Strauss (1943) and Grant (1946) Railway Arbitration Tribunals. Member of delegn to London to discuss Mineral Royalties (1949) and Constitution (1950 and 1951); Member of Northern Rhodesia delegation to Closer Association Conference at Victoria Falls, 1951. MLC, N Rhodesia, 1938, MEC 1940–53. Chm. Unofficial Members Assoc. 1946–53. Federation of Rhodesia and Nyasaland: Minister of Transport, Communications and Posts, 1953–56; Leader of the House and Deputy Prime Minister, 1955–56; Prime Minister and Minister of External Affairs, 1956–63 (also Minister of Defence, 1956–59). Heavy-weight boxing champion of the Rhodesias, 1926–28. *Publication:* Welensky's 4000 Days, The Life and Death of the Federation of Rhodesia and Nyasaland, 1964; *relevant publications:* The Rhodesian, by Don Taylor; Welensky's Story, by Garry Allighan; The Welensky Papers, by Dr J. R. T. Wood. *Recreation:* gardening. *Address:* Shaftesbury House, Milldown Road, Blandford Forum, Dorset DT11 7DE. *Club:* Farmers'.

WELLAND, Colin, (Colin Williams); actor, playwright; *b* 4 July 1934; *s* of John Arthur Williams and Norah Williams; *m* 1962, Patricia Sweeney; one *s* three *d*. *Educ:* Newton-le-Willows Grammar Sch.; Bretton Hall Coll.; Goldsmiths' Coll., London (Teacher's Dip. in Art and Drama). Art teacher, 1958–62; entered theatre, 1962; Library Theatre, Manchester, 1962–64; television, films, theatre, 1962–. Films (actor): Kes; Villain; Straw Dogs; Sweeney; (original screenplay): Yanks, 1978; Chariots of Fire, 1980 (won Oscar, Evening Standard and Broadcasting Press Guild Awards, 1982); Twice in a Lifetime, 1986; A Dry White Season, 1989. Plays (author): Say Goodnight to Grandma, St Martin's, 1973; Roll on Four O'clock, Palace, 1981. Award winning TV plays include: Roll on Four O'clock, Kisses at 50, Leeds United, Jack Point, Your Man from Six Counties. Best TV Playwright, Writers Guild, 1970, 1973 and 1974; Best TV Writer, and Best Supporting Film Actor, BAFTA Awards, 1970; Broadcasting Press Guild Award (for writing), 1973. *Publications:* Northern Humour, 1982; plays: Roomful of Holes, 1972; Say Goodnight to Grandma, 1973. *Recreations:* sport, theatre, cinema, politics, dining out. *Address:* c/o Peters, Fraser & Dunlop, 5th Floor, The Chambers, Chelsea Harbour, Lots Road, SW10 0XF.

WELLBELOVED, James; Commercial Consultant; writer and broadcaster on foreign and domestic affairs; Director General, National Kidney Research Fund, since 1985; *b* 29 July 1926; *s* of Wilfred Henry Wellbeloved, Sydenham and Brockley (London), and Paddock Wood, Kent; *m* 1948, Mavis Beryl Ratcliff; two *s* one *d*. *Educ:* South East London Technical College. Boy seaman, 1942–46. Contested (SDP/Alliance) Erith and Crayford, 1987. MP (Lab 1965–81, SDP 1981–83) Erith and Crayford, Nov. 1965–1983; Parly Private Secretary: Minister of Defence (Admin), 1967–69; Sec. of State for Foreign and Commonwealth Affairs, 1969–70; an Opposition Whip, 1972–74; Parly Under-Sec. of State for Defence (RAF), MoD, 1976–79. UK Rep., North Atlantic Assembly, 1972–76, 1979–82. Dep. Chm., London MPs Parly Gp, 1970–81; Chairman: River Thames Gp; All Party Parly Camping and Caravanning Gp, 1967–74; Nat. Whitley Council, MoD, 1976–79; Member: Ecclesiastical Cttee, 1971–76; RACS Political Purposes Cttee, 1973–83; PLP Liaison Cttee, 1974–78; Defence Council, 1976–79; Unrelated Live Transplant Regulatory Authority, 1990–; Vice Chm., Labour Party Defence Gp, 1970–81. Contested, 1983, Prospective Parly Cand., 1985 (SDP) Erith and Crayford. Dir, Assoc. of Former MPs, 1983–. Nat. Vice-Pres., Camping and Caravanning Club, 1974–. Former

Governor, Greenwich Hosp. Sch. *Publication:* Local Government, 1971. *Recreations:* camping, travel. *Address:* Craigdon House, Lesney Park, Erith, Kent DA8 3DS.

WELLBY, Rear-Adm. Roger Stanley, CB 1958; DSO 1940; DL; Retired; lately Head of UK Services Liaison Staff in Australia and Senior Naval Adviser to UK High Commissioner, 1956–59; *b* 28 Apr. 1906; *o s* of Dr Stanley Wellby and Marian Schwann; *m* 1936, Elaine, *d* of late Sir Clifford Heathcote-Smith; three *s. Educ:* RNC, Dartmouth. Qualified as Torpedo Officer, 1931; Commander, 1939; Special Service in France, 1940 (DSO, Croix de Guerre); Captain, 1947; Imperial Defence College; Rear-Adm. 1956. Dep. Comr-in-Chief, St John Ambulance Brigade, 1963–71; Comr, St John Ambulance Brigade, Bucks, 1971–75. DL Bucks 1972. KStJ 1966. *Recreation:* hockey, for Navy. *Address:* Oakengrove, Hastoe, Tring HP23 6LY. *T:* Tring (044282) 3233.

WELLER, Dr Thomas Huckle; Richard Pearson Strong Professor of Tropical Public Health, Harvard University, 1954–85, Emeritus 1985 (Head, Department of Tropical Public Health, 1954–81); Director Center for Prevention of Infectious Diseases, Harvard School of Public Health, 1966–81; *b* 15 June 1915; *s* of Carl V. and Elsie H. Weller; *m* 1945, Kathleen R. Fahey; two *s* two *d. Educ:* University of Michigan (AB, MS); Harvard (MD). Fellow, Departments of Comparative Pathology and Tropical Medicine and Bacteriology, Harvard Medical School, 1940–41; Intern, Children's Hosp., Boston, 1941–42. Served War, 1942–45: 1st Lieut to Major, Medical Corps, US Army. Asst Resident in Medicine, Children's Hosp., 1946; Fellow, Pediatrics, Harvard Medical School, 1947; Instructor, Dept Tropical Public Health, Harvard School of Public Health, 1948; Assistant Professor, 1949; Associate Professor, 1950. Asst Director, Research Div. of Infectious Diseases, Children's Medical Center, Boston, 1949–55; Dir, Commission on Parasitic Diseases, Armed Forces Epidemiological Bd, 1953–59, Mem. 1959–72; Mem. Trop. Med. and parasitology study sect., US Public Health Service, 1953–56. Diplomate, American Board of Pediatrics, 1948; Amer. Acad. of Arts and Sciences, 1955; National Academy of Sciences, USA. Consultant on tropical medicine and infectious diseases to foundations and industries, 1985–. Hon. FRSTM&H, 1987. Hon. LLD Michigan, 1956; Hon. DSc: Gustavus Adolphus Coll., 1975; Univ. of Mass Med. Sch., 1986; Hon. LHD Lowell, 1977. Mead Johnson Award of Amer. Acad. of Pediatrics (jointly), 1954; Kimble Methodology Award (jointly), 1954; Nobel Prize Physiology or Medicine (jointly), 1954; Ledlie Prize, 1963; United Cerebral Palsy Weinstein-Goldenson Award, 1974; Bristol Award, Infectious Diseases Soc. of America, 1980. *Publications:* numerous scientific papers on *in vitro* cultivation of viruses and on helminth infections of man. *Recreations:* gardening, photography. *Address:* 56 Winding River Road, Needham, Mass 02192, USA. *Club:* Harvard (Boston).

WELLER, Walter; Principal Conductor and Music Director, Royal Scottish Orchestra, since 1992; Principal Guest Conductor, National Orchestra of Spain, since 1987; *b* 30 Nov. 1939; *s* of Walter and Anna Weller; *m* 1966, Elisabeth Samohyl; one *s. Educ:* Realgymnasium, Vienna; Akademie für Musik, Vienna (degree for violin and piano). Founder of Weller Quartet, 1958–69; Member, Vienna Philharmonic, 1958–69. First Leader, 1960–69; Conductor, Vienna State Opera, 1969–75; Guest Conductor with all main European and American Orchestras, also in Japan and Israel, 1973–; Chief Conductor, Tonkünstler Orch., Vienna, 1974–77; Principal Conductor and Artistic Adviser, Royal Liverpool Philharmonic Orch., 1977–80, Guest Conductor Laureate, 1980–; Principal Conductor, RPO, 1980–85. Many recordings (Grand Prix du disque Charles Cros). Medal of Arts and Sciences, Austria, 1968. *Recreations:* magic, model railway, sailing, swimming, stamp-collecting, ski-ing. *Address:* c/o Harrison-Parrott Ltd, 12 Penzance Place, W11 4PA.

WELLESLEY, family name of **Earl Cowley** and of **Duke of Wellington.**

WELLESLEY, Julian Valerian; Chairman, Eastbourne District Health Authority, since 1990 (Member, since 1986); *b* 9 Aug. 1933; *s* of late Gerald Valerian Wellesley, MC, and Elizabeth Thornton Harvey; *m* 1965, Elizabeth Joan Hall; one *s* one *d*; three step *d. Educ:* Royal Naval Colleges, Dartmouth (schol.) and Greenwich. Royal Navy, 1947–61: America and West Indies, 1955–56; Far East, 1957–58; Navigation Specialist, 1959. Joined Charles Barker, 1961: a Dir, 1963; Dep. Chm., 1975; Chm., Charles Barker Group, 1978–83; Consultant, TSB Gp, 1984; Director: Horizon Travel, 1984–87; Chatsworth Food Ltd, 1986–90; E. & R. Garrould Ltd, 1988–90. Cttee Mem., Assoc. of Lloyd's Mems, 1985–91. Vice-Chm., Wealden Cons. Assoc., 1988–91. *Recreations:* family, music, reading, playing tennis, watching cricket. *Address:* Tidebrook Manor, Wadhurst, Sussex TN5 6PD. *Clubs:* Brooks's; Sussex.

WELLINGS, Sir Jack (Alfred), Kt 1975; CBE 1970; Chairman, 1968–87, Managing Director, 1963–84, The 600 Group Ltd; Chairman: On Line Business and Scientific Systems Ltd, since 1984; Craigmore House Ltd, since 1985; *b* 16 Aug. 1917; *s* of Edward Josiah and Selina Wellings; *m* 1946, Greta, *d* of late George Tidey; one *s* two *d. Educ:* Selhurst Grammar Sch.; London Polytechnic. Vice-Pres., Hawker Siddeley (Canada) Ltd, 1954–62; Dep. Man. Dir, 600 Group Ltd, 1962. Member: NCB, 1971–77; NEB, 1977–79; part-time Mem., British Aerospace, 1980–87; non-exec. Dir, Clausing Corp., USA, 1982–84. *Address:* Boundary Meadow, Collum Green Road, Stoke Poges, Bucks SL2 4BB. *T:* Fulmer (02816) 2978.

WELLINGS, Victor Gordon, QC 1973; President of the Lands Tribunal, since 1989 (Member, since 1973); Deputy Judge of the High Court, since 1975; *b* 19 July 1919; *e s* of late Gordon Arthur Wellings, solicitor, and Alice Adelaide Wellings (now Mrs Alice Adelaide Poole); *m* 1948, Helen Margaret Jill Lovell; three *s. Educ:* Reading Sch.; Exeter Coll., Oxford (MA). Called to Bar, Gray's Inn, 1949; practised 1949–73. War service, 1940–46; Captain Indian Army, 17th Dogra Regt; Intell. Corps, India; Captain, TARO, 1949–. *Publications:* Editor, Woodfall, The Law of Landlord and Tenant, 28th edn, 1978 (Jt Editor 26th and 27th edns, 1963 and 1968), and other works on same subject. *Recreations:* golf, fishing. *Address:* Cherry Tree Cottage, Whitchurch Hill, Pangbourne, Berks RG8 7PT. *T:* Pangbourne (0734) 842918. *Club:* United Oxford & Cambridge University.

WELLINGTON, 8th Duke of, *cr* 1814; **Arthur Valerian Wellesley,** KG 1990; LVO 1952; OBE 1957; MC 1941; DL; Baron Mornington, 1746; Earl of Mornington, Viscount Wellesley, 1760; Viscount Wellington of Talavera and Wellington, Somersetshire, Baron Douro, 1809; Earl of Wellington, Feb. 1812; Marquess of Wellington, Oct. 1812; Marquess Douro, 1814; Prince of Waterloo, 1815, Netherlands; Count of Vimeiro, Marquess of Torres Vedras and Duke of Victoria in Portugal; Duke of Ciudad Rodrigo and a Grandee of Spain, 1st class; *b* 2 July 1915; *s* of 7th Duke of Wellington, KG, and Dorothy Violet (*d* 1956), *d* of Robert Ashton, Croughton, Cheshire; *S* father, 1972; *m* 1944, Diana Ruth, *o d* of Maj.-Gen. D. F. McConnel; four *s* one *d. Educ:* Eton; New Coll., Oxford. Served War of 1939–45 in Middle East (MC), CMF and BLA. Lt-Col Comdg Royal Horse Guards, 1954–58; Silver Stick-in-Waiting and Lt-Col Comdg the Household Cavalry, 1959–60; Comdr 22nd Armoured Bde, 1960–61; Comdr RAC 1st (Br.) Corps, 1962–64; Defence Attaché, Madrid, 1964–67, retired; Col-in-Chief, The Duke of Wellington's Regt, 1974–; Hon. Col 2nd Bn, The Wessex Regt, 1974–80. Director: Massey Ferguson Holdings Ltd, 1967–89; Massey Ferguson Ltd, 1973–84. President: Game Conservancy, 1976–81 (Dep. Pres., 1981–87); SE Branch, Royal British Legion, 1978; BSJA, 1980–82; Rare Breeds Survival Trust, 1984–87; Council for Environmental Conservation, 1983–87; Atlantic Salmon Trust, 1983–. Vice-Pres., Zool Soc. of London, 1983–89; Mem. Council, RASE, 1976–85. HM's Rep. Trustee, Bd of Royal Armouries, 1983–; Trustee, WWF (UK), 1985–90. Hampshire CC 1967–74; DL Hants, 1975. Governor of Wellington Coll., 1964–; Chm., Pitt Club. OStJ. Officier, Légion d'Honneur (France); Kt Grand Cross: Order of St Michael of the Wing (Portugal), 1984; Order of Isabel the Catholic (Spain), 1986. *Heir: s* Marquess of Douro, *qv. Address:* Stratfield Saye House, Basingstoke, Hants RG27 0AS; Apsley House, 149 Piccadilly, W1V 9FA. *Club:* Buck's.

WELLINGTON (NZ), Archbishop of, (RC), since 1979; **His Eminence Cardinal Thomas Stafford Williams,** DD; Metropolitan of New Zealand; *b* 20 March 1930; *s* of Thomas Stafford Williams and Lillian Maude Kelly. *Educ:* Holy Cross Primary School, Miramar; SS Peter and Paul Primary School, Lower Hutt; St Patrick's Coll., Wellington; Victoria University Coll., Wellington; St Kevin's Coll., Oamaru; Holy Cross Coll., Mosgiel; Collegio Urbano de Propaganda Fide, Rome (STL); University Coll., Dublin (BSocSc); Hon. DD. Assistant Priest, St Patrick's Parish, Palmerston North, 1963–64; Director of Studies, Catholic Enquiry Centre, Wellington, 1965–70; Parish Priest: St Anne's Parish, Leulumoega, W Samoa, 1971–75; Holy Family Parish, Porirua, NZ, 1976–79. Cardinal, 1983. *Address:* Viard, 21 Eccleston Hill, Wellington 1, New Zealand. *T:* 4961 795.

WELLINGTON (NZ), Bishop of; *see* New Zealand, Primate and Archbishop of.

WELLINGTON, Peter Scott, CBE 1981; DSC; PhD; ARCS; FLS; FIBiol; FRAgS; Director, National Institute of Agricultural Botany, 1970–81; *b* 20 March 1919; *er s* of late Robert Wellington, MBE, MC; *m* 1947, Kathleen Joyce, *widow* of E. H. Coombe; one *s* one *d. Educ:* Kelly Coll.; Imperial Coll. of Science. BSc 1946. Observer, Fleet Air Arm, 1940–45 (Lt-Comdr (A) RNVR). Research Asst 1948–52, Chief Officer 1953–61, Official Seed Testing Stn for England and Wales; Asst Dir 1961–68, Dep. Dir 1968–69, Nat. Inst. of Agricultural Botany. Vice-Pres., Internat. Seed Testing Assoc., 1953–56 (Chm. Germination Cttee, 1956–70); Chief Officer, UK Variety Classification Unit, 1965–70; Chm., Technical Working Group, Internat. Convention for Protection of Plant Varieties, 1966–68; Mem., Governing Body, Nat. Seed Develt Orgn Ltd, 1982–87. *Publications:* papers on germination of cereals and weeds, seed-testing and seed legislation. *Recreations:* gardening, walking, reading. *Address:* Colescus, Gorran Haven, St Austell, Cornwall. *T:* Mevagissey (0726) 842065.

WELLS, Dean of; *see* Lewis, Very Rev. R.

WELLS, Archdeacon of; *see* Thomas, Ven. C. E.

WELLS, Dr Alan Arthur, OBE 1982; FRS 1977; FEng 1978; Director-General, The Welding Institute, 1977–88; *s* of Arthur John Wells and Lydia Wells; *m* 1950, Rosemary Edith Alice Mitchell; four *s* one *d. Educ:* City of London Sch.; Univ. of Nottingham (BScEng); Clare Coll., Cambridge (PhD). MIMechE, Hon. FWeldI. British Welding Res. Association: Asst Dir, 1956; Dep. Dir (Scientific), 1963; Queen's Univ. of Belfast: Prof. of Struct. Science, 1964; Head of Civil Engrg Dept, 1970–77; Dean, Faculty of Applied Science and Technol., 1973–76. MRIA 1976. Hon. Dr, Faculty of Engrg, Univ. of Gent, 1972; Hon. DSc Glasgow, 1982; Hon. DScEng QUB, 1986. *Publications:* Brittle Fracture of Welded Plate (jtly), 1967; res. papers on welding technol. and fracture mechanics. *Recreation:* handyman about the house and garden. *Address:* The Welding Institute, Abington Hall, Abington, Cambs CB1 6AL. *T:* Cambridge (0223) 891162. *Club:* Athenæum.

WELLS, Bowen; MP (C) Hertford and Stortford, since 1983 (Hertford and Stevenage, 1979–83); *b* 4 Aug. 1935; *s* of Reginald Laird Wells and Agnes Mary Wells (*née* Hunter); 1975, Rennie Heyde; two *s. Educ:* St Paul's School; Univ. of Exeter (BA Hons); Regent St Polytechnic School of Management (Dip. Business Management). National Service, RN (promoted to Sub Lt), 1954–56. Schoolmaster, Colet Court, 1956–57; sales trainee, British Aluminium, 1957–58; Univ. of Exeter, 1958–61; Commonwealth Development Corporation, 1961–73: Personal Asst to Regional Controller and Ind. Relations Manager, 1962–65; Company Sec. and Ind. Relations Manager, Guyana Timbers, 1965–67; Manager, Guyana Housing and Develt Co., Guyana Mortgage Finance Co. and Cane Farming Develt Corp., 1967–71; Sen. Exec. for Subsidiary and Associated Develt Finance Co., 1971–73; Owner Manager, Substation Group Services Ltd, 1973–79. PPS to Min. of State for Employment, 1982–83. Member: For. Affairs Select Cttee, 1981–; European Legislation Select Cttee, 1983–; Chairman: UN Parly Gp, 1983–; British-Caribbean Gp; Jt Hon. Sec., Parly Cons. Trade and Industry Gp, 1984–91 (Vice-Chm., 1983–84); Sec., All Party Overseas Develt Gp., 1984–; Sec., Cons. Envmt Cttee, 1991–; Mem., British-American Gp, 1985. Mem., UK Br. Exec., CPA, 1984–. Trustee, Industry and Parlt Trust, 1985–. Gov., Inst. of Development Studies, 1980–. *Recreations:* music, walking, gardening cooking, sailing. *Address:* House of Commons, SW1A 0AA. *T:* 071–219 5154.

WELLS, Brigid; *see* Wells, J. B. E.

WELLS, Sir Charles Maltby, 2nd Bt *cr* 1944; TD 1960; *b* 24 July 1908; *e s* of 1st Bt, and Mary Dorothy Maltby (*d* 1956); *S* father, 1956; *m* 1935, Katharine Boulton, *d* of Frank Boteler Kenrick, Toronto; two *s. Educ:* Bedford School; Pembroke College, Cambridge. Joined RE (TA), 1933; Capt. 1939; served War of 1939–45: 54th (EA) Div., 1939–41; Lt-Col 1941; 76th Div., 1941–43; British Army Staff, Washington, 1943–45. *Heir: s* Christopher Charles Wells [*b* 12 Aug. 1936; *m* 1st, 1960, Elizabeth Florence Vaughan (marr. diss. 1983), *d* of I. F. Griffiths, Outremont, Quebec; two *s* two *d*; 2nd, 1985, Lynda Anne Cormack; one *s*]. *Address:* Apt 507, 350 Lonsdale Road, Toronto, Ont, Canada.

WELLS, Prof. David Arthur; Professor of German, Birbeck College, University of London, since 1987; *b* 26 April 1941; *s* of Arthur William Wells and Rosina Elizabeth (*née* Jones). *Educ:* Christ's Hosp., Horsham; Gonville and Caius Coll., Cambridge; Univs of Strasbourg, Vienna and Münster. Mod. and Med. Langs Tripos, BA 1963, Tiarks Studentship 1963–64, MA, PhD Cantab 1967. Asst Lectr 1966–67, Lectr 1967–69, in German, Univ. of Southampton; Lectr in German, Bedford Coll., Univ. of London, 1969–74; Sec., London Univ. Bd of Staff Examiners in German, 1973–74; Tutor, Nat. Extension Coll., Cambridge, 1966–74; Prof. of German, QUB, 1974–87. Lecture tour of NZ univs, 1975. Mem., Managing Body, Oakington Manor Jun. Mixed and Infant Sch., London Bor. of Brent, 1972–74; Hon. Sec., Mod. Humanities Res. Assoc., 1969–; Hon. Treas., Assoc. for Literary and Linguistic Computing, 1973–78; Sec.-Gen., Internat. Fedn for Modern Langs and Lits, 1981–. Editor, MHRA Ann. Bull. of Modern Humanities Research Assoc., 1969–; Jt Editor, The Year's Work in Modern Language Studies, 1976– (Editor, 1982). FRSA 1983. *Publications:* The Vorau Moses and Balaam: a study of their relationship to exegetical tradition, 1970; The Wild Man from the Epic of Gilgamesh to Hartmann von Aue's Iwein, 1975; A Complete Concordance to the Vorauer Bücher Moses (Concordances to the Early Middle High German Biblical Epic), 1976; contribs to MHRA Style Book: Notes for Authors and Editors, 1971, 3rd edn 1981; articles, monographs and reviews in learned jls. *Recreations:* travel, theatre, music. *Address:*

Department of German, Birkbeck College, 43 Gordon Square, WC1H 0PD. *T:* 071–631 6103; 128 Belgrave Road, SW1. *T:* 071–834 6558.

WELLS, David George; Regional Chairman, British Gas plc, South Eastern, since 1988; *b* 6 Aug. 1941; *s* of George Henry Wells and Marian (*née* Trolley); *m* 1967, Patricia Ann Fenwick; two *s*. *Educ:* Market Harborough Grammar Sch.; Reading Univ. (BA). FCA 1966. Hancock, Gilbert & Morris, 1962–67; Esso Chemical Ltd, 1967–69; joined Gas Council, 1969; Investment Accountant (Investment Appraisal), 1970–73; British Gas Corporation: Chief Accountant, Admin, 1973–76; Chief Investment Accountant, 1976; Dir of Finance, SE Reg., 1976–83; Dep. Chm., W Midlands Reg., 1983–88. Director: Metrogas Bldg Soc., 1978–86 (Dep. Chm., 1979–83); Port Greenwich Ltd, 1989–. Chm., S London Trng and Enterprise Council, 1989–. CIGasE 1988; CBIM 1990. *Recreations:* walking, reading, photography, gardening. *Address:* British Gas plc South Eastern, Katharine Street, Croydon, Surrey CR9 1JU. *T:* 081–688 4466.

WELLS, Doreen Patricia, (Marchioness of Londonderry); dancer and actress; Ballerina of the Royal Ballet, 1955–74; *m* 9th Marquess of Londonderry, *qv*; two *s*. *Educ:* Walthamstow; Bush Davies School; Royal Ballet School. Engaged in Pantomime, 1952 and 1953. Joined Royal Ballet, 1955; became Principal Dancer, 1960; has danced leading roles in Noctambules, Harlequin in April, Dance Concertante, Sleeping Beauty, Coppelia, Swan Lake, Sylvia, La Fille mal Gardée, Two Pigeons, Giselle, Invitation, Rendezvous, Blood Wedding, Raymonda, Concerto, Nutcracker, Romeo and Juliet, Concerto No 2 (Ballet Imperial); has created leading roles in Toccata, La Création du Monde, Sinfonietta, Prometheus, Grand Tour; now playing leading roles in musical shows. Adeline Genée Gold Medal, 1954. *Recreations:* classical music, reading, theatre-going, aikido.

WELLS, Prof. George Albert, MA, BSc, PhD; Professor of German, Birkbeck College, University of London, 1968–88, now Emeritus; *b* 22 May 1926; *s* of George John and Lilian Maud Wells; *m* 1969, Elisabeth Delhey. *Educ:* University College London (BA, MA German; PhD Philosophy; BSc Geology). Lecturer in German, 1949–64, Reader in German, 1964–68, University Coll. London. Hon. Associate, Rationalist Press Assoc., 1989 (Dir, 1974–89). Mem., Acad. of Humanism, 1983– (Humanist Laureate, 1983). *Publications:* Herder and After, 1959; The Plays of Grillparzer, 1969; The Jesus of the Early Christians, 1971; Did Jesus Exist?, 1975, 2nd edn 1986; Goethe and the Development of Science 1750–1900, 1978; The Historical Evidence for Jesus, 1982; The Origin of Language: aspects of the discussion from Condillac to Wundt, 1987; (ed and contrib.) J. M. Robertson (1856–1933), Liberal, Rationalist and Scholar, 1987; Religious Postures, 1988; Who Was Jesus? a critique of the New Testament record, 1989; articles in Jl of History of Ideas, Jl of English and Germanic Philology, German Life and Letters, Question, Trivium, Wirkendes Wort. *Recreation:* walking. *Address:* 35 St Stephen's Avenue, St Albans, Herts AL3 4AA. *T:* St Albans (0727) 51347.

WELLS, Lt-Col Herbert James, CBE 1958; MC 1918; FCA 1934; JP; DL; *b* 27 March 1897; *s* of late James J. Wells, NSW; *m* 1926, Rose Hamilton (*d* 1983), *d* of late H. D. Brown, Bournemouth; no *c*. *Educ:* NSW. Chartered Accountant; Consultant (formerly Sen. Partner), Amsdon Cossart & Wells. Surrey CC: Alderman, 1960; Vice-Chm., 1959–62; Chm., 1962–65. JP Surrey 1952 (Chm., Magistrates' Ct, Wallington, 1960–70); DL 1962, High Sheriff 1965, Surrey. A General Comr for Income Tax. Freeman, City of London. Former Pres. Brit. Red Cross, Carshalton and Sutton Division; former Member, Surrey T&AFA, retired 1968; Chairman, Queen Mary's Hospital for Children, Carshalton, 1958–60; Member, Carshalton UDC, 1945–62 (Chm. 1950–52 and 1955–56). Served European War, 1914–18 with Aust. Inf. and Aust. Flying Corps in Egypt and France (MC); served War of 1939–45. DUniv Surrey, 1975. *Recreations:* football, hockey, tennis, squash, now golf. *Address:* 17 Oakhurst Rise, Carshalton Beeches, Surrey SM5 4AG. *T:* 081–643 4125. *Club:* Royal Automobile.

WELLS, Jack Dennis; Assistant Director, Central Statistical Office, 1979–88; *b* 8 April 1928; *s* of late C. W. Wells and H. M. Wells (*née* Clark); *m* 1st, 1953, Jean Allison; one *s* one *d*; 2nd, 1987, Cynthia Palmer. *Educ:* Hampton Grammar Sch.; Polytechnic of Central London. AIS 1955. Ministry of Fuel and Power, 1947; Royal Air Force, 1947–49; Min. of (Fuel and) Power, 1949–69; Private Secretary to Paymaster General, 1957–59; Chief Statistician, Dept of Economic Affairs, 1969; Min. of Technology, 1969; HM Treasury, 1970; Dept of (Trade and) Industry, 1971–79. Pres., CS Aviation Assoc., 1988–. Past Chairman, Old Hamptonians Assoc. *Publications:* contribs to Long Range Planning, Economic Trends, Statistical News, Review of Income and Wealth, Jl of Banking and Finance, BIEC Yearbook. *Recreations:* flying, cricket, jazz, travel. *Clubs:* Civil Service, MCC.

WELLS, (Jennifer) Brigid (Ellen), (Mrs Ian Wells); JP; Member, Broadcasting Complaints Commission, since 1986; *b* 18 Feb. 1928; *d* of Dr Leonard John Haydon, TD, MA Cantab, MB BCh and Susan Eleanor Haydon (*née* Richmond), actress; *m* 1962, Ian Vane Wells; three *d*. *Educ:* schools in UK, USA, Canada; Edinburgh Univ.; Lady Margaret Hall, Oxford (scholar; BA Mod. Hist.). Commonwealth Relations Office, 1949; UK High Commn, NZ, 1952–54; Private Sec. to Parly Under-Sec. of State, CRO, 1954–56; MAFF, 1956–62; teaching: LCC, 1962–63; Haringey, 1967; Camden Sch. for Girls, 1969–75 (to Head of Dept); Head of Dept, St David's and St Katharine's, Hornsey, 1975–77; Headmistress, Brighton and Hove High Sch., GPDST, 1978–88. Mem., Local Radio Council, 1980–82; Chairman: Educn Cttee, GSA, 1987–88; SE Region, GSA, 1984–86; CSSB, 1989–. Project Manager (USA), GAP, 1989–; Mem., British Atlantic Council; Governor, Woldingham Sch., 1989–; Dep. Chm., Friends of GPDST, 1989–. JP Inner London, 1972–77, Brighton, 1980–. *Publications:* articles in learned jls. *Recreations:* decorating, dressmaking, travel. *Address:* 107 Surrenden Road, Brighton BN1 6WB. *T:* Brighton (0273) 503668.

WELLS, John Campbell; writer, actor and director; *b* 17 Nov. 1936; *s* of Eric George Wells and Dorothy Amy Thompson; *m* 1982, Teresa (*née* Chancellor). *Educ:* Eastbourne Coll.; St Edmund Hall, Oxford. Taught: English at Landerziehungsheim Schondorf am Ammersee, 1958–59; French and German at Eton, 1961–63; Co-Editor, Private Eye, 1964–67; Afterthought column, The Spectator, 1966–68. *Author of: revues, etc (also performer):* Never Too Late, 1960, Late Night Final, 1961 (both jtly), Edinburgh Fest.; A Man Apart (jtly), 1968, Changing Scenes, 1969, BBC Radio; Charlie's Grants (jtly), 1970, Up Sunday, 1973–74, The End of the Pier Show (jtly), 1975, BBC TV; Return to Leeds (jtly), Yorkshire TV, 1974; In the Looking Glass (jtly), 1976; *plays:* (with Claud Cockburn) Listen to the Knocking Bird, Nottingham Playhouse, 1965; (with Richard Ingrams) Mrs Wilson's Diary, Th. Royal, Stratford East, transf. Criterion, 1968; The Projector, 1970, and Cranford, 1970, Th. Royal, Stratford East; (with Barry Fantoni) Lionel, New London, 1977; (with Julius Gellner) The Immortal Haydon, Mermaid, 1978; The Peace, Scottish Opera Go Round, 1978; (with Robert Morley) A Picture of Innocence, Brighton, 1979; Anyone for Denis?, Whitehall, 1981–82 (also title rôle); Alice in Wonderland, Lyric, Hammersmith, 1986; *television plays:* The Scriblerus Club, 1967; Voltaire in England, 1968; Orpheus in the Underground, 1977; The Arnolfini Marriage, 1978; *radio play adaptations:* Alice in Wonderland, 1978; Alice Through the Looking Glass, 1980; *translations:* Danton's Death, 1971, The Marriage of Figaro, 1974, NT; The Barber of Seville, and A Mother's Guilt, 1984, BBC Radio; Women All Over, Edinburgh, 1984; La Vie Parisienne, Scottish Opera, 1986 (also dir, Glasgow, 1987); The Magic Flute, City of Birmingham Touring Opera, 1988; The Merry Widow, Scottish Opera, 1989. *Actor:* An Italian Straw Hat, Lyric, Hammersmith, 1961; Murderous Angels, Paris, 1971; Private Lives, Newcastle, 1972; Jumpers, 1973, Design for Living, 1974, Nottingham Playhouse; Bartholomew Fair, Round House, 1978; Greystoke (film), 1984; The Philanthropist, Chichester Fest., 1985; Rude Health, Channel Four, 1985–86; Bartholomew Fair, NT, 1988; Frontiers—East/West Germany, BBC TV, 1990; Dunrulin', BBC TV, 1990; *director:* (with Jonathan Miller) Candide, Glasgow, 1988; The Mikado, D'Oyly Carte tour, 1989; The Bold Fisherman, TVS, 1991. *Publications:* (with Richard Ingrams) Mrs Wilson's Diary, 1964–70 and 1974–76; The Exploding Present, 1971; (with John Fortune) A Melon for Ecstacy, 1971; (with Richard Ingrams) The Dear Bill Letters, 1980–; Anyone for Denis?, 1982; Masterpieces, 1982; Fifty Glorious Years, 1984; Rude Words: a history of the London Library, 1991. *Recreations:* walking, talking. *Address:* 1A Scarsdale Villas, W8 6PT. *T:* 071–937 0534.

WELLS, Prof. John Christopher, PhD; FIL; Professor of Phonetics, since 1988 and Head of Department of Phonetics and Linguistics, since 1990, University College London; *b* 11 March 1939; *s* of Rev. Philip Cuthbert Wells and Winifred May (*née* Peaker). *Educ:* St John's Sch., Leatherhead; Trinity Coll., Cambridge (BA 1960; MA 1964); University Coll., London (MA 1962; PhD 1971). FIL 1982. University College London: Asst Lectr in Phonetics, 1962–65; Lectr, 1965–82; Reader, 1982–88. Sec., Internat. Phonetic Assoc., 1973–86; Pres., World Esperanto Assoc., 1989–; Mem., Esperanto Acad., 1971–. Editor, Jl Internat. Phonetic Assoc., 1971–87. Contribs to radio and TV programmes. *Publications:* Concise Esperanto and English Dictionary, 1969; (with G. Colson) Practical Phonetics, 1971; Jamaican Pronunciation in London, 1973; (jtly) Jen Nia Mondo 1, 1974 (trans. Italian, Icelandic, Swedish, Finnish; (jtly) Jen Nia Mondo 2, 1977; Lingvistikaj aspektoj de Esperanto, 1978, 2nd edn 1989 (trans. Danish; Accents of English (three vols and cassette), 1982; Geiriadur Esperanto/Kimra vortaro, 1985; (pronunciation editor) Universal Dictionary, 1987; (pronunciation editor) Hutchinson Encyclopedia, 8th edn 1988, 9th edn 1990; Longman Pronunciation Dictionary, 1990; articles in learned jls and collective works. *Recreations:* reading, walking, running. *Address:* Department of Phonetics and Linguistics, University College London, Gower Street, WC1E 6BT. *T:* 071–380 7175; 5 Poplar Road, SW19 3JR. *T:* 081–542 0302. *Club:* Esperanto.

WELLS, Sir John (Julius), Kt 1984; *b* 30 March 1925; *s* of A. Reginald K. Wells, Marlands, Sampford Arundel, Som; *m* 1948, Lucinda Meath-Baker; two *s* two *d*. *Educ:* Eton; Corpus Christi College, Oxford (MA). War of 1939–45: joined RN as ordinary seaman, 1942; commissioned, 1943, served in submarines until 1946. Contested (C) Smethwick Division, General Election, 1955. MP (C) Maidstone, 1959–87. Chairman: Cons. Party Horticulture Cttee, 1965–71, 1973–87; Horticultural sub-Cttee, Select Cttee on Agriculture, 1968; Parly Waterways Group, 1974–80; Vice-Chm., Cons. Party Agriculture Cttee, 1970; Mem., Mr Speaker's Panel of Chairmen, 1974. Hon. Freeman, Borough of Maidstone, 1979. Kt Comdr, Order of Civil Merit (Spain), 1972; Comdr, Order of Lion of Finland, 1984. *Recreations:* country pursuits. *Address:* Mere House Barn, Mereworth, Kent; Acheillie, Rogart, Sutherland.

WELLS, Malcolm Henry Weston, FCA; Chairman, BWD Securities plc, since 1987; Deputy Chairman, Carclo Engineering Group PLC, since 1987 (Director, since 1982); *b* 26 July 1927; *s* of late Lt-Comdr Geoffrey Weston Wells; *m* 1952, Elizabeth A. Harland, *d* of late Rt Rev. M. H. Harland, DD; one *s* one *d*. *Educ:* Eton Coll. ACA 1951, FCA 1961. Served RNVR, 1945–48. Peat, Marwick Mitchell, 1948–58; Siebe Gorman and Co. Ltd, 1958–63; Charterhouse Japhet, 1963–80 (Chm., 1973–80); Dir, Charterhouse Gp, 1971–80; Chairman: Charterhouse Petroleum PLC, 1977–82; Granville Business Expansion Funds, 1983–; London rep., Bank in Liechtenstein, 1981–85; Director: Bank in Liechtenstein (UK) Ltd, 1985–90; Nat. Home Loans Corp., 1989–. Mem., CAA, 1974–77. Mem. Solicitors' Disciplinary Tribunal, 1975–81. *Recreation:* sailing. *Address:* Holmbush House, Findon, West Sussex BN14 0SY. *T:* Findon (0903) 873630. *Clubs:* City of London; West Wittering Sailing.

WELLS, Petrie Bowen; *see* Wells, B.

WELLS, Richard Burton, QPM 1987; Chief Constable, South Yorkshire Police, since 1990; *b* 10 Aug. 1940; *s* of Walter Percival Wells and Daphne Joan Wells (*née* Harris); *m* 1970, Patricia Ann Smith; one *s* one *d*. *Educ:* Sir Roger Manwood's Grammar Sch., Sandwich; Priory Sch. for Boys, Shrewsbury; St Peter's Coll., Oxford (Open Exhibnr 1959; BA 1962; MA 1965); principal educn, 28 yrs with the Metropolitan Police. Constable, Bow Street, 1962–66; Sergeant, Notting Hill, 1966–68; Special Course, Police Staff Coll., 1966–67; Inspector, Leman St and Hendon, 1968–73; Chief Inspector, Notting Hill, 1973–76; Supt, Hampstead, 1976–79; Chief Supt, Hammersmith and New Scotland Yard, 1979–82; Sen. Command Course, Police Staff Coll., 1981; Comdt, Hendon Training Sch., 1982–83; Dep. Asst Comr, Dir of Public Affairs, New Scotland Yard, 1983–88; Dep. Asst Commissioner, OC NW London, 1986–90. *Publications:* (contrib.) The Roots of Urban Unrest, ed Benyon and Solomos, 1987; contrib. Cropwood Conf., and Die Streife Jl. *Recreations:* hockey, squash, walking, painting (watercolour, gloss and emulsion), photography, philately. *Address:* South Yorkshire Police HQ, Snig Hill, Sheffield S3 8LY. *T:* Sheffield (0742) 768522.

WELLS, Ven. Roderick John; Archdeacon of Stow, since 1989; *b* 17 Nov. 1936; *s* of Leonard Arthur and Dorothy Alice Wells; *m* 1969, Alice Louise Scholl; one *s* two *d*. *Educ:* Durham Univ. (BA Hons Theol.); Hull Univ. (MA). Insurance clerk, 1953–55 and 1957–58. RAF, 1955–57 (Radar Mechanic). Asst Master, Chester Choir School, 1958–59; Asst Curate, St Mary at Lambeth, 1965–68, Priest-in-Charge 1968–71; Rector of Skegness, 1971–78; Team Rector, West Grimsby Team Ministry (Parish of Great and Little Coates with Bradley), 1978–89; Area Dean of Grimsby and Cleethorpes, 1983–89. *Recreations:* music (pianist and organist), walking, geology. *Address:* The Vicarage, Hackthorn, Lincoln LN2 3PF. *T:* Welton (0673) 60382.

WELLS, Ronald Alfred, OBE 1965; BSc, FRSC, FIMM; retired; *b* 11 February 1920; *s* of Alfred John Wells and Winifred Jessie (*née* Lambert); *m* 1953, Anne Brebner Lanshe; two *s*. *Educ:* Birkbeck College, London; Newport Technical College. Service with Government Chemist, 1939–40; Royal Naval Scientific Service, 1940–47; Joined Nat. Chemical Laboratory, 1947; Mem. UK Scientific Mission, Washington, 1951–52; Head of Radio-chemical Group, 1956; Head of Div. of Inorganic and Mineral Chemistry, 1963; Deputy Director, Nov. 1963; Director of National Chemical Laboratory, 1964; Dir of Research, TBA Industrial Products Ltd, 1965–70, Jt Man. Dir, 1970–77; Man. Dir, AMFU Ltd (Turner & Newall), 1977–81; Gp Scientist, Turner & Newall, 1981–83; industrial consultant, 1983–87. Director: Salford Univ. Industrial Centre Ltd, 1981–82; Rochdale Private Surgical Unit, 1975–81; non-exec. Dir, Eversave (UK) Ltd, 1984–85. Mem. Council, Royal Inst. Chemistry, 1965–68. *Publications:* numerous contribs to Inorganic Chromatography and Extractive Metallurgy. *Recreations:* gardening, golf, mineralogy. *Address:* Westbury, 19 First Avenue, Charmandean, Worthing, Sussex BN14 9NJ. *T:* Worthing (0903) 33844.

WELLS, Mrs Stanley; see Hill, S. E.

WELLS, Prof. Stanley William; Professor of Shakespeare Studies, and Director of the Shakespeare Institute, University of Birmingham, since 1988; General Editor of the Oxford Shakespeare since 1978; *b* 21 May 1930; *s* of Stanley Cecil Wells and Doris Wells; *m* 1975, Susan Elizabeth Hill, *qv*; two *d* (and one *d* decd). *Educ*: Kingston High Sch., Hull; University Coll., London (BA); Shakespeare Inst., Univ. of Birmingham (PhD). Fellow, Shakespeare Inst., 1962–77: Lectr, 1962; Sen. Lectr, 1971; Reader, 1973–77; Hon. Fellow, 1979–88; Head of Shakespeare Dept, OUP, 1978–88. Sen. Res. Fellow, Balliol Coll., Oxford, 1980–88. Consultant in English, Wroxton Coll., 1964–80. Dir, Royal Shakespeare Theatre Summer Sch., 1971–; Pres., Shakespeare Club of Stratford-upon-Avon, 1972–73. Member: Council, Malone Soc., 1967–; Exec. Council, 1976–, F and GP Cttee, 1991, Royal Shakespeare Theatre (Gov., 1974–, Vice Chm. of Govs, 1991); Exec. Cttee, Shakespeare's Birthplace, 1976–78, 1988– (Trustee, 1975–81, 1984–; Vice Chm. Trustees, 1990–). Governor, King Edward VI Grammar Sch. for Boys, Stratford-upon-Avon, 1973–77. Guest lectr, British and overseas univs; British Acad. Annual Shakespeare Lecture, 1987; Hilda Hulme Meml Lecture, 1987; first annual Globe Lecture, 1990. Hon. DLitt Furman Univ., SC, 1978. Associate Editor, New Penguin Shakespeare, 1967–77; Editor, Shakespeare Survey, 1980–. *Publications*: (ed) Thomas Nashe, Selected Writings, 1964; (ed, New Penguin Shakespeare): A Midsummer Night's Dream, 1967, Richard II, 1969, The Comedy of Errors, 1972; Shakespeare, A Reading Guide, 1969 (2nd edn 1970); Literature and Drama, 1970; (ed, Select Bibliographical Guides): Shakespeare, 1973 (new edn 1990), English Drama excluding Shakespeare, 1975; Royal Shakespeare, 1977, 2nd edn 1978; (compiled) Nineteenth-Century Shakespeare Burlesques (5 vols), 1977; Shakespeare: an illustrated dictionary, 1978, 2nd edn 1985; Shakespeare: the writer and his work, 1978; (ed with R. L. Smallwood) Thomas Dekker, The Shoemaker's Holiday, 1979; (with Gary Taylor) Modernizing Shakespeare's Spelling, with three studies in the text of Henry V, 1979; Re-Editing Shakespeare for the Modern Reader, 1984; (ed) Shakespeare's Sonnets, 1985; (ed with Gary Taylor *et al*) The Complete Oxford Shakespeare, 1986; (ed) The Cambridge Companion to Shakespeare Studies, 1986; (with Gary Taylor *et al*) William Shakespeare: a textual companion, 1987; An Oxford Anthology of Shakespeare, 1987; contrib. Shak. Survey, Shak. Qly, Shak. Jahrbuch, Theatre Notebook, Stratford-upon-Avon Studies, TLS, etc. *Recreations*: music, the countryside. *Address*: Midsummer Cottage, Church Lane, Beckley, Oxford. *T*: Stanton St John (086735) 252; 38 College Street, Stratford-upon-Avon, Warwicks. *T*: Stratford-upon-Avon (0789) 296047.

WELLS, Thomas Leonard; Agent General for Ontario in the United Kingdom, since 1985; *b* 2 May 1930; *s* of Leonard Wells and Lilian May Butler; *m* 1954, Audrey Alice Richardson; one *s* two *d*. *Educ*: University of Toronto. Advertising Manager: Canadian Hosp. Jl, 1951–61; Canadian Med. Assoc. Jl, 1961–67; Chm., Scarborough, Ont Bd of Educn, 1961, 1962; MLA (Progressive C) for Scarborough N, Ontario, 1963–85; Minister: without Portfolio (responsible for Youth Affairs), 1966–69; of Health, 1969–71; of Social and Family Services, 1971–72; of Education, 1972–78; of Intergovtl Affairs, 1978–85; Govt House Leader, Ont, 1980–85. Hon. Fellow, Ont Teachers' Fedn, 1976. Hon. DLitt Univ. of Windsor, Ont, 1985. Freeman, City of London, 1985; Mem., Guild of Freemen of the City of London, 1987–. CLJ 1984. Confederation Medal, Canada, 1967; Silver Jubilee Medal, 1977. *Recreations*: photography, walking, theatre, cinema. *Address*: Ontario House, 21 Knightsbridge, SW1X 7LY. *T*: 071–245 1222; 6/12 Reeves Mews, W1Y 3PB. *T*: 071–629 6983. *Clubs*: Royal Automobile, Royal Over-Seas League, Commonwealth Trust, United Wards; Albany, Empire (Toronto).

WELLS, Thomas Umfrey, MA; Headmaster, Wanganui Collegiate School, New Zealand, 1960–80; *b* 6 Feb. 1927; *s* of Athol Umfrey and Gladys Colebrook Wells; *m* 1953, Valerie Esther Brewis; two *s* one *d*. *Educ*: King's College, Auckland, New Zealand; Auckland University (BA); (Orford Studentship to) King's College, Cambridge. BA 1951; MA 1954. Assistant Master, Clifton College, 1952–60 (Senior English Master, 1957–60). Pres., NZ Assoc. of Heads of Independent Secondary Schs, 1972–75. Member: Univs Entrance Bd, 1972–80; HMC; Tongariro Forest Park Promotion Cttee, 1984–87; Taumarunui and Dist Promotion and Develt Council, 1985–; Chm., CKC Visual Arts Trust, 1986–; Wanganui River Floats Coalition, 1987–; Taumarunui Community Arts Council, 1987–; Trustee: Avonlea, 1984–; Outdoor Pursuits Centre, Tawhiti-kuri, 1985–90; Taumarunui Museum Trust, 1987–. Synodsman, 1985–, Mem. Standing Cttee, 1989–, Waikato Dio. Pres., Taumarunui Cricket Club Assoc., 1984–86, Patron, 1986–; Mem., Rotary Club of Wanganui, 1961–80 (Pres., 1979–80), of Taumarunui, 1980–; Chm., Dist 993 Rotaract Cttee, 1983–85. *Recreations*: reading, theatre, cricket (Cambridge Blue, 1950), tennis, fishing; formerly Rugby football (Cambridge Blue, 1951). *Address*: PO Box 48, Owhango, King Country, New Zealand. *Clubs*: MCC; Hawks (Cambridge); Wanganui, Rotary of Taumarunui (NZ).

WELLS, William Henry Weston, FRICS; Chairman, Chesterton, London, since 1984 (Partner, since 1965); Chairman, Royal Free Hospital Trust, since 1990; *b* 3 May 1940; *s* of Sir Henry Wells, CBE, and Lady Wells; *m* 1966, Penelope Jean Broadbent; two *s* (and one *s* decd). *Educ*: Radley Coll.; Magdalene Coll., Cambridge (BA). Joined Chestertons, 1959; Chairman: Land and House Property Corporation, 1977; Frincon Holdings Ltd, 1977–87. Director: London Life Assoc., 1984–89; AMP UK Bd, 1989–. Chm., Hampstead HA, 1982–90. Member: Board of Governors, Royal Free Hosp., 1968–74; Camden and Islington AHA, 1974–82; Chm., Special Trustees of Royal Free Hosp., 1979–; Mem. Council, Royal Free Hosp. Sch. of Medicine, 1977–91; Hon. Treas., RCN, 1988–. *Recreations*: family, philately, gardening. *Club*: Boodle's.

WELMAN, Douglas Pole, CBE 1966; *b* 22 June 1902; *s* of late Col Arthur Pole Welman and late Lady Scott; *m* 1st, 1929, Denise, *d* of Charles Steers Peel; one *d*; 2nd, 1946, Betty Marjorie, *d* of late Henry Huth. *Educ*: Tonbridge Sch.; Faraday House Engineering Coll. DFH, CEng, FIMechE, FIEE, CIGasE. Electrical and Mechanical Engineering career at home and abroad, West Indies, 1928–32; Consulting Practice, 1932–37; Man. Dir of Foster, Yates and Thom Limited, Heavy Precision Engineers, 1937–50; Chairman or Member of number of wartime committees in Lancashire including Armaments Production, Emergency Services Organisation, and Ministry of Production; went to Ministry of Aircraft Production at request of Minister as Director of Engine Production, 1942; Deputy Director-General, 1943; Control of Directorate-Gen. including Propeller and Accessory Production, 1944; Part Time Member North Western Gas Board, 1949, Chairman, 1950–64; Chairman, Southern Gas Board, 1964–67; Member, Gas Council, 1950–67; Chm. and Man. Dir, Allspeeds Holdings Ltd, 1967–72. Member, Ct of Govs, Univ. of Manchester Inst. of Sci. and Techn., 1956–64, 1968–72 (Mem. Coun., 1960–64, 1968–72). CStJ 1968 (OStJ 1964). FRSA. *Publications*: articles and papers on company management. *Recreations*: sailing, fishing. *Address*: 11 St Michael's Gardens, St Cross, Winchester SO23 9JD. *T*: Winchester (0962) 868091. *Club*: Royal Thames Yacht.

WELSBY, John Kay, CBE 1990; Chief Executive, British Railways Board, since 1990 (Board Member, since 1987); *b* 26 May 1938; *s* of late Samuel and Sarah Ellen Welsby; *m* 1964, Jill Carole Richards; one *s* one *d*. *Educ*: Heywood Grammar Sch.; Univ. of Exeter (BA); Univ. of London (MSc). FCIT. Govt Economic Service, 1966–81; British Railways

Board: Dir, Provincial Services, 1982–84; Managing Dir, Procurement, 1985–87. *Publications*: articles on economic matters. *Recreations*: walking, music, swimming. *Address*: British Railways Board, Euston House, 24 Eversholt Street, NW1 1DZ.

WELSBY, Rev. Canon Paul Antony; Canon Residentiary and Vice-Dean of Rochester Cathedral, 1966–88, Canon Emeritus since 1988; Chaplain to the Queen, 1980–90; *b* 18 Aug. 1920; *m* 1948, Cynthia Mary Hosmer; one *d*. *Educ*: Alcester Grammar Sch.; University Coll., Durham (MA); Lincoln Theological Coll.; Univ. of Sheffield (PhD). Curate at Boxley, Kent, 1944–47; Curate, St Mary-le-Tower, Ipswich, 1947–52; Rector of Copdock with Washbrook, 1952–66; Rural Dean of Samford, 1964–66. Director of Post-Ordination Training for Dio. of Rochester, 1966–88; Examining Chaplain to Bp of Rochester, 1966–88, Personal Chaplain 1988–90. Member, Church Assembly, 1964–70, General Synod, 1970–80; Chm., House of Clergy at Gen. Synod and Prolocutor of Convocation of Canterbury, 1974–80. *Publications*: A Modern Catechism, 1956; Lancelot Andrewes, 1958; How the Church of England Works, 1960, new edn, 1985; The Unwanted Archbishop, 1962; The Bond of Church and State, 1962; Sermons and Society, 1970; A History of the Church of England 1945–80, 1984; contrib. Theology. *Recreations*: reading detective fiction, visiting National Trust properties. *Address*: 20 Knights Ridge, Pembury, Kent TN2 4HP. *T*: Pembury (089282) 3053.

WELSH, Andrew Paton; MP (SNP) Angus East, since 1987; *b* 19 April 1944; *s* of William and Agnes Welsh; *m* 1971, Sheena Margaret Cannon; one *d*. *Educ*: Univ. of Glasgow. MA (Hons) History and Politics; DipEd, 1980. Teacher of History, 1972–74; Lectr in Public Admin and Economics, Dundee Coll. of Commerce, 1979–83; Sen. Lectr in Business and Admin. Studies, Angus Technical Coll., 1983–87. MP (SNP) South Angus, Oct. 1974–1979; SNP Parly Chief Whip, 1978–79, 1987–; SNP Spokesman on: Housing, 1974–78; Self Employed Affairs and Small Businesses, 1975–79, 1987–; Agriculture, 1976–79, 1987–; Local Govt, 1987–; SNP Exec. Vice Chm. for Admin, 1979–87; SNP Vice-Pres., 1987–. Contested (SNP) Angus E, 1983. Mem., Angus District Council, 1984–87; Provost of Angus, 1984–87. *Recreations*: music, horse riding, languages. *Address*: Community Centre, Marketgate, Arbroath, Angus DD11 1HR. *T*: Arbroath (0241) 74522. *Club*: Glasgow University Union.

WELSH, Frank Reeson; writer; Director, Grindlays Bank, 1971–85; *b* 16 Aug. 1931; *s* of F. C. Welsh and D. M. Welsh; *m* 1954, Agnes Cowley; two *s* two *d*. *Educ*: Gateshead and Blaydon Grammar Schools; Magdalene Coll., Cambridge (schol.; MA). With John Lewis Partnership, 1954–1958; CAS Group, 1958–64; Man. Dir, William Brandt's Sons & Co. Ltd, 1965–72; Chairman: Hadfields Ltd, 1967–79; Jensen Motors Ltd, 1968–72; Cox & Kings, 1972–76; Dir, Henry Ansbacher & Co., 1976–82. Member: British Waterways Board, 1975–81; Gen. Adv. Council, IBA, 1976–80; Royal Commn on Nat. Health Service, 1976–79; Health Educn Council, 1978–80. Dir, Trireme Trust, 1983–. Vis. Lectr and Alcoa Schol., Graduate Sch. of Business Studies, Univ. of Tennessee, Knoxville, 1979–85. CBIM. *Publications*: The Profit of the State, 1982; (contrib.) Judging People, 1982; The Afflicted State, 1983; First Blood, 1985; (with George Ridley) Bend'Or, Duke of Westminster, 1985; Uneasy City, 1986; Building the Trireme, 1988; Companion Guide to the Lake District, 1989. *Recreation*: sailing. *Clubs*: United Oxford & Cambridge University, Savile.

WELSH, Michael Collins; MP (Lab) Doncaster North, since 1983 (Don Valley, 1979–83); *b* 23 Nov. 1926; *s* of Danny and Winnie Welsh; *m* 1950, Brenda Nicholson; two *s*. *Educ*: Sheffield Univ. (Dept of Extramural Studies, Day Release Course, three years); Ruskin Coll., Oxford. Miner from age of 14 years. Member, Doncaster Local Authority, 1962–. *Address*: House of Commons, SW1A 0AA. *Club*: Carcroft Village Workingmen's (Carcroft, near Doncaster).

WELSH, Michael John; Member (C) Lancashire Central, European Parliament, since 1979; *b* 22 May 1942; *s* of Comdr David Welsh, RN, and Una Mary (*née* Willmore); *m* 1963, Jennifer Caroline Pollitt; one *s* one *d*. *Educ*: Dover Coll.; Lincoln Coll., Oxford (BA (Hons) Jurisprudence). Proprietors of Hays Wharf Ltd, 1963–69; Levi Strauss & Co. Europe Ltd, 1969–79 (Dir of Market Development, 1976). Chm., Cttee for Social Affairs and Employment, Eur. Parlt, 1984–87. Chm., Positive Europe Gp, 1988–. *Recreations*: amateur drama, sailing, rough walking. *Address*: Watercrook, 181 Town Lane, Whittle le Woods, Chorley, Lancs PR6 8AG. *T*: Chorley (02572) 76992. *Club*: Carlton.

WELSH, Maj.-Gen. Peter Miles, OBE 1983; MC 1967; President, Regular Commissions Board, 1983–85; *b* 23 Dec. 1930; *s* of William Miles Moss O'Donnel Welsh and Mary Edith Margaret Gertrude Louise Welsh (*née* Hearn); *m* 1974, June Patricia McCausland (*née* Macadam); two step *s* one step *d*. *Educ*: Winchester College; RMA Sandhurst. Commissioned, KRRC, 1951; Kenya Regt, 1958–60; student, Staff Coll., 1961; Malaya and Borneo, 1965–66; Royal Green Jackets, 1966; JSSC, 1967; Instructor, Staff Coll., 1968–71; CO 2 RGJ, 1971–73; Comd 5 Inf. Bde, 1974–76; RCDS, 1977; HQ BAOR, 1978–80; Brig., Light Div., 1980–83. *Recreations*: shooting, fishing, vegetable gardening, cooking, golf. *Address*: c/o Lloyds Bank, Maidenhead, Berks. *Clubs*: MCC, Free Foresters, I Zingari, Jesters; Berks Golf.

WELTY, Eudora; Gold Medal for the Novel, Amer. Acad. and Inst. of Arts and Letters, 1972; National Medal for Literature, 1980; Presidential Medal of Freedom, 1980. *Publications*: A Curtain of Green, 1943; The Robber Bridegroom, 1944; The Wide Net, 1945; Delta Wedding, 1947; Golden Apples, 1950; The Ponder Heart, 1954; The Bride of Innisfallen, 1955; The Shoe Bird, 1964; Losing Battles, US 1970, UK 1982; One Time, One Place, 1971; The Optimist's Daughter, 1972 (Pulitzer Prize, 1973); The Eye of the Story, 1979; The Collected Stories of Eudora Welty, 1980; One Writer's Beginnings, 1984. *Address*: 1119 Pinehurst Street, Jackson, Miss 39202, USA.

WEMYSS, 12th Earl of *cr* 1633, **AND MARCH**, 8th Earl of *cr* 1697; **Francis David Charteris**, KT 1966; Lord Wemyss of Elcho, 1628; Lord Elcho and Methil, 1633; Viscount Peebles, Baron Douglas of Neidpath, Lyne and Munard, 1697; Baron Wemyss of Wemyss (UK), 1821; President, The National Trust for Scotland, 1967–91 (Chairman of Council, 1946–69); Lord Clerk Register of Scotland and Keeper of the Signet, since 1974; *b* 19 Jan. 1912; *s* of late Lord Elcho (killed in action, 1916) and Lady Violet Manners (she *m* 2nd, 1921, Guy Holford Benson (decd), and *d* 1971), 2nd *d* of 8th Duke of Rutland; *S* grandfather, 1937; *m* 1940, Mavis Lynette Gordon, BA (*d* 1988), *er d* of late E. E. Murray, Hermanus, Cape Province; one *s* one *d* (and one *s* and one *d* decd). *Educ*: Eton; Balliol College, Oxford. Assistant District Commissioner, Basutoland, 1937–44. Served with Basuto Troops in Middle East, 1941–44. Lieut, Queen's Body Guard for Scotland, Royal Company of Archers; Lord High Comr to Gen. Assembly of Church of Scotland, 1959, 1960, 1977; Chairman: Scottish Cttee, Marie Curie Meml Foundn, 1952–86; Royal Commn on Ancient and Historical Monuments, Scotland, 1949–84; Scottish Churches Council, 1964–71; Hon. Pres., The Thistle Foundn; Mem., Central Cttee, WCC, 1961–75; Mem., Royal Commn on Historical Manuscripts, 1975–85. Consultant, Wemyss and March Estates Management Co. Ltd; formerly Director: Standard Life Assurance Co. Ltd; Scottish Television Ltd. Lord-Lieut, E Lothian, 1967–87. Hon. LLD St Andrews, 1953; DUniv Edinburgh, 1983. *Heir*: *s* Lord Neidpath, *qv*. *Address*: Gosford

House, Longniddry, East Lothian EH32 0PX. *Club:* New (Edinburgh).
See also D. H. Benson, Baron Charteris of Amisfield.

WEMYSS, Rear-Adm. Martin La Touche, CB 1981; Clerk to the Brewers' Company, since 1981; *b* 5 Dec. 1927; *s* of Comdr David Edward Gillespie Wemyss, DSO, DSC, RN, and late Edith Mary Digges La Touche; *m* 1st, 1951, Ann Hall (marr. diss. 1973); one *s* one *d*; 2nd, 1973, Elizabeth Loveday Alexander; one *s* one *d*. *Educ:* Shrewsbury School. CO HMS Sentinel, 1956–57; Naval Intell. Div., 1957–59; CO HMS Alliance, 1959–60; CO Commanding Officers' Qualifying Course, 1961–63; Naval Staff, 1963–65; CO HMS Cleopatra, 1965–67; Naval Asst to First Sea Lord, 1967–70; CO 3rd Submarine Sqdn, 1970–73; CO HMS Norfolk, 1973–74; Dir of Naval Warfare, 1974–76; Rear-Adm., 1977; Flag Officer, Second Flotilla, 1977–78; Asst Chief of Naval Staff (Ops), 1979–81. *Recreations:* sailing, shooting. *Address:* The Old Post House, Emberton, near Olney, Bucks. *T:* Bedford (0234) 713838. *Clubs:* White's, Army and Navy.

WEN, Eric Lewis; freelance writer and music producer; Editor, The Musical Times, 1988–90; *b* 18 May 1953; *s* of Adam and Mimi Wen; *m* 1989, Louise Anne, *d* of B. L. Barder, *qv*; one *d*. *Educ:* Columbia Univ. (BA); Yale Univ. (MPhil); Cambridge Univ. Lecturer: Guildhall Sch. of Music, 1978–84; Goldsmiths' Coll., Univ. of London, 1980–84; Mannes Coll. of Music, NY, 1984–86; Editor, The Strad, 1986–89. *Publications:* (contrib.) Schenker Studies, 1989; (contrib.) Trends in Schenkerian Research, 1990; (ed) The Fritz Kreisler Collection, 1990; (contrib.) Cambridge Companion to the Violin, 1992; contrib. various music jls. *Recreations:* music, chess, cooking, unintentional humour. *Address:* 35 St George Street, W1R 9FA. *T:* 071–408 2458.

WENBAN-SMITH, Nigel; *see* Wenban-Smith, W. N.

WENBAN-SMITH, William, CMG 1960; CBE 1957; *b* 8 June 1908; *o s* of late Frederick Wenban-Smith, Worthing; *m* 1935, Ruth Orme, *e d* of late S. B. B. McElderry, CMG; three *s* two *d*. *Educ:* Bradfield; King's Coll., Cambridge (MA). Colonial Administrative Service, 1931–61: Cadet, Zanzibar, 1931; Administrative Officer, Grade II, 1933; Asst DO, Tanganyika, 1935; DO, 1943; Sen. DO, 1951 (acted on various occasions as Resident Magistrate, Comr for Co-op. Development, Provincial Comr, and Sec. for Finance); Dir of Establishments, 1953; Minister for Social Services, 1958; Minister for Education and Labour, 1959–61. Chairman, Public Service Commission and Speaker, Legislative Council, Nyasaland, 1961–63. HM Diplomatic Service, Kuala Lumpur, 1964–69. *Publication:* Walks in the New Forest, 1975. *Recreations:* music, gardening. *Address:* Lane End, School Lane, Lymington, Hants SO41 9EJ. *T:* Lymington (0590) 679343. *Club:* Commonwealth Trust.
See also W. N. Wenban-Smith.

WENBAN-SMITH, (William) Nigel, CMG 1991; HM Diplomatic Service; High Commissioner to Malaŵi, since 1990; *b* 1 Sept. 1936; *s* of William Wenban-Smith, *qv*; *m* 1st, 1961, Charlotte Chapman-Andrews; two *s* two *d*; 2nd, 1976, Charlotte Susanna Rycroft (*d* 1990); two *s*. *Educ:* King's Sch., Canterbury; King's Coll., Cambridge (BA). National Service, RN. Plebiscite Supervisory Officer, Southern Cameroons, 1960–61; Asst Principal, CRO, 1961–65 (Private Sec. to Parly Under Sec., 1963–64); Second Sec., Leopoldville, 1965–67; First Sec. and (1968) Head of Chancery, Kampala, 1967–70; FCO, 1970–74; Dublin, 1975; Commercial Sec., Brussels, 1976–78; Commercial Counsellor, Brussels, 1978–80; on loan to Cabinet Office, 1980–82; Hd of E Africa Dept and Comr, British Indian Ocean Territory, FCO, 1982–85; National Defence Coll. of Canada, 1985–86; Deputy High Comr, Ottawa, 1986–89. *Recreations:* walking, gardening. *Address:* c/o Foreign and Commonwealth Office, King Charles Street, SW1A 2AF.

WENDT, Henry; Chairman, SmithKline Beecham, since 1989; *b* 19 July 1933; *s* of Henry Wendt and Rachel L. (*née* Wood); *m* 1956, Holly Peterson; one *s* one *d*. *Educ:* Princeton Univ. (AB 1955). Joined SmithKline & French Labs, 1955: various positions in Internat. Div.; Pres., 1976–82; Chief Exec. Officer, 1982–87; Chm., 1987–89 (merger of SmithKline Beckman and Beecham, 1989). Director: Arjo Wiggins Appleton plc, 1990–; Allergan Inc., 1989–; Beckman Instruments Inc., 1989–; Atlantic Richfield Co., 1987–. Trustee: Amer. Enterprises Inst.; Philadelphia Museum of Art. *Recreations:* sailing, flyfishing, tennis, viticulture. *Address:* c/o SmithKline Beecham, SB House, Great West Road, Brentford, Middx TW7 4BN. *T:* 081–560 5151. *Clubs:* Flyfishers'; Philadelphia (Philadelphia); River, Links (NYC).

WENDT, Robin Glover; DL; Secretary, Association of County Councils, since 1989; *b* 7 Jan. 1941; *er s* of William Romilly Wendt and late Doris May (*née* Glover), Preston, Lancs; *m* 1965, Prudence Ann Dalby; two *d*. *Educ:* Hutton GS, Preston; Wadham Coll., Oxford Univ. (BA 1962). Asst Principal 1962, Principal 1966, Min. of Pensions and Nat. Insurance; Principal Private Sec. to Sec. of State for Social Services, 1970; Asst Sec., DHSS, 1972; Dep. Sec., 1975, Chief Exec., 1979–89, Cheshire CC; Clerk of Cheshire Lieutenancy, 1979–90. Member: Social Security Adv. Cttee, 1982–; PCFC, 1989–; Council, RIPA, 1989–. DL Cheshire, 1990. *Publications:* various articles and reviews on public service issues. *Recreations:* music, swimming, following sport, travel. *Address:* 28 Church Lane, Upton, Chester CH2 1DJ.

WENHAM, Brian George; media consultant and journalist; *b* 9 Feb. 1937; *s* of late George Frederick Wenham and of Harriet Wenham, London; *m* 1966, Elisabeth Downing, *d* of Keith and Margery Woolley; two *d*. *Educ:* Royal Masonic Sch., Bushey; St John's Coll., Oxon. Television journalist, Independent Television News, 1962–69; Editor, Panorama, BBC, 1969–71; Head of Current Affairs Gp, 1971–78; Controller, BBC 2, 1978–82; Dir of Programmes, BBC TV, 1983–86; Man. Dir, BBC Radio, 1986–87. FRTS 1986. *Publication:* (ed) The Third Age of Broadcasting, 1982. *Address:* Red Cottage, Wey Road, Weybridge, Surrey. *T:* Weybridge (0932) 843313.

WENNER, Michael Alfred; HM Diplomatic Service, retired; President, Wenner Communications Co. (formerly Wenner Trading Co.), since 1982; *b* 17 March 1921; *s* of Alfred E. Wenner and of Simone Roussel; *m* 1st, 1950, Gunilla Cecilia Ståhle (*d* 1986), *d* of Envoyé Nils K. Ståhle, CBE, and Birgit Olsson; four *s*; 2nd, 1990, Holly (Raven) Adrianne Johnson, *d* of Adrian W. Johnson and Ophelia A. Matley. *Educ:* Stonyhurst; Oriel College, Oxford (Scholar). Served E Yorks Regt, 1940; Lancs Fusiliers and 151 Parachute Bn, India, 1941–42; 156 Bn, N Africa, 1943; No 9 Commando, Italy and Greece, 1944–45. Entered HM Foreign Service, 1947; 3rd Sec., Stockholm, 1948–51; 2nd Sec., Washington, 1951–53; Foreign Office, 1953–55; 1st Sec., Tel Aviv, 1956–59; Head of Chancery, La Paz, 1959–61, and at Vienna, 1961–63; Inspector of Diplomatic Establishments, 1964–67; Ambassador to El Salvador, 1967–70. Former Commercial Advr, Consulate-Gen. of Switzerland in Houston. *Publication:* Advances in Controlled Droplet Application, Agrichemical Age, 1979. *Recreations:* fly-fishing, old maps, choral singing, elocution. *Address:* 8277 Kingsbrook No 255, Houston, Texas 77024, USA. *T:* (713) 465 9169; Laythams Farm, Slaidburn, Clitheroe, Lancs BB7 3AJ. *T:* Slaidburn (02006) 677.

WENT, Ven. John Stewart; Archdeacon of Surrey, since 1989; *b* 11 March 1944; *s* of Douglas and Barbara Went; *m* 1968, Rosemary Evelyn Amy (*née* Dunn); three *s*. *Educ:* Corpus Christi Coll., Cambridge (1st Cl Classics Pt I, starred 1st Theology Pt II; MA). Curate, Emmanuel, Northwood, Mddx, 1969–75; Vicar, Holy Trinity, Margate, 1975–83; Vice-Principal, Wycliffe Hall, Oxford, 1983–89. Chm., Diocesan Council for Unity and Mission, Guildford, 1990–. *Recreations:* music, photography, crosswords. *Address:* Tarawera, 71 Boundstone Road, Rowledge, Farnham, Surrey GU10 4AT. *T:* Frensham (025125) 3987.

WENTWORTH, Maurice Frank Gerard, CMG 1957; OBE 1946; *b* 5 Nov. 1908; *s* of F. B. Wentworth, Finchley, N3; *m* 1962, Belinda Margaret, *d* of late B. S. Tatham and Mrs Tatham, Mickleham, Surrey; one *s* one *d*. *Educ:* Haileybury; University Coll., London (BA). Military Service, 1939–46, Lieutenant-Colonel. Gold Coast: Inspector of Schools, 1930; Sen. Education Officer, 1945; Principal, Teacher Training Coll., Tamale, 1946; Administrative Officer Class I, 1951; Permanent Secretary, 1953; Establishment Secretary, 1954–57 (Ghana Civil Service); Chairman: Public Service Commission: Sierra Leone, 1958–61; E African High Commn, 1961–64; Appointments Officer, ODM, 1964–73. *Address:* Quarry Hill, Todber, Sturminster Newton, Dorset DT10 1HY.

WENTWORTH, Stephen; Under Secretary and Head of Livestock Products Group, Ministry of Agriculture, Fisheries and Food, since 1989; *b* 23 Aug. 1943; *s* of Ronald Wentworth, OBE and Elizabeth Mary Wentworth (*née* Collins); *m* 1970, Katharine Laura Hopkinson; three *d*. *Educ:* King's College Sch., Wimbledon; Merton Coll., Oxford (MA, MSc). Ministry of Agriculture, Fisheries and Food, 1967–; seconded: to CSSB, 1974; to FCO, as First Sec., UK Perm. Repn to EEC, Brussels, 1976; Head of Beef Div., 1978; to Cabinet Office, 1980; Head of: Milk Div., 1982; European Communities Div., 1985; Under-Sec. and Head of Meat Gp, 1986. *Address:* Ministry of Agriculture, Fisheries and Food, Whitehall Place, SW1A 2HH.

WERNER, Alfred Emil Anthony; Chairman, Pacific Regional Conservation Center, 1975–82, retired; *b* 18 June 1911; *o s* of late Professor Emil Alphonse Werner, Dublin; *m* 1939, Marion Jane Davies; two *d*. *Educ:* St Gerard's School, Bray; Trinity College, Dublin. MSc (Dublin Univ.) and ARIC 1936; MA (Dublin) and DPhil (Univ. of Freiburg im Breisgau) 1937; Hon. ScD (Dublin) 1971. Lecturer in Chemistry, TCD, 1937; Reader in Organic Chemistry, TCD, 1946; Research Chemist, National Gallery, 1948; Principal Scientific Officer, British Museum Research Laboratory, 1954, Keeper, 1959–75. Prof. of Chemistry, Royal Acad., 1962–75. FSA 1958; FMA 1959 (President, 1967); MRIA 1963. Pres., International Institute for the Conservation of Artistic and Historic Works, 1971 (Hon. Treasurer, 1962). *Publications:* The Scientific Examination of Paintings, 1952; (with H. Roosen-Runge) Codex Lindisfarnensis, Part V, 1961; (with H. J. Plenderleith) The Conservation of Antiquities and Works of Art, 1972; Dufy, 1987; articles in scientific and museum journals. *Recreations:* chess, travelling. *Address:* Smalls Farm, Groton, Colchester, Essex CO6 5EG. *T:* Boxford (0787) 210231; 11/73 South Street, Bellerive, Tas 7018, Australia. *T:* (002) 44 69 59. *Club:* Athenæum.

WERNER, Ronald Louis, AM 1980; MSc, PhD; company director; President, New South Wales Institute of Technology, 1974–86; Emeritus Professor, University of Technology, Sydney, since 1988; *b* 12 Sept. 1924; *s* of Frank Werner and Olive Maude Werner; *m* 1948, Valerie Irene (*née* Bean); two *s* one *d*. *Educ:* Univ. of New South Wales (BSc (1st Cl. Hons; Univ. Medal); MSc, PhD). FRACI. Sen. Lectr, 1954–60, Associate Prof., 1961–67, Head of Dept of Phys. Chemistry, 1964–67, Univ. of New South Wales; Dep. Dir, 1967–68, Director, 1968–73, NSW Inst. of Technology. Chm., NSW Advanced Educn Bd, 1969–71; Trustee, Mus. of Applied Arts and Scis, 1973–86 (Pres., Bd of Trustees, 1976–84); Chairman: Conf. of Dirs of Central Insts of Technology, 1975–; ACDP, 1982–83; Member: Science and Industry Forum, Aust. Acad. of Science, 1971–76; Council for Tech. and Further Educn, 1970–85; Hong Kong UPGC, 1972–90; NSW Bicentennial Exhibition Cttee, 1985–88; Adv. Council, Univ. of Western Sydney, 1986–88; Governor, College of Law, 1972–76. Director: NRMA Life Ltd, 1985–; NRMA Travel Ltd, 1986–; Open Road Publishing Co., 1986–; NRMA Sales & Service, 1986–. Councillor, Nat. Roads and Motorists Assoc., 1977–. DUniv Univ. of Tech., Sydney, 1988. *Publications:* numerous papers in scientific jls. *Recreations:* yachting, golf. *Address:* 13 Capri Close, Clareville, NSW 2107, Australia.

WERNHAM, Prof. Richard Bruce, MA Oxon; Professor of Modern History, Oxford University, 1951–72; Fellow of Worcester College, Oxford, 1951–72; now Professor and Fellow Emeritus; *b* 11 Oct. 1906; *o s* of Richard George and Eleanor Mary Wernham; *m* 1939, Isobel Hendry Macmillan (*d* 1987), Vancouver BC; one *d*. *Educ:* Newbury Grammar School; Exeter College, Oxford. Research Asst, Inst. of Historical Research, London Univ., 1929–30; Temp. Asst, Public Record Office, 1930–32; Editor, PRO, State Papers, Foreign Series. 1933–; Lecturer in Modern History, University Coll., London, 1933–34; Fellow of Trinity College, Oxford, 1934–51, Senior Tutor, 1940–41 and 1948–51; University Lecturer in Modern History, Oxford, 1941–51; Examiner in Final Honour School of Modern History, Oxford, 1946–48. Vis. Professor: Univ. of S Carolina, 1958; Univ. of California, Berkeley, 1965–66; Una's Lectr, Berkeley, 1978. Served in RAF, 1941–45. *Publications:* Before the Armada: the Growth of English Foreign Policy 1485–1558, 1966; The Making of Elizabethan Policy, 1980; After the Armada: Elizabethan England and the Struggle for Western Europe 1588–95, 1984; Calendars of State Papers, Foreign Series, Elizabeth; (ed) Vol III, New Cambridge Modern History: The Counter-Reformation and Price Revolution, 1559–1610, 1968; (ed) Expedition of Sir John Norris and Sir Francis Drake to Spain and Portugal, 1589, 1988; articles in English Hist. Review, History, Trans Royal Hist. Soc., Encyclopædia Britannica. *Address:* 63 Hill Head Road, Hill Head, Fareham, Hants PO14 3JL.

WESIERSKA, Mrs George; *see* Walder, Ruth C.

WESIL, Dennis; *b* 18 Feb. 1915; *e s* of Jack and Polly Wesil, London; *m* 1941, Kathleen, *d* of H. S. McAlpine; two *d*. *Educ:* Central Foundation Sch.; University Coll., London. Entered London telephone service as Asst Supt of Traffic, 1937; PO Investigation Branch, 1941; Asst Postal Controller, 1947; Principal, PO Headqrtrs, 1953; Dep. Chief Inspector of Postal Services, 1961; Asst Sec. in charge of Postal Mechanisation Branch, 1963; Dep. Dir, NE Region (GPO), 1966; Director: NE Postal Region, 1967; London Postal Region, 1970–71; Sen. Dir, Posts, PO, 1971–75. Mem., PO Management Bd, 1975. *Recreations:* reading, golf. *Address:* 2 Stoneleigh, Martello Road South, Poole, Dorset BH13 7HQ. *T:* Canford Cliffs (0202) 707304.

WESKER, Arnold, FRSL 1985; playwright; director; Founder Director of Centre Fortytwo, 1961 (dissolved 1970); Chairman, British Centre of International Theatre Institute, 1978–82; President, International Playwrights' Committee, 1979–83; *b* 24 May 1932; *s* of Joseph Wesker and Leah Perlmutter; *m* 1958, Dusty Bicker; two *s* two *d*. *Educ:* Upton House School, Hackney. Furniture Maker's Apprentice, Carpenter's Mate, 1948; Bookseller's Asst, 1949 and 1952; Royal Air Force, 1950–52; Plumber's Mate, 1952; Farm Labourer, Seed Sorter, 1953; Kitchen Porter, 1953–54; Pastry Cook, 1954–58. Former Mem., Youth Service Council. Hon. LittD UEA, 1989. Author of plays: The Kitchen, produced at Royal Court Theatre, 1959, 1961 (filmed, 1961); Trilogy of plays (Chicken Soup with Barley, Roots, I'm Talking about Jerusalem) produced Belgrade Theatre (Coventry), 1958–60, Royal Court Theatre, 1960; Chips with Everything, Royal Court, 1962, Vaudeville, 1962 and Plymouth Theatre, Broadway, 1963; The Four

Seasons, Belgrade Theatre (Coventry) and Saville, 1965; Their Very Own and Golden City, Brussels and Royal Court, 1966 (Marzotto Drama Prize, 1964); The Friends, Stockholm and London, 1970 (also dir); The Old Ones, Royal Court, 1972; The Wedding Feast, Stockholm, 1974, Leeds 1977; The Journalists, Coventry (amateur), 1977, Yugoslav TV, 1978, Germany, 1981; The Merchant, subseq. entitled Shylock, Stockholm and Aarhus, 1976, Broadway, 1977, Birmingham, 1978; Love Letters on Blue Paper, Nat. Theatre, 1978 (also dir); Fatlips (for young people), 1978; Caritas (Scandinavian Project commission), 1980, Nat. Theatre, 1981; Sullied Hand, 1981, Edinburgh Festival and Finnish TV, 1984; Four Portraits (Japanese commn), Tokyo, 1982, Edinburgh Festival, 1984; Annie Wobbler, Suddeutscher Rundfunk, Germany, Birmingham and New End Theatre, 1983, Fortune Theatre, 1984, New York, 1986; One More Ride on the Merry-Go-Round, Leicester, 1985; Yardsale, Edinburgh Fest. and Stratford-on-Avon (RSC Actors' Fest.), 1985 (also dir); When God Wanted A Son, 1986; Whatever Happened to Betty Lemon (double-bill with Yardsale), Lyric Studio, 1987 (also dir); Little Old Lady (for young people), Sigtuna, Sweden, 1988; Beorhtel's Hill, Towngate, Basildon, 1989; Lady Othello (film script), 1980. *Television:* (first play) Menace, 1963; Breakfast, 1981; (adapted) Thieves in the Night, by A. Koestler, 1984; (adapted) Diary of Jane Somers, by Doris Lessing, 1989. *Radio:* Yardsale, 1984; Bluey (Eur. Radio Commn), Cologne Radio 1984, BBC Radio 3, 1985. *Publications:* Chicken Soup with Barley, 1959; Roots, 1959; I'm Talking about Jerusalem, 1960; The Wesker Trilogy, 1960; The Kitchen, 1961; Chips with Everything, 1962; The Four Seasons, 1966; Their Very Own and Golden City, 1966; The Friends, 1970; Fears of Fragmentation (essays), 1971; Six Sundays in January, 1971; The Old Ones, 1972; The Journalists, 1974 (in Dialog; repr. 1975); Love Letters on Blue Paper (stories), 1974, 2nd edn 1990; (with John Allin) Say Goodbye! You May Never See Them Again, 1974; Words—as definitions of experience, 1976; The Wedding Feast, 1977; Journey Into Journalism, 1977; Said the Old Man to the Young Man (stories), 1978; The Merchant, 1978; Fatlips (for young people), 1978; The Journalists, a triptych (with Journey into Journalism and A Diary of the Writing of The Journalists), 1979; Caritas, 1981; The Merchant, 1983; Distinctions, 1985; Yardsale, 1987; Whatever Happened to Betty Lemon, 1987; Little Old Lady, 1988; Shoeshine, 1989; Collected Plays: vols 1 and 5, 1989, vols 2, 3, 4 and 6, 1990. *Address:* 37 Ashley Road, N19 3AG.

WESLEY, Mary; *see* Siepmann, M. A.

WESSEL, Robert Leslie, OBE 1969; *b* 21 Oct. 1912; *s* of late H. L. Wessel, Copenhagen, Denmark; *m* 1936, Dora Elizabeth, *d* of G. C. G. Gee, Rothley, Leics; two *s* two *d. Educ:* Malvern College. Entered N. Corah & Sons Ltd, 1932, Chm., 1957–69, retired. Served War of 1939–45, 44th Searchlight Regt RATA, 1939–41. Chairman: Nat. Youth Bureau, 1972–76; Youth Service Information Centre, 1968–72; Nat. Coll. for training Youth Leaders, 1960–70. Member: Council of Industrial Soc. (Chm., 1969–72); Cttee of Management, RNLI, 1974–82; Pro-Chancellor, Loughborough University of Technology, 1969–78; Group Chairman, Duke of Edinburgh's Conference, 1956. Mem., N and E Midlands Regional Bd, Lloyds Bank Ltd, 1962–78; Dir, Loughborough Consultants Ltd, 1970–78. FBIM; FIWM. Hon. DTech Loughborough, 1978. Mem., Worshipful Co. of Framework Knitters (Master, 1969–70). *Recreations:* painting, photography, music, travel. *Address:* 12 St Elmo Court, Sandhills Road, Salcombe, South Devon TQ8 8JP. *T:* Salcombe (0548) 842456.

WEST; *see* Sackville-West, family name of Baron Sackville.

WEST, Christopher Robin; District General Manager, Portsmouth and South East Hampshire Health Authority, since 1984; Member, Audit Commission, since 1990; *b* 26 April 1944; *s* of George Edward Harry West and of late Queenie (*née* Rickwood); *m* 1970, Lesley Jane Dadd; two *s. Educ:* Sir James Smith's Grammar Sch., Camelford, Cornwall; Durham Univ. (MSc). AHSM. Health Service appointments: Bristol, 1965–66; Torquay, 1966–67; Sunderland, 1967–68; Asst Hosp. Sec., Westminster Hosp., 1968–72; Asst Clerk, Bd of Govs, Guy's Hosp., 1972–75; Regl Management Services Officer and Head of Strategic Planning, Oxford RHA, 1975–78; Area Administrator, Wilts AHA, 1978–82; Portsmouth and SE Hants HA, 1982–84. *Publications:* Education for Senior NHS Management, 1975 (Chm., Business Graduates Assoc. Report); (jtly) Industrial Relations: in search for a system, 1979; (jtly) Health Care in the United Kingdom, 1982; (jtly) Walk, don't run, 1987; (jtly) Day Care, Surgery, Anaesthesia and Management, 1989; articles in various jls. *Recreations:* sailing, photography, cricket, ornithology, reading, gardening, an interest in all things related to Cornwall. *Address:* c/o District Offices, St Mary's Hospital, Portsmouth, Hants PO3 6AD. *T:* Portsmouth (0705) 866600.

WEST, David Arthur James; Assistant Under Secretary of State (Naval Personnel), Ministry of Defence, 1981–84, retired; *b* 10 Dec. 1927; *s* of Wilfred West and Edith West (*née* Jones). *Educ:* Cotham Grammar Sch., Bristol. Executive Officer, Air Ministry, 1946; Higher Executive Officer, 1955; Principal, 1961; Assistant Secretary, 1972; Asst Under Sec. of State, 1979. *Address:* 66 Denton Road, East Twickenham TW1 2HQ. *T:* 081–892 6890.

WEST, David Thomson, CBE 1982; *b* 10 March 1923; *m* 1958, Marie Sellar; one *s* one *d. Educ:* Malvern Coll.; St John's Coll., Oxford. Served in RNVR, 1942–45; HM Diplomatic Service, 1946–76; served in Foreign Office, Office of Comr General for UK in SE Asia, HM Embassies, Paris, Lima, and Tunis; Counsellor, 1964; Commercial Inspector, 1965–68; Counsellor (Commercial) Berne, 1968–71; Head of Export Promotion Dept, FCO, 1971–72; seconded to Civil Service Dept as Head of Manpower Div., 1972–76; transf. to Home Civil Service, 1976, retired 1983. *Address:* 7 St Paul's Place, N1 2QE. *T:* 071–226 7505. *Club:* Garrick.

WEST, Prof. Donald James; Professor of Clinical Criminology 1979–84, now Emeritus, and Director 1981–84, University of Cambridge Institute of Criminology; Fellow of Darwin College, Cambridge, 1967–91, now Emeritus; Hon. Consultant Psychiatrist, National Health Service, 1961, retired; *b* 9 June 1924; *s* of John Charles and Jessie Mercedes West. *Educ:* Merchant Taylors' Sch., Crosby; Liverpool Univ. (MD). LittD Cambridge. FRCPsych. Research Officer, Soc. for Psychical Research, London, and pt-time graduate student in psychiatry, 1947–50; in hospital practice in psychiatry, 1951–59; Sen. Registrar, Forensic Psychiatry Unit, Maudsley Hosp., 1957–59; Inst. of Criminology, Cambridge, 1960–. Leverhulme Emeritus Fellow, 1988–89. Vice Pres., 1981–, and former Pres., British Soc. of Criminology; Pres., Soc. for Psychical Research, 1963–65, 1984–87; Chm., Forensic Section, World Psychiatric Assoc., 1983–89; Chm., Streetwise Youth, 1986–. *Publications:* Psychical Research Today, 1954 (revd edn 1962); Eleven Lourdes Miracles (med. inquiry under Parapsych. Foundn Grant), 1957; The Habitual Prisoner (for Inst. of Criminology), 1963; Murder followed by Suicide (for Inst. of Criminology), 1965; The Young Offender, 1967; Homosexuality, 1968; Present Conduct and Future Delinquency, 1969; (ed) The Future of Parole, 1972; (jtly) Who Becomes Delinquent?, 1973; (jtly) The Delinquent Way of Life, 1977; Homosexuality Re-examined, 1977; (ed, jtly) Daniel McNaughton: his trial and the aftermath, 1977; (jtly) Understanding Sexual Attacks, 1978; Delinquency: its roots, careers and prospects, 1982; Sexual Victimisation, 1985; Sexual Crimes and Confrontations, 1987; (jtly) Children's Sexual Encounters with Adults, 1990; various contribs to British Jl of Criminology, Jl of Adolescence. *Recreations:* travel, parapsychology. *Address:* 32 Fen Road, Milton, Cambridge CB4 6AD. *T:* Cambridge (0223) 860308; 11 Queen's Gate Gardens, SW7. *T:* 071–581 2875.

WEST, Edward Mark, CMG 1987; Special Representative of Director-General, Food and Agriculture Organization of the United Nations, since 1990; *b* 11 March 1923; *m* 1948, Lydia Hollander; three *s. Educ:* Hendon County Sch.; University Coll., Oxford (MA). Served RA (W/Lieut), 1943; ICU BAOR (A/Captain), 1945. Asst Principal, Colonial Office, 1947; Private Sec., PUS, Colonial Office, 1950–51, Principal, 1951–58; Head of Chancery, UK Commn, Singapore, 1958–61; Private Secretary to Secretary of State, Colonial Affairs, 1961–62; Private Secretary to Secretary of State for Commonwealth and Colonial Affairs, 1963; Asst Sec., ODM, 1964–70; Food and Agriculture Organization: Director, Programme and Budget Formulation, 1970; Asst Dir-Gen., Administration and Finance Dept, 1974; Asst Dir-Gen., Programme and Budget Formulation, 1976; Dep, Dir-Gen. of Orgn, 1982–86. *Address:* 10 Warwick Mansions, Cromwell Crescent, SW5 9QR.

WEST, Rt. Rev. Francis Horner, MA; *b* 9 Jan. 1909; *o s* of Sydney Hague and Mary West, St Albans, Herts; *m* 1947, Beryl Elaine, 2nd *d* of late Rev. W. A. Renwick, Smallbridge, Rochdale; one *s* one *d. Educ:* Berkhamsted School; Magdalene Coll. and Ridley Hall, Cambridge. Exhibitioner, Magdalene, Cambridge; MA 1934; Curate St Agnes, Leeds, 1933–36; Chaplain, Ridley Hall, Cambridge, 1936–38; Vicar of Starbeck, Yorks, 1938–42. Served War of 1939–45, as CF with BEF, MEF, CMF and SEAC, 1939–46 (despatches, 1945); Director of Service Ordination Candidates, 1946–47; Vicar of Upton, Notts, 1947–51; Archdeacon of Newark, 1947–62; Vicar of East Retford, 1951–55; Bishop Suffragan of Taunton, 1962–77; Prebendary of Wells, 1962–77; Rector of Dinder, Somerset, 1962–71. Select Preacher, Cambridge Univ., 1962. Visitor, Croft House School, 1968–79. *Publications:* Rude Forefathers, The Story of an English Village, 1600–1666, 1949, reprinted 1989; The Great North Road in Nottinghamshire, 1956; Sparrows of the Spirit, 1957; The Country Parish Today and Tomorrow, 1960; F. R. B.: a portrait of Bishop F. R. Barry, 1980; The Story of a Wiltshire Country Church, 1987. *Recreations:* writing, gardening. *Address:* 11 Castle Street, Aldbourne, Marlborough, Wilts SN8 2DA. *T:* Marlborough (0672) 40630.

WEST, Lt-Col George Arthur Alston-Roberts-, CVO 1988; DL; Comptroller, Lord Chamberlain's Office, 1987–90 (Assistant Comptroller, 1981–87); an Extra Equerry to the Queen, since 1982; *b* 1937; *s* of Major W. R. J. Alston-Roberts-West, Grenadier Guards (killed in action 1940) and late Mrs W. R. J. Alston-Roberts-West; *m* 1970, Hazel, *d* of late Sir Thomas Cook and of Lady Cook. *Educ:* Eton Coll.; RMA, Sandhurst. Commissioned into Grenadier Guards, Dec. 1957; served in England, Northern Ireland, Germany and Cyprus; retired, 1980. DL Warwicks, 1988. *Address:* Atherstone Hill Farm, Atherstone-on-Stour, Stratford-on-Avon, Warwicks CV37 8NF. *Clubs:* Boodle's, Pratt's.

WEST, Rt. Hon. Henry William, PC (N Ire) 1960; Leader, Ulster Unionist Party, 1974–79; *b* 27 March 1917; *s* of late W. H. West, JP; *m* 1956, Maureen Elizabeth Hall; four *s* three *d. Educ:* Enniskillen Model School; Portora Royal School. Farmer. MP for Enniskillen, NI Parlt, 1954–72; Mem. (U), Fermanagh and S Tyrone, NI Assembly, 1973–75; Parly Sec. to Minister of Agriculture, 1958; Minister of Agriculture, 1960–67, and 1971–72; MP (UUUC) Fermanagh and South Tyrone, Feb.-Sept. 1974; Mem. (UUUC), for Fermanagh and South Tyrone, NI Constitutional Convention, 1975–76. N Ireland representative on British Wool Marketing Board, 1950–58; President, Ulster Farmers' Union, 1955–56. High Sheriff, Co. Fermanagh, 1954. *Address:* Rossahilly House, Enniskillen, Northern Ireland. *T:* Enniskillen (0365) 3060.

WEST, Prof. John Clifford, CBE 1977; PhD, DSc; FEng; FIEE; FRGS; Vice-Chancellor and Principal, University of Bradford, 1979–89; *b* 4 June 1922; *s* of J. H. West and Mrs West (*née* Ascroft); *m* 1946, Winefride Mary Turner; three *d. Educ:* Hindley and Abram Grammar School; Victoria Univ., Manchester. PhD 1953, DSc 1957. Matthew Kirtley Entrance Schol., Manchester Univ., 1940. Electrical Lieutenant, RNVR, 1943–46. Lecturer, University of Manchester, 1946–57; Professor of Electrical Engineering, The Queen's University of Belfast, 1958–65; University of Sussex: Prof. of Electrical and Control Engineering, 1965–78; Founder Dean, Sch. of Applied Scis, 1965–73, Pro-Vice-Chancellor, 1967–71; Dir, Phillips' Philatelic Unit, 1970–78. Director, A. C. E. Machinery Ltd, 1966–79. Member: UGC, 1973–78 (Chm., Technology Sub-Cttee, 1973–78); Science Res. Council Cttee on Systems and Electrical Engineering, 1963–67; Science Res. Council Engrg Bd, 1976–79; Vis. Cttee, Dept of Educn and Science, Cranfield; Civil Service Commn Special Merit Promotions Panel, 1966–72; Naval Educn Adv. Cttee, 1965–72; Crawford Cttee on Broadcasting Coverage, 1973–74; Inter-Univ. Inst. of Engrg Control, 1967–83 (Dir, 1967–70); Chairman: Council for Educnl Technology, 1980–85; Educn Task Gp, IStructE, 1988–89. Pres., IEE, 1984–85 (Dep. Pres. 1982–84); Chm., Automation and Control Div., IEE, 1970–71. Treasurer, Yorkshire Cancer Res. Campaign, 1989–. Chm., Internat. Commn on Higher Educn, Botswana, 1990. Member: Royal Philatelic Soc., 1960–; Sociedad Filatélica de Chile, 1970–; Chm., British Philatelic Council, 1980–81; Trustee, Nat. Philatelic Trust, 1989–. FRPSL, 1970–; Hon. FInstMC 1984. Hon. DSc Sussex, 1988; DUniv Bradford, 1990. Hartley Medal, Inst. Measurement and Control, 1979. *Publications:* Textbook of Servomechanisms, 1953; Analytical Techniques for Non-Linear Control Systems, 1960; papers in Proc. IEE, Trans Amer. IEE, Brit. Jl of Applied Physics, Jl of Scientific Instruments, Proc. Inst. Measurement and Control. *Recreations:* philately, postal history. *Address:* 6 Park Crescent, Guiseley, Leeds LS20 8EL. *T:* Guiseley (0943) 72605. *Clubs:* Athenæum, Commonwealth Trust.

WEST, Kenneth, CChem, FRSC; Deputy Chairman, ICI Fibres Division, 1980–84 (Technical Director, 1977–80); *b* 1 Sept. 1930; *s* of Albert West and Ethel Kirby (*née* Kendall); *m* 1980, Elizabeth Ann Borland (*née* Campbell); one step *s*, and three *d* by a previous marriage. *Educ:* Archbishop Holgate's Grammar Sch., York; University Coll., Oxford (BA). Customer Service Manager, ICI Fibres, 1960; Res. and Engrg Manager, FII, 1967; Director: South African Nylon Spinners, Cape Town, 1970; Fibre Industries Inc., N Carolina, 1974; Man. Dir, TWA, 1984–85; Dir, Water Res. Council, 1984–85. Dir, Seahorse Internat. Ltd, 1987–89. FRSA. *Recreations:* sailing, flying, music, whisky. *Address:* Stone Ridge, Niton Undercliff, Ventnor, Isle of Wight PO38 2LY. *T:* Isle of Wight (0983) 730846. *Clubs:* Yorkshire Aeroplane; Lymington Town Sailing.

WEST, Martin Litchfield, DPhil; FBA 1973; Senior Research Fellow, All Souls College, University of Oxford, since 1991; *b* 23 Sept. 1937; *s* of Maurice Charles West and Catherine Baker West (*née* Stainthorpe); *m* 1960, Stephanie Roberta Pickard (*see* S. R. West); one *s* one *d. Educ:* St Paul's Sch.; Balliol Coll., Oxford (MA 1962; DPhil 1963). Chancellor's Prizes for Latin Prose and Verse, 1957; Hertford and de Paravicini Schols, 1957; Ireland Schol., 1957; Conington Prize, 1965. Woodhouse Jun. Research Fellow, St John's Coll., Oxford, 1960–63; Fellow and Praelector in Classics, University Coll., Oxford, 1963–74; Prof. of Greek, Bedford Coll., then at RHBNC, London Univ., 1974–91. Corresp. Mem., Akademie der Wissenschaften zu Göttingen, 1991. Editor of Liddell and Scott's Greek-English Lexicon, 1965–81. *Publications:* Hesiod, Theogony (ed), 1966; Fragmenta Hesiodea (ed with R. Merkelbach), 1967; Early Greek Philosophy and the Orient, 1971; Sing Me, Goddess, 1971; Iambi et Elegi Graeci (ed), 1971–72; Textual Criticism and Editorial Technique, 1973; Studies in Greek Elegy and Iambus, 1974; Hesiod, Works and Days (ed), 1978; Theognidis et Phocylidis fragmenta, 1978; Delectus ex Iambis et Elegis Graecis, 1980; Greek Metre, 1982; The Orphic Poems, 1983; Carmina Anacreontea, 1984; The Hesiodic Catalogue of Women, 1985; Euripides, Orestes (ed), 1987; Introduction to Greek Metre, 1987; Hesiod (trans.), 1988; Aeschyli Tragoediae, 1990; Studies in Aeschylus, 1991; articles in classical periodicals. *Recreation:* strong music. *Address:* All Souls College, Oxford OX1 4AL.

WEST, Michael Charles B.; *see* Beresford-West.

WEST, Morris (Langlo), AM 1985; novelist; *b* Melbourne, 26 April 1916; *s* of Charles Langlo West and Florence Guilfoyle Hanlon; *m* Joyce Lawford; three *s* one *d*. *Educ:* Melbourne Univ. (BA 1937). Taught modern langs and maths, NSW and Tas, 1933–39. Served, Lieutenant, AIF, South Pacific, 1939–43. Sec. to William Morris Hughes, former PM of Australia, 1943. FRSL; Fellow World Acad. of Art and Science. Hon. DLitt, Univ. of Santa Clara, 1969; Hon. DLitt Mercy Coll., NY, 1982. Internat. Dag Hammarskjold Prize (Grand Collar of Merit), 1978. *Publications:* Gallows on the Sand, 1955; Kundu, 1956; Children of the Sun, 1957; The Crooked Road, 1957 (Eng.: The Big Story); The Concubine, 1958; Backlash, 1958 (Eng.: The Second Victory); The Devil's Advocate, 1959 (National Brotherhood Award, National Council of Christians and Jews 1960; James Tait Black Memorial Prize, 1960; RSL Heinemann Award, 1960; filmed 1977); The Naked Country, 1960; Daughter of Silence (novel), 1961, (play), 1961; The Shoes of the Fisherman, 1963; The Ambassador, 1965; The Tower of Babel, 1968; The Heretic, a Play in Three Acts, 1970; (with R. Francis) Scandal in the Assembly, 1970; Summer of the Red Wolf, 1971; The Salamander, 1973; Harlequin, 1974; The Navigator, 1976; Proteus, 1979; The Clowns of God, 1981 (Universe Literary Prize, 1981); The World is Made of Glass, 1983 (play 1984); Cassidy, 1986; Masterclass, 1988; Lazarus, 1990. *Address:* c/o Maurice Greenbaum, Rosenman Colin, 575 Madison Avenue, New York, NY 10022, USA. *Clubs:* Australian, Royal Prince Alfred Yacht (Sydney).

WEST, Nigel; *see* Allason, R. W. S.

WEST, Norman; Member (Lab) Yorkshire South, European Parliament, since 1984; *b* 26 Nov. 1935; *m*; two *s*. *Educ:* Barnsley; Sheffield Univ. Miner. Mem., South Yorks CC (Chm., Highways Cttee; Mem., anti-nuclear working party). Member: NUM; CND. Mem., Energy, Research and Technology Cttee, European Parlt, 1984–. *Address:* 43 Coronation Drive, Birdwell, Barnsley, South Yorks.

WEST, Peter; BBC television commentator/anchorman, 1950–86; commentaries for radio, 1947–85; Chairman, West Nally Group (sports marketing), 1971–83; *b* 12 Aug. 1920; *s* of Harold William and Dorcas Anne West; *m* 1946, Pauline Mary Pike; two *s* one *d*. *Educ:* Cranbrook Sch.; RMC, Sandhurst. Served War of 1939–45: Duke of Wellington's Regt. TV/Radio commentaries every year: on Test matches, 1952–86; on Wimbledon, 1955–82; on Rugby Union, 1950–85; Olympics, 1948–60–64–68–72–76. Rugby Football Correspondent of The Times, 1971–82. TV shows: Chairman of: Why?, 1953; Guess my Story, 1953–54–55. Introduced: At Home, 1955; First Hand and It's Up to You, 1956–57; Box Office, 1957; Come Dancing, 1957–72 (incl.); Be Your Own Boss and Wish You Were Here, 1958; Get Ahead, 1958–62; Good Companions, 1958–62; First Years at Work (Schs TV), 1958–69 (incl.); Miss World, 1961–66 (incl.); Facing West (HTV, Bristol), 1986–88. Children's TV: introd.: Question Marks, 1957; Ask Your Dad, 1958; What's New?, 1962–63–64. Radio: introd.: What Shall We Call It?, 1955; Sound Idea, 1958; Morning Call, 1960–61; Treble Chance, 1962; Sporting Chance, 1964; Games People Play, 1975. *Publications:* The Fight for the Ashes, 1953; The Fight for the Ashes, 1956; Flannelled Fool and Muddied Oaf (autobiog.), 1986; Clean Sweep, 1987; Denis Compton—Cricketing Genius, 1989. *Recreation:* gardening. *Address:* The Paddock, Duntisbourne Abbotts, Cirencester, Glos GL7 7JW. *T:* Miserden (028582) 380.

WEST, Prunella Margaret Rumney, (Mrs T. L. West); *see* Scales, Prunella.

WEST, Prof. Richard Gilbert, FRS 1968; FSA; FGS; Fellow of Clare College, Cambridge, since 1954; Professor of Botany, University of Cambridge, 1977–91; *b* 31 May 1926; *m* 1st, 1958; one *s*; 2nd, 1973, Hazel Gristwood; two *d*. *Educ:* King's School, Canterbury; Univ. of Cambridge. Cambridge University: Demonstrator in Botany, 1957–60; Lecturer in Botany, 1960–67; Dir, Subdept of Quaternary Research, 1966–87; Reader in Quaternary Research, 1967–75; Prof. of Palaeoecology, 1975–77. Member: Council for Scientific Policy, 1971–73; NERC, 1973–76; Ancient Monuments Bd for England, 1980–84. Darwin Lecturer to the British Association, 1959; Lyell Fund, 1961, Bigsby Medal, 1969, Lyell Medal, 1988, Geological Society of London. Hon. MRIA. *Publications:* Pleistocene Geology and Biology, 1968, 2nd edn 1977; (jtly) The Ice Age in Britain, 1972, 2nd edn 1981; The Pre-glacial Pleistocene of the Norfolk and Suffolk coasts, 1980; Pleistocene Palaeoecology of Central Norfolk, 1991. *Address:* 3A Woollards Lane, Great Shelford, Cambs. *T:* Cambridge (0223) 842578; Clare College, Cambridge.

WEST, Prof. Richard John, FRCP; Medical Postgraduate Dean to South Western Region, and Hon. Professor, University of Bristol, since 1991; *b* 8 May 1939; *s* of late Cecil J. West and of Alice B. West (*née* Court); *m* 1962, Jenny Winn Hawkins; one *s* two *d*. *Educ:* Tiffin Boys' Sch.; Middlesex Hospital Medical School (MB, BS, MD, DCH, DObstRCOG). FRCP 1979. Research Fellow, Inst. of Child Health, London, 1971–73; Sen. Registrar, Hosp. for Sick Children, London, 1973–74; Lectr, Inst. of Child Health, 1974–75; Sen. Lectr, 1975–91, Dean, 1982–87, St George's Hosp. Med. Sch.; Consultant Paediatrician, St George's Hosp., 1975–91. Member: Wandsworth HA, 1981–82, 1989–90; SW Thames RHA, 1982–88. Member: Governing Body: Inst. of Med. Ethics, 1985– (Gen. Sec., 1989–); Tiffin Boys' Sch., 1983–86; Wimbledon High Sch., 1988–. *Publications:* Family Guide to Children's Ailments, 1983; Royal Society of Medicine Child Health Guide, 1991; research papers on metabolic diseases, incl. lipid disorders. *Recreations:* windmills, medical history, medical education. *Address:* University of Bristol Medical Postgraduate Department, Canynge Hall, Whiteladies Road, Bristol BS8 2PR. *T:* Bristol (0272) 732688.

WEST, Dr Stephanie Roberta, FBA 1990; Senior Research Fellow in Classics and Librarian, Hertford College, Oxford, since 1990; *b* 1 Dec. 1937; *d* of Robert Enoch Pickard and Ruth (*née* Batters); *m* 1960, Martin Litchfield West, *qv*; one *s* one *d*. *Educ:* Nottingham High Sch. for Girls; Somerville Coll., Oxford (1st cl. Classics Mods 1958, 1st cl. Lit. Hum. 1960; Gaisford Prize for Greek Verse Composition 1959; Ireland Scholar 1959, Derby Scholar 1960); MA 1963, DPhil 1964, Oxon. Oxford University: Mary Ewart Res. Fellow, Somerville Coll., 1965–67; Lecturer: in Classics, Hertford Coll., 1966–90; in Greek, Keble Coll., 1981–. Mem. Council, GPDST, 1974–87. *Publications:* The Ptolemaic Papyri of Homer, 1967; Omero, Odissea 1 (libri I–IV), 1981; (with A. Heubeck and J. B. Hainsworth) A commentary on Homer's Odyssey 1, 1988; articles and reviews in learned jls. *Recreations:* opera, curious information. *Address:* 42 Portland Road, Oxford OX2 7EY. *T:* Oxford (0865) 56060.

WEST, Prof. Thomas Summers, CBE 1988; FRS 1989; FRSE, FRSC; Director, Macaulay Institute for Soil Research, Aberdeen, 1975–87; Honorary Research Professor, University of Aberdeen, 1983–87, now Emeritus; *b* 18 Nov. 1927; *s* of late Thomas West and Mary Ann Summers; *m* 1952, Margaret Officer Lawson, MA; one *s* two *d*. *Educ:* Tarbat Old Public Sch., Portmahomack; Royal Acad., Tain; Aberdeen Univ. (BSc 1st Cl. Hons Chemistry, 1949); Univ. of Birmingham (PhD 1952, DSc 1962). FRSC (FRIC 1962); FRSE 1979. Univ. of Birmingham: Sen. DSIR Fellow, 1952–55; Lectr in Chem., 1955–63; Imperial Coll., London: Reader in Analytical Chem., 1963–65; Prof. of Analytical Chem., 1965–75. Royal Society: Mem., British National Cttee for Chem., and Chm., Analytical Sub-cttee, 1965–82; Mem., Internat. Cttee, 1990–. Sec. Gen., IUPAC, 1983–91 (Pres., Analytical Div., 1977–79); Pres., Soc. for Analytical Chem., 1969–71; Chm., Finance Cttee, ICSU, 1990–; Mem., British Nat. Cttee for IUPAC, RSC, 1990–; Hon. Sec., Chemical Soc., 1972–75 (Redwood Lectr, 1974); Hon. Member: Bunseki Kagakukai (Japan), 1981; Fondation de la Maison de la Chimie (Paris), 1985. Meldola Medal, RIC, 1956; Instrumentation Medal, 1976, and Gold Medal, 1977, Chemical Soc.; Johannes Marcus Medal for Spectroscopy, Spectroscopic Soc. of Bohemia, 1977. *Publications:* Analytical Applications of Diamino ethane tetra acetic acid, 1958, 2nd edn 1961; New Methods of Analytical Chemistry, 1964; Complexometry with EDTA and Related Reagents, 1969. *Recreations:* gardening, motoring, reading, music, fishing. *Address:* 31 Baillieswells Drive, Bieldside, Aberdeen AB1 9AT. *T:* Aberdeen (0224) 868294.

WEST, Timothy Lancaster, CBE 1984; actor and director; *b* 20 Oct. 1934; *s* of late Harry Lockwood West and Olive Carleton-Crowe; *m* 1st, 1956, Jacqueline Boyer (marr. diss.); one *d*; 2nd, 1963, Prunella Scales, *qv*; two *s*. *Educ:* John Lyon Sch., Harrow; Regent Street Polytechnic. Entered profession as asst stage manager, Wimbledon, 1956; first London appearance, Caught Napping, Piccadilly, 1959; Mem., RSC, 1964–66; Prospect Theatre Co., 1966–72: Dr Samuel Johnson, Prospero, Bolingbroke, young Mortimer in Edward II, King Lear, Emerson in A Room with a View, Alderman Smuggler in The Constant Couple, and Holofernes in Love's Labour's Lost; Otto in The Italian Girl, 1968; Gilles in Abelard and Heloise, 1970; Robert Hand in Exiles, 1970; Gilbert in The Critic as Artist, 1971; Sir William Gower in Trelawny (musical), Bristol, 1972; Falstaff in Henry IV Pts I and II, Bristol, 1973; Shpigelsky in A Month in the Country, Chichester, 1974 (London, 1975); Brack in Hedda Gabler, RSC, 1975; Iago in Othello, Nottingham, 1976; with Prospect Co.: Harry in Staircase, 1976, Claudius in Hamlet, storyteller in War Music, and Enobarbus in Antony and Cleopatra, 1977; Ivan and Gottlieb in Laughter, and Max in The Homecoming, 1978; with Old Vic Co.: Narrator in Lancelot and Guinevere, Shylock in The Merchant of Venice, 1980; Beecham, Apollo, 1980, NZ, 1983, Dublin, 1986; Uncle Vanya, Australia, 1982; Stalin in Master Class, Leicester, 1983, Old Vic, 1984; Charlie Mucklebrass in Big in Brazil, 1984; The War at Home, Hampstead, 1984; When We Are Married, Whitehall, 1986; The Sneeze, Aldwych, 1988; Bristol Old Vic: The Master Builder, 1989; The Clandestine Marriage, Uncle Vanya, 1990; James Tyrone, in Long Day's Journey into Night, 1991, also at NT. *Directed:* plays for Prospect Co., Open Space, Gardner Centre, Brighton, and rep. at Salisbury, Bristol, Northampton and Cheltenham; own season, The Forum, Billingham, 1973; Artistic Dir, Old Vic Co., 1980–81. *Television includes:* Richard II, 1969; Edward II, and The Boswell and Johnson Show, 1970; Horatio Bottomley, 1972; Edward VII, 1973; Hard Times, 1977; Crime and Punishment, Churchill and the Generals, 1979 (RTS Award); Brass, 1982–84, 1990; The Last Bastion, 1984; The Nightingale Saga, Tender is the Night, 1985; The Monocled Mutineer, The Good Doctor Bodkin Adams, 1986; What the Butler Saw, Harry's Kingdom, The Train, When We Are Married, Breakthrough at Reykjavik, 1987; Strife, A Shadow on the Sun, The Contractor, 1988; Blore, MP, Beecham, 1989; Survival of the Fittest, 1990. *Films:* The Looking-Glass War, 1968; Nicholas and Alexandra, 1970; The Day of the Jackal, 1972; Hedda, 1975; Joseph Andrews, and The Devil's Advocate, 1976; William Morris, 1977; Agatha, and The 39 Steps, 1978; The Antagonists, 1980; Murder is Easy, and Oliver Twist, 1981; Cry Freedom, 1986; Consuming Passions, 1987. Compiles and dir. recital progs; sound broadcaster. Director in Residence, Univ. of WA, 1982; Director: All Change Arts Ltd; World Student Drama Trust. Member: Arts Council Drama Panel, 1974–76, and Touring Cttee, 1978–80; Council, LAMDA, 1980–; Governor, Bristol Old Vic Trust, 1986–91. *Recreations:* theatre history, travel, music, old railways. *Address:* c/o James Sharkey Associates Ltd, 15 Golden Square, W1. *Club:* Garrick.

WEST, Prof. William Dixon, CIE 1947; ScD, FGS, FNA (Geol.); Emeritus Professor of Applied Geology, University of Saugar; *b* 1901; *s* of Arthur Joseph West. *Educ:* King's Sch., Canterbury; St John's Coll., Cambridge (BA; ScD). Former Director, Geological Survey of India; former Vice-Chancellor, Univ. of Saugar. Lyell Medal, Geological Soc. of London, 1950; Wadia Medal, Indian Nat. Science Acad., 1983. *Address:* Department of Applied Geology, Doctor Harisingh Gour Vishwavidyalaya, Sagar, Madhya Pradesh 470003, India.

WEST CUMBERLAND, Archdeacon of; *see* Packer, Ven. J. R.

WEST HAM, Archdeacon of; *see* Stevens, Ven. T. J.

WEST INDIES, Archbishop of, since 1986; **Most Rev. Orland Ugham Lindsay;** Bishop of the North-Eastern Caribbean and Aruba (formerly Antigua), since 1970; *b* 24 March 1928; *s* of Hubert and Ida Lindsay; *m* 1959, Olga Daphne (*née* Wright); three *s*. *Educ:* Culham Coll., Oxon (Teachers' Cert.); St Peter's Coll., Jamaica; McGill Univ. BD (London) 1957. RAF, 1944–47. Teacher, Franklyn Town Govt School, Jamaica, 1949–52; Asst Master, Kingston College, 1952–53. Deacon 1956, priest 1957; Asst Curate, St Peter's Vere, Jamaica, 1956–57; Asst Master, Kingston Coll., 1958–67, Chaplain 1962–63; Priest-in-Charge, Manchioneal Cure, Jamaica, 1960; Chaplain, Jamaica Defence Force, 1963–67; Principal, Church Teachers' Coll., Mandeville, 1967–70. Sec. to Jamaica Synod, 1962–70. Hon. DD Berkeley Divinity School, 1978. *Recreations:* jazz music, photography. *Address:* Bishop's Lodge, PO Box 23, St John's, Antigua. *T:* (office and home) (809) 462 0151, (direct line) (809) 462 2091, *Fax:* (809) 462 2090.

WEST-RUSSELL, His Honour Sir David (Sturrock), Kt 1986; President of Industrial Tribunals for England and Wales, 1984–91; *b* 17 July 1921; *o s* of late Sir Alexander West-Russell and late Agnes West-Russell (*née* Sturrock); *m* Christine (*née* Tyler); one *s* two *d*. *Educ:* Rugby; Pembroke Coll., Cambridge. Served war: Buffs, 1940; commissioned Queen's Own Cameron Highlanders, 1941; Parachute Regt, 1942–46; N Africa, Italy, France, Greece, Norway and Palestine (despatches, Major). Management Trainee, Guest Keen and Nettlefold, 1948–50; Harmsworth Law Scholar, 1952; called to Bar, Middle Temple, 1953, Bencher, 1986; SE Circuit; Dep. Chm., Inner London Quarter Sessions, 1966–72; Circuit Judge, 1972; Sen. Circuit Judge, Inner London Crown Court, 1979–82, Southwark Crown Court, 1983–84. Mem., Departmental Cttee on Legal Aid in Criminal Proceedings, 1964–65. Comr (NI Emergency Provisions Act), 1974–80; Chairman: Lord Chancellor's Adv. Cttee on Appts of Magistrates for Inner London, 1976–87; Home Sec's Adv. Bd on Restricted Patients, 1985–91; Inner London Probation Cttee, 1988–89 (Mem., 1979–89); Member: Lord Chancellor's Adv. Cttee on the Trng of Magistrates, 1980–85; Judicial Studies Bd, 1980–84, 1987–90; Parole Bd, 1980–82; Parole Review Cttee, 1987–88. Pres., Inner London Magistrates' Assoc., 1979–85; Jt Pres., Council of HM Circuit Judges, 1985. *Recreations:* town gardening, country walking. *Address:* 24 Hamilton Terrace, NW8. *T:* 071–286 3718. *Club:* Garrick.

WESTALL, Robert Atkinson; freelance author; *b* 7 Oct. 1929; *s* of Robert Atkinson Westall and Maggie Alexandra Leggett; *m* 1958, Jean Underhill; (one *s* decd). *Educ:* Tynemouth High Sch.; Durham Univ. (1st Cl. Hons Fine Art); London Univ. (Slade Dip.). National Service, L-Corp. Royal Signals, Egypt, 1953–55. Art Master: Erdington Hall Sec. Mod. Sch., 1957–58; Keighley Boys Grammar Sch., 1958–60; Hd of Art, Hd of Careers, Sir John Deane's Coll., Cheshire, 1960–85; antique dealer, 1985–86. Dir, Telephone Samaritans of Mid-Cheshire, 1966–75. Carnegie Medal, 1975, 1980; Horn Book Award (American), 1976, 1981; Preis der Leseratten (German), 1988. *Publications: for children:* The Machine-Gunners, 1975; The Wind Eye, 1976; The Watch House, 1977; The Devil on the Road, 1978; Fathom Five, 1979; Scarecrows, 1980; Break of Dark, 1981; The Haunting of Chas McGill, 1982; Futuretrack Five, 1983; The Cats of Seroster, 1984; Rachel and the Angel, 1986; Urn Burial, 1986; Ghosts and Journeys, 1986; The Creature in the Dark, 1987; Ghost Abbey, 1988; Blitzcat, 1989; Old Man on a Horse, 1989; The Call and Other Stories, 1989; Echoes of War, 1989; A Walk on the Wild Side, 1989; The Kingdom by the Sea, 1990; The Promise, 1990; Stormsearch, 1990; If Cats Could Fly, 1990; Yaxley's Cat, 1991; The Christmas Cat, 1991; The Stories of Muncaster Cathedral 1991; *for adults:* Antique Dust, 1989; *non-fiction:* The Children of the Blitz, 1985. *Recreations:* cats, Gothic architecture, local history, film, is still a practising sculptor, religion and the supernatural. *Address:* c/o Macmillan Publishers, 4 Little Essex Street, WC2R 3LF.

WESTALL, Rupert Vyvyan Hawksley, MA Cantab; Lieutenant Commander RN (retired); Head Master, Kelly College, Tavistock, Devon, 1939–59; *b* 27 July 1899; *s* of late Rev. William Hawksley Westall and Adela Clara Pope; *m* 1925, Sylvia G. D. Page (*d* 1979); two *s* three *d*. *Educ:* RN Colleges Osborne and Dartmouth; Queens' College, Cambridge. Royal Navy, 1912–22; served European War, 1914–18; served in HMS Goliath, HMS Canada, HMS Ure and four years in The Submarine Service; Service on East African Station and Gallipoli, 1914–15, Jutland, China Station; Queens' College, Cambridge, 1922–26 (Exhibitioner and schol.; MA 1926, 1st division first part, 2nd class 2nd part History Tripos); Training College for Schoolmasters, Cambridge, 1925–26; VI form and Careers Master, Blundell's School, 1926–34; Head Master West Buckland School, 1934–38. *Address:* Penrose, 9 Kimberley Place, Falmouth, Cornwall TR11 3QL. *T:* Falmouth (0326) 313238.

WESTBROOK, Eric Ernest, CB 1981; painter and writer; *b* 29 Sept. 1915; *s* of Ernest James and Helen Westbrook; *m* 1st, 1942, Ingrid Nyström; one *d*; 2nd, 1964, Dawn Sime. *Educ:* Alleyn's Sch., Dulwich; various schools of art. Lecturer for Arts Council of Gt Britain, 1943; Director, Wakefield City Art Gallery, Yorks, 1946; Chief Exhibitions Officer, British Council, 1949; Director: Auckland City Art Gallery, NZ, 1952–55; National Gallery of Victoria, Melbourne, Aust., 1956–73; Director (Permanent Head), Ministry for the Arts, Victoria, 1973–80, retired. Hon. LLD Monash, 1974. Chevalier de l'Ordre des Arts et Lettres (France), 1972; Palmes Académiques, 1989. *Publications:* Birth of a Gallery, 1968; various articles and reviews in arts and museum pubns. *Recreations:* music, gardening. *Address:* Houghton Park, Odgers Road, Castlemaine, Vic 3450, Australia. *T:* (054) 724171.

WESTBROOK, Michael John David, OBE 1988; composer, pianist and band-leader; *b* 21 March 1936; *s* of Philip Beckford Westbrook and Vera Agnes (*née* Butler); *m* 1976, Katherine Jane (*née* Duckham), singer, songwriter and painter; one *s* one *d* of previous marriage. *Educ:* Kelly Coll., Tavistock; Plymouth Coll. of Art (NDD); Hornsey Coll. of Art (ATD). Formed first band at Plymouth Art Sch., 1958; moved to London, 1962, and has since led a succession of groups incl. The Mike Westbrook Brass Band, formed with Phil Minton in 1973, The Mike Westbrook Orch., 1974–, and trio (with Kate Westbrook and Chris Biscoe) A Little Westbrook Music, formed in 1982. Has toured extensively in Britain and Europe, and performed in Australia, Canada and NY. Has written commissioned works for fests in Britain, France and other European countries, composed music for theatre, radio, TV and films, and made numerous LPs. Principal compositions/recordings include: Marching Song, 1967; Metropolis, 1969; Tyger: a celebration of William Blake (with Adrian Mitchell), 1971; Citadel/Room 315, 1974; On Duke's Birthday (dedicated to the memory of Duke Ellington), 1984; Bean Rows and Blues Shots (saxophone concerto), 1991; TV scores incl. Caught on a Train, 1983; film score: Moulin Rouge, 1990; with Kate Westbrook: concert works incorporating European poetry and folk song, notably The Cortège, for voices and jazz orch., 1979, and London Bridge is Broken Down, for voice, jazz orch. and chamber orch., 1987; also a succession of music-theatre pieces, including: Mama Chicago, 1978; Westbrook-Rossini, 1984; The Ass (based on poem by D. H. Lawrence), 1985; Pier Rides, 1986; Quichotte (opera), 1989. *Recreation:* work. *Address:* c/o Laurence Aston, PO Box 354, Reading RG2 7JB.

WESTBROOK, Sir Neil (Gowanloch), Kt 1988; CBE 1981; Chairman, Trafford Park Estates PLC; *b* 21 Jan. 1917; *s* of Frank and Dorothy Westbrook; *m* 1945, Hon. Mary Joan Fraser, *o d* of 1st Baron Strathalmond, CBE; one *s* one *d*. *Educ:* Oundle Sch.; Clare Coll., Cambridge (MA). FRICS. Served War of 1939–45: Sapper, 1939; Actg Lt-Col 1945 (despatches). Member: Council, CBI North West Region, 1982–88 (Chairman: NW Inner Cities Studies Gp, 1985; NW Working Party on Derelict Land Clearance, 1986); Inst. of Directors Greater Manchester Branch Cttee, 1972–86. Treas., Manchester Conservative Assoc., 1964–73, Dep. Chm., 1973–74, Chm., 1974–83; Chairman: Greater Manchester Co-ordinating Cttee, NW Area Cons. Assoc., 1977–86; Exchange Div. Cons. Assoc., 1973; Manchester Euro South Cons. Assoc., 1978–84; Member: NW Area F and GP Cttee, Cons. Party, 1974–87; Nat. Union Exec. Cttee, 1975–81; Cons. Bd of Finance, 1984–87. Mem., Manchester City Council, 1949–71; Dep. Leader 1967–69; Lord Mayor 1969–70. Chm., North Western Art Galleries and Museums Service, 1965–68; Mem., Exec. Cttee, Museums Assoc., 1965–69. Pres., Central Manchester Br., Arthritis and Rheumatism Council, 1970. Member: Duke of Edinburgh's Award Scheme Cttee, Manchester Area, 1972–75; Bd, Manchester YMCA, 1960–73. Mem., Chartered Auctioneers & Estate Agents Agricl Cttee, 1949–70; Mem., ABCC Rating Cttee, 1971–74. *Recreations:* football, fishing, horse racing. *Address:* c/o Trafford Park Estates PLC, Estate Office, Trafford Park, Manchester M17 1AU. *Clubs:* Carlton; Manchester Tennis and Racquets.

WESTBROOK, Roger, CMG 1990; HM Diplomatic Service; Ambassador to Zaire, since 1991; *b* 26 May 1941; *e s* of Edward George Westbrook and Beatrice Minnie Westbrook (*née* Marshall). *Educ:* Dulwich Coll.; Hertford Coll., Oxford (MA Modern History). Foreign Office, 1964; Asst Private Sec. to Chancellor of Duchy of Lancaster and Minister of State, FO, 1965; Yaoundé, 1967; Rio de Janeiro, 1971; Brasilia, 1972; Private Sec. to Minister of State, FCO, 1975; Head of Chancery, Lisbon, 1977; Dep. Head, News Dept, FCO, 1980; Dep. Head, Falkland Is Dept, FCO, 1982; Overseas Inspectorate, FCO, 1984; High Comr, Negara Brunei Darussalam, 1986–91. *Recreations:* doodling, sightseeing, theatre, reading, dining. *Address:* c/o Foreign and Commonwealth Office, SW1A 2AH. *Club:* Travellers'.

WESTBURY, 5th Baron, *cr* 1861; **David Alan Bethell,** MC 1942; DL; *b* 16 July 1922; *s* of Captain The Hon. Richard Bethell (*d* 1929; *o c* of 3rd Baron); *S* brother, 1961; *m* 1947, Ursula Mary Rose James, CBE; two *s* one *d*. *Educ:* Harrow. 2nd Lieut 1940, Capt. 1944, Scots Guards. Equerry to the Duke of Gloucester, 1946–49. DL N Yorks, formerly NR Yorks, 1973. GCStJ 1988 (KStJ 1977). *Heir: s* Hon. Richard Nicholas Bethell, MBE 1979 [*b* 29 May 1950; *m* 1975, Caroline Mary (marr. diss. 1990), *d* of Richard Palmer; one *s* two *d*. *Educ:* Harrow; RMA Sandhurst. Major Scots Guards, retired]. *Address:* Barton Cottage, Malton, North Yorkshire YO17 0AT. *T:* Malton (0653) 692293.

WESTBURY, Prof. Gerald, OBE 1990; FRCP, FRCS; Professor of Surgery 1982–89, and Dean, 1986–Sept. 1992, Institute of Cancer Research, now Emeritus Professor; Hon. Consultant Surgeon, Royal Marsden Hospital, 1982–89; *b* 29 July 1927; *s* of Lew and Celia Westbury; *m* 1965, Hazel Frame; three *d*. *Educ:* St Marylebone Grammar Sch.; Westminster Med. Sch., Univ. of London (MB, BS (Hons) 1949); FRCS 1952; FRCP 1976. House Surg., Westminster and Royal Northern Hosps, 1949–50; RAF Med. Service, 1950–52; RSO, Brompton Hosp., 1952–53; Registrar and Sen. Registrar, Westminster Hosp., 1953–60; Fellow in Surgery, Harvard Med. Sch., 1957; Cons. Surg., Westminster Hosp., 1960–82 (Hon. Cons. Surgeon, 1982–89); Hon. Cons. in Surgery to the Army, 1980–89. Pres., British Assoc. of Surgical Oncology, 1989–Dec. 1992. Examiner, Univs of London, Edinburgh, Cambridge, Hong Kong; Hunterian Prof., RCS, 1963; Honyman Gillespie Lectr, Univ. of Edinburgh, 1965; Semon Lectr and Haddow Lectr, RSM, 1982; Gordon-Taylor Lectr, RCS, 1989. Walker Prize, RCS, 1990. *Publications:* medical articles and contribs to text books. *Recreations:* music, bird watching. *Club:* Athenæum.

WESTCOTT, Prof. John Hugh, DSc(Eng), PhD, DIC; FRS 1983; FEng, FCGI, FInstD; Emeritus Professor of Control Systems, and Senior Research Fellow, Imperial College of Science and Technology; Chairman: Feedback plc; Churchill Controls Ltd; *b* 3 Nov. 1920; *s* of John Stanley Westcott and Margaret Elisabeth Westcott (*née* Bass); *m* 1950, Helen Fay Morgan; two *s* one *d*. *Educ:* Wandsworth Sch.; City and Guilds Coll., London; Massachusetts Inst. of Technology. Royal Commission for the Exhibition of 1851 Senior Studentship; Apprenticeship BTH Co., Rugby. Radar Research and Develt Estabt, 1941–45; Lectr, Imperial Coll., 1950; Reader, 1956; Prof., 1961; Head of Computing and Control Dept, 1970–79. Control Commn for Germany, 1945–46. Consultant to: Bataafsche Petroleum Maatschappij (Shell), The Hague, Holland, 1953–58; AEI, 1955–69; ICI, 1965–69; George Wimpey & Son, 1975–80; Westland plc, 1983–85. Chm., Control and Automation Div., Instn of Electrical Engrs, 1968–69. Mem., Exec. Council of Internat. Fedn of Automatic Control, 1969–75; Chm., United Kingdom Automation Council, 1973–79; Pres., Inst. of Measurement and Control, 1979–80. Mem., Adv. Council, RMCS, 1986–; Governor, Kingston Polytechnic, 1974–80. Hon. FIEE; Hon. FInstMC. *Publications:* An Exposition of Adaptive Control, 1962; monographs and papers, mainly on Control Systems and related topics. *Recreations:* gardening, reading. *Address:* (home) Broadlawns, 8 Fernhill, Oxshott, Surrey KT22 0JH; Department of Electrical Engineering, Imperial College, SW7 2BT. *T:* 071–589 5111.

WESTENRA, family name of **Baron Rossmore.**

WESTERMAN, Sir (Wilfred) Alan, Kt 1963; CBE 1962 (OBE 1957); EdD; MAEcon; Chairman, Australian Industry Development Corporation, 1971–83; *b* NZ, 25 March 1913; *s* of W. J. Westerman, Sydney, NSW; *m* 1969, Margaret, *d* of late B. H. White. *Educ:* Knox Grammar School; Universities of Tasmania, Melbourne and Columbia. Chairman, Commonwealth Tariff Board, 1958–60; Sec., Dept of Trade and Industry, Canberra, 1960–71. Director: Ampol Ltd; Philips Industries Holdings Ltd; Oak Systems of Australia Pty Limited; Chm., Stevedoring Industry Consultative Council, 1978–. *Recreation:* tennis. *Clubs:* Commonwealth (Canberra); Athenæum (Melbourne); Union (Sydney).

WESTHEIMER, Prof. Gerald, FRS 1985; Professor of Neurobiology, and Head of Division of Neurobiology, since 1989, University of California, Berkeley (Professor of Physiology, 1967–89); *b* Berlin, 13 May 1924; *s* of late Isaac Westheimer and Ilse Westheimer (*née* Cohn). *Educ:* Sydney Tech. Coll. (Optometry dip. 1943, Fellowship dip. 1949); Univ. of Sydney (BSc 1947); Ohio State Univ. (PhD 1953); postdoctoral training at Marine Biol. Lab., Woods Hole, 1957 and at Physiolog. Lab., Cambridge, 1958–59. Australian citizen, 1945; practising optometrist, Sydney, 1945–51; faculties of Optometry Schools: Univ. of Houston, 1953–54; Ohio State Univ., 1954–60; Univ. of California, Berkeley, 1960–67. Associate: Bosch Vision Res. Center, Salk Inst., 1984–; Neurosciences Res. Program, NY, 1985–; Chairman: Visual Scis Study Sect., NIH, 1977–79; Bd of Scientific Counsellors, Nat. Eye Inst., 1981–83; Bd of Editors, Vision Research, 1986–91; service on numerous professional Cttees. Fellow or Member, scientific socs, UK and overseas. Lectures: Sackler, in Med. Sci., Tel Aviv Univ., 1989; Perception, Eur. Conf. on Visual Perception, 1989; D. O. Hebb, McGill Univ., Canada, 1991. Hon. DSc: New South Wales, 1988; SUNY, 1990. Tillyer Medal, Optical Soc. of America, 1978; Proctor Medal, Assoc. for Res. in Vision and Ophthalmology, 1979; von Sallmann Prize, Coll. of Physicians and Surgeons, Columbia Univ., 1986; Prentice Medal, Amer. Acad. of Optometry, 1986; Bicentennial Medal, Aust. Optometric Assoc., 1988. *Publications:* research articles in sci. and professional optometric and ophth. jls; edtl work for sci. jls. *Recreations:* chamber music (violin), foundation and history of sensory physiology. *Address:* 582 Santa Barbara Road, Berkeley, Calif 94707, USA.

WESTLAKE, Prof. Henry Dickinson; Hulme Professor of Greek in the University of Manchester, 1949–72, now Professor Emeritus; *b* 4 Sept. 1906; *s* of C. A. Westlake and Charlotte M. Westlake (*née* Manlove); *m* 1940, Mary Helen Sayers; one *s* one *d*. *Educ:* Uppingham School; St John's College, Cambridge (Scholar). Strathcona Student, 1929; Assistant Lecturer, University College, Swansea, 1930–32; Fellow of St John's College, Cambridge, 1932–35; Assistant Lecturer, University of Bristol, 1936–37; Lecturer, King's College, Newcastle, 1937–46; Administrative Assistant, Ministry of Home Security, 1941–44; Reader in Greek, University of Durham, 1946–49; Dean of the Faculty of Arts, Univ. of Manchester, 1960–61; Pro-Vice-Chancellor, 1965–68. *Publications:* Thessaly in the Fourth Century BC, 1935; Timoleon and his relations with tyrants, 1952; Individuals in Thucydides, 1968; Essays on the Greek Historians and Greek History, 1969; Studies in Thucydides and Greek History, 1989; articles and reviews in learned periodicals. *Address:* West Lodge, Manor Farm Road, Waresley, Sandy, Bedfordshire SG19 3BX. *T:* Gamlingay (0767) 50877.

WESTLAKE, Peter Alan Grant, CMG 1972; MC 1943; *b* 2 Feb. 1919; *s* of A. R. C. Westlake, CSI, CIE, and late Dorothy Louise (*née* Turner) *m* 1943, Katherine Spackman (*d* 1990); two *s*. *Educ:* Sherborne; Corpus Christi Coll., Oxford; Military College of Science. Served with 1st Regt RHA (Adjt 1942), and on the staff (despatches). HM Foreign Service (now Diplomatic Service), 1946–76: served in Japan and at Foreign Office; Joint Services Staff College, 1954; Israel, 1955; Japan, 1957; Administrative Staff Coll., 1961; Counsellor: Foreign Office, 1961; Washington, 1965; British High Commn, Canberra, 1967–71; Minister, Tokyo, 1971–76. Pres., Asiatic Soc. of Japan, 1972–74. UK Comr-General, Internat. Ocean Expo, Okinawa, 1975. BD Wales 1981, MSc Wales, 1981; Deacon, Church in Wales, 1981, Priest 1982. FRAS. Order of the Rising Sun, Japan. *Address:* 53 Church Street, Beaumaris, Anglesey.

WESTMACOTT, Richard Kelso; Chairman: Hoare Govett Ltd, 1975–90; Security Pacific Hoare Govett (Holdings) Ltd, 1985–90; *b* 20 Feb. 1934; *s* of Comdr John Rowe Westmacott, RN and Ruth Pharazyn; *m* 1965, Karen Husbands; one *s* one *d*. *Educ:* Eton College. Royal Navy, 1952–54. Hoare & Co., 1955; Mem., Stock Exchange, 1960. *Recreations:* sailing, shooting. *Address:* 9 Alexander Square, SW3 2AY. *Clubs:* White's; Royal Yacht Squadron.

WESTMEATH, 13th Earl of, *cr* 1621; **William Anthony Nugent;** Baron Delvin, by tenure temp. Henry II; by summons, 1486; Senior Master, St Andrew's School, Pangbourne, 1980–88; *b* 21 Nov. 1928; *s* of 12th Earl of Westmeath and Doris (*d* 1968), 2nd *d* of C. Imlach, Liverpool; *S* father, 1971; *m* 1963, Susanna Margaret, *o d* of J. C. B. W. Leonard, *qv*; two *s*. *Educ:* Marlborough Coll. Captain, RA, retired. Staff of St Andrew's Sch., Pangbourne, 1961–88. *Heir: s* Hon. Sean Charles Weston Nugent, *b* 16 Feb. 1965. *Address:* Farthings, Rotten Row Hill, Bradfield, Berks. *T:* Bradfield (0734) 744426.

WESTMINSTER, 6th Duke of, *cr* 1874; **Gerald Cavendish Grosvenor;** DL; Bt 1622; Baron Grosvenor, 1761; Earl Grosvenor and Viscount Belgrave, 1784; Marquess of Westminster, 1831; commissioned Queens Own Yeomanry, 1973, Captain 1979, Major 1985; *b* 22 Dec. 1951; *s* of 5th Duke of Westminster, TD, and Viola Maud (*d* 1987), *d* of 9th Viscount Cobham, KCB, TD; *S* father, 1979; *m* 1978, Natalia, *d* of Lt-Col H. P. J. Phillips; one *s* two *d*. *Educ:* Harrow. MRICS. Director: Claridges Hotel Ltd; Sun Alliance & London Group; Sutton Ridge Pty Ltd; Maritime Trust; Marcher Sound Ltd; Cutty Sark Soc.; Grosvenor Estate Hldgs; NW Business Leadership Team Ltd; Westminster Christmas Appeal Trust Ltd. Governor: Royal Agricl Soc. of England; Internat. Students' Trust, 1977; Chester Teacher Training Coll., 1979; Cawthorne's Endowed Sch., 1981; Pro-Chancellor, Univ. of Keele, 1986–. President: London Tourist Bd, 1980–; NW Industrialists' Council, 1979–; Chester City Conservative Assoc., 1977–; London Fedn of Boys' Clubs, 1984–; St John's Ambulance, London Dist, 1983–; RNIB, 1986–; Arthritis Care, 1987–; Spastics Soc., 1985–; Royal Soc. of British Dairy Farmers, 1987–; Game Conservancy; London Fedn of Boys' Clubs; Abbeyfield Soc., 1989–. Member, Committee: Rural Target Team, Business in the Community; N Amer. Adv. Gp, BOTB; Nat. Army Mus.; Prince's Youth Business Trust; US Inf. Agency; Winston Churchill Meml Trust. Patron: Worcs CCC (Pres., 1984–86); British Holstein Soc.; British Kidney Patients Assoc.; Dyslexia Inst., 1989–. Trustee: Civic Trust, 1983–; Civic Trust for the NW; TSB Foundn for England and Wales; Grosvenor Estate; Lambeth Fund; Westminster Abbey Trust; Westminster Foundn; Westminster Housing Trust. Gov., Harrow Sch., 1987–. Freeman: Chester, 1973; England, 1979; City of London, 1980. Liveryman: GAPAN; Gunmakers' Co.; Weavers' Co.; Armourers and Braziers' Co.; Marketors' Co.; Goldsmiths' Co.; Fishmongers' Co. FRSA; FRAS; FCIM. CStJ 1987. DL Cheshire, 1982. *Heir: s* Earl Grosvenor, *qv*. *Address:* Eaton Hall, Chester, Cheshire CH4 9ET. *Clubs:* Brooks's, Cavalry, MCC; Royal Yacht Squadron.

WESTMINSTER, Archbishop of, (RC), since 1976; **His Eminence Cardinal (George) Basil Hume;** *b* 2 March 1923; *s* of Sir William Hume, CMG, FRCP. *Educ:* Ampleforth Coll.; St Benet's Hall, Oxford; Fribourg Univ., Switzerland. Ordained priest 1950. Ampleforth College: Senior Modern Language Master, 1952–63; Housemaster, 1955–63; Prof. of Dogmatic Theology, 1955–63; Magister Scholarum of the English Benedictine Congregation, 1957–63; Abbot of Ampleforth, 1963–76. Cardinal, 1976. President: RC Bishops' Conf. of England and Wales, 1979–; Council of European Bishops' Confs, 1979–86; (jtly) Churches Together in England, 1990–; Mem. Council for Secretariat of Internat. Synod of Bishops, 1978–87. Hon. Bencher, Inner Temple, 1976. Hon. DD: Cantab, 1979; Newcastle upon Tyne, 1979; London, 1980; Oxon, 1981; York, 1982; Kent, 1983; Durham, 1987; Collegio S Anselmo, Rome, 1987; Hull, 1989; Hon. DHL: Manhattan Coll., NY, 1980; Catholic Univ. of America, 1980. *Publications:* Searching for God, 1977; In Praise of Benedict, 1981; To Be a Pilgrim, 1984; Towards a Civilisation of Love, 1988. *Address:* Archbishop's House, Westminster, SW1P 1QJ.

WESTMINSTER, Auxiliary Bishops of, (RC); *see* Crowley, Rt Rev. J. P.; Guazzelli, Rt Rev. V.; Harvey, Rt Rev. P. J. B.; Mahon, Rt Rev. G. T.; and O'Brien, Rt Rev. J. J.

WESTMINSTER, Dean of; *see* Mayne, Very Rev. M. C. O.

WESTMORLAND, 15th Earl of *cr* 1624; **David Anthony Thomas Fane,** KCVO 1970; DL; Baron Burghersh, 1624; late RHG; Master of the Horse, since 1978; Director: Sotheby Parke Bernet Group, since 1965 (Deputy Chairman, 1979, Chairman, 1980–82); Sotheby Holdings Inc., since 1983; Sotheby Advisory Board, since 1987; *b* 31 March 1924; *e s* of 14th Earl of Westmorland and Hon. Diana Lister (*d* 1983), *widow* of Capt. Arthur Edward Capel, CBE, and *y d* of 4th Baron Ribblesdale; *S* father 1948; *m* 1950, Jane, *d* of Lt-Col Sir Roland Lewis Findlay, 3rd Bt, and Barbara Joan, *d* of late Maj. H. S. Garrard; two *s* one *d*. Served War of 1939–45 (wounded); resigned from RHG with hon. rank of Captain, 1950. A Lord in Waiting to the Queen, 1955–78. DL Glos, 1991. *Heir: s* Lord Burghersh, *qv*. *Address:* Kingsmead, Didmarton, Badminton, Avon; 26 Laxford House, Cundy Street, SW1. *Clubs:* Buck's, White's.

WESTMORLAND AND FURNESS, Archdeacon of; *see* Peat, Ven. L. J.

WESTOLL, James, DL; *b* 26 July 1918; *s* of late James Westoll, Glingerbank, Longtown; *m* 1946, Sylvia Jane Luxmoore, MBE, *d* of late Lord Justice Luxmoore, Bilsington, Kent; two *s* two *d*. *Educ:* Eton; Trinity College, Cambridge (MA). Served War of 1939–45: Major, The Border Regiment (despatches). Called to Bar, Lincoln's Inn, 1952. Member, NW Electricity Board, 1959–66; Deputy Chm., Cumberland Quarter Sessions, 1960–71; Cumberland County Council: CC 1947; CA 1959–74; Chm., 1958–74; Chm., Cumbria Local Govt Reorganisation Jt Cttee, 1973; Chm., Cumbria CC, 1973–76. DL 1963, High Sheriff 1964, Cumberland. Warden, 1973–75, Master, 1983–84, Clothworkers' Company. Hon. LLD Leeds, 1984. KStJ 1983. *Recreations:* gardening, shooting. *Address:* Dykeside, Longtown, Carlisle, Cumbria CA6 5ND. *T:* Longtown (0228) 791235. *Clubs:* Boodle's, Farmers'; County and Border (Carlisle).

WESTOLL, Prof. Thomas Stanley, BSc, PhD Dunelm; DSc Aberdeen; FRS 1952; FRSE, FGS, FLS; J. B. Simpson Professor of Geology, University of Newcastle upon Tyne (formerly King's College, Newcastle upon Tyne, University of Durham), 1948–77, now Emeritus; Chairman of Convocation, Newcastle upon Tyne University, 1979–89; *b* W Hartlepool, Durham, 3 July 1912; *e s* of Horace Stanley Raine Westoll; *m* 1st, 1939, Dorothy Cecil Isobel Wood (marr. diss. 1951); one *s*; 2nd, 1952, Barbara Swanson McAdie. *Educ:* West Hartlepool Grammar School; Armstrong (later King's) Coll., Univ. of Durham; University College, London. Senior Research Award, DSIR, 1934–37; Lecturer in Geology, Univ. of Aberdeen, 1937–48. Leverhulme Emeritus Res. Fellow, 1977–79. Alexander Agassiz Visiting Professor of Vertebrate Paleontology, Harvard University, 1952; Huxley Lectr, Univ. of Birmingham, 1967. J. B. Tyrell Fund, 1937, and Daniel Pidgeon Fund, 1939, Geological Soc. of London. President: Palæontological Assoc., 1966–68; Section C, British Assoc. for Advancement of Science, Durham, 1970; Geological Soc., 1972–74; Mem. Council, Royal Soc., 1966–68. Corr. Mem., Amer. Museum of Natural History; Hon. Life Mem., Soc. of Vertebrate Paleontology, USA, 1976. Hon. LLD Aberdeen, 1979. Murchison Medal, Geol. Soc. London, 1967; Clough Medal, Geol Soc. of Edinburgh, 1977; Linnean Gold Medal (Zool.), 1978. *Publications:* (ed) Studies on Fossil Vertebrates, 1958; (ed, with D. G. Murchison) Coal and Coal-bearing Strata, 1968; (ed, with N. Rast) Geology of the USSR, by D. V. Nalivkin, 1973; numerous papers and monographs on vertebrate anatomy and palæontology and geological topics, in several journals. *Recreations:* photography and numismatics. *Address:* 21 Osborne Avenue, Newcastle upon Tyne NE2 1JQ. *T:* 091–281 1622.

WESTON, Bertram John, CMG 1960; OBE 1957; retired from the public service; Estate Factor to British Union Trust Ltd, 1964–81; *b* 30 March 1907; *o s* of late J. G. Weston, Kennington, Kent; *m* 1932, Irene Carey; two *d*. *Educ:* Ashford Grammar School; Sidney Sussex College, Cambridge (MA); Pretoria University, SA (MSc, Agric); Cornell University, USA (Post Grad.). Horticulturist, Cyprus, 1931; Asst Comr, Nicosia (on secondment), 1937; Administrative Officer, 1939. War Service, 1940–43 (Major). Commissioner for development and post-war construction, Cyprus, 1943; Commissioner, 1946; Administrative Officer Class I, 1951; Senior Administrative Officer, 1954; Senior Commissioner, 1958; Government Sec., St Helena, 1960–63; acted as Governor and C-in-C, St Helena, at various times during this period. *Recreations:* lawn tennis, gardening, watching cricket and other sports. *Address:* 10 Westfield Close, Uphill, Weston-super-Mare BS23 4XQ. *Club:* Commonwealth Trust.

WESTON, Bryan Henry; Chairman: Manweb plc (formerly Merseyside and North Wales Electricity Board), since 1985; The National Grid Holding, since 1991; *b* 9 April 1930; *s* of Henry James Weston and Rose Grace Weston; *m* 1956, Heather West; two *s* two *d*. *Educ:* St George Grammar School, Bristol; Bristol, Rutherford and Oxford Technical Colleges. CEng, MIEE; MBIM. South Western Electricity Board: Commercial Manager, 1973–75; Bd Mem., 1975; Exec. Mem., 1975–77; Dep. Chm., Yorkshire Electricity Bd, 1977–85. *Recreations:* caravanning, walking, gardening. *Address:* Fountainhead Cottage, Brassey Green, near Tarporley, Cheshire. *T:* Tarporley (0829) 733523.

WESTON, Rear-Adm. Charles Arthur Winfield, CB 1978; Admiral President, RN College, Greenwich, 1976–78; Appeals Secretary, King Edward VII's Hospital for Officers, 1979–87; *b* 12 July 1922; *s* of late Charles Winfield Weston and of Edith Alice Weston; *m* 1946, Jeanie Findlay Miller; one *s* one *d*. *Educ:* Merchant Taylors' Sch. Entered RN as Special Entry Cadet, 1940; HM Ships: Glasgow, 1940; Durban, 1942; Staff of C-in-C Mediterranean, as Sec. to Captain of the Fleet, 1944–45 (despatches 1945); Sec. to Cdre in Charge Sheerness, 1946–47, to Flag Captain Home Fleet, HMS Duke of York, 1947–48; Loan Service, RAN, 1948–50; HM Ships: St Vincent, 1952–53; Ceres, 1954–55; Decoy, 1956; Sec. to DCNP (Trng and Manning), 1957–58, to DG Trng, 1959; CO HMS Jufair, 1960; Supply Officer, St Vincent, 1961–62; Sec. to Fleet Comdr Far East Fleet, 1963–64, to Second Sea Lord, 1965–67; sowc 1968; Chief Staff Officer (Q) to C-in-C Naval Home Comd, 1969–70; DNPTS, 1971; Director Defence Admin Planning Staff, 1972–74; Dir of Quartering (Navy), 1975. ADC to the Queen, 1976. Rear-Adm. 1976. Liveryman, Shipwrights' Co., 1979–. *Recreations:* cricket, golf, gardening, music. *Address:* Westacre, Liphook, Hants GU30 7NY. *T:* Liphook (0428) 723337. *Clubs:* MCC, Army and Navy.

WESTON, Christopher John; Chairman and Chief Executive: Phillips Son & Neale, since 1972; Glendining & Co., and subsidiaries, since 1972; *b* 3 March 1937; *s* of Eric Tudor Weston and Evelyn Nellie Weston; *m* 1969, Josephine Annabel Moir; one *d*. *Educ:* Lancing Coll. FIA (Scot.). Director: Phillips, 1964–; Foreign and Colonial Investment Trust PLC (formerly F & C Pacific Investment Trust), 1984–; Headline Book Publishing PLC, 1986–; Foreign & Colonial Enterprise Trust plc, 1987–; Foreign & Colonial Ventures Advisors Ltd, 1988–; Bradford Peters (Holdings) Ltd, 1978–. Pres., Soc. of Fine Art Auctioneers, 1987– (Chm., 1973–87). Liveryman, Painters-Stainers' Co. FRSA (Mem. Council, 1985). *Recreations:* theatre, music. *Address:* 101 New Bond Street, W1Y 0AS. *T:* 071–629 6602. *Club:* Oriental.

WESTON, Rev. David Wilfrid Valentine; Domestic Chaplain to the Bishop of Carlisle, since 1989; *b* 8 Dec. 1937; *s* of late Rev. William Valentine Weston and late Mrs Gertrude Hamilton Weston; *m* 1984, Helen Strachan Macdonald, *d* of James and Barbara Macdonald; two *s*. *Educ:* St Edmund's Sch., Canterbury. Entered Nashdom Abbey, 1960; deacon, 1967, priest, 1968; Novice Master, 1969–74; Prior, 1971–74; Abbot, 1974–84; Curate, St Peter's, Chorley, 1984–85; Vicar, St John the Baptist, Pilling, 1985–89. Freeman, City of London; Liveryman of Salters' Co. *Address:* The Chaplain's House, Rose Castle, Dalston, Carlisle, Cumbria CA5 7BZ.

See also Ven. F. V. Weston.

WESTON, Ven. Frank Valentine; Archdeacon of Oxford and a Canon of Christ Church, Oxford, since 1982; *b* 16 Sept. 1935; *s* of William Valentine Weston and Gertrude Hamilton Weston; *m* 1963, Penelope Brighid, *d* of Marmaduke Carver Middleton Athorpe, formerly of Dinnington, Yorks; one *s* two *d*. *Educ:* Christ's Hospital; Queen's Coll., Oxford; Lichfield Theological Coll. BA 1960, MA 1964. Curate, St John the Baptist, Atherton, Lancs, 1961–65; Chaplain, 1965–69, Principal, 1969–76, College of the Ascension, Selly Oak, Birmingham; Vice-Pres., Selly Oak Colls, 1973–76; Principal and Pantonian Prof., Edinburgh Theological Coll., 1976–82. Court of Assistants, Salters' Co. Governor: Christ's Hosp.; Tudor Hall Sch.; St Augustine's Upper Sch., Oxford. *Publications:* (contrib.) Quel Missionnaire, 1971; (contrib.) Gestalten der Kirchengeschichte, 1984. *Recreations:* wine, persons and song; exploring the countryside. *Address:* Archdeacon's Lodging, Christ Church, Oxford OX1 1DP. *T:* Oxford (0865) 276185.

See also Rev. D. W. V. Weston.

WESTON, Galen; *see* Weston, W. G.

WESTON, Garfield Howard, (Garry); Chairman: Associated British Foods plc, since 1967; Fortnum and Mason, since 1978; British Sugar PLC; *b* 28 April 1927; *s* of late Willard Garfield Weston and Reta Lila Howard; *m* 1959, Mary Ruth, *d* of late Major-Gen. Sir Howard Kippenberger; three *s* three *d*. *Educ:* Sir William Borlase School, Marlow; New College, Oxford; Harvard University (Economics). Man. Director: Ryvita Co. Ltd, 1951; Weston Biscuit Co., Aust., 1954; Vice-Chairman, Associated British Foods Ltd, 1960; Chm., George Weston Holdings Ltd, 1978. *Recreations:* gardening, tennis, walking. *Address:* Weston Centre, Bowater House, 68 Knightsbridge, SW1X 7LR. *T:* 071–589 6363. *Club:* Lansdowne.

WESTON, Geoffrey Harold, CBE 1975; FHSM; retired; Deputy Health Service Commissioner for England, Scotland and Wales, 1977–82; *b* 11 Sept. 1920; *s* of George and Florence Mary Weston; *m* 1953, Monica Mary Grace Comyns; three *d*. *Educ:* Wolverhampton Sch. War Service, 1940–46. Gp Sec., Reading and Dist Hosp. Management Cttee, 1955–65; Board Sec., NW Metropolitan Regional Hosp. Bd, 1965–73; Regional Administrator, NW Thames RHA, 1973–76. Member: Salmon Cttee, 1963–65; Whitley Councils: Mem. Management side of Optical Council, 1955–65, and of Nurses and Midwives Council, 1966–76; Mem., Working Party on Collab. between Local Govt and Nat. Health Service, 1973–74. Inst. of Health Service Administrators: Mem., Nat. and Reg. Councils, 1959–78 (Vice-Chm. of Council, 1968, Chm. 1969, Pres. of Inst., 1970).

Bd Mem., London and Provincial Nursing Services Ltd, 1973–90; Member: Mental Health Review Tribunal, 1982–; Oxford RHA, 1983–89; Trustee, Goring Day Centre, 1978–89. Vice-Chm., Goring Decorative and Fine Art Soc., 1990– (Treas., 1987–89). Parish Councillor, 1979–87. *Recreations:* travel, dining with friends. *Address:* 15 Hill Gardens, Streatley, near Reading, Berks RG8 9QF. *T:* Goring on Thames (0491) 872881. *Club:* Royal Air Force.

WESTON, John; *see* Weston, P. J.

WESTON, Dr John Carruthers; General Manager, Northampton Development Corporation, 1969–77. *Educ:* Univ. of Nottingham. Admiralty Research, 1940–46; Plessey Co., 1946–47; Building Research Station, 1947–64; Chief Exec. Operational Div., Nat. Building Agency, 1964–65; Dir, Building Research Station, MPBW, 1966–69. *Recreations:* gardening, music, walking, reading and living.

WESTON, John Pix, BSc(Eng), BSc(Econ); CEng, FIEE, FBIM; investment consultant, since 1984; *b* 3 Jan. 1920; *s* of John Pix Weston and Margaret Elizabeth (*née* Cox); *m* 1948, Ivy (*née* Glover); three *s*. *Educ:* King Edward's Sch., Birmingham, 1931–36; Univ. of Aston, 1946–50 (BSc(Eng), Hons); Univ. of London (LSE), 1954–57 (BSc(Econ), Hons). CEng 1953, FIEE 1966; FSS 1958; FREconS 1958; FBIM 1977. City of Birmingham: Police Dept, 1936–39; Electricity Supply Dept, 1939–48; Midlands Electricity Bd, 1948–50; English Electricity Co., 1950–51; NW Elec. Bd, 1951–58; Eastern Elec. Bd, 1958–60; Dep. Operating Man., Jamaica Public Services Co., 1960–61; Principal Asst Engr, Midlands Elec. Bd, 1961–64; Asst Ch. Commercial Officer, S of Scotland Elec. Bd, 1964–66; Sen. Econ. Adviser to Mrs Barbara Castle, MoT, 1966–69; Sen. Econ. and Chartered Engr, IBRD, 1968–70; Michelin Tyre Co., France, 1970–72; Dir of Post Experience Courses, Open Univ., 1972–75; Dir Gen., RoSPA, 1975–77; Gen. Sec., Birmingham Anglers' Assoc., 1977; Industrial Develt Officer, Argyll and Bute, 1977–79; Health, Safety and Welfare Officer, Newcastle Polytechnic, and Central Safety Advr, Northants CC, 1979; Chief Admin. Officer and Clerk to Governors, W Bromwich Coll. of Comm. and Tech., 1979–85. Hon. Sec. and Treasurer, Assoc. of Coll. Registrars and Administrators (W Midlands), 1982–85. Council Mem., Midlands Counties Photographic Fedn, 1984–86; Hon. Prog., Competition and Outings Sec. and Council Mem., Birmingham Photographic Soc., 1981–86; MIES 1963; Mem., Assoc. of Public Lighting Engrs, 1962. Chm., Upper Marlbrook Residents' Assoc., 1982–87; Asst Treasurer, Laugharne Cons. Assoc., 1990–. Member: Narbeth and Dist Probus Club, 1988–; St Clears Probus Club, 1989– (Pres., 1990–91); Tenby Probus Club, 1990–. Page Prize, IEE, 1950; Rosebery Prize, Univ. of London, 1957. SBStJ 1962. *Publications:* papers, reports and other contribs on electricity, highways, educn (espec. function and progress of the Open University), safety, etc, to public bodies, congresses and conferences, UK and abroad. *Recreations:* cine photography, gardening, swimming, fell walking. *Address:* Brook Mill & Woodside, Brook, Pendine, Dyfed. *T:* Laugharne (0994) 427477. *Clubs:* Farmers', St John House; Birmingham Press.

WESTON, John William, CB 1979; Principal Assistant Solicitor, Board of Inland Revenue, 1967–80; *b* 3 Feb. 1915; *s* of Herbert Edward Weston, MA, and Emma Gertrude Weston; *m* 1943, Frances Winifred (*née* Johnson); two *s* one *d*. *Educ:* Berkhamsted Sch., Herts. Solicitor, 1937. Joined Inland Revenue, 1940; Sen. Legal Asst, 1948; Asst Solicitor, 1954. *Recreation:* golf. *Address:* 5 Dickerage Road, Kingston Hill, Surrey. *T:* 081–942 8130.

WESTON, Dame Margaret (Kate), DBE 1979; BScEng (London); CEng, MIEE, FINucE; FMA; CBIM; Director of the Science Museum, 1973–86; *b* 7 March 1926; *o c* of late Charles Edward and Margaret Weston. *Educ:* Stroud High School; College of Technology, Birmingham (now Univ. of Aston). Engineering apprenticeship with General Electric Co. Ltd, followed in 1949 by development work, very largely on high voltage insulation problems. Joined Science Museum as an Assistant Keeper, Dept of Electrical Engineering and Communications, 1955; Deputy Keeper, 1962; Keeper, Dept of Museum Services, 1967–72. Member: Ancient Monuments Bd for England, 1977–84; 1851 Commission, 1987–; Museums and Galleries Commission, 1988–; Steering Gp, Museum in Docklands, 1986–. Member: SE Elec. Bd, 1981–90; BBC Sci. Consultative Gp, 1986–89. Chm., Horniman Public Mus. and Public Park Trust, 1990–; Trustee: Hunterian Collection, 1981–; Brooklands, 1987–. Governor, Imperial Coll., 1974–90 (FIC 1975); Governor and Mem. Management Cttee, Ditchley Foundn, 1984–. Pres., Assoc. of Railway Preservation Socs, 1985–. FMA 1976; Sen. Fellow, RCA, 1986; FRSA (Mem. Council, 1985–90). Hon. Fellow, Newnham Coll., Cambridge, 1986. Hon. DEng Bradford, 1984; Hon. DSc: Aston, 1974; Salford, 1984; Leeds, 1987; Loughborough, 1988; DUniv Open 1987. *Address:* 7 Shawley Way, Epsom, Surrey KT18 5NZ. *T:* Burgh Heath (0737) 355885.

WESTON, Sir Michael Charles Swift, KCMG 1991; CVO 1979; HM Diplomatic Service; Ambassador to Kuwait, since 1990; *b* 4 Aug. 1937; *s* of late Edward Charles Swift Weston and of Kathleen Mary Weston (*née* Mockett); *m* 1959, Veronica Anne Tickner; two *s* one *d*. *Educ:* Dover Coll.; St Catharine's Coll., Cambridge (Exhibitioner). BA, MA. Joined HM Diplomatic Service, 1961; 3rd Sec., Kuwait, 1962; 2nd Sec., FCO, 1965; 1st Secretary: Tehran, 1968; UK Mission, New York, 1970; FCO, 1974; Counsellor, Jedda, 1977; RCDS, 1980; Counsellor (Information), Paris, 1981; Counsellor, Cairo, 1984; Head of Southern European Dept, FCO, 1987. *Recreations:* tennis, squash. *Club:* United Oxford & Cambridge University.

WESTON, (Philip) John, CMG 1985; HM Diplomatic Service; Ambassador and UK Permanent Representative to North Atlantic Council, since 1991; *b* 13 April 1938; *s* of late Philip George Weston and Edith Alice Bray (*née* Ansell); *m* 1967, Margaret Sally Ehlers; two *s* one *d*. *Educ:* Sherborne; Worcester Coll., Oxford. 1st Cl. Hons, Honour Mods Classics and Lit. Hum. Served with Royal Marines, 1956–58. Entered Diplomatic Service, 1962; FO, 1962–63; Treasury Centre for Admin. Studies, 1964; Chinese Language student, Hong Kong, 1964–66; Peking, 1967–68; FO, 1969–71; Office of UK Permanent Representative to EEC, 1972–74; Asst Private Sec. to Sec. of State for Foreign and Commonwealth Affairs (Rt Hon. James Callaghan, Rt Hon. Anthony Crosland), 1974–76; Counsellor, Head of EEC Presidency Secretariat, FCO, 1976–77; Vis. Fellow, All Souls Coll., Oxford, 1977–78; Counsellor, Washington, 1978–81; Hd Defence Dept, FCO, 1981–84; Asst Under-Sec. of State, FCO, 1984–85; Minister, Paris, 1985–88; Dep. Sec. to Cabinet, Cabinet Office, 1988–89 (on secondment); Dep. Under-Sec. of State (Defence), FCO, 1989–90; Political Dir, FCO, 1990–91. *Recreations:* fly-fishing, poetry, running, chess. *Address:* c/o Foreign and Commonwealth Office, SW1. *Club:* United Oxford & Cambridge University.

WESTON, W(illard) Galen, OC 1990; Chairman, since 1974, and President, since 1978, George Weston Ltd, Toronto; *b* England, 29 Oct. 1940; *s* of W. Garfield Weston and Reta Lila (*née* Howard); *m* 1966, Hilary Mary Frayne; one *s* one *d*. Chairman: Loblaw Companies Ltd; Holt Renfrew & Co. Ltd; Brown Thomas Group Ltd (Eire); Weston Foods Ltd; Weston Resources Ltd; Vice-Chm., Fortnum & Mason plc (UK); Chm. and Pres., Wittington Investments Ltd; Director: Canadian Imperial Bank of Commerce; Associated British Foods plc (UK). President and Trustee: W. Garfield Weston Foundation; Lester B. Pearson Coll. of Pacific; United World Colls of Canada Inc.; Pres., Royal Agricl Winter Fair, Toronto. Hon. LLD Univ. of Western Ont. *Recreations:* polo, tennis. *Address:* Suite 2001, George Weston Ltd, 22 St Clair Avenue East, Toronto, Ont M4T 2S3, Canada. *T:* 416 922 2500, *Fax:* 416 922 4394. *Clubs:* Toronto, York (Toronto); Guards' Polo; Lyford Cay (Bahamas).

WESTON, Rear-Adm. William Kenneth, CB 1956; OBE 1945; RN retired; *b* 8 November 1904; *s* of late William Weston; *m* 1934, Mary Ursula Shine; one *s* two *d*. *Educ:* RNC Osborne and Dartmouth. RNEC Keyham; RNC Greenwich. Served on staff of Flag Officer Destroyers, Pacific, 1945–46; Admiralty District Engineer Overseer, NW District, 1951–54; Staff of C-in-C Plymouth, 1954–58; retired, 1958. Court of Assistants of the Worshipful Company of Salters, 1959, Master, 1963, resigned 1989. *Address:* Brackleyways, Hartley Wintney, Hants. *T:* Hartley Wintney (025126) 2546. *Club:* Naval and Military.

WESTWELL, Alan Reynolds, MSc; CEng, MIMechE, MIProdE; FCIT; Managing Director and Chief Executive, Greater Manchester Buses Ltd, since 1990; *b* 11 April 1940; *s* of Stanley Westwell and Margaret (*née* Reynolds); *m* 1967, Elizabeth Aileen Birrell; two *s* one *d*. *Educ:* Old Swan Coll.; Liverpool Polytechnic (ACT Hons); Salford Univ. (MSc 1983). Liverpool City Transport Dept: progressively, student apprentice, Technical Asst, Asst Works Manager, 1956–67; Chief Engineer: Southport Corporation Transport Dept, 1967–69; Coventry Corp. Transport Dept, 1969–72; Glasgow Corp. Transport Dept, 1972–74; Director of Public Transport (responsible for bus/rail, airport, harbours), Tayside Regional Council, 1974–79; Dir Gen., Strathclyde PTE, 1979–86; Chm., 1987–90, Man. Dir and Chief Exec., 1986–90, Strathclyde Buses Ltd. Professional Advr, COSLA, 1976–86. President: Scottish Council of Confedn of British Road Passenger Transport, 1982–83 (Vice-Pres., 1981–82); Bus and Coach Council, Scotland, 1982–83; Bus and Coach Council, UK, 1989–90 (Vice Pres., 1985–88; Sen. Vice-Pres., 1988–89). Member: Parly Road Transport Cttee, 1986–; Cttee, Internat. Metropolitan Railways Cttee, 1979–86; Internat. Traffic and Urban Planning, 1986–. Chm., IMechE, Automobile Div., Scottish Centre, 1982–84; Mem. Council, CIT, 1986–89 (Chm. Scottish Centre, 1983–84); former Mem., Internat. Union of Public Transport. *Publications:* various papers. *Recreations:* golf, swimming, tennis, music, model making, reading. *Address:* 6 Amberley Drive, Hale, Cheshire WA15 0DT. *T:* 061–980 3551.

WESTWOOD, family name of **Baron Westwood.**

WESTWOOD, 2nd Baron, *cr* 1944, of Gosforth; **William Westwood;** Company Director; *b* 25 Dec. 1907; *s* of 1st Baron and Margaret Taylor Young (*d* 1916); *S* father 1953; *m* 1937, Marjorie, *o c* of Arthur Bonwick, Newcastle upon Tyne; two *s*. *Educ:* Glasgow; JP Newcastle upon Tyne, 1949. Dir of several private companies. Hon. Vice-Pres., Football Association, 1981 (Vice-Pres., 1974–81); Life Mem., Football League, 1981. FRSA; FCIS. *Heir:* *s* Hon. William Gavin Westwood [*b* 30 Jan. 1944; *m* 1969, Penelope, *er d* of Dr C. E. Shafto, Newcastle upon Tyne; two *s*]. *Address:* 55 Moor Court, Westfield, Gosforth, Newcastle upon Tyne NE3 4YD.

WESTWOOD, Rt. Rev. William John; *see* Peterborough, Bishop of.

WETHERED, Julian Frank Baldwin; Director General, Royal Society for the Prevention of Accidents, since 1990; *b* 9 Nov. 1929; *s* of late Comdr Owen Francis McTier Wethered, RN retd and Betty (*née* Baldwin); *m* 1st, 1952, Britt Eva Hindmarsh (marr. diss. 1971); one *s* one *d*; 2nd, 1973, Antonia Mary Ettrick Roberts; two *s*. *Educ:* Eton Col.; Jesus Coll., Cambridge (BA Hons Hist. 1952; MA). National Service, RM, HMS Diadem, 1948–49. Trainee, Expandite Ltd, 1952–54; Sales Rep., Remington Rand, 1955–56; Thomas De La Rue and Co.: trainee, 1956; Mem., PA Study Team, 1957; Printing Preliminaries Manager, Currency Div., 1958–62; Special Rep., Africa, 1963–67; Manager, Banknote Printing Co., 1968–69; Regl Manager, FE, 1970–75; Associate Dir of Sales, Africa and FE, 1976–83; Regl Dir, FE, De La Rue Co. plc, 1984–88; Associate Dir of Sales, Thomas De La Rue & Co., 1989. Pres., British Business Assoc. of Singapore, 1988. FInstD; FRSA. *Recreations:* sailing, riding, the arts. *Address:* Cadley House, near Marlborough, Wilts SN8 4NE. *T:* Marlborough (0672) 513407. *Club:* Travellers'

WETHERELL, Alan Marmaduke, PhD; FRS 1971; Senior Physicist, CERN (European Organisation for Nuclear Research), Geneva, since 1963 (Division Leader, Experimental Physics Division, 1981–84); *b* 31 Dec. 1932; *s* of Marmaduke and Margaret Edna Wetherell; *m* 1957, Alison Morag Dunn (*d* 1974); one *s*. *Educ:* Univ. of Liverpool (BSc, PhD). Demonstrator in Physics, Univ. of Liverpool, 1956–57; Commonwealth Fund Fellow, California Inst. of Technology, Pasadena, Calif., 1957–59; Physicist, CERN, 1959–63. Vis. Prof., Dept of Physics, Univ. of Liverpool, 1981–. *Publications:* scientific papers in: Proc. Phys. Soc. (London), Proc. Roy. Soc. (London), Physical Review, Physical Review Letters, Physics Letters, Nuovo Cimento, Nuclear Physics, Nuclear Instruments and Methods, Yadernaya Fizika, Uspekhi Fizicheski Nauk. *Recreations:* skiing, water skiing. *Address:* 27 Chemin de la Vendee, 1213 Petit Lancy, Geneva, Switzerland. *T:* 022 928742.

WETHERELL, Gordon Geoffrey; HM Diplomatic Service: Counsellor and Deputy Head of Mission, Warsaw, since 1988; *b* 11 Nov. 1948; *s* of Geoffrey and Georgette Maria Wetherell; *m* 1981, Rosemary Anne Myles; four *d*. *Educ:* Bradfield Coll., Berks; New Coll., Oxford (BA 1969; MA 1975); Univ. of Chicago (MA 1971). Joined HM Diplomatic Service, 1973; FCO, 1973–74; E Berlin, 1974–77; First Sec., FCO, 1977; UK Delegn to Comprehensive Test Ban Negotiations, Geneva, 1977–80; New Delhi, 1980–83; FCO, 1983–85; on secondment to HM Treasury, 1986–87; Asst Head, European Communities Dept (External), FCO, 1987–88. *Recreations:* reading, travel, Manchester United Football Club. *Address:* c/o Foreign and Commonwealth Office, King Charles Street, SW1A 2AH. *Club:* United Oxford & Cambridge University.

WETTON, Philip Henry Davan; HM Diplomatic Service; Consul-General, Milan, since 1990; *b* 21 Sept. 1937; *s* of late Eric Davan Wetton, CBE and Kathleen Valerie Davan Wetton; *m* 1983, Roswitha Kortner. *Educ:* Westminster; Christ Church, Oxford (MA). Unilever Ltd, 1958–65; FCO, 1965–68; served Tokyo, Osaka and FCO, 1968–73; Head of Division, later Director, Secretariat of Council of Ministers of European Communities, 1973–83; Counsellor, Seoul, 1983–87; FCO, 1987–90. *Recreations:* rowing, music, astronomy. *Address:* c/o Foreign and Commonwealth Office, SW1.

WETZEL, Dave; Director, London Dial-a-Ride Users' Association, since 1989; *b* 9 Oct. 1942; *s* of Fred Wetzel and Ivy Donaldson; *m* 1973, Heather Allman; two *d*. *Educ:* Spring Grove Grammar Sch.; Southall Technical Coll., Ealing Coll., and the Henry George Sch. of Social Sciences (part-time courses). Student apprentice, 1959–62; Bus Conductor/Driver, 1962–65, Bus Official, 1965–69, London Transport; Br. Manager, Initial Services, 1969–70; Pilot Roster Officer, British Airways, 1970–74 (ASTMS Shop Steward); Political Organiser, Co-operative Soc., 1974–81; Member (Lab) for Hammersmith N, GLC, 1981–86 (Transport Cttee Chair, 1981–86); Mem. (Lab) Hounslow Borough Council, 1964–68, 1986– (Dep. Leader and Chair, Environmental Planning, 1986–87; Leader, 1987–91). Chair, Labour Land Campaign, 1982–. Pres., Transport Studies Soc., 1991–Sept. 1992. Editor, Civil Aviation News, 1978–81. *Recreations:* politics, Esperanto, camping. *Address:* Civic Centre, Lampton Road, Hounslow, Middlesex TW3 4DN. *T:* 081–862 5025. *Club:* Feltham Labour.

WEYMES, John Barnard, OBE 1975; HM Diplomatic Service, retired; Managing Director, Cayman Islands News Bureau, Grand Cayman, 1981–83; *b* 18 Oct. 1927; *s* of William Stanley Weymes and Irene Innes Weymes; *m* 1978, Beverley Pauline Gliddon; three *c* (by a previous marr.). *Educ:* Dame Allan's Sch., Newcastle upon Tyne; King's Coll., Durham Univ., Newcastle upon Tyne. Served HM Forces, 1945–48. Foreign Office, 1949–52; 3rd Sec., Panama City, 1952–56; 2nd Sec., Bogotá, 1957–60; Vice-Consul, Berlin, 1960–63; Dep-Consul, Tamsui, Taiwan, 1963–65; 1st Sec., FCO, 1965–68; Prime Minister's Office, 1968–70; Consul, Guatemala City, 1970–74; 1st Sec., FCO, 1974–77; Consul-Gen., Vancouver, 1977–78; Ambassador to Honduras, 1978–81. *Recreations:* outdoor sport, partic. cricket; chess, reading. *Address:* Nuthatches, Balcombe Green, Sedlescombe, Battle, E Sussex TN33 0QL. *T:* Sedlescombe (0424) 870455. *Clubs:* MCC, Middlesex County Cricket; Sedlescombe Cricket.

WEYMOUTH, Viscount; Alexander George Thynn; Director: Cheddar Caves, since 1956; Longleat Enterprises, since 1964; *b* 6 May 1932; *s* of Marquess of Bath, *qv*; *m* 1969, Anna Gael Gyarmathy; one *s* one *d*. *Educ:* Eton College; Christ Church, Oxford (BA, MA). Lieutenant in the Life Guards, 1951–52, and in Royal Wilts Yeomanry, 1953–57. Contested (Wessex Regionalist): Westbury, Feb. 1974; Wells, 1979; contested (Wessex Regionalist and European Federal Party) Wessex, European Election 1979. Pres., Verulam Inst., 1976–86. Permanent exhibn of murals (painted 1964–69, opened to public 1973), in private apartments at Longleat House. Record, I Play the Host, singing own compositions, 1974. *Publications:* (as Alexander Thynn) (before 1976 Alexander Thynne) The Carry-cot, 1972; Lord Weymouth's Murals, 1974; A Regionalist Manifesto, 1975; The King is Dead, 1976; Pillars of the Establishment, 1980. *Heir: s* Hon. Ceawlin Henry Laszlo Thynn, *b* 6 June 1974. *Address:* Longleat, Warminster, Wilts BA12 7NN. *T:* Warminster (0985) 844300.

WHADDON, Baron *cr* 1978 (Life Peer), of Whaddon in the County of Cambridgeshire; **(John) Derek Page;** Director, Cambridge Chemical Co. Ltd, since 1962; Chairman: Daltrade, since 1983; Skorimpex-Rind, since 1985; Britpol Chemicals, since 1989; *b* 14 Aug. 1927; *s* of John Page and Clare Page (*née* Maher); *m* 1st, 1948, Catherine Audrey Halls (*d* 1979); one *s* one *d*; 2nd, 1981, Angela Rixson. *Educ:* St Bede's College, Manchester; London University. External BSc (Soc.). MP (Lab) King's Lynn, 1964–70; contested (Lab) Norfolk NW, Feb. 1974. Mem., Council of Management, CoSIRA, 1975–82; Mem., E Anglia Economic Planning Council, 1975–80. Golden Insignia of Order of Merit (Poland), 1989. *Recreation:* private pilot. *Address:* The Old Vicarage, Whaddon, Royston, Herts. *T:* Cambridge (0223) 207209. *Club:* Reform.

WHALE, John Hilary; Editor, Church Times, since 1989; *b* 19 Dec. 1931; *s* of Rev. Dr John Seldon Whale, *qv*; *m* 1957, Judith Laurie Hackett; one *s*. *Educ:* Winchester; Corpus Christi College, Oxford. BA Lit Hum 1955, MA 1958. Lieut, Intelligence Corps, 1950–51 (Nat. Service). Writing, acting and teaching, 1954–58; Section Anglaise, French radio, Paris, 1958–59; ITN, 1960–69: Political Corresp., 1963–67; US Corresp., Washington, 1967–69; Sunday Times, 1969–84: political staff, 1969–79; Religious Affairs Corresp., 1979–84; Asst Editor, 1981–84; leader-writer throughout; Head of Religious Programmes, BBC TV, 1984–89. Dir, London programme, Univ. of Missouri Sch. of Journalism, 1980–83. Churchwarden, St. Mary's, Barnes, 1976–81. *Publications:* The Half-Shut Eye, 1969; Journalism and Government, 1972; The Politics of the Media, 1977; One Church, One Lord, 1979 (Winifred Mary Stanford Prize, 1980); (ed) The Pope from Poland, 1980; Put it in Writing, 1984; (contrib.) Why I am Still an Anglican, 1986; The Future of Anglicanism, 1988; contribs to books, quarterlies, weeklies. *Address:* 28 St James's Walk, Clerkenwell, EC1R 0AP. *T:* 071–253 1008.

WHALE, Rev. John Seldon, MA (Oxon); DD (Glasgow); *b* 19 Dec. 1896; *s* of Rev. John Whale and Alice Emily Seldon; *m* Mary, *d* of Rev. H. C. Carter, MA; two *s* two *d* (and one *s* decd). *Educ:* Caterham School, Surrey; St Catherine's Society and Mansfield College, Oxford; 1st Class Hons Sch. of Mod. Hist. 1922; Magdalene College, Cambridge, 1933. Minister of Bowdon Downs Congregational Church, Manchester, 1925–29; Mackennal Professor of Ecclesiastical History, Mansfield College, Oxford, and Tutor in Modern History, St Catherine's, 1929–33; President of Cheshunt College, Cambridge, 1933–44; Headmaster of Mill Hill School, 1944–51; Visiting Professor of Christian Theology, Drew Univ., Madison, NJ, USA, 1951–53. Moderator of Free Church Federal Council, 1942–43; Select Preacher, Univ. of Cambridge, 1943, 1957; Warrack Lecturer, 1944; Russell Lecturer (Auburn and New York), 1936 and 1948; Alden Tuthill Lecturer, Chicago, 1952; Greene Lecturer, Andover, 1952; Currie Lecturer, Austin, Texas, 1953; Hill Lectr, St Olaf Coll., Minnesota, 1954; Visiting Lecturer, Univ. of Toronto, 1957; Danforth Scholar, USA, 1958; Sir D. Owen Evans Lectures, Aberystwyth, 1958. Visiting Professor, Univ. of Chicago, 1959; Senior Fellow of Council of Humanities, Princeton Univ., 1960. *Publications:* The Christian Answer to the Problem of Evil, 1936; What is a Living Church?, 1937; This Christian Faith, 1938; Facing the Facts, 1940; Christian Doctrine, 1941; The Protestant Tradition, 1955; Victor and Victim: the Christian doctrine of Redemption, 1960; Christian Reunion: historic divisions reconsidered, 1971; The Coming Dark Age, 1973 (Eng. trans. of Roberto Vacca's Il Medioevo Prossimo Venturo, 1972). *Address:* Wild Goose, Widecombe-in-the-Moor, Newton Abbot, S Devon TQ13 7TY. *T:* Widecombe-in-the-Moor (03642) 260.

See also *J. H. Whale.*

WHALEN, Geoffrey Henry, CBE 1989; FIMI, FIPM; Managing Director, since 1984, and Deputy Chairman, since 1990, Peugeot Talbot Motor Co. Ltd; *b* 8 Jan. 1936; *s* of Henry and Mabel Whalen; *m* 1961, Elizabeth Charlotte; two *s* three *d*. *Educ:* Magdalen College, Oxford. MA Hons Modern History. National Coal Board, Scotland (industrial relations), 1959–66; Divl Personnel Manager, A. C. Delco Div., General Motors, Dunstable, 1966–70; British Leyland, 1970–78; Personnel Dir, Leyland Cars, 1975–78; Personnel Dir, Rank Hovis McDougall Bakeries Div., 1978–80; Personnel and Indust. Rel. Dir, Talbot Motor Co., 1980–81, Asst Man. Dir, 1981–84. Vice Pres., SMMT, 1991– (Pres., 1988–90; Dep Pres., 1990–91); Vice Pres., Inst. of Motor Industry, 1986–; Chm., Coventry and Warwicks TEC, 1990–. FCGI; CBIM. 1987 Midlander of the Year Award, Bass Mitchells & Butlers Ltd, 1988. Chevalier de la Légion d'Honneur (France), 1990. *Address:* Victoria Lodge, 8 Park Crescent, Abingdon, Oxon OX14 1DF. *Club:* United Oxford & Cambridge University.

WHALLEY, John Mayson, FRTPI; FRIBA; PPLI; Senior Partner, Derek Lovejoy Partnership, since 1968; *b* 14 Sept. 1932; *s* of George Mayson Whalley and Ada Florence Cairns; *m* 1966, Elizabeth Gillian Hide; one *s* two *d*. *Educ:* Grammar Sch., Preston; Univ. of Liverpool (BArch, 1st Cl. Hons; MCivic Des.); Univ. of Pennsylvania (MLandscape Arch). Sir Charles Reilly Medal and Prize for thesis design, 1956; Leverhulme and Italian Govt Fellowships for study in Scandinavia and Univ. of Rome, 1957; Fulbright Schol., 1958; Manchester Soc. of Architects Winstanley Fellowship, 1965. Asst architect to Sir Frederick Gibberd, Harlow, 1956; architect/landscape architect: Oskar Stonorov, Philadelphia, 1958–60; Grenfell Baines and Hargreaves Building Design Partnership, Preston, 1960–62; Associate, Derek Lovejoy & Associates, 1963–68. Chm., NW Region, RIBA, 1984–85; President: Manchester Soc. of Architects, 1980–81; Landscape Inst., 1985–87. Civic Trust awards: W Burton Power Stn, 1968; Cheshire Constabulary HQ, 1969; Rochdale Canal, 1973; design competitions 1st prizes: Cergy-Pontoise, 1970; La Courneuve, Paris, 1972; Liverpool Anglican Cathedral precinct, 1982; Urban Park, Vitoria-Gasteiz; Garden Festivals: Liverpool, 1982; Stoke-on-Trent, 1983; Glasgow, 1985. Civic Trust awards assessor, 1970–; UN Tech. Expert, Riyadh, 1975. Mem., Order of Architectes de France; FRSA. Contribs to radio and TV. *Publications:* Selected Architects Details, 1958; articles in professional jls. *Recreations:* jazz, salmon fishing, photography, cricket, good wine and food. *Address:* Derek Lovejoy and Partners, Arkwright House, Parsonage Gardens, Manchester M3 2LE. *T:* 061–834 8825; Dilworth House, Longridge, Preston, Lancs PR3 3ST. *T:* Longridge (0772) 783262. *Clubs:* Landsdowne; St James's (Manchester).

WHALLEY, Richard Carlton; Chairman, Ewden Associates Ltd, since 1981; *b* Quetta, India, 4 July 1922; *s* of Frederick Seymour Whalley, MC, FCGI, MIMechE, and Gwendolen, *d* of Sir William Collingwood; *m* 1945, Mary Christian Bradley; two *s* twin *d*. *Educ:* Shrewsbury Sch.; 151 OCTU, Aldershot. Served War: Private, Royal Berkshire Regt, 1940; commissioned 2nd Lieut, Royal Corps of Signals, 1942; Captain and Adjt, 2nd Div. Signals, India, Assam, Burma, 1942–45 (despatches). War Office, AG II (O), 1945–48; GHQ Singapore, 1948–51. Vulcan Foundry Ltd: Asst Sec., 1952–58; Commercial Manager, 1958–60; Dep. Gen. Manager, 1960–65; Manager, English Electric Diesel Engine Div., 1965–67; Dir and Gen. Manager, Glacier Metal Co., 1968–70. 1970–78: Dep. Chm. and Managing Dir, Millspaugh Ltd; Chm. and Managing Dir, C. A. Harnden Ltd, Westbury Engrg Ltd, Hargreaves & Jennings Ltd, and T. Rowbottom Ltd; Director: Bertram-Scott Ltd; Sulzer Bros (UK) Ltd; Mem., Bd of British Shipbuilders (with special responsibility for personnel, indust. relations, and trng), 1978–80. Chairman: F. & M. Ducker Ltd, 1981–84; A. Spafford & Co. Ltd, 1981–82; Pennine Plastics Ltd, 1981–82; Eaton and Booth Ltd, 1984–87; (also Chief Exec.) Eaton and Booth Rolling Mills Ltd, 1984–87; John King and Co. Ltd, 1985–87; Director: Estridge & Ropner Ltd, 1981–84; Sheffield Photoco, 1983–84; Dep. Chm., Malacarp Group, 1982–84. *Recreations:* rowing, walking. *Address:* Sunnybank Farm, Bolsterstone, Sheffield S30 5ZL. *T:* Sheffield (0742) 883116. *Clubs:* National Liberal; Sheffield (Sheffield); London Rowing.

WHALLEY, Prof. William Basil; Professor of Chemistry and Head of Department of Pharmaceutical Chemistry, School of Pharmacy, 1961–82, now Emeritus Professor of Chemistry, University of London; *b* 17 Dec. 1916; *s* of William and Catherine Lucy Whalley; *m* 1945, Marie Agnes Alston; four *s* one *d*. *Educ:* St Edward's College, Liverpool; Liverpool University. BSc Hons 1938; PhD 1940; DSc 1952; FRIC 1950. MOS and ICI 1940–45. Lecturer, 1946–55, Sen. Lectr, 1955–57, Reader, 1957–61, in Organic Chemistry, at Liverpool University. *Publications:* contrib. on organic chemistry to several books: *eg* Heterocyclic Compounds, Vol. 7, Edited R. C. Elderfield, Wiley (New York); many pubns in Jl of Chem. Soc., Jl Amer. Chem. Soc., etc. *Recreations:* music and mountaineering. *Address:* 9 Peaks Hill, Purley, Surrey CR8 3JG. *T:* 081–668 2244.

WHALLEY, Maj.-Gen. William Leonard, CB 1985; Project Director, Corby City Technology College, since 1989; Colonel Commandant, Royal Army Ordnance Corps, since 1986; *b* 19 March 1930; *m* 1955, Honor Mary (*née* Golden); one *d*. *Educ:* Sir William Turner's Sch., Coatham. Joined Army (Nat. Service), 1948; sc 1962; Commander, RAOC, 1st Div., 1968–71; Dir of Ordnance Services, BAOR, 1980–83; Dir Gen. of Ordnance Services, MoD, 1983–85. Life Vice-Pres., Army Boxing Assoc. (Chm., 1983–85). Chm., Little Aston Br., Conservative Assoc., 1987–. *Recreations:* bridge, computers, cabinet making. *Address:* Midland Bank, 8 High Street, Sutton Coldfield, West Midlands B72 1XB.

WHALLEY-TOOKER, Hyde Charnock, MA, LLM (Cantab), MA (Oxon); Emeritus Fellow of Downing College, Cambridge (Fellow, 1927–67, and Senior Tutor, 1931–47); University Lecturer in Law, 1931–67; *b* 1 Sept. 1900; *o s* of Edward Whalley-Tooker; *m* 1935, Frances (*d* 1987), *er d* of late Thomas Halsted; one *d*. *Educ:* Eton; Trinity Hall, Cambridge; Balliol College, Oxford; Law Tripos Part I, Class I, 1921; Part II, Class I, 1922. *Address:* 5 Wilberforce Road, Cambridge. *T:* Cambridge (0223) 350073.

WHARNCLIFFE, 5th Earl of, *cr* 1876; **Richard Alan Montagu Stuart Wortley;** Baron Wharncliffe 1826; Viscount Carlton 1876; *b* 26 May 1953; *s* of Alan Ralph Montagu-Stuart-Wortley (*d* 1986) and of Virginia Anne, *d* of W. Martin Claybaugh; *S* cousin, 1987; *m* 1979, Mary Elizabeth Reed; two *s*. *Heir: s* Viscount Carlton, *qv*. *Address:* 270 Main Street, Cumberland, Maine 04021, USA.

WHARTON, Baroness, 11th in line, *cr* 1544–5; **Myrtle Olive Felix Robertson, (Ziki);** *b* 20 Feb. 1934; *d* of David George Arbuthnot (*d* 1985) and Baroness Wharton, 10th in line (*d* 1974); *S* to Barony of mother (called out of abeyance, 1990); *m* 1958, Henry McLeod Robertson; three *s* one *d*. *Recreations:* animal welfare, photography, skiing, opera. *Heir: s* Hon. Myles Christopher David Robertson, *b* 1 Oct. 1964. *Address:* c/o House of Lords, SW1A 0PW.

WHARTON, Michael Bernard; author and journalist; 'Peter Simple' Columnist, Daily and Sunday Telegraph, since 1957; *b* 19 April 1913; *s* of Paul Nathan and Bertha Wharton; *m* 1st, 1936, Joan Atkey (marr. diss. 1947); one *s*; 2nd 1952, Catherine Mary Derrington (marr. diss. 1972); one *d*; 3rd, 1974, Susan Moller. *Educ:* Bradford Grammar Sch.; Lincoln Coll., Oxford. Army service, Royal Artillery and General Staff, 1940–46. Scriptwriter and Producer, BBC, 1946–56; (with Colin Welch) writer of Peter Simple column, Daily Telegraph, 1957–60. *Publications: as Michael Wharton:* (ed) A Nation's Security, 1955; Sheldrake (novel), 1958; The Missing Will (autobiog.), 1984; A Dubious Codicil (autobiog.), 1991; editor and mainly writer of twelve anthologies of Peter Simple column, 1963–87; *under pseudonym Simon Crabtree:* Forgotten Memories, 1941; Hector Tumbler Investigates, 1943. *Recreations:* walking, gardening, Celtic studies. *Address:* Forge Cottage, Naphill Common, High Wycombe, Bucks HP14 4SU. *T:* Naphill (024024) 3454.

WHATLEY, Prof. Frederick Robert, FRS 1975; Sherardian Professor of Botany, Oxford University, 1971–91; Fellow of Magdalen College, Oxford, since 1971; *b* 26 Jan. 1924; *s* of Frederick Norman Whatley and Maud Louise (*née* Hare); *m* 1951, Jean Margaret Smith Bowie; two *d*. *Educ:* Bishop Wordsworth's Sch., Salisbury; (Scholar) Selwyn Coll., Cambridge University (BA, PhD). Benn W. Levy Student, Cambridge, 1947. Sen. Lectr. in Biochemistry, Univ. of Sydney, 1950–53; Asst Biochemist, Univ. of California at Berkeley, 1954–58; Associate Biochemist, 1959–64; Guggenheim Fellowship (Oxford and Stockholm), 1960; Prof. of Botany, King's Coll., London, 1964–71. Vis. Fellow, ANU, 1979. *Publications:* articles and reviews in scientific jls. *Address:* Magdalen College, Oxford OX1 4AU.

WHATLEY, William Henry Potts, OBE 1986; General Secretary, Union of Shop Distributive and Allied Workers, 1979–85; *b* 16 Dec. 1922; *s* of Arthur John and Ethel Whatley; *m* 1946, Margaret Ann Harrison. *Educ:* Gosforth Secondary School. Clerk, CWS, Newcastle upon Tyne, 1938; War Service, RAF, War of 1939–45; Area Organiser,

USDAW, Bristol, 1948; National Officer, 1966; Chief Organising Officer, 1976; Member: TUC General Council, 1979–85; TUC Economic Cttee, 1979; Pres., EURO-FIET, 1982–87. *Recreations:* gardening, reading. *Address:* 72 St Martin's Road, Ashton-on-Mersey, Sale, Cheshire. *T:* 061–973 3772.

WHEADON, Richard Anthony; Principal, Elizabeth College, Guernsey, 1972–88, retired; *b* 31 Aug. 1933; *s* of Ivor Cecil Newman Wheadon and Margarita Augusta (*née* Cash); *m* 1961, Ann Mary (*née* Richardson); three *s. Educ:* Cranleigh Sch. Balliol Coll., Oxford. MA (Physics). Commissioned RAF, 1955 (Sword of Honour); Air Radar Officer, 1955–57; Asst Master, Eton Coll., 1957–66; Dep. Head Master and Head of Science Dept, Dauntsey's Sch., 1966–71. Mem., Wilts Educn Cttee's Science Adv. Panel, 1967–71. Rowed bow for Oxford, 1954, for GB in European Championships and Olympic Games, 1956; Captain RAF VIII, 1956 and 1957; Olympic Selector and Nat. Coach, 1964–66. Contingent Comdr, Dauntsey's Sch. CCF, 1969–70. *Publication:* The Principles of Light and Optics, 1968. *Recreations:* French horn, photography, electronics, singing, sailing, words. *Address:* L'Enclos Gallienne, Rue du Court Laurent, Torteval, Guernsey, Channel Islands. *T:* Guernsey (0481) 64988.

WHEARE, Thomas David, MA; Headmaster of Bryanston School, since 1983; *b* 11 Oct. 1944; *s* of late Sir Kenneth Wheare, CMG, FBA, and of Lady (Joan) Wheare; *m* 1977, Rosalind Clare Spice; two *d. Educ:* Dragon Sch.; Magdalen College Sch., Oxford; King's Coll., Cambridge (BA, MA); Christ Church, Oxford (DipEd). Assistant Master, Eton College, 1967–76; Housemaster of School House, Shrewsbury School, 1976–83. FRSA 1989. *Recreations:* music, reading. *Address:* Bryanston School, Blandford, Dorset DT11 0PX. *T:* Blandford (0258) 452728.

WHEAT, Rev. Fr Charles Donald Edmund, SSM; Vicar, All Saints', Middlesbrough, since 1988; *b* 17 May 1937; *s* of Charles and Alice Wheat. *Educ:* Kelham Theol Coll.; Nottingham Univ. (BA); Sheffield Univ. (MA). Curate, St Paul's, Arbourthorne, Sheffield, 1962–67; licensed, Dio. Southwell, 1967–70; Mem., SSM, 1969–; Chaplain, St Martin's Coll., Lancaster, 1970–73; Prior, SSM Priory, Sheffield, 1973–75; Curate, St John, Ranmoor and Asst Chaplain, Sheffield Univ., 1975–77, Chaplain 1977–80; Provincial, English Province, 1981–91, Dir, 1982–89, SSM. Mem., Gen. Synod, 1975–80. *Recreations:* reading, watching soap operas. *Address:* All Saints' Vicarage, Grange Road, Middlesbrough TS1 2LR. *T:* Middlesbrough (0642) 245035.

WHEATCROFT, Stephen Frederick, OBE 1974; Director, Aviation and Tourism International Ltd, since 1983; *b* 11 Sept. 1921; *s* of late Percy and Fanny Wheatcroft; *m* 1st, 1943, Joy (*d* 1974), *d* of late Cecil Reed; two *s* one *d*; 2nd, 1974, Alison, *d* of late Arnold Dessau; two *s. Educ:* Latymer Sch., N9; London Sch. of Economics. BSc(Econ) 1942. Served War, Pilot in Fleet Air Arm, 1942–45. Commercial Planning Manager, BEA, 1946–53; Simon Research Fellow, Manchester Univ., 1953–55; private practice as Aviation Consultant, 1956–72; retained as Economic Adviser to BEA. Commns for Govts of: Canada, India, W Indies, E African Community, Afghanistan; Consultant to World Bank; Assessor to Edwards Cttee on British Air Transport in the Seventies; Mem. Bd, British Airways (Dir of Economic Develt), 1972–82. Governor, London Sch. of Economics. FRAeS, FCIT (Pres., 1978–79); FAIAA. *Publications:* Economics of European Air Transport, 1956; Airline Competition in Canada, 1958; Air Transport Policy, 1966; Air Transport in a Competitive European Market, 1986; European Liberalisation and World Air Transport, 1990; articles in professional jls. *Recreation:* travel. *Address:* (office) 33 Park Walk, SW10 0AJ. *T:* 071–352 4150. *Club:* Reform.

WHEATLEY, Alan Edward, FCA; Senior Partner, Price Waterhouse (London Office), since 1985; *b* 23 May 1938; *s* of late Edward and of Margaret Wheatley (*née* Turner); *m* 1962, Marion Frances (*née* Wilson); two *s* one *d. Educ:* Ilford Grammar School. Chartered Accountant. Norton Slade, 1954–60, qualified 1960; joined Price Waterhouse, 1960; admitted to partnership, 1970; Mem., Policy Cttee, 1981–. Non-exec. Dir, EBS Investments (Bank of England sub.), 1977–90; Govt Dir, Cable & Wireless, 1981–84, non-exec. Dep. Chm., 1984–85. Member: British Steel plc (formerly British Steel Corp.), 1984–; Ind. Develt Adv. Bd, 1985–. Governor, Solefield School, 1985–. *Recreations:* golf, tennis, badminton, bridge. *Address:* Highcroft, Kippington Road, Sevenoaks, Kent. *T:* Sevenoaks (0732) 453088. *Club:* Wildernesse (Seal, Kent).

WHEATLEY, Rear-Adm. Anthony, CB 1988; General Manager, National Hospital for Neurology and Neurosurgery, Queen Square, since 1988; *b* 3 Oct. 1933; *yr s* of Edgar C. Wheatley and late Audrey G. Barton Hall; *m* 1962, Iona Sheila Haig; one *d. Educ:* Berkhamsted School. Entered RN Coll., Dartmouth, 1950; RNEC, Manadon, 1953–57; HMS Ceylon, 1958-60; HMS Ganges, 1960–61; HMS Cambrian, 1962–64; Staff of RNEC, Manadon, 1964–67; Staff of Comdr British Navy Staff, Washington, 1967–69; HMS Diomede, 1970–72; Staff of C-in-C Fleet, 1972–74; Exec. Officer, RNEC Manadon, 1975–76; MoD Procurement Exec., 1977–79; British Naval Attaché, Brasilia, 1979–81; RCDS course 1982; HMS Collingwood (in Command), 1982–85; Flag Officer, Portsmouth, Naval Base Comdr and Head of Establishment of Fleet Maintenance and Repair Orgn, Portsmouth, 1985–87. *Recreations:* cricket, golf, music. *Address:* 2 Claridge Court, Munster Road, SW6 4EY. *Clubs:* Army and Navy; Free Foresters, Incogniti.

WHEATLEY, Rev. Canon Arthur; Priest in Charge of St Columba's, Grantown-on-Spey and St John's, Rothiemurchus, since 1983; *b* 4 March 1931; *s* of George and Elizabeth Wheatley; *m* 1959, Sheena Morag Wilde; two *s* two *d. Educ:* Alloa Academy; Coates Hall Theol Coll., Edinburgh. Deacon 1970, priest 1970, Dio. Brechin; 1st Curate's title, St Salvador's with St Martin's, Dundee, 1970–71; Curate in Charge, St Ninian's Mission, Dundee, 1971–76; Rector of Holy Trinity, Elgin with St Margaret's Church, Lossiemouth, Dio. Moray, Ross and Caithness, 1976–80; Canon of St Andrew's Cathedral, 1978–80; Provost, 1980–83; Canon of Inverness Cathedral, 1985–. Episcopalian Chaplain to HM Prison, Porterfield, 1980–; Anglican Chaplain to RAF Unit, Grantown-on-Spey, 1984–. *Recreations:* shooting, fishing, bee keeping. *Address:* St Columba's Rectory, Grant Road, Grantown-on-Spey, Moray PH26 3ER.

WHEATLEY, Derek Peter Francis, QC 1981; Barrister-at-Law; Chief Legal Adviser to Lloyds Bank, 1976–89; Member, Joint Law Society/Bar Council Working Party on Banking Law, since 1976; *b* 18 Dec. 1925; 3rd *s* of late Edward Pearse Wheatley, company director, and Gladys Wheatley; *m* 1955, Elizabeth Pamela, *d* of John and Gertrude Reynolds; two *s* one *d. Educ:* The Leys Sch., Cambridge; University Coll., Oxford (MA). Served War of 1939–45, Army, 1944–47: (short univ. course, Oxford, 1944); commissioned into 8th King's Royal Irish Hussars, 1945, Lieut. University Coll., Oxford, 1947–49; called to the Bar, Middle Temple, 1951; Deputy Coroner: to the Royal Household, 1959–64; for London, 1959–64; Recorder of the Crown Court, 1972–74. Member: Commercial Court Cttee, 1976–90; Senate of Inns of Court and the Bar, 1975–78, 1982–85; Exec. Cttee, Bar Council, 1982–85; Bar Council, 1986–90 (Member: Professional Standards Cttee, 1986–88; F and GP Cttee, 1988–); Vice-Pres., Bar Assoc. for Commerce, Finance and Industry, 1986– (Chm., 1982–83). Chm., Legal Cttee, Cttee of London and Scottish Bankers, 1985–87. *Publications:* articles in legal jls and The Times, etc. *Recreation:* sailing. *Address:* 3 Gray's Inn Place, Gray's Inn, WC1. *T:* 071–831 8441; Three The Wardrobe, Old Palace Yard, Richmond, Surrey. *T:* 081–940 6242. *Clubs:* Bar Yacht, Little Ship.

WHEATLEY, John Derek; Director General, The Sports Council, 1983–88; *b* 24 July 1927; *s* of Leslie Sydney and Lydia Florence Wheatley; *m* 1956, Marie Gowers; one *s* one *d. Educ:* Sir Thomas Rich's Sch., Gloucester; Loughborough Coll., 1944–46 (Teacher's Cert.); Carnegie College of Physical Educn, 1952–53 (DipPE). Served RAF, 1946–52; Surrey Education Authority, 1953–54; Central Council of Physical Recreation: London and SE, 1954–58; Secretary, Northern Ireland, 1959–69; Principal Regional Officer, SW, 1970–72; Sports Council: Regional Director, SW, 1972–80; Director of Administrative Services, Headquarters, 1980–83. Mem., Nat. Rivers Authy, 1989–. Chm., Nat. Small-Bore Rifle Assoc., 1989–. *Recreations:* gardening, bee keeping. *Address:* 1 Argyll Court, 82–84 Lexham Gardens, W8 5JB.

WHEATLEY, Hon. John Francis; Sheriff of Tayside Central and Fife at Perth, since 1980 (at Dunfermline, 1979–80); *b* 9 May 1941; *s* of Rt Hon. John Thomas Wheatley (Baron Wheatley) and Agnes Nichol; *m* 1970, Bronwen Catherine Fraser; two *s. Educ:* Mount St Mary's Coll., Derbyshire; Edinburgh Univ. (BL). Called to the Scottish Bar, 1966; Standing Counsel to Scottish Develt Dept, 1971; Advocate Depute, 1975. *Recreations:* gardening, music. *Address:* Braefoot Farmhouse, Crook of Devon, Fossoway, Kinross-shire. *T:* Fossoway (05774) 212.

WHEATLEY, Ven. Paul Charles; Archdeacon of Sherborne and Priest in Charge of West Stafford with Frome Billet, since 1991; *b* 27 May 1938; *s* of Charles Lewis and Doris Amy Wheatley; *m* 1963, Iris Mary Lacey; two *s* one *d. Educ:* Wycliffe Coll.; St John's Coll., Durham (BA 1961); Lincoln Theol Coll. Ordained deacon 1963, priest 1964; Curate, Bishopston, Bristol, 1963–68; Youth Chaplain, dio. of Bristol, 1968–73; Team Rector, Dorcan, Swindon, 1973–79; Rector, Ross, Hereford, 1979–81; Team Rector, Ross with Brampton Abbots, Bridstow, Peterstow, 1979–91; Prebendary, Hereford Cathedral, 1987–91; Ecumenical Officer, Hereford, 1987–91; Hon. Canon, Salisbury Cathedral, 1991–. *Recreations:* travel, gardening, opera, model railways. *Address:* The Rectory, West Stafford, Dorchester, Dorset DT2 8AB. *T:* Dorchester (0305) 64637.

WHEATON, Rev. Canon David Harry; Vicar of Christ Church, Ware, since 1986; Chaplain to the Queen, since 1990; *b* 2 June 1930; *s* of Harry Wheaton, MBE, and Kathleen Mary (*née* Frost); *m* 1956, Helen Joy Forrer; one *s* two *d. Educ:* Abingdon Sch.; St John's Coll., Oxford (Exhibnr; MA); London Univ. (BD (London Bible Coll.)); Oak Hill Theol Coll. NCO, Wiltshire Regt, 1948–49. Deacon, 1959; priest, 1960; Tutor, Oak Hill Coll., 1954–62; Rector of Ludgershall, Bucks, 1962–66; Vicar of St Paul, Onslow Square, S Kensington, 1966–71; Chaplain, Brompton Chest Hosp., 1969–71; Principal Oak Hill Theol Coll., 1971–86; RD of Hertford, 1988–91. Hon. Canon, Cathedral and Abbey Church of St Alban, 1976. *Publications: contributed to:* Baker's Dictionary of Theology, 1960; New Bible Dictionary, 1962; New Bible Commentary (rev.), 1970; Evangelical Dictionary of Theology, 1984; Here We Stand, 1986; Restoring the Vision, 1990. *Recreations:* walking, carpentry and do-it-yourself. *Address:* Christ Church Vicarage, 15 Hanbury Close, Ware, Herts SG12 7BZ. *T:* Ware (0920) 463165.

WHEELDON, Rt. Rev. Philip William, OBE 1946; *b* 20 May 1913; *e s* of late Alfred Leonard Wheeldon and late Margaret Proctor Wheeldon (*née* Smith); *m* 1966, Margaret Redfearn. *Educ:* Clifton Coll., Bristol; Downing Coll., Cambridge; Westcott House Theological Coll. BA 1935, MA 1942. Deacon, 1937; Priest, 1938; Farnham Parish Church, Dio. Guildford, 1937–39; Chaplain to the Forces, 1939–46; Chaplain, 1st Bn Coldstream Guards, 1939–42; Senior Chaplain, 79th Armoured Div., 1942–43; Dep. Asst Chaplain-Gen. 12th Corps, 1943–45; 8th Corps, 1945–46; Hon. Chaplain to the Forces, 1946–; Domestic Chaplain to Archbishop of York, 1946–49, Hon. Chaplain, 1950–54; General Sec., CACTM, 1949–54; Prebendary of Wedmore II in Wells Cathedral, 1952–54; Suffragan Bishop of Whitby, 1954–61; Bishop of Kimberley and Kuruman, 1961–65; resigned, 1965; an Asst Bishop, Dio. Worcester, 1965–68; Bishop of Kimberley and Kuruman, 1968–76. Hon. Asst Bishop, Diocese of Worcester 1976–77, Diocese of Wakefield 1977–85. *Recreations:* music, gardening. *Address:* 11 Toothill Avenue, Brighouse, West Yorks HD6 3SA.

WHEELER, Sir Anthony; *see* Wheeler, Sir H. A.

WHEELER, Captain Arthur Walter, RN retd; CEng; Keeper, HMS Belfast, 1983–88; *b* 18 Oct. 1927; *s* of Walter Sidney Wheeler and Annie Ethel Marsh; *m* 1st, 1957, Elizabeth Jane Glendinning Bowman (marr. diss. 1968); two *s*; 2nd, 1968, Mary Elvis Findon; one *s. Educ:* Woodhouse Sch., Finchley; HMS Fisgard, Torpoint; RN Engineering Coll., Manadon. FIMechE, MIMarE. Joined Royal Navy as artificer apprentice, 1943; served in cruiser Birmingham, 1947–50. Progressively, Sub Lieut 1950 to Captain 1974. Served in frigate Palliser and aircraft carriers Bulwark, Hermes and Ark Royal 1954–74; Sea Trng Staff at Portland, 1961–63; MoD, Ship Dept, 1966–70 and 1975–78; CSO(Engrg) to Flag Officer Third Flotilla, 1979–80; HMS Daedalus in comd, 1980–82, retired. *Recreations:* painting and drawing, music and opera, books, English history, walking. *Address:* c/o Lloyds Bank, Bath Capital & Counties Branch, 47 Milsom Street, Bath BA1 1DX. *T:* (home) Shawbury (0939) 250662.

WHEELER, Arthur William Edge, CBE 1979 (OBE 1967); Chairman, Foreign Compensation Commission, since 1983; *b* 1 Aug. 1930; *e s* of Arthur William Wheeler and Rowena (*née* Edge); *m* 1956, Gay; two *s* one *d. Educ:* Mountjoy Sch.; Trinity Coll., Dublin (Reid Prof.'s Prize, MA, LLB). Called to the Irish Bar, King's Inns, 1953; called to the Bar, Gray's Inn, 1960. Crown Counsel, Nigeria, 1955; Legal Sec. (Actg), Southern Cameroons, and Mem. Exec. Council and House of Assembly, 1958; Principal Crown Counsel, Fedn of Nigeria, 1961; Northern Nigeria: Dep. Solicitor Gen., 1964; Dir of Public Prosecutions, 1966; High Court Judge, 1967; Chief Judge (formerly Chief Justice), Kaduna State of Nigeria, 1975; Comr for Law Revision, northern states of Nigeria, 1980. Mem., Body of Benchers, Nigeria, 1975; Associate Mem., Commonwealth Parly Assoc. *Recreations:* sport (university colours for hockey and assoc. football; Nigerian hockey internat.), music. *Address:* c/o Foreign Compensation Commission, Room 3/56, Old Admiralty Building, Whitehall, SW1A 2AF. *Club:* Commonwealth Trust.

WHEELER, Charles (Cornelius-); journalist and broadcaster, since 1940; *b* 26 March 1923; *s* of late Wing-Comdr Charles Cornelius-Wheeler, RFC and RAFVR, and Winifred (*née* Rees); *m* 1961, Dip Singh; two *d. Educ:* Cranbrook School. Began journalism as tape-boy, Daily Sketch, 1940. Served War, Royal Marines, 1942–46; Captain 1944 (despatches NW Europe). Sub-editor, BBC Latin American Service, 1947–49; German Service Correspondent in Berlin, 1950–53; Talks writer, European Service, 1954–56; Producer, Panorama, 1956–58; S Asia Correspondent, 1958–62; Berlin Corresp., 1962–65; Washington Corresp., 1965–68; Chief Correspondent: USA, 1969–73; Europe, 1973–76; BBC Television News, 1977; Panorama, 1977–79; Newsnight, 1980–. Documentaries include: The Kennedy Legacy, 1970; Battle for Berlin, 1985; The Road to War (series), 1989; Bloody Sunday in Tbilisi, 1989; Beyond Reasonable Doubt, 1990. TV Journalist of the Year, RTS, 1988; Internat. Documentary Award, RTS, 1989; James Cameron Meml

Award, 1990. *Publication:* The East German Rising (with Stefan Brant), 1955. *Recreations:* gardening, travel. *Address:* 10A Portland Road, W11.

WHEELER, Prof. David John, FRS 1981; Professor of Computer Science, Cambridge University, since Oct. 1978; Fellow of Darwin College, Cambridge, since 1967; *b* 9 Feb. 1927; *s* of Arthur William Wheeler and Agnes Marjorie (*née* Gudgeon); *m* 1957, Joyce Margaret Blackler. *Educ:* Camp Hill Grammar Sch., Birmingham; Hanley High Sch., Stoke on Trent; Trinity Coll., Cambridge. Research Fellow, Trinity Coll., Cambridge, 1951–57; Visiting Asst Prof., Univ. of Illinois, USA, 1951–53; Asst Director of Research, Cambridge Univ., 1956–66; Reader in Computer Science, Cambridge Univ., 1966–78. *Publication:* The Preparation of Programs for an Electronic Digital Computer, 1951. *Address:* 131 Richmond Road, Cambridge CB4 3PS. *T:* Cambridge (0223) 351319.

WHEELER, Frank Basil, CMG 1990; HM Diplomatic Service; Ambassador to Ecuador, since 1989; *b* 24 April 1937; *s* of late Harold Gifford Wheeler and Winifred Lucy Wheeler (*née* Childs); *m* 1st, 1959, Catherine Saunders Campbell (*d* 1979); one *s*; 2nd, 1984, Alyson Ruth Lund (*née* Powell) (marr. diss. 1989); 3rd, 1991, Susana Plaza Larrea. *Educ:* Mill Hill Sch. HM Forces, 1956–58. HM Foreign Service, 1958–: Foreign Office, 1958–61; Third Sec. (Commercial), Moscow, 1961–63; Asst Private Sec. to Minister of State, FO, 1963–65; Second Sec. (Commercial), Berne, 1965–67; First Sec., FO (later FCO), 1967–72; Wellington, 1972–75; FCO, 1975–77; Counsellor and Head of Chancery, Prague, 1977–79; Inspector, 1979–82; Head of Personnel Policy Dept, FCO, 1982–84; Counsellor and Head of Chancery, UK Delegn to NATO, Brussels, 1984–86; Counsellor, on loan to DTI, 1986–89. *Recreations:* music, tennis. *Address:* c/o Foreign and Commonwealth Office, SW1A 2AH.

WHEELER, Sir Frederick (Henry), AC 1979; Kt 1967; CBE 1962 (OBE 1952); Secretary to the Treasury, Australia, 1971–79; *b* 9 Jan. 1914; *s* of late A. H. Wheeler; *m* 1939, Peggy Hilda (*d* 1975), *d* of Basil P. Bell; one *s* two *d*. *Educ:* Scotch College; Melbourne University (BCom). State Savings Bank of Victoria, 1929–39; Treasury: Research Officer, 1939; Economist, 1944; Asst Sec., 1946; First Asst Sec., 1949–52; Treasurer Comptroller, ILO, Geneva, 1952–60; Chm., Commonwealth Public Service Bd, Canberra, 1961–71; Member: Aust. delegn to various British Commonwealth Finance Ministers' Conferences; Austr. Delegn Bretton Woods Monetary Conf.; UN Civil Service Adv. Bd, 1969–72; Commonwealth Govt Defence Review Cttee, 1981–82. Director: Amatil Ltd, 1979–84; Alliance Holdings Ltd, 1979–86. Dir, Winston Churchill Meml Trust (Aust.), 1965–. *Address:* 9 Charlotte Street, Red Hill, ACT 2603, Australia. *T:* 2959 888. *Clubs:* (Pres. 1966–69) Commonwealth (Canberra); Royal Canberra Golf.

WHEELER, Rt. Rev. Monsignor Gordon; *see* Wheeler, W. G.

WHEELER, Sir (Harry) Anthony, Kt 1988; OBE 1973; RSA, FRIBA; President, Royal Scottish Academy, 1983–90; Consultant, Wheeler & Sproson, Architects and Planning Consultants, Edinburgh and Kirkcaldy, since 1986 (Senior Partner, 1954–86); *b* 7 Nov. 1919; *s* of Herbert George Wheeler and Laura Emma Groom; *m* 1944, Dorothy Jean Campbell; one *d*. *Educ:* Stranraer High Sch.; Royal Technical Coll., Glasgow; Glasgow School of Art; Univ. of Strathclyde (BArch). RIBA, DipTP, MRTPI. Glasgow Sch. of Architecture, 1937–48 (war service, Royal Artillery, 1939–46); John Keppie Scholar and Sir Rowand Anderson Studentship, 1948; RIBA Grissell Gold Medallist, 1948, and Neale Bursar, 1949. Assistant: to City Architect, Oxford, 1948; to Sir Herbert Baker & Scott, London, 1949; Sen. Architect, Glenrothes New Town, 1949–51; Sen. Lectr, Dundee Sch. of Arch., 1952–58; commenced private practice in Fife, 1952. Principal works include: Woodside Shopping Centre and St Columba's Parish Church, Glenrothes; Reconstruction of Giles Pittenweem; Redevelopment of Dysart and of Old Buckhaven; Town Centre Renewal, Grangemouth; Students' Union, Univ. of St Andrews; Hunter Building, Edinburgh Coll. of Art; St Peter's Episcopal Ch., Kirkcaldy. Member: Royal Fine Art Commn for Scotland, 1967–86; Scottish Housing Adv. Cttee, 1971–75; Trustee, Scottish Civic Trust, 1970–83; Pres., Royal Incorpn of Architects in Scotland, 1973–75; Vice-Pres., RIBA, 1973–75. RSA 1975 (ARSA 1963; Treasurer, 1978–80; Sec., 1980–83); Hon. RA 1991. 22 Saltire Awards and Commendations for Housing and Reconstruction; 12 Civic Trust Awards and Commendations. *Publications:* articles on civic design and housing in technical jls. *Recreations:* making gardens, sketching and water colours, fishing, music and drama. *Address:* Hawthornbank House, Dean Village, Edinburgh EH4 3BH. *T:* 031–225 2334. *Clubs:* New, Scottish Arts (Edinburgh).

WHEELER, Air Chief Marshal Sir (Henry) Neil (George), GCB 1975 (KCB 1969; CB 1967); CBE 1957 (OBE 1949); DSO 1943; DFC 1941 (Bar 1943); AFC 1954; *b* 8 July 1917; *s* of late T. H. Wheeler, South African Police; *m* 1942, Elizabeth, *d* of late W. H. Weightman, CMG; two *s* one *d*. *Educ:* St Helen's College, Southsea, Hants. Entered Royal Air Force College, Cranwell, 1935; Bomber Comd, 1937–40; Fighter and Coastal Comds, 1940–45; RAF and US Army Staff Colls, 1943–44; Cabinet Office, 1944–45; Directing Staff, RAF Staff Coll., 1945–46; FEAF, 1947–49; Directing Staff, JSSC, 1949–51; Bomber Comd, 1951–53; Air Min., 1953–57. Asst Comdt, RAF Coll., 1957–59; OC, RAF Laarbruch, 1959–60; IDC, 1961; Min. of Defence, 1961–63; Senior Air Staff Officer, HQ, RAF Germany (2nd TAF), Sept. 1963–66; Asst Chief of Defence Staff (Operational Requirements), MoD, 1966–67, Deputy Chief of Defence Staff, 1967–68; Commander, FEAF, 1969–70; Air Mem. for Supply and Organisation, MoD, 1970–73; Controller, Aircraft, MoD Procurement Exec., 1973–75. ADC to the Queen, 1957–61. Director: Rolls-Royce Ltd, 1977–82; Flight Refuelling (Holdings) Ltd, 1977–85. Chm., Anglo-Ecuadorian Soc., 1986–88. Vice-Pres., Air League; Liveryman, GAPAN, 1980, Master, 1986–87. FRAeS; CBIM. *Address:* Boundary Hall, Cooksbridge, Lewes, East Sussex BN8 4PT. *Clubs:* Royal Air Force, Flyfishers'.

WHEELER, Sir John (Daniel), Kt 1990; JP; DL; MP (C) Westminster North, since 1983 (City of Westminster, Paddington Division, 1979–83); *b* 1 May 1940; *s* of late Frederick Harry Wheeler and of Constance Elsie (*née* Foreman); *m* 1967, Laura Margaret Langley; one *s* one *d*. *Educ:* county sch., Suffolk; Staff Coll., Wakefield. Home Office: Asst Prison Governor, 1967–74; Res. Officer (looking into causes of crime and delinquency and treatment of offenders), 1974–76; Dir-Gen., BSIA, 1976–88 (Hon. Mem., 1990). Dir, National Supervisory Council for Intruder Alarms, 1977–88. Chairman: Nat. Inspectorate of Security Guard Patrol and Transport Services, 1982–; Security Systems Inspectorate, 1987–90. Non-Exec. Dir, Hunterprint Group PLC and other cos. Prospective Parly Candidate, City of Westminster, Paddington, 1976–79. Member: Home Office Standing Cttee on Crime Prevention, 1976–85; Home Office Steering Cttee on Crime Prevention, 1986–; Cons. Party National Adv. CPC Cttee, 1978–80; Home Affairs Select Cttee, 1979– (Chm., 1987–); Chairman: Home Affairs Sub-Cttee, Race Relations and Immigration, 1980–87; Residential Burglary Working Gp, 1986–87; All Party Penal Affairs Gp, 1986– (Vice-Chm., 1979–86); Vice-Chairman: Cons. Urban and New Towns Cttee, 1980–83; Cons. Home Affairs Cttee, 1987–90 (Jt Sec., 1980–87); British Pakistan Parly Gp, 1987–; Chm., Cons. Greater London Area Members' Cttee, 1983–90 (Jt Sec., 1980–83). Mem., Lloyd's, 1986–. Mem. Council, Order of St John for London, 1990–; Vice Pres., Paddington Div., St John Ambulance, 1990–. OStJ 1991. JP Inner London, 1978; DL Greater London, 1989. Freeman, City of London, 1987. *Publications:* Who Prevents Crime?, 1980; (jtly) The Standard Catalogue of the Coins of the British Commonwealth, 1642 to present day, 1986. *Recreation:* enjoying life. *Address:* House of Commons, SW1A 0AA. *T:* 071–219 4615. *Club:* Carlton.

WHEELER, Sir John (Hieron), 3rd Bt *cr* 1920; formerly Chairman, Raithby, Lawrence & Co. Ltd, retired 1973; *b* 22 July 1905; 2nd *s* of Sir Arthur Wheeler, 1st Bt; *S* brother, Sir Arthur (Frederick Pullman) Wheeler, 1964; *m* 1929, Gwendolen Alice (*née* Oram); two *s*. *Educ:* Charterhouse. Engaged in Print. Served War of 1939–45, Trooper, RTR, 1941–45. After the war, returned to printing. *Recreations:* whittling, dry stone walling. *Heir:* *s* John Frederick Wheeler [*b* 3 May 1933; *m* 1963, Barbara Mary, *d* of Raymond Flint, Leicester; two *s* one *d*]. *Address:* 39 Morland Avenue, Leicester LE2 2PF. *Club:* Wig and Pen.

WHEELER, Hon. Sir Kenneth (Henry), Kt 1976; JP; Speaker of the Victorian Parliament, Australia, 1973–79; *b* 7 Sept. 1912; *s* of William Henry Wheeler and Alma Nellie Wheeler; *m* 1934, Hazel Jean Collins; one *s* one *d*. *Educ:* Mernda State Sch., Vic. Grazier and retail dairyman for 19 years. Municipal Councillor, 1950–59; Mayor, City of Coburg, Vic., 1955–56; elected to Parliament of Victoria for Essendon, 1958. Member: CPA; Victorian Parly Former Mems Assoc.; Life Mem., Coburg FC. Life Governor: Essendon Hosp.; Essendon Lions Club. *Recreations:* golf, football, exhibition of horses. *Address:* 955 Mt Alexander Road, Essendon, Melbourne, Vic 3040, Australia. *Clubs:* Essendon; Coburg Rotary; Royal-Park Golf; Royal Automobile of Victoria.

WHEELER, Air Vice-Marshal Leslie William Frederick; Independent Inspector for Public Inquiries and Chairman of Appointments Boards for Civil Service Commissioners and Ministry of Defence, since 1984; *b* 4 July 1930; *s* of late George Douglas Wheeler and of Susan Wheeler; *m* 1960, Joan, *d* of late Harry Carpenter and of Evelyn Carpenter; two *d*. *Educ:* Creighton School, Carlisle. Commnd, 1952; Egypt and Cyprus, 1954–56; Specialist in Signals, 1958; Aden, 1958–60; V-force (Valiants), 1961–65; India (Staff Coll.), 1965–66; Headquarters Signals Command, 1966–69; OC 360 Sqdn, 1970–72; Dir, RAF Staff Coll., 1972–74; Electronic Warfare and Recce Operations, MoD, 1975–77; Stn Comdr, RAF Finningley, 1977–79; Air Cdre Policy & Plans, Headquarters RAF Support Comd, 1979–83; Dir-Gen., Personal Services (RAF), MoD, 1983–84, retired. *Recreations:* walking, reading, DIY, philately. *Address:* c/o Midland Bank, Brampton, Cumbria. *Club:* Royal Air Force.

WHEELER, Michael Mortimer, QC 1961; *b* Westminster, 8 Jan. 1915; *o s* of late Sir Mortimer Wheeler, CH, CIE, MC, TD, and late Tessa Verney Wheeler, FSA; *m* 1939, Sheila, *e d* of late M. S. Mayou, FRCS; two *d*. *Educ:* Dragon School, Oxford; Rugby School; Christ Church, Oxford. Barrister: Gray's Inn, 1938; Lincoln's Inn, 1946 (Bencher 1967; Treasurer, 1986); Dep. High Court Judge (Chancery Div.), 1972–89. Served throughout War of 1939–45, with RA (TA) in UK and Italy (Lt-Col 1945; despatches); TD 1961. *Address:* 114 Hallam Street, W1N 5LW. *T:* 071–580 7284. *Clubs:* Garrick, MCC.

WHEELER, Sir Neil; *see* Wheeler, Sir H. N. G.

WHEELER, Maj.-Gen. (retd) Richard Henry Littleton, CB 1960; CBE 1953; *b* 2 Nov. 1906; *s* of Maj. Henry Littleton Wheeler, CB, DSO, and Vera Gillum Webb; *m* 1941, Iris Letitia Hope; one *d*. *Educ:* Uppingham; RMA, Woolwich. 2nd Lt RA, 1926. Served War of 1939–45, 50th Division. Lt-Col 1942; Brigadier 1950; HQ Northern Army Group, 1958–61; Maj.-Gen. 1959. Col Comdt RA, 1963–71. *Recreations:* riding, music. *Address:* Manor Farm, Knighton, Sherborne, Dorset DT9 6QU. *Club:* Army and Navy.

WHEELER, Maj.-Gen. Roger Neil, CBE 1983; Assistant Chief of the General Staff, Ministry of Defence, since 1990; *b* 16 Dec. 1941; *s* of Maj.-Gen. T. N. S. Wheeler, CB, CBE; *m* 1980, Felicity Hares; three *s* one *d* by former marriage. *Educ:* All Hallows Sch., Devon. Early Army service in Borneo and ME, 1964–70; Bde Major, Cyprus Emergency, 1974; Mem., Lord Carver's Staff, Rhodesia talks, 1977; Bn Comd, Belize, Gibraltar, Berlin and Canada, 1979–82; COS, Falkland Is, June–Dec. 1982; Bde Comd, BAOR, 1985–86; Dir, Army Plans, 1987–89; Comdr, 1st Armoured Div., BAOR, 1989–90. *Recreations:* fly-fishing, cricket, shooting, ornithology. *Clubs:* Army and Navy; Stragglers of Asia CC, Devon Dumplings CC.

WHEELER, (Selwyn) Charles (Cornelius-); *see* Wheeler, C. C.

WHEELER, Rt. Rev. (William) Gordon, MA Oxon; Hon. DD Leeds; Bishop Emeritus of Leeds; *b* 5 May 1910; *o s* of late Frederick Wheeler and Marjorie (*née* Upjohn). *Educ:* Manchester Gram. Sch.; University Coll. and St Stephen's House, Oxford; Beda Coll., Rome. Curate, St Bartholomew's, Brighton, 1933; Curate, St Mary and All Saints, Chesterfield, 1934; Asst Chaplain, Lancing Coll., 1935. Received into Roman Catholic Church at Downside, 1936; Beda Coll., Rome, 1936–40; ordained priest, 1940; Asst St Edmund's, Lower Edmonton, 1940–44; Chaplain of Westminster Cathedral and Editor of Westminster Cathedral Chronicle, 1944–50; Chaplain to the Catholics in the University, London, 1950–54, and Ecclesiastical Adviser to the Union of Catholic Students, 1953–60; Privy Chamberlain to HH The Pope, 1952; Hon. Canon of Westminster, 1954, Administrator of Cathedral, 1954–65; Created Domestic Prelate to HH Pope Pius XII, 1955; Grand Cross Conventual Chaplain to the British Association of the Sovereign and Military Order of Malta, 1986; Coadjutor Bishop of Middlesbrough, 1964–66; present at 2nd Vatican Council, Rome, 1964 and 1965; Bishop of Leeds, 1966–85. *Publications:* In Truth and Love (memoirs), 1990; edited and contributed to Homage to Newman, 1945; Richard Challoner, 1947; The English Catholics, etc.; contribs to Dublin Review, The Tablet, Clergy Review, etc. *Address:* College of the Blessed Virgin, 62 Headingley Lane, Leeds, W Yorks LS6 2BX.

WHEELER, William Henry, CMG 1959; PhD (London); Chairman, Mark Laboratories Ltd, since 1960; *b* Petersfield, Hants, 5 March 1907; *s* of John William and Ellen Wheeler; *m* 1937, Mary Inkpen; no *c*. *Educ:* St Catharine's Coll., Cambridge (BA); Imperial Coll. of Science (DIC). Beit Memorial Research Fellow, Imperial Coll., 1931. Man. British Automatic Refrigerators, London, 1935; Government Scientific Service, 1937; Dir, Guided Weapons Research & Development, 1950; Head of UK Ministry of Supply Staff and Scientific Adviser to UK High Commission, Australia, 1955; Director of Explosives Research, Waltham Abbey, 1959. Man. Dir, 1961–82, and Dep. Chm., 1968–82, Urquhart Engineering Co. Ltd; Chairman: Urquhart Engineering Co. (Pty) Ltd, 1971–82; Urquhart Engineering GmbH, 1973–82; Dep. Chm., Steam and Combustion Engineering Ltd, 1973–82; Chm., Process Combustion Corp., USA, 1970–82. *Publications:* papers on Combustion and Detonation in Proc. and Trans. Royal Society, and on Rocket Propellants in Nature, Proc. of Inst. of Fuel and Instn of Chemical Engineers; papers on the Mechanism of Cavitation Erosion for DSIR and American Soc. of Mechanical Engineers. *Recreation:* private research laboratory. *Address:* 9 Bulstrode Court, Oxford Road, Gerrards Cross, Bucks SL9 7RR.

WHEELER-BOOTH, Michael Addison John; Clerk of the Parliaments, since 1991; *b* 25 Feb. 1934; *s* of Addison James Wheeler and Mary Angela Wheeler-Booth (*née*

Blakeney-Booth); *m* 1982, Emily Frances Smith; one *s* two *d*. *Educ:* Leighton Park Sch.; Magdalen Coll., Oxford (Exhibnr; MA). Clerk, Parliament Office, House of Lords, 1960; seconded as Private Secretary to Leader of House and Government Chief Whip, 1965; seconded as Jt Sec., Inter-Party Conference on House of Lords Reform, 1967; Clerk of the Journals, 1970–74, 1983–90; Chief Clerk, Overseas and European Office, 1972, Principal Clerk, 1978; Reading Clerk, 1983; Clerk Asst, 1988. *Address:* Northfields, Sandford St Martin, Oxon OX5 4AG. *T:* Great Tew (060883) 632; 11 Dewhurst Road, W14 0ET. *T:* 071–602 0838. *Club:* Brooks's.

WHELAN, Michael John, MA, PhD, DPhil; FRS 1976; Reader in the Physical Examination of Materials, Department of Materials, University of Oxford, since 1966; Fellow of Linacre College, Oxford, since 1967; *b* 2 Nov. 1931; *s* of William Whelan and Ellen Pound. *Educ:* Farnborough Grammar Sch.; Gonville and Caius Coll., Cambridge. FInstP. Fellow of Gonville and Caius Coll., 1958–66; Demonstrator in Physics, Univ. of Cambridge, 1961–65; Asst Dir of Research in Physics, Univ. of Cambridge, 1965–66. *Publications:* (co-author) Electron Microscopy of Thin Crystals, 1965; Worked Examples in Dislocations, 1990; numerous papers in learned jls. *Recreation:* gardening. *Address:* 18 Salford Road, Old Marston, Oxford OX3 0RX. *T:* Oxford (0865) 244556.

WHELAN, Terence Leonard; Editor, Ideal Home Magazine, since 1977; *b* 5 Dec. 1936; *s* of Thomas James and Gertrude Beatrice Whelan; *m* 1972, Margaret Elizabeth Bowen; two *s* one *d*. *Educ:* Oakfield Secondary School. NDD 1955; MSTD 1972. Studied Graphic Design at Beckenham College of Art, 1953–56. Art Editor, Publishers, Condé Nast, working on Vogue Pattern Book, Vogue South Africa and British Vogue, 1959–68; gained a number of Design and Art Direction awards during this period; Art Editor, 1968–74, Asst Editor/Art Director, 1974–77, Ideal Home magazine. Editor of the Year, Special Interest Section, British Soc. of Magazine Editors, 1988. *Publications:* writer and broadcaster on home improvements. *Recreation:* classical guitar. *Address:* Ideal Home Magazine, King's Reach Tower, Stamford Street, SE1. *T:* 071–261 6474.

WHELDON, Juliet Louise; Legal Secretary to the Law Officers, since 1989; *b* 26 March 1950; *d* of John Wheldon and Ursula Mabel Caillard. *Educ:* Sherborne School for Girls; Lady Margaret Hall, Oxford (1st Cl. Hons Mod. Hist.). Called to the Bar, Gray's Inn, 1975. Treasury Solicitor's Dept, 1976–83; Law Officers Dept, 1983–84; Treasury Solicitor's Dept, 1984–86; Asst Legal Sec. to the Law Officers, 1986–87; Hd of Central Adv. Div., Treasury Solicitor's Dept (Under-Sec.), 1987–89. *Address:* c/o Legal Secretariat to the Law Officers, Attorney General's Chambers, 9 Buckingham Gate, SW1E 6JP.

WHELER, Sir Edward (Woodford), 14th Bt *cr* 1660, of City of Westminster; Company Secretary, Robert Lewis (St James's) Ltd, 1981–90; *b* 13 June 1920; *s* of Sir Trevor Wood Wheler, 13th Bt, and Margaret Idris (*d* 1987), *y d* of late Sir Ernest Birch, KCMG; *S* father, 1986; *m* 1945, Molly Ashworth, *e d* of Thomas Lever, Devon; one *s* one *d*. *Educ:* Radley College. Joined Army (RA), 1940; commnd Royal Sussex Regt, 1941; attached 15 Punjab Regt, IA, 1941–45; BAOR, 1945–47. Oversea Audit Service, Uganda and Ghana, 1948–58; Automobile Association of East Africa, Kenya, 1958–70; Benson & Hedges Ltd, 1971–81, Director 1979–81. Liveryman, Co. of Pipe Makers and Tobacco Blenders, 1980; Freeman, City of London, 1980. *Heir: s* Trevor Woodford Wheler [*b* 11 April 1946; *m* 1974, Rosalie Margaret, *d* of late Ronald Thomas Stunt; two *s*].

WHELON, Charles Patrick Clavell; a Recorder of the Crown Court, since 1978; *b* 18 Jan. 1930; *s* of Charles Eric Whelon and Margaret Whelon; *m* 1968, Prudence Mary (*née* Potter); one *s* one *d*. *Educ:* Wellington Coll.; Pembroke Coll., Cambridge (MA Hons). Called to Bar, Middle Temple, 1954. Liveryman of Vintners' Co., 1952–. *Recreations:* gardening, cartooning. *Address:* 2 Harcourt Buildings, Temple, EC4. *T:* 071–353 2112; Russets, Pyott's Hill, Old Basing, Hants RG24 0AP. *T:* Basingstoke (0256) 469964.

WHENT, Gerald Arthur, CBE 1989; Chief Executive, Racal Telecom plc, since 1988; *b* 1 March 1927; *m* 1st, Coris Dorothy (*née* Bellman-Thomas); one *s* one *d*; 2nd, Sarah Louise (*née* Donaldson); two step *s* one step *d*. *Educ:* St Mary's College, Southampton. Dent Allcroft & Co.: Management Trainee, 1952; Asst Div. Manager, 1957; Div. Manager, 1959–62; Plessey Co.: Dept Manager, 1962; Div. Gen. Manager, 1966–69; Dir, Racal Recorders, 1970–72; Man. Dir, Racal Comsec, 1973–76; Man. Dir, Racal-Tacticom, 1977–80; Chm. and Man. Dir, Racal Radio Group, 1980–85; Dir, Racal Electronics plc, 1982–; Chm. and Chief Exec., Racal Telecommunications Group, 1983–88. *Recreations:* golf, ski-ing, horse riding, chess, bridge. *Address:* The Bothy, Horris Bank, Horris Hill, Newtown Common, Newbury, Berks RG15 9DF. *T:* Newbury (0635) 42855.

WHETSTONE, Rear-Adm. Anthony John, CB 1982; Deputy Secretary, Defence Press and Broadcasting Committee, since 1987; Chairman of Trustees, Royal Navy Submarine Museum, since 1990; *b* 12 June 1927; *s* of Albert Whetstone; *m* 1951, Elizabeth Stewart Georgeson; one *s* two *d*. *Educ:* King Henry VIII School, Coventry. Joined RN, 1945; specialised in submarines, 1949; Commanded: HMS Sea Scout, 1956–57; HMS Artful, 1959–61; HMS Repulse, 1968–70; HMS Juno, 1972–73; HMS Norfolk, 1977–78; Flag Officer Sea Training, 1978–80; Asst Chief of Naval Staff (Operations), 1981–83. Director-General: Cable TV Assoc., 1983–86; Nat. Television Rental Assoc., 1983–87. Sec., Special Trustees for St George's Hosp., 1988–91. Pres., Submarine Old Comrades Assoc., 1988–. FBIM 1979. *Recreations:* hill walking, fishing, amateur dramatics (Chm., Civil Service Drama Fedn). *Address:* 17 Anglesey Road, Alverstoke, Hants PO12 2EG. *Club:* Army and Navy.

See also N. K. Whetstone.

WHETSTONE, (Norman) Keith, OBE 1983; VRD; journalist and editorial consultant; *b* 17 June 1930; *yr s* of Albert and Anne Whetstone; *m* 1952, Monica Joan Clayton, Leamington Spa; three *s*. *Educ:* King Henry VIII Sch., Coventry. Served Royal Navy, 1949–50, 1951–52; Lt Comdr (S) RNVR, retired, 1965. Coventry Evening Telegraph, 1950–51; Western Morning News, 1952–55; Birmingham Post, 1955–58; Coventry Evening Telegraph, 1958–63; Editor, Cambridge Evening News, 1964–70; Editor, Coventry Evening Telegraph, 1970–80; Editor-in-Chief: Birmingham Evening Mail series, 1980–84; Birmingham Post and Birmingham Evening Mail series, 1984–86; Dir, Birmingham Post & Mail Ltd, 1980–86. Nat. Pres., Guild of British Newspaper Editors, 1976–77. Mem. Press Council, 1980–86. *Recreations:* theatre, Rugby football, golf, squash. *Address:* Tudor Cottage, Benton Green Lane, Berkswell, Coventry CV7 7AY. *T:* Berkswell (0676) 32323. *Club:* Quadrant (Coventry).

See also A. J. Whetstone.

WHEWAY, Albert James; Director, Hogg Robinson Travel Ltd, since 1976; *b* 6 April 1922; *s* of Albert and Alice Wheway; *m* 1st, 1946, Joan Simpson; 2nd, 1984, Susannah Mary Gray (*née* Luesby). *Educ:* Kimberworth School, Rotherham. Cooper Bros (later Cooper Lybrand), 1946–53; S. G. Warburg, 1953–57; industry, 1957–63; Ionian Bank, 1963–70; internat. industry and commerce, 1970–; Chm., Hogg Robinson Group plc, 1983–87. *Recreations:* art collecting, music. *Address:* Beaumont, Duddington, near Stamford, Lincs PE9 3QE. *T:* Duddington (078083) 237; Bilancia, Cappella Alta, Lucca, Italy. *T:* 0583 39 44 73.

WHEWELL, Prof. Charles Smalley, PhD; Professor of Textile Industries, University of Leeds, 1963–77, Emeritus Professor 1977 (Professor of Textile Technology, 1954–63, Head of Department, 1963–75); *b* 26 April 1912; *m* 1937, Emma Stott, PhD; one *s*. *Educ:* Grammar School, Darwen, Lancs; University of Leeds (BSc, PhD). Research Chemist, Wool Industries Research Association, 1935–37. University of Leeds, 1937–77: Lecturer in Textile Chemistry; Lecturer in Textile Finishing; Senior Lecturer in Textile Chemistry; Reader in Textile Finishing; Pro-Vice-Chancellor, 1973–75. Pres., Textile Inst., 1977–79. Hon. Liveryman, Clothworkers' Company, 1970. Hon. Fellow: Huddersfield Polytechnic, 1977; Textile Inst., 1979 (Hon. Life Mem., 1987). Textile Institute Medal, 1954; Warner Memorial Medal, 1960; Textile Institute Service Medal, 1971; Distinguished Service Award, Indian Inst. of Technol., Delhi, 1985. *Publications:* contrib. to: Chambers's Encyclopædia; Encyclopædia Britannica; British Wool Manual; Waterproofing and Water-repellency; Chemistry of Natural Fibres, ed Asquith, 1977; Oxford History of Technology, ed Williams; Jl Soc. of Dyers and Colourists; Jl Textile Inst. *Recreations:* music (organ), travel. *Address:* 8 Weetwood Avenue, Leeds LS16 5NF. *T:* Leeds (0532) 751654.

WHICHER, Peter George, CEng; FRAeS; MIEE; Consultant, Logica, since 1985; *b* 10 March 1929; *o s* of late Reginald George Whicher and Suzanne (*née* Dexter); *m* 1962, Susan Rosemary Strong (*d* 1989); one *s* one *d*. *Educ:* Chichester High School. BSc(Eng) London 1948; CEng, MIEE 1957. STC, 1948–51; Flying Officer, RAF, 1951–53; Min. of Aviation, 1953; Principal Expert in Telecommunications, Eurocontrol Agency, Paris, 1962–64; Cabinet Office, 1964–66; Asst Dir, Telecommunications R & D, and Manager, Skynet Satellite Communications Project, Min. of Technology, 1967–71; Superintendent, Communications Div., RAE, 1971–73; Dir, Air Radio, MoD(PE), 1973–76; RCDS, 1977; Dir, Defence Sci. (Electronics), MoD, 1978–81; Dep. Dir, RAE, 1981–84. FRAeS 1985. *Publications:* papers for professional instns. *Recreations:* sailing, innovation, arts. *Address:* Logica, 68 Newman Street, W1. *Club:* Royal Ocean Racing.

WHICKER, Alan Donald; television broadcaster (Whicker's World); writer; *b* 2 Aug. 1925; *o s* of late Charles Henry Whicker and late Anne Jane Cross. *Educ:* Haberdashers' Aske's Sch. Capt., Devonshire Regt; Dir, Army Film and Photo Section, with 8th Army and US 5th Army. War Corresp. in Korea, Foreign Corresp., novelist, writer and radio Broadcaster. Joined BBC TV, 1957: Tonight programme (appeared nightly in filmed reports from around the world, studio interviews, outside broadcasts, Eurovision, and Telstar, incl. first Telstar two-way transmission at opening of UN Assembly, NY, 1962); TV Series: Whicker's World, 1959–60; Whicker Down Under, 1961; Whicker on Top of the World!, 1962; Whicker in Sweden, Whicker in the Heart of Texas, Whicker Down Mexico Way, 1963; Alan Whicker Report series: The Solitary Billionaire (J. Paul Getty), etc; wrote and appeared in own series of monthly documentaries on BBC 2, subseq. repeated on BBC 1, under series title, Whicker's World, 1965–67 (31 programmes later shown around the world); BBC radio programmes and articles for The Listener, etc; left BBC, 1968. Various cinema films, incl. The Angry Silence. Mem., successful consortium for Yorkshire Television, 1967. Contrib. a documentary series to ITV, 1968. Completed 16 Documentaries for Yorkshire TV during its first year of operation, incl. Whicker's New World Series, and Specials on Gen. Stroessner of Paraguay, Count von Rosen, and Pres. Duvalier of Haiti; Whicker in Europe; Whicker's Walkabout; Broken Hill—Walled City; Gairy's Grenada; documentary series, World of Whicker; Whicker's Orient; Whicker within a Woman's World, 1972; Whicker's South Seas, Whicker way out West, 1973; Whicker's World, series on cities, 1974–77; Whicker's World—Down Under, 1976; Whicker's World: US, 1977 (4 progs); India, 1978 (7 progs); Indonesia, 1979; California, 1980 (6 progs); Peter Sellers Meml programme, 1980; Whicker's World Aboard the Orient Express, 1982; Around Whicker's World in 25 Years (3 YTV retrospect. progs), 1982; BBC TV, 1982–; Whicker's World—the First Million Miles (6 retrospect. progs), 1982; Whicker's World—a Fast Boat to China (4 QE2 progs), 1984; Whicker! (10 talk shows), 1984; Whicker's World—Living with Uncle Sam (10 progs), 1985; Whicker's World—Living with Waltzing Matilda (10 progs), 1987–88; Whicker's World—Hong Kong (8 progs), 1990. BBC Radio: Chm., Start the Week; Whicker's Wireless World (3 series), 1983; Various awards, 1963–, incl. Screenwriters' Guild, best Documentary Script, 1963; Guild of Television Producers and Directors Personality of the Year, 1964; Silver Medal, Royal Television Soc., 1968; Dumont Award, Univ. of California, 1970; Best Interview Prog. Award, Hollywood Festival of TV, 1973; Dimbleby Award, BAFTA, 1978; TV Times Special Award, 1978. FRSA 1970. *Publications:* Some Rise by Sin, 1949; Away—with Alan Whicker, 1963; Best of Everything, 1980; Within Whicker's World: an autobiography, 1982; Whicker's Business Traveller's Guide (with BAA), 1983; Whicker's New World, 1985; Whicker's World Down Under, 1988; Sunday newspaper columns; contrib. various internat. pubns. *Recreations:* people, photography, writing, travel, and reading (usually airline timetables). *Address:* Le Gallais Chambers, St Helier, Jersey.

WHIFFEN, David Hardy, MA, DPhil (Oxon), DSc (Birmingham); FRS 1966; FRSC; Professor of Physical Chemistry, 1968–85, Head of School of Chemistry, 1978–85, Pro-Vice-Chancellor, 1980–83, University of Newcastle upon Tyne (Dean of Science, 1974–77); *s* of late Noël H. and Mary Whiffen; *m* Jean P. Bell; four *s*. *Educ:* Oundle School; St John's College, Oxford (Scholar). Sometime Commonwealth Fund Fellow, Sen. Student of Commn for 1851 Exhibition. Formerly: Lectr in Chemistry, Univ. of Birmingham; Supt, Molecular Science Div., NPL. Vice-Chm., Newcastle HA, 1983–85 (Mem., Newcastle AHA, 1978–82, Newcastle HA, 1982–85). Pres., Faraday Div., RSC, 1981–83. *Publications:* Spectroscopy, 1966; The Royal Society of Chemistry: the first 150 years, 1991; papers in scientific jls.

WHINNEY, Rt. Rev. Michael Humphrey Dickens; Assistant Bishop, Diocese of Birmingham, since 1988; *b* 8 July 1930; *s* of late Humphrey Charles Dickens Whinney and Evelyn Lawrence Revell Whinney (*née* Low); great-great-grandson of Charles Dickens; *m* 1958, Veronica (*née* Webster); two *s* one *d*. *Educ:* Charterhouse; Pembroke Coll., Cambridge (BA 1955, MA 1958); Ridley Hall, Cambridge; General Theological Seminary, NY (STM 1990). National Service commission, RA, 1949 (served in 5th Regt, RHA and Surrey Yeo. Queen Mary's Regt). Articled clerk to Chartered Accountants, Whinney Smith & Whinney (now Ernst Young), 1950–52. Curate, Rainham Parish Church, Essex, 1957–60; Head, Cambridge University Mission Settlement, Bermondsey, 1960–67, Chaplain, 1967–72; Vicar, St James' with Christ Church, Bermondsey, 1967–73; Archdeacon and Borough Dean of Southwark, 1973–82; Bishop Suffragan of Aston, 1982–85; Bishop of Southwell, 1985–88. *Address:* Moorcroft, 3 Moor Green Lane, Moseley, Birmingham B13 8NE.

WHIPPLE, Prof. Fred Lawrence; Senior Scientist, Smithsonian Astrophysical Observatory, since 1973; Director, Smithsonian Institution Astrophysical Observatory, 1955–73; Phillips Professor of Astronomy, Harvard University, 1968–77; *b* 5 Nov. 1906; *s* of Harry Lawrence Whipple and Celestia Whipple (*née* MacFarland); *m* 1st, 1928, Dorothy Woods (divorced 1935); one *s*; 2nd, 1946, Babette Frances Samelson; two *d*. *Educ:* Long Beach High School, Calif; UCLA; Univ. of California, Berkeley. Lick Observatory Fellow, 1930–31; Staff Member, Harvard Univ., 1931–; Instructor,

1932–38; Lecturer, 1938–45; Assoc. Prof., 1945–50; Professor, 1950–77; Chm. Dept of Astronomy, 1949–56. US Nat. Cttee of Internat. Geophysical Year: Chm. Techn. Panel on Rocketry, 1955–59; Member: Techn. Panel on Earth Satellite Program, 1955–59; Working Group on Satellite Tracking and Computation, 1955–58; Scientific Advisory Bd to USAF, 1953–62; Cttee on Meteorology, Nat. Acad. of Sciences, Nat. Research Coun., 1958–61; Special Cttees on Space Techn., Nat. Advisory Cttee for Aeronautics, 1958–63 (now NASA), US; Space Sciences Working Group on Orbiting Astronomical Observatories, Nat. Acad. of Sciences (Mem. Nat. Acad. of Sciences, 1959–); Advisory Panel to Cttee on Sci. and Astronautics of US House of Representatives, 1960–73; Amer. Philosophical Soc., Philadelphia; Amer. Acad. of Arts and Sciences, Boston; New York Acad. of Science, NY; several technical societies. Associate, Royal Astronomical Soc., 1970–. Benjamin Franklin Fellow, RSA, 1968–. Editor: Smithsonian Contributions to Astrophysics, 1956–73; Planetary and Space Science, 1958–. Hon. degrees: MA, Harvard Univ., 1945; DSc, Amer. Internat. Coll., 1958; DLitt, North-eastern Univ., 1961; DS: Temple Univ., 1961; Arizona, 1979; LLD, CW Post Coll. of Long Island Univ., 1962. J. Lawrence Smith Medal of Nat. Acad. of Sciences, 1949; Donohue Medals, 1932, 1933, 1937, 1940, 1942 (received two medals that year); Presidential Certificate of Merit, 1948; Exceptional Service Award, US Air Force Scientific Adv. Bd, 1960; Space Flight Award, Amer. Astron. Soc., 1961; President's Award for Distinguished Federal Civilian Service, 1963; Space Pioneers Medallion, 1968; NASA Public Services Award, 1969; Kepler Medal, AAAS, 1971; Nat. Civil Service League's Civil Service Award, 1972; Henry Medal, Smithsonian Instn, 1973; Alumnus of the Year Award, UCLA, 1976; Gold Medal, Royal Astronomical Soc., 1983; Bruce Gold Medal, Astronomical Soc. of Pacific, 1986; other foreign awards. Depicted on postal stamp, Mauritania, 1986 (in recognition of contribn to understanding of comets, and to commemorate Halley's Comet). *Publications:* Earth, Moon and Planets, 1942, 3rd edn 1968; Orbiting the Sun, 1981; The Mystery of Comets, 1985; many technical papers in various astronomical and geophysical journals and books; popular articles in magazines and in Encyclopædia Britannica. *Recreation:* cultivation of roses. *Address:* Smithsonian Astrophysical Observatory, 60 Garden Street, Cambridge, Mass 02138, USA. *T:* 617–864—7383.

WHIPPMAN, Michael Lewis, PhD; Under Secretary, Home, Transport and Education Group, HM Treasury, since 1990; *b* 20 Sept. 1938; *s* of Matthew Whippman and Adelina Whippman (*née* Abrahams); *m* 1967, Constance Baskett; two *d.* *Educ:* King Edward VII Sch.; Univ. of the Witwatersrand; Clare Coll., Cambridge (PhD). Res. Fellow 1963–65, Asst Prof. 1965–71, Univ. of Pennsylvania; Sen. Res. Fellow, Univ. of Helsinki, 1971–73; Principal 1973, Asst Sec. 1980, Under Sec., 1988, DHSS. Fellow, Amer. Phys. Soc., 1971. *Publications:* papers in Phys. Rev., Annals of Physics, Il Nuovo Cimento, etc. *Recreations:* opera, arguing. *Address:* HM Treasury, Parliament Street, SW1P 3AG.

WHISHAW, Anthony Popham Law, RA 1989 (ARA 1980); *b* 22 May 1930; *s* of Robert Whishaw and Joyce (*née* Wheeler); *m* 1957, Jean Gibson; two *d.* *Educ:* Tonbridg Sch.; Chelsea Sch. of Art (Higher Cert); Royal College of Art (ARCA). Travelling Schol., RCA; Abbey Minor Schol.; Spanish Govt Schol.; Abbey Premier Schol., 1982; Lorne Schol., 1982–83. John Moores Minor Painting Prize, 1982; (jtly) 1st Prize, Hunting Group Art Awards, 1986. *One-Man Exhibns:* Libreria Abril, Madrid, 1957; Rowland Browse and Delbranco, London, 1960, 1961, 1963, 1965, 1968; ICA, 1971; New Art Centre, 1972; Folkestone Arts Centre, 1973; Hoya Gall., London, 1974; Oxford Gall., Oxford, 1974; ACME, London, 1978; Newcastle upon Tyne Polytech. Gall., 1979; (with Martin Froy) New Ashgate Gall., Farnham, 1979; Nicola Jacobs Gall., London 1981; From Landscape, Kettle's Yard, Cambridge, Ferens Gall., Hull, Bede Gall., Jarrow, 1982–84; Works on Paper, Nicola Jacobs Gall., 1983; Paintings, Nicola Jacobs Gall., 1984; Mappin Art Gall., Sheffield, 1985; Large Paintings, RA 1986; Reflections after Las Meninas (touring): Royal Acad., and Hatton Gall., Newcastle upon Tyne, 1987; Mead Gall., Warwick Univ., John Hansard Gall., Southampton Univ., and Spacex Gall., Exeter, 1988; Infaust Gall., Shanghai and Hamburg, 1989. *Group Exhibns:* Gimpel Fils, AIA Gall., Café Royal Centen., Towards Art (RCA), Camden Arts Centre, London, Ashmoleum Mus., Oxford, 1957–72; Brit. Drawing Biennale, Teesside, 1973; British Landscape, Graves Art Gall., Sheffield, Chichester Nat. Art, 1975; Summer Exhibn, RA, 1974–81; British Painting, 1952–77, RA, 1977; London Group, Whitechapel Open, 1978, A Free Hand, Arts Council (touring show), 1978; The British Art Show, Arts Council (touring), Recent Arts Council Purchases and Awards, Serpentine Gall., First Exhibition, Nicola Jacobs Gall., Tolly Cobbold (touring), 55 Wapping Artists, London, 1979; Four Artists, Nicola Jacobs Gall., Sculpture and Works on Paper, Nicola Jacobs, Wapping Open Studios, Hayward Annual, Hayward Gall., Whitechapel Open, Whitechapel Gall., John Moore's Liverpool Exhibn 12, 1980, Exhibn 13, 1982, Walker Art Gall., Liverpool; London Gp, S London Art Gall., Wapping Artists, 1981; Images for Today, Graves Art Gall., Sheffield, 1982; Nine Artists (touring), Helsinki, 1983; Tolly Cobbold/Eastern Arts Fourth (touring), 1983; Three Decades 1953–83, RA, 1983; Romantic Tradition in Contemporary British Painting (touring), Murcia and Madrid, Spain, and Ikon Gall., Birmingham, 1988. *Works in Collections:* Arts Council of GB, Tate Gall., Coventry Art Gall., Leicester Art Gall., Nat. Gall. of Wales, Sheffield City Art Galls, Financial Times, Shell-BP, Museo de Bahia, Brazil, Nat. Gall. of Victoria, Melb., Seattle Mus. of Art, Bank of Boston, Chantrey Bequest, W Australia Art Gall., Bayer Pharmaceuticals, DoE, Nat. Westminster Bank, Power Art Gall., Aust. European Parlt, Ferens Art Gall, Museum, Murcia, Spain. *Recreations:* chess, badminton. *Address:* 7a Albert Place, Victoria Road, W8 5PD. *T:* 071–937 5197.

WHISHAW, Sir Charles (Percival Law), Kt 1969; solicitor (retired); *b* 29 October 1909; 2nd *s* of late Montague Law Whishaw and Erna Louise (*née* Spies); *m* 1936, Margaret Joan (*d* 1989), *e d* of late Col T. H. Hawkins, CMG, RMLI; one *s* two *d.* *Educ:* Charterhouse; Worcester College, Oxford. Called to Bar, Inner Temple, 1932; Solicitor, 1938; Partner in Freshfields, 1943–74. Trustee, Calouste Gulbenkian Foundn, 1956–81. Member: Iron and Steel Holding and Realisation Agency, 1953–67; Council, Law Soc., 1967–76. Comdr, Order of Prince Henry (Portugal), 1981. *Address:* Clare Park, near Farnham, Surrey GU10 5DT. *T:* Aldershot (0252) 851333, 850681.

WHISTLER, Maj.-Gen. Alwyne Michael Webster, CB 1963; CBE 1959; retired, 1965; *b* 30 Dec. 1909; *s* of Rev. W. W. Whistler and Lilian Whistler (*née* Meade), Elsted, Sussex; *m* 1936, Margaret Louise Michelette, *d* of Brig.-Gen. Malcolm Welch, CB, CMG, JP, Stedham, Sussex; one *s* two *d.* *Educ:* Gresham's Sch., Holt; RMA Woolwich. 2nd Lt Royal Signals, 1929; served in India, 1932–44; War of 1939–45: Staff Coll., Camberley, 1944; Burma Campaign, 19 and 25 Indian Divs and XII Army, 1944–45 (despatches twice). ADPR, Berlin, 1946; GSO1 (Military Adviser), Military Governor of Germany, 1946–48; AQMG, War Office, 1949–50; JSSC 1950; Comdg Royal Signals, 3 Div., 1951–54; Col GS, War Office, 1955–57; Col Q Far ELF, 1957–58; Comdr Corps Royal Signals, 1 (British) Corps, BAOR, 1959–60; Signal Officer-in-Chief, War Office, 1960–62; Chairman, British Joint Communications Board, Ministry of Defence, 1962–64; Assistant Chief of the Defence Staff (Signals), 1964–65. Hon. Col Princess Louise's Kensington Regt (41st Signals) TA, 1963–66; Col Commandant, Royal Corps of Signals, 1964–68; Hon. Col 32nd (Scottish) Signal Regiment (V), 1967–72. Princess Mary Medal, Royal Signals Instn, 1978. Master of Fox Hounds, Nerbudda Vale Hunt, 1938–40. *T:* Wareham (09295) 2605.

WHISTLER, Laurence, CBE 1973 (OBE 1955); FRSL; engraver on glass; writer; *b* 21 Jan. 1912; *s* of Henry Whistler and Helen (*née* Ward); *yr b* of late Rex Whistler; *m* 1st, 1939, Jill (*d* 1944), *d* of Sir Ralph Furse, KCMG, DSO; one *s* one *d*; 2nd, 1950, Theresa (marr. diss.), *yr sister* of Jill Furse; one *s* one *d*; 3rd, 1987, Carol Dawson, *d* of John Dudley Groves, *qv.* *Educ:* Stowe; Balliol College, Oxford (Hon. Fellow 1974). BA Oxon (MA 1985). Chancellor's Essay Prize, 1934. Served War of 1939–45: private soldier, 1940; commissioned in The Rifle Brigade, 1941; Captain 1942. King's Gold Medal for Poetry, 1935 (first award); Atlantic Award for Literature, 1945. First Pres., Guild of Glass Engravers, 1975–80. *Work on glass includes:* goblets, etc, in point-engraving and drill, and engraved church windows and panels at: Sherborne Abbey; Moreton, Dorset; Checkendon, Oxon; Ilton, Som; Eastbury, Berks (window to Edward and Helen Thomas); Guards' Chapel, London; Stowe, Bucks; St Hugh's Coll., Oxford; Ashmansworth, Berks; Steep, Hants (windows to Edward Thomas); Hannington, Hants; Yalding, Kent (windows to Edmund Blunden); Thornham Parva, Suffolk; Salisbury Cathedral; Curry Rivel, Som; Wootton St Lawrence, Hants. *Exhibitions:* Agnews, Bond Street, 1969; Marble Hill, Twickenham, 1972; Corning Museum, USA, 1974; Ashmolean, 1976, 1985. *Publications include:* Sir John Vanbrugh (biography), 1938; The English Festivals, 1947; Rex Whistler, His Life and His Drawings, 1948; The World's Room (Collected Poems), 1949; The Engraved Glass of Laurence Whistler, 1952; Rex Whistler: The Königsmark Drawings, 1952; The Imagination of Vanbrugh and his Fellow Artists, 1954; The View From This Window (poems), 1956; Engraved Glass, 1952–58; The Work of Rex Whistler (with Ronald Fuller), 1960; Audible Silence (poems), 1961; The Initials in the Heart: the story of a marriage, 1964, rev. edn 1975; To Celebrate Her Living (poems), 1967; Pictures on Glass, 1972; The Image on the Glass, 1975; Scenes and Signs on Glass, 1985; The Laughter and the Urn: the life of Rex Whistler, 1985; Enter (poems), 1987. *Address:* Cox's and Kings Branch, Lloyds Bank, 7 Pall Mall, SW1Y 5NA.

WHISTON, Peter Rice, RSA 1977; ARIBA; FRIAS; Consultant Architect, since 1977; *b* 19 Oct. 1912; *s* of Thomas Whiston and Marie Barrett; *m* 1947, Kathleen Anne Parker (*d* 1983); one *s* four *d.* *Educ:* Holy Cross Acad.; Sch. of Architecture, Edinburgh Coll. of Art. RIBA Silver Medallist for Recognised Schs, 1937. Served War, Staff Captain RE, 1940–45. Articled, City Architect, Edinburgh, 1930–35; Partner, Dick Peddie McKay & Jamieson, 1937–38; Chief Architect, SSHA, 1946–49; Sen. Lectr, Sch. of Architecture, ECA, 1950–69; Dir, Arch. Conservation Studies, at Heriot Watt Univ., 1969–77. Visiting Lectr at Internat. Centre for Conservation, Rome, 1971; Ecclesiological Practice, 1950–77. *Works include:* Cistercian Abbey at Nunraw; St Margaret's, St Mark's and St Paul's, Edin.; St Columba, Cupar; St Mary Magdalene's, Perth; St Ninian's and St Leonard's, Dundee; Our Lady, Mother of the Church, Edin.; Corpus Christi, Glasgow; St Mark's, Rutherglen; St Bernadette's, Tullibody. Awarded Papal Knighthood of St Gregory for Services to Architecture, (KSG), 1969. *Recreations:* travel, sketching, painting. *Address:* 14 Grange Court, Edinburgh. *T:* 031–668 2720.

WHITAKER, Benjamin Charles George; author; Director, Gulbenkian Foundation (UK), since 1988; *b* 15 Sept. 1934; 3rd *s* of late Maj.-Gen. Sir John Whitaker, 2nd Bt, CB, CBE, and late Lady Whitaker (*née* Snowden), Babworth, Retford, Notts; *m* 1964, Janet Alison Stewart; two *s* one *d.* *Educ:* Eton; New Coll., Oxford. BA (Modern History). Called to Bar, Inner Temple, 1959 (Yarborough-Anderson Scholar). Practised as Barrister, 1959–67. Extra-mural Lectr in Law, London Univ., 1963–64. MP (Lab) Hampstead, 1966–70; PPS to Minister of: Overseas Development, 1966; Housing and Local Govt, 1966–67; Parly Sec., ODM, 1969–70. Exec. Dir, Minority Rights Group, 1971–88. Member: UN Human Rights Sub-Commn, 1975–88 (Vice-Chm., 1979); Goodman Cttee on Charity Law Reform, 1974–76; UK Nat. Commn for UNESCO, 1978–85; Speaker's Commn on Citizenship, 1989–90; Chairman: UN Working Gp on Slavery, 1976–78; Defence of Literature and Arts Soc., 1976–82; City Poverty Cttee, 1971–83. Judge, NCR Book Award, 1990. *Publications:* The Police, 1964; (ed) A Radical Future, 1967; Crime and Society, 1967; Participation and Poverty, 1968; Parks for People, 1971; (ed) The Fourth World, 1972; The Foundations, 1974; The Police in Society, 1979; (contrib.) Human Rights and American Foreign Policy, 1979; UN Report on Slavery, 1982; (ed) Teaching about Prejudice, 1983; A Bridge of People, 1983; (ed) Minorities: a question of human rights?, 1984; UN Report on Genocide, 1985; The Global Connection, 1987; (contrib.) The United Kingdom—The United Nations, 1990; Gen. Editor, Sources for Contemporary Issues series (7 vols), 1973–75. *Address:* 13 Elsworthy Road, NW3.

See also Sir James Whitaker, Bt.

WHITAKER, David Haddon, OBE 1991; Chairman, J. Whitaker & Sons, Ltd, since 1982 (Editorial Director, 1980–91); Director, since 1968, and Chairman, since 1982, Standard Book Numbering Agency; Director, Teleordering Ltd, since 1983; *b* 6 March 1931; *s* of late Edgar Haddon Whitaker, OBE and of Mollie Marian, *y d* of George and Louisa Seely; *m* 1st, 1959, Veronica Wallace (decd); two *s* two *d*; 2nd, 1976, Audrey Miller (marr. diss.). *Educ:* Marlborough; St John's Coll., Cambridge. Joined family firm of publishers, J. Whitaker & Sons, Ltd, 1955; Dir, 1966; Editor, The Bookseller, 1977–79. Member: Adv. Panel, Internat. Standard Book Numbering Agency (Berlin), 1979–; Adv. Panel, Registrar for Public Lending Right, 1983– (Chm., 1989–); Standing Cttee on Technology, Booksellers' Assoc., 1984–89; Library and Information Services Council, 1985–89. Chairman: Soc. of Bookmen, 1984–86; Book Trade Electronic Data Interchange Standards Cttee, 1987–90. Hon. Vice-Pres., LA, 1990. *Recreations:* reading, walking. *Address:* 30 Jenner House, Hunter Street, WC1N 1BL. *T:* 071–837 8109. *Clubs:* Garrick, Thames Rowing; Leander (Henley-on-Thames).

WHITAKER, Sir James Herbert Ingham, 3rd Bt, *cr* 1936; Vice-Chairman, Halifax Building Society, since 1973; *b* 27 July 1925; *s* of late Maj.-Gen. Sir John Whitaker, 2nd Bt, CB, CBE, and Lady Whitaker (*née* Snowden); *S* father 1957; *m* 1948, Mary Elisabeth Lander Urling Clark (*née* Johnston), *widow* of Captain D. Urling Clark, MC; one *s* one *d.* *Educ:* Eton. Coldstream Guards, 1944. Served in North West Europe. Retired, 1947. Dir, Governing Body, Atlantic College. High Sheriff of Notts, 1969–70. *Recreation:* shooting. *Heir:* *s* John James Ingham Whitaker, BSc, FCA, AMIEE [*b* 23 October 1952; *m* 1981, Janey, *d* of L. J. R. Starke, New Zealand; one *s* three *d*]. *Address:* Babworth Hall, Retford, Notts. *T:* Retford (0777) 703454; Auchnafree, Dunkeld, Perthshire. *Club:* Boodle's.

See also B. C. G. Whitaker.

WHITAKER, Sheila; Director, London Film Festival, since 1987; *b* 1 April 1936; *d* of Hilda and Charles Whitaker. *Educ:* Cathays High Sch. for Girls, Cardiff; Kings Norton Grammar Sch. for Girls, Birmingham; Univ. of Warwick (BA Hons). Secretarial and admin. posts in commerce and industry, 1956–68; Chief Stills Officer, National Film Archive, 1968–74; Univ. of Warwick, 1975–78; Dir, Tyneside Cinema, Tyneside Film Festival, Newcastle upon Tyne, 1979–84; Head, Programming, NFT, 1984–90. Founder and Co-Editor, Writing Women, 1981–84; Gen. Editor, Tyneside Publications, 1984. *Publications:* contribs to Framework, Screen. *Recreations:* reading, swimming, occasional cycling. *Address:* 8 Stonefield Mansions, Cloudesley Square, N1 0HS. *T:* 071–837 1054. *Club:* Groucho.

WHITAKER, Thomas Kenneth; Chancellor, National University of Ireland, since 1976; Member, Council of State, Ireland; Joint Chairman, Anglo-Irish Encounter,

1983–89; President, Royal Irish Academy, 1985–87; *b* 8 Dec. 1916; *s* of Edward Whitaker and Jane O'Connor; *m* 1941, Nora Fogarty; five *s* one *d*. *Educ:* Christian Brothers' Sch., Drogheda; London Univ. (External Student; BScEcon, MScEcon). Irish CS, 1934–69 (Sec., Dept of Finance, 1956–69); Governor, Central Bank of Ireland, 1969–76; Dir, Bank of Ireland, 1976–85. Dir, Arthur Guinness Son & Co. Ltd, 1976–84. Chairman: Bord na Gaeilge, 1975–78; Agency for Personal Service Overseas, 1973–78; Mem., Seanad Éireann, 1977–82. Pres., Econ. and Social Res. Inst.; Chm. Council, Dublin Inst. for Advanced Studies. Hon. DEconSc National Univ. of Ireland, 1962; Hon. LLD: Univ. of Dublin, 1976; Queen's Univ. of Belfast, 1980; Hon. DSc NUU, 1984. Commandeur de la Légion d'Honneur, France, 1976. *Publications:* Financing by Credit Creation, 1947; Economic Development, 1958; Interests, 1983. *Recreations:* fishing, golf, music. *Address:* 148 Stillorgan Road, Donnybrook, Dublin 4, Ireland. *T:* Dublin 2693474.

WHITBREAD, Samuel Charles, JP; Chairman, Whitbread plc, since 1984; Lord-Lieutenant of Bedfordshire, since 1991; *b* 22 Feb. 1937; *s* of late Major Simon Whitbread; *m* 1961, Jane Mary Hayter; three *s* one *d*. *Educ:* Eton College. Beds and Herts Regt, 1955–57. Joined Board, Whitbread & Co., 1972, Dep. Chm., Jan. 1984. Director: Whitbread Investment Co., 1977–; Sun Alliance Gp, 1989–. Chm., Mid-Beds Conservative Assoc., 1969–72 (Pres., 1986–91). President: Shire Horse Soc., 1990–; E of England Agricl Soc., 1991–March 1992; St John Council for Beds, 1991–; Beds TA&VRA, 1991–; Vice-Pres., E Anglia TA&VRA, 1991–. Bedfordshire: JP, 1969–83, 1991; High Sheriff, 1973–74; DL, 1974; County Councillor, 1974–82. *Recreations:* shooting, travel, photography, music. *Address:* Southill Park, Biggleswade, Beds SG18 9LL. *T:* Hitchin (0462) 813272. *Club:* Brooks's.

WHITBREAD, William Henry, TD; MA Cantab; Past President, Whitbread and Company, Ltd, 1972–79 (Chairman, 1944–71, Managing Director, 1927–68); Chairman, Whitbread Investment Co. Ltd, 1956–77; Vice-President of the Brewers' Society (Chairman, 1952–53); Past-Master, Brewers' Company; Vice-Pres. Inst. of Brewing (Chm. Res. Cttee, 1948–52); *b* 22 Dec. 1900; *s* of late Henry William Whitbread, Norton Bavant, Wiltshire; *m* 1st, 1927, Ann Joscelyne (*d* 1936), *d* of late Samuel Howard Whitbread, CB, Southill, Beds; two *s* one *d*; 2nd, 1941, Betty Parr, *d* of Samuel Russell, ICS; one *s* two *d*. *Educ:* Eton; Corpus Christi College, Cambridge. Lovat Scouts, 1920–41; served War of 1939–45: Lovat Scouts, 1939–41; Reconnaissance Corps, 1941–45; Parachutist. Chm. Parliamentary Cttee, Brewers' Society, 1948–52. Director: Barclays Bank Ltd, 1958–73; Eagle Star Insurance Co., 1958–74. Member Governing Body Aldenham School, 1929–61 (Chairman, 1948–58). President: BSJA, 1966–68; Shire Horse Soc., 1971–72; Member: National Hunt Committee, 1956–68; Jockey Club, 1968–; Hurlingham Club Polo Committee, 1932–45; Master, Trinity Foot Beagles, 1921–23. *Recreations:* shooting, fishing and sailing. *Address:* Hazelhurst, Bunch Lane, Haslemere, Surrey; The Heights, Kinlochewe, Ross-shire; Farleaze, near Malmesbury, Wilts. *Clubs:* Brooks's, Pratt's, Royal Thames Yacht; Royal Yacht Squadron.

See also J. F. Doble, Sir L. H. J. Tollemache, Bt.

WHITBY, Bishop Suffragan of, since 1983; **Rt. Rev. Gordon Bates;** *b* 16 March 1934; *s* of Ernest and Kathleen Bates; *m* 1960, Betty (*née* Vaux); two *d*. *Educ:* Kelham Theological Coll. (SSM). Curate of All Saints, New Eltham, 1958–62; Youth Chaplain in Gloucester Diocese, 1962–64; Diocesan Youth Officer and Chaplain of Liverpool Cathedral, 1965–69; Vicar of Huyton, 1969–73; Canon Residentiary and Precentor of Liverpool Cathedral and Diocesan Director of Ordinands, 1973–83. Mem., House of Bishops, Gen. Synod, 1988–. *Recreations:* golf, music, writing. *Address:* Handyside, 60 West Green, Stokesley, Cleveland TS9 5BD. *T:* Stokesley (0642) 710390. *Club:* Commonwealth Trust.

WHITBY, Charles Harley, QC 1970; a Recorder of the Crown Court, Western Circuit, since 1972; *b* 2 April 1926; *s* of late Arthur William Whitby and Florence Whitby; *m* 1981, Eileen Scott. *Educ:* St John's, Leatherhead; Peterhouse, Cambridge. Open Schol., Peterhouse, 1943; served RAFVR, 1944–48; BA (History) 1st cl. 1949, MA 1951. Called to Bar, Middle Temple, 1952; Bencher, 1977; Mem. Bar Council, 1969–71, 1972–78. Mem., Criminal Injuries Compensation Bd, 1975–. Chm. Council, St John's Sch., Leatherhead, 1985– (Mem., 1977–). *Publications:* contrib. to Master and Servant in Halsbury's Laws of England, 3rd edn, Vol. 25, 1959 and Master and Servant in Atkin's Encyclopaedia of Court Forms, 2nd edn, Vol. 25, 1962. *Recreations:* golf, watching soccer, boating, fishing, swimming, theatre, cinema. *Address:* 12 King's Bench Walk, Temple, EC4Y 7EL. *T:* 071–583 0811. *Clubs:* United Oxford & Cambridge University, Royal Automobile (Steward, 1985–), Garrick; Woking Golf.

WHITBY, Mrs Joy; Director, Grasshopper Productions Ltd; *b* 27 July 1930; *d* of James and Esther Field; *m* 1954, Anthony Charles Whitby (*d* 1975); three *s*. *Educ:* St Anne's Coll., Oxford. Schools Producer, BBC Radio, 1956–62; Children's Producer, BBC Television, 1962–67; Executive Producer, Children's Programmes, London Weekend Television, 1967–70; freelance producer and writer, 1970–76; Head of Children's Programmes, Yorkshire TV, 1976–85. Dir, Bd of Channel 4, 1980–84; Member: Adv. Panel for Youth, Nat. Trust, 1985–89; Bd, Unicorn Theatre, 1987–. Devised for television: Play School, 1964; Jackanory, 1965; The Book Tower, 1979; Under the Same Sky (EBU Drama Exchange), 1984. Independent film productions: Grasshopper Island, 1971; A Pattern of Roses, 1983; Emma and Grandpa, 1984; East of the Moon, 1988; The Angel and the Soldier Boy, 1989. BAFTA Award and Prix Jeunesse: for Play School, 1965; for The Book Tower, 1980 (also BAFTA Award, 1983); Eleanor Farjeon Award for Services to Children's Books, 1979. *Publications:* Grasshopper Island, 1971; Emma and Grandpa (4 vols), 1984.

WHITBY, Professor Lionel Gordon, FRSE, FRCP, FRCPE, FRCPath, FIBiol; Professor of Clinical Chemistry, University of Edinburgh, 1963–91, Emeritus Professor since 1991; Biochemist-in-charge, Royal Infirmary of Edinburgh, 1963–91; *b* 18 July 1926; *s* of late Sir Lionel Whitby, CVO, MC, MD, FRCP, Regius Prof. of Physic and Master of Downing Coll., Cambridge; *m* 1949, Joan Hunter Sanderson; one *s* two *d*. *Educ:* Eton; King's Coll., Cambridge; Middlesex Hosp. MA, PhD, MD, BChir. Fellow of King's College, Cambridge, 1951–55; W. A. Meek Schol., Univ. of Cambridge, 1951; Murchison Schol., RCP, 1958; Rockefeller Trav. Res. Fellow, Nat. Insts of Health Bethesda, Md, USA, 1959. Registrar and Asst Lectr in Chem. Path., Hammersmith Hosp. and Postgrad. Med. Sch. of London, 1958–60; Univ. Biochemist to Addenbrooke's Hosp., 1960–63, and Fellow of Peterhouse, 1961–62, Cambridge; Univ. of Edinburgh: Dean of Faculty of Medicine, 1969–72 and 1983–86; Curator of Patronage, 1978–91; Vice-Principal, 1979–83. Member: Standing Adv. Cttee, Lab. Services, SHHD, 1965–72; Laboratory Develt Adv. Group, DHSS, 1972–76; Scientific Services Adv. Gp, SHHD, 1974–77; Screening Sub-Cttee of Standing Medical Adv. Cttee, 1975–81; Training Cttee, RCPath, 1977–79; Med. Lab. Technicians Bd, 1978–; GMC, 1986–; Adv. Council, British Library, 1986–. Guest Lectr, Amer. Chem. Soc., 1966; Vis. Prof. of Chemical Pathology, RPMS, 1974. Vice-Pres., RSE, 1983–86. Trustee, Nat. Library of Scotland, 1982–. *Publications:* (ed jointly) Principles and Practice of Medical Computing, 1971; (jointly) Lecture Notes on Clinical Chemistry, 1975, 4th edn 1988; (jtly) Multiple Choice Questions on Clinical Chemistry, 1981; scientific papers on flavinglucosides, catecholamines and metabolites, several aspects of clin. chem., and early detection of disease by chemical tests. *Recreations:* gardening, photography. *Address:* 51 Dick Place, Edinburgh EH9 2JA. *T:* 031–667 4358.

WHITE, family name of **Barons Annaly** and **White of Hull** and **Baronesses James of Holland Park** and **White.**

WHITE, Baroness *cr* 1970 (Life Peer), of Rhymney, Monmouth; **Eirene Lloyd White;** a Deputy Speaker, House of Lords, 1979–89; *b* 7 Nov. 1909; *d* of late Dr Thomas Jones, CH; *m* 1948, John Cameron White (*d* 1968). *Educ:* St Paul's Girls' Sch.; Somerville Coll., Oxford. Ministry of Labour officer, 1933–37 and 1941–45; Political Correspondent, Manchester Evening News, 1945–49; contested (Lab) Flintshire, 1945; MP (Lab) East Flint, 1950–70. Nat. Exec. Cttee of the Labour Party, 1947–53, 1958–72, Chm. 1968–69; Parly Secretary, Colonial Office, 1964–66; Minister of State for Foreign Affairs, 1966–67; Minister of State, Welsh Office, 1967–70; Chm., Select Cttee on Eur. Communities, and Principal Dep. Chm. of Cttees, H of L, 1979–82; Dep. Chm., Parly Scientific Cttee, 1986–89. Member: Royal Commn on Environmental Pollution, 1974–81; British Waterways Bd, 1974–80. Governor: National Library of Wales, 1950–70; Brit. Film Inst. and National Film Theatre, 1959–64; Indep. Mem. Cinematograph Films Council, 1946–64. Chairman, Fabian Society, 1958–59; President: Nursery School Assoc., 1964–66; Council for Protection of Rural Wales, 1974–89; former Pres., Nat. Council of Women (Wales); Lord President's nominee, Council, UCW, Aberystwyth, 1973–77, Court (elected), 1977–85; Member: UGC, 1977–80; Council, UCNW Bangor, 1977–80; Council, UWIST, Cardiff, 1981– (Chm., 1983–88; Pres., 1987–88); Chairman: Internat. Cttee, Nat. Council of Social Service, 1973–77; Coleg Harlech, 1974–84; Adv. Cttee on Oil Pollution at sea, 1974–78; Land Authority for Wales, 1975–80; Dep. Chm., Metrication Bd, 1972–76; Vice-President: Commonwealth Countries League; Commonwealth Youth Exchange Council, 1976–79; Council for National Parks, 1985–; TCPA, 1983–91. Hon. Mem., RTPI, 1987; Hon. Fellow: Somerville College, Oxford, 1966; Univ. of Wales, Cardiff, 1989. Hon. LLD: Wales, 1979; Queen's Univ., Belfast, 1981; Bath, 1983. *Publication:* The Ladies of Gregynog, 1985. *Address:* 64 Vandon Court, Petty France, SW1H 9HF. *T:* 071–222 5107; Treberfydd, Bwlch, Powys LD3 7PX. *T:* Brecon (0874) 730911. *Club:* Commonwealth Trust.

WHITE OF HULL, Baron *cr* 1991 (Life Peer), of Hull in the County of Humberside; **Vincent Gordon Lindsay White,** KBE 1979; Chairman, Hanson Industries, since 1983; *b* 11 May 1923; *s* of late Charles White and Lily May (*née* Wilson); *m* 1974, Virginia Anne; one *s* (and two *d* by a former marriage). *Educ:* De Aston Sch., Lincs. Served War, 1940–46: SOE, Force 136, Captain. Chairman, family publishing business, Welbecson Ltd, 1947–65; Dep. Chm., Hanson Trust Ltd, 1965–73; Special Commn to open Hanson Trust's opportunities overseas, 1973–83. Mem. Bd and Chm., Internat. Cttee, Congressional Award, 1984–; Chm., Zoological Soc. of London Develt Trust, 1989–; Member: Council for Police Rehabilitation Appeal, 1985–; Bd of Dirs, Shakespeare Theatre, Folger Library, Washington, 1985–; Council, City of Technology Colls Trust Ltd, 1987–. Bd Mem., British Airways, 1989–. Governor, BFI, 1982–84. Hon. Fellow, St Peter's Coll., Oxford, 1984. Hon. DSc(Econ), Hull, 1988. Nat. Voluntary Leadership Award, Congressional Award 1984; (with Lord Hanson) Aims of Industry Free Enterprise Award, 1985; People to People Internat. Award, 1986. *Recreations:* flying (holder of helicopter licence), riding, skiing, tennis. *Address:* 410 Park Avenue, New York, NY 10022, USA. *T:* (212) 759–8477. *Clubs:* Special Forces; Brook, Explorers' (New York).

WHITE, Adrian N. S.; *see* Sherwin-White.

WHITE, Aidan Patrick; General Secretary, International Federation of Journalists, since 1987; *b* 2 March 1951; *s* of Thomas White and Kathleen Ann McLaughlin. *Educ:* King's Sch., Peterborough. Dep. Gp Editor, Stratford Express, 1977–79; journalist, The Guardian, 1980–87. Mem., Press Council, 1978–80. National Union of Journalists: Mem. Exec. Council, 1974, 1976, 1977; Treasurer, 1984–86; Chm., National Newspapers Council, 1981. Vice-Chm., Campaign for Press and Broadcasting Freedom, 1983–84. *Address:* 92 Quilter Street, E2. *T:* 071–739 3598.

WHITE, Alan, CMG 1985; OBE 1973; HM Diplomatic Service, retired; Ambassador to Chile, 1987–90; *b* 13 Aug. 1930; *s* of William White and Ida (*née* Hall); *m* 1st, 1954, Cynthia Maidwell; two *s* one *d*; 2nd, 1980, Clare Corley Smith. SSC Army 1954 (Capt.); Hong Kong, 1959–63; MoD (Central), 1965; First Sec., FO (later FCO), 1966; Mexico City, 1969; First Sec., UK Disarmament Delegn, Geneva, 1974; Counsellor (Commercial), Madrid, 1976; Counsellor and Head of Chancery, Kuala Lumpur, 1980–83; Hd, Trade Relns and Exports Dept, FCO, 1983–85; Ambassador to Bolivia, 1985–87. *Recreations:* reading, travel. *Address:* c/o Foreign and Commonwealth Office, SW1. *Club:* Royal Automobile.

WHITE, Prof. Alan Richard, BA, PhD; Ferens Professor of Philosophy in the University of Hull, 1961–89; *b* Toronto, Canada, 9 Oct. 1922; *s* of late George Albert White and Jean Gabriel Kingston; *m* 1st, 1948, Eileen Anne Jarvis; one *s* two *d*; 2nd, 1979, Enid Elizabeth Alderson. *Educ:* Midleton College and Presentation College, Cork; Trinity College, Dublin. Dublin: Schol. and 1st class Moderator in Classics, 1st class Moderator in Mental and Moral Science; Boxing Pink; President of the 'Phil'; Univ. Student in Classics and Dep. Lecturer in Logic, 1945–46; Asst Lecturer, Lecturer, Sen. Lecturer in Philosophy, Univ. of Hull, 1946–61, Dean of Arts, 1969–71, Pro-Vice-Chancellor, 1976–79. Visiting Professor: Univ. of Maryland, 1967–68, 1980; Temple Univ., 1974; Simon Fraser Univ., 1983; Univ. of Delaware, 1986; Bowling Green State Univ., Ohio, 1988; Special Prof., Univ. of Nottingham, 1986–. Secretary, Mind Assoc., 1960–69, Pres., 1972. Pres., Aristotelian Soc., 1979–80. 42nd Dublin Rifles (LDF), 1941–45. *Publications:* G. E. Moore: A Critical Exposition, 1958; Attention, 1964; The Philosophy of Mind, 1967; (ed) The Philosophy of Action, 1968; Truth, 1970; Modal Thinking, 1975; The Nature of Knowledge, 1982; Rights, 1984; Grounds of Liability, 1985; Methods of Metaphysics, 1987; The Language of Imagination, 1990; Misleading Cases, 1991; articles in philosophical journals. *Recreations:* dilettantism and odd-jobbery. *Address:* 77 Newfield Road, Sherwood, Nottingham NG5 1HF. *T:* Nottingham (0602) 605078.

WHITE, Rev. Barrington Raymond; Senior Research Fellow and Tutor in Ecclesiastical History, Regent's Park College, Oxford, since 1989 (Principal, 1972–89); *b* 28 Jan. 1934; *s* of Raymond Gerard and Lucy Mildred White; *m* 1957, Margaret Muriel Hooper; two *d*. *Educ:* Chislehurst and Sidcup Grammar Sch.; Queens' Coll., Cambridge (BA Theol, MA); Regent's Park Coll., Oxford (DPhil). Ordained, 1959; Minister, Andover Baptist Church, 1959–63; Lectr in Ecclesiastical History, Regent's Park Coll., Oxford, 1963–72. First Breman Prof. of Social Relations, Univ. of N Carolina at Asheville, 1976. FRHistS 1973. *Publications:* The English Separatist Tradition, 1971; Association Records of the Particular Baptists to 1660, Part I, 1971, Part II, 1973, Part III, 1974; Authority: a Baptist view, 1976; Hanserd Knollys and Radical Dissent, 1977; contrib. Reformation, Conformity and Dissent, ed R. Buick Knox, 1977; The English Puritan Tradition, 1980; contrib. Biographical Dictionary of British Radicals in the Seventeenth Century, ed Greaves and Zaller, 1982–84; The English Baptists of the Seventeenth Century, 1983; contribs to Baptist Qly, Jl of Theological Studies, Jl of Ecclesiastical History, Welsh Baptist Studies. *Recreation:* recorded music. *Address:* Regent's Park College, Oxford.

WHITE, Bryan Oliver; HM Diplomatic Service, retired; consultant on Latin American affairs; *b* 3 Oct. 1929; *s* of Thomas Frederick White and Olive May Turvey; *m* 1958, Helen McLeod Jenkins; one *s* two *d*. *Educ:* The Perse Sch.; Wadham Coll., Oxford (Lit.Hum.). HM Forces, 1948–49; FO, 1953; Kabul, Vienna, Conakry, Rio de Janeiro, the Cabinet Office, and Havana, 1953–79; Counsellor, Paris, 1980–82; Head of Mexico and Central America Dept, FCO, 1982–84; Ambassador to Honduras and (non-resident) to El Salvador, 1984–87; Consul-Gen., Lyon, 1987–89. *Recreation:* the Romance languages. *Address:* 45 Westminster Palace Gardens, SW1P 1RR. *Club:* Cercle de l'Union (Lyon).

WHITE, Byron R(aymond); Associate Justice of the Supreme Court of the United States since 1962; *b* Fort Collins, Colorado, 8 June 1917; *s* of Alpha White, Wellington, Colorado; *m* 1946, Marion Lloyd Stearns, *d* of Dr Robert L. Stearns; one *s* one *d*. *Educ:* Wellington High Sch.; Univ. of Colorado; Oxford Univ. (Rhodes Scholar); Yale Univ. Law Sch (before and after War). Served War of 1939–45: USNR, Naval Intell., Pacific (two Bronze Stars). Law Clerk to Chief Justice of the United States, 1946–47; law practice in Denver, Colorado, 1947–60, with firm of Lewis, Grant, Newton, Davis and Henry (later Lewis, Grant and Davis). Dep. Attorney-Gen., 1961–62. Phi Beta Kappa, Phi Gamma Delta. As a Democrat, he was a prominent supporter of John F. Kennedy in the Presidential campaign of 1960. *Recreations:* ski-ing, paddle tennis, fishing. *Address:* US Supreme Court, 1 First Street NE, Washington, DC 20543, USA.

WHITE, Prof. Cedric Masey, DSc(Eng), PhD; Professor Emeritus, University of London, 1966; Consultant for River and Coastal projects; *b* 19 Oct. 1898; *s* of Joseph Masey White, Nottingham; *m* 1st, 1921, Dorothy F. Lowe; 2nd, 1946, Josephine M. Ramage (*d* 1991); one *d*. *Educ:* privately; University College, Nottingham. Served European War, in Tank Corps, 1917–19. Lecturer in Civil Engineering, Univ. of London, King's Coll., 1927–33; Reader in Civil Engineering, and Asst Prof. in Imperial Coll. of Science and Technology, 1933–45; Responsible for work of Hawksley Hydraulic Lab., 1933–66; Professor of Fluid Mechanics and Hydraulic Engineering, 1946–66. Completed various investigations for Admiralty, WO, MAP, etc, during War of 1939–45, and investigations of proposed river-structures for Hydro-Power here and abroad, 1946–56. Founder Member, Hydraulic Research Bd, 1946–51, 1959–67; sometime member of Research Committees of Instn of Civil Engineers; delegation on Hydrology to Internat. Union of Geodesy and Geophysics, 1939, 1948, 1951; Member: Council of British Hydromechanics Research Assoc., 1949–59; Internat. Assoc. for Hydraulic Research, 1947–59. Hon. ACGI, 1951. *Publications:* various engineering reports and scientific papers, chiefly on the motion of air and water. *Address:* Marsh Hill Farm, RR4, Stirling, Ont K0K 3E0, Canada.

WHITE, Christopher John, PhD; FBA 1989; Director, Ashmolean Museum, Oxford, since 1985; Fellow of Worcester College, Oxford, since 1985; *b* 19 Sept. 1930; *s* of late Gabriel Ernest Edward Francis White, CBE and Elizabeth Grace Ardizzone; *m* 1957, Rosemary Katharine Desages; one *s* two *d*. *Educ:* Downside Sch.; Courtauld Institute of Art, London Univ. BA (Hons) 1954, PhD 1970. Served Army, 1949–50; commnd, RA, 1949. Asst Keeper, Dept of Prints and Drawings, British Museum, 1954–65; Director, P. and D. Colnaghi, 1965–71; Curator of Graphic Arts, Nat. Gall. of Art, Washington, 1971–73; Dir of Studies, Paul Mellon Centre for Studies in British Art, 1973–85; Adjunct Prof. of History of Art, 1976–85; Associate Dir, Yale Center for British Art, 1976–85. Dutch Govt Schol., 1956; Hermione Lectr, Alexandra Coll., Dublin, 1959; Adjunct Prof., Inst. of Fine Arts, New York Univ., 1973 and 1976; Conference Dir, European-Amer. Assembly on Art Museums, Ditchley Park, 1975; Visiting Prof., Dept of History of Art, Yale Univ., 1976. Dir, Burlington Magazine, 1981–. Reviews Editor, Master Drawings, 1967–80. *Publications:* Rembrandt and his World, 1964; The Flower Drawings of Jan van Huysum, 1965; Rubens and his World, 1968; Rembrandt as an Etcher, 1969; (jtly) Rembrandt's Etchings: a catalogue raisonné, 1970; Dürer: the artist and his drawings, 1972; English Landscape 1630–1850, 1977; The Dutch Paintings in the Collection of HM The Queen, 1982; (ed) Rembrandt in Eighteenth Century England, 1983; Rembrandt, 1984; Peter Paul Rubens: man and artist, 1987 (Eugène Baie Prize, 1983–87); (jtly) Drawing in England from Hilliard to Hogarth, 1987; (jtly) Rubens in Oxford, 1988; (jtly) One Hundred Old Master Drawings from the Ashmolean Museum, 1991; film (script and commentary), Rembrandt's Three Crosses, 1969; various exhibn catalogues; contribs to Burlington Mag., Master Drawings, etc. *Recreation:* husbandry. *Address:* 39 St Giles, Oxford OX1 3LW. *T:* Oxford (0865) 512289; 14 South Villas, NW1 9BS. *T:* 071–485 9148; Shingle House, St Cross, Harleston, Norfolk IP20 0NT. *T:* St Cross (098682) 264.

WHITE, Sir Christopher (Robert Meadows), 3rd Bt *cr* 1937, of Boulge Hall, Suffolk; *b* 26 Aug. 1940; *s* of Sir (Eric) Richard Meadows White, 2nd Bt, and Lady Elizabeth Mary Gladys (*d* 1950), *o d* of 6th Marquess Townshend; *S* father, 1972; *m* 1st, 1962, Anne Marie Ghislaine (marr. diss. 1968), *yr d* of Major Tom Brown, OBE; 2nd, 1968, Dinah Mary Sutton (marr. diss. 1972), Orange House, Heacham, Norfolk; 3rd, 1976, Ingrid Carolyn Jowett, *e d* of Eric Jowett, Great Baddow; two step *s*. *Educ:* Bradfield Coll., Berks. Imperial Russian Ballet School, Cannes, France, 1961; schoolmaster, 1961–72; Professore, Istituto Shenker, Rome, and Scuola Specialisti Aeronauta, Macerata, 1962–63; Housemaster, St Michael's Sch., Ingoldisthorpe, Norfolk, 1963–69. Hon. Pres., Warnborough House, Oxford, 1973–. Lieutenant, TA, Norfolk, 1969. *Recreations:* dogs, vintage cars, antiques.

WHITE, Christopher Stuart Stuart-; *see* Stuart-White.

WHITE, David Harry, DL; Chairman, Nottingham Health Authority, since 1986; Director, 1980–90, a Deputy Chairman, 1986–90, National Freight Consortium; *b* 12 Oct. 1929; *s* of late Harry White, OBE, FCA, and Kathleen White; *m* 1971, Valerie Jeanne White; one *s* four *d*. *Educ:* Nottingham High Sch.; HMS Conway. Master Mariner's F. G. Certificate. Sea career, apprentice to Master Mariner, 1946–56; Terminal Manager, Texaco (UK) Ltd, 1956–64; Operations Manager, Gulf Oil (GB) Ltd, 1964–68; Asst Man. Dir, Samuel Williams Dagenham, 1968–70; Trainee to Gp Managing Director, British Road Services Ltd, 1970–76; Group Managing Director: British Road Services, 1976–82; Pickfords, 1982–84; NFC Property Gp, 1984–87; Chm., NFC Trustees, 1986–; Director (non-executive): BR Property Bd, 1985–87; Y. J. Lovell Ltd, 1987–; European Leisure PLC, 1991–. Chairman: Nottingham Develt Enterprise, 1987–; Bd of Governors, Nottingham Polytechnic, 1989–. Trustee, Djanogly City Technology Coll., 1989–. County Chm., Notts County Branch, King George's Fund for Sailors, 1985–; Hon-Pres., Notts County Branch, RSPCA, 1987–. Governor, Nottingham High Sch., 1987–. DL Notts, 1989. *Recreations:* football supporter (Forest), walking. *Address:* Whitehaven, 6 Croft Road, Nottingham NG12 4BW. *Club:* Royal Automobile.

WHITE, David Thomas, (Tom), CBE 1990; Principal and Chief Executive, National Children's Home, since 1990; *b* 10 Oct. 1931; *s* of Walter Henry White and Annie White; *m* 1956, Eileen May Moore; two *d* (and one *s* decd). *Educ:* Council Primary and Maesydderwen Grammar Sch., Ystradgynlais, Swansea Valley; University Coll., Swansea (Social Sci.); London School of Economics (Social Work). Clerical Officer, CS, 1947–54; National Service, RAF, 1951–53. Social work and management posts, Devon CC, 1957–61; Dep. Children's Officer, Monmouthshire, 1961–65; Dep. County Children's Officer, Lancs, 1965–70; Dir of Social Services, Coventry, 1970–85; Dir of Social Work, Nat. Children's Home, 1985–90. Past President: Assoc. of Child Care Officers; Assoc. of Directors of Social Services; Gov., Nat. Inst. of Social Work, 1973–. *Publication:* (contrib.) Social Work, the Media and Public Relations, 1991. *Recreations:* gardening, golf, walking. *Address:* (home) 102 Kenilworth Road, Coventry CV4 7AH. *T:* Coventry (0203) 419949; (office) 85 Highbury Park, N5 1UD. *T:* 071–226 2033. *Club:* Coventry Golf (Finham, Coventry).

WHITE, Derek Leslie; HM Diplomatic Service; High Commissioner to Kiribati, since 1990; *b* 18 April 1933; *s* of John William and Hilda White; *m* 1989, Elisabeth Denise Marcelle Lemoine; one *d* from previous marr. *Educ:* Catshill Secondary Sch., Bromsgrove; RAF Apprentice Sch. Served RAF, 1950–63. For. Office (later HM Diplomatic Service), 1963; served Helsinki, Sofia, Algiers; Vice Consul, Tripoli, 1970; FCO, 1972; Commercial Officer, Baghdad, 1975, Second Sec., 1977; Port Louis, 1979; Antananarivo, 1983; FCO, 1984, First Sec., 1985; Consul, Marseilles and Principality of Monaco, 1986; FCO, 1989. *Recreations:* sailing, cooking, music. *Address:* c/o Foreign and Commonwealth Office, SW1A 2AH.

WHITE, Sir Dick (Goldsmith), KCMG 1960; KBE 1955 (CBE 1950; OBE 1942); formerly attached to Foreign and Commonwealth Office, retired 1972; *b* 20 Dec. 1906; *s* of Percy Hall White and Gertrude White (*née* Farthing); *m* 1945, Kathleen Bellamy; two *s*. *Educ:* Bishops Stortford Coll.; Christ Church, Oxford (Hon. Student, 1981); Universities of Michigan and California, USA. US Legion of Merit, Croix de Guerre (France). *Club:* Garrick.

See also J. A. White.

WHITE, Edward George, OBE 1976; HM Diplomatic Service, retired; *b* 30 June 1923; *s* of late George Johnson White, OBE, ISO, and Edith Birch; *m* 1st, 1945, Sylvia Shears; two *d*; 2nd, 1966, Veronica Pauline (*née* Crosling). *Educ:* Bec Secondary Sch., London SW. Served RAF, 1941–47. Various consular and diplomatic appts in Guatemala, USA, Madagascar, Burma, Thailand and India; Dep. Head of Finance Dept, FCO, 1976–78; Counsellor (Admin), Bonn, 1978–79. Specialist Adviser, Foreign Affairs Cttee, H of C, 1980–87. *Address:* 7 Crosslands, Thurlestone, Kingsbridge, Devon TQ7 3TF. *T:* Kingsbridge (0548) 560236.

WHITE, (Edward) Martin (Everatt); Chairman, The Curlew Partnership Ltd, since 1990; *b* 22 Feb. 1938; *s* of Frank and Norah White; *m* 1969, Jean Catherine Armour; one *s* one *d*. *Educ:* Priory Boys' Grammar Sch., Shrewsbury; King's Coll., Cambridge (MA). Solicitor. Asst Solicitor, Lancs County Council, 1962–65; Sen. Asst Solicitor, then Asst Clerk, then Principal Asst Clerk, Kent County Council, 1965–72; Dep. Chief Exec., Somerset County Council, 1972–74; Chief Executive: Winchester City Council, 1974–80; Bucks County Council, 1980–88; Nat. Assoc. of Citizens Advice Bureaux, 1988–90. *Recreations:* gardening, walking, other outdoor pursuits. *Address:* The Spinney, Sevenacres, Chilton Road, Long Crendon, Bucks HP18 9DU. *T:* Long Crendon (0844) 208914.

WHITE, Frank John; His Honour Judge White; a Circuit Judge, since 1974; *b* 12 March 1927; *s* of late Frank Byron White and Marie-Thérèse Renée White; *m* 1953, Anne Rowlandson, MBE, *d* of late Sir Harold Gibson Howitt, GBE, DSO, MC; two *s* two *d*. *Educ:* Reading Sch.; King's Coll., London. LLB, LLM (London). Sub-Lt, RNVR, 1945–47; called to the Bar, Gray's Inn, 1951; Mem., General Council of the Bar, 1969–73; Dep. Chm., Berkshire QS, 1970–72; a Recorder of the Crown Court, 1972–74. Pres., Council of HM Circuit Judges, 1990–91. Member: Lord Chancellor's Adv. Cttee on Legal Aid, 1977–83; Judicial Studies Bd, 1985–89; County Court Rule Cttee, 1991–. *Publication:* Bench Notes and Exercises for Assistant Recorders, 1988. *Recreations:* walking, photography. *Address:* 8 Queen's Ride, SW13 0JB. *T:* 081–788 8903; Blauvac, Vaucluse, France. *Clubs:* Athenæum, Roehampton.

WHITE, Frank Richard, JP; executive director and industrial relations adviser; Director, National Training College, GMB (formerly General, Municipal, Boilermakers and Allied Trades Union), since 1988; *b* Nov. 1939; *m*; three *c*. *Educ:* Bolton Tech. Coll. Member: Bolton CC, 1963–74; Greater Manchester CC, 1973–75; Bolton DC, 1986–. Member: GMB; IPM; Inst. of Management Services. Contested (Lab): Bury and Radcliffe, Feb. 1974; Bury North, 1983; Bolton NE, 1987. MP (Lab) Bury and Radcliffe, Oct. 1974–1983; PPS to Minister of State, Dept of Industry, 1975–76; Asst Govt Whip, 1976–78; Opposition Whip, 1980–82; opposition spokesman on church affairs, 1980–83. Chairman: All Party Paper Industry Gp, 1979–83; NW Lab Gp, 1979–83; Mem., NW Regional Exec., Labour Party, 1986–88. *Address:* 4 Ashdown Drive, Firwood Fold, Bolton, Lancs BL2 3AX.

WHITE, Sir Frederick William George, KBE 1962 (CBE 1954); PhD; FAA 1960; FRS 1966; Chairman, Commonwealth Scientific and Industrial Research Organization, 1959–70 (Deputy Chairman, 1957, Chief Executive Officer, 1949–57); *b* 26 May 1905; *s* of late William Henry White; *m* 1932, Elizabeth Cooper; one *s* one *d*. *Educ:* Wellington College, New Zealand; Victoria University College, Univ. of New Zealand (MSc 1928); Cambridge Univ. (PhD 1932). Postgrad. Schol. in Science, Univ. of NZ and Strathcona Schol., St John's Coll., Cambridge; Research in Physics, Cavendish Laboratory, 1929–31; Asst Lecturer in Physics, Univ. of London, King's Coll., 1931–36; Professor of Physics, Canterbury University Coll., NZ, 1937; Member, British Empire Cancer Campaign Soc., Canterbury Branch Cttee, 1938; Radio Research Cttee, DSIR NZ, 1937; Advisor to NZ Govt on radar research, 1939; seconded to Aust. CSIR, 1941; Chm., Radiophysics Adv. Bd, 1941; Chief, Div. of Radiophysics, 1942. Exec. Officer, 1945, Mem., Exec. Cttee, 1946, CSIR Aust. Radio Research Bd, 1942; Scientific Adv. Cttee, Aust. Atomic Energy Commn, 1953; FInstP; Fellow Aust. Instn of Radio Engrs. Hon. DSc: Monash Univ.; ANU; Univ. of Papua and New Guinea. *Publications:* Electromagnetic Waves, 1934; scientific papers on nature of ionosphere over NZ, on propagation of radio waves, and on songs of Australian birds (1985–87). *Recreation:* fishing. *Address:* 57 Investigator Street, Red Hill, Canberra, ACT 2603, Australia. *T:* 957424.

WHITE, Air Vice-Marshal George Alan, CB 1984; AFC 1973; FRAeS; Commandant, Royal Air Force Staff College, 1984–87; Chairman, Ground Air Training Systems (Cyprus) Ltd, since 1987; *b* 11 March 1932; *s* of James Magee White and Evangeline (*née* Henderson); *m* 1955, Mary Esmé (*née* Magowan); two *d*. *Educ:* Queen's Univ., Belfast; University of London (LLB). Pilot, 1956; served in RAF Squadrons and OCUs, 1956–64; RAF Staff College, 1964; HQ Middle East Command, 1966–67; 11 Sqn, 1968–70; 5 Sqn, 1970–72; Nat. Defence Coll., 1972–73; in command, RAF Leuchars, 1973–75; Royal Coll. of Defence Studies, 1976; Dir of Ops (Air Defence and Overseas), 1977–78; SASO No 11 Group, 1979–80; Air Cdre Plans, HQ Strike Comd, 1981–82; Dep. Comdr, RAF Germany, 1982–84. FRAeS 1985. *Recreations:* sailing, hill walking, bridge. *Address:* PO Box 2048, Paphos, Cyprus. *Club:* Royal Air Force.

WHITE, Sir George (Stanley James), 4th Bt *cr* 1904, of Cotham House, Bristol; JP; FSA; clockmaker and horological consultant; Keeper of the Collection of the Worshipful Company of Clockmakers, since 1988; *b* 4 Nov. 1948; *s* of Sir George Stanley Midelton

White, 3rd Bt, and of Diane Eleanor, *d* of late Bernard Abdy Collins, CIE; *S* father, 1983; *m* 1st, 1974; one *d*; 2nd, 1979, Elizabeth Jane, *d* of Sir Reginald Verdon-Smith, *qv*; one *s* one *d*. *Educ:* Harrow School. Member: Nat. Art Collections Fund Cttee (Avon Br.), 1985–; Gloucester Diocesan Adv. Cttee for Care of Churches, 1985– (Clocks Advr, 1986–); Council, Bristol and Glos Archaeological Soc., 1987– (Vice-Chm., 1989–). Liveryman, Co. of Clockmakers, 1986. High Sheriff, Avon, 1989; JP 1991. FSA 1988. *Publications:* (with E. J. White) St Mary's Church, Hawkesbury, 1980; English Lantern Clocks, 1989; contrib. Antiquaries' Jl, Antiquarian Horology, etc. *Heir: s* George Philip James White, *b* 19 Dec. 1987.

WHITE, Maj.-Gen. Gilbert Anthony, MBE 1944; *b* 10 June 1916; *s* of Cecil James Lawrence White and Muriel (*née* Collins); *m* 1939, Margaret Isabel Duncan Wallet; two *d*. *Educ:* Christ's Hosp., Horsham. Member of Lloyd's, 1938. Joined TA Artists Rifles, 1937; TA Commn, E Surrey Regt, 1939; served BEF, 1940, N Africa, 1943–44, Italy, 1944–45; Staff Coll., 1944; Instructor, Staff Coll., Haifa, 1946; with UK Delegn to UN, 1946–48; served on Lord Mountbatten's personal staff in MoD, 1960–61; idc 1965; BAOR, 1966–69; Chief, Jt Services Liaison Orgn, Bonn, 1969–71; retd 1971. Mem. Council, Guide Dogs for the Blind, 1971–. *Recreations:* golf, racing. *Address:* Speedwell, Tekels Avenue, Camberley, Surrey GU15 2LB. *T:* Camberley (0276) 23812. *Club:* Army and Navy.

WHITE, Harold Clare, MBE 1967; HM Diplomatic Service, retired; Consul-General, Seattle, 1976–79; *b* 26 Oct. 1919; *s* of Alfred John White and Nora White; *m* 1951, Marie Elizabeth Richardson; two *d*. *Educ:* Grammar Sch., Warrington. Served War, Royal Signals, 1939–45. GPO, 1937–39 and 1946; FO, 1947; Third Sec., Djakarta, 1951; FO, 1955; Vice-Consul, Piraeus, Kirkuk, San Francisco, and Durban, 1957–64; 1st Secretary: Kinshasa, 1964; Kuala Lumpur, 1968; FCO, 1972; Dep. Consul-Gen., Chicago, 1974. *Recreations:* cricket, golf. *Address:* 31 Stuart Avenue, Eastbourne, East Sussex BN21 1UR. *T:* Eastbourne (0323) 31148. *Club:* Civil Service.

WHITE, Sir Harold (Leslie), Kt 1970; CBE 1962; MA; FLAA; FAHA; FASSA; National Librarian, National Library of Australia, Canberra, 1947–70; *b* Numurkah, Vic, 14 June 1905; *s* of late James White, Canterbury, Vic; *m* 1930, Elizabeth (MBE), *d* of Richard Wilson; two *s* two *d*. *Educ:* Wesley College, Melbourne; Queen's College, University of Melbourne (Fellow, 1988–). Commonwealth Parliamentary Library, 1923–67; National and Parliamentary Librarian, 1947–67. Visited US as Carnegie Scholar, 1939, and as first Australian under "Leaders and Specialists programme" of Smith Mundt Act, 1950. Represented Australia at various overseas Conferences, 1939–69. Chairman, Standing Cttee, Aust. Advisory Council on Bibliographical Services, 1960–70; Member: various Aust. cttees for UNESCO; Aust. Nat. Film Bd; UNESCO Internat. Cttee on Bibliography, Documentation and Terminology, 1961–64; Nat. Meml Cttee, 1975–; Chm., Adv. Cttee, Australian Encyclopaedia, 1970–87; Governor, Australian Film Inst., 1958–77; Hon. Vice Pres., Library Assoc. of UK, 1970–. H. C. L. Anderson Award, Library Assoc. of Australia, 1983. *Publications:* (ed) Canberra: A Nation's Capital; contribs to various jls. *Address:* 27 Mugga Way, Canberra, ACT 2603, Australia.

WHITE, Sir Henry Arthur Dalrymple D.; *see* Dalrymple-White.

WHITE, Vice-Adm. Sir Hugo Moresby, KCB 1991; CBE 1985; Flag Officer Scotland and Northern Ireland, since 1991; *b* 22 Oct. 1939; *s* of late Hugh Fortescue Moresby White, CMG and of Betty Sophia Pennington White; *m* 1966 Josephine Mary Lorimer Pedler; two *s*. *Educ:* Dragon School; Nautical Coll., Pangbourne; Britannia RN Coll., Dartmouth. HMS Blackpool, 1960; submarine training, 1961; HM Submarines Tabard, Tiptoe, Odin, 1961–65; Long Navigation Course, HMS Dryad, 1966; Navigator, HMS Warspite, 1967; First Lieut, HMS Osiris, 1968–69; in Comd, HMS Oracle, 1969–70; Staff, BRNC Dartmouth, 1971–72; Submarine Sea Training, 1973–74; in Comd, HMS Salisbury (cod war), 1975–76; Naval Sec.'s Dept, 1976–78; Naval Plans, 1978–80; in Comd, HMS Avenger (Falklands) and 4th Frigate Sqn, 1980–82; Principal Staff Officer to Chief of Defence Staff, 1982–85; in Comd, HMS Bristol and Flag Captain, 1985–87; Flag Officer Third Flotilla, and Comdr Anti-Submarine Warfare Striking Force, 1987–88; ACNS, 1988–91. *Recreations:* sailing, travelling, gardening. *Address:* c/o Naval Secretary, Old Admiralty Building, Spring Gardens, SW1. *Club:* Army and Navy.

WHITE, Ian; Member (Lab) Bristol, European Parliament, since 1989; Partner, McCarthy and White, solicitors. *Address:* (office) 34 High Street, Thornbury, Bristol BS12 2AJ. *T:* Thornbury (0454) 413696.

WHITE, James; Managing Director, Glasgow Car Collection Ltd, since 1959; *m*; one *s* two *d*. *Educ:* Knightswood Secondary School. Served Eighth Army, War of 1939–45 (African and Italian Stars; Defence Medal). MP (Lab) Glasgow (Pollok), 1970–87. Mem. Commonwealth Parly Assoc. Delegns, Bangladesh, 1973, Nepal, 1981. *Address:* 23 Alder Road, Glasgow G43 2UU.

WHITE, James; author and art historian; Professor of History of Painting, Royal Hibernian Academy, since 1968; *b* 16 Sept. 1913; *s* of Thomas John White and Florence Coffey; *m* 1941, Agnes Bowe; three *s* two *d*. *Educ:* Belvedere Coll., Dublin; privately in European museums and collections. Art Critic: Standard, 1940–50; Irish Press, 1950–59; Irish Times, 1959–62. Curator, Municipal Gallery of Modern Art, Dublin, 1960–64; Director, Nat. Gallery of Ireland, 1964–80. Chm., Irish Arts Council, 1978–84; Hon. Sec., Royal Dublin Soc., 1986–. Ext. Lectr in History of Art, University Coll., Dublin, 1955–77; Visiting Lectr in Univs and Socs in GB, Italy, USA, Canada. Trustee, Chester Beatty Library of Oriental Art, Dublin. Radio and Television contribs: BBC, RTE, and in the USA. Irish Comr to Biennale at Venice and at Paris on various occasions; Organiser of Exhibns in Dublin, London, Paris, etc., incl. Paintings from Irish Collections, 1957. Corresp. Mem., Real Academia de Bellas Artes de San Fernando, 1975. Hon. LLD NUI, 1970. Arnold K. Henry Medal of RCS of Ireland. Chevalier, Légion d'Honneur, 1974; Order of Merit, Govt of Italy, 1977; Commander of the Order of Merit, Federal Republic of Germany, 1983. *Publications:* Irish Stained Glass (with Michael Wynne), 1963; The National Gallery of Ireland, 1968; Jack B. Yeats, 1971; John Butler Yeats and the Irish Renaissance, 1972; Masterpieces of the National Gallery of Ireland, 1978; Pauline Bewick: painting a life, 1985; monographs on Louis Le Brocquy, George Campbell, Brian Bourke; contributor to: Apollo, Art News, Studio, Connoisseur, Blackfriars, Manchester Guardian, The Furrow, Doctrine and Life, Art Notes, Merian, Werk, Das Munster, Hollandsche Art, La Biennale, La Revue Française, Il Milione, Encyclopaedia of Art, etc. *Recreations:* golf, swimming, gardening, bridge. *Address:* 15 Herbert Park, Ballsbridge, Dublin 4. *T:* 683723. *Club:* Kildare Street and University (Dublin).

WHITE, James, CA; Chairman, Ashley Group plc, since 1988; *b* 22 Oct. 1937; *s* of John and Helen White; *m* 1961, Mary Jardine; two *d*. *Educ:* Wishaw High Sen. Secondary Sch. CA (Scotland) 1961. Operations Dir (UK), SKF, 1961–70; Main Bd Dir, Lex Service PLC, 1970–79; Chief Exec., 1980–90, Chm., 1989–90, Bunzl PLC. Director: Lucas Industries plc, 1985–; Redland PLC, 1986–; Beecham Group plc, 1986–89; Smithkline Beecham PLC, 1989–. *Recreations:* golf, athletics, gardening. *Address:* Ashley Group plc, 47 Park Lane, W1Y 3LB. *Club:* St Stephen's Constitutional.

WHITE, James Ashton V.; *see* Vallance White.

WHITE, John Alan; Deputy Chairman, Associated Book Publishers Ltd, 1963–68 (Managing Director, 1946–62); former Director: British Publishers Guild Ltd; Eyre & Spottiswoode Ltd; Chapman & Hall Ltd; Book Centre Ltd; *b* 20 June 1905; *e s* of Percy Hall White and Gertrude (*née* Farthing); *m* 1st, Marjorie Lovelace Vincent (*d* 1958); two *s*; 2nd, Vivienne Rosalie Musgrave. *Educ:* Bishops Stortford College. President, Publishers' Association, 1955–57; Chairman, National Book League, 1963–65. *Recreations:* reading, gardening. *Address:* Hayfield House, College Road, Cork, Ireland. *T:* Cork 271519. *Club:* Garrick.

See also Sir Dick Goldsmith White.

WHITE, Rev. Canon John Austin; Canon of Windsor, since 1982; *b* 27 June 1942; *s* of Charles White and Alice Emily (*née* Precious). *Educ:* The Grammar Sch., Batley, W Yorkshire; Univ. of Hull (BA Hons); College of the Resurrection, Mirfield. Assistant Curate, St Aidan's Church, Leeds, 1966–69; Asst Chaplain, Univ. of Leeds, 1969–73; Asst Director, post ordination training, Dio. of Ripon, 1970–73; Chaplain, Northern Ordination Course, 1973–82. *Publications:* (with Julia Neuberger) A Necessary End: attitudes to death, 1991; various articles. *Recreations:* medieval iconography, drama, Italy, cooking. *Address:* 8 The Cloisters, Windsor Castle SL4 1NJ. *T:* Windsor (0753) 860409.

WHITE, Hon. Sir John (Charles), Kt 1982; MBE (mil.) 1942; Judge of High Court of New Zealand, retired 1981, sat as retired Judge, 1982–84; *b* 1 Nov. 1911; *s* of Charles Gilbert White and Nora Addison Scott White; *m* 1st, 1943, Dora Eyre Wild (*d* 1982); one *s* three *d*; 2nd, 1987, Margaret Elspeth Maxwell Fletcher. *Educ:* Wellesley Coll., Wellington; John McGlashan Coll., Dunedin; Victoria University Coll., Wellington; Univ. of New Zealand (LLM Hons). Barrister and Solicitor of Supreme Court of New Zealand. Judge's Associate, 1937–38; served War, Middle East, Greece, Crete, Italy, 1940–45, final rank Major; formerly Dominion Vice-Pres., New Zealand Returned Services Assoc.; Private practice as barrister and solicitor, Wellington, 1945–66; Pres., Wellington Law Soc., Vice-Pres., NZ Law Soc., 1966; QC and Solicitor General of New Zealand, 1966; Judge of the Supreme Court (now High Court), 1970, retd 1981; Judge Advocate General of Defence Forces, 1966–87. Actg Chief Justice, Solomon Islands, 1984. Pres., Solomon Is Court of Appeal, 1985–87. Royal Comr, Inquiry into 1982 Fiji Gen. Election, 1983. Asst Editor, Sim's Practice & Procedure, 9th edn, 1955, and 10th edn 1966. *Recreations:* formerly Rugby, cricket, tennis, golf, bowls. *Address:* 23 Selwyn Terrace, Wellington 1, New Zealand. *T:* 725–502. *Clubs:* Wellington; Dunedin; Melbourne.

WHITE, Prof. John Edward Clement Twarowski, CBE 1983; FSA; Durning-Lawrence Professor of the History of Art, University College, London, since 1971 (Vice-Provost, 1984–88); *b* 4 Oct. 1924; *s* of Brigadier A. E. White and Suzanne Twarowska; *m* 1950, Xenia Joannides. *Educ:* Ampleforth College; Trinity College, Oxford; Courtauld Institute of Art, University of London. Served in RAF, 1943–47. BA London 1950; Junior Research Fellow, Warburg Inst., 1950–52; PhD Lond. 1952; MA Manchester 1963. Lectr in History of Art, Courtauld Inst., 1952–58; Alexander White Vis. Prof., Univ. of Chicago, 1958; Reader in History of Art, Courtauld Inst., 1958–59; Pilkington Prof. of the History of Art and Dir of The Whitworth Art Gallery, Univ. of Manchester, 1959–66; Vis. Ferens Prof. of Fine Art, Univ. of Hull, 1961–62; Prof. of the History of Art and Chm., Dept of History of Art, Johns Hopkins Univ., USA, 1966–71. Member: Adv. Council of V&A, 1973–76; Exec. Cttee, Assoc. of Art Historians, 1974–81 (Chm., 1976–80); Art Panel, Arts Council, 1974–78; Vis. Cttee of RCA, 1977–86; Armed Forces Pay Review Body, 1986–; Chm., Reviewing Cttee on Export of Works of Art, 1976–82 (Mem., 1975–82). Trustee, Whitechapel Art Gall., 1976– (Vice-Chm., 1985–). Membre Titulaire, 1983–, Membre du Bureau, 1986–, Comité International d'Histoire de l'Art. *Publications:* Perspective in Ancient Drawing and Painting, 1956; The Birth and Rebirth of Pictorial Space, 1957, 3rd edn 1987 (Italian trans. 1971); Art and Architecture in Italy, 1250–1400, 1966, 2nd edn 1987; Duccio: Tuscan Art and the Medieval Workshop, 1979; Studies in Renaissance Art, 1983; Studies in Late Medieval Italian Art, 1984; articles in Art History, Art Bulletin, Burlington Magazine, Jl of Warburg and Courtauld Institutes. *Address:* Department of The History of Art, University College, Gower Street, WC1E 6BT; (home) 25 Cadogan Place, SW1. *Club:* Athenæum.

WHITE, John Sampson, AO 1982; CMG 1970; Secretary to the Governor, South Australia, 1976–82; *b* 9 June 1916; *s* of late W. J. White; *m* 1941, Dorothy G., *d* of late E. J. Griffin; one *s* one *d*. *Educ:* Black Forest Primary and Adelaide High Schs. AASA. Attorney-General's Dept, 1933–61. Served War, 2nd AIF, 1941–45, Captain. Asst Sec., Industries Develt Cttee, 1950, Sec., 1951–61; Sec., Land Agents' Bd, 1951–61; Sec. to Premier, SA, 1961–65; Mem., SA Superannuation Fund Bd, 1961–74; Sec., Premier's Dept, SA, 1965–74; Agent-Gen. for SA, 1974–76; Comr of Charitable Funds, 1964–74. Member: State Exec. Cttee, Meals on Wheels Inc., 1982–; Exec. Cttee, SA Br., Victoria League for Commonwealth Friendship, 1982–; Bd of Dirs, Service to Youth Council, 1982–84; Casino Supervisory Authy, 1983–86. Mem., Council of Governors, Presb. Girls' Coll., 1958–73. Freeman, City of London. *Recreations:* swimming, tennis. *Address:* 4 Evans Avenue, Mitcham, SA 5062, Australia. *Clubs:* Adelaide, Naval, Military and Air Force, Sturt (Adelaide).

WHITE, John William, CMG 1981; DPhil; FRSC; FAA; Professor of Physical and Theoretical Chemistry, Australian National University, Canberra, since 1985; *b* Newcastle, Australia, 25 April 1937; *s* of late George John White and of Jean Florence White; *m* 1966, Ailsa Barbara, *d* of A. A. and S. Vise, Southport, Qld; one *s* three *d*. *Educ:* Newcastle High Sch.; Sydney Univ. (MSc); Lincoln Coll., Oxford (1851 Schol., 1959; MA, DPhil). ICI Fellow, Oxford Univ.; Research Fellow, Lincoln Coll., 1962; University Lectr, Oxford, 1963–85, Assessor, 1981–82; Fellow, St John's Coll., Oxford, 1963–85 (Vice-Pres. 1973). Neutron Beam Coordinator, AERE, Harwell, 1974; Asst Director, 1975, Director 1977–80, Institut Laue-Langevin, Grenoble. Argonne Fellow, Argonne Nat. Lab. and Univ. of Chicago, 1985; Christensen Fellow, St Catherine's Coll., Oxford, 1991. Pres., Soc. of Crystallographers, Aust., 1989–. Chm., Dirs' Adv. Council, Intense Pulsed Neutron Source, Argonne Nat. Lab., and Univ of Chicago, 1989–. Lectures: Tilden, Chemical Soc., 1975; Liversidge, Sydney Univ., 1985; Hinshelwood, Oxford Univ., 1991; Foundn, Assoc. of Asian Chemical Socs, 1991. Member of Council: Epsom Coll., 1981–85; Wycliffe Hall, Oxford, 1983–85. FRSC 1982; FRACI 1985; FAIP 1986; FAA 1991. Marlow Medal, Faraday Soc., 1969. *Publications:* various contribs to scientific jls. *Recreations:* family, squash, skiing. *Address:* 2 Spencer Street, Turner, ACT 2601, Australia. *T:* Canberra 486836.

WHITE, Sir John (Woolmer), 4th Bt *cr* 1922; *b* 4 Feb. 1947; *s* of Sir Headley Dymoke White, 3rd Bt and of Elizabeth Victoria Mary, *er d* of late Wilfrid Ingram Wrightson; *S* father, 1971; *m* 1987, Joan Borland; one *s*. *Educ:* Hurst Court, Hastings; Cheltenham College. *Heir: s* Kyle Dymoke Wilfrid White, *b* 16 March 1988. *Address:* Salle Park, Norwich, Norfolk NR10 4SG.

WHITE, Lawrence John, CMG 1972; formerly Assistant Secretary, Board of Customs and Excise, 1961–75, retired; *b* 23 Feb. 1915; *s* of Arthur Yirrell White and Helen Christina White; *m* 1936, Ivy Margaret Coates; one *s*. *Educ:* Banbury Grammar Sch.

Joined Customs and Excise, 1933; Commonwealth Relations Office, 1948–50; Customs and Excise, 1951–75. *Recreations:* reading, walking. *Address:* Peach Tree Cottage, Fifield, Oxon OX7 6HL. *T:* Shipton under Wychwood (0993) 830806.

WHITE, Sir Lynton (Stuart), Kt 1985; MBE (mil.) 1943; TD 1950; DL; Chairman, Hampshire County Council, 1977–85; *b* 11 Aug. 1916; 2nd *s* of Sir Dymoke White, 2nd Bt, JP, DL; *m* 1945, Phyllis Marie Rochfort Worley, *er d* of Sir Newnham Arthur Worley, KBE; four *s* one *d*. *Educ:* Harrow; Trinity College, Cambridge (MA 1938). Associate RIBA, 1947–82. TA 1939, as 2nd Lieut RA; served War of 1939–45: UK, 1939–40; Far East, 1940–45 (despatches, 1943); Hon. Lieut-Col RA, TA, 1946; TARO, 1948–71. Member Hampshire CC, 1970; Vice-Chm., 1976. DL Hants 1977. *Address:* Oxenbourne House, East Meon, Petersfield, Hants GU32 1QL.

WHITE, Martin; *see* White, E. M. E.

WHITE, Michael Simon; theatre and film producer; *b* 16 Jan. 1936; *s* of Victor R. and Doris G. White; *m* 1965, Sarah Hillsdon (marr. diss. 1973); two *s* one *d*; 2nd, 1985, Louise M. Moores, *d* of late Nigel Moores; one *s*. *Educ:* Lyceum Alpinum, Zuoz, Switzerland; Pisa University; Sorbonne, Paris. Asst to Sir Peter Daubeny, 1956–61; *stage:* London productions include: Rocky Horror Show; Sleuth; America Hurrah; Oh, Calcutta!; The Connection; Joseph and the Amazing Technicolor Dreamcoat; Loot; The Blood Knot; A Chorus Line; Deathtrap; Annie; Pirates of Penzance; On Your Toes; The Mystery of Edwin Drood; Metropolis; Bus Stop; *films:* include: Monty Python and the Holy Grail; Rocky Horror Picture Show; My Dinner with André; Ploughman's Lunch; Moonlighting; Strangers's Kiss; The Comic Strip Presents; The Supergrass; High Season; Eat the Rich; White Mischief; The Deceivers; Nuns on the Run; Robert's Movie; The Pope Must Die. *Publication:* Empty Seats, 1984–. *Recreations:* art, ski-ing, racing. *Address:* 13 Duke Street, St James's, SW1. *T:* 071–839 3971.

WHITE, Neville Helme; Stipendiary Magistrate for Humberside, since 1985; *b* 12 April 1931; *s* of Noel Walter White and Irene Helme White; *m* 1958, Margaret Jennifer Catlin; two *s* one *d*. *Educ:* Newcastle-under-Lyme High School. RAF, 1949–51. Partner, Grindey & Co., Solicitors, Stoke-on-Trent, 1960–85. Pres., N Staffs Law Soc., 1980–81. *Recreations:* music, walking, gardening, reading, all sports, paintings. *Address:* 20 Waltham Lane, Beverley, North Humberside HU17 8HB.

WHITE, Norman Arthur, PhD; CEng, FIMechE; Eur Ing; Director and Principal Executive, Norman White Associates, since 1972; *b* Hetton-le-Hole, Durham, 11 April 1922; *s* of late Charles Brewster White and Lillian Sarah (*née* Finch); *m* 1st 1944, Joyce Marjorie Rogers (*d* 1982); one *s* one *d*; 2nd, 1983, Marjorie Iris Rushton. *Educ:* Luton Tech. Coll. (HNC); Manchester Inst. of Sci. and Technol. (AMCT Hons); London Univ. (BSc Eng (Hons)); Univ. of Philippines (MSc); London Polytechnic (DMS); Harvard Business Sch. (grad. AMP 1968); LSE (PhD 1973). CEng; MRAeS; FInstPet; FInstE; FIMechE; FIMM. Industrial apprentice, George Kent, and D. Napier & Son; Flight Test Engr, Mil. Aircraft develt, 1943–45. Joined Royal Dutch/Shell Gp, 1945; Petroleum Res. Engr, Thornton Res. Centre, 1945–51; Tech. Manager, Shell Co. of Philippines, 1951–55; Shell International Petroleum: Div. Hd, later Dep. Manager, Product Develt Dept, 1955–61; special assignments in various countries, 1961–63; Gen. Manager, Lubricants, Bitumen and LPG Divs, 1963–66; Dir of Marketing Develt, 1966–68; Chief Exec., New Enterprises Div., London and The Hague, 1968–72; Chm. and Dir, Shell oil and mining cos, UK and overseas, 1963–72. Established Norman White Associates (specialists in technology based enterprises and international resources), 1972; Energy Advr, Hambros Bank, 1972–76; Chm./Dir, various petroleum exploration and prodn cos in UK, Netherlands, Canada and USA, 1974–88; Chairman: KBC Advanced Technologies, 1979–90; Tesel plc, 1983–85 (Dir, 1980–85); Ocean Thermal Energy Conversion Systems, 1982–; Process Automation and Computer Systems, 1985–; Andaman Resources plc, 1986–90; Technology Transfer Centre Surrey Ltd, 1990–; Delta Media Solutions Ltd, 1990–; Transnational Satellite Educn Centre, 1991–; Director: Environmental Resources, 1973–87; Henley Centre for Forecasting, 1974– (Dep. Chm., 1974–87); Kelt Energy plc (formerly Petranol), 1985–88 (Chm., 1986–87); Com-Tek Resources, Denver, 1988–. Mem., Parly and Scientific Cttee, House of Commons, 1977–83, 1987–. World Energy Council, Member: British Nat. Cttee, 1977–88; Conservation Commn, 1979–87; Internat. Exec. Assembly, 1987–; World Petroleum Congress: Chm., British Nat. Cttee, 1987– (Dep. Chm., 1977–87); Permanent Council, 1979–; Treasurer, 1983–91; Chm., Develt Cttee, 1989–; Member: Bd and World Council, Internat. Road Fedn, Geneva and Washington, 1964–72; UK CAA Cttee of Enquiry on Flight Time Limitations (Bader Cttee), 1972–73; Internat. Energy/Petroleum Delegn to USSR, Rumania, E Germany, Japan, Korea, India, Mexico, Argentina and Brazil, 1979–; Royal Soc./Inst. of Petroleum Delegn to People's Republic of China, 1985; Chm., China Technical Exchange Cttee, 1985–89. Visiting Professor: Arthur D. Little Management Educn Inst., Boston, USA, 1977–79; ASC, Henley, 1979–89 (Vis. Fellow 1976–79); Manchester Business Sch., 1981–90 (Vis. Industrial Dir 1971–81); City Univ., 1990– (ext. examnr, 1983–89); Vis. Lectr, RCDS, 1981–85. London University: Member: Senate, 1974–87; External Council, 1974–84; Governing Bd, Commerce Degree Bureau, 1975–84; Academic Adv. Bd in Engrg, 1976–85; Collegiate Council, 1984–87; Cttee of Mangt, Inst. of US Studies, 1984–; Mem., Council of Mining and Metallurgical Instns, 1981–87; Member Council: Inst. of Petroleum, 1975–81 (Vice-Pres., 1978–81); IMechE, 1980–85, 1987–91 (Chm., Engrg Management Div., 1980–85, Southern Br., 1987–89); Founder Chm., Jt Bd for Engrg Management, 1990–. FRSA 1944; FBIM; MRI; Mem., RIIA; Founder Mem., British Inst. of Energy Econs. Associate, St George's House, Windsor Castle, 1972. Governor: King Edward VI Royal Grammar Sch., Guildford, 1976–; Reigate Grammar Sch., 1976–. Freeman, City of London, 1983; Liveryman: Worshipful Co. of Engineers, 1984; Co. of Spectacle Makers, 1986; Mem., Guild of Freemen, 1986. *Publications:* Financing the International Petroleum Industry, 1978; The International Outlook for Oil Substitution to 2020, 1983; (contrib.) Handbook of Engineering Management, 1988; contribs to professional jls in UK, Philippines and Canada, on fluid mechanics, petroleum utilization, energy resources, R&D management, project financing and engrg management. *Recreations:* family and various others in moderation, country and coastal walking, wild life, browsing, international affairs, comparative religions, domestic odd-jobbing. *Address:* 9 Park House, 123–125 Harley Street, W1N 1HE. *T:* 071–935 7387, *Fax:* 071–935 5573; Green Ridges, Downside Road, Guildford, Surrey GU4 8PH. *T:* Guildford (0483) 67523. *Clubs:* Athenæum, City Livery, Inst. of Directors; Harvard Business (USA).

WHITE, Adm. Sir Peter, GBE 1977 (KBE 1976; CBE 1960; MBE 1944); Associate Director, Business in the Community, since 1988; *b* 25 Jan. 1919; *s* of William White, Amersham, Bucks; *m* 1947, Audrey Eileen (*d* 1991), *d* of Ernest Wallin, Northampton; two *s*. *Educ:* Dover College. Secretary: to Chief of Staff, Home Fleet, 1942–43; to Flag Officer Comdg 4th Cruiser Sqdn, 1944–45; to Asst Chief of Naval Personnel, 1946–47; to Flag Officer, Destroyers, Mediterranean, 1948–49; to Controller of the Navy, 1949–53; to C-in-C Home Fleet and C-in-C Eastern Atlantic, 1954–55; Naval Asst to Chm. BJSM, Washington, and UK Rep. of Standing Group, NATO, 1956–59; Supply Officer, HMS Adamant, 1960–61; Dep. Dir of Service Conditions and Fleet Supply Duties, Admty, 1961–63; idc 1964; CO HMS Raleigh, 1965–66; Principal Staff Officer to Chief of Defence Staff, 1967–69; Dir-Gen. Fleet Services, 1969–71; Port Admiral, Rosyth, 1972–74; Chief of Fleet Support, 1974–77. Consultant, Wilkinson Match Ltd, 1978–79; Associate Dir, The Industrial Soc., 1980–88. Underwriting Member of Lloyd's, 1979–. Chm., Officers Pension Society, 1982–90. Mem. Foundn Cttee, Gordon Boys' Sch., 1979–89.

WHITE, Raymond Walter Ralph, CMG 1982; Chairman: BP New Zealand, 1984–91; NZ Advisory Board, Westpac Banking Corporation, since 1991; Australian Guarantee Corporation (New Zealand) Ltd, since 1991; *b* 23 June 1923; *s* of Henry Underhill White and Ethel Annie White; *m* 1946, Nola Colleen Adin; one *s* two *d*. *Educ:* Palmerston North Technical High Sch.; Victoria Univ. FCA 1981; FCIS 1968; FBINZ 1982. Dep. Governor, 1967–77, Governor, 1977–82, Reserve Bank of NZ. Director: NZ Guardian Trust Co., 1983–; Alcan Australia Ltd, 1988–; NZ Adv. Bd, ICI, 1990–. *Recreations:* golf, tennis, gardening. *Address:* 63 Chatsworth Road, Silverstream, New Zealand. *T:* Wellington 282084. *Club:* Wellington (NZ).

WHITE, Captain Richard Taylor, DSO 1940 (Bars 1941 and 1942); RN retired; *b* 29 Jan. 1908; *s* of Sir Archibald White, 4th Bt and *heir-pres.* to Sir Thomas White, *qv*; *m* 1936, Gabrielle Ursula Style; three *s* two *d*. *Educ:* RN College, Dartmouth. Served War of 1939–45 (DSO and two Bars). Retired 1955. *Address:* Tilts House, Boughton Monchelsea, Maidstone, Kent ME17 4JE.

WHITE, Prof. Robert Stephen, FGS; Professor of Geophysics, Cambridge University, since 1989; Fellow of St Edmund's College, Cambridge, since 1988; *b* 12 Dec. 1952; 2nd *s* of James Henry White and Ethel Gladys (*née* Cornick); *m* 1976, Helen Elizabeth (*née* Pearce); one *s* one *d*. *Educ:* Market Harborough and West Bridgford Comprehensive Schs; Emmanuel Coll., Cambridge (Sen. Schol., 1972–74; Bachelor Schol., 1974–77; BA, MA, PhD). FRAS 1979; FGS 1989. Research Assistant: Berkeley Nuclear Labs, CEGB, 1970–71; Dept of Geodesy and Geophysics, Cambridge, 1978; postdoctoral schol., Woods Hole Oceanographic Instn, USA, 1978–79; Res. Fellow, Emmanuel Coll., Cambridge, 1979–82; Sen. Asst in Res., 1981–85, Asst Dir of Res., 1985–89, Dept of Earth Scis, Cambridge Univ. Cecil and Ida H. Green Schol., Scripps Instn of Oceanography, UCSD, USA, 1987; Guest Investigator, Woods Hole Oceanographic Instn, 1988. Bigsby Medal, Geol Soc., 1991. *Publications:* papers in many internat. jls. *Recreations:* building and flying radio-controlled model gliders, walking. *Address:* Bullard Laboratories, Madingley Road, Cambridge CB3 0EZ. *T:* Cambridge (0223) 333400.

WHITE, Robin Bernard G.; *see* Grove-White.

WHITE, Roger, FSA 1986; Secretary, Georgian Group, since 1984; *b* 1 Sept. 1950; *s* of Geoffrey and Zoë White. *Educ:* Ifield Grammar School; Christ's College, Cambridge (1st class Hons, Hist. of Art Tripos); Wadham College, Oxford. GLC Historic Buildings Div., 1979–83. *Publications:* John Vardy, 1985; contribs to Architectural Hist., Jl of Garden Hist., Country Life. *Recreation:* visiting and writing about historic buildings. *Address:* The Georgian Group, 37 Spital Square, E1 6DY. *T:* 071–377 1722.

WHITE, Roger Lowrey, JP; Managing Director, Research Information Services (Westminster) Ltd, since 1975; Associate Director, Cargill Attwood International, since 1971; *b* 1 June 1928; *o s* of late George Frederick White and Dorothy Jeanette White; *m* 1962, Angela Mary (*née* Orman), company director. *Educ:* St Joseph's Coll., Beulah Hill. National Vice-Chm., Young Conservatives, 1958–59; Founder Mem., Conservative Commonwealth Council; Mem. Council, London Borough of Bromley, 1964–68. MP (C) Gravesend, 1970–Feb. 1974. Gen. Comr of Taxes, 1991–. Member: Asthma Research Council, 1973–; London Crime Stoppers Bd, 1989–. Freeman, City of London, 1953; Liveryman, Worshipful Co. of Makers of Playing Cards, 1975–; JP Inner London Area, 1965; Chm., E Central Div. of Inner London Magistrates, 1989– (Dep. Chm., 1986–89). *Recreations:* golf, fishing. *Address:* 74 Clifton Court, Aberdeen Place, NW8 8HX. *Clubs:* Carlton, English-Speaking Union, City Livery.

WHITE, Stephen Fraser; consulting engineer; *b* 13 May 1922; *s* of Robert and Iola White; *m* 1953, Judith Hamilton Cox; two *s* one *d*. *Educ:* Friars, Bangor; Nottingham Univ. BSc; FICE, MIWES, MIStructE. War Service in Indian Electrical and Mechanical Engineers, discharged 1947. G. H. Hill and Sons, Consulting Civil Engineers, 1947–59; Cardiff Corporation, 1959–62; Engineering Inspector, Min. of Housing and Local Govt, 1962–70; Dir of Water Engineering, Dept of the Environment, 1970–77; Sen. Technical Advr to Nat. Water Council, 1977–83. *Recreations:* golf, bridge. *Address:* Rosehill, 4 Goodens Lane, Great Doddington, Northants NN9 7TY.

WHITE, Terence de Vere, FRSL; *b* 29 April 1912; *s* of Frederick S. de Vere White, LLD, and Ethel (*née* Perry); *m* 1st, 1941, Mary O'Farrell (marr. diss. 1982); two *s* one *d*; 2nd, 1982, Hon. Victoria Glendinning, *qv*. *Educ:* St Stephen's Green Sch., Dublin; Trinity Coll., Dublin (BA, LLB). Admitted solicitor, 1933. Mem. Council, Incorporated Law Society, retd 1961. Literary Editor, The Irish Times, 1961–77. Vice-Chm., Board of Governors, National Gallery of Ireland; Trustee: National Library, 1946–79; Chester Beatty Library, 1959–80; Dir, Gate Theatre, 1969–81. Mem., Irish Academy of Letters, 1968; Hon. RHA 1968; Hon. Prof. of Literature, RHA, 1973; FRSL 1981; Mem., Aosdána, 1989. *Publications:* The Road of Excess, 1945; Kevin O'Higgins, 1948; The Story of the Royal Dublin Society, 1955; A Fretful Midge, 1957; A Leaf from the Yellow Book, 1958; An Affair with the Moon, 1959; Prenez Garde, 1962; The Remainder Man, 1963; Lucifer Falling, 1965; The Parents of Oscar Wilde, 1967; Tara, 1967; Leinster, 1968; Ireland, 1968; The Lambert Mile, 1969; The March Hare, 1970; Mr Stephen, 1971; The Anglo-Irish, 1972; The Distance and the Dark, 1973; The Radish Memoirs, 1974; Big Fleas and Little Fleas, 1976; Chimes at Midnight, 1977; Tom Moore, 1977; My Name is Norval, 1978; Birds of Prey, 1980; Johnnie Cross, 1983; Chat Show, 1987; contribs to 19th Century, Cambridge Review, Horizon, The Spectator, NY Times, Sunday Telegraph. *Recreation:* formerly riding. *Address:* Davis Cottage, Torriano Cottages, NW5 2TA. *Clubs:* Garrick, Academy.

WHITE, Air Vice-Marshal Terence Philip, CB 1987; CEng, FIEE; at leisure; *b* 1 May 1932; *s* of Horace Arthur White and Evelyn Annie White (*née* Simpson); *m* 1956, Sheila Mary (*née* Taylor); three *d*. *Educ:* Wellingborough Technical Inst,; Rugby Coll. of Technology and Arts; RAF Engineering College. Electrical engineering apprentice, 1948–53; Junior Design Engineer, BTH Co., 1953; commissioned RAF Signals Officer, 1954–56; RAF Permt commn, Elect. Engr, 1957; attached RAAF, 1958–60; RAF weapons, communications and radar appts, 1963–67; OC Wing, RAF, Fylingdales, 1967–70; RAF Staff Coll., 1971; commanded RAF N Luffenham, 1972–74; Mem., RCDS, 1975; Senior Elect. Engr, HQ RAF Strike Command, 1976–77; Dir, Engineering Policy MoD (Air), 1978–80; Air Officer, Engrg and Supply, HQ RAF Germany, 1981–82; AOC Maintenance Units and AO Maintenance, RAF Support Comd, 1983–87. *Publications:* contribs to RAF and professional jls. *Recreations:* rough shooting, antique and house restoration. *Address:* c/o Midland Bank, Grantham, Lincs. *Club:* Royal Air Force.

WHITE, Thomas Anthony B.; *see* Blanco White.

WHITE, Sir Thomas Astley Woollaston, 5th Bt, *cr* 1802; JP; Hon. Sheriff for Wigtownshire, since 1963; *b* 13 May 1904; *s* of Sir Archibald Woollaston White, 4th Bt, and late Gladys Becher Love, *d* of Rev. E. A. B. Pitman; *S* father, 1945; *m* 1935, Daphne Margaret, *er d* of late Lt-Col F. R. I. Athill, CMG; one *d*. *Educ*: Wellington College. FRICS. JP Wigtownshire, 1952. *Heir*: *b* Capt. Richard T. White, *qv*. *Address*: Ha Hill, Torhousemuir, Wigtown, Newton Stewart DG8 9DJ. *T*: Wigtown (09884) 2238.

WHITE, Tom; *see* White, D. T.

WHITE, Willard Wentworth; singer, actor; *b* 10 Oct. 1946; *s* of Egbert and Gertrude White; *m* 1972, Gillian Jackson; three *s* ond *d*. *Educ*: Excelsior High Sch., Kingston, Jamaica; Juilliard Sch. of Music. BM. Guest singer, recitalist and recording artist, UK and overseas; singing rôles include Sarastro, Osmin, Sprecher, Leporello, Banquo, King Philip, Grand Inquisitor, Ferrando, Wotan, Klingsor, Hunding, Fafner, King Henry, Orestes, Porgy, Golaud; *stage*: title rôle, Othello, RSC, 1989. Prime Minister of Jamaica's Medal of Appreciation, 1987. *Address*: c/o Harrison Parrott, 12 Penzance Place, W11 4PA.

WHITE, William Kelvin Kennedy, CMG 1983; HM Diplomatic Service, retired; *b* 10 July 1930; *y s* of late Kennedy White, JP, Caldy, Cheshire, and Violet White; *m* 1957, Susan Margaret, *y d* of late R. T. Colthurst, JP, Malvern, Worcs; three *s*. *Educ*: Birkenhead Sch.; Merton Coll., Oxford. HM Forces, 1949–50, 2nd Lieut Manchester Regt; Lieut 13th (Lancs) Bn, Parachute Regt, TA, 1950–54. Entered HM Foreign (later Diplomatic) Service, 1954; Foreign Office, 1954–56, attending UN Gen. Assemblies, 1954 and 1955; 3rd Sec., Helsinki, 1956–57; 2nd Sec., Commissioner-General's Office, Singapore, 1957–61; 2nd Sec., then 1st Sec., FO, 1961–66; 1st Sec. (Commercial), Stockholm, 1966–69; 1st Sec., then Counsellor and Head of Republic of Ireland Dept, FCO, 1969–74; Counsellor, New Delhi, 1974–77; Head of South Asian Dept, FCO, 1978–80; Minister, Canberra, 1980–81; Dep. Chief Clerk and Chief Inspector, FCO, 1982–84; High Comr to Zambia, 1984–87; Ambassador to Indonesia, 1988–90. Mem. Council, Univ. of Surrey. *Address*: Church Farm House, North Moreton, near Didcot, Oxon OX11 9BA. *Club*: Moreton CC.

WHITE-THOMSON, Very Rev. Ian Hugh; Dean of Canterbury, 1963–76; *b* 18 December 1904; *m* 1954, Wendy Ernesta Woolliams; two *s* two *d*. *Educ*: Harrow; Oxford. Deacon, 1929; Priest, 1930; Curacy, St Mary's, Ashford, Kent, 1929–34; Rector of S Martin's with St Paul's, Canterbury, 1934–39; Chaplain to Archbishops of Canterbury, 1939–47; Vicar of Folkestone, 1947–54; Archdeacon of Northumberland and Canon of Newcastle, 1955–63; Chaplain to King George VI, 1947–52, to the Queen, 1952–63; Examining Chaplain to Bishop of Newcastle, 1955–63. Hon. Canon of Canterbury Cathedral, 1950. Governor, Harrow School, 1947–62, 1965–70. Freeman, City of Canterbury, 1976. Hon. DCL Univ. of Kent at Canterbury, 1971. *Address*: Camphill, Harville Road, Wye, Ashford, Kent TN25 5EY. *T*: Wye (0233) 812210.

WHITEHEAD, Edward Anthony, (Ted); playwright; theatre and film reviewer; *b* 3 April 1933; *s* of Edward Whitehead and Catherine Curran; *m* 1st, 1958, Kathleen Horton (marr. diss. 1976); two *d*; 2nd, 1976, Gwenda Bagshaw. *Educ*: Christ's Coll., Cambridge (MA). Military Service, King's Regt (Infantry), 1955–57. *TV plays*: Under the Age; The Peddler; The Proofing Session; *TV adaptations*: The Detective; Jumping the Queue; The Life and Loves of a She-Devil; Firstborn; The Free Frenchman; Murder East, Murder West; The Cloning of Joanna May; *stage adaptation*: The Dance of Death. Evening Standard Award, and George Devine Award, 1971; BAFTA Award, 1986; American Cable Entertainments Award, 1987. *Publications*: The Foursome, 1972; Alpha Beta, 1972; The Sea Anchor, 1975; Old Flames, 1976; The Punishment, 1976; Mecca, 1977; World's End, 1981; The Man Who Fell in Love with his Wife, 1984. *Recreations*: soccer, pubs, music. *Address*: c/o Jenne Casarotto, 2nd Floor, National House, 60–66 Wardour Street, W1V 3HP. *T*: 071–287 4450.

WHITEHEAD, Frank Ernest; Deputy Director (Statistics), Office of Population Censuses and Surveys, 1987–89; *b* 21 Jan. 1930; *s* of Ernest Edward Whitehead and Isabel Leslie; *m* 1961, Anne Gillian Marston; three *s*. *Educ*: Leyton County High School; London School of Economics. BSc (Econ). National Service, RAF, 1948–49. Rio Tinto Co. Ltd, 1952–54; Professional Officer, Central Statistical Office, Fedn of Rhodesia and Nyasaland, 1955–64; Statistician, General Register Office, 1964–68; Chief Statistician, Min. of Social Security, later DHSS, 1968–77; Head of Social Survey Div., Office of Population Censuses and Surveys, 1977–82; Under Secretary, 1982; Dep. Dir, OPCS, 1982–87. Vice-Pres., Royal Statistical Soc., 1988–89 (Council, 1987–). *Publications*: Social Security Statistics: Reviews of United Kingdom Statistical Sources, Vol. II (ed W. F. Maunder), 1974; contribs to Statistical News, Population Trends. *Recreations*: family history, unskilled garden labour. *Address*: Queensmead, Pilgrims Way, Kemsing, Kent TN15 6XA.

WHITEHEAD, His Honour (Garnet) George (Archie), DFC 1944; a Circuit Judge, 1977–89; *b* 22 July 1916; *s* of late Archibald Payne Whitehead and Margaret Elizabeth Whitehead; *m* 1946, Monica (*née* Watson); two *d*. *Educ*: Wisbech. Admitted Solicitor, 1949. Served War, 1939–45, RAF, Pilot, Bomber Comd and Transport Comd; demob. as Flt Lt, 1 Jan. 1947. Articled to Edmund W. Roythorne, MBE, Solicitor, Spalding. Formerly Senior Partner, Roythorne & Co., Solicitor, Boston, Lincs (Partner, 1950–77); a Recorder of the Crown Court, 1972–77. Formerly Alderman, Boston Borough Council; Mayor of Boston, 1969–70. Reader, Diocese of Lincoln. *Recreations*: photography, walking. *Address*: 15 Burton Close, Boston, Lincs PE21 9QW. *T*: Boston (0205) 364977.

WHITEHEAD, George Sydney, CMG 1966; LVO 1961; HM Diplomatic Service, retired; re-employed in Foreign and Commonwealth Office (Security Department), 1976–81; *b* 15 Nov. 1915; *s* of William George and Annie Sabina Whitehead; *m* 1948, Constance Mary Hart (*née* Vale); one *d* (and one step *d*). Educ: Harrow County Sch.; London Sch. of Economics. India Office, 1934. Armed Forces (Royal Artillery), 1940–45. Private Sec. to Parly Under-Sec. of State for India and Burma, 1945–46; British Embassy, Rangoon, 1947; CRO 1948–52; British High Commn, Canberra, 1952–55; Counsellor, British High Commn, Calcutta, 1958–61; Inspector, Commonwealth Service, 1961–64; Inspector, Diplomatic Service, 1965; Head of Asia Economic Dept, CO, 1966–67; Head of Commonwealth Trade Dept, CO, 1967–68; Head of Commodities Dept, FCO, 1968–69; Dep. High Comr and Minister (Commercial), Ottawa, 1970–72; Asst Under-Sec. of State, 1972–75, Dep. Chief Clerk, 1973–75, FCO. Vice-Pres., RIPA, 1985– (Mem. Council, 1977–84). *Recreations*: gardening, reading, walking. *Address*: 399 Pinner Road, Harrow, Mddx. *T*: 081–427 5872. *Clubs*: Civil Service, Commonwealth Trust, Middlesex County Cricket.

WHITEHEAD, Graham Wright, CBE 1977; President, Jaguar Cars Inc., since 1983; Chairman, Jaguar Canada Inc., Ontario, since 1983; Director: Jaguar Cars Ltd, since 1982; Jaguar plc, since 1984; *m* Gabrielle Whitehead, OBE; one *s* one *d*. Joined Wolseley Motors, 1945; moved to US, 1959; Pres., BL Motors Inc., later Jaguar Rover Triumph Inc., NJ, 1968–83; Chm., Jaguar Rover Triumph Canada Inc., Ont, 1977–83. President: British-American Chamber of Commerce, NY, 1976–78; British Automobile Manufacturers Assoc., NY; St George's Soc. of NY; Governor, Nat. Assoc. of Securities Dealers, 1987–90. *Address*: 20 Meadow Place, Old Greenwich, Conn 06870, USA. *Club*: Riverside Yacht (Conn).

WHITEHEAD, Dr John Ernest Michael, FRCPath; Director of Public Health Laboratory Service, 1981–85; *b* 7 Aug. 1920; *s* of Dr Charles Ernest Whitehead and Bertha Whitehead; *m* 1946, Elizabeth Bacchus (*née* Cochran); one *s* one *d*. *Educ*: Merchant Taylors' Sch.; Gonville and Caius Coll., Cambridge (MA); St Thomas's Hosp. Med. Sch. (MB BChir, DipBact). Jun. Ho. appts, St Thomas' Hosp., 1944–47; Lectr in Bacteriology, St Thomas's Hosp. Med. Sch., 1948–51; Travelling Fellowship, State Serum Inst., Copenhagen, 1949–50; Asst Bacteriologist, Central Public Health Laboratory, 1952–53; Dep. Dir, Public Health Lab., Sheffield, 1953–58; Dir, Public Health Lab., Coventry, 1958–75; Cons. Microbiologist, Coventry Hosps, 1958–75; Dep. Dir, Public Health Laboratory Service, 1975–81. Hon. Lecturer: Univ. of Sheffield, 1954–58; Univ. of Birmingham, 1962–75. Vice-Pres., RCPath, 1983–86; Member: Adv. Cttee on Dangerous Pathogens, 1981–85; Adv. Cttee on Irradiated and Novel Foods, 1982–86; Expert Adv. Gp on AIDS, 1985; Consultant Advr in Microbiol., DHSS, 1982–85; Specialist Advr to H of C Agric. Cttee, 1988–91, to H of C Social Services Cttee, 1989–90; Temporary Adviser and Chm., Working Gp on Safety Measures in Microbiology, WHO, 1976–82; Chm., Working Gp on Organisation and Administration of Public Health Laboratory Services, Council of Europe, 1977–79. *Publications*: chapters in The Pathological Basis of Medicine, ed R. C. Curran and D. G. Harnden, 1974; papers and reviews in med. microbiology in various med. and scientific jls. *Recreations*: house and garden maintenance, skiing, modern languages. *Address*: Martins, Lee Common, Great Missenden, Bucks HP16 9JP. *T*: The Lee (0494) 837. *Club*: Athenæum.

WHITEHEAD, Sir John (Stainton), KCMG 1986 (CMG 1976); CVO 1978; HM Diplomatic Service; Ambassador to Japan, since 1986; *b* 20 Sept. 1932; *s* of late John William and Kathleen Whitehead; *m* 1964, Carolyn (*née* Hilton); two *s* two *d*. *Educ*: Christ's Hospital; Hertford Coll., Oxford (MA; Hon. Fellow 1991). HM Forces, 1950–52; Oxford, 1952–55; FO, 1955–56; 3rd Sec., later 2nd Sec., Tokyo, 1956–61; FO, 1961–64; 1st Sec., Washington, 1964–67; 1st Sec. (Economic), Tokyo, 1968–71; FCO, 1971–76, Head of Personnel Services Dept, 1973–76; Counsellor, Bonn, 1976–80; Minister, Tokyo, 1980–84; Dep. Under-Sec. of State (Chief Clerk), FCO, 1984–86. Trustee, Monteverdi Choir and Orchestra, 1991. *Recreations*: music, travel, golf, tree-felling, walking, chess. *Address*: British Embassy, 1 Ichiban-cho, Chiyoda-ku, Tokyo 100, Japan; Bracken Edge, High Pitfold, Hindhead, Surrey. *T*: Hindhead (0428) 604162. *Clubs*: Beefsteak, United Oxford & Cambridge University; Liphook Golf (Hants).

WHITEHEAD, Phillip; writer and television producer; Chairman, Consumers' Association, since 1990; *b* 30 May 1937; adopted *s* of late Harold and Frances Whitehead; *m* 1967, Christine, *d* of T. G. Usborne; two *s* one *d*. *Educ*: Lady Manners' Grammar Sch., Bakewell; Exeter Coll., Oxford. President, Oxford Union, 1961. BBC Producer, 1961–67, and WEA Lecturer, 1961–65; Editor of This Week, Thames TV, 1967–70. Guild of TV Producers Award for Factual Programmes, 1969. Vice-Chm., Young Fabian Group, 1965; Chm., Fabian Soc., 1978–79 (Centenary Dir, 1983–84). Chairman: New Society Ltd, 1986; Statesman and Nation Publications Ltd, 1985–90; Director: Goldcrest Film and Television Hldgs Ltd, 1984–87; Brook Productions, 1986–. Member: Annan Cttee on Future of Broadcasting, 1974–77; Council, Consumers' Assoc., 1982–. Vis. Fellow, Goldsmiths' Coll., Univ. of London, 1985–; MacTaggart Lectr, Edinburgh Internat. Television Festival, 1987. MP (Lab) Derby N, 1970–83; Front bench spokesman on higher educn, 1980–83 and on the arts, 1982–83; Member: Procedure Cttee, 1977–79; Select Cttee on Home Affairs, 1979–81; PLP Liaison Cttee, 1975–79; Council of Europe Assembly, 1975–80. Contested (Lab): W Derbys, 1966, Derby N, 1983, 1987. Member: NUJ; NUR. Times columnist, 1983–85; Presenter, Credo series, LWT, 1983–84. FRSA 1983. *Publications*: (jtly) Electoral Reform: time for change, 1982; (contrib.) Fabian Essays in Socialist Thought, 1984; The Writing on the Wall, 1985; (jtly) Stalin, a time for judgment, 1990. *Recreations*: walking, cinema, old model railways. *Address*: Mill House, Rowsley, Matlock, Derbys. *T*: Matlock (0629) 732659.

WHITEHEAD, Sir Rowland (John Rathbone), 5th Bt, *cr* 1889; *b* 24 June 1930; *s* of Major Sir Philip Henry Rathbone Whitehead, 4th Bt, and 1st wife Gertrude, *d* of J. C. Palmer, West Virginia, USA; *S* father, 1953; *m* 1954, Marie-Louise, *d* of Arnold Christian Gausel, Stavanger, Norway; one *s* one *d*. *Educ*: Radley; Trinity Hall, Cambridge (BA). Late 2nd Lieutenant RA. Chairman: Trustees, Rowland Hill Benevolent Fund, 1982–; Exec. Cttee, Standing Council of the Baronetage, 1984–87; Trustee, Baronets' Trust, 1984– (founder Chm., 1984–89). Governor, Appleby Grammar Sch., 1964–. Liveryman, Worshipful Co. of Fruiterers'; Freeman, City of London. *Recreations*: poetry and rural indolence. *Heir*: *s* Philip Henry Rathbone Whitehead [*b* 13 Oct. 1957; *m* 1987, Emma, *d* of Captain A. M. D. Milne Home. Late Welsh Guards]. *Address*: Sutton House, Chiswick Mall, W4 2PR. *T*: 071–994 2710; Walnut Tree Cottage, Fyfield, Lechlade, Glos GL7 3NT. *Club*: Arts.

WHITEHEAD, Ted; *see* Whitehead, E. A.

WHITEHEAD, Prof. Thomas Patterson, CBE 1985; MCB, FRCPath, FRSC; Professor of Clinical Chemistry, University of Birmingham, 1968–87, retired; Consultant Biochemist, Queen Elizabeth Medical Centre, 1960–87; *b* 7 May 1923; *m* 1947, Doreen Grace Whitton, JP; two *s* one *d*. *Educ*: Salford Royal Technical Coll.; Univ. of Birmingham (PhD). Biochemist to S Warwickshire Hospital Gp, 1950–60. Dean, Faculty of Medicine and Dentistry, Birmingham Univ., 1984–87. Dir, Wolfson Research Laboratories, 1972–84. Council Mem., Med. Research Council, 1972–76; Mem., Health Service Research Bd, 1973–75; Chairman: Div. of Path. Studies, Birmingham, 1974–80; Board of Undergraduate Med. Educn, Birmingham, 1982–84; W Midlands RHA Res. Cttee, 1982–86; DHSS Adv. Cttee on Assessment of Laboratory Standards, 1969–84; W Midlands RHA Scientific Services Cttee, 1984–86; Member: Adv. Bd, CS Occupational Health Service, 1988–; Med. Adv. Panel on Driving and Alcohol and Substance Abuse, Dept of Transport, 1989–. Chief Scientific Advr, BUPA Med. Res., London, 1987–91; Consultant to: BUPA Medical Centre, London, 1969–91; BUPA Hosps, London, 1983–91; BUPA Med. R&D, 1991–; Centro Diagnostico Italiano, Milan, 1972–; WHO, Geneva, 1974–86; JS Pathology Services, London, 1983–. Pres., Assoc. of Clinical Biochemists, 1981–83; Mem. Council, RCPath, 1982–84. Hon. MRCP 1985. Kone Award Lectr, 1983. Wellcome Prize, 1972; Dade Award, Geneva, 1975; Disting. Internat. Services Award, Internat. Fedn of Clinical Chemistry, 1987; Rank Prize for Opto-Electronics, 1991. *Publications*: Quality Control in Clinical Chemistry, 1976; papers in med. and scientific jls. *Recreation*: growing and exhibiting sweet peas. *Address*: 70 Northumberland Road, Leamington Spa CV32 6HB. *T*: Leamington Spa (0926) 421974. *Club*: Athenæum.

WHITEHORN, John Roland Malcolm, CMG 1974; a Deputy Director-General, Confederation of British Industries, 1966–78; *b* 19 May 1924; *s* of late Alan and Edith Whitehorn; *m* 1st, 1951, Josephine (*née* Plummer) (marr. diss. 1973; she *d* 1990); no *c*; 2nd, 1973, Marion FitzGibbon (*née* Gutmann). *Educ*: Rugby Sch. (Exhbnr); Trinity Coll., Cambridge (Exhbnr). Served War, 1943–46, RAFVR (Flying Officer). Joined FBI, 1947;

Dep. Overseas Dir, 1960; Overseas Dir, 1963; Overseas Dir, CBI, 1965–68; Dir, Mitchell Cotts plc, 1978–86; Consultant Dir, Lilly Industries, 1978–89. Member: BOTB, 1975–78; Bd, British Council, 1968–82; Gen. Adv. Council, BBC, 1976–82. *Address:* Casters Brook, Cocking, near Midhurst, W Sussex GU29 0HJ. *T:* Midhurst (0730) 813537. *Club:* Reform.

See also Katharine Whitehorn.

WHITEHORN, Katharine Elizabeth, (Mrs Gavin Lyall); Columnist, The Observer, since 1960 (Associate Editor, 1980–88); *b* London; *d* of late A. D. and E. M. Whitehorn; *m* 1958, Gavin Lyall, *qv*; two *s. Educ:* Blunt House; Roedean; Glasgow High School for Girls, and others; Newnham Coll., Cambridge. Publisher's Reader, 1950–53; Teacher-Secretary in Finland, 1953–54; Grad. Asst, Cornell Univ., USA, 1954–55; Picture Post, 1956–57; Woman's Own, 1958; Spectator, 1959–61. Member: Latey Cttee on Age of Majority, 1965–67; BBC Adv. Gp on Social Effects of Television, 1971–72; Board, British Airports Authority, 1972–77; Council, RSocMed, 1982–85. Director: Nationwide Building Soc., 1983–; Nationwide Anglia Estate Agents, 1987–90. Rector, St Andrews Univ., 1982–85. Hon. LLD St Andrews, 1985. *Publications:* Cooking in a Bedsitter, 1960; Roundabout, 1961; Only on Sundays, 1966; Whitehorn's Social Survival, 1968; Observations, 1970; How to Survive in Hospital, 1972; How to Survive Children, 1975; Sunday Best, 1976; How to Survive in the Kitchen, 1979; View from a Column, 1981; How to Survive your Money Problems, 1983. *Recreation:* river boat. *Address:* c/o The Observer, Chelsea Bridge House, Queenstown Road, SW8 4NN. *T:* 071–627 0700.

See also J. R. M. Whitehorn.

WHITEHOUSE, Dr David Bryn; Deputy Director, The Corning Museum of Glass, Corning, USA, since 1988 (Chief Curator, 1984–88); *b* 15 Oct. 1941; *s* of Brindley Charles Whitehouse and Alice Margaret Whitehouse; *m* 1st, 1963, Ruth Delamain Ainger; one *s* two *d*; 2nd, 1975, Elizabeth-Anne Ollemans; one *s* two *d. Educ:* King Edward's Sch., Birmingham; St John's Coll., Cambridge. MA, PhD; FSA; FRGS. Scholar, British Sch. at Rome, 1963–65; Wainwright Fellow in Near Eastern Archaeology, Univ. of Oxford, 1966–73; Dir, Siraf Expedn, 1966–73; Dir, British Inst. of Afghan Studies, 1973–74; Dir, British Sch. at Rome, 1974–84. President: Internat. Union of Institutes, 1980–81; Internat. Assoc. for Hist. of Glass, 1991– (Mem. Management Cttee, 1988–); Mem. Council, Internat. Assoc. for Classical Archaeology, 1974–84. Corresp. Mem., German Archaeological Inst.; Academician, Accademia Fiorentina dell'Arte del Disegno; Fellow: Pontificia Accademia Romana di Archeologia; Accademia di Archeologia, Lettere e Belle Arti, Naples. Ed., Jl of Glass Studies, 1988–. *Publications:* (jtly) Background to Archaeology, 1973; (jtly) The Origins of Europe, 1974; (with Ruth Whitehouse) Archaeological Atlas of the World, 1975; (ed jtly) Papers in Italian Archaeology I, 1978; Siraf III: The Congregational Mosque, 1980; (with David Andrews and John Osborne) Papers in Italian Archaeology III, 1981; (with Richard Hodges) Mohammed, Charlemagne and the Origins of Europe, 1983; (jtly) Glass of the Caesars, 1987; Glass of the Roman Empire, 1988; The Medieval Pottery of Central and Southern Italy, 1991; many papers in Iran, Antiquity, Med. Archaeol., Papers of Brit. Sch. at Rome, Jl of Glass Studies, etc. *Address:* The Corning Museum of Glass, One Museum Way, Corning, NY 14830–2253, USA. *T:* (607) 937 5371. *Club:* Athenæum.

WHITEHOUSE, David Rae Beckwith; QC 1990; a Recorder, since 1987; *b* 5 Sept. 1945; *s* of David Barry Beckwith Whitehouse, MA, MD, FRCS, FRCOG and late Mary Beckwith Whitehouse, JP; *m* 1971, Linda Jane, *d* of Eric Vickers, CB and Barbara Mary Vickers; one *s. Educ:* Ellesmere College; Choate Sch., Wallingford, Conn., USA; Trinity College, Cambridge (MA). English-Speaking Union Scholarship, 1964. Called to the Bar, Gray's Inn, 1969; practice, SE Circuit. *Recreations:* the arts, esp. architecture and music; yoga, walking. *Address:* 3 Raymond Buildings, Gray's Inn, WC1R 5BH. *T:* 071–831 3833.

WHITEHOUSE, Mary, CBE 1980; Honorary General Secretary, National Viewers' and Listeners' Association, 1965–80, President since 1980; freelance journalist, broadcaster; *b* 13 June 1910; *d* of James and Beatrice Hutcheson; *m* 1940, Ernest R. Whitehouse; three *s. Educ:* Chester City Grammar Sch.; Cheshire County Training Coll. Art Specialist: Wednesfield Sch., Wolverhampton, 1932–40; Brewood Grammar Sch., Staffs, 1943; Sen. Mistress, and Sen. Art Mistress, Madeley Sch., Shropshire, 1960–64. Co-founder, "Clean up TV campaign", 1964. *Publications:* Cleaning Up TV, 1966; "Who Does She Think She Is?", 1971; Whatever Happened to Sex?, 1977; A Most Dangerous Woman?, 1982; Mightier than the Sword, 1985. *Recreations:* reading, gardening, walking. *Address:* Ardleigh, Colchester, Essex CO7 7RH. *T:* Colchester (0206) 230123.

WHITEHOUSE, Walter Alexander; Professor of Theology, University of Kent, 1965–77; Master of Eliot College, University of Kent, 1965–69, and 1973–75; *b* 27 Feb. 1915; *e s* of Walter and Clara Whitehouse, Shelley, near Huddersfield; *m* 1st, 1946, Beatrice Mary Kent Smith (*d* 1971); 2nd, 1974, Audrey Ethel Lemmon. *Educ:* Penistone Gram. Sch.; St John's Coll., Cambridge; Mansfield Coll., Oxford. Minister of Elland Congregational Church, 1940–44; Chaplain at Mansfield College, Oxford, 1944–47; Reader in Divinity, Univ. of Durham, 1947–65. Principal of St Cuthbert's Soc., Univ. of Durham, 1955–60; Pro-Vice-Chancellor of Univ., and Sub-Warden, 1961–64. Minister at High Chapel, Ravenstonedale, 1977–82. Mem. (Lab), Glos CC, 1989–. Hon. DD Edinburgh, 1960. *Publications:* Christian Faith and the Scientific Attitude, 1952; Order, Goodness, Glory (Riddell Memorial Lectures), 1959; The Authority of Grace, 1981. *Address:* 37 Cotswold Green, Stonehouse, Glos GL10 2ET.

WHITELAW, family name of **Viscount Whitelaw.**

WHITELAW, 1st Viscount *cr* 1983, of Penrith in the County of Cumbria; **William Stephen Ian Whitelaw,** KT 1990; CH 1974; MC; PC 1967; DL; farmer and landowner; *b* 28 June 1918; *s* of late W. A. Whitelaw and Mrs W. A. Whitelaw, Monkland, Nairn; *m* 1943, Cecilia Doriel, 2nd *d* of late Major Mark Sprot, Riddell, Melrose, Roxburghshire; four *d. Educ:* Winchester Coll.; Trinity Coll., Camb. Reg. Officer, Scots Guards; Emergency Commn, 1939; resigned Commn, 1947. MP (C) Penrith and the Border Div. of Cumberland, 1955–83; PPS to Chancellor of the Exchequer, 1957–58 (to Pres. of BOT, 1956); Asst Govt Whip, 1959–61; a Lord Comr of the Treasury, 1961–62; Parly Sec., Min. of Labour, July 1962–Oct. 1964; Chief Opposition Whip, 1964–70; Lord Pres. of Council and Leader, House of Commons, 1970–72; Secretary of State for: N Ireland, 1972–73; Employment, 1973–74; Chm., Conservative Party, 1974–75; Dep. Leader of the Opposition and spokesman on home affairs, 1975–79; Home Secretary, 1979–83; Lord President of the Council and Leader, H of L, 1983–88. Visiting Fellow, Nuffield Coll., Oxford, 1970–. DL Dunbartonshire, 1952–66; DL Cumbria, formerly Cumberland, 1967. *Publication:* The Whitelaw Memoirs, 1989. *Recreations:* golf, shooting. *Heir:* none. *Address:* Ennim, Penrith, Cumbria. *Clubs:* White's, Carlton (Chm., 1986–); Royal and Ancient (Captain 1969–70).

See also Earl of Swinton.

WHITELAW, Billie, CBE 1991; actress; *b* 6 June 1932; *d* of Perceval and Frances Whitelaw; *m* Robert Muller, writer; one *s. Educ:* Thornton Grammar Sch., Bradford. Appeared in: *plays:* Hotel Paradiso, Winter Garden, 1954 and Oxford Playhouse, 1956; Progress to the Park, Theatre Workshop and Saville, 1961; England our England, Prince's, 1962; Touch of the Poet, Venice and Dublin, 1962; National Theatre, 1963–65: Othello, London and Moscow; Hobson's Choice; Beckett's Play; Trelawny of the Wells; The Dutch Courtesan; After Haggerty, Criterion, 1971; Not I, Royal Court, 1973 and 1975; Alphabetical Order, Mayfair, 1975; Footfalls, Royal Court, 1976; Molly, Comedy, 1978; Happy Days, Royal Court, 1979; The Greeks, Aldwych, 1980; Passion Play, Aldwych, 1981; Rockaby and Enough, NY, 1981, with Footfalls, 1984, NT 1982, Riverside, 1986, Adelaide Fest., 1986, Purchase Fest., NY, 1986; Tales from Hollywood, NT, 1983; Who's Afraid of Virginia Woolf?, Young Vic, 1987; *films:* No Love for Johnny; Charlie Bubbles; Twisted Nerve; The Adding Machine; Start the Revolution Without Me; Leo the Last; Eagle in a Cage; Gumshoe; Frenzy; Night Watch; The Omen; Leopard in the Snow; The Water Babies; An Unsuitable Job for a Woman; Slayground; Shadey; The Chain; The Dressmaker; Maurice; Joyriders; The Krays; *television:* No Trams to Lime Street; Lena Oh My Lena; Resurrection; The Skin Game; Beyond the Horizon; Anna Christie; Lady of the Camelias; The Pity of it all; Love on the Dole; A World of Time; You and Me; Poet Game; Sextet (8 plays); Napoleon and Love (9 plays: Josephine); The Fifty Pound Note (Ten from the Twenties); The Withered Arm (Wessex Tales); The Werewolf Reunion (2 plays); Two Plays by Samuel Beckett; Not I; Eustace and Hilda (2 plays); The Serpent Son; Happy Days (dir. by Beckett); Private Schulz; Last Summer's Child; A Tale of Two Cities; Jamaica Inn; Camille; Old Girlfriends; The Secret Garden; Imaginary Friends (mini-series); The Picnic; Three Beckett plays; The 15 Streets; Lorna Doone; Duel of Love; A Murder of Quality; The Cloning of Joanna May; *radio plays:* The Master Builder; Hindle Wakes; Jane Eyre; The Female Messiah; Alpha Beta; The Cherry Orchard; Vassa Zhelyezhova; Filumena. Lectr on Beckett at US Univs of Santa Barbara, Stanford and Denver, 1985, at Balliol Coll., Oxford, 1986. Silver Heart Variety Club Award, 1961; TV Actress of Year, 1961, 1972; British Academy Award, 1968; US Film Critics Award, 1968; Variety Club of GB Best Film Actress Award, 1977; Evening News Film Award as Best Actress, 1977; Sony Best Radio Actress Award, 1987; Evening Standard Film Award for Best Actress, 1988. Hon. DLitt Bradford 1981. *Recreation:* pottering about the house. *Address:* c/o Duncan Heath Associates Ltd, 162 Wardour Street, W1.

WHITELAW, Prof. James Hunter, FEng 1991; FIMechE; Professor of Convective Heat Transfer, Imperial College, London, since 1974; *b* 28 Jan. 1936; *s* of James Whitelaw and Jean Ross Whitelaw (*née* Scott); *m* 1959, Elizabeth Shields; three *s. Educ:* Univ. of Glasgow (BSc 1957; PhD 1961); DSc London 1981. Res. Associate, Brown Univ., 1961–63; Lectr, Imperial Coll., 1963–69; Reader, Imperial Coll., 1969–74. Editor, Experiments in Fluids, 1983–. DSc *hc* Lisbon, 1980. *Publications:* (jtly) Data and Formulae Handbook, 1967, 2nd edn 1976; (jtly) Principles and Practice of Laser-Doppler Anemometry, 1976, 2nd edn 1981; (jtly) Engineering Calculation Methods for Turbulent Flow, 1981; ed. 17 vols proc., and published over 300 papers in learned jls, incl. Jl of Fluid Mechanics, Experiments in Fluids, proc. of learned socs. *Recreations:* gardening, music. *Address:* 149a Coombe Lane West, Kingston-upon-Thames, KT2 7DH. *T:* 081–942 1836.

WHITELEY, family name of **Baron Marchamley.**

WHITELEY, Maj.-Gen. Gerald Abson, CB 1969; OBE 1952; *b* 4 March 1915; *s* of late Harry Whiteley, Walton Park, Bexhill; *m* 1943, Ellen Hanna (*d* 1973). *Educ:* Worksop Coll.; Emmanuel Coll., Cambridge (MA). Solicitor, 1938. Commissioned, RA, 1940; Maj., DJAG's Staff, ME, 1942–45. AAG, Mil. Dept, JAG's Office, WO, 1945–48; Asst Dir of Army Legal Services: FARELF, 1948–51; WO, 1952–53; Northern Army Gp, 1953–54; MELF, 1954–57; BAOR, 1957–60; Dep. Dir of Army Legal Services, BAOR, 1960–62; Col, Legal Staff, WO, 1962–64; Dir of Army Legal Services, MoD, 1964–69. *Recreations:* photography, walking. *Address:* 8 Kemnal Park, Haslemere, Surrey GU27 2LF. *T:* Haslemere (0428) 2803. *Club:* Army and Navy.

WHITELEY, Sir Hugo Baldwin H.; *see* Huntington-Whiteley.

WHITELEY, Gen. Sir Peter (John Frederick), GCB 1979 (KCB 1976); OBE 1960; DL; Lieutenant-Governor and Commander-in-Chief, Jersey, 1979–84; *b* 13 Dec. 1920; *s* of late John George Whiteley; *m* 1948, Nancy Vivian, *d* of late W. Carter Clayden; two *s* two *d. Educ:* Bishop's Stortford Coll.; Bembridge Sch.; Ecole des Roches. Joined Royal Marines, 1940; 101 Bde, 1941; HMS: Resolution, 1941; Renown, 1942; HMNZS Gambia, 1942; seconded to Fleet Air Arm, 1946–50; Adjt 40 Commando, 1951; Staff Coll., Camberley, 1954; Bde Major 3rd Commando Bde, 1957; Instructor, Staff Coll., Camberley, 1960–63; CO 42 Commando, 1965–66 (despatches, Malaysia, 1966); Col GS Dept of CGRM, 1966–68; Nato Defence Coll., 1968; Comdr 3rd Commando Bde, 1968–70; Maj.-Gen. Commando Forces, 1970–72; C of S, HQ Allied Forces Northern Europe, 1972–75; Commandant General, Royal Marines, 1975–77; C-in-C Allied Forces Northern Europe, 1977–79. Col Comdt, RM, 1985–87; Hon. Col, 211 (Wessex) Field Hosp. RAMC (Volunteers), TA, 1985–90. Member: Council, Union Jack Club, 1985–91; Bd of Dirs, Theatre Royal, Plymouth, 1988–; Pres., W Devon Area, 1985–87, Pres., Devon, 1987–, St John's Ambulance Bde. Trustee, Jersey Wildlife Preservation Trust. Governor: Bembridge Sch., 1981–; Kelly Coll., 1985–; St Michael's Sch., Tavistock, 1985–89. Member: Royal Commonwealth Soc., 1981–; Anglo Norse Soc., 1980–; Anglo Danish Soc., 1980–; Jersey Soc. in London, 1984–. Liveryman, Fletchers' Co., 1982; Guild of Freemen of City of London: Mem. Ct of Assistants, 1980–; Master, 1987–88. DL Devon, 1987. CBIM. KStJ 1980; Chevalier, Ordre de la Pléaiade, Assoc. of French Speaking Parliaments, 1984. *Publications:* contribs to Jane's Annual, NATO's Fifteen Nations, RUSI Jl, Nauticus. *Recreations:* music, photography, painting, wood carving, sailing, dogs. *Clubs:* Anchorites; Royal Marines Sailing, Royal Naval Sailing Assoc.

WHITELEY, Samuel Lloyd; Deputy Chief Land Registrar, 1967–73; Legal Assistant to the Clerk to the Haberdashers' Company 1973–78, Freeman, 1978; *b* 30 April 1913; *s* of Rev. Charles Whiteley and Ann Letitia Whiteley; *m* 1939, Kathleen Jones (*d* 1988); two *d. Educ:* George Dixon Sch.; Birmingham Univ. LLB (Hons) 1933. Admitted Solicitor, 1935; HM Land Registry, 1936; seconded Official Solicitor's Dept, 1939; RAF, 1940–46; HM Land Registry, 1946–73. *Recreation:* sport, as a reminiscent spectator. *Address:* 8 Stonehaven Court, Knole Road, Bexhill, Sussex. *T:* Bexhill (0424) 213191.

WHITEMAN, Elizabeth Anne Osborn, DPhil; FRHistS, FSA; JP; Tutor in Modern History 1946–85, Fellow 1948–85, and Vice-Principal 1971–81, Lady Margaret Hall, Oxford; *b* 10 Feb. 1918; *d* of Harry Whitmore Whiteman and Dorothy May (*née* Austin). *Educ:* St Albans High Sch.; Somerville Coll., Oxford (MA 1945, DPhil 1951). FRHistS 1954; FSA 1958. Served War, WAAF, 1940–45: served in N Africa and Italy (mentioned in despatches, 1943). Rep. of Women's Colls, Oxford Univ., 1960–61. Member: Hebdomadal Council, Oxford Univ., 1968–85; Academic Planning Bd, Univ. of Warwick, 1961–65; UGC, 1976–83. Trustee, Ruskin Sch. of Drawing, 1974–77. JP City of Oxford, 1962. *Publications:* (contrib.) Victoria County History, Wilts, Vol. III, 1956; (contrib.) New Cambridge Modern History, Vol. V, 1961; (contrib.) From Uniformity to Unity, ed Chadwick and Nuttall, 1962; (ed with J. S. Bromley and P. G. M. Dickson, and contrib.) Statesmen, Scholars and Merchants: Essays in eighteenth-century History presented to Dame Lucy Sutherland, 1973; (ed with Mary Clapinson) The Compton

Census of 1676, 1986; contrib. hist. jls. *Address:* 5 Observatory Street, Oxford OX2 6EW. *T:* Oxford (0865) 511009.

WHITEMAN, Prof. John Robert, PhD; FIMA; Vice Principal, since 1991, and Professor of Numerical Analysis, since 1981, Brunel University; Director, Brunel Institute of Computational Mathematics, since 1976; *b* 7 Dec. 1938; *s* of Robert Whiteman and Rita (*née* Neale); *m* 1964, Caroline Mary Leigh; two *s* (one *d* decd). *Educ:* Bromsgrove Sch.; Univ. of St Andrews (BSc); Worcester Coll., Oxford (DipEd); Univ. of London (PhD). FIMA 1970. Sen. Lectr, RMCS, Shrivenham, 1963–67; Assistant Professor: Univ. of Wisconsin, 1967–68; Univ. of Texas, Austin, 1968–70; Reader in Numerical Analysis, Brunel Univ., 1970–76; Richard Merton Gästprofessor, Univ. of Münster, 1975–76; Hd of Dept of Maths and Statistics, Brunel Univ., 1982–90. Visiting Professor: Univ. of Pisa, 1975; Univ. of Kuwait, 1986; Texas A & M Univ., 1986, 1988, 1989, 1990; Univ. of Stuttgart, 1989. Lectures: Geary, City Univ., 1986; Robert Todd Gregory, Univ. of Texas, Austin, 1990; Collatz Gedenkkolloquium, Hamburg Univ, 1991. Mem., SERC Maths Cttee, 1981–86 and Science Bd, 1989–91. Editor, Numerical Methods for Partial Differential Equations, 1985–; Member, Editorial Board: Computer Methods in Applied Mechanics and Engrg; Communications in Applied Numerical Methods; Internat. Jl for Numerical Methods in Fluids; Jl of Mathematical Engrg in Industry; Jl of Engrg Analysis. *Publications:* (ed) The Mathematics of Finite Elements and Applications, vols 1–7, 1973, 1976, 1979, 1982, 1985, 1988, 1991; numerous works on numerical solution of partial differential equations, particularly finite element methods. *Recreations:* walking, swimming, golf, orchestral and choral music. *Address:* Institute of Computational Mathematics, Brunel University, Uxbridge, Middx UB8 3PH. *T:* Uxbridge (0895) 274000.

WHITEMAN, Peter George; QC 1977; barrister-at-law; a Recorder, since 1989; Attorney and Counselor at Law, State of New York; Professor of Law, University of Virginia, since 1980; Member, Faculty of Laws, Florida University, since 1977; *b* 8 Aug. 1942; *s* of David Whiteman and Betsy Bessie Coster; *m* 1971, Katherine Ruth (*née* Ellenbogen); two *d*. *Educ:* Warwick Secondary Modern Sch.; Leyton County High Sch.; LSE (LLB, LLM with Distinction). Called to the Bar, Lincoln's Inn, 1967, Bencher, 1985. Lectr, London Univ., 1966–70. Visiting Professor: Virginia Univ., 1978; Univ. of California at Berkeley, 1980. Mem. Cttee, Unitary Tax Campaign (UK), 1982–. Pres., Dulwich Village Preservation Soc., 1987–; Chm., Dulwich against the Rail Link, 1988–. Mem., Cttee Dulwich Picture Gall., 1989–. FRSA. Mem. Bd, Univ. of Virginia Jl of Internat. Law, 1981–. *Publications:* Whiteman on Capital Gains Tax, 1967, 4th edn 1988; Whiteman on Income Tax, 1971, 3rd edn 1988; contrib. British Tax Encyc. *Recreations:* tennis, squash, mountain-walking, jogging, croquet. *Address:* 101 Dulwich Village, SE21 7BJ. *T:* 081–299 0858; (chambers) 071–936 3131; University of Virginia School of Law, Charlottesville, Va 22901, USA. *T:* (804) 924–3996.

WHITEMAN, Ven. Rodney David Carter; Archdeacon of Bodmin, since 1989; Priest-in-charge of Cardinham with Helland, since 1989; *b* Par, Cornwall, 6 Oct. 1940; *s* of Leonard Archibald Whiteman and Sybil Mary (*née* Morshead); *m* 1969, Christine Anne Chelton; one *s* one *d*. *Educ:* St Austell Grammar School; Pershore Coll. of Horticulture; Ely Theological Coll. Deacon 1964, priest 1965; Curate of Kings Heath, Birmingham, 1964–70; Vicar: St Stephen, Rednal, Birmingham, 1970–79; St Barnabas, Erdington, 1979–89; RD of Aston, 1981–89; Hon. Canon of Birmingham Cathedral, 1985–89; Hon. Canon of Truro Cathedral, 1989–. *Recreations:* gardening, music, historic buildings and monuments, walking. *Address:* The Rectory, Cardinham, Bodmin, Cornwall PL30 4BL. *T:* Cardinham (020882) 614.

WHITEMORE, Hugh John; dramatist; *b* 16 June 1936; *s* of Samuel George Whitemore and Kathleen Alma Whitemore (*née* Fletcher); *m* 1st, Jill Brooke (marr. diss.); 2nd, 1976, Sheila Lemon; one *s*. *Educ:* King Edward VI School, Southampton; RADA. *Stage:* Stevie, Vaudeville, 1977; Pack of Lies, Lyric, 1983; Breaking the Code, Haymarket, 1986, transf. Comedy, 1987 (Amer. Math. Soc. Communications Award, 1990); The Best of Friends, Apollo, 1988; *television:* plays and dramatisations include: Elizabeth R (Emmy award, 1970); Cider with Rosie (Writer's Guild award, 1971); Country Matters (Writer's Guild award, 1972); Dummy (RAI Prize, Prix Italia, 1979); Concealed Enemies (Emmy award, Neil Simon Jury award, 1984); The Final Days, 1989; *films:* Stevie, 1980; The Return of the Soldier, 1982; 84 Charing Cross Road, 1986 (Scriptor Award, Los Angeles, 1988); UTZ, 1991. *Publications:* (contrib) Elizabeth R, 1972; Stevie, 1977, new edn 1984; (contrib.) My Drama School, 1978; (contrib.) Ah, Mischief!, 1982; Pack of Lies, 1983; Breaking the Code, 1986; The Best of Friends, 1988. *Recreations:* music, movies, reading. *Address:* c/o Judy Daish Associates, 83 Eastbourne Mews, W2 6LQ. *T:* 071–262 1101. *Clubs:* Dramatists', Groucho.

WHITEOAK, John Edward Harrison, MA, CIPFA; County Treasurer, Cheshire County Council, since 1981; *b* 5 July 1947; *s* of Frank Whiteoak, farmer, and Marion Whiteoak; *m* 1st, 1969, Margaret Elizabeth Blakey (decd); one *s* two *d*; 2nd, 1983, Karen Lynne Wallace Stevenson, MB ChB, BSc; two *d*. *Educ:* Sheffield Univ. (MA). CIPFA 1971. Various positions in local govt, 1966–76 (Skipton RDC and UDC, Solihull CBC and MBC); Asst County Treasurer, Cleveland CC, 1976–79; Dep. County Treasurer, Cheshire CC, 1979–81. Financial Advr, ACC, 1984–. Member: Soc. of County Treasurers, 1981–; Accounting Standards Cttee, 1984–87. Chartered Institute of Public Finance and Accountancy: Mem., Technical Cttee, 1986–87; Mem., Accounting Panel, 1984–87 (Chm., 1987); Chm., Financial Reporting Panel, 1991. Lord of the Manors of Huntington and Cheaveley. *Publications:* various local government journals. *Recreations:* social golf, tennis, snooker. *Address:* Huntington Hall, Huntington, Chester CH3 6EA. *T:* (home) Chester (0244) 312901; (business) Chester (0244) 602000. *Club:* City (Chester).

WHITESIDE, Prof. Derek Thomas, PhD; FBA 1975; University Professor of History of Mathematics and Exact Sciences, Cambridge, since 1987; *b* 23 July 1932; *s* of Ernest Whiteside and Edith (*née* Watts); *m* 1962, Ruth Isabel Robinson; one *s* one *d*. *Educ:* Blackpool Grammar Sch.; Bristol Univ. (BA); Cambridge Univ. (PhD). Leverhulme Research Fellow, 1959–61; DSIR Research Fellow, 1961–63; Research Asst, 1963–72, Asst Dir of Research, 1972–76, University Reader in History of Mathematics, 1976–87, Univ. of Cambridge. Hon. DLitt Lancaster, 1987. Médaille Koyré, Académie Internat. d'Histoire des Sciences, 1968; Sarton Medal, Amer. History of Sci. Soc., 1977. *Publications:* Patterns of Mathematical Thought in the later Seventeenth Century, 1961; (ed) The Mathematical Papers of Isaac Newton, 1967–; (ed) The Preliminary Manuscripts for Isaac Newton's 1687 Principia: 1684–1686 (in facsimile), 1989; articles in Brit. Jl Hist. Science, Jl for Hist. of Astronomy, etc. *Recreation:* looking into space creatively. *Address:* Department of Pure Mathematics and Mathematical Statistics, 16 Mill Lane, Cambridge CB2 1SB.

WHITFIELD, family name of **Baron Kenswood.**

WHITFIELD, Adrian; QC 1983; a Recorder of the Crown Court since 1981; *b* 10 July 1937; *s* of Peter Henry Whitfield and Margaret Mary Burns; *m* 1st, 1962, Lucy Caroline Beckett (marr. diss.); two *d*; 2nd, 1971, Niamh O'Kelly; one *s* one *d*. *Educ:* Ampleforth Coll.; Magdalen Coll., Oxford (Demy; MA). 2nd Lieut, KOYLI (Nat. Service), 1956–58. Called to the Bar, Middle Temple, 1964, Bencher 1990; Member of Western Circuit. *Publications:* contribs on legal matters in medical and dental pubns. *Recreations:* reading, carpentry, country pursuits. *Address:* 47 Faroe Road, W14 0EL. *T:* 071–603 8982; 3 Serjeants' Inn, EC4Y 1BQ *T:* 071–353 5537.

WHITFIELD, Alan; Road Programme Director, Department of Transport, since 1989; *b* 19 April 1939; *s* of John J. Whitfield and Annie Fothergill-Rawe; *m* 1964, Sheila Carr; two *s*. *Educ:* Consett Grammar Sch., Durham; Sunderland and Newcastle Colls of Advanced Technology. MICE 1968; MIMunE 1969; FIHT 1984. Surveyor/Engr, NCB, 1956–62; Engrg Asst, Northumberland CC, 1962–70; Department of Transport: Main Grade Engr, 1970–73; Prin. Professional, 1973–76; Suptg Engr, 1976–80; Dep. Dir, Midlands Road Construction Unit, 1980–83; Dir (Transport), W Midlands Reg. Office, 1983–89; Regl Dir, Eastern Region, DoE and Dept of Transport, 1989. *Publications:* papers on cost benefit analysis, centrifugal testing soils, road design and construction, etc. to IHT, ICE, Inst. Geo. Sci., etc. *Recreations:* bridge, golf, music. *Address:* (office) RPD/MWU, Friars House, Coventry; 2 Marsham Street, SW1P 3EB; 102 Lillington Road, Leamington Spa, Warwickshire CV32 6LW. *T:* Leamington Spa (0926) 420760. *Club:* Royal Automobile.

WHITFIELD, Prof. Charles Richard, MD; FRCOG; FRCPGlas; Regius Professor of Midwifery in the University of Glasgow, since Oct. 1976; *b* 21 Oct. 1927; *s* of Charles Alexander and Aileen Muriel Whitfield; *m* 1953, Marion Douglas McKinney; one *s* two *d*. *Educ:* Campbell Coll., Belfast; Queen's Univ., Belfast (MD). House Surg. and Ho. Phys. appts in Belfast teaching hospitals, 1951–53; Specialist in Obstetrics and Gynaecology, RAMC (Lt-Col retd), 1953–64; Sen. Lectr/Hon. Reader in Dept of Midwifery and Gynaecology, Queen's Univ., Belfast, 1964–74; Consultant to Belfast teaching hosps, 1964–74; Prof. of Obstetrics and Gynaecology, Univ. of Manchester, 1974–76. Chm., Subspecialty Bd, RCOG, 1984–. *Publications:* (ed) Dewhurst's Obstetrics and Gynaecology for Postgraduates, 4th edn 1985; papers on perinatal medicine, pregnancy anaemia and other obstetric and gynaec. topics in med. and scientific jls. *Recreations:* food, travel, sun-worship. *Address:* Redlands, 23 Thorn Road, Bearsden, Glasgow G61 4BS.

WHITFIELD, Rev. George Joshua Newbold; General Secretary, Church of England Board of Education, 1969–74; *b* 2 June 1909; *s* of late Joshua Newbold and Eva Whitfield; *m* 1937, Dr Audrey Priscilla Dence, *d* of late Rev. A. T. Dence; two *s* two *d*. *Educ:* Bede Gram. Sch., Sunderland; King's Coll., Univ. of London; Bishops' Coll., Cheshunt. BA 1st cl. Hons, Engl. and AKC, 1930 (Barry Prizeman); MA 1935. Asst Master, Trin. Sch., Croydon, 1931–34; Sen. Engl. Master: Doncaster Gram. Sch., 1934–36; Hymers Coll., Hull, 1937–43; Headmaster: Tavistock Gram. Sch., 1943–46; Stockport Sch., 1946–50; Hampton Sch., 1950–68 (Whitfield Building opened 1990). Chief Examr in Engl., Univ. of Durham Sch. Exams Bd, 1940–43. Deacon, 1962; Priest, 1963. Member: Duke of Edinburgh's Award Adv. Cttee, 1960–66; Headmasters' Conf., 1964–68; Corporation of Church House, 1974–; Pres., Headmasters' Assoc., 1967; Chm., Exeter Diocesan Educn Cttee, 1981–88. *Publications:* (ed) Teaching Poetry, 1937; An Introduction to Drama, 1938; God and Man in the Old Testament, 1949; (ed) Poetry in the Sixth Form, 1950; Philosophy and Religion, 1955; (jtly) Christliche Erziehung in Europa, Band I, England, 1975. *Recreations:* gardening, photography. *Address:* Bede Lodge, 31A Rolle Road, Exmouth, Devon EX8 2AW. *T:* Exmouth (0395) 274162. *Club:* Athenæum.

WHITFIELD, John; Solicitor, family firm of Whitfield Son and Hallam, of Batley, Dewsbury and Mirfield, since 1965; *b* 31 Oct. 1941; *s* of Sydney Richard Whitfield and Mary Rishworth Whitfield; *m* 1967, Mary Ann Moy; three *s*. *Educ:* Sedbergh Sch.; Leeds Univ. (LLB). MP (C) Dewsbury, 1983–87. Contested (C) Dewsbury, 1987; Prospective Parly Cand., Dewsbury. Director: Ashwood Chemicals Ltd; Thomas Carr Ltd. *Address:* The Old Rectory, Badsworth, Pontefract WF9 1AF. *T:* Pontefract (0977) 645420. *Clubs:* Headingley Football; Mirfield Constitutional; Tanfield Angling.

WHITFIELD, John Flett, JP, DL; Chairman, Surrey Police Authority, 1985–89; Chairman of Police Committee, Association of County Councils, 1985–88; *b* 1 June 1922; *s* of John and Bertha Whitfield; *m* 1946, Rosemary Elisabeth Joan Hartman; two *d*. *Educ:* Epsom Coll., Surrey. Served War, King's Royal Rifle Corps, 1939–46. HM Foreign Service, 1946–57; Director, Materials Handling Equipment (GB) Ltd, 1957–61; London Director, Hunslet Holdings Ltd, 1961–64. Director, Sunningdale Golf Club, 1973–77. Councillor: Berkshire CC, 1961–70; Surrey CC, 1970–89 (Chm., 1981–84). Contested (C) Pontefract, General Election, 1964. JP Berkshire 1971–, Chm. Windsor County Bench, 1978–80; DL Surrey 1982, High Sheriff, 1985–86. Chm., Surrey Univ. Council, 1986–88 (Vice-Chm., 1983–86). *Recreations:* golf, foreign languages, bookbinding. *Address:* 4 Holiday House, Sunningdale, Berks SL5 9RW. *T:* Ascot (0344) 20997. *Clubs:* Royal and Ancient Golf of St Andrews; Royal Cinque Ports Golf; Sunningdale Golf; Rye Golf.

WHITFIELD, Professor John Humphreys; Serena Professor of Italian Language and Literature in the University of Birmingham, 1946–74; *b* 2 Oct. 1906; *s* of J. A. Whitfield; *m* 1936, Joan Herrin, ARCA (Lectr in Design Sch., RCA, 1928–36); two *s*. *Educ:* Handsworth Grammar School; Magdalen College, Oxford. William Doncaster Scholar, Magdalen Coll., 1925–29; Double First Class Hons in Mod. Langs, 1928, 1929; Paget Toynbee Prizeman, 1933. Asst Master, King Edward VII School, Sheffield, 1930–36; University Lecturer in Italian, Oxford University, 1936–46; Awarder to Oxford and Cambridge Schools Examination Bd, 1940–68. Part-time Temporary Assistant Civil Officer, Naval Intelligence Department, 1943. Chairman, Society for Italian Studies, 1962–74; Senior editor of Italian Studies, 1967–74. President: Dante Alighieri Society (Comitato di Birmingham), 1957–75; Assoc. of Teachers of Italian, 1976–77. Hon. Fellow, Inst. for Advanced Res. in the Humanities, Univ. of Birmingham, 1984–87. Barlow Lecturer on Dante, University College, London, 1958–59, Barlow Centenary Lecture, 1977; Donald Dudley Meml Lecture, Birmingham, 1980. Edmund G. Gardner Memorial Prize, 1959; Amedeo Maiuri Prize (Rome), 1965; Serena Medal for Italian Studies, British Acad., 1984. Commendatore, Ordine al Merito della Repubblica Italiana, 1972 (Cavaliere Ufficiale, 1960). *Publications:* Petrarch and the Renascence, 1943 (NY, 1966); Machiavelli, 1947 (NY, 1966); Petrarca e il Rinascimento (tr. V. Capocci, Laterza), 1949; Dante and Virgil, 1949; Giacomo Leopardi, 1954 (Italian tr. 1964); A Short History of Italian Literature, 1962 (Pelican, 1960, 5th edn 1980); The Barlow Lectures on Dante, 1960; Leopardi's Canti, trans. into English Verse, 1962; Leopardi's Canti, ed with Introduction and notes, 1967, rev. edn 1978; Discourses on Machiavelli, 1969; The Charlecote Manuscript of Machiavelli's Prince, facsimile edn with an Essay on the Prince, 1969; Castiglione: The Courtier, ed with introduction, 1974; Guarini: Il Pastor Fido, ed bilingual edn with introduction, 1976; Painting in Naples from Caravaggio to Giordano (trans. of Italian texts), 1982; articles and reviews contrib. to Modern Language Review, Italian Studies, History, Medium Aevum, Comparative Literature, Problemi della Pedagogia, Le parole e le Idee, Encyclopædia Britannica, Chambers's Encyclopædia, Hutchinson's Encyclopædia, Concise Encyclopædia of the Italian Renaissance, etc. *Festschrift:* Essays in Honour of John Humphreys Whitfield, 1975. *Address:* 2 Woodbourne Road, Edgbaston, Birmingham B15 3QH. *T:* 021–454 1035.
See also R. Whitfield.

WHITFIELD, June Rosemary, (Mrs T. J. Aitchison), OBE 1985; actress; *b* 11 Nov. 1925; *d* of John Herbert Whitfield and Bertha Georgina Whitfield; *m* 1955, Timothy John Aitchison; one *d*. *Educ:* Streatham Hill High School; RADA (Diploma 1944). Revue, musicals, pantomime, TV and radio; worked with Arthur Askey, Benny Hill, Frankie Howerd, Dick Emery, Bob Monkhouse, Leslie Crowther, Ronnie Barker; first worked with Terry Scott in 1969; *radio:* series include: Take It From Here (with Dick Bentley and Jimmy Edwards, 1953–60; The News Huddlines (with Roy Hudd and Chris Emmett), 1984–; *films:* Carry on Nurse, 1959; Carry on Abroad, 1972; Bless This House, 1972; Carry on Girls, 1973; *television:* series include: Fast and Loose (with Bob Monkhouse), 1954; Faces of Jim (with Jimmy Edwards), 1962, 1963; Beggar My Neighbour, 1966, 1967; Scott On . . . (with Terry Scott), 1969–73; Happy Ever After, 1974; Terry and June, 1979–87; Cluedo, 1990; *stage:* An Ideal Husband, Chichester, 1987; Ring Round the Moon, Chichester, 1988; Over My Dead Body, Savoy, 1989; Babes in the Wood, Croydon, 1990. Freeman, City of London, 1982. *Address:* c/o April Young, The Clockhouse, 6 St Catherine's Mews, Milner Street, SW3 2PU. *T:* 071–584 1274.

WHITFIELD, Dr Michael, CChem, FRSC; Director and Secretary, Marine Biological Association, since 1987; Deputy Director, Plymouth Marine Laboratory, since 1988; *b* 15 June 1940; *s* of Arthur and Ethel Whitfield; *m* 1961, Jean Ann Rowe (*d* 1984); one *s* three *d*. *Educ:* Univ. of Leeds (BSc 1st cl. Hons Chem.; PhD Chem.). Research Scientist, CSIRO Div. of Fisheries and Oceanography, Cronulla, NSW, 1964–69; Vis. Res. Fellow, KTH Stockholm, 1969, Univ. of Liverpool, 1970; Res. Scientist, Marine Biolog. Assoc., 1970–87. *Publications:* Ion-selective electrodes for the analysis of natural waters, 1970; Marine Electrochemistry, 1981; Tracers in the Ocean, 1988; Light and Life in the Sea, 1990; numerous papers in professional jls. *Recreations:* hill walking, bird watching. *Address:* The Laboratory, Citadel Hill, Plymouth PL1 2PB. *T:* Plymouth (0752) 669762.

WHITFIELD, Prof. Roderick; Professor of Chinese and East Asian Art, University of London, and Head of Percival David Foundation of Chinese Art, since 1984; *b* 20 July 1937; *s* of John Humphreys Whitfield, *qv*; *m* 1st, 1963, Frances Elizabeth Oldfield, PhD (marr. diss 1983), *e d* of late Prof. R. C. Oldfield and Lady Kathleen Oldfield; one *s* two *d*; 2nd, 1983, Youngsook Pak, PhD, art historian, *e d* of Pak Sang-Jon, Seoul. *Educ:* Woodbourne Acad.; King Edward's Sch., Birmingham; Sch. of Oriental and African Studies (Civil Service Interpreter, 2nd cl.); St John's Coll., Cambridge (BA Hons 1960, Oriental Studies Tripos); Princeton Univ. (MA 1963, PhD 1965). Research Associate and Lectr, Princeton, 1965–66; Research Fellow, St John's Coll., Cambridge, 1966–68; Asst Keeper I, Dept of Oriental Antiquities, British Museum, 1968–84. Trustee, Inst. of Buddhist Studies, 1987–. *Publications:* In Pursuit of Antiquity: Chinese paintings of Ming and Ch'ing dynasties in collection of Mr and Mrs Earl Morse, 1969; The Art of Central Asia: the Stein collection at the British Museum, 3 vols, 1983–85; (ed) Treasures from Korea, 1984; (ed) Korean Art Treasures, 1986; (ed) Early Chinese Glass, 1988; Caves of the Thousand Buddhas, 1990; articles in Asiatische Studien, Buddhica Britannica, Orientations and other jls. *Address:* 7 St Paul's Crescent, NW1 9XN. *T:* 071–267 2888.

WHITFIELD LEWIS, Herbert John; *see* Lewis, H. J. W.

WHITFORD, Hon. Sir John (Norman Keates), Kt 1970; Judge of the High Court, Chancery Division, 1970–88; *b* 24 June 1913; *s* of Harry Whitford and Ella Mary Keates; *m* 1946, Rosemary, *d* of John Barcham Green and Emily Paillard; four *d*. *Educ:* University College School; Munich University; Peterhouse, Cambridge. President, ADC. Called to the Bar: Inner Temple, 1935; Middle Temple, 1946 (Bencher 1970). Served with RAFVR, 1939–44: Wing Comdr, 1942; Chief Radar Officer and Dep. Chief Signals Officer, Air Headquarters Eastern Mediterranean; Advisor on patents and information exchanged for war purposes, HM Embassy, Washington, 1944–45. QC 1965. Member of Bar Council, 1968–70. Chm., Departmental Cttee on Law Relating to Copyright and Designs, 1974–76. *Address:* 140 High Street, West Malling, Kent ME19 6NE.

WHITHAM, Prof. Gerald Beresford, FRS 1965; Charles Lee Powell Professor of Applied Mathematics, at the California Institute of Technology, Pasadena, Calif, since 1983; *b* 13 Dec. 1927; *s* of Harry and Elizabeth Ellen Whitham; *m* 1951, Nancy (*née* Lord); one *s* two *d*. *Educ:* Elland Gram. Sch., Elland, Yorks; Manchester University. PhD Maths, Manchester, 1953. Lectr in Applied Mathematics, Manchester Univ., 1953–56; Assoc. Prof., Applied Mathematics, New York Univ., 1956–59; Prof., Mathematics, MIT, 1959–62; Prof. of Aeronautics and Maths, 1962–67, Prof. of Applied Maths, 1967–83, CIT. FAAAS 1959. Wiener Prize in Applied Mathematics, 1980. *Publications:* Linear and Nonlinear Waves, 1974; Lectures on Wave Propagation, 1979; research papers in Proc. Roy. Soc., Jl Fluid Mechanics, Communications on Pure and Applied Maths. *Address:* Applied Mathematics 217–50, California Institute of Technology, Pasadena, California 91125, USA.

WHITING, Alan; Under Secretary, Finance and Resource Management Division, Department of Trade and Industry, since 1989; *b* 14 Jan. 1946; *s* of Albert Edward and Marjorie Irene Whiting; *m* 1968, Annette Frances Pocknee; two *s* two *d*. *Educ:* Acklam Hall Grammar Sch., Middlesbrough; Univ. of East Anglia (BA Hons); University College London (MSc Econ). Research Associate and Asst Lectr, Univ. of East Anglia, 1967; Cadet Economist, HM Treasury, 1968; Economic Asst, DEA, and Min. of Technology, 1969; Economist, EFTA, Geneva, 1970; Economist, CBI, 1972; Economic Adviser, DTI, 1974; Sen. Econ. Adviser, 1979; Industrial Policy Div., Dept of Industry, 1983–85; Under Sec., 1985. *Publications:* (jtly) The Trade Effects of EFTA and the EEC 1959–1967, 1972; (ed) The Economics of Industrial Subsidies, 1975; articles in economic jls. *Recreations:* building, gardening, music, sailing. *Address:* c/o Department of Trade and Industry, Ashdown House, 123 Victoria Street, SW1E 6RB. *Club:* Littleton Sailing.

WHITING, Rev. Peter Graham, CBE 1984; Minister, Beechen Grove Baptist Church, since 1985; *b* 7 Nov. 1930; *s* of Rev. Arthur Whiting and late Mrs Olive Whiting; *m* 1960, Lorena Inns; two *s* three *d*. *Educ:* Yeovil Grammar Sch.; Irish Baptist Theol Coll., Dublin. Ordained into Baptist Ministry, 1956. Minister, King's Heath, Northampton, 1956–62; commnd RAChD, 1962; Regtl Chaplain, 1962–69 (Chaplain to 1st Bn The Parachutte Regt, 1964–66); Sen. Chaplain, 20 Armd Bde and Lippe Garrison, BAOR, 1969–72; Staff Chaplain, HQ BAOR, 1973–74; Sen. Chaplain, 24 Airportable Bde, 1974–75; Dep. Asst Chaplain Gen., W Midland Dist, Shrewsbury, 1975–78 (Sen. Chaplain, Young Entry Units, 1976–78); Asst Chaplain Gen., 1st British Corps, BAOR, 1978–81; Dep. Chaplain Gen. to the Forces (Army), 1981–84. QHC 1981–85. *Address:* 264 Hempstead Road, Watford, Herts WD1 3LY. *T:* (office) Watford (0923) 241858; (home) Watford (0923) 53197.

WHITLAM, Hon. (Edward) Gough, AC 1978; QC 1962; Member: Executive Board of Unesco, 1985–89 (Australian Ambassador to Unesco, 1983–86); Constitutional Commission, 1986–88; Prime Minister of Australia, 1972–75; *b* 11 July 1916; *s* of late H. F. E. Whitlam, Australian Crown Solicitor and Aust. rep. on UN Human Rights Commission; *m* 1942, Margaret Elaine, AO, *d* of late Mr Justice Dovey, NSW Supreme Court; three *s* one *d*. *Educ:* University of Sydney. BA 1938; LLB 1946. RAAF Flight Lieut, 1941–45. Barrister, 1947; MP for Werriwa, NSW, 1952–78; Mem., Jt Parly Cttee on Constitutional Rev., 1956–59; Leader, 1973 and 1975, Dep. Leader, 1977, Constnl Conventions; Deputy Leader, Aust. Labor Party, 1960, Leader, 1967–77; Leader of the Opposition, 1967–72 and 1976–77; Minister for Foreign Affairs, 1972–73. Vis. Fellow, 1978–81, First Nat. Fellow, 1980–81, ANU; Fellow, Univ. of Sydney Senate, 1981–83, 1986–89; Vis. Prof., Harvard Univ., 1979. Chairman: Australia–China Council, 1986–91; Australian Nat. Gall., 1987–90. Pres., Australian Sect, Internat. Commn of Jurists, 1982–83. Mem. of Honour, IUCN, 1988. Hon. DLitt: Sydney, 1981; Wollongong, 1989; Hon. LLD Philippines, 1974. Silver Plate of Honour, Socialist Internat., 1976; Mem. of Honour, World Conservation Union, 1988. *Publications:* The Constitution *versus* Labor, 1957; Australian Foreign Policy, 1963; Socialism within the Constitution, 1965; Australia, Base or Bridge?, 1966; Beyond Vietnam: Australia's Regional Responsibility, 1968; An Urban Nation, 1969; A New Federalism, 1971; Urbanised Australia, 1972; Australian Public Administration and the Labor Government, 1973; Australia's Foreign Policy: New Directions, New Definitions, 1973; Road to Reform: Labor in Government, 1975; The New Federalism: Labor's Programs and Policies, 1975; Government of the People, for the People—by the People's House, 1975; On Australia's Constitution, 1977; Reform During Recession, 1978; The Truth of the Matter, 1979, 2nd edn 1983; The Italian Inspiration in English Literature, 1980; A Pacific Community, 1981; The Cost of Federalism, 1983; The Whitlam Government 1972–75, 1985; International Law-Making, 1989; Australia's Administrative Amnesia, 1990; Living with the United States: British Dominions and New Pacific States, 1990; National and International Maturity, 1991. *Address:* 100 William Street, Sydney, NSW 2011, Australia.
See also N. R. Whitlam.

WHITLAM, Michael Richard; Director-General, The British Red Cross Society, since 1991; *b* 25 March 1947; *s* of late Richard William Whitlam and Mary Elizabeth Whitlam (*née* Land); *m* 1968, Anne Jane McCurley; two *d*. *Educ:* Morley Grammar Sch.; Tadcaster Grammar Sch.; Coventry Coll. of Educn, Univ. of Warwick (Cert. of Educn); Home Office Prison Dept Staff Coll. (Qual. Asst Governor Prison Dept); Cranfield Coll. of Technology (MPhil 1988). Biology teacher, Ripon, 1968–69; Asst Governor, HM Borstal, Hollesley Bay and HM Prison, Brixton, 1969–74; Dir, Hammersmith Teenage Project, NACRO, 1974–78; Dep. Dir/Dir, UK ops, Save the Children Fund, 1978–86; Chief Exec., RNID, 1986–90. Chm., Sound Advantage plc. Member: Exec. Council, Howard League, 1974–84; Community Alternative Young Offenders Cttee, NACRO, 1979–82; Exec. Council, Nat. Children's Bureau, 1980–86; Bd, City Literary Inst.; Chairman: London Intermediate Treatment Assoc., 1980–83; Assoc. of Chief Execs of Nat. Voluntary Orgns, 1988–. *Publications:* numerous papers on juvenile delinquency and charity management. *Recreations:* painting, walking, keeping fit, family activities, voluntary organisations, politics. *Address:* (office) 9 Grosvenor Crescent, SW1X 7EJ.

WHITLAM, Nicholas Richard; Chairman, Mountarrow Wines Pty Ltd; Managing Director, Whitlam Turnbull & Co. Ltd, 1987–90; *b* 6 Dec. 1945; *s* of Hon. (Edward) Gough Whitlam, *qv*; *m* 1973, Sandra Judith Frye; two *s* one *d*. *Educ:* Sydney High Sch.; Harvard Univ. (AB Hons); London Graduate Sch. of Business Studies (MSc). Morgan Guaranty Trust Co., 1969–75; American Express Co., 1975–78; Banque Paribas, 1978–80; Comr, Rural Bank of New South Wales, 1980–81, then Man. Dir, State Bank of New South Wales, 1981–87. Board Member: Aust. Graduate Sch. of Management, 1982– (Chm., 1988–); Aust. Trade Commn, 1985–; Aust. Sports Foundn, 1986–; Trustee, Sydney Cricket and Sports Ground, 1984–88. *Recreations:* swimming, cycling. *Address:* 27 Underwood Street, Paddington, NSW 2021, Australia. *T:* (02) 387–3155. *Clubs:* Brooks's; Hong Kong; Tattersall's (Sydney)

WHITLEY, Elizabeth Young, (Mrs H. C. Whitley); social worker and journalist; *b* 28 Dec. 1915; *d* of Robert Thom and Mary Muir Wilson; *m* 1939, Henry Charles Whitley (Very Rev. Dr H. C. Whitley, CVO; *d* 1976); two *s* two *d* (and one *s* decd). *Educ:* Laurelbank School, Glasgow; Glasgow University. MA 1936; courses: in Italian at Perugia Univ., 1935, in Social Science at London School of Economics and Glasgow School of Social Science, 1938–39. Ran Girls' Clubs in Govan and Plantation, Glasgow, and Young Mothers' Clubs in Partick and Port Glasgow; Vice-Chm. Scottish Association of Girls' Clubs and Mixed Clubs, 1957–61, and Chm. of Advisory Cttee, 1958–59. Broadcast regular programme with BBC (Scottish Home Service), 1953. Member: Faversham Committee on AID, 1958–60; Pilkington Committee on Broadcasting, 1960–62. Columnist, Scottish Daily Express. Adopted as Parly candidate for SNP by West Perth and Kinross, 1968. *Publications:* Plain Mr Knox, 1960; The Two Kingdoms: the story of the Scottish covenanters, 1977; descriptive and centenary articles for Scottish papers, particularly Glasgow Herald and Scotland's Magazine. *Recreations:* reading, gardening. *Address:* The Glebe, Southwick, by Dumfries. *T:* Southwick (038778) 276.

WHITLEY, John Reginald; His Honour Judge Whitley; a Circuit Judge, since 1986; *b* 22 March 1926; *o s* of late Reginald Whitley and of Marjorie Whitley (*née* Orton); *m* 1966, Susan Helen Kennaway; one *d*. *Educ:* Sherborne Sch.; Corpus Christi Coll., Cambridge. Served War, Army, Egypt, Palestine, 1944–48; commissioned, KRRC, 1945. Called to the Bar, Gray's Inn, 1953; Western Circuit, 1953; a Recorder, 1978–86. *Recreation:* golf. *Address:* Kingsrod, Friday's Hill, Kingsley Green, near Haslemere, Surrey GU27 3LL.

WHITLEY, Air Marshal Sir John (René), KBE 1956 (CBE 1945); CB 1946; DSO 1943; AFC 1937, Bar, 1956; *b* 7 September 1905; *s* of late A. Whitley, Condette, Pas de Calais, France; *m* 1st, 1932, Barbara Liscombe (*d* 1965); three *s* (and one *s* decd); 2nd, 1967, Alison (*d* 1986), *d* of Sir Nigel Campbell and *widow* of John Howard Russell; three step *s*. *Educ:* Haileybury. Entered Royal Air Force with a short-service commission, 1926; Permanent Commission, 1931; served in India, 1932–37; served in Bomber Command, 1937–45, as a Squadron Comdr, Station Comdr, Base Comdr and AOC 4 Group; HQ ACSEA Singapore, 1945; HQ India and Base Comdr, Karachi, 1946–47; Director of Organisation (Establishments), Air Ministry, 1948 and 1949; Imperial Defence College, 1950; AOA, 2nd Tactical Air Force, 1951 and 1952; AOC No 1 (Bomber) Group, 1953–56; Air Member for Personnel, 1957–59; Inspector-General, RAF, 1959–62; Controller, RAF Benevolent Fund, 1962–68, retd. *Address:* 2 Woodside Close, Woodside Avenue, Lymington SO41 8FH. *T:* Lymington (0590) 676920. *Clubs:* Royal Air Force; Royal Lymington Yacht.

WHITLEY, Oliver John; Managing Director, External Broadcasting, British Broadcasting Corporation, 1969–72, retired; *b* 12 Feb. 1912; *s* of Rt Hon. J. H. Whitley, and Marguerite (*née* Marchetti); *m* 1939, Elspeth Catherine (*née* Forrester-Paton); four *s* one *d*. *Educ:* Clifton Coll.; New Coll., Oxford. Barrister-at-Law, 1935; BBC, 1935–41. Served in RNVR, 1942–46; Coastal Forces and Combined Ops. BBC 1946–: seconded to Colonial Office, 1946–49; Head of General Overseas Service, 1950–54; Assistant Controller, Overseas Services, 1955–57; Appointments Officer, 1957–60; Controller, Staff Training and Appointments, 1960–64; Chief Assistant to Dir-Gen., 1964–68. Valiant for Truth Award, Order of Christian Unity, 1974. *Recreations:* reading and gardening. *Address:* Greenacre, Ganavan Road, Oban, Argyll PA34 5TU. *T:* Oban (0631) 62555.

WHITLOCK, William Charles; *b* 20 June 1918; *s* of late George Whitlock and Sarah Whitlock, Sholing, Southampton; *m* 1943, Jessie Hilda, *d* of George Reardon of Armagh;

five s. Educ: Itchen Gram. Sch.; Southampton Univ. Army Service, 1939–46. Apptd full-time Trade Union Officer, Area Organiser of Union of Shop, Distributive and Allied Workers, 1946. President, Leicester and District Trades Council, 1955–56; President, Leicester City Labour Party, 1956–57; President, North-East Leicester Labour Party, 1955–56, and 1958–59. Member East Midlands Regional Council of Labour Party, 1955–67, Vice-Chairman 1961–62, Chairman 1962–63. MP (Lab) Nottingham N, Oct. 1959–1983; Opposition Whip, House of Commons, 1962–64; Vice-Chamberlain of the Household, 1964–66; Lord Comr of Treasury, March 1966–July 1966; Comptroller of HM Household, July 1966–March 1967; Dep. Chief Whip and Lord Comr of the Treasury, March–July 1967; Under Sec. of State for Commonwealth Affairs, 1967–68; Parly Under-Sec. of State, FCO, 1968–69. Contested (Lab) Nottingham N, 1983. DPhil hc Ukranian Free Univ., 1986. Address: 51 Stoughton Road, Stoneygate, Leicester.

WHITMORE, Sir Clive (Anthony), GCB 1988 (KCB 1983); CVO 1983; Permanent Under-Secretary of State, Home Office, since 1988; b 18 Jan. 1935; s of Charles Arthur Whitmore and Louisa Lilian Whitmore; m 1961, Jennifer Mary Thorpe; one s two d. Educ: Sutton Grammar Sch., Surrey; Christ's Coll., Cambridge (BA). Asst Principal, WO, 1959; Private Sec. to Permanent Under-Sec. of State, WO, 1961; Asst Private Sec. to Sec. of State for War, 1962; Principal, 1964; Private Sec. to Permanent Under-Sec. of State, MoD, 1969; Asst Sec., 1971; Asst Under-Sec. of State (Defence Staff), MoD, 1975; Under Sec., Cabinet Office, 1977; Principal Private Sec. to the Prime Minister, 1979–82; Dep. Sec., 1981; Permanent Under-Sec. of State, MoD, 1983–88. Recreations: gardening, listening to music. Address: 50 Queen Anne's Gate, SW1H 9AT.

WHITMORE, Sir John (Henry Douglas), 2nd Bt cr 1954; b 16 Oct. 1937; s of Col Sir Francis Henry Douglas Charlton Whitmore, 1st Bt, KCB, CMG, DSO, TD, and of Lady Whitmore (née Ellis Johnsen); S father 1961; m 1st, 1962, Gunilla (marr. diss. 1969), e d of Sven A. Hansson, OV, KLH, Danderyd, and o d of Mrs Ella Hansson, Stockholm, Sweden; one d; 2nd, 1977, Diana Elaine, e d of Fred A. Becchetti, California, USA; one s. Educ: Stone House, Kent; Eton; Sandhurst; Cirencester. Active in personal development and social change; professional racing driver; business trainer and sports psychologist. Publications: The Winning Mind, 1987; Superdriver, 1988. Recreations: ski-ing, squash. Heir: s Jason Whitmore, b 26 Jan. 1983. Address: Southfield, Leigh, near Tonbridge TN11 8PJ. Club: British Racing Drivers.

WHITNEY, John Norton Braithwaite; Chairman, The Really Useful Group plc, since 1990 (Managing Director, 1989–90); b 20 Dec. 1930; s of Dr Willis Bevan Whitney and Dorothy Anne Whitney; m 1956, Roma Elizabeth Hodgson; one s one d. Educ: Leighton Park Friends' Sch. Radio producer, 1951–64; formed Ross Radio Productions, 1951, and Autocue, 1955; founded Radio Antilles, 1963; Man. Dir, Capital Radio, 1973–82; Dir Gen., IBA, 1982–89. Mem. Bd, Royal National Theatre, 1982–; Non-Exec. Chm., Trans World Communications, 1991–; Founder Dir, Sagitta Prodns, 1968–82; Director: Duke of York's Theatre, 1979–82; Consolidated Productions (UK) Ltd, 1980–82; Friends' Provident Life Office, 1982– (Chm., Friends' Provident Stewardship Trust, 1985–). Chm. and Co-founder, Local Radio Assoc., 1964; Chm., Assoc. of Indep. Local Radio Contractors, 1973, 1974, 1975 and 1980. Wrote, edited and devised numerous television series, 1956–82. Founded Recidivists Anonymous Fellowship Trust, 1962; Chm., Sony Radio Awards Cttee, 1991–; Vice Chm., Japan Festival 1991, 1991– (Chm., Festival Media Cttee, 1991); Member: Films, TV and Video Adv. Cttee, British Council, 1983–89; RCM Centenary Develt Fund (formerly Appeals Cttee), 1982– (Chm., Media and Events Cttee, 1982–); Royal Jubilee Trusts Industry and Commerce Liaison Cttee, 1986– (Mem., Admin. Council of Trusts, 1981–85); Member: Council: Royal London Aid Society, 1966–90; TRIC, 1979– (Pres., 1985–86); Fairbridge Drake Soc. (formerly Drake Fellowship), 1981–; Intermediate Technol. Gp, 1982–85; Member: Council for Charitable Support, 1989–; Bd, Open Coll., 1987–89. Pres., London Marriage Guidance Council, 1983–90; Vice President: Commonwealth Youth Exchange Council, 1982–85; RNID, 1988–; Chairman of Trustees: Soundaround (National Sound Magazine for the Blind), 1981–; Artsline, 1983–; Trustee, Venture Trust, 1982–86; Patron, MusicSpace Trust, 1990–; Gov., English Nat. Ballet (formerly London Festival Ballet), 1989–; Chm., Theatre Investment Fund, 1990–. Fellow and Vice Pres., RTS, 1986–89; Member: BAFTA; SWET. FRSA; Hon. FRCM. Recreations: chess, photography, sculpture. Address: 10 Wadham Gardens, NW3 3DP. T: 071–586 9490. Clubs: Garrick, Pilgrims.

WHITNEY, Raymond William, OBE 1968; MP (C) Wycombe, Bucks, since April 1978; b 28 Nov. 1930; o s of late George Whitney, Northampton; m 1956, Sheila Margot Beswick Prince; two s. Educ: Wellingborough Sch.; RMA, Sandhurst; London Univ. (BA (Hons) Oriental Studies). Commnd Northamptonshire Regt, 1951; served in Trieste, Korea, Hong Kong, Germany; seconded to Australian Army HQ, 1960–63; resigned and entered HM Diplomatic Service, 1964; First Sec., Peking, 1966–68; Head of Chancery, Buenos Aires, 1969–72; FCO, 1972–73; Dep. High Comr, Dacca, 1973–76; FCO, 1976–78, Hd of Information Res. Dept and Hd of Overseas Inf. Dept, 1976–78. PPS to Treasury Ministers, 1979–80; Parly Under-Sec. of State, FCO, 1983–84, DHSS, 1984–86. Vice-Chm., Cons. Employment Cttee, 1980–83; Chm., Cons. For. Affairs Cttee, 1981–83; Mem., Public Accounts Cttee, 1981–83; Chairman: Parly Latin-America Cttee, 1987–; Council for Defence Information, 1987–. Chairman: Mountbatten Community Trust (formerly Mountbatten Training), 1987–; The Cable Corp., 1989–; Windsor Cable TV, 1989–. Publications: National Health Crisis—a modern solution, 1988; articles on Chinese and Asian affairs in professional jls. Recreations: theatricals (performing, producing and writing), tennis, bridge, walking, wind-surfing. Address: The Dial House, Sunninghill, Berks SL5 0AG. T: Ascot (0344) 23164.

WHITSEY, Fred; Gardening Correspondent, Daily Telegraph, since 1971; b 18 July 1919; m 1947, Patricia Searle. Educ: outside school hours, and continuously since then. Assistant Editor, Popular Gardening, 1948–64, Associate Editor, 1964–67, Editor, 1967–82. Gardening correspondent, Sunday Telegraph, 1961–71. Gold Veitch Meml Medal, RHS, 1979; VMH 1986. Publications: Sunday Telegraph Gardening Book, 1966; Fred Whitsey's Garden Calendar, 1985; Garden for All Seasons, 1986; contribs to Country Life, The Garden, and The Gardener. Recreations: gardening, music. Address: Avens Mead, 20 Oast Road, Oxted, Surrey RH8 9DU.

WHITSON, Thomas Jackson, OBE 1985; Commandant, Scottish Police College, 1987–91; b 5 Sept. 1930; s of Thomas and Susan Whitson; m 1953, Patricia Marion Bugden; two s. Educ: Knox Acad., Haddington. RN, 1949–56. Lothian and Peebles Police, 1956–75: Police Constable, 1956; Detective Constable, 1959; Detective Sergeant, 1966; Inspector, 1969; Chief Inspector, 1972; Superintendent, 1974; Lothian and Borders Police, 1975–80: Chief Superintendent, 1976; Dep. Chief Constable, Central Scotland Police, 1980–87. Recreations: golf, curling. Address: 12 Plewlandscroft, South Queensferry EH30 9RG.

WHITTAKER, Air Vice-Marshal David, CB 1988; MBE 1967; Air Officer Administration and Air Officer Commanding Directly Administered Units, RAF Support Command, 1986–89, retired; b 25 June 1933; s of Lawson and Irene Whittaker; m 1956, Joyce Ann Noble; two s. Educ: Hutton Grammar School. Joined RAF, 1951; commissioned

1952; served No 222, No 3, No 26 and No 1 Squadrons, 1953–62; HQ 38 Group, 1962–63; HQ 24 Bde, 1963–65; Comd Metropolitan Comms Sqdn, 1966–68; RAF Staff Coll., 1968; Asst Air Adviser, New Delhi, 1969–70; RAF Leeming, 1971–73; Coll. of Air Warfare, 1973; Directing Staff, RNSC Greenwich, 1973–75; Staff of CDS, 1975–76; DACOS (Ops), AFCENT, 1977–80; RCDS 1980; Defence and Air Adviser, Ottawa, 1983–86. Recreations: fishing, gardening, travel. Address: Seronera, Copgrove, Harrogate, North Yorks. T: Boroughbridge (0423) 340459. Club: Royal Air Force.

WHITTAKER, Geoffrey Owen, OBE 1984 (MBE 1962); Governor of Anguilla, 1987–89; retired 1990; b 10 Jan. 1932; s of late Alfred James Whittaker and Gertrude (née Holvey); m 1959, Annette Faith Harris; one s and one d. Educ: Nottingham High Sch.; Bristol Univ. (BA). Auditor: Tanganyika, 1956–58; Dominica, 1958–60; Principal Auditor, Windward Is, 1960–64; Dir of Audit, Grenada, 1964–67; Audit Adviser, British Honduras, 1967–69; Colonial Treas., St Helena, 1970–75; Financial Sec. and Actg Governor, Montserrat, 1975–78; Financial Sec., British Virgin Is, 1978–80; Admin Officer, Hong Kong, 1980–87; Finance Br., 1980–83; Principal Asst Sec., Lands and Works Br., 1983–85; Gen. Man., Hong Kong Industrial Estates Corp., 1985–87. Recreations: music, Rugby football, heraldry. Address: Palmer's Piece, Hall Lane, Ashley, near Market Harborough, Leics. T: Medbourne Green (085883) 312.

WHITTAKER, Stanley Henry, FCA; Director of Finance and Planning, British Railways Board, 1988–91; b 14 Sept. 1935; s of Frederick Whittaker and Gladys Margaret (née Thatcher); m 1959, Freda Smith; two s. Educ: Bec School. ACA 1958, FCA 1969; ACMA 1971. Articled clerk, G. H. Attenborough & Co., Chartered Accountants, 1953–57; Sen. Assistant, Slater, Chapman & Cooke, 1960–62; Partner, Tiplady, Brailsford & Co., 1962–65; Finance Manager, NCB, 1965–68; British Railways: Finance Manager, 1968–74; Corporate Budgets Manager, 1974–78; Sen. Finance Manager, 1978–80; Chief Finance Officer, Western Reg., 1980–82; Director: Budgetary Control, 1982–86; Finance Develt, 1986–87; Group Finance, 1987–88. Recreations: ski-ing, industrial archaeology, travel. Address: 10 Hazel Gardens, Sonning Common, Reading, Berks RG4 9TF. T: Reading (0734) 723659.

WHITTALL, Harold Astley, CBE 1978; CEng; Chairman: B.S.G. International Ltd, since 1981; Ransomes plc (formerly Ransome, Sims & Jefferies Ltd), since 1983 (Director since 1979; Deputy Chairman, 1981–83); Turriff Corporation, since 1986 (Deputy Chairman, 1985–86); b 8 Sept. 1925; s of Harold and Margaret Whittall; m 1952, Diana Margharita Berner. Educ: Handsworth Grammar Sch., Birmingham; Handsworth and Birmingham Technical Colls. Gen. Manager, Belliss & Morcom, 1962; Managing Dir, Amalgamated Power Engineering, 1968, Chm., 1977–81; Director: LRC Internat., 1982–85; APV (formerly APV Baker and APV Hldgs), 1982–; Sykes Pickervant, 1987–; Inchcape Insurance Hldgs, 1988–90. Pres., Engineering Employers' Fedn, 1976–78; Chairman: Engrg ITB, 1985–91; ETA, 1990–; British Iron and Steel Consumers Council, 1987–91. Address: Brook Farmhouse, Whelford, near Fairford, Glos GL7 4DY. T: Cirencester (0285) 712393. Clubs: Royal Automobile, St James'.

WHITTALL, Michael Charlton, CMG 1980; OBE 1963; HM Diplomatic Service; Counsellor, Foreign and Commonwealth Office, 1973–91; b 9 January 1926; s of Kenneth Edwin Whittall and Edna Ruth (née Lawson); m 1953, Susan Olivia La Fontaine one d. Educ: Rottingdean; Rugby; Trinity Hall, Cambridge. Served RAF, 1944–48. Foreign Office, 1949; Salonika, 1949; British Middle East Office, 1952; Vice-Consul, Basra, 1953; FO, 1955; Second Secretary, Beirut, 1956; FO, 1958; First Secretary, Amman, 1959. Recreations: railways (GWR), birdwatching, photography. Address: c/o Royal Bank of Scotland, Kirkland House, Whitehall, SW1.

WHITTAM, Prof. Ronald, FRS 1973; Emeritus Professor, Leicester University, since 1983 (Professor of Physiology, 1966–83); b 21 March 1925; e s of Edward Whittam and May Whittam (née Butterworth), Oldham, Lancs; m 1957, Christine Patricia Margaret, 2nd d of Canon J. W. Lamb; one s one d. Educ: Council and Technical Schools, Oldham; Univs of Manchester and Sheffield and King's College, Cambridge. BSc 1st Class Hons (Manchester); PhD (Sheffield and Cambridge); MA (Oxon). Served RAF, 1943–47. John Stokes Fellow, Dept of Biochem., Univ. of Sheffield, 1953–55; Beit Memorial Fellow, Physiological Lab., Cambridge, 1955–58; Mem. Scientific Staff, MRC Cell Metabolism Research Unit, Oxford, 1958–60; Univ. Lectr in Biochemistry, Oxford, 1960–66; Bruno Mendel Fellow of Royal Society, 1965–66; Dean of Fac. of Science, Leicester Univ., 1979–82. Mem. Editorial Bd of Biochem. Jl, 1963–67; Hon. Sec., 1969–74, Hon. Mem., 1986, Physiological Soc.; Mem. Biological Research Bd of MRC, 1971–74, Co-Chm., 1973–74; Member: Biological Sciences Cttee, UGC, 1974–82; Educn Cttee, Royal Soc., 1979–83; Chm., Biological Educn Cttee, Royal Soc. and Inst Biol., 1974–77. Foundn Governor, St Thomas More Sch., Leicester, 1989–. Publications: Transport and Diffusion in Red Blood Cells, 1964; scientific papers dealing with cell membranes. Recreation: walking. Address: 9 Guilford Road, Leicester LE2 2RD. T: Leicester (0533) 707132.

WHITTAM SMITH, Andreas; Editor, since 1986, and Chief Executive, since 1987, The Independent; b 13 June 1937; s of Canon J. E. Smith and Mrs Smith (née Barlow); m 1964, Valerie Catherine, d of late Wing Comdr J. A. Sherry and of Mrs N. W. H. Wyllys; two s. Educ: Birkenhead Sch., Cheshire; Keble Coll., Oxford (BA) (Hon. Fellow, 1987). With N. M. Rothschild, 1960–62; Stock Exchange Gazette, 1962–63; Financial Times, 1963–64; The Times, 1964–66; Dep. City Editor, Daily Telegraph, 1966–69; City Editor, The Guardian, 1969–70; Editor, Investors Chronicle and Stock Exchange Gazette, and Dir, Throgmorton Publications, 1970–77; City Editor, Daily Telegraph, 1977–85; Dir, Newspaper Publishing PLC, 1986–. Hon. Fellow, UMIST, 1989. Wincott award, 1975; Journalist of the Year, British Press Awards, 1987; Editor of the Year, Granada TV What the Papers Say award, 1989. Recreations: music, history. Address: 40 City Road, EC1Y 2DB. Club: Garrick.

WHITTELL, James Michael Scott, OBE 1984; British Council Director (formerly Representative), Nigeria, since 1989; b 17 Feb. 1939; s of late Edward Arthur Whittell and Helen Elizabeth Whittell (née Scott); m 1962, Eleanor Jane Carling; three s. Educ: Gresham's School, Holt; Magdalen College, Oxford (MA, BSc); Manchester Univ. Teaching, Sherborne School, 1962–68, Nairobi School, 1968–72; British Council: Ibadan, Nigeria, 1973–76; Enugu, Nigeria, 1976–78; Director General's Dept, 1978–81; Rep., Algiers, 1981–85; Sec. to the British Council and Head of Dir Gen's Dept, 1985–88. Recreations: walking, mountaineering, books, music. Address: British Council, 10 Spring Gardens, SW1A 2BN. Clubs: Travellers', Alpine.

WHITTEMORE, Ernest William, MM 1944 and Bar 1945; Under-Secretary, Department of Health and Social Security, 1973–76; b 31 Aug. 1916; s of late Ernest William Whittemore and Hilda Whittemore; m 1942, Irene Mollie Hudson; two d. Educ: Raine's Sch., Stepney; King's Coll., London. BA Hons English. Receiver's Office, New Scotland Yard, 1934–35; Min. of Health, 1935–45; Royal Artillery, 1942–46; Min. of Nat. Insce (and successor depts), 1945–76. Recreations: bibliomania, travel, sweet peas. Address: 39 Montalt Road, Woodford Green, Essex IG8 9RS. T: 081–504 7028.

WHITTERIDGE, Prof. David, FRS 1953; FRSE 1951; Waynflete Professor of Physiology, University of Oxford, 1968–79, now Emeritus Professor; *b* 22 June 1912; 2nd *s* of Walter and late Jeanne Whitteridge; *m* 1938, Gweneth, Hon. FRCP, *d* of S. Hutchings; three *d*. *Educ*: Whitgift School, Croydon; Magdalen College, Oxford (1st cl. Physiology Finals, 1934); King's College Hospital. BSc 1936; BM, BCh 1937; DM 1945; FRCP 1966. Beit Memorial Fellowship, 1940; Schorstein Research Fellow, 1944; Fellow by Special Election, Magdalen College, Oxford, 1945–50; University Demonstrator in Physiology, Univ. of Oxford, 1944–50; Prof. of Physiology, Univ. of Edinburgh, 1950–68. Fellow of Magdalen Coll., Oxford, 1968–79, Hon. Fellow, 1979. Leverhulme Vis. Prof., Univ. Delhi, 1967 and 1973; Lectures: Sherrington, RSM, 1972; Victor Horsley Meml, BMA, 1972; Bowman, OSUK, 1977; Bayliss Starling, Physiolog. Soc., 1979; G. Parr Meml, EEG Soc., 1980; K. N. Seneviratue Meml Oration, Physiol Soc. of Sri Lanka, 1987. Mem. Bd of Trustees, Nat. Lib. of Scotland, 1966–70. Physiological Society: Sec., 1947–51; Foreign Sec., 1980–86; Hon. Mem., 1982. Vice-Pres., RSE, 1956–59. Hon. Mem., Assoc. of British Neurologists, 1984; Foreign FNA, 1982. Feldberg Prize, Feldberg Foundn, 1962. *Publications*: One hundred years of Congresses of Physiology, 1989; papers on physiological topics in Jl Physiol., Brain, etc. *Address*: Winterslow, Lincombe Lane, Boar's Hill, Oxford OX1 5DZ. *T*: Oxford (0865) 735211.
    See also R. A. Furtado, Sir G. C. Whitteridge.

WHITTERIDGE, Sir Gordon (Coligny), KCMG 1964 (CMG 1956); OBE 1946; HM Diplomatic Service, retired; *b* 6 Nov. 1908; *s* of late Walter Randall and Jeanne Whitteridge, Croydon; *m* 1st, 1938, Margaret Lungley (*d* 1942; one *s* one *d* decd 1942); 2nd, 1951, Jane (*d* 1979), twin *d* of Frederick J. Driscoll, Brookline, Mass, USA; one *s*; 3rd, 1983, Mrs Jill Stanley (*née* Belcham). *Educ*: Whitgift School, Croydon; Fitzwilliam Coll., Cambridge. Joined Consular Service, 1932; one of HM Vice-Consuls, Siam, 1933; Vice-Consul, Batavia, 1936; Acting Consul, Batavia, 1937, 1938, and 1939; Acting Consul, Medan, Sept. 1941–Feb. 1942. Employed at Foreign Office from June, 1942; promoted Consul (Grade II), Foreign Office, 1944, Consul, 1945. 1st Secretary, Moscow, 1948–49; Consul-General Stuttgart, 1949–51; Counsellor/Consul-Gen., 1950; Counsellor, Bangkok, 1951–56 (Chargé d'Affaires in 1952, 1953, 1954, 1955); Consul-Gen., Seattle, Wash., 1956–60; HM Consul-General, Istanbul, 1960–62; Ambassador: to Burma, 1962–65; to Afghanistan, 1965–68; retired, 1968. Chm., Anglo-Thai Soc., 1971–76; Hon. Treasurer: Soc. for Afghan Studies, 1972–83; Soc. for S Asian Studies, 1983–85. (Lay) Mem., Immigration Appeal Tribunal, 1970–81. *Publication*: Charles Masson of Afghanistan, 1986. *Recreations*: music, history. *Address*: Stonebank, Blighton Lane, The Sands, near Farnham, Surrey GU10 1PU. *Club*: Travellers'.
    See also R. A. Furtado, Prof. D. Whitteridge.

WHITTICK, Richard James; Assistant Under-Secretary of State, Home Office, 1967–72; *b* 21 August 1912; *s* of Ernest G. Whittick and Grace M. Shaw; *m* 1938, Elizabeth Mason; two *s*. *Educ*: George Heriot's School; Edinburgh University. British Museum (Natural History), 1936; Home Office, 1940; Principal Private Secretary to Home Secretary, 1952–53; Assistant Secretary, 1953. *Recreations*: gardening, photography (FRPS 1988). *Address*: Coombe Cottage, Coombe, Sherborne, Dorset DT9 4BX. *T*: Sherborne (0935) 814488.

WHITTINGDALE, John Flasby Lawrance, OBE 1990; Private Secretary to Rt Hon. Margaret Thetcher, since 1990; *b* 16 Oct. 1959; *s* of John Whittingdale and Margaret Esmé Scott Napier; *m* 1990, Ancilla Campbell Murfitt. *Educ*: Sandroyd Sch.; Winchester Coll.; University Coll. London (BScEcon). Head of Political Section, Conservative Research Dept, 1982–84; Special Adviser to Sec. of State for Trade and Industry, 1984–87; Manager, N. M. Rothschild & Sons, 1987; Political Sec. to the Prime Minister, 1988–90. *Recreations*: cinema, music. *Club*: Reform.

WHITTINGHAM, Charles Percival, BA, PhD Cantab; Head of Department of Botany, Rothamsted Experimental Station, 1971–82; *b* 1922; *m* 1946, Alison Phillips; two *d*. *Educ*: St John's College, Cambridge. Professor of Botany, London University, at Queen Mary College, 1958–64; Head of Dept of Botany, 1967–71, and Prof. of Plant Physiology, 1964–71, Imperial Coll., Univ of London; Dean, Royal Coll. of Science, 1969–71; Hon. Dir, ARC Unit for Plant Physiology, 1964–71. Vis. Prof., Univ. of Nottingham, 1978. *Publications*: Chemistry of Plant Processes, 1964; (with R. Hill) Photosynthesis, 1955; The Mechanism of Photosynthesis, 1974; contrib. to scientific journals. *Recreations*: music, travel. *Address*: Red Cottage, The Green, Brisley, Dereham, Norfolk.

WHITTINGTON, Charles Richard, MC 1944; Chamberlain of London, 1964–1973; *b* 8 March 1908; *er s* of late Charles Henry Whittington, Stock Exchange, and Vera Whittington; *m* 1938, Helen Irene Minnie (*d* 1990), *d* of late Lieutenant-Colonel J. E. Hance, RHA; one *s* four *d*. *Educ*: Uppingham School. Served War of 1939–45. Member of The Stock Exchange, London, 1931–64. Liveryman Mercers' Company, 1931; Mem. of Court of Common Council for Ward of Broad Street, 1939–64; one of HM Lieutenants, City of London, 1964–73. *Recreation*: gardening. *Address*: Wood Cottage, Brampton Bryan, Bucknell, Salop SY7 0DH. *T*: Bucknell (05474) 291.

WHITTINGTON, Prof. Geoffrey; Price Waterhouse Professor of Financial Accounting, since 1988, Fellow of Fitzwilliam College, 1966–72 and since 1988, Cambridge University; *b* 21 Sept. 1938; *s* of Bruce Whittington and Dorothy Gwendoline Whittington (*née* Gent); *m* 1963, Joyce Enid Smith; two *s*. *Educ*: Dudley Grammar Sch.; LSE (Leverhulme Schol.; BSc Econ). MA, PhD Cantab. FCA. Chartered Accountancy training, 1959–62; research posts, Dept of Applied Econ., Cambridge, 1962–72; Dir of Studies in Econs, Fitzwilliam Coll., Cambridge, 1967–72; Prof. of Accountancy and Finance, Edinburgh Univ., 1972–75; University of Bristol: Prof. of Accounting and Finance, 1975–88; Head of Dept of Econs, 1981–84; Dean, Faculty of Social Scis, 1985–87. Part-time Econ. Adviser, OFT, 1977–83; part-time Mem., Monopolies and Mergers Commn, 1987–; Academic Advr, Accounting Standards Bd, 1990–. *Publications*: Growth, Profitability and Valuation (with A. Singh), 1968; The Prediction of Profitability, 1971; Inflation Accounting, 1983; (with D. P. Tweedie) The Debate on Inflation Accounting, 1984; (ed jtly) Readings in the Concept and Measurement of Income, 1986; contribs to jls and books in accounting, economics and finance. *Recreations*: music, squash, badminton, walking, usual academic pursuits of reading my own books and laughing at my own jokes. *Address*: Faculty of Economics and Politics, Sidgwick Avenue, Cambridge CB3 9DD. *T*: Cambridge (0223) 335200.

WHITTINGTON, Prof. Harry Blackmore, FRS 1971; Woodwardian Professor of Geology, Cambridge University, 1966–83; *b* 24 March 1916; *s* of Harry Whittington and Edith M. (*née* Blackmore); *m* 1940, Dorothy E. Arnold; no *c*. *Educ*: Handsworth Gram. Sch.; Birmingham University. Commonwealth Fund Fellow, Yale Univ., 1938–40; Lectr in Geology, Judson Coll., Rangoon, 1940–42; Prof. of Geography, Ginling Coll., Chengtu, W China, 1943–45; Lectr in Geology, Birmingham Univ., 1945–49; Harvard Univ.: Vis. Lectr, 1949–50; Assoc. Prof. of Geology, 1950–58; Prof. of Geology, 1958–66. Trustee: British Museum (Nat. History), 1980–89; Uppingham Sch., 1983–91. Hon. Fellow, Geol Soc. of America, 1983. Hon. AM, Harvard Univ., 1950. Medal, Paleontol Soc., USA, 1983; Lyell Medal, Geological Soc., 1986; Mary Clark Thompson Medal, US Nat. Acad of Scis, 1990. *Publications*: The Burgess Shale, 1985; articles in Jl of Paleontology, Bulletin Geol. Soc. of Amer., Quarterly Jl Geol. Soc. London, Phil. Trans. Royal Soc., etc. *Address*: 20 Rutherford Road, Cambridge CB2 2HH. *Club*: Geological.

WHITTINGTON, Joseph Basil, OBE 1981; HM Diplomatic Service, retired; HM Consul-General, Rotterdam, 1977–80; *b* 24 Oct. 1921; *s* of Joseph and Margaret Whittington; *m* 1947, Hazel Joan Rushton; two *s* one *d*. *Educ*: Cotton Coll., North Staffs; St Philip's Grammar Sch., Birmingham. Post Office, 1938–48. Served Army, 1940–46; Captain, Royal Artillery. Regional Boards for Industry, 1948–52; Bd of Trade, 1952–64; Asst Trade Commissioner, Jamaica, 1953–55; Bahamas and Bermuda, 1955–57 and Jamaica, 1957–58; Trade Commissioner, Johannesburg, 1958–62 and Toronto, 1963–67; transf. to Diplomatic Service, 1964; Head of Chancery, First Sec. (Commercial) and Consul, Liberia, 1968–70; First Sec. (Economic/Commercial), Zambia, 1970–73 and Malta, 1974–77. *Recreations*: gardening, golf, walking. *Address*: Heathcote, Darlington Road, Bath BA2 6NL. *T*: Bath (0225) 461697.

WHITTINGTON, Thomas Alan, CB 1977; TD 1986; Circuit Administrator, North Eastern Circuit, 1974–81; *b* 15 May 1916; *o s* of late George Whittington, JP and Mary Elizabeth Whittington; *m* 1939, Audrey Elizabeth, *y d* of late Craven Gilpin, Leeds; four *s*. *Educ*: Uppingham Sch.; Leeds Univ. (LLB). Commnd W Yorks Regt (Leeds Rifles) TA, 1937, serving War of 1939–45 in UK and 14th Army in India (Major). Solicitor of Supreme Court, 1945; Clerk of the Peace, Leeds, 1952–70; Senior Partner, Marklands, Solicitors, Leeds, 1967–70, Consultant, 1981–; Under-Sec., Lord Chancellor's Office, 1970; Circuit Administrator, Northern Circuit, 1970–74. *Recreations*: fishing, gardening. *Address*: The Cottage, School Lane, Collingham, Wetherby LS22 5BQ. *T*: Collingham Bridge (0937) 573881.

WHITTINGTON-SMITH, Marianne Christine, (Mrs C. A. Whittington-Smith); *see* Lutz, M. C.

WHITTLE, Air Cdre Sir Frank, OM 1986; KBE 1948 (CBE 1944); CB 1947; Comdr, US Legion of Merit, 1946; RDI 1985; FRS 1947; FEng; MA Cantab; RAF, retired; *b* 1 June 1907; *s* of M. Whittle; *m* 1930, Dorothy Mary Lee (marr. diss. 1976); two *s*; *m* 1976, Hazel S. Hall. *Educ*: Leamington Coll.; No 4 Apprentices' Wing, RAF Cranwell; RAF Coll., Cranwell; Peterhouse, Cambridge (Mechanical Sciences Tripos, BA 1st Cl. Hons). No 4 Apprentices' Wing, RAF Cranwell, 1923–26; Flight Cadet, RAF Coll., Cranwell, 1926–28 (Abdy-Gerrard-Fellowes Memorial Prize); Pilot Officer, 111 (Fighter) Sqdn, 1928–29; Flying Instructors' Course, Central Flying Sch., 1929; Flying Instructor, No 2 Flying Training Sch., RAF Digby, 1930; Test Pilot, Marine Aircraft Experimental Estab., RAF Felixstowe, 1931–32; RAF Sch. of Aeronautical Engrg, Henlow, 1932–34; Officer i/c Engine Test, Engine Repair Section, Henlow, 1934 (6 mths); Cambridge Univ., 1934–37 (Post-Graduate year, 1936–37); Special Duty List, attached Power Jets Ltd for develt of aircraft gas turbine for jet propulsion, 1937–46; War Course, RAF Staff Coll., 1943; Technical Adviser to Controller of Supplies (Air), Min. of Supply, 1946–48; retd RAF, 1948. Hon. Technical Adviser: Jet Aircraft, BOAC, 1948–52; Shell Gp, 1953–57; Consultant, Bristol Siddeley Engines/Rolls Royce on turbo drill project, 1961–70. Mem. Faculty, US Naval Acad., Annapolis, Maryland, 1977–. Partnered late Flt-Lt G. E. Campbell in Crazy Flying RAF Display, Hendon, 1930; 1st flights of Gloster jet-propelled aeroplane with Whittle engine, May 1941. Freeman of Royal Leamington Spa, 1944. Hon. FRAeS; Hon. FAeSI; Hon. FIMechE; Founder Fellow, Fellowship of Engineering, 1976. Hon. Mem., Franklin Inst.; Hon. FAIAA; Hon. Mem., Société Royale Belge des Ingénieurs; Hon. Foreign Mem., Amer. Acad. Arts and Scis, 1976; For. Assoc., US Nat. Acad. of Engrg, 1978; Hon. Fellow, Soc. of Experimental Test Pilots, USA; Hon. MEIC. Hon. Fellow, Peterhouse. Hon. DSc: Oxon; Manchester; Leicester; Bath; Warwick; Exeter; Cranfield Inst. of Technology, 1987; Hon. LLD Edinburgh; Hon. ScD Cantab; Hon. DTech: Trondheim; Loughborough, 1987. James Alfred Ewing Medal, ICE, 1944; Gold Medal, RAeS, 1944; James Clayton Prize, IMechE, 1946; Daniel Guggenheim Medal, USA, 1946; Kelvin Gold Medal, 1947; Melchett Medal, 1949; Rumford Medal, Royal Soc., 1950; Gold Medal, Fedn Aeronautique Internat., 1951; Churchill Gold Medal, Soc. of Engineers, 1952; Albert Gold Medal, Soc. of Arts, 1952; Franklin Medal, USA, 1956; John Scott Award, 1957; Goddard Award, USA, 1965; Coventry Award of Merit, 1966; International Communications (Christopher Columbus) Prize, City of Genoa, 1966; Tony Jannus Award, Greater Tampa Chamber of Commerce, 1969; James Watt Internat. Gold Medal, IMechE, 1977; Nat. Air and Space Mus. Trophy, 1986; (first) Prince Philip Medal, Fellowship of Engrg, 1991. *Publications*: Jet, 1953; Gas Turbine Aero-Thermodynamics, 1981. *Clubs*: Royal Air Force; Wings (New York).

WHITTLE, Kenneth Francis, CBE 1987; CEng, FIEE; Chairman, South Western Electricity Board, 1977–87; *b* 28 April 1922; *s* of Thomas Whittle and May Whittle; *m* 1945, Dorothy Inskip; one *s* one *d*. *Educ*: Kingswood Sch., Bath; Faculty of Technol., Manchester Univ. (BScTech). Served War, Electrical Lieut, RNVR, 1943–46. Metropolitan Vickers Elec. Co. Ltd, 1946–48; NW Div., CEGB, 1948–55; North West Electricity Board: various posts, 1955–64; Area Commercial Officer, Blackburn, 1964–69; Manager, Peak Area, 1969–71; Manager, Manchester Area, 1971–74; Chief Commercial Officer, 1974–75; Dep. Chm., Yorks Elec. Bd, 1975–77. Chairman: British Electrotechnical Approvals Bd, 1985–; British Approvals Bd for Telecommunications, 1985–. *Recreation*: golf. *Address*: 8 Cambridge Road, Clevedon, Avon BS21 7HX. *T*: Clevedon (0272) 874017.

WHITTLE, Prof. Peter, FRS 1978; Churchill Professor of Mathematics of Operational Research, University of Cambridge, since 1967; Senior Fellow, Science and Engineering Research Council, since 1988; *b* 27 Feb. 1927; *s* of Percy Whittle and Elsie Tregurtha; *m* 1951, Käthe Hildegard Blomquist; three *s* three *d*. *Educ*: Wellington Coll., New Zealand. Docent, Uppsala Univ., 1951–53; employed New Zealand DSIR, 1953–59, rising to Senior Principal Scientifc Officer; Lectr, Univ. of Cambridge, 1959–61; Prof. of Mathematical Statistics, Univ. of Manchester, 1961–67. Mem., Royal Soc. of NZ, 1981–. Hon. DSc Victoria Univ. of Wellington, NZ, 1987. *Publications*: Hypothesis Testing in Time Series Analysis, 1951; Prediction and Regulation, 1963; Probability, 1970; Optimisation under Constraints, 1971; Optimisation over Time, 1982; Systems in Stochastic Equilibrium, 1986; Risk-sensitive Optimal Control, 1990; contribs to Jl Roy. Statistical Soc., Proc. Roy. Soc., Jl Stat. Phys, Systems and Control Letters. *Recreation*: house maintenance. *Address*: 268 Queen Edith's Way, Cambridge; Statistical Laboratory, University of Cambridge.

WHITTLE, Stephen Charles; Head of Religious Programmes, BBC Television, since 1989; *b* 26 July 1945; *s* of Charles William Whittle and Vera Lillian Whittle (*née* Moss); *m* 1988, Claire Walmsley. *Educ*: St Ignatius College, Stamford Hill; University College London (LLB Hons). Asst Editor, New Christian, 1968–70; Communications Officer, World Council of Churches, Geneva, 1970–73; Editor, One World, WCC, 1973–77; Asst Head, Communications Dept, WCC, 1975–77; BBC: Sen. Producer, Religious Programmes, Manchester, 1977–82; Producer, Newsnight, 1982; Editor, Songs of Praise and Worship, 1983–89. Freeman, City of London, 1990. *Publications*: Tickling Mrs Smith, 1970; contribs to One World and The Tablet. *Recreations*: cinema, theatre, music, reading, exercise. *Address*: BBC Television Centre, Wood Lane, W12 7RJ. *T*: 081–576 7589.

WHITTOME, Sir (Leslie) Alan, Kt 1991; *b* 18 Jan. 1926; *s* of Leslie Whittome and Beryl Treherne-Thomas; *m* 1984, Duncan Eleanor Woods Moose Ripley; two *d* by previous marr. *Educ*: Marlborough Coll.; Pembroke Coll., Cambridge (MA). Capt., RAC, 1944–48. Bank of England, 1951–64; Dep. Chief Cashier; International Monetary Fund: Dir, European Dept, 1964–86; Dir, ETR, 1986–90; Special Advr to Man. Dir, 1990–91. *Address*: Box 108, RR2, Lovettsville, Va 22080, USA. *T*: (703) 822 9030.

WHITTON, Cuthbert Henry; *b* 18 Feb. 1905; *s* of Henry and Eleanor Whitton; *m* 1938, Iris Elva Moody; one *d*. *Educ*: St Andrew's College, Dublin; Dublin University. Malayan Civil Service, 1929; Colonial Legal Service, 1939; Puisne Judge, Federation of Malaya, 1951; Puisne Judge, Supreme Court, Singapore, 1954; Foreign Compensation Commn, Legal Dept, 1959–71. *Recreations*: golf, gardening. *Address*: 5 Marsham Lodge, Marsham Lane, Gerrards Cross, Bucks SL9 7AB. *T*: Gerrards Cross (0753) 885608. *Clubs*: Commonwealth Trust; Kildare Street and University (Dublin).

WHITTON, Prof. Peter William; Deputy Vice-Chancellor, University of Melbourne, 1979–84, retired; *b* 2 Sept. 1925; *s* of William Whitton and Rosa Bungay; *m* 1950, Mary Katharine White; two *s* three *d*. *Educ*: Latymer Upper Sch., London; Southampton Univ. (BScEng); Imperial College of Science and Technology, London (DIC, PhD); ME Melbourne 1965. FIE(Aust). Engineering Cadet, English Electric Co., Preston, 1942–46; Wireless Officer, Royal Signals, Catterick and Singapore, 1946–48; Sen. Lectr in Mech. Engrg, Univ. of Melbourne, 1953–56; Head, Engrg Sect., ICI Metals Div. Research Dept, Birmingham, 1956–60; Foundation Prof. and Dean, Faculty of Engrg, Univ. of the West Indies, 1960–64; University of Melbourne: Prof. of Mech. Engrg, 1965–77, Emeritus Prof., 1977–; Dean, Faculty of Engrg, 1966; Principal, Royal Melbourne Inst. of Technology, 1977–78. *Publications*: various papers on metal forming, in Proc. IMechE, London, and Jl of Inst. of Metals, London. *Recreations*: reading, golf. *Address*: 425 Beach Road, Beaumaris, Victoria 3193, Australia.

WHITTUCK, Gerald Saumarez, CB 1959; *b* 13 Oct. 1912; *s* of late Francis Gerald Whittuck; *m* 1938, Catherine McCrea; two *s*. *Educ*: Cheltenham; Clare Coll., Cambridge. Air Ministry, 1935; Private Secretary to Secretary of State, 1944–46; Asst Under-Secretary of State: Air Ministry, 1955–63; War Office, 1963–64; MoD, 1964–71; Dir, Greenwich Hosp., 1971–74. Mem., Royal Patriotic Fund Corp., 1971–74. *Address*: 15A Greenaway Gardens, NW3 7DH. *T*: 071–435 3742.

WHITTY, John Lawrence; General Secretary, Labour Party, since 1985; *b* 15 June 1943; *s* of Frederick James and Kathleen May Whitty; *m* 1969, Tanya Margaret (marr. diss. 1986); two *s*. *Educ*: Latymer Upper School; St John's College, Cambridge (BA Hons Economics). Hawker Siddeley Aviation, 1960–62; Min. of Aviation Technology, 1965–70; Trades Union Congress, 1970–73; General, Municipal, Boilermakers and Allied Trade Union (formerly GMWU), 1973–85. *Recreations*: theatre, cinema, swimming. *Address*: 94 Broomwood Road, SW11 6LA. *T*: 071–228 8412.

WHITWAM, Derek Firth, CEng, FRINA; RCNC; quality engineering consultant, since 1988; *b* 7 Dec. 1932; *s* of Hilton and Marion Whitwam; *m* 1954, Pamela May (*née* Lander); one *s* one *d*. *Educ*: Royds Hall Sch., Huddersfield; Royal Naval Coll., Dartmouth; Royal Naval Engineering Coll., Manadon; Royal Naval Coll., Greenwich. Work on ship design, MoD (N) Bath, 1957–65; Rosyth Dockyard, 1965–68; Singapore Dockyard, 1968–70; DG Ships Bath, 1970–77; RCDS 1978; Production Manager, Rosyth Dockyard, 1979–80; Gen. Manager, Portsmouth Dockyard, 1981–84; Principal Dir of Planning and Policy, Chief Exec. Royal Dockyards, 1984–85; Dir of Quality Assurance, MoD, 1985–88. *Publications*: papers for Trans Royal Inst. of Naval Architects. *Recreations*: golf, music, walking. *Address*: 10 Woodlands Park, Lower Swainswick, Bath BA1 7BQ.

WHITWELL, Stephen John, CMG 1969; MC; HM Diplomatic Service, retired; *b* 30 July 1920; *s* of Arthur Percy Whitwell and Marion Whitwell (*née* Greenwood). *Educ*: Stowe; Christ Church, Oxford. Coldstream Guards, 1941–47; joined HM Foreign Service (now Diplomatic Service), 1947; served: Tehran, 1947; FO, 1949; Belgrade, 1952; New Delhi, 1954; FO, 1958; Seoul, 1961. Polit. Adv. to C-in-C Middle East, Aden, 1964; Counsellor, Belgrade, 1965; Ambassador to Somalia, 1968–70; Head of East-West Contacts Dept, FCO, 1970–71. *Recreations*: reading, painting, looking at buildings. *Address*: Jervis Cottage, Aston Tirrold, Oxon. *Club*: Travellers'.

WHITWORTH, Francis John; Chairman, Merchant Navy Officers' Pension Fund Trustees, since 1987; Member, Economic and Social Committee of the European Communities, since 1986; *b* 1 May 1925; *s* of late Captain Herbert Francis Whitworth, OBE, RNVR, and Helen Marguerite Whitworth (*née* Tait); *m* 1956, Auriol Myfanwy Medwyn Hughes; one *s* one *d*. *Educ*: Charterhouse (Jun. Schol.); Pembroke Coll., Oxford (Holford Schol.; MA Jurisprudence 1949). FBIM 1980 (MBIM 1967). Served War, Royal Marines, 1943–46. Called to Bar, Middle Temple, 1950. Joined Cunard Steam-Ship Co., 1950; Personnel Director, 1965, Managing Dir Cunard Line, 1968, Group Admin Dir, 1969; joined British Shipping Fedn as Dep. Dir, Industrial Relations, 1972; Dep. Dir-Gen., Gen. Council of British Shipping, 1980–87; Dir, Internat. Shipping Fedn, 1980–88; Mem., Nat. Maritime Bd, 1962–87. Chairman: Internat. Cttee of Passenger Lines, 1968–71; Atlantic Passenger Steamship Conf., 1970–71; Employers' Gp, Jt Maritime Commn of ILO, 1980–88; Employers' Gp, Internat. Maritime (Labour) Conf. of ILO, 1986–87; Social Affairs Cttee, Comité des Assocs d'Armateurs des Communautés Européennes, 1983–88; Nat. Sea Training Schs, 1980–87; Member: Industrial Tribunals for England and Wales, 1978–; Council, Marine Soc., 1988–; Council, Missions to Seamen, 1988–. *Recreations*: racing, opera, music, cricket. *Address*: The Old School House, Farley Chamberlayne, Romsey, Hants SO51 0QR. *T*: Braishfield (0794) 68538. *Club*: United Oxford & Cambridge University.

WHITWORTH, Group Captain Frank, QC 1965; a Recorder of the Crown Court, 1972–82; *b* 13 May 1910; *o s* of late Daniel Arthur Whitworth, Didsbury, Manchester; *m* 1st, 1939, Mary Lucy (*d* 1979), *o d* of late Sir John Holdsworth Robinson, JP, Bingley, Yorks; no *c*; 2nd, 1980, Mrs Irene Lannon (*d* 1991). *Educ*: Shrewsbury Sch.; Trinity Hall, Cambridge. Served with RAFVR (Special Duties), 1940–45, retired. Called to Bar, Gray's Inn, 1934. Member of Dorking and Horley RDC, 1939–68. Contested (C) St Helens, 1945. Judge of Courts of Appeal of Jersey and Guernsey, 1971–80. Master, Clockmakers' Co., 1962 and 1971. Trustee, Whiteley Village Homes, 1963. *Publications*: miscellaneous verse and articles. *Recreation*: farming. *Address*: Little Manor House, Westcott, near Dorking, Surrey. *T*: Dorking (0306) 889966; 13 King's Bench Walk, Temple, EC4. *T*: 071–353 7204. *Club*: United Oxford & Cambridge University.

WHITWORTH, Hugh Hope Aston, MBE 1945; Lay Assistant to the Archbishop of Canterbury, 1969–78; *b* 21 May 1914; *s* of Sidney Alexander Whitworth and Elsie Hope Aston; *m* 1st, 1944, Elizabeth Jean Boyes (*d* 1961); two *s* one *d*; 2nd, 1961, Catherine Helen Bell (*d* 1986). *Educ*: Bromsgrove Sch.; Pembroke Coll., Cambridge (BA). Indian Civil Service, Bombay Province, 1937–47; Administrator, Ahmedabad Municipality, 1942–44; Collector and District Magistrate, Nasik, 1945–46; Board of Trade, 1947–55;

Scottish Home Dept, 1955; Asst Sec., 1957; Under-Sec., Scottish Home and Health Dept, 1968–69. *Recreations*: travel, gardening. *Address*: 47 Orford Gardens, Strawberry Hill, Twickenham, Mddx TW1 4PL. *T*: 081–892 4672. *Club*: Commonwealth Trust.

WHITWORTH, Maj.-Gen. Reginald Henry, CB 1969; CBE 1963; MA; *b* 27 Aug. 1916; 2nd *s* of late Aymer William Whitworth and late Alice (*née* Hervey), Eton College; *m* 1946, June Rachel, *o d* of late Sir Bartle Edwards, CVO, MC, and of Daphne, MBE, *d* of late Sir Cyril Kendall Butler, KBE; two *s* one *d*. *Educ*: Eton; Balliol College, Oxford, 1st cl. Hons, Modern History, 1938; Laming Travelling Fellow, Queen's Coll., Oxford, 1938–39. 2nd Lt Grenadier Guards, 1940; War Service in N Africa and Italy, 1943–45; GSO2, 78 Division, 1944; Bde Major, 24 Guards Brigade, 1945–46; GSO2, Staff College, Camberley, 1953–55; comdg 1st Bn Grenadier Guards, 1956–57; GSO1, SHAPE, 1958–59; Sen. Army Instructor, JSSC, 1959–61; Comdr Berlin Infantry Bde Gp, 1961–63; DMS 1, Ministry of Defence, 1964–66; GOC: Yorkshire District, 1966–67; Northumbrian District, 1967–68; Chief of Staff, Southern Command, 1968–70. Bursar and Official Fellow, Exeter College, Oxford, 1970–81. Gov., St Mary's, Wantage (Chm.). Chm., Army Museums Ogilby Trust; Trustee, Historic Churches Preservation Trust. Bronze Star, USA, 1945. *Publications*: Field Marshal Earl Ligonier, 1958; Famous Regiments: the Grenadier Guards, 1974; Gunner at Large, 1988. *Recreations*: riding, fishing, military history. *Address*: Abbey Farm, Goosey, Faringdon, Oxon SN7 8PA. *T*: Faringdon (0367) 710252. *Club*: Army and Navy.

WHITWORTH-JONES, Anthony; General Director (formerly General Administrator), Glyndebourne Festival Opera, since 1989; *b* 1 Sept. 1945; *s* of Henry Whitworth-Jones and Patience Martin; *m* 1974, Camilla (*née* Barlow); one *d*. *Educ*: Wellington College. Mem., Inst. of Chartered Accountants of Scotland. Thomson McLintock & Co., 1970–72; Administrative Dir, London Sinfonietta, 1972–81; Administrator, Glyndebourne Touring Opera and Opera Manager, Glyndebourne Festival Opera, 1981–89. *Recreations*: enjoying the spirit and countryside of Wales, listening to music other than opera, contemporary art, golf. *Address*: 81 St Augustine's Road, NW1 9RR. *T*: 071–485 6736.

WHYBREW, Edward Graham, (Ted); Director, Personnel and Staff Development, Employment Department Group, since 1989; *b* 25 Sept. 1938; *s* of Ernest Whybrew and Winifred (*née* Castle); *m* 1967, Julia Helen Baird; one *s* two *d*. *Educ*: Hertford Grammar Sch.; Balliol Coll., Oxford (BA 1961); Nuffield Coll., Oxford. Economist: NEDO, 1963; DEA, 1964–69; Dept of Employment, 1969–77; Asst Sec., Employment, Trng and Industrial Relations, 1977–85, Under Sec., Industrial Relations Div., 1985–89, Dept of Employment. *Publication*: Overtime Working in Great Britain, 1968. *Recreations*: cricket, horse riding, gardening.

WHYTE, Very Rev. James Aitken; Moderator of the General Assembly of the Church of Scotland, 1988–89; Professor of Practical Theology and Christian Ethics, University of St Andrews, 1958–87; *b* 28 Jan. 1920; 2nd *s* of late Andrew Whyte, Leith, and late Barbara Janet Pittillo Aitken; *m* 1942, Elisabeth (*d* 1988), *er d* of Rev. G. S. Mill, MA, BSc, Kalimpong, India; two *s* one *d*. *Educ*: Daniel Stewart's Coll., Edinburgh; University of Edinburgh (Arts and Divinity), MA 1st Cl. Hons Phil., 1942. Ordained, 1945; Chaplain to the Forces, 1945–48; Minister of: Dunollie Road, Oban, 1948–54; Mayfield, Edinburgh, 1954–58. St Andrews University: Dean, Faculty of Divinity, 1968–72; Principal, St Mary's Coll., 1978–82. Guest Lectr, Inst. for the Study of Worship and Religious Architecture, Birmingham, 1965–66; Lectures: Kerr, Univ. of Glasgow, 1969–72; Croall, Univ. of Edinburgh, 1972–73; Margaret Harris, Univ. of Dundee, 1990. Pres., Soc. for Study of Theol., 1983–84. Hon. LLD Dundee, 1981; Hon DD St Andrews, 1989. *Publications*: (ed jtly) Worship Now: Vol. 1, 1972, Vol. 2, 1989; contributor to various dictionaries, composite volumes, journals, etc. *Address*: 13 Hope Street, St Andrews, Fife. *Club*: New (Edinburgh).

WHYTE, John Stuart, CBE 1976; MSc(Eng); FEng 1980; FIEE; CBIM; Chairman, GPT (International) Ltd, 1988–90; *b* High Wycombe, 20 July 1923; *s* of late William W. Whyte and Ethel K. Whyte; *m* 1951, E. Joan M. (*née* Budd); one *s* one *d*. *Educ*: The John Lyon Sch., Harrow; Northampton Polytechnic, London Univ. BSc(Eng) (Hons), MSc(Eng). Post Office Radio Laboratory, Castleton, Cardiff, 1949–57; PO Research Station, Dollis Hill: Sen. Exec. Engr, 1957–61; Asst Staff Engr, 1961–65. Asst Sec., HM Treasury, 1965–68; Dep. Dir of Engrg, PO, 1968–71; Dir, Operational Programming, PO, 1971–75; Dir of Purchasing and Supply, 1975–76, Sen. Dir of Develt, 1977–79, Dep. Man. Dir, 1979–81, PO Telecommunications; Engr-in-Chief, Man. Dir (major systems), and Mem. Main Bd, British Telecom, 1981–83; Dir, British Telecommunications Systems Ltd, 1979–83; Chm., Astronet Corp., 1984–85; Pres., 1984–85, Chm., 1985–86, Stromberg Carlson Corp; Chm., Plessey Telecommunications (Internat.) Ltd, 1983–85; Dep. Chm., Plessey Telecommunications and Office Systems Ltd, 1985–88. Manager, Royal Instn, 1971–74 (Vice-Pres., 1972, 1973, 1974), Mem. Cttee of Visitors, 1975–78 (Chm., 1977–78), Chm., Membership Cttee, 1975–77. Mem., Nat. Electronics Council, 1977– (Mem. Exec. Cttee, 1977–; Dep. Chm., 1980–); Mem. Council, ERA, 1977–83. President: Instn of PO Electrical Engrs, 1977–82; Instn of British Telecommunications Engrs, 1982–83 (Hon. Mem., 1984); Mem. Council, IEE, 1980–84 (Vice-Pres., 1981–84; Chm. Professional Bd, 1981–84). Governor, Internat. Council for Computer Communication, 1985–91. Liveryman, Scientific Instrument Makers' Co. Freeman, City of London, 1979. Leader, British Hinku Expedn, 1979; Pres., Assoc. of British Members of Swiss Alpine Club, 1988–90. *Publications*: various articles and papers in professional telecommunications jls. *Recreations*: mountaineering, photography, opera. *Address*: Wild Hatch, Coleshill Lane, Winchmore Hill, Amersham, Bucks HP7 0NT. *T*: Amersham (0494) 722663. *Clubs*: Alpine; Swiss Alpine (Berne).

WHYTE, (John) Stuart Scott, CB 1986; Under Secretary, Department of Health and Social Security, 1978–86; *b* 1 April 1926; *er s* of late Thomas and Mysie Scott Whyte, Sandycove, Co. Dublin; *m* 1950, Jocelyn Margaret, *o d* of late George Hawley, CBE, Edinburgh; two *s* one *d*. *Educ*: St Andrew's Coll., Dublin; Trinity Coll., Univ. of Dublin. BA 1947; LLB 1948. Asst Principal, Dept of Health for Scotland, 1948; Principal, 1955; Principal Private Sec. to Sec. of State for Scotland, 1959; Asst Sec., Scottish Develt Dept, 1962; Asst Sec., Cabinet Office, 1969; Asst Under-Sec. of State, Scottish Office, 1969–74; Under Sec., Cabinet Office, 1974–78. *Address*: 27 The Circus, Bath, Avon BA1 2EU. *T*: Bath (0225) 339612; La Bâtisse, Bonin, 47120 Duras, France. *T*: 53.83.70.31.

WHYTE, Stuart Scott; see Whyte, J. S. S.

WIBBERLEY, Prof. Gerald Percy, CBE 1972; Ernest Cook Professor of Countryside Planning in the University of London, University College/Wye College, 1969–82; *b* 15 April 1915; *m* 1st, 1943, Helen Yeomans (*d* 1963); one *d*; 2nd, 1972, Peggy Samways. *Educ*: King Henry VIII Grammar Sch., Abergavenny; Univs of Wales, Oxford and Illinois, USA. BSc, MS, PhD. Asst Lectr, Univ. of Manchester, 1940–41; E Sussex Agricultural Cttee: Dist Officer, 1941–43; Asst Exec. Officer, 1943–44; Min. of Agriculture: Asst Rural Land Utilisation Officer, 1944–49; Research Officer, Land Use, 1949–54; Univ. of London, Wye Coll.: Head of Dept of Economics, 1954–69, also Reader in Agricultural Economics, 1958–62; Prof. of Rural Economy, 1963–69; Fellow 1985. Dir, CoSIRA, 1968–86; Mem., Nature Conservancy Council, 1973–80; Pres.,

British Agricl Econs Soc., 1975–76. Chm., Rural Planning Services Ltd, 1972–82. Hon. Associate Mem. TPI, 1949–67; Hon. Mem., RTPI, 1967–. Hon. DSc Bradford, 1982. *Publications:* Agriculture and Urban Growth, 1959; (part author): The Agricultural Significance of the Hills, 1956; Land Use in an Urban Environment, 1960; Outdoor Recreation in the British Countryside, 1963; An Agricultural Land Budget for Britain 1965–2000, 1970; The Nature and Distribution of Second Homes in England and Wales, 1973; (jtly) Planning and the Rural Environment, 1976; Countryside Planning: a personal evaluation, 1982; Gipsy Sites — the present position, 1986; contributor to Jls of: Agricl Economics, Land Economics, Town and Country Planning. *Recreations:* music, altering old houses, arguing about rural affairs. *Address:* Vicarage Cottage, 7 Upper Bridge Street, Wye, near Ashford, Kent TN25 5AW. *T:* Wye (0233) 812377. *Club:* Farmers'.

WIBLIN, Derek John; Under Secretary, Principal Establishment and Finance Officer, Crown Prosecution Service, since 1988; *b* 18 March 1933; *s* of late Cyril G. H. Wiblin and of Winifred F. Wiblin (*née* Sandford); *m* 1960, Pamela Jeanne Hamshere; one *s* one *d*. *Educ:* Bishopshalt School, Hillingdon; Birmingham University (BSc Hons Chem 1954). RAF, 1954–57. Courtaulds Ltd, 1957–58; joined DSIR Building Research Station, 1958; Civil Service Commission, 1967–71; DoE, 1971–79; Ports Div., Dept of Transport, 1979–81; Estabs Div., DoE, 1981–83; Under Sec., Principal Estabt and Finance Officer, Lord Chancellor's Dept, 1984–88. *Recreations:* making violins, collecting books. *Address:* (office) 4–12 Queen Anne's Gate, SW1H 9AZ. *T:* 071–273 8114. *Club:* Royal Air Force.

WICKBERG, Gen. Erik E.; Comdr of the Order of Vasa (Sweden), 1970; General of the Salvation Army, 1969–74; *b* 6 July 1904; *s* of David Wickberg, Commissioner, Salvation Army, and Betty (*née* Lundblad); *m* 1929, Ens. Frieda de Groot (*d* 1930); *m* 1932, Captain Margarete Dietrich (*d* 1976); two *s* two *d*; *m* 1977, Major Eivor Lindberg. *Educ:* Uppsala; Berlin; Stockholm. Salvation Army Internat. Training Coll., 1924–25, and Staff Coll., 1926; commissioned, 1925; appts in Scotland, Berlin, London; Divisional Commander, Uppsala, 1946–48; Chief Secretary, Switzerland, 1948–53; Chief Secretary, Sweden, 1953–57; Territorial Commander, Germany, 1957–61; Chief of the Staff, Internat. HQ, London, 1961–69; elected General of the Salvation Army, July 1969; assumed international leadership, Sept. 1969. Hon. LLD Choong Ang Univ., Seoul, 1970. Order of Moo-Koong-Wha, Korea, 1970; Grosses Verdienstkreuz, Germany, 1971; The King's golden medal (Sweden), 1980. *Publications:* In Darkest England Now, 1974; Inkallad (autobiography, in Swedish), 1978; Uppdraget (The Charge: my way to preaching, in Swedish), 1990; articles in Salvation Army periodicals and Year Book. *Recreations:* reading, fishing, chess. *Address:* c/o The Salvation Army, Box 5090, 10242 Stockholm, Sweden.

WICKENS, Prof. Alan Herbert, OBE 1980; FEng, FIMechE; Professor of Dynamics, Department of Mechanical Engineering, Loughborough University of Technology, since 1989; *b* 29 March 1929; *s* of late Herbert Leslie Wickens and of Sylvia Wickens; *m* 1st, 1953, Eleanor Joyce Waggott (*d* 1984); one *d*; 2nd, 1987, Patricia Anne McNeil. *Educ:* Ashville Coll., Harrogate; Loughborough Univ. of Technol. (DLC Eng, BScEng London, 1951; DSc Loughborough, 1978). CEng, FIMechE 1971; MRAeS. Res. Engr, Sir W. G. Armstrong Whitworth Aircraft Ltd, Coventry, 1951–55; Gp Leader, Dynamics Analysis, Canadair Ltd, Montreal, 1955–59; Head of Aeroelastics Section, Weapons Res. Div., A. V. Roe & Co., Ltd, Woodford, 1959–62; British Rail: Supt, Res. Dept, 1962–67; Advanced Projs Engr, 1967–68; Dir of Advanced Projs, 1968–71; Dir of Labs, 1971–78; Dir of Research, 1978–84; Dir of Engrg Develt and Research, 1984–89. Industrial Prof. of Transport Technol., Loughborough Univ. of Technol., 1972–76. Pres., Internat. Assoc. of Vehicle System Dynamics, 1981–86; Chm., Office of Res. and Experiments, Union Internationale de Chemins de fer, 1988–90. Mem., Amer. Inst. Aeronautics and Astronautics, 1958. FBIS; FRSA. Hon. Fellow, Derbyshire Coll. of Higher Educn, 1984. Hon. DTech CNAA, 1978; Hon. Dr Open Univ, 1980. George Stephenson Res. Prize, IMechE, 1966; (jtly) MacRobert Award, 1975. *Publications:* papers on dynamics of railway vehicles, high speed trains and future railway technology, publ. by IMechE, Amer. Soc. of Mech. Engrs, Internat. Jl of Solids and Structures, and Jl of Vehicle System Dynamics. *Recreations:* gardening, travel, music. *Address:* Ecclesbourne Farmhouse, Ecclesbourne Lane, Idridgehay, Derbys DE4 4JB. *T:* Cowers Lane (077389) 368. *Club:* Royal Air Force.

WICKERSON, Sir John (Michael), Kt 1987; Partner, Ormerod, Wilkinson (formerly Ormerod, Morris & Dumont), since 1962; President, Law Society, 1986–87; *b* 22 Sept. 1937; *s* of Walter and Ruth Wickerson; *m* 1963, Shirley Maud Best; one *s*. *Educ:* Christ's Hospital; London University (LLB). Admitted solicitor, 1960; Mem. Council, Law Society, 1969 (Chm., Contentious Business Cttee; Vice-Pres., 1985–86). Member: Matrimonial Causes Rules Cttee, 1982–86; Royal Commn on Criminal Justice, 1991–. Pres., London Criminal Courts Solicitors Assoc., 1980–81. Dir, R. Mansell Ltd, 1987–. Hon. Member: Amer. Bar Assoc., 1986; Canadian Bar Assoc., 1986; NZ Law Soc., 1987. *Publication:* Motorist and the Law, 1975, 2nd edn 1982. *Recreation:* golf. *Address:* c/o Ormerod, Wilkinson, 10 High Street, Croydon, Surrey CR9 2BH. *T:* 081–686 3841.

WICKES, Charles G.; *see* Goodson-Wickes.

WICKHAM, Daphne Elizabeth, (Mrs J. K. A. Alderson); a Metropolitan Stipendiary Magistrate, since 1989; *b* 31 Augt. 1946; *d* of late Major Harry Temple Wickham and of Phyllis Wickham (*née* Roycroft); *m* 1983, John Keith Ameers Alderson. *Educ:* Sydenham High Sch.; Chislehurst and Sidcup Girls' Grammar School. Called to the Bar, Inner Temple, 1967. *Recreation:* laughter. *Address:* 3 Temple Gardens, Temple, EC4Y 9AU. *T:* 071–353 3102.

WICKHAM, Rt. Rev. Edward Ralph; Assistant Bishop, Diocese of Manchester, since 1982; *b* 3 Nov. 1911; *s* of Edward Wickham, London; *m* 1944, Dorothy Helen Neville Moss, *d* of Prof. Kenneth Neville Moss, Birmingham; one *s* two *d*. *Educ:* University of London (BD); St Stephen's House, Oxford. Deacon, 1938; Priest, 1939; Curate, Christ Church, Shieldfield, Newcastle upon Tyne, 1938–41; Chaplain, Royal Ordnance Factory, Swynnerton, 1941–44; Curate-in-charge, Swynnerton, 1943–44; Diocesan Missioner to Industry, Sheffield, 1944–59; Hon. Chaplain to Bishop of Sheffield, 1950–59; Canon Residentiary, Sheffield, 1951–59; Bishop Suffragan of Middleton, 1959–82. Sir H. Stephenson Fellow, Sheffield University, 1955–57. Chm. Working Party, Gen. Synod Industrial Cttee, 1977 (report: Understanding Closed Shops); Chairman: Bd for Social Responsibility Working Party on The Future of Work, 1980; Royal Soc. of Arts Industry Year 1986 Churches' Cttee, 1985–86. Chm. Council, and Pro-Chancellor, Salford Univ., 1975–83. FRSA 1986. Hon. DLitt Salford, 1973. *Publications:* Church and People in an Industrial City, 1957; Encounter with Modern Society, 1964; Growth & Inflation, 1975; Growth, Justice and Work, 1985; contributions to: Theology, The Ecumenical Review, Industrial Welfare, etc. *Recreations:* mountaineering, rock-climbing. *Address:* 12 Westminster Road, Eccles, Manchester M30 9HF. *T:* 061–789 3144.

WICKHAM, Glynne William Gladstone; Professor of Drama, University of Bristol, 1960–82, now Emeritus; Dean of Faculty of Arts, 1970–72; *b* 15 May 1922; *s* of W. G. and Catherine Wickham; *m* 1954, Marjorie Heseltine (*née* Mudford); two *s* one *d*. *Educ:* Winchester College; New College, Oxford. Entered RAF, 1942; commissioned as Navigator, 1943; discharged as Flt Lt, 1946. BA, 1947; DPhil, 1951 (Oxon); President of OUDS, 1946–47. Asst Lecturer, Drama Dept, Bristol Univ., 1948; Senior Lecturer and Head of Dept, 1955. Worked sporadically as actor, script-writer and critic for BBC, from 1946; attended General Course in Broadcasting, BBC Staff Trg Sch., 1953. Travelled in America on Rockefeller Award, 1953. Visiting Prof., Drama Dept, State Univ. of Iowa, 1960; Ferens Vis. Prof. of Drama, Hull Univ., 1969; Vis. Prof. of Theatre History, Yale Univ., 1970; Killam Res. Prof., Dalhousie Univ., 1976–77; S. W. Brooks Vis. Prof., Univ. of Qld, 1983; Vis. Prof. in British Studies (Drama), Univ. of the South, Sewanee, 1984; Adjunct Prof. (Arts and Letters), Univ. of Notre Dame (London Campus), 1987–; Hon. Prof., Univ. of Warwick, 1990–. Lectures: G. F. Reynolds Meml, Univ. of Colorado, 1960; Judith E. Wilson, in Poetry and Drama, Cambridge, 1960–61; Festvortrag, Deutsche Shakespeare Gesellschaft, 1973; Shakespeare, British Acad., 1984; British Council, in Europe, annually 1969–79. Directed: Amer. première, The Birthday Party, for Actors' Workshop, San Francisco, 1960; world première, Wole Soyinka's Brother Jero's Metamorphosis, 1974. Consultant to Finnish National Theatre and Theatre School on establishment of Drama Department in Univ. of Helsinki, 1963. Governor of Bristol Old Vic Trust, 1963–83; Vandyck Theatre, Bristol Univ., renamed Glynne Wickham Studio Theatre, 1983. Consultant to Univ. of E Africa on establishment of a Sch. of Drama in University Coll., Dar-es-Salaam, Tanzania, 1965; Dir, Theatre Seminar, for Summer Univ., Vaasa, Finland, 1965; External Examr to Sch. of Drama in Univ. of Ibadan, Nigeria, 1965–68. Chm., Nat. Drama Conf., Nat. Council of Social Service, 1970–76; Chm., and Chief Exec., Radio West plc (ILR Bristol), 1979–83; Pres., Soc. for Theatre Research, 1976–; Member: Adv. Cttee, British Theatre Museum, 1974–77; Culture Adv. Panel, UK Nat. Commn to UNESCO, 1984–86. Mem., Edit. Cttee, Shakespeare Survey, 1974–; Chairman: Adv. Bd, Theatre Research International, 1975–; Gen. Edit. Bd, Theatre in Europe: documents and sources, 1979–. Trustee, St Deiniol's Residential Library, Hawarden, 1985–; Dir, Bd of Internat. Shakespeare Globe Centre, 1986–. Hon. DLitt: Loughborough, 1984; Univ. of the South, Sewanee, 1984. *Publications:* Early English Stages 1300–1660, Vol. I (1300–1576), 1959, 2nd edn 1980; Vol. II (1576–1660, Pt 1), 1962; Vol. II (Pt 2), 1972; Vol. III, 1981; Editor: The Relationship between Universities and Radio, Film and Television, 1954; Drama in a World of Science, 1962; Gen. Introd. to the London Shakespeare, 6 vols (ed J. Munro), 1958; Shakespeare's Dramatic Heritage, 1969; The Medieval Theatre, 1974, 3rd edn 1987; English Moral Interludes, 1975, 2nd edn 1985; A History of the Theatre, 1985. *Recreations:* gardening and travel. *Address:* 6 College Road, Clifton, Bristol BS8 3JB. *T:* Bristol (0272) 34918. *Club:* Garrick.

WICKHAM, William Rayley; His Honour Judge Wickham; a Circuit Judge, since 1975; *b* 22 Sept. 1926; *s* of late Rayley Esmond Wickham and late Mary Joyce Wickham; *m* 1957, Elizabeth Mary (*née* Thompson); one *s* two *d*. *Educ:* Sedbergh Sch.; Brasenose Coll., Oxford (MA, BCL). Served War of 1939–45, Army, 1944–48. Called to Bar, Inner Temple, 1951. Magistrate, Aden, 1953; Chief Magistrate, Aden, 1958; Crown Counsel, Tanganyika, 1959; Asst to Law Officers, Tanganyika, 1961–63; practised on Northern Circuit, 1963–75; a Recorder of the Crown Court, 1972–75. *Recreations:* fell walking, music, amateur dramatics. *Address:* Queen Elizabeth II Law Courts, Liverpool.

WICKINS, David Allen; *b* 15 Feb. 1920; *s* of Samuel Wickins and Edith Hannah Robinson; *m* 1969, Karen Esther Young; one *s* five *d*. *Educ:* St George's College, Weybridge. Trained as chartered accountant with Deloitte & Co., attached to Johannesburg Consolidated Investment Co. and moved to S Africa, 1938, to work on audits for Rhodesian copper mines and sawmills. War of 1939–45: S African Naval Forces (18 months with Eastern Fleet); seconded to RN; served with UK Coastal Forces. Founded, Feb. 1946, Southern Counties Car Auctions, later The British Car Auction Group. Former Chairman: Attwoods plc; Group Lotus plc; Expedier Leisure plc. *Recreations:* tennis, golf, sailing. *Clubs:* St James's, Royal Thames Yacht; Sunningdale Golf; Wentworth Golf.

WICKRAMASINGHE, Prof. Nalin Chandra, PhD, ScD; Professor of Applied Mathematics and Astronomy in the School of Mathematics, University of Wales College of Cardiff, since 1988 (Professor and Head of Department of Applied Mathematics and Astronomy, University College, Cardiff, 1973–88); *b* 20 Jan. 1939; *s* of Percival Herbert Wickramasinghe and Theresa Elizabeth Wickramasinghe; *m* 1966, Nelum Priyadarshini Pereira; one *s* two *d*. *Educ:* Royal Coll., Colombo, Sri Lanka; Univ. of Ceylon (BSc); Univ. of Cambridge (MA, PhD, ScD). Commonwealth Scholar, Trinity Coll., Cambridge, 1960; Powell Prize for English Verse, 1961; Jesus College, Cambridge: Research Fellow, 1963–66; Fellow, 1967–73; Tutor, 1970–73; Staff Mem., Inst. of Theoretical Astronomy, Univ. of Cambridge, 1968–73. Visiting Professor: Vidyodaya Univ. of Ceylon, Univ. of Maryland, USA, Univ. of Arizona, USA, Univ. of Kyoto, Japan, 1966–70; Univ. of W Ontario, 1974, 1976; UNDP Cons. and Scientific Advisor to President of Sri Lanka, 1970–81; Dir, Inst. of Fundamental Studies, Sri Lanka, 1982–83. Collaborator with Prof. Sir Fred Hoyle, and propounder with Hoyle of the theory of the space origin of life and of microorganisms. Dag Hammarskjöld Gold Medal in science, Académie Diplomatique de la Paix, 1986; Scholarly Achievement Award, Inst. of Oriental Philosophy, Japan, 1989; Mijazaki Award for Scientific Excellence, 1990. *Publications:* Interstellar Grains, 1967; (with F. D. Kahn and P. G. Mezger) Interstellar Matter, 1972; Light Scattering Functions for Small Particles with Applications in Astronomy, 1973; The Cosmic Laboratory, 1975; (with D. J. Morgan) Solid State Astrophysics, 1976; (with Daisaku Ikeda) Emergent Perspectives for 2000 AD, 1981; Fundamental Studies and the Future of Science, 1984; (with F. Hoyle and J. Watkins) Viruses from Space, 1986; (with F. Hoyle): Lifecloud: the origin of life in the universe, 1978; Diseases From Space, 1979; The Origin of Life, 1980; Evolution From Space, 1981; Space Travellers, the Bringers of Life, 1981; From Grains to Bacteria, 1984; Living Comets, 1985; Archaeopteryx, the Primordial Bird: a case of fossil forgery, 1986; Cosmic Life Force, 1987; Theory of Cosmic Grains, 1991; over 250 articles and papers in astronomical and scientific jls; contributor to anthologies of Commonwealth Poetry, incl. Young Commonwealth Poets '65, ed P. L. Brent, 1965. *Recreations:* photography, poetry—both writing and reading, history and philosophy of science. *Address:* School of Mathematics, University of Wales College of Cardiff, Senghenydd Road, Cardiff CF2 4AG. *T:* Cardiff (0222) 752146, *Fax:* Cardiff (0222) 753173. *Club:* Icosahedron Dining (Cardiff).

WICKREME, A. S. K.; *see* Kohoban-Wickreme.

WICKREMESINGHE, Dr Walter Gerald, CMG 1954; OBE 1949; *b* 13 Feb. 1897; *s* of Peter Edwin Wickremesinghe and Charlotte Catherine Goonetilleka; *m* 1931, Irene Amelia Goontilleka; two *s* two *d*. *Educ:* Royal College, Colombo; Ceylon Medical College; London University (the London Hospital); Harvard University (School of Public Health). Licentiate in Medicine and Surgery (Ceylon), 1921; MRCS, LRCP, 1923; Master of Public Health (Harvard), 1926; Dr of Public Health (Harvard), 1927. Director of Medical and Sanitary Services, Ceylon, 1948–53. Chief Delegate from Ceylon at WHO. Assembly and Executive board, Geneva, 1952; Mem. UN Health Planning Mission to Korea, 1952; WHO Consultant, Manila, 1965; Chairman, Committee of Inquiry into Mental Health Services, Ceylon, 1966. (Hon.) FAPHA 1952. OStJ. *Publications:* contributions to Brit. Med. Jl; Ceylon Med. Jl; Trans. Soc. of Med. Officers of Health, Ceylon; Amer. Jl of Public Health. *Recreations:* golf, tennis, riding, swimming.

Address: 48 Buller's Lane, Colombo 7, Sri Lanka. *T:* Colombo 81374. *Clubs:* Otter Aquatic, Royal Colombo Golf (Colombo); Nuwara Eliya Golf, Nuwara Eliya Hill; (Life Mem.) Health Dept Sports.

WICKS, Allan, CBE 1988; Organist, Canterbury Cathedral, 1961–88; *b* 6 June 1923; *s* of late Edward Kemble Wicks, priest, and Nancie (*née* Murgatroyd); *m* 1955, Elizabeth Kay Butcher; two *d. Educ:* Leatherhead; Christ Church, Oxford. Sub-organist, York Minster, 1947; Organist, Manchester Cathedral, 1954. MusDoc Lambeth, 1974; Hon. DMus Kent, 1985. *Address:* The Old Farm House, Lower Hardres, Canterbury, Kent CT4 5NR. *T:* Petham (022770) 253.

WICKS, David Vaughan, RE 1961 (ARE 1950); Technical Artist, Bank of England Printing Works, 1954–79, retired, Consultant, 1979–85; *b* 20 Dec. 1918; British; *m* 1948, Margaret Gwyneth Downs; one *s* one *d* (and one *s* decd). *Educ:* Wychwood, Bournemouth; Cranleigh School, Surrey. Polytechnic School of Art, 1936, silver medal for figure composition, 1938, 1939. Radio Officer, Merchant Navy, 1940–46. Royal College of Art, Engraving School, 1946–49, Diploma, ARCA Engraving. Taught Processes of Engraving at RCA, 1949–54. *Recreations:* gardening, bowls.

WICKS, Geoffrey Leonard; Metropolitan Stipendiary Magistrate, since 1987; *b* 23 July 1934; *s* of late Leonard James Wicks and Winifred Ellen Wicks; *m* 1st, 1959, Catherine Margaret Shanks (marr. diss. 1977); one *s* one *d;* 2nd, 1978, Maureen Evelyn Neville. *Educ:* Tollington Sch., N10; Law Society's Sch. of Law, London. Admitted Solicitor, 1957. National Service, RASC, 1957–59. Asst Solicitor, LCC, 1959–60; Asst Solicitor, 1960–61, Partner, 1961–79 (Abu Dhabi office, 1978), Oswald Hickson, Collier & Co., Solicitors, London, Chesham, Amersham, Slough; Principal, Geoffrey Wicks & Co., Solicitors, Chesham, Hemel Hempstead, 1979–82; Partner, Iliffes, Solicitors, London, Chesham, 1982–87. Member: Chesham Round Table, 1962–75 (Chm. 1968–69, Area Chm. Area 42, 1972–73); Chesham Rotary Club, 1974–77. *Recreations:* walking, photography, roses, sheep rearing, theatre, cinema. *Address:* c/o Inner London Magistrates Court Service, North West Wing, Bush House, Aldwych, WC2. *T:* 071–836 9331.

WICKS, Sir James (Albert), Kt 1978; JP; Wanganui Computer Centre Privacy Commissioner, 1978–83; Acting District Court Judge, 1980–81; *b* 14 June 1910; *s* of Henry James Wilmont Wicks and Melanie de Rohan Wicks (*née* Staunton); *m* 1942 Lorna Margaret de la Cour; one *s* one *d. Educ:* Christchurch Boys' High Sch.; Canterbury Univ., NZ. LLM (Hons) Univ. of New Zealand. Admitted Barrister and Solicitor of Supreme Court of NZ, 1932; Notary Public, 1951; Lectr in Trustee Law, Canterbury Univ., 1946–55; in practice as barrister and solicitor (in Christchurch), 1945–61; Mem. Council, Canterbury Dist Law Soc., 1954–61. Stipendiary Magistrate, 1961–78. JP 1963; Chairman: Magistrates' Courts' Rules Cttee, 1967–78; NZ Magistrates' Exec., 1973–78; Dept of Justice's Editorial Bd, 1968–78; Chairman: various Appeal Boards and Statutory Cttees, 1965–78; Teachers' Disciplinary Bd, 1978–82; Cttee of Inquiry into the Administration of the Electoral Act, 1979; Public Service Appeal Bd, 1982; conducted inquiry into alleged improper political interference in administration of the State Services Commn, 1986; Mem. Bd of Dirs, Nat. Soc. on Alcoholism and Drug Dependence, NZ Inc., 1985–88. Consultant to Govt of Niue on legal, judicial and law enforcement systems and policies, 1983. *Publications:* papers to Australian Inst. of Criminology, Feb. 1974, and Commonwealth Magistrates' Conf., Kuala Lumpur, Aug. 1975; contribs to NZ Law Jl, Commonwealth Judicial Jl. *Address:* 29 Glen Road, Kelburn, Wellington 5, New Zealand. *T:* 759–204. *Club:* Canterbury (Christchurch, NZ).

WICKS, Nigel Leonard, CVO 1989; CBE 1979; Second Permanent Secretary (Finance), HM Treasury, since 1989; *b* 16 June 1940; *s* of late Leonard Charles and Beatrice Irene Wicks; *m* 1969, Jennifer Mary (*née* Coveney) three *s. Educ:* Beckenham and Penge Grammar Sch.; Portsmouth Coll. of Technology; Univ. of Cambridge (MA); Univ. of London (MA). The British Petroleum Co. Ltd, 1958–68; HM Treasury, 1968–75; Private Sec. to the Prime Minister, 1975–78; HM Treasury, 1978–83; Economic Minister, British Embassy, Washington, and UK Exec. Dir, IMF and IBRD, 1983–85; Principal Private Sec. to the Prime Minister, 1985–88. Mem. Bd, BNOC, 1980–82. *Address:* HM Treasury, Parliament Street, SW1P 3AG.

WICKS, Rt. Rev. Ralph Edwin, OBE 1982; ED 1964; Bishop of the Southern Region, Diocese of Brisbane, 1985–88; *b* 16 Aug. 1921; *s* of Charles Thomas Wicks and Florence Maud Wicks (*née* White); *m* 1946, Gladys Hawgood (*d* 1981); one *s* one *d*; 1988, Patricia Henderson. *Educ:* East State Sch. and State High Sch., Toowoomba, Qld; St Francis Theological Coll., Brisbane, Qld (LTh). Mem., Qld Public Service (Educn Dept), 1936–41; Theological Student, 1941–44; Asst Curate: Holy Trinity Ch., Fortitude Valley, Brisbane, 1944–47; St James' Ch., Toowoomba, Qld, 1947–48; Rector: Holy Trinity Ch., Goondiwindi, Qld, 1949–54; Holy Trinity Ch., Fortitude Valley, Brisbane, 1954–63; St James' Church, Toowoomba, Qld, 1963–72; Asst Bishop of Brisbane, 1973; Rector of St Andrew's Parish, Caloundra, and Commissary to Archbishop of Brisbane, 1983–85. Hon. Canon of St John's Cath., Brisbane, 1968; Archdeacon of Darling Downs, Qld, 1973. Chaplain to the Australian Army, 1949–70. *Recreations:* reading, gardening, music. *Address:* PO Box 303, Coolum Beach, Qld 4573, Australia.

WICKSTEAD, Cyril; Chairman, Eastern Electricity Board, 1978–82; Member, Electricity Council, 1978–82; *b* 27 Sept. 1922; *s* of John William and Mary Caroline Wickstead; *m* 1948, Freda May Hill; two *s. Educ:* Rowley Regis Central Sch.; City of Birmingham Commercial Coll. FCIS; CBIM. Served War, Royal Navy (Lieut RNVR), 1942–46. Midland Electric Corporation for Power Distribution Ltd: various positions, 1937–42; Asst Sec., 1946–48; Midlands Electricity Board: Sec., S Staffs and N Worcs Sub-Area, 1948–59; Dep. Sec. of Bd, 1959–63; Sec., 1964–72; Dep. Chm., 1972–77. Freeman, City of London, 1979. *Recreations:* walking, music, gardening, sport. *Address:* Ryton, Brook Street, Dedham, Colchester, Essex CO7 6AD.

WIDDAS, Prof. Wilfred Faraday, MB, BS; BSc; PhD; DSc; Professor of Physiology in the University of London, and Head of the Department of Physiology, Bedford College, 1960–81, now Professor Emeritus; *b* 2 May 1916; *s* of late Percy Widdas, BSc, mining engineer, and Annie Maude (*née* Snowdon); *m* 1940, Gladys Green (*d* 1983); one *s* two *d. Educ:* Durham School; University of Durham College of Medicine and Royal Victoria Infirmary, Newcastle upon Tyne. MB, BS 1938; BSc 1947; PhD 1953; DSc 1958. Assistant in General Practice, 1938–39. Served in RAMC, 1939–47; Deputy Assistant Director-General Army Medical Services, War Office (Major), 1942–47. Research Fellow, St Mary's Hospital Medical School, 1947–49; Lecturer and Sen. Lecturer in Physiology, St Mary's Hospital Medical School, 1949–55; Senior Lecturer in Physiology, King's College, 1955–56; University Reader in Physiology at King's College, 1956–60. FRSocMed. Member: Royal Institution of Gt Britain; Physiological Society. *Publications:* Membrane Transport of Sugars, chapter in Carbohydrate Metabolism and its Disorders; Permeability, chapter in Recent Advances in Physiology; also papers on similar topics in (chiefly) Jl of Physiology. *Recreations:* tennis, golf. *Address:* 67 Marksbury Avenue, Kew Gardens, Richmond, Surrey TW9 4JE. *T:* 081–876 6374.

WIDDECOMBE, Ann Noreen; MP (C) Maidstone, since 1987; *b* 4 Oct. 1947; *d* of James Murray Widdecombe, *qv. Educ:* La Sainte Union Convent, Bath; Univ. of Birmingham; Lady Margaret Hall, Oxford (BA Hons, MA). Marketing, Unilever, 1973–75; Senior Administrator, Univ. of London, 1975–87. Contested (C): Burnley, 1979; Plymouth, Devonport, 1983. PPS to Tristan Garel-Jones, MP, Nov. 1990; Parly Under Sec. of State, Dept of Social Security, 1990–. *Publication:* Layman's Guide to Defence, 1984. *Recreations:* riding, reading; researching Charles II's escape. *Address:* 9 Tamar House, Kennington Lane, SE11 4XA. *T:* 071–735 5192; Kloof Cottage, Sutton Valence, Maidstone, Kent. *T:* Maidstone (0622) 843868.

WIDDECOMBE, James Murray, CB 1968; OBE 1959; Director-General, Supplies and Transport (Naval), Ministry of Defence, 1968–70, retired; *b* 7 Jan. 1910; *s* of late Charles Frederick Widdecombe and late Alice Widdecombe; *m* 1936, Rita Noreen Plummer; one *s* one *d. Educ:* Devonport High Sch. Asst Naval Armament Supply Officer, Portsmouth, Holton Heath and Chatham, 1929–35; Dep. Naval Armt Supply Officer, Chatham, 1936; OC, RN Armt Depot, Gibraltar, 1936–40; Naval Armt Supply Officer: Admty, 1940–43; Levant, 1943–44. Capt. (SP) RNVR. Sen. Armt Supply Officer: Staff of C-in-C, Med., 1944–46; Admty, 1946–50; Asst Dir of Armt Supply, Admty, 1950–51, and 1956–59; Suptg Naval Armt Supply Officer, Portsmouth, 1951–53; Prin. Naval Armt Supply Officer, Staff of C-in-C, Far East, 1953–56; Dep. Dir of Armt Supply, Admiralty, 1959–61; Dir of Victualling, Admty, 1961–66; Head of RN Supply and Transport Service, MoD, 1966–68; special duties, Management Services, MoD, 1970–73. Gen. Sec., CS Retirement Fellowship, 1973–79. FBIM; FInstPS. *Recreations:* golf, gardening, amateur dramatics. *Address:* 1 Manor Close, Haslemere, Surrey GU27 1PP. *T:* Haslemere (0428) 642899. *Clubs:* Hindhead Golf (Pres.), Navy Department Golfing Society.

See also A. N. Widdecombe.

WIDDICOMBE, David Graham; QC 1965; a Recorder, since 1985; *b* 7 Jan. 1924; *s* of Aubrey Guy Widdicombe and Margaret (*née* Puddy); *m* 1961, Anastasia Cecilia (*née* Leech) (marr. diss. 1983); two *s* one *d. Educ:* St Albans Sch.; Queen's Coll., Cambridge (BA 1st cl. Hons; LLB 1st cl. Hons; MA). Called to the Bar, Inner Temple, 1950, Bencher, 1973; Attorney at Law, State Bar of California, 1986. Mem., Cttee on Local Govt Rules of Conduct, 1973–74; Chairman: Oxfordshire Structure Plan Examination in Public, 1977; Cttee of Inquiry into Conduct of Local Authority Business, 1985–86. *Publication:* (ed) Ryde on Rating, 1968–83. *Address:* 2 Mitre Court Buildings, Temple, EC4Y 7BX. *T:* 071–583 1380; 5 Albert Terrace, NW1 7SU. *T:* 071–586 5209. *Clubs:* Athenæum, Garrick.

WIDDOWS, Air Commodore Charles; *see* Widdows, Air Commodore S. C.

WIDDOWS, Roland Hewlett, CB 1989; a Deputy Special Commissioner of Income Tax and Chairman (part-time) of Value Added Tax Tribunals, since 1990; *b* 14 Aug. 1921; *s* of late A. E. Widdows, CB; *m* 1945, Diana Gweneth, *d* of late E. A. Dickson, Malayan Civil Service; two *s* one *d. Educ:* Stowe Sch.; Hertford Coll., Oxford (MA). Served in Royal Navy, Coastal Forces, 1941–45. Called to Bar, Middle Temple, 1948; entered Inland Revenue Solicitor's Office, 1951; Asst Solicitor, 1963; on staff of Law Commission, 1965–70; Lord Chancellor's Office, 1970–77; Under Secretary, 1972; Special Comr of Income Tax, 1977–90, Presiding Comr, 1984–90. *Recreation:* sailing. *Address:* 1 Chaucer Drive, Milford-on-Sea, Hants SO41 0SS. *T:* Lymington (0590) 644661. *Club:* United Oxford & Cambridge University.

WIDDOWS, Air Commodore (Stanley) Charles, CB 1959; DFC 1941 (despatches twice); RAF retired; People's Deputy, States of Guernsey, 1973–79; *b* 4 Oct. 1909; *s* of P. L. Widdows, Southend, Bradfield, Berkshire; *m* 1939, Irene Ethel, *d* of S. H. Rawlings, Ugley, Essex; two *s. Educ:* St Bartolomew's School, Newbury; No 1 School of Technical Training, RAF, Halton; Royal Air Force College, Cranwell. Commissioned, 1931; Fighting Area, RAF, 1931–32; RAF Middle East, Sudan and Palestine, 1933–37; Aeroplane and Armament Experimental Estab., 1937–40; OC 29 (Fighter) Sqdn, 1940–41; OC RAF West Malling, 1941–42; Gp Capt., Night Ops, HQ 11 and 12 Gp, 1942; SASO, No 85 (Base Defence) Gp, 1943–44, for Operation Overlord; Gp Capt. Organisation, HQ, Allied Expeditionary Air Force, 1944; OC, RAF Wahn, Germany, 1944–46; RAF Instructor, Sen. Officers War Course, RNC, Greenwich, 1946–48; Fighter Command, 1948–54: SASO HQ No 12 Gp; Chief Instructor, Air Defence Wing, School of Land/Air Warfare; Sector Commander, Eastern Sector. Imperial Defence College, 1955; Director of Operations (Air Defence), Air Ministry, 1956–58. Baulwick Rep., RAF Benevolent Fund. Vice-Pres., Guernsey Scout Assoc. *Address:* Les Granges de Beauvoir, Rohais, St Peter Port, Guernsey, CI. *T:* Guernsey (0481) 720219. *Club:* Royal Channel Islands Yacht.

WIDDOWSON, Dr Elsie May, CBE 1979; FRS 1976; Department of Medicine, Addenbrooke's Hospital, Cambridge, 1972–88; *b* 21 Oct. 1906; *d* of Thomas Henry Widdowson and Rose Widdowson. *Educ:* Imperial Coll., London (BSc, PhD); DSc London 1948. Courtauld Inst. of Biochemistry, Mddx Hosp., 1931–33; KCH, London, 1933–38; Cambridge University: Dept of Exper. Medicine, 1938–66; Infant Nutrition Res. Div., 1966–72. President: Nutrition Soc., 1977–80; Neonatal Soc., 1978–81; British Nutrition Foundn, 1986–. Hon. DSc Manchester, 1974. James Spence Medal, British Paediatric Assoc., 1981; 2nd Bristol-Myers Award for Distinguished Achievement in Nutrition Res., 1982; 1st European Nutrition Award, Fedn of European Nutrition Socs, 1983; Rank Prize Funds Prize for Nutrition, 1984; McCollum Award, E. V. McCollum Commemorative Cttee, USA, 1985; Atwater Award, USA Agricl Res. Service, 1986; Nutritia Internat. Award, Nutricia Res. Foundn, 1988. *Publications:* (with R. A. McCance) The Composition of Foods, 1940 (2nd edn 1967); (with R. A. McCance) Breads White and Brown: Their Place in Thought and Social History, 1956; contrib. Proc. Royal Soc., Jl Physiol., Biochem. Jl, Brit. Jl Nut., Arch. Dis. Child., Lancet, BMJ, Nature, Biol. Neonate, Nut. Metabol., and Ped. Res. *Address:* Orchard House, 9 Boot Lane, Barrington, Cambridge CB2 5RA. *T:* Cambridge (0223) 870219.

WIDDOWSON, Prof. Henry George; Professor of Education, University of London, at Institute of Education, since 1977; *b* 28 May 1935; *s* of George Percival Widdowson and Edna Widdowson; *m* 1966, Dominique Dixmier; two *s. Educ:* Alderman Newton's Sch., Leicester; King's Coll., Cambridge (MA); Univ. of Edinburgh (PhD). Lectr, Univ. of Indonesia, 1958–61; British Council Educn Officer, Sri Lanka, 1962–63; British Council English Language Officer, Bangladesh, 1963–64, 1965–68; Lectr, Dept of Linguistics, Univ. of Edinburgh, 1968–77. Chm., English Teaching Adv. Cttee, British Council, 1982–; Mem., Kingman Cttee of Inquiry into Teaching of English Language, 1986–88. Editor, Jl of Applied Linguistics, 1980–85. *Publications:* Stylistics and the Teaching of Literature, 1975, Japanese edn 1989; Teaching Language as Communication, 1978, French edn 1981, Ital. edn 1982; Explorations in Applied Linguistics I, 1979; Learning Purpose and Language Use, 1983, Italian edn 1986; Explorations in Applied Linguistics II, 1984; (with Randolph Quirk) English in the World, 1985; Aspects of Language Teaching, 1990; editor of series: English in Focus; Communicative Grammar; Language Teaching: a scheme for teacher education; papers in various jls. *Recreations:* poetry, rumination, walking. *Address:* 151 Sheen Road, Richmond upon Thames, Surrey TW9 1YS. *T:* 081–948 0854.

WIDDUP, Malcolm, CB 1979; retired 1981; Under-Secretary, HM Treasury, 1971–80; *b* 9 May 1920; *s* of John and Frances Ellen Widdup; *m* 1947, Margaret Ruth Anderson; one *s* one *d*. *Educ:* Giggleswick Sch.; Trinity Coll., Oxford (MA). Served War, Army, RA and Staff, 1940–45. Ministry of Food, 1946–53; HM Treasury, 1953–55; Cabinet Office, 1955–57; HM Treasury, 1957–60; Min. of Health, 1960–62; HM Treasury, 1962–66; UK Delegn to OECD, 1966–68; HM Treasury, 1968–80; Sen. Clerk, House of Lords, 1980–81. *Recreations:* gardening, bridge, bowling.

WIESEL, Prof. Elie; Andrew W. Mellon Professor in the Humanities, Boston University, since 1976; *b* 30 Sept. 1928; naturalised US citizen, 1963; *m* 1969, Marion Erster; one *s* one *d*. *Educ:* The Sorbonne, Univ. of Paris. Distinguished Prof. of Judaic Studies, City Coll., City Univ. of New York, 1972–76; Dist. Vis. Prof. of Literature and Philosophy, Florida Internat. Univ., 1982; Henry Luce Vis. Scholar in the Humanities and Social Thought, Whitney Humanities Center, Yale Univ., 1982–83. Founder, Elie Wiesel Foundn for Humanity, 1987. Chairman: US Holocaust Meml Council, 1980–86; US President's Commn on the Holocaust, 1979–80; Adv. Bd, World Union of Jewish Students, 1985–; Member, Board of Directors: Nat. Cttee on Amer. Foreign Policy, 1983– (Special Award, 1987); Internat. Rescue Cttee, 1985–; Hebrew Arts Sch.; HUMANITAS; Member, Board of Trustees: Amer. Jewish World Service, 1985–; Yeshiva Univ., 1977; Member, Board of Governors: Tel-Aviv Univ., 1976–; Haifa Univ., 1977–; Oxford Centre for Postgrad. Hebrew Studies, 1978–; Mem. Adv. Bd, Andrei Sakharov Inst.; Fellow: Jewish Acad. of Arts and Sciences; Amer. Acad. of Arts and Sciences, 1986; Member: Amnesty Internat.; Writers Guild of America (East); Authors' Guild; Writers and Artists for Peace in ME; Royal Norwegian Soc. of Sciences and Letters, 1987; Hon. Life Mem., Foreign Press Assoc., 1985. Holds hon. degrees from univs and colls. Elie Wiesel Chair in Judaic Studies endowed at Connecticut Coll., 1990. Nobel Peace Prize, 1986; other awards include: Anatoly Shcharansky Humanitarian Award, 1983; Congressional Gold Medal of Achievement, 1984; Achievement Award, Israel, 1987. Grand Officier de la Légion d'Honneur, France, 1990 (Commandeur, 1984); Grand Cross, Order of the Southern Cross, Brazil, 1987. *Publications:* Night (memoir), 1960; The Jews of Silence (personal testimony), 1966; Legends of Our Time, 1968; One Generation After, 1971; Souls on Fire: portraits and legends of the Hasidic masters, 1972; Messengers of God: portraits and legends of Biblical heroes, 1976; A Jew Today, 1978; Four Hasidic Masters, 1978; Images from the Bible, 1980; Le Testament d'un Poète Juif Assassiné, 1980 (Prix Livre-Inter, and Bourse Goncourt, France, 1980; Prix des Bibliothèquaires, France, 1981); Five Biblical Portraits, 1981; Paroles d'étranger, 1982; Somewhere a Master, 1982; The Golem, 1983; Signes d'Exode, 1985; Against Silence: the voice and vision of Elie Wiesel (collected shorter writings, ed Irving Abrahamson), 3 vols, 1985; Job ou Dieu dans la Tempête (dialogue and commentary with Josy Eisenberg), 1986; The Nobel Address, 1987; (jtly) The Six Days of Destruction, 1988; Silences et Mémoire d'hommes, 1989; From the Kingdom of Memory (reminiscences), 1990; Evil and Exile (dialogues with Philippe-Michael de Saint-Chéron), 1990; (with John Cardinal O'Connor) A Journey of Faith, 1990; *novels:* Dawn, 1961; The Accident, 1962; The Town beyond the Wall, 1964; The Gates of the Forest, 1966; A Beggar in Jerusalem, 1970; The Oath, 1973; The Testament, 1980; The Fifth Son, 1985 (Grand Prix de la Littérature, Paris); Twilight, 1988; L'Oublié, 1989; *cantatas:* Ani Maamin, 1973; A Song for Hope, 1987; *plays:* Zalmen, or the Madness of God, 1975; The Trial of God, 1979. *Address:* Boston University, 745 Commonwealth Avenue, Boston, Mass 02215, USA. *Club:* PEN.

WIESEL, Prof. Torsten Nils, MD; Head of Laboratory of Neurobiology, Rockefeller University, since 1983; *b* 3 June 1924; *s* of Fritz S. Wiesel and Anna-Lisa Wiesel (*née* Bentzer); *m* 1st, 1956, Teeri Stenhammar (marr. diss. 1970); 2nd, 1973, Ann Yee (marr. diss. 1981); one *d*. *Educ:* Karolinska Inst., Stockholm (MD 1954). Instructor, Dept of Physiol., Karolinska Inst., 1954–55; Asst, Dept of Child Psychiatry, Karolinska Hosp., Stockholm, 1954–55; Fellow in Ophthalmol., 1955–58, Asst Prof. of Ophthalmic Physiol., 1958–59, Johns Hopkins Univ. Med. Sch., Baltimore; Harvard Medical School: Associate in Neurophysiol. and Neuropharmacol., 1959–60; Asst Prof., 1960–67; Prof. of Physiol., 1967–68; Prof. of Neurobiol., 1968–74; Chm., Dept of Neurobiol., 1973–82; Robert Winthrop Prof. of Neurobiol., 1974–83. Lectures: Ferrier, Royal Soc., 1972; Grass, Soc. for Neurosci., 1976. Member: Amer. Physiol Soc.; AAAS; Amer. Acad. of Arts and Scis; Amer. Philosophical Soc.; Soc. for Neurosci. (Pres. 1978–79); Nat. Acad. of Scis; Swedish Physiol Soc.; Foreign Mem., Royal Soc., 1982; Hon. Mem., Physiolog. Soc., 1982. Hon. AM Harvard Univ., 1967; Hon. MD Linköping, 1982; Hon. Dr of Med. and Surg. Ancona Univ., 1982; Hon. DSc Pennsylvania, 1982. Awards and Prizes: Dr Jules C. Stein, Trustees for Research to Prevent Blindness, 1971; Lewis S. Rosenstiel, Brandeis Univ., 1972; Friedenwald, Assoc. for Res. in Vision and Ophthalmology, 1975; Karl Spencer Lashley, Amer. Phil. Soc., 1977; Louisa Gross Horwitz, Columbia Univ., 1978; Dickson, Pittsburgh Univ., 1979; Ledlie, Harvard Univ., 1980; Soc. for Scholars, Johns Hopkins Univ., 1980; Nobel Prize in Physiology or Medicine, 1981. *Publications:* (contrib.) Physiological and Biochemical Aspects of Nervous Integration, 1968; (contrib.) The Organization of the Cerebral Cortex, 1981; contribs to professional jls, symposia and trans of learned socs. *Address:* Rockefeller University, 1230 York Avenue, New York, NY 10021, USA. *T:* (212) 570–7661. *Club:* Harvard (Boston).

WIESNER, Dr Jerome Bert; President Emeritus, since 1980, and Institute Professor Emeritus, since 1985, Massachusetts Institute of Technology (Dean of Science, 1964–66; Provost, 1966–71; President, 1971–80; Institute Professor, 1980–85); *b* 30 May 1915; *s* of Joseph and Ida Friedman Wiesner; *m* 1940, Laya Wainger; three *s* one *d*. *Educ:* University of Michigan, Ann Arbor, Michigan. PhD in electrical engineering, 1950. Staff, University of Michigan, 1937–40; Chief Engineer, Library of Congress, 1940–42; Staff, MIT Radiation Lab., 1942–45; Staff, Univ. of Calif Los Alamos Lab., 1945–46; Asst Prof. of Electrical Engrg, MIT, 1946; Associate Prof. of Electrical Engrg, 1947; Prof. of Electrical Engrg, 1950–64; Dir, Res. Lab. of Electronics, 1952–61. Special Assistant to the President of the USA, for Science and Technology, The White House, 1961–64; Director, Office of Science and Technology, Exec. Office of the President, 1962–64; Chm., Tech. Assessment Adv. Council, Office of Tech. Assessment, US Congress, 1976–78. Member, Board of Directors: Faxon Co.; MacArthur Foundn; Consultants for Management, Inc.; Internat. Foundn for the Survival and Develt of Humanity. *Publications:* Where Science and Politics Meet, 1965; contrib.: Modern Physics for the Engineer, 1954; Arms Control, Disarmament and National Security, 1960; Arms Control, issues for the Public, 1961; Lectures on Modern Communications, 1961; technical papers in: Science, Physical Rev., Applied Physics, Scientific American, Proc. Inst. Radio Engineers, etc. *Recreations:* photography, boating. *Address:* Massachusetts Institute of Technology, Building E15–207, Cambridge, Mass 02139, USA. *T:* 253–2800. *Clubs:* Cosmos (Washington, DC); Commercial, St Botolph's (Boston); Century, Harvard Club of New York City (NY).

WIGAN, Sir Alan (Lewis), 5th Bt *cr* 1898; *b* 19 Nov. 1913; second *s* of Sir Roderick Grey Wigan, 3rd Bt, and Ina (*d* 1977), *o c* of Lewis D. Wigan, Brandon Park, Suffolk; *S* brother, 1979; *m* 1950, Robina, *d* of Sir Iain Colquhoun, 7th Bt, KT, DSO; one *s* one *d*. *Educ:* Eton; Magdalen College, Oxford. Commissioned Suppl. Reserve, KRRC, 1936; served with KRRC, 1939–46; wounded and taken prisoner, Calais, 1940. Director, Charrington & Co. (Brewers), 1939–70. Master, Brewers' Co., 1958–59. *Recreations:* shooting, fishing, golf. *Heir:* *s* Michael Iain Wigan [*b* 3 Oct. 1951; *m* 1st, 1984, Frances (marr. diss. 1985), *d* of late Flt-Lt Angus Barr Faucett and of Mrs Antony Reid; 2nd, 1989, Julia, *d* of John de Courcy Ling, *qv*; one *s*]. *Address:* Badingham House, Badingham, Woodbridge, Suffolk. *T:* Badingham (072875) 664; Moorburn, The Lake, Kirkcudbright. *Club:* Army and Navy.

WIGDOR, Lucien Simon, CEng, MRAeS; President, L. S. Wigdor Inc., New Hampshire, since 1984; Managing Director, L. S. Wigdor Ltd, since 1976; *b* Oct. 1919; *s* of William and Adèle Wigdor; *m* 1951, Marion Louise, *d* of Henry Risner; one *s* one *d*. *Educ:* Highgate Sch.; College of Aeronautical Engineering. Served War, RAF, early helicopter pilot, 1940–46 (Sqn Ldr); Operational Research, BEA: Research Engr, 1947–51; Manager, Industrial and Corporate Develt, Boeing Vertol Corp., USA, 1951–55; Managing Dir, Tunnel Refineries Ltd, 1955–69, Vice-Chm., 1969–72; Corporate Consultant, The Boeing Company, 1960–72; Dep. Dir-Gen., CBI, 1972–76; Chief Exec., Leslie & Godwin (Holdings) Ltd, 1977–78, Dir 1977–81; Chm., Weir Pumps Ltd, 1978–81; Director: The Weir Group, 1978–81; Rothschild Investment Trust, 1977–82; Zambian Engineering Services Ltd, 1979–84; Rothschild Internat. Investments SA, 1981–82. Special Adviser on Internat. Affairs, Bayerische Hypotheken-SPTund Wechsel-SPTBank AG, 1981–83; Consultant: Lazard Bros, 1982–84; Manufacturing and Financial Services Industries (L. S. Wigdor Inc.), 1984–. *Publications:* papers to Royal Aeronautical Soc., American Helicopter Soc. *Recreations:* ski-ing, experimental engineering. *Address:* Indian Point, Little Sunapee Road, PO Box 1035, New London, New Hampshire 03257, USA. *T:* (603) 526 4456, *Fax:* (603) 526 4963. *Club:* Royal Air Force.

WIGGHAM, Hon. (Edward) Barrie, CBE 1991; JP; Secretary for Civil Service, Hong Kong Government, since 1990; Member, Governor's Executive Council, since 1989; *b* 1 March 1937; *s* of Edward and Agnes Wiggham; *m* 1961, Mavis Mitson; two *d* (one *s* decd). *Educ:* Woking Grammar Sch.; Queen's Coll., Oxford (MA Mod. Langs). Hong Kong Government: Admin. Officer, 1961–63; Dist Officer, New Territories, 1963–71; postings in finance, econ., security and information branches, 1971–79; Comr for Recreation and Culture, 1979–83; Regl Sec., 1983–86; seconded to British Embassy, Peking, 1986; Sec., General Duties, 1986–90. JP Hong Kong, 1973. *Recreations:* music, people. *Address:* c/o Government Secretariat, Lower Albert Road, Hong Kong. *Clubs:* Commonwealth Trust; Hong Kong, Foreign Correspondents, United Services (Hong Kong).

WIGGIN, Alfred William, (Jerry Wiggin); TD 1970; MP (C) Weston-super-Mare since 1969; *b* 24 Feb. 1937; *e s* of late Col Sir William H. Wiggin, KCB, DSO, TD, DL, JP, and late Lady Wiggin, Worcestershire; *m* 1964, Rosemary Janet (marr. diss. 1982), *d* of David L. D. Orr; two *s* one *d*. *Educ:* Eton; Trinity Coll., Cambridge. 2nd Lieut, Queen's Own Warwickshire and Worcestershire Yeomanry (TA), 1959; Major, Royal Yeomanry, 1975–78. Contested (C), Montgomeryshire, 1964 and 1966. PPS to Lord Balniel, at MoD, later FCO, 1970–74, and to Ian Gilmour, MoD, 1971–72; Parly Sec., MAFF, 1979–81; Parly Under-Sec. of State for Armed Forces, MoD, 1981–83. Chm., Select Cttee on Agriculture, 1987–. Jt Hon. Sec., Conservative Defence Cttee, 1974–75; Vice-Chm., Conservative Agricultural Cttee, 1975–79; Chm., West Country Cons. Gp, 1978–79. Promoted Hallmarking Act, 1973. Chm., Economic Cttee, North Atlantic Assembly, 1990–. *Address:* House of Commons, SW1A 0AA. *T:* 071–219 4522; The Court, Axbridge, Somerset BS26 2BN. *T:* Axbridge (0934) 732527. *Clubs:* Beefsteak, Pratt's; Royal Yacht Squadron.

WIGGIN, Jerry; *see* Wiggin, A. W.

WIGGIN, Sir John (Henry), 4th Bt *cr* 1892; MC 1946; DL; Major, Grenadier Guards, retired; *b* 3 March 1921; *s* of Sir Charles Richard Henry Wiggin, 3rd Bt, TD, and Mabel Violet Mary (*d* 1961), *d* of Sir William Jaffray, 2nd Bt; *S* father, 1972; *m* 1st, 1947, Lady Cecilia Evelyn Anson (marr. diss. 1961; she *d* 1963), *yr d* of 4th Earl of Lichfield; two *s*; 2nd, 1963, Sarah, *d* of Brigadier Stewart Forster; two *s*. *Educ:* Eton; Trinity College, Cambridge. Served War of 1939–45 (prisoner-of-war). High Sheriff, 1976, DL 1985, Warwicks. *Heir:* *s* Charles Rupert John Wiggin, Major, Grenadier Guards [*b* 2 July 1949; *m* 1979, Mrs Mary Burnett-Hitchcock; one *s* one *d*. *Educ:* Eton]. *Address:* Honington Hall, Shipston-on-Stour, Warwicks CV36 5AA. *T:* Shipston-on-Stour (0608) 61434.

WIGGINS, (Anthony) John; Deputy Secretary, Department of Education and Science, since 1988; *b* 8 July 1938; *s* of late Rev. Arthur Wiggins and of Mavis Wiggins (*née* Brown); *m* 1962, Jennifer Anne Walkden; one *s* one *d*. *Educ:* Highgate Sch.; The Hotchkiss Sch., Lakeville, Conn, USA; Oriel Coll., Oxford (MA). Assistant Principal, HM Treasury, 1961; Private Sec. to Permanent Under Sec., Dept of Economic Affairs, 1964–66; Principal: Dept of Economic Affairs, 1966–67; HM Treasury, 1967–69; Harkness Fellow, Harvard Univ., 1969–71 (MPA 1970); Asst Sec., HM Treasury 1972–79; Principal Private Sec. to Chancellor of the Exchequer, 1980–81; Under Sec., Dept of Energy, 1981–84 (Mem. of BNOC, 1982–84); Under Sec., Cabinet Office, 1985–87; Under Sec., DES, 1987–88. Sec. to Royal Opera House Develt Bd, 1987– (Sec. to cttees, 1982–87). *Recreations:* mountaineering, skiing, opera. *Address:* Department of Education and Science, Sanctuary Buildings, Great Smith Street, SW1. *Club:* Alpine.

WIGGINS, Prof. David, FBA 1978; Professor of Philosophy, Birkbeck College, University of London, since 1989; *b* 8 March 1933; *s* of late Norman Wiggins and of Diana Wiggins (*née* Priestley); *m* 1979, Jennifer Hornsby. *Educ:* St Paul's Sch.; Brasenose Coll., Oxford. BA 1955; MA 1958. Asst Principal, Colonial Office, London 1957–58. Jane Eliza Procter Vis. Fellow, Princeton Univ., 1958–59; Lectr, 1959, then Fellow and Lecturer, 1960–67, New College, Oxford; Prof. of Philosophy, Bedford Coll., Univ. of London, 1967–80; Fellow and Praelector in Philosophy, University Coll., Oxford, 1981–89. Visiting appointments: Stanford, 1964 and 1965; Harvard, 1968 and 1972; All Souls College, 1973; Princeton, 1980; New York Univ., 1988; Fellow, Center for Advanced Study in the Behavioral Sciences, Stanford, 1985–86. Mem., Indep. Commn on Transport, 1973–74; Chm., Transport Users' Consultative Cttee for the South East, 1977–79. Mem., Institut International de Philosophie. *Publications:* Identity and Spatio-Temporal Continuity, 1967; Truth, Invention and the Meaning of Life, 1978; Sameness and Substance, 1980; Needs, Values, Truth: essays in the philosophy of value, 1986; philosophical articles in Philosophical Review, Analysis, Philosophy, Synthèse, Phil Qly; articles on environmental and transport subjects in Spectator, Times, Tribune.

WIGGINS, John; *see* Wiggins, A. J.

WIGGINS, Rt. Rev. Maxwell Lester; Bishop of Victoria Nyanza, 1963–76; retired; *b* 5 Feb. 1915; *s* of Herbert Lester and Isobel Jane Wiggins; *m* 1941, Margaret Agnes (*née* Evans); one *s* two *d*. *Educ:* Christchurch Boys' High Sch., NZ; Canterbury University College, NZ (BA). Asst Curate, St Mary's, Merivale, NZ, 1938; Vicar of Oxford, NZ, 1941; CMS Missionary, Diocese Central Tanganyika, 1945; Head Master, Alliance Secondary Sch., Dodoma, 1948; Provost, Cathedral of Holy Spirit, Dodoma, 1949; Principal, St Philip's Theological Coll., and Canon of Cathedral of Holy Spirit, Dodoma, 1954; Archdeacon of Lake Province, 1956; Asst Bishop of Central Tanganyika, 1959;

Asst Bishop of Wellington, 1976–81; Pres., NZ CMS, 1986– (Gen. Sec., 1982–83). Sen. ChLJ, 1982–. *Address:* 42 Otara Street, Christchurch 5, New Zealand.

WIGGLESWORTH, Gordon Hardy; Consultant, Alan Turner Associates, architects, planning and development consultants, since 1988 (Director, 1984–88); *b* 27 June 1920; *m* 1952, Cherry Diana Heath; three *d. Educ:* Highgate; University Coll., London; Architectural Association. ARIBA; AADipl. Served War of 1939–45: Royal Engineers, 1941–46. Architectural Assoc., 1946–48; private practice and Univ. of Hong Kong, 1948–52; private practice: London, 1952–54; Hong Kong, 1954–56; London, 1956–57. Asst Chief Architect, Dept of Education and Science, 1957–67; Dir of Building Develt, MPBW, later DoE, 1967–72; Principal Architect, Educn, GLC (ILEA), 1972–74; Housing Architect, GLC, 1974–80. FRSA. *Address:* 53 Canonbury Park South, N1 2JL. *T:* 071–226 7734.

WIGGLESWORTH, Sir Vincent (Brian), Kt 1964; CBE 1951; MA, MD, BCh Cantab; FRS 1939; FRES; Retired Director, Agricultural Research Council Unit of Insect Physiology (1943–67); Quick Professor of Biology, University of Cambridge, 1952–66; Fellow of Gonville and Caius College; *b* 17 April 1899; *s* of late Sidney Wigglesworth, MRCS; *m* 1928, Mabel Katherine (*d* 1986), *d* of late Col Sir David Semple, IMS; three *s* one *d. Educ:* Repton; Caius Coll., Cambridge (Scholar); St Thomas' Hosp. 2nd Lt RFA, 1917–18, served in France; Frank Smart Student of Caius College, 1922–24; Lecturer in Medical Entomology in London School of Hygiene and Tropical Medicine, 1926; Reader in Entomology in University of London, 1936–44; Reader in Entomology, in University of Cambridge, 1945–52. Fellow, Imperial College, London, 1977. Hon. Member: Royal Entomological Soc.; Physiological Soc.; Soc. Experimental Biology; Assoc. Applied Biology; International Confs of Entomology; Soc. of European Endocrinologists; Royal Danish Academy of Science; Amer. Philosophical Soc.; US Nat. Academy of Sciences; American Academy of Arts and Sciences; Kaiserliche Deutsche Akademie der Naturforscher, Leopoldina; Deutsche Entomologische Gesellschaft; Amer. Soc. of Zoologists; American Entomol. Soc.; USSR Acad. of Sciences; All-Union Entomol. Soc.; Entomol. Soc. of India; Société Zoologique de France; Société Entomologique de France, Société Entomologique d'Egypte; Entomological Society of the Netherlands; Schweizerische Entomologische Gesellschaft; Indian Academy of Zoology; Corresponding Member: Accademia delle Scienze dell' Istituto di Bologna; Société de Pathologie Exotique; Entomological Soc. of Finland; Dunham Lecturer, Harvard, 1945; Woodward Lecturer, Yale, 1945; Croonian Lecturer, Royal Society, 1948; Messenger Lecturer, Cornell, 1958; Tercentenary Lecturer, Royal Society, 1960. Hon. FRCP 1989. DPhil (*hc*) University, Berne; DSc (*hc*): Paris, Newcastle and Cambridge. Royal Medal, Royal Society, 1955; Swammerdam Medal, Soc. Med. Chir., Amsterdam, 1966; Gregor Mendel Gold Medal, Czechoslovak Acad. of Science, 1967; Frink Medal, Zoological Soc., 1979; Wigglesworth Medal, Royal Entomological Soc., 1981. *Publications:* Insect Physiology, 1934; The Principles of Insect Physiology, 1939; The Physiology of Insect Metamorphosis, 1954; The Life of Insects, 1964; Insect Hormones, 1970; Insects and the Life of Man, 1976; numerous papers on comparative physiology. *Address:* 14 Shilling Street, Lavenham, Suffolk. *T:* Lavenham (0787) 247293.

See also W. R. B. Wigglesworth.

WIGGLESWORTH, William Robert Brian; Deputy Director General of Telecommunications, since 1984; *b* 8 Aug. 1937; *s* of Sir Vincent Wigglesworth, *qv*; *m* 1969, Susan Mary, *d* of late Arthur Baker, JP, Lavenham; one *s* one *d. Educ:* Marlborough; Magdalen College, Oxford (BA). Nat. Service, 2nd Lieut, Royal Signals, 1956–58. Ranks, Hovis McDougall Ltd, 1961–70: trainee; Gen. Manager, Mother's Pride Bakery, Cheltenham; PA to Group Chief Exec.; Gen. Manager, Baughans of Colchester; Board of Trade, 1970; Fair Trading Div., Dept of Prices and Consumer Protection, 1975; Posts and Telecommunications Div., 1978, Inf. Tech. Div., 1982, Dept of Industry. *Recreations:* fishing, gardening, history. *Address:* Office of Telecommunications, Export House, 50 Ludgate Hill, EC4M 7JJ. *T:* 071–822 1604.

WIGHT, James Alfred, OBE 1979; FRCVS; practising veterinary surgeon, since 1939; author, since 1970; *b* 3 Oct. 1916; *s* of James Henry and Hannah Wight; *m* 1941, Joan Catherine Danbury; one *s* one *d. Educ:* Hillhead High Sch.; Glasgow Veterinary Coll. FRCVS 1982. Started in general veterinary practice in Thirsk, Yorks, 1940, and has been there ever since with the exception of war-time service with the RAF. Began to write at the ripe age of 50 and quite unexpectedly became a best-selling author of books on his veterinary experiences which have been translated into all European languages and many others, incl. Japanese. Hon. Member: British Vet. Assoc., 1975; British Small Animal Vet. Assoc., 1989. Hon. DLitt Heriot-Watt, 1979; Hon. DVSc Liverpool, 1983. *Publications:* (as James Herriot): If Only They Could Talk, 1970; It Shouldn't Happen to a Vet, 1972; All Creatures Great and Small, (USA) 1972; Let Sleeping Vets Lie, 1973; All Things Bright and Beautiful, (USA) 1973; Vet in Harness, 1974; Vets Might Fly, 1976; Vet in a Spin, 1977; James Herriot's Yorkshire, 1979; The Lord God Made Them All, 1981; The Best of James Herriot, 1982; James Herriot's Dog Stories, 1985; Blossom Comes Home, 1988; The Market Square Dog, 1989; *for children:* Moses the Kitten, 1984; Only One Woof, 1985; The Christmas Day Kitten, 1986; Bonny's Big Day, 1987. *Recreations:* music, dog-walking. *Address:* Mire Beck, Thirlby, Thirsk, Yorks YO7 2DJ.

WIGHT, Robin; Chairman, WCRS; Joint Chairman, Eurocom Advertising, since 1989; *b* 6 July 1944; *s* of late Brig. I. L. Wight and of C. P. Wight; *m* (marr. diss.); two *s* one *d. Educ:* Wellington Coll.; St Catharine's Coll., Cambridge. Copywriter: Robert Sharp and Partners, 1966; CDP and Partners, 1967; Creative Director: Richard Cope and Partners, 1968; Euro Advertising, 1968; Creative Partner, Wight, Collins, Rutherford, Scott, 1979. Marketing Adviser to Rt Hon. Peter Walker, 1982–84. Contested (C) Bishop Auckland, 1987. *Publication:* The Day the Pigs Refused to be Driven to Market, 1972. *Recreations:* horseriding, oenology. *Address:* 13 Horbury Crescent, W11 3NF. *T:* 071–221 3378.

WIGHTMAN, Very Rev. William David; Provost of St Andrew's Cathedral, Aberdeen, since 1991; Priest in charge of St Ninian, Aberdeen, since 1991; *b* 29 Jan. 1939; *s* of William Osborne Wightman and Madge Wightman; *m* 1963, Karen Elizabeth Harker; two *s* two *d. Educ:* Univ. of Birmingham (BA Hons Theol.); Wells Theol Coll. Ordained deacon, 1963; priest, 1964; Curate: St Mary and All Saints, Rotherham, 1963–67; St Mary, Castlechurch, Stafford, 1967–70; Vicar: St Aidan, Buttershaw, Bradford, 1970–76; St John the Evangelist, Cullingworth, Bradford, 1976–83; Rector: St Peter, Peterhead, 1983–91; St John Longside, St Drostan, Old Deer and All Saints, Strichen, 1990–91; Chaplain, HM Prison, Peterhead, 1989–91; Dir, Training for Ministry, Dio. of Aberdeen and Orkney, 1989–. Hon. Canon, Christ Church Cathedral, Hartford, Conn, USA, 1991. *Recreations:* fishing, choral music, swimming, gardening. *Address:* 15 Morningfield Road, Aberdeen AB2 4AP. *T:* Aberdeen (0224) 314765. *Club:* Blue Feather (Peterhead).

WIGHTWICK, Charles Christopher Brooke, MA; educational consultant, 1991; *b* 16 Aug. 1931; *s* of Charles Frederick Wightwick and Marion Frances Wightwick (*née* Smith); *m* 1st, 1955, Pamela Layzell (marr. diss. 1986); one *s* two *d*; 2nd, 1986, Gillian Rosemary Anderson (*née* Dalziel). *Educ:* St Michael's, Otford Court; Lancing Coll.; St Edmund Hall, Oxford. BA 1954, MA 1958. Asst Master, Hurstpierpoint Coll., 1954–59; Head of German, Denstone Coll., 1959–65; Head of Languages, then Director of Studies, Westminster Sch., 1965–75; Head Master, King's College Sch., Wimbledon, 1975–80; HM Inspector of Schs, 1980–91; Staff Inspector for Mod. Langs, 1988. *Publication:* (co-author) Longman Audio-Lingual German, 3 vols., 1974–78. *Recreations:* photography, computer programming, running, judo, language. *Address:* 19 Nottingham Road, SW17 7EA. *T:* 081–767 6161.

WIGLEY, Dafydd; MP (Plaid Cymru) Caernarfon since Feb. 1974; President, Plaid Cymru, 1981–84; industrial economist; *b* April 1943; *s* of Elfyn Edward Wigley, former County Treasurer, Caernarfonshire CC; *m* Elinor Bennett (*née* Owen), *d* of late Emrys Bennett Owen, Dolgellau; one *s* one *d* (and two *s* decd). *Educ:* Caernarfon Grammar Sch.; Rydal Sch., Colwyn Bay; Manchester Univ. Ford Motor Co., 1964–67; Chief Cost Accountant and Financial Planning Manager, Mars Ltd, 1967–71; Financial Controller, Hoover Ltd, Merthyr Tydfil, 1971–74. Mem., Merthyr Tydfil Borough Council, 1972–74. Vice-Chm., Parly Social Services Gp, 1985–88; Mem., Select Cttee on Welsh Affairs, 1983–87. Sponsor, Disabled Persons Act, 1981. Vice-Pres., Nat. Fedn of Industrial Develt Authorities, 1981–. Mem., Nat. Cttee for Electoral Reform. Pres., Spastic Soc. of Wales, 1985–90. Pres. (unpaid), S Caernarfonshire Creamery. Pres., Caernarfon Town FC, 1987–. *Publication:* An Economic Plan for Wales, 1970. *Address:* House of Commons, SW1A 0AA.

WIGMORE, James Arthur Joseph; His Honour Judge Wigmore; a Circuit Judge, since 1990; *b* 7 Aug. 1928; *s* of Sqdn-Ldr Arthur J. O. Wigmore, MB, and Kathleen (*née* Jowett); *m* 1966, Diana, *d* of Comdr H. J. Holemans, RN; three *d. Educ:* Downside Sch.; Royal Military Acad., Sandhurst; English Coll., Rome. BSc, PhL, STL. Served Royal Signals, 1946–52, commnd 1948. Lectured in Philosophy: Downside Abbey, 1960–63; Oscott Coll., 1963–66. Called to the Bar, Inner Temple, 1971; Dep. Coroner, Bristol, 1976–88; a Recorder, 1989. *Club:* Naval and Military.

WIGNER, Prof. Eugene P(aul); Thomas D. Jones Professor of Mathematical Physics of Princeton University, 1938–71, retired; *b* 17 Nov. 1902; *s* of Anthony and Elizabeth Wigner; *m* 1st, 1936, Amelia Z. Frank (*d* 1937); 2nd, 1941, Mary Annette Wheeler (*d* 1977); one *s* one *d*; 3rd, 1979, Eileen C. P. Hamilton. *Educ:* Technische Hochschule, Berlin, Dr Ing. 1925. Asst and concurrently Extraordinary Prof., Technische Hochschule, Berlin, 1926–35; Lectr, Princeton Univ., 1930, half-time Prof. of Mathematical Physics, 1931–36; Prof. of Physics, Univ. of Wisconsin, 1936–38. Mem. Gen. Adv. Cttee to US Atomic Energy Commn, 1952–57, 1959–64; Director: Nat. Acad. of Sciences Harbor Project for Civil Defense, 1963; Civil Defense Project, Oak Ridge Nat. Lab., 1964–65. Pres., Amer. Physical Soc., 1956 (Vice-Pres., 1955); Member: Amer. Physical Soc.; Amer. Assoc. of Physics Teachers; Amer. Math. Soc.; Amer. Nuclear Soc.; Amer. Assoc. for Adv. of Scis; Sigma Xi; Franklin Inst.; German Physical Soc.; Royal Netherlands Acad. of Science and Letters, 1960; Foreign Mem., Royal Soc., 1970; Corresp. Mem. Acad. of Science, Göttingen, 1951; Austrian Acad. Sciences, 1968; Nat. Acad. Sci. (US); Amer. Philos. Soc.; Amer. Acad. Sci. Hon. Mem., Eötvös Lorand Soc., Hungary, 1976. Citation, NJ Sci. Teachers' Assoc., 1951. US Government Medal for Merit, 1946; Franklin Medal, 1950; Fermi Award, 1958; Atoms for Peace Award, 1960; Max Planck Medal of German Phys. Soc., 1961; Nobel Prize for Physics, 1963; George Washington Award, Amer. Hungarian Studies Assoc., 1964; Semmelweiss Medal, Amer. Hungarian Med. Assoc., 1965; US Nat. Medal for Science, 1969; Pfizer Award, 1971; Albert Einstein Award, 1972; Wigner Medal, 1978. Holds numerous hon. doctorates. *Publications:* Nuclear Structure (with L. Eisenbud), 1958; The Physical Theory of Neutron Chain Reactors (with A. M. Weinberg), 1958; Group Theory (orig. in German, 1931), English trans., NY, 1959 (trans. Hungarian, Russian, 1979); Symmetries and Reflections, 1967 (trans. Hungarian, Russian, 1971); Survival and the Bomb, 1969. *Address:* 8 Ober Road, Princeton, NJ 08540, USA. *T:* 609–924–1189. *Club:* Cosmos (Washington, DC).

WIGODER, family name of **Baron Wigoder.**

WIGODER, Baron *cr* 1974 (Life Peer), of Cheetham in the City of Manchester; **Basil Thomas Wigoder,** QC 1966; Chairman, British United Provident Association, since 1981; *b* 12 Feb. 1921; *s* of late Dr P. I. Wigoder and Mrs R. R. Wigoder, JP, Manchester; *m* 1948, Yoland Levinson; three *s* one *d. Educ:* Manchester Gram. Sch.; Oriel Coll., Oxford (Open Scholar, Mod. Hist.; MA 1946). Served RA, 1942–45. Pres. Oxford Union, 1946. Called to Bar, Gray's Inn, 1946, Master of the Bench, 1972, Vice-Treas., 1988, Treas., 1989. A Recorder of the Crown Court, 1972–84. BoT Inspector, Pinnock Finance (GB) Ltd, 1967. Member: Council of Justice, 1960–; Gen. Council of the Bar, 1970–74; Crown Court Rules Cttee, 1971–77; Council on Tribunals, 1980–86; Home Office Adv. Cttee on Service Candidates, 1984–; Chm., Health Services Bd, 1977–80; a Tribunal Chm., Securities Assoc., 1988–. Chm., Liberal Party Exec., 1963–65; Chm., Liberal Party Organising Cttee, 1965–66; Liberal Chief Whip, House of Lords, 1977–84 (Dep. Whip, 1976–77). Contested (L): Bournemouth, 1945 and by-election, Oct. 1945; Westbury, 1959 and 1964. Vice-President: Nuffield Hosps, 1981–; Statute Law Soc., 1984–90; Mem. Court, Nene Coll., 1982–90; Trustee, Oxford Union Soc., 1982–. *Recreations:* cricket, music. *Address:* House of Lords, SW1A 0PW. *Clubs:* National Liberal, MCC.

WIGRAM, family name of **Baron Wigram.**

WIGRAM, 2nd Baron, *cr* 1935, of Clewer; **George Neville Clive Wigram,** MC 1945; JP; DL; *b* 2 Aug. 1915; *s* of Clive, 1st Baron Wigram, PC, GCB, GCVO, CSI, and Nora Mary (*d* 1956), *d* of Sir Neville Chamberlain, KCB, KCVO; *S* father 1960; *m* 1941, Margaret Helen (*d* 1986), *yr d* of late General Sir Andrew Thorne, KCB, CMG, DSO; one *s* two *d. Educ:* Winchester and Magdalen College, Oxford. Page of Honour to HM King George V, 1925–32; served in Grenadier Guards, 1937–57: Military Secretary and Comptroller to Governor-General of New Zealand, 1946–49; commanded 1st Bn Grenadier Guards, 1955–56. Governor of Westminster Hospital, 1967. JP Gloucestershire, 1959, DL 1969. *Heir: s* Major Hon. Andrew (Francis Clive) Wigram, MVO, late Grenadier Guards [*b* 18 March 1949; *m* 1974, Gabrielle Diana, *y d* of late R. D. Moore; three *s* one *d*]. *Address:* Poulton Fields, Cirencester, Gloucestershire GL7 5SS. *T:* Cirencester (0285) 851250. *Club:* Cavalry and Guards.

WIGRAM, Rev. Canon Sir Clifford Woolmore, 7th Bt, *cr* 1805; Vicar of Marston St Lawrence with Warkworth, near Banbury, 1945–83, also of Thenford, 1975–83; Non-Residentiary Canon of Peterborough Cathedral, 1973–83, Canon Emeritus since 1983; *b* 24 Jan. 1911; *er s* of late Robert Ainger Wigram and Evelyn Dorothy, *d* of C. W. E. Henslowe; *S* uncle, 1935; *m* 1948, Christobel Joan Marriott (*d* 1983), *d* of late William Winter Goode. *Educ:* Winchester; Trinity Coll., Cambridge. Asst Priest at St Ann's, Brondesbury, 1934–37; Chaplain Ely Theological College, 1937. *Heir: b* Maj. Edward Robert Woolmore Wigram, Indian Army [*b* 19 July 1913; *m* 1944, Viva Ann, *d* of late Douglas Bailey, Laughton Lodge, near Lewes, Sussex; one *d. Educ:* Winchester; Trinity Coll., Cambridge. Attached 2nd Batt. South Staffordshire Regt, Bangalore, 1935; Major, 19th KGO Lancers, Lahore, 1938]. *Address:* 2 Mold Cottages, Marston St Lawrence, Banbury, Oxon OX17 2DB.

WIGRAM, Derek Roland, MA, BSc (Econ.); Headmaster of Monkton Combe School, near Bath, 1946–68; *b* 18 Mar. 1908; *er s* of late Roland Lewis Wigram and of Mildred (*née* Willock); *m* 1944, Catharine Mary, *d* of late Very Rev. W. R. Inge, KCVO, DD, former Dean of St Paul's; one *s* one *d*. *Educ:* Marlborough Coll.; Peterhouse, Cambridge (Scholar). 1st Class Hons Classical Tripos, 1929; 2nd Class Hons Economics and Political Science, London, 1943; Assistant Master and Careers Master, Whitgift School, Croydon, 1929–36; House Master and Careers Master, Bryanston School, 1936–46. Hon. Associate Mem., Headmasters' Conf. (Chm., 1963–64); Vice-Pres., CMS (Chm., Exec. Cttee, 1956–58, 1969–72); Patron, Oxford Conf. in Education; Vice Pres. and Trustee of Lee Abbey; Founder Mem., Coll. of Preachers, 1962. Bishops' Inspector of Theological Colls (Mem. Archbishops' Commn, 1970–71). *Publication:* (Jt Editor) Hymns for Church and School, 1964. *Address:* 23 The Pastures, Westwood, Bradford on Avon, Wilts BA15 2BH. *T:* Bradford on Avon (02216) 2362.

WIIN-NIELSEN, Aksel Christopher, Fil.Dr; Professor, Geophysical Institute, University of Copenhagen, since 1988; *b* 17 Dec. 1924; *s* of Aage Nielsen and Marie Petre (*née* Kristoffersen); *m* 1953, Bente Havsteen (*née* Zimsen); three *d*. *Educ:* Univ of Copenhagen (MSc 1950); Univ. of Stockholm (Fil.Lic. 1957; Fil.Dr 1960). Danish Meteorol Inst., 1952–55; Staff Member: Internat. Meteorol Inst., Stockholm, 1955–58; Jt Numerical Weather Prediction Unit, Suitland, Md, USA, 1959–61; Asst Dir, Nat. Center for Atmospherical Research, Boulder, Colorado, 1961–63; Prof., Dept of Atmospheric and Oceanic Sci., Univ. of Michigan, 1963–73; Dir, European Centre for Medium-Range Weather Forecasts, Reading, 1974–79; Sec.-Gen., WMO, 1980–83; Dir, Danish Meteorol Office, 1984–87. Pres., European Geophysical Soc., 1988–90; Vice-Pres., Danish Acad. of Technical Scis, 1989– (Mem., 1984–); Member: Finnish Acad. of Arts and Scis; Royal Swedish Acad. of Sci.; Danish Royal Soc., 1986–; Hon. Mem., RMetS. Hon. DSc: Reading, 1982; Copenhagen, 1986. Buys Ballot Medal, Royal Netherlands Acad., 1982; Wihuri Internat. Prize, Finland, 1983. *Publications:* Dynamic Meteorology, 1970; over 100 scientific publications. *Recreation:* tennis. *Address:* Solbakken 6, 3230 Graested, Denmark.

WILBERFORCE, family name of **Baron Wilberforce.**

WILBERFORCE, Baron, *cr* 1964 (Life Peer); **Richard Orme Wilberforce,** PC 1964; Kt 1961; CMG 1956; OBE 1944; a Lord of Appeal in Ordinary, 1964–82; Fellow, All Souls College, Oxford, since 1932; *b* 11 Mar. 1907; *s* of late S. Wilberforce; *m* 1947, Yvette, *d* of Roger Lenoan, Judge of Court of Cassation, France; one *s* one *d*. *Educ:* Winchester; New College, Oxford. Called to the Bar, 1932; served War, 1939–46 (Hon. Brig.); Under Sec., Control Office Germany and Austria, 1946–47; returned to Bar, 1947; QC 1954; Judge of the High Court of Justice (Chancery Division), 1961–64; Bencher, Middle Temple, 1961. Chm. Exec. Council, Internat. Law Assoc., 1966–88; Mem., Permanent Court of Arbitration; President: Fédération Internationale du Droit Européen, 1978; Appeal Tribunal, Lloyd's of London, 1983–87. Jt Pres., Anti-Slavery Soc.; Vice-President: (jt) RCM; David Davies Meml Inst. Chancellor, Univ. of Hull, 1978–; University of Oxford: High Steward, 1967–90; Visitor: Wolfson Coll., 1974–90; Linacre Coll., 1983–90; Hon. Fellow: New Coll., 1965; Wolfson Coll., 1991. Hon. FRCM. Hon. Comp. Royal Aeronautical Society. Hon. Mem., Scottish Faculty of Advocates, 1978. Hon. DCL Oxon, 1968; Hon. LLD: London, 1972; Hull, 1973; Bristol, 1983. Diplôme d'Honneur, Corp. des Vignerons de Champagne. US Bronze Star, 1944. *Publications:* The Law of Restrictive Trade Practices, 1956; articles and pamphlets on Air Law and International Law. *Recreations:* the turf, travel, opera. *Address:* House of Lords, SW1A 0PW. *Club:* Athenæum.

WILBERFORCE, William John Antony, CMG 1981; HM Diplomatic Service, retired; *b* 3 Jan. 1930; *s* of late Lt-Col W. B. Wilberforce and Cecilia (*née* Dormer); *m* 1953, Laura Lyon, *d* of late Howard Sykes, Englewood, NJ; one *s* two *d*. *Educ:* Ampleforth; Christ Church, Oxford. Army National Service, 2nd Lieut KOYLI, 1948–49. HM Foreign Service, 1953; served: Oslo, 1955–57; Berlin, 1957–59; Ankara, 1962–64; Abidjan, 1964–67; Asst Head of UN (Econ. and Social) Dept, 1967–70, and of Southern European Dept, 1970–72; Counsellor, 1972–74, and Head of Chancery, 1974–75, Washington; Hd of Defence Dept, FCO, 1975–78; Asst Under-Sec., RCDS, 1979; Leader of UK Delegn to Madrid Conf. on Security and Cooperation in Europe Review Meeting, with rank of Ambassador, 1980–82; High Comr in Cyprus, 1982–88. Hon. DHum Wilberforce, 1973. *Recreations:* the turf, travel, gardening. *Address:* Markington Hall, Harrogate HG3 3PQ. *T:* Ripon (0765) 677356. *Club:* Athenæum.

WILBRAHAM; *see* Bootle-Wilbraham, family name of Baron Skelmersdale.

WILBRAHAM, Sir Richard B.; *see* Baker Wilbraham.

WILCOCK, Christopher Camplin; Head of Electricity Division, Department of Energy, since 1991 (Head of Electricity Division A, 1988–91); *b* 13 Sept. 1939; *s* of Arthur Camplin Wilcock and Dorothy (*née* Haigh); *m* 1965, Evelyn Clare Gollin; two *d*. *Educ:* Berkhamsted and Ipswich Schs; Trinity Hall, Cambridge (BA 1st Cl. Hons; MA). FO, 1962–63; MECAS, 1963–64; 3rd Sec., Khartoum, 1964–66; FO, 1966–68; 2nd Sec., UK Delegn to NATO, 1968–70; FO, 1970–72; Hosp. Bldg Div., DHSS, 1972–74; Petroleum Prodn, subseq. Continental Shelf Policy Div., Dept of Energy, 1974–78, Asst Sec. 1976; Electricity Div., 1978–81; on secondment to Shell UK Ltd, 1982–83; Hd of Finance Br., Dept of Energy, 1984–86; Dir of Resource Management (Grade 4), 1986–88; Grade 3, 1988. Order of the Two Niles, Fifth Cl. (Sudan), 1965. *Recreations:* reading, history, cinema. *Address:* Department of Energy, 1 Palace Street, SW1E 5HE.

WILCOCK, Prof. William Leslie; consultant in industrial instrumentation; Professor of Physics, University College of North Wales, Bangor, 1965–82, now Emeritus; *b* 7 July 1922. *Educ:* Manchester Univ. (BSc, PhD). Instrument Dept, RAE, 1943–45. Asst Lectr in Physics, 1945–48, Lectr, 1950–56, Manchester Univ.; DSIR Res. Fellow, St Andrews Univ., 1948–50; Reader in Instrument Technol., 1956–61, in Applied Physics, 1961–65, Imperial Coll. of Science and Technology, London. Arnold O. Beckman Award, Instrument Soc. of Amer., 1977. Mem., SERC, 1981–85. *Publications:* (contrib.) Principles of Optics, 1959; Advances in Electronics and Electron Physics, vols 12–16 (ed jtly), 1960–61; numerous papers in scientific jls. *Address:* Fferm Felin Hen, Y Felin Hen, Bangor, Gwynedd LL57 4BB.

WILCOX, Albert Frederick, CBE 1967; QPM 1957; Chief Constable of Hertfordshire, 1947–69, retired; *b* 18 April 1909; *s* of late Albert Clement Wilcox, Ashley Hill, Bristol; *m* 1939, Ethel, *d* of late E. H. W. Wilmott, Manor House, Whitchurch, Bristol; one *s* two *d*. *Educ:* Fairfield Grammar School, Bristol. Joined Bristol City Police, 1929; Hendon Police Coll., 1934; Metropolitan Police, 1934–43. Served Allied Mil. Govt, Italy and Austria (Lt-Col), 1943–46. Asst Chief Constable of Buckinghamshire, 1946. Cropwood Fellowship, Inst. of Criminology, Cambridge, 1969. Pres. Assoc. of Chief Police Officers, Eng. and Wales, 1966–67; Chm. of Management Cttee, Police Dependents' Trust, 1967–69. Regional Police Commander (designate), 1962–69. Member, Parole Board, 1970–73. Criminological Res. Fellowship, Council of Europe, 1974–76. Barrister-at-Law, Gray's Inn, 1941. Mem. Edit. Bd, Criminal Law Review, 1972–86. *Publication:* The Decision to Prosecute, 1972. *Address:* 34 Roundwood Park, Harpenden, Herts.

WILCOX, David John Reed; His Honour Judge David Wilcox; a Circuit Judge, since 1985; *b* 8 March 1939; *s* of Leslie Leonard Kennedy Wilcox and Margaret Ada Reed Wilcox (*née* Rapson); *m* 1962, Wendy Feay Christine Whiteley; one *s* one *d*. *Educ:* Wednesbury Boys' High Sch.; King's Coll., London (LLB Hons). Called to the Bar, Gray's Inn, 1962. Directorate, Army Legal Services (Captain): Legal Staff, 1962–63; Legal Aid, Far East Land Forces, Singapore, 1963–65. Crown Counsel, Hong Kong, 1965–68; Member, Hong Kong Bar, 1968; in practice, Midland and Midland and Oxford Circuits, 1968–85; a Recorder of the Crown Court, 1979–85. Chm., Nottingham Friendship Housing Assoc., 1970–75. *Recreations:* reading, gardening, travel. *Address:* c/o Crown Court, The Castle, Lincoln.

WILCOX, Rev. Rt. David Peter; *see* Dorking, Bishop Suffragan of.

WILCOX, Desmond John; independent television producer/reporter; journalist and author; *b* 21 May 1931; *e s* of late John Wallace Wilcox and of Alice May Wilcox; *m* 1st (marr. diss.); one *s* two *d*; 2nd, 1977, Esther Rantzen, *qv*; one *s* two *d*. *Educ:* Cheltenham Grammar Sch.; Christ's Coll., London; Outward Bound Sea Sch. Sail training apprentice, 1947; Deckhand, Merchant Marine, 1948; Reporter, weekly papers, 1949; commissioned Army, National Service, 1949–51; News Agency reporter, 1951–52; Reporter and Foreign Correspondent, Daily Mirror, incl. New York Bureau and UN, 1952–60; Reporter, This Week, ITV, 1960–65; joined BBC 1965: Co-Editor/Presenter, Man Alive, 1965; formed Man Alive Unit, 1968; Head of General Features, BBC TV, 1972–80; Writer/Presenter, Americans, TV documentary, 1979; Presenter/Chm., Where it Matters, ITV discussion series, 1981; Producer/Presenter BBC TV series: The Visit, 1982, 1984–87 (TV Radio Industries Club Award for Best Documentary, 1984, 1986), 1989–; The Marriage, 1986; Presenter, 60 Minutes, BBC TV, 1983–84. Man. Dir, Wilcox Bulmer Productions Ltd, 1987–; Chm., Network One Ltd, 1989–. Trustee: Conservation Foundn, 1982–; Walk Again Limb Kinetics, 1984–; Tinbergen Trust (Autistic treatment), 1988–; Mem. of Bd, Disfigurement Guidance Centre, 1988–. SFTA Award for best factual programme series, 1967; Richard Dimbleby Award, SFTA, for most important personal contrib. in factual television, 1971. *Publications:* (jtly) Explorers, 1975; Americans, 1978; (with Esther Rantzen) Kill the Chocolate Biscuit: or Behind the Screen, 1981; (with Esther Rantzen) Baby Love, 1985; Return Visit, 1991. *Recreations:* riding, gardening, television. *Address:* Wilcox Bulmer, 12 Cambridge Court, 210 Shepherds Bush Road, W6 7NL. *T:* 071–602 9811; (agents) Noel Gay Artists, 19 Denmark Street, WC2H 8NA. *T:* 071–836 3941. *Clubs:* Arts, BBC, Groucho.

WILCOX, Esther Louise, (Mrs Desmond Wilcox); *see* Rantzen, E. L.

WILCOX, Judith Ann, (Lady Wilcox); Chairman, National Consumer Council, since 1990; *d* of John and Elsie Freeman; *m* 1st, 1961, Keith Davenport; one *s*; 2nd, 1986, Sir Malcolm George Wilcox, CBE (*d* 1986). *Educ:* St Dunstan's Abbey, Devon; St Mary's Convent, Wantage; Plymouth Polytechnic. Management of family business, High Street trading, Devon, 1960–70; Financial Director: Capstan Foods, Devon, 1970–78; Channel Foods, Cornwall, 1980–88; Pres. Dir Gen., Pêcheries de la Morinie, France, 1988–90; Partner, Morinie et Cie, France, 1990–. Member: Nat. Cttee for Develt of Nat. Curriculum in England and Wales; Money Advice Trust, FHA; Adv. Gp on Eco-labelling, DoE; former Member: Electricity Consumers Council; Area Manpower Boards for Devon and Cornwall; ITEC in Cornwall; Cornwall Cttee for Disabled. Mem. Council, Inst. of Dirs; FBIM. FRSA. *Recreations:* sailing, birdwatching, flyfishing, calligraphy. *Address:* 9 West Eaton Place, SW1X 8LT. *Clubs:* Reform, Annabel's; St Mawes Sailing.

WILD, Dr David; Director of Public Health, South West (Teaching) Regional Health Authority, 1989–90, retired; Director (non-executive), Worthing District Health Authority, since 1990; *b* 27 Jan. 1930; *s* of Frederick and Lena Wild; *m* 1954, Dr Sheila Wightman; one *s* one *d*. *Educ:* Manchester Grammar Sch.; Univ. of Manchester (MB, ChB); Univ. of Liverpool (DPH; FFCM, DMA). Deputy County Medical Officer, 1962, Area Medical Officer, 1974, West Sussex; Regional MO, 1982–86, Dir of Prof. Services, 1986–89, SW (Teaching) RHA. Editor (with Dr Brian Williams), Community Medicine, 1978–84. *Publications:* contribs Jl Central Council of Health Educn, Medical Officer. *Recreation:* conversation. *Address:* 16 Brandy Hole Lane, Chichester, Sussex PO19 4RY. *T:* Chichester (0243) 527125; 13 Surrendale Place, W9. *T:* 071–289 7257.

WILD, David Humphrey; His Honour Judge Wild; a Circuit Judge, since 1972; *b* 24 May 1927; *s* of John S. Wild and Edith Lemarchand; *m* 1963, Estelle Grace Prowett, *d* of James Marshall, Aberdeen and Malaya; one *s*. *Educ:* Whitgift Middle Sch., Croydon. Served War of 1939–45, Royal Navy, 1944–48. Called to Bar, Middle Temple, 1951. Practised, London and SE Circuit, 1951–58, Midland Circuit, 1958–72; resident judge, Cambridge Crown Court, 1973–84. Councillor, Oundle and Thrapston RDC, 1968–72. Mem., St Catharine's Coll., Cambridge, 1973. *Publication:* The Law of Hire Purchase, 1960 (2nd edn, 1964). *Clubs:* Naval and Military, Savile, Sette of Odd Volumes.

WILD, Major Hon. Gerald Percy, AM 1980; MBE 1941; Company Director; Agent-General for Western Australia in London, 1965–71; *b* 2 Jan. 1908; *m* 1944, Virginia Mary Baxter; two *s* one *d*. *Educ:* Shoreham Gram. Sch., Sussex; Chivers Acad., Portsmouth, Hants. Served War of 1939–45 (despatches, MBE): Middle East, Greece, Crete, Syria, New Guinea and Moratai, Netherlands East Indies (Major). Elected MLA for Western Australia, 1947; Minister for Housing and Forests, 1950–53; Minister for Works and Water Supplies and Labour (WA), 1959–65. JP Perth (WA), 1953. *Recreations:* golf, tennis, cricket, football. *Address:* 80 Culeenup Road, North Yunderup, WA 6208, Australia. *T:* (095) 376191. *Clubs:* East India, Devonshire, Sports and Public Schools; West Australian Turf (WA).

WILD, Very Rev. John Herbert Severn, MA Oxon; Hon. DD Durham, 1958; Dean of Durham, 1951–73, Dean Emeritus, since 1973; *b* 22 Dec. 1904; *e s* of Right Rev. Herbert Louis Wild and Helen Christian, *d* of Walter Severn; *m* 1945, Margaret Elizabeth Everard, *d* of G. B. Wainwright, OBE, MB. *Educ:* Clifton Coll.; Brasenose College, Oxford (Scholar); represented Oxford against Cambridge at Three Miles, 1927; Westcott House, Cambridge. Curate of St Aidan, Newcastle upon Tyne, 1929–33; Chaplain-Fellow of University College, Oxford, 1933–45; Master, 1945–51; Hon. Fellow, 1951–; Select Preacher, Univ. of Oxford, 1948–49. Church Comr, 1958–73. ChStJ, 1966–. *Recreations:* fishing, walking. *Address:* Deacons Farmhouse, Rapps, Ilminster, Somerset TA19 9LG. *T:* Ilminster (0460) 53398. *Club:* United Oxford & Cambridge University.

WILD, Dr John Paul, AC 1986; CBE 1978; FRS 1970; FAA 1962; FTS 1978; Chairman, Very Fast Train Joint Venture, since 1986; Chairman and Chief Executive, Commonwealth Scientific and Industrial Research Organization, 1978–85 (Associate Member of Executive, 1977; Chief, Division of Radiophysics, 1971); *b* 1923; *s* of late Alwyn Howard Wild and late Bessie Delafield (*née* Arnold); *m* 1948, Elaine Poole Hull; two *s* one *d*. *Educ:* Whitgift Sch.; Peterhouse, Cambridge (Hon. Fellow 1982). ScD 1962. Radar Officer in Royal Navy, 1943–47; joined Research Staff of Div. of Radiophysics, 1947, working on problems in radio astronomy, esp. of the sun, later also radio navigation (Interscan aircraft landing system). Dep. Chm., 1973–75, 1980–82, Chm., 1975–80,

Anglo-Australian Telescope Bd; Mem. Bd, Interscan (Australia) Pty Ltd, 1978–84. For. Hon. Mem., Amer. Acad. of Arts and Scis, 1961; For. Mem., Amer. Philos. Soc., 1962; Corresp. Mem., Royal Soc. of Scis, Liège, 1969; For. Sec., Australian Acad. of Science, 1973–77. Hon. FIE(Aust), 1991; Hon. FRSA 1991. Hon. DSc: ANU, 1979; Newcastle (NSW), 1982. Edgeworth David Medal, 1958; Hendryk Arctowski Gold Medal, US Nat. Acad. of Scis, 1969; Balthasar van der Pol Gold Medal, Internat. Union of Radio Science, 1969; 1st Herschel Medal, RAS, 1974; Thomas Ranken Lyle Medal, Aust. Acad. of Science, 1975; Royal Medal, Royal Soc., 1980; Hale Medal, Amer. Astronomical Soc., 1980; ANZAAS Medal, 1984; Hartnett Medal, RSA, 1988. *Publications:* numerous research papers and reviews on radio astronomy in scientific jls. *Address:* RMB, 338 Sutton Road, via Queanbeyan, NSW 2620, Australia. *T:* (06) 2383348.

WILD, John Vernon, CMG 1960; OBE 1955; Colonial Administrative Service, retired; *b* 26 April 1915; *m* 1st, 1942, Margaret Patricia Rendell (*d* 1975); one *d* (one *s* decd); 2nd, 1976, Marjorie Mary Lovatt Robertson. *Educ:* Taunton School; King's College, Cambridge. Senior Optime, Cambridge Univ., 1937; Cricket Blue, 1938. Colonial Administrative Service, Uganda: Assistant District Officer, 1938; Assistant Chief Secretary, 1950; Establishment Secretary, 1951; Administrative Secretary, 1955–60; Chairman, Constitutional Committee, 1959. Teacher and Lectr in Mathematics, 1960–76. *Publications:* The Story of the Uganda Agreement; The Uganda Mutiny; Early Travellers in Acholi. *Recreations:* golf, gardening. *Address:* Maplestone Farm, Brede, near Rye, East Sussex TN31 6EP. *T:* Brede (0424) 882261. *Club:* Rye Golf.

WILD, Prof. Raymond, DSc, PhD; CEng, FIMechE, FIProdE; Principal, Henley, The Management College, since 1990; *b* 24 Dec. 1940; *s* of Alice Wild and Frank Wild; *m* 1965, Carol Ann Mellor; one *s* one *d*. *Educ:* Stockport College; Bradford University (PhD (Management), MSc (Eng), MSc (Management)). DSc Brunel, 1988; WhF. Engineering apprentice, Crossley Bros, 1957–62, design engineer, 1962–63, research engineer, 1963–65; postgrad. student, Bradford Univ., 1965–66; production engineer, English Electric, 1966–67; Res. Fellow then Senior Res. Fellow, Bradford Univ., 1967–73; Dir of Grad. Studies, Admin. Staff Coll., Henley, 1973–77, Mem., Senior Staff, Henley Management Coll., 1973–; Brunel University: Dir, Special Engineering Programme, 1977–84; Hd, Dept of Engrg and Management Systems, 1977–86; Hd, Dept of Prodn Technology, 1984–86; Hd, Dept of Manufacturing and Engrg Systems, 1986–89; Pro-Vice-Chancellor, 1988–89. CBIM, FRSA. Editor-in-Chief, Internat. Jl of Computer Integrated Manufacturing Systems, 1988–. *Publications:* The Techniques of Production Management, 1971; Management and Production, 1972, trans. Greek 1984; (with A. B. Hill and C. C. Ridgeway) Women in the Factory, 1972; Mass Production Management, 1972; (with B. Lowes) Principles of Modern Management, 1972; Work Organization, 1975; Concepts for Operations Management, 1977; Production and Operations Management, 1979, 4th edn 1989; Operations Management: a policy framework, 1980; Essentials of Production and Operations Management, 1980, 3rd edn 1990; (ed) Management and Production Readings, 1981; Read and Explain (4 children's books on technology), 1982 and 1983, trans. French, Swedish, German, Danish; How to Manage, 1983, USA edn 1985; (ed) International Handbook of Production and Operations Management, 1989; (ed) Technology and Management, 1990; papers in learned jls. *Recreations:* writing, do it yourself, restoring houses, travel. *Address:* Broomfield, New Road, Shiplake, Henley on Thames, Oxon RG9 3LA. *T:* Wargrave (0734) 404102.

WILD, Robert; Director, Project Underwriting Group, Export Credits Guarantee Department, since 1989; *b* 19 April 1932; *s* of Thomas Egan Wild and Janet Wild; *m* 1955, Irene Whitton Martin; two *d*. *Educ:* King Edward VII Sch., Lytham. Board of Trade, 1950; Export Credits Guarantee Dept, 1959. *Recreations:* bird watching, archaeology, reading. *Address:* Export Credits Guarantee Department, 2 Exchange Tower, Harbour Exchange Square, E14 9GS. *T:* 071–512 7008. *Club:* Overseas Bankers'.

WILDE, Derek Edward, CBE 1978; Vice Chairman, 1972–77, and Director, 1969–83, Barclays Bank Ltd; Deputy Chairman, Charterhouse Group, 1980–83; *b* 6 May 1912; *s* of late William Henry Wilde and Ethel May Wilde; *m* 1940, Helen, *d* of William Harrison; (one *d* decd). *Educ:* King Edward VII School, Sheffield. Entered Barclays Bank Ltd, Sheffield, 1929; General Manager, 1961; Sen. General Manager, 1966–72. Dir, Yorkshire Bank Ltd, 1972–80; Chairman: Keyser Ullmann Holdings, 1975–81; Charterhouse Japhet, 1980–81. Governor, Midhurst Med. Res. Inst., 1970–85. Fellow, Inst. of Bankers (Hon. Fellow 1975). Hon. DLitt Loughborough, 1980. *Recreation:* gardening. *Address:* Ranmoor, Smarts Hill, Penshurst, Kent. *T:* Penshurst (0892) 870228.

WILDE, Peter Appleton; HM Diplomatic Service, retired; *b* 5 April 1925; *m* 1950, Frances Elisabeth Candida Bayliss; two *s*. *Educ:* Chesterfield Grammar Sch.; St Edmund Hall, Oxford. Army (National Service), 1943–47; Temp. Asst Lectr, Southampton, 1950; FO, 1950; 3rd Sec., Bangkok, 1951–53; Vice-Consul, Zürich, 1953–54; FO, 1954–57; 2nd Sec., Baghdad, 1957–58; 1st Sec., UK Delegn to OEEC (later OECD), Paris, 1958–61; 1st Sec., Katmandu, 1961–64; FO (later FCO), 1964–69; Consul-Gen., Lourenço Marques, 1969–71; Dep. High Comr, Colombo, 1971–73. Mem., Llanfihangel Rhosycorn Community Council, 1974–83. Member: Management Cttee, Carmarthenshire Pest Control Soc. Ltd, 1974–82; Council, Royal Forestry Soc., 1977–86; Regional Adv. Cttee, Wales Conservancy, Forestry Commn, 1985–87 (Mem., Regional Adv. Cttee, S Wales Conservancy, 1983–85). *Recreation:* forestry. *Address:* Nantyperchyll, Gwernogle, Carmarthen, Dyfed SA32 7RR. *T:* Brechfa (0267) 202241.

WILDENSTEIN, Daniel Leopold; art historian; President, Wildenstein Foundation Inc., since 1964; Chairman, Wildenstein & Co Inc., New York, since 1968 (Vice-President, 1943–59, President, 1959–68); Vice-President, Florence Gould Foundation, since 1983; *b* Verrières-le-Buisson, France, 11 Sept. 1917; *s* of Georges Wildenstein; *m* 1939, Martine Kapferer (marr. diss. 1968); two *s*; *m* 1978, Sylvia Roth. *Educ:* Cours Hattemer; Sorbonne (LèsL 1938). Gp Sec., French Pavilion, World's Fair, 1937; went to US, 1940; with Wildenstein & Co. Inc., New York, 1940–; Director: Wildenstein & Co. Inc., London, 1963–; Wildenstein Arte, Buenos Aires, 1963–. Dir, Gazette des Beaux Arts, 1963–; Dir of Activities, Musée Jacquemart-André, Paris, 1956–62; Musée Chaalis, Institut de France, Paris, 1956–62; organiser of art competitions (Hallmark art award). Mem., French Chamber of Commerce in US (Conseiller), 1942–; Founder (1947) and Mem, Amer. Inst. of France (Sec.). Mem., Institut de France (Académie des Beaux-Arts), 1971; Membre du Haut Comité du Musée de Monaco. *Publications:* Claude Monet, vol. 1, 1975, vols 2 and 3, 1979, vol. 4, 1985; Edouard Manet, vol. 1, 1976, vol. 2, 1977; Gustave Courbet, vol. 1, 1977, vol. 2, 1978. *Recreation:* horse racing (leading owner, 1977). *Address:* 48 avenue de Rumine, 1007 Lausanne, Switzerland; (office) 57 rue La Boétie, 75008 Paris, France. *T:* 45 63 01 00. *Clubs:* Brooks's; Turf and Field, Madison Square Garden (New York); Cercle de Deauville, Tir au Pigeon (Paris); Jockey (Buenos Aires).

WILDING, Richard William Longworth, CB 1979; Head of Office of Arts and Libraries, Cabinet Office, 1984–88; *b* 22 April 1929; *er s* of late L. A. Wilding; *m* 1954, Mary Rosamund de Villiers; one *s* two *d*. *Educ:* Dragon Sch., Oxford; Winchester Coll.; New Coll., Oxford (MA). HM Foreign Service, 1953–59; transf. to Home Civil Service, 1959; Principal, HM Treasury, 1959–67; Sec., Fulton Cttee on Civil Service, 1966–68; Asst Sec., Civil Service Dept, 1968–70; Asst Sec., Supplementary Benefits Commn, DHSS, 1970–72; Under-Sec., Management Services, 1972–76, Pay, 1976, CSD; Deputy Secretary: CSD, 1976–81; HM Treasury, 1981–83. Review of Structure of Arts Funding in England, 1989; Review of Redundant Churches Fund, 1990. Trustee, Nat. Museums and Galleries on Merseyside, 1989–. *Publications:* (with L. A. Wilding) A Classical Anthology, 1954; Key to Latin Course for Schools, 1966; The Care of Redundant Churches, 1990; articles in Jl Public Administration, Social Work Today, Studies. *Recreations:* music, gardening. *Address:* 14 The Lodge, Kensington Park Gardens, W11 3HA. *T:* 071–727 6880. *Club:* Athenæum.

WILDISH, Vice-Adm. Denis Bryan Harvey, CB 1968; Director General of Personal Services and Training (Naval), 1970–72, retired; *b* 24 Dec. 1914; *s* of late Rear-Adm. Sir Henry William Wildish, KBE, CB; *m* 1941, Leslie Henrietta Jacob; two *d*. *Educ:* RNC Dartmouth; RNEC. Entered Royal Navy, 1928; Comdr 1948; Capt. 1957; Rear-Adm. 1966; Vice-Adm. 1970. Dir of Fleet Maintenance, 1962–64; Commodore Naval Drafting, 1964–66; Adm. Supt, HM Dockyard, Devonport, 1966–70. *Recreations:* cricket, painting. *Address:* 78 Grenehurst Way, Petersfield, Hants GU31 4AZ. *Clubs:* Army and Navy, MCC.

WILDSMITH, Brian Lawrence; artist and maker of picture books for young children; *b* 22 Jan. 1930; *s* of Paul Wildsmith and Annie Elizabeth Oxley; *m* 1955, Aurelie Janet Craigie Ithurbide; one *s* three *d*. *Educ:* de la Salle Coll.; Barnsley Sch. of Art; Slade Sch. of Fine Arts. Art Master, Selhurst Grammar School for Boys, 1954–57; freelance artist, 1975–. Production design, illustrations, titles and graphics for first USA-USSR Leningrad film co-production of the Blue Bird. Kate Greenaway Medal, 1962; Soka Gakkai Japan Educn Medal, 1988. *Publications:* ABC, 1962; The Lion and the Rat, 1963; The North Wind and the Sun, 1964; Mother Goose, 1964; 1; 2; 3;, 1965; The Rich Man and the Shoemaker, 1965; The Hare and the Tortoise, 1966; Birds, 1967; Animals, 1967; Fish, 1968; The Miller the Boy and the Donkey, 1969; The Circus, 1970; Puzzles, 1970; The Owl and the Woodpecker, 1971; The Twelve Days of Christmas, 1972; The Little Wood Duck, 1972; The Lazy Bear, 1973; Squirrels, 1974; Pythons Party, 1974; The Blue Bird, 1976; The True Cross, 1977; What the Moon Saw, 1978; Hunter and his Dog, 1979; Animal Shapes, 1980; Animal Homes, 1980; Animal Games, 1980; Animal Tricks, 1980; The Seasons, 1980; Professor Noah's Spaceship, 1980; Bears Adventure, 1981; The Trunk, 1982; Cat on the Mat, 1982; Pelican, 1982; The Apple Bird, 1983; The Island, 1983; All Fall Down, 1983; The Nest, 1983; Daisy, 1984; Who's Shoes, 1984; Toot Toot, 1984; Give a Dog a Bone, 1985; Goats Trail, 1986; My Dream, 1986; What a Tail, 1986; If I Were You, 1987; Giddy Up . . ., 1987; Carousel, 1988; The Christmas Story, 1989; The Snow Country Prince, 1990; The Cheery Tree, 1991; The Princess and the Moon, 1991. *Recreations:* squash, tennis, music (piano). *Address:* 11 Castellaras, 06370 Mouans-Sartoux, France. *T:* (93) 75.24.11. *Club:* Reform.

WILEMAN, Margaret Annie, MA; Honorary Fellow since 1973 (President (formerly Principal), 1953–73), Hughes Hall, Cambridge; *b* 19 July 1908; *e d* of Clement Wileman and Alice (*née* Brinson). *Educ:* Lady Margaret Hall, Oxford, and the University of Paris. Scholar of Lady Margaret Hall, Oxford, 1927; First in Hons School of Mod. Langs, 1930; Zaharoff Travelling Scholar, 1931; Assistant, Abbey School, Reading, 1934; Senior Tutor, Queen's College, Harley Street, 1937; Lecturer, St Katherine's Coll., Liverpool, 1940; Resident Tutor, Bedford College, Univ. of London, 1944–53; Univ. Lectr, and Dir of Women Students, Dept of Educn, Cambridge Univ., 1953–73. *Address:* 5 Drosier Road, Cambridge CB1 2EY. *T:* Cambridge (0223) 351846. *Club:* University Women's.

WILES, Prof. Andrew John, PhD; FRS 1989; Professor of Mathematics, Princeton University, 1980–88 and since 1990. *Educ:* Clare Coll., Cambridge (MA 1977; PhD 1980); MA Oxon 1988. Sometime Fellow, Clare Coll., Cambridge; Royal Society Research Professor in Maths and Professorial Fellow of Merton Coll., Oxford University, 1988–90. (Jtly) Jun. Whitehead Prize, London Math. Soc., 1988. *Address:* Department of Mathematics, Princeton University, Fine Hall, Washington Hall, Princeton, NJ 08544, USA.

WILES, Sir Donald (Alonzo), KA 1984; CMG 1965; OBE 1960; Consultant to Barbados National Trust, since 1985; *b* 8 Jan. 1912; *s* of Donald Alonzo Wiles and Millicent Wiles; *m* 1938, Amelia Elsie Pemberton; two *d*. *Educ:* Harrison Coll., Barbados; Univs of London, Toronto, Oxford. Member of Staff of Harrison College, Barbados, 1931–45; Public Librarian, Barbados, 1945–50; Asst Colonial Secretary, Barbados, 1950–54; Permanent Secretary, Barbados, 1954–60; Administrator, Montserrat, 1960–64; Administrative Sec., Da Costa & Musson Ltd, 1965–79. Exec. Dir, Barbados Nat. Trust, 1980–84. *Recreations:* swimming, hiking, tennis. *Address:* Casa Loma, Sunrise Drive, Pine Gardens, St Michael, Barbados. *T:* 426–6875.

WILES, Rev. Prof. Maurice Frank, FBA 1981; Canon of Christ Church, Oxford, and Regius Professor of Divinity, 1970–91; *b* 17 Oct. 1923; *s* of late Sir Harold Wiles, KBE, CB, and Lady Wiles; *m* 1950, Patricia Margaret (*née* Mowll); two *s* one *d*. *Educ:* Tonbridge School; Christ's College, Cambridge. Curate, St George's, Stockport, 1950–52; Chaplain, Ridley Hall, Cambridge, 1952–55; Lectr in New Testament Studies, Ibadan, Nigeria, 1955–59; Lectr in Divinity, Univ. of Cambridge, and Dean of Clare College, 1959–67; Prof. of Christian Doctrine, King's Coll., Univ. of London, 1967–70; Bampton Lectr, Univ. of Oxford, 1986. FKC 1972. *Publications:* The Spiritual Gospel, 1960; The Christian Fathers, 1966; The Divine Apostle, 1967; The Making of Christian Doctrine, 1967; The Remaking of Christian Doctrine, 1974; (with M. Santer) Documents in Early Christian Thought, 1975; Working Papers in Doctrine, 1976; What is Theology?, 1976; Explorations in Theology 4, 1979; Faith and the Mystery of God, 1982 (Collins Biennial Religious Book Award, 1983); God's Action in the World, 1986. *Address:* Christ Church, Oxford.

WILES, Prof. Peter John de la Fosse, FBA 1990; Professor of Russian Social and Economic Studies, University of London, 1965–85, now Emeritus; *b* 25 Nov. 1919; *m* 1st, 1945, Elizabeth Coppin (marr. diss., 1960); one *s* two *d*; 2nd, 1960, Carolyn Stedman. *Educ:* Lambrook Sch.; Winchester Coll.; New Coll., Oxford. Royal Artillery, 1940–45 (despatches twice; mainly attached Intelligence Corps). Fellow, All Souls Coll., Oxford, 1947–48; Fellow, New Coll., Oxford, 1948–60; Prof., Brandeis Univ., USA, 1960–63; Research Associate, Institutet för Internationell Ekonomi, Stockholm, 1963–64. Visiting Professor: Columbia Univ., USA, 1958; City Coll. of New York, 1964 and 1967; Collège de France, 1972; Ecole des Sciences Politiques, 1979; Univ. of Windsor, Ont., 1986. *Publications:* The Political Economy of Communism, 1962; Price, Cost and Output (2nd edn), 1962; Communist International Economics, 1968; (ed) The Prediction of Communist Economic Performance, 1971; Economic Institutions Compared, 1977; Die Parallelwirtschaft, 1981; (ed) The New Communist Third World, 1981; (ed with Guy Routh) Economics in Disarray, 1985. *Recreations:* simple. *Address:* 23 Ridgmount Gardens, WC1.

WILFORD, Sir (Kenneth) Michael, GCMG 1980 (KCMG 1976; CMG 1967); HM Diplomatic Service, retired; *b* Wellington, New Zealand, 31 Jan. 1922; *yr s* of late George

McLean Wilford and late Dorothy Veronica (*née* Wilson); *m* 1944, Joan Mary, *d* of Captain E. F. B. Law, RN; three *d*. *Educ:* Wrekin College; Pembroke College, Cambridge. Served in Royal Engineers, 1940–46 (despatches). Entered HM Foreign (subseq. Diplomatic) Service, 1947; Third Sec., Berlin, 1947; Asst Private Secretary to Secretary of State, Foreign Office, 1949; Paris, 1952; Singapore, 1955; Asst Private Sec. to Sec. of State, Foreign Office, 1959; Private Sec. to the Lord Privy Seal, 1960; served Rabat, 1962; Counsellor (Office of British Chargé d'Affaires) also Consul-General, Peking, 1964–66; Visiting Fellow of All Souls, Oxford, 1966–67; Counsellor, Washington, 1967–69; Asst Under Sec. of State, FCO, 1969–73; Dep. Under Sec. of State, FCO, 1973–75; Ambassador to Japan, 1975–80. Director: Lloyds Bank Internat., 1982–85; Lloyds Merchant Bank Ltd, 1986–87; Adviser, Baring Internat. Investment Management, 1982–90. Chm., Royal Soc. for Asian Affairs, 1984–; Hon. Pres., Japan Assoc., 1981–. *Recreations:* golf, gardening. *Address:* Brook Cottage, Abbotts Ann, Andover, Hants SP11 7DS. *T:* Andover (0264) 710509.

WILHELM, Most Rev. Joseph Lawrence, DD, JCD; former Archbishop of Kingston, Ontario, (RC); *b* Walkerton, Ontario, 16 Nov. 1909. *Educ:* St Augustine's Seminary, Toronto; Ottawa Univ., Ottawa, Ont. Ordained priest, Toronto, 1934. Mil. Chaplain to Canadian Forces, 1940–46 (MC, Sicily, 1943). Auxiliary Bishop, Calgary, Alberta, 1963–66; Archbishop of Kingston, Ont, 1967–82. Hon. DD Queen's Univ., Kingston, Ont, 1970. *Address:* The Anchorage, Belleville, Ont, Canada.

WILKES, Prof. Eric, OBE (civil) 1974 (MBE (mil.) 1943); DL; FRCP, FRCGP, FRCPsych; Professor of Community Care and General Practice, Sheffield University, 1973–83, now Emeritus; *b* 12 Jan. 1920; *s* of George and Doris Wilkes; *m* 1953, Jessica Mary Grant; two *s* one *d*. *Educ:* Royal Grammar Sch., Newcastle upon Tyne; King's Coll., Cambridge (MA); St Thomas' Hosp., SE1 (MB, BChir). Lt-Col, Royal Signals, 1944. General Medical Practitioner, Derbyshire, 1954–73. High Sheriff of S Yorkshire, 1977–78. Med. Director, St Luke's Nursing Home, later St Luke's Hospice, Sheffield, 1971–86; Hon. Consultant, Centre for Palliative and Continuing Care, Trent RHA, 1989–. Chairman: Sheffield and Rotherham Assoc. for the Care and Resettlement of Offenders, 1976–83; Sheffield Council on Alcoholism, 1976–83; Prevention Cttee, Nat. Council on Alcoholism, 1980–83; Trinity Day Care Trust, 1979–83; Sheffield Victim Support Scheme, 1983–84; Mem., Nat. Cancer sub cttee, 1979–88; Pres., Inst. of Religion and Medicine, 1982–83; Trustee, Help the Hospices, 1984– (Co-Chm., 1984–; Chm., Trng and Educn Sub-Cttee, 1984–89). DL Derbys, 1984. Hon. Fellow, Sheffield City Polytechnic, 1985. Hon. MD Sheffield, 1986. *Publications:* The Dying Patient, 1982; Long-Term Prescribing, 1982; various chapters and papers, mainly on chronic and incurable illness. *Recreations:* gardening, fishing, natural history. *Address:* Curbar View Farm, Calver, Sheffield S30 1XR. *T:* Hope Valley (0433) 31291.

WILKES, Prof. John Joseph, FSA; FBA 1986; Professor of Archaeology of the Roman Provinces, University of London, since 1974; *b* 12 July 1936; *s* of Arthur Cyril Wilkes and Enid Cecilia Eustance; *m* 1980, Dr Susan Walker; one *s*. *Educ:* King Henry VIII Grammar Sch., Coventry; Harrow County Grammar Sch.; University Coll. London (BA); Univ. of Durham (St Cuthbert's Society) (PhD). FSA 1969. Research Fellow, Univ. of Birmingham, 1961–63; Asst Lectr in History and Archaeology, Univ. of Manchester, 1963–64; Lectr in Roman History, 1964–71, Sen. Lectr 1971–74, Univ. of Birmingham. Chm., Faculty of Archaeology, Hist. and Letters, British Sch. at Rome, 1979–83. Vis. Fellow, Inst. of Humanistic Studies, Pennsylvania State Univ., 1971. Mem., Ancient Monuments Bd for Scotland, 1981–. Vice-Pres., Soc. for Promotion of Roman Studies, 1978; Pres., London and Middx Archaeological Soc., 1982–85. Corresp. Mem., German Archaeol Inst., 1976. Governor, Mus. of London, 1981–. Editor, Britannia, 1980–84. *Publications:* Dalmatia (Provinces of Roman Empire series), 1969; (jtly) Diocletian's Palace: joint excavations in the southeast quarter, Pt 1, Split, 1972; (ed jtly) Victoria County History of Cambridgeshire, vol. VII, Roman Cambridgeshire, 1978; Rhind Lectures (Edinburgh), 1984; Diocletian's Palace, Split (2nd Ian Saunders Meml Lecture, expanded), 1986; (jtly) Strageath: excavations within the Roman Fort 1973–1986, 1989; papers, excavation reports and reviews in learned jls of Britain, Amer., and Europe. *Recreations:* listening to music, watching Association football. *Address:* Institute of Archaeology, 31–34 Gordon Square, WC1H 0PY. *T:* 071–387 6052.

WILKES, Maurice Vincent, MA, PhD; FRS 1956; FEng 1976; FIEE; FBCS; Consultant on Research Strategy, Olivetti Research Directorate, since 1990 (Member for Research Strategy, Olivetti Research Board, 1980–86); Head of the Computer Laboratory, Cambridge (formerly Mathematical Laboratory), 1970–80; Professor of Computer Technology, 1965–80, now Emeritus Professor; Fellow of St John's College, since 1950; *b* 26 June 1913; *s* of late Vincent J. Wilkes, OBE; *m* 1947, Nina Twyman; one *s* two *d*. *Educ:* King Edward's School, Stourbridge; St John's College, Cambridge. Mathematical Tripos (Wrangler). Research in physics at Cavendish Lab.; Univ. Demonstrator, 1937. Served War of 1939–45, Radar and Operational Research. Univ. Lecturer and Acting Dir of Mathematical Laboratory, Cambridge, 1945; Dir of Mathematical Laboratory, 1946–70. Computer Engr, Digital Equipment Corp., USA, 1980–86; Adjunct Prof. of Computer Sci. and Elect. Engrg, MIT, 1981–85. Member: Measurement and Control Section Committee, IEE, 1956–59; Council, IEE, 1973–76; First President British Computer Soc., 1957–60, Distinguished Fellow 1973. Mem. Council, IFIP, 1960–63; Chm. IEE E Anglia Sub-Centre, 1969–70; Turing Lectr Assoc. for Computing Machinery, 1967. Foreign Hon. Mem., Amer. Acad. of Arts and Sciences, 1974; Foreign Corresponding Mem., Royal Spanish Acad. of Sciences, 1979; Foreign Associate: US Nat. Acad. of Engrg, 1977; US Nat. Acad. of Scis, 1980. Hon. DSc: Newcastle upon Tyne, 1972; Hull, 1974; Kent, 1975; City, 1975; Amsterdam, 1978; Munich, 1978; Bath, 1987; Hon. DTech Linköping, 1975. Harry Goode Award, Amer. Fedn of Inf. Processing Socs, 1968; Eckert-Mauchly Award, Assoc. for Computing Machinery and IEEE Computer Soc., 1980; McDowell Award, IEEE Computer Soc., 1981; Faraday Medal, IEE, 1981; Pender Award, Univ. of Pennsylvania, 1982; C & C Prize, Foundn for C & C Promotions, Tokyo, 1988. *Publications:* Oscillations of the Earth's Atmosphere, 1949; (joint) Preparations of Programs for an Electronic Digital Computer, Addison-Wesley (Cambridge, Mass), 1951, 2nd edn 1958; Automatic Digital Computers, 1956; A Short Introduction to Numerical Analysis, 1966; Time-sharing Computer System, 1968, 3rd edn 1975; (jtly) The Cambridge CAP Computer and its Operating System, 1979; Memoirs of a Computer Pioneer, 1985; papers in scientific jls. *Address:* Olivetti Research Ltd, 24a Trumpington Street, Cambridge CB2 3NJ. *T:* Cambridge (0223) 343300. *Club:* Athenæum.

WILKES, Ven. Michael Jocelyn James P.; *see* Paget-Wilkes.

WILKES, Lt-Gen. Sir Michael (John), KCB 1991; CBE 1988 (OBE 1980); Commander United Kingdom Field Army and Inspector General of the Territorial Army, since 1990; *b* 11 June 1940; *s* of late Lt-Col Jack Wilkes, OBE, MC and of Phyllis Wilkes; *m* 1966, Anne Jacqueline Huelin; two *s*. *Educ:* King's Sch., Rochester; RMA Sandhurst. Commnd RA, 1960; joined 7 Para Regt, RHA, 1961; served ME Troop, Comdr Special Forces, 1964–67, Radfan, S Arabia, Borneo; Staff Coll., 1971–72; Bde Major RA, HQ3 Armd Div., 1973–74; Battery Comdr Chestnut Troop, 1 RHA (BAOR), 1975–76, CO, 1977–79; Mil. Asst to CGS, 1980–81; COS, 3 Armd Div., 1982–83; Comdr, 22 Armd Bde, 1984–85; Arms Dir, MoD, 1986–88; GOC 3 Armd Div., 1988–90. *Recreations:* sailing, ski-ing, hill walking, travelling. *Clubs:* Travellers', Special Forces.

WILKES, Richard Geoffrey, CBE 1990 (OBE (mil.) 1969); TD 1959; DL; FCA; Director, Cassidy, Davis Holdings Ltd, since 1989; Partner, Price Waterhouse, Chartered Accountants, 1969–90; *b* 12 June 1928; *s* of Geoffrey W. Wilkes and Kathleen (*née* Quinn); *m* 1953, Wendy Elaine, *d* of Rev. C. Ward; one *s* three *d*. *Educ:* Repton (Exhibnr). ACA 1952; FCA 1957. Partner, Bolton Bullivant, Chartered Accountants, Leicester, 1953–69. Pres., Leics and Northants Soc. of Chartered Accountants, 1967–68; Mem. Council, Inst. of Chartered Accountants in England and Wales, 1969–90 (Dep. Pres., 1979–80; Pres., 1980–81); Chairman: UK Auditing Practices Cttee, 1976–78; CA Compensation Scheme, 1990–; International Federation of Accountants: UK Rep; Mem. Council, 1983–87; Dep. Pres., 1985–87; Pres., 1987–90; Mem., Internat. Auditing Practices Cttee, 1978–79; Adviser on self-regulation, Lloyd's of London, 1983–85. Governor, CARE for the Mentally Handicapped, 1972–. Commnd RHA, 1947; served TA, RA and Royal Leics Regt, 1948–69; CO 4/5th Bn Royal Leics Regt (TA), 1966–69; Col TAVR E Midlands Dist, 1969–73; ADC (TAVR) to the Queen, 1972–77. Dep. Hon. Col, Royal Anglian Regt (Leics), 1981–88; Vice Chm., E Midlands TA&VRA, 1980–89 (Chm., Leics Co. Cttee, 1980–89); Chm., E Midlands TAVRA Employers Liaison Cttee, 1990–. Comdt, Leics Special Constab., 1972–79. Mem., Court, Worshipful Co. of Chartered Accountants in England and Wales, 1977– (Master, 1991–92). DL Leics, 1967. Internat. Award, ICA, 1990. *Recreations:* shooting, sailing. *Address:* The Hermitage, Swingbridge Street, Foxton, Market Harborough, Leics LE16 7RH. *T:* East Langton (085884) 213. *Club:* Army and Navy.

WILKIE, Prof. Douglas Robert, FRS 1971; Jodrell Research Professor of Physiology, in the University of London, 1979–88, now Emeritus Research Professor; *b* 2 Oct. 1922; *m* 1949, June Rosalind Hill (marr. diss. 1982); one *s*. *Educ:* Medical Student, University Coll. London, 1940–42 (Fellow, 1972); Yale Univ. (MD), 1942–43; University Coll. Hosp., MB, BS, 1944, MRCP 1945; FRCP 1972. Lectr, Dept of Physiology, UCL, 1948; Inst. of Aviation Medicine, Farnborough (Mil. Service), 1948–50; London University: Locke Research Fellowship (Royal Soc.), UCL, 1951–54; Readership in Experimental Physiology, UCL, 1954–65; Prof. of Experimental Physiology, 1965–69; Jodrell Prof., and Head of Physiology Dept, UCL, 1969–79. SRC Sen. Res. Fellowship, 1978. *Publications:* Muscle, 1968; contribs to learned jls, etc, mainly research on energetics of muscular contraction, and attempts to make thermodynamics simpler, recently, application of nuclear magnetic resonance in medicine. *Recreations:* sailing, friends, photography. *Address:* 2 Wychwood End, Stanhope Road, N6 5ND. *T:* 071–272 4024.

WILKIN, (Frederick) John, CBE 1978 (OBE 1968); DFM 1943; Chairman, The Wickenby Register (12 and 626 Squadrons Association), since 1983; Member of Council, National Incorporated Beneficent Society, since 1968; *b* 15 Aug. 1916; *s* of late George Wilkin and Rosetta Christina Wilkin; *m* 1st, 1943, Marjorie Joan Wilson (*d* 1972); one *d*; 2nd, 1975, Laura Elizabeth Eason; one *s* one *d*. *Educ:* Southwark Central Sch.; Morley Coll., London. Served RAF, 1940–46: Navigator (12, 101 and 156 Sqdns); Permanent Award Pathfinder Badge. Asst Accountant, House of Commons, 1955, Chief Accountant, 1962–80; Secretary: House of Commons Members' Fund, 1962–81; Parliamentary Contributory Pensions Fund, 1965–80; Head of Admin Dept, House of Commons, 1980–81. Associate Mem. of Special Trustees, Charing Cross and Westminster Hosps, 1979–91; Vice-Chm., Hammersmith and Fulham DHA, 1982–83. Mem., Guild of Freemen of City of London. *Recreations:* gardening, watching sport; formerly cricket, cycling, table tennis. *Address:* 14 Forest Ridge, Beckenham, Kent BR3 3NH. *T:* 081–650 5261. *Clubs:* Royal Air Force, Pathfinder.

WILKINS, Sir Graham John, (Bob), Kt 1980; Director, Eastern Electricity, since 1990; Chairman, THORN EMI, 1985–89, retired (Chief Executive, 1985–87); President, Beecham Group Ltd, 1984–89 (Chairman and Chief Executive, 1975–84); *b* 22 Jan. 1924; *s* of George William and Anne May Wilkins; *m* 1st, 1945, Daphne Mildred Haynes; 2nd, 1990, Helen Catherine McGregor. *Educ:* Yeovil Sch.; University Coll., South West of England, Exeter (BSc). Dir and Vice-Pres., Beecham (Canada) Ltd, 1954–59; C. L. Bencard Ltd, and Beecham Research Labs Ltd: Asst Man. Dir, 1959; Man. Dir, 1960; Dir, Beecham Pharmaceutical Div., 1962–64; Beecham Group Ltd: Dir and Chm., Pharmaceutical Div., 1964–72; Man. Dir (Pharmaceuticals), 1972; Exec. Vice-Chm., 1974; Chm., ICC UK, 1985–89 (Vice Chm., 1984–85); Director: Beecham Inc., 1967–86; Hill Samuel Gp Ltd, 1977–87; THORN EMI (formerly Thorn Electrical Industries) Ltd, 1978–89; Rowntree, 1985–88 (Dep. Chm., 1988). Mem., Doctors' and Dentists' Remuneration Rev. Bd, 1980–90 (Chm., 1986–90). Vice-Chm., Proprietary Assoc. of GB, 1966–68; President: Assoc. of Brit. Pharmaceutical Industry, 1969–71 (Vice-Pres., 1968–69); European Fedn of Pharmaceutical Industries Assoc., 1978–82; Chm., Medico-Pharmaceutical Forum, 1971–73 (Vice-Chm., 1969–70). Mem., BOTB, 1977–80. Pres., Advertising Assoc., 1983–89. Mem. Council, Sch. of Pharmacy, London Univ., 1984– (Chm., 1987–). Hon. FRCP 1984. *Publications:* various papers on pharmaceutical industry. *Recreations:* golf, theatre-going. *Address:* Alceda, Walton Lane, Shepperton-on-Thames, Mddx TW17 8LQ.

WILKINS, John Anthony Francis; Editor of The Tablet, since 1982; *b* 20 Dec. 1936; *s* of Edward Manwaring Wilkins and Ena Gwendolen Francis. *Educ:* Clifton Coll., Bristol (Scholar); Clare Coll., Cambridge (State Scholar, 1954; Major Scholar and Foundn Scholar; Classical Tripos 1959, Theol Tripos 1961; BA 1961). Served 1st Bn Glos Regt, 1955–57 (2nd Lieut). Planning Div., Marine Dept, Head Office of Esso Petroleum, London, 1962–63; Asst Editor: Frontier, 1964–67; The Tablet, 1967–72; features writer, BBC External Services, 1972–81; Producer, Radio 4, 1978. Ondas Radio Prize, 1973. *Recreation:* ornithology. *Address:* The Tablet, 48 Great Peter Street, SW1P 2HB. *T:* 071–222 7462.

WILKINS, Prof. Malcolm Barrett, FRSE 1972; Regius Professor of Botany, since 1970 and Chairman, School of Biological Sciences, since 1988, University of Glasgow (Dean, Faculty of Science, 1984–87); *b* 27 Feb. 1933; *s* of Barrett Charles Wilkins and Eleanor Mary Wilkins (*née* Jenkins); *m* 1959, Mary Patricia Maltby; one *s* (one *d* decd). *Educ:* Monkton House Sch., Cardiff; King's Coll., London. BSc 1955; PhD London 1958; AKC 1958; DSc 1972. Lectr in Botany, King's Coll., London, 1958–64; Rockefeller Foundn Fellow, Yale Univ., 1961–62; Research Fellow, Harvard Univ., 1962–63; Lectr in Biology, Univ. of East Anglia, 1964–65; Prof. of Biology, Univ. of East Anglia, 1965–67; Prof. of Plant Physiology, Univ. of Nottingham, 1967–70. Darwin Lectr, British Assoc. for Advancement of Science, 1967. Member: Biol. Sci. Cttee of SRC, 1971–74; Governing Body: Hill Farming Res. Orgn, 1971–80; Scottish Crops Research Inst, 1974–89; Glasshouse Crops Res. Inst., 1979–88; W of Scotland Agricl Coll., 1983–; Exec. Cttee, Scottish Field Studies Assoc.; British Nat. Cttee for Biology, 1977–82; Life Science Working Gp, ESA, 1983–89 (Chm., 1987–89); Microgravity Adv. Cttee, ESA, 1985–89; NASA Lifesat Science Cttee, 1986–91. Mem. Council, RSE, 1989–. Trustee, Royal Botanic Gdn, Edinburgh, 1990–. Corresp. Mem., Amer. Soc. of Plant Physiologists, 1985. Dir, West of Scotland Sch. Co.; Chm., Laurel Bank Sch. Co. Ltd. Cons. Editor in Plant Biology, McGraw-Hill Publishing Co., 1968–80; Managing Editor, Planta, 1977–. *Publications:*

(ed) The Physiology of Plant Growth and Development, 1969; (ed) Advanced Plant Physiology, 1984; Plantwatching, 1988; (ed) Plant Biology (series), 1981–; papers in Jl of Experimental Botany, Plant Physiology, Planta, Nature, Proc. Royal Soc. *Recreations:* sailing, fishing, model engineering. *Address:* Department of Botany, The University, Glasgow G12 8QQ. *T:* 041–330 4450. *Club:* Caledonian.

WILKINS, Maurice Hugh Frederick, CBE 1963; MA, PhD; FRS 1959; Professor of Bio-physics, 1970–81, Emeritus Professor of Biophysics since 1981, and Fellow, since 1973, King's College, University of London; Director, Medical Research Council Cell Biophysics Unit, 1974–80 (Deputy Director, 1955–70, Director, 1970–72, Biophysics Unit; Director Neurobiology Unit, 1972–74); *b* 15 Dec. 1916; *s* of late Edgar Henry Wilkins and of Eveline Constance Jane (*née* Whittaker), both of Dublin; *m* 1959, Patricia Ann Chidgey; two *s* two *d*. *Educ:* King Edward's Sch., Birmingham: St John's College, Cambridge (Hon. Fellow, 1972). Research on luminescence of solids at Physics Department, Birmingham University, with Ministry of Home Security and Aircraft Production, 1938; PhD 1940; Manhattan Project (Ministry of Supply), Univ. of California (research on separation of uranium isotopes by mass spectrograph), 1944; Lectr in Physics, St Andrews Univ., 1945; MRC Biophysics Unit in Physics Department, King's College, London, 1946; Hon. Lecturer in the sub-department of Biophysics, 1958; Prof. of Molecular Biology, King's Coll., 1963–70. President: British Soc. for Social Responsibility in Science, 1969–; Food and Disarmament Internat., 1984–. Hon. Mem., Amer. Soc. of Biological Chemists, 1964; For. Hon. Mem., Amer. Acad. of Arts and Scis, 1970. Albert Lasker Award, Amer. Public Health Assoc., 1960. Hon. LLD Glasgow, 1972. (Jt) Nobel Prize for Medicine, 1962. *Publications:* papers in scientific journals on luminescence and topics in bio-physics, *eg* molecular structure of nucleic acids and structure of nerve membranes. *Address:* 30 St John's Park, SE3. *T:* 081–858 1817.

WILKINS, Lt-Gen. Sir Michael (Compton Lockwood), KCB 1985; OBE 1975; Lieutenant-Governor and Commander-in-Chief, Guernsey, since 1990; *b* 4 Jan. 1933; *s* of Eric Wilkins and Lucy (*née* Lockwood); *m* 1960, Anne Catherine (*née* Skivington); one *s* two *d*. *Educ:* Mill Hill School. Joined Royal Marines, 2nd Lieut, 1951; 40 Commando RM, 1954–56; Special Boat Sqdn, 1957–61; 41 Commando RM, 1961–62; RM Eastney, 1962–64; sc 1965; GSO2 (Ops) 17 Division, 1966–67; Plans Division, Naval Staff, 1968–69; Bde Major 3 Commando Bde, 1970–71; Directing Staff, Army Staff Coll., 1972–73; CO 40 Commando RM, 1974–75; NATO Defence Coll., 1976; Director of Drafting and Records, 1977–78; Comdr 3 Commando Bde, 1979–80; COS to Comdt Gen. RM, 1981–82; Maj.-Gen. Commando Forces RM, 1982–84; Comdt Gen., RM, 1984–87, retd. Hon. Col, Exeter Univ. OTC, 1990. KStJ 1990. *Recreations:* country pursuits. *Club:* Army and Navy.

WILKINS, Nancy; barrister-at-law; *b* 16 June 1932; three *s* one *d*. *Educ:* School of St Helen and St Katharine, Abingdon, Berkshire. Called to the Bar, Gray's Inn, Nov. 1962; in practice, Midland Circuit, 1962–85; Dep. Circuit Judge, 1974–78; a Recorder, 1978–85; practised in solicitors' office, 1986–90; retired. *Publication:* An Outline of the Law of Evidence (with late Prof. Sir Rupert Cross), 1964, 5th edn 1980. *Recreation:* writing my memoirs. *Address:* 11 Well Cross, Edith Weston, Rutland LE15 8HG; c/o Segaria SL, Carretera Les Marines, Playa Centro 91, Setla, Denia, Spain.

WILKINSON, Rev. Canon Alan Bassindale, PhD; lecturer, writer and honorary priest, Portsmouth Cathedral, since 1988; *b* 26 Jan. 1931; *s* of late Rev. J. T. Wilkinson, DD; *m* 1975, Fenella Holland; two *s* one *d* of first marriage. *Educ:* William Hulme's Grammar Sch., Manchester; St Catharine's Coll., Cambridge; College of the Resurrection, Mirfield. MA 1958, PhD 1959 (Cambridge). Deacon, 1959; Priest, 1960; Asst Curate, St Augustine's, Kilburn, 1959–61; Chaplain, St Catharine's Coll., Cambridge, 1961–67; Vicar of Barrow Gurney and Lecturer in Theology, College of St Matthias, Bristol, 1967–70; Principal, Chichester Theol. Coll., 1970–74; Canon and Prebendary of Thorney, 1970–74, Canon Emeritus, 1975; Warden of Verulam House, Dir of Training for Auxiliary Ministry, dio. of St Albans, 1974–75; Lectr in Theology and Ethics, Crewe and Alsager Coll. of Higher Educn, 1975–78; Dir of Training, Diocese of Ripon, 1978–84; Hon. Canon, Ripon Cathedral, 1984; Priest-in-Charge, Darley with Thruscross and Thornthwaite, 1984–88. Hulsean Preacher, 1967–68; Select Preacher, Oxford Univ., 1982. Mem., Bd of Educn, Gen. Synod, 1981–85; Vice-Chm., Leeds Marriage and Personal Counselling Service, 1981–83. Governor: SPCK, 1982–; Coll. of Ripon and York St John, 1985–88. *Publications:* The Church of England and the First World War, 1978; Would You Believe It?, 1980; More Ready to Hear, 1983; Christian Choices, 1983; Dissent or Conform?, 1986; Chesterton and the Modernist Crisis, 1990; contributor to: Cambridge Sermons on Christian Unity, 1966; Catholic Anglicans Today, 1968; A Work Book in Popular Religion, 1986; also to: Faith and Unity, Sobornost, Preacher's Quarterly, London Quarterly Holborn Review, Theology, Clergy Review, New Fire, Church Times, Chesterton Review, Internat. Christian Digest. *Recreations:* gardening, walking, cinema, Victorian architecture. *Address:* Hope Cottage, 27 Great Southsea Street, Portsmouth PO5 3BY. *T:* Portsmouth (0705) 825788.

WILKINSON, Alexander Birrell; Sheriff of Glasgow and Strathkelvin, since 1991; *b* 2 Feb. 1932; *o s* of late Captain Alexander Wilkinson, MBE, The Black Watch and Isabella Bell Birrell; *m* 1965, Wendy Imogen, *d* of late Ernest Albert Barrett and R. V. H. Barrett; one *s* one *d*. *Educ:* Perth Academy; Univs of St Andrews and Edinburgh. Walker Trust Scholar 1950, Grieve Prizeman in Moral Philosophy 1952, MA(Hons Classics) 1954, Univ. of St Andrews. National Service, RAEC, 1954–56. Balfour Keith Prizeman in Constitutional Law 1957, LLB (with distinction) 1959, Univ. of Edinburgh. Admitted to Faculty of Advocates, 1959; in practice at Scottish bar, 1959–69; Lecturer in Scots Law, Univ. of Edinburgh, 1965–69; Sheriff of Stirling, Dunbarton and Clackmannan at Stirling and Alloa, 1969–72; Prof. of Private Law, 1972–86, and Dean of Faculty of Law, 1974–76 and 1986, Univ. of Dundee; Sheriff of Tayside, Central and Fife at Falkirk, 1986–91. Chancellor: Dio. of Brechin, 1982–; Dio. of Argyll and the Isles, 1985–. Chairman: Central Scotland Marriage Guidance Council, 1970–72; Scottish Marriage Guidance Council, 1974–77; Legal Services Gp, Scottish Assoc. of CAB, 1979–83. *Publications:* (ed jtly) Gloag and Henderson's Introduction to the Law of Scotland, 8th edn 1980, 9th edn 1987; The Scottish Law of Evidence, 1986; articles in legal periodicals. *Recreations:* collecting books and pictures, reading, travel. *Address:* 25 Glencairn Crescent, Edinburgh EH12 5BT. *T:* 031–346 1797. *Club:* New (Edinburgh).

WILKINSON, Prof. Andrew Wood, CBE 1979; ChM (Edinburgh); FRCSE; FRCS; Emeritus Professor of Pædiatric Surgery, University of London; Surgeon, Hospital for Sick Children, Great Ormond Street, since 1958; Hon. Consultant Pædiatric Surgeon, Post-graduate Medical School, Hammersmith, and Queen Elizabeth Hospital for Children; Civilian Consultant in Pediatric Surgery to RN; *b* 19 April 1914; *s* of Andrew W. and Caroline G. Wilkinson; *m* 1941, Joan Longair Sharp; two *s* two *d*. *Educ:* Univ. of Edinburgh. MB, ChB, Edin., 1937; ChM; (1st cl. hons and gold medal for thesis), 1949; FRCS Edin. 1940; FRCS Eng. 1959. Surg. specialist, Lt-Col RAMC, 1942–46. Syme Surgical Fellowship, Univ. of Edinburgh, 1946–49; Senior University Clinical Tutor in Surgery, 1946–51; Lecturer in Surgery, University of Edinburgh and Assistant Surgeon, Deaconess Hosp., Edinburgh, 1951–53; Sen. Lectr in Surgery, Univ. of Aberd. and Asst Surg., Roy. Inf. and Roy. Aberd. Hosp. for Sick Children, 1953–58; Nuffield Prof. of Paediatric Surgery, Inst. of Child Health, 1958–79. Dir, Internat. Sch. of Med. Scis, Ettore Majorana Foundn, 1970–. Royal College of Surgeons of Edinburgh: Mem. Council, 1964–73; Vice-Pres., 1973–76; Pres., 1976–79; Founder and Mem., Appeal Cttee, 1978–. Member: Armed Forces Med. Adv. Bd; Nat. Med. Consultative Cttee. Examr Primary and Final FRCS Ed.; Past Examiner: Univ. Glasgow, DCH London; Primary FRCSEng. Lectures: Tisdall, Canadian Med. Assoc., 1966; Mason Brown Meml, 1972; Forshall, 1979; Simpson Smith Meml, 1980; Tan Sri Datu Ismail Oration, Kuala Lumpur, 1980. Hunterian Prof., RCS, 1965. Visiting Prof. Univ. of Alexandria, 1965, Albert Einstein Coll. of Medicine, 1967. Member: Bd of Governors, Hosp. for Sick Children, 1972–80; Cttee of Management, Inst. of Child Health, 1959–79. Founder Mem., Scottish Surgical Pædiatric Soc.; Hon. Mem., and Past Pres., British Assoc. of Pediatric Surgeons, 1970–72 (Denis Browne Gold Medal, 1981). FRSocMed (Pres. Open Section, 1974–76). Hon. FRCSI; Hon. FRACS; Hon. FCPS (Pakistan); Hon. FCPS (S Africa); Hon. Fellow: Brasilian Soc. Pædiatric Surgery; Yugoslavian Pediatric Surgical Soc.; Greek Pædiatric Surgical Soc.; Amer. Acad. Pediatrics; Italian Pediatric Surgical Soc.; Pediatric Surgical Soc. of Ecuador; Hong Kong Surgical Soc.; Amer. Coll. Surgeons; Hon. Member: Neonatal Soc.; BPA; Peruvian Socs Pediatrics and Pædiatric Surgery; Hellenic Surgical Soc.; Assoc. of Surgeons of India; Corresp. Member: Scandinavian Pediatric Surgical Assoc.; Sicilian Calabrian Soc. of Pædiatric Surgery. *Publications:* Body Fluids in Surgery, 1955, 4th edn 1973 (Japanese edn, 1978); Recent Advances in Pædiatric Surgery, 1963, 3rd edn 1974 (Spanish edn, 1977); Parenteral Feeding, 1972; (jtly) Research in Burns, 1966; (ed jtly) Metabolism and the Response to Injury, 1976; Early Nutrition and Later Development, 1976; (jt) Placental Transport, 1978; Inflammatory Bowel Disease, 1980; Investigation of Brain Function, 1981; Immunology of Breast Feeding, 1981; chapters, articles and reviews in various books, and surgical and other jls. *Recreations:* fishing, gardening, cooking, eating. *Address:* Auchenbrae, Rockcliffe, Dalbeattie, Kirkcudbrightshire DG5 4QF. *Club:* New (Edinburgh).

WILKINSON, Christopher Richard; Head of Division, Directorate General for Telecommunications, Information Industries and Innovation, Commission of the European Communities, since 1983; *b* 3 July 1941; *s* of Rev. Thomas Richard Wilkinson and Winifred Frances Wilkinson (*née* Steel); *m* 1965, Marie-Françoise Courthieu (marr. diss. 1990); one *s* one *d*. *Educ:* Hymers Coll., Kingston upon Hull; Heath Grammar Sch., Halifax; Selwyn Coll., Cambridge (MA). Commonwealth Economic Cttee, 1963–65; OECD, Paris and Madrid, 1965–66; World Bank, Washington DC and Lagos, 1966–73; EEC: Head of Div., Directorate Gen. for Regional Policy, 1973–78; Head of Div., Directorate Gen. for Internal Market and Industrial Affairs, 1978–82. Vis. Fellow, Center for Internat. Affairs, Harvard Univ., 1982–83. Vice-Pres., European School Parents Assoc., Brussels, 1974, 1976–77. *Recreations:* mountain walking, gardening, cooking. *Address:* rue Charles Quint 55, B-1040 Brussels, Belgium; 81 Old Bank Road, Mirfield, West Yorkshire.

WILKINSON, Clive Victor; Chairman, Sandwell District Health Authority; *b* 26 May 1938; *s* of Mrs Winifred Jobson; *m* 1961, Elizabeth Ann Pugh; two *d*. *Educ:* Four Dwellings Secondary Sch., Quinton; Birmingham Modern Sch. Birmingham City Council: Member, 1970–84; Leader, 1973–76 and 1980–82; Leader of Opposition, 1976–80, 1982–84. Dir, Nat. Exhibn Centre, 1973–84; Financial and Commercial Dir, Birmingham Rep. Theatre, 1983–87. Chm., CoSIRA, 1977–80; Dep. Chairman: AMA, 1974–76; Redditch Develt Corp., 1977–81. Member: Develt Commn, 1977–86; Electricity Consumers Council, 1977–80; Audit Commn, 1987–; Black Country Develt Commn, 1989–; Midlands Industrial Assoc. (formerly Chm.). Chairman: Birmingham Civil Housing Assoc., 1979–; Customer Services Cttee, Severn Trent Region, Office of Water Services, 1990–. Mem. Council, Univ. of Birmingham, 1974–84. Trustee, Bournville Village Trust, 1982–. Hon. Alderman, City of Birmingham, 1984. *Recreations:* watching Birmingham City Football Club, playing squash. *Address:* 53 Middle Park Road, Birmingham B29 4BH. *T:* 021–475 1829.

WILKINSON, David Anthony; Head of Science Branch, Department of Education and Science, since 1989; *b* 27 Nov. 1947; *s* of Ambrose Wilkinson and Doreen (*née* Durden); *m* 1973, Meryl, *d* of Edison and Margaret Pugh; three *d*. *Educ:* Boteler Grammar Sch., Warrington; Wigan and District Mining and Technical Coll.; Bedford Coll., Univ. of London (BA History); London School of Economics; Moscow State Univ. Department of Education and Science, 1974–: Hd of Inf. Br., 1987–88; Dep. Dir of Establishments, 1988–89; Under Sec., 1989–. *Address:* c/o Department of Education and Science, Sanctuary Buildings, Great Smith Street, SW1. *Club:* Wimbledon Squash and Badminton.

WILKINSON, Sir D. G. B.; *see* Wilkinson, Sir Graham.

WILKINSON, David Lloyd; Chief Executive and General Secretary, Cooperative Union, since 1975; *b* 28 May 1937; *m* 1960; one *s* one *d*. *Educ:* Royds Hall Grammar Sch. ACIS; CSD. *Address:* 2 Old House, Marsden, Huddersfield HD7 6AS. *T:* Huddersfield (0484) 844580.

WILKINSON, Sir Denys (Haigh), Kt 1974; FRS 1956; Vice-Chancellor, University of Sussex, 1976–87 (Emeritus Professor of Physics, 1987); *b* Leeds, Yorks, 5 September 1922; *o s* of late Charles Wilkinson and Hilda Wilkinson (*née* Haigh); *m* 1st, 1947, Christiane Andrée Clavier (marriage dissolved, 1967); three *d*; 2nd, 1967, Helen Sellschop; two step *d*. *Educ:* Loughborough Gram. Sch.; Jesus Coll. Cambridge (Fellow, 1944–59, Hon. Fellow 1961). BA 1943, MA, PhD 1947, ScD 1961. British and Canadian Atomic Energy Projects, 1943–46; Univ. Demonstrator, Cambridge, 1947–51; Univ. Lecturer, 1951–56; Reader in Nuclear Physics, Univ. of Cambridge, 1956–57; Professor of Nuclear Physics, Univ. of Oxford, 1957–59; Prof. of Experimental Physics, Univ. of Oxford, 1959–76, Head of Dept of Nuclear Physics, 1962–76; Student, Christ Church, Oxford, 1957–76, Emeritus Student, 1976, Hon. Student, 1979. Dir, Internat. Sch. of Nuclear Physics, Erice, Sicily, 1975–83. Mem. Governing Board of National Institute for Research in Nuclear Science, 1957–63 and 1964–65; Member: SRC, 1967–70; Wilton Park Acad. Council, 1979–83; Council, ACU, 1980–87; Royal Commn for the Exhibn of 1851, 1983–90 (Chm., Science Scholarships Cttee, 1983–90); British Council, 1987– (Chm., Sci. Adv. Panel and Cttee, 1977–86); Chairman: Nuclear Physics Board of SRC, 1968–70; Physics III Cttee, CERN, Geneva, 1971–75; Radioactive Waste Management Adv. Cttee, 1978–83; Pres., Inst. of Physics, 1980–82; Vice-Pres., IUPAP, 1985–. Lectures: Welch, Houston, 1957; Scott, Cambridge Univ., 1961; Rutherford Meml, Brit. Physical Soc., 1962; Graham Young, Glasgow Univ., 1964; Queen's, Berlin, 1966; Silliman, Yale Univ., 1966; Cherwell-Simon, Oxford Univ., 1970; Distinguished, Utah State Univ., 1971, 1983, 1988; Goodspeed-Richard, Pennsylvania Univ., 1973 and 1986; Welsh, Toronto Univ., 1975; Tizard Meml, Westminster Sch., 1975; Lauritsen Meml, Cal. Tech., 1976; Herbert Spencer, Oxford Univ., 1976; Schiff Meml, Stanford Univ., 1977; Racah Meml, Hebrew Univ. Jerusalem, 1977; Cecil Green, Univ. of BC, 1978; Distinguished, Univ. of Alberta, 1979; Wolfson, Oxford Univ., 1980; Waterloo-Guelph Distinguished, Guelph Univ., 1981; Herzberg, Ottawa, 1984; Solly Cohen Meml, Hebrew Univ., Jerusalem, 1985; Peter Axel Meml, Univ. of Illinois, 1985; Breit Meml, Yale Univ., 1987; Moon, Birmingham Univ., 1987; Rochester, Durham Univ., 1988; Pegram, Brookhaven Nat.

Lab., 1989; W. B. Lewis Meml, Chalk River, Ont, 1989; Humphry Davy, Académie des Sciences, Paris, 1990; Rutherford Meml, Royal Soc., 1991. Walker Ames Prof., Univ. of Washington, 1968; Battelle Distinguished Prof., Univ. of Washington, 1970–71. For. Mem., Royal Swedish Acad. of Scis, 1980; Mem. Acad. Europaea, 1990. Holweck Medal, British and French Physical Socs, 1957; Rutherford Prize, British Physical Soc., 1962; Hughes Medal, Royal Society, 1965; Bruce-Preller Prize, RSE, 1969; Bonner Prize, American Physical Soc., 1974; Royal Medal, Royal Soc., 1980; Guthrie Medal and Prize, Inst. of Physics, 1986; Gold Medal, Centro Cultura Scientifica Ettore Majorana, Sicily, 1988. Hon. Mem., Mark Twain Soc, 1978. Hon. DSc: Saskatchewan, 1964; Utah State, 1975; Guelph, 1981; Queen's, Kingston, 1987; William and Mary, Va, 1989; Hon. FilDr Uppsala, 1980; Hon. LLD Sussex, 1987. Comm. Bontemps Médoc et Graves, 1973. *Publications:* Ionization Chambers and Counters, 1951; (ed) Isospin in Nuclear Physics, 1969; (ed) Progress in Particle and Nuclear Physics, 1978–84; (ed jtly) Mesons in Nuclei, 1979; Our Universes, 1991; papers on nuclear physics and bird navigation. *Recreations:* mediæval church architecture and watching birds. *Address:* Gayles Orchard, Friston, Eastbourne, East Sussex BN20 0BA. *T:* East Dean (0323) 423333.

WILKINSON, Elizabeth Mary, PhD; FBA 1972; Professor of German, University College London, 1960–76, now Emeritus; *b* 17 Sept. 1909; *d* of Frank Wilkinson and Martha E. Gilleard, Keighley, Yorks. *Educ:* Whalley Range High Sch., Manchester; Bedford Coll., London (BA, PhD; Hon. Fellow 1985); DipEd Oxford. Vis. Prof., Univ. of Chicago, 1955; first Virginia C. Gildersleeve Prof., Barnard Coll., Columbia Univ., 1958; Prof.-at-Large of Cornell Univ., 1967–. President: English Goethe Soc., 1974–86; Modern Language Assoc., GB, 1964; Hon. Mem., Modern Language Assoc. of America, 1965. Governor, Bedford Coll., London. Korresp. Mitglied, Akademie der Wissenschaften zu Göttingen, 1973; Deutsche Akad. für Sprache und Dichtung, 1976. Hon. LLD Smith Coll., Mass, 1966; Hon. DLitt Kent, 1971. Medaille in Gold des Goethe-Instituts, 1965; Preis für Germanistik im Ausland der Deutschen Akad. für Sprache und Dichtung, 1974. German Editor, Notebooks of Samuel Taylor Coleridge, 1950–62 (vols 1 and 2); Editor, publications of the English Goethe Soc., 1951–70. *Publications:* Thomas Mann's Tonio Kröger, 1943; (with L. A. Willoughby) Schiller's Kabale und Liebe, 1944; J. E. Schlegel: A German Pioneer in Aesthetics, 1945, German edn 1973 (Wissenschaftliche Buchges.) (J. G. Robertson Prize); Edward Bullough's Aesthetics, 1957; (with L. A. Willoughby) Goethe: Poet and Thinker, 1962 (German edn 1974); (with L. A. Willoughby) Schiller: On the Aesthetic Education of Man, 1967 (German edn 1977); Goethe Revisited, 1983; contrib. on Goethe to Encyclopædia Britannica, 1963 and subsq. edns. *Address:* 33 Queen Court, Queen Square, WC1N 3BB.

WILKINSON, Prof. Sir Geoffrey, Kt 1976; FRS 1965; Sir Edward Frankland Professor of Inorganic Chemistry, University of London, 1956–88, now Emeritus; Senior Research Fellow, Imperial College, since 1988; *b* 14 July 1921; *s* of Henry and Ruth Wilkinson; *m* 1951, Lise Sølver, *o d* of Rektor Prof. Svend Aa. Schou, Copenhagen; two *d. Educ:* Todmorden Secondary Sch (Royal Scholar, 1939); Imperial Coll., London; USA. Junior Scientific Officer, Nat. Res. Council, Atomic Energy Div., Canada, 1943–46; Research Fellow: Radiation Lab., Univ. of Calif, Berkeley, Calif, USA, 1946–50; Chemistry Dept, Mass Inst. of Technology, Cambridge, Mass, USA, 1950–51; Asst Prof. of Chemistry, Harvard Univ., Cambridge, Mass, 1951–56; Prof. of Inorganic Chemistry at Imperial Coll., Univ. of London, 1956, Sir Edward Frankland Prof. 1978. Arthur D. Little Visiting Prof., MIT, 1967; Lectures: William Draper Harkins' Meml, Univ. of Chicago, 1968; Leermakers, Wesleyan Univ., 1975; First Mond, Chem. Soc., 1980; First Sir Edward Frankland, RSC, 1983. John Simon Guggenheim Fellow, 1954. Foreign Member: Roy. Danish Acad. of Science and Arts (math.-phys section), 1968; Amer. Acad. of Arts and Sciences, 1970; Foreign Assoc., Nat. Acad. of Scis, 1975; Centennial Foreign Fellow, Amer. Chem. Soc., 1976. Hon. Fellow: Lady Margaret Hall, Oxford, 1984; UMIST, 1989. Hon. DSc: Edinburgh, 1975; Granada, 1976; Columbia, 1978; Bath, 1980; Essex, 1989. American Chem. Soc. Award in Inorganic Chemistry, 1965; Lavoisier Medal, Société Chimique de France, 1968; Chem. Soc. Award for Transition Metal Chemistry, 1972; (jtly) Nobel Prize for Chemistry, 1973; Consejero de Honor, Spanish Council for Scientific Res., 1974; Hiroshima Univ. Medal, 1978; Royal Medal, Royal Soc., 1981; Galileo Medal, Univ. of Pisa, 1983; Longstaff Medal, RSC, 1987; Medal, Univ. of Camerino, Italy, 1989; Messel Medal, SCI, 1990. Hon. Citizen Award, Todmorden Town Council, 1990. *Publications:* (jtly) Advanced Inorganic Chemistry: a Comprehensive Text, 1962, 5th edn 1988; Basic Inorganic Chemistry, 1976, 2nd edn 1987; numerous in Physical Review, Journal of the American Chemical Society, etc. *Address:* Chemistry Department, Imperial College, SW7 2AY. *T:* 071–589 5111.

WILKINSON, Geoffrey Crichton, CBE 1986; AFC; Chief Inspector of Accidents (Aircraft), 1981–86; *b* 7 Nov. 1926; *s* of Col W. E. D. Wilkinson and Mrs E. K. Wilkinson; *m* 1958, Virginia Mary Broom; two *d. Educ:* Bedford Sch. Graduate, Empire Test Pilots Sch.; FRAES. Royal Indian Mil. Coll., 1943–44; served RN, 1944–47; aeronautical engrg course, 1948; served RAF, 1949–59 (Air Force Cross, 1956); Turner and Newall, 1959–61; Mercury Airlines, 1961–65; Accidents Investigation Br., 1965–86. Air Medal, USA, 1953. *Recreations:* sailing, skiing, music. *Address:* Buckingham House, 50 Hyde Street, Winchester, Hants SO23 7DY. *T:* Winchester (0962) 865823. *Clubs:* Royal Air Force; Royal Air Force Yacht (Hamble).

WILKINSON, Sir Graham, 3rd Bt *cr* 1941; Managing Director, S.E.I.C. Services (UK) Ltd, 1985–89; *b* 18 May 1947; *s* of Sir David Wilkinson, 2nd Bt, DSC, and of Sylvia Anne, *d* of late Professor Bosley Alan Rex Gater; *S* father, 1972; *m* 1977, Sandra Caroline, *d* of Dr Richard Rossdale; two *d. Educ:* Millfield; Christ Church, Oxford. Orion Royal Bank Ltd, 1971–85 (Dir 1979–85); Non-Exec. Dir, Galveston-Houston Co., USA, 1986–89. OStJ 1976. *Club:* Royal Yacht Squadron.

WILKINSON, Heather Carol, (Mrs Nigel Wilkinson); *see* Hallett, H. C.

WILKINSON, Jeffrey Vernon; Director, Alan Patricof Associates, since 1986; Chairman and Chief Executive Officer, Rotaprint Industries Ltd, since 1988; *b* 21 Aug. 1930; *s* of late Arthur Wilkinson and Winifred May Allison; *m* 1955, Jean Vera Nurse; two *d. Educ:* Mathew Humberstone Foundation Sch.; King's Coll., Cambridge (MA); Sorbonne. FBCS, CBIM. Joined Joseph Lucas as graduate apprentice, 1954; Director, CAV, 1963; Director and General Manager, Diesel Equipment, CAV, 1967; Director: Simon Engineering, 1968; Joseph Lucas, 1974; Gen. Manager, Lucas Electrical, 1974; Divisional Man. Dir, Joseph Lucas Ltd, 1978; Jt Gp Man. Dir, Lucas Industries plc, 1979–84. Chairman: Automotive Components Manufacturers, 1979–84; Plastics Processing EDC, 1985–87; Mem. Council and Exec., SMMT, 1979–84. Liveryman, Wheelwrights Company, 1971–. *Recreations:* water-skiing, swimming, reading, theatre, art. *Address:* Hillcroft, 15 Mearse Lane, Barnt Green, Birmingham B45 8HG. *T:* 021–445 1747.

WILKINSON, John Arbuthnot Du Cane; MP (C) Ruislip Northwood, since 1979; *b* 23 Sept. 1940; 2nd *s* of late Denys Wilkinson and Gillian Wilkinson, Eton College; *m* 1st, 1969 (marr. diss. 1987); one *d*; 2nd, 1987, Cecilia Cienfuegos, *d* of Raul Cienfuegos, Santiago, Chile; one *s. Educ:* Eton (King's Scholar); RAF Coll., Cranwell; Churchill Coll., Cambridge (2nd cl. Hons Mod. Hist.; MA). Flight Cadet, RAF Coll., Cranwell, 1959–61 (Philip Sassoon Meml Prize, qualified French Interpreter); commnd 1961; Flying Instructor, No 8 FTS, Swinderby, 1962. Churchill Coll., Cambridge, Oct. 1962–65. Trooper, 21st Special Air Service Regt (Artists'), TA, 1963–65; rejoined RAF 1965; Flying Instructor, RAF Coll., Cranwell, 1966–67; Tutor, Stanford Univ.'s British Campus, 1967; ADC to Comdr 2nd Allied Tactical Air Force, Germany, 1967; resigned RAF, 1967. Head of Universities' Dept, Conservative Central Office, 1967–68; Aviation Specialist, Cons. Research Dept, 1969; Senior Administration Officer (Anglo-French Jaguar Project), Preston Div., British Aircraft Corp., 1969–70; Tutor, Open Univ., 1970–71; Vis. Lectr, OCTU RAF Henlow, 1971–75; Chief Flying Instructor, Skywork Ltd, Stansted, 1974–75; Gen. Manager, General Aviation Div., Brooklands Aviation Ltd, 1975–76; PA to Chm., BAC, 1975–77; Senior Sales Executive, Eagle Aircraft Services Ltd, 1977–78; Sales Manager, Klingair Ltd, 1978–79. MP (C) Bradford W, 1970–Feb. 1974; Chm., Cons. Parly Aviation Cttee, 1983–85 (Jt Sec., 1972–74; Vice-Chm., 1979); Vice-Chm., Cons. Parly Defence Cttee, 1983–85, 1990– (Sec., 1972–74 and 1980–81); Member Select Committee on: Race Relations and Immigration, 1972–74; Sci. and Technol., 1972–74; Defence, 1987–90; contested (C) Bradford W, Feb. and Oct. 1974; PPS to Minister of State for Industry, 1979–80, to Sec. of State for Defence, 1981–82; Chairman: Anglo-Asian Cons. Soc., 1979–82; European Freedom Council, 1982–; Cons. Space Sub Cttee, 1986–90 (Vice-Chm., 1983–85). Chm., Horn of Africa Council, 1984–88. Delegate to Council of Europe (Chm., Space Sub-Cttee, 1984–88) and WEU (Chm., Cttee on Scientific, Technological and Aerospace Questions, 1986–89), 1979–90. Chm., EMC Communications Ltd, 1984–. Parly Industrial Fellow, GKN plc, 1989–90. Institute of Directors. HQA Pakistan, 1989. *Publications:* (jtly) The Uncertain Ally, 1982; British Defence: a blueprint for reform, 1987; pamphlets and articles on defence and politics. *Recreation:* flying. *Address:* c/o House of Commons, SW1.

See also R. D. Wilkinson, Sir W. H. N. Wilkinson.

WILKINSON, John Francis; *b* 2 Oct. 1926; *s* of late Col W. T. Wilkinson, DSO, and Evelyn S. Wilkinson (*née* Ward); *m* 1951, Alison, *d* of late Hugh and Marian Malcolm; two *s* one *d. Educ:* Wellington Coll.; Edinburgh Univ. Naval Short Course, 1944–45; Cambridge and London Univs Colonial Course, 1947–48. Served Royal Navy (Fleet Air Arm trainee pilot, 1945), 1945–47; HM Colonial Service, N Nigeria, 1949; Asst District Officer, Bida, 1949; Asst Sec., Lands and Mines, Kaduna, 1950; Private Sec. to Chief Comr, N Nigeria, 1951; transf. to Nigerian Broadcasting Corp., 1952; Controller: Northern Region, 1952–56; National Programme, Lagos, 1956–58; joined BBC African Service as African Programme Organiser, 1958; East and Central African Programme Organiser, 1961; BBC TV Production Trng Course and attachment to Panorama, 1963; Asst Head, 1964, Head, 1969, BBC African Service; attachment to Horizon, 1972; Head of Production and Planning, BBC World Service, 1976; Secretary of the BBC, 1977–80; Dir, Public Affairs, BBC, 1980–85. Dir, 1986–90, Trustee, 1990–, The One World Broadcasting Trust. Chm. of Governors, Centre for Internat. Briefing, Farnham Castle, 1977–87, Vice-Pres., 1987–. Vice-Pres., Royal African Soc., 1978–82. MUniv Open, 1989. *Publications:* Broadcasting in Africa, in African Affairs (Jl of Royal African Soc.), 1972; contrib. to Broadcasting in Africa, a continental survey of radio and television, 1974. *Recreations:* sailing, occasional golf. *Address:* Compass Cottage, Box, Minchinhampton, near Stroud, Glos GL6 9HD. *T:* Stroud (0453) 833072. *Club:* Commonwealth Trust.

WILKINSON, Dr John Frederick, FRCP, MD (Gold Medal), ChB, BSc (1st Cl. Hons Chem.), MSc, PhD Manchester, DSc (Hon.) Bradford; CChem, FRSC; author; Consulting Physician; Consulting Haematologist, United Manchester Hospitals; late Director of Department of Hæmatology, University and Royal Infirmary of Manchester; late Reader in Hæmatology, and Lecturer in Systematic Medicine, Univ. of Manchester; late Hon. Consulting Hæmatologist, The Christie Cancer Hospital, Holt Radium Institute and The Duchess of York Hospital for Babies, Manchester; Hon. Fellow and Editor, Manchester Medical Society; formerly President, European Hæmatological Soc.; Life Councillor, International Hæmatological Soc.; *b* Oldham, 10 June 1897; *s* of John Frederick Wilkinson, Oldham and Stockport, and Annie, *d* of late Reverend E. Wareham, DD, Rector of Heaton Mersey; *m* 1964, Marion Crossfield, Major, WRAC. *Educ:* Arnold School, Blackpool; University of Manchester; Manchester Royal Infirmary. Served European War, 1916–19, RNAS, RN, and later attached Tank Corps, France; also served on Vindictive at Zeebrugge, 1918, and ballotted for Victoria Cross award; Chemical Research Manchester University, 1919–28; Medical Research since 1929; Regional Transfusion Officer, and Regional Adviser on Resuscitation, Ministry of Health, NW Region, 1940–46. Graduate Scholarship (Chemistry), 1920; Dalton Research Scholarship; Sir Clement Royds Research Fellowship; Medical (Graduate) Scholarship, 1923; Hon. Demonstrator in Crystallography; Research Asst in Physiology; Sidney Renshaw Physiology Prizeman; Gold Medal for Dissertation in Med., 1931, University of Manchester. RCP Lectures: Oliver Sharpey, 1948; Samuel Gee, 1977. Worshipful Society of Apothecaries, London: Liveryman, 1948; Osler Lectr, 1981; Hon. Fellow 1982 (Faculty of History and Philosophy of Medicine and Pharmacy). Freeman City of London, 1949. Hon. DSc Bradford, 1976. *Publications:* scientific and medical publications since 1920 in English and foreign journals, etc. Sections on Blood Diseases, Anæmias and Leukæmias in British Encyclopædia of Medical Practice, 1936, 1950 and yearly supplements since 1951, and in Encyclopædia of General Practice, 1964; Section on Emergencies in Blood Diseases, in Medical Emergencies, 1948 to date; ed Modern Trends in Diseases of the Blood, 1955, 1975; The Diagnosis and Treatment of Blood Diseases, 1973; ed, Section in Clinical Surgery, 1967; articles on antiques, Old English and continental apothecaries' drug jars, etc, in miscellaneous medical and art jls, 1970–. *Recreations:* motoring, antiques, travel, zoos, tropical fish keeping, lecturing, scouting since 1908. *Address:* Mobberley Old Hall, Knutsford, Cheshire WA16 7AB. *T:* Mobberley (056587) 2111.

WILKINSON, Rev. Keith Howard; Headmaster, Berkhamsted School, since 1989; *b* 25 June 1948; *s* of Kenneth John Wilkinson and Grace Winifred (*née* Bowler); *m* 1972, Carolyn Gilbert; two *d. Educ:* Beaumont Leys Coll.; Gateway Sch., Leicester; Univ. of Hull (BA Hons); Emmanuel Coll., Cambridge (Lady Romney Exhibnr, MA status); Westcott House, Cambridge. Hd of Religious Studies, Bricknell High Sch., 1970–72; Hd of Faculty (Humanities), Kelvin Hall Comprehensive Sch., Kingston upon Hull, 1972–74; Deacon 1976; Priest 1977; Asst Priest, St Jude, Westwood, Peterborough, 1977; Asst Master and Chaplain, Eton Coll., Windsor, 1979–84; Sen. Chaplain and Hd of Religious Studies, Malvern Coll., 1984–89; Sen. Tutor, Malvern Coll., 1988–89. *Publications:* various articles and reviews. *Recreations:* films, drama, music, walking, buildings and building, ecology. *Address:* Wilson House, The School, Castle Street, Berkhamsted, Herts HP4 2BE. *T:* Berkhamsted (0442) 864827. *Club:* East India.

WILKINSON, Leon Guy, FCIB; a General Commissioner of Income Tax, City of London, since 1989; part-time Member, VAT Tribunal, since 1989; *b* 6 Nov. 1928; *s* of Thomas Guy and Olive May Wilkinson; *m* 1953, Joan Margaret; one *s* one *d. Educ:* Bude Grammar Sch. CMS Oxon. Lloyds Bank: Regional Gen. Man., N and E Midlands, 1976–79; Asst Gen. Man., 1979–83; Gen. Man. (Finance), 1984–86; Chief Financial Officer, 1986–88. *Recreations:* sports, country pursuits. *Address:* Astons, Bishops Down Park Road, Tunbridge Wells, Kent TN4 8XR. *T:* Tunbridge Wells (0892) 541184. *Clubs:* MCC, Royal Over-Seas League; Nevill Golf (Tunbridge Wells).

WILKINSON, Rear-Adm. Nicholas John; Senior Military Member, Defence Organisation Study and Project Team, since 1991; *b* 14 April 1941; *s* of Lt-Col Michael Douglas Wilkinson, RE and Joan Mary Wilkinson (*née* Cosens); *m* 1969, Penelope Ann Stephenson; three *s* one *d*. *Educ:* English School, Cairo; Cheltenham College; BRNC Dartmouth. Served HM Ships Venus, Vidal and Hermes, 1960–64; RN Air Station, Arbroath, 1964–65; HMS Fife, 1965–67; Asst Sec. to Vice-Chief of Naval Staff, 1968–70; HMS Endurance, 1970–72; Army Staff Course, 1973 (Mitchell Prizewinner); Clyde Submarine Base, 1974–75; Sec. to ACNS (Policy), 1975–77; HMS London, 1977–78; Asst Dir, Naval Officer Appts (SW), 1978–80; Trng Comdr, HMS Pembroke, 1980–82; NATO Defence Coll., Rome, 1982–83; MA to Dir, NATO Internat. Mil. Staff, 1983–85; RCDS, 1986; Dir, Defence Logistics, 1986; Sec. to First Sea Lord, 1989–90. *Publications:* articles in The Naval Review. *Recreations:* RN Volunteer Bands, swimming, cricket, opera, jazz, eating in the Perigord. *Address:* c/o Naval Secretary, Old Admiralty Building, SW1A 2BE; c/o Cox's and King's, 7 Pall Mall, SW1Y 5NA. *Club:* MCC.

WILKINSON, Rt. Hon. Sir Nicolas Christopher Henry B.; *see* Browne-Wilkinson.

WILKINSON, Nigel Vivian Marshall; QC 1990; *b* 18 Nov. 1949; *s* of John Marshall Wilkinson and Vivien Wilkinson; *m* 1974, Heather Carol Hallett; two *s*. *Educ:* Charterhouse; Christ Church, Oxford (Holford exhibnr; MA). Called to the Bar, Middle Temple, 1972; Astbury Scholar, 1972; Midland and Oxford Circuit, 1972–. *Recreations:* cricket, golf, theatre. *Address:* 2 Crown Office Row, Temple, EC4Y 7HJ. *T:* 071–353 9337. *Clubs:* Vincent's (Oxford); I Zingari, Butterflies CC, Invalids CC, Armadillos CC, Rye Golf, Woking Golf.

WILKINSON, Prof. Paul; Professor of International Relations, University of St Andrews, since 1990; Director, Research Institute for the Study of Conflict and Terrorism, since 1989; *b* 9 May 1937; *s* of late Walter Ross Wilkinson and of Joan Rosemary (*née* Paul); 1960, Susan; two *s* one *d*. *Educ:* Lower School of John Lyon; University Coll., Swansea, Univ. of Wales (BA (jt Hons Mod. Hist. and Politics), MA; Hon. Fellow, 1986). Royal Air Force regular officer, 1959–65. Asst Lecturer in Politics, 1966–68, Lectr in Politics, 1968–75, Sen. Lectr in Politics, 1975–77, University Coll., Cardiff; Reader, Univ. of Wales, 1978–79; Prof., Internat. Relations, 1979–89, Hd, Dept of Politics and Internat. Relations, 1985–89, Univ. of Aberdeen. Member: IBA Scottish Adv. Cttee, 1982–85; Academic Adv. Bd, Hughenden Foundn, 1986–. Special Consultant, CBS Broadcasting Co., USA, 1986–; Security Advr, Internat. Foundn of Airline Passengers Assocs, 1988–. Editorial Adviser, Contemporary Review, 1980–; Mem., Editorial Board, Conflict Quarterly, 1980–; Gen. Editor, Key Concepts in International Relations, 1980–; Jt Editor, Terrorism and Political Violence Jl, 1988–. *Publications:* Social Movement, 1971; Political Terrorism, 1974; Terrorism versus Liberal Democracy, 1976; Terrorism and the Liberal State, 1977, rev. edn 1986; (jtly) Terrorism: theory and practice, 1978; (ed) British Perspectives on Terrorism, 1981; The New Fascists, 1981, rev. edn 1983; Defence of the West, 1983; (jtly) Contemporary Research on Terrorism, 1987; Lessons of Lockerbie, 1989; contribs to wide range of jls in Britain, USA and Canada. *Recreations:* modern art, poetry, walking. *Address:* Department of International Relations, North Street, St Andrews, Fife. *T:* St Andrews (0334) 76161. *Club:* Savile.

WILKINSON, Sir Peter (Allix), KCMG 1970 (CMG 1960); DSO 1944; OBE 1944; HM Diplomatic Service, retired; *b* 15 April 1914; *s* of late Captain Osborn Cecil Wilkinson (killed in action, 1915) and Esmé, *d* of late Sir Alexander Wilson; *m* 1945, Mary Theresa (*d* 1984), *d* of late Algernon Villiers; two *d*. *Educ:* Rugby; Corpus Christi Coll., Cambridge. Commissioned in 2nd Bn Royal Fusiliers, 1935; active service in Poland (despatches), France, ME, Italy, Balkans and Central Europe; commanded No 6 Special Force (SOE), 1943–45; retired with rank of Lieut-Colonel, 1947. Entered HM Foreign Service, appointed 1st Secretary at British Legation, Vienna, 1947; 1st Secretary at British Embassy, Washington, 1952; Secretary-General of Heads of Government Meeting at Geneva, 1955; Counsellor, HM Embassy, Bonn, 1955; Counsellor, Foreign Office, 1960–63; Under-Secretary, Cabinet Office, 1963–64; Senior Civilian Instructor at the Imperial Defence Coll., 1964–66; Ambassador to Vietnam, 1966–67; Under-Secretary, Foreign Office, 1967–68; Chief of Administration, HM Diplomatic Service, 1968–70; Ambassador to Vienna, 1970–71; Consultant, Cabinet Office, 1972–73. Cross of Valour (Poland), 1940; Order of White Lion (IV Class) (Czechoslovakia), 1945; Order of Jugoslav Banner (Hon.), 1984. *Recreations:* gardening, sailing, fishing. *Address:* 28 High Street, Charing, Kent TN27 0HX. *T:* Charing (023371) 2306. *Clubs:* White's, Army and Navy.

WILKINSON, Sir Philip (William), Kt 1988; FCIB; Director: National Power PLC, since 1990; National Westminster Bank PLC, 1979–90 (Deputy Chairman, 1987–90); HandelsBank NatWest, 1983–90 (Deputy Chairman, 1987–90); British Aerospace PLC, 1987–91; *b* 8 May 1927; *m* 1951, Eileen Patricia (*née* Malkin); one *s* two *d*. *Educ:* Leyton County High School. With Westminster Bank, later National Westminster Bank, 1943–90; Chief Executive, Lombard North Central Ltd, 1975; General Manager, Related Banking Services Division, 1978; Dir, 1979–90; Dep. Group Chief Executive, 1980; Group Chief Executive, 1983–87; Chm., NatWest Investment Bank, 1987–89; Director: Internat. Westminster Bank, 1982–90; Nat. Westminster Bank, USA, 1987–90. Former Mem., Bd of Banking Supervision, Bank of England; a Vice-Pres., Chartered Inst. of Bankers, 1989–. Dir, ENO, 1987–. Mem. Council, Imperial Cancer Res. Fund, 1990–. Trustee, Baptist Building Fund, 1987–. Freeman, City of London, 1969. *Recreations:* golf and watching sport. *Address:* Pine Court, Whichert Close, Knotty Green, Beaconsfield, Bucks HP9 2TP. *Club:* Royal Automobile.

WILKINSON, Rev. Canon Raymond Stewart; Rector of Solihull, 1971–87; Chaplain to the Queen, 1982–89; Hon. Canon of Birmingham, since 1976; *b* 5 June 1919; *s* of Sidney Ewart and Florence Miriam Wilkinson; *m* 1945, Dorothy Elinor Church; four *s*. *Educ:* Luton Grammar Sch.; King's Coll., London (AKC); Bishop's Coll., Cheshunt. Curate of Croxley Green, 1943–45; Vicar: S Oswald's, Croxley Green, 1945–50; Abbot's Langley, 1950–61; Rector of Woodchurch, 1961–71; Proctor in Convocation and Mem., Church Assembly, 1964–71. Member, various educnl governing bodies. *Publications:* To the More Edifying, 1952; The Church and Parish of Abbot's Langley, 1955; My Confirmation Search Book, 1962, 10th edn 1982; An Adult Confirmation Candidate's Handbook, 1964, 6th edn 1984; Gospel Sermons for Alternative Service Book, 1983; Learning about Vestments and Altar Serving, 1984; A Pocket Guide for Servers, 1985; The Essence of Anglicanism, 1986. *Recreations:* producing, acting in and conducting Gilbert and Sullivan operas; church architecture, organising youth holidays. *Address:* 42 Coten End, Warwick, CV34 4NP. *T:* Warwick (0926) 493510. *Clubs:* Commonwealth Trust, Royal Society of Arts.

WILKINSON, Richard Denys; HM Diplomatic Service; Counsellor (Information), Paris, since 1988; *b* 11 May 1946; *y s* of late Denys and Gillian Wilkinson; *m* 1982, Maria Angela Morris; two *s* one *d*. *Educ:* Eton Coll. (King's Schol.); Trinity Coll., Cambridge (MA, MLitt, Wace Medallist); Ecole Nat. des Langues Orientales Vivantes, Univ. de Paris; Ecole des Langues Orientales Anciennes, Inst. Catholique de Paris. Hayter Postdoctoral Fellow in Soviet Studies, SSEES, London, 1971; joined Diplomatic Service, 1972: Madrid, 1973; FCO, 1977; Vis. Prof., Univ. of Michigan, Ann Arbor, 1980; FCO, 1980; Ankara, 1983; Mexico City, 1985. *Publications:* articles and reviews in learned jls. *Recreations:* sightseeing, oriental studies. *Address:* c/o Foreign and Commonwealth Office, SW1. *Club:* United Oxford & Cambridge University.

See also J. A. D. Wilkinson, *Sir* W. H. N. Wilkinson.

WILKINSON, Robert Purdy, OBE 1990; Director of Surveillance, The Stock Exchange, 1984–90; Director of Enforcement, The Securities Association, 1987–90; *b* 23 Aug. 1933; *s* of Robert Purdy and Lily Ingham Wilkinson; *m* 1957, June (*née* Palmer); two *d*. *Educ:* Univ. of Durham (BA). Kleinwort Sons & Co., 1958–62; Estabrook & Co., 1962–64; Partner, W. I. Carr Sons & Co., 1966–81. Stock Exchange: Mem. Council, 1978–81; Cttee Chm., 1980–81; Stock Exchange Inspector, 1981–84. Testified US Congress Special Cttee, 1988. *Publications:* contrib. to French Society of Investment Jl; various articles on securities regulation and insider dealing. *Recreations:* walking, ski-ing, looking after an old house. *Address:* Bessels House, Bessels Green, Sevenoaks, Kent TN13 2PS. *T:* Sevenoaks (0732) 457782.

WILKINSON, Sir William (Henry Nairn), Kt 1989; Chairman, Nature Conservancy Council, 1983–91; *b* 22 July 1932; *e s* of late Denys and Gillian Wilkinson, of Eton College; *m* 1964, Katharine Louise Frederica, *er d* of late F. W. H. Loudon and of Lady Prudence Loudon; one *s* two *d*. *Educ:* Eton Coll. (King's Schol.); Trinity Coll., Cambridge (Major Scholar; MA). Royal Society for the Protection of Birds: Mem. Council, 1970–76, 1977–83; Hon. Treasurer, 1971–76; Vice-Pres., 1991; Council of the Game Conservancy, 1976–83 (Vice-Chm., 1981–83); Vice-President: Plantlife, 1991; Kent Trust for Nature Conservation, 1991. Chm., TSL Thermal Syndicate plc, 1984–88 (Dir, 1976–88); Director: Kleinwort Benson Ltd, 1973–85; John Mowlem and Co. plc, 1977–87; Mem., CEGB, 1986–89. Mem. Council, Winston Churchill Meml Trust, 1985–. FRSA. *Publications:* papers for ornithological conferences. *Recreations:* ornithology, opera and music, archaeology. *Address:* 119 Castelnau, Barnes, SW13 9EL; Pill House, Llanmadoc, Gower, West Glamorgan SA3 1DB. *Club:* Brooks's.

See also J. A. D. Wilkinson, R. D. Wilkinson.

WILKINSON, Dr William Lionel, CBE 1987; FRS 1990; FEng 1980; Deputy Chief Executive, British Nuclear Fuels Ltd, since 1986 (Deputy Director, 1979–84; Technical Director, 1984–86); Director, Allied Colloids plc, since 1990; *b* 16 Feb. 1931; *s* of Lionel and Dorothy Wilkinson; *m* 1955, Josephine Anne Pilgrim; five *s*. *Educ:* Christ's Coll., Cambridge. MA, PhD, ScD; FIChemE. Salters' Res. Schol., Christ's Coll., Cambridge, 1953–56; Lectr in Chem. Engrg, UC Swansea, 1956–59; UKAEA Production Gp, 1959–67; Prof. of Chem. Engrg, Univ. of Bradford, 1967–79. Vis. Prof. of Chemical Engrg, Imperial Coll., London, 1980–. Member: SERC, 1981–85; ACOST, 1990–. Pres., IChemE, 1980. *Publications:* Non-Newtonian Flow, 1960; contribs to sci. and engrg jls on heat transfer, fluid mechanics, polymer processing and process dynamics. *Recreations:* sailing, fell-walking. *Address:* Tree Tops, Legh Road, Knutsford, Cheshire WA16 8LP. *T:* Knutsford (0565) 53344. *Club:* Athenæum.

WILKS, Jean Ruth Fraser, CBE 1977; Chairman of Council and Pro-Chancellor, Birmingham University, 1985–89; *b* 14 April 1917; *d* of Mark Wilks. *Educ:* North London Collegiate Sch.; Somerville Coll., Oxford (MA; Hon. Fellow, 1985). Assistant Mistress: Truro High Sch., 1940–43; James Allen's Girls' Sch., Dulwich, 1943–51; Head Mistress, Hertfordshire and Essex High Sch., Bishop's Stortford, Hertfordshire, 1951–64; Head Mistress, King Edward VI High Sch. for Girls, Birmingham, 1965–77. Pres., Assoc. of Head Mistresses, 1972–74; Member: Public Schools Commn, 1968–70; Governing Council of Schools Council, 1972–75; Adv. Council on Supply and Trng of Teachers, 1973–78; Educn Cttee, Royal Coll. of Nursing, 1973–79; University Authorities Panel, 1982–89. University of Birmingham: Mem. Council, 1971–89; Life Mem. Court, 1977; Chm., Academic Staffing Cttee, 1978–85; Dep. Pro-Chancellor, 1979–85. Hon. Fellow, Somerville Coll., 1985 (Pres. ASM, 1982–85); Chm. Governors, Ellerslie, Malvern, 1982–. FCP 1978. Hon. LLD Birmingham, 1986. *Address:* 4 Hayward Road, Oxford OX2 8LW. *Club:* Naval and Military.

WILKS, Jim; *see* Wilks, Stanley David.

WILKS, Stanley David, (Jim Wilks), CB 1979; MIEx; Director: Hadson Petroleum International, since 1981; Hadson Corporation (USA), since 1985; Strategy International, since 1990 (Consultant Director, 1981–89); *b* 1 Aug. 1920; *m* 1947, Dorothy Irene Adamthwaite; one *s* one *d*. *Educ:* Polytechnic Sch., London. Royal Armoured Corps, 1939–46; service with 48th Bn, Royal Tank Regt; 3rd Carabiniers, Imphal, 1944. Home Office, 1946–50; Board of Trade, later Dept of Trade and Industry, 1950–80: posts included 1st Sec., British Embassy, Washington, 1950–53; GATT, non-ferrous metals, ECGD, airports policy; Chief Exec., BOTB, 1975–80. Deputy Chairman, Technology Transfer Gp, 1981–89; Trade Network Internat., 1989 (Chm., Export Network, 1986–89); Director: Matthew Hall Internat. Develt, subseq. Matthew Hall Business Develt, 1981–89; Associated Gas Supplies, 1988–90; Regl Dir, James Hallam, 1984–. Vice-Chm., Internat. Tin Council, 1968–69; Chm., Tech. Help for Exporters Management Cttee, BSI, 1982–88. Chm., UK Wayfarer Assoc., 1982–89. MIEx 1981. *Recreations:* dinghy racing, water-skiing. *Address:* 6 Foxgrove Avenue, Beckenham, Kent BR3 2BA. *Clubs:* Royal Over-Seas League, Civil Service, Lloyd's Yacht; Medway Yacht (Rochester); Tamesis (Kingston).

WILL, Ronald Kerr; Deputy Keeper of Her Majesty's Signet, 1975–83; formerly Senior Partner, Dundas & Wilson, CS, Edinburgh; *b* 22 March 1918; 3rd *s* of late James Alexander Will, WS and late Bessie Kennedy Salmon, Dumfries; *m* 1953, Margaret Joyce, *d* of late D. Alan Stevenson, BSc, FRSE; two *s*. *Educ:* Merchiston Castle Sch.; Edinburgh Univ. Commnd King's Own Scottish Borderers, 1940; served with 1st Bn and in Staff appts (despatches); psc; GSO2. Writer to the Signet, 1950. Director: Scottish Equitable Life Assce Soc., 1965–88 (Chm., 1980–84); Scottish Investment Trust PLC, 1963–88; Standard Property Investment PLC, 1972–87. Mem. Council on Tribunals, 1971–76 and Chm. of Scottish Cttee, 1972–76. Governor, Merchiston Castle Sch., 1953–76. *Recreations:* shooting, fishing. *Address:* Chapelhill Cottage, Dirleton, East Lothian EH39 5HG. *T:* Dirleton (062085) 338. *Club:* New (Edinburgh).

WILLACY, Michael James Ormerod, CBE 1989; Procurement Adviser, HM Treasury, since 1991; *b* 7 June 1933; *s* of James and Marjorie Willacy (*née* Sanders); *m* 1st, 1961, Merle Louise de Lange; two *s* one *d*; 2nd, 1985, Victoria Stuart John; three *s* one *d*. *Educ:* Taunton Sch., Somerset. FInstPS. Purchasing Agent, Shell Venezuela, 1964–73; Procurement Advr, Shell Internat., The Hague, 1974–77; Supt., Shell Stanlow, 1978–80; Manager, Shell Wilmslow, 1981–83; Gen. Man., Shell UK Materials Services, 1983–85; Dir, Central Unit on Purchasing, HM Treasury, 1985–90. Chairman: Macclesfield Chamber of Commerce, 1981–83; Macclesfield Business Ventures, 1982–83. Old Tauntonian Association: Gen. Sec., 1978–91; Pres., 1988–89; Vice-Pres., 1990–. *Recreations:* golf, travel, gardening. *Address:* Lower Barn, Coarsewell, Ugborough, Ivybridge, Devon PL21 0HP. *T:* Gara Bridge (0548) 82536. *Clubs:* Commonwealth Trust; Old Tauntonian Association (Taunton).

WILLAN, Edward Gervase, CMG 1964; HM Diplomatic Service, retired; Ambassador to Czechoslovakia, 1974–77; *b* 17 May 1917; *er s* of late Captain F. G. L. Willan, RNR; *m* 1944, Mary Bickley Joy, *d* of late Lieut-Colonel H. A. Joy, IAOC. *Educ:* Radley; Pembroke Coll., Cambridge (Exhibitioner, MA). Indian Civil Service, 1939–47; 2nd Secretary (from 1948, 1st Secretary) on staff of UK High Commissioner, New Delhi, 1947–49; appointed to HM Diplomatic Service, 1948; Foreign Office, 1949–52; 1st Secretary, HM Embassy, The Hague, 1953–55; 1st Secretary, HM Legation, Bucharest, 1956–58 (Chargé d'Affaires, 1956, 1957 and 1958); Head of Communications Dept, FO, 1958–62; Political Adviser to Hong Kong Government, 1962–65; Head of Scientific Relations Dept, FO, 1966–68; Minister, Lagos, 1968–70; Ambassador at Rangoon, 1970–74. *Recreations:* walking, gardening. *Address:* Cherry Tree Cottage, Shappen Hill, Burley, Hants BH24 4AH. *Club:* United Oxford & Cambridge University.

WILLAN, Prof. Thomas Stuart, MA, BLitt, DPhil; FBA 1991; Professor of Economic History, University of Manchester, 1961–73, now Emeritus; *b* 3 Jan. 1910; 3rd *s* of Matthew Willan and Jane (*née* Stuart); unmarried. *Educ:* Queen Elizabeth's Sch., Kirkby Lonsdale; The Queen's Coll., Oxford. Asst Lecturer, School of Economics and Commerce, Dundee, 1934–35; University of Manchester: Asst Lecturer in History, 1935–45; Lecturer in History, 1945–47; Senior Lecturer in History, 1947–49; Reader in History, 1949–61. *Publications:* River Navigation in England, 1600–1750, 1936; The English Coasting Trade, 1600–1750, 1938; (ed with E. W. Crossley) Three Seventeenth-century Yorkshire Surveys, 1941; The Navigation of the Great Ouse between St Ives and Bedford in the Seventeenth Century, 1946; The Navigation of the River Weaver in the Eighteenth Century, 1951; The Muscovy Merchants of 1555, 1953; The Early History of the Russia Company, 1553–1603, 1956; Studies in Elizabethan Foreign Trade, 1959; (ed) A Tudor Book of Rates, 1962; The Early History of the Don Navigation, 1965; An Eighteenth-Century Shopkeeper, Abraham Dent of Kirkby Stephen, 1970; The Inland Trade, 1976; Elizabethan Manchester, 1980; articles in English Historical Review, Economic History Review, etc. *Address:* 3 Raynham Avenue, Didsbury, Manchester M20 0BW. *T:* 061–445 4771. *Club:* Penn.

WILLATT, Sir Hugh, Kt 1972; Secretary General of the Arts Council of Great Britain, 1968–75 (Member, 1958–68); *b* 25 April 1909; *m* 1945, Evelyn Gibbs (*d* 1991), ARE, ARCA, (Rome Scholar); no *c*. *Educ:* Repton; Pembroke Coll., Oxford (MA). Admitted a Solicitor, 1934; Partner, Hunt, Dickins and Willatt, Nottingham, and later Partner in Lewis, Silkin & Partners, Westminster. Served War of 1939–45, in RAF. Member BBC Midland Regional Adv. Council, 1953–58; Member Arts Council Drama Panel, 1955–68 (Chairman, 1960–68); Chm. Bd, Nat. Opera Studio, 1977–; Member Board: National Theatre, 1964–68; Mercury Trust Ltd (Ballet Rambert) (Chm.), 1961–67; Nottingham Theatre Trust Ltd, 1949–60; Riverside Studios, Hammersmith (Chm., 1976–82); Visiting Arts Unit (Chm., 1977–83); English Stage Co. (Royal Court Theatre), 1976–. Trustee, Shakespeare's Birthplace, 1968–. FRSA 1974. Hon. MA, University of Nottingham. *Address:* 4 St Peter's Wharf, Hammersmith Terrace, W6 9UD. *Clubs:* Garrick, Arts.

WILLCOCK, Kenneth Milner, QC 1972; **His Honour Judge Willcock;** a Circuit Judge, since 1972. MA; BCL. Called to Bar, Inner Temple, 1950. Dep. Chm., Somerset QS, 1969–71; a Recorder of the Crown Court, 1972. *Address:* Queen Elizabeth Building, Temple, EC4Y 9BS.

WILLCOCK, Prof. Malcolm Maurice; Professor of Latin, 1980–91, and Vice-Provost, 1988–91, University College London; *b* 1 Oct. 1925; *s* of late Dr Maurice Excel Willcock and Evelyn Clarice Willcock (*née* Brooks); *m* 1957, Sheena Gourlay; four *d*. *Educ:* Fettes Coll.; Pembroke Coll., Cambridge (MA). Served Royal Air Force, 1944–47. Research Fellow, Pembroke Coll., Cambridge, 1951–52; Sidney Sussex College: Fellow, 1952–65; Sen. Tutor, 1962–65; University of Lancaster: first Professor of Classics, 1965–79; Principal, Bowland Coll., 1966–79; Pro-Vice-Chancellor, 1975–79. *Publications:* ed, Plautus, Casina, 1976; Companion to the Iliad, 1976; ed, Iliad of Homer, vol. 1 (Books I–XII) 1978, vol. 2 (Books XIII–XXIV) 1984; ed, Plautus, Pseudolus, 1987. *Recreation:* bridge. *Address:* 1 Lancaster Avenue, SE27. *T:* 081–761 5615.

WILLCOCKS, Sir David (Valentine), Kt 1977; CBE 1971; MC 1944; Musical Director of the Bach Choir since 1960; General Editor, OUP Church Music, since 1961; *b* 30 Dec. 1919; *s* of late T. H. Willcocks; *m* 1947, Rachel Gordon, *d* of late Rev. A. C. Blyth, Fellow of Selwyn Coll., Cambridge; one *s* two *d* (and one *s* decd). *Educ:* Clifton Coll.; King's Coll., Cambridge (MA; MusB). Chorister, Westminster Abbey, 1929–33; Scholar, Clifton Coll., 1934–38; FRCO, 1938; Scholar at College of St Nicolas (RSCM), 1938–39; Organ Scholar, King's Coll., Cambridge, 1939–40; Open Foundation Scholarship, King's Coll., Cambridge, 1940; Stewart of Rannoch Scholarship, 1940. Served War of 1939–45, 5th Bn DCLI, 1940–45. Organ Scholar, King's Coll., Cambridge, 1945–47; Fellow of King's Coll., Cambridge, 1947–51, Hon. Fellow, 1979–; Organist of Salisbury Cathedral, 1947–50; Master of the Choristers and Organist, Worcester Cathedral, 1950–57; Fellow and Organist, King's Coll., Cambridge, 1957–73; Univ. Lectr in Music, Cambridge Univ., 1957–74; Univ. Organist, Cambridge Univ., 1958–74; Dir, RCM, 1974–84. Conductor: Cambridge Philharmonic Soc., 1947; City of Birmingham Choir, 1950–57; Bradford Festival Choral Soc., 1957–74; Cambridge Univ. Musical Soc., 1958–73. President: RCO, 1966–68; ISM, 1978–79; Old Cliftonian Soc., 1979–81; Nat. Fedn of Music Socs, 1980–89. Mem. Council, Winston Churchill Trust, 1980–90. Freeman, City of London, 1981. FRSCM 1965; FRCM 1971; FRNCM 1977; FRSAMD 1982; Hon. RAM 1965; Hon. FTCL 1976; Hon. GSM 1980; Hon. FRCCO 1967. Hon. MA Bradford, 1973; Hon. DMus: Exeter, 1976; Leicester, 1977; Westminster Choir Coll., Princeton, 1980; Bristol, 1981; St Olaf Coll., Minnesota, 1991; Hon. DLitt Sussex, 1982; Hon. Dr of Sacred Letters, Trinity Coll., Toronto, 1985. *Publications:* miscellaneous choral and instrumental works. *Address:* 13 Grange Road, Cambridge CB3 9AS. *T:* Cambridge (0223) 359559. *Clubs:* Athenæum, Arts.

WILLCOX, James Henry, CB 1988; Clerk of Public Bills, House of Commons, 1982–88, retired; *b* 31 March 1923; *s* of George Henry and Annie Elizabeth Willcox; *m* 1st, 1950, Winsome Rosemarie Adèle Dallas Ross (*d* 1984); one *s* one *d*; 2nd, 1985, Pamela, *widow* of Col John Lefroy Knyvett. *Educ:* St George's Coll., Weybridge; St John's Coll., Oxford (Schol.; MA). Served RNVR, 1942–45. Assistant Clerk, House of Commons, 1947; Sen. Clerk, 1951; Clerk of Standing Committees, 1975–76; Clerk of Overseas Office, 1976–77; Clerk of Private Bills, Examiner of Petitions for Private Bills and Taxing Officer, 1977–82. *Recreations:* walking, gardening. *Address:* Ibthorpe Farm House, Ibthorpe, near Andover, Hants SP11 0BN. *T:* Hurstbourne Tarrant (026476) 575. *Club:* Garrick.

WILLEBRANDS, His Eminence Cardinal Johannes Gerardus Maria; President, Vatican Secretariat for Promoting Christian Unity, 1969–89, now President Emeritus; Archbishop of Utrecht and Primate of Holland, 1975–83; *b* Netherlands, 4 Sept. 1909. *Educ:* Warmond Seminary, Holland; Angelicum, Rome (Dr Phil.). Priest, 1934; Chaplain, Begijnhof Church, Amsterdam, 1937–40; Prof. of Philosophy, Warmond, 1940; Director, 1945; Pres., St Willibrord Assoc., 1946; organised Catholic Conf. on Ecumenical Questions, 1951; Sec., Vatican Secretariat for Promoting Christian Unity, 1960; Titular Bishop of Mauriana, 1964; Cardinal, 1969; Cardinal with the Title of St Sebastian, Martyr, 1975. Hon. Dr of Letters: Notre Dame Univ.; St Louis Univ.; St Olaf Coll., USA; St Thomas' Coll., St Paul's, Minn, 1979; Assumption Coll., Worcester, Mass, 1980; Hon. Dr of Theology: Catholic Univ. of Louvain, 1971; Leningrad Theological Acad, 1973; Catholic Univ., Lublin, Poland, 1985; Hon. DD Oxon, 1987; Hon. DTheol Catholic Univ., München, 1987; Hon. DH Hellenic Coll./Holy Cross Orthodox Sch. of Theol., Brookline, Mass, 1989; Hon. DTheol St Michael's Univ. Coll., Toronto, 1990. *Publications:* Oecuménisme et Problèmes Actuels; Mandatum Unitatis, Beiträge zur Oekumene, 1989; reports on the ecumenical situation and articles on inter-church relationships. *Address:* Via dell'Erba 1, I-00193–Rome, Italy.

WILLESDEN, Area Bishop of; *no new appointment at time of going to press.*

WILLESEE, Hon. Donald Robert; Member of Senate for Western Australia, 1949–75; *b* 14 April 1916; *m*; four *s* two *d*. *Educ:* Carnarvon, Western Australia. Special Minister of State, Minister assisting Prime Minister, Minister assisting Minister for Foreign Affairs and Vice-Pres. of Exec. Council, 1972–73; Minister for Foreign Affairs, 1973–75; Leader of Opposition in the Senate, 1966–67; Deputy Leader of Opposition in Senate, 1969–72; Deputy Leader of Govt in Senate, 1972. *Recreation:* swimming. *Address:* 5 Walton Place, Quinns Rock, WA 6030, Australia.

WILLETT, Archibald Anthony; Investment Chairman, Cable & Wireless Pension Funds, since 1984; *b* 27 Jan. 1924; *s* of Reginald Beckett Willett and Mabel Alice (*née* Plaister); *m* 1948, Doris Marjorie Peat; one *d* (one *s* decd). *Educ:* Oswestry High Sch.; Southall Grammar School. Lloyds Bank Ltd, 1940; Great Western Railway Co., 1941–42 and 1947–48; RAF (Signals Branch), 1942–47; Cable & Wireless Ltd, 1948–77; Dir, 1967–77; Dep. Man. Dir, 1971–72; Man. Dir, 1973–77. Bursar and Fellow, St Antony's Coll., Oxford, 1977–84, Fellow Emeritus 1984. MA Oxon 1977; FCIS 1963. *Recreations:* home and garden, walking, bowls, trout fishing. *Address:* St Antony's College, Oxford OX2 6JF. *Clubs:* Royal Automobile; Exiles' (Twickenham).

WILLETT, Prof. Frank, CBE 1985; FRSE 1979; Hon. Senior Research Fellow, Hunterian Museum, University of Glasgow, since 1990; *b* 18 Aug. 1925; *s* of Thomas Willett and Frances (*née* Latham); *m* 1950, Mary Constance Hewitt; one *s* three *d*. *Educ:* Bolton Municipal Secondary Sch.; University Coll., Oxford. MA (Oxon); Dip. Anthropology (Oxon). War damage clerk, Inland Revenue, 1940; RAF Linguist, Japanese, 1943–44. Keeper, Dept of Ethnology and Gen. Archaeology, Manchester Museum, 1950–58; Hon. Surveyor of Antiquities, Nigerian Federal Govt, 1956–57, 1957–58; Archaeologist and Curator, Mus. of Ife Antiquities, Nigerian Fed. Govt, 1958–63; Supply Teacher, Bolton Educn Cttee, 1963–64; Leverhulme Research Fellow, 1964; Research Fellow, Nuffield Coll., Oxford, 1964–66; Prof. of Art History, African and Interdisciplinary Studies, Northwestern Univ., Evanston, Ill, USA, 1966–76; Dir and Titular Prof., Hunterian Mus. and Art Gall., Glasgow, 1976–90. Vis. Fellow, Clare Hall, Cambridge, 1970–71. Hon. Corresp. Member, Manchester Literary and Philosophical Soc., 1958–. *Publications:* Ife in the History of West African Sculpture, 1967, rev. edn, Ife: une Civilisation Africaine, 1971; African Art: An Introduction, 1971, rev. 1977; (with Ekpo Eyo) Treasures of Ancient Nigeria, 1980; articles in Encyc. Britannica, Man, Jl of Afr. Hist., Afr. Arts, Africa, Jl of Nigerian Historical Soc., Odu, SA Archaeol Bull., Archæometry; many conf. reports and chapters in several books. *Recreations:* relaxing, baiting architects. *Address:* Hunterian Museum, University of Glasgow, Glasgow G12 8QQ. *T:* 041–339 8855. *Club:* Commonwealth Trust.

WILLETT, Prof. Frederick John, AO 1984; DSC 1944; consultant in education administration; *b* 26 Feb. 1922; *s* of E. Willett; *m* 1949, Jane Cunningham Westwater; one *s* two *d*. *Educ:* Fitzwilliam House, Cambridge. MA (Cambridge), MBA (Melb.). Observer, Fleet Air Arm, Atlantic, Mediterranean, Indian and Pacific theatres, 1939–46; served with British Naval Liaison Mission, Washington, 1942–43. Asst Director of Research in Industrial Management, Univ. of Cambridge, 1957–62; Sidney Myer Prof. of Commerce and Business Administration, 1962–72, now Emeritus, and Pro Vice-Chancellor, 1966–72, University of Melbourne; Vice-Chancellor, Griffith Univ., Qld, 1972–84; Academic Dir, Graduate Sch., Bangkok Univ., 1986–89. Mem., Aust.-China Council, 1979–82; Chm., Indonesian Social Sciences Project, 1983–86. Hon. LLD Melbourne, 1973; Hon. DEcon Qld, 1983; DUniv Griffith, 1983. FAIM. *Publications:* many articles and papers. *Address:* 2 Yallaroo Drive, Blackmans Bay, Tas 7052, Australia. *Club:* Queensland (Brisbane).

WILLETTS, Bernard Frederick, PhD; CEng, FIMechE; CBIM; Deputy Chairman and Managing Director, International Development Corporation Ltd, since 1988; Non-Executive Director, Trinity International Holdings, 1976–91; *b* 24 March 1927; *s* of James Frederick Willetts and Effie Hurst; *m* 1952, Norah Elizabeth Law; two *s*. *Educ:* Birmingham Central Grammar Sch.; Birmingham Univ. (BSc); Durham Univ. (MSc, PhD). Section Leader, Vickers-Armstrong (Engineers) Ltd, 1954–58; Massey-Ferguson (UK) Ltd: Chief Engineer, 1959; Director, Engineering, 1962; Director, Manufacturing, 1965; Dep. Managing Director, 1967; Plessey Co. Ltd: Group Managing Director, Telecommunications, 1968; Main Board Director, 1969; Dep. Chief Exec., 1975–78; Vickers Ltd: Asst Managing Director, 1978; Man. Dir, 1980–81; Dep. Chief Exec., Dubai Aluminium Co. Ltd, 1981–88. Vice-Pres., Instn of Production Engineers, 1979–82. *Recreations:* gardening, golf, stamp collecting. *Address:* Suna Court, Pearson Road, Sonning-on-Thames, Berkshire. *T:* Reading (0734) 695050. *Clubs:* Lansdowne; Parkstone Yacht.

WILLETTS, David Lindsay; Director of Studies, Centre for Policy Studies, since 1987; *b* 9 March 1956; *s* of John Roland Willetts and Hilary Sheila Willetts; *m* 1986, Hon. Sarah Harriet Ann, *d* of Lord Butterfield, *qv*; one *d*. *Educ:* King Edward's Sch., Birmingham; Christ Church, Oxford (BA 1st cl. Hons PPE). Res. Asst to Nigel Lawson, MP, 1978; HM Treasury, 1978–84: Pvte Sec. to Financial Sec., 1981–82; Principal Monetary Policy Div., 1982–84; Prime Minister's Downing Street Policy Unit, 1984–86. Consultant Dir, Cons. Res. Dept, 1987–. Director: Retirement Security Ltd, 1988–; Electra Corporate Ventures Ltd, 1988–. Mem., Social Security Adv. Cttee, 1989–. Member: Parkside HA, 1988–90; Lambeth, Lewisham and Southwark FPC, 1987–90. Prosp. Parly Cand. (C), Havant, 1989–. *Publications:* Reforming the Health Service, 1989; Happy Families?; four points to a Conservative family policy, 1991; contrib. to Kavanagh and Seldon (ed), The Thatcher Effect, 1989; paper, The Role of the Prime Minister's Policy Unit, 1987 (Haldane Medal, RIPA). *Recreations:* swimming, reading. *Address:* c/o Centre for Policy Studies, 8 Wilfred Street, SW1E 6PL. *T:* 071–828 1176.

WILLIAMS; *see* Rees-Williams, family name of Baron Ogmore.

WILLIAMS, family name of **Baron Williams of Elvel.**

WILLIAMS OF ELVEL, Baron *cr* 1985 (Life Peer), of Llansantffraed in Elvel in the County of Powys; **Charles Cuthbert Powell Williams,** CBE 1980; Deputy Leader of the Opposition, since 1989, opposition spokesman on Trade and Industry, since 1986 and on Defence, since 1990, House of Lords; *b* 9 Feb. 1933; *s* of late Dr Norman Powell Williams, DD, and Mrs Muriel de Lérisson Williams (*née* Cazenove); *m* 1975, Jane Gillian (*née* Portal), DL, JP; one step *s*. *Educ:* Westminster Sch.; Christ Church, Oxford (MA);

LSE. British Petroleum Co. Ltd, 1958–64; Bank of London and Montreal, 1964–66; Eurofinance SA, Paris, 1966–70; Baring Brothers and Co. Ltd, 1970–77 (Man. Dir, 1971–77); Chm., Price Commn, 1977–79; Man. Dir 1980–82, Chm. 1982–85, Henry Ansbacher & Co. Ltd; Chief Exec., Henry Ansbacher Holdings PLC, 1982–85. Parly Candidate (Lab), Colchester, 1964. Opposition spokesman on Energy, H of L, 1988–90. Founder Mem, Labour Econ. Finance and Taxation Assoc. (Vice-Chm., 1975–77, 1979–83). Director: Pergamon Holdings Ltd, 1985–91; Mirror Group Newspapers Ltd, 1985–91, Mirror Group Newspapers PLC, 1991–; Chm., Acoustignide Ltd, 1989–. President: Campaign for Protection of Rural Wales, 1989–; Fedn of Industrial Develt Assocs, 1990–. *Recreations:* cricket (Oxford Univ. CC, 1953–55, Captain 1955; Essex CCC, 1953–59); music, real tennis. *Address:* 48 Thurloe Square, SW7 2SX. *T:* 071–581 1783; Pant-y-Rhiw, Llansantffraed in Elvel, Powys LD1 5RH. *Clubs:* Reform, MCC.

WILLIAMS, Prof. Alan Frederick, PhD; FRS 1990; Director, Medical Research Council Cellular Immunology Unit, since 1977; Professor of Immunology, and Fellow of Brasenose College, University of Oxford, since 1990; *b* 25 May 1945; *s* of Walter Alan and Mary Elizabeth Williams; *m* 1967, Rosalind Margaret Wright; one *s* one *d*. *Educ:* Box Hill High Sch., Melbourne; Melbourne Univ. (BAgrSc); Adelaide Univ. (PhD Biochem). Departmental Demonstrator, Biochemistry Dept, Oxford Univ., 1970–72; Jun. Research Fellow, Linacre Coll., Oxford, 1970–72; Staff Member, MRC Immunochemistry Unit, Oxford, 1972–77. Mem., Eur. Molecular Biology Orgn, 1984–. Hon. Member: Amer. Assoc. of Immunologists, 1989; Scandinavian Soc. of Immunology, 1990. *Publications:* contribs to biochemistry and immunology scientific jls. *Recreations:* gardening, modern art. *Address:* Sir William Dunn School of Pathology, University of Oxford, Oxford OX1 3RE. *T:* Oxford (0865) 275595.

WILLIAMS, Prof. Alan Harold; Professor in the Department of Economics, University of York, since 1968; *b* 9 June 1927; *s* of Harold George Williams and Gladys May Williams (*née* Clark); *m* 1953, June Frances Porter; two *s* one *d*. *Educ:* King Edward's, Birmingham; Univ. of Birmingham (BCom). Lecturer, Exeter Univ., 1954–63; Sen. Lectr and Reader, Univ. of York, 1964–68. Visiting Lecturer: MIT, 1957–58; Princeton, 1963–64; Director of Economic Studies, HM Treasury Centre for Administrative Studies, 1966–68. Member: Yorkshire Water Authority, 1973–76; DHSS Chief Scientists Research Cttee, 1973–78; Royal Commission on the NHS, 1976–78; various SSRC Cttees and Panels, 1973–; Nat. Water Council, 1980–83. Hon. DPhil Lund, 1977. *Publications:* Public Finance and Budgetary Policy, 1963; (with Robert Anderson) Efficiency in the Social Services, 1975; (with Robert Sugden) Principles of Practical Cost-Benefit Analysis, 1978; articles in Economica, Jl of Political Econ., Jl of Public Econs, Nat. Tax Jl, Jl of Health Econ., BMJ and elsewhere; numerous conf. papers on various aspects of public expenditure appraisal, esp. health and health care. *Recreations:* music, walking, teasing.

WILLIAMS, Rt. Hon. Alan John, PC 1977; MP (Lab) Swansea West since 1964; *b* 14 Oct. 1930; *m* 1957, Mary Patricia Rees, Blackwood, Mon; two *s* one *d*. *Educ:* Cardiff High Sch.; Cardiff College of Technology; University College, Oxford. BSc (London); BA (Oxon). Lecturer in economics, Welsh College of Advanced Technology; Free-lance Journalist. Joined Labour Party, 1950. Member: NATFHE (formerly of ATTI), 1958–; Fabian Society; Co-operative Party; National Union of Students delegation to Russia, 1954. Advr, Assoc. of First Div. Civil Servants, 1982–. Contested (Lab) Poole, 1959. PPS to Postmaster General, 1966–67; Parly Under-Sec., DEA, 1967–69; Parly Sec., Min. of Technology, 1969–70; Opposition Spokesman on Consumer Protection, Small Businesses, Minerals, 1970–74; Minister of State: Dept of Prices and Consumer Protection, 1974–76; DoI, 1976–79; Opposition spokesman on Wales, 1979–80; Shadow Minister for CS, 1980–83; opposition spokesman on: trade and industry, 1983–87; Wales, 1987–89; Dep. Shadow Leader of the House, 1983–89 and 1988–89; Shadow Sec. of State for Wales, 1987–88. Chairman, Welsh PLP, 1966–67; Delegate, Council of Europe and WEU, 1966–67; Mem. Public Accts Cttee, 1966–67; Jt Chm., All-Party Minerals Cttee, 1979–86. Sponsored by TSSA (Mem., 1984–). *Address:* House of Commons, SW1; Hill View, 96 Plunch Lane, Limeslade, Swansea. *Club:* Clyne Golf.

WILLIAMS, Alan Lee, OBE 1973; Warden and Chief Executive, Toynbee Hall, since 1987; *b* 29 Nov. 1930; *m* 1974, Jennifer Ford. *Educ:* Roan Sch., Greenwich; Ruskin Coll., Oxford. National Service, RAF, 1951–53; Oxford, 1954–56; National Youth Officer, Labour Party, 1956–62; MP (Lab) Hornchurch, 1966–70, Havering, Hornchurch, Feb. 1974–1979; PPS to Sec. of State for Defence, 1969–70, 1976; PPS to Sec. of State for NI, 1976–78; Dir-Gen., English-Speaking Union, 1979–86. Chm., Parly Lab. Party Defence Cttee, 1976–79; Member: FO Adv. Cttee on Disarmament and Arms Control, 1975–79; Adv. Council on Public Records, 1977–84; Chm., Delegn to 4th Cttee of UN, NY, 1969; Chm., Transport on Water Assoc.; Deputy Director, European Movement, 1970–71, Treasurer, 1972–79; Dir, British Atlantic Cttee, 1972–74, Chm., 1980–83; Vice Pres., European-Atlantic Gp, 1983–; Chairman: Peace Through NATO, 1983–; European Working Gp of Internat. Centre for Strategic and Internat. Studies, Washington DC, 1987– (Mem., 1974–); Member: RUSI, 1968–; Trilateral Commn, 1976–; Council, Council for Arms Control, 1982–; British Bd, British-American Project, 1983–. Freeman: City of London, 1969; Co. of Watermen and Lightermen, 1952–. DLitt (*hc*) Schiller Internat. Univ., 1987. FRSA. *Publications:* Radical Essays, 1966; Europe or the Open Sea?, 1971; Crisis in European Defence, 1973; The European Defence Initiative: Europe's bid for equality, 1985; The Decline of Labour and the Fall of the SDP, 1989; Fabian Soc. pamphlet on East/West Détente; Toynbee Hall briefing, Islamic Resurgence, 1991. *Recreations:* reading, history, walking. *Address:* Toynbee Hall, Commercial Street, E1 6LS. *T:* 071–247 6943. *Clubs:* Reform, Pilgrims.

WILLIAMS, Dr Alan Wynne; MP (Lab) Carmarthen, since 1987; *b* 21 Dec. 1945; *s* of Tom and Mary Hannah Williams; *m* 1973, Marian Williams. *Educ:* Carmarthen Grammar School; Jesus College, Oxford. BA Chem. 1st cl. hons; DPhil. Senior Lecturer in Environmental Science, Trinity College, Carmarthen, 1971–87. *Recreations:* reading, watching sport. *Address:* Cwmaber, Alltycnap Road, Carmarthen, Dyfed SA33 5BL. *T:* Carmarthen (0267) 235825.

WILLIAMS, Sir Alastair Edgcumbe James D., *see* Dudley-Williams.

WILLIAMS, Albert; General Secretary, Union of Construction, Allied Trades and Technicians, since 1985; President, European Federation of Building and Woodworkers, since 1988; *b* 12 Feb 1927; *s* of William Arthur Williams and Phyllis Williams (*née* Barnes); *m* 1954, Edna Bradley; two *s*. *Educ:* Houldsworth School, Reddish; Manchester School of Building (1st and 2nd year Union of Lancs and Cheshire Insts Certs of Training). Apprentice bricklayer, Manchester City Corp., 1941; Armed Forces, 1944–48; bricklaying for various contractors; Member: Exec., Amalgamated Union of Building Trade Workers, 1958–; Exec., Council of UCATT, 1971–; Construction Ind. Trng Bd, 1979–; Gen. Council, TUC, 1986–; Dir, Bldg and Civil Engrg Holidays Scheme Management Ltd, 1979–; Operatives' Side Sec., Nat. Jt Council for Building Industry, 1984–. *Recreations:* poetry and work. *Address:* UCATT House, 177 Abbeville Road, SW4 9RL. *T:* 071–622 2442.

WILLIAMS, (Albert) Trevor; management scientist; *b* 7 April 1938; *s* of Ben and Minnie Williams; *m* 1st, 1970, Mary Lynn Lyster; three *s*; 2nd, 1978, Deborah Sarah Fraser Duncan (*née* Milne); one *s*. *Educ:* King George V Sch., Southport; Queens' Coll., Cambridge (MA); Cranfield Institute of Technology (MSc). Rotary Foundation Fellow, Univ. of Ghana, 1961–62; Business Operations Research Ltd: Director, 1965–68; various academic appointments, 1968–82, including: Sen. Lectr and Vis. Professor, Graduate School of Business, Cape Town Univ.; Sen. Research Fellow, Sussex Univ.; Vis. Associate Prof., Wisconsin Univ.; Vis. Prof., INSEAD; taught corporate strategy at Hong Kong Univ., 1989 (Hon. Prof.), at LSE, 1990–91. Dir, Novy Eddison and Partners, 1971–74; Dep.-Dir for Futures Research, Univ. of Stellenbosch, 1974–78; Dep. Chief Scientific Officer, Price Commission, 1978–79; Advisor on Technology Projects, Scottish Development Agency, 1979; Dir, Henley Centre for Forecasting, 1980–81. Consultant, Sen. Industrial Advr and Team Manager, Monopolies and Mergers Commn, 1982–90. *Publication:* A Guide to Futures Studies, 1976. *Recreations:* walking, reading. *Address:* Bodenham House, Dinedor, Hereford HR2 6LQ. *T:* Holme Lacy (0432) 870243; 13 Highcroft, 170 Highgate Road, NW5 1EJ. *Clubs:* Athenæum, Institute of Directors.

WILLIAMS, Alexander, CB 1991; FInstP; Government Chemist, 1987–91; *b* 30 March 1931; *s* of Henry and Dorothy Williams; *m* 1957, Beryl Wynne Williams (*née* Williams); one *s*. *Educ:* Grove Park Grammar Sch., Wrexham; University College of North Wales, Bangor (BSc). National Service, REME, 1953–55; Monsanto Chemicals, 1955–56; Southern Instruments, Camberley, 1956–59; National Physical Laboratory: Div. of Radiation Science, 1959–78; Head, Div. of Mechanical and Optical Metrology, 1978–81; Under Sec., Res. and Technology Policy Div., DTI 1981–87. Dir, Assoc. of Official Analytical Chemists, 1989–. *Publications:* A Code of Practice for the Detailed Statement of Accuracy (with P. J. Campion and J. E. Burns), 1973; numerous papers on measurements of radio-activity etc, to Internat. Jl of Applied Radiation and Isotopes, Nucl. Instruments and Methods, etc. *Recreations:* bell-ringing, music, opera, walking.

WILLIAMS, Sir Alwyn, Kt 1983; PhD; FRS 1967; FRSE, MRIA, FGS; Principal and Vice-Chancellor of University of Glasgow, 1976–88, Hon. Senior Research Fellow in Geology, since 1988; *b* 8 June 1921; *s* of D. Daniel Williams and E. May (*née* Rogers); *m* 1949, E. Joan Bevan; one *s* one *d*. *Educ:* Aberdare Boys' Grammar Sch.; University College of Wales, Aberystwyth. PhD Wales. Fellow, Univ. of Wales, 1946–48. Harkness Fund Fellow at US National Museum, Washington, DC, 1948–50; Lecturer in Geology in University of Glasgow, 1950–54; Prof. of Geology, 1954–74, Pro-Vice-Chancellor, 1967–74, Queen's Univ. of Belfast; Lapworth Prof. of Geology, and Head of Dept, Univ. of Birmingham, 1974–76. Pres., Palaeontological Assoc., 1968–70. Trustee, British Museum (Nat. History), 1971–79, Chm. of Trustees, 1974–79. Member: Equip. and Phys. Sci. sub-cttees, UGC, 1974–76; NERC, 1974–76; Adv. Council, British Library, 1975–77; Scottish Tertiary Educn Adv. Council, 1983–87; Adv. Bd for the Res. Councils, 1985–88; Chairman: Cttee on Nat. Museums and Galls in Scotland, 1979–81; Cttee on Scottish Agricl Colls, 1989; Scottish Hospitals Endowment Res. Trust, 1989–; Vice-Chm., Cttee of Vice-Chancellors and Principals, 1979–81. Dir, Scottish Daily Record & Sunday Mail Ltd, 1984–90. Pres., Royal Soc. of Edinburgh, 1985–88. FRSAMD 1988. Hon. Fellow, Geol Soc. of America, 1970–; For. Mem., Polish Academy of Sciences, 1979–; Hon. Associate, BM (Nat. Hist.), 1981–; Hon. FRCPS; Hon. FDS RCPS; Hon. DSc: Wales, 1974; Belfast, 1975; Edinburgh, 1979; Hon. LLD: Strathclyde, 1982; Glasgow, 1988; Hon. DCL Oxford, 1987. Bigsby Medal, 1961, Murchison Medal, 1973, Geol Soc.; Clough Medal, Edin. Geol. Soc., 1976; T. Neville George Medal, Glasgow Geol. Soc., 1984. *Publications:* contrib. to Trans Royal Socs of London and Edinburgh, Jl Geological Society; Geological Magazine; Washington Acad. of Sciences; Geological Societies of London and America; Palaeontology; Journal of Paleontology, etc. *Address:* Department of Geology and Applied Geology, The University, Glasgow G12 8QQ; 25 Sutherland Avenue, Pollokshields, Glasgow G41 4HG. *T:* 041–427 0589.

WILLIAMS, Anna Maureen, (Mrs G. H. G. Williams); *see* Worrall, A. M.

WILLIAMS, Sir Arthur (Dennis Pitt), Kt 1991; Chairman, Williams Holdings Ltd, since 1965; *b* 15 Oct. 1928; *s* of Arthur Henry Williams and Dora Ruth Williams; *m* 1st, 1951, Ngaire; three *s* two *d*; 2nd, 1989, Jeanne; one *s*. *Educ:* Salmerston; Margate College. Served RN, 1944–46. Apprentice carpenter, 1942–44 and 1946–47; carpenter, NZ, 1951–53; builder, 1953–, and property owner. Govt Appointee, Govt Property Services Ltd, 1991. Fellow: NZ Inst. of Builders; Aust. Inst. of Builders; NZ Inst. of Management. NZ Commemorative Medal, 1990. *Recreations:* horse breeding and racing. *Address:* Cranbrook, Cranbrook Grove, Waikanae, New Zealand. *T:* (business) 063647739, *Fax:* 063647605. *Club:* Wellesley (Wellington, NZ).

WILLIAMS, Arthur Vivian, CBE 1969; General Manager and Solicitor, Peterlee (New Town) Development Corporation, 1948–74, and of Aycliffe (New Town) Development Corporation, 1954–74; *b* 2 Jan. 1909; *s* of N. T. and Gwendolen Williams; *m* 1937, Charlotte Moyra (*d* 1985), *d* of Dr E. H. M. Milligan; three *s* one *d*. *Educ:* William Hulme's Grammar Sch., Manchester; Jesus Coll., Oxford. MA (Oxon). Admitted as Solicitor, 1936; Dep. Town Clerk of Finchley, 1938–41; Town Clerk of Bilston, 1941–46; Town Clerk and Clerk of the Peace, Dudley, 1946–48. *Address:* 7 Majestic Court, Spring Grove, Harrogate HG1 2HT. *T:* Harrogate (0423) 568451.

WILLIAMS, Hon. Atanda F.; *see* Fatayi-Williams.

WILLIAMS, Rev. Austen; *see* Williams, Rev. S. A.

WILLIAMS, Basil Hugh G.; *see* Garnons Williams.

WILLIAMS, Prof. Bernard Arthur Owen, FBA 1971; White's Professor of Moral Philosophy, and Fellow of Corpus Christi College, University of Oxford, since 1990; Monroe Deutsch Professor of Philosophy, University of California, Berkeley, since 1988; *b* 21 Sept. 1929; *s* of late O. P. D. Williams, OBE and of H. A. Williams; *m* 1955, Shirley Vivienne Teresa Brittain Catlin (*see* Rt. Hon. S. V. T. B. Williams) (marr. diss. 1974); one *d*; *m* 1974, Patricia Law Skinner; two *s*. *Educ:* Chigwell Sch., Essex; Balliol Coll., Oxford (Hon. Fellow 1984). BA (Oxon) 1951; MA 1954. Fellow of All Souls Coll., Oxford, 1951–54; RAF (Gen. Duties Br.), 1951–53; Fellow of New Coll., Oxford, 1954–59; Vis. Lectr, Univ. Coll. of Ghana, 1958–59; Lectr in Philosophy, Univ. Coll., London, 1959–64; Professor of Philosophy, Bedford College, London, 1964–67 (Hon. Fellow 1985); Knightbridge Prof. of Philosophy, Cambridge, 1967–79; Fellow, 1967–79 and 1987, Provost, 1979–87, King's Coll., Cambridge. Visiting Professor: Princeton Univ., USA, 1963; Harvard Univ., 1973; Univ. of California, Berkeley, 1986; Sather Prof. of Classics, Univ. of Calif, Berkeley, 1989; Vis. Fellow, Inst. of Advanced Studies, ANU, 1969; Sen. Vis. Fellow, Princeton, 1978, 1991. Member: Public Schools Commn, 1965–70; Royal Commn on Gambling, 1976–78; Chairman: Cttee on Obscenity and Film Censorship, 1977–79; Fitzwilliam Mus. Syndicate, 1984–87. Dir, English Nat. Opera (formerly Sadler's Wells Opera), 1968–86. Foreign Hon. Mem., Amer. Acad. of Arts and Sciences, 1983. Hon. LittD Dublin, 1981; Hon. DLitt Aberdeen, 1987. Author and presenter, What is Truth? series, Channel 4, 1988. *Publications:* (ed with A. C. Montefiore) British Analytical Philosophy, 1966; Morality, 1972; Problems of the Self, 1973; A

Critique of Utilitarianism, 1973; Descartes: The Project of Pure Enquiry, 1978; Moral Luck, 1981; (ed with A. K. Sen) Utilitarianism and Beyond, 1982; Ethics and the Limits of Philosophy, 1985; articles in philosophical jls, etc. *Recreation:* music, particularly opera. *Address:* Corpus Christi College, Oxford OX1 4JF; Department of Philosophy, University of California, Berkeley, Calif 94720, USA.

WILLIAMS, Betty; *see* Williams, Elizabeth.

WILLIAMS, Prof. Sir Bruce (Rodda), KBE 1980; Titular Professor of the University of Sydney, since 1967 (Vice-Chancellor and Principal, 1967–81); Visiting Fellow, Australian National University, 1987, 1988 and 1990; *b* 10 January 1919; *s* of late Reverend W. J. Williams and Helen Baud; *m* 1942, Roma Olive Hotten; five *d. Educ:* Wesley College; Queen's College, University of Melbourne (BA 1939). MA Adelaide 1942; MA(Econ) Manchester, 1963. FASSA 1968. Lecturer in Economics, University of Adelaide, 1939–46 and at Queen's University of Belfast, 1946–50; Professor of Economics, University College of North Staffordshire, 1950–59; Robert Otley Prof., 1959–63, and Stanley Jevons Prof., 1963–67, Univ. of Manchester; Dir, Technical Change Centre and Vis. Prof., Imperial Coll., London, 1981–86. Secretary and Joint Director of Research, Science and Industry Committee, 1952–59. Member, National Board for Prices and Incomes, 1966–67; Econ. Adviser to Minister of Technology, 1966–67; Member: Central Advisory Council on Science and Technology, 1967; Reserve Bank Board, 1969–81; Chairman: NSW State Cancer Council, 1967–81; Australian Vice Chancellors Cttee, 1972–74; Aust. Govt Cttee of Inquiry into Educn and Trng, 1976–79; (Australian) Review of Discipline of Engrg, 1987–88; Dep. Chm., Parramatta Hosps Bd, 1979–81. Editor, The Sociological Review, 1953–59, and The Manchester Sch., 1959–67. President Economics Section of British Assoc., 1964. Hon. FIE(Aust) 1989. Hon. DLitt: Keele, 1973; Sydney, 1982; Hon. DEcon Qld, 1980; Hon. LLD: Melbourne, 1981; Manchester, 1982; Hon. DSc Aston, 1982. Kirby Meml Award, IProdE, 1988. *Publications:* The Socialist Order and Freedom, 1942; (with C. F. Carter): Industry and Technical Progress, 1957, Investment in Innovation, 1958, and Science in Industry, 1959; Investment Behaviour, 1962; Investment Proposals and Decisions, 1965; Investment, Technology and Growth, 1967; (ed) Science and Technology in Economic Growth, 1973; Systems of Higher Education: Australia, 1978; Education, Training and Employment, 1979; Living with Technology, 1982; (ed) Knowns and Unknowns in Technical Change, 1985; Attitudes to New Technologies and Economic Growth, 1986; Review of the Discipline of Engineering, 1988; The Effect of New Funding Methods on British Universities, 1991. *Address:* 106 Grange Road, W5 3PJ. *Club:* Athenæum.

WILLIAMS, Campbell (Sherston); *see under* Smith, Campbell (Sherston).

WILLIAMS, Catrin Mary, FRCS; Consultant Ear, Nose and Throat Surgeon, Clwyd Health Authority (North), 1956–86; Chairman, Wales Council for the Deaf, 1986–88; *b* 19 May 1922; *d* of late Alderman Richard Williams, JP, Pwllheli, and Mrs Margaret Williams; unmarried. *Educ:* Pwllheli Grammar Sch.; Welsh National Sch. of Medicine (BSc 1942, MB, BCh 1945). FRCS 1948. Co-Chm., Women's National Commn, 1981–83; Pres., Medical Women's Fedn, 1973–74; Founding Vice-Pres., Gymdeithas Feddygol Gymraeg (Welsh Med. Soc.), 1975–79; Vice-Chm., Meniere's Soc., 1986–90, Chm., 1990–; Member: Council and Exec. Cttee, RNID, 1986–; Exec. Cttee, Wales Council for the Disabled, 1988–; Procedure Advr, Med. Women's Internat. Assoc., 1984–. *Recreations:* reading, embroidery. *Address:* Gwrych House, Abergele, Clwyd LL22 8EU. *T:* Abergele (0745) 832256.

WILLIAMS, Cecil Beaumont, CHB 1980; OBE 1963; Executive Director, Da Costa & Musson Ltd, Barbados, since 1980; *b* 8 March 1926; *s* of George Cuthbert and Violet Irene Williams; *m* 1952, Dorothy Marshall; two *s* one *d. Educ:* Harrison Coll., Barbados; Durham Univ.; Oxford Univ. BA, DipEd. Asst Master, Harrison Coll., 1948–54. Asst Sec., Govt Personnel Dept, and Min. of Trade, Industry and Labour (Barbados), 1954–56; Permanent Secretary: Min. of Educn, 1958; Min. of Trade, Industry and Labour, 1958–63; Dir, Economic Planning Unit, 1964–65; Manager, Industrial Develt Corp., 1966–67; High Comr to Canada, 1967–70; Permanent Sec., Min. of External Affairs, 1971–74; Ambassador to USA and Perm. Rep. to OAS, 1974–75; High Comr in UK, 1976–79. *Recreations:* music, tennis, reading, gardening. *Address:* Moonshine Hall, St George, Barbados.

WILLIAMS, Rear-Adm. Charles Bernard, CB 1980; OBE 1967; Flag Officer Medway and Port Admiral Chatham, 1978–80, retired; *b* 19 Feb. 1925; *s* of Charles Williams and Elizabeth (*née* Malherbe); *m* 1946, Patricia Mary, *d* of Henry Brownlow Thorp and Ellen Thorp; one *s* one *d. Educ:* Graeme Coll., Grahamstown, SA; Royal Naval Engineering Coll., Plymouth. Served in HM Ships Nigeria, Hornet, Triumph, 1946–53; in charge: Flight deck trials unit, 1953; Naval Wing, Nat. Gas Turbine Estabt, 1956; Sen. Engr, HMS Cumberland, 1958; in charge Admiralty Fuel Experimental Station, 1960; Comdr 1960; Engineer Officer, HMS London, 1962; Staff Engr, Flag Officer ME, 1964; Duty Comdr, Naval Ops MoD (N), 1967; Captain 1969; Dep. Manager, Portsmouth Dockyard, 1969; Supt, Clyde Submarine Base, 1972; Captain, HMS Sultan, 1975; Rear-Adm. 1978. *Recreations:* sailing (Chm., Whitbread Round the World Race, 1981–90), walking, music. *Address:* Green Shutters, Montserrat Road, Lee-on-Solent PO13 9LT. *T:* Lee-on-Solent (0705) 550816. *Clubs:* Royal Yacht Squadron; Royal Ocean Racing; Royal Southern Yacht; Royal Naval Sailing Association (Life Vice Cdre); Lee-on-Solent Sailing; Royal London Yacht (Hon. Mem.); Cruising Association of South Africa (Life Mem.).

WILLIAMS, Rt. Rev. Christopher; *see* Williams, Rt Rev. J. C. R., Bishop of The Arctic.

WILLIAMS, Dr Cicely Delphine, CMG 1968; retired (except on demand); *b* 2 Dec. 1893; *d* of James Rowland Williams, Kew Park, Jamaica (Dir of Educn, Jamaica) and Margaret E. C. Williams (*née* Farewell). *Educ:* Bath High Sch. for Girls; Somerville Coll., Oxford (Hon. Fellow, 1979); King's Coll. Hosp. DM, FRCP, DTM&H. Colonial Med. Service: appts, 1929–48. WHO Adv. in Maternal and Child Health, 1948–51; Research on Vomiting Sickness, 1951–53; Sen. Lectr in Nutrition, London, 1953–55; consulting visits to various countries, 1955–59; Visiting Professor: of Maternal and Child Health, Amer. Univ. of Beirut, 1959–64; Tulane Sch. of Public Health, New Orleans, 1971–; Adv. in Trng Progrs, Family Planning Assoc., 1964–67. Lectures: Milroy, RCP, 1958; Blackfan, Harvard Med. Sch., 1973; Balgopal Oration, Paediatric Soc., Katmandu, Nepal, 1981; Speaker, Pakistan Paediatric Assoc., 1982. Emeritus Professor of Maternal and Child Health, Nursing and Nutrition, Tulane Sch. of Public Health, 1974. Hon. FRSM 1976; Hon. Fellow: King's Coll. Hosp. Medical Sch, 1978; Green Coll., Oxford, 1985. Hon. DSc: Univ. of WI; Univ. of Maryland; Univ. of Tulane; Smith Coll., Northampton, Mass. James Spence Meml Medal, Br. Paed. Assoc., 1965; Goldberger Award in Clin. Nutrition, Amer. Med. Assoc., 1967; Dawson-Williams Award in Paediatrics, BMA (jt), 1973; Galen Medal, Worshipful Soc. of Apothecaries, London, 1984. Order of Merit, Jamaica, 1975. *Publications:* chapters in: Diseases of Children in the Tropics, 1954; Sick Children, 1956; The Matrix of Medicine, 1958; (with D. B. Jelliffe) Mother and Child Health: delivering the services, 1972; contrib. to: The Lancet, Archives of Diseases in Childhood (which reissued, 1982, as 'perhaps the most important ever published in the Archives', her paper A Nutritional Disease of Childhood, 1933), Tropical Pediatrics, etc. *Recreations:* people and solitude. *Address:* Highfield, The Common, Marlborough, Wilts SN8 1DL. *T:* Marlborough (0672) 52671. *Club:* Commonwealth Trust.

WILLIAMS, Clifford; Associate Director, Royal Shakespeare Company, since 1963; *b* 30 Dec. 1926; *s* of George Frederick Williams and Florence Maud Williams (*née* Gapper); *m* 1st, 1952, Joanna Douglas (marr. diss. 1959); no *c*; 2nd, 1962, Josiane Eugenie Peset; two *d. Educ:* Highbury County Grammar Sch. Acted in London (These Mortals, Larissa, Wolves and Sheep, Great Catherine), and repertory theatres, 1945–48; founded and directed Mime Theatre Company, 1950–53; Dir of Productions: at Marlowe Theatre, Canterbury, 1955–56; at Queen's Theatre, Hornchurch, 1957. Directed at Arts Theatre, London: Yerma, 1957; Radio Rescue, 1958; Dark Halo, Quartet for Five, The Marriage of Mr Mississippi (all in 1959); Moon for the Misbegotten, The Shepherd's Chameleon, Victims of Duty (all in 1960); The Race of Adam, Llandaff Festival, 1961. Joined Royal Shakespeare Company, 1961; Directed: Afore Night Come, 1962; The Comedy of Errors, 1963. Productions for RSC in Stratford and London: The Tempest, The Representative, The Comedy of Errors (revival), 1963; Richard II, Henry IV Pts I and II (co-dir), Afore Night Come (revival), The Jew of Malta, 1964; The Merchant of Venice, The Jew of Malta (revival), The Comedy of Errors (revival), 1965; The Meteor, Twelfth Night, Henry IV Pts I and II (co-dir, revivals), 1966; Doctor Faustus, 1968; Major Barbara, 1970; The Duchess of Malfi, 1971; The Comedy of Errors (revival), 1972; The Taming of the Shrew, A Lesson in Blood and Roses, 1973; Cymbeline (co-dir), 1974; The Mouth Organ, Too True to be Good, 1975; Wild Oats, 1976, 1979; Man and Superman, 1977; The Tempest, 1978; The Love-Girl and the Innocent, 1981; The Happiest Days of Your Life, 1984; Il Candelaio, 1986; The Beaux' Stratagem, 1988. Other productions include: Our Man Crichton, 1964, and the Flying Dutchman, 1966, in London; The Gardener's Dog, 1965, and The Merry Wives of Windsor, 1967, for the Finnish National Theatre; Volpone at Yale Univ., 1967; Othello, for Bulgarian Nat. Theatre, Soldiers, New York and London, 1968; Dido and Aeneas, Windsor Festival, Famine, English Stage Soc., 1969; As You Like It, 1967, and Back to Methuselah, 1969, both for the Nat. Theatre of GB; The Winter's Tale, 1969, for Yugoslav Nat. Theatre; Sleuth, London, NY and Paris, 1970; Oh! Calcutta!, London and Paris, 1970; Emperor Henry IV, New York, 1973; As You Like It (revival), New York, What Every Woman Knows, London, Emperor Henry IV, London, 1974; Murderer, London, 1975; Mardi-Gras, London, Carte Blanche, London, 1976; Stevie, The Old Country, Rosmerholm, London, 1977; The Passion of Dracula, London, 1978; Richard III, Mexican Nat. Theatre, 1979; Threepenny Opera, 1979, and The Love-Girl and the Innocent, 1980, Aalborg; Born in the Gardens, London, 1980; Overheard, London, To Grandmother's House We Go, NY, The Carmelites, Aalborg, 1981; Othello, Bad Hersfeld, Chapter 17, London, 1982; Richard III, Madrid, Merry Wives of Windsor, USA, Scheherazade, Festival Ballet, 1983; Pack of Lies, London, 1983, NY, 1985; A Child's Christmas in Wales (revival), USA, 1983; Rise and Fall of the City of Mahagonny, Aalborg, 1984; Aren't We All?, London, 1984, NY, 1985; The Cherry Orchard, Tokyo, 1984; Measure for Measure, Norrköping, St Joan, British tour, 1985; Legends, USA, 1986; Breaking the Code, London, 1986, NY, 1987; Aren't We All?, Australia, 1986; The Importance of Being Earnest, Copenhagen, 1987; A Chorus of Disapproval, British tour, Richard II, London, 1988; Richard III, London, Song at Nightfall, Dorset Music Fest., Wheel of Fire, Mérida Fest., Spain, 1989; Bellman's Opera, Stockholm, 1990; A Slight Hangover, British tour, Painting Churches, Southampton, Denmark, 1991. Also directed plays for the Arena Theatre, Triumph Theatre Co., Theatre Workshop, Guildford, Oxford, Coventry, Toronto, Los Angeles, Washington, Houston, Johannesburg, Edinburgh Festival; Malvern Festival; Dir, Man and Superman (film), 1986. Mem. Welsh Arts Council, 1963–72; Chairman: Welsh Nat. Theatre Co., 1968–72; British Theatre Assoc., 1977–90; Chm., British Children's Theatre Assoc., 1968–71; Governor, Welsh Coll. of Music and Drama, 1981–90. Associate Artist of Yugoslav Nat. Theatre, 1969; FTCL. *Publications:* (ed) John O'Keeffe, Wild Oats, 1977; *plays:* The Disguises of Arlecchino, 1951; The Sleeping Princess, 1953; The Goose Girl, 1954; The Secret Garden, 1955; (with Donald Jonson) Stephen Dedalus, 1956; (with Daphne du Maurier) Rebecca, 1989; *translations:* Ionesco, The Duel, Double Act, 1979; Pirandello, As You Desire Me, 1981; Chekhov, The Cherry Orchard, 1981. *Recreations:* motor boating, water-ski-ing. *Address:* 62 Maltings Place, Bagleys Lane, SW6 2BY; 12 Chemin Cambarnier Nord, 06560 Opio, Valbonne, France.

WILLIAMS, Colin; *see* Welland, C.

WILLIAMS, Colin Hartley; Head of Corporate Communications, National Westminster Bank, since 1990 (Chief Press Relations Manager, 1983–90); *b* 7 Dec. 1938; *s* of late Gwilym Robert Williams and Margaret (*née* Hartley); *m* 1964, Carolyn (*née* Bulman); one *s* two *d. Educ:* Grangefield Grammar Sch., Stockton-on-Tees; University College of Wales, Aberystwyth (BA). Journalist: Evening Gazette, Middlesbrough, 1960–63; Today Magazine, Odhams Press, 1964; Daily Sketch, 1964–66; Senior Lecturer, International Press Inst., Nairobi, 1967–68; Corporate and Public Relations Executive, 1969–74; Press Officer, Corporation of City of London, 1975–76; Asst Dir, City Communications Centre, 1977, Exec. Dir, 1979–83; Exec. Dir, Cttee on Invisible Exports, 1982–83. *Publications:* articles on labour management, financial and communication topics. *Recreations:* writing, wine, golf. *Address:* 84 Clare Road, Prestwood, near Great Missenden, Bucks HP16 0NU. *T:* Great Missenden (02406) 4464.

WILLIAMS, Cyril Robert, CBE 1945; *b* 11 May 1895; *s* of Rev. F. J. Williams, MA; *m* 1928, Ethel Winifred Wise; two *d. Educ:* Wellington College, Berks; New College, Oxford. Dist Loco. Supt, Khartoum, Sudan Rlys, 1923; Asst Mech. Engineer (Outdoor), 1924; Loco. Running Supt, 1927; Works Manager, 1932; Asst Chief Mech. Engineer, 1936; Deputy General Manager, 1939; General Manager, 1941. JP Somerset, 1947–69. *Recreation:* philately. *Address:* Ballacree, Somerton, Somerset TA11 6RW. *T:* Somerton (0458) 72408.

WILLIAMS, Dafydd Wyn J.; *see* Jones-Williams.

WILLIAMS, Prof. David, FRS 1984; Professor of Mathematical Statistics and Professorial Fellow, Clare College, Cambridge University, 1985–Sept. 1992; Professor of Mathematical Sciences, Bath University, from Oct. 1992; *b* 9 April 1938; *s* of Gwyn Williams and Margaret Elizabeth Williams; *m* 1966, Sheila Margaret Harrison; two *d. Educ:* Jesus College, Oxford (DPhil); Grey College, Durham. Instructor, Stanford Univ., 1962; Lectr, Durham Univ., 1963; Shell Research Lectr, Statistical Lab., and Res. Fellow, Clare Coll., Cambridge, 1966; Lectr, 1969, Prof. of Maths, 1972, University Coll., Swansea. Vis. Fellow, Bath Univ., 1991–92. Hon. Fellow, UC, Swansea, 1991–. *Publications:* Diffusions, Markov processes, and martingales, vol. 1, Foundations, 1979, vol. 2 (with L. C. G. Rogers), Itô calculus, 1987; papers in Séminaire de probabilités and other jls. *Recreations:* music, cycling, walking. *Address:* 7 Moss Drive, Haslingfield, Cambridge CB3 7JB. *T:* Cambridge (0223) 872194; (from Oct. 1992) c/o Mathematical Sciences Department, University of Bath, Claverton Down, Bath BA2 7AY.

WILLIAMS, Adm. Sir David, GCB 1977 (KCB 1975); DL; Governor and Commander-in-Chief, Gibraltar, 1982–85; a Gentleman Usher to The Queen, 1979–82, an Extra Gentleman Usher, since 1982; Chairman of Council, Missions to Seamen, since 1989; *b*

22 Oct. 1921; 3rd *s* of A. E. Williams, Ashford, Kent; *m* 1947, Philippa Beatrice Stevens; two *s*. *Educ:* Yardley Court Sch., Tonbridge; RN College, Dartmouth. Cadet, Dartmouth, 1935. Graduate, US Naval War Coll., Newport, RI. Served War of 1939–45 at sea in RN. Qual. in Gunnery, 1946; Comdr, 1952; Captain, 1960; Naval Asst to First Sea Lord, 1961–64; HMS Devonshire, 1964–66; Dir of Naval Plans, 1966–68; Captain, BRNC, Dartmouth, 1968–70; Rear-Adm. 1970; Flag Officer, Second in Command Far East Fleet, 1970–72; Vice-Adm. 1973; Dir-Gen. Naval Manpower and Training, 1972–74; Adm. 1974; Chief of Naval Personnel and Second Sea Lord, 1974–77; C-in-C Naval Home Comd, and ADC to the Queen, 1977–79, retired. Pres., Ex Services Mental Welfare Soc., 1979–91. Member: Commonwealth War Graves Commn, 1980–89 (Vice Chm., 1985–89); Museums and Galleries Commn, 1987–. Hon. Liveryman, Fruiterers' Co.; KStJ 1982. FRSA. DL Devon, 1981. *Recreations:* sailing, tennis, gardening. *Address:* Brockholt, Strete, Dartmouth, Devon TQ6 0RR. *Clubs:* Army and Navy; Royal Dart Yacht; RN Sailing Association; Royal Yacht Squadron.

WILLIAMS, Rear-Adm. David Apthorp, CB 1965; DSC 1942; *b* 27 Jan. 1911; *s* of Thomas Pettit Williams and Vera Frederica Dudley Williams (*née* Apthorp); *m* 1951, Susan Eastlake, 3rd *d* of late Dr W. H. Lamplough and *widow* of Surg. Cdr H. de B. Kempthorne, RN; one *s* two step *d*. *Educ:* Cheltenham College; Royal Naval Engineering College, Keyham. Joined RN, 1929. Served War, Engineer Officer, HMS Hasty, 1939–42 (DSC, despatches four times), 2nd Destroyer Flotilla, Med. Fleet, S Atlantic Stn, Home Fleet, E Med. Fleet; Sen. Engineer, HMS Implacable, 1942–45, Home Fleet, and 1st Aircraft Carrier Sqdn, British Pacific Fleet, Comdr (E) 1945; Capt. 1955; Rear-Adm. 1963; Dir Gen. Aircraft, Admiralty, 1962–64; Dir Gen., Aircraft (Naval), Ministry of Defence, 1964–65; retired list, 1965. CEng, MIMechE. *Recreations:* various. *Address:* 3 Ellachie Gardens, Alverstoke, Hants PO12 2DS. *T:* Gosport (0705) 583375. *Club:* Army and Navy.

WILLIAMS, David Barry, TD 1964; QC 1975; **His Honour Judge David Williams;** a Circuit Judge, since 1979; Deputy Senior Judge (non-resident), Sovereign Base Areas, Cyprus, since 1983; Designated Resident Judge, Swansea Crown Court, since 1984; *b* 20 Feb. 1931; *s* of Dr W. B. Williams and Mrs G. Williams, Garndiffaith, Mon; *m* 1961, Angela Joy Davies; three *s* one *d*. *Educ:* Cardiff High Sch. for Boys; Wellington Sch., Somerset; Exeter Coll., Oxford (MA). Served with South Wales Borderers, 1949–51, 2nd Bn Monmouthshire Regt (TA), 1951–67, retired (Major). Called to Bar, Gray's Inn, 1955; Wales and Chester Circuit, 1957. A Recorder of the Crown Court, 1972–79; Asst Comr, Local Govt Boundary Commn for Wales, 1976–79; Comr for trial of Local Govt election petitions, 1978–79; Liaison Judge for W Glamorgan, 1983–87. A Pres., Mental Health Review Tribunals, 1983–. Chm., Legal Affairs Cttee, Welsh Centre for Internat. Affairs, 1980–89; Mem., Court and Council, Univ. of Wales Coll. of Cardiff, 1989– (Mem., Court, University Coll., Cardiff, 1980–89); Vice-Pres., UWIST, 1985–89 (Mem. Court and Council, 1981–89; Vice-Chm. Council, 1983–89). *Recreations:* mountain walking, Rugby football. *Address:* 52 Cyncoed Road, Cardiff CF2 6BH. *Clubs:* Army and Navy; Cardiff and County (Cardiff).

WILLIAMS, David Carlton, PhD; retired; President and Vice-Chancellor, University of Western Ontario, 1967–77; *b* 7 July 1912; *s* of John Andrew Williams and Anna Williams (Carlton); *m* 1943, Margaret Ashwell Carson; one *s* one *d*. *Educ:* Gordon Bell and Kelvin High Schs; Univ. of Manitoba, Winnipeg (BA); Univ. of Toronto (MA, PhD, Psych.). Special Lectr in Psychology, Univ. of Toronto, 1946; Associate Prof. of Psychology, Univ. of Manitoba, 1947; Prof. and Head, Dept of Psychology, Univ. of Manitoba, 1948; Prof. of Psychology, Univ. of Toronto, 1949–58 (Cons. to Toronto Juvenile Ct Clinic, 1951–58); Dir of Univ. Extension, Univ. of Toronto, 1958; a Dir, John Howard Soc., Toronto, 1956–67; Mem., Royal Commn on Govt Organization, 1961; Chm., Ontario Commn on Freedom of Information and Individual Privacy, 1977. Vice-Pres., Univ. of Toronto, for Scarborough and Erindale Colls, 1963–67. Principal of Scarborough Coll., Univ. of Toronto, 1963; Principal of Erindale Coll., Univ. of Toronto, 1965. Dir, Assoc. of Univs and Colls of Canada, 1970–; Chairman: Council of Ontario Univs, 1970–73; Bd, University Hosp., London, Ont, 1984–86; London Teaching Hosps Council, 1990–. Mem., Ontario Press Council, 1990–. Hon. LLD: Univ. of Manitoba, 1969; Univ. Windsor, 1977; Univ. of Western Ontario, 1977; Toronto Univ., 1977. *Publications:* The Arts as Communication, 1963; University Television, 1965. *Recreations:* photography, music, swimming, fishing. *Address:* Apt 407, 1201 Richmond Street, London, Ontario N6A 3L6, Canada. *T:* (519) 433–1436. *Clubs:* University, London Hunt and Country (London, Ont); York (Toronto).

WILLIAMS, David Claverly, CVO 1970; CBE 1977; *b* 31 July 1917; *s* of late Rev. Canon Henry Williams, OBE, and late Ethel Florence Williams; *m* 1944, Elizabeth Anne Fraser; three *d*. *Educ:* Christ's Coll., Christchurch, NZ; Victoria Univ. of Wellington. Professional Exam. in Public Administration. Inland Revenue Dept, 1936–39. Served War, 2NZEF, Pacific and Middle East, 1939–46. NZ Forest Service, 1946–60; Official Sec. to the Governor-General of NZ, 1960–77; Sec./Manager, The Wellington Club (Inc.), 1978–82. *Address:* 4 Huia Road, Days Bay, Eastbourne, New Zealand. *Clubs:* Wellington (Wellington).

WILLIAMS, Sir David (Glyndwr Tudor), Kt 1991; Vice-Chancellor, Cambridge University, 1989–Sept. 1992; President, Wolfson College, University of Cambridge, since 1980; Rouse Ball Professor of English Law, Cambridge University, since 1983; *b* 22 Oct. 1930; *s* of late Tudor Williams, OBE (Headmaster of Queen Elizabeth Grammar Sch., Carmarthen, 1929–55), and late Anne Williams; *m* 1959, Sally Gillian Mary Cole; one *s* two *d*. *Educ:* Queen Elizabeth Grammar Sch., Carmarthen; Emmanuel Coll., Cambridge (MA, LLB, Hon. Fellow 1984). LLM Calif. Nat. Service, RAF, 1949–50. Called to the Bar, Lincoln's Inn, 1956, Hon. Bencher, 1985. Commonwealth Fund Fellow of Harkness Foundn, Berkeley and Harvard, 1956–58; Lecturer: Univ. of Nottingham, 1958–63; Univ. of Oxford, 1963–67 (Fellow of Keble Coll.); Emmanuel College, Cambridge: Fellow, 1967–80; Sen. Tutor and Tutor for Admissions, 1970–76; Reader in Public Law, Cambridge Univ., 1976–83. Vis. Fellow, ANU, Canberra, 1974; Allen, Allen and Hemsley Vis. Fellow, Law Dept, Univ. of Sydney, 1985. Pres., Nat. Soc. for Clean Air, 1983–85; Chm., Animal Procedures Cttee, 1987–90. Member: Clean Air Council, 1971–79; Royal Commn on Environmental Pollution, 1976–83; Commn on Energy and the Environment, 1978–81; Council on Tribunals, 1972–82; Justice/All Souls Cttee on Adminstrative Law, 1978–88; Berrill Cttee of Investigation, SSRC, 1982–83; Marre Cttee on Future of Legal Profession, 1986–88; Univ. Comr, 1988–; Hon. DLitt: William Jewell Coll., 1984; Loughborough Univ. of Technology, 1988; Hon. LLD: Hull, 1989; Sydney 1990; Nottingham, 1991. *Publications:* Not in the Public Interest, 1965; Keeping the Peace, 1967; articles in legal jls. *Address:* Wolfson College, Cambridge CB3 9BB. *T:* Cambridge (0223) 335900.

WILLIAMS, Sir David Innes, Kt 1985; MD, MChir Cambridge, FRCS; President, Royal Society of Medicine, since 1990; Consulting Urologist: Hospital for Sick Children, Great Ormond Street (Urologist, 1952–78); St Peter's Hospital, London (Surgeon, 1950–78); *b* 12 June 1919; *s* of late Gwynne E. O. Williams, MS, FRCS; *m* 1944, Margaret Eileen Harding; two *s*. *Educ:* Sherborne Sch.; Trinity Hall, Cambridge; Univ. College Hospital (Hon. Fellow, 1986). RAMC, 1945–48 (Major, Surg. Specialist). Urologist, Royal Masonic Hosp., 1963–72; Civilian Consultant Urologist to RN, 1974–84; Dir, BPMF, 1978–86, Pro-Vice-Chancellor, 1985–87, Univ. of London. Mem., 1975–91, Chm., 1982–91, Council, ICRF; Chm., Council for Postgrad. Med. Educn in England and Wales, 1985–88. Mem., Home Sec's Adv. Cttee on Cruelty to Animals, 1975–79. Mem., GMC, 1979–89 (Chm., Overseas Cttee, 1981–88); Vice-Pres., RCS, 1983–85 (Mem. Council, 1974–86; Mem. Jt Consultants Cttee, 1983–85; Hon. Medal, 1987); Pres., BMA, 1988–89. FRSocMed (Past Pres., Urology Sect.); Hon. Member: British Assoc. Paediatric Surgeons (Denis Browne Medal, 1977); British Assoc. Urological Surgeons (Past Pres.; St Peter's Medal, 1967); Assoc. Française d'Urologie; Amer. Surgical Assoc.; British Paediatric Assoc.; Amer. Acad. Pediatrics (Urology Medal, 1986). Hon. FACS 1983; Hon. FRCSI 1984; Hon. FDSRCS. *Publications:* Urology of Childhood, 1958; Paediatric Urology, 1968, 2nd edn 1982; Scientific Foundations of Urology, 1976, 2nd edn 1982; various contributions to medical journals. *Address:* (office) Imperial Cancer Research Fund, Lincoln's Inn Fields, PO Box 123, WC2A 3PX; 66 Murray Road, SW19 4PE. *T:* 081–879 1042; The Old Rectory, East Knoyle, Salisbury, Wilts. *T:* East Knoyle (074783) 0255.

WILLIAMS, Dr David Iorwerth, FRCP, FKC; Dean, King's College Hospital Medical School, 1966–77, now Dean Emeritus and Fellow; former Consultant in Dermatology, King's College Hospital; Consultant to Kuwait Health Office, London; *b* 7 May 1913; *s* of William Tom Williams and Mabel Williams (*née* Edwards); *m* 1939, Ethel Margaret Wiseman; one *s* (one *d* decd). *Educ:* Dulwich Coll. (Jun. and Sen. Scholar); King's College Hosp. Med. Sch. Warneford and Raymond Gooch Scholar; MB, BS 1938; FRCP 1953; AKC 1934; FKC 1977. RAMC, 1940–46, Lt-Col. Member: BMA; Brit. Assoc. of Dermatology (Past Pres. and Past Sec., Hon. Mem. 1979); Royal Soc. of Med. (Past Pres. Dermatology Section); West Kent Medico-Chirurgical Soc. (Past Pres.); Hon. (or Foreign) Member: American, Austrian, Danish, French and S African Dermatological Socs. Gold Medal of Brit. Assoc. of Dermatology, 1965. *Publications:* articles in various med. jls over last 40 yrs. *Recreations:* my stroke, music. *Address:* 28 South Row, SE3 0RY. *T:* 081–852 7060.

WILLIAMS, David John; *b* 10 July 1914; *s* of late James Herbert Williams and late Ethel (*née* Redman); unmarried. *Educ:* Lancing College; Christ Church, Oxford (MA). Called to Bar, Inner Temple, 1939. Postgrad. Dip. in Social Anthropology, LSE, 1965. Served War of 1939–45, Royal Artillery. Practised as Barrister, Norwich, 1946–51; Resident Magistrate, Tanganyika, 1951–56; Senior Resident Magistrate, 1956–60; Judge of High Court of Tanganyika, 1960–62; Lord Chancellor's Office, 1966–79. *Recreations:* the arts and travelling. *Address:* 10e Thorney Crescent, Morgan's Walk, SW11 3TR. *Clubs:* Travellers', Hurlingham.

WILLIAMS, David John; Chief Constable, Surrey Constabulary, since 1991 (Deputy Chief Constable, 1989–91); *b* 7 April 1941; *s* of late John Isaac Williams and of Edith (*née* Stoneham); *m* 1962, Johanna Murphy; two *s*. *Educ:* Ystalyfera Grammar Sch.; University Coll. London (LLB Hons). Called to the Bar, Middle Temple, 1977. Metropolitan Police, 1960–84; FBI Nat. Acad., 1982; on secondment to Home Office Inspectorate, 1983; Herts Constabulary, 1984–89. Queen's Commendation for Bravery, 1976; Police Long Service and Good Conduct Medal, 1982. *Recreations:* music, Rugby football, countryside walking, keeping fit. *Address:* Surrey Constabulary HQ, Mount Browne, Sandy Lane, Guildford, Surrey GU3 1HG. *T:* Guildford (0483) 571212.

WILLIAMS, (David John) Delwyn; solicitor and company director; *b* 1 Nov. 1938; *s* of David Lewis Williams and Irena Violet Gwendoline Williams; *m* 1963, Olive Elizabeth Jerman; one *s* one *d*. *Educ:* Welshpool High School; University College of Wales, Aberystwyth. LLB. Solicitor and company director. MP (C) Montgomery, 1979–83; former Member: Select Cttee on Wales; Statutory Instruments Cttee; Jt Sec., All-Party Leisure and Recreation Industry Cttee. Contested (C) Montgomery, 1983; Prospective Parly Cand. (C) Clwyd SW, 1989–. Mem., British Field Sports Soc. *Recreations:* race horse owner; cricket, golf, small bore shooting. *Address:* Frondeg, Guilsfield, Welshpool, Powys SY21 9NQ. *T:* Welshpool (0938) 3400.

WILLIAMS, David Lincoln; Chairman and Managing Director, Costa Rica Coffee Co. Ltd, since 1988; Chairman: Allied Profiles Ltd, since 1981; Cox (Penarth) Ltd, since 1987; *b* 10 Feb. 1937; *s* of Lewis Bernard Williams and Eileen Elizabeth Cadogan; *m* 1959, Gillian Elisabeth, *d* of Dr William Phillips; one *s* one *d*. *Educ:* Cheltenham College. Served RA Gibraltar, 1955–57. Chairman: Allied Windows (S Wales) Ltd, 1971–85; Cardiff Broadcasting PLC, 1979–84; Chm. and Man. Dir, John Williams of Cardiff PLC, 1983–88 (Dir, 1968–88). President, Aluminium Window Assoc., 1971–72. Member: CBI Welsh Council, 1986–89; Welsh Arts Council, 1987–(Chm., Music Cttee, 1988–). Chm., Vale of Glamorgan Festival, 1978–; Nat. Chm., Friends of Welsh National Opera, 1980–. FInstD. Freeman, City of London, 1986; Liveryman, Founders' Co., 1986. *Recreations:* opera, skiing, fine weather sailing. *Address:* Rose Revived, Llantrithyd, Cowbridge, S Glam CF7 7UB. *T:* Bonvilston (0446) 781357. *Club:* Cardiff and County (Cardiff).

WILLIAMS, David Oliver; General Secretary, Confederation of Health Service Employees, 1983–87; *b* 12 March 1926; *m* 1949, Kathleen Eleanor Jones, Dinorwic; two *s* five *d* (and one *s* decd). *Educ:* Brynrefail Grammar Sch.; North Wales Hospital, Denbigh (RMN 1951). COHSE: full-time officer, Regional Secretary, Yorkshire Region, 1955; National Officer, Head Office, 1962; Sen. National Officer, 1969; Asst General Secretary, 1964. Chairman: Nurses and Midwives Whitley Council Staff Side, 1977–87; General Whitley Council Staff Side, 1974–87. Jubilee Medal, 1977. *Recreations:* walking, birdwatching, swimming, music. *Address:* 1 King's Court, Beddington Gardens, Wallington, Surrey SM6 0HR. *T:* 081–647 6412.

WILLIAMS, Air Vice-Marshal David Owen C.; *see* Crwys-Williams.

WILLIAMS, Prof. David Raymond; Professor of Applied Chemistry, University of Wales, Cardiff, since 1977; *b* 20 March 1941; *s* of Eric Thomas and Amy Gwendoline Williams; *m* 1964, Gillian Kirkpatrick Murray; two *d*. *Educ:* Grove Park Grammar Sch., Wrexham, Clwyd; Univ. of Wales, Bangor (BSc (1st Cl. Hons Chemistry); PhD). NATO Postdoctoral Fellowship, Univ. of Lund, 1965–66; Lectr in Chemistry, Univ. of St Andrews, 1966–77. Chm., Sci. Adv. Cttee, British Council, 1986–; Member: Radioactive Waste Management Adv. Cttee, DoE, 1980–; Cttee on Medical Aspects of Radiation in the Environment, DHSS, later Dept of Health, 1985–89. Jeyes Silver Medal, RSC, 1987; Wolfson Foundn Res. Award, 1988. *Publications:* The Metals of Life, 1970; An Introduction to Bioinorganic Chemistry, 1976; The Principles of Bioinorganic Chemistry, 1977; Laboratory Introduction to Bioinorganic Chemistry, 1979; Analysis Using Glass Electrodes, 1984; 300 res. papers. *Recreations:* cycling, swimming, other outdoor pursuits, public speaking. *Address:* School of Chemistry and Applied Chemistry, University of Wales College of Cardiff, PO Box 912, Cardiff CF1 3TB. *T:* Cardiff (0222) 372647.

WILLIAMS, David Wakelin, (Lyn), MSc, PhD; CBiol, FIBiol; retired as Director, Department of Agriculture and Fisheries for Scotland, Agricultural Scientific Services, 1963–73; *b* 2 Oct. 1913; *e s* of John Thomas Williams and Ethel (*née* Lock); *m* 1948,

Margaret Mary Wills, BSc, *d* of late Rev. R. H. Wills; one *s*. *Educ:* Rhondda Grammar School, Porth; University College, Cardiff. Demonstrator, Zoology Dept, Univ. Coll., Cardiff, 1937–38; Lectr in Zoology and Botany, Tech. Coll., Crumlin, Mon., 1938–39; research work on nematode physiology, etc. (MSc, PhD), 1937–41; biochemical work on enzymes (Industrial Estate, Treforest), 1942–43. Food Infestation Control Inspector (Min. of Food), Glasgow; Sen. Inspector, W Scotland, 1945; Scotland and N Ireland, 1946. Prin. Scientific Officer, Dept Agriculture for Scotland, 1948; Sen. Prin. Scientific Officer, 1961; Dep. Chief Scientific Officer (Director), 1963. Chairman, Potato Trials Advisory Cttee, 1963–; FIBiol 1966 (Council Mem. Scottish Br., 1966–69). MBIM, 1970–76. *Publications:* various papers, especially for the intelligent layman, on the environment, and on pest control and its side effects. *Recreations:* writing, music, Hi-Fi, photography, computing. *Address:* 8 Hillview Road, Edinburgh EH12 8QN. *T:* 031–334 1108.

WILLIAMS, Delwyn; *see* Williams, D. J. D.

WILLIAMS, Sir Denys (Ambrose), Kt 1987; Gold Crown of Merit, Barbados, 1981; Chief Justice of Barbados, since 1987; *b* 12 Oct. 1929; *s* of George Cuthbert and Violet Irene Williams; *m* 1954, Carmel Mary Coleman; two *s* four *d*. *Educ:* Combermere and Harrison College, Barbados; Worcester College, Oxford (BCL, MA). Called to the Bar, Middle Temple, 1954. Asst Legal Draftsman, Barbados, 1957; Asst to Attorney General, 1959; Asst Legal Draftsman, Fedn of West Indies, 1959; Senior Parly Counsel, Barbados, 1963; Judge of the Supreme Court, 1967. *Recreations:* horse racing, tennis, walking. *Address:* No 9, Garrison, St Michael, Barbados. *T:* (609) 4271164. *Clubs:* Carlton, Barbados Turf (Barbados).

WILLIAMS, Derek Alfred H.; *see* Hutton-Williams.

WILLIAMS, Derrick; *see* Williams, R. D.

WILLIAMS, Sir Dillwyn; *see* Williams, Sir E. D.

WILLIAMS, Doiran George; Chairman of Medical Appeal Tribunals, since 1987; *b* 27 June 1926; *s* of Rev. Dr Robert Richard Williams and Dilys Rachel Williams; *m* 1st, 1949, Flora Samitz (decd); one *s* one *d*; 2nd, 1977, Maureen Dorothy Baker; one *d*. *Educ:* Hereford Cathedral Sch.; Colwyn Bay Grammar Sch.; Liverpool Coll.; John F. Hughes Sch., Utica, NY. Served Army (Infantry), 1944–47. Called to the Bar, Gray's Inn, 1952; practised in Liverpool, 1952–58; Dept of Dir of Public Prosecutions, 1959, Asst Dir, 1977–82, Principal Asst Dir of Public Prosecutions, 1982–86. Sec., Liverpool Fabian Soc., 1956–58. Reader: Liverpool Dio., 1953–58; London Dio., 1959–63; Southwark Dio., 1963–88; Hereford Dio., 1988–; Member: Southwark Dio. Synod, 1971–73; Southwark Readers' Bd, 1977–88. *Recreations:* arts, mountains, sport, wine. *Address:* Howberry, Whitbourne, Hereford and Worcester WR6 5RZ.

WILLIAMS, Sir Donald Mark, 10th Bt *cr* 1866; *b* 7 Nov. 1954; *s* of Sir Robert Ernest Williams, 9th Bt, and of Ruth Margaret, *d* of Charles Edwin Butcher, Hudson Bay, Saskatchewan, Canada; *S* father, 1976; *m* 1982, Denise, *o d* of Royston H. Cory; one *d* (one *s* decd). *Educ:* West Buckland School, Devon. *Heir: b* Barton Matthew Williams, *b* 21 Nov. 1956. *Address:* Upcott House, Barnstaple, N Devon.

WILLIAMS, Douglas, CB 1977; CVO 1966; Deputy Secretary, Ministry of Overseas Development (later Overseas Development Administration), 1973–77, retired; *b* 14 May 1917; *s* of late James E. Williams and Elsie Williams; *m* 1948, Marie Jacquot; no *c*. *Educ:* Wolverhampton Sch.; Exeter Coll., Oxford. Served War, 1939–46 (despatches): Major, RA. Colonial Office, 1947; Principal, 1949; Colonial Attaché, Washington, 1956–60; Asst Sec., Colonial Office, 1961; transferred to ODM (later ODA), 1967, Under-Sec., 1968–73. Member: Bd, Crown Agents, 1978–84; EEC Econ. and Social Cttee, 1978–82; Governing Council, ODI, 1979–85. Trustee, Help the Aged and associated charities, 1984– (Chm. of Exec. Cttee, 1985–87, Chm., Overseas Cttee, 1987–88); Mem. Exec. Cttee, David Davies Meml Inst. of Internat. Studies, 1986–. *Publications:* The Specialized Agencies and the United Nations: the system in crisis, 1987; contrib. to United Kingdom—United Nations, 1990; articles on human rights and economic development, British colonial history. *Address:* 14 Gomshall Road, Cheam, Sutton, Surrey. *T:* 081–393 7306. *Clubs:* Commonwelath Trust, United Oxford & Cambridge University.

WILLIAMS, Dudley Howard, PhD, ScD; FRS 1983; Reader in Organic Chemistry, University of Cambridge, since 1974; Fellow of Churchill College, since 1964; *b* 25 May 1937; *s* of Lawrence Williams and Evelyn (*née* Hudson); *m* 1963, Lorna Patricia Phyllis, *d* of Anthony and Lorna Bedford; two *s*. *Educ:* Grammar Sch., Pudsey, Yorks; Univ. of Leeds (state schol.; BSc, PhD); MA, ScD Cantab. Post-doctoral Fellow and Research Associate, Stanford Univ., Calif, 1961–64; Sen. Asst in Research, 1964–66, Asst Dir of Research, 1966–74, Univ. of Cambridge. Nuffield Vis. Lectr, Sydney Univ., 1973; Dist. Vis. Lectr, Texas A & M Univ., 1986; Visiting Professor: Univ. of California, Irvine, 1967, 1986 and 1989; Univ. of Cape Town, 1972; Univ. of Wisconsin, 1975; Univ. of Copenhagen, 1976; ANU, 1980. Lectures: Arun Guthikonda Meml Award, Columbia Univ., 1985; Rover, Ohio State Univ., 1989; Foundn, Univ. of Auckland, 1991; Pacific Coast, 1991. Mem. Acad. Europaea. Meldola Medal, RIC, 1966; Corday-Morgan Medal, 1968; Tilden Medal and Lectr, 1983; Structural Chemistry Award, 1984, Bader Award, 1991, RSC. *Publications:* Applications of NMR in Organic Chemistry, 1964; Spectroscopic Methods in Organic Chemistry, 1966, 4th edn 1987; Mass Spectrometry of Organic Compounds, 1967; Mass Spectrometry—Principles and Applications, 1981; papers in chemical and biochemical jls. *Recreations:* music, squash. *Address:* 7 Balsham Road, Fulbourn, Cambridge CB1 5BZ. *T:* Cambridge (0223) 880592.

WILLIAMS, Sir Edgar (Trevor), Kt 1973; CB 1946; CBE 1944; DSO 1943; DL; Emeritus Fellow, Balliol College, Oxford, since 1980; a Radcliffe Trustee, since 1960; Governor, St Edward's School, Oxford, since 1960; a Freeman of Chester; *b* 20 Nov. 1912; *e s* of late Rev. J. E. Williams; *m* 1938, Monica, *d* of late Professor P. W. Robertson; one *d*; *m* 1946, Gillian, *yr d* of late Major-General M. D. Gambier-Parry, MC; one *s* one *d*. *Educ:* Tettenhall College; KES, Sheffield; Merton College, Oxford (Chambers Postmaster, 1931–34; First Class, Modern History, 1934; Harmsworth Senior Scholar, 1934–35; Junior Research Fellow, 1937–39; MA 1938; Hon. Fellow, 1964–). FRHistS 1947. Asst Lectr, Univ. of Liverpool, 1936. Served War of 1939–45 (despatches thrice); 2nd Lieut (SRO), 1st King's Dragoon Guards, 1939; Western Desert, 1941; GSO1, Eighth Army (North Africa, 1942–43, Sicily and Italy, 1943); Brig., Gen. Staff I, 21st Army Gp, 1944–45; Rhine Army, 1945–46; Officer, US Legion of Merit, 1945; UN Security Council Secretariat, 1946–47. Fellow, Balliol Coll., Oxford, 1945–80; Warden, Rhodes House, 1952–80; Sec., Rhodes Trust, 1959–80; a Pro-Vice-Chancellor, Oxford Univ., 1968–80. Editor, DNB, 1949–80. Mem., Devlin Nyasaland Commn, 1959; UK Observer, Rhodesian elections, 1980. Trustee, Nuffield Provincial Hosps Trust, 1963–91 (Chm., 1966–88). DL Oxfordshire, 1964–. President, OUCC, 1966–68 (Sen. Treasurer, 1949–61); Hon. Mem., American Hosp. Assoc., 1971. Hon. Fellow: Queen Elizabeth House, Oxford, 1975; Wolfson Coll., Oxford, 1981. Hon. LLD: Waynesburg Coll., Pa, 1947; Univ. of Windsor, Ontario, 1969; Hon. LHD, Williams Coll., Mass, 1965; Hon. PdD, Franklin and Marshall Coll., Pa, 1966; Hon. DLitt: Warwick, 1967; Hull, 1970; Mt Allison, NB, 1980; Liverpool, 1982; Hon. LittD: Swarthmore Coll., Pa, 1969; Sheffield, 1981. *Festschrift:* Oxford and the Idea of Commonwealth (ed A. F. Madden and D. K. Fieldhouse), 1982. *Address:* 94 Lonsdale Road, Oxford OX2 7ER. *T:* Oxford (0865) 515199. *Clubs:* Athenæum, Savile; MCC; Vincent's (Oxford).

WILLIAMS, Maj.-Gen. Edward Alexander Wilmot, CB 1962; CBE 1958; MC 1940; DL; *b* 8 June 1910; *s* of late Captain B. C. W. Williams, DL, JP, Herringston, Dorchester and late Hon. Mrs W. M. Williams (*er d* of 2nd Baron Addington); *m* 1943, Sybilla Margaret, *er d* of late Colonel O. A. Archdale, MBE, late The Rifle Brigade, West Knighton House, Dorchester; one *s* three *d*. *Educ:* Eton; Royal Military College. 2nd Lieut 60th Rifles, 1930; Adjutant, 2nd Battalion (Calais), 1938–39. Served War of 1939–45; commanded 1st Bn 60th Rifles, 1944; mentioned in despatches, 1945; US Armed Forces Staff Coll. (course 1), 1947; Bt Lieut-Col, 1950; Directing Staff, Joint Services Staff College, 1950–52; commanded 2nd Bn 60th Rifles, 1954–55; Comdr 2nd Infantry Brigade, 1956–57; Imperial Defence College, 1958; Brigadier Author, War Office, 1959. GOC 2nd Div. BAOR, 1960–62: Chief of Staff, GHQ Far East Land Forces, May-Nov. 1962; General Officer Commanding Singapore Base District, 1962–63; Chairman, Vehicle Cttee, Min. of Defence, 1964; retired 1965; Colonel Commandant, 2nd Bn The Royal Green Jackets (The King's Royal Rifle Corps), 1965–70. DL Dorset, 1965; High Sheriff of Dorset, 1970–71. *Recreations:* fishing, shooting. *Address:* Herringston, Dorchester, Dorset DT2 9PU. *T:* Dorchester (0305) 264122. *Clubs:* Army and Navy, Pratt's, Lansdowne; Royal Dorset Yacht.

WILLIAMS, Prof. Sir (Edward) Dillwyn, Kt 1990; FRCP; FRCPath; Professor of Pathology, University of Wales College of Medicine, since 1969; Consultant Pathologist, Cardiff, since 1969; *b* 1 April 1929; *s* of Edward Williams and Ceinwen Williams (*née* James); *m* 1st, 1954, Ruth Hill; one *s* two *d* (and one *s* decd); 2nd, 1976, Olwen Williams; one *s* one *d*. *Educ:* Christ's Coll., Cambridge (MA, MD; Hon. Fellow, 1991); London Hospital Med. Coll. Jun. appts, London Hosp. and RPMS; successively Lectr, Sen. Lectr, Reader, in Morbid Anatomy, RPMS; Vice-Provost, Univ. of Wales Coll. of Medicine, 1982–84. Res. Fellowship, Harvard Univ., 1962–63. Pres., RCPath, 1987–90; Hd and Prin. Investigator of WHO's Internat. Reference Centre for Endocrine Tumours, 1972–; Chm., Welsh Sci. Adv. Cttee, 1985–; Mem., GMC, 1987–90. Corresp. Mem., Amer. Thyroid Assoc.; Pres., Thyroid Club of GB, 1987–90. *Publications:* International Histological Classification of Tumours: histological typing of endocrine tumours, 1980; Pathology and Management of Thyroid Disease, 1981; Current Endocrine Concepts, 1982; numerous contribs to learned jls in field of endocrine pathology and carcinogenesis. *Recreations:* natural history in general, birdwatching in particular, mountain walking. *Address:* Orchard House, Boverton Road, Boverton, near Llantwit Major, South Glamorgan CF6 9UH. *T:* Llantwit Major (0446) 796403. *Club:* Reform.

WILLIAMS, Air Cdre Edward Stanley, CBE 1975 (OBE 1968); defence consultant; *b* 27 Sept. 1924; *s* of late William Stanley Williams and Ethel Williams; *m* 1947, Maureen Donovan; two *d*. *Educ:* Wallasey Central Sch.; London Univ. Sch. of Slavonic and E European Studies; St John's Coll., Cambridge (MPhil (Internat. Relations), 1982). Joined RAF, 1942; trained in Canada; service in flying boats, 1944; seconded BOAC, 1944–48; 18 Sqdn, Transport Comd, 1949; Instr, Central Navigation Sch., RAF Shawbury, 1950–52; Russian Language Study, 1952–54; Flying Appts MEAF, A&AEE, 216 Sqdn Transport Comd, 1954–61; OC RAF Element, Army Intell. Centre, 1961–64; Asst Air Attaché, Moscow, 1964–67; first RAF Defence Fellow, UCL, 1967–68; comd Jt Wing, Sch. of Service Intell., 1968–71; Chief, Target Plans, HQ Second ATAF, 1971–73; Chief Intell. Officer, HQ British Forces Near East, 1973–75; comd Jt Air Reconn. Intell. Centre, 1976–77; Defence and Air Attaché, Moscow, 1978–81, retired RAF, 1981. *Publications:* The Soviet Military, 1986; Soviet Air Power: prospects for the future, 1990; various articles in professional jls. *Recreations:* Russian studies, walking, photography. *Address:* c/o Midland Bank, 2 Liscard Way, Wallasey, Merseyside L44 5TR. *Club:* Royal Air Force.

WILLIAMS, Hon. Sir Edward (Stratten), KCMG 1983; KBE 1981; Chairman, Queensland Corrective Services Commission Board, since 1989; *b* 29 Dec. 1921; *s* of Edward Stratten and Zilla Claudia Williams; *m* 1949, Dorothy May Murray; three *s* four *d* (and one *s* decd). *Educ:* Yungaburra State Sch., Qld; Mt Carmel Coll., Charters Towers, Qld; Univ. of London (LLB Hons). Served RAAF, UK and Aust., 1942–46. Barrister-at-Law, 1946; QC (Australia) 1965; Justice of Supreme Court of Qld, 1971–84. Chairman, Parole Board of Qld, 1976–83; Royal Commissioner, Aust. Royal Commn of Inquiry into Drugs, 1977–80; Member, Internat. Narcotics Control Board (UN), 1982–87. Comr-Gen., Expo 88, Brisbane, 1984–88; Director: Elders IXL Ltd, 1984–; Aust. Hydrocarbons NL, 1985–. Chairman, Commonwealth Games Foundn Brisbane (1982), 1976–83. Pres., Playground and Recreation Assoc. of Qld, 1971–. Mem., Anti-Cancer Council, 1983–, Trustee, 1987–, Queensland Cancer Fund. Australian of the Year, 1982; Queenslander of the Year, 1983. *Publications:* Report of Australian Royal Commission of Inquiry into Drugs and associated reports. *Recreations:* horse racing, gardening, golf. *Address:* 150 Adelaide Street East, Clayfield, Queensland 4011, Australia. *T:* 2624802. *Clubs:* Brisbane, United Services, Queensland Turf (Chairman, 1980–), Rugby Union, BATC, Tattersall's, Albion Park Trotting, Far North Queensland Amateur Turf (all Queensland).

See also Sir H. S. Williams.

WILLIAMS, Edward Taylor, CMG 1962; MICE; retired as General Manager, Malayan Railway; civil engineering railway consultant with Kennedy Henderson Ltd (formerly Henderson, Busby partnership), consulting engineers and economists, since 1965; *b* Bolton, Lancashire, 15 October 1911; *s* of Edward and Harriet Williams; *m* 1940, Ethel Gertrude Bradley (*d* 1983); one step *s* one step *d*. *Educ:* Accrington Grammar School; Manchester College of Technology. LMS Rly, pupil engineer, 1929–36; Sudan Rly, Asst Civil Engr, 1936–38; Metropolitan Water Board, Civil Engr, 1939–41; Malayan Rly, 1941–62 (Gen. Man. 1959–62); Rly Advr, Saudi Govt Railroad, 1963–65. Interned in Singapore, in Changi and Sime Road, 1941–45. *Recreation:* travel. *Address:* 8 Cromartie Point, Livermead, Torquay, Devon TQ2 6QY. *T:* Torquay (0803) 606393.

WILLIAMS, Elizabeth, (Betty), (Mrs J. T. Perkins); working for peace, since 1976; *b* 22 May 1943; *m* 1st, 1961, Ralph Williams (marr. diss.); one *s* one *d*; 2nd, 1982, James T. Perkins. *Educ:* St Dominic's Grammar School. Office Receptionist. Leader, NI Peace Movement, 1976–78. Hon. LLD, Yale Univ., 1977; Hon. HLD, Coll. of Sienna Heights, Michigan, 1977. Nobel Peace Prize (jtly), 1976; Carl-von-Ossietsky Medal for Courage, 1976. *Recreation:* gardening.

WILLIAMS, Evelyn Faithfull M.; *see* Monier-Williams.

WILLIAMS, Sir Francis (John Watkin), 8th Bt *cr* 1798; QC 1952; *b* Anglesey, 24 Jan. 1905; *s* of Col Lawrence Williams, OBE, DL, JP (*d* 1958) (*gs* of 1st Bt); *S* brother, 1971; *m* 1932, Brenda, *d* of Sir John Jarvis, 1st Bt; four *d*. *Educ:* Malvern College; Trinity Hall, Cambridge. Barrister of Middle Temple, 1928. Served War of 1939–45; Wing Comdr, RAFVR. Recorder of Birkenhead, 1950–58; Recorder of Chester, 1958–71; Chm., Anglesey QS, 1960–71 (Dep. Chm., 1949–60); Chm., Flint QS, 1961–71 (Dep Chm., 1953–61); Dep. Chm., Cheshire QS, 1952–71; a Recorder of the Crown Court, 1972–74. Hon. Mem., Wales and Chester Circuit, 1986. JP Denbighshire, 1951–74; Chm. Medical

Appeal Tribunal for N Wales Areas, 1954–57; High Sheriff: of Denbighshire, 1957, of Anglesey, 1963. Chancellor, Diocese of St Asaph, 1966–83. Freeman of City of Chester, 1960. *Heir: half-b* Lawrence Hugh Williams [*b* 25 Aug. 1929; *m* 1952, Sara Margaret Helen, 3rd *d* of Sir Harry Platt, 1st Bt; two *d*]. *Address:* Llys, Middle Lane, Denbigh, Clwyd. *T:* Denbigh (074571) 2984. *Club:* United Oxford & Cambridge University.

See also Sir Charles Kimber, Bt.

WILLIAMS, Francis Julian, CBE 1986; JP; DL; Member of Prince of Wales' Council, Duchy of Cornwall, 1969–85; *b* 16 April 1927; 2nd *s* of late Alfred Martyn Williams, CBE, DSC; *m* Delia Fearne Marshall, *e d* of Captain and Mrs Campbell Marshall, St Mawes; two *s*. *Educ:* Eton; Trinity Coll., Cambridge (BA). RAF, 1945–48. Chm., Cambridge Univ. Conservative Assoc;, 1950; Pres., Cambridge Union, 1951. Contested (C) All Saints Div. of Birmingham, 1955. Mem., Devon and Cornwall Cttee, Lloyds Bank, 1971–. Succeeded to Caerhays, 1955. Pres., Cornwall Cricket Club. Mem., Cornwall CC, 1967–89 (Vice-Chm., 1974; Chm., 1980–89). JP 1970, DL 1977, Cornwall. *Recreation:* gardening. *Address:* Caerhays Castle, Gorran, St Austell, Cornwall. *T:* Truro (0872) 501250. *Clubs:* Brooks's, White's.

WILLIAMS, Frank Denry Clement, CMG 1956; *b* 3 May 1913; *s* of Frank Norris Williams and Joanna Esther Williams; *m* 1941, Traute Kahn; no *c*. *Educ:* Leighton Park School, Reading; London School of Economics (BSc Econ.). Cadet, Colonial Administrative Service, 1946; Asst Financial Sec., Nigeria, 1952; Financial Secretary: Jamaica, 1954; Federation of Nigeria, 1956; Economic Adviser, Federation of Nigeria, 1957–58; Permanent Secretary, Prime Minister's Dept, Fedn of The W Indies, 1958–62; Financial Sec., The Gambia, 1962–65. *Recreations:* walking, languages. *Address:* 51 The Priory, London Road, Brighton, Sussex BN1 8QT.

WILLIAMS, Prof. Gareth Howel, JP; Professor of Chemistry, University of London, 1967–84 (Head of Department of Chemistry, Bedford College, 1967–84), now Emeritus Professor; *b* 17 June 1925; *s* of Morgan John and Miriam Williams, Treherbert, Glam; *m* 1955, Marie, BA, *yr d* of William and Jessie Mary Mitchell, Wanlockhead, Dumfriesshire; one *s* one *d*. *Educ:* Pentre Grammar Sch.; University Coll., London. BSc, PhD, DSc London; FRSC. Asst Lectr, then Lectr in Chemistry, King's Coll., Univ of London, 1947–60; Research Fellow, Univ. of Chicago, 1953–54; Reader in Organic Chemistry, Birkbeck Coll., Univ. of London, 1960–67. Vis. Lectr, Univ. of Ife, Nigeria, 1965; Rose Morgan Vis. Prof., Univ. of Kansas, 1969–70; Vis. Prof., Univ. of Auckland, NZ, 1977. External Examr: Univ. of Rhodesia, 1967–70; Univ. of Khartoum, 1967–73, 1976–80; City Univ., 1968–74; Univ. of Surrey, 1974–76; Brunel Univ., 1980–85. Chm., London Welsh Assoc., 1987–90. JP Brent, 1979 (Dep. Chm., 1989–). *Publications:* Homolytic Aromatic Substitution, 1960; Organic Chemistry: a conceptual approach, 1977; (Editor) Advances in Free-Radical Chemistry, Vol. I, 1965, Vol. II, 1967, Vol. III, 1969, Vol. IV, 1972, Vol. V, 1975, Vol. VI, 1980; numerous papers in Jl Chem. Soc. and other scientific jls. *Recreation:* music. *Address:* Hillside, 22 Watford Road, Northwood, Mddx HA6 3NT. *T:* Northwood (09274) 25297. *Club:* Athenæum.

WILLIAMS, Prof. Gareth Lloyd; Professor of Educational Administration, Institute of Education, University of London, since 1984; *b* 19 Oct. 1935; *s* of Lloyd and Katherine Enid Williams; *m* 1960, Elizabeth Ann Peck; two *s* one *d*. *Educ:* Creeting St Mary; Framlingham; Cambridge Univ. (MA). Res. Officer, Agricl Econs Res. Inst., Oxford Univ., 1959–62; Res. Fellow, OECD, Athens, 1962–64; Principal Administrator, OECD, Paris, 1964–68; Associate Dir, Higher Educn Res. Unit, LSE, 1968–73; Prof. of Educnl Planning, Univ. of Lancaster, 1973–84. Vis. Prof., Melbourne Univ., 1981–82. Specialist Adviser to Arts and Educn Sub-Cttee to House of Commons Cttee on Expenditure, 1972–76; Consultant to OECD, ILO, UNESCO, and World Bank. Member: Council, Policy Studies Inst., 1979–85; Governing Council for Soc. for Res. into Higher Educn, 1970– (Chm., 1978–80, 1986–88). Mem. Bd, Red Rose Radio PLC, 1981–. FRSA 1982. *Publications:* (with Greenaway) Patterns of Change in Graduate Employment, 1973; (with Blackstone and Metcalf) The Academic Labour Market in Britain, 1974; Towards Lifelong Learning, 1978; (with Zabalza and Turnbull) The Economics of Teacher Supply, 1979; (with Woodhall) Independent Further Education, 1979; (with Blackstone) Response to Adversity, 1983; Higher Education in Ireland, 1985; (with Woodhall and O'Brien) Overseas Students and their Place of Study, 1986. *Address:* 11 Thornfield, Ashton Road, Lancaster. *T:* Lancaster (0524) 66002.

WILLIAMS, Sir Gareth R.; *see* Rhys Williams, Sir A. G. L. E.

WILLIAMS, Gareth Wyn; QC 1978; a Recorder of the Crown Court, since 1978; *b* 5 Feb. 1941; *s* of Albert Thomas Williams and Selina Williams; *m* 1962, Pauline Clarke; one *s* two *d*. *Educ:* Rhyl Grammar Sch.; Queens' Coll., Cambridge (Open Schol. (History) 1958; Univ. Prize, Jurisprudence 1962; Foundn Schol. 1964; LLB (1st Cl.) 1964; MA 1965). Called to the Bar, Gray's Inn, 1965; Leader, Wales and Chester Circuit, 1987–89. Mem., 1986–, Vice Chm., 1991–, Bar Council. *Address:* Farrars Building, Temple, EC4Y 7BD. *T:* 071–583 9241.

WILLIAMS, Geoffrey Guy; Group Executive Director, Standard Chartered plc, since 1990; *b* 12 July 1930; *s* of late Captain Guy Williams, OBE, and Mrs Margaret Williams (*née* Thomas). *Educ:* Blundell's Sch.; Christ's Coll., Cambridge (MA, LLM). Slaughter and May, Solicitors, 1952–66, Partner 1961; Dir, J. Henry Schroder Wagg & Co. Ltd, 1966–90, Vice-Chm. 1974, Dep. Chm., 1977–90. Chm., National Film Finance Corp., 1976–85 (Dir, 1970). Director: Bass plc, 1971–; Schroders plc, 1976–90; John Brown plc, 1977–85. Chm., Issuing Houses Assoc., 1979–81. Public Works Loan Comr, 1990–. *Recreations:* reading, theatre, cinema. *Address:* 18G Eaton Square, SW1W 9DD. *T:* 071–235 5212. *Club:* Brooks's.

WILLIAMS, (George Haigh) Graeme; QC 1983; barrister; a Recorder of the Crown Court, since 1981; *b* 5 July 1935; *s* of Dr Leslie Graeme Williams and Joan Haigh Williams (*née* Iago); *m* 1963, Anna Maureen Worrall, *qv*; two *d*. *Educ:* Tonbridge Sch. (Scholar); Brasenose Coll., Oxford (MA). Nat. Service, RA, 1953–55. Called to the Bar, Inner Temple, 1959. *Address:* 13 King's Bench Walk, Temple, EC4Y 7EN. *T:* 071–353 7204.

WILLIAMS, George Mervyn, CBE 1977; MC 1944; TD; Vice Lord-Lieutenant of Mid Glamorgan, since 1986; Chairman, Williams & Morgan Ltd; *b* 30 Oct. 1918; *yr s* of late Owain Williams and late Mrs Williams; *m* 1st, 1940, Penelope (marr. diss. 1946), *d* of late Sir Frank Mitchell, KCVO; 2nd, 1950, Grizel Margaretta Cochrane, DStJ, *d* of late Major Walter Stewart, DSO; one *s*. *Educ:* Radley Coll. Served Royal Fusiliers, N Africa and Italy, 1939–46; Major, British Military Mission to Greece, 1945. Great Universal Stores, 1946–49; Christie-Tyler PLC: Sales Dir, 1949; Man. Dir, 1950–80; Chm., 1959–85; Director: Lloyds Bank plc, 1972–77; Lloyds Bank UK Management Ltd, 1975–85; Chm., S Wales Regl Bd, Lloyds Bank, 1977–87. Dir, Kitaqawa Europe Ltd. Governor, United World Coll. of Atlantic, 1980–88. JP 1965–70, High Sheriff 1966, DL 1967–86, Glamorgan. CStJ. *Address:* Llanharan House, Llanharan, Mid Glamorgan CF7 9A. *T:* Llantrisant (0443) 226253; Craig y Bwla, Crickhowell, Powys NP8 1SU. *T:* Crickhowell (0873) 810413. *Clubs:* Brooks's; Cardiff and County (Cardiff).

WILLIAMS, George W.; *see* Wynn-Williams.

WILLIAMS, Prof. Glanmor, CBE 1981; FBA 1986; Professor of History, 1957–82, University College of Swansea; Chairman, Ancient Monuments Board (Wales), since 1983; *b* 5 May 1920; *s* of Daniel and Ceinwen Williams, Dowlais, Glam; *m* 1946, Margaret Fay Davies; one *s* one *d*. *Educ:* Cyfarthfa Grammar Sch., Merthyr Tydfil; Univ. Coll. of Wales, Aberystwyth. MA 1947; DLitt 1962. Univ. Coll. of Swansea: Asst Lectr in History, 1945; Sen. Lectr, 1952; a Vice-Principal, 1975–78. Nat. Governor, BBC, for Wales, 1965–71; Chm., Royal Commn on Ancient and Historical Monuments in Wales, 1986–90 (Mem., 1962–90); Member: Historic Bldgs Council for Wales, 1962–; British Library Bd, 1973–80 (Chm., Adv. Council, 1981–85); Adv. Council on Public Records, 1974–82; Welsh Arts Council, 1978–81; Council, Nat. Museum of Wales, 1983–90; Chm., Welsh Folk-Museum Cttee, 1987–90. Vice-Pres., UCW Aberystwyth, 1986–. Chm., Pantyfedwen Foundations, 1973–79; Pres., Cambrian Arch. Assoc., 1980. FRHistS 1954 (Vice-Pres., 1979–83); FSA 1978. *Publications:* Yr Esgob Richard Davies, 1953; The Welsh Church, 1962; Owen Glendower, 1966; Welsh Reformation Essays, 1967; (ed) Glamorgan County History, vol II 1984, vol. III 1971, vol. IV 1974, vol. V 1980, vol. VI 1988; Religion, Language and Nationality in Wales, 1979; Grym Tafodau Tân, 1984; Henry Tudor and Wales, 1985; Wales 1415–1642, 1987; (ed) Swansea: an illustrated history, 1990; (ed) The Celts and the Renaissance, 1990; contrib. to: History, Welsh History Review, etc. *Recreations:* gramophone, cine-photography. *Address:* 11 Grosvenor Road, Swansea. *T:* Swansea (0792) 204113.

WILLIAMS, Glanville Llewelyn, QC 1968; FBA 1957; Fellow of Jesus College, Cambridge, 1955–78, Hon. Fellow, 1978, and Rouse Ball Professor of English Law in the University of Cambridge, 1968–78 (Reader, 1957–65; Professor, 1966); *b* 15 Feb. 1911; *s* of late B. E. Williams, Bridgend, Glam; *m* 1939, Lorna Margaret, *d* of late F. W. Lawfield, Cambridge; one *s*. *Educ:* Cowbridge; University College of Wales, Aberystwyth; St John's Coll., Cambridge. Called to the Bar, 1935; PhD (Cantab), 1936; Research Fellow of St John's Coll., 1936–42; LLD (Cantab), 1946; Reader in English Law and successively Professor of Public Law and Quain Professor of Jurisprudence, University of London, 1945–55. Carpentier Lecturer in Columbia Univ., 1956; Cohen Lecturer in Hebrew University of Jerusalem, 1957; first Walter E. Meyer Visiting Research Professor, New York Univ., 1959–60; Charles Inglis Thompson Guest Professor, University of Colorado, 1965; Vis. Prof., Univ. of Washington, 1969. Special Consultant for the American Law Institute's Model Penal Code, 1956–58; Member: Standing Cttee on Criminal Law Revision, 1959–80; Law Commn's Working Party on Codification of Criminal Law, 1967; Cttee on Mentally Abnormal Offenders, 1972. Pres., Abortion Law Reform Assoc., 1962–; Vice-Pres., Voluntary Euthanasia, 1985–. Hon. Bencher, Middle Temple, 1966. Fellow, Galton Inst.; For. Hon. Mem., Amer. Acad. of Arts and Sci., 1985. Ames Prize, Harvard, 1963; (joint) Swiney Prize, RSA, 1964. Hon. LLD: Nottingham, 1963; Wales, 1974; Glasgow, 1980; Sussex, 1987; Hon. DCL Durham, 1984. *Publications:* Liability for Animals, 1939; chapters in McElroy's Impossibility of Performance, 1941; The Law Reform (Frustrated Contracts) Act (1943), 1944; Learning the Law, 1st edn 1945, 11th edn 1982; Crown Proceedings, 1948; Joint Obligations, 1949; Joint Torts and Contributory Negligence, 1950; Speedhand Shorthand, 1952, 8th edn 1980; Criminal Law; The General Part, 1st edn 1953, 2nd edn 1961; The Proof of Guilt, 1st edn 1955, 3rd edn 1963; The Sanctity of Life and the Criminal Law, American edn 1956, English edn 1958; The Mental Element in Crime, 1965; (with B. A. Hepple) Foundations of the Law of Tort, 1976, 2nd edn 1984; Textbook of Criminal Law, 1978, 2nd edn 1983; articles in legal periodicals. *Address:* Merrion Gate, Gazeley Lane, Cambridge CB2 2HB. *T:* Cambridge (0223) 841175.

WILLIAMS, Rev. Dr Glen Garfield; General Secretary, Conference of European Churches, 1968–87, retired 1988; *b* 14 Sept. 1923; *s* of John Archibald Douglas Williams and Violet May (*née* Tucker); *m* 1945, Velia Cristina (*née* Baglio). *Educ:* Newport High Sch.; Universities of Wales (Cardiff), London, Tübingen. Military Service, 1943–47. Univ. studies, 1947–55. Minister, Dagnall Street Baptist Church, St Albans, 1955–59; European Area Secretary, World Council of Churches, Geneva, 1959–68. Vis. Prof. of Church History, Presbyterian Theological Seminary, Austin, Texas, 1987. Hon. DTh Budapest, 1975; Hon. DD Bucharest, 1981. Order of St Vladimir, 1976, and St Sergius, 1979, Russian Orthodox Church; Order of St Mary Magdalene, 1980, Polish Orthodox Church; Order of St Augustine, C of E, 1986; Order of SS Cyril and Methodius, Bulgarian Orthodox Church, 1987. *Publications:* contrib. to Handbook on Western Europe, 1967, etc; numerous articles, mainly in Continental journals. *Recreations:* travel, reading, archæology. *Address:* 139 Rue de Lausanne, 1202 Geneva, Switzerland. *T:* (022) 731.30.16. *Club:* Athenæum.

WILLIAMS, Graeme; *see* Williams, George H. G.

WILLIAMS, Air Vice-Marshal Graham Charles, AFC 1970 and Bar 1975; FRAeS; Commandant General, RAF Regiment and Director General of Security (RAF), 1989–91; *b* 4 June 1937; *s* of Charles Francis Williams and Molly (*née* Chapman); *m* 1962, Judith Teresa Ann Walker; one *s* one *d*. *Educ:* Marlborough College; RAF College, Cranwell. FRAeS 1984. 54 Sqn, 229 OCU, 8 Sqn, Empire Test Pilots' School, A Sqn, A&AEE, 1958–70; RAF Staff Coll., 1971; OC 3 Sqn, Wildenrath, 1972–74; Junior Directing Staff (Air), RCDS, 1975–77; OC RAF Brüggen, 1978–79; Group Captain Ops, HQ RAF Germany, 1980–82; CO Experimental Flying Dept, RAE, 1983; Comdt, Aeroplane and Armament Exptl Estabt, 1983–85; Dir, Operational Requirements, MoD, 1986; ACDS, Operational Requirements (Air), 1986–89. Harmon Internat. Trophy for Aviators, USA, 1970. *Recreations:* squash (Pres. RAFSRA), golf. *Address:* c/o Lloyds Bank, Wilton, Hants SP2 0HU. *Club:* Royal Air Force.

WILLIAMS, Air Vice-Marshal Harold Guy L.; *see* Leonard-Williams.

WILLIAMS, Harri Llwyd H.; *see* Hudson-Williams.

WILLIAMS, Rev. Harry Abbott; Community of the Resurrection, since 1969; *b* 10 May 1919; *s* of late Captain Harry Williams, RN, and Annie Williams. *Educ:* Cranleigh Sch.; Trinity Coll., Cambridge; Cuddesdon Coll., Oxford. BA 1941; MA 1945. Deacon, 1943; Priest, 1944. Curate of St Barnabas, Pimlico, 1943–45; Curate of All Saints, Margaret Street, 1945–48; Chaplain and Tutor of Westcott House, Cambridge, 1948–51; Fellow of Trinity Coll., Cambridge, 1951–69; Dean of Chapel, 1958–69, and Tutor, 1958–68; Exam. Chaplain to Bishop of London, 1948–69. Mem., Anglican delegation to Russian Orthodox Church, Moscow, 1956; Select Preacher, Univ. of Cambridge, 1950, 1958, 1975; Hulsean Preacher, 1962, 1975; Select Preacher, Univ. of Oxford, 1974. Licensed to officiate in Dio. of Ely, 1948–, Dio. of Wakefield, 1979–. *Publications:* Jesus and the Resurrection, 1951; God's Wisdom in Christ's Cross, 1960; The Four Last Things, 1960; The True Wilderness, 1965; True Resurrection, 1972; Poverty, Chastity and Obedience: the true virtues, 1975; Tensions, 1976; Becoming What I Am, 1977; The Joy of God, 1979; Some Day I'll Find You (autobiog.), 1982; contribs to: Soundings, 1962; Objections to Christian Belief, 1963; The God I Want, 1967. *Recreations:* idleness and religion. *Address:* House of the Resurrection, Mirfield, West Yorks WF14 0BN.

WILLIAMS, Helen Elizabeth Webber, MA; High Mistress of St Paul's Girls' School, since 1989; *b* 28 April 1938; *o d* of Alwyn and Eleanor Thomas; *m* 1962, Dr Peter Williams (marr. diss. 1974); one *s* one *d*. *Educ:* Redland High Sch., Bristol; Girton Coll., Cambridge (MA; DipEd). Assistant English Mistress: St Paul's Girls' Sch., 1962–63; St George's Sch., Edinburgh, 1963–64; Edinburgh University: Asst Lectr, Dept of English, 1964–67; Lectr in English and Dir of Studies, Faculty of Arts, 1967–78; Headmistress, Blackheath High Sch., 1978–89. Member: Governing Body, SOAS, 1988–; Council, City Univ. *Publication:* (ed) T. S. Eliot: The Wasteland, 1968. *Recreations:* music, drama, cookery, gardening. *Address:* 48 Rowan Road, W6 7DU.

WILLIAMS, Ven. Henry Leslie; Archdeacon of Chester, 1975–88; *b* 26 Dec. 1919; *m* 1949, Elsie Marie; one *s*. *Educ:* Bethesda Gram. Sch.; St David's Coll., Lampeter (BA); St Michael's Coll., Llandaff. Deacon 1943, priest 1944, Bangor; Curate of Aberdovey, 1943–45; St Mary's, Bangor, 1945–48; Chaplain, HMS Conway, 1948–49; Curate, St Mary-without-the-Walls, Chester, 1949–53; Vicar of Barnston, Wirral, 1953–84. RD of Wirral North, 1967–75; Hon. Canon of Chester Cathedral, 1972–75. Mem., General Synod, 1978–80, 1985–88. CF (TA), 1953–62. *Recreations:* fly-fishing, bee-keeping. *Address:* 1 Bartholomew Way, Westminster Park, Chester CH4 7RJ. *T:* Chester (0244) 675296.

WILLIAMS, Sir (Henry) Sydney, Kt 1983; OBE 1978; company director; *b* 10 Jan. 1920; *s* of Edward Stratten Williams and Zilla Williams (*née* McHugh); *m* 1940, Joyce Veronica Meldon; four *s*. *Educ:* Mt Carmel Coll., Charters Towers, Qld, Aust. Served 7th Aust. Div. Cavalry Regt, ME and PNG, 1940–45; 51st Inf. Bn (Far North Qld Regt), 1947–57, Lt-Col Comd 1954–57. Chm., Air Queensland Ltd (formerly Bush Pilots Airways Ltd), 1960–86; Chairman: Willtrac Pty Ltd, 1964–; Lizard Island Pty Ltd, 1970–86; Director: Carlton & United Breweries (NQ) Ltd, 1964–; Placer Pacific Ltd, 1986–90. Member: Queensland Art Gall., 1981–; Cairns Port Authority, 1982–; Life Mem., Cairns RSSAILA; Trustee, WWF, 1981–; Councillor, Enterprise Australia, 1980–; Pres., Far North Queensland Amateur Turf Club, 1959–; past Dep. Chm., Australian Tourist Commn; past Pres., Cairns Legacy Club. Hon. Col, 51st Infantry Bn (Far North Qld Regt), 1987–; Patron, Light Horse Assoc. Ltd, Qld, 1989–. *Recreations:* fishing, bowls, golf. *Address:* 14 Bellevue Crescent, Edge Hill, Cairns, Queensland, Australia. *T:* 531489. *Clubs:* North Queensland (Townsville); United Services, Brisbane (Brisbane).
See also Hon. Sir Edward Williams.

WILLIAMS, Hilary a'Beckett E.; *see* Eccles-Williams.

WILLIAMS, Hubert Glyn, AE 1944; a Recorder of the Crown Court, 1974–77; Senior Partner, Blake, Lapthorn, Rea & Williams, Solicitors, Portsmouth and District, 1973–83; *b* 18 Dec. 1912; *s* of John Christmas Williams and Florence Jane Williams (*née* Jones); *m* 1952, Audrey Elizabeth Righton; one *s* one *d*. *Educ:* Ruthin. Admitted solicitor, 1934 (2nd cl. Hons). Served War of 1939–45 (Sqdn Ldr; AE): AAF, 1939–41; RAFVR, 1941–45; UK, Egypt, E Africa, Palestine. Pres., Hampshire Inc. Law Soc., 1977–78. *Recreation:* cricket. *Address:* Twenty Nine, The Avenue, Alverstoke, Gosport, Hants PO12 2JS. *T:* Gosport (0705) 583058. *Club:* MCC.

WILLIAMS, Hugo Mordaunt; writer; *b* 20 Feb. 1942; *s* of Hugh Williams, actor and playwright, and Margaret Vyner; *m* 1965, Hermine Demoriane; one *d*. *Educ:* Eton College. Asst Editor, London Magazine, 1961–70; television critic, 1983–88, and poetry editor, 1984–, New Statesman; theatre critic, The Sunday Correspondent, 1989–. Henfield Writer's Fellowship, Univ. of East Anglia, 1981. Awards (for poetry): Eric Gregory, 1965; Cholmondeley, 1970; Geoffrey Faber Memorial Prize, 1979. *Publications: poems:* Symptoms of Loss, 1965; Sugar Daddy, 1970; Some Sweet Day, 1975; Love-Life, 1979; Writing Home, 1985; Selected Poems, 1989; Self-Portrait With A Slide, 1990; *travel:* All the Time in the World, 1966; No Particular Place to Go, 1981. *Address:* 3 Raleigh Street, N1 8NW. *T:* 071–226 1655.

WILLIAMS, Ian Malcolm Gordon, CBE 1960 (OBE 1954; MBE 1945); *b* 7 May 1914; *s* of late Thomas and Mabel Williams. *Educ:* Tatterford Sch., Norfolk; Leeds Univ.; Gonville and Caius Coll., Cambridge. President, Leeds University Students' Union, 1939. Volunteered Military Service, Sept. 1939; Officer Cadet, 123 OCTU; Commnd Royal Regt of Artillery, March 1940; NW Frontier of India and Burma, 1940–45, as Major, RA, and Mountain Artillery, Indian Army (despatches, MBE). Staff Officer, Hong Kong Planning Unit, 1946; Adjutant, Hong Kong Defence Force, 1946. Entered Colonial Administrative Service, 1946; was District Officer and Asst Colonial Secretary, Hong Kong, 1946–49; at Colonial Office, 1949–51; Senior Asst Secretary, Secretariat, Cyprus, 1951–53; Commissioner: of Paphos, 1953–55, of Larnaca, 1955–57, of Limassol, 1957–60; Chief Officer, Sovereign Base Areas of Akrotiri and Dhekelia, 1960–64; Member Administrator's Advisory Board; UK Chairman, Joint Consultative Board, 1960–64; Min. of Technology, 1965–67; DoE, 1967–71; Programme Dir, UN/Thai Programme for Drug Abuse Control in Thailand, 1972–79. Comdr, Most Noble Order of the Crown of Thailand, 1981. *Recreations:* art, Cypriot archæology, swimming. *Address:* White House, Adderbury, near Banbury, Oxfordshire. *Club:* East India, Devonshire, Sports and Public Schools.

WILLIAMS, Prof. James Gordon, FEng 1982; Professor of Polymer Engineering, since 1975 and Head of Department of Mechanical Engineering, since 1990, Imperial College, London; *b* 13 June 1938; *s* of John William and Eira Williams; *m* 1960, Ann Marie Joscelyne; two *s* one *d*. *Educ:* Imperial Coll. (BScEng, PhD, DScEng); FCGI. RAE, Farnborough, 1956–61; Imperial College: Asst Lectr, 1962–64; Lectr, 1964–70; Reader, 1970–75. *Publications:* Stress Analysis of Polymers, 1973, 2nd edn 1981; Fracture Mechanics of Polymers, 1984. *Recreations:* gardening, mountains (walking and ski-ing), golf. *Address:* Mechanical Engineering Department, Imperial College, Exhibition Road, South Kensington, SW7. *T:* 071–225 8976.

WILLIAMS, (James) Vaughan, DSO 1942; OBE 1959; TD 1947; JP; Lord-Lieutenant for the County of West Glamorgan, 1985–87; *b* 25 Oct. 1912; *s* of James Vaughan Williams, Merthyr Tydfil; *m* 1938, Mary Edith Jones (*d* 1972), *d* of G. Bryn Jones, OBE, JP, Merthyr Tydfil; two *d*. Local Govt Service, 1930–39. Commnd RE (TA), 1934; served War of 1939–45, BEF, France, Egypt, Italy, Berlin (despatches 1942 and 1943); psc 1946; Lt-Col TA, 1947–59; Hon. Col 53rd (W) Div. RE, 1959–67. Mem. Wales TA&VRA, 1968; Vice-Chm. Glam TA&VR Cttee, 1968; Pres., Dunkirk Veteran Assoc.; Past President, Swansea Branch, Royal British Legion; Scout Council West Glamorgan; West Glam Council St John of Jerusalem; West Glam SSAFA; Royal Engrs Assoc. Past Chm., S Wales Assoc. ICE. DL Glam 1959; HM Lieut, W Glam, 1974–85; JP Glamorgan 1975. KStJ 1979. *Recreations:* travel, gardening. *Address:* 5 The Grove, Mumbles, Swansea, West Glamorgan. *T:* Swansea (0792) 368551. *Club:* Bristol Channel Yacht.

WILLIAMS, John, AO 1987; OBE 1980; guitarist; *b* Melbourne, 24 April 1941. Studied with father, Segovia and at the Accademia Musicale Chigiana, Siena and RCM, London; since when has given many recitals, concerts, made TV and radio appearances worldwide, and recordings of both solo guitar, and chamber and orchestral music. Mem., Sky, 1979–84. Artistic Dir, South Bank Summer Music, 1984 and 1985; Artistic Dir, Melbourne Arts Fest., 1987. Hon. FRCM; Hon. FRNCM. *Recreations:* people, living, chess, table-tennis, music. *Address:* c/o Harold Holt Ltd, 31 Sinclair Road, W14.

WILLIAMS, John Brinley, OBE 1988; FCIT; Managing Director, Associated British Ports (formerly British Transport Docks Board), 1985–89 (Board Member, 1980–89; Joint Managing Director, 1982–85); *b* 18 Aug. 1927; *s* of late Leslie Williams and of Alice Maud Williams; *m* 1951, Eileen (*née* Court) one *s* one *d*. *Educ:* Eveswell Sch., Newport. Asst Manager, Cardiff Docks, 1963–65; Commercial and Development Asst to Chief Docks Manager, South Wales Ports, 1965–67; Docks Manager: Cardiff and Penarth Docks, 1968–72; Hull Docks, 1972–75; Port Director: South Wales Ports, 1976–78; Southampton, 1978–82. *Recreations:* Rugby, open air pursuits. *Address:* Maes-y-Coed, Oakwood Road, Chandler's Ford, Hants. *T:* Chandler's Ford (0703) 69522.

WILLIAMS, (John Bucknall) Kingsley; solicitor; *b* 28 July 1927; *s* of Charles Kingsley Williams and Margaret Elizabeth (*née* Bucknall); *m* 1961, Brenda (*née* Baldwin); two *s*. *Educ:* Kingswood Sch., Bath; Trinity Hall, Cambridge (MA, LLB). Partner, Dutton Gregory & Williams, Solicitors, Winchester, 1956–91. Chm., Wessex RHA, 1975–82. Member: Winchester City Council, 1966–73; Hampshire CC, 1971–73; Assoc. of County Councils, 1973–75; Chm., NHS Supply Council, 1980–82. Vice-Chm., Council, Southampton Univ., 1976–87, Chm., 1987–; Chm. of Governors, Winchester Sch. of Art, 1986–. *Address:* Danesacre, Worthy Road, Winchester, Hants SO23 7AD. *T:* Winchester (0962) 852594, *Fax:* Winchester (0962) 869883.

WILLIAMS, Ven. John Charles; Archdeacon of Worcester, 1975–80, now Archdeacon Emeritus; Residentiary Canon of Worcester Cathedral, 1975–80; *b* 17 July 1912; *s* of William and Edith Williams; *m* 1940, Agnes Mildred Hutchings, MA; one *s* one *d*. *Educ:* Cowbridge Sch.; St David's University Coll., Lampeter; University College, Oxford. Asst Curate, Christ Church, Summerfield, Birmingham, 1937–39; Asst Curate, Hales Owen, in charge of St Margaret's, Hasbury, 1939–43; Vicar: Cradley Heath, Staffs, 1943–48; Redditch, Worcs, 1948–59. Surrogate, 1951–71; Rural Dean of Bromsgrove, 1958–59; Rector, Hales Owen, 1959–70; Archdeacon of Dudley, 1968–75; Vicar of Dodderhill, 1970–75. Hon. Canon, Worcester Cathedral, 1965–75; Examng Chaplain to Bishop of Worcester, 1969–80; Dir, Worcester Diocesan Central Services, 1974–75; Director of Ordination Candidates, 1975–79. Substitute Chaplain, HM Prison Long Lartin, Evesham, 1982–. *Publication:* One Hundred Years, 1847–1947; A History of Cradley Heath Parish. *Recreations:* history of architecture, sailing. *Address:* The Old Vicarage, Norton with Lenchwick, Evesham, Worcs WR11 4TL. *Clubs:* Oxford University Occasionals, United Oxford & Cambridge University.

WILLIAMS, John Charles, PhD; FEng 1990; FIEE; Secretary and Chief Executive, Institution of Electrical Engineers, since 1989; *b* 17 July 1938; *s* of Frank and Miriam Williams; *m* 1968, Susan Winifred Williams; one *s* one *d*. *Educ:* Queen Mary Coll. (BScEng (1st Cl. Hons); PhD). Philips Research Labs, 1964–78; GEC Marconi Space and Defence Systems, Stanmore, 1978–80; GEC Central Res. Labs, Wembley, 1980–82; GEC Marconi Res. Centre, Gt Baddow, 1982–88. *Recreations:* traditional jazz, contract bridge, walking his dog, gardening, listening to his family play classical music. *Address:* c/o Institution of Electrical Engineers, Savoy Place, WC2R 0BL. *T:* 071–240 1871.

WILLIAMS, John Eirwyn F.; *see* Ffowcs Williams.

WILLIAMS, Prof. John Ellis Caerwyn, FBA 1978; FSA; Professor of Irish, University College of Wales, Aberystwyth, 1965–79, now Professor Emeritus; Director of Centre for Advanced Welsh and Celtic Studies, Aberystwyth, 1978–85; *b* 17 Jan. 1912; *s* of John R. Williams and Maria Williams; *m* 1946, Gwen Watkins. *Educ:* Ystalyfera Int. County Sch.; University Coll. of N Wales, Bangor (BA Hons: Latin 1933, Welsh 1934; MA); Nat. Univ. of Ireland, Dublin; TCD; United Theol Coll., Aberystwyth (BD 1944); Theol Coll., Bala. Research Lectr, UC of N Wales, Bangor, 1937–39; Fellow, Univ. of Wales, 1939–41; Lectr, 1945–51, Sen. Lectr, 1951–53, Prof. of Welsh, 1953–65, UC of N Wales. Leverhulme Fellow, 1963–64; Vis. Prof. Celtic, UCLA, 1968; Summer Sch., Harvard, 1968; Lectures: O'Donnell, in Celtic Studies, Oxford Univ., 1979–80; Dr Daniel Williams, Aberystwyth, 1983; Sir John Morris Jones, Oxford, 1983; R. T. Jenkins, Bangor, 1983. Pres., Welsh Acad., 1989– (Chm., 1965–75); Mem., Council for Name Studies in GB and Ireland, 1965–. Cons. Editor, Univ. of Wales Welsh Dict. Fasc. xxiii-; Chm., Editorial Cttee, Welsh Acad. Dict., 1976–; Editor: Y Traethodydd, 1965–; Ysgrifau Beirniadol, i-xvii; Studia Celtica, i-xxv; Llên y Llenor, 1983–; Llyfryddiaeth yr Iaith Gymraeg, 1988. FSA 1975; Hon. MRIA 1990; Hon. DLitt: Celt., Univ. of Ireland, 1967; Univ. of Wales, 1983. Derek Allen Prize, British Acad., 1985. *Publications:* trans., Ystorïau ac Ysgrifau Pádraic Ó Conaire, 1947; trans., Yr Ebol Glas, 1954; Traddodiad Llenyddol Iwerddon, 1958; trans., Aderyn y Gwirionedd, 1961; Edward Jones, Maes-y-Plwm, 1963; ed, Llên a Llafar Môn, 1963; trans., I. Williams, Canu Taliesin (Poems of Taliesin), 1968; The Court Poet in Medieval Ireland, 1972; Y Storïwr Gwyddeleg a'i Chwedlau, 1972; Beirdd y Tywysogion—Arolwg 1970, in Llên Cymru, and separately 1972; ed, Literature in Celtic Countries, 1971; trans. Jakez Riou, An Ti Satanazet (Diawl yn y Tŷ), 1972; Canu Crefyddol y Gogynfeirdd (Darlith Goffa Henry Lewis), 1976; The Poets of the Welsh Princes, 1978; Cerddi'r Gogynfeirdd i Wragedd a Merched, 1979; (with Máirín Ní Mhuiríosa) Traidisiún Liteartha Na nGael, 1979; Geiriadurwyr y Gymraeg yng nghyfnod y Dadeni, 1983; (with Patrick Ford) The Irish Literary Tradition, 1992; contribs to Encyclopaedia Britannica, Princeton Encyclopedia of Poetry and Poetics, Bull. Bd of Celt. Studies, Celtica, Études Celt., Llên Cymru, etc. *Recreation:* walking. *Address:* University College of Wales, Aberystwyth SY23 2AX. *T:* Aberystwyth (0970) 623177; Iwerydd, 6 Pant-y-Rhos, Aberystwyth, Dyfed SY23 3QE. *T:* Aberystwyth (0970) 612959.

WILLIAMS, Prof. John Eryl Hall; Professor Emeritus of Criminology with Special Reference to Penology, London School of Economics, University of London; *b* 21 Sept. 1921; *s* of late Edward Hall Williams and Kitty Hall Williams; *m* 1951, Constance Mary Evans. *Educ:* Barry County Sch.; University Coll. of Wales, Aberystwyth (LLB 1942, LLM 1953). Called to the Bar, Middle Temple, 1949. Lectr, Dept of Law, University Coll. of Hull, 1946–50; LSE: Lectr, Law Dept, 1950–59; Reader in Criminology, 1959; Prof. of Criminology with Special Reference to Penology, 1984–86. Vis. Associate Prof., NY Univ. Sch. of Law, 1955–56; Senior Fellow and Vis. Lectr, Yale Law Sch., 1965–66. Mem., Parole Bd, 1970–72, 1976–78. Pres., British Soc. of Criminology, 1970–72; Sec.-Gen., Internat. Soc. for Criminology, 1974–79, Vice-Pres., 1985–; Mem., Criminological Scientific Council, Council of Europe, 1985–89. Hon. LLD JFK Univ., Calif., 1981. Jt Editor, British Jl of Criminology, 1966–79. *Publications:* The English Penal System in Transition, 1970; Changing Prisons, 1975; (with L. H. Leigh) The Management of the Prosecution Process in Denmark, Sweden and The Netherlands, 1981; Criminology and Criminal Justice, 1982; (ed) The Role of the Prosecutor, 1988; (ed jtly) Punishment, Custody and the Community: reflections and comments on the Green Paper, 1989. *Recreations:* landscape painting, foreign travel. *Address:* Law Department, London School of Economics and Political Science, Houghton Street, Aldwych, WC2A 2AE. *T:* 071–405 7686.
See also R. H. Williams.

WILLIAMS, John Griffith; QC 1985; a Recorder of the Crown Court, since 1984; *b* 20 Dec. 1944; *s* of Griffith John Williams, TD and Alison Williams; *m* 1971, Mair Tasker Watkins, *d* of Rt Hon. Sir Tasker Watkins, *qv;* two *d. Educ:* King's School, Bruton; The Queen's College, Oxford (MA). Served 4th Bn, RWF (TA), 1965–68; Welsh Volunteers (TAVR), 1968–71 (Lieut). Called to the Bar, Gray's Inn, 1968. Mem., Bar Council, 1990–. *Recreation:* golf. *Address:* 144 Pencisely Road, Llandaff, Cardiff CF5 1DR. *T:* Cardiff (0222) 562981. *Clubs:* Army and Navy; Cardiff and County (Cardiff); Royal Porthcawl Golf.

WILLIAMS, Rev. John Herbert, LVO 1989; Chaplain to the Royal Victorian Order and Chaplain of the Queen's Chapel of the Savoy, 1983–89; Chaplain to the Queen, 1988–89; *b* 15 Aug. 1919; *s* of Thomas and Mary Williams; *m* 1948, Joan Elizabeth (*née* Morgan); one *s Educ:* St David's Coll., Lampeter (BA Hons); Salisbury Theological Coll. Deacon 1943; priest 1944; Curate: Blaenavon (Gwent), 1943–46; Llanishen, Cardiff, 1946–48; Priest in Charge, Rogerstone (Gwent), 1948–51; Asst Chaplain, HM Prison, Manchester, 1951; Chaplain, HM Prison: Holloway, 1952; Birmingham, 1957; Wormwood Scrubs, 1964; South East Regional Chaplain, 1971; Deputy Chaplain General, Home Office Prison Dept, 1974–83; Priest-in-Ordinary to the Queen, 1980–83. *Recreations:* Rugby, classical music/opera, Francophile. *Address:* 18 Coombe Lane West, Kingston-upon-Thames. *T:* 081–942 1196. *Clubs:* Zion College, City Livery.

WILLIAMS, (John) Kyffin, OBE 1982; DL; RA 1974 (ARA 1970); *b* 9 May 1918; *s* of Henry Inglis Wynne Williams and Essyllt Mary Williams (*née* Williams). *Educ:* Shrewsbury Sch.; Slade Sch. of Art. Sen. Art Master, Highgate Sch., 1944–73. One-man shows: Leicester Galleries, 1951, 1953, 1956, 1960, 1966, 1970; Colnaghi Galleries, 1948, 1949, 1965, 1970; Thackeray Gall., biennially 1975–. Retrospective exhibn, Nat. Mus. of Wales, Mostyn Art Gall., Llandudno and Glynn Vivian Art Gall., Swansea, 1987. Pres., Royal Cambrian Acad., 1969–76. Winston Churchill Fellow, 1968; Hon. Fellow: University Coll. of Swansea, 1989; UCNW, 1991. DL Gwynedd 1985. Hon. MA Wales, 1973. Medal, Hon. Soc. of Cymmrodorion, 1991. *Publications:* Across the Straits (autobiog.), 1973; A Wider Sky (autobiog.), 1991. *Recreations:* the countryside, sport. *Address:* Pwllfanogl, Llanfairpwll, Gwynedd LL61 6PD. *T:* Llanfairpwll (0248) 714693.

WILLIAMS, John Leighton; QC 1986; a Recorder of the Crown Court, since 1985; *b* 15 Aug. 1941; *s* of Reginald John Williams and Beatrice Beynon; *m* 1969, Sally Elizabeth Williams; two *s. Educ:* Neath Boys' Grammar School; King's College London (LLB); Trinity Hall, Cambridge (MA). Called to the Bar, Gray's Inn, 1964. Mem., Criminal Injuries Compensation Bd, 1987–. *Address:* Farrar's Building, Temple, EC4Y 7BD. *T:* 071–583 9241.

WILLIAMS, Sir (John) Leslie, Kt 1974; CBE 1970; Chairman, Civil Service Appeal Board, 1977–78 (Deputy Chairman, 1973–77); Secretary General, Civil Service National Whitley Council (Staff Side), 1966–73; *b* 1 Aug. 1913; *s* of Thomas Oliver Williams and Mary Ellen Williams; *m* 1937, Florrie Read Jones; one *s. Educ:* Grove Park Grammar Sch., Wrexham, N. Wales. Civil Servant, 1931–46. Society of Civil Servants: Asst Secretary, 1947–49; Dep. General Secretary, 1949–56; General Secretary, 1956–66. Royal Institute of Public Administration: Executive Council Member, 1955–74; Chairman, 1968; Vice-Pres., 1974–84. Member Board of Governors: Nat. Hospitals for Nervous Diseases, 1962–82 (Chm., 1974–82); Hospital for Sick Children, 1976–81; Member: NW Metropolitan Regional Hospital Board, 1963–65; (part-time) UKAEA, 1970–80; Adv. Council, Civil Service Coll., 1970–76; (part-time) Pay Bd, 1974; Royal Commn on Standards of Conduct in Public Life, 1974–76; Armed Forces Pay Review Body, 1975–80; (part-time) Independent Chm., Conciliation Cttees NJC for Civil Air Transport, 1974–77; Standing Commn on Pay Comparability, 1979–80; London Adv. Gp on NHS, 1980–81. *Recreations:* cricket, gardening, music. *Address:* 73 Millside, Stalham, Norwich NR12 9PB. *T:* Stalham (0692) 82557.

WILLIAMS, John Melville; QC 1977; a Recorder, since 1986; *b* 20 June 1931; *o s* of late Baron Francis-Williams and late Lady (Jessie Melville) Francis-Williams; *m* 1955, Jean Margaret, *d* of Harold and Hilda Lucas, Huddersfield; three *s* one *d. Educ:* St Christopher Sch., Letchworth; St John's Coll., Cambridge (BA). Called to the Bar, Inner Temple, 1955, Bencher, 1985. Counsel to NUJ; a legal assessor to GMC; first Pres., Assoc. of Personal Injury Lawyers, 1990–; Mem., Indep. Review Body Under New Colliery Review Procedure, 1985–. *Recreations:* mountain scrambling and walking, indifferent golf. *Address:* Deers Hill, Sutton Abinger, near Dorking, Surrey RH5 6PS. *T:* Dorking (0306) 730331; Cnoclochan, Scourie, by Lairg, Sutherland; 15 Old Square, Lincoln's Inn, WC2A 3UH. *T:* 071–831 0801, *Fax:* 071–405 1387.

WILLIAMS, John M(eredith), CBE 1988; Chairman, Welsh Development Agency, 1982–88; *b* 20 Oct. 1926; *s* of Gwynne Evan Owen Williams and Cicely Mary Innes; *m* 1953, Jean Constance (*née* Emerson); two *d. Educ:* Sherborne Sch., Dorset; Trinity Hall, Cambridge. Dir, BOC Gp, 1969–78; Chm., Newman Industries Ltd, 1980–82; Director: Stone-Platt Industries Ltd, 1981–82; Harland and Wolff Ltd, 1982–89. Mem., Milk Marketing Bd, 1984–. *Address:* 95 Hurlingham Court, Ranelagh Gardens, SW6 3UR. *T:* 071–731 0686; Victuals Grove, St Briavels, Lydney, Glos. *T:* Dean (0594) 530494. *Clubs:* Hurlingham, Himalayan.

WILLIAMS, Rt. Rev. Monsignor John Noctor, CBE 1989; Prelate of Honour, 1985; Principal Roman Catholic Chaplain (Army), 1985–89, retired; Vicar General, 1986; *b* 9 Aug. 1931; *s* of Thomas Williams and Anne Williams (*née* Noctor). *Educ:* St Anselm's Grammar School, Birkenhead; Ushaw College, Durham. Curate: St Laurence's, Birkenhead, 1956; St Joseph's, Sale, 1958; Sacred Heart, Moreton, 1958; Our Lady's, Birkenhead, 1959–66. Army, Chaplains' Dept, 1966; 7 Armd Bde, 1966; Singapore, 1969; 6 Armd Bde, 1971; UN, Cyprus, 1972; Senior Chaplain: Hong Kong, 1976; 1 Div., 1978; N Ireland, 1980; HQ BAOR, 1982; SE District, 1984. *Recreations:* bridge, golf, motoring. *Address:* St Michaels, Scotland Street, Ellesmere, Shropshire SY12 0ED. *Clubs:* Sandiway Golf, Worplesdon Golf, Delamere Forest Golf.

WILLIAMS, John Peter Rhys, MBE 1977; FRCSEd; Consultant in Trauma and Orthopaedic Surgery, Princess of Wales Hospital, Bridgend, since 1986; *b* 2 March 1949; *s* of Peter Williams, MB, BCh and Margaret Williams, MB, BCh; *m* 1973, Priscilla Parkin, MB, BS, DObst, RCOG, DA; one *s*; three *d. Educ:* Bridgend Grammar School; Millfield; St Mary's Hosp. Med. School. MB, BS London 1973; LRCP, MRCS, 1973; Primary FRCS 1976; FRCSEd 1980. University Hosp., Cardiff, Battle Hosp., Reading, St Mary's Hosp., London, 1973–78; Surgical Registrar, 1978–80, Orthopaedic Registrar, 1980–82, Cardiff Gp of Hosps; Sen. Orthopaedic Registrar, St Mary's Hosp., London, 1982–86. Played Rugby for Bridgend, 1967–68, 1976–79 (Captain, 1978–79), 1980–81, for London Welsh, 1968–76; 1st cap for Wales, 1969 (Captain, 1978); British Lions tours, 1971, 1974; a record 55 caps for Wales, to 1981; won Wimbledon Lawn Tennis Junior Championship, 1966. *Publication:* JPR (autobiog.), 1979. *Recreations:* sport and music. *Address:* Llansannor Lodge, Llansannor, near Cowbridge, South Glamorgan. *Clubs:* Wig and Pen; Lord's Taverners'.

WILLIAMS, Sir John (Robert), KCMG 1982 (CMG 1973); HM Diplomatic Service, retired; Chairman, Board of Governors, Commonwealth Institute, 1984–87; *b* 15 Sept. 1922; *s* of late Sydney James Williams, Salisbury; *m* 1958, Helga Elizabeth, *d* of Frederick Konow Lund, Bergen; two *s* two *d. Educ:* Sheen County School; Fitzwilliam House, Cambridge (Hon. Fellow 1984). Served War of 1939–45, with 1st Bn King's African Rifles in East Africa and Burma Campaign (Captain). Joined Colonial Office as Asst Principal, 1949; First Secretary, UK High Commission, New Delhi, 1956; Commonwealth Relations Office, 1958; Deputy High Commissioner in North Malaya, 1959–63; Counsellor, New Delhi, 1963–66; Commonwealth Office, 1966; Private Sec. to Commonwealth Secretary, 1967; Diplomatic Service Inspectorate, 1968; High Comr, Suva, 1970–74; Minister, Lagos, 1974–79 and concurrently Ambassador (non-resident) to Benin, 1976–79; Asst. Under-Sec. of State, FCO, 1979; High Comr in Kenya, 1979–82; Perm. British Rep. to UN Environment Prog. and to UN Centre for Human Settlements, 1979–82. Mem. Gen. Council, Royal Over-Seas League, 1983–87. Chm., Salisbury and S Wilts Museum, 1989–. *Recreations:* music, gardening. *Address:* Eton House, Hanging Langford, Salisbury SP3 4NN. *Club:* United Oxford & Cambridge University.

WILLIAMS, John Towner; composer of film scores; *b* 8 Feb. 1932. *Educ:* Juilliard Sch., NY. Conductor, Boston Pops Orchestra, 1980–84. Hon. DMus: Berklee Coll. of Music, Boston, 1980; St Anselm Coll., Manchester, NH, 1981; Boston Conservatory of Music, 1982; Hon. DHL S Carolina, 1981; Hon. Dr of Fine Arts Northeastern Univ. (Boston), 1981; Hon. DMus, William Woods Coll., USA, 1982. Awards include Oscars for: Fiddler on the Roof (filmscore arrangement), 1971; Jaws, 1976; Star Wars, 1978; E.T., 1983; 14 Grammies, 2 Emmys and many other awards; 16 Academy Award nominations. *Composer of film scores:* The Secret Ways, 1961; Diamond Head, 1962; None but the Brave, 1965; How to Steal a Million, 1966; Valley of the Dolls, 1967; The Cowboys, 1972; The Poseidon Adventure, 1972; Tom Sawyer, 1973; Earthquake, 1974; The Towering Inferno, 1974; Jaws, 1975; Jaws 2, 1976; The Eiger Sanction, 1975; Family Plot, 1976; Midway, 1976; The Missouri Breaks, 1976; Raggedy Ann and Andy, 1977; Black Sunday, 1977; Star Wars, 1977; Close Encounters of the 3rd Kind, 1977; The Fury, 1978; Superman, 1978; Dracula, 1979; The Empire Strikes Back, 1980; Raiders of the Lost Ark, 1981; E. T. (The Extra Terrestial), 1982; Return of the Jedi, 1983; Indiana Jones and the Temple of Doom, 1984; Empire of the Sun, 1988; many TV films. *Address:* 20th Century Fox, Music Department, PO Box 900, Beverly Hills, Calif 90213, USA.

WILLIAMS, Rev. John Tudno, PhD; Professor of Biblical Studies, United Theological College, Aberystwyth, since 1973; Moderator of the Free Church Federal Council, March 1990–91; *b* 31 Dec. 1938; *s* of Rev. Arthur Tudno Williams and late Primrose (*née* Hughes Parry); *m* 1964, Ina Lloyd-Evans; one *s* one *d. Educ:* Liverpool Inst. High School; Colfe's GS, Lewisham; Jesus Coll., Oxford (MA); UCW, Aberystwyth (PhD); United Theol Coll., Aberystwyth. Ordained as Welsh Presbyterian Minister, 1963; Minister in Borth, Cards, 1963–73; Part-time Lecturer: United Theol Coll., 1966–73; UCW (Religious Studies), 1976–87; Tutor responsible for Religious Studies, external degree through medium of Welsh, UCW, 1984–; Dean, Aberystwyth and Lampeter Sch. of Theology, 1985–87. Secretary: Theology Section, Univ. of Wales Guild of Graduates, 1967–; Educn Cttee, Gen. Assembly of Presbyterian Church of Wales, 1979–; Bd of Trustees, Davies Lecture, 1983–. Examiner in religious studies and member of various educn cttees. Mem., Aberystwyth Town Council, 1979–87. *Publications:* Cewri'r Ffydd (Heroes of the Faith), 1974, 2nd edn 1979; Problem Dioddefaint a Llyfr Job (The Problem of Suffering and the Book of Job), 1980; contrib. to: Studia Biblica, 1978, Vol. ii 1980; C. H. Dodd, The Centenary Lectures, 1985; Yr Epistol Cyntaf at y Corinthiaid (Commentary on I Corinthians), 1991; articles in Welsh jls. *Recreations:* music (singing), Welsh language and culture. *Address:* United Theological College, Aberystwyth, Dyfed SY23 2LT. *T:* Aberystwyth (0970) 624574. *Club:* Penn.

WILLIAMS, Dame Judi; *see* Dench, Dame J. O.

WILLIAMS, Kingsley; *see* Williams, J. B. K.

WILLIAMS, Kyffin; *see* Williams, John K.

WILLIAMS, Sir Leonard, KBE 1981; CB 1975; Director-General for Energy, Commission of the European Communities, 1976–81; *b* 19 Sept. 1919; *m* Anne Taylor Witherley; three *d. Educ:* St Olave's Grammar Sch.; King's Coll., London. Inland Revenue, 1938. War Service (RA), 1940–47. Ministry of Defence, 1948; NATO, 1951–54; Min. of Supply (later Aviation), 1954; Min. of Technology (later DTI), 1964; IDC 1966; Dep. Sec., 1973; Dept of Energy, 1974–76. *Address:* Blue Vines, Bramshott Vale, Liphook, Hants GU30 7PZ.

WILLIAMS, Leonard Edmund Henry, CBE 1981; DFC 1944; President, Nationwide Anglia Building Society, since 1989 (Chairman, 1987–88); *b* 6 Dec. 1919; *s* of William Edmund Williams; *m* 1946, Marie Harries-Jones; four *s* one *d. Educ:* Acton County Grammar School. FCA, FCBSI, IPFA; FRSA; CBIM. RAF, 1939–46. Acton Borough Council, 1935–39, Chief Internal Auditor 1946–49; Asst Accountant, Gas Council, 1949–53; Nationwide Building Society: Finance Officer, 1954–61; Dep. Gen. Man., 1961–67; Chief Exec., 1967–81; Dir, 1975–87; Chm., 1982–87. Director: Y. J. Lovell (Hldgs) plc, 1982–89; Peachey Property Corp. plc, 1982–88; Dep. Chm., BUPA Ltd, 1988–90 (Governor, 1982–88); Mem., Housing Corp., 1976–82. Chm., Building Socs Assoc., 1979–81 (Dep. Chm., 1977–79); Pres., Metrop. Assoc. of Building Socs, 1989– (Chm., 1972–73). Pres., Chartered Building Socs Inst., 1969–70. Hon. Life Mem., Internat. Union of Building Socs and Savings Assocs. *Publication:* Building Society Accounts, 1966. *Recreations:* golf, reading. *Address:* The Romanys, Albury Road, Burwood Park, Walton-on-Thames, Surrey KT12 5DY. *T:* Walton-on-Thames (0932) 242758. *Clubs:* Royal Air Force, Arts, City Livery.

WILLIAMS, Sir Leslie; *see* Williams, Sir J. L.

WILLIAMS, Ven. Leslie Arthur, MA; Archdeacon of Bristol, 1967–79; *b* 14 May 1909; *s* of Arthur and Susan Williams; *m* 1937, Margaret Mary, *d* of Richard Crocker; one *s* one *d. Educ:* Knutsford; Downing Coll., Cambridge. Curate of Holy Trinity, Bristol, 1934–37; Licensed to officiate, St Andrew the Great, Cambridge, 1937–40; Curate in Charge, St Peter, Lowden, Chippenham, 1940–42; Chaplain, RAFVR, 1942–46; Curate, Stoke Bishop, 1946–47; Vicar: Corsham, Wilts, 1947–53; Bishopston, Bristol, 1953–60; Stoke Bishop, Bristol, 1960–67. Rural Dean of Clifton, 1966–67; Hon. Canon of Bristol, 1958. *Recreation:* gardening. *Address:* St Monica Home, Westbury on Trym, Bristol BS9 3UN. *Clubs:* Hawks (Cambridge); Savage (Bristol).

WILLIAMS, Lyn; *see* Williams, D. W.

WILLIAMS, Martin John, CVO 1983; OBE 1979; HM Diplomatic Service; Head of South Asian Department, Foreign and Commonwealth Office, since 1990; *b* 3 Nov. 1941; *s* of John Henry Stroud Williams and Barbara (*née* Benington); *m* 1964, Susan Dent; two *s. Educ:* Manchester Grammar Sch.; Corpus Christi Coll., Oxford (BA). Joined Commonwealth Relations Office, 1963; Private Sec. to Permanent Under Secretary, 1964; Manila, 1966; Milan, 1970; Civil Service College, 1972; FCO, 1973; Tehran,

1977; FCO, 1980; New Delhi, 1982; Rome, 1986. Mem., Royal Commonwealth Society. *Recreations:* music, gardening. *Address:* c/o Foreign and Commonwealth Office, King Charles Street, SW1A 2AH.

WILLIAMS, Sir Max; *see* Williams, Sir W. M. H.

WILLIAMS, Dr Michael, FBA 1989; Reader in Geography, since 1990, Fellow of Oriel College and Lecturer, St Anne's College, since 1978, University of Oxford; *b* 24 June 1935; *s* of Benjamin Williams and Ethel (*née* Marshell); *m* 1955, Eleanore Lerch; two *d*. *Educ:* Emmanuel Grammar Sch.; Dynevor Grammar Sch., Swansea; Swansea UC (BA 1956; PhD 1960; DLitt 1991); St Catharine's Coll., Cambridge (DipEd 1960). Deptl Demonstrator in Geography, Swansea, 1957–60; University of Adelaide: Lectr in Geog., 1960–66; Sen. Lectr, 1966–69; Reader, 1970–77; Lectr in Geog., Oxford Univ., 1978–89. Visiting Professor: Univ. of Wisconsin-Madison, 1973; Univ. of Chicago, 1989; Vis. Lectr, UCL, 1966, 1973. Mem., State Commn on Uniform Regl Boundaries, SA, 1974–75; Chm., Histl Geog. Res. Gp, Inst. of British Geographers, 1983–86; Sec., Inst. of Aust. Geographers, 1969–72; Pres., SA Br., RGS, 1975–76 (Ed. of Procs, 1962–70); Ed., Trans of Inst. of British Geographers, 1983–88. John Lewis Gold Medal, RGS, SA, 1979; Lit. Prize, Adelaide Fest. of Arts, 1976; Hidy Award, Forest Hist. Soc., Durham, NC, 1987 (Hon. Fellow, 1990). *Publications:* South Australia from the Air, 1969; The Draining of the Somerset Levels, 1970; The Making of the South Australian Landscape, 1974; (ed jtly) Australian Space, Australian Time, 1975; The Changing Rural Landscape of South Australia, 1977, 2nd edn 1991; Americans and their Forests, 1989; (ed) Wetlands: a threatened landscape, 1991; (ed) Planet Management, 1991; edited vols of essays; contribs to geogl and histl jls. *Recreations:* walking, music. *Address:* Westgates, Vernon Avenue, Harcourt Hill, Oxford OX2 9AU. *T:* Oxford (0865) 243725.

WILLIAMS, Rev. Michael Joseph; Principal of the Northern Ordination Course, since 1989; President, Northern Federation for Training in Ministry, since 1991; *b* 26 Feb. 1942; *s* of James and Edith Williams; *m* 1971, Mary Miranda Bayley; one *s* one *d*. *Educ:* St John's College, Durham (BA in Philosophy 1968). Apprentice Mechanical Engineer, then Engineer, with W & T Avery, Birmingham, 1958–63 (HNC in Mech. Eng 1962). Deacon 1970, priest 1971; Curate, then Team Vicar, St Philemon, Toxteth, 1970–78; Director of Pastoral Studies, St John's Coll., Durham, 1978–88. Hon. Tutor in Pastoral Theology, Univ. of Manchester, 1990–. *Publications:* The Power and the Kingdom, 1989; regular contribs to Anvil. *Address:* Luther King House, Brighton Grove, Rusholme, Manchester M14 5JP.

WILLIAMS, Michael Leonard; actor; Associate Artist, Royal Shakespeare Company, since 1966; *b* 9 July 1935; *s* of Michael Leonard Williams and Elizabeth (*née* Mulligan); *m* 1971, Judith Olivia Dench (*see* Dame Judi Dench); one *d*. *Educ:* St Edward's Coll., Liverpool; RADA (Coronation Scholar). Début, Nottingham Playhouse, 1959; London début, Celebration, Duchess Theatre, 1961; joined RSC, 1963; rôles include: Puck in A Midsummer Night Dream, Filch in The Beggar's Opera, Eichmann in The Representative, 1963; Oswald in King Lear (also NY), Pinch in The Comedy of Errors, Kokol in Marat/Sade, Lodowick in The Jew of Malta, 1964; Dromio of Syracuse in The Comedy of Errors, Guildenstern in Hamlet, Herald in Marat/Sade (also NY), 1965; Arthur in Tango, 1966; Petruchio in The Taming of the Shrew, Orlando in As You Like It, 1967; Fool in King Lear, Troilus in Troilus and Cressida, 1968; Charles Courtly in London Assurance, 1970; Bassanio in The Merchant of Venice, Ferdinand in The Duchess of Malfi, title rôle in Henry V, 1971; Mole in Toad of Toad Hall, 1972; Stellio in Content to Whisper, 1973; Private Meek in Too True to be Good, 1975; title rôle in Schweyk in the Second World War, Dromio in The Comedy of Errors (musical version), Autolycus in The Winter's Tale, Fool in King Lear, 1976; title rôle in national tour, Quartermaine's Terms, 1982; Bob in Pack of Lies, Lyric, 1983; George in Two Into One, Shaftesbury, 1984; Charles Pooter in Mr and Mrs Nobody, Garrick, 1986; George in Out of Order, Shaftesbury, 1990; *films* include: The Marat/Sade, 1966; Eagle in a Cage, 1969; Dead Cert, 1974; In Search of Alexander the Great, 1980; Enigma, 1981; Educating Rita, 1982; *television* includes: Elizabeth R, 1971; A Raging Calm, The Hanged Man, 1974; My Son, My Son, 1978; Love in a Cold Climate, 1980; Quest of Eagles, 1980; A Fine Romance, 1980–81, 1982; Blunt, 1986; Double First, 1988; Angel Voices, 1989; Can you hear me thinking?, 1990. Chm., Catholic Stage Guild, 1977–87. *Recreations:* family, tennis, pottering, gardening. *Address:* c/o Michael Whitehall Ltd, 125 Gloucester Road, SW7 4TE. *T:* 071–244 8466. *Club:* Garrick.

WILLIAMS, Prof. Michael Maurice Rudolph; consultant engineer; Professor of Nuclear Engineering, University of Michigan, 1987–89; Professor of Nuclear Engineering, 1970–86, now Emeritus, and Head of Department, 1980–86, Queen Mary College, London University; *b* 1 Dec. 1935; *s* of late M. F. Williams and G. M. A. Denton; *m* 1958, Ann Doreen Betty; one *s* one *d*. *Educ:* Ewell Castle Sch.; Croydon Polytechnic; King's Coll., London; Queen Mary Coll., London. BSc, PhD, DSc; CEng; Fellow, Instn Nuclear Engrs (Vice-Pres., 1971); FInstP. Engr with Central Electricity Generating Board, 1962; Research Associate at Brookhaven Nat. Lab., USA, 1962–63; Lectr, Dept of Physics, Univ. of Birmingham, 1963–65; Reader in Nuclear Engrg, Queen Mary Coll., London Univ., 1965–70. Mem., Adv. Cttee on Safety of Nuclear Installations, 1983–86. Chm. of Governors, Ewell Castle Sch., 1976–79. Exec. Editor, Annals of Nuclear Energy. Fellow American Nuclear Soc. *Publications:* The Slowing Down and Thermalization of Neutrons, 1966; Mathematical Methods in Particle Transport Theory, 1971; Random Processes in Nuclear Reactors, 1974; Aerosol Science, 1991; contribs to Proc. Camb. Phil. Soc., Nucl. Science and Engrg, Jl Nuclear Energy, Jl Physics. *Address:* 2A Lytchgate Close, South Croydon, Surrey CR2 0DX.

WILLIAMS, Sir Michael O.; *see* Williams, Sir Osmond.

WILLIAMS, Nicholas James Donald; *b* 21 Oct. 1925; *s* of late Nicholas Thomas Williams and Daisy Eustace (*née* Hollow); *m* 1st, 1947, Dawn Vyvyan (*née* Hill); one *s* one *d*; 2nd, 1955, Sheila Mary (*née* Dalgety); two *s* one *d*. *Educ:* St Erbyn's Sch., Penzance; Rugby Sch. (Scholar). Admitted Solicitor 1949. Served Royal Marines, 1943–47 (Captain). Partner, Nicholas Williams & Co., Solicitors, London, 1950; Senior Partner, Surridge & Beecheno, Solicitors, Karachi, 1955; Burmah Oil Co. Ltd: Legal Adviser, 1961; Co-ordinator for Eastern ops, 1963; Dir, 1965; Asst Man. Dir, 1967; Man. Dir and Chief Exec., 1969–75; Man. Dir and Chief Exec., Don Engineering, 1977–84. Director: Flarebay Ltd, 1978–85; EBC Gp PLC, 1986–90; Ranvet Ltd, 1986–. *Recreation:* sailing. *Address:* Purlieus Farmhouse, Ewen, Cirencester, Glos. *Clubs:* Royal Ocean Racing; Royal Cornwall Yacht.

WILLIAMS, Nicholas John S.; *see* Sims-Williams.

WILLIAMS, Nigel Christopher Ransome, CMG 1985; HM Diplomatic Service; Ambassador to Denmark, since 1989; *b* 29 April 1937; *s* of Cecil Gwynne Ransome Williams and Corinne Belden (*née* Rudd). *Educ:* Merchant Taylors' Sch.; St John's Coll., Oxford. Joined Foreign Service and posted to Tokyo, 1961; FO, 1966; Private Secretary: to Minister of State, 1968; to Chancellor of Duchy of Lancaster, 1969; UK Mission to UN, New York, 1970; FCO, 1973; Counsellor (Economic), Tokyo, 1976; Cabinet Office, 1980; Hd of UN Dept, FCO, 1980–84; Minister, Bonn, 1985–88. *Address:* c/o Foreign and Commonwealth Office, SW1.

WILLIAMS, Noel Ignace B.; *see* Bond-Williams.

WILLIAMS, Norman; *see* Williams, R. N.

WILLIAMS, Sir Osmond, 2nd Bt, *cr* 1909; MC 1944; JP; *b* 22 April 1914; *s* of late Captain Osmond T. D. Williams, DSO, 2nd *s* of 1st Bt, and Lady Gladys Margaret Finch Hatton, *o d* of 13th Earl of Winchilsea; *S* grandfather, 1927; *m* 1947, Benita Mary, *yr d* of late G. Henry Booker, and late Mrs Michael Burn; two *d*. *Educ:* Eton; Freiburg Univ. Royal Scots Greys, 1935–37, and 1939–45; served Palestine, Africa, Italy and NW Europe. Chm., Quarry Tours Ltd (Llechwedd slate caverns), 1973–77. Vice-Chm., Amnesty Internat. (British Sect.), 1971–74. Trustee: Internat. Prisoners of Conscience Fund; Festiniog Rly Trust; Mem., Merioneth Park Planning Cttee, 1971–74. Governor, Rainer Foundn Outdoor Pursuits Centre, 1964–76. JP 1960 (Chairman of the Bench, Ardudwy-uwch-Artro, Gwynedd, 1974–84). Chevalier, Order of Leopold II with Palm; Croix de Guerre with Palm (Belgium), 1940. *Recreations:* music, travelling. *Heir:* none. *Address:* Borthwen, Penrhyndeudraeth, Gwynedd LL48 6EN. *Club:* Travellers'.

WILLIAMS, Owen Lenn; retired; Regional Financial and Development Adviser, St Vincent, West Indies, 1976–78; *b* 4 March 1914; *s* of Richard Owen Williams and Frances Daisy Williams (*née* Lenn); *m* 1959, Gisela Frucht. *Educ:* St Albans Sch.; London University. Asst Principal, Export Credit Guarantee Dept, 1938; Asst Principal, Treasury, 1939; UK High Commn, Ottawa, 1941; Principal, Treasury, 1945; Asst Treasury Representative, UK High Commn, New Delhi, 1953; Treasury Rep., UK High Commn, Karachi, 1955; Economic and Financial Adviser, Leeward Islands, 1957; Perm. Sec., Min. of Finance, Eastern Nigeria, 1959; Asst Sec., Treasury, 1962; Counsellor, UK Delegn to OECD, 1968–73; Gen. Fiscal Adviser to Minister of Finance, Sierra Leone, 1974–75. *Recreations:* music, travel. *Address:* c/o National Westminster Bank, Caxton House, SW1. *Club:* Reform.

WILLIAMS, Paul Glyn; consultant, since 1983; joined Hogg Robinson Career Services, 1991; *b* 14 Nov. 1922; *s* of late Samuel O. Williams and Esmée I. Williams (*née* Cail); *m* 1947, Barbara Joan Hardy (marr. diss. 1964); two *d*; *m* 1964, Gillian Foote, *e d* of A. G. Howland Jackson, Elstead, Surrey, and of Mrs E. J. Foote and step *d* of late E. J. Foote, Estoril, Portugal; one *d*. *Educ:* Marlborough; Trinity Hall, Cambridge (MA). MP (C) Sunderland South, (C 1953–57, Ind. C 1957–58, C 1958–64). Chairman, Monday Club, 1964–69. Chm. and Man. Dir, Mount Charlotte Investments, 1966–77; Chm., Backer Electric Co., 1978–87. Director: First South African Cordage, 1947–54; Hodgkinson Partners Ltd, PR consultants, 1956–64; Transair, 1955–62; Minster Executive, 1977–83; Henry Sykes, 1980–83; consultant, P-E Internat. plc, 1983–91. FInstD; FBIM. *Address:* 65 Perrymead Street, SW6 3SN. *T:* 071–731 0045. *Clubs:* Boodle's, Institute of Directors.

WILLIAMS, Paul H.; *see* Hodder-Williams.

WILLIAMS, Dr Paul Randall, FInstP; Director, Rutherford Appleton Laboratory, Science and Engineering Research Council, since 1987; *b* 21 March 1934; *s* of Fred and Eileen Westbrook Williams; *m* 1957, Marion Frances Lewis; one *s* one *d*. *Educ:* Baines' Grammar School; Loughborough College (BSc London external); Liverpool Univ. (PhD). DLC. ICI Research Fellow, Liverpool Univ., 1957; Research Physicist, British Nat. Bubble Chamber, 1958–62; Rutherford Lab., SRC, 1962–79 (Dep. Div. Head, Laser Div., 1976–79); Science and Engineering Research Council: Head, Astronomy, Space and Radio Div., 1979–81; Head, Engineering Div., 1981–83; Dep. Dir, Rutherford Appleton Lab., 1983–87. Local Preacher, Methodist Church. *Recreations:* sailing, choral singing, ski-ing. *Address:* 5 Tatham Road, Abingdon, Oxon OX14 1QB. *T:* Abingdon (0235) 524654.

WILLIAMS, Penry Herbert; Fellow and Tutor in Modern History, New College, Oxford, since 1964; *b* 25 Feb. 1925; *s* of late Douglas Williams and Dorothy Williams (*née* Murray); *m* 1952, June Carey Hobson, *d* of late George and Kathleene Hobson; one *s* one *d*. *Educ:* Marlborough Coll.; New Coll., Oxford, 1947–50; St Antony's Coll., Oxford, 1950–51. MA, DPhil Oxon. Served Royal Artillery, 1943–45, Royal Indian Artillery, 1945–47. Asst Lecturer in History, 1951–54, Lectr, 1954–63, Sen. Lectr, 1963–64, Univ. of Manchester. Sexual Harrassment Officer and Dir, Graduate Studies, Faculty of Modern History, Univ. of Oxford, 1989–90. Fellow of Winchester Coll., 1978. Jt Editor, English Historical Review, 1982–90. *Publications:* The Council in the Marches of Wales under Elizabeth I, 1958; Life in Tudor England, 1963; The Tudor Regime, 1979, paperback 1981; (ed, with John Buxton) New College, Oxford 1379–1979, 1979; contribs to learned jls. *Address:* New College, Oxford OX1 3BN; 53 Park Town, Oxford OX2 6SL. *T:* Oxford (0865) 57613.

WILLIAMS, Peter F.; *see* Firmston-Williams.

WILLIAMS, Peter H.; *see* Havard-Williams.

WILLIAMS, Peter Keegan; HM Diplomatic Service; Ambassador to Socialist Republic of Vietnam, since 1990; *b* 3 April 1938; *s* of William Edward Williams and Lilian (*née* Spright); *m* 1969, Rosamund Mary de Worms; two *d*. *Educ:* Calday Grange Grammar Sch.; Collège de Marcq-en-Baroeul (Nord); Univ. de Lille; Pembroke Coll., Oxford (MA). Joined Diplomatic Service, 1962; language student, MECAS, Lebanon, 1962; Second Sec., Beirut, 1963, Jedda, 1964; Commonwealth Office, 1967; First Sec., FCO, 1969; Director, Policy and Reference Div., British Information Services, New York, 1970; First Sec., FCO, 1973; First Sec., Head of Chancery and Consul, Rabat, 1976 (Chargé d'Affaires, 1978 and 1979); Counsellor, GATT, UK Mission, Geneva, 1979–83 (Chm. Panel, USA/Canada, 1980–81; Chm., Cttee on Finance, 1981–83); Ambassador, People's Democratic Republic of Yemen, 1983–85; Hd of UN Dept, FCO, 1986–89; RCDS, 1989. *Recreations:* wine, walking. *Address:* c/o Foreign and Commonwealth Office, SW1. *Clubs:* Travellers', United Oxford & Cambridge University.

WILLIAMS, Peter Lancelot, OBE 1971; editor, writer on dance, designer; chairman of committees on dance; *b* 12 June 1914; *s* of Col G. T. Williams and Awdrie Elkington. *Educ:* Harrow Sch.; Central Sch. of Art and Design, London. Dress designer with own business, 1934–39; Transport Officer, Civil Defence (Falmouth Div.), 1939–45; Head Designer, Jantzen Ltd, 1945–47; stage designer, 1947–. Arts Council of Great Britain, 1965–80: served on most panels with connections with ballet and music; resp. for ballet sect. on Opera and Ballet Enquiry, 1966–69 (led to develt of dance theatre throughout GB); Chm., Dance Advisory Cttee (formerly Dance Theatre Cttee), 1973–80. Chairman: Brit. Council's Drama Adv. Cttee, 1976–81; (also Founder), Dancers Pensions and Resettlement Fund, 1975–; Creative Dance Artists Ltd, 1979–; Royal Ballet Benevolent Fund 1984–; Gov., Royal Ballet, 1986–; Mem., most cttees concerned with dance: Royal Acad. of Dancing, Cecchetti Soc. Asst Editor, Ballet, 1949–50; Founder Editor/Art Dir, Dance and Dancers, 1950–80; Ballet Critic, Daily Mail, 1950–53; Dance Critic, The Observer, 1982–83 (Deputy, 1970–). *Publications:* Masterpieces of Ballet Design, 1981; contrib. articles, mainly on dance and theatre, to newspapers and magazines in GB and internationally. *Address:* Tredrea, Perranarworthal, Truro, Cornwall; 47A Limerston Street, SW10 0BL.

WILLIAMS, Peter Michael, PhD; Chief Executive, since 1985, Chairman, since 1991, Oxford Instruments Group plc (Managing Director, 1983–85); *b* 22 March 1945; *s* of Cyril Lewis and Gladys Williams; *m* 1970, Jennifer Margaret Cox; one *s. Educ:* Hymers College, Hull; Trinity College, Cambridge. MA, PhD. Mullard Research Fellow, Selwyn College, Cambridge, 1969–70; Lectr, Dept of Chemical Engineering and Chemical Technology, Imperial College, 1970–75; VG Instruments Group, 1975–82 (Dep. Man. Dir, 1979–82); Oxford Instruments Group plc, 1982–. Supernumerary Fellow, St John's Coll., Oxford, 1988–. Mem., Physics Bd, CNAA, 1983–86. Guardian Young Business Man of the Year, 1986. *Publications:* numerous contribs to jls relating to solid state physics. *Recreations:* ski-ing, gardening. *Address:* Yew Cottage, Old Boars Hill, Oxford OX1 5JJ. *T:* Oxford (0865) 739470.

WILLIAMS, Dr Peter Orchard, CBE 1991; FRCP; Director: The Wellcome Trust, 1965–91; Wellcome Institute for the History of Medicine, 1981–83; *b* 23 Sept. 1925; *s* of Robert Orchard Williams, CBE, and Agnes Annie Birkinshaw; *m* 1949, Billie Innes Brown; two *d. Educ:* Caterham Sch.; Queen's Royal College, Trinidad; St John's Coll., Cambridge (MA); St Mary's Hospital Medical School. MB, BChir 1950; MRCP 1952; FRCP 1970. House Physician, St Mary's Hospital, 1950–51; Registrar, Royal Free Hospital, 1951–52; Medical Specialist, RAMC, BMH Iserlohn, 1954; Medical Officer, Headquarters, MRC, 1955–60; Wellcome Trust: Asst and Dep. Scientific Secretary, 1960–64; Scientific Secretary, 1964–65. Vice-Pres., Royal Soc. of Tropical Med. and Hygiene, 1975–77, Pres., 1991–; Member: Nat. Council of Soc. Services Cttee of Enquiry into Charity Law and Practice, 1974–76; BBC, IBA Central Appeals Adv. Cttee, 1978–83; DHSS Jt Planning Adv. Cttee, 1986–; Chairman: Foundations Forum, 1977–79; Assoc. of Med. Res. Charities, 1974–76, 1979–83; Hague Club (European Foundns), 1981–83. Hon. Fellow, LSHTM, 1986. Hon. DSc Birmingham, 1989. Hon. DM Nottingham, 1990. Mary Kingsley Medal for Services to Tropical Medicine, Liverpool Sch. of Trop. Med., 1983. *Publications:* Careers in Medicine, 1952; papers in scientific journals. *Recreations:* gardening, travel, golf. *Address:* Symonds House, Symonds Street, Winchester SO23 9JS.

WILLIAMS, Sir Peter W.; *see* Watkin Williams.

WILLIAMS, Sir Philip; *see* Williams, Sir R. P. N.

WILLIAMS, Raymond Lloyd, CBE 1987; DPhil, DSc; CChem, FRSC; Director, Metropolitan Police Laboratory, 1968–87; Visiting Professor in Chemistry, University of East Anglia, since 1968; *b* Bournemouth, 27 Feb. 1927; *s* of late Walter Raymond Williams and Vera Mary Williams; *m* 1956, Sylvia Mary Lawson Whitaker; one *s* one *d. Educ:* Bournemouth Sch.; St John's Coll., Oxford (schol.). Gibbs Univ. Schol. 1948, BA 1st Cl. Hons Nat Sci-Chem, MA, DPhil, DSc Oxon. Research Fellow, Pressed Steel Co., 1951–53; Commonwealth Fund Fellow, Univ. of California, Berkeley, 1953–54; progressively, Sen. Res. Fellow, Sen. Scientific Officer, Principal Sci. Officer, Explosives R&D Estab., 1955–60; PSO, Admiralty Materials Lab., 1960–62; Explosives R&D Establishment: SPSO, 1962; Supt, Analytical Services Gp, 1962–65; Supt, Non-metallic Materials Gp, 1965–68. External Examiner: Univ. of Strathclyde, 1983–85; KCL, 1986–88. Vis. Lectr, Univ. of Lausanne, 1989; Lectures: Theophilus Redwood, RSC, 1984; Schools, RSC, 1988; Public, RSC, 1990. Jt Editor: Forensic Science International, 1978–; Forensic Science Progress, 1984–. Pres., Forensic Science Soc., 1983–85; Hon. Mem., Assoc. of Police Surgeons of GB, 1980. *Publications:* papers in scientific jls on spectroscopy, analytical chemistry, and forensic science. *Recreations:* lawn tennis (played for Civil Service and Oxfordshire: representative colours), squash rackets, carpentry. *Address:* 9 Meon Road, Bournemouth, Dorset BH7 6PN. *T:* Bournemouth (0202) 423446.

WILLIAMS, (Reginald) Norman, CB 1982; Assistant Registrar of Friendly Societies, since 1984; *b* 23 Oct. 1917; *s* of Reginald Gardnar Williams and Janet Mary Williams; *m* 1956, Hilary Frances West; two *s. Educ:* Neath Grammar Sch.; Swansea Univ. Served War: Captain RA and later Staff Captain HQ 30 Corps, 1940–46. Solicitor in private practice, 1947–48. Dept of Health and Social Security (formerly Min. of Nat. Insurance): Legal Asst, 1948; Sen. Legal Asst, 1959; Asst Solicitor, 1966; Principal Asst Solicitor, 1974; Under Sec., 1977–82. Member of Law Society. *Recreations:* golf, photography, reading. *Address:* Brecon, 23 Castle Hill Avenue, Berkhamsted, Herts HP4 1HJ. *T:* Berkhamsted (0442) 865291.

WILLIAMS, (Richard) Derrick, MA (Cantab); Principal, Gloucestershire College of Arts and Technology, 1981–89; *b* 30 March 1926; *s* of Richard Leslie Williams and Lizzie Paddington; *m* 1949, Beryl Newbury Stonebanks; four *s. Educ:* St John's Coll., Cambridge. Asst Master, Lawrence Sherrif Sch., Rugby, 1950–51; Lectr, University Coll., Ibadan, Nigeria, 1951–52; Adult Tutor, Ashby-de-la-Zouch Community Coll., Leicestershire, 1952–54; Further Educn Organising Tutor, Oxfordshire, 1954–60; Asst Educn Officer: West Suffolk, 1960–65; Bristol, 1965–67; Dep. Chief Educn Officer, Bristol, 1967–73; Chief Educn Officer, County of Avon, 1973–76; Dir, Glos Inst. of Higher Educn, 1977–80. *Recreations:* cricket, music. *Address:* Goldington, Evesham Road, Cheltenham, Glos; Glan y Nant, Bryniau, Brithdir, Dolgellau, Gwynedd.

WILLIAMS, Richard Hall; Under Secretary, Agriculture Department, Welsh Office, Cardiff, 1981–86; Deputy Chairman, Local Government Boundary Commission for Wales, since 1989; *b* 21 Oct. 1926; *s* of late Edward Hall Williams and Kitty Hall Williams; *m* 1949, Nia Wynn (*née* Jones); two *s* two *d. Educ:* Barry Grammar Sch., Glamorgan; University College of Wales, Aberystwyth (BScEcon Hons). Career within Welsh Office included service in Health and Economic Planning Groups before entering Agriculture Dept, 1978. Treasurer, Ministerial Bd, Presbyterian Church of Wales, 1986–. *Recreation:* enjoying all things Welsh. *Address:* Argoed, 17 West Orchard Crescent, Llandaff, Cardiff CF5 1AR. *T:* Cardiff (0222) 562472.
See also J. E. H. Williams.

WILLIAMS, Sir Robert (Evan Owen), Kt 1976; MD, FRCP, FRCPath; FFPHM; Director, Public Health Laboratory Service, 1973–81; Chairman, Advisory Committee on Genetic Manipulation, Health and Safety Executive, 1984–86 (Chairman, Genetic Manipulation Advisory Group, 1981–84); *b* 30 June 1916; *s* of Gwynne Evan Owen Williams and Cicely Mary (*née* Innes); *m* 1944, Margaret (*née* Lumsden) (*d* 1990); one *s* two *d. Educ:* Sherborne Sch., Dorset; University College, London and University College Hospital. Assistant Pathologist, EMS, 1941–42; Pathologist, Medical Research Council Unit, Birmingham Accident Hospital, 1942–46; on staff Public Health Laboratory Service, 1946–60 (Director, Streptococcus, Staphylococcus and Air Hygiene Laboratory, 1949–60); Prof. of Bacteriology, Univ. of London, at St Mary's Hosp. Med. Sch., 1960–73, Dean 1967–73. Mem. MRC, 1969–73. Pres., RCPath, 1975–78. Fellow, UCL, 1968. Hon. FRCPA, 1977; Hon. MD Uppsala, 1972; Hon. DSc Bath, 1977. *Publications:* (jt author) Hospital Infection, 1966; Microbiology for the Public Health, 1985; numerous publications in journals on bacteriological and epidemiological subjects. *Recreation:* horticulture. *Address:* Little Platt, Plush, Dorchester, Dorset DT2 7RQ. *T:* Piddletrenthide (03004) 320. *Club:* Athenæum.

WILLIAMS, Prof. Robert Hughes, (Robin), FRS 1990; CPhys, FInstP; Professor and Head of Physics Department, University of Wales College of Cardiff, since 1984; *b* 22 Dec. 1941; *s* of Emrys and Catherine Williams; *m* 1967, Gillian Mary Harrison; one *s* one *d. Educ:* Bala Boys' Grammar Sch.; University College of North Wales, Bangor (BSc, PhD, DSc). Res. Fellow, Univ. of Wales, 1966–68; Lectr, then Reader and Prof., New University of Ulster, 1968–83. Visiting Professor: Max Planck Inst., Stuttgart, 1975; Xerox Res. Labs, Palo Alto, USA, 1979; IBM Res. Labs, Yorktown Heights, USA, 1982. Silver Medal, British Vacuum Council, 1988; Max Born Medal and Prize, German Physics Soc. and Inst. of Physics, 1989. *Publications:* Metal-Semiconductor Contacts (with E. H. Rhoderick), 1988; over 200 pubns in field of solid state physics and semiconductor devices. *Recreations:* walking, fishing, soccer. *Address:* Dolwerdd, Trerhyngyll, Cowbridge, S Glamorgan CF7 7TN. *T:* Cowbridge (0446) 773402.

WILLIAMS, Prof. Robert Joseph Paton, DPhil; FRS 1972; Senior Research Fellow, Wadham College, Oxford, since 1991 (Fellow, since 1955); Royal Society Napier Research Professor at Oxford, 1974–91; *b* 25 Feb. 1926; *m* 1952, Jelly Klara (*née* Büchli); two *s. Educ:* Wallasey Grammar Sch.; Merton Coll., Oxford (MA, DPhil). FRSC. Rotary Foundn Fellow, Uppsala, 1950–51; Jun. Res. Fellow, Merton Coll., Oxford, 1951–55; Lectr, 1955–73, Reader in Inorganic Chemistry, 1973–74, Univ. of Oxford. Associate, Peter Bent Brigham Hosp., Boston, USA; Commonwealth Fellow, Mass, 1965–66. Liversidge Lectr, Chem. Soc., 1979; Commem. Lectr, Biochem. Inst., Univ. of Zurich, 1981; Bakerian Lectr, Royal Soc., 1981. President: Chem. Sect., BAAS, 1985–86; Dalton Div., RSC, 1991–. Foreign Member: Acad. of Science, Portugal, 1981; Royal Soc. of Science, Liège, 1981; Royal Swedish Acad. of Sciences, 1983; Czechoslovak Acad. of Science, 1989. Hon. DSc: Liège, 1980; Leicester, 1985. Tilden Medal, Chem. Soc., 1970; Keilin Medal, Biochem. Soc., 1972; Hughes Medal, Royal Soc., 1979; Chaire Bruylants Medal, Louvain, 1979; Krebs Medal, Europ. Biochem. Soc., 1985; Linderstrøm-Lang Medal, Carlsberg Foundn, Copenhagen, 1986; Sigillum Magnum (Medal), Univ. of Bologna, 1987; Heyrovsky Medal, Internat. Union of Biochem., 1988; Frederick Gowland Hopkins Medal, Biochem. Soc., 1990. *Publications:* (with C. S. G. Phillips) Inorganic Chemistry, 1965; (jtly) Nuclear Magnetic Resonance in Biology, 1977; (ed jtly) New Trends in Bio-Inorganic Chemistry, 1978; (with S. Mann and J. Webb) Biomineralization, 1989; (with J. J. R. Frausto da Silva) The Biological Chemistry of the Elements, 1991; papers in Jl Chem. Soc., biochemical jls, etc. *Recreation:* walking in the country. *Address:* Wadham College, Oxford OX1 3QR. *T:* Oxford (0865) 242564.

WILLIAMS, Robert Martin, CB 1981; CBE 1973; retired; Chairman, State Services Commission, New Zealand, 1975–81; *b* 30 March 1919; *s* of late Canon Henry Williams; *m* Mary Constance, *d* of late Rev. Francis H. Thorpe; one *s* two *d. Educ:* Christ's Coll., NZ; Canterbury University College, NZ; St John's Coll., Cambridge. MA. 1st Class Hons Mathematics, Univ. Sen. Schol., Shirtcliffe Fellow, NZ, 1940; BA, 1st Class Hons Mathematics Tripos, Cantab, 1947; PhD Math. Statistics, Cantab, 1949. Mathematician at Radar Development Laboratory, DSIR, NZ, 1941–44; Member UK Atomic Group in US, 1944–45; Member, 1949–53, Director, 1953–62, Applied Mathematics Laboratory, DSIR, NZ; Harkness Commonwealth Fellow and Vis. Fellow, at Princeton Univ., 1957–58; State Services Commissioner, NZ Public Service, 1963–67; Vice-Chancellor: Univ. of Otago, Dunedin, 1967–73; ANU, 1973–75. Mem., NZ Metric Adv. Bd, 1969–73. Mem., Internat. Statistical Inst., 1961–. Chairman: Cttee of Inquiry into Educnl TV, 1970–72; Policy Cttee, Dictionary of NZ Biography, 1983–90. Pres., NZ Book Council, 1989–. Carnegie Travel Award, 1969. Hon. LLD Otago, 1972. *Publications:* papers mainly on mathematical statistics and related topics. *Address:* 21 Wadestown Road, Wellington, New Zealand. *Club:* Wellington (Wellington, NZ).

WILLIAMS, Sir (Robert) Philip (Nathaniel), 4th Bt *cr* 1915; *b* 3 May 1950; *s* of Sir David Philip Williams, 3rd Bt and of Elizabeth Mary Garneys, *d* of late William Ralph Garneys Bond; *S* father, 1970; *m* 1979, Catherine Margaret Godwin, *d* of Canon Cosmo Pouncey, Tewkesbury; one *s* three *d. Educ:* Marlborough; St Andrews Univ. MA Hons. *Heir: s* David Robert Mark Williams, *b* 31 Oct. 1980. *Address:* Bridehead, Littlebredy, Dorchester, Dorset. *T:* Long Bredy (0308) 482232. *Club:* MCC.

WILLIAMS, Robin; *see* Williams, Robert H.

WILLIAMS, Maj.-Gen. Robin Guy, CB 1983; MBE 1969; retired; Chief Executive, Auckland Division, Cancer Society of New Zealand (Inc.), since 1988; Chairman, Bell Helicopter (BH) Pacific, since 1988; *b* 14 Aug. 1930; *s* of John Upham and Margaret Joan Williams; *m* 1953, Jill Rollo Tyrie; one *s* two *d. Educ:* Nelson Coll., New Zealand. psc(UK) 1963, jssc(AS) 1972, rcds(UK) 1976. Commissioned RMC, Duntroon, 1952; 1 Fiji Inf. Regt Malaya, 1953–54; Adjt/Coy Comd 2 NZ Regt Malaya, 1959–61 Chief Instructor Sch. of Inf. (NZ), 1964–65; BM 28 Comwel Inf. Bde, Malaysia, 1965–68; CO 1 Bn Depot (NZ), 1969; CO 1 RNZIR (Singapore), 1969–71; GSO1 Field Force Comd (NZ), 1972–73; CofS Field Force Comd (NZ), 1973–74; Col SD, Army GS, 1974–75; Comd Field Force, 1977–79; ACDS (Ops/Plans), 1979–81; DCGS 1981; CGS, 1981–84. Vice-Chm., 1985–86, Chm., 1986–88, Operation Raleigh, NZ; Chief Exec., Order of St John (NZ), 1986–87. *Recreations:* golf, swimming, walking. *Address:* 71 Shore Road, Remuera, Auckland 5, New Zealand. *T:* 520–1547. *Clubs:* Wellington (NZ); Northern (Auckland); Auckland Golf (Middlemore, NZ).

WILLIAMS, Sir Robin (Philip), 2nd Bt, *cr* 1953; Insurance Broker since 1952; Lloyd's Underwriter, 1961; 2nd Lieut, retired, RA; *b* 27 May 1928; *s* of Sir Herbert Geraint Williams, 1st Bt, MP, MSc, MEngAssoc, MInstCE; *S* father 1954; *m* 1955, Wendy Adèle Marguerite, *o d* of late Felix Joseph Alexander, London and Hong Kong; two *s. Educ:* Eton Coll.; St John's Coll., Cambridge (MA). 2nd Lieut, Royal Artillery, 1947. Vice-Chairman, Federation of Univ. Conservative and Unionist Assocs, 1951–52; Acting Chairman, 1952; Chairman of Bow Group (Conservative Research Society), 1954. Called to Bar, Middle Temple, 1954; Chm., Anti-Common Market League, 1969; Dir, Common Market Safeguards Campaign, 1973–76; Hon. Sec., Campaign for an Independent Britain, 1989–. Councillor, Haringey, 1968–74. *Publication:* Whose Public Schools?, 1957. *Heir: s* Anthony Geraint Williams, *b* 22 Dec. 1958. *Address:* 1 Broadlands Close, Highgate, N6 4AF.

WILLIAMS, Dr Roger Stanley, FRCP, FRCS; Consultant Physician, King's College Hospital and Director, Institute of Liver Studies (formerly Liver Research Unit), King's College School of Medicine and Dentistry (formerly King's College Hospital and Medical School), since 1966; Consultant, Liver Research Unit Trust, since 1974; Hon. Consultant in medicine to the Army, since 1988; *b* 28 Aug. 1931; *s* of Stanley George Williams and Doris Dagmar Clatworthy; *m* 1st, 1954, Lindsay Mary Elliott (marr. diss. 1977); two *s* three *d*; 2nd, 1978, Stephanie Gay de Laszlo; one *s* two *d. Educ:* St Mary's Coll., Southampton; London Hosp. Med. Coll., Univ. of London. MB, BS (Hons), MD; LRCP, MRCP, FRCP 1966; MRCS, FRCS 1988; FRCPE 1990; FRACP 1991. House appointments and Pathology Asst, London Hospital, 1953–56; Jun. Med. Specialist, Queen Alexandra Hospital, Millbank, 1956–58; Medical Registrar and Tutor, Royal Postgrad.

Med. Sch., 1958–59; Lectr in Medicine, Royal Free Hospital, 1959–65; Consultant Physician, Royal South Hants and Southampton General Hospital, 1965–66. Member: Adv. Gp on Hepatitis, DHSS, 1980–; Transplant Adv. Panel, DHSS, 1974–83; WHO Scientific Gp on Viral Hepatitis, Geneva, 1972. Rockefeller Travelling Fellowship in Medicine, 1962; Legg Award, Royal Free Hosp. Med. Sch., 1964; Melrose Meml Lecture, Glasgow, 1970; Goulstonian Lectr, RCP, 1970; Searle Lecture, Amer. Assoc. for the Study of Liver Diseases, 1972; Sir Ernest Finch Vis. Prof., Sheffield, 1974; Fleming Lecture, Glasgow Coll. of Physicians and Surgeons, 1975; Sir Arthur Hurst Meml Lecture, British Soc. of Gastroênterology, 1975; Skinner Lecture, Royal Coll. of Radiologists, 1978; Albert M. Snell Meml Lecture, Palo Alto Med. Foundn, 1981; Datta Meml Oration, India, 1984. Member: European Assoc. for the Study of the Liver, 1966– (Cttee Mem., 1966–70; Pres., 1983); Harveian Soc. of London (Sec., Councillor and Vice-Pres., 1963–70, Pres., 1974–75); British Assoc. for Study of Liver (formerly Liver Club) (Sec. and Treasurer, 1968–71; Pres., 1984–86); Royal Soc. of Medicine (Sec. of Section, 1969–71); British Soc. of Gastroenterology (Pres., 1989). *Publications:* (ed) Fifth Symposium on Advanced Medicine, 1969; edited jointly: Immunology of the Liver, 1971; Artificial Liver Support, 1975; Immune Reactions in Liver Disease, 1978; Drug Reactions and the Liver, 1981; Variceal Bleeding, 1982; Antiviral Agents in Chronic Hepatitis B Virus Infection, 1985; author of over 1000 scientific papers, review articles and book chapters. *Recreations:* tennis, sailing, opera. *Address:* Reed House, Satchell Lane, Hamble, Hants. *T:* Southampton (0703) 453747; 8 Eldon Road, W8. *T:* 071–937 5301. *Clubs:* Saints and Sinners, Royal Ocean Racing; Royal Yacht Squadron (Cowes).

WILLIAMS, Ronald Millward, CBE 1990; DL; Member, Essex County Council, since 1970 (Chairman, 1983–86); *b* 9 Dec. 1922; *s* of George and Gladys Williams; *m* 1943, Joyce; one *s* two *d*. *Educ:* Leeds College of Technology. Electrical Engineer, then Industrial Eng Superintendent, Mobil Oil Co. Ltd, 1954–82. Member: Benfleet Urban Dist Council, 1960–74 (Chm. 1963–66, 1972–74); Castle Point Dist Council, 1974–87 (Chm. 1980–81; Leader, 1981–87); Leader Cons. Gp, Essex County Council: 1977–83, 1986–87; Chm., County Highways Cttee, 1989–. Chm., Southend Health Authority, 1982–90, Southend Health Care Services, NHS Trust, 1990–. Chm., SE Essex Abbeyfield Soc., 1983–88. DL Essex 1983. *Recreations:* supporter, football, cricket, bowls, tennis; video filming of countryside. *Address:* 41 Poors Lane, Hadleigh, Benfleet, Essex SS7 2LA. *T:* Southend on Sea (0702) 559565.

WILLIAMS, Ronald William; Senior Adviser, Coopers & Lybrand Deloitte (formerly Coopers & Lybrand Associates), since 1986; Director, Office of Manpower Economics, 1980–86 (on secondment); *b* 19 Dec. 1926; *yr s* of late Albert Williams and Katherine Teresa Williams (*née* Chilver). *Educ:* City of London Sch.; Downing Coll., Cambridge (BA, LLB). RN, 1945–48. Iraq Petroleum Co. Ltd, 1956–58; Philips Electrical Industries Ltd, 1958–64; Consultant, later Sen. Consultant, PA Management Consultants Ltd, 1964–69; Asst Sec., NBPI, 1969–71; Sen. Consultant, Office of Manpower Economics, 1971–73; Asst Sec., CSD, 1973–80 (UK Govt rep., ILO Tripartite Conf. on Public Servs, 1975); Under Sec. 1980; HM Treasury, 1982; Dept of Employment, 1986. *Recreations:* music, visual arts. *Address:* 126 Defoe House, Barbican, EC2Y 8DN. *T:* 071–638 5456.

WILLIAMS, Rev. Prof. Rowan Douglas, FBA 1990; Lady Margaret Professor of Divinity, and Canon of Christ Church, Oxford, since 1986; *b* 14 June 1950; *s* of Aneurin Williams and Nancy Delphine Williams; *m* 1981, Hilary Jane Paul; one *d*. *Educ:* Dynevor School, Swansea; Christ's College, Cambridge (BA 1971, MA 1975); Christ Church and Wadham College, Oxford (DPhil 1975; DD 1989). Lectr, College of the Resurrection, Mirfield, 1975–77; Chaplain, Tutor and Director of Studies, Westcott House, Cambridge, 1977–80; Cambridge University: Univ. Lectr in Divinity, 1980–86; Fellow and Dean of Clare Coll., 1984–86. Hon. Asst Priest, St George's, Cambridge, 1980–83; Canon Theologian, Leicester Cathedral, 1981–. Examining Chaplain to Bishop of Manchester, 1987–. *Publications:* The Wound of Knowledge, 1979; Resurrection, 1982; The Truce of God, 1983; (with Mark Collier) Beginning Now: peacemaking theology, 1984; Arius: heresy and tradition, 1987; (ed) The Making of Orthodoxy, 1989; Teresa of Avila, 1991; contribs to Theologische Realencyklopädie, Jl of Theological Studies, Downside Review, Eastern Churches Review, Sobornost, New Blackfriars. *Recreations:* music, fiction, languages. *Address:* Priory House, Christ Church, Oxford.

WILLIAMS, Roy, CB 1989; Deputy Secretary, Department of Trade and Industry, since 1984; *b* 31 Dec. 1934; *s* of Eric Williams and Ellen Williams; *m* 1959, Shirley, *d* of Captain and Mrs O. Warwick; one *s* one *d*. *Educ:* Liverpool Univ. (1st Cl. BA Econs). Asst Principal, Min. of Power, 1956; Principal, 1961; Harkness Commonwealth Fellow, Univs of Chicago and Berkeley, 1963–64; Principal Private Sec., Minister of Power and subseq. Paymaster Gen., 1969; Asst Sec., DTI, 1971; Principal Private Sec., Sec. of State for Industry, 1974; Under-Sec., DoI, later DTI, 1976–84. *Address:* Darl Oast, The Street, Ightham, Sevenoaks, Kent TN15 9HH. *T:* Borough Green (0732) 883944.

WILLIAMS, Rev. Samuel Lewis; Minister, St Columba's United Reformed Church, Gosport, since 1991; *b* 8 Jan. 1934; *s* of Thomas John Williams and Miriam Mary Williams (*née* West); *m* 1958, Mary Sansom (*née* Benjamin); one *s* one *d*. *Educ:* Pagefield College Public Day School, Newport, Gwent; Memorial Coll. (Congregational), Brecon. Local government officer, 1950–52; RAF, 1952–55; theol. training, 1955–58. Ordained Congregational (URC) Minister, 1958; Mill Street Congregational Church, Newport, Gwent, 1958–63; Bettws Congregational Church, 1963–68; Llanvaches Congregational Church, 1966–68; Free Churches Chaplain, St Woolas Hosp., Newport, 1964–68. Entered RN as Chaplain, 1968; served HMS: Seahawk, 1968–69; Hermes, 1969–70; Raleigh, 1970–71; Seahawk, 1971–73; Daedalus, 1973–74; served Malta, 1974–76; C-in-C Naval Home Comd staff, 1977–81; HMS Sultan, 1981–84; Flag Officer Scotland and NI staff, 1984–86; HMS Heron, 1986; Prin. Chaplain (Navy), Ch. of Scotland and Free Churches, 1986–91; RN retired, 1991. QHC, 1986–91. *Recreations:* oil painting, golf, hill walking, music, gardening, Rugby. *Address:* 18 Brodrick Avenue, Gosport, Hants PO12 2EN. *T:* Gosport (0705) 581114.

WILLIAMS, Rt. Hon. Shirley Vivien Teresa Brittain, PC 1974; Co-founder, Social Democratic Party, 1981, President, 1982–88; *b* 27 July 1930; *d* of late Prof. Sir George Catlin, and late Mrs Catlin, (Vera Brittain); *m* 1st, 1955, Prof. Bernard Arthur Owen Williams (marr. diss. 1974), *qv*; one *d*; 2nd, 1987, Prof. Richard Elliott Neustadt. *Educ:* eight schools in UK and USA; Somerville Coll., Oxford (scholar; MA), Hon. Fellow, 1970; Columbia Univ., New York (Smith-Mendt Scholar). General Secretary, Fabian Soc., 1960–64 (Chm., 1980–81). Contested: (Lab) Harwich, Essex, 1954 and 1955, and Southampton Test, 1959; (SDP) Crosby, 1984; (SDP/Alliance) Cambridge, 1987. MP: (Lab) Hitchin, 1964–74; (Lab) Hertford and Stevenage, 1974–79; (first-elected SDP MP) Crosby, Nov. 1981–1983; PPS, Minister of Health, 1964–66; Parly Sec., Min. of Labour, 1966–67; Minister of State: Education and Science, 1967–69; Home Office, 1969–70; Opposition spokesman on: Social Services, 1970–71, on Home Affairs, 1971–73; Prices and Consumer Protection, 1973–74; Sec. of State for Prices and Consumer Protection, 1974–76; Sec. of State for Educn and Science, 1976–79; Paymaster General, 1976–79. Chm., OECD study on youth employment, 1979. Mem., Labour Party Nat. Exec. Cttee, 1970–81. Visiting Fellow, Nuffield College, Oxford, 1967–75; Fellow, PSI, 1979–85; Visiting Faculty, Internat. Management Inst., Geneva, 1979–; Fellow, Inst. of Politics, Harvard, 1979–80 (Mem., Sen. Adv. Council, 1986–); Director: Turing Inst., Glasgow, 1985–; Learning by Experience Trust, 1986–. Godkin Lectr, Harvard, 1980; Rede Lectr, Cambridge, 1980; Janeway Lectr, Princeton, 1981. Hon. DEd CNAA, 1969; Hon. Dr Pol. Econ.: Univ. of Leuven, 1976; Radcliffe Coll., Harvard, 1978; Leeds, 1980; Bath, 1980; Hon. LLD: Sheffield, 1980; Southampton, 1981; Hon. DLitt Heriot-Watt, 1980; Hon. DSc Aston, 1981. *Publications:* Politics is for People, 1981; Jobs for the 1980s; Youth Without Work, 1981; (jtly) Unemployment and Growth in the Western Economies, 1984; A Job to Live, 1985. *Recreations:* music, hill walking. *Address:* c/o SLD, 4 Cowley Street, SW1.

WILLIAMS, Rev. (Sidney) Austen, CVO 1980; Vicar of St Martin-in-the-Fields, 1956–84; Chaplain to the Queen's Household, 1961–82, Extra Chaplain since 1982; a Prebendary of St Paul's Cathedral, since 1973; *b* 23 Feb. 1912; *s* of Sidney Herbert and Dorothy Williams; *m* 1945, Daphne Joan McWilliam; one *s* one *d*. *Educ:* Bromsgrove School; St Catharine's College, Cambridge (MA); Westcott House, Cambridge. Curate of St Paul, Harringay, 1937–40. Chaplain, Toc H, France and Germany, 1940–48 (POW, 1940–44). Curate of: All Hallows, Barking by the Tower, 1945–46; St Martin-in-the-Fields, 1946–51; Vicar of St Albans, Westbury Park, Clifton, Bristol, 1951–56. Freeman of the City of London, 1977. *Recreations:* photography, ornithology. *Address:* 37 Tulsemere Road, SE27. *T:* 081–670 7945.

WILLIAMS, Susan Elizabeth; Regional Director of Nursing and Quality Assurance, West Midlands Regional Health Authority, since 1988; *b* 30 Oct. 1942; *d* of Ernest George Fost and Kathleen Beatrice Maud Fost; *m* 1st, 1964, Dennis Norman Carnevale (decd); one *s* one *d*; 2nd, 1977, Keith Edward Williams. *Educ:* Grammar School for Girls, Weston-super-Mare; Wolverhampton Polytechnic (Post-grad. DipPsych); Bristol Royal Hosps (RSCN, RGN, RNT); BEd (Hons), DipN London. Ward Sister, Royal Hosp. for Sick Children, Bristol, 1972–76; Nurse Tutor, Salop Area Sch. of Nursing, 1976–80; Sen. Tutor, Dudley AHA, 1980–83; Reg. Nurse (Educn and Res.), W Midlands RHA, 1983–87; Chief Nurse Advr/Dir of Nurse Educn, Bromsgrove and Redditch HA, 1987–88. *Recreations:* hill walking, photography, reading, listening to music, foreign travel. *Address:* West Midlands Regional Health Authority, Arthur Thomson House, 146 Hagley Road, Birmingham B16 9PA. *T:* 021–456 1444.

WILLIAMS, Mrs Susan Eva, MBE 1959; Lord-Lieutenant of South Glamorgan, 1985–90; *b* 17 Aug. 1915; *d* of Robert Henry Williams and Dorothy Marie Williams; *m* 1950, Charles Crofts Llewellyn Williams (*d* 1952). *Educ:* St James's, West Malvern. WAAF, 1939–45. JP 1961, High Sheriff 1968, DL 1973, Glamorgan; Lieut, S Glam, 1981–85. DStJ 1990. *Recreation:* National Hunt racing. *Address:* Caercady, Welsh St Donats, Cowbridge, S Glamorgan CF7 7ST. *T:* Cowbridge (0446) 772346.

WILLIAMS, Sir Sydney; *see* Williams, Sir Henry S.

WILLIAMS, Prof. Thomas Eifion Hopkins, CBE 1980; CEng; Research Professor of Civil Engineering, University of Southampton, since 1983 (Professor of Civil Engineering, 1967–83); *b* 14 June 1923; *s* of David Garfield Williams and Annie Mary Williams (*née* Hopkins), Cwmtwrch, Brecon; *m* 1947, Elizabeth Lois Davies; one *s* two *d*. *Educ:* Ystradgynlais Grammar Sch.; Univ. of Wales (BSc, MSc); Univ. of Durham (PhD). FICE, MIStructE, FIHT, FCIT, FRSA. Research Stressman, Sir W. G. Armstrong-Whitworth Aircraft, 1945; Asst Engr, Trunk Roads, Glam CC, 1946; Asst Lectr Civil Engrg, UC Swansea, 1947; Lectr in Civil Engrg, King's Coll., Univ. of Durham, 1948; Resident Site Engr, R. T. James & Partners, 1952; Post-doctoral Visitor, Univ. of California at Berkeley, 1955; Vis. Prof., Civil Engrg, Northwestern Univ., 1957; Sen. Lectr, Reader and Prof. of Civil and Transport Engrg, King's Coll., Univ. of Durham (subseq. Univ. of Newcastle upon Tyne), 1958–67. Chairman: Civil Engrg EDC, 1976–78; Standing Adv. Cttee on Trunk Rd Assessment, Dept of Transport, 1980–87 (Mem., Adv. Cttee, 1977–80); Member: EDC Civil Engrg, 1967–76; Transport Cttee, SRC; Roads Engrg Bd, ICE; British Nat. Cttee, PIARC; Council and Transp. Engrg Bd, Inst. Highway Engrs (Pres. 1979–80); Public Policy Cttee, RAC, 1981–. Visitor, TRRL, 1982–88 (Mem., Adv. Cttee on Traffic and Safety, 1977–80); Special Advisor, H of L Select Cttee on European Transport, 1989. Mem. Council, Church Schools Co., 1982–90. *Publications:* (Editor) Urban Survival and Traffic, 1961; Capacity, in Traffic Engineering Practice, 1963; Prediction of Traffic in Industrial Areas, 1966; Autostrade: Strategia, di sviluppo industriale e la vitalita delle nostre citta, 1965; Inter-City VTOL: Potential Traffic and Sites, 1969; Mobility and the Environment, 1971; (ed) Transportation and Environment: policies, plans and practice, 1973; Integrated Transport: developments and trends, 1976; Air, Rail and Road Inter-City Transport Systems, 1976; Land Use, Highways and Traffic, 1977; Motor Vehicles in a Changing World, 1978; Traffic Engineering 1960–81, 1981; Transport Policy: facts; frameworks; econometrics, 1983; Assessment of Urban Roads, 1986; contribs to Proc. ICE, Highway Engrs, IMunE, Road International, Traffic Engrg and Control, Segnalazioni Stradali, OTA/PIARC Confs. *Recreation:* music. *Address:* Willowdale, Woodlea Way, Ampfield, Romsey, Hants SO51 9DA. *T:* Chandler's Ford (0703) 253342. *Club:* Royal Automobile.

WILLIAMS, His Eminence Cardinal Thomas Stafford; *see* Wellington (NZ), Archbishop of, (RC).

WILLIAMS, Trevor; *see* Williams, A. T.

WILLIAMS, Trevor Illtyd, MA, BSc, DPhil, CChem, FRSC, FRHistS; scientific writer and historian; *b* 16 July 1921; *s* of Illtyd Williams and Alma Mathilde Sohlberg; *m* 1st, 1945 (marriage dissolved, 1952); 2nd, 1952, Sylvia Irène Armstead; four *s* one *d*. *Educ:* Clifton College; Queen's College, Oxford (scholar and exhibnr). Nuffield Research Scholar, Sir William Dunn Sch. of Pathology, Oxford, 1942–45; Endeavour: Deputy Editor, 1945–54; Editor, 1954–74, 1977– (Consulting Scientific Editor, 1974–76); Editor, Outlook on Agriculture, 1982–89. Academic Relations Advr, ICI Ltd, 1962–74. Chm., Soc. for the Study of Alchemy and Early Chemistry, 1967–86; Jt Editor, Annals of Science, 1966–74; Chairman: World List of Scientific Periodicals, 1966–88; Adv. Cttee on the Selection of Low-priced Books for Overseas, 1982–84; Member: Steering Cttee, English Language Book Soc., 1984–90; Adv. Council, Science Museum, 1972–84; Council, University Coll., Swansea, 1965–83. Vis. Fellow, ANU, 1981; Leverhulme Fellow, 1985. Dexter Award, Amer. Chem. Soc., for contribs to the history of chemistry, 1976. *Publications:* An Introduction to Chromatography, 1946; Drugs from Plants, 1947; (ed) The Soil and the Sea, 1949; The Chemical Industry Past and Present, 1953; The Elements of Chromatography, 1954; (ed, jtly) A History of Technology, 1954–58; (with T. K. Derry) A Short History of Technology, 1960; Science and Technology (Ch. III, Vol. XI, New Cambridge Mod. History); (rev. edn) Alexander Findlay's A Hundred Years of Chemistry, 1965; (ed) A Biographical Dictionary of Scientists, 1968; Alfred Bernhard Nobel, 1973; James Cook, 1974; Man the Chemist, 1976; (ed) A History of Technology, Vols VI and VII: The Twentieth Century, 1978; (ed) Industrial Research in the United Kingdom, 1980; A History of the British Gas Industry, 1981; A Short History of Twentieth Century Technology, 1982; (ed) European Research Centres, 1982; Florey: penicillin and after, 1984; The Triumph of Invention, 1987; Robert Robinson, Chemist

Extraordinary, 1990; Science: invention and discovery in the twentieth century, 1990; numerous articles on scientific subjects, especially history of science and technology. *Recreations:* gardening, hill walking. *Address:* 20 Blenheim Drive, Oxford OX2 8DG. *T:* Oxford (0865) 58591. *Club:* Athenæum.

WILLIAMS, Vaughan; *see* Williams, J. V.

WILLIAMS, Walter Gordon Mason, CB 1983; FRICS; Vice President, London Rent Assessment Panel, since 1984; *b* 10 June 1923; *s* of Rees John Williams, DSO and Gladys Maud Williams; *m* 1950, Gwyneth Joyce Lawrence; two *d*. *Educ:* Cardiff High Sch. FRICS. Joined Valuation Office, Inland Revenue, 1947; Superintending Valuer (N Midlands), 1969–73; Asst Chief Valuer, 1973–79; Dep. Chief Valuer, 1979–83. *Address:* 33A Sydenham Hill, SE26 6SH. *T:* 081–670 8580.

WILLIAMS, Prof. William David, MA, DPhil; Professor of German, Liverpool University, 1954–80; *b* 10 March 1917; *s* of William Williams and Winifred Ethel Williams (*née* Anstey); *m* 1946, Mary Hope Davis; one *s* one *d*. *Educ:* Merchant Taylors' School; St John's Coll., Oxford (MA, DPhil). Served War of 1939–45, with Sudan Defence Force, Middle East, and as Liaison Officer with Polish Army in Italy; Asst Lecturer in German, Leeds Univ., 1946; Lecturer in German, Oxford Univ., 1948–54; Pro-Vice-Chancellor, Liverpool Univ., 1965–68. *Publications:* Nietzsche and the French, 1952; The Stories of C. F. Meyer, 1962; reviews, etc, in Modern Language Review, and Erasmus. *Recreation:* gardening. *Address:* Strangers Corner, 5 Summerfield Rise, Goring-on-Thames, near Reading, Berks RG8 0DS. *T:* Goring-on-Thames (0491) 872603.

WILLIAMS, Sir (William) Max (Harries), Kt 1983; solicitor; Senior Partner, Clifford Chance, 1989–91 (Joint Senior Partner, 1987–89); *b* 18 Feb. 1926; *s* of Llwyd and Hilary Williams; *m* 1951, Jenifer, *d* of late Rt Hon. E. L. Burgin, LLD, and Mrs Burgin, JP; two *d*. *Educ:* Nautical Coll., Pangbourne. Served 178 Assault Field Regt RA, Far East (Captain), 1943–47. Admitted Solicitor, 1950. Sen. Partner, Clifford Turner, 1984–87. Mem. Council, 1962–85, Pres., 1982–83, Law Society. Mem., Crown Agents for Oversea Govts and Administration, 1982–86; Lay Mem., Stock Exchange Council, 1984–. Director: Royal Insurance plc, 1985–; 3i Group plc, 1988– (Chm. Audit Cttee, 1991–); Garden Pension Trustees Ltd, 1990–; Royal Insurance Co. of Canada, 1991–. Chm., Review Bd for Govt Contracts, 1986–; Member: Royal Commission on Legal Services, 1976–79; Cttee of Management of Inst. of Advanced Legal Studies, 1980–86; Council, Wildfowl Trust (Hon. Treasurer, 1974–80). Pres., City of London Law Soc., 1986–87. Mem., Amer. Law Inst., 1985–; Hon. Member: Amer. Bar Assoc.; Canadian Bar Assoc. Master, Solicitors' Co., 1986–87. Hon. LLD Birmingham, 1983. *Recreations:* golf, fishing, ornithology. *Address:* 19 New Bridge Street, EC4V 6BY. *T:* 071–353 0211. *Clubs:* Garrick, Flyfishers'; Mid-Herts Golf.

WILLIAMS, William Thomas, OBE 1980; ARCS; PhD, DSc (London); DIC; FIBiol; FLS; FAA 1978; with Australian Institute of Marine Science, Cape Ferguson, Townsville, 1980–85; pianoforte teacher (LMus Australia), since 1973; *b* 18 Apr. 1913; *o s* of William Thomas and Clara Williams. *Educ:* Stationers' Company's School, London; Imperial College of Science and Technology. Demonstrator in Botany, Imperial College, 1933–36; Lecturer in Biology, Sir John Cass' College, 1936–40. Served War, 1940–46; RA (Sjt), RAOC (2/Lt), REME (T/Major). Lecturer in Botany, Bedford College, London, 1946–51; Professor of Botany, University of Southampton, 1951–65; CSIRO Division of Computing Research, Canberra, Australia, 1966–68; Div. of Tropical Pastures, Brisbane, 1968–73; Chief Res. Scientist, CSIRO, 1970–73; with Townsville Lab., CSIRO, 1973–80. Sometime Secretary of Society for Experimental Biology, and of Sherlock Holmes Society of London. Past Editor, Journal of Experimental Botany. Hon. DSc Queensland, 1973. *Publications:* The Four Prisons of Man, 1971; (ed) Pattern Analysis in Agricultural Science, 1976; over 150 papers on plant physiology, numerical taxonomy and statistical ecology in scientific journals. *Recreations:* music, drinking beer. *Address:* 10 Surrey Street, Hyde Park, Townsville, Qld 4812, Australia. *T:* (077) 794596.

WILLIAMS, Col William Trevor, FCIS; Director General, Engineering Industries Association, since 1981; *b* 16 Oct. 1925; *s* of Francis Harold and Ellen Mabel Williams, Newton Manorbier; *m* 1951, Elizabeth, *d* of late Brig. Arthur Goldie; two *s* two *d*. *Educ:* Darwin Coll., Univ. of Kent (MA). FBIM, MCIT. Commissioned in Infantry, 1945; regimental service, India and Malaya, to 1949; seconded to Guyanese Govt, 1964, 1965; Commander, Maritime Air Regt, Far East, 1967–69; Project Office, National Defence Coll., 1970–71; Adviser, Ethiopian Govt, 1971–72; Col Q BAOR, 1973–76 (Chm., Berlin Budget Cttee); Head of Secretariat, MoD, 1976–77; Director, SATRA, 1979–80. *Publications:* military. *Recreations:* golf, photography. *Address:* 15 Mill Lane, Lower Harbledown, Canterbury. *T:* Canterbury (0227) 768170.

WILLIAMS, Yvonne Lovat; Secretary, Monopolies and Mergers Commission, 1974–79, retired; *b* 23 Feb. 1920; *d* of late Wendros Williams, CBE and Vera Lovat Williams. *Educ:* Queenswood Sch., Hatfield; Newnham Coll., Cambridge. BA History 1941, MA 1946. Temp. Civil Servant, BoT, 1941–46; Asst Principal, BoT, 1946–48, Principal 1948–56; Treasury, 1956–58; BoT, 1958–63; Asst Sec., BoT, Min. Tech., DTI, 1963–73. *Recreations:* visiting friends, theatres and old places. *Address:* Flat 16, The Limes, 34–36 Linden Gardens, W2 4ET. *T:* 071–727 9851.

WILLIAMS-BULKELEY, Sir Richard Harry David, 13th Bt, *cr* 1661; TD; JP; Lord Lieutenant of Gwynedd, 1974–83 (HM Lieutenant for the County of Anglesey, 1947–74); Member: Anglesey County Council, 1946–74 (Chairman, 1955–57); Mayor of Beaumaris, 1949–51; *b* 5 Oct. 1911; *s* of late Maj. R. G. W. Williams-Bulkeley, MC, and late Mrs V. Williams-Bulkeley; *S* grand-father, 1942; *m* 1938, Renée Arundell, *yr d* of Sir Thomas L. H. Neave, 5th Bt; two *s*. *Educ:* Eton. Served with 9th and 8th Bns Royal Welch Fusiliers, 1939–44, 2nd in Command of both Battalions and with Allied Land Forces South East Asia, specially employed, 1944–Sept. 1945, Lt-Col Comdt, Anglesey and Caernarvonshire Army Cadet Force, 1946–47 (resigned on appointment as HM Lieut). CStJ. *Recreations:* shooting, golf, hunting. *Heir: s* Richard Thomas Williams-Bulkeley [*b* 25 May 1939; *m* 1964, Sarah Susan, *er d* of Rt Hon. Sir Henry Josceline Phillimore, OBE; twin *s* one *d*]. *Address:* Plâs Meigan, Beaumaris, Gwynedd. *T:* Beaumaris (0248) 810345. *Club:* Army and Navy.

WILLIAMS-WYNN, Sir (David) Watkin, 11th Bt *cr* 1688, of Gray's Inn; DL; *b* 18 Feb. 1940; *s* of Sir Owen Watkin Williams-Wynn, 10th Bt, CBE and Margaret Jean (*d* 1961), *d* of late Col William Alleyne Macbean, RA; *S* father, 1988; *m* 1st, 1967, Harriet Veryan Elspeth (marr. diss. 1981), *d* of Gen. Sir Norman Tailyour, KCB, DSO; two *s* twin *d*; 2nd, 1983, Victoria Jane Dillon, *d* of late Lt-Col Ian Dudley De-Ath, DSO, MBE; twin *s*. *Educ:* Eton. Lt Royal Dragoons, 1958–63; Major Queen's Own Yeomanry, 1970–77. DL 1970, High Sheriff, 1990, Clwyd. *Recreations:* foxhunting and other field sports. *Heir: s* Charles Edward Watkin Williams-Wynn, *b* 17 Sept. 1970. *Address:* Plas-yn-Cefn, St Asaph, Clwyd LL17 0EY, N Wales. *T:* St Asaph (0745) 582200. *Club:* Cavalry and Guards.

WILLIAMS-WYNNE, Col John Francis, CBE 1972; DSO 1945; JP; FRAgS; Vice Lord-Lieutenant of Gwynedd, 1980–85 (Lieutenant, 1974–80; HM Lieutenant of Merioneth, 1957–74); Constable of Harlech Castle since 1964; *b* 9 June 1908; *s* of late Major F. R. Williams-Wynn, CB, and late Beatrice (*née* Cooper); *m* 1938, Margaret Gwendolen, DL Gwynedd, *d* of late Rev. George Roper and late Mrs G. S. White; one *s* two *d*. *Educ:* Oundle; Magdalene College, Cambridge (MA Mech. Sciences). Commissioned in RA 1929; served NW Frontier, 1936; served War of 1939–45; psc Camberley; Brigade Major, RA 2 Div., 1940–41; 2 i/c 114 Fd Regt, 1942; GSO2 HQ Ceylon Comd, 1942; comd 160 Jungle Field Regt, RA, 1943–44; GSO1, GHQ India, 1945; GSO1, War Office, 1946–48; retd 1948; comd 636 (R Welch) LAA Regt, RA, TA, 1951–54; Subs. Col 1954. Hon. Col 7th (Cadet) Bn RWF, 1964–74. Contested (C) Merioneth, 1950. JP 1950, DL 1953, VL 1954, Merioneth. Chairman, Advisory Cttee, Min. of Agric. Experimental Husbandry Farm, Trawscoed, 1955–76. Part-time mem., Merseyside and N Wales Electricity Bd, 1953–65; National Parks Comr, 1961–66; Forestry Comr, 1963–65; Member: Regional Adv. Cttee N Wales Conservancy Forestry Commission, 1950–63; County Agric. Exec. Cttee, 1955–63 and 1967–71; Gwynedd River Board, 1957–63; Forestry Cttee of GB, 1966–76; Home Grown Timber Advisory Cttee, 1966–76; Prince of Wales's Cttee for Wales, 1970–79; President: Timber Growers Organisation, 1974–76; Royal Welsh Agric. Soc., 1968 (Chm. Council, 1971–77); Chairman: Agricl Adv. Cttee, BBC Wales, 1974–79; Flying Farmers' Assoc., 1974–. Pres., Merioneth Br., CLA, 1979–. Member: Airline Users Cttee, CAA, 1973–79; Sch. of Agric. Cttee, University Coll. N Wales, 1982–. Chm. and Man. Dir, Cross Foxes Ltd. *Recreations:* farming, forestry and flying. *Address:* Peniarth, Tywyn-Merioneth, Gwynedd. *T:* Tywyn (0654) 710328. *Clubs:* Army and Navy, Pratt's.

See also Hon. D. A. C. Douglas-Home.

WILLIAMSON, family name of **Baron Forres.**

WILLIAMSON, Andrew George; Director of Social Services, Devon County Council, since 1990; *b* 29 Feb. 1948; *s* of Albert and Jocelyn Williamson; *m* 1972, Mary Eleanor White; one *s* one *d*. *Educ:* Southern Grammar Sch., Portsmouth; Oxford Poly. (Dip. in Social Work; CQSW); Birmingham Univ. (Advanced Management Develt Prog., 1982). Residential Child Care, Portsmouth, 1967; Child Care Officer, Hants, 1969; social work management positions in Northumberland and Wandsworth; Asst Dir of Social Services, East Sussex, 1983; Dep. Dir, West Sussex, 1986. *Recreations:* reading, cricket, music, theatre. *Address:* 33 St Leonards Road, Exeter, Devon EX2 4LR. *T:* Exeter (0392) 73936.

WILLIAMSON, Brian; *see* Williamson, R. B.

WILLIAMSON, David Francis, CB 1984; Secretary-General, Commission of the European Communities, since 1987; *b* 8 May 1934; *s* of late Samuel Charles Wathen Williamson and Marie Eileen Williamson (*née* Denney); *m* 1961, Patricia Margaret Smith; two *s*. *Educ:* Tonbridge Sch.; Exeter Coll., Oxford (MA). Entered Min. of Agriculture, Fisheries and Food, 1958; Private Sec. to Permanent Sec. and to successive Parly Secs, 1960–62; HM Diplomatic Service, as First Sec. (Agric. and Food), Geneva, for Kennedy Round Trade Negotiations, 1965–67; Principal Private Sec. to successive Ministers of Agric., Fisheries and Food, 1967–70; Head of Milk and Milk Products Div., Marketing Policy Div. and Food Policy Div., 1970–74; Under-Sec., Gen. Agricultural Policy Gp, 1974–76, EEC Gp, 1976–77; Dep. Dir Gen., Agriculture, European Commn, 1977–83; Dep. Sec., 1982; Cabinet Office, 1983–87. *Address:* Secretariat-General, Commission of the European Communities, Rue de la Loi 200, 1049 Brussels, Belgium.

WILLIAMSON, David Theodore Nelson, FRS 1968; Group Director of Engineering, Rank Xerox Ltd, 1974–76; Director, Xerox Research (UK) Ltd, 1975–76; retired; *b* 15 Feb. 1923; *s* of David Williamson and Ellie (*née* Nelson); *m* 1951, Alexandra Janet Smith Neilson; two *s* two *d*. *Educ:* George Heriot's Sch., Edinburgh; Univ. of Edinburgh. MO Valve Co. Ltd, 1943–46; Ferranti Ltd, Edinburgh, 1946–61; pioneered numerical control of machine tools, 1951; Manager, Machine Tool Control Div., 1959–61; Work on sound reproduction: Williamson amplifier, 1947, Ferranti pickup, 1949; collab. with P. J. Walker in developt of first wide-range electrostatic loud-speaker, 1951–56; Dir of Res. and Develt, Molins Ltd, 1961–74. Member: NEL Metrology and Noise Control Sub cttee, 1954–57; NEL Cttee on Automatic Design and Machine Tool Control, 1964–66; Min. of Technology Working Party on Computer-Aided Design, 1967; Penny Cttee on Computer-Aided Design, 1967–69; Steering Cttee, IAMTACT, 1967–69; SRC Mech. and Prod. Engrg Cttee, 1965–69; SRC Control Panel, 1966–69; Mech. Engrg EDC, 1968–74; SRC Engrg Bd, 1969–75; Adv. Cttee for Mech. Engrg, 1969–71; Court, Cranfield Inst. of Technology, 1970–79; Council and Exec. Cttee, British Hydrodynamics Research Assoc., 1970–73; Design Council (formerly CoID) Engrg Design Adv. Cttee, 1971–75; Council for Scientific Policy, 1972–73; Science Mus. Adv. Cttee, 1972–79; SRC Manufrg Technology Cttee, 1972–75 (Chm.); Mech. Engrg and Machine Tool Requirements Bd, DTI subseq. DoI, 1973–76; Council, Royal Soc., 1977–78. Hon. DSc: Heriot-Watt, 1971; Edinburgh, 1985. *Publications:* contrib. to: Electronic Engineers' Reference Book, 1959; Progress in Automation, 1960; Numerical Control Handbook, 1968; papers and articles on engrg subjects; NEDO Discussion Paper No 1, 1971. James Clayton Lecture, IMechE, 1968. *Recreations:* music, photography. *Address:* Villa Belvedere, La Cima 10, Tuoro-sul-Trasimeno, 06069 Pg, Umbria, Italy. *T:* (075) 826285.

WILLIAMSON, Dame (Elsie) Marjorie, DBE 1973; MSc, PhD (London); Principal, Royal Holloway College, University of London, 1962–73; *b* 30 July 1913; *d* of late Leonard Claude Williamson and Hannah Elizabeth Cary. *Educ:* Wakefield Girls' High School; Royal Holloway College. Demonstrator in Physics, Royal Holloway College, University of London, 1936–39; Lecturer in Physics, University College of Wales, Aberystwyth, 1939–45; Lecturer in Physics, Bedford Coll., Univ. of London, 1945–55; Principal, St Mary's Coll., Univ. of Durham, 1955–62; Deputy Vice-Chancellor, Univ. of London, 1970–71, 1971–72. Fellow, Bedford Coll., Univ. of London, 1975. A Manager, The Royal Instn, 1967–70, 1971–74. Mem., Commonwealth Scholarship Commn, 1975–83. *Publications:* papers in various scientific periodicals. *Recreations:* music, gardening. *Address:* Priory Barn, Lower Raydon, Ipswich, Suffolk IP7 5QT. *T:* Hadleigh (0473) 824033.

WILLIAMSON, Frank Edger, QPM 1966; *b* 24 Feb. 1917; *s* of John and late Mary Williamson; *m* 1943, Margaret Beaumont; one *d*. *Educ:* Northampton Grammar Sch. Manchester City Police, 1936–61; Chief Constable: Carlisle, 1961–63; Cumbria Constabulary, 1963–67; HM Inspector of Constabulary, 1967–72. OStJ 1967. *Address:* Eagle Cottage, Alderley Park, Nether Alderley, Macclesfield, Cheshire SK10 4TD. *T:* Alderley Edge (0625) 583135.

WILLIAMSON, (George) Malcolm, FCIB; Group Managing Director, Standard Chartered Bank, since 1991 (Group Executive Director, Banking, 1989–91); *b* 27 Feb. 1939; *s* of George and Margery Williamson; *m* 1963, Pamela (*née* Williams); one *s* one *d*. *Educ:* Bolton School. FIB. Barclays Bank: Local Director, 1980; Asst Gen. Manager, 1981; Regional Gen. Manager, 1983–85; Bd Mem., Post Office, and Man. Dir, Girobank plc, 1985–89. *Recreations:* mountaineering, golf, chess. *Address:* Martyr Worthy Place, Martyr Worthy, Winchester SO21 1AW. *Clubs:* Rucksack, Pedestrian (Manchester).

WILLIAMSON, Hazel Eleanor, (Mrs H. C. J. Marshall); QC 1988; *b* 14 Jan. 1947; *d* of Geoffrey Briddon and Nancy Nicholson; *m* 1st, 1969, Robert Hector Williamson (marr. diss. 1980); 2nd, 1983, Harvey Christopher John Marshall; one step *s. Educ:* Wimbledon High Sch; St Hilda's Coll., Oxford (BA Jurisprudence). Atkin Scholar, Gray's Inn. Called to the Bar, Gray's Inn, 1972. *Recreations:* gardening, opera, occasional off-shore sailing. *Address:* 13 Old Square, Lincoln's Inn, WC2A 3UA. *T:* 071–404 4800. *Club:* CWIL.

WILLIAMSON, Dr Hugh Godfrey Maturin; Reader in Hebrew and Aramaic, 1989–92, and Fellow of Clare Hall, 1985–92, Cambridge University; Regius Professor of Hebrew, and Student of Christ Church, Oxford, from April 1992; *b* 15 July 1947; *s* of Thomas Broadwood Williamson and Margaret Frances (*née* Davy); *m* 1971, Julia Eiluned Morris; one *s* two *d. Educ:* Rugby Sch.; Trinity Coll., Cambridge (BA 1st cl. Hons Theol., 1969; MA); St John's Coll., Cambridge; PhD 1975, DD 1986, Cantab. Cambridge University: Asst Lectr in Hebrew and Aramaic, 1975–79; Lectr, 1979–89. *Publications:* Israel in the Books of Chronicles, 1977; 1 and 2 Chronicles, 1982; Ezra, Nehemiah, 1985; Ezra and Nehemiah, 1987; Annotated Key to Lambdin's Introduction to Biblical Hebrew, 1987; (ed jtly) The Future of Biblical Studies, 1987; (ed jtly) It is Written: essays in honour of Barnabas Lindars, 1988; contrib. to learned jls incl. Vetus Testamentum, Jl of Theol Studies, Jl of Biblical Lit., Jl of Semitic Studies, Jl for Study of OT, Palestine Exploration Qly, Zeitschrift für die alttestamentliche Wissenschaft, Oudtestamentische Studiën. *Recreations:* sea angling, model yacht sailing. *Address:* 7 Chester Road, Southwold, Suffolk IP18 6LN. *T:* Southwold (0502) 722319.

WILLIAMSON, Prof. James, CBE 1985; FRCPE; Professor of Geriatric Medicine, University of Edinburgh, 1976–86, now Emeritus; Co-Director, Royal College of Physicians of Edinburgh/Bayer Research Unit, since 1988; *b* 22 Nov. 1920; *s* of James Mathewson Williamson and Jessie Reid; *m* 1945, Sheila Mary Blair; three *s* two *d. Educ:* Wishaw High Sch., Lanarkshire; Univ. of Glasgow (MB ChB 1943); FRCPE 1959 (MRCPE 1949). Training in general medicine, incl. two years in general practice, later specialising in respiratory diseases, then in medicine of old age; Consultant Physician, 1954–73; Prof. of Geriatric Medicine in newly established Chair, Univ. of Liverpool, 1973–76. Pres., British Geriatrics Soc., 1986–88; Chm., Age Concern Scotland, 1987–90. Hon. DSc Rochester, USA, 1989. *Publications:* chapters in various textbooks; numerous articles in gen. med. jls and in jls devoted to subject of old age. *Recreations:* walking, reading. *Address:* 14 Ann Street, Edinburgh EH4 1PJ. *T:* 031–332 3568.

WILLIAMSON, Marshal of the Royal Air Force Sir Keith (Alec), GCB 1982 (KCB 1979); AFC 1968; Chief of the Air Staff, 1982–85; Air ADC to the Queen, 1982–85; *b* 25 Feb. 1928; *s* of Percy and Gertrude Williamson; *m* 1953, Patricia Anne, *d* of W/Cdr F. M. N. Watts; two *s* two *d. Educ:* Bancroft's Sch., Woodford Green; Market Harborough Grammar Sch.; RAF Coll., Cranwell. Commissioned, 1950; flew with Royal Australian Air Force in Korea, 1953; OC 23 Sqdn, 1966–68; Command, RAF Gütersloh, 1968–70; RCDS 1971; Dir, Air Staff Plans, 1972–75; Comdt, RAF Staff Coll., 1975–77; ACOS (Plans and Policy), SHAPE, 1977–78; AOC-in-C, RAF Support Comd, 1978–80; AOC-in-C, RAF Strike Command and C-in-C, UK Air Forces, 1980–82. *Recreation:* golf. *Address:* c/o National Westminster Bank, Fakenham, Norfolk.

WILLIAMSON, Malcolm; *see* Williamson, G. M.

WILLIAMSON, Malcolm Benjamin Graham Christopher, CBE 1976; composer, pianist, organist; Master of the Queen's Music, since 1975; *b* 21 Nov. 1931; *s* of Rev. George Williamson, Sydney, Australia; *m* 1960, Dolores Daniel; one *s* two *d. Educ:* Barker Coll., Hornsby, NSW; Sydney Conservatorium. Composer-in-Residence, Westminster Choir Coll., Princeton, NJ, 1970–71. Pres., Royal Philharmonic Orch., 1977–82. Ramaciotti Medical Research Fellow, Univ. of NSW, 1982–83; Vis. Prof. of Music, Strathclyde Univ., 1983–86. President: Beauchamp Sinfonietta, 1972–; Birmingham Chamber Music Soc., 1975–; Univ. of London Choir, 1976–; Sing for Pleasure, 1977–; British Soc. for Music Therapy, 1977–. Hon. DMus: Westminster Choir Coll., Princeton, NJ, 1970 (Hon. Fellow, 1971); Melbourne, 1982; Sydney, 1982; DUniv Open, 1983. Hon. AO 1987. *Compositions include: orchestral:* seven symphonies; Santiago de Espada Overture; Sinfonia Concertante; Sinfonietta; Concerto Grosso; Symphonic Variations; Fiesta; Ochre; Fanfarade; In Thanksgiving Sir Bernard Heinze; Himna Titu; *string orchestra:* Epitaphs for Edith Sitwell; Lament in memory of Lord Mountbatten of Burma; Ode for Queen Elizabeth; Symphony No 7; Lento for Strings; *concertos:* three Piano Concertos; Organ Concerto; Violin Concerto; Concerto for Two Pianos; Harp Concerto; *ballets:* The Display, 1964; Sun into Darkness, 1966; Astarte, 1974; Heritage, 1985; *operas:* Our Man in Havana, 1963; The Violins of Saint-Jacques, 1966; Lucky Peter's Journey, 1969; *chamber operas:* English Eccentrics, 1964; The Happy Prince, 1965; Julius Caesar Jones, 1965; Dunstan and the Devil, 1967; The Growing Castle, 1968; The Red Sea, 1972; *operatic sequence:* The Brilliant and the Dark, 1969; *cassations (mini-operas):* The Moonrakers; Knights in Shining Armour; The Snow Wolf; Genesis; The Stone Wall; The Winter Star; The Glitter Gang; The Terrain of the Kings; The Valley and the Hill; Le Pont du Diable; *vocal:* A Vision of Beasts and Gods; Celebration of Divine Love; Three Shakespeare Songs; Six English Lyrics; From a Child's Garden; Pietà; White Dawns; *symphonic song cycles:* Hammarskjöld Portrait, 1974; Les Olympiques, 1976; Tribute to a Hero, 1981; Next Year in Jerusalem—Poems of Jorge Luis Borges, 1985; *choral:* Symphony for Voices; In Place of Belief; The Death of Cuchulain; Love the Sentinel; The Musicians of Bremen; Canticle of Fire; The World at the Manger; *chorus with orchestra:* Symphony No 3 (The Icy Mirror), 1972; Ode to Music, 1973; Mass of Christ the King, 1977 (to celebrate the Queen's Silver Jubilee); A Pilgrim Liturgy—Cantata, 1984; Songs for a Royal Baby, 1985; *chamber music:* Variations for Cello and Piano; Concerto for Wind Quintet and Two Pianos; Serenade for Flute, Piano and String Trio; Pas de Quatre for Woodwind Quartet and Piano; Piano Quintet; Piano Trio; Champion Family Album; *piano:* two Sonatas; seven books of Travel Diaries; Five Preludes; Sonata for two Pianos; Ritual of Admiration; Himna Titu; *organ:* Fons Amoris; Resurgence du Feu; Symphony for Organ; Vision of Christ-Phoenix; Little Carols of the Saints; Peace Pieces; Mass of a Medieval Saint; The Lion of Suffolk; Mass of the People of God; *church music:* masses, cantatas, anthems, psalms, hymns. *Recreation:* reading. *Address:* Campion Press, Sandon, Buntingford, Herts SG9 0QW.

WILLIAMSON, Dame Marjorie; *see* Williamson, Dame E. M.

WILLIAMSON, Sir Nicholas Frederick Hedworth, 11th Bt, *cr* 1642; *b* 26 Oct. 1937; *s* of late Maj. William Hedworth Williamson (killed in action, 1942) and Diana Mary, *d* of late Brig.-Gen. Hon. Charles Lambton, DSO (she *m* 2nd, 1945, 1st Baron Hailes, PC, GBE, CH); *S* uncle, 1946. *Address:* Abbey Croft, Mortimer, Reading, Berks RG7 3PE. *T:* Mortimer (0734) 332324.

WILLIAMSON, Nicol; actor; *b* Hamilton, Scotland, 14 Sept. 1938. Dundee Rep. Theatre, 1960–61; Royal Court: That's Us, Arden of Faversham, 1961; A Midsummer Night's Dream, Twelfth Night, 1962; Royal Shakespeare Company, 1962; Nil Carborundum, The Lower Depths, Women Beware Women; Spring Awakening, Royal Court, 1962; Kelly's Eye, The Ginger Man, Royal Court, 1963; Inadmissible Evidence, 1964, 1978, Royal Court, Wyndham's 1965 (Evening Standard Best Actor Award), NY 1965 (NY Drama Critics Award); A Cuckoo in the Nest, Waiting for Godot, Miniatures, 1964; Sweeney Agonistes, Globe, 1965; Diary of a Madman, Duchess, 1967; Plaza Suite, NY, 1968; Hamlet, Round House, 1969 (Evening Standard Best Actor Award), NY and US tour, 1969; Midwinter Spring, Queen's, 1972; Circle in the Square, Uncle Vanya, NY, 1973; Royal Shakespeare Company, 1973–75: Corialanus, Midwinter Spring, Aldwych, 1973; Twelfth Night, Macbeth, Stratford 1974, Aldwych 1975; dir and title role, Uncle Vanya, Other Place, Stratford, 1974; Rex, NY, 1975; Inadmissible Evidence, NY, 1981; Macbeth, NY, 1983; The Entertainer, NY, 1983; The Lark, USA, 1983; The Real Thing, NY, 1985. *Films:* Inadmissible Evidence, 1967; The Bofors Gun, 1968; Laughter in the Dark, 1968; The Reckoning, 1969; Hamlet, 1970; The Jerusalem File, 1971; The Wilby Conspiracy, 1974; The Seven Per Cent Solution, 1975; The Cheap Detective, The Goodbye Girl, Robin and Marion, 1977; The Human Factor, 1979; Excalibur, Venom, 1980; I'm Dancing as Fast as I Can, 1981; Return to Oz, 1984; Black Widow, 1986. *Television:* The Word, 1977; Macbeth, BBC Shakespeare series, 1982; Christopher Columbus, 1983; Lord Mountbatten—the Last Viceroy, 1985; Passion Flower, 1985. *Address:* c/o ICM, 388–396 Oxford Street, W1.

WILLIAMSON, Nigel; Diary Editor, The Times, since 1990; *b* 4 July 1954; *s* of Neville Albert and Anne Maureen Williamson; *m* 1976, Magali Patricia Wild; two *s. Educ:* Chislehurst and Sidcup Grammar School; University College London. Tribune: Journalist, 1982–84; Literary Editor, 1984; Editor, 1984–87; Editor: Labour Party News, 1987–89; New Socialist, 1987–89; political reporter, The Times, 1989–90. *Publications:* The SDP (ed), 1982; The New Right, 1984. *Recreations:* opera, cricket, gardening. *Address:* High Beeches, 60 Sutherland Avenue, Biggin Hill, Westerham, Kent. *T:* Westerham (0959) 71127. *Clubs:* St James's; Charlton Athletic Football; Skyliners Cricket.

WILLIAMSON, Peter Roger; HM Diplomatic Service; Counsellor, Foreign and Commonwealth Office, since 1988; *b* 20 April 1942; *s* of Frederick W. and Dulcie R. Williamson; *m* 1977, Greta Helen Clare Richards; one *s* one *d. Educ:* Bristol Grammar Sch.; St John's Coll., Oxford (MA). Journalist and teacher, Far East, 1965–66; joined FCO, 1966; Kuala Lumpur, 1970; 1st Sec., FCO, 1973; Hong Kong, 1975; FCO, 1979; Counsellor, Kuala Lumpur, 1985–88. *Recreations:* squash, tennis, travel, theatre. *Address:* c/o Foreign and Commonwealth Office, SW1. *Club:* Lake (Kuala Lumpur).

WILLIAMSON, Richard Arthur; Director, Midland Region, Crown Prosecution Service, 1987–89; *b* 9 Jan. 1932; *s* of George Arthur and Winifred Mary Williamson; *m* 1957, Christina Elizabeth, *d* of Harry Godley Saxton, Worksop, Notts, and Helena Saxton; two *s. Educ:* King Edward VI Grammar Sch., East Retford; Sheffield Univ. (statutory year). Solicitor, 1956. National Service, RN (Sub-Lieut), 1956–58. Asst Solicitor, Lancs CC, 1958–61; Sen. Asst Solicitor, Lincs (Lindsey) CC, 1961–65; private practice, Partner in Hetts, Solicitors, Scunthorpe, 1965–76; Prin. Prosecuting Solicitor, Greater Manchester, 1976–83; Chief Prosecuting Solicitor, Lincs, 1983–85; Asst Hd of Field Management, Crown Prosecution Service, 1985–87. Prosecuting Solicitors Soc. of England and Wales: Mem. Exec. Council, 1978–85; Treas., 1978–85; Chm., Hds of Office, 1984–85. *Recreations:* family, theatre, gardening. *Address:* The Lookout, Back Street, Alkborough, near Scunthorpe, South Humberside DN15 9JN. *T:* Scunthorpe (0724) 720843.

WILLIAMSON, Prof. Robert, FRCP, FRCPath; Professor of Biochemistry, St. Mary's Hospital Medical School, University of London, since 1976; *b* 14 May 1938; *s* of John and Mae Williamson; *m* 1962, Patricia Anne Sutherland; one *s* one *d. Educ:* Bronx High School of Science, NY; Wandsworth Comprehensive School; University College London (BSc, MSc, PhD). FRCP 1990. Lectr, Univ. of Glasgow, 1963–67; Sen. Scientist (Molecular Biol.), Beatson Inst. for Cancer Research, Glasgow, 1967–76. Sen. Fellow, Carnegie Instn of Washington, Baltimore,1972–73. External Examnr, Malaysia, Saudi Arabia. Member: UK Genetic Manipulation Adv. Cttee, 1976–; Grants Cttees, MRC, Cancer Research Campaign, Action Research for Crippled Child, Cystic Fybrosis Research Trust. Hon. MRCP 1986. Hon. MD Turku, 1987. Wellcome Award, Biochem. Soc., 1983. *Publications:* (ed) Genetic Engineering, vol. 1, 1981, vol. 2, 1982, vol. 3, 1982, vol. 4, 1983; articles in Nature, Cell, Procs of US Nat. Acad. of Scis, Biochemistry, Nucleic Acids Research. *Recreations:* reading, sport. *Address:* Department of Biochemistry & Molecular Genetics, St Mary's Hospital Medical School, Norfolk Place, W2 1PG. *T:* 071–723 1252.

WILLIAMSON, (Robert) Brian, CBE 1989; Chairman, Gerrard & National Holdings PLC, since 1989 (Managing Director, 1978–89); *b* 16 Feb. 1945; *m* 1986, Diane Marie Christine de Jacquier de Rosée. *Educ:* Trinity College, Dublin (MA). Personal Asst to Rt Hon. Maurice Macmillan (later Viscount Macmillan), 1967–71; Editor, International Currency Review, 1971; Chairman: LIFFE, 1985–88; GNI Ltd, 1985–89; Director: Fleming Internat. High Income Investment Trust plc, 1990–; Court, Bank of Ireland, 1990–; Member: Bd, Bank of Ireland Britain Hldgs, 1986–90; Council, 1985–88, Council, Eur. Cttee, 1988–90, British Invisible Exports Council; Securities and Investments Bd, 1986–. Mem. HAC, commissioned 1975. Contested (C) Sheffield Hillsborough, Feb. and Oct. 1974; prosp. parly cand., Truro, 1976–77. *Address:* 23 Paultons Square, SW3. *Club:* Kildare and University (Dublin).

WILLIAMSON, Rt. Rev. Robert Kerr; *see* Southwark, Bishop of.

WILLIAMSON, Prof. Robin Charles Noel, FRCS; Professor and Director of Surgery, Royal Postgraduate Medical School, University of London and Hammersmith Hospital, since 1987; *b* 19 Dec. 1942; *s* of James Charles Frederick Lloyd Williamson and Helena Frances Williamson (*née* Madden); *m* 1967, Judith Marjorie (*née* Bull); three *s. Educ:* Rugby School; Emmanuel College, Cambridge; St Bartholomew's Hosp. Med. Coll. MA, MD, MChir (Cantab). Surgical Registrar, Reading, 1971–73; Sen. Surgical Registrar, Bristol, 1973–75; Res. Fellow, Harvard, 1975–76; Consultant Sen. Lectr, Bristol, 1977–79; Prof. of Surgery, Univ. of Bristol, 1979–87. Mem., Cell Biology and Disorders Bd, MRC, 1987–. Fulbright-Hays Sen. Res. Scholar, USA, 1975; Sen. Penman Vis. Fellow, South Africa, 1985; Paul Grange Vis. Fellow, Univ. of Monash, 1986; Hunterian Prof., RCS, 1981–82; Raine Vis. Prof., Univ. of Western Australia, 1983; Richardson Prof., Mass Gen. Hosp., 1985; Visiting Professor: Univ. of Lund, Sweden, 1985; Univ. of Hong Kong, 1987; Johnson and Johnson Vis. Prof., Univ. of Calif, San Francisco, 1989; Edwin Tooth Guest Prof., Royal Brisbane Hosp., Qld, 1989. Lectures: Arris and Gale, RCS, 1977–78; Finlayson Meml, RCPSG, 1985; Sir Gordon Bell Meml, RACS, NZ, 1988. Moynihan Fellow, Assoc. of Surgeons, 1979. Pres., Pancreatic Soc. of GB and Ireland, 1984–85; Chm., Educn Cttee, British Soc. of Gastroenterology, 1981–87; Sec. Gen., World Assoc. of Hepatopancreatobiliary Surgery, 1990– (Treas., 1986–90). Examiner, Primary FRCS, 1981–87. Hallett Prize, RCS, 1970; Research Medal, British Soc. of Gastroenterology, 1982. Sen. Ed., British Jl of Surgery, 1991– (Co. Sec., 1983–91). *Publications:* (ed jtly): Colonic Carcinogenesis, 1982; General Surgical Operations, 2nd edn 1987; Emergency Abdominal Surgery, 1990; Surgical Management, 1991; numerous papers in surgical and med. jls. *Recreations:* travel, military uniforms and history. *Address:* The Barn, 88 Lower Road, Gerrards Cross, Bucks SL9 8LB. *T:* Gerrards Cross (0753) 889816. *Club:* United Oxford & Cambridge University.

WILLIAMSON, Prof. Stephen; Professor of Engineering, Cambridge, since 1989; Fellow, St John's College, Cambridge, since 1990; *b* 15 Dec. 1948; *s* of Donald Williamson and Patricia K. M. Williamson (*née* Leyland); *m* 1970, Zita Mellor; one *s* two *d*. *Educ:* Burnage Grammar Sch., Manchester; Imperial Coll. of Science and Technology (BScEng, ACGI, PhD, DIC; DScEng 1989). Lectr in Engineering, Univ. of Aberdeen, 1973–81; Sen. Lectr, 1981–85, Reader, 1985–89, Dept of Electrical Engineering, Imperial College. FCGI 1989. *Publications:* papers relating to induction machines. *Recreations:* reading, walking. *Address:* Cambridge University Engineering Department, Trumpington Street, Cambridge CB2 1PZ. *T:* Cambridge (0233) 332664.

WILLING, Maria Paula Figueiroa, (Mrs Victor Willing); *see* Rego, Paula.

WILLINK, Sir Charles (William), 2nd Bt *cr* 1957; *b* 10 Sept. 1929; *s* of Rt Hon. Sir Henry Urmston Willink, 1st Bt, MC, QC (*d* 1973), and Cynthia Frances (*d* 1959), *d* of H. Morley Fletcher, MD, FRCP; *S* father, 1973; *m* 1954, Elizabeth, *d* of Humfrey Andrewes, Highgate, London; one *s* one *d*. *Educ:* Eton College (scholar); Trinity College, Cambridge (scholar; MA, PhD). Assistant Master: Marlborough College, 1952–54; Eton College, 1954–85 (Housemaster, 1964–77). FRSA. *Publications:* (ed) Euripides' Orestes, 1986; articles in Classical Quarterly. *Recreations:* bridge, field botany, music (bassoon). *Heir: s* Edward Daniel Willink, *b* 18 Feb. 1957. *Address:* 20 North Grove, Highgate, N6 4SL. *T:* 081–340 3996.

WILLIS, family name of **Baron Willis.**

WILLIS, Baron, *cr* 1963, of Chislehurst (Life Peer); **Edward Henry Willis;** FRTS; FRSA; playwright (as Ted Willis); Director: World Wide Pictures, since 1967; Vitalcall Ltd, since 1983; *b* London, 13 Jan. 1918; *m* 1944, Audrey Hale; one *s* one *d*. *Educ:* Tottenham Central School. *Plays include:* Hot Summer Night, New, 1957; God Bless the Guv'nor, Unity, 1959; Woman in a Dressing Gown, 1962; A Slow Roll of Drums, 1964; Queenie, 1967; Mr Polly, 1977; Doctor on the Boil, 1978; Stardust, 1983; Cat and Mouse, 1985; Old Flames, 1986; Tommy Boy, 1988; Intent to Kill, 1990; The Killing Edge, 1991; A Home for Animals, 1991; *Television scripts:* Dixon of Dock Green Series, 1953–75; Sergeant Cork, 1963–67; Knock on any Door, 1964; Crime of Passion, 1970; Hunter's Walk, 1973; Black Beauty, 1979; Buckingham Palace Connection, 1981; Eine Heim für Tiere (Germany), 1984; Racecourse, 1987; *Films include:* Woman in a Dressing Gown, 1958 (Berlin Award); Flame in the Streets (play, Hot Summer Night), 1961; Bitter Harvest, 1963; A Long Way to Shiloh, 1969; Maneater, 1979; The Iron Man, 1983; Mrs Harris MP, 1984; Mrs Harris Goes to New York, 1985; The Left-Handed Sleeper, 1986; Mrs Harris Goes to Moscow, 1986; Mrs Harris Goes to Monte Carlo, 1987; Mrs Harris Goes to Majorca, 1990. President, Writers Guild of GB, 1958–68, 1976–79, Life Pres., 1988; Mem., Sports Council, 1971–73. Awards include: Writers' Guild Zita, 1966, 1974; Internat. Writers' Guild Distinguished Writing, 1972; Variety Club of GB for Distinguished Service, 1974; Pye TV for Outstanding Service, 1983; RSA Silver Medal, 1966. *Publications:* Woman in a Dressing Gown and other TV plays, 1959; Whatever Happened to Tom Mix? (autobiography), 1970; Evening All (autobiog.), 1991; *novels:* Death May Surprise Us, 1974; The Left-Handed Sleeper, 1975; Man-eater, 1976; The Churchill Commando, 1977; The Buckingham Palace Connection, 1978 (Current Crime Cup); The Lions of Judah, 1979; The Naked Sun, 1980; The Most Beautiful Girl in the World, 1981; Spring at the Winged Horse, 1983; A Problem for Mother Christmas (children's novel), 1986; The Green Leaves of Summer, 1987; The Bells of Autumn, 1990. *Recreations:* tennis, Association football. *Address:* 5 Shepherds Green, Chislehurst, Kent BR7 6PB. *Club:* Garrick.

WILLIS, Charles Reginald; Director, Tiverton Gazette & Associated Papers Ltd, since 1971; Member, Press Council, 1967; *b* 11 June 1906; *s* of Charles and Marie Willis, Tiverton, Devon; *m* 1929, Violet Stubbs; one *d*. *Educ:* Tiverton Grammar Sch. Tiverton Gazette, 1922–27; North Western Daily Mail, 1927–29; Evening Chronicle, Newcastle upon Tyne, 1929–1935; Evening Chronicle, Manchester, 1935–42; Empire News, London, 1942–43; The Evening News, London, 1943 (Editor, 1954–66); Dir, Associated Newspapers Ltd, 1961–71; Editorial Dir, Harmsworth Publications, 1967–70. *Recreation:* cricket. *Address:* Howden Heyes, Ashley, Tiverton, Devon EX16 5PB. *T:* Tiverton (0884) 254829.

WILLIS, Hon. Sir Eric (Archibald), KBE 1975; CMG 1974; Executive Director, Arthritis Foundation of Australia (NSW), since 1984; *b* 15 Jan. 1922; *s* of Archibald Clarence Willis and Vida Mabel Willis (*née* Buttenshaw); *m* 1st, 1951, Norma Dorothy Thompson (*née* Knight) (marr. diss.); two *s* one *d*; 2nd, 1982, Lynn Anitra Ward (*née* Roberts). *Educ:* Murwillumbah High Sch., NSW; Univ. of Sydney (BA Hons). MLA (Liberal) for Earlwood, NSW, 1950–78; Dep. Leader, NSW Parly Liberal Party, 1959–75, Leader, 1976–77; Minister for Labour and Industry, Chief Secretary and Minister for Tourism, 1965–71; Chief Sec. and Minister for Tourism and Sport, 1971–72; Minister for Education, 1972–76; Premier and Treasurer, 1976; Leader of the Opposition, NSW Parlt, 1976–77. Exec. Sec., Royal Australian Coll. of Ophthalmologists, 1978–83. *Recreation:* reading. *Address:* 5/94 Kurraba Road, Neutral Bay, NSW 2089, Australia. *T:* (02) 9093432; (office) 64 Kippax Street, Surry Hills, NSW 2010, Australia. *T:* (02) 281 1611.

WILLIS, Frank William; Director of Advertising and Sponsorship, Independent Television Commission, since 1991; *b* 6 April 1947; *s* of Prof. F. M. Willis and J. C. Willis; *m* 1972, Jennifer Carol Arnold; two *d*. *Educ:* Bradford Grammar School; Magdalen Coll., Oxford (BA, BPhil). HM Diplomatic Service, 1971; Moscow, 1972–74; Ecole Nationale d'Administration, 1974–75; First Sec., FCO, 1975–79; Dept of Trade, later DTI, 1980; Asst Sec., Consumer Affairs Div., DTI, 1984; Controller of Advertising, IBA, 1987–90. *Recreations:* shopping in Muswell Hill, moors and mountains, wine. *Address:* ITC, 70 Brompton Road, SW3 1EY. *T:* 071–584 7011.

WILLIS, Gaspard; *see* Willis, R. W. G.

WILLIS, Vice-Adm. Sir (Guido) James, KBE 1981; AO 1976; Chief of Naval Staff, Department of Defence, Australia, 1979–82, retired; *b* 18 Oct. 1923; *s* of late Jack Rupert Law Willis and Théa Willis; *m* 1976, Marjorie J. Rogers. *Educ:* Wesley Coll., Melbourne; Royal Australian Naval Coll. Imperial Defence Coll., 1967; Director General Operations and Plans, 1968–71; CO HMAS Melbourne, 1971–72; DDL Project Director, 1972–73; Chief of Naval Personnel, 1973–75; Chief of Naval Material, 1975–76; Asst Chief of Defence Force Staff, 1976–78; Flag Officer Commanding HMA Fleet, 1978–79. Commander 1956, Captain 1962, Rear-Adm. 1973, Vice-Adm. 1979. *Address:* 5 Roebuck Street, Red Hill, ACT 2603, Australia. *T:* (06) 239 7108.

WILLIS, Sir James; *see* Willis, Sir G. J.

WILLIS, His Honour John Brooke; a Circuit Judge (formerly County Court Judge), 1965–80; Barrister-at-Law; *b* 3 July 1906; *yr s* of William Brooke Willis and Maud Mary Willis, Rotherham; *m* 1929, Mary Margaret Coward (marr. diss., 1946); one *s* one *d*; *m* 1964, Terena Ann Steel (formerly Hood); two *d*. *Educ:* Bedford Modern Sch.; Sheffield Univ. Called to the Bar, Middle Temple, 1938, North Eastern Circuit. Served War of 1939–45. RAFVR, 1940–45, Sqdn Leader. Recorder, Rotherham, 1955–59, Huddersfield, 1959–65; Dep. Chm., W Riding of Yorks QS, 1958–71. Chairman, Medical Appeal Tribunal under the National Insurance (Industrial Injuries) Acts, 1953–65. *Address:* 14 Larchwood, Woodlands Drive, Rawdon, Leeds LS19 6JZ.

WILLIS, Maj.-Gen. John Brooker, CB 1981; independent defence and marketing consultant; *b* 28 July 1926; *s* of late William Noel Willis and of Elaine Willis; *m* 1959, Yda Belinda Jane Firbank; two *s* two *d*. *Educ:* privately, until 1941; Redhill Technical Coll. ptsc, jssc. Enlisted in Royal Navy (Fleet Air Arm) as Trainee Pilot; basic training in USA, 1944; returned to UK, transf. to Indian Army, attended Armoured OTS Ahmed Nagar, 1945; commnd 1947, joined 10th Royal Hussars; attended 13 Technical Staff Course, RMCS, 1958–60; Bt Lt-Col 1965, in comd 10th Hussars Aden and BAOR; GSO1 (Armour) DS RMCS, 1968–69; Col GS MGO Secretariat, MoD, 1969–71; Dep. Comdt, RAC Centre, 1971–74; Sen. Officers' War Course, Greenwich, 1974; Dir, Projects (Fighting Vehicles), 1974–77; Dir Gen., Fighting Vehicles and Engr Equipment, 1977–81, retd. *Recreations:* golf, gardening, aviation, amateur dramatics. *Address:* c/o Lloyds Bank, 26 Hammersmith Broadway, W6 7AH. *Club:* Army and Navy.

WILLIS, Air Vice Marshal John Frederick, CB 1991; CBE 1988; Director General of Training, Royal Air Force, since 1991; *b* 27 Oct. 1937; *s* of F. A. and K. E. Willis; *m* 1959, Merrill Thewliss; three *s* two *d*. *Educ:* Dulwich Coll.; RAF Coll., Cranwell. Entered RAF, 1955; comnd, 1958; Pilot, 83/44/9/Sqdns (Vulcan), 1958–64; Flying Instr, 1964–67; Officer and Aircrew Selection Centre, 1967–69; Staff Coll., 1970; Chief Flying Instr, Vulcan OCU, Flt Comdr/Sqdn Comdr, 27 Sqdn, 1971–77; Policy Div., Air Force Dept, MoD, 1977–82; Stn Comdr, Akrotiri, Cyprus, 1982–84; Briefing Officer to CAS, 1984–85; SHAPE, 1985–88; ACDS (Policy and Nuclear), 1989–90. *Recreations:* walking, reading, model making. *Address:* Ministry of Defence, Adastral House, Theobalds Road, WC1X 8RU. *T:* 071–430 7290. *Club:* Royal Air Force.

WILLIS, John Trueman, DFM 1942; housing consultant; Director: Kingdomwide Housing Trust, since 1982; Kingdomwide Ltd, since 1981; Kingdomwide Development Ltd, since 1982; *b* 27 Oct. 1918; *s* of Gordon and Ethel Willis, Headington, Oxford; *m* 1947, Audrey Joan, *d* of Aubrey and Gertrude Gurden, Headington, Oxford; one *s* one *d*. *Educ:* Oxford High Sch., Oxford. Estates Management, Magdalen Coll., Oxford, 1935–36; Industrial Trng, Lockheed Hydraulic Brake Co., Leamington Spa, 1937–38. Served War of 1939–45: Pilot on 14 Sqdn RAF Middle East, 1940–42; PoW Stalag Luft III, Germany, 1943–45. Estates Management, 1946–64, Estates Sec., 1953–65, Magdalen Coll., Oxford; Rent Officer for Oxford, 1965–67; Sec. Housing Societies Charitable Trust, 1968–69; Director: Shelter, 1971–72 (Housing Dir, 1969–70); Liverpool Housing Trust, 1973–75; Castle Rock Housing Assoc., 1976–78. Member: NEDO Housing Strategy Cttee, 1975–78; Management Cttee, Kingdomwide Housing Assoc. Ltd, 1986–. Promoted housing conf., Planning for Home Work, 1984. ICSA. *Publication:* Housing and Poverty Report, 1970. *Recreations:* diminishing. *Address:* 36 Kings Court, The Kings Gap, Hoylake, Wirral, Merseyside L47 1JE. *T:* 051–632 3873.

WILLIS, Joseph Robert McKenzie, CB 1952; CMG 1946; Deputy Chairman, Board of Inland Revenue, 1957–71; *b* 18 March 1909; 2nd *s* of Charles Frederick Willis and Lucy Alice McKenzie; *m* 1945, Elizabeth Browning, *er d* of James Ewing; one *s* one *d*. *Educ:* Eton; Christ Church, Oxford. Entered Inland Revenue Dept, 1932; Under Secretary, Central Economic Planning Staff, Treasury, 1948–49; Commissioner of Inland Revenue, 1949; Student of Imperial Defence Coll., 1948. Professorial Res. Fellow and Vis. Prof., Bath Univ., 1972–79. Specialist advr to Select Cttee on Wealth Tax, 1975. *Publications:* (with C. T. Sandford and D. J. Ironside): An Accessions Tax, 1973; An Annual Wealth Tax, 1975; (with P. J. W. Hardwick) Tax Expenditures in the United Kingdom, 1978. *Address:* Bunbury, Lower Shiplake, Henley-on-Thames, Oxon RG9 3PD. *T:* Wargrave (0734) 402726.

WILLIS, Rear-Adm. Kenneth Henry George, CB 1981; Director General, Home Farm Trust Ltd, Bristol, 1982–88, retired; *m*; three *d*. *Educ:* Royal Naval Engineering Coll.; Royal Naval Coll.; Jesus Coll., Cambridge (BA 1949). Joined RN 1944; served at sea and in shore weapons depts; Resident Officer, Polaris Executive, Clyde Submarine Base, 1965–68; i/c training, HMS Collingwood, 1969–70; Asst Dir, Underwater Weapon Dept, 1970; sowc 1974; Dep. Dir, RN Staff Coll., Greenwich, 1975–76, Dir, 1976; CO HMS Collingwood, 1976–79; C of S to C-in-C, Naval Home Command, 1979–81, retired. MInstD. FRSA. *Address:* c/o Barclays Bank, 1 Manvers Street, Bath, Avon. *Clubs:* Combe Grove Manor Country, Bath and County (Bath).

WILLIS, Norman David; General Secretary, Trades Union Congress, since 1984; *b* 21 Jan. 1933; *s* of Victor J. M. and Kate E. Willis; *m* 1963, Maureen Kenning; one *s* one *d*. *Educ:* Ashford County Grammar Sch.; Ruskin and Oriel Colls, Oxford, 1955–59 (Hon. Fellow, Oriel Coll., 1984). Employed by TGWU, 1949; Nat. Service, 1951–53; PA to Gen. Sec., TGWU, 1959–70; Nat. Sec., Research and Educn, TGWU, 1970–74; TUC: Asst Gen. Sec., 1974–77, Dep. Gen. Sec., 1977–84. Councillor (Lab) Staines UDC, 1971–74. Member: NEDC, 1984–; Council, ODI, 1985–; Council, Motability, 1985–; Chm., Nat. Pensioners' Convention Steering Cttee, 1979–; Vice-President: IMS, 1985–; ICFTU, 1984–; WEA, 1985–; Trades Union Adv. Cttee to OECD, 1986–; Pres., ETUC, 1991– (Vice-Pres., 1984–91). Member: Exec. Bd, UNICEF, 1986–90; Council for Charitable Support, 1988–; Trustee: Duke of Edinburgh's Commonwealth Study Conf., 1986–; Anglo-German Foundn for the Study of Industrial Soc., 1986–; Council, Prince of Wales Youth Business Trust, 1986–; Patron, West Indian Welfare (UK) Trust, 1986–. Vice-Pres., Poetry Soc. Hon. Mem., Writers' Guild of GB. *Recreations:* painting, poetry, natural history, architecture, canals. *Address:* TUC, Congress House, Great Russell Street, WC1B 3LS.

WILLIS, (Robert William) Gaspard, MA; Founder and Headmaster of Copford Glebe School, 1958–69, Principal, 1969–72, retired; *b* 22 Nov. 1905; *s* of Rev. W. N. Willis, founder and Headmaster for 38 years of Ascham St Vincent's, Eastbourne, and Sophia Caroline Baker; *m* 1930, Ernestine Ruth Kimber; two *s* two *d*. *Educ:* Ascham St Vincent's, Eastbourne; Eton Coll. (Foundation Scholar); Corpus Christi Coll., Cambridge (Scholar). Assistant Master at Malvern Coll., Worcs, 1927–39 (Mathematics and Classics); Senior Mathematical Master at The King's School, Macclesfield, Cheshire, 1939–41; Headmaster of Sir William Turner's School (Coatham School), Redcar, 1941–53; Headmaster of English High School for Boys, Istanbul, Turkey, 1953–57. Hon. Fellow, Huguenot Soc. of London. Hon. Life Mem., Gainsborough's House Soc., Sudbury. Reader, 1935–. *Publication:* A Centenary History of Ascham 1889–1989, 1989. *Recreation:* golf. *Address:* 8 Links View, Newton Green, Sudbury, Suffolk CO10 0QT. *T:* Sudbury (0787) 72522. *Clubs:* Royal Over-Seas League; Newton Green Golf.

WILLIS, His Honour Roger Blenkiron, TD; a Circuit Judge (formerly County Court Judge), 1959–81; *b* 22 June 1906; *s* of late William Outhwaite Willis, KC, and Margaret Alice (*née* Blenkiron); *m* 1933, Joan Eleanor Amy Good (*d* 1990); two *d*. *Educ:* Charterhouse School; Emmanuel Coll., Cambridge. Barrister, Inner Temple, Nov. 1930. Joined Middlesex Yeomanry (TA), 1938. Served War of 1939–45. *Address:* 18 Turners Reach House, 9 Chelsea Embankment, SW3. *Clubs:* Garrick, MCC.

WILLIS, Stephen Murrell; His Honour Judge Willis; a Circuit Judge, since 1986; *b* 21 June 1929; *s* of late John Henry Willis and late Eileen Marian (*née* Heard), Hadleigh, Suffolk; *m* 1st, 1953, Jean Irene Eve; one *s* three *d*; 2nd, 1975, Doris Florence Davies (*née* Redding); two step *d*. *Educ:* (chorister) Christ Church Cathedral, Oxford; Bloxham Sch. (scholar). Admitted solicitor, 1955; Partner: Chamberlin Talbot & Bracey, Lowestoft and Beccles, Suffolk, 1955–63; Pearless, de Rougemont & Co., East Grinstead, Sussex, 1964–85; a Recorder, 1980–85. Founded The Suffolk Singers, 1960; Founder and Director, The Prodigal Singers and Gallery Band, 1964–. *Compositions:* mediaeval song settings for radio and theatre plays. *Recording:* (with The Prodigal Singers) Christmas Tree Carols. *Recreations:* performing early music, sailing, travel. *Address:* The Law Courts, Altyre Road, Croydon CR9 5AB. *Club:* Noblemen and Gentlemen's Catch.

WILLIS, Ted; *see* Willis, Baron.

WILLISON, Lt-Gen. Sir David (John), KCB 1973; OBE 1958; MC 1945; Chief Royal Engineer, 1977–82; Consultant, County Natwest Investment Bank, since 1985; President, Western Area, Hampshire, St John's Ambulance, since 1987; Chairman, Royal Engineers Widows Society, since 1987; *b* 25 Dec. 1919; *s* of Brig. A. C. Willison, DSO, MC; *m* 1941, Betty Vernon Bates (*d* 1989); one *s* two *d*. *Educ:* Wellington; RMA Woolwich. 2/Lt RE, 1939; OC 17 and 246 Field Cos, 1944–45; Staff Coll., Camberley 1945; Brigade Major, Indian Inf. Brigade, Java, 1946; Malaya, 1947; WO, 1948–50; OC 16 Field Co., Egypt, 1950–52; GHQ MELF, 1952–53; OC, RE Troops, Berlin, 1953–55; Directing Staff, Staff Coll., Camberley, 1955–58; AQMG (Ops), HQ British Forces Aden, 1958–60; CO, 38 Engr Regt, 1960–63; Col GS MI/DI4, MoD, 1963–66; idc 1966; BGS (Intell.), MoD, 1967–70; BGS (Intell. and Security)/ACOS, G2, HQ NORTHAG, 1970–71; Dir of Service Intelligence, MoD, 1971–72; Dep. Chief Defence Staff (Int.), 1972–75; Dir Gen. of Intelligence, MoD, 1975–78. Col Comdt RE, 1973–82. Consultant on Internat. Affairs, Nat. Westminster Bank Gp, 1980–84. Freeman, City of London, 1981. *Recreations:* sailing, shooting. *Address:* Long Barton, Lower Pennington Lane, Lymington, Hampshire. *Clubs:* Naval and Military; Royal Lymington Yacht.

WILLISON, Sir John (Alexander), Kt 1970; OBE 1964; QPM 1968; DL; *b* 3 Jan. 1914; *s* of John Willison Gow Willison and Mabel Willison, Dalry, Ayrshire; *m* 1947, Jess Morris Bruce. *Educ:* Sedbergh School. Joined City of London Police, 1933; served with RNVR, 1943–46; Chief Constable: Berwick, Roxburgh and Selkirk, 1952–58; Worcestershire Constabulary, 1958–67; West Mercia Constabulary, 1967–74. DL Worcs 1968. KStJ 1973. *Address:* Ravenhills Green, Lulsley, near Worcester.

WILLMAN, John; writer and journalist; *b* 27 May 1949; *s* of John Willman and Kate Willman (*née* Thornton); *m* 1978, Margaret Shanahan; one *s* two *d*. *Educ:* Bolton Sch.; Jesus Coll., Cambridge (MA); Westminster Coll., Oxford (CertEd). Teacher, Brentford Sch. for Girls, Brentford, Mddx, 1972–76; Financial Researcher, Money Which?, 1976–79; Editor, Taxes and Assessment (Inland Revenue Staff Fedn pubn), 1979–83; Pubns Manager, Peat, Marwick, Mitchell & Co., 1983–85; Gen. Sec., Fabian Soc., 1985–89; Jt Editor, New Socialist, 1989; Editor, Consumer Policy Review. *Publications:* Make Your Will, 1989; Labour's Electoral Challenge, 1989; Sorting Out Someone's Will, 1990; The Which? Guide to Planning and Conservation, 1990; Lloyds Bank Tax Guide, 1991; Work for Yourself, 1991; contributor to books on finance, economics and taxation; numerous articles. *Recreation:* rethinking socialism. *Address:* 33 Reservoir Road, SE4 2NU. *T:* 071–639 3845, *Fax:* 071–277 7615.

WILLMER, Prof. (Edward) Nevill, ScD; FRS 1960; Emeritus Professor of Histology, University of Cambridge, since 1969; Fellow of Clare College since 1936; *b* 15 Aug. 1902; 5th *s* of Arthur W. Willmer, Birkenhead; *m* 1939, Henrietta Noreen (Penny), 2nd *d* of H. Napier Rowlatt; two *s* two *d*. *Educ:* Birkenhead Sch.; Corpus Christi Coll., Oxford (Hon. Fellow, 1983). BA (Oxon) 1924; MA (Oxon) 1965; MSc (Manchester) 1927; ScD (Cambridge) 1944. Demonstrator and Assistant Lecturer in Physiology, Manchester, 1924–29; Lecturer in Histology, Cambridge, 1930–48; Reader, 1948–65, Prof., 1966–69. Editor, Biological Reviews, 1969–80. *Publications:* Tissue Culture, 1934; Retinal Structure and Colour Vision, 1946; Cytology and Evolution, 1960, 2nd edn 1970; (ed) Cells and Tissues in Culture, vols 1 and 2, 1965, vol. 3, 1966; Old Grantchester, 1976; The River Cam, 1979; Waen and the Willmers, 1988; contrib. physiological and biological journals. *Recreations:* painting, gardening, walking. *Address:* Yew Garth, Grantchester, Cambridge CB3 9ND. *T:* Cambridge (0223) 840360.
See also B. J. Davenport.

WILLMER, John Franklin, QC 1967; *b* 30 May 1930; *s* of Rt Hon. Sir (Henry) Gordon Willmer, OBE, TD and of Barbara, *d* of Sir Archibald Hurd; *m* 1st, 1958, Nicola Ann Dickinson (marr. diss. 1979); one *s* three *d*; 2nd, 1979, Margaret Lilian, *d* of Chester B. Berryman. *Educ:* Winchester; Corpus Christi Coll., Oxford. National Service, 2nd Lieut, Cheshire Regt, 1949–50; TA Cheshire Regt, 1950–51; Middlesex Regt, 1951–57 (Captain). Called to Bar, Inner Temple, 1955, Bencher, 1975. A Gen. Comr of Income Tax for Inner Temple, 1982. Member: panel of Lloyd's Arbitrators in Salvage Cases, 1967; panel from which Wreck Commissioners appointed, 1967–79, reapptd 1987–. *Recreation:* walking. *Address:* Flat 4, 23 Lymington Road, NW6 1HZ. *T:* 071–435 9245. *Club:* United Oxford & Cambridge University.

WILLMER, Nevill; *see* Willmer, E. N.

WILLMORE, Prof. (Albert) Peter, FRAS; Professor of Space Research, University of Birmingham, since 1972; *b* 28 April 1930; *s* of Albert Mervyn Willmore and Kathleen Helen Willmore; *m* 1st, 1963, Geraldine Anne Smith; two *s*; 2nd, 1972, Stephanie Ruth Alden; one *s* one *d*. *Educ:* Holloway Sch.; University Coll. London (BSc, PhD). Research interests: fusion res., AERE, 1954–57; upper atmosphere, using sounding rockets and satellites, esp. Ariel I (launched 1962), UCL, 1957–70; X-ray astromony, using sounding rockets and satellites, UCL, 1970–72, Univ. of Birmingham, 1972–. Tsiolkowski Medal, USSR, 1987. *Publications:* approx. 100 papers in learned jls, together with many other articles and reviews. *Recreations:* music, playing the violin (though this may not be music), literature, Bronze Age history, travel, sailing. *Address:* 38 Grove Avenue, Moseley, Birmingham B13 9RY. *T:* 021–449 2616.

WILLMOTT, Dennis James, CBE 1988; QFSM 1981; Group Contingency Manager, Avon Rubber plc, since 1988; *b* 10 July 1932; *s* of James Arthur Willmott and Esther Winifred Maude Willmott (*née* Styles); *m* 1958, Mary Patricia Currey; three *s*. *Educ:* St Albans County Grammar School. MIFireE. Regular Army Service, East Surrey Regt, 1950–51, Royal Norfolk Regt, 1951–57. London, Bucks, Hants and Isle of Wight Fire Brigades, 1957–74; Dep. Chief Officer, Wilts Fire Brigade, 1974–76; Chief Staff Officer, 1976–81, Dep. Chief Officer, 1981–83, London Fire Brigade; Chief Fire Officer, Merseyside Fire Brigade, 1983–88. Mem., Kennet DC. Mem., Wilts Archaeol and Nat. Hist. Soc. *Recreation:* walking. *Address:* 27 Highlands, Potterne, Devizes, Wilts SN10 5NS. *T:* Devizes (0380) 725672. *Clubs:* Conservative (Devizes); Royal British Legion (Potterne).

WILLMOTT, Maj.-Gen. Edward George, CB 1990; OBE 1979; CEng, FICE; Chief Executive, Construction Industry Training Board, since 1991; *b* 18 Feb. 1936; *s* of late T. E. Willmott and E. R. Willmott (*née* Murphy); *m* 1960, Sally Penelope (*née* Banyard); two *s* one *d*. *Educ:* Gonville and Caius Coll., Cambridge (MA). FICE 1989; CEng 1990. Commissioned RE 1956; psc 1968; active service, N Borneo 1963, N Ireland 1971, 1972, 1977; comd 8 Field Sqdn, 1971–73; 23 Engr Regt, 1976; 2 Armd Div. Engr Regt, 1977–78; 30 Engr Bde, 1981–82; RCDS 1983; Dep. Comdt RMCS, 1984–85; Vice-Pres. (Army), Ordnance Bd, 1985–86; Pres., Ordnance Bd, 1986–88; Dir Gen., Weapons (Army), 1988–90. Col Comdt, RE, 1987–. Pres., Instn of Royal Engrs, 1987–90. *Recreations:* sailing, gardening. *Address:* c/o Lloyds Bank plc, 125 Colmore Row, Birmingham. *Club:* Institute of Directors.

WILLMOTT, Prof. John Charles, CBE 1983; PhD; Professor of Physics, University of Manchester, 1964–89 (Director of the Physical Laboratories, 1967–89; a Pro-Vice-Chancellor, 1982–85; Adviser to Vice-Chancellor on Research Exploitation, since 1988); *b* 1 April 1922; *s* of Arthur George Willmott and Annie Elizabeth Willmott; *m* 1952, Sheila Madeleine Dumbell; two *s* one *d*. *Educ:* Bancroft's Sch., Woodford; Imperial Coll. of Science and Technol. (BSc, PhD). ARCS. Lectr in Physics, Liverpool Univ., 1948–58, Sen. Lectr, 1958–63, Reader, 1963–64. Member: SERC (formerly SRC), 1978–82; Science for Stability Cttee, NATO, 1987–. *Publications:* Tables of Coefficients for the Analysis of Triple Angular Correlations of Gamma-rays from Aligned Nuclei, 1968; Atomic Physics, 1975; articles on nuclear structure in learned jls. *Address:* 37 Hall Moss Lane, Bramhall, Cheshire SK7 1RB. *T:* 061–439 4169.

WILLMOTT, Peter; Senior Fellow, Policy Studies Institute, since 1983; Visiting Fellow, Department of Social Studies and Administration, London School of Economics, since 1988 (Visiting Professor of Social Policy and Administration, 1983–88); Hon. Research Fellow, Bartlett School of Architecture and Planning, University College London, since 1983; *b* 18 Sept. 1923; *s* of Benjamin Merriman Willmott and Dorothy Willmott (*née* Waymouth); *m* 1948, Phyllis Mary Noble; two *s*. *Educ:* Tollington Sch., London; Ruskin Coll., Oxford. BSc (Soc) (external) London. Research Asst, Labour Party, 1948–54; Institute of Community Studies: Res. Officer, 1954–60; Dep. Dir, 1960–64; Co-Dir, 1964–78; Chm., 1978–. Dir, Centre for Environmental Studies, 1978–80; Head of Central Policy Unit, GLC, 1981–83; Vis. Prof., Bartlett Sch. of Architecture and Planning, UCL, 1972–83. Vis. Prof., Ecole Pratique des Hautes Etudes, Paris, 1972; Regents' Lectr, Univ. of California, 1982. Hon. LitD Univ. of Orleans, 1990. Editor, Policy Studies, 1988–. *Publications:* (with Michael Young) Family and Kinship in East London, 1957; (with Michael Young) Family and Class in a London Suburb, 1960; The Evolution of a Community, 1963; Adolescent Boys of East London, 1966; (with Michael Young) The Symmetrical Family, 1973; (ed) Sharing Inflation? Poverty Report, 1976; (with Graeme Shankland and David Jordan) Inner London: policies for dispersal and balance, 1977; (with Charles Madge) Inner City Poverty in Paris and London, 1981; (with Roger Mitton and Phyllis Willmott) Unemployment, Poverty and Social Policy in Europe, 1983; Community in Social Policy, 1984; Social Networks, Informal Care and Public Policy, 1986; Friendship Networks and Social Support, 1987; (with Alan Murie) Polarisation and Social Housing, 1988; Community Initiatives: patterns and prospects, 1989. *Address:* 27 Kingsley Place, N6 5EA. *T:* 081–348 3958.

WILLOCHRA, Bishop of, since 1987; **Rt. Rev. William David Hair McCall;** *b* 29 Feb. 1940; *s* of late Rt Rev. Theodore Bruce McCall, ThD, Bishop of Wangaratta, and Helen Christie McCall; *m* 1969, Marion Carmel le Breton; two *s* three *d*. *Educ:* Launceston and Sydney Grammar Schools; Saint Michael's House, Crafers. Deacon 1963, priest 1964, dio. Riverina; Assistant Curate: St Alban's, Griffith, 1963–64; St Peter's, Broken Hill, 1965–67; Priest-in-charge, Barellan-Weethalle, 1967–73; Rector: St John's, Corowa, 1973–78; St George's, Goodwood, 1978–87; Pastoral Chaplain, St Barnabas' Theol Coll., 1980–87. *Recreations:* reading, walking. *Address:* Bishop's House, Gladstone, SA 5473, Australia. *T:* (086) 622057.

WILLOTT, Brian; *see* Willott, W. B.

WILLOTT, (William) Brian, PhD; Head of Financial Services Division, Department of Trade and Industry, since 1987; *b* 14 May 1940; *s* of Dr William Harford Willott and Dr Beryl P. M. Willott; *m* 1970, Alison Leyland Pyke-Lees; two *s* two *d*. *Educ:* Trinity Coll., Cambridge (MA, PhD). Research Associate, Univ. of Maryland, USA, 1965–67; Asst Principal, Board of Trade, 1967–69; Principal: BoT, 1969–73; HM Treasury, 1973–75; Asst Sec., Dept of Industry, 1975–78; Secretary: Industrial Development Unit, DoI, 1978–80; NEB, 1980–81; Chief Exec., British Technology Gp (NEB and NRDC), 1981–84; Head of IT Div., DTI, 1984–87. *Recreations:* music, reading, ancient history, gardening. *Address:* Department of Trade and Industry, 10–18 Victoria Street, SW1.

WILLOUGHBY, family name of **Baron Middleton.**

WILLOUGHBY DE BROKE, 21st Baron *cr* 1491; **Leopold David Verney;** *b* 14 Sept. 1938; *s* of 20th Baron Willoughby de Broke, MC, AFC, AE and Rachel (*d* 1991), *d* of Sir Bourchier Wrey, 11th Bt; *S* father, 1986; *m* 1965, Petra, 2nd *d* of Sir John Aird, 3rd Bt, MVO, MC; three *s*. *Educ:* Le Rosey; New College, Oxford. *Heir:* *s* Hon. Rupert Greville Verney, *b* 4 March 1966. *Address:* Ditchford Farm, Moreton-in-Marsh, Glos.

WILLOUGHBY DE ERESBY, Baroness (27th in line), *cr* 1313; **Nancy Jane Marie Heathcote-Drummond-Willoughby;** *b* 1 Dec. 1934; *d* of 3rd Earl of Ancaster, KCVO, TD, and Hon. Nancy Phyllis Louise Astor (*d* 1975), *d* of 2nd Viscount Astor; *S* to barony of father, 1983. *Heir:* *co-heiresses:* Lady Catherine Mary Clementina Hume [*b* 25 Sept. 1906; *m* 1st, 1935, John St Maur Ramsden (marr. diss. 1947), *s* of Sir John Frecheville Ramsden 6th Bt; one *d*; 2nd, 1948, Charles Wedderburn Hume (*d* 1974)]; Lady Priscilla Aird [*b* 29 Oct. 1909; *m* 1939, Col Sir John Renton Aird, 3rd Bt, MVO, MC; one *s* three *d*]. *Address:* Grimsthorpe, Bourne, Lincs PE10 0LZ. *T:* Edenham (077832) 222.

WILLOUGHBY, Ven. David Albert; Archdeacon of the Isle of Man, since 1982; Vicar of St George's with All Saints, Douglas, since 1980; *b* 8 Feb. 1931; *s* of John Robert and Jane May Willoughby; *m* 1959, Brenda Mary (*née* Watson); two *s*. *Educ:* Bradford Grammar School; St John's Coll., Univ. of Durham (BA, Dip. Theol.). Assistant Curate: St Peter's, Shipley, 1957–60; Barnoldswick with Bracewell, 1960–62; Rector of St Chad's, New Moston, Manchester, 1962–72; Vicar of Marown, Isle of Man, 1972–80; Rural Dean of Douglas, 1980–82. Chaplain, Noble's Hospital, Douglas, 1980–; Mem. Gen. Synod, 1982–; Church Commissioner for IOM, 1982–. *Recreations:* motor cycling, competition singing and involvement in light entertainment. *Address:* St George's with All Saints Vicarage, 16 Devonshire Road, Douglas, Isle of Man. *T:* Douglas (0624) 675430.

WILLOUGHBY, Kenneth James; *b* 6 Nov. 1922; *y s* of late Frank Albert Willoughby and late Florence Rose (*née* Darbyshire); *m* 1943, Vera May Dickerson; one *s* one *d*. *Educ:* Hackney Downs (Grocers') Sch.; Selwyn Coll., Cambridge. Tax Officer, Inland Revenue, 1939; Royal Engineers, UK, Egypt, Italy, Austria, Greece, 1941–47 (despatches, Captain); Asst Auditor, Exchequer and Audit Dept, 1947; Asst Prin., Min. of Civil Aviation, 1949; Asst Private Sec. to Minister of Civil Aviation, 1950; Private Sec. to Perm. Sec., 1951; Principal, Min. of Transport (and later, Civil Aviation), 1951; Sec., Air Transport Adv.

Council, 1957–61; Asst Sec., Min. of Aviation, 1962; Under-Secretary: Min. of Technology, 1968–70; DTI, 1970–74. *Recreations:* gardening, music, reading. *Address:* 84 Douglas Avenue, Exmouth, Devon EX8 2HG. *T:* Exmouth (0395) 271175.

WILLOUGHBY, Rt. Rev. Noel Vincent; *see* Cashel and Ossory, Bishop of.

WILLOUGHBY, Roger James; Clerk of Private Bills, House of Commons, since 1988; *b* 30 Sept. 1939; *s* of late Hugh Lloyd Willoughby and Gerd Willoughby; *m* 1970, Veronica, *d* of Frank and Elisabeth Lepper. *Educ:* Shrewsbury Sch.; Balliol Coll., Oxford (BA). A Clerk in the House of Commons, 1962–; Dep. Principal Clerk, 1975; Sec. to UK Delegn to European Parlt, 1976; Clerk of Home Affairs Cttee, 1979; Clerk of Supply, Public Bill Office, 1984. *Recreations:* literature, cricket, walking in solitary places, bonfires. *Address:* 35 Defoe Avenue, Kew, Richmond, Surrey TW9 4DS. *T:* 081–876 1718.

WILLS, family name of **Baron Dulverton.**

WILLS, Arthur William, OBE 1990; DMus (Dunelm), FRCO (CHM), ADCM; composer; Organist, Ely Cathedral, 1958–90; *b* 19 Sept. 1926; *s* of Violet Elizabeth and Archibald Wills; *m* 1953, Mary Elizabeth Titterton; one *s* one *d. Educ:* St John's Sch., Coventry. Sub. Organist, Ely Cathedral, 1949; Director of Music, King's School, Ely, 1953–65; Prof., Royal Academy of Music, 1964. Mem. Council, RCO, 1966–; Examr to Royal Schs of Music, 1966–. Recital tours in Canada, Europe, USA, Australia and New Zealand; recording artist. Hon. RAM, Hon. FLCM, FRSCM. *Publications:* (contrib.) English Church Music, 1978; Organ, 1984; numerous musical compositions include: *organ:* Sonata, Trio Sonata, Christmas Meditations, Prelude and Fugue (Alkmaar), Tongues of Fire, Variations on Amazing Grace, Symphonia Eliensis, Concerto (organ, strings and timpani), The Fenlands (symphonic suite for brass band and organ), Etheldreda Rag (organ or piano); *brass band:* Overture: A Muse of Fire; *guitar:* Sonata, Pavane and Galliard, Hommage à Ravel, Four Elizabethan Love Songs (alto and guitar), Moods and Diversions, The Year of the Tiger, Suite Africana, Concerto Lirico for Guitar Quartet; Concerto for guitar and organ; *chamber:* Sacrae Symphoniae: Veni Creator Spiritus; *piano:* Sonata; *choral:* Missa Eliensis, The Child for Today (carol sequence), The Light Invisible (double choir, organ and percussion), Missa in Memoriam Benjamin Britten, An English Requiem, Jerusalem Luminosa (choir and organ), Ely (part-song for treble voices), Caedmon: a children's cantata; *vocal:* When the Spirit Comes (four poems of Emily Brontë), The Dark Lady (eight Shakespeare Sonnets); *opera:* '1984'; *orchestra:* Symphony No 1 in A minor. *Recreations:* travel, antique collecting, Eastern philosophy. *Address:* 26 New Barns Road, Ely, Cambs CB7 4PN. *T:* Ely (0353) 662084.

WILLS, Brian Alan, PhD; FPS, CChem, FRSC; Chief Pharmacist, Department of Health (formerly of Health and Social Security), 1978–89, retired; *b* 17 Feb. 1927; *s* of late William Wills and Emily (*née* Hibbert); *m* 1955, Barbara Joan Oggelsby; one *d. Educ:* Univ. of Nottingham (BPharm); PhD (London). FPS 1972 (MPS 1949); FRSC (FRIC 1967, ARIC 1957); CChem 1975. Lecturer in Pharmaceutics, Sch. of Pharmacy, Univ. of London, 1951–57; Head of Research and Control Dept, Allen & Hanburys (Africa) Ltd, Durban, S Africa, 1957–62; Head of Control Div., Allen & Hanburys Ltd, London, E2, 1962–78. Member: British Pharmacopoeia Commn, 1973–; UK delegn to European Pharmacopoeia Commn, 1975–; UK delegn to Council of Europe Public Health Cttee (Partial Agreement) on Pharmaceutical Questions, 1979–89; WHO Expert Adv. Panel on Internat. Pharmacopoeia and Pharmaceutical Preparations, 1979–89. Vis. Professor: Univ. of Bath, 1979–83; Univ. of Bradford, 1984–. Member: Jt Formulary Cttee for British Nat. Formulary, 1979–89; Pharmacy Working Party, Nat. Adv. Body for Local Authy Higher Educn, 1982–89; Bd of Studies in Pharmacy, London Univ., 1979–87; Council, Sch. of Pharmacy, London Univ., 1981–89. Hon. Auditor, RPSGB, 1990–. Mem. Ct of Assts, Soc. of Apothecaries of London, 1987–. *Publications:* papers on sterilisation and disinfection and on the preservation, stability and quality control of pharmaceutical preparations. *Address:* 8 Graces Maltings, Akeman Street, Tring, Herts HP23 6DL. *T:* Tring (044282) 4217.

WILLS, Colin Spencer, FCA; Chairman, Visual Arts Office of Great Britain and Northern Ireland, since 1990; Director, Breadwinners (London) Ltd, since 1987; *b* 25 June 1937; *s* of Sir John Spencer Wills, *qv. Educ:* Eton; Queens' Coll., Cambridge (MA). FCA 1967. Qualified, 1962; worked in USA, 1963–64; Rediffusion Television, 1964–68; Dep. Gen. Man., ATV Network, Birmingham, 1968–69; employed by British Electric Traction, 1970–88 as Managing Director: Humphries Holdings plc, 1977–85; A-R Television, 1972–88; Director: Thames Television, 1970–91; Euston Films, 1972–91; Wembley Stadium, 1974–84; BAFTA, 1980–. Gov., English Nat. Ballet, 1988–. *Recreations:* music, opera, travel, country pursuits. *Address:* 12 Campden Hill Square, W8 7LB. *T:* 071–727 0534; Old Brick Farm, Burwash, East Sussex. *T:* Burwash (0435) 234. *Club:* White's.
See also N. K. S. Wills.

WILLS, Sir David; *see* Wills, Sir H. D. H.

WILLS, Sir (David) Seton, 5th Bt *cr* 1904, of Hazelwood and Clapton-in-Gordano; FRICS; *b* 29 Dec. 1939; *s* of Major George Seton Wills (*d* 1979) (*yr s* of 3rd Bt) and Lilah Mary, *y d* of Captain Percy Richard Hare; *S* uncle, 1983; *m* 1968, Gillian, twin *d* of A. P. Eastoe; one *s* three *d. Educ:* Eton. *Heir: s* James Seton Wills, *b* 24 Nov. 1970. *Address:* Eastridge House, Ramsbury, Marlborough, Wilts SN8 2HJ.

WILLS, Dean Robert, AM 1986; Chairman and Managing Director, Coca-Cola Amatil Ltd (formerly Amatil Ltd), since 1984 (Director, since 1975; Deputy Chairman, 1983–84); *b* 10 July 1933; *s* of Walter William Wills and Violet Wills (*née* Kent); *m* 1955, Margaret Florence Williams, *d* of E. G. Williams; one *s* two *d. Educ:* Sacred Heart Coll., S. Aust.; SA Inst. of Technology. AASA. Dir, 1974, Man. Dir, 1977, Chm., 1983–89, W. D. & H. O. Wills (Australia) Ltd; Chm., Australian Eagle Insurance Co., 1986–89. Member: Business Council of Aust., 1984– (Vice Pres., 1987–88, Pres., 1988–90); Bd of Aust. Graduate Sch. of Management, Univ. of NSW, 1985–. Pres., Med. Foundn, 1991–; Trustee, Mus. of Applied Arts and Sciences (Powerhouse Mus.), NSW, 1986–90. *Recreations:* tennis, classic cars. *Address:* 71 Macquarie Street, Sydney, NSW 2000, Australia. *T:* (02) 259–6666. *Clubs:* American National, Pymble Golf (Sydney).

WILLS, Helen; *see* Roark, H. W.

WILLS, Sir (Hugh) David (Hamilton), Kt 1980; CBE 1971 (MBE 1946); TD 1964; DL; *b* 19 June 1917; 2nd *s* of late Frederick Noel Hamilton Wills and of Margery Hamilton Sinclair; *m* 1949, Eva Helen, JP, *d* of late Major A. T. McMorrough Kavanagh, MC; one *s* one *d. Educ:* Eton; Magdalen Coll., Oxford. Served War of 1939–45 with Queen's Own Cameron Highlanders (TA): France 1940, Aruba 1941; GSO 3 (Ops) GHQ Home Forces, 1942–43; GSO 2 (Ops) Southern Command, 1943–44. Chairman of Trustees, Rendcomb Coll., 1955–83; Chm., Ditchley Foundation, 1972–83; Mem. Governing Body, Atlantic Coll., 1963–73, 1980–. High Sheriff Oxfordshire 1961, DL 1967. *Recreations:* fishing, sailing. *Address:* Sandford Park, Sandford St Martin, Oxford OX5 4AJ. *T:* Great Tew (060883) 238. *Clubs:* Boodle's, Ends of the Earth.

WILLS, Sir John Spencer; Kt 1969; FCIT; Chairman, British Electric Traction Co. Ltd, 1966–82 (Director, 1939–82, Managing Director, 1946–73, Deputy Chairman, 1951–66); Director and Chairman: National Electric Construction Co. Ltd, since 1945; Birmingham and District Investment Trust Ltd, since 1946; Electrical & Industrial Investment Co. Ltd, since 1946; *b* 10 Aug. 1904; *s* of Cedric Spencer Wills and Cécile Charlotte; *m* 1936, Elizabeth Drusilla Alice Clare Garcke; two *s. Educ:* Cleobury Mortimer Coll., Shropshire; Merchant Taylors' Sch., London. Asst to Secs, British Traction Co. Ltd and British Automobile Traction Ltd, 1922–23; Sec., Wrexham and Dist Transport Co. Ltd, 1924–26; Gen. Manager, E Yorks Motor Services Ltd, 1926–31, Dir and Chm., 1931–65; Chm., Birmingham & Midland Motor Omnibus Co. Ltd, 1946–68; Dir, 1947–73, Dep. Chm., 1953–71, Monotype Corp. Ltd; Man. Dir, 1947–67, Chm., 1947–78, Broadcast Relay Service Ltd, later Rediffusion Ltd; Chm., Associated-Rediffusion Ltd, later Rediffusion Television Ltd, 1954–78; Director and Chairman: E Midland Motor Services Ltd, 1931–44; Yorks Woollen Dist Transport Co. Ltd, 1931–43; Hebble Motor Services Ltd, 1932–45; Yorks Traction Co. Ltd, 1932–46; Mexborough & Swinton Traction Co. Ltd, 1933–47; Western Welsh Omnibus Co. Ltd, 1933–60; Crosville Motor Services Ltd, 1933–41; Ribble Motor Services Ltd, 1942–47; N Western Road Car Co. Ltd, 1943–45; S Wales Transport Co. Ltd, Swansea Improvements & Tramways Co. Ltd, 1943–46; Devon Gen. Omnibus and Touring Co. Ltd, 1946–47; Man. Dir, British and Foreign Aviation Ltd and Great Western and Southern Air Lines Ltd, 1938–42; Director: Olley Air Service Ltd, Channel Air Ferries Ltd, West Coast Air Services Ltd, Air Booking Co. Ltd, 1938–42; Air Commerce Ltd, 1939–42; Yorks Electric Power Co., 1942–48; Wembley Stadium Ltd, 1960–82 (Chm., 1965–82). Chm., Hull and Grimsby Sect., Incorp. Secs' Assoc. (now CIS), 1929–31; Member of Council: BET Fedn, 1933 (Pres., 1946–79); Public Road Transport Assoc. (formerly Public Transport Assoc.), 1943–68 (Chm., 1945–46; Hon. Mem., 1969), subseq. Confedn of British Road Passenger Transport Ltd (Hon. Mem., 1975); FCIT (Henry Spurrier Meml Lectr, 1946, Pres., 1950–51); Chairman: Omnibus Owners' Assoc., 1943–44; Nat. Council for Omnibus Industry, 1944–45 (Mem. 1940–66); Standing Cttee, Air Transport Sect., London Chamber of Commerce, 1953–65 (Mem. 1943; Dep. Chm. 1949). Governor, Royal Shakespeare Theatre, Stratford upon Avon, 1946–74; Mem. Council, Royal Opera House Soc., 1962–74; Trustee, LSO Trust, 1962–68; Vice-Patron, Theatre Royal Windsor Trust, 1965–. Member, UK Council, European Movement, 1966–. *Recreations:* complete idleness; formerly: flying, swimming, ski-ing, tennis, riding, shooting; continued occupations: forestry and farming. *Address:* Beech Farm, Battle, East Sussex. *T:* Battle (04246) 2950. *Clubs:* Naval and Military, East India, Devonshire, Sports, and Public Schools.
See also C. S. Wills, N. K. S. Wills.

WILLS, Sir John Vernon, 4th Bt, *cr* 1923; TD; FRICS; JP; Lord-Lieutenant and Custos Rotulorum of Avon, since 1974; Chairman: Bristol and West Building Society, since 1988 (Director, since 1969, Vice-Chairman, since 1982); Bristol Waterworks Co., since 1986 (Director, 1964–73; Deputy Chairman, 1983–86); Director, Bristol Evening Post, since 1973 (Deputy Chairman, since 1978); Deputy Chairman, Bristol United Press, since 1980; *b* 3 July 1928; *s* of Sir George Vernon Proctor Wills, 2nd Bt, and Lady Nellie Jeannie, ARRC, JP, *y d* of late J. T. Rutherford, Abergavenny; *S* brother 1945; *m* 1953, Diana Veronica Cecil (Jane), *o d* of Douglas R. M. Baker, Winsford, Somerset; four *s. Educ:* Eton. Served Coldstream Guards, 1946–49; Lt-Col Comdg N Somerset and Bristol Yeomanry, 1965–67; Bt Col 1967; now TARO. Hon. Col, 37th (Wessex and Welsh) Signal Regt, T&AVR, 1975–87; Hon. Capt., RNR, 1988. Chm., Wessex Water Auth., 1973–82; Mem., Nat. Water Council, 1973–82; Chm., Bristol Marketing Bd, 1984–86. Local Dir, Barclays Bank, 1981–87. Pro-Chancellor, Univ. of Bath, 1979–. Pres., Royal Bath and West Southern Counties Soc., 1980. Member of Somerset CC. JP 1962, DL 1968, High Sheriff, 1968, Somerset. KStJ 1978. Hon. LLD Bristol, 1986. *Heir: s* David James Vernon Wills, *b* 2 Jan. 1955. *Address:* Langford Court, near Bristol, Avon BS18 7DA. *T:* Wrington (0934) 862338. *Club:* Cavalry and Guards.

WILLS, Nicholas Kenneth Spencer, FCA; Chairman, BET plc, since 1991 (Managing Director, 1982–91; Chief Executive, 1985–91); *b* 18 May 1941; *s* of Sir John Spencer Wills, *qv*; *m* 1st, 1973, Hilary Ann (marr. diss. 1983), *d* of N. C. Flood; two *s* two *d*; 2nd, 1985, Philippa Trench Casson, *d* of Rev. D. Casson; one *d. Educ:* Rugby Sch.; Queens' Coll., Cambridge (MA; Hon. Fellow, 1990). Binder Hamlyn & Co., 1963–67; Morgan Grenfell, 1967–70; Managing Director: Birmingham & Dist Investment Trust, 1970–91; Electrical & Industrial Investment, 1970–91; National Electric Construction, 1971–91; Chairman: Argus Press Hldgs, 1974–83; Electrical Press, 1974–83; Boulton & Paul plc, 1979–84; Initial plc, 1979–87; BET Building Services Ltd, 1984–87; Director: BET plc, 1975–; Bradbury, Agnew & Co. Ltd, 1974–83; National Mutual Life Assce Soc., 1974–85; St George Assce Co. Ltd, 1974–81; Colonial Securities Trust Co. Ltd, 1976–82; Cable Trust Ltd, 1976–77; Globe Investment Trust plc, 1977–90; Drayton Consolidated, 1982–; American Chamber of Commerce (UK), 1985– (Vice-Pres., 1988–); United World Colls (Internat.) Ltd, 1987–; Advr, City and West End, National Westminster Bank, 1982–91; Adv. Bd, Charterhouse Buy-Out Funds, 1990–. Member: Council, CBI, 1987– (Member: Overseas Cttee, 1987–90; Public Expenditure Task Force, 1988; Economic and Financial Policy Cttee, 1991–); Council, Business in the Community, 1987–; Adv. Bd, Fishman-Davidson Center for Study of Service Sector, Wharton Sch., Univ. of Pennsylvania, 1988–. Mem. Adv. Council, 1988–, Hon. Treas., 1989–, Prince's Youth Business Trust; Chm., Internat. Fedn of Keystone Youth Orgns Internat. Trustees, 1990–. Treasurer and Churchwarden, Church of St Bride, Fleet Street, 1978–; Asst, Worshipful Co. of Haberdashers', 1981–. CBIM; FCIM; FCT; FRSA. *Recreations:* shooting, trying to farm in the Highlands. *Address:* Stratton House, Stratton Street, Piccadilly, W1X 6AS. *T:* 071–629 8886. *Clubs:* White's, Royal Automobile, City Livery; Clyde Cruising.
See also C. S. Wills.

WILLS, Peter Gordon Bethune, TD 1967; Chairman, Security Settlements (Options) Ltd (formerly Sheppards and Chase (Options) Ltd), since 1978; *b* 25 Oct. 1931; *s* of P. L. B. Wills and E. W. Wills (*née* Stapleton); *m* 1st, Linda Hutton; two *s* one *d*; 2nd, Faith Hines. *Educ:* Malvern Coll.; Corpus Christi Coll., Cambridge, 1952–55 (MA). National Service with Royal Inniskilling Fusiliers, N Ireland and Korea, 1950–52; TA, London Irish Rifles, 1952–67. Joined Sheppards & Co. (later Sheppards and Chase), 1955, Partner, 1960–85; Chm., Sheppards Moneybrokers Ltd, 1985–89. Member, Stock Exchange Council, 1973–87 (Dep. Chm., 1979–82; Chm., Money Brokers' Cttee, 1985–89). Director: Wills Group plc, 1969–87 (Vice Chm.); BAII Holding, 1986–89; The Securities Assoc., 1986–89; London Clear, 1987–89. *Recreations:* collecting mangles. *Address:* 54 Frant Road, Tunbridge Wells, Kent TN2 5LJ. *Club:* Brooks's.

WILLS, Sir Seton; *see* Wills, Sir D. S.

WILLSON, Douglas James, CBE 1953; TD; *b* 30 Oct. 1906; *s* of late Ernest Victor Willson and late Mary Willson; *m* 1942, Morna Josephine, *d* of Stanley Hine; one *d. Educ:* Bishop's Stortford Coll., Herts. Admitted Solicitor, 1928; joined Customs and Excise, 1928. Served War, 1939–45, Lieut-Colonel, RA. Solicitor for Bd of Customs and Excise,

1963–71. *Publications:* Titles Purchase Tax and Excise in Halsbury's Encyclopædia of Laws of England, 3rd edn; Willson & Mainprice on Value Added Tax. *Recreations:* gardening and bird watching. *Address:* Dove Cottage, West Farleigh, Kent. *T:* Maidstone (0622) 812203.

WILLSON, Prof. (Francis Michael) Glenn; Vice-Chancellor, 1978–84, Emeritus Professor, since 1985, Murdoch University, Western Australia; Visiting Professor, University of California, Santa Cruz, since 1985; *b* 29 Sept. 1924; *s* of late Christopher Glenn Willson and late Elsie Katrine (*née* Mattick); *m* 1945, Jean (*née* Carlyle); two *d*. *Educ:* Carlisle Grammar Sch.; Manchester Univ. (BA Admin); Balliol and Nuffield Colls Oxford (DPhil, MA). Merchant Navy, 1941–42; RAF, 1943–46; BOAC 1946–47. Research Officer, Royal Inst. of Public Admin, 1953–60; Res. Fellow, Nuffield Coll., Oxford, 1955–60; Lectr in Politics, St Edmund Hall, Oxford, 1958–60; Prof. of Govt, UC Rhodesia and Nyasaland, 1960–64; Dean, Faculty of Social Studies, UC Rhodesia and Nyasaland, 1962–64; Univ. of California, Santa Cruz: Prof. of Govt/Politics, 1965–74; Provost of Stevenson Coll., 1967–74; Vice-Chancellor, College and Student Affairs, 1973–74; Warden, Goldsmiths' Coll., London, 1974–75; Principal of Univ. of London, 1975–78. *Publications:* (with D.N. Chester) The Organization of British Central Government 1914–56, 2nd edn 1914–64, 1968; Administrators in Action, 1961; contrib. Public Admin, Polit. Studies, Parly Affairs, etc. *Address:* 32 Digby Mansions, Hammersmith Bridge Road, W6 9DF.

WILLSON, John Michael, CMG 1988; HM Diplomatic Service, retired; High Commissioner in Zambia, 1988–90; *b* 15 July 1931; *e s* of late Richard and Kathleen Willson; *m* 1954, Phyllis Marian Dawn, *o c* of late William and Phyllis Holman Richards, OBE; two *s* two *d*. *Educ:* Wimbledon Coll.; University Coll., Oxford (MA); Trinity Hall, Cambridge. National Service, 1949–51. HM Colonial Service, N Rhodesia, 1955–64; Min. of Overseas Development, 1965–70 (seconded to British High Commn, Malta, 1967–70); joined HM Diplomatic Service, 1970; British Consulate-General, Johannesburg, 1972–75; FCO (W Indian and N American Depts), 1975–78; Special Counsellor for African Affairs, 1978; Secretary-General, Rhodesian Independence Conf., 1979; Salisbury (on staff of Governor of Rhodesia), 1979–80; Counsellor, Bucharest, 1980–82; Ambassador to Ivory Coast, Burkina (formerly Upper Volta) and Niger, 1983–87; seconded to RCDS, 1987. Mem., Adv. Bd, Africa Business and Investment, 1990–. *Recreations:* gardening, photography, music. *Address:* c/o C. Hoare & Co., 37 Fleet Street, EC4P 4DQ; PO Box 3476, Halfway House, 1685, South Africa. *Club:* Commonwealth Trust.

WILMINGTON, Joseph (Robert); JP; Chairman and Managing Director, Wilmington Employment Agencies Ltd, since 1966; *b* 21 April 1932; *s* of Joseph R. Wilmington and Magtilda Susanna Wilmington; *m* Anne; two *s*. *Educ:* Alsop High Sch., Liverpool; London Sch. of Economics. Mem., Liverpool City Council, 1962; Past Chm., Liverpool Liberal Party, 1965–67; Chairman: Personnel Cttee, Liverpool City Council; Markets Cttee, Liverpool City Council; Chief Whip; Lord Mayor of Liverpool, 1974–75. Chm., NW Fedn of Employment Consultants; Mem. Nat. Exec., Fedn of Employment Consultants; Mem. Inst. Employment Consultants. JP Liverpool, 1976. *Recreations:* koi keeping, music and the arts. *Address:* Jordaan, South Drive, Sandfield Park, Liverpool L12 1LH.

WILMOT, David, QPM 1989; Chief Constable, Greater Manchester Police, since 1991; *b* 12 March 1943; *m* Ann Marilyn (*née* Dore). *Educ:* Southampton Univ. (BSc). Lancashire Constabulary, 1962; Merseyside Police, 1974; W Yorkshire Police, 1983; Deputy Chief Constable, Greater Manchester Police, 1987. *Address:* Greater Manchester Police, PO Box 22 (S West PDO), Chester House, Boyer Street, Manchester M16 0RE. *T:* 061–872 5050.

WILMOT, Sir Henry Robert, 9th Bt *cr* 1759; *b* 10 April 1967; *s* of Sir Robert Arthur Wilmot, 8th Bt, and of Juliet Elvira, *e d* of Captain M. N. Tufnell, RN; *S* father, 1974. *Heir:* *b* Charles Sacheverel Wilmot, *b* 13 Feb. 1969. *Address:* 12 Saxe-Coburg Place, Edinburgh EH3 5BR.

WILMOT, Sir John Assheton E.; *see* Eardley-Wilmot.

WILMOT, Robb; *see* Wilmot, R. W.

WILMOT, Robert William, (Robb Wilmot), CBE 1985; Chairman, Wilmot Enterprises Ltd, since 1984; Founder, 1985, and Director, European Silicon Structures, ES2; Director, Octagon Industries Ltd, since 1986; Founder and Chairman, Organisation and System Innovations Ltd, OASiS, since 1986; Founder and Director, MOVID Inc., since 1987; *b* 2 Jan. 1945; *s* of Thomas Arthur William Wilmot and Frances Mary Hull; *m* 1969, Mary Josephine Sharkey; two *s*. *Educ:* Royal Grammar Sch., Worcester; Nottingham Univ. BSc (1st cl. Hons) Electrical Engrg. Texas Instruments, 1966–81: European Technical Dir, France, 1973–74; Div. Dir, USA, 1974–78; Man. Dir, 1978–81; Asst Vice Pres., 1980; International Computers (ICL): Man. Dir, 1981–83; Chief Exec., 1983–84; Chm., 1985. Partner, Euroventures UK and Ireland Programme, 1987–; Director: Headland Gp PLC (formerly Comproft Hldgs PLC), 1987–; Alphameric PLC, 1990–; Founder and Chm., POQET Inc., 1988–. Council Mem., Centre of Business Strategy, London Business Sch., 1987–. Hon. DSc: Nottingham, 1983; City, 1984; Cranfield, 1988. *Recreations:* music, theatre, walking, vintage boats. *Address:* The White House, Bolney Road, Lower Shiplake, Henley-on-Thames, Oxon RG9 3PA. *T:* Wargrave (0734) 4252.

WILMOT-SITWELL, Peter Sacheverell; Chairman, S. G. Warburg, Akroyd, Rowe & Pitman, Mullens Securities Ltd, since 1990 (Joint Chairman, 1986–90); *b* 28 March 1935; *s* of late Robert Bradshaw Wilmot-Sitwell and Barbara Elizabeth Fisher; *m* 1960, Clare Veronica Cobbold (LVO 1991); two *s* one *d*. *Educ:* Eton Coll.; Oxford Univ., 1955–58 (BA, MA). Commnd Coldstream Guards, 1953–55. Trainee, Hambros Bank Ltd, 1958–59; Partner 1959–82, Sen. Partner 1982–86, Rowe & Pitman. Dir (non-exec.), W. H. Smith Ltd, 1987–. *Recreations:* shooting, golf, tennis. *Address:* Portman House, Dummer, near Basingstoke, Hants RG25 2AD. *Clubs:* White's, Pratt's; Swinley Forest (Ascot).

WILMOTT, Peter Graham; Director-General (Customs and Indirect Taxation), Commission of the European Communities, since 1990; *b* 6 Jan. 1947; *s* of John Joseph Wilmott and Violet Ena Wilmott; *m* 1969, Jennifer Carolyn Plummer; two *d*. *Educ:* Hove Grammar Sch.; Trinity Coll., Cambridge (MA). Asst Principal, Customs and Excise, 1968; Second Sec., UK Delegn to EEC, Brussels, 1971; Principal, Customs and Excise, 1973; First Sec., UK Perm. Rep's Office to EEC, Brussels, 1977; Asst to UK Mem., European Ct of Auditors, Luxembourg, 1980; Asst Sec., Customs and Excise, 1983; a Comr of Customs and Excise, 1988. *Recreation:* travelling in France.

WILMSHURST, Jon Barry; Under Secretary, Economic and Social Division, Overseas Development Administration, since 1990; *b* 25 Oct. 1936; *s* of Edwin and Sylvia Wilmshurst (*née* Munson); *m* 1960, June Taylor; four *d*. *Educ:* Beckenham and Penge Grammar Sch.; Manchester Univ. (BA Econ.). Statistician, Fedn of Rhodesia and Nyasaland, 1960–63; Inst. of Economic and Social Research, 1964; Statistician and Economic Adviser, ODA, 1964–71; Senior Economic Adviser: ODA, 1971–79; Dept of Transport, 1979–83; Monopolies and Mergers Commn, 1983–85; ODA, 1985–90. *Recreations:* golf, gardening. *Address:* Overseas Development Administration, 94 Victoria Street, SW1E 5JL. *Club:* Langley Park Golf.

WILMSHURST, Michael Joseph; HM Diplomatic Service, retired; *b* 14 Sept. 1934; *s* of Mr and Mrs E. J. Wilmshurst; *m* 1958, Mary Elizabeth Kemp; one *s* one *d*. *Educ:* Latymer Upper Sch.; Christ's Coll., Cambridge. BA 1959. Entered Foreign Service, 1953. 2nd Lieut, Royal Signals, 1953–55. Asst Private Sec. to Foreign Secretary, 1960–62; 2nd Sec., The Hague, 1962–65; 1st Sec. (Commercial), Bogota, 1965–67; Western European Dept, FCO, 1968–70; 1st Sec. (Commercial), Cairo, 1970–73; Asst Head of Energy Dept, FCO, 1974–75; Asst Head of Energy and Arms Control and Disarmament Depts, 1975–77; Counsellor and Head of Joint Nuclear Unit, FCO, 1977–78; Consul, Guatemala City, 1978–81; Sabbatical, Stiftung Wissenschaft und Politik, Ebenhausen, 1982; UK Permanent Rep. to IAEA, UNIDO and UN, Vienna, 1982–87; seconded to IAEA, Vienna as Dir of External Relns, 1987; retd from HM Diplomatic Service, 1989, from IAEA, 1991. *Publications:* Nuclear Non-Proliferation: can the policies of the Eighties prove more successful than those of the Seventies?, 1982; (contrib.) The International Nuclear Non-Proliferation System: challenges and choices, 1984. *Recreation:* reading. *Address:* 7 East Street, Southwold, Suffolk IP18 6EH.

WILSEY, Lt-Gen. Sir John (Finlay Willasey), KCB 1991; CBE 1985 (OBE 1982); General Officer Commanding and Director of Military Operations, Northern Ireland, since 1990; *b* 18 Feb. 1939; *s* of Maj.-Gen. John Harold Owen Wilsey, CB, CBE, DSO and of Beatrice Sarah Finlay Wilsey; *m* 1975, Elizabeth Patricia Nottingham; one *s* one *d*. *Educ:* Sherborne Sch.; RMA Sandhurst. Commissioned, Devonshire and Dorset Regt, 1959; regtl service in Cyprus, Libya, British Guyana, Germany, Malta, UK; Instructor, RMA, 1967–68; Great Abbai (Blue Nile) Expedition, 1968; Staff Coll., 1973, Defence Policy Staff, MoD, 1974–75; Co. Comdr, 1976–77, BAOR and NI (despatches 1976); Directing Staff, Staff Coll., 1978–79; Comd 1st Bn Devonshire and Dorset Regt, 1979–82 (despatches 1981); COS, HQ NI, 1982–84; Comdr 1st Inf. Brigade, 1984–86; RCDS 1987; COS, HQ UKLF, 1988–90. Rep. Col Comdt, ACC, 1989–; Col, Devonshire and Dorset Regt, 1990–. Mem., Scientific Exploration Soc. *Publication:* (contrib.) Seaford House Papers, 1987. *Recreations:* ski-ing, fishing, expeditions and collecting water colours. *Address:* c/o Lloyds Bank, 9 Broad Street, St Helier, Jersey, CI. *Club:* Army and Navy.

WILSHIRE, David; MP (C) Spelthorne, since 1987; *b* 16 Sept. 1943; *m* 1967, Margaret Weeks; one *s* (and one *d* decd). *Educ:* Kingswood School, Bath; Fitzwilliam College, Cambridge. Partner, Western Political Research Services, 1979–; Co-Director, Political Management Programme, Brunel Univ., 1986–91. Leader, Wansdyke DC, 1981–87. *Recreations:* gardening, grape growing, wine making. *Address:* 55 Cherry Orchard, Staines, Middx. *T:* Staines (0784) 450822.

WILSON; *see* McNair-Wilson.

WILSON, family name of **Barons Moran, Nunburnholme, Wilson, Wilson of Langside** and **Wilson of Rievaulx.**

WILSON, 2nd Baron, *cr* 1946, of Libya and of Stowlangtoft; **Patrick Maitland Wilson;** *b* 14 Sept. 1915; *s* of Field-Marshal 1st Baron Wilson, GCB, GBE, DSO, and Hester Mary (*d* 1979), *d* of Philip James Digby Wykeham, Tythrop House, Oxon; *S* father 1964; *m* 1945, Violet Storeen (*d* 1990), *d* of late Major James Hamilton Douglas Campbell, OBE. *Educ:* Eton; King's College, Cambridge. Served War of 1939–45 (despatches). *Heir:* none. *Address:* c/o Barclays Bank, Cambridge.

WILSON OF LANGSIDE, Baron *cr* 1969 (Life Peer); **Henry Stephen Wilson,** PC 1967; QC (Scot.) 1965; *b* 21 March 1916; *s* of James Wilson, Solicitor, Glasgow, and Margaret Wilson (*née* Young); *m* 1942, Jessie Forrester Waters; no *c*. *Educ:* High School, Glasgow; Univ. of Glasgow (MA, LLB). Joined Army, 1939; Commd 1940; Regl Officer, HLI and RAC, 1940–46. Called to Scottish Bar, 1946; Advocate-Depute, 1948–51. Sheriff-Substitute: Greenock, 1955–56; Glasgow, 1956–65; Solicitor-General for Scotland, 1965–67; Lord Advocate, 1967–70; Dir, Scottish Courts Administration, 1971–74; Sheriff Principal of Glasgow and Strathkelvin, 1975–77. Contested (Lab) Dumfriesshire, 1950, 1955, W Edinburgh, 1951; Mem. SDP, 1981–. *Recreations:* hill walking, gardening. *Address:* Dunallan, Kippen, Stirlingshire FK8 3HL. *T:* Kippen (078687) 210. *Club:* Western (Glasgow).

WILSON OF RIEVAULX, Baron *cr* 1983 (Life Peer), of Kirklees in the County of West Yorkshire; **James Harold Wilson;** KG 1976; OBE 1945; PC 1947; FRS 1969; *b* 11 March 1916; *s* of late James Herbert and Ethel Wilson, Huddersfield, Yorks (formerly of Manchester); *m* 1940, Gladys Mary, *d* of Rev. D. Baldwin, The Manse, Duxford, Cambridge; two *s*. *Educ:* Milnsbridge Council Sch. and Royds Hall Sch., Huddersfield; Wirral Grammar Sch., Bebington, Cheshire; Jesus Coll., Oxford (Gladstone Memorial Prize, Webb Medley Economics Scholarship, First Class Hons Philosophy, Politics and Economics). Lecturer in Economics, New Coll., Oxford, 1937; Fellow of University Coll., 1938; Praelector in Economics and Domestic Bursar, 1945. Dir of Econs and Stats, Min. of Fuel and Power, 1943–44. MP (Lab) Ormskirk, 1945–50, Huyton, Lancs, 1950–83; Parly Sec. to Ministry of Works, 1945–March 1947; Sec. for Overseas Trade, March-Oct. 1947; Pres., BoT, Oct. 1947–April 1951; Chairman: Labour Party Exec. Cttee, 1961–62; Public Accounts Cttee, 1959–63; Leader, Labour Party, 1963–76; Prime Minister and First Lord of the Treasury, 1964–70, 1974–76; Leader of the Opposition, 1963–64, 1970–74. Chairman: Cttee to Review the Functioning of Financial Instns, 1976–80; British Screen Adv. Council, 1985–. Pres., Royal Statistical Soc., 1972–73. An Elder Brother of Trinity House, 1968. Hon. Fellow, Jesus and University Colleges, Oxford, 1963. Hon. Freeman, City of London, 1975. Hon. Pres., Great Britain-USSR Assoc., 1976–. Pres., Royal Shakespeare Theatre Co., 1976–85. Chancellor, Bradford Univ., 1966–85. Hon. LLD: Lancaster, 1964; Liverpool, 1965; Nottingham, 1966; Sussex, 1966; Hon. DCL, Oxford, 1965; Hon. DTech., Bradford, 1966; DUniv: Essex, 1967; Open, 1974. *Publications:* New Deal for Coal, 1945; In Place of Dollars, 1952; The War on World Poverty, 1953; The Relevance of British Socialism, 1964; Purpose in Politics, 1964; The New Britain (Penguin), 1964; Purpose in Power, 1966; The Labour Government 1964–70, 1971; The Governance of Britain, 1976; A Prime Minister on Prime Ministers, 1977; Final Term: the Labour Government 1974–76, 1979; The Chariot of Israel, 1981; Harold Wilson Memoirs 1916–64, 1986. *Address:* House of Lords, SW1.

WILSON, Prof. Alan Geoffrey; Professor of Urban and Regional Geography, since 1970, Vice-Chancellor, since 1991, University of Leeds (Pro-Vice-Chancellor, 1989–91); *b* 8 Jan. 1939; *s* of Harry Wilson and Gladys (*née* Naylor). *Educ:* Corpus Christi Coll., Cambridge (MA). Scientific Officer, Rutherford High Energy Lab., 1961–64; Res. Officer, Inst. of Econs and Statistics, Univ. of Oxford, 1964–66; Math. Adviser, MoT, 1966–68; Asst Dir, Centre for Environmental Studies, London, 1968–70. Mem., Kirklees AHA, 1979–82; Vice-Chm., Dewsbury HA, 1982–85. Vice-Chm. Environment and Planning Cttee, ESRC, 1986–88. Gill Meml Award, RGS, 1978; Honours Award, Assoc. of Amer. Geographers, 1987. *Publications:* Entropy in Urban and Regional Modelling, 1970; Papers in Urban and Regional Analysis, 1972; Urban and Regional Models in Geography and

Planning, 1974; (with M. J. Kirkby) Mathematics for Geographers and Planners, 1975, 2nd edn 1980; (with P. H. Rees) Spatial Population Analysis, 1977; (ed with P. H. Rees and C. M. Leigh) Models of Cities and Regions, 1977; Catastrophe Theory and Bifurcation: applications to urban and regional systems, 1981; (jtly) Optimization in Locational and Transport Analysis, 1981; Geography and the Environment: Systems Analytical Methods, 1981; (with R. J. Bennett) Mathematical Methods in Geography and Planning, 1985. *Recreations:* writing, dog walking, miscellaneous fads. *Address:* Vice-Chancellor's Office, University of Leeds, Leeds LS2 9JT. *T:* Leeds (0532) 333000. *Club:* Athenæum.

WILSON, Sir Alan (Herries), Kt 1961; FRS 1942; Chairman, Glaxo Group Ltd, 1963–73; *b* 2 July 1906; *o s* of H. and A. Wilson; *m* 1934, Margaret Constance Monks (*d* 1961); two *s*. *Educ:* Wallasey Gram. Sch.; Emmanuel College, Cambridge. Smith's Prize, 1928; Adams Prize, 1931–32; Fellow of Emmanuel College, Cambridge, 1929–33; Fellow and Lecturer of Trinity College, Cambridge, 1933–45; University Lecturer in Mathematics in the University of Cambridge, 1933–45; joined Courtaulds Ltd, 1945; Man. Dir, 1954; Dep. Chm., 1957–62. Dir, Internat. Computers (Hldgs) Ltd, 1962–72. Chairman: Committee on Coal Derivatives, 1959–60; Committee on Noise, 1960–63; Nuclear Safety Adv. Committee, 1965–66; Central Adv. Water Cttee, 1969–74; Dep. Chm. and pt-time Mem., Electricity Council, 1966–76; Member: Iron and Steel Board, 1960–67; UGC, 1964–66; President: Inst. of Physics and Physical Soc., 1963–64; Nat. Society for Clean Air, 1965–66; Aslib, 1971–73. Chm. Governing Body, Nat. Inst. of Agricultural Engrg, 1971–76; Chm., Bd of Governors, Bethlem Royal and Maudsley Hosps., 1973–80. Prime Warden, Goldsmiths Co., 1969–70. Hon. Fellow: Emmanuel College, Cambridge; St Catherine's College, Oxford; UMIST. Hon. FIChemE; Hon. FInstP; Hon. FIMA. Hon. DSc: Oxford; Edinburgh. *Publications:* The Theory of Metals, 1936, 2nd edition 1953; Semi-conductors and Metals, 1939; Thermo-dynamics and Statistical Mechanics, 1957; many papers on atomic physics. *Address:* 65 Oakleigh Park South, Whetstone, N20 9JL. *T:* 081–445 3030. *Club:* Athenæum.

WILSON, Alan Martin; QC 1982; a Recorder of the Crown Court, since 1979; *b* 12 Feb. 1940; *s* of late Joseph Norris Wilson and Kate Wilson; *m* 1st, 1966, Pauline Frances Kibart (marr. diss. 1975); two *d*; 2nd, 1976, Julia Mary Carter; one *d*. *Educ:* Kilburn Grammar Sch.; Nottingham Univ. (LLB Hons). Called to the Bar, Gray's Inn, 1963; Dep. Circuit Judge, 1978. *Recreations:* shooting, sailing, poetry. *Address:* 1 Serjeant's Inn, EC4Y 1LL; Langland House, Peopleton, near Pershore, Worcs WR10 2EE. *Clubs:* Sloane; Bar Yacht.

WILSON, Alastair James Drysdale; QC 1987; *b* 26 May 1946; *s* of A. Robin Wilson and Mary Damaris Wilson; *m* (marr. diss.); one *s* two *d*. *Educ:* Wellington College; Pembroke College, Cambridge. Called to the Bar, Middle Temple, 1968. *Recreations:* gardening, restoring old buildings. *Address:* 3 Pump Court, EC4Y 7AJ; Vanbrugh Castle, Greenwich, SE10 8XQ.

WILSON, Alexander, CBE 1986; FLA; freelance library and information consultant, since 1986; Director General, British Library Reference Division, 1980–86; *b* 12 Feb. 1921; *s* of late William Wilson and Amelia Wilson; *m* 1949, Mary Catherin Traynor; two *s*. *Educ:* Bolton County Grammar Sch. FLA 1950; Hon. FLA 1984. Served War, RAF, 1941–46. Librarian at Bolton, Harrogate, Taunton, and Swindon, 1946–52; Dir of Library and Cultural Services, Dudley and later Coventry, 1952–72; Dir, Cheshire Libraries and Museums Service, 1972–79. Member: Library Adv. Council (England), 1971–74; British Library Bd, 1974–86. Pres., LA, 1986. Mem., Harold Macmillan Trust, 1986–. Fellow, Birmingham Polytechnic, 1989. Hon. DLit Sheffield, 1989. *Publications:* contrib. books and periodicals on libraries and other cultural services. *Recreations:* walking, listening to music, lecturing and writing on professional subjects. *Address:* 1 Brockway West, Tattenhall, Chester CH3 9EZ.

WILSON, Lt-Gen. Sir (Alexander) James, KBE 1974 (CBE 1966; MBE 1948); MC 1945; Chief Executive, Tobacco Advisory Council, 1983–85 (Chairman, 1977–83); Director: Standard Commercial Corporation, since 1983; Standard Wool, since 1987; *b* 13 April 1921; *s* of Maj.-Gen. Bevil Thomson Wilson, CB, DSO, and of Florence Erica, *d* of Sir John Starkey, 1st Bt; *m* 1958, Hon. Jean Margaret Paul, 2nd *d* of 2nd Baron Rankeillour; two *s*. *Educ:* Winchester Coll.; New Coll., Oxford (BA, Law). Served War of 1939–45, North Africa and Italy, Rifle Bde (despatches); Adjt, IMA Dehra Dun, 1945–47; PS to C-in-C Pakistan, 1948–49; Co. Comdr, 1st Bn Rifle Bde, BAOR 1949 and 1951–52, Kenya 1954–55 (despatches); psc 1950; Bde Major 11th Armd Div., BAOR, 1952–54; Instr, Staff Coll. Camberley, 1955–58; 2nd in comd 3rd Green Jackets, BAOR, 1959–60; GSO1 Sandhurst, 1960–62; CO 1st Bn XX Lancs Fus, 1962–64; Chief of Staff, UN Force in Cyprus, 1964–66 (Actg Force Comdr, 1965–66); Comdr, 147 Inf. Bde TA, 1966–67; Dir of Army Recruiting, MoD, 1967–70; GOC NW District, 1970–72; Vice Adjutant General, MoD, 1972–74; GOC SE District, 1974–77. Dep. Col (Lancashire), RRF, 1973–77, Col, 1977–82; Hon. Col, Oxford Univ. OTC, 1978–82. Col Commandant: Queen's Division, 1974–77; RAEC, 1975–79; Royal Green Jackets, 1977–81. Mem., Marketing Council, Drake Beam Morin (UK), 1990–. Chm., Council, RUSI, 1973–75. Member: Sports Council, 1973–82; Council, CBI, 1977–85; Pres., Army Cricket Assoc., 1973–76; Vice-Pres., Army Football Assoc., 1973–76, Chm., 1976–77, Pres., 1977–82; Hon. Vice-Pres., FA, 1976–82. Chm., Crown and Manor Club, Hoxton, 1977–; Vice Pres., NABC, 1990– (Vice Chm., 1977–90); President: Notts Assoc. of Boys and Keystone Clubs, 1986–; Broadway Foundn, 1989–. Association Football Correspondent, Sunday Times, 1957–90; Review Editor, Army Quarterly, 1985–. *Publications:* articles and book reviews on mil. subjects. *Recreations:* cricket, Association football. *Address:* 151 Rivermead Court, SW6 3SF. *T:* 071–736 7228. *Clubs:* Travellers', MCC; Notts CC.

WILSON, Air Marshal Sir Andrew; *see* Wilson, Air Marshal Sir R. A. F.

WILSON, Andrew James; *see* Wilson, Snoo.

WILSON, Andrew N.; author; Literary Editor, Evening Standard, since 1990; *b* 27 Oct. 1950; *s* of late N. Wilson and of Jean Dorothy Wilson (*née* Crowder); *m* 1971, Katherine Duncan-Jones (marr. diss. 1990); two *d*. *Educ:* Rugby; New College, Oxford (MA). Chancellor's Essay Prize, 1971, and Ellerton Theological Prize, 1975. Asst Master, Merchant Taylors' Sch., 1975–76; Lectr, St Hugh's Coll. and New Coll., Oxford, 1976–81; Literary Ed., Spectator, 1981–83. FRSL 1981. *Publications: novels:* The Sweets of Pimlico, 1977 (John Llewellyn Rhys Memorial Prize, 1978); Unguarded Hours, 1978; Kindly Light, 1979; The Healing Art, 1980 (Somerset Maugham Award, 1981; Arts Council National Book Award, 1981; Southern Arts Prize, 1981); Who was Oswald Fish?, 1981; Wise Virgin, 1982 (W. H. Smith Literary Award, 1983); Scandal, 1983; Gentlemen in England, 1985; Love Unknown, 1986; Stray, 1987; Incline Our Hearts, 1988; A Bottle in the Smoke, 1990; Daughters of Albion, 1991; *non fiction:* The Laird of Abbotsford, 1980 (John Llewellyn Rhys Memorial Prize, 1981); A Life of John Milton, 1983; Hilaire Belloc, 1984; How Can We Know?, 1985; (jtly) The Church in Crisis, 1986; The Lion and the Honeycomb, 1987; Penfriends from Porlock, 1988; Tolstoy, 1988 (Whitbread Biography Award); Eminent Victorians, 1989; C. S. Lewis, a biography, 1990; Against Religion, 1991. *Address:* 91 Albert Street, NW1 7LX.

WILSON, Andrew Thomas, CMG 1982; Chief Natural Resources Adviser, Overseas Development Administration, 1983–87, retired; *b* 21 June 1926; *s* of John Wilson, farmer, and Gertrude (*née* Lucas); *m* 1954, Hilda Mary (*née* Williams); two *d*. *Educ:* Cowley Sch.; Leeds Univ. (BSc); St John's Coll., Cambridge (DipAg); Imperial College of Tropical Agriculture (DTA). Colonial Service/HMOCS, Northern Rhodesia/Zambia, 1949–66: Agricultural Officer, 1949; Chief Agricl Officer, 1959; Chief Agricl Research Officer, 1961; Dep. Director of Agriculture, 1963; ODM/ODA: Agricl Adviser, British Development Div. in the Caribbean, 1967; FCO: Agricl Adviser, Nairobi and Kampala, 1969; ODM/ODA: Agricl Adviser, E Africa Development Div., 1974; Agricl Adviser, Middle East Development Div., 1976; Head of British Develt Div. in S Africa, 1979. *Recreations:* sport, gardening. *Address:* Beechwood House, Great Hockham, Thetford, Norfolk IP24 1NY. *Clubs:* Farmers'; Nairobi (Kenya).

WILSON, Sir Anthony, Kt 1988; FCA; Member, Review Body on Top Salaries, since 1989; Chairman, Joint Disciplinary Scheme of UK Accountancy Profession, since 1990; Head of Government Accountancy Service and Accounting Adviser to HM Treasury, 1984–88; *b* 17 Feb. 1928; *s* of late Charles Ernest Wilson and Martha Clarice Wilson (*née* Mee); *m* 1955, Margaret Josephine Hudson; two *s* one *d*. *Educ:* Giggleswick School. Royal Navy, 1946–49. John Gordon Walton & Co., 1945–46 and 1949–52; Price Waterhouse, 1952, Partner, 1961–84; HM Treasury, 1984–88. Non-exec. Dir, Capita Gp plc, 1989–. Member: UK Govt Production Statistics Adv. Cttee, 1972–84; Accounting Standards Cttee, 1984–88; Auditing Practices Cttee, 1987–88; Council, Inst. of Chartered Accountants in England and Wales, 1985–88. Mem. Management Cttee, SW Regl Arts Assoc., 1983– (Chm., 1988–); Member: English Ceramic Circle, 1983–; Northern Ceramic Soc., 1976–89. Pres., Chandos Chamber Choir, 1986–88; Chm., Dorset Opera, 1988–; Dir, Opera-80 Ltd, 1989–. Court, Needlemakers' Co.; Liveryman, Chartered Accountants' Co. FRSA 1983. *Recreations:* fishing, gardening, golf, collecting pottery. *Address:* The Barn House, 89 Newland, Sherborne, Dorset DT9 3AG. *T:* Sherborne (0935) 815674. *Club:* Reform.

WILSON, Anthony Joseph, (Joe); Member (Lab) North Wales, European Parliament, since 1989; *b* 6 July 1937; *s* of Joseph Samuel Wilson and Eleanor Annie (*née* Jones); *m* 1959, June Mary Sockett; one *s* two *d*. *Educ:* Birkenhead Sch.; Loughborough Coll. (DLC); Univ. of Wales (BEd Hons). National Service, RAPC, 1955–57. Teacher: Vauvert Sec. Mod. Sch., Guernsey, 1960–64; Les Beaucamps Sec. Mod. Sch., Guernsey, 1964–66; Man., St Mary's Bay Sch. Journey Centre, Kent, 1966–69; Lectr in PE, Wrexham Tech. Coll., subseq. N Wales Inst. of Higher Educn, 1969–89. *Recreations:* basketball, camping. *Address:* 79 Ruabon Road, Wrexham, North Wales LL13 7PU. *T:* Wrexham (0978) 352808.

WILSON, Maj.-Gen. Arthur Gillespie, CBE 1955; DSO 1946; *b* 29 Sept. 1900; *s* of late Charles Wilson, originally of Glasgow, Scotland; *m* 1st, 1927, Edna D. L. Gibson (*d* 1940); no *c*; 2nd, 1953, Shirley H. Cruickshank, *d* of late Colin Campbell, Queenscliff, Victoria, Australia; no *c*. *Educ:* North Sydney Boys' High School, NSW, Australia; Royal Military College, Duntroon, Australia. Commissioned Aust. Staff Corps, 1921; served India with various Brit. and IA Artillery Units, 1924; commanded Roy. Aust. Artillery, Thursday Island, 1926–28; Staff College, Quetta, 1935–36; GSO3, AHQ 1938; continued to serve in various appts at AHQ until joined AIF 1940; GSO1 HQ AIF UK and then Assistant Mil. Liaison Officer, Australian High Commissioner's Office, UK, until 1943, when returned to Australia; served with AIF New Guinea Philippines and Borneo, 1943–45; DDSD(o) Land Headquarters, 1944–45; commanded British Commonwealth Base BCOF Japan, 1946–47; served various appts AHQ and HQ Eastern Command, 1947–52; Aust. Army Rep., UK, 1953–54; GOC, Central Command, Australia, 1954–57; retired 1957. *Address:* Leahurst Cottage, Crafers, South Australia 5152, Australia. *Club:* Naval, Military and Air Force (Adelaide).

WILSON, Prof. Arthur James Cochran, FRS 1963; Professor of Crystallography, Department of Physics, Birmingham University, 1965–82, now Emeritus; *b* 28 November 1914; *o s* of Arthur A. C. and Hildegarde Gretchen (*née* Geldert) Wilson, Springhill, Nova Scotia, Canada; *m* 1946, Harriett Charlotte, BSc, PhD, Sociologist (*née* Friedeberg); two *s* one *d*. *Educ:* King's Collegiate School, Windsor, Nova Scotia, Canada; Dalhousie University, Halifax, Canada (MSc); Massachusetts Institute of Technology (PhD); Cambridge University (PhD). 1851 Exhibition Scholar, 1937–40. Res. Asst, Cavendish Lab., Cambridge, 1940–45; Lecturer, 1945, and Senior Lecturer, 1946, in Physics, University College, Cardiff; Professor of Physics, University College, Cardiff, 1954–65. Visiting Professor: Georgia Inst. of Technology, 1965, 1968, 1971; Univ. of Tokyo, 1972. Editor of Structure Reports, 1948–59; Editor of Acta Crystallographica, 1960–77; Assoc. Editor, Proc. Royal Society, 1978–83; Editor of International Tables for Crystallography, 1982–. Member: Exec. Cttee, Internat. Union of Crystallography, 1954–60 and 1978–81 (Vice-Pres., 1978–81); ICSU Abstracting Bd (now Internat. Council for Scientific and Technical Information), 1971–77, 1980–86 (Vice-Pres.). *Publications:* X-ray Optics, 1949 (Russian edn 1951, 2nd edn 1962); Mathematical Theory of X-ray Powder Diffractometry, 1963 (French edn 1964, German edn 1965); Elements of X-ray Crystallography, 1970; (with L. V. Azároff and others) X-ray Diffraction, 1974; (ed jtly) Crystallographic Statistics: Progress and Problems, 1982; (ed) Structure and Statistics in Crystallography, 1985; (ed jtly) Direct Methods, Macromolecular Methods and Crystallographic Statistics, 1987; (ed and contrib.) International Tables for Crystallography, Vol. C, 1991; numerous papers in Proc. Phys. Soc., Proc. Roy. Soc., Acta Cryst., etc. *Address:* Crystallographic Data Centre, University Chemical Laboratory, Cambridge CB2 1EW.

WILSON, Austin Peter; Assistant Under Secretary of State, since 1981; Northern Ireland Office, since 1988; *b* 31 March 1938; *s* of Joseph and Irene Wilson; *m* 1962, Norma Louise, *y d* of D. R. Mill; one *s* two *d*. *Educ:* Leeds Grammar Sch.; St Edmund Hall, Oxford (BA). Entered Home Office, 1961; Private Secretary to Minister of State, 1964–66; Principal, 1966; Secretary, Deptl Cttee on Death Certification and Coroners (Brodrick Cttee), 1968–71; Asst Sec., 1974, Prison Dept; seconded to N Ireland Office, 1977–80; Asst Under Secretary of State, Criminal Justice Dept, 1981; Hd of Community Progs and Equal Opportunities Dept, 1982–86, Equal Opportunities and Gen. Dept, 1986–87, Police Dept, 1987–88, Home Office. *Recreations:* theatre, walking, exploring France. *Address:* Northern Ireland Office, Old Admiralty Building, SW1. *T:* 071–210 3000.

WILSON, Vice-Adm. Sir Barry (Nigel), KCB 1990; Deputy Chief of Defence Staff (Programmes and Personnel), since 1989; *b* 5 June 1936; *s* of Rear-Adm. G. A. M. Wilson, CB, and of Dorothy Wilson; *m* 1961, Elizabeth Ann (*née* Hardy); one *s* one *d*. *Educ:* St Edward's Sch., Oxford; Britannia Royal Naval Coll. Commanded: HMS Mohawk, 1973–74; HMS Cardiff, 1978–80; RCDS 1982; Dir Navy Plans, 1983–85; Flag Officer Sea Training, 1986–87; ACDS (Progs), 1987–89. Chm., Bede House, Bermondsey, 1990. *Recreations:* campanology, gardening. *Address:* c/o Naval Secretary, Old Admiralty Building, Whitehall, SW1. *T:* 071–218 9000.

WILSON, Lt-Col Blair Aubyn S.; *see* Stewart-Wilson.

WILSON, Brian David Henderson; MP (Lab) Cunninghame North, since 1987; *b* 13 Dec. 1948; *s* of late John Forrest Wilson and of Marion MacIntyre; *m* 1981, Joni Buchanan; one *d*. *Educ:* Dunoon Grammar School; Dundee Univ. (MA Hons); University College Cardiff (Dip. Journalism Studies). Publisher and founding editor, West Highland Free Press, 1972–. Front bench spokesman on Scottish Affairs, 1988–. First winner, Nicholas Tomalin Meml Award, 1975. *Publications:* Celtic: a century with honour, 1988; contribs to Guardian, Glasgow Herald, Scotland on Sunday, etc. *Address:* House of Commons, SW1A 0AA; 37 Main Street, Kilbirnie, Ayrshire. *T:* (office) Kilbirnie (0505) 682847; 22 Glebe Road, Beith, Ayrshire. *T:* Beith (05055) 4783; Miavaig House, Isle of Lewis. *T:* Timsgarry (085175) 357.

WILSON, Prof. Brian Graham; Vice-Chancellor, University of Queensland, since 1979; *b* 9 April 1930; *s* of Charles Wesley Wilson and Isobel Christie (*née* Ferguson); *m* 1st, 1959, Barbara Elizabeth Wilkie; two *s* one *d*; 2nd, 1978, Margaret Jeanne Henry; 3rd, 1988, Joan Patricia Opdebeeck; one *s*. *Educ:* Queen's Univ., Belfast (BSc Hons); National Univ. of Ireland (PhD Cosmic Radiation). Post-doctoral Fellow, National Research Council, Canada, 1955–57; Officer in Charge, Sulphur Mt Lab., Banff, 1957–60, Associate Res. Officer, 1959–60; Associate Prof. of Physics, Univ. of Calgary, 1960–65, Prof., 1965–70, Dean of Arts and Science, 1967–70; Prof. of Astronomy and Academic Vice-Pres., Simon Fraser Univ., 1970–78. FTS 1990. Hon. LLD Calgary, 1984. *Publications:* numerous, on astrophysics, in learned jls. *Recreations:* golf, swimming. *Address:* 55 Walcott Street, St Lucia, Queensland 4067, Australia. *T:* (07)870 8757. *Club:* Brisbane.

WILSON, Brian Harvey, CBE 1972 (MBE 1944); solicitor, retired; Town Clerk and Chief Executive, London Borough of Camden, 1965–77; *b* 4 Sept. 1915; *o s* of Sydney John Wilson, MC, and Bessie Mildred (*née* Scott); *m* 1941, Constance Jane (*née* Gee); one *s*. *Educ:* Manchester Grammar Sch.; (Exhibitioner) Corpus Christi Coll., Cambridge (MA, LLB). Chief Asst Solicitor, Warrington, 1946–48; Dep. Town Clerk: Grimsby, 1948–53; Ilford, 1953–56; Town Clerk, Hampstead, 1956–65 (now Camden). Hon. Clerk to Housing and Works Cttee, London Boroughs Assoc., 1965–79; Chm., Metropolitan Housing Trust, 1978–85. Chm., Royal Inst. of Public Administration, 1973–75. Member: Uganda Resettlement Board, 1972–73; DoE Study Gp on Agrément, 1978. Chairman: Public Examn, Glos Structure Plan, 1980; Indep. Inquiry into death of Maria Mehmedagi, 1981; GLC Independent Inquiry into financial terms of GLC housing transferred to London Boroughs and Districts, 1984–85. *Address:* Old Housing, Fifield, Oxon. *T:* Shipton-under-Wychwood (0993) 830695.

WILSON, Brian William John Gregg, MA; Deputy Head, St Mary's School, Wantage, since 1989; *b* 16 June 1937; *s* of late Cecil S. and Margaret D. Wilson; *m* 1969, Sara Remington (*née* Hollins); two *d*. *Educ:* Sedbergh Sch., Yorks; Christ's Coll., Cambridge (MA). NI short service commn, RIrF, 1955–57. Asst Master, Radley Coll., 1960–65; Housemaster, King's Sch., Canterbury, 1965–73; Dir of Studies, Eastbourne Coll., 1973–76; Headmaster, Campbell Coll., Belfast, 1977–87. Project Manager, Navan Fort Initative Gp, 1987–88. Member: Central Religious Adv. Cttee, BBC/ITV, 1982–86; Management Cttee, NISTRO, 1980–87. Hon. Sec., Ancient History Cttee, JACT, 1967–77. *Publications:* (with W. K. Lacey) Res Publica, 1970; (with D. J. Miller) Stories from Herodotus, 1973. *Recreations:* fives, squash, golf, cricket, hockey, etc; translating, theology, stock market, drama. *Address:* 44 Alfredston Place, Wantage, Oxon OX12 8DL.

WILSON, Rt. Rev. Bruce Winston; *see* Bathurst (NSW), Bishop of.

WILSON, Bryan Ronald, PhD, DLitt; Reader in Sociology, University of Oxford, since 1962; Fellow, since 1963, and Domestic Bursar, since 1989, All Souls College, Oxford (Sub-Warden, 1988–90); *b* 25 June 1926. *Educ:* University Coll., Leicester (BSc Econ London); London Sch. of Economics (PhD); MA, DLitt Oxon. Lectr in Sociology, Univ. of Leeds, 1955–62. Commonwealth Fund Fellow (Harkness), 1957–58; Fellow, Amer. Council of Learned Socs, 1966–67; Visiting Professor or Fellow, Universities of: Louvain, 1976,1982, 1986; Toronto, 1978; Melbourne (Ormond Coll.), 1981; Queensland, 1986; California, Santa Barbara, 1987. Pres., Conf. Internat. de sociologie religieuse, 1971–75. Sen. Treasurer, Oxford Union Soc., 1983–91. Hon. DLitt Soka Univ., Japan, 1985. *Publications:* Sects and Society, 1961; Religion in Secular Society, 1966; (ed) Patterns of Sectarianism, 1967; The Youth Culture and the Universities, 1970; (ed) Rationality, 1970; Religious Sects, 1970; Magic and the Millenium, 1973; (ed) Education, Equality and Society, 1975; The Noble Savages, 1975; Contemporary Transformations of Religion, 1976; (ed) The Social Impact of New Religious Movements, 1981; Religion in Sociological Perspective, 1982; (with Daisaku Ikeda) Human Values in a Changing World, 1984; (ed with Brenda Almond) Values: a symposium, 1988; The Social Dimensions of Sectarianism, 1990; contribs to learned jls. *Address:* All Souls College, Oxford OX1 4AL. *T:* Oxford (0865) 279290.

WILSON, Catherine Mary, (Mrs P. J. Wilson), FMA, FSA; Director, Norfolk Museums Service, since 1991; *b* 10 April 1945; *d* of Arthur Thomas Bowyer and Kathleen May (*née* Hawes); *m* 1968, Peter John Wilson. *Educ:* Windsor County Grammar Sch. FMA 1984 (AMA 1972); FSA 1990. Museum Asst, Lincoln City Museums, 1964; Curator, Museum of Lincolnshire Life, 1972; Asst Dir (Museums), Lincs CC, 1983. *Recreations:* industrial archaeology, vernacular architecture, all local history. *Address:* Castle Museum, Norwich, Norfolk NR1 3JU. *Club:* Norfolk (Norwich).

WILSON, Brig. Charles Edward T.; *see* Tryon-Wilson.

WILSON, Sir Charles Haynes, Kt 1965; MA Glasgow and Oxon; Principal and Vice-Chancellor of University of Glasgow, 1961–76; *b* 16 May 1909; 2nd *s* of late George Wilson and Florence Margaret Hannay; *m* 1935, Jessie Gilmour Wilson; one *s* two *d*. *Educ:* Hillhead High School; Glasgow Univ.; Oxford Univ. Glasgow University Faulds Fellow in Political Philosophy, 1932–34. Lecturer in Political Science, London School of Economics, 1934–39; Fellow and Tutor in Modern History, Corpus Christi College, Oxford, 1939–52. Junior Proctor, 1945; Faculty Fellow, Nuffield College. Visiting Professor in Comparative Government at Ohio State Univ., 1950; Principal, The University College of Leicester, 1952–57; Vice-Chancellor, Univ. of Leicester, 1957–61. Chairman: Commn on Fourah Bay Coll., Sierra Leone, 1957; Miners' Welfare Nat. Schol. Scheme Selec. Cttee, 1959–64; Acad. Planning Bd for Univ. of E Anglia, 1960; Member: Academic Planning Cttee and Council of UC of Sussex, 1958; Acad. Adv. Cttee, Royal Coll. of Science and Technology, Glasgow (now Univ. of Strathclyde), 1962; British Cttee of Selection for Harkness Fellowships of Commonwealth Fund, 1962–67; Heyworth Cttee on Social Studies, 1962; Acad. Planning Bd, Univ. of Stirling, 1964; Chairman, Cttee of Vice-Chancellors and Principals, 1964–67; Chm., Assoc. of Commonwealth Univs, 1966–67 and 1972–74. Mem., Museums and Galleries Commn (formerly Standing Commn on Museums and Galleries), 1976–83. Hon. Fellow: Corpus Christi Coll., Oxford, 1963; LSE, 1965. Hon. LLD: Glasgow, 1957; Leicester, 1961; Rhodes Univ., 1964; Queen's Univ., Kingston, Ont, 1967; Ohio State Univ., 1969; Pennsylvania, 1975; Hon. DLitt: Strathclyde, 1966; NUU, 1976; Heriot-Watt, 1977; Hon. DCL East Anglia, 1966. Comdr, St Olav (Norway), 1966; Chevalier, Legion of Honour, 1976. *Address:* Whinnymuir, Dalry, Castle Douglas DG7 3TT. *T:* Dalry (06443) 218. *Club:* Royal Scottish Automobile.

WILSON, Charles Martin; Managing Director and Editor-in-chief, The Sporting Life, since 1990; Editorial Director, Mirror Group Newspapers plc, since 1991; *b* 18 Aug. 1935; *s* of Adam and Ruth Wilson; *m* 1st, 1968, Anne Robinson (marr. diss. 1973); one *d*; 2nd, 1980, Sally Angela O'Sullivan, *qv*; one *s* one *d*. *Educ:* Eastbank Academy, Glasgow. News Chronicle, 1959–60; Daily Mail, 1960–71; Dep. Northern Editor, Daily Mail, 1971–74; Asst Editor, London Evening News, 1974–76; Editor, Glasgow Evening Times, Glasgow Herald, Scottish Sunday Standard, 1976–82; The Times: Exec. Editor, 1982; Dep. Editor, 1983; Editor, 1985–90; Internat. Develts Dir, News Internat. plc, 1990. *Recreations:* reading, horse racing. *Address:* Mirror Group Newspapers plc, 33 Holborn Circus, EC1P 1DQ. *Club:* Reform.

WILSON, (Christopher) David, CBE 1968; MC 1945; Chairman: Southern Television Ltd, 1976–81 (Managing Director, 1959–76); Southstar Television International, 1976–81; Beaumont (UK) Ltd, 1979–81; *b* 17 Dec. 1916; *s* of late James Anthony Wilson, Highclere, Worplesdon, Surrey; *m* 1947, Jean Barbara Morton Smith; no *c*. *Educ:* St George's Sch., Windsor; Aldenham. Served War of 1939–45: Captain RA, in India, Middle East and Italy. Business Manager, Associated Newspapers Ltd, 1955–57; Dir, Associated Rediffusion Ltd, 1956–57; Gen. Manager, Southern Television Ltd, 1957–59; Chm., ITN Ltd, 1969–71. Mem. Council, Southampton Univ., 1980–89; Vice-Pres., Southern Arts Assoc.; Trustee, Chichester Festival Theatre Trust Ltd. FCA 1947. *Recreations:* sailing, music. *Address:* Little Croft, Upham, Hants SO3 1JH. *T:* Durley (04896) 204; La Marina Española 14[4], Javea, Alicante, Spain. *Clubs:* MCC; Royal Southern Yacht.

WILSON, Christopher Maynard, DIC, PhD; Chairman: LCE Computer Maintenance Ltd, since 1987; Barlec Richfield, since 1990; Director: Radiodetection Ltd, since 1987; J. W. Sharman Ltd, since 1989; *b* 19 Dec. 1928; *s* of late George Henry Cyril Wilson and of Adelaide Flora Marie Wilson; *m* 1953, Elizabeth Ursula Canning; one *s* two *d*. *Educ:* King Edward VII Sch., Sheffield; Worksop Coll., Notts; Imperial Coll., London Univ. (BSc, ARCS, DIC, PhD). National Service, RAF, 1947–49. Ferranti Computers, 1953–63; Ferranti merged with ICT, 1963, ICT merged with English Electric Computers to become ICL, 1968; Manager, UK Sales, 1968–70; Director: Marketing and Product Strategy, 1970–72; Internat. Div., 1972–77; Man. Dir, International Computers Ltd, 1977–81; Chm., Exxel Consultants Ltd, 1982–86; Man. Dir, Ansafone Corp., 1984–86. *Recreations:* squash, tennis, gardening, golf. *Address:* Tiles Cottage, Forest Road, Winkfield Row, near Bracknell, Berks RG12 6NR.

WILSON, Clifford; Professor of Medicine, University of London, at the London Hospital and Director, Medical Unit, The London Hospital, 1946–71, now Emeritus Professor; *b* 27 Jan. 1906; *m* 1936, Kathleen Hebden; one *s* one *d*. *Educ:* Balliol College, Oxford. Brackenbury Scholar, Balliol Coll., Oxford, 1924; 1st Class Oxford Final Hons School of Nat. Sciences, 1928; BM BCh 1933; DM 1936. MRCS 1931; FRCP 1951 (MRCP 1946). House Physician, etc., London Hospital, 1931–34; Rockefeller Travelling Fellow, 1934–35; Research Fellow, Harvard Univ.; Asst Director, Medical Unit, London Hosp., 1938; Univ. Reader in Medicine, London Hosp., 1940; Major RAMC, Medical Research Section, 1942–45. President Renal Association, 1963–64. Examiner MRCP, 1960–; Censor, RCP, 1964–66; Senior Censor and Senior Vice-Pres., 1967–68. Dean, Faculty of Medicine, Univ. of London, 1968–71. Hon. Fellow, London Hosp. Medical Coll., 1986. *Publications:* sections on renal diseases and diseases of the arteries in Price's Text Book of Medicine; papers on renal disease, hypertension, arterial disease and other medical subjects, 1930–70. *Address:* The White Cottage, Woodgreen, Fordingbridge, Hants SP6 2BD.

WILSON, Clive Hebden; Under Secretary, Priority Health Services Division, Department of Health, since 1990; *b* 1 Feb. 1940; *s* of Joseph and Irene Wilson; *m* 1976, Jill Garland Evans; two *d*. *Educ:* Leeds Grammar Sch.; Corpus Christi Coll., Oxford. Joined Civil Service, 1962; Ministry of Health: Asst Principal, 1962–67; Asst Private Sec. to Minister of Health, 1965–66; Principal, 1967–73; Assistant Secretary: DHSS, 1973–77; Cabinet Office, 1977–79; DHSS, 1979–82; Under Sec., DHSS, later DoH, 1982–; Dir of Estabs (HQ), 1982–84; Child Care Div., 1984–86; Children, Maternity, Prevention Div., 1986–87; Medicines Div., 1987–90. *Recreations:* walking, gardening.

WILSON, Prof. Colin Alexander St John, RA 1991 (ARA 1990); FRIBA; Professor of Architecture, Cambridge University, 1975–89, now Emeritus Professor; Fellow, Pembroke College, Cambridge, since 1977; Architect (own private practice); *b* 14 March 1922; *yr s* of late Rt Rev. Henry A. Wilson, CBE, DD; *m* 1st, 1955, Muriel Lavender (marr. diss. 1971); 2nd, 1972, Mary Jane Long; one *s* one *d*. *Educ:* Felsted Sch.; Corpus Christi Coll., Cambridge, 1940–42 (MA); Sch. of Architecture, London Univ., 1946–49 (Dip. Lond.). Served War, RNVR, 1942–46. Asst in Housing Div., Architects Dept, LCC, 1950–55; Lectr at Sch. of Architecture, Univ. of Cambridge, 1955–69; Fellow, Churchill Coll., Cambridge, 1962–71. Practised in assoc. with Sir Leslie Martin, 1955–64: on bldgs in Cambridge (Harvey Court, Gonville and Caius Coll.; Stone Building, Peterhouse); Univ. of Oxford, Law Library; Univ. of Leicester, Science Campus; Univ. of London, Royal Holloway Coll. In own practice Buildings include: Extension to Sch. of Architecture, Cambridge; Research Laboratory, Babraham; Extension to British Museum; Library for QMC; Meml Library for Bishop Wilson Sch., Spring Field; The British Library, St Pancras (commenced construction, 1982); various residences; Projects for Liverpool Civic and Social Centre, and Group Headquarters and Research Campus for Lucas Industries Ltd. Vis. Critic to Yale Sch. of Architecture, USA, 1960, 1964 and 1983; Bemis Prof. of Architecture, MIT, USA, 1970–72. Member: Fitzwilliam Mus. Syndicate, 1985–89; Arts Council of GB, 1990–. Trustee: Tate Gall., 1973–80; Nat. Gall., 1977–80. *Publications:* articles in: The Observer; professional jls in UK, USA, France, Spain, Japan, Germany, Norway, Italy, Switzerland, Finland, etc. *Address:* 31A Grove End Road, NW8. *T:* 071–286 8306; (office) Colin St John Wilson & Partners, Highbury Crescent Rooms, 70 Ronalds Road, N5 1XW. *T:* 071–354 2030.

WILSON, Colin Henry; author; *b* Leicester, 26 June 1931; *s* of Arthur Wilson and Annetta Jones; *m* Dorothy Betty Troop; one *s*; *m* Joy Stewart; two *s* one *d*. *Educ:* The Gateway Secondary Technical School, Leicester. Left school at 16. Laboratory Asst (Gateway School), 1948–49; Civil Servant (collector of taxes), Leicester and Rugby, 1949–50; national service with RAF, AC2, 1949–50. Various jobs, and a period spent in Paris and Strasbourg, 1950; came to London, 1951; various labouring jobs, long period in plastic factory; returned to Paris, 1953; labouring jobs in London until Dec. 1954, when began writing The Outsider: has since made a living at writing. Visiting Professor: Hollins Coll., Va, 1966–67; Univ. of Washington, Seattle, 1967; Dowling Coll., Majorca, 1969; Rutgers Univ., NJ, 1974. Plays produced: Viennese Interlude; The Metal Flower Blossom; Strindberg. *Publications:* The Outsider, 1956; Religion and the Rebel, 1957; The Age of Defeat, 1959; Ritual in the Dark, 1960; Adrift in Soho, 1961; An Encyclopædia of Murder, 1961; The Strength to Dream, 1962; Origins of the Sexual Impulse, 1963; The Man without a Shadow, 1963; The World of Violence, 1963; Rasputin and the Fall of the Romanovs, 1964; The Brandy of the Damned (musical essays), 1964; Necessary Doubt, 1964; Beyond the Outsider, 1965; Eagle and Earwig, 1965; The Mind Parasites, 1966; Introduction to The New Existentialism, 1966; The Glass Cage, 1966; Sex and the Intelligent Teenager, 1966; The Philosopher's Stone, 1968; Strindberg (play), 1968;

Bernard Shaw: A Reassessment, 1969; Voyage to a Beginning, 1969; Poetry and Mysticism, 1970; The Black Room, 1970; A Casebook of Murder, 1970; The God of the Labyrinth, 1970; Lingard, 1970; (jtly) The Strange Genius of David Lindsay, 1970; The Occult, 1971; New Pathways in Psychology, 1972; Order of Assassins, 1971; Tree by Tolkien, 1973; Hermann Hesse, 1973; Strange Powers, 1973; The Schoolgirl Murder Case, 1974; Return of the Lloigor, 1974; A Book of Booze, 1974; The Craft of the Novel, 1975; The Space Vampires, 1976 (filmed as Lifeforce, 1985); Men of Strange Powers, 1976; Enigmas and Mysteries, 1977; The Geller Phenomenon, 1977; Mysteries, 1978; Mysteries (play), 1979; The Quest for Wilhelm Reich, 1979; The War Against Sleep: the philosophy of Gurdjieff, 1980; Starseekers, 1980; Frankenstein's Castle, 1981; (ed with John Grant) The Directory of Possibilities, 1981; Poltergeist!, 1981; Access to Inner Worlds, 1982; The Criminal History of Mankind, 1983; (with Donald Seaman) Encyclopaedia of Modern Murder, 1983; Psychic Detectives, 1983; The Janus Murder Case, 1984; The Essential Colin Wilson, 1984; The Personality Surgeon, 1985; Spider World: the tower, 1987; (with Damon Wilson) Encyclopedia of Unsolved Mysteries, 1987, 1989; Spider World: the delta, 1987; (ed with Ronald Duncan) Marx Refuted, 1987; Aleister Crowley: the nature of the beast, 1987; (with Robin Odell) Jack the Ripper: summing up and verdict, 1987; The Magician from Siberia, 1988; The Misfits: a study of sexual outsiders, 1988; Beyond the Occult, 1988; Written in Blood, 1989; (with Donald Seaman) The Serial Killers, 1990; Mozart's Journey to Prague (play), 1991; contribs to: The Times, Literary Review, Audio, etc. *Recreations:* collecting gramophone records, mainly opera; mathematics. *Address:* Tetherdown, Trewallock Lane, Gorran Haven, Cornwall. *Club:* Savage.

WILSON, Maj.-Gen. Dare; *see* Wilson, Maj.-Gen. R. D.

WILSON, David; *see* Wilson, C. D.

WILSON, Sir David, 3rd Bt *cr* 1920; solicitor; *b* 30 Oct. 1928; *s* of Sir John Mitchell Harvey Wilson, 2nd Bt, KCVO, and Mary Elizabeth (*d* 1979), *d* of late William Richards, CBE; *S* father, 1975; *m* 1955, Eva Margareta, *e d* of Tore Lindell, Malmö, Sweden; two *s* one *d*. *Educ:* Deerfield Acad., Mass., USA; Harrow School; Oriel Coll., Oxford (Brisco Owen Schol.). Barrister, Lincoln's Inn, 1954–61; admitted Solicitor, 1962; Partner in Simmons & Simmons, EC2, 1963–. *Heir: s* Thomas David Wilson [*b* 6 Jan. 1959; *m* 1984, Valerie, *er d* of Vivian Stogdale, Shotover, Oxford; two *s*]. *Address:* Tandem House, Queen's Drive, Oxshott, Leatherhead, Surrey KT22 0PH. *Clubs:* Arts; Royal Southern Yacht.

WILSON, Sir David (Clive), GCMG 1991 (KCMG 1987; CMG 1985); PhD; Governor and Commander-in-Chief, Hong Kong, since 1987; *b* 14 Feb. 1935; *s* of Rev. William Skinner Wilson and Enid Wilson; *m* 1967, Natasha Helen Mary Alexander; two *s*. *Educ:* Trinity Coll., Glenalmond; Keble Coll., Oxford (schol., MA); PhD London 1973. National Service, The Black Watch, 1953–55; entered Foreign Service, 1958; Third Secretary, Vientiane, 1959–60; Language Student, Hong Kong, 1960–62; Second, later First Secretary, Peking, 1963–65; FCO, 1965–68; resigned, 1968; Editor, China Quarterly, 1968–74; Vis. Scholar, Columbia Univ., New York, 1972; rejoined Diplomatic Service, 1974; Cabinet Office, 1974–77; Political Adviser, Hong Kong, 1977–81; Hd, S European Dept, FCO, 1981–84; Asst Under-Sec. of State, FCO, 1984–87. Oxford Univ. Somaliland Expedn, 1957; British Mt Kongur Expedn (NW China), 1981. Hon. LLD Aberdeen, 1990; Hon. DLitt Sydney, 1991. KStJ 1987. *Recreations:* mountaineering, ski-ing, reading. *Address:* Government House, Hong Kong. *Clubs:* Athenæum, Alpine; Hong Kong (Hong Kong).

WILSON, Sir David (Mackenzie), Kt 1984; FBA 1981; Director of the British Museum, 1977–91; *b* 30 Oct. 1931; *e s* of Rev. Joseph Wilson; *m* 1955, Eva, *o d* of Dr Gunnar Sjögren, Stockholm; one *s* one *d*. *Educ:* Kingswood Sch.; St John's Coll., Cambridge (LittD; Hon. Fellow, 1985); Lund Univ., Sweden. Research Asst, Cambridge Univ., 1954; Asst Keeper, British Museum, 1954–64; Reader in Archaeology of Anglo-Saxon Period, London Univ., 1964–71; Prof. of Medieval Archaeology, Univ. of London, 1971–76; Jt Head of Dept of Scandinavian Studies, UCL, 1973–76 (Hon. Fellow, 1988). Slade Prof., Cambridge, 1985–86. Member: Ancient Monuments Bd for England, 1976–84; Historic Bldgs and Monuments Commn, 1990–. Governor, Museum of London, 1976–81; Trustee: Nat. Museums of Scotland, 1985–87; Nat. Museums of Merseyside, 1986–. Crabtree Orator 1966. Member: Royal Swedish Acad. of Sci.; Royal Acad. of Letters, History and Antiquities, Sweden; German Archaeological Inst.; Royal Gustav Adolf's Acad. of Sweden; Royal Soc. of Letters of Lund; Vetenskapssocieteten, Lund; Royal Soc. of Sci. and Letters, Gothenburg; Royal Soc. of Sci., Uppsala; Royal Norwegian Soc. of Sci. and Letters; FSA; Hon. MRIA; Hon. Mem., Polish Archaeological and Numismatic Soc.; Hon. FMA. Sec., Soc. for Medieval Archaeology, 1957–77; Pres., Viking Soc., 1968–70; Pres., Brit. Archaeological Assoc., 1962–68. Mem. Council, Nottingham Univ., 1988–. Hon. Fil.Dr Stockholm; Hon. Dr Phil: Aarhus; Oslo; Hon. DLitt: Liverpool; Nottingham; Leicester; Hon LLD Pennsylvania. Félix Neuburgh Prize, Gothenburg Univ., 1978. Order of Polar Star, 1st cl. (Sweden), 1977. *Publications:* The Anglo-Saxons, 1960, 3rd edn 1981; Anglo-Saxon Metalwork 700–1100 in British Museum, 1964; (with O. Klindt-Jensen) Viking Art, 1966; (with G. Bersu) Three Viking Graves in the Isle of Man, 1969; The Vikings and their Origins, 1970, 2nd edn 1980; (with P. G. Foote) The Viking Achievement, 1970; (with A. Small and C. Thomas) St Ninian's Isle and its Treasure, 1973; The Viking Age in the Isle of Man, 1974; (ed) Anglo-Saxon Archaeology, 1976; (ed) The Northern World, 1980; The Forgotten Collector, 1984; Anglo-Saxon Art, 1984; The Bayeux Tapestry, 1985; The British Museum: purpose and politics, 1989. *Address:* The Lifeboat House, Castletown, Isle of Man. *T:* Castletown (0624) 822800. *Club:* Athenæum.

WILSON, David William; Chairman, Wilson Bowden PLC, since 1987; *b* 5 Dec. 1941; *s* of Albert Henry Wilson and Kathleen May Wilson; *m* 1st, 1964, Ann Taberner; one *s* one *d*; 2nd, 1985, Laura Isobel Knifton; two *s*. *Educ:* Ashby Boys' Grammar Sch.; Leicester Polytechnic. Created from scratch what is now Wilson Bowden PLC. *Recreations:* farming, fox hunting. *Address:* Lowesby Hall, Lowesby, Leics LE7 9DD. *T:* Hungarton (053750) 321.

WILSON, Des; General Election Campaign Director, Liberal Democrats, since 1990; *b* 5 March 1941; *s* of Albert H. Wilson, Oamaru, New Zealand; *m* 1985, Jane Dunmore; one *s* one *d* by a previous marriage. *Educ:* Waitaki Boys' High Sch., New Zealand. Journalist-Broadcaster, 1957–67; Director, Shelter, Nat. Campaign for the Homeless, 1967–71; Head of Public Affairs, RSC, 1974–76; Editor, Social Work Today, 1976–79; Dep. Editor, Illustrated London News, 1979–81; Chm., 1981–85, Project Advr, 1985–89, CLEAR (Campaign for Lead-Free Air). Chairman: Friends of the Earth (UK), 1982–86; Campaign for Freedom of Information, 1984–91; Citizen Action, 1983–91; Parents Against Tobacco, 1990. Member: Nat. Exec., Nat. Council for Civil Liberties, 1971–73; Cttee for City Poverty, 1972–73; Bd, Shelter, 1982– (Trustee, 1982–86); Trustee, Internat. Year of Shelter for the Homeless (UK), 1985–87. Columnist, The Guardian, 1968–70; Columnist, The Observer, 1971–75; regular contributor, Illustrated London News, 1972–85. Contested (L) Hove, 1973, 1974; Liberal Party: Mem. Council, 1973–74 and 1984–85; Mem., Nat. Exec., 1984–85; Pres., 1986–87; Pres., NLYL, 1984–85; Mem. Federal Exec., SLD, 1988. *Publications:* I Know It Was the Place's Fault, 1970; Des Wilson's Minority Report (a diary of protest), 1973; So you want to be Prime Minister: a personal view of British politics, 1979; The Lead Scandal, 1982; Pressure, the A to Z of Campaigning in Britain, 1984; (ed) The Environmental Crisis, 1984; (ed) The Secrets File, 1984; The Citizen Action Handbook, 1986; Battle for Power — Inside the Alliance General Election Campaign, 1987; Costa Del Sol (novel), 1990; Campaign (novel), 1992. *Address:* 46 Arundel Street, Brighton, Sussex.

WILSON, Sir Donald; *see* Wilson, Sir R. D.

WILSON, Dr Douglas George, CB 1984; Chief Government Medical Officer, Queensland, 1968–84, retired 1984; Senior Lecturer in Forensic Medicine, University of Queensland, since 1968; *b* 21 Jan. 1924; *s* of William John Wilson and Mary Catherine Mitchell; *m* 1951, Heloise, *d* of J. J. McCormack; one *s*. *Educ:* St Joseph's College, Nudgee, Qld. MB BS Qld 1952; DPH Sydney 1965; Dip. Med. Jurisp., Soc. of Apothecaries of London, 1975. War service, 2nd AIF, 1942–44; RAAMC, 1953. Resident MO, Brisbane Gen. Hosp., 1952–53; private practice, Caloundra, 1954–65; Dep. MOH, NSW Dept of Public Health, 1965–67. Founder Dep. Chm., Qld Road Safety Council Res. Cttee, 1975–; Mem., Traffic Adv. Cttee, 1968–84; Dep. Chm. Med. Div. and Mem. Internat. Med. Commn, XII Commonwealth Games, Brisbane, 1982. Nat. Health and MRC Travelling Fellowship in Forensic Medicine, 1975; Fulbright Sen. Schol. in Traffic Medicine, Central Missouri State Univ., 1978. Member: British Acad. of Forensic Scis; Forensic Sci. Soc.; Internat. Assoc. for Accident and Traffic Medicine; Aust. and Pacific Area Police Med. Officers' Assoc. Foundation Chairman: Sunshine Coast Br., Arthritis Foundn of Aust., 1985; Qld Estuarine Res. Gp, 1985. Gold Medal, Internat. Assoc. for Accident and Traffic Medicine, 1985. SBStJ 1978. *Publications:* Rationale of the Determination of Blood Alcohol Concentration by Breath Analysis (Training Manual), 1968; numerous papers on alcohol, drugs and traffic safety, forensic subjects in learned jls. *Recreations:* swimming, boating, golf, tropical fruit farming. *Address:* 3 Alfred Street, Caloundra, Qld 4551, Australia. *T:* (071) 91 1610. *Clubs:* University of Queensland (Brisbane); Caloundra Golf, Caloundra Power Boat, Caloundra Returned Services.

WILSON, Lt-Col Eric Charles Twelves, VC 1940; retired; *b* 2 October 1912; *s* of Rev. C. C. C. Wilson; *m* 1943, Ann (from whom he obtained a divorce, 1953), *d* of Major Humphrey Pleydell-Bouverie, MBE; two *s*; *m* 1953, Angela Joy, *d* of Lt-Col J. McK. Gordon, MC; one *s*. *Educ:* Marlborough; RMC, Sandhurst. Commissioned in East Surrey Regt, 1933; seconded to King's African Rifles, 1937; seconded to Somaliland Camel Corps, 1939; Long Range Desert Gp, 1941–42; Burma, 1944; seconded to N Rhodesia Regt, 1946; retd from Regular Army, 1949; Admin Officer, HM Overseas Civil Service, Tanganyika, 1949–61; Dep. Warden, London House, 1962, Warden, 1966–77. Hon. Sec., Anglo-Somali Soc., 1972–77 and 1988–90. *Publication:* Stowell in the Blackmore Vale, 1986. *Recreation:* country life. *Address:* Woodside Cottage, Stowell, Sherborne, Dorset. *T:* Templecombe (0963) 70264.

WILSON, Frank Richard, CMG 1963; OBE 1946; Controller of Administration, Commonwealth Development Corporation, 1976–80; retired HMOCS Oct. 1963; *b* 26 Oct. 1920; *er s* of late Sir Leonard Wilson, KCIE and the late Muriel Wilson; *m* 1947, Alexandra Dorothy Mary (*née* Haigh); two *s*. *Educ:* Oundle Sch.; Trinity Hall, Cambridge (1939–40 only). Commnd Indian Army, 1941; retired as Lieut-Col, 1946. Joined Colonial Administrative Service (later HMOCS) in Kenya, 1947; District Comr, 1950–56; Private Sec. to the Governor, 1956–59; Provincial Comr, Central Province, 1959–63; Civil Sec., Central Region, 1963. With Commonwealth Develt Corp., 1964–80. *Address:* Chelsea House, Mickleton, Chipping Campden, Glos GL55 6SD.

WILSON, Geoffrey; Chairman, Wells, O'Brien & Co., since 1972; *b* 11 July 1929; *m* 1962, Philomena Mary Kavanagh; one *s* one *d*. *Educ:* Bolton County Grammar Sch.; Univ. of Birmingham; Linacre Coll., Oxford. PE Consulting Group, 1958–63; British Railways, 1963–71; Mem., BR Bd, 1968–71, Chief Exec. (Railways), 1971. Member: Council, Royal Inst. of Public Admin, 1970–71; Council, Inst. of Transport, 1970–71. *Recreations:* golf, gardening, painting. *Address:* 10 Montpellier Grove, Cheltenham, Glos GL50 2XB.

WILSON, Geoffrey Alan; Chairman, Greycoat plc, since 1985; *b* 19 Feb. 1934; *s* of Lewis Wilson and Doris Wilson (*née* Shrier); *m* 1963, Marilyn Helen Freedman; one *s* two *d*. *Educ:* Haberdashers' Aske's School; College of Estate Management. FRICS. 2nd Lieut RA, 1955–56. Private practice, 1957–60; Director: Amalgamated Investment & Property Co., 1961–70; Sterling Land Co., 1971–73 (and co-founder); Greycoat, 1976– (and co-founder). Mem., W Metropolitan Conciliation Cttee, Race Relations Bd, 1969–71; Trustee: ORT Trust, 1980–; Public Art Develt Trust, 1990–. *Recreations:* reading, architecture, art, film. *Address:* Greycoat plc, Leconfield House, Curzon Street, W1Y 8AS. *T:* 071–491 8688. *Clubs:* Reform, Royal Automobile.

WILSON, Hon. Geoffrey Hazlitt, CVO 1989; FCA, FCMA; Chairman, Delta plc, since 1982; *b* 28 Dec. 1929; *yr s* of 1st Baron Moran, MC, MD, FRCP, and Lady Moran, MBE; *m* 1955, Barbara Jane Hebblethwaite; two *s* two *d*. *Educ:* Eton; King's Coll., Cambridge (BA Hons). JDipMA. Articled to Barton Mayhew (now Ernst & Whinney), 1952; Chartered Accountant 1955; joined English Electric, 1956; Dep. Comptroller, 1965; Financial Controller (Overseas), GEC, 1968; joined Delta Group as Financial Dir, Cables Div., 1969; elected to Main Board as Gp Financial Dir, 1972; Jt Man. Dir, 1977; Dep. Chief Executive, 1980; Chief Exec., 1981–88. Director: Blue Circle Industries plc, 1980–; Drayton English & International Trust, 1978–; W Midlands and Wales Regl Bd, Nat. Westminster Bank PLC, 1985– (Chm., 1990–); Southern Electric plc (formerly Southern Electricity), 1989–; Vicarage Motorcars, 1989–; Johnson, Matthey plc, 1990–; UK Adv. Bd, National Westminster Bank, 1990–. Member: Council, Inst. of Cost and Management Accountants, 1972–78; Accounting Standards Cttee, 1978–79; Inflation Accounting Steering Gp, 1976–80; London Metal Exchange, 1982–; Engrg Industries Council, 1985–; Chm., 100 Gp of Chartered Accountants, 1979–80 (Hon. Mem., 1985). Mem. Management Bd, Engineering Employers Fedn, 1979–83 (Vice-Pres., 1983–86 and 1990–; Dep. Pres., 1986–90); Chm., EEF Cttee on Future of Wage Bargaining, 1980; Dep. Pres., 1986–87, Pres., 1987–88, BEAMA; Member: Administrative Council, Royal Jubilee Trusts, 1979–88, Hon. Treas., 1980–89; Council, Winchester Cathedral Trust, 1985–; Council, St Mary's Hosp. Med. Sch., 1985–88. CBIM. Mem. Ct of Assistants, Chartered Accountants' Co., 1982–, Master, 1988–89. *Recreations:* family, reading, walking, ski-ing, vintage cars. *Address:* Delta plc, 1 Kingsway, WC2B 6XF. *T:* 071–836 3535. *Clubs:* Boodle's, Royal Automobile.

WILSON, Sir Geoffrey Masterman, KCB 1969 (CB 1968); CMG 1962; Chairman, Oxfam, 1977–83; *b* 7 April 1910; 3rd *s* of late Alexander Cowan Wilson and Edith Jane Brayshaw; *m* 1st, 1946, Julie Stafford Trowbridge (marr. diss. 1979); two *s* two *d*; 2nd, 1989, Stephanie Stainsby (*née* Ross). *Educ:* Manchester Grammar School; Oriel College, Oxford. Chairman, Oxford Univ. Labour Club, 1930; Pres., Oxford Union, 1931. Harmsworth Law Scholar, Middle Temple, 1931; called to Bar, Middle Temple, 1934. Served in HM Embassy, Moscow, and Russian Dept of Foreign Office, 1940–45. Cabinet

Office, 1947; Treasury, 1948; Director, Colombo Plan Technical Co-operation Bureau, 1951–53; Under-Secretary, Treasury, 1956–58; Deputy Head of UK Treasury Delegn and Alternate Exec. Dir for UK, Internat. Bank, Washington, 1958; Vice-President, International Bank, Washington, 1961–66; Deputy Secretary, ODM, 1966–68, Permanent Secretary, 1968–70; Dep. Sec.-Gen. (Economic), Commonwealth Secretariat, 1971. Chm., Race Relations Bd, 1971–77. Hon. Fellow: Wolfson Coll., Cambridge, 1971; Inst. of Develt Studies, Brighton, 1981. *Address:* 4 Polstead Road, Oxford.

See also Prof. J. E. Meade.

WILSON, Geoffrey Studholme, CMG 1961; Commissioner of Police, Tanganyika Police Force, 1958–62; *b* 5 June 1913; *s* of late J. E. S. Wilson; *m* 1936, Joy Noel, *d* of Capt. C. St G. Harris-Walker; two *s*. *Educ:* Radley College. Joined Hong Kong Police, 1933; Commissioner of Police, Sarawak Constabulary, 1953–58. King's Police Medal, 1950. OStJ 1961. *Recreations:* golf, fishing, sailing. *Address:* British Bank of the Middle East, Falcon House, Curzon Street, W1Y 8AA. *Club:* Hong Kong (Hong Kong).

WILSON, George; *see* Wilson, W. G.

WILSON, George Pritchard Harvey, CMG 1966; JP; Chairman, Victorian Inland Meat Authority, 1973–77 (Deputy Chairman, 1970–73); *b* 10 March 1918; *s* of late G. L. Wilson; *m* 1945, Fay Hobart Duff; two *s* one *d*. *Educ:* Geelong Grammar School. Nuffield Scholar (Farming), 1952. Council Member, Monash University, 1961–69; Royal Agricultural Society of Victoria: Councillor, 1950; President, 1964–73; Trustee, 1968–. Member: Victoria Promotion Cttee, 1968–81; Victoria Economic Develt Corp., 1981–82. Chm., Australian Nuffield Farming Scholars Assoc., 1973–89; Hon. Trustee, UK Nuffield Farming Scholarship Trust, 1989. JP 1957. *Recreation:* fishing. *Address:* Wilson House, Berwick, Victoria 3806, Australia. *T:* Berwick 7071271. *Clubs:* Melbourne, Royal Automobile Club of Victoria (Melbourne).

WILSON, Gerald Robertson, CB 1991; Secretary, Scottish Office Education Department, since 1988; *b* 7 Sept. 1939; *s* of Charles Robertson Wilson and Margaret Wilson (*née* Early); *m* 1963, Margaret Anne, *d* of late John S. and Agnes Wight; one *s* one *d*. *Educ:* Holy Cross Academy, Edinburgh; University of Edinburgh. MA. Asst Principal, Scottish Home and Health Dept, 1961–65; Private Sec. to Minister of State for Scotland, 1965–66; Principal, Scottish Home and Health Dept, 1966–72; Private Sec. to Lord Privy Seal, 1972–74, to Minister of State, Civil Service Dept, 1974; Asst Sec., Scottish Economic Planning Dept, 1974–77; Counsellor, Office of the UK Perm. Rep. to the European Communities, Brussels, 1977–82; Asst Sec., Scottish Office, 1982–84; Under Sec., Industry Dept for Scotland, 1984–88. *Recreation:* music. *Address:* c/o Scottish Office Education Department, New St Andrew's House, Edinburgh EH1 3SY. *Clubs:* Commonwealth Trust; New (Edinburgh).

WILSON, (Gerald) Roy; Under Secretary and Deputy Director of Savings, Department for National Savings, 1986–89, retired; *b* 11 Jan. 1930; *s* of late Fred Wilson and Elsie Wilson (*née* Morrison); *m* 1st, 1965, Doreen Chadderton (*d* 1990); one *s* one *d*; 2nd, 1990, Patricia Henderson (*née* Ive). *Educ:* High School, Oldham. Min. of Works, 1947; HM Stationery Office, 1949; Post Office Savings Dept, 1957; PO HQ, 1963; National Girobank, 1966; Dept for National Savings, 1969–89; Controller, Savings Certificate and SAYE Office, Durham, 1978–86. FBIM; Mensa. *Recreations:* swimming, and its organisation and teaching, reading, drawing, photography, watching other sports. *Address:* 48 Ancroft Garth, High Shincliffe, Durham DH1 2UD. *Clubs:* Civil Service; Durham Rotary, Durham Probus, Dunelm (Durham); Durham City Swimming, Durham City Cricket.

WILSON, Gilbert; *b* 2 March 1908; *s* of J. E. Wilson; *m* 1934, Janet Joy Turner; two *d*. *Educ:* Auckland Grammar School. Served with 2nd NZEF, Middle East, 1940–43. Joined National Bank of New Zealand, 1924; joined Reserve Bank of New Zealand, 1935; Dep. Chief Cashier, 1948–53; Chief Cashier, 1953–56; Dep. Governor, 1956–62; Governor, 1962–67; also Alternate Governor for New Zealand of International Monetary Fund, 1962–67. *Address:* 41 Mere Road, Taupo, New Zealand.

WILSON, Gillian Brenda, (Mrs Kenneth Wilson); *see* Babington-Browne, G. B.

WILSON, Gordon; *see* Wilson, Robert G.

WILSON, Gordon Wallace, CB 1986; Under Secretary, Ministry of Agriculture, Fisheries and Food, 1975–86, retired; *b* 14 July 1926; *s* of late John Wallace Wilson and of Mrs Joyce Elizabeth Grace Sherwood-Smith; *m* 1951, Gillian Maxwell (*née* Wood); three *s*. *Educ:* King's Sch., Bruton; Queen's Coll., Oxford (BA PPE). Entered Civil Service (War Office), 1950; Principal Private Sec. to Sec. of State for War, 1962; Asst Sec., MoD, 1964; Dir, Centre of Admin Studies, HM Treasury, 1965; Asst Sec., DEA, 1968; HM Treasury, 1969. *Recreations:* tennis, carpentry, gardening, sketching. *Address:* 61 Ottways Lane, Ashtead, Surrey KT21 2PS. *T:* Ashtead (0372) 272898.

WILSON, Graeme McDonald, CMG 1975; British Civil Aviation Representative (Far East), 1964–81, retired; *b* 9 May 1919; *s* of Robert Linton McDonald Wilson and Sophie Hamilton Wilson (*née* Milner); *m* 1968, Yabu Masae; three *s*. *Educ:* Rendcomb Coll., Glos; Schloss Schule Salem, Germany; Lincoln Coll., Oxford; Gray's Inn, London. Served in Fleet Air Arm, 1939–46. Joined Home Civil Service, 1946. Private Sec. to Parly Sec., Min. of Civil Aviation, 1946–49; Planning 1, 1949–53; Dep. UK Rep. on Council of ICAO, 1953–56; Lt-Comdr (A) (O) (Ph) (q) RCNR, 1954; Internat. Relations 1, Min. of Transport and Civil Aviation, 1956–61; Asst Sec. Interdependence, Exports and Electronics, Min. of Aviation, 1961–64; seconded to Foreign Service as Counsellor and Civil Air Attaché, at twelve Far Eastern posts, 1964. Ford Foundn Fellow, Nat. Translation Center, Austin, Texas, 1968–69. UN Expert on Air Services Agreements, 1984. *Publications:* Face At The Bottom Of The World: translations of the modern Japanese poetry of Hagiwara Sakutaro, 1969; (trans., with Ito Aiko) I Am a Cat, 1971; (trans., with Atsumi Ikuko) Three Contemporary Japanese Poets, 1972; (trans., with Ito Aiko) Ten Nights of Dream, 1973; Nihon no Kindaishi to Gendaishi no Dai Yon-sho: Hagiwara Sakutaro, 1974; (trans., with Ito Aiko) I Am a Cat II, 1979; (trans., with Ito Aiko) I Am a Cat III, 1985; From the Morning of the World (trans. of selected Japanese poems from the Manyōshū of 759), 1991; articles on East Asian literature and poems (mostly Japanese, Chinese, Vietnamese and Korean trans). *Address:* 42 Cranford Avenue, Exmouth, Devon. *T:* Exmouth (0395) 264786. *Clubs:* Naval; PEN Club of Japan (Tokyo).

WILSON, Guy Murray, MA; FSA; Master of the Armouries, since 1988; *b* 18 Feb. 1950; *s* of late Rowland George Wilson and Mollie (*née* Munson; later Mrs Youngs); *m* 1972, Pamela Ruth McCredie; two *s* two *d*. *Educ:* New Coll., Oxford (MA); Manchester Univ. (Dip. Art, Gallery and Museum Studies). FSA 1984. Joined Royal Armouries, 1972; Keeper of Edged Weapons, 1978; Dep. Master of the Armouries, 1981. Member: British Commn for Military History, 1978–; Adv. Cttee on History Wreck Sites, 1981–; Arms and Armour Soc. of GB, 1973–; Arms and Armour Soc. of Denmark, 1978–; Meyrick Soc., 1980–. *Publications:* Treasures of the Tower: Crossbows, 1975; (with A. V. B. Norman) Treasures from the Tower of London, 1982; contribs to museum and exhibn catalogues and to Jl of Arms and Armour Soc., Internat. Jl of Nautical Archaeol., Connoisseur, Burlington, Country Life, Museums Jl, Guns Rev., etc. *Recreations:* theatre, music, reading, walking. *Address:* 15 St Fabians Drive, Chelmsford, Essex CM1 2PR; 8 Tower Green, HM Tower of London, EC3N 4AB.

WILSON, Harold; His Honour Judge Harold Wilson; a Circuit Judge, since 1981 (Midland and Oxford Circuit); *b* 19 Sept. 1931; *s* of late Edward Simpson Wilson; *m* 1973, Jill Ginever, *d* of late Charles Edward Walter Barlow; one step *s* one step *d*; three *s* one *d* by previous marriage. *Educ:* St Albans Sch.; Sidney Sussex Coll., Cambridge (State Scholar; MA). Commnd service, RAF, RAFVR, RAuxAF, 1950–disbandment. Administrative Trainee, KCH, 1954–56; Schoolmaster, 1957–59. Called to the Bar, Gray's Inn, 1958 (Holker Exhbr; runner-up, Lee Essay Prize, 1959); Oxford Circuit, 1960–70 (Circuit Junior, 1964–65); Midland and Oxford Circuit, 1971–75; Dep. Chm., Monmouthshire Quarter Sessions, 1970; a Recorder, Midland and Oxford Circuit, 1971–75; Chm. of Industrial Tribunals, Birmingham, 1976–81; Resident Judge, Coventry Crown Ct, 1983–; Liaison Judge, 1986–; Hon. Recorder of Coventry, 1986–; designated Care Centre Judge, Coventry, 1991–. Pres., Transport Tribunal, 1991–; Chm., Coventry Reparation Unit Adv. Cttee, 1991–. Member: Matrimonial Causes Rules Cttee, 1984–88; W Midlands Probation Cttee, 1985–. *Recreations:* watching rugby football, reading and listening to music. *Address:* 2 Harcourt Buildings, Temple, EC4Y 9DB. *T:* 071–353 6961. *Club:* Royal Air Force.

WILSON, Harold Arthur Cooper B.; *see* Bird-Wilson.

WILSON, Harry; *see* Wilson of Langside, Baron.

WILSON, Henry Braithwaite; Assistant Under-Secretary of State, Home Office, 1963–71; *b* 6 Aug. 1911; *s* of Charles Braithwaite Wilson and Ellen Blanche Hargrove; *m* 1936, Margaret Bodden; two *s* two *d*. *Educ:* Leighton Park School; Lincoln College, Oxford. Editorial work for Joseph Rowntree Social Service Trust, 1933–40; Sub-Warden, Toynbee Hall, 1940–41; Home Office: Temp. Administrative Asst, 1941–44; Sec., Departmental Cttee on War Damaged Licensed Premises and Reconstruction, 1942–44; Principal, 1944 (estab. 1946); Asst Sec., 1956. *Address:* Arran, Yew Tree Road, Grange over Sands, Cumbria LA11 7AA. *T:* Grange (05395) 33488.

WILSON, Henry Moir, CB 1969; CMG 1965; MBE 1946; PhD, BSc, FRAeS; *b* 3 Sept. 1910; 3rd *s* of late Charles Wilson, Belfast; *m* 1937, Susan Eveline Wilson; one *s* three *d*. *Educ:* Royal Belfast Academical Institution, Queen's Univ., Belfast. Apprentice in Mech. Eng, Combe Barbour, Belfast, 1927–31; QUB, 1927–31 (part-time) and 1931–34 (full-time); BSc with 1st Class Hons in Elect. Eng, 1932; PhD 1934 (Thesis on High Voltage Transients on Power Transmission Lines). College Apprentice, Metropolitan-Vickers, Manchester, 1934–35. Joined RAF Educational Service, 1935; commissioned RAFVR, 1939; Senior Tutor, RAF Advanced Armament Course, Ft. Halstead, 1943–46; Senior Educ. Officer, Empire Air Armament School, Manby (Acting Wing Comdr), 1946–47. Joined Ministry of Supply, 1947, as Senior Principal Sci. Officer, Supt Servo Div., Guided Projectile Estab., Westcott, 1947; Supt Guidance and Control Div. Guided Weapons Dept, RAE, 1947–49; Head of Armament Dept, RAE, 1949–56. Dep. Chief Sci. Officer, 1952; Chief Scientific Officer, 1956; Director-General, Aircraft Equipment Research and Devel., Ministry of Aviation, 1956–62; Head, Defence Research and Development Staff, British Embassy, Washington, DC, 1962–65; Dep. Chief Scientist (Army), 1965–66, Chief Scientist (Army), 1967–70; Dir, SHAPE Tech. Centre, 1970–75. Hon. DSc QUB, 1971. *Recreations:* golf, gardening. *Address:* 7 Carlinwark Drive, Camberley, Surrey GU15 3TX.

WILSON, Prof. Henry Wallace, PhD; CPhys, FInstP; FRSE; physicist; Director, Scottish Universities' Research and Reactor Centre, 1962–85; Personal Professor of Physics, Strathclyde University, 1966–85, now Emeritus; *b* 30 Aug. 1923; *s* of Frank Binnington Wilson and Janet (*née* Wilson); *m* 1955, Fiona McPherson Martin, *d* of Alfred Charles Steinmetz Martin and Agnes Mary (*née* McPherson); three *s*. *Educ:* Allan Glen's Sch., Glasgow; Glasgow Univ. (BSc, PhD Physics). AInstP 1949, FInstP 1962; FRSE 1963. Wartime work as Physicist, Explosives Res. Div., ICI, Ardeer. Asst Lectr, Natural Philosophy Dept, Glasgow Univ., 1947–51; post-doctoral Res. Fellow, Univ. of Calif, Berkeley, 1951–52; Lectr, Nat. Phil. Dept, Glasgow Univ., 1952–55; Leader of Physical Measurements Gp, UKAEA, Aldermaston, 1955–62 (Sen. Principal Scientific Officer, 1958). Hon. Scientific Advr, Nat. Mus. of Antiquities of Scotland, 1969. Mem., Nuclear Safety Cttee, 1964–89, and Consultant, SSEB; Mem., Radioactive Substances Adv. Cttee, 1966–70. Inst. of Physics: Mem. Council, 1970–71; Chm., Scottish Br., 1969–71; mem. several cttees; Royal Soc. of Edinburgh: Mem. Council, 1966–69, 1976–79; Vice Pres., 1979–81. Member: Brit. Nuclear Energy Soc.; British Mass Spectrometry Soc. (Chm., 1977–79). *Publications:* contributions to: Alpha, Beta and Gamma-ray Spectroscopy, ed K. Siegbahn, 1965; Activation Analysis, ed Lenihan and Thomson, 1965; Modern Aspects of Mass Spectrometry, ed R. I. Reed, 1968; Encyclopaedic Dictionary of Physics, ed J. Thewlis, 1973; (ed) Nuclear Engineering sect., Chambers' Science and Technology Dictionary, gen. ed. P. M. B. Walker, 1988; papers on radioactivity, low energy nuclear physics, meson physics, mass spectrometry, isotope separation, effects of radiation, and reactor physics, in Phil. Mag., Nature, Phys. Rev., Proc. Phys. Soc., etc. *Recreations:* sailing, hill-walking, industrial archaeology, photography. *Address:* Ashgrove, The Crescent, Busby, Glasgow G76 8HT. *T:* 041–644 3107. *Club:* Caledonian (Edinburgh).

WILSON, Ian D.; *see* Douglas-Wilson.

WILSON, Ian Matthew, CB 1985; Secretary of Commissions for Scotland, since 1987; *b* 12 Dec. 1926; *s* of Matthew Thomson Wilson and Mary Lily Barnett; *m* 1953, Anne Chalmers (*d* 1991); three *s*. *Educ:* George Watson's Coll.; Edinburgh Univ. (MA). Asst Principal, Scottish Home Dept, 1950; Private Sec. to Perm. Under-Sec. of State, Scottish Office, 1953–55; Principal, Scottish Home Dept, 1955; Asst Secretary: Scottish Educn Dept, 1963; SHHD, 1971; Asst Under-Sec. of State, Scottish Office, 1974–77; Under Sec., Scottish Educn Dept, 1977–86. *Address:* 1 Bonaly Drive, Edinburgh EH13 0EJ. *T:* 031–441 2541.

WILSON, Sir James; *see* Wilson, Sir A. J.

WILSON, Brig. James, CBE 1986; Director, Edinburgh Old Town Trust, 1987–90; Chief Executive, Livingston Development Corporation, 1977–87; *b* 12 March 1922; *s* of late Alexander Robertson Wilson and Elizabeth Wylie Wilson (*née* Murray); *m* 1949, Audrie Veronica, *er d* of late A. W. and O. V. Haines; three *d*. *Educ:* Irvine Royal Academy; Edinburgh Academy; Aberdeen Univ. Commissioned RA, 1941; served War with 71 (West Riding) Field Regt, N Africa and Italy, 1941–45; Instructor, Sch. of Artillery, India, 1945–47; Adjt, Sussex Yeo., 1948–49; active service in Malaya and ME, 1950–53; psc 1954; DAQMG, War Office, 1955–57; Instructor, Staff Coll., 1959–61; CO, 439 (Tyne) Light Air Defence Regt, 1964–67; AQMG, Northern Comd, 1967–68; Col GS SD, HQ BAOR, 1969–71; AMA and DCBAS, Washington, 1972–73; DQMG, HQ UKLF, 1974–77. Member: Executive Council, TCPA (Scotland), 1977–87; Edin. Univ. Careers Adv. Cttee, 1982–86; Scottish Cttee, Inst. of Dirs, 1983–86; Dir, Edinburgh Chamber of Commerce, 1979–82. Mem., Royal Artillery Council for Scotland, 1979–; Chairman: W Lothian SSAFA, 1983–; E Scotland SSAFA Cttee, 1986–; RA Assoc.

(Scotland), 1987–. FBIM 1980. *Recreations:* golf, sailing, bridge. *Address:* 2 The Gardens, Aberlady, East Lothian EH32 0SF. *T:* Aberlady (08757) 583. *Clubs:* Army and Navy; New (Edinburgh); Hon. Co. of Edinburgh Golfers.

WILSON, Dr James Maxwell Glover, FRCP, FRCPE, FFPHM; Senior Principal Medical Officer, Department of Health and Social Security, 1972–76; *b* 31 Aug. 1913; *s* of late James Thomas Wilson and Mabel Salomons; *m* Lallie Methley; three *s. Educ:* King's College Choir Sch., Cambridge; Oundle Sch.; St John's Coll., Cambridge; University College Hosp., London. MA, MB, BChir (Cantab). Clinical appts, London and Cambridge, 1937–39. Served War, RAMC (Major, 6th Airborne Div.), 1939–45. Hospital appts, London and Edinburgh, 1945–54; medical work on tea estates in India, 1954–57; Medical Staff, Min. of Health (later DHSS), concerned with the centrally financed research programme, 1957–76; Sen. Res. Fellow, Inf. Services Div., Common Services Agency, Scottish Health Service, 1976–81. Lectr (part-time), Public Health Dept, London Sch. of Hygiene and Tropical Med., 1968–72. *Publications:* (with G. Jungner) Principles and Practice of Screening for Disease (WHO), 1968; contribs to med. jls, mainly on screening for disease. *Recreations:* reading, walking, conservation. *Address:* Millhill House, 77 Millhill, Musselburgh, Midlothian EH21 7RP. *T:* 031–665 5829.

WILSON, James Noel, ChM, FRCS; retired; Consultant Orthopædic Surgeon: Royal National Orthopædic Hospital, London (Surgeon i/c Accident Unit, RNOH Stanmore), 1955–84; National Hospitals for Nervous Diseases, Queen Square and Maida Vale, 1962–84; Teacher of Orthopædics, Institute of Orthopædics, University of London; retired; *b* Coventry, 25 Dec. 1919; *s* of Alexander Wilson and Isobel Barbara Wilson (*née* Fairweather); *m* 1945, Patricia Norah McCullough; two *s* two *d. Educ:* King Henry VIII Sch., Coventry; University of Birmingham. Peter Thompson Prize in Anatomy, 1940; Sen. Surgical Prize, 1942; Arthur Foxwell Prize in Clinical Medicine, 1943; MB, ChB 1943; MRCS, LRCP, 1943; FRCS 1948; ChM (Birmingham) 1949; House Surgeon, Birmingham General Hospital, 1943; Heaton Award as Best Resident for 1943. Service in RAMC, Nov. 1943–Oct. 1946, discharged as Captain; qualified as Parachutist and served with 1st Airborne Division. Resident surgical posts, Birmingham General Hospital and Coventry and Warwickshire Hospital, 1947–49; Resident Surgical Officer, Robert Jones and Agnes Hunt Orthopædic Hospital, Oswestry, 1949–52; Consultant Orthopædic Surgeon to Cardiff Royal Infirmary and Welsh Regional Hospital Board, 1952–55. Prof. of Orthopaedics, Addis Ababa Univ., 1989. Watson-Jones Lectr, RCS, 1988. Pres., 1979–84, Chm. UK Region, 1984–, World Orthopaedic Concern; Vice-Chm., Impact (UK) Foundn; Pres., Orthopaedic Section, RSocMed, 1982–83; former Mem. Brit. Editorial Bd, Jl of Bone and Joint Surgery; Sen. Fellow, and formerly Editorial Sec., British Orthopædic Assoc. (BOA Travelling Fellowship to USA, 1954); FRSocMed. Life Mem., Bangladesh Orthopaedic Soc.; Hon. Mem., Egyptian Orthopaedic Assoc. *Publications:* (ed) Watson Jones Fractures and Joint Injuries, 6th edn 1982; former contributor, Butterworth's Operative Surgery; chapters and articles on orthopædic subjects to various books and journals. *Recreations:* golf, reluctant gardening, photography. *Address:* The Chequers, Waterdale, near Watford, Herts. *T:* Garston (0923) 672364. *Club:* Royal Society of Medicine.

WILSON, Air Vice-Marshal James Stewart, CBE 1959; Hon. Civil Consultant in Preventive Medicine to the Royal Air Force, since 1983; *b* 4 Sept. 1909; *s* of late J. Wilson, Broughty Ferry, Angus, and late Helen Fyffe Wilson; *m* 1937, Elizabeth Elias; one *s* (and one *s* decd). *Educ:* Dundee High Sch.; St Andrews Univ. (MB, ChB). DPH (London) 1948; FFCM(RCP) 1974. House Surgeon, Dundee Royal Infirmary, 1933; House Surgeon, Arbroath Infirmary, 1934; Commissioned Royal Air Force, 1935. Served North Africa, 1942–45. Director Hygiene and Research, Air Ministry, London, 1956–59; Principal Medical Officer, Flying Training Command, 1959–61; Director-General of Medical Services, Royal Australian Air Force, 1961–63. QHP 1961–65; Principal Medical Officer, Bomber Command, 1963–65, retired. Special Adviser in Epidemiology and Applied Entomology, Inst. of Community Medicine, RAF Halton, 1965–83. *Publications:* articles (jointly) on respiratory virus infections, in medical journals. *Recreations:* golf, fishing, shooting. *Address:* Eucumbene, Buckland, Aylesbury, Bucks. *T:* Aylesbury (0296) 630062. *Club:* Royal Air Force.

WILSON, Sir James (William Douglas), 5th Bt *cr* 1906; farmer; *b* 8 Oct. 1960; *s* of Captain Sir Thomas Douglas Wilson, 4th Bt, MC, and of Pamela Aileen, *d* of Sir Edward Hanmer, 7th Bt; *S* father, 1984; *m* 1985, Julia Margaret Louise, fourth *d* of J. C. F. Mutty, Mulberry Hall, Melbourne, Cambs; one *s* one *d. Educ:* London Univ. (BA Hons French). *Heir: s* Thomas Edward Douglas Wilson, *b* 15 April 1990. *Address:* Lillingstone Lovell Manor, Buckingham MK18 5BQ. *T:* Lillingstone Dayrell (02806) 643.

WILSON, Joe; *see* Wilson, A. J.

WILSON, Sir John (Foster), Kt 1975; CBE 1965 (OBE 1955); Director, Royal Commonwealth Society for the Blind, 1950–83, Vice-President 1983; Senior Consultant, United Nations Development Programme, since 1983; President, International Agency for the Prevention of Blindness, 1974–83; *b* 20 Jan. 1919; *s* of late Rev. George Henry Wilson, Buxton, Derbys; *m* 1944, Chloe Jean McDermid, OBE 1981; two *d. Educ:* Worcester College for the Blind; St Catherine's, Oxford (MA Jurisprudence, Dipl. Public and Social Administration; Hon. Fellow, 1984). Asst Secretary, Royal National Inst. for the Blind, 1941–49; Member, Colonial Office Delegation investigating blindness in Africa, 1946–47. Proposed formation of Royal Commonwealth Society for Blind; became its first Director, 1950; extensive tours in Africa, Asia, Near and Far East, Caribbean and N. America, 1952–67; world tours, 1958, 1963, 1978; formulated Asian plan for the Blind 1963, and African Plan for the Blind, 1966. Internat. Member of World Council for Welfare of Blind and Hon. Life Mem., World Blind Union; Founder Member, National Fedn of Blind (President, 1955–60); Pres., Internat. Agency for the Prevention of Blindness, 1974–83. Helen Keller International Award, 1970; Lions Internat. Humanitarian Award, 1978; World Humanity Award, 1979; Albert Lasker Award, 1979. *Publications:* Blindness in African and Middle East Territories, 1948; Ghana's Handicapped Citizens, 1961; Travelling Blind, 1963; (ed) World Blindness and its Prevention, 1980; various on Commonwealth affairs, rehabilitation and blindness. *Recreations:* current affairs, travel, writing, tape-recording, wine-making. *Address:* 22 The Cliff, Roedean, Brighton, East Sussex BN2 5RE. *T:* Brighton (0273) 607667. *Club:* Commonwealth Trust.

WILSON, Sir John Gardiner, Kt 1982; CBE 1972; Chairman, Australian Paper Manufacturers Ltd, 1978–84; *b* 13 July 1913; *s* of J. S. Wilson; *m* 1944, Margaret Louise De Ravin; three *d. Educ:* Melbourne Grammar Sch.; Clare Coll., Cambridge (MA 1935). Served RAE, AIF, 1939–46, Col. With J. S. Wilson & Co., actuaries and sharebrokers, 1934–39; Mem., Melbourne Stock Exchange, 1935–47; joined Australian Paper Manufacturers, 1947: Dep. Man. Dir, 1953–59; Man. Dir, 1959–78. Former Director: Vickers Australia; Vickers Cockatoo Dockyard Pty. *Address:* 6 Woorigoleen Road, Toorak, Vic 3142, Australia. *Clubs:* Melbourne, Australian, Royal Melbourne Golf (Melbourne).

WILSON, Prof. John Graham; Cavendish Professor of Physics, 1963–76 (Professor, 1952–63), Pro-Vice-Chancellor, 1969–71, University of Leeds; now Emeritus Professor; *b* 28 April 1911; *er s* of J. E. Wilson, Hartlepool, Co. Durham; *m* 1938, Georgiana Brooke, *o d* of Charles W. Bird, Bisley, Surrey; one *s* one *d. Educ:* West Hartlepool Secondary Sch.; Sidney Sussex Coll., Cambridge. Member of teaching staff, University of Manchester, 1938–52; Reader in Physics, 1951. University of York: Member, Academic Planning Board, 1960–63; Member of Council, 1964–84; Chairman, Joint Matriculation Board, 1964–67. DUniv York, 1975; Hon. DSc Durham, 1977. *Publications:* The Principles of Cloud Chamber Technique, 1951. Editor of Progress in Cosmic Ray Physics, 1952–71; (with G. D. Rochester), Cloud Chamber Photographs of the Cosmic Radiation, 1952. Papers on cosmic ray physics, articles in jls. *Recreation:* gardening. *Address:* 23 Newall Hall Park, Otley, West Yorks LS21 2RD. *T:* Otley (0943) 465184.

WILSON, Ven. John Hewitt, CB 1977; Canon Emeritus of Lincoln Cathedral, since 1980; Rector of The Heyfords with Rousham and Somerton, diocese of Oxford, since 1981; *b* 14 Feb. 1924; 2nd *s* of John Joseph and Marion Wilson; *m* 1951, Gertrude Elsie Joan Weir; three *s* two *d. Educ:* Kilkenny Coll., Kilkenny; Mountjoy Sch., Dublin; Trinity Coll., Dublin. BA 1946, MA 1956. Curate, St George's Church, Dublin, 1947–50. Entered RAF, 1950: RAF Coll., Cranwell, 1950–52; Aden, 1952–55; RAF Wittering, 1955–57; RAF Cottesmore, 1957–58; RAF Germany, 1958–61; Staff Chaplain, Air Ministry, 1961–63; RAF Coll., Cranwell, 1963–66; Asst Chaplain-in-Chief: Far East Air Force, 1966–69; Strike command, 1969–73; Chaplain-in-Chief, RAF, 1973–80. QHC 1973–80. *Recreations:* Rugby football, tennis, gardening, theatre. *Address:* Glencree, Philcote Street, Deddington, Banbury, Oxon OX15 0TB. *T:* Deddington (0869) 38903. *Club:* Royal Air Force.

WILSON, John James, FIEE; CBIM; Chairman, London Electricity plc (formerly London Electricity Board), since 1986; *b* 16 Feb. 1932; *s* of Norval John Wilson and Edna May (*née* Smith); *m* 1961, Connie Catherina Boldt Salomonsson; one *s. Educ:* Royal Grammar Sch., Worcester; College of Technology, Birmingham (BSc). Successive engineering appts, Midlands Electricity Bd, Southern Electricity Bd, 1955–68; Southern Electricity Board: Dist Manager, Swindon, 1968–69; Dist Manager, Reading, 1969–72; Area Manager, Portsmouth, 1972–77; Midlands Electricity Board: Chief Engineer, 1977–79; Dep. Chairman, 1979–82; Chairman, 1982–86. *Recreations:* golf, gardening.

WILSON, Sir John (Martindale), KCB 1974 (CB 1960); a Vice-President, Civil Service Retirement Fellowship, since 1982; *b* 3 Sept. 1915; *e s* of late John and Kate Wilson; *m* 1941, Penelope Beatrice, *e d* of late Francis A. Bolton, JP, Oakamoor, Staffs; one *s* one *d. Educ:* Bradfield Coll.; Gonville and Caius Coll., Cambridge. BA (Cantab), 1st Class Law Trip., 1937; MA 1946. Asst Principal, Dept of Agriculture for Scotland, 1938; Ministry of Supply, 1939; served War, 1939–46 (despatches) with Royal Artillery in India and Burma; Private Sec. to Minister of Supply, 1946–50; Asst Sec., 1950; Under-Sec., 1954; Cabinet Office, 1955–58; MoD, 1958–60; Dep. Sec., Min. of Aviation, 1961–65; Dep. Under-Sec. of State, MoD, 1965–72; Second Permanent Under-Sec. of State (Admin), MoD, 1972–75. Chairman: Crown Housing Assoc., 1975–78; CS Appeal Bd, 1978–81 (Dep. Chm., 1975–78); Civil Service Retirement Fellowship, 1978–82. *Recreation:* gardening. *Address:* Bourne Close, Bourne Lane, Twyford, near Winchester, Hants SO21 1NX. *T:* Twyford (0962) 713488. *Club:* Army and Navy.

WILSON, Dr John Murray, MBE 1964; Controller, Home Division, British Council, 1985–86; *b* 25 July 1926; *s* of Maurice John and Mary Ellen Wilson (*née* Murray); *m* 1957, Audrey Miriam Simmons; one *s* one *d. Educ:* Selwyn Avenue Junior, Highams Park; Bancroft's School, Essex; St John's College, Oxford (MA Botany 1952; DPhil 1957; *prox. acc.* Christopher Welch Scholarship 1951). Served RAF, 1945–48. British Council, 1955–86: Science Dept, 1955–58; Chile, 1958–62; Brazil, 1962–66; India, 1966–71; Dep. Rep./Sci. Officer, Italy, 1971–74; Sci. Officer, Germany, 1974–79; Dep. Rep., Germany, 1979–81; Dep. Controller, Home Div., 1981–85. *Publications:* (with J. L. Harley) papers in New Phytologist. *Recreations:* gardening, photography, messing about. *Address:* c/o Personnel Records, The British Council, 10 Spring Gardens, SW1A 2BN.

WILSON, John Spark, CBE 1979 (OBE 1969); Assistant Commissioner, Traffic and Technical Support Department, Metropolitan Police, 1977–82, retired; Director, Security and Investigation Service, T. Miller & Co., 1982–87; *b* 9 May 1922; *s* of John Wilson and Elizabeth Kidd Wilson; *m* 1948, Marguerite Chisholm Wilson; two *s* one *d. Educ:* Logie Central Sch., Dundee. Joined Metropolitan Police, 1946; Special Branch, 1948–67; Detective Chief Supt, 1968; Comdr, 1969; went to Wales re Investiture of Prince of Wales, 1969; Dep. Asst Comr (CID), 1972; Asst Comr (Crime), 1975. *Recreations:* football, Rugby, boxing.

WILSON, Prof. John Stuart Gladstone, MA, DipCom; Professor of Economics and Commerce in the University of Hull, 1959–82, now Emeritus Professor; Head of Department, 1959–71, and 1974–77; *b* 18 Aug. 1916; *s* of Herbert Gladstone Wilson and Mary Buchanan Wilson (*née* Wylie); *m* 1943, Beryl Margaret Gibson, *d* of Alexander Millar Gibson and Bertha Noble Gibson; no *c. Educ:* University of Western Australia. Lecturer in Economics: University of Tasmania, 1941–43; Sydney, 1944–45; Canberra, 1946–47; LSE, 1948–49. Reader in Economics, with special reference to Money and Banking, Univ. of London, 1950–59; Dean, Faculty of Social Sciences and Law, Univ. of Hull, 1962–65; Chairman, Centre for S-E Asian Studies, Univ. of Hull, 1963–66. Hackett Research Student, 1947; Leverhulme Research Award, 1955. Economic Survey of New Hebrides on behalf of Colonial Office, 1958–59; Consultant, Trade and Payments Dept, OECD, 1965–66; Consultant with Harvard Advisory Development Service in Liberia, 1967; headed Enquiry into Sources of Capital and Credit to UK Agriculture, 1970–73; Consultant, Directorate Gen. for Agric., EEC, 1974–75; Specialist Adviser, H of C Select Cttee on Nationalised Industries, 1976; Consultant, Cttee on Financial Markets, OECD, 1979–81; Dir, Centre for Jt Study of Economics, Politics and Sociology, 1980–82; SSRC Grant for comparative study of banking policy and structure, 1977–81; Leverhulme Emeritus Fellow, 1983–84. Mem. Cttee of Management, Inst. of Commonwealth Studies, London, 1960–77, Hon. Life Mem., 1980; Governor, SOAS, London, 1963–92. Member: Yorkshire Council for Further Education, 1963–67; Nat. Advisory Council on Education for Industry and Commerce, 1964–66; Languages Bd, CNAA, 1978–83. Société Universitaire Européenne de Recherches Financières: Mem., Steering Cttee, 1964–69; Sec.-Gen., 1968–72; Mem. Council, 1970–91; Pres., 1973–75; Vice-Pres., 1977–83. Editor, Yorkshire Bulletin of Economic and Social Research, 1964–67; Mem., Editorial Adv. Bd, Modern Asian Studies, 1966–89. *Publications:* French Banking Structure and Credit Policy, 1957; Economic Environment and Development Programmes, 1960; Monetary Policy and the Development of Money Markets, 1966; Economic Survey of the New Hebrides, 1966; (ed with C. R. Whittlesey) Essays in Money and Banking in Honour of R. S. Sayers, 1968, repr. 1970; Availability of Capital and Credit to United Kingdom Agriculture, 1973; (ed with C. F. Scheffer) Multinational Enterprises—Financial and Monetary Aspects, 1974; Credit to Agriculture—United Kingdom, 1975; The London Money Markets, 1976, 2nd edn 1989; (ed with J. E. Wadsworth and H. Fournier) The Development of Financial Institutions in Europe, 1956–1976, 1977; Industrial Banking: a comparative survey, 1978; Banking Policy and Structure: a comparative analysis, 1986; (ed) Managing Bank Assets and Liabilities, 1988; contributions to: Banking in the British Commonwealth (ed R. S. Sayers), 1952; Banking in Western Europe (ed R. S. Sayers), 1962; A Decade of the Commonwealth, 1955–64, ed W. B. Hamilton and others, 1966; International Encyclopaedia of the Social Sciences; Encyclopaedia Britannica, 15th edn; Economica, Economic Journal, Journal of Political Econ., Economic Record, Banca Nazionale del Lavoro Quarterly Rev. *Recreations:* gardening, theatre, art galleries, travel, photography. *Address:* Department of Economics and Commerce, The University, Hull, North Humberside HU6 7RX. *Club:* Reform.

WILSON, (John) Tuzo, CC (Canada) 1974 (OC 1970); OBE 1946; FRS 1968; FRSC 1949; Chancellor, York University, Toronto, 1983–86; Professor of Geophysics, University of Toronto, 1946–74, Emeritus Professor, 1977; Director-General, Ontario Science Centre, 1974–85; *b* Ottawa, 24 Oct. 1908; *s* of John Armitstead Wilson, CBE, and Henrietta L. Tuzo; *m* 1938, Isabel Jean Dickson; two *d*. *Educ:* Ottawa; Universities of Toronto (Governor-General's medal, Trinity Coll., 1930; Massey Fellow, 1930), Cambridge (ScD), and Princeton (PhD). Asst Geologist, Geological Survey of Canada, 1936–46; Principal, Erindale Coll., Univ. of Toronto, 1967–74. Regimental service and staff appointments, Royal Canadian Engrs, UK and Sicily, 1939–43; Director, Opl. Research, Nat. Defence HQ, Ottawa (Colonel), 1944–46. President, International Union of Geodesy and Geophysics, 1957–60; Visiting Prof.: Australian Nat. Univ., 1950 and 1965; Ohio State Univ., 1968; California Inst. of Technology, 1976. Member Nat. Research Council of Canada, 1957–63; Member Defence Res. Board, 1958–64. Canadian Delegation to Gen. Ass., UNESCO, 1962, 1964, 1966. President: Royal Society of Canada, 1972–73; Amer. Geophysical Union, 1980–82. Overseas Fellow, Churchill Coll., Cambridge, 1965; Trustee, Nat. Museums of Canada, 1967–74. Hon. Fellow: Trinity Coll., University of Toronto, 1962; St John's Coll., Cambridge, 1981; Hon. FRSE 1986. Foreign Associate, Nat. Acad. of Sciences, USA, 1968; Foreign Hon. Mem., Amer. Acad. of Arts and Sciences; For. Mem., Royal Swedish Acad. of Sciences, 1981; Associé, Académie Royale de Belgique, 1981. Holds hon. doctorates and hon. or foreign memberships and medals, etc, in Canada and abroad. Vetlesen Prize, Columbia Univ., 1978; Britannica Award, 1986. *Publications:* One Chinese Moon, 1959; Physics and Geology (with J. A. Jacobs and R. D. Russell), 1959; IGY Year of the New Moons, 1961; (ed) Continents Adrift, 1972; Unglazed China, 1973; (ed) Continents Adrift and Continents Aground, 1976; scientific papers. *Recreation:* travel. *Address:* 27 Pricefield Road, Toronto, Ont M4W 1Z8, Canada. *T:* 923–4244. *Clubs:* Arts and Letters, York (Toronto).

WILSON, John Veitch D.; *see* Drysdale Wilson.

WILSON, John Warley; His Honour Judge John Wilson; a Circuit Judge, since 1982; *b* 13 April 1936; *s* of late John Pearson Wilson and Nancy Wade Wilson (*née* Harston); *m* 1962, Rosalind Mary Pulford. *Educ:* Warwick Sch.; St Catharine's Coll., Cambridge (MA). Called to the Bar, Lincoln's Inn, 1960, in practice, 1960–82; a Recorder of the Crown Court, 1979–82. Dep. Chairman, West Midlands Agricultural Land Tribunal, 1978–82. *Recreations:* gardening, National Hunt racing. *Address:* Victoria House, Farm Street, Harbury, Leamington Spa CV33 9LR. *T:* Harbury (0926) 612572.

WILSON, Rt. Rev. John Warwick; Bishop of the Southern Region (Assistant Bishop, Diocese of Melbourne), since 1985; *b* 12 July 1937; *s* of Walter and Norma Wilson; *m* 1963, Jill Brady; two *d*. *Educ:* Bathurst Coll., NSW; Ridley Coll., Parkville, Victoria (ThL, ThSchol); London Univ. (BD (Hons)); Yale Univ. (STM); Duke Univ. (PhD). Educn Officer, Papua New Guinea, 1957–59. Ordained deacon and priest, 1964; Asst, St Cyprian's, Narrabri, 1964–67; Vicar, St Andrew, Tingha, 1967–68; Priest in charge, St John's Henderson, North Carolina, USA, 1969–72; Lectr in OT, Ridley Coll., 1973–85. *Publications:* The Old Testament and Christian Living, 1981, 2nd edn 1985; Ezekiel: God's Communicator, 1990. *Recreations:* reading, music, cinema. *Address:* St Paul's Cathedral Buildings, 209 Flinders Lane, Melbourne, Vic 3000, Australia. *T:* (03) 653 4220.

WILSON, Joseph Albert; Secretary to the Cabinet, Sierra Leone Government, 1968; Barrister-at-Law; *b* 22 Jan. 1922; *e s* of late George Wilson; *m* 1947, Esther Massaquoi; two *s* four *d* (and one *s* decd). *Educ:* St Edward's Secondary Sch., Freetown, Sierra Leone; University of Exeter, (DPA); Middle Temple. Graded Clerical Service, Sierra Leone Government, 1941–47; family business, 1948–51; Secretary, Bonthe District Council, 1951–59; Administrative Officer, Sierra Leone Government, rising to rank of Cabinet Secretary, 1959; High Comr from Sierra Leone to UK, 1967–68. Manager (Special Duties), SLST Ltd, 1959; Dir, National Diamond Mining Co. (Sierra Leone) Ltd. Mem., Court of Univ. of Sierra Leone. *Recreations:* tennis, golf. *Address:* 14 Syke Street, Brookfields, Freetown, Sierra Leone. *T:* 2590.

WILSON, Mrs (Katherine) Muriel (Irwin), OBE 1985; Chairman and Chief Executive, Equal Opportunities Commission for Northern Ireland, 1981–84; *b* 3 Dec. 1920; *d* of Francis Hosford and Martha Evelyn (*née* Irwin); *m* 1949, William George Wilson; one *s*. *Educ:* Methodist Coll., Belfast; The Queen's University of Belfast (DPA); MBIM. Northern Ireland Civil Service, 1939–49; N Ireland Health Service, 1949–73: Eastern Special Care Management Cttee (Services for the Mentally Handicapped): Asst Sec., 1963–71; Gp Sec. and Chief Admin. Officer, 1971–73; Asst Chief Admin. Officer (Personnel and Management Services), Northern Health and Social Services Board, 1973–81. Chm. NI Div., 1977–79, National Vice-Pres. 1979–81, United Kingdom Fedn of Business and Professional Women; Member: Bd, Labour Relations Agency (NI), 1976–81; Fair Employment Agency for NI, 1981–84; NI Adv. Cttee, IBA, 1978–83; NI Council, RIPA, 1985–88; Women's Forum, NI, 1990–. Dir, Ulster Telethon Trust, 1989–. Chairman, Board of Governors: Glenravel Special Sch., Belfast, 1987–; Hill Croft Sch., Newtownabbey, 1987–89. *Recreations:* swimming, reading.

WILSON, Prof. Kenneth Geddes, PhD; Professor of Physics, and Director, Ohio State Supercomputer Center, Ohio State University, since 1989; *b* 8 June 1936; *s* of Edgar Bright Wilson and Emily Fisher Buckingham; *m* 1982, Alison Brown. *Educ:* Harvard Univ. (AB); Calif Inst. of Technol. (PhD). Cornell University: Asst Prof. of Physics, 1963; Prof. of Physics, 1963–88; Dir, Center for Theory and Simulation in Sci. and Engrg, 1985–88. Hon. PhD: Harvard, 1981; Chicago, 1976. Nobel Prize for Physics, 1982. *Publications:* (ed jtly) Broken Scale Invariance and the Light Cone, 1971; Quarks and Strings on a Lattice, 1975; (contrib.) New Pathways in High Energy Physics, Vol. II 1976; (contrib.) New Developments in Quantum Field Theory and Statistical Mechanics, 1977; (contrib.) Recent Developments in Gauge Theories, 1980; contrib. Jl of Math. Phys, Nuovo Cimento, Acta Phys. Austriaca, Phys Rev., Jl of Chem. Phys, Comm. Math. Phys, Phys Reports, Advances in Maths, Rev. of Mod. Phys, Scientific American; symposia and conf. papers. *Address:* Department of Physics, Ohio State University, 174 West 18th Avenue, Columbus, Ohio 43210–1106, USA. *T:* (614) 292–2876, (614) 292–5193.

WILSON, Rev. Canon L(eslie) Rule; Hon. Canon of Holy Cross Cathedral, Geraldton, since 1966; *b* 19 July 1909; *y s* of late Rev. John and Mary Adelaide Wilson; *m* 1984, Mrs Margaret Nunns, *widow* of R. C. Nunns, Stocksfield. *Educ:* Royal Grammar Sch., Newcastle upon Tyne; University College, Durham; Edinburgh Theological College. Asst Priest, Old St Paul's, Edinburgh, 1934–36; Rector of Fort William, 1936–42, with Nether Lochaber and Portree, 1938–42; Canon of Argyll and The Isles, 1940–42; Education Officer, 1942–45; Welfare Officer, SEAC (Toc H), 1945–46; Vicar of Malacca, Malaya, 1946–50; Principal Probation Officer, Federation of Malaya, 1950–52; Vicar of Kuching, Sarawak, 1952–55; Provost and Canon of St Thomas' Cathedral, Kuching, 1955–59; Rector of Geraldton, W Australia, 1960–64; Dean of Geraldton, 1964–66 (Administrator, Diocese of NW Australia, 1966); Archdeacon of Carpentaria, 1966–67; Rector of Winterbourne Stickland with Turnworth and Winterbourne Houghton, 1967–69; Vicar of Holmside, 1969–74; retired 1974; permission to officiate, Diocese of Durham, 1975–. Commissary for Bp of NW Australia, 1966–83. Founder and Chairman, Parson Woodforde Society, 1968–75 (Hon. Life Pres., 1975). *Recreations:* reading, genealogy. *Address:* 11 Norwich Close, Great Lumley, Chester-le-Street, Co. Durham DH3 4QL. *T:* Durham (091) 3892366.

WILSON, Leslie William, JP; Director-General, Association of Special Libraries and Information Bureaux (Aslib), 1950–78, retired; *b* 26 Sept. 1918; *s* of Harry Wilson and Ada Jane Wilson; *m* 1942, Valerie Jones; one *s* two *d*. *Educ:* Cambridgeshire High Sch.; Trinity Hall, Cambridge (Open Scholar, MA Mod. Langs). Army Service, India, 1940–46. Foreign Editor, Times Educnl Supplement, 1946–50. Hon. Fellow, Internat. Fedn for Documentation, 1978; Hon. Member: Inst. of Information Scientists, 1977; US Special Libraries Assoc., 1978; Aslib, 1978. JP Mddx, 1971. *Address:* 6 Queensberry House, Friars Lane, Richmond, Surrey TW9 1NT. *T:* 081–948 0421.

WILSON, Lynn Anthony; Chairman, Wilson (Connolly) Holdings PLC, since 1982; Director of 24 subsidiary companies; *b* 8 Dec. 1939; *s* of Connolly Thomas Wilson and Frances (*née* Chapman); *m* 1964, Judith Helen Mann; two *s*. *Educ:* Oakham Sch., Rutland. FCIOB; CBIM. Wilson Builders (N'pton) Ltd, 1957; Man. Dir, Wilson (Connolly) Holdings, on flotation, 1966. Nat. Pres., House Builders Fedn, 1981. Pres., Old Oakhamian Club, 1988; Trustee, Oakham Sch., 1983–. Chm., Northants CCC, 1990– (Mem. Cttee, 1971–80; Treas., 1974–79). *Recreations:* cricket, golf, horseracing, shooting. *Address:* c/o Wilson (Connolly) Holdings PLC, Thomas Wilson House, Tenter Road, Moulton Park, Northampton NN3 1QJ. *T:* Northampton (0604) 790909. *Clubs:* Farmers', MCC; Northants CC.

WILSON, Sir Mathew John Anthony, 6th Bt *cr* 1874, of Eshton Hall, Co. York; OBE 1979 (MBE 1971); MC 1972; *b* 2 Oct. 1935; *s* of Anthony Thomas Wilson (*d* 1979; 2nd *s* of Sir Mathew Richard Henry Wilson, 4th Bt) and Margaret (*d* 1980), *d* of late Alfred Holden; *S* uncle, 1991; *m* 1962, Janet Mary, *e d* of late E. W. Mowll, JP; one *s* one *d*. *Educ:* Trinity Coll. Sch., Ontario. Brig. KOYLI, retired 1983. Exec. Dir, Wilderness Foundn (UK), 1983–85. Former Vice-Pres., Internat. Wilderness Leadership Foundn. *Heir:* *s* Mathew Edward Amcotts Wilson, *b* 13 Oct. 1966.

WILSON, Michael Anthony, FRCGP; Principal in general practice, Strensall, since 1961; *b* 2 June 1936; *s* of Charles Kenneth Wilson and late Bertha Wilson; *m* 1959, Marlene (*née* Wilson); two *s*. *Educ:* Roundhay Grammar Sch., Leeds; Medical Sch., Univ. of Leeds (MB ChB 1958). DObst RCOG 1961; MRCGP 1965, FRCGP 1980. British Medical Association: Chm., Gen. Med. Services Cttee, 1984–90 (Dep. Chm., 1979–84); Pres., Yorkshire Regional Council, 1975–79; Mem. Council, 1977–90; Fellow, 1979. Member: GMC, 1989–; Standing Med. Adv. Cttee to DHSS, 1967–69, 1978–90 (Dep. Chm., 1986–90); NHS Clinical Standards Adv. Gp, 1990–; Med. Protection Soc. Adv. Bd, 1990–; Code of Practice Cttee, Assoc. of British Pharmaceutical Industry, 1990–; Jt Consultants Cttee, 1991–. *Recreations:* golf, Rotary. *Address:* Longueville, Mill Hill, Huntington, York YO3 9PY. *T:* York (0904) 768861. *Club:* East India.

WILSON, Michael Sumner; Chief Executive, J Rothschild Assurance, since 1992; Sole Proprietor of Sumner Wilson & Co.; *b* 5 Dec. 1943; *s* of Peter and Margaret Wilson; *m* 1975, Mary Drysdale; one *d*. *Educ:* St Edward's School, Oxford. Equity & Law, 1963–68; Abbey Life, 1968–71; Allied Dunbar (Hambro Life until 1985, when name was changed), 1971–91: Exec. Dir, 1973; Board Dir, 1976; Dep. Man. Dir, 1982; Man. Dir, 1984; Gp Chief Exec., 1988–91. Dir, BAT Industries, 1989–91. *Recreations:* tennis, racing. *Address:* Warrens Gorse, near Cirencester, Glos GL7 7JD. *T:* Cirencester (0285) 83229. *Club:* Raffles.

WILSON, Mrs Muriel; *see* Wilson, K. M. I.

WILSON, Nicholas Allan Roy; QC 1987; a Recorder, since 1987; *b* 9 May 1945; *s* of Roderick Peter Garratt Wilson and Dorothy Anne Wilson (*née* Chenevix-Trench); *m* 1974, Margaret (*née* Higgins); one *s* one *d*. *Educ:* Bryanston School; Worcester College, Oxford (BA 1st cl. hons Jurisp. 1966). Eldon Scholar, 1967. Called to the Bar, Inner Temple, 1967. *Address:* Queen Elizabeth Building, Temple, EC4Y 9BS. *T:* 071–583 7837.

WILSON, Nigel Guy, FBA 1980; Fellow and Tutor in Classics, Lincoln College, Oxford, since 1962; *b* 23 July 1935; *s* of Noel Wilson and Joan Lovibond. *Educ:* University Coll. Sch.; Corpus Christi Coll., Oxford (1st Cl. Classics (Mods) 1955; 1st Cl. Lit. Hum. 1957; Hertford Scholar 1955; Ireland and Craven Scholar 1955; Derby Scholar 1957). Lectr, Merton Coll., Oxford, 1957–62. Jt Editor, Classical Rev., 1975–87. Ospite Linceo, Scuola normale superiore, Pisa, 1977; Visiting Professor: Univ. of Padua, 1985; Ecole Normale Supérieure, Paris, 1986. Gaisford Lectr, 1983. Gordon Duff Prize, 1968. *Publications:* (with L. D. Reynolds) Scribes and Scholars, 1968, 3rd edn 1991; An Anthology of Byzantine Prose, 1971; Medieval Greek Bookhands, 1973; St Basil on the Value of Greek Literature, 1975; Scholia in Aristophanis Acharnenses, 1975; (with D. A. Russell) Menander Rhetor, 1981; Scholars of Byzantium, 1983; (with Sir Hugh Lloyd-Jones) Sophoclea, 1990; (ed with Sir Hugh Lloyd-Jones) Sophocles: Fabulae, 1990; articles and reviews in various learned jls. *Recreations:* bridge, squash, real tennis. *Address:* Lincoln College, Oxford OX1 3DR. *T:* Oxford (0865) 279794, *Fax:* 279802.

WILSON, Norman George, CMG 1966; Commercial Director, ICI of Australia Ltd, 1972–73; Deputy Chairman, Fibremakers Ltd, 1972–73; *b* 20 Oct. 1911; *s* of P. Wilson; *m* 1939, Dorothy Gwen, *d* of late Sir W. Lennon Raws; one *s* two *d*. *Educ:* Melbourne University (BCE). Joined ICI Australia Ltd, 1935: Exec. positions, 1936–48; General Manager, Dyes and Plastics Group, 1949–54; Director, 1959–73; Managing Director: Dulux Pty Ltd, 1954–62; Fibremakers Ltd, 1962–72. Business Adviser to Dept of Air, and Dep. Chm. Defence Business Board, Commonwealth Government, 1957–76; Chairman Production Board, Dept of Manufacturing Industries, Commonwealth Government, 1960–76. Mem., Export Develt Council, Dept of Trade and Industry, Commonwealth Govt, 1966–72. Mem. Bd, Victorian Railways, 1973–83; Dep. Chm., Victorian Conservation Trust, 1973–83; Foundn Pres., Australia/Britain Soc., Vic, 1971–76. FInstD, FAIM. *Recreation:* farming. *Address:* The Highlands, Kerrie, Romsey, Vic 3434, Australia. *T:* 054 270232. *Clubs:* Australian (Melbourne); Melbourne Cricket, Victoria Racing.

WILSON, Prof. Peter Northcote, CBE 1987; FRSE; Science Director, Edinburgh Centre for Rural Research, since 1990; *b* 4 April 1928; *s* of Llewellyn W. C. M. Wilson and F. Louise Wilson; *m* 1950, Maud Ethel (*née* Bunn); two *s* one *d*. *Educ:* Whitgift School; Wye College, Univ. of London (BSc (Agric), MSc, PhD); Univ. of Edinburgh (Dip.

Animal Genetics). CBiol, FIBiol; FRSE 1987. Lectr in Agriculture, Makerere Coll., UC of E Africa, 1951–57; Sen. Lectr in Animal Production, Imperial Coll. of Tropical Agriculture, 1957–61; Prof. of Agriculture, Univ. of W Indies, 1961–64; Senior Scientist, Unilever Res. Lab., 1964–68; Agricl Dir, SLF Ltd (Unilever), 1968–71; Chief Agricl Advr, BOCM Silcock Ltd (Unilever), 1971–83; Prof. of Agric. and Rural Economy and Hd of Sch. of Agric., Univ. of Edinburgh, 1984–90; Principal, East of Scotland Coll. of Agric., 1984–90. Vis. Prof. Univ. of Reading, 1975–83. Pres., Brit. Soc. of Animal Production, 1977; Vice-Pres., Inst. of Biol., 1977–79. Sec.-Gen., Council of Scottish Agricl Colls, 1985–86 (Mem. Exec. Bd, Scottish Agricl Colls, 1987–90). Chm., Frank Parkinson Agricl Trust, 1980–. FRSA. *Publications:* Agriculture in the Tropics, 1965, 2nd edn 1980; Improved Feeding of Cattle and Sheep, 1981; numerous papers in learned jls. *Recreations:* hill walking, photography, foreign travel, philately. *Address:* 8 St Thomas' Road, Edinburgh EH9 2LQ. *T:* 031–667 3182. *Club:* Farmers'.

WILSON, Philip Alexander P.; *see* Poole-Wilson.

WILSON, Quintin Campbell, OBE 1975; HM Inspector of Constabulary for Scotland, 1975–79; *b* 19 Nov. 1913; *s* of William Wilson and Mary (*née* Cowan); *m* 1939, Adelia Campbell Scott; two *s*. *Educ:* Barr Primary Sch.; Girvan High Sch. Halifax Borough Police, April 1936; Ayrshire Constabulary, Nov. 1936; Chief Supt, Police Research and Planning Branch, Home Office, London, 1965; Dep. Chief Constable, Ayrshire, 1966; Chief Constable, Ayrshire, 1968–75. *Recreation:* golf. *Address:* 15 Portmark Avenue, Alloway, Ayr KA7 4DN. *T:* Alloway (0292) 43034.

WILSON, Prof. Raymond; Professor of Education, 1968–89, now Emeritus, Chairman of School of Education, 1969–76 and 1980–89, University of Reading; *b* 20 Dec. 1925; *s* of John William Wilson and Edith (*née* Walker); *m* 1950, Gertrude Mary Russell; two *s* one *d*. *Educ:* London Univ. (BA English, 1st Cl.). Teacher, secondary schs, 1950–57; English Master, subseq. Chief English Master, Dulwich Coll., 1957–65; Lectr, Southampton Univ., 1965–68. *Publications:* numerous textbooks and anthologies; papers on English language and literature, philosophy of education, and the humanities; occasional poet and writer of fiction. *Recreations:* walking, natural history. *Address:* 7 Northfield Court, Northfield Close, Henley-on-Thames, Oxon RG9 2LH. *T:* Henley (0491) 575395. *Club:* Commonwealth Trust.

WILSON, Sir Reginald (Holmes), Kt 1951; BCom; FCIT; CBIM; Scottish Chartered Accountant; Director of business and finance companies; *b* 1905; *o s* of Alexander Wilson and Emily Holmes Wilson; *m* 1st, 1930, Rose Marie von Arnim; one *s* one *d*; 2nd, 1938, Sonia Havell. *Educ:* St Peter's Sch., Panchgani; St Lawrence, Ramsgate; London Univ. BCom. Partner in Whinney Murray & Co., 1937–72; HM Treasury, 1940; Principal Assistant Secretary, Ministry of Shipping, 1941; Director of Finance, Ministry of War Transport, 1941; Under-Secretary, Ministry of Transport, 1945; returned to City, 1946; Joint Financial Adviser, Ministry of Transport, 1946; Member of Royal Commission on Press, 1946; Vice-Chairman, Hemel Hempstead Development Corporation, 1946–56; Adviser on Special Matters, CCG, 1947. Comptroller BTC, 1947, Member BTC, 1953, Chm. E Area Board, 1955–60, Chm. London Midland Area Board, 1960–62; Dep. Chm. and Man. Dir, Transport Holding Co., 1962–67; Chairman: Transport Holding Co., 1967–70; Nat. Freight Corp., 1969–70; Transport Develt Gp, 1971–74 (Dep. Chm., 1970–71); Thos Cook & Son Ltd, 1967–76. Mem., Cttee of Enquiry into Civil Air Transport, 1967–69. Chm., Bd for Simplification of Internat. Trade Procedures, 1976–79. Award of Merit, Inst. Transport, 1953; President, Inst. Transport, 1957–58. Governor, LSE, 1954–58; Chairman, Board of Governors: Hospitals for Diseases of the Chest, 1960–71; National Heart Hospital, 1968–71; National Heart and Chest Hospitals, 1971–80; Chm., Cardiothoracic Inst., 1960–80; UK Rep., Council of Management, Internat. Hosp. Fedn, 1973–79. *Publications:* various papers on transport matters. *Recreations:* music, walking. *Address:* 49 Gloucester Square, W2 2TQ. *Clubs:* Athenæum, Oriental.

WILSON, Prof. Richard Middlewood; Professor of English Language, University of Sheffield, 1955–73; *b* 20 Sept. 1908; *e s* of late R. L. Wilson, The Grange, Kilham, Driffield, E Yorks; *m* 1938, Dorothy Muriel, *y d* of late C. E. Leeson, Eastgate House, Kilham, Driffield; one *d*. *Educ:* Woodhouse Grove School; Leeds University. Asst Lecturer, Leeds Univ., 1931, Lecturer, 1936; Senior Lecturer and Head of Dept of English Language, Sheffield Univ., 1946. *Publications:* Sawles Warde, 1939; Early Middle English Literature, 1939; (with B. Dickins) Early Middle English Texts, 1951; The Lost Literature of Medieval England, 1952; (with D. J. Price) The Equatorie of the Planetis, 1955; articles and reviews. *Recreation:* cricket. *Address:* 9 Endcliffe Vale Avenue, Sheffield S11 8RX. *T:* Sheffield (0742) 663431.

WILSON, Richard Thomas James, CB 1991; Deputy Secretary (Industry), HM Treasury, since 1990; *b* 11 Oct. 1942; *s* of late Richard Ridley Wilson and Frieda Bell (*née* Finlay); *m* 1972, Caroline Margaret, *y d* of Rt Hon. Sir Frank Lee, GCMG, KCB and of Lady Lee; one *s* one *d*. *Educ:* Radley Coll.; Clare Coll., Cambridge (Exhibnr; BA 1964, LLB 1965). Called to the Bar, Middle Temple, 1965. Joined BoT as Asst Principal, 1966; Private Sec. to Minister of State, BoT, 1969–71; Principal: Cabinet Office, 1971–73; Dept of Energy, 1974; Asst Sec., 1977–82; Under Sec., 1982; Prin. Estabt and Finance Officer, Dept of Energy, 1982–86; on loan to Cabinet Office (MPO), 1986–87; Dep. Sec., Cabinet Office, 1987–90. *Address:* c/o HM Treasury, Parliament Street, SW1P 3AG.

WILSON, Sir Robert, Kt 1989; CBE 1978; FRS 1975; Perren Professor of Astronomy, since 1972, and Head of Department of Physics and Astronomy, since 1987, University College London; *b* 16 April 1927; *s* of Robert Graham Wilson and Anne Wilson; *m* 1986, Fiona (*née* Nicholson). *Educ:* King's Coll., Univ. of Durham; Univ. of Edinburgh. BSc (Physics) Dunelm, 1948; PhD (Astrophysics), Edin., 1952. SSO, Royal Observatory, Edinburgh, 1952–57; Research Fellow, Dominion Astrophysical Observatory, Canada, 1957–58; Leader of Plasma Spectroscopy Gp, CTR Div., Harwell, 1959–61; Head of Spectroscopy Div., Culham Laboratory, 1962–68; Dir, Science Research Council's Astrophysics Research Unit, Culham, 1968–72; Dean, Faculty Sci., UCL, 1982–85. Member: SERC, 1985–89; NERC, 1985–88; Chairman: British National Cttee for Space Res., 1983–88; Anglo-Australian Telescope Bd, 1986–89; James Clerk Maxwell Telescope Bd, 1987–. Foreign Mem., Société Royale des Sciences, Liège; Vice-Pres., Internat. Astronomical Union, 1979–85; Trustee, Internat. Acad. of Astronautics, 1985; Mem., COSPAR Bureau, 1986–90. Hon. Fellow, UCL, 1990. (Jtly) Herschel Medal, RAS, 1986; Science Award, Internat. Acad. of Astronautics, 1987; President Reagan's Award for design excellence (on behalf of UK team on the Internat. Ultraviolet Explorer), 1988. *Publications:* papers in many jls on: optical astronomy, plasma spectroscopy, solar physics, ultraviolet astronomy. *Address:* Department of Physics and Astronomy, University College London, Gower Street, WC1E 6BT. *T:* 071–380 7154.

WILSON, Sir (Robert) Donald, Kt 1987; DL; farmer; Chairman: Mersey Regional Health Authority, since 1982; Electricity Consultative Council (North West), since 1981; *b* 6 June 1922; *s* of John and Kate Wilson; *m* 1946, E. Elizabeth Ellis. *Educ:* Grove Park Sch., Wrexham, Clwyd. Served RAF, 1940–46. Tyre industry, 1946–60; farming, 1954–; Director of various farming and property companies; Member of Lloyd's, 1970–; Board Mem. (part-time), North West Electricity Bd (NORWEB), 1981–. Chairman: Ayrshire Cattle Soc., 1966–67; Cheshire Br., CLA, 1980–82; Nat. Staff Cttee, Admin, Catering and Other Services, 1983–85. Vice-Chm. Governors, Cheshire Coll. of Agric., 1980–84. High Sheriff, Cheshire, 1985–86, DL, 1987. FRSA 1986. *Recreations:* fishing, shooting. *Address:* The Oldfields, Pulford, Chester, Cheshire CH4 9EJ. *T:* Rossett (0244) 570207. *Clubs:* Farmers'; City (Chester).

WILSON, (Robert) Gordon; solicitor in private practice; *b* 16 April 1938; *s* of R. G. Wilson; *m* 1965, Edith M. Hassall; two *d*. *Educ:* Douglas High Sch.; Edinburgh Univ. (BL). Scottish National Party: Nat. Sec., 1963–71; Exec. Vice-Chm., 1972–73; Sen. Vice-Chm., 1973–74; Dep Leader, 1974–79; Nat. Convener (formerly Chm.), 1979–90. Contested (SNP) Dundee E, 1987. MP (SNP) Dundee E, Feb. 1974–1987. Parly Spokesman: on Energy, 1974–79; on Home Affairs, 1975–76; on Devolution (jt responsibility), 1976–79. Rector, Dundee Univ., 1983–86. Chm., Marriage Counselling (Tayside) (formerly Dundee Marriage Guidance Council), 1989–. Gov., Dundee Inst. of Technology, 1991–. Hon. LLD Dundee, 1986. *Recreations:* reading, walking, photography, sailing. *Address:* 48 Monifieth Road, Broughty Ferry, Dundee DD5 2RX. *T:* Dundee (0382) 79009.

WILSON, Robert Julian, (Robin), MA; Headmaster, Trinity School of John Whitgift, Croydon, since 1972; *b* 6 July 1933; *s* of late Prof. Frank Percy Wilson, FBA, and Joanna Wilson (*née* Perry-Keene); *m* 1957, Caroline Anne (*née* Maher); two *d* (and one *s* one *d* decd). *Educ:* St Edward's Sch., Oxford; Trinity Coll., Cambridge (MA). Lektor, Univ. of Münster, Westphalia, 1955–58; Assistant Master: St Peter's, York, 1958–62; Nottingham High Sch. (Hd of English), 1962–72. Cttee, HMC, 1987–; Vice-Chm., Academic Policy Cttee, 1990–; Univ. of London Schools Exam. Bd, 1990. FRSA 1982. *Publications:* Bertelsmann Sprachkursus English (jtly), 1959; (ed) The Merchant of Venice, 1971; articles on the teaching of English. *Recreations:* drama, travel, ski-ing, golf. *Address:* 22 Beech House Road, Croydon, Surrey CR0 1JP. *T:* 081–686 1915. *Clubs:* East India, Devonshire, Sports and Public Schools; Addington Golf.

WILSON, Prof. Robert McLachlan, FBA 1977; Professor of Biblical Criticism, University of St Andrews, 1978–83; *b* 13 Feb. 1916; *er s* of Hugh McL. Wilson and Janet N. (*née* Struthers); *m* 1945, Enid Mary, *d* of Rev. and Mrs F. J. Bomford, Bournemouth, Hants; two *s*. *Educ:* Greenock Acad.; Royal High Sch., Edinburgh; Univ. of Edinburgh (MA 1939, BD 1942); Univ. of Cambridge (PhD 1945). Minister of Rankin Church, Strathaven, Lanarkshire, 1946–54; Lectr in New Testament Language and Literature, St Mary's Coll., Univ. of St Andrews, 1954, Sen. Lectr, 1964, Prof., 1969–78. Vis. Prof., Vanderbilt Divinity Sch., Nashville, Tenn, 1964–65. Pres., Studiorum Novi Testamenti Societas, 1981–82. Hon. Mem., Soc. of Biblical Literature, 1972–. Associate Editor, New Testament Studies, 1967–77, Editor 1977–83; Mem., Internat. Cttee for publication of Nag Hammadi Codices, and of Editorial Bd of Nag Hammadi Studies monograph series. Hon. DD Aberdeen, 1982. Burkitt Medal for Biblical Studies, British Academy, 1990. *Publications:* The Gnostic Problem, 1958; Studies in the Gospel of Thomas, 1960; The Gospel of Philip, 1962; Gnosis and the New Testament, 1968; (ed) English trans., Hennecke-Schneemelcher, NT Apocrypha: vol. 1, 1963 (3rd edn 1991); vol. 2, 1965 (2nd edn 1974); (ed) English trans., Haenchen, The Acts of the Apostles, 1971; (ed) English trans., Foerster, Gnosis: vol. 1, 1972; vol. 2, 1974; (ed and trans., jtly) Jung Codex treatises: De Resurrectione, 1963, Epistula Jacobi Apocrypha, 1968, Tractatus Tripartitus, pars I, 1973, partes II et III, 1975; (ed) Nag Hammadi and Gnosis, 1978; (ed) The Future of Coptology, 1978; (ed jtly) Text and Interpretation, 1979; (ed) English trans., Rudolph, Gnosis, 1983; Commentary on Hebrews, 1987; articles in British, Amer. and continental jls. *Recreation:* golf. *Address:* 10 Murrayfield Road, St Andrews, Fife KY16 9NB. *T:* St Andrews (0334) 74331.

WILSON, Robert Peter; Chief Executive, RTZ Corporation plc, since 1991; *b* 2 Sept. 1943; *s* of late Alfred Wilson and Dorothy (*née* Mathews); *m* 1975, Shirley Elisabeth Robson; one *s* one *d*. *Educ:* Epsom Coll.; Sussex Univ. (BA); Harvard Business Sch. (AMP). With Dunlop Ltd, 1966–67; Mobil Oil Co. Ltd, 1967–70; RTZ Corporation plc, 1970–, Dir, Main Bd, 1987–. Non-Exec. Dir, CRA Ltd (Australia), 1990–. *Recreations:* theatre, opera, tennis. *Address:* 6 St James's Square, SW1Y 4LD. *T:* 071–930 2399.

WILSON, Dr Robert Woodrow; Head, Radio Physics Research Department, AT&T Bell Laboratories, since 1976; *b* 10 Jan. 1936; *s* of Ralph Woodrow Wilson and Fannie May Willis; *m* 1958, Elizabeth Rhoads Sawin; two *s* one *d*. *Educ:* Rice Univ. (BA Physics, 1957); Calif Inst. of Technol. (PhD 1962). Post-doctoral Fellowship, Calif Inst. of Technol., 1962–63; Mem. Technical Staff, Bell Labs, Holmdel, NJ, 1963–76. Member: Phi Beta Kappa; Amer. Acad. of Arts and Sciences, 1978; US Nat. Acad. of Science, 1979. Hon. degrees: Monmouth Coll., 1979; Jersey City State Coll., 1979; Thiel Coll., 1980. Henry Draper Award, 1977; Herschel Award, RAS, 1977; (jtly) Nobel Prize for Physics, 1978. *Publications:* contrib. to Astrophys. Jl. *Recreations:* running, skiing. *Address:* 9 Valley Point Drive, Holmdel, NJ 07733, USA. *T:* (201) 671–7807.

WILSON, Robin; *see* Wilson, R. J.

WILSON, Robin Lee, FEng 1986; Director, Travers Morgan Ltd, Consultants, since 1988; *b* 4 March 1933; *s* of late Henry Eric Wilson, OBE and Catherine Margaret Wilson; *m* 1956, Gillian Margaret, *d* of late L. J. N. Kirkby and Margaret Kirkby; one *s* two *d*. *Educ:* Glenalmond College; Univ. of Glasgow (BSc Eng. 1955). FICE 1966; FIHT 1966; MConsE 1966; MCIT 1984. Joined R. Travers Morgan & Partners, 1956, Partner, 1966, Sen. Partner, 1985, Gp Chm., 1988–91; Chairman: New Builder Publications Ltd, 1989–; Thomas Telford Ltd, publishers, 1990–. Member Council: ICE, 1977–80, 1983–86, 1987– (Pres., 1991–Nov. 1992); ACE, 1985–88; Construction Industry Council, 1990–; Glenalmond Coll., 1985–. Minister's nominee, SE Council for Sport and Recreation, 1987–90. Coopers Hill Meml Prize, ICE, 1989; Instn of Highways and Transportation Award, 1990. *Publications:* papers in learned jls on highway engineering and related subjects. *Recreations:* sailing, golf. *Address:* The Grove House, Little Bognor, Pulborough, Sussex RH20 1JT. *T:* Fittleworth (079882) 569. *Clubs:* Royal Thames Yacht, City Livery; Itchenor Sailing, West Sussex Golf.

WILSON, Rodney Herbert William; Director, Department of Film, Video and Broadcasting, Arts Council of Great Britain, since 1986; *b* 21 June 1942; *s* of Herbert Herman Wilson and Vera Anne Faulkner. *Educ:* Windsor Grammar Sch. for Boys; Berkshire Coll. of Art (Intermediate Diploma); Camberwell Sch. of Art (NDD); Hornsey Coll. of Art (ATD). Asst Lectr, Loughborough Coll. of Art, 1965–69; Film Officer, 1970, Head of Film Section, 1980, Arts Council of GB. Member: Film, Video and Television Adv. Cttee, British Council, 1983–; Council, Edinburgh Film Festival, 1984–. Exec. Producer for Arts Council Films, 1970–, including: Lautrec (Palm d'Or, Cannes, 1975); Monet in London (BAFTA Best Factual Film, 1975); Tom Philips (Grierson Award, 1977); Ubu (Golden Bear, Berlin, 1979); Give Us This Day (Grierson Award, 1983); Shadows from Light (Best Film, Montreal, 1984); Steve Reich: a new musical language (Best TV Arts Film, Rio de Janeiro, 1987); Jacob Epstein: rebel angel (Best TV Arts Film, Montreal, 1988). BFI Award for Ind. Film, 1984. *Recreations:* walking, squash, doodling, photography. *Address:* 35a Jacksons Lane, N6 5SR.

WILSON, Rt. Rev. Roger Plumpton, KCVO 1974; DD (Lambeth), 1949; Clerk of the Closet to the Queen, 1963–75; Hon. Assistant Bishop, Diocese of Bath and Wells, since 1974; *b* 3 Aug. 1905; *s* of Canon Clifford Plumpton Wilson, Bristol, and Hester Marion Wansey; *m* 1935, Mabel Joyce Avery, Leigh Woods, Bristol; two *s* one *d*. *Educ:* Winchester Coll. (Exhibitioner); Keble Coll., Oxford (Classical Scholar). Hon. Mods in Classics 1st Class, Lit. Hum. 2nd Class, BA 1928; MA 1932. Classical Master, Shrewsbury Sch., 1928–30, 1932–34; Classical Master, St Andrew's Coll., Grahamstown, S Africa, 1930–32. Deacon, 1935; Priest, 1936; Curacies: St Paul's, Prince's Park, Liverpool, 1935–38; St John's, Smith Square, SW1, 1938–39; Vicar of South Shore, Blackpool, 1939–45; Archdeacon of Nottingham and Vicar of Radcliffe on Trent, 1945–49; also Vicar of Shelford (in plurality), 1946–49; Bishop of Wakefield, 1949–58; Bishop of Chichester, 1958–74. Chm., Church of England Schools Council, 1957–71; Mem., Presidium, Conf. of European Churches, 1967–74. *Recreations:* Oxford University Authentics Cricket Club, Oxford University Centaurs Football Club, golf. *Address:* Kingsett, Wrington, Bristol BS18 7NH. *T:* Wrington (0934) 862464. *Club:* Commonwealth Trust.

WILSON, Sir Roland, KBE 1965 (CBE 1941); Kt 1955; Chairman: Commonwealth Banking Corporation, 1966–75; Qantas Airways Ltd, 1966–73; Wentworth Hotel, 1966–73; Director: The MLC Ltd, 1969–79; ICI Australia, 1967–74; economic and financial consultant; *b* Ulverstone, Tasmania, 7 April 1904; *s* of Thomas Wilson; *m* 1930, Valeska (*d* 1971), *d* of William Thompson; *m* 1975, Joyce, *d* of Clarence Henry Chivers. *Educ:* Devonport High School; Univ. of Tasmania; Oriel College, Oxford; Chicago University. Rhodes Scholar for Tasmania, 1925; BCom 1926, Univ. of Tasmania; Dipl. in Economics and Political Science 1926, and DPhil 1929, Oxon; Commonwealth Fund Fellow, 1928, and PhD 1930, Chicago. Pitt Cobbett Lecturer in Economics, Univ. of Tasmania, 1930–32; Director of Tutorial Classes, Univ. of Tasmania, 1931–32; Asst Commonwealth Statistician and Economist, 1932; Economist, Statistician's Branch, Commonwealth Treasury, 1933; Commonwealth Statistician and Economic Adviser to the Treasury, Commonwealth of Australia, 1936–40 and 1946–51; Sec. to Dept Labour and Nat. Service, 1941–46; Chairman Economic and Employment Commission, United Nations, 1948–49. Secretary to Treasury, Commonwealth of Australia, 1951–66; Member Bd: Commonwealth Bank of Australia, 1951–59; Reserve Bank of Australia, 1960–66; Qantas Empire Airways, 1954–66; Commonwealth Banking Corp., 1960–75. Hon. Fellow, Acad. of Social Scis in Australia, 1972. Hon. LLD Tasmania, 1969. Distinguished Fellow Award, Econ. Soc. of Australia, 1988. *Publications:* Capital Imports and the Terms of Trade, 1931; Public and Private Investment in Australia, 1939; Facts and Fancies of Productivity, 1946. *Address:* 64 Empire Circuit, Forrest, Canberra, ACT 2603, Australia. *T:* 295–2560. *Club:* Commonwealth (Canberra).

WILSON, Air Marshal Sir (Ronald) Andrew (Fellowes), (Sir Sandy), KCB 1991 (CB 1990); AFC 1978; Commander-in-Chief, RAF Germany and Commander Second Allied Tactical Air Force, since 1991; *b* 27 Feb. 1941; *s* of Ronald Denis Wilson and Gladys Vera Groombridge; *m* 1979, Mary Christine Anderson; one *d* and one step *s* one step *d*. *Educ:* Tonbridge Sch.; RAF Coll., Cranwell. Flying Instr, 1963–65; No 2 Sqn, 1966–68; ADC to C-in-C, RAF Germany, 1967–68; Flt Comdr No 2 Sqn, 1968–72; RAF Staff Coll., 1973; HQ STC, 1974–75; CO No 2 Sqn, 1975–77; Air Plans, MoD, 1977–79; CO RAF Lossiemouth, 1980–82; Air Cdre Falkland Islands, 1982–83; Central Staff, MoD, 1983–85; Dir Ops Strike, MoD, 1985; Dir Air Offensive, MoD, 1986–87; SASO, HQ, RAF Strike Comd, 1987–89; AOC No 1 Group, 1989–91; Comdr, British Forces during Op. Granby, ME, Aug.–Dec. 1990. Freeman, City of London, 1966; Liveryman, 1970, Mem. Court, 1984–87, Worshipful Co. of Skinners. Mem., British Ski Council, 1986. FBIM 1986. *Recreations:* ski-ing, golf, photography, antique restoration. *Address:* c/o Royal Bank of Scotland, Holts Branch, Whitehall, SW1. *Club:* Royal Air Force.

WILSON, Maj.-Gen. (Ronald) Dare, CBE 1968 (MBE 1949); MC 1945; MA Cantab; DL; retired; current interests farming and forestry; *b* 3 Aug. 1919; *s* of Sydney E. D. Wilson and Dorothea, *d* of George Burgess; *m* 1973, Sarah, *d* of Sir Peter Stallard, *qv*; two *s*. *Educ:* Shrewsbury Sch.; St John's Coll. Cambridge. Commissioned into Royal Northumberland Fusiliers, 1939; served War, 1939–45: BEF 1940, ME and NW Europe (MC, despatches 1946); 6th Airborne Div., 1945–48; 1st Bn Parachute Regt, 1949; MoD, 1950; Royal Northumberland Fusiliers: Korea, 1951; Kenya, 1953; GSO2, Staff Coll., Camberley, 1954–56; AA&QMG, 3rd Div., 1958–59; comd 22 Special Air Service Regt, 1960–62; Canadian Nat. Defence Coll., 1962–63; Col GS 1(BR) Corps BAOR, 1963–65; comd 149 Infantry Bde (TA), 1966–67; Brig. 1966; Brig., AQ ME Comd, 1967; Maj.-Gen. 1968; Dir, Land/Air Warfare, MoD, 1968–69; Dir, Army Aviation, MoD, 1970–71. Exmoor Nat. Park Officer, 1974–78. Formerly Consultant to Fedn of Nature and Nat. Parks of Europe. Speaker for E-SU in USA. Church Warden, Church of St George, Morebath, Devon. Helicopter and light aircraft pilot; Mem., Army Cresta Run Team and Army Rifle VIII; captained British Free-Fall Parachute Team, 1962–65; Chm., British Parachute Assoc., 1962–65. Mem. Council, Cambridge Soc., 1989–. FRGS. DL Somerset, 1979. Royal Humane Soc. Award, 1953; Royal Aero Club Silver Medal, 1967. *Publications:* Cordon and Search, 1948, reissued USA, 1984; contribs to military jls. *Recreations:* country pursuits, travelling, winter sports. *Address:* Combeland, Dulverton, Somerset TA22 9LJ. *Club:* Flyfishers'.

WILSON, Hon. Sir Ronald (Darling), AC 1988; KBE 1979; CMG 1978; Justice of the High Court of Australia, 1979–89; Chancellor, Murdoch University, since 1980; President: Uniting Church in Australia, 1988–91; Human Rights and Equal Opportunity Commission, since 1990; *b* 23 Aug. 1922; *s* of Harold Wilson and Jean Ferguson Wilson (*née* Darling); *m* 1950, Leila Amy Gibson Smith; three *s* two *d*. *Educ:* Geraldton State School; Univ. of Western Australia (LLB Hons; Hon. LLD 1980); Univ. of Pennsylvania (LLM). Assistant Crown Prosecutor, Western Australia, 1954–59; Chief Crown Prosecutor, WA, 1959–61; Crown Counsel, WA, 1961–69; QC 1963; Solicitor General, WA, 1969–79. Moderator, Presbyterian Church in Western Australia, 1965; Moderator, WA Synod, Uniting Church in Australia, 1977–79. Hon. DEd Keimyung Univ., Korea, 1989. *Address:* 6B Atkins Road, Applecross, WA 6153, Australia.

WILSON, Ronald Marshall, CBE 1982; sole proprietor, Ronnie Wilson, Chartered Surveyors, since 1983; Chairman, Nightingale Secretariat PLC, since 1985; *b* 6 March 1923; *s* of Marshall Lang Wilson and Margaret Wilson Wilson; *m* 1948, Marion Robertson Scobie (marr. diss. 1985); two *s*. *Educ:* Sedbergh; London Univ. (BSc Estate Management 1950). Served War of 1939–45: North Irish Horse; Court Orderly Officer, Wüppertal War Crimes Trial, 1946. Partner, Bell-Ingram, Chartered Surveyors, 1957–83. Dir, Control Securities plc, 1986–. Royal Institution of Chartered Surveyors: Mem. General Council, 1973–; President, 1979–80; Mem. Land Agency and Agricl Divisional Council, 1970–77 (Chm., 1974–75); Chm., Internat. Cttee, 1976–78. *Publications:* articles on technical and professional subjects, incl. Planning in the Countryside. *Recreations:* golf, fishing, shooting. *Address:* Gable Cottage, 12 Britwell Road, Watlington, Oxon OX9 5JS. *T:* (049161) 3015. *Club:* Farmers'.

WILSON, Roy; *see* Wilson, G. R.

WILSON, Roy Vernon, CEng, MICE; Director, Eastern Region, Property Services Agency, Department of the Environment, 1980–82; *b* 23 July 1922; *s* of late Alfred Vincent Wilson and Theresa Elsie Wilson; *m* 1951, Elsie Hannah Barrett; three *s*. *Educ:* Cheadle Hulme Sch.; Manchester Univ. (BScTech Hons). Served Royal Engineers, 1942–44. Civil Engineer, local govt, 1945–51; Harlow Develt Corp., 1951–54; Air Ministry Works Directorate: Warrington, 1954–59; Newmarket, 1959–62; Germany, 1962–65; District Works Officer: Wethersfield, 1965–67; Mildenhall, 1967–72; Area Officer, Letchworth (PSA), 1972–76; Regional Director, Cyprus (PSA), 1976–79; Chief Works Officer, Ruislip, 1979. *Recreations:* lacrosse (earlier years), golf, tennis. *Address:* 12 Diomed Drive, Great Barton, Bury St Edmunds, Suffolk IP31 2TD. *Club:* Civil Service.

WILSON, Sally Angela, (Mrs Charles Wilson); *see* O'Sullivan, S. A.

WILSON, Samuel; Lord Mayor of Belfast, June 1986–87; *b* 4 April 1953; *s* of Alexander and Mary Wilson. *Educ:* Methodist Coll., Belfast; The Queen's Univ., Belfast (BScEcon; PGCE). Teacher of Economics, 1975–83; Researcher in N Ireland Assembly, 1983–86. Councillor, Belfast CC, 1981–; Press Officer for Democratic Unionist Party, 1982–. *Publications:* The Carson Trail, 1982; The Unionist Case—The Forum Report Answered, 1984. *Recreations:* reading, motor cycling, windsurfing. *Address:* 19 Jocelyn Gardens, Belfast. *T:* Belfast (0232) 59934.

WILSON, Air Marshal Sir Sandy; *see* Wilson, Air Marshal Sir R. A. F.

WILSON, Sandy; composer, lyric writer, playwright; *b* 19 May 1924; *s* of George Walter Wilson and Caroline Elsie (*née* Humphrey). *Educ:* Elstree Preparatory School; Harrow School; Oriel College, Oxford (BA Eng. Lit.). Contributed material to Oranges and Lemons, Slings and Arrows, 1948; wrote lyrics for touring musical play Caprice, 1950; words and music for two revues at Watergate Theatre, 1951 and 1952; (musical comedy) The Boy Friend for Players' Theatre, 1953, later produced in West End and on Broadway, 1954, revival, Comedy, 1967 (also directed), revival, Old Vic, 1984; (musical play) The Buccaneer, 1955; Valmouth (musical play, based on Firbank's novel), Lyric, Hammersmith and Savile Theatre, 1959, New York, 1960, revival, Chichester, 1982; songs for Call It Love, Wyndham's Theatre, 1960; Divorce Me, Darling! (musical comedy), Players' Theatre, 1964, Globe, 1965; music for TV series, The World of Wooster, 1965–66; music for As Dorothy Parker Once Said, Fortune, 1969; songs for Danny la Rue's Charley's Aunt (TV), 1969; wrote and performed in Sandy Wilson Thanks the Ladies, Hampstead Theatre Club, 1971; His Monkey Wife, Hampstead, 1971; The Clapham Wonder, Canterbury, 1978; Aladdin, Lyric, Hammersmith, 1979. *Publications:* This is Sylvia (with own illustrs), 1954; The Boy Friend (with own illustrs), 1955; Who's Who for Beginners (with photographs by Jon Rose), 1957; Prince What Shall I Do (illustrations, with Rhoda Levine), 1961; The Poodle from Rome, 1962; I Could Be Happy (autobiog.), 1975; Ivor, 1975; Caught in the Act, 1976; The Roaring Twenties, 1977. *Recreations:* visiting the National Film Theatre and writing musicals. *Address:* 2 Southwell Gardens, SW7 4SB. *T:* 071–373 6172. *Club:* Players' Theatre.

WILSON, Snoo; writer, since 1969; *b* 2 Aug. 1948; *s* of Leslie Wilson and Pamela Mary Wilson; *m* 1976, Ann McFerran; two *s* one *d*. *Educ:* Bradfield Coll.; Univ. of East Anglia (BA English and American Studies). Associate Director, Portable Theatre, 1970–75; Dramaturge, Royal Shakespeare Co., 1975–76; Script Editor, Play for Today, 1976; Associate Prof. of Theatre, Univ. of Calif at San Diego, 1987. Henfield Fellow, Univ. of E Anglia, 1978; US Bicentennial Fellow in Playwriting, 1981–82. *Filmscript:* Shadey, 1986; *opera:* (adapted) Gounod's La Colombe, 1983. *Publications: plays:* Layby (jtly), 1972; Pignight, 1972; The Pleasure Principle, 1973; Blowjob, 1974; Soul of the White Ant, 1976; England England, 1978; Vampire, 1978; The Glad Hand, 1978; A Greenish Man, 1978; The Number of the Beast, 1982; Flaming Bodies, 1982; Grass Widow, 1983; Loving Reno, 1983; Hamlyn, 1984; More Light, 1987; Callas, 1990, etc; *novels:* Spaceache, 1984; Inside Babel, 1985; *opera:* Orpheus in the Underworld (new version), 1984; *musical:* 80 Days, 1988. *Recreations:* beekeeping, space travel. *Address:* 41 The Chase, SW4 0NP.

WILSON, Stanley John, CBE 1981; FCIS; Chairman, Burmah Oil (South Africa) (Pty) Ltd, since 1982; Managing Director, 1975–82 and Chief Executive, 1980–82, The Burmah Oil Co. Ltd; *b* 23 Oct. 1921; *s* of Joseph Wilson and Jessie Cormack; *m* 1952, Molly Ann (*née* Clarkson); two *s*. *Educ:* King Edward VII Sch., Johannesburg Witwatersrand Univ. CA (SA); ASAA, ACMA; FCIS 1945; CBIM; FInst Pet. 1945–73: Chartered Accountant, Savory & Dickinson; Sec. and Sales Man., Rhodesian Timber Hldgs; Chm. and Chief Exec. for S Africa, Vacuum Oil Co.; Reg. Vice Pres. for S and E Asia, Mobil Petroleum; Pres., Mobil Sekiyu; Pres., subseq. Reg. Vice Pres. for Europe, Mobil Europe Inc.; Pres., Mobil East Inc., and Reg. Vice Pres. for Far East, S and SE Asia, Australia, Indian Sub-Continent, etc, 1973–75. Underwriting Mem. of Lloyd's. Freeman, City of London; Liveryman, Basketmakers' Co. FRSA. *Recreations:* golf, shooting, fishing. *Address:* The Jetty, PO Box 751, Plettenberg Bay, Cape Province, 6600, South Africa. *T:* Plettenberg Bay 9624. *Clubs:* City of London, Royal Automobile; Royal & Ancient Golf; Tidworth Garrison Golf; City (Cape Town); Rand (Johannesburg); Heresewentien (SA).

WILSON, Stanley Livingstone, CMG 1966; DSO 1943; Visiting Surgeon, Dunedin Hospital, 1937–66, Hon. Consulting Surgeon, Dunedin Hospital, since 1966; *b* 17 April 1905; *s* of Robert and Elizabeth Wilson; *m* 1930, Isabel, *d* of William Kirkland; two *s* one *d*. *Educ:* Dannevirke High School; University of Otago. Univ. Entrance Schol., 1923; MB, ChB 1928; FRCS 1932; FRACS 1937. Resident Surgeon, Dunedin Hosp., Royal Northern and St Mary's Hosps, London, 1929–37. NZ Medical Corps, Middle East; Solomons, 1940–44; OC 2 NZ Casualty Clearing Station, Pacific, 1943–44. President, Otago BMA, 1948; Council, RACS 1951–63 (President, 1961–62). Examiner in Surgery, Univ. of Otago, 1952–65; Court of Examiners, RACS, 1948–60; Mem., Otago Hosp. Bd, 1965–74. Hon. Fellow, American Coll. of Surgeons, 1963. Hon. DSc Otago, 1975. *Recreation:* golf. *Address:* 27 Burwood Avenue, Dunedin, NW1, New Zealand. *T:* 741.061. *Club:* Dunedin (Dunedin).

WILSON, Prof. Thomas, OBE 1945; FBA 1976; FRSE 1980; Adam Smith Professor of Political Economy, University of Glasgow, 1958–82; Hon. Fellow, London School of Economics, 1979; *b* 23 June 1916; *s* of late John Bright and Margaret G. Wilson, Belfast; *m* 1943, Dorothy Joan Parry, MVO 1945; one *s* two *d*. *Educ:* Methodist College and Queen's University, Belfast; London School of Economics. Mins of Economic Warfare and Aircraft Production, 1940–42; Prime Minister's Statistical Branch, 1942–45. Fellow of University College, Oxford, 1946–58; Faculty Fellow of Nuffield College, Oxford, 1950–54; Vis. Fellow, All Souls Coll., Oxford, 1974–75; Editor, Oxford Economic Papers, 1948–58. Vice-Chm., Scottish Council's Cttee of Inquiry into the Scottish Economy, 1960–61; Nuffield Foundation Visiting Prof., Univ. of Ibadan, 1962. Economic Consultant to Govt of N Ireland, 1964–65, 1968–70; to Sec. of State for Scotland, 1963–64 and 1970–83; Shipbuilding Industry Cttee, 1965; Assessor, DoE, 1984–85. Dir, Scottish Mutual Assce Soc., 1966–87 (Chm., 1978–81). DUniv Stirling, 1982. *Publications:* Fluctuations in Income and Employment, 1941; (ed) Ulster under Home Rule, 1955; Inflation, 1960; Planning and Growth, 1964; (ed) Pensions, Inflation and Growth, 1974; (ed with A. S. Skinner) Essays on Adam Smith, 1975; (ed with A. S. Skinner) The Market and the State, 1976; The Political Economy of Inflation (British Acad. Keynes Lecture), 1976; (with D. J. Wilson) The Political Economy of the Welfare State, 1982; Inflation, Unemployment and the Market, 1985; Ulster—Conflict and Consent, 1989. *Recreations:* sailing, hill walking. *Address:* 1 Chatford House, The Promenade, Clifton, Bristol BS8 3NG. *T:* Bristol (0272) 730741. *Club:* Athenæum.

WILSON, Thomas Marcus; Assistant Under-Secretary, Ministry of Defence (Procurement Executive), 1971–73; retired; *b* 15 April 1913; *s* of Reverend C. Wilson; *m* 1939, Norah Boyes (*née* Sinclair) (*d* 1984); no *c*. *Educ:* Manchester Grammar School; Jesus College, Cambridge. Asst Principal, Customs and Excise, 1936; Private Secretary: to Board of Customs and Excise, 1939; to Chm. Bd, 1940; Principal, 1941; lent to Treasury, 1942; lent to Office of Lord President of Council, 1946; Asst Sec., 1947; seconded: Min. of Food, 1949; Min. of Supply, 1953, Under-Sec., 1962, and Prin. Scientific and Civil Aviation Adv. to Brit. High Comr in Australia, also Head of Defence Research and Supply Staff, 1962–64; Under-Secretary: Min. of Aviation, 1964–67; Min. of Technology, 1967–70; Min. of Aviation Supply, 1970–71; MoD, 1971–73. *Recreations:* reading, music, painting and travel, especially in France. *Address:* Flat 6, 21 Queen Square, Bath BA1 2HX.

WILSON, Timothy Hugh, FSA; Keeper of Western Art, Ashmolean Museum, Oxford, since 1990; Professorial Fellow, Balliol College, Oxford, since 1990; *b* 8 April 1950; *s* of late Col Hugh Walker Wilson and of Lilian Rosemary (*née* Kirke); *m* 1984, Jane Lott; one *s* one *d*. *Educ:* Winchester Coll.; Mercersburg Acad., USA; Corpus Christi Coll., Oxford (BA 1973; MA); Warburg Inst., London Univ. (MPhil 1976); Dept of Museum Studies, Leicester Univ. FSA 1989. Res. Asst, Dept of Weapons and Antiquities, Nat. Maritime Mus., Greenwich, 1977–79; Asst Keeper (Renaissance collections), Dept of Medieval and Later Antiquities, BM, 1979–90. Fellow, Harvard Univ. Center for Renaissance Studies, Villa I Tatti, Florence, 1984; Hon. Fellow, Royal Soc. Painter-Printmakers, 1991. *Publications:* (jtly) The Art of the Jeweller, 1984; Flags at Sea, 1986; Ceramic Art of the Italian Renaissance, 1987; Maiolica, 1989; (ed) Italian Renaissance Pottery, 1991; articles in Apollo, Burlington Mag., Faenza, Jl Warburg and Courtauld Insts, etc; contribs exhibition catalogues. *Recreations:* cycling, board-games, second-hand bookshops. *Address:* Balliol College, Oxford OX1 3BJ; 6 Longworth Road, Oxford OX2 6RA. *T:* Oxford (0865) 511029.

WILSON, William; DL; *b* 28 June 1913; *s* of Charles and Charlotte Wilson; *m* 1939, Bernice Wilson; one *s*. *Educ:* Wheatley St Sch.; Cheylesmore Sch.; Coventry Jun. Technical School. Qual. as Solicitor, 1939. Entered Army, 1941; served in N Africa, Italy and Greece; demobilised, 1946 (Sergeant). Contested (Lab) Warwick and Leamington, 1951, 1955, March 1957, 1959. MP (Lab) Coventry S, 1964–74, Coventry SE, 1974–83; Mem., Commons Select Cttee on Race Relations and Immigration, 1970–79. Mem., Warwicks CC, 1958–70 (Leader Labour Group), re-elected 1972. DL County of Warwick, 1967. *Recreations:* gardening, theatre, watching Association football. *Address:* Avonside House, High Street, Barford, Warwickshire CV35 8BU. *T:* Barford (0926) 624278.

WILSON, Prof. William Adam; Lord President Reid Professor of Law, University of Edinburgh, since 1972; *b* 28 July 1928; *s* of Hugh Wilson and Anne Adam. *Educ:* Hillhead High Sch., Glasgow; Glasgow Univ. MA 1948, LLB 1951. Solicitor, 1951. Lectr in Scots Law, Edinburgh Univ., 1960, Sen. Lectr 1965. Dep. Chm., Consumer Protection Adv. Cttee, 1974–82. FRSE 1991. *Publications:* (with A. G. M. Duncan) Law of Trusts, Trustees and Executors, 1975; Introductory Essays on Scots Law, 1978, 2nd edn 1984; Law of Debt, 1981, 2nd edn 1991; articles in legal jls. *Address:* 2 Great Stuart Street, Edinburgh EH3 6AW. *T:* 031–225 4958.

WILSON, William Desmond, OBE 1964 (MBE 1954); MC 1945; DSC (USA) 1945; HM Diplomatic Service, retired; Deputy High Commissioner, Kaduna, Nigeria, 1975–81; *b* 2 Jan. 1922; *s* of late Crozier Irvine Wilson and Mabel Evelyn (*née* Richardson); *m* 1949, Lucy Bride; two *s*. *Educ:* Royal Belfast Acad. Instn; QUB; Trinity Coll., Cambridge. Joined Indian Army, 1941; served with 10 Gurkha Rifles, India and Italy, 1942–46 (Major). Colonial Admin. Service: Northern Nigeria, 1948–63 (MBE for Gallantry, 1954); retd as Permanent Sec.; joined Foreign (subseq. Diplomatic) Service, 1963; First Sec., Ankara, 1963–67; UN (Polit.) Dept, FO, 1967; First Sec. and Head of Chancery, Kathmandu, 1969–74; Counsellor, 1975; Sen. Officers' War Course, RNC Greenwich, 1975. *Recreations:* shooting, riding. *Address:* The Spinney, Forge Hill, Pluckley, Kent TN27 0SJ. *T:* Pluckley (023384) 300. *Club:* East India.

WILSON, (William) George, OBE 1960; Associate Director, PA Consulting Group, since 1989; *b* 19 Feb. 1921; *s* of late William James Wilson and late Susannah Wilson; *m* 1948, Freda Huddleston; three *s*. Min. of Health, 1939. Served War, Army, in India and Ceylon, 1940–46. Min. of Nat. Insurance, 1947; Asst Principal, Colonial Office, 1947; Principal, CO, 1950–57 (Adviser, UK Delegn to UN Gen. Assembly, 1951); Financial Sec., Mauritius, 1957–60; Asst Sec., MoH, 1962; Consultant, Hosp. Design and Construction, Middle East and Africa, 1968–70; Asst Sec., DHSS, 1971; Under-Sec., DHSS, 1972–81. Chm., Paul James & George Wilson Ltd, Health Service Devélt Advrs, 1986–89 (Dir, 1983–86). *Recreation:* gardening. *Address:* Clarghyll Hall, Alston, Cumbria CA9 3NF. *Club:* Commonwealth Trust.

WILSON, Rt. Rev. William Gilbert; *see* Kilmore, Elphin and Ardagh, Bishop of.

WILSON, William Lawrence, CB 1967; OBE 1954; retired as Deputy Secretary, Department of the Environment, now Consultant; *b* 11 Sept. 1912; *s* of Joseph Osmond and Ann Wilson; *m* C. V. Richards; two *s*. *Educ:* Stockton on Tees Secondary School; Constantine College, Middlesbrough. BSc (London), FIMechE, Whitworth Prizeman. Apprentice, ICI Billingham 1928–33; Technical Asst, ICI, 1933–36; Assistant Engineer, HMOW, 1937; subsequently Engineer, 1939; Superintending Engineer, (MOW) 1945; Assistant Chief Engineer, 1954; Chief Engineer, 1962; Deputy Secretary, MPBW later DoE, 1969–73. Pres., Assoc. of Supervising Electrical Engineers. FRSA; Hon. FCIBSE. Coronation Medal. *Publications:* papers on Radioactive Wastes; contrib. to World Power Conference, USSR and USA. *Recreations:* cricket, fishing, watching all forms of sport. *Address:* Oakwood, Chestnut Avenue, Rickmansworth, Herts WD3 4HB. *T:* Rickmansworth (0923) 774419.

WILSON, William Napier M.; *see* Menzies-Wilson.

WILSON-BARNETT, Prof. Jenifer, (Mrs M. R. Trimble); Professor and Head of Department of Nursing Studies, King's College, London, since 1986; *b* 10 Aug. 1944; adopted by Edith M. Barnett and Barbara M. Wilson; *m* 1975, Michael Robert Trimble. *Educ:* Chichester High School for Girls; St George's Hosp., London (student nurse), 1963–66; Univ. of Leicester, 1967–70 (BA Politics); Edinburgh Univ., 1970–72 (MSc); Guy's Hosp. Med. Sch., London (PhD 1977). FRCN 1984. Staff Nurse, 1966, Nursing Sister, 1972–74, St George's Hosp.; Researcher, Guy's Hosp., 1974–77; Chelsea College: Lectr in Nursing, 1977; Sen. Lectr, 1983; Reader and Hd of Dept, 1984. *Publications:* Stress in Hospital: patients' psychological reactions to illness and health care, 1979; (with Morva Fordham) Recovery from Illness, 1982; Patient Teaching, 1983; Nursing Research: ten studies in patient care, 1983; Nursing Issues and Research in Terminal Care, 1988; Patient Problems: a research base for nursing care, 1988; (with Sarah Robinson) Direction in Nursing Research, 1989. *Recreations:* ski-ing, music, clothes-shopping, writing, 'singing'. *Address:* Department of Nursing Studies, Cornwall House Annexe, Waterloo Road, SE1. *Clubs:* Royal Automobile, Royal College of Nursing, Royal Society of Medicine.

WILSON-JOHNSON, David Robert; baritone; *b* 16 Nov. 1950; *s* of Sylvia Constance Wilson and Harry Kenneth Johnson. *Educ:* Wellingborough School; British Institute, Florence; St Catharine's College, Cambridge (BA Hons 1973); Royal Acad. of Music. NFMS Award, 1977; Gulbenkian Fellowship, 1978–81. Royal Opera House, Covent Garden: We Come to the River (début), 1976; Billy Budd, 1982; L'Enfant et les Sortilèges, 1983; Le Rossignol, 1983; Les Noces, Boris Godunov, 1984; Die Zauberflöte, 1985; Werther, Turandot, 1987; Madam Butterfly, 1988; title rôle, St François d'Assise (Messiaen), 1988–89; Wigmore Hall recital début, 1977; BBC Proms début, 1981; Paris Opera début (Die Meistersinger), 1989; US début, Cleveland Orch., 1990; appearances at Glyndebourne, Edinburgh, and other UK and overseas venues; numerous recordings. FRAM 1988 (Hon. ARAM 1982). *Recreations:* swimming, slimming, gardening and growing walnuts at Dordogne house. *Address:* 28 Englefield Road, N1 4ET. *T:* 071–254 0941.

WILSON JONES, Prof. Edward, FRCP, FRCPath; Professor of Dermatopathology, Institute of Dermatology, University of London, since 1974 (Dean, 1980–89); *b* 26 July 1926; *s* of Percy George Jones and Margaret Louisa Wilson; *m* 1952, Hilda Mary Rees; one *s* one *d*. *Educ:* Oundle Sch.; Trinity Hall, Cambridge (MB, BChir 1951); St Thomas' Hosp., London. FRCP 1970; FRCPath 1975. National Service, Army, 1953–54. House Surgeon (Ophthalmic), St Thomas' Hosp., 1951; House Physician (Gen. Medicine), St Helier Hosp., Carshalton, 1951–52; House Physician (Neurology and Chest Diseases), St Thomas' Hosp., 1955; Registrar (Gen. Medicine), Watford Peace Meml Hosp., 1955–57; Registrar (Derm.), St Thomas' Hosp., 1957–60; Inst. of Dermatology, St John's Hosp. for Diseases of the Skin: Sen. Registrar (Derm.), 1960–62; Sen. Registrar (Dermatopath.), 1962–63; Sen. Lectr (Dermatopath.), 1963–74; Hon. Consultant, St John's Hosp. for Diseases of Skin, 1974–. *Publications:* (contrib.) Textbook of Dermatology, ed Rook, Wilkinson and Ebling, 3rd edn 1979; articles on dermatopath. subjects in British Jl of Derm., Arch. of Derm., Acta Dermatovenereologica, Dermatologica, Clin. and Exptl Derm., Histopath., and in Human Path. *Recreation:* art history. *Address:* Institute of Dermatology, St John's Dermatology Centre, South Wing, Block 7a, St Thomas' Hospital, SE1 7EH.

WILTON, 7th Earl of, *cr* 1801; **Seymour William Arthur John Egerton;** Viscount Grey de Wilton, 1801; *b* 29 May 1921; *s* of 6th Earl and Brenda (*d* 1930), *d* of late Sir William Petersen, KBE; *S* father, 1927; *m* 1962, Mrs Diana Naylor Leyland. *Heir:* (by special remainder) *kinsman* Baron Ebury, *qv*. *Address:* The Old Vicarage, Castle Hedingham, Halstead, Essex CO9 3EZ. *Club:* White's.

WILTON, Andrew; *see* Wilton, J. A. R.

WILTON, Sir (Arthur) John, KCMG 1979 (CMG 1967); KCVO 1979; MC 1945; MA; HM Diplomatic Service, retired; *b* 21 Oct. 1921; *s* of Walter Wilton and Annetta Irene Wilton (*née* Perman); *m* 1950, Maureen Elizabeth Alison Meaker; four *s* one *d*. *Educ:* Wanstead High School; Open Schol., St John's Coll., Oxford, 1940. Commissioned, Royal Ulster Rifles, 1942; served with Irish Brigade, N Africa, Italy and Austria, 1943–46. Entered HM Diplomatic Service, 1947; served Lebanon, Egypt, Gulf Shaikhdoms, Roumania, Aden, and Yugoslavia; Dir, Middle East Centre for Arabic Studies, Shemlan, 1960–65; Ambassador to Kuwait, 1970–74; Asst Under-Sec. of State, FCO, 1974–76; Ambassador to Saudi Arabia, 1976–79. Dir, London House for Overseas Graduates, 1979–86. Chm., Arab-British Centre, 1981–86; Pres., Plymouth Br., ESU, 1991– (Vice-Pres., 1988–91); Trustee, Arab-British Chamber Charitable Foundn, 1989–. Gov., Hele Sch., Plympton, 1988–. FRSA 1982. Hon. LLD New England Coll., NH, 1986. *Recreations:* reading, gardening. *Address:* Legassick House, 69 Fore Street, Plympton St Maurice, Plymouth PL7 3NA.

WILTON, (James) Andrew (Rutley); Keeper of British Art, Tate Gallery, since 1989; *b* 7 Feb. 1942; *s* of Herbert Rutley Wilton and Mary Cecilia Morris (*née* Buckerfield); *m* 1976, Christina Frances Benn (marr. diss.); one *s*. *Educ:* Dulwich Coll.; Trinity Coll., Cambridge (MA). Assistant Keeper: Walker Art Gallery, Liverpool, 1965; Dept of Prints and Drawings, BM, 1967; Curator of Prints and Drawings, Yale Center for British Art, 1976; Asst Keeper, Turner Collection, BM, 1981; Curator, Turner Collection, Tate Gallery, 1985. *Publications:* Turner in Switzerland (with John Russell), 1976; British Watercolours 1750–1850, 1977; The Wood Engravings of William Blake, 1977; The Life and Work of J. M. W. Turner, 1979; The Art of Alexander and John Robert Cozens, 1979; William Pars: journey through the Alps, 1979; Turner and the Sublime, 1980; Turner Abroad, 1982; Turner in his Time, 1987; Painting and Poetry, 1990; contribs to arts magazines. *Recreations:* cooking, walking, architecture, drawing, music. *Address:* Tate Gallery, SW1P 4RG. *Club:* Athenæum.

WILTON, Sir John; *see* Wilton, Sir A. J.

WILTS, Archdeacon of; *see* Smith, Ven. B. J.

WILTSHIRE, Earl of; Christopher John Hilton Paulet; *b* 30 July 1969; *s* and *heir* of Marquess of Winchester, *qv*.

WILTSHIRE, Edward Parr, CBE 1965; HM Diplomatic Service, retired; *b* 18 Feb. 1910; 2nd *s* of late Major Percy Wiltshire and Kathleen Olivier Lefroy Parr Wiltshire, Great Yarmouth; *m* 1942, Gladys Mabel Stevens; one *d*. *Educ:* Cheltenham College; Jesus College, Cambridge. Entered Foreign Service, 1932. Served in: Beirut, Mosul, Baghdad, Tehran, Basra, New York (one of HM Vice-Consuls, 1944); promoted Consul, 1945; transf. Cairo, 1946 (Actg Consul-Gen., 1947, 1948); transf. Shiraz (having qual. in Arabic, and subseq. in Persian); Consul, Port Said, 1952; 1st Sec. and Consul: Baghdad, 1952, Rio de Janeiro, 1957; promoted Counsellor, 1959; Political Agent, Bahrain, 1959–63; Consul-General, Geneva, 1963–67; Dir, Diplomatic Service Language Centre, London, 1967–68; worked for Council for Nature (Editor, Habitat), 1968–69; Consul, Le Havre, 1969–75. Hon. Associate, BM (Nat. Hist.), 1980. *Publications:* The Lepidoptera of Iraq, 1957; A Revision of the Armadini, 1979. *Recreations:* music, entomology. *Address:* Wychwood, High Road, Cookham, Berks SL6 9JS.

WILTSHIRE, Sir Frederick Munro, Kt 1976; CBE 1970 (OBE 1966); FTS 1976; Managing Director: Wiltshire File Co. Pty Ltd, Australia, 1938–77; Wiltshire Cutlery Co. Pty Ltd, 1959–77; Director: Repco Ltd, 1966–81; Australian Paper Manufacturers Ltd, 1966–83; *b* 1911; *m* 1938, Jennie L., *d* of F. M. Frencham; one *d*. Chm., Dept of Trade and Industry Adv. Cttee on Small Businesses, 1968; Chm., Cttees of Inquiry, etc. Mem., Executive, CSIRO, 1974–78. Past Pres., Aust. Industries Develt Assoc.; Member, Manufacturing Industries Adv. Council, 1957–77 (Vice-Pres. 1972); Industrial Member, Science and Industry Forum of Aust. Acad. of Science, 1967–80; FAIM (Councillor,

1955–59). *Address:* 38 Rockley Road, South Yarra, Vic 3141, Australia. *Clubs:* Athenæum (Melbourne); Kingston Heath Golf (Aust.).

WIMALASENA, Nanediri; Governor, Province of Sabaragamuwa, Sri Lanka, since 1988; *b* 22 March 1914; *m* 1938, Prema Fernando; one *s* two *d*. *Educ:* Ananda Coll., Colombo; Ceylon University Coll.; Ceylon Law Coll. Attorney-at-Law. Elected member, Kandy Municipal Council, 1946, remaining a member for an unbroken period of 21 years; Dep. Mayor of Kandy, 1946; Mayor of City of Kandy, 1963. Elected Member of Parliament for Senkadagala: March-July 1960; again, 1965, then re-elected 1970–May 1977; Dep. Minister of Finance, 1965–70. High Comr for Sri Lanka in London, 1977–80. Dep. Dir Gen., Greater Colombo Econ. Commn of Sri Lanka, 1981–88. *Recreations:* tennis, hiking. *Address:* 55 Ward Place, Colombo 7, Sri Lanka.

WIMBORNE, 3rd Viscount, *cr* 1918; **Ivor Fox-Strangways Guest;** Baron Wimborne, 1880; Baron Ashby St Ledgers, 1910; Bt 1838; Chairman, Harris and Dixon Holdings Ltd, since 1976; *b* 2 Dec. 1939; *s* of 2nd Viscount and of Dowager Viscountess Wimborne; *S* father, 1967; *m* 1st, 1966, Victoria Ann (marr. diss. 1981), *o d* of late Col Mervyn Vigors, DSO, MC; one *s*; 2nd, 1983, Mrs Venetia Margaret Barker, *er d* of Richard Quarry; one *d*. *Educ:* Eton. Chairman: Harris & Dixon Ltd, 1972–76 (Man. Dir, 1967–71); Harris & Dixon Group of Cos, 1977–; Dep. Chm., Ermitage Group. Jt Master, Pytchley Hounds, 1968–76. *Heir: s* Hon. Ivor Mervyn Vigors Guest, *b* 19 Sept. 1968. *Clubs:* Travellers', Cercle Interalliée, Polo (Paris).

WIMBUSH, Rt. Rev. Richard Knyvet; an Assistant Bishop, Diocese of York, since 1977; *b* 18 March 1909; *s* of late Rev. Canon J. S. Wimbush, Terrington, Yorks, and late Judith Isabel Wimbush, *d* of Sir Douglas Fox; *m* 1937, Mary Margaret (*d* 1989), *d* of Rev. E. H. Smith; three *s* one *d*. *Educ:* Haileybury Coll.; Oriel Coll., Oxford; Cuddesdon Coll. 2nd cl. Classical Mods 1930; BA 1st cl. Theol. 1932; MA 1935. Deacon, 1934; Priest, 1935; Chaplain, Cuddesdon Coll., Oxon, 1934–37; Curate: Pocklington, Yorks, 1937–39; St Wilfrid, Harrogate, 1939–42. Rector, Melsonby, Yorks, 1942–48; Principal, Edinburgh Theological Coll., 1948–63; Bishop of Argyll and the Isles, 1963–77; Primus of the Episcopal Church in Scotland, 1974–77; Priest-in-charge of Etton with Dalton Holme, dio. York, 1977–83. Canon of St Mary's Cathedral, Edinburgh, 1948–63; Exam. Chap. to Bp of Edinburgh, 1949–62; Select Preacher, Oxford Univ., 1971. *Recreations:* gardening, walking. *Address:* 5 Tower Place, York YO1 1RZ. *T:* York (0904) 641971. *Club:* New (Edinburgh).

WINCH, Prof. Donald Norman, FBA 1986; FRHistS; Professor, History of Economics, University of Sussex, since 1969; *b* 15 April 1935; *s* of Sidney and Iris Winch; *m* 1983, Doreen Lidster. *Educ:* Sutton Grammar Sch.; LSE (BSc Econ 1956); Princeton Univ. (PhD 1960). FRHistS 1987. Vis. Lectr, Univ. of California, 1959–60; Lectr in Economics, Univ. of Edinburgh, 1960–63; University of Sussex: Lectr, 1963–66; Reader, 1966–69; Dean, Sch. of Social Scis, 1968–74; Pro-Vice-Chancellor (Arts and Social Studies), 1986–89. Visiting Fellow: Sch. of Social Sci., Inst. for Advanced Study, Princeton, 1974–75; King's Coll., Cambridge, 1983; History of Ideas Unit, ANU, 1983; Vis. Prof., Tulane Univ., 1984. Publications Sec., Royal Economic Soc., 1971–; Review Editor, Economic Jl, 1976–83. *Publications:* Classical Political Economy and Colonies, 1965; James Mill: selected economic writings, 1966; Economics and Policy, 1969; (with S. K. Howson) The Economic Advisory Council 1930–1939, 1976; Adam Smith's Politics, 1978; (with S. Collini and J. W. Burrow) That Noble Science of Politics, 1983; Malthus, 1987. *Address:* University of Sussex, Brighton BN1 9QN. *T:* Brighton (0273) 678028.

WINCHESTER, 18th Marquess of, *cr* 1551; **Nigel George Paulet;** Baron St John of Basing, 1539; Earl of Wiltshire, 1550; Premier Marquess of England; *b* 23 Dec. 1941; *s* of George Cecil Paulet (*g g g s* of 13th Marquess) (*d* 1961), and Hazel Margaret (*d* 1976), *o d* of late Major Danvers Wheeler, RA, Salisbury, Rhodesia; *S* kinsman, 1968; *m* 1967, Rosemary Anne, *d* of Major Aubrey John Hilton; two *s* one *d*. *Heir: s* Earl of Wiltshire, *qv*. *Address:* 6A Main Road, Irene 1675, Transvaal, South Africa.

WINCHESTER, Bishop of, since 1985; **Rt. Rev. Colin Clement Walter James;** *b* 20 Sept. 1926; *yr s* of late Canon Charles Clement Hancock James and Gwenyth Mary James; *m* 1962, Margaret Joan, (Sally), Henshaw; one *s* two *d*. *Educ:* Aldenham School; King's College, Cambridge (MA, Hons History); Cuddesdon Theological College. Assistant Curate, Stepney Parish Church, 1952–55; Chaplain, Stowe School, 1955–59; BBC Religious Broadcasting Dept, 1959–67; Religious Broadcasting Organizer, BBC South and West, 1960–67; Vicar of St Peter with St Swithin, Bournemouth, 1967–73; Bishop Suffragan of Basingstoke, 1973–77; Canon Residentiary of Winchester Cathedral, 1973–77; Bishop of Wakefield, 1977–85. Member of General Synod, 1970–; Chairman: Church Information Cttee, 1976–79; C of E's Liturgical Commn, 1986–. Chm., BBC and IBA Central Religious Adv. Cttee, 1979–84. President: Woodard Corp., 1978–; RADIUS, 1980–. Chm., USPG, 1985–88. *Recreations:* theatre, travelling. *Address:* Wolvesey, Winchester, Hants SO23 9ND. *T:* Winchester (0962) 854050.

WINCHESTER, Dean of; *see* Beeson, Very Rev. T. R.

WINCHESTER, Archdeacon of; *see* Clarkson, Ven. A. G.

WINCHESTER, Ian Sinclair, CMG 1982; HM Diplomatic Service, retired; *b* 14 March 1931; *s* of late Dr Alexander Hugh Winchester, FRCS(Ed), and Mary Stewart (*née* Duguid); *m* 1957, Shirley Louise Milner; three *s*. *Educ:* Lewes County Grammar Sch., Sussex; Magdalen Coll., Oxford. Foreign Office, 1953; Third Sec. (Oriental), Cairo, 1955–56; FO, 1956–60; Asst Political Agent, Dubai, 1960–62; Actg Political Agent, Doha, 1962; First Sec. (Inf.), Vienna, 1962–65; First Sec. (Commercial), Damascus, 1965–67; FO (later FCO), 1967–70; Counsellor, Jedda, 1970–72; Counsellor (Commercial), Brussels, 1973–76; FCO, 1976–81; Minister, Jedda, 1982–83; Asst Under-Sec. of State (Dir of Communications and Technical Services), FCO, 1985–89. *Address:* 134 College Road, SE19 1XD.

WINCHILSEA, 16th Earl of, *cr* 1628, **AND NOTTINGHAM,** 11th Earl of, *cr* 1681; **Christopher Denys Stormont Finch Hatton,** Bart 1611; Viscount Maidstone, 1623; Bart English, 1660; Baron Finch, 1674; Custodian of Royal Manor of Wye; *b* 17 Nov. 1936; *er s* of 15th Earl and Countess Gladys Széchényi (*d* 1978) (who obtained a divorce, 1946; she *m* 1954, Arthur Talbot Peterson), 3rd *d* of Count László Széchényi; *S* father, 1950; *m* 1962, Shirley, *e d* of late Bernard Hatfield, Wylde Green, Sutton Coldfield; one *s* one *d*. *Heir: s* Viscount Maidstone, *qv*. *Address:* South Cadbury House, Yeovil, Somerset.

WINCKLES, Kenneth, MBE 1945; business consultant; Director, Dowson-Shurman Associates Ltd, since 1988; *b* 17 June 1918; *s* of Frank and Emily Winckles; *m* 1941, Peggy Joan Hodges; one *s* one *d*. *Educ:* Lower School of John Lyon, Harrow. FCA. Served War, Army, 1939–46, demobilised Lt-Col. Company Secretary, Scribbans-Kemp Ltd, 1947–48; Rank Organisation, 1948–67: Director and Gp Asst Managing Dir; Managing Dir, Theatre Div.; Dir, Southern Television Ltd; Dir, Rank-Xerox Ltd; Chm., Odeon Theatres (Canada) Ltd; Chm., Visnews Ltd. Chm. and Man. Dir, United Artists Corp, 1967–69; Man. Dir, Cunard Line Ltd, 1969–70; Dir, Hill Samuel Gp Ltd, 1971–80; Dep. Chm., ITL Information Technology plc, 1981–89. Director: Horserace Totalisator Bd, 1974–76; CAA, 1978–80. *Publications:* The Practice of Successful Business Management, 1986; Funding Your Business, 1988. *Recreations:* swimming, gardening, music. *Address:* Moor House, Fishers Wood, Sunningdale, Ascot, Berks SL5 0JF. *T:* Ascot (0344) 24800.

WINDEYER, Sir Brian (Wellingham), Kt 1961; FRCP, FRCS, FRCSE, FRSM, FRCR, DMRE; Vice-Chancellor, University of London, 1969–72; Professor of Radiology (Therapeutic), Middlesex Hospital Medical School, University of London, 1942–69; Dean, Middlesex Hospital Medical School, 1954–67; formerly Director: Meyerstein Institute of Radiotherapy, Middlesex Hospital; Radiotherapy Department, Mount Vernon Hospital; Cons. Adviser in Radiotherapy to Ministry of Health; *b* 7 Feb. 1904; *s* of Richard Windeyer, KC, Sydney, Australia; *m* 1st, 1928, Joyce Ziele, *d* of Harry Russell, Sydney; one *s* one *d*; 2nd, 1948, Elspeth Anne, *d* of H. Bowrey, Singapore; one *s* two *d*. *Educ:* Sydney C of E Grammar Sch.; St Andrew's Coll., Univ. of Sydney. Sydney Univ. Rugby Team, 1922–27; combined Australian and NZ Univs Rugby Team, 1923; coll. crew, 1922–26. MB, BS Sydney, 1927; FRCSE 1930; DMRE Cambridge, 1933; FFR (now FRCR) 1940; FRCS (ad eundem) 1948; MRCP 1957. Formerly House Physician, House Surgeon and Radium Registrar, Royal Prince Alfred Hosp., Sydney; Asst, Fondation Curie, Paris, 1929–30; Middlesex Hospital: Radium Officer, 1931; MO i/c Radiotherapy Dept, 1936; Medical Comdt, 1940–45; Dir, EMS Radiotherapy Dept, Mt Vernon Hosp., 1940–46; Dean, Faculty of Medicine, Univ. of London, 1964–68. Skinner Lectr, Faculty of Radiologists, 1943 (Pres. of Faculty, 1949–52); Hunterian Prof., RCS, 1951. Pres., Radiology Section, RSM, 1958–59. Chairman: Radio-active Substances Adv. Cttee, 1961–70; Nat. Radiological Protection Bd, 1970–78; Academic Council, Univ. of London, 1967–69; Matilda and Terence Kennedy Inst. of Rheumatology, 1970–77; Inst. of Educn, Univ. of London, 1974–83; Council, RSA, 1973–78. Member: Royal Commn on Med. Educn; Grand Council and Exec. Cttee, British Empire Cancer Campaign; British Inst. of Radiology (late Mem. Council); Med. Soc. of London; MRC, 1958–62 and 1968–71; Clinical Research Bd, 1954–62 (Chm., 1968); a Vice Pres., Royal Surgical Aid Soc. (formerly Chm.). Co-opted Mem. Council, RCS, to rep. radiology, 1948–53. Former Chm., Throgmorton Club. Mem. Court, 1963–78, Master, 1972–73, Apothecaries' Soc. Hon. Mem., Amer. Radium Soc., 1948. Hon. FRACS, 1951; Hon. FCRA (now FRACR) 1955; Hon. FACR 1966. Hon. DSc: British Columbia, 1952; Wales, 1965; Cantab, 1971; Hon. LLD Glasgow, 1968; Hon. MD Sydney, 1979. *Publications:* various articles on cancer and radiotherapy. *Recreations:* golf, gardening. *Address:* 9 Dale Close, St Ebbe's, Oxford OX1 1TU. *T:* Oxford (0865) 242816. *Club:* Athenæum.

WINDHAM, William Ashe Dymoke; Chairman, Skelmersdale Development Corporation, 1979–85; (Deputy Chairman, 1977); *b* 2 April 1926; *s* of late Lt-Col Henry Steuart Windham and Marjory Russell Dymock; *m* 1956, Alison Audrey, *d* of late Maj. P. P. Curtis and Ellinor Kidston; two *s* one *d*. *Educ:* Bedford; Christ's Coll., Cambridge (schol.; MA). CEng, MIChemE. Gen. Manager, Runcorn Div., Arthur Guinness Son & Co. (GB), 1972–84. Mem., Runcorn Develt Corp., 1975–77. Chm., Halton Dist Sports Council, 1973–76; first Chm., Halton Sports and Recreational Trust, 1975–81; Mem., Cttee of Management Henley Royal Regatta, 1973–; rowed for: Cambridge, 1947 and 1951; England, Empire Games, 1950; GB, European Championships, 1950 and 1951 (Gold Medal); Olympic Games, 1952. Chm., Gt Budworth Church Restoration Trust, 1982–84. *Recreations:* shooting, fishing. *Address:* Parc Gwynne, Glasbury-on-Wye, via Hereford HR3 5LL. *T:* Glasbury (0497) 847289. *Clubs:* Hawks (Cambridge); Leander (Henley).

WINDHAM, Brig. William Russell S.; *see* Smijth-Windham.

WINDLE, Terence Leslie William, CBE 1991; Director, Directorate General for Agriculture, European Commission, 1980–91; *b* 15 Jan. 1926; *s* of Joseph William Windle and Dorothy Windle (*née* Haigh); *m* 1957, Joy Winifred Shield; one *s* two *d*. *Educ:* Gonville and Caius College, Cambridge (MA); London University (Colonial Course). Colonial/HMOCS: Nigeria, 1951–59; Zambia, 1959–69 (Under Sec., Min. of Natural Resources and Tourism); Home Civil Service, MAFF, 1969–73; Commn of EC, 1973–91. *Address:* rue du Fond Agny 20, 1380 Lasne, Belgium. *T:* (2) 633 4410.

WINDLESHAM, 3rd Baron, *cr* 1937; **David James George Hennessy,** CVO 1981; PC 1973; Bt 1927; Principal, Brasenose College, Oxford, since 1989; Chairman, Trustees of the British Museum, since 1986 (Trustee, since 1981); *b* 28 Jan. 1932; *s* of 2nd Baron Windlesham; *S* father, 1962; *m* 1965, Prudence Glynn (*d* 1986); one *s* one *d*. *Educ:* Ampleforth; Trinity Coll., Oxford (MA; Hon. Fellow 1982). Chairman, Bow Group, 1959–60, 1962–63; Member, Westminster City Council, 1958–62. Minister of State, Home Office, 1970–72; Minister of State for Northern Ireland, 1972–73; Lord Privy Seal and Leader of the House of Lords, 1973–74. Mem., Cttee of Privy Counsellors on Ministerial Memoirs, 1975. Man. Dir, Grampian Television, 1967–70. Jt Man. Dir, 1974–75, Man. Dir, 1975–81, Chm., 1981, ATV Network; Director: The Observer, 1981–89; W. H. Smith Gp, plc, 1986–. Chm., The Parole Bd, 1982–88. Vice-Pres., Royal Television Soc., 1977–82. Jt Dep. Chm., Queen's Silver Jubilee Appeal, 1977; Dep. Chm., The Royal Jubilee Trusts, 1977–80; Chairman: Oxford Preservation Trust, 1979–89; Oxford Society, 1985–88; Mem, Museums and Galleries Commn, 1984–86. Ditchley Foundation: Governor and Mem., Council of Management, 1983–; Vice-Chm., 1987–; Trustee: Charities Aid Foundn, 1977–81; Community Service Volunteers, 1981–. Vis. Fellow, All Souls Coll., Oxford, 1986. *Publications:* Communication and Political Power, 1966; Politics in Practice, 1975; Broadcasting in a Free Society, 1980; Responses to Crime, 1987; (with Richard Rampton) The Windlesham/Rampton Report on Death on the Rock, 1989. *Heir: s* Hon. James Hennessy, *b* 9 Nov. 1968. *Address:* Brasenose College, Oxford OX1 4AJ.

WINDSOR, Viscount; Ivor Edward Other Windsor-Clive; *b* 19 Nov. 1951; *s* and *heir* of 3rd Earl of Plymouth, *qv*; *m* 1979, Caroline, *d* of Frederick Nettlefold and Hon. Mrs Juliana Roberts; two *s* one *d*. *Educ:* Harrow; Royal Agricl Coll., Cirencester. Co-founder, and Dir, Centre for the Study of Modern Art, 1973. *Recreation:* cricket. *Heir: s* Hon. Robert Other Ivor Windsor-Clive, *b* 25 March 1981. *Address:* The Stables, Oakly Park, Ludlow, Shropshire.

WINDSOR, Dean of; *see* Mitchell, Very Rev. P. R.

WINDSOR-CLIVE, family name of **Earl of Plymouth.**

WINFIELD, Dr Graham, CBE 1991; Chief Executive, Overseas Division, BOC Group, 1979–89; *b* 28 May 1931; *s* of Josiah and Gladys Winfield; *m* 1959, Olive Johnson; three *s* one *d*. *Educ:* Univ. of Liverpool (BSc, PhD Chemistry). Chemist, Min. of Supply, 1956–57; Lectr, Univ. of Liverpool, 1957–58; Chief Chemist, later Develt Manager, Ciba ARL, 1958–62; Develt Manager, MaxMeyer Co., Milan, 1962–63; BOC Group, 1963–: R&D, marketing, gen. management; Chief Exec., Metals Div. UK, 1969–74; Chief Exec., Gases Div. UK, 1974–79. Non-exec. Dir., Baker Perkins Group, 1984–87. Mem., ESRC, 1985–90; Chm., Post Grad. Trng Bd, 1987–90. *Publications:* numerous papers in pure and applied chemistry. *Recreations:* golf, bridge, music, reading. *Address:* Milford, Chinnor Road, Bledlow Ridge, near High Wycombe, Bucks HP14 4AL. *T:* Bledlow Ridge (024027) 216.

WINFIELD, Peter Stevens, FRICS; Senior Partner, Healey & Baker, London, Amsterdam, Brussels, New York, Paris, St Helier, Jersey, 1975–88, Consultant, since 1988; *b* 24 March 1927; *s* of late Harold Stevens Winfield and Susan Cooper; *m* 1955, Mary Gabrielle Kenrick; four *s* two *d*. *Educ:* Sloane Sch., Chelsea; West London College of Commerce. Served Royal Artillery, 1944–48. Joined Healey & Baker, 1951. Governor, Guy's Hospital, 1973–74, Special Trustee, 1974–; Chairman: London Auction Mart Ltd, 1980– (Dir, 1970–); Letinvest plc, 1987–; Director: Manders (Holdings) plc, 1987–; Osprey Management Co. Ltd, 1989–. Member: Lloyd's of London, 1978–; Property Investment Cttee of Save & Prosper Gp Ltd, 1980–; Horserace Totalisator Bd, 1981–. Dir, Kingston Theatre Trust, 1990–. Liveryman: Worshipful Company of Farriers, 1967–; Worshipful Company of Feltmakers, 1972–, Asst to the Court, 1979–, Master, 1990–91. *Recreations:* horseracing, cricket. *Address:* 29 St George Street, W1A 3BG. *T:* 071–629 9292. *Clubs:* Buck's, Royal Automobile, City Livery, United & Cecil, MCC, Turf.

WING, Prof. John Kenneth, CBE 1990; MD, PhD; DPM; FRCPsych; Director of Research Unit, Royal College of Psychiatrists, since 1989; Professor of Social Psychiatry, Institute of Psychiatry and London School of Hygiene and Tropical Medicine, 1970–89, now Emeritus Professor, University of London; *b* 22 Oct. 1923. *Educ:* Strand Sch.; University College London (MB, BS, MD, PhD). Served RNVR, 1942–46, Lieut (A). Dir, MRC Social Psychiatry Unit, 1965–89. Mem., MRC, 1985–89 (Chm., Neurosciences Bd, 1985–87; Chm., Health Services Res. Cttee, 1987–89). Hon. Consultant Psychiatrist, Maudsley and Bethlem Royal Hosp., 1960–89. Advr to H of C Social Services Cttee, 1984–85 and 1990. Hon. MD Heidelberg, 1977. *Publications:* (ed) Early Childhood Autism, 1966, 2nd edn 1975 (trans. Italian 1970, German 1973); (with G. W. Brown) Institutionalism and Schizophrenia, 1970; (with J. E. Cooper and N. Sartorius) Description and Classification of Psychiatric Symptoms, 1974 (trans. German 1978, French 1980, Japanese 1981); Reasoning about Madness, 1978 (trans. Portuguese 1978, German 1982, Italian 1983); ed, Schizophrenia: towards a new synthesis, 1978; ed (with R. Olsen), Community Care for the Mentally Disabled, 1979; (with J. Leach) Helping Destitute Men, 1979; (ed jtly) What is a Case?, 1981; (ed jtly) Handbook of Psychiatric Rehabilitation, 1981; (with L. G. Wing) Psychoses of Uncertain Aetiology, vol. III of Cambridge Handbook of Psychiatry, 1982; (ed) Contributions to Health Services Planning and Research, 1989. *Address:* Royal College of Psychiatrists, 17 Belgrave Square, SW1X 8PG. *T:* 071–235 2351.

WINGATE, Captain Sir Miles (Buckley), KCVO 1982; FNI; Deputy Master and Chairman of the Board of Trinity House, London, 1976–88, retired; *b* 17 May 1923; *s* of Terrence Wingate and Edith Wingate; *m* 1947, Alicia Forbes Philip; three *d*. *Educ:* Taunton Grammar Sch.; Southampton and Prior Park Coll., Somerset. Master Mariner. Apprenticed to Royal Mail Lines Ltd, 1939; first Comd, 1957; elected to Bd of Trinity House, 1968. Commonwealth War Graves Comr, 1986–91. Vice-President: Seamen's Hosp. Soc., 1980–; Royal Alfred Seafarers Soc., 1980–; British Maritime Charitable Foundn, 1983–; Pres., Internat. Assoc. of Lighthouse Authorities, 1985–88 (Vice-Pres., 1980–85); Dep. Chm., Gen. Council, King George's Fund for Sailors, 1983; Mem., Cttee of Management, RNLI, 1976–; Council, Missions to Seamen, 1982–. Liveryman: Hon. Co. of Master Mariners, 1970–; Shipwrights' Co., 1977–90; Freeman, Watermen and Lightermen's Co., 1984. Governor, Pangbourne Coll., 1982–. *Recreation:* golf. *Address:* Trinity House, Tower Hill, EC3N 4DH. *T:* 071–480 6601. *Club:* Hove Deep Sea Anglers.

WINGFIELD, family name of **Viscount Powerscourt.**

WINGFIELD DIGBY; *see* Digby.

WINGFIELD DIGBY, Very Rev. Richard Shuttleworth, MA; Dean of Peterborough, 1966–80, Dean Emeritus since 1980; *b* 19 Aug. 1911; *s* of late Everard George Wingfield Digby and Dorothy (*née* Loughnan); *m* 1936, Rosamond Frances, *d* of late Col W. T. Digby, RE; two *s* one *d*. *Educ:* Nautical Coll., Pangbourne; Royal Navy; Christ's Coll., Cambridge; Westcott House, Cambridge. BA 1935; MA 1939. Asst Curate of St Andrew's, Rugby, 1936–46. Chaplain to the Forces (4th Cl. Emergency Commn), 1940–45; POW, 1940–45. Vicar of All Saints, Newmarket, 1946–53; Rector of Bury, Lancs, 1953–66; Rural Dean of Bury, 1962–66. Pres. and Chm., Bury Trustee Savings Bank, 1953–66; Dep. Chm., Trustee Savings Bank Assoc., North-West Area, 1965–66. Hon. Canon of Manchester Cathedral, 1965; Hon. Chaplain to Regt XX, The Lancs Fusiliers, 1965. Chm. C of E Council for Places of Worship, 1976–81. *Recreations:* walking, dry stone walling. *Address:* Byways, Higher Holton, near Wincanton, Somerset BA9 8AP. *T:* Wincanton (0963) 32137. *Club:* Army and Navy.

WINGFIELD DIGBY, Ven. Stephen Basil, MBE 1944; Archdeacon of Sarum, 1968–79; Canon Residentiary, 1968–79, and Treasurer, 1971–79, Salisbury Cathedral; *b* 10 Nov. 1910; *m* 1940, Barbara Hatton Budge (*d* 1987); three *s* one *d*. *Educ:* Marlborough Coll.; Christ Church, Oxford; Wycliffe Hall, Oxford. Asst Master, Kenton Coll., Kenya, 1933–36; Curate, St Paul's, Salisbury, 1936–38; Priest-in-Charge, St George's, Oakdale, Poole, 1938–47. CF (temp.), 1939–45; SCF, 7th Armoured Div., 1943–45. Vicar of Sherborne with Castleton and Lillington, 1947–68. RD of Sherborne and Canon of Salisbury Cathedral, 1954–68. *Recreations:* fishing, gardening. *Address:* The Old Rectory, Nunton, Salisbury, Wilts. *T:* Salisbury (0722) 327479.

WINKELMAN, Joseph William, RE 1982 (ARE 1979); RWA 1990 (ARWA 1983); free-lance painter-printmaker, since 1971; President, Royal Society of Painter-Etchers and Engravers, since 1989; Chairman, Oxford Art Society, since 1987; *b* 20 Sept. 1941; *s* of George William Winkelman and Cleo Lucretia (*née* Harness); *m* 1969, Harriet Lowell Belin; two *d*. *Educ:* Univ. of the South, Sewanee, Tenn (BA English 1964); Wharton School of Finance, Univ. of Pennsylvania; Univ. of Oxford (Cert. of Fine Art 1971). Royal Society of Painter-Etchers and Engravers: Hon. Sec., 1982; Vice-Pres., 1986; Fellow: Printmakers' Council of GB, 1978; Royal Soc. of British Artists, 1981. Sometime tutor for: Sch. of Architecture, Oxford Polytechnic; Ruskin Sch. of Drawing, Oxford Univ.; Dept for External Studies, Oxford Univ. *Recreations:* gardening, hill walking. *Address:* The Hermitage, 69 Old High Street, Headington, Oxford OX3 9HT. *T:* Oxford (0865) 62839.

WINKLEY, Dr Stephen Charles, MA; Headmaster, Uppingham School, since 1991; *b* 9 July 1944; *e s* of late George Winkley and Eunice Winkley (*née* Golding); *m* 1st, 1968, Georgina Smart; two *s*; 2nd, 1983, Jennifer Burt; one *d*. *Educ:* St Edward's School, Oxford; Brasenose College, Oxford (MA 1967; DPhil 1973). Asst Master, Cranleigh Sch., 1969–85; Second Master, Winchester College, 1985–91. *Recreations:* music, water colours. *Address:* Headmaster's House, Spring Back Way, Uppingham, Rutland LE15 9QE. *T:* Uppingham (0572) 822688.

WINKS, Prof. Robin W(illiam Evert), MA, PhD; Randolph W. Townsend Professor of History, and John B. Madden Master of Berkeley College, Yale University, since 1957; *b* 5 Dec. 1930; *s* of Evert McKinley Winks and Jewell Sampson; *m* 1952, Avril Flockton, Wellington, NZ; one *s* one *d*. *Educ:* Univ. of Colorado (BA Hons 1952, MA 1953); Victoria Univ., NZ (Cert. 1952); Johns Hopkins Univ. (PhD 1957). Dir, Office of Special Projects and Foundns, Yale Univ., 1974–76. Chm., Council of Masters, Yale Univ., 1978–84, 1986–88. Smith-Mundt Prof., Univ. of Malaya, 1962; Vis. Prof., Univ. of Sydney, 1963; Vis. Fellow, Inst. of Commonwealth Studies, 1966–67; Guggenheim Fellow, 1976–77; Vis. Prof. of Economics, Univ. of Stellenbosch, 1983; Fellow, Amer. Sch. for Research, 1985 and 1991; George Eastman Vis. Prof., Oxford Univ., Sept. 1992–93. Cultural Attaché, Amer. Embassy, London, 1969–71; Advisor to Dept of State, 1971–. Chm., Nat. Park Service Adv. Bd, 1981–83; Trustee, Nat. Parks and Conservation Assoc., 1985–. Mem. Council on For. Relations. FRHistS; Fellow, Explorers' Club, 1986. Hon. MA Yale 1967; Hon. DLitt: Univ. of Nebraska, 1976; Univ. of Colorado, 1987. *Publications:* Canada and the United States, 1960, 3rd edn 1988; The Cold War, 1964, 2nd edn 1977; Historiography of the British Empire-Commonwealth, 1966; Malaysia, 1966, 2nd edn 1979; Age of Imperialism, 1969; Pastmasters, 1969; The Historian as Detective, 1969; The Blacks in Canada, 1971; Slavery, 1972; An American's Guide to Britain, 1977, 3rd edn 1987; Other Voices, Other Views, 1978; The Relevance of Canadian History, 1979, 2nd edn 1988; Western Civilization, 1979; Detective Fiction, 1980; The British Empire, 1981; Modus Operandi, 1982; History of Civilization, 1984; Cloak and Gown, 1987; Asia in Western Language Fiction, 1990; Frederick Billings: a life, 1991; articles in Amer. Hist. Rev. *Recreations:* travel, conservation, detective fiction. *Address:* 7321 Yale Station, New Haven, Conn 06520, USA. *Clubs:* Athenæum, Royal Commonwealth Trust; Yale (NY); Explorers'.

WINN, family name of **Barons Headley** and **St Oswald.**

WINNER, Prof. Harold Ivor, MA, MD, FRCP, FRCPath; Professor of Medical Microbiology, University of London, at Charing Cross Hospital Medical School, 1965–83, now Emeritus; Consulting Microbiologist, Charing Cross Hospital, (Consultant Microbiologist, 1954–83); *b* 1 June 1918; *y s* of late Jacob Davis and Janet Winner; *m* 1945, Nina (*d* 1986), *e d* of Jacques and Lily Katz; two *s*. *Educ:* St Paul's Sch.; Downing Coll., Cambridge (Maj. Schol.); University College Hospital Medical School. 1st class hons, Nat. Scis Tripos Cambridge, 1939. House Surgeon, Addenbrooke's Hospital, Cambridge, 1942; served RAMC, 1942–44; Asst Pathologist, EMS, 1945–48 and NW Group Laboratory, Hampstead, 1948–50; Lecturer, Sen. Lecturer, and Reader in Bacteriology, Charing Cross Hospital Medical Sch., 1950–64; Mem. School Council, 1967–69 and 1977–83. Member: Univs' Cttee on Safety, 1981–; Adv. Cttee on Dangerous Pathogens, 1981–84. Examiner: Examining Board in England, 1962–77; Royal Coll. of Surgeons, 1971–76; Royal Coll. of Pathologists, 1975–; universities at home and overseas. Founder Fellow and Archivist, RCPath; formerly Pres. and Hon. Editor, Section of Pathology, and Vice-Pres., Sect. of Comparative Medicine, RSM; Chm., Med. Scis Historical Soc., 1982–83; Vis. Prof., Guest Lectr and corresp. Mem., various univs and medical insts at home and overseas. *Publications:* Candida albicans (jointly), 1964; Symposium on Candida Infections (jointly), 1966; Microbiology in Modern Nursing, 1969; Microbiology in Patient Care, 1973, 2nd edn 1978; Louis Pasteur and Microbiology, 1974; chapters in medical books; papers in medical, scientific and nursing journals. *Recreations:* listening to music, looking at pictures and buildings, gardening, travel. *Address:* 48 Lyndale Avenue, NW2 2QA. *T:* 071–435 5959.

WINNER, Michael Robert; Chairman: Scimitar Films Ltd, Michael Winner Ltd, Motion Picture and Theatrical Investments Ltd, since 1957; *b* 30 Oct. 1935; *s* of late George Joseph and Helen Winner. *Educ:* St Christopher's Sch., Letchworth; Downing Coll., Cambridge Univ. (MA). Film critic and Fleet Street journalist and contributor to: The Spectator, Daily Express, London Evening Standard, etc. Panellist, Any Questions, BBC radio. Entered Motion Pictures, 1956, as Screen Writer, Asst Director, Editor. Mem. Council, Directors' Guild of Great Britain, 1983–, Chief Censorship Officer 1983–. Films include: Play It Cool (Dir), 1962; The Cool Mikado (Dir and Writer), 1962; West Eleven (Dir), 1963; The System (Prod. and Dir), 1963; You Must Be Joking (Prod., Dir, Writer), 1965; The Jokers (Prod., Dir, Writer), 1966; I'll Never Forget What's 'isname (Prod. and Dir), 1967; Hannibal Brooks (Prod., Dir, Writer), 1968; The Games (Prod. and Dir), 1969; Lawman (Prod. and Dir), 1970; The Nightcomers (Prod. and Dir), 1971; Chato's Land (Prod. and Dir), 1971; The Mechanic (Dir), 1972; Scorpio (Prod. and Dir), 1972; The Stone Killer (Prod. and Dir), 1973; Death Wish (Prod. and Dir), 1974; Won Ton Ton The Dog That Saved Hollywood (Prod. and Dir), 1975; The Sentinel (Prod., Dir, Writer), 1976; The Big Sleep (Prod., Dir, Writer), 1977; Firepower (Prod., Dir), 1978; Death Wish Two (Prod., Dir, Writer), 1981; The Wicked Lady (Prod., Dir, Writer), 1982; Scream for Help (Prod., Dir), 1984; Death Wish Three (Prod. and Dir), 1985; Appointment with Death (Prod., Dir, Writer), 1988; A Chorus of Disapproval (Prod., Dir, Jt screenplay writer), 1989; Bullseye! (Prod., Dir, jt screenplay writer), 1990. Theatre productions: The Tempest, Wyndhams, 1974; A Day in Hollywood A Night in the Ukraine, 1978. Founder and Chm., Police Meml Trust, 1984–. *Recreations:* walking around art galleries, museums, antique shops, being difficult. *Address:* 6/8 Sackville Street, W1X 1DD. *T:* 071–734 8385.

WINNICK, David Julian; MP (Lab) Walsall North, since 1979; *b* Brighton, 26 June 1933; *s* of late Eugene and Rose Winnick; *m* 1968, Bengi Rona (marr. diss.), *d* of Tarik and Zeynep Rona. *Educ:* secondary school; London Sch. of Economics (Dip. in Social Admin). Army National Service, 1951–53. Branch Secretary, Clerical and Administrative Workers' Union, 1956–62 (now APEX); Mem. Exec. Council, 1978–88, Vice-Pres., 1983–88, APEX. Advertisement Manager, Tribune, 1963–66. Employed by a voluntary organisation, 1970–79. Chm., UK Immigrants Adv. Service, 1984–90. Contested (Lab) Harwich, 1964; MP (Lab) Croydon South, 1966–70; contested (Lab): Croydon Central, Oct. 1974; Walsall N, Nov. 1976. Member: Select Cttee on the Environment, 1979–83; Home Affairs Cttee, 1983–87; Select Cttee on Procedure, 1989–. Member: Willesden Borough Council, 1959–64; London Borough of Brent Council, 1964–66 (Chairman, Children Cttee, 1965–66). Contributor to socialist and trade union journals. *Recreations:* walking, cinema, theatre, reading. *Address:* House of Commons, SW1A 0AA.

WINNIFRITH, Sir (Alfred) John (Digby), KCB 1959 (CB 1950); *b* 16 Oct. 1908; *s* of Rev. B. T. Winnifrith; *m* 1935, Lesbia Margaret (*d* 1981), *d* of late Sir Arthur Cochrane, KCVO; two *s* one *d*. *Educ:* Westminster School; Christ Church, Oxford. Entered Board of Trade, 1932; transferred to HM Treasury, 1934; Asst Sec., War Cabinet Office and Civil Sec., Combined Operations HQ, 1942–44, till return to HM Treasury; Third Secretary, HM Treasury, 1951–59; Permanent Secretary, Ministry of Agriculture, Fisheries and Food, 1959–67; Dir-Gen., National Trust, 1968–70. Trustee, British Museum (Natural History), 1967–72; Member: Royal Commn on Environmental Pollution, 1970–73; Commonwealth War Graves Commn, 1970–83; Hops Marketing Board, 1970–78. Hon. ARCVS 1974. *Address:* Hallhouse Farm, Appledore, Kent. *T:* Appledore (023383) 264.

See also C. B. Winnifrith.

WINNIFRITH, Charles Boniface; Principal Clerk of the Table Office, House of Commons, since 1989; *b* 12 May 1936; *s* of Sir John Winnifrith, *qv*; *m* 1962, Josephine Poile, MBE (*d* 1991); one *s* two *d*. *Educ:* Tonbridge Sch.; Christ Church, Oxford (MA). 2nd Lieut, RAEC, 1958–60. Joined Dept of the Clerk of the House of Commons, 1960; Second Clerk of Select Cttees, 1983; Clerk of Select Cttees, 1987. Mem., General Synod of C of E, 1970–90. Governor, Ashford Sch., Kent, 1973–. *Recreations:* cricket, American soap opera. *Address:* Cliffe Cottage, St Margaret's-at-Cliffe, Kent CT15 6BJ. *T:* Dover (0304) 853280. *Club:* MCC.

WINNING, Most Rev. Thomas J.; *see* Glasgow, Archbishop of, (RC).

WINNINGTON, Sir Francis Salwey William, 6th Bt, *cr* 1755; Lieut, late Welsh Guards; *b* 24 June 1907; *er s* of late Francis Salwey Winnington, *e s* of 5th Bt and Blanch, *d* of Commander William John Casberd-Boteler, RN; *S* grandfather, 1931; *m* 1944, Anne, *o d* of late Captain Lawrence Drury-Lowe; one *d.* *Educ:* Eton. Served War of 1939–45 (wounded, prisoner). Owns 4700 acres. *Heir: b* Colonel Thomas Foley Churchill Winnington, MBE, Grenadier Guards [*b* 16 Aug. 1910; *m* 1944, Lady Betty Marjorie Anson, *er d* of 4th Earl of Lichfield; two *s* two *d*]. *Address:* Brockhill Court, Shelsley Beauchamp, Worcs. *Club:* Cavalry and Guards.
See also Viscount Campden.

WINNINGTON-INGRAM, Edward John; Managing Director, Mail Newspapers Plc (formerly Associated Newspapers Group), 1986–89, retired; *b* 20 April 1926; *s* of Rev. Preb. Edward Francis and Gladys Winnington-Ingram; *m* 1st, 1953, Shirley Lamotte (marr. diss. 1968); two *s*; 2nd, 1973, Elizabeth Linda Few Brown. *Educ:* Shrewsbury; Keble Coll., Oxford (BA). Served RN (Sub-Lieut), 1944–47. Joined Associated Newspapers, 1949; Circulation Manager, Daily Mail, 1960–65; Gen. Manager, Daily Mail Manchester, 1965–70; helped create Northprint Manchester Ltd, a jt printing consortium with Manchester Guardian and Evening News and Associated, 1969; Dir, Associated Newspapers, 1971; Managing Director: Harmsworth Publishing, 1973; Mail on Sunday, 1982; Dir, Associated Newspapers Holdings, 1983; non-executive Director: NAAFI, 1987–; Burlington Gp, 1988–. *Recreations:* tennis, shooting, beagling, gardening, music, defending the 1662 Prayer Book. *Address:* Old Manor Farm, Cottisford, Brackley, Northants NN13 5SW. *T:* Finmere (02804) 367. *Clubs:* Buck's, Roehampton.

WINNINGTON-INGRAM, Prof. Reginald Pepys, FBA 1958; Professor of Greek Language and Literature in the University of London (King's College), 1953–71, now Professor Emeritus; Fellow of King's College, since 1969; *b* 22 Jan. 1904; *s* of late Rear-Admiral and late Mrs C. W. Winnington-Ingram; *m* 1938, Mary, *d* of late Thomas Cousins. *Educ:* Clifton Coll., Trinity Coll., Cambridge. BA 1925; MA 1929; Scholar of Trinity Coll., 1922, Fellow, 1928–32; 1st Class Classical Tripos, Part I, 1923; Waddington Schol., 1924; 1st Class Classical Tripos, Part II, 1925; Charles Oldham Classical Schol., 1926. Asst Lecturer and Lecturer, University of Manchester, 1928, 1930 and 1933; Reader in Classics, University of London (Birkbeck College), 1934–48. Temp. Civil Servant, Ministry of Labour and National Service, 1940–45 (Asst Secretary, 1944); Professor of Classics in the University of London (Westfield Coll.), 1948–53; J. H. Gray Lectures, Cambridge Univ., 1956. Vis. Prof., Univ. of Texas at Austin, 1971, 1973; Vis. Aurelio Prof., Boston Univ., 1975. President, Society for the Promotion of Hellenic Studies, 1959–62 (Hon. Secretary, 1963–82, Hon. Mem., 1983). Director, University of London Inst. of Classical Studies, 1964–67. Hon. DLitt: Glasgow, 1969; London, 1985. *Publications:* Mode in Ancient Greek Music, 1936; Euripides and Dionysus, 1948; (ed) Aristides Quintilianus, *De Musica*, 1963; Sophocles: an interpretation, 1980; Studies in Aeschylus, 1983; contribs to classical and musical journals, dictionaries, etc. *Recreation:* music. *Address:* 12 Greenhill, NW3 5UB. *T:* 071–435 6843. *Club:* Athenæum.

WINSHIP, Peter James Joseph, QPM 1990; Assistant Commissioner (Management Support and Strategy Department), Metropolitan Police, since 1989; *b* 21 July 1943; *s* of late Francis Edward Winship and Iris May (*née* Adams); *m* 1st, 1963, Carol Ann McNaughton; two *s* one *d*; 2nd, 1989, Janet Mary Bird; one *d.* *Educ:* Bicester Grammar Sch.; St John's Coll., Oxford (BA Eng. Lang. and Lit.; MA). Oxfordshire Constabulary, 1962; Sergeant to Supt, Thames Valley Police, 1968–79; Graduate, FBI Acad., 1980; Chief Supt, Metropolitan Police, 1982; Asst Chief Constable, Thames Valley Police, 1984; Dep. Asst Comr, Policy & Planning, 1987, No 1 Area HQ, 1988, Metropolitan Police. Member: Exec. Council, London Fedn of Boys' Clubs, 1988–; Exec. Cttee, Royal Humane Soc.; Chairman: Met. Police Shooting Club, 1987–; Met. Police Flying Club, 1988–. FBIM. *Publications:* articles in police jls and other periodicals on professionally related subjects, travel, and treatment of police in literature; essay on delinquency and social policy (Queen's Police Gold Medal, Essay Competition, 1969). *Recreations:* reading, riding, gardening, music. *Address:* New Scotland Yard, Broadway, SW1H 0BG. *T:* 071–230 1212.

WINSKILL, Air Commodore Sir Archibald (Little), KCVO 1980 (CVO 1973); CBE 1960; DFC 1941 and Bar 1943; AE 1944; Extra Equerry to The Queen; *b* 24 Jan. 1917; *s* of late James Winskill; *m* 1947, Christiane Amilie Pauline, *d* of M. Bailleux, Calais, France; one *s* one *d.* War of 1939–45: Fighter Pilot: Battle of Britain; European and North African Theatres. Post-war: Air Adviser to Belgian Govt; Station Cmdr, RAF Turnhouse and Duxford; Gp Capt. Ops Germany; Air Attaché, Paris; Dir of Public Relations, MoD (RAF); Captain of the Queen's Flight, 1968–82. Pres., Queen's Flight Assoc. Liveryman, GAPAN, 1978–; Freedom of City of London, 1978. MRAeS. *Recreation:* golf. *Address:* Anchors, Coastal Road, West Kingston Estate, East Preston, West Sussex BN16 1SN. *T:* Rustington (0903) 775439. *Club:* Royal Air Force.
See also C. J. R. Meyer.

WINSTANLEY, family name of **Baron Winstanley.**

WINSTANLEY, Baron *cr* 1975 (Life Peer), of Urmston in Greater Manchester; **Michael Platt Winstanley;** TV and radio broadcaster, author, journalist, columnist, medical practitioner; Chairman, Countryside Commission, 1978–80; *b* Nantwich, Cheshire, 27 Aug. 1918; *e s* of late Dr Sydney A. Winstanley; *m* 1st, 1945, Nancy Penney (marr. diss. 1952); one *s*; 2nd, 1955, Joyce M. Woodhouse; one *s* one *d.* *Educ:* Manchester Grammar Sch.; Manchester Univ. President, Manchester Univ. Union, 1940–41; Captain, Manchester Univ. Cricket Club, 1940–42; Captain Combined English Univs Cricket Team, 1941; Ed. University magazine, 1941–42. MRCS LRCP, 1944. Resident Surgical Officer, Wigan Infirmary, 1945; Surgical Specialist, RAMC, 1946; GP, Urmston, Manchester, 1948–66; MO, Royal Ordnance Factory, Patricroft, 1950–66; Treasury MO and Admiralty Surgeon and Agent, 1953–66; Member Lancs Local Med. Cttee, 1954–66; Member Lancs Exec. Council, 1956–65. Spokesman for Manchester Div. of BMA, 1957–65. Member Liberal Party Council, 1962–66. Contested (L) Stretford, 1964; MP (L) Cheadle, 1966–70; MP (L) Hazel Grove, Feb.-Sept. 1974. Chairman Liberal Party Health Cttee, 1965–66; Liberal Party Spokesman on health, Post Office and broadcasting. TV and radio broadcaster, 1957–; own series on Indep. TV and BBC. Member: BBC Gen. Adv. Council, 1967–70; Post Office Bd, 1978–80; Water Space Amenity Commn, 1980–82. President: Fluoridation Soc., 1984–; Gingerbread, 1984–; Birth Control Campaign, 1984–; Chm., Groundwork Trust, 1980–. A Dep. Pro-Chancellor, Univ. of Lancaster, 1986–. *Publications:* Home Truths for Home Doctors, 1963; The Anatomy of First-Aid, 1966; The British Ombudsman, 1970; Tell Me, Doctor, 1972; Know Your Rights, 1975; cricket columnist, Manchester Evening News, 1964–65; weekly personal column, Manchester Evening News, 1970–76; articles on current affairs, health, etc. *Recreations:* cricket; golf; playing the bagpipes. *Address:* Hare Hall, Dunnerdale, Broughton-in-Furness, Cumbria. *Clubs:* National Liberal, Authors'.

WINSTANLEY, Rt. Rev. Alan Leslie; *see* Peru and Bolivia, Bishop of.

WINSTANLEY, John, MC 1944; TD 1951; FRCS, FCOphth; Hon. Consultant Ophthalmic Surgeon, St Thomas' Hospital, since 1983 (Ophthalmic Surgeon, 1960–83); *b* 11 May 1919; 3rd *s* of late Captain Bernard Joseph Winstanley and Grace Taunton; *m* 1959, Jane Frost; one *s* two *d.* *Educ:* Wellington Coll., Berks; St Thomas's Hosp. Med. Sch. (MB, BS 1951). FRCS 1957; FCOphth 1988. Served 4th Bn Queen's Own Royal West Kent Regt, 1937–46 (despatches BEF, 1940). Resident med. appts, St Thomas' and Moorfields Eye Hosps, 1951–56; Chief Clin. Asst, Moorfields Eye Hosp., 1956–60; Sen. Registrar, St Thomas' Hosp., 1956–60; recog. teacher of ophthalmol., St Thomas' Hosp., 1960–83; Ophth. Surg., Lewisham and Greenwich Health Dists, 1959–70; Hon. Ophthalmic Surgeon: Royal Hosp., Chelsea, 1963–85; Queen Alexandra's Mil. Hosp., Millbank, 1966–72; Queen Elizabeth Mil. Hosp., Woolwich, 1972–83. Hon. Civilian Consultant in Ophthalmol. to MOD (Army), 1971–83. Examiner in Ophthalmology (DipOphth of Examining Bd of RCP and RCS, 1968–72; Mem. Court of Examiners, RCS, 1972–78). FRSM 1963 (Vice-Pres., Sect. of Ophth., 1979); Member: Ophthal. Soc. UK, 1958–88 (Hon. Sec. 1966–68, Vice-Pres. 1980–83); Faculty of Ophthalmologists, 1958–88, Mem. Council, 1973–85, Vice-Pres., 1979–85; Mem. Council, Medical Protection Soc., 1979–90. Liveryman, Soc. of Apothecaries, 1965 (Mem. Livery Cttee, 1982). *Publications:* chapter, Rose's Medical Ophthalmology, 1983; papers on ophthalmic topics and med. hist. in med. jls. *Recreations:* shooting, fishing, medical history. *Address:* The Churchill Clinic, 80 Lambeth Road, SE1 7PW. *T:* 081–928 5633; 10 Pembroke Villas, The Green, Richmond, Surrey TW9 1QF. *T:* 081–940 6247. *Clubs:* Army and Navy, Flyfishers'.

WINSTON, Clive Noel; Assistant Director, Federation Against Copyright Theft Ltd, 1985–88; *b* 20 April 1925; *s* of George and Alida Winston; *m* 1952, Beatrice Jeanette; two *d.* *Educ:* Highgate Sch.; Trinity Hall, Cambridge (BA). Admitted solicitor, 1951. Joined Metropolitan Police, 1951; Dep. Solicitor, Metropolitan Police, 1982–85. Chairman, Union of Liberal and Progressive Synagogues, 1981–85 (Vice-Pres., 1985–); Treas., Eur. Bd, World Union of Progressive Judaism, 1990–. *Recreations:* golf, gardening.

WINSTON, Prof. Robert Maurice Lipson, FRCOG; Professor of Fertility Studies, University of London at the Institute of Obstetrics and Gynaecology, Royal Postgraduate Medical School, since 1987; Consultant Obstetrician and Gynaecologist: Hammersmith Hospital, since 1978; Royal Masonic Hospital, since 1988; *b* 15 July 1940; *s* of late Laurence Winston and of Ruth Winston-Fox, *qv*; *m* 1973, Lira Helen Feigenbaum; two *s* one *d.* *Educ:* St Paul's Sch., London; London Hosp. Med. Coll., London Univ. (MB, BS 1964). MRCS, LRCP 1964; FRCOG 1983 (MRCOG 1971). Jun. posts, London Hosp., 1964–66; Registrar and Sen. Registrar, Hammersmith Hosp., 1970–74; Wellcome Res. Sen. Lectr, Inst. of Obs and Gyn., 1974–78; Sen. Lectr, Hammersmith Hosp., 1978–81; Reader in Fertility Studies, RPMS, 1982–86. Vis. Prof., Univ. of Leuven, Belgium. 1976–77; Prof. of Gyn., Univ. of Texas at San Antonio, 1980–81; Clyman Vis. Prof., Mt Sinai Hosp., New York, 1985. Member, Steering Cttee, WHO: on Tubal Occlusion, 1975–77; on Ovum Transport, 1977–78. Pres., Internat. Fallopius Soc., 1987–. Chm., Progress (all-party parly campaign for res. into human reprodn), 1988–. Founder Mem., British Fertility Soc., 1975–; Hon. Member: Georgian Obs Soc., 1983–; Pacific Fertility Soc., 1983–; Spanish Fertility Soc., 1985–. Presenter, Your Life in their Hands, BBC TV, 1979–; Member, Editorial Board: Internat. Jl of Microsurgery, 1981–; Clinical Reproduction and Fertility, 1985–. *Publications:* Reversibility of Sterilization, 1978; (jtly) Tubal Infertility, 1981; Infertility, a Sympathetic Approach, 1987; scientific pubns on human and experimental reproduction. *Recreations:* theatre (directed award-winning Pirandello production, Each in his Own Way, Edinburgh Fest., 1969), broadcasting, music, wine. *Address:* 11 Denman Drive, NW11 6RE. *T:* 081–455 7475.

WINSTON-FOX, Mrs Ruth, JP; Co-Chairman, Women's National Commission, 1979–81 (Member, since 1971); *b* 12 Sept. 1912; *d* of Major the Rev. Solomon Lipson, Hon. SCF, and Tilly Lipson (*née* Shandel); *m* 1st, 1938, Laurence Winston (*d* 1949); two *s* one *d*; 2nd, 1960, Goodwin Fox (*d* 1974). *Educ:* St Paul's Girls' Sch.; London Univ. BSc Household and Social Sci.; Home Office Child Care Cert. Mental Hosps Dept and Child Care Dept, LCC, 1936–39; Dep. Centre Organiser, WVS, Southgate, 1941–45; Southgate Borough Council: Member, 1945–65; Alderman, 1955–65; Mayor of Southgate, 1958–59, Dep. Mayor, 1959–61; Sen. Officer, Adoptions Consultant, Social Services Dept, Herts CC, 1949–77. Member: London Rent Assessment Panel and Tribunals, 1975–; Review Cttee for Secure Accommodation, London Borough of Enfield, 1982–; Bd of Deputies of British Jews, 1960– (Chm. Educn Cttee, 1974–80; voluntary nat. organiser, exhibn Jewish Way of Life, 1978–); Vice-Pres., Internat. Council of Jewish Women, 1974– (Chairman: Status of Women Cttee, 1966–75; Inter-Affiliate Travel Cttee, 1975–81); Mem. Governing Body, World Jewish Congress, 1981–; Co-Chm., Jewish Community Exhibn Centre, 1984–. Founder, one of first Day Centres for the Elderly in GB, Ruth Winston House, Southgate Old People's Centre, opened by Princess Alexandra, 1961, and again, 1972; Vice-President: Southgate Old People's Welfare Cttee, 1974–; Southgate Horticultural Soc.; President: League of Jewish Women, 1969–72; First Women's Lodge, England, 1972–74; Enfield Marriage Guidance Council, 1984–. JP Mddx Area GLC, 1954–. *Publications:* articles only. *Recreations:* five grandchildren, travel, voluntary service. *Address:* 4 Morton Crescent, Southgate, N14 7AH. *T:* 081–886 5056. *Clubs:* University Women's, Bnai Brith.
See also R. M. L. Winston.

WINSTONE, Dame Dorothy (Gertrude), DBE 1990; CMG 1976; *b* 23 Jan. 1919; *d* of Stanley Fowler and Constance May Fowler (*née* Sherwin); *m* 1941, Wilfrid Frank Winstone; three *s* one *d.* *Educ:* Auckland Girls' Grammar Sch.; Auckland Teachers' Coll.; Auckland University Coll. (BA, DipEd 1940). Primary School Teacher, 1938; Asst Mistress, Seddon Memorial Tech. Coll., 1939–45; voluntary community worker, 1945–. Hon. LLD Univ. of Auckland, 1983; Member Emerita, NZ Fedn of Univ. Women, 1973; Life Mem., Nat. Council of Women of NZ, 1980; Adelaide Ristori Medal, Centro Culturale Italiano, 1975. *Recreations:* reading, gardening, 13 grandchildren. *Address:* 17 Tuhaere Street, Auckland 5, New Zealand. *T:* 09 5203407.

WINT, Dr Arthur Stanley, OJ 1989; CD 1973; MBE 1954; FRCS; private medical practitioner; Doctor and Surgeon in charge, Linstead General Hospital, Jamaica, 1978–85; *b* 25 May 1920; *s* of John Samuel Wint and Hilda Wint; *m* 1949, Norma Wint (*née* Marsh); three *d.* *Educ:* Calabar High School; Excelsior College, Jamaica; St Bartholomew's Medical School. MB BS; FRCS. Served RAF, 1942–47; Medical School, 1947–53. Participated in international athletics, 1936–53; Olympics 1948: Gold medal, 400 m; Silver medal, 800 m; Olympics 1952: Gold medal, 4x400 m Relay; Silver medal, 800 m. Medical Practitioner, 1953–73. Jamaican High Comr in the UK, 1974–78. FICS 1972; DMJ (Clin), 1975. Hon. DLitt Loughborough, 1982. *Recreations:* badminton, swimming, walking. *Address:* 21 King Street, Linstead, St Catherine, Jamaica, WI. *Club:* Polytechnic Harriers.

WINTER, Rt. Rev. Allen Ernest; *b* 8 Dec. 1903; *o s* of Ernest Thomas and Margaret Winter, Malvern, Vic; *m* 1939, Eunice Eleanor, 3rd *d* of Albert and Eleanor Sambell; three *s* two *d. Educ:* Melbourne C of E Grammar School; Trinity Coll., Univ. of Melbourne (BA 1926, MA 1928); University Coll., Oxford (BA 1932, MA 1951); Australian College of Theology (ThL 1927, ThD 1951 iur. dig.). Deacon, 1927, priest, 1928, Melbourne; Curate, Christ Church, S Yarra, 1927–29; on leave, Oxford, 1929–32; Curate, St James', Ivanhoe, 1932–35; Minister of Sunshine, 1935–39; Incumbent of St Luke's, Brighton, Melb., 1939–48; Chaplain, AIF, 1942–46; Incumbent of Christ Church, Essendon, 1948–49; Canon-Residentiary and Rector of All Saints' Cathedral, Bathurst, 1949–51; Bishop of St Arnaud, 1951–73; Chaplain, St John's Coll., Morpeth, NSW, 1974. *Address:* Lis Escop, 34 Malvern Grove, North Caulfield, Vic 3161, Australia. *T:* 03–509–2554.

WINTER, Charles Milne, CBE 1990; FIBScot; Group Chief Executive, Royal Bank of Scotland Group plc, since 1985 (Director, since 1981); *b* 21 July 1933; *s* of David and Annie Winter; *m* 1957, Audrey Hynd; one *s* one *d. Educ:* Harris Acad., Dundee. FIBScot 1979. Served RAF, 1951–53. Joined The Royal Bank of Scotland, 1949; Exec. Dir, 1981–86; Man. Dir, 1982–85; Dep. Gp Chief Exec., 1985. Dir, Williams & Glyn's Bank, 1982–85 (Man. Dir, March-Oct. 1985). Pres., Inst. of Bankers in Scotland, 1981–83; Vice-Pres., Edinburgh Chamber of Commerce and Manufactures, 1987–; Chairman: Cttee of Scottish Clearing Bankers, 1983–85, 1989–; Inter-Alpha Gp Steering Cttee, 1986–87. *Recreations:* golf, choral music. *Clubs:* New (Edinburgh), Royal and Ancient Golf (St Andrews).

WINTER, Rev. David Brian; Priest-in-Charge of Ducklington, since 1989; Bishop's Officer for Evangelism, Diocese of Oxford, since 1989; *b* 19 Nov. 1929; *s* of Walter George Winter and Winifred Ella Winter; *m* 1961, Christine Ellen Martin; two *s* one *d. Educ:* Machynlleth County Sch.; Trinity County Grammar Sch., Wood Green; King's Coll., Univ. of London (BA, PGCE). Nat. Service, RAF, 1948–50. Teacher: Ware CE Secondary Sch., 1954–58; Tottenham County Grammar Sch., 1958–59; Editor, Crusade, 1959–70; freelance writer and broadcaster, 1970–71; BBC: Producer, Religious Broadcasting, 1971–75, Sen. Producer, 1975–82; Hd of Religious Progs, Radio, and Dep. Hd, Religious Broadcasting, 1982–87; Hd of Religious Broadcasting, 1987–89. Chm., Arts Centre Gp, 1976–82. Hon. Asst Curate, St Paul and St Luke, Finchley, 1987–89. *Publications:* Ground of Truth, 1964; New Singer, New Song (biog. of Cliff Richard), 1967; (with S. Linden) Two a Penny, 1968; Closer than a Brother, 1971; Hereafter, 1972; (ed) Matthew Henry's Commentary on the New Testament, 1974; After the Gospels, 1977; But this I can believe, 1980; The Search for the Real Jesus, 1982; Truth in the Son, 1985; Living through Loss, 1985; Walking in the Light (confessions of St Augustine), 1986; Believing the Bible, 1987; Battered Bride, 1988. *Recreations:* watching cricket and writing about it, fish-keeping, talking. *Address:* The Rectory, 6 Standlake Road, Ducklington, Witney, Oxon OX8 7XG. *T:* Witney (0993) 776625.

WINTER, Frederick Thomas, CBE 1963; racehorse trainer, 1964–87, retired; *b* 20 Sept. 1926; *s* of late Frederick Neville Winter and Ann (*née* Flanagan); *m* 1956, Diana Pearson; three *d* (incl. twins). *Educ:* Ewell Castle. Served as Lieut, 6th Bn Para. Regt, 1944–47. Jockey, Flat, 1939–42; National Hunt jockey, 1947–64. *Recreations:* golf, gardening. *Address:* Montague House, Eastbury, Newbury, Berks RG16 7JL.

WINTER, Prof. Gerald Bernard, FDS RCS; Professor and Head of Department of Children's Dentistry, since 1966, Dean and Director of Studies since 1983, Institute of Dental Surgery, University of London; *b* 24 Nov. 1928; *s* of Morris Winter and Edith (*née* Malter); *m* 1960, Brigitte Eva Fleischhacker; one *s* one *d. Educ:* Coopers' Company's Sch.; London Hospital Med. Coll. (BDS, MB BS); DCH London. Ho. Surg./Ho. Phys., London Hosp. Med. Coll., 1955–59; Lectr in Children's Dentistry, Royal Dental Hosp., London, 1959–62; Cons. Dent. Surg., Eastman Dental Hosp., 1962–. Hon. Sec. 1962–65, Pres. 1970–71, Brit. Paedodontic Soc.; Hon. Gen. Sec., Internat. Assoc. of Dentistry for Children, 1971–79; Founder Chm., Brit. Soc. of Dentistry for the Handicapped, 1976–77. *Publications:* A Colour Atlas of Clinical Conditions in Paedodontics (with R. Rapp), 1979; many chapters and sci. papers. *Recreations:* theatre, music, gardening. *Address:* Institute of Dental Surgery, Eastman Dental Hospital, Gray's Inn Road, WC1X 8LD. *T:* 071–837 3646; (private) 1 Hartfield Close, Elstree, Herts. *T:* 081–953 3403.

WINTER, Gregory Paul, FRS 1990; Member of staff, Medical Research Council Laboratory of Molecular Biology, since 1981 and Deputy Director, Interdisciplinary Research Centre for Protein Engineering, since 1990; Senior Research Fellow, Trinity College, Cambridge, since 1991; *b* 14 April 1951; *m* Fiona Jane Winter. *Educ:* Royal Grammar Sch., Newcastle-upon-Tyne; Trinity College, Cambridge (BA Natural Scis 1973; MA; PhD 1976). Postgrad. studies in protein chem., Cambridge, 1973–76; Fellow, Trinity College, Cambridge (structure of genes and influenza virus), 1976–80; MRC–LMB (protein and antibody engineering), 1981–. Novo Biotechnology Award, Denmark, 1986; Colworth Medal, Biuochem. Soc., 1986; Behring Prize, FRG, 1989; Louis Jeantet Foundn for Medicine, Switzerland, 1989; Pfizer Award, 1989; Milano Award, Italy, 1990. *Publications:* articles in learned jls on protein and gene structure, enzymes, viral proteins and antibodies. *Recreation:* helping to found a Biotech company (Cambridge Antibody Technology). *Address:* Medical Research Council Laboratory of Molecular Biology, Hills Road, Cambridge CB2 2QH.

WINTERBOTTOM, family name of **Baron Winterbottom.**

WINTERBOTTOM, Baron, *cr* 1965 (Life Peer), of Clopton in the county of Northampton; **Ian Winterbottom;** Former Chairman: Dynavest Ltd; Anglo Global Limited; *b* 6 April 1913; *s* of G. H. Winterbottom, Horton House, Northants, and Georgina MacLeod; *m* 1st, 1939, Rosemary Mills (marr. diss. 1944); one *s*; 2nd, 1944, Irene Eva, (Ira), Munk; two *s* one *d. Educ:* Charterhouse; Clare Coll., Cambridge. Worked in textile and engineering trades in Manchester, Derby, and Bamberg and Cologne, Germany. Captain Royal Horse Guards; served War of 1939–45, NW European Campaign; ADC and subsequently Personal Assistant to Regional Commissioner, Hamburg, 1946–49. MP (Lab) Nottingham Central, 1950–55; Parly Under Sec. of State, Royal Navy, MoD, 1966–67; Parly Sec., MPBW, 1967–68; Parly Under-Sec. of State, RAF, MoD, 1968–70; opposition spokesman on defence, 1970–74; a Lord in Waiting (Govt Whip), 1974–78; spokesman on: defence, 1974–78; trade and industry, 1976–78; resigned from Govt, 1978; Founder Mem., SDP. Deleg., UN Trusteeship Council, 1974; Founder Mem., House of Lords All-Party Defence Study Gp; Member: Parly and Scientific Cttee; CPA; Anglo-Nigerian Soc. Director: Winterbottom Bookcloth Co., 1955–57; Venesta Internat., 1957–66, 1970–74 (Chm., 1972–74); Chairman: Centurion Housing Association, 1980–; Collins Aircraft Co., 1980–; Consultant, C. Z. Scientific Instruments Ltd, 1980–. *Recreations:* birdwatching, music. *Address:* Lower Farm, Fossbury, Marlborough, Wilts SN8 3NJ. *T:* Oxenwood (026489) 269. *Club:* Athenæum.

WINTERBOTTOM, Michael, MA, DPhil; FBA 1978; Fellow and Tutor in Classics, Worcester College, Oxford, since 1967; Reader in Classical Languages, University of Oxford, since 1990; *b* 22 Sept. 1934; *s* of Allan Winterbottom and Kathleen Mary (*née* Wallis); *m* 1st, 1963, Helen Spencer (marr. diss. 1983); two *s*; 2nd, 1986, Nicolette Janet Streatfeild Bergel. *Educ:* Dulwich Coll.; Pembroke Coll., Oxford. 1st Cl. Hon. Mods and Craven Schol., 1954; 1st Cl. Lit. Hum. and Derby Schol., 1956; Domus Sen. Schol., Merton Coll., 1958–59; Research Lectr, Christ Church, 1959–62. MA 1959, DPhil 1964 (Oxon). Lectr in Latin and Greek, University Coll. London, 1962–67. Dhc Besançon, 1985. *Publications:* (ed) Quintilian, 1970; (with D. A. Russell) Ancient Literary Criticism, 1972; Three Lives of English Saints, 1972; (ed and trans.) The Elder Seneca, 1974; (ed with R. M. Ogilvie) Tacitus, *Opera Minora*, 1975; (ed and trans.) Gildas, 1978; Roman Declamation, 1980; (ed with commentary) The Minor Declamations ascribed to Quintilian, 1984; (with D. C. Innes) Sopatros the Rhetor, 1988; (with M. Brett and C. N. L. Brooke) rev. edn of Charles Johnson (ed), Hugh the Chanter, 1990; articles and reviews in jls. *Recreations:* travel and plans for travel, hill walking, under-gardening. *Address:* 172 Walton Street, Oxford OX1 2HD. *T:* Oxford (0865) 515727.

WINTERBOTTOM, Sir Walter, Kt 1978; CBE 1972 (OBE 1963); retired; *b* 31 March 1913; *s* of James Winterbottom and Frances Holt; *m* 1942, Ann Richards; one *s* two *d. Educ:* Chester Coll. of Educn; Carnegie Coll. of Physical Educn. Schoolmaster, Oldham; Lectr, Carnegie Coll. of Phys. Educn; Wing Comdr, RAF, 1939–45; Dir of Coaching and Manager of England Team, Football Assoc., 1946–62; Gen. Sec., Central Council of Physical Recreation, 1963–72; Dir, The Sports Council, 1965–78. *Publications:* technical, on association football. *Recreations:* golf, bowls. *Address:* 15 Orchard Gardens, Cranleigh, Surrey GU6 7LG. *T:* Cranleigh (0483) 271593.

WINTERFLOOD, Brian Martin; Managing Director, Winterflood Securities Ltd, since 1988; *b* 31 Jan. 1937; *s* of Thomas G. Winterflood and Doris M. Winterflood; *m* 1966, Doreen Stella McCartney; two *s* one *d. Educ:* Fray's Coll., Uxbridge. Greener Dreyfus & Co., 1953–55. National Service, 1955–57. Bisgood Bishop & Co. Ltd, 1957–85: Partner, 1967–71; Dir, 1971–81; Man. Dir, 1981–85; Man. Dir, County Bisgood, 1985–86; County NatWest Securities Ltd: Dir, 1986–87; Exec. Dir, 1987–88, resigned, 1988. Dir, Union Discount Co. of London, 1991–. Vice Pres., Rehabilitation and Med. Res. Trust, 1989–; Jt Chm., Cttee of USM Initiative, Prince's Youth Bus. Trust, 1989–. Mem., Inst. of Directors, 1972–. *Recreations:* family, travel. *Address:* Knollys House, 5th Floor, 47 Mark Lane, EC3R 7QH. *T:* 071–621 0004.

WINTERSGILL, Dr William, FFPHM; Specialist in Community Medicine, York Health Authority, since 1984; Examining Medical Officer (part-time), Department of Health, since 1989; Member, Research and Advisory Committee, Cambridge Applied Nutrition, Toxicology and Biosciences Ltd, since 1984; *b* 20 Dec. 1922; *s* of Fred Wintersgill and May Wintersgill; *m* 1952, Iris May Holland; three *d. Educ:* Barnsley Holgate Grammar Sch.; Leeds Medical Sch., Univ. of Leeds (MB, ChB). MRCGP, MFCM; FFCM 1983. House Surgeon, 1948, and Registrar, 1948–49, Pontefract Infirmary; Principal, Gen. Practice, Snaith, Yorks, 1950–66; Dept of Health and Social Security (formerly Min. of Health): Reg. MO, 1967–70; SMO, 1970–72; PMO, 1972–76; SPMO, 1976–84. Pt-time MO, Cttee on Safety of Medicines, 1987–; Mem., Health Adv. Service Vis. Team, 1987–; Dist Med. Advr, 1987–88. Chm., British Assoc. of Community Physicians, 1985–. *Recreations:* gardening, antique collecting (silver especially), playing the piano, painting, old buildings. *Address:* 2 The Old Orchard, Easingwold, York. *T:* Easingwold (0347) 21561.

WINTERTON, 7th Earl, *cr* 1766 (Ireland); **Robert Chad Turnour;** Baron Winterton, *cr* 1761 (Ireland); Viscount Turnour, 1766 (Ireland); Royal Canadian Air Force; *b* 13 Sept. 1915; *s* of Cecil Turnour (*d* 1953), Saskatoon, Sask.; *S* kinsman, 1962; *m* 1st, 1941, Kathleen Ella (*d* 1969), *d* of D. B. Whyte; 2nd, 1971, Marion Eleanor, *d* of late Arthur Phillips. *Educ:* Nutana Coll., Canada. Joined RCAF, 1940; with Canadian NATO Force Sqdn, Sardinia, 1957–58. *Heir: nephew* Donald David Turnour [*b* 1943; *m* 1968, Jill Pauline, *d* of late J. G. Esplen; two *d*]. *Address:* 1326 55th Street, Delta, BC V4M 3K3, Canada.

WINTERTON, (Jane) Ann; MP (C) Congleton, since 1983; *b* 6 March 1941; *d* of Joseph Robert Hodgson and Ellen Jane Hodgson; *m* 1960, Nicholas R. Winterton, *qv*; two *s* one *d. Educ:* Erdington Grammar Sch. for Girls. Mem., Agric. Select Cttee, 1987–. *Recreations:* music, theatre, tennis, ski-ing. *Address:* Whitehall Farm, Newbold Astbury, Congleton, Cheshire CW12 3NH.

WINTERTON, Nicholas Raymond; MP (C) Macclesfield since Sept. 1971; *b* 31 March 1938; *o s* of late N. H. Winterton, Lysways House, Longdon Green, near Rugeley, Staffs; *m* 1960, Jane Ann Hodgson (*see* J. A. Winterton); two *s* one *d. Educ:* Bilton Grange Prep. Sch.; Rugby Sch. Commnd 14th/20th King's Hussars, 1957–59. Sales Exec. Trainee, Shell-Mex and BP Ltd, 1959–60; Sales and Gen. Manager, Stevens and Hodgson Ltd, Birmingham (Co. engaged in sale and hire of construction equipment), 1960–71. Chairman: CPC Cttee, Meriden Cons. Assoc., 1966–68; Midland Branch, Contractors Mech. Plant Engrs Assoc., 1968–69. Member: W Midlands Cons. Council, 1966–69, 1971–72; Central Council, Nat. Union of Cons. and Unionist Assocs, 1971–72. Contested (C) Newcastle-under-Lyme, Oct. 1969, 1970. Chm., Select Cttee on Health, 1991–. Joint Vice-Chairman: Anglo Danish Parly Gp; All Party Parly British Swedish Gp; Treasurer: All Party Parly British Indonesian Gp; All Party Parly Anglo-Austrian Gp; Chairman: All Party Parly Textile Gp; All Party Parly British Namibia Gp; All Party Parly Gp for Paper and Board Industry; Vice Chairman: British South Africa Parly Gp, 1983–89; UK Falkland Is Gp; Cons. Parly Sports and Recreation Cttee, 1979–84; Mem., H of C Chairmen's Panel, 1987–. Member: Exec. Cttee, Anglo-Austrian Soc., 1987–; Nat. Adv. Cttee, Duke of Edinburgh Award Scheme. County Councillor, Atherstone Div. Warwickshire CC, 1967–72. President: Macclesfield Fermain Club; Poynton Community Centre; N Staffs Polytechnic Conservative Assoc.; Wigan Young Conservatives; Vice-President: NW Area Young Conservative Assoc.; Macclesfield and Congleton District Scout Council; Cheshire Scout Assoc.; Upton Priory Youth Centre, Macclesfield; E Cheshire Hospice. Hon. Mem., Macclesfield Lions Club; Hon. Life Mem., Macclesfield Rugby Union Football Club; Pres., Macclesfield Hockey Club; Patron: Macclesfield and District Sheep Dog Trials Assoc; Internat. Centre for Child Studies. President, Macclesfield Branch: Riding for the Disabled; Multiple Sclerosis Soc.; Trustee, NW Liver Res. Fund. Pres., Bollington Light Opera Gp; Life Mem., Poynton Gilbert and Sullivan Soc. Liveryman, Weavers' Co.; Freeman of the City of London. *Recreations:* Rugby football, squash, hockey, tennis, swimming, horse riding. *Address:* Whitehall Farm, Mow Lane, Newbold Astbury, Congleton, Cheshire CW12 3NH. *Clubs:* Cavalry and Guards, Lighthouse.

WINTLE, Rev. Canon Ruth Elizabeth; Parish Deacon, St John-in-Bedwardine, and Diocesan Director of Ordinands, Worcester, since 1984; *b* 30 Sept. 1931; *d* of John Wintle and Vera (*née* Lane). *Educ:* Clarendon Sch., Malvern, and Abergele, Wales; Westfield Coll., London (BA Hons French 1953); St Hugh's Coll., Oxford (MA Theol. 1972); St Michael's House, Oxford (IDC 1966). Teacher, St Hilda's Sch., Jamaica, 1953–60; Travelling Sec., Inter-Varsity Fellowship and Technical Colls Christian Fellowship, 1960–63; Accredited Lay Worker, St Andrew's Church, N Oxford, 1967–69; Tutor, St John's Coll., Durham, 1969–74; Deaconess (C of E), 1972; Selection Sec., ACCM, 1974–83; Organiser, Internat. Diakonia Conf., Coventry, 1983; ordained Deacon, 1987;

Hon. Canon, Worcester Cathedral, 1987. *Recreations:* reading, driving, ornithology. *Address:* 72 Henwick Road, Worcester WR2 5NT. *T:* Worcester (0905) 422841.

WINTON, Alexander, QFSM 1987; HM Chief Inspector of Fire Services for Scotland, since 1990; *b* 13 July 1932; *s* of Alexander and Jean Winton; *m* 1957, Jean Dowie; two *s*. MIFireE. Fireman, Perth, 1958–64; Station Officer: Perth, 1964–67; Lancashire, 1967–69; Assistant Divisional Officer: E Riding, 1969–72; Angus, 1972–73; Divisional Officer III: Angus, 1973–75; Tayside, 1975–76; Divl Comdr (DOI), Tayside, 1976–80; Temp. Sen. Divl Officer, 1980–81; Dep. Firemaster, 1981–85; Firemaster, Tayside Fire Bde, 1985–89. *Recreations:* golf, curling, reading. *Address:* 5 Ferndale Drive, Broughty Ferry, Dundee DD5 3DB. *T:* Dundee (0382) 78156.

WINTON, Walter; Keeper, Department of Electrical Engineering, Telecommunications and Loan Circulation, Science Museum, 1976–80; *b* 15 May 1917; *m* 1942, Dorothy Rickard; two *s* one *d*. *Educ:* Glossop Grammar Sch.; Manchester Univ. (BSc and Teacher's Diploma). Royal Ordnance Factories, Chemist, 1940–45. Taught Science, Harrow County and Greenford, 1945–50; Assistant and Deputy Keeper, Science Museum, 1950–67; Keeper: Dept of Loan Circulation, Mining and Marine Technol., 1968–73; Dept of Museum Services, 1973; Dept of Mechanical and Civil Engrg and Loan Circulation, 1973–76. *Publications:* contrib. to journals. *Recreations:* Scottish dancing, sailing, fell-walking. *Address:* The Old Workhouse, Harefield, Middlesex UB9 6NE. *T:* Harefield (0895) 822103.

WINTOUR, Anna, (Mrs David Shaffer); Editor, US Vogue, since 1988; *b* 3 Nov. 1949; *d* of Charles Wintour, *qv*; *m* 1984, Dr David Shaffer; one *s* one *d*. *Educ:* Queen's College Sch., London; North London Collegiate Sch. Dep. Fashion Editor, Harpers and Queen Magazine, 1970–76; Fashion Editor, Harpers Bazaar, NY, 1976–77; Fashion and Beauty Editor, Viva Mag., 1977–78; Contributing Editor for Fashion and Style, Savvy Mag., 1980–81; Sen. Editor, New York Mag., NY, 1981–83; Creative Dir, US Vogue, 1983–86; Editor-in-Chief, Vogue, 1986–87; Editor, House and Garden, New York, 1987–88. *Address:* 25 Ladbroke Square, W11; 45 MacDougal Street, New York, NY 10014.

WINTOUR, Audrey Cecelia; *see* Slaughter, A. C.

WINTOUR, Charles Vere, CBE 1978 (MBE (mil.) 1945); journalist; *b* 18 May 1917; *s* of late Maj.-Gen. F. Wintour, CB, CBE; *m* 1st, 1940, Eleanor Trego Baker (marr. diss. 1979), *er d* of Prof. R. J. Baker, Harvard Univ.; two *s* two *d* (and one *s* decd); 2nd 1979, Mrs Audrey Slaughter, *qv*. *Educ:* Oundle Sch.; Peterhouse, Cambridge. BA 1939; MA 1946. Royal Norfolk Regt, 1940; GSO2 Headquarters of Chief of Staff to the Supreme Allied Commander (Designate) and SHAEF, 1943–45 (despatches). Joined Evening Standard, 1946: Dep. Editor, 1954–57; Editor, 1959–76 and 1978–80; Managing Dir, 1978–79; Chm., 1968–80; Asst Editor, Sunday Express, 1952–54; Managing Editor, Daily Express, 1957–59, Managing Dir, 1977–78; Editor: Sunday Express Magazine, 1981–82; UK Press Gazette, 1985–86; Editorial Consultant, London Daily News, 1986–87; Ombudsman, Sunday Times, 1990–. Director: Evening Standard Co. Ltd, 1959–82; Express (formerly Beaverbrook) Newspapers Ltd, 1964–82; TV-am (News) Ltd, 1982–84; Wintour Publications, 1984–85. Mem., Press Council, 1979–81; Pres., Media Soc., 1989–91. Croix de Guerre (France) 1945; Bronze Star (US) 1945. *Publications:* Pressures on the Press, 1972; The Rise and Fall of Fleet Street, 1989. *Recreations:* theatre-going, reading newspapers. *Address:* 60 East Hatch, Tisbury, Wilts SP3 6PH. *T:* Tisbury (0747) 870880. *Club:* Garrick.
See also A. Wintour.

WINYARD, Dr Graham Peter Arthur, FRCP; FFCM; Regional Medical Director and Director of Public Health, Wessex Regional Health Authority, since 1990; *b* 19 Jan. 1947; *s* of Lyonel Arthur Winyard and Dorothy Elizabeth Payne; *m* 1979, Sandra Catherine Bent; one *s* two *d*. *Educ:* Southend High Sch.; Hertford Coll., Oxford (MA); Middlesex Hosp. (BM, BCh). Ho. Phys., Middlesex Hosp., Ho. Surg., Ipswich Hosp., 1972; Sen. House Officer, United Oxford Hosps, 1973–75; Registrar in Community Medicine, 1975–77; Provincial Health Officer, Madang, PNG, 1977–79; Sen. Registrar in Community Medicine, Oxford RHA, and Lectr, LSHTM, 1979–82; Dist MO, Lewisham and N Southwark HA, 1982–87; SPMO, DHSS, later Dept of Health, 1987–90. *Publications:* various on med. care in med. jls. *Recreations:* family, gardening, DIY, music. *Address:* 15 Clifton Road, Winchester SO22 5BP. *T:* Winchester (0962) 54682.

WISBECH, Archdeacon of; *see* Fleming, Ven. D.

WISDOM, Prof. Arthur John Terence Dibben, MA; Professor of Philosophy, University of Oregon, 1968–72; Fellow of Trinity College, Cambridge; *b* 1904; *s* of Rev. H. C. Wisdom and Edith S. Wisdom. *Educ:* Aldeburgh Lodge School; Fitzwilliam House (now College), Cambridge (Hon. Fellow, Fitzwilliam Coll., 1978). BA 1924; MA 1934. Lecturer in Moral Sciences, Trinity Coll., Cambridge; Prof. of Philosophy, Cambridge Univ., 1952–68. DU Essex, 1978. *Publications:* Other Minds, 1952; Philosophy and Psycho-Analysis, 1952; Paradox and Discovery, 1966. Contributions to Mind and to Proceedings of the Aristotelian Society. *Address:* 154 Stanley Road, Cambridge.

WISDOM, Norman; Actor/Comedian; has starred regularly on stage and screen, since 1952. First film Trouble in Store, in 1953 (winning an Academy Award) since which has starred in 19 major films in both England and America; two Broadway awards for stage musical, Walking Happy; numerous Royal Performances, both film and stage. *Recreations:* all sports. *Address:* c/o Eric Glass Ltd, 28 Berkeley Square, W1X 6HD.

WISE, family name of **Baron Wise.**

WISE, 2nd Baron, *cr* 1951, of King's Lynn; **John Clayton Wise;** farmer; *b* 11 June 1923; *s* of 1st Baron Wise and of Kate Elizabeth (*d* 1987), *e d* of late John Michael Sturgeon; *S* father, 1968; *m* 1946, Margaret Annie, *d* of Frederick Victor Snead, Banbury; two *s*. *Heir:* *s* Hon. Christopher John Clayton Wise, PhD, BSc Hons [*b* 19 March 1949. *Educ:* Norwich School; Univ. of Southampton. Plant Scientist]. *Address:* Martlets, Blakeney, Norfolk NR25 7NP.

WISE, Mrs Audrey; MP (Lab) Preston, since 1987; *d* of George and Elsie Crawford Brown; *m* John Wise; one *s* one *d*. Shorthand typist. MP (Lab) Coventry South West, Feb. 1974–1979. Contested (Lab) Woolwich, 1983. Mem., Labour Party NEC, 1982–87. Pres., USDAW, 1991–. *Publications:* Women and the Struggle for Workers' Control, 1973; Eyewitness in Revolutionary Portugal, 1975. *Recreations:* family life, camping, walking, reading. *Address:* House of Commons, SW1A 0AA.

WISE, Derek; *see* Wise, R. D.

WISE, Prof. Douglass, OBE 1980; FRIBA; Director, Institute of Advanced Architectural Studies, University of York, since 1975; *b* 6 Nov. 1927; *s* of Horace Watson Wise and Doris Wise; *m* 1958, Yvonne Jeannine Czeiler; one *s* one *d*. *Educ:* King's Coll., Newcastle, Durham Univ. (BArch; DipTP). Lecturer in Architecture, 1959–65, Prof. of Architecture, 1965–69, Head of Dept of Architecture, 1969–75, Newcastle Univ. Principal, Douglass Wise & Partners, Architects, 1959–. RIBA: Chm., Moderators, 1969–75; Chm., Examinations Cttee, 1969–75; Mem. Council, 1976–79; Chm., Heads of Schools Cttee, 1971–73; Mem. Bd of Management, North Eastern Housing Assoc., 1967–76 (Vice-Chm., 1974–76); Mem. Council, Newcastle Polytechnic, 1974–77; past Mem. Council, Senate and Court, Newcastle Univ.; Governor, Building Centre Trust, London, 1976–. *Publications:* contribs to various technical jls on housing, continuing educn and architectural theory. *Recreations:* painting, natural history. *Address:* The Institute of Advanced Architectural Studies, The King's Manor, York YO1 2EP. *T:* York (0904) 433987.

WISE, Ernie; *see* Wiseman, Ernest.

WISE, Prof. Michael John, CBE 1979; MC 1945; PhD; FRGS; Emeritus Professor of Geography, University of London; *b* Stafford, 17 August 1918; *s* of Harry Cuthbert and Sarah Evelyn Wise; *m* 1942, Barbara Mary, *d* of C. L. Hodgetts, Wolverhampton; one *d* one *s*. *Educ:* Saltley Grammar School, Birmingham; University of Birmingham. BA (Hons Geography) Birmingham, and Mercator Prize in Geography, 1939; PhD Birmingham, 1951. Served War, Royal Artillery, 80th LAA Regt, 1941–44, 5th Bn The Northamptonshire Regt, 1944–46, in Middle East and Italy; commissioned, 1941, Major, 1944. Assistant Lecturer, Univ. of Birmingham, 1946–48, Lecturer in Geography, 1948–51; London School of Economics: Lecturer in Geography, 1951–54; Sir Ernest Cassel Reader in Economic Geography, 1954–58; Prof. of Geography, 1958–83; Pro-Director, 1983–85; Hon. Fellow, 1988. Chm., Departmental Cttee of Inquiry into Statutory Smallholdings, 1963–67; Mem., Dept of Transport Adv. Cttee on Landscape Treatment of Trunk Roads, 1971–90 (Chm., 1981–90). Mem., UGC for Hong Kong, 1966–73. Recorder, Sect. E, Brit. Assoc. for Advancement of Science, 1955–60 (Pres., 1965); President: Inst. of British Geographers, 1974 (Hon. Mem., 1989); IGU, 1976–80 (Vice-Pres., 1968–76); Geographical Assoc., 1976–77 (Hon. Treasurer, 1967–76, Hon. Mem., 1983); Mem., SSRC, 1976–82; Chm., Council for Extra-Mural Studies, Univ. of London, 1976–83; Chm., Exec. Cttee, Assoc. of Agriculture, 1972–83 (Vice-Pres., 1983–); Mem. Adv. Cttees, UN Univ., 1976–82; Hon. Sec., RGS, 1963–73, Vice-Pres., 1975–78, Hon. Vice-Pres., 1978–80, 1983–, Pres., 1980–82. Chm., Birkbeck Coll., 1983–89 (Governor, 1968–89; Fellow, 1989); Mem. Delegacy, Goldsmiths' Coll., 1984–88. Erskine Fellow, Univ. of Canterbury, NZ, 1970. Hon. Life Mem., Univ. of London Union, 1977. Hon. Member: Geog. Soc. of USSR, 1975; Assoc. of Japanese Geographers, 1980; Geog. Soc. of Mexico, 1984; Geog. Soc. of Poland, 1986; Membre d'Honneur, Société de Géographie, 1983. FRSA. Hon. FLI 1991. DUniv Open, 1978; Hon. DSc Birmingham, 1982. Received Gill Memorial award of RGS, 1958; RGS Founder's Medal, 1977; Alexander Körösi Csoma Medal, Hungarian Geographical Soc., 1980; Tokyo Geographical Soc. Medal, 1981; Lauréat d'Honneur, IGU, 1984. *Publications:* Hon. Editor, Birmingham and its Regional Setting, 1951; A Pictorial Geography of the West Midlands, 1958; General Consultant, An Atlas of Earth Resources, 1979; General Consultant, The Great Geographical Atlas, 1982; (consultant and contrib.) The Ordnance Survey Atlas of Great Britain, 1982; numerous articles on economic and urban geography. *Recreations:* music, gardening. *Address:* 45 Oakleigh Avenue, N20. *T:* 081–445 6057. *Club:* Athenæum.

WISE, Peter Anthony Surtees; Assistant Commissioner (Commercial), Hong Kong Government Office, London, since 1978; also Representative for Commercial Relations with Austria and the Nordic Countries, since 1980 (formerly non-resident Counsellor (Hong Kong Trade Affairs), Helsinki, Oslo, Stockholm, Vienna); *b* 26 June 1934; *s* of late J. A. S. (Tony) Wise and Lenore Dugdale; *m* 1956, Elizabeth Muirhead Odhams; two *s*. *Educ:* Royal Naval College, Dartmouth. Served Royal Navy, 1948–56 (invalided). Marconi Instruments Ltd, 1956–60; Vickers Ltd, 1961–74; First Secretary, later Counsellor (Hong Kong Affairs), UK Mission, Geneva, 1974–78. *Address:* Field House, Boxford, Berks RG16 8DN. *T:* Boxford (048838) 302. *Club:* Hong Kong (Hong Kong).

WISE, Very Rev. Randolph George, VRD 1964; Dean of Peterborough, 1981–Feb. 1992; *b* 20 Jan. 1925; *s* of George and Agnes Lucy Wise; *m* 1951, Hazel Hebe Simpson; four *d*. *Educ:* St Olave's and St Saviour's Grammar School; Queen's Coll., Oxford (MA); Lincoln Theological Coll.; Ealing Technical Coll. (DMS). Served RNVR, 1943–47. Assistant Curate: Lady Margaret, Walworth, 1951–53; Stocksbridge, Sheffield, 1953–55; Vicar of Lady Margaret, Walworth, 1955–60; Vicar of Stocksbridge, 1960–66; Bishop of London's Industrial Chaplaincy, 1966–76; Guild Vicar, St Botolph, Aldersgate, 1972–76; Rector of Notting Hill, 1976–81. Member of Plaisterers' Company. *Recreations:* music, sculling. *Address:* (until Feb. 1992) The Deanery, Peterborough PE1 1XS. *T:* Peterborough (0733) 62780; (from March 1992) 2 Derwent Drive, Oakham, Leics LE15 6SA. *Club:* Naval.

WISE, (Reginald) Derek, CBE 1977; Partner, Wise & Mercer, Paris, since 1983; *b* 29 July 1917; *s* of Reginald and Rita Wise; *m* 1957, Nancy Brenta Scialoya; two *s* one *d*. *Educ:* St Paul's Sch. Admitted solicitor, 1947. Served War of 1939–45, RA and Intell. Partner, Theodore Goddard, Paris, 1957–82. Legal Adviser, British Embassy, Paris, 1962–. *Address:* 203 bis Boulevard St Germain, 75007 Paris, France. *T:* 4222.07.94. *Club:* Travellers' (Paris).

WISEMAN, Prof. Donald John, OBE 1943; DLit; FBA 1966; FSA; Professor of Assyriology in the University of London, 1961–82, Emeritus 1982; *b* 25 Oct. 1918; *s* of Air Cdre Percy John Wiseman, CBE, RAF; *m* 1948, Mary Catherine, *d* of P. O. Ruoff; three *d*. *Educ:* Dulwich College; King's College, London. BA (London); AKC, McCaul Hebrew Prize, 1939; FKC 1982. Served War of 1939–45, in RAFVR. Ops, 11 Fighter Group, 1939–41; Chief Intelligence Officer, Mediterranean Allied Tactical Air Forces with Rank of Group Capt., 1942–45. Heap Exhibitioner in Oriental Languages, Wadham Coll., Oxford, 1945–47; MA 1949. Asst Keeper, Dept of Egyptian and Assyrian, later Western Asiatic, Antiquities, British Museum, 1948–61. Epigraphist on archæological excavations at Nimrud, Harran, Rimah; Jt Dir of British School of Archæology in Iraq, 1961–65, Chm. 1970–88, Vice-Pres., 1988–. Pres., Soc. for Old Testament Studies, 1980; Chm., Tyndale House for Biblical Research, Cambridge, 1957–86. Corresp. Mem., German Archæological Inst., 1961. Editor, Journal IRAQ, 1953–78; Joint Editor, Reallexion der Assyriologie, 1959–83. Bronze Star (USA), 1944. *Publications:* The Alalakh Tablets, 1953; Chronicles of Chaldaean Kings, 1956; Cuneiform Texts from Cappadocian Tablets in the British Museum, V, 1956; Cylinder-Seals of Western Asia, 1958; Vassal-Treaties of Esarhaddon, 1958; Illustrations from Biblical Archæology, 1958; Catalogue of Western Asiatic Seals in the British Museum, 1963; Peoples of Old Testament Times, 1973; Archaeology and the Bible, 1979; Essays on the Patriarchal Narratives, 1980; Nebuchadrezzar and Babylon, 1985; contrib. to journals. *Address:* Low Barn, 26 Downs Way, Tadworth, Surrey KT20 5DZ. *T:* Tadworth (0737) 813536.

WISEMAN, Ernest, OBE 1976; **(Ernie Wise);** *b* 27 Nov. 1925; *s* of Harry and Connie Wiseman; *m* 1953, Doreen Blyth. *Educ:* Council School. Career in show business: radio, variety, TV, films. First double act (with E. Morecambe), at Empire Theatre, Liverpool, 1941; first broadcast, 1943; BBC and ITV television series, 1955–84 (Soc. of Film and Television Arts Best Light Entertainment Award, 1973); series sold to Time Life, USA, 1980; Morecambe and Wise Tribute Show, Bring Me Sunshine, 1984; The Best of Morecambe and Wise, BBC, 1984; What's My Line, 1985; Too Close for Comfort,

1985; Los Angilla's, 1985; *stage:* The Mystery of Edwin Drood, Savoy, 1987; Run for Your Wife, Criterion, 1988; *films:* The Intelligence Men, 1964; That Riviera Touch, 1965; The Magnificent Two, 1966; (for TV) Night Train to Murder, 1983. *Awards:* BAFTA (formerly SFTA), 1963, 1971, 1972, 1973, 1977; Silver Heart, 1964; Water Rats, 1970; Radio Industries, 1971, 1972; Sun Newspaper, 1973; Sun, 1974; Water Rats Distinguished Services, 1974; TV Times Hall of Fame Award, 1980–81; Commendation, 1981, Special Mention, 1982, HM Queen Mother's Award, Keep Britain Tidy; Best Dressed Man Award, 1983; Variety Club of GB award for work for deprived children, 1983; TV Times Award, 1985. Telethon for Children's Charity, NZ, 1985. Freeman, City of London, 1976. *Publications:* (with E. Morecambe): Eric and Ernie: an autobiography of Morecambe and Wise, 1973; Scripts of Morecambe and Wise, 1974; Morecambe and Wise Special, 1977; There's No Answer to That, 1981; Still on My Way to Hollywood (autobiog.), 1990. *Recreations:* boating, tennis, swimming, jogging. *Address:* Thames Television, Teddington Lock, TW11 9NT.

WISEMAN, Sir John William, 11th Bt, *cr* 1628; *b* 16 March 1957; *o s* of Sir William George Eden Wiseman, 10th Bt, and Joan Mary, *d* of late Arthur Phelps, Harrow; *S* father, 1962; *m* 1980, Nancy, *d* of Casimer Zyla, New Britain, Conn; two *d*. *Educ:* Millfield Sch.; Univ. of Hartford, Conn, USA. *Heir: kinsman* Thomas Alan Wiseman [*b* 8 July 1921; *m* 1946, Hildemarie Domnik; (one *s* one *d* decd)]. *Address:* 395 North Road, Sudbury, Mass 01776, USA.

WISEMAN, Prof. Timothy Peter, DPhil; FSA; FBA 1986; Professor of Classics, University of Exeter, since 1977; *b* 3 Feb. 1940; *s* of Stephen Wiseman and Winifred Agnes Wiseman (*née* Rigby); *m* 1962, Doreen Anne Williams. *Educ:* Manchester Grammar Sch.; Balliol Coll., Oxford (MA 1964; DPhil 1967). FSA 1977. Rome Schol. in Classical Studies, British Sch. at Rome, 1962–63; University of Leicester: Asst Lectr in Classics, 1963–65; Lectr, 1965–73; Reader in Roman History, 1973–76. Vis. Associate Prof., Univ. of Toronto, 1970–71; Lansdowne Lectr, Univ. of Victoria (BC), 1987; Whitney J. Oates Fellow, Princeton, 1988. Hon. DLitt Durham, 1988. *Publications:* Catullan Questions, 1969; New Men in the Roman Senate, 1971; Cinna the Poet, 1974; Clio's Cosmetics, 1979; (with Anne Wiseman) Julius Caesar: The Battle for Gaul, 1980; (ed) Roman Political Life, 1985; Catullus and his World, 1985; Roman Studies Literary and Historical, 1987; Flavius Josephus: death of an emperor, 1991; Talking to Virgil, 1991. *Address:* Classics Department, The University, Exeter EX4 4QH. *T:* Exeter (0392) 264201.

WISHART, Maureen; *see* Lehane, M.

WISTRICH, Enid Barbara, PhD; Reader in Public Administration, Middlesex Polytechnic, since 1991 (Principal Lecturer, 1979–91); *b* 4 Sept. 1928; *d* of Zadik Heiber and Bertha Brown; *m* 1950, Ernest Wistrich, *qv*; two *c* (and one *c* decd). *Educ:* Froebel Institute Sch.; Brackley High Sch.; St Paul's Girls' Sch.; London School of Economics (BScEcon, PhD). Research Asst, LSE, 1950–52; Instructor, Mt Holyoke Coll., Mass, USA, 1952–53; Research Officer, Royal Inst. of Public Administration, 1954–56; Sen. Res. Officer, LSE, 1969–72; NEDO, 1977–79. Vis. Lectr, Univ. of Waikato, NZ, 1989. Councillor (Lab): Hampstead Metropolitan Bor. Council, 1962–65; London Bor. of Camden, 1964–68 and 1971–74; GLC, ILEA, 1973–77. Mem., Hampstead Community Health Council, 1984– (Chm., 1986–88). Governor: British Film Inst., 1974–81 (also Actg Chm., 1977–78); National Film Sch., 1978–82. Chm. of Governors, Heathlands Sch. for Autistic Children, 1976–86. *Publications:* Local Government Reorganisation: the first years of Camden, 1972; I Don't Mind the Sex, It's the Violence: film censorship explored, 1978; The Politics of Transport, 1983; articles in Political Qly, Local Government Studies, Jl of Media Law and Practice, Teaching Public Administration, etc. *Recreations:* experiencing the arts, admiring nature, fussing round the family. *Address:* 37B Gayton Road, NW3 1UB. *T:* 071–435 8796.

WISTRICH, Ernest, CBE 1973; Director, European Movement (British Council), 1969–86; *b* 22 May 1923; *s* of Dr Arthur and Mrs Eva Wistrich; *m* 1950, Enid Barbara (*née* Heiber), *qv*; two *c* (and one *c* decd). *Educ:* Poland; University Tutorial Coll., London. Served in RAF, 1942–46; Timber Merchant, 1946–67; Dir, Britain in Europe, 1967–69; Councillor, Hampstead Borough Council, 1959–65; Camden Borough Council, Alderman 1964–71, Councillor 1971–74; Chm., Camden Cttee for Community Relations, 1964–68; Mem., Skeffington Cttee on Public Participation in Planning, 1968–69. Contested (Lab): Isle of Thanet, 1964; Hendon North, 1966; Cleveland, 1979; contested (SDP) London Central, 1984, European Parly elections. Editor of various jls, incl. The European, 1986–88. *Publications:* After 1992: the United States of Europe, 1989; contrib. Into Europe, Facts, New Europe and other jls. *Recreations:* music, walking. *Address:* 37B Gayton Road, NW3 1UB. *T:* 071–435 8796.

WITHALL, Maj.-Gen. William Nigel James, CB 1982; Marketing Director, and Member, Board of Directors, Singer Link-Miles Ltd, since 1985 (Consultant, 1984); *b* 14 Oct. 1928; *s* of late Bernard Withall and Enid (*née* Hill); *m* 1952, Pamela Hickman; one *s* one *d*. *Educ:* St Benedict's; Birmingham Univ. (Civil Engrg degree). Commnd RE, 1950; served in Hong Kong, Gulf States, Aden, Germany and India; Staff Coll., 1961; Sqdn Comd, 73 Fd Sqdn, 1964–66; Jt Services Staff Coll., Latimer, 1967; Mil. Asst to MGO, 1968–70; CO 26 Engr Regt, BAOR, 1970–72; Bde Comd, 11 Engr Bde, 1974–76; NDC, India, 1977; No 259 Army Pilots Course, 1978; Dir, Army Air Corps, 1979–83. Col Comdt RE, 1984–. Chm., Army Football Assoc., 1980–81; Pres., Army Cricket Assoc., 1981–83; Hon. Life Vice Pres., Aircrew Assoc., 1986. Freeman, City of London, 1981; Liveryman, GAPAN, 1981. *Recreations:* cricket, squash, all games, reading, walking. *Address:* c/o Barclays Bank, High Street, Andover, Hants. *Clubs:* City Livery, MCC.

WITHERINGTON, Giles Somerville Gwynne; Chairman, 1982–87, Member of Council, since 1980, Save the Children Fund; *b* 7 June 1919; *s* of Iltid Gwynne Witherington and Alice Isabel Gage Spicer; *m* 1951, Rowena Ann Spencer Lynch; one *s* three *d*. *Educ:* Charterhouse; University Coll., Oxford (MA). War Service, Royal Artillery, UK, N Africa, Italy, 1939–46 (despatches). Joined Spicers Ltd, 1946, Jt Managing Director, 1960; joined Reed International Ltd: Director, 1963; Dep. Chm., 1976; retired, 1982. Mem. Council, 1984–, Chm. of Trustees of the Friends, 1984–, Textile Conservation Centre. Hon. LLD Birmingham, 1983. *Recreations:* shooting, gardening, modern art, travel. *Address:* Bishops, Widdington, Saffron Walden, Essex CB11 3SQ; Flat 2, 11 Netherton Grove, SW10 9TQ. *Club:* Arts.

WITHEROW, David Michael Lindley; Deputy Managing Director, BBC World Service, since 1989; *b* 19 July 1937; *s* of Dr James Witherow and Greta (*née* Roberts); *m* 1960, Ragnhild Kadow (separated 1988); two *d*. *Educ:* King Edward's Sch., Birmingham (Foundn Schol.); Pembroke Coll., Cambridge (BA Hons 1960). Nat. service, RCS, 1955–57. Press Assoc., 1960–63; BBC, 1963–: Ext. Services News, 1963–77, Editor, 1973–77; Editor, Weekly Progs, TV News, 1977–79; Chief Assistant, Regions, 1980; Head, then Gen. Manager, Monitoring Service, Caversham, 1980–85; Controller, Resources and Admin, Ext. Services, 1985–89. *Recreations:* travel, music, crime fiction. *Address:* 43 Hillfield Court, Belsize Avenue, NW3 4BJ. *T:* 071–431 1880. *Club:* Commonwealth Trust.

WITHERS, Googie, (Mrs John McCallum), AO 1980; Actress since 1932; *b* Karachi, India, 12 March 1917; *d* of late Captain E. C. Withers, CBE, CIE, RIM, and late Lizette Catherine Wilhelmina van Wageningen; *m* 1948, John Neil McCallum, *qv*; one *s* two *d*. *Educ:* Fredville Park, Nonnington, Kent; Convent of the Holy Family, Kensington. Started as dancer in Musical Comedy. First film contract at age of 17; has acted in over 50 pictures, starring in 30. *Films include:* One of our Aircraft is Missing; The Silver Fleet; On Approval; Loves of Joanna Godden; It Always Rains on Sunday; White Corridors; Nickel Queen. *Plays include:* They Came to a City; Private Lives; Winter Journey; The Deep Blue Sea; Waiting for Gillian; Janus. Stratford on Avon Season, 1958: Beatrice in Much Ado About Nothing; Gertrude in Hamlet. The Complaisant Lover, New York, 1962; Exit the King, London, 1963; Getting Married, Strand, 1967; Madame Renevsky in The Cherry Orchard, Mrs Cheveley in An Ideal Husband, 1972; Lady Kitty in The Circle, Chichester Festival Theatre, 1976, Haymarket, 1977 (nominated for SWET best actress award), Toronto, 1978; Lady Bracknell in The Importance of Being Earnest, Chichester, 1979; Time and the Conways, Chichester, 1983; Lady Sneerwell in The School for Scandal, Duke of York's, 1984 (also European tour); The Chalk Garden, Chichester, 1986; Hay Fever, Ring Round the Moon, Chichester, 1988. Tours: 1959, Australia and NZ with: Roar Like a Dove, The Constant Wife and Woman in a Dressing Gown; 1964, excerpts Shakespeare (Kate, Margaret of Anjou, Beatrice, Portia, Rosalind, Cleopatra); 1965, Australia and NZ, with Beekman Place; 1968, Australia, with Relatively Speaking; 1969–70, Australia and NZ, with Plaza Suite; 1978–80, Australia, NZ and Far East, with The Kingfisher; 1981, UK tour, The Cherry Orchard, The Skin Game, Dandy Dick; 1984–85, UK and Australia, Stardust; 1987, Far East, Middle East and Gulf, with The Kingfisher; 1989–90, Australia and UK tour, The Cocktail Hour. TV appearances in drama including The Public Prosecutor; Amphitryon 38; The Deep Blue Sea (Best Actress, 1954); Last Year's Confetti, Court Circular, 1971; Knightsbridge, 1972; The Cherry Orchard, 1973; series Within These Walls, 1974–76 (Best Actress of the Year, 1974); Time after Time (TV film), 1985 (Best Actress ACE Award, USA, 1988); Hotel du Lac (TV film), 1985; Northanger Abbey (TV film), 1986; Ending Up, 1989. *Recreations:* music, travel, reading, interior decorating. *Address:* 1740 Pittwater Road, Bay View, NSW 2104, Australia; c/o Coutts & Co., 440 Strand, WC2.

WITHERS, John Keppel Ingold D.; *see* Douglas-Withers.

WITHERS, Rt. Hon. Reginald (Greive), PC 1977; Senator (L) for Western Australia, 1966–87; Lord Mayor of Perth, Western Australia, since 1991; *b* 26 Oct. 1924; *s* of late F. J. Withers and I. L. Greive; *m* 1953, Shirley Lloyd-Jones; two *s* one *d*. *Educ:* Bunbury; Univ. of WA (LLB). Barrister-at-law 1953. Served War, RAN, 1942–46. Councillor, Bunbury Municipal Council, 1954–56; Mem., Bunbury Diocesan Council, 1958–59, Treasurer, 1961–68. State Vice-Pres., Liberal and Country League of WA, 1958–61, State Pres., 1961–65; Mem., Federal Exec. of Liberal Party, 1961–65; Fed. Vice-Pres., Liberal Party, 1962–65. Govt Whip in Senate, 1969–71; Leader of Opposition in Senate, 1972–75; Special Minister of State, Minister for Capital Territory, Minister for Media, and Minister for Tourism and Recreation, Nov.-Dec. 1975; Vice-Pres. of Exec. Council, Leader of Govt in Senate, and Minister for Admin. Services, 1975–78. Sec., SW Law Soc., 1955–68. *Recreations:* swimming, reading, painting. *Address:* 23 Malcolm Street, West Perth, WA 6005, Australia. *T:* (09)324 1322.

WITHERS, Roy Joseph, CBE 1983; FEng 1983; Vice Chairman, Davy Corporation plc, since 1983; Chairman, Transmark, since 1987 (Director, since 1978); *b* 18 June 1924; *s* of Joseph Withers and Irene Ada Withers (*née* Jones); *m* 1947, Pauline M. G. Johnston; four *s*. *Educ:* T School, Kingston upon Thames; Trinity College, Cambridge (1st. cl. Hons Mech. Scis Tripos). ICI, 1948–55; Humphreys & Glasgow, 1955–63; Engineering Dir, then Man. Dir, Power-Gas Corp. (subsid. of Davy Corp.), 1963–71; Chief Exec., Davy Powergas International, 1972–73; Man. Dir, Davy Corp., 1973–83. Director: A. Monk & Co., 1983–88; Vosper Thornycroft (Hldgs), 1985– (Chm., 1985–90). Mem., BOTB, 1983–86; Chm., Overseas Projects Board, 1983–86. Hon. FIChemE. *Recreations:* painting, golf, walking. *Address:* Wheelwrights Cottage, Bramshaw, Lyndhurst, Hants SO4 7JB. *T:* Lyndhurst (0703) 812543. *Clubs:* Carlton; Hampstead Golf, Bramshaw Golf.

WITHERS, Rupert Alfred; Director, Dalgety Ltd, 1969–83 (Deputy Chairman and Managing Director, 1969–71; Chairman, 1972–77); *b* 29 Oct. 1913; *o s* of late Herbert Withers, FRAM and Marguerite (*née* Elzy); *m*; three *d*. *Educ:* University College School. Fellow Institute of Chartered Accountants, 1938. Secretary and Chief Accountant, Gloster Aircraft Co. Ltd, 1940–44; a Senior Partner of Urwick Orr & Partners Ltd until 1959; Man. Dir, Ilford Ltd, 1959–64; Chm. and Chief Executive, 1964–68. *Recreations:* music, books, theatre. *Address:* 11K Stuart Tower, Maida Vale, W9. *T:* 071–286 8706. *Club:* Savile.

WITHY, George; retired journalist; Assistant Editor (night), Liverpool Echo, 1972–89; *b* Birkenhead, 15 May 1924; *er s* of George Withy and Alma Elizabeth Withy (*née* Stankley); *m* 1950, Dorothy Betty, *e c* of Bertram Allen and Dorothy Gray, Northfield, Birmingham; two *d*. *Educ:* Birkenhead Park High Sch. Served War, Royal Artillery, Britain and NW Europe, 1942–47. Trainee and Reporter, Birkenhead News, 1940; Chief Reporter, Redditch Indicator, 1948; District Reporter, Birmingham Post and Mail, 1950; Editor, Redditch Indicator, 1952. Joined Liverpool Daily Post 1960: successively Sub-Editor, Dep. Chief Sub-Editor, Asst News Editor, Chief Sub-Editor. Chief Sub-Editor, Liverpool Echo, 1970. Inst. of Journalists, 1962: successively Sec. and Chm., Liverpool District; Convenor, NW Region; Chm., Salaries and Conditions Bd, 1973–89; Vice-Pres. and then Pres., 1975; Fellow 1975. Chm., Nat. Council for the Trng of Journalists, 1974, 1982 (Mem., 1970; Vice-Chm., 1973, 1981; Chm., North-West Adv. Trng Cttee, 1974–76, 1983–85); Mem., Newspaper Trng Cttee, Printing and Publishing Industry Trng Bd; Mem., Press Council, 1973–79. *Recreations:* writing on Rugby Union football, gardening, reading, philately. *Address:* 3 Woodside Road, Irby, Wirral, Merseyside L61 4UL. *T:* 051–648 2809.

WITNEY, Kenneth Percy, CVO; *b* 19 March 1916; *s* of late Rev. Thomas and of Dr Myfanwy Witney, S India; *m* 1947, Joan Tait; one *s* one *d*. *Educ:* Eltham Coll.; Wadham Coll., Oxford (Schol.). BA Hons Mod. History, 1938; MA 1975; DipArch 1990. Min. of Home Security, 1940; Private Sec. to Parly Under-Sec., 1942–44; Home Office, 1945; Asst Private Sec. to Home Sec., 1945–47; Colonial Office (Police Div.), 1955–57; Asst Sec., Home Office, 1957; Asst Under-Sec. of State, Home Office, 1969–76. Special Consultant to Royal Commn on Gambling, 1976–78. Chm., Kent Fedn of Amenity Socs, 1982–85. *Publications:* The Jutish Forest, 1976; The Kingdom of Kent, 1982; contribs to Econ. Hist. Rev., Archaeologia Cantiana, Agricl Hist. Rev. *Recreations:* local history, gardening. *Address:* 1 Loampits Close, Tonbridge, Kent. *T:* Tonbridge (0732) 352971; 37 Paradise Row, Sandwich, Kent.

WITT, Rt. Rev. Howell Arthur John; Bishop of Bathurst, 1981–89; *b* 12 July 1920; *s* of Thomas Leyshon Witt and Harriet Jane Witt; *m* 1949, Gertrude Doreen Edwards; three *s* two *d*. *Educ:* Newport Sec. Sch.; Leeds Univ.; Coll. of the Resurrection, Mirfield. Deacon 1944; Priest 1945. Asst Curate of: Usk, Mon, 1944–47; St George's, Camberwell, 1948–49; Chaplain, Woomera, S Australia, 1949–54; Rector, St Mary Magdalene's,

Adelaide, 1954–57; Priest in charge of Elizabeth, 1957–65; Missioner of St Peter's Coll. Mission, 1954–65; Bishop of North-West Australia, 1965–81. *Publication:* Bush Bishop (autobiography), 1980. *Recreation:* script writing. *Address:* Unit 20, DGV, 99 McCabe Street, Mosman Park, WA 6012, Australia. *Club:* Public Schools (Adelaide).

WITTE, Prof. William, FRSE; Professor of German in the University of Aberdeen, 1951–77; *b* 18 Feb. 1907; *o s* of W. G. J. and E. O. Witte; *m* 1937, Edith Mary Stenhouse Melvin; one *s* one *d.* *Educ:* Universities of Breslau, Munich, Berlin. MA, DLit (London); PhD (Aberdeen); FRSE 1978. Assistant, Department of German: Aberdeen, 1931–36; Edinburgh, 1936–37; Lecturer, Department of German, Aberdeen, 1937; Head of Dept, 1945; Reader in German, 1947. Gold Medal, Goethe Inst., 1971. Cross of the Order of Merit (Federal Republic of Germany), 1974. *Publications:* Modern German Prose Usage, 1937; Schiller, 1949; ed Schiller's Wallenstein, 1952; ed Two Stories by Thomas Mann, 1957; Schiller and Burns, and Other Essays, 1959; ed Schiller's Wallensteins Tod, 1962; ed Schiller's Maria Stuart, 1965; ed Goethe's Clavigo, 1973; contributions to collective works; articles in Modern Language Review, German Life and Letters, Oxford German Studies, Publications of the English Goethe Society, Publications of the Carlyle Soc., Aberdeen Univ. Rev., Wisconsin Monatshefte, Schiller-Jahrbuch, Forum for Modern Language Studies, Encyclopædia Britannica, etc. *Recreation:* gardening. *Address:* 41 Beechgrove Terrace, Aberdeen AB2 4DS. *T:* Aberdeen (0224) 643799.

WITTEVEEN, Dr (Hendrikus) Johannes, Commander, Order of Netherlands Lion; Commander, Order of Orange Nassau; Board Member: Royal Dutch Petroleum Co., 1971–73 and 1978–89; Robeco, 1971–73 and since 1979 (Adviser, 1971–73); Nationale-Nederlanden, since 1979; *b* Zeist, Netherlands, 12 June 1921; *m* 1949, Liesbeth de Vries Feyens; two *s* one *d.* *Educ:* Univ. Rotterdam (DrEcons). Central Planning Bureau, 1947–48; Prof., Univ. Rotterdam, 1948–63; Mem. Netherlands Parlt, First Chamber, 1959–63 and 1971–73, and Second Chamber, 1965–67; Minister of Finance, Netherlands, 1963–65 and 1967–71; First Deputy Prime Minister, 1967–71; Managing Director, IMF, 1973–78. Chm., Group of Thirty, 1979–85, Hon. Chm., 1985–; Member: Internat. Council, Morgan Guaranty Trust Co. of NY, 1978–85; European Adv. Council, General Motors, 1978–91; Bd Mem., Thyssen-Bornemisza NV, 1978–86; Advr for Internat. Affairs, Amro Bank, Amsterdam, 1979–90. Grand Cross, Order of Crown (Belgium); Order of Oak Wreath (Luxemburg); Order of Merit (Fed. Republic Germany). *Publications:* Loonshoogte en Werkgelegenheid, 1947; Growth and Business Cycles, 1954; articles in Economische Statistische Berichten, Euromoney. *Recreation:* hiking. *Address:* 2243 HL Wassenaar, Waldeck Pyrmontlaan 15, The Netherlands.

WITTON-DAVIES, Ven. Carlyle; Archdeacon Emeritus of Oxford, since 1985; *b* 10 June 1913; *s* of late Prof. T. Witton Davies, DD, and Hilda Mabel Witton Davies (*née* Everett); *m* 1941, Mary Rees, BA, *o d* of late Canon W. J. Rees, St Asaph, Clwyd; three *s* four *d.* *Educ:* Friars School, Bangor; University College of N Wales, Bangor; Exeter College, Oxford; Cuddesdon College, Oxford; Hebrew University, Jerusalem. Exhib., University Coll. of N Wales, Bangor, 1930–34; BA (Wales), 1st Cl. Hons Hebrew, 1934; BA (Oxon), 2nd Cl. Hons Theology, 1937; Junior Hall Houghton Septuagint Prize, Oxford, 1938, Senior, 1939; MA (Oxon), 1940; Deacon, 1937, Priest, 1938, St Asaph; Assistant Curate, Buckley, 1937–40; Subwarden, St Michael's College, Llandaff, 1940–44; Examining Chaplain to Bishop of Monmouth, 1940–44; Adviser on Judaica to Anglican Bishop in Jerusalem, 1944–49; Examining Chaplain to Bishop in Jerusalem, 1945–49; Canon Residentiary of Nazareth in St George's Collegiate Church, Jerusalem, 1947–49; Dean and Precentor of St David's Cathedral, 1949–57; Examining Chaplain to Bishop of St David's, 1950–57; Chaplain, Order of St John of Jerusalem, 1954–; Archdeacon of Oxford and Canon of Christ Church, Oxford, 1957–82, Sub Dean, 1972–82 (Student Emeritus of Christ Church, 1982–); Examining Chaplain to Bishop of Oxford, 1965–82. Chairman, Council of Christians and Jews, 1957–78 (Vice-Pres., 1978–); Mem., Archbishops' Commn on Crown Appointments, 1962–64; Censor Theologiae, Christ Church, 1972–75, 1978–80; Member, Convocation of Canterbury, and Church Assembly/General Synod of C of E, 1957–75, 1978–80. First recipient, Sir Sigmund Sternberg Award, 1979. *Publications:* Journey of a Lifetime, 1962; (part translated) Martin Buber's Hasidism, 1948; (translated) Martin Buber's The Prophetic Faith, 1949; contrib. to Oxford Dictionary of the Christian Church, 1957; contrib. to The Mission of Israel, 1963. *Recreations:* music, lawn tennis, swimming, travel. *Address:* 199 Divinity Road, Oxford OX4 1LS. *T:* Oxford (0865) 247301.

WITTY, (John) David, CBE 1985; Director, Great Portland Estates PLC, since 1987; Lawyer Member, London Rent Assessment Panel, since 1984; *b* 1 Oct. 1924; *s* of late Harold Witty and Olive Witty, Beverley; *m* 1955, Doreen Hanlan; one *s.* *Educ:* Beverley Grammar Sch.; Balliol Coll., Oxford (MA). Served War, RN, 1943–46. Asst Town Clerk, Beverley, 1951–53; Asst Solicitor: Essex CC, 1953–54; Hornsey, 1954–60; Dep. Town Clerk: Kingston upon Thames, 1960–65; Merton, 1965–67; Asst Chief Exec., Westminster, 1967–77, Chief Exec., 1977–84. Hon. Sec., London Boroughs Assoc., 1978–84. Chm., London Enterprise Property Co., 1984–85. Order of Infante D. Henrique (Portugal), 1978; Order of Right Hand (Nepal), 1980; Order of King Abdul Aziz (Saudi Arabia), 1981; Order of Oman, 1982; Order of Orange-Nassau, 1982. *Recreation:* golf. *Address:* 14 River House, The Terrace, Barnes, SW13 0NR.

WIX, Ethel Rose; Special Commissioner of Income Tax, 1977–86; *b* 1 Nov. 1921; *d* of Michael Wix and Anna Wix (*née* Snyder). *Educ:* Henrietta Barnett Sch.; Cheltenham Ladies' Coll.; University Coll. London (BA Hons 1942); Hull University Coll. (Cert Ed 1943). Special Operations Executive, 1944–45; lived in S Africa, 1948–54; work for S African Inst. of Race Relations, 1950–54; Africa Bureau, London, 1955–56; Solicitor of Supreme Court, 1960; Partner, Herbert Oppenheimer, Nathan & Vandyk, 1960–75; General Commissioner of Income Tax, 1976–78. Mem., Arbitrators Panel, The Securities Assoc. Consumer Arbitration Scheme, 1988–. Member: Exec. Cttee, Jewish Mus., 1987– (Hon. Treas., 1987–89); Exec. Cttee, Inst. of Jewish Affairs, 1990–; Liby Cttee, Oxford Centre for Postgrad. Hebrew Studies, 1990–. Mem. Council: Richmond Fellowship, 1975–85; Trinity Hospice, Clapham, 1981–90; Cheltenham Ladies' Coll., 1983– (Vice-Chm., 1990–); St Christopher's Hospice, 1985–; Clifton Coll., 1987–; Governor, Warwick Schs Foundn, 1988–90. *Publications:* papers on Cost of Living, 1951, and Industrial Feeding Facilities, 1953, for S African Inst. of Race Relations; summary of Royal Commn Report on E Africa, 1956, for Africa Bureau. *Recreations:* reading, cooking, theatre. *Address:* 5 Phillimore Gardens, W8 7QG. *T:* 071–937 8899. *Clubs:* Reform, University Women's, Special Forces.

WODEHOUSE, family name of **Earl of Kimberley.**

WODEHOUSE, Lord; John Armine Wodehouse; Principal Systems Programmer, Glaxo, since 1987 (Systems Programmer, since 1979); *b* 15 Jan. 1951; *s* and *heir* of 4th Earl of Kimberley, *qv*; *m* 1973, Hon. Carol Palmer, (Rev. Lady Wodehouse), MA (Oxon), PGCE, *er d* of 3rd Baron Palmer, OBE; one *s* one *d.* *Educ:* Eton; Univ. of East Anglia. BSc (Chemistry) 1973; MSc (Physical Organic Chemistry) 1974. FRSA. Research Chemist, Glaxo, 1974–79. Chm., UK Info Users Gp, 1981–83. Fellow, British Interplanetary Soc., 1984 (Associate Fellow, 1981–83). MBCS 1988. *Recreations:* interest in spaceflight, photography, computing, fantasy role playing games. *Heir:* *s* David Simon John Wodehouse, *b* 10 Oct. 1978. *Address:* Derry House, North End, Henley-on-Thames, Oxon RG9 6LQ.

WOGAN, Michael Terence, (Terry); jobbing broadcaster; *b* 3 Aug. 1938; *s* of late Michael Thomas and Rose Wogan; *m* 1965, Helen Joyce; two *s* one *d.* *Educ:* Crescent Coll., Limerick, Ireland; Belvedere Coll., Dublin. Joined RTE as Announcer, 1963, Sen. Announcer, 1964–66; various programmes for BBC Radio, 1965–67; Late Night Extra, BBC Radio, 1967–69; The Terry Wogan Show, BBC Radio One, 1969–72, BBC Radio Two, 1972–84; television shows include: Lunchtime with Wogan, ATV; BBC: Come Dancing; Song for Europe; The Eurovision Song Contest; Children in Need; Wogan's Guide to the BBC; Blankety-Blank; Wogan. Awards include: Pye Radio Award, 1980; Radio Industries Award (Radio Personality 3 times; TV Personality, 1982, 1984, 1985, 1987); TV Times TV Personality of the Year (10 times); Daily Express Award (twice); Carl Alan Award (3 times); Variety Club of GB: Special Award, 1982; Showbusiness Personality, 1984; Radio Personality of last 21 yrs, Daily Mail Nat. Radio Awards, 1988. *Publications:* Banjaxed, 1979; The Day Job, 1981; To Horse, To Horse, 1982; Wogan on Wogan, 1987; Wogan's Ireland, 1988. *Recreations:* tennis, golf, swimming, reading, writing. *Address:* c/o Jo Gurnett, 2 New Kings Road, SW6 4SA. *Clubs:* Lord's Taverners; London Irish Rugby Football; Temple Golf (Henley-on-Thames).

WOLEDGE, Brian, FBA 1989; Emeritus Professor of French Language and Literature, University of London; Fielden Professor of French, University College, London, 1939–71; Hon. Research Fellow, University College London; *b* 16 Aug. 1904; *m* 1933, Christine Mary Craven; one *s* one *d.* *Educ:* Leeds Boys' Modern School; University of Leeds. BA (Leeds) 1926; MA (Leeds) 1928; Docteur de l'Université de Paris, 1930; Asst Lecturer in French, University College, Hull, 1930–32; Lecturer in French, University of Aberdeen, 1932–39. Visiting Andrew Mellon Professor of French, University of Pittsburg, 1967. Docteur *hc* de l'Université d'Aix-Marseille, 1970. *Publications:* L'Atre périlleux; études sur les manuscrits, la langue et l'importance littéraire du poème, 1930; L'Atre périlleux, roman de la Table ronde (Les Classiques français du moyen âge 76), 1935; Bibliographie des romans et nouvelles en prose française antérieurs à 1500, 1954, repr. 1975, Supplement 1975; The Penguin Book of French Verse, Vol. 1, To the Fifteenth Century, 1961; Répertoire des premiers textes en prose française, 842–1210 (with H. P. Clive), 1964; La Syntaxe des substantifs chez Chrétien de Troyes, 1979; Commentaire sur Yvain (Le Chevalier au Lion) de Chrétien de Troyes, Vol. 1, 1986, Vol. 2, 1988. *Address:* 28a Dobbins Lane, Wendover, Aylesbury, Bucks HP22 6DH. *T:* Wendover (0296) 622188.

WOLF, Prof. Peter Otto, FEng; FICE; FIWEM; FRMetS; FASCE; Consultant; Professor and Head of Department of Civil Engineering, 1966–82, The City University, London, now Professor Emeritus; *b* 9 May 1918; *s* of Richard Wolf and Dora (*née* Bondy); *m* 1st, 1944, Jennie Robinson; two *s* one *d*; 2nd, 1977, Janet Elizabeth Robertson. *Educ:* University of London (BScEng). Assistant under agreement to C. E. Farren, Cons. Engr, 1941–44; Civilian Asst, a Dept of the War Office, 1944–45; Engineer (Chief Designer, Loch Sloy Project), under James Williamson, Cons. Engr, 1945–47; Engineer for Mullardoch Dam (Affric Project), John Cochrane & Sons Ltd, 1947–49; Imperial College of Science and Technology: Lectr in Fluid Mechanics and Hydraulic Engrg, 1949–55; Reader in Hydrology in Univ. of London, 1955–66. Private consultancy, London, 1950–. Chm., Cttee on Flood Protection Res., MAFF, 1984–85; Vice-Chm., Standing Cttee on Natural Hazards, Hazards Forum, 1990–. Visiting Professor: Stanford Univ., Calif, 1959–60, 1961–64; Cornell Univ., 1963. Pres., British Hydrol Soc., 1987–89. Hon. Mem., BHRA, 1984–. Hon. DrIng Technological Univ. of Dresden, 1986. *Publications:* trans. and ed, Engineering Fluid Mechanics, by Charles Jaeger, 1956; papers in Proc. ICE, Jl IWE, UNESCO Reports, UNESCO Nature and Resources, Proc. Internat. Water Resources Assoc., etc. *Recreations:* classical music, reading, ski-ing, sailing, walking. *Address:* 69 Shepherds Hill, N6 5RE. *T:* 081–340 6638. *Club:* Athenæum.

WOLFE, William Cuthbertson; Member, SNP National Council, since 1991; *b* 22 Feb. 1924; *s* of late Major Tom Wolfe, TD, and Katie Cuthbertson; *m* 1953, Arna Mary, *d* of late Dr Melville Dinwiddie, CBE, DSO, MC; two *s* two *d.* *Educ:* Bathgate Academy; George Watson's Coll., Edinburgh. CA. Army service, 1942–47, NW Europe and Far East; Air OP Pilot. Hon. Publications Treas., Saltire Society, 1953–60; Scout County Comr, West Lothian, 1960–64; Hon. Pres. (Rector), Students' Assoc., Heriot-Watt Univ., 1966–69. Contested (SNP): West Lothian, 1962, 1964, 1966, 1970, Feb. and Oct. 1974, 1979; North Edinburgh, Nov. 1973; Chm., SNP, 1969–79, Pres., 1980–82. Treas., Scottish CND, 1982–85; Sec., Scottish Poetry Liby, 1985–91. *Publication:* Scotland Lives, 1973. *Address:* Burnside Forge, Burnside Road, Bathgate, W Lothian EH48 4PU. *T:* Bathgate (0506) 54785.

WOLFENDALE, Prof. Arnold Whittaker, PhD, DSc; FRS 1977; FInstP, FRAS; Professor of Physics, University of Durham, since 1965; Astronomer Royal, since 1991; *b* 25 June 1927; *s* of Arnold Wolfendale and Doris Wolfendale; *m* 1951, Audrey Darby; twin *s.* *Educ:* Univ. of Manchester (BSc Physics 1st Cl. Hons 1948, PhD 1953, DSc 1970). FInstP 1958; FRAS 1973. Asst Lectr, Univ. of Manchester, 1951, Lectr, 1954; Univ. of Durham: Lectr, 1956; Sen. Lectr, 1959; Reader in Physics, 1963; Head of Dept, 1973–77, 1980–83, 1986–89. Vis. Lectr, Univ. of Celon, 1952; Vis. Prof., Univ. of Hong Kong, 1977–78. Lectures: H. C. Bhuyan Meml, Gauhati Univ., 1978; B. B. Roy Meml, Calcutta Univ., 1978; Norman Lockyer, Exeter Univ., 1978; E. A. Milne, Oxford Univ., 1982; Rochester, Durham Univ., 1990. Home Office, Civil Defence, later Regl Scientific Advr, 1956–84. Chm., Northern Reg. Action Cttee, Manpower Services Commn's Job Creation Prog., 1975–78; Mem., SERC, 1988– (Chm., APS Bd). Chm., Cosmic Ray Commn, IUPAP, 1982–84. Pres., RAS, 1981–83. Pres., Durham Univ. Soc. of Fellows, 1988–; For. Fellow, INSA, 1990; Indian Nat. Acad. Scis. Hon. DSc: Univ. of Potchefstroom for Christian Higher Educn, 1989; Univ. of Lodz, 1989. Silver Jubilee Medal, 1977; Univ. of Turku Medal, 1987. *Publications:* Cosmic Rays, 1963; (ed) Cosmic Rays at Ground Level, 1973; (ed) Origin of Cosmic Rays, 1974; (ed jtly and contrib.) Origin of Cosmic Rays, 1981; (ed) Gamma Ray Astronomy, 1981; (ed) Progress in Cosmology, 1982; (with P. V. Ramana Murthy) Gamma Ray Astronomy, 1986; (with F. R. Stephenson) Secular Solar and Geomagnetic Variations in the last 1,000 years, 1988; original papers on studies of cosmic radiation and aspects of astrophysics. *Recreations:* walking, gardening, foreign travel. *Address:* Ansford, Potters Bank, Durham. *T:* Durham (091) 3845642.

WOLFF, Prof. Heinz Siegfried, FIBiol; Director, Brunel Institute for Bioengineering, Brunel University, since 1983; *b* 29 April 1928; *s* of Oswald Wolff and Margot (*née* Saalfeld); *m* 1953, Joan Eleanor Stephenson; two *s.* *Educ:* City of Oxford Sch.; University Coll. London (BSc(Hons)Physiology) (Fellow, 1987). National Institute for Medical Research: Div. of Human Physiology, 1954–62; Hd, Div. of Biomedical Engrg, 1962–70; Hd, Bioengrg Div., Clinical Res. Centre of MRC, 1970–83. European Space Agency: Chm., Life Science Working Gp, 1976–82; Mem., Sci. Adv. Cttee, 1978–82; Chm., Microgravity Adv. Cttee, 1982–91. Chm., Microgravity Panel, Brit. Nat. Space Centre, 1986–87. Pres., Sch. Natural Sci. Soc., 1988–. FRSA; Hon. Fellow, Ergonomics Soc., 1991. *Television series:* BBC TV Young Scientist of the Year (contributor), 1968–81; BBC2: Royal Instn Christmas Lectures, 1975; Great Egg Race, 1978–; Great Experiments,

1985–86. Harding Award, Action Res. for the Crippled Child/RADAR, 1989. *Publications:* Biomedical Engineering, 1969 (German, French, Japanese and Spanish trans, 1970–72); about 120 papers in sci. jls and contribs to books. *Recreations:* working, lecturing to children, dignified practical joking. *Address:* Brunel Institute for Bioengineering, Brunel University, Uxbridge, Mddx UB8 3PH.

WOLFF, Michael, PPCSD; FRSA; Chairman, Addison Design Consultants, since 1987; Member, Board of Trustees, the Hunger Project, since 1979; *b* 12 Nov. 1933; *s* of Serge Wolff and Mary (*née* Gordon); *m* 1st, 1976, Susan Kent (marr. diss.); one *d*; 2nd, 1989, Martha Newhouse. *Educ:* Gresham's Sch., Holt, Norfolk; Architectural Association Sch. of Architecture. Designer: Sir William Crawford & Partners, 1957–61; BBC Television, 1961–62; Main Wolff & Partners, 1964–65; with Wolff Olins Ltd as a founder and Creative Director, 1965–83. President: D & AD, 1971; SIAD, then CSD, 1985–87. *Recreations:* enjoying a family, seeing. *Address:* 9 Cumberland Gardens, WC1. *T:* 071–833 0007; (office) 60 Britton Street, EC1M 5NA. *T:* 071–250 1887.

WOLFF, Prof. Otto Herbert, CBE 1985; MD, FRCP; Nuffield Professor of Child Health, University of London, 1965–85, now Emeritus Professor; Dean of the Institute of Child Health, 1982–85; *b* 10 Jan. 1920; *s* of Dr H. A. J. Wolff; *m* 1952, Dr Jill Freeborough; one *s* one *d*. *Educ:* Peterhouse, Cambridge; University College Hospital, London. Lieut and Capt. RAMC, 1944–47. Resident Medical Officer, Registrar and Sen. Med. Registrar, Birmingham Children's Hospital, 1948–51; Lecturer, Sen. Lectr, Reader, Dept of Pædiatrics and Child Health, Univ. of Birmingham, 1951–64. Senator, London Univ.; Representative of London Univ. on GMC. Past Pres., British Pædiatric Assoc.; Member: Royal Society of Medicine; American Pædiatric Society; New York Academy of Sciences; Amer. Academy of Pediatrics; European Soc. for Paediatric Research; European Soc. for Paediatric Gastroenterology; Deutsche Akad. der Naturforscher Leopoldina. Corresp. Member: Société Française de Pédiatrie; Société Suisse de Pédiatrie; Osterreichische Gesellschaft für Kinderheilkunde; Società Italiana di Pediatria; Deutsche Gesellschaft für Kinderheilkunde; Fellow, Indian Acad. of Pediatrics. Chm. of Trustees, Child-to-Child Charity, 1989–. Dawson Williams Meml Prize, BMA, 1984; Medal, Assoc. Française pour le Dépistage et la Prévention des Maladies Métaboliques et des Handicaps de l'Enfant, 1986; Harding Award, Action Res. for Crippled Child, 1987; James Spence Medal, BPA, 1988. *Publications:* chapter on Disturbances of Serum Lipoproteins in Endocrine and Genetic Diseases of Childhood (ed L. I. Gardner); chapter on Obesity in Recent Advances in Paediatrics (ed David Hull); articles in Lancet, British Medical Journal, Archives of Disease in Childhood, Quarterly Jl of Medicine, etc. *Recreation:* music. *Address:* 53 Danbury Street, N1 8LE. *T:* 071–226 0748.

WOLFF, Rosemary Langley; Member, Police Complaints Authority, since 1985 (Member, Police Complaints Board, 1977–85); *b* 10 July 1926; *er d* of late A. C. V. Clarkson; *m* 1956, Michael Wolff, JP (*d* 1976); two *d*. *Educ:* Haberdashers' Aske's Sch. Mem., Community Relations Commn, 1973–77. Manager of various primary schs in North Kensington and Tower Hamlets, 1963–; Governor, City College; Chm., Conservative Contact Group, 1973–77; Mem., Managing Cttee, Working Ladies' Guild. *Address:* 13 Holland Park, W11 3TH. *T:* 071–727 9051.

WOLFSON, family name of **Barons Wolfson** and **Wolfson of Sunningdale.**

WOLFSON, Baron *cr* 1985 (Life Peer), of Marylebone in the City of Westminster; **Leonard Gordon Wolfson,** Bt 1962; Kt 1977; Chairman, since 1972, and Founder Trustee, since 1955, Wolfson Foundation; Chairman: Great Universal Stores, since 1981 (Managing Director, 1962; Director, 1952); Burberrys Ltd, since 1978; *b* 11 Nov. 1927; *s* of Sir Isaac Wolfson, 1st Bt, FRS (*d* 1991) and Edith Specterman (*d* 1981); *m* 1949, Ruth (marr. diss. 1991), *d* of E. A. Sterling; four *d*; *m* 1991, Estelle, *widow* of Michael Jackson, FCA. *Educ:* King's School, Worcester. Hon. Fellow: St Catherine's Coll., Oxford; Wolfson Coll., Cambridge; Wolfson Coll., Oxford; Worcester Coll., Oxford; UCL; LSHTM 1985; QMC 1985; Imperial Coll., 1991. Trustee, Imperial War Mus., 1988–. Patron, Royal College of Surgeons, 1976; Hon. FRCS 1988; Hon. FRCP 1977; Hon. FBA 1986. Hon. DCL: Oxon, 1972; East Anglia, 1986; Hon. LLD: Strathclyde, 1972; Dundee, 1979; Cantab, 1982; London, 1982; Hon. DSc: Hull, 1977; Wales, 1984; Hon. PhD: Tel Aviv, 1971; Hebrew Univ., 1978; Weizmann Inst., 1988; Hon. DHL Bar Ilan Univ., 1983; DUniv Surrey, 1990. Winston Churchill Award, 1989. *Recreations:* history, economics. *Heir* (to baronetcy): none. *Address:* Universal House, 251 Tottenham Court Road, W1A 1BZ.

WOLFSON OF SUNNINGDALE, Baron *cr* 1991 (Life Peer), of Trevose in the County of Cornwall; **David Wolfson,** Kt 1984; Chairman, Next plc, since 1990; *b* 9 Nov. 1935; *s* of Charles Wolfson and Hylda Wolfson; *m* 1st, 1962, Patricia E. Rawlings, *qv* (marr. diss. 1967); 2nd, 1967, Susan E. Davis; two *s* one *d*. *Educ:* Clifton Coll.; Trinity Coll., Cambridge (MA); Stanford Univ., California (MBA). Great Universal Stores, 1960–78, Director 1973–78; Secretary to Shadow Cabinet, 1978–79; Chief of Staff, Political Office, 10 Downing Street, 1979–85. Chm., Alexon Group PLC (formerly Steinberg Group PLC), 1982–86; non-executive Director: Stewart Wrightson Holdings PLC, 1985–87; Next, 1989–. Hon. Fellow, Hughes Hall, Cambridge, 1989. Hon. FRCR 1978; Hon. FRCOG 1989. *Recreations:* golf, bridge. *Clubs:* Portland; Sunningdale; Woburn Golf.

WOLFSON, Sir Brian (Gordon), Kt 1990; Chairman, Wembley PLC, since 1986; Chairman, National Training Task Force (formerly Training Commission, then Training Agency), since 1988; *b* 2 Aug. 1935; *s* of Gabriel and Eve Wolfson; *m* 1958, Helen, *d* of late Lewis Grodner; one *s* one *d*. *Educ:* Liverpool Coll.; Liverpool Univ. Joined Granada Group, 1961, Jt Man. Dir, 1967–70; Chm., Anglo Nordic Holdings, 1976–87; Director: Kepner Tregoe Inc., USA, 1980–; Charles Ede Ltd, London, 1971–. Vice-Pres., BIM, 1988– (Chm., 1986–88). First non-North American World Pres., Young Presidents' Orgn, 1979–80; Mem., NEDC, 1989– (Chm., Cttee on leisure, 1987). University of Pennsylvania: Mem. Adv. Bd, Wharton Center for Internat. Management Studies, 1980–; Bd, Wharton Exec. Library, Wharton Sch., 1980–; Bd, Joseph H. Lauder Inst., 1983–. FBIM 1969, CBIM 1970; Fellow, Inst BE. Hon. DBA, 1989. *Recreations:* archaeological digs, making wildlife films. *Address:* Wembley PLC, The Wembley Stadium, Wembley HA9 0DW.

WOLFSON, (Geoffrey) Mark; MP (C) Sevenoaks, since 1979; Partner, John Adair and Associates, since 1988; *b* 7 April 1934; *s* of late Captain V. Wolfson, OBE, VRD, RNR, and Dorothy Mary Wolfson; *m* 1965, Edna Webb (*née* Hardman); two *s*. *Educ:* Eton Coll.; Pembroke Coll., Cambridge (MA). Served Royal Navy, 1952–54; Cambridge, 1954–57; Teacher in Canada, 1958–59; Warden, Brathay Hall Centre, Westmorland, 1962–66; Head of Youth Services, Industrial Soc., 1966–69; Hd of Personnel, 1970–85, Dir, 1973–88, Hambros Bank. PPS to Minister of State for NI, 1983–84, to Minister of State for Defence Procurement, 1984–85, to Minister of State for Armed Forces, 1987–88. Officer, Cons. Backbench Employment Cttee, 1981–83. Mem., Parly Human Rights Delegn to Nicaragua, 1982, El Salvador and Baltic States, 1990. FRSA 1990.

WOLFSON, Mark; *see* Wolfson, G. M.

WOLKIND, Jack, CBE 1978; Chairman, London World Trade Centre, since 1991; *b* 16 Feb. 1920; *s* of Samuel and Golda Wolkind; *m* 1945, Bena Sternfeld; two *s* one *d*. *Educ:* Mile End Central Sch.; King's Coll., London. LLB Hons, LLM (London). Admitted Solicitor, 1953. Army service to 1945. Dep. Town Clerk and Solicitor, Stepney Borough Council, 1952–65; Chief Exec. (formerly Town Clerk), Tower Hamlets, 1964–85; Chief Exec., St Katharine by the Tower Ltd, 1990–91 (Dir, 1985–). Mem., London Residuary Body. Indep. Mem., Kessler Foundn, 1986–; Chm., Claredale Housing Assoc. Ltd, 1987–. Governor: Toynbee Hall, 1981–; QMC, Univ. of London, 1981–90 (Hon. Fellow, 1985). FRSA 1980; Fellow, City of London Poly., 1985. *Recreations:* reading, music. *Address:* International House, 1 St Katharine's Way, E1 9UN. *Club:* City Livery.

WOLLHEIM, Prof. Richard Arthur, FBA 1972; Mills Professor, University of California, Berkeley, since 1985; Professor of Philosophy and the Humanities, University of California, Davis, since 1989; Emeritus Grote Professor in the University of London; *b* 5 May 1923; *s* of Eric Wollheim; *m* 1st, 1950, Anne, *yr d* of Lieutenant-Colonel E. G. H. Powell (marr. diss. 1967); two *s*; 2nd, 1969, Mary Day, *er d* of Robert S. Lanier, NYC; one *d*. *Educ:* Westminster School; Balliol College, Oxford (MA). Served in the Army, N Europe, 1942–45 (POW during Aug. 1944). Assistant Lecturer in Philosophy, University College, London, 1949; Lecturer, 1951; Reader, 1960; Grote Prof. of Philosophy of Mind and Logic in Univ. of London, 1963–82; Prof. of Philosophy, Columbia Univ., 1982–85. Visiting Professor: Columbia Univ., 1959–60, 1970; Visva-Bharati Univ., Santiniketan, India, 1968; Univ. of Minnesota, 1972; Graduate Centre, City Univ. of NY, 1975; Univ. of California, Berkeley, 1981; Harvard Univ., 1982; Sarah Lawrence Coll., 1987; Univ. of Guelph, 1988; Washington Univ., St Louis, 1989. Lectures: Power, Univ. of Sydney, 1972; Leslie Stephen, Univ. of Cambridge, 1979; William James, Harvard Univ., 1982; Andrew W. Mellon, Nat. Gall., Washington, 1984; Cassirer, Yale Univ. Pres., Aristotelian Soc., 1967–68; Vice-Pres., British Soc. of Aesthetics, 1969–. Mem., American Acad. of Arts and Scis, 1986. Hon. Affiliate, British Psychoanalytical Soc. *Publications:* F. H. Bradley, 1959, rev. edn 1969; Socialism and Culture, 1961; On Drawing an Object (Inaugural Lecture), 1965; Art and its Objects, 1968, 2nd edn with suppl. essays, 1980; A Family Romance (fiction), 1969; Freud, 1971; On Art and the Mind (essays and lectures), 1973; The Good Self and the Bad Self (Dawes Hicks lecture), 1976; The Sheep and the Ceremony (Leslie Stephen lecture), 1979; The Thread of Life, 1984; Painting as an Art, 1987; On Painting and the Self (essays and lectures), 1992; edited: F. H. Bradley, Ethical Studies, 1961; Hume on Religion, 1963; F. H. Bradley, Appearance and Reality, 1968; Adrian Stokes, selected writings, 1972; Freud, a collection of critical essays, 1974; J. S. Mill, Three Essays, 1975; (with Jim Hopkins) Philosophical Essays on Freud, 1982; articles in anthologies, philosophical and literary jls. *Address:* 20 Ashchurch Park Villas, W12 9SP; 1814 Marin Avenue, Berkeley, Calif 94707, USA.

WOLLONGONG, Bishop of; *see* Goodhew, Rt Rev. R. H.

WOLMER, Viscount; William Lewis Palmer; *b* 1 Sept. 1971; *s* and *heir* of 4th Earl of Selborne, *qv*. *Educ:* Eton Coll. *Address:* Temple Manor, Selborne, Alton, Hants GU34 3LR.

WOLPERT, Prof. Lewis, CBE 1990; DIC, PhD; FRS 1980; Professor of Biology as Applied to Medicine, University College and Middlesex School of Medicine, University College London (formerly at Middlesex Hospital Medical School), since 1966; *b* 19 Oct. 1929; *s* of William and Sarah Wolpert; *m* 1961; two *s* two *d*. *Educ:* King Edward's Sch., Johannesburg; Univ. of Witwatersrand (BScEng); Imperial Coll., London (DIC); King's Coll., London (PhD). Personal Asst to Director of Building Research Inst., S African Council for Scientific and Industrial Research, 1951–52; Engineer, Israel Water Planning Dept, 1953–54; King's College, London: Asst Lectr in Zoology, 1958–60; Lectr in Zoology, 1960–64; Reader in Zoology, 1964–66; Hd of Dept of Biology as Applied to Medicine, later Dept of Anatomy and Biology as Applied to Medicine, Middlesex Hosp. Med. Sch., 1966–87. MRC: Mem. Council, 1984–88; Mem., 1982–88, Chm., 1984–88, Cell Bd; Chm., Scientific Inf. Cttee, Royal Soc., 1983–; Chm., Biology Concerted Action Cttee, EEC, 1988–; President: British Soc. for Cell Biology, 1985–; Inst. of Information Scientists, 1986–87. Lectures: Steinhaus, Univ. of California at Irvine, 1980; van der Horst, Univ. of Witwatersrand, Johannesburg, 1981; Bidder, Soc. for Experimental Biology, Leicester, 1982; Swirling, Dana-Faber, Boston, 1985; Lloyd-Roberts, RCP, 1986; Royal Instn Christmas Lectures, 1986; R. G. Williams, Univ. of Pennsylvania, 1988; Bernal, Birkbeck Coll., 1989; Radcliffe, Warwick Univ., 1990; Redfearn, Leicester, 1991; Wade, Southampton, 1991. Presenter, Antenna, BBC2, 1987–88; interviews with scientists, Radio 3, 1981–; documentaries: The Dark Lady of DNA; The Virgin Fathers of the Calculus. Hon. MRCP, 1986. Scientific Medal, Zoological Soc., 1968. *Publications:* A Passion for Science (with A. Richards), 1988; Triumph of the Embryo, 1991; articles on cell and developmental biology in scientific jls. *Recreation:* tennis. *Address:* Department of Anatomy and Developmental Biology, University College and Middlesex School of Medicine, Cleveland Street, W1P 6DB.

WOLRIGE-GORDON, Patrick; *b* 10 Aug. 1935; *s* of late Captain Robert Wolrige-Gordon, MC and Joan Wolrige-Gordon; *m* 1962, Anne, *o d* of late Peter D. Howard and Mrs Howard; one *s* two *d*. *Educ:* Eton; New College, Oxford. MP (C) Aberdeenshire East, Nov. 1958–Feb. 1974. Liveryman Worshipful Company of Wheelwrights, 1966. *Recreations:* reading, golf, music. *Address:* Ythan Lodge, Newburgh, Aberdeenshire. *Club:* Royal Over-Seas League.

See also John MacLeod of MacLeod.

WOLSELEY, Sir Charles Garnet Richard Mark, 11th Bt, *cr* 1628; Consultant, Smiths Gore, Chartered Surveyors, since 1987 (Associate Partner, 1974; Partner, 1979–87); *b* 16 June 1944; *s* of Capt. Stephen Garnet Hubert Francis Wolseley, Royal Artillery (*d* 1944, of wounds received in action), and of Pamela, *yr d* of late Capt. F. Barry and Mrs Lavinia Power, Wolseley Park, Rugeley, Staffs; *S* grandfather, Sir Edric Charles Joseph Wolseley, 10th Bt, 1954; *m* 1st, 1968, Anita Maria (marr. diss. 1984), *er d* of late H. J. Fried, Epsom, Surrey; one *s* three *d*; 2nd, 1984, Mrs Imogene Brown. *Educ:* St Bede's School, near Stafford; Ampleforth College, York. FRICS. *Recreations:* shooting, fishing, gardening. *Heir:* *s* Stephen Garnet Hugo Charles Wolseley, *b* 2 May 1980. *Address:* Wolseley Park, Rugeley, Staffs WS15 2TU. *T:* Rugeley (0889) 582346. *Clubs:* Farmers', Shikar; English XX Rifle (Bisley).

WOLSELEY, Sir Garnet, 12th Bt, *cr* 1744–45 (Ireland); emigrated to Ontario, Canada, 1951; *b* 27 May 1915; *s* of late Richard Bingham and Mary Alexandra Wolseley; *S* cousin (Rev. Sir William Augustus Wolseley), 1950; *m* 1950, Lillian Mary, *d* of late William Bertram Ellison, Wallasey. *Educ:* New Brighton Secondary Sch. Served War of 1939–45, Northants Regt, Madagascar, Sicily, Italy and Germany. Boot Repairer Manager, 1946. *Heir:* *kinsman* James Douglas Wolseley [*b* 17 Sept. 1937; *m* 1st, 1965, Patricia Lynn (marr. diss. 1971), *d* of William R. Hunter; 2nd, 1984, Mary Anne, *d* of Thomas G. Brown]. *Address:* 73 Dorothy Street, Brantford, Ontario, Canada. *T:* 753–7957.

WOLSTENCROFT, Alan, CB 1961; Director, 1974–87, and Chairman, 1979–84, National Counties Building Society; *b* 18 Oct. 1914; *yr s* of late Walter and Bertha Wolstencroft; *m* 1951, Ellen, *d* of late W. Tomlinson. *Educ:* Lancaster Royal Grammar

Sch.; Caius Coll., Cambridge (MA 1st Cl. Classical Tripos). Assistant Principal, GPO, 1936. Served War of 1939–45: Royal Engineers (Postal Section), France and Middle East. Principal GPO, 1945; Assistant Secretary, GPO, 1949; Secretary, Independent Television Authority, 1954; General Post Office: Director of Personnel, 1955; Director of Postal Services, 1957; Director of Radio Services, 1960–64; Deputy Director General, 1964–67; Man. Dir Posts, 1967, Posts and GIRO, 1968; Adviser on Special Projects to Chm. of Post Office Corporation, 1969–70; Sec. to Post Office, 1970–73; retired. *Address:* Green Court, 161 Long Lane, Tilehurst, Reading RG3 6YW.

WOLSTENHOLME, Sir Gordon (Ethelbert Ward), Kt 1976; OBE (mil.) 1944; MA, MB, BChir; MRCS, FRCP, FIBiol; Founder and Chairman, Action in International Medicine, since 1988; *b* Sheffield, 28 May 1913; *m* 1st; one *s* two *d*; 2nd; two *d*. *Educ:* Repton; Corpus Christi Coll., Cambridge; Middlesex Hosp. Med. Sch. Served with RAMC, 1940–47 (OBE); France, UK, ME and Central Mediterranean; specialist and advr in transfusion and resuscitation; OC Gen. Hosp. in Udine and Trieste; Dir, Ciba Foundn, 1949–78; Harveian Librarian, RCP, 1979–89; Fellow, Green Coll., Oxford, 1986–90. Mem., GMC, 1973–83; Chm., Genetic Manipulation Adv. Gp, 1976–78. Founder Mem. 1954, Treasurer 1955–61, Mem. Exec. Bd 1961–70, UK Cttee for WHO; Organizer and Advr, Haile Selassie I Prize Trust, 1963–74; Advr, La Trinidad Med. Centre, Caracas, 1969–78. Royal Society of Medicine: Hon. Sec. 1964–70; Pres. Library (Sci. Res) Sect., 1968–70; Chm. Working Party on Soc's Future, 1972–73; Pres., 1975–77, 1978; Zoological Society: Scientific Fellow and Vice-Pres.; Member: Finance Cttee, 1962–69; Council, 1962–66, 1967–70, 1976–80; Chm., Nuffield Inst. for Comparative Medicine, 1969–70; Chm. Governors, Inst. for Res. into Mental and Multiple Handicap, 1973–77. Founder Mem. 1950, Hon. Treasurer 1956–69, Renal Assoc. of GB; Chm. Congress Prog. Cttee, 1962–64, Mem. Finance Cttee 1968–72, Internat. Soc. for Endocrinology; Trustee and Mem. Res. Bd, Spastics' Soc., 1963–67; Founder Chm., European Soc. for Clinical Investigation, 1966–67 (Boerhaave Lectr, 1976); Mem. Council 1969–75, Sponsor 1976–, Inst. for Study of Drug Dependence; Dir, Nuffield Foundn Inquiry into Dental Educn, 1978–80; Chairman: Dental Res. Strategy Gp, 1986–89; Oral and Dental Res. Trust, 1989–. Member: Council, Westfield Coll., London Univ., 1965–73; Planning Bd, University College at Buckingham, 1969. Chm., Anglo-Ethiopian Soc., 1967–70. Emeritus Mem. Ct of Assistants, Soc. of Apothecaries, 1988– (Mem., 1969–88; Master, 1979–80; Chm., Faculty of Hist. and Philosophy of Med. and Pharmacy, 1973–75; Visitor, 1975–78); Chm., Skin Diseases Res. Fund, 1980–85. Vis. Prof., UCSD, 1982, 1983, 1984. Dir, IRL Press Ltd, 1980–88. Trustee, Foulkes Foundn; Trustee, 1978–90, Chm. Acad. Bd, 1978–88, St George's Univ. Sch. of Med., Grenada. Mem. Bd, Dahlem Konferenzen, 1978–90. Vice-Pres., ASLIB, 1979–82. Pres., Brit. Soc. Hist. Medicine, 1983–85. Patron, FRAME, 1977–. Hon. Life Governor, Middlesex Hosp., 1938. Fellow UCL, 1991; FRSA 1979. Hon. FACP, 1975; Hon. FDSRCS 1991; Hon. Fellow: Hunterian Soc., 1975 (Orator 1976); Royal Acad. of Med. in Ireland, 1976; European Soc. for Clinical Investigation, 1979; RSocMed, 1982; Faculty of Hist. Med. Pharm., 1982. Hon. Member: Swedish Soc. of Endocrinology, 1955; Soc. of Endocrinology, 1959; Swiss Acad. of Med. Sciences, 1975; Assoc. Med. Argentina, 1977; Internat. Assoc. for Dental Res., 1984; Osler Club, 1986 (Orator, 1986); Foreign Mem., Swedish Med. Soc., 1959; Hon. For. Mem., Amer. Acad. of Arts and Scis, 1981. Hon. LLD Cambridge, 1968; Hon. DTech Brunel, 1981; Hon. MD Grenada, 1982. Linnaeus Medal, Royal Swedish Acad. Sci., 1977; Pasteur Medal, Paris, 1982; Gold Medal: Perugia Univ., 1961; (class 1A) Italian Min. of Educn, 1961. Tito Lik, 1945; Chevalier, Légion d'Honneur, 1959; Star of Ethiopia, 1966. *Publications:* (ed) Ciba Foundation vols, 1950–78; Royal College of Physicians: Portraits, vol. I (ed with David Piper), 1964, vol. II (ed with John Kerslake), 1977; (ed with Valerie Luniewska) Munk's Roll, vol. VI, 1982, vol. VII, 1984, vol. VIII, 1989; (jtly) Portrait of Irish Medicine, 1984. *Recreations:* walking, photography. *Address:* 10 Wimpole Mews, W1M 7TF. *T:* 071–486 3884.

WOLSTENHOLME, Roy; County Treasurer, Surrey County Council, since 1988; *b* 1 Jan. 1936; *m* 1959, Mary R. Wolstenholme; one *s* two *d*. *Educ:* Stretford Grammar Sch.; Manchester College of Commerce. Stretford Bor. Council, 1952–61; Worcs CC, 1961–63; Worthing Bor. Council, 1963–65; Glos CC, 1965–68; Holland (Lincs) CC, 1968–74; Lincs CC, 1974–77; County Treas., Northumberland CC, 1977–88. *Recreations:* music, walking, gardening, *Address:* Surrey County Council, PO Box 5, County Hall, Kingston upon Thames KT1 2EA. *T:* 081–541 9200. *Club:* Royal Over-Seas League.

WOLTERS, Gwyneth Eleanor Mary; a Commissioner of Inland Revenue, 1971–78; *b* 21 Nov. 1918; *d* of late Prof. and Mrs A. W. Wolters. *Educ:* Abbey Sch., Reading; Reading Univ.; Newnham Coll., Cambridge (Class. Tripos; Hilda Richardson Prize). Temp. Admin. Asst, Min. of Works, 1941–47; Asst Principal, 1947–49, Principal, 1949–57, Asst Sec., 1957–71, Inland Revenue. *Address:* 45 Albert Road, Caversham, Reading. *T:* Reading (0734) 472605.

WOLTON, Harry; QC 1982; a Recorder, since 1985; *b* 1 Jan. 1938; *s* of late Harry William Wolton and Dorothy Beatrice Wolton; *m* 1971, Julie Rosina Josephine Lovell (*née* Mason); three *s*. *Educ:* King Edward's Sch., Birmingham; Univ. of Birmingham. Called to the Bar, Gray's Inn, 1969. *Recreations:* gardening, family, farming. *Address:* Armscote Farm, Armscote, Stratford upon Avon, Warwickshire CV37 8DQ. *T:* Ilmington (060882) 234; 10 St Luke's Street, Chelsea, SW3. *T:* 071–352 5056.

WOLTZ, Alan Edward; Chairman, London International Group, since 1985 (Chief Executive, 1985–91); *b* 29 Feb. 1932; *s* of Robert Woltz and Rose Woltz Katz; *m* 1977, Barbara Howell; three *s* one *d*. *Educ:* Dwight Morrow High Sch., Eaglewood, NJ; Wagner Coll., Staten Is, NY. Served US Army, Korea, 1952–54. Schmid Laboratories Inc.: Exec. Vice-Pres., 1971–74; Pres., 1974–78; Pres., LRC N America, 1978–79; Man. Dir and Chief Exec., London Internat. Gp, 1979–85. *Recreations:* golf, swimming. *Address:* London International Group, 35 New Bridge Street, EC4V 6BJ. *T:* 071–489 1977. *Clubs:* Wentworth Golf; Metropolitan (NY).

WOLVERHAMPTON, Bishop Suffragan of, since 1985; **Rt. Rev. Christopher John Mayfield;** *b* 18 Dec. 1935; *s* of Dr Roger Bolton Mayfield and Muriel Eileen Mayfield; *m* 1962, Caroline Ann Roberts; two *s* one *d*. *Educ:* Sedbergh School; Gonville and Caius Coll., Cambridge (MA 1961); Linacre House, Oxford (Dip. Theology). Deacon 1963, priest 1964, Birmingham; Curate of St Martin-in-the-Bull Ring, Birmingham, 1963–67; Lecturer at St Martin's, Birmingham, 1967–71; Chaplain at Children's Hospital, Birmingham, 1967–71; Vicar of Luton, 1971–80 (with East Hyde, 1971–76); RD of Luton, 1974–79; Archdeacon of Bedford, 1979–85. MSc Cranfield, 1984. *Recreations:* marriage, evangelism, walking. *Address:* 61 Richmond Road, Merridale, Wolverhampton WV3 9JH. *T:* Wolverhampton (0902) 23008.

WOLVERSON COPE, F(rederick); *see* Cope.

WOLVERTON, 7th Baron *cr* 1869; **Christopher Richard Glyn,** FRICS; *b* 5 Oct. 1938; *s* of 6th Baron Wolverton, CBE and of Audrey Margaret, *d* of late Richard Stubbs; *S* father, 1988; *m* 1st, 1961, Carolyn Jane (marr. diss. 1967), *yr d* of late Antony N. Hunter; two *d*; 2nd, 1975, Mrs Frances S. E. Stuart Black (marr. diss. 1989). *Educ:* Eton. *Heir: b* Hon. Andrew John Glyn [*b* 30 June 1943; *m* 1st, 1965, Celia Laws (marr. diss. 1986); one *s* one *d*; 2nd, 1986, Wendy Carlin; one *d*]. *Address:* 97 Hurlingham Road, SW6.

WOMBWELL, Sir George (Philip Frederick), 7th Bt *cr* 1778; *b* 21 May 1949; *s* of Sir (Frederick) Philip (Alfred William) Wombwell, 6th Bt, MBE, and late Ida Elizabeth, *er d* of Frederick J. Leitch; *S* father, 1977; *m* 1974, (Hermione) Jane, *e d* of T. S. Wrightson; one *s* one *d*. *Educ:* Repton. *Heir: s* Stephen Philip Henry Wombwell, *b* 12 May 1977. *Address:* Newburgh Priory, Coxwold, York YO6 4AS.

WOMERSLEY, (Denis) Keith, CBE 1974; HM Diplomatic Service, retired; *b* 21 March 1920; *s* of late Alfred Womersley, Bradford, Yorks, and late Agnes (*née* Keighley); *m* 1955, Eileen Georgina (*d* 1990), *d* of late George and Margaret Howe. *Educ:* Christ's Hospital; Caius Coll., Cambridge (Hons, MA). Served War, HM Forces, 1940–46. Entered Foreign (later Diplomatic) Service, 1946; Foreign Office, 1948, Control Commn Germany, 1952; Vienna, 1955; Hong Kong, 1957, FO, 1960; Baghdad, 1962; FO, 1963; Aden, 1966; Beirut, 1967; FCO, 1969–71; Bonn, 1971–74; Counsellor, FCO, 1974–77. FRSA 1976. Gov., Christ's Hosp., 1991–. *Recreations:* violin-playing, photography, Abbeyfield Soc. work. *Club:* Christ's Hospital (Horsham).

WOMERSLEY, Keith; *see* Womersley, D. K.

WOMERSLEY, Sir Peter (John Walter), 2nd Bt *cr* 1945; JP; Personnel Manager, SmithKline Beecham; *b* 10 November 1941; *s* of Capt. John Womersley (*o s* of 1st Bt; killed in action in Italy, 1944), and of Betty, *d* of Cyril Williams, Elstead, Surrey; *S* grandfather, 1961; *m* 1968, Janet Margaret Grant; two *s* two *d*. *Educ:* Aldro; Charterhouse; RMA, Sandhurst. Entered Royal Military Academy (Regular Army), 1960; Lt, King's Own Royal Border Regt, 1964, retd 1968. JP 1991. *Publication:* (with Neil Grant) Collecting Stamps, 1980. *Heir: s* John Gavin Grant Womersley, *b* 7 Dec. 1971. *Address:* Broomfields, Goring Road, Steyning, W Sussex BN44 3GF.

WONFOR, Andrea Jean; Director, Channel Television, since 1987; Controller, Arts and Entertainment, Channel Four Television, since 1990 (Deputy Director of Programmes, 1989); *b* 31 July 1944; *d* of George Duncan and Audrey Joan Player; *m* 1st, 1967, Patrick Masefield (marr. diss. 1973); one *d*; 2nd, 1974, Geoffrey Wonfor; one *d*. *Educ:* Simon Langton Girls School, Canterbury; New Hall, Cambridge (BA). Graduate trainee, Granada Television, 1966–67; Tyne Tees Television: Researcher, 1969; Director, 1973; Head of Children's and Young People's Programmes, 1976; Dir of Progs, 1983–87. Man. Dir, Zenith North, 1988–90. Mem., Bd of Govs, BFI, 1989–. FRTS 1991. *Recreations:* reading, music. *Address:* Fell Pasture, Ingoe, Matfen, Northumberland NE20 0SP. *T:* Stamfordham (0661) 886487.

WONG Kin Chow, Michael; Hon. Mr Justice Wong; Judge of the High Court, Hong Kong, since 1985; Chairman, Release Under Supervision Board, since 1988; *b* 16 Aug. 1936; *s* of late Wong Chong and Au Ting; *m* 1963, Mae (*née* Fong); two *s* two *d*. *Educ:* Univ. of Liverpool (LLB Hons 1961). Called to the Bar, Middle Temple, 1962; private practice, Hong Kong, 1962–65; Hong Kong Government: Crown Counsel, Legal Dept, 1966–69; Senior Crown Counsel, 1969–72; Asst Principal Crown Counsel, 1973; Presiding Officer, Labour Tribunal, 1973–75; Asst Registrar, Supreme Court, 1975–77; District Judge, 1977. *Address:* Supreme Court, Hong Kong. *T:* 5–8254429. *Clubs:* Chinese, Royal Hong Kong Jockey, Kowloon Cricket (Hong Kong).

WONTNER, Sir Hugh (Walter Kingwell), GBE 1974; Kt 1972; CVO 1969 (MVO 1950); President, The Savoy Hotel plc, since 1990; Chairman: Claridge's and the Berkeley Hotels, London, since 1948; Lancaster Hotel, Paris, since 1973; Chairman and Managing Director, The Savoy Theatre, since 1948; Director, Forest Mere, since 1977; Clerk of the Royal Kitchens, since 1953, and a Catering Adviser in the Royal Household, since 1938; Underwriting Member of Lloyd's, since 1937; *b* 22 Oct. 1908; *er s* of Arthur Wontner, actor-manager; *m* 1936, Catherine, *o d* of Lieut T. W. Irvin, Gordon Highlanders (*d* of wounds, France, 1916); two *s* one *d*. *Educ:* Oundle and in France. On staff of London Chamber of Commerce, 1927–33; Asst Sec., Home Cttee, Associated Chambers of Commerce of India and Ceylon, 1930–31; Sec., London Cttee, Burma Chamber of Commerce, 1931; Gen. Sec., Hotels and Restaurants Assoc. of Great Britain, 1933–38; Asst to Sir George Reeves-Smith at The Savoy, 1938–41; Director, The Savoy Hotel Ltd, 1940–88, Man. Dir, 1941–79, Chm., 1948–84. Chm., Eurocard International, 1964–78. Sec., Coronation Accommodation Cttee, 1936–37, Chm., 1953; a British delegate, Internat. Hotel Alliance, 1933–38; Pres., Internat. Hotel Assoc., 1961–64, Mem. of Honour, 1965–. Chairman: Exec. Cttee, British Hotels and Rests Assoc., 1957–60 (Vice-Chm., 1952–57; Vice-Chm. of Council, 1961–68; Chm., London Div., 1949–51); Chm. of Council, British Hotels, Restaurants and Caterers Assoc., 1969–73; London Hotels Information Service, 1952–56; Working Party, Owners of Historic Houses open to the public, 1965–66; Historic Houses Cttee, BTA, 1966–77. Member: Historic Buildings Council, 1968–73; British Heritage Cttee, 1977–; Heritage of London Trust, 1980–; Barbican Centre Cttee, 1979–84; Board of BTA, 1950–69; LCC Consultative Cttee, Hotel and Restaurant Technical School, 1933–38; Court of Assistants, Irish Soc., 1967–68, 1971–73; Vis. Cttee, Holloway Prison, 1963–68. Governor: University Coll. Hosp., 1945–53 (Chm., Nutrition Cttee, 1945–52); Christ's Hosp., 1963. Trustee: College of Arms Trust; Southwark Cathedral Develt Trust; D'Oyly Carte Opera Trust; Morden Coll., Blackheath; Chm., Temple Bar Trustees; Vice Pres., The Pilgrims. Liveryman: Worshipful Co. of Feltmakers, 1934– (Master, 1962–63 and 1973–74); Clockmakers, 1967– (Warden, 1971–; Master, 1975–76); Hon. Liveryman: Worshipful Co. of Launderers', 1970; Plaisterers, 1975; Chancellor, The City Univ., 1973–74; one of HM Lieuts and a JP for the City of London, 1963–80, Chief Magistrate, 1973–74; Freeman of the City, 1934, Alderman for Broad Street Ward, 1963–79, Sheriff, 1970–71; Lord Mayor of London, 1973–74. Hon. Citizen, St Emilion, 1974; Freeman of the Seychelles, 1974. Order of Cisneros, Spain, 1964; Officer, L'Etoile Equatoriale, 1970; Médaille de Vermeil, City of Paris, 1972; Ordre de l'Etoile Civique, 1972; Officier du Mérite Agricole, 1973; Comdr, Nat. Order of the Leopard, Zaire, 1974; Knight Comdr, Order of the Dannebrog, 1974; Order of the Crown of Malaysia, 1974; Knight Comdr, Royal Swedish Order of the Polar Star, 1980. KStJ 1973 (OStJ 1971). Hon. DLitt 1973. *Recreations:* genealogy, acting. *Address:* 1 Savoy Hill, WC2. *T:* 071–836 1533. *Clubs:* Garrick, City Livery.

WOOD, family name of **Earl of Halifax** and **Baron Holderness.**

WOOD, Alan John, CBE 1971; Tan Sri (Malaysia) 1972; Assistant Director, Delaware River Port Authority, Port Operations Division (formerly World Trade Division), Camden, NJ, USA, since 1983; *b* 16 Feb. 1925; *s* of late Lt-Col Maurice Taylor Wood, MBE; *m* 1950 (marr. diss.); one *s* one *d*; *m* 1978, Marjorie Anne (*née* Bennett). *Educ:* King Edward VI Royal Grammar Sch., Guildford, Surrey, UK. Served Army, 1943–47; demobilised rank Captain. Various exec. and managerial positions with Borneo Motors Ltd, Singapore and Malaya, 1947–64 (Dir, 1964); Dir, Inchcape Bhd, 1968–73, Exec. Dep. Chm. 1973–74; Exec. Vice Pres., Sowers, Lewis, Wood Inc., Old Greenwich, Conn, 1975–78; Gen. Man., India, Singer Sewing Machine Co., 1979–82. Pres., Malaysian Internat. Chamber of Commerce, 1968–72; Chairman: Nat. Chambers of Commerce of

Malaysia, 1968 and 1972; Internat. Trade Cttee, Chamber of Commerce of Southern NJ, 1990–. Panglima Setia Mahkota (Hon.), 1972. *Recreation:* tennis. *Address:* 34 Treaty Drive, Wayne, Pa 19087, USA. *Clubs:* Oriental; Lake (Kuala Lumpur); Penang (Penang).

WOOD, Sir Alan Marshall M.; *see* Muir Wood.

WOOD, Alfred Arden, CBE 1988; TD 1960; FRIBA, FRTPI; architect and town planner; *b* 8 Sept. 1926; *s* of late Henry Arden Wood, AMIMechE, and Victoria Wood (*née* Holt); *m* 1957, Dorinda Rae (*née* Hartley) (*d* 1990); one *s* one *d*. *Educ:* Ashville Coll., Harrogate; Harrogate Grammar Sch.; Hertford Coll., Oxford; Leeds Schs of Architecture and Town Planning. Dip. and Dip. with Dist. Served 8th Royal Tank Regt, Leeds Rifles TA and Westminster Dragoons TA, 1944–62. Architect, Stockholm CC, Harlow New Town, W Riding CC, Leeds CC, Glasgow Corp., partner in private practice, 1951–65; City Planning Officer, Norwich, 1965–72; County Planner, Hereford and Worcester CC, 1972–73; County Architect and Planner, W Midlands CC, 1973–84; Head of Area Conservation, English Heritage, 1984–87. Buildings and other works include: housing in Harlow, Leeds and Glasgow, 1953–65; conservation, 1965–72, and first pedestrianisation in UK, Norwich, 1967; conservation, Jewellry Quarter, Birmingham, 1980–84; Birmingham Internat. Airport, 1984. Chm., Design Panel, Sheffield Develt Corp., 1989–; Member: Historic Buildings Council for England, 1969–84; RTPI Council, 1969–75; UK Exec. European Architectural Heritage Year, 1975 (Chm., Heritage Grants Cttee); Preservation Policy Gp, 1967–70; Environmental Bd, 1975–78; Comr, Indep. Transport Commn, 1972–74. Prof., Centre for the Conservation of Historic Towns and Bldgs, Katholieke Univ., Leuven, Belgium, ex Coll. of Europe, Bruges, 1976–86; External Examiner at several univs; adviser, at various times, Council of Europe, Strasbourg, and OECD, Paris; various lecture tours and conf. addresses in Europe and N America. Civic Trust awards, 1969, 1971. *Publications:* contributions to jls of learned societies. *Recreations:* cities, buildings, travel, trams, trains, music, many wines. *Address:* The Hall Barn, Dunley, Worcestershire DY13 0TX.

WOOD, Andrew Marley, CMG 1986; HM Diplomatic Service; Minister, Washington, since 1989; *b* 2 Jan. 1940; *s* of Robert George Wood; *m* 1st, 1972, Melanie LeRoy Masset (*d* 1977); one *s*; 2nd, 1978, Stephanie Lee Masset; one *s* one *d*. *Educ:* Ardingly Coll.; King's Coll., Cambridge (MA 1965). Foreign Office, 1961; Moscow, 1964; Washington, 1967; FCO, 1970; seconded to Cabinet Office, 1971; First Sec., FCO, 1973; First Sec. and Hd of Chancery, Belgrade, 1976; Counsellor, 1978; Hd of Chancery, Moscow, 1979; Hd of W European Dept, 1982, Hd of Personnel Operations Dept, 1983, FCO; Ambassador to Yugoslavia, 1985–89. *Address:* c/o Foreign and Commonwealth Office, SW1A 2AH.

WOOD, Sir Anthony John P.; *see* Page Wood.

WOOD, Anthony Richard; HM Diplomatic Service, retired; *b* 13 Feb. 1932; *s* of late Rev. T. J. Wood and of Phyllis Margaret (*née* Bold); *m* 1966, Sarah Drew (marr. diss. 1973); one *s* one *d*. *Educ:* St Edward's Sch.; Worcester Coll., Oxford (BA). HM Forces, 1950–52. British Sch. of Archaeology in Iraq, Nimrud, 1956; joined HM Foreign Service, 1957; served: Beirut, 1957; Bahrain, 1958; Paris, 1959; Benghazi, 1962; Aden, 1963; Basra, 1966; Tehran, 1970; Muscat, 1980; Counsellor, FCO, 1984–87. *Recreations:* walking, singing. *Clubs:* Army and Navy, Royal Green Jackets.

WOOD, Ven. Arnold; Warden, Community of the Epiphany, since 1985; Archdeacon of Cornwall and Canon Residentiary (Librarian), Truro Cathedral, 1981–88; Archdeacon and Canon Emeritus, 1988; *b* 24 Oct. 1918; *s* of Harry and Annie Wood; *m* 1945, Dorothy Charlotte Tapper; two *d*. *Educ:* Holy Trinity School, Halifax; London Univ. (Dip. Economics). Commissioned, RASC, 1939–49. Legal Adviser and Man. Director, CMI Engineering Co. Ltd, 1949–63; student, Clifton Theological Coll., 1963–65; Curate, Kirkheaton, W Yorks, 1965–67; Vicar, Mount Pellon, W Yorks, 1967–73; Rector of Lanreath and Vicar of Pelynt, 1973–81; Rural Dean, West Wivelshire, dio. Truro, 1976–81. Mem., General Synod, 1985–88. Gen. Comr of Income Tax, 1977–. *Recreations:* walking, bowls, music. *Address:* Cobblers, Quethiock, Liskeard, Cornwall PL14 3SQ. *T:* Liskeard (0579) 44788. *Club:* Commonwealth Trust.

WOOD, Charles; Chief Executive, London Borough of Brent, since 1986; *b* 16 May 1950; *s* of Sir Frank Wood, KBE, CB and Lady (Olive May) Wood (*née* Wilson); *m* Carolyn Hall; three *s* two *d*. *Educ:* King's College London (BSc Hons); Polytechnic of Central London (DipTP). Engineer, GLC, 1971–76; Planner, and Dep. Dir of Housing, London Borough of Hammersmith and Fulham, 1976–82; Dir of Develt, London Borough of Brent, 1982–86. *Recreations:* walking, tennis. *Address:* Brent Town Hall, Forty Lane, Wembley, HA9 9HX.

WOOD, Charles Gerald, FRSL 1984; writer for films, television and the theatre, since 1962; *b* 6 Aug. 1932; *s* of John Edward Wood, actor and Catherine Mae (*née* Harris), actress; *m* 1954, Valerie Elizabeth Newman, actress; one *s* one *d*. *Educ:* King Charles I Sch., Kidderminster; Birmingham Coll. of Art. Corp., 17/21st Lancers, 1950–55; Factory worker, 1955–57; Stage Manager, advertising artist, cartoonist, scenic artist, 1957–59; Bristol Evening Post, 1959–62. Member: Drama Adv. Panel, South Western Arts, 1972–73; Council, BAFTA, 1991–. Consultant to Nat. Film Develt Fund, 1980–82. *Wrote plays:* Prisoner and Escort, John Thomas, Spare, (Cockade), Arts Theatre, 1963; Meals on Wheels, Royal Court, 1965; Don't Make Me Laugh, Aldwych, 1966; Fill the Stage with Happy Hours, Nottingham Playhouse, Vaudeville Theatre, 1967; Dingo, Bristol Arts Centre, Royal Court, 1967; H, National Theatre, 1969; Welfare, Liverpool Everyman, 1971; Veterans, Lyceum, Edinburgh, Royal Court, 1972; Jingo, RSC, 1975; Has 'Washington' Legs?, Nat. Theatre, 1978; Red Star, RSC, 1984; Across from the Garden of Allah, Comedy, 1986; adapted Pirandello's Man, Beast and Virtue, Nat. Theatre, 1989. *Screenplays include:* The Knack, 1965 (Grand Prix, Cannes; Writers Guild Award for Best Comedy); Help!, 1965; How I Won the War, 1967; The Charge of the Light Brigade, 1968; The Long Day's Dying, 1969; Cuba, 1980; Wagner, 1983; Red Monarch, 1983; Puccini, 1984; Tumbledown, 1988 (Prix Italia, RAI Prize, 1988; BAFTA, Broadcasting Press Guild and RTS awards, 1989); Shooting the Hero, 1991; *adapted:* Bed Sitting Room, 1973; Man, Beast and Virtue, 1989. Numerous television plays incl. Prisoner and Escort, Drums Along the Avon, Drill Pig, A Bit of a Holiday, A Bit of an Adventure, Do As I Say, Love Lies Bleeding, Dust to Dust; creator of Gordon Maple in series, Don't Forget to Write; Company of Adventurers (series for CBC), 1986; My Family and Other Animals (series for BBC), 1987; The Settling of the Sun, 1987. Evening Standard Awards, 1963, 1973. *Publications:* plays: Cockade, 1965; Fill the Stage with Happy Hours, 1967; Dingo, 1967; H, 1970; Veterans, 1972; Has 'Washington' Legs?, 1978; Tumbledown, 1987; Man, Beast and Virtue, 1990. *Recreations:* military and theatrical studies; gardening. *Address:* c/o Jane Annakin, William Morris (UK) Ltd, 31/32 Soho Square, W1V 5DG. *T:* 071–434 2191. *Clubs:* Royal Over-Seas League, British Playwrights' Mafia.

WOOD, Rear Adm. Christopher Lainson, CB 1991; Assistant Chief of the Defence Staff, Operational Requirements (Sea Systems), 1988–91; *b* 9 Feb. 1936; *s* of Gordon and Eileen Wood; *m* 1962, Margot Price; two *s* one *d*. *Educ:* Pangbourne College. FBIM; MNI. Seaman Officer, RN, 1954; joined submarine service, 1958; CO's qualifying course, 1966; in comd, HMS Ambush, 1966–68; JSSC, 1970; nuclear submarine training, 1971; in comd, HMS Warspite, 1971–73; Staff of FO Submarines, 1973–75; Staff of Dir, Naval Op. Requirements, 1975–77; Underwater Weapons Acceptance, 1978–81; Dep. Dir, Naval Op. Requirements, 1981–83; Dir Gen., Underwater Weapons, 1983–85; Dir Gen., Fleet Support, 1986–88. *Recreations:* reading, outdoor pursuits, sailing, fishing, sporting interests, community and church work. *Address:* c/o Lloyds Bank, Cox's & King's Branch, PO Box 1190, 7 Pall Mall, SW1Y 5NA. *Club:* Institute of Directors (Associate Mem.).

WOOD, Rt. Rev. Clyde Maurice; *see* Northern Territory (Australia), Bishop of the.

WOOD, David; actor, playwright, composer, theatrical producer and director; *b* 21 Feb. 1944; *s* of Richard Edwin Wood and Audrey Adele Wood (*née* Fincham) *m* 1975, Jacqueline Stanbury; two *d*. *Educ:* Chichester High Sch. for Boys; Worcester Coll., Oxford. BA (Hons). Acted with OUDS and ETC at Oxford; first London appearance in ETC prodn, Hang Down Your Head and Die (also co-writer), Comedy, 1964; later performances include: A Spring Song, Mermaid, 1964; Dr Faustus (OUDS), 1966; Four Degrees Over, Edinburgh Festival and Fortune, 1966 (also contrib. lyrics and sketches); repertory, 1966–69; RSC's After Haggerty, Aldwych 1970, and Criterion 1971; A Voyage Round My Father, Greenwich, 1970, Toronto, 1972; Me Times Me, tour, 1971; Mrs Warren's Profession, 1972, and revue Just the Ticket, 1973, Thorndike, Leatherhead; The Provok'd Wife, Greenwich, 1973; Jeeves, Her Majesty's, 1975; Terra Nova, Chichester, 1980. *Films include:* If . . . , 1968; Aces High, 1975; Sweet William, 1978; North Sea Hijack, 1979. *TV series include:* Mad Jack, Fathers and Sons, Cheri, Disraeli, The Avengers, Van der Valk, Danger UXB, Huntingtower, Enemy at the Door, Jackanory, Jim'll Fix It, When the Boat Comes In, The Brack Report, Tricky Business. Various revues in collaboration with John Gould; music and lyrics, The Stiffkey Scandals of 1932, Queen's, 1967; with John Gould formed Whirligig Theatre, touring children's theatre company, 1979; has directed one of own plays on tour and at Sadler's Wells Theatre, annually 1979–; has performed David Wood Magic and Music Show in theatres all over UK, incl. Polka Theatre, Arts Theatre and Purcell Room, 1983–. Formed, jointly: Verronmead Ltd, indep. TV producing co., 1983; Westwood Theatrical Productions Ltd, 1986. *TV series scripts:* Chips' Comic; Chish 'n' Fips; Seeing and Doing; The Gingerbread Man; *screenplays:* Swallows and Amazons, 1974; Back Home, 1989; Tide Race, 1989. *Publications: musical plays for children:* (with Sheila Ruskin) The Owl and the Pussycat went to see . . . , 1968; (with Sheila Ruskin) Larry the Lamb in Toytown, 1969; The Plotters of Cabbage Patch Corner, 1970; Flibberty and the Penguin, 1971; The Papertown Paperchase, 1972; Hijack over Hygenia, 1973; Old Mother Hubbard, 1975; The Gingerbread Man, 1976; Old Father Time, 1976; (with Tony Hatch and Jackie Trent) Rock Nativity, 1976; Nutcracker Sweet, 1977; Mother Goose's Golden Christmas, 1977; Tickle, 1978; Babes in the Magic Wood, 1978; There Was an Old Woman . . . , 1979; Cinderella, 1979; Aladdin, 1981; (with Dave and Toni Arthur) Robin Hood, 1981; Dick Whittington and Wondercat, 1981; Meg and Mog Show, 1981; The Ideal Gnome Expedition, 1982; Jack and the Giant, 1982; The Selfish Shellfish, 1983; (with ABBA and Don Black) Abbacadabra, 1984; (with Dave and Toni Arthur) Jack the Lad, 1984; (with Peter Pontzen) Dinosaurs and all that Rubbish, 1985; The Seesaw Tree, 1986; The Old Man of Lochnagar (based on book by HRH the Prince of Wales), 1986; (with Dave and Toni Arthur) The Pied Piper, 1988; Save the Human, 1990; The BFG (based on book by Roald Dahl), 1991; *books for children:* The Gingerbread Man, 1985; (with Geoffrey Beitz) The Operats of Rodent Garden, 1984; (with Geoffrey Beitz) The Discorats, 1985; Chish 'n' Fips, 1987; Play-Theatres, 1987; Sidney the Monster, 1988; (with Richard Fowler) Happy Birthday, Mouse, 1991 (USA 1990); Save the Human, 1991; articles in Drama, London Drama. *Recreations:* writing, conjuring, collecting old books. *Address:* c/o Margaret Ramsay Ltd, 14A Goodwin's Court, St Martin's Lane, WC2. *T:* 071–240 0691. *Club:* Green Room.

WOOD, Sir David (Basil) H.; *see* Hill-Wood.

WOOD, Maj.-Gen. Denys Broomfield, CB 1978; Independent Inquiry Inspector, since 1984; General Commissioner for Taxes, since 1986; *b* 2 Nov. 1923; *s* of late Percy Neville Wood and Meryl Broomfield; *m* 1948, Jennifer Nora Page, *d* of late Air Cdre William Morton Page, CBE; one *s* two *d*. *Educ:* Radley; Pembroke Coll., Cambridge. MA: CEng, FIMechE. Commissioned into REME, 1944; war service in UK and Far East, 1944–47; Staff Captain, WO, 1948–49; Instructor, RMA, Sandhurst, 1949–52; Staff Coll., 1953; DAA&QMG, 11 Infantry Bde, 1955–57; OC, 10 Infantry Workshop, Malaya, 1958–60; jssc 1960; Directing Staff, Staff Coll., 1961–63; Comdr, REME, 3rd Div., 1963–65; Operational Observer, Viet Nam, 1966–67; Col GS, Staff Coll., 1967–69; idc 1970; Dir, Administrative Planning, 1971–73; Dep. Military Sec. (2), 1973–75; Dir of Army Quartering, 1975–78. Exec. Sec., 1978–82, Sec., 1982–84, CEI. Col Comdt, REME, 1978–84. Lay Mem., Law Soc. Adjudication Cttee, 1986–. FRSA. *Recreations:* walking, gardening, reading. *Address:* Elmtree House, Hurtmore, Godalming, Surrey GU7 2RA. *T:* Godalming (0483) 416936. *Club:* Army and Navy.

WOOD, Derek Alexander; QC 1978; a Recorder, since 1985; Principal, St Hugh's College, Oxford, since 1991; *b* 14 Oct. 1937; *s* of Alexander Cecil Wood and Rosetta (*née* Lelyveld); *m* 1961, Sally Teresa Clarke, *d* of Lady Elliott and step *d* of Sir Norman Elliott, *qv*; two *d*. *Educ:* Tiffin Boys' Sch., Kingston-upon-Thames; University Coll., Oxford (MA, BCL). Called to the Bar, Middle Temple, 1964, Bencher, 1986. Dept of the Environment: Mem., Adv. Gp on Commercial Property Develt, 1975–78; Mem., Property Adv. Gp, 1978–; Mem., Working Party on New Forms of Social Ownership and Tenure in Housing, 1976; Dept of Transport: Chm., Standing Adv. Cttee on Trunk Road Assessment, 1987–. Dep. Chm., Soc. of Labour Lawyers, 1978–90. Chm., Chislehurst Constituency Labour Party, 1972–76, 1979–84. Mem. Council, London Bor. of Bromley, 1975–78. Fellow, CAAV, 1988. *Recreation:* music. *Address:* 30 Westmoreland Place, SW1V 4AE. *T:* 071–821 0236; St Hugh's College, Oxford OX2 6LE. *Clubs:* Athenæum, Royal Automobile, Architecture; Kent Valuers' (Hon. Mem.).

WOOD, Prof. Derek Rawlins, FIBiol; Dean of Faculty of Medicine and Professor of Applied Pharmacology, University of Leeds, 1969–86, now Professor Emeritus; *b* 16 May 1921; *s* of Frederick Charles Wood and Ruth Dorothy (*née* Rawlins); *m* 1945, Mary Elizabeth Caldwell; two *s* two *d* (and one *s* decd). *Educ:* Wm Hulme's Grammar Sch., Manchester; Brasenose Coll. and Radcliffe Infirmary, Oxford. BM BCh, BSc, MA Oxford. House Physician, Radcliffe Inf., 1945; Demonstrator, Pharmacology, Oxford, 1945–46; Lectr 1946, Sen. Lectr 1952–57, Pharmacology, Univ. of Sheffield; J. H. Hunt Travelling Schol., 1949; J. H. Brown Fellow, Pharmacol., Yale, 1955–56; Associate Prof., Pharmacol., McGill Univ., 1957–60; Prof. and Head of Dept of Pharmacol., Univ. of Leeds, 1960–69. Hon. Sec., 1952–57, Hon. Treas., 1964–70, Brit. Pharmacol. Soc.; Member: Stag Jt Commn on Classification of Proprietary Remedies, 1964–69; British Nat. Formulary Cttee, 1967–74; Adv. Commn on Pesticides, 1968–70; Brit. Pharmacopoeia Commn, 1969–79; GMC, 1969–86; Gen. Dental Council, 1971–86; Leeds Reg. Hosp. Bd, 1969–74; Bd of Governors, United Leeds Hosps, 1969–74; Leeds AHA (T), 1974–82; Leeds DHA, West and East, 1982–84. Exec. Sec., University Hosps Assoc., 1988– (Chm., 1978–81). Mem. Court: Univs of Bradford, 1970–, and Sheffield, 1966–79. Hon. MPS. *Publications:* Dental Pharmacology and Therapeutics (with L. E.

Francis), 1961; contribs to Brit. Jl Pharmacol., Jl Physiol., and others. *Recreations:* gardening, music. *Address:* 5 Spring Terrace, Lothersdale, Keighley, W Yorks BD20 8HA. *T:* Cross Hills (0535) 632593.

WOOD, Dudley Ernest; Secretary, Rugby Football Union, since 1986; *b* 18 May 1930; *s* of Ernest Edward and Ethel Louise Wood; *m* 1955, Mary Christina Blake; two *s*. *Educ:* Luton Grammar School; St Edmund Hall, Oxford (BA Modern Languages). ICI 1954; Petrochemicals and Plastics Division, ICI: Overseas Manager, 1977–82; Sales and Marketing Manager, 1982–86. Rugby Football: Oxford Blue, 1952, 1953; played for Bedford, Rosslyn Park, Waterloo, Streatham-Croydon, East Midlands; Hon. Life Mem., Squash Rackets Assoc., 1984. *Recreations:* Rugby Football, squash, dog breeding (golden retriever), travel, Middle East affairs. *Address:* Rugby Football Union, Twickenham, Middx TW1 1DZ. *T:* 081–892 8161. *Clubs:* East India, Royal Over-Seas League.

WOOD, Prof. Edward James; Professor of Latin, University of Leeds, 1938–67, Professor Emeritus, 1967; Pro-Vice-Chancellor, University of Leeds, 1957–59; *b* 3 Sept. 1902; *s* of James M. A. Wood, Advocate in Aberdeen; *m* 1933, Marion Grace Chorley; one *s* one *d*. *Educ:* Aberdeen Grammar School; Aberdeen University; Trinity College, Cambridge. Lectr in Classics, Manchester University, 1928; Professor of Latin, Aberystwyth, 1932. *Publications:* contributions to: Classical Review, Gnomon. *Address:* The Towans, Berrow Road, Burnham-on-Sea, Somerset TA8 2EZ. *T:* Burnham-on-Sea (0278) 782762.

WOOD, Eric; Finance Director (formerly Finance Officer), University of Bristol, 1979–91; *b* 22 Sept. 1931; *s* of Herbert Francis and Eva Wood; *m* 1955, Erica Twist; three *d*. *Educ:* West Hartlepool Grammar Sch.; Blandford Grammar Sch.; St Peter's Coll., Oxford (MA). IPFA. National Service, Army, 1950–51. Finance Depts, Cheshire, Durham and Notts County Councils, 1954–65; Finance Dept, London Transport, 1965–67; Asst Treasurer, GLC, 1967–73; Dir, CIPFA, 1973–79. *Publications:* articles in prof. accountancy press. *Recreations:* skiing, squash. *Address:* 14 Alexandra Road, Clifton, Bristol BS8 2DD. *T:* Bristol (0272) 730881.

WOOD, Francis Gordon, FIA; Deputy Chief General Manager, Prudential Assurance Co. Ltd, 1982–85; non-Executive Director, Prudential Corporation, 1985–90 (Director, 1984); *b* 30 Oct. 1924; *s* of Francis R. and Florence A. Wood; *m* 1950, Margaret Parr; two *d*. *Educ:* Alleyne's Grammar School, Stone, Staffs. ACII. Prudential Assurance Co. Ltd, 1941–85; Dir, 1981. *Recreation:* golf. *Address:* 6 Matching Lane, Bishop's Stortford, Herts CM23 2PP. *T:* Bishop's Stortford (0279) 652197.

WOOD, Frank; His Honour Judge Wood; Resident Judge, Sovereign Base Areas of Akrotiri and Dhekelia, since 1986; *b* 10 June 1929; *s* of late Robert Wood and Marjorie Edith Park Wood (*née* Senior); *m* 1951, Diana Mae Shenton; two *s* one *d*. *Educ:* Berkhamsted; RMA Sandhurst. Called to the Bar, Lincoln's Inn, 1969. Commissioned RASC, 1949–52. Bechuanaland Protectorate Police, 1953–65 (Supt 1965), Acting Dist Comr, 1957–58, 1959–60; Crown Counsel, Bechuanaland, 1965–66, State Counsel, 1966–67; Magistrate, Seychelles, 1970, Sen. Magistrate, 1974; Puisne Judge and Justice of Appeal, Seychelles, 1977–85, Acting Chief Justice, 1982–84; Chief Justice and Justice of Appeal, Solomon Islands, 1985–86; Justice of Appeal, Vanuatu, 1985–87. Chancellor, Dio. of Seychelles, 1973–84. Mem. Council, Commonwealth Magistrates' Assoc., 1973–77. *Publication:* Sovereign Base Areas Law Reports 1960–87, 1988. *Recreations:* riding, shooting, sailing, philately. *Address:* Judge's Chambers, HM Court, Episkopi, BFPO 53; The Barn, Ewyas Harold, Hereford HR4 9BH. *Clubs:* Commonwealth Trust; Joint Services Saddle (Episkopi).

WOOD, Sir Frederick (Ambrose Stuart), Kt 1977; Hon. Life President, Croda International Ltd, since 1987 (Managing Director, 1953–85, Executive Chairman, 1960–85, non-executive Chairman, 1985–86); *b* 30 May 1926; *s* of Alfred Phillip Wood, Goole, Yorkshire, and Patras, Greece, and Charlotte Wood (*née* Barnes), Goole, Yorkshire, and Athens, Greece; *m* 1947, J. R. (Su) King; two *s* one *d*. *Educ:* Felsted Sch., Essex; Clare Coll., Cambridge. Served War, Sub-Lt (A) Observer, Fleet Air Arm, 1944–47. Trainee Manager, Croda Ltd, 1947–50; Pres., Croda Inc., New York, 1950–53. Chm., Nat. Bus Co., 1972–78. Mem., 1973–78, Chm., 1979–83, NRDC; Chm. NEB, 1981–83; Chm., British Technology Gp, 1981–83. Mem., Nationalised Industries Chms' Gp, 1975–78. Chm. British Sect., Centre Européen d'Entreprise Publique, 1976–78. Hon. LLD Hull, 1983. *Address:* Plaster Hill Farm, Churt, Surrey. *T:* Headley Down (0428) 712134.

WOOD, Maj.-Gen. Harry Stewart, CB 1967; TD 1950; *b* 16 Sept. 1913; *e s* of late Roland and Eva M. Wood; *m* 1939, Joan Gordon, *d* of Gordon S. King; two *s* (and one *s* decd). *Educ:* Nautical Coll., Pangbourne. Civil Engineer (inc. articled trg), 1931–39. Commnd RA (TA), 1937. Served War of 1939–45: Regimental Service, Sept. 1939–June 1944; subseq. Technical Staff. Dep. Dir of Artillery, Min. of Supply (Col), 1958–60; Dep. Dir of Inspection (Brig.), 1960–62; Sen. Mil. Officer, Royal Armament Research and Development Estab. (Brig.), 1962–64; Vice-President, Ordnance Board, 1964–66, President, 1966–67. Maj.-Gen. 1964; retd, 1967. Legion of Merit, degree of Legionnaire (USA), 1947. *Recreations:* home and garden, motor sport. *Address:* Brook House, Faygate, near Horsham, Sussex RH12 4SS. *T:* Faygate (0293) 851342.

WOOD, Sir Henry (Peart), Kt 1967; CBE 1960; Principal, Jordanhill College of Education, Glasgow, 1949–71, retired; *b* 30 Nov. 1908; *s* of T. M. Wood, Bedlington, Northumberland; *m* 1937, Isobel Mary, *d* of W. F. Stamp, Carbis Bay, Cornwall; one *s* two *d*. *Educ:* Morpeth Grammar Sch.; Durham University. BSc 1930, MSc 1934, Durham; MA 1938, MEd 1941, Manchester. Lecturer, Manchester University, 1937–44; Jordanhill College of Education: Principal Lecturer, 1944–46; Vice-Principal, 1947–49. Part-time Lectr, Glasgow Univ., 1972–78; Assessor in Educn, Strathclyde Univ., 1972–82; Vis. Prof. in Educn, Strathclyde Univ., 1978–84. Hon. LLD: Glasgow, 1972; Strathclyde, 1982. *Address:* 15a Hughenden Court, Hughenden Road, Glasgow G12 9XP. *T:* 041–334 3647.

See also R. F. M. Wood.

WOOD, Humphrey; *see* Wood, J. H. A.

WOOD, Ian Clark, CBE 1982; Chairman since 1981, and Managing Director since 1967, John Wood Group plc; Chairman, J. W. Holdings Ltd, since 1981; *b* 21 July 1942; *s* of John Wood and Margaret (*née* Clark); *m* 1970, Helen Macrae; three *s*. *Educ:* Aberdeen Univ. (BSc Psychology, First Cl. Hons). Joined John Wood Group, 1964. Dir, Royal Bank of Scotland, 1988–. Chairman: Aberdeen Beyond 2000, 1986–90; Grampian Enterprise, 1990–. Member: Aberdeen Harbour Bd, 1972–90; Sea Fish Industry Authority, 1981–87; Offshore Industry Adv. Bd, 1988–; Offshore Industry Export Adv. Gp, 1988–; Bd, Scottish Develt Agency, 1984–90; Scottish Econ. Council, 1987–; Scottish Sub-Cttee, UGC, subseq. UFC, 1988–; Nat. Trng Task Force, 1991–. CBIM 1983. Hon. LLD Aberdeen, 1984. Silver Jubilee Medal, 1977. *Recreations:* family, squash, reading, art. *Address:* Marchmont, 42 Rubislaw Den South, Aberdeen AB2 6BB. *T:* Aberdeen 313625.

WOOD, John; actor. *Educ:* Bedford Sch.; Jesus Coll., Oxford (Pres. OUDS). Old Vic Co., 1954–56; Camino Real, Phoenix, 1957; The Making of Moo, Royal Court, 1957; Brouhaha, Aldwych, 1958; The Fantasticks, Apollo, 1961; Rosencrantz and Guildenstern are Dead, NY, 1967; Exiles, Mermaid, 1970; joined Royal Shakespeare Company, 1971; Enemies, The Man of Mode, Exiles, The Balcony, Aldwych, 1971; The Comedy of Errors, Stratford, 1972; Julius Caesar, Titus Andronicus, Stratford, 1972, Aldwych, 1973; Collaborators, Duchess, 1973; A Lesson in Blood and Roses, The Place, 1973; Sherlock Holmes, Travesties (Evening Standard Best Actor Award, 1974; Tony Award, 1976), Aldwych, 1974, NY, 1974; The Devil's Disciple, Ivanov, Aldwych, 1976; Death Trap, NY, 1978; Undiscovered Country, Richard III, Nat. Theatre, 1979; Piaf, Wyndham's, 1980; The Provok'd Wife, Nat. Theatre, 1980; Royal Shakespeare Co.: The Tempest, 1988; The Man Who Came to Dinner, The Master Builder, 1989; King Lear, Love's Labours Lost, 1990. *Television:* A Tale of Two Cities, Barnaby Rudge, 1964–65; The Victorians, 1965; The Duel, 1966. *Films:* Nicholas and Alexandra, 1971; Slaughterhouse Five, 1972; War Games, 1983. *Address:* c/o Royal Shakespeare Company, Barbican Centre, Silk Street, EC2Y 8DS.

WOOD, John, CB 1989; Director of Public Prosecutions, Hong Kong, since 1990; *b* 11 Jan. 1931; *s* of Thomas John Wood and Rebecca Grand; *m* 1958, Jean Iris Wood; two *s*. *Educ:* King's College Sch., Wimbledon. Admitted Solicitor, 1955. Director of Public Prosecutions: Legal Assistant, 1958; Sen. Legal Asst, 1963; Asst Solicitor, 1971; Asst Director, 1977; Principal Asst Dir, 1981; Dep. Dir., 1985–87; Head of Legal Services, Crown Prosecution Service, 1986–87; Dir of Serious Fraud Office, 1987–90. *Recreations:* cricket, Rugby football, badminton, music, theatre. *Address:* Attorney General's Chambers, Queensway Government Offices, 66 Queensway, Hong Kong.

WOOD, John Edwin, PhD; consultant; *b* 24 July 1928; *s* of late John Stanley Wood and Alice (*née* Hardy); *m* 1953, Patricia Edith Wilson Sheppard (marr. diss. 1978); two *s* two *d*. *Educ:* Darlington Grammar Sch.; Univ. of Leeds (BSc, PhD). Joined Royal Naval Scientific Service at HM Underwater Countermeasures and Weapons Estabt, 1951; Admiralty Underwater Weapons Estabt, 1959; Head of Acoustic Research Div., 1968; Head of Sonar Dept, 1972; Admiralty Surface Weapons Establishment: Head of Weapons Dept, 1976; Head of Communications, Command and Control Dept, 1979; Chief Scientist (Royal Navy), and Director General Research (A), 1980; joined Sperry Gyroscope (subseq. British Aerospace), Bracknell, 1981; Exec. Dir, BAe, Bristol, 1984–88; Dir of Underwater Engrg, BAe Dynamics Div., 1988–90. Pres., Gp 12, Council of British Archaeology, 1984–. *Publications:* Sun, Moon and Standing Stones, 1978, 2nd edn 1980; papers and book reviews in technical and archaeological jls. *Recreations:* archaeology, fell-walking. *Address:* 7 Pennant Hills, Bedhampton, Havant, Hants PO9 3JZ. *T:* Havant (0705) 471411.

WOOD, (John) Humphrey (Askey); a Managing Director, Consolidated Gold Fields plc, 1979–89; Non-Executive Deputy Chairman, Vinten Group plc, since 1991; non-executive director of cos; *b* 26 Nov. 1932; *s* of late Lt-Col Edward Askey Wood and Irene Jeanne Askey Wood; *m* 1st, 1965, Jane Holland; one *s*; 2nd, 1981, Katherine Ruth Stewart Reardon (*née* Peverley); one step *s* one step *d*. *Educ:* Abberley Hall; Winchester College; Corpus Christi College, Cambridge. MA (Mech. Scis). De Havilland Aircraft Co. Ltd, 1956; Hawker Siddeley Aviation Ltd, 1964, Dir and Gen. Manager, Manchester, 1969–76; Man. Dir, Industrial and Marine Div., Rolls-Royce Ltd, 1976–79; Chm., Amey Roadstone Corp., 1979–86. Director: Gold Fields of South Africa Ltd, 1986–89; Blue Tee Corp., 1986–89; Non-Exec. Director: Birse Gp plc, 1989–; Albrighton plc, 1990–. Vice-Pres., Nat. Council of Building Material Producers, 1985–89. Mem. Council, CBI, 1983–89. *Recreations:* fly fishing, sailing, painting. *Address:* Albyn House, 239 New King's Road, SW6 4XG. *T:* 071–731 5092.

WOOD, Hon. Sir John (Kember), Kt 1977; MC 1944; **Hon. Mr Justice Wood;** a Judge of the High Court of Justice, Family Division, since 1977; President, Employment Appeal Tribunal, since 1988 (Judge, 1985–88); *b* Hong Kong, 8 Aug. 1922; *s* of John Roskruge Wood and Gladys Frances (*née* Kember); *m* 1952, Kathleen Ann Lowe; one *s* one *d*. *Educ:* Shrewsbury Sch.; Magdalene Coll., Cambridge. Served War of 1939–45: Rifle Brigade, 1941–46; ME and Italy; PoW, 1944. Magdalene Coll., 1946–48. Barrister (Lincoln's Inn), 1949, Bencher, 1977; QC 1969; a Recorder of the Crown Court, 1975–77. Vice-Chm., Parole Bd, 1987–89 (Mem. 1986–89). *Recreations:* sport, travel. *Address:* Royal Courts of Justice, WC2. *Clubs:* Garrick, MCC; Hawks (Cambridge).

WOOD, J(ohn) Laurence; Keeper, Department of Printed Books, British Library, 1966–76; retired; *b* 27 Nov. 1911; *s* of J. A. Wood and Clara Josephine (*née* Ryan); *m* 1947, Rowena Beatrice Ross; one *s* one *d*. *Educ:* Bishop Auckland; Merton Coll., Oxford (BA); Besançon; Paris. Lecteur, Univ. of Besançon, 1934; Asst Cataloguer, British Museum, 1936; seconded to Foreign Office, 1941; Asst Keeper, British Museum, 1946; Deputy Keeper, 1959. Editor, Factotum, 1978–. *Publications:* (trans.) The French Prisoner, Garneray, 1957; (trans.) Contours of the Middle Ages, Genicot, 1967. *Recreation:* bookbinding. *Address:* 88 Hampstead Way, NW11 7XY. *T:* 081–455 4395.

WOOD, John Peter; freelance gardening journalist and broadcaster; *b* 27 March 1925; *s* of Walter Ralph Wood and Henrietta Martin; *m* 1956, Susan Maye White; one *s* one *d*. *Educ:* Grove Park Grammar Sch.; Seale Hayne Agricultural Coll. (NDH and Dip. in Hort., of College). FIHort 1986. Served War, 1943–46. Horticultural studies, 1946–52; Amateur Gardening: Asst Editor, 1952–66; Dep. Editor, 1966–71; Editor, 1971–86; Cons. Editor, 1986–89. *Publications:* Amateur Gardening Handbook—Bulbs, 1957; Amateur Gardening Picture Book—Greenhouse Management, 1959. *Recreations:* gardening, choral singing. *Address:* 1 Charlton House Court, Charlton Marshall, Blandford, Dorset DT11 9NT. *T:* Blandford (0258) 454653.

WOOD, Joseph Neville, (Johnnie), CBE 1978; Director General, The General Council of British Shipping, 1975–78; *b* 25 October 1916; *o s* of late Robert Hind Wood and Emily Wood, Durham; *m* 1st, 1944, Elizabeth May (*d* 1959); three *d*; 2nd, 1965, Josephine Samuel (*née* Dane) (*d* 1985); 3rd, 1986, Frances Howarth (*née* Skeer). *Educ:* Johnston School, Durham; London School of Economics. Entered Civil Service (Board of Trade), 1935; Ministry of War Transport, 1940; jssc 1950; Ministry of Transport: Asst Sec., 1951; Far East Representative, 1952–55; Under-Sec., 1961; Chief of Highway Administration, 1967–68. Joined Chamber of Shipping of the UK, 1968, Dep. Dir, 1970, Dir, 1972–78. Mem., Baltic Exchange, 1968–; Director: Finance for Shipping Ltd, 1978–82; Ship Mortgage Finance Co. Ltd, 1978–83. Mem. Chichester DC, 1979–91. Vice Pres., Shipwrecked Fishermen and Mariners Royal Benevolent Soc., 1989– (Dep. Chm., 1983–89). FCIT 1976. Freeman, City of London, 1978. Officier, Ordre de Mérite Maritime, 1950. *Recreation:* gardening. *Address:* Barbers Cottage, Heyshott, Midhurst, Sussex. *T:* Midhurst 814282.

WOOD, Kenneth Maynard; consultant; *b* 4 Oct. 1916; *s* of late Frederick Cavendish Wood and Agnes Maynard; *m* Patricia Rose; two *s* two *d* (by previous marriage), and three step *s*. *Educ:* Bromley County School. Cadet, Merchant Navy, 1930–34; electrical and mechanical engineering, 1934–37; started own company radio, television and radar development, 1937–39; sold business and joined RAF, transferred for development of electronic equipment, 1939–46; started Kenwood Manufacturing Co. Ltd, 1946; Managing Director, 1946 until take-over by Thorn Electrical Industries Ltd, 1968; Chm. and Man. Dir, Dawson-Keith Group of Companies, 1972–80; Chm, Hydrotech Systems

Ltd, 1984–87. Fellow, Inst. of Ophthalmology. *Recreation:* golf. *Address:* Dellwood Cottage, Wheatsheaf Enclosure, Liphook, Hants GU30 7EH. *T:* Liphook (0428) 723108.

WOOD, Leonard George, CBE 1978; Director of Parent Board, 1965–80, and Group Director, Music, 1966–78, EMI Ltd; *s* of Leonard George Wood and Miriam (*née* Barnes); *m* 1936, Christine Florence Reason (*d* 1978). *Educ:* Bishopshalt Sch., Hillingdon, Mddx; London Univ. (BCom). Served War, RAF: Sgt, Airfield Controller, 1943; commnd Flying Control Officer, 1944–46. Asst Record Sales Manager, UK, EMI Ltd, 1939, Record Sales Man., 1947; EMI Records Ltd: Gen. Man., 1957; Man. Dir, 1959–66; Chm., 1966–78; EMI Ltd: Gp Divl Dir, 1961; Gp Asst Man. Dir, 1973–77. Internat. Fedn of Producers of Phonograms and Videograms: Chm. Council, 1968–73; Pres., 1973–76; Vice Pres. and Mem. Bd, 1967–81, Emeritus Vice-Pres., 1981–82; Mem. Bd, IFPI (Secretariat) Ltd, 1979–81. Chm., Record Merchandisers Ltd, 1975–81; Dep. Chm., Phonographic Performance Ltd, 1967–80; Hon. Pres., Brit. Phonographic Industry, 1980– (Chm., 1973–80); Governor, Brit. Inst. of Recorded Sound, 1974–78; Trustee, British Record Industry Trust, 1989–. FRSA 1971–85. *Publication:* paper to RSA on growth and develt of recording industry. *Address:* Lark Rise, 39 Howards Thicket, Gerrards Cross, Bucks SL9 7NT. *T:* Gerrards Cross (0753) 884233.

WOOD, Leslie Walter; General Secretary, Union of Construction, Allied Trades and Technicians, 1978–85, retired; Member, TUC General Council, 1979–85; *b* 27 Nov. 1920; *s* of Walter William Wood and Alice Bertha Wood (*née* Clark); *m* 1945 Irene Gladys Emery; two *d.* *Educ:* Birmingham Central Technical Coll.; Ruskin Coll., Oxford. Apprenticed carpenter and joiner, 1935; RAF, 1939–45; Asst Workers' Sec., Cadbury's Works Council, 1948–49; full time employment in Union, 1953–85; Asst Gen. Sec., Amalgamated Soc. of Woodworkers, 1962. Mem. Council, ACAS, 1980–85. *Publication:* A Union to Build (history of Building Trades Unionism), 1979. *Recreations:* golf, swimming, bridge. *Address:* 67 Chestnut Grove, South Croydon, Surrey. *T:* 081–657 7852.

WOOD, Rt. Rev. Mark; *see* Wood, Rt Rev. S. M.

WOOD, Mark William; Editor-in-Chief, Reuters, since 1989; *b* 28 March 1952; *s* of Joseph Hatton Drew Wood and Joyce Wood; *m* 1986, Helen Lanzer; one *d.* *Educ:* Univs of Leeds (BA Hons), Warwick (MA) and Oxford. Joined Reuters, 1976; corresp. in Vienna, 1977–78, East Berlin, 1978–81, Moscow, 1981–85; Chief Corresp., West Germany, 1985–87; Editor, Europe, 1987–89. Director: Visnews, 1989–; Reuters Hldgs, 1990–. *Recreations:* German literature, ski-ing. *Address:* c/o Reuters, 85 Fleet Street, EC4P 4AJ. *T:* 071–250 1122.

WOOD, Sir Martin (Francis), Kt 1986; OBE 1982; FRS 1987; DL; Deputy Chairman, Oxford Instruments Group plc (Founder, 1959, Chairman, until 1983); Fellow, Wolfson College, Oxford, since 1967; *b* 1927; *s* of Arthur Henry Wood and Katharine Mary Altham (*née* Cumberlege); *m* 1955, Audrey Buxton (*née* Stanfield); one *s* one *d* and one step *s* one step *d.* *Educ:* Gresham's; Trinity Coll., Cambridge (MA); Imperial Coll. (RSM) (BSc); Christ Church, Oxford (MA). Nat. Service, Bevin Boy, S Wales and Derbyshire coalfields, 1945–48. NCB, 1953–55; Sen. Res. Officer, Clarendon Lab., Oxford Univ., 1956–69. Chm., Nat. Commn for Superconductivity, SERC/DTI, 1987–; Member: Adv. Bd for Res. Councils, 1983–89; ACOST, 1990–. Dir, Celltech Ltd, and other cos; Technical Consultant, African Med. and Res. Foundn; Founder: Northmoor Trust (for nature conservation); Oxford Trust (for encouragement of study and application of science and technol.). Hon. Fellow UMIST, 1989. Hon. DSc Cranfield Inst. of Technol., 1983; Hon. DTech Loughborough Univ. of Technol., 1985. Mullard Medal, Royal Soc., 1982. DL 1985. *Address:* c/o Oxford Instruments Group plc, Eynsham, Oxford OX8 1TL.

WOOD, Rt. Rev. Maurice Arthur Ponsonby, DSC 1944; MA; RNR; an Hon. Assistant Bishop, Diocese of London, since 1985, and Diocese of Oxford, since 1989; Resident Priest of Englefield, since 1987; *b* 26 Aug. 1916; *o s* of late Arthur Sheppard Wood and of Jane Elspeth Dalzell Wood (*née* Piper); *m* 1st, 1947, Marjorie (*née* Pennell) (*d* 1954); two *s* one *d*; 2nd, 1955, M. Margaret (*née* Sandford); two *s* one *d.* *Educ:* Monkton Combe Sch.; Queens' Coll., Cambridge (MA); Ridley Hall, Cambridge. Deacon, 1940; priest, 1941; Curate, St Paul's, Portman Square, 1940–43. Royal Naval Chaplain, 1943–47 (still Chap. to Commando Assoc.); attached RM Commandos, 1944–46; Chaplain, RNR, 1971–. Rector, St Ebbe's, Oxford, 1947–52; Vicar and RD of Islington, and Pres. Islington Clerical Conf., 1952–61; Principal, Oak Hill Theological Coll., Southgate, N14, 1961–71; Prebendary of St Paul's Cathedral, 1969–71; Bishop of Norwich, 1971–85; Abbot of St Benet's, 1971–85. Proctor in Convocation of Canterbury and Mem. House of Clergy and Gen. Synod of Church of England (formerly Church Assembly), 1954–85 (House of Bishops, 1971–85); Member: Archbishops' Council on Evangelism, 1972–85; Church Comrs' Houses Cttee, 1980–85; Lords and Commons Family and Child Protection Gp, 1980–. Chairman: Theological Colls Principals' Conf., 1970–71; Norfolk Water Safety Assoc, 1966–71; Norwich RSPCA, 1971–85; The Manson Trust (India), 1984– (and Trustee); Order of Christian Unity, 1986–; Pres., Hildenborough Hall Christian Conf. Centre, 1970–85; Vice-President: Bible Churchmen's Missionary Soc.; Boys' Brigade, 1986– (Chm., Anglican Council); Trustee: Mary Whitehouse Trust, 1986–90; Riding Lights Theatre Co., 1986–; Parly Christian Fellowship Trust, 1989–; Council Member: Wycliffe Hall, Oxford, 1981–; British Atlantic Council, 1985–88; Commonwealth Human Ecology Council, 1986–. Governor: Monkton Combe Sch., Bath; Gresham's Sch., Holt, 1971–85; St Helen's Sch., Abingdon, 1989–; Visitor: Langley Sch., Norfolk, 1980–89; Luckley-Oakfield Sch., 1990–. Chaplain, Weavers' Co., 1986–. Mission work with Dr Billy Graham in Tokyo, Toronto, Virginia, Osaka, Boston, Amsterdam. Mem., House of Lords, 1975–85. *Publications:* Like a Mighty Army, 1956; Comfort in Sorrow, 1957; Your Suffering, 1959; Christian Stability, 1968; To Everyman's Door, 1968; Into the Way of Peace, 1982; This is our Faith, 1985. *Recreations:* swimming, painting, (still) supporting Norwich City FC. *Address:* St Mark's House, Englefield, near Reading, Berks RG7 5EP. *T:* Reading (0734) 302227. *Club:* Commonwealth Trust.

WOOD, Norman, CBE 1965; Director: Co-operative Wholesale Society Ltd, 1942–64; Manchester Ship Canal Co., 1954–64; Associated British Foods Ltd, 1964–75, retired; *b* 2 Oct. 1905; *m* 1st, 1933, Ada Entwisle (*d* 1974); two *s* one *d*; 2nd, 1976, Nita Miller. *Educ:* Bolton Co. Grammar Sch.; Co-operative Coll. Nat. Exec. Co-operative Party, and Central Board of Co-operative Union, 1934; Ministry of Information, 1939; Chocolate and Sugar Confectionery War-time Assoc., 1942; British Tourist and Holidays Board (later BTA), 1947–70 (Dep. Chm., 1964–67); Plunkett Foundation, 1948– (Vice-Pres. 1972–); Cake and Biscuit Alliance, 1948; Wheat Commission, 1950; Domestic Coal Consumers Council, 1950; Coronation Accommodation Cttee, 1952. Member: British and Irish Millers, 1950–64; White Fish Authority, 1959–63; Food Res. Adv. Cttee, 1961–65; DTI Japan Trade Adv. Cttee, 1971–; Exec. Mem., British Food Export Council, 1970–75. Chairman: Food and Drink Cttee, British Week, Toronto, 1967, Tokyo, 1969; Chm., ten Food and Drink Missions to Hong Kong and Japan, 1968–76; Dir, Fedn of Agricl Co-ops (UK) Ltd, 1975–; Mem., Lab Party Study Gp on Export Services and Organisation, 1974; Founder Mem., SDP; Pres., Epsom & Ewell Area Party, SDP, 1986–. *Recreations:* walking, music. *Address:* 17 Wallace Fields, Epsom, Surrey KT17 3AX. *T:* 081–393 9052. *Club:* Oriental.

WOOD, Peter Edric; Chairman (part-time), Huddersfield Health Authority, since 1982; Member, Audit Commission, since 1990; *b* 17 July 1929; *s* of Edric Wood and Ruby (*née* Revill); *m* 1952, Barbara Evans; one *s* three *d.* *Educ:* RAF Coll.; Bradford Univ. (MSc); Open Univ. (BA). DipEE. RAF, 1946–61. With ICI, 1961–82; Lectr (part-time), Manchester Univ., 1982–84; Sen. Teaching Fellow (part-time), Leeds Univ., 1984–89. *Recreations:* reading, walking, golf. *Address:* 9 Abbey Close, Hade Edge, Holmfirth, Huddersfield HD7 1RT. *T:* Holmfirth (0484) 686977.

WOOD, Peter (Lawrence); theatrical and television director; *b* 8 Oct. 1928; *s* of Frank Wood and Lucy Eleanor (*née* Meeson). *Educ:* Taunton School; Downing College, Cambridge. Resident Director, Arts Theatre, 1956–57; Associate Dir, NT, 1978–89. Director: The Iceman Cometh, Arts, 1958; The Birthday Party, Lyric, Hammersmith, 1958; Maria Stuart, Old Vic, 1958; As You Like It, Stratford, Canada, 1959; The Private Ear and The Public Eye, Globe, 1962, Morosco, New York, 1963; Carving a Statue, Haymarket, 1964; Poor Richard, Helen Hayes Theatre, New York, 1964; Incident at Vichy, Phœnix, 1966; The Prime of Miss Jean Brodie, Wyndham's, 1966; White Liars, and Black Comedy, 1968; In Search of Gregory (film), 1968–69; Design for Living, Los Angeles, 1971; Jumpers, Burgtheater, Vienna, 1973, Billy Rose Theatre, NY, 1974; Dear Love, Comedy, 1973; Macbeth, LA, 1975; The Mother of Us All (opera), Santa Fé, 1976; Long Day's Journey into Night, LA, 1977; Cosi Fan Tutte, Santa Fé, 1977; She Stoops to Conquer, Burgtheater, Vienna, 1978; Night and Day, Phoenix, 1978, NY, 1979; Il Seraglio, Glyndebourne, 1980, 1988; Don Giovanni, Covent Garden, 1981; Macbeth, Staatsoper, Vienna, 1982; The Real Thing, Strand, 1982; Orione (opera), Santa Fé, 1983; Orion, King's Theatre, Edinburgh, 1984; Jumpers, Aldwych, 1985; Wildfire, Phoenix, 1986; Otello, Staatsoper, Vienna, 1987; Les Liaisons Dangereuses, LA, 1988; Hapgood, Aldwych, 1988, LA, 1989; The Silver King, Chichester, 1990; Map of the Heart, Globe, 1991; *Royal Shakespeare Company:* Winter's Tale, 1960; The Devils, 1961; Hamlet, 1961; The Beggar's Opera, 1963; Co-Dir, History Cycle, 1964; Travesties, 1974 (NY, 1975); The Strange Case of Dr Jekyll and Mr Hyde, 1991; *National Theatre:* The Master Builder, 1964; Love for Love, 1965 (also Moscow); Jumpers, 1972; The Guardsman, The Double Dealer, 1978; Undiscovered Country, 1979; The Provok'd Wife, 1980; On the Razzle, 1981; The Rivals, 1983; Rough Crossing, 1984; Love for Love, 1985; Dalliance, 1986; The Threepenny Opera, 1986; The American Clock, 1986; The Beaux Strategem, 1989; The School for Scandal, 1990; *Television:* Hamlet, USA, 1970; Long Day's Journey Into Night, USA, 1973; Shakespeare, episode I, 1976; Double Dealer, 1980; The Dog it was that Died, 1988. *Recreation:* gastronomic pursuits. *Address:* The Old Barn, Batcombe, Somerset.

WOOD, Philip, OBE 1979; Under Secretary, Department of Transport, since 1986; *b* 30 June 1946; *s* of late Frank and Eleanor Wood; *m* 1971, Dilys Traylen Smith; one *s.* *Educ:* Queen Elizabeth Grammar Sch., Wakefield; Queen's Coll., Oxford. Entered Civil Service, 1967; Min. of Transport, 1967–70; DoE, 1970–75; a Private Sec. to the Prime Minister, 1975–79; Dept of Transport, 1979–: Sec. to Armitage Inquiry into Lorries and the Envmt, 1980; seconded to BRB, 1986–88. *Address:* Department of Transport, 2 Marsham Street, SW1P 3EB.

WOOD, (René) Victor; Director: Sun Life Corp. plc, since 1986; Wemyss Development Co. Ltd, since 1982; *b* 1925; *e s* of late Frederick Wood and Jeanne Wood (*née* Raskin); *m* 1950, Helen Morag, *o d* of late Dr David S. Stewart. *Educ:* Jesus Coll., Oxford (BA). FFA. Chief Exec., 1969–79, Chm. 1974–79, Hill Samuel Insurance and Shipping Holdings Ltd; Chm., Lifeguard Assurance, 1976–84. Director: Haslemere Estates, 1976–86; Coalite Gp, 1977–89; Chandros Insce Co., 1979–89; Colbourne Insce Co., 1980–90; Criterion Insce Co., 1984–90; Scottinvest SA, 1985–; Wemyss Hotels France SA, 1985–; Les Résidences du Colombier SA, 1985–; Domaine de Rimauresq SARL, 1985–. Vice-Pres., British Insurance Brokers' Assoc., 1981–84. *Publications:* (with Michael Pilch): Pension Schemes, 1960; New Trends in Pensions, 1964; Pension Scheme Practice, 1967; Company Pension Schemes, 1971; Managing Pension Schemes, 1974; Pension Schemes, 1979. *Address:* Little Woodbury, Newchapel, near Lingfield, Surrey RH7 6HR. *T:* Lingfield (0342) 832054.

WOOD, Prof. Richard Frederick Marshall, RD 1976; FRCSG, FRCS; Professor of Surgery, St Bartholomew's Hospital Medical College, University of London, and Hon. Consultant Surgeon, City and Hackney Health District, since 1984; *b* 6 Jan. 1943; *s* of Sir Henry Peart Wood, *qv*; *m* 1968, Christine Crawford Smith Jamieson; two *s.* *Educ:* Glasgow Acad.; Univ. of Glasgow (MB ChB 1967, MD 1976); MA Oxon 1981. FRCS 1972; FRCSG 1972. Surgeon Lt-Comdr, RNR, 1973–. Jun. surgical appts at Western Infirmary, Glasgow, 1967–74; Lectr and Sen. Lectr in Surgery, Univ. of Leicester, 1974–81; Hon. Consultant Surgeon, Leics AHA, 1977; Clinical Reader in Surgery and Fellow of Green Coll., Oxford Univ., and Hon. Consultant Surgeon, Oxford AHA, 1981–84. Vis. Fellow, Peter Bent Brigham Hosp., Boston, 1980; Hunterian Prof., RCS, 1985. Mem., Management Cttee, UK Transplant Service, 1980–. Sec., Surgical Res. Soc., 1987–. Fellow, Assoc. of Surgeons of GB; Member Editorial Board: British Jl of Surgery; Transplantation. *Publications:* Renal Transplantation: a clinical handbook, 1983; Surgical Aspects of Haemodialysis, 1983; papers and chapters in textbooks on transplantation, and surgical topics. *Recreations:* music, sailing. *Address:* 25 Turney Road, Dulwich, SE21. *T:* 081–670 2658.

WOOD, Rt. Rev. Richard James; Hon. Assistant Bishop of York, since 1985; *b* 25 Aug. 1920; *s* of Alexander and Irene Wood; *m* 1st, 1946, Elsa Magdalena de Beer (*d* 1969); one *s* one *d* (twins); 2nd, 1972, Cathleen Anne Roark; two *d.* *Educ:* Oldham Hulme Grammar School; Regent St Polytechnic; Wells Theological Coll. Electrical Officer, RAF, then with Ceylon Fire Insurance Assoc. Curate, St Mary's, Calne, 1952–55; Curate, St Mark's Cathedral, George, S Africa, 1955–58; Rector, Christ Church, Beaufort West, 1958–62; Vicar of St Andrew's, Riversdale, 1962–65; Chaplain, S African Defence Force, 1965–68; Asst, St Alban's, E London, 1968; Rector of St John's, Fort Beaufort, 1969–71; Rector of Keetmanshoop, dio. Damaraland, 1971; Priest-in-Charge of Grace Church and St Michael's, Windhoek and Canon of St George's Cathedral, 1972; Vicar Gen. and Suffragan Bishop of Damaraland, 1973–75; expelled by S Africa, 1975; Hon. Asst Bishop of Damaraland, 1976–; Sec. to The Africa Bureau, 1977; Priest-in-Charge of St Mary, Lowgate, Hull, Chaplain to Hull Coll. of Higher Education and Hon. Asst Bishop of York, 1978–79; at St Mark's Theolog. Coll., Dar es Salaam, 1979–83; Interim Rector: St Matthew's, Wheeling, W Virginia, 1983–84; Trinity, Martinsburg, W Virginia, 1984–85. Hon. Life Mem., Hull Univ. Student Union. *Recreations:* general home interests.

WOOD, Robert Eric, CBE 1972; Director, City of Leicester Polytechnic, 1969–73; *b* 6 May 1909; *e s* of Robert and Emma Wood; *m* 1935, Beatrice May Skinner (*d* 1983); one *s* one *d.* *Educ:* Birkenhead Inst.; Liverpool Univ. BSc 1st cl. hons, MSc; FInstP. Lectr and Demonstrator, Liverpool Univ., 1930; Lecturer: Borough Road Trng Coll., 1931; Kingston Techn. Coll., 1934; Woolwich Polytechnic, 1939; Head of Physics Dept, Wigan Techn. Coll., 1942; Principal: Grimsby Techn. Coll., 1947; Leicester Regional Coll. of Technology, 1953. Assoc. of Principals of Technical Instns: Hon. Sec., 1960–65; Pres.,

1965–66; Chm., Interim Cttee of Polytechnic Directors, 1969–70; Mem. Council, CNAA, 1964–70; Mem., Council for Techn. Educn and Trng in Overseas Countries, 1962–66; Vice-Chm., Nat. Adv. Council on Educn for Industry and Commerce, 1967–72. Hon. FCFI. *Address:* Capler, Peppers Lane, Burton Lazars, Melton Mowbray, Leics. *T:* Melton Mowbray (0664) 64576.

WOOD, Air Vice-Marshal Robert Henry, OBE 1977; Regional Director, Fortis Aviation Group; *b* 24 Jan. 1936; *s* of Jack Cyril Wood and May Doris Wood; *m* 1957, Amy Cameron Wright; one *s* two *d. Educ:* Maldon Grammar School; cfs, psc, ndc, rcds. Commnd RAF, 1956; served Nos 617 and 88 Sqns, 1957–63; CFS, 1965–67; No 44 Sqn, 1967–69; attended Indian Staff Coll., 1970; MA to COS Far East Command, Singapore, 1970–71; PSO to Air Sec., 1972; NDC, Latimer, 1973; OC 51 Sqn, 1974; MoD Policy and Plans Dept, 1977; OC RAF Cranwell, 1978; OC RAF Linton-on-Ouse, 1979; Gp Capt. Flying Trng, HQ RAFSC, 1981–83; Dir Personal Services 1 (RAF), 1983–85; RCDS, 1985; Dep. Comdt, RAF Staff Coll., Bracknell, 1986; AOC and Comdt, RAF Coll., Cranwell, 1987–89; retd 1990. *Recreations:* golf, riding. *Club:* Royal Air Force.

WOOD, Robert Noel; psychotherapist; *b* 24 Dec. 1934; *s* of Ernest Clement Wood, CIE and Lucy Eileen Wood; *m* 1962, Sarah Child (marr. diss. 1981); one *s* one *d. Educ:* Sherborne Sch.; New Coll., Oxford (BA Hons PPE); LSE (Rockefeller Student; Certif. in Internat. Studies). Nat. Service Commn, RHA, 1953–55. Dep. Res. Dir, Internat. Div., Economist Intelligence Unit Ltd, 1959–65; Inst. of Econs and Statistics, Oxford, 1965–70; Sen. Economist, Min. of Econ. Affairs and Develt Planning, Tanzania, 1966–69; Econ. Advr, ODM, 1970; Dir of Studies, Overseas Develt Inst., 1970–74; Adviser to House of Commons Select Cttee on Overseas Develt, 1973–74; Dir, Overseas Develt Inst., 1974–82. Jungian analysis, 1982–90; full Mem., Inst. of Psychotherapy and Counselling. Chm., Friends of the Union Chapel, 1983–87; Mem., Religious Soc. of Friends (Quakers), 1982–. Gov., Quintin Kynaston Sch., 1974–86. *Publications:* contrib. Bull. Oxford Inst. of Econs and Statistics, ODI Rev. *Recreations:* Victorian artists, listening to music, singing, swimming, walking, Arsenal football club, poetry, Jung. *Address:* 19 Baalbec Road, N5 1QN. *T:* 071–226 4775.

WOOD, Rt. Rev. Roland Arthur; *see* Saskatoon, Bishop of.

WOOD, Prof. Ronald Karslake Starr, FRS; Professor of Plant Pathology, Imperial College, University of London, since 1964; *s* of Percival Thomas Evans Wood and Florence Dix Starr; *m* 1947, Marjorie Schofield; one *s* one *d. Educ:* Ferndale Grammar Sch.; Imperial College. Royal Scholar, 1937; Forbes Medal, 1941; Huxley Medal, 1950. Research Asst to Prof. W. Brown, 1941; Directorate of Aircraft Equipment, Min. of Aircraft Production, 1942; London University: Lectr, Imperial Coll., 1947; Reader in Plant Pathology, 1955; Prof. of Plant Pathology, 1964; Head of Dept of Pure and Applied Biol., Imperial Coll., 1981–84. Commonwealth Fund Fellow, 1950; Research Fellow, Connecticut Agric. Experiment Stn, 1957. Mem. Council, British Mycological Soc., 1948; Sec., Assoc. of Applied Biologists; Mem., 1949, Chm., 1987–, Biological Council; Mem., Parly and Scientific Cttee; Consultant, Nat. Fedn of Fruit and Potato Trades, 1955; Mem. Council, Inst. of Biology, 1956; Chm., Plant Pathology Cttee, British Mycological Soc.; Mem. Governing Body, Nat. Fruit and Cider Inst., Barnes Memorial Lectr, 1962; Sec., First Internat. Congress of Plant Pathology, 1965; Mem. Governing Body: East Malling Research Stn, 1966 (Vice-Chm.); Inst. for Horticultural Res., 1987; Pres., Internat. Soc. for Plant Pathology, 1968 (Hon. Mem., 1988); Mem., Nat. Cttee for Biology, 1978; Chm., British Nat. Sub-Cttee for Botany, 1978; Dean, RCS, 1975–78; Founder Pres. and Hon. Mem., British Soc. for Plant Pathol., 1987. Scientific Dir, NATO Advanced Study Institute, Pugnochiuso, 1970, Sardinia, 1975, Cape Sounion, 1980; Consultant, FAO/UNDP, India, 1976. Fellow, Amer. Phytopathological Soc., 1972; Corres. Mem., Deutsche Phytomedizinische Gesellschaft, 1973. Otto-Appel-Denkmünster, 1978. Thurburn Fellow, Univ. of Sydney, 1979; Sir C. V. Raman Prof., Univ. of Madras, 1980; Regents' Lectr, Univ. of California, 1981. *Publications:* Physiological Plant Pathology, 1967; (ed) Phytotoxins in Plant Diseases, 1972; (ed) Specifity in Plant Diseases, 1976; (ed) Active Defence Mechanisms in Plants, 1981; (ed) Plant Diseases: infection, damage and loss, 1984; numerous papers in Annals of Applied Biology, Annals of Botany, Phytopathology, Trans British Mycological Soc. *Recreation:* gardening. *Address:* Pyrford Woods, Pyrford, near Woking, Surrey. *T:* Byfleet (09323) 43827.

WOOD, Maj.-Gen. Roy; Director General of Military Survey, Ministry of Defence, since 1990; *b* 14 May 1940; *s* of Alec and Lucy Maud Wood; *m* 1963, Susan Margaret Croxford; two *s. Educ:* Farnham Grammar Sch.; Welbeck College; RMA; Cambridge Univ. (MA); University College London (MSc 1971). FRICS; FRGS. Commissioned RE 1960; Mapping Surveys, Sarawak, Sierra Leone and Sabah, 1964–70; Instructor, Sch. of Military Survey, 1972–75; MoD, 1975–77; OC 14 Topo. Sqn, BAOR, 1977–79; CO Mapping and Charting Estabt, 1979–81; Defense Mapping Agency, USA, 1981–83; MoD, 1984; Comdr, 42 Survey Engr Gp, 1985–87; Dir, Military Survey, 1987–90. FBIM. *Publications:* articles on surveying and mapping in professional and technical jls. *Recreations:* orienteering, hill walking, travel. *Address:* Ministry of Defence, Elmwood Avenue, Feltham, Middx TW13 7AH. *T:* 081–890 3622. *Club:* Geographical.

WOOD, Sir Russell (Dillon), KCVO 1985 (CVO 1979; MVO 1975); VRD 1964; Lt-Comdr, RNR; Deputy Treasurer to the Queen, 1969–85; an Extra Gentleman Usher to the Queen, since 1986; *b* 16 May 1922; *s* of William G. S. Wood, Whitstable, Kent, and Alice Wood; *m* 1948, Jean Violet Yelwa Davidson, *d* of late Alan S. Davidson, Lenham, Kent; one *s* three *d. Educ:* King's Sch., Canterbury. Fleet Air Arm Pilot, 1940–46 (despatches twice). Qual. as Chartered Accountant, 1951; financial management career with major public companies, 1951–68. *Recreations:* private flying, sailing, shooting. *Address:* The Old Forge, Dunwich, Suffolk IP17 3DU. *T:* Westleton (072873) 595. *Clubs:* Army and Navy; East Anglian Flying, Aldeburgh Yacht.

WOOD, Sam, MSc; Director of Statistics and Business Research, Post Office, 1965–72, retired; *b* 10 Oct. 1911; *m* 1940, Lucy Greenhalgh Whittaker; two *d. Educ:* Glossop Grammar School, Derbyshire; University of Manchester. Gaskell Open Scholarship, Derbyshire Major Scholarship, 1929; BSc (1st cl. Hons) Maths; Bishop Harvey Goodwin Research Scholarship, 1932; MSc 1933. Civil Service: GPO, 1933–34; National Assistance Board, 1934–43; Min. of Aircraft Production, 1943–46; Treasury, 1946–50; GPO: Statistician, 1950; Chief Statistician, 1954. *Publications:* articles in Jl of Inst. of Statisticians, British Jl of Industrial Relations. *Address:* Flat 1, The Rookery, East Avenue, Benton, Newcastle upon Tyne NE12 9PH.

WOOD, Rt. Rev. (Stanley) Mark; *b* 21 May 1919; *s* of Arthur Mark and Jane Wood; *m* 1947, Winifred Ruth, *d* of Edward James Toase; three *s* two *d. Educ:* Pontypridd County School; University College, Cardiff; College of the Resurrection, Mirfield. BA (2nd cl. Greek and Latin), Wales. Curate at St Mary's, Cardiff Docks, 1942–45; Curate, Sophiatown Mission, Johannesburg, 1945–47; Rector of Bloemhof, Transvaal, 1947–50; Priest in charge of St Cyprian's Mission, Johannesburg, 1950–55; Rector of Marandellas, Rhodesia, 1955–65; Dean of Salisbury, Rhodesia, 1965–70; Bishop of Matabeleland, 1971–77; Asst Bishop of Hereford, 1977–81; Archdeacon of Ludlow, 1982–83; Bishop Suffragan of Ludlow, 1981–87. *Address:* Glen Cottage, The Norton, Tenby, Dyfed SA70 8AG. *T:* Tenby (0834) 3463.

WOOD, Terence Courtney, CMG 1989; HM Diplomatic Service; Minister, Rome, since 1987; *b* 6 Sept. 1936; *s* of Courtney and Alice Wood; *m* 1st, 1962, Kathleen Mary Jones (marr. diss. 1981); one *s* one *d*; 2nd, 1982, Diana Humphreys-Roberts. *Educ:* King Edward VI Sch., Chelmsford; Trinity Coll., Cambridge. BA Hons 1960. RA, 1955–57 (2nd Lieut). Information Officer, FBI (later CBI), 1963–67; entered HM Diplomatic Service, 1968; Foreign Office, 1968–69; 1st Sec., Rome, 1969–73; FCO, 1973–77; Counsellor (Economic and Commercial), New Delhi, 1977–81; Political Advr and Hd of Chancery, Brit. Mil. Govt, Berlin, 1981–84; Hd of S Asian Dept, FCO, 1984–86; Vis. Fellow, Center for Internat. Affairs, Harvard Univ., 1986–87. sowc, Royal Naval Coll., Greenwich, 1977. *Recreations:* music, painting. *Address:* c/o Foreign and Commonwealth Office, SW1. *Club:* Travellers'.

WOOD, Timothy John Rogerson; MP (C) Stevenage, since 1983; an Assistant Government Whip, since 1990; *b* 13 Aug. 1940; *s* of Thomas Geoffrey Wood and Norah Margaret Annie (*née* Rogerson); *m* 1969, Elizabeth Mary Spencer; one *s* one *d. Educ:* King James's Grammar Sch., Knaresborough, Yorks; Manchester Univ. (BSc Maths). Joined Ferranti Ltd as Lectr in Computer Programming, 1962; joined ICT Ltd (later ICL), 1963; subseq. involved in develt of ICL systems software; Sen. Proj. Management Consultant advising on introdn of large computer systems, 1977; Sen. Proj. Manager on application systems, 1981; resigned from ICL, 1983. PPS to: Minister for Armed Forces, 1986–87; Minister of State, 1987–89, Sec. of State, 1989–90, Northern Ireland; Chm., Wokingham Cons. Assoc., 1980–83; Vice Chairman: National Assoc. of Cons. Graduates, 1975–76; Thames Valley Euro Constituency Council, 1979–83; Member: Bow Gp, 1962– (Mem. Council, 1968–71); Bracknell DC, 1975–83 (Leader, 1976–78); Bd, Bracknell Develt Corp., 1977–82. *Publications:* Bow Group pamphlets on educn, computers in Britain, and the Post Office. *Recreations:* gardening, chess, reading. *Address:* House of Commons, SW1A 0AA. *T:* 071–219 3601.

WOOD, Victor; *see* Wood, R. V.

WOOD, Victoria; writer and comedienne; *b* 19 May 1953; *d* of Stanley and Helen Wood; *m* 1980, Geoffrey Durham; one *d. Educ:* Bury Grammar School for Girls; Univ. of Birmingham (BA Drama, Theatre Arts). Performed regularly on television and radio as singer/songwriter, 1974–78. First stage play, Talent, performed at Crucible Th., Sheffield, 1978; TV production of this, broadcast, 1979 (3 National Drama awards, 1980); wrote Good Fun, stage musical, 1980; wrote and performed, TV comedy series: Wood and Walters, 1981–82; Victoria Wood As Seen On TV, 1st series 1985 (Broadcasting Press Guilds Award; BAFTA Awards, Best Light Entertainment Prog., Best Light Entertainment Perf.), 2nd series 1986 (BAFTA Award, Best Light Entertainment Prog.), Special, 1987 (BAFTA Best Light Entertainment Prog.); An Audience with Victoria Wood, 1988 (BAFTA Best Light Entertainment Prog., BAFTA Best Light Entertainment Perf.); Victoria Wood, 1989. Appeared in stage revues, Funny Turns, Duchess Th., 1982, Lucky Bag, Ambassadors, 1984; Victoria Wood, Palladium, 1987; Victoria Wood Up West, 1990. Variety Club BBC Personality of the Year, 1987. Hon. DLitt Lancaster, 1989. *Publications:* Victoria Wood Song Book, 1984; Up to you, Porky, 1985; Barmy, 1987; Mens Sana in Thingummy Doodah, 1990. *Recreations:* walking and talking. *Address:* c/o Richard Stone, 25 Whitehall, SW1. *T:* 071–839 6421.

WOOD, Walter; Town Clerk, City of Birmingham, 1972–74; *b* Bolton, 11 Jan. 1914; *s* of Walter Scott Wood; *m* 1939, Hilda Maude, *d* of Albert Forrester; two *s. Educ:* Canon Slade Sch., Bolton; Victoria Univ., Manchester (LLB). Served with RAF, 1940–45. Admitted solicitor, 1937 (Daniel Reardon and Clabon prizeman); legal associate member, RTPI, 1948; Asst Solicitor, Bradford, 1937. Swansea, 1939; Dep. Town Clerk, Grimsby, 1947; Principal Asst Solicitor, Sheffield, 1948; Asst Town Clerk, Birmingham, 1952; Dep. Town Clerk, Birmingham, 1960. Panel Inspector, DoE, 1974–85. Governor, Solihull Sch., 1974–84. Pres., Birmingham Law Soc., 1976. Pres., West Midland Rent Assessment Panel, 1980–84. *Recreations:* swimming, philately. *Address:* 43 Sandgate Road, Hall Green, Birmingham B28 0UN. *T:* 021–744 1195.

WOOD, Rt. Rev. Wilfred Denniston; *see* Croydon, Bishop Suffragan of.

WOOD, Sir William (Alan), KCVO 1978; CB 1970; Second Crown Estate Commissioner, 1968–78; Ombudsman, Mirror Group Newspapers, 1985–89; Chairman, London and Quadrant Housing Trust, 1980–89; *b* 8 Dec. 1916; *m* 1st, 1943, Zoë (*d* 1985), *d* of Rev. Dr D. Frazer-Hurst; two *s* two *d*; 2nd, 1985, Mrs Mary Hall (*née* Cowper). *Educ:* Dulwich Coll.; Corpus Christi Coll., Cambridge (Scholar). Ministry of Home Affairs, N. Ireland, 1939. Lieut, RNVR, 1942–46. Ministry of Town and Country Planning, 1946; Minister's Private Secretary, 1951; Principal Regional Officer (West Midlands), Ministry of Housing and Local Government, 1954; Asst Secretary, 1956; Under-Secretary, 1964–68. Chm. Council, King Alfred Sch., 1966–78, Pres. 1978–. *Address:* 93 Crawford Street, W1H 1AT. *T:* 071–724 0685; Maplewood, 40 Picklers Hill, Abingdon, Oxon OX14 2BB. *T:* Abingdon (0235) 520515. *Club:* Athenæum.

WOODALL, Alec; *b* 20 Sept. 1918; *m* 1950; one *s* one *d. Educ:* South Road Elementary School. Colliery official. MP (Lab) Hemsworth, Feb. 1974–1987. PPS to Sec. of State for Trade, 1976–78. *Address:* 2 Grove Terrace, Hemsworth, West Yorkshire WF9 4BQ. *T:* Hemsworth (0977) 613897.

WOODARD, Rear-Adm. Robert Nathaniel; Flag Officer Royal Yachts, since 1990; *b* 13 Jan. 1939; *s* of Francis Alwyne Woodard and Catherine Mary Woodard (*née* Hayes); *m* 1963, Rosamund Lucia, *d* of Lt-Col D. L. A. Gibbs, DSO and Lady Hilaria Gibbs (*née* Edgcumbe); two *s* one *d. Educ:* Lancing College. Joined Royal Navy as Cadet, 1958; specialised in flying; served HM Ships Ark Royal, Eagle, Victorious, Bulwark in 800, 801, 845, 846 and 848 Sqns (active service Malaya, Borneo); Commands: 771 Sqn, 1973–74; 848 Sqn, 1974–75; HMS Amazon, 1978–80; HMS Glasgow, 1983–84; HMS Osprey, 1984–86; MoD Op. Requirements, 1986–88; comd. Clyde Submarine Base, 1989–90. Dir, Woodard (Western Div.) plc; Fellow Western Div., Woodard Corp. Governor: King's Coll., Taunton; St Clare's, Penzance; King's Hall, Pyrland. *Recreations:* shooting, fishing, painting, sailing. *Address:* HM Yacht Britannia, BFPO Ships. *Clubs:* Commonwealth Trust; Royal Cornwall Yacht, Port Navas Yacht.

WOODBINE PARISH, Sir David (Elmer), Kt 1980; CBE 1964; Chairman, City and Guilds of London Institute, 1967–79, Life Vice-President, 1979; *b* 29 June 1911; *o s* of late Walter Woodbine Parish and Audrey Makins; *m* 1939, Mona Blair McGarel, BA (Arch), ARIBA (*d* 1991), *o d* of late Charles McGarel Johnston, Glynn, Co. Antrim; two *d. Educ:* Sandroyd; Eton; Lausanne, Switzerland. Chm. and Man. Dir, Holliday and Greenwood Ltd, 1953–59 (Dir., 1937–59); Chm., Bovis Ltd, 1959–66; Dep. Chm., Marine and General Mutual Life Assurance Soc., 1976–86 (Dir, 1971–86). Chm., Jt Mission Hosp. Equip. Bd (ECHO), 1973–78. President: London Master Builders Assoc., 1952; Nat. Fedn of Building Trades Employers, 1960; Vice-Pres., Internat. Fedn of European Contractors of Building and Public Works, 1967–71; Member: Regional Adv. Council for Technological Educn, London and Home Counties, 1952–69; Architects Registration

Council, 1952–72; Nat. Adv. Council for Educn in Industry and Commerce, 1953–78; BIM Council, 1953–62, Bd of Fellows, 1966–72; Nat. Council for Technological Awards, 1955–61; Bd of Building Educn, 1955–66; Building Res. Bd, 1957–60; Industrial Training Council, 1958–64; Council, British Employers' Confedn, 1959–65; Council Foundn for Management Educn, 1959–65; British Productivity Council, 1961–70 (Chm., Educn and Trng Cttee, 1963–70); Human Sciences Cttee (SRC), 1963–66; Construction Industry Training Bd, 1964–70. Chairman: UK Nat. Cttee, Internat. Apprentice Competition, 1962–70; MPBW Working Party on Res. and Information, 1963; Nat. Examinations Bd for Supervisory Studies, 1964–73; Mem., Nat. Jt Consult. Cttee of Architects, Quantity Surveyors and Builders, 1958–70 (Chm. 1966–68); Chm., Dept of Health and Social Security Cttee of Inquiry on Hosp. Building Maintenance and Minor Capital Works, 1968–70; Member: Court, Russia Co., 1937–84; Court, City Univ., 1967–72; Bd of Governors, The Polytechnic, Regent Street, 1967–70; Court, Polytechnic of Central London, 1970–76; Governing Body, Imperial Coll. of Science and Technology, 1971–81. Vice-Chm., Bd of Governors, St Thomas' Hosp., 1967–74 (Chm., Rebuilding Cttee, 1968–76); Chairman: Council, St Thomas's Hosp. Med. Sch., 1970–82; St Thomas' Dist Educn Adv. Council, 1974–81; Florence Nightingale Museum Trust, 1982–86; Member: Nightingale Fund Council, 1974–84; Bd of Governors, Bethlem Royal Hosp. and Maudsley Hosp., 1975–78; Council of Governors, Utd Medical and Dental Schs of Guy's and St Thomas's Hosps, 1982–85. Chm., Sussex Area, Royal Sch. of Church Music, 1981–85. Master, Clothworkers' Co., 1974–75 (Warden, 1962–64; Chm., Angel Court Develt, 1969–80). Mem. Bd of Governors, Clothworkers' Foundation, 1977–. FCIOB (FIOB 1940); FRSA 1953; CBIM (FBIM 1957). Fellow, Imperial Coll., 1976; Hon. FCGI 1979. Hon. LLD Leeds, 1975. *Publications:* contribs to technical jls concerned with construction. *Recreations:* travel and music. *Address:* The Glebe Barn, Pulborough, West Sussex RH20 2AF. *T:* Pulborough (07982) 2613. *Club:* Boodle's.

WOODCOCK, Dr George, FRGS; Editor, Canadian Literature, 1959–77; author; *b* 8 May 1912; *s* of Samuel Arthur Woodcock and Margaret Gertrude Woodcock (*née* Lewis); *m* 1949, Ingeborg Hedwig Elisabeth Linzer. *Educ:* Sir William Borlase's Sch., Marlow. Editor, Now, London, 1940–47; freelance writer, 1947–54; Lectr in English, Univ. of Washington, 1954–56; Lectr, Asst Prof. and finally Associate Prof. of English, Univ. of British Columbia, 1956–63; Lectr in Asian Studies, Univ. of British Columbia, 1966–67. At the same time continued writing books and talks; also plays and documentaries for Canadian Broadcasting Corporation. Prepared a series of nine documentary films for CBC, on South Pacific, 1972–73. Hon. LLD: Victoria, 1967; Winnipeg, 1975; Hon. DLitt: Sir George Williams Univ., 1970; Univ. of Ottawa, 1974; Univ. of British Columbia, 1977. John Simon Guggenheim Fellow, 1950; Canadian Govt Overseas Fellow, 1957; Canada Council: Killam Fellow, 1970; Senior Arts Fellow, 1975. Governor-General's Award for Non-Fiction, 1967; Molson Prize, 1973; UBC Medal for Popular Biography, 1973 and 1976. FRSC 1968, FRGS 1971. *Publications:* William Godwin, 1946; The Anarchist Prince, 1950; Proudhon, 1956; To the City of the Dead, 1956; Selected Poems, 1967; Anarchism, 1962; Faces of India, 1964; The Greeks in India, 1966; The Crystal Spirit: a study of George Orwell, 1966; Canada and the Canadians, 1970; Dawn and the Darkest Hour, 1971; Gandhi, 1971; Rejection of Politics, 1972; Herbert Read, 1972; Who Killed the British Empire?, 1974; Gabriel Dumont, 1975; Notes on Visitations, 1975; South Sea Journey, 1976; Peoples of the Coast, 1977; Thomas Merton, Monk and Poet, 1978; Two Plays, 1978; The Canadians, 1980; The World of Canadian Writing, 1980; The George Woodcock Reader, 1980; The Mountain Road, 1981; Confederation Betrayed, 1981; Taking It to the Letter, 1981; Letter to the Past, 1982; Collected Poems, 1983; British Columbia: a celebration, 1983; Orwell's Message, 1984; Strange Bedfellows, 1985; The Walls of India, 1985; The University of British Columbia, 1986; Northern Spring, 1987; Beyond the Blue Mountains, 1987; The Social History of Canada, 1988; The Caves in the Desert, 1988; The Marvellous Century, 1988; Powers of Observation, 1989; A History of British Columbia, 1990; Anarchist Essays, 1991; Tolstoy at Yasnaya Polyana, 1991; also many articles. *Recreation:* travel. *Address:* 6429 McCleery Street, Vancouver, BC V6N 1G5, Canada. *T:* 604–266–9393. *Club:* Faculty (Vancouver).

WOODCOCK, Gordon, FCA, CIPFA; County Treasurer of Staffordshire, 1973–83. Served War, Royal Navy, 1942–46. City Treasurer's Dept: Birmingham, 1937–42 and 1946–54; Stoke-on-Trent, 1954–73; City Treasurer of Stoke-on-Trent, 1971–73.

WOODCOCK, Sir John, Kt 1989; CBE 1983; QPM 1976; CBIM; HM Chief Inspector of Constabulary, since 1990; *b* 14 Jan. 1932; *s* of late Joseph Woodcock and of Elizabeth May Woodcock (*née* Whiteside); *m* 1953, Kathleen Margaret Abbott; two *s* one *d*. *Educ:* Preston, Lancs, elementary schs; Preston Technical Coll. Police cadet, Lancashire Constabulary, 1947–50; Army Special Investigation Branch, 1950–52; Constable to Chief Inspector, Lancashire Constabulary, 1952–65; Supt and Chief Supt, Bedfordshire and Luton Constabulary, 1965–68; Asst Chief Constable, 1968–70, Dep. Chief Constable, 1970–74, Gwent Constabulary; Dep. Chief Constable, Devon and Cornwall Constabulary, 1974–78; Chief Constable: N Yorkshire Police, 1978–79; S Wales Constabulary, 1979–83; HM Inspector of Constabulary, Wales and Midlands, 1983–90. Intermed. Comd Course, Police Coll., 1965, Sen. Comd Course, 1968; Study, Bavarian Police, 1977; European Discussion Centre, 1977; Internat. Police Course (Lectr), Sicily, Rome, 1978; FBI, Nat. Exec., Washington, 1981; Study, Royal Hong Kong Police, 1989. Vice-Pres., Welsh Assoc. of Youth Clubs, 1981–87; Chm., South Wales Cttee, Royal Jubilee and Prince's Trusts, 1983–85; Member: Admin. Council, Royal Jubilee Trusts, 1981–85; Prince's Trust Cttee for Wales, 1981–85; Mem., Governing Body, World College of the Atlantic, 1980–85. OStJ 1981; KSG 1984. *Recreations:* squash, badminton, walking, golf. *Address:* Home Office, Queen Anne's Gate, SW1H 9AT. *Club:* Hon. Member, Swansea Lions.

WOODCOCK, John Charles; cricket writer; *b* 7 Aug. 1926; *s* of late Rev. Parry John Woodcock and Norah Mabel Woodcock (*née* Hutchinson). *Educ:* Dragon Sch.; St Edward's Sch., Oxford; Trinity Coll., Oxford (MA; OUHC *v* Cambridge, 1946, 1947). Manchester Guardian, 1952–54; Cricket Correspondent to The Times, 1954–87, and to Country Life, 1962–91; Editor, Wisden Cricketers' Almanack, 1980–86; has covered 36 Test tours, 1950–87, to Australia, 16 times, S Africa, W Indies, New Zealand, India and Pakistan. Mem., MCC Cttee, 1988–91. Sports Journalist of the Year, British Press Awards, 1987. *Publications:* The Ashes, 1956; (with E. W. Swanton) Barclay's World of Cricket, 1980 (Associate Editor, 2nd edn 1986, Consultant Editor, 3rd edn, 1986). *Recreations:* the countryside, golf. *Address:* The Curacy, Longparish, near Andover, Hants SP11 6PB. *T:* Longparish (026472) 259. *Clubs:* MCC, Flyfishers'; Vincent's (Oxford); St Enodoc Golf.

WOODCOCK, Michael, (Mike), JP; MP (C) Ellesmere Port and Neston, since 1983; *b* 10 April 1943; *s* of Herbert Eric Woodcock and Violet Irene Woodcock; *m* 1969, Carole Ann (*née* Berry); one *s* one *d*. *Educ:* Queen Elizabeth's Grammar Sch., Mansfield, Notts; DLitt IMCB, 1988. Successively: Accountant, Personnel Officer, Management Development Adviser, Head of Small Business Development Unit, Consultant, Vice-Pres. of US Corp., Founder of four UK companies. Underwriting Mem. of Lloyd's, 1984–. Parly Advr, Chamber of Coal Traders, 1985–. JP Mansfield, Notts, 1971. *Publications:* People at Work, 1975; Unblocking Your Organisation, 1978; Team Development Manual, 1979 (UK and USA); Organisation Development Through Teambuilding, 1981 (UK and USA); The Unblocked Manager, 1982 (UK and USA); 50 Activities for Self Development, 1982 (UK and USA); Manual of Management Development, 1985; 50 Activities for Teambuilding, 1989; 50 Activities for Unblocking Your Organisation, 1990; The Self Made Leader, 1990. *Recreation:* walking. *Address:* House of Commons, SW1. *Club:* Farmers'.

WOODCOCK, Thomas, FSA; Somerset Herald, since 1982; *b* 20 May 1951; *s* of Thomas Woodcock, Hurst Green, Lancs, and Mary, *d* of William Woodcock, Holcombe, Lancs. *Educ:* Eton; University Coll., Durham (BA); Darwin Coll., Cambridge (LLB). FSA 1990. Called to Bar, Inner Temple, 1975. Research Assistant to Sir Anthony Wagner, Garter King of Arms, 1975–78; Rouge Croix Pursuivant, 1978–82. *Publication:* (with John Martin Robinson) The Oxford Guide to Heraldry, 1988. *Address:* 47 Regents Park Road, NW1 7SY. *T:* 071–722 5166; College of Arms, Queen Victoria Street, EC4V 4BT. *T:* 071–236 3634. *Club:* Travellers'.

WOODFIELD, Sir Philip (John), KCB 1983 (CB 1974); CBE 1963; Member, Royal Commission on Criminal Justice, since 1991; Chairman, Irish Soldiers and Sailors Land Trust, since 1986; Staff Counsellor for the Security and Intelligence Services, since 1987; *b* 30 Aug. 1923; *s* of late Ralph and Ruth Woodfield; *m* 1958, Diana Margaret, *d* of Sydney and Margaret Herington; three *d*. *Educ:* Alleyn's Sch., Dulwich; King's Coll., London. Served War of 1939–45: Royal Artillery, 1942–47 (Captain). Entered Home Office, 1950; Asst Private Secretary to Home Secretary, 1952; Federal Government of Nigeria, 1955–57; Home Office, 1957–60; Private Secretary to the Prime Minister, 1961–65; Asst Sec. 1965–67, Asst Under-Sec. of State, 1967–72, Home Office; Deputy Sec., NI Office, 1972–74, Home Office, 1974–81; Perm. Under-Sec. of State, NI Office, 1981–83. Secretary to: Commonwealth Immigration Mission, 1965; Lord Mountbatten's inquiry into prison security, Nov.-Dec. 1966; Chairman: Scrutiny of Supervision of Charities, 1987; Review of British Transport Police, 1987–88. Chm., London and Metropolitan Gout Staff Commn, 1984–91. *Recreation:* music. *Address:* c/o Lloyds Bank, 6 Pall Mall, SW1. *Clubs:* Garrick, Beefsteak.

WOODFORD, Air Vice-Marshal Anthony Arthur George, CB 1989; Assistant Chief of Staff Policy, Supreme Headquarters Allied Powers Europe, since 1989; *b* 6 Jan. 1939; *s* of Arthur and May Woodford; *m* 1965, Christine Barbara Tripp; one *s* two *d*. *Educ:* Haberdashers' Aske's Hampstead School; RAF College, Cranwell. BA Hons Open Univ. 1978. Commissioned pilot, 1959; served Nos 12, 44, 53, 101 Sqns and 4017th CCTS USAF; Asst Air Attaché, British Embassy, Washington, 1978–81; Comdr RAF St Mawgan, 1982–83; Comdr British Forces Ascension Island, 1982; ADC to the Queen, 1982–83; RCDS 1984; HQ Strike Command: Air Cdre Plans, 1985–87; AOA, 1987–89. *Address:* Ministry of Defence, Whitehall, SW1A 2HB. *Club:* Royal Air Force.

WOODFORD, Colin Godwin Patrick; His Honour Judge Woodford; a Circuit Judge, since 1991; *b* 30 Jan. 1934; *s* of late Reginald Godwin Woodford and of Cecilia Mary Agnes (*née* Green); *m* 1st, 1955, Julia Mary Howe (marr. diss. 1976); two *s* one *d*; 2nd, 1978, Jane Ellen Woolston; one *d*. *Educ:* St Joseph's Coll., Beulah Hill, W Norwood; St Joseph's Coll., Ipswich; University Coll. London (LLB). Baker and confectioner, 1949–52; RAF, 1952–54; local govt Treasurer's Dept, 1954; Constable to Chief Inspector, Essex Constabulary, 1954–72; called to the Bar, Middle Temple, 1972; Barrister, London and E Anglia, 1972–91. *Recreations:* computer studies, sailing, reading. *Address:* The Law Courts, Bishopsgate, Norwich NR3 1CR.

WOODFORD, Maj.-Gen. David Milner, CBE 1975; retired; Member, Lord Chancellor's Panel of Inspectors, since 1988; *b* 26 May 1930; *s* of late Major R. M. Woodford, MC, and Marion Rosa Woodford (*née* Gregory); *m* 1959, Mary E. Jones (marr. diss. 1987). *Educ:* Prince of Wales Sch., Nairobi; Wadham Coll., Oxford. psc, jsdc, rcds. National Service, then Regular, 1st Royal Fusiliers, Korea, 1953, then Regtl service, Egypt, Sudan, UK, 1953–55; ADC/GOC Berlin, 1956–58; Adjt and Co. Comd 1RF, Gulf, Kenya, Malta, Cyprus, Libya, UK, 1958–61; GSO3 Div./Dist, UK, 1962; sc Camberley, 1963; GSO2 MO 1, then MA/VCGS, 1964–66; Co. Comd 1RF, BAOR, UK, Gulf and Oman, 1966–68; GSO1 (DS) Staff Coll., 1968–70; CO 3 RRF, Gibraltar, UK, N Ireland, 1970–72; Col GS NEARELF (Cyprus), 1972–75; Comd 3 Inf. Bde (N Ireland), 1976–77; Dep. Col, RRF, 1976–81; RCDS 1978; D Comd and COS SE Dist, UK, 1979–80; Dir Army Training, 1981–82; Sen. Army Mem., RCDS, 1982–84; Comdt, JSDC, 1984–86. Col RRF, 1982–86. *Recreations:* literary, historical; passionate golfer. *Address:* c/o Regimental Headquarters, The Royal Regiment of Fusiliers, HM Tower of London, EC3N 4AB. *Clubs:* Army and Navy, New Zealand Golf.

WOODFORD, (Frederick) Peter, PhD; FRCPath; CChem, FRSC; Chief Scientific Officer, Department of Health (formerly of Health and Social Security), since 1984; *b* 8 Nov. 1930; *s* of Wilfrid Charles Woodford and Mabel Rose (*née* Scarff); *m* 1964, Susan Silberman, NY; one *d*. *Educ:* Lewis Sch., Pengam, Glam; Balliol Coll., Oxford (Domus Exhibnr; BA (Hons Chem.) 1952; MA 1955); PhD Leeds 1955. FRCPath 1984; CChem, FRSC 1990. Res. Fellow, Leiden Univ., 1958–62; Vis. Scientist/Lectr, Univ. of Tennessee Med. Sch. and NIH, USA, 1962–63; Guest Investigator, Rockefeller Univ., NY, 1963–71; Scientific Historian, Ciba Foundn, and Scientific Associate, Wellcome Trust, 1971–74; Exec. Dir, Inst. for Res. into Mental and Multiple Handicap, 1974–77; PSO (Clin. Chem.), DHSS, 1977–84. Managing/Executive Editor: Jl of Atherosclerosis Res., 1960–62; Jl of Lipid Res., 1963–69; Procs of Nat. Acad. of Scis, USA, 1970–71. Waverley Gold Medal for scientific writing, 1955; Meritorious Award, Council of Biology Editors, USA, 1984. *Publications:* Scientific Writing for Graduate Students, 1969, 4th edn 1986; Medical Research Systems in Europe, 1973; The Ciba Foundation: an analytic history 1949–1974, 1974; Writing Scientific Papers in English, 1975; articles on scientific writing, lipids of the arterial wall, editing of biomed. jls, prevention and treatment of handicapping disorders, screening for spina bifida, quality in pathology labs, costing and ethics in clin. chem. *Recreations:* chamber music (pianist), gardening, opera. *Address:* 1 Akenside Road, NW3 5BS. *Club:* Athenæum.

WOODGATE, Joan Mary, CBE 1964; RRC 1959; Matron-in-Chief, Queen Alexandra's RN Nursing Service, 1962–66, retired; *b* 30 Aug. 1912; *d* of Sir Alfred Woodgate, CBE, and Louisa Alice (*née* Digby). *Educ:* Surbiton High Sch., Surrey. Trained at St George's Hospital, 1932–36, Sister, 1937–38; Queen Charlotte's Hospital, 1936. Joined QARNNS, 1938; served Middle East and Far East; HM Hospital Ship, Empire Clyde, 1945–47; HM Hospital Ship, Maine, 1953–54; Principal Matron: RNH Haslar, 1959–61; RNH Malta, 1961–62. OStJ 1959; QHNS, 1962–64. Member, Commonwealth War Graves Commn, 1966–83. *Recreations:* gardening, country pursuits. *Address:* Tiptoe, near Lymington, Hants SO41 6FS. *Club:* English-Speaking Union.

WOODHALL, David Massey; Chief Executive, Commission for New Towns, 1982–April 1992; *b* 25 Aug. 1934; *s* of Douglas J. D. and Esme Dorothy Woodhall; *m* 1954, Margaret A. Howarth; two *s*. *Educ:* Bishop Holgate's Sch., Barnsley; Royds Hall, Huddersfield; Henley Administrative Staff Coll. Dip. Leeds Sch. of Architecture and Town Planning. West Riding CC, 1951–60; Cumberland CC, 1960–63;

Northamptonshire CC, 1963–82: County Planning Officer, 1971–80; Asst Chief Executive, 1980–82. *Recreations:* motor-racing, fell walking, food and wine. *Address:* 5 Kylestrome House, Cundy Street, SW1W 9JT. *T:* 071–730 0989.

WOODHAM, Professor Ronald Ernest; Professor of Music, Reading University, 1951–77; *b* 8 Feb. 1912; *s* of Ernest Victor Woodham, Beckenham, Kent; *m* 1949, Kathleen Isabel, *e d* of P. J. Malone; three *s. Educ:* Sherborne Sch.; Royal College of Music, London; Christ Church, Oxford. BA, DMus; FRCO, ARCM. Assistant Director of Music, Bradfield Coll., 1936. Served in RASC, in Middle East and Italy, 1939–45 (despatches). Acting Director of Music, Bradfield Coll., 1946; Director of Music, Sherborne Sch., 1946; Cramb Lecturer in Music, Glasgow Univ., 1947–51. *Address:* 8 Sutton Gardens, St Peter Street, Winchester, Hants SO23 8HP.

WOODHAMS, Ven. Brian Watson; Archdeacon of Newark, 1965–79, Archdeacon Emeritus since 1980; Hon. Canon of Southwell Minister, 1960–79; Rector of Staunton with Flawborough and Kilvington, 1971–79; *b* 16 Jan. 1911; *s* of Herbert and Florence Osmond Woodhams; *m* 1941, Vera Charlotte White; one *s. Educ:* Dover Coll.; Oak Hill Theological Coll.; St John's Coll., University of Durham. LTh 1934, BA 1936, Durham. Deacon, 1936; Priest, 1937. Curate: St Mary Magdalene, Holloway, 1936–39; St James-the-Less, Bethnal Green, 1939–41; Christ Church, New Malden, i/c of St John, New Malden, 1941–43; Vicar: St Mark, Poplar, 1943–45; St James-the-Less, Bethnal Green, 1945–50; St Jude's, Mapperley, Nottingham, 1950–65; Farndon with Thorpe-by-Newark, 1965–71. Proctor in York Convocation, 1955–65. Chairman, Southwell Diocesan Board of Women's Work, 1966–79. Bishop's Hon. Chaplain to Retired Clergy, dio. of Southwell, 1980–. *Recreations:* children's and refugee work; joys and problems of retirement; interested in sport (local FA football referee). *Address:* 2 Lunn Lane, Collingham, Newark, Notts NG23 7LP. *T:* Newark (0636) 892207.

WOODHEAD, Vice-Adm. Anthony Peter; Deputy Supreme Allied Commander Atlantic, since 1991; *b* 30 July 1939; *s* of Leslie and Nancy Woodhead; *m* 1964, Carol; one *s* one *d. Educ:* Leeds Grammar Sch.; Conway; BRNC Dartmouth. Seaman Officer; Pilot, 1962; Aircraft Carriers, Borneo Campaign; CO, HM Ships Jupiter, 1974, Rhyl, 1975; NDC 1976; Naval Plans Div., MoD, 1977; CSO to Flag Officer, Third Flotilla, 1980; COS to FO Comdg Falklands Task Force, 1982; Captain, Fourth Frigate Sqdn, 1983; RCDS 1984; Dir, Naval Ops, 1985; CO HMS Illustrious, 1986; Flag Officer: Flotilla Two, 1988; Flotilla One, 1989. *Recreations:* tennis, antique restoration. *Address:* c/o Naval Secretary, Old Admiralty Building, Whitehall, SW1. *Club:* Royal Navy of 1765 and 1785.

WOODHEAD, David James; National Director, Independent Schools Information Service, since 1985; *b* 9 Nov. 1943; *s* of Frank and Polly Woodhead; *m* 1974, Carole Underwood; two *s. Educ:* Queen Elizabeth Grammar Sch., Wakefield; Univ. of Leicester (BA Hons history, politics and English). Journalist: Cambridge Evening News (educn corresp.), 1965; Sunday Telegraph, 1968; ILEA Press Office: Press Officer, 1975; Chief Press Officer, 1978. Trustee, Jt Educnl Trust. FRSA. Editl Dir, The ISIS Magazine. *Publications:* Choosing Your Independent School, annually, 1985–; (ed) Good Communications Guide, 1986, 2nd edn 1989; numerous newspaper and magazine articles. *Recreations:* family, opera, classical music, travel, countryside. *Address:* Independent Schools Information Service, 56 Buckingham Gate, SW1E 6AG. *T:* 071–630 8796.

WOODHEAD, (Susan) Jane, (Mrs D. C. Woodhead); Building Societies Ombudsman, since 1991; *b* 6 March 1954; *d* of John Darroll Angus and Greta Geraldine Angus; *m* 1978, Donald Christopher Woodhead; two *d* (one *s* decd). *Educ:* Beaconsfield Girls' High Sch.; Bristol Univ. (LLB). Admitted as solicitor, 1978. Asst solicitor, private practice, 1980–82; Legal Asst, Insurance Ombudsman Bureau, 1983–89; Sen. Legal Officer, Office of Building Socs Ombudsman, 1989–91. *Publications:* contrib. legal periodicals. *Recreations:* reading, France. *Address:* Grosvenor Gardens House, 35–37 Grosvenor Gardens, SW1X 7AW. *T:* 071–931 0044.

WOODHOUSE, family name of **Baron Terrington.**

WOODHOUSE, Ven. Andrew Henry, DSC 1945; MA; Archdeacon of Hereford and Canon Residentiary, Hereford Cathedral, 1982–91; *b* 30 Jan. 1923; *s* of H. A. Woodhouse, Dental Surgeon, Hanover Square, W1, and Woking, Surrey, and Mrs P. Woodhouse; unmarried. *Educ:* Lancing Coll.; The Queen's Coll., Oxford. MA 1949. Served War, RNVR, 1942–46 (Lieut). Oxford, 1941–42 and 1946–47; Lincoln Theological Coll., 1948–50. Deacon, 1950; Priest, 1951; Curate of All Saints, Poplar, 1950–56; Vicar of St Martin, West Drayton, 1956–70; Rural Dean of Hillingdon, 1967–70; Archdeacon of Ludlow and Rector of Wistanstow, 1970–82. *Recreations:* photography, walking. *Address:* Orchard Cottage, Bracken Close, Woking, Surrey GU22 7HD. *T:* Guildford (0483) 760671. *Club:* Naval.

WOODHOUSE, Rt. Hon. Sir (Arthur) Owen, KBE 1981; Kt 1974; DSC 1944; PC 1974; Founding President, Law Commission, New Zealand, 1986–91; a Judge of the Supreme Court, New Zealand, 1961–86; a Judge of the Court of Appeal, 1974–86, President of the Court of Appeal, 1981–86; *b* Napier, 18 July 1916; *s* of A. J. Woodhouse and W. J. C. Woodhouse (*née* Allen); *m* 1940, Margaret Leah Thorp; four *s* two *d. Educ:* Napier Boys' High Sch.; Auckland Univ. (LLB). Served War of 1939–45, Lt-Comdr in RNZNVR on secondment to RN; service in MTBs; liaison officer with Yugoslav Partisans, 1943; Asst to Naval Attaché, HM Embassy Belgrade, 1945. Joined Lusk, Willis & Sproule, barristers and solicitors, 1946; Crown Solicitor, Napier, 1953; appointed Judge of Supreme Court, 1961. Chm., Royal Commn on Compensation and Rehabilitation in respect of Personal Injury in NZ, 1966–67, and of inquiry into similar questions in Australia, 1973–74. Hon. LLD: Victoria Univ. of Wellington, 1978; Univ. of York, Toronto, 1981. *Recreations:* music, golf. *Address:* Box 2590, Wellington, New Zealand. *Clubs:* Northern (Auckland); Hawkes Bay (Napier); Wellesley, Wellington (Wellington).

WOODHOUSE, Ven. (Charles) David (Stewart); Archdeacon of Warrington, since 1981; Vicar of St Peter's, Hindley, since 1981; *b* 23 Dec. 1934; *s* of Rev. Hector and Elsie Woodhouse. *Educ:* Silcoates School, Wakefield; Kelham Theological College. Curate of St Wilfrid's, Halton, Leeds, 1959–63; Youth Chaplain, Kirkby Team Ministry, Diocese of Liverpool, 1963–66; Curate of St John's, Pembroke, Bermuda, 1966–69; Asst Gen. Secretary, CEMS, 1969–70; Gen. Sec., 1970–76; Rector of Ideford, Ashcombe and Luton and Domestic Chaplain to Bishop of Exeter, 1976–81. Hon. Canon, Liverpool Cathedral, 1983. *Address:* The Vicarage, Wigan Road, Hindley, Lancs WN2 3DF. *T:* Wigan (0942) 55505.

WOODHOUSE, Hon. (Christopher) Montague, DSO 1943; OBE 1944; MA (Oxon); *b* 11 May 1917; 2nd *s* of 3rd Baron Terrington, KBE; *b* and *heir-pres.* to 4th Baron Terrington, *qv; m* 1945, Lady Davina, *d* of 2nd Earl of Lytton, KG, PC, GCSI, GCIE, and *widow* of 5th Earl of Erne; two *s* one *d. Educ:* Winchester; New Coll., Oxford (Craven and Hertford Schols, Gaisford Prizeman; Hon. Fellow, 1982). First Cl. Hon. Mods, 1937; First Class Lit. Hum., 1939; MA 1947; Lord Justice Holker Schol. Gray's Inn, 1939; enlisted RA, 1939, commissioned 1940; Colonel, Aug. 1943, in command of Allied Military Mission to Greek Guerillas in German-occupied Greece (despatches twice, DSO,

OBE, Officer of Legion of Merit (USA), Commander of Order of the Phoenix, with Swords (Greece)). Served in HM Embassy, Athens, 1945, Tehran, 1951; Secretary-General, Allied Mission for Observing Greek Elections, 1946; worked in industry 1946–48; Asst Secretary, Nuffield Foundation, 1948–50; Foreign Office, 1952; Director-General, RIIA, and Dir. of Studies, 1955–59; MP (C) Oxford, 1959–66 and 1970–Sept. 1974; Parliamentary Secretary, Ministry of Aviation, 1961–62; Joint Under-Secretary of State, Home Office, July 1962–Oct. 1964. Dir, Educn and Training, CBI, 1966–70. President, Classical Assoc., 1968; Chm. Council, RSL, 1977–86. Fellow of Trinity Hall, Cambridge, 1950; Visiting Fellow, Nuffield Coll., Oxford, 1956; Vis. Prof., King's Coll., London, 1978. FRSL 1951. Special Mem., Acad. of Athens, 1980. *Publications:* Apple of Discord, 1948; One Omen, 1950; Dostoievsky, 1951; The Greek War of Independence, 1952; Britain and the Middle East, 1959; British Foreign Policy since the Second World War, 1961; Rhodes (with late J. G. Lockhart), 1963; The New Concert of Nations, 1964; The Battle of Navarino, 1965; Post-War Britain, 1966; The Story of Modern Greece, 1968; The Philhellenes, 1969; Capodistria: the founder of Greek independence, 1973; The Struggle for Greece (1941–1949), 1976; Something Ventured, 1982; Karamanlis: the restorer of Greek democracy, 1982; The Rise and Fall of the Greek Colonels, 1985; Gemistos Plethon: the last of the Hellenes, 1986; numerous articles, translations, broadcasts. *Address:* Willow Cottage, Latimer, Bucks HP5 1TW. *T:* Little Chalfont (0494) 762627.

WOODHOUSE, Ven. David; *see* Woodhouse, Ven. C. D. S.

WOODHOUSE, James Stephen; Headmaster, Lancing College, since 1981; *b* 21 May 1933; *s* of late Rt Rev. J. W. Woodhouse, sometime Bishop of Thetford, and late Mrs K. M. Woodhouse; *m* 1957, Sarah, *d* of late Col Hubert Blount, Cley, Norfolk; three *s* one *d. Educ:* St Edward's Sch.; St Catharine's Coll., Cambridge. BA (English) Cantab, 1957; MA 1961. Nat. Service, 14th Field Regt RA, 1953. Asst Master, Westminster Sch., 1957; Under Master and Master of the Queen's Scholars, 1963; Headmaster, Rugby Sch., 1967–81. Chairman: NABC Religious Adv. Cttee, 1971–; Bloxham Project, 1972–77; Head Masters' Conf., 1979; Joint Standing Cttee of HMC, IAPS and GSA, 1981–86; Vice-Chm., E-SU Schoolboy Scholarship Cttee, 1973–77. *Recreations:* sailing, music, hill walking. *Address:* The Old Farmhouse, Lancing College, Lancing, West Sussex BN15 0RW.

WOODHOUSE, Prof. John Henry, PhD; Professor of Geophysics, and Fellow of Worcester College, Oxford, since 1989; *b* 15 April 1949; *s* of G. B. Woodhouse. *Educ:* Southall Grammar Sch.; Bristol Univ. (BSc 1970); King's Coll., Cambridge (MA, PhD 1975). Fellow, King's Coll., Cambridge, 1974–78; Vis. Asst Res. Geophysicist, Inst. of Geophysics and Planetary Physics, Univ. of Calif., San Diego, 1976–77; Asst Prof., 1978–80, Associate Prof., 1980–83, Prof. of Geophysics, 1983–89, Harvard Univ. Chm., Commn on Seismological Theory, Internat. Assoc. of Seismol. and Physics of Earth's Interior, 1983–87. Fellow, Amer. Geophys. Union (McElwane Award, 1984). Associate Ed., Jl of Geophysical Res., 1979–81. *Publications:* many contribs to learned jls. *Address:* Worcester College, Oxford OX1 2HB.

WOODHOUSE, Prof. John Robert; Fiat Serena Professor of Italian Studies, Oxford, and Fellow, Magdalen College, since 1990; *b* 17 June 1937; *s* of Horace Woodhouse and Iris Evelyn Pewton; *m* 1967, Gaynor Mathias. *Educ:* King Edward VI Grammar School, Stourbridge; Hertford College, Oxford (MA, DLitt); Univ. of Pisa; PhD Wales. Asst Lectr in Italian, Univ. of Aberdeen, 1961–62; British Council Scholar, Scuola Normale Superiore, Pisa, 1962–63; Asst Lectr and Lectr, UCNW, Bangor, 1963–66; Lectr and Sen. Lectr, Univ. of Hull, 1966–73; Oxford University: Univ. Lectr in Italian and Fellow of St Cross Coll., 1973–84; Lectr at Jesus Coll., 1973, St Edmund Hall, 1975, Brasenose Coll., 1976; Fellow, 1984–90, Supernumerary Fellow, 1991, Pembroke Coll. Mem., Exec. Cttee, Soc. for Italian Studies, 1979–85. Harvard Old Dominion Foundn Fellow, Villa I Tatti, 1969; Founding Mem., Centro Studi Dannunziani, Pescara, 1979; Mem., Accad. lett. ital. dell'Arcadia, 1980; Socio Correspondente, Accademia della Crusca, 1991; Sen. Res. Fellow, Center for Medieval and Renaissance Studies, UCLA, 1985; Fellow: Huntington Liby, Calif., 1986; Newberry Liby, Chicago, 1988. Editor (Italian), Modern Language Review, 1984–; Mem., Editl Bd, Italian Studies, 1987–91. Cavaliere Ufficiale, Order of Merit (Italy), 1991. *Publications:* Italo Calvino: a reappraisal and an appreciation of the trilogy, 1968; (ed) Italo Calvino, Il barone rampante, 1970; (ed) V. Borghini, Scritti inediti o rari sulla lingua, 1971; (ed) V. Borghini, Storia della nobiltà fiorentina, 1974; Baldesar Castiglione, a reassessment of the Cortegiano, 1978; (ed) G. d'Annunzio, Alcyone, 1978; (ed with P. R. Horne) G. Rossetti, Lettere familiari, 1983; (ed jtly) G. Rossetti, Carteggi, I, 1984, II, 1988, III, 1991; (ed jtly) The Languages of Literature in Renaissance Italy, 1988; From Castiglione to Chesterfield: the decline of the courtier's manual, 1991; articles in learned jls. *Recreations:* gardening, hill walking. *Address:* Magdalen College, Oxford OX1 4AU.

WOODHOUSE, Hon. Montague; *see* Woodhouse, Hon. C. M.

WOODHOUSE, Rt. Hon. Sir Owen; *see* Woodhouse, Rt Hon. Sir A. O.

WOODHOUSE, Ven. Samuel Mostyn Forbes; Archdeacon of London and Canon Residentiary of St Paul's, 1967–78, Archdeacon Emeritus and Canon Emeritus, 1978; Archdeacon to Retired Clergy, Bath and Wells, since 1978; Retired Clergy Association, since 1980; *b* 28 April 1912; *s* of Rev. Major James D. F. Woodhouse, DSO, and Elsie Noel Woodhouse, Water, Manaton, Devon; *m* 1939, Patricia Daniel; two *s* one *d. Educ:* Shrewsbury; Christ Church, Oxford; Wells Theological Coll. BA 1934; MA 1942. Deacon, 1936, Priest, 1937, Diocese of Blackburn; Curate, Lancaster Priory, 1936–39. Chaplain to the Forces (Army), 1939–45 (despatches thrice). Vicar, Holy Trinity, South Shore, Blackpool, 1945–49; Vicar of Leominster, 1949–57; Rural Dean of Leominster, 1956–57; Rector of Bristol City Parish Church (St Stephen's), 1957–67. *Recreations:* painting, architecture. *Address:* Under Copse Cottage, Redhill, Wrington, Bristol BS18 7SH. *T:* Wrington (0934) 862711. *Clubs:* Leander; Vincent's (Oxford).

WOODLEY, Ven. Ronald John; Archdeacon of Cleveland, 1985–91, Emeritus since 1991; *b* 28 Dec. 1925; *s* of John Owen Woodley and Maggie Woodley; *m* 1959, Patricia Kneeshaw; one *s* two *d. Educ:* Montagu Road School, Edmonton; St Augustine's Coll., Canterbury; Bishops' Coll., Cheshunt. Deacon 1953, priest 1954; Curate: St Martin, Middlesbrough, 1953–58; Whitby, 1958–61; Curate in Charge 1961–66, and Vicar 1966–71, The Ascension, Middlesbrough; Rector of Stokesley, 1971–85; RD of Stokesley, 1977–84. Canon of York, 1982–. *Recreations:* gardening, walking. *Address:* Brierton House, 52 South Parade, Northallerton, N Yorks DL7 8SL. *T:* Northallerton (0609) 778818.

WOODLOCK, Jack Terence; Under-Secretary, Department of Health and Social Security, 1969–79, retired; *b* 10 July 1919; *s* of late James Patrick and Florence Woodlock; *m* 1941, Joan Mary Taylor; three *s* one *d. Educ:* Bromley Grammar School. Entered Civil Service, 1936; served in Royal Artillery, 1939–45; Ministry of Health, 1945; Asst Principal 1946; Principal 1950; Principal Private Sec. to Minister, 1958–59; Asst Sec. 1959. *Recreation:* historical studies. *Address:* 9 Berens Way, Chislehurst, Kent BR7 6RH. *T:* Orpington (0689) 22895.

WOODROFFE, Most Rev. George Cuthbert Manning, KBE 1980 (CBE 1973); MA, LTh; Archbishop of West Indies, 1980–86; Bishop of Windward Islands, 1969–86, retired; *b* 17 May 1918; *s* of James Manning Woodroffe and Evelyn Agatha (*née* Norton); *m* 1947, Aileen Alice Connell; one *s* one *d* (and one *s* decd). *Educ:* Grenada Boys' Secondary School; Codrington Coll., Barbados. Clerk in Civil Service, Grenada, 1936–41; Codrington Coll. (Univ. of Durham), 1941–44; Deacon 1944; Priest 1945; Asst Priest, St George's Cath., St Vincent, 1944–47; Vicar of St Simon's, Barbados, 1947–50; Rector: St Andrew, 1950–57; St Joseph, 1957–62; St John, 1962–67; Rural Dean of St John, Barbados, 1965–67; Sub-Dean and Rector of St George's Cathedral, St Vincent, Windward Islands, 1967–69. Vice-Chm., Anglican Consultative Council, 1974. Chm., Vis. Justices St Vincent Prisons, 1968–76. Mem., Prerogative of Mercy Cttee, St Vincent, 1969–86. Member: Bd of Educn, Barbados, 1964–67; National Trust of St Vincent, 1967– (Chm., 1972–82); Council, Univ. of the West Indies, 1980–83; Chm., Bd of Governors, Alleyne Sch., Barbados, 1951–57. Hon. DD Nashotah House, USA, 1980; Hon. LLD Univ. of the West Indies, 1981. *Recreations:* music, driving, detective tales and novels, military band music. *Address:* PO Box 919, Murray Road, St Vincent, West Indies. *T:* St Vincent 809 45 61277. *Club:* Commonwealth Trust.

WOODROFFE, Jean Frances, (Mrs J. W. R. Woodroffe), CVO 1953; *b* 22 Feb. 1923; *d* of late Capt. A. V. Hambro; *m* 1st, 1942, Capt. Hon. Vicary Paul Gibbs, Grenadier Guards (killed in action, 1944), *er s* of 4th Baron Aldenham; one *d* (and one *d* decd); 2nd, 1946, Rev. Hon. Andrew Charles Victor Elphinstone (*d* 1975), 2nd *s* of 16th Lord Elphinstone, KT; one *s* (*see* 18th Lord Elphinstone) one *d*; 3rd, 1980, Lt-Col John William Richard Woodroffe (*d* 1990). Lady-in-Waiting to the Queen as Princess Elizabeth, 1945; Extra Woman of the Bedchamber to the Queen, 1952–. *Address:* Maryland, Worplesdon, Guildford, Surrey GU3 3RB. *T:* Worplesdon (0483) 232629.

WOODROOFE, Sir Ernest (George), Kt 1973; PhD, FInstP, FIChemE; *b* 6 Jan. 1912; *s* of late Ernest George Woodroofe and Ada (*née* Dickinson); *m* 1st, 1938, Margaret Downes (*d* 1961); one *d*; 2nd, 1962, Enid Grace Hutchinson Arnold. *Educ:* Cockburn High Sch.; Leeds Univ. Staff of Loders & Nucoline Ltd, 1935–44; Staff of British Oil & Cake Mills Ltd, 1944–50; Mem., Oil Mills Executive of Unilever Ltd, 1951–55; Director of British Oil & Cake Mills Ltd, 1951–55; Head of Research Division of Unilever Ltd, 1955–61; Director: United Africa Co. Ltd, 1961–63; Unilever NV, 1956–74; Chm., Unilever Ltd, 1970–74 (Dir, 1956–74; Vice-Chm., 1961–70); Trustee, Leverhulme Trust, 1962–82 (Chm., 1974–82). President, International Society for Fat Research, 1962. Member Cttee of Enquiry into the Organisation of Civil Science, 1962–63; A Vice-Pres., Soc. of Chemical Industry, 1963–66; Member: Tropical Products Inst. Cttee, 1964–69; Council for Nat. Academic Awards, 1964–67; Cttee of Award of the Commonwealth Fund, 1965–70; Royal Commn for the Exhibn of 1851, 1968–84; British Gas Corp., 1973–81. Director: Schroders Ltd, 1974–89; Burton Group Ltd, 1974–83; Guthrie Corp. Ltd, 1974–82. Chairman: Review Body on Doctors' and Dentists' Remuneration, 1975–79; CBI Research Cttee, 1966–69. Governor, London Business Sch., 1970–75 (Dep. Chm., 1973–75). Hon. ACT Liverpool, 1963; Hon. Fellow, University of Manchester Inst. of Science and Technology, 1968; Hon. LLD Leeds, 1968; DUniv Surrey, 1970; Hon. DSc: Cranfield, 1974; Liverpool, 1980. Vis. Fellow, Nuffield Coll., Oxford, 1972–80. Comdr, Order of Orange Nassau (Netherlands), 1972. *Recreation:* fishing. *Address:* 44 The Street, Puttenham, Surrey. *T:* Guildford (0483) 810977. *Club:* Athenæum.

WOODROW, David, CBE 1979; retired solicitor; *b* 16 March 1920; *s* of late Sydney Melson Woodrow and late Edith Constance (*née* Farmer); *m* 1st, 1950, Marie-Armande (marr. diss.; she *d* 1989), *d* of late Benjamin Barrios, KBE, and late Lady Ovey; two *d*; 2nd, 1983, Mary Miley, *d* of late Rupert Alexander Whitamore and Sally Whitamore. *Educ:* Shrewsbury; Trinity Coll., Oxford (MA). Commnd Royal Artillery, 1940; served SE Asia; POW Java and Japan, 1942–45. Admitted Solicitor, 1949. Chairman: Reading and District HMC, 1966–72; Oxford Regional Hosp. Bd, 1972–74; RHA, 1973–78; NHS Nat. Staff Cttee, Administrative and Clerical Staff, 1975–79. *Recreations:* painting and looking at pictures. *Address:* Dobsons, Brightwell-cum-Sotwell, Wallingford, Oxon OX10 0RH. *T:* Wallingford (0491) 36170. *Club:* Leander (Henley-on-Thames).

WOODROW, Gayford William; HM Diplomatic Service, retired; Consul, Algeciras, 1982–85; *b* 21 Feb. 1922; *s* of William Alexander Woodrow and Charlotte Louise (*née* Ellis); *m* 1946, Janine Suzanne Marcelle Jannot; one *s*. *Educ:* Brockley County School. Served War, RAF, 1941–46. Foreign Office, 1946; Caracas, 1949; Vice Consul: Barcelona, 1952; Panama, 1954; Consul: Cairo, 1960; Alexandria, 1961; First Sec. and Consul, Warsaw, 1962; Consul: Valencia, 1965; Jerusalem, 1969; First Sec., Ottawa, 1976; Consul General, Tangier, 1978–80; Asst, Consular Dept, FCO, 1980–81. *Recreations:* walking, swimming, history. *Address:* Apartment 3, Pitt House, Chudleigh, Devon TQ13 0EL.

WOODRUFF, Prof. Alan Waller, CMG 1978; OBE 1989; Professor of Medicine, University of Juba, Sudan, since 1981; Wellcome Professor of Clinical Tropical Medicine, London School of Hygiene and Tropical Medicine, 1952–81; Hon. Consultant in Tropical Diseases to: the Army, 1956–81; British Airways, 1962–89; *b* 27 June 1916; *s* of late William Henry Woodruff, Sunderland, and Mary Margaret Woodruff; *m* 1946, Mercia Helen, *d* of late Leonard Frederick Arnold, Dorking, and Amy Elizabeth Arnold; two *s* one *d*. *Educ:* Bede Collegiate Sch., Sunderland; Durham Univ. MB, BS 1939, MD 1941, Durham; DTM&H England, 1946; PhD London, 1952; FRCP 1953; FRCPE 1960. House Physician and House Surgeon, Royal Victoria Infirmary, Newcastle upon Tyne, 1939–40; MO and Med. Specialist, RAFVR, 1940–46; Med. Registrar, Royal Victoria Infirmary, Newcastle upon Tyne, 1946–48; Sen. Lectr in Clinical Tropical Medicine, London Sch. of Hygiene and Trop. Medicine, 1948–52; First Asst, 1948–52, Physician, 1952–81, Hosp. for Tropical Diseases, University Coll. Hosp., London; Lectr in Tropical Medicine, Royal Free Hosp. Sch. of Medicine, 1952–81; William Julius Mickle Fellow, Univ. of London, 1959. Lectures: Goulstonian, RCP, 1954; Lettsomian, Med. Soc. of London, 1969; Watson-Smith, RCP, 1970; Halliburton Hume, Newcastle-upon-Tyne, 1981. Orator, Reading Pathological Soc., 1976. Member: WHO Expert Adv. Panel on Parasitic Diseases, 1963–88; Med. Cttee of Overseas Develt Administration; Visiting Professor at Universities: Alexandria, 1963; Ain Shams, Cairo, 1964; Baghdad, 1966, 1968, 1971, 1974; Mosul, 1977–79; Basrah, 1973–74; Makerere, 1973; Khartoum, 1974, 1978; Benghazi, 1976–80. Mem., Assoc. of Physicians of GB and Ireland; President: Durham Univ. Soc., 1963–73; Royal Soc. of Tropical Medicine and Hygiene, 1973–75; Medical Soc. of London, 1975–76; Section of History of Medicine, Royal Soc. Med., 1977–79. Hon. Mem., Burma Med. Assoc., 1966; Hon. Mem., Société de Pathologie Exotique, Paris; Hon. Associate Mem., Soc. Belge de Médecine Tropicale, 1965; Hon. Mem., Brazilian Soc. of Tropical Medicine; Hon. Fellow, Canadian Soc. of Tropical Medicine and International Health, 1976. Katherine Bishop Harman Prize, BMA, 1951; Cullen Prize, RCPE, 1982. Hon. RE 1979. Gold Medal of Univ. of Pernambuco, Brazil, 1980. *Publications:* (with S. Bell) A Synopsis of Infectious and Tropical Diseases, 1968 (with S. G. Wright), 3rd edn 1987; (ed) Alimentary and Haematological Aspects of Tropical Disease, 1970; (ed) Medicine in the Tropics, 1974, 2nd edn 1984; sections in: Paediatrics for the Practitioner (ed Gaisford and Lightwood); Price's Textbook of Medicine; contribs to BMJ, Lancet, Trans Royal Soc. Trop. Medicine and Hygiene, W African Med. Jl, E African Med. Jl, Newcastle Med. Jl, Practitioner, Clinical Science, Proc. Nutrition Soc., etc. *Recreation:* engraving. *Address:* 122 Ferndene Road, SE24 0BA. *T:* 071–274 3578; University of Juba, PO Box 82, Juba, Sudan. *Clubs:* Athenæum; Sunderland (Sunderland).

WOODRUFF, Harry Wells, CMG 1966; retired, 1972; *b* 31 Oct. 1912; *s* of Leonard Wells Woodruff and Rosina Woodruff; *m* 1938, Margaret Bradley; one *d*. *Educ:* Reigate Grammar Sch.; London Univ. Trade Comr, Johannesburg, 1946–51; Trade Comr and Economic Adviser to High Commissioner: Salisbury, 1951–55; Kuala Lumpur, 1957–61; Commercial Counsellor, Canberra, 1962–66; Economic Adviser to Foreign Office, 1966–68; Asst Sec., Dept of Trade and Industry (formerly Bd of Trade), 1968–72. *Publication:* (jointly) Economic Development in Rhodesia and Nyasaland, 1955. *Recreation:* painting. *Address:* 387 Sandbanks Road, Poole, Dorset.

WOODRUFF, Prof. Sir Michael (Francis Addison), Kt 1969; FRS 1968; FRCS; DSc, MS (Melbourne); Emeritus Professor of Surgery, University of Edinburgh, and Surgeon, Edinburgh Royal Infirmary, 1957–76; Director, Nuffield Transplantation Surgery Unit, Edinburgh, 1968–76; *b* 3 April 1911; *s* of late Prof. Harold Addison Woodruff and Margaret Ada (*née* Cooper); *m* 1946, Hazel Gwenyth Ashby; two *s* one *d*. *Educ:* Wesley Coll., Melbourne; Queen's Coll., University of Melbourne. MB, BS (Melbourne) 1937, MD 1940, MS 1941; FRCS 1946. Captain, Australian Army Medical Corps, 1940–46. Tutor in Surgery, Univ. of Sheffield, 1946–48; Senior Lecturer in Surgery, Univ. of Aberdeen, 1948–52; Hunterian Prof., RCS, 1952; Travelling Fellow, WHO, 1949; Prof. of Surgery, Univ. of Otago, Dunedin, NZ, 1953–56; Prof. of Surgery, Univ. of Edinburgh, 1957–76. Pres., Transplantation Soc., 1972–74. A Vice-Pres., Royal Soc., 1979. Associé Etranger, Académie de Chirurgie, 1964; Hon. Fellow American Surgical Assoc., 1965; Korrespondierendem Mitglied, Deutsche Gesellschaft für Chirurgie; Hon. FACS 1975; Hon. FRCPE 1982. Lister Medal, 1969; Gold Medal, Soc. of Apothecaries, 1974. *Publications:* (Joint) Deficiency Diseases in Japanese Prison Camps, 1951; Surgery for Dental Students, 1954; Transplantation of Tissues and Organs, 1960; (essays) On Science and Surgery, 1977; The Interaction of Cancer and Host, 1980; Cellular Variation and Adaptation in Cancer, 1990; articles on surgical topics and on experimental tissue transplantation. *Recreations:* music, sailing. *Address:* The Bield, 506 Lanark Road, Juniper Green, Edinburgh EH14 5DH. *Clubs:* Athenæum; New (Edinburgh); Royal Forth Yacht.

WOODRUFF, Philip; *see* Mason, Philip.

WOODRUFF, William Charles, CBE 1985; FRAeS; *b* 14 Aug. 1921; *s* of late Thomas and Caroline Woodruff; *m* 1st, 1946, Ethel May Miles (*d* 1981); one *s* one *d*; 2nd, 1987, Olivia Minerva Henson. *Educ:* St George's, Ramsgate. RAF, 1941–46: Navigator/Observer, 1409 Flight; POW Germany, 1943–45. Seconded Air Min., 1945, and later Min. of Civil Aviation for Air Traffic Control planning; various air traffic control appts at Hurn, Northolt, Southern Centre, Heston and MTCA Hdqrs, 1946–56; Air Traffic Control Officer i/c Heathrow, 1956–62; Sec. of Patch Long-term Air Traffic Control Planning Group, 1960–61; Dep. Dir, 1962–67, Dir, 1967–69, Civil Air Traffic Ops; National Air Traffic Services: Jt Field Comdr, 1969–74; Dep. Controller, 1974–77; Controller, 1977–81. Assessor, Stanstead/Heathrow Airports Public Inquiries, 1981–84; Specialist Advr, H of C Transport Select Cttee on Air Safety, 1988–89. Guild of Air Traffic Control Officers: Clerk, 1952–56; Master, 1956. *Publications:* articles on aviation subjects. *Address:* Great Oaks, 36 Court Road, Ickenham, Uxbridge, Middx UB10 8TF. *T:* Ruislip (0895) 639134.

WOODS, Brian; His Honour Judge Woods; a Circuit Judge, since 1975; *b* 5 Nov. 1928; *yr s* of late E. P. Woods, Woodmancote, Cheltenham; *m* 1957, Margaret, *d* of late F. J. Griffiths, Parkgate, Wirral; three *d*. *Educ:* City of Leicester Boys' Sch.; Nottingham Univ. (LLB 1952). National Service, RAF, 1947–49. Called to the Bar, Gray's Inn, 1955; Midland Circuit; Dep. Chm., Lincs (Lindsey) QS, 1968. Chancellor, Diocese of Leicester, 1977–79; Reader, dio. of Leicester, 1970–79, dio. of Lichfield, 1978–. Member Council: S Mary and S Anne's Sch., Abbots Bromley, 1977–; Ellesmere Coll., 1983–84. Mem., Law Adv. Cttee, Nottingham Univ., 1979–; a Legal Mem., Trent Region Mental Health Review Tribunal, 1983–. Fellow, Midland Div., Woodard Corp., 1979–. *Recreations:* daughters, musical music, taking photographs. *Address:* c/o Circuit Administrator, 2 Newton Street, Birmingham B4 7LU.

WOODS, Maj.-Gen. Charles William, CB 1970; MBE 1952; MC 1944; Chairman, Douglas Haig Memorial Homes, 1975–87; *b* 21 March 1917; *s* of late Captain F. W. U. Woods and of Mrs M. E. Woods, Gosbrook House, Binfield Heath, Henley-on-Thames; *m* 1940, Angela Helen Clay; one *d* (one *s* decd). *Educ:* Uppingham Sch.; Trinity Coll., Cambridge (MA). Commnd into Corps of Royal Engineers, 1938; served War of 1939–45, N Africa, Sicily, Italy, NW Europe (D Landings with 50th Div.); Staff Coll., Camberley, 1946; served in Korea, 1951–52; comd 35 Corps Engineer Regt, BAOR, 1959–60; Dep. Military Secretary, 1964–67; Dir of Manning (Army), 1967–70. Col Comdt, RE, 1973–78. Chm., RE Assoc., 1971–77. *Recreations:* sailing, ski-ing. *Address:* 6 Grove Pastures, Lymington, Hants SO41 9RG. *T:* Lymington (0590) 673445. *Clubs:* Naval and Military, Royal Ocean Racing, Royal Cruising, Ski Club of Great Britain; Royal Lymington Yacht, Royal Engineer Yacht, Island Sailing (Cowes).

WOODS, Christopher Matthew, CMG 1979; MC 1945; HM Diplomatic Service, retired; Special Operations Executive Adviser, Foreign and Commonwealth Office, 1982–88; *b* 26 May 1923; *s* of Matthew Grosvenor Woods; *m* 1954, Gillian Sara Rudd (*d* 1985); four *s* one *d*. *Educ:* Bradfield Coll.; Trinity Coll., Cambridge. HM Forces, KRRC and SOE, 1942–47; Foreign Office, 1948; served Cairo, Tehran, Milan, Warsaw, Rome; FO, later FCO, 1967. *Address:* 10 St John's Street, Woodbridge, Suffolk IP12 1EB. *T:* Woodbridge (0394) 387881. *Club:* Special Forces.

WOODS, Sir Colin (Philip Joseph), KCVO 1977; CBE 1973; QPM 1980; Director and Consultant, Securicor and Securicor International, since 1982; Director, Caravan Club and Touring Club of Great Britain, since 1986; *b* London, 20 April 1920; *s* of late Michael Woods, Sub-divisional Inspector, Metropolitan Police; *m* 1941, Gladys Ella May (*née* Howell); one *d*. *Educ:* LCC Primary and Secondary Schs; Finchley Grammar Sch. Served War, in 60th Rifles and RUR, 1939–46. Metropolitan Police: Constable, through ranks, to Dep. Comdr; Commander, Traffic Dept, 1966–67; Head of Management Services, 1968; Comdt, National Police Coll., 1969–70; Asst Comr (Traffic Dept), 1970; Asst Comr (Crime), 1972; Dep. Comr, 1975–77; HM Chief Inspector of Constabulary, 1977–79; Comr, Australian Federal Police, 1979–82. Chm. Council, BSIA, 1987–. *Recreations:* walking, gardening, caravanning. *Address:* Doversmead, Littleworth Road, The Sands, Farnham, Surrey GU10 1JW. *T:* Runfold (02518) 2514.

WOODS, Elisabeth Ann; Head of Finance, Department of Social Security, since 1988; *b* 27 Oct. 1940; *d* of Norman Singleton, *qv*; *m* 1976, James Maurice Woods. *Educ:* South Hampstead High Sch.; Girton Coll., Cambridge (BA Hons Cl. 1 Modern Languages, 1963). Asst Principal, Min. of Pensions and Nat. Insurance, 1963–69 (Asst Private Sec. to the Minister, and Private Sec. to Permanent Sec.); Principal, DHSS, 1969–76 (Sec. to Cttees on Nursing and on Allocation of Resources to Health Authorities); Asst Sec.,

DHSS, 1976–88 (responsible for mental handicap policy, later for liaison with RHAs, finally for aspects of supplementary benefit); seconded to HM Treasury, 1980–82; Grade 3, DHSS Central Resource Management, 1988. *Recreations:* cycling, reading, cooking. *Address:* Department of Social Security, Richmond House, 79 Whitehall, SW1A 2NS. *T:* 071-210 5126.

WOODS, Most Rev. Frank, KBE 1972; Archbishop of Melbourne, 1957–77; Primate of Australia, 1971–77; *b* 6 April 1907; *s* of late Rt Rev. E. S. Woods, DD, Bishop of Lichfield; *m* 1936, Jean Margaret Sprules; two *s* two *d.* *Educ:* Marlborough; Trinity Coll., Cambridge. Deacon, 1931; priest, 1932; Curate of Portsea Parish Church, 1932–33; Chaplain, Trinity Coll., Cambridge, 1933–36; Vice-principal, Wells Theological Coll., 1936–39; Chaplain to the Forces, 1939–45; Vicar of Huddersfield, 1945–52; Suffragan Bishop of Middleton, 1952–57. Proctor in Convocation, 1946–51; Chaplain to the King, 1951–52; Chaplain, Victoria Order of St John, 1962. Hon. Fellow, Trinity Coll., Melbourne, 1981. Hon. DD Lambeth, 1957; Hon. LLD Monash, 1979. *Recreation:* walking. *Address:* 18 Victoria Road, Camberwell, Vic 3124, Australia. *Clubs:* Melbourne, Australian (Melbourne).
See also Rt Rev. R. W. Woods.

WOODS, Maj.-Gen. Henry Gabriel, CB 1979; MBE 1965; MC 1945; General Officer Commanding North East District, 1976–80, retired; Vice Lord-Lieutenant, North Yorkshire, since 1985; Secretary, St William's Foundation, since 1984; *b* 7 May 1924; *s* of late G. S. Woods and F. C. F. Woods (*née* McNevin); *m* 1953, Imogen Elizabeth Birchenough Dodd; two *d.* *Educ:* Highgate Sch.; Trinity Coll., Oxford (MA 1st Cl. Hons Mod. History). FBIM. psc, jssc, rcds. Commnd 5th Royal Inniskilling Dragoon Guards, 1944; served NW Europe, 1944–45; Korea, 1951–52; Adjt, 1952–53; Sqdn Leader, 1954–55 and 1960–62; Army Staff Coll., 1956; Jt Services Staff Coll., 1960; Mil. Asst to Vice CDS, MoD, 1962–64; comd 5th Royal Inniskilling Dragoon Gds, 1965–67; Asst Mil. Sec. to C-in-C BAOR, 1968–69; Comdt, RAC Centre, 1969–71; RCDS, 1972; Mil. Attaché, Brit. Embassy, Washington, 1973–75. Head, Centre for Industrial and Educnl Liaison (W and N Yorks), 1980–87. Chairman: SATRO Panel, 1982–83; W and N Yorks Regl Microelectronics Educn Programme, 1982–86; Yorks and Humberside Industry/Educn Council, 1982–87; Bradford and W Yorks Br., BIM, 1982–84; N Yorks Scouts, 1982–; Yorks Region, Royal Soc. of Arts, 1982–; Vice Chm., W Yorks Br. Exec. Cttee, Inst. of Dirs, 1985–91; Mem., Yorks Br. Exec. Cttee, British Assoc. for Advancement of Sci., 1982–87. Mem. Council, Univ. of Leeds, 1980–. Chm., 5th Royal Inniskilling Dragoon Guards Regtl Assoc. Pres. York and Humberside Br., Royal Soc. of St George, 1986–88. Member: Co. of Merchants of Staple of England; Merchant Adventurers of the City of York. DL N Yorks, 1984. FRSA. Hon. DLitt Bradford, 1988. Officier, Ordre de Léopold, Belgium, 1965. *Publication:* Change and Challenge: the story of 5th Royal Inniskilling Dragon Guards, 1978. *Recreations:* hunting, fencing, sailing, military history. *Address:* Grafton House, Tockwith, York YO5 8PY. *T:* Tockwith (0423) 358735. *Clubs:* Cavalry and Guards; Ends of the Earth (UK section); Trinity Society, Oxford Society.

WOODS, Ivan; *see* Woods, W. I.

WOODS, Dr John David, CBE 1991; Director of Marine and Atmospheric Science, Natural Environment Research Council, since 1986; Member, Robert Hooke Institute for Atmospheric Research, Oxford University, since 1986; *b* 26 Oct. 1939; *s* of late Ronald Ernest Goff Woods and of Ethel Marjorie Woods; *m* 1971, Irina, *y d* of Bernd von Arnim and Elizabeth Gräfin Platen-Hallermund; one *s* one *d.* *Educ:* Imperial College, Univ. of London. BSc Physics 1961, PhD 1965. Research Asst, Imperial Coll., 1964–66; Sen., later Principal, Research Fellow, Meteorol Office, 1966–72; Prof. of Physical Oceanography, Southampton Univ., 1972–77; Ordinarius für Ozeanographie, Christian Albrechts Universität und Direktor Regionale Ozeanographie, Kiel Institut für Meereskunde, Beamter auf Lebenzeit Schleswig-Holstein, 1977–86. Vis. Prof. Atmospheric Scis, Miami Univ., 1969. Member: NERC, 1979–82; Meteorol Res. Cttee, Meteorol Office, 1976–77, 1987–. Council Member: Underwater Assoc., 1967–72 (Hon. life mem., 1987); RMetS, 1972–75; RGS, 1975–77, 1987–; Member, international scientific committees for: Global Atmospheric Research Prog., 1976–79; Climate Change and the Ocean, 1979–84; World Climate Research Prog., 1980–86; World Ocean Circulation Experiment, 1983–89 (Chm., 1984–86); Internat. Geosphere Biosphere Prog., 1987–91. Mem., Academia Europaea, 1988. Lectures: Iselin, Harvard, 1989; Linacre, Oxford, 1991; Adye, Fellowship of Engrg, 1991. Hon. DSc Liège, 1980. L. G. Groves Prize, MoD, 1968; Medal of Helsinki Univ., 1982. *Publications:* (with J. Lythgoe) Underwater Science, 1971; (with E. Drew and J. Lythgoe) Underwater Research, 1976; papers on atmospheric physics and oceanography in learned jls. *Recreations:* underwater swimming, history. *Address:* 30 Feilden Grove, Oxford OX3 0DU. *T:* Oxford (0865) 69342. *Club:* Athenæum.

WOODS, Rev. Canon John Mawhinney; *b* 16 Dec. 1919; *s* of Robert and Sarah Hannah Woods. *Educ:* Edinburgh Theological College. Deacon 1958, for St Peter's, Kirkcaldy, Fife; priest, 1959; Rector of Walpole St Peter, Norfolk, 1960–75; Provost, St Andrew's Cathedral, Inverness, 1975–80; Rector of The Suttons with Tydd, 1980–85; Canon of Inverness, 1980–. *Address:* Sudbury House, 1 Purfleet Place, King's Lynn, Norfolk PE30 1JH. *T:* King's Lynn (0553) 775599.

WOODS, Prof. Leslie Colin, BE, MA, DPhil, DSc; Professor of Mathematics (Theory of Plasma), University of Oxford, 1970–90, now Emeritus Professor; Fellow of Balliol College, Oxford, 1970–90, Emeritus Fellow, since 1991; *b* Reporoa, NZ, 6 Dec. 1922; *s* of A. B. Woodhead, Sandringham, NZ; *m* 1st, 1943; five *d*; 2nd, 1977; 3rd, 1990, Suzanne Griffiths. *Educ:* Auckland Univ. Coll.; Merton Coll., Oxford. Fighter pilot, RNZAF, Pacific Area, 1942–45. Rhodes Schol., Merton Coll., Oxford, 1948–51; Scientist (NZ Scientific Defense Corps) with Aerodynamics Div., NPL Mddx, 1951–54; Senior Lectr in Applied Maths, Sydney Univ., 1954–56; Nuffield Research Prof. of Engineering, Univ. of New South Wales, 1956–60; Fellow and Tutor in Engrg Science, Balliol Coll., Oxford, 1960–70; Reader in Applied Maths, Oxford, 1964–70. Chm., Mathematical Inst., Oxford, 1984–89. Hon. DSc Auckland, 1983. *Publications:* The Theory of Subsonic Plane Flow, 1961; Introduction to Neutron Distribution Theory, 1964; The Thermodynamics of Fluid Systems, 1975; Principles of Magnetoplasma Dynamics, 1987; many research papers in aerodynamics and plasma physics in Proc. Royal Soc., Physics of Fluids, etc. *Recreations:* music, gardening. *Address:* Balliol College, Oxford OX1 3BJ.

WOODS, Maurice Eric; Regional Chairman, Industrial Tribunals (Bristol), since 1990; *b* 28 June 1933; *s* of late Leslie Eric Woods and of Winifred Rose Woods (*née* Boniface); *m* 1956, Freda Pauline Schlosser; two *s* two *d.* *Educ:* Moulsham Secondary Modern Sch., Chelmsford. LLB London. Solicitor. Clerk with Essex CC, 1948–51; National Service (Army), 1951–53; Police Constable, Essex Police Force, 1954–59; Claims Asst, Cornhill Insurance, 1959–61; Solicitors Clerk and Articled Clerk with Barlow Lyde and Gilbert, 1961–65; private practice, 1965–84; Dep. County Court Registrar, 1977–84; Chairman: Suppl. Benefit Appeal Tribunals and Social Security Appeal Tribunals, 1981–84; Industrial Tribunals, Bristol, 1984–90. *Recreations:* music, travel. *Address:* Regional Office of Industrial Tribunals, Prince House, 43–51 Prince Street, Bristol BS1 4PE. *T:* Bristol (0272) 298261.

WOODS, Rt. Rev. Robert Wilmer, KCMG 1989; KCVO 1971; MA; Assistant Bishop, Diocese of Gloucester, since 1982; Prelate of the Most Distinguished Order of St Michael and St George, 1971–89; *b* 15 Feb. 1914; *s* of late Edward Woods, Bishop of Lichfield, and Clemence (*née* Barclay); *m* 1942, Henrietta Marion (JP 1966), *d* of late K. H. Wilson; two *s* three *d.* *Educ:* Gresham's Sch., Holt; Trinity Coll., Cambridge. Asst Sec., Student Christian Movement, 1937–42; Chaplain to the Forces, 1942–46 (despatches, 1944); Vicar of South Wigston, Leicester, 1946–51; Archdeacon of Singapore and Vicar of St Andrew's Cathedral, 1951–58; Archdeacon of Sheffield and Rector of Tankersley, 1958–62; Dean of Windsor, 1962–70; Domestic Chaplain to the Queen, 1962–70; Register of the Most Noble Order of the Garter, 1962–70; Bishop of Worcester, 1970–81. Secretary, Anglican/Methodist Commn for Unity, 1965–74; Member: Council, Duke of Edinburgh's Award Scheme, 1968; Public Schools Commn, 1968–70; Governor, Haileybury Coll.; Pres, Queen's Coll., Birmingham, and Chm. Council, 1970–85; Chairman: Windsor Festival Co., 1969–71; Churches Television Centre, 1969–79; Dir, Christian Aid, 1969. Chm., Birmingham and Hereford and Worcester Bd, MSC, 1976–83. Visitor, Malvern Coll., 1970–81. *Publication:* Robin Woods: an autobiography, 1986. *Recreations:* shooting, painting. *Address:* Torse End, Tirley, Gloucester GL19 4EU. *T:* Tirley (045278) 327.
See also Most Rev. F. Woods.

WOODS, Timothy Phillips, MA, DPhil; Head of History, Trent College, since 1985; *b* 24 Dec. 1943; *s* of late Arthur Phillips Woods and of Katherine Isabella Woods; *m* 1969, Erica Lobb. *Educ:* Cordwalles Prep. Sch., Natal; Michaelhouse Sch., Natal; Rhodes Univ. (BA Hons, MA; UED); Oxford Univ. (DPhil). Cape Province Rhodes Scholar, 1968; Felsted School: Asst Master, 1971; Head of History, 1975; Headmaster, Gresham's Sch. 1982–85. *Recreations:* cricket, hockey, squash, gardening, music, history and architecture of cathedrals. *Address:* 63 Curzon Street, Long Eaton, Nottingham NG10 4FG. *T:* Nottingham (0602) 720927. *Club:* Vincent's (Oxford).

WOODS, (William) Ivan; 3rd *s* of late William and Anna Woods, Annaghmore, Co. Armagh; *m* (1st wife *d* 1965); one *s* one *d*; 2nd, 1966, Florence Margaret, *o d* of late William and Florence Sloan, Ach-na-mara, Donaghadee, Co. Down; one *s* two *d.* *Educ:* Ranelagh Sch., Athlone; Mountjoy Sch., Dublin. Accountant, Min. of Finance for N Ire., 1962; N Ire. Govt Liaison Officer in London, 1963; Dir of Office of Parliamentary Commissioner for Administration, NI, 1969; Dir of Office of Commissioner for Complaints, NI, 1969; Dep. Sec., Dept of Finance for NI, 1973–76. Sec., Milibern Trust, 1976–79. *Recreations:* golf, sailing. *Address:* 112 Warren Road, Donaghadee, Co. Down BT21 0PQ. *T:* Donaghadee (0247) 883568. *Clubs:* Portaferry Sailing, Mitchels GA (Co. Down).

WOODSTOCK, Viscount; Timothy Charles Robert Noel Bentinck; Count of the Holy Roman Empire; actor; *b* 1 June 1953; *s* and *heir* of Earl of Portland, *qv*; *m* 1979, Judith Ann, *d* of John Robert Emerson; two *s.* *Educ:* Harrow; Univ. of East Anglia (BA Hons). Trained Bristol Old Vic Theatre Sch. Winner BBC Drama Schs Radio Competition, 1978. London theatre appearances include: Pirates of Penzance, Theatre Royal, Drury Lane, 1982; Reluctant Heroes, Theatre of Comedy, 1984; Hedda Gabler, King's Head Theatre, 1990; *radio:* David Archer in The Archers; over 75 plays; *films:* North Sea Hijack, 1979; Pirates of Penzance, 1981; Winter Flight, 1985; *television* includes: By the Sword Divided, 1983; Square Deal, 1989; Made in Heaven, 1990; composer of theme music for Easy Money, BBC TV, 1984. Inventor of The Hippo (child-carrying device). HGV licence. *Recreations:* songwriting, ski-ing, swimming, house renovation, computers. *Heir:* *s* Hon. William Jack Henry Bentinck, *b* 19 May 1984.

WOODWARD, Hon. Sir (Albert) Edward, Kt 1982; OBE 1969; Chancellor, University of Melbourne, since 1990; *b* 6 Aug. 1928; *s* of Lt-Gen. Sir Eric Winslow Woodward, KCMG, KCVO, CB, CBE, DSO, and Amy Freame Woodward (*née* Weller); *m* 1950, Lois Thorpe; one *s* six *d.* *Educ:* Melbourne C of E Grammar Sch.; Melbourne Univ. (LLM). Practising barrister, 1953–72; QC 1965; Judge: Australian Industrial Court and Supreme Court of Australian Capital Territory, 1972–90; Federal Ct of Australia, 1977–90. Chairman, Armed Services Pay Inquiry, 1972; Royal Commissioner: Aboriginal Land Rights, 1973–75; into Australian Meat Industry, 1981–82; President: Trade Practices Tribunal, 1974–76; Defence Force Discipline Appeal Tribunal, 1988–90; Director-General of Security, 1976–81. Chairman: Victorian Dried Fruits Bd, 1963–72; Nat. Stevedoring Industry Conf. and Stevedoring Industry Council, 1965–72; Australian Defence Force Academy Council, 1985–; Schizophrenia Australia Foundn, 1985–. Mem. Council, Melbourne Univ., 1973–76, 1986–; Chm. Council, Camberwell Grammar Sch., 1983–87. Hon. LLD New South Wales, 1986. *Address:* 63 Tivoli Road, South Yarra, Victoria 3141, Australia. *T:* (03) 826 8404.

WOODWARD, Barry; His Honour Judge Woodward; a Circuit Judge, since 1990; *s* of Wilfred and Mary Hannah Woodward; *m* 1963, Patricia Holland; two *d.* *Educ:* Sheffield Univ. (LLM). Called to the Bar, Gray's Inn, 1970. Teaching positions, 1961–70; practice on Northern Circuit, 1970–84; Chm., Industrial Tribunals, Manchester Region, 1984; a Recorder, 1988. *Recreations:* ski-ing, windsurfing, any other sporting activity that time and fitness permits, messing with classic motor cars. *Address:* Courts of Justice, Crown Square, Manchester. *T:* 061-832 8393.

WOODWARD, Prof. C(omer) Vann; Sterling Professor of History, Yale University, 1961–77, now Emeritus Professor; *b* 13 Nov. 1908; *s* of Hugh Allison Woodward and Bess (*née* Vann); *m* 1937, Glenn Boyd MacLeod; one *s.* *Educ:* Emory Univ. (PhB); Universities of Columbia (MA), North Carolina (PhD). Asst Professor of History, University of Florida, 1937–39; Visiting Asst Professor of History, University of Virginia, 1939–40; Assoc. Professor of History, Scripps Coll., 1940–43; Assoc. Professor of History, Johns Hopkins University, 1946; Professor of American History, Johns Hopkins Univ., 1947–61. Served with US Naval Reserve, 1943–46. Commonwealth Lecturer, UCL, 1954; Harold Vyvyan Harmsworth Professor of American History, University of Oxford, 1954–55. Corresp. Fellow: British Academy, 1972, RHistS, 1978. Member: American Academy of Arts and Sciences (Vice-Pres., 1988–89); American Philosophical Society; Amer. Acad. of Arts and Letters; American Historical Assoc. (President, 1969); Orgn of American Historians (President, 1968–69). Hon. MA Oxon, 1954; hon. doctoral degrees from univs of Arkansas, Brandeis, Cambridge, Colgate, Columbia, Emory, Henderson, Johns Hopkins, Michigan, N Carolina, Northwestern, Pennsylvania, Princeton, Rutgers, Washington and Lee, William and Mary, and Rhodes Coll. Literary Award, Amer. Acad. and Inst. of Arts and Letters, 1954; Gold Medal for History, 1990. *Publications:* Tom Watson: Agrarian Rebel, 1938; The Battle for Leyte Gulf, 1947; Origins of the New South (1877–1913), 1951 (Bancroft Prize, 1952); Reunion and Reaction, 1951; The Strange Career of Jim Crow, 1955; The Burden of Southern History, 1960; American Counterpoint, 1971; Thinking Back, 1986; The Future of the Past, 1989; The Old World's New World, 1991; (ed) The Comparative Approach to American History, 1968; (ed) Mary Chesnut's Civil War, 1981 (Pulitzer Prize, 1982). *Address:* 83 Rogers Road, Hamden, Conn 06517, USA.

WOODWARD, Hon. Sir Edward; *see* Woodward, Hon. Sir A. E.

WOODWARD, Edward, OBE 1978; actor and singer, since 1946; *b* 1 June 1930; *s* of Edward Oliver Woodward and Violet Edith Woodward; *m* 1st, 1952, Venetia Mary Collett; two *s* one *d*; 2nd, 1987, Michele Dotrice; one *d*. *Educ:* Kingston Coll.; RADA. *Stage:* Castle Theatre, Farnham, 1946; appeared for some years in rep. cos throughout England and Scotland; first appearance on London stage, Where There's a Will, Garrick, 1955; Mercutio in Romeo and Juliet, and Laertes in Hamlet, Stratford, 1958; Rattle of a Simple Man, Garrick, 1962; Two Cities (musical), 1968; Cyrano in Cyrano de Bergerac, and Flamineo in The White Devil, Nat. Theatre Co., 1971; The Wolf, Apollo, 1973; Male of the Species, Piccadilly, 1975; On Approval, Theatre Royal Haymarket, 1976; The Dark Horse, Comedy, 1978; starred in and directed Beggar's Opera, 1980; Private Lives, Australia, 1980; The Assassin, Greenwich, 1982; Richard III, Ludlow Fest., 1982; has appeared in 3 prodns in NY; *films:* Becket, 1966; File on the Golden Goose, 1968; Hunted, 1973; Sitting Target, Young Winston, The Wicker Man, 1974; Stand Up Virgin Soldiers, 1977; Breaker Morant, 1980; The Appointment, 1981; Who Dares Wins, Forever Love, Merlin and the Sword, 1982; Champions, 1983; Christmas Carol, 1984; King David, Uncle Tom's Cabin, 1986; Mister Johnson, 1990. Over 2000 TV prodns, inc. Callan (TV series and film, and in Wet Job, 1981); The Trial of Lady Chatterley, Blunt Instrument, 1980; Churchill: The Wilderness Years, 1981; The Equalizer (series), 1985–89; Codename Kyril, 1987; Hunted, 1988; The Man in the Brown Suit, 1988; Hands of a Murderer, or The Napoleon of Crime, 1990; Over My Dead Body (series), 1990; In Suspicious Circumstances (series), 1991; 12 long-playing records (singing), 3 records (poetry) and 10 talking book recordings. Many national and internat. acting awards. *Recreations:* boating, geology. *Address:* c/o Eric Glass Ltd, 28 Berkeley Square, W1X 6HD. *T:* 071–629 7162, *Fax:* 071–499 6780. *Clubs:* Garrick, Green Room, Wellington.

WOODWARD, Geoffrey Frederick, RIBA; jssc; Assistant Director General of Design Services, Property Services Agency, Department of the Environment, 1983–84; *b* 29 June 1924; *s* of Joseph Frederick and Edith Mary Woodward; *m* 1953, Elizabeth Marjory McCubbin; four *s*. *Educ:* Wirral Grammar School for Boys; Trinity College, Cambridge Univ.; School of Architecture, Liverpool Univ. (BArch). Architects' Dept: Hertfordshire CC, 1952–56; British Transport Commn, 1956–60; Directorate of Army Works, 1960–63; Directorate of Research & Development, Min. of Public Building and Works, 1963–67; Directorate of Works (Married Quarters), MPBW, 1967–70; Directorate of Works (Navy Home), PSA, 1970–71; Director of Works (Navy Home), PSA, 1971–75; Director, Directorate General of Design Services, Design Office, 1975–78; Under Sec., PSA, DoE, 1978; Dir of Architectural Services, 1978–81; Dir, Diplomatic and Post Office Services, 1981–83. jssc 1963. *Recreations:* motoring, walking. *Address:* Little Orchard, Cuddington Way, Cheam, Sutton, Surrey SM2 7JA. *T:* 081–643 1964.

WOODWARD, Adm. Sir John (Forster), GBE 1989; KCB 1982; Commander-in-Chief, Naval Home Command, 1987–89; Flag Aide-de-Camp to the Queen, 1987–89; *b* Penzance, Cornwall, 1 May 1932; *s* of late T. Woodward and M. B. M. Woodward; *m* 1960, Charlotte Mary McMurtrie; one *s* one *d*. *Educ:* Royal Naval College, Dartmouth. Under training, Home Fleet, until 1953; Submarine Specialist, serving in HMS Sanguine, Porpoise, Valiant, and commanding HMS Tireless, Grampus and Warspite, from 1953; Min. of Defence and senior training posts, from 1971, plus comd HMS Sheffield, 1976–77; Director of Naval Plans, 1978–81; Flag Officer, First Flotilla, 1981–83, Sen. Task Gp Comdr, S Atlantic, during Falklands Campaign, Apr.-July 1982; Flag Officer, Submarines, and Comdr, Submarines Eastern Atlantic, 1983–84; Dep. Chief of Defence Staff (Commitments), 1985–87. Hon. Liveryman, Glass Sellers' Co., 1982. *Recreations:* sailing, philately, skiing. *Address:* c/o The Naval Secretary, Ministry of Defence, Old Admiralty Building, Whitehall, SW1. *Club:* Royal Yacht Squadron (Cowes).

WOODWARD, Rev. Max Wakerley; Methodist Minister, retired 1973; *b* 29 Jan. 1908; *s* of Alfred Woodward, Methodist Minister, and Mabel (*née* Wakerley); *m* 1934, Kathleen May Beaty; three *s* one *d*. *Educ:* Orme Sch., Newcastle; Kingswood Sch., Bath; Handsworth Coll., Birmingham. Missionary to Ceylon, 1929–42; Chaplain, Royal Navy, 1942–46; Minister: Leamington Spa, 1946–50; Finsbury Park, 1950–54; Harrow, 1954–58; Wesley's Chapel, London, 1958–64; Secretary, World Methodist Council, 1964–69; Minister, Bromley, Kent, 1969–73. Exchange Preacher, Univ. Methodist Church, Baton Rouge, La, 1957. Dir, Methodist Newspaper Co. Ltd, 1962–84. *Publication:* One At London, 1966. *Recreations:* gardening, stamp collecting. *Address:* 6a Field End Road, Pinner, Mddx HA5 2QL. *T:* 081–429 0608.

WOODWARD, Shaun Anthony; Director of Communications, Conservative Party, since 1991; *b* 26 Oct. 1958; *s* of Dennis George Woodward and Joan Lillian (*née* Nunn); *m* 1987, Camilla Davan, *e d* of Hon. Timothy Sainsbury, *qv*; one *s* one *d*. *Educ:* Bristol Grammar Sch.; Jesus Coll., Cambridge (MA). Parly Lobbyist, Nat. Consumer Council, 1981–82; BBC TV: Researcher, That's Life!, 1982–85; Producer: Newsnight, 1985–87; Panorama, 1988–89; Editor, That's Life!, 1989–91; Researcher, Lost Babies, 1983; Producer: Drugwatch, 1985; The Gift of Life!, 1987. *Publications:* (with Ron Lacey) Tranquillisers, 1983; (with Esther Rantzen) Ben: the story of Ben Hardwick, 1985; (with Sarah Caplin) Drugwatch, 1986. *Recreations:* opera, tennis, reading, gardening, family. *Club:* Vanderbilt.

WOODWARD, William Charles; QC 1985; a Recorder, since 1989; *b* 27 May 1940; *s* of Wilfred Charles Woodward and Annie Stewart Woodward (*née* Young); *m* 1965, Carolyn Edna Johns; two *s* one *d*. *Educ:* South County Junior Sch.; Nottingham High Sch.; St John's Coll., Oxford (BA Jurisp). Marshall to Sir Donald Finnemore, Michaelmas 1962. Called to the Bar, Inner Temple, 1964; pupillage with Brian J. Appleby, QC; Midland and Oxford Circuit, 1964–; Head of Chambers, 24 The Ropewalk, Nottingham, 1986–. Member: Nottingham Univ. Law Adv. Cttee; E Midlands Area Cttee, Law Soc.; Cttee, and Founder Mem., Notts Medico-Legal Soc. *Recreations:* family, friends, holidays. *Address:* (chambers): 24 The Ropewalk, Nottingham NG1 5EF. *T:* Nottingham (0602) 472581, *Fax:* Nottingham (0602) 476532; 22 Old Buildings, Lincoln's Inn, WC2A 3UR. *Clubs:* Pre War Austin Seven; Nottingham and Notts United Services.

WOOF, Robert Edward; Member and former official, National Union of Mineworkers; *b* 24 Oct. 1911; *m* Mary Bell (*d* 1971); one *d*. *Educ:* Elementary School. Began work in the mines at an early age, subsequently coal face worker. Member of the Labour Party, 1937–; MP (Lab) Blaydon, Co. Durham, Feb. 1956–1979. Member Durham County Council, 1947–56. *Address:* 10 Ramsay Road, Chopwell, Newcastle upon Tyne NE17 7AG.

WOOF, Robert Samuel, PhD; Reader in English Literature, University of Newcastle upon Tyne, since 1971; Director, Wordsworth Trust, Dove Cottage, Grasmere, since 1989; *b* 20 April 1931; *s* of William Woof and Annie (*née* Mason); *m* 1958, Pamela Shirley Moore; two *s* two *d*. *Educ:* Lancaster Royal Grammar School; Pembroke College, Oxford (MA); University of Toronto (PhD). Goldsmith Travelling Fellow, 1953–55; Lectr, Univ. of Toronto, 1958–61; University of Newcastle: Lord Adams of Ennerdale Fellow, 1961–62; Lectr, 1962; Leverhulme Fellow, 1983–84. Vice-Chm., Northern Arts Assoc., 1974–81; Hon. Keeper of Collections, Trustees of Dove Cottage, Grasmere, 1974–.

Hon. Sec. and Treasurer, 1978–. Mem., 1982–88, Rep., 1988–, Arts Council: Vice-Chm., 1982–88, acting Chm, 1985–86; Drama Panel; Chm., Literature Panel, 1984–88 (Vice-Chm., 1983–84). *Publications:* (ed) T. W. Thompson, Wordsworth's Hawkshead, 1970; The Wordsworth Circle, 1979; (with Peter Bicknell) The Discovery of the Lake District 1750–1810, 1982; (with Peter Bicknell) The Lake District Discovered 1810–50, 1983; Thomas De Quincey: an English opium-eater 1785–1859, 1985; (with David Thomason) Derwentwater, the Vale of Elysium, 1986; The Artist as Evacuee, 1987; (with Jonathan Wordsworth and Michael C. Jaye) William Wordsworth and the Age of English Romanticism, 1987; Matthew Arnold, a Centennial Exhibition, 1988; Byron: a dangerous romantic?, 1989. *Recreations:* the arts, the Lake District. *Address:* 4 Burdon Terrace, Jesmond, Newcastle upon Tyne NE2 3AE. *T:* 091–281 2680; The Wordsworth Trust, Dove Cottage, Grasmere, Cumbria LA22 9SH. *T:* Grasmere (09665) 544/580.

WOOL, Dr Rosemary Jane, FRCPsych; Director, Prison Medical Services, since 1989. *Educ:* University of London (Charing Cross Hospital Medical School). MB BS, DPM, DRCOG. *Address:* Home Office Prison Department, Cleland House, Page Street, SW1P 4LN.

WOOLARD, Edgar Smith; Chairman and Chief Executive Officer, Du Pont, since 1989; *b* 15 April 1934; *s* of Edgar S. Woolard and Mamie (Boone) Woolard; *m* 1956, Peggy Harrell; two *d*. *Educ:* North Carolina State Univ. (BSc Indust. Eng. 1956). Joined Du Pont 1957; industrial engineer, Kinston, NC, 1957–59; group supervisor, industrial engrg, 1959–62; supervisor, manufg sect., 1962–64; planning supervisor, 1964–65; staff asst to Prodn Manager, Wilmington, 1965–66; product supt, Old Hickory, Tenn, 1966–69; engrg supt, 1969–70; Asst Plant Manager, Camden, SC, 1970–71; Plant Manager, 1972–73; Dir of products marketing div., Wilmington, 1973–75; Man. Dir, textile marketing div., 1975–76; corp. plans dept, 1976–77; Gen. Dir, products and planning div., 1977–78; Gen. Manager, 1978–81, Vice-Pres., 1981–83, textile fibers; Exec. Vice President, 1983–85; Vice Chm., 1985–87. Director: Citicorp; IBM Corp.; N Carolina Textile Foundn; Jt Council on Economic Educn; Seagram Co.; Member: Bd of Trustees, Winterthur Mus. and Bd of Govs of its Corporate Council; Bd of Trustees, N Carolina State Univ.; Med. Center of Delaware; Protestant Episcopal Theol Seminary, Virginia; Exec. Cttee, Delaware Roundtable; Bretton Woods Cttee; World Affairs Council; Policy Cttee, Business Roundtable. *Address:* Du Pont, 1007 Market Street, Wilmington, Delaware 19898, USA.

WOOLDRIDGE, Ian Edmund, OBE 1991; Sports Columnist, Daily Mail, since 1972; BBC Television documentary reporter and writer; *b* 14 Jan. 1932; *s* of late Edmund and Bertha Wooldridge; *m* 1st, Veronica Ann Churcher; three *s*; 2nd, Sarah Margaret Chappell Lourenço. *Educ:* Brockenhurst Grammar School. New Milton Advertiser, 1948; Bournemouth Times, 1953; News Chronicle, 1956; Sunday Dispatch, 1960; Daily Mail, 1961. Columnist of Year, 1975 and 1976; Sportswriter of Year, 1972, 1974, 1981, 1989, in British Press Awards; Sportswriter of the Year, Sports Council Awards, 1987, 1988. *Publications:* Cricket, Lovely Cricket, 1963; (with Mary Peters) Mary P, 1974; (with Colin Cowdrey) MCC: The Autobiography of a Cricketer, 1976; The Best of Wooldridge, 1978; Travelling Reserve, 1982; Sport in the Eighties, 1989. *Recreations:* travel, golf, Beethoven and dry Martinis. *Address:* 11 Collingham Gardens, SW5 0HS. *Club:* Scribes.

WOOLF, Geoffrey; General Secretary, National Association of Teachers in Further and Higher Education, since 1989; *b* 15 April 1944. *Educ:* Polytechnic of Central London (BSc Econ). Lecturer in History, Southgate Technical College, 1974–89. *Recreation:* politics. *Address:* 18 Selborne Road, Southgate, N14 7DH. *T:* 081–882 0785.

WOOLF, Harry, PhD; Professor, Institute for Advanced Study, Princeton, USA, since 1976 (Director, 1976–87); *b* 12 Aug. 1923; *s* of Abraham Woolf and Anna (*née* Frankman); *m*; two *s* two *d*. *Educ:* Univ. of Chicago (BS Physics and Maths 1948; MA Physics and History 1949); Cornell Univ. (PhD Hist. of Science 1955). Served US Army, 1943–46. Instructor: Boston Univ., Mass, 1953–55; Brandeis Univ., Waltham, Mass, 1954–55; Univ. of Washington, Seattle: Asst Prof., Associate Prof., and Prof., 1955–61; Johns Hopkins University: Prof., Hist. of Science Dept, 1961–76 (Chm. of Dept, 1961–72); Provost, 1972–76; Princeton University: Mem. Adv. Council, Depts of Philosophy, 1980–84, and of Comparative Lit., 1982–86. Pres., Chm. of Bd, Johns Hopkins Program for Internat. Educn in Gynecology and Obstetrics, Inc., 1973–76, Trustee 1976–; Mem. Adv. Bd, Smithsonian Research Awards, 1975–79; Member: Vis. Cttee Student Affairs, MIT, 1973–77; Corporation Vis. Cttee, Dept of Linguistics and Philosophy, MIT, 1977–83; Nat. Adv. Child Health and Human Develt Council, NIH, 1977–80; Mem. Vis. Cttee, Research Center for Language Sciences, Indiana Univ., 1977–80; Trustee: Associated Universities Inc., Brookhaven Nat. Laboratories, Nat. Radio Astronomy Observatory, 1972–82; Hampshire Coll., Amherst, Mass, 1977–81; Merrill Lynch Cluster C Funds, 1982–; Trustee-at-Large, Univs Research Assoc. Inc., Washington, DC (Fermi Nat. Accelerator Lab.), 1978–91, Chm. Bd 1979–89. Member: Corp. Visiting Cttee for Dept of Physics, MIT, 1979–85; Council on Foreign Relations Inc., 1979–; Adv. Panel, WGBH, NOVA, 1979–; Internat. Research and Exchanges Bd, NY, 1980–; Scientific Adv. Bd, Wissenschaftskolleg zu Berlin, 1981–87; Board of Directors: Alex. Brown Mutual Funds, Inc., Baltimore, 1981–; W. Alton Jones Cell Science Center, 1982–86; Westmark Corp., 1987–. Member: Adv. Council, Dept of Comparative Literature, Princeton Univ., 1982–; Adv. Council, Nat. Science Foundn, 1984–89; Bd of Trustees, Rockefeller Foundn, 1984–; Dir-at-large, Amer. Cancer Soc., 1982–86. Member: Académie Internat. d'Histoire des Sciences; Amer. Philosoph. Soc.; Phi Beta Kappa; Sigma Xi (also Bicentennial Lectr, 1976). Editor, ISIS Internat. Review, 1958–64; Associate Editor, Dictionary of Scientific Biog., 1970–80; Mem. Editl Bd, Interdisciplinary Science Revs, 1975–; Mem. Editl Adv. Bd, The Writings of Albert Einstein, 1977–. Fellow, Amer. Acad. of Arts and Scis; FAAAS. Hon. DSc: Whitman Coll., 1979; Amer. Univ., Washington DC, 1982; Hon. LHD: Johns Hopkins Univ., 1983; St Lawrence Univ., 1986. *Publications:* The Transits of Venus: a study in eighteenth-century science, 1959, repr. 1981; (ed) Quantification: essays in the history of measurement in the natural and social sciences, 1961; (ed) Science as a Cultural Force, 1964; (ed and contrib.) Some Strangeness in the Proportion: a centennial symposium to celebrate the achievements of Albert Einstein, 1980; (ed) The Analytic Spirit: essays in the history of science, 1981. *Address:* Institute for Advanced Study, Princeton, NJ 08540, USA. *T:* (609) 734–8018. *Club:* Century Association (New York).

WOOLF, Rt. Hon. Sir Harry (Kenneth), Kt 1979; PC 1986; **Rt. Hon. Lord Justice Woolf;** a Lord Justice of Appeal, since 1986; *b* 2 May 1933; *s* of late Alexander Woolf and Leah Woolf (*née* Cussins); *m* 1961, Marguerite Sassoon, *d* of George Sassoon; three *s*. *Educ:* Fettes Coll.; University Coll., London (LLB; Fellow, 1981). Called to Bar, Inner Temple, 1954; Bencher, 1976. Commnd (Nat. Service), 15/19th Royal Hussars, 1954; seconded Army Legal Services, 1955; Captain 1955. Started practice at Bar, 1956. A Recorder of the Crown Court, 1972–79; Jun. Counsel, Inland Revenue, 1973–74; First Treasury Junior Counsel (Common Law), 1974–79; a Judge of the High Court of Justice, Queen's Bench Div., 1979–86; Presiding Judge, SE Circuit, 1981–84. Held inquiry into prison disturbances, 1990, Part II with Judge Tumin, report 1991. Member: Senate, Inns of Court and Bar, 1981–85 (Chm., Accommodation Cttee, 1982–85); Bd of Management, Inst. of Advanced Legal Studies, 1985– (Chm., 1986–); Chairman: Lord Chancellor's Adv. Cttee on Legal Educn., 1986–; Mddx Adv. Cttee on Justices of the Peace, 1986–90; President: Assoc. of Law Teachers, 1985–89; Anglo-Jewish Archives, 1985–89; Central Council of Jewish Social Services, 1987–; SW London Magistrates Assoc., 1987–. Trustee, Butler Trust, 1991–. Gov., Oxford Centre for Postgrad. Hebrew Studies, 1989–. Hon. Mem., SPTL, 1988. *Publication:* Protecting the Public: the new challenge (Hamlyn Lecture), 1990. *Address:* Royal Courts of Justice, Strand, WC2. *Clubs:* Garrick, Royal Automobile.

WOOLF, Sir John, Kt 1975; film and television producer; Founder and Chairman, Romulus Films Ltd, since 1948; Managing Director, since 1967 and Chairman, since 1982, British & American Film Holdings Plc; Director, First Leisure Corporation Plc, since 1982; *s* of Charles M. and Vera Woolf; *m* 1955, Ann Saville; two *s*. *Educ:* Institut Montana, Switzerland. War of 1939–45 (Bronze Star (USA), 1945): Asst Dir, Army Kinematography, War Office, 1944–45. Co-founder and Executive Director, Anglia TV Group PLC, 1958–83. Member: Cinematograph Films Council, 1969–79; Bd of Governors, Services Sound & Vision Corp. (formerly Services Kinema Corp.), 1974–83; Mem. Exec. Council and Trustee, Cinema and Television Benevolent Fund. Freeman, City of London, 1982. FRSA 1978. Films produced by Romulus Group include: The African Queen, Pandora and the Flying Dutchman, Moulin Rouge, I am a Camera, Carrington VC, Beat the Devil, Story of Esther Costello, Room at the Top, Wrong Arm of the Law, The L-Shaped Room, Term of Trial, Life at the Top, Oliver!, Day of the Jackal, The Odessa File (Romulus prodns have won 12 Oscars in various categories). TV productions for Anglia include over 100 Tales of the Unexpected. Personal awards include: British Film Academy Award for Best Film of 1958: Room at the Top; Oscar and Golden Globe for Best Film of 1969: Oliver!; special awards for contribution to British film industry from Cinematograph Exhibitors Assoc., 1969, Variety Club of GB, 1974. *Address:* 214 The Chambers, Chelsea Harbour, SW10 0XF. *T:* 071–376 3791, *Fax:* 071–352 7457.

WOOLF, John Moss, CB 1975; Deputy Chairman of the Board of Customs and Excise, and Director-General (Customs and Establishments), 1973–78; *b* 5 June 1918; *o s* of Alfred and Maud Woolf; *m* 1940, Phyllis Ada Mary Johnson (*d* 1990); one *d*. *Educ:* Drayton Manor Sch.; Honourable Society of Lincoln's Inn. Barrister-at-law, 1948. War Service, 1939–46 (Captain, RA). Inland Revenue, 1937. Asst Principal, Min. of Fuel and Power, 1948; HM Customs and Excise, 1950: Principal, 1951; Asst Sec., 1960; Chm., Valuation Cttee, Customs Cooperation Council, Brussels, 1964–65; National Bd for Prices and Incomes, 1965; Under-Secretary, 1967; Asst Under-Sec. of State, Dept of Employment and Productivity, 1968–70; HM Customs and Excise: Comr, 1970; Dir of Establishments and Organisation, 1971–73. Advr on Price Problems, Govt of Trinidad & Tobago, 1968. Assoc. of First Div. Civil Servants: Mem. of Exec. Cttee, 1950–58 and 1961–65; Hon. Sec., 1952–55; Chm., 1955–58 and 1964–65; Mem., Civil Service National Whitley Council (Staff Side), 1953–55. Leader of Review Team to examine responsibilities of the Directors of the Nat. Museums and Galleries, 1978–79; Review of Organisation and Procedures of Chancery Div. of High Court, 1979–81; Overseas Adviser to CEGB, 1979–82. Commandeur d'Honneur, Ordre du Bontemps de Médoc et des Graves, 1973; Hon. Borgenerális (Hungary), 1974. *Publications:* Report on Control of Prices in Trinidad and Tobago (with M. M. Eccleshall), 1968; Report of the Review Body on the Chancery Division of the High Court (with Lord Oliver of Aylmerton and R. H. H. White), 1981. *Recreations:* reading, gardening. *Address:* West Lodge, 113 Marsh Lane, Stanmore, Mddx HA7 4TH. *T:* 081–952 1373. *Club:* Civil Service.

WOOLFORD, Harry Russell Halkerston, OBE 1970; Consultant, formerly Chief Restorer, National Gallery of Scotland; *b* 23 May 1905; *s* of H. Woolford, engineer; *m* 1932, Nancy Philip; one *d*. *Educ:* Edinburgh. Studied art at Edinburgh Coll. of Art (Painting and Drawing) and RSA Life School (Carnegie Travelling Scholarship, 1928), London, Paris and Italy; afterwards specialized in picture restoration. FMA; FIIC. Hon. Mem., Assoc. of British Picture Restorers, 1970. Hon. MA Dundee, 1976. *Address:* 7a Barntongate Avenue, Barnton, Edinburgh EH4 8BD. *T:* 031–339 6861. *Club:* Scottish Arts.

WOOLFSON, Mark; Consultant and Director of Consortium, Pollution Control Consultants, 1972–89; a Partner, Posford Duvivier (formerly Posford Pavry & Partners), 1976–89; retired, 1990; *b* 10 Nov. 1911; *s* of Victor Woolfson and Sarah (*née* Kixman); *m* 1940, Queenie Carlis; two *d*. *Educ:* City of London. Student Engr, Lancashire Dynamo & Crypto, until 1936; Engr, ASEA Electric Ltd, 1936–40; War Service, RNVR, 1940–46 (Lt-Comdr); MPBW, later DoE, 1946–71, Chief Mech. and Electr. Engineer, 1969–71. FIMechE, FIEE. *Publications:* papers in Jls of Instns of Civil, Mechanical and Elect. Engrs. *Recreations:* tennis, gardening, golf. *Address:* 3 Runnelfield, Harrow, Mddx. *T:* 081–422 1599.

WOOLFSON, Prof. Michael Mark, FRS 1984; FRAS; FInstP; Professor of Theoretical Physics, University of York, since 1965; *b* 9 Jan. 1927; *s* of Maurice and Rose Woolfson; *m* 1951, Margaret (*née* Frohlich); two *s* one *d*. *Educ:* Jesus College, Oxford (MA); UMIST (PhD, DSc). Royal Engineers, 1947–49. Research Assistant: UMIST, 1950–52; Cavendish Lab., Cambridge, 1952–54; ICI Fellow, Univ. of Cambridge, 1954–55; Lectr, 1955–61, Reader, 1961–65, UMIST; Head of Dept. of Physics, Univ. of York, 1982–87. Hughes Medal, Royal Soc., 1986. *Publications:* Direct Methods in Crystallography, 1961; An Introduction to X-Ray Crystallography, 1970; The Origin of the Solar System, 1989; papers in learned jls. *Recreations:* gardening, wine making. *Address:* 124 Wigton Lane, Leeds LS17 8RZ. *T:* Leeds (0532) 687890.

WOOLHOUSE, Prof. Harold William; Director, Waite Agricultural Research Institute, University of Adelaide, since 1990; *b* 12 July 1932; *s* of William Everson Woolhouse and Frances Ella Woolhouse; *m* 1959, Leonie Marie Sherwood; two *s* one *d*. *Educ:* Univ. of Reading (BSc); Univ. of Adelaide (PhD). Lecturer and Sen. Lectr, Sheffield Univ., 1960–69; Professor of Botany, Leeds Univ., 1969–80; Dir, John Innes Inst., and Prof. of Biological Scis, UEA, 1980–86; Dir of Res., AFRC Inst. of Plant Sci. Res., and Hon. Prof., UEA, 1987–90. Vis. Professor, USC, Los Angeles, 1968; Andrew D. White Professor at Large, Cornell Univ., 1983–89. Hon. DSc UEA, 1990. *Publications:* research papers on plant senescence, photosynthesis, metal toxicity and tolerance, and physiology of adaptation. *Recreations:* poetry, music, poultry breeding, gardening. *Address:* Old Sun House, 65 Damgate Street, Wymondham, Norfolk NR18 0BH; Waite Agricultural Research Institute, University of Adelaide, Glen Osmond, SA 5064, Australia. *T:* 61–8–372–2201.

WOOLHOUSE, Prof. John George, CBE 1988; Professor of Education, and Director of Centre for Education and Industry, University of Warwick, since 1988; *b* 17 June 1931; *s* of George Francis Woolhouse and Doris May Woolhouse (*née* Webber); *m* 1958, Ruth Carolyn Harrison; two *s* one *d*. *Educ:* Chichester High Sch. for Boys; Ardingly Coll; Brasenose Coll., Univ. of Oxford (MA). FBIM; MIPM. Rolls-Royce Ltd, 1954–72: Dir, Rolls-Royce and Associates, 1965–68; Co. Educn and Trng Officer, 1968–72; Asst Dir, Kingston Polytechnic and Dir, Kingston Regl Management Centre, 1972–78; Dir Atkins Planning, W. S. Atkins Gp Consultants, and Hd of Human Resources Develt, 1978–82; Dir, Technical and Vocational Educn Initiative, MSC, 1983–86; Dir of Educn Progs, MSC, 1986–87. Chm., Assoc. of Regional Management Centres, 1977–78. Hon. FIIM. *Publications:* chapters in: The Training of Youth in Industry, 1966; The Management Development Handbook, 1973; Gower Handbook of Management, 1983. *Recreations:* travel, music, boating, fishing. *Address:* Ivy Farm House, Ivy Farm Lane, Coventry CV4 7BW. *Club:* Royal Air Force.

WOOLLAM, John Victor; Barrister-at-Law; *b* 14 Aug. 1927; *s* of Thomas Alfred and Edie Moss Woollam; *m* 1964, Lavinia Rosamond Ela, *d* of S. R. E. Snow; two *s*. *Educ:* Liverpool Univ. Called to the Bar, Inner Temple. Contested (C) Scotland Div. of Liverpool, 1950; MP (C) W Derby Div. of Liverpool, Nov. 1954–Sept. 1964; Parliamentary Private Sec. to Minister of Labour, 1960–62. *Recreation:* philately. *Address:* Naishes Farm, Danes Hill, Dalwood, Axminster, E Devon EX13 7HB. *T:* Axminster (0297) 33516.

WOOLLASTON, Sir (Mountford) Tosswill, Kt 1979; painter (abandoned other occupations, 1966); *b* 11 April 1910; *s* of John Reginald Woollaston and Charlotte Kathleen Frances (*née* Tosswill); *m* 1936, Edith Winifred Alexander; three *s* one *d*. *Educ:* Huinga Primary; Stratford (NZ) Secondary; brief brushes with art schools, Christchurch, 1931; King Edward Technical Coll., Dunedin, 1932. Member, The Group, Christchurch, 1935–; a few private but enthusiastic supporters; work featured in Art in New Zealand, 1937. Doldrums, 1950s; Auckland City Art Gallery began purchasing work, 1958, other galleries followed; overseas travel grant, NZ Arts Council, 1961; reputation increased. Govt purchases for embassies overseas, early sixties; Peter McLeavey, Dealer, Wellington, took over selling, 1967. *Publications:* The Faraway Hills (Auckland City Art Gall. Associates), 1962; ERUA (48 drawings of a boy, with text—Paul), 1966; Sage Tea (autobiog.), 1981. *Recreation:* gardening. *Address:* RD3, Motueka, New Zealand. *T:* Motueka 88425.

WOOLLCOMBE, Rt. Rev. Kenneth John; an Assistant Bishop, Diocese of Worcester, since 1989; *b* 2 Jan. 1924; *s* of late Rev. E. P. Woollcombe, OBE, and Elsie Ockenden Woollcombe; *m* 1st, 1950, Gwendoline Rhona Vyvien Hodges (*d* 1976); three *d*; 2nd, 1980, Rev. Juliet Dearmer; one *d*. *Educ:* Haileybury Coll., Hertford; St John's Coll., Oxford; Westcott House, Cambridge. Sub-Lieut (E) RNVR, 1945. Curate, St James, Grimsby, 1951; Fellow, Chaplain and Tutor, St John's Coll., Oxford, 1953, Hon. Fellow, 1971; Professor of Dogmatic Theology, General Theological Seminary, New York, 1960; Principal of Episcopal Theological Coll., Edinburgh, 1963; Bishop of Oxford, 1971–78; Asst Bishop, Diocese of London, 1978–81; Canon Residentiary of St Paul's, 1981–89, Precentor 1982–89. Chm., SPCK, 1973–79; Mem., Central Cttee, World Council of Churches, 1975–83; Chm., Churches' Council for Covenanting, 1978–82; Co-Chm., English Anglican-RC Cttee, 1985–88; Judge in Court of Ecclesiastical Causes Reserved, 1984–89. Hon. Chaplain, 1978–87, Hon. Liveryman, 1986, Glass Sellers' Co. STD Univ. of the South, Sewanee, USA, 1963; Hon. DD Hartford, Conn, 1975. *Publications:* (contrib.) The Historic Episcopate, 1954; (jointly) Essays on Typology, 1957. *Address:* 4 Flax Piece, Upton Snodsbury, Worcester WR7 4PA.

WOOLLETT, Maj.-Gen. John Castle, CBE 1957 (OBE 1955); MC 1945; MA Cantab; FICE; Principal Planning Inspector, Department of the Environment, 1971–81; *b* 5 Nov. 1915; *o s* of John Castle Woollett and Lily Bradley Woollett, Bredgar, Kent; *m* 1st, 1941, Joan Eileen Stranks (marr. diss., 1957); two *s* (and one *s* decd); 2nd, 1959, Helen Wendy Willis; two step *s*. *Educ:* St Benedict's Sch.; RMA Woolwich; St John's Coll., Cambridge. Joined RE, 1935; 23 Field Co., 1938–40 (BEF, 1939–40); 6 Commando, 1940–42; Major Comdg 16 Field Sqdn and 16 Assault Sqdn RE, 1942–45 (BLA, 1944–45); Student, Staff Coll., Camberley, 1946; DAAG and GSO2, Brit. Service Mission to Burma, 1947–50; Major Comdg 51 Port Sqdn RE, 1950; Instructor, Staff Coll., Camberley, 1950–53; Lt-Col Comdg 28 Field Engr Regt, 1954–55 (Korea); Bt Lt-Col 1955; Comdr Christmas Is, 1956–57; GSO1, Northern Army Gp, 1957–59; Col GS, US Army Staff Coll., Fort Leavenworth, 1959–61; DQMG (Movements), BAOR, 1962–64; Brig. Comdg Hants Sub District and Transportation Centre, RE, 1964–65; Sch. of Transport, 1965–66; Dep. Engr-in-Chief, 1966–67; Maj.-Gen., Chief Engineer, BAOR, 1967–70, retired. Col Comdt, RE, 1973–78. Pres., Instn of RE, 1974–79. *Recreations:* cruising, shooting. *Address:* 42 Rhinefield Close, Brockenhurst, Hants. *Clubs:* Army and Navy, Royal Ocean Racing, Royal Cruising; Island Sailing (Cowes), Royal Lymington Yacht.

WOOLLEY, David Rorie, QC 1980; barrister-at-law; a Recorder of the Crown Court, since 1982; *b* 9 June 1939; *s* of Albert and Ethel Woolley. *Educ:* Winchester Coll.; Trinity Hall, Cambridge (BA Hons Law). Called to the Bar, Middle Temple, 1962, Bencher, 1988. Vis. Scholar, Wolfson Coll., Cambridge, 1982–87. Inspector, DoE inquiry into Nat. Gall. extension, 1984. *Publications:* Town Hall and the Property Owner, 1965; contribs to various legal jls. *Recreations:* opera, mountaineering, real tennis. *Address:* 1 Sergeants' Inn, EC4Y 1NH. *T:* 071–583 1355. *Clubs:* MCC; Swiss Alpine.

WOOLLEY, John Maxwell, MBE 1945; TD 1946; Clerk, Merchant Taylors' Company, and Clerk to The Governors, Merchant Taylors' School, 1962–80; *b* 22 March 1917; *s* of Lt-Col Jasper Maxwell Woolley, IMS (Retd) and Kathleen Mary Woolley (*née* Waller); *m* 1952, Esme Adela Hamilton-Cole; two *s*. *Educ:* Cheltenham College; Trinity College, Oxford. BA (Oxon) 1938, MA (Oxon) 1962. Practising Solicitor, 1950–55; Asst Clerk, Merchant Taylors' Company, 1955–62. Hon. Mem. CGLI, 1991. *Address:* Flat 27, 15 Grand Avenue, Hove, E Sussex BN3 2NG. *T:* Brighton (0273) 733200. *Club:* Hove.

WOOLLEY, (John) Moger; Chairman: Dolphin Packaging, since 1990; CHB Group, since 1991; *b* 1 May 1935; *s* of Cyril Herbert Steele Woolley and Eveline Mary May Woolley; *m* 1960, Gillian Edith Millar; one *s* one *d*. *Educ:* Taunton Sch.; Bristol Univ., 1956–59 (BSc). National Service, 1954–56. Various management positions, DRG plc, 1959–89, Chief Exec., 1985–89. Non-Executive Director: Staveley Industries; Bristol Water Co.; United Bristol Hosp. Trust. *Recreations:* cricket, hockey, golf, gardening. *Address:* Matford House, Northwoods, Winterbourne, Bristol BS17 1RS. *T:* Winterbourne (0454) 772180. *Clubs:* Naval and Military; Merchant Venturers' (Bristol).

WOOLLEY, Roy Gilbert; His Honour Judge Woolley; a Circuit Judge, since 1976; *b* 28 Nov. 1922; *s* of John Woolley and Edith Mary Woolley; *m* 1953, Doreen, *d* of Humphrey and Kathleen Morris; two *s* two *d*. *Educ:* Overton and Marchwiel Primary Schs; Deeside Secondary Sch.; UCL (LLB Hons 1949). Served War, 1939–45, Air Gunner, RAF. Christopher Tancred Student, Lincoln's Inn, 1948; called to the Bar, 1951; Wales and Chester Circuit; Recorder, 1975. Reader: Diocese of Chester, 1955–; Diocese of Lichfield, 1977–. Member: Lichfield Diocesan Synod, 1988–; General Synod of C of E, 1990–; Legal Adv. Commn of C of E, 1991–. *Recreations:* outdoor pursuits, incl. horse riding, gardening; interested in music, poetry, art and antique furniture. *Address:* Henlle Hall, St Martins, Oswestry, Salop SY10 7AX. *T:* Oswestry (0691) 661257.

WOOLLEY, Russell; *see* Woolley, A. R.

WOOLMAN, (Joseph) Roger; Director, Legal Division, Office of Fair Trading, since 1988; *b* 13 Feb. 1937; *s* of late Maurice Wollman and Hilda Wollman; *m* 1973, Elizabeth, *d* of late Eric Ingham; one *s* one *d*. *Educ:* Perse School, Cambridge; Trinity Hall, Cambridge (Exhibnr; BA (Law Tripos), MA). Solicitor, 1974; Legal Asst, Office of Fair Trading, 1976; Senior Legal Asst, Dept of Trade, 1978; Asst Solicitor, DTI, 1981; Under Sec. (Legal), DTI, 1985. *Clubs:* Reform; Hampstead Golf.

WOOLMER, Kenneth John; Director of MBA Programmes, School of Business and Economic Studies, Leeds University; Principal in Halton Gill Associates, consultants on central and local government relations; Marketing Consultant to Trades Union Unit Trust; *b* 25 April 1940; *s* of Joseph William and Gertrude May Woolmer; *m* 1961, Janice Chambers; three *s*. *Educ:* Gladstone Street County Primary, Rothwell, Northants; Kettering Grammar Sch.; Leeds Univ. (BA Econs). Research Fellow, Univ. of West Indies, 1961–62; Teacher, Friern Rd Sec. Mod. Sch., London, 1963; Lecturer: Univ. of Leeds (Economics), 1963–66; Univ. of Ahmadu Bello, Nigeria, 1966–68; Univ. of Leeds, 1968–79. Councillor: Leeds CC, 1970–78; West Yorkshire MCC, 1973–80 (Leader, 1975–77; Leader of Opposition, 1977–79). Chairman, Planning and Transportation Cttee, Assoc. of Metropolitan Authorities, 1974–77. Contested (Lab) Batley and Spen, 1983, 1987. MP (Lab) Batley and Morley, 1979–83; Opposition spokesman on trade, shipping and aviation, 1981–83; Mem., Select Cttee on Treasury and Civil Service, 1980–81; Chm., 1981, Vice-Chm., 1982, PLP Economics and Finance Gp. Dir, Leeds United AFC, 1991–. *Address:* 8 Ancaster Crescent, Leeds LS16 5HS.

WOOLRYCH, Prof. Austin Herbert, FBA 1988; Professor of History, University of Lancaster, 1964–85, now Emeritus; *b* 18 May 1918; *s* of Stanley Herbert Cunliffe Woolrych and May Gertrude (*née* Wood); *m* 1941, Muriel Edith Rolfe (*d* 1991); one *s* one *d*. *Educ:* Westminster Sch.; Pembroke Coll., Oxford (BLitt, MA). Served War, RAC, 1939–46: commnd RTR, 1940; Captain 1943. Lectr in History, subseq. Sen. Lectr, Univ. of Leeds, 1949–64; Pro-Vice-Chancellor, Univ. of Lancaster, 1971–75. Vis. Fellow, All Souls Coll., Oxford, 1981–82; Commonwealth Vis. Fellow to univs in Australia and NZ, 1983. Hon. DLitt Lancaster, 1986. *Publications:* Battles of the English Civil War, 1961; Oliver Cromwell, 1964; (introd) Complete Prose Works of John Milton, vol 7, 1980; Commonwealth to Protectorate, 1982; England without a King, 1983; Soldiers and Statesmen, 1987; articles and reviews in jls and symposia. *Recreations:* walking, travel, opera. *Address:* Patchetts, Caton, Lancaster LA2 9QN. *T:* Caton (0524) 770477.

WOOLSEY, Rt. Rev. Gary Frederick; *see* Athabasca, Bishop of.

WOOLTON, 3rd Earl of, *cr* 1956; **Simon Frederick Marquis;** Baron Woolton, 1939; Viscount Woolton, 1953; Viscount Walberton, 1956; *b* 24 May 1958; *s* of 2nd Earl of Woolton and of Cecily Josephine (now Countess Lloyd George of Dwyfor), *e d* of Sir Alexander Gordon Cumming, 5th Bt; *S* father, 1969; *m* 1987, Hon. Sophie Frederika, *o d* of Baron Birdwood, *qv*.; one *d*. *Educ:* Eton College; St Andrews Univ. (MA Hons). Merchant banker, S. G. Warburg & Co. Ltd, 1982–88; Dir, The Art Collection Ltd, 1990–. Mem. Cttee, Tayside Reg., Game Conservancy. Trustee, Woolton Charitable Trust. Freeman, Skinners' Co. *Recreations:* gardening, golf, field sports. *Address:* Glenogil, by Forfar, Angus DD8 3SX; 79 Alderney Street, SW1V 4HF. *Clubs:* White's, Brooks's, MCC; New (Edinburgh); Royal and Ancient.

WOOLVERTON, Kenneth Arthur; Head of Latin America, Caribbean and Pacific Department, Overseas Development Administration of the Foreign and Commonwealth Office, 1985–86; *b* 4 Aug. 1926; *s* of Arthur Eliott Woolverton and Lilian Woolverton; *m* 1957, Kathleen West; one *s*. *Educ:* Orange Hill Grammar Sch. Colonial Office, 1950–61; CRO, 1961–66 (2nd Sec., Jamaica); Min. of Overseas Development, 1966–79; Hd of Middle East Develt Div., ODA, 1979–81; Hd of British Develt Div. in the Caribbean, ODA, 1981–84. *Recreations:* photography, archaeology, sailing. *Address:* 47 Durleston Park Drive, Great Bookham, Surrey. *T:* Bookham (0372) 454055. *Club:* Farmers'.

WOOLWICH, Bishop Suffragan of, since 1984; **Rt. Rev. (Albert) Peter Hall;** *b* 2 Sept. 1930; *s* of William Conrad Hall and Bertha Gladys Hall; *m* 1957, Valerie Jill Page; two *s*. *Educ:* Queen Elizabeth Grammar School, Blackburn; St John's Coll., Cambridge (MA Mod. Langs); Ridley College, Cambridge. Deacon 1955, priest 1956; Curate: St Martin, Birmingham, 1955–60; St Mary Magdalene, Avondale, Zimbabwe, 1960; Rector of Avondale, Zimbabwe, 1963–70; Rector of Birmingham, 1970–84. *Recreations:* squash, mountain walking. *Address:* 8B Hillyfields Crescent, Brockley, SE4 1QA. *T:* 081–469 0013.

WOON, Peter William; *b* 12 Dec. 1931; *s* of Henry William Woon and Gwendoline Constance Woon; *m* 1969, Diana Jean Ward; two *s*. *Educ:* Christ's Hospital. 2nd Lieut Royal Signals, 1954–56; Reporter, Bristol Evening Post, 1949–54 and 1956–58; air corresp., Daily Express, 1958–61; BBC: reporter, 1961–66; Asst Editor, TV News, 1966–69; Editor, Radio News, 1969–75; Head of Information, 1975–77; Editor, News and Current Affairs, radio, 1977–80; Editor, TV News, 1980–85; Head, Ops, N America, 1985–88. *Recreations:* theatre, sailing. *Address:* 1 Quay Street, Lymington, Hants SO41 9AS. *T:* Lymington (0590) 672912.

WOOSNAM, Charles Richard; a Forestry Commissioner, since 1986; *b* 4 Aug. 1925; *s* of late Ralph William Woosnam and Kathleen Mary Woosnam (*née* Evan-Thomas); *m* 1950, Patricia Rodney Carruthers; two *s* two *d*. *Educ:* Winchester; Pembroke Coll., Cambridge. BA Estate Management. FRICS. Commissioned 15th/19th The King's Royal Hussars, 1943–47, served Europe and Palestine; with Land Agents Strutt and Parker, Builth Wells office, 1950–63; set up own Land Agency partnership, Woosnam & Tyler, 1964. Member: Valuation Panel, Agricultural Mortgage Corp., 1962–; Welsh Water Authy, 1973–76 (Chm., Fisheries Adv. Cttee); Exec. Cttee, Timber Growers UK (formerly Timber Growers England & Wales), 1976–86 (Dep. Chm., England and Wales; Chm., Finance Cttee); Home Grown Timber Adv. Cttee, Forestry Commn, 1981–86; Chm., CLA Game Fair Local Cttee, 1976. High Sheriff, Powys, 1985–86. *Recreations:* shooting, fishing. *Address:* Cefnllysgwynne, Builth Wells, Powys. *T:* Builth Wells (0982) 552237. *Club:* Army and Navy.

WOOSTER, Clive Edward Doré; consultant; *b* 3 Nov. 1913; *s* of Edward Doré Wooster; *m*; two *s*; *m* 1970, Patricia Iris (formerly Dewey). *Educ:* Private School, Southend-on-Sea. Private offices, 1930–40; War Service, Captain RA, 1940–46. Local Authority Offices and LCC, 1946–51; Ministry of Education, 1951–58; University Grants Cttee, 1958–59; Works Directorate, War Office, 1959–63; Dir of Building Management, MPBW, 1963–69; Dep. Chief Architect, Min. of Housing and Local Govt, 1969; Dir, Housing Develt, DoE, 1972–74, retired. RIBA Technical Standards Cttee, 1960–64; RIBA Building Controls Panel Chairman, 1960–63; RIBA Management Handbook Cttee, 1963–67; RIBA Council, 1970–72. *Publications:* Lectures on architectural and building management subjects; contrib. to professional journals. *Address:* 141 Harefield Road, Rickmansworth, Herts WD3 1PB. *T:* Rickmansworth (0923) 775401.

WOOTTON, Godfrey; *see* Wootton, N. G.

WOOTTON, Gordon Henry; His Honour Judge Wootton; a Circuit Judge, since 1980; *b* 23 April 1927; *s* of William Henry Wootton and Winifred Beatrice Wootton; *m* 1st, 1953, Camilla Bowes (marr. diss. 1979); two *s*; 2nd, 1979, Eileen Mary North. LLB Hons. Captain, RE, 1947. Called to the Bar, Middle Temple, 1952; Resident Magistrate, Uganda, 1954–62; a Recorder of the Crown Court, 1975–80. *Address:* Beech-Hurst, Abbotswood, Greenhill, Evesham, Worcs WR11 4NS.

WOOTTON, Ian David Phimester, MA, MB, BChir, PhD, FRSC, FRCPath, FRCP; Professor of Chemical Pathology, Royal Postgraduate Medical School, University of London, 1963–82; *b* 5 March 1921; *s* of D. Wootton and Charlotte (*née* Phimester); *m* 1946, Veryan Mary Walshe; two *s* two *d*. *Educ:* Weymouth Grammar School; St John's College, Cambridge; St Mary's Hospital, London. Research Assistant, Postgraduate Med. School, 1945; Lecturer, 1949; Sen. Lecturer, 1959; Reader, 1961. Consultant Pathologist to Hammersmith Hospital, 1952. Member of Medical Research Council Unit, Cairo, 1947–48; Major, RAMC, 1949; Smith-Mundt Fellow, Memorial Hosp., New York, 1951. Chief Scientist (Hosp. Scientific and Technical Services), DHSS, 1972–73. *Publications:* Microanalysis in Medical Biochemistry, 1964, ed 6th edn, 1982; Biochemical Disorders in Human Disease, 1970; papers in medical and scientific journals on biochemistry and pathology. *Recreations:* carpentry, boating, beekeeping. *Address:* Cariad Cottage, Cleeve Road, Goring, Oxon RG8 9DB. *T:* Goring-on-Thames (0491) 873050.

WOOTTON, (Norman) Godfrey; Stipendiary Magistrate for Merseyside, since 1976; *b* 10 April 1926; *s* of H. N. and E. Wootton, Crewe, Cheshire. *Educ:* The Grammar Sch., Crewe; Liverpool Univ. (LLB). Called to Bar, Gray's Inn, 1951. Joined Northern Circuit, 1951. A Recorder of the Crown Court, 1972. *Recreations:* travel, photography. *Address:* Magistrates' Court, Dale Street, Liverpool L2 2JQ. *Club:* Athenæum (Liverpool).

WOOTTON, Ronald William, CBE 1991; Assistant Secretary, Overseas Development Administration, 1976–91; *b* 7 April 1931; *s* of William George and Lilian Wootton; *m* 1954, Elvira Mary Gillian Lakeman; one *s* one *d*. *Educ:* Christ's College, Finchley. Served Royal Signals, 1950–52. Colonial Office, 1952–63; Commonwealth Relations Office, 1963–65; ODM/ODA, 1965–91; Head of British Develt Div. in the Pacific, 1982–85. *Address:* 16 The Heath, Chaldon, Surrey CR3 5DG. *T:* Caterham (0883) 344903.

WOOZLEY, Prof. Anthony Douglas, MA; University Professor Emeritus of Philosophy and Law, University of Virginia, since 1983; *b* 14 Aug. 1912; *o s* of David Adams Woozley and Kathleen Lucy Moore; *m* 1937, Thelma Suffield (marr. diss. 1978), *e d* of late Frank Townshend, Worcester; one *d*. *Educ:* Haileybury College; Queen's College, Oxford. Open Scholar, Queen's College, 1931–35; 1st Cl. Class. Hon. Mods, 1933; 1st Cl. Lit. Hum., 1935; John Locke Schol., 1935. Served War, 1940–46 (despatches); commissioned King's Dragoon Guards, 1941; served N Africa, Italy, Greece, Egypt, Syria, Palestine; Major. Fellow of All Souls College, 1935–37; Fellow and Praelector in Philosophy, Queen's Coll., 1937–54; Librarian, 1938–54; Tutor, Queen's College, 1946–54; University Lecturer in Philosophy, 1947–54; Senior Proctor, 1953–54; Prof. of Moral Philosophy, Univ. of St Andrews, 1954–67; University of Virginia: Prof. of Philosophy, 1966; Commonwealth Prof. of Philosophy, 1974–77; Commonwealth Prof. and Univ. Prof. of Philosophy and Law, 1977–83. Editor of The Philosophical Quarterly, 1957–62; Editor, Home University Library, 1962–68. Visiting Professor of Philosophy: Univ. of Rochester, USA, 1965; Univ. of Arizona, 1972. *Publications:* (ed) Thomas Reid's Essays on the Intellectual Powers of Man, 1941; Theory of Knowledge, 1949; (with R. C. Cross) Plato's Republic: a Philosophical Commentary, 1964; (ed) John Locke's Essay Concerning Human Understanding, 1964; Law and Obedience, 1979; articles and reviews in Mind, etc. *Address:* 655 Kearsarge Circle, Charlottesville, Va 22903, USA.

WORCESTER, Marquess of; Henry John Fitzroy Somerset; ARICS; *b* 22 May 1952; *s* and *heir* of 11th Duke of Beaufort, *qv*; *m* 1987, Tracy Louise, *yr d* of Hon. Peter Ward and Hon. Mrs Claire Ward; one *s*. *Educ:* Eton; Cirencester Agricultural College. With Morgan Grenfell Laurie Ltd (formerly Michael Laurie & Partners), London, 1977; subseq. with Franc Warwick. *Recreations:* hunting, shooting, golf, tennis, skiing, rock music. *Heir:* *s* Earl of Glamorgan, *qv*. *Club:* Turf.

WORCESTER, Bishop of, since 1982; **Rt. Rev. Philip Harold Ernest Goodrich;** *b* 2 Nov. 1929; *s* of late Rev. Canon Harold Spencer Goodrich and Gertrude Alice Goodrich; *m* 1960, Margaret Metcalfe Bennett; four *d*. *Educ:* Stamford Sch.; St John's Coll., Cambridge (MA); Cuddesdon Theological Coll. Curate, Rugby Parish Church, 1954–57; Chaplain, St John's Coll., Cambridge, 1957–61; Rector of the South Ormsby Group of Parishes, 1961–68; Vicar of Bromley, 1968–73; Diocesan Director of Ordinands, Rochester, 1974–82; Bishop Suffragan of Tonbridge, 1974–82. *Recreations:* gardening, music, walking, looking at buildings. *Address:* Bishop's House, Hartlebury Castle, Kidderminster, Worcs DY11 7XX. *Club:* United Oxford & Cambridge University.

WORCESTER, Dean of; *see* Jeffery, Very Rev. R. M. C.

WORCESTER, Archdeacon of; *see* Bentley, Ven. F. W. H.

WORCESTER, Robert Milton; Chairman, since 1973 and Managing Director, since 1969, Market & Opinion Research International (MORI) Ltd; Visiting Professor, City University, since 1990; *b* 21 Dec. 1933; *s* of late C. M. and Violet Ruth Worcester, of Kansas City, Mo, USA; *m* 1st, 1958, Joann (*née* Ransdell); two *s*; 2nd, 1982, Margaret Noel (*née* Smallbone). *Educ:* Univ. of Kansas (BSc). Consultant, McKinsey & Co., 1962–65; Controller and Asst to Chm., Opinion Research Corp., 1965–68. Past Pres., World Assoc. for Public Opinion Research. Vice Pres., Internat., Social Science Council, UNESCO, 1989–. Trustee: WWF (UK); Natural History Mus. Develt Trust; Member: Exec. Cttee, Pilgrims'; Programme Cttee, Ditchley Foundn. Consultant: The Times; Sunday Times; Economist. Frequent broadcaster and speaker on British and Amer. politics. FRSA; MBIM. Co-Editor, Internat. Jl of Public Opinion Research. *Publications:* edited: Consumer Market Research Handbook, 1971, 3rd edn 1986; (with M Harrop) Political Communications, 1982; Political Opinion Polling: an international review, 1983; (with Lesley Watkins) Private Opinions, Public Polls, 1986; (with Eric Jacobs) We British, 1990; British Public Opinion: history and methodology of political opinion polling in Great Britain, 1991; Typically British, 1991; contrib. The Times; papers in tech. and prof. jls. *Recreations:* choral music (St Bartholomew's Hospital Choir), gardening, scuba diving. *Address:* 32 Old Queen Street, SW1H 9HP. *T:* 071–222 0232. *Club:* Reform.

WORDIE, Sir John (Stewart), Kt 1981; CBE 1975; VRD 1963; barrister-at-law; *b* 15 Jan. 1924; *s* of late Sir James Mann Wordie, CBE, Hon. LLD, and of Lady Wordie (*née* Henderson); *m* 1955, Patricia Gladys Kynoch, Keith, Banffshire, *d* of Lt-Col G. B. Kynoch, CBE, TD, DL; four *s*. *Educ:* Winchester Coll.; St John's Coll., Cambridge (MA; LLM). Served RNVR, 1942–46. Comdr RNR, 1967; Comdr London Div. RNR, 1969–71. Cambridge, 1946–49; Called to the Bar, Inner Temple, 1950; in practice at the Bar, 1951–86. Chairman: Burnham and Pelham Cttees, 1966–87; Soulbury Cttee, 1966–; Wages Councils; Mem., Agricultural Wages Bd for England and Wales, 1974–; Dep. Chm. and Mem., Central Arbitration Cttee, 1976–; Mem. Council, ACAS, 1986–90. Chm., Nat. Jt Council for Lectures in Further Educn, 1980–. Mem. Court of Assistants, Salters' Co., 1971–, Master, 1975. *Recreations:* shooting, sailing and boating, athletics, tennis. *Address:* Shallows Cottage, The Shallows, Breamore, Fordingbridge, Hants SP6 2AG. *T:* Downton (0725) 22432. *Clubs:* Travellers', Army and Navy, Royal Ocean Racing; Hawks (Cambridge); Royal Tennis Court (Hampton Court); Clyde Corinthian Yacht.

WORDLEY, Ronald William; Chairman, The Buckingham Group (Winslow Press) Ltd, since 1987; Director, BCS Developments Ltd, since 1989; Managing Director, 1978–87, Chairman, 1985–86, HTV Ltd; *b* 16 June 1928; *s* of William Wordley and Elizabeth Anne Hackett; *m* 1953, Pamela Mary Offord; two *s* one *d* (and one *s* decd). *Educ:* Barnet Grammar Sch.; City of London Coll.; RMA, Sandhurst. Regular Army Officer: 2/Lieut RA, 1948; regtl duty, UK, Far East and Europe; Liaison Officer, RM Commando Bde, 1951, Captain; Air OP Pilot, 1953; Army Light Aircraft Sch., 1955; seconded Army Air Corps Cadre, 1957; resigned commn, 1958. Unilever (United Africa Co.), 1958–59; Anglia Television Ltd: Sales Exec., 1959; Gen. Sales Manager, 1962; Dep. Sales Controller, 1964; joined Harlech Consortium as Sales Controller, 1967; Sales Dir on bd of HTV Ltd, 1971. Director: Instock Ltd; Independent Television Publications Ltd; (also Mem. Council), Independent Television Cos Assoc. Ltd; HTV Gp plc; HTV Equipment Ltd; HTV Property Ltd., 1971–87. Hon. Patron, Royal Regt of Wales, 1986–91. Mem., Inst. of Marketing; FRSA 1983; FInstD 1986. *Recreations:* music, travel, golf, swimming. *Address:* 6 Spring Leigh, Leigh Woods, Bristol, Avon BS8 3PG. *T:* (office) Bicester (0869) 244644; TSDY Tirion II, Quay 11, Berth 14, Port de La Rague, Theoule-sur-Mer 06590, France. *Clubs:* Clifton (Bristol); Bristol and Clifton Golf.

WORDSWORTH, Barry; conductor; Musical Director of the Royal Ballet and of the Birmingham Royal Ballet, since 1991; *b* 20 Feb. 1948; *s* of Ronald and Kathleen Wordsworth; *m* 1970, Ann Barber; one *s*. *Educ:* Royal College of Music. Conductor, Royal Ballet, 1974–84; Music Dir, Sadler's Wells Opera, 1982–84, New Sadler's Wells Opera; Musical Dir and Prin. Conductor, Brighton Philharmonic Orch., 1989–; Prin. Conductor, BBC Concert Orch., 1989–. Joint winner, Sargent Conductor's Prize, 1970; Tagore Gold Medal, RCM, 1970. *Recreations:* swimming, photography, cooking. *Address:* c/o Marygate Management, 13 Cotswold Mews, 12–16 Battersea High Street, SW11 3JE.

WORKMAN, Charles Joseph, TD 1966; Part-time Chairman: Industrial Tribunals for Scotland, since 1986; Social Security Appeal Tribunals, since 1986; *b* 25 Aug. 1920; *s* of Hugh William O'Brien Workman and Annie Shields; *m* 1949, Margaret Jean Mason; one *s* two *d*. *Educ:* St Mungo's Acad., Glasgow; Univ. of Glasgow (MA 1950, LLB 1952). Admitted solicitor, 1952. Served War, 1939–45: France, Belgium, Holland, Germany; commnd Second Fife and Forfar Yeomanry, RAC, 1942; Captain, 1945; served Intell. Corps TA and TAVR, 1954–69; Bt Lt-Col 1969; Hon. Col, Intell. and Security Gp (V), 1977–86. Entered Office of Solicitor to Sec. of State for Scotland as Legal Asst, 1955; Sen. Legal Asst, 1961; Asst Solicitor, 1966; Dep. Solicitor to Sec. of State, 1976; Dir, Scottish Courts Administration, 1978–82; Senior Dep. Sec. (Legal Aid), Law Soc. of Scotland, 1982–86. Chm., Public Service and Commerce Gp, Law Soc. of Scotland, 1977–78. Founder Mem., Edinburgh Chamber Music Trust, 1977–. *Publication:* (contrib.) The Laws of Scotland: Stair Memorial Encyclopaedia, vol. 2, 1987. *Recreations:* hill walking, swimming, music. *Address:* Green Lane Cottage, Lasswade, Midlothian EH18 1HE. *Club:* New (Edinburgh).

WORKMAN, Robert Little, CB 1974; Under-Secretary, HM Treasury, 1967–74; *b* 30 Oct. 1914; *s* of late Robert Workman and Jesse Little; *m* 1940, Gladys Munroe Foord; two *d*. *Educ:* Sedbergh Sch.; Clare Coll., Cambridge. Economist, Export Credits Guarantee Dept, 1938–49; HM Treasury: Principal, 1949–59; Asst Secretary, 1959–66. Member, St Pancras Borough Council, 1945–49. *Recreations:* building and the visual arts. *Address:* Flatts Farm, Hawstead, Bury St Edmunds, Suffolk IP29 5NW. *T:* Sicklesmere (028486) 497.

WORKMAN, Timothy; a Metropolitan Stipendiary Magistrate, since 1986; a Chairman, Inner London Juvenile Panel, since 1989; *b* 18 Oct. 1943; *s* of Gordon and late Eileen Workman; *m* 1971, Felicity Ann Caroline Western; one *s* one *d*. *Educ:* Ruskin Grammar Sch., Croydon. Probation Officer, Inner London, 1967–69; admitted Solicitor, 1969; Solicitor, subseq. Partner, C. R. Thomas & Son, later Lloyd Howorth & Partners, Maidenhead, 1969–85. *Recreations:* ski-ing, pottery. *Address:* Orchard House, Fleet Hill, Finchampstead, Berks RG11 4LA. *T:* Eversley (0734) 733315. *Club:* Medico-Legal.

WORLOCK, Most Rev. Derek John Harford; *see* Liverpool, Archbishop of, (RC).

WORMALD, Brian Harvey Goodwin, MA; University Lecturer in History, Cambridge, 1948–79; Fellow of Peterhouse, 1938–79, Emeritus Fellow 1979; *b* 24 July 1912; *s* of late Rev. C. O. R. Wormald and Mrs A. W. C. Wormald (*née* Brooks); *m* 1946, Rosemary, *d* of E. J. B. Lloyd; four *s*. *Educ:* Harrow; Peterhouse, Cambridge (Scholar). BA 1934 (1st Class Hons Hist. Tripos, Parts I and II); Members Prize (English Essay), 1935; Strathcona Research Student, St John's College, 1936–38; Prince Consort Prize, 1938; MA 1938. Chaplain and Catechist, Peterhouse, 1940–48; Dean, 1941–44; Tutor, 1952–62. Select Preacher, Cambridge, 1945 and 1954. Junior Proctor, 1951–52. Received into Catholic Church, 1955. *Publication:* Clarendon: Politics, History and Religion, 1951. *Address:* c/o Peterhouse, Cambridge CB2 1RD. *Club:* Travellers'.

WORMALD, Maj.-Gen. Derrick Bruce, DSO 1944; MC 1940, Bar 1945; Director-General of Fighting Vehicles and Engineer Equipment, Ministry of Defence, 1966–70, retired; *b* 28 April 1916; 2nd *s* of late Arthur and Veronica Wormald; *m* 1953, Betty Craddock; two *d*. *Educ:* Bryanston Sch.; RMA Sandhurst. Commnd into 13/18 Royal Hussars (QMO), 1936; served in India, 1936–38, BEF, 1939–40 and BLA, 1944–45; Comd, 25th Dragoons, India, 1945–47; Staff Coll., Quetta, 1947; War Office, 1948–50; Comdr, 1st Armoured Car Regt of Arab Legion, 1951–52; Comdr Arab Legion Armoured Corps, 1953–54; jssc 1955; GSO1, 11th Armoured Div., 1956; Comd, 3rd The King's Own Hussars, 1956, and The Queen's Own Hussars, 1958; Comdr, Aden Protectorate Levies, 1959–61; Comdr, Salisbury Plain Sub District, 1962–65. Col, 13th/18th Royal Hussars (QMO), 1974–79. Order of El Istiqlal (Jordan), 1953. *Recreations:* shooting, fishing, sailing. *Address:* Ballards, Wickham Bishops, Essex CM8 3JJ. *T:* Maldon (0621) 891218. *Club:* Cavalry and Guards.

WORMALD, Dame Ethel (May), DBE 1968; DL; *b* 19 Nov. 1901; *d* of late John Robert Robinson, Journalist, Newcastle upon Tyne; *m* 1923, Stanley Wormald, MA, MEd, BSc (decd); two *s*. *Educ:* Whitley Bay High Sch.; Leeds Univ. (BA, DipEd). Liverpool City Councillor, 1953–67; Lord Mayor of Liverpool, 1967–68. President, Assoc. of Education Cttees, 1961–62; Chairman, Liverpool Education Cttee, 1955–61, and 1963–67. JP Liverpool, 1948–71; DL Lancaster, 1970, Merseyside, 1974. *Address:* 17 Rhes James, Bethesda, Gwynedd LL57 3RA. *T:* Bethesda (0248) 601800.

WORMALD, Peter John, CB 1990; Director, Office of Population Censuses and Surveys, and Registrar General for England and Wales, since 1990; *b* 10 March 1936; *s* of late H. R. and G. A. Wormald; *m* 1962, Elizabeth North; three *s*. *Educ:* Doncaster Grammar Sch.; The Queen's Coll., Oxford (MA). Assistant Principal, Min. of Health, 1958, Principal, 1963; HM Treasury, 1965–67, Asst Sec., 1970; Under Sec., DHSS, 1978; Dep. Sec., Dept of Health (formerly DHSS), 1987. *Recreations:* music, golf, contract bridge. *Address:* Office of Population Censuses and Surveys, St Catherine's House, 10 Kingsway, WC2B 6JP. *Club:* United Oxford & Cambridge University.

WÖRNER, Dr Manfred; Secretary-General of NATO, since 1988; *b* Stuttgart, 24 Sept. 1934; *s* of Carl Wörner; *m* 1982, Elfriede (*née* Reinsch); one *s* of previous marriage. *Educ:* Univ. of Heidelberg; Univ. of Paris; Univ. of Munich (Dr jur). Lawyer, 1957. Joined CDU, 1956; CDU State Parly Advr, Baden Württemberg, 1962–64; Mem., Bundestag, 1965–88; Minister of Defence, FRG, 1982–88. Dep. Chm., CDU Parly Gp, 1969–71; CDU/CSU Bundestag Parliamentary Party: Chm., Defence Working Gp, 1972–76; Dep. Chm., 1980–82; Chm., Bundestag Defence Cttee, 1976–80. *Address:* NATO Headquarters, Brussels 1110, Belgium.

WORRALL, Alfred Stanley, CBE 1983 (OBE 1975); *b* 28 Jan. 1912; *s* of Rev. Sidney A. Worrall and Margaret Worrall (*née* White); *m* 1936, Mary Frances Marshall; one *s* two *d* (and one *s* decd). *Educ:* King Edward's Sch., Bath; St Catharine's Coll., Cambridge (Schol.; MA); BD London. Teaching posts at St George's Sch., Bristol, 1935–38, Leeds Grammar Sch., 1938–49; war service in Non-combatant Corps (bomb disposal) and coal mining, 1941–46; Headmaster: Rock Ferry High Sch., 1949–57; Sir Thomas Rich's Sch., 1957–61; Methodist Coll., Belfast, 1961–74, retired. Member, Methodist Conference, 1955, 1959, 1961–64, also of the Conf. in Ireland, 1966–83. Pres., Ulster Headmasters' Assoc., 1966–68; Chairman: BBC Religious Adv. Council, N Ireland, 1968–73; Arts Council of N Ire., 1974–82; New Ulster Movement, 1974–79; Chm. of Governors, Stranmillis Coll. of Educn, 1974–83; Mem., Radio Telefis Eireann Authority, Dublin, 1979–83; Chm., Libr. and Inf. Services Council, NI, 1982–83. Hon. Life Mem., SHA, 1980. Hon. LLD QUB, 1974. *Publications:* (with Cahal B. Daly) Ballymascanlon: a venture in Irish inter-church dialogue, 1978; (with Eric Gallagher) Christians in Ulster 1968–80, 1982; (trans.) Origène, by H. Crouzel, 1989. *Recreations:* travel, enjoyment of the arts. *Address:* 27 Selly Park Road, Birmingham B29 7PH. *T:* 021–471 5140.

WORRALL, Anna Maureen, (Mrs G. H. G. Williams); QC 1989; a Recorder, since 1987; *m* 1964, G. H. Graeme Williams, *qv*; two *d*. *Educ:* Hillcrest Sch., Bramhall; Loreto Coll., Llandudno; Manchester Univ. Called to the Bar, Middle Temple, 1959; in practice, 1959–63 and 1971–; Lectr in Law, Holborn Coll. of Law, Language and Commerce, 1964–69; Dir, ILEA Educnl Television Service, 1969–71. *Recreations:* theatre, music, cooking, walking, riding, travel. *Address:* Cloisters, Pump Court, Temple, EC4Y 7AA. *T:* 071–583 0303. *Club:* Network.

WORRALL, Denis John, PhD; MP (Democratic Party) Berea (Durban), South Africa, since 1989; Chief Executive, Omega Investment Research Ltd; *b* 29 May 1935; *s* of Cecil John Worrall and Hazel Worrall; *m* 1965, Anita Ianco; three *s*. *Educ:* Univ. of Cape Town (BA Hons, MA); Univ. of South Africa (LLB); Cornell Univ. (PhD). Teaching and research positions, Univs of Natal, S Africa, Ibadan, Witwatersrand, California, Cornell; Rearch Prof. and Dir, Inst. of Social and Economic Research, Rhodes Univ., 1973. Senator, 1974; elected to Parlt, 1977; Chm., Constitutional Cttee, President's Council, 1981; Ambassador: to Australia, 1983–84; to the UK, 1984–87. Advocate of Supreme Court of S Africa. *Publication:* South Africa: government and politics, 1970. *Recreations:* tennis, reading, music. *Address:* PO Box 5455, Cape Town, 8000, South Africa.

WORSFOLD, Reginald Lewis, CBE 1979; Member for Personnel, British Gas Corporation (formerly Gas Council), 1973–80, retired; *b* 18 Dec. 1925; *s* of Charles S. and Doris Worsfold; *m* 1st, 1952, Margot Kempell (marr. diss. 1974); one *s* one *d*; 2nd, 1982, Christine McKeown. *Educ:* School of Technology, Art and Commerce, Oxford; London Sch. of Economics. MIPM. Served War of 1939–45: Lieut 44 Royal Marine Commandos, 1943–46. Organising Commissioner, Scout Council of Nigeria, 1947–49; Personnel Manager: British European Airways, 1953–65; W Midlands Gas Bd, 1965–69; Gas Council: Dep. Personnel Dir, 1969–70; Personnel Dir, 1970–72. *Recreations:* sailing, camping, music. *Address:* Beck House, 43 Wychwood Grove, Chandler's Ford, Hants SO5 1FQ. *T:* Chandler's Ford (0703) 269873.

WORSKETT, Prof. Roy, RIBA; MRTPI; consultant architect and town planner; Partner, Architectural Planning Partnership, Horsham, 1982–85; *b* 3 Sept. 1932; *s* of Archibald Ellwood Worskett and Dorothy Alice Roffey; two *s* one *d*. *Educ:* Collyer's Sch., Horsham; Portsmouth Sch. of Architecture. MRTPI 1975; RIBA 1955. Architect's Dept, LCC, 1957–60; Architect, Civic Trust, London, 1960–63; Historic Areas Div., DoE (formerly MPBW), 1963–74; City Architect and Planning Officer, Bath City Council, and Prof. of Urban Conservation, Sch. of Architecture, Bath Univ., 1974–79; Consultant Head, Conservation Section, Crafts Council, 1979–82. Consultant Architect: Bath CC, 1979–83; Salisbury DC, 1980–; Brighton Palace Pier, 1987–; London boroughs of Lambeth, Kensington and Chelsea, and Richmond, 1988–; Consultant: Ford Foundn in India, 1982–; Council of Europe, 1984–; Nat. Audit Office, 1987; evidence to Public Inquiries at Mansion House, for City of London, and at County Hall, London, 1984–. Chm., Conservation Cttees, Crafts Adv. Cttee, 1974–79; Member: Heritage Educn Group, 1976–88; Council for Urban Study Centres, TCPA, 1977–80; Council of Management, Architectural Heritage Fund, 1977–. Pres., Urban Design Gp, 1983–84. Vis. Prof., Internat. Centre for Conservation, Rome, 1972–. *Publications:* The Character of Towns, 1968; articles in architect. and planning magazines. *Recreation:* looking and listening in disbelief. *Address:* 32 Smithbarn, Horsham, Sussex RH13 6EB. *T:* Horsham (0403) 54208.

WORSLEY, Lord; George John Sackville Pelham; *b* 9 Aug. 1990; *s* and *heir* of 8th Earl of Yarborough, *qv*.

WORSLEY, Francis Edward, (Jock); Chairman, Financial Training Co. Ltd, since 1972; *b* 15 Feb. 1941; *s* of late Francis Arthur Worsley and Mary Worsley; *m* 1962, Caroline Violet (*née* Hatherell); two *s* two *d*. *Educ:* Stonyhurst College. FCA. Articled, Barton, Mayhew & Co., 1959–64; with Anderson Thomas Frankel, Chartered Accountants, 1964–69; Financial Training Co., 1969–. Dir, Lautro, 1990–. Pres., Inst. of Chartered Accountants in England and Wales, 1988–89 (Vice-Pres., 1986–87, Dep. Pres., 1987–88); Mem., Building Socs Commn, 1991–. *Recreations:* tennis, wine, cooking. *Address:* 136/142 Bramley Road, W10 6SR. *T:* 081–960 4421. *Club:* Carlton.

WORSLEY, Air Cdre Geoffrey Nicolas Ernest T. C.; *see* Tindal-Carill-Worsley.

WORSLEY, Jock; *see* Worsley, F. E.

WORSLEY, Sir Marcus; *see* Worsley, Sir W. M. J.

WORSLEY, Michael Dominic Laurence; QC 1985; *b* 9 Feb. 1926; *s* of Paul Worsley and Magdalen Teresa Worsley; *m* 1962, Pamela (*née* Philpot) (*d* 1980); one *s* (and one *s* decd); *m* 1986, Jane, *d* of Percival and Mary Sharpe. *Educ:* Bedford School; Inns of Court School of Law. RN 1944–45. Lived in Africa, 1946–52; called to the Bar, Inner Temple, 1955, Bencher, 1980; Standing Prosecuting Counsel to Inland Revenue, 1968–69; Treasury Counsel at Inner London Sessions, 1969–71; Junior Treasury Counsel, 1971–74, Senior Treasury Counsel, 1974–84, CCC. *Recreations:* music, travelling. *Address:* 6 King's

Bench Walk, Temple, EC4Y 7DR. *T:* 071–583 0410. *Clubs:* Garrick, Lansdowne; Thomas More Society.

WORSLEY, Paul Frederick; QC 1990; a Recorder, since 1987; *b* 17 Dec. 1947; *s* of Eric Worsley, MBE, GM and Sheila Mary Worsley (*née* Hoskin); *m* 1974, Jennifer Ann, JP, *d* of late Ernest Avery; one *s* one *d. Educ:* Hymers College, Hull; Mansfield College, Oxford (MA). Called to the Bar, Middle Temple, 1970 (Astbury Scholar); practised NE Circuit, 1970–. *Recreations:* Spy prints, Whitby, opera, preaching. *Address:* Park Court Chambers, 40 Park Cross Street, Leeds LS1 2QH. *T:* Leeds (0532) 433277; 2 Harcourt Buildings, Temple, EC4Y 9BD. *T:* 071–353 1394. *Club:* Yorkshire (York).

WORSLEY, Gen. Sir Richard (Edward), GCB 1982 (KCB 1976); OBE 1964; Pilkington Brothers, 1982–86; Chairman: Western Provident Assoc., since 1989; Electro-Optical Division, Pilkington Group, 1984–86 (Chief Executive, 1982–86); Barr and Stroud, 1982–86; Pilkington PE, 1982–86; *b* 29 May 1923; *s* of H. H. K. Worsley, Grey Abbey, Co. Down; *m* 1st, 1959, Sarah Anne Mitchell; one *s* one *d*; 2nd, 1980, Caroline, Duchess of Fife, *er d* of Baron Forteviot, *qv. Educ:* Radley Coll. Served War: commissioned into Rifle Bde, 1942, Middle East and Italian Campaigns, 1942–45. Instr, RMA Sandhurst, 1948–51; Malayan Emergency, 1956–57; Instr, Staff Coll., Camberley, 1958–61; CO, The Royal Dragoons, 1962–65; Comdr, 7th Armoured Bde, 1965–67; Imperial Defence Coll., 1968; Chief of Staff, Far East Land Forces, 1969–71; GOC 3rd Div., 1972–74; Vice-QMG, MoD, 1974–76; GOC 1 (Br) Corps, 1976–78; QMG, 1979–82. Freeman: City of London, 1983; Glass Sellers' Co., 1984. *Recreations:* shooting, ornithology. *Address:* c/o Barclays Bank, 27 Regent Street, SW1. *Club:* Cavalry and Guards.

WORSLEY, Sir (William) Marcus (John), 5th Bt *cr* 1838; JP; Deputy Chairman, The National Trust, since 1986; Lord-Lieutenant of North Yorkshire, since 1987; *b* 6 April 1925; *s* of Colonel Sir William Arthington Worsley, 4th Bt, and Joyce Morgan (*d* 1979), *d* of Sir John Fowler Brunner, 2nd Bt; *S* father, 1973; *m* 1955, Hon. Bridget Assheton, *d* of 1st Baron Clitheroe, PC, KCVO; three *s* one *d. Educ:* Eton; New Coll., Oxford. Green Howards, 1943–47 (Lieut seconded to Royal West African Frontier Force). BA Hons (Oxford) Modern History, 1949. Programme Assistant, BBC European Service, 1950–53. Contested (C) Keighley, 1955; MP (C) Keighley, 1959–64, Chelsea, 1966–Sept. 1974; Parliamentary Private Secretary: to Minister of Health, 1960–61; to Minister without Portfolio, 1962–64; to Lord President of the Council, 1970–72. Second Church Estates Commissioner, 1970–74; a Church Commissioner, 1976–84. Pres., Royal Forestry Soc. of England, Wales and N Ireland, 1980–82 (Vice-Pres., 1976–80); National Trust: Chm., Yorks Reg. Cttee, 1969–80; Chm., Properties Cttee, 1980–90. Hon. Col, 2nd Bn, Yorkshire Volunteers, 1988–. JP 1957 (Chm., Malton Bench, 1983–90), DL 1978–87, North Yorks; High Sheriff of North Yorks, 1982. KStJ 1987. *Recreations:* walking, reading. *Heir: s* William Ralph Worsley, ARICS [*b* 12 Sept. 1956; *m* 1987, Marie-Noëlle, *yr d* of Bernard H. Dreesmann; one *d*]. *Address:* Hovingham Hall, York YO6 4LU. *T:* Hovingham (0653) 628206. *Clubs:* Boodle's; Yorkshire (York).

WORSTHORNE, Sir Peregrine (Gerard), Kt 1991; writer; Editor, Comment Section, Sunday Telegraph, 1989–91; *b* 22 Dec. 1923; *s* of Col Koch de Gooreynd, OBE (who assumed surname of Worsthorne by deed poll, 1921), and Baroness Norman, CBE; *m* 1950, Claude Bertrand de Colasse (*d* 1990); one *d*; *m* 1991, Lady Lucinda, *d* of Viscount Lambton, *qv. Educ:* Stowe; Peterhouse, Cambridge (BA); Magdalen Coll., Oxford. Commnd Oxf. and Bucks LI, 1942; attached Phantom, GHQ Liaison Regt, 1944–45. Sub-editor, Glasgow Herald, 1946; Editorial staff: Times, 1948–53; Daily Telegraph, 1953–61; Deputy Editor, Sunday Telegraph, 1961–76, Associate Editor, 1976–86, Editor, 1986–89. *Publications:* The Socialist Myth, 1972; Peregrinations: selected pieces, 1980; By the Right, 1987. *Recreations:* tennis, reading. *Address:* 74A Kensington Church Street, W8; The Old Rectory, Hedgerley, Bucks SL2 3UY. *T:* Slough (0753) 646167. *Clubs:* Beefsteak, Garrick, Pratt's.

See also S. P. E. C. W. Towneley.

WORSWICK, (George) David (Norman), CBE 1981; FBA 1979; Director, National Institute of Economic and Social Research, 1965–82; *b* 18 Aug. 1916; *s* of Thomas Worswick, OBE, and Eveline (*née* Green); *m* 1940, Sylvia, *d* of A. E. Walsh, MBE; one *s* two *d* (and one *s* decd). *Educ:* St Paul's Sch.; New Coll., Oxford (Scholar). Final Hons (Maths), 1937; Dipl. in Economics and Political Science, 1938. Research staff, Oxford Univ. Institute of Statistics, 1940–60; Fellow and Tutor in Economics, Magdalen Coll., Oxford, 1945–65 (Sen. Tutor, 1955–57; Vice-President, 1963–65; Emeritus Fellow, 1969). Vis. Prof. of Economics, MIT, 1962–63. Mem., SSRC, 1966–70. President: Sect. F, British Assoc., 1971; Royal Econ. Soc., 1982–84. Hon. DSc City, 1975. *Publications:* Joint Editor: The British Economy 1945–50, 1952; The British Economy in the 1950's, 1962; (ed) The Free Trade Proposals, 1960; (jt) Profits in the British Economy 1909–1938, 1967; (ed) Uses of Economics, 1972; (ed) The Concept and Measurement of Involuntary Unemployment, 1976; (jt ed) Keynes and the Modern World, 1983; Unemployment: a problem of policy, 1991; articles in academic jls. *Address:* 25 Beech Croft Road, Oxford OX2 7AY. *T:* Oxford (0865) 52486. *Club:* United Oxford & Cambridge University.

See also R. D. Worswick.

WORSWICK, Dr Richard David; Government Chemist and Chief Executive, Laboratory of the Government Chemist, since 1991; *b* 22 July 1946; *s* of (George) David (Norman) Worswick, *qv*; *m* 1970, Jacqueline Brigit Isobel Adcock; three *d. Educ:* New College, Oxford (BA Hons Nat. Sci. 1969; MA 1972; DPhil 1972). SRC post-doctorate res. asst, Inorganic Chem. Lab., Oxford, 1972–73; Res. Admin, Boots Co., Nottingham, 1973–76; Harwell Lab., UKAEA, 1976–91: marketing and planning, 1976–85; Head, Res. Planning and Inf. Services, 1985–87; Head, Safety Branch, 1988; Head, Envtl and Med. Scis Div., 1988–90; Dir, Process Technology and Instrumentation, AEA Industrial Technology, 1990–91. *Publications:* research papers in sci. jls. *Recreations:* listening to music, playing the violin, gardening. *Address:* Laboratory of the Government Chemist, Queen's Road, Teddington, Middx TW11 0LY. *T:* 081–943 7300.

WORTH, George Arthur, MBE; JP; Farmer and Landowner; *b* 3 May 1907; *s* of late Arthur Hovendon Worth; *m* 1935, Janet Maitland, *d* of late Air Chief Marshal Sir A. M. Longmore, GCB, DSO; two *s* two *d. Educ:* Marlborough Coll.; Sidney Sussex Coll., Cambridge. Served War of 1939–45, RAF. JP Parts of Holland, Lincs, 1939; High Sheriff of Lincolnshire, 1948–49; DL Lincs, 1950–73. *Address:* 5 Church Lane, Manton, Oakham, Leics.

See also H. B. H. Carlisle.

WORTH, Irene, Hon. CBE 1975; actress; *b* 23 June 1916. *Educ:* University of California, Los Angeles (BE). Antoinette Perry Award for distinguished achievement in the Theatre, 1965. First appeared as Fenella in Escape Me Never, New York, 1942; debut on Broadway as Cecily Harden in The Two Mrs Carrolls, Booth Theatre, 1943. Studied for six months with Elsie Fogerty, 1944–45. Subsequently appeared frequently at Mercury, Bolton's, Q, Embassy, etc. Parts include: Anabelle Jones in Love Goes to Press, Duchess Theatre, 1946 (after Embassy); Ilona Szabo in The Play's the Thing, St James's, 1947 (after tour and Lyric, Hammersmith); Eileen Perry in Edward my Son, Lyric, 1948; Lady Fortrose in Home is Tomorrow, Cambridge Theatre, 1948; Olivia Raines in Champagne for Delilah, New, 1949; Celia Coplestone in The Cocktail Party, New, 1950 (after Edinburgh Festival, 1949; Henry Miller Theatre, New York, 1950); Desdemona in Othello, Old Vic, 1951; Helena in Midsummer Night's Dream, Old Vic, 1952; Catherine de Vausselles in The Other Heart, Old Vic, 1952; Lady Macbeth in Macbeth, Desdemona in Othello, Helena in Midsummer Night's Dream, Catherine de Vausselles in The Other Heart, Old Vic tour of S Africa, 1952; Portia in The Merchant of Venice, Old Vic, 1953; Helena in All's Well That Ends Well and Queen Margaret in Richard III, First Season Shakespeare Festival Theatre, Stratford, Ont, Canada, 1953; Frances Farrar in A Day By The Sea, Haymarket, 1953–54; Alcestis in A Life in the Sun, Edinburgh Festival, 1955; leading rôles in: The Queen and the Rebels, Haymarket, 1955; Hotel Paradiso, Winter Garden, 1956; Mary Stuart, Phœnix Theatre, NY, 1957, Old Vic, 1958; The Potting Shed, Globe Theatre, London, 1958; Rosalind in As You Like It, Shakespeare Festival Theatre, Stratford, Ont, 1959; Albertine Prine in Toys in the Attic, Hudson Theatre, New York, 1960 (NY Newspaper Guild Page One Award); Season at Royal Shakespeare Theatre, Stratford, 1962; Goneril in King Lear, Aldwych, 1962; Doctor Mathilde von Zahnd in The Physicists, Aldwych, 1963; Clodia Pulcher in The Ides of March, Haymarket, 1963; World tour of King Lear for Royal Shakespeare Company, 1964; Alice in Tiny Alice, Billy Rose Theatre, New York, 1965 (Tony award 1965), Aldwych, 1970; Hilde in A Song at Twilight, Anne in Shadows of the Evening, Anna-Mary in Come into the Garden Maud (Noël Coward Trilogy), Queen's, 1966 (Evening Standard Award); Hesione Hushabye in Heartbreak House, Chichester and Lyric, 1967 (Variety Club of GB Award, 1967); Jocasta in Seneca's Oedipus, National Theatre, 1968; Hedda in Hedda Gabler, Stratford, Ont, 1970; worked with internat. Co. for Theatre Res., Paris and Iran, 1971; Notes on a Love Affair, Globe, 1972; Madame Arkadina, The Seagull, Chichester, 1973; Hamlet, Ghosts, The Seagull, Greenwich, 1974; Sweet Bird of Youth, Lake Forest, Washington, New York, 1975 (Tony Award, 1975; Jefferson Award, 1975); The Cherry Orchard, NY, 1977 (Drama Desk Award, 1977); Happy Days, NY, 1979; The Lady from Dubuque, NY, 1980; L'Olimpiade, Edinburgh Fest., 1982; The Chalk Garden, NY, 1982; The Physicists, Washington, 1983; The Golden Age, NY, 1984; Coriolanus, Nat. Theatre, 1984; The Bay at Nice, Nat. Theatre, 1986; You Never Can Tell, Haymarket, 1987; Volumnia in Coriolanus, Public Theatre, NY, 1988–89; Lake Forest, Ill, productions: Misalliance, 1976; Old Times, 1977; After the Season, 1978; Lost in Yonkers, NY, 1991 (Tony Award, 1991). *Films:* Orders to Kill, 1957 (British Film Academy Award for Best Woman's Performance, 1958); The Scapegoat, 1958; King Lear (Goneril), 1970; Nicholas and Alexandra, 1971; Eye Witness, 1980; Deathtrap. Daily Mail National Television Award, 1953–54, and has subseq. appeared on television and acted with CBC Television in NY and Canada; Coriolanus (BBC Shakespeare series), 1984. Hon. Dr Arts Tufts Univ., 1980; Hon. DFA Queen's Coll., NY, 1986. Whitbread Anglo-American Award for Outstanding Actress, 1967; NY Theatre Hall of Fame, 1979; Obie Award for sustained achievement in the theatre, 1989. *Recreation:* music. *Address:* c/o ICM, Sam Cohn, 40 West 57th Street, New York, NY 10019, USA.

WORTH, Prof. Katharine Joyce; Professor of Drama and Theatre Studies in the University of London at Royal Holloway and Bedford New College, 1985–87, now Emeritus (at Royal Holloway College, 1978–85); *b* 4 Aug. 1922; *d* of George and Elizabeth Lorimer; *m* 1947, George Worth; two *s* one *d. Educ:* Bedford Coll., Univ. of London (BA English, MA res. degree, PhD). Lectr in drama and theatre history (pt-time), Central Sch. of Speech and Drama and for Univ. of London Dept of Extra-Mural Studies, 1948 intermittently until 1963; Lectr 1964–74, Reader 1974–78, in English Lit., RHC; Hon. Fellow, RHBNC, 1990. Leverhulme Professorial Fellowship, 1987–89. Vis. Prof., KCL, 1987–. Hon. Pres., Consortium for Drama and Media in Higher Educn, 1987–; Co-editor, Theatre Notebook, 1987–. Prodns of Beckett's TV play, Eh Joe, and his radio plays, Words and Music, Embers and Cascando, 1972–84 (music for Words and Music and Cascando by Humphrey Searle); stage adaptation of Samuel Beckett's Company, perf. Edinburgh, Belfast, London and NY, 1987–88. *Publications:* Revolutions in Modern English Drama, 1973; (ed) Beckett the Shape Changer, 1975; The Irish Drama of Europe: from Yeats to Beckett, 1978; Oscar Wilde, 1983; Maeterlinck's Plays in Performance, 1985; (critical edn): W. B. Yeats: Where There is Nothing, and, W. B. Yeats and Lady Gregory: The Unicorn from the Stars, 1987; Waiting for Godot and Happy Days: text and performance, 1990; many articles and reviews on modern drama in symposia and in English, Irish and Amer. jls, incl. Modern Drama, TLS, Irish Univ. Rev., Th. Notebook, etc. *Recreations:* foreign travel, theatre, art galleries, walking in the country. *Address:* 48 Elmfield Avenue, Teddington, Mddx TW11 8BT. *T:* 081–977 5778.

WORTHINGTON, Anthony, (Tony); MP (Lab) Clydebank and Milngavie, since 1987; *b* 11 Oct. 1941; *s* of Malcolm and Monica Worthington; *m* 1966, Angela Oliver; one *s* one *d. Educ:* LSE (BA Hons); Univ. of Glasgow (MEd). Lecturer, Social Policy and Sociology: HM Borstal, Dover, 1962–66; Monkwearmouth Coll. of Further Educn, Sunderland, 1967–71; Jordanhill Coll. of Educn, Glasgow, 1971–87. Councillor, Strathclyde Region, 1974–87 (Chm., Finance Cttee, 1986–87). Mem., Home Affairs Select Cttee, 1987–89. Opposition front bench spokesman on educn and employment in Scotland, 1989–. Chm., Labour Campaign for Criminal Justice, 1987–89. *Recreations:* running, gardening, arts, sailing. *Address:* 24 Cleddans Crescent, Hardgate, Clydebank. *T:* Duntocher (0389) 73195. *Club:* Clydebank Athletic.

WORTHINGTON, Edgar Barton, CBE 1967; MA, PhD; environmental consultant; *b* 13 Jan. 1905; *s* of Edgar Worthington and Amy E. Beale; *m* 1st, 1930, Stella Desmond Johnson (*d* 1978); three *d*; 2nd, 1980, Harriett Stockton, Cape Cod. *Educ:* Rugby; Gonville and Caius Coll., Cambridge. Expeditions to African Lakes, 1927–31; Balfour Student, 1930–33, and Demonstrator in Zoology, Cambridge Univ., 1933–37; Scientist for the African Research Survey, 1934–37; Mungo Park Medal, RSGS, 1939; Director of Laboratories and Secretary of Freshwater Biological Assoc., Windermere, 1937–46; Scientific Adviser to Middle East Supply Centre, 1943–45; Development Adviser, Uganda, 1946; Scientific Secretary to Colonial Research Council, 1946–49, to E Africa High Commission, 1950–51; Secretary-General to Scientific Council for Africa South of the Sahara, 1951–55; Deputy Director-General (Scientific) Nature Conservancy, 1957–65; Scientific Dir, Internat. Biological Programme, 1964–74; Pres., Cttee on Water Res. of Internat. Council of Scientific Unions, 1973–77. Order of Golden Ark (Netherlands), 1976; Member of Honour, IUCN, 1978. *Publications:* (with Stella Worthington) Inland Waters of Africa, 1933; Science in Africa, 1938; Middle East Science, 1946; Development Plan for Uganda, 1947; (with T. T. Macan) Life in Lakes and Rivers, 1951, rev. edn 1973; Science in the Development of Africa, 1958; (ed) Man-made Lakes: problems and environmental effects, 1973; Evolution of the IBP, 1975; (ed) Arid Land Irrigation: problems and environmental effects, 1976; The Nile, 1978; The Ecological Century, 1983; official reports and papers in scientific journals. *Recreations:* field sports and farming. *Address:* Colin Godmans, Furner's Green, Uckfield, East Sussex TN22 3RR. *T:* Chelwood Gate (082574) 322. *Clubs:* Athenæum, Farmers'.

WORTHINGTON, Air Vice-Marshal (Retired) Sir Geoffrey (Luis), KBE 1960 (CBE 1945); CB 1957; idc; psa; Director-General of Equipment, Air Ministry, 1958–61, retired; *b* 26 April 1903; *s* of late Commander H. E. F. Worthington, RN; *m* 1931, Margaret Joan (*d* 1989), *d* of late Maj.-Gen. A. G. Stevenson, CB, CMG, DSO; two *s* one *d. Educ:* HMS Conway; Eastbourne Coll. RAF Coll., Cranwell, 1921. BA Open 1988. Joined RAF, 1922; resigned 1924; re-joined, 1926, in Stores Branch; RAF Staff Coll., 1934. Served War of 1939–45 (despatches, CBE): HQ Maintenance Comd, 1939–43; Air Cdre, 1943; HQ AEAF, 1944; SHAEF, 1944–45; Air Comd, Far East, 1945–47; Director of Equipment B, Air Ministry, 1948–49; idc 1950; Director of Equipment D, Air Ministry, 1951–53; AOC No 42 Group, Maintenance Comd, 1954–55; Air Vice-Marshal, 1956; AOC No 40 Group, 1955–58. Comdr US Legion of Merit, 1955. *Address:* 30 Brickwall Close, Burnham-on-Crouch, Essex CM0 8HB. *T:* Maldon (0621) 782388. *Clubs:* Royal Air Force; Royal Burnham Yacht.

WORTHINGTON, George Noel; His Honour Judge Worthington; a Circuit Judge, since 1979; *b* 22 June 1923; *s* of late George Errol Worthington and Edith Margaret Boys Worthington; *m* 1954, Jacqueline Kemble Lightfoot, 2nd *d* of late G. L. S. Lightfoot and Mrs Lightfoot; one *s* one *d* (and one *s* decd). *Educ:* Rossall Sch., Lancashire. Served War of 1939–45 in Royal Armoured Corps, 1941–46. Admitted a solicitor, 1949; a Recorder of the Crown Court, 1972–79. Liveryman, Wax Chandlers' Co. *Recreation:* gardening. *Clubs:* Athenæum; Border and County (Carlisle).

WÖSSNER, Dr Mark Matthias; President and Chief Executive Officer, Bertelsmann AG, since 1983. *Educ:* Stuttgart Technical University (DrIng). Management Asst, Bertelsmann AG, Gütersloh, 1968; Mohndruck (Bertelsmann largest printing operation): Production Manager, 1970; Technical Dir, 1972; Gen. Manager, 1974; Mem. Exec. Bd, Bertelsmann, 1976; Dep. Chm. of Bd, 1981, Chm., 1983. *Address:* Bertelsmann AG, Postfach 5555, 4830 Gütersloh, Germany. *T:* 05241/80–0.

WOUK, Herman; author, US; *b* New York, 27 May 1915; *s* of Abraham Isaac Wouk and Esther Wouk (*née* Levine); *m* 1945, Betty Sarah Brown; two *s* (and one *s* decd). *Educ:* Townsend Harris High Sch.; Columbia Univ. (AB). Radio script writer, 1935–41; Vis. Professor of English, Yeshiva Univ., 1952–57; Presidential consultative expert to the United States Treasury, 1941. Served United States Naval Reserve, 1942–46, Deck Officer (four campaign stars). Member Officers' Reserve Naval Services. Trustee, College of the Virgin Islands, 1961–69. Hon. LHD Yeshiva Univ., New York City, 1954; Hon. DLit: Clark Univ., 1960; American Internat. Coll., 1979; Hon. PhD Bar-Ilan, 1990. Columbia University Medal for excellence, 1952; Alexander Hamilton Medal, Columbia Univ., 1980; Berkeley Medal, Univ. of Calif, 1984; Golden Plate Award, Amer. Acad. of Achievement, 1986; Lone Sailor Award, US Navy Meml Foundn, 1987; Kazetnik Award, Yad Vashem, 1990. *Publications: novels:* Aurora Dawn, 1947; The City Boy, 1948; The Caine Mutiny (Pulitzer Prize), 1951; Marjorie Morningstar, 1955; Youngblood Hawke, 1962; Don't Stop The Carnival, 1965; The Winds of War, 1971 (televised 1983); War and Remembrance, 1978 (televised 1989); Inside, Outside (Washington Book Award), 1985; *plays:* The Traitor, 1949; The Caine Mutiny Court-Martial, 1953; Nature's Way, 1957; *non-fiction:* This Is My God, 1959. *Address:* c/o BSW Literary Agency, 3255 N Street, NW, Washington, DC 20007, USA. *Clubs:* Cosmos, Metropolitan (Washington); Bohemian (San Francisco); Century (New York).

WRAGG, Prof. Edward Conrad; Director, Exeter University School of Education, since 1978; *b* 26 June 1938; *s* of George William and Maria Wragg; *m* 1960, Judith (*née* King); one *s* two *d*. *Educ:* King Edward VII Grammar Sch., Sheffield; Durham Univ. (BA Hons German Cl. 1; Postgrad. CertEd, Cl. 1); Leicester Univ. (MEd); Exeter Univ. (PhD). Asst Master, Queen Elizabeth Grammar Sch., Wakefield, 1960–64; Head of German, Wyggeston Boys' Sch., Leicester, 1964–66; Lectr in Education, Exeter Univ., 1966–73; Prof. of Educn, Nottingham Univ., 1973–78; Prof. of Educn and Dir of Sch. of Educn, Exeter Univ., 1978–. Pres., British Educnl Research Assoc., 1981–82; Specialist Adviser, Parliamentary Select Cttee, 1976–77; Chairman: School Broadcasting Council for UK, 1981–86; Educnl Broadcasting Council for UK, 1986–87; BBC Regl Adv. Council for South and West, 1989–; Member: Educnl Res. Bd, SSRC, 1974–78; Educn Sub-Cttee, UGC, 1981–89. Specialist Advr in Educn, UFC, 1989–. Presenter of radio and TV series and items on education, including Chalkface (Granada), Crisis in Education (BBC), The Education Roadshow (BBC), The Education Programme (BBC), Pebble Mill at One (BBC). Editor, Research Papers in Education, 1986–. FCP 1988. DUniv Open, 1989. *Publications:* Teaching Teaching, 1974; Teaching Mixed Ability Groups, 1976; Classroom Interaction, 1976; A Handbook for School Governors, 1980; Class Management and Control, 1981; A Review of Teacher Education, 1982; Swineshead Revisited, 1982; Classroom Teaching Skills, 1984; Pearls from Swineshire, 1984; The Domesday Project, 1985; Education: an action guide for parents, 1986; Teacher Appraisal, 1987; Education in the Market Place, 1988; The Wragged Edge, 1988; Parents and Schools, 1989; Riches from Wragg, 1990; frequent contributor to Guardian, Times Educnl Supp. (regular columnist), Times Higher Educn Supp., Observer, Independent, Good Housekeeping. *Recreations:* football playing, watching and coaching; cooking, running, writing, music. *Address:* 14 Doriam Close, Exeter EX4 4RS. *T:* Exeter (0392) 77052.

WRAGG, John, RA 1991 (ARA 1983); sculptor; *b* 20 Oct. 1937; *s* of Arthur and Ethel Wragg. *Educ:* York Sch. of Art; Royal Coll. of Art. *Work in Public Collections:* Israel Mus., Jerusalem; Tate Gall.; Arts Council of GB; Arts Council of NI; Contemp. Art Soc.; Wellington Art Gall., NZ; work in private collections in GB, America, Canada, France and Holland. *One-man Exhibitions:* Hanover Gall., 1963, 1966 and 1970; Galerie Alexandre Iolas, Paris, 1968; York Fest., 1969; Bridge Street Gall., Bath, 1982; Quinton Green Fine Art, London, 1985; *Exhibitions:* Lords Gall., 1959; L'Art Vivant, 1965–68; Arts Council Gall., Belfast, 1966; Pittsburgh Internat., 1967; Britische Kunst heute, Hamburg, Fondn Maeght, and Contemp. Art Fair, Florence, 1968; Bath Fest. Gall., 1977; Artists Market, 1978; Biennale di Scultura di Arese, Milan, and King Street Gall., Bristol, 1980; Galerie Bollhagen Worpswede, N Germany, 1981 and 1983. Sainsbury Award, 1960; Winner of Sainsbury Sculpture Comp., King's Road, Chelsea, 1966; Arts Council Major Award, 1977. *Relevant Publications:* chapters and articles about his work in: Neue Dimensionen der Plastic, 1964; Contemporary British Artists, 1979; British Sculpture in the Twentieth Century, 1981; Studio Internat., Art & Artiste, Sculpture Internat., Arts Rev., and The Artist. *Recreation:* walking. *Address:* 4 Lansdowne Terrace, Morris Lane, Devizes, Wilts SN10 1NX. *T:* Devizes (0380) 5819.

WRAIGHT, Sir John (Richard), KBE 1976; CMG 1962; HM Diplomatic Service, retired; company consultant and company director, since 1976; *b* 4 June 1916; *s* of late Richard George Wraight; *m* 1947, Marquita Elliott. *Educ:* Selhurst Grammar Sch.; London Univ. extension courses. Served War of 1939–45 with Honourable Artillery Company and RHA, Western Desert and Libya; Ministry of Economic Warfare Mission in the Middle East, Cairo, 1944. Economic Warfare Adviser, HQ Mediterranean Allied Air Forces, Italy, June-Dec. 1944. Worked in City of London, 1933–39; Foreign Office, 1945; Special Assistant to Chief of UNRRA Operations in Europe, 1946. Entered Foreign (subseq. Diplomatic) Service, 1947; British Embassy: Athens, 1948; Tel Aviv, 1950; Washington, 1953; Asst Head of Economic Relations Dept, Foreign Office, 1957; Counsellor (Commercial): Cairo, 1959; Brussels and Luxembourg, 1962 (UK Comr on Tripartite Commn for Restitution of Monetary Gold, Brussels, 1962–68); Minister and Consul-General, Milan, 1968–73; Ambassador to Switzerland, 1973–76. Internat. consultant to Phillips & Drew, 1976–88. Pres., Greater London SW Scout County, 1977–. Commander of the Order of the Crown (Belgium), 1966. *Publications:* The Food Situation in Austria, 1946; The Swiss and the British, 1987; The Swiss in London, 1991. *Recreations:* music, gardening, birdwatching. *Address:* c/o Lloyds Bank plc, 16 St James's Street, SW1.

WRAN, Hon. Neville Kenneth, AC 1988; QC (NSW) 1968; Chairman, Commonwealth Scientific Industrial Research Organisation, since 1986; Premier of New South Wales, 1976–86. *Educ:* Fort Street Boys' High Sch., Sydney; Sydney Univ. (LLB). Solicitor before admission to Bar of NSW, 1957. Joined Australian Labor Party, 1954, Nat. Pres., 1980–86. Elected to Legislative Council, 1970; Dep. Leader of Opposition, 1971; Leader of Opposition, Legislative Council, 1972; MLA for Bass Hill, Nov. 1973–1986; Leader of Opposition, Dec. 1973–76. Is especially interested in law reform, civil liberties, industrial relations, conservation and cultural matters. Mem., NSW Bar Assoc. Chm., Turnbull and partners (formerly Whitlam Turnbull & Co.), investment bankers, 1987–. Chm., Lionel Murphy Foundn. Mem., Centennial Park Trust. FRSA 1990. *Recreations:* reading, walking, swimming, tennis. *Address:* GPO Box 4545, Sydney, NSW 2001, Australia. *Clubs:* Sydney Labor (Hon. Life Mem.); University and Schools.

WRATTEN, Donald Peter; Director, National Counties Building Society, since 1985; *b* 8 July 1925; *er s* of late Frederick George and Marjorie Wratten; *m* 1947, Margaret Kathleen (*née* Marsh); one *s* one *d*. *Educ:* Morehall Elem. Sch. and Harvey Grammar Sch., Folkestone; London Sch. of Economics. Storehand, temp. clerk, meteorological asst (Air Min.), 1940–43; service with RAF Meteorological Wing, 1943–47. LSE, 1947–50. Joined Post Office, 1950; Private Sec. to Asst Postmaster Gen., 1955–56; seconded to Unilever Ltd, 1959; Private Sec. to Postmaster Gen., 1965–66; Head of Telecommunications Marketing Div., 1966–67; Director: Eastern Telecommunications Region, 1967–69; Exec. Dir, Giro and Remittance Services, 1969–74 (Sen. Dir, 1970–74); Sen. Dir, Data Processing Service, 1974–75; Sen. Dir, Telecom Personnel, 1975–81. Member: Industrial Adv. Panel, City Univ. Business Sch., 1974–81 (Chm., 1977–81); Court, Cranfield Inst. of Technology, 1976–81; Business Educn Council, 1977–83; Council: Intermediate Technology Develt Gp, 1982–85; Internat. Stereoscopic Union, 1987–; Vice-Chm., Stereoscopic Soc., 1990–. Chm., Radlett Soc. & Green Belt Assoc., 1989–. *Publication:* The Book of Radlett and Aldenham, 1990. *Recreations:* travel, topography, photography, consumer affairs, do-it-yourself. *Address:* 10 Homefield Road, Radlett, Herts WD7 8PY. *T:* Radlett (0923) 854500.

WRATTEN, Air Marshal Sir William (John), KBE 1991 (CBE 1982); CB 1991; AFC 1973; FRAeS; Director General, Saudi Armed Forces Project, since 1992; *b* 15 Aug. 1939; *s* of William Wellesley Wratten and Gwenneth Joan (*née* Bourne); *m* 1963, Susan Jane Underwood; two *s* two *d*. *Educ:* Chatham House Grammar Sch., Ramsgate; RAF Coll., Cranwell. OC, RAF Coningsby, 1980–82; Sen. RAF Officer, Falkland Is, 1982; RCDS, 1983; Dir, Operational Requirements (RAF), MoD, 1984–86; SASO, HQ 1 Gp, 1986–89; AOC No 11 Gp, 1989–91; Air Comdr British Forces ME, and Dep. to Comdr (on attachment), Nov. 1990–March 1991. *Recreation:* golf. *Club:* Royal Air Force.

WRAXALL, 2nd Baron, *cr* 1928, of Clyst St George, Co. Devon; **George Richard Lawley Gibbs;** DL; *b* 16 May 1928 (for whom Queen Mary was sponsor); *er s* of 1st Baron and Hon. Ursula Mary Lawley, OBE 1945, RRC (*d* 1979), *e d* of 6th Baron Wenlock; *S* father 1931. *Educ:* Eton; RMA Sandhurst. Coldstream Guards, 1946–53; 2nd Lieut, 1948; Actg Captain, 1953; Captain, RARO, 1954; Lieut North Somerset Yeomanry/44 Royal Tank Regt (TA), Dec. 1958; Captain, 1962; Major, 1965; retired 1967. Chairman: N Somerset Conservative Assoc., 1970–74; Avon County Scout Council, 1976–; N Somerset Yeo. Regtl Assoc., 1989– (Trustee, 1970–); Pres., Assoc. of Professional Foresters, 1991; Vice-Pres. and Trustee, Woodspring Cons. Assoc., 1984–; Council Mem., Royal Bath and West Show, 1955–89. Mem., Exec. Cttee, Woodard Corporation, 1983–; Chm. Governors, St Katherine's Sch., Avon, 1976–81; Fellow, Woodard Schs (Western Div.), 1979–. Patron, N Somerset Agricl Soc., 1988–. DL Avon, 1974. *Heir: b* Hon. Sir Eustace Hubert Beilby Gibbs, *qv*. *Address:* Tyntesfield, Wraxall, Bristol, Avon BS19 1NU. *T:* Flax Bourton (0275) 462923. *Clubs:* Royal Automobile, Cavalry and Guards; Clifton (Bristol).

WRAXALL, Sir Charles (Frederick Lascelles), 9th Bt *cr* 1813; Assistant Accountant, 1987–89; *b* 17 Sept. 1961; *s* of Sir Morville William Lascelles Wraxall, 8th Bt, and of Lady (Irmgard Wilhelmina) Wraxall; *S* father, 1978; *m* 1983, Lesley Linda, *d* of William Albert and Molly Jean Allan; one *s*. *Educ:* Archbishop Tenison's Grammar School, Croydon. *Recreations:* stamp and postcard collection, watching football. *Heir: s* William Nathaniel Lascelles Wraxall, *b* 3 April 1987.

WRAY, Prof. Gordon Richard, FRS 1986; FEng 1980; Eur Ing; Fellowship of Engineering Professor in Principles of Engineering Design, Engineering Design Institute, Loughborough University of Technology, since 1988; *b* 30 Jan. 1928; *s* of Joseph and Letitia Wray (*née* Jones); *m* 1954, Kathleen Senior; one *s* one *d*. *Educ:* Bolton Tech. Coll., Univ. of Manchester (BScTech, MScTech, PhD); DSc Loughborough; FIMechE, FTI; FRSA. Engineering apprentice, Bennis Combustion, Bolton, 1943; Design draughtsman, Dobson & Barlow, Bolton, 1946; Sir Walter Preston Scholar, Univ. of Manchester, 1949; Develt Engineer, Platts (Barton), 1952; Lectr in Mech. Engrg, Bolton Tech. Coll., 1953; Lectr in Textile Engrg, UMIST, 1955; Loughborough University of Technology: Reader, 1966–70, Prof. and Hd of Dept, 1970–88, Dept of Mech. Engrg; Dir, Engrg Design Inst., 1988–91. Springer Vis. Prof., Univ. of California, Berkeley, 1977. Lectures: Brunel, BAAS, 1980; Thomas Hawksley Meml, IMechE, 1989. Member: DoI Chief Scientist's Requirements Bd, 1974–75; CEI/CSTI Interdisciplinary Bd, 1978–83; SEFI Cttee on Innovation, Brussels, 1980–82; Royal Soc. Working Gp on Agricl Engrg, 1981–82; SERC Applied Mechanics Cttee, 1982–85; Fellowship of Engrg Working Party on DoI Requirements Bds, 1982; SERC Working Party on Engrg Design, 1983; Royal Soc. Sectional Cttee 4 (i), 1986–89; Cttee, Engrg Profs Conf., 1986–88; Royal Soc. Mullard Award Cttee, 1986–; Royal Soc./SERC Industrial Fellowships Panel, 1986–89; Chm., Engrg Council/Design Council Wkg Party on Attaining Competences in Engrg Design, 1989–91. First recipient of title European Engineer (Eur Ing), Paris, 1987. Mem. Council, IMechE, 1964–67 (Chm., Manip. and Mech. Handling Machinery Gp, 1969–71). Chm., Judging Panel, William Lee Quatercentenary Technology Prize, 1989. Hon. MIED 1990. IMechE Prizes: Viscount Weir, 1959; Water Arbitration, 1972; James Clayton, 1975; Warner Medal, Textile Inst., 1976; S. G. Brown Award and Medal, Royal Soc., 1978; Engrg Merit Award, ASME, 1977. *Publications:* (contrib.) Textile Engineering Processes, ed Nissan, 1959; Modern Yarn Production from Man-made Fibres, 1960; Modern Developments in Weaving Machinery, 1961; An Introduction to the Study of Spinning, 3rd edn 1962; (contrib.) Contemporary Textile Engineering, ed Happey, 1982; Design or Decline; a national emergency?, 1990; numerous papers to learned jls. *Recreations:* fell-walking, photography, theatre, music, gardening, DIY. *Address:* Stonestack, Rempstone, Loughborough, Leics LE12 6RH. *T:* Wymeswold (0509) 880043.

WRAY, James; MP (Lab) Glasgow, Provan, since 1987; *b* 28 April 1938; *m*; one *s* two *d*. Heavy goods vehicle driver. Mem., Strathclyde Regl Council, 1976–. President: Scottish Fedn of the Blind, 1987 (Vice Pres., 1986); St Enoch's Drug Centre; Scottish Ex-Boxers'

Assoc.; Gorbals United FC. Mem., TGWU. *Address:* Robin Hill Cott, Hazelden Road, Newton Mearns, Glasgow G77 6RR; House of Commons, SW1A 0AA.

WRENBURY, 3rd Baron, *cr* 1915; **Rev. John Burton Buckley;** Partner, Thomson Snell and Passmore, 1974–90; *b* 18 June 1927; *s* of 2nd Baron and Helen Malise (*d* 1981), 2nd *d* of late His Honour John Cameron Graham of Ballewan, Stirlingshire; *S* father, 1940; *m* 1st, 1956, Carolyn Joan Maule (marr. diss., 1961), *o d* of Lt-Col Ian Burn-Murdoch, OBE, of Gartincaber, Doune, Perthshire; 2nd, 1961, Penelope Sara Frances, *o d* of Edward D. Fort, The White House, Sixpenny Handley, Dorset; one *s* two *d*. *Educ:* Eton Coll.; King's Coll., Cambridge. Deputy Legal Adviser to the National Trust, 1955–56; Partner, Freshfield's, Solicitors, 1956–74. Ordained Deacon in Church of England, 1990. *Recreations:* golf, campanology, bagpipes. *Heir: s* Hon. William Edward Buckley, *b* 19 June 1966. *Address:* Oldcastle, Dallington, near Heathfield, East Sussex. *T:* Rushlake Green (0435) 830400. *Club:* Oriental.

WREXHAM, Bishop of, (RC), since 1987: **Rt. Rev. James Hannigan;** *b* Co. Donegal, 15 July 1928. Ordained pritest, 1954. Bishop of Menevia 1983–87. Chm., Catholic Educn Council, 1984– . *Address:* Bishop's House, Sontley Road, Wrexham, Clwyd LL13 7EW. *T:* Wrexham (0978) 262726.

WREY, Sir (Castel Richard) Bourchier, 14th Bt, *cr* 1628; *b* 27 March 1903; *s* of late Edward Castel Wrey and Katharine Joan, *d* of Rev. John Dene; *S* uncle, 1948; *m* 1946, Alice Sybil, *d* of Dr Lubke, Durban, S Africa; two *s*. *Educ:* Oundle. Served War of 1939–45; 2nd Lieut, RASC (Supp. Res.), France, 1939–40 (invalided); joined RN as ordinary seaman, 1940; Lieut, RNVR, 1942. *Heir: s* George Richard Bourchier Wrey [*b* 2 Oct. 1948; *m* 1981, Lady Caroline Lindesay-Bethune, *d* of 15th Earl of Lindsay; two *s* one *d*]. *Address:* Hollamoor Farm, Tawstock, Barnstaple, N Devon; 511 Currie Road, Durban, South Africa.

WRIGGLESWORTH, Sir Ian (William), Kt 1991; Deputy Chairman, John Livingston & Sons Ltd, since 1987; Director: Fairfield Industries Ltd, since 1987; CIT Research Ltd, since 1987; Divisional Director, Smiths Industries PLC; *b* Dec. 1939; *s* of Edward and Elsie Wrigglesworth; *m* Patricia Truscott; two *s* one *d*. *Educ:* Stockton Grammar Sch.; Stockton-Billingham Technical Coll; Coll. of St Mark and St John, Chelsea. Formerly: Personal Assistant to Gen. Sec., NUT; Head of Research and Information Dept of Co-operative Party; Press and Public Affairs Manager of National Giro. Contested (SDP/Alliance) Stockton South, 1987. MP (Lab and Co-op, 1974–81, SDP, 1981–87) Teesside, Thornaby, Feb. 1974–1983, Stockton South, 1983–87. PPS to Mr Alec Lyon, Minister of State, Home Office, 1974; PPS to Rt Hon. Roy Jenkins, Home Secretary, 1974–76; Opposition spokesman on Civil Service, 1979–80; SDP spokesman on industry, 1981, on home affairs, 1982, on industry and economic affairs, 1983–87. Pres., Liberal Democrats, 1988–90. *Address:* Fairfield Industries Ltd, 24 Buckingham Gate, SW1E 6LB. *T:* 071–828 8323. *Clubs:* Reform, Institute of Directors.

WRIGHT, Alan John; a Master of the Supreme Court, Supreme Court Taxing Office, 1972–91; *b* 21 April 1925; *s* of late Rev. Henry George Wright, MA and Winifred Annie Wright; *m* 1952, Alma Beatrice Ridding; two *s* one *d*. *Educ:* St Olave's and St Saviour's Grammar Sch., Southwark; Keble Coll., Oxford. BA 1949, MA 1964. Served with RAF, India, Burma and China, 1943–46. Solicitor 1952; in private practice with Shaen Roscoe & Co., 1952–71; Legal Adviser to Trades Union Congress, 1955–71. Lay Reader, Southwark dio., 1989–. *Recreations:* Germanic studies, walking, travel, youth work, foreign languages. *Address:* 21 Brockley Park, Forest Hill, SE23 1PT.

WRIGHT, Alec Michael John, CMG 1967; *b* Hong Kong, 19 Sept. 1912; *s* of Arthur Edgar Wright and Margery Hepworth Chapman; *m* 1948, Ethel Surtees; one *d*. *Educ:* Brentwood Sch. ARICS 1934; ARIBA 1937. Articled pupil followed by private practice in London. Joined Colonial Service, 1938; appointed Architect in Hong Kong, 1938. Commissioned Hong Kong Volunteer Defence Force, 1941; POW in Hong Kong, 1941–45. Chief Architect, Public Works Dept, Hong Kong, 1950; Asst Director of Public Works, 1956; Dep. Director, 1959; Director, 1963–69; Commissioner for Hong Kong in London, 1969–73. *Address:* 13 Montrose Court, Exhibition Road, SW7 2QG. *T:* 071–584 4293. *Club:* Hong Kong (Hong Kong).

See also Sir Denis Wright.

WRIGHT, Hon. Alison Elizabeth, JP; Director General, British Invisibles, since 1991; Member, Commonwealth Development Corporation, since 1984; *b* 5 Jan. 1945; *d* of Baron Franks, *qv*; *m* 1973, Stanley Harris Wright, *qv*. *Educ:* Headington School, Oxford; Downe House, Newbury; St Anne's College Oxford (BA PPE). Research Officer, Overseas Development Institute, 1965–69; research in Spain, 1970–72; business advr on Spain and Portugal, 1972–80; Managing Consultant, Ernst & Whinney, then Ernst & Young, 1988–90. Member: Heilbron Cttee on Law of Rape, 1975; Top Salaries Review Body, Nov. 1984, resigned April 1985; Council, Overseas Develt Inst., 1988–. JP Inner London 1978; Mem., Inner London Exec. Cttee, Magistrates' Assoc., 1980–82. *Publications:* The Less Developed Countries in World Trade (with M. Zammit Cutajar), 1969; The Spanish Economy 1959–1976, 1977; contribs to Economist Intelligence Unit and other publications. *Recreations:* reading, theatre. *Address:* British Invisibles, Windsor House, 39 King Street, EC2V 8DQ. *T:* 071–600 1198.

WRIGHT, Sir Allan Frederick, KBE 1982; farmer; Chairman: Mair & Co.; R. G. Robinson Produce Ltd; Applefields Ltd; Director: Farmers' Mutual Insurance Group; NZ Railways Corporation; NZ Skin Pool Co-operative; Southpower; Earnscleugh Orchards; Trigon Industries Ltd; *b* Darfield, 25 March 1929; *s* of Quentin A. Wright; *m* 1953, Dorothy June Netting; three *s* two *d*. *Educ:* Christ's Coll., Christchurch. Nat. Pres., Young Farmers' Clubs, 1957–58; President: N Canterbury Federated Farmers, 1971–74; Federated Farmers of NZ, 1977–81 (formerly Sen. Nat. Vice-Pres.). Mem., NZ Cricket Bd of Control, 1967–; Manager, NZ Cricket Team to England, 1983. Chancellor, Lincoln Univ. (Chm. Council, Lincoln Coll., 1985–, Mem., 1974–). *Recreations:* cricket (played for N Canterbury), rugby, golf. *Address:* Annat, RD Sheffield, Canterbury, New Zealand.

WRIGHT, Dr Anne Margaret; Rector and Chief Executive, Sunderland Polytechnic, since 1990; *b* 26 July 1946; *d* of Herbert and Florence Holden; *m* 1970, Martin Wright; one *d*. *Educ:* Holy Trinity Indep. Grammar Sch., Bromley; King's Coll., London (BA Hons English I, 1967; Inglis Teaching Studentship, 1967–68; PhD 1970). Lectr in English, Lancaster Univ., 1969–71; Lectr, then Sen. Lectr, Principal Lectr and Reader in Modern English Studies, Hatfield Poly., 1971–84; British Acad. Res. Award, Univ. of Texas at Austin, 1979; Registrar for Arts and Humanities, CNAA, 1984–86; Dep. Rector (Academic), Liverpool Poly, 1986–90. Member: English Studies Bd, 1978–84, Arts and Humanities Res. Sub-Cttee, 1979–84, CNAA; Council, Northern Examining Assoc., 1989–; Cttee I of Cttee for Internat. Co-op. in Higher Educn, British Council, 1990–. Chm., Wearside Common Purpose, 1990–; Director: Everyman Theatre, Liverpool, 1988–90; The Wearside Opportunity, 1991–; Northern Sinfonia, 1991–. *Publications:* (ed jtly) Heartbreak House: a facsimile of the revised typescript, 1981; Literature of Crisis 1910–1922, 1984; Bernard Shaw's Saint Joan, 1984; articles in jls and entries in dictionaries of lit. biog. *Recreations:* singing, theatre, opera, the arts. *Address:* Langham Tower, Ryhope Road, Sunderland SR2 7EE. *T:* 091–515 2000.

WRIGHT, Arthur Francis Stevenson, MBE 1945; FRIBA, FRIAS; architect principal in private practice, since 1949, consultant, since 1983; *b* 15 Feb. 1918; *s* of Arthur and Alice Wright; *m* 1946, Catherine Grey Linton; one *d*. *Educ:* Morgan Academy; College of Art, Dundee (DipArch 1948). Served War, Royal Engineers (Major), 1940–46. FRIBA 1956; FRIAS 1954 (Pres., 1975–77); FCIOB (FIOB 1974); FCIArb (FIArb 1976). Chm., Jt Standing Cttee of Architects, Surveyors and Builders in Scotland, 1973–75. *Recreations:* fishing, golf. *Address:* Thorvale, Castlegate, Ceres, Fife KY15 5NG.

WRIGHT, (Arthur Robert) Donald, OBE 1984; *b* 20 June 1923; *s* of late Charles North Wright and Beatrice May Wright; *m* 1948, Helen Muryell Buxton; two *s* three *d*. *Educ:* Bryanston Sch.; Queens' Coll., Cambridge. War Service (commnd 1943), NW Europe (despatches) and India, 1942–46. Taught at: University Coll. Sch., 1948–50; The Hill School, Pennsylvania, 1950; Leighton Park School, 1950–52; Marlborough College (Housemaster), 1953–63; Headmaster, Shrewsbury Sch., 1963–75. Chm., HMC, 1971. Appointments' Sec. to Archbishops of Canterbury and York, 1975–84 and Sec., Crown Appointments Commn, 1977–84. A Chm., Civil Service Comrs' Interview Panel, 1984–. Chm., Council, Benenden Sch., 1976–86; Governor, King's Coll. Sch., Wimbledon, 1981–. *Publications:* (ed) Neville Cardus on Music: a centenary collection, 1988; (ed and contrib.) Walter Hamilton: a portrait, 1991. *Recreations:* music, writing. *Address:* Mill Barn, Coulston, near Westbury, Wilts BA13 4NY.

WRIGHT, Beatrice Frederika, (Lady Wright); Vice-President, Royal National Institute for the Deaf, since 1978; Co-Founder, Hearing Dogs for the Deaf, 1982 (President, 1983–88); *b* New Haven, Connecticut; *d* of Mr and Mrs F. Roland Clough; *m* 1st, 1932, John Rankin Rathbone (Flight Lieut, RAFVR, MP, killed in action, 1940); one *s* one *d*; 2nd, 1942, Paul Hervé Giraud Wright (*see* Sir Paul Wright); one *d*. *Educ:* Ethel Walker School, Simsbury, Conn; Radcliffe College, Oxford. MP (U) Bodmin Div. of Cornwall, 1941–45. *Address:* 62 Westminster Gardens, Marsham Street, SW1P 4JG.

See also J. R. Rathbone.

WRIGHT, Rt. Rev. Benjamen; Assistant Bishop, diocese of Perth (Goldfields Region), since 1988; *b* 15 March 1952; *s* of Clarice and Herbert Wright; *m* 1966, Annette Jennifer Dunne; two *s* one *d*. *Educ:* Slade Sch., Warwick, Qld; Murdoch Univ., Perth (ThL, BA). Anglican Ministry, 1964–. *Recreations:* fishing, gardening. *Address:* Bishopsbourne, 41 Ward Street, Kalgoorlie, WA 6430, Australia.

WRIGHT, Billy; *see* Wright, W. A.

WRIGHT, Claud William, CB 1969; Deputy Secretary, Department of Education and Science, 1971–76; *b* 9 Jan. 1917; *s* of Horace Vipan Wright and Catherine Margaret Sales; *m* 1947, Alison Violet Readman; one *s* four *d*. *Educ:* Charterhouse; Christ Church, Oxford (MA). Assistant Principal, War Office, 1939; Private, Essex Regiment, 1940; 2nd Lieut, KRRC, 1940; War Office, rising to GSO2, 1942–45; Principal, War Office, 1944; Min. of Defence: Principal, 1947; Asst Sec., 1951; Asst Under-Sec. of State, 1961–68; Dep. Under-Sec. of State, 1968–71. Chm., Cttee on Provincial Museums and Galleries, 1971–73. Research Fellow, Wolfson Coll., Oxford, 1977–83. Lyell Fund, 1947, R. H. Worth Prize, 1958, Prestwich Medal, 1987, Geological Society of London; Foulerton Award, Geologists Association, 1955; Stamford Raffles Award, Zoological Society of London, 1965; Phillips Medal, Yorks Geol. Soc., 1976; Strimple Award, Paleontol Soc., USA, 1988. President, Geologists Assoc., 1956–58. Hon. Associate, British Museum (Nat. Hist.), 1973; fil.Dr *hc* Uppsala, 1979; Hon. DSc Hull, 1987. *Publications:* (with W. J. Arkell *et al*) vol. on Ammonites, 1957, (with W. K. Spencer) on Starfish, 1966, in Treatise on Invertebrate Palaeontology; (with J. S. H. Collins) British Cretaceous Crabs, 1972; (with W. J. Kennedy) Ammonites of the Middle Chalk, 1981; (with W. J. Kennedy) Ammonites of the Lower Chalk, pt I, 1984, pt II, 1987, pt III, 1990; (with A. B. Smith) British Cretaceous Echinoidea, pt I, 1988, pt II, 1990; papers in geological, palaeontological and archaeological journals. *Recreations:* palaeontology, natural history, gardening, archæology. *Address:* Old Rectory, Seaborough, Beaminster, Dorset DT8 3QY. *T:* Broadwindsor (0308) 68426. *Club:* Athenæum.

WRIGHT, David John, LVO 1990; HM Diplomatic Service; Ambassador to the Republic of Korea, since 1990; *b* 16 June 1944; *s* of J. F. Wright; *m* 1968, Sally Ann Dodkin; one *s* one *d*. *Educ:* Wolverhampton Grammar Sch.; Peterhouse, Cambridge (MA). Third Secretary, FO, 1966; Third Sec., later Second Sec., Tokyo, 1966–72; FCO, 1972–75; Ecole Nationale d'Administration, Paris, 1975–76; First Sec., Paris, 1976–80; Private Sec. to Secretary of the Cabinet, 1980–82; Counsellor (Economic), Tokyo, 1982–85; Head of Personnel Services Dept, FCO, 1985–88; Dep. Private Sec. to HRH the Prince of Wales, 1988–90 (on secondment). *Recreations:* running, cooking, military history. *Address:* c/o Foreign and Commonwealth Office, SW1. *Club:* United Oxford & Cambridge University.

WRIGHT, Sir Denis (Arthur Hepworth), GCMG 1971 (KCMG 1961; CMG 1954); HM Diplomatic Service, retired; *b* 23 March 1911; *s* of late A. E. Wright, Hong Kong, and Margery Hepworth Chapman, York; *m* 1939, Iona Craig, Bolney, Sussex; no *c*. *Educ:* Brentwood School; St Edmund Hall, Oxford, Hon. Fellow 1972. Asst Advertising Manager to Gallaher & Co. (Tobacco Manufacturers), 1935–39. Employed from outbreak of war as Vice-Consul on economic warfare work at HM Consulate at Constantza (Roumania), 1939–41. Vice-Consul-in-charge of HM Consulate at Trebizond (Turkey), 1941–43; Acting-Consul-in-charge of HM Consulate, Mersin (Turkey), 1943–45; First Secretary (Commercial) to HM Embassy, Belgrade, 1946–48; Superintending Trade Consul at Chicago for Middle-Western Region of USA, 1949–51; Head of Economic Relations Department in the Foreign Office, 1951–53; appointed Chargé d'Affaires, Tehran, on resumption of diplomatic relations with Persia, Dec. 1953; Counsellor, HM Embassy, Tehran, 1954–55; Asst Under-Sec., FO, 1955–59; Ambassador to Ethiopia, 1959–62; Asst Under-Sec., FO, 1962; Ambassador to Iran, 1963–71. Dir, Shell Transport & Trading Co., Standard Chartered Bank, and Mitchell Cotts Gp, 1971–81. Governor, Oversea Service, Farnham Castle, 1972–86; Mem. Council, British Inst. of Persian Studies, 1973– (Pres., 1978–87); Pres., Iran Soc., 1989– (Chm., 1976–79). Hon. Fellow St Antony's Coll., Oxford, 1976. Sir Percy Sykes Meml Medal, RSAA, 1990. *Publications:* Persia (with James Morris and Roger Wood), 1969; The English Amongst the Persians, 1977; The Persians Amongst the English, 1985. *Address:* Duck Bottom, 15 Flint Street, Haddenham, Aylesbury, Bucks HP17 8AL. *Club:* Travellers'.

See also A. M. J. Wright.

WRIGHT, Desmond Garforth, QC 1974; *b* 13 July 1923; *s* of late Arthur Victor Wright and Doris Greensill; *m* 1952, Elizabeth Anna Bacon; one *s* one *d*. *Educ:* Giggleswick; Royal Naval Coll., Greenwich; Worcester Coll., Oxford (MA). Cholmondley Scholar of Lincoln's Inn. Served War of 1939–45: RNVR, 1942–46. Staff of Flag Officer Malaya Forward Area, 1946. Called to Bar, Lincoln's Inn, 1950, Bencher, 1981. *Publication:* Wright on Walls, 1954. *Recreations:* cartology, conversation, skiing on snow. *Address:* 1 Atkin Building, Gray's Inn, WC1R 5BQ. *T:* 071–404 0102.

WRIGHT, Donald; *see* Wright, A. R. D.

WRIGHT, Mrs Edmund Gordon; *see* Cross, H. M.

WRIGHT, Sir Edward (Maitland), Kt 1977; MA, DPhil, LLD, DSc; FRSE; Research Fellow, University of Aberdeen, since 1976; *b* 1906; *s* of M. T. Wright, Farnley, Leeds; *m* 1934, Elizabeth Phyllis (*d* 1987), *d* of H. P. Harris, Bryn Mally Hall, N Wales; one *s*. *Educ:* Jesus Coll. and Christ Church, Oxford; Univ. of Göttingen. Master, Chard School, Somerset, 1923–26; Scholar, Jesus College, Oxford, 1926–30; Senior Scholar, Christ Church, 1930–33; Lecturer, King's College, London, 1932–33; Lecturer, Christ Church, 1933–35; Flt Lieut, RAFVR, 1941–43; Principal Scientific Officer, Air Ministry, 1943–45; Prof. of Mathematics, 1935–62, Vice-Principal, 1961–62, Principal and Vice-Chancellor, 1962–76, Univ. of Aberdeen. Member: Anderson Cttee on Grants to Students, 1958–60; Hale Cttee on Univ. Teaching Methods, 1961–64; Scottish Universities Entrance Bd, 1948–62 (Chm. 1955–62); Royal Commission on Medical Education, 1965–67. Vice-Pres., RUSI, 1969–72. Associate Editor, Math. Abstracts, 1950–; Hon. Editor, Jl Graph Theory, 1983–. Hon. LLD: St Andrews, 1963; Pennsylvania, 1975; Aberdeen, 1978; Hon. DSc Strathclyde, 1974. Hon. Fellow, Jesus College, Oxford, 1963. Macdougall-Brisbane Prize, RSE, 1952; Sen. Berwick Prize, London Math. Soc., 1978. Gold Medal of the Order of Polonia Restituta of the Polish People's Republic, 1978. *Publications:* Introduction to the Theory of Numbers (with Professor G. H. Hardy), 1938, 5th edn 1979; mathematical papers in scientific journals. *Address:* 16 Primrosehill Avenue, Cults, Aberdeen. *T:* Aberdeen (0224) 861185. *Club:* Caledonian.

WRIGHT, Eric; Regional Director, Yorkshire and Humberside Region, Department of Trade and Industry, since 1985; *b* 17 Nov. 1933; *s* of Alec Wright and Elsie (*née* Worthington); *m* 1955, Pauline Sutton; three *s* (and one *s* decd). *Educ:* Wolstanton Grammar Sch.; Keble Coll., Oxford (BA 1st Cl. Hons Mod. Hist.). 2nd Lieut RASC, 1955–57. Ministry of Fuel and Power, 1957–65; Civil Service Commission, 1965–67; Min. of Technology, 1968–70; Sloan Fellow, London Business Sch., 1970–71; Principal Private Sec. to Secretary of State, DTI, 1971–72; Dept of Trade, 1972–77; Dept of Industry, 1977–83, Under Sec., 1979. *Recreations:* music, tennis, chess. *Address:* 25 Queen Street, Leeds LS1 2TW. *T:* Leeds (0532) 338200.

WRIGHT, Eric David, CB 1975; Deputy Under-Secretary of State, Home Office, and Director-General, Prison Service, 1973–77; *b* 12 June 1917; *s* of Charles Henry and Cecelia Wright; *m* 1944, Doris (*née* Nicholls); one *s*. *Educ:* Ealing County Grammar School. Joined War Office, 1935; Principal, 1945; seconded to Dept of the Army, Australia, 1951; Asst Secretary, 1955; Command Secretary, BAOR, 1955–58; Imperial Defence College, 1964; Asst Under-Sec. of State, MoD, 1965; on loan to Home Office, Police Dept, 1970–73. Mem., Parole Bd, 1978–83. Chm., Hillingdon CHC, 1988–90. *Address:* 32 Valley Road, Rickmansworth, Herts WD3 4DS.

WRIGHT, Prof. Esmond; Emeritus Professor of American History, University of London, since 1983; Vice-President, Automobile Association, since 1985 (Vice-Chairman and Hon. Treasurer, 1971–85; Chairman, Drive Publications, 1980–85); *b* 5 Nov. 1915; *m* 1945, Olive Adamson. *Educ:* University of Durham (Open Entrance Schol.); Univ. of Virginia (Commonwealth Fund Fellow). War Service, 1940–46, demobilised as Lt-Col, 1946. Glasgow Univ., 1946–67; Prof. of Modern History, 1957–67. MP (C) Glasgow, Pollok, March 1967–1970; Dir, Inst. of US Studies and Prof. of American History, Univ. of London, 1971–83; Principal, Swinton Cons. Coll., 1972–76. Chm., Border TV, 1981–85 (Vice-Chm., 1976–81). Founder-Mem., British Association for American Studies (Chm., 1965–68). Mem., Marshall Aid Commemoration Commn, 1966–83; Vice-Chm., British Road Fedn, 1981–85. FRHistS; FRSA (Franklin Medal, 1988). Hon. LHD Pennsylvania, 1983; Hon. DLitt New Brunswick, 1984. *Publications:* A Short History of our own Times, 1951; George Washington and the American Revolution, 1957; The World Today, 1961, 4th edn 1978; Fabric of Freedom, 1961, 2nd edn 1978; (ed) Illustrated World History, 1964; Benjamin Franklin and American Independence, 1966; (ed) Causes and Consequences of the American Revolution, 1966; (ed) American Themes, 1967; American Profiles, 1967; (ed) Benjamin Franklin, a profile, 1970; A Time for Courage, 1971; A Tug of Loyalties, 1974; Red, White and True Blue, 1976; (with A. G. Nicolson) Europe Today, 1979; The Great Little Madison (British Academy Lecture), 1981; The Fire of Liberty, 1983; (ed) History of the World: Pre-History to Renaissance, 1985, The Last Five Hundred Years, 1986; Franklin of Philadelphia, 1986; Franklin: his life as he wrote it, 1989; articles in periodicals. *Address:* Radleigh House, Masham, N Yorks HG4 4EF. *Club:* Athenæum.

WRIGHT, Georg Henrik von, GCVO (Hon.); MA; Research Professor in the Academy of Finland, 1961–86; *b* Helsingfors, 14 June 1916; *s* of Tor von Wright and Ragni Elisabeth Alfthan; *m* 1941, Maria Elisabeth von Troil, CVO (Hon.); one *s* one *d*. *Educ:* Svenska Normallyceum, Helsingfors; Helsingfors Univ. Helsingfors University: Lectr and Acting Prof. of Philosophy, 1943–46; Prof. of Philosophy, 1946–61 (also in Univ. of Cambridge, 1948–51); Prof. at Large, Cornell Univ., 1965–77; Chancellor of Abo Academy, 1968–77; Visiting Professor: Cornell Univ., 1954 and 1958; Univ. Calif., Los Angeles, 1963; Univ. Pittsburg, 1966; Univ. Karlsruhe, 1975; Lectures: Shearman Meml, University Coll., London, 1956; Gifford, Univ. of St Andrews, 1959–60; Tarner, Trinity Coll., Cambridge, 1969; Woodbridge, Columbia Univ., 1972; Nellie Wallace, Univ. of Oxford, 1978; Tanner, Helsingfors Univ., 1984. President: Internat. Union of History and Philosophy of Science, 1963–65; Acad. of Finland, 1968–69; Philosophical Soc. of Finland, 1962–73; Institut International de Philosophie, 1975–78. Fellow: Finnish Soc. of Sciences (Pres., 1966–67, Hon. Fellow 1978); New Soc. of Letters, Lund; Royal Swedish Academy of Sciences; Royal Soc. of Letters, Lund; British Academy; Royal Swedish Academy of Letters, History and Antiquities; Finnish Acad. of Sciences; Royal Danish Acad. of Sciences and Letters; Royal Acad. of Arts and Sciences, Uppsala; Norwegian Acad. of Science and Letters; Royal Acad. of Science, Trondheim; European Acad. of Arts, Sciences and Humanities; World Acad. of Arts and Scis; Serbian Acad. of Scis and Arts; Hon. Foreign Mem., Amer. Acad. of Arts and Sciences. Sometime Fellow, Trinity College, Cambridge, Hon. Fellow 1983. Hon. degrees: Helsingfors Univ. (doctor of pol. sci.); Univ. of Liverpool (DLitt); doctor of philosophy: Univ. of Lund; Univ. of Bologna; Abo Acad.; Turku Univ. (doctor of philosophy, doctor of law); Saint Olaf Coll., Northfield, Minn. (doctor of humane letters); Tampere Univ. (doctor of soc. sci.); Univ. of Buenos Aires; Univ. of Salta. Wilhuri Foundn Internat. Prize, 1976; Alexander von Humboldt Foundn Forschungspreis, 1986; Gold Medal, Swedish Acad., 1986. *Publications:* The Logical Problem of Induction, 1941, rev. edn 1957; Den logiska Empirismen, 1943; Über Wahrscheinlichkeit, 1945; A Treatise on Induction and Probability, 1951; An Essay in Modal Logic, 1951; Logical Studies, 1957; The Varieties of Goodness, 1963; The Logic of Preference, 1963; Norm and Action, 1963; An Essay in Deontic Logic, 1968; Time, Change, and Contradiction, 1969; Explanation and Understanding, 1971; Causality and Determinism, 1974; Freedom and Determination, 1980; Wittgenstein, 1982; Philosophical Papers I-III, 1983–84; Vetenskapen och förnuftet, 1986; Intellectual Autobiography, in The Philosophy of Georg Henrik von Wright, 1989. *Address:* 4 Skepparegatan, Helsingfors, Finland.

WRIGHT, George Henry, MBE 1977; Regional Secretary, Wales, Transport and General Workers Union, since 1972; Vice-Chairman, Wales Co-operative Development Centre, since 1985 (Chairman, 1983–85); *b* 11 July 1935; *s* of William Henry and Annie Louisa Wright; *m* 1956, Margaret Wright; two *d*. *Educ:* Tinkers Farm Sch., Birmingham. Car worker, 1954–65. T&GWU: District Officer, West Bromwich, 1966–68; District Secretary, Birmingham, 1968–72. Gen. Sec., Wales TUC, 1974–84 (Chm., 1989–90). Member: MSC Wales, 1976–88; Employment Appeal Tribunal, 1985–; Welsh Trng Adv. Gp, 1989–. *Recreations:* fishing, gardening. *Address:* 5 Kidwelly Court, Caerphilly, Mid Glamorgan, Wales. *T:* Caerphilly (0222) 885434.

WRIGHT, George Paul; Chief Superintendent, Royal Signals and Radar Establishment, Ministry of Defence, Baldock, 1976–80; *b* 27 April 1919; *s* of late George Maurice Wright, CBE, and of late Lois Dorothy Wright (*née* Norburn); *m* 1957, Jean Margaret Reid, *d* of Lt-Col Charles Alexander Reid Scott, DSO and Marjorie Reid Scott (*née* Mackintosh); one *s* one *d*. *Educ:* Bishops Stortford Coll.; Magdalen Coll., Oxford. BA 1948, MA 1951; FInstP. Admty Signal Estabt, 1939–45; Services Electronics Research Lab., 1945–57; Dept of Physical Research, Admty, 1957–63; Services Electronics Research Lab., 1963–76 (Dir, 1972–76). *Recreations:* music, sailing, gardening. *Address:* Tilekiln Farmhouse, Earls Colne, Colchester, Essex CO6 2JR. *T:* Earls Colne (0787) 222432. *Clubs:* United Oxford & Cambridge University, Civil Service; Blackwater Sailing (Maldon).

WRIGHT, Gerard, QC 1973; *b* 23 July 1929; *s* of Leo Henry and Catherine M. F. Wright; *m* 1950, Betty Mary Fenn; one *s* two *d*. *Educ:* Stonyhurst Coll.; Lincoln Coll., Oxford (BA, BCL). Served in Army, 1947–49, rank T/Captain. Called to Bar, Gray's Inn, 1954 (Arden Scholar, Barstow Scholar); Northern Circuit. KHS 1974; KCHS 1979; Auxiliaire de l'Hospitalité de Notre Dame de Lourdes, 1982, Titulaire 1985. *Publication:* Test Tube Babies—a Christian view (with others), 1984. *Recreations:* skiing, sailing. *Address:* 1 King's Court, Hoylake, Merseyside L47 1JE. *T:* 051–632 5566; 3rd Floor, Peel House, 5–7 Harrington Street, Liverpool L2 9XN.

WRIGHT, Graeme Alexander; Editor, Wisden Cricketers' Almanack, since 1986; *b* 23 April 1943; *s* of Alexander John Wright and Eileen Margaret (*née* Hanlon). *Educ:* St Patrick's Coll., Wellington, NZ; St Patrick's High Sch., Timaru, NZ; Univ. of Canterbury, Christchurch, NZ. Copywriter, NZ Broadcasting Corp., 1965–67; Sub-editor, BSI, 1968–69; Editor and writer, Publicare Ltd, 1969–72; Managing Editor, Queen Anne Press, 1973–74; freelance editor and writer, 1974–; Dir, John Wisden & Co. Ltd, 1983–86. *Publications:* (with Phil Read) Phil Read, 1977; The Illustrated Handbook of Sporting Terms, 1978; Olympic Greats, 1980; (with George Best) Where do I go from here?, 1981; (with Patrick Eagar): Test Decade 1972–1982, 1982; Botham, 1985; (with Joe Brown) Brown Sauce, 1986; Merrydown: forty vintage years, 1988. *Recreations:* reading, music, letter-writing, travelling. *Address:* c/o John Wisden & Co. Ltd, 25 Down Road, Merrow, Guildford, Surrey GU1 2PY. *Club:* MCC.

WRIGHT, Prof. H(enry) Myles; FRIBA; FRTPI; Lever Professor of Civic Design, University of Liverpool, 1954–75; now Emeritus Professor; University Planning Consultant, 1957–77; *b* 9 June 1908; *s* of H. T. Wright, Gosforth, Newcastle upon Tyne; *m* 1939, Catharine Noble (*d* 1981), *y d* of Very Rev. H. N. Craig, Dean of Kildare; two *d*. *Educ:* Fettes College, Edinburgh (Foundationer); King's College, Newcastle upon Tyne; St John's College, Cambridge. Assistant in various private offices, 1930–35; Asst Editor, The Architects' Journal, and in private practice, 1935–40; Partner in firm of Sir William Holford, 1948–54; principally engaged on planning proposals for Cambridge and Corby New Town. Member British Caribbean Federal Capital Commn, 1956. *Publications:* The Planner's Notebook, 1948; Cambridge Planning Proposals, 1950, and Corby New Town (with Lord Holford), 1952; Land Use in an Urban Environment (Editor and contributor), 1961; The Dublin Region: Preliminary and Final Reports, 1965 and 1967; Lord Leverhulme's Unknown Venture, 1982; other technical publications. *Recreations:* walking, reading. *Address:* 9 Pine Hey, Neston, S Wirral, Cheshire L64 3TJ.

WRIGHT, Hugh Raymond, MA; Chief Master, King Edward's School, Birmingham, since 1991; *b* 24 Aug. 1938; *s* of Rev. Raymond Blayney Wright and Alice Mary Wright (*née* Hawksworth); *m* 1962, Jillian Mary McIldowie Meiklejohn; three *s*. *Educ:* Kingswood Sch., Bath; The Queen's Coll., Oxford (Bible Clerk; MA Lit. Hum.). Asst Master, Brentwood Sch., 1961–64; Cheltenham Coll., 1964–79: Hd of Classics, 1967–72; Housemaster, Boyne House, 1971–79; Headmaster: Stockport Grammar Sch., 1979–85; Gresham's School, Holt, 1985–91. Chm., NW Dist, HMC, 1983; Chm., HMC Community Service Sub-Cttee, 1985–90 (Mem., 1980–90); Mem., Admty Interview Bd Panel, 1982–. FRSA 1984. *Publication:* film strips and notes on The Origins of Christianity and the Medieval Church, 1980. *Recreations:* music, theatre, hill walking, wildfowl, gardening, Rugby football, tennis. *Address:* King Edward's School, Birmingham B15 2UA. *T:* 021–472 1672. *Club:* East India.

WRIGHT, Prof. Jack Clifford, MA, BA; Professor of Sanskrit in the University of London, at the School of Oriental and African Studies, since 1964; *b* 5 Dec. 1933; *s* of late Jack and Dorothy Wright, Aberdeen; *m* 1958, Hazel Chisholm (*née* Strachan), Crathes, Banchory; one *s*. *Educ:* Robert Gordon's Coll., Aberdeen; Univ. of Aberdeen (MA Hons in French and German, 1955)); University of Zürich; Univ. of London (BA Hons in Sanskrit, 1959). Lectr in Sanskrit, 1959–64, Head, Dept of Indology and Mod. Langs and Lits of S Asia, 1970–83, SOAS, Univ. of London. *Address:* School of Oriental and African Studies, University of London, WC1E 7HP.

WRIGHT, Hon. James Claude, Jr; Speaker, US House of Representatives, 1987–89; *b* 22 Dec. 1922; *s* of James C. Wright and Marie Wright (*née* Lyster); *m* 1972, Betty Hay; one *s* three *d* by former marr. *Educ:* Weatherford College, Univ. of Texas. Served US Army Air Force, 1941–45 (DFC, Legion of Merit). Mem., Texas Legislature, 1947–49; Mayor of Weatherford, Texas, 1950–54; Mem., US House of Representatives for Fort Worth, 1955–89; Dep. Democratic Whip to 1976; Majority Leader, 1976–87; former Mem. of Committees: Budget, Public Works and Transportation; Govt Operations; Highway Beautification (Chm.). Former lay minister, Presbyterian Church. *Publications:* You and Your Congressman, 1965; The Coming Water Famine, 1966; Of Swords and Plowshares, 1968; (jtly) Congress and Conscience, 1970; Reflections of a Public Man, 1984. *Address:* 9A10 Federal Building, 819 Taylor Street, Fort Worth, Texas 76102, USA.

WRIGHT, Adm. Jerauld, DSM (US) (twice); Silver and Bronze Star Medals; Legion of Merit (US); USN retired; US Ambassador to Nationalist China, 1963–65; *b* Amherst, Mass., 4 June 1898; *s* of Gen. William Mason Wright and Marjorie R. (Jerauld) Wright; *m* 1938, Phyllis B. Thompson; one *s* one *d*. *Educ:* US Naval Academy. Ensign, USN, 1917; promoted through grades to Admiral, 1954, Executive Staff of US Naval Academy; operational staff appointments for N African, Sicilian and Italian landings; Mem., Gen. Mark Clark's Expedition to North Africa, 1942; Comd British Sub. HMS Seraph in evacuation of Gen. Henri Giraud from S France to Gibraltar, 1942; Staff Adv. to Sir Andrew B. Cunningham, RN, in N African invasion, 1942; Staff Comdr, 8th Fleet in Sicily and Salerno landings, 1943. Comdr, USS Santa Fe, Pacific, 1943–44; Comdr Amphibious Group Five, 1944–45; Comdr Cruiser Div. Six, 1945; Asst Chief of Naval Operations for Fleet Readiness, 1945–48; Comdr. Amphibious Force, US Atlantic Fleet,

1949–51; US Rep. NATO Standing Group, Washington, 1951–52; C-in-C US Naval Forces, E Atlantic and Medit., 1952–54; Supreme Allied Commander, Atlantic, and C-in-C Western Atlantic Area, NATO, 1954–60; C-in-C Atlantic (US Unified Command), and C-in-C Atlantic Fleet, 1954–60. Pres. US Naval Inst., 1959. Holds Hon. doctorates in Laws and Science. Awarded foreign decorations. *Address:* (home) 4101 Cathedral Avenue, Washington, DC 20016, USA. *Clubs:* Metropolitan, Alibi, Chevy Chase (Washington); Knickerbocker, Brook (New York).

WRIGHT, Joe Booth, CMG 1979; HM Diplomatic Service, retired; Ambassador to Ivory Coast, Upper Volta and Niger, 1975–78; *b* 24 Aug. 1920; *s* of Joe Booth Wright and Annie Elizabeth Wright; *m* 1st, 1945, Pat (*née* Beaumont); one *s* two *d*; 2nd, 1967, Patricia Maxine (*née* Nicholls). *Educ:* King Edward VI Grammar Sch., Retford; Univ. of London. BA Hons, French. GPO, 1939–47. Served War, HM Forces: RAOC, Intelligence Corps, 1941–46. Entered Foreign Office, 1947; FO, 1947–51; Vice-Consul, Jerusalem, 1951; Consul, Munich, 1952, and Basra, 1954; Dep. Consul, Tamsui, 1956; FO, 1959–64; Consul, Surabaya, 1964; Consul, Medan, 1965–67; First Sec. (Information), Nicosia, 1968; Head of Chancery and Consul, Tunis, 1968–71; Consul-General: Hanoi, 1971–72; Geneva, 1973–75. Mem., Inst. of Linguists and Translators' Guild, 1982–. FRSA 1987. *Publications:* Francophone Black Africa Since Independence, 1981; Zaire Since Independence, 1983; Paris As It Was, 1985. *Recreations:* cricket, film-going, music, Chinese painting. *Address:* 29 Brittany Road, St Leonards-on-Sea, East Sussex TN38 0RB. *Club:* Royal Over-Seas League.

WRIGHT, Captain John, DSC 1944; RN (retd); General Manager, HM Dockyard, Devonport, 1972–77; *b* 30 April 1921; *s* of Percy Robert and Lucy Ada Wright; *m* 1946, Ethel Lumley Sunderland; one *s* two *d*. *Educ:* Liverpool Univ. (Part I for BSc). MIEE; Silver Medal, City and Guilds. Served War: RNVR, 1942; 16th Destroyer Flotilla, 1942; HMS Birmingham, 1943; HMS Diadem, 1943. Devonport Gunnery Sch., 1946; HMS Collingwood, 1948; BJSM, USA, 1951; Admiralty Surface Weapons Estabt, 1952; HMS Cumberland, 1956; Naval Ordnance Div., 1958; British Naval Staff, USA, 1960; Polaris Technical Dept, 1964; HM Dockyard, Chatham, 1968; RN retd 1972. Gen. Manager, Marconi Space and Defence Systems Ltd, Portsmouth, 1981–82; Asst Man. Dir and Gen. Manager, Marconi Underwater Systems, 1982–84. *Recreations:* fishing, gardening. *Address:* Oakdene, 21 Blackbrook Park Avenue, Fareham, Hants PO15 5JN. *T:* Fareham (0329) 280512.

WRIGHT, John Hurrell C.; *see* Collier-Wright.

WRIGHT, John Keith; JP; economic and financial consultant; Under Secretary, Overseas Development Administration, Foreign and Commonwealth Office (formerly Ministry of Overseas Development), 1971–84; *b* 30 May 1928; *s* of late James Wright and Elsie Wright, Walton-on-Thames, Surrey; *m* 1958, Thérèse Marie Claire, *er d* of René Aubenas, Paris. *Educ:* Tiffins' Sch.; King's Coll., Cambridge (MA Hist., 1950; Dipl. in Economics, 1954; Gladstone Memorial Prize, 1954); Yale Univ. OEEC, Paris: Economics and Statistics Directorate, 1951–52; Agriculture and Food Directorate, 1954–56; UK Atomic Energy Authority, 1956–61; Chief Scientific Adviser's staff, MoD, 1961–66 (UK Delegn to 18 Nation Disarmament Conf., 1962–64); Sen. Econ. Adviser, CRO, 1966–68; Head of Economists Dept and subseq. Dir (Economic), FCO, 1968–71. Chm., Economists' Panel, First Division Assoc., 1973–75. Dir, Sadlers Wells (Trading) Ltd, 1983–. Mem., Social Security Appeals Tribunal, Central London, 1985–. Member: Court of Governors, London Sch. of Hygiene and Tropical Medicine, 1979–81; Councils, Queen Elizabeth Coll., 1982–85, King's Coll., 1984–, Univ. of London; Bd of Visitors, Canterbury Prison, 1987–. Trustee, Thomson Foundn, 1985–. JP Dover and East Kent, 1983–. Has exhibited at Royal Academy. *Publications:* articles on economic subjects and on nuclear strategy. *Recreations:* economic and military history, music, amateur radio (G4IOL). *Address:* Laurie House, Airlie Gardens, W8 7AW; Bowling Corner, Sandwich, Kent. *Clubs:* Athenæum, Beefsteak.

WRIGHT, Hon. Sir (John) Michael, Kt 1990; **Hon. Mr Justice Wright;** a Judge of the High Court of Justice, Queen's Bench Division, since 1990; *b* 26 Oct. 1932; *s* of Prof. John George Wright, DSc, MVSc, FRCVS, and Elsie Lloyd Razey; *m* 1959, Kathleen, *er d* of F. A. Meanwell; one *s* two *d*. *Educ:* King's Sch., Chester; Oriel Coll., Oxford. BA Jurisprudence 1956, MA 1978. Served Royal Artillery, 1951–53. Called to Bar, Lincoln's Inn (Tancred Student), 1957, Bencher 1983; QC 1974; a Recorder, 1974–90; Leader, SE Circuit, 1981–83; Chm. of the Bar, 1983–84 (Vice-Chm., 1982–83). Member: Bar Council, 1972–73; Senate of the Four Inns of Court, 1973–74; Senate of the Inns of Court and the Bar, 1975–84. Mem. Supreme Court Rules Cttee, 1973–74. Legal Assessor to the Disciplinary Cttee, RCVS, 1983–90; Vice-Chm., Appeal Cttee, ICA, 1989–90. Hon. Member: American Bar Assoc.; Canadian Bar Assoc. *Recreations:* books, music. *Address:* c/o Royal Courts of Justice, Strand, WC2.

WRIGHT, Sir (John) Oliver, GCMG 1981 (KCMG 1974; CMG 1964); GCVO 1978; DSC 1944; HM Diplomatic Service, retired; King of Arms, Most Distinguished Order of St Michael and St George, since 1987; *b* 6 March 1921; *m* 1942, Lillian Marjory Osborne; three *s*. *Educ:* Solihull School; Christ's College, Cambridge (MA; Hon. Fellow 1981; pre-elected Master, May 1982, resigned July 1982). Served in RNVR, 1941–45. Joined HM Diplomatic Service, Nov. 1945; served: New York, 1946–47; Bucharest, 1948–50; Singapore, 1950–51; Foreign Office, 1952–54; Berlin, 1954–56; Pretoria, 1957–58. Imperial Defence College, 1959. Asst Private Sec. to Sec. of State for Foreign Affairs, 1960; Counsellor and Private Sec., 1963; Private Sec. to the Prime Minister, 1964–66 (to Rt Hon. Sir Alec Douglas-Home, and subseq. to Rt Hon. Harold Wilson); Ambassador to Denmark, 1966–69; seconded to Home Office as UK Rep. to NI Govt, Aug. 1969–March 1970; Chief Clerk, HM Diplomatic Service, 1970–72; Dep. Under-Sec. of State, FCO, 1972–75; Ambassador to Federal Republic of Germany, 1975–81; retired, then re-apptd, Ambassador to Washington, 1982–86. Director: Siemens Ltd, 1981–82; Amalgamated Metal Corp., April-July 1982; Savoy Hotel plc, 1987–; General Technology Systems Inc., 1990–. Distinguished Vis. Prof., Univ. of S Carolina, 1986–90; Clark Fellow, Cornell Univ., 1987; Lewin Vis. Prof., Washington Univ., St Louis, 1988. Pres., German Chamber of Industry and Commerce, London, 1989–. Bd Mem., British Council, 1981–82, 1986–90. Trustee: British Museum, 1986–91; Internat. Shakespeare Globe Centre, 1986–; Chm., British Königswinter Conf. Steering Cttee, 1987–; Co-Chm., Anglo-Irish Encounter, 1986–91. Gov., Reigate Grammar Sch., 1987– (Chm., 1990–). Hon. DHL Univ. of Nebraska, 1983; Hon. DL Rockford Coll., Ill, 1985. Grand Cross, German Order of Merit, 1978. *Recreations:* theatre, gardening. *Address:* Burstow Hall, near Horley, Surrey. *T:* Horley (0293) 783494. *Club:* Travellers'.

WRIGHT, Joseph, OBE 1978; FRPharmS; FCIS; Secretary (Chief Executive), National Pharmaceutical Association (formerly National Pharmaceutical Union), 1961–81; *b* 7 Jan. 1917; *s* of late Thomas Wright and Margaret (*née* Cardwell); *m* 1942, Margaretta May Hart Talbot, BA, MRPharmS; two *s* two *d*. *Educ:* Blackpool Boys' Grammar Sch.; Chelsea Polytechnic. Dip., Chem. and Druggist and PhC examinations. Called to the Bar, Middle Temple, 1952. In retail pharmacy, 1933–47, incl. 4 years apprenticeship in Blackpool, with subseq. experience in London. Served war, RAF, commnd wireless navigator, Coastal Comd. On staff, Pharm. Section, Min. of Health, 1947–48; joined NPU, 1948: Asst Sec., 1949, Dep. Sec., 1955, Sec. and Manager, 1961; Dir, NPA Gp, 1971 (Gp comprises Nat. Pharm. Assoc. Ltd, Chemists' Def. Assoc. Ltd, Pharmacy Mutual Insce Co. Ltd, Pharm. and Gen. Prov. Soc., NPU Ltd (t/a NPA Sces), NPU Holdings Ltd). Director: NPU Holdings Ltd, 1965–81; NPU Ltd, 1971–81; Indep. Chemists Marketing Ltd, 1972–81; NPU Marketing Ltd, 1966–81; Member: Standing Pharm. Adv. Cttee, 1964–82; Poisons Bd, 1963–84; Panel of Fellows of Pharm. Soc., 1965–82; Gen. Practice Sub-Cttee, PSGB, 1963–81; Bd, Nat. Chamber of Trade, 1973–82; Trade & Professional Alliance, 1975–81; Legislation & Taxation Cttee, Nat. Ch. of Trade, 1964–81; Adviser to Pharm. Services Negotiating Cttee, 1977–81. Hon. Life Mem., S African Retail Chem. and Druggists Assoc., 1974; Distinguished Service Award, Pharmacy Guild of Aust., 1978. Charter Gold Medal of Pharmaceutical Soc. of GB, 1980. Liveryman, Worshipful Soc. of Apoth. of London, 1978–. Freedom of City of London. *Recreations:* reading, travel, amateur radio (G0AJO) and—intermittently—grandchildren. *Address:* 116 Wynchgate, Winchmore Hill, N21 1QU. *T:* 081–886 1645.

WRIGHT, Judith, (Mrs J. P. McKinney); writer; *b* 31 May 1915; *d* of late Phillip Arundell Wright, CMG, and Ethel Mabel (*née* Bigg); *m* J. P. McKinney; one *d*. *Educ:* NSW Correspondence Sch.; New England Girls' Sch.; Sydney Univ. Secretarial work, 1938–42; Univ. Statistician (Univ. of Queensland), 1945–48. Creative Arts Fellow, ANU, 1974; Australia Council Senior Writers' Fellowship, 1977. Dr of Letters (Hon.): Univ. of New England, 1963; Univ. of Sydney, 1976; Monash Univ., 1977; ANU, 1981; Univ. of NSW, 1985; Griffith Univ., 1988; Univ. of Melbourne, 1988. Encyclopædia Britannica Writer's Award, 1965; Robert Frost Medallion, Fellowship of Australian Writers, 1975; Asan World Prize, Asan Meml Assoc., 1984. FAHA 1970. *Publications: verse:* The Moving Image, 1946; Woman to Man, 1950; The Gateway, 1953; The Oxford Book of Australian Verse, 1954; New Land New Language (anthology), 1956; The Two Fires, 1955; Birds, 1960; Five Senses, 1963; The Other Half, 1966; Collected Poems, 1971; Alive, 1972; Fourth Quarter, 1976; The Double Tree, 1978; Phantom Dwelling, 1985; A Human Pattern, 1990; *prose:* The Generations of Men, 1955; Preoccupations in Australian Poetry, 1964; The Nature of Love, 1966; Because I Was Invited, 1975; Charles Harpur, 1977; The Coral Battleground, 1977; The Cry for the Dead, 1981; We Call for a Treaty, 1985; Born of The Conquerors, 1991; four books for children; also critical essays and monographs. *Recreation:* gardening. *Address:* PO Box 93, Braidwood, NSW 2622, Australia.

WRIGHT, Kenneth Campbell, CMG 1987; OBE 1973; PhD; HM Diplomatic Service, retired; Director, British Invisibles (formerly British Invisible Exports Council), since 1989; *b* 31 May 1932; *s* of James Edwin Wright and Eva Rebecca Wright (*née* Sayers) *m* 1958, Diana Yolande Binnie; one *s* two *d*. *Educ:* George Heriot's Sch., Edinburgh; Univs of Edinburgh (MA 1st Cl. Hons Mod Langs, PhD) and Paris (LèsL). Short-service commission, Royal Air Force, 1957–60. Lecturer, Inst. Politique Congolais and Lovanium Univ., Congo (Zaire), 1960–63; Lectr, later Sen. Lectr, Dept of Modern Languages, Univ. of Ghana, 1963–65; entered HM Diplomatic Service, 1965; FO, 1965–68; First Sec., Bonn, 1968–72; FCO, 1972–75; First Sec., later Counsellor, UK Permanent Representation to the European Communities, Brussels, 1975–79; FCO, 1979–82; Counsellor, Paris, 1982–85; FCO, 1985–89. Dir, City Communications Centre, 1989, until merger with BIEC. *Recreations:* people, places, books. *Address:* c/o British Invisibles, Windsor House, 39 King Street, EC2V 8DQ. *Club:* Athenæum.

WRIGHT, Lance Armitage, RIBA; Associate Director, International Committee of Architectural Critics, since 1978; *b* 25 Dec. 1915; *s* of Edmund Lancelot Wright and Elizabeth Helen (*née* Bonser); *m* 1942, Susan Melville Foster; two *s* two *d*. *Educ:* Haileybury; University Coll. London; Architectural Assoc. Sch. Architect in private practice, 1946–73; Registrar, Royal West of England Academy Sch. of Architecture, 1950–53; Technical Editor, The Architects Journal, 1954; Editor, The Architectural Review, 1973–80. Chevalier, Order of St Gregory the Great, 1971. *Publication:* (with D. A. C. A. Boyne) Architects Working Details, vols 4–15, 1953–69. *Address:* 18 Holly Hill, Hampstead, NW3 6SE.

WRIGHT, Prof. Margaret S.; *see* Scott Wright.

WRIGHT, Martin; Policy Development Officer, Victim Support, since 1988; *b* 24 April 1930; *s* of late Clifford Kent Wright and Rosalie Wright, Stoke Newington; *m* 1957, Louisa Mary Nicholls; three *s* two *d*. *Educ:* Repton; Jesus Coll., Oxford. Librarian, Inst. of Criminology, Cambridge, 1964–71; Dir, Howard League for Penal Reform, 1971–81; NAVSS, later Victim Support, 1985–, Information Officer, to 1988. Chm., Lambeth Mediation Service, 1989–; Vice-Chm., Forum for Initiatives in Reparation and Mediation, 1988–89. ALA 1960. *Publications:* (ed) The Use of Criminological Literature, 1974; Making Good: Prisons, Punishment and Beyond, 1982; (ed jtly) Mediation and Criminal Justice, 1988; Justice for Victims and Offenders: a restorative response to crime, 1991. *Recreation:* suggesting improvements. *Address:* 19 Hillside Road, SW2 3HL. *T:* 081–671 8037.

WRIGHT, Hon. Sir Michael; *see* Wright, Hon. Sir J. M.

WRIGHT, Michael Thomas; writer and lecturer on architecture, fine arts and conservation; *b* 10 Dec. 1936; *o c* of Thomas Manning Wright and Hilda Evelyn Wright (*née* Whiting); *m* 1st, 1964, Jennifer Olga Angus (marr. diss. 1990), 2nd *d* of C. B. Angus, Singapore; two *s*; 2nd, 1990, Wendelina Elisabeth Pascall (*née* van Manen). *Educ:* Bristol Grammar Sch.; Gonville and Caius Coll., Cambridge (MA); Trinity Coll., Dublin. Member, Honourable Society of Gray's Inn. Churchwarden, St Michael's Parish Church, Highgate, 1974–79; Chm., Highgate Soc., 1985–87; Dir, Nat. Heritage Meml Fund, 1987–88. Judge, RICS/The Times Conservation Awards, 1976–89, 1991. Lectr, NADFAS, 1989. Member: DoE Working Party on Rural Settlements; Cttee, SPAB, 1987–; Trustee, Lutyens Trust, 1986–. Formerly: Financial Analyst, Ford Motor Co. Asst Sec., Town Planning Inst.; Editor, Town Planning Inst. Jl; Asst Editor, Country Life; Managing Editor, Journal of Royal Inst. of British Architects; Dep. Editor, Country Life; Publisher: Country Life, 1984–87 (Editor, 1973–84, Editor in Chief, 1980–84); Practical Woodworking, 1985–87; Television, 1985–87; Editor in Chief and Publisher, Antique Dealer and Collectors' Guide, 1982–87; Editorial Consultant, Country Life Books, 1978–86. FRSA 1980. JP Haringey, 1986–89. *Publications:* contrib. articles to: TPI Jl; RIBA Jl; Water Space; Country Life; Homes and Gardens. *Recreations:* music, tennis, walking; participation in local amenity society work. *Address:* Doverhay, Woollard Lane, Whitchurch, near Bristol, Avon BS14 0QS. *T:* Whitchurch (0272) 838201. *Club:* Travellers'.

WRIGHT, Prof. Nicholas Alcwyn, MD, PhD, DSc; FRCPath; Professor of Histopathology, Royal Postgraduate Medical School, since 1980; Director of Clinical Research, Imperial Cancer Research Fund, since 1991; *b* 24 Feb. 1943; *s* of late Glyndwr Alcwyn Wright and Hilda Lilian (*née* Jones); *m* 1966, Vera Matthewson; one *s* one *d*. *Educ:* Bristol Grammar Sch.; Durham Univ. (MB BS 1965); Newcastle Univ. (MD 1974; PhD 1975; DSc 1984); MA (Oxon) 1979. FRCPath 1986. University of Newcastle upon Tyne: Demonstrator in Pathology, 1966–71; Res. Fellow, 1971–74; Lectr in

Pathology, 1974–76; Sen. Lectr, 1976–77; Clinical Reader in Pathology, Univ. of Oxford, 1977, Nuffield Reader, 1978; Fellow, Green Coll., Oxford, 1979–80; Dir of Histopathology, Hammersmith Hosp., 1980–; Imperial Cancer Research Fund: Asst Dir, 1988; Associate Dir, 1989; Dep. Dir, 1990; Dir, Histopathology Unit, 1988–. Mem. Council: RCPath, 1982, 1986, 1990; British Soc. for Gastroenterology, 1986, 1990. Editor, Cell and Tissue Kinetics, 1980–87. Lectures: Avery Jones, Central Middx Hosp., 1989; Kettle, RCPath, 1990; Showering, Southmead Hosp., 1991; Morson, British Soc. Gastroenterology, 1991. *Publications:* Introduction to Cell Population Kinetics, 1977; (ed) Psoriasis: cell proliferation, 1982; The Biology of Epithelial Cell Populations, 1984; (ed) Colorectal Cancer, 1989; (ed) Oxford Textbook of Pathology, 1991; (ed) Clinical Aspects of Cell Proliferation, 1991. *Recreations:* Rugby football, cricket, squash, military history, cooking. *Address:* Department of Histopathology, Royal Postgraduate Medical School, Hammersmith Hospital, Du Cane Road, W12 0NN. *T:* 081–740 3292; Imperial Cancer Research Fund, Lincoln's Inn Fields, WC2A 3PX. *T:* 071–242 0200. *Club:* Athenæum.

WRIGHT, Sir Oliver; *see* Wright, Sir J. O.

WRIGHT, Sir Patrick (Richard Henry), GCMG 1989 (KCMG 1984; CMG 1978); HM Diplomatic Service, retired; Permanent Under-Secretary of State and Head of the Diplomatic Service, 1986–91; *b* 28 June 1931; *s* of late Herbert H. S. Wright and of Rachel Wright (*née* Green), Haslemere, Surrey; *m* 1958, Virginia Anne Gaffney; two *s* one *d. Educ:* Marlborough; Merton Coll. (Postmaster), Oxford (MA; Hon. Fellow, 1987). Served Royal Artillery, 1950–51; joined Diplomatic Service, 1955; Middle East Centre for Arabic Studies, 1956–57; Third Secretary, British Embassy, Beirut, 1958–60; Private Sec. to Ambassador and later First Sec., British Embassy, Washington, 1960–65; Private Sec. to Permanent Under-Sec., FO, 1965–67; First Sec. and Head of Chancery, Cairo, 1967–70; Dep. Political Resident, Bahrain, 1971–72; Head of Middle East Dept, FCO, 1972–74; Private Sec. (Overseas Affairs) to Prime Minister, 1974–77; Ambassador to: Luxembourg, 1977–79; Syria, 1979–81; Dep. Under-Sec. of State, FCO, 1982–84; Ambassador to Saudi Arabia, 1984–86. Dir, British Petroleum Co., 1991–. Gov., Wellington Coll., 1991–. KStJ 1990. *Recreations:* music, philately, walking. *Address:* c/o Barclays Bank, 1 Pall Mall East, SW1Y 5AX. *Club:* United Oxford & Cambridge University.

WRIGHT, Sir Paul (Hervé Giraud), KCMG 1975 (CMG 1960); OBE 1952; FRSA; HM Diplomatic Service, retired; Chairman: Irvin Great Britain Ltd, 1979–88; British American Arts Association, 1983–88; Member Council, Trusthouse Forte, since 1987; *b* 12 May 1915; *o s* of late Richard Hervé Giraud Wright; *m* 1942, Beatrice Frederika Rathbone (*see* Beatrice Wright), *widow* of Flt-Lt J. R. Rathbone, MP; one *d. Educ:* Westminster. Employed by John Lewis Partnership Ltd, 1933–39. Served HM Forces, War of 1939–45; Major, KRRC; HQ 21 Army Group, 1944–45 (despatches). Contested (L) NE Bethnal Green, 1945. Asst Dir, Public Relations, National Coal Bd, 1946–48; Dir, Public Relations, Festival of Britain, 1948–51. HM Foreign Service: Paris and New York, 1951–54; Foreign Office, 1954–56; The Hague, 1956–57; Head of Information, Policy Dept in FO, 1957–60; Cairo, 1960–61; UK Delegn to N Atlantic Council, 1961–64; Minister (Information), Washington, 1965–68, and Dir-Gen., British Inf. Services, NY, 1964–68; Ambassador to Congo (Kinshasa) and to Republic of Burundi, 1969–71; Ambassador to the Lebanon, 1971–75. Special Rep. of Sec. of State for Foreign and Commonwealth Affairs, 1975–78. Chm., British Lebanese Assoc., 1987–90. Hon. Sec. Gen., London Celebrations Cttee for Queen's Silver Jubilee, 1977; Vice-Chm., The American Fest., 1985; Pres., Elizabethan Club, 1988–; Governor, Westminster Cathedral Choir School, 1981–. Hon. RCM. Kt of the Order of the Cedar of Lebanon, 1990. *Publication:* A Brittle Glory (autobiog.), 1986. *Address:* 62 Westminster Gardens, Marsham Street, SW1P 4JG. *Club:* Garrick.

WRIGHT, Penelope Ann, (Mrs D. C. H. Wright); *see* Boys, P. A.

WRIGHT, Peter, CBE 1988 (OBE 1982); Chief Constable, South Yorkshire Police, 1983–90; *b* Stockport, 21 July 1929; *s* of Henry Wright and late Elizabeth (*née* Burton); *m* 1950, Mary Dorothea (*née* Stanway); one *s. Educ:* Edgeley Roman Catholic Sch.; Stockport Technical School. RN, 1947–49. Manchester City Police, 1954, to Chief Superintendent, Greater Manchester, 1975; Asst Chief Constable, 1975–79, Dep. Chief Constable, 1979–82, Merseyside. Mem., Parole Review Cttee, 1987–88. Pres., ACPO, 1988–89. *Recreations:* walking, gardening. *Address:* c/o South Yorkshire Police, Snig Hill, Sheffield S3 8LY. *T:* Sheffield (0742) 78522. *Club:* Commonwealth Trust.

WRIGHT, Peter Michael, FRCO(CHM); Organist and Director of Music, Southwark Cathedral, since 1989; *b* 6 March 1954; *s* of Dudley Cyril Brazier Wright and Pamela Deirdre (*née* Peacock). *Educ:* Highgate Sch. (Music Schol.); Royal Coll. of Music (Exhibnr; ARCM); Emmanuel Coll., Cambridge (Organ Schol.; MA). LRAM. Sub-Organist, Guildford Cathedral, and Music Master, Royal Grammar Sch., Guildford, 1977–89. Conductor: Guildford Chamber Choir, 1984–; Surrey Festival Choir, 1987–. Freelance conductor, recitalist (organ), adjudicator and broadcaster. *Recreations:* travel, theatre, reading, good food. *Address:* 52 Bankside, SE1 9JE. *T:* 071–261 1291.

WRIGHT, Peter Robert, CBE 1985; Director, The Birmingham (formerly Sadler's Wells) Royal Ballet, since 1977; *b* 25 Nov. 1926; *s* of Bernard and Hilda Mary Wright; *m* 1954, Sonya Hana; one *s* one *d. Educ:* Bedales School; Leighton Park Sch. Dancer: Ballet Jooss, 1945–47, 1951–52; Metropolitan Ballet, 1947–49; Sadler's Wells Theatre Ballet, 1949–51, 1952–56; Ballet Master, Sadler's Wells Opera, and Teacher, Royal Ballet Sch., 1956–58; freelance choreographer and teacher, 1958–61; Ballet Master and Asst Dir, Stuttgart Ballet, 1961–63; BBC Television Producer, 1963–65; freelance choreographer, 1965–69; Associate Dir, Royal Ballet, 1969–77. Special Prof., Sch. of Performance Studies, Birmingham Univ., 1990. Governor: Royal Ballet Sch., 1976–; Sadler's Wells Theatre, 1987–. FBSM (Conservatoire Fellow), 1991. *Creative Works:* Ballets: A Blue Rose, 1957; The Great Peacock, 1958; Musical Chairs, 1959; The Mirror Walkers, 1962; Quintet, 1962; Namouna, 1963; Designs for Dancers, 1963; Summer's Night, 1964; Danse Macabre, 1964; Variations, 1964; Concerto, 1965; Arpege, 1974; El Amor Brujo, 1975; Summertide, 1976; own productions of classics: Giselle: Stuttgart, 1966; Cologne, 1967; Royal Ballet, 1968 and 1985; Canadian National Ballet, 1970; Munich, 1976; Dutch National Ballet, 1977; Houston, Texas, 1979; Frankfurt, 1980; Rio de Janeiro, Brazil, 1982; Winnipeg, 1982; Tokyo, 1989; The Sleeping Beauty: Cologne, 1968; Royal Ballet, 1968; Munich, 1974; Dutch National Ballet, 1981; Sadler's Wells Royal Ballet, 1984; Coppelia: Royal Ballet, 1976; Sadler's Wells Royal Ballet, 1979; Swan Lake: Sadler's Wells Royal Ballet, 1981; Munich, 1984; Birmingham Royal Ballet, 1991; Nutcracker: Royal Ballet, 1984, Birmingham Royal Ballet, 1990. Hon. DMus London, 1990. Evening Standard Award for Ballet, 1982; Queen Elizabeth II Coronation Award, Royal Acad. of Dancing, 1990. *Recreations:* ceramics, gardening. *Address:* The Birmingham Royal Ballet, Birmingham Hippodrome, Thorp Street, Birmingham B5 4AU.

WRIGHT, Maj.-Gen. Richard Eustace John G.; *see* Gerrard-Wright.

WRIGHT, Sir Richard (Michael) C.; *see* Cory-Wright.

WRIGHT, Robert Anthony Kent, QC 1973; *b* 7 Jan. 1922; *s* of Robert and Eva Wright; *m* 1956, Gillian Elizabeth Drummond Hancock. *Educ:* Hilton Coll., Natal, S Africa; St Paul's Sch., London; The Queen's Coll., Oxford (MA). Indian Army, 1942–46, Major. Oxford, 1946–48. Called to Bar, Lincoln's Inn, 1949, Bencher 1979. *Recreations:* music, sailing, golf, walking. *Address:* Erskine Chambers, 30 Lincoln's Inn Fields, WC2A 3PF. *T:* 071–242 5532. *Clubs:* National Liberal; Bosham Sailing (Bosham); Island Sailing (Cowes); Royal Wimbledon Golf (Wimbledon).

WRIGHT, Rt. Rev. Roderick; *see* Argyll and the Isles, Bishop of, (RC).

WRIGHT, Very Rev. Ronald (William Vernon) Selby, CVO 1968; TD; DD; FRSE; FSA Scotland; JP; Minister Emeritus of the Canongate (The Kirk of Holyroodhouse), Edinburgh, and of Edinburgh Castle (Minister, 1936–77); Extra Chaplain to the Queen in Scotland, 1961–63 and since 1978 (Chaplain, 1963–78); Chaplain to The Queen's Bodyguard for Scotland, Royal Company of Archers, since 1973; *b* 12 June 1908; *s* of late Vernon O. Wright, ARCM, and late Anna Gilberta, *d* of Major R. E. Selby; unmarried. *Educ:* Edinburgh Academy; Melville Coll.; Edinburgh Univ. (MA; Hon. DD 1956); New Coll. Edinburgh. Warden, St Giles' Cathedral Boys' Club, 1927–36, and Canongate Boys' Club (formerly St Giles'), 1937–78. Cadet Officer, The Royal Scots, 1927–31; Student-Asst at St Giles' Cathedral, 1929–36; Asst Minister of Glasgow Cathedral, 1936; Warden of first Scottish Public Schools' and Clubs' Camp, 1938; Chaplain to 7th/9th (Highlanders) Bn The Royal Scots, 1938–42 (France, 1940), 1947–49; Senior Chaplain to the Forces: 52nd (Lowland) Div., 1942–43; Edinburgh Garrison, 1943; Middle East Forces, 1943–44; NE London, 1944; 10th Indian Div., CMF, 1944–45 (despatches); Hon. SCF, 1945–. Special Preacher, Oxford Univ., 1944; Select Preacher, Cambridge Univ., 1947; Visiting Preacher: Aberdeen Univ., 1946, 1953, 1965, 1973; St Andrews Univ., 1951, 1956, 1967, 1973; Glasgow Univ., 1955, 1973; Edinburgh Univ., 1959; Birmingham Univ., 1959; Hull Univ., 1967; Dundee Univ., 1973. Chaplain to, the Lord High Comr, 1959, and 1960. Conducted numerous series of religious broadcasts for BBC as Radio Padre, toured for War Office and BBC all Home Comds in 1942 and 1943 and MEF, 1943–44; toured transit camps etc in Italy, Austria, S Germany, etc, 1945; toured, for Church of Scotland: India, 1972; for HM Forces: Hong Kong 1973; Singapore, 1973. Moderator, Presbytery of Edinburgh, 1963; Moderator, Gen. Assembly of the Church of Scotland, 1972–73. Chm., Edinburgh and Leith Old People's Welfare Council, 1956–69; Extraordinary Dir, The Edinburgh Academy, 1973–; Hon. Church of Scotland Chaplain to: Fettes Coll., 1957–60, 1979– (Hon. Mem., 1983); Loretto Sch., 1960–84 (Hon. Old Lorettonian, 1976); Edinburgh Acad., 1966–73; Hon. Mem. Cargilfield Sch., 1985; Chaplain to: Governor of Edinburgh Castle, 1937–91; Merchant Co. of Edinburgh, 1973–82; ChStJ 1976; President: Scottish Church Soc., 1971–74; Scottish Assoc. of Boys Clubs; Vice-Pres., Old Edinburgh Club; Hon. Pres. Scottish Churches FA; Patron, Lothian Amateur FA. Mem. Edinburgh Educn Cttee, 1960–70. JP Edinburgh, 1963. Cross of St Mark, 1970. *Publications:* Asking Why (with A. W. Loos), 1939; The Average Man, 1942; Let's Ask the Padre, 1943; The Greater Victory, 1943; The Padre Presents, 1944; Small Talks, 1945; Whatever the Years, 1947; What Worries Me, 1950; Great Men, 1951; They Looked to Him, 1954; Our Club, 1954; The Kirk in the Canongate, 1956; The Selfsame Miracles, 1957; Our Club and Panmure House, 1958; Roses in December, 1960; The Seven Words, 1964; An Illustrated Guide to the Canongate, 1965; Take up God's Armour, 1967; The Seven Dwarfs, 1968; Haply I May Remember, 1970; In Christ We Are All One, 1972; Seven Sevens, 1977; Another Home, 1980; edited and contributed to Asking Them Questions, 1936; A Scottish Camper's Prayer Book, 1936; I Attack, 1937; Asking Them Questions-Second Series, 1938; Front Line Religion, 1941; Soldiers Also Asked, 1943; Asking Them Questions-Third Series, 1950; Asking Them Questions (a Selection), 1953; The Beloved Captain: Essays by Donald Hankey, 1956; (with L. Menzies and R. A. Knox) St Margaret, Queen of Scotland, 1957; A Manual of Church Doctrine (with T. F. Torrance), 1960; Fathers of the Kirk, 1960; Asking Them Questions, a new series, 1972, 1973; contrib. to Chambers's Encyclopædia, DNB, etc. Editor, Scottish Forces' Magazine (quarterly), 1941–76. *Recreation:* after trying to run Boys' Clubs and Camps, 1927–78 and a busy parish, now enjoying a busy retirement. *Address:* The Queen's House, 36 Moray Place, Edinburgh EH3 6BX. *T:* 031–226 5566. *Clubs:* Athenæum; New (Hon. Mem.) (Edinburgh).

WRIGHT, Roy Kilner; Deputy Editor, The London Standard (formerly Evening Standard), 1979–88; *b* 12 March 1926; *s* of Ernest Wright and Louise Wright; *m* 1st (marr. diss.); two *d*; 2nd, 1969, Jane Barnicoat (*née* Selby). *Educ:* elementary sch., St Helens, Lancs. Jun. Reporter, St Helens Reporter, 1941; Army Service; Sub-Editor: Middlesbrough Gazette, 1947; Daily Express, Manchester, 1951; Daily Mirror, London, 1952; Features Editor, Daily Express, London; Dep. Editor, Daily Express, 1976, Editor, 1976–77; Dir, Beaverbrook Newspapers, 1976–77; Senior Asst Editor, Daily Mail, 1977. *Address:* Girards, Broadchalke, Salisbury, Wilts SP5 5HL. *T:* Salisbury (0722) 780385.

WRIGHT, Roy William, CBE 1970; MIEE; Director, 1957–85, Deputy Chairman and Deputy Chief Executive, 1965–75, The Rio Tinto-Zinc Corporation; Director: Davy Corporation Ltd, 1976–85; A. P. V. Holdings Ltd, 1976–85; Transportation Systems and Market Research, 1978–85; *b* 10 Sept. 1914; *s* of late Arthur William Wright; *m* 1939, Mary Letitia, *d* of late Llewelyn Davies; two *d. Educ:* King Edward VI Sch., Chelmsford; Faraday House Coll., London. Served War of 1939–45, S African Navy and RN in S Atlantic, N Atlantic and Arctic; Lt-Comdr 1944. Joined Rio Tinto Co. Ltd, 1952; Man. Dir, Rio Tinto Canada, 1956; Director: Rio Tinto Co. Ltd, 1957; Lornex Mining Co., Vancouver, 1970–79; Rio Algom Ltd, Toronto, 1960–80; Palabora Mining Co., Johannesburg, 1963–80; Rio Tinto South Africa Ltd, Johannesburg, 1960–79. Chairman: Process Plant Expert Cttee, Min. of Technology, 1968; Econ. Develt Cttee for Electronics Industry, NEDO, 1971–76. *Address:* Cobbers, Forest Row, East Sussex RH18 5JZ. *T:* Forest Row (034282) 2009. *Clubs:* Athenæum, Royal Automobile; Toronto (Toronto).

WRIGHT, Rt. Rev. Royston Clifford; *see* Monmouth, Bishop of.

WRIGHT, Hon. Ruth Margaret; *see* Richardson, Hon. R. M.

WRIGHT, Sheila Rosemary Rivers; *b* 22 March 1925; *d* of Daniel Rivers Wright and Frances Grace Wright; *m* 1949, Ronald A. Gregory; two *c.* Social Science Cert. 1951; BScSoc London External 1956. Personnel Officer, 1951–57; Social Worker, 1957–74. Councillor: Birmingham CC, 1956–78; West Midlands CC, 1973–81. MP (Lab) Birmingham, Handsworth, 1979–83. Member, Birmingham Reg. Hosp. Bd and W Midlands RHA, 1966–80. *Address:* 41 Beaudesert Road, Birmingham B20 3TQ. *T:* 021–554 9840.

WRIGHT, Shirley Edwin McEwan; corporate consultant; *b* 4 May 1915; *s* of Alfred Coningsby Wright and Elsie Derbyshire; *m* 1939, Dora Fentem; one *s* three *d. Educ:* Herbert Strutt Sch., Belper; Coll. of Technology, Manchester; Univ. of Sheffield. BEng, CEng, FIMechE. Metropolitan Vickers, 1932, ICI Explosives Div., 1938; Asst Chief Engr, ICI Nobel Div., 1955; Dir, Irvine Harbour Bd, 1962; Engrg and Techn Dir, ICI Nobel Div., 1965; Pres., Philippine Explosives Corp., 1970; Chief Exec., Livingston Develt Corp., 1972–77; Dir, Premix-Fibreglass, 1978–80. *Recreations:* cricket, golf. *Address:* Hazeldene, West Kilbride, Ayrshire. *T:* West Kilbride (0294) 822659.

WRIGHT, Stanley Harris; Director: Wolstenholme Rink Plc, since 1980 (Chairman, 1982–91); Stadium Ltd, since 1989; *b* 9 April 1930; *er s* of John Charles Wright and Doris Wright; *m* 1st, 1957, Angela Vivien Smith (marr. diss. 1973); one *s*; 2nd, 1973, Alison Elizabeth Franks (*see* Hon. A. E. Wright). *Educ:* Bolton Sch.; Merton Coll., Oxford (Postmaster); 1st cl. hons PPE. Nat. Service, Manchester Regt, 1948–49. Asst Principal, BoT, 1952–55; 2nd Sec., UK Delegn to OEEC, Paris, 1955–57; Principal, HM Treasury, 1958–64; 1st Sec. (Financial), British Embassy, Washington, 1964–66; Asst Sec., HM Treasury, 1966–68; Lazard Bros & Co. Ltd 1969 and 1970 (Dir 1969); Under-Sec., HM Treasury, 1970–72. Exec. Dir, Lazard Bros & Co. Ltd, 1972–81; Exec. Chm., International Commercial Bank Plc, 1981–83; Non-Executive Director: Wilkinson Match Ltd, 1974–81; Scripto Inc., 1977–81; Law Land Co., 1979–81; Royal Trust Bank, 1984–88; Royal Trust Asset Management (UK Holdings) Ltd, 1987–88; James Ferguson Holdings Plc, 1987–88; Partner, Price Waterhouse and Partners, 1985–88. Chm., British Bankers Assoc. Fiscal Cttee, 1974–80; Member: Layfield Cttee on Local Government Finance, 1974–76; Armstrong Cttee on Budgetary Reform, 1979–80; (and Dir of Studies), CBI Wkg Pty on Tax Reform, 1984–85; CS Commn Final Selection Bd, 1986–; Panel for Financial Services Tribunal, 1988–91; Mem. Council, and Treas., QMW, London, 1989– (Mem. Council, 1977–89, Hon. Treas., 1987–89, Westfield Coll.). *Recreations:* various. *Address:* 6 Holly Place, NW3 6QU. *Clubs:* Reform, MCC.

WRIGHT, Stephen John Leadbetter; HM Diplomatic Service; Counsellor (External Relations), UK Permanent Representation to European Commission, Brussels, since 1991; *b* 7 Dec. 1946; *s* of J. H. Wright, CBE and Joan Wright; *m* 1970, Georgina Susan Butler; one *s* one *d*. *Educ:* Shrewsbury Sch.; The Queen's Coll., Oxford (BA Mod. History, 1968). HM Diplomatic Service, 1968; Havana, 1969–71; CS Coll., 1971–72; FCO, 1972–75; British Information Services, NY, 1975–80; UK Permanent Repn to EC, Brussels, 1980–84; FCO, 1984–85; seconded to Cabinet Office, 1985–87; Counsellor and Hd of Chancery, New Delhi, 1988–91. *Recreations:* photography, birdwatching, books. *Address:* c/o Foreign and Commonwealth Office, King Charles Street, SW1A 2AH.

WRIGHT, Prof. Verna, FRCP; Professor of Rheumatology, University of Leeds, since 1970; Consultant Physician in Rheumatology, Leeds Area Health Authority (A) Teaching, and Yorkshire Regional Health Authority, since 1964; Co-Director, Bioengineering Group for Study of Human Joints, University of Leeds, since 1964; *b* 31 Dec. 1928; *s* of Thomas William and Nancy Eleanor Wright; *m* 1953, Esther Margaret Brown; five *s* four *d*. *Educ:* Bedford Sch.; Univ. of Liverpool (MB ChB 1953, MD 1956). FRCP 1970 (MRCP 1958). House Officer, Broadgreen Hosp., Liverpool, 1953–54; Sen. Ho. Officer, Stoke Mandeville Hosp., 1954–56; Research Asst, Dept of Clin. Medicine, Univ. of Leeds, 1956–58; Research Fellow, Div. of Applied Physiology, Johns Hopkins Hosp., Baltimore, 1958–59; Lectr, Dept of Clin. Med., Univ. of Leeds, 1960–64; Sen. Lectr, Dept of Medicine, Univ. of Leeds, 1964–70. Adv. Fellow to World Fedn of Occupational Therapists, 1980–. President: Heberden Soc., 1976–77; British Assoc. for Rheumatology and Rehabilitation, 1978–80; Soc. for Research in Rehabilitation, 1978; Soc. for Back Pain Research, 1977–79; Chm., Standing Cttee for Academic Develt and Res., Arthritis and Rheumatism Council, 1989–. Member, Johns Hopkins Soc. for Scholars, USA, 1978–. Lectures: Casson Meml, Assoc. of Occupational Therapists, 1979; John Gibson Flemming, Royal Infirmary, Glasgow, 1984; Phillip Ellman, RSocMed, 1985; Kodama Meml, Japanese Rheumatism Assoc., Tokyo, 1986; C. W. Stewart Meml, Maryland Univ., 1988; John Matheson Shaw, RCPE, 1988; Heberden Oration, British Soc. of Rheumatology, 1985. Hon. Member: Canadian Rheumatism Assoc., 1978; Brazilian Soc. for Rheumatology, 1978; Hellenic Soc. of Rheumatology, 1981; Amer. Rheumatism Assoc., 1985. Elizabeth Fink Award, Nat. Ankylosing Spondylitis Soc., 1987. *Publications:* Lubrication and Wear in Joints, 1969; (with J. M. H. Moll) Seronegative Polyarthritis, 1976; Clinics in Rheumatic Diseases: Osteoarthrosis, 1976; (with I. Haslock) Rheumatism for Nurses and Remedial Therapists, 1977; (with D. Dowson) Evaluation of Artificial Joints, 1977; (with D. Dowson) Introduction to the Biomechanics of Joints and Joint Replacement, 1981; The Relevance of Christianity in a Scientific Age, 1981; (with H. A. Bird) Applied Drug Therapy of the Rheumatic Diseases, 1982; Topical Reviews in Rheumatic Disorders, vol. 2, 1982; Clinics in Rheumatic Diseases: osteoarthritis, 1982; Clinics in Rheumatic Diseases: measurement of joint movement, 1982; Bone and Joint Disease in the Elderly, 1983; (with R. A. Dickson) Integrated Clinical Science: musculo-skeletal disease, 1984; Personal Peace in a Nuclear Age, 1985; Arthritis and Joint Replacement (family doctor bklt), 1987; Pain, Clinical Rheumatology, International Practice and Research, 1987; (jtly) Diagnostic Picture Tests in Rheumatology, 1987. *Recreations:* interdenominational Christian youth work, voracious reader. *Address:* Inglehurst, Park Drive, Harrogate HG2 9AY. *T:* Harrogate (0423) 502326.

WRIGHT, William Ambrose, (Billy Wright), CBE 1959; Consultant, Central Independent Television Ltd, 1985–89 (Controller of Sport, 1982–85; Head of Sport and Outside Broadcasts, ATV Network Ltd, 1966–81); *b* 6 Feb. 1924; *m* 1958, Joy Beverley; two *d*, and one step *s*. *Educ:* Madeley Secondary Modern Sch. Professional Footballer; became Captain, Wolverhampton Wanderers Football Club; played for England 105 times; Captain of England 90 times; Manager of Arsenal Football Club, 1962–66. FA Cup Winners medal; 3 Football League Winners Medals. Director: Wolverhampton Wanderers FC; Midlands Cable Ltd; Telford Telecommunications Ltd. *Publications:* Captain of England; The World's my Football Pitch. *Recreations:* golf, cricket. *Address:* 26 Farnham Close, Whetstone, N20.

WRIGHT, Prof. William David, ARCS, DIC, DSc; Professor of Applied Optics, Imperial College of Science and Technology, 1951–73; *b* 6 July 1906; *s* of late William John Wright and Grace Elizabeth Ansell; *m* 1932, Dorothy Mary Hudson (*d* 1990); two *s*. *Educ:* Southgate County Sch.; Imperial Coll. Research engineer at Westinghouse Electric and Manufacturing Co., Pittsburgh, USA, 1929–30; research and consultant physicist to Electric and Musical Industries, 1930–39. Lecturer and Reader in Technical Optics Section, Imperial Coll., 1931–51. Kern Prof. of Communications, Rochester Inst. of Technol., USA, 1984–85. Chm. Physical Soc. Colour Group, 1941–43; Vice-Pres., Physical Soc., 1948–50; Sec., International Commn for Optics, 1953–66; Chairman: Physical Soc. Optical Group, 1956–59; Colour Group (GB), 1973–75; Pres., International Colour Assoc., 1967–69. Hon. DSc: City Univ., 1971; Waterloo, Canada, 1991. *Publications:* The Perception of Light, 1938; The Measurement of Colour, 4th edn, 1969; Researches on Normal and Defective Colour Vision, 1946; Photometry and the Eye, 1950; The Rays are not Coloured, 1967. About 80 original scientific papers, mainly dealing with colour and vision. *Address:* 25 Craig Mount, Radlett, Herts WD7 7LW. *T:* Radlett (0923) 855306.

WRIGHTSON, Sir (Charles) Mark (Garmondsway), 4th Bt *cr* 1900; Director, Hill Samuel & Co. Ltd, since 1984; *b* 18 Feb. 1951; *s* of Sir John Garmondsway Wrightson, 3rd Bt, TD, and of Hon. Rosemary, *y d* of 1st Viscount Dawson of Penn, GCVO, KCB, KCMG, PC; *S* father, 1983; *m* 1975, Stella Virginia, *d* of late George Dean; three *s*. *Educ:* Eton; Queens' Coll., Cambridge (BA 1972). Called to the Bar, Middle Temple, 1974. Joined Hill Samuel & Co. Ltd, 1977. *Heir: s* Barnaby Thomas Garmondsway Wrightson, *b* 5 Aug. 1979. *Address:* 39 Westbourne Park Road, W2.

WRIGLEY, Edward Anthony, (Tony), PhD; FBA 1980; Senior Research Fellow, All Souls College, Oxford, since 1988; Fellow of Peterhouse, Cambridge, since 1958; *b* 17 Aug. 1931; *s* of Edward Ernest Wrigley and Jessie Elizabeth Wrigley; *m* 1960, Maria Laura Spelberg; one *s* three *d*. *Educ:* King's Sch., Macclesfield; Peterhouse, Cambridge (MA, PhD). William Volker Res. Fellow, Univ. of Chicago, 1953–54; Lectr in Geography, Cambridge, 1958–74; Tutor, Peterhouse, 1962–64; Sen. Bursar, 1964–74; Co-Dir, Cambridge Gp for History of Population and Social Structure, 1974–; Prof. of Population Studies, LSE, 1979–88. Pres., Manchester Coll., Oxford, 1987–. Mem., Inst. for Advanced Study, Princeton, 1970–71; Hinkley Vis. Prof., Johns Hopkins Univ., 1975; Tinbergen Vis. Prof., Erasmus Univ., Rotterdam, 1979. Pres., British Soc. for Population Studies, 1977–79; Chm., Population Investigation Cttee, 1984–90; Treas., British Acad., 1989–. Editor, Economic History Review, 1986–. *Publications:* Industrial Growth and Population Change, 1961; (ed) English Historical Demography, 1966; Population and History, 1969; (ed) Nineteenth Century Society, 1972; (ed) Identifying People in the Past, 1973; (ed with P. Abrams) Towns in Societies, 1978; (with R. S. Schofield) Population History of England, 1981; (ed jtly) The Works of Thomas Robert Malthus, 1986; People, Cities and Wealth, 1987; Continuity, Chance and Change, 1988. *Recreations:* gardening, violin making. *Address:* 13 Sedley Taylor Road, Cambridge CB2 2PW. *T:* Cambridge (0223) 247614.

WRIGLEY, Air Vice-Marshal Henry Bertram, CB 1962; CBE 1956; DL; Senior Technical Staff Officer, Royal Air Force Fighter Command, 1960–64, retired; Sales Manager Air Weapons, Hawker Siddeley Dynamics, 1964–76; *b* 24 Nov. 1909; *s* of Frederick William Wrigley and Anne Jeffreys, Seascale, Cumberland; *m* 1935, Audrey (*d* 1987), *d* of C. S. Boryer, Portsmouth; one *d*. *Educ:* Whitehaven Grammar Sch.; RAF Coll., Cranwell. 33 Squadron, 1930; HMS Glorious 1931; HMS Eagle, 1933; long Signals Course, 1934; various signals appointments until 1937; RAF Signals Officer, HMS Glorious, 1938; served War of 1939–45, X Force, Norway, 1940; Fighter Command, 1940–43; HQ South East Asia, 1943–46; RAF Staff Coll., 1946; comd Northern Signals Area, 1947–50; jssc 1950; Inspector, Radio Services, 1950–52; Chief Signals Officer, 2nd TAF, 1952–54; Director of: Signals (I), Air Ministry, 1954–57; Guided Weapons (Air), Min. of Aviation, 1957–60. DL, Hertfordshire, 1966. *Recreation:* gardening. *Address:* Boonwood, Turpin's Chase, Oaklands Rise, Welwyn, Herts. *T:* Welwyn (043871) 5231. *Club:* Royal Air Force.

WRIGLEY, Prof. Jack, CBE 1977; Professor of Education, 1967–88, and Deputy Vice-Chancellor, 1982–88, University of Reading, now Professor Emeritus; *b* 8 March 1923; *s* of Harry and Ethel Wrigley; *m* 1946, Edith Baron; two *s*. *Educ:* Oldham High Sch.; Manchester Univ. BSc, MEd (Manch.); PhD (Queen's, Belfast). Asst Mathematics Teacher: Stretford Grammar Sch., 1946–47; Chadderton Grammar Sch., 1948–50; Research Asst, Manchester Univ., 1950–51; Lectr in Educn: Queen's Univ., Belfast, 1951–57; Univ. of London Inst. of Educn, 1957–62; Research Adviser, Curriculum Study Gp in Min. of Educn, 1962–63; Prof. of Educn, Univ. of Southampton, 1963–67; Dir of Studies, Schools Council, 1967–75. Member: Bullock Cttee on Teaching of Reading and other uses of English, 1972–74; SSRC, Mem. Council and Chm. Educnl Res. Bd, 1976–81. Specialist Adviser, H of C Select Cttee on Educn, Sci., and Arts, 1989–90. *Publications:* (ed) The Dissemination of Curriculum Development, 1976; Values and Evaluation in Education, 1980; contrib. learned jls. *Recreations:* chess (Ulster Chess Champion, 1957), theatre, foreign travel. *Address:* Valley Crest, Thrushwood, Keswick, Cumbria CA12 4PG. *T:* Keswick (07687) 71146.

WRIGLEY, Michael Harold, OBE 1971; HM Diplomatic Service; retired; *b* 30 July 1924; *e s* of Edward Whittaker Wrigley and Audrey Margaret Wrigley; *m* 1950, Anne Phillida Brewis; two *s* two *d*. *Educ:* Harrow; Worcester Coll., Oxford. Served War of 1939–45: Rifle Brigade, 1943–47. HM Diplomatic Service, 1950; served HM Embassies: Brussels, 1952–54; Bangkok, 1956–59; Office of Commissioner-Gen. for South-East Asia, Singapore, 1959–60; HM Embassy, Bangkok (again), 1961–64 and 1966–71; Counsellor, Kuala Lumpur, 1971–74; Counsellor, FCO, 1974–76. Mem., North Yorkshire CC, 1977–85. *Recreations:* shooting, racing. *Address:* Ganton Hall, Scarborough, N Yorks YO12 4NT. *T:* Sherburn (0944) 70223. *Clubs:* White's, Turf, Jockey; Royal Bangkok Sports (Bangkok).

WRIGLEY, Tony; *see* Wrigley, E. A.

WRINTMORE, Eric George; His Honour Judge Wrintmore; a Circuit Judge, since 1984; *b* 11 June 1928; *s* of Rev. F. H. and Muriel Wrintmore; *m* 1951, Jean Blackburn; two *s* one *d*. *Educ:* Stationers' Company's Sch.; King's Coll. London (LLB Hons). Called to Bar, Gray's Inn, 1955; full-time Chm., Industrial Tribunals, 1971; Regional Chm., Industrial Tribunals, 1976–84; a Dep. Circuit Judge, 1980–83; a Recorder, 1983–84. *Recreations:* sailing, squash, golf. *Address:* The Crown Court, The Court House, Southgate, Chichester, Sussex PO19 1SX. *Clubs:* Chichester Yacht; Ifield Golf and Country.

WRIXON-BECHER, Major Sir William F.; *see* Becher.

WROATH, John Herbert; His Honour Judge Wroath; a Circuit Judge, since 1984; *b* 24 July 1932; *s* of Stanley Wroath and Ruth Ellen Wroath; *m* 1959, Mary Bridget Byrne; two *s* one *d*. *Educ:* Ryde Sch., Ryde, IoW. Admitted Solicitor, 1956; private practice, 1958–66; Registrar, Isle of Wight County Court, 1965; County Prosecuting Solicitor, 1966; full-time County Court Registrar, 1972; a Recorder of the Crown Court, 1978–84. *Recreations:* sailing, bowling, reading, painting. *Address:* 8 Tides Reach, Birmingham Road, Cowes, Isle of Wight PO31 7NU. *T:* Isle of Wight (0983) 293072. *Clubs:* Royal London Yacht; Cowes Island Sailing (Cowes).

WROE, David Charles Lynn; Director of National Accounts, and Deputy Director, Central Statistical Office, since 1991; *b* 20 Feb. 1942; *m* 1966, Susan Higgitt; three *d*. *Educ:* Reigate Grammar Sch.; Trinity Coll., Cambridge (MA); Trinity Coll., Oxford (Cert. Statistics); Birkbeck Coll., London (MSc). Min. of Pensions and National Insurance, 1965–68; Central Statistical Office, 1968–70, 1973–75, 1976–82; secondment to Zambian Govt, 1971–72; Secretariat of Royal Commission on Distribution of Income and Wealth, 1975–76; Under Sec., Regional Policy Directorate, 1982–86, Dir of Stats, 1982–91, Under Sec., Housing Monitoring and Analysis, 1986–91, DoE. *Address:* Central Statistical Office, Great George Street, SW1P 3AQ.

WRONG, Henry Lewellys Barker, CBE 1986; Director: Spencer House (St James's) Ltd, since 1991 (Chairman, 1989–91); European Arts Foundation, since 1989; *b* Toronto, Canada, 20 April 1930; *s* of Henry Arkel Wrong and Jean Barker Wrong; *m* 1966, Penelope Hamilton Norman; two *s* one *d*. *Educ:* Trinity Coll., Univ. of Toronto (BA). Stage and business administration, Metropolitan Opera Assoc., New York, 1952–64; Director Programming, National Arts Center, Ottawa, 1964–68; Director: Festival Canada Centennial Programme, 1967; Barbican Centre, 1970–90. Member: Royal Opera House Trust, 1989–; Adv. Cttee, ADAPT (Access for Disabled People to Arts Premises Today). Trustee, Henry Moore Foundn, 1990. Freeman, City of London, 1970; Liveryman, Fishmongers' Co., 1987. FRSA 1988. Hon. DLitt City, 1985. Centennial Medal, Govt of Canada, 1967. Officier, Ordre Nat. du Mérite (France), 1985. *Address:*

Yew Tree House, Much Hadham, Herts SG10 6AJ. *T:* Much Hadham (027984) 2106. *Clubs:* Mark's; Badminton and Rackets (Toronto).

WROTTESLEY, family name of **Baron Wrottesley.**

WROTTESLEY, 6th Baron *cr* 1838; **Clifton Hugh Lancelot de Verdon Wrottesley;** Bt 1642; *b* 10 Aug. 1968; *s* of Hon. Richard Francis Gerard Wrottesley (*d* 1970) (2nd *s* of 5th Baron) and of Georgina Anne (who *m* 1982, Lt-Col Jonathan L. Seddon-Brown), *er d* of Lt-Col Peter Thomas Clifton, *qv; S* grandfather, 1977. *Educ:* Eton. *Heir:* half-uncle Hon. Stephen John Wrottesley [*b* 21 Dec. 1955; *m* 1982, Mrs Roz Fletcher (*née* Taylor); two *d*]. *Address:* 57 Rostrevor Road, SW6 5AR.

WROUGHTON, Philip Lavallin; Chairman and Chief Executive, C. T. Bowring & Co. Ltd, since 1988; Director, Marsh & McLennan Companies Inc., since 1988; *b* 19 April 1933; *s* of Michael Lavallin Wroughton and Elizabeth Angela Wroughton (*née* Rate); *m* 1957, Catriona Henrietta Ishbel MacLeod; two *d. Educ:* Eton Coll. Nat. Service, 1951–53, 2nd Lieut KRRC. Price Forbes & Co. Ltd, 1954–61; C. T. Bowring & Co. Ltd, 1961–. High Sheriff, Berks, 1977. *Recreations:* shooting, racing. *Address:* Woolley Park, Wantage, Oxon OX12 8NJ. *T:* Chaddleworth (04882) 214. *Club:* White's.

WU Shu-Chih, Hon. Alex, CBE 1983 (OBE 1973); JP; company director; Chairman, Fidelity Management Ltd, since 1965; Vice-Chairman, Dai Nippon Printing Co. (HK) Ltd, since 1973 (Managing Director, 1964–73); *b* 14 Sept. 1920; *s* of Wu Chao-Ming and Yeh Huei-Cheng; *m* 1946; three *s* three *d. Educ:* National South West Associated Univ., Kunming, China. Director: Hong Kong Ferry Co. Ltd, 1976–; Hong Kong Aircraft Engineering Co. Ltd, 1983–; Longman Group (Far East) Ltd, 1984–; Nat. Electronics (Consolidated) Ltd, 1984–; K. Wah Stones (Holdings) Ltd, 1986–; Consultant: General Association Hong Kong Ltd, 1980–; Austdairy Ltd, 1987– (Dir, 1983–87); Omisa Oil Management, SA, 1987–90; China Daily, 1988–; Proprietor, Sino-Scottish Trading Co., 1960–; Publisher, Sino-American Publishing Co., 1960–. Chairman: Supplementary Med. Professions Council, 1981–89; Printing Industry Trng Bd, 1967–89; Council for the Performing Arts, 1982–89; Council, Hongkong Acad. for Performing, 1982–86; Vice-Chairman: Hong Kong Trade Develt Council, 1974–83; Vocational Trng Council, 1982–89; Nominating Cttee, Stock Exchange of Hong Kong Ltd, 1989–; Member: Hong Kong Heart Foundn Ltd, 1975–; Aviation Adv. Bd, 1980–89; Med. Sub-Cttee, Univ. and Polytechnic Grants Cttee, 1983–89; Hong Kong Indust. Estates Corp., 1984–89; Adv. Cttee on China–Hong Kong Trade Develt Council, 1985–; Hong Kong Inst. for Promotion of Chinese Culture, 1985–; Bd of Governors, Hong Kong Philharmonic Soc. Ltd, 1978–. Pres., Hongkong Jun. Chamber of Commerce, 1960; Hon. Pres., Hong Kong Printers Assoc., 1983–. MLC Hong Kong, 1975–85. JP Hong Kong, 1973. Fellow, Hong Kong Management Assoc., 1983; FBIM 1979; FInstD 1980; FIOP 1984. *Recreations:* classical music, Western and Peking opera, tennis, soccer, swimming, contract bridge. *Address:* 14/F, Hart House, 12–14 Hart Avenue, Tsimshatsui, Kowloon, Hong Kong. *T:* 3–668789. *Clubs:* Hong Kong, Rotary of Hong Kong; Royal Hong Kong Jockey; Royal Hong Kong Golf.

WULSTAN, Prof. David; Gregynog Professor of Music, University College of Wales, Aberystwyth, since 1983; *b* 18 Jan. 1937; *s* of Rev. Norman and (Sarah) Margaret Jones; *m* 1965, Susan Nelson Graham; one *s. Educ:* Royal Masonic Sch., Bushey; Coll. of Technology, Birmingham; Magdalen Coll., Oxford (Academical Clerk, 1960; Burrowes Exhibr, 1961; Mackinnon Sen. Schol., 1963; Fellow by examination, 1964). MA, BSc, BLitt; ARCM. Lectr in History of Music, Magdalen Coll., Oxford, 1968–78; also at St Hilda's and St Catherine's Colls; Vis. Prof., Depts of Near Eastern Studies and Music, Univ. of California, Berkeley, 1977; Statutory (Sen. Lectr), University Coll., Cork, 1979, Prof. of Music, 1980–83. Dir, Clerkes of Oxenford (founded 1961); appearances at Cheltenham, Aldeburgh, York, Bath, Flanders, Holland, Krakow, Zagreb, Belgrade Fests, BBC Proms; many broadcasts and TV appearances, gramophone recordings; also broadcast talks, BBC and abroad. *Publications:* Septem Discrimina Vocum, 1983; Tudor Music, 1985; editor: Gibbons, Church Music, Early English Church Music, vol. 3, 1964, vol. 27, 1979; Anthology of Carols, 1968; Anthology of English Church Music, 1971; Play of Daniel, 1976; Victoria, Requiem, 1977; Tallis, Puer Natus Mass, 1977; Coverdale Chant Book, 1978; Sheppard, Complete Works, 1979–; Weelkes, Ninth Service, 1980; many edns of anthems, services etc; entries in Encyclopédie de Musique Sacrée, 1970; chapter in A History of Western Music, ed Sternfeld, 1970; articles and reviews in learned jls. *Recreations:* badminton, tennis, cooking, eating. *Address:* Tŷ Isaf, Llanilar, near Aberystwyth, Dyfed SY23 4NP. *T:* Llanilar (09747) 229.

WUTTKE, Hans A., Dr jur; German banker, retired; advisor; Executive Vice President and Chief Executive, International Finance Corporation (World Bank Group), 1981–84; *b* Hamburg, 23 Oct. 1923; *m*; two *s* two *d; m* 1982, Jagoda M. Buić. *Educ:* Univs of Cologne and Salamanca. Dresdner Bank AG, 1949–54; Daimler-Benz AG, 1954–61; Partner, M. M. Warburg-Brinckmann, Wirtz and Co., Hamburg, 1961–75; Executive Director, S. G. Warburg and Co. Ltd, London, 1962–75; Man. Dir, Dresdner Bank AG, Frankfurt, 1975–80; Chm., Deutsch-Süd-Amerikanische Bank AG, 1975–80. Mem. Board several European companies; Mem. Bd, German Development Co., Cologne, 1962–80; Chairman: East Asia Assoc., 1963–73; Comité Européen pour le Progrès Economique et Social (CEPES), 1976–. *Address:* 77 Cadogan Square, SW1X 0DY; (office) 6 Edith Grove, SW10 0NW. *T:* 071–376 5163, *Fax:* 071–376 5643; 38 Quai d'Orléans, Paris 75004, France.

WYATT, family name of **Baron Wyatt of Weeford.**

WYATT OF WEEFORD, Baron *cr* 1987 (Life Peer), of Weeford in the county of Staffordshire; **Woodrow Lyle Wyatt;** Kt 1983; Chairman, Horserace Totalisator Board, since 1976; *b* 4 July 1918; *y s* of late Robert Harvey Lyle Wyatt and Ethel Morgan; *m* 1957, Lady Moorea Hastings (marr. diss., 1966), *e d* of 15th Earl of Huntingdon and Cristina, *d* of the Marchese Casati, Rome; one *s; m* 1966, Veronica, *widow* of Baron Dr Laszlo Banszky Von Ambroz; one *d. Educ:* Eastbourne Coll.; Worcester Coll., Oxford, MA. Served throughout War of 1939–45 (despatches for Normandy); Major, 1944. Founder and Editor, English Story, 1940–50; Editorial Staff, New Statesman and Nation, 1947–48; Weekly Columnist: Reynolds News, 1949–61; Daily Mirror, 1965–73; Sunday Mirror, 1973–83; News of the World, 1983–; fortnightly columnist, The Times, 1983–. Began Panorama with Richard Dimbleby, 1955; under contract BBC TV, 1955–59; introduced non-heat-set web offset colour printing to England, 1962. MP (Lab) Aston Div. of Birmingham, 1945–55, Bosworth Div. of Leicester, 1959–70; Member of Parly Delegn to India, 1946; Personal Asst to Sir Stafford Cripps on Cabinet Mission to India, 1946; Parly Under-Sec. of State, and Financial Sec., War Office, May–Oct. 1951. Contested (Lab) Grantham Div. of Lincolnshire, 1955. Mem. Council, Zoological Soc. of London, 1968–71, 1973–77. *Publications:* (ed with introd.) English Story, 10 vols, 1940–50; The Jews at Home, 1950; Southwards from China, 1952; Into the Dangerous World, 1952; The Peril in Our Midst, 1956; Distinguished for Talent, 1958; (ed with introd.) 69 Short Stories by O'Henry, 1967; Turn Again, Westminster, 1973; The Exploits of Mr Saucy Squirrel, 1976; The Further Exploits of Mr Saucy Squirrel, 1977; What's Left of the Labour Party?, 1977; To the Point, 1981; Confessions of an Optimist (autobiog.), 1985;

(ed with introd.) The Way We Lived Then: the English story in the 1940s, 1989. *Address:* House of Lords, SW1A 0PW.

WYATT, (Alan) Will; Managing Director, BBC Network Television, since 1991; *b* 7 Jan. 1942; *s* of Basil Wyatt and Hettie Evelyn (*née* Hooper); *m* 1966, Jane Bridgit Bagenal; two *d. Educ:* Magdalen College Sch., Oxford; Emmanuel Coll., Cambridge. Trainee reporter, Sheffield Telegraph, 1964; Sub-Editor, BBC Radio News, 1965; moved to BBC television, 1968; Producer: Late Night Line Up, In Vision, The Book Programme, B. Traven—a mystery solved, *et al*, 1970–77; Asst Hd of Presentation (Programmes), 1977; Hd of Documentary Features, 1981; Hd of Features and Documentaries Gp, 1987; Asst Man. Dir, BBC Network Television, 1988. Chm., BBC Guidelines on Violence, 1983, 1987; Director: BARB, 1989–91; BBC Subscription TV, 1990–; BBC Enterprises, 1991–. Governor, London Inst., 1990–. *Publication:* The Man Who Was B. Traven, 1980. *Recreations:* fell walking, horse racing. *Address:* 38 Abinger Road, W4 1EX. *T:* 081–995 8557.

WYATT, Arthur Hope, CMG 1980; HM Diplomatic Service, retired; re-employed in Foreign and Commonwealth Office, since 1990; *b* 12 Oct. 1929; *s* of Frank and Maggie Wyatt, Anderton, Lancs; *m* 1957, Barbara Yvonne, *d* of Major J. P. Flynn, late Indian Army; two *d. Educ:* Bolton School. Army, 1947–50; FO, 1950–52; 3rd Sec., Ankara, 1952–56; 2nd Sec., Phnom Penh, 1956–58; 2nd Sec., Ankara, 1958–61; FO, 1962–66; 1st Sec., Bonn, 1966–70; FCO, 1970–72; Counsellor and Head of Chancery, Lagos, 1972–75; Dep. High Comr, Valletta, 1975–76; Diplomatic Service Inspector, 1977–79; Counsellor (Econ. and Comm.) and Consul-Gen., Tehran, 1979–80; Counsellor, Ankara, 1981–84; Minister, Lagos, 1984–86; High Comr to Ghana and Ambassador (non-resident) to Togo, 1986–89. *Recreations:* golf, football, bridge, stamp collecting. *Address:* 44 Baronsmede, W5 4LT. *T:* 081–579 0782.

WYATT, (Christopher) Terrel, FEng, FICE, FIStructE; Chairman and Chief Executive, W. S. Atkins Ltd, since 1987; *b* 17 July 1927; *s* of Lionel Harry Wyatt and Audrey Vere Wyatt; *m* 1970, Geertruida; four *s. Educ:* Kingston Grammar Sch.; Battersea Polytechnic (BScEng); Imperial Coll. (DIC). FICE 1963; FIStructE 1963; FEng 1980. Served RE, 1946–48. Charles Brand & Son Ltd, 1948–54; Richard Costain Ltd, 1955–87: Dir, 1970–87; Gp Chief Exec., 1975–80; Dep. Chm., 1979–80; Chm., Costain Group PLC, 1980–87. *Recreation:* sailing. *Address:* Lower Hawksfold, Fernhurst, near Haslemere, Surrey GU27 3NR. *T:* Haslemere (0428) 54538.

WYATT, David Joseph, CBE 1977; Director, International Division, British Red Cross Society, since 1985 (Acting Director General, Jan.–July 1990); HM Diplomatic Service, 1949–85; *b* 12 Aug. 1931; *s* of late Frederick Wyatt and Lena (*née* Parr); *m* 1st, 1957, Annemarie Angst (*d* 1978); two *s* one *d;* 2nd, 1990, Dr Wendy Baron, *qv. Educ:* Leigh Grammar Sch. National Service, RAF, 1950–52. Entered Foreign Service, 1949; Berne, 1954; FO, 1957–61; Second Sec., Vienna, 1961; First Sec., Canberra, 1965; FCO, 1969–71; First Sec., Ottawa, 1971; Counsellor, 1974; seconded Northern Ireland Office, Belfast, 1974–76; Counsellor and Head of Chancery, Stockholm, 1976–79; Under Sec. on loan to Home Civil Service, 1979–82; UK Mission to UN during 1982 General Assembly (personal rank of Ambassador); Minister and Dep. Comdt, British Mil. Govt, Berlin, 1983–85. FRSA 1991. *Address:* c/o British Red Cross Society, 9 Grosvenor Crescent, SW1.

WYATT, Gavin Edward, CMG 1965; *b* 12 Jan. 1914; *s* of Edward A. Wyatt and Blanche M. Muller; *m* 1950, Mary Mackinnon, *d* of John Macdonald, Oban; one *s* one *d. Educ:* Newton Abbot Grammar Sch. CEng, FIEE 1951; FIMechE 1962. Engineer and Manager, East African Power & Lighting Co. Ltd, Tanganyika and Kenya, 1939–57; Chief Exec. Officer and General Manager, Electricity Corp. of Nigeria, 1957–62; Man. Director, East Africa Power & Lighting Co. Ltd, 1962–64; World Bank, 1965–76, retired as Dir, Projects Dept, Europe, Middle East and North Africa Region. *Recreations:* gardening, viticulture, oenology. *Address:* Holne Bridge Lodge, Ashburton, South Devon TQ13 7NW.

WYATT, Terrel; see Wyatt, C. T.

WYATT, Wendy, (Mrs D. J. Wyatt); see Baron, O. W.

WYATT, Will; see Wyatt, A. W.

WYETH, Andrew Newell; artist; landscape painter; *b* 12 July 1917; *s* of Newell and Caroline Wyeth; *m* 1940, Betsy Merle James; two *s. Educ:* privately. First one man exhibn, William Macbeth Gall., NY, 1937; subsequent exhibitions include: Doll & Richards, Boston, 1938, 1940, 1942, 1944; Cornell Univ., 1938; Macbeth Gall., 1938, 1941, 1943, 1945; Art Inst. of Chicago, 1941; Museum of Modern Art, NYC, 1943; Dunn Internat. Exhibn, London, 1963; one man exhibns: M. Knoedler and Co., NYC, 1953, 1958; MIT, Cambridge, 1966; The White House, Washington DC, 1970; Tokyo, 1974; retrospectives: Metropolitan Museum, NY, 1976; RA, 1980 (1st by living American artist); Tokyo, 1974, 1979. Member: Nat. Inst. of Arts and Letters (Gold Medal, 1965); Amer. Acad. of Arts and Sciences; Amer. Acad. of Arts and Letters (Medal of Merit, 1947); Académie des Beaux-Arts, 1977; Hon. Mem., Soviet Acad. of the Arts, 1978. Presidential Medal of Freedom, 1963; Einstein Award, 1967. Hon. AFD: Colby Coll., Maine, 1954; Harvard, 1955; Dickinson, 1958; Swarthmore, 1958; Nasson Coll., Maine, 1963; Temple Univ., 1963; Maryland, 1964; Delaware, 1964; Northwestern Univ., 1964; Hon. LHD Tufts, 1963. *Publication:* The Helga Paintings, 1987. *Address:* Chadds Ford, Pa 19317, USA.

WYFOLD, 3rd Baron, *cr* 1919, of Accrington; **Hermon Robert Fleming Hermon-Hodge,** ERD 1990; 3rd Bt, *cr* 1902; Director, Robert Fleming Holdings, 1949–85, retired; formerly director other companies; *b* 26 June 1915; *s* of 2nd Baron and Dorothy (*d* 1976), *e d* of late Robert Fleming, Joyce Grove, Oxford; *S* father, 1942. *Educ:* Eton; Le Rosey, Switzerland. Captain, Grenadier Guards (RARO), 1939–65. *Heir:* none. *Address:* c/o Robert Fleming Holdings, 25 Copthall Avenue, EC2R 7DR. *T:* 071–638 5858. *Clubs:* Carlton, Pratt's; Metropolitan (New York).

WYKEHAM, Air Marshal Sir Peter, KCB 1965 (CB 1961); DSO 1943 and Bar 1944; OBE 1949; DFC 1940 and Bar 1941; AFC 1951; technical consultant, since 1969; *b* 13 Sept. 1915; *s* of Guy Vane and Audrey Irene Wykeham-Barnes; family changed name by Deed Poll, 1955, from Wykeham-Barnes to Wykeham; *m* 1949, Barbara Priestley, RIBA, AADip., *d* of late J. B. Priestley, OM; two *s* one *d. Educ:* RAF Halton. Commissioned, 1937; served with fighter sqns, 1937–43 (commanded Nos 73, 257 and 23 sqns); commanded fighter sectors and wings, 1943–45; Air Ministry, 1946–48; Test Pilot, 1948–51; seconded to US Air Force, Korea, 1950; commanded fighter stations, 1951–53; NATO, 1953–56; staff appointments, 1956–59; AOC No 38 Gp, RAF, 1960–62; Dir, Jt Warfare Staff, Min. of Defence, Aug. 1962–64. Comdr, FEAF, 1964–66; Dep. Chief of Air Staff, 1967–69. Chm., Wykehams Ltd; Partner, Anglo-European Liaison. FRAeS 1968; FBIM. Chevalier, Order of Dannebrog, 1945; US Air Medal, 1950. *Publications:* Fighter Command, 1960; Santos-Dumont, 1962. *Recreations:* sailing, writing. *Address:* Green Place, Stockbridge, Hampshire. *Club:* Royal Automobile.

WYKES, James Cochrane, MA (Cantab); *b* 19 Oct. 1913; *m* 1938, Cecile Winifred Graham, *e d* of J. Graham Rankin; one *s* one *d*. *Educ:* Oundle Sch.; Clare Coll., Cambridge (Open Exhibn in Classics). Asst Master, Loretto Sch., 1935–51; Headmaster, St Bees Sch., 1951–63; Head of Educational Broadcasting, ATV Network, 1963–66; Inner London Education Authority: Dir of Television, 1966–75; Television Adviser, 1975–78. Chm., Nat. Educnl Closed Circuit Television Assoc., 1970–72. Served War of 1939–45: Black Watch (RHR), 1940–44. *Publication:* Caesar at Alexandria, 1951. *Recreations:* walking, fishing, ornithology, music. *Address:* 36 Crimple Meadows, Pannal, Harrogate, N Yorks HG3 1EN. *T:* Harrogate (0423) 870307. *Club:* New (Edinburgh).

WYLD, Martin Hugh; Chief Restorer, National Gallery, since 1979; *b* 14 Sept. 1944; *s* of John Wyld and Helen Leslie Melville; one *s* one *d*. *Educ:* Harrow School. Assistant Restorer, National Gallery, 1966. *Recreation:* travel. *Address:* 21 Grafton Square, SW4 0DA. *T:* 071–720 2627. *Clubs:* Colony Room, MCC.

WYLDBORE-SMITH, Maj.-Gen. Sir (Francis) Brian, Kt 1980; CB 1965; DSO 1943; OBE 1944; General Officer Commanding, 44th Division (TA) and Home Counties District, 1965–68; *b* 10 July 1913; *s* of Rev. W. R. Wyldbore-Smith and Mrs D. Wyldbore-Smith; *m* 1944, Hon. Molly Angela Cayzer, *d* of 1st Baron Rotherwick; one *s* four *d*. *Educ:* Wellington Coll.; RMA, Woolwich. Served Middle East, Italy, France and Germany, 1941–45; Military Adviser to CIGS, 1947–49; GSO1, 7 Armoured Div., 1951–53; Comd 15/19 King's Royal Hussars, 1954–56; IDC 1959; BGS Combat Development, 1959–62; Chief of Staff to Commander-in-Chief, Far East Command, 1962–64. Col, 15/19 Hussars, 1970–77. *Recreations:* hunting, shooting. *Address:* Grantham House, Grantham, Lincs NG31 6SS. *T:* Grantham (0476) 64705. *Clubs:* Buck's, Naval and Military.

WYLIE, Rt. Hon. Lord; Norman Russell Wylie, PC 1970; VRD 1961; a Senator of the College of Justice in Scotland, 1974–90; *b* 26 Oct. 1923; *o s* of late William Galloway Wylie and late Mrs Nellie Smart Wylie (*née* Russell), Elderslie, Renfrewshire; *m* 1963, Gillian Mary, *yr d* of late Dr R. E. Verney, Edinburgh; three *s*. *Educ:* Paisley Grammar Sch.; St Edmund Hall, Oxford (Hon. Fellow, 1975); Univs of Glasgow and Edinburgh. BA (Oxon) 1948; LLB (Glasgow) 1951. Admitted to Faculty of Advocates, 1952; QC (Scotland) 1964. Appointed Counsel to Air Ministry in Scotland, 1956; Advocate-Depute, 1959; Solicitor-General for Scotland, April-Oct. 1964. MP (C) Pentlands Div., Edinburgh, Oct. 1964–Feb. 1974; Lord Advocate, 1970–74. Trustee, Carnegie Trust for Univs of Scotland, 1976–; Chm., Scottish Nat. Cttee, English-Speaking Union of the Commonwealth, 1978–84. Served in Fleet Air Arm, 1942–46; subseq. RNR; Lt-Comdr, 1954. *Recreations:* shooting, sailing. *Address:* 30 Lauder Road, Edinburgh EH9 2JF. *T:* 031–667 8377. *Clubs:* New (Edinburgh); Royal Highland Yacht.

WYLIE, Sir Campbell, Kt 1963; ED; QC; *b* NZ, 14 May 1905; *m* 1933, Leita Caroline Clark (*d* 1984); no *c*. *Educ:* Dannevirke High Sch.; Auckland Grammar Sch.; Univ. of New Zealand. LLM 1st Class hons (Univ. of New Zealand), 1928; Barrister and Solicitor (New Zealand), 1928; Barrister-at-law, Inner Temple, 1950. Was in private practice, New Zealand, until 1940. War service, 1940–46 (despatches). Crown Counsel, Malaya, 1946; Senior Federal Counsel, 1950; Attorney-General: Barbados, 1951; British Guiana, 1955; The West Indies, 1956; Federal Justice, Supreme Court of The West Indies, 1959–62; Chief Justice, Unified Judiciary of Sarawak, N Borneo and Brunei, 1962–63; Chief Justice, High Court in Borneo, 1963–66; Law Revision Commissioner, Tonga, 1966–67; Chief Justice, Seychelles, 1967–69; Comr for Law Revision and Reform, Seychelles, 1970–71. QC 1952 (Barbados), 1955 (British Guiana). *Address:* Unit No 80, Heron Court, 98 Bayview Street, Runaway Bay, Qld 4216, Australia. *T:* 075–372398.

WYLIE, Prof. Christopher Craig; F. J. Quick Professor of Biology, since 1988, and Fellow of Darwin College, since 1989, Cambridge University; *b* 15 Sept. 1945; *s* of Joseph and Edna Wylie; *m* 1st, 1969, Christine Margaret Hall; 2nd, 1976, Janet Heasman; three *s* one *d*. *Educ:* Chislehurst and Sidcup County Grammar School for Boys; University College London (BSc, 1st cl. Hons Anatomy 1966; PhD 1971). Lectr in Anatomy, University College London, 1969; St George's Hosp. Med. School: Sen. Lectr in Anatomy, 1975; Reader, 1983; Prof., 1985. Vis. Asst Prof. in Biology, Dartmouth Coll., 1975; Vis. Associate Prof. of Anatomy, Harvard Med. Sch., 1981. Editor in Chief, Development (internat. jl of develt biol.), 1987–. *Publications:* numerous research articles in sci. jls of biology. *Recreations:* relaxing with the family, racket sports. *Address:* 48 High Street, Great Shelford, Cambridge CB2 5EH. *T:* Cambridge (0223) 842434.

WYLIE, Derek; *see* Wylie, W. D.

WYLIE, Rt. Hon. Norman Russell; *see* Wylie, Rt Hon. Lord.

WYLIE, (William) Derek, FRCP, FRCS, FFARCS; Consulting Anaesthetist, St Thomas' Hospital, SE1; Consultant Anaesthetist, The Royal Masonic Hospital, 1959–82; Dean, St Thomas's Hospital Medical School, 1974–79; Adviser in Anaesthetics to the Health Service Commissioner, 1974–79; *b* 24 Oct. 1918; *s* of Edward and Mabel Wylie, Huddersfield; *m* 1945, Margaret Helen, 2nd *d* of F. W. Toms, Jersey, CI (formerly Dep. Inspector-Gen., Western Range, Indian Police); one *s* two *d* (and one *s* decd). *Educ:* Uppingham Sch.; Gonville and Caius Coll., Cambridge (MA; MB, BChir); St Thomas's Hosp. Med. Sch. MRCP 1945, FFARCS 1953, FRCP 1967, FRCS 1972. Resident posts at St Thomas' Hosp., 1943–45. Served RAFVR, 1945–47, Wing Comdr. Apptd Hon. Staff, St Thomas' Hosp., 1946; Consultant, 1948; Sen. Cons. Anaesthetist, 1966–79; Cons. Anaesthetist, The National Hosp. for Nervous Diseases, 1950–67. Examiner: FFARCS, 1959–72; FFARCSI, 1966–78. Mem., Bd of Faculty of Anaesthetists, RCS, 1960–70 (Dean, 1967–69; Vice-Dean, 1965–66; Bernard Johnson Adviser in Postgraduate Studies, 1959–67; Faculty Medal, 1984); Mem. Council, RCS, 1967–69; FRSM (Mem. Council, 1962–72; Hon. Treas., 1964–70; Pres., Section of Anaesthetics, 1963); Mem., Bd of Governors, St Thomas' Hosp., 1969–74; Mem. Council, Med. Defence Union, 1962–92, Pres., 1982–88. Jenny Hartmann Lectr, Basle Univ., 1961; Clover Lectr and Medallist, RCS(Eng), 1974. Pres., Assoc. of Anaesthetists of GB and Ireland, 1980–82, Hon. Mem., 1984 (John Snow Silver Medal, 1988). Hon. Citizen of Dallas, USA, 1963; Hon. FFARCSI, 1971; Hon. FFARACS, 1984. Henry Hill Hickman Medal, RSM, 1983. *Publications:* The Practical Management of Pain in Labour, 1953; A Practice of Anaesthesia, 3rd edn, 1972 (jtly with Dr H. C. Churchill-Davidson); papers in specialist and gen. med. jls. *Recreations:* reading, travel, philately. *Address:* St John's Cottage, Nursery Lane, Fairwarp, Uckfield, East Sussex TN22 3BD. *T:* Nutley (082571) 2822. *Club:* Royal Automobile.

WYLLIE, Prof. Peter John, PhD; FRS 1984; Professor of Geology, California Institute of Technology, since 1983 (Chairman, Division of Geological and Planetary Sciences, 1983–87); *b* 8 Feb. 1930; *s* of George William and Beatrice Gladys Wyllie (*née* Weaver); *m* 1956, Frances Rosemary Blair; two *s* one *d* (and one *d* decd). *Educ:* Univ. of St Andrews. BSc 1952 (Geology and Physics); BSc 1955 (1st cl. hons Geology); PhD 1958 (Geology). Glaciologist, British W Greenland Expdn, 1950; Geologist, British N Greenland Expdn, 1952–54; Asst Lectr in Geology, Univ. of St Andrews, 1955–56; Research Asst, 1956–58, Asst Prof. of Geochemistry, 1958–59, Pennsylvania State Univ.; Research Fellow in Chemistry, 1959–60, Lectr in Exptl Petrology, 1960–61, Leeds Univ.; Associate Prof. of Petrology, Pennsylvania State Univ., 1961–65 (Acting Head, Dept Geochem. and Mineralogy, 1962–63); University of Chicago: Prof. of Petrology and Geochem., 1965–77; Master Phys. Scis, Collegiate Div., Associate Dean of Coll. and of Phys. Scis Div., 1972–73; Homer J. Livingston Prof., 1978–83; Chm., Dept of Geophysical Scis, 1979–82. Louis Murray Vis. Fellow, Univ. of Cape Town, 1987. Pres., Internat. Mineralogical Assoc., 1986–90. Foreign Associate, US Nat. Acad. of Scis, 1981; Fellow: Amer. Acad. of Arts and Scis, 1982; Amer. Geophys. Union; Geol Soc. Amer.; Mineral Soc. Amer., 1965; Corresponding Fellow, Edin. Geol Soc., 1985–; Foreign Fellow: Indian Geophys. Union, 1987; Indian Nat. Sci. Acad., 1991; Foreign Mem., USSR Acad. of Scis, 1988. Hon. Mem., Mineralogical Soc. of GB and Ireland, 1986–. Hon. DSc St Andrews, 1974. Polar Medal, 1954; Wollaston Medal, Geol Soc. of London, 1982; Abraham-Gottlob-Werner Medal, German Mineral Soc., 1987. *Publications:* Ultramafic and Related Rocks, 1967; The Dynamic Earth, 1971; The Way the Earth Works, 1976; numerous papers in sci. jls. *Address:* 2150 Kinclair Drive, Pasadena, Calif 91107, USA. *T:* 818–791–9164. *Club:* Arctic (Cambridge).

WYLLIE, Robert Lyon, CBE 1960; DL; JP; FCA; *b* 4 March 1897; *s* of Rev. Robert Howie Wyllie, MA, Dundee; *m* 1924, Anne, *d* of Thomas Rutherford, Harrington, Cumberland; two *d*. *Educ:* Hermitage Sch., Helensburgh; Queen's Park Sch., Glasgow. Served European War, 1914–18, with Lothians and Border Horse (France). Chartered Accountant, 1920; FCA 1949. Dir, Ashley and Rock Ltd, 1966–90. Life Vice-President, Cumberland Development Council Ltd. Formerly Chairman: W Cumberland Industrial Develt Co. Ltd; W Cumberland Silk Mills Ltd; Cumberland Dévelt Council Ltd; Whitehaven & Dist Disablement Advisory Cttee, and Youth Employment Cttee; Vice-Chm. W Cumberland Hosp. Management Cttee; Hon. Treas., NW Div., YMCA. JP 1951; DL Cumbria (formerly Cumberland), 1957–84. OStJ 1976. *Recreation:* fishing. *Address:* The Cottage, Papcastle, Cockermouth, Cumbria CA13 0LA. *T:* Cockermouth (0900) 823292.

WYLLIE, William Robert Alexander; Chairman and Chief Executive, Asia Securities Ltd, Hong Kong, since 1971; Chairman, Asia Securities International Ltd, since 1987; *b* 9 Oct. 1932; *s* of Robert Wyllie and Marion Margaret Rae (*née* McDonald); *m* 1988, Rhonda Noreen (*née* McGrath); two *s* one *d* from previous marr. *Educ:* Scarborough State Sch., Perth, W Australia; Perth Technical Coll. (qual. Automobile and Aeronautical Engrg). MIRTE. Sen. Exec./Br. Manager, Wearne Bros Ltd, Malaysia/Singapore, 1953–64; Man. Dir, Harpers Internat. Ltd, Hong Kong, 1964–73; Chm. and Chief Exec., China Engineers Holdings Ltd, Hong Kong, 1973–75; Deputy Chairman and Chief Executive: Hutchison Internat. Ltd, Hong Kong, 1975–Dec. 1977; Hutchison Whampoa Ltd, Hong Kong, Jan. 1978–June 1979 (Chm. and Chief Exec., 1979–80). FInstD 1980. *Recreations:* power boating, water skiing, Scuba diving, restoration of vintage cars. *Address:* Asia Securities International Ltd, 17/F One Pacific Place, 88 Queensway, Hong Kong. *T:* (office) 8105500; (home) 8094946. *Clubs:* Hong Kong, American, Shek O Country, Royal Hong Kong Jockey, Royal Hong Kong Yacht (Hong Kong); Clearwater Bay Golf and Country.

WYMAN, John Bernard, MBE 1945; FRCS; FFARCS; Consultant Anaesthetist, Westminster Hospital, 1948–81; Dean, Westminster Medical School, 1964–81 (Sub-Dean, 1959–64); *b* 24 May 1916; *s* of Louis Wyman and Bertha Wyman; *m* 1948, Joan Dorothea Beighton; three *s* one *d*. *Educ:* Davenant Foundn Sch., London; King's Coll., London (Fellow 1980); Westminster Med. Sch. MRCS, LRCP 1941; DA 1945; FFARCS 1953; FRCS 1981. Military Service, 1942–46: Major RAMC; N Africa, Italy and India. Cons. Anaesthetist, Woolwich War Memorial Hospital Hosp., 1946–64; formerly Hon. Anaesthetist, Italian Hosp. Hunterian Prof., RCS, 1953. Member: Bd of Governors, Westminster Hosp., 1959–74; Sch. Council, Westminster Med. Sch., 1959–81; Croydon AHA, 1974–75; Kensington and Chelsea and Westminster AHA, 1975–81. *Publications:* chapters in med. text books and papers in gen. and specialist jls on anaesthesia and med. educn. *Recreation:* gardening. *Address:* Chilling Street Cottage, Sharpthorne, Sussex. *T:* Sharpthorne (0342) 810281. *Club:* Savage.

WYNDHAM, family name of **Baron Egremont and Leconfield.**

WYNDHAM-QUIN, family name of **Earl of Dunraven.**

WYNESS, James Alexander Davidson; Joint Senior Partner, Linklaters & Paines, since 1991; *b* 27 Aug. 1937; *s* of late Dr James Alexander Davidson Wyness and of Millicent Margaret (*née* Beaton); *m* 1966, Josephine Margaret Worsdell; three *d*. *Educ:* Stockport Grammar Sch.; Emmanuel Coll., Cambridge (MA, LLB). National Service, 2 Lieut, RA. Articled Clerk, A. F. & R. W. Tweedie, 1964–66 (qualified 1965); Linklaters & Paines, 1966–: Partner, 1970–87; Managing Partner, 1987–91. Non-Exec. Dir, Bowthorpe Holdings plc, 1979–. Mem., Law Soc. Mem., Co. of City of London Solicitors. Vice-Pres., Saracens FC (RFU) (Captain, 1962–65); Mddx RFU; London Div. RFU. *Recreations:* visiting France, growing vegetables, Rugby football, reading. *Address:* Linklaters & Paines, Barrington House, 59–67 Gresham Street, EC2V 7JA. *T:* 071–606 7080.

WYNFORD, 8th Baron, *cr* 1829; **Robert Samuel Best;** MBE 1953; DL; Lt-Col Royal Welch Fusiliers; *b* 5 Jan. 1917; *e s* of 7th Baron and Evelyn (*d* 1929), *d* of late Maj.-Gen. Sir Edward S. May, KCB, CMG; *S* father, 1943; *m* 1941, Anne Daphne Mametz, *d* of late Maj.-Gen. J. R. Minshull Ford, CB, DSO, MC; one *s* two *d*. *Educ:* Eton; RMC, Sandhurst. 2nd Lieut, RWF, 1937; served BEF; GHQ Home Forces; North Africa (Croix de Guerre); Egypt; Italy; wounded, 1944; Instructor, Staff College, 1945–46; War Office, 1947–49; OC Depot, RWF, 1955–57; Instructor Joint Service Staff Coll., 1957–60; RARO 1960. DL Dorset, 1970. *Heir:* *s* Hon. John Philip Best [*b* 23 Nov. 1950; *m* 1981, Fenella Christian Mary, *o d* of Arthur Reginald Danks; one *s* one *d*]. *Address:* Wynford House, Wynford Eagle, Dorchester, Dorset DT2 0ER. *TA* and *T:* Maiden Newton (0300) 20241. *Club:* Army and Navy.

WYNGAARDEN, James Barnes, MD; FRCP; Foreign Secretary, National Academy of Sciences, Washington, since 1990; *b* 19 Oct. 1924; *s* of Martin Jacob Wyngaarden and Johanna Kempers Wyngaarden; *m* 1946, Ethel Dean Vredevoogd (marr. diss. 1976); one *s* four *d*. *Educ:* Calvin College; Western Michigan University; University of Michigan. MD 1948; FRCP 1984. Investigator, NIH, 1953–56; Associate Prof. of Medicine, Duke Univ. Med. Center, 1956–61; Prof. of Medicine, Duke Univ. Med. Sch., 1961–65; Chairman, Dept of Medicine: Univ. of Pennsylvania Med. Sch., 1965–67; Duke Univ. Med. Sch., 1967–82; Dir, NIH, 1982–89; Assoc. Dir, Life Scis, Exec. Office of the President, 1989–90. Hon. DSc: Michigan, 1980; Ohio, 1984; Illinois, 1985; George Washington, 1986; S Carolina, 1989; Western Michigan, 1989; Hon. PhD Tel Aviv, 1987. *Publications:* (ed jtly) The Metabolic Basis of Inherited Disease, 1960, 5th edn 1983; (with O. Sperling and A. DeVries) Purine Metabolism in Man, 1974; (with W.N. Kelley) Gout and Hyperuricemia, 1976; (with L. H. Smith) Review of Internal Medicine; a self-assessment guide, 1979, 3rd edn 1985; (ed jtly) Cecil Textbook of Medicine, 15th edn 1979 to 19th edn 1992. *Recreations:* tennis, ski-ing, painting. *Address:* National Academy of Sciences, 2101 Constitution Avenue, NW, Washington, DC 20418, USA. *T:* (202) 334 2800.

WYNN, family name of **Baron Newborough.**

WYNN, Arthur Henry Ashford; Adviser on Standards, Department of Trade and Industry (formerly Ministry of Technology), 1965–71; *b* 22 Jan. 1910; *s* of late Prof. William Henry Wynn, MD, MSc; *m* 1938, Margaret Patricia Moxon; three *s* one *d*. *Educ:* Oundle Sch.; Trinity Coll., Cambridge (Entrance Scholar, Nat. Science and Mathematics; MA). Barrister-at-Law, Lincoln's Inn, 1939; Director of Safety in Mines Research Establishment, Ministry of Fuel and Power, 1948–55; Scientific Member of National Coal Board, 1955–65; Member: Advisory Council on Research and Development, Ministry of Power, 1955–65; Safety in Mines Research Advisory Board, 1950–65; Exec. Cttee, British Standards Institution, 1966–71; Advisory Council on Calibration and Measurement, 1967–71; Chairman: Standing Joint Cttee on Metrication, 1966–69; Adv. Cttee on Legal Units of Measurement, 1969–71. *Publications:* (with Margaret Wynn): The Protection of Maternity and Infancy in Finland, 1974; The Right of Every Child to Health Care in France, 1974; Nutrition Counselling in Canada, 1975; Prevention of Handicap of Perinatal Origin in France, 1976; Prevention of Preterm Birth, 1977; Prevention of Handicap and Health of Women, 1979; Prevention of Handicap of Early Pregnancy Origin, 1981; Lead and Human Reproduction, 1982; The Case for Preconception Care, 1991. *Address:* 9 View Road, N6. *T:* 081–348 1470.

WYNN, Sir (David) Watkin W.; *see* Williams-Wynn.

WYNN, Terence; Member (Lab) Merseyside East, European Parliament, since 1989; *b* 27 June 1946; *s* of Ernest Wynn and Lily (*née* Hitchen); *m* 1967, Doris Ogden; one *s* one *d*. *Educ:* Leigh Technical Coll.; Riversdale Technical Coll., Liverpool (OND); Liverpool Polytechnic (Combined Chief Engrs Cert); Salford Univ. (MSc Manpower Studies and Industrial Relns 1984). Seagoing Marine Engr Officer, MN, 1962–74; Engr Surveyor, ICI, Runcorn, 1975–76; Ship Repair Man., Manchester Dry Docks, 1976–78; Trng Advr, Shipbuilding ITB, 1978–82; Sen. Trng Exec., Marine Trng Assoc., 1982–89. Methodist local preacher, 1978–. *Recreation:* Rugby League supporter. *Address:* 34 Holden Brook Close, Leigh, Lancs WN7 2HL. *Club:* Hindley Green Labour.

WYNN, Terence Bryan; Director, More Publicity, since 1990; Editor, Brentwood News, since 1990; *b* 20 Nov. 1928; *o s* of late Bernard Wynn and Elsie Wynn (*née* Manges); unmarried. *Educ:* St Cuthbert's Grammar Sch., Newcastle upon Tyne. Started as jun. reporter with Hexham Courant, Northumberland, 1945; Blyth News, 1947–48; Shields Evening News, 1948–50; Sunderland Echo, 1950–53; Reporter with Daily Sketch, 1953–58; News Editor, Tyne Tees Television, 1958, then Head of News and Current Affairs, 1960–66; Editorial Planning, BBC Television News, 1966–67; Sen. Press and Information Officer with Land Commn, 1967–71; Sen. Inf. Officer, HM Customs and Excise, 1971–72; Editor, The Universe, 1972–77; Editor, Liberal News, and Head of Liberal Party Orgn's Press Office, 1977–83; Regl Press Officer, MSC, COI, London and SE Region, 1983–85; Editor, Your Court (house jl of Lord Chancellor's Dept), 1985–88. Helped to found and first Editor of Roman Catholic monthly newspaper, Northern Cross. Chm., Catholic Writers' Guild, 1967–70 (Hon. Vice-Pres., 1970); Judge for British Television News Film of the Year Awards, 1961–64; Mem. Mass Media Commn, RC Bishops' Conf. of England and Wales, 1972–83. *Publication:* Walsingham, a modern mystery play, 1975. *Recreations:* reading, writing, talking. *Address:* Bosco Villa, 30 Queen's Road, South Benfleet, Essex SS7 1JW. *T:* South Benfleet (0268) 792033.

WYNN-WILLIAMS, George, MB, BS London; FRCS; FRCOG; Surgeon, Chelsea Hospital for Women; Consulting Obstetrician to City of Westminster; Consulting Gynæcologist, Chelsea Hospital for Women; Consulting Obstetric Surgeon, Queen Charlotte's Hospital; Consulting Gynæcologist to the Civil Service; Teacher in Gynæcology and Obstetrics, London University; *b* 10 Aug. 1911; *er s* of William Wynn-Williams, MRCS, LRCP, and Jane Anderson Brymer, Caernarvon, N Wales; *m* 1943, Penelope, *o d* of 1st and last Earl Jowitt of Stevenage, PC, and Lesley McIntyre; two *s* one *d*. *Educ:* Rossall; King's Coll.; Westminster Hospital. MRCS, LRCP 1937; MB, BS (London) 1937; MRCOG 1941; FRCS 1943; FRCOG 1967. Alfred Hughes Anatomy Prize, King's Coll.; Chadwick Prize in Clinical Surgery, Forensic Medicine and Public Health Prizes, Westminster Hospital. Various appointments 1937–41; Chief Asst and Surgical Registrar and Grade I Surgeon, EMS, 1941–45; Acting Obst. and Gynæcol. Registrar, Westminster Hosp., 1941–46; Surgeon-in-Charge, Mobile Surg. Team to Portsmouth and Southampton, June-Oct. 1944; Chief Asst, Chelsea Hosp. for Women, 1946–47; Obst. Registrar, Queen Charlotte's Hosp., 1946–50; Cons. Obstetrician, Borough of Tottenham; Cons. Gynæcologist, Weir Hosp. Surgical Tutor, Westminster Hosp., 1941–46; Obst. and Gynæcol. Tutor, Westminster Hosp., 1941–48; Lectr and Demonstrator to Postgrad. Students, Queen Charlotte's Hosp., 1946–50; Lectr to Postgrad. Students, Chelsea Women's Hosp., 1946–; Examiner, Central Midwives' Board; Recognized Lectr of London Univ.; Assoc. Examiner in Obst. and Gynæcol., Worshipful Co. of Apothecaries. Woodhull Lectr, Royal Instn, 1978. Member: BMA; Soc. for Study of Fertility; The Pilgrims. FRSM. *Publications:* (jtly) Queen Charlotte's Text Book of Obstetrics; contributions to medical journals, including Human Artificial Insemination, in Hospital Medicine, 1973; Infertile Patients with Positive Immune Fluorescent Serum, 1976; Spermatazoal Antibodies treated with Condom Coitus, 1976; The Woodhull Lecture on Infertility and its Control, 1978. *Recreations:* tennis, shooting, fishing. *Address:* 48 Wimpole Street, W1M 7DG. *T:* 071–487 4866; 39 Hurlingham Court, SW6; The Hall, Wittersham, Isle of Oxney, Kent. *Clubs:* Hurlingham, Chelsea Arts, English-Speaking Union, Oriental; Rye Golf.

WYNNE, Prof. Charles Gorrie, FRS 1970; BA, PhD; Senior Visiting Fellow, Cambridge University Institute of Astronomy, since 1988; *b* 18 May 1911; *s* of C. H. and A. E. Wynne; *m* 1937, Jean Richardson; one *s* one *d* (and one *s* decd). *Educ:* Wyggeston Grammar Sch., Leicester; Exeter Coll., Oxford (Scholar). Optical Designer, Taylor Taylor & Hobson Ltd, 1935–43; Wray (Optical Works) Ltd, 1943–60, latterly Director; Dir, Optical Design Gp, 1960–78, and Sen. Res. Fellow, 1978–87, Imperial Coll., London; Prof. of Optical Design, Univ. of London, 1969–78, now Emeritus. Vis. Prof. Univ. of Durham, 1987–90. Dir, IC Optical Systems, 1970– (Chm., 1975–88). Hon. Sec. (business), Physical Soc., 1947–60; Hon. Sec., Inst. of Physics and Physical Soc., 1960–66. Editor, Optica Acta, 1954–65. Thomas Young Medal, Inst. of Physics, 1971; Gold Medal, Royal Astronomical Soc., 1979; Rumford Medal, Royal Soc., 1982. *Publications:* scientific papers on aberration theory and optical instruments in Proc. Phys. Soc., Mon. Not. RAS, Astrophys. Jl, Optica Acta, etc. *Address:* 4 Holben Close, Barton, Cambs CB3 7AQ. *T:* Cambridge (0223) 263098.

WYNNE, David; sculptor, since 1949; *b* Lyndhurst, Hants, 25 May 1926; *s* of Comdr Charles Edward Wynne and Millicent (*née* Beyts); *m* 1959, Gillian Mary Leslie Bennett (*née* Grant) (*d* 1990); two *s*, and one step *s* one step *d*. *Educ:* Stowe Sch.; Trinity Coll., Cambridge. FZS; FRSA. Served RN, 1944–47: minesweepers and aircraft carriers (Sub-Lieut RNVR). No formal art training. First exhibited at Leicester Galls, 1950, and at Royal Acad., 1952. One-man Exhibitions: Leicester Galls, 1955, 1959; Tooth's Gall., 1964, 1966; Temple Gall., 1964; Findlay Galls, New York, 1967, 1970, 1973; Covent Garden Gall., 1970, 1971; Fitzwilliam Museum, Cambridge, 1972; Pepsico World HQ, New York, 1976; Agnew's Gall., 1983; retrospective, Cannizaro House, 1980; also various mixed exhibns. Large works in public places: Magdalen Coll., Oxford; Malvern Girls' Coll.; Civic Centre, Newcastle upon Tyne; Lewis's, Hanley; Ely Cathedral; Birmingham Cath.; Church of St Paul, Ashford Hill, Berks; Ch. of St Thomas More, Bradford-on-Avon; Mission Ch., Portsmouth; Fountain Precinct, Sheffield; Bowood House, Wilts; Risen Christ and 2 seraphim, west front of Wells Cathedral, 1985; Abbey Gdns, Tresco, Isles of Scilly; London and environs: Albert Bridge; British Oxygen Co., Guildford; Cadogan Place Gardens and Cadogan Sq.; Crystal Palace Park; Guildhall; Longbow House; St Katharine-by-the-Tower; Taylor Woodrow; Wates Ltd, Norbury; also London Road, Kingston-upon-Thames; Elmsleigh Centre, Staines; IPC HQ, Sutton; St Raphael's Hospice, Cheam, Surrey; Central Park, Watford; USA: Ambassador Coll., Texas, and Ambassador Coll., Calif; Atlantic Richfield Oil Co., New Mexico; Lakeland Meml Hosp., Wis; First Fed. Savings, Mass; Pepsico World HQ, Purchase, NY; Playboy Hotel and Casino, Atlantic City, NJ; Sarasota, Fla; Mayo Foundation, Minn; Sherman, Texas; Ritz Carlton, Rancho Mirage, Calif; also Perth, WA, and Place Camelotti, Geneva, 1988. Bronze portrait heads include: Sir Thomas Beecham, 1956; Sir John Gielgud, 1962; Yehudi Menuhin, 1963; The Beatles, 1964; Kokoschka, 1965; Sir Alec Douglas-Home, 1966; Robert, Marquess of Salisbury, 1967; The Prince of Wales, 1969; Lord Baden-Powell, 1971; Virginia Wade, 1972; The Queen, 1973; King Hassan of Morocco, 1973; Air Chief Marshal Lord Dowding, 1974; The Begum Aga Khan, 1975; Pele, 1976; Lord Hailsham, 1977; Prince Michael of Kent, 1977; Earl Mountbatten of Burma, 1981; Paul Daniels, 1982; Jackie Stewart, 1982; Portrait Figures: Arnold Palmer, 1983; Björn Borg, 1984; other sculptures: Fred Perry, AELTC, 1984; Shergar and jockey, 1981; Shareef Dancer and groom, 1984; Cresta Rider, St Moritz, 1985; Two Dolphins, Provence, France, 1986. Designed: Common Market 50 pence piece of clasped hands, 1973; King Hassan, for Moroccan coinage, 1973; the Queen's Silver Jubilee Medal, 1977 (with new effigy of the Queen wearing St Edward's Crown). *Publication:* The Messenger, a sculpture by David Wynne, 1982. *relevant publications:* T. S. R. Boase, The Sculpture of David Wynne 1949–1967, 1968; Graham Hughes, The Sculpture of David Wynne 1968–1974, 1974. *Recreations:* active sports, poetry, music. *Address:* Rushmere, 12 South Side, SW19 4TL. *T:* 081–946 1514. *Clubs:* Garrick, Queen's; Village (Wimbledon); Leander (Henley-on-Thames); 1st and 3rd Trinity Boat; St Moritz Tobogganing; The Royal Tennis Court (Hampton Court Palace).

WYNNE, Col J. F. W.; *see* Williams-Wynne.

WYNNE-EDWARDS, Vero Copner, CBE 1973; MA, DSc; FRS 1970; FRSE, FRSC; Regius Professor of Natural History, University of Aberdeen, 1946–74, Vice Principal, 1972–74; *b* 4 July 1906; 3rd *s* of late Rev. Canon John Rosindale Wynne-Edwards and Lilian Agnes Streatfeild; *m* 1929, Jeannie Campbell, *e d* of late Percy Morris, Devon County Architect; one *s* one *d*. *Educ:* Leeds Grammar Sch.; Rugby Sch.; New Coll., Oxford. 1st Class Hons in Natural Science (Zoology), Oxford, 1927; Senior Scholar of New Coll., 1927–29; Student Probationer, Marine Biological Laboratory, Plymouth, 1927–29; Assistant Lecturer in Zoology, Univ. of Bristol, 1929–30; Asst Prof. of Zoology, McGill Univ., Montreal, 1930–44; Associate Prof., 1944–46. Canadian representative, MacMillan Baffin Island expedition, 1937; Canadian Fisheries Research Board expeditions to Mackenzie River, 1944, and Yukon Territory, 1945; Baird Expedition to Central Baffin Island, 1950. Visiting Prof. of Conservation, University of Louisville, Kentucky, 1959, Commonwealth Universities Interchange Fellow New Zealand, 1962; Leverhulme Emeritus Fellowship, 1978–80. Jt Editor, Journal of Applied Ecology, 1963–68. Member: Nature Conservancy, 1954–57; Red Deer Commn (Vice-Chm.), 1959–68; Royal Commn on Environmental Pollution, 1970–74; President: British Ornithologists' Union, 1965–70; Scottish Marine Biological Assoc., 1967–73; Section D, British Assoc., 1974; Chairman: NERC, 1968–71; DoE and Scottish Office Adv. Cttees on Protection of Birds, 1970–78; Scientific Authority for Animals, DoE, 1976–77. For. Mem., Societas Scientiarum Fennica, 1965; Hon. Mem., British Ecological Soc., 1977. Hon. FIBiol 1980. Hon. DUniv Stirling, 1974; Hon. LLD Aberdeen, 1976. Godman-Salvin Medal, British Ornithologists' Union, 1977; Neill Prize, RSE, 1977; Frink Medal, Zoological Soc., 1980. *Publications:* Animal Dispersion in relation to social behaviour, 1962; Evolution through Group Selection, 1986; (contrib.) Leaders in the Study of Animal Behaviour, ed D. A. Dewsbury, 1985; scientific papers on ornithology (esp. oceanic birds), animal populations. *Recreation:* natural history. *Address:* Ravelston, William Street, Torphins, via Banchory, Aberdeenshire AB31 4JR.

WYNNE MASON, Walter, CMG 1967; MC 1941; *b* 21 March 1910; *y s* of late George and Eva Mason, Wellington, NZ; *m* 1945, Freda Miller, *d* of late Frederick and Lilian Miller, Woodford, Essex; two *s* one *d*. *Educ:* Scots Coll., NZ; Victoria University College, NZ (MA). NZ Govt Education Service 1934–39; served (2nd NZEF in War of 1939–45, UK, Greece, Crete, Libya; NZ War Histories, 1946–48; NZ Diplomatic Service, Paris and London, 1949–54; Commonwealth War Graves Commission: Chief, Middle East, 1954–56; Dep. Dir-Gen., 1956–70; Mem., Sec. of State for Environment's panel of independent Inspectors, 1972–77; retired 1978. *Publications:* Prisoners of War, 1954; (with Philip Longworth and Edmund Blunden) The Unending Vigil: a history of the Commonwealth War Graves Commission, 1967. *Recreations:* lawn tennis, theatre, music. *Address:* Keene House, 10 Hillier Road, Guildford, Surrey GU1 2JQ. *T:* Guildford (0483) 572601.

X

XENAKIS, Iannis; composer, architect, civil engineer; Professor, Université de Paris I (Panthéon-Sorbonne), 1973–89, now Emeritus; *b* Athens, 29 May 1922; *s* of Clearchos Xenakis and Fotini Pavlou; *m* 1953, Françoise Gargouïl; one *d. Educ:* Athens Polytechnic Inst.; Ecole Normale de Musique, Paris; Gravesano; Paris Conservatoire; studied with Milhaud, Scherchen, Messiaen; studied engineering, Athens. DèsL Sorbonne, 1976. Fought in Greek Resistance, war of 1939–45, sentenced to death; exile, France, 1947; with Le Corbusier as engineer and architect, 1947–60. Numerous musical compositions through introd. of mass concept of music, stochastic music, symbolic music, through probability calculus and set theory, including instrumental, electro-acoustic and computerized works; designer of pavilions and spectacles. Numerous academic appts, including Associate Prof., Indiana Univ., Bloomington, USA, 1967–72. Member: Centre Nat. de Recherche Scientifique; Acad. des Beaux Arts, 1983; Nat. Inst. of Arts and Letters; Akademie der Kunste, Berlin and Munich, 1983; For. Mem., Swedish Royal Acad. of Music, 1989; Hon. mem.: Amer. Acad. of Arts and Letters, 1975; Scottish Soc. of Composers, 1987–. Hon. DMus: Edinburgh, 1989; Glasgow, 1990. Maurice Ravel Gold Medal, 1974; Beethoven Prize (FRG), 1977. Officier, Ordre des Arts et des Lettres (France), 1981; Chevalier, Légion d'honneur (France), 1982; Officier, Ordre National du Mérite (France), 1985. *Compositions include: orchestral:* Métastasis, 1954; Stratégie, 1962; Terretektorh, 1966; Nomos Gamma, 1968; Kraanberg (ballet score), 1969; Antikhthon 1971; Erikhthon (pno and orch.), 1974; Noomena, 1974; Jonchaies, 1977; Lichens, 1984; Alax, 1985; Keqrops (pno and orch.), 1986; Horos, 1986; Ata, 1987; Kyania, 1990; Dox-Orkh (violin and orch.), 1991; *vocal and orchestral:* Cendrées, 1973; Anemoessa, 1979; Aïs, 1980, Nekuia, 1981; Kassandra: Oresteïa II, 1987; *Choral:* Oresteïa, 1966; Medea, 1967; Pour la Paix, 1982; *instrumental ensemble:* Atrées, 1960; Eonta, 1963; N'Shima, 1975; Thallein, 1984; Jalons, 1986; Waarg, 1988; *solo instrumental:* Nomos Alpha ('cello), 1966; Persephassa (perc.), 1969; Gmeeoorh (organ), 1974; Khoaï (hpchd), 1976; Pléïades (perc.), 1978; Komboï (hpchd and perc.), 1981; Tetras (strings), 1983; Naama (hpchd), 1984; Tetora (strings), 1990; *electro-acoustic:* Bohor, 1962; Hibiki Hana Ma, 1970; Persepolis, 1971; Polytope de Cluny, 1972; La Légende d'Eer, 1977; Voyage Absolu des Unari vers Andromède, 1989. *Publications:* Musiques Formelles, 1963 (Formalized Music, 1970); Musique Architecture, 1970; Xenakis, les Polytopes, 1975; Arts and Sciences: Alloys, 1979. *Address:* 17 rue Victor Massé, F-75009 Paris, France.

Y

YACOUB, Prof. Magdi Habib, FRCS; Professor of Cardiothoracic Surgery, National Heart and Lung Institute (formerly Cardiothoracic Institute), at Royal Brompton National Heart and Lung Hospital (formerly Brompton Hospital), since 1986; Consultant Cardiothoracic Surgeon, Harefield Hospital, Hillingdon; *b* Cairo, 16 Nov. 1935; *m*; one *s* two *d. Educ:* Cairo University, FRCS, FRCSE, FRCSGlas, 1962; LRCP 1966. Former Asst Prof. of Cardiothoracic Surgery, Chicago Univ.; Cardiac Surgeon, Harefield Hosp., 1969. Has developed innovations in heart and heart-lung transplants. Mem., Soc. Thoracic Surgeons; FRSocMed. *Publications:* papers on pulmonary osteoarthropath, aortic valve homografts, surgical treatment of ischaemic heart disease, valve repairs, and related subjects.

YALE, David Eryl Corbet, FBA 1980; Reader in English Legal History, Cambridge University, since 1969; Fellow, Christ's College, since 1950; *b* 31 March 1928; *s* of Lt-Col J. C. L. Yale and Mrs Beatrice Yale (*née* Breese); *m* 1959, Elizabeth Ann, *d* of C. A. B. Brett, Belfast; two *s. Educ:* Malvern Coll., Worcs; Queens' Coll., Cambridge (BA 1949, LLB 1950, MA 1953). Called to the Bar, Inner Temple, 1951; Asst Lectr and Lectr in Law, Cambridge Univ., 1952–69. Literary Dir, Selden Soc. *Publications:* various, mainly in field of legal history. *Recreation:* fishing. *Address:* Christ's College, Cambridge CB2 3BU. *T:* Cambridge (0223) 334900.

YALOW, Rosalyn Sussman, PhD; Senior Medical Investigator, Veterans Administration, since 1972; *b* 19 July 1921; *d* of Simon Sussman and Clara (*née* Zipper); *m* 1943, Aaron Yalow; one *s* one *d. Educ:* Hunter Coll., NYC (AB Physics and Chemistry, 1941); Univ. of Ill, Urbana (MS Phys. 1942, PhD Phys. 1945). Diplomate, Amer. Bd of Radiol., 1951. Asst in Phys., Univ. of Ill, 1941–43, Instr, 1944–45; Lectr and Temp. Asst Prof. in Phys., Hunter Coll., 1946–50. Veterans Admin Hospital, Bronx, NY: Consultant, Radioisotope Unit, 1947–50; Physicist and Asst Chief, Radioisotope Service, 1950–70 (Actg Chief, 1968–70); Chief, Nuclear Medicine Service, 1970–80; Dir, Solomon A. Berson Res. Lab. 1973–; Chm., Dept of Clin. Scis, Montefiore Hosp. and Med. Center, Bronx, NY, 1980–85; Chief, VA Radioimmunoassay Ref. Lab., 1969–. Consultant, Lenox Hill Hosp., NYC, 1952–62. Res. Prof., Dept of Med., Mt Sinai Sch. of Med., 1968–74, Distinguished Service Prof., 1974–79; Distinguished Prof.-at-Large, Albert Einstein Coll. of Med., Yeshiva Univ., NY, 1979–85, Prof. Emeritus, 1985–; Solomon A. Berson Distinguished Prof.-at-Large, Mt Sinai Sch. of Medicine, City Univ. of NY, 1986–. IAEA Expert, Instituto Energia Atomica, Brazil, 1970; WHO Consultant, Radiation Med. Centre, India, 1978; Sec., US Nat. Cttee on Med. Physics, 1969–72; Member: President's Study Gp on Careers for Women, 1966–67; Med. Adv. Bd, Nat. Pituitary Agency, 1968–71; Endocrinol. Study Sect., Nat. Insts of Health, 1969–72; Cttee for Evaluation of NPA, Nat. Res. Council, 1973–74; Council, Endocrine Soc., 1974–80 (Koch Award, 1972; Pres., 1978); Bd of Dirs, NY Diabetes Assoc., 1974–77. Member: Editorial Adv. Council, Acta Diabetologica Latina, 1975–77; Ed. Adv. Bd, Encyclopaedia Universalis, 1978–; Ed. Bd, Mt Sinai Jl of Medicine, 1976–79; Ed. Bd, Diabetes, 1976–79. Fellow: NY Acad. of Sciences (Chm., Biophys. Div., 1964–65; A. Cressy Morrison Award in Nat. Sci., 1975); Radiation Res. Soc.; Amer. Assoc. of Physicists in Med.; Biophys. Soc.; Amer. Endocrine Assoc. (Eli Lilly Award), 1961; Commemorative Medallion, 1972; Banting Medal, 1978; Rosalyn S. Yalow Res. and Develt Award estabd 1978); Amer. Physiol. Soc.; Soc. of Nuclear Med. Associate Fellow in Phys., Amer. Coll. of Radiol. Member: Nat. Acad. of Sciences; Amer. Acad. Arts and Sciences; Foreign Associate, French Acad. of Medicine. Hon. DSc and Hon. DHumLett from univs and med. colls in the US, France, Argentina, Canada. Nobel Prize in Physiology or Medicine, 1977; VA Exceptional Service Award, 1975 and 1978; Nat. Medal of Sci., 1988. Has given many distinguished lectures and received many awards and prizes from univs and med. socs and assocs. *Publications:* over 400 papers and contribns to books, research reports, proceedings of conferences and symposia on radioimmunoassay of peptide hormones and related subjects, since 1950. *Address:* VA Medical Center, Bronx, NY 10468, USA. *T:* (212) 579 1644.

YAMAZAKI, Toshio; Corporate Advisor, Mitsubishi Corporation, Tokyo, since 1988; Japanese Ambassador to the Court of St James's, 1985–88; retired; *b* 13 Aug. 1922; *s* of Takamaro Yamazaki and Konoe Yamazaki; *m* 1955, Yasuko Arakawa; one *s* one *d. Educ:* Tokyo University (Faculty of Law). 2nd Sec., Japanese Embassy, London, 1955–59; Dir, British Commonwealth Div., European and Oceanic Affairs Bureau, Min. of Foreign Affairs, 1962–64; Counsellor, Permt Mission to UN, New York; 1964–67; Dir, Financial Affairs Div., Minister's Secretariat, Min. of Foreign Affairs, 1967–70; Dep. Dir-Gen., Treaties Bureau, 1970; Minister, Washington, 1971–74; Dir-Gen., Amer. Affairs Bureau, Min. of Foreign Affairs, 1974–77; Dep. Vice-Minister for Admin, 1978–80; Ambassador to Egypt, 1980–82, to Indonesia, 1982–84. Chm., Japan-British Soc., Tokyo, 1988–. Order of Republic, 1st cl. (Egypt), 1982; Banda 2nd cl., Orden del Aguila Azteca (Mexico), 1978; Grosses Verdienstkreuz mit Stern (FRG), 1979. *Recreation:* golf. *Address:* 9-1-506 Sanban-Cho, Chiyoda-Ku, Tokyo 102, Japan. *T:* 03–3288–1458. *Clubs:* Tokyo (Tokyo); Tokyo Golf.

YAMEY, Prof. Basil Selig, CBE 1972; FBA 1977; Professor of Economics, University of London, 1960–84, now Emeritus; Member (part-time), Monopolies and Mergers Commission, 1966–78; *b* 4 May 1919; *s* of Solomon and Leah Yamey; *m* 1948, Helen Bloch (*d* 1980); one *s* one *d. Educ:* Tulbagh High Sch.; Univ. of Cape Town; LSE. Lectr in Commerce, Rhodes Univ., 1945; Senior Lectr in Commerce, Univ. of Cape Town, 1946; Lectr in Commerce, LSE, 1948; Associate Prof. of Commerce, McGill Univ., 1949; Reader in Economics, Univ. of London, 1950. Dir, Private Bank and Trust Co. Ltd, 1989–. Managing Trustee, IEA, 1986–91. Trustee: National Gall., 1974–81; Tate Gall., 1979–81; Member: Council, National Trust, 1979–81; Museums and Galls Commn, 1983–84; Cinematograph Films Council, 1969–73. Mem. Committee of Management: Courtauld Inst., 1981–84; Warburg Inst., 1981–84; Mem., Governing Body, London Business Sch., 1965–84. *Publications:* Economics of Resale Price Maintenance, 1954; (jt editor) Studies in History of Accounting, 1956; (with P. T. Bauer) Economics of Under-developed Countries, 1957; (jt editor) Capital, Saving and Credit in Peasant Societies, 1963; (with H. C. Edey and H. Thomson) Accounting in England and Scotland, 1543–1800, 1963; (with R. B. Stevens) The Restrictive Practices Court, 1965; (ed) Resale Price Maintenance, 1966; (with P. T. Bauer) Markets, Market Control and Marketing Reform: Selected Papers, 1968; (ed) Economics of Industrial Structure, 1973; (jt editor) Economics of Retailing, 1973; (jt editor) Debits, Credits, Finance and Profits, 1974; (with B. A. Goss) Economics of Futures Trading, 1976; Essays on the History of Accounting, 1978; (jt editor) Stato e Industria in Europa: Il Regno Unito, 1979; Further Essays on the

History of Accounting, 1983; Arte e Contabilità, 1986; Análisis Económico de los Mercados, 1987; Art and Accounting, 1989; articles on economics, economic history and law in learned journals. *Address:* 36 Hampstead Way, NW11 7JL. *T:* 081–455 5810.

YANG, Chen Ning; physicist, educator; Einstein Professor and Director, Institute for Theoretical Physics, State University of New York at Stony Brook, New York, since 1966; *b* Hofei, China, 22 Sept. 1922; *s* of Ke Chuen Yang and Meng Hwa Lo; *m* 1950, Chih Li Tu; two *s* one *d.* Naturalized 1964. *Educ:* National Southwest Associated Univ., Kunming, China (BSc), 1942; University of Chicago (PhD), 1948. Institute for Advanced Study, Princeton, NJ: Member, 1949–55; Prof. of Physics, 1955–65; several DSc's from universities. Member of Board: Rockefeller Univ., 1970–76; AAAS, 1976–80; Salk Inst., 1978–; Ben Gurion Univ.; Member: Amer. Phys. Soc.; Nat. Acad. Sci.; Amer. Philos. Soc., Sigma Xi; Brazilian, Venezuelan and Royal Spanish Acads of Sci. Nobel Prize in Physics, 1957; Einstein Commemorative Award in Sciences, 1957; Rumford Prize, 1980; Nat. Medal of Science, 1986. *Publications:* contrib. to Physical Review, Reviews of Modern Physics. *Address:* (home) 14 Woodhull Cove, Setauket, New York 11733, USA; (office) State University of New York at Stony Brook, NY 11790, USA.

YANG SHANGKUN; President of the People's Republic of China, since 1988; *b* Tongnan County, Sichuan Province, 1907; *m* Li Bozhao (decd), playwright. *Educ:* Sun Yat-sen Univ., Moscow. Joined Communist Youth League, 1925, and Communist Party, 1926; formerly: Head of Propaganda Department: All-China Fedn of Trade Unions, Shanghai (also Sec. of Party Orgn); Communist Party's Jiangsu Provincial Cttee; Communist Party's Central Cttee; Editor, Red China newspaper; Dep. Head, Communist Party's sch., Jiangxi; Dir, Political Dept, First Front Army of Red Army; Dep. Dir, Gen. Pol Dept, Red Army; Pol Commisar, Third Red Army Corps; Long March, Oct. 1934–Oct. 1935; Chinese Communist Party's Central Committee: successively: Sec., N Bureau, 1937; Sec.-Gen., Mil. Commn, 1945; Dir, Gen. Office; Dep. Sec.-Gen.; Alternate Mem. of Secretariat; Mem. Secretariat, Guangdong Provincial Party Cttee; removed from posts and imprisoned during Cultural Revolution, 1966–76; successively: Second Sec., Guangdong Provincial Party Cttee; Vice-Gov., Guangdong; First Sec., Guangzhou City Party Cttee; Chm., Guangzhou City Revolutionary Cttee; Vice-Chm. and Sec.-Gen., Standing Cttee, Nat. People's Congress, 1980; Exec. Vice-Chm., 1982–, First Vice-Chm., 1989–, Mil. Commn of Party Central Cttee (Sec.-Gen., 1980–81); Mem., Pol Bureau, 1982–. *Recreations:* sports, especially swimming. *Address:* Office of the President, Zhongnanhai, Beijing, People's Republic of China.

YANG, Hon. Sir Ti Liang, Kt 1988; **Hon. Mr Justice Yang;** Chief Justice of Hong Kong, since 1988; President of the Court of Appeal of Negara Brunei Darussalam, since 1988; *b* 30 June 1929; *s* of late Shao-nan Yang and Elsie (*née* Chun); *m* 1954, Eileen Barbara (*née* Tam); two *s. Educ:* The Comparative Law Sch. of China; Soochow Univ., Shanghai; UCL (LLB Hons 1953; Fellow 1989). Called to the Bar (with honours), Gray's Inn, 1954, Hon. Bencher, 1988. Magistrate, Hong Kong, 1956; Sen. Magistrate, 1963; Rockefeller Fellow, London Univ., 1963–64; District Judge, Dist Court, 1968; Judge of the High Court, Hong Kong, 1975; Justice of Appeal, Hong Kong, 1980. Chairman: Kowloon Disturbances Claims Assessment Bd, 1966, Compensation Bd, 1967; Commn of Inquiry into the Rainstorm Disasters, 1972; Commn of Inquiry into the Leung Wing-sang Case, 1976; Commn of Inquiry into the MacLennan Case, 1980; Mem., Law Reform Commn, 1980– (Chm., Sub-cttee on law relating to homosexuality, 1980). Mem., Chinese Lang. Cttee (Chm. Legal Sub-cttee), 1970. Vice Chm., Hong Kong Sea Cadet Corps; Hon. President: Hong Kong Scouts Assoc.; Hong Kong Discharged Prisoners' Aid Soc.; Soc. Against Child Abuse. Chairman: University and Polytechnic Grants Cttee, 1981–84; Hong Kong Univ. Council, 1985–. Hon. LLD Chinese Univ. of Hong Kong, 1984; Hon. DLitt Hong Kong Univ., 1991. SPMB Negara Brunei Darussalam, 1990; Order of Chivalry, First Class. *Recreations:* philately, reading, walking, oriental ceramics, travelling, music. *Address:* Supreme Court, Hong Kong. *T:* Hong Kong 8254601; Flat 45, Grove Hall Court, 2–4 Hall Road, St John's Wood, NW8. *Clubs:* Athenæum; Hong Kong, Hong Kong Country, Royal Hong Kong Jockey (Hong Kong).

YANKOV, Alexander; Professor of International Law, Sofia State University, 1968; *b* 22 June 1924; *m* 1949, Eliza; one *s* one *d. Educ:* Sofia State Univ. Law Sch. (PhD Internat. Law); Hague Acad. of Internat. Law. Asst Prof. of Internat. Law, 1951–54, Associate Prof. 1957–64, Sofia State Univ. Sec., Internat. Union of Students, Prague, 1954–57; Counsellor, Perm. Mission of Bulgaria to UN, mem. delegns to sessions of UN Gen. Assembly, 1965–68; Vice-Chm., UN Cttee on Peaceful Uses of Sea-bed, 1968–73; Ambassador of Bulgaria to Court of St James's, 1972–76; Dep. Minister for Foreign Affairs, 1976; Ambassador and Perm. Rep. to UN, 1977–80. Mem., Perm. Court of Arbitration at The Hague, 1971; Mem. Court of Arbitration to Bulgarian Chamber of Commerce, 1970–. Mem., Bulgarian Nat. Assembly, 1986–91; Minister of Science and Higher Education, 1989–90. Vice-Pres., Bulgarian Acad. of Scis., 1986–. Pres., 8th Assembly, IMCO, 1973–75; Head of Bulgarian Delegn, 3rd UN Conf. on Law of the Sea; Chm., 3rd Cttee, UN Conf. on Law of the Sea, NY 1973, Caracas 1974, Geneva 1975, NY 1976, 1977, 1982; Chm., 4th Cttee, London Conf. on Marine Pollution by Ships, 1973; Vice-Chm., Intergovtl Oceanographic Commn, UNESCO, 1987–91; Member: Exec. Council, Internat. Law Assoc., 1973–; Internat. Law Commn, 1977–. Order 9 Sept. 1944, 1959; Order of Freedom of the People, 1960; Order of Cyril and Methodius, 1962; Order of People's Republic of Bulgaria, 1974 (all Bulgaria). *Publications:* The European Collective Security System, 1958; Reservations to the Declaration of Acceptance of Compulsory Jurisdiction of the International Court of Justice, 1961; The Peace Treaty with the Two German States and its Legal Effects, 1962; Principles of International Law as Applied to the Treaty Practice of Bulgaria, 1964; The United Nations: Legal Status and International Personality, 1965; Exploration and Uses of the Sea-bed: a new legal framework, 1970; United Nations Declaration on Principles of Friendly Relations and Progressive Development of International Law, 1971; United Nations and Development of International Trade Law, 1971, etc. *Recreations:* theatre, swimming. *Address:* Sofia State University, Ruski 15, Sofia, Bulgaria; Complex Lenin, Block 73, 1111–Sofia, Bulgaria.

YAPP, Sir Stanley Graham, Kt 1975; Chairman, West Midlands County Council, 1983–84 (Leader, 1973–77; Vice-Chairman, 1982–83); Member, Birmingham City Council, later Birmingham District Council, 1961–77 (Leader, 1972–74); *s* of late William and of Elsie Yapp; *m* 1961, Elisbeth Wise (marr. diss.); one *d*; *m* 1974, Carol Matheson (marr. diss.); one *s*; *m* 1983, Christine Horton. Member, West Midlands Economic Planning Council (Chm., Transport Cttee); Member many bodies both local and national, inc.: Vice-Chm. LAMSAC; Member: Local Govt Trng Board; Nat. Jt Councils on pay and conditions; AMA; BR Adv. Bd, Midlands and N Western Reg., 1977–79; Chm., West Midlands Planning Authorities Conf., 1973–75, Vice-Chm. 1975–77. Governor, BFI, 1977–79. FBIM. *Publications:* contribs to Local Government Chronicle, Municipal Journal, Rating and Valuation. *Recreations:* astronomy, reading walking. *Address:* 172 York Road, Hall Green, Birmingham B28 8LE.

YARBOROUGH, 8th Earl of, *cr* 1837; **Charles John Pelham;** Baron Yarborough, 1794; Baron Worsley, 1837; *b* 5 Nov. 1963; *o s* of 7th Earl of Yarborough and Ann, *d* of late John Herbert Upton; *S* father, 1991; *m* 1990, Anna-Karin Zecevic, *d* of George Zecevic; one *s. Heir: s* Lord Worsley, *qv. Address:* Brocklesby Park, Habrough, South Humberside DN37 8PL.

YARBURGH-BATESON; *see* de Yarburgh-Bateson, family name of Baron Deramore.

YARDE-BULLER, family name of **Baron Churston.**

YARDLEY, Prof. David Charles Miller; Chairman, Commission for Local Administration in England, since 1982; *b* 4 June 1929; *s* of late Geoffrey Miller Yardley and Doris Woodward Yardley (*née* Jones); *m* 1954, Patricia Anne Tempest Olver; two *s* two *d. Educ:* The Old Hall Sch., Wellington; Ellesmere Coll., Shropshire; Univ. of Birmingham (LLB, LLD); Univ. of Oxford (MA, DPhil). Called to Bar, Gray's Inn, 1952. RAF Flying Officer (nat. service), 1949–51. Bigelow Teaching Fellow, Univ. of Chicago, 1953–54; Fellow and Tutor in Jurisprudence, St Edmund Hall, Oxford, 1953–74, Emeritus Fellow, 1974–; CUF Lectr, Univ. of Oxford, 1954–74; Sen. Proctor, Univ. of Oxford, 1965–66; Barber Prof. of Law, Univ. of Birmingham, 1974–78; Head of Dept of Law, Politics and Economics, Oxford Poly., 1978–80; Rank Foundn Prof. of Law, University Coll. at Buckingham, 1980–82. Visiting Prof. of Law, Univ. of Sydney, 1971. Constitutional Consultant, Govt of W Nigeria, 1956; Chm., Thames Valley Rent Tribunal, 1963–82; Vice-Pres., Cambs Chilterns and Thames Rent Assessment Panel, 1966–82; Oxford City Councillor, 1966–74; Chairman: Oxford Area Nat. Ins. Local Appeal Tribunal, 1969–82; Oxford Preservation Trust, 1989–. Chm. of Governors, St Helen's Sch., Abingdon, 1967–81. FRSA. Freeman, City of Oxford, 1989. *Publications:* Introduction to British Constitutional Law, 1960, 7th edn, 1990; A Source Book of English Administrative Law, 1963, 2nd edn, 1970; The Future of the Law, 1964; Geldart's Elements of English Law, 7th edn, 1966–10th edn (as Geldart's Introduction to English Law), 1991; Hanbury's English Courts of Law, 4th edn, 1967; Hanbury and Yardley, English Courts of Law, 5th edn, 1979; Principles of Administrative Law, 1981, 2nd edn, 1986; (with I. N. Stevens) The Protection of Liberty, 1982. *Recreations:* lawn tennis, squash racquets, opera, cats. *Address:* 9 Belbroughton Road, Oxford OX2 6UZ. *T:* Oxford (0865) 54831. *Club:* Royal Air Force.

YARMOUTH, Earl of; Henry Jocelyn Seymour; *b* 6 July 1958; *s* and *heir* of 8th Marquess of Hertford, *qv*; *m* 1990, Beatriz, *d* of Jorge Karam.

YARNOLD, Rev. Edward John, SJ; DD; Tutor in Theology, Campion Hall, Oxford, since 1964 (Master, 1965–72; Senior Tutor, 1972–74); *b* 14 Jan. 1926; *s* of Edward Cabré Yarnold and Agnes (*née* Deakin). *Educ:* St Michael's Coll., Leeds; Campion Hall, Oxford (MA); Heythrop College (STL). Taught classics at St Francis Xavier's Coll., Liverpool, 1954–57; ordained, 1960; taught classics at St Michael's Coll., Leeds, 1962–64; Res. Lectr, Oxford Univ., 1991–. Sarum Lectr, Univ. of Oxford, 1972–73; Lectr (part-time), Heythrop Coll., London, 1978–80; Vis. Prof., Univ. of Notre Dame, 1982–. Assoc. Gen. Sec., Ecumenical Soc. of Blessed Virgin Mary, 1975–; Mem., Anglican-Roman Catholic Internat. Commn, 1970–81 and 1983–91; Pres., Catholic Theol. Assoc. of GB, 1986–88. Order of St Augustine, 1981. *Publications:* The Theology of Original Sin, 1971; The Awe-Inspiring Rites of Initiation, 1972; The Second Gift, 1974; (with H. Chadwick) Truth and Authority, 1977; (ed jtly and contrib.) The Study of Liturgy, 1978; They are in Earnest, 1982; Eight Days with the Lord, 1984; (ed jtly and contrib.) The Study of Spirituality, 1986; In Search of Unity, 1989; Time for God, 1991; articles in learned jls. *Recreations:* opera, cricket. *Address:* Campion Hall, Oxford OX1 1QS. *T:* Oxford (0865) 726811 or 240861, *Fax:* Oxford (0865) 798001.

YARNOLD, Patrick; HM Diplomatic Service; Consul-General, Hamburg, since 1990; *b* 21 March 1937; *s* of late Leonard Francis Yarnold and Gladys Blanche Yarnold (*née* Merry); *m* 1961, Caroline, *er d* of late Andrew J. Martin; two *d. Educ:* Bancroft's School. HM Forces, 1955–57. Joined HM Foreign (now Diplomatic) Service, 1957; served: FO, 1957–60; Addis Ababa, 1961–64; Belgrade, 1964–66; FO (later FCO), 1966–70; 1st Sec., Head of Chancery, Bucharest, 1970–73; 1st Sec. (Commercial), Bonn, 1973–76; FCO, 1976–79; Counsellor (Economic and Commercial), Brussels, 1980–83; Consul-Gen., Zagreb, 1983–85; Counsellor and Head of Chancery, Belgrade, 1985–87; Hd of Defence Dept, FCO, 1987–90. *Recreations:* travel, photography, walking, genealogy, local history, Chinese cooking, etc. *Address:* c/o Foreign and Commonwealth Office, SW1A 2AH.

YARRANTON, Peter George; Chairman, Sports Council, since 1989; General Manager, Lensbury Club, since 1978; *b* 30 Sept. 1924; *s* of late Edward John Yarranton and Norah Ellen (*née* Atkins); *m* 1947, Mary Avena (*née* Flowitt); one *s* one *d. Educ:* Willesden Technical Coll. Prelim. ARIBA. Joined RAF, 1942; commnd 1944; Flying Officer, 1945; Flt Lieut, 1949; voluntarily retd, 1957. Shell Mex & BP Ltd: management trainee, 1957–58; Ops Officer, Reading, 1958–61; UK Indust. Relations Officer, 1961–63; i/c Indust. Relations, 1963–66; Manager, Indust. Relations, 1966–69; Regional Ops Manager, SE Region, 1969–75; Manager, Plant and Engrg, Distbn Div., Shell UK Oil, 1975–77. Founder Dir, London Docklands Arena Ltd, 1984–; Governor: Sports Aid Foundn, 1989–; London Marathon Ltd, 1989–; Trustee, Golden Globe Charity Trust, 1990–. Mem., Recreation Managers Assoc., 1979–; Pres., Rugby Football Union, 1991–July 1992 (Public Relations Advr to the Union, 1983–91; Vice Pres., 1989–91); President: Mddx County RFU, 1986–88; Lensbury RFC; Wasps FC, 1982–85; England Internat. (5 caps), Rugby Union Football: *v* Ireland, New Zealand and Wales, 1954, Scotland and France 1955; played for and captained Barbarians, London, Mddx, Wasps, British Combined Services, and RAF Rugby Clubs; formerly: Mem., London and Mddx Premier Swimming and Water Polo Teams; Captain, RAF Swimming and Water Polo Teams. Freeman, City of London, 1977; Liveryman, Worshipful Co. of Gold and Silver Wyre Drawers, 1977 (Mem., Court of Assts, 1987). FBIM 1980; FIPM 1975. Mem. Editorial Bd, Rugby World and Post, 1983–. *Recreations:* all sports, indoor and outdoor, particularly Rugby, soccer, cricket, swimming, water polo and sub-aqua diving. *Address:* Lensbury Club, Broom Road, Teddington, Mddx TW11 9NU. *T:* 081–977 8821; 2 Sunnydale Villas, Durlston Road, Swanage, Dorset BH19 2HY. *Clubs:* East India, Royal Air Force, Rugby, Cricketers.

YARROW, Dr Alfred, FFPHM; Honorary Member, Epidemiology Unit, Ministry of Health, Jerusalem, since 1987; *b* 25 May 1924; *s* of Leah and step *s* of Philip Yarrow; *m* 1953, Sheila Kaufman; two *d. Educ:* Hackney Downs Grammar Sch.; Edinburgh Univ. (MB, ChB); London Sch. of Hygiene and Trop. Medicine (Hons DPH). Foundn FFCM (now FFPHM) 1972. Dep. Area MO, Tottenham and Hornsey, 1955–60; Area MO, SE Essex, 1960–65; MOH, Gateshead, 1965–68; Dir, Scottish Health Educn Unit, 1968–73; SMO, 1973–77, SPMO, 1977–84, DHSS. Temp. Consultant, WHO, 1975–76. Brit. Council Lectr, 1975; Council of Europe Fellow, 1978. *Publications:* So Now You Know About Smoking, 1975; Politics, Society and Preventive Medicine, 1986; scientific papers on demography, epidemiology, preventive medicine and health educn. *Recreations:* lawn bowls, travelling, reading. *Address:* 9/4 Nof Harim, Jerusalem 96190, Israel. *T:* 438792.

YARROW, Sir Eric Grant, 3rd Bt, *cr* 1916; MBE (mil.) 1946; DL; Chairman, Clydesdale Bank PLC, 1985–91 (Director 1962–91, Deputy Chairman, 1975–85); Director: Standard Life Assurance Co., 1958–91; National Australia Bank Ltd, 1987–91; *b* 23 April 1920; *o s* of Sir Harold Yarrow, 2nd Bt and 1st wife, Eleanor Etheldreda (*d* 1934); *S* father, 1962;

m 1st, 1951, Rosemary Ann (*d* 1957), *yr d* of late H. T. Young, Roehampton, SW15; (one *s* decd); 2nd, 1959, Annette Elizabeth Françoise (marr. diss. 1975), *d* of late A. J. E. Steven, Ardgay; three *s* (including twin *s*); 3rd, 1982, Mrs Joan Botting, *d* of late R. F. Masters, Piddinghoe, Sussex. *Educ:* Marlborough Coll.; Glasgow Univ. Served apprenticeship, G. & J. Weir Ltd. Served Burma, 1942–45; Major RE, 1945. Asst Manager Yarrow & Co., 1946; Dir, 1948; Man. Dir, 1958–67; Chm., 1962–85; Pres., Yarrow PLC, 1985–87. Mem. Council, RINA, 1957–; Vice-Pres., 1965; Hon. Vice-Pres., 1972. Mem., General Cttee, Lloyd's Register of Shipping, 1960–87; Prime Warden, Worshipful Co. of Shipwrights, 1970; Deacon, Incorporation of Hammermen of Glasgow, 1961–62; Retired Mem. Council, Institution of Engineers & Shipbuilders in Scotland; Mem. Council, Inst. of Directors, 1983–90. Pres., Scottish Convalescent Home for Children, 1957–70; Hon. Pres., Princess Louise Scottish Hospital at Erskine, 1986– (Chm., 1980–86). President: Smeatonian Soc. of Civil Engineers, 1983; Marlburian Club, 1984; Scottish Area, Burma Star Assoc., 1990–; Chm., Blythe Sappers, 1989. DL Renfrewshire, 1970. OStJ. *Recreations:* golf, shooting, family life. *Heir: g s* Ross William Grant Yarrow, *b* 14 Jan. 1985. *Address:* Cloak, Kilmacolm, Renfrewshire PA13 4SD. *T:* Kilmacolm (050587) 2067. *Clubs:* Army and Navy; Royal Scottish Automobile.

YARWOOD, Michael Edward, OBE 1976; entertainer, since 1962; *b* 14 June 1941; *s* of Wilfred and Bridget Yarwood; *m* 1969, Sandra Burville; two *d*. *Educ:* Bredbury Secondary Modern Sch., Cheshire. First television appearance, 1963; *BBC TV:* Three of a Kind, 1967; Look—Mike Yarwood, and Mike Yarwood in Persons (series), 1971–82; *ATV:* Will the Real Mike Yarwood Stand Up? (series), 1968; *Thames:* Mike Yarwood in Persons, 1983–84; Yarwood's Royal Variety Show, the Yarwood Chat Show, and Mike Yarwood in Persons, 1986. Royal Variety performances, 1968, 1972, 1976, 1981, 1987. Variety Club of Gt Britain award for BBC TV Personality of 1973; Royal Television Society award for outstanding creative achievement in front of camera, 1978. Mem., Grand Order of Water Rats, 1968. *Publications:* And This Is Me, 1974; Impressions of my life (autobiog.), 1986. *Recreations:* golf, tennis. *Address:* Oxshott, Surrey. *Club:* Lord's Taverners.

YASS, Irving; Under Secretary, Department of Transport, since 1982; *b* 20 Dec. 1935; *s* of late Abraham and Fanny Yass; *m* 1962, Marion Leighton; two *s* one *d*. *Educ:* Harrow County Grammar School for Boys; Balliol Coll., Oxford (Brackenbury Schol.; BA). Assistant Principal, Min. of Transport and Civil Aviation, 1958; Private Sec. to Joint Parliamentary Secretary, 1960; HM Treasury, 1967–70; Asst Secretary, Dept of the Environment, 1971; Secretary, Cttee of Inquiry into Local Govt Finance, 1974–76; Dept of Transport, 1976–. *Address:* Department of Transport, 2 Marsham Street, SW1. *T:* 071–276 6089.

YASSUKOVICH, Stanislas Michael, Hon. CBE 1991; Director, Merrill Lynch Europe Ltd (Chairman, 1985–89); Chairman: Flextech plc, since 1989; Cragnotti & Partners Capital Investment UK, since 1991; *b* 5 Feb. 1935; *s* of Dimitri and Denise Yassukovich; *m* 1961, Diana (*née* Townsend); two *s* one *d*. *Educ:* Deerfield Academy; Harvard University. US Marine Corps, 1957–61. Joined White, Weld & Co., 1961: posted to London, 1962; Branch Manager, 1967; General Partner, 1969; Managing Director, 1969; European Banking Co. Ltd: Managing Director, 1973; Group Dep. Chm., 1983. Sen. Advr, Merrill Lynch & Co., 1989–90; Dir, Merrill Lynch Europe Ltd, 1985–90 (Chm., 1985–89); Director: Bristol & West Building Soc., 1991–; ABC Internat. Bank, 1991–. Jt Dep. Chm., Internat. Stock Exchange, 1986–89; Chm., Securities Assoc., 1988–91. Chm., City Res. Project, 1991–. *Publications:* articles in financial press. *Recreations:* hunting, shooting, polo. *Address:* Cragnotti & Partners, 25 St James's Street, SW1A 1HG. *T:* 071–839 3551. *Clubs:* Buck's, Turf; Travellers' (Paris); Brook, Union (New York).

YATES, Alfred, CBE 1983; FBPsS; Director, National Foundation for Educational Research in England and Wales, 1972–83; *b* 17 Nov. 1917; *s* of William Oliver Yates and Frances Yates; *m* 1st, 1943, Joan Mary Lawrence-Fellows (*d* 1987); one *s* one *d*; 2nd, 1989, Elsie Roberts. *Educ:* Farnworth Grammar Sch.; Sheffield Univ. (BA); Oxford Univ. (MA); QUB (MEd). FBPsS 1957. Served War, Army, 1940–46: Captain, REME. Schoolmaster, Launceston Coll., Cornwall, 1939–40; Lectr, QUB, 1946–51; Sen. Res. Officer, NFER, 1951–59; Sen. Tutor, Dept of Educnl Studies, Oxford Univ., 1959–72. FCP 1981. *Publications:* Admission to Grammar Schools, 1957; Grouping in Education, 1966; An Introduction to Educational Measurement, 1968; The Role of Research in Educational Change, 1971; The Organisation of Schooling, 1971. *Recreations:* reading, theatre, watching Association football and cricket. *Address:* 14 Craighall Road, Bolton BL1 7HH. *T:* Bolton (0204) 595642.

YATES, Anne; see Yates, E. A.

YATES, Edgar; see Yates, W. E.

YATES, (Edith) Anne, (Mrs S. J. Yates), CBE 1972; *b* 21 Dec. 1912; *d* of William Blakeman and Frances Dorothea (*née* Thacker); *m* 1935, Stanley James Yates (*d* 1990); two *s* one *d*. *Educ:* Barrs' Hill Girls' Sch., Coventry. County Councillor, 1955–, County Alderman, 1966, Notts; Chm., Notts CC, Feb. 1968–March 1974. Mem., BTEC Bd for Distribution, Hotel and Catering and Leisure Services, 1984–. Chairman: Midlands Tourist Bd, 1971–76; E Midlands Sports Council, 1972–77; Indep. Chm., Nat. Cttee on Recreation Management Trng, 1976–82 (Yates Report, 1984); Member: Sports Council, 1971–74; E Midlands Council of Sport and Recreation, 1977–82; MSC, 1974–76; East Midlands Regional MSC, 1977–82; English Tourist Bd, 1975–78; Nat. Water Council, 1973–79 (Chm., Water Training Cttee, 1973–79). Life Vice Pres., Inst. of Trading Standards Admin, 1965. Chm., Notts Internat. Rowing Regatta, 1987–90; Chm., Sports Aid Foundn (E Midlands), 1990–. *Recreations:* reading, music, theatre. *Address:* Manor Close, Rolleston, Newark, Notts. *T:* Southwell (0636) 813362.

YATES, Frank, CBE 1963; ScD; FRS 1948; Honorary Scientist, Rothamsted Experimental Station, since 1968 (formerly Head of Statistics Department and Agricultural Research Statistical Service, and Deputy Director); *b* 1902; *s* of Percy and Edith Yates, Didsbury, Manchester; *m* 1939, Pauline (*d* 1976), *d* of Vladimir Shoubersky; *m* 1981, Ruth, *d* of William James Hunt, Manchester. *Educ:* Clifton; St John's Coll., Cambridge. Research Officer and Mathematical Adviser, Gold Coast Geodetic Survey, 1927–31; Rothamsted Experimental Station, 1931, Dept of Statistics, 1933, Agric. Res. Statistical Service, 1947, Dep. Dir, 1958; Scientific Adviser to various Mins, UNO, FAO, 1939–; Wing Comdr (Hon.) RAF, 1943–45; Mem. UN Sub-Commn on Statistical Sampling, 1947–52. Sen. Res. Fellow, Imperial Coll., 1969–74; Sen. Vis. Fellow, Imperial Coll., 1974–77. Pres., British Computer Society, 1960–61; Pres., Royal Statistical Society, 1967–68. Royal Medal of the Royal Society, 1966. Hon. DSc London, 1982. *Publications:* Design and Analysis of Factorial Experiments, 1937; (with R. A. Fisher) Statistical Tables for Biological, Medical and Agricultural Research, 1938 (6th edn 1963); Sampling Methods for Censuses and Surveys, 1949 (4th edn 1981); Experimental Design: Selected Papers, 1970. Numerous scientific papers. *Recreation:* mountaineering. *Address:* Stackyard, Rothamsted, Harpenden, Herts AL5 2BQ. *T:* Harpenden (0582) 712732.

YATES, Ian Humphrey Nelson, CBE 1991; Director, 1989–90, Chief Executive, 1975–90, The Press Association Ltd; *b* 24 Jan. 1931; *s* of James Nelson Yates and Martha (*née* Nutter); *m* 1956, Daphne J. Hudson, MCSP; three *s*. *Educ:* Lancaster Royal Grammar Sch.; Canford Sch., Wimborne. Royal Scots Greys, Germany and ME (National Service Commn), 1951–53. Management Trainee, Westminster Press Ltd, 1953–58 (Westmorland Gazette, and Telegraph & Argus, Bradford); Asst to Man. Dir, King & Hutchings Ltd, Uxbridge, 1958–60; Bradford and District Newspapers: Asst Gen. Man., 1960; Gen. Man., 1964; Man. Dir, 1969–75; Dir, Westminster Press Planning Div., 1969–75. Chairman: Universal News Services Ltd, 1988–; Tellex Monitors Ltd, 1988–; CRG Communications Gp Ltd, 1990–. President: Young Newspapermen's Assoc., 1966; Yorks Newspaper Soc., 1968. Member: Council, Newspaper Soc., 1970–75; Council, Commonwealth Press Union, 1977–; Pres., Alliance of European News Agencies, 1987–88 (Chm., New Media Cttee, 1984–89). FRSA 1989. *Recreations:* walking, reading, theatre. *Address:* Woodbury, 11 Holmwood Close, East Horsley, Surrey. *T:* East Horsley (04865) 3873.

YATES, Ivan R., CBE 1982; FEng 1983; industrial consultant; Deputy Chief Executive (Engineering), 1986–90, Deputy Managing Director (Aircraft), 1985–90, Director, 1982–90, British Aerospace PLC; *b* 22 April 1929; *m* 1967, Jennifer Mary Holcombe; one *s* one *d*. *Educ:* Liverpool Collegiate Sch.; Liverpool Univ. (BEng 1st Class Hons). FIMechE; FRAeS 1968; FAIAA 1984; CBIM. Graduate Apprentice, English Electric, Preston, 1950, Chief Project Engr, 1959; Project Manager, Jaguar, 1966; British Aircraft Corporation: Special Dir, Preston Div., 1970; Dir, Preston, Warton Div., 1973; Dir, Aircraft Projects, 1974; Director: SEPECAT SA, 1976; Panavia GmbH, 1977; Eurofighter GmbH, 1986–90; British Aerospace: Man. Dir, Warton, 1978; Dir of Engrg and Project Assessment, Aircraft Gp, 1981; Chief Exec., Aircraft Gp, 1983–86. Vis. Prof. in Design, Cambridge Univ., 1991–. Mem., Technology Requirements Bd, 1985–. Pres., 1988–89, Dep. Pres., 1989–90, SBAC; Mem. Council, RAeS, 1986–91. Member: Design Council, 1990; Council, RUSI. Commissioner, Royal Commn for Exhibn of 1851, 1990. Mem. Council, Imperial Coll., 1991–. FRSA 1985 (Mem., Manufacture and Commerce Cttee). Hon. DSc: Loughborough, 1989; City, 1991. British Silver Medal, 1979, Gold Medal, 1985, RAeS. *Publications:* various papers and lectures. *Recreations:* walking, ski-ing, painting, music. *Fax:* (office) Guildford (0483) 303994. *Club:* Athenæum.

YATES, Rt. Rev. John; head of the Archbishop of Canterbury's staff (with title of Bishop at Lambeth), since 1991; *b* 17 April 1925; *s* of late Frank and late Edith Ethel Yates; *m* 1954, Jean Kathleen Dover; one *s* two *d*. *Educ:* Battersea Grammar School; Blackpool Grammar School; Jesus College, Cambridge (MA). RAFVR (Aircrew), 1943–47; University of Cambridge, 1947–49; Lincoln Theological College, 1949–51. Curate: Christ Church, Southgate, 1951–54; Tutor and Chaplain, Lincoln Theological College, 1954–59; Vicar, Bottesford-with-Ashby, 1959–65; Principal, Lichfield Theological College, 1966–72; Bishop Suffragan of Whitby, 1972–75; Bishop of Gloucester, 1975–91. Chm., Gen. Synod Bd for Social Responsibility, 1987–91. *Address:* Lambeth Palace, SE1 7JU.

YATES, Peter (James); film director/producer and theatre director; *b* 24 July 1929; *s* of Col Robert L. Yates and Constance Yates; *m* 1960, Virginia Pope; two *s* one *d* (and one *d* decd). *Educ:* Charterhouse; Royal Academy of Dramatic Art. Entered film industry, 1956. *Films directed:* Summer Holiday, 1962; One Way Pendulum, 1964; Robbery, 1966; Bullitt, 1968; John and Mary, 1969; Murphy's War, 1970; The Hot Rock, 1971; The Friends of Eddie Coyle, 1972; For Pete's Sake, 1973; Mother, Jugs and Speed, 1975; The Deep, 1976; Breaking Away (dir and prod.), 1979 (nominated 1980 Academy Awards, Director and Producer); The Janitor (dir and prod.), 1980; Krull, 1982; The Dresser (dir and prod.), 1983 (nominated 1984 Academy Awards, Dir and Producer); Eleni, 1985; The House on Carroll Street (dir and prod.), 1986; Suspect, 1987; An Innocent Man, 1989. *Theatre directed:* The American Dream, Royal Court, 1961; The Death of Bessie Smith, (London) 1961; Passing Game, (New York) 1977; Interpreters, (London) 1985. *Recreations:* tennis, sailing, skiing. *Address:* c/o CAA, 9830 Wilshire Boulevard, Los Angeles, Calif 90212–1825, USA. *Club:* Garrick.

YATES, William; The Administrator of Christmas Island, Indian Ocean, 1982–83; *b* 15 September 1921; *er s* of late William Yates and of Mrs John T. Renshaw, Burrells, Appleby, Westmorland; *m* 1st, 1946, Hon. Rosemary (marr. diss. 1955), *yr d* of 1st Baron Elton; two *d* (one *s* decd); 2nd, 1957, Camilla, *d* of late E. W. D. Tennant, Orford House, Ugley, Bishop's Stortford; four *s*. *Educ:* Uppingham; Hertford Coll., Oxford. Served War, 1940–45, North Africa and Italy; Captain The Bays, 1945. Shropshire Yeomanry, 1956–67. Appointed Legal Officer to report on State lands in Department of Custodian's Office in Tripoli, Libya, 1951. MP (C) The Wrekin Division of Shropshire, 1955–66. Myron Taylor Lectures in International Affairs, Cornell Univ., USA, 1958 and 1966. MP (L) Holt, Vic, Aust. Commonwealth, 1975–80; Mem. Liberal Party Parly Cttee for Defence and Foreign Affairs, 1975–80; Mem., Cttee of Privileges, House of Representatives, 1977–80. Mem., Inst. of Internat. Affairs, Victoria. *Address:* The Old House, Old Tallangatta, Vic 3700, Australia. *Clubs:* Cavalry and Guards; Commonwealth (Canberra).

YATES, Prof. (William) Edgar, MA, PhD; Professor of German, University of Exeter, since 1972; *b* 30 April 1938; *s* of Douglas Yates and Doris Yates (*née* Goode); *m* 1963, Barbara Anne Fellowes; two *s*. *Educ:* Fettes Coll. (Foundn Schol.); Emmanuel Coll., Cambridge (Minor Open Schol.; MA, PhD). 2nd Lieut, RASC, 1957–58. Lectr in German, Univ. of Durham, 1963–72; University of Exeter: Hd of Dept of German, 1972–86; Dep. Vice-Chancellor, 1986–89. Vice-Chm., Conf. of Univ. Teachers of German, 1991–. Member: Cttee, Modern Humanities Res. Assoc., 1980–; Council, English Goethe Soc., 1984–; Council, Internat. Nestroy-Gesellschaft, 1986–. Germanic Editor, MLR, 1981–88; Modern German Editor, MHRA Texts and Dissertations, 1984–. Gov., Exeter Sch., 1986–. J. G. Robertson Prize, Univ. of London, 1975. *Publications:* Grillparzer: a critical introduction, 1972; Nestroy: satire and parody in Viennese popular comedy, 1972; Humanity in Weimar and Vienna: the continuity of an ideal, 1973; Tradition in the German Sonnet, 1981; (ed) Hofmannsthal: Der Schwierige, 1966; (ed) Grillparzer: Der Traum ein Leben, 1968; (ed) Nestroy: Stücke 12–14 (Hist.-krit. Ausgabe), 1981–82, Stücke 34, 1989, Stücke 18/1, 1991; (ed jtly) Viennese Popular Theatre, 1985; (ed jtly) Grillparzer und die europäische Tradition, 1987; numerous articles on Austrian literary and cultural history, on German literature of the Biedermeier period, and on German lyric poetry. *Recreation:* music. *Address:* 7 Clifton Hill, Exeter EX1 2DL. *T:* Exeter (0392) 54713.

YATIM, Datuk Rais, DSNS (Malaysia) 1978; Advocate and Solicitor of the High Court of Malaya; Minister of Foreign Affairs, Malaysia, 1986–87; *b* 15 April 1942; *s* of Yatim Tahir and Siandam Boloh; *m* 1975, Datin Masnah; two *s* one *d*. *Educ:* Language Inst., Kuala Lumpur; Northern Illinois Univ.; Univ. of Singapore. DipEd; LLB (Hons); DipPsych. Language teacher, 1966–68. Parly Sec., Min. of Youth, 1974; Dep. Law Minister, 1976; Chief Minister, State of Negeri Sembilan, 1978–82; Minister of Land Regl Develt, 1982–84; Minister of Information, 1984–86. Returned to law practice in Kuala Lumpur, 1988–. Pres., Malaysia's Anti-Drug Assoc., 1976–87. Mem., MG Owners' Club, Swavesey. *Publication:* Faces in the Corridors of Power: a pictorial depiction of

Malaysians in power and authority, 1987. *Recreations:* photography, jogging, travel. *Address:* (residence) 41 Road 12, Taman Grandview, Ampang Jaya, 68000 Ampang, Selangor Darul Ehsan, Malaysia. *T:* 03–4569621. *Club:* Darul Ehsan Recreational (Kuala Lumpur).

YAXLEY, John Francis, CBE 1990; Commissioner, Hong Kong Government, London, since 1989; *b* 13 Nov. 1936; *s* of Rev. Canon R. W. and Dorothy Yaxley; *m* 1960, Patricia Anne Scott; one *s*. *Educ:* Hatfield Coll., Durham Univ. (BA Hons). National Service, 1958–60. HMOCS, 1961–, New Hebrides, Solomon Islands, Hong Kong; Dep. Financial Sec., Hong Kong Govt, 1987–89. *Publication:* The Population of the New Hebrides (with Dr Norma McArthur), 1968. *Recreations:* walking, birdwatching, history. *Address:* Hong Kong Government Office, 6 Grafton Street, W1X 3LB. *T:* 071–499 9821. *Clubs:* Commonwealth Trust, Royal Over-Seas League.

YEATES, W(illiam) Keith, MD, MS; FRCS; FRCSEd (without examination); Honorary Consultant Urologist, Newcastle Health Authority, since 1985 (Consultant Urologist, 1951–85); Hon. Senior Lecturer, Institute of Urology, University of London, since 1981; Chairman, Intercollegiate Board in Urology, 1984–88; *b* 10 March 1920; *s* of William Ravensbourne Yeates and Winifred (*née* Scott); *m* 1946, Jozy McIntyre Fairweather; one *s* one *d*. *Educ:* Glasgow Academy; Whitley Bay Grammar Sch.; King's Coll., Newcastle, Univ. of Durham. Consultant Advr in Urology, DHSS, 1978–84. Chm., Specialist Adv. Cttee in Urology, Jt Cttee on Higher Surgical Trng, RCS, 1984–86. Visiting Professor: Universities of: Baghdad, 1974, 1978; California, LA, 1976; Texas, Dallas, 1976; Delhi, 1977; Cairo, 1978; Kuwait, 1980; Guest Prof., New York section, Amer. Urolog. Assoc., 1977, 1985; Principal Guest Lectr, Urolog. Soc. of Australasia, 1977; Guest Lecturer: Italian Urolog. Assoc., 1978; Yugoslavian Urolog. Assoc., 1980; Vis. Lectr, Rio de Janeiro, 1975. Senior Member: Internat. Soc. of Urology, 1986– (Mem., 1958–86); European Assoc. of Urology, 1986– (Foundn Mem., 1974–86); Hon. Member: Urolog. Soc. of Australasia, 1977–; Canadian Urological Assoc., 1981–; British Assoc. of Urolog. Surgeons, 1985–. President: N of England Surgical Soc., 1971–72; British Assoc. of Urological Surgeons, 1980–82 (Vice-Pres., 1978–80, St Peter's Medal, 1983). British Journal of Urology: Editor, 1973–78; Chm., Editorial Cttee, 1978–84; Consulting Editor, 1985–90. *Publications:* various papers, chapters in text books on Urology, particularly on bladder dysfunction and male infertility. *Address:* 22 Castleton Grove, Jesmond, Newcastle upon Tyne NE2 2HD. *T:* 091–2814030; 71 King Henry's Road, NW3 3QU. *T:* 071–586 7633.

YEEND, Sir Geoffrey (John), AC 1986; Kt 1979; CBE 1976; FAIM; consultant; Chancellor, Australian National University, since 1990; Director: AMATIL Ltd, since 1986; ALCAN Australia Ltd, since 1986; Canberrra Advance Bank (formerly Civic Advance Bank), since 1987; Menzies Memorial Trust, since 1986; Mercantile Mutual Holdings Ltd, since 1988; Australian Capital Television Ltd, since 1989; *b* 1 May 1927; *s* of Herbert Yeend; *m* 1952, Laurel, *d* of L. G. Mahoney; one *d* one *s*. *Educ:* Canberra High Sch.; Melbourne Univ. (Canberra University Coll.) (BCom). Served RAE, AIF, 1945–46. Dept of Post War Reconstruction, 1947–49; Prime Minister's Dept, 1950–86, incl.: Private Sec. to Prime Minister (Sir Robert Menzies), 1952–55; Asst Sec., Aust. High Commn, London, 1958–61; Dep. Sec., 1972–77; Head of Dept and Sec. to Cabinet, 1978–86; Mem., Defence Cttee, 1978–86. Mem. and leader of Aust. delegns to internat. confs. Mem., Adv. Council on Aust. Archives, 1985–87. Nat. Vice Pres., and Pres., ACT, Multiple Sclerosis Soc. of Aust., 1989–. Pro-Chancellor, ANU, 1988–90. Aust. Eisenhower Fellow, 1971. FAIM 1982. International Hockey Federation: Councillor, 1959–66; Vice-Pres., 1967–76; Member of Honour, 1979; Trustee, 1988. Patron, Woden Valley Choir, 1980–; Vice-Patron: Australian Nat. Eisteddfod, 1983–; Australian Volleyball Assoc. *Recreations:* golf, fishing. *Address:* 1 Loftus Street, Yarralumla, ACT 2600, Australia. *T:* 062 813266. *Clubs:* Commonwealth (Canberra); Royal Canberra Golf.

YELLOWLEES, Sir Henry, KCB 1975 (CB 1971); Chief Medical Officer, Department of Health and Social Security, Department of Education and Science and Home Office, 1973–83; *b* 1919; *s* of late Henry Yellowlees, OBE, Psychiatrist of Bath. *Educ:* Stowe Sch.; University Coll., Oxford. MA, BM, BCh Oxon 1950. FRCP 1971 (MRCP 1966, LRCP 1950); FFCM 1972; FRCS 1983 (MRCS 1950). Pilot, RAF, 1941–45. Resident Med. Officer, Mddx Hosp., London, 1951–54; Asst Senior Med. Officer, South West Regional Hosp. Bd, 1954–59; Dep. Sen. Admin. Med. Officer, North West Metropolitan Regional Hosp. Bd, 1959–63; Principal Med. Officer, Min. of Health, 1963–65 (seconded); Senior Principal Med. Officer, 1965–67 (established); Dep. Chief Med. Officer, 1967–72, 2nd Chief Med. Officer, 1972–73, Dept of Health and Social Security. Consultant, MoD, 1985; Occasional Consultant, European Reg., WHO, 1985–. Chm., WHO Commn to investigate health care of Bulgarian citizens arriving in Turkey, 1989. Member: Medical Research Council, 1974–83; Gen. Medical Council, 1979–89; Health Services Supervisory Bd, 1983; Council, BMA, 1986–; Council, British Nutrition Foundn, 1973–. Hon. FRCP Glasgow, 1974; Hon. FRCPsych, 1977; Fellow Brit. Inst. of Management, 1974–83; Vice-Pres., Mental After-Care Assoc.; Hon. Mem., Nat. Assoc. of Clinical Tutors. *Address:* 43 Sandwich House, Sandwich Street, WC1H 9PR.

YELSTIN, Boris Nikolayevich; President, Russian Federation, since 1990; *b* 1 Feb. 1931. *Educ:* Urals M. Kirov Polytechnic Inst. Engineer, 1955–68; joined Communist Party, 1961; engaged in work for Communist Party, 1968–; First Sec., Dist Central Cttee, Sverdlosk, 1976; Mem., Party Central Cttee, 1981; Sec., Central Cttee, 1985–86; First Sec., Moscow Party Cttee, 1985–87; Candidate Mem., Politburo, 1986–88; First Dep. Chm., State Cttee for Construction, 1988–89; Mem., Congress of People's Deputies, 1989–. *Publication:* Against the Grain (autobiog.), 1990. *Address:* c/o The Kremlin, Moscow, USSR.

YEMM, Prof. Edmund William, BA, MA, DPhil Oxon; Melville Wills Professor of Botany, University of Bristol, 1955–74, Emeritus Professor 1974; *b* 16 July 1909; *s* of William H. Yemm and Annie L. Brett; *m* 1935, Marie Solari; one *s* three *d*. *Educ:* Wyggeston School, Leicester; Queen's College, Oxford. Foundation, Schol., Queen's Coll., 1928; Christopher Welch Schol., 1931. Major, REME, 1942–45. Research Fellow, Queen's Coll., 1935–38; Lecturer, Univ. of Bristol, 1939–49; Reader in Botany, Univ. of Bristol, 1950–55; Pro-Vice-Chancellor, Bristol Univ., 1970–73. Fellowship, Rockefeller Foundation, 1954; Vis. Prof., Western Reserve Univ., 1966–67. *Publications:* scientific papers in Proc. Royal Soc., New Phytologist, Biochemical Jl, Jl of Ecology, Jl of Experimental Botany. *Recreations:* cricket, gardening; formerly football (Oxford Univ. Assoc. Football Blue, 1929–31). *Address:* The Wycke, 61 Long Ashton Road, Bristol BS18 9HW. *T:* Long Ashton (0272) 392258.

YENTOB, Alan; Controller, BBC2, since 1988; *b* 11 March 1947; *s* of Isaac Yentob and Flora Yentob (*née* Khazam). *Educ:* King's School, Ely; Univ. of Grenoble; Univ. of Leeds (LLB). BBC general trainee, 1968; producer/director, 1970–; arts features, incl. Omnibus; Editor, Arena, 1978–85; Co-Editor, Omnibus, 1985; Hd of Music and Arts, BBC TV, 1985–88. Member: Bd of Directors, Riverside Studios, 1984–91; BFI Production Board, 1985–; Council, English Stage Co., 1990–. Gov., Nat. Film School, 1988–. Hon. Fellow: RCA, 1987; RIBA, 1991. *Recreations:* swimming, books. *Address:* 99 Blenheim Crescent, W11.

YEO, Diane Helen; Charity Commissioner, since 1989; *b* 22 July 1945; *d* of Brian Harold Pickard, FRCS and Joan Daisy Pickard; *m* 1970, Timothy Stephen Kenneth Yeo, *qv*; one *s* one *d*. *Educ:* Blackheath High Sch.; London Univ.; Institut Français de Presse. BBC Radio, 1968–74; Africa Educnl Trust, 1974–79; Girl Guides' Assoc., 1979–82; YWCA, 1982–85; Director: Inst. of Charity Fundraising Managers, 1985–88; Charity Appointments, 1985–; Consultant, Centre for Voluntary Organisation, LSE, 1988–; Chm., Charity Commn Trng Cttee, 1990–; Member: Nathan Cttee on Effectiveness and the Voluntary Sector, 1989–90; NCVO Trustee Trng Wkg Party, 1990–. FRSA. *Publications:* contribs to professional jls. *Recreations:* tennis, swimming, photography, piano. *Address:* Charity Commission, St Albans House, Haymarket, SW1Y 4QX.

YEO, Douglas; Director, Shell Research Ltd, Thornton Research Centre, 1980–85; *b* 13 June 1925; *s* of Sydney and Hylda Yeo; *m* 1947, Joan Elisabeth Chell; two *d*. *Educ:* Secondary Sch., St Austell; University Coll., Exeter (BSc London). Expedn on locust control, Kenya, 1945. HMOCS, 1948–63; Tropical Pesticides Research Inst., Uganda and Tanzania, 1948–61 (Scientific Officer, 1948–51, Sen. Scientific Officer, 1951–57, Prin. Scientific Officer, 1957–61). Internat. African Migratory Locust Control Organisation, Mali: on secondment, 1958, 1960; Dir and Sec. Gen., 1961–63. Shell Research Ltd: Research Dir, Woodstock Agricultural Research Centre, 1963–69, Dir, 1969–76; Dir, Biosciences Lab., Sittingbourne, 1976–80. Mem. Council, RHBNC, London Univ., 1985–90. FIBiol. *Publications:* papers in Bulletin Ent. Res., Bull. WHO, Anti-Locust Bull., Qly Jl Royal Met. Soc., Jl Sci. Fd. Agric., Plant Protection Confs, etc. *Recreations:* sailing, hill walking, fishing. *Address:* Tremarne, Tremarne Close, Feock, Truro TR3 6SB. *Club:* Royal Corinthian Yacht (Burnham on Crouch).

YEO, Kok Cheang, CMG 1956; MD; MB; BS; DPH; DTM&H; *b* 1 April 1903; *s* of Yeo Kim Hong; *m* Florence, *d* of late Sir Robert Ho-tung, KBE; one *s* two *d*. *Educ:* Hong Kong University; Cambridge University; London School of Hygiene and Tropical Medicine. MB, BS, Hong Kong, 1925, MD, 1930; DTM&H (England) 1927; DPH, Cambridge, 1928. Assistant Medical Officer of Health, Hong Kong, 1928; Lecturer and Examiner in public health, Hong Kong University, 1936–37; Official JP 1938; Chinese Health Officer, senior grade, 1939–47; Deputy Director of Health Services, and Vice-Chairman of Urban Council, 1947–50; Deputy Director of Medical and Health Services, 1950–52; member of Legislative Council, Hong Kong, 1951–57; Director of Medical and Health Services, Hong Kong, 1952–58; Professor of Social Medicine, Hong Kong University, 1953–58; retd 1958. *Address:* 16 Saxonwood Court, Market Road, Battle, East Sussex TN33 0XA.

YEO, Timothy Stephen Kenneth; MP (C) Suffolk South, since 1983; Parliamentary Under Secretary of State, Department of the Environment, since 1990; *b* 20 March 1945; *s* of late Dr Kenneth John Yeo and Norah Margaret Yeo; *m* 1970, Diane Helen Pickard (*see* D. H. Yeo); one *s* one *d*. *Educ:* Charterhouse; Emmanuel Coll., Cambridge (Open Exhibnr; MA 1971). Asst Treas., Bankers Trust Co., 1970–73; Director, Worcester Engineering Co. Ltd, 1975–86. Dir, Spastics Soc., 1980–83, Mem., Exec. Council, 1984–86. PPS to Sec. of State for Home Dept, 1988–89, to Sec. of State for Foreign Affairs, 1989–90; Mem., Social Services Select Cttee, 1985–88. Jt Sec., Cons. Pty Finance Cttee, 1984–87. Hon. Treasurer, International Voluntary Service, 1975–78. Trustee: African Palms, 1970–85; Tanzania Development Trust, 1980–; Chm., Tadworth Court Trust, 1983–90. *Publication:* Public Accountability and Regulation of Charities, 1983. *Recreation:* skiing. *Address:* House of Commons, SW1A 0AA. *T:* 071–219 3000. *Clubs:* Carlton; Sudbury Conservative (Sudbury); Royal St George's (Sandwich).

YEOMAN, Maj.-Gen. Alan, CB 1987; Director, Army Sport Control Board, since 1988; *b* 17 Nov. 1933; *s* of George Smith Patterson Yeoman and Wilhelmina Tromans Elwell; *m* 1960, Barbara Joan Davies; two *s* one *d*. *Educ:* Dame Allan's School, Newcastle upon Tyne. Officer Cadet, RMA Sandhurst, 1952; commnd Royal Signals, 1954; served Korea, Malaysia, Singapore, Cyprus, UK, BAOR and Canada, 1954–70 (Staff Coll., 1963); CO 2 Div. Sig. Regt, BAOR, 1970–73; HQ 1 (BR) Corps, BAOR, 1973–74; MoD, 1974–77; Col AQ, HQLF Cyprus, 1978–79; Comd Trng Gp, Royal Signals and Catterick Garrison, 1979–82; Brig. AQ, HQ 1 (BR) Corps, BAOR, 1982–84; Comd Communications, BAOR, 1984–87; retd 1988. Col Comdt, Royal Corps of Signals, 1987–. Hon. Col, 37th (Wessex and Welsh) Signal Regt, T & AVR, 1987–. *Recreations:* golf, cricket, ski-ing. *Address:* c/o Lloyds Bank, Catterick Garrison, North Yorks. *Clubs:* Army and Navy, MCC.

YEOMAN, Prof. Michael Magson, PhD; FRSE; Regius Professor of Botany, since 1978, Vice-Principal, since 1988, Curator of Patronage, since 1988, University of Edinburgh; *b* 16 May 1931; *s* of Gordon Yeoman and Mabel Ellen (*née* Magson), Newcastle upon Tyne; *m* 1962, Erica Mary Lines; two *d*. *Educ:* Gosforth Grammar Sch.; King's Coll., Univ. of Durham (BSc 1952, MSc 1954, PhD 1960); FRSE 1980. National Service, Royal Corps of Signals, 1954–56. Demonstrator in Botany, King's Coll., Newcastle upon Tyne, 1957–59; Edinburgh University: Lectr in Botany, 1960; Sen. Lectr, 1968; Reader, 1973; Dean, Fac. of Science, 1981–84. Vis. Prof., NENU, Changchung, China, 1986–. Chm., Univs Council for Adult and Continuing Educn (Scotland), 1989–. Member: Governing Bodies, Nat. Vegetable Res. Stn and Scottish Plant Breeding Stn, 1978–82; SERC Biological Scis Cttee, 1982–85; SERC Biotechnology Management Cttee, 1983–85; British Nat. Cttee for Biology, 1981–89. Governor: East of Scotland Coll. of Agriculture, 1984–; Scottish Crops Res. Inst., 1986–89. Trustee, Edinburgh Botanic Gdn (Sibbald) Trust, 1986–. Mem. Council, RSE, 1985– (Fellowship Sec., 1986–). Mem., Editorial Bds of Jl of Experimental Botany, 1981–85, Plant Science Letters, 1974–83, and New Phytologist (Trustee). *Publications:* (ed) Cell Division in Higher Plants, 1976; (jtly) Laboratory Manual of Plant Cell and Tissue Culture, 1982; (ed) Plant Cell Technology, 1986; contrib. scientific jls; chapters, articles and revs in books. *Recreations:* military history, photography, gardening, walking. *Address:* 9 Glenlockhart Valley, Edinburgh EH14 1DE. *T:* 031–443 8540.

YEOMAN, Philip Metcalfe, MD; FRCS; Consultant Orthopaedic Surgeon, Bath, 1964–88, retired; *b* 29 April 1923; *s* of William Yeoman, MD and Dorothy Young; *m* 1947, Idonea Evelyn Mary Scarrott; two *s* one *d*. *Educ:* Sedbergh; Cambridge (MA, MB BChir, MD); University Coll. Hosp. London. Flight Lieut, RAF Hosp., Ely, 1950–52. Lectr, Inst. of Orthopaedics, 1959–64. Member: Pensions Appeal Tribunals, 1986–; Professional and Linguistic Assessment Bd, 1987–. External Examr in Surg., Univ. of Liverpool. Mem. Council, RCS, 1984– (Mem., Court of Examrs, 1980–; Hunterian Prof., 1983); Vice-Pres., British Orthopaedic Assoc., 1984–85 (Robert Jones Gold Medal, 1963; North American Travelling Fellow, 1964; Mem. Council, 1981–84); President: Section of Orthopaedics, RSocMed, 1983; North American Travelling Fellows, 1981–83. Mem., Internat. Skeletal Soc. Hugh Owen Thomas Meml Lectr, Liverpool, 1988. *Publications:* chapters on peripheral nerve injuries, brachial plexus injuries, bone tumours, surgical management of rheumatoid arthritis of the cervical spine. *Recreations:* golf, gardening.

Address: Broadmead, Monkton Combe, near Bath BA2 7JE. *T*: Limpley Stoke (022122) 3294. *Club*: Army and Navy.

YEOMANS, Richard Millett, CEng, FIEE; FIMechE; Chief Executive, Scottish Nuclear Ltd, since 1989; *b* 19 July 1932; *s* of late Maj. Richard J. Yeomans and Lillian (*née* Spray); *m* 1957, Jennifer Margaret Wingfield Pert; three *s* one *d*. *Educ*: Durban, SA; Cornwall Tech. Coll. CEng; FIEE; FIMechE. Student apprentice, CEGB, 1948. Lt, REME, 1953–55. CEGB power stations, 1955–67; South of Scotland Electricity Board: Dep. Manager, Longannet Power Stn, 1971–75; Manager, Inverkip Power Stn, 1975–77; Manager, Hunterston A&B Nuclear Power Stns, 1977–80; Generation Engineer (Nuclear), 1980–87; Chief Engineer, 1987–89. *Recreations*: sailing, golf, gardening. *Address*: Ashcraig, Skelmorlie, Ayrshire PA17 5HB. *T*: Greenock (0475) 520298.

YERBURGH, family name of **Baron Alvingham.**

YERBURGH, John Maurice Armstrong; Vice Lord-Lieutenant of Dumfries and Galloway (District of Stewartry), since 1990; Chairman, Daniel Thwaites, since 1966 (Director, since 1947); *b* 23 May 1923; *e s* of late Major Guy Yerburgh (*d* 1926), OBE, Belgian Croix de Guerre, Italian Croce di Guerra and Lady (Hilda Violet Helena) Salisbury-Jones, *e d* of Rt Hon. Sir Maurice de Bunsen, Bt, GCMG, GCVO, CB; *m* 1973, Ann Jean Mary, *d* of N. P. Maclaren, Brooklands, Crocketford, Dumfries; one *s* four *d*. *Educ*: Eton; Magdalene College, Cambridge (BA). Commissioned Irish Guards 1943; served with 2nd Bn, France, Holland, Belgium, Germany; retired 1947 with rank of Captain. Contested (C) Blackburn, 1959 and 1963. Chm., S of Scotland Regional Adv. Cttee, Forestry Commn, 1972–87; Governor, Cumbria College of Agriculture and Forestry, 1975–89; Shire Horse Society: Pres., 1983–84; Dep. Pres., 1988. DL Dumfries 1989. *Recreations*: shooting, fishing, trees. *Address*: Barwhillanty, Parton, Castle Douglas, Kirkcudbrightshire DG7 3NS. *T*: Parton (06447) 237.

YERBY, Frank Garvin; novelist; *b* 5 September 1916; *s* of Rufus Garvin Yerby and Wilhelmina Smythe; *m* 1956, Blanca Calle Pérez; two *s* two *d* of former marriage. *Educ*: Haines Institute; Paine College; Fisk Univ.; Univ. of Chicago. Teacher, Florida Agricultural and Mechanical Coll., 1939; Southern Univ. (Baton Rouge, Louisiana), 1940–41; War work: laboratory technician, Ford Motor Company, Detroit, 1941–44; Ranger Aircraft, New York, 1944–45; writer since 1944; O. Henry Award for short story, 1944. *Publications*: The Foxes of Harrow, 1946; The Vixens, 1947; The Golden Hawk, 1948; Pride's Castle, 1949; Floodtide, 1950; A Woman Called Fancy, 1951; The Saracen Blade, 1952; The Devil's Laughter, 1953; Benton's Row, 1954; The Treasure of Pleasant Valley, 1955; Captain Rebel, 1956; Fairoaks, 1957; The Serpent and the Staff, 1958; Jarrett's Jade, 1959; Gillian, 1960; The Garfield Honor, 1961; Griffin's Way, 1962; The Old Gods Laugh, 1964; An Odor of Sanctity, 1965; Goat Song, 1967; Judas, My Brother, 1968; Speak Now, 1969; The Man from Dahomey, 1970; The Girl from Storyville, 1972; The Voyage Unplanned, 1974; Tobias and the Angel, 1975; A Rose for Ana María, 1976; Hail the Conquering Hero, 1977; A Darkness at Ingraham's Crest, 1978; Western, 1983; Devilseed, 1984; McKenzie's Hundred, 1985. *Recreations*: photography, painting. *Address*: c/o Wm Morris Agency, 1350 Avenue of the Americas, New York, NY 10019, USA. *Clubs*: Authors Guild (New York); Real Sociedad Hipica Española (Madrid).

YEVTUSHENKO, Yevgeny Aleksandrovich; poet, novelist, film director, film actor, photographer; Member, Congress of People's Deputies of USSR, since 1989; *b* 18 July 1933; *m*; five *s*; *m* 4th, 1986, Maria Novikova. *Educ*: Moscow Literary Inst., 1952–56 (expelled). Has visited 93 countries; Vice-Pres., Russian PEN, 1990–; Hon. Mem., Amer. Acad. of Arts and Scis, 1987; hon. degrees from numerous Univs. Film actor: Take Off, 1979 (silver prize, Moscow Internat. film fest.); film director: Kindergarten, 1984; Stalin's Funeral, 1990. *Publications*: *in Russian*: Scouts of the Future, 1952; The Third Snow, 1955; The Highway of Enthusiasts, 1956; The Promise, 1959; The Apple, 1960; A Sweep of the Arm, 1962; Tenderness, 1962; Mail Boat, 1966; Bratsk Power Station, 1967; Kazan's University, 1971; A Father's Hearing, 1975; Morning People, 1978; Talent is not a Miracle by Chance (essays), 1980; Wild Berries Places (novel), 1981; Mother and Neutron Bomb and other poems, 1983; Almost at the End, 1986; A Wind of Tomorrow (essays), 1987; Selected Poetry, 3 vols, 1987; words to Shostakovich's 13th Symphony and Execution of Stepan Razin Oratorio; *in English*: Zima Junction, 1961; A Precocious Autobiography, 1963; Bratsk Power Station, 1966; Stolen Apples, 1972; From Desire to Desire, 1976; The Face Behind the Face, 1979; Dove in Santiago, 1982; Invisible Threads (photography), 1981; Wild Berries (novel), 1984; Ardabiola (novel), 1985; Almost at the End, 1987; Divided Twins (photography), 1987; Last Attempt, 1988; Politics—everybody's privilege (essays), 1990. *Address*: Moskovskay Oblast, Peredelkino, Gogolia 1, 142783 PO Michyrinskoe, USSR.

YOCKLUNN, Sir John (Soong Chung), KCVO 1977; Kt 1975; Chief Librarian, Monash University College, Gippsland (formerly Gippsland Institute of Advanced Education), since 1983; *b* Canton, China, 5 May 1933; *s* of late Charles Soong Yocklunn and Wui Sin Yocklunn, formerly of W Australia; *m* 1981, Patricia Ann Mehegan. *Educ*: Perth Modern Sch.; Northam High Sch., W Australia; Univ. of W Australia (BA); Aust. Nat. Univ. (BA); Univ. of Sheffield (MA). ALA; ALAA. Dept of the Treasury, Canberra, 1959–63; Nat. Library of Australia, Canberra, 1964–67; Librarian-in-Charge, Admin Coll. of Papua New Guinea, Port Moresby, 1967–69; Exec. Officer, Public Service Board of Papua New Guinea, 1969–70; Librarian, Admin Coll., 1970–72; Principal Private Sec. to Chief Minister, 1972–73; study in UK, under James Cook Bicentenary Schol., 1973–74; on return, given task of organising a national library; Sen. Investigation Officer, Public Services Commn, 1974–77; Asst Sec. (Library Services), Dept of Educn (National Librarian of PNG), 1978–83. Chm., PNG Honours and Awards Cttee, 1975–83; Advr on Honours to PNG Govt, 1984–85; Consultant on estabt of new honours system, 1985–86. Vice-Pres., Pangu Pati, 1968–72; Nat. Campaign Manager for Pangu Pati for 1972 general elections in Papua New Guinea; Treasurer, Pangu Pati, 1973–80. Asst Dir, Visit of Prince of Wales to PNG, 1975; Dir, Visits of the Queen and Prince Philip to PNG, 1977 and 1982. Australian Library and Information Association: Chm., Gippsland Regional Gp, 1984–; Mem., Vict. Br. Council, 1986–; rep. on Commonwealth Library Assoc., 1988–91; Mem. Exec. Cttee, Vict. Div., Aust. Council for Library and Inf. Servs, 1989–. Mem. Adv. Council, CARE Aust., 1988–. Trustee, 1986–, Chm. of Friends, 1985–88, Management Cttee, 1990–, Mus. of Chinese Australian Hist. *Publications*: The Charles Barrett Collection of Books relating to Papua New Guinea, 1967, 2nd edn 1969; articles on librarianship, etc., in various jls. *Recreations*: book collecting, languages, cooking. *Address*: Monash University College, Churchill, Victoria 3842, Australia. *T*: (office) (051) 22 6420; (home) (051) 34 8303.

YOFFEY, Joseph Mendel, DSc, MD, FRCS; Visiting Professor, Hebrew University of Jerusalem, since 1969; Professor of Anatomy, University of Bristol, 1942–67, now Professor Emeritus; *b* 10 July 1902; *s* of Rabbi Israel Jacob Yoffey and Pere Jaffe; *m* 1940, Betty Gillis, LLB; three *d*. *Educ*: Manchester Grammar School; Univ. of Manchester. Leech Research Fellow, University of Manchester, 1926–27; Research Scholar, BMA, 1928–29; House Surgeon, Manchester Royal Infirmary, 1929–30; Asst Lectr in Anatomy, Univ. of Manchester, 1930; Senior Lectr in Anatomy, University College of South Wales and Monmouthshire, Cardiff; Hunterian Prof., RCS England, 1933 and 1940; Fellow of Rockefeller Foundn, 1937–39. Visiting Professor: Univ. of Washington, 1958; Univ. of Calif., San Francisco, 1967–68; John Curtin Sch. of Medical Research, ANU, 1968–69. Hon. Life Mem., Reticulendotheliol Soc., 1978; Hon. Mem., Amer. Assoc. of Anatomists, 1980. John Hunter Triennial Medal, RCS, 1968. Hon. LLD Manchester, 1973. Knight First Class of the Order of the Dannebrog (Denmark), 1959. *Publications*: Quantitative Cellular Hæmatology, 1960; Bone Marrow Reactions, 1966; (with Dr F. C. Courtice) Lymphatics, Lymph and the Lymphomyeloid Complex, 1970; Bone Marrow in Hypoxia and Rebound, 1973; (with M. Tavassoli) Bone Marrow: structure and function, 1983; numerous scientific papers. *Recreations*: music, walking, modern Hebrew. *Address*: 1 Rehov Degania, Beth Hakerem, Jerusalem, Israel. *T*: Jerusalem 525738.

YONG NYUK LIN; Member, Presidential Council for Minority Rights, Singapore; *b* Seremban, Malaya, 24 June 1918; *s* of late Yong Thean Yong and Chen Shak Moi; *m* 1939, Kwa Geok Lan; two *d*. *Educ*: Raffles Coll., Singapore. Science Master, King George V Sch., Seremban, Malaya, 1938–41; with Overseas Assurance Corp., Singapore, 1941 (resigned, as Gen. Manager, 1958). Legislative Assemblyman, Singapore, 1959–65, MP 1965–79; Minister for Educn, 1959–63; Chm., Singapore Harbour Bd, 1961–62; Minister for: Health, 1963–68; Communications, 1968–75; Minister without Portfolio, 1975–76; High Comr in London, 1975–76. Chm., Singapore Land/Marina Centre Development Private Ltd, 1980–86. *Address*: 50 Oei Tiong Ham Park, Singapore 1026.

YONGE, Dame (Ida) Felicity (Ann), DBE 1982 (MBE 1958); Special Adviser in Government Chief Whip's Office, 1979–83; *b* 28 Feb. 1921; *d* of Comdr W. H. N. Yonge, RN, and Kathleen Yonge. *Educ*: Convent of the Holy Child, St Leonard's-on-Sea. Served WRNS (2nd Officer), 1940–46. Purser's Office, P&OSN Co., 1947–50; Private Secretary: to Chairman of the Conservative Party, 1951–64; to Leader of the Opposition, 1964–65; to Opposition Chief Whip, 1965–70 and 1974–79; to Leader of House of Commons, 1970–74. *Recreations*: gardening, bridge. *Address*: 58 Leopold Road, Wimbledon, SW19 7JF.

YORK, Archbishop of, since 1983; **Most Rev. and Rt. Hon. John Stapylton Habgood,** PC 1983; MA, PhD; *b* 23 June 1927; *s* of Arthur Henry Habgood, DSO, MB, BCh, and Vera (*née* Chetwynd-Stapylton); *m* 1961, Rosalie Mary Anne Boston; two *s* two *d*. *Educ*: Eton; King's Coll., Cambridge (Hon. Fellow, 1986); Cuddesdon Coll., Oxford. Univ. Demonstrator in Pharmacology, Cambridge, 1950–53; Fellow of King's Coll., Cambridge, 1952–55; Curate of St Mary Abbots, Kensington, 1954–56; Vice-Principal of Westcott House, Cambridge, 1956–62; Rector of St John's Church, Jedburgh, 1962–67; Principal of Queen's College, Birmingham, 1967–73; Bishop of Durham, 1973–83. Hulsean Preacher, Cambridge Univ., 1987–88. Moderator, Church and Society Sub-Unit, WCC, 1983–91. Pro-Chancellor, Univ. of York, 1985–90. Hon. DD: Durham, 1975; Cambridge, 1984; Aberdeen, 1988; Huron, 1990; Hull, 1991. *Publications*: Religion and Science, 1964; A Working Faith, 1980; Church and Nation in a Secular Age, 1983; Confessions of a Conservative Liberal, 1988. *Recreations*: painting, DIY. *Address*: Bishopthorpe, York YO2 1QE. *Club*: Athenæum.

YORK, Dean of; *see* Southgate, Very Rev. J. E.

YORK, Archdeacon of; *see* Austin, Ven. G. B.

YORK, Christopher, DL; *b* 27 July 1909; *s* of late Col Edward York; *m* 1934, Pauline Rosemary, *d* of late Sir Lionel Fletcher, CBE; one *s* three *d*. *Educ*: Eton; RMC Sandhurst. Joined The Royal Dragoons, India, 1930; retired, 1934, on to Supplementary Reserve; rejoined Regt, 1939, rank Major; joined Land Agents Soc., 1934, and passed examinations, acting as Land Agent until elected MP; MP (U) Harrogate Division, 1950–54 (Ripon Division of the West Riding, 1939–50); DL West Riding of Yorkshire, later N Yorkshire, 1954; High Sheriff of Yorkshire, 1966. Pres., RASE, 1979. Hon. Fellow, Royal Veterinary Coll., 1971. *Recreation*: writing. *Address*: South Park, Long Marston, York YO5 8LL. *TA* and *T*: Rufforth (090483) 357. *Clubs*: Boodle's, Carlton; Yorkshire (York).

YORK, Michael, (Michael York-Johnson); actor; *b* 27 March 1942; *s* of Joseph Johnson and Florence Chown; *m* 1968, Patricia Frances McCallum. *Educ*: Hurstpierpoint College; Bromley Grammar School; University College, Oxford (BA). *Stage*: Dundee Repertory Theatre, 1964; National Theatre Co., 1965; Outcry, NY, 1973; Bent, NY, 1980; Cyrano de Bergerac, Santa Fe, 1981; *films*: The Taming of the Shrew, Accident, 1966; Romeo and Juliet, 1967; Cabaret, England Made Me, 1971; The Three Musketeers, 1973; Murder on the Orient Express, 1974; Logan's Run, 1975; The Riddle of the Sands, 1978; Success is the Best Revenge, 1984; Dawn, 1985; Vengeance, 1986; The Secret of the Sahara, Imbalances, 1987; The Joker, Midnight Blue, The Return of the Musketeers, 1988; The Prodigal Father, 1991; *television*: Jesus of Nazareth, 1976; A Man Called Intrepid, 1978; For Those I Loved, 1981; The Weather in the Streets, The Master of Ballantrae, 1983; Space, 1984; The Far Country, 1985; Are you my Mother, 1986; Ponce de Leon, 1987; Knots Landing, The Four Minute Mile, The Lady and the Highwayman, The Heat of the Day, 1988; The Hunt for Stolen War Treasure, Till We Meet Again, 1989; The Night of the Fox, 1990; The Road to Avonlea, 1991. Chm., Calif Youth Theatre, 1987. Hon. DFA Univ. of S Carolina. *Publications*: (contrib.) The Courage of Conviction, 1986; (contrib.) Voices of Survival, 1987; Travelling Player (autobiog.), 1991. *Recreations*: travel, music, collecting theatrical memorabilia.

YORK, Susannah; actress and writer; *b* 9 Jan. 1942; *d* of William Fletcher and Joan Bowring; *m* 1960, Michael Wells (marr. diss. 1976); one *s* one *d*. *Educ*: Marr Coll., Troon, Scotland; RADA, London. *Films* include: The Greengage Summer, 1961; Freud, 1962; Tom Jones, 1963; A Man for All Seasons, 1966; The Killing of Sister George, 1968; They Shoot Horses, Don't They, 1969; Zee and Co., 1971; Images, 1972; Superman, 1978; Golden Gate Murders, 1979; Alice, 1980; Superman 2, 1984; A Christmas Carol, Mio My Mio, 1986; Bluebeard; Just Ask for Diamonds, 1988; Melancholia, 1989; Barbarblu Barbarblu; Little Women. *Theatre* includes: Wings of a Dove, 1964; A Singular Man, 1965; The Maids, 1974; Peter Pan, 1977; The Singular Life of Albert Nobbs, 1978; Hedda Gabler, New York 1981, London 1982; Agnes of God, 1983; The Human Voice (own trans. of Cocteau), 1984; Fatal Attraction, Haymarket, 1985; The Apple Cart, Haymarket, 1986; The Women, Old Vic, 1986; The Glass Menagerie (tour), 1989. TV series We'll Meet Again, 1982. *Publications*: In Search of Unicorns, 1973, rev. edn 1984; Larks Castle, 1975, rev. edn, 1985; (ed) The Big One, 1984. *Recreations*: family, writing, gardening, reading, houses, riding, languages, travelling, theatre, cinema, walking. *Address*: c/o Jeremy Conway, Eagle House, 109 Jermyn Street, SW1Y 6HB.

YORK-JOHNSON, Michael; *see* York, M.

YORKE, family name of **Earl of Hardwicke.**

YORKE, David Harry Robert, FRICS; Senior Partner, since 1984 and Group Chairman, since 1989, Weatherall Green & Smith, Chartered Surveyors (Partner, since 1961); *b* 5 Dec. 1931; *s* of late Harry Yorke and of Marie Yorke, Minera, N Wales; *m* 1955, Patricia Gwynneth Fowler-Tutt; one *d*. *Educ*: Dean Close Sch., Cheltenham; College of Estate

Management. FRICS 1966 (ARICS 1956). Articled to Tregear & Sons, 1948–54. 2nd Lieut RA, 1955–56. Weatherall Green & Smith, 1960–. Dir, London Auction Mart, 1981–. Mem., Bristol Develt Corp., 1988–; Dir, British Waterways Bd, 1988–. Mem., Management Cttee, Shroder Exempt Property Unit Trust, 1989–. Royal Institution of Chartered Surveyors: Mem., Gen. Council, 1978–; Pres., Gen. Practice Div., 1981–82; Pres., 1988–89; Chm., RICS Insurance Services, 1991–. Mem. Council, British Property Fedn, 1990–. Pres., British Chapter, Internat. Real Estate Fedn, 1974. Mem. Council, Donkey Breed Soc., 1975. Freeman, City of London, 1979; Liveryman, Co. of Chartered Surveyors, 1979. *Publications:* (contrib.) The Third Cuckoo, 1985; contribs to property professional jls. *Recreations:* crossword puzzles, narrow boating, swimming, occasional cookery. *Address:* Holford Manor, North Chailey, Sussex BN8 4DU. *T:* Wivelsfield Green (044484) 277. *Club:* Buck's.

YORKSHIRE, EAST RIDING, Archdeacon of; *see* Buckingham, Ven. H. F.

YOUARD, Richard Geoffrey Atkin; The Investment Referee, since 1989; *b* 27 Jan. 1933; *s* of Geoffrey Bernard Youard, MBE and Hon. Rosaline Joan Youard (*née* Atkin); *m* 1960, Felicity Ann Morton; one *s* two *d. Educ:* Bradfield Coll., Berks; Magdalen Coll., Oxford (BA Jurisprudence). Admitted Solicitor, 1959. Commnd (2nd Lieut) RA, 1952 (Nat. Service); Lieut TA, 1954. Slaughter and May, London: Articled Clerk, 1956–59; Asst Solicitor, 1959–68; Partner, 1968–89. Inspector, DTI, 1987–. Hon. Sen. Res. Fellow, KCL, 1988–. Chairman: Nat. Fedn of Consumers Groups, 1968; Cttee of Inquiry, Accountants Jt Disciplinary Scheme, 1989–; Mem., Home Office Cttee on London Taxicab and Car Hire Trade, 1967. Clerk to Governors, Bradfield Coll., 1968–89, Governor, 1989–. *Publications:* (contrib.) Sovereign Borrowers, 1984; (contrib.) Current Issues of International Financial Law, 1985; (jtly) Butterworths Banking Documents, 1986; (contrib.) Butterworths Banking and Financial Law Review, 1987; contribs on legal aspects of internat. finance to Jl of Business Law, Euromoney and Internat. Financial Law Review. *Recreations:* gardening, electronics (holder of Amateur Transmitting Licence), beekeeping, map collecting, reading, jazz, playing the trumpet/cornet. *Address:* 12 Northampton Park, N1 2PJ. *T:* 071–226 8055. *Club:* Garrick.

YOUDS, His Honour Edward Ernest; a Circuit Judge, Bedford, 1972–85; *b* 21 Nov. 1910; *s* of late Edward Youds. *Educ:* Birkenhead Sch.; Magdalene Coll., Cambridge. BA, LLB (Hons) Cantab. Called to Bar, Gray's Inn, 1936. Practised on Northern Circuit as Barrister-at-law. Served 1940–45, France and Germany (despatches, 1945). Dep. Chm., Lancs County Sessions, 1961–66; County Court Judge, 1966–69; Puisne Judge, High Court, Uganda, 1969–72.

YOUELL, Rev. Canon George; *b* 23 Dec. 1910; *s* of late Herbert Youell, Beccles; *m* 1st, 1936, Gertrude Barron (*d* 1982), *d* of late J. Irvine, West Hartlepool; two *s* three *d*; 2nd, 1983, Mary Nina, *d* of late Revd H. G. Phillipson. *Educ:* Beccles; St Michaels; Hartley Coll., Manchester; St Stephen's House, Oxford; Univ. of Keele (MA 1969). Ordained, 1933; Curate, St John's, Chester, 1933; Clerical Dir of Industrial Christian Fellowship, 1937; chaplain attached to 2nd Bn Grenadier Guards (BEF and Guards Armoured Div.), 1939; Sen. Chaplain to Forces: Nigeria, 1942; Woolwich and SE London, 1944; Nigeria and Gold Coast, 1945; Rector of Ightfield with Calverhall, Salop, 1947; Rural Dean of Leek, 1952–56; Vicar of Leek, 1952–61; Archdeacon of Stoke-upon-Trent, 1956–70; Vicar of Horton, Leek, 1968–70; Chaplain, Univ. of Keele, 1961–68; Hon. Canon, Lichfield Cathedral, 1967–70; Canon Residentiary of Ely Cathedral, 1970–81; Vice-Dean and Treas., 1973–81. *Publications:* Africa Marches, 1949; contributor on colonial and sociological affairs to the Guardian, 1947–51. *Recreations:* fell walking, gardening. *Address:* 6 St Mary's Court, Ely, Cambs CB7 4HQ.

YOUENS, Ven. Archdeacon John Ross, CB 1970; OBE 1959; MC 1946; Chaplain to the Queen 1969–84; Senior Treasurer, Corporation of the Sons of the Clergy, 1982–84; *b* 29 Sept. 1914; *e s* of late Canon F. A. C. Youens; *m* 1940, Pamela Gordon Lincoln (*née* Chandler); one *s* (two *d* decd). *Educ:* Buxton Coll.; Kelham Theological Coll. Curate of Warsop, Notts, 1939–40. Commissioned RA Chaplains' Dept, 1940; Aldershot and SE Comd, 1940–42; Sen. Chaplain: 59 Inf. Div., 1942; Chatham, 1943; 2nd Army Troops, June 1944; Guards Armd Div., Nov. 1944–45; 3rd Inf. Div. in Egypt and Palestine, 1945–48; 7th Armd Div. in Germany, 1948–50; Aldershot, 1950–51; DACG, Egypt, 1951–53; Tripoli, 1953–54; Sen. Chaplain, RMA Sandhurst, 1955–58; DACG, Gibraltar, 1958–60; ACG War Office, 1960–61, Rhine Army, 1961–66; Chaplain General to the Forces, 1966–74; Archdeacon Emeritus, 1974. Dep. Chairman, Keston Coll., Centre for the Study of Religion and Communism (Mem. Council, 1975–84). *Address:* King Edward VII Convalescent Home, Osborne House, East Cowes, Isle of Wight PO32 6JY. *Clubs:* Cavalry and Guards (Hon. Mem.), MCC.

YOUENS, Sir Peter (William), Kt 1965; CMG 1962; OBE 1960; *b* 29 April 1916; 2nd *s* of late Canon F. A. C. Youens; *m* 1943, Diana Stephanie (*d* 1990), *d* of Edward Hawkins, Southacre, Norfolk; two *d. Educ:* King Edward VII's School, Sheffield; Wadham College, Oxford. MA (Oxon), 1938. Joined Colonial Administrative Service; naval service, 1939–40. Sub-Lt, Cadet S. L., 1939; Asst Dist Comr, 1942; Dist Comr, 1948; Colony Comr and Member, Sierra Leone Legislative Council, 1950; Asst Sec., Nyasaland, 1951; Dep. Chief Sec., 1953–63; Secretary to the Prime Minister and to the Cabinet, Malawi, 1964–66 (Nyasaland, 1963–64); Mem., Nyasaland Legislative Council, 1954–61. Retired, 1966. Exec. Dir, Lonrho Ltd, 1966–69, Non-Exec. Dir, 1980–81, Exec. Dir, 1981–; Partner, John Tyzack & Partners Ltd, 1969–81. *Address:* Hill View, Primrose Hill Road, NW3. *Clubs:* East India, Devonshire, Sports and Public Schools; Vincent's (Oxford).

YOUNG, family name of **Baron Kennet, Baroness Young** and **Barons Young of Dartington** and **Young of Graffham.**

YOUNG; *see* Hughes-Young, family name of Baron St Helens.

YOUNG, Baroness *cr* 1971 (Life Peer), of Farnworth in the County Palatine of Lancaster; **Janet Mary Young;** PC 1981; DL; *b* 23 Oct. 1926; *d* of John Norman Leonard Baker and Phyllis Marguerite Baker (*née* Hancock); *m* 1950, Geoffrey Tyndale Young; three *d. Educ:* Dragon School Oxford, Headington School, and in America; St Anne's Coll., Oxford; MA (Politics, Philosophy and Economics); Hon. Fellow, 1978. Baroness in Waiting (Govt Whip), 1972–73; Parly Under-Sec. of State, DoE, 1973–74; Minister of State, DES, 1979–81; Chancellor, Duchy of Lancaster, 1981–82; Leader of House of Lords, 1981–83; Lord Privy Seal, 1982–83; Minister of State, FCO, 1983–87. A Vice-Chm., Cons. Party Organisation, 1975–83, Dep. Chm., 1977–79. Co-Chm., Women's Nat. Commn, 1979–83. Councillor Oxford City Council, 1957; Alderman, 1967–72; Leader of Conservative Group, 1967–72. Director: UK Provident Instn, 1975–79; Nat. Westminster Bank, 1987–; Marks and Spencer Plc, 1987–. Mem., BR Adv. Bd, Western Reg., 1977–79. Mem., West End Hand-in-Hand Bd, Commercial Union, 1991–. Chairman: ISJC, 1989–; GBGSA, 1989–. A Vice-President: W India Cttee, 1987–; Assoc. of Dist Councils, 1990–. Member: Council of Management, Ditchley Foundn, 1990–; Court, Cranfield Inst. of Technology, 1991–. DL Oxon, 1989. Hon. FICE. Hon. DCL Mt Holyoke Coll., 1982. *Recreation:* music. *Address:* House of Lords, SW1A 0PW.

YOUNG OF DARTINGTON, Baron *cr* 1978 (Life Peer), of Dartington in the County of Devon; **Michael Young,** BSc (Econ), MA, PhD; Director, Institute of Community Studies since 1953; Deputy Chairman, Dartington Hall, since 1980 (Trustee, since 1942); *b* 9 Aug. 1915; father a musician, mother a writer; *m* 1st, 1945, Joan Lawson; two *s* one *d*; 2nd, 1960, Sasha Moorsom; one *s* one *d. Educ:* Dartington Hall Sch.; London Univ. Barrister, Gray's Inn. Dir of Political and Economic Planning, 1941–45; Sec., Research Dept, Lab. Party, 1945–51. Chairman: Social Science Research Council, 1965–68; Dartington Amenity Research Trust, 1967–; Internat. Extension Coll., 1970–; Nat. Consumer Council, 1975–77; Mutual Aid Centre, 1977–; Coll. of Health, 1983–90; Health Information Trust, 1987–; Argo Venture, 1984–; Open Coll. of the Arts, 1987–; Open Sch., 1989–; Dir, Mauritius Coll. of the Air, 1972; Member: Central Adv. Council for Education, 1963–66; NEDC, 1975–78; Policy Cttee, SDP, 1981–83; President: Consumer's Assoc., 1965– (Chm., 1956–65); National Extension Coll., 1971– (Chm., 1962–71); Adv. Centre for Educn, 1976– (Chm., 1959–76); Birkbeck Coll., London Univ., 1989–. Chm., Tawney Soc., 1982–84. Fellow, Churchill Coll., Cambridge, 1961–66; Vis. Prof. of Extension Educn, Ahmadu Bello Univ., Nigeria, 1974; Regents' Lectr, UCLA, 1985. Hon. LittD Sheffield, 1965; DUniv Open, 1973; Hon. DLitt: Adelaide, 1974; Keele, 1991; Hon. LLD Exeter, 1982. Hon. Fellow: LSE, 1978; Plymouth Polytechnic, 1980; QMC, 1983. *Publications:* Family and Kinship in East London (with Peter Willmott), 1957; The Rise of the Meritocracy, 1958; (with Peter Willmott) Family and Class in a London Suburb, 1960; Innovation and Research in Education, 1965; (with Patrick McGeeney) Learning Begins at Home, 1968; (ed) Forecasting and the Social Sciences, 1968; (with Peter Willmott) The Symmetrical Family, 1973; (ed) The Poverty Report, 1974 and 1975; (with Marianne Rigge) Mutual Aid in a Selfish Society, 1979; (with others) Distance Teaching for the Third World, 1980; The Elmhirsts of Dartington—the creation of an Utopian Community, 1982; (with Marianne Rigge) Revolution From Within: co-operatives and co-operation in British industry, 1983; Social Scientist as Innovator, 1984; The Metronomic Society, 1988; (ed with Tom Schuller) The Rhythms of Society, 1988; (with Tom Schuller) Life After Work—the arrival of the ageless society, 1991. *Recreation:* painting. *Address:* 18 Victoria Park Square, E2 9PF.

YOUNG OF GRAFFHAM, Baron *cr* 1984 (Life Peer), of Graffham in the County of W Sussex; **David Ivor Young;** PC 1984; Executive Chairman, Cable and Wireless, since 1990; Director, Salomon Inc., since 1990; *b* 27 Feb. 1932; *s* of late Joseph and of Rebecca Young; *m* 1956, Lita Marianne Shaw; two *d. Educ:* Christ's Coll., Finchley; University Coll., London (LLB Hons; Fellow, 1988). Admitted solicitor, 1956. Exec., Great Universal Stores Ltd, 1956–61; Chairman: Eldonwall Ltd, 1961–75; Manufacturers Hanover Property Services Ltd, 1974–84; Dir, Town & City Properties Ltd, 1972–75. Chairman: British ORT, 1975–80, Pres., 1980–82; Admin. Cttee, World ORT Union, 1980–84. Dir, Centre for Policy Studies, 1979–82 (Mem., Management Bd, 1977); Mem., English Industrial Estates Corp., 1980–82; Chm., Manpower Services Commn, 1982–84. Industrial Adviser, 1979–80, Special Adviser, 1980–82, DoI; Minister without Portfolio, 1984–85; Sec. of State for Employment, 1985–87; Sec. of State for Trade and Industry, 1987–89; Dep. Chm., Cons. Party, 1989–90. Mem., NEDC, 1982–89. Pres., Jewish Care, 1990–; Chairman: Internat. Council of Jewish Social and Welfare Services, 1981–84; Bd of Govs, Oxford Centre for Postgrad. Hebrew Studies, 1989–. Dir, Royal Opera House Trust, 1990–. Hon. FRPS, 1981. *Publication:* The Enterprise Years: a businessman in the Cabinet, 1990. *Recreations:* golf, fishing, photography. *Address:* c/o 88 Brook Street, W1. *Clubs:* Savile; West Sussex Golf.

See also B. A. Rix.

YOUNG, Prof. Alec David, OBE 1964; MA; FRS 1973; FEng 1976; Professor and Head of the Department of Aeronautical Engineering, Queen Mary College, London University, 1954–78, now Emeritus; Vice-Principal, Queen Mary College, 1966–78; *b* 15 Aug. 1913; *s* of Isaac Young and Katherine (*née* Freeman); *m* 1st, 1937, Dora Caplan (*d* 1970); two *s* one *d*; 2nd, 1971, Rena Waldmann (*née* Szafer). *Educ:* Caius Coll., Cambridge. Wrangler, Mathematical Tripos, 1935. Research Student in Aeronautics, Cambridge, 1935–36; Mem. of staff, Aerodynamics Dept, Royal Aircraft Estab., 1936–46; College of Aeronautics: Senior Lectr and Dep. Head of Dept of Aerodynamics, 1946–50; Prof. and Head of Dept of Aerodynamics, 1950–54. Dean, Faculty of Engineering, Univ. of London, 1962–66; Mem. Senate, Univ. of London, 1970–78. Mem. various Cttees of Aeronautical Research Council, Chm. of Council, 1968–71. Exec. Sec., Internat. Council of Aeronautical Scis, 1987–90. Chm., Bd of Direction, Von Karman Institute for Fluid Dynamics, 1964; Mem., Advisory Bd, RAF Coll., Cranwell, 1966. Gold Medal, 1972, Royal Aeronautical Soc. (Past Chm., Aerodynamics Data Sheets Cttee); FRAeS, 1951, Hon. FRAeS 1984. Ludwig Prandtl Ring, Deutsche Gesellschaft für Luft-und Raumfahrt, 1976; Von Karman Medal, AGARD, 1979. Commandeur de l'Ordre de Leopold, 1976. Fellow: QMC, 1980; AIAA, 1987. Editor, Progress in Aerospace Sciences, 1983–. *Publications:* (jtly) An Elementary Treatise on the Mechanics of Fluids, 1960, 2nd edn 1970; (jtly) Aircraft Excrescence Drag, 1981; Boundary Layers, 1989; various, of Aeronautical Research Council, Coll. of Aeronautics Reports series; articles in Aeronautical Quarterly and Jl of Royal Aeronautical Soc., Quarterly Jl of Mechanics and Applied Mathematics, and Aircraft Engineering. *Recreations:* drama, sketching, etching. *Address:* 70 Gilbert Road, Cambridge CB4 3PD. *T:* Cambridge (0223) 354625.

YOUNG, Alexander, FRNCM; retired as free-lance concert and opera singer; Head of Department of Vocal Studies, Royal Northern College of Music, Manchester, 1973–86; *b* London; *m* 1948, Jean Anne Prewett; one *s* one *d. Educ:* secondary; (scholar) Royal Coll. of Music, London; studied in London with late Prof. Pollmann, of Vienna State Academy. FRNCM 1977. Served War, HM Forces, 1941–46. Has regular engagements with the BBC and has sung in the USA, Canada, and most European countries, as well as frequently in Britain. First operatic rôle (tenor), as Scaramuccio in Strauss' Ariadne, Edin. Fest., with Glyndebourne Opera, 1950; parts at Glyndebourne, and began broadcasting for BBC, 1951 (subseq. incl. opera, oratorio, recitals, light music, etc). First appearances: with English Opera Group, world Première of Lennox Berkeley's opera, A Dinner Engagement, 1954; also appeared at Royal Festival Hall, several times with Sir Thomas Beecham, in Mozart Requiem; at Sadler's Wells Opera, as Eisenstein in Die Fledermaus, 1959, and subsequently in many roles such as: Ramiro in La Cenerentola; title role in Count Ory; Almaviva in The Barber of Seville; notable roles include: Tom in Stravinsky's Rake's Progress (which he created for British audiences); David in Die Meistersinger; title role in Mozart's Idomeneo. At Covent Garden sang in: Strauss's Arabella; Britten's A Midsummer Night's Dream. Oratorio roles include: Evangelist in Bach Passions; Elgar's Dream of Gerontius; Britten's War Requiem. Was regularly engaged by Welsh National Opera and Scottish Opera. Many commercial recordings, especially of Handel oratorios and operas, as well as The Rake's Progress conducted by the composer. Lieder recitals a speciality. *Recreations:* railway modelling, stamp collecting, photography.

YOUNG, Andrew; Mayor of Atlanta, Georgia, 1982; *b* New Orleans, La, 12 March 1932; *s* of Andrew J. Young and Daisy Fuller; *m* 1954, Jean Childs; one *s* three *d. Educ:* Howard Univ., USA; Hartford Theological Seminary. Ordained, United Church of Christ, 1955; Pastor, Thomasville, Ga, 1955–57; Associate Dir for Youth Work, Nat. Council of Churches, 1957–61; Admin. Christian Educn Programme, United Church of Christ,

1961–64; Mem. Staff, Southern Christian Leadership Conf., 1961–70; Exec. Dir, 1964–70; Exec. Vice-Pres., 1967–70; elected to US House of Representatives from 5th District of Georgia, 1972 (first Black Congressman from Georgia in 101 years); re-elected 1974 and 1976; US Ambassador to UN, 1977–79. Chairman: Atlanta Community Relations Commn, 1970–72; National Democratic voter registration drive, 1976; during 1960s organized voter registration and community develt programmes. Holds numerous hon. degrees and awards. *Address:* c/o The Office of the Mayor, 68 Mitchell Street SW, Atlanta, Georgia 30303, USA.

YOUNG, Dr Andrew Buchanan, FRCPE, FFPHM; Deputy Chief Medical Officer, Scottish Office Home and Health Department, since 1989; *b* 11 Aug. 1937; *s* of Alexander and Elizabeth Young; *m* 1965, Lois Lilian Howarth; one *s* one *d.* *Educ:* Falkirk High School; Edinburgh Univ. (MB ChB). DTM&H. Supt, Presbyterian Church of E Africa Hosps, Kenya, 1965–72; Fellow in Community Medicine, Scottish Health Service, 1972–75; Scottish Home and Health Department: MO 1975; SMO 1978; PMO 1985. Dir, Edinburgh Medical Missionary Soc. *Recreations:* singing in choirs, reading. *Address:* 6 Queen's Crescent, Edinburgh EH9 2AZ. *T:* 031–667 6627.

YOUNG, Barbara Scott; Chief Executive, Royal Society for the Protection of Birds, since 1991; *b* 8 April 1948; *d* of George Young and Mary (*née* Scott). *Educ:* Perth Acad.; Edinburgh Univ. (MA Classics); Strathclyde Univ. (Diploma Sec. Sci.); DipHSM, 1971. Various posts, finally Sector Administrator, Greater Glasgow Health Bd, 1973–78; Dir of Planning and Develt, St Thomas' Health Dist, 1978–79; Dist Gen. Administrator, NW Dist, Kensington and Chelsea and Westminster AHA, 1979–82; Dist Administrator, Haringey HA, 1982–85; District General Manager: Paddington and N Kensington HA, 1985–88; Parkside HA, 1988–91. Member: BBC Gen. Adv. Cttee, 1985–88; Cttee, King's Fund Inst., 1986–90; Delegacy, St Mary's Hosp. Med. Sch., 1991–. Pres., Inst. of Health Services Management, 1987–88. Internat. Fellow, King Edward VII Hosp. Fund Coll., 1985–87 and 1990. Trustee, Wytham Hall, 1990–. FRSA. *Publications:* (contrib.) What Women Want, 1990; (contrib.) Medical Negligence, 1990; articles in Hosp. Doctor. *Recreations:* obsessive cinema going, gardening. *Address:* Royal Society for the Protection of Birds, The Lodge, Sandy, Beds SG19 2DL. *T:* Sandy (0767) 680551.

YOUNG, Bertram Alfred, OBE 1980; dramatic critic, since 1964, and arts editor, 1971–77, The Financial Times; *b* 20 Jan. 1912; *y* (twin) *s* of Bertram William Young and Dora Elizabeth Young (*née* Knight); unmarried. *Educ:* Highgate. Served with Artists Rifles, 1930–35, and Lancs Fusiliers, KAR and Staff, 1939–48; Asst Editor, Punch, 1949–62; Dramatic Critic, Punch, 1962–64. Mem., British Council Drama Adv. Cttee, 1973–83; Pres., Critics' Circle, 1978–80. Hon. Kentucky Col, 1980. *Publications:* Tooth and Claw, 1958; How to Avoid People, 1963; Bechuanaland, 1966; Cabinet Pudding, 1967; Colonists from Space, 1979; The Mirror up to Nature, 1982; The Rattigan Version, 1986; author of about 20 radio plays broadcast 1938–49. *Recreation:* music (consumer only). *Address:* Clyde House, Station Street, Cheltenham GL50 3LX. *T:* Cheltenham (0242) 581485. *Club:* Garrick.

YOUNG, Air Vice-Marshal Brian Pashley, CB 1972; CBE 1960 (OBE 1944); Commandant General, RAF Regiment, 1968–73; *b* 5 May 1918; *s* of Kenneth Noel Young and Flora Elizabeth Young, Natal, S Africa; *m* 1942, Patricia Josephine, *d* of Thomas Edward Cole, Bedford; three *s* two *d.* *Educ:* Michaelhouse, Natal, SA; RAF Coll., Cranwell. Fighter Comd, UK and France, 1938–40 (wounded); Hosp., 1941–42; Coastal Comd, N Ire and Western Isles, 1942–43; Aden and Persian Gulf, 1944; Staff Coll., Haifa, 1945; Middle East, 1946–47; Air Min., 1948–50; Bomber Comd HQ No 1 Gp, Hemswell/Gaydon, 1951–57; HQ Bomber Comd, 1958–60; NATO, Fontainebleau, Asst Chief of Staff, Intelligence, 1960–62; IDC 1963; AOC, Central Reconnaisance Estabt, 1964–67. Planning Inspector, DoE, 1973–83. Rep. RAF: athletics, 1939, Rugby, 1947–48. *Address:* Chapel Walk House, The Street, Didmarton, Glos. *Club:* Royal Air Force.

YOUNG, Sir Brian (Walter Mark), Kt 1976; MA; Chairman, Christian Aid, 1983–90; *b* 23 Aug. 1922; *er s* of late Sir Mark Young, GCMG and Josephine (*née* Price); *m* 1947, Fiona Marjorie, *o d* of late Allan, 16th Stewart of Appin, and Marjorie (*née* Ballance); one *s* two *d.* *Educ:* Eton (King's Schol.); King's College, Cambridge (Schol.). Served in RNVR, mainly in destroyers, 1941–45. First class hons in Part I, 1946, and Part II, 1947, of Classical Tripos; Porson Prize, 1946; Winchester Reading Prize, 1947; BA 1947; MA 1952. Assistant Master at Eton, 1947–52; Headmaster of Charterhouse, 1952–64; Dir, Nuffield Foundn, 1964–70; Dir-Gen., IBA (formerly ITA), 1970–82. Member: Central Advisory Council for Education, 1956–59 (Crowther Report); Central Religious Adv. Cttee of BBC and ITA, 1960–64; Bd of Centre for Educn Develt Overseas, 1969–72; Arts Council of GB, 1983–88; Exec. Cttee, British Council of Churches, 1983–90; Chm., Associated Bd of the Royal Schs of Music, 1984–87. Pres., British and Foreign Sch. Soc., 1991–. A Managing Trustee, Nuffield Foundn, 1978–90; Trustee: Lambeth Palace Liby, 1984–; Imperial War Mus., 1985–. Hon. RNCM, 1987. Hon. DLitt Heriot-Watt, 1980. *Publications:* Via Vertendi, 1952; Intelligent Reading (with P. D. R. Gardiner), 1964; The Villein's Bible: stories in Romanesque carving, 1990. *Recreations:* music, travel, history, problems. *Address:* Hill End, Woodhill Avenue, Gerrards Cross, Bucks SL9 8DJ. *T:* Gerrards Cross (0753) 887793.

YOUNG, Christopher Godfrey; His Honour Judge Young; a Circuit Judge, since 1980; *b* 9 Sept. 1932; *s* of the late Harold Godfrey Young, MB, ChB, and Gladys Mary Young; *m* 1969, Jeanetta Margaret (*d* 1984), *d* of Halford and Dorothy Vaughan; one *s.* *Educ:* Bedford Sch.; King's Coll., Univ. of London (LLB Hons 1954). Called to the Bar, Gray's Inn, 1957; Midland and Oxford Circuit, 1959; a Recorder of the Crown Court, 1975–79. Mem., Parole Bd, 1990–. Chm., Maidwell with Draughton Parish Council, 1973–76. *Recreations:* music, natural history, gardening. *Address:* Stockshill House, Duddington, near Stamford, Lincs PE9 3QQ.

YOUNG, Colin, OBE 1976; Director, National Film and Television School of Great Britain, since 1970; *b* 5 April 1927; *s* of Colin Young and Agnes Holmes Kerr Young; *m* 1st, 1960, Kristin Ohman; two *s*; 2nd, 1987, Constance Yvonne Templeman; one *s* one *d.* *Educ:* Bellahouston Academy, Glasgow; Univs of Glasgow, St Andrews and California (Los Angeles). Theatre and film critic, Bon Accord, Aberdeen, 1951; cameraman, editor, writer, director, 1953–; producer, 1967–; UCLA (Motion Pictures): Instructor, 1956–59; Asst Prof., 1959–64; Assoc. Prof., 1964–68; Prof., 1968–70, Head, Motion Picture Div., Theater Arts Dept, UCLA, 1964–65; Chm., Dept of Theater Arts, 1965–70. Res. Associate, Centre Nat. de Recherche Scientifique, Paris, 1984 and 1987; Andrew W. Mellon Vis. Prof. in Humanities, Rice Univ., Houston, Texas, 1985–86. Vice-Chm., 1972–76, Chm., 1976–, Edinburgh Film Festival; Governor, BFI, 1974–80. Member: Arts Council Film Cttee, 1972–76; Public Media Panel, Nat. Endowment for Arts, Washington, 1972–77; Gen. Adv. Council, BBC, 1973–78; Council of Management, BAFTA, 1974–81; Exec. Cttee, Centre International de Liaison des Ecoles de Cinéma et de Télévision, 1974– (Pres., 1980–); Nat. Film Finance Corp., 1979–85. Consultant, Goldcrest Films & Television Ltd, 1985–86. FBKS 1975. Chm., Cttee on Educational Policy, UCLA, 1968–69. London Editor, Film Quarterly, 1970– (Los Angeles Editor, 1958–68). Michael Balcon Award, BAFTA, 1983. Chevalier de l'Ordre des Arts et des Lettres (France), 1987. *Publications:* various articles in collections of film essays including Principles of Visual Anthropology, 1975; experimental film essay for Unesco, 1963; ethnographic film essay for Unesco, 1966; contribs to Film Quarterly, Sight and Sound, Jl of Aesthetic Education, Jl of the Producers Guild of America, Kosmorama (Copenhagen), etc. *Address:* National Film and Television School, Beaconsfield, Bucks.

YOUNG, David Edward Michael, QC 1980; a Recorder, since 1987; *b* 30 Sept. 1940; *s* of George Henry Edward Young and Audrey Young; *m* 1968, Ann de Bromhead; two *d.* *Educ:* Monkton Combe Sch.; Hertford Coll., Oxford (MA). Called to the Bar, Lincoln's Inn, 1966, Bencher, 1989; practising at Chancery Bar, specialising in indust. property work. Chm., Plant Varieties and Seeds Tribunal, 1987–. *Publications:* (co-ed) Terrell on the Law of Patents, 12th edn 1971, 13th edn 1982; Passing Off, 1985, 2nd edn 1989. *Recreations:* tennis, country pursuits, ski-ing. *Address:* 6 Pump Court, Temple, EC4Y 7AR.

YOUNG, (David) Junor; HM Diplomatic Service; Deputy High Commissioner, Karachi, since 1991; *b* 23 April 1934; *m* 1954, Kathleen Brooks; two *s* two *d.* *Educ:* Robert Gordon's College. Joined Foreign Office, 1951; served Berlin, Ankara, South Africa, DSAO, Port Louis, Belgrade, 1951–75; Consul (Comm.), Stuttgart, 1978–81; First Sec., Kampala, 1981–84; Consul Gen., Hamburg, 1984–86; Counsellor (Commercial), Bonn, 1986–88; High Comr, Solomon Is, 1988–90. *Recreations:* fishing, shooting. *Address:* c/o Foreign and Commonwealth Office, SW1A 2AH. *Club:* Naval and Military.

YOUNG, Rt. Rev. David Nigel de Lorentz; *see* Ripon, Bishop of.

YOUNG, Lt-Gen. Sir David (Tod), KBE 1980; CB 1977; DFC 1952; Chairman, Cairntech Ltd, Edinburgh, since 1983; GOC Scotland and Governor of Edinburgh Castle, 1980–82; *b* 17 May 1926; *s* of late William Young and Davina Tod Young; *m* 1st, 1950, Joyce Marian Melville (*d* 1987); two *s*; 2nd, 1988, Joanna Myrtle Oyler (*née* Torin). *Educ:* George Watson's Coll., Edinburgh. Commissioned, The Royal Scots (The Royal Regt), 1945 (Col, 1975–80). Attached Glider Pilot Regt, 1949–52; Bt Lt-Col, 1964; Mil. Asst to Dep. Chief of Gen. Staff, MoD, 1964–67; commanded 1st Bn The Royal Scots (The Royal Regt), 1967–69; Col Gen. Staff, Staff Coll., 1969–70; Comdr, 12th Mechanized Bde, 1970–72; Dep. Mil. Sec., MoD, 1972–74; Comdr Land Forces, NI, 1975–77; Dir of Infantry, 1977–80. Col Comdt: Scottish Div., 1980–82; UDR, 1986–91; Hon. Col, NI Regt AAC, 1988. Pres., ACFA, Scotland, 1984–. HM Comr, Queen Victoria Sch., Dunblane, 1984–. Chm., St Mary's Cathedral Workshop Ltd, 1986–. Chm. Scottish Cttee, Marie Curie Meml Foundn, 1986– (Mem., 1983–); Governor, St Columba's Hospice, Edinburgh, 1986–. *Recreations:* golf, shooting, spectator of sports. *Address:* c/o Adam & Co. plc, 22 Charlotte Square, Edinburgh EH2 4DF. *Clubs:* Royal Scots, New (Edinburgh).

YOUNG, David Tyrrell; Deputy Chairman, Touche Ross, since 1990; *b* 6 Jan. 1938; *s* of Tyrrell F. Young and Patricia M. Young (*née* Spicer); *m* 1965, Madeline Helen Celia Philips; three *d.* *Educ:* Charterhouse. Trained as Chartered Accountant, Gérard van de Linde & Son, 1955–60; James Edward Dangerfield, 1961–65; joined Spicer & Pegler, later Spicer & Oppenheim, 1965 (merged with Touche Ross, 1990): Partner 1968; Managing Partner, 1982; Sen. Partner, 1988–90. Mem. Council, Inst. of Chartered Accountants in England and Wales, 1979–82. Mem. Court, Fishmongers' Co., 1981–. *Recreations:* golf, tennis, limited gardening. *Address:* Overhall, Ashdon, Saffron Walden, Essex CB10 2JH. *T:* Saffron Walden (0799) 84556. *Clubs:* City of London, Honourable Artillery Company; Royal St George's Golf, Royal Worlington Golf.

YOUNG, David Wright; MP (Lab) Bolton South East, since 1983 (Bolton East, Feb. 1974–1983); teacher; *b* Greenock, Scotland. *Educ:* Greenock Academy; Glasgow Univ.; St Paul's Coll., Cheltenham. Head of History Dept; subseq. insurance executive. Joined Labour Party, 1955; contested: South Worcestershire, 1959; Banbury, 1966; Bath, 1970. PPS to Sec. of State for Defence, 1977–79. Member: Select Cttee on Employment, 1982–; Public Accts Commn, 1983–. Formerly Alderman, Nuneaton Borough Council; Councillor, Nuneaton District Council. Chm., Coventry East Labour Party, 1964–68. Member: TGWU; Co-operative Party. Is especially interested in comprehensive educn, defence, pensions, economics. *Recreations:* reading, motoring. *Address:* House of Commons, SW1A 0AA.

YOUNG, Donald Anthony, CEng, FIGasE; CBIM; Managing Director, National Transmission, British Gas plc, since 1991; *b* 23 June 1933; *s* of Cyril Charles Young and Sarah Young; *m* 1960, June (*née* Morrey); two *d.* *Educ:* Stockport Secondary Sch. FIGasE 1969. National Service, 2nd Lieut REME, 1953–55. North Western Gas Bd, 1949–60; E Midlands Gas Bd, 1960–68; Gas Council Terminal Manager, Bacton Natural Gas Reception Terminal, 1968–70; Gas Council Plant Ops Engr, 1970–73; Asst Dir (Ops), Prodn & Supply Div., British Gas HQ, 1973–77; Regional Dep. Chm., N Thames Gas, 1977–79; Dir (Operations), Prodn & Supply Div., British Gas HQ, 1979–83; Regional Chairman: Southern Reg., British Gas Corp., subseq. British Gas plc Southern, 1983–89; British Gas plc West Midlands, 1989–91. CBIM 1986. *Recreations:* gardening, walking. *Address:* c/o British Gas plc, Rivermill House, 152 Grosvenor Road, SW1V 3JL.

YOUNG, Edward Preston, DSO 1944; DSC 1943; writer and retired book designer; *b* 17 Nov. 1913; *m* 1st, 1945, Diana Lilian Graves (marr. diss.); two *d*; 2nd, 1956, Mary Reoch Cressall. *Educ:* Highgate Sch. Served War, 1940–45: RNVR; entered submarine service 1940 (despatches, DSC); first RNVR officer to command operational submarine, 1943 (DSO, Bar to DSC); temp. Commander RNVR, 1945. Man. Dir, Rainbird Publishing Gp Ltd, 1970–73. *Publications:* One of Our Submarines, 1952; Look at Lighthouses, 1961; The Fifth Passenger, 1962; Look at Submarines, 1964. *Address:* 15 Maple Walk, Rustington, W Sussex.

YOUNG, Eric, OBE 1976; HM Diplomatic Service, retired; Editor, Control Risks Information Services, since 1984; *b* 16 Nov. 1924; *s* of late Robert Young, MBE, and Emily Florence Young, Doncaster; *m* 1949, Sheila Hutchinson; three *s* one *d.* *Educ:* Maltby Grammar Sch.; Sheffield Univ. (BA 1948). Served War, RN, 1943–46. Editorial staff: Sheffield Telegraph, 1948; Western Morning News, 1951; Daily Dispatch, 1952; Manchester Guardian, 1953; PRO, NCB, Manchester, 1958; Dep. Dir, UK Inf. Office, Tanganyika and Zanzibar, 1960; First Secretary: (Inf.), Dar es Salaam, 1961; (Aid), Kaduna, 1963; Commonwealth Office (later FCO), 1967; Madras, 1969; Head of Chancery, Reykjavik, 1973 (Hd of Brit. Interests Section, French Embassy, during breach of diplomatic relations, 1976); Dep. High Comr, Bombay, 1977; High Comr, Seychelles, 1980–83. *Recreations:* music, books, hill walking in England and France. *Address:* c/o Midland Bank, 11 Stamford New Road, Altrincham, Cheshire WA14 1BW.

See also Air Vice-Marshal G. Young.

YOUNG, Frieda Margaret, OBE 1969; HM Diplomatic Service, retired; *b* 9 April 1913; *d* of Arthur Edward Young. *Educ:* Wyggeston Grammar Sch., Leicester; Wycombe Abbey Sch., Bucks; and in France and Germany. Home Office, 1937–39; Min. of Home Security, 1939–41; MOI 1941–44; Paris 1944–48; Tehran 1948–51; Vienna 1951–54; FO 1954–57; First Secretary and Consul, Reykjavik, 1957–59; Consul, Cleveland, 1959–62; FO 1962–65; Consul, Bergen, 1965–68; Consul-General, Rotterdam, 1968–73. *Recreations:* travel, bird-watching. *Address:* 6 Lady Street, Lavenham, Suffolk.

YOUNG, Gavin David, FRSL, FRGS; foreign correspondent, author and traveller; *b* 24 April 1928; *s* of Lt-Col Gavin David Young and Daphne, *yr d* of Sir Leolin Forestier-Walker, Bt, KBE. *Educ:* Rugby; Trinity Coll., Oxford (MA). FRSL 1987; FRGS 1989. National Service, Lieut, Welsh Guards, 1946–48; served Palestine, 1947–48. Lived with Marsh Arabs of S Iraq, 1952–54; at large in SW Arabia (Hejaz, Tihama and Asir), with Desert Locust Control, 1954–56; foreign corresp. with The Observer, 1959–90, covering wars, etc, in Algeria, Cuba, Nagaland, Congo, Middle East, Kurdistan, Yemen, Bangladesh, Angola, Vietnam, Cambodia; Observer's corresp. in NY, 1962–63, Paris, 1967. *Publications:* Return to the Marshes, 1977; Iraq: land of two rivers, 1979; Slow Boats to China, 1981; Slow Boats Home, 1985; Worlds Apart, 1987; Beyond Lion Rock, 1988; In Search of Conrad, 1991; contribs to jls and magazines. *Recreations:* travel in remote places, reading, walking, music, talking late. *Address:* c/o Weil, 49 Earls Court Road, W8 6EE. *T:* 071–937 3538. *Clubs:* Brooks's, Beefsteak, Cavalry and Guards, Pratt's, Travellers'; Foreign Correspondents' (Hong Kong).

YOUNG, Gavin Neil B.; *see* Barr Young.

YOUNG, George Bell, CBE 1976; Managing Director, East Kilbride Development Corporation, 1973–90 (and Stonehouse, 1973–77); *b* 17 June 1924; *s* of late George Bell Young and late Jemima Mackinlay; *m* 1946, Margaret Wylie Boyd (decd); one *s*; *m* 1979, Joyce Marguerite McAteer. *Educ:* Queens Park, Glasgow. MIEx 1958; FInstM 1984 (MInstM 1969); CBIM 1988 (FBIM 1982). RNVR, 1942–45, Lieut (destroyers and mine-sweepers). Journalist and Feature Writer, Glasgow Herald, 1945–48; North of Scotland Hydro-Electric Board, 1948–52; Chief Exec. (London), Scottish Council (Development and Industry), 1952–68 (Founder Fellow, 1986); Gen. Man., E Kilbride Develt Corp., 1968–73. Pres., Lanarks Br., BIM, 1985; Chm., BIM Scotland, 1988–91. Mem. Council, Nat. Trust for Scotland, 1974–79; Dir, Royal Caledonian Schools, 1957–85; Chm., East Kilbride and District National Savings Cttee, 1968–78; Trustee, Strathclyde Scanner Campaign; Scottish Chm., British Heart Foundn, 1975–79 (Mem., East Kilbride Cttee, 1970–; Pres., Scottish Appeal, 1980–). Hon. Vice-Pres., East Kilbride Dist Sports Council, 1984. Chm., E Kilbride Cttee, Order of St John, 1972–88 (CStJ 1979). Mem., Amer. Inst. of Corporate Asset Managers, 1985. Member: Saints and Sinners Club of Scotland (Hon. Sec., 1982–89; Chm., 1990); Royal Glasgow Inst. of the Fine Arts; The Merchants House of Glasgow; Mem. Scotland Cttee, Nat. Children's Homes, 1980–88. FRSA 1968. Freeman, East Kilbride, 1990. *Recreations:* reading, travel. *Address:* 4 Newlands Place, East Kilbride, Lanarkshire. *Clubs:* Caledonian; Royal Scottish Automobile (Glasgow).

YOUNG, Sir George (Samuel Knatchbull), 6th Bt, *cr* 1813; MP (C) Ealing, Acton, since Feb. 1974; Minister of State, Department of the Environment, since 1990; *b* 16 July 1941; *s* of Sir George Young, 5th Bt, CMG, and Elisabeth (*née* Knatchbull-Hugessen); *S* father 1960; *m* 1964, Aurelia Nemon-Stuart, *er d* of late Oscar Nemon, and of Mrs Nemon-Stuart, Boar's Hill, Oxford; two *s* two *d*. *Educ:* Eton; Christ Church, Oxford (Open Exhibitioner); MA Oxon, MPhil Surrey. Economist, NEDO, 1966–67; Kobler Research Fellow, University of Surrey, 1967–69; Economic Adviser, PO Corp., 1969–74. Councillor, London Borough of Lambeth, 1968–71; Mem., GLC, for London Borough of Ealing, 1970–73. An Opposition Whip, 1976–79; Parly Under Sec. of State, DHSS, 1979–81, DoE, 1981–86; Comptroller of HM Household, 1990. Chm., Acton Housing Assoc., 1972–79. Dir, Lovell Partnerships Ltd, 1987–90. Trustee, Guinness Trust, 1986–90. *Publications:* Accommodation Services in the UK 1970–1980, 1970; Tourism, Blessing or Blight?, 1973. *Recreations:* squash, bicycling. *Heir: s* George Horatio Young, *b* 11 Oct. 1966. *Address:* House of Commons, SW1A 0AA.

YOUNG, Gerard Francis, CBE 1967; DL; CEng, FIMechE; HM Lord-Lieutenant and Custos Rotolurum, for South Yorkshire, 1974–85; *b* 5 May 1910; *s* of Smelter J. Young, MICE, and Edith, *d* of Sir John Aspinall, Pres. ICE and Pres. IMechE; *m* 1937, Diana Graham Murray, MA, BSc, JP, *d* of Charles Graham Murray, MD; two *s* three *d*. *Educ:* Ampleforth College. Engrg Apprentice, LNER, Doncaster. Entered family firm, The Tempered Spring Co. Ltd (later Tempered Group Ltd), 1930; Dir, 1936; Man. Dir, 1942; Chm., 1954–78. Dir, 1958, Chm., 1967–80, Sheffield Area Board, Sun Alliance & London Insurance Group; Dir, National Vulcan Engineering Insce Group, 1962–79. Member: Nat. Bd for Prices and Incomes, 1968–71; Top Salaries Review Body, 1971–74; Armed Forces Pay Review Body, 1971–74; Gen. Comr of Income Tax, 1947–74 (Chm., Don Div., 1968–74). Dir, Crucible Theatre Trust Ltd, 1967–75; Sec., Assoc. of Christian Communities in Sheffield, 1940–46; Chm., Radio Hallam Ltd, 1973–79; Trustee, Sheffield Town Trust (Town Collector, 1978–81); Chm., J. G. Graves Charitable Fund, 1974–85; Chm., Freshgate Foundn, 1979–86; Mem., Finance Bd, RC Dio. of Hallam, 1981–. President: Council of St John, South and West Yorks, 1979–85; Yorks Volunteers Council, 1980–81; TAVRA Yorks & Humberside, 1983–85 (Vice-Pres., 1974–82). Univ. of Sheffield: Mem. Council, 1943; Treas., 1947–51; Pro-Chancellor, 1951–67; Chm., 1956–67; Life Mem. of Court, 1983. Mem. Bd of Govs, United Sheffield Hosps, 1948–53 (Chm. of Finance Cttee, 1948–50); Chm., Royal Hosp., 1951–53. Master, Company of Cutlers in Hallamshire, 1961–62. JP Sheffield, 1950–85. High Sheriff of Hallamshire, 1973–74; DL West Riding of Yorks, 1974. Hon. LLD Sheffield, 1962. KStJ 1976; GCSG 1974. *Recreations:* gardening, 13 grandchildren. *Address:* 69 Carsick Hill Crescent, Sheffield S10 3LS. *T:* Sheffield (0742) 302834. *Club:* Sheffield (Sheffield).
See also H. J. S. Young.

YOUNG, Air Vice-Marshal Gordon, CBE 1963; retired; *b* 29 May 1919; *s* of late Robert Young, MBE, and late Emily Florence Young, Doncaster; *m* 1943, Pamela Doris Weatherstone-Smith; two *d*. *Educ:* Maltby Grammar School; Sheffield Univ. Served War of 1939–45, Flying Boat Ops S Atlantic and Western Approaches (despatches); Air Min., 1945–47; Asst Air Attaché, Moscow, 1949–52; OC No 204 Sqdn, 1954–55; RAF Staff Coll., 1956; OC Flying Wing, RAF St Mawgan, 1958–60; Asst Chief, Comdrs-in-Chief Mission to Soviet Forces in Germany, 1960–63; OC RAF Wyton, 1963–65; Air Attaché, Bonn, 1966–68; SASO Coastal Command, 1968–69; COS No 18 (M) Gp, 1969–71. *Recreation:* bird-watching (MBOU 1969). *Address:* PO Box 24, Bath, Ont K0H 1G0, Canada. *T:* 613–352–3498. *Club:* Royal Air Force.
See also Eric Young.

YOUNG, Hon. Sir Harold (William), KCMG 1983; Senator for South Australia, 1967–83, President of the Senate, 1981–83, retired; *b* 30 June 1923; *s* of Frederick James Garfield Young and Edith Mabel Scott; *m* 1952, Eileen Margaret Downing; two *s* two *d*. *Educ:* Prince Alfred Coll., Adelaide. Wheat farmer and grazier prior to entering Parliament. Government Whip in the Senate, 1971–72; Opposition Whip, 1972–75; Shadow Spokesman on the Media, 1975; Chm., Govt Members' Cttee on National Resources, Energy and Trade, 1976–81; Senate: Temp. Chm. of Cttees, 1976–81; Chm., Select Cttee on Offshore Petroleum Resources; Mem., Estimates Cttees; Member: Jt Foreign Affairs and Defence Cttee; Library Cttee; Jt Statutory Cttee on Public Works; Jt House Cttee; Jt Chm., New Parlt House Cttee, 1981–83. Order of Diplomatic Service Merit (Korea), 1982. *Address:* 32 Greenwood Grove, Urrbrae, SA 5064, Australia.

YOUNG, Hugo John Smelter; journalist; *b* 13 Oct. 1938; *s* of Gerard Francis Young, *qv*; *m* 1966, Helen Mason (*d* 1989); one *s* three *d*; *m* 1990, Lucy Waring. *Educ:* Ampleforth Coll.; Balliol Coll., Oxford (MA Jurisprudence). Yorkshire Post, 1961; Harkness Fellow, 1963; Congressional Fellow, US Congress, 1964; The Sunday Times, 1965–84: Chief Leader Writer, 1966–77; Political Editor, 1973–84; Jt Dep. Editor, 1981–84; Political Columnist, The Guardian, 1984–; Dir, The Tablet, 1985–. Chm., Scott Trust, 1989–. Columnist of the Year: British Press Awards, 1980, 1983, 1985; Granada TV What the Papers Say Awards, 1985. *Publications:* (jtly) The Zinoviev Letter, 1966; (jtly) Journey to Tranquillity, 1969; The Crossman Affair, 1974; (jtly) No, Minister, 1982; (jtly) But, Chancellor, 1984; (jtly) The Thatcher Phenomenon, 1986; One of Us, 1989, rev. edn 1991. *Address:* c/o The Guardian, 119 Farringdon Road, EC1.

YOUNG, Ian Robert, OBE 1985; PhD; FRS 1989; FEng 1988; Senior Research Fellow, Hirst Research Centre, GEC plc, since 1981; *b* 11 Jan. 1932; *s* of John Stirling Young and Ruth Muir Young (*née* Whipple); *m* 1956, Sylvia Marianne Whewell Ralph; two *s* one *d*. *Educ:* Sedbergh Sch., Yorkshire; Aberdeen Univ. (BSc, PhD). FIEE. Hilger & Watts Ltd, 1955–59; Evershed & Vignoles Ltd (and affiliates), 1959–76; EMI Ltd, 1976–81; GEC plc, 1981–. Vis. Prof. of Radiology, RPMS, 1986. Hon. FRCR, 1990. *Publications:* over 100 papers in Proc. IEE, Magnetic Resonance in Medicine, Magnetic Resonance Imaging, Jl Magnetic Resonance, Computer Assisted Tomography, etc; 40 separate patents. *Recreations:* bird watching, hill walking, brick laying. *Address:* Church Hill Cottage, West Overton, near Marlborough, Wilts SN8 4ER. *T:* Marlborough (0672) 86615.

YOUNG, James Edward D.; *see* Drummond Young.

YOUNG, Jimmy; *see* Young, L. R.

YOUNG, John Allen, CBE 1975; Chairman and Managing Director, Young & Co.'s Brewery, since 1962; *b* 7 Aug. 1921; *e s* of late William Allen Young and of Joan Barrow Simonds; *m* 1951, Yvonne Lieutenant, Liège; one *s*. *Educ:* Nautical Coll., Pangbourne; Corpus Christi Coll., Cambridge (BA Hons Econs). Served War, 1939–45: Lt-Comdr (A) RNVR; comd 888 Naval Air Sqdn (despatches). Runciman Ltd, 1947; Moor Line, 1949; Young & Co.'s Brewery, 1954–. Chairman: Foster-Probyn Ltd; Cockburn & Campbell; RI Shipping Ltd. Gen. Comr of Taxes, 1965–. President: London Carthorse Parade Soc., 1957–68; Shire Horse Soc., 1963–64 (Treas., 1962–73); Greater London Horse Show, 1972–74; Battersea Scouts, 1974–86. Chairman: Bd of Governors, Nat. Hosps for Nervous Diseases, 1982–86 (Mem. Bd, 1972–86; Chm. Finance, 1974–82); Nat. Hosps Develt Foundn, 1984–; Dep. Chm., Inst. of Neurology, 1982–86 (Chm., Jt Res. Adv. Cttee, 1973–82); Governor, Chalfont Centre for Epilepsy, 1983–; Mem. Bd of Management, Royal Hosp. and Home, Putney, 1990–. Trustee: Licensed Trade Charities Trust, 1984–; Clapham Junction Disaster Fund, 1989–. Freeman, City of London, 1986. *Recreations:* music, sailing. *Address:* Moonsbrook Cottage, Wisborough Green, West Sussex. *T:* Wisborough Green (0403) 700355. *Club:* Royal Yacht Squadron (Cowes).

YOUNG, Sir John (Kenyon Roe), 6th Bt *cr* 1821; Senior Buyer; *b* 23 April 1947; *s* of Sir John William Roe Young, 5th Bt, and Joan Minnie Agnes (*d* 1958), *d* of M. M. Aldous; *S* father, 1981; *m* 1977, Frances Elise, *o d* of W. R. Thompson; one *s* one *d*. *Educ:* Hurn Court; Napier College. Joined RN, 1963; transferred to Hydrographic Branch, 1970; qualified Hydrographic Surveyor, 1977; retired from RN, 1979; attended Napier Coll., 1979–80. Mem. Hydrographic Soc. *Recreations:* Rugby, golf. *Heir: s* Richard Christopher Roe Young, *b* 14 June 1983. *Address:* Bolingey, 159 Chatham Road, Maidstone, Kent ME14 2ND.

YOUNG, Hon. Sir John (McIntosh), AC 1989; KCMG 1975; Lieutenant-Governor of Victoria, Australia, since 1974; Chief Justice of the Supreme Court of Victoria, 1974–91; *b* Melbourne, 17 Dec. 1919; *s* of George David Young, Glasgow, and Kathleen Mildred Young, Melbourne; *m* 1951, Elisabeth Mary, *yr d* of late Dr Edward Wing Twining, Manchester; one *s* two *d*. *Educ:* Geelong Grammar Sch.; Brasenose Coll., Oxford (MA; Hon. Fellow, 1991); Inner Temple; Univ. of Melbourne (LLB). Served War: Scots Guards, 1940–46 (Captain 1943); NW Europe (despatches), 1945. Admitted Victorian Bar, 1948; Associate to Mr Justice Dixon, High Court of Australia, 1948; practice as barrister, 1949–74; Hon. Sec., Victorian Bar Council, 1950–60; Lectr in Company Law, Univ. of Melbourne, 1957–61; Hon. Treas., Medico Legal Soc. of Vic., 1955–65 (Vice-Pres., 1966–68; Pres., 1968–69). QC (Vic.) 1961; admitted Tasmanian Bar, 1964, QC 1964; NSW Bar, 1968, QC 1968; Consultant, Faculty of Law, Monash Univ., 1968–74. Mem., Bd of Examiners for Barristers and Solicitors, 1969–72; Mem. Council, Geelong Grammar Sch., 1974; President: Victorian Council of Legal Educn and Victoria Law Foundn, 1974–91; Scout Assoc. of Australia, 1986–89 (Vice-Pres., 1985; Pres., Victorian Br., 1974–87); Chief Scout of Australia, 1989–; Pres., St John Council for Victoria, 1975–82; GCStJ 1991 (KStJ 1977); Chancellor, Order of St John in Australia, 1982–91. Hon. Col, 4th/19th Prince of Wales's Light Horse, 1978–; Rep. Hon. Col, RAAC, 1986–; Hon. Air Cdre, No 21 (City of Melbourne) Sqn, RAAF, 1986–. Hon. LLD: Monash, 1986; Melbourne, 1989. *Publications:* (co-author) Australian Company Law and Practice, 1965; articles in legal jls. *Recreations:* riding, golf. *Address:* 17 Sorrett Avenue, Malvern, Victoria 3144, Australia. *T:* (03) 822 6259. *Clubs:* Cavalry and Guards; Melbourne, Australian (Melbourne).

YOUNG, John Richard Dendy; Attorney of Supreme Court, South Africa, since 1984; *b* 4 Sept. 1907; 5th *s* of James Young and Evelyn Maud Hammond; *m* 1946, Patricia Maureen Mount; four *s* two *d*. *Educ:* Hankey, Cape Province, SA; Humansdorp, CP, SA; University, South Africa (External). Joined Public Service, S Rhodesia, 1926; resigned to practise at Bar, 1934; joined Military Forces, 1940; active service, North Africa, Sicily and Italy; commissioned in the field; demobilised, 1945. QC 1948; MP Southern Rhodesia, 1948–53; Member Federal Assembly, 1953–56; Judge of the High Court of Rhodesia, 1956–68; Chief Justice, Botswana, 1968–71; Advocate of Supreme Court of SA, 1971–84; Sen. Counsel, 1979–84; Judge of Appeal, Lesotho, Swaziland, Botswana, 1979–84. *Recreations:* swimming, walking. *Address:* 8 Tulani Gardens, Greenfield Road, Kenilworth, Cape, 7700, South Africa.

YOUNG, John Robert Chester; Chief Executive and Director, The Securities and Futures Authority (formerly The Securities Association), since 1987; *b* 6 Sept. 1937; *s* of Robert Nisbet Young and Edith Mary (*née* Roberts); *m* 1963, Pauline Joyce; one *s* one *d* (and one *s* decd). *Educ:* Bishop Vesey's Grammar Sch.; St Edmund Hall, Oxford Univ.; Gray's Inn, London. Joined Simon & Coates, members of the Stock Exchange, 1961; Partner, 1965; Dep. Sen. Partner, 1976; International Stock Exchange (formerly Stock Exchange): Mem. Council, 1978–82; Dir of Policy and Planning, 1982–87; Vice-Chm., Managing Bd, 1987–90; Divisional Dir (non-exec.), Primary Markets Bd, 1990–. Formerly internat. athlete, Rugby player and England Rugby selector. *Recreations:* cooking, Rugby football. *Address:* The Securities and Futures Authority, Stock Exchange Building, Old Broad Street, EC2N 1EQ. *T:* 071–256 9000. *Clubs:* Harlequins (Trustee), Vincent's.
See also L. Botting.

YOUNG, John Robertson, (Rob), CMG 1991; HM Diplomatic Service; Minister, British Embassy, Paris, since 1991; *b* 21 Feb. 1945; *s* of late Francis John Young and of Marjorie Elizabeth Young; *m* 1967, Catherine Suzanne Françoise Houssait; one *s* two *d*.

Educ: King Edward VI Sch., Norwich; Leicester Univ. (BA 1st Cl. Hons, French). Entered FCO, 1967; MECAS, Lebanon, 1968; Third Sec., Cairo, 1970; Second Sec., FCO, 1972; Private Sec. to Minister of State, 1975; First Sec., Paris, 1977; Asst Head, Western European Dept, FCO, 1982; Counsellor, Damascus, 1984; Head of Middle East Dept, FCO, 1987. *Recreations:* music, sailing, acting. *Address:* c/o Foreign and Commonwealth Office, SW1A 2AH. *Club:* Cruising Association.

YOUNG, John Zachary, MA; FRS 1945; Professor of Anatomy, University College, London, 1945–74, now Emeritus, Hon. Fellow, 1975; engaged in research at Oxford University, Marine Biology Station, Plymouth, and Duke Marine Laboratory, Beaufort, N Carolina; *b* 18 March 1907; *s* of Philip Young and Constance Maria Lloyd; *m* Phyllis Heaney; one *s* one *d*; *m* Raymonde Parsons; one *d*. *Educ:* Wells House, Malvern Wells; Marlborough Coll.; Magdalen Coll., Oxford (Demy). Senior Demy, Magdalen Coll., 1929, Christopher Welch Scholar, 1928, Naples Biological Scholar, 1928, 1929; Fellow of Magdalen Coll., Oxford, 1931–45 (Hon. Fellow, 1975); University Demonstrator in Zoology and Comparative Anatomy, Oxford, 1933–45; Rockefeller Fellow, 1936. Fullerton Professor of Physiology, Royal Institution, 1958–61. Pres., Marine Biol Assoc., 1976–86. Foreign Member: Amer. Acad. of Arts and Scis; Amer. Philosophical Soc.; Accademia dei Lincei. Hon. FBA 1986. Hon. DSc: Bristol, 1965; McGill, 1967; Durham, 1969; Bath, 1973; Duke, 1978; Oxford, 1979; Hon. LLD: Glasgow, 1975; Aberdeen, 1980. Royal Medal, Royal Society, 1967; Linnean Gold Medal, 1973; Jan Swammerdam Medal, Amsterdam Soc. for Natural Scis and Medicine, 1980. *Publications:* The Life of Vertebrates, 1950, 3rd edn 1981; Doubt and Certainty in Science, 1951; The Life of Mammals, 1957; A Model of the Brain, 1964 (lectures); The Memory System of the Brain, 1966; An Introduction to the Study of Man, 1971; The Anatomy of the Nervous System of *Octopus vulgaris*, 1971; Programs of the Brain, 1978; Philosophy and the Brain, 1987; scientific papers, mostly on the nervous system. *Recreation:* walking. *Address:* 1 The Crossroads, Brill, Bucks HP18 9TL. *T:* Brill (0844) 237412; Department of Experimental Psychology, South Parks Road, Oxford OX1 3UD. *T:* Oxford (0865) 271444, *Fax:* (0865) 310447.

YOUNG, Joyce Jean, SRN, RMN; Regional Nursing Officer, Oxford, since 1984; *b* 16 Nov. 1936; *d* of Leslie Cyril and Frances May Lyons. *Educ:* Cowes High School, Isle of Wight. General Nurse training, Essex County Hosp., Colchester, 1955–58; Mental Nurse training, Severalls Hosp., Colchester, 1959–60; Ward Sister posts, gen. and psych. hosps, 1960–70; Clinical Nurse Advr, Hosp. Adv. Service, 1970–72; Regl Nurse Advr, SE Metrop. Hosp. Bd for Mental Illness, Mental Handicap and Elderly Services, 1972–74; Dist Nursing Officer, Tunbridge Wells Health Dist., 1974–80; Chief Nursing Officer, Brighton HA, 1980–84. Nursing Advisor to Social Services Select Cttee, 1985–; Mem., Broadmoor Hosp. Management Bd, 1987–. *Publications:* (contrib.) Impending Crisis of Old Age (Nuffield Provincial Trust), 1981; articles in Nursing Times and Nursing Mirror. *Recreations:* gardening, wild life. *Address:* c/o Oxford Regional Health Authority, Old Road, Headington, Oxford OX3 7LF.

YOUNG, Junor; *see* Young, D. J.

YOUNG, Kenneth Middleton, CBE 1977; Deputy Chairman, Post Office Corporation, since 1990; Chairman: Subscription Services Ltd, since 1988; Post Office Counters Ltd, since 1990; *b* 1 Aug. 1931; *s* of Cyril W. D. Young and Gwladys Middleton Young; *m* 1958, Brenda May Thomas; one *s* one *d*. *Educ:* Neath Grammar Sch.; University Coll. of Wales, Aberystwyth (Hon. Fellow, 1991); Coll. of Science and Technology, Univ. of Manchester. BA (Hons) 1952; Diploma in Personnel Management, 1954. Pilot Officer/Navigator, General Duties (Aircrew), RAF, 1952–54. Asst Personnel Manager, Elliott-Automation Ltd, 1955–59; Collective Agreements Manager, later Salary Administration Manager, Massey-Ferguson (UK) Ltd, 1959–64; Personnel Adviser, Aviation Div., Smiths Industries Ltd, 1964–66; Group Personnel Manager, General Electric Company Ltd, and Dir, GEC (Management) Ltd, 1966–71; Post Office Corporation: Bd Mem., 1972– (formerly for Personnel and Corporate Resources and, during 1987, also as Man. Dir, Royl Mail Parcels); Vice-Chm., 1986–90; Acting Chm. during 1989; Chm., Girobank PLC, 1989–90. Member: Management Bd, Engineering Employers Fedn, 1971; CBI Employment Policy Cttee, 1978–84; Employment Appeal Tribunal, 1985–; BIC Target Team on Business/Educn Partnerships, 1988–89; Trustee, Post Office Pension Funds, 1989–. Member: Council, Inst. of Manpower Studies, 1980–86; London Business Sch. Liaison Cttee, 1982–89; Chm. Bd of Govs, SW London Coll., 1991. CBIM; FIPM. *Recreations:* photography; Wales Rugby; Chelsea Football Club. *Address:* Post Office Headquarters, 30 St James's Square, SW1Y 4PY.

YOUNG, Leslie, DSc (London), PhD; FRSC; Professor of Biochemistry in the University of London, and Head of the Department of Biochemistry, St Thomas's Hospital Medical School, London, SE1, 1948–76, now Professor Emeritus; Hon. Consultant, St Thomas' Hospital; *b* 27 Feb. 1911; *o c* of John and Ethel Young; *m* 1939, Ruth Elliott; one *s*. *Educ:* Sir Joseph Williamson's Mathematical Sch., Rochester; Royal College of Science, London; University College, London. Sir Edward Frankland Prize and Medal of Royal Institute of Chemistry, 1932; Bayliss-Starling Memorial Scholar in Physiology, University Coll., London, 1933–34; Asst Lectr in Biochemistry, University College, London, 1934–35; Commonwealth Fund Fellow in Biochemistry at Washington Univ. Medical School and Yale Univ., USA, 1935–37; Lectr in Biochemistry, University Coll., London, 1937–39; Assoc. Prof. of Biochemistry, Univ. of Toronto, 1939–44; chemical warfare research for the Dept of Nat. Defence, Canada, 1940–46; Prof. of Biochemistry, Univ. of Toronto, 1944–47; Reader in Biochemistry, University Coll., London, 1947–48. Hon. Sec., The Biochemical Soc., 1950–53; Vice-Pres., The Royal Institute of Chemistry, 1964–66; Mem., Bd of Governors, St Thomas' Hosp., 1970–74; Chm. of Council, Queen Elizabeth Coll., London Univ., 1975–80, Hon. Fellow, 1980. FKC 1980. *Publications:* (with G. A. Maw) The Metabolism of Sulphur Compounds, 1958; papers on chem. and biochem. subjects in various scientific journals. *Address:* 23 Oaklands Avenue, Esher, Surrey KT10 8HX. *T:* 081–398 1262. *Club:* Athenæum.

YOUNG, Sir Leslie (Clarence), Kt 1984; CBE 1980; DL; Director: Swiss Pioneer Life (formerly Pioneer Mutual Insurance Co.), since 1986; Britannia Cable Systems Wirral plc, since 1990; *b* 5 Feb. 1925; *s* of late Clarence James Young and of Ivy Isabel Young; *m* 1949, Muriel Howard Pearson; one *s* one *d*. *Educ:* London School of Economics (BScEcon). Courtaulds Ltd: held range of senior executive appts, incl. chairmanship of number of gp companies, 1948–68; J. Bibby & Sons Ltd, 1968–86: Managing Director, J. Bibby Agriculture Ltd, 1968; Chm. and Man. Dir, J. Bibby Food Products Ltd, 1970; Gp Man. Dir, 1970, Dep. Chm. and Man. Dir, 1977, Chm., 1979–86, J. Bibby & Sons Ltd. Director: Bank of England, 1986–90; National Westminster Bank, 1986–90 (Regl Dir, 1979–90, Chm., 1986–90, Northern Regl Bd); Sibec Developments PLC 1988–91. Chairman: NW Regional Council, CBI, 1976–78; NW Industrial Development Board, 1978–81; Merseyside Develt Corp., 1981–84; British Waterways Bd, 1984–87. Trustee, Civic Trust for the North West, 1978–83. Non-Exec. Dir, Granada Television Ltd, 1979–84. Chm. Trustees, Nat. Museums and Galls on Merseyside, 1986–. Member Council: N of England Zoological Soc., 1979–85; Royal Liverpool Philharmonic Soc., 1980–. DL Merseyside, 1983. Hon. Col, Liverpool Univ. OTC, 1989–. Hon. LLD Liverpool, 1988. *Recreations:* fly-fishing, walking, shooting. *Address:* Overwood, Vicarage Lane, Burton, South Wirral L64 5TJ. *T:* 051–336 5224. *Clubs:* Royal Automobile; Artists' (Liverpool).

YOUNG, Leslie Ronald, (Jimmy Young), OBE 1979; Presenter, Jimmy Young Programme, BBC Radio Two, since 1973 (Radio One, 1967–73); *b* 21 Sept.; *s* of Frederick George Young and Gertrude Woolford; *m* 1st, 1946, Wendy Wilkinson (marr. diss.); one *d*; 2nd, 1950, Sally Douglas (marr. diss.). *Educ:* East Dean Grammar Sch., Cinderford, Glos. RAF, 1939–46. First BBC radio broadcast, songs at piano, 1949; pianist, singer, bandleader, West End, London, 1950–51; first theatre appearance, Empire Theatre, Croydon, 1952; regular theatre appearances, 1952–; first radio broadcast introd. records, Flat Spin, 1953; BBC TV Bristol, Pocket Edition series, 1955; first introd. radio Housewives' Choice, 1955; BBC radio series, incl.: The Night is Young, 12 o'clock Spin, Younger Than Springtime, Saturday Special, Keep Young, Through Till Two, 1959–65; presented progs, Radio Luxembourg, 1960–68. BBC TV: series, Jimmy Young Asks, 1972; The World of Jimmy Young, 1973. First live direct BBC broadcasts to Europe from Soviet Union, Jimmy Young Programme, 16 and 17 May 1977; Jimmy Young Programmes broadcast live from Egypt and Israel, 9 and 12 June 1978, from Zimbabwe-Rhodesia, 9 and 10 Aug. 1979; Host for Thames TV of first British Telethon, 2nd and 3rd Oct. 1980; Jimmy Young Programmes live from Tokyo, 26th, 27th and 28th May 1981, from Sydney, 4–8 Oct. 1982, from Washington DC, 3–7 Oct. 1983. ITV series: Whose Baby?, 1973; Jim's World, 1974; The Jimmy Young Television Programme, 1984–87. Hit Records: 1st, Too Young, 1951; Unchained Melody, The Man From Laramie, 1955 (1st Brit. singer to have 2 consec. no 1 hit records); Chain Gang, More, 1956; Miss You, 1963. Weekly Column, Daily Sketch, 1968–71. Hon. Mem. Council, NSPCC, 1981–. Freeman, City of London, 1969. Variety Club of GB Award, Radio Personality of the Year, 1968; Sony Award, Radio Personality of the Year, 1985; Sony Radio Awards Roll of Honour, 1988; Jimmy Young Programme: BBC Current Affairs Prog. of the Year, Daily Mail Nat. Radio Awards, 1988; Radio Prog. of the Year, TV and Radio Inds Club Award, 1989. Silver Jubilee Medal, 1977. *Publications:* Jimmy Young Cookbook: No 1, 1968; No 2, 1969; No 3, 1970; No 4, 1972; (autobiogs) JY, 1973, Jimmy Young, 1982; contrib. magazines, incl. Punch, Woman's Own. *Address:* c/o Broadcasting House, Portland Place, W1A 1AA. *Clubs:* Wig and Pen; Wigan Rugby League Social.

YOUNG, Neil; *see* Young, R. N.

YOUNG, Sir Norman (Smith), Kt 1968; formerly Chairman: Pipelines Authority of South Australia; South Australian Brewing Co. Ltd; South Australian Oil and Gas Corporation Pty Ltd; News Ltd; Elder Smith Goldsbrough Mort Ltd; Bradmill Ltd; *b* 24 July 1911; *s* of Thomas and Margaret Young; *m* 1936, Jean Fairbairn Sincock; two *s* one *d*. *Educ:* Norwood High Sch.; University of Adelaide. Member: Adelaide City Council, 1949–60; Municipal Tramways Trust, 1951–67 (Dep. Chairman); Royal Commn on Television, 1953–54; Bankruptcy Law Review Cttee, 1956–62. Fellow, Inst. of Chartered Accountants, 1933; FASA, 1932; Associate in Commerce, University of Adelaide, 1930. *Publication:* Bankruptcy Practice in Australia, 1942. *Address:* 522 Greenhill Road, Hazelwood Park, SA 5006, Australia. *T:* 79–1684.

YOUNG, Priscilla Helen Ferguson, CBE 1982; Director, Central Council for Education and Training in Social Work, 1971–86; retired; *b* 25 Nov. 1925; *d* of Fergus Ferguson Young and Helen Frances Graham (*née* Murphy). *Educ:* Kingsley Sch., Leamington Spa; Univ. of Edinburgh (MA). Social Worker: London Family Welfare Assoc., 1947–51; Somerset CC Children's Dept, 1951–53; Oxford City Children's Dept, 1953–58 (Dep. Children's Officer); Child and Family Services, Portland, Me, USA, 1958–61; Lectr/Sen. Lectr, Sch. of Social Work, Univ. of Leicester, 1961–71. Nat. Chairperson, Family Service Units, 1987–. Hon. Fellow, Sheffield City Polytechnic, 1977. Hon. DLitt Ulster, 1987. *Publication:* The Student and Supervision in Social Work Education, 1967.

YOUNG, Sir Richard (Dilworth), Kt 1970; BSc, FIMechE; CBIM; Chairman, Boosey & Hawkes Ltd, 1979–84 (Deputy Chairman, 1978–79); Director: The Rugby Group PLC (formerly Rugby Portland Cement Co.), 1968–89; Commonwealth Finance Development Corp. Ltd, 1968–86; Warwick University Science Park Ltd, since 1983; Retirement Securities Ltd, since 1983; *b* 9 April 1914; *s* of Philip Young and Constance Maria Lloyd; *m* 1951, Jean Barbara Paterson Lockwood, *d* of F. G. Lockwood; four *s*. *Educ:* Bromsgrove; Bristol Univ. Joined Weldless Steel Tube Co. Ltd, 1934; served with Tube Investments companies in production and engineering capacities until 1944; Representative of TI in S America and Man. Dir of Tubos Britanicos (Argentina) Ltda, 1945–50; Man. Dir of TI (Export) Ltd, 1950–53; Sales Dir of TI Aluminium Ltd, 1953–56; Asst to Chm. of Tube Investments Ltd, 1957–60; Dir, 1958; Asst Man. Dir, 1959; Man. Dir, 1961–64; Chairman: Park Gate Iron & Steel Co., 1959–64; Raleigh Industries Ltd, 1960–64; Alfred Herbert Ltd: Dep. Chm., 1965–66; Chm., 1966–74; Director: Ingersoll Milling Machine Co., USA, 1967–71; Ingersoll Engineers Inc., 1976–86. Member: Council BIM, 1960–65; Council, CBI, 1967–74; Council, IMechE, 1969–76; Adv. Cttee on Scientific Manpower, 1962–65; SSRC, 1973–75; Council, Warwick Univ., 1966–89; Central Adv. Council on Science and Technol., 1967–70; SRC Engineering Bd, 1974–76. Freeman, City of London, 1987. Hon. DSc Warwick, 1987. *Address:* Bearley Manor, Bearley, near Stratford-on-Avon, Warwickshire. *T:* Stratford-on-Avon (0789) 731220. *Club:* Athenæum.

YOUNG, Rob; *see* Young, J. R.

YOUNG, Robert; Director, Beauford plc, since 1990; *b* 27 March 1944; *s* of Walter Horace Young and Evelyn Joan Young; *m* 1965, Patricia Anne Cowin; one *s* one *d* (and one *s* decd). *Educ:* Magdalen College, Oxford (BA Hons 1965). Graduate apprentice, Rolls-Royce, 1965; IBM UK, 1969–71; Rolls-Royce Motors, 1971–81: Man. Dir, Military Engine Div., 1977–79; Dir and Gen. Manager, Diesel Div., 1979–81; Vickers, 1981–85 (Group Commercial Dir, 1981–83); Man. Dir, Crane Ltd, 1985–88; Chief Exec., Plastics Div., McKechnie plc, 1989–90. Member: Central Policy Review Staff, 1983; No 10 Policy Unit, 1983–84; CBI W Midlands Regional Council, 1980–81 (Chm., CBI Shropshire, 1981); Monopolies and Mergers Commn, 1986. FInstD. *Recreations:* Mozart, railways, cats, photography. *Address:* 54 Fordhook Avenue, Ealing, W5 3LR. *Club:* Institute of Directors.

YOUNG, Sir Robert Christopher M.; *see* Mackworth-Young.

YOUNG, Robert Henry; Consultant Orthopædic Surgeon, St George's Hospital, SW1, 1946–68; Hon. Consultant, St Peter's Hospital, Chertsey, 1939–68; *b* 6 Oct. 1903; *s* of James Allen Young and Constance Barrow Young; *m* 1st, 1929, Nancy Willcox; 2nd, 1961, Norma, *d* of Leslie Williams; two *s*. *Educ:* Sherborne Sch.; Emmanuel Coll., Cambridge; St Thomas' Hospital, SE1. *Publications:* numerous articles in leading medical journals. *Address:* Milestone Farm, Ash, near Martock, Somerset TA12 6PD. *Clubs:* United Oxford & Cambridge University, Buck's.

YOUNG, Robin Urquhart; Under Secretary, Environment Policy, Department of the Environment, since 1989; *b* 7 Sept. 1948; *s* of Col Ian U. Young and Mary Young. *Educ:* Fettes Coll., Edinburgh; University Coll., Oxford (BA 1971). Joined DoE, 1973; Private

Sec. to Parly Sec., Planning and Local Govt, 1976; Private Sec. to Minister of Housing, 1980–81; Local Govt Finance, 1981–85; Private Sec. to successive Secs of State, 1985–88; Under Sec., Housing, 1988–89. Dir (non-exec.), Bovis Construction Ltd, 1989–. *Recreations:* squash, tennis, cinema. *Address:* Department of the Environment, 2 Marsham Street, SW1P 3EB.

YOUNG, (Roderic) Neil; Investment Consultant, since 1989; *b* 29 May 1933; *s* of late Dr F. H. Young and of S. M. Young (*née* Robinson); *m* 1962, Gillian Margaret Salmon; two *s* one *d*. *Educ:* Eton; Trinity College, Cambridge (MA). FCA. 2nd Lieut Queen's Own Royal West Kent Regt, 1952–53. Howard Howes & Co., 1956–59; Fenn & Crosthwaite, 1960–63; Brown Fleming & Murray, 1964–68; Director: Murray Johnstone, 1969–70; Kleinwort Benson, 1971–88. Director: Brunner Investment Trust; Malvern UK Index Trust; Aberdeen Petroleum; London and SE Bd, Bradford and Bingley Bldg Soc. Almoner, Christ's Hospital. City of London: Mem., Court of Common Council, 1980; Alderman, Ward of Bread Street, 1982–; Sheriff, 1991. *Recreations:* gardening, shooting, DIY, golf. *Address:* Pembury Hall, Pembury, Kent TN2 4AT. *T:* Pembury (089282) 2971. *Club:* City Livery.

YOUNG, Roger; Chief Executive, Scottish Hydro-Electric plc, since 1988; *b* 14 Jan. 1944; *s* of Arnold and Margaret Young; *m* 1970, Susan Neilson; one *s* two *d*. *Educ:* Gordonstoun Sch.; Edinburgh Univ. (BSc Engrg); Cranfield Business Sch. (MBA). Rolls-Royce Ltd, 1961–72; Alidair Ltd, 1972–73; Wavin Plastics Ltd, 1973–76; Aurora Holdings Ltd, 1976–80; Low & Bonar plc, 1980–88. *Recreations:* family, hill walking. *Address:* Scottish Hydro-Electric plc, 16 Rothesay Terrace, Edinburgh EH3 7SE. *Club:* Caledonian.

YOUNG, Sir Roger (William), Kt 1983; MA; STh, LHD, FRSE; Principal of George Watson's College, Edinburgh, 1958–85; *b* 15 Nov. 1923; *yr s* of late Charles Bowden Young and Dr Ruth Young, CBE; *m* 1950, Caroline Mary Christie; two *s* two *d*. *Educ:* Dragon Sch., Oxford; Westminster Sch. (King's Scholar); Christ Church, Oxford (Scholar). Served War of 1939–45, RNVR, 1942–45. Classical Mods, 1946, Lit Hum 1948. Resident Tutor, St Catharine's, Cumberland Lodge, Windsor, 1949–51; Asst Master, The Manchester Grammar Sch., 1951–58. 1st Class in Archbishop's examination in Theology (Lambeth Diploma), 1957. Participant, US State Dept Foreign Leader Program, 1964. Scottish Governor, BBC, 1979–84. Member: Edinburgh Marriage Guidance Council, 1960–75; Scottish Council of Christian Educn Movement, 1960–81 (Chm., 1961–67; Hon. Vice-Pres., 1981–85); Gen. Council of Christian Educn Movement, 1985– (Vice-Pres., 1989–); Management Assoc., SE Scotland, 1965–85; Educational Research Bd of SSRC, 1966–70; Court, Edinburgh Univ., 1967–76; Public Schools Commn, 1968–70; Consultative Cttee on the Curriculum, 1972–75; Adv. Cttee, Scottish Centre for Studies in Sch. Administration, 1972–75; Royal Soc. of Edinburgh Dining Club, 1972–; Scottish Adv. Cttee, Community Service Volunteers, 1973–78; Edinburgh Festival Council, 1970–76; Independent Schs Panel of Wolfson Foundn, 1978–82; Gen. Adv. Council of BBC, 1978–79; Scottish Council of Independent Schs, 1978–85; Royal Observatory Trust, Edin., 1981–; Council, RSE, 1982–85. Hon. Sec., Headmasters' Assoc. of Scotland, 1968–72, Pres., 1972–74; Chairman: HMC, 1976; BBC Consult. Gp on Social Effects of TV, 1978–79; Bursary Bd, Dawson International Ltd, 1977–85; Bath Film Soc., 1990–; Dep. Chm., GBA, 1988–. Trustee: Campion Sch., Athens, 1984–91; Wells Cathedral Sch., 1987–; Chm. Council, Cheltenham Ladies' Coll., 1986–; Member, Governing Body: Westminster Sch., 1986–; Royal Sch., Bath, 1987–. Conducted Enquiry on Stirling Univ., 1973. Hon. LHD, Hamilton Coll., Clinton, NY, 1978. *Publications:* Lines of Thought, 1958; Everybody's Business, 1968; Everybody's World, 1970; Report on the Policies and Running of Stirling University 1966–1973, 1973. *Recreations:* gardening, photography, climbing, golf, knitting. *Address:* 11 Belgrave Terrace, Bath, Avon BA1 5JR. *T:* Bath (0225) 336940. *Club:* East India.

YOUNG, Sheriff Sir Stephen Stewart Templeton, 3rd Bt, *cr* 1945; Sheriff of North Strathclyde at Greenock, since 1984; advocate; *b* 24 May 1947; *s* of Sir Alastair Young, 2nd Bt, and Dorothy Constance Marcelle (*d* 1964), *d* of late Lt-Col Charles Ernest Chambers, and *widow* of Lt J. H. Grayburn, VC, 43rd LI; *S* father, 1963; *m* 1974, Viola Margaret Nowell-Smith, *d* of Prof. P. H. Nowell-Smith, *qv* and Perilla Thyme (she *m* 2nd, Lord Roberthall, KCMG, CB); two *s*. *Educ:* Rugby; Trinity Coll., Oxford; Edinburgh Univ. Voluntary Service Overseas, Sudan, 1968–69. Sheriff of Glasgow and Strathkelvin, March-June 1984. *Heir:* *s* Charles Alastair Stephen Young, *b* 21 July 1979. *Address:* Glen Rowan, Shore Road, Cove, Dunbartonshire G84 0NU.

YOUNG, Thomas Nesbitt; HM Diplomatic Service; Director of Trade Promotion, British High Commission, Canberra, since 1990; *b* 24 July 1943; *s* of Sir Frank Young, FRS and Lady Young; *m* 1971, Elisabeth Ann Shepherdson Hick; one *s* one *d*. *Educ:* The Leys Sch., Cambridge; Pembroke Coll., Oxford (BA Hons Chem., MA). Teaching, Kigezi Coll., Kabale, Uganda, 1962; joined HM Diplomatic Service, 1966; Ankara, 1969–71; Madrid, 1972–76; Head of Chancery, Ankara, 1979–80; Dep. Dir of Trade Develt, NY, 1981; First Sec., Washington, 1981–84; Asst Head, Nuclear Energy Dept, FCO, 1984–86; Dep. High Comr, Accra, 1987–90. *Address:* c/o Foreign and Commonwealth Office, King Charles Street, SW1A 2AH.

YOUNG, Wayland; *see* Kennet, Baron.

YOUNG, William Hilary, CMG 1957; HM Diplomatic Service, retired; Ambassador to Colombia 1966–70; *b* 14 Jan. 1913; *s* of late Rev. Arthur John Christopher Young and Ethel Margaret (*née* Goodwin); *m* 1st, 1946, Barbara Gordon Richmond, *d* of late Gordon Park Richmond; one *s* one *d*; 2nd, 1986, Virginia, *widow* of Sir Ivo Stourton, CMG, OBE, KPM. *Educ:* Marlborough Coll.; Emmanuel Coll., Cambridge. Entered Consular Service, 1935; served HM Legation, Tehran, 1938–41; Foreign Office, 1941–45; 1st Secretary, 1945; Berlin (Political Division, Control Commission), 1945–48; HM Legation, Budapest, 1948–50; attached to IDC, 1951; Counsellor: UK High Commn, New Delhi, 1952–54; Foreign Office, 1954–57; Minister, Moscow, 1957–60; Senior Civilian Instructor, IDC, 1960–62; Minister, British Embassy, Pretoria and Cape Town, 1962–65; Fellow, Harvard University Center for Internat. Affairs, 1965–66. *Address:* The Old Bakery, Kimpton, Andover, Hants SP11 8NU.

YOUNG, Hon. William Lambert, JP; High Commissioner for New Zealand in UK, 1982–85; concurrently Ambassador to Ireland and High Commissioner in Nigeria, 1982–85; *b* 13 Nov. 1913; *s* of James Young and Alice Gertrude Annie Young; *m* 1946, Isobel Joan Luke; one *s* four *d*. *Educ:* Wellington Coll. Commenced work, 1930; spent first 16 yrs with farm servicing co., interrupted by War Service, N Africa with Eighth Army, 1940–43; took over management of wholesale distributing co. handling imported and NZ manufactured goods; Gen. Man. of co. manufg and distributing radios, records, electronic equipment and owning 32 retail stores, 1956; purchased substantial interest in importing and distributing business, 1962. MP (National) Miramar, 1966–81; Minister of Works and Develt, 1975–81; introduced Women's Rights of Employment Bill, 1975. Formerly Chairman: National Roads Bd; National Water and Soil Authority; NZ Fishing Licensing Authority. Formerly: Director: Johnsons Wax of NZ Ltd (subsid. of USA Co.); Howard Rotovator Co. Ltd; AA Mutual Insurance Co.; J. J. Niven Ltd; NZ Motor Bodies Ltd; Trustee, Wellington Savings Bank. Pres., Star Boating Club, 1981–; Mem. Council, NZ Amateur Rowing Assoc., 1984–87. Life Mem., AA of Wellington (Mem. Council, 1976–). JP 1962. *Address:* 3/28 Oriental Terrace, Oriental Bay, Wellington 1, New Zealand. *T:* (04) 801 8030. *Club:* Wellington (Wellington, NZ).

YOUNG, Sir William Neil, 10th Bt, *cr* 1769; Head of Investment Management, Saudi International Bank, since 1988; *b* 22 Jan. 1941; *s* of Captain William Elliot Young, RAMC (killed in action 27 May 1942), and Mary, *d* of late Rev. John Macdonald; *S* grandfather, 1944; *m* 1965, Christine Veronica Morley, *o d* of late R. B. Morley, Buenos Aires; one *s* one *d*. *Educ:* Wellington Coll.; Sandhurst. Captain, 16th/5th The Queen's Royal Lancers, retired 1970. Dir, Kleinwort Benson International Investment Ltd, 1982–87. *Recreations:* ski-ing, sailing, tennis, shooting. *Heir:* *s* William Lawrence Elliot Young, *b* 26 May 1970. *Address:* 22 Elm Park Road, SW3. *Clubs:* Cavalry and Guards; Hong Kong (Hong Kong).

YOUNG-HERRIES, Sir Michael Alexander Robert; *see* Herries.

YOUNGER, family name of **Viscount Younger of Leckie.**

YOUNGER OF LECKIE, 3rd Viscount, *cr* 1923; **Edward George Younger;** OBE 1940; 3rd Bt of Leckie, *cr* 1911; Lord-Lieutenant, Stirling and Falkirk (formerly of County of Stirling), 1964–79; Colonel, Argyll and Sutherland Highlanders (TA); *b* 21 Nov. 1906; *er s* of 2nd Viscount and Maud (*d* 1957), *e d* of Sir John Gilmour, 1st Bt; *S* father 1946; *m* 1930, Evelyn Margaret, MBE (*d* 1983), *e d* of late Alexander Logan McClure, KC; three *s* one *d*. *Educ:* Winchester; New Coll., Oxford. Served War of 1939–45 (OBE). *Heir:* *s* Hon. George (Kenneth Hotson) Younger, *qv*. *Address:* Leckie, Gargunnock, Stirling. *T:* Gargunnock (078686) 281. *Club:* New (Edinburgh).

See also Hon. R. E. G. Younger.

YOUNGER, Maj.-Gen. Allan Elton, DSO 1944; OBE 1962; MA; Director-General, Royal United Services Institute for Defence Studies, 1976–78; *b* 4 May 1919; *s* of late Brig. Arthur Allan Shakespear Younger, DSO, and late Marjorie Rhoda Younger (*née* Halliley); *m* 1942, Diana Lanyon; three *d*. *Educ:* Gresham's; RMA Woolwich; Christ's Coll., Cambridge. Commnd RE, 1939; France and Belgium, 1940; France, Holland and Germany, 1944–45; Burma, 1946–47; Malaya, 1948; Korea, 1950–51; RMA Sandhurst, 1954–57; Bt Lt-Col 1959; comd 36 Corps Engineer Regt in UK and Kenya, 1960–62; Instructor US Army Comd and Gen. Staff Coll., Fort Leavenworth, 1963–66; Programme Evaluation Gp, 1966–68; Chief Engr, Army Strategic Comd, 1968–69; COS, HQ Allied Forces Northern Europe, Oslo, 1970–72; Sen. Army Mem., Directing Staff, RCDS, 1972–75. Col Comdt, RE, 1974–79. Member Council: British Atlantic Cttee; Lord Kitchener Nat. Meml Fund. Silver Star (US), 1951. *Publications:* contribs to RUSI Jl, Military Review (USA). *Recreation:* gardening. *Club:* Army and Navy.

YOUNGER, Charles Frank Johnston, DSO 1944; TD 1952; *b* 11 Dec. 1908; *s* of late Major Charles Arthur Johnston Younger, King's Dragoon Guards; *m* 1935, Joanna, *e d* of late Rev. John Kyrle Chatfield, BD, MA, LLB; one *d*. *Educ:* Royal Naval Coll., Dartmouth. Served Royal Navy, 1926–37; resigned commn to enter William Younger & Co. Ltd, Brewers, Edinburgh, 1937. Served War of 1939–45 (despatches, DSO); RA (Field), 15th Scottish Division, 1939–41; 17th Indian Light Div., Burma, 1942–45; commanded 129th Lowland Field Regt, RA, 1942–45 and 278th Lowland Field Regt RA (TA), 1946–52 (Lt-Col). Director: William Younger & Co. Ltd, 1945–73; Scottish & Newcastle Breweries Ltd, 1946–73; Dir, Bank of Scotland, 1960–79. Vice Pres., Brewers' Soc., 1964– (Chm., 1963–64; Chairman: Parly Cttee, 1961–63; Survey Cttee, 1967–75). Chm., Scottish Union & National Insurance Co., 1954–57, 1966–68, Dep. Chm., 1968–79; Dir, Norwich Union and Associated Cos, 1966–79, Vice-Chm., 1976–79. Chm., Scottish Adv. Bd, 1976–80. UK deleg. to EFTA Brewing Ind. Council, 1964–73; Mem. Council, CBI, 1965–73. Mem., Worshipful Company of Brewers. Mem., Royal Company of Archers (Queen's Body Guard for Scotland). Freeman of the City of London. *Recreations:* country pursuits. *Address:* Painsthorpe Hall, Kirby Underdale, York Y04 1RQ. *T:* Bishop Wilton (07596) 342. *Clubs:* Boodle's, Pratt's.

See also Earl of Halifax.

YOUNGER, Rt. Hon. George (Kenneth Hotson), TD 1964; PC 1979; DL; MP (C) Ayr, since 1964; Chairman: Royal Bank of Scotland, since 1990 (Director, since 1989; Deputy Chairman, 1990); Royal Bank of Scotland Group, since 1991; *b* 22 Sept. 1931; *e s* and *heir* of 3rd Viscount Younger of Leckie, *qv*; *m* 1954, Diana Rhona, *er d* of Captain G. S. Tuck, RN, Little London, Chichester, Sussex; three *s* one *d*. *Educ:* Cargilfield Sch., Edinburgh; Winchester Coll.; New Coll., Oxford. Commnd in Argyll and Sutherland Highlanders, 1950; served BAOR and Korea, 1951; 7th Bn Argyll and Sutherland Highlanders (TA), 1951–65; Hon. Col, 154 (Lowland) Transport Regt, RCT, T&AVR, 1977–85. Director: George Younger & Son Ltd, 1958–68; J. G. Thomson & Co. Ltd, Leith, 1962–66; Maclachlans Ltd, 1968–70; Tennant Caledonian Breweries Ltd, 1977–79. Contested (U) North Lanarkshire, 1959; Unionist Candidate for Kinross and West Perthshire, 1963, but stood down in favour of Sir A. Douglas-Home. Scottish Conservative Whip, 1965–67; Parly Under-Sec. of State for Develt, Scottish Office, 1970–74; Minister of State for Defence, 1974; Sec. of State for Scotland, 1979–86; Sec. of State for Defence, 1986–89. Chm., Conservative Party in Scotland, 1974–75 (Dep. Chm., 1967–70); Pres., Nat. Union of Cons. and Unionist Assocs, 1987–88. Pres., Royal Highland and Agricl Soc., 1990; Chairman: Royal Anniversary Trust, 1990; Romanian Orphanage Trust, 1990. Brig., Queen's Body Guard for Scotland (Royal Company of Archers). DL Stirlingshire, 1968. *Recreations:* music, tennis, sailing, golf. *Address:* c/o House of Commons, SW1. *Clubs:* Caledonian; Highland Brigade.

See also Hon. R. E. G. Younger.

YOUNGER, Maj.-Gen. Sir John William, 3rd Bt *cr* 1911; CBE 1969 (MBE 1945); Commissioner-in-Chief, St John Ambulance Brigade, 1980–85; *b* 18 Nov. 1920; *s* of Sir William Robert Younger, 2nd Bt, and of Joan Gwendoline Johnstone (later Mrs Dennis Wheatley; she *d* 1982); *S* father, 1973; *m* 1st, 1948, Mrs Stella Jane Dodd (marr. diss. 1952), *d* of Rev. John George Lister; one *s* one *d*; 2nd, 1953, Marcella Granito, Princess Pignatelli Di Belmonte (*d* 1989), *d* of Prof. Avv. R. Scheggi; 3rd, 1991, Anne Henrietta Maria St Paul Seely, *o d* of Horace George St Paul Butler. *Educ:* Canford Sch.; RMC Sandhurst. Served War 1939–45, Middle East (PoW) (MBE); 2nd Lt, Coldstream Gds, 1939; Lt Col 1959; AQMG, HQ London Dist, 1961–63; Col 1963; AAG, War Office, 1963–65; Brig. 1967; Dep. Dir, Army Staff Duties, MoD, 1967–70; Dir of Quartering (A), MoD, 1970–73; Maj.-Gen. 1971; Dir, Management and Support of Intelligence, 1973–76. Chm. or Mem., various Civil Service Commn and Home Office Interview Bds. Dep. Comr, St John Ambulance Bde, London (Prince of Wales's) Dist, 1978. KStJ 1980. *Recreations:* reading, photography, travel. *Heir:* *s* Julian William Richard Younger, [*b* 10 Feb. 1950; *m* 1981, Deborah Ann Wood; one *s*]. *Address:* 23 Cadogan Square, SW1X 0HU. *Club:* Boodle's.

YOUNGER, Hon. Robert Edward Gilmour; Sheriff of Tayside, Central and Fife, since 1982; *b* 25 Sept. 1940; third *s* of 3rd Viscount Younger of Leckie, *qv*; *m* 1972, Helen Jane Hayes; one *s* one *d*. *Educ:* Cargilfield Sch., Edinburgh; Winchester Coll.; New Coll., Oxford (MA); Edinburgh Univ. (LLB); Glasgow Univ. Advocate, 1968; Sheriff of

Glasgow and Strathkelvin, 1979–82. *Recreation:* out of doors. *Address:* Old Leckie, Gargunnock, Stirling, Scotland FK8 3BN. *T:* Gargunnock (078686) 213.
See also Rt. Hon. G. K. H. *Younger.*

YOUNGER, Sir William McEwan, 1st Bt, *cr* 1964, of Fountainbridge; DSO 1942; DL; Chairman: Scottish & Newcastle Breweries Ltd, 1960–69 (Managing Director, 1960–67); The Second Scottish Investment Trust Company Ltd, 1965–75; *b* 6 Sept. 1905; *y s* of late William Younger, Ravenswood, Melrose; *m* 1st, 1936, Nora Elizabeth Balfour (marr. diss., 1967); one *d*; 2nd, 1983, June Peck. *Educ:* Winchester; Balliol Coll., Oxford (Hon. Fellow 1984). Served War of 1939–45 (despatches, DSO); Western Desert, 1941–43; Italy, 1943–45; Lt-Col, RA. Hon. Sec., Scottish Unionist Assoc., 1955–64; Chm., Conservative Party in Scotland, 1971–74. Mem. Queen's Body Guard for Scotland. Director: British Linen Bank, 1955–71; Scottish Television, 1964–71; Chm., Highland Tourist (Cairngorm Development) Ltd, 1966–78. DL Midlothian, later City of Edinburgh, 1956–84. *Recreations:* mountaineering and fishing. *Heir:* none. *Address:* Little Hill Cottage, Harpsden, Henley-on-Thames, Oxon RG9 4HR. *T:* Henley-on-Thames (0491) 574339; 27 Moray Place, Edinburgh EH3 6DA. *T:* 031–225 8173. *Clubs:* Carlton, Alpine; New (Edinburgh).

YOUNGSON, Prof. Alexander John, CBE 1987; Emeritus Professor, Australian National University, since 1980; *b* 28 Sept. 1918; *s* of Alexander Brown, MA, MB, ChB and Helen Youngson; *m* 1948, Elizabeth Gisborne Naylor; one *s* one *d. Educ:* Aberdeen Grammar Sch.; Aberdeen Univ. Pilot, Fleet Air Arm, 1940–45. MA Aberdeen Univ., 1947; Commonwealth Fellow, 1947–48. Lecturer, University of St Andrews, 1948–50; Lecturer, University of Cambridge, 1950–58; Prof. of Political Economy 1963–74, and Vice-Principal, 1971–74, Univ. of Edinburgh; Dir, Res. Sch. of Social Scis, ANU, 1974–80; Prof. of Econs, Univ. of Hong Kong, 1980–82. Chm., Royal Fine Art Commn for Scotland, 1983–90 (Mem., 1972–74). Hon. FRIAS 1984. DLitt Aberdeen Univ., 1952. *Publications:* The American Economy, 1860–1940, 1951; Possibilities of Economic Progress, 1959; The British Economy, 1920–1957, 1960; The Making of Classical Edinburgh, 1966; Overhead Capital, 1967; After the Forty-Five, 1973; Beyond the Highland Line, 1974; Scientific Revolution in Victorian Medicine, 1979; (ed) China and Hong Kong: the economic nexus, 1983; The Prince and the Pretender, 1985; Urban Development and the Royal Fine Art Commission, 1990; contrib. to various journals devoted to economics and economic history. *Recreation:* gardening. *Address:* Flat 2, The Warren, Hummel Road, Gullane, E Lothian.

YOUNIE, Edward Milne, OBE 1978; HM Diplomatic Service, retired; Consultant, Trefoil Associates, since 1983; *b* 9 Feb. 1926; *s* of John Milne and Mary Dickie Younie; *m* 1st, 1952, Mary Groves (*d* 1976); 2nd, 1979, Mimi Barkley. *Educ:* Fettes Coll. (Scholar); Gonville and Caius Coll., Cambridge (Scholar) (BA Hons). RN, 1944–46. HM Colonial Service, Tanganyika, 1950–62; FCO, 1963; Johannesburg, 1964–67; Blantyre, 1967–69; First Secretary: Lagos, 1972–76; Nairobi, 1977–79; Salisbury, 1979–81 (Counsellor, 1980); FCO, 1981–82. *Recreations:* golf, tennis, music. *Address:* Glebe House, Kippen, Stirling FK8 3DY. *Club:* Brooks's.

YOUNSON, Maj.-Gen. Eric John, OBE 1952; BSc; CEng, FRAeS, FBIM, FIIM, FRSA; industrial consultant; *b* 1 March 1919; *o s* of late Ernest M. Younson, MLitt, BCom, Jarrow; *m* 1946, Jean Beaumont Carter, BA; three *d. Educ:* Jarrow Grammar Sch.; Univ. of Durham; Royal Military Coll. of Science. Served War of 1939–45: commissioned, RA, 1940; UK and NW Europe (despatches). Directing Staff, RMCS, 1953–55; Atomic Weapons Research Estab., 1957–58; Attaché (Washington) as rep. of Chief Scientific Adviser, 1958–61; Head of Defence Science 3, MoD, 1961–63; Dep. Dir of Artillery,

1964–66; Dir of Guided Weapons Trials and Ranges, Min. of Technology, 1967–69; Vice-Pres., Ordnance Board, 1970–72, Pres., 1972–73, retired 1973; Sen. Asst Dir, Central Bureau for Educnl Visits and Exchanges, 1973–74; Dep. Dir, SIMA, 1974–78; Sec.-Gen., EUROM, 1975–77; Clerk to Worshipful Co. of Scientific Instrument Makers, 1976–87 (Hon. Liveryman and Clerk Emeritus, 1987). Freeman, City of London, 1981. *Publications:* The Worshipful Company of Scientific Instrument Makers: history, 1988; articles on gunnery and scientific subjects in Service jls; occasional poetry. *Recreations:* photography, electronics. *Address:* 7 Pondwick Road, Harpenden, Herts AL5 2HG. *T:* Harpenden (0582) 715892.

YUDKIN, John, MA, PhD, MD, BCh (Cambridge); BSc (London); FRCP, FRSC, FIBiol; Professor of Nutrition, University of London, at Queen Elizabeth College, 1954–71, Emeritus Professor, since 1971; *b* 8 August 1910; 3rd *s* of Louis and Sarah Yudkin, London; *m* 1933, Emily Himmelweit; three *s. Educ:* Hackney Downs (formerly Grocers' Company) School, London; Chelsea Polytechnic; Christ's Coll., Cambridge; London Hospital. Research in Biochemical Laboratory, Cambridge, 1931–36; Research in Nutritional Laboratory, Cambridge, 1938–43; Benn Levy Research Student, 1933–35; Grocers' Company Research Scholar, 1938–39; Sir Halley Stewart Research Fellow, 1940–43; Dir of Medical Studies, Christ's Coll., Cambridge, 1940–43; Prof. of Physiology, Queen Elizabeth Coll., 1945–54; Fellow, Queen Elizabeth Coll., London (now KCL), 1976. William Julius Mickle Fellow for Medical Res., London Univ., 1961–62. Responsible for introd. first comprehensive univ. courses leading to Bachelor and Master degrees in nutrition, 1953. *Publications:* This Slimming Business, 1958; The Complete Slimmer, 1964; Changing Food Habits, 1964; Our Changing Fare, 1966; Pure, White and Deadly, 1972, 2nd edn 1986; This Nutrition Business, 1976; A-Z of Slimming, 1977; Penguin Encyclopaedia of Nutrition, 1985; The Sensible Person's Guide to Weight Control, 1990; numerous articles on biochemistry and nutrition in scientific and medical journals. *Address:* 20 Wellington Court, Wellington Road, St John's Wood, NW8 9TA. *T:* 071–586 5586.

YUKAWA, Morio, Hon. GCVO; Japanese diplomatist; *b* 23 Feb. 1908; *m* 1940, Teiko Kohiyama; two *s. Educ:* Tokyo Imperial Univ. (Law Dept). Joined Diplomatic Service, and apptd Attaché, London, 1933; Dir, Trade Bureau of Economic Stabilization Bd (Cabinet), 1950; Dir, Econ. Affairs Bureau (For. Min.), 1951; Counsellor, Paris, 1952; Dir, Internat. Co-op. Bureau (For. Min.), 1954; again Dir, Econ. Affairs Bureau, 1955; Ambassador to The Philippines, 1957–61; Dep. Vice-Minister (For. Min.), 1961–63; Ambassador to Belgium, 1963–68; concurrently Ambassador to Luxembourg and Chief of Japanese Mission to European Economic Community, 1964–68; Ambassador to Court of St James's, 1968–72. Grand Master of Ceremonies, Imperial Household, Tokyo, 1973–79. First Order of Sacred Treasure and many other decorations, inc. Hon. GCVO 1971. *Publications:* articles and brochures, principally on historical subjects. *Recreations:* golf, theatre, history and biography. *Address:* Sanbancho Hilltop, 5–10 Sanbancho, Chiyoda-ku, Tokyo, Japan. *Clubs:* Tokyo, Nihon, Gakushikai (Tokyo); Hodogaya Country (Yokohama).

YUKON, Bishop of, since 1981; **Rt. Rev. Ronald Curry Ferris;** *b* 2 July 1945; *s* of Herald Bland Ferris and Marjorie May Ferris; *m* 1965, Janet Agnes (*née* Waller); two *s* four *d. Educ:* Toronto Teachers' Coll. (diploma); Univ. of W Ontario (BA); Huron Coll., London, Ont. (MDiv). Teacher, Pape Avenue Elem. School, Toronto, 1965; Principal Teacher, Carcross Elem. School, Yukon, 1966–68. Incumbent, St Luke's Church, Old Crow, Yukon, 1970–72; Rector, St Stephen's Memorial Church, London, Ont., 1973–81. Hon. DD, Huron Coll., London, Ont., 1982. *Address:* Box 4247, Whitehorse, Yukon Y1A 3T3, Canada.

Z

ZACHARIAH, Joyce Margaret; Secretary of the Post Office, 1975–77; *b* 11 Aug. 1932; *d* of Robert Paton Emery and Nellie Nicol (*née* Wilson); *m* 1978, George Zachariah. *Educ:* Earl Grey Sch., Calgary; Hillhead High Sch., Glasgow; Glasgow Univ. (MA 1st cl. Hons French and German, 1956). Post Office: Asst Principal, 1956; Private Sec. to Dir Gen., 1960; Principal, 1961; Asst Sec., 1967; Dir, Chairman's Office, 1970. *Address:* 8 Berkeley Square, Grand Avenue, Worthing, West Sussex BN11 5AF.

See also E. J. Emery.

ZACHAROV, Prof. Vasilii, (Basil), PhD, DSc; consultant; Director of Information Processing, International Organization for Standardization, Geneva, since 1989; *b* 2 Jan. 1931; *s* of Viktor Nikiforovich Zakharov and Varvara Semyenovna (*née* Krzak); *m* 1959, Jeanne (*née* Hopper) one *s* one *d*. *Educ:* Latymer Upper Sch.; Univ. of London (BSc: Maths 1951, Phys 1952; MSc 1958; PhD 1960; DIC 1960; DSc 1977). Research in Computer systems and applications, Birkbeck Coll., 1953–56; digital systems development, Rank Precision Instruments, 1956–57; Research Fellow, Imperial Coll., 1957–60; Physicist, European Organisation for Nuclear Res. (CERN), Geneva, 1960–65; Reader in Experimental Physics, Queen Mary Coll., London, 1965–66; Head of Computer Systems and Electronics Div., as Sen. Principal Sci. Officer, SRC Daresbury Laboratory, 1966–69, Dep. Chief Sci. Officer, 1970–78; Dir, London Univ. Computing Centre, 1978–80, and Prof. of Computing Systems, 1979–80; Sen. Associate, CERN, Geneva, 1981–83; Invited Prof., Univ. of Geneva, 1984–87. Vis Scientist: JINR Dubna, USSR, 1965; CERN, 1971–72; Consultant to AERE Harwell, 1965; Vis. Prof. of Physics, QMC London, 1968; Vis. Prof., Westfield Coll., 1974–78. Member, SRC Comp. Sci. Cttee, 1974–77. *Publications:* Digital Systems Logic, 1968, and other books; scientific papers in professional jls on photoelectronics, computer systems, elementary particle physics and computer applications. *Recreations:* collecting Russian miscellanea, skiing, shooting, amateur radio; grape growing, wine making, wine drinking. *Address:* The Firs, Oldcastle, Cheshire SY14 7NE.

ZAHEDI, Ardeshir; Ambassador of Iran to the United States, 1959–61 and 1973–79; Ambassador of Iran to Mexico, 1973–76; *b* Tehran, 16 Oct. 1928; *s* of General Fazlollah and Khadijeh Zahedi; *m* 1957, HIH Princess Shahnaz Pahlavi (marr. diss., 1964); one *d*. *Educ:* American Coll. of Beirut; Utah State Univ. (BS). Treasurer, Jt Iran-American Commn, and Asst to Dir of Point 4 Program, 1950; took part in revolution led by Gen. Zahedi which overthrew Mossadegh, 1953; Special Adviser to Prime Minister, 1953; Chamberlain to HIM the Shahanshah of Iran, 1954–59; Head of Iranian Students Program, 1959–60; Head of Mission representing Iran at 150th Anniv. Celebrations in Argentina, 1960; Ambassador of Iran to the Court of St James's, 1962–66; Foreign Minister of Iran, 1967–71. Represented Iranian Govt: at signing of Treaty banning Nuclear Tests, London, 1963; at Independence Celebrations, Bahamas, 1973. Hon. Doctorates: Utah State Univ., 1951; Chungang Univ. of Seoul, 1969; East Texas State, 1973; Kent State Univ., 1974; St Louis Univ., 1975. Holds decorations from Iran and 23 other countries incl. Iranian Taj with Grand Cordon First Class, 1975. *Recreations:* hunting, shooting.

ZAHIRUDDIN bin Syed Hassan, Tun Syed, SMN, PSM, DUNM, SPMP, JMN, PJK; Governor of Malacca, 1975; *b* 11 Oct. 1918; *m* 1949, Toh Puan Halimah, *d* of Hj. Mohd. Noh; five *s* five *d*. *Educ:* Malay Coll., Kuala Kangsar; Raffles Coll., Singapore (Dip.Arts). Passed Cambridge Sch. Cert. Malay Officer, Tanjong Malim, etc, 1945–47; Dep. Asst Dist Officer, 1948; Asst Dist Officer, 1951–54; 2nd Asst State Sec., Perak, 1955; Registrar of Titles and Asst State Sec. (Lands), Perak, 1956; Dist Officer, Batang Padang, Tapah, 1957; Dep. Sec., Public Services Commn, 1958; Principal Asst Sec. (Service), Fedn Estabt Office, Kuala Lumpur, 1960; State Sec., Perak, 1961; Permanent Sec.: Min. of Agric. and Co-operatives, Kuala Lumpur, 1963; Min. of Educn, Kuala Lumpur, 1966; Dir-Gen., Public Services Dept, Kuala Lumpur, 1969; retd, 1972. High Comr for Malaysia in London, 1974–75. Chm., Railway Services Commn, Kuala Lumpur, 1972–. Chairman: Special Cttee on Superannuation in the Public Services, 1972, and Statutory Bodies; Bd of Governors, Malay Coll., Kuala Kangsar; Interim Council of Nat. Inst. of Technology; Central Bd. Vice-Pres., Subang Nat. Golf Club, 1972–74. Hon. GCVO 1974. *Recreation:* golf. *Address:* Seri Melaka, Malacca, Malaysia.

ZAIDI, Bashir Husain, Syed, CIE 1941; Padma Vibhushan 1976; Director of several industrial concerns; *b* 1898; *s* of Syed Shaukat Husain Zaidi; *m* 1937, Qudsia Abdullah (*d* 1960); two *s* one *d*. *Educ:* St Stephen's College, Delhi; Cambridge University. Called to Bar, Lincoln's Inn, 1923; served Aligarh Univ., 1923–30; entered Rampur State service, 1930; Chief Minister Rampur State, UP, 1936–49; Member: Indian Constituent Assembly, 1947–49, Indian Parliament, 1950–52, Indian Delegation to Gen. Assembly of UN, 1951; Indian Parliament (Lok Sabha), 1952–57; (Rajya Sabha) 1964–70; Govt of India's Commn of Inquiry on Communal Disturbances, 1967–69. Chm., Associated Journals Ltd, 1952–77. Vice-Chancellor, Aligarh Muslim University, 1956–62. Leader, Good Will Mission to 9 Afro-Asian countries, 1964; Leader, Cultural Delegn to participate in Afghan Independence Week celebrations, 1965. Trustee: HEH the Nizam's Trusts, 1962–; Youth Hostels Assoc. of India, 1970–. Member: Governing Body, Dr Zakir Husain Coll., New Delhi, 1974–; Ct, Aligarh Muslim Univ., 1983–. DLitt *hc:* Aligarh 1964; Kanpur, 1974. *Address:* Zaidi Villa, Jamianagar, New Delhi, India. *T:* 631648.

ZAMBONI, Richard Frederick Charles, FCA; Managing Director, 1979–89 and a Vice-Chairman, 1986–89, Sun Life Assurance Society plc; Chairman, Avon Enterprise Fund PLC, since 1990 (Director, since 1984); *b* 28 July 1930; *s* of Alfred Charles Zamboni and Frances Hosler; *m* 1960, Pamela Joan Marshall; two *s* one *d*. *Educ:* Monkton House Sch., Cardiff. Gordon Thomas & Pickard, Chartered Accountants, 1948–54; served Royal Air Force, 1954–56; Peat Marwick Mitchell & Co., 1956–58; British Egg Marketing Board, 1959–70, Chief Accountant, from 1965; Sun Life Assurance Society plc, 1971–89, Director, 1975–89; Chairman: Sun Life Investment Management Services, 1985–89; Sun Life Trust Management, 1985–89; Sun Life Direct Marketing, 1986–89. Deputy Chairman: Life Offices' Assoc., 1985 (Mem., Management Cttee, 1981–85); Assoc. of British Insurers, 1986–88 (Dep. Chm., 1985–86, Chm., 1986–88, Life Insurance Council); Member: Council, Chartered Insurance Inst., 1983–85; Life Assurance and Unit Trust Regulatory Orgn's steering gp, 1985–86; Hon. Treasurer, Insurance Institute of London, 1982–85. Member, Management Cttee, Effingham Housing Assoc. Ltd, 1980–86; Chm., Council of Management, Grange Centre for the Handicapped, 1991–. Pres., Insurance Offices RFU, 1985–87. *Recreations:* ornithology, gardening, tennis. *Address:* Long Meadow, Beech Avenue, Effingham, Leatherhead, Surrey KT24 5PH. *T:* Bookham (0372) 458211.

ZAMYATIN, Leonid Mitrofanovich; Soviet Ambassador to the Court of St James's, 1986–91; *b*. Nizhni Devitsk, 9 March 1922; *m* 1946; one *d*. *Educ:* Moscow Aviation Inst.; Higher Diplomatic School. Mem., CPSU, 1944–, Mem. Central Cttee, 1976–; Min. of Foreign Affairs, 1946; First Sec., Counsellor on Political Questions, USSR Mission to UN, 1953–57; Soviet Dep. Rep., Preparatory Cttee, later Bd of Governors, IAEA, 1957–59; Soviet Rep., IAEA, 1959–60; Dep. Head, American Countries Dept, Min. of Foreign Affairs, 1960–62; Head of Press Dept, 1962–70; Mem., Collegium of Ministry, 1962–70; Dir-Gen., TASS News Agency, 1970–78, Govt Minister, 1972–; Dep. to USSR Supreme Soviet, 1970; Chief, Dept of Internat. Inf., Central Cttee, CPSU, 1978–86. Mem., Commn for Foreign Relations, Soviet of Nationalities, 1974–. Lenin Prize 1978; USSR Orders and medals incl. Order of Lenin (twice). *Address:* c/o Soviet Embassy, 13 Kensington Palace Gardens, W8 4QX. *T:* 071–229 3620.

ZANDER, Prof. Michael; Professor of Law, London School of Economics, since 1977; *b* 16 Nov. 1932; *s* of Dr Walter Zander and Margaret Magnus; *m* 1965, Betsy Treeger; one *d* one *s*. *Educ:* Royal Grammar Sch., High Wycombe; Jesus Coll., Cambridge (BA Law, double 1st Cl. Hons; LLB 1st Cl. Hons; Whewell Scholar in Internat. Law); Harvard Law Sch. (LLM). Solicitor of the Supreme Court. National Service, RA, 1950–52, 2nd Lieut. Cassel Scholar, Lincoln's Inn, 1957, resigned 1959; New York law firm, 1958–59; articled with City solicitors, 1959–62; Asst Solicitor with City firm, 1962–63; London Sch. of Economics: Asst Lectr, 1963; Lectr, 1965; Sen. Lectr, 1970; Reader, 1970; Convener, Law Dept, 1984–88. Legal Correspondent, The Guardian, 1963–87. *Publications:* Lawyers and the Public Interest, 1968; (ed) What's Wrong with the Law?, 1970; (ed) Family Guide to the Law, 1971 (2nd edn 1972); Cases and Materials on the English Legal System, 1973 (6th edn 1991); (with B. Abel-Smith and R. Brooke) Legal Problems and the Citizen, 1973; Social Workers, their Clients and the Law, 1974 (3rd edn 1981); A Bill of Rights?, 1975 (3rd edn 1985); Legal Services for the Community, 1978; (ed) Pears Guide to the Law, 1979; The Law-Making Process, 1980 (3rd edn 1989); The State of Knowledge about the English Legal Profession, 1980; The Police and Criminal Evidence Act 1984, 1985 (2nd edn 1990); A Matter of Justice: the legal system in ferment, 1988 (rev. edn 1989); articles in Criminal Law Rev., Mod. Law Rev., Law Soc.'s Gazette, New Law Jl, Solicitors' Jl, Amer. Bar Assoc. Jl, New Society, etc. *Recreation:* the cello. *Address:* 12 Woodside Avenue, N6 4SS. *T:* 081–883 6257.

ZANZIBAR AND TANGA, Bishop of; *see* Tanzania, Archbishop of.

ZARNECKI, Prof. George, CBE 1970; MA, PhD; FSA; FBA 1968; Professor of History of Art, University of London, 1963–82, now Emeritus Professor (Reader, 1959–63); Deputy Director, Courtauld Institute of Art, 1961–74; *b* 12 Sept. 1915; *m* 1945, Anne Leslie Frith; one *s* one *d*. *Educ:* Cracow Univ. MA Cracow Univ., 1938; PhD Univ. of London, 1950. Junior Asst, Inst. of History of Art, Cracow Univ., 1936–39. Served war of 1939–45 as lance-corporal in Polish Army; in France, 1939–40 (Polish Cross of Valour and Croix de Guerre, 1940); prisoner of war, 1940–42; interned in Spain, 1942–43; in Polish Army in UK, 1943–45. On staff of Courtauld Institute of Art, Univ. of London, 1945–82, Hon. Fellow, 1986. Slade Professor of Fine Art, Univ. of Oxford, 1960–61. Vice-President: Soc. of Antiquaries of London, 1968–72; British Soc. of Master Glass Painters, 1976–90; British Archaeol Assoc., 1979–; British Academy: Member: Corpus Vitrearum Medii Aevi Cttee, 1956–85; Publications Cttee, 1978–84; Corpus of Romanesque Sculpture in Britain and Ireland, 1988–; Chm., Corpus of Anglo-Saxon Sculpture Cttee, 1979–84. Member: Conservation Cttee, Council for Places of Worship, 1969–75; Royal Commn on Historical Monuments, 1971–84; Arts Sub-Cttee of UGC, 1972–77; Sub-Cttee for Higher Doctorates, CNAA, 1978–82; Chm., Working Cttee organizing Arts Council exhibition, English Romanesque Art 1066–1200, 1984. Mem., Inst. for Advanced Study, Princeton, 1966. Hon. Mem., Royal Archaeol Inst., 1985. Hon. DLitt: Warwick, 1978; East Anglia, 1981; Hon. LittD Dublin, 1984. Gold Medal, Soc. of Antiquaries, 1986. Gold Medal of Merit (Poland), 1978. *Publications:* English Romanesque Sculpture 1066–1140, 1951; Later English Romanesque Sculpture 1140–1210, 1953; English Romanesque Lead Sculpture, 1957; Early Sculpture of Ely Cathedral, 1958; Gislebertus, sculpteur d'Autun, 1960 (English edn, 1961); Romanesque Sculpture at Lincoln Cathedral, 1964; La sculpture à Payerne, Lausanne, 1966; 1066 and Architectural Sculpture (Proceedings of Brit. Acad.), 1966; Romanik (Belser Stilgeschichte, VI), 1970 (English edn, Romanesque Art, 1971); The Monastic Achievement, 1972; (contrib.) Westminster Abbey, 1972; Art of the Medieval World, 1975 (trans. Chinese, 1991); Studies in Romanesque Sculpture, 1979; Romanesque Lincoln, 1988; articles in archaeological journals. *Address:* 22 Essex Park, N3 1NE. *T:* 081–346 6497.

ZEALLEY, Christopher Bennett; Chairman: Dartington and Co. Group plc (formerly White Hart Holdings PLC); Charity Appointments Ltd, since 1988; *b* 5 May 1931; *s* of Sir Alec Zealley and Lady Zealley (*née* King); *m* 1966, Ann Elizabeth Sandwith; one *s* one *d*. *Educ:* Sherborne Sch.; King's Coll., Cambridge (MA Law). Commnd RNVR, 1953; ICI Ltd, 1955–66; IRC, 1967–70; Dir, Dartington Hall Trust, 1970–88. Chairman:

Public Interest Research Centre, 1972–; Social Audit Ltd, 1972–. Mem. Council, Assoc. for Consumer Res. (formerly Consumers' Assoc.), 1976– (Chm., 1977–82). Trustee, Charities Aid Foundn, 1982–90. Director: JT Group Ltd; Grant Instruments Ltd; Good Food Club Ltd. Chairman: Dartington Coll. of Art, 1973–; Dartington Summer Sch. of Music, 1980–. *Recreation:* music. *Address:* Sneydhurst, Broadhempston, Totnes, Devon TQ9 6AX. *Club:* Naval.

ZEALLEY, Dr Helen Elizabeth, FRCPEd, FFPHM; Director of Public Health and Chief Administrative Medical Officer, Lothian Health Board, since 1988; *b* 10 June 1940; *d* of late Sir John Howie Flint Brotherston and of Lady Brotherston; *m* 1965, Dr Andrew King Zealley; one *s* one *d*. *Educ:* St Albans High Sch. for Girls; Edinburgh Univ. (MB, ChB 1964; MD 1968). FRCPEd 1987; FFPHM 1980. Formerly Consultant in Public Health Medicine with a special interest in the health of children; Exec. Mem., Lothian Health Bd, 1991–. Member: Council, RCPE, 1989–; Bd, Faculty of Public Health Medicine, 1989–. Kentucky Colonel, 1961. *Recreations:* family, sailing, ski-ing, WHO health for all movement. *Address:* Viewfield House, 12 Tipperlinn Road, Edinburgh EH10 5ET. *T:* 031–447 5545.

ZEEMAN, Sir Erik Christopher, Kt 1991; PhD; FRS 1975; Principal, Hertford College, Oxford, since 1988; *b* 4 Feb. 1925; *s* of Christian Zeeman and Christine Zeeman (*née* Bushell); *m* 1960, Rosemary Gledhill; three *s* two *d*. *Educ:* Christ's Hospital; Christ's Coll., Cambridge (MA, PhD; Hon. Fellow, 1989). Commonwealth Fellow, 1954; Fellow of Gonville and Caius Coll., Cambridge, 1953–64; Lectr, Cambridge Univ., 1955–64; Prof., and Dir of Maths Res. Centre, Warwick Univ., 1964–88. Sen. Fellow, SRC, 1976–81. Visiting Prof. at various institutes, incl.: IAS; Princeton; IHES, Paris; IMPA, Rio; Royal Instn; also at various univs, incl.: California, Florida, Pisa. Hon. Dr, Strasbourg. *Publications:* numerous research papers on topology, dynamical systems, and applications to biology and the social sciences, in various mathematical and other jls. *Recreation:* family. *Address:* Hertford College, Oxford OX1 3BW.

ZEFFIRELLI, G. Franco (Corsi); opera, film and theatrical producer and designer since 1949; *b* 12 February 1923. *Educ:* Florence. Designer: (in Italy): A Streetcar Named Desire; Troilus and Cressida; Three Sisters. Has produced and designed numerous operas at La Scala, Milan, 1952–, and in all the great cities of Italy, at world-famous festivals, and in UK and USA; *operas include:* Lucia di Lammermoor, Cavalleria Rusticana, and Pagliacci (Covent Garden, 1959, 1973); Falstaff (Covent Garden, 1961); L'Elisir D'Amore (Glyndebourne, 1961); Don Giovanni, and Alcina (Covent Garden, 1962); Tosca, Rigoletto (Covent Garden, 1964, 1966, 1973, Metropolitan, NY, 1985); Don Giovanni (Staatsoper-Wien, 1972); Otello (Metropolitan, NY, 1972); Antony and Cleopatra (Metropolitan, NY, 1973); Otello (La Scala, 1976); La Bohème (Metropolitan, NY, 1981); Turandot (La Scala, 1983, 1985, Metropolitan, NY, 1987); *stage:* Romeo and Juliet (Old Vic, 1960); Othello (Stratford-on-Avon), 1961; Amleto (National Theatre), 1964; After the Fall (Rome), 1964; Who's Afraid of Virginia Woolf (Paris), 1964, (Milan), 1965; La Lupa (Rome), 1965; Much Ado About Nothing (National Theatre), 1966; Black Comedy (Rome), 1967; A Delicate Balance (Rome), 1967; Saturday, Sunday, Monday (Nat. Theatre), 1973; Filumena, Lyric, 1977; *films:* The Taming of the Shrew, 1965–66; Florence, Days of Destruction, 1966; Romeo and Juliet, 1967; Brother Sun, Sister Moon, 1973; Jesus of Nazareth, 1977; The Champ, 1979; Endless Love, 1981; La Traviata, 1983; Cavalleria Rusticana, 1983; Otello, 1986; The Young Toscanini, 1988; Hamlet, 1991. Produced Beethoven's Missa Solemnis, San Pietro, Rome, 1971. *Publication:* Zeffirelli (autobiog.), 1986. *Address:* c/o Ken McReddie Ltd, 91 Regent Street, W1R 7TB; Via due Macelli 31, Rome.

ZEHETMAYR, John Walter Lloyd, OBE 1991; VRD 1963; FICFor; Senior Officer for Wales and Conservator South Wales, Forestry Commission, 1966–81, retired; Member, Brecon Beacons National Park Committee, since 1982; Chairman, Forestry Safety Council, since 1986; *b* 24 Dec. 1921; *s* of late Walter Zehetmayr and late Gladys Zehetmayr; *m* 1945, Isabell (Betty) Neill-Kennedy; two *s* one *d*. *Educ:* St Paul's, Kensington; Keble Coll., Oxford (BA). Served RNVR, 1942–46 (despatches); now Lt Cdr RNR retired. Forestry Commission: Silviculturist, 1948–56; Chief Work Study Officer, 1956–64; Conservator West Scotland, 1964–66. Member: Prince of Wales' Cttee, 1970–89; Brecon Beacons Nat. Park Cttee, 1982–91. *Publications:* Experiments in Tree Planting on Peat, 1954; Afforestation of Upland Heaths, 1960; The Gwent Small Woods Project 1979–84, 1985; Forestry in Wales, 1985. *Recreations:* garden, conservation, skiing. *Address:* The Haven, Augusta Road, Penarth, S Glam CF6 2RH.

ZEIDLER, Sir David (Ronald), AC 1990; Kt 1980; CBE 1971; FAA 1985; FRACI; FIChemE; FIEAust; FTS; Chairman and Managing Director, ICI Australia, 1973–80, retired; *s* of Otto William and Hilda Maude Zeidler; *m* 1943, June Susie Broadhurst; four *d*. *Educ:* Scotch Coll., Melbourne; Melbourne Univ. (MSc). FTS 1976; FIEAust 1988. CSIRO, 1941–52; joined ICI Australia, 1952: Research Manager, 1953; Development Manager, 1959; Controller, Dyes and Fabrics Gp, 1962; Dir, 1963; Man. Dir, 1971; Dep. Chm., 1972. Chm., Metal Manufactures Ltd, 1980–88; Director: Amatil Ltd, 1979–89; Broken Hill Pty Co. Ltd, 1978–88; Commercial Bank of Australia Ltd, 1974–82; Westpac Banking Corp., 1982–91 (Dep. Chm., 1989–91); Australian Foundation Investment Co. Ltd, 1982–90; past Director: ICI New Zealand Ltd; IMI Australia Ltd. Vice-Pres., Walter and Eliza Hall Inst. of Med. Res., 1972–89; Dep. Chm., Queen's Silver Jubilee Trust, 1977–88. Chairman: Govt Inquiry into Elec. Generation and Power Sharing in SE Aust., 1980–81; Defence Industry Cttee, 1981–84; Member, or past Mem., cttees concerned with prof. qualifications, defence industry, educn and trng, internat. business co-operation. Member: Aust.-Japan Businessmen's Co-operation Cttee, 1978–80; Aust.-NZ Businessmen's Council Ltd, 1978–80; Sir Robert Menzies Meml Trust, 1978–80; Council, Aust. Acad. of Technol Scis, 1979–88 (Vice-Pres., 1970–71; Pres., 1983–88); Council, Science Museum of Victoria, 1964–82; Commerce and Industry Cttee, 1978–85, and Defence Industry Cttee, 1977–84 (Chm., 1981–84), Victorian Div. of Aust. Red Cross Soc.; Inst. of Dirs; Royal Society, Victoria; Royal Soc. for Encouragement of Arts Manuf. and Commerce in London; Cook Society. Director: Schizophrenia Aust. Foundn, 1986–; Aust. Bicentennial Multicultural Foundn, 1988–; Vict. Govt Strategic Res. Foundn, 1988– (Dep. Chm., 1990–). Governor, Ian Clunies Ross Meml Foundn, 1984–. *Recreations:* tennis, ski-ing, golf. *Address:* 45/238 The Avenue, Parkville, Victoria 3052, Australia. *T:* 387 5720. *Clubs:* Melbourne, Australian (Melb. and Sydney), Commonwealth (Canberra), Sciences.

ZEKI, Prof. Semir, FRS 1990; Professor of Neurobiology, University College London, since 1981; *b* 8 Nov. 1940; *m* 1967, Anne-Marie Claire Blestel; one *d* one *s*. *Educ:* University College London (BSc Anat. 1964; PhD 1967). Asst Lectr, UCL, 1966–67; Res. Associate, St Elizabeth's Hosp., Washington DC, 1967–68; Asst Prof., Univ. of Wisconsin, 1968–69; Lectr in Anatomy, UCL, 1969–75; Henry Head Res. Fellow, Royal Soc., 1975–80; Reader in Neurobiology, UCL, 1980–81. Visiting Professor: Duke Univ., 1977; Ludwig Maximillians Univ., Munich, 1982–87; Univ. of California, Berkeley, 1984; St Andrews, 1985. Lectures: Edridge Green, RCS, 1987; G. L. Brown, Physiol Soc., 1988; first Dist. in Neurosci., Edinburgh Univ., 1989; David Marr, Cambridge Univ., 1989; Perception, European Conf. of Visual Perception, 1990; Halliburton, KCL, 1991. Mem., Neuroscience Res. Program and Neurosci. Inst., NY, 1985–. MRI, 1985; Mem., Academia Europaea, 1990. Hon. Mem., Italian Primatological Assoc., 1988. Minerva Foundn Prize, USA, 1985; Prix Science pour l'Art, LVMH, Paris, 1991. *Publications:* articles on vision and the brain in professional jls. *Recreations:* reading (esp. about the darker side of man), music, deep sleep. *Address:* Anatomy Department, University College London, WC1E 6BT. *T:* 071–380 7187.

ZELLICK, Prof. Graham John, PhD; Principal, Queen Mary and Westfield College, University of London, and Professor of Law in the University of London, since 1991; *b* 12 August 1948; *s* of R. H. and B. Zellick; *m* 1975, Jennifer Temkin, LLM, Barrister, Prof. of Law and Dean, Sch. of Law, Univ. of Buckingham; one *s* one *d*. *Educ:* Christ's Coll., Finchley; Gonville and Caius Coll., Cambridge (MA, PhD); Stanford Univ. Ford Foundn Fellow, Stanford Law Sch., 1970–71; Queen Mary College, later Queen Mary and Westfield College, London: Lectr, 1971–78; Reader in Law, 1978–82; Prof. of Public Law, 1982–88; Dean of Faculty of Laws, 1984–88; Head, Dept of Law, 1984–90; Drapers' Prof. of Law, 1988–91; Gov., 1983–89; Mem. Council, 1989–; Sen. Vice-Principal and Acting Principal, 1990–91; University of London: Dean, Faculty of Laws, 1986–88; Mem. Senate, 1985–; Dep. Chm., Academic Council, 1987–89. Vis. Fellow, Centre of Criminology, 1978–79, and Vis. Prof. of Law, 1975, 1978–79, Toronto Univ.; Vis. Scholar, St John's Coll., Oxford, 1989. Lectures: Noel Buxton, NACRO, 1983; Webber, Jews' Coll., London, 1986; Sir Gwilym Morris, UWIST, Cardiff, 1986; Wythe, Coll. of William and Mary, Va, 1989. Member: Council and Exec. Cttee, Howard League for Penal Reform, 1973–82; Jellicoe Cttee on Bds of Visitors of Prisons, 1973–75; Sub Cttee on Crime and Criminal Justice, 1984–88, and Sub Cttee on Police Powers and the Prosecution Process, 1985–88, ESRC; Lord Chancellor's Legal Aid Adv. Cttee, 1985–88; Newham Dist Ethics Cttee, 1985–86; Data Protection Tribunal, 1985–; Lord Chancellor's Adv. Cttee on Legal Educn, 1988–90; Chairman: Prisoners' Advice and Law Service, 1984–89; Legal Cttee, All-Party Parly War Crimes Gp, 1988–; Dep. Chm., Justice Cttee on Prisoners' Rights, 1981–83. Chairman: Cttee of Heads of Univ. Law Schs, 1988–90; Disciplinary Appeals Cttee, Univ. of London Sch. Examinations Bd, 1988–; Mem., CVCP, 1991–. Member: Council: Univ. Coll. Sch., 1983–; West London Synagogue, 1990–; City and East London Confedn for Medicine and Dentistry, 1991–; St Bartholomew's Hosp. Med. Coll., 1991–; Council of Govs, London Hosp. Med. Coll., 1991–; Court of Governors: Polytechnic of Central London, 1973–77; Polytechnic of N London, 1986–89; Gov., Pimlico Sch., 1973–77; Chm., Lawyers' Gp, 1984–89, and Trustee, 1985–87, Tel Aviv Univ. Trust. FBIM; FRSA 1991. JP Inner London (N Westminster), 1981–85. Editor: European Human Rights Reports, 1978–82; Public Law, 1981–86; Member of Editorial Board: British Jl of Criminology, 1980–90; Public Law, 1981–91; Howard Jl of Criminal Justice, 1984–87; Civil Law Library, 1987–. *Publications:* Justice in Prison (with Sir Brian MacKenna), 1983; (ed) The Law Commission and Law Reform, 1988; (contrib.) Halsbury's Laws of England, 4th edn 1982; contribs to collections of essays, pamphlets, the national press, and professional and learned periodicals incl. British Jl of Criminology, Civil Justice Quarterly, Criminal Law Rev., Modern Law Rev., Public Law, Univ. of Toronto Law Jl, William and Mary Law Rev. *Address:* Queen Mary and Westfield College, E1 4NS. *T:* 071–975 5001; 14 Brookfield Park, NW5 1ER. *T:* 071–485 8219; 34 Mixbury, Oxon. *T:* Finmere (0280) 848295. *Club:* Reform.

ZEMAN, Prof. Zbyněk Anthony Bohuslav; Research Professor in European History, since 1982, and Professorial Fellow of St Edmund Hall, since 1983, Oxford University; *b* Prague, 18 Oct. 1928; *s* of late Jaroslav and Růžena Zeman; *m* 1956, Sarah Anthea Collins (separated); two *s* one *d*. *Educ:* London and Oxford Universities. BA (Hons) London, DPhil Oxon. Research Fellow, St Antony's Coll., Oxford, 1958–61, and Mem. editorial staff, The Economist, 1959–62; Lectr in Modern History, Univ. of St Andrews, 1962–70; Head of Research, Amnesty International, 1970–73; Director, East-West SPRL (Brussels) and European Cooperation Research Gp, 1974–76; Prof. of Central and SE European Studies and Dir, Comenius Centre, Lancaster Univ., 1976–82. Vis. Prof. of Hist., Charles Univ., Prague, 1990–91. Hon. Fellow, Österreichisches Ost-und Südosteuropa-Institut, 1988–89. *Publications* include: The Break-up of the Habsburg Empire 1914–1918, 1961; Nazi Propaganda, 1964; (with W. B. Scharlau) The Merchant of Revolution, A Life of Alexander Helphand (Parvus), 1965; Prague Spring, 1969; A Diplomatic History of the First World War, 1971; (ed jtly) International Yearbook of East-West Trade, 1975; The Masaryks, 1976; (jtly) Comecon Oil and Gas, 1977; Selling the War: art and propaganda in the Second World War, 1978; Heckling Hitler: caricatures of the Third Reich, 1984; Pursued by a Bear: the making of Eastern Europe, 1989; The Making and Breaking of Communist Europe, 1991. *Recreations:* skiing, squash, cooking. *Address:* St Edmund Hall, Oxford.

ZENINED, Abdesselam, Hon. GCVO 1987; Moroccan Ambassador to the Court of St James's, 1987–91; *b* 15 Dec. 1934; *m* 1960; one *s* two *d*. *Educ:* Bordeaux Univ.; Sorbonne. Carnegie scholarship, Inst. des Hautes Etudes Internat., Geneva, 1962. Ministry of Foreign Affairs, Morocco, 1959; Min. of Information, 1967; MP 1977–80; Minister of Tourism, 1979–80; Ambassador to Iraq, 1980–85. *Address:* c/o Ministry of Foreign Affairs, avenue Franklin Roosevelt, Rabat, Morocco. *Club:* Ambassadors'.

ZETLAND, 4th Marquess of, *cr* 1892; **Lawrence Mark Dundas;** Bt 1762; Baron Dundas, 1794; Earl of Zetland, 1838; Earl of Ronaldshay (UK), 1892; *b* 28 Dec. 1937; *e s* of 3rd Marquess of Zetland, DL and of Penelope, *d* of late Col Ebenezer Pike, CBE, MC; *S* father, 1989; *m* 1964, Susan, 2nd *d* of late Guy Chamberlin, Oatlands, Wrington Hill, Wrington, Bristol, and late Mrs Chamberlin; two *s* two *d*. *Educ:* Harrow School; Christ's College, Cambridge. Late 2nd Lieut, Grenadier Guards. *Heir: s* Earl of Ronaldshay, *qv*. *Address:* Copt Hewick Hall, Ripon, N Yorks HG4 5DE. *T:* Ripon (0765) 603946. *Clubs:* All England Lawn Tennis and Croquet, Jockey.

ZETTER, Paul Isaac, CBE 1981; Chairman, Zetters Group Ltd, since 1972; *b* 9 July 1923; *s* of late Simon and Esther Zetter; *m* 1954, Helen Lore Morgenstern; one *s* one *d*. *Educ:* City of London Sch. Army, 1941–46. Family business, 1946–; became public co., 1965. Chm., Southern Council for Sport and Recreation, 1985–87; Member: Sports Council, 1985–87; National Centres Bd, Sports Council, 1987–88; Governor, 1975–, and Hon. Vice-Pres., 1985–, Sports Aid Foundation (Chm., 1976–85). Trustee, Thames Salmon Trust, 1988–. Pres., John Carpenter Club, 1987–88. Mem., Glovers' Co., 1981–; Freeman, City of London, 1981. *Publication:* It Could Be Verse, 1976. *Recreations:* varied water sports, walking, writing. *Address:* 86 Clerkenwell Road, EC1P 1ZS. *Club:* Royal Automobile.

ZETTERBERG, Christer; President and Chief Executive Officer, AB Volvo, since 1990; *b* 2 Nov. 1941; *m* 1966, Inger Mathson; three *d*. MBA 1967. Officer, Royal Swedish Navy Reserve, 1964. Svenska Cellulosa AB, 1968–76 (Manager, Pulp Sales and Head, Pulp Div.); President: Calor-Celsius, 1976–80; Tibnor, 1980–83; Holmens Bruk, 1983–88; Pres. and Chief Exec. Officer, PKBanken, 1988–90. *Address:* AB Volvo, S-405 08 Gothenburg, Sweden. *T:* 46 31 59 00 90.

ZETTERLING, Mai Elizabeth; actress, films and stage; film director; writer; *b* 24 May 1925; *d* of Joel and Lina Zetterling; *m* 1st, 1944, Tutte Lemkow; one *s* one *d*; 2nd, 1958,

David John Hughes (marr. diss. 1977). *Educ:* Stockholm, Sweden. Graduate of Royal Theatre School of Drama, Stockholm. First appeared as Cecilia in Midsummer Dream in the Workhouse, Blanche Theatre, Stockholm, Oct. 1941. Stage successes (all at Royal Theatre, Stockholm) include: Janet in St Mark's Eve; Agnes in The Beautiful People; Brigid in Shadow and Substance; Maria in Twelfth Night; Nerissa in Merchant of Venice; Electra in Les Mouches; Adela in House of Bernarda. First appearance in London, as Hedwig in The Wild Duck, St Martin's, Nov. 1948; subsequently Nina in The Seagull, Lyric, Hammersmith, and St James's, 1949; Eurydice in Point of Departure, Lyric, Hammersmith and Duke of York's, 1950; Karen in The Trap, Duke of York's, 1952; Nora Helmer in A Doll's House, Lyric, Hammersmith, 1953; Poppy in The Count of Clérambard, Garrick, 1955; Thérèse Tard in Restless Heart, St James's, 1957; Tekla in Creditors, Lyric, Hammersmith, 1959, etc. *Swedish films* include: Frenzy, Iris, Rain Follows Dew, Music in the Dark, A Doll's House, Swinging on a Rainbow. *English films* include: Frieda, The Bad Lord Byron, Quartet, Portrait from Life, Lost People, Blackmailed, Hell is Sold Out, Tall Headlines, Desperate Moment, Faces in the Dark, Offbeat, The Main Attraction, and Only Two Can Play, Scrubbers. *United States films* include: Knock on Wood, Prize of Gold, and Seven Waves Away. Director of documentary films for BBC; Dir and Prod and co-writer with David Hughes of short film The War Game; 1st Award at Venice for Narrative Shorts, 1963; Director: Swedish full-length films, Alskande Par, (Eng.) Loving Couples, 1965; Night Games, 1966 (and *see infra*); Dr Glas, 1968; Flickorna, (Eng.) The Girls, 1968; Writer and Director: Visions of Eight (Olympics film), USA, 1972; Vincent the Dutchman, (award 1973); We Have Many Names (and actress), Sweden, 1975; The Moon is a Green Cheese, Sweden, 1976; The Native Squatter (for Canadian TV), Sweden, 1977; Lady Policeman (Granada TV documentary), 1979; Of Seals and Men (with Greenland trade dept), 1979; Love, Canada, 1980; Love and Marriage (Canadian TV documentary); (dir and co-writer) Scrubbers, 1981 (feature film, England); Amorosa (feature film, Sweden), 1989; starring in film, The Witches, 1990. Dir and Deviser, Playthings, Vienna English Theatre, New Half Moon Theatre, 1980. *Publications:* The Cat's Tale (with David Hughes), 1965; Night Games (novel), 1966; Shadow of the Sun (short stories), 1975; Bird of Passage (novel), 1976; Rains Hat (children's book), 1979; Ice Island (novel), 1979; All Those Tomorrows (autobiog.), 1985. *Recreations:* gardening, cooking, philosophical ESP, alchemy. *Address:* c/o Jeny Casarotto Ltd, National House, 60–66 Wardour Street, W1V 3HP.

ZHAO ZIYANG; General Secretary, Central Committee, Chinese Communist Party, 1987–89; *b* Huaxian County, Henan Prov., 1919; *m*; four *s* one *d*. Joined Chinese Communist Youth League, 1932, Chinese Communist Party, 1938; held various posts, S China Sub-Bureau of Central Cttee, Guangdong Provincial Cttee, and Cttee of Inner Mongolia Autonomous Reg., 1950–74; First Sec. of Provincial Cttee and Chm. of Revolutionary Cttee, Guangdong, 1974, Sichuan, 1975–80; First Political Commissar, Chengdu Mil. Reg., Chinese People's Liberation Army, 1976–80; Vice-Chm., 5th Nat. Cttee, Chinese People's Political Consultative Conf., 1978–80; Vice Premier, State Council, 1980, Premier, 1980–87. Mem., 10th Central Cttee, Chinese Communist Party, 1973; Alternate Mem., 1977, Mem., 1979, Mem. Standing Cttee, 1980, Political Bureau, and Vice Chm., 1981, 11th Central Cttee; Mem., 1982, and Mem. Standing Cttee, 1982, Political Bureau, 12th Central Cttee. *Address:* c/o Secretariat, Chinese Communist Party, Beijing, People's Republic of China.

ZHUKOV, Georgi Alexandrovich; Hero of Socialist Labour (1978); Orders of: Lenin (2); October Revolution; Red Banner of Labour (2); Red Star; Great Patriotic War, Grade 2; Friendship of Peoples; Joliot-Curie Medal; Columnist of Pravda, since 1962; Member Presidium, World Peace Council, since 1974; Vice-President, Soviet-American Institute, since 1961; President, Society USSR-France, since 1958; Secretary, Moscow writing organization, since 1970; *b* 1908. *Educ:* Lomonosov Inst., Moscow. Corresp.: local papers in Lugansk, Kharkov, 1927–32; Komsomolskaya Pravda, 1932–46 (Mem. Editorial Bd); Pravda in Paris, 1947–52; Foreign Editor of Pravda, 1952–57; Chairman, USSR Council of Ministers' State Committee for Cultural Relations with Foreign Countries, 1957–62. Mem., Central Auditing Cttee of CPSU, elected by XX, XXII, XXIII and XXIV Congresses of CPSU, 1956–89; Alternate Mem., Central Cttee of CPSU, elected by XXV, XXVI and XXVII Congresses of CPSU, 1976–89; Mem., Foreign Relations Cttee, USSR Supreme Soviet, 1966–89; MP, 1962–89; Chm., Soviet–French Parly Gp, 1966–89. Prizes: Lenin (for Journalism); Vorovsky; Union of Soviet Journalists; internat. organization of journalists. *Publications:* Border, 1938; Russians and Japan, 1945; Soldier's Life, 1946; American Notes (essays), 1947; The West After War, 1948; Three Months in Geneva, 1954; Taming Tigers, 1961; Japan, 1962; Meetings in Transcarpathia, 1962; One MIG from a Thousand, 1963, 2nd edn 1979; These Seventeen Years, 1963; Silent Art, 1964; The People of the Thirties, 1964; Vietnam, 1965; America, 1967; The People of the Forties, 1968, 2nd edn 1975; From Battle to Battle: letters from the ideological front, 1970; Chilean Diary, 1970; The USA on the Threshold of the Seventies, 1970; The People in the War (about Vietnam), 1972; 33 Visas, 1972; Times of Great Changes, 1973; Alex and others, 1974; Poisoners, 1975; The War: the beginning and the end, 1975; Letters from Rambouillet, 1975; European Horizons, 1975; Thirty Conversations with TV Viewers, 1977; Town's Beginning, 1977; Thoughts of Unthinkable, 1978; Society without Future, 1978; The Tale of Dirty Tricks, 1978; Roots, 1980; Pioneer Builders, 1982; Steep Steps, 1983 (English edn 1987); Journey through Indo-China, 1984; Journalists, 1984 (Chinese edn 1988); Where is peace—there life, 1985; Lack of Spirit, 1985; Dogs of War, 1986; Soldier's Thoughts, 1987; USSR–USA: the seventy years long way, 1988; Selected Works in Two Volumes, 1989. *Address:* 24 Pravda Street, Moscow, USSR.

ZIEGLER, Henri Alexandre Léonard, Ingénieur Général Air; Grand Officier, Légion d'Honneur; Croix de Guerre (1939–45); Rosette de la Résistance; Hon. CBE; Hon. CVO; Legion of Merit (US); French Aviation Executive; *b* Limoges, 18 Nov. 1906; *s* of Charles Ziegler and Alix Mousnier-Buisson; *m* 1932, Gillette Rizzi; three *s* one *d*. *Educ:* Collège Stanislas, Paris; Ecole Polytechnique (Grad.); Ecole Nationale Supérieure de l'Aéronautique. Officer-Pilot in French Air Force, 1928 (5000 hours); Tech. Officer, Min. of Aviation, 1929; Dep. Dir of Flight Test Centre, 1938; Foreign Missions: Gt Britain, USA, Germany, Poland, USSR. War of 1939–45: Dep. Buying Mission, USA, Dec. 1939; French Resistance, 1941–44; Col and Chief of Staff, Forces Françaises de l'Intérieur (London), 1944. Dir-Gen., Air France, 1946–54. Dir of Cabinet: of J. Chaban-Delmas (Min. of Public Works, Transport and Tourism), 1954; of Gen. Cormiglion-Molignier (Min. of Public Works), 1955–56; Admin. Dir-Gen., Ateliers d'aviation Louis Breguet, 1957–67. Pres. Dir-Gen., Sud Aviation, 1968; Pres. Dir-Gen., Soc. Nationale Industrielle Aérospatiale, 1970–73; Pres., Airbus Industrie, 1970–74. Pres., Air Alpes, 1961–76; Pres., Forum Atomique Européen, 1956–60; Admin. Inst. du Transport Aérien, 1969–77; Pres., Union Syndicale des Industries Aérospatiales, 1971–74. Mem., Amicale des anciens des essais en vol. Hon. Fellow, Soc. of Experimental Test Pilots; Hon. FRAeS. *Publication:* La Grande Aventure de Concorde, 1976. *Recreation:* alpinism. *Address:* 55 boulevard Lannes, 75116 Paris, France. *T:* 45.04.61.53. *Club:* Aéro-Club de France (Paris).

ZIEGLER, Philip Sandeman, CVO 1991; author; *b* 24 Dec. 1929; *s* of Major Colin Louis Ziegler, DSO, DL, and Mrs Dora Ziegler (*née* Barnwell); *m* 1st, 1960, Sarah Collins; one *s* one *d*; 2nd, 1971, Mary Clare Charrington; one *s*. *Educ:* Eton; New Coll., Oxford (1st Cl. Hons Jurisprudence; Chancellor's Essay Prize). Entered Foreign Service, 1952; served in Vientiane, Paris, Pretoria and Bogotá; resigned 1967; joined William Collins and Sons Ltd, 1967, Editorial Dir 1972, Editor-in-Chief, 1979–80. Chairman: The London Library, 1979–85; Soc. of Authors, 1988–90. FRSL 1975; FRHS 1979. Hon. DLitt Westminster Coll., Fulton, 1988. *Publications:* Duchess of Dino, 1962; Addington, 1965; The Black Death, 1968; William IV, 1971; Omdurman, 1973; Melbourne, 1976 (W. H. Heinemann Award); Crown and People, 1978; Diana Cooper, 1981; Mountbatten, 1985; Elizabeth's Britain 1926 to 1986, 1986; The Sixth Great Power: Barings 1762–1929, 1988; King Edward VIII, 1990; *edited:* the Diaries of Lord Louis Mountbatten 1920–1922, 1987; Personal Diary of Admiral the Lord Louis Mountbatten 1943–1946, 1988; From Shore to Shore: the diaries of Earl Mountbatten of Burma 1953–1979, 1989. *Address:* 22 Cottesmore Gardens, W8 5PR. *T:* 071–937 1903; Picket Orchard, Ringwood, Hants. *T:* Ringwood (0425) 473258. *Club:* Brooks's.

ZIENKIEWICZ, Prof. Olgierd Cecil, CBE 1989; FRS 1979; FEng 1979; Professor and Head of Civil Engineering Department, 1961–88, and Director, Institute for Numerical Methods in Engineering, 1976–88, University of Wales at Swansea, now Professor Emeritus; UNESCO Professor of Numerical Methods in Engineering, Universidad Politécnica de Cataluña, Barcelona; J. Walter Professor of Engineering, University of Texas, Austin; *b* Caterham, 18 May 1921; *s* of Casimir Zienkiewicz and Edith Violet (*née* Penny); *m* 1952, Helen Jean (*née* Fleming), Toronto; two *s* one *d*. *Educ:* Katowice, Poland; Imperial Coll., London. BSc (Eng); ACGI; PhD; DIC; DSc (Eng); DipEng; FICE; FASCE. Consulting engrg, 1945–49; Lectr, Univ. of Edinburgh, 1949–57; Prof. of Structural Mechanics, Northwestern Univ., 1957–61. Naval Sea Systems Comd Res. Prof., Monterey, Calif, 1979–80; Chalmers Jubilee Prof., Gothenburg, 1990. Hon. Founder Mem., GAMNI, France. Chairman: Cttee on Analysis and Design, Internat. Congress of Large Dams; Jt Computer Cttee, Instn of Civil Engineers. Mem. Council, ICE, 1972–75 (Chm., S Wales and Mon. Br.); Telford Premium, ICE, 1963–67. Pres., Internat. Assoc. Computational Mechanics, 1986–90. General Editor, Internat. Jl Numerical Methods in Engineering; Member Editorial Board: Internat. Jl Solids and Structures; Internat. Jl Earthquakes and Structural Mechanics; Internat. Jl Rock Mechanics, Numerical and Analytical Methods in Geomechanics. For. Associate, US Nat. Acad. of Engrg, 1981; For. Mem., Polish Acad. of Sci., 1985. Hon. Prof., Dalian Inst. of Technology, China, 1987; Hon. Dr, Lisbon, 1972; Hon. DSc: NUI, 1975; Northwestern Univ., Illinois, 1984; Chalmers Univ. of Technology, Gothenburg, 1987; Univ. of Technol., Warsaw, 1989; Technical Univ., Krakow, 1989; Hon. DTech Norwegian Inst. of Technol., Trondheim, 1985; Hon. DSci Free Univ., Brussels, 1982; Hon. LLD Dundee, 1987. FCGI 1979. James Clayton Fund Prizes, IMechE, 1967, 1973; James Alfred Ewing Medal, ICE, 1980; Newmark Medal, ASCE, 1980; Worcester Reed Warner Medal, ASME, 1980; Gauss Medal, Acad. of Science, Braunschweig, West Germany, 1987; Royal Medal, Royal Soc., 1990. *Publications:* Stress Analysis, 1965; Rock Mechanics, 1968; Finite Element Method, 1967, 4th edn 1989; Optimum Design of Structures, 1973; Finite Elements in Fluids, 1975; Numerical Methods in Offshore Engineering, 1977; Finite Elements and Approximation, 1983; numerous papers in Jl ICE, Jl Mech. Sci., Proc. Royal Soc., Internat. Jl of Num. Methods in Engrg, etc. *Recreations:* sailing, skin-diving. *Address:* 29 Somerset Road, Langland, Swansea SA3 4PG. *T:* Swansea (0792) 368776. *Clubs:* Athenæum; Rotary (Mumbles); Mumbles Yacht.

ZIJLSTRA, Jelle; Central Banker; President, Netherlands Bank, 1967–81; Member, Supervisory Board, Royal Dutch Petroleum, since 1982; *b* 27 Aug. 1918; *s* of Ane Zijlstra and Pietje Postuma; *m* 1946, Hetty Bloksma; two *s* three *d*. *Educ:* Netherlands Sch. of Economics. Asst, Netherlands Sch. of Economics, 1945; Prof., Theoretical Economics, 1948–52; Prof., Public Finance, 1963–66, Free Univ. of Amsterdam; Minister of Economic Affairs, 1952–58; of Finance, 1959–63; Prime Minister, 1966–67. Mem., Chm. Board, and Pres., BIS, 1967–82; Governor, IMF, 1967–81. *Publications:* Planned Economy, 1947; The Velocity of Money and its Significance for the Value of Money and for Monetary Equilibrium, 1948; Economic Order and Economic Policy, 1952. *Recreations:* sailing, ski-ing. *Address:* Park Oud Wassenaar, flat 44, 2243 BX Wassenaar, Netherlands.

ZILKHA, Selim Khedoury; Chairman and Chief Executive Officer (also sole owner), Zilkha Energy Co., Houston, Texas, since 1987; *b* 7 April 1927; *s* of Khedoury Aboodi Zilkha and Louise (*née* Bashi); *m* (marr. diss.); one *s* one *d*. *Educ:* English Sch., Heliopolis, Egypt; Horace Mann Sch. for Boys, USA; Williams Coll., USA (BA Major Philos.). Dir, Zilkha & Sons Inc., USA, 1947–87; Chm. and Man. Dir, Mothercare Ltd and associated cos, 1961–82; Dir, Habitat Mothercare Gp, 1982; Chairman: Amerfin Co. Ltd, GB, 1955–68; Spirella Co. of Great Britain Ltd, 1957–62; Chm./Jt Man. Dir, Lewis & Burrows Ltd, 1961–64; Chairman and Chief Executive Officer: Towner Petroleum Co., Houston, 1983–85; SKZ Inc., Houston, 1986. *Recreations:* bridge, backgammon, golf, tennis, horse racing. *Address:* 750 Lausanne Road, Los Angeles, Calif 90077, USA. *Clubs:* Portland; Sunningdale Golf; Travellers' (Paris).

ZIMAN, Prof. John Michael, FRS 1967; Emeritus Professor of Physics, University of Bristol, 1988; Director, Science Policy Support Group, since 1986; *b* 16 May 1925; *s* of late Solomon Netheim Ziman, ICS, retired, and Nellie Frances Ziman (*née* Gaster); *m* 1951, Rosemary Milnes Dixon; two adopted *s* two adopted *d*. *Educ:* Hamilton High Sch., NZ; Victoria University Coll., Wellington, NZ; Balliol Coll., Oxford. Junior Lectr in Mathematics, Oxford Univ., 1951–53; Pressed Steel Co. Ltd Research Fellow, Oxford Univ., 1953–54; Lectr in Physics, Cambridge Univ., 1954–64; Fellow of King's Coll., Cambridge, 1957–64; Editor of Cambridge Review, 1958–59; Tutor for Advanced Students, King's Coll., Cambridge, 1959–63; University of Bristol: Prof. of Theoretical Physics, 1964–69; Melville Wills Prof. of Physics, 1969–76; Dir, H. H. Wills Physics Lab., 1976–81; Henry Overton Wills Prof. of Physics, 1976–82. Vis. Prof., Dept of Social and Economic Studies, 1982–87, Dept of Humanities, 1982–, Imperial Coll., London. Rutherford Memorial Lectr in India and Pakistan, 1968. Chairman: Council for Science and Society, 1976–90; European Assoc. for Study of Science and Technology, 1982–86; Member: Scientific Council, Internat. Centre for Theoretical Physics, Trieste, 1970–79; CNAA, 1982–87. Hon. DSc Victoria Univ. of Wellington, NZ, 1985. Jt Editor, Science Progress, 1965–. *Publications:* Electrons and Phonons, 1960; Electrons in Metals, 1963; (with Jasper Rose) Camford Observed, 1964; Principles of the Theory of Solids, 1965; Public Knowledge, 1968; Elements of Advanced Quantum Theory, 1969; The Force of Knowledge, 1976; Reliable Knowledge, 1978; Models of Disorder, 1979; Teaching and Learning about Science and Society, 1980; Puzzles, Problems and Enigmas, 1981; An Introduction to Science Studies, 1984; (with Paul Sieghart and John Humphrey) The World of Science and the Rule of Law, 1986; Knowing Everything about Nothing, 1987; numerous articles in scientific jls. *Address:* Science Policy Support Group, 22 Henrietta Street, WC2E 8NA. *T:* 071–836 6515.

ZINNEMANN, Fred; Film Director since 1934; *b* Austria, 29 April 1907; *s* of Dr Oskar Zinnemann, Physician and Anna F. Zinnemann; *m* 1936, Renée Bartlett; one *s*. *Educ:* Vienna Univ. (Law School). First film, The Wave (documentary) directed for Mexican Govt, 1934; initiated, with others, school of neo-realism in American cinema, directing among other films: The Seventh Cross, 1943; The Search, 1948; The Men, 1949; Teresa, 1950; High Noon, 1951; Member of the Wedding, 1952; From Here to Eternity, 1953.

Later films include: Oklahoma!, 1956; The Nun's Story, 1959; The Sundowners, 1960; Behold a Pale Horse, 1964; A Man for All Seasons, 1966; The Day of the Jackal, 1973; Julia, 1977; Five Days One Summer, 1982. Member: Amer. Film Inst. (co-founder and ex-trustee); Acad. of Motion Picture Arts; Directors' Guild of America (2nd Vice-Pres., 1960–64); Hon. Pres., Directors' Guild of Great Britain, 1983–87. Fellow: BAFTA, 1978; BFI, 1990. Awards include: Academy Award, Los Angeles, 1951, 1954, 1967; Film Critics' Award, NY, 1952, 1954, 1960, 1967; Golden Thistle Award, Edinburgh, 1965; Moscow Film Festival Award, 1965; D. W. Griffith Award, 1970; Donatello Award, Florence, 1978; US Congressional Lifetime Achievement Award, 1987. Gold Medal of City of Vienna, 1967. Order of Arts and Letters, France, 1982. *Publication:* article on directing films, Encyclopædia Britannica. *Recreations:* mountain climbing, chamber music. *Address:* 128 Mount Street, W1Y 5HA. *T:* 071–499 8810. *Club:* Sierra (San Francisco).

ZOBEL de AYALA, Jaime; Chairman and President, Ayala Corporation, since 1983; Chairman, Bank of the Philippine Islands, since 1985; *b* 18 July 1934; *s* of Alfonso Zobel de Ayala and Carmen Pfitz y Herrero; *m* 1958, Beatriz Miranda; two *s* five *d*. *Educ:* La Salle, Madrid; Harvard Univ. (BA, Arch. Scis). Lt Col, Philippine Air Force (Res.). Philippire Ambassador to the Court of St James's and concurrently to Scandinavian countries 1970–74. Mem., Camera Club of the Philippines, 1978–; Associate, RPS, 1984. Hon. D of Business Management De La Salle Univ., 1985; Hon. LLD Univ. of Philippies, 1991. Comendador de la Orden del Mérito Civil, Spain, 1968; Chevalier des Arts et œs Lettres, 1980. *Recreation:* photography. *Address:* Ayala Corporation, Makati, Metro Nanila 1200, Philippines. *Clubs:* White's; Fox (Harvard).

ZOLEVEKE, Sir Gideon (Asatori Pitabose), KBE 1983 (MBE 1968); retired as public servant, 973 and as politician, 1980; farmer since 1980; *b* 3 Aug. 1922; *s* of Pita Pitabose and Mat Taburana; *m* 1954, Melody Sukuluta'a Watanamae; three *s* three *d* (and one *s* decd). *Euc:* primary schs, Solomon Is; secondary sch. and tertiary educn, Fiji. Dip. in Surgeryınd Medicine, Fiji Sch. of Medicine, Suva; DCMHE London. Served British Solomoıls Protectorate Defence Force, 1942–45 (Pacific Stars). Govt MO, 1951–62; Sen. Health Eucn Officer, 1962–73; Mem., Governing Council, 1973–74 (Chm., Works and Public tilities); MLA, 1974–78 (Backbencher, 1975–76); Minister of: Works and Public tilities, 1974–75; Home Affairs, April-July 1975; Educn, July-Nov. 1975; Agricultre and Lands, 1976–78; Health and Med. Services, 1978–80. Mem. and leader, various pvt delegns, 1953–. Mem., Solomon Is Public Service Commn, 1981–; Chm., Solomoris Electricity Authy Bd of Management, 1983–. Founder and first Pres., Solomon Is Med.)fficers Assoc., 1952–69; President: W Pacific Br.,BMA, 1961–70; Choiseul People's ssoc., 1955–71; Civil Servants Assoc., British Solomon Is Protectorate, 1966–67; Solomors Br., BRCS, 1974–78 (BRCS award, 1978; Life Mem., 1982); Solomon Is Red Cross, 178–82; St John's Primary Sch., Rove, Honiara, 1968–76; Honiara Club, 1963–68Foundn Mem., 1967–, Pres. and Chm., 1980–, Sir Winston Churchill Trust Fund, Somon Is. *Publications:* A Man from Choiseul (autobiog.), 1980; (contrib.) Lands in the Somon Islands, 1982; (contrib.) Solomon Island Politics, 1983. *Recreations:* writing, ading. *Address:* Kaiti Hill, PO Box 243, Honiara, Solomon Islands. *T:* Honiara 22927.

ZOUCHE 8th Baron, *cr* 1308, of Haryngworth; **James Assheton Frankland;** Bt 1660; companyirector; President, Multiple Sclerosis Society of Victoria, 1981–84; *b* 23 Feb. 1943; *s* oflajor Hon. Sir Thomas William Assheton Frankland, 11th Bt, and Mrs Robert Pardoe (*d*972), *d* of late Captain Hon. Edward Kay-Shuttleworth; *S* to father's Btcy 1944; *S* gndmother, 17th Baroness Zouche, 1965; *m* 1978, Sally Olivia, *y d* of R. M. Barton, Bgay, Suffolk; one *s* one *d*. *Educ:* Lycée Jaccard, Lausanne. Served 15/19th the King's Rol Hussars, 1963–68. *Heir:* *s* Hon. William Thomas Assheton Frankland [*b* 23 July 1984*Address:* The Abbey, Charlton Adam, Somerton, Somerset TA11 7BE. *Clubs:* Cavalry a Guards; Melbourne (Melbourne).

ZSÖGÖD, za B. G.; *see* Grosschmid-Zsögöd, G. B.

ZUCKER, enneth Harry, QC 1981; **His Honour Judge Zucker;** a Circuit Judge, since 198 4 March 1935; *s* of Nathaniel and Norma Zucker; *m* 1961, Ruth Erica, *y d* of Dr H. dno; one *s* one *d*. *Educ:* Westcliff High Sch.; Exeter Coll., Oxford, 1955–58 (MA). Seid in Royal Air Force, 1953–55. Bacon Scholar, Gray's Inn, 1958; called to Bar, Grayın, 1959; Atkin Scholar, Gray's Inn, 1959. A Recorder, 1982–89. *Recreations:* reading, vking, photography.

ZUCKERMN, family name of **Baron Zuckerman.**

ZUCKERMN, Baron *cr* 1971 (Life Peer), of Burnham Thorpe, Norfolk; **Solly Zuckerm,** OM 1968; KCB 1964 (CB 1946); Kt 1956; MA, MD, DSc; MRCS, FRCP; FR943, FIBiol, Hon. FRCS, Hon. FPS; President, British Industrial Biological Research Aciation, since 1974; *b* Cape Town, 1904; *m* 1939, Lady Joan Rufus Isaacs, *er d* of 2nd Mquess of Reading; one *s* one *d*. *Educ:* S African College Sch.; Univ. of Cape Town (Limann Scholar); University Coll. Hosp., London (Goldsmid Exhibnr). Demonstra of Anatomy, Univ. of Cape Town, 1923–25; Union Res. Scholar, 1925; Res. Anatcst to Zoological Soc. of London and Demonstrator of Anatomy, UCL, 1928–32; l Associate and Rockefeller Res. Fellow, Yale Univ., 1933–34; Beit Meml Res. Fellov934–37, Univ. Demonstrator and Lectr in Human Anatomy, 1934–45, Oxford Ur, William Julius Mickle Fellow, Univ. of London, 1935; Hunterian Prof., Royal Coll Surgeons, 1937; Sands Cox Prof. of Anatomy, Univ. of Birmingham, 1943–68, nProf. Emeritus; Professor-at-Large, Univ. of E Anglia, 1969–74, now Prof. Emeritus. tor, Bedford Coll., 1968–85 (Hon. Fellow, 1989). Scientific Adviser, Combined erations HQ; Scientific Advr on planning, AEAF, MAAF, SHAEF, 1939–46 (Gapt. (Hon.) RAF, 1943–46); Member: Min. of Works Sci. Cttee, 1945–47; Cttee on Fu Sci. Policy (Barlow Cttee), 1946–48; Min. of Fuel and Power Sci. Adv. Cttee, 1948; Associate Mem., Ordnance Bd, 1947–69, Dep. Chm., Adv. Council on Sci. Policy, 8–64; Mem., Agricl Res. Council, 1949–59; Chairman: Cttee on Sci. Manpower, 0–64; Natural Resources (Technical) Cttee, 1951–64; UK Delegate, Nato Science Ctte957–66; Mem., BBC Gen. Adv. Council, 1957–62; Chairman: Cttee on Managemend Control of Research and Develt, 1958–61; Defence Research Policy Cttee, 1960- Chief Scientific Adviser: to Sec. of State for Defence, 1960–66; to HM Govt, 1964- Chm., Central Adv. Cttee for Science and Technology, 1965–70; UK Delegate on disarmament working gps, 1966–71; Trustee, British Museum (Natural History), 1977; Chm., Hosp. Sci. and Tech. Services Cttee, 1967–68; Mem., Royal Commn onrironmental Pollution, 1970–74; Chm., Commn on Mining and the Environmen71–72; Mem., WHO Adv. Cttee on Med. Research, 1973–77. President: Parly and Sttee, 1973–76; Assoc., of Learned and Professional Soc. Publishers, 1973–77; FaPreservation Soc., 1974–81; Zoological Soc. of London, 1977–84 (Hon. Sec., 1955–7on. Fellow, 1984); Bath Inst. of Med. Engrg, 1980–. Lectures: Gregynog, UC Wales, 1 Mason, Univ. of Birmingham, 1957; Caltech Commencement, 1959; Lees Knowlcambridge, 1965; Maurice Lubbock, Oxford, 1967; Maurice Bloch, Glasgow, 19Trueman Wood, RSA, 1969; Compton, MIT, 1972; Edwin Stevens, RoySocMed,4; Romanes, Oxford, 1975; Rhodes, S Africa, 1975; Jubilee, Imperial Coll., 1982; Lane, Clare Coll., Cambridge, 1983; Keith Morden Meml, Portland State Univ., 1985. Fellow, University College, London; Fellow Commoner, Christ's College, Cambridge. Hon. Member: Academia das Ciencias, Lisboa; Anatomical Soc.; Physiological Soc.; Soc. for Endocrinology; Foreign Member: Amer. Philosophical Soc., Amer. Acad. of Arts and Sciences; Assoc. Mem. (Emeritus), Ordnance Bd. Dr *hc* Bordeaux, 1961; Hon. DSc: Sussex, 1963; Jacksonville, USA, 1964; Bradford, 1966; Hull, 1977; Columbia, USA, 1977; East Anglia, 1980; Reading, 1984; Hon. LLD: Birmingham, 1970; St Andrews, 1980. Gold Medal, Zoological Soc. of London, 1971. Medal of Freedom with Silver Palm (USA); Chevalier de la Lègion d'Honneur. *Publications:* The Social Life of Monkeys and Apes, 1932, 2nd edn 1981; Functional Affinities of Man, Monkeys and Apes, 1933; (ed, anonymous) Science in War, 1940; A New System of Anatomy, 1961, 2nd edn, 1981; (ed) The Ovary, 2 vols, 1962, 2nd edn 1977; Scientists and War, 1966; Beyond the Ivory Tower, 1970; (ed) Great Zoos of the World, 1980; Science Advisers, Scientific Advisers and Nuclear Weapons, 1980; Nuclear Illusion and Reality, 1982; Star Wars in a Nuclear World, 1986; *autobiography:* From Apes to Warlords, 1978; Monkeys, Men and Missiles, 1988; contribs to scientific jls since 1925. *Address:* University of East Anglia, Norwich NR4 7TJ. *Clubs:* Beefsteak, Brooks's.

ZUCKERMAN, Prof. Arie Jeremy, MD, DSc; FRCP, FRCPath; Professor of Microbiology in the University of London, since 1975, and Dean, Royal Free Hospital School of Medicine, since 1989; *b* 30 March 1932. *Educ:* Birmingham Univ. (BSc 1953; MSc 1962; DSc 1973); London Univ. (MB BS 1957; MD 1963; DipBact 1965). MRCS, LRCP, 1957; DObst, RCOG, 1958; MRCPath 1965, FRCPath 1977; MRCP 1977, FRCP 1982. Ho. Surg., Royal Free Hosp., 1957–58; Ho. Phys., 1958, Casualty Surg. and Admissions Officer, 1958–59, Whittington Hosp.; Medical Branch, RAF, 1959–62: Unit MO and Tutor in Aviation Medicine, Advanced Flying Sch., 1959–60; Epidemiol Res. Lab., PHLS, 1960–62; seconded to Dept of Pathol., Guy's Hosp. Med. Sch., 1962–65; Sen. Registrar, PHLS, 1963–65; London School of Hygiene and Tropical Medicine: Sen. Lectr, Dept of Bacteriol. and Immunol., 1965–68; Reader in Virology, 1968–72; Prof. of Virology, 1972–75; Dir, Dept of Med. Microbiol., 1975–88. Hon. Consultant Microbiologist: UCH, 1982–89; Royal Free Hosp., 1989–; Hon. Consultant Virologist: Charing Cross Hosp., 1982–; NE Thames Regl Blood Transfusion Centre, Brentwood, 1970–. World Health Organisation: Consultant on hepatitis, 1970–; Mem., Expert Adv. Panel on Virus Diseases, 1974–89; Dir, Collaborating Centre for Ref. and Res. on Viral Diseases, 1990–; Dir, Collaborating Centre for Ref. and Res. on Viral Hepatitis, London, 1974–. Non-exec. Dir, Royal Free Hampstead NHS Trust, 1990–. Stewart Prize, BMA, 1981. Editor: Jl of Med. Virology, 1976–; Jl of Virological Methods, 1979–. *Publications:* Virus Diseases of the Liver, 1970; Hepatitis-associated Antigen and Viruses, 1972, 2nd edn as Human Viral Hepatitis, 1975 (trans. Japanese, 1980); (with C. R. Howard) Hepatitis Viruses of Man, 1979 (trans. Japanese, 1981); A Decade of Viral Hepatitis: abstracts 1969–1979, 1980; (ed) Viral Hepatitis: clinics in tropical medicine and communicable diseases, 1986; (ed jtly) Principles and Practice of Clinical Virology, 1987, 2nd edn 1990 (trans. Italian, 1992); (ed) Viral Hepatitis and Liver Disease, 1988; (ed) Recent Developments in Prophylactic Immunization, 1989; (ed) Viral Hepatitis, 1990 (trans. Spanish, 1991); contribs to many learned jls. *Address:* Royal Free Hospital School of Medicine, Rowland Hill Street, Hampstead, NW3 2PF. *T:* 071–794 0500.

ZUKERMAN, Pinchas; concert violinist; *b* Tel Aviv, Israel, 16 July 1948; *s* of Jehuda and Miriam Zukerman; *m* 1985, Tuesday Weld, actress; two *d* by previous *m*. *Educ:* Juilliard School of Music. Début, USA, 1963, Europe, 1970. Violin soloist with every major orchestra in USA and Europe; tours of USA, Europe, Israel, Scandinavia, Australia; extensive recordings. Music Director: South Bank Festival, 1978–80; St Paul Chamber Orch., 1980–87. First prize, Leventritt Internat. Violin Competition, 1967. *Recreation:* tennis. *Address:* c/o Shirley Kirshbaum & Associates, 711 West End Avenue, New York, NY 10025, USA. *T:* (212) 222–4843.

ZUNTZ, Prof. Günther, FBA 1956; DrPhil (Marburg); Emeritus Professor, Manchester University; Professor of Hellenistic Greek, 1963–69; *b* 28 Jan. 1902; *s* of Dr Leo Zuntz and Edith (*née* Bähring); *m* 1947, Mary Alyson Garratt; two *s* one *d*. *Educ:* Bismarck-Gymnasium, Berlin-Wilmersdorf; Berlin, Marburg, Göttingen and Graz Universities. Teacher, Odenwaldschule, 1924–26; Teacher, Marburg Gymnasium and Kassel Gymnasium, 1926–32; worked for Monumenta Musicae Byzantinae, in Copenhagen, 1935–39, in Oxford, 1939–47; Librarian, Mansfield College, Oxford, 1944–47; Senior Lecturer, Manchester University, 1947–55 (Reader, 1955–63). Corresponding Member: Oesterreich. Akad. der Wissenschaften, 1974; Heidelberger Akademie der Wissenschaften, 1985. Dr.phil *hc* Tübingen, 1983. *Publications:* Hölderlins Pindar-Übersetzung, 1928; (with C. Höeg) Prophetologium, i-vi, 1939–71; The Ancestry of the Harklean New Testament, 1945; The Text of the Epistles, 1953; The Political Plays of Euripides, 1955, corrected repr., 1963; The Transmission of the Plays of Euripides, 1965; Persephone, 1971; Opuscula Selecta, 1972; Ein griechischer Lehrgang, 3 vols, 1983, revd edn 1991 (trans. A Greek Course, 1992); Drei Kapitel zur Griechischen Metrik, 1984; Aion, Gott des Römerreichs, 1989; articles in many learned journals. *Recreation:* music. *Address:* 1 Humberstone Road, Cambridge CB4 1JD. *T:* Cambridge (0223) 357789.

ZUNZ, Sir Gerhard Jacob, (Sir Jack), Kt 1989; FEng 1983; Consultant, Ove Arup Partnership and Ove Arup & Partners, since 1989; *b* 25 Dec. 1923; *s* of Wilhelm Zunz and Helene (*née* Isenberg); *m* 1948, Babs Maisel; one *s* two *d*. *Educ:* Athlone High Sch., Johannesburg; Univ. of the Witwatersrand (BScCivEng); FICE, FIStructE. War service, Egypt and Italy, with SA Artillery, 1943–46. Asst Engr, Alpheus, Williams & Dowse, 1948–50; Structural and Civil Engr with Ove Arup & Partners, London, 1950–54; Co-founder and Partner, Ove Arup & Partners (S Africa), 1954–61; Ove Arup & Partners: Associate Partner, 1961–65; Sen. Partner, and Partner in all overseas partnerships, 1965–77; Dir and Chm., 1977–84; Co-Chm., Ove Arup Partnership, and Dir, Ove Arup & Partners, 1984–89. Industrial Fellow Commoner, Churchill Coll., Cambridge, 1967–68; former mem., various cttees associated with the construction industry. Hon. FRIBA 1990; FCGI 1990. Oscar Faber Silver Medal (jtly, with Sir Ove Arup), 1969; IStructE Gold Medal, 1988. *Publications:* (some jtly) number of technical papers to learned socs, incl. papers on Sydney Opera House and Hongkong & Shanghai Bank. *Recreations:* theatre, music, golf, tribal art. *Address:* 2A Drax Avenue, Wimbledon, SW20 0EH. *T:* 081–947 1537.

ZURENUO, Rt. Rev. Sir Zurewe (Kamong), Kt 1981; OBE 1971; Head Bishop of Evangelical Lutheran Church of Papua New Guinea, 1973–82; *b* 5 July 1920; *s* of Zurenuo and Kbasung (previously the people took only one name and were known by none other); *m* 1941, Eleju; two *s* three *d* (and one *s* decd). *Educ:* Lutheran Mission schools (8 years in formal schools and 2 years teacher trng). Began teaching in Lutheran Schools, 1939, interrupted by illness, 1946; also did pastoral work; became Church Secretary of Sattelberg Circuit of Lutheran Church, 1953, and was elected General Secretary of Evangelical Lutheran Church of New Guinea, 1962; ordained, 1966. Instrumental in leading the church from mission status to indigenous church status; played a leading role in writing the constitution of the church; active in community affairs and inter-church relations; Chairman, Melanesian Council of Churches, 1970–73; established Lae City Christian Council, 1972 (Chm., 1972–82). *Address:* Evangelical Lutheran Church of Papua New Guinea, PO Box 80, Lae, Papua New Guinea.